No Longer the Property of
Hayner Public Library District

For Reference

Not to be taken from this room

A SUPPLEMENT TO THE

OXFORD ENGLISH DICTIONARY

A SUPPLEMENT TO THE OXFORD ENGLISH DICTIONARY

EDITED BY

R. W. BURCHFIELD

VOLUME III · O–Scz

OXFORD
AT THE CLARENDON PRESS
1982

HAYNER PUBLIC LIBRARY DISTRICT
ALTON, ILLINOIS

Oxford University Press, Walton Street, Oxford OX2 6DP
London Glasgow New York Toronto
Delhi Bombay Calcutta Madras Karachi
Kuala Lumpur Singapore Hong Kong Tokyo
Nairobi Dar es Salaam Cape Town
Melbourne Auckland
and associates in
Beirut Berlin Ibadan Mexico City Nicosia

© *Oxford University Press 1982*

Published in the United States by
Oxford University Press, New York

All rights reserved. No part of this publication may be reproduced, stored in a retrieval system, or transmitted, in any form or by any means, electronic, mechanical, photocopying, recording, or otherwise, without the prior permission of Oxford University Press

British Library Cataloguing in Publication Data
A Supplement to the Oxford English Dictionary
Vol. 3: O–Scz
1. English language–Dictionaries
I. Burchfield, R. W.
II. The Oxford English Dictionary
423 PE 1625

ISBN 0–19–861124–2

Library of Congress Cataloging in Publication Data (*Revised*)
Main entry under title:
A Supplement to the Oxford English dictionary.
CONTENTS: v. 1. A–G.—v. 2. H–N.—v. 3. O–Scz.
1. English language—Dictionaries. I. Burchfield, Robert W.
II. Title: Oxford English dictionary.
PE1625.N53 1933 Suppl. 423 82–6411
ISBN 0–19–861115–3 (*v. 1*) *AACR2*

Typesetting by the University Press, Oxford, William Clowes & Sons Ltd., Beccles, and Latimer Trend Ltd., Plymouth
Printed in Great Britain by
Thomson Litho Ltd., East Kilbride, and bound at the University Press, Oxford

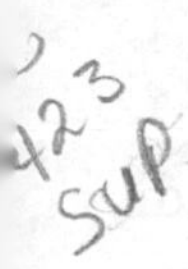

AAG-6578

PREFACE

IN her *Personal Pleasures* (1935) Rose Macaulay notes that on a blank page at the beginning of her copy of the 1933 *Supplement to the OED* she recorded emendations, corrections, additions, and earlier uses of words.

> To amend so great a work gives me pleasure; I feel myself one of its architects; I am Sir James Murray, Dr. Bradley, Sir William Craigie, Dr. Onions . . .
>
> If there is a drawback to this pure pleasure of doing good to a dictionary, I have not yet found it. Except that, naturally, it takes time.

With the publication of this volume we have now reached the three-quarter mark, proportionately about as far as the point reached by Dr Murray on the *OED* itself before he died in 1915. We are now preparing the fourth and last volume, and it should be ready for publication in 1985. It would not be prudent to start congratulating ourselves yet—no major lexicographical project has been brought to its last word without the final agonies of a marathon runner—but the glittering prize of completion now seems to be within sight at last.

The letter S—the longest one in the alphabet—needed to be divided. Calculations of various kinds were made and in the end it was decided to make the division at *Scythism*, though it is a word of no great account, in order to balance the size of the third and fourth volumes. The fourth and final volume will begin with an entry for the ancient and productive word *sea*.

We have continued to follow the main lines of policy described in the first two volumes, but with changes of emphasis or detail here and there in order to take into account the events of the later part of the past decade, the research interests of scholars in various subjects, and the vicissitudes of the OED Department and of my own life.

During the 1970s the markedly linguistic descriptivism of the post-war years was to some extent brought into question. Infelicities of language, whether in the spoken or the written word, were identified and assailed by a great many people who seemed to believe that the English language itself was in a period of decline. Regular columns largely concerned with verbal error appeared (and many of them continue to appear) in *The Times* (Mr Philip Howard), the *New York Times Sunday Magazine* (Mr William Safire), the *New Statesman* ('This English'), *Encounter* ('In the Margin'), the New Zealand *Listener* (Professor I. A. Gordon), and many other newspapers and journals. The House of Lords devoted a session to the subject on 21 November 1979 and another on 28 January 1981, in the course of which eloquent voices were raised against the use of modish words like *ongoing*, *relevant*, and *viable*.[1]

My own views on these great issues were expressed in several publications[2] and in many lectures and broadcasts—broadly that 'the English language is alive and well, in the right hands'.

> Expressions like *right on* and *hopefully* bring out the worst and the best in men and women. They stand as emblems of social and political divisions within our society. These and other elements lying strewn in the disputed territory of our language are at any given time not numerous but are charged with a significance that goes far beyond the mere linguistic. If you are tempted to fulminate against them, or to feel uneasy about them, bear in mind that the English language has been in the hands of linguistic conservatives and linguistic radicals for more than a thousand years and that, far from bleeding to death from past crudities and past wounds, it can be used with majesty and power, free of all fault, by our greatest writers.[3]

One small legacy of these great debates is that here and there in the present volume I have found

1 The text of these debates is recorded in the relevant issues of Hansard.

2 Especially in *The Quality of Spoken English on BBC Radio* (BBC, 1979), *The Spoken Language as an Art Form: an Autobiographical Approach* (English-Speaking Union, New York, 1981), and *The Spoken Word: a BBC Guide* (BBC, 1981).

3 *The Spoken Language as an Art Form*, p. 17.

myself adding my own opinions about the acceptability of certain words or meanings in educated use. Users of the dictionary may or may not find these editorial comments diverting: they have been added (adapting a statement by John Ray in 1691) 'as oil to preserve the mucilage from inspissation'.

The volume has been prepared in circumstances of great adversity, though not without many mitigating factors. The editorial staff remained more or less constant in number but very different in constitution as some moved away to other posts and others took charge of other projects within the Department. Also, in 1977, we left our 'shabby Victorian villa', 40 Walton Crescent, and moved to 37a St. Giles', a splendid spacious Georgian mansion in central Oxford, with all the disruption brought about by such a move. We lost our printers, William Clowes & Co. Ltd., Beccles, after they had set the letters O and P for this volume. The closing down of their hot-metal department in 1980 delayed the printing of Volume III by six months before new printers were found and the material was transferred to Plymouth or to Oxford. The Department embarked on many other projects, including new editions of nearly all the Oxford dictionaries below the level of the *OED* itself, and completed a number of new dictionaries including the *Oxford Paperback Dictionary* (1979); three dictionaries closely related to it, including the *Oxford American Dictionary* (1980) and the *St. Michael Oxford Dictionary* (1981); the *Oxford Minidictionary* (1981); and several school dictionaries. My governance, at various removes, of these projects inevitably delayed the completion of the third volume of the Supplement. The Oxford University Press found itself locked in internal debates and wrangles about ways and means of surviving in difficult trading conditions. Trading profits turned into trading losses and unpleasantnesses occurred as those responsible for the management of affairs found themselves in inevitable dispute with the unions. The Department could not stand aside and pretend that it existed in an ivory tower of its own choice. The words *picket* and *picketer* are dealt with in this volume: all of us encountered the fact of picketing at intervals while this volume was in preparation. We continued to receive sustained and invaluable assistance from many outside scholars and institutions (see below) but suffered a grievous blow when G. and C. Merriam Co. decided in 1977 that they could no longer help us, as they had in the past, by supplying from their files earlier examples of words than those held in our own files. This volume contains numerous examples of the type '1934 in WEBSTER'[4] because this great American dictionary house felt obliged to cancel an arrangement that I had made with Dr Philip Gove, the Editor of *Webster's Third New International Dictionary*, in 1968.

These adversities have left their mark but the pleasures of historical lexicography remain as a source of endless delight and can be observed in the pages that follow. The burgeoning of the word *O.K.* in its numerous spellings and variations; the engaging curiosities of the letter Q (this with X the letter always dealt with at greatest speed by lexicographers); the words of Yiddish, German, Greek, and Italian origin beginning with *sch-*, a vigorous group if ever there was one; the numerous Chinese loanwords or loan translations—for example, *pipa*, *putonghua*, *Little Red Book*, *running dog*, and *scorched earth*—with the Chinese originals expressed in the revolutionary (and one hopes permanent) Pinyin transliteration system; and the numberless entries with *post-*, *pre-*, *pro-*, and *re-* as their first elements. Those who wish to explore the volume further rather than simply use it as a work of occasional reference may derive pleasure (according to taste) under at any rate some of the following assorted entries: *oung*, v. (of an elephant: to drag logs along a stream); *parp* (invented apparently by Enid Blyton); *person*, sb. 2 f (as in *chairperson*); *Pip, Squeak, and Wilfred; pneumonoultramicroscopicsilicovulcanoconiosis* (a factitious word of 45 letters); *Princeton-First Year* (Auden); *puddle-duck* (an earlier use than that in Beatrix Potter's famous work); controversial words like *piccaninny*, *Sambo*, and *Scientology; scripophily* (one of numerous invented words for various collecting habits); and *scrolloping* (Virginia Woolf).

[4] See, for example, the entries for *phrasally*, *retrain* (verb), *rewire* (noun), *rubbernecker*, *sales clerk*, and *sales force*.

Some new areas of vocabulary or doctrine that I have explored myself have been dealt with in several papers published elsewhere.[5]

A new feature of this volume is the inclusion of a table showing how we have transliterated foreign scripts—not always, unfortunately, with complete success. I am grateful to Dr J. B. Sykes (in particular), Sir Edward Playfair, Mr T. F. Hoad, and the late Mr. N. A. M. Rankin for very considerable assistance while it was being prepared.

Inevitably and sadly a number of people associated with the Supplement have not survived to see the publication of the third volume. The following contributors or outside consultants have died since Volume II was published in 1976: Professor J. A. W. Bennett (my former tutor), Dr E. J. Bowen, Dr R. S. Cahn, Professor B. Foster, Dr R. A. Hunter, Professor W. S. Mackie, Dr K. P. Oakley, N. A. M. Rankin (from the Dictionary Department itself), the Revd H. E. G. Rope (aged 97), and Nicolaas Van Blerk. Special mention should be made of Dr Douglas Leechman (who died in July 1980) and Professor W. S. Avis (who died in December 1979): there can scarcely be any Canadian item in the Supplement that has not benefited from the work of these two great men. Perhaps the most devastating blow of all came when Mr Gordon Murray, a member of the editorial staff, died in June 1981 at the age of 32.

Major contributors of quotations in the period 1976–80 included the following: †Professor W. S. Avis, G. Charters, G. Chowdharay-Best, C. Collier, Mrs J. Harker, Dom Sylvester Houédard, W. Kings, Miss M. Laski, †Dr D. Leechman, Mrs D. McColl, Mrs J. M. Marson, †E. H. Mart, Mrs M. Y. Offord, Sir Edward Playfair, F. Shapiro, Mrs V. Smith, and Mrs G. M. Spriggs. Of these Miss Laski and Mr Chowdharay-Best contributed approximately 30,000 quotations each, and all the others named supplied between 1,000 and 10,000 quotations each. Indispensable batches of quotations from fiction, including detective fiction, and from works in the whole area of domestic and social life were received from Miss Laski. Our treatment of exotic vocabulary from, for example, the Far East, the Pacific, and the language of politics would have been less thorough without the contributions of Mr Chowdharay-Best, of Asia Minor and the Middle East without those of Sir Edward Playfair, and of American card and board games, and of some other specialized areas, without those of Mr Shapiro.

The outside proof-readers, generously industrious and helpful throughout the preparation of Volume III, were Professor A. R. Duckert, M. W. Grose, T. F. Hoad, Miss Marghanita Laski, Mrs M. Y. Offord, and Professor E. G. Stanley.

The outside consultants to whom we have repeatedly turned while the volume was being prepared were: Dr G. C. Ainsworth, A. J. Augarde, †Professor W. S. Avis, Dr R. P. Beckinsale, Professor A. J. Bliss, Dr S. Bradbury, Dr Jean Branford, †Dr R. S. Cahn, Sir A. K. Cairncross, Professor F. G. Cassidy, Miss Chan Yin-Ling, Miss P. Cooray, Dr J. Cortés, Professor G. N. C. Crawford, Professor S. Deas, P. G. Embrey, D. F. Foxon, R. B. Freeman, W. K. V. Gale, P. G. W. Glare, Dr I. Goddard, R. Hall, R. E. Hawkins, Dr M. H. Hey, M. T. Heydeman, Professor Elizabeth (Carr) Holmes, †Dr R. A. Hunter, Dr D. M. Jackson, P. Jarrett, Dr Russell Jones, Dr N. R. Ker, Dr W. J. Kirwin, Professor K. Koike, Professor J. Leech, †Dr D. Leechman, Professor B. Lennox, Dr A. Loveless, Dr D. J. Mabberly, Professor R. I. McDavid Jr, Dr R. S. McGregor, Professor J. B. McMillan, Dr L. V. Malakhovski, Dr F. H. C. Marriott, R. D. Meikle, D. D. Murison, †Dr K. P. Oakley, I. and P. Opie, Professor C. Rabin, Professor R. H. Robins,

[5] 'Names of Types of Oil Wells: an Aspect of Short-Term Historical Lexicography', in *Feestbundel F. de Tollenaere* (Leiden, 1977); 'Aspects of Short-Term Historical Lexicography', in *Second Round Table on Historical Lexicography* (delivered in Leiden in 1977, published 1980), pp. 271–86; 'Further Aspects of Short-Term Historical Lexicography', in *James B. McMillan: Essays in Linguistics by his Friends and Colleagues* (University of Alabama Press, 1977), pp. 115–31; 'On that Other Great Dictionary', in *Encounter*, May 1977, pp. 47–50; *The Fowlers: their Achievements in Lexicography and Grammar* (Presidential Address to the English Association, 1979); Preface to a facsimile edition of Samuel Johnson's *Dictionary of the English Language* (London, 1979); 'Dictionaries and Ethnic Sensibilities', in L. Michaels and C. Ricks, *The State of the Language* (University of California Press, 1980), pp. 15–23.

Valuable papers by two of my departmental colleagues were also published in *Exeter Linguistic Studies*, Vol. IV (1979): L. S. Burnett, 'Lexicographical Problems in the Treatment of some Linguistic Terms in a Supplement to the OED'; and S. J. Raphael, 'The Treatment of the Terminology of Natural History in the Oxford English Dictionaries'.

Professor N. G. Sabbagha, R. Scruton, Dr J. B. Sykes, Miss Tao Jie, Professor G. Treitel, G. W. Turner, J. O. Urmson, Professor T. G. Vallance, Dr R. L. Venezky, the Revd Canon Professor M. F. Wiles, and Dr D. R. Woodall. Many others have given us advice and comments on individual entries.

This third volume contains about 18,750 Main Words divided into some 28,000 senses. There are about 8,500 defined Combinations within the articles and some 4,500 undefined Combinations. The illustrative quotations are estimated to number 142,500.

Finally, the Editor would like to record his personal indebtedness to many individual scholars and institutions: Mrs L. S. Burnett and Dr W. R. Trumble, who made signal editorial contributions to the Supplement before they started work on a new edition of the *Shorter Oxford English Dictionary* in 1980; similarly Dr R. E. Allen, who succeeded Dr J. B. Sykes as editor of the *Concise Oxford Dictionary* and *Pocket Oxford Dictionary* in 1981; my other Senior Editors, Mr A. M. Hughes (for Science), Miss Sandra Raphael (for Natural History and Library Research), and, in more recent times, Mr E. S. C. Weiner and Mr J. A. Simpson; the library research staff who have managed to overcome the adversities now strewn in the path of anyone constantly using great libraries, and in particular Miss V. M. Salusbury (until she left in 1977), Miss J. L. Harley (retired 1980), and others who worked in London and in America far from the editorial headquarters in Oxford; Mr J. Paterson for his resolution of many difficult bibliographical problems within the inevitable limits of time; my hosts in Chicago and New York in July 1978 when I startled them and many others by suggesting in a lecture to the American Library Association that American and British English were drifting apart and that one day interpreters would be needed;[6] Liverpool University for their munificence in conferring an Honorary D.Litt. on me in 1978; those who welcomed me in China in May 1979, especially Mr Chen Yuan of the Commercial Press, Peking, and my interpreter, Miss Tao Jie, Peking University; and my hosts in seven cities in the United States in October 1980 when I gave a series of lectures on the English language at the invitation of the English-Speaking Union. Above all, I have continued to build up my indebtedness to those whom I see daily and who have given me superlative support and succour over the last six years, my colleagues and assistants on the Dictionary staff itself.

Oxford R.W.B.
October 1981

[6] The lecture was printed with the title 'The Point of Severance: English in 1776 and Beyond', in *Encounter*, October 1978, pp. 129–33.

CONTENTS

VOLUME III

EDITORIAL STAFF xi

KEY TO THE PRONUNCIATION xiii

LIST OF ABBREVIATIONS, SIGNS, ETC. xiv

PROPRIETARY NAMES xv

TRANSLITERATION OF FOREIGN SCRIPTS xvi

A SUPPLEMENT TO THE OXFORD ENGLISH DICTIONARY, O–Scz 1

EDITORIAL STAFF

The dates given after the names indicate when each person joined the editorial staff of this dictionary. The letter P precedes the names of those who worked as part-timers.

Senior Editors (General):	R. E. ALLEN	1974–80
	LESLEY S. BURNETT	1974–80
	J. A. SIMPSON	1976–
	E. S. C. WEINER	1977–
Senior Editor (Science):	A. M. HUGHES	1968–
Senior Editor (Natural History and Library Research):	SANDRA RAPHAEL	1969–
Assistant Editor (Bibliographical Collation):	J. PATERSON	1975–

Editorial Assistants

E. C. DANN	1963–	A. HODGSON	1976–
ADRIANA P. ORR	1966–	YVONNE L. WARBURTON	1976–
DEBORAH D. HONORÉ		JULIA C. SWANNELL	1976–
(*formerly* COWEN)	1970–	D. J. EDMONDS	1977–80
JOYCE L. HARLEY	1970–80	PF. D. HAYES	1977–
ROSEMARY J. SANSOME	1975–80	†G. MURRAY	1977–81
N. S. WEDD	1975–81	P. R. HARDIE	1977–80
D. R. HOWLETT	1975–9	ELIZABETH M. KNOWLES	1977–
W. R. TRUMBLE	1975–80	C. F. KEMP	1978–81
EDITH BONNER		ROSAMUND E. MOON	1979–81
(*formerly* ROGERSON)	1976–	AMANDA J. BURRELL	1979–

Members of the editorial staff received valuable part-time assistance from the following outside helpers: Grace M. Briggs (1959–), Rita G. Keckeissen (1968–), Daphne Gilbert-Carter (1975–), and Sally Hinkle (1977–), the first-named in Oxford and the others in New York, Washington, and Boston respectively.

Mr Kemp and Mrs Burrell (both based in London), Mrs Orr (in Washington), and Miss Harley, Miss Warburton, and Miss Knowles (all in Oxford) were mainly concerned with research (especially for 'first uses') and with the verification of quotations. Mr Wedd, Dr Trumble, and Mr Murray dealt with scientific terms, and Mrs Honoré with terms in the Social Sciences. Mr Edmonds assisted with the reading of proofs. All other Editorial Assistants named above undertook general editorial work.

Among those who assisted for relatively short periods with the editorial work of Volume III as part of the regular staff were the following: Veronica M. Salusbury (1966–77), J. Claire Nicholls (1974–7), PMarguerite Y. Offord (1974–9), P. J. Broadhead (1977–8), J. S. Wood (1978–80), and Wendy H. Archer (1980–1).

New members of the editorial staff who (from 1980) assisted with the final stages of Volume III were Dr D. B. W. Birk, M. A. Mabe, and Della J. Thompson. Mrs Honoré worked part-time from mid-1980.

Secretarial and clerical assistants: Beta Cotmore (1974–9), Anne Whear (1975–), Katherine A. Shock (1978–9), D. Ann Baker (1978–81), Afra E. Singer (1979–81), and Karin C. E. Vines (1981–).

KEY TO THE PRONUNCIATION

THE pronunciations given are those in use in the educated speech of southern England (the so-called 'Received Standard'), and the keywords given are to be understood as pronounced in such speech.

I. *Consonants and Semi-Consonants*

b, d, f, k, l, m, n, p, t, v, z *have their usual English values*

g as in *go* (gō^{u}).
h ... *ho!* (hō^{u}).
r ... run (rɒn), terrier (te·riəɹ).
ɹ ... her (hə̄ɹ), farther (fā·ɹðəɹ).
s ... see (sī), success (sɒ̆kse·s).
w ... *wear* (wē^{ə}ɹ).
hw... *when* (hwen).
y ... *yes* (yes).

þ as in thin (þin), bath (bɑþ).
ð ... then (ðen), bathe (bē^{i}ð).
ʃ ... shop (ʃǫp), dish (diʃ).
tʃ ... chop (tʃǫp), ditch (ditʃ).
ʒ ... vision (vi·ʒən), déjeuner (deʒöne).
dʒ ... judge (dʒɒdʒ).
ŋ ... singing (si·ŋiŋ), think (þiŋk).
ŋg ... finger (fi·ŋgəɹ).

(FOREIGN AND NON-SOUTHERN)

ṅ as in French nasal, environ (aṅviroṅ).
l^{y} ... It. serraglio (serā·l^{y}o).
n^{y} ... It. signore (sin^{y}ō·re).
χ ... Ger. ach (aχ), Sc. loch (lǫχ), Sp. frijoles (frī·χoles).
χ^{y} ... Ger. ich (iχ^{y}), Sc. nicht (niχ^{y}t).
γ ... North Ger. sagen (zā·γĕn).
γ^{y} ... Ger. legen, regnen (lē·γ^{y}ĕn, rē·γ^{y}nĕn).
k^{y} ... Afrikaans baardmannetjie (bā·rtmanək^{y}i).

The reversed r (ɹ) and small 'superior' letters (pe·rĕm^{p}təri) are used to denote elements that may be omitted either by individual speakers or in particular phonetic contexts.

II. *Vowels*

The symbol ¯ placed over a vowel-letter denotes length.

The incidence of main stress is shown by a raised point (·) after the vowel-symbol, and a secondary stress by a double point (:) as in *callithumpian* (kæ:līþɒ·mpiăn).

The stressed vowels a, æ, e, i, o, u become obscured with loss of stress, and the indeterminate sounds thus arising, and approximating to the 'neutral' vowel ə, are normally printed ă, æ̆, ĕ, ĭ, ŏ, ŭ.

A break ˌ is used to indicate syllable-division when necessary to avoid ambiguity.

ORDINARY

a as in Fr. *à la* mode (a la mod').
ai ... *aye*=yes (ai), Isaiah (əizai·ă).
æ ... man (mæn).
ɑ ... pass (pɑs), chant (tʃɑnt).
ɑu ... loud (lɑud), now (nɑu).
ɒ ... cut (kɒt), son (sɒn).
e ... yet (yet), ten (ten).
‖e ... Fr. attaché (ataʃe).
‖ę ... Fr. chef (ʃęf).
ə ... ever (e·vəɹ), nation (nē^{i}·ʃən).
əi ... *I*, *eye* (əi), bind (bəind).
‖ə ... Fr. tour de force (tūrdəfors).
i ... sit (sit), mystic (mistik).
i ... Psyche (səi·ki), react (riˌæ·kt).
o ... achor (ē^{i}·koɹ), morality (moræ·lĭti).
oi ... oil (oil), boy (boi).
o ... hero (hī^{ə}·ro), zoology (zoˌǫ·lŏdʒi).
ǫ ... what (hwǫt), watch (wǫtʃ).
ǫ,ǫ̀* ... got (gǫt), soft (sǫ̀ft)*.
‖ö ... Ger. Köln (köln).
‖ö ... Fr. peu (pö).
u ... full (ful), book (buk).
iu ... duration (diurē^{i}·ʃən).
u ... unto (ɒ·ntu), frugality (fru-).
iu ... Matthew (mæ·þiu), virtue (və̄·ɹtiu).
‖ü ... Ger. Müller (mü·lĕr).
‖ü ... Fr. dune (dün).
^{ə} (see ī^{ə}, ē^{ə}, ō^{ə}, ū^{ə}) } see Vol. I of Dict., p.
$^{i, u}$ (see ē^{i}, ō^{u}) } xxxiv, note 3.
' as in able (ē^{i}·b'l), eaten (ī·t'n) = voice-glide.

LONG

ā as in alms (āmz), bar (bāɹ).
ɒ̄ ... curl (kɒ̄ɹl), fur (fɒ̄ɹ).
ē (ē^{ə}) ... there (ðē^{ə}ɹ), pear, pare (pē ɹ).
ē (ē^{i}) ... rein, rain (rē^{i}n), they (ðē^{i}).
‖ę̄ ... Fr. faire (fę̄r').
ə̄ ... fir (fə̄ɹ), fern (fə̄ɹn), earth (ə̄ɹþ).
ī (ī^{ə}) ... bier (bī^{ə}ɹ), clear (klī^{ə}ɹ).
ī ... thief (þīf), see (sī).
ō (ō^{ə}) ... boar, bore (bō^{ə}ɹ), glory (glō^{ə}·ri).
ō (ō^{u}) ... so, sow (sō^{u}), soul (sō^{u}l).
ǭ ... walk (wǭk), wart (wǭɹt).
ǭ ... short (ʃǭɹt), thorn (þǭɹn).
‖ȫ ... Fr. cœur (kȫr).
‖ȫ ... Ger. Goethe (gȫtĕ), Fr. jeûne (ʒȫn).
ū (ū^{ə}) ... poor (pū^{ə}ɹ), moorish (mū^{ə}·riʃ).
iū, ^{i}ū ... pure (piū^{ə}ɹ), lure (l^{i}ū^{ə}ɹ).
ū ... two moons (tū mūnz).
iū, ^{i}ū ... few (fiū), lute (l^{i}ūt).
‖ǖ ... Ger. grün (grǖn), Fr. jus (ʒǖ).

OBSCURE

ă as in amœba (ămī·bă).
æ̆ ... accept (æ̆kse·pt), maniac (mē^{i}·niæ̆k).
ɒ̆ ... datum (dē^{i}·tɒ̆m).
ĕ ... moment (mō^{u}·mĕnt), several (se·vĕrăl).
ĕ ... separate (*adj.*) (se·părĕt).
ė ... added (æ·dėd), estate (ėstē^{i}·t).
ĭ ... vanity (væ·nĭti).
ĭ ... remain (rĭmē^{i}·n), believe (bĭlī·v).
ŏ ... theory (þī·ŏri).
ŏ ... violet (vəi·ŏlėt), parody (pæ·rŏdi).
ǫ̆ ... *au*thority (ǫ̆þǫ·rĭti).
ǫ̆ ... connect (kǫ̆ne·kt), amazon (æ·măzǫ̆n).
iŭ, ^{i}ŭ verdure (və̄·ɹdiŭɹ), measure (me·ʒ^{i}ŭɹ).
ŭ ... altogether (ǭltŭge·ðəɹ).
iŭ ... circular (sə̄·ɹkiŭlăɹ).

* Words such as *soft, cloth, cross* are often still pronounced with (ǭ) by Southern speakers in England but the pronunciation with ǫ is now more usual.

‖ Only in foreign (or earlier English) words.

LIST OF ABBREVIATIONS, SIGNS, ETC.

Some abbreviations here listed in italics are occasionally, for the sake of clarity, printed in roman type, and vice versa.

a. (in Etym.)	adoption of, adopted from
a (as *a* 1850)	*ante*, 'before', 'not later than'
a.	adjective
abbrev.	abbreviation (of)
abl.	ablative
absol.	absolute, -ly
Abstr.	Abstract(s)
acc.	accusative
ad. (in Etym.)	adaptation of
Add.	Addenda
adj.	adjective
adv.	adverb
advb.	adverbial, -ly
(Advt.),	advertisement
Aeronaut.	in Aeronautics
AF., AFr.	Anglo-French
Afr.	Africa, -n
Agric.	in Agriculture
Alb.	Albanian
Amer.	American
Amer. Ind.	American Indian
Anat.	in Anatomy
Anglo-Ind.	Anglo-Indian
Anglo-Ir.	Anglo-Irish
Anthrop., Anthropol.	in Anthropology
Antiq.	in Antiquities
aphet.	aphetic, aphetized
app.	apparently
Arab.	Arabic
Aram.	Aramaic
Arch., Archit.	in Architecture
arch.	archaic
Archæol.	in Archæology
Arm.	Armenian
assoc.	association
Astr.	in Astronomy
Astrol.	in Astrology
attrib.	attributive, -ly
Austral.	Australian
A.V.	Authorized Version
bef.	before
Bibliogr.	in Bibliography
Biochem.	in Biochemistry
Biol.	in Biology
Bot.	in Botany
Bulg.	Bulgarian
c (as *c* 1700)	*circa*, 'about'
c. (as 19th c.)	century
Canad.	Canadian
Cat.	Catalan
catachr.	catachrestically
Celt.	Celtic
Cent. Dict.	*Century Dictionary*
Cf., cf.	*confer*, 'compare'
Ch.	Church
Chem.	in Chemistry
Cinemat., Cinematogr.	in Cinematography
cl. L.	classical Latin
cogn. w.	cognate with
collect.	collective, -ly
colloq.	colloquial, -ly
comb.	combined, -ing
Comb.	Combinations
Comm.	in Commercial usage
Communic.	in Communications
comp.	compound, composition
compar.	comparative
compl.	complement
Conch.	in Conchology
concr.	concrete, -ly
conj.	conjunction
cons.	consonant
const.	construction, construed with
corresp.	corresponding (to)
cpd.	compound
Cryst.	in Crystallography
Da.	Danish
D.A.	*Dictionary of Americanisms*
D.A.E.	*Dictionary of American English*
dat.	dative
def.	definite, -ition
deriv.	derivative, -ation
derog.	derogatory
dial.	dialect, -al
Dict.	Dictionary; *spec.*, the *Oxford English Dictionary*
dim.	diminutive
D.O.S.T.	*Dictionary of the Older Scottish Tongue*
Du.	Dutch
E.	East
Eccl.	in Ecclesiastical usage
Ecol.	in Ecology
Econ.	in Economics
ed.	edition
E.D.D.	*English Dialect Dictionary*
Educ.	in Education
e.g.	*exempli gratia*, 'for example'
Electr.	in Electricity
ellipt.	elliptical, -ly
Embryol.	in Embryology
e.midl.	east midland (dialect)
Eng.	English
Engin.	in Engineering
Ent.	in Entomology
erron.	erroneous, -ly
esp.	espccially
et al.	*et alii*, 'and others'
etc.	et cetera
Ethnol.	in Ethnology
etym.	etymology
euphem.	euphemistically
exc.	except
f. (in Etym.)	formed on
f. (in subordinate entries)	form of
F.	French
fem. (*rarely* f.)	feminine
fig.	figurative, -ly
Finn.	Finnish
fl.	*floruit*, 'flourished'
Fr.	French
freq.	frequent, -ly
Fris.	Frisian
Funk's Stand. Dict.	*Funk and Wagnalls Standard Dictionary*
G.	German
Gael.	Gaelic
Gaz.	Gazette (in names of newspapers)
gen.	genitive
gen.	general, -ly
Geogr.	in Geography
Geol.	in Geology
Geom.	in Geometry
Geomorphol.	in Geomorphology
Ger.	German
Gmc.	Germanic
Goth.	Gothic
Gr.	Greek
Gram.	in Grammar
Heb.	Hebrew
Her.	in Heraldry
Herb.	among herbalists
Hind.	Hindustani
Hist.	in History
hist.	historical
Hort.	in Horticulture
Ibid.	*Ibidem*, 'in the same book or passage'
Icel.	Icelandic
Ichthyol.	in Ichthyology
id.	*idem*, 'the same'
i.e.	*id est*, 'that is'
IE.	Indo-European
imit.	imitative
Immunol.	in Immunology
imp.	imperative
impers.	impersonal
impf.	imperfect
ind.	indicative
indef.	indefinite
inf.	infinitive
infl.	influenced
int.	interjection
intr.	intransitive
Introd.	Introduction
Ir.	Irish
irreg.	irregular, -ly
It.	Italian
J., (J.)	Johnson's *Dictionary* (quoted from)
(Jam.)	Jamieson, *Scottish Dict.*
Jap.	Japanese
joc.	jocular, -ly
l.	line
L.	Latin
lang.	language
Let., Lett.	letter, letters
LG.	Low German
lit.	literal, -ly
Lit.	Literary
Lith.	Lithuanian
LXX	Septuagint
Mal.	Malay, Malayan
Manuf.	in Manufacture, -ing
masc. (*rarely* m.)	masculine
Math.	in Mathematics
MDu.	Middle Dutch
ME.	Middle English
Mech.	in Mechanics
Med.	in Medicine
med.L.	medieval Latin
Metaph.	in Metaphysics
Meteorol.	in Meteorology
MHG.	Middle High German
midl.	midland (dialect)
Mil.	in military usage
Min.	in Mineralogy
MLG.	Middle Low German
mod.	modern
mod.L.	modern Latin
(Morris),	E. E. Morris's *Austral English* (quoted from)
Mus.	in Music
Mythol.	in Mythology
N.	North
N. Amer.	North America, -n
N. & Q.	*Notes and Queries*
Nat. Hist.	in Natural History
Naut.	in Nautical language
Neurol.	in Neurology
neut. (*rarely* n.)	neuter
NF., NFr.	Northern French
nom.	nominative
north.	northern (dialect)
Norw.	Norwegian
N.T.	New Testament
Nucl.	Nuclear
Numism.	in Numismatics
N.Z.	New Zealand
obj.	object
obl.	oblique
Obs., obs.	obsolete
occas.	occasional, -ly
Oceanogr.	in Oceanography
OE.	Old English (= Anglo-Saxon)
OF., OFr.	Old French
OFris.	Old Frisian
OHG.	Old High German

OIr.	Old Irish
ON.	Old Norse (Old Icelandic)
ONF.	Old Northern French
Ophthalm.	in Ophthalmology
opp.	opposed (to), the opposite (of)
Opt.	in Optics
orig.	origin, -al, -ally
Ornith.	in Ornithology
OS.	Old Saxon
OSl.	Old (Church) Slavonic
O.T.	Old Testament
p.	page
Palæogr.	in Palæography
Palæont.	in Palæontology
pa. pple.	passive or past participle
(Partridge),	E. Partridge's *Dictionary of Slang and Unconventional English* (quoted from)
pass.	passive, -ly
pa. t.	past tense
Path.	in Pathology
perh.	perhaps
Pers.	Persian
pers.	person, -al
Petrogr.	in Petrography
Petrol.	in Petrology
(Pettman),	C. Pettman's *Africanderisms* (quoted from)
pf.	perfect
Pg.	Portuguese
Pharm.	in Pharmacology
Philol.	in Philology
Philos.	in Philosophy
phonet.	phonetic, -ally
Photogr.	in Photography
phr.	phrase
Phys.	in Physics, physical; (*rarely*) in Physiology
Physiol.	in Physiology
pl.	plural; plate
poet.	poetic, -al
Pol.	Polish
Pol.	in Politics
Pol. Econ.	in Political Economy
pop.	popular, -ly
poss.	possessive
ppl. a., ppl. adj.	participial adjective
pple.	participle
Pr.	Provençal
prec.	preceding (word or article)
pred.	predicative
pref.	prefix
pref., Pref.	preface
prep.	preposition
pres.	present
priv.	privative
prob.	probably
pron.	pronoun
pronunc.	pronunciation
prop.	properly
Pros.	in Prosody
Prov.	Provençal
pr. pple.	present participle
Psych., *Psychol.*	in Psychology
Q.	Quarterly (in names of periodicals)
quot(s).	quotation(s)
q.v.	*quod vide*, 'which see'
R.	Royal (in names of periodicals, etc.)
Radiol.	in Radiology
R. C. Ch.	Roman Catholic Church
redupl.	reduplicating
refash.	refashioned, -ing
refl., refl.	reflexive
reg.	regular
rel.	related (to)
repr.	representative, representing
Rhet.	in Rhetoric
Rom.	Roman, Romance, Romanic
Rum.	Rumanian
Russ.	Russian
S.	South
S. Afr.	South Africa, -n
sb.	substantive
sc.	*scilicet*, 'understand' or 'supply'
Sc., *Scot.*	Scotch, Scottish
Sci.	(in) Science, scientific
Sc. Nat. Dict.	*Scottish National Dictionary*
Ser.	series
sing.	singular
Skr.	Sanskrit
Slav.	Slavonic
S.N.D.	*Scottish National Dictionary*
Sociol.	in Sociology
Sp.	Spanish
sp.	spelling
spec.	specific, -ally
(Stanf.),	*Stanford Dictionary of Anglicised Words and Phrases* (quoted from)
subj.	subject, subjunctive
subord. cl.	subordinate clause
subseq.	subsequent, -ly
subst.	substantively
suff.	suffix
superl.	superlative
Suppl.	Supplement
Surg.	in Surgery
s.v.	*sub voce*, 'under the word'
Sw.	Swedish
s.w.	south-western (dialect)
syll.	syllable
Syr.	Syrian
techn.	technical, -ly
Tel.	Telegraph (in names of newspapers)
Telegr.	in Telegraphy
Teleph.	in Telephony
(Th.),	Thornton's *American Glossary* (quoted from)
Theatr.	in the Theatre, theatrical
Theol.	in Theology
Tokh.	Tokharian
tr., transl.	translation (of)
trans.	transitive
transf.	transferred sense
Trig.	in Trigonometry
Turk.	Turkish
Typog., *Typogr.*	in Typography
ult.	ultimate, -ly
unkn.	unknown
U.S.	United States
usu.	usual, -ly
v., vb.	verb
var(r)., vars.	variant(s) of
vbl. sb.	verbal substantive
Vet., *Vet. Sci.*	in Veterinary Science
viz.	*videlicet*, 'namely'
v. str., or *w.*	verb strong, or weak
vulg.	vulgar
W.	Welsh; West
wd.	word
Webster	*Webster's (New International) Dictionary*
WGmc.	West Germanic
w.midl.	west midland (dialect)
WS.	West Saxon
(Y.),	Yule & Burnell's *Hobson-Jobson* (quoted from)
Zoogeogr.	in Zoogeography
Zool.	in Zoology

Signs and Other Conventions

Before a word or sense

† = obsolete
‖ = not naturalized, alien
¶ = catachrestic and erroneous uses (see Dict., Vol. I, p. xxi)

In the listing of Forms

1 = before 1100
2 = 12th c. (1100 to 1200)
3 = 13th c. (1200 to 1300), etc.
5–7 = 15th to 17th century. (See General Explanations, Dict., Vol. I, p. xxx)

In the etymologies

* indicates a word or form not actually found, but of which the existence is inferred
:– = normal development of

The printing of a word in SMALL CAPITALS indicates that further information will be found under the word so referred to.

In cross-references * indicates that the word or sense referred to is in the Supplement.

After the number of a sense * and ** (etc.) indicate new senses which are not directly related to the senses so numbered in the main body of the Dictionary, but which have to be inserted within the existing numerical sequence because of the custom in the Dictionary of placing the Combinations at the conclusion of each article.

. . indicates an omitted part of a quotation.

PROPRIETARY NAMES

THIS Supplement includes some words which are or are asserted to be proprietary names or trade marks. Their inclusion does not imply that they have acquired for legal purposes a non-proprietary or general significance nor any other judgement concerning their legal status. In cases where the editorial staff have established in the records of the Patent Offices of the United Kingdom and of the United States that a word is registered as a proprietary name or trade mark this is indicated, but no judgement concerning the legal status of such words is made or implied thereby.

TRANSLITERATION OF FOREIGN SCRIPTS

The lists below show the schemes of transliteration used in this Supplement for the most commonly occurring languages that have not adopted the Roman alphabet.

Arabic: (omitted), ب b, ت t, ث ṯ, ج j, ح ḥ, خ ḵ, د d, ذ ḏ, ر r, ز z, س s, ش š, ص ṣ, ض ḍ, ط ṭ, ظ ẓ, ع ʿ, غ ġ, ف f, ق ḳ, ك k, ل l, م m, ن n, ه h, ة (omitted), و w, ى y; ʾ ʾ; vowels a, i, u, ā, ī, ū.

Chinese: Wade–Giles system without tone-numbers; in Volumes III and IV Pinyin.

Hebrew: א ʾ, ב b, ג g, ד d, ה h, ו w, ז z, ח ḥ, ט ṭ, י y, כ k, ל l, מ m, נ n, ס s, ע ʿ, פ p, צ ṣ, ק q or ḳ, ר r, שׂ ś, שׁ sh or š, ת t;
spirant consonants underlined or with added h; doubled consonant for *daghesh forte*;

vowels a, e, i, o, u; long vowels with macron or circumflex according as written defective or *plene*; shva and reduced vowels superscript or omitted.

Japanese: 'Modified Hepburn' system, British Standard 4812: 1972.

Russian: А а a, Б б b, В в v, Г г g, Д д d, Е е e, Ж ж zh, З з z, И и i, Й й ĭ, К к k, Л л l, М м m, Н н n, О о o, П п p, Р р r, С с s, Т т t, У у u, Ф ф f, Х х kh, Ц ц ts, Ч ч ch, Ш ш sh, Щ щ shch, Ъ ъ ″, Ы ы ȳ, Ь ь ′, Э э é, Ю ю yu, Я я ya.

Sanskrit: अ a, आ ā, इ i, ई ī, उ u, ऊ ū, ऋ ṛ, ॠ ṝ, ऌ ḷ, ए e, ऐ ai, ओ o, औ au, ं ṃ, ः ḥ, क k, ख kh, ग g, घ gh, ङ ṅ, च c, छ ch, ज j, झ jh, ञ ñ, ट ṭ, ठ ṭh, ड ḍ, ढ ḍh, ण ṇ, त t, थ th, द d, ध dh, न n, प p, फ ph, ब b, भ bh, म m, य y, र r, ल l, व v, श ś, ष ṣ, स s, ह h; post-consonantal vowels -ा -ā, ि- -i, -ी -ī, ु -u, ू -ū, ृ -ṛ, -ॄ -ṝ, ॢ -ḷ, े -e, ै -ai, -ो -o, -ौ -au.

NOTES

Arabic: ْ (sukūn) omitted
ّ (šadda) doubled consonant

Assimilate l of definite article.
Hyphenate article to noun.
Diphthongs aw, ay; nunation an, in, un.
Extra letters in Persian p, ch, zh, g; s, t, z, s̱, ẕ, ż replace ṣ, ṭ, ẓ, ṯ, ḏ, ḍ; vowels include e, o.
Extra letters in Urdu ṭ, ḍ, ṛ.
This is for classical Arabic; colloquial forms may include further letters, e.g. ə at *FELLAGHA.

Hebrew: also for Aramaic and Yiddish.

Japanese: n is assimilated before b, m, p (*kombu*, not *konbu*).

Russian: stress generally marked by acute accent on vowel; stressed ȳ written ý́.

Sanskrit: bare stem used (dictionary form); -a is not written in devanagari.
Also for Hindi.

O

O. Add: **4*.** [orig. denoting absence: cf. O *sb.*[1]] In *Hæmatology*, designating absence of the A and B agglutinogens of the ABO blood group system; hence (and now usu.) used to designate the blood group of individuals lacking these two agglutinogens; also, more widely, used to designate the allele involved in determining this blood group.

1926 LANDSTEINER & WITT in *Jrnl. Immunol.* XI. 242 It has been pointed out by one of the writers..that the isoagglutinin reactions of human blood can be possibly explained by the simple assumption of only two different agglutinogens and agglutinins. Designating these by α and β, and the agglutinogens by A and B, the following symbols are obtained for the blood groups: I $-\alpha, \beta$; II A, β; III B, α; IV A, B $-$; if we include the factors A^1 and α^1 in the scheme, and if O and o signify the absence of agglutinogens or agglutinins, then the signs are: I O α, β, α^1; II A, β, and A, A^1, β; III B, α, α^1; IV A, B, o. **1927** [see *A II. 7]. **1929** L. H. SNYDER *Blood Grouping* i. 3 To try to obviate the confusion still existing from a reversal of groups I and IV in the two systems, a new system of nomenclature, based on the agglutinophyllic [*sic*] capacity of the cells, has been suggested. In this system, Jansky's group IV is known as *AB*, having the two agglutinogens A and B. Group III, containing agglutinogen B, is known as group *B*, group II as group *A*, and group I, containing neither agglutinogen, as group *O*. **1948** C. C. STURGIS *Hematol.* xxiii. 825 These characteristics in the erythrocytes may be present singly or together, or they can be absent. If the absence of these isogglutinable substances is designated as O, then there are four possibilities: namely, groups, O, A, B, and AB. **1958** J. B. MIALE *Lab. Med.: Hematol.* vi. 319 The O gene, when carried by both chromosomes, determines phenotype O. **1966** *Listener* 6 Oct. 493/1 Mr and Mrs H's blood was found to belong to group O, while Clive's blood was found to belong to group A2. **1968** PASSMORE & ROBSON *Compan. Med. Stud.* I. xxvi. 17/1 Every person has a pair of chromosomes each of which carries the A, B or O gene. **1969** J. H. GREEN *Basic Clin. Physiol.* vi. 34/2 The remainder of the population (46 per cent.) have neither A nor B on their red cells, and they are said to be Group O.

5. b. O.A.P., old age pensioner; (also formerly old age pension); O.E. (examples); also, Old Etonian; OF. (examples); OHG. (examples); ON. (examples).

1708 J. KERSEY *Dict. Anglo-Britannicum* Pref., *O.F.*, Old French. **1864** R. MORRIS *Early Eng. Allit. Poems* p. xxxvi, The preposition *from* never occurs in the following poems; it is replaced by *fro* (Northumbrian *fra*, O.N. *frá*). **1868** —— *Old Eng. Homilies* I. p. lvi, In Gothic we find plural forms in *-a*, as *worda*, &c., which are certainly older than the O.E. forms *word*, &c. *Ibid.* 312 Cp. the O.N. *lát*, *læti*. **1884** O.E. [used s.v. A *adj.*[1]]. **1884** O.H.G., O.N. [used s.v. A *adv.*]. **1887** W. W. SKEAT *Princ. Eng. Etymol.* 1st Ser. x. 172 The G. *trieb* (drove) is a modern form. The O.H.G. was *dreib* or *treib*. **1891** *Ibid.* 2nd ser. iii. 43 Lat. *u*..was sometimes long, as in Lat. *nūllum*, and sometimes short, as in Lat. *mŭltum*; and was developed accordingly. Hence O.F. *nul* (nyl) and *moult* (mult). **1901** G. FRANKAU *Eton Echoes* 48 Or pass to hear them say with eyes askance 'The siding ass! Suppose he's some O.E.' **1912** R. W. CHAMBERS *Widsith* 191 Kluge has pointed out that this form of the name corresponds to the O.N. *Atli*, as against the M.H.G. *Etzel*, O.H.G. *Ezzilo*. **1914** C. MACKENZIE *Sinister St.* II. III. i. 516 Come and have coffee with me after hall. One or two O.E.'s are coming in, but you won't mind? **1927** *Englische Studien* 10 Nov. 81 ON. *lifr* occurs in Norwegian river-names. **1934** M. K. POPE *From Lat. to Mod. Fr.* II. xi. 172 In educated Parisian speech the denasalisation of O.F. *ã* appears to have begun in the later sixteenth century. **1936** J. BUCHAN *Island of Sheep* vi. 112 He wore white linen breeches, a smartly cut flannel coat, and an O.E. tie. **1940** W. O. ROSS *M. E. Sermons* p. xxix, *S* appears very rarely for OE. *sc*. **1942** PARTRIDGE *Dict. Abbrev.* 70/1 *O.A.P.*, Old Age Pension(s). **1959** P. BULL *I know Face* x. 186 The O.A.P.s were very angry indeed, at not only having to witness *Waiting for Godot*, but also having to pay twelve pennies for the privilege. **1959** M. SCHLAUCH *Eng. Lang. in Mod. Times* i. 29 The [pronoun] forms which sprang from the OE and ON datives later assumed the function of accusatives as well. **1970** B. M. H. STRANG *Hist. English* iv. 274 A few native formations are calques on OF prepositions. **1972** M. L. SAMUELS *Linguistic Evol.* ii. 25 One of the best known of irreversible consonant-changes is that of voiceless plosives to fricatives or affricates, as in..OHG [p, t, k] > [pf, ts, kx]. **1972** E. J. DOBSON *Eng. Text of Ancrene Riwle* p. cxlix, OE (ON) *ā* is normally spelt *o*. **1973** 'B. GRAEME' *Two & Two* xiv. 139 'What about the Rexalls?' 'Apart from being O.A.P.s, I know nothing.' **1973** *Listener* 7 June 777/1 Tony sports an OE tie. **1976** *Evening Post* (Nottingham) 15 Dec. 19/7 (Advt.), Gamston Kennels (Est 1926)..Pedigree puppies ..Labradors, O.E. sheepdogs, Pekes, Poodles.

c. O.B.E., (Officer of the) Order of the British Empire; O.D.C., Order of Discalced Carmelites; O.M., Order of Merit; also by metonymy, a member of this Order; O.M.I. (see quot. 1907); O.P., Order of Preachers; O.S.A., Order of Saint Augustine; O.S.B. (examples); O.S.F.(C.), Order of Saint Francis (, Capuchin).

1798 J. MILNES *Life Challoner* 32 That zealous orthodox prelate..whose loss we at the present moment deplore, the Right Reverend Bishop Walmesley, O.S.B. *Ibid.*, Another person for whom he had deservedly the greatest respect and regard was the Rev. Pacificus Baker, O.S.F. **1839** *Dublin Rev.* May 556 English sermons were delivered by the Rev. Dr. Wiseman, F. Hughes, O.S.F., and the Rev. Messrs. McGill and Kyan. **1865** *Cath. Directory* p. lxii, Rev. F. Lawrence (Praxmarer), O.S.F.C. **1891** *Cath. Times* 6 Mar. 2/7 Very Rev. Dr Keane, O.P. **1903** *Who's Who* 760 Keppel, Hon. Sir Harry, G.C.B.; cr. 1857; O.M. **1907** *Cath. Encycl.* I. 28/1 *O.M.I.*, Oblati Mariæ Immaculatæ—Oblate Fathers of Mary Immaculate. *Ibid.*, *O.P.*, Ordo Prædicatorum—Dominicans. *Ibid.*, *O.S.A.*, Ordo (Eremitarum) Sancti Augustini—Augustinians. **1917** O.B.E. [see M.B.E. s.v. *M 5]. **1922** JOYCE *Ulysses* 312 Amongst the clergy present were..the rev. P. J. Cleary, O.S.F.; the rev. L. J. Hickey, O.P.; the very rev. Fr. Nicholas, O.S.F.C.; the very rev. B. Gorman, O.D.C.;.. the rev. T. Brangan, O.S.A.;..the rev. B. R. Slattery, O.M.I.; [etc.]. **1923** *Cornh. Mag.* June 765 A Captain and an O.B.E. **1937** B. JARRETT *Eng. Dominicans* (rev. ed.) 186 Consecrated Bishop of Tiberiopolis by Pope Benedict XIII, O.P. **1955** *Times* 9 Aug. 4/7 A person of the highest character, who served with distinction in both world wars and received the O.B.E. **1955** *Essays in Crit.* V. 430 Od's life, need an O.M. swear to the truth of an epigram? **1955** 'D. KNOWLES' *Relig. Orders in Eng.* II. 390/1 Ashbourne, Thomas, OSA. **1957** *Oxf. Dict. Chr. Ch.* 235/1 In England and Ireland they [*sc.* the Capuchins] sign O.S.F.C. ('Ordinis Sancti Francisci Capuccinorum'). **1963** I. WILKES *Brit. Init. & Abbrev.* 82/1 *ODC*, Order of Discalced Carmelites, 41, Kensington Church Street, London, W.8. **1969** I. & P. OPIE *Children's Games* p. xvi, We have also to thank Father Damian Webb O.S.B. **1972** *Bookseller* 2 Dec. 2543 (Advt.), Sister Mary Joyce O.P.

d. O. and M., organization and methods; OAO *Forces' slang*, one and only; OAO, orbiting astronomical observatory; O.A.S., on active service; O.A.S., Organisation de l'Armée Secrète, an organization opposed to Algerian independence from France; O.A.S., Organization of American States; O.A.U., Organization of African Unity; OB, obstetrics, obstetric, or obstetrician (*U.S.*); OB, order of battle; O.B., outside broadcast; O.B.U., One Big Union; O.C., officer commanding; OCR, optical character recognition; O.C.T.U., officer cadet(s') training unit; also *Octu* (ǫ·ktu); O.D. (*U.S.*) officer of the day; olive drab; O.D., ordinary seaman; O.D., Ordnance datum; OD, organization development; O.D., o.d., outside diameter; O.D. *slang* (orig. *U.S.*), overdose; so as *v. intr.*, to take an overdose; O.D.'d, overdosed, dead of an overdose; O.D.V. *joc.*, eau-de-vie; O.E.C.D., Organization for Economic Co-operation and Development; O.E.D., Oxford English Dictionary; O.E.E.C., Organization for European Economic Co-operation; O.E.O. (*U.S.*), Office of Economic Opportunity; OGO, orbiting geophysical observatory; O.H.C., ohc., overhead camshaft; O.H.M.S., on His (or Her) Majesty's Service; O.H.V., o.h.v., overhead valve; O.K., see *O.K. *a.*, *sb.*, and *v.* (as main entry); O level, Ordinary level (of the General Certificate of Education examination); hence *O leveller*; O.N.C., Ordinary National Certificate; o.n.o., or near(est) offer; O.O.W., Officer of the Watch; O.P. (*b*) (earlier and later examples); (*d*) (examples); (*e*) observation post (also *O. Pip*); OPEC (ōu·pek), Organization of Petroleum-Exporting Countries; O.P.M., other people's money (*U.S. slang*); O.P.M., output per man; O.R., OR, operational research; O.R., other ranks; O.R.T.F., Office de Radiodiffusion-Télévision Française, formerly the state television and radio service of France; O.S., ordinary seaman; O.S., Ordnance Survey; O.S., outsize; OSHA, Occupational Safety and Health Act (or Administration) (*U.S.*); OSO, orbiting solar observatory; OSO, Ordnance Survey Office; O.S.S. (*U.S.*), Office of Strategic Services; OTB, off-track betting (*U.S.*); O.T.C., Officers' Training Corps; O.T.C., Organization for Trade Co-operation; OTC, over the counter; O.T.U., Operational Training Unit; O.U., Open University; O.U.D.S., Oxford University Dramatic Society; cf. also *OUDS; O.V.R.A. [see quot. 1961], the secret police of Fascist Italy.

1958 *Daily Mail* 3 July 4/3 Modern business techniques using 'work study' and the 'O. and M.' treatment (Organisation and Methods), can prove 'a considerable help to us in the hospitals'. **1965** *New Statesman* 7 May 707/2 An O & M survey should swiftly be initiated to decide what dead wood needs to be cut out. **1971** K. GOTTSCHALK in B. de Ferranti *Living with Computer* v. 46 Groups concerned with efficiency in the office are sometimes called organization and methods (O & M) groups. **1936** *Nat. Geogr. Mag.* June 778/2 Or she may be the OAO—the One and Only. **1967** *Everybody's Mag.* (Austral.) 18 Jan. 36/2 In each war, a new vocabulary is created. Today, in Vietnam, Australians are again catching up on American Army slang... All would refer to a special girlfriend as their OAO—one and only. Probably, the OAO was met on skirt patrol. **1962** F. I. ORDWAY et al. *Basic Astronautics* iv. 119 An OAO is seen in Fig. 4.2. **1971** *McGraw-Hill Yearbk. Sci. & Technol.* 300 Although the first OAO malfunctioned, the second one (launched on Dec. 7, 1968) has..produced a wealth of important new astronomical data. **1928** BLUNDEN *Undertones of War* 178, I remember your superscriptions, 'O.A.S.' and 'B.E.F.'. **1962** *Listener* 4 Jan. 10/2 An O.A.S. bomb. **1963** *Times* 14 Mar. 16/2 Algeria at the period when O.A.S. terrorism was at its height. **1973** C. EGLETON *Seven Days to Killing* vii. 78 He was an Algerian colonist..and the French police had long been satisfied that he had never been connected with the OAS. **1949** *Ann. Organization Amer. States* I. No. 1. (title-page), Charter of the OAS. **1972** *Buenos Aires Herald* 3 Feb. 7/6 The juridical commission of the Organization of American States (OAS) has condemned the sending of British troops to Honduras. **1974** *Greenville* (S. Carolina) *News* 22 Apr. 3/5 Kissinger was asked why he had not mentioned Cuba in a speech Saturday to the Organization of American States (OAS) meeting in Atlanta. **1964** *Ann. Reg. 1963* 322 Organisation of African Unity (O.A.U.). Established at Conference of African Heads of State at Addis Ababa, 22–26 May 1963. **1971** *Sunday Nation* (Nairobi) 11 Apr. 7/1 The announcement had little to do with any assumed prevailing trends among members of the OAU. **1944** DORLAND & MILLER *Med. Dict.* (ed. 20) 1005/1 *O.B.*, abbreviation for *obstetrics*. **1967** *Boston Globe* 21 May 9/3 Sitting in an office for an OB check. *Ibid.* 9/4 A two hour wait in the OB's office. **1972** *Daily Colonist* (Victoria, B.C.) 29 Feb. 2/1 My last checkup with my OB doctor revealed a fibroid tumor. **1946** CHANDLER & ROBB *Front-Line Intelligence* xii. 137 O/B (Order of Battle) is a military science whose mission is to determine: (1) How strong the enemy is, [etc.]. **1950** *Tactics & Techniques Infantry* (U.S.) II. ii. 312 The order of battle (OB) team. **1971** *Combat Intelligence* (U.S. Dept. Army, Field Manual 30-5) vii. 7-1 Order of battle (OB) is the identification, strength, command structure, and disposition of the personnel, units, and equipment of any military force. **1975** tr. *Melchior's Sleeper Agent* (1976) III. 192 He'd sent him on to the Corps OB team, to see if there was anything in the latest Order of Battle book. **1927** *B.B.C. Handbk. 1928* 143/1 Outside Broadcast Features... Every O.B. of the simplest..nature necessitates the provision of two complete telephone line circuits..between the site of the performance and the Station Control Room. **1960** *Punch* 17 Feb. 251/1 Oh, I agree, it's [television is] splendid for sport and O.B.s. **1971** R. BUSBY *Deadlock* xiii. 200 You'd think he was the bloody big white chief instead of an OB technician. **1919** *Camp Worker* (Vancouver) 17 May 5/3 At Medicine Hat the Federated Railway Trades have unanimously endorsed the O.B.U. **1931** 'D. STIFF' *Milk & Honey Route* 210 *O.B.U.*, One Big Union. The ideal of the soap boxers. **1977** *Guardian Weekly* 11 Sept. 10/2 The Industrial Workers of the World... In Canada its counterpart was called the OBU, One Big Union..an attempt to prevent divisions in the labour movement by creating a single trade union. **1904** *N.Y. World Mag.* 1 May 6/5 'O.C.' is the officer in charge. **1917** F. M. FORD *Let.* 19 Feb. (1965) 84 It suits me better to write: 'O.C. Canadous will detail a fatigue party of 1 NCO & 10 men at 4:30 a.m.' **1928** T. E. LAWRENCE *Let.* 2 May (1938) 600 Also [you will inherit] my copyrights which now no longer include *Revolt in the Desert*: but you will be O.C. *The Seven Pillars*. **1967** G. F. FIENNES *I tried to run a Railway* iii. 25 He had been a gunner himself and had warned the O.C. of the 15 inch crew. **1966** *Computer Jrnl.* IX. 224/2 We decided to experiment to see what limitations, if any, O.C.R. would place on our stationery design. **1970** *Brit. Printer* July 57/1 The alphabet itself does not have any practical OCR use at all. **1942** E. WAUGH *Put out More Flags* ii. 121 'O.C.T.U. candidates,' said the company sergeant-major. **1972** D. MCLACHLAN *No Case for Crown* iv. 56 He reminded me sometimes of a sergeant who gave me hell in my O.C.T.U. **1929** *Papers Mich. Acad. Sci., Arts & Lett.* X. 311 *O.D.*, I, the officer of the day; II, olive drab. **1966** *Sunday Times* (Colour Suppl.) 4 Dec. 73/2 GI Jargon *OD*, officer of the day, or olive drab (both the colour and the uniforms themselves, e.g. 'I'm wearing my ODs tonight'). **1915** *Recruiter's Bull.* (U.S.) June 17/2 Two O.D. shirts you next slip in, A pair of shoes goes in between. **1975** tr. *Melchior's Sleeper Agent* (1976) III. 173 He was clad only in his OD shorts and undershirt. **1916** 'TAFFRAIL' *Pincher Martin* i. 7 'Strumbles,' he said, ''ere's another O.D. come to join your mess.' **1962** GRANVILLE *Dict. Sailors' Slang* 83/1 *O.D.* Naval colloquialism for ordinary seaman. *OS* or *Ord* is the official abbreviation. **1926** J. MALCOLM *Agric. Surveying* v. 123 The datum adopted in the Ordnance Survey of Great Britain, denoted by the letters O.D., was what was considered in 1844 to be mean sea level at Liverpool... The new datum is mean sea level at Newlyn. **1956** *Railway Mag.* Mar. 185/2 The top of the wall at the Barmouth end is 35 ft. above Ordnance Datum, dropping to 28 ft. above O.D. at the slipway. **1972** L. ALCOCK *By South Cadbury* ii. 25 Roughly one quarter of the hill-top, lying above four hundred and ninety feet O.D., forms a broad summit ridge. **1972** *Times* 5 June 22/6 OD. not infrequently causes strong reactions among managers. **1976** BLAKE & MOUTON (*title*) Diary of an OD man.

1930 Walker & Crocker *Piping Handbk.* iv. 293 In sizes 14 in. and upward pipe is designated by its outside diameter (O.D.) and the wall thickness is specified. **1963** H. R. Clauser *Encycl. Engin. Materials* 120/1 Nonferrous castings are produced commercially in o.d.'s ranging from about 1 in. to 6 ft. **1967** *Electronics* 6 Mar. 15/2 (Advt.), The screw-on has an OD of only $\frac{1}{8}$ inch with a mated length of only one inch. **1960** R. G. Reisner *Jazz Titans* 162 *O.D.*, an overdose of narcotics. **1971** *Black World* Apr. 38/1 A truly brilliant Black filmmaker goes into his grave at 24..an O.D. takes him, he loses a battle of several years—the 'stuff' wins. **1972** *Telegraph* (Brisbane) 17 Oct. 70/6 A fatal dosage of drugs—*O.D.* (*successful overdose*). **1970** S. O'Callaghan *Drug Addiction in Britain* xii. 151 Diana has O.D.'d and she's dead. **1969** R. De Sola *Abbrev. Dict.* (rev. ed.) 196/1 *Od'd*, overdosed (dope addict). **1973** *Black World* Aug. 55/1 The garbage collectors found Little Prez in the alley near Six-trey, OD'd away, layin' there cool and stiff. **1839** *Picayune* (New Orleans) in *Spirit of Times* (N.Y.) 5 Oct. 368/3 Why, that in French, is nothing but O.D.V. **1886** H. Baumann *Londinismen* 124/1 *O.D.V.*,..Branntwein, Spiritus. **1965** *Acronyms & Initialisms Dict.* (Gale Research Co.) 530 *ODV*, taken from pronunciation of French eau-de-vie and used to refer to brandy. **1960** *Times* 25 Nov. 10/7 The 20 members of O.E.C.D. are the 18 full members of O.E.E.C., together with the United States and Canada. **1971** *Power Farming* Mar. 15/1 European standards, issued by the Organization for Economic Co-operation and Development (O.E.C.D.) and the European Committee of Associations of Manufacturers of Agricultural Machinery (C.E.M.A.). **1898** Morris *Austral English* p. xviii, The practice of the 'O.E.D.' has been followed in this respect. **1962** *New Yorker* 10 Mar. 132/2 The compositor..who began setting type for the O.E.D. in 1884 and was still at it when the last volume came off the presses in 1928. **1973** *Daily Tel.* 20 Oct. 11/5 The word *hoax*..at present connotes more of the mischief than of the humour mentioned in the O.E.D.'s leisurely definition. **1976** *Times* 15 Apr. 13/8 'Fanatical', in the strict OED sense of the word, is surely..appropriate..to describe those serried ranks. **1948** *News Chron.* 13 Sept. 1/2 The job they were doing had been given them by O.E.E.C. **1964** *Listener* 13 Aug. 222/2, I was nearly four years chairman of what was then called the O.E.E.C. **1965** *Economist* 17 Apr. 297/1 The testimony of..the head of the Office of Economic Opportunity, revived the emotions of last year, when Congress established the OEO. **1974** *Black Panther* 16 Mar. 4/3 Congressman Dellums is co-sponsor of a tax reform measure that will work to the same end and has fought to save the programs that were funded through the Office of Economic Opportunity (OEO). **1961** *Sat. Rev.* (U.S.) 6 May 71/3 (Advt.), Each spacecraft in the OGO series will be capable of carrying up to 50 selected scientific experiments in a single flight. **1969** *Times* 4 June 5/1 The satellite being prepared for launch tomorrow..is the sixth and last of Orbiting Geophysical Observatories (OGO). **1974** *McGraw-Hill Yearbk. Sci. & Technol.* 346/2 Figure 2 shows an altitude-density profile through the plasmasphere measured by the *Ogo 5* satellite. **1932** O.H.C. [see O.H.V. below]. **1954** P. H. Smith *Design & Tuning of Competition Engines* iv. 57 The merits of the double o.h.c. arrangement lie mainly in the substitution of rotary for reciprocating motion right up to the valves. **1977** *Drive* Sept.–Oct. 113/1 *Ohc*, overhead camshaft. **1895** *Brewer's Dict. Phr. & Fable* (new ed.) 904/2 *O.H.M.S.*, On His (or Her) Majesty's Service. **1907** *Yesterday's Shopping* (1969) 338/2 In accordance with the provisions of the Post Office Protection Acts, Envelopes with 'O.H.M.S.' or 'On His Majesty's Service', will only be supplied to those persons who have authority to use them. **1952** L. Durrell *Spirit of Place* (1969) 115, I think one or two white lined notebooks, official Foreign Office Stationery labelled OHMS. **1972** P. Cleife *Slick & Dead* I. i. 17 Nearly all the flying I've done has been O.H.M.S. I don't think I go much on civil operations. **1932** F. J. Camm *Motor Car Upkeep* i. 15 (*caption*) Three common types of Valve Gear: Side-by-side, overhead valve (O.H.V.), operated by rocker, and overhead valves (O.H.C.), operated by camshaft. **1958** *Engineering* 28 Feb. 265/1 It is a two-door all-steel saloon of unit construction with..a flat twin air-cooled o.h.v. 600 c.c. four-stroke engine. **1968** Burdett & Ellis *Motor Vehicle Mechanics' Course* II. v. 102 The filling of the cylinder is much improved by this design, particularly where the O.H.V. is placed towards the other side of the chamber. **1949** *Joint Matric. Board Exam. for G.C.E. 1951* 6 If a language is to be specially approved..at the O level. **1959** *Times* 3 June 8/1 O level in any subject was 'very O'. **1974** *Times* 6 July 21/3 (Advt.), Expense account—plus £25 for an 'O' level man 17–22. **1961** *Listener* 26 Oct. 659/2 The £6-odd offered (per week) by banks and post offices, etc., to sixteen-year-old 'O' levellers. **1949** *Educ. in 1948*, 44 (*caption*) in *Parl. Papers 1948–9* (Cmd. 7724) XIV. 345 O.N.C. **1962** in H. O. Beecheno *Introd. Business Stud.* p. iii, Mr. Beecheno has written a comprehensive introduction to the commercial world. It is intended particularly for the ONC and HNC student. **1977** P. Carter *Under Goliath* xv. 79 'Our Billy got the G.C.E.,' I said. '*And* the O.N.C. He is going in for the Higher National now.' **1958** *Listener* 6 Nov. 732/1 'O.o.o' means 'one owner only', whereas 'o.n.o.' means 'or near offer'. **1973** *Country Gentlemen's Mag.* Mar. 183/1 Coffee set, thirteen pieces, £5 o.n.o. plus postage. **1977** *Drive* Sept.–Oct. 113/1 *Ono*, or nearest offer. **1923** *Man. Seamanship* (Admiralty) II. ii. 48 Any man discovering a fire..is to send a message to the O.O.W. immediately. **1958** *Spectator* 1 Aug. 169/3, I hear that the archaic and old-fashioned Officer of the Watch (briefly, OOW) is to be changed to Period Progress and Procedure Organiser and Overseer. **1790** T. Wilkinson *Mem.* II. 226 So, on their not complying with my expectations and proposals, we parted with mutual disdain, rage, and anger at O.P. and P.S. **1919** Wodehouse *My Man Jeeves* 45 Lady Malvern was a hearty..female,..measuring about six feet from the O.P. to the Prompt Side. **1933** O.P. [see *flood *sb.* 6*]. **1859** G. Simpson *Let.* 19 Nov. in *Geo. Eliot Lett.* (1954) III. 209 He says you tell him Clerical Scenes is O.P. **1921** A. Bennett *Let.* 4 Sept. (1966) I. 296 It seems to me that.. *The Old Wives' Tale* ought not to be o.p. **1916** F. M. Ford *Let.* 23 Aug. (1965) 69 George V..really was in some danger. At least he was in an O.P. that was being shelled fairly heavily. **1972** L. Lamb *Picture Frame* ii. 20 Gerry's no fool, but we don't think our o.p. has been rumbled. **1960** *Times* 15 Sept. 11/4 The conference adopted the (Iraq) proposal to establish an 'Organization of Petroleum-Exporting Countries'...The five participating states are founder-members of O.P.E.C. **1975** *Petroleum Economist* Aug. 282/1 For eighteen months the problem of OPEC's surplus oil revenues has occupied the minds of western statesmen, bankers and economists. **1916** *War Illustr.* 7 Oct. 185/1 A French 'O-Pip' in the Hills. **1919** J. Masefield *Battle of Somme* 88 Some of them were quite good trees, and we had an O. Pip in one of them (artillery observation post). **1943** Hunt & Pringle *Service Slang* 49 *O pip*, an Observation Post of the Field Artillery. ['Pip' stood for 'P' in the services' phonetic alphabet.] **1901** 'J. Flynt' *World of Graft* iv. 169 It cost me nothing to play the game, because I played it with O.P.M. (other people's money). **1969** *Time* 15 Aug. 60 No institution manages more 'O.P.M.', or Other People's Money, than Manhattan's 116-year-old United States Trust Co. **1946** J. Jewkes in *Manch. Sch. Econ. & Social Stud.* XIV. 4 Of two industries that with the higher O.P.M. is not necessarily the more efficient. *Ibid.* 5 O.P.M. may always be increased by installing new machinery but it may be the quickest way to the bankruptcy court. **1969** *New Scientist* 5 June 543 The UK with much higher R & D spending..had only a third of Japan's growth in output per man (OPM) employed. **1953** *Operational Research Q.* IV. 72 The evolution of O.R...is reflected by the number of publications. **1960** *Times* 17 Mar. 2/7 We shall require evidence of experience in either O.R. or cybernetics. **1964** T. W. McRae *Impact of Computers on Accounting* v. 118 A good number of O.R. problems can be solved by using nothing more powerful than a desk calculator. **1969** J. Argenti *Managem. Techniques* 107 Courses on OR designed for managers. **1942** Partridge *Dict. Abbrev.* 72/1 O.R., other ranks, i.e. ranks other than officers. **1947** J. Bertram *Shadow of War* vii. ii. 217 The heavy work in the camp was done by N.C.O.s and O.R.s., known as 'camp-employed'. **1967** J. Porter *Chinks in Curtain* xv. 147, I..tried to invoke the officer/O.R. relationship. **1964** *Economist* 30 May 945/2 The new [French] broadcasting service will be called ORTF, *Office de Radiodiffusion Télévision Française.* **1969** *Listener* 27 Mar. 410/2 The ORTF is never happier than with the state visit to Paris of the President of some French-speaking African statelet. **1977** *Rep. Comm. Future of Broadcasting* ii. 15 In France, years of feuding between government and broadcasters led in 1974 to the dissolution of the ORTF. **1894** *Gloss. Terms Evidence R. Comm. Labour* 60/1 in *Parl. Papers 1893–4* (C. 7063) XXXVIII. 411, *O.S.*, an abbreviation for 'ordinary seaman'. **1908** *Army & Navy Gaz.* 7 Nov. 1066/1 The two marines, a stoker, and an O.S. caged like rats in a trap. **1914** C. F. Tweney *Dict. Naval & Mil. Terms* 164 *O.S.*, Ordinary Seaman; one who has undergone training as a ship's boy, but who is not fully qualified as a seaman. **1962** O.S. [see O.D. above]. **1962** *Punch* 10 Oct. 534/3 A good submarine forest, marked on the OS map. **1971** A. Hunter *Gently at Gallop* ii. 20 At the summit of the rise.. stood an O.S. triangulation pedestal. **1907** *Yesterday's Shopping* (1969) 768/1 O.S. Night Dresses... O.S. Chemises. **1927** *Daily Express* 3 Nov. 7 Forty inches at the hips would be O.S. A woman with 60 inches at the hips would be O.O.S., or extra outsize. **1973** *Country Gentlemen's Mag.* Mar. 184/1 For sale owing to loss of weight, full length O.S. evening dress, deep mauve velvet ..will accept £15. **1971** *New Acronyms & Initialisms* (Gale Research Co.) 56/1 *OSHA*, Occupational Safety and Health Act (1970). *OSHA*, Occupational Safety and Health Administration (Department of Labor). **1975** V. Bush (*title*) Safety in the construction industry: OSHA. **1976** G. & H. Matwes (*title*) A retailer's guide to OSHA. **1938** *Times* 2 Feb. 18/1 He could say that it would launch the O.S.O. on a new programme. **1962** *Daily Tel.* 8 Mar. 19/6 Yesterday the American National Aeronautics and Space Administration launched..the first of a new series of satellites, the orbiting solar observatories. The first was called OSO–1. **1971** *McGraw-Hill Yearbk. Sci. & Technol.* 301 Each OSO contains instruments that monitor the UV and x-ray radiation emitted by the entire solar disk. **1943** *Newsweek* 25 Jan. 26/2 OSS is the planning agency in psychological warfare for the Joint Chiefs of Staff. **1972** K. Benton *Spy in Chancery* viii. 83 We were together in Italy at the end of the war. I was in the OSS and he'd switched over to MI 6. **1964** *Horsemen's Jrnl.* Jan. 69/2 The political sponsors of the bill have figures and plans on how to 'cut-up' the tax dollar taken through O.T.B. **1971** *New Yorker* 31 July 65 Seems that the OTB computers that are linked with those at the race track developed a colic or something, and wagers at the fourteen shops around town had to be recorded manually. **1975** *Ibid.* 16 June 101/2 The OTB shops around town took in $2,442,589, of which $1,649,591 was bet on the Belmont. **1909** *Captain* XXI. p. xiv/1 Senior Divisions of the O.T.C. **1974** 'M. Innes' *Mysterious Commission* xiv. 124 He had also done rather well in what, during his public-school days, had still been called the O.T.C. **1955** *Times* 12 Aug. 8/6 The United States Congress rose without voting on President Eisenhower's proposal for entry into the O.T.C., and it cannot now be dealt with until next year. **1965** *Acronyms & Initialisms Dict.* (Gale Research Co.) 543 *OTC*, over-the-counter (Pharmacy). **1974** M. C. Gerald *Pharmacol.* ii. 20 Nonprescription (over-the-counter, OTC) sleep-facilitating products. **1976** *National Observer* (U.S.) 4 Sept. 1/3 Fourteen prescription remedies—mostly antihistamines—be sold as nonprescription, or over-the-counter (OTC) drugs. **1942** *R.A.F. Jrnl.* 3 Oct. 31 At last O.T.U. and the introduction to real aircraft. **1966** Gurnett & Kyte *Cassell's Dict. Abbrev.* 163/1 *O.T.U.*, Operational Training Unit. **1969** *Guardian* 23 July 9/3 Milton Keynes, seat of the OU from September. **1975** *Times* 28 Aug. 12/5 The OU campus seems to have a strangely insular attitude... Town and gown seldom mix. **1886** *Oxford Tatler* 15 May 35/2 No one will be surprised to hear the O.U.D.S. does not intend to put another play on the stage this term. **1959** *Oxf. Univ. Gaz.* 9 Mar. 740/2 An O.U.D.S. producer might be a clear bet for the B.B.C., a bridge and chess expert for data-processing. **1976** J. Cooper *Harriet* ii. 18 She'd seen him..in the OUDS production of *Cat on a Hot Tin Roof.* **1930** *Times* 4 Dec. 15/3 All these arrests are said to have been made by the 'O.V.R.A.', a special section of the police, dependent directly on the Ministry of the Interior. These letters are supposed in some quarters to stand for 'Organizzazione di Vigilanza Riservata sulle Associazione', whereas other persons explain the last two initials as standing for 'Repressione di Anti-Fascismo'. **1941** W. Graham *Night Journey* viii. 98 Supposing the Gestapo cut their agreement with Bonini and communicate with the O.V.R.A. **1958** *Listener* 21 Aug. 278/3 The O.V.R.A. (or Italian secret police) was by no means incompetent. **1961** C. F. Delzell *Mussolini's Enemies* i. 41 The first of these sections was the OVRA, established late in 1927 as a 'special inspectorate' with headquarters in Milan, but soon extended throughout the country. The precise meaning of the initials is still uncertain, according to the knowledgeable Guido Leto, who headed the dread agency from 1938 until 1943. [Note] Three interpretations have been suggested: 'Organizzazione di Vigilanza e Repressione dell'Antifascismo ('Organization for Vigilance and Repression of Anti-Fascism'); Organo di Vigilanza dei Reati Antistatali ('Organ of Vigilance for Anti-State Crimes'); and Opera Volontaria di Repressione Antifascista ('Voluntary Agency for Anti-Fascist Repression').

e. In *Chem. o-* (usu. italic) signifies *ortho-* (Ortho- 2 b).

1889 G. M'Gowan tr. *Bernthsen's Text-bk. Org. Chem.* xvi. 310 Thus, *o*-diamido-benzene is that one which results from the reduction of *o*-dinitro-benzene. **1926** A. Davidson *Intermediates for Dyestuffs* v. 109 *o*-Tolidine is used in making azo dyes of the same types as those derived from benzidine. **1968** R. O. C. Norman *Princ. Org. Synthesis* xi. 387 The use as a protective group is illustrated by the synthesis of *o*-nitroaniline. **1971** [see *m*- s.v. *M 5].

6. Used with reference to the shape of the letter, as *O-ring*, a gasket (usu. in the form of a ring) with a circular cross-section.

1955 J. Yarwood *High Vacuum Technique* (ed. 3) i. 60 In many ways, the best solution is the 'o' ring gasket made of rubber or, preferably, oil-resisting neoprene cord, of circular cross-section. **1959** H. Barnes *Oceanogr. & Marine Biol.* iv. 182 The sphere [*sc.* the Deep Sea Benthograph] has five openings, the largest of which is a 15-in. diameter access door closed by a cast steel plate bolted in place and sealed by two neoprene O-rings. **1971** C. M. Blow *Rubber Technol. & Manuf.* x. 443 The O-ring is very widely used, though some designers prefer the rectangular, D, or delta sections. **1975** G. Anderson *Coring* iv. 77 The pycnometer has a breech-locked lid which utilizes an 'O' ring for pressure sealing.

O, *sb.*[1] Add: **2.** Also *Comb.*

1917 'H. H. Richardson' *Fortunes R. Mahony* iii. iii. 196 He stood o-mouthed and absent-minded.

3. Name of one of several gauges of track in model railways: specifically 32 mm.; so *O gauge.* Also *OO*, $16\frac{1}{2}$ mm., *OOO* 10 mm., etc.

1905 W. Ives *Something for Boys* 3 *Rails, crossings, switches*, with automatic lock action. No. O gauge, $1\frac{3}{8}$ in. **1922** *Everyday Science* Nov. 441/1 (*heading*) No. OO gauge model 'table' railways. *Ibid.*, I am pleased to see that a small gauge, i.e., 'oo' gauge, railway, is to be placed on the market shortly. **1924** H. Greenly *Model Railways* i. 3 A plan is given of Mr. H. L. Stevens' No. O gauge railway. *Ibid.* vi. 103 *No. OO Gauge 'Table' Railways.*—This standard gauge has been recently introduced by the writer..to provide for those who are limited in space to that of an ordinary dining-room table...The actual gauge is 16 mm. ($\frac{5}{8}$ in.). **1932** P. Bloomfield *Imaginary Worlds* ii. 34 Pretending..that our O gauge railway round the nursery floor is really the line taken by the 'Flying Scotsman'. **1967** C. J. Freezer *Model Railway Terminol.* 3, O. Gauge: 32 mm. Scale: 7 mm. Limited commercial support, but..in a flourishing condition. *Ibid.*, OO. Gauge: 16·5 mm. Scale: 4 mm. The most popular gauge in Britain. Fully supported commercially with ample selection of models.

-o, *suffix*[2]. Perh. connected with O *int.* 3 and reinforced by the final syllable of abbrev. forms such as Compo, Hippo, Photo, etc. The use of the suffix is widespread in English-speaking countries but nowhere more so than in Australia (e.g. *afto*, *arvo, *Commo, etc.).

a. Forming colloq. or slang equivalents added as a final syllable to (*a*) shortened forms of sbs., as *ag(g)ro* [f. *aggr(avation* or *aggr(ession*], *ammo, *beano, *combo, *compo[2], *metho[1], etc.; (*b*) sbs., as *boyo, *bucko, *kiddo, etc.; (*c*) adjs., as *cheapo*, *deado.*

1967 J. Burke *Till Death us do Part* ii. 31 You can buy that cheapo, cos no one wants it. **1969** *It* 13–25 June 16/2 Hustle the bread from whatever source you can... If all the above sounds like too much aggro don't..go and..run your benefit event in conjunction with an existing club. *Ibid.* 10–23 Oct. 10/1 At the moment kids are split up into different subcultural groups which have been driven by the system into a permanent state of aggro with each other. **1969** *Daily Mail* 8 Nov. 8/3 How do we get past him, man? Like he might start some agro. **1970** *Observer* 11 Jan. 28/2 Hippies and aggro-boys may look collectively and individually startling, pretty or repulsive according to tribal loyalty. **1973** A. Hunter *Gently French* iii. 29, I gets hold of the bastard and tries to pull him up. Then I sees he's bloody deado. **1973** M. Amis *Rachel Papers* 65 It wasn't day-to-day aggro, nor the drooped, guilty, somehow sexless disgruntlement I had seen overtake many relationships. **1977** 'E. Crispin' *Glimpses of Moon* xi. 215 It was possible to judge..that his aggro was strictly verbal.

b. Forming personal (chiefly occupational) sbs. from non-personal sbs., as *bottle-o(h, *milko, *wino, etc.

c. Forming sbs. from adjs., as *PINKO, *WEIRDO, etc.

d. As a meaningless ending in other words, as *BILLY-O, **good-o*, *CHEERIO, *right*(*y*)*o*, etc.

oaf[2]. Abbrev. of *OFAY. *U.S.*

1941 J. Smiley *Hash House Lingo* 40 *Oaf*, white person (used by negroes).

oa·fishly, *adv.* [f. Oafish *a.* + -ly[2].] In an oafish or stupid manner.

1876 F. K. Robinson *Gloss. Whitby* 134/1 *Oafishly, oafly*, absurdly; foolishly. **1908** A. S. M. Hutchinson *Once aboard Lugger* I. vii. 38 The driver becomes temporarily idiot—stands us oafishly silent. **1958** P. Kemp *No Colours or Crest* vii. 137, I stared back oafishly at him from under the brim of my hat.

oafo (ōu·fo). *slang.* [f. Oaf + *-o[2].] A lout or hooligan. Also *attrib.*

1959 C. MacInnes *Absolute Beginners* 39, I eyed the oafo. *Ibid.* 184 The oafo lot went off laughing. **1962** R. Cook *Crust on its Uppers* i. 25 The middle classes..the working classes..not to mention the oafos.

oak. Add: **8. a.** *oak-scroll, -thicket.* **c.** *oak framed* adj. **d.** *oak-pale, -trunked* adjs.

1953 E. Simon *Past Masters* I. 47 On the walls..two oak-framed prints. **1977** *Times* 15 Oct. 8/2 The house.. had..an oak-framed porch. **1922** Joyce *Ulysses* 6 His fair oakpale hair stirring slightly. **1874** G. M. Hopkins *Jrnls. & Papers* (1959) 245 A beautiful spray-off of the dead oak-scrolls. **1846–7** Thoreau *Walden* (1957) 186 Pine woods and oak-thickets. **1934** Dylan Thomas *Let.* 21 Sept. (1966) 268 No One more welcome than the oak-trunked maestro—.

9. oak barren *U.S.* (earlier example); **oak cist, coffin** (see quot. 1957); **oak flat** *U.S.*, a level expanse of ground bearing a growth of oaks; **oakleaf braid** (see quots.); **oakleaf jar** (see quot. 1960); **oak-mast** (earlier example); **oak moss,** the lichen *Evernia prunastri* or one closely related to it, often found growing on oak trees and used to produce an aromatic extract; also the extract itself; also *attrib.*; **oak-opening** (earlier and later examples); **oak-pruner** *U.S.*, a longicorn beetle *Elaphidion villosum*, the larva of which mines down the centre of hardwood twigs, causing them to snap; now usually called the twig pruner; **oak room,** an oak-panelled room; **oak towel** *slang* (see quot.); **oak wilt** *U.S.*, a disease of oaks and certain other trees produced by the fungus *Ceratocystis fagacearum*, which causes the wilting and death of foliage and eventually kills affected trees; **oak yard** *U.S.*, an enclosure in which oaks are grown.

1811 *Weekly Reg.* 12 Oct. 101/2 Our oak barrens and underwooded plains may be profitably applied to sheep. **1937** E. V. Gordon tr. *Shetelig & Falk's Scand. Archaeol.* 146 Of similar type is the other well-known form of Norse bronze-age grave, the 'oak cist', a coffin made from a thick trunk of oak, split and hollowed out. **1968** G. Jones *Hist. Vikings* I. i. 19 The tannin of the 'oak cists' of Denmark, the very flesh and fell of the wearers. **1937** E. V. Gordon tr. *Shetelig & Falk's Scand. Archaeol.* 147 The complete picture of this personal equipment is obtained from the oak coffins mentioned earlier. **1957** T. C. Lethbridge *Gogmagog* viii. 132 Occasionally in Britain and more frequently in Denmark human bodies are found buried in what are known as 'oak coffins'. These are not coffins in the ordinary sense; but are large sections of tree trunks, split lengthwise and hollowed out to contain the body. **1964** W. L. Goodman *Hist. Woodworking Tools* 10 The remarkable wooden folding stool found with an oak-coffin burial at Guldhoj in Jutland. *a* **1816** B. Hawkins *Sk. Creek Country* (1848) 29 Oak flats, red and post oak,..on its left side. **1849** E. Chamberlain *Indiana Gazetteer* (ed. 3) 381 Beech and oak flats, which are adapted only to grass. **1954** *N. & Q.* June 273/1 *Oakleaf braid.*—This is the black braid supplied for hats of senior police officials and also used by St. John Ambulance. **1957** *Textile Terms & Definitions* (Textile Inst.) (ed. 3) 70 *Oakleaf braid*, a woven narrow fabric having a conventional oakleaf and acorn and border Jacquard design, now always black... It is used as a hatband for officials such as Police Inspectors. **1903** H. Wallis (*title*) Oak-leaf Jars: A fifteenth century Italian Ware showing Moresco Influence. **1960** R. G. Haggar *Conc. Encycl. Cont. Pott. & Porc.* 334/1 *Oak-leaf jars*, Tuscan fifteenth century maiolica drug pots painted with an oak-like..leaf decoration. **1849** E. Chamberlain *Indiana Gazetteer* (ed. 3) 17 Oak and beech mast is found in such quantities as to contribute largely both to feeding and fattening hogs. **1921** A. L. Smith *Lichens* x. 418 French perfumers extract an excellent perfume from *Evernia prunastri*.. known as 'Mousse des Chênes' (Oak moss), and it appears that the plants which grow on oak contain more perfume than those which live on other trees. **1921** *Times Lit. Suppl.* 25 Aug. 542/4 The oak-moss lichen is used as a basis for perfumes, the thallus on being soaked in spirit yielding a sweet and persistent odour. **1966** J. S. Cox *Illustr. Dict. Hairdressing* 104/2 Oak Moss Resin. Obtained from tree lichens, especially oak; used in perfumery. **1967** M. E. Hale *Biol. Lichens* iv. 59 These 'oak mosses' accumulated silicon, phosphorus, magnesium, iron and aluminium to a significant degree. **1975** F. Kennett *Hist. Perfume* vii. 148 The main ingredients of it [*sc.* Poudre de Chypre] are oakmoss (extracted from a species of lichen and still commonly used in perfumery, by the name *mousse de chêne*), rose-water, musk, civet, and a little sandalwood. **1830** J. M'Call in *Wisconsin State Hist. Soc. Coll.* (1892) XII. 185 From that up, on the right bank, it is oak openings. **1833** C. F. Hoffman *Winter in West* (1835) I. 142 At a sudden turning of the path, I came at once upon the 'oak openings'. **1839** C. M. Kirkland *New Home* xx. 133 The 'grubs' present a most formidable hindrance to all gardening efforts in the 'oak-openings'. **1848** J. F. Cooper *Oak Openings* I. i. 10 Giving their appellation to this particular species of native forest, under the name of 'Oak Openings'. **1882** *Econ. Geol. Illinois* II. vi. 104 There is an intermediate district occupied by oak-openings. **1970** *Daily Progress* (Charlottesville, Va.) 24 May 4/1 Trees and shrubs grew along the streams, on wooded knolls or ridges, and in occasional 'oak openings'. **1819** *Mass. Agric. Repository & Jrnl.* V. 308 From the effect of its labours, it may be called the oak pruner. **1838** *Mass. Zool. Survey Rep.* 92 The oak-pruner, so named by Prof. Peck, inhabits the white and black oaks. **1862** *Rep. Comm. Patents: Agric. 1861* (U.S. Dept. Agric.) 615 The black and white oak trees are infested with..the 'Oak-pruner'. **1899** D. Sharp in *Cambr. Nat. Hist.* VI. v. 286 *Elaphidion villosum* is called the oak-pruner in North America. **1849** Thackeray *Pendennis* I. xxiii. 213 On the other side [of the hall] the oak room. **1922** Joyce *Ulysses* 154 In the supper room or oakroom of the mansion house. **1971** D. Francis *Bonecrack* iii. 34 The account books.. are in the oak room. **1889** Farmer *Americanisms* 396/1 *Oak towel*..a stout oaken stick. There is an allusion here to 'wiping' or 'dressing one down'. **1942** *Bull. Wisconsin Agric. Exper. Stat.* No. 455. 75/1 Oak wilt, a disease now ravaging many fine Southern Wisconsin woodlots, is caused by a certain fungus. *Ibid.* 76/1 Thus far there is no way of controlling oak wilt. **1944** B. W. Henry et al. in *Phytopathology* XXXIV. 163 The present paper presents evidence on the significance, symptoms, and cause of a disease called oak wilt. **1957** J. M. Haller *Tree Care* ix. 148 The oak wilt came into prominence about seven years ago, spreading rapidly through the midwestern states. **1959** P. P. Pirone *Tree Maintenance* (ed. 3) xvi. 346 The oak wilt fungus appears to be most infectious early in the growing season. **1969** *New Scientist* 28 Aug. 430/2 They inoculate the weed oaks with the organism that causes oakwilt disease, *Ceratocystis fagacearum*. **1835** R. M. Bird *Hawks of Hawk-Hollow* II. v. 52 His father..had suddenly checked his horse at the entrance of the little oak-yard.

oaken, *a.* **4.** *oakenshaw* (further example).

1903 A. E. Housman 'The Oracles' in *Venture* I. 39 When winds were in the oakenshaws.

oa·kery. *U.S. rare.* [f. Oak + -ery.] An oak yard.

1838 C. Gilman *Recoll. Southern Matron* xxx. 213 Turning suddenly, he bounded over the fence into papa's oakery.

oa·kiness. [f. Oaky *a.*] The quality of being oaky.

1863 'G. Hamilton' *Gala-Days* 128 [In] the English Church..there is a general tone of oakiness, solid, substantial, sincere.

oak land, oak-land. Chiefly *U.S.* [Oak 8.] Land bearing a growth of oak-trees.

c **1658** in *Early Rec. Lancaster, Mass.* (1884) 271 Thare is another peice of upland..Sum part pine Land & partly oak Land. *Ibid.*, Sum part of it [is]..oake land. **1737** J. Wesley *Jrnl.* 2 Dec. (1909) I. 401 The land is of four sorts —pine-barren, oak-land, swamp, and marsh. **1751,** etc. [in Dict. s.v. Oak 8]. **1811** *Weekly Reg.* 28 Dec. 302/1 It was a piece of dry oak land. **1837** W. Jenkins *Ohio Gazetteer* 187 The soil of Franklin is, what is generally called oak land, being a mixture of clay, sand and gravel. **1849** E. Chamberlain *Indiana Gazetteer* (ed. 3) 209 The oak land is more extensive than the beech.

oaky, *a.* Add: **1.** *oaky-looking* adj.

1921 D. H. Lawrence *Sea & Sardinia* 165 Curious slim oaky-looking trees.

2. (Earlier example.)

a **1816** B. Hawkins *Sk. Creek Country* (1848) 62 The good land spreads out for four or five miles on both sides of the creek, with oaky woods.

-oan (ŏăn, ōu·ăn), *suffix. Min.* [f. *-o* (in Ferro-, -ous c, as against Ferri-, -ic 1 b) + *-i)an 2.] Used like *-ian 2, but denoting a lower valency than that suffix (see quot.).

1930 [see *-ian 2].

oar, *sb.* Add: **5. a.** (Further examples.) Also, *to get, shove*, etc., *one's oar in.* The primary sense is 'to interfere, to be (or become) meddlesome'.

1630 R. Brathwait *Eng. Gentleman* i. 11 Youth.. putting his oare in every mans boat. **1731** C. Coffey *Devil to Pay* I. ii. 12, I will govern my own House without your putting in an Oar. **1890** Barrère & Leland *Dict. Slang* II. 92/2 '*To shove in an oar*', to intermeddle, or give an opinion unasked. **1908** J. H. Shinn *Pioneers Arkansas* xxxii. 258 The idea is always to do the other fellow before he does you, and if he does get his oar in first, come back with remark called for brevity, 'The Retort Courteous'. **1916** 'Taffrail' *Pincher Martin* vii. 109 'It ain't fit an' proper fur gals o' your age to go abart unpertected like.'.. 'And who asked you to put your oar in, Mister Billings?' **1946** K. Tennant *Lost Haven* (1947) xiv. 224 He would probably go on talking all the morning, if a bloke didn't put in his oar. *Ibid.* 226 Look here, Dip. You're shoving in your oar, so I'll just tell you what I'm up against. **1968** J. R. Ackerly *My Father & Myself* ix. 87 One who preferred to stand outside of life and observe it not (as he would have phrased it) to 'put one's oar in'. **1977** *Film & Television Technician* Mar. 5/1 The more that the workers stick their oar into the administration of actual film production the more they will weaken their strength in negotiation for the improvement of wages and terms of employment. **1978** J. Anderson *Angel of Death* i. 6 Senior police officers couldn't go around saying things like that... He'd better get his oar in first.

6. oar-fish (examples); **oar-lop** now *obs.*, a lop-eared rabbit with its ears sticking out at right angles to its head; (the form *oar-lap* appears to be an error arising from the misprint in the source of quot. 1868).

1860 J. Richardson *Yarrell's Hist. Brit. Fishes* (2nd Suppl.) 27 (*heading*) Banks's oar-fish. **1880** A. C. L. G. Günther *Introd. Study Fishes* II. 522 They [*sc. Regalecus* species] are frequently called..'Oar-fishes', from their two ventral fins, which have a dilatation at their extremity not unlike the blade of an oar. **1925** J. T. Jenkins *Fishes Brit. Isles* 120 The name Oar-fish is derived from the presence of the two pelvic fins, which are..something like the blade of an oar. **1959** A. Hardy *Open Sea* II. iv. 76 The oar-fish *Regalecus glesne*.. is world-wide in distribution... It is the largest of the so-called ribbon-fish and..it looks almost like one's idea of the mythical sea-serpent. **1972** *N.Z. News* 31 May 3/2 Two small boys rowing their boat in the Otago Harbour.. bumped into a comparatively rare oar fish, 10 feet long and weighing about 100 pounds... Only about a dozen of the species, Regalecus pacificus, have been washed up on the New Zealand coast in the past 100 years. Oar fish are a deep-water variety. **1854** 'E. S. Delamer' *Pigeons & Rabbits* 136 The Oar-lop is the next stage of deflection, when the ears extend horizontally outwards on each side, forming a line that is more or less straight, giving the idea of a pair of oars which a waterman is resting out of the water. **1868** [see Lop *sb.*[7]]. **1872** C. Rayson *Rabbits* III. xiii. 71 The 'oar-lop'..is not fit for exhibition purposes. **1912** G. A. Townsend *Pract. Rabbit Keeping* vii. 62 If both ears stood out from the head at right angles, the rabbit was an 'Oar Lop'. **1933** F. L. Washburn *Rabbit Bk.* (ed. 2) ii. 55 The term 'oar-lop' was used to express the condition where the ears are horizontal.

oarlock. Add: Also *attrib.* in *oarlock seat.*

1874 J. W. Long *Amer. Wild-Fowl Shooting* 85 Both may row, if two sets of oarlock-seats are provided.

oarsman. (Earlier example.)

1811 *Weekly Reg.* I. xiv. 245/1 They certainly possess great dexterity as oarsmen.

oar-weed, now the usual spelling of Ore-weed; = *LAMINARIA. (Later examples.)

1917 *Chambers's Jrnl.* July 473/1 The 'oar weed' variety of seaweed..contains considerable supplies of potash. **1922** Joyce *Ulysses* 45 He climbed over the sedge and eely oarweeds. **1954** *New Biol.* XVII. 102 The broad oar-weeds, the Laminarias,..occupy the shore at low-water mark of spring tides and at greater depth. **1971** C. L. Duddington *Beginner's Guide to Seaweeds* iii. 47 The oarweeds (genus *Laminaria*) are large seaweeds that grow in the sublittoral zone, from just below low-tide mark down to a depth of about fifteen feet. The oarweeds are perennial plants. *Ibid.*, The oarweeds have a varied history of usefulness, first in the old kelp burning industry ..and later as a source of alginic acid and alginates.

oat, *sb.* Add: **4. d.** *to feel one's oats*, to be lively; to feel important, to display one's self-importance. *colloq.* (orig. *U.S.*).

1831 *Boston Even. Transcript* 22 Dec. 1/1 Whether the pony felt his oats,..He took a frightful canter. **1833** A. Lawrence *Diary & Corr.* (1855) 126 We both 'feel our oats' and our youth. **1843** T. C. Haliburton *Attaché* 1st Ser. II. 157 You know that, and you feel your oats, as well as any one. **1869** P. T. Barnum *Struggles & Triumphs* i. 33 My father..installed me as clerk in this country store. Of course I 'felt my oats'. **1897** C. M. Flandrau *Harvard Episodes* 85, I suppose he was feeling his oats when he captained his class eleven. **1959** *Listener* 5 Nov. 770/1 The new influences and pressures within a colony that was 'feeling its oats'. **1971** D. Lees *Rainbow Conspiracy* i. 17 The Manchester circulation is nudging the one and a half million a day mark and they are beginning to feel their oats.

e. *off one's oats* colloq., off one's food.

1890 Kipling in *Lippincott's Monthly Mag.* Aug. 254 I'm a bit restless and off my oats. **1898** *Bulletin* (Sydney) 17 Dec. (Red Page), The horse is a power in Australia, and a few choice expressions spring from horses..*out of collar* aptly describes out of work; *off his oats*, sickness or a state of offishness. **1930** Wodehouse *Very Good, Jeeves!* iv. 98 The poor kid, who's quite off her oats about him. **1949** D. M. Davin *Roads from Home* II. ii. 99 What's the matter, John? Off your oats this morning? **1977** J. Fleming *Every Inch a Lady* I. i. 5 It's not like to put me off me oats..but it's been a nasty day.

f. *one's oats*, sexual gratification. *slang.*

1923 J. Manchon *Le Slang* 209 *To have one's oats*, faire des bêtises avec une femme, courir la gueuse. **1941** Baker *Austral. Slang* 50 *Oats from* (*a woman*), *get one's*, to coit with a woman. **1961** X. Herbert *Soldiers' Women* 265 There's nothing makes a hot-shot sheik like that so mad as being asked to pay for his oats. **1965** W. Dick *Bunch of Ratbags* 188, I was kissing her excitedly and passionately. You're doin' O.K., Cookie, you're gonna get your oats tonight for sure, I thought to myself. **1968** A. Diment *Bang Bang Birds* v. 65 Despite her lovely body it was her face that had me hooked... I like to watch something pretty..when collecting my oats. **1976** P. Hill *Hunters* vii. 90 She wouldn't let you have your oats... You wanted to go to bed with her..she wouldn't have it. **1978** J. Wainwright *Jury People* xxxvi. 108 This wife he was lumbered with. Okay—he loved her... But, even *he* wanted his oats, occasionally. He was human.

5*. oats and chaff *Rhyming slang*, a footpath.

1857 'Ducange Anglicus' *Vulgar Tongue* 14 *Oats and chaff*,..footpath. **1935** A. J. Pollock *Underworld Speaks* 82/1 *Oats and chaff*, footpath.

6. *oat-bag, -straw* (earlier examples).

1851 A. O. Hall *Manhattaner* 5 It was a modest commercial plain..with..bits of machinery, and ploughs, and oat bags, and hay bales. *a* **1650** D. Calderwood *Hist.*

Kirk (1842–9) VI. 27 A scheaffe of oat straw was sold for fourtie shillings in Edinburgh. **1850** *Rep. Comm. Patents: Agric. 1849* (U.S. Dept. Agric.) 380 Getting no other food in winter but a scanty supply of oat-straw. **1859** A. CARY *Pict. Country Life* i. 7 [He] lay..with a bundle of oat-straw for his pillow.

b. oat burner *N. Amer. colloq.*, a horse; **oat cell** *Med.*, a small oval cell with little cytoplasm and an oval, densely staining nucleus which is characteristic of a type of carcinoma of the lung (formerly regarded as a sarcoma); freq. *attrib.* in *oat-cell carcinoma, tumour*, etc.; hence **oat-celled** *a.*, containing such cells; **oat(s opera** = *OATER².

1941 *Sun* (Baltimore) 21 July 11/4 There isn't a galloper in the lot who can say 'I'm the boss', so your milkman's oat burner might do just as well as any of 'em. **1952** *Daily News* (N.Y.) 20 Aug. C 11/4 When the time comes..that even an oat-burner must sport a tax stamp on its stem or stern. **1973** B. BROADFOOT *Ten Lost Years* v. 50 Them oatburners never broke down. **1903** W. S. L. BARLOW *Elem. Path. Anat. & Histol.* I. ix. 190 (*heading*) Oat cell Sarcoma. **1926** *Jrnl. Path. & Bacteriol.* XXIX. 244 In obvious carcinomata of the lung 'oat cells' have been found in addition to the more readily recognisable carcinoma cells. **1956** MAYER & MAIER *Pulmonary Carcinoma* iv. 96 Among anaplastic tumors belong the 'oat cell' carcinomas, called 'reserve cell' by some. **1957** A. I. SPRIGGS *Cytol. of Effusions* vi. 24 One of the most characteristic types of malignant cell is the oat-cell, so named after its appearance in histological sections. **1966** WRIGHT & SYMMERS *Systemic Path.* I. x. 418/1 The finding of tubules in 'oat-cell' tumours..should not affect the histological diagnosis. **1972** *Brit. Jrnl. Dis. Chest* LXVI. 164 Oat cell carcinomas have a more sinister prognosis. **1926** *Jrnl. Path. & Bacteriol.* XXIX. 244 The so-called 'oat-celled Sarcoma' of the posterior mediastinum is a medullary carcinoma of the bronchi. **1948** R. A. WILLIS *Path. Tumours* xix. 369 'Oat-celled' or spindle-celled structure ..is common in bronchial carcinoma. **1942** BERREY & VAN DEN BARK *Amer. Thes. Slang* § 608/9 *Western picture*, ..oats opera. **1947** *Richmond* (Virginia) *Times-Dispatch* 2 May 10/1 Roy Rogers, Gene Autry and other oat opera stars.

oat, *v.* (Earlier and later examples.)

1732 B. LYNDE *Diary* 9 May (1880) 26 Next morning.. dined at Hampton;..thence to Greenland, where oated, and for 2 horses and drink, 2s. **1741** *Ibid.* 27 Oct. 121 Breakfasted and oated our 3 horses, at Deacon Tucker's. **1855** P. T. BARNUM *Life* 70 Old 'Bob' was duly oated and watered.

oater² (ōᵘ·təɹ). Chiefly *U.S.* = **horse opera*.

1951 GREEN & LAURIE *Show Biz* 570/1 *Oater*, Western film. **1961** A. BERKMAN *Singers' Gloss. Show Business* 64 *Oater*, Western film. **1969** M. PEI *Words in Sheep's Clothing* (1970) iii. 22 'Western'..along with its synonyms, 'horse opera', 'oater'. **1975** *Radio Times* 10 Jan. 10/1 Borden (*Red River*) Chase wrote this expansive oater [sc. *Lone Star*] for Clark Gable.

oath, *sb.* Add: **1.** *under oath*, on or upon oath.

1712 [see UNDER *prep.* 14 b]. **1851** R. GLISAN *Jrnl. Army Life* (1874) viii. 83 He was then under oath not to drink for six months.

c. *my* (*colonial*, etc.) *oath*, a mild expletive or exclamation: yes! of course! upon my word! *Austral.* and *N.Z. slang.*

1859 H. KINGSLEY *Recoll. G. Hamlyn* II. vi. 94 'You're not fit company for any man except the hangman,' said Tom,..'Oh my — — (colonial oath!)' said the other; 'oh my — — cabbage tree!' **1895** J. KIRBY *Old Times in Bush* x. 143 The snake..made a hoop of hisself, and then, my oath, he did go. **1896** H. LAWSON *While Billy Boils* 203 (*title*) His colonial oath. *Ibid.*, 'My oath!' he replied... 'My blooming oath!' **1899** *Bulletin* (Sydney) 25 Feb. (Red Page), I don't mean the variety whose conversation consists of expectoration and 'Yer' or 'My — oath'. **1916** J. B. COOPER *Coo-oo-ee* i. 11 Ain't that like a woman with a man? My oath it is! I know 'em. **1925** H. H. COOK *Far Flung* 12 'Perhaps ye'll square up?'..'My oath!' cried the debtor. **1928** 'BRENT OF BIN BIN' *Up Country* xv. 255 'My—Colonial oath!' echoed Erroll. **1941** *Coast to Coast 1941* 45 'Who said I was going to give you a quid anyway?' 'You did.' 'My oath I didn't.' **1946** E. G. WEBBER *Johnny Enzed in Italy* 36 'All this us der merry laugh gives, no?' I said. 'My oath!' said the Bloke. 'My colonial oath!' **1952** M. TRIPP *Faith is Windsock* i. 7 'Pay twenties and twenty-ones.' 'My oath!' Bergen threw his cards (a king and a six) face down on the table. **1969** *Melbourne Truth* 12 July 3/4 Whitton, with his ear close to the receiver, listened to the reply. It was: 'My bloody oath I will.' **1974** N. MARSH *Black as he's Painted* iii. 73 'And that's when your headache really sets in, is it, Fred?' 'My oath! Well, take a look at it.' **1977** J. WAINWRIGHT *Do Nothin'* xi. 185 My oath—those couple of hours were some session.

5. *oath-breaker* (later example), *-keeper*, *-taking* (later examples); *oath-bound* adj. (later example); **oath-helper** = COMPURGATOR 1 b; hence *oath-helping* vbl. sb.

1939 W. B. YEATS *Last Poems* 8 That all are oath-bound men. *a* **1973** J. R. R. TOLKIEN *Silmarillion* (1977) ix. 83 For so sworn, good or evil, an oath may not be broken, and it shall pursue oathkeeper and oathbreaker to the world's end. **1891** Oath-helper [used s.v. COMPURGATOR 1 b]. **1902** *Encycl. Brit.* XXVIII. 331/1 One of the two litigants must prove his case, by his body in battle,.. or by an oath with oath-helpers. **1943** F. M. STENTON *Anglo-Saxon Eng.* ix. 312 It is probable that in the earliest time a man's 'oath-helpers' had been chosen exclusively from among his kin. *Ibid.* 313 Ine of Wessex orders that every person accused of homicide, whatever his status, must include at least one man of high rank among his oath-helpers. **1970** FOOTE & WILSON *Viking Achievement* xi. 375 After the man accused had made his statement on oath, then each of his oath-helpers swore that they believed his oath to be honest. **1973** A. HARDING *Law Courts Med. Eng.* 25 The Normans let the parties fight an actual physical battle, but the Anglo-Saxons preferred trial by ordeal or by oath-helping. *a* **1973** Oath-keeper [see *oath-breaker* above]. **1960** *News Chron.* 9 July 1/3 The Mau Mau oath-taking ceremonies. **1961** *Guardian* 29 Mar. 2/1 Recent reports of Mau-Mau oath-taking in Kenya.

oathing, *vbl. sb.* (Later examples.)

1961 *Guardian* 12 May 5/5, I don't attribute the oathing to the party. *Ibid.* 7 June 11/4 The oathing ceremonies at Meru last month when more than a thousand people took an undisclosed oath. **1969** *Daily Tel.* 9 Sept. 20/6 To a Christian, secret oathing is repugnant and unacceptable. *Ibid.*, Secret oathing ceremonies.

oatmeal. Add: **2*.** A greyish-fawn colour resembling that of oatmeal. Also *attrib.* or as *adj.*

1927 *Daily Express* 2 May 7 Colours: Beige, Oatmeal, [etc.]. **1935** A. CHRISTIE *Three Act Tragedy* III. ix. 188 The room..had walls of a rather drab oatmeal colour. **1939–40** *Army & Navy Stores Catal.* 636/2 All wool flannels. ..Oatmeal Shade. **1951** 'C. CARNAC' *It's her own Funeral* i. 10 The dark panelling made a good background to her oatmeal suit. **1951** *Catal. of Exhibits, South Bank Exhib, Festival of Britain* 58/2 Woman's oatmeal glacé gloves **1960** *House & Garden* May 61/2 Settee..covered in oatmeal tweed. **1961** *Guardian* 1 Feb. 7/5 Colours were pale green, oatmeal, navy. **1963** *Times* 27 Feb. 12/5 Contrasting cravats of silk or organza set off soft oatmeal or sand tones, pale *tilleul* greens, navy, black, off-white. **1970** [see *KINGFISHER 3]. **1973** 'R. MACLEOD' *Burial in Portugal* iii. 69 An oatmeal sports coat.

3. *oatmeal bread, stout*; **oatmeal mush** *U.S.*, porridge made with oatmeal; **oatmeal soap**, soap containing oatmeal as a mild abrasive.

1943 A. SIMON *Conc. Encycl. Gastron.* IV. 83/1 Oatmeal bread. **1974** R. B. PARKER *God save Child* (1975) xii. 86 He put a plate of sliced turkey..and a loaf of oatmeal bread on the table. **1883** H. P. SPOFFORD in *Harper's Mag.* Aug. 465/1 You've been the means of starving me.. on oatmeal mush. **1903** S. CLAPIN *New Dict. Amer.* 291 Oatmeal-mush. **1890–91** *T. Eaton & Co. Catal.* Fall & Winter 42 Colgate's soaps—oatmeal, [etc.]. **1897** *Sears, Roebuck Catal.* 19/1 (*heading*) 'Oat Meal' Toilet Soap. *c* **1938** *Fortnum & Mason Price List* 54/1 Soaps... Violet Oatmeal. **1977** *Honey* Nov. 55/2 Friction cleaning is most effective on blackheads... You can use Boots No 7. very mild oatmeal and lavender soap 89p. **1926–7** *Army & Navy Stores Catal.* 64/1 Oatmeal Stout (recommended for its tonic properties) doz. 9/-. **1976** J. B. HILTON *Gamekeeper's Gallows* iii. 26 If he wins, he always takes it [*sc.* a rabbit] a bottle of oatmeal stout home.

Oaxacan (o,æksā·kăn), *a.* [f. *Oaxaca* (see below) + -AN.] Of or pertaining to the southern Mexican state of Oaxaca.

1934 A. HUXLEY *Beyond Mexique Bay* 263 Our Oaxacan friend, Don Manuel, invited us one evening to join this endless procession. **1977** *Dædalus* Summer 88 This early Oaxacan elite was distinctly less sophisticated than the Olmec aristocracy of the neighboring Mexican Gulf Coast country.

ob., abbrev. of L. *obiit*, died: add examples.

1890 BARRÈRE & LELAND *Dict. Slang* II. 93/1 *Ob* (Winchester College), for *obit.* **1952** D. BALSDON *Freshman's Folly* iii. 141 The highly complexioned countenance of the Reverend Nathaniel Blunt, S.T.P., ob. 1782. **1978** C. JONES et al. *Study of Liturgy* II. i. vii. 57 *The Apostolic Tradition*, ascribed by many scholars to Hippolytus, the schismatic bishop of Rome (ob. A.D. 236, 237?).

ob (ǫb). A representation of a pronunciation of the word OF *prep.*, supposed to occur esp. in the speech of American Blacks.

1839 *Bentley's Misc.* VI. 263 He said de Queen ob Sheba wab a dark lady, may be bery dark. **1846** *Negro Singer's Own Bk.* 5, I am glad ob it, for my part. *Ibid.* 23 One day just at de set ob sun,..When de work war did an done. *Ibid.* 29, I tell you ob a scrape I had wid a gal. **1848** S. C. FOSTER *Old Uncle Ned* (*song*) 3 He had no wool on de top ob de head. **1851** —— *Ring de Banjo* (*song*) 4 Den come again, Susanna, By de gas-light ob de moon; We'll tum de old piano When de banjo's out ob tune. **1882** *Judge* (N.Y.) 30 Dec. 10/3 Money am de root ob all ebil. **1891** C. TOWNSEND *Negro Minstrels* 22 He..drank a gallon ob tangle foot. **1893** M. A. OWEN *Voodoo Tales* 168 Hit am er powdeh mek outen de same hef' ob snails an' lizuhds. **1893** K. MACKAY *Out Back* (ed. 2) III. viii. 288 'Any fella longa tribe ob my sister, Queen Victoria, friend longa mine,' replied the black-fellow. **1895** BANKS & SMILEY in A. Dundes *Mother Wit* (1973) 256/2 Three bottles sittin' in de road, one ob dem full. **1950** R. AMES in *Ibid.* 492/1 In de fork ob de branch. **1974** R. B. PARKER *Godwulf Manuscript* vii. 55 Ah is a member ob de press, baby.

oba (ǫ·bă). *W. Afr.* Also **obba.** [Yoruba.] The title of the ruler of the ancient West African kingdom of Benin, now part of Nigeria, whose power used to be absolute. Now revived as the title of a local chief.

1903 H. L. ROTH *Great Benin* xi. 118 The Obba kindly promised to send a messenger round with orders. **1906** R. E. DENNETT *At Back of Black Man's Mind* xvii. 175 The OBA's throne or chair was placed on a platform of mud three steps above the ordinary level of the ground. **1926** P. A. TALBOT *Peoples S. Nigeria* I. iv. 155 The land of Southern Nigeria, including the kingdom of Benin, was discovered by Ruy de Sequeira. The Portuguese were presented by the Obba with..carved wooden platters. **1936** J. U. EGHAREVBA *Short Hist. Benin* i. 8 The oracle declared..the senior wife of the Oba, to be the cause. **1957** W. M. HAILEY *Afr. Survey* (rev. ed.) ii. 35 The Yoruba kingdoms in Nigeria were..highly centralized...The rulers, generally known as Obas, were traditionally sacred persons. **1967** W. SOYINKA *Kongi's Harvest* 4 When an Oba stops the procession And squats on the wayside, It's on an urgent matter. **1972** R. N. HENDERSON *King in Every Man* I. ii. 43 The first king or oba, Eweka I, whose regalia came from the Yoruba city of Ife. **1975** *Times* 16 July 77/5 A massive Benin bronze head of an oba. **1976** *Nigerian Herald* 20 July 4/5 The Deji suggested that a law should be made by the federal military government to leave the selection and appointment of obas and chiefs to those who were versed in the custom culture of the community concerned as a means to curb chieftaincy wranglings in the country. **1976** *Sunday Times* (Lagos) 1 Aug. 24/3 It is the turn of this ruling house to provide an Oba for the town.

Obanian (obēⁱ·niăn), *a.* *Archæol.* [f. the name of the Scottish burgh of *Oban*, Strathclyde (formerly Argyllshire).] Applied to a culture of the mesolithic period for which most evidence is found in the neighbourhood of Oban. Also as *sb.*, the Obanian culture or a person living in this culture.

1942 H. L. MOVIUS *Irish Stone Age* II. iii. 180 With the changing environment certain new forms were evolved to meet the new needs, but lack of flint or other easily worked rocks hampered cultural progress. It is proposed to call this culture the *Obanian*, after the type site in Argyllshire. *Ibid.*, The Obanian was discovered in 1879 by Symington Grieve (1883) at Caisteal-nan-Gillean, a large kitchen-midden 150 feet in diameter on the Island of Oronsay, Argyllshire. *Ibid.*, At Caisteal-nan-Gillean a large series of stone, bone and antler implements was found, typical of the Obanian culture. **1957** V. G. CHILDE *Dawn European Civilization* (ed. 6) i. 5 On the south-west coast of Scotland..the industry..is distinctive enough to be regarded as a new culture, 'the Obanian', not certainly descended from the French Azilian. **1958** *Proc. Soc. Antiquaries Scot.* LXXXIX. 91 (*heading*) Notes on the Obanian with special reference to antler- and bone-work. **1959** *Chambers's Encycl.* V. 452/1 The contents of the middens show that the Obanians hunted red and roe deer [etc.]. **1963** *Field Archaeol.* (Ordnance Survey) (ed. 4) 24 The Obanians are found on the west coast and in the islands. **1963** E. S. WOOD *Collins Field Guide Archaeol.* iv. 52 The old description of the Obanian culture, based on hunting, and on fish and molluscs, as a movement of the mesolithic people called Azilian, from south-west Europe, no longer holds. **1970** BRAY & TRUMP *Dict. Archaeol.* 165/1 *Obanian culture*... The sites are rock-shelters, and also shell middens on post-glacial raised beaches. The way of life was adapted to coastal conditions. Flintwork is scarce, but diagnostic tools include barbed spears and stone limpet-picks.

obba, var. *OBA.

obbligato, *a.* Add: (Example of *transf.* use.)

1861 GEO. ELIOT *Let.* 13 Apr. (1954) III. 405 Don't think about reading Silas Marner, just because it is come out. I hate obligato reading and obligato talk about my books.

B. *sb.* Also *transf.*

1888 KIPLING *Departmental Ditties* (ed. 3) 58 A Wagner *obbligato, scherzo*, double-hand *staccato*, Played..by the clacking tonga-bar. **1921** G. HOPKINS *City in Foreground* i. 15 He took the easiest way, which was to supply a gentle *obbligato* to the inspired melody of his companion's speech. **1955** *Times* 21 May 6/5 Lady Megan..was wreathed in smiles and her chuckle was a frequent obbligato. **1972** A. ROUDYBUSH *Sybaritic Death* (1974) ix. 82 Her complaints..formed a sort of obbligato to their drive.

obbo (ǫ·bo). *slang.* Also **obo.** [Abbrev. of OBSERVATION: cf.*-O²]. Observation, esp. in police work. In military use *ellipt.* for *observation balloon.*

1925 FRASER & GIBBONS *Soldier & Sailor Words* 212 *Obbo*, observation balloon. **1933** C. E. LEACH *On Top of Underworld* 9, I am still 'on the trail', like you, and my thoughts hark back to the long weary days and nights of 'obbo' (observation) and shadowing. **1940** PARTRIDGE *Slang* 192 An observation balloon is an *obbo* or a *sausage*. **1968** BUSBY & HOLTHAM *Main Line Kill* vi. 68 Now I got a fix on the place I got to do some obo first. Get the lie of the land. **1972** 'B. GRAEME' *Tomorrow's Yesterday* xi. 117 We're keeping a man, suspected of robbery..under obbo. **1973** D. LEES *Rape of Quiet Town* iv. 68, I went to keep obo for a bit.

obclude, var. OCCLUDE *v.*

1894 *Proc. Zool. Soc.* 434 Only about half the iris is visible, and even some part of the lens is obcluded.

obduct, *v.* Restrict † *Obs.* to sense in Dict. and add: **2.** *Geol.* To cause to undergo obduction. Hence **obdu·cted** *ppl. a.*

1971 R. G. COLEMAN in *Jrnl. Geophysical Res.* LXXVI. 1216/2 Parts of the oceanic crust have been overthrust (obducted) onto thin continental edges. **1974** *Nature* 1 Mar. 38/2 The ophiolites of west Newfoundland and the Burlington Peninsula represent obducted oceanic lithosphere. *Ibid.* 20 Sept. 259/1 With the development of actual collision between continental blocks a period of tectogenesis and orogenesis (uplift) results in F_3 flexuring of the subducted lithosphere, slivers of which are consequently overthrust (obducted) on to the 'active' continental block.

obduction. Restrict † *Obs.* to sense in Dict. and add: **2.** *Geol.* The movement of a lithospheric plate sideways and upwards over the margin of an adjacent plate.

1971 R. G. COLEMAN in *Jrnl. Geophysical Res.* LXXVI. 1216/2 According to Davies.., the ophiolites represent a slab of oceanic crust and mantle emplaced in Cretaceous or Eocene time by overthrusting (obduction) oceanic crust onto the continental crust. **1972** *Rep. 24th Internat. Geol. Congr.* III. 409 The obduction zone is..an upthrust of the oceanic crust and mantle..mostly of a marginal sea (small ocean basin). **1972** *Nature* 31 Mar. 222/2 The Alpine orogeny culminated with the collision between the continental plates of Eurasia and Africa and was probably preceded by subduction or obduction of the Tethyan plate along the European continental margin. **1975** *Ibid.* 20 Feb. 615/2 Ophiolite emplacement is integrally associated with plate subduction, either by the accretion of oceanic crust on to the wall of the upper plate (in oceanic trenches) or by the bodily thrusting (obduction) of the oceanic crust on to a continental margin.

obeah. Add to etym.: 'Also the base of Twi *ɔ-bayifó*, witch, wizard, sorcerer (more literally sorcery-man, "obeah-man", since *-fó* means *person*).' (Cassidy & Le Page *Dict. Jamaican Eng.* 1967).

2. Delete 'and formerly' and read 'a form of which survives in the West Indies and neighbouring countries'. (Earlier and later examples.)

1760 *Jrnls. Assembly Jamaica* 16 Dec. (1798) V. 245/1 The engrossed bill to remedy the evils arising from irregular assemblies of slaves..and for preventing the practice of *obeah*. **1930** J. J. WILLIAMS *Hebrewisms W. Afr.* 17 The word Obeah itself is really the Ashanti Obayifo, a witch or rather more properly,..a wizard, being derived from bayi, sorcery. **1934** J. RHYS *Voy. in Dark* III. iv. 192 Anne Chewett used to say that it's haunted and obeah—she had been in gaol for obeah. **1934** *Times Lit. Suppl.* 19 July 502/4 On the subject of obia (which a Jamaican negro will never mention) they are quite unreserved. **1954** *Caribbean Q.* III. I. 5 Obeah has been prohibited by law, and is always spoken of with a laugh; but the laughter is..never sneering. **1957** *Times Lit. Suppl.* 2 May 237/3 You have also to reckon with *obeah* (in the shape of a mongrel puppy) with the other candidate Preacher, who wickedly distorts the slogan 'Vote Harbans or Die'. **1963** G. J. MCCALL in A. Dundes *Mother Wit* (1973) 420/1 'Hoodoo'..corresponding to *vodun* ('voodoo') and *obeah* in Haiti.

3. (Later examples.)

1917 *Chambers's Jrnl.* Apr. 248/1 No treasure was found, and the Obeahman had disappeared just when he was most wanted to counsel and guide. **1934** J. RHYS *Voy. in Dark* III. iv. 192 Obeah-women who dig up dead people. **1970** J. BROWN *Un-Melting Pot* vii. 99 Though St Lucia is 92 per cent Catholic,..obeah beliefs and practices still pervade its whole fabric of life. **1973** *Sunday Express* (Trinidad & Tobago) 1 Apr. (Suppl.) 12/2 Sometimes they would visit Rattan, the famed obeah man..and ask him to cast a good spell on them. **1974** *Practitioner* Dec. 848 An Obeahman or Obeahwoman may also be consulted about social matters, including a child's education.

obeah *v.* (later example); **obeahism** (later examples).

1902 *Chambers's Jrnl.* Feb. 82/1 The vitality of *obeahism* is surprising. **1949** *Caribbean Q.* I. II. 45 Mr. Waugh manages to feature an immigrant London crooner ..and an obeahed French colonial official, in his treatment of..St. Lucia, Dominica, and Martinique. **1972** *Guardian* 6 Dec. 13/1 Obeahism, the Jamaican form of voodooism..that originated in Haiti.

obeche (obī·tʃī). [Bini name in Nigeria.] A large West African tree, *Triplochiton scleroxylon*, of the family Sterculiaceæ, found in lowland forests; also its light-coloured timber. Also *attrib.*

1908 H. N. THOMPSON in *Kew Bull.* 195 'Satinwood', 'Obeche'...At the Liverpool Market..it was classified as Satinwood...It is a very common tree. **1934** *Jrnl. R. Aeronaut Soc.* XXXVIII. 56 One of the most remarkable instances of clean fracture is in the West African Obeche. .. This wood is relatively new to commerce, and is being used..for motor-body work. **1956** *Handbk. Hardwoods* (Forest Prod. Res. Lab.) 171 Obeche grows to a height of 150 ft... Obeche is nearly white to pale straw in colour with no clear distinction between sapwood and heartwood. **1958** *Archit. Rev.* CXXIV. 41/1 The wall is of a natural obeche timber. **1965** W. SOYINKA *Road* 27 And high class timber kid. High class. Golden walnut. Obeche. Ironwood. **1971** *Country Life* 1 Apr. 731/2 My obeche wood decoys have been admired a great deal in the five or six years since I made them. **1972** *Timber Trades Jrnl.* 13 May 47/2 Among the species displayed by Lathams were two hardwoods—guarea and obeche—which were comparatively unknown at the time [*sc.* 1925].

obedience. Add: **5. obedience class, test, trial,** a competition designed to test a dog's obedience; **obedience training,** the process of teaching a dog to obey orders; hence (as a back-formation) **obedience-train** *v.*

1930 E. C. ASH *Practical Dog Bk.* ii. 21 Obedience classes are held at Cruft's Show, and are always an occasion of considerable interest. **1936** J. Z. RINE *Dog Owner's Manual* xii. 195 We see these blue ribbon dogs carrying off prizes also in obedience tests. **1961** J. HOLMES (*title*) Obedience training for dogs. **1971** 'L. EGAN' *Malicious Mischief* (1972) i. 15 'If your dog had been obedience-trained he would not have been stolen so easily... An obedience-trained dog is impossible to steal or poison.'.. 'Obedience training? What does that mean?' **1945** C. L. B. HUBBARD *Observer's Bk. Dogs* 105 The breed [*sc.* the Monkey Terrier] is surprisingly intelligent and..should do well in Obedience Trials. **1971** 'L. EGAN' *Malicious Mischief* (1972) iii. 40 Most of the big bench shows have obedience trials.

obedient, *a.* (*sb.*) Add: **5. obedient plant** = *PHYSOSTEGIA.

1948 F. PERRY *Herbaceous Border* v. 103 *P[hysostegia] virginiana*, sometimes known as the Obedient Plant because the individual sage-like blossoms on the flower spikes may be moved from side to side and remain as placed. **1971** J. RAVEN *Botanist's Garden* xi. 201 A curious plant, of better value perhaps for the entertainment it affords children than for beauty, called the obedient plant or *Physostegia virginiana*.

obeisantly, *adv.* (Later example.)

1902 *Westm. Gaz.* 2 July 2/3, I..came in turn Of him myself obeisantly to learn.

obelia (obī·liă). [mod.L. (Peron & Lesueur 1809, in *Ann. du Muséum d'Hist. Nat.* XIV. 355), f. Gr. ὀβελ-ός + -IA[1].] A marine colony-forming coelenterate of the genus so called, belonging to the class Hydrozoa.

1868 T. HINCKS *Hist. Brit. Hydroid Zoophytes* I. 148 Some of his [*sc.* Edward Forbes's] species are only various stages of one and the same *Obelia*. **1897** PARKER & HASWELL *Text-bk. Zool.* I. iv. 118 Obelia is a common zoophyte occurring in the form of a delicate, whitish or light brown, almost fur-like growth on the wooden piles of piers and wharfs. **1927** HALDANE & HUXLEY *Animal Biol.* ix. 179 If an ordinary hydroid polyp like Obelia be kept in the laboratory, the hydranths, or separate organized individuals of the colony, will (unless the water is well aerated artificially) show a curious series of changes. **1974** A. SILVERSTEIN *Biol. Sciences* 178/2 *Obelia*, a typical colonial coelenterate, has a number of specialized feeding polyps and reproductive polyps, growing in a branchlike arrangement.

obelion. Substitute for etym.: [ad. F. *obélion* (P. Broca 1875, in *Bull. de la Soc. d'Anthrop. de Paris* X. 356), f. Gr. ὀβελιαῖος sagittal (given in Broca's paper as ὀβελαῖος): see *-ION[2].] Hence also **obe·lial** *a.*

1890 H. ALLEN *Clin. Study Skull* 52 The parietal foramina lie on the sides and serve as guides to this the obelial portion.

obeliscoid (ǫbĭli·skoid), *a.* [f. OBELISK + -OID.] Resembling an obelisk in form; obelisk-shaped; obeliscal.

1877 W. R. COOPER *Short Hist. Egypt. Obelisks* v. 25 An obeliscoid monolith originally erected by Osirtesen. **1901** A. J. EVANS in *Jrnl. Hellenic Stud.* XXI. 173 The obeliskoid pillar of the Cretan ring.

obelisk, *sb.* (*a.*) **B.** as *adj.* For † *Obs.* read 'rare', and add later example.

1922 JOYCE *Ulysses* 45 Their pushedback chairs, my obelisk valise, around a board of abandoned platters.

obeophone (ōu·biofōun). [first element uncertain + *-PHONE.] A type of orchestrina (ORCHESTRINA a) (see quot. 1927). (*Disused.*)

1927 H. E. WORTHAM *O. Browning* xiii. 234 For the performance of chamber music he possessed a number of *orchestrine di camera*, familiarly known as 'obeophones', which represented the wood-wind, or even supplemented the strings. **1940** V. WOOLF *Roger Fry* ii. 49 The host himself pedalled away at the obeophone.

oberek (obe·rėk). [Polish.] A lively Polish dance in triple time, related to the mazurka.

1938 *Oxf. Compan. Mus.* 624/2 *Oberek*, a type of Polish dance. **1952** H. WOLSKA *Dances of Poland* 33 Oberek. *Region*—Mazovia... *Character*—Gay and vigorous. *Formation*—Couple Dance. **1958** [see *KRAKOWIAK]. **1976** *Times* 23 July 11/3 The Mazowszc Song and Dance Company from Poland..whirl through oberek and mazurka, polka and Krakowiak.

obertas (obēə·ɹtäs). Also **obertass.** [Polish.] = *OBEREK.

1889 GROVE *Dict. Mus.* IV. 733/1 *Obertas*, this is described in the 'Encyklopedyja Powszechna'..as the most popular of Polish national dances. **1895** L. GROVE et al. *Dancing* vii. 234 The *Obertas*, one of the most popular of national dances, is a variation of the *Mazur*. **1938** *Oxf. Compan. Mus.* 270/1 It [*sc.* a drabant] began with a solemn march and then changed to an Obertass. **1944** W. APEL *Harvard Dict. Mus.* 500/1 Chopin's Mazurka op. 56, no. 2 is in the character of an obertas. **1954** *Grove's Dict. Mus.* (ed. 5) V. 641/2 The Obertas or Oberek.

obey, *v.* Add: **1. f.** Naut. phr. *obey orders, if (though) you break owners*, obey orders, even when they are wrong.

1840 R. H. DANA *Two Yrs. before Mast* xvii. 92 It almost broke our poor darky's heart when he heard that Bess [a pet pig] was to be taken ashore... 'Obey orders, if you break owners!' said he..and lent a hand to get her over the side. **1849** H. MELVILLE *Redburn* I. vi. 57 The motto is, 'Obey orders, though you break owners'. **1915** J. E. PATTERSON *Epistles from Deep Seas* xiv. 300 There was the unwritten shipboard law: 'Obey orders, even if you break owners.' **1924** R. CLEMENTS *Gipsy of Horn* iii. 50 What could be sounder than 'Obey orders, if you break owners'—meaning, do as you're told, even if you know it's wrong.

obeyance. Delete † *Obs.* and add later examples.

1921 C. E. MULFORD *Bar-20 Three* x. 118 The obeyance of the order might possibly be accepted by the crowd as grounds for justification. **1939** JOYCE *Finnegans Wake* III. 540 Obeyance from the townsmen spills felixity by the toun. **1950** *Tablet* 9 Dec. 504/1 Erecting pointed arches in blind obeyance of mechanical efficiency.

‖ **obi**[3] (ōu·bi). *W. Afr.* [Igbo.] In Nigeria, a native hut.

1931 *Discovery* May 154/1 The more important natives have what is called an *obi* house, which is practically a shrine to the family gods and ancestors. **1937** C. K. MEEK *Law & Authority in Nigerian Tribe* iii. 62 It [*sc.* a wooden pillar] is fixed inside the householder's *obi* (entrance hut) facing outwards. **1958** C. ACHEBE *Things fall Apart* ix. 69 'Where do you sleep with your wife, in your *obi* or in her own hut?' asked the medicine-man. **1962** —— in F. Ademola *Reflections* 24 Their grand-father..was waiting in his Obi when his grand-children arrived.

‖ **obi**[4] (ōu·bi). *W. Afr.* Also **Obi.** [Ibo: see quot. 1958.] A king of the Onitsha people of Nigeria.

1937 C. K. MEEK *Law & Authority in Nigerian Tribe* x. 219 At Onitsha it was a capital offence for any one to have sexual relations with a wife of the Obi. **1958** J. S. COLEMAN *Nigeria* i. 28 The *obi* (an Ibo term—of likely Yoruba origin—for king or chief) was appointed by the Oba of Benin. **1973** *Times Lit. Suppl.* 9 Mar. 258/3 It is these sons who today are trying to rediscover..their ancient customs and, in particular, those relating to the office of King (Obi) of Onitsha.

Obie (ōu·bi). *U.S. Theatr.* [repr. pronunc. of *OB*, colloq. abbrev. *OFF-BROADWAY *a.* and *sb.*] One of a number of annual awards for off-Broadway experimental theatre productions. Also *attrib.*

1967 *National Observer* (U.S.) 10 Apr. 20/1 Last year several 'Obies', the prize theater awards normally reserved for the stalwarts of Off-Broadway, were given to OOB [*sc.* off-off-Broadway] veterans, among them actor Kevin O'Connor and playwright Sam Shepard. **1970** *Time* 12 Jan. 37 Meanwhile he was acting (six Broadway shows, 25 off-Broadway), collecting two Obies for off-Broadway performances, [etc.]. **1972** *Village Voice* (N.Y.) 1 June 54/2 Sharon Thie's play with its Open Theatre performers, including Sharon Gans (Obie winner for her performance as November). **1973** *Black World* Apr. 20/2 The next Proscenium production of Black significance was Derek Walcott's Obie Award-winning *Dream On Monkey Mountain*.

obit, *sb.* **1. b.** Delete *arch.* and add: (Later examples.) In mod. *colloq.* (esp. *journalists'*) use usu. regarded as an abbrev. of OBITUARY *sb.*

1874 *Athenæum* 12 Sept. 353 The sub-editor of a New York daily newspaper wrote to me begging me to send him the proper materials for the construction of an obit. He said it was the custom of his journal to keep obits in readiness. **1899** C. PLUMMER *Two Saxon Chrons. Parallel* II. p. lxiv, Then comes a period, 893–958, during which E and F are almost barren, containing only a few obits, [etc.]. **1901** FARMER & HENLEY *Slang* (1902) V. 85/1 *Obit*..(journalists') an obituary notice. **1935** *Atlantic Monthly* Jan. 43 (*title*) Obit for E. Harris. **1953** *N.Y. Times* 9 Aug. 8/3 This is not the obit page. **1957** D. BETHURUM *Homilies of Wulfstan* 64 Wulfstan's obit is marked in MS Hatton 113, in an Ely calendar, and in the E and F *Chronicle*, 1023. **1964** W. R. NASH *How Newspapers Work* iv. 74 The 'obits'..are revised at regular intervals. **1972** *Daily Tel.* (Colour Suppl.) 11 Aug. 5/1 The obituarists polish their obits. **1975** B. MEGGS *Matter of Paradise* (1976) IV. iv. 96 Doc had been given a very nice obit coverage on page 42.

obiter, *adj.* and *sb.* Add: (Later examples.) As *sb.* = *obiter dictum*.

1927 *Daily Tel.* 19 July 9/2 Lord Justice Scrutton recalled a recent obiter by Mr. Justice Eve to the effect that [etc.]. **1957** G. SCHWARZENBERGER *Internat. Law* (ed. 3) I. xxiv. 437 The Commission's observations..were strictly *obiter dicta*. As, however, the reformulation of Article 18 ..followed the line taken in this Award, the view expressed by the Commission, though *obiter*, deserves not to pass unnoticed. **1959** 'W. HAGGARD' *Venetian Blind* ii. 24 Mr Justice Downderry refused an injunction. He did more. He made it very clear that his remarks were *obiter*, but he was exquisitely acidulous.

obitual, *a.* and *sb.* Add: **A.** *adj.* (Further U.S. example.)

1893 *Nation* (N.Y.) 30 Nov. 406/3 Obitual days constitute an important, distinctive, and ever recurrent feature in the proceedings of our national Legislature.

obituarian (obi:tiu,ēə·riăn). *U.S.* [f. OBITUARY + -IAN.] = OBITUARIST.

1909 in *Cent. Dict.* Suppl. II. 882/3 There is one characteristic story to be told about Robert Louis Stevenson which his obituarians have missed, probably because they knew nothing about it. **1971** *Sat. Rev.* (U.S.) 6 Nov. 44/3 Alden Whitman is the obituarian for The New York Times.

obituarist. Add: (Later examples.)

1905 M. BEERBOHM *Around Theatres* (1953) 399 The obituarists seem hardly to do justice to the intensely interesting personality of Irving in private life. **1930** A. HUXLEY *Brief Candles* 4 'Metaphysically and artistically a cretin.' 'The obituarist doesn't seem to be of your opinion.' **1961** P. FLEMING *Bayonets to Lhasa* 295 'The man' wrote one of his obituarists 'was greater than his message.' **1972** [see *OBIT *sb.* 1 b]. **1974** *Punch* 3 Apr. 550/3 He joins the staff of this magazine as assistant obituarist. **1978** P. SUTCLIFFE *Oxf. Univ. Press* III. iii. 82 When he died in 1904 *The Times* obituarist attributed his failure to write in later life to the fact that he was unmethodical.

obituarize *v.*, also *trans.*

1969 *Observer* 21 Dec. 28/2 Stand by for a barrage of TV programmes obituarising the Sixties. **1972** *Times Lit. Suppl.* 31 Mar. 352/2 Evelyn Waugh, obituarizing Duggan, wrote [etc.].

obituary, *sb.* and *a.* Add: **A.** *sb.* **1.** (Later example.)

1952 *Latin Liturg. MSS.* (Exhib. Guide, Bodl. Libr.) 35 *Obituary* (and martyrology) Secular; cathedral of St. Ethelbert, Hereford; mid-14th century.

obituarily *adv.*: delete *rare*⁻⁰ and add examples.

1889 G. B. SHAW *London Music 1888–89* (1937) 61 Madame Ilma de Murska is dead; and an ungrateful world is describing her obituarily as a person remarkable for a compass that extended to F in alt. **1902** *Westm. Gaz.* 1 Aug. 1/3 Whatever may happen 'obituarily' or otherwise ..to the organisation and officials making these 'distri-uutions', they have not ceased. **1974** *Daily Tel.* (Colour Suppl.) 22 Feb. 7/3 Perhaps the generation of the Seventies, will be willing to accept the notion of dressing the deceased (obituarily) in the same garments he wore in life, gravy stains and all.

object, *sb.* Add: **3. c.** *object of art* = *objet d'art* (*OBJET 3). Also *object of art and virtu* (see sense *3 d and cf. *OBJET 6).

1862 E. HALL *Diary* 5 June in O. A. Sherrard *Two Victorian Girls* (1966) 294 Went..to a private view of objects of art at South Kensington..the Wedgwood ware exquisite. **1863** MRS. GASKELL *Dark Night's Work* x. 180 The beautiful pictures and other objects of art in the house. **1879** C. SCHREIBER *Jrnl.* 6 Dec. (1911) II. 250 As an object of art, it is vile, but in an antiquarian point of view, most curious. **1894** G. DU MAURIER *Trilby* I. I. 66 I've brought you these objects of art and virtu to make the peace with you. **1918** A. BENNETT *Roll Call* I. viii. 152 The perfunctory accents in which she had catalogued her objects of art. **1925** CONRAD *Suspense* II. ii. 96 Cosmo looked at it with appreciation, as if it had been an object of art. **1973** W. JUST *Congressman who loved Flaubert* 119 The columnist treated Caroline as a singular object of art, a serene and delicate event.

d. *object of virtu* (see VIRTU, VERTU 1 c). (Further examples.)

1914 A. HUXLEY *Let.* 13 May (1969) 59, I hope things at Eastbourne are more or less settled now...I gather that 27 will fairly burst with bits of objects of vertu and utility. **1970** S. J. PERELMAN *Baby, it's Cold Inside* 54 The objects of virtu rifled from a hundred auction rooms. **1971** *Daily Tel.* 11 May 10/5 The sale, of miniatures and objects of vertu brought £15,919. **1974** *Ibid.* 9 May 6/8 The sale of miniatures, gold watches, enamels and objects of vertu, totalled £37,294.

5. *the object of the exercise*: see *EXERCISE *sb.* 8 h.

b. *no object*, not a thing aimed at or regarded as important to obtain. Freq. also used of distance, expense, etc., not taken into account or forming no obstacle.

See C. T. Onions in *S.P.E. Tract* (1930) XXXVI. 531–4. **1782** *Morning Herald* 20 May 4/2 (Advt.), A Gentlewoman..wishes to superintend the family of a single Gentleman or Lady..and salary will be no object. **1796** *Deb. Congress U.S.* 7 Apr. (1849) 878/2 Enjoying..unexampled prosperity,..the expense of completing the frigates could be no object to the country. **1800** *Morning Herald* 4 Jan. 4/2 (Advt.), Wanted, in Chatham-place or New Bridge-street, a roomy convenient House... Rent no object, if the house is agreeable. **1855** *Poultry Chron.* III. 67/2 Where every convenience is obtainable, and expense no object. *a* **1864** R. S. SURTEES *Mr. F. Romford's Hounds* (1865) i. 4 Money! Money would be no object to him! He'd give anything for a good horse! **1871** *English Mechanic* 20 Jan. 431/1 The colour of the solder is no object, as the joint will be hidden. **1873** J. H. BEADLE *Undevel. West* XXXV. 762 With one team to each family (time being no object to such people) it cost them nothing to move. **1886** *Encycl. Brit.* XX. 228/1 Only those travel who travel by necessity, or to whom money is no object. **1891** MRS. J. H. RIDDELL *Mad Tour* 3 The time when distance was, as the advertisements say, 'no object'. **1909** 'O. HENRY' *Roads of Destiny* iv. 62 She..gave her *a la carte* to fit me out—money no object. **1916** G. B. SHAW *Pygmalion* I. 116 *I'm* going home in a taxi... Eightpence aint no object to me, Charlie. **1926** A. BENNETT *Lord Raingo* II. lxxii. 326 'I'm thinking of going back to town now, sir.. Unless of course you'd like me to stay.' 'No object in staying,' Sam murmured, as if in disgust. **1930** *London Mercury* Nov. 45 Distance being no object..scenes in Siam can be.. transmitted. **1956** B. HOLIDAY *Lady sings Blues* (1973) xiv. 121 We looked for the best private sanatorium around. Money was no object. **1964** R. BRADDON *Year Angry Rabbit* xii. 109 Each side, having already bankrupted itself to finance this war, declared that money was no object.

7. (Examples of *object clause.*) Also *object-case* = ACCUSATIVE *a.* 1; *object complement*, a word, usu. a noun or adjective, which complements the object of a verb, expressing the state or condition of the object at the time of, or resulting from, the action; cf. **objective complement*; *object-pronoun*, a pronoun, esp. a relative pronoun, which is the object of a verb or which introduces an object clause.

1870 W. W. GOODWIN *Elem. Greek Gram.* III. 167 Object clauses depending on verbs signifying *to strive for, to care for, to effect*, regularly take the future indicative after both primary and secondary tenses. **1885** Object clause [used s.v. ASK *v.* 5 a]. **1904** C. T. ONIONS *Adv. Eng. Syntax* 92 The large majority of verbs took the Accusative as Object, and thus there was a tendency for the Accusative to become the universal Object-case. **1906** G. R. CARPENTER *Eng. Gram.* ii. 25 An object complement is a noun or adjective completing the meaning of a transitive verb. **1927** E. A. SONNENSCHEIN *Soul of Grammar* 10 There is no ambiguity in sentences like the following, though the object-case has the same *form* as the subject-case: 'the lion beat the unicorn'. **1957** R. W. ZANDVOORT *Handbk. Eng. Gram.* III. vi. 165 *What*..may introduce a subject clause, an object clause. **1960** T. F. MUSTANOJA *M.E. Syntax* I. 205 Non-expression of the object-pronoun in a relative clause has not been attested in OE. **1963** F. T. VISSER *Hist. Syntax Eng. Lang.* I. iv. 550 Since these added adjectives or nouns do not affect the meaning of the verb, but are merely adjuncts to the object the term 'object complement' or 'objective complement' ..seems preferable to the appellation 'predicative adjunct'. **1964** *English Studies* XLV. 386 The rapidly developing 'periphrastic genitive', in which object-case pronouns *h-r* and *h-m* (after *of*) contrasted. **1966** *Ibid.* XLVII. 55 Of special importance is the absence of the relative object-pronoun (e.g. *The spirits I have raised* abandon me), one of the most frequent idioms in coll. English. *Ibid.* 253 A third argument against calling the *that*-clause an object clause is that it lacks the noun characteristic of forming prepositional adjuncts.

10. *object-directed* adj. (so *object-directedness*); **object chart,** a chart for use in object lessons; **object choice** *Psychol.*, something external to the ego chosen as a desirable object; **object-lesson** (earlier and later examples of *fig.* use); **object libido** *Psycho-anal.*, that part of psychic energy which is directed to objects other than the ego; **object love,** love for something external to the ego or self; **object program** *Computers*, a program into which some other program is translated by an assembler or compiler; cf. *OBJECT LANGUAGE 3; **object-relation, -relationship** *Psychol.*, a relationship felt, or the emotional energy directed, by the self or ego towards a chosen object; also *attrib.*; **object-system,** the system of teaching by object-lessons; **object-teaching** (examples); **object-white** *Billiards*, the white object-ball; **object word,** a word which designates an object or material thing; *spec.* in the theories of Bertrand Russell, a word the meaning of which can be learnt independently of the rest of the linguistic system; **object-world,** the world external to the self, apprehended through the objects in it.

1872 *Rep. Indian Affairs 1871* (U.S.) 306 A new and original series of 'object charts' gotten up expressly for the Indians of Oregon by myself. **1920** *Internat. Jrnl. Psycho-Anal.* I. 137 Such motivation of the homosexual object-choice must be by no means uncommon. **1948** M. KLEIN *Contrib. Psycho-Anal.* 121 His homosexual object choice at the narcissistic level. **1965** P. L. GIOVACCHINI in B.L. Greene *Psychother. Marital Disharmony* 43 The spouse, representing a heterosexual object choice, would ideally be associated with ego transactions. **1960** W. V. QUINE *Word & Object* vii. 239 Some of us are carried away by the object-directed pattern of our thinking. **1973** *Jrnl. Genetic Psychol.* CXXII. 264 Six categories of object-directed behavior. **1963** A. KENNY *Action, Emotion & Will* 195 How..can Brentano say that object-directedness is peculiar to psychological phenomena? **1881** 'MARK TWAIN' *Prince & Pauper* xii. 115 In the times of which we are writing, the Bridge furnished 'object lessons' in English history. **1936** N. STREATFEILD *Ballet Shoes* xi. 180 It was an object lesson she might remember always. **1977** *Early Music* July 401/3 Saul Novak gives an object-lesson in linear analysis for early music. **1920** *Internat. Jrnl. Psycho-Anal.* I. 170 Paraphrenia differs from the psychoneuroses in that the object-libido is re-converted into ego-libido. **1933** A. A. BRILL in S. Lorand *Psycho-Anal. Today* 108 We thus distinguish an ego libido and an object libido. **1955** J. STRACHEY et al. tr. *Freud's Compl. Psychol. Wks.* XVIII. 257 The transformation of object-libido into narcissism necessarily carried along with it a certain degree of desexualization. **1964** H. HARTMANN *Ess. Ego Psychol.* x. 185 It has sometimes been said..that the loss of object libido destroys the repressions. **1918** E. JONES *Papers on Psycho-Anal.* (ed. 2) xviii. 332 The transference..like every 'object love', has its deepest root in the repressed parent-complex. **1924** J. RIVIERE et al. tr. *Freud's Coll. Papers* II. 83 The sexual instinct passes on from auto-erotism to object-love. **1938** *Times Lit. Suppl.* 26 Feb. 132/4 The stage of 'object-love', when the moral superego takes charge and the ego is no longer coercive but submissive. **1968** A. H. MODELL (*title*) Object love and reality. **1959** M. H. WRUBEL *Primer of Programming* vi. 128 At the end of the assembly or translation phase.., the programmer is presented with a machine-language deck [of cards] called the 'object program'. **1970** O. DOPPING *Computers & Data Processing* xix. 304 In the most common systems for automatic coding, the translation from source program to object program is done in a separate computer run, called the compilation run. **1968** L. BREGER in J. Marmor *Mod. Psychoanal.* 47 The concept of 'object relation' (that is, the idea that there is a fixed quantity of energy in a more or less closed system, so that if libido is 'invested' in one object it is 'unavailable' for other purposes). **1968** R. & G. BLANCK *Marriage & Pers. Devel.* vi. 70 Persons on the need-gratifying level of object relations can change partners..readily. **1970** *Jrnl. Analytical Psychol.* XV. I. 7 True object relations are the goal of our efforts towards insight into our emotions. **1926** *Brit. Jrnl. Med. Psychol.* VI. 292 The hetero-sexual stage, which is the most complete form of allo-erotic object relationship. **1946** *Internat. Jrnl. Psycho-Anal.* XXVII. 31/2 From the point of view of object-relationship psychology, explicit pleasure-seeking represents a deterioration of behaviour. **1974** K. LAMBERT in M. Fordham et al. *Technique in Jungian Analysis* III. 312 This annuls the 'object relationship' between the patient and the analyst. **1869** C. L. BRACE *New West* vi. 75 The improvement which we have sought so much to bring before the public in New York..—the 'Object System'—has already been adopted here. **1878** *Harper's Mag.* Mar. 607/2 This school is too large for strictly Kindergarten Teaching; but the 'object system'..was the one adopted. **1860** H. BARNARD (*title*) Object teaching and oral lessons on social science and common things. **1945** C. V. GOOD *Dict. Educ.* 411/2 *Teaching, object*, a method of elementary-school teaching derived from the work of Pestalozzi in Europe and introduced into the United States at the Westfield, Massachusetts, State Teachers' College in 1848 and at Oswego, New York, in 1861. **1904** MANNOCK & MUSSABINI *Billiards Expounded* I. iii. 97 To enable the object-ball to go on to the baulk cushion and return up by the object-white. **1907** *Westm. Gaz.* 19 June 7/2 He got the red ball against the top cushion,..and..the object-white against the side cushion. **1914** L. BLOOMFIELD *Introd. Study Lang.* iv. 111 The explicit predication of quality or action is impossible for languages in which every word expresses an object... In these languages the sentence consists of one or more object-words. **1940** B. RUSSELL *Inquiry into Meaning & Truth* 80 'Object words' are defined, logically, as words having meaning in isolation, and, psychologically, as words which have been learnt without its being necessary to have previously learnt any other words. **1953** *Mind* LXII. 10 Harm has been done by the well-meaning distinction between object words and logical words... An object word such as 'table'..has meaning in isolation from other words. **1954** E. BRANTH tr. *H. Spang-Hanssen's Recent Theories Nature of Lang. Sign* in *Travaux du Cercle Ling. de Copenhague* IX. 75 Even in the presence of an object, an object-word will only have an extremely vague 'meaning' if it did not—through its oppositions—concentrate its meaning on a particular 'property' in the object. **1964** E. A. NIDA *Toward Sci. Transl.* iv. 62 Basically there are four principal functional classes of lexical symbols: object words, event words, abstracts, and relationals. **1880** G. M. HOPKINS *Sermons & Devotional Writings* (1959) II. i. 127 Part of this world of objects, this object-world, is also part of the very self in question. **1904** W. JAMES *Coll. Ess. & Rev.* (1920) 446 There is..no account of the fact (which I assume the writers to believe in) that different subjects share a common object-world. **1934** W. TEMPLE *Nature, Man & God* I. vi. 135 That discussion will be primarily concerned neither with the inner life of mind, conceived as separate from environment, nor with the object-world which mind apprehends and contemplates, but with the inter-relation of these two. **1948** M. KLEIN *Contrib. Psycho-Anal.* 313 By being internalized, people, things, situations and happenings..cannot be verified by the means of perception which are available in connection with the tangible and palpable object-world. **1964** GOULD & KOLB *Dict. Social Sci.* 313/2 Our understanding and its object-world.

object, *v.* Add: **4. b.** Also with direct speech. (Later examples.)

1972 D. BLOODWORTH *Any Number can Play* xvi. 154 'But it would have been..a pointed piece of skin,' objected Green. **1974** *Listener* 3 Oct. 423/2 Mr Johnston objected: 'But we already have..a shop stewards' movement.'

objectant. Delete † *Obs. rare* and add: In recent use as a legal term in the U.S.

1972 *N.Y. Law Jrnl.* 22 Aug. 6/4 The proponent or the objectant seeks an examination of the adverse party before trial. **1973** *Ibid.* 19 July 13/5 In view of the failure of the objectant to proceed with this matter, his objections are denied.

objectifiable (ǫbdʒe·ktifəi:ăb'l), *a.* [f. OBJECTIFY *v.* + -ABLE.] That is capable of being objectified.

1925 C. D. BROAD *Mind & its Place* vi. 306 To be 'epistemologically objectifiable' means to be capable of corresponding to the epistemological object of some referential situation.

objectification. (Further examples.)

1883 HALDANE & KEMP tr. *Schopenhauer's World as Will & Idea* I. II. 121 (*heading*) The objectification of the will. **1927** A. N. WHITEHEAD *Symbolism* (1928) i. 30 Thus 'objectification' itself is an abstraction. **1931** W. R. B. GIBSON tr. *Husserl's Ideas* II. ii. 123 Thanks to this objectification we find facing us in the natural setting.. not natural things merely, but values and practical objects of every kind. **1963** J. MACQUARRIE *Twentieth-Century Relig. Thought* xii. 203 Berdyaev goes further..in his antipathy to objectification, which he identifies with the fall of man. **1971** E. B. ASHTON tr. *Jaspers's Philos.* III. i. 8 Metaphysical objectifications of transcendence.

objectified, *ppl. a.*, **objectifying,** *vbl. sb.* (Later examples.)

1927 A. N. WHITEHEAD *Symbolism* (1928) i. 30 No actual thing is 'objectified' in its 'formal' completeness. **1931** W. R. B. GIBSON tr. *Husserl's Ideas* II. ii. 122 The intentional object first becomes an apprehended object through a distinctively 'objectifying' turn of thought. **1940** S. C. PEPPER in P. A. Schilpp *Philos. Santayana* 229 The expression of moral and political greatness, however, is the satisfaction of interests quite different from objectified pleasure. **1977** R. WILLIAMS *Marxism & Lit.* II. ii. 86 Here society is the objectified (unconscious and unwilled) general process.

objectifier (ǫbdʒe·ktifəi:əɹ). [f. OBJECTIFY *v.* + -ER[1].] That which objectifies or makes objective.
1956 J. D. MABBOTT in H. D. Lewis *Contemp. Brit. Philos.* (ser. 3) 307 Morality has to be sustained by conviction and conviction is a great objectifier.

objection. Add: **1. a., b.** *spec.* in *Horse Racing.*
1898 *Encycl. Sport* II. 228/1 All disputes, objections, and appeals referred to or brought before the Stewards of the Jockey Club for their decision, shall be decided by the three Stewards. **1930** *Daily Express* 6 Oct. 17/6 An objection to Kippit Lore on behalf of Ferry Maid was overruled. **1977** 'J. LE CARRÉ' *Hon. Schoolboy* vii. 165 Objection!.. Where's the Stewards..? That horse was pulled!

objective, *a.* and *sb.* Add: **A.** *adj.* **3. a.** (Earlier and later examples.)
1838 J. S. MILL in *London & Westm. Rev.* Aug. 496 An essentially *objective* people, like those of Northern and Central Italy. **1967** H. ARENDT *Orig. Totalitarianism* (new ed.) xii. 423 The Jews in Nazi Germany or the descendants of the former ruling classes in Soviet Russia were not really suspected of any hostile action; they had been declared 'objective' enemies of the regime in accordance with its ideology.

7. b. *objective complement* = *object complement* (*OBJECT *sb.* 7).
1870 C. P. MASON *Eng. Gram.* (ed. 14) 127 When the verb is transitive, and in the active voice, the complement of the predicate stands in the attributive relation to the object of the verb; as, 'He dyed the cloth red.'.. This kind of complement may be termed the *Objective Complement,* inasmuch as it is closely connected with the object of the verb. **1897** CLARKE & MULLER *Class Bk. Eng. Gram.* 219 The name *Objective Complement* would be applied by some Grammarians [to 'captain' in the sentence 'They elected *James captain*']. **1945** M. M. BRYANT *Functional Eng. Gram.* xii. 132 In 'They made him chairman'..the second complement is called an objective complement. *Ibid.*, In the sentence 'The frost turned the leaves red', the objective complement is of a somewhat different nature, since here the word *red* is an adjective rather than a noun. **1963** [see *OBJECT *sb.* 7].

B. *sb.* **5.** *attrib.*, as **objective function,** in linear programming, the function that it is desired to maximize or minimize.
1949 *Econometrica* XVII. 207 The optimum feasible program is that feasible program which maximizes a specified linear objective function. **1958** RILEY & GASS *Linear Programming* i. 5 The linear-programming problem has a linear function of the variables to aid in choosing a solution to the problem. This linear combination of the variables, called the objective function, must be optimized by the selected solution. **1969** D. C. HAGUE *Managerial Econ.* I. i. 16 We shall find that the aim of the business is set out in what is called an objective function—a name which indicates its purpose exactly.

objective correlative. [f. OBJECTIVE *a.* 2b + CORRELATIVE *sb.* 1.] Term applied by T. S. Eliot to the technique in art of representing or evoking a particular emotion by the presentation of physical symbols of it, as surroundings, situations, sets of objects, etc., which become indicative of that emotion and are associated with it.
[**1850** W. ALLSTON *Lect. Art, & Poems* 16 No possible modification in the degrees or proportion of these elements [*sc.* air, earth, heat, water] can change the specific form of a plant... So, too, is the external world to the mind; which needs, also, as the condition of its manifestation, its objective correlative.] **1919** T. S. ELIOT in *Athenæum* 26 Sept. 941/1 The only way of expressing emotion in the form of art is by finding an 'objective correlative'; in other words, a set of objects, a situation, a chain of events which shall be the formula of that *particular* emotion; such that when the external facts, which must terminate in sensory experience, are given, the emotion is immediately evoked. **1946** *Sewanee Rev.* LIV. 301 In that Eliot proposes the objective correlative, 'he accepts with the vast majority of his contemporaries the modern dogma that the artist is primarily concerned with emotion'. **1947** T. S. ELIOT *Milton* 7 Two or three phrases of my coinage—like 'objective correlative'—which have had a success in the world astonishing to their author. **1951** H. KENNER *Poetry E. Pound* viii. 66 It is easy to see why the objective correlative, the image as sensory equivalent of an emotion, the Aristotelian equation of a poem with an action, and Eliot's claim that emotions the poet has never experienced will serve his turn as well as familiar ones, should seem in such eyes impossibly muddle-headed. **1955** D. DAVIE *Articulate Energy* vii. 86 The use of the objective correlative, the invention of a fable or an 'unreal' landscape. **1957** WIMSATT & BROOKS *Lit. Crit.* 676 A realization that Winters' conception of poetry, like Eliot's, is ultimately 'dramatic' need not impugn the useful distinction between motive (the reason for an emotion) and objective correlative (the symbol of an emotion). **1962** T. P. DUNNING in Davis & Wrenn *Eng. & Medieval Stud.* 168 The pagan element of the story is superbly handled by Chaucer as an essential feature of his *inventum*, or objective correlative. **1963** N. FRYE *Romanticism Reconsidered* 3 Some belief of which Romantic poetry is supposed to form the objective correlative. **1964** J. B. LEISHMAN *Rilke's New Poems* 9 An essentially expounding poet..might still be continuously engaged in a search for ever new 'objective correlatives' for old and unchanged convictions. **1966** K. AMIS *Anti-Death League* II. 176 This communicability..can work via an outward symbol or artefact, so that state-of-mind produces object which in turn produces state-of-mind. There are obvious analogies here with aesthetic theory, in particular with Eliot's notion of the objective correlative. **1971** *Times Lit. Suppl.* 31 Dec. 1629/4 In all these poems the objective correlative was utterly unsatisfactory from any partisan political point of view.

objectively, *adv.* Add: **3.** (Earlier examples.)
1796 [see SUBJECTIVELY *adv.* 4]. **1798** A. F. M. WILLICH *Elem. Critical Philos.* 6 Our knowledge is called objectively true, in so far as objects must be perceived by every other being, in the same manner in which we represent them to ourselves.

objectivism. Add: (Earlier and later examples.)
1854 GEO. ELIOT tr. *Feuerbach's Essence Christianity* xxi. 203 Belief in revelation is the culminating point of religious objectivism. *Ibid.* xxiii. 224 Religious objectivism has two passives, two modes in which God is thought. **1954** *Mind* LXIII. 265 'Objectivism'..is so ambiguous that there are very few ethical theories which cannot claim to be in some sense 'objectivist'. **1966** tr. *Kotarbinski's Gnosiology* ii. 68 The gap within idealist views between objectivism and subjectivism. **1972** PICCONE & HANSEN tr. *Paci's Function of Sci.* ii. 27 According to Husserl the struggle between objectivism and transcendentalism gives us the 'meaning' of the history of the modern spirit.

b. A derogatory term used in communist theory to describe an objective attitude towards existing conditions and acceptance of working within their limitations, as opposed to the concern for changing them according to revolutionary theories. So **objectivist.**
1933 T. B. H. BRAMELD *Philos. Approach to Communism* xi. 156 An objectivism which tends to deny the significance of conscious men. **1957** R. N. C. HUNT *Guide to Communist Jargon* 99 Objectivism is thus the opposite of 'party-mindedness', and is a serious offence. **1960** tr. *Lenin's Coll. Wks.* I. 401 The objectivist speaks of 'insurmountable historical tendencies'; the materialist speaks of the class which 'directs' the given economic system. **1972** tr. *Marx's On Hist. Materialism* 708 He [*sc.* Lenin] exposed their attempts to devoid Marxism of its revolutionary content and showed that their views were based on bourgeois objectivism which justified capitalism and glossed over class contradictions.

objectivity. (Later examples.)
1950 W. H. BARBER tr. *Jolivet's Introd. Kierkegaard* III. ii. 98 'Objectivity', whose idolatrous worship has been propagated by the modern nationalists, might equally well be defined as 'positivity'. **1957** R. MAY et al. *Existence* i. 25 He [*sc.* Kierkegaard] was convinced not only that the goal of 'pure objectivity' is impossible but that even if it were possible it would be undesirable. **1966** K. HARTMANN *Sartre's Ontology* i. 7 Thus, the phenomena would cease to be moments of myself and would take on 'objectivity'. **1969** R. STRACHAN tr. *Malet's Thought R. Bultmann* i. 19 In its objectivity the other is only an extension of myself.

objectivization (ǫbdʒe:ktivəizēⁱ·ʃən). [n. of action from OBJECTIVIZE *v.*: see -ATION.] The action or condition of making or becoming objective; an instance of this; something external in which an idea, principle, etc., is expressed concretely.
1929 [see *EXPRESSIONISM]. **1944** S. PUTNAM tr. *E. da Cunha's Rebellion in Backlands* ii. 144 It [*sc.* Canudos] was the objectivization of a tremendous insanity. **1965** D. A. LOWRIE tr. *Berdyaev's Christian Existentialism* ii. 33 The objectivization of the criterion of truth usually means that that is transferred to another's consciousness and conscience. **1969** W. GLEN-DOEPEL tr. *Metz's Theol. of World* III. 126 The de-privatization and de-existentialization, or, to put it positively, the 'new objectivization' of the Christian message. **1970** R. J. HOLLINGDALE tr. *Schopenhauer's Ess. & Aphorisms* 59 The will's objectivization.

objectivize, *v.* Add: Hence **obje·ctivized** *ppl. a.*
1965 D. A. LOWRIE tr. *Berdyaev's Christian Existentialism* ii. 34 Objectivized knowledge in all its levels is withdrawn from the existential subject, that is from man.

object language. [OBJECT *sb.* + LANGUAGE *sb.*] **1.** A language described or analysed in terms of another language (known as the metalanguage).
1935 *Mind* XLIV. 501 Formal syntax requires a language of which it is the syntax. This language is called the 'object-language' (*Objektsprache*) in distinction from the syntax language. **1937** A. SMEATON tr. *Carnap's Logical Syntax of Lang.* 4 We are concerned with two languages: in the first place with the language which is the object of our investigation—we shall call this the *object-language*—and, secondly, with the language in which we speak *about* the syntactical forms of the object-language. **1946** C. MORRIS *Signs, Lang. & Behavior* 179 So if we talked about French in English, French would be the object language and English the metalanguage. **1947** A. J. AYER *Thinking & Meaning* 26, I am using English in a twofold aspect, as an object-language and as a meta-language in which I speak about the object-language. **1947** R. CARNAP *Meaning & Necessity* i. 4 In order to speak *about* any *object language*..we need a *metalanguage.* **1965** B. MATES *Elem. Logic* ii. 36 In the case of a Greek grammar written in English, Greek is the object-language and English is the metalanguage. **1977** J. LYONS *Semantics* I. i. 10 We may say that the language being described is the object-language and the language which is used to make the descriptive statements is the metalanguage.

2. In the theories of Bertrand Russell: a language consisting only of words having meaning in isolation.
1940 B. RUSSELL *Inquiry into Meaning & Truth* iv. 63 There must..be a language of lowest type... I shall call this sometimes the 'object-language', sometimes the 'primary language'. **1954** E. BRANTH tr. *H. Spang-Hanssen's Recent Theories Nature of Lang. Sign* in *Travaux du Cercle Ling. de Copenhague* IX. 76 Object-words form an object-language, which is the primary languagei n a language hierarchy. **1963** J. LYONS *Structural Semantics* iv. 54, I do not accept..that there is a basic 'object-language', the elements of which are learnt in isolation and to which the rest of the vocabulary can be reduced.

3. *Computers.* A language into which a program is translated by an assembler or compiler. Cf. *object program* (*OBJECT *sb.* 10).
1961 LEEDS & WEINBERG *Computer Programming Fund.* ii. 49 Just as in language translation, a type of dictionary is employed in translating from the source language to the object language. **1970** P. M. SHERMAN *Techniques Computer Programming* vi. 109 The result of the translation process is an object program in an object language or machine language.

objectly (ǫ·bdʒėktli), *adv.* [f. OBJECT *sb.* + -LY[2].] Objectively.
1925 *Blackw. Mag.* Dec. 786/1 He saw himself objectly as a felon with the mark of Cain.

o·bjectness. [f. OBJECT *sb.* + -NESS.] The state or quality of being objective or perceptible.
1933 *Mind* XLII. 510 This second relation..is a relation neither to the material object nor to 'objectness'. **1973** J. ELSOM *Erotic Theatre* ix. 179 The laws concerning static nakedness exactly illustrated the idea of 'objectness'. **1975** *Russ. Rev.* (N.Y.) XXXIV. 272 In futurism, in cubism, space is almost always cultivated, but its form, being connected with objectness, does not convey, even to the imagination, the presence of world space; its space is limited by the space which is shared by the things on the earth.

‖ **objet** (ǫbʒe). [Fr., = object.] **1.** An object which is displayed as an ornament.
1857 A. MATHEWS *Tea-Table Talk* I. 98 Every part of it [*sc.* the house] abounded in pretty things—*objets*, as they are sometimes called, which her visitors were strictly forbidden to touch. **1960** *Good Housekeeping* Feb. 60/2 For some people a collection is worthwhile only if the pieces are rare... For others, the pleasure lies, quite simply, in possessing a number of more ordinary *objets* which intrigue, amuse or otherwise delight the owner. **1970** V. C. CLINTON-BADDELEY *No Case for Police* vii. 136 All those lamentable *objets* on the window-sills. **1973** *Listener* 6 Sept. 319/3 The sights and textures of bourgeois existence: the plush, the antimacassars, the *objets* in the home and in the shops.

2. One who is the object of (someone's) attentions or affection. Cf. OBJECT *sb.* 4. *rare.*
1847 THACKERAY *Van. Fair* (1848) xv. 132 Find out who is the *objet*, Briggs. I'll set him up in a shop. **1877** L. W. M. LOCKHART *Mine is Thine* (1878) II. xviii. 33 He ..protested,..against being 'swindled' into further association with the *objet aimé* for the present.

3. *objet d'art* (ǫbʒe dār), a small artistic object; a curio; a precious and finely worked ornament. Also *transf.* Also *objet d'art et de vertu* (see sense 6 below and VIRTU, VERTU 1c in Dict.). Cf. *object of art* (*and virtu*) (*OBJECT *sb.* 3c).
1865 'OUIDA' *Strathmore* II. xx. 236 Cachemires, sables, flowers, objets d'art, were scattered over it. **1866** MRS. GASKELL *Wives & Daughters* II. x. 98 The various little tables, loaded with 'objets d'art' (as Mrs. Gibson delighted to call them) with which the drawing room was crowded. **1872** C. SCHREIBER *Jrnl.* 27 Mar. (1911) I. 145 We were surprised..to find a house containing 3 rooms entirely hung with pictures, in which were a few unimportant objets d'art. **1883** E. W. HAMILTON *Diary* 29 Jan. (1972) II. 395 Mentmore..certainly is a gorgeous place, full of *objets d'art* and choice articles of furniture. **1913** W. LAWRENCE *Let.* 14 Oct. in T. E. Lawrence *Lett.* (1938) 159 Great collectors of objets d'art. **1921** M. CORELLI *Secret Power* xxii. 267 The ceremony..has become a mere show of dressed-up manikins and womenkins, many of the latter being mere *objets d'art,*—stands for the display of millinery. **1931** *N. & Q.* 5 Sept. 175/1, I should be much obliged for any notes of the mention of platinum—as *objet d'art*, precious possession, gift, jewel or the like—in literature. **1939** O. LANCASTER *Homes Sweet Homes* 38 *Objets d'art et de vertu* had been collected by rich men since the end of the seventeenth century. **1940** N. MARSH *Surfeit of Lampreys* (1941) v. 72 The jewellery and *objets-d'art* idea seemed a capital one. **1955** *Times* 27 May 14/3, I have seen him start from his chair and literally explode from the room, scattering priceless *objets d'art* to right and left. **1965** A. NICOL *Truly Married Woman* 17 He turned over the pages with the hopeless air of a connoisseur examining an objet d'art. **1973** G. SIMS *Hunters Point* xiii. 119 Buchanan knew nothing of fine wines or *objets d'art* but he considered himself a connoisseur of loneliness. **1974** K. CLARK *Another Part of Wood* vi. 257 At Portland Place they [*sc.* the author's children] were hidden away at the top of the house and brought down to be exhibited as *objets d'art* to our friends.

4. *objet de luxe* (see *DE LUXE *adj. phr.*), an especially fine or sumptuous article of value, a luxury article.
1881 C. C. HARRISON *Woman's Handiwork* III. 149 This was chiefly for the chambers of royal palaces—screens,

then as now, being *objets de luxe* in the literal sense. **1934** *Burlington Mag.* Sept. 125/2 Cabinets and boxes covered with tortoise-shell veneer..are among the many 'objets de luxe' brought from India to Europe and now found in old collections. **1941** [see *BÆTYL]. **1956** K. CLARK *Nude* i. 8 A few *objets de luxe*, like the Veroli Casket. **1976** *Times Lit. Suppl.* 12 Mar. 290/2 To trace the changing fortunes of Ruritanian royalty, through the dispersal of their Fabergé objets de luxe.

5. *objet trouvé* (lit. 'found object', pl. *objets trouvés*), an object found or picked up at random and presented as a rarity or a work of art. Also *transf.* and *fig.*

1937 AUDEN & MACNEICE *Lett. from Iceland* xvii. 243 The Surrealists shall have J. A. Smith as an Objet Trouvé in disguise. **1940** GRAVES & HODGE *Long Week-End* xx. 352 The similarity between '*objets trouvés*'..and the neo-Victorian knick-knack collecting habit. **1956** M. LASKI in *Pick of Today's Short Stories* VII. 121 *Collages* were countered by *montages*, *objets trouvés* by *objets faits*. **1959** P. & L. MURRAY *Dict. Art & Artists* 112 *Found object* (*objet trouvé*), in Surrealist theory an object of any kind, such as a shell found on a walk, can be a work of art; and such 'Found Objects' have been exhibited. **1962** *Listener* 6 Sept. 350/2 He was far ahead of his time. In the eighteen-nineties he was working on *objets trouvés*, in his case coals from his fire. **1967** L. DEIGHTON *Expensive Place* v. 34 An *objet trouvé* is a piece of driftwood or a fine stone—it's something in which an artist has found and seen otherwise unnoticed beauty. **1970** *New Yorker* 17 Oct. 159/2 Mr. Berio allows that he has treated the Mahler movement as an *objet trouvé*. **1973** *Guardian* 17 Oct. 7/8 The City's food... Among *objets trouvés* were a screw in a cheese and tomato roll, a brass rivet in a Chelsea bun. **1974** *Sunday Times* 14 July 28/2 He [*sc.* Lord Goodman] plonked himself down, a volunteer *objet-trouvé*, and was given a studiously informal treatment.

6. *objet de vertu* (or *virtu*), a spurious transl. into French of *object of virtu* (see VIRTU, VERTU 1 c), after *objet d'art* above. (The required meaning of *vertu* does not exist in French.) Also in phr. *objet d'art et de vertu*.

1939 [see sense 3 above]. **1947** M. MCCARTHY in *Partisan Rev.* XIV. 63 Lady Windermere's fan becomes an *objet de virtu* as powerful as Desdemona's handkerchief. **1954** 'N. BLAKE' *Whisper in Gloom* II. x. 139 Mr. Borch was in search of information rather than *objets de vertu*. **1961** *Connoisseur* Dec. p. xlvi, *Objets de Vertu* and fine Works of Art. **1974** *Times* 7 Dec. 14/7 His main interests are *objets de vertu* and antique weapons.

‖ **oblast** (ǫ·blast). [Russ.] A second-order administrative subdivision in Imperial Russia and the U.S.S.R.; a Russian province or region. Also *attrib.* Cf. *KRAY.

1886 *Encycl. Brit.* XXI. 69/2 *Oblasts*, or provinces. **1911** *Ibid.* XXIII. 875/2 For purposes of provincial administration Russia is divided into 78 governments (*guberniya*), 18 provinces (*oblast*) and 1 district (*okrug*). **1934** WEBSTER s.v. *Soviet*, They [*sc.* the soviets].. send deputies to the higher soviet congresses: *volosts* (rural district),..*oblasts* (regional), and the congresses of the constituent republics. **1936** *Nature* 23 May 843/1 They [*sc.* the soviets] in their turn send delegates to the rayons, above which are the oblasts. **1938**, etc. [see *KRAY]. **1951** *Ann. Reg. 1950* 202 The unsatisfactory condition of agriculture in the *oblast* was attributed to organizational deficiencies... N. S. Patolichev..had spent the previous two years in the comparatively obscure post of *oblast* party Secretary. **1955** *Times* 23 Aug. 6/3 Every credit is given to those oblast and individual state and collective farms which fulfil..the plan. **1964** *New Statesman* 6 Mar. 353/1 Interference at the district level by agricultural departments of the town or village council has been superseded by 'guidance' at the *oblast* (regional) level. **1964** *Economist* 13 June 1264/2 The first oil was struck in the Tyumen oblast only in 1960. **1976** *Survey* Spring 57 He embarked on a successful career in party administration, attaining the rank of *oblast* First Secretary.

‖ **oblietjie** (ǫbli·kʸi). *S. Afr.* Also **oubl(i)etje.** [Afrikaans, f. F. *oublie* wafer (see OBLEY) + *-tjie* (dim. ending).] A type of wafer-thin teacake.

1890 *Hilda's Where is it? of Recipes* (ed. 2) 243 See also 'obletjes', Scones and Cakes, Puffs and Sandwiches. **1904** *Ibid.* (new ed.) 153 (Pettman), *Obletjes* (or *Oubliès*). An old-fashioned recipe for tea cakes brought to the Cape by the French refugees. **1912** *Northern News* 27 Aug. (Pettman), The one word I feel sure of is *oublietje*, that delicious, crisp, wafer-like pastry to be invariably found at bazaars in the districts settled by the Huguenots. **1947** *Cape Times* 26 Apr. 14/4 The old South African confectionery oblietjies, which the King so much enjoyed. **1947** L. G. GREEN *Tavern of Seas* viii. 65 She also served the rolled wafer tea cakes called oblietjies, made with cinnamon and white wine—a Huguenot contribution to Cape cookery. **1950** M. MASSON *Birds of Passage* vii. 69 The cook they employed..would turn out a number of delicious local confections which included wafer thin teacakes, known as oublietjes.

obligate, *v.* **3. a.** and **5.** Add: In later use chiefly *dial.* and *U.S. colloq.*

1888 'C. E. CRADDOCK' *Despot of Broomsedge Cove* 146 The parson..was 'obligated' to go down to the Settlement. **1900** S. R. CROCKETT *Little Anna Mark* xl. 340 When she came to New Milns she was obligated to go to the Scots kirk with Sir James. **1898** J. MACMANUS *Bend of Road* 73 I'll be happy to obligate ye. **1919** F. HURST *Humoresque* 226 She thought maybe..I'd go over to her place for Wednesday-night supper for a change. You know how a girl like Clara gets to feeling obligated. **1955** C. MCCULLERS in *Mademoiselle* Nov. 134/1 'I can't stay but just a minute,' John said. 'I'm obligated to sell those tickets. I have to eat and run.' **1963** *PMLA* LXXVIII. IV. ii. 11/1 Many of them felt obligated to turn out teaching materials as a kind of *quid pro quo* for their $350 stipend. **1970** N. ARMSTRONG et al. *First on Moon* ix. 212 The foreman..has to side with his mechanics because he is obligated to a schedule. **1975** *N.Y. Times* 29 Nov. 26/1 President Ford is obligated early next month to report to Congress on the 'progress' of negotiations looking toward a Cyprus settlement.

obligately (ǫ·bligĕtli), *adv. Biol.* [f. OBLIGATE *ppl. a.* + -LY².] Out of necessity, because restricted to such a mode of life or such environmental conditions.

1952 [see *SAPROBE]. **1955** *New Biol.* XVIII. 54 These nitrogen-fixing bacteria were found to differ strikingly in that *Clostridium* is obligately anaerobic, i.e. able to grow only in the absence of oxygen. **1967** *Oceanogr. & Marine Biol.* V. 194 An obligately psychrophilic marine bacterium. **1971** [see *HALOPHILIC *a.*]. **1974** *Nature* 18 Oct. 574/2 Whether a symbiotic association is mutualistic or obligately parasitic.

obligative, *a.* Add: **2.** *Gram.* Of a verb form, mood, etc.: implying obligation. Hence as *sb.*

1877 W. D. WHITNEY *Essent. Eng. Gram.* v. 122 With *must* and *ought* (*to*) we make forms which may be called *obligative*, 'implying obligation': thus, *I must give*, *I ought to give*. **1968** J. LYONS *Introd. Theoret. Linguistics* vii. 309 The distinction between the 'obligative' and the 'inferential' sense associated with the auxiliary verb *must* in English is neutralized in a non-past sentence like *He must come regularly*. *Ibid.*, There is a further distinction within the 'obligative' in English, which has to do with the acceptance or fulfilment of the obligation. **1974** W. P. LEHMANN *Proto-Indo-Europ. Syntax* iv. 105 The PIE subjunctive may resemble in meaning an obligative. *Ibid.* 131 In time the obligative meaning of the subjunctive came to be subsidiary to its function of indicating subordination.

obligatorily, *adv.* (Later examples.)

1942 PARTRIDGE *Usage & Abusage* 346/2 *Vari-coloured* and *variegated* are, the first obligatorily, the second preferably, to be used of or in reference to colour. **1961** *Amer. Speech* XXXVI. iii. 163 Postnominal modifiers can be shifted out beyond the noun obligatorily. **1975** T. P. WHITNEY tr. *Solzhenitsyn's Gulag Archipel.* II. III. i. 15 Camps for forced labor were obligatorily created.

oblige, *v.* Add: **6. d.** *intr.* and *trans.* To act as a charwoman (for); to provide with domestic help. *euphem.*

1933 D. C. PEEL *Life's Enchanted Cup* xix. 259 The mother took in washing and went out to 'oblige' and earned roughly 22s. a week and some of her food. **1937** E. GARNETT *Family from One End St.* i. 13 She occasionally did odd work to 'oblige' Mrs. Theobald, the Vicar's wife. **1958** J. CANNAN *And be a Villain* iii. 51 I'm not in service. I oblige by the hour. **1963** A. LUBBOCK *Austral. Roundabout* 165 Twice a week a lady came to 'oblige' in the house. **1972** 'A. ARMSTRONG' *One Jump Ahead* i. 8 A bachelor who..paid well and wasn't too fussy..was a far better proposition than some others she had 'obliged'.

obliger. Add: **2. b.** One who obliges (sense *6 d); a charwoman. *euphem.*

1959 T. GIRTIN *Unnatural Break* 107, I thought that it was a bit odd the tea-things not being cleared away. I mean that looks as if they hadn't got an obliger. **1960** P. COLERIDGE *Running Footsteps* 63, I was agreeably surprised to be confronted by an elderly obliger, trailing a floor-mop.

oblique, *a.* (*sb.*) Add: **B.** *sb.* **3.** = *oblique case* (see OBLIQUE *a.* 5).

1695 WHEELER *Royal Gram. Reformed* vii. 26 *Qui* standing alone as a personal Relative is Englished *who* in the Nominatives, and *whom* in the Obliques. **1939** *Language* XV. 81 The obliques regularly have -äs. **1961** R. B. LONG *Sentence & its Parts* 494 Obliques such as the *insist* of *she insists on paying*.

4. *Photogr.* A photograph taken at an oblique angle.

1942 *R.A.F. Jrnl.* 27 June 10 The second photograph is an earlier oblique of a similar type of *Sperrbrecher*. **1955** E. WAUGH *Officers & Gentlemen* II. i. 158 Guy, have you still got those obliques of 'Badger'?.. Bung 'em back to GHQ. **1958** C. B. SMITH *Evidence in Camera* i. 19 The other two [cameras]—one on either side—were at an angle to take obliques. **1970** M. KELLY *Spinifex* ii. 48 Oosterman bracing the Newman cine-camera, F.245 aimed for obliques.

5. An oblique line, *spec.* a sloping virgule.

1961 in WEBSTER. **1965** W. S. ALLEN *Vox Latina* 9 Phonemic symbols..are conventionally set between obliques, e.g. /t/. **1973** A. H. SOMMERSTEIN *Sound Pattern Anc. Greek* i. 7, I follow the practice of Chomsky and Halle, who say..that they use obliques 'for representations in which the features are functioning as classificatory devices'.

obli·teratingly, *adv.* [f. OBLITERATING *ppl. a.* + -LY².] In an obliterating manner; so as to obliterate.

1904 H. G. WELLS *Food of Gods* I. iii. 56 He scarcely remembers the leap he must have made..so obliteratingly hot and swift did his impressions rush upon him.

obliteration. Add: **1.** Also *attrib.*, as *obliteration bombing*: heavy bombing intended to destroy a target completely.

1943 *Spectator* 24 Sept. 289/2 (*heading*) 'Obliteration' bombing. *Ibid.* 8 Oct. 337/2 The question of 'obliteration bombing'..raises more difficulties than Mr. Johnstone envisages. **1944** *Sat. Rev. Lit.* (U.S.) 8 Apr. 14/1 Vera Brittain, has become the spearhead of a movement.. directed against the mass air attacks of enemy cities, which she describes as 'obliteration bombings'. **1945** L. MUMFORD *City Devel.* (1946) 173 This failure would still be serious..even if obliteration bombing had not been practised.

obliterative, *a.* Add: **2.** *Zool.* **obliterative coloration, shading** = *COUNTERSHADING.

1909 [see *COUNTERSHADING]. **1926** W. P. PYCRAFT *Camouflage in Nature* vi. 66 This type of coloration he [*sc.* A. H. Thayer] designated 'obliterative coloration'. **1940** H. B. COTT *Adaptive Coloration in Animals* I. iii. 39 The appearance of obliterative shading can be..reproduced by means of patterns..rather than by the more usual method of graded ground colour. **1964** A. L. THOMSON *New Dict. Birds* 139/2 Graded coloration, ranging from darkest on the back to lightest on the under parts, neutralises relief and thus renders the solid body as an apparently flat surface. Obliterative shading forms a basis for the coloration of nearly all cryptic birds, whether or not they carry a super-imposed pattern.

obliterator (ǫ̆bli·tĕreⁱtǫ̆ɹ). [f. OBLITERATE *v.* + -OR¹.] One who or a thing which obliterates.

1895 HARDY *Jude* I. i. 7 In place of it a tall new building ..had been erected..by a certain obliterator of historic records. **1900** *Pall Mall Gaz.* 18 Apr. 3/2 Fire was an obliterator of evil deeds more sure than any other.

oblivia·lity. *rare.* [f. OBLIVIAL *a.* + -ITY.] Liability to be forgotten.

1905 E. F. BENSON *Image in Sand* i. 5 You certainly did not [meet him], or you would remember. Mr. Henderson has absolutely none of the quality of obliviality.

oblivion. 2. (Later example.)

1912 GALSWORTHY *Inn of Tranquility* 128 Handwrought bronze sconces and a band of metal bordering, all blackened with oblivion.

oblivious, *a.* **1.** ¶ Read: Unaware or unconscious of. Const. *of* or (esp.) *to*. Add further examples. No longer regarded as *erron.*

1926 W. DE LA MARE *Connoisseur* 173 Above them, as if entirely oblivious to their ranting, a glazed King Edward VII stared stolidly out of a Christmas lithograph. **1960** C. DAY LEWIS *Buried Day* v. 84, I stayed indoors all day for several days, oblivious to the damp heat of Falmouth.., re-living battles I had never fought. **1970** *Daily Tel.* (Colour Suppl.) 17 Apr. 54/3 For a man who has lived here all his life Makinen is oddly oblivious to the city's history.

obliviscible (ǫblivi·sib'l), *a.* [f. L. *oblīvīsci* to forget + -IBLE.] Able or likely to be forgotten.

1905 *N.Y. Times* 12 Aug. II. 526/4 The sonnets he [*sc.* Swinburne] wrote about those poets, so obliviscible, excepting by himself.

Oblomov, Oblomoff (ǫ·blomǫf). The name of a character in Ivan Goncharov's novel 'Oblomov' (1855), represented as inactive, weak-willed, and procrastinating: used allusively. Hence **Oblomovism** (ǫblōᵘ·moviz'm, ǫ·blomǫ̆viz'm), conduct resembling that of Oblomov; sluggishness, inertia.

1902 *Encycl. Brit.* XXIX. 29/2 Dobroluboff said of it, '..something of Oblomoff is to be found in every one of us'. Peesareff..declared that 'Oblomoffism'..'is an illness fostered by the nature of the Slavonic character and the life of Russian society.' **1924** *Psyche* V. 55 This type of introversion..is known in Russia as 'Oblomovism'. **1925** I. A. RICHARDS *Princ. Lit. Crit.* vii. 52 Most people in the same day are Bonaparte and Oblomov by turns. **1942** *Penguin New Writing* XII. 62 Thompson had been sinking towards semi-starvation, I to the insidious Oblomovism of the country. **1957** A. G. MEYER *Leninism* ix. 214 Oblomovism—the behavior of Oblomov, pathetic hero of Goncharov's novel of the same name, who prefers to contemplate and discuss the universe, including his own predicament, instead of taking an active part in solving his problems and participating in life. **1970** *Harper's Mag.* Oct. 44 Friends hint there may be a touch of Oblomovism combined with whatever real ills his aging flesh may be heir to.

obnoxity (ǫ̆bnǫ·ksĭti). [f. as OBNOXIOUS *a.* + -ITY.] An obnoxious, objectionable, or offensive person or thing; an object of aversion.

1924 LAWRENCE & SKINNER *Boy in Bush* xx. 282 The parlour was the coolest place for the meat. Easu shifted the red obnoxity, wire cover and all, to the top of a cupboard. *c* **1925** D. H. LAWRENCE *Virgin & Gipsy* (1930) iii. 38 That widow of a knighted doctor, a harmless person indeed, had become an obnoxity in their lives.

obnubilated, *ppl. a.* (Earlier and later examples.)

1658 [see *ADIAPHANOUS *a.*]. **1939** E. POUND *Let.* 7 Nov. (1971) 330, I loathe and always have loathed Indian art... Obnubilated, short curves, muddle, jungle, etc.

‖ **obo** (ǭᵘ·bo). [Native word.] In Mongolia, a ritual cairn of stones.

Quot. 1923 may be a different word.

1923 G. COLLINS *Valley of Eyes Unseen* 58 The *obo* consists of slabs of slate..inscribed all over with Tibetan characters. **1934** H. HASLUND *Tents in Mongolia* vi. 59 We passed by two colossal heaps of stones, which the caravan men called *obos*. *Ibid.*, The two obo were..

erected at the point where the caravan route crosses the boundary between Inner and Outer Mongolia. **1936** P. FLEMING *News from Tartary* v. 134 There were also prayer flags and a good many *obos*, which are cairns of stones with a wide range of superstitious significance. **1970** C. R. BAWDEN in L. Ligeti *Mongolian Studies* 65 The worship of the mountains and *obos* (ritual cairns).

obo, var. *OBBO.

oboe. Add: Now usu. with pronunc. (ō͡u·bo). **3.** (With capital initial.) The name of a radar system for guiding military aircraft in which two ground stations interrogate a transponder in the aircraft to identify it and determine its position, which information is then transmitted to the aircraft. Also *attrib.* and *Comb.*

1945 *Daily Mirror* 15 Aug. 4/2 Next came 'Gee', the bombing beam which guided our radar-equipped bombers on to their targets, and the even more accurate 'Oboe'. **1946** *R.A.F. Jrnl.* May 169 'Oboe'-controlled Mosquito aircraft were assigned to the marking of targets. **1947** CROWTHER & WHIDDINGTON *Science at War* I. 59 The Oboe pathfinders started later and were faster... The pathfinder was under Oboe control, while approaching the target, for about ten minutes. **1974** *Encycl. Brit. Macropædia* XV. 371/1 The extreme accuracy of Oboe, H, or Shoran was not needed for guiding a plane between airfields on a friendly mission.

oboe (ō͡u·bo), *v. rare.* [f. the sb.] *trans.* To sound in the tone of an oboe.

1923 A. HUXLEY *Antic Hay* i. 8 Like an oboe, Mr. Pelvey intoned: 'The Lord be with you.'..those words, good Lord! that Mr. Pelvey was oboeing out of existence.

‖**oboe da caccia** (ō·boe dă ka·tʃiă). Also **oboe di caccia.** Pl. **oboi.** [It., lit. 'hunting oboe'.] An old form of oboe, a fifth lower in pitch than the ordinary instrument. Cf. TENOROON.

1876 STAINER & BARRETT *Dict. Mus. Terms* 317/2 The oboe d'amore, which was also called *oboe luonga*, produced a delicate and sweet tone, while the *oboe da caccia* corresponded to the tenoroon oboe, or corno inglese. **1880** GROVE *Dict. Mus.* II. 489/1 Two important movements.. in Haydn's Stabat mater are scored for two oboi di caccia obligati. **1938** *Oxf. Compan. Mus.* 627/1 Bach does not make much sole use of the normal hautboy... The oboe d'amore and the oboe da caccia were the instruments to which he gave a solo position in his cantatas, &c. **1963** *Listener* 21 Mar. 532/2 No oboi da caccia in *Qui tollis*.

‖**oboe d'amore** (ō·boe damō·re). Pl. **oboes, oboi.** [It., lit. 'oboe of love'.] An old form of oboe with a pitch a minor third below that of the ordinary oboe.

1876 [see prec.]. **1885** G. B. SHAW *How to become Mus. Critic* (1960) 62 The renovation of the obsolete *oboe d'amore* (love-hautboy)..proved very successful. **1930** [see *FLÛTE-À-BEC]. **1962** *Listener* 27 Dec. 1109/2 Oboe d'amore and two bassoons. **1976** *Gramophone* July 199/3 Scored only for strings and two oboi d'amore, it has some of the most remarkable writing in all Bach's church cantatas.

‖**obosom** (obō͡u·sǫm). 9 **b-.** Pl. **abosom.** [Ashanti.] In the religious system of the Ashanti peoples of Ghana, a general name for any of the many gods inferior to the Supreme Being.

1853 B. CRUICKSHANK *Eighteen Yrs. on Gold Coast* II. vi. 129 From the Souman, or idol of individuals, we come to the Boossum of a family or town, which frequently has no material representation. This..does not so much represent the god of an individual as a family god, or, more universally still, the god of a people. **1887** A. B. ELLIS *Tshi-Speaking Peoples of Gold Coast* ii. 18 They [*sc.* the local deities] are very numerous... The general name for these deities is *Bohsŭm*. **1916** R. S. RATTRAY *Ashanti Proverbs* i. 30 A *suman* would seem to derive its power from the *abosom*, just as the *obosom* in turn gains its own from *Onyankōpɔ̆ṅ*. **1923** —— *Ashanti* ii. 54 The great *obosom* (god) of all Ashanti is the Tano River, from which are derived countless of 'his children' as lesser *abosom*... Tano is considered as the 'son of the Supreme God'. **1960** M. J. FIELD *Search for Security* I. ii. 47 The Supreme God (called *Onyame* in Ashanti) is aloof... The *abosom* are the active, approachable executives of the Supreme God. The *abosom* are popularly referred to as 'the little gods', but each one is treated, in daily practice, as though he were omnipotent, omniscient and omnipresent. **1970** P. OLIVER *Savannah Syncopators* 30 The occasions which I was privileged to attend, culminating in a cult or 'fetish' dance for a local *obosom*, or protective spirit, were simple and moving.

oboy. *U.S.* = *BOY *sb.*[1] 9.

1963 T. PYNCHON *V.* xvi. 429 'Oboy, oboy,' said Fat Clyde wearily. **1966** —— *Crying of Lot 49* vi. 181 Oboy... they'd call her names, proclaim her..as a redistributionist and pinko.

O'Brienism (obrəi·əniz'm). [f. the name of William *O'Brien*, Irish patriot (1852–1928) + -ISM.] The conduct or anti-union policy of William O'Brien, esp. in the British Parliament about 1900 and 1901. **O'Bri·enite,** a supporter of William O'Brien.

1889 *Globe & Traveller* 18 Feb. 1/2 (*heading*) O'Brienism. **1900** *Westm. Gaz.* 22 Oct. 2/2 Mr. Redmond accepts ..the new situation caused by the triumph of the O'Brienites and the defeat of the Healyites. *Ibid.* 24 Dec. 3/1 O'Brienism is an equivalent term for constitutional anarchy. **1911** *Q. Rev.* July 241 The realists come from the north, east, and south, the strongholds of Unionism and O'Brienism.

obruchevite (ǫbrū·tʃĕvəit). *Min.* [ad. Russ. *obruchevit*, f. the name of V. A. *Obruchev* (1863–1956), Russian geologist: see -ITE[1].] A mineral containing appreciable proportions of yttrium and uranium that was orig. regarded as a member of the pyrochlore group (see quot. 1977).

1955 *Internat. Conf. Peaceful Uses Atomic Energy* (United Nations) *U.S.S.R.: Sci. & Techn. Exhib.* 9 These classes of minerals include..obruchevite. **1959** *Mineral. Abstr.* XIV. 54/1 In 1945 E. I. Nefedov discovered in a pegmatite vein in the Alakuztti region (N.W. Karelia) a peculiar metamict tantalo-niobate, which he classed with ellsworthite. In 1949 A. A. Beus after a study of this mineral called it obruchevite in honour of V. A. Obruchev. ..Obruchevite replaces albite and infills cracks in quartz. It occurs in association with garnet and other minerals as nests and irregular masses up to 5 cm. in diameter. **1966** Z. LERMAN tr. *Vlasov's Geochem. & Mineral. Rare Elements* II. 509 The mode of occurrence of obruchevite and its mineral paragenesis show that it forms during the latest stages of the replacement process. **1977** *Amer. Mineralogist* LXII. 407/1 [Report of the Subcommittee on Pyrochlore Nomenclature of the IMA Commission on New Minerals and Mineral Names.] Synonyms, doubtful and discredited names, and species not belonging to the pyrochlore group... *Obruchevite* (Kalita, 1957) is a name later shown to have been given to two different species (Gorzhevskaya and Sidorenko, 1969). One of these, brown obruchevite, after heating to 700°C, crystallized to the samiresite S phase... The other, black obruchevite, was subsequently renamed yttropyrochlore (Kupriyanova, 1970, unpublished). The Soviet Union's Commission of New Minerals (KNM) and Mineralogical Terminology have recommended the name *yttropyrochlore* replace this type of *obruchevite*.

obs, slang abbrev. OBSERVATION. Cf. *OBBO.

1943 *R.A.F. Jrnl.* Aug. 32 The Met. Officer has sent his obs through each hour in the usual way. **1970** O. NORTON *Dead on Prediction* v. 99 Hurry up. I'm keeping obs.

obscene, *a.* **1.** Delete 'Now somewhat *arch.*' and substitute 'Now restored to general use'. (Later examples.)

1875 'MARK TWAIN' *Sk. New & Old* 148 The obscene Tumble-Bug. **1915** A. HUXLEY *Let.* 1 Feb. (1969) 65 Practically speaking, Sligger and myself are the only two possible people left alive in Oxford; even the few possibilities of last term have now vanished, leaving only a sort of obscene riff-raff. **1923** A. BENNETT *Riceyman Steps* I. x. 44 The three-story houses (with areas and basements) were all alike... The fronts of the door-steps were green with vegetable growth... The areas, except one or two, were obscene. The Square..was merely decrepit, foul and slatternly. **1936** 'N. BLAKE' *Thou Shell of Death* i. 7 The shop windows, too, are piled with that diversity of obscene knick-knacks which nothing but the spirit of universal goodwill could surely tolerate. **1974** 'J. GRAHAM' *Bloody Passage* i. 19 Vietnam was the most obscene episode of the century. **1974** *Greenville* (S. Carolina) *News* 23 Apr. 1/8 Energy officials have already predicted that first-quarter oil profits will be 'embarrassingly high' or 'whoppers'. Sen. Henry Jackson, D-Wash., has said they'll be 'almost obscene'. **1974** *Observer* 1 Sept. 1/7 The result..was another defeat for the image of football. In six hours of running skirmishes, 55 people were arrested; but what was particularly obscene was the mindlessness of the 3,000 or 4,000 youths who took part. **1977** *Time* 19 Dec. 19/2 Something in the very robustness of Germany's economy seemed to the terrorists and their sympathizers profoundly obscene.

2. (Later examples.)

1959 *Act 7 & 8 Eliz. II* c. 66 §1 An article shall be deemed to be obscene if its effect..is, if taken as a whole, such as to tend to deprave and corrupt persons who are likely..to read, see or hear the matter contained or embodied in it. **1964** *Daily Tel.* 11 Dec. 26/2 Appeal Court judges ruled..that not only sex, but drug addiction, made a book obscene and depraved. **1972** *N.Y. Law Jrnl.* 31 Oct. 14/9 U.S.A. v. Various Articles of Obscene Merchandise.

obscenely, *adv.* **a.** Delete (*arch.*) and add later examples.

1922 F. SCOTT FITZGERALD *Beautiful & Damned* II. i. 157 This cowardice sprang out, became almost obscenely evident, then faded. **1964** R. CHURCH *Voyage Home* viii. 178 In those uncrowded years..England was less obscenely populated. **1974** *Times* 9 Apr. 14/3 Broadmoor's forbidding buildings are obscenely overcrowded.

obscenity. Add: **a.** (Later examples.)

1971 J. TREVELYAN in *Mind & Mental Health* Winter 6/1 My own inclination is to apply the word 'pornography' to written or visual material concerned solely with sex, and the word 'obscenity' as a more general term covering pornography and also other things, especially violence. This view was held by D. H. Lawrence who suggested that obscenity was a matter of personal opinion, whereas pornography was something specific; he defined it as making sex dirty for money. **1972** *Police Rev.* 1 Dec. 1557/1 Mr. Chuter Ede..asked the Commissioner whether the Yard's obscenity squad—as it was then—were judges of literature and art?

b. Delete *Obs.* or *arch.* (Later examples.)

1940 *Times* 19 Apr. 7/2 What one American newspaper stigmatizes as the 'obscenity' of the attack upon Norway. **1970** *Times* 21 Mar. 3/1 The obscenity of racial hatred has been vigorously propagated over the last few years. **1975** *New Yorker* 25 Aug. 31/3 We had said 'so long' to the U.S.A., had bade farewell to..the obscenity of American life in our time. **1977** 'E. MCBAIN' *Long Time no See* xiii. 217 One-third of all the homicides committed in this city involved a victim and a murderer who didn't even *know* each other... Perfect strangers..locked in the ultimate intimate obscenity.

obscurancy. For *rare*[-1] read *rare.* (Later example.)

1970 *Nature* 1 Nov. 448/2 Throughout these early years, *Nature* offered its 'leadership' support against obscurancy and obstruction in high places.

obscura·ntic, *a.* [f. OBSCURANT *sb.* and *a.* + -IC.] Opposed to enquiry or enlightenment. So **obscura·nticism** = OBSCURANTISM. Also **obscuranti·stic** *a.*

1926 *Contemp. Rev.* Nov. 661 The book..is full of warnings which sometimes are obvious and sometimes obscurantic. **1927** *Ibid.* Feb. 208 It would not be a work of truth or of love, but of well-meaning though mischievous obscuranticism. **1934** *Amer. Speech* IX. 278/1 The moralists..are in reality ensuring that the minds of the young will develop into the same welter of obscurantistic obsessions as their own. **1941** F. MATTHIESSEN *Amer. Renaissance* XIV. iv. 653 Where Hawthorne's criticism runs no risk of being obscurantistic is in his portrait of Hollingsworth.

obscuration. 1. (Further transf. examples.)

1904 *Rep. Joint Comm. Phonetic Eng. Alphabet* (U.S.) ii. 12 In unstressed syllables the sounds undergo a change which, in the lack of a better name, may be called 'obscuration'. The quality and extent of this obscuration vary somewhat with the style of the discourse, the idiosyncrasy of the speaker and the nature of the neighboring consonants. **1935** J. S. KENYON *Amer. Pronunc.* (ed. 6) 101 Not all of these pairs of stressed and stressless vowels represent the same historical stage of obscuration of the unaccented vowel. **1962** A. C. GIMSON *Introd. Pronunc. Eng.* vii. 142 As a general rule, weak accent in OE led to the obscuration of short vowels and the shortening of long vowels.

obscure, *a.* Add: **4. b.** *spec.* of a vowel sound, weak and centralized; reduced. (Further examples.)

[**1568** T. SMITH *De Recta et Emendata Linguæ Anglicæ Scriptione Dialogus* 14 Si Galli suum habent fœmininum obscurum, siue fuscum *e*, quod in fine dictionis positum, propè nihil sonat, auditur tamen, & apud illos est frequentissimum, nostræ linguæ prorsus incognitum. **1653** J. WALLIS *Grammatica Linguæ Anglicanæ* i. 6 Eodem loci..formatur Gallorum *e* fœmininum; sono nempe obscuro. *Ibid.* 7 Ibidem etiam... Sonatur *ǒ*, vel *ŭ*, obscurum.] **1665** O. PRICE *Vocal Organ* B3[v] The ,*e*, is twofold. 1. Clear; as in let... 2. Obscure, onely when *e* is short before *r*, as in her, liberty, brother, father, merchant. *Ibid.* B4 The short ŭ, and obscure *ǒ*, are formed in the throat, yet narrower then *è*. **1695** *Writing Scholar's Compan.* x. 36, o, is obscure, like (oo) or short (u)..before (m) as, *come* [etc.]. **1892** W. W. SKEAT *Primer Eng. Etymol.* ii. 25 In the A. S. *Dūn-stān*..the *ā* has been shortened, and is now obscure. **1904** *Rep. Joint Comm. Phonetic Eng. Alphabet* (U.S.) iii. 30 The obscure [ə] is the goal to which the most of the other vowels tend when not supported by the stress. **1909** O. JESPERSEN *Mod. Eng. Gram.* I. ix. 249 Portuguese short *a* is an obscure vowel. **1924** J. S. KENYON *Amer. Pronunc.* 107 Naturalness..is gained only by observing the normal relation between strest and unstrest syllables, distinct and obscure vowels. **1967** J. D. O'CONNOR *Better Eng. Pronunc.* v. 106 In initial position, as in..*attempt*,..*account*,..*observe*, you must again keep it very short and very obscure.

obscure, *v.* **1.** Delete †.

c. Add to def.: *spec.* to articulate (a vowel) in a weaker, more centralized position. (Earlier and later examples.)

a **1637** JONSON *Eng. Gram.* (1640) I. iii. 36 Where it [*sc.* e] endeth a last Syllable,..it either soundeth flat... Or, it passeth away obscur'd, like the faint *i.* as in these, *Written..divel*, &c. *a* **1790** B. FRANKLIN *Autobiogr.* in *Writings* (1905) I. 358, I found his voice distinct till I came near Front Street, when some noise in that street obscur'd it. **1924** J. S. KENYON *Amer. Pronunc.* 108 The student should rid himself of a common misconception; namely, that the obscuring of certain consonants and vowels owing to lack of stress on syllables or words is the result of a corruption of good English. **1934** *S.P.E. Tract* XXXIX. 621 'Short *e*'. This is rarely raised to [i], and never, except before *-r*, obscured to [ə]. **1934** S. ROBERTSON *Devel. Mod. Eng.* (1936) vii. 230 Obscuring and loss of formerly distinctive vowel sounds, and dropping of consonants in phonetically difficult combinations.., are both to be found in Old English. **1935** J. S. KENYON *Amer. Pronunc.* (ed. 6) 90 The vowels of unaccented syllables have gradually become obscured to a sound quite different in resonance, or quality, from what they had formerly been. **1962** A. C. GIMSON *Introd. Pronunc. Eng.* vi. 80 Vowels under weak accent are increasingly obscured to [ə] or [ɪ], or are elided.

obscured, *ppl. a.* Add: **2.** *Phonetics.* Of a vowel sound: having a neutral, centralized articulation; weakened; reduced.

1925 G. P. KRAPP *Eng. Lang. in Amer.* II. 250 Difficulty was expressed in disposing of this unstressed and obscured vowel. **1934** M. K. POPE *From Latin to Mod. French* v. 119 The obscured neutral vowel in use in Modern English is buccal and central, the one in Modern French is a slightly rounded front sound. **1935** J. S. KENYON *Amer. Pronunc.* (ed. 6) 90 The same spelling is kept for the obscured vowel that was used to spell it before it became obscured. **1962** A. C. GIMSON *Introd. Pronunc. Eng.* vii. 120 As the great variety of spellings indicates, /ə/ may represent the reduced (obscured, 'schwa') form of any vowel or diphthong in an unaccented position.

obscu·ringly, *adv.* [-LY².] In an obscuring manner; so as to obscure.

1902 *New Liberal Rev.* Aug. 317 The Celtic fringes hang obscuringly over our eyes, as fringes do under befeathered hats in the Old Kent Road.

obscurist (ǒbskiūᵊ·rist). [f. OBSCURE *a.* or *v.* + -IST.] = OBSCURANTIST *sb.*

1925 *Chambers's Jrnl.* Mar. 196/1 He is no faddist or eccentric, no obscurist of any kind, but one who catches at charms in human life and paints them.

‖ **obscurum per obscurius** (ǫbskiūᵊ·rǒm pɜɪ ǫbskiūᵊ·riǒs), *phr.* [Late L., lit. the unclear (explained) by means of the more unclear.] An unclear argument or proposition (expressed) in terms of one that is even less clear; such an explanation. (Cf. *IGNOTUM PER IGNOTIUS.)

[**1616** W. CLERK *Withals's Dict. Eng. & Lat.* (rev. ed.) 574 *Obscurum per obscurius.* I am as wise as I was before.] **1892** C. A. M. FENNELL *Stanford Dict.* 580/1 *Obscūrum per obscūrius*, phr.: Late Lat.: the obscure by the more obscure. **1949** K. DAVIS *Human Society* viii. 202 At its best it was an explanation *obscurum per obscurius.* **1952** G. SARTON *Hist. Sci.* I. viii. 200 Herodotus..was already combining Pythagorean ideas with Egyptian, Orphic, and Bacchic ones, and he mixed up the story of Pythagoras with that of Zalmoxis, thus explaining *obscurum per obscurius.* **1959** *Listener* 8 Jan. 58/1 Alexander's attempt to describe certain other relations in nature on the analogy of this may seem like an attempt to explain *obscurum per obscurius.*

obsequent (ǫ·bsǐkwěnt, ǫbsī·kwěnt), *a.*² *Geomorphol.* [f. OB- + *-sequent* in CONSEQUENT, SUBSEQUENT *adjs.*] Of a stream, stream valley, or drainage pattern: having a course or character opposite to that of a consequent stream, stream valley, or drainage pattern, i.e. against the direction of dip of the strata. Hence as *sb.*, an obsequent stream.

1895 W. M. DAVIS in *Geogr. Jrnl.* V. 134 Its escarpment face sheds short, back-flowing streams into the longitudinal subsequent valley that has been developed along the weak underlying stratum: and, even at the risk of multiplying terms unduly, I would suggest that these streams be called obsequent, as their direction is opposed to that of the initial consequent streams. *Ibid.* 145 Such obsequents are represented by the Ousel and Ivel farther east. **1902** H. J. MACKINDER *Britain & Brit. Seas* 121 The Little Ouse of East Anglia is also an obsequent. **1954** W. D. THORNBURY *Princ. Geomorphol.* v. 114 Obsequent valleys drain in a direction opposite to the original consequent valleys. **1968** R. W. FAIRBRIDGE *Encycl. Geomorphol.* 288/2 (*caption*) Evolution of subsequent (plus obsequent and resequent) drainage system. *Ibid.* 1187/1 Obsequents were originally defined as streams having a direction opposite to that of the consequent streams in their vicinity. Usually, however, the term is interpreted to mean merely a stream flowing against the direction of dip.

b. Of a fault-line scarp or a related feature: having (as a result of differential erosion) a relief the reverse of that originally produced by the faulting.

1913 W. M. DAVIS in *Bull. Geol. Soc. Amer.* XXIV. 198 If it descends toward the relatively uplifted side, as must be the case when weaker rocks occur on that side, it may be called an obsequent scarp. **1954** W. D. THORNBURY *Princ. Geomorphol.* x. 260 If..the erosional topography is opposite to the original fault-produced topography, the mountain blocks would be obsequent tilt block mountains, the basins would be obsequent tilt block valleys, and the bounding scarps would be obsequent fault-line scarps. **1970** R. J. SMALL *Study of Landforms* iii. 103 An 'obsequent' fault-line scarp faces in the opposite direction to the original fault-scarp.

observabi·lity. [f. OBSERVABLE *a.* + -ITY.] The quality of being observable; observable character or state; capacity for being seen.

1934 *Philos. Rev.* XLIII. 137 The simplest case of verifiability—observability at will. **1944** *Mind* LIII. 220 The new positivist principle..does not say anything at all about the observability or non-observability of the facts asserted or denied in P. **1956** E. H. HUTTEN *Lang. Mod. Physics* iv. 154 A numerical limit to the observability of microscopic events. **1968** R. A. LYTTLETON *Mysteries Solar Syst.* iv. 120 It may happen that two periods of observability occur as different parts of its path on opposite sides of perihelion bring the comet into the night sky. **1974** *Nature* 8 Feb. 352/2 It has been argued that the observability of the scattered waves is closely related to the presence of a caustic. **1974** M. HESSE *Struct. Sci. Inference* i. 9 Most accounts of the observation language were dependent on circular definitions of observability and its cognates.

observable, *sb.* **2.** Delete † *Obs. rare* and add: Something that can be perceived more or less directly; something that is knowable through the senses. (Later examples.)

1954 A. J. AYER *Philos. Ess.* i. 9 It may be left open what situations are to count as being observable; whether, for example, we are to treat such objects as electrons as being directly accessible to observation, or only such common-sense objects as chairs and tables, or only sense-data. Whatever decision may be taken..we are..likely to be left with some descriptive expressions which do not signify observables. **1959** *Listener* 1 Oct. 520/1 According to Dingle, the observables of a science must be potentially observable 'by all normal people'. **1963** J. LYONS *Structural Semantics* i. 1 We must reject any theory of semantics the terms of which neither refer to observables nor are reducible to observables. **1964** *Philos.* XXXIX. 262 If one supposes observables to be ontologically fundamental then models appear gratuitous. **1965** P. CAWS *Philos. of Sci.* viii. 52 The concepts which science borrows from the knowledge and experience of ordinary men..yield principally substantive and adjectival constructs directly linked to perception. Constructs having this direct link will be called observables. **1968** J. J. C. SMART *Between Sci. & Philos.* v. 143 The instrumentalist..would agree with the operationist in holding that in science no statements are made about entities other than macroscopic observables.

b. *Physics.* A quantity that can (in principle) be measured.

1930 P. A. M. DIRAC *Princ. Quantum Mech.* ii. 25 In quantum mechanics it is more convenient to deal with something that refers to one particular time instead of to all times, analogous to the value of a classical variable at a particular instant of time. We shall call such a quantity an observable. **1955** W. PAULI *Niels Bohr* 38 All physical observables are represented by Hermitian operators. **1966** C. G. HEMPEL *Philos. of Nat. Sci.* vi. 74 These wavelengths are not observables in the ordinary sense of the word. **1974** H. CLARK *First Course Quantum Mech.* iii. 54 In quantum mechanics..not all the observables of a system can be measured simultaneously. If some observable is measured, this act of measurement may disturb the system and change the value of some other observable... The disturbance in a classical system..can in principle be allowed for exactly but not in quantum physics. **1975** *Nature* 31 Jan. 315/1 Body temperature, enzyme activity, leaf movement, neural firing, mitotic index or other convenient observables typically persist in regular up and down periods of about 24-h, even in ostensibly constant conditions.

observant, *a.* Add: **1. b.** Acting in accordance with the precepts of behaviour associated with a particular religion, esp. Judaism.

1902 *Daily Chron.* 2 Oct. 7/1 To-day observant Jews throughout the world celebrate the commencement of their New Year. *Ibid.* Even the less observant..hasten to the Synagogue to-day to listen to the mystic sound of the Ram's Horn trumpets. **1905** *Westm. Gaz.* 25 Mar. 3/2 Someone will be suggesting [giving up] linen collars next—in which case the really Lenten-observant man will look like nothing so much as a burglar. **1972** C. POTOK *My Name is Asher Lev* i. 36 The stores that were run by observant Jews were all closed on Shabbos. **1975** *Times Lit. Suppl.* 21 Nov. 1392/5 An observant Jew..declined to join a prominent Berlin literary club because he would eat only kosher food.

Observantine. Add: Also *attrib.* or as *adj.*

a **1773** A. BUTLER *Lives Saints* (1779) IV. 208 He [*sc.* St. James of Sclavonia] embraced with great fervour the humble and penitential state of a lay-brother among the Observantin Franciscan friars at Bitecto, a small town nine miles from Bari. **1930** F. J. EBLE tr. *Grisar's Martin Luther* ii. 51 The vicar..jeopardized the canonical and disciplinary autonomy of the Observantine monasteries entrusted to his care. **1932** *Times Lit. Suppl.* 9 June 425/2 A fifteenth-century bard who joined the order at the time when the Observantine reform was making great headway in Ireland.

observation. **2.** Delete † *Obs.* and add later example.

1911 W. J. LOCKE *Glory of Clementina Wing* xxii. 277 The daily calls to inquire after her health and happiness had grown to be a sacred observation.

10. *observation balloon, deck, gallery, platform, post, room, terrace, vehicle, window*; *observation-based* adj; (in Philos.) *observation basis, report, term* (see quots.); **observation-car** (earlier and later examples); **observation officer** = *OBSERVER 4 b; **observation-sentence** *Philos.*, in a scientific theory, a sentence that reports, or directly relates to, observed phenomena (opp. *theoretical sentence*); **observation-statement,** an observation-sentence, or the utterance of one; **observation ward** (see quot. 1927).

1909 *London Mag.* Sept. 15/2 He made numerous ascents in captive observation balloons. **1917** F. STARK *Let.* 16 Oct. (1974) I. 49 We had a great time.., going to call on a Major..who looks after the observation balloons in this sector. **1950** *Gloss. Aeronaut. Terms* (*B.S.I.*) I. 46 *Observation balloon*, a balloon fitted with a basket or car to carry passengers. **1965** *Language* XLI. 212 The value of observation-based description. **1965** P. CAWS *Philos. of Sci.* xxiv. 182 The observation basis must consist of carefully formulated protocol sentences. **1872** *Harper's Mag.* May 876/1 You look out of the open 'observation car' as you sweep down from a height of 7000 feet. **1880** 'E. LEATHES' *Actor Abroad* 177 An observation car, which is roomy, comfortable, and roofless is attached to the end of the train on leaving Sacramento. **1936** WODEHOUSE *Laughing Gas* ii. 17 These observation cars, in case you don't know, are where the guard's van is on an English train. **1973** *Guardian* 17 Mar. 14/4 The 'Rheingold' from Basle to Amsterdam..has a vista-dome observation car. **1951** A. C. CLARKE *Sands of Mars* iii. 21 He..hurried out to the observation deck, wondering what happened to Earth overnight. **1976** E. P. BENSON *Bulls of Ronda* vii. 51 Rafael Durán stood on the observation deck of the airport, watching the plane. **1951** Observation gallery [see *LINER *sb.*² 8 c]. **1904** *Daily Chron.* 22 June 9/3 The aim of the Japs..was deadly true, and the observation officers were able to see, through their field-glasses, men falling in every direction. **1922** Observation officer [see *flying officer* s.v. *FLYING *vbl. sb.* 3]. **1974** *Times* 23 Jan. 16/8 [Mr Arthur Harold Stevens] won the MC in 1916 for great courage under fire as an observation officer. **1906** F. LYNDE *Quickening* 29 At the rear of the string of Pullmans was a private car, with a deep observation platform. **1943** J. S. HUXLEY *TVA* xv. 127 The operation building for the navigation lock..contains control machinery.., and observation platform. **1957** D. ROBINS *Noble One* x. 103 She could imagine him climbing up the ladders to the observation platforms on the tree tops. **1909** *Westm. Gaz.* 17 Sept. 3/1 The way of this little bird is to sit on its observation post. **1914** *Daily Express* 28 Sept. 4/5 The damage to the cathedral was the inevitable result of the French using the cathedral as an observation post. **1937** KOESTLER *Spanish Testament* II. 276 At eight the prisoners came out into the courtyard again, and I took up my observation post. **1959** *Listener* 26 Mar. 553/1 In the extreme, as in modern totalitarianism, all 'observation posts' are available only to the duly qualified. **1974** K. ROYCE *Trap Spider* vii. 124, I could see the entrance... I had as good an observation post as any. **1964** *Amer. Philos. Q.* I. 251/1 The observation report can be a singular statement that contradicts the law. **1974** M. HESSE *Struct. Sci. Inference* i. 35 The 'meaning' of observation reports is 'theory-laden'. **1970** *Guardian* 14 Feb. 8/2 Observation rooms for looking down into the studios. **1936** R. CARNAP in *Philos. of Sci.* III. 429 My testing of any sentence..refers back ultimately to my own observation-sentences. **1940** A. J. AYER *Found. Empirical Knowl.* ii. 86 Some observation-sentence should be derivable. **1964** I. SCHEFFLER *Anat. Inquiry* 135 Their vocabulary was appropriate, enabling derivation from observation-sentences. **1970** W. V. QUINE *Philos. of Logic* i. 5 Usually observation sentences are..individually responsive to observation. This is what distinguishes observation sentences from theoretical sentences. **1946** A. J. AYER *Lang., Truth & Logic* (ed. 2) 11 My principle..I shall restate here..using the phrase 'observation-statement' in place of 'experiential proposition', to designate a statement 'which records an actual or possible observation'. **1951** *Mind* LX. 19 Such observation statements as 'The hydrogen-oxygen mixture in this glass vessel when ignited changed into water vapour'. **1961** E. NAGEL *Struct. of Sci.* xi. 348 Singular statements that either formulate the outcome of observations..or describe the overt procedures..we shall call..'observation statements'. **1966** *Philos.* XLI. 260 Various views..were held about observation-statements. **1965** P. CAWS *Philos. of Sci.* xi. 78 Terms which name percepts we have agreed to call observation terms, since they refer to what is directly observed. **1974** M. HESSE *Struct. Sci. Inference* i. 10 The allegedly clear and distinct character of the observation terms. **1968** *N.Y. City* (Michelin Tire Corp.) 129 An observation terrace..offers a splendid view of the airport. **1972** *Police Rev.* 10 Nov. 1444/1 They merge into almost any background—and for this reason they are the colours selected for Police observation vehicles. **1927** W. E. COLLINSON *Contemp. Eng.* 58 If there is doubt as to the presence of the disease in the patient when in hospital, he may be put in an observation ward. **1961** C. COCKBURN *View from West* i. 7 This ward..had..been built..probably as an observation ward for children. **1897** KIPLING *Capt. Cour.* ix. 193 The secretary and typewriter sat together..by the plate-glass observation window at the rear end. **1974** P. DICKINSON *Poison Oracle* i. 7 Wesley Morris stared at Dinah [*sc.* an ape] through the observation window.

observationalism. Delete *rare* and add: Also, the doctrine that observation, rather than theory, is the basis of science. Hence **observa·tionalist** *a.* (*sb.*), adhering to observationalism; practising observational as opp. to theoretical work; also, one who adheres to observationalism. Also **observationa·lity,** closeness to the level of observation; non-theoreticality.

1951 *Mind* LX. 44 The inductive account of scientific method, which is an alternative way of stating observationalism, postulated..the cautious generalization which must not go beyond the data. *Ibid.* 46 A consequence of observationalist presuppositions. **1960** W. V. QUINE *Word & Object* 42 We may speak of degrees of observationality. **1966** *Philos.* XLI. 360 Opposition to dogmatic observationalism should not develop into dogmatic anti-observationalism. **1973** *Sci. Amer.* May 12/3 Sclater..writes that McKenzie 'is the theoretician and I am the observationalist'.

observationally, *adv.* Add: (Further examples.) Also, with regard to observation.

1930 A. S. EDDINGTON *Rotation of Galaxy* 13 The effect on the apparent angular motion..remains always on the verge of what is detectable observationally. **1964** *Philos. Rev.* LXXIII. 203 We cannot observationally verify the speaker's claims. **1976** *Nature* 26 Feb. 628/2 Observationally one requires better high resolution, far-infrared and molecular maps and a near-infrared search for the dust-enshrouded protostars in the H II regions before the vastly complex physics and mechanics of these birth-places of stars can be understood fully.

observe, *sb.* Add: † **3.** *Sc.* A division of a sermon.

1833 W. L. MACKENZIE *Sk. Canada & U.S.* 8, I went to hear Doctor McLeod, a steadfast Presbyterian of the old school. There..the discourse is divided and subdivided into heads and observes in true covenanting fashion.

observer. Add: **3. c.** A person who observes without participating; *spec.* (*a*) one who attends a conference, display, etc., to note the proceedings; (*b*) one posted to an area of conflict to note events, supervise a cease-fire, etc.; also *attrib.*, as *observer force, group.*

1925 A. TOYNBEE *Survey Internat. Affairs 1920–23* 10 Several meetings were attended by an American observer. **1949** *Ann. Reg. 1948* 292 The U.N. Balkans Commission.. sent observers to watch the fighting there. **1958** *Observer* 10 Aug. 4/6 Any measures.., in addition to the original observer group, which would serve to ensure the territorial integrity and political independence of Lebanon. **1962** *Rep. Comm. Broadcasting 1960* 188 in *Parl. Papers 1961–2* (Cmnd. 1753) IX. 259 The three advertising organisations which now appoint one representative and one observer to the Committee formerly appointed two representatives each. **1970** *Guardian* 13 Jan. 9/8 The French and the Pope have already called for a new observer force. **1977** *Times* 9 Dec. 1/3 Sir David attended the inquest in Pretoria as an independent observer at the invitation of the Association of Law Societies of South Africa.

4. b. One whose duty it is to make military observations; *esp.* (*a*) a member of an artillery group trained to identify the target; (*b*) a person trained to notice and identify aircraft, or carried in an aeroplane († or other aircraft) to note the enemy's position, etc.; *spec.* as a rank in an air force; also *attrib.*, as *observer company, corps, flight, officer.*

[**1854** C. TOMLINSON *Cycl. Useful Arts* I. 16/1 Scarcely had the observer reached the height of 3,000 feet, than he observed..a thin vapour.] **1870** tr. *F. Marion's Wonderful Balloon Ascents* III. iv. 215 The soldiers of the enemy, all who saw the observer watching them.., came to the idea that they could do nothing without being seen. **1903** *Heavy Artill. Training* 36 If the target is not visible from the guns or ground quite close to them,..two observers are required. **1906** *Strand Mag.* May 515/1 The first of these was Mr. E. T. Fetch, accompanied by Mr. Krarup as observer, on a twelve-horse-power single cylinder Packard car. **1910** *Blackw. Mag.* Feb. 209/1 The service of an aeroplane, especially if..it could carry a military observer as well as the pilot, would be invaluable. **1914** *Field Artill. Training* ix. 325 The observer, having located the position of the target and conveyed the information to the artillery commander..receives from him the signal 'Observe for line'. **1914** *Daily Express* 28 Aug. 2/6 (*heading*) Observer flights. **1916** H. BARBER *Aeroplane Speaks* 50 Quickly the Observer climbs into his seat in front of the Pilot. **1928** C. F. S. GAMBLE *Story N. Sea Air Station* xiii. 226 During this year [1916] the rank of Observer Officer was created. **1932** *Flight* 22 July 677/2 It is very necessary to see, at least once a year, how the Observer Corps is functioning. **1940** *War Illustr.* 5 Jan. p. ii/3 Parker.. was a Group Commander in the Observer Companies of the Royal Defence Corps, which was founded in 1916. **1954** P. K. KEMP *Fleet Air Arm* 52 During 1916, the Admiralty opened a special school for training observers and instituted a new rank of Observer Officer. **1977** J. CLEARY *High Road to China* i. 26 The Bristol Fighter..carried two guns, one fired straight ahead by the pilot and the other able to be fired in a complete circle by the observer.

c. Used *attrib.* with reference to the effect of subjective factors on the accuracy or veracity of scientific observations.

1959 *Times Lit. Suppl.* 31 July 441/2 Proper consideration of evidence, allowance for observer-error, the clarification of language as a communicative medium—these.. are the barriers which stand between us and the irrational abyss. **1970** G. GREER *Female Eunuch* 90 It takes another psychiatrist to explain to her the function of observer bias. **1971** *Brit. Med. Bull.* XXVII. 6/1 Observer variability has also been shown to be a significant factor in errors in blood-pressure readings. *Ibid.* 8/1 There was little evidence to suggest variation between observers or observer bias.

obsession. Add: **3.** (Later examples.)

1901 G. B. SHAW *Three Plays for Puritans* Pref. p. xvii, The English novelist, like the starving tramp who can think of nothing but his hunger, seems to be unable to escape from the obsession of sex. **1908** YEATS & GREGORY *Unicorn from Stars* II. 56 There is another kind of inspiration, or rather an obsession or possession. **1916** G. B. SHAW *Androcles & Lion* Pref. p. lxxviii, The mass of mankind..are concerned almost to obsession with sex. **1922** JOYCE *Ulysses* 130 The Roman, like the Englishman who follows in his footsteps, brought to every new shore on which he set his foot..only his cloacal obsession.

b. *Psychol.* An idea or image that repeatedly intrudes upon the mind of a person against his will and is usually distressing (in psycho-analytic theory attributed to the subconscious effect of a repressed emotion or experience).

1901 C. A. MERCIER *Psychol.* 368 Obsessions are extremely varied in character. **1913** E. JONES *Papers on Psycho-Anal.* v. 126 Twenty years ago Janet separated obsessions and phobias under the title of 'psychasthenia'. **1924** J. RIVIERE et al. tr. *Freud's Coll. Papers* I. vii. 129 Two components are found in every obsession: (1) an idea that forces itself upon the patient: (2) an associated emotional state. **1958** M. ARGYLE *Relig. Behaviour* xii. 165 The similarities and differences between rituals and obsessions. **1976** SMYTHIES & CORBETT *Psychiatry* vi. 82 If we see some particularly horrible disaster, most people find it very hard to get it 'out of their minds'. An image of horror keeps coming back unwanted and the person has to struggle to get it out of consciousness. More trivial examples are tunes that keep running through one's head or fears that one might forget one's lines in a play... These are examples of mild obsessions—unwanted thoughts and images that crowd into consciousness in spite of all attempts to keep them out.

obsessional, *a.* Add: **2. a.** Characterized by or caused by an obsession (sense 3 or *3 b).

1909 *Cent. Dict.* Suppl., *Obsessional*.., pertaining to or of the nature of obsession. **1913** E. JONES *Papers on Psycho-Anal.* v. 126 Krafft-Ebing maintained the independence of obsessional states. **1940** *Mind* XLIX. 370 Thus with obsessional duties, 'I must go and make sure I have turned out the lights, turned off the taps,..made sure of security'. **1952** V. GOLLANCZ *My Dear Timothy* i. 11 Breathless delight in ease and comfort, and an obsessional drive not merely to work but..'to work extra'. **1954** M. FORTES in E. E. Evans-Pritchard *Inst. Primitive Society* vii. 89 There are the individuals with obsessional and paranoiac fears whose fantasies about themselves.. sound like morbid caricatures of primitive beliefs. **1973** R. LEWIS *Of Singular Purpose* vi. 139 There was only one word to describe Paul Mercereau's interest in Van Rijk. It was obsessional.

b. *obsessional neurosis*: in psychoanalytic theory, a psychoneurosis in which obsessional thoughts resulting from a regression of the libido lead to neurotic or compulsive behaviour. So *obsessional neurotic*, a person suffering from an obsessional neurosis.

1918 E. JONES *Papers on Psycho-Anal.* (ed. 2) xxx. 515 A detailed study of the obsessional neurosis. **1924** J. RIVIERE et al. tr. *Freud's Coll. Papers* I. viii. 153 Hysteria's close association with the female sex and..the preference of the male for the obsessional neurosis. **1926** [see *ISOLATION 2 b]. **1939** E. GLOVER *Psycho-Anal.* II. x. 78 The obsessional neurotic, like the hysteric, recognizes the irrationality of his symptoms. **1942** [see *DE-EMOTIONALIZE *v.*]. **1968** C. RYCROFT *Crit. Dict. Psychoanal.* 103 According to classical theory, the psychopathology of obsessional neurosis centres round regression to the anal-sadistic stage.

obse·ssional, *sb.* [f. the adj.] Someone whose personality is dominated by an obsession.

1928 [see *DIDDUMS]. **1945** *Brit. Jrnl. Psychol.* XXXV. 41 As a group, the obsessionals are distinctly more intelligent than the others. **1963** *Listener* 14 Mar. 474/3 The *soi-disant* realist was really just a neurotic old obsessional with an eye for detail. **1972** E. K. LEDERMANN *Existential Neurosis* ii. 13 Obsessionals and reactive depressives showed high sedation thresholds. **1978** P. PORTER *Cost of Seriousness* 43 Dangerous modes In all weather when obsessionals walk To a favourite spur above the land.

obsessionally (ǫbse·ʃənăli), *adv.* [f. OBSESSIONAL *a.* + -LY^2.] In an obsessional manner.

1961 J. DAWSON *Ha-Ha* vi. 126, I noticed the cracks between each board, and followed each one, uneasily, obsessionally, till it ran into the wall. **1961** *John o' London's* 12 Oct. 407/2 He *cares* for the theatre; passionately, obsessionally. **1966** P. GREEN tr. *Escarpit's Novel Computer* viii. 102 Fermigier never suspected a thing, though he was an obsessionally jealous man by nature. **1973** A. ROY *Sable Night* xvi. 167 The two men..had their attention almost obsessionally occupied.

obsessionist (ǫbse·ʃənist). [f. OBSESSION + -IST.] One who is obsessed, or subject to obsession, by a fixed idea.

1921 *Glasgow Herald* 24 June 8/4 The canards of the anti-waste obsessionists. **1928** *Daily Express* 6 Dec. 10/5, I once sat in a train for five hours opposite an obsessionist, who played chess with himself on a miniature board.

obsessive (ǫbse·siv), *a.* [f. OBSESS *v.* 3 + -IVE.] Of or pertaining to obsession; liable to obsess; obsessing. So as *sb.*, a person characterized by obsessive behaviour.

1911 I. H. CORIAT *Abnormal Psychol.* II. vi. 281 One of the most common of these obsessive states is what is known as the obsession of self-consciousness. **1918** A. E. DAVIS *Hypnotism* I. 46 A frequent cause of..obsessive thoughts, is the feeling of shame or regret arising out of bad habits. **1926** J. I. SUTTIE tr. *Ferenczi's Further Contrib. Theory & Technique Psycho-Anal.* xviii. 232 The individual suffering from obsessive ideas is really substituting thought for action. **1966** *Listener* 17 Mar. 414/1 Of the medical obsessives I particularly liked Maurice Denham as Bloomfield Bonington. **1969** N. W. PIRIE *Food Resources* iii. 104 In 1939 many of us argued that protein supplies would be the main problem in feeding Britain in war-time. We were stigmatized as obsessives. **1973** T. & R. MILLON *Abnormal Behav.* (1974) III. xiii. 296 Obsessive thoughts are intrusive ideas which the person cannot block from consciousness. **1975** R. HILL *April Shroud* xii. 154 'I've got some rushes here. You want to see them?' Like all obsessives, he could not doubt the answer.

b. *obsessive-compulsive* adj. Psychol., applied to a disorder in which an obsession results in the compulsion to perform repeatedly meaningless acts; also *fig.*; so as *sb.*, a person whose compulsive behaviour is due to obsessive thoughts.

1927 HENDERSON & GILLESPIE *Text-bk. Psychiatry* xiv. 399 'Obsessive-compulsive' state is applied to a..condition in which the preoccupation issues in motor acts of an apparently trifling or meaningless kind. **1941** S. H. KRAINES *Therapy Neuroses & Psychoses* i. 26 Hysteria and obsessive-compulsive neurosis in which states symbolic symptoms are more common. **1960** *Cambr. Rev.* 7 May 509/1 Of 100 severe reactions among students..the schizophrenic were the most frequent (34)... There were ..7 obsessive-compulsives. **1965** *New Statesman* 24 Sept. 426/1 [Ronald] Reagan has been associated with the obsessive-compulsive faction of the Republican right. **1970** *Jrnl. Gen. Psychol.* LXXXII. 175 Schizophrenics, obsessive-compulsives, and depressed persons have a high level of health anxiety.

obsessively (ǫbse·sivli), *adv.* [f. *OBSESSIVE *a.* + -LY^2.] In an obsessive manner; insistently, beyond reason.

1949 M. MEAD *Male & Female* xv. 296 The picture can be obsessively elaborated. **1969** *Sunday Times* 2 Nov. 51/3 Expressions of a mind almost obsessively in pursuit of unification. **1971** *Physics Bull.* June 332/3 Each side.. can select instances which demonstrate its point and.. can obsessively ignore others which demonstrate the opposite. **1977** P. DICKINSON *Walking Dead* IV. i. 252 The Captain continued to flick obsessively at the wheel.

obse·ssiveness. [f. as prec. + -NESS.] The quality of being obsessive.

1961 in WEBSTER. **1966** *Listener* 8 Sept. 366/3 Mr Storey portrayed very accurately that brand of obsessiveness which salesmen call enthusiasm.

obsidianite (ǫbsi·diănəit). *Geol.* [f. OBSIDIAN + -ITE^1.] = *TEKTITE.

1898 R. H. WALCOTT in *Proc. R. Soc. Victoria* XI. 23 As long as this uncertainty exists, some other name would be more appropriate, and I suggest and will refer to them in this paper as 'obsidianites'. **1909** [see *AUSTRALITE]. **1933** *Nature* 28 Jan. 117/1 Small, curiously shaped pieces of.. glass have long been known from certain regions, and have been called moldavites from the Moldau River in Bohemia..; australites or obsidianites from Australia; [etc.]. **1963** J. A. O'KEEFE *Tektites* i. 1 Earlier writers referred to tektites as obsidianites.

obsolesce, *v.* For *rare*—^{1} read *rare*. Add later examples.

1934 G. B. SHAW *On Rocks* 160 The lists of crimes and penalties will obsolesce like the doctors' lists of diseases and medicines. **1950** *N.Y. Times* 12 Nov. 96/2 (Advt.), New New a thousand times New (we'd rather die than obsolesce). **1975** *Amer. Speech 1972* XLVII. 261 *Exolinguistics* has never become a standard term in either linguistics or anthropology, but it has persisted in both periodicals and books for twenty years, and it refuses to obsolesce.

obsolescence. Add: **1. b.** *spec.* of machinery or similar assets. Also *attrib.* See also **planned obsolescence*.

1887 GARCKE & FELLS *Factory Accounts* v. 93 This increased production may be due to certain parts being of a more permanent type than others and added to stock with less risk of obsolescence. **1913** R. J. PORTERS *Pitman's Dict. Book-Keeping* 330 Any loss sustained through obsolescence is charged to Profit and Loss. **1930** *Economist* 25 Jan. 163/2 In steelworks the question of obsolescence and the need for replacement of plant depend, partly, on the present condition of the plant and partly [etc.]. **1930** HUTCHINSON & LOVELL *Short Dict. Legal Terms* 87 *Obsolescence*. Where machinery is lessened in value not by mere usage or lapse of time, but by the fact that improved machinery is being brought into use, then this lessened value is termed obsolescence as distinguished from depreciation. **1957** CLARK & GOTTFRIED *University Dict. Business & Finance* 245/1 *Obsolescence*, with respect to an asset, the loss in value brought about through improvements in technology, changes in public taste, or a falling off in demand. **1959** JOWITT *Dict. Eng. Law* II. 1257/2 *Obsolescence allowance*, a charge allowed in determining profits for taxation purposes [etc.]. **1962** [see *built-in* (*b*) s.v. *BUILT *ppl. a.* 1 b]. **1966** *New Statesman* 28 Jan. 140/2 We have set up an obsolescence reserve of £1,500,000.

obsole·scing, *ppl. a.* [f. OBSOLESCE *v.* + -ING^2.] That is becoming obsolete.

1916 E. V. LUCAS *Cloud & Silver* 71 The Mayor..still clung to the steadily obsolescing topper. **1953** *Sun* (Baltimore) 23 Oct. 2/7 This sort of conversion [of gun turrets] is, in fact, under way, with other heavy 'obsolescing' types.

obsolete, *v.* Delete 'Now *rare*' and add later (chiefly N.Amer.) examples.

1944 *Amer. Speech* XIX. 234/1 A number of new laws and regulations..will almost certainly obsolete anything we might have given you during the past couple of months. **1945** in *Amer. Speech* (1948) XXIII. 70/1 The pressure of today's events has obsoleted many filing systems. **1960** [see *PRE-TEEN *a.*]. **1961** *Flight* 3 Feb. 154/3, I have read Sir Percy Hunting's paper... It is competent, commendable stuff, marred only by the inclusion of..some Americanisms... For example: obsoleting, envisioned, peppercorn rentals, fiscal, transportation. **1967** *Technology Week* 23 Jan. 100/1 (Advt.), The new gas turbine engine that's out to obsolete the diesel. **1972** *Fortune* Jan. 52/3 Increasing emphasis upon service and repair of existing equipment, rather than mindlessly obsoleting it. **1975** *Sci. Amer.* Feb. 39/1 (Advt.), Our precoated sheet failed to obsolete the glass TLC plate. **1975** *Listener* 11 Dec. 788/2 (American speaker) News reporting on the hour or the half-hour—when only part of the earlier news had been obsoleted—meant a great deal of repetition. **1977** *Islander* (Victoria, B.C.) 1 May 13/1 Wire is being obsoleted in communication today.

obstacle, *sb.* Add: **3. obstacle course** (see quot. 1961); also *transf.* and *fig.*

1961 WEBSTER s.v., *Obstacle course n*, a military training area filled with obstacles (as hurdles, fences, walls, ditches) that must be surmounted. **1973** *Black Panther* 31 Mar. 14/3 Could you describe some of the more known programs used in 'boot camp' such as the obstacle course and the firing range? **1976** J. WAINWRIGHT *Who goes Next?* 145 As an obstacle course the yard was a nothing. **1977** *New Yorker* 27 June 26/1 Then he picked two miracles attributed..to Neumann..and started them over what Father Litz called the Vatican obstacle course.

obstinancy. (Later example.)
1894 B. THOMSON *Diversions of Prime Minister* xiii. 213 The steadfastness of their followers was obstinancy under the lash of persecution.

obstreperous, *a.*, **obstreperously,** *adv.* Add: Further examples of illiterate forms.
Quot. 1922 is *ellipt.* for 'obstreperous mouth'.
1824 J. WIGHT *Mornings at Bow St.* 155 They were forthwith conveyed to the watch-house, and there they conducted themselves so '*obstropolously*', that the constable of the night found it necessary to have them put down below. **1922** JOYCE *Ulysses* 420 Hark! Shut your obstropolos.

obstruct, *v.* Add: **2. b.** Cricket. *obstructing the field* (formerly, *the ball*): an expression used to denote the manner of dismissal of a batsman who, in the umpire's opinion, wilfully hindered a fieldsman or interfered with the ball in order to avoid being caught, stumped, etc.
1877 C. BOX *Eng. Game Cricket* 456 Obstructing the Ball.—A man may be given out, but seldom is on such an account. **1905** *Laws of Cricket* § 26 The striker is out..if under pretence of running, or otherwise, either of the batsmen wilfully prevent a ball from being caught;—'Obstructing the field'. **1912** A. A. LILLEY *Twenty-Four Years Cricket* v. 57 As the ball struck it [*sc.* the bat] and fell to the ground, I pushed it further along with my bat, and Wheeler..gave me out. The point upon which he gave his decision was for obstructing the field.

c. In various games: to impede (a player) in a manner which constitutes an offence.
1895 H. F. BATTERSBY *Hockey* vii. 131 A player shall not run in between his opponent and the ball so as to obstruct him. **1953** *Association Football* ('Know the Game' Series) 33/2 If an opponent is obstructing a player, the player may charge him. **1969** *F.A. Guide to Laws of Game* 144 He is obstructing or interfering with an opponent. **1974** *Rules of Game* 163/3 An indirect free kick is awarded..for intentionally obstructing an opponent while not attempting to play the ball, in order to prevent him reaching it.

obstruction. Add: **2. b.** *spec.* in *Law.*
1908 *Encycl. Laws Eng.* (ed. 2) X. 116 *Obstruction.* This term is used in law mainly in two senses: (1) Interference with public or private rights or easements, particularly of light, way, navigation, or watercourse; (2) interference with officers of justice in the execution of their duty. **1910** *Daily Chron.* 18 Sept. 1/7 The conviction of two men for obstructing the police. After the evidence of two witnesses denying the statements made by the policemen when the obstruction charge was being considered, [etc.]. **1933** P. MACDONALD *Mystery of Dead Police* v. 41 My car's outside Savarin's... There's a bobby by it. He wants me for obstruction.

c. *spec.* as an offence in various games.
1923 H. E. HASLAM *How to play Hockey* xiii. 81 Turning on the ball incurs a penalty on the score of obstruction. **1935** *Encycl. Sports* 521/2 Charging and Obstruction... A player who is not running for the ball must not charge or obstruct an opponent not holding the ball. **1950** *Men's Hockey* ('Know the Game' Series) 18/1 A penalty bully is awarded..[for] a bad case of obstruction in front of goal. **1953** *Association Football* ('Know the Game' Series) 33/1 Should the obstruction take the form of a personal foul.. then the foul is penalised by a direct free kick. **1969** *F.A. Guide to Laws of Game* 197 Indirect free-kick for obstruction. **1974** *Rules of Game* 163/2 A direct free kick..is awarded for the following intentional fouls..: charging from behind (unless the opponent is guilty of obstruction).

5. obstruction light *Aeronaut.* (see quot. 1960).
1934 *Jrnl. R. Aeronaut. Soc.* XXXVIII. 728 The Air Ministry specified the number and type of obstruction lights which had to be fitted to each mast. **1960** *Guide Civil Land Aerodrome Lighting* (*B.S.I.*) 9 *Obstruction light*, a light indicating the presence of an obstruction.

obstru·ctionary, *a. rare.* [f. OBSTRUCTION + -ARY[1].] Tending or disposed to obstruct.
1934 W. DE LA MARE *Froward Child* 13 He was not always too anxious as to what kind of self was being so obstructionary. **1975** *New Yorker* 27 Oct. 77/1 There were rules, not of Herr Kautz's making, that guaranteed us a coeducational clubroom and occasional dances, but he was always around in a silently obstructionary manner, operating the turntable, serving the punch, watching.

obstructionism. Delete *rare*—[1] and add later examples.
1941 W. S. CHURCHILL *Second World War* (1950) III. 752 Please report to me any signs of obstructionism. **1955** *Times* 9 Aug. 11/4 Obstructionism is a game two can play. What is required to solve the difficulty is sincerity on both sides. **1964** S. BRITTAN *Treasury under Tories* ii. 61 He would not dream of indulging in the narrow-minded obstructionism of some of his predecessors. **1977** *Time* 5 Sept. 35/1 O'Neill made it clear to Georgia's crusty John Flynt, chairman of the ethics committee, that neither he nor Jaworski would tolerate any obstructionism.

obstructionist. (Later examples.)
1934 C. LAMBERT *Music Ho!* IV. 242 They were.. obstructionist rather than constructionist. **1965** [see *FILIBUSTER *sb.* 4]. **1966** M. R. D. FOOT *SOE in France* ii. 11 Petty obstructionists of this kind lay about SOE's path all its life, and some have pursued it since its winding-up. **1975** *New Yorker* 26 May 94/2 The late nineteen-forties, when another President got himself returned to office by blaming nearly everything that was wrong with the country on an obstructionist Congress controlled by the opposing party.

obstruent, *a.* and *sb.* Add: **A.** *adj.* (Later examples.)
1945 R. HARGREAVES *Enemy at Gate* 27 Cold, flabby, capricious, obstruent, and quite femininely vindictive, he was a creature of almost supernal selfishness, timidity and irresolution. **1973** J. WAINWRIGHT *Pride of Pigs* 70 The object of the exercise was to demolish any obstruent bushel likely to get in the way of *his* particular light.

B. *sb.* **c.** *Phonetics.* Also *erron.* **obstruant.** A fricative or plosive speech sound. Also *attrib.* and *Comb.*
1942 *Language* XVIII. 13 The first member of a cluster of two obstruents (stop or spirant) is voiceless. **1952** W. P. LEHMANN *Proto-Indo-European Phonol.* ii. 7 We then arrive at three classes of phonemes: 1. those which may not function as syllabics will be called obstruents. **1955** C. F. HOCKETT *Man. Phonol.* 97 A number of obstruent systems include no symmetric set at all. **1956** J. WHATMOUGH *Language* iii. 36 Sounds which are partially or completely stopped at some point—between the larynx and the lips (these are known as obstruents), e.g. *p:k*, or *f:χ*. **1962** *Word* XVIII. 312 Postvocalic consonants cluster in exactly the opposite direction, right to left, with privilege of occurrence of more than one consonant from an obstruent group, as many as three lenes or four fortes, but never a lenis after a fortis. **1963** ERVIN & MILLER in J. A. Fishman *Readings Sociol. of Lang.* (1968) 71 Vowel distinctions are learned first. The order of acquisition for the remaining features is: (*a*) vowels *vs.* consonants; (*b*) sonorants *vs.* articulated obstruants [etc.]. **1965** N. CHOMSKY *Aspects of Theory of Syntax* iv. 168 If the second consonant is a liquid, the first must be an obstruent. **1969** *Language* XLV. 248 We may symbolize the elements involved as C (any obstruent), R (any 'resonant' or semivowel) and V (any vowel). **1970** *Canad. Jrnl. Linguistics* XV. 122 Two examples [of persistent rule] are the well known devoicing of the final obstruants in German..and the loss of final /n/ in Livonian. **1973** A. H. SOMMERSTEIN *Sound Pattern Anc. Greek* ii. 26 The derivation of [n] from /nt/ is by Obstruent Dropping. **1975** *Language* LI. 528, I observed that the alternation between distinctively paired obstruents such as [p-b, t-d, k-g] had to be stated as a morphophonemic regularity. **1977** *Trans. Philol. Soc. 1975* 4 It is clear that a certain class of obstruent-final stems has the property of having inflected forms where the stem-final obstruents differ in voicing from those in the simplex forms.

obtainability (ǒbtēⁱ:năbi·lĭti). [f. OBTAINABLE *a.*: see -ITY.] The quality or state of being obtainable; capability of being obtained.
1932 H. H. PRICE *Perception* vii. 177 The existence or obtainability of the other sense-data. **1933** *Mind* XLII. 294, I fail to distinguish these merely entertained and probably false (in any case unverifiable) propositions as to the present and simultaneous actuality of the, as yet, unsensed sense, from that believed and probably true one as to their successive obtainability. **1971** *Analysis* XXXII. 55 The obtainability of the conditional.

obtrusively, *adv.* (Earlier example.)
1817 COLERIDGE *Biog. Lit.* I. x. 191, I have seen gross intolerance shewn in support of tolerance; sectarian antipathy most obtrusively displayed.

obtrusiveness. (Earlier example.)
a **1817** JANE AUSTEN *Persuasion* (1818) IV. x. 213 He stood, as opposed to Captain Wentworth, in all his own unwelcome obtrusiveness.

obtundent, *a.* and *sb.* (Later examples.)
1898 H. H. BURCHARD *Text-bk. Dental Path. & Therapeutics* VII. 538 Under the head of obtundents are included those agents which are applied locally to benumb the terminals of sensory nerves. **1908** J. D. PATTERSON in C. N. Johnson *Text-bk. Operative Dentistry* xxviii. 460 Obtundents. For the purpose of obtunding, many preparations have been advocated and many methods advised. **1930** W. H. O. MCGEHEE *Text-bk. Operative Dentistry* xxiv. 700 An Obtundent Paste devised by Doctor J. Lewis Blass..used with splendid results. **1961** MACDOUGALL & NIXON *Guide to Dental Therapeutics* viii. 115 When drugs are applied locally to relieve pain, they are referred to as local anaesthetics or obtundents.

Ob-Ugrian (ǫb,ū-griăn). [f. *Ob*, the name of a Siberian river + UGRIAN *a.* and *sb.*] A Finno-Ugric linguistic group of Siberia related to Hungarian. So **Ob-Ugric** *a.* and *sb.*
1933 L. BLOOMFIELD *Language* iv. 68 *Ob-Ugrian*, consisting of *Ostyak*..and *Vogule*. **1954** PEI & GAYNOR *Dict. Linguistics* 151 *Ob-Ugrian*, a language group (consisting of Ostyak and Vogul) which with Hungarian constitutes the Ugric branch of the Finno-Ugric (or Uralic) subfamily of the Ural-Altaic family of languages. **1955** B. COLLINDER *Fenno-Ugric Vocab.* p. xi, Vogul, Ostyak, and Hungarian are called Ugric languages; vg and os are called Ob-Ugric. *Ibid.* p. xiv, I made up my mind to quote even such words as occur only in Ugric and Permian, nay, even in Ob-Ugric and Permian. **1975** G. F. CUSHING tr. *Hajdu's Finno-Ugrian Lang. & Peoples* iii. 119 Ob-Ugrian is the collective name for the languages and peoples known as Vogul (Man'si) and Ostyak (Chanti).

obverse, *a.* and *sb.* Add: **A.** *adj.* **4.** *Logic.* Of a proposition: obtained from another proposition by the process of obversion.
1870 A. BAIN *Logic* I. 110 To each of the four Propositional Forms..there is an obverse form. **1917** J. WELTON *Groundwork of Logic* v. 79 In no case is there any loss in the range of application in the obverse proposition.

B. *sb.* **3.** (Earlier example.)
1870 A. BAIN *Logic* I. 110 No men are gods. The obverse is..all men are no-gods.

obversion. 2. (Earlier example.)
1870 A. BAIN *Logic* I. 110 In affirming one thing, we must be prepared to deny the opposite: 'the road is level', 'it is not inclined', are not two facts, but the same fact from its other side. This process is named *Obversion.*

obvert, *v.* **3.** (Earlier example.)
1870 A. BAIN *Logic* I. 110 Obvert the predicate, and prefix the sign of negation.

obverted, *ppl. a.* (Further example.)
1870 A. BAIN *Logic* I. 115 These obverted forms are Particular Affirmatives, and are therefore converted simply.

obvertend. (Earlier example.)
1886 P. K. RAY *Text-bk. Deductive Logic* (ed. 2) III. ii. 129 The given proposition may be called the *Obvertend.*

obviation. Add: **2.** The use, in some American Indian languages, of the obviative (see next).
1927 L. BLOOMFIELD in *Internat. Jrnl. Amer. Linguistics* IV. 191 Although obviation is confined to animate nouns.., verbs have obviative forms also for inanimate actors. **1974** P. H. VOORHIS *Introd. Kickapoo Lang.* 45 A noun and a pronoun agreeing with it in gender, number, and obviation are used to form statements of the identity of the noun and pronoun. **1976** *Language* LII. 519 Obviation is analysed as a dimension of contrast within the 3rd person.

obviative (ǫ·bviătiv, -ēⁱtiv). [ad. F. *obviatif*, f. OBVIATE *v.* + -IVE.] A grammatical category of the Algonquian family of N. Amer. Indian languages that marks a third person as subordinate to another, animate, third person in a given context. Also, a similar category in certain other languages. Also *attrib.* or as *adj.*
[**1866** J. A. CUOQ *Études Philologiques sur Quelques Langues Sauvages de L'Amérique* I. ii. 43 *De L'Obviatif.* Quand dans une phrase, se *rencontrent* deux 3èmes personnes de première classe, l'une *sujet* et l'autre régime de la phrase, la personne–régime se met à *l'obviatif. Ibid.*, Si le nom de la personne *dominante* se trouve exprimé, on le met à l'obviatif simple.] **1877** *Trans. Amer. Philol. Assoc. 1876* VII. 150 When two nouns (or a noun and a pronoun) in the third person are introduced in the same sentence, one as a subject and the other as the object of a verb, the latter takes the *obviative*—or second third-personal-form. **1899** *Proc. Amer. Philos. Soc.* XXXVIII. 186 In *pŏhĕgŭnŭl* and the following word, we have the ending *-ŭl* of the obviative, or accus[ative] of the third person, which appears in all the Algic idioms. **1922** L. BLOOMFIELD in *Amer. Jrnl. Philol.* XLIII. 276 He arrived at no clear statement of such features as the 'obviative' (the peculiar subsidiary third person of Algonquian grammar). **1927** —— in *Amer. Speech* II. 438/2 In inflection, Menomini, like the other Algonquian languages, has an *obviative* form for subsidiary third persons. **1958** *Archivum Linguisticum* X. II. 171 Distinction..of Proximate and Obviative, a common Algonquian distinction. **1965** *Canad. Jrnl. Linguistics* X. 80 The use of the obviative in Kutenai. **1976** *Language* LII. 519 The 3rd person in Cree includes two dimensions of contrast: proximate/obviative and animate/inanimate.

obvious, *a.* Add: **4. c.** quasi-sb., *the obvious*: something which is obvious; plain or manifest inferences, remarks, details, facts, etc.
1903 K. D. WIGGIN *Rebecca* (1904) i. 10 Their steadfast gaze..had the effect of looking directly through the obvious to something beyond. **1919** M. K. BRADBY *Psycho-Anal.* xiii. 175 The work of the artist who consciously and deliberately descends to the obvious..is uninteresting. **1976** G. MCDONALD *Confess, Fletch* (1977) iii. 19 You do the obvious and stop in at the first singles bar you come to.

oca. Add: Also **oka.** (Further examples.)
1885 W. MILLER tr. *Vilmorin-Andrieux's Veget. Garden* 355 The Oka-plant is easily propagated from the tubers. **1950** *N.Z. Jrnl. Agric.* May 471/3 The oka plant.., a native of Peru,..produces tubers which can be used as vegetables. **1966** *New Scientist* 9 June 643/1 Quinoa, papa-lisa, oka and isaño are plants [in Bolivia] which produce crops with higher nutritive value and protein content than wheat, maize and rice. **1972** Y. LOVELOCK *Vegetable Bk.* 221 The young leaves and flowers of the Spanish-American *oca*..are used in soups and as a pot-herb, and the flowers serve as a kind of vinegar substitute in salads. It is cultivated, however, for the sake of its egg-sized tubers, which are an important staple in Mexico and the Andean states.

Occam's razor: see RAZOR *sb.* 1 b in Dict. and Suppl.

occasion, *sb.*[1] Add: **1.** *to rise to the occasion*: see RISE *v.* 15 b.

occasional, *a.* (*sb.*) Add: **2. b.** (Further examples.)
1829 H. C. ROBINSON *Diary* 13 Aug. (1967) 102 [Goethe] remarked..that *occasional* poems are among the best poems when the poet takes care to retain all the spirit of the occasion. **1834** G. CRABBE JUN. in *Poet. Wks.*

G. Crabbe I. i. 15 His father took in a periodical work.. which contained, at the end of each number, a sheet of 'occasional poetry'. **1891** F. Locker-Lampson *Lyra Elegantiarum* (rev. ed.) p. x, In his [*sc.* the Editor's] judgment Occasional Verse should be short, graceful, refined, and fanciful, not seldom distinguished by chastened sentiment, and often playful. **1932** Chadwick & Kershaw *Growth of Lit.* I. 25 Both poems [sc. *Deor* and *Widsith*]..contain passages describing what purport to be personal experiences of the authors, and which—at least in the case of *Deor*—approximate to 'occasional' poetry. **1965** M. Spark *Mandelbaum Gate* i. 11 He..had before the war published a volume of his own occasional verses. **1976** S. Hynes *Auden Generation* v. 140 Lehmann's *The Noise of History* and Spender's *Vienna*..*are* occasional: like..'Easter 1916' and Auden's elegy on Yeats—they mythologize history.

c. (Earlier and further examples.)

1749 J. Cleland *Mem. Woman Pleasure* II. 91 Mrs. Cole had prepar'd my spark and me an occasional field-bed, to which we retired. **1771** Smollett *Humph. Cl.* III. 25 At night, half a dozen occasional beds are ranged.. along the wall. **1857** Dickens & Collins *Lazy Tour* i. in *Househ. Words* 3 Oct. 316/1 A little round occasional table in a window.

B. *sb.* **2.** (Earlier and later examples.)

1867 'Mark Twain' *Lett. to Publishers* (1967) 13, I am on the N.Y. Tribune staff here as an 'occasional', among other things. **1908** *Westm. Gaz.* 10 Dec. 6/1 (*heading*) Oxford University v. Oxford Occasionals. **1977** 'J. Le Carré' *Hon. Schoolboy* v. 112 He never got round to blowing [*sc.* betraying] the Occasionals...the Occasionals were filed..in a separate archive.

occidental, *a.* Add: **2.** Also, of, belonging to, or characteristic of, the western United States.

1809 E. A. Kendall *Travels Northern Parts U.S.* II. 28 Among the natural forest-trees, are the button-wood or occidental plane, the spruce-fir and the locust-tree. **1846** *Knickerbocker* XXVII. 471 'I.L. of this vicinity,' writes an occidental correspondent, 'had carried the knife for a long time.' **1933** E. C. Jaeger *Calif. Deserts* v. 57 The occidental harvester (*P[ogonomyrmex] occidentalis*) is a large, reddish ant building conspicuous mounds of pebbles.

B. *sb.* **2.** An artificial language, based chiefly on the Romance languages, invented by E. J. de Wahl (1867–1948), an Estonian, in 1922.

1926 *Encycl. Brit.* III. 906/2 Mr. E. de Wahl..finally produced Occidental, 'comprehensible at first sight to 10,000,000 educated Europeans without preliminary study'. To write or speak it is less easy than to read it, variety being dearly bought by the introduction of irregularities. **1928** O. Jespersen *Internat. Lang.* I. 26, I have read articles and received letters, chiefly in Ido, but also in Esperanto and Occidental, written from not a few countries. **1934** S. Robertson *Devel. Mod. Eng.* (1936) iv. 89 Jespersen now feels that there are enough points of similarity among the leading projects looking toward an international language—including Esperanto,..Occidental, and his own creation, Novial—to justify the hope that a single adequate International Auxiliary Language will some day emerge. **1949** M. Pei *Story of Language* (1952) vi. iii. 441 The twentieth century has continued the tradition [of creating artificial languages], with..Occidental.., Monding, and a host of others.

occidentalist. Add: **c.** One who advocates or uses the artificial language called Occidental.

1946 H. Jacob *On Choice of Common Lang.* iii. 40 The Occidentalists were the most critical.

occipito-. Add: **occipito-a·ngular** (see quot. 1890); **occipito-ante·rior,** denoting that form of vertex presentation in child-birth in which the occiput is directed away from the sacrum of the mother; **occipito-poste·rior,** denoting that form of vertex presentation in child-birth in which the occiput is directed towards the sacrum of the mother.

1890 *Cent. Dict., Occipito-angular*, pertaining to or common to the occipital lobe and the angular convolution. **1898** Occipito-angular [see *corticipetal *a.*]. **1831** C. D. Meigs tr. *Velpeau's Elem. Treat. Midwifery* v. 290 The English accoucheurs..bestow the title of natural labour only upon the occipito-anterior position, while according to them, the occipito-posterior position belongs to the class of preternatural labour. **1974** Passmore & Robson *Compan. Med. Stud.* III. 11/1 (*caption*) Vertex presentation, left occipito-anterior position, well flexed. **1831** Occipito-posterior [see *occipito-anterior* above]. **1971** *Brit. Med. Bull.* XXVII. 49/1 Impaired performance was associated with toxaemia, occipitoposterior presentation and delivery in an ambulance.

Occitan (ǫ·ksităn, ‖ ǫksitaṅ). [Fr.] **a.** Old Provençal, the *langue d'Oc.* **b.** Modern Provençal; *spec.* (see quot. 1974). Also *attrib.* or as *adj.* Also **Occitanian** (ǫksitēi·niăn) *sb.* and *a.*

1940 M. Belgion tr. *de Rougemont's Passion & Society* II. vi. 90 The whole of the Occitanian, Petrarchian, and Dantesque lyric has but a single theme—love. **1957** *Archivum Linguisticum* IX. II. 107 *Uniō* thrives in French, the adjoining fringe of Occitanian, and Franco-Provençal. **1960** [see *Languedocian *a.* and *sb.*]. **1961** P. Green tr. *Oldenbourg's Massacre at Montségur* i. 18 Languedoc itself, the area where the Occitan dialect was spoken, was not a major Power. **1964** G. Price in *Archivum Linguisticum* XVI. 34 In the twelfth and thirteenth centuries, Occitan—or Provençal, as it is more usually known—was one of the major European literary languages. *Ibid.*, The whole Occitan-speaking area, from the Alps to the Pyrenees. **1970** *Times Lit. Suppl.* 8 Jan. 40/2 Occitanian or Provençal (raised again to the status of a literary language by the efforts of the Felibrige). **1971** P. Wolff *Western Languages* v. 147 The years around 1100 also show the sudden appearance of lyrical poetry in Occitan, first made known in written form by the Duke troubadour William of Aquitaine (1071–1127). **1972** W. B. Lockwood *Panorama Indo-European Lang.* 33 Provençal survives today in certain rural localities... Provençal is sometimes termed Occitan. ..**1974** R. A. Hall *External Hist. Romance Lang.* 26 Modern Provençal has had two main standard varieties: i. That of the lower Rhône valley and the French Riviera.., often called 'Mistralien'... ii. 'Occitan', a somewhat different variety with its base in the usage of Languedoc. Much, but not all, of the difference between 'Mistralien' and 'Occitan' lies in orthographical details.

occlude, *v.* Add: **2.** Also, to cover or hide; *spec.* to cover (an eye) so as to block its sight. (Further examples.)

1909 H. G. Wells *Tono-Bungay* I. ii. 74 In the middle was the brown coffin end,..half occluded by the vicar's Oxford hood. **1921** *Amer. Jrnl. Ophthalm.* IV. 239/1 The choice of the eye to be covered is usually determined by finding out which eye the patient uses for pointing or aiming at a distant object, and occluding the other, or if one eye is defective, by occluding that. **1932** *Ibid.* XV. 321/1 The nondominant eye is occluded by having its spectacle lens replaced..by a black patch. **1963** Hirsch & Wick *Vision of Children* (1964) vii. 223 For suppression or for amblyopia with central (foveal) fixation, the preferred eye is usually occluded (direct occlusion). **1975** *Nature* 6 Feb. 406/1 During early childhood amblyopia can be cured by simple treatments such as by occluding the good eye for a period.

3. *intr. Dentistry.* Of a tooth: to come into contact with a tooth or teeth of the other set.

1888 E. S. Talbot *Irregularities of Teeth* I. v. 64 When the first permanent molars in both jaws have erupted so that they occlude, this will prevent forward progression. *Ibid.* 65 The anterior teeth do not occlude, and when the jaws are closed quite a space is observed. **1913** A. Hopewell-Smith *Introd. Dental. Anat. & Physiol* xi. 233 The teeth in Man do not..occlude by means of their cusps, but by a perfect system of interdigitation. **1974** Geiger & Hirschfeld *Minor Tooth Movement* (ed. 3) ii. 41 The mesiobuccal cusp of the maxillary first molar occludes with the buccal groove of the mandibular first molar in centric occlusion.

4. *trans. Chem.* To carry (a substance) out of solution by occlusion (sense *5); to trap within growing crystals of a precipitate.

1920 *Chem. Abstr.* XIV. 3030 Ca and Mg compds. are occluded in the pptn. of Fe‴ by NH_4OH. **1929** L. P. Hammett *Solutions of Electrolytes* I. iii. 40 Cadmium sulfide carries down or occludes barium sulfide, although the latter is a very soluble substance. **1930** W. T. Hall *Textbk. Quantitative Analysis* xi. 141 If the barium sulfate adsorbs or occludes ferric sulfate, the latter will lose SO_3 upon ignition. **1950** Kolthoff & Sandell *Textbk. Quantitative Inorg. Analysis* (rev. ed.) viii. 111 If the incorporated material fits in the crystal lattice of the precipitate (host crystal), it is occluded in the form of *mixed* crystals or a solid solution. **1952** Diehl & Smith *Quantitative Analysis* ii. 33 Precipitates that occlude the mother liquor seriously should be dissolved and reprecipitated under such conditions that little foreign material..is present in the solution.

5. *intr. Meteorol.* Of a front or frontal system: to undergo occlusion (sense *7).

1940 N. Shaw *Forecasting Weather* (ed. 3) xxviii. 583 There is a further supply of warm air available to provide a warm sector in the new formation, which runs through a life-history..and in due course occludes. **1955** W. J. Saucier *Princ. Meteorol. Analysis* ix. 270/1 The front occludes further, and meantime the cyclonic circulation becomes larger and more symmetric. **1969** S. Petterssen *Introd. Meteorol.* (ed. 3) xiii. 212 During the further development, the cold front overtakes the warm front and the system is said to occlude.

occluded, *ppl. a.* (s.v. Occlude *v.*). Add: *spec.* in *Meteorol.*, applied to a front or frontal system in which a cold front has caught up with a warm front.

1922 Bjerknes & Solberg in *Geofysiske Publikationer* III. I. 4 The remaining part of the warm sector near the centre also disappears fairly soon, so that the cyclone on the ground only consists of cold air... For this type we have chosen the name 'occluded cyclones'. **1934** D. Brunt *Physical & Dynamical Meteorol.* xviii. 324 When a depression has become occluded, the cold front trails behind the depression. **1941** B. Haurwitz *Dynamic Meteorol.* xv. 315 In this situation the occluded cyclone can increase its kinetic energy again. **1955** [see *occlusion 7]. **1970** F. W. Cole *Introd. Meteorol.* xii. 266 If an occluded front is well advanced in development, the warm-front portion may have little or no effect on the ensuing weather.

occluder (ǫklū·dəɹ). *Ophthalm.* [f. Occlud(e *v.* + -er¹.] Any device designed to occlude an eye.

1930 *Brit. Jrnl. Ophthalm.* XIV. 520 Many varieties of occluder..have been devised. **1949** S. Duke-Elder *Text-bk. Ophthalm.* IV. xlv. 3917 For older children who can be trusted not to peep round it, a simple occluder of metal..or rubber..may be attached to the spectacles... These should be replaced by strapping on a tie-on occluder during the night. **1974** *Nature* 11 Oct. 506/2 One eye was centred on a projection perimeter (the other eye was always covered with a plasticine occluder).

occlusal (ǫklū·săl), *a. Dentistry.* [f. L. *occlūs-*, ppl. stem of *occlūd-ere* to Occlude + -al.] Of, pertaining to, or involved in occlusion (sense *3); *spec.* applied to the surface of a tooth that comes into contact with a tooth in the other jaw in occlusion.

1897 S. H. Guildford in E. C. Kirk *Amer. Text-bk. Operative Dentistry* vi. 142 Cavities upon the occlusal surface are very accessible and in full view. *Ibid.* 143 The occlusal surface of an upper first or second molar presents two points liable to decay. **1939** I. Hirschfeld *Toothbrush* i. 2 (*caption*) Mandible of Australian aboriginal, showing advanced occlusal wear. **1951** J. M. Schweitzer *Oral Rehabilitation* xxxi. 623 The question of whether natural teeth should have flat occlusal surfaces..or occlusal surfaces that have cusps. **1974** P. E. Dawson (*title*) Evaluation, diagnosis, and treatment of occlusal problems.

Hence **occlu·sally** *adv.*, from or on an occlusal surface.

1912 B. E. Lischer *Princ. & Methods Orthodontics* xiii. 202 An arm extended from the alignment wire..is made from an ordinary tube hook and prevented from dropping occlusally, or being forced gingivally, by flattening the alignment wire with a file along its lingual surface. **1946** Tylman & Peyton *Acrylics* xvi. 408/2 Inlay wax is then added occlusally to the thin casting, the occlusal plane is determined, and finally the occlusal surfaces and contour are carved in the wax. **1969** *Gloss. Terms Dentistry (B.S.I.)* 72 *Occlusally approaching clasp*, a clasp originating on the occlusal side of the survey line and terminating in the infra-bulge area.

occlusion. Add: **3.** *Dentistry.* The position assumed by the two sets of teeth relative to each other when the mouth is closed; the state of having the jaws closed and the teeth in contact.

1880 N. W. Kingsley *Treat. Oral Deformities* xxi. 525 In extreme pain (except in cases where the patient is suffering from periodontitis, when the occlusion of the jaws intensifies the suffering), the teeth are brought together with great force. **1904** V. H. Jackson *Orthodontia & Orthopædia of Face* 198 The opening of the bite in any manner with apparatus, if continued for a considerable time, is likely to prove detrimental to the occlusion. **1962** Blake & Trott *Periodontology* xv. 156 In the European it is usual to find that during lateral movements to either side molar and pre-molar teeth of one side remain in occlusion, while contact is completely lost on the other side. **1974** Harty & Roberts *Restorative Procedures Practising Dentist* xii. 167 It is very important that the occlusion is studied and corrected before any fixed or removable prosthesis is made.

4. *Phonetics.* The act of closing, or the period of closure of, the breath passage during the articulation of an orally-released consonant, or of the mouth passage during the articulation of a nasal consonant.

1906 *Mod. Lang. Rev.* I. iv. 346 'Occlusion', was, if I remember aright, used by Wilkins in the seventeenth century, but this hardly justifies the employment of such a pedantic term instead of 'stoppage', 'closure', or 'stop'. **1926** *Germanic Rev.* I. I. 58 Here, 'occlusion' in the glottis does not mean glottal stop, but the partial occlusion in the articulation of voice sounds. **1935** J. S. Kenyon *Amer. Pronunc.* (ed. 6) 51 This initial contact for any sound that has contact is called the closure, or occlusion, and the end of the contact is called the opening, or release. **1943** *Amer. Speech* XVIII. 39 In pronouncing such phrases as 'Hello, Pete!'..a British speaker ordinarily articulates the vowel of the final syllable, lifts his tongue to make the closure for the final consonant (applosion), holds it there from eight to twelve hundredths of a second (occlusion), and then breaks the closure with a sharp downward snap of the tongue which produces a clear 'pop' (explosion). **1966** B. Trnka *Phonol. Analysis Present-Day Stand. Eng.* (rev. ed.) ii. 11 In producing *l*, the tip of the tongue forms an occlusion against the alveolar ridge.

5. *Chem.* A kind of co-precipitation (see quots.); the trapping of foreign material by growing crystals of a precipitate.

1920 *Chem. Abstr.* XIV. 3029 (*heading*) The occlusion of lime and magnesia by ferric oxide. **1929** L. P. Hammett *Solutions of Electrolytes* I. iii. 40 Analytical separations are ..never quite as satisfactory..because of the existence of occlusion. **1932** [see *co-precipitation]. **1942** W. Rieman et al. *Quantitative Analysis* (ed. 2) xvii. 244 The phenomenon [*sc.* coprecipitation] has also been called contamination, inclusion, occlusion, and adsorption. The last two terms should not be used as synonyms for coprecipitation because they denote certain mechanisms that apply to some but not all cases of coprecipitation. **1947** *Jrnl. Chem. Education* XXIV. 597/1 The term *occlusion* has been used to refer to contamination of a precipitate by the incorporation into the body of it during its formation of foreign substances whether or not the latter give rise to mixed crystal formation (solid solution)... It has been used to include both solid solution phenomena and contamination of the precipitate by adsorption..; it has been used to indicate contamination by basic salts and other substances not adsorbed and not in solid solution..; and I have heard a noted analytical chemist reserve the term to indicate the contamination of a precipitate by mechanically trapped solute or solvent ions or molecules. No doubt one could locate other senses in which *occlusion* has been used; the term is almost omnivorous. **1966** E. M. Rattenbury *Introd. Titrimetric & Gravimetric Anal.* vii. 146 Sometimes water or mother liquor is imprisoned by occlusion. **1969** E. S. Gilreath *Elem. Quantitative Chem.* x. 138 Occlusion is a form of coprecipitation in which impurities are enclosed..within the lattice structure of a crystalline precipitate. *Ibid.*, Contamination by occlusion..can produce serious errors in gravimetric analysis.

6. *Ophthalm.* The covering of an eye so as to block its sight.

1920 *Brit. Jrnl. Ophthalm.* IV. 146 (*heading*) The influence of prolonged monocular occlusion in revealing errors of the muscle balance. **1973** *Nature* 26 Jan. 288/2 The technique of monocular occlusion has long been used by ophthalmologists in the therapeutic treatment of such conditions as strabismus (squint) amd amblyopia.

7. *Meteorol.* The overtaking of the warm front of a depression by the cold front, so that the body of warm air between them is forced upwards off the earth's surface by two wedges of cold air; also, the occluded front so formed.

1922 BJERKNES & SOLBERG in *Geofysiske Publikationer* III. I. 6 No boundary surface results when both branches meet during the occlusion of the cyclone. *Ibid.*, The occlusion then assumes the character of a cold front with a rather narrow rain zone. **1934** D. BRUNT *Physical & Dynamical Meteorol.* xviii. 311 The occlusion begins at the centre, where the cold front has a shorter path to cover before overtaking the warm front. *Ibid.*, There will still be a warm sector in the upper air for some time after occlusion has taken place at the surface. **1941** B. HAURWITZ *Dynamic Meteorol.* xv. 314 The part of the front where the cold front has caught up is called the occlusion. **1944** HEWSON & LONGLEY *Meteorol. Theoret. & Appl.* xvi. 277 The rate of occlusion in several types of frontal depressions may be discussed qualitatively. **1955** W. J. SAUCIER *Princ. Meteorol. Analysis* ix. 270/1 The cold front overtakes the warm front, resulting in an occluded front (or occlusion). **1974** *Encycl. Brit. Macropædia* V. 394/2 There still is a belt of thick cloud and rain along the line of the old occlusion.

occlusive, *a.* Add: (Further examples.) Also, characterized by occlusion.

1961 *Lancet* 22 July 192/1 Of three techniques for treating the stump [of the umbilicus]—standard non-occlusive spirit technique, antibiotic or antiseptic non-occlusive technique, and occlusive technique with or without antibiotics—they showed the last to be the most reliable and the most effective. **1972** *Where* May/June 135/2 The sheath, the various occlusive caps, even chemical contraceptives do provide some barrier to the spread of germs from one person to another. **1974** PASSMORE & ROBSON *Compan. Med. Stud.* III. xvii. 16/2 The most important cause of occlusive arterial disease is atherosclerosis.

B. *sb. Phonetics.* A consonant sound produced with stoppage of breath by the organs of speech; a stop with suppression of the explosive sound.

1902 [see *AFFRICATE *v.*]. **1943** *Amer. Speech* XVIII. 39 The only audible expression of the final consonant..is the cutting-off of the preceding vowel sound by the raising of the tongue to make the closure... The explosive stop here becomes what may most conveniently be termed a simple occlusive. **1976** *Archivum Linguisticum* VII. 183 He cannot add *H_3 and a third series of guttural occlusives to the number of fallen consonantal phonemes he has postulated.

occluso- (ǫklū·so), comb. form of *OCCLUSAL *a.* or OCCLUSION (sense *3), as in **occluso-cervi·cal, occlusogi·ngival** *adjs.*

1923 DORLAND *Med. Dict.* (ed. 12) 755/1 Occlusocervical. **1962** J. E. H. FOWLER *Heinemann Mod. Dict. Dental Students* 182/1 *Occlusocervical*, relating to the occlusal surface and the neck of a tooth. **1940** J. OSBORNE *Dental Mech.* xii. 136 The brush should be run in an occluso-gingival direction. **1963** C. R. COWELL et al. *Inlays, Crowns, & Bridges* iii. 14 Measuring the occluso-gingival depth on the side of the tooth.

occult, *a.* (*sb.*) Add: **1. c.** *Med.* Of a disease or bodily process: †inexplicable, obscure; unaccompanied by any readily discernible signs or symptoms. *occult blood*, blood abnormally present in some material (esp. fæces) but too scanty to be readily recognized; so *occult bleeding* [tr. G. *okkulte(magen)-blutung* (I. Boas 1901, in *Deutsch. med. Wochenschr.* 16 May 315/2)].

[**1690** S. BLANCKAERT *Lexicon Novum Medicum* 450 *Occulti morbi*... Angl. Hiden disease.] **1809** R. CARMICHAEL *Ess. Effects of Carbonate upon Cancer* iv. 292 Three of these lucky people had occult cancers of the breast, and a fourth had an occult cancer of the lip. **1820** R. HOOPER *Lexicon Medicum* (ed. 4) 623/2 *Occult quality*, a term that has been much used by writers that had not clear ideas of what they undertook to explain; and which served therefore only for a cover to their ignorance. **1854** W. E. SWAINE tr. *Rokitausky's Man. Path. Anat.* I. ix. 260 This process takes place either in the depths of the growth,..as so-termed occult cancer; or upon the free surface of the body or of a mucous cavity, as so-called apert or open cancer. **1872** D. C. BLACK *On Functional Dis. Renal Organs* ii. 108 The condition to which Dr. Barnes has applied the term occult menstruation... Owing to the imperforate condition of the hymen, the menstrual flux accumulates in the *cul de sac*..formed by the upper portion of the vagina. **1904** *Progressive Med.* IV. 24 Occult blood is constantly found in cancer of the gastrointestinal tract. *Ibid.*, Occult bleeding in the cases of ulcer was most frequently observed when the patient had recently complained of pain in the stomach. **1905** G. R. BUTLER *Diagnostics of Internal Med.* (ed. 2) I. xii. 147 'Occult' blood is a term applied to blood in the fæces (or stomach contents) which is in such small quantity that it can not be recognised by the eye, or is so altered as not to be identified by the microscope. **1936** E. N. CHAMBERLAIN *Symptoms & Signs Clin. Med.* xii. 387 The most important chemical test applicable in the clinic room is that for occult blood. **1961** R. D. BAKER *Essent. Path.* xvii. 458 Occult carcinoma of the prostate is a frequent finding at autopsy in persons who have died from other causes. **1962** *Lancet* 1 Dec. 1145/1 Orthotoluidine sampling of these motions was strongly positive for occult blood. **1973** *Q. Jrnl. Med.* XLII. 125 (*heading*) Occult rickets and osteomalacia amongst the Asian immigrant population. **1973** *Lancet* 4 Aug. 262/1 Occult bleeding in the alimentary tract.

occult, *v.* Add: **a.** (Later examples.)

1957 A. MACNAB *Bulls of Iberia* vi. 61 In both the *gaonera* and the *mariposa* the man's body is fully exposed in front of the bull's face, and not occulted by the cloth lure. **1977** 'E. CRISPIN' *Glimpses of Moon* v. 76 The platform for the legs competition..had a wooden screen designed to occult the competititors from the groin upwards.

c. *intr.* Of a lighthouse light: to be cut off from view as part of its cycle of light and dark.

1880, 1892 [implied in OCCULTING *ppl. a.*]. **1902** *Encycl. Brit.* XXVI. 464/1 The light occults every ten seconds,.. the occultations being actuated by a double valve arrangement. **1964** J. MASTERS *Trial at Monomoy* i. 15 Close on the north the lighthouse tower edged into the view... That light occulted every four seconds.

Hence **occu·lter,** an apparatus for occulting lights.

1902 *Encycl. Brit.* XXX. 256/1 This light shows, instead of one prolonged flash at intervals of one minute, as would be produced by the apparatus in the absence of a gas occulter, a group of short flashes.

occultist. Add: Also *attrib.*

1902 *Encycl. Brit.* XXX. 275/1 Cabalistic, occultist, Indian, and modern spiritualistic ideas and formulas. **1977** R. L. WOLFF *Gains & Losses* iv. 316 Charles Maurice Davies['s]..book *The Great Secret* (1896)..was published anonymously. His occultist leanings were, however, well known.

occupance. Delete *rare* and add: *spec.* in *Geogr.*, the inhabiting and modification of an area by man. (Further examples.)

1932 *Sci. Monthly* XXXV. 266/1 France..is strikingly an aggregation of '*pays*', each of which has its distinctive character stamped upon every aspect of the natural environment and upon every form of human occupance thereof. **1934** *Ann. Assoc. Amer. Geogr.* XXIV. 81 Occupance is..defined as the process of occupying or living in an area, and the transformations of the initial landscape which result. *Ibid.*, Occupance refers not only to..economic activities but also to other activities..such as the construction of buildings, roads, and so on. The word includes also the results as well as the process of living in an area. **1974** F. EMERY *Oxfordsh. Landscape* i. 35 People who could cultivate the land with digging-sticks in order to grow cereals, covering the ground..with a 'slash-and-burn' or shifting occupance of the kind we still meet today in certain forest environments.

occupancy. Add: **3. b.** *Teleph.* The proportion of the time during which a circuit or device is handling calls.

1933 *Post Office Electr. Engineers' Jrnl.* XXVI. 269 (*caption*) Probabilities *P* for a delay exceeding *t* holding times when there are *n* switches with occupancy *a*. **1960** R. SYSKI *Introd. Congestion Theory Teleph. Syst.* i. 10 The traffic carried (or handled) refers to the changing patterns of occupancy conditions in the group. *Ibid.* vi. 365 The limit in (*4.6*) exists provided the traffic intensity ('occupancy')..is less than unity.

c. The proportion of accommodation occupied or used.

1974 *Economist* 7 Sept. 51 The 'France' has had a 77 per cent occupancy rate on the North Atlantic run and a 91 per cent rate on winter cruises. **1975** *Daily Tel.* 11 Dec. 9/6 If airlines did not overbook, planes would go out 40 per cent. full instead of the 70 per cent. occupancy needed to give a profit. **1977** *Daily Tel.* 2 Dec. 10/7 Hotels in large towns outside London experienced a similar increased occupancy this year. **1977** *Time* 19 Dec. 61/3 The 27,400-acre complex..sports three Disney hotels, with an occupancy rate of about 97%.

‖**occupatio** (ǫkiŭpē·ʃio, -pā·tio). *Rhet.* [L. (see OCCUPATION).] = PRETERITION 3.

1586 [see PARALIPSIS]. **1928** C. S. BALDWIN *Medieval Rhetoric & Poetic* x. 296 The rehearsal of all the conventionally appropriate *loci* of description at the funeral of Arcite (A2919–2966) sounds to modern ears impatient, if not sarcastic. But, after all, the whole long passage is the 'colour' *occupatio* (præteritio). The shorter *occupatio* in the Squire's Tale (F63–75) suggests sarcasm less by itself than in its connection with lines 32–40 and 401–408. **1933** F. N. ROBINSON *Compl. Wks. Chaucer* 772/2 It should be added that the rhetorical figure here employed —the refusal to describe or narrate, technically known as 'occupatio'—is very common with Chaucer. **1957** C. MUSCATINE *Chaucer & French Tradition* vi. 177 Though Chaucer omits a great deal of the tale originally told by Boccaccio in the *Teseida*, he frequently resorts to the rhetorical device of *occupatio* to summarize in detail events or descriptions in such a way as to shorten the story without lessening weight and impressiveness. **1968** J. A. W. BENNETT *Chaucer's Bk. of Fame* ii. 94 But the didactic bird is not to be thwarted utterly, and launches.. into an *occupatio* summarizing the lore in Ovid's *Fasti* that would have enabled the poet to identify such constellations as Lyra, Gemini, and the Pleiades. **1975** *Times Lit. Suppl.* 28 Feb. 213/4 'Do not describe the total horror, the full degree of despair that rushes into your head, your brain and emotions...', and so on. The device used to be known as *occupatio.*

occupation. Add: **1. b.** *spec.*, by Germany and her allies during the war of 1939–45; usu., the period during which a country was held by German, etc., troops, or the state of being held by such troops.

1940 A. HUXLEY *Let.* 7 July (1969) 455 Jehanne was out of Paris during the occupation. **1957** *Times Lit. Suppl.* 27 Dec. 783/3 The particular man whose life has been conditioned by the hot North African sun and the cold chill of the Occupation. **1972** *Guardian* 9 Sept. 12/4 The programme is..divided into three parts... There is life under the occupation..as drawn from experience in occupied Europe.

7. Also, in military uses, as *occupation army, forces, troops;* in archæological use, as *occupation floor, layer, level, scatter, site.* Also **occupation centre,** an establishment where occupational therapy is practised or where the mentally handicapped are trained or employed; **occupation disease,** an occupational disease; **occupation neurosis** *Med.*, a painful and disabling spasm affecting muscles used more than normally because of the person's occupation; **occupation number** *Physics*, the number of particles in a system that are in any given state.

1918 E. S. FARROW *Dict. Mil. Terms* 414 Occupation Army, an army that remains in possession of a newly conquered country, retaining it as a kind of hostage, until peace is signed and the war indemnity paid. **1976** T. ALLBEURY *Only Good German* xiv. 100 A goon on each staircase and the lift doors padlocked... It's like an occupation army. **1940** FRAZER & STALLYBRASS *Text-bk. Public Health* (ed. 10) xix. 440 If the home conditions are good and the defective's condition is suitable he may attend at an occupation centre where simple occupational training can be given. **1958** [see *day-hospital* s.v. *DAY *sb.* 23 a]. **1965** PETERS & KINNAIRD *Health Services Admin.* vii. 255 The [Education] Authorities establish training and occupation centres for the lower grades of the mentally handicapped who cannot take education in ordinary educational subjects. **1900** DORLAND *Med. Dict.* 209/1 Occupation-disease. **1901** *Brit. Med. Jrnl.* 17 Aug. 405/1 (*heading*) The medical profession and the control of occupation diseases. **1930** F. B. YOUNG *Jim Redlake* III. iii. 326 Overcrowding, short commons, adulterated food, occupation diseases—they're all just words in a newspaper. **1959** J. D. CLARK *Prehist. S. Afr.* plate 4 (*caption*) Handaxes, cleavers, and waste flakes of evolved Chelles-Acheul culture on occupation floors. **1971** W. TUCKER *This Witch* ii. 20 The native beer was vile... The occupation forces did their drinking elsewhere. **1953** R. J. C. ATKINSON *Field Archaeol.* (ed. 2) i. 39 The chief use of such detectors is in the excavation of graves and occupation-layers in which metal objects may be expected to occur. **1935** *Discovery* Nov. 343/1 Further excavations..have brought to light older occupation-levels and hearth-marks. **1888** W. R. GOWERS *Man. Dis. Nervous Syst.* II. v. 656 The term 'occupation neuroses', adopted from the German ('Beschaftigungs-neurosen'), is a convenient designation for a group of maladies in which certain symptoms are excited by the attempt to perform some often-repeated muscular action, commonly one that is involved in the occupation of the sufferer... The most frequent symptom is spasm. **1911** *Jrnl. Nerv. & Mental Dis.* XXXVIII. 107 An occupation neurosis is literally a fatigue cramp, and is characterized by spasms of muscles concerned in special movements, and brought on whenever these special movements, such as writing, are attempted. **1958** SYKES & BELL tr. *Landau & Lifshitz' Quantum Mech.* ix. 215 Let us seek to construct a mathematical formalism in which the occupation numbers..of the states (and not the co-ordinates of the particles) play the part of independent variables. **1974** G. REECE tr. *Hund's Hist. Quantum Theory* xiii. 180 Jordan was thus entitled to express his hope of a quantum wave theory of matter in which the numbers of particles would be the occupation numbers N_r of the discrete quantum wave states. **1954** S. PIGGOTT *Neolithic Cultures* ix. 271 The occupation-scatter of small sherds and flints. **1939** *Oxoniensa* IV. 6 The region between Oxford and Northampton is notoriously, but probably deceptively, barren of occupation-sites. **1948** *N.Y. Jrnl. American* (Sunday Mail ed.) 9 May 1/7 Police and U.S. occupation troops are prepared for bloodshed. **1975** R. L. DUNCAN *Dragons at Gate* (1976) iv. 32 On the day of the surrender, before the Occupation troops could arrive, Takaeshi..set out into Tokyo Bay, and blew himself up.

occupational, *a.* (s.v. OCCUPATION). Add: (Further examples.) *occupational disease*, (a) disease to which a particular occupation renders a person especially liable; also *joc.*; *occupational hazard, risk*, a risk accepted as part of a particular occupation; also *joc.*; *occupational therapy*, an activity, mental or physical, prescribed as an aid to recovery from disease or injury or for mental patients; so *occupational therapist*, someone skilled in supervising or trained to supervise such activity.

1901 *Brit. Med. Jrnl.* 17 Aug. 412/2 A number of valuable papers upon occupational diseases. **1915** G. E. BARTON in *Trained Nurse & Hospital Rev.* Mar. 138 (*heading*) Occupational therapy. **1919** —— (*title*) Teaching the sick; a manual of occupational therapy and re-education. **1919** J. L. GARVIN *Econ. Found. Peace* 328 These occupational federations acted independently of each other. **1922** *Jrnl. Mental Sci.* LXVIII. 192 The *personnel* comprises a chief and five assistant trained occupational therapists. **1923** *Ibid.* LXIX. 126 The occupational centre or 'curative workshop' serves more or less as a proving ground. **1926** B. WEBB *My Apprenticeship* iii. 129 Personal vanity..was an 'occupational disease' of entertaining and being entertained. **1934** H. C. WARREN *Dict. Psychol.* 184/2 *Occupational hierarchy*, the serial arrangement of occupational groups according to average intelligence. **1937** *Discovery* May 144/1 The excavation..showed a mound that had already been abandoned by 1500 B.C., and 20 occupational levels below it. **1944** M. LASKI *Love on Supertax* iv. 51 You're insured against occupational risks. **1949** W. L. WARNER in M. Fortes *Social Struct.* 4 Interviews..are taken from informants..from several occupational groups. **1951** R.

FIRTH *Elem. Social Organiz.* iv. 138 A worker's choice of employment is guided by his wife's attitude to the conditions of his work, its cleanliness, occupational risks, or security. **1952** 'VIGILANS' *Chamber of Horrors* 94 *Occupational hazard*, a risk necessarily run in one's work. **1956** S. GIBBONS *Here be Dragons* xvii. 235, I don't think I shall marry if I'm asked. There's too much occupational risk. **1956** B. GOOLDEN *At Foot of Hills* ix. 202 Are you the young man who wants to see over the occupational therapy department? **1959** *Listener* 15 Oct. 614/1 Exile has been regarded as an occupational hazard for poets in particular ever since Plato denied them rights of citizenship in his republic. *Ibid.* 10 Dec. 1041/3 As a museum man himself, Mr. Baxandall will be aware of.. that occupational disease of his profession which might be called 'collector's greediness'. **1959** B. WOOTTON *Social Sci. & Social Path.* ii. 48 Whether, on balance, prisoners are likely to exalt or to debase their occupational level is anybody's guess. **1971** *Times* 6 Sept. 7/8 The Department of Employment has occupational guidance services throughout the country. **1973** *Times* 13 Jan. 19/7 Occupational pension scheme is one established by an employer for the benefit of his employees, and wholly paid for by him and (frequently, but not necessarily) his employees. *Ibid.* 1 June 24/1 (Advt.), For further information please contact the Head Occupational Therapist. **1974** *Encycl. Brit. Micropædia* VII. 470/2 Occupational therapy provides not only training in daily living activities but also aids that make eating, dressing, and toilet less fatiguing for the sick or elderly. **1974** PASSMORE & ROBSON *Compan. Med. Stud.* III. 76/1 Asbestos has become an increasingly important occupational hazard. *Ibid.*, This led to a false sense of security about occupational disease in coal mining until 1920.

Hence **occupa·tionally** *adv.*

1952 C. P. BLACKER *Eugenics* vii. 141 That there existed a group of occupationally unstable persons who are in continuous receipt of public assistance had been well recognized since the time of Charles Booth. **1971** D. CRYSTAL *Linguistics* 132 Do they occur in certain occupationally restricted uses of language only, such as journalese? **1973** *Daily Tel.* 18 Aug. 8/1 The Council, sitting in Star Chamber, publicly ordered anyone not occupationally resident in London to leave the City forthwith.

occupa·tionalism. [-ISM.] Occupational character or conduct; professionalism.

1927 E. BARKER *National Character* iv. 96 It is true that a new and qualifying factor has been added to the national temper by the growth of occupationalism.

occupied, *ppl. a.* Add: Esp. of countries held by Germany and her allies during the war of 1939–45; of parts of countries under military occupation.

1940 R. W. B. CLARKE *Britain's Blockade* 7 The division of France into 'occupied' and 'non-occupied' territory is nothing more than a device to relieve the Germans of the administrative difficulties created by the millions of refugees, [etc.]. **1940** A. HUXLEY *Let.* 9 Oct. (1969) 459 There is practically no communication between occupied France and the USA. **1941** *Times Lit. Suppl.* 18 Oct. 514/1 (*heading*) In occupied Belgium. **1965** M. SPARK *Mandelbaum Gate* vii. 280 'So far as I know she's still in Israel—' Joe Ramdez clapped his hands over his ears.. 'Occupied Palestine,' Freddy said with deference. **1973** L. SNELLING *Heresy* I. i. 8 In Paris, capital of Occupied France, in the abnormally hot summer of nineteen-forty.

occupying, *ppl. a.* Add: **occupying power**, a state whose army occupies (part of) a foreign country; used *spec.* with ref. to the occupation of Germany after the war of 1939–45.

1946 *Ann. Reg. 1945* 452/1 (Index) Germany,.. Legislation by occupying powers. **1959** *Observer* 22 Mar. 1/2 Nuclear weapons.. would be in the hands of the occupying Powers and never pass into German control. **1965** A. J. P. TAYLOR *Eng. Hist. 1914–45* xvi. 594 The Allied leaders.. reached agreement of a kind over the reparations which each of the occupying Powers could exact from its zone of Germany. **1975** J. CLEARY *Safe House* i. 26 The need to show the Occupying Powers that.. they were not going to favour Nazis and ex-Nazis.

occurrence. Add: **5.** *attrib.*, as **occurrence(s book,** a record of events kept at a police station, drawn from the diaries of police officers.

1929 J. MOYLAN *Scotland Yard* vi. 138 Occurrence Books are kept at all stations, so that there may be a complete daily record of all occurrences, etc., at the station or within the area assigned to it. **1955** M. GILBERT *Sky High* v. 72 Everything that a policeman hears, sees and does goes down in the Occurrences Book. **1966** L. SOUTHWORTH *Felon in Disguise* xi. 158 The Inspector was about to complete his Occurrence Book entries. **1972** M. GILBERT *Body of Girl* xi. 103 It would have been in the Occurrence Book... Where are the 'O' books kept?

occurrency. Restrict †*Obs.* to sense in Dict. and add: **b.** = OCCURRENCE 2.

1935 G. K. ZIFF *Psycho-Biol. of Lang.* (1936) 289 Relative frequency of occurrency of meaning. **1967** *Oceanogr. & Marine Biol.* V. 283 Most of the clusters defined by joint occurrency of species have a given geographical distribution.

ocean, *sb.* (*a.*) Add: **3. a.** Also *pl.* Lots *of.* (Further examples.)

1840 *Spirit of Times* 25 Apr. 85/3 The leader of this predatory band had oceans of money which he looked to when he sat down, and then crammed his greasy wallet back into his pocket. **1886** H. BAUMANN *Londinismen* 123/2 He's got oceans o' money. **1926** *Amer. Mercury* Dec. 465/1 She is a flaming flamboyant blonde with oceans of stuff. **1952** M. LASKI *Village* ii. 36 Poor People's children.. had oceans of pocket-money because Poor People didn't understand the value of money.

b. Phr. *ocean of being.*

1652 N. CULVERWEL *Worth of Souls* in *Lt. Nature* [II]. 201 All beings they are within the souls Horizon... It can take in the several drops of Being, and it can take in much of the Ocean of Being. **1690** LOCKE *Essay Hum. Und.* I. i. 3 We let loose our thoughts into the vast ocean of Being. **1931** G. F. STOUT *Mind & Matter* 14 Knowledge of this type.. leaves us adrift on the ocean of being, with oars indeed, but without rudder or compass.

4. a. *ocean-blue, -deep, -flood, -floor* (misprinted *flood* in Dict.), *front, -green,* (nonce-wd.) *-inn, liner* (examples), *-side, -song*; **b.** *oceanflowing* adj.; objective, as *ocean-cleaving, -dividing* adjs.

1842 W. C. BRYANT *Child's Funeral* in *Fountain* 62 Flowers of the morning—red, or ocean-blue. **1936** *Times* 6 Jan. 11/3 It is in a number of good colours, including ocean-blue. *a* **1926** R. CAMPBELL *Golden Shower* in *Coll. Poems* (1957) II. 21 The ocean-cleaving whale. **1926** J. PEDERSEN *Israel* I. II. 463 He is overwhelmed by the surges of death.. and desires to be pulled up from the *t*ᵉ*hōmōth* of the earth, its ocean-deep. **1966** 'J. HACKSTON' *Father clears Out* 43 His diving-dress would enable a diver to go down to the very depths of the ocean-deep. **1954** W. FAULKNER *Fable* 232 The mutual rage and fear of the three ocean-dividing nations themselves. *a* **1957** R. CAMPBELL tr. *F. Garcia Lorca's He died of Love* in *Coll. Poems* (1960) III. 78 The ocean-flood of perjured oaths Was thundering. **1820** SHELLEY *Ode to Liberty* v, in *Prometh. Unb.* 211 The ocean-floors Pave it. **1884** [in Dict.]. **1968** *Times* 3 Oct. 13/3 The ocean floor is spreading out from the Mid-Atlantic Ridge at a rate of between one and three centimetres a year. **1974** L. DEIGHTON *Spy Story* xix. 202 The ship sank to the ocean floor. **1922** JOYCE *Ulysses* 656 Confluent oceanflowing rivers with their tributaries and transoceanic currents. **1934** WEBSTER, Ocean front. **1963** *New Yorker* 8 June 104 Your own ocean-front cottages. **1975** R. L. SIMON *Wild Turkey* (1976) xxii. 159 We headed.. onto the street by the pier... We were alone on the ocean front. **1922** JOYCE *Ulysses* 253 By bronze, by gold, in oceangreen of shadow. **1976** *Yorkshire Even. Press* 9 Dec. 20/2 (Advt.), 1973 L 144 saloon de luxe, ocean green, black trim, two bar, wing mirrors, push button radio. **1851** H. MELVILLE *Moby Dick* II. ii. 7 His casual stopping-places and ocean-inns, so to speak. **1939** T. S. ELIOT *Family Reunion* I. i. 41 These ocean liners With all their swimming baths and gymnasiums. **1964** M. MCLUHAN *Understanding Media* II. x. 94 People used to say that an ocean liner might as well be a hotel in a big city. **1974** W. GARNER *Big Enough Wreath* 154 Like a power-boat brought under the bows of an ocean liner. **1934** WEBSTER, Oceanside. **1962** J. D. MACDONALD *Girl, Gold Watch & Everything* vi. 71 These [rooms] interconnect so this whole oceanside can be turned into a big suite. **1975** *Sat. Rev.* (U.S.) 3 May 62/3 Immaculate oceanside apartments. **1922** JOYCE *Ulysses* 261 Lips that.. hummed.. the oceansong.

c. ocean greyhound (later examples); **oceanless** *a.* (*nonce-wd.*) devoid of or lacking an ocean; **ocean-line** (only Melville) = *ocean-lane*; **ocean pipe-fish,** a pipe-fish, *Entelurus æquoreus,* found in oceanic waters of north-western Europe; = *snake pipe-fish* (SNAKE *sb.* 11 b); **ocean spray** *N. Amer.*, a shrub of western North America, *Holodiscus discolor,* of the family Rosaceæ, sometimes included in the genus *Spiræa*, and distinguished by curving branches bearing large panicles of small white flowers; **ocean wave,** rhyming slang for 'shave'.

1913 F. H. BURNETT *T. Tembarom* xl. 519 An ocean greyhound had landed the pair at the dock. **1967** *Economist* 23 Sept. 1109/1 Ironically, the airlines which once had only speed to offer against the one-time ocean greyhounds, can now anticipate the lounges, cinemas, etc., which until the jumbo jets get going remain one of the few prerogatives of the ocean liners. **1941** T. S. ELIOT *Dry Salvages* ii. 9 We cannot think of a time that is oceanless. **1851** H. MELVILLE *Moby Dick* II. ii. 5 The sperm whales .. mostly swim in *veins*, as they are called; continuing their way along a given ocean-line with.. undeviating exactitude. **1865** J. COUCH *Hist. Fishes Brit. Islands* IV. 358, I have possessed a male of the acknowledged Ocean Pipefish which in length measured twenty-six inches. **1925** J. T. JENKINS *Fishes Brit. Isles* 372/2 Ocean pipe-fish. **1906** *Contrib. U.S. Nat. Herbarium* XI. 330 Schizonotus discolor... Ocean spray. **1940** *Oregon: End of Trail* 20 In the spring and early summer.. sweet syringa, ocean spray, and Douglas spirea form streamside thickets of riotous blossom. **1971** *Islander* (Victoria, B.C.) 28 Mar. 12/2 A rod made from a seasoned spirea (ocean spray), a common shrub around Victoria. **1928** M. C. SHARPE *Chicago May* 287/2 *Ocean waves* [sic], shave. **1934** *John o' London's Weekly* 9 June 353/1, I 'as my ocean wave an' when I've got my mince-pie properly open I goes down the apples and pears.

Also **oceaner,** (*b*) an ocean-going vessel.

1879 W. WHITMAN *Specimen Days* (1882–3) 136 The proud, steady, noiseless cleaving of the grand oceaner down the bay.

Oceana (ōuʃi,ēi·nă). The name of Harrington's ideal state, applied by J. A. Froude to the British Maritime Empire.

[**1656** J. HARRINGTON (*title*) The Common-Wealth of Oceana.] **1886** J. A. FROUDE *Oceana* 395 If Oceana is to be hereafter governed by a federal parliament, such a parliament will grow when the time is ripe for it. **1899** J. MILNE *Romance of Pro-Consul* ix. 87 He was being set to the straightening-out of some twist in Oceana, to the healing of a sore which threatened one of her limbs.

oceanarium (ōuʃiănēᵊ·riŏm). orig. *U.S.* Pl. **-ia.** [f. OCEAN *sb.* (*a.*) + *-arium*, after AQUARIUM.] An establishment having a pool in which large sea-creatures can be kept and observed, esp. for public entertainment.

1944 E. B. MARKS *They All had Glamour* 440 The aquarium of other days is now slated to be the oceanarium. **1955** *Sci. News Let.* 2 Apr. 211 (*caption*) A puzzled fisherman hauled the strange fish in in his shad net off the northern coast of Florida and it was identified by scientists at the oceanarium at Marineland, Fla. **1962** *Times* 15 Feb. 15/5 This is the usual training manœuvre for any type of animal in circuses and in oceanaria. **1972** *Village Voice* (N.Y.) 1 June 21/5 In exploiting the killer whale for the amusement of the crowds, the oceanarium people exploded two myths about Shamu's sisters and brothers of the sea. **1977** *Time* 4 July 28/3 In San Diego, 55 miles from Disneyland, is Sea World, the best-planned, best-stocked oceanarium in the U.S.

oceanaut (ōu·ʃiănǭt). [f. OCEAN *sb.* (*a.*) + *-naut*, after *AQUANAUT.] One who lives for a period at the bottom of the sea in an underwater 'house'.

1962 *Daily Tel.* 7 Sept. 1/5 This cylinder will be pierced in the middle by a large chimney, through which our two oceanauts will pass. **1967** *Ibid.* 30 Jan. 10/6 Cousteau looks forward to training oceanauts for completely new tasks like servicing and even laying deep underwater pipe lines for oil companies, as well as carrying out research on the almost unknown marine life found at such depths.

oceanic, *a.* Add: **1. b.** Pertaining to or inhabiting those regions of the open sea beyond the edge of a continental shelf.

1877 H. N. MOSELEY in *Q. Jrnl. Microsc. Sci.* XVII. 24 The present oceanic form is placed in the genus Stylochus on account of the position of the tentacles. **1902** *Encycl. Brit.* XXXIII. 936/2 The majority of the oceanic epiplankton appears to be stenothermal. **1909** [see *holoplankton* s.v. *HOLO-]. **1942** H. U. SVERDRUP et al. *Oceans* viii. 278 The oceanic province has an upper lighted zone and a lower dark zone. **1953** E. PALMER tr. *Ekman's Zoogeogr. Sea* xiv. 312 The coastal organisms.. are termed neritic and they are contrasted with the open-sea organisms; the latter are often called simply oceanic, but this term is less exact. **1974** LUCAS & CRITCH *Life in Oceans* i. 24 The pelagic division is divided into the region inshore of the continental edge, known as the 'neritic province', and the remainder, called the 'oceanic province'. In the oceanic province some aspects of the environment may change with level.

2. a. (Later example.)

1977 *Language* LIII. 391 One must at all times bear in mind, however, that this [*sc.* the philosophy of history] is a field of oceanic proportions.

b. *oceanic feeling*: a phrase used in a communication with Freud by R. Rolland (1866–1944), French writer and philosopher, in describing the longing for something vast and eternal of which he and others felt aware, and which he suggested as a possible source of religious feelings, but Freud interpreted as probably the nostalgia of the psyche for the ego-completeness of infancy; so *oceanic longing*.

1930 J. RIVIERE tr. *Freud's Civilization & its Discontents* i. 8 It is a feeling which he would like to call a sensation of 'eternity', a feeling as of something limitless, unbounded, something 'oceanic'... I cannot discover this 'oceanic' feeling in myself. *Ibid.* 21 The 'oceanic' feeling, which I suppose seeks to reinstate limitless narcissism... I can imagine that the oceanic feeling could become connected with religion later on. **1944** O. FENICHEL in *Psychoanal. Rev.* XXXI. 145 The masochist behaves masochistically because he has an oceanic longing for being united with a greater unity. **1949** KOESTLER *Insight & Outlook* xiii. 194 The general occurrence of the oceanic feeling, of the tendency towards cosmic self-transcendence, is a fact. **1967** *Philos. Rev.* LXXVI. 207 Correlates.. may be lacking when we come to the experiencing of oceanic feelings. **1971** P. BALOGH *Freud* x. 109 The feeling described by Romain Rolland of being mystically identified with the universe Freud called an oceanic feeling.

3. (Later examples.)

1937 *Discovery* Oct. 303/2 The origins of the Oceanic peoples and the remarkable affinities of culture between them and the Naga tribes of Assam. **1971** L. A. BOGER *Dict. World Pott. & Porc.* 248/1 In a general sense Oceanic pottery is primarily a woman's craft. **1974** S. MARCUS *Minding the Store* (1975) xiv. 288 They then proceeded to duplicate the same systematic approach to pre-Columbian terracottas and Oceanic sculpture.

4. Of a climate: influenced by proximity to a large body of water and hence having a relatively small diurnal and annual range of temperature and relatively great precipitation.

1877 A. GEIKIE *Elem. Lessons Physical Geogr.* v. 351 An insular or oceanic climate is one where the difference between summer and winter temperature is reduced to a minimum, and where there is a copious supply of moisture from the large water-surface. **1902** *Encycl. Brit.* XXX. 710/2 A globe whose surface is dotted with land and water, so uniformly intermixed that there can be no chance for the existence of distinct areas of continental and oceanic climates. **1922** W. G. KENDREW *Climates of Continents* xxix. 215 The east of the British Isles has a continental rather than oceanic rainfall régime. **1957** G. E. HUTCHINSON *Treat. Limnol.* I. vii. 443 The distinction between oceanic and continental climatic regimes. **1974** *Encycl. Brit. Macropædia* IV. 726/1 The differences between oceanic (or maritime) and continental climates, though operative in all latitudes, are most apparent in middle latitudes.

oceanicity (ōuʃiăni·sĭti). [f. OCEANIC *a.* + -ITY.] The extent to which a particular climate is oceanic; the state of being or having an oceanic climate.

1946 *Proc. Prehist. Soc.* XII. 3 Conditions of lesser oceanicity such as are encountered for instance in the great central plain of Ireland. **1950** *Jrnl. Ecol.* XXXVIII. 335 A. Mann (1929) suggested using as a measure of the degree of oceanicity of climates an index of hygrothermy. **1950** F. E. ZEUNER *Dating Past* (ed. 2) 394 The Theory relies on periods of increased and decreased oceanicity of the climate coupled with favourable physiographic conditions. **1974** *Nature* 17 May 211/1 The term 'oceanicity' traditionally has conveyed to ecologists the impression of a climate with a low amplitude fluctuation in seasonal temperature and a high annual precipitation.

oceanite (ōu·ʃiănəit). *Petrogr.* [ad. F. *océanite* (A. Lacroix *Minéral. de Madagascar* (1923) III. iii. 49), f. *océan* OCEAN *sb. (a.)*, from the abundance of the rock on islands in the Pacific + *-ite* -ITE[1].] Any of various basalts which are very rich in olivine.

[**1923** *Mineral. Abstr.* II. 146 New rock-names are doréite, kivite, and océanite.] **1926** G. W. TYRRELL *Princ. Petrol.* vi. 131 (*caption*) Oceanite (ultrabasic olivine-rich 'basalt'). **1967** HESS & POLDERVAART *Basalts* I. 201 An increase in olivine and clinopyroxene in the alkali basalts (at the expense of plagioclase) leads to the development of melanocratic lavas (alkaline picrite-basalts, 'oceanites', and ankaramites). **1971** *Nature* 8 Oct. 406/2 The area includes both aa and pahoehoe lava flows which are olivine basalt, basalt, or oceanite in composition.

oceanity (ōuʃi,æ·nĭti). [ad. G. *oceanität* (W. Zenker *Der thermische Aufbau d. Klimate* (1895) II. 122): see OCEAN *sb. (a.)* + -ITY.] = *OCEANICITY.

1922 [see *CONTINENTALITY]. **1924** *Geogr. Jrnl.* LXIV. 43 A station near the coast will thus show marked 'continentality' or 'oceanity' of climate, according as the prevailing wind is from the land or from the sea. **1944** V. CONRAD *Methods in Climatol.* xvii. 195 It is always better to speak of continentality than of 'oceanity'. **1959** R. E. HUSCHKE *Gloss. Meteorol.* 402 *Oceanity*, same as oceanicity.

oceanization (ōuʃiănəizēi·ʃən). *Geol.* [f. OCEAN *sb. (a.)* + -IZATION.] The conversion of continental crust into the much thinner and petrologically distinct oceanic crust.

1960 *Jrnl. Geophysical Res.* LXV. 4128/2 We must do our best to find an explanation of this 'oceanization' of the earth's crust. **1961** *Jrnl. Geol.* LXIX. 653/1 The statement that the 'sial' may be transformed into oceanic crust which leads to the 'oceanization' of a certain part of the earth's surface seems to be quite reasonable. **1973** *Nature* 22 June 434/1 Subsidence being attributed variously to crustal warping associated with orogenic compression, subcrustal erosion, oceanization (and that very recently). **1975** *Ibid.* 6 Feb. 396/2 The Soviet tectonician Belousov has gone so far as to invoke extensive 'oceanisation' of continental crust to account for the ocean basins.

oceanography. Delete '*c* 1880' in etym. and substitute for def.: The science dealing with the physical and biological properties and phenomena of the ocean. Cf. OCEANOLOGY in Dict. and Suppl. (Earlier and later examples.)

1859 M. F. MAURY *Physical Geogr. Sea* (rev. ed.) xx. 330 'Text-book of Oceanography for the Use of the Imperial Naval Academy', by Dr. August Jilek, Vienna, 1857. **1931** H. B. BIGELOW *Oceanogr.* i. 8 The other [factor] is the growth of an economic demand that oceanography afford practical assistance to the sea fisheries. **1955** *Sci. News Let.* 27 Aug. 142/1 Explorers of the ocean depths have been turning up so many new peaks, ridges, basins, seamounts and other underwater landmarks that naming them all has become a major problem in the flourishing science of oceanography. **1970** D. A. ROSS *Introd. Oceanogr.* i. 3 Most oceanographers have divided oceanography into four main parts: (1) chemical oceanography; (2) biological oceanography; (3) physical oceanography; and (4) marine geology and geophysics. **1977** *Times Lit. Suppl.* 18 Nov. 1348/3 The only basic research programmes in which he was closely involved were..for high-energy physics, materials research and oceanography.

oceanological (ōuʃiănŏlǫ·dʒikăl), *a.* [f. OCEANOLOGY: see -LOGICAL.] Of or pertaining to oceanology.

1969 *New Scientist* 20 Feb. 382/1 A final element in oceanological development..is the promised White Paper. **1970** R. BARTON *Oceanology Today* vii. 187 Cooperation in oceanological endeavor is not confined to agreement between nations as to who owns what. **1975** *Nature* 2 Oct. 353/1 This will include atmospheric sounding, the investigation of deep-level ice cores.., oceanological investigation in the Drake Straits, [etc.].

oceanologist (ōuʃiănǫ·lŏdʒist). [f. as prec. + -IST.] An expert or specialist in oceanology.

1954 *Deep-Sea Research* II. 86 Any oceanologist could conceive an ideal plan, but when the problem of money is introduced, restrictions are needed. **1972** *Daily Tel.* 22 Mar. 7 (*caption*) The Russian research ship Professor Subov, 6,681 tons, which is making a three-day visit to London... The crew and team of oceanologists and meteorologists spent the day sightseeing.

oceanology. Delete *rare*—⁰ and add: In mod. use freq. given a broader meaning than *oceanography* (see quots. 1969[1], 1973). (Examples.)

1898 *Ann. Rep. Board of Regents Smithsonian Inst. 1896* 295 This brings us to the equally important question of oceanology, which should comprise a complete knowledge not only of the surface currents in the Arctic seas, but also surface and deep-sea temperatures, [etc.]. **1955** *Deep-Sea Research* II. 247 The use of the words 'Oceanology' and 'Oceanologist' was well and truly pondered in days past. Today they are little used save in Russia. **1956** *Ibid.* IV. 68 In 1949 the R/V *Vitjaz* of the Institute of Oceanology of the Academy of Sciences of the U.S.S.R. started its investigations. **1969** *Nature* 1 Mar. 804/2 A brief explanation is required of the word 'oceanology'... In the early days it was often used synonymously with 'oceanography' to mean marine science... It is now often used to mean marine technology, and although it has no precise definition, is usually taken to exclude conventional naval architecture. [**1969** *Ibid.* 13 Dec. 1049/2 Much of what passes for oceanography is nothing more than the straightforward use of the sea for such things as fishing and transport.] **1970** R. BARTON *Oceanology Today* i. 12 The project becomes even more valuable when looked at in terms of the lessons..that will be learned across the whole field of oceanology, from offshore oil exploration to physiological research in diving. **1973** HICKLING & BROWN *Seas & Oceans* p. viii, Sea or ocean science is nowadays called *oceanography*, or by an even newer word, *oceanology*, coined in the 1960s. Some like to differentiate between the use of these terms, using *oceanography* to describe the more academic aspects of ocean science, and *oceanology* to describe modern ocean technology, including the political, legal, financial and economic aspects of the seas and oceans.

ochlophobia (ǫklǫfōu·biă). [f. Gr. ὄχλο-ς crowd + -PHOBIA: see OCHLOPHOBIST.] A morbid aversion to crowds. Hence **ochlopho·bic** *a.*

1894 GOULD *Dict. Med.* 884/2 Ochlophobia. **1929** C. CONNOLLY *Let.* Nov. in *Romantic Friendship* (1975) 330, I have had ochlophobia lately. **1976** R. PERRY *One Good Death* x. 157 [He] preferred to work in greater privacy. It could even be that he was ochlophobic like Toller, the Austrian killer.

ochlospecies (ǫ·klospī:sīz, spī:ʃīz). *Taxonomy.* [f. as prec. + SPECIES.] (See quot. 1967.)

1962 F. WHITE in D. Nichols *Taxon. & Geogr.* 79 Such species cannot be satisfactorily subdivided and could conveniently be distinguished from monotypic and polytypic species by calling them *ochlo*-species. **1967** *Gardens' Bull.* XXII. 6 White has coined the useful and appropriate term ochlospecies for species showing a complex reticulate pattern of variation. **1972** G. T. PRANCE in *Flora Neotropica* IX. 109 *Licania heteromorpha* is a good example of an ochlospecies.

ochone (oχōu·n), *int.* (*sb.*) Also **och hone.** Repr. an Anglo-Irish form of OHONE *int.* (*sb.*). Also as *v. intr.*

1829 G. GRIFFIN *Collegians* III. xxxiii. 54 I'm ashamed o' myself, to be always..moaning and ochoning, among the neighbours. *c* **1850** in R. Ward *Penguin Bk. Austral. Ballads* (1964) 52 The trees grew so thick I couldn't find it, ochone,..So bothered and lost was poor Paddy Malone. **1855** [see OHONE *int.* (*sb.*) b]. **1861** TROLLOPE *Tales of All Countries* (ser. 1) 67, I could plainly hear poor Larry's head strike against the stone floor. 'Ochone, ochone!' he cried at the top of his voice. **1884** D. BOUCICAULT *Shaughraun* 20/1 Och hone!—my darlin' boy, it will be a grand day for you, but your poor ould mother will be left alone..och-o-o-hone! **1913** W. B. YEATS *Countess Cathleen* in *Poems* 68 Ochone! The treasure room is broken in. **1919** G. B. SHAW *O'Flaherty V.C.* in *Heartbreak House* 186 Ochone! ochone! my son's turned agen me. Oh, whatll I do at all at all? **1920** F. SCOTT FITZGERALD *This Side of Paradise* (1921) *A Lament for a Foster Son*... Ochone He is gone from me the son of my mind. **1939** JOYCE *Finnegans Wake* 277 His sevencoloured's soot (Ochone! Ochonal!). **1977** *Irish Democrat* Mar. 6/3 When Sarsfield sailed away I wept as I heard the wild ochone.

Ochrana, var. *OKHRANA.

ochre, *sb.* Add: **4.** *ochre-yellow* (examples); **ochre-grave** (see quot.); also *attrib.*

1928 PEAKE & FLEURE *Steppe & Sown* 20 In the early type of kurgan are found skeletons..buried in a contracted position, the bones covered with red ochre. These..are now known as the ochre-graves. *Ibid.* 26 The ochre-grave folk. **1957** V. G. CHILDE *Dawn Europ. Civilization* (ed. 6) ix. 149 (*heading*) The Ochre Grave Cultures of the Pontic Steppes. *Ibid.* 157 The beginnings of the Ochre Grave culture should go back well into the third millenium. **1899** Ochre yellow [see *hæmochromatosis* s.v. *HÆMO-, HEMO-]. **1952** A. G. L. HELLYER *Sanders' Encycl. Gardening* (ed. 22) 121 *Dayana*, ochre-yellow, lip white and brown.

ochro, var. OKRO, OKRA. (Examples.)

1952 S. SELVON *Brighter Sun* v. 82 Neighbour ask me bringam dry ochro seed for she to plant. **1953** G. LAMMING *In Castle of my Skin* xiv. 274 Slicing the ochroes was ..painstaking. The prickly surface irritated the skin, and the slices fell off on the hand in a slimy mess. **1971** *Advocate-News* (Barbados) 17 Sept. (Guyana Suppl.) p. ii/2 Now the Liliputians have completed planting of ground provisions, pumpkins, ochroes, blackeye peas, celery, bora and such permanent crops as breadfruit, citrus and breadnut.

ochronosis. Substitute for entry s.v. OCHRO-: (ōukrŏnōu·sis). *Path.* [mod.L. (R. Virchow 1866, in *Arch. f. path. Anat. u. Physiol.* XXXVII. 218), f. Gr. ὠχρός pale yellow + νόσος disease + -OSIS.] An abnormal brown pigmentation of tissue, notably cartilage, esp. when a symptom of the metabolic disorder alkaptonuria and resulting from the accumulation of polymerized homogentisic acid.

1867 *Half-Yearly Abstr. Med. Sci.* XLV. 28 Virchow proposes to call this affection ochronosis. **1876** [in Dict. s.v. OCHRO-]. **1906** *Lancet* 6 Jan. 26/1 The urine of his patient.., who had the blackening of cartilages which constitutes ochronosis, was brown when passed. **1948** W. A. D. ANDERSON *Path.* iv. 88 Phenol poisoning, due to absorption of phenol from surgical dressings, has been reported to cause a pigmentation similar to ochronosis. **1962** C. A. CLARKE *Genetics for Clinician* xiii. 156 Alkaptonuria... In addition to the urinary abnormality..there is pigmentation of cartilage and ligaments (ochronosis). **1970** *Nature* 21 Nov. 770/1 Adults with alcaptonuria develop a destructive arthritis secondary to the deposition of a melanin-like pigment in their connective tissues, especially skin, tendon and cartilage (ochronosis).

Hence **ochrono·tic** *a.* [-OTIC].

1922 *Arch. Internal Med.* XXIX. 737 Hanseman observed diffuse and granular ochronotic pigment in the tissues. **1961** *Arthritis & Rheumatism* IV. 137 (*heading*) Studies on the pathogenesis of ochronotic arthropathy.

ochrous, *a.* (Earlier examples of U.S. form.)

1806 WEBSTER, *Ocherous*,..like or containing ocher. **1828** —— s.v. *Ocherous matter*, an ocherous color. **1869** *Rep. Comm. Agric. 1868* (U.S. Dept. Agric.) 427 The pasture..hardening in some such manner as 'hard-pan' forms in ocherous soil.

ocker (ǫ·kəɹ), *sb.*[2] *Austral. slang.* Also **Ocker.** [The name of a character in a series of Australian television sketches by Ron Frazer: used earlier as a colloquial variant of names like *Oscar* and *O'Connor*.] A rough, uncultivated, or aggressively boorish Australian. Also *attrib.* or as *adj.*

[**1959**: see *NAUGHTY *sb.* 2.] **1971** G. JOHNSTON *Cartload of Clay* 71 The big man would be a good player, a vigorous clubman, a hearty participant in the companionship of the club bar. He was a type Julian had sometimes talked to him about, what the boy called an 'Ocker'. **1973** *Sunday Sun* (Brisbane) 1 July 21/5 His cigarette commercials were the next step in his career. And once again the ocker image worked wonders. **1973** *Nation Rev.* (Melbourne) 24–30 Aug. 1430/4 (Advt.), Sydney Femme, 27, bored by ozzie ockers and oedipal neurotics, desires to develop dynamic dalliance with..male human beings. **1974** *Sydney Morning Herald* 24 Apr. 6 That image, of the RSL itself as a sabre-rattling élitist organisation with an over-privileged influence on governments, and of RSL members themselves as beer-swilling, 'pokey-playing' Ockers, has, executives believe, faded if not totally evaporated. **1975** *TV Times* (Austral.) 12 Apr. 10 The cult of the ocker is sweeping Australia. **1976** *Telegraph* (Brisbane) 30 July 42/1 It is no use telling Australians to wake up; it is not in the ocker character.

Hence **o·ckerdom,** ockers collectively. Also **o·ckerism,** over-assertive boorishness, uncultivated behaviour.

1974 P. PORTER in *Australian* 5 Oct. 13 The new Australian boorishness is known as Ockerism, from a slob-like character called Ocker in a television series, the embodiment of oafish, blinkered self-satisfaction. **1975** M. HARRIS in *Ibid.* 18 Jan. 18 The resurgence of an aggressive Australian ockerdom was coincident with the first election of the Whitlam Government and the discovery of a 'new nationalism'. **1977** *Sunday Times* 23 Jan. 30/8 It is seen as a defeat for the spirit of ockerism (that is, being blatantly Australian).

Ockham's razor: see *RAZOR *sb.* 1 b.

o'clock. Used, in various contexts specifying direction, esp. with reference to the target in shooting, to give bearings corresponding to the positions of the numerals on a clock face, from the standpoint of one facing twelve o'clock. (Cf. quot. 1797 s.v. CLOCK *sb.*[1] 4.)

1904 W. WINANS *Hints on Revolver Shooting* iv. 33 When the hind sight comes to the level of your eyes.., the front sight will be seen through the middle of the 'U' pointed at the bottom of the bull's-eye, the top of the front sight just touching it at 'six o'clock'. **1913** A. G. FULTON *Notes on Rifle Shooting* 15 If the bull can be seen without much difficulty a 6 o'clock aim is probably the best. **1918** E. S. FARROW *Dict. Mil. Terms* 415 *O'clock*, a term employed to indicate, by means of the divisions on the dial of the clock, the location of a hit on the target or the direction from which the wind may be blowing, as a 7 o'clock, 4 or 5 o'clock wind. **1932** J. A. BARLOW *Elements of Rifle Shooting* iv. 47 Allowances for a constant strength of wind blowing from a varying o'clock, vary according to the length of the perpendicular drawn from the hour on the clock face to the 6–12 o'clock diameter. **1943** C. H. WARD-JACKSON *Piece of Cake* 44 *O'clock*. Used thus, 'Ten bandits at 6 o'clock' means ten enemy aircraft immediately below the recipient of the message. **1948** A. M. TAYLOR *Lang. World War II* (rev. ed.) 141 *O'clock*, term used largely by fliers in designating directions, e.g. 'twelve o'clock' indicates straight ahead; 'three o'clock' directly to the right, etc. **1967** B. KNOX *Blacklight* ii. 48 The lamp continued. 'They say we have it at about our ten o'clock sir.' **1970** M. KELLY *Spinifex* vii. 119 'Black rock. Eight o'clock. One hundred metres!' He'd instinctively ranged artillery in another war. **1972** *National Observer* (U.S.) 27 May 19/1 He says the hands should grasp the wheel at 3 and 9 o'clock. **1973** *Country Life* 25 Oct. 1292/1 From its position at twelve o'clock, the dog begins the critical 'lift'.

ocote (ǒko·te). [Amer. Sp., f. Nahuatl *ocotl* torch.] A resinous Mexican pine, *Pinus montezumæ*, or its wood; also = PITCH-PINE. Also *attrib.*

[**1858** G. GORDON *Pinetum* 211 It [sc. *Pinus teocote*] is the 'de'ocote' or 'Pino de'ocote' (candle wood) of the Mexicans. **1861** E. B. TYLOR *Anahuac* 336/2 *Ocote* (Aztec, *ocotl*), a pine-tree, pine-torch.] **1908** H. GADOW *Through Southern Mexico* iii. 50 The forest consists mainly of the long-leaved *Pinus liophylla* and the 'ocote' or *Pinus montezumae*, which much resembles our Scotch fir. **1926** D. H. LAWRENCE *Plumed Serp.* vii. 129 The boy.. sat apart watching the two ocote torches. **1927** —— *Mornings in Mexico* 10 There is a resinous smell of ocote wood. **1938** *Amer. Speech* XIII. 113 The name [*ocotillo*] is a derivative of Mexican-Spanish *ocote*, a word also applied to pitch-pines or the wood they yield.

ocotillo (ōukotī·yo). *U.S.* Also **ocetilla, ocochilla, ocotilla.** [Amer. Sp., dim. of *OCOTE.] A spiny shrub, *Fouquiera splendens*, of the family Fouquieraceæ, native to the south-western United States and Mexico and bearing narrow, inconspicuous leaves and panicles of red flowers. Also *attrib.*

1856 in *Dict. Americanisms*, Aside from the grass, there is a shrub called the..*Ocetilla.* **1864** *Harper's Mag.* Nov. 697/2 Passing through some dense thickets of mesquit and ocochilla, the struggling family found themselves at the foot of a rocky bluff. **1883** *Ibid.* Mar. 491/1 The houses consist of a frame-work of cottonwood or ocotilla wattles. *Ibid.* 502/2 The ocotilla is simply a wattle of sticks.. waiting to be cut down and turned into palings. **1893** *Nation* (N.Y.) 7 Sept. 169/3 Walking-sticks made of the porous ocotillo cactus. **1915** L. H. BAILEY *Stand. Cycl. Hort.* III. 1271/1 Ocotillo..is a conspicuous object in the deserts from Texas westward,..the rod-like stiff canes looking like lifeless sticks in dry weather and in its season crowned with masses of showy bloom. **1948** *Natural Hist.* Apr. 181 The Ocotillo is frankly red, adding its flaming tips to every dry stick that looked dead a week ago. **1966** MRS. L. B. JOHNSON *White House Diary* 3 Apr. (1970) 381 The ocotillo..looks like about a dozen long coach whips stuck into the ground, spraying out in a weeping fashion. **1976** *San Antonio* (Texas) *Express-News* 27 Nov. 1B/5 'You know the *ocotillo*,' Ben said, pointing out the cactus that looks like five or six spiny, 10-foot pieces of rope snaking up into the air.

-ocracy. Add: (Further examples as *sb.*) Now used generically to denote any form of government or domination to which a word in *-ocracy* can be applied.

1831 C. C. F. GREVILLE *Mem.* (1874) II. xiii. 112 It has elicited a strong Conservative demonstration, and proved that out of the rabble-ocracy (for everything is in *ocracy* now) his power is anything but unlimited. **1894** G. B. SHAW in *Fortn. Rev.* Apr. 489 Social-Democracy, like all other '-ocracies', will have a great deal more trouble with its idle and worthless members than with its able ones. **1928** —— *Intelligent Woman's Guide Socialism* xliii. 166 If it be still necessary to call the rich an ocracy of any kind, they must be called a plutocracy. **1963** F. W. FREY in L. W. Pye *Communications & Political Devel.* xvii. 299 Movement towards 'democracy'..or whatever one's preferred..'ocracy' happens to be.

octa-. Add: **b. octade·canol**, any of the alcohols with the formula $C_{18}H_{37}OH$; spec. *normal* (or *n-*) *octadecanol*, a crystalline primary alcohol which is present in whale and dolphin oils, also called stearyl alcohol; **octape·ptide**, any peptide composed of eight amino-acid residues.

1914 *Jrnl. Chem. Soc.* CV. 2233 The acetates of the dextrorotatory carbinols from ethylbutylcarbinol (γ-heptanol) on to ethylpentadecylcarbinol (γ-octadecanol) are all of negative rotation. **1949** E. CHAIN in H. W. Florey et al. *Antibiotics* II. xvii. 709 Antifoam reagent (3 per cent. octadecanol in lard oil). **1970** *Chem. & Physics Lipids* IV. 246 The major long-chain alcohols found in heart and brain tissues are hexadecanol, octadecanol and octadecenol. **1931** *Chem. Rev.* VIII. 390 Curtius..found that when his triglycylglycine ester was heated to 100°C. *in vacuo* it was converted into an insoluble infusible material having the composition $—NHCH_2CO—$. He assigned to this material the structure of a cyclic octapeptide, but a much more highly polymeric open chain structure seems more probable. **1957** *Science* 3 May 886/1 (*heading*) Synthesis and pharmacology of the octapeptide angiotonin. **1972** *Lancet* 17 June 1320/1 The superb work of Wieland and his school established that the toxins are either cyclic heptapeptides or octapeptides.

octahedrally (ǫktăhī·drăli), *adv.* [f. OCTAHEDRAL, OCTO- *a.* + -LY².] In an octahedral shape or arrangement.

1872 *Geol. Mag.* IX. 356 The octahedrally crystallized magnetic particles do not contain any traces of nickel. **1947** *Q. Rev. Chem. Soc.* I. 253 Half of the metal ions are surrounded, approximately octahedrally, by four oxygen atoms of AsO_4 (or PO_4) ions and by two OH ions. **1970** *Nature* 11 Apr. 141/2 It is a reasonable guess that the molecules around the ion are disposed octahedrally.

octahedrite. Add: **2.** An iron meteorite which shows a Widmanstätten structure on etching due to intimate intergrowths of plates of kamacite with narrow borders of tænite oriented parallel to the faces of a regular octahedron.

1916 *Mineral. Mag.* XVIII. 42 (*table*) Nickel-poor octahedrites. **1944** C. PALACHE et al. *Dana's Syst. Min.* (ed. 7) I. 120 A similar structureless aspect can be obtained in an octahedrite by prolonged heating at about 900°. **1974** *Encycl. Brit. Micropædia* VII. 477/2 Besides nickel-iron, major minerals in octahedrites are troilite and schreibersite.

octal (ǫ·ktăl), *a.* and *sb.* [f. OCT- + -AL.] **A.** *adj.* **1.** *Electronics.* Applied to valve bases and plugs (and the corresponding sockets) having a standard circular arrangement of eight pins with a central moulded key for determining the orientation.

1936 *Wireless World* 20 Nov. 557 (*heading*) 8-pin base (octal) connections. **1943** C. L. BOLTZ *Basic Radio* x. 165 Then from America came the international octal base, with eight pins symmetrically arranged in a circle. **1961** *Engineering* 14 July 42/4 The unit is constructed as a plug-in module..connecting with associated circuits through a standard octal plug. **1976** *Gramophone* Feb. 1403/1 At the left is an octal valve socket designed for use with a matching transformer when a moving coil cartridge is used.

2. *Math.* and *Computers.* Pertaining to or being a system of numerical notation that employs 8 rather than 10 as the base.

1948 *Math. Tables & Other Aids to Computation* III. 295 Binary numbers are set into the keyboard in the octal (radix 8) notation. **1962** T. C. BARTEE et al. *Theory & Design Digital Machines* 307 In the octal system the sequence 624 represents the sum $6 \times 8^2 + 2 \times 8^1 + 4 \times 8^0$ which is equal to the sequence 404 in the decimal system. **1963** *Rep. Comm. Inquiry Decimal Currency* 4 in *Parl. Papers 1962–3* (Cmnd. 2145) XI. 195 If..we have in mind electronic rather than human computers, a case can be made for counting in eights—an octal system—because this can be related more easily to the binary system used by such computers. **1973** *Nature* 27 Apr. 620/1 The octal system is widely used in listing machine instruction programs for small computers, where groups of six octal digits are written in place of sixteen to eighteen binary digits.

B. *sb.* The octal system; rarely *pl.*

1948 *Math. Tables & Other Aids to Computation* III. 295 The conversions octal-binary and binary-octal are very elementary. **1961** EVANS & PERRY *Programming & Coding* iii. 89 The two representations ·101010101 in binary, and ·525 in octal, are different representations of the same magnitude. **1961** *Times* 28 Dec. 9/5 (*heading*) Thinking in octals. Advantages over decimals. **1967** KLERER & KORN *Digital Computer User's Handbk.* I. ii. 39 Since $2^3 = 8^1$, a binary series of digits may be converted to octal by grouping the binary digits into three to left or right of the decimal point. Thus the binary integer $(1001011011)_2 = (1\ 001\ 011\ 011)_2 = (1133)_8$. **1977** D. BAGLEY *Enemy* xxxi. 253 This gadget is working in octal instead of decimal... Many computers work in octal internally.

o:ctame·thylcy:clote:trasilo·xane. *Chem.* [f. OCTA- + METHYL + CYCLO- + TETRA- + *SILOXANE.] A colourless oily liquid that is a cyclic tetramer, $[(CH_3)_2SiO]_4$, and an intermediate in the manufacture of many silicones.

1946 M. J. HUNTER et al. in *Jrnl. Amer. Chem. Soc.* LXVIII. 361/1 When a few drops of concentrated sulfuric acid are added to a quantity, say 10 c.c., of octamethyl*cyclo*tetrasiloxane, $[(CH_3)_2SiO]_4$, there is no marked change in appearance or temperature. **1962** BARRY & BECK in Stone & Graham *Inorg. Polymers* v. 216 The slow addition of dimethyldichlorosilane to excess water at 15 to 20°C yields a mixture consisting of 0·5% hexamethylcyclotrisiloxane (D_3), 42·0% octamethylcyclotetrasiloxane (D_4), 6·7% decamethylcyclopentasiloxane (D_5), [etc.]. **1970** *Encycl. Polymer Sci. & Technol.* XII. 503 Almost all strong inorganic alkalis and most quaternary ammonium hydroxides and phosphonium hydroxides will polymerize octamethylcyclotetrasiloxane to a high-molecular-weight polymer.

octane. Add: **1. b.** *ellipt.* for *octane number*, esp. with prefixed numeral, e.g. *105 octane*, or adj., e.g. *high octane.*

1932, etc. [see *high-octane* s.v. *HIGH *a.* 22 a]. **1935** *Oil & Gas Jrnl.* 4 July 16/1 Until this spring, 87 octane gasoline was the highest quality used for commercial take-offs. **1954** [see *ISOOCTANE b]. **1960** J. B. HILL in V. B. Guthrie *Petroleum Products Handbk.* iv. 20 A particular gasoline may have a Research octane of 88 and a Motor octane of 78. **1966** *McGraw-Hill Encycl. Sci. & Technol.* III. 309/2 High octane gasoline burns in the same manner and with the same flame velocity as low octane gasoline. **1973** J. LEASOR *Host of Extras* vii. 136 Adrenalin surged round my body like 105 octane petrol.

2. *attrib.* and *Comb.*, as (sense *1 b) *octane-booster, -quality*; *octane-scented* adj., **octane number, rating**, a number indicating the anti-knock properties of a motor or aviation fuel, equal (for numbers below 100) to the percentage by volume of isooctane in an isooctane/normal heptane mixture of equivalent performance (see also quot. 1966).

1971 *New Scientist* 5 Aug. 323/1 Those spokesmen of the oil industry who have been arguing that alkyl lead (added to petrol as an octane-booster..) is not a health hazard. **1931** *Automobile Engineer* Aug. 308/3 Lead tetra-ethyl is the only other practical alternative to cracked spirits as a means of raising the anti-knock value of motor spirit to an octane number of 70 or more (this now being the prime consideration of a premium gasoline or petrol). **1933** *Flight* 4 May 408/1 The British Air Ministry is, rightly or wrongly, taking its time over considering the matter of octane number. **1966** *McGraw-Hill Encycl. Sci. & Technol.* IX. 273/1 Fuels with octane numbers above 100 are usually rated by finding the number of milliliters of tetraethyllead required per gallon of isooctane to give the same resistance to detonation as the fuel sample. **1972** PATTERSON & HENEIN *Emissions from Combustion Engines* ii. 63 The octane number of the fuels on the market is about 94 for regular gasoline and 100 for premium gasoline. **1959** R. J. HENGSTEBECK *Petroleum Processing* i. 3 The octane quality of a gasoline may be rated differently by different engines. **1940** A. W. JUDGE *Aircraft Engines* I. v. 114 If it was found that a mixture of 78 per cent. of iso-octane and 22 per cent. of heptane matched the particular fuel under test in 'knocking' qualities the fuel in question would be said to have an octane rating of 78. **1959** R. J. HENGSTEBECK *Petroleum Processing* i. 3 Octane ratings above 100 are proportional to their performance potentials. **1972** *Daily Tel.* 15 Mar. 11/7 Lead has been used in growing quantities to raise the octane rating of petrol, allowing modern engines to make more efficient use of the fuel. **1946** *R.A.F. Jrnl.* May 151 Newly-arrived from the octane-scented atmosphere of Station life and full of inspiration.

octanoic (ǫktănōu·ik), *a.* *Chem.* [f. OCTAN(E + *-OIC.] = CAPRYLIC *a.*

1909 *Jrnl. Chem. Soc.* XCVI. II. 1378/1 (Index), Octanoic acid, ε-hydroxy-, and its lactone. **1940** T. P. HILDITCH *Chem. Constitution Nat. Fats* iii. 99 In the milk fats of sheep and goats.., the proportions of octanoic and decanoic (caprylic and capric) acids are much greater and approach, or even exceed, that of butyric acid in cow milk fats. **1972** *Materials & Technol.* V. ix. 244 $CH_3(CH_2)_6COOH$, octanoic acid, was first described in 1844 by Lerch who isolated it from butter.

Hence **octano·ate**, the anion, or an ester or salt, of octanoic acid; **o·ctanoyl**, the radical $CH_3(CH_2)_6CO—$ present in octanoic acid; also called *caprylyl.*

1945 *Jrnl. Biol. Chem.* CLXI. 416 Of the tested fatty acids octanoate was the most reactive under these conditions. **1949** *Union Internat. Chim. Pure et Appl., Compt. Rend.* XV. 145 Rule 58.3... Octanoyl. Replacing 'capryloyl' and 'caprylyl'. **1954** A. WHITE et al. *Princ. Biochem.* xviii. 482 The reaction sequence..by which octanoate might give rise to acetoacetate. **1973** *Agric. & Biol. Chem.* (Tokyo) XXXVII. 2713/2 During this acylation process with *n*-octanoyl chloride, esterification of two OH groups of 2 moles of Thr contained in a colistin nonapeptide molecule was possible. **1974** *Acta Crystallogr.* XXX. B. 2913/2 Copper(II) octanoate was prepared by adding copper carbonate to an excess of solution of octanoic acid in ethanol.

octanol (ǫ·ktănǫl). *Chem.* [f. as prec. + -OL.] Any saturated aliphatic monohydric alcohol containing eight carbon atoms, $C_8H_{17}OH$, of which many isomeric forms exist; *esp.* the primary straight-chain alcohol (*n-* or 1-octanol), or the secondary alcohol, $CH_3(CH_2)_5$-$CH(OH)CH_3$ (2-octanol), both of which are colourless odoriferous liquids used chiefly in the perfume and plastic industries; octyl alcohol.

1905 *Jrnl. Chem. Soc.* LXXXVIII. I. 573 δ-Octanol is a mobile liquid with a pleasant odour which boils at 71° under 10 mm. pressure. **1932** *Physical Rev.* XL. 830 The series consists of twenty-one octanols which differ from one another only in the relative positions of a methyl and hydroxyl group along the chain. **1947** KIRK & OTHMER *Encycl. Chem. Technol.* I. 317, 1-Octanol..is a colorless liquid with a penetrating odor. *Ibid.*, The technical grades of 2-octanol are used as solvents for many resins and in some protective formulations to improve flow and leveling. **1950** I. MELLAN *Industr. Solvents* (ed. 2) xi. 511 Commercial *n*-octanol is derived synthetically from coconut oil. **1975** J. M. TEDDER et al. *Basic Org. Chem.* V. xii. 450 Long chain fatty alcohols (mainly octanol and decanol) are used to inhibit terminal bud growth and hence stimulate branching in many plant species.

octantal, *a.* (s.v. OCTANT). Add: **b.** Vanishing once in each octant of the compass.

1928 L. S. PALMER *Wireless Princ. & Pract.* xii. 472 Any error of this nature occurring twice in each quadrant is termed an octantal error. **1954** *Electronic Engin.* XXVI. 39/1 Marconi's have developed a unique fixed (non-rotating) aerial with low octantal error.

octaploid, var. *OCTOPLOID *a.* (*sb.*).

octapole, var. *OCTUPOLE.

Octateuch. Add: (Later examples.) Also, a manuscript or edition of the Octateuch.

1967 R. L. S. BRUCE-MITFORD *Art of Codex Amiatinus* 9 They may be read as follows: OCT·LIB LEG.. (i.e. eight books of the Octateuch and the Law..). **1976** *Amer. N. & Q.* XV. 61/2 The Octateuch of Vatopédi, going back to the thirteenth century and considered one of the most valuable of the five known octateuchs. **1977** D. CUPITT in J. Hick *Myth of God Incarnate* vii. 143 A miniature in the Smyrna Octateuch.

octavalent (ǫktăvēi·lěnt), *a.* *Chem.* Also (now *rare*) **octo-.** [f. OCTA-, OCTO- + L. *vălent-em*, pres. pple. of *valēre* to be worth.] Characterized by a valency of eight.

1880 Octovalent [see PER-[1] 5 b]. **1909** J. N. FRIEND *Theory of Valency* xvii. 117 Osmium apparently functions as an octavalent atom in the tetroxide OsO_4, as does ruthenium in RuO_4. **1950** N. V. SIDGWICK *Chem. Elements* II. 1458 There are a fair number of octovalent osmium compounds. **1973** S. E. LIVINGSTONE in J. C. Bailar et al. *Comprehensive Inorg. Chem.* III. xliii. 1209 The octavalent state [of osmium] is more stable than that of ruthenium.

Hence **octava·lency**, the property of being octavalent.

1925 *Ann. Rep. Progr. Chem.* XXI. 54 These facts are held to confirm the octavalency of osmium.

octave, *sb.* (*a.*) Add: **3. f.** (Further examples.)

1923 GLAZEBROOK *Dict. Appl. Physics* IV. 891/2 The continuous spectrum was thus extended to thirty-nine times the wave-length of sodium yellow, or five octaves into the infra-red. **1960** [see *INFRA-RED *a.* and *sb.* B]. **1961** BERKNER & ODISHAW *Sci. in Space* i. 3 Even if we add the radio-frequency window to the narrow light-wave window, the sum gives astronomy about twenty octaves.. of the electromagnetic spectrum with which to investigate the universe from the Earth.

4. b. *law of octaves* (earlier and later examples).

1865 J. A. R. NEWLANDS in *Chem. News* 18 Aug. 83/2 This peculiar relationship I propose to provisionally term the 'Law of Octaves'. **1932** J. N. FRIEND *Text-bk. Physical Chem.* I. xvi. 330 According to Newlands' Law of Octaves, when the elements are arranged in the order of increasing atomic weights, the first and last of any eight consecutive elements possess similar properties. **1965** D. ABBOTT *Inorg. Chem.* i. 31 In 1864 Newlands put forward his Law of Octaves, in which he likened the classification of elements to the musical scale.

8. octave key, a key on a wind-instrument used to produce a note an octave higher than the note that is being fingered.

1880 GROVE *Dict. Mus.* II. 487/1 In more modern instruments [*sc.* oboes] a second octave-key has been introduced..which is usually lifted on reaching A above the stave. **1911** *Encycl. Brit.* XXIV. 274/1 The first 15 semitones are obtained by opening successive keys, the rest of the compass by means of octave keys enabling the performer to sound the harmonic octave of the fundamental scale. **1957** A. C. BAINES *Woodwind Instrum.* iv. 106 With full automatic octave keys, the G♯ key, when pressed, holds down ring III.

octavic (ǫktēi·vik), *a.* and *sb.* *Math.* [f. L. *octāv-us* eighth + -IC.] **A.** *adj.* Of the eighth order or degree. **B.** *sb.* An octavic polynomial or curve.

1854 *Cambr. & Dublin Math. Jrnl.* IX. 94 The biquadratic and octavic function of x, y, $(x, y)^4$, $(x, y)^8$. **1879** *Amer. Jrnl. Math.* II. 251 For the first four orders there is but one such block, for the quintic and the sextic two, for the seventhic five, for the octavic three, and for the 9ic and 10ic four. **1897** *Nature* 11 Nov. 47/1 More general forms of octavic curves with six double points.

octet, octette. Add: **3. b.** A stable group of eight electrons in an electron shell of an atom.

1919 I. LANGMUIR in *Jrnl. Amer. Chem. Soc.* XLI. 888 After the very stable pairs..the next most stable arrangement of electrons is the group of 8 such as forms the outside layer in atoms of neon and argon. We shall call this stable group of 8 electrons the 'octet'. **1927** N. V. SIDGWICK *Electronic Theory of Valency* x. 175 The trivalent elements, having incomplete octets, strive to complete them by co-ordination. **1965** D. ABBOTT *Inorg. Chem.* ii. 70 Some atoms can remain stable when surrounded by more than an octet of electrons (they expand their octets).

c. *Nuclear Physics.* A multiplet (sense *b) of eight sub-atomic particles.

1961 in GELL-MANN & NE'EMAN *Eightfold Way* (1964) i. 13 The most important prediction is..that the eight baryons should all have the same spin and parity and that the pseudoscalar and vector mesons should form 'octets', with possible additional 'singlets'. **1962** *Physical Rev.* CXXV. 1068/2 The baryons, as well as the mesons, can form octets and singlets. **1963** [see *NONET 2]. **1968** M. S. LIVINGSTON *Particle Physics* xii. 213 Here [*sc.* in SU(3) theory] the basic octet of states is identified with the nucleon, the Σ-particle triplet, the Λ^0 particle, and the Ξ-particle doublet.

octic (ǫ·ktik), *a.* and *sb.* *Math.* [f. L. *octo* eight + -IC.] = *OCTAVIC *a.* and *sb.*

1877 *Encycl. Brit.* VI. 726/1 ϕ is not expressible as the square root of an octic function of θ. **1916** G. A. MILLER et al. *Theory & Applic. Finite Groups* i. 4 The Octic Group. There are eight movements of a plane which transform into itself a square situated in this plane. **1938** *Duke Math. Jrnl.* IV. 285 Normal octics with the group $G(2, 2, 2)$. **1978** *Amer. Math. Monthly* LXXXV. 470 (*heading*) Rational octic and higher reciprocity laws.

‖ **octli** (ōu·ktli). [Mex. Sp.] = PULQUE.

1845 *Encycl. Metrop.* XVI. 528/1 The most favourite spirit of the Mexicans is *pulque* or *octli*, a thick ropy juice which flows from a wounded agave or maguey. **1883** *Encycl. Brit.* XVI. 213/1 The juice extracted by tapping the great aloe before flowering was fermented into an intoxicating drink about the strength of beer, *octli*, by the Spaniards called *pulque*. **1914** T. A. JOYCE *Mexican Archaeol.* ii. 43 This awakening after heavy sleep..connected the octli gods with the waxing and waning of vegetation and the moon. **1938** *Times Lit. Suppl.* 5 Mar. 157/1 Other mistakes relate to the preparation of the fermented drink 'octli'.

octo-. Add: **o·ctode** *Radio* [*-ODE[2]], any thermionic valve with eight electrodes, some of which have been used as frequency changers in superheterodyne receivers; **octofoil** *a.* (later example); **octora·diant** *a.* = *octoradial* adj.; **o·ctose** [a. G. *octose* (E. Fischer 1890, in *Ber. d. Deut. Chem. Ges.* XXIII. 934): see -OSE[2]], any monosaccharide having eight carbon atoms in the molecule.

1934 A. W. HASLETT *Radio round World* 191 There are many more complicated types of valve, ranging up to the octode which has eight different components instead of only three. **1943** *Electronic Engin.* XV. 339 Table A shows the more important frequency changers..and it may be noted that three of these, the pentode, the octode and the heptode mixer, owe some of their success to their high anode impedance. **1961** *Amat. Radio Handbk.* (ed. 3) ii. 58/2 When provided with an additional grid used as a suppressor it [*sc.* the heptode] was referred to as an octode. **1958** *Times* 11 Dec. 12/4 An octofoil plain salver. **1911** BEERBOHM *Zuleika D.* xviii. 271 He affixed to his breast the octoradiant star, so much larger and more lustrous than any actual star in heaven. **1890** Octose [see *heptose* s.v. *HEPTA-]. **1931** R. J. WILLIAMS *Introd. Biochem.* iii. 26 Aldoheptoses, octoses, nonoses and a decose have been made synthetically. **1962** D. J. BELL in Florkin & Mason *Comparative Biochem.* III. vii. 297 The first natural octose, D-glycero-D-mannoctulose..has recently been isolated from an aqueous extract of the Californian avocado.

October. Add: **3. October Revolution,** name given to the revolution in which the Provisional Government in Russia was overthrown by the Bolsheviks in 1917 on 25 October Old Style (7 November New Style). Also *transf.*

1917 *Times* 13 Dec. 8/4 The October revolution, having broken the power of the capitalists and landlords,..set up a 'Government' of People's Commissioners. **1925** P. A. SOROKIN *Sociol. of Revolution* xvii. 390 Since the latter party included the workmen, the enormous mass of soldiers.., and the peasants..the October revolution was becoming inevitable. **1932** M. EASTMAN tr. *Trotsky's Hist. Russ. Revolution* I. 17 In the historic conditions which formed Russia..we ought to be able to find the premises both of the February revolution and of the October revolution which replaced it. **1952** E. H. CARR *Bolshevik Rev.* II. xvi. 71 Even before the October revolution conditions in Petrograd..were particularly acute. **1965** *Guardian* 14 Oct. 10/2 Russian visitors..might.. conclude that our October Revolution is still to come. **1965** B. PEARCE tr. *Preobrazhensky's New Economics* 77 It would be no exaggeration to say that the most interesting and exciting question since the October revolution of 1917 ..is the question of what the Soviet system is. **1974** tr. *Sniečkus's Soviet Lithuania* 56 The October Revolution opened up a new era in mankind's social progress.

Octoberist, -brist. Restrict *nonce-wd.* to sense in Dict. and add: **2.** (Chiefly in form *Octobrist.*) **a.** [Russ. *oktyabríst.*] In Russian politics, a member of the League of the 17 October 1905 Old Style (30 October New Style), formed in response to the Imperial Constitutional Manifesto of the same date. Also *attrib.* or as *adj.*

1906 *Daily Chron.* 10 Apr. 3/6 Count Peter Heyden, of the Octoberist party. **1906** *Westm. Gaz.* 29 Aug. 2/2 One of the chief questions in Russia has been whether the Octobrists would join the Reactionaries or make terms with the Constitutional Democrats. **1912** D. M. WALLACE *Russia* (rev. ed.) xxxix. 738 The weak point in the present Assembly is that the Octobrists—the moderate party which accepts the famous October manifesto in its natural sense, and wishes to co-operate with the Government in legislative work—do not possess an absolute majority. **1958** *Times Lit. Suppl.* 10 Jan. 14/3 The majority of the *zemstva* liberals found themselves on the side of the more left-wing Kadets, and only the minority among the Octobrists. *a* **1967** A. RANSOME *Autobiogr.* (1976) xxii. 195 Pares was intimate with Gutchkov of the Octobrists.

b. [Russ. *oktyabryónok.*] A member of a Russian communist organization founded in 1925 for young people below the normal age of the 'Pioneers' (see *PIONEER *sb.* 3 c).

1929 S. N. HARPER *Civic Training in Soviet Russia* iv. 66 A widening of the scope of the movement also came in 1925... The Pioneers were given the task of working among their younger brothers and sisters and of organizing them into groups of 'Little Octobrists', in honour of the Bolshevik revolution of October 1917. **1935** S. & B. WEBB *Soviet Communism* I. v. 401 The Pioneers were given the task of bringing their younger brothers and sisters, as young as eight years old, into groups of Little Octobrists. By 1926 the two junior organisations had over two million members (1,800,000 Pioneers and 250,000 Octobrists). **1959** D. W. TREADGOLD *20th Cent. Russia* III. xviii. 288 The Little Octobrists for children eight to eleven years of age, the Pioneers..and the Komsomol..were together designed to produce adults who accepted the fundamental ideological commitments and values of the Party proper. **1960** A. KASSOF in C. E. Black *Transformation Russ. Society* v. 485 The Octobrists..includes members from seven through nine years of age. *Ibid.* 496 Of particular significance was the recent decision to re-establish the Octobrists for children younger than Pioneer age. **1974** T. P. WHITNEY tr. *Solzhenitsyn's Gulag Archipel.* I. I. viii. 333 It was just such a well-nourished little imp that our Octobrist child—Law—began to grow.

octonary, *a.* Add: *spec.* = *OCTAL *a.* 1. (Further examples.)

1891 *Bull. N.Y. Math. Soc.* I. 5 The distinction between numbers of the form $4n+1$ and those of the form $4n+3$ is of great importance in the theory of numbers, and in the octonary system it would be obvious at a glance to which of these classes a given uneven number belongs. **1957** D. D. MCCRACKEN *Digital Computer Programming* iii. 33 The simple reason for the use of octal (also sometimes called octonary) numbers is that the conversion from binary to octal can be carried out mentally. **1963** L. SCHULTZ *Digital Processing* i. 22 Requiring eight symbols, the octal (sometimes, 'octonary') system proves to be a convenient means of expressing a binary value in a number approximately one-third the length of the binary number.

octopamine (ǫktōu·pămīn). *Biochem.* [f. OCTOP(US + AMINE, the compound having been first identified in salivary extracts from an octopus.] A weakly sympathomimetic amine, $HO{\cdot}C_6H_4{\cdot}CHOH{\cdot}CH_2NH_2$, which under the action of monoamine oxidase inhibitors may accumulate in nerves in place of the closely related noradrenaline, thereby inhibiting the transmission of nerve impulses and causing vasoconstriction; 1-(3-hydroxyphenyl)-2-aminoethanol.

1948 V. ERSPAMER in *Acta Pharmacol.* IV. 245 It is suggested that the parent substance of the adrenaline-like principle in the salivary extracts should be called 'Octopamine'. **1952** *Nature* 1 Mar. 376/1 Having identified octopamine as norsynephrine, it was obvious to expect that hydroxyoctopamine could be identified as..noradrenaline. This assumption was confirmed experimentally. **1970** PASSMORE & ROBSON *Compan. Med. Stud.* II. xv. 32/2 Octopamine is a much weaker adrenergic receptor activator than noradrenaline and replacement by it of a portion of the noradrenaline released by nerve stimulation could result in a diminished response of the effector tissue. **1972** FLORKIN & BRICTEUX-GRÉGOIRE in Florkin & Scheer *Chem. Zool.* VII. x. 323 Octopamine may result from the decarboxylation of *p*-hydroxyphenylserine.., but it is known that octopamine may also result from the oxidation of tyramine... Octopamine itself can be oxidized into..noradrenaline.

octo·pian, *a.* [f. OCTOP(US + -IAN.] Suggestive of an octopus; = OCTOPEAN *a.* Also **octo·pic** [-IC], **o·ctopine** [-INE[1]], *adjs.*

1914 CHESTERTON *Flying Inn* 248 The Captain prepared to swing himself on to one of the octopine branches [of a tree]. **1922** C. E. MONTAGUE *Disenchantment* i. 11 He had..struck..a crate, from which some octopian beast.. had reached out at him. **1968** *Punch* 6 Nov. 667/3 The sight of a Breton fisherman pulling the suckers off a live octopic leg.

octoploid (ǫ·ktŏploid), *a.* (*sb.*) *Biol.* Also **octa-**. [f. OCTO- + *-PLOID.] (Made up of somatic cells) containing eight sets of chromosomes. Also as *sb.*, an octoploid organism.

1925 C. C. HURST *Experiments in Genetics* xxxviii. 542 By successive losses of septets the decaploid species would give rise to an octoploid species, the octoploid to a hexaploid species, the hexaploid to a tetraploid species. **1931** *Genetics* XVI. 462 The octoploid may be considered as having a replication of eight basically similar genoms. **1943** *Hereditas* XXIX. 193 (*heading*) Notes on octaploid *Solanum punæ* plant. **1961** *Lancet* 26 Aug. 488/1 The finding of 8 sex-chromatin bodies in an octaploid XXXY cell can be predicted from the above formula. **1973** *Nature* 11 May 87/2 Triploids.., artificial tetraploids and octoploids were all found to synthesize orientin isomers. **1974** *Sci. Amer.* Aug. 73/2 If a hexaploid wheat (*T. aestivum*) is crossed with rye, the result is an octoploid triticale.

Hence **o·ctoploidy**, the state or condition of being octoploid.

1934 *Gen. Program 3rd Pittsburgh Meeting Amer. Assoc. Adv. Sci.* 34 Octoploidy and diploidy in *Miastor americana*. **1948** *Jrnl. Heredity* XXXIX. 42/1 Instead of abrupt doublings of the chromosome number as in mitosis, there is therefore a gradual change from diploidy to tetraploidy, from tetraploidy to octoploidy and so on. **1970** AMBROSE & EASTY *Cell Biol.* 496 (Index), Octoploidy.

octopole, var. *OCTUPOLE.

octupole (ǫ·ktupōul). *Physics.* Also **octa-, octo-**. [f. *octu-* (in OCTUPLE *a.* (*sb.*), OCTUPLET: cf. *QUADRUPOLE), OCTA-, OCTO- + POLE *sb.*[2]] A multipole of order $l=3$. Freq. *attrib.* or as *adj.* Cf. *MULTIPOLE *sb.*

1929 P. DEBYE *Polar Molecules* ii. 26 The next configuration, constructed by a displacement of the quadrupole in an arbitrary direction, will give the octupole. **1950** D. HALLIDAY *Introd. Nucl. Physics* ii. 57 Gamma-emission processes can be classified as to multipole order; we speak, for example, of dipole, quadrupole, octopole, and still higher-order transitions. **1954** *Physical Rev.* XCIV. 1799 (*heading*) Hyperfine structure of In^{115}. Evidence of a nuclear octupole moment. **1961** A. ABRAGAM *Princ. Nucl. Magnetism* vi. 170 The existence of magnetic octopoles has been established by atomic beam methods. **1970** G. K. WOODGATE *Elem. Atomic Struct.* ix. 166 The only multipole (2^k-pole) moments which do not vanish are: magnetic dipole ($k=1$), electric quadrupole ($k=2$), magnetic octupole ($k=3$), electric hexadecapole ($k=4$), etc. **1971** *Nature* 27 Aug. 609/1 The magnetic dipole and octapole and electric quadrupole moments all appear to vanish as $(Z_\odot+1)^{-2}$ as $Z_\odot$, the redshift of light coming from the centre of the disk, goes to infinity.

octopush (ǫ·ktŏpuʃ). [f. OCTO(PUS + PUSH *sb.*[1]] A game of underwater hockey (see quots.). Hence **o·ctopusher,** one who plays octopush.

1970 *Times* 18 Feb. 11 Octopush..is a new form of underwater hockey... The game is played by teams of six.

. . The object of the game is to propel or shovel the puck . . along the bottom of the pool and into the opponents' gull [*sc.* goal]. **1971** *Observer* 23 May 19/2 (*caption*) Octopush . . the name of the game for skindivers. Players try to push a lead puck (called a squid) through the other team's goal (gulley). **1973** *Sunday Mail* (Brisbane) 7 Jan. 2/3 Octopush . . is played like underwater hockey. The teams, in flippers and face masks, but no oxygen tanks, play in a pool six feet deep. Instead of hockey sticks they use pushers,—shaped something like a rake with a blade where the prongs should be. **1973** *Telegraph* (Brisbane) 7 Mar. 3/2 Not mermaids but octopushers . . are members of the Safari Women's team which plays the new game of octopush—diving to push a lead weight along the bottom of a swimming pool into the opposing team's goal.

oculism (ǫ·kiŭliz'm). *rare.* [f. L. *ocul-us* eye + -ISM; after OCULIST.] The business of an oculist; knowledge of defects of vision, diseases of the eye, etc., and the remedies.

1909 W. BOOTH in H. Begbie *Life W. Booth* (1920) II. 433 The gentleman . . was a doctor and . . he knew something of oculism.

oculist. Add: **3.** *Comb.* **oculist-stamp** (also *oculist's stamp*), the more usual name among antiquaries for *medicine seal, stamp* (MEDICINE *sb.*[1] 6 a).

1778 *Gentl. Mag.* XLVIII. 509 An inscription on an oculist's stamp. **1851** *Monthly Jrnl. Med. Sci.* XII. 42 Above sixty Roman oculist-stamps have been now discovered in different parts of western Europe. **1886** *Guide Exhib. Galleries Brit. Mus.* 200 Roman Implements, such as steelyards and their weights, oculists' stamps, locks and keys. **1954** R. SUTCLIFF *Eagle of Ninth* viii. 87 An oculist's stamp is a talisman to carry a man safely where a Legion could not go.

oculo-. Add: **oculo-agra·vic** *a.* [f. **oculogravic* with insertion of A- 14], applied to an illusion of an apparent upward movement of objects in the visual field that is experienced when the effective force acting on a person is reduced; **oculogra·vic** *a.* [L. *grav-is* heavy], applied to an illusion of apparent tilting that is experienced when a person undergoes an acceleration that causes the effective force acting on him to change direction; **oculogy·ral** *a.* [Gr. γῦρ-ος ring, circle], applied to an illusion of apparent rotation that is experienced during or just after rotational accelerations of the body; **oculogy·ric** *a.* [Gr. γῦρ-ος ring, circle], relating to or involving the turning of the eyeball in its socket; *oculogyric crisis*, an attack involving the involuntary movement of the eyeball to an exaggerated position, usu. with the gaze directed upwards, and the maintenance of this position for a period.

1958 GERATHEWOHL & STALLINGS in *Jrnl. Aviation Med.* XXIX. 504 We predicted an apparent motion under conditions of reduced gravity which would be opposite in direction to the one observed at increased accelerative force. This hypothetical phenomenon, which may be observed best in the zero-gravity state, is called the oculo-agravic illusion. **1961** H. G. ARMSTRONG *Aerospace Med.* xv. 232/1 The authors attribute the oculoagravic illusion to an otolith response and noted that the direction of apparent movement of the image was the opposite of that expected from the previous work . . on the oculogravic illusion. **1968** R. A. WEALE *From Sight to Light* vi. 117 The oculo-agravic illusion has been studied by means of the apparent movement of an after-image. **1947** A. GRAYBIEL et al. in *Jrnl. Exper. Psychol.* XXXVII. 170 The oculo-gravic illusion refers to the apparent displacement of an object in space which may be observed when the sensory receptors in the otolith organs are stimulated by an accelerative force which forms a resultant vector with the force of gravity. **1968** R. A. WEALE *From Sight to Light* vi. 116 The oculogravic phenomenon was accompanied by a downward turn of the eyes as acceleration increased and if no fixation light was provided. **1946** GRAYBIEL & HUPP in *Jrnl. Aviation Med.* XVII. 3/1 If . . visual cues are reduced by darkness, relatively weak stimulation of the labyrinth may cause strong illusions of apparent motion which may persist after all other sensations of rotation have disappeared. To this visual phenomenon, produced in this manner, we have applied the term 'oculo-gyral illusion'. **1953** R. A. McFARLAND *Human Factors Air Transportation* iv. 192/1 The oculogyral illusion has its origin in the stimulation of the vestibular mechanism rather than in the eye alone. **1968** R. A. WEALE *From Sight to Light* vi. 115 The astronaut Glenn reported on the oculogyral effect that he experienced in orbit. **1922** STEDMAN *Med. Dict.* (ed. 7) 690 *Oculogyric*, ophthalmogyric, oculomotor. **1927** *Jrnl. Neurol. & Psychopath.* VIII. 27 Other features may . . be present, such as oculogyric crises or respiratory disorders. **1954** S. DUKE-ELDER *Parsons' Dis. Eye* (ed. 12) xxvii. 461 (*caption*) The cerebral ocular motor connections. . . OGA, oculo-gyric area; OGT, oculo-gyric tract. **1973** DUKE-ELDER & WYBAR in S. Duke-Elder *Syst. Ophthalm.* VI. xii. 846 The most typical spasm of vertical movements is seen in oculogyric crises, a striking phenomenon wherein spasmodic deviations of the eyes occur in any direction but usually upwards and less frequently downwards, lasting from a few seconds to some hours.

odalisque. Add: (Further examples.) Also *transf.* and *fig.*

1798 [see *domestic slave* s.v. *DOMESTIC *a.* 2 a]. **1834** R. H. BARHAM *Let.* 26 June (1870) I. v. 239 My seraglio of twelve elderly odalisques certainly does, now and then, furnish me with a job in the way of composing differences which will occasionally arise even in their well-regulated minds. **1903** G. B. SHAW *Let.* 8 May (1972) II. 322 What you want is a repertory of plays which you can carry on your own shoulders, and in which you cannot come into competition with the young odalisques of the west end. *a* **1915** JOYCE *Giacomo Joyce* (1968) 14 She leans back against the pillowed wall: odalisque-featured in the luxurious obscurity. **1926** A. BENNETT *Lord Raingo* I. v. 21 Withal she was no odalisque. She tried to improve herself, to make herself interesting to him. **1938** *Times* 18 Feb. 19/1 Evening gowns include such opposite styles as the odalisque type, with a transparent dancing skirt in black over a gown in gold lamé. **1967** *Listener* 16 Mar. 366/1 Is the creation of a cubist odalisque 'of consequence', and the devoutly humble production of an ikon not?

odd, *a.* (*sb.*) and *adv.* Add: **A.** *adj.* **2. b.** (Further examples.)

1955 J. A. WHEELER in W. Pauli *Niels Bohr* 166 The spontaneous fission rates of nuclei of odd mass number are observed to be slower than the rates for the corresponding even nuclei. **1966** *Mathematical Rev.* XXXI. 36/1 Matrices *M* of even order behave somewhat differently from those of odd order. **1970** O. DOPPING *Computers & Data Processing* ii. 50 The most common form of redundancy check is the parity check, in which the value of a check bit is determined by the parity (odd or even) of the number of ones in the unit to be checked.

f. *Physics.* Having odd parity.

1930 *Physical Rev.* XXXVI. 617 In the case of homonuclear molecules . . any electron state may be either 'odd' or even. An electron state of a homonuclear molecule is said to be odd if the electronic factor of 4 changes sign on reflection in the midpoint of the line joining the nuclei, even, if it does not change sign. [*Note*] The use of 'odd' and 'even' in this sense was introduced by Hund. . . The words . . are applied by Kronig, in a sense different from that used by Hund, to the *complete* 4 function of any molecule, homonuclear or heteronuclear. **1940** *Ibid.* LVIII. 104/1 The nearest one could come . . would be to assume for the correct wave function a linear combination of two wave functions. . . These would correspond, respectively, to an even and odd state of the core. **1961** *Encycl. Dict. Physics* II. 786/2 Homonuclear molecules . . can have even (*g*) orbitals (*g* for 'gerade') and odd (*u*) orbitals (*u* for 'ungerade') which are, respectively, symmetric and antisymmetric with respect to interchange of the nuclei.

4. d. Add to def.: or *odds.*

1930 *Times* 25 Mar. 24/1 The balance-sheet shows a loan from the bankers of the company as at December 31 of £118,413 odds.

4*. *Math.* Of a function of one variable: having the property that changing the sign of the argument changes the sign, but not the magnitude, of the function (i.e. $f(-x) = -f(x)$).

1886 A. G. GREENHILL *Differential & Integral Calculus* ii. 80 f*x* is an odd function, so that $f(-x) = -fx$. **1899** F. G. TAYLOR *Introd. Differential & Integral Calculus* xi. 106 A function of *x* is said to be even when it is not altered . . on changing *x* into −*x*; it is said to be odd when it is altered in sign, but not in magnitude. **1946** *Ann. Computation Lab. Harvard Univ.* I. 17 This feature is especially valuable when dealing with the interpolation of odd functions. **1969** A. M. HOWATSON *Princ. Appl. Electricity* iv. 74 Some waveforms . . can be represented either by an even or by an odd function according to the choice of origin of *θ*. Others can be even but not odd . . or odd but not even.

8. a. (Later examples.)

1930 *Daily Tel.* 1 Dec. 9/3 The 'odd' heavy tweed skirt that is worn in the English country can be left behind. **1949** D. M. DAVIN *Roads from Home* III. i. 210 He'd still be able to save the odd quid. **1959** *Times Lit. Suppl.* 7 Aug. p. ix/4 An endearing wizard liable to irritability and the odd fit of despair. **1973** G. MOFFAT *Deviant Death* i. 18 [He] could have made scarcely enough money from book reviews and the odd feature on country life to pay his petrol bill.

d. (Earlier and later examples.) *odd job* (earlier and later examples), *odd-jobber*, *odd-job man* (later and *fig.* examples); also *odd-jobs man*; *odd-job* v. intr., to do odd jobs; *odd-jobbing* vbl. sb.; *odd-timer*, *odd work.*

1743 W. ELLIS *Mod. Husbandman* Oct. xxii. 149 The Odd-man's Wages is from fifty Shillings, to four Pounds a Year. *c* **1770** in de Vries & Fryer *Venus Unmasked* (1967) 33 Miss E. P. . . . R . . has not received her stated allowance; is therefore obliged, in order to keep up appearances, to do *odd jobs.* **1798** J. WOODFORDE *Diary* 24 Nov. (1931) V. 148 Paid John Buck, Blacksmith, for divers odd Jobbs for the Year 1798 the Sum of 2.14.10. **1853** MRS. GASKELL *Ruth* II. iii. 64 Just try for a day to think of all the odd jobs as to be done well. **1859** DICKENS *T. Two Cities* III. ix. 206 A gentleman like yourself wot I've had the honour of odd jobbing till I'm grey at it. **1860** —— *Gt. Expect.* (1861) I. vii. 90, I was . . odd-boy about the forge. **1861** MRS. BEETON *Bk. Househ. Managem.* 964 Where a single footman, or odd man, is the only male servant then . . he is required to make himself generally useful. **1863** *All Year Round* 11 July 472/2 Either can rest occasionally by employing an 'odd man', of whom there are several . . ready to do 'odd' work. **1897** E. L. VOYNICH *Gadfly* 190, I lived by odd-jobbing for the blacks on the sugar plantations. **1905** Odd-man [see *DOORMAN 2]. **1909** J. R. WARE *Passing Eng.* 186/1 *Odd job man*, modified description of the Shyster, who professes to do anything and only does his employer. **1915** R. BROOKE *Let.* 20 Apr. (1968) 681 Ian Hamilton . . asked me if I'd like to be attached to his staff as a sort of 'galloper' and odd-jobber —'A.D.C.'. **1916** H. G. WELLS *Mr. Britling* I. i. 28 They become villa parasites and odd-job men. **1925** A. S. M. HUTCHINSON *One Increasing Purpose* I. xviii. 113 She's an odd-timer on Miss Marr's typist staff. **1933–4** WITTGENSTEIN *Blue & Brown Bks.* (1958) 44 We are tempted to describe the use of important 'odd-job' words as though they were words with regular functions. **1938** D. SMITH *Dear Octopus* I. 22 Just a sort of receptionist and general odd-jobber. **1940** L. MACNEICE *Last Ditch* 25 He was not able to read or write, He did odd jobs on gentlemen's places, Cutting the hedge or hoeing the drive. **1944** F. CLUNE *Red Heart* 32 He taught, biked, and odd-jobbed his way around Great Britain for a year. **1948** in D. M. Davin *N.Z. Short Stories* (1953) 195 The odd-jobs man who was also the cowman and gardener at the homestead. **1973** A. CHRISTIE *Postern of Fate* II. ii. 69 I've done odd jobbing, you know. **1977** *Private Eye* 4 Mar. 20/2 (Advt.), Carpentry, cleaning, electrics, decorating, gardening, handy persons, odd jobbers.

9. b. *odd bod* (freq. in *pl.*) [*BOD].

1955 [see *BOD]. **1966** *Courier-Mail* (Brisbane) 15 Sept. 1/7 A family of 12 self-styled 'odd bods' is immigrating to Spain because Australia is 'too conventional'. **1976** 'J. ROFFMAN' *Why Someone had to Die* 78 Anyone would, except you who have an inborn bias toward the odd bods in society.

D. *Comb.* **1. a.** *odd-shaped* (later examples).

1921 W. DE LA MARE *Crossings* 54 He . . carries an odd-shaped fiddle. **1967** KARCH & BUBER *Offset Processes* ii. 34 Products include paper and board too large for conventional presses (over 80 inches), odd-shaped objects, posters, [etc.]. **1977** P. D. JAMES *Death of Expert Witness* III. 169 The gathering of those odd-shaped pieces of information . . which, in the end, would click together to form a picture.

b. *odd-looking* (later examples), *-sounding* (later examples).

1876 'GEO. ELIOT' *Dan. Der.* III. v. xxxviii. 135 Spectators would be likely to think of him as an odd-looking Jew. **1976** J. B. HILTON *Gamekeeper's Gallows* ii. 23 Beresford was curious to know what this odd-looking character was carrying. **1853** MRS. GASKELL *Cranford* vii. 131 There she sat, as stately and composed as though we had never heard that odd-sounding cough. **1942** PARTRIDGE *Usage & Abusage* (1947) 15/1 *Admittable* is rare and odd-sounding for *admissible.*

c. the adj. with a sb., forming an attrib. phr., as *odd-number*, *-order*, *-parity.*

1922 F. F. POTTER *Teaching of Arithmetic* xvii. 325 The simple odd-number series. **1957** L. FOX *Numerical Solution Two-Point Bound. Probl.* vi. 141 This too is connected with the use of central differences for even-order equations, but of mean central differences for odd-order equations. **1962** *Gloss. Terms Automatic Data Processing* (*B.S.I.*) 33 When the numbers of ones (or zeros) is required to be odd the check is called an odd parity check, and when even an even parity check. **1967** *Bodl. Libr. Rec.* VIII. 3 The second drawback is the use of an odd-parity code, with seven-hole punching necessary for a plain tape-feed.

2. odd-and-end (earlier example); **odd-even** *a. Nuclear Physics*, (*a*) of or pertaining to nuclei of odd mass number and those of even mass number; (*b*) applied to nuclei containing an odd number of protons and an even number of neutrons; **odd-gaits, -gates** *local* [GATE *sb.*[2] 9 b], odd, strange, out of the way; **odd man out**, (*b*) a person or thing differing from all others of a group in some respect; **odd-odd** *a. Nuclear Physics*, (*a*) of or pertaining to nuclei of odd mass number only; (*b*) applied to nuclei containing an odd number of protons and an odd number of neutrons.

1846 J. BROWN *Lett.* (1912) 90, I have no continuity and thoroughness of thought, . . and my style, if style it can be called, is the piebaldest, oddandendest. **1936** *Physical Rev.* XLIX. 897/1 The transitions are of the odd-even type. **1949** GAMOW & CRITCHFIELD *Theory of Atomic Nucleus* iv. 88 $\delta_A = 0$ for even-even nuclei, $= 1$ for odd-even nuclei, $= 2$ for odd-odd nuclei. **1955** J. A. WHEELER in W. Pauli *Niels Bohr* 166 Odd-even differences in spontaneous fission. The spontaneous fission rates of nuclei of odd mass number are observed to be slower than the rates for the corresponding even nuclei. **1970** G. K. WOODGATE *Elem. Atomic Struct.* ix. 195 The tentative explanation of this phenomenon, called odd-even staggering, is beyond the scope of this discussion. **1906** KIPLING *Puck of Pook's Hill* 263 Won'erful odd-gates place—Romney Marsh. **1957** H. HALL *Parish's Dict. Sussex Dial.* 88/2 *Oddgaits*, extraordinary. 'It's an odd-gaits sort of place.' **1928** F. W. CROFTS *Sea Mystery* xvi. 263 Mrs. Berlyn as hostess would reasonably be the odd man out when the change was made from snooker to billiards. **1935** MRS. BELLOC LOWNDES *Let.* 10 Aug. (1971) 129 Rex Whistler . . is rather 'odd man out', though he is so quiet and unassuming that everyone likes him. **1945** F. L. GREEN (*title*) Odd man out. **1958** *Times* 29 Nov. 9/1 Here . . is the fallen foe [*sc.* the pike]; not merely our foe, but . . the odd man out in Nature and in the sporting Canon. **1969** in Halpert & Story *Christmas Mumming in Newfoundland* 33 These settlements are 'odd men out'; at odds with outside economic forces. **1970** *Guardian* 19 Nov. 11/4 The products . . would look odd men out in a formal setting. **1973** *Listener* 15 Nov. 658/1 Eight of the present nine members of the EEC voted in favour, the odd man out being . . Denmark. **1936** *Physical Rev.* XLIX. 897/1 The transition is of an odd-odd or even-even type. **1937** *Ibid.* LI. 951/2 The condition . . for the instability of odd-odd nuclei should read $g + 2g_\sigma < g_m$. **1956** *Proc. Physical Soc.* A. LXIX. 635 (*heading*) The magnetic moments of odd-odd nuclei.

oddball (ǫ·dbǭl). *colloq.* (orig. *U.S.*). Also **odd-ball, odd ball.** [f. ODD *a.* + BALL *sb.*[1]] An eccentric person; a person of unconventional views or habits. Also *attrib.* or as *adj.*, eccentric, exceptional, peculiar.

1948 *Amer. Speech* XXIII. 221 *Odd Ball* . . connoted that the individual's strangeness was not the result of prison camp experiences. **1953** Berrey & Van den Bark *Amer. Thes. Slang* (1954) § 411/2 Peculiar or eccentric person..oddball, odd-fellow, odd stick. *Ibid.* § 454/3 Social dud or bore; 'drip'..oddball, ooly-drooly, pain. **1956** W. H. Whyte *Organization Man* (1957) ix. 123 There are exceptions, but one must be a very odd ball to be one. **1956** Wallis & Blair *Thunder Above* (1959) xvi. 158 A phlegmatic odd-ball in a world of make-believe. **1957** *Time* 2 Sept. 23/2 Officialdom in Saigon thought that the threat of rebellions by the country's fanatic, odd-ball religious groups was ended at last. **1959** *Washington Post* 19 Oct. B. 10/6 Life aboard a submarine has its oddball moments. **1968** *Canad. Antiques Collector* Dec. 10/1 The classic tradition was too strong at the end of the 18th c. for any but obvious odd balls to find a 'better way' of building their houses. **1969** *Daily Mail* 15 Jan. 5/4 If that burn-time was not correct we could have gone into all sort of odd-ball orbits. **1971** C. Fick *Danziger Transcript* (1973) 41 They had been oddball friends since Harvard. **1973** M. Truman *Harry S. Truman* xvi. 331 Earlier in 1946 an oddball broke into the National Gallery and cut a hole in Dad's portrait. **1974** *Peace News* 15 Mar. 10 It's always been very much an odd ball way of doing it. **1974** D. Sears *Lark in Clear Air* ii. 27 The oddest of a family where odd-balls were not the exception.

Oddfellow, Odd-fellow. (Earlier and later examples.)

1795 in R. Humphreys *Mem. J. Decastro* (1824) 247 As many Grands and Brothers of the Odd Fellows, Bucks, Masonic and other Lodges. **1800** *Sporting Mag.* XVI. 59/1 A Member of the Odd Fellows. **1951** McWhiney & Simkins in A. Dundes *Mother Wit* (1973) 594/2 This mummery manifests itself in numerous other secret organizations such as the Odd Fellows, the Masons, and the Knights of Columbus. **1970** *New Yorker* 14 Nov. 175/1 Members of the Independent Order of Odd Fellows stuck to their symbol of an axe left cleaving into a realistic log. **1977** P. D. James *Death of Expert Witness* i. 16 A ticket for the local Oddfellows' hop.

Oddfellowship. (Later U.S. examples.)

1907 C. E. Jackson *Poet Wildey* 11 It is the Independent Order of Odd Fellows, or if you like the term better, American Odd Fellowship. **1972** *Fairbanks* (Alaska) *Daily News-Miner* 3 Nov. 7/7 Odd Fellowship..is a benevolent, fraternal order banded together for mutual benefit.

odditorium (ǫditōᵊ·riɒ̆m). [f. Oddit(y + -orium.] A shop or venue for the display or retailing of oddities. Also *transf.*

1914 R. & E. Shackleton *Four on Tour* 182 We happened upon an 'odditorium', a delightful name adopted by a very shabby shop in a very narrow lane [in Kingston-upon-Thames] where we found some very attractive bits of old silver and china. **1933** *Sun* (Baltimore) 16 Dec. 10/6 Mr. Miller..manages the Ripley Believe It or Not 'odditorium' at Horticulture Hall, which contains thirty-nine oddities. **1940** *Time* 26 Feb. 42/2 Sanka Coffee's Tuesday-night odditorium of the air.

oddlings (ǫ·dliŋz), *sb. pl.* [f. Odd *a.* + -ling[1].] = Oddments *sb. pl.*

1854– in *Eng. Dial. Dict.* **1900** *Windsor Mag.* XI. 354 A hundred odd bits, that's all—but they are a manufacturer's oddlings.

odd lot (ǫ·d lǫt). [f. Odd *a.* + Lot *sb.*] **1.** An incomplete set or random mixture (of articles of commerce).

1897 *Sears, Roebuck Catal.* 173/1 The pants are not the size to fit the coats and vests. We then throw them into what we call our 'Odd Lots', or mixed suits. **1931** C. Maughan *Markets of London* 105 Parcels of five bags or less are known as 'odd lots' and are sold separately at the end of the auctions, with the exception of pea-berries, which are sold irrespective of the size of the lots.

2. *U.S. Stock Exchange.* Used *attrib.* of transactions involving numbers of shares smaller than is normally dealt in. Hence **odd-lotter.**

1929 *Times* 1 Nov. 22/5 The list generally moved up under heavy accumulation of standard issues, together with reports of a tremendous volume of odd-lot bargain buying. **1939** C. O. Hardy (*title*) Odd-lot trading on the New York Stock Exchange. **1968** *Economist* 28 May 94/1 The unit trust investor is not quite an odd-lotter—the American term for a small investor. **1970** *Washington Post* 30 Sept. D. 10/3 Odd lot transactions by principal dealers. **1976** *National Observer* (U.S.) 28 Feb. 8/4 But odd-lot figures..suggest that small investors were, on balance, selling in November and December of 1972 and in January of 1973. *Ibid.*, There is some statistical evidence that odd-lotters have been wrong far too often in the past.

odds, *sb.* Add: **2. c.** *What's the odds?* (earlier and later examples); *it makes no odds* (later examples).

1826 *Sessions Papers* 11 Dec. 86/1, I asked Jackson whose they were—he said, 'What odds; they are mine.' **1840** Thackeray *Shabby Genteel Story* ix, in *Fraser's Mag.* Oct. 410/1 Suppose I do die,..what's the odds? Caroline doesn't care for me. **1855** Geo. Eliot in *Ibid.* June 699/1 'What's the odds, so long as one can sleep?' is your *formule de la vie.* **1890** Kipling *Soldiers Three* 79 'Wot's the odds as long as you're 'appy?' said Ortheris. **1923** D. H. Lawrence *Kangaroo* xvi. 345 That sense of sardonic tolerance, endurance. 'What's the odds, boys?' **1967** N. Freeling *Strike Out* 84 You do neo-expressionism, or..neo-whatever-you-like, it makes no odds,..you'd still be up against the machine. **1973** 'M. Underwood' *Reward for Defector* xxii. 158 What's the difficulty?.. Not that it makes any odds.

4. d. Phr. *to ask* (or † *beg*) *no odds*: to desire no advantage; to seek no favour. *U.S.*

1806 *Baltimore Even. Post* 5 Mar. 2/2 (Th.), No odds he begs Of any beast that walks upon four legs. **1834** *Vermont Free Press* 7 June (Th.), A Varmounter never uses a dog... Give him a gun, and he asks no odds. **1894** *Congress. Rec.* 29 May 5447/1 South Dakota asks no odds of any State of the Union.

e. *over the odds*, past the limit, above a generally agreed rate.

1922 'Sapper' *Black Gang* xviii. 306, I admit it seems a bit over the odds, but every word I've told you is gospel. **1930** —— *Finger of Fate* 103, I admit..that to be called a damned Englishman by Pedro Gonsalvez is a bit over the odds. **1972** *Which?* Feb. 50/1 You could even pay more than the list prices. We found some of the tools being sold for perhaps a pound or so over the odds. **1972** *Listener* 28 Dec. 897/2 Sir Michael Swann, the new Chairman of the BBC's Board of Governors..felt that Alf Garnett went 'over the odds' occasionally. **1974** 'D. Craig' *Dead Liberty* xxxi. 187 His..means of pushing his conscience underground was by paying a little over the odds.

5. b. Phr. *to shout the odds* (see quot. 1925).

1925 Fraser & Gibbons *Soldier & Sailor Words* 257 *To shout the odds*, to talk too much: to brag: to grumble. **1958** F. Norman *Bang to Rights* i. 10 He was still shouting the odds about this blag which was..nothing but a dirty great romance. **1960** L. Cooper *Accomplices* ii. i. 76 There are always a few bloody fools who shout the odds about British justice and fair trials. **1967** *Sunday Times* 15 Oct. 9 For years he's shouted the odds about the Scouse way of life. **1973** 'J. Patrick' *Glasgow Gang Observed* xv. 131 He still shouts the odds fae the windae when there's a ba'le [*sc.* battle] oan. 'Get *right* intae it, Tim,' he says.

6. b. *by all odds*, by far. *U.S.*

1866 W. D. Howells *Venetian Life* 50 By all odds, the loungers at Florian's were the most interesting. **1951** J. P. Marquand *Melville Goodwin* x. 163 Lee said that McClellan was the best Union general he fought against by all odds.

7. b. *odds and sods* (orig. Services' slang): see quots. 1930 and 1948; now in gen. use as a variant of *odds and ends.*

1930 Brophy & Partridge *Songs & Slang 1914–1918* 143 *Odds and Sods*, 'details' attached to Battalion Headquarters for miscellaneous offices: batmen, sanitary men, professional footballers and boxers on nominal duties, etc. *a* **1935** T. E. Lawrence *Mint* (1955) ii. ix. 125 Ten minutes late for dinner. Odds and sods to eat. **1941** *Argus* (Melbourne) *Week-End Mag.* 15 Nov. 1/4 *Odds-and-sods*, men not attached to a particular unit. **1944** *Penguin New Writing* XX. 44 The section was mixed up with the Police and one or two odds and sods as usual. **1948** Partridge *Dict. Forces Slang* 130 *Odds and sods*, men on miscellaneous duties. Men not classified. Members of other denominations than Roman Catholic, Church of England and Presbyterian. (Army.) (2) In the Navy, the rank and file—the *hoi polloi*—of the lower-deck. **1950** G. Wilson *Brave Company* xiii. 193 Add three-inch mortar, four-point-two inch mortar, Vickers and all the odds and sods. **1955** E. Waugh *Officers & Gentlemen* i. vi. 64 They left me behind with the other odds and sods. **1971** B. W. Aldiss *Soldier Erect* 205 We've got precious little strike-power..—the Assam Regiment,..a few odds and sods of the Burma Regiment, and our friends and allies of the Nepalese army! **1975** *Time Out* 26 Sept. 57/4 Although Tolkien's planned preface to the poems was never realised, his son Christopher has created one mostly out of his father's odds and sods—a radio talk plus notes. **1976** A. Hill *Summer's End* iv. 61 Beyond these were oblong-shaped archway bricks, chimney-cowlings, roof-tiles and other odds and sods I couldn't put names to.

8. odds-on *a.* (later and *fig.* examples); also (occas. without hyphen) as *adv.* and as *sb.*, the state of betting when odds are less than 1:1; an odds-on favourite.

1917 [see *Aussie *sb.* and *a.* 2]. **1923** Wodehouse *Inimitable Jeeves* xiii. 153 'Something's gone wrong with the favourite.' 'Which is the favourite, sir?' 'Mr. Heppenstall. He's gone to odds on.' **1926** E. Wallace *More Educated Evans* x. 222 Six successive odds-on chances. **1928** *Daily Mail* 31 July 11/4 The favourite.. started at heavy odds-on. **1941** Baker *Dict. Austral. Slang* 50 *An odds-on*, an odds-on favourite. **1945** J. B. Blair in *Coast to Coast 1944* 136 It seemed odds on that Wang would stop a bullet. **1955** *Times* 11 May 5/1 Lions Love..was made odds-on for the race for two-year-old fillies. **1962** D. Francis *Dead Cert* i. 7 Admiral, the odds-on certainty who had lost his first race for two years. **1972** *Guardian* 5 Dec. 13/4 In one area near Poona there have been 22 drought years in the past 30... There, as in other places, it is a two to one odds-on probability. **1973** [see *nap *v.*[4]]. **1976** H. Tracy *Death in Reserve* xix. 147 'Odds on they've gone to France.' said Phoenix. 'He'd have enough fuel.'

odds, *v.* Add: **2.** *slang.* To elude, to evade.

1958 F. Norman *Bang to Rights* ii. 52, I used to go to church every Sunday only because I couldn't odds it. **1970** G. F. Newman *Sir, You Bastard* iv. 124, I can't odds being mixed up in crime.

oddside (ǫ·dsəid). *Founding.* [f. Odd *a.* + Side *sb.*[1]]. A temporary cope, usu. made of sand or plaster of Paris, in which part of a pattern is bedded while the final mould is made of the upper, exposed portion.

1836 W. H. Smith *Birmingham* iii. 33 The patterns still lie on the sand of the 'odd side', as it is termed. **1903** *Work* 11 July 364/1 It is necessary, when the mould is commenced, either to block up the half of the flask to a level with the parting line on the pattern, or to sink the same into a bed of sand as far as its greatest diameter. This bed of sand is known as a match or 'oddside', and it has importance as a time-saver. **1928** W. Rawlinson *Mod. Foundry Operations* xiii. 177 The use of oddsides eliminates the necessity of making a joint in the moulding operation, as is the case when moulding with a loose pattern. **1960** R. Lister *Decorative Cast Ironwork* ii. 45 When the plaster has set, the sections are removed and placed aside, and the bottom section placed in another oddside. **1972** P. R. Beeley *Foundry Technol.* viii. 351 Where a flat parting plane intersects the pattern, moulding is simplified by providing a split pattern and dispensing with the oddside.

ode. Add: **1.** *spec.* A short Old English poem, esp. *The Battle of Brunanburh.*

1770 T. Percy tr. *Mallet's Northern Antiquities* II. 196 Compare the Anglo-Saxon Ode on Athelstan's Victory, preserved in the Saxon Chronicle. **1798** S. Henshall *Saxon & Eng. Lang.* 39 The first specimen we shall exhibit is the conclusion of a Saxon Ode on a Victory of King Athelstan's. **1807** S. Turner *Hist. Anglo-Saxons* (ed. 2) II. 323 It will be sufficient to add to the already copious specimens of the Anglo-Saxon poetry, the following Ode, which is appended to the menology. **1847** F. Madden *Laȝamon's Brut* I. p. xxiii, No one can read his descriptions of battles and scenes of strife without being reminded of the Ode on Æthelstan's victory at Brunanburh. **1871** H. Sweet in W. C. Hazlitt *Warton's Hist. Eng. Poetry* II. 7 There are only two poems of any merit to which we can assign with any certainty a southern origin. These are the ode on the battle of Brunanburh, and the narrative of the battle of Maldon, which were, no doubt, composed immediately after the events they record.

3. *ode-metre.*

1901 *Academy* 14 Dec. 585/2 That so-called 'irregular' ode-metre which they [*sc.* Patmore and Henley] use in common.

-ode[2], formative element repr. Gr. ὁδός way, path, first used in *anode, cathode, electrode,* and later in the names of thermionic valves with a specified number of electrodes, as *diode, triode, tetrode,* etc. (with two, three, four electrodes); (certain of these latter—e.g. *diode, hexode*—were orig. coined directly from the Gr. to describe forms of multiplex telegraphy).

odeon (ōᵘ·diǫ̆n). [*ad.* Gr. ᾠδεῖον a building for musical performances.] **1.** Also **odeion** (odəi·ǫ̆n). = Odeum.

1902 Anderson & Spiers *Archit. Greece & Rome* vii. 117 No Greek example exists of the Odeon. *Ibid.* 280 *Odeon*, a circular building in which rehearsals and musical contests took place in Greece. **1908** W. R. Lethaby *Greek Buildings* iv. 196 The rotundas at Olympia..must have been covered by low cones. So must the Odeon and the Skias at Athens. **1909** A. Marquand *Greek Archit.* vi. 355 The Odeion (ᾠδεῖον), or music hall, was designed for musical contests and rehearsals of plays. **1961** L. Mumford *City in Hist.* Note to plate 12, What modern town.. can point to..as many handsome examples of bath, theater, odeon? **1977** *Jrnl. R. Soc. Arts* CXXXV. 485/2 The Department of Antiquities..is now excavating an Odeon.

2. (With capital initial.) The name of any of numerous cinemas in a chain built by Oscar Deutsch or his company in the 1930s. Hence in wider use, any cinema, esp. of similar lavish architectural style. Also *attrib.* and as *adj.*, designating this style.

1937 Klingender & Legg *Money behind Screen* 46 *Odeon Theatres, Ltd.*—Is a private company registered in October, 1933 with £100 capital... In November, 1936, the Odeon group of companies was increased by Cinema Ground Rents & Properties, Ltd... The object of the concern is stated to be primarily that of acquiring new sites for Odeon cinemas. **1946** J. P. Mayer *Sociol. of Film* iv. 51 Between August 1944 and June 1945 I spent approximately twenty Saturday mornings in the Odeon and Gaumont British Children's Cinema Clubs. **1952** A. Wood *Mr. Rank* v. 87 People on holiday..would go into an Odeon because it would remind them of the Odeon at home. *Ibid.* 88 Beginning modestly.., Deutsch by 1937 had raised the total number of Odeons to over 200... His cinemas were all built to sumptuous standards, with the aim of providing something more luxurious than the rest. .. The Odeon cinemas became almost a symbol of the British way of life in the 1930s. **1954** J. Betjeman *Few Late Chrysanthemums* 40 An Odeon flashes fire Where stood their villa. **1960** C. MacInnes *Mr. Love & Justice* 224 The two girls carried on..joint excursions to their respective Odeons. **1964** *New Statesman* 10 Apr. 576/3 The whole occasion, with its foamy seats, Odeon hues and ice-cream girls, is organised to resemble film-going as closely as possible. **1970** Collins & Dodd *Perishers Bk. 8* 4 Maisie..still finds Marlon attractive in a repulsive sort of way, especially when he wears his Odeon Admiral's uniform. **1972** H. C. Rae *Shooting Gallery* ii. 243 It was the cinema, an Odeon in the heart of Glasgow, big and modern and comfortable. **1977** *Times* 12 Feb. 7/3 M. Barrier designed his own restaurant under the influence of *fin-de-siècle*, early Odeon, and fifties tubular.

odiferous. Delete 'obs.' and add later examples.

1851 V. Lush *Jrnl.* 8 Aug. (1971) 83 It looked marvellously strange to see so rough a looking man taking up bottle after bottle with all the air of a connoisseur, and at last after much deliberation selecting those which seemed to his olfactory nerves the most odiferous. **1977** *Fanfare* (Toronto) 6 July 3/1 German barbers worked busily for years on odiferous brews to suppress the dangerous shade.

Odissi (odi·si). *India.* [f. the place-name *Orissa*, Skr. *oḍra*.] A style of Indian dance, believed to be one of the oldest in India, originating in the eastern state of Orissa. Also called *Orissi.

1965 E. Bhavnani *Dance in India* vi. 49 The classical dance as practised in Orissa, a State on the mid-north-eastern coast of India, is known as Orissi or Odissi. **1967** Singha & Massey *Indian Dancer* xxv. 203 Odissi did not escape a decline any more than the other dances of India. .. Odissi draws upon several ancient texts in Sanskrit and Oriya. *Ibid.* 205 Although Odissi recitals are nowadays given on the stage, they are nevertheless essentially a form of worship in which the dancer performs an act of adoration. **1971** *Femina* (Bombay) 30 Apr. 29/1 A student of Hindustani classical music, she knows many Oriya songs and is in demand in Bombay to accompany young Odissi dancers. **1972** *Daily Tel.* 26 Apr. 14/4 Her Odissi section could hardly have been more different. In this quintessentially feminine style, she showed the ancient thrice-bent sculptural positions as well as a wide variety of spins.

odium. Add: **e.** (Earlier and later examples of *odium theologicum*.) Also, by imitation, *odium academicum* (academic), *archæologicum* (archæological), *biologicum* (biological), *ethicum* (ethical), *philologicum* (philological), *philosophicum* (philosophical), *scholasticum* (scholarly).

[**1673** J. Flavel *Fountain of Life* xxx. 414 Strigelius desired to die, that he might be freed *ab implacabilibus odiis theologorum*, from the implacable strifes of contending Divines.] **1734** 'Philalethes Cantabrigiensis' *Geometry No Friend to Infidelity* 13 This is the very method which the *Odium Theologicum*, the intemperate zeal of Divines has always pursued. *a* **1866** J. Grote *Exam. Utilitarian Philos.* (1870) 9 The 'odium ethicum' is even more unreasonable than the 'odium theologicum'. **1946** *Mind* LV. 98, I am accused of indulging in 'quixotic denunciations' of Spinoza, and of being actuated by a spirit of *odium philosophicum* against his memory. **1959** *Listener* 10 Sept. 405/2 The *odium biologicum* which it now seems scarcely possible for the acknowledged biologist wholly to avoid. *Ibid.* 29 Oct. 743/3 A kind of *odium archaeologicum* has been added to an *odium theologicum*. **1962** *Ibid.* 10 May 821/1 The lay public is now familiar with the wars of the learned... With Professor Dumond we are involved in something more than *odium academicum*. **1963** *Times* 14 Feb. 15/1 The question, then, arises whether the college to which he belongs and the cause of education in Oxford are to be sacrificed to the *odium theologicum* of a few infatuated dignitaries. **1970** *Language* XLVI. 246 The public will not change, and we will continue to suffer from the odium philologicum unless we can find a way of establishing more friendly communication. **1973** *Times Lit. Suppl.* 30 Mar. 347/4 Does not conceal her *odium scholasticum* at being anticipated by Firbank's bibliographer and first biographer. **1974** *Times* 21 Mar. (Art & Antiques Suppl.) p. iii/2 No punches are pulled in the book reviews, which are often filled with *odium scholasticum*, as one expert dissects the researches of another. *Ibid.* 9 Nov. 13/6 The *odium theologicum* that often characterises academic debate.

odometer. Add: Now *esp.* one in a motor vehicle. (Further examples.)

1913 *Collier's* 11 Jan. II. 57/1 The Corbin-Brown Speedometer records speed accurately... Its hand is steady; its odometer absolutely dependable. **1962** *Which? Car Suppl.* Jan. 28/2 We measured the accuracy of speedometer, mileage recorder (odometer) and fuel level gauge. **1968** *Chicago Tribune* 9 July 1. 12/1 He went out the next week-end in his sportscar and, using the auto's odometer, plotted running courses from his home. **1969** B. Weil *Dossier IX* v. 34 He checked the odometer which he had zeroed at the Porte de Versailles. Three more kilometres, then a right turn. **1972** *Drive* Spring 84 Cruising speed was restricted to 55 mph in deference to the 90,000 miles already clocked up on the broken odometer.

ödometer: see *œdometer.

odontology. (Later examples.)

1911 *Chambers's Jrnl.* June 375/1 The British Medical Association has recently founded a Section of Odontology. **1966** G. Gustafson (*title*) Forensic odontology. **1974** *Encycl. Brit. Macropædia* XI. 814/1 Other specialties on which the courts frequently require expert opinion include forensic odontology.

odorant, *a.* Restrict 'Now *rare*' to sense in Dict. and add: **B.** *sb.* Also **odourant.** An odoriferous substance; *spec.* one used to impart a desired odour to a product. Also *attrib.*

1944 R. W. Moncrieff *Chemical Senses* viii. 166 Reactions to odorants are usually mild and undefined, a sniff, a drawing away, or..disgust. **1952** Kirk & Othmer *Encycl. Chem. Technol.* VIII. 142 Biacetyl has been used as an odorant for butter, cream, milk, margarine.., cheese, coffee, confectionery.., ice cream mixes, and tobacco. **1971** *Nature* 24 Sept. 231/1 Theories of olfaction are thus legion; all attempt to answer the central question as to what properties of the odourant molecules are responsible for the wide variety of odour quality. **1972** *Materials & Technol.* V. xiv. 526 In microcellular soling mixes,.. odorants which confer the odour of leather to the soles are frequently incorporated.

† **odoriferent** (ōudŏri·fĕrĕnt). *Obs. rare*$^{-1}$. [f. med.L. *odōriferens* (see Odoriferant *a.*).] = *odorant *sb.*

1858 G. A. Sala *Journey Due North* viii. 130 These boots have a peculiar..odour..of myrrh, frankincense, sandalwood, benzoin, and other odoriferents.

odorimeter (ōudŏri·mĭtəɹ). [f. L. *odor*, *odōri-* Odour + -meter.] An instrument for measuring the intensity of odours.

1898 *Amer. Jrnl. Psychol.* X. 85 We are indebted to Dr. Zwaardemaker for the words 'olfactometry' and 'olfactometer'.., 'odorimetry' and 'odorimeter'. **1966** *New Scientist* 29 Dec. 726/3 The odorimeter is well adapted for plant control, for the regular injections of plasticizer can be made to coincide with the repeated inspection of batches being deodorized.

Hence **odorime·tric** *a.*, of or pertaining to odorimetry; **odori·metry,** the measurement of the intensity of odours.

1898 *Amer. Jrnl. Psychol.* X. 85 Odorimetry is a 'side issue' of olfactometry. **1917** *Jrnl. Exper. Psychol.* II. 437 The preceding odorimetric method..enables one to stimulate the nose continuously for any desired time by means of an air current containing a known proportion of odorous molecules. **1922** *Perfumery & Essent. Oil Rec.* XIII. 5/2 Odorimetry..enables us to compare this value with fortuitous smells. **1935** *Bull. Neurol. Inst. N.Y.* IV. 15 (*heading*) Theoretical considerations, significance for quantitative and qualitative odorimetry and olfactometry. **1972** *Biol. Abstr.* LIV. 349/2 (*heading*) Odorimetric appraisal of polymers used in the construction of sealed chambers.

odoriphore (ōu·dŏrifōəɹ). Also **odorophore.** [ad. G. *odoriphor* (H. Zwaardemaker *Die Physiol. des Geruchs* (1895) xiv. 240), f. as prec.: see -phore.] = *osmophore 1.

1919 *Physiol. Abstr.* IV. 13 Adsorption is..but the first step [in olfaction], on which follows the solution of the odorous substance and its odorophore in the lipoids of the epithelial cell. **1922** *Ibid.* VII. 174 The natural groups of odours..are characterised by the presence, number, size, and arrangement of odoriphore groups. **1944** R. W. Moncrieff *Chemical Senses* xii. 306 Zwaardemaker considered that odour was dependent on the presence of odoriphores, special chemical groups, each of which was responsible for a special odour.

Hence **odoripho·ric** *a.*

1944 R. W. Moncrieff *Chemical Senses* xii. 307 Odoriphoric groups. **1968** W. McCartney *Olfaction & Odours* 169 That odorous energy is molecular-vibratory..seemed to him [*sc.* A. Heyninx] the sole admissible view and on it he reached the following conclusions:..4. The specific vibrations of the 'odoriphoric' groups of the odorous molecules cause the olfactory mucous membrane..to vibrate.

odorivector (ōu·dŏrivektəɹ). [ad. F. *odorivecteur* (A. Heyninx *Essai d'Olfactique physiol.* (1919) i. 2), f. as prec. + F. *vecteur* Vector.] Any substance the molecules of which stimulate the olfactory system.

1926 *Nature* 24 Apr. 591/2 The quality of the sensation depends on the molecular structure of the odorivector. **1964** *Ann. N.Y. Acad. Sci.* CXVI. 431 The final result of interaction of the odorivector molecules with the olfactory area is a modification in the electrical activity of the nerve cells which communicate with the sensors. **1967** J. W. Johnston in T. Hayashi *Olfaction & Taste II.* 46 It is problematical whether there are pure odorivectors that stimulate one type of sensor unit.

odour. Add: **4. b.** (Earlier and later examples.) Also without qualifying adj.

1835 Dickens *Let.* 16 Dec. (1965) I. 106 As the Tories are the principal party here, *I* am in no very good odour in the town. **1954** N. Mitford *Mme de Pompadour* xviii. 230 In 1760 St. Germain fell into bad odour with the police and Choiseul sent him packing. **1977** *Bulletin* (Sydney) 22 Jan. 33/1 There is no doubt that the Daoud affair, which has brought France into such odour abroad including a call for the boycott of French goods in the United States, was the result of conflicting interests between French diplomats and French security services.

6. *odour-reek*; *odour-free*, *-laden*, *-proof* adjs.; **odour-blindness,** an inability to perceive a particular smell or range of smells.

1931 *Eugenical News* July 106/1 Some were thus 'blind' to fragrance in the red flowers though perceiving fragrance in the pink while others were just reversed in their odor 'blindness'. **1973** *Nature* 23 Mar. 271/2 Three types of odour-blindness or specific anosmia have been studied. **1955** *Jrnl. Appl. Physiol.* VIII. 341/2 The odorant.. introduced through an ultramicroburette was vaporized into the odor-free test room by an atomizing jet of odor-free air. **1962** W. D. Hislop in H. W. Chatfield *Sci. Surface Coatings* xviii. 531 Use can be made of catalytic oxidation to treat the exhaust and render it odour-free. **1885** W. B. Yeats in *Dublin Univ. Rev.* Apr. 58/1 Dreaming in their soft odour-laden sleep. **1900** —— *Shadowy Waters* 44 Where time is drowned in odour-laden winds. **1934** Webster, Odorproof. **1950** *Amer. Jrnl. Psychol.* LXIII. 433 The need for rigorous experimental controls for smell soon became apparent. A large odor-proof globe..was first thought of. **1951** M. McLuhan *Mech. Bride* (1967) 62/1 A special caste of robots, who would care for the victims of such necessities in germ- and odor-proof laboratories. **1960** *Farmer & Stockbreeder* 1 Mar. 55/3 The odour-proof film minimizes the risk of contamination. **1932** W. Faulkner *Light in August* viii. 187 The odorreek of all anonymous men.

odourant, var. *odorant *sb.*

odourless. Add: Hence **o·dourlessness,** the condition of being without odour.

1890 *Retrospect Med.* CII. 149 The odourlessness of Aristol..renders the drug most useful in the treatment of soft chancre. **1901** *Westm. Gaz.* 24 Dec. 9/1 We would again lay stress on the odourlessness; it is a whale, not a smelt. **1963** W. Summer *Methods Air Deodorization* iii. 101 The simultaneous olfaction of two selected and matched odours will cause the psychological effect of odourlessness. **1968** [see *osmoceptor].

odum (odū·m). [Native name in Ghana.] = *iroko.

1920 *Nature* 29 July 692/1 Another valuable wood is that labelled Odum..which has also been exported as Iroko, sometimes falsely termed African teak... It possesses none of the qualities of teak with the exception of a superficial resemblance in colour. **1959** A. Abbs *Ashanti Boy* i. 34 The thick, odum stick he kept beside his bed. *Ibid.* 38 Low easy-chairs made of local mahogany or odum wood. **1962** *Listener* 6 Sept. 359/2 The big odum tree near the school park [in Ghana].

œcology, œcological, now written **ecology, ecological.** Cf. *ecological, ecology. (Examples of **œcological.**) So **œco·logist** (obs. var. *ecologist).

1893 J. S. Burdon-Sanderson in *Nature* 14 Sept. 465/1 Whether with the œcologist we regard the organism in relation to the world, or with the physiologist as a wonderful complex of vital energies, the two branches have this in common. **1899** *Natural Sci.* July 11 One of the most important oecological studies which has yet appeared in the United States. **1909** E. Warming *Oecol. Plants* p. v, I have given my views on oecological classification in a more comprehensive and detailed manner.

‖ **œcumene** (īkiu·menĭ). Also **ecumene, oik(o)umene.** [a. Gr. οἰκουμένη (see Œcumenic *a.*).] The inhabited world as known to the ancient Greeks; the Greeks and their neighbours regarded in the context of development in human society. Also *transf.*, the inhabited world (or a part of it) as known to or embraced by a later civilization.

1911 E. C. Semple *Influences Geogr. Environment* vi. 171 Humanity's area of distribution and historical movement we call the Oikoumene. **1926** M. T. Bingham tr. *P. Vidal de la Blache's Princ. Human Geogr.* 18 Ocean solitudes long divided inhabited countries (oikoumenes). *Ibid.* ii. 49 Recent conquests by the *oikoumene*. **1941** *Antiquity* XV. 6 By reinstating the archaeological evidence the continuum of the oikumene, made explicit in the medieval travellers' narratives, could be displayed as an enlargement of one already implied in the Bronze Age by the 24th century B.C. **1946** V. Ehrenberg *Aspects Anc. World* iii. 32 Greeks and Romans alike regarded the inhabited earth, the *oecumene*, as an area round the Mediterranean. **1953** *Ann. Assoc. Amer. Geogr.* XLIII. 92 Distribution of people in its..global scale, involves dividing the land portions of the earth into permanently inhabited as compared with uninhabited, or temporarily inhabited, parts. The terms ecumene and non-ecumene have been employed to represent these two major subdivisions. **1956** A. Toynbee *Historian's Approach to Relig.* 214 The political partition of the *Oikoumenê* into sixty or seventy self-governing parochial states. **1962** B. Lewis in Lewis & Holt *Historians of Middle East* xvi. 182 It [*sc.* the common stock of Muslim universal history] appears chiefly in the general introductory matter, leading up to the establishment of the Islamic oecumene. **1967** *Economist* 18 Nov. 742/2 Should the political scientist make change itself his theme? And if so, in an interdependent world, can the boundaries of his study be less than the *oikumene* itself? **1967** H. R. Friis *Pacific Basin* ii. 20 Eratosthenes..was like other philosophers before him concerned with the extent of the inhabited world—the *oikoumene*. **1972** D. M. Nicol *Last Centuries of Byzantium* v. 78 The paterfamilias, the head of the Christian family or *oikoumene*, was the emperor in Constantinople.

œcumenic, -ical, -icalism, -icality, -ically, -icity, see *ecumenic, -ical, etc.

Œdipal (ī·dipăl), *a.* *Psychol.* [f. Œdip(us + -al.] Characterized by an Oedipus complex; of or pertaining to the desire felt for a parent of the opposite sex.

1939 H. V. Dicks *Clin. Stud. Psychopathol.* v. 79 The analysis was devoted to working out the Oedipal, strongly sexualized, love for him. **1950** E. Frenkel-Brunswik in T. Wiesengrund-Adorno et al. *Authoritarian Personality* ix. 316 The problem of homosexuality relates to the different ways of failure in resolving the Oedipal conflict. **1960** *New Left Rev.* Nov.–Dec. 69/1 They interpreted the assassination in Oedipal terms, Trotsky being ..the hated father-substitute. **1967** T. Stoppard *Rosencrantz & Guildenstern* ii. 59 He at last confronts his mother and in a scene of provocative ambiguity (*a somewhat oedipal embrace*) begs her to repent. **1972** *Jrnl. Social Psychol.* LXXXVI. 157 The less dramatic resolution of the Oedipal complex experienced by females causes them to have a weaker superego than males. **1975** C. Dennis *Somebody just grabbed Annie!* 132 There was nothing Oedipal in his sleeping habits. He was just able to relax more easily in his old room.

Œdipean, *a.* (Later examples.)

1876 *Spectator* 9 Sept. 1131/2 The Œdipean trilogy of Sophocles. **1972** P. H. Kocher *Master of Middle-Earth* (1973) iii. 43 In striving to avert a danger he thinks he sees lying ahead he may take the very measures which are necessary to bring it about. All finite knowledge about the future is cursed by this Oedipean paradox.

Œdipode·an, *a.* [f. Gr. Οἰδιπόδειος of Oedipus + -an.] **a.** Of or pertaining to Oedipus or his family. **b.** = *Œdipal *a.*

1947 E. F. WATLING *Sophocles' Theban Plays* 13 Each of the three plays deals with a situation in the Oedipodean family history. **1959** S. NEILL *Genuinely Human Existence* x. 239 The Laian situation precedes the Oedipodean situation. **1968** H. J. SCHONFIELD *Those Incredible Christians* xiii. 202 Athenagoras similarly speaks of the heathen charges of 'atheism, Thyestean feasts and Oedipodean intercourse'.

Œdipus. Add: **2.** *Psychol.* Used *attrib.* in *Œdipus legend, love object, phantasy, phase, situation, theory*, with reference to the psycho-analytic interpretation given to Sophocles' play *Œdipus Tyrannus* (in which Oedipus unknowingly kills his father and marries his mother) by Freud, and seen by him to exemplify the desires felt for the parent of the opposite sex by a child at an early stage of sexual development.

1910 *Amer. Jrnl. Psychol.* XXI. 97 The illustration of the attitude of son to parent is..transpicuous in the Œdipus legend. **1913** E. JONES *Papers on Psycho-Anal.* xviii. 381 (*heading*) Note on the Œdipus Saving Phantasy. **1926** J. I. SUTTIE tr. *Ferenczi's Further Contrib. Theory & Technique Psycho-Anal.* ix. 112 The patient..was here realizing sexual intercourse displaced 'from below upwards' (from the 'Oedipus phantasy'). **1943** H. READ *Educ. through Art* vi. 179 It is the Oedipus situation which gives rise to those idealistic tendencies in humanity which we know as religion, morality, custom, etc. **1957** N. FRYE *Anat. Crit.* iii. 181 A kind of comic Oedipus situation in which the hero replaces his father as a lover. **1963** A. HERON *Towards Quaker View of Sex* 59 That acceptance which would permit the Oedipus phase to be 'worked through'. **1964** M. ARGYLE *Psychol. & Social Probl.* i. 19 The Oedipus theory has been found not to be universal. **1972** H. L. MUSLIN in S. C. Post *Moral Values & Superego Concept* v. 109 Guilt as a result of the introjection of the Oedipus love objects.

b. Œdipus complex, the name given by Freud to the complex of emotions which he found were aroused in a child by its subconscious sexual desire for the parent of the opposite sex, which, if not resolved naturally, may lead to repression, guilt feelings, and an inability to form normal emotional or sexual relationships. Cf. *ELECTRA.

1910 E. JONES in *Amer. Jrnl. Psychol.* XXI. 72 (*heading*) The Œdipus-complex as an explanation of Hamlet's mystery. **1920** S. FREUD in *Internat. Jrnl. Psycho-Anal.* I. 133 The girl had quietly passed through the normal stage of the feminine Oedipus complex, and had..begun to replace her father by a brother slightly older than herself. **1925** G. B. SHAW *Let.* 22 Feb. in J. Barrymore *Confessions of Actor* (1926) 122 [In 'Hamlet'] You..offer ..a demonstration of that very modern discovery called the Œdipus complex, thereby adding a really incestuous motive on Hamlet's part. **1927** [see *ELECTRA]. **1942** KOESTLER *Yogi & Commissar* (1945) I. i. 9 He believes that all the pests of humanity, including constipation and the Oedipus complex, can and will be cured by Revolution. **1951** M. MCLUHAN *Mech. Bride* (1967) 76/2 Did I give my baby an Oedipus complex? **1965** T. S. SZASZ *Ethics of Psychoanal.* I. iii. 50 According to classical analysis, he [*sc.* the psychoanalyst] teaches the patient about his early family situation, the Oedipus complex..transference, and resistance. **1969** *Listener* 17 Apr. 543/3 'I have to tell you, madam,' the psychiatrist said, 'that your son is suffering from an Oedipus complex.' 'What does it matter,' she replied, 'so long as he loves his mum?' **1971** J. Z. YOUNG *Introd. Study Man* i. 4 Psychoanalysis..has revealed some startling features of our lives, but 'man is more than his Oedipus complex'. **1973** *Jrnl. Genetic Psychol.* CXXII. 156 The basic dynamics of the feminine 'Oedipus' complex are already fairly well known.

c. Œdipus effect, a term derived from that part of the legend of Oedipus which evidences the self-fulfilling nature of a prophecy or prediction (see quot. 1957).

1957 K. R. POPPER *Poverty of Historicism* i. 13, I suggest the name '*Oedipus effect*' for the influence of the prediction upon the predicted event..whether this influence tends to bring about the predicted event, or whether it tends to prevent it. **1961** A. FLEW *Hume's Philos. of Belief* vii. 152 Hume is here in his own way taking note of the particular sort of feedback which has recently been given the mnemonically useful label *Oedipus effect.* **1972** I. C. JARVIE *Concepts & Society* iv. 124 By our belief in them [*sc.* class beliefs] and an acute Oedipus effect, they verify themselves. **1974** *Brit. Jrnl. Pol. Sci.* IV. 255 It is precisely this research perspective which in a dialectical fashion lends strength to an objection based on the Oedipus effect.

œdometer (īdǫ·mĭtəɹ). Also (*rare*) **ödometer.** [f. Gr. οἴδ-ημα swelling, swollen condition + -OMETER.] A device for measuring the swelling of a gel when water is absorbed or the compressibility of soil.

1915 W. W. TAYLOR *Chem. Colloids* xi. 158 Reinke used the oedometer, by means of which he measured the pressure of imbibition, to determine the velocity of the process. **1926** C. TERZAGHI in *Colloid Symposium Monograph* IV. 73 My own tests performed with coarse grained sands, by using a method which in every respect corresponds to the Ödometer method for measuring the swelling pressure of gels. **1938** *Nature* 24 Sept. 584/2 From the results of tests made with the Terzaghi oedometer together with calculation of the distribution of pressure from the building, it is possible to estimate the amount of settlement to be expected. **1969** LAMBE & WHITMAN *Soil Mech.* ix. 116 In the oedometer test, stress is applied to the soil specimen along the vertical axis, while strain in the horizontal directions is prevented.

‖**œil-de-perdrix** (öidəpę̄rdrī). [Fr., lit. 'partridge-eye'.] **1.** In French pottery and porcelain, a design of dotted circles, usu. on a coloured background, first used *circa* 1760 on Sèvres porcelain.

1865 F. B. PALLISER *Hist. Lace* iv. 70 The lovely diapered ground recalls the may-flower of the Dresden and the oeil-de-perdrix of the Sèvres china of that time. **1925** W. W. WORSTER tr. *E. Hannover's Pott. & Porc.* III. 276 Next to the monochrome grounds, a favourite method was ..that of dotting the porcelain over with some little simple design repeated without a break in the manner of textiles. One of these was the famous *œil-de-perdrix* pattern, consisting of tiny circles or double circles dotted in green or blue and reserved in white on a monochrome or dotted ground. **1953** F. TILLEY *Litchfield's Pott. & Porc.* (ed. 6) vi. 234 The names of some other decorations [on Sèvres work] occur in various catalogues and inventories: thus the *œil de perdrix*, the well-known partridge eye-pattern. **1971** *Canad. Antiques Collector* Feb. 16/2 The rim has a light blue ground upon which is the oeil-de-perdrix pattern leaving three oval reserves.

b. A similar design used as a ground in lace-making (see quots.).

1891 A. S. COLE *Suppl. Descr. Catal. Specimens Lace S. Kensington Mus.* 23 The pattern consists of tape-like stems..with a coarse ground of 'oeil de perdrix' devices or irregular little hexagons. *Ibid.* 31 The scheme of pattern consists of a series of oval compartments.., on an oeil-de-perdrix ground. **1899** A. M. SHARP *Point & Pillow Lace* vi. 148 This Lace [*sc.* Flemish Mechlin] is sometimes grounded with an ornamental 'réseau', instead of one in the usual hexagonal shape, called 'Fond de néige' or 'Œil de perdrix'. **1953** M. POWYS *Lace & Lace-Making* xi. 207 (*heading*) Fond de Neige, so-called Oeil de Perdrix. An elaborate ground, often used as a filling. **1960** H. HAYWARD *Antique Coll.* 178/2 Other grounds were sometimes used such as the *œil de perdrix.*

2. Applied to wines which are pink or pale red in colour. Hence *ellipt.* as *sb.*

1872 E. BRADDON *Life in India* viii. 305 If he required ..anything from Holloway's pills to œil de perdrix champagne..he was compelled to lay in such a stock as would carry him through. **1920** G. SAINTSBURY *Notes on Cellar-Bk.* v. 80 The true *œil-de-perdrix* tint is not..'synthetically' attainable. *Ibid.* xii. 188 A glass, filled with *œil-de-perdrix* wine. **1959** W. JAMES *Word-Bk. Wine* 135 *Œil de perdrix.* A partridge-eye wine is a pink wine; the term is applied to pink champagnes, light-coloured sparkling burgundies, and to some wines made from a mixture of red and white grapes. **1966** *Country Life* 6 Oct. 820/1 In 1784 'L' Oeil de Perdrix Celleroy', presumably what we would now call pink champagne, fetched 48s. as against 38s. for ordinary Celleroy. **1971** *Times* 29 Mar. (Switzerland Suppl.) p. iii/6 From Neuchâtel..comes the best-known rosé, Oeil de Perdrix.

œllacherite (öla·kərəit). *Min.* [f. the name of J. *Œllacher* (b. 1804), Hungarian chemist + -ITE[1].] A white or pink variety of muscovite containing a significant proportion of barium.

1867 J. D. DANA in *Amer. Jrnl. Sci.* XCIV. 256 (*table*) Œllacherite. [*Note*] Œllacher's margarite from Pfitschthal [Tyrol]. **1933** *Amer. Mineralogist* XVIII. 30 A massive pink mineral with obscure cleavage..appeared under the microscope to have a micaceous texture and had about the optical characters of muscovite... The varietal name oellacherite is given by Dana to this barium-muscovite. **1949** *Chem. Abstr.* XLIII. 6120 The discovery of a previously unknown mineral in the mountains of Kara-Tau in Kazakhstan is reported... The chem. compn. corresponds to œllacherite in which a part of the Al_2O_3 is isomorphically displaced by V_2O_3. **1962** W. A. DEER et al. *Rock-Forming Min.* III. 14 It is probable that roscoelite and oellacherite are distinct chemical and structural species and that there is not a complete series between each of them and muscovite.

œno-. Add: **œ·nocyte** (also † **-cyth**) *Ent.* [ad. G. *oenocyth* (H. R. von Wielowiejski 1886, in *Zeitschr. f. wissensch. Zool.* XLIII. 515): see -CYTE], a large, probably secretory, wine-coloured cell of insects that is often grouped into glands and is produced in the epidermis, either remaining there or migrating elsewhere (esp. to the fat body); **œnocy·toid** *Ent.* [ad. F. *œnocytoïde* (E. Poyarkoff 1910, in *Arch. d'Anat. microsc.* XII. 344)], a large, round, non-phagocytic cell, similar in appearance to an œnocyte, that occurs in the hæmolymph of some insects; **œnophil** (ī·nofil), **œnophile** (ī·nofəil) [Gr. -φιλος loving] = *œnophilist*; so **œnophi·lic** *a.*, wine-loving.

1886 *Jrnl. R. Microsc. Soc.* 964 The second kind of cell is, in consequence of its colour, called the 'œnocyth'; these were found arranged in groups, or were very small, or formed rows, or plexiform plates or larger complexes or plates. **1891** *Ibid.* 587 Prof. V. Graber discusses the complex tissue found in the body-cavity of most insects. It includes..the yellow 'œnocytes', which Wielowiejski finds to be usually arranged in segmental groups. **1970** *Nature* 7 Nov. 581/1 Oenocytes, sometimes called abdominal endocrine glands, are the cells most probably interacting with the prothoracic glands in the control of moulting. **1925** A. D. IMMS *Gen. Textbk. Entomol.* I. 125 The leucocytes exist in several forms and four types..are recognized by Hollande..as being present in most insects... These are—(1) Proleucocytes... (2) Phagocytes. .. (3) Granular leucocytes... (4) Œnocytoids. **1969** R. F. CHAPMAN *Insects* xxxiii. 676 Oenocytoids are found in Coleoptera, Lepidoptera and some Diptera and Heteroptera. **1974** *Nature* 29 Nov. 391/2 Five cell types were identified in the haemolymph of *G*[*alleria*] *mellonella*; prohaemocytes, plasmatocytes, granular cells, spherule cells and oenocytoids. **1930** *New Statesman* 28 June 366/1 Professor Saintsbury, an oenophile who is free from the snobbish contempt his kind affect for whisky. **1961** C. WILLOCK *Death in Covert* iii. 68 This man, who described himself as an oenophil, believed that wine was the only fit alcoholic drink. **1962** *Punch* 6 June 869/2 For not-too-adventurous oenophiles I commend Ice Peach Wine. **1969** *New Scientist* 13 Feb. 357/2 Scientific oenophiles would not need the sometimes drastic oversimplification of scientific matters. **1976** *Times* 5 May 16/8 British Transport Hotels invited distinguished oenophiles to sip and sniff their way through a representative selection of English wines. **1957** *Times Lit. Suppl.* 20 Dec. 778/2 Merely a salon volume designed for presentation to oenophilic friends.

Oerlikon (ō·ɹlikǫn). Also **oerlikon.** [Name of the suburb of Zurich where the guns are manufactured.] The proprietary name used by Werkzeugmaschinenfabrik Oerlikon Buhrle & Co. for guns and fittings manufactured by them; usu. *ellipt.* for an Oerlikon light anti-aircraft cannon.

1944 *R.A.F. Jrnl.* Aug. 272 (*caption*) Battleship..; carries..a varying number of Oerlikons.., sometimes sixty. **1949** S. P. LLEWELLYN *Troopships* 31 Their forward and after decks cluttered with..pom-poms, oerlikons, and improvised wash-houses, the troopships cleared Wellington heads. **1970** *Trade Marks Jrnl.* 7 Oct. 1667/2 Oerlikon... Guns and parts and fittings therefor.. ammunition for cannon; apparatus..for launching rockets; and rockets (missiles). Dieter Buhrle and Charlotte Buhrle-Schalk, trading as Werkzeugmaschinenfabrik Oerlikon Buhrle & Co.,..Zurich,..Switzerland; manufacturers and merchants. **1973** D. LEES *Rape of Quiet Town* x. 165 The frigate..sprayed the sub with Oerlikon fire.

oersted (ə·ɹsted). *Physics.* [f. the name of H. C. *Oersted* (1777–1851), Danish physicist.]

† **a.** (Written **oerstedt.**) (See quots.) *Obs.*

1879 J. D. EVERETT *Units & Physical Constants* xi. 139 The practical unit of current is the current due to an electromotive force of 1 volt working through a resistance of 1 ohm. It is called a current of 1 weber per second. Its theoretical value is 1 weber per second = 1/10 of the C.G.S. unit of current. In the 'Testing Instructions of the Indian Telegraph Department' it is called the Oerstedt. **1885** W. WILLIAMS *Man. Telegr.* 206 The unit current..has already been described as the Ampère or Oerstedt.

† **b.** The electromagnetic unit of reluctance in the C.G.S. system, defined as one gilbert per maxwell. (In the International System of Units replaced by the reciprocal heury, equal to approximately $1{\cdot}26 \times 10^{-8}$ gilberts per maxwell.) *Obs.*

1893 [see *GILBERT[2]]. **1896** M. MACLEAN *Physical Units* 92 The committee on Notation of the Chamber of Delegates of the International Electrical Congress of 1893 in Chicago recommended that—unit field intensity, unit magnetic induction, and unit magnetising force be each called a Gauss; unit flux of magnetic force a Weber; unit magneto-motive force a Gilbert; and unit reluctance or magnetic resistance an Oersted. **1903** *Electr. World & Engin.* XLI. 1010/2 For practical work..the magnetic reluctance of a cubic centimeter of all non-magnetic materials..is the same as that of an air-pump vacuum. This unit of reluctance is called the 'oersted'. **1931** S. R. WILLIAMS *Magn. Phenomena* i. 46 The oersted of reluctance corresponds to the ohm of resistance.

c. The electromagnetic unit of magnetic field strength in the C.G.S. system, equal to the field strength produced at a distance of one centimetre by a unit magnetic pole or a thin straight wire carrying half an e.m.u. (i.e. five amp.) of current; one maxwell per square centimetre. Cf. GAUSS in Dict. and Suppl. (In the International System of Units the oersted is replaced by the ampere per metre, equal to $4\pi \times 10^{-3}$ (approximately 0·0126) oersted.)

1930 *Engineering* 25 July 113/2 At the meeting of the International Electrotechnical Commission..it was.. recommended that the names of maxwell, gauss, oersted and gilbert should be applied to the C.G.S. units for magnetic flux, flux density, magnetic field intensity and magneto-motive force respectively. **1938** R. W. LAWSON tr. *Hevesy & Paneth's Man. Radioactivity* (ed. 2) ii. 26 By means of deflexion experiments in very strong magnetic fields (23,000 oersteds) a fine structure of the α-particles from thorium C..has been detected. **1959** *Sci. News* LI. 17 For instance, at a temperature of 0·01° K a magnetic field of the order of 100,000 oersted is needed in order to achieve the necessary nuclear alignment for the subsequent cooling by demagnetization. **1962** [see *GAUSS]. **1963** JERRARD & MCNEILL *Dict. Sci. Units* 97 The earth's magnetic field has a magnetizing force of the order 0·2 to 0·3 oersted. **1974** *Nature* 16 Aug. 535/2 Few, if any [geomagneticians] have really cared whether their magnetometers have measured *B* or *H*; the gauss, the c.g.s. unit of *B*, has by usage become totally interchangeable with the oersted, the c.g.s. unit of *H*. **1976** *Ibid.* 26 Feb. 652/1 All 36 specimens were submitted to magnetic study, including alternating field treatment up to 850 oersted.

œsophago-. Add: Also **esophago-, œso:-phagoga·stric** *a.*, pertaining to both the œsophagus and the stomach.

1954 *Amer. Jrnl. Surg.* LXXXVIII. 330/2 The procedure could be considered for esophagogastric resection for gastric and esophageal varices secondary to portal hypertension and cirrhosis. **1971** *Nature* 9 July 117/1 The stomach was isolated between ligatures at the oesophagogastric and gastro-duodenal junctions.

œstradiol (īs-, estrădəi·ǫl). *Biochem.* Also (*U.S.*) **estr-**. [f. *ŒSTRA(NE + DI-[2] + -OL.] The most active known naturally occurring œstrogenic hormone in mammals, $C_{18}H_{22}(OH)_2$, which is formed in the ovarian follicles, controls the growth of the female sexual organs and some functions of the uterus, and is used, e.g., in treating the menopausal syndrome and conditions associated with hypoplasia of the genital tract.

1934 K. DAVID et al. in *Biochem. Jrnl.* XXVIII. 1366 The increased oestrogenic potency of these substances is associated with an increased effect on the seminal vesicles. Oestradiol is about twice as oestrogenic as oestrone. **1951** A. GROLLMAN *Pharmacol. & Therapeutics* xxvi. 579 Estradiol is also marketed in the form of its benzoic acid ester in which form its activity is greatly enhanced. **1955** *Sci. News Let.* 17 Sept. 179/3 Drs. Emil Witsch and C. Y. Chang..told..that they were able to change male Xenopus toads into egg-laying females..under the influence of a female hormone, estradiol. **1968** *Times* 4 Oct. 9/2 Injections of male or female sex hormones, testosterone or oestradiol, prevent the shedding of old antlers.

œstral (ī·s-, e·străl), *a.* Also (*U.S.*) **estral.** [f. ŒSTR(US + -AL.] = ŒSTROUS *a.*

1883 *Brit. Med. Jrnl.* 10 Mar. 446/2 The 'œstral' products had never found vent from the uterus. *Ibid.*, The lower animals do certainly have an 'œstral' discharge. **1972** *Biol. Abstr.* LIV. 6236/1 (*heading*) Change in the estral cycle of white rats..exposed to the..effect of gasoline..vapors.

œstrane (ī·s-, e·strēin). *Biochem.* Also (*U.S.*) **estr-**. [f. *ŒSTR(IN + -ANE.] (See quot. 1933.)

1933 N. K. ADAM et al. in *Nature* 5 Aug. 205/2 The parent saturated hydrocarbon of the œstrin group, $C_{18}H_{30}$, containing the sterol skeleton with one methyl group but without the side chain, may be termed 'œstrane'. **1947** H. SELYE *Textbk. Endocrinol.* i. 71/2 A side-chain at C_{17} does not necessarily decrease folliculoid activity in the estrane series and..it may even increase it. **1973** *Biochemistry* (Easton, Pa.) XII. 2221/1 All neutral and charged derivatives of estrane and androstane inhibit hydrolysis of *bovine* albumin.

œstrin (ī·s-, e·strin). *Biochem.* Also (*U.S.*) **estr-**. [f. ŒSTR(US + -IN[1].] Any of various preparations of œstrogenic material; an œstrogen, *spec.* œstrone.

1926 PARKES & BELLERBY in *Jrnl. Physiol.* LXI. 573 We suggest that 'oestrin' or some such term..should be applied to the oestrus-producing principle of the ovary. **1933** [see prec.]. **1935** B. HARROW in Harrow & Sherwin *Textbk. Biochem.* xxx. 756 The true theelin or estrin, as well as several related compounds, has been isolated in the chemically pure form. **1938** *Ann. Reg. 1937* 348 Oestrin, styryl blue, the acenaphthene derivatives and squalene can act as efficient evocators in embryological induction. **1970** W. B. YAPP *Introd. Animal Physiol.* (ed. 3) viii. 293 Collectively all are called oestrins or oestrogens; they are steroids.

œstriol (ī·s-, e·stri,ǫl). *Biochem.* Also (*U.S.*) **estr-**. [f. *ŒS(TRANE + TRI- + -OL.] An œstrogenic hormone, $C_{18}H_{21}(OH)_3$, which is one of the metabolic products of œstradiol and is produced in the placenta during pregnancy.

1933 N. K. ADAM et al. in *Nature* 5 Aug. 206/1 The full chemical names of two important derivatives..are 3,16,17-trihydroxy 1,3,5-œstratriene, and 3-hydroxy 17-keto 1,3,5-œstratriene. These names, though suitable for chemical literature, are cumbrous for general and biological use. We suggest as common names, for use where the chemical nature of the principle has been identified, 'œstriol' for the trihydroxy compound, and 'œstrone' for the keto-hydroxy compound. **1950** L. LEVIN in S. Soskin *Progr. Clin. Endocrinol.* xi. 410 The separation of estriol from estrone on the basis of the somewhat greater acid dissociation of estriol. **1958** *Sci. News* XLVII. 88 Oestrone has also been obtained from palm kernel extracts, and oestriol from female willow flower. **1968** *New Scientist* 22 Feb. 399/3 Measurement of the mother's oestriol excretion is a guide to the well-being of both the foetus and the placenta that nourishes it.

œstrogen (ī·s-, e·strǒdʒěn). *Med.* Also (*U.S.*) **estro-**. [f. ŒSTR(US + -O + -GEN.] Any natural or synthetic substance which can produce or maintain the secondary female sex characteristics in a mammal and which initiates certain bodily changes associated with the menstrual or œstrous cycle.

1927 *Official Gaz.* (U.S. Patent Office) 22 Nov. 788/1 Parke, Davis & Company, Detroit, Michigan...*Estrogen.* .. Extract of gland tissue for use in the treatment of various types of ovarian disfunctions. Claims use since May 25, 1927. **1928** *Endocrinology* XII. 151 (*heading*) Estrogen, a new sex hormone. **1936** *Jrnl. Amer. Med. Assoc.* 10 Oct. 1223/2 'Estrogen' is a registered trade mark belonging to Parke, Davis and Company... This firm has commendably agreed to relinquish its proprietary rights in the name on its adoption by the Council as a generic term. **1943** *Endeavour* II. 29/2 This soon led..to the synthesis of artificial oestrogens of extraordinary potency. **1951** A. GROLLMAN *Pharmacol. & Therapeutics* xxvi. 583 Diethylstilbestrol and other estrogens exert an ameliorative effect in carcinoma of the prostate and in certain cases of mammary carcinoma occuring in post-menopausal women. **1960** *Which?* Feb. 24/1 Oestrogens, originally, seem to have been incorporated into face creams without any direct *evidence* that they could affect the skin. **1968** PASSMORE & ROBSON *Compan. Med. Stud.* I. xxxvii. 11/1 The principal ovarian hormones..fall into three broad functional categories, oestrogens, progestagens and androgens. **1968** *Times* 28 Nov. 14/4 Most oral contraceptive pills contain both a progestogen and an oestrogen—another type of ovarian hormone which is thought to be responsible for most of the side effects, such as changes of weight. **1974** *Nature* 12 Apr. 616/2 The role of oestrogens in male reproduction remains an enigma.

b. *attrib.* and *Comb.*, as *œstrogen effect, excretion, ointment, pill, therapy; œstrogen-induced, -secreting, -treated* adjs.

1957 *Times* 2 Dec. (Agric. Suppl.) p. vi/4 A source of greater fear to those familiar with oestrogen effects is the inhalation of dust from a concentrated premix. **1972** *Endocrinology* XCI. 1273 (*heading*) Early estrogen effects on lipid metabolism in the rat uterus. **1946** *Nature* 24 Aug. 276/2 The significance of androgen and oestrogen excretion in the urine in relation to ageing. **1972** *Brit. Vet. Jrnl.* CXXVIII. 565 Urinary oestrogen excretion has been studied during the oestrus cycle in a variety of domestic animals. **1956** *Nature* 10 Mar. 478/2 Progesterone ..prevents oestrogen-induced abdominal fibroids. **1960** *Which?* Feb. 24/2 In aged women..it was claimed that treatment with oestrogen ointment had an effect. **1972** F. WARNER *Maquettes* 44 Oestrogen-pills on prescription. **1948** L. MARTIN *Clin. Endocrinol.* ix. 191 Œstrogen-secreting ovarian tumours composed of cells resembling those of the membrane granulosa of the Graafian follicle. *Ibid.* 170 Prolonged œstrogen therapy causes hypertrophy of the uterus and endometrium and enlargement of the breasts. **1974** *Jrnl. Amer. Med. Assoc.* 4 Feb. 522/1 Patients with preexisting hyperlipemia should probably not receive estrogen therapy. **1957** *A.M.A. Arch. Path.* LXIV. 595/2 Stratified squamous epithelium may be produced in the uterus of estrogen-treated rats by two separate..methods.

œstrogenic (īs-, estrǒdʒe·nik), *a.* Also (*U.S.*) **estro-**. [f. prec. + -IC.] Of the nature of, or having the actions of, an œstrogen.

1930 *Endocrinology* XIV. 101 Estrogenic material has been obtained from follicular fluid. **1938** *Ann. Reg. 1937* 348 Knowledge [was] advanced of the relation between molecular structure and the oestrogenic activity of the sex hormones. **1951** A. GROLLMAN *Pharmacol. & Therapeutics* xxvi. 579 The naturally occurring estrogenic substances have been displaced in therapeutics to a large extent by a number of cheaper synthetic compounds. **1957** *Times* 2 Dec. (Agric. Suppl.) p. ii/7 Recently, fresh developments have taken place in the use of oestrogenic hormones such as stilboestrol and hexoestrol for beef production both in the United States and in this country. **1965** LEE & KNOWLES *Animal Hormones* iii. 52 Whether oestrogenic substances are secreted by the testes [of reptiles] has yet to be clarified.

Hence **œstroge·nically,** *adv.*, as regards œstrogenic properties; **œstrogeni·city,** œstrogenic property.

1930 *Endocrinology* XIV. 389 A relationship between estrogenicity and the portion of a plant used as a source of extract. **1935** *Jrnl. Biol. Chem.* CXII. 425 In the commercial extraction of theelin and theelol from human pregnancy urine, an acidic, nitrogenous, crystalline substance may be separated from the crude extract. Preliminary Allen-Doisy tests showed this compound to be estrogenically inert. **1966** *Internat. Jrnl. Fertility* XI. 399 Both norethynodrel and norethisterone are active as a result of their estrogenicity. **1968** A. WHITE et al. *Princ. Biochem.* (ed. 4) xliv. 948 They are estrogenically active when given orally.

œstrogenized (ī·strǒdʒěnəizd), *a.* *Med.* Also (chiefly *U.S.*) **estr-**. [f. *ŒSTROGEN + -IZE + -ED[1].] Treated with œstrogen. Also **œ:strogeniza·tion,** the action or result of treating with œstrogen.

1946 *Nature* 20 July 96/1 The mobilization of lipochrome..in the serum of œstrogenized or actively laying fowl must..be familiar to all who have prepared phospholipid extracts from the sera of such birds. **1961** *Proc. 4th Nat. Cancer Conf.* (U.S.) 42/1 The lymphoid neoplasms that follow chronic estrogenization in some strains of mice. **1974** *Brain Res.* LXXX. 152 (*heading*) Inhibitory effect of neonatal estrogenization on the incorporation of $[^3H]$lysine in the Purkinje cells of the adult male and female rat. **1975** *Nature* 5 June 498/1 The oestrogenised pituitary glands, without bromocryptine, stored less and released more prolactin.

œstrone (ī·s-, e·strōun). *Biochem.* Also (*U.S.*) **estr-**. [f. *ŒSTR(ANE + -ONE.] An œstrogenic hormone, $C_{18}H_{22}O_2$, obtained from the urine of pregnant women and mares with actions and uses similar to those of œstradiol.

1933 [see *ŒSTRIOL]. **1951** A. GROLLMAN *Pharmacol. & Therapeutics* xxvi. 579 Several preparations of amorphous concentrates of pregnancy urine or placental tissue, which consist principally of estrone sulfate, are prepared commercially for oral use. **1958** *Sci. News* XLVII. 87 Oestrone was the first naturally occurring oestrogen to be isolated in pure crystalline form. **1968** R. O. C. NORMAN *Princ. Org. Synthesis* xix. 651 There are four asymmetric carbon atoms in oestrone, so that there are eight enantiomorphic pairs of stereoisomers, all of which have been synthesized.

œstrous, *a.* Add: Also (*U.S.*) **estrous.** Add to def.: in heat; *œstrous cycle,* the cyclic series of changes preceding, including, and following œstrus that takes place in most female mammals and involves esp. the reproductive and endocrine systems. (Earlier and later examples.)

1900 *Q. Jrnl. Microsc. Sci.* XLIV. 60 The sexual season of all mammals is evidenced by a series of phenomena which constitute, in the absence of the male, one œstrous cycle (monœstrous mammals) or a series of œstrous cycles (polyœstrous mammals). **1904** *Phil. Trans. R. Soc.* B. CXCVI. 47 (*heading*) The œstrous cycle and the formation of the corpus luteum in the sheep. *Ibid.* 73 (*heading*) Number of follicles discharging at an œstrous period. **1920** *Lancet* 2 Oct. 727/1 Under well-regulated food conditions the œstrous cycle in the guinea-pig is almost uniformly 16–17 days in duration. **1963** A. HERON *Towards Quaker View of Sex* 54 In most mammals, the oestrous cycle of the female, hormone-controlled, is an important factor. **1972** *Science* 5 May 519/1 Estrous rhythms and ovulation pattern had been reversed by substituting darkness for daylight. **1975** *Sci. Amer.* May 57/1 He [*sc.* a young male lion]..will mate if he encounters an unattended estrous female.

œstrual, *a.* Delete *rare*—[0] and add examples. **œstruation** (examples).

1859 J. C. DALTON *Treat. Human Physiol.* II. v. 471 The ripening and discharge of the egg are accompanied by a peculiar condition of the entire system, known as the 'rutting' condition, or 'œstruation'. **1883** *Brit. Med. Jrnl.* 3 Mar. 398/1 Observation of wild animals..shows that, after a definite period of quiescence, œstruation, or the 'rut', invariably recurs at epochs which strictly conform to some multiple of weeks. **1924** *Amer. Jrnl. Physiol.* LXVIII. 294 (*heading*) The effect of pubescence, oestruation and menopause on the voluntary activity in the albino rat. *Ibid.* 303 The oestrual cycles became more and more irregular..as the animals approached the end of their sexual life. **1936** *Ibid.* CXVI. 5 Oestrual behavior in cats represents a specific pattern of response. **1961** *Nature* 16 Dec. 1043 (*heading*) Variations in the nuclear deoxyribonucleic acid content in the adrenal cortex of the female white rat during the œstrual cycle.

œstrum. 2. b. (Later examples.)

1878 G. FLEMING *Text-bk. Vet. Obstetr.* 55 The rutting, heat, œstrum, or venereal œstrum of animals is analogous to 'menstruation' in woman. **1900** [see *OESTRUS 2 b]. **1925** [see *ACCEPTANCE 1 b]. **1939** *Brit. Birds* XXXII. 251 The 'false œstrum' which temporarily affects so many birds during this period. **1963** JUBB & KENNEDY *Path. Domestic Animals* I. i. 11/1 Oestrum may not occur, or be irregular.

œstrus. Add: Also (*U.S.*) **estrus. 2. b.** In mod. use: The rut or heat (HEAT *sb.* 13) of female mammals, or the period during which this lasts.

1900 *Q. Jrnl. Microsc. Sci.* XLIV. 6 Œstrus may be a brief period and exist for only a few hours. *Ibid.*, The period of œstrus is referred to by various writers as 'Brunst', 'rut', 'heat', 'season', 'brim', or 'œstrum'. *Ibid.* 17 The duration of the œstri. **1904** *Phil. Trans. R. Soc.* B. CXCVI. 67 Œstrus was noted in a Black-faced ewe. **1963** A. HERON *Towards Quaker View of Sex* 54 In the baboon.. females in oestrus will mate with other males if their overlord's attention is temporarily distracted. **1974** *Encycl. Brit. Macropædia* VIII. 1083/1 Estrogens are substances that evoke the cyclical onset of heat, or estrus, during which the animal is sexually active and receptive to the male. **1974** *Country Life* 12 Dec. 1853/1 There was mention of what is termed 'synchronised oestrus'. By the use of drugs cows are induced to come in season at a prearranged time.

‖**œuf en cocotte** (ǒf aṅ kokǫ·t). Also **œuf cocotte.** Pl. **œufs (en) cocotte(s).** [Fr., lit. 'egg in cocotte': see *COCOTTE 2.] An egg cooked in a cocotte, *spec.* in *pl.*, a French dish of eggs baked in butter in individual cocottes or ramekins and served thus.

1900 *French Cookery for Eng. Homes* 142 Eggs with Sweet Herbs (*Oeufs en cocottes aux fines hérbes* [sic]). Colour in 1½ oz. of butter, some chopped onions, mushrooms, and parsley... Pour over each egg a teaspoonful of good raw cream. **1909** C. H. SENN *New Cent. Cookery Bk.* (ed. 3) xxx. 690 *Oeufs en Cocottes.* 6 to 8 eggs, a little butter, 1 tablespoonful..parsley, 6 to 8 dessertspoonfuls cream... Dish up and serve in the pipkin pans. **1960** E. DAVID *French Provincial Cooking* 190, I always thought *œufs en cocotte* were soft. **1962** G. Z. STONE *Althea* (1964) 70 Eggs should be either very soft or thoroughly cooked,.. that was what was the matter with *oeufs en cocotte.* **1963** I. FLEMING *On H.M. Secret Service* ii. 27 In England he lived on grilled soles, oeufs cocotte and cold roast beef. **1966** *Observer* (Colour Suppl.) 25 Sept. 45/3 Perhaps the perfect egg dish is *oeufs en cocotte.* **1974** *She* Jan. 83/2 Dined at home. *Oeufs en cocotte* and grouse.

‖**œuvre** (ǒvr). [Fr., = work.] A work of art, music, or literature; the corpus of work produced by an artist, composer, or writer, considered as a whole. Cf. CHEF D'ŒUVRE in Dict. and Suppl. Hence *œuvre-catalogue,* a catalogue of an artist's complete work; *œuvre de vulgarisation,* a work conveying knowledge of an academic or esoteric subject for the popular taste.

1875 GEO. ELIOT *Let.* 10 Oct. in J. W. Cross *George Eliot's Life* (1885) III. xvii. 264 Our unprinted matter, our *œuvres inédites*, were safe. **1889** E. DOWSON *Let.* 31 July (1967) 97 If I can only shake off Cursitor St I will go to the oeuvre like one oclock. **1890** —— *Let.* 10 or 11 June (1967) 153 The bêtise of a public which boycotts his oeuvre & buys Chomondley's pretty little ineptiae. **1898** C. PHILLIPS *Later Work of Titian* iii. 66 The technical execution of these canvases, the treatment of landscape in the former would lead the writer to place them some years farther on still in the *œuvre* of the master. **1917** R. Fry in *Burlington Mag.* Aug. 61/2 A better opportunity for a general study of Cézanne's *oeuvre* than any other book. **1934** T. S. Eliot *Eliz. Ess.* 136 Even without an *œuvre*, some dramatists can effect a satisfying unity and significance of pattern in single plays. **1938** W. S. Maugham *Summing Up* 184 A body of work, an *œuvre*, is the result of long-continued and resolute effort. **1958** *Listener* 2 Oct. 540/1 The spreading abroad of his [*sc.* Palestrina's] bulky *oeuvre* gained considerably from the attentions of the romantics. **1959** *Ibid.* 20 Aug. 289/1 Were they in fact *oeuvres de vulgarisation* or attempts to stimulate craftsmen to new formal conquests? **1962** *Economist* 14 Apr. 141/3 An *oeuvre de vulgarisation* to bring his fifteen volume history..before a wider public. **1965** *New Statesman* 16 July 92/1 Only four oil-paintings before 1913 are listed in his oeuvre-catalogue. **1974** *Listener* 17 Jan. 66/2 A television serial which should incorporate the Palliser oeuvre entire. **1976** *Publishers Weekly* 15 Mar. 57/2 The author tells his engaging tale with disarming simplicity and the illustrator's pictures do justice to the *oeuvre*. **1976** *Times* 16 July 12/1 Raymond Lister at Cambridge..is currently working on an oeuvre catalogue for [Samuel] Palmer. **1978** *Times Lit. Suppl.* 25 Aug. 950/2 His oeuvre is the perfect place of exercise for..jocular pedantry.

of, *prep.* Add: **4. c.** *N. Amer.* and *dial.* In expressing the time: from or before (a specified hour); = To *prep.* 6 b. Also *ellipt.*

1817 T. Dean *Jrnl.* 31 May in *Indiana Hist. Soc. Publ.* (1918) VI. 278 At 15 minutes of 10 A.M. Paul Dick arrived. **1857** M. J. Holmes *Meadow Brook* v. 64 Five minutes of nine, and round the corner at the foot of the hill appeared a group of children. **1912** in *Sc. Nat. Dict.* (1965) VI. 466/3 It is a quarter of twelve. **1972** H. MacInnes *Message from Málaga* xix. 264, I have to leave by a quarter of four—at the latest. **1973** D. MacKenzie *Postscript to Dead Let.* 22 It was a quarter-of-seven. **1976** I. Levin *Boys from Brazil* iv. 135 'Can I go with you?' 'Sure... I leave at five of.'

43. b. (Further examples.) Freq. in phrases expressing surprise at something or someone unexpected.

1848 A. Jameson in G. Macpherson *Mem. Life A. Jameson* (1878) ix. 254, I ran to Ireland, of all places in the world. **1896** *Month* May 135 'I should like it of all things,' said his sister. **1906** W. Churchill *Coniston* I. xiv. 178 'Well, of all people, Cynthia Wetherell!' he cried. *c* **1921** D. H. Lawrence *Mr. Noon* i. in *Mod. Lover* (1934) 175 'Well, of all the idle scawd-rags!' he said as he entered with the tray. **1926** D. O. Stewart *Mr. & Mrs. Haddock in Paris* x. 266 'Maybe you would like to take a little rest—perhaps at a nice, comfortable movie.' 'Well, of all things, Will Haddock!' **1953** A. Huxley *Let.* 17 Aug. (1969) 683 It is to appear serially—of all places—in *Esquire*—which is at present engaged in serving God and Mammon. **1956** S. Beckett *Waiting for Godot* I. 40 (*He fumbles in his pockets.*)..What have I done with my spray? (*He fumbles.*) Well, of all the—— (*he looks up, consternation on his features. Faintly.*) I can't find my pulverizer! **1958** W. Plomer *At Home* ii. 38 He actually filled a glass with (of all things, on a black November afternoon) ginger beer.

d. (Later examples.) Also used (with repetition of the sb.) to denote a person who shows strong (*spec.* national) characteristics.

1895 G. A. Sala *Life* (ed. 2) I. vi. 64 Morris Barnett.. was a remarkably clever man—a Hebrew of the Hebrews, with a pronounced musical faculty. **1976** *Times* 15 May 14/7 Tévic the Milkman is a Jew of the Jews in character and behaviour, yet his problems are not peculiarly Jewish. **1976** *Lancet* 13 Nov. 1094/2 A Scot of Scots, he was born in 1912 and was educated at St Andrews and Edinburgh Universities.

47. d. Typical or characteristic of (a particular period).

1923 H. Simpson (*title of play*) A man of his time. **1940** M. K. Tippett (*title of oratorio*) A child of our time. **1965** *Listener* 11 Nov. 760/1 It is a highly original picture, but like any work of art it has roots. It is absolutely of its time: all the enthusiasms of those last pre-war years are contained in it at boiling point. **1968** *Ibid.* 4 July 9/2 The 'Four' were very much of the 1890s.

52. b. (Later examples.)

1867 'E. Kirke' *On Border* iii. 67, I don't forget..how you worked of nights. **1891** Barrie *Little Minister* III. xl. 156 So long as women sit up of nights listening for a footstep. **1897** J. L. Allen *Choir Invisible* xvii. 252 You have holiday of Saturdays. I have not, you see.

of (ǫv, əv), joc. (being erroneous in Received Standard) or dial. var. Have *v.* (representing the unstressed pronunc. of *have*, esp. in such phrases as *could have, might have, must have*, and *would have*).

1837 W. Tayler *Diary* 10 May in J. Burnett *Useful Toil* (1974) II. 181 Soposing seven hundred and sixty [servants] to of advertised and the same number not to of advertised. **1844** *Southern Lit. Messenger* X. 486/2, I never would of married in the world, ef I couldn't of got jist exactly suited. **1854** M. J. Holmes *Tempest & Sunshine* viii. 115, I don't see why in the old Harry he couldn't of lived. **1913** C. Mackenzie *Sinister St.* I. I. iv. 60 Mrs. Frith used to talk about 'people as gave theirselves airs which they had no business to of done.' **1916** [see *fair *sb.*[2] 1 c]. **1924** A. S. Neill *Dominie's Five* ii. 31 If Neill had been 'ere, 'e could of told us. **1931** E. Linklater *Juan in Amer.* II. iv. 79 There's no beer-racket in Paris or Rome, and even if there had been I wouldn't of tried to muscle in on it. *Ibid.* III. iii. 226 If I hadn't of worked nights on a correspondence course I'd of been firing a furnace still. **1945** A. Kober *Parm Me* 26 I'm certainly glad to of made your acquaintance. **1946** K. Tennant *Lost Haven* (1947) i. 19 There might have been a time when I thought Kelly was too hard on the kids, and ..I might of been glad when he went off with that bloody moll. *Ibid.* xiii. 202 She must of forgot. **1957** [see *blower[1] 3 e]. **1959** [see *dozer[2]]. **1977** *New Yorker* 6 June 56/3 Sometimes I get to thinking that I could of raised up four girls and worn out a couple of saddles.

ofay (ōu·fēi). *U.S. slang* (chiefly used by Blacks). [Orig. unknown: the balance of probability is that it is a word of African origin (but the precise attribution in quot. 1932 lacks foundation). The suggestion that it is Pig Latin for *foe* seems no more than an implausible guess.] In the use of American Blacks: an offensive term for 'a white person'. Also *attrib.* or as *adj.* Cf. *fay *sb.*[4]

1925 *Inter-State Tattler* 6 Mar. 8 We hear that 'Booker Red' has three ofays on his staff. **1926** [see *dicty *a.*]. **1927** *Amer. Mercury* Dec. 392 Ugly people there are, certainly, but the percentage of beautiful folk is unquestionably larger than among the ofay brethren. **1932** *Africa* V. 506 The last of the five words contributed indirectly by Ibibio to the English language is *Offay*... The root of the word appears to come from the Ibibio *Afia*, white or light-coloured. Hence in Harlem *Offay* means any light-coloured person and therefore a European. **1936** Mencken *Amer. Lang.* (ed. 4) v. 214 The word *ofay*, which may have come from the French *au fait* (signifying mastery), is in general use in the Negro press of the United States to designate a white person. **1940** *New Republic* 7 Oct. 472 When he goes downtown to this civil-service office, they take him for ofay... One of them young ofay chicks what clerk down there, she even tries to flirt with him. **1946** *Variety* 23 Oct. 114 Boys start out with a Negro spiritual, with their inflection and harmony making it racially authentic, although they're ofay. **1952** M. Steen *Phoenix Rising* iii. 70 'Dey run him out.' 'What for?' Karl sounded bored. 'Got after Harry's ofay chick—' **1956** B. Holiday *Lady sings Blues* (1973) v. 52 Most of the ofays, the white people, who came to Harlem those nights were looking for atmosphere. *Ibid.* ix. 89 'What will people think?' is a big deal in ofay circles. **1968** M. Richler *Cocksure* iv. 25 Was she amused by his dilemma? His ofay dilemma. **1971** *Black World* Apr. 62, I was attendant in the ofay ladies lounge. **1971** B. Malamud *Tenants* 48 Who are those cats, brothers or ofays? *Ibid.* 74 The black replies. 'No ofay motherfucker can put himself in *my* place.' **1977** *Amer. Speech* 1975 L. 89 That this word [*sc.* Yoruba *oje*] could have been brought to the United States by slaves is altogether possible... Thus *ofay* may be taken as a word said for self-protection in times of threat, which was then transferred to the source of threat, and so came to mean 'whiteman'.

off, *adv., prep., adj.*, and *sb.*[1] Add: **A.** *adv.* **1. b.** (Further examples.)

1629, etc. [see Buy *v.* 7 a]. **1902** G. H. Lorimer *Lett. Merchant* xiv. 203 By the time the real weather comes along everybody has guessed wrong and knocked the market off a cent or two. **1934** G. B. Shaw *On Rocks* I. 25 You have to buy him off with a scrap of dole. **1971** *Nature* 30 Apr. 604/1 Halfway through the book, the reasons why the rapid development of fluidics in the early 1960s has tended to fall off recently become clear.

e. *they're off* (occas. *they are off*): a colloq. phrase indicating that a race has started; *to be off and running*: to be making good progress.

1833 *Mirror of Lit.* 27 July 59/2 *They are off!* 'No, no'—cries one jockey whose horse turned his tail to the others. **1846** 'Sylvanus' *Pedestrian & Other Reminisc.* xxiv. 227 The horses are paraded, the flag is dropped—'they're off!' is repeated by twenty thousand tongues. **1872** B. Jerrold *London* viii. 74 *Clear the course!*... A flutter goes through the sea of heads on the Grand Stand... *They're off!* **1928** E. O'Neill *Strange Interlude* VIII. 288 They're off!..Navy and Washington are leading—Gordon's third. **1967** *Boston Herald* 1 Apr. 1/1 Although he has not announced it officially, Wallace appears to be off and running for the presidency. **1970** Wilson & Michaels tr. *Charrière's Papillon* vi. 211 We were off and running.

f. *ellipt.*, = off one's head (Head *sb.* 34): (somewhat) crazy. *colloq.* or *dial.*

1866 W. Gregor *Dial. Banffshire* in *Trans. Philol. Soc.* 215 *Aff*, to be, to be deranged; as, 'He wiz lang jummlet; bit he's *aff* athegeethir noo.' **1887** *Lantern* (New Orleans) 9 Apr. 3/2 Humor him as he was a little off. **1904** W. H. Smith *Promoters* i. 8 I've sometimes thought you were a trifle visionary, but I never considered you seriously off. **1927** W. E. Collinson *Contemp. Eng.* 116 Mental debility finds adequate expression in a whole series: he's not all there, a bit off (the top), he's off his chump. **1975** B. Wood *Killing Gift* II. i. 47 He was an old man, after all; perhaps he was just a little off... 'No, gentlemen, I'm not senile.'

g. In bad condition; wrong, abnormal, odd; *spec.* (*a*) of a horse or athlete: not in good condition or form; off-form; (*b*) of food: stale, sour, contaminated; (*c*) of social behaviour: unacceptable; ill-mannered; esp. in phr. (*it's*) *a bit off*.

Not always clearly distinguishable from sense 2 c.

1846 *Spirit of Times* 18 Apr. 91/1 He had endurance and speed enough to make a good race in any crowd, when 'all right', but then, he [*sc.* a horse] was liable to be oftener 'off' than otherwise. **1868** H. Woodruff *Trotting Horse* xxxvi. 300 When a trotter wins with great ease,..it is assumed, not that the loser was 'off', but that the winner is greatly superior. **1902** G. H. Lorimer *Lett. Merchant* xvi. 231, I may be off in sizing this thing up, because it's a little out of my line. **1916** 'Taffrail' *Pincher Martin* ix. 153 'S'pose I'd best be makin' a move, though,' he added ruefully. 'Bit orf, I calls it!' **1922** J. Cannan *Misty Valley* 58 Audrey had taken them sailing, but she had upset the boat, and they had drifted down stream, clinging to the sail, saying that it was a bit off. Whereafter they would go down to the pier and knit jumpers. **1941** E. Bowen *Look at Roses* 68 'Your caller sounded to me a bit off.' 'Oh, Mrs. Massey's had bad news. She..didn't feel well.' **1951** C. Armstrong *Black-Eyed Stranger* (1952) xiv. 117 Ambielli's got principles. They are a little off, slightly out of whack, you know. **1952** R. Finlayson *Schooner came to Atia* 140 Meat that tasted 'off'. **1953** K. Amis *Lucky Jim* v. 56 It was rather rude, all the same. I could see Mrs. Neddy thought it was a bit off. **1960** 'A. Burgess' *Right to Answer* ii. 23 That tomato juice is a bit off. Been in the tin too long. **1966** 'W. Cooper' *Mem. New Man* II. v. 155 It *is* just a teentsy-weentsy bit off, isn't it, darling, not to let you know he was coming. **1974** *Listener* 24 Jan. 102/1 Something was a little off with the mechanism, so the feeder-belt chewed up the baggage in transit.

3. d. *Theatr.* = *off stage *adv.* Also *transf.* and *fig.*

1774 [see Stage *sb.* 5]. **1775** T. Campbell *Diary* 4 Mar. (1947) 44 The players..stood their ground for a long time—but were at length hissed off. *Ibid.*, Mr. Vernon attempted to speak, but he wd not be heared—still the cry was off, off. **1805** T. Dibdin in G. Colman *John Bull* p. i, To whom, thus midway placed, I say, be kind, John Bull before, Oh, spare John Bull behind (*pointing off.*). **1836** Dickens *Sk. Boz* 1st Ser. II. 255 'But you must take care you don't knock a wing down...' 'I shall fall with my head "off", and then I can't do any harm.' *c* **1863** T. Taylor *Ticket-of-Leave Man* I. 7 The Bellevue Tea Gardens,..ornamental orchestra and concert room... Music heard off. **1909** 'I. Hay' *Man's Man* vi. 83 Portentous trampings 'off' announced the return of the glee-party. **1923** *Referee* 12 Aug. 3/3 The leopardess..was heard to roar a good deal 'off',..making her only appearance [on the stage]—in a cage. **1924,** etc. [see *noise *sb.* 3 c]. **1954** T. S. Eliot *Confid. Clerk* I. 27 *Lady Elizabeth Mulhammer's voice off*: Just open that case, I want something out of it. **1965** *New Statesman* 7 May 739/1 The elaborate framework of posh voices off intoning fragments of letters.

e. Of an item of food: deleted from the menu; not available. *colloq.*

[**1870** D. J. Kirwan *Palace & Hovel* x. 154 On 'off' days they have soup and thick gruel for breakfast.] **1902** Farmer & Henley *Slang* V. 89/2 'Chops is hoff' = 'there are no more chops to-day'. **1933** [see *bawl *v.* 3 c]. **1953** 'M. Innes' *Christmas at Candleshoe* ii. 24 The celerity with which the less unpalatable dishes are prone to be 'off' in English hotels. **1966** N. Freeling *Dresden Green* II. 123 Sorry sir, said the waitress in the teashop, the pudding's *off*. We can do you a nice ice-cream though. **1974** D. Chantler *Man who Followed* II. 60 Tell the waiters..the Tutti-Frutti is off.

4. d. Away or free from one's work, school, service, etc.

1861 J. O'Neil *Diary* 1 Apr. in J. Burnett *Useful Toil* (1974) I. 78 At Low Moor there is a great many off. There is above a hundred looms standing. **1882** J. D. McCabe *New York* 384 Then begins five hours' patrol..after which he is 'off'. **1883,** etc. [see *day off* s.v. *day *sb.* 19]. **1885,** etc. [see *night *sb.* 5 a]. **1916** B. Ruck *Girls at his Billet* xviii. 242, I am sure your auntie..would be quite agreeable to letting us have the afternoon off for the ceremony. **1940** F. Sargeson *Man & Wife* (1944) 21 Of course Sally wasn't off for long. And they gave her a rise. **1970** 'D. Halliday' *Dolly & Cookie Bird* v. 74, I was..bedding the avocados in lettuce. Anne-Marie was off but Helmuth did the last stages. *Ibid.* viii. 128 It was Anne-Marie's afternoon off.

6. b. Of stocks, shares, etc.: lower in value or price (by a specified amount or numbered points).

1929 *Times* 30 Oct. 14/1 Duke Power 'opened' at 130 off 39½ points, Newhaven Railway at 90 off 18. **1931** *Daily Express* 21 Sept. 14/4 Japanese bonds were only slightly off. **1964** *Financial Times* 12 Mar. 21/5 Belfast Ropework were 6d off to 35s 6d. **1977** *Times* 19 Nov. 17/5 By the close the *FT* Index was just 0·5 off at 480·5.

c. with ellipsis of *taken*. Of retail commodities: reduced in price by a specified amount.

1965 *New Statesman* 9 Apr. 562/1 Don't be put off by the fact that both packets also say '3d off'. **1966** 'J. Ashford' *Consider Evidence* i. 5 Tomato soup was being sold at threepence a tin off. **1968** 'J. Le Carré' *Small Town in Germany* v. 71 Don't matter what you fancy: radios, dish-washers, cars; he'll get you a bit off, like.

7. b. (Further examples.) Also *colloq.*

1824 J. Wight *Mornings at Bow St.* 21 Two young men ..were charged by a watchman with having 'bother'd him on his *bate*,' and refused to 'go along off of it when he *tould* 'em.' **1843** T. C. Haliburton *Attaché* 1st Ser. II. xii. 210 The groom has stole her oats, forgot to give her water, and let her make a supper sometimes off of her nasty, mouldy, filthy beddin'. **1884** 'Mark Twain' *Huck. Finn* vi. 32 I'd borrow two or three dollars off of the judge for him. *a* **1922** T. S. Eliot *Waste Land Drafts* (1971) 5 The reputation the place gets, off of a few barflies. **1962** F. Norman *Guntz* i. 15, I got hold of this very very old typewriter off of a friend of mine. *Ibid.* iii. 24 After his secretary had picked him off of the floor he got on the blower to his accounts department. **1965** T. Parker *Five Women* i. 45 They'll thieve off-of anyone and jump in bed with anyone. **1974** J. Stubbs *Painted Face* xxiii. 284 Get off of me, will you, sir?

13. Used with a preceding numeral to represent a quantity in production or manufacture, esp. *one off* (see *one 29* b).

1934, etc. [see *one 29 b]. **1947** Crowther & Whiddington *Science at War* 49 Manufacturers found it very difficult to give up mass production, in order to make the 200 or so sets 'off'. **1970** *Cabinet Maker & Retail Furnisher* 30 Oct. 205/2 Without barrier coats mould breakdown can start after 60 units off. **1973** *Physics Bull.* Apr. 238/2 (Advt.), Kienzle printers. 6 off, surplus to manufacturing requirements.

B. *prep.* **5. b.** (Further examples.) Also, having lost interest in; averse to; *off form*: in bad form; *off one's game*: see *GAME *sb.* 6 f.

Transfer quot. 1894 in Dict. to sense 1 b.

1807 SCOTT *Let.* 14 Mar. (1932) I. 359 This principle that the pursuers are entitled to have their time compensated when they were *bona fide* off work. **1853** MRS. GASKELL *Cranford* iv. 74, I had a note to say her mistress was 'very low and sadly off her food'. **1889** E. DOWSON *Let.* 16 Nov. (1967) 117 You are perhaps right in being 'off' Gortsachoff's though the cooking is less deleterious than Pinolis. **1909** W. B. YEATS *Let.* 10 Dec. (1954) 544 She seemed as eager as ever about the play. I had thought she was off it. **1910** *Ibid.* 8 Jan. 546, I have not touched the long play but will come to it fresh from being so long off it. **1912** C. MATHEWSON *Pitching in a Pinch* vii. 142 The Chicago pitchers were away off form in the series. **1913** C. MACKENZIE *Sinister St.* I. II. xviii. 452 He said he was 'off girls' at the moment. **1929** E. BOWEN *Last Sept.* xxiv. 308 'What about their bungalow?' 'Oh, that was just an idea; they are quite off it.' **1973** 'H. CARMICHAEL' *Too Late for Tears* xiii. 153 I'm off my food, that's all.

9. In combs. with *the* and a sb., used *attrib.* or as *adj.*, as **off-the-course,** occurring away from a race-course; **off-the-face,** of a hat: not covering or shading any part of the face; **off-the-job,** (*a*) done or happening away from one's work; (*b*) unemployed; **off-the-rack** = **off-the-peg*; **off-the-road,** located, operated, or occurring away from roads; **off-the-shelf,** obtained from stock; ready-made; also *fig.* Also *off-the-cuff, off-the-map, off-the-peg, off-the-shoulder*; see these sbs.

1961 *Times* 2 June 22/2 She makes a tremendous off-the-course bet. **1908** *Sears, Roebuck Catal.* 1036/2 Pretty 'off the face' hat for children. **1953** *News Chron.* 2 June 1/4 The Queen Mother, in a white feathered gown and off-the-face white hat. **1962** *Guardian* 3 Oct. 8/2 Off-the-job training of men over 25 for semi-skilled work. **1967** *Time* 21 July 51 Some sort of new company-financed plan enabling an off-the-job worker to maintain 'his normal living standard' for up to a year. **1970** *Times* 9 Feb. 19 The off-the-job study is essential because it removes the pressures and distractions of the shop-floor. **1970** *Capital Times* (Madison, Wisconsin) 21 Feb. (Green Sheet Sect.) 4/2 An off-the-rack mod suit. **1974** H. WAUGH *Parrish for Defence* (1975) xxxvii. 173 The dress wasn't made for it [*sc.* her figure]. That was the trouble with off-the-rack clothes. **1975** 'A. THACKERAY' *One Way Ticket* i. 24 He wore off-the-rack clothes. **1962** *Guardian* 4 Oct. 14/2 Off-the-road training grounds for learner drivers. **1973** *Country Life* 18 Oct. 1172/2 Another type of off-the-road transport is the all-terrain vehicle, or ATV. **1966** *Electronics* 17 Oct. 38 The fact that its roll in a normal ocean is only 1° means that off-the-shelf, land-rated equipment can be used. **1971** *Engineering* Apr. 88 (Advt.), No chance of errors and 'off-the-shelf' service.

C. *adj.* **2. a.** Also *off lead, leader, ox* (also *fig.*, a clumsy or stubborn person), *wheeler.*

1807 *Balance* (Hudson, N.Y.) 25 Aug. 267 (Th.), We behold a clumsy, awkward off ox trying the tricks of a kitten. **1823** J. F. COOPER *Pioneers* I. iv. 51, I knew just the spot where to touch the off-leader. **1848** J. R. LOWELL *Biglow Papers* 1st Ser. 90 Ez to the answerin' o' questions, I'm an off ox at bein' druv. **1887** E. CUSTER *Tenting on Plains* xii. 354 The old reliability of a mule-team is the off-wheeler. **1890** KIPLING *Barrack-Room Ballads* (1892) 35 Two's off-lead 'e answered to the name o' *Snarleyow*. **1910** J. HART *Vigilante Girl* x. 140 An iron 'jockey-stick' ran from the near leader's hames to the off-leader's bit. **1915** *Dialect Notes* IV. 209 My grandfather was always an off-ox. **1933** *Daily Progress* (Charlottesville, Va.) 1 Apr. 4/3, I don't know him from Adam's (or God's) off-ox.

b. (Earlier and later examples.) Also of a ball or hit on this side, or a batsman who hits the ball in this direction; **off-cutter,** a cutter (see *CUTTER *sb.*[1] 5 b (*b*)) that turns from the off side.

1773 in G. B. Buckley *Fresh Light on 18th Cent. Cricket* (1935) 61 Having run a considerable number of notches from off-strokes. **1816** W. LAMBERT *Instr. & Rules Cricket* 31 Wide Bowling..should be directed at the off side of the wicket. **1836** *New Sporting Mag.* July 195 Crossing the leg over at off-balls is another rule that I should like to see more men adopt. *Ibid.*, The mode of handling the bat, for 'On hitting' must be similar to what is requisite for 'Off hitting'. **1836** E. JESSE *Angler's Rambles* 298 His off-hits between point and slip, were the admiration of the club. **1851** J. PYCROFT *Cricket Field* vii. 151 A good off-hitter should send the ball according to its pitch, not to one point only, but to three or four. **1854** *Ibid.* (ed. 2) 117 A bat brought forward from the centre stump to a ball Off or to leg, must..form an angle sufficient to make Off or On hits. **1885** *J. Lillywhite's Cricketers' Compan.* 91 Mr. W. H. Woodhouse..a brilliant off-hitter. **1888** A. G. STEEL in Steel & Lyttelton *Cricket* iii. 183 Left-handed batsmen are notoriously strong and powerful in their off hitting. **1895** H. G. HUTCHINSON *P. Steele* i. 28 This off-ball Peter..drove..so hard..that [etc.]. **1900** P. F. WARNER *Cricket in Many Climes* 182 Blanckenberg..made some very good off-side strokes. **1904** F. C. HOLLAND *Cricket* 9 Nearly all off strokes can be classed under one of the four principal hits—the off drive, the cut drive, the square cut, and the late cut. **1955** *Times* 5 July 4/2 Singh..was making his off-cutters seem more sinister than one feels they really were. **1956** R. ALSTON *Test Commentary* xiii. 114 Benaud packed the off-side. **1966** [see *CUTTER *sb.*[1] 5 b].

c. *off-verse* [tr. G. *Abvers*]: the second half-line of a line of Old English verse. Cf. *on-verse* (*ON *a.* 1 b).

1935 K. MALONE in *ELH* II. 291 The chief function of alliteration in OE poetry is that of binding together the two halves (i.e. the on- and off-verses) of the so-called long line. **1953** [see *ICTUS 1]. **1953** *Speculum* XXVIII. 451 In the on-verse position *Béowulf* 2795 has *Wuldorcyninge* and in the off-verse position *eorþ-, héah- þéodcyninges*, also *Frīs-cyninge*, and *sǣ-cyninga*. **1963** F. P. MAGOUN in Brown & Foote *Early Eng. & Norse Stud.* 134 These verses tend to be used as off-verses. **1970** *Rev. Eng. Stud.* XXI. 134 The Anglo-Saxon poets apparently preferred beginning new clauses with the off-verse.

4. (Earlier and further examples.) Also said of a shorter period of time to denote an interval of leisure or relaxation, and of a day, night, etc., when one does not feel fit or when one's performance is not up to the usual standard. Also *transf.*

1826 F. REYNOLDS *Life & Times* I. iv. 151 On Mrs. Siddons's nights, Mr. Harris (being sure of an overflow from Drury-lane,) only put up his weakest bills, reserving the strongest for his *off nights*. **1843** *Knickerbocker* XXII. 325 After an 'off night' when I was allowed to stay in town. **1875** *All Year Round* 3 Apr. 23/1 That estimable lady.. had arranged those meetings on the quiet off-evenings. **1876** 'MARK TWAIN' *Old Times Mississippi* 25 The 'off-watch' was just turning in, and I heard some brutal laughter from them. **1880** *Inter-Ocean* (Chicago) 28 May 8/3 Peters had an 'off' day. **1905** G. B. SHAW *Let.* 3 Jan. (1972) II. 487, I had quiet literary offnights at the New Shakespear Society under F. J. Furnival, and breezy literary offnights at the Browning Society. **1908** *Sketch* 11 Sept. 340/2 Rhodes had an 'off-day' and could do nothing. **1913** A. G. BRADLEY *Other Days* v. 161 On the rare off-days [we] raided such crows and magpies' nests as we could find. **1928** *Weekly Dispatch* 18 Mar. 2/4 He'd never have picked up that skill in the Lagos Lagoon in the few off-watches he'd get from a branch-boat. **1929** *Star* 21 Aug. 5/2 It was certainly Elder's off-night. He was not feeling in the best of form. **1930** F. E. BAILY *It won't do any Harm* xiii. 260 You happened to ask me when I was in what I call an off-moment. **1932** E. E. REYNOLDS *Nansen* i. 9. There was plenty of fun as well as hard work. One account of an off-hour is worth extracting as illustrating Nansen's geniality in whatever company he might find himself. **1946** R. LEHMANN *Gipsy's Baby* 28 She was having a bit of an off-day, unfortunately. **1959** *Manch. Guardian* 24 July 4/2 Tolstoy or Balzac in an off-moment might be almost anyone. **1959** T. GRIFFITH *Waist-High Culture* (1960) 169 Such doubts arise in us all, at least on our off days. **1969** *Guardian* 21 Aug. 3/6 On off-days he tends his private camellias and on off-nights listens to Mozart and The Three B's. **1974** *Melody Maker* 13 Apr. 48 Everyone has their off nights and so the one who's feeling better helps the other one. **1976** *National Observer* (U.S.) 17 Jan. 19/2 Dr. Moskowitz is passionate about reading, theater, music, and writing, which is her newest off-hours activity.

b. *off year*, in the U.S., a year in which there is a Congressional election but no Presidential election. Also *attrib.*

1873 B. A. HINSDALE *Let.* 17 Oct. in *Garfield-Hinsdale Lett.* (1949) 247 About one half is lost because it is the 'off year' in politics. **1906** *N.Y. Even. Post* 5 Nov. 4 In this off-year election. **1950** *Manch. Guardian Weekly* 24 Aug. 15 A full-dress State election in an 'off-year', that is a year when there is no Presidential election. **1972** *Times* 27 Dec. 5/7 Soon after he succeeded to the Presidency the Republicans, in the off-year elections of 1946, won both Houses of Congress.

6. Corresponding to or producing the state (of an electrical device) of being off (OFF *adv.* 4 b).

1899 J. PIGG *Railway 'Block' Signalling* vii. 363 In the 'off' position of the signal arm the switch makes such contacts as passes a 'holding down' current from the battery at the local station. **1935** D. L. SAYERS *Gaudy Night* xvi. 327 The switch..stood in the 'Off' position, and she struck it down. **1960** *Practical Wireless* XXXVI. 425/2 A two-pole toggle switch..could be used in the S1 position thus isolating the mains completely from the equipment when the switch is in the 'off' position. **1975** L. DEIGHTON *Yesterday's Spy* vii. 52 Schlegel bashed the 'off' button and the music ended with a loud click.

7. *Physiol.* Of, pertaining to, or exhibiting the electrical activity that occurs briefly in some optic nerve fibres in vertebrates when illumination of the retina ceases.

1903 F. GOTCH in *Jrnl. Physiol.* XXIX. 393 The third or terminal portion is a second rise due to the sudden change from light to darkness; this I propose for brevity to term the OFF effect. *Ibid.* 401 The rate of development of the OFF change. *Ibid.* 403 In no instance is the OFF delay greater than the ON. **1934** *Ibid.* LXXXI. 26 The increase in P III and its rapid return at 'off' account for the increased off-effect of the light-adapted eye. **1941** S. H. BARTLEY *Vision* xii. 287 The off-response first appears when the light flash is very short. **1948** *Jrnl. Physiol.* CVII. 57 Of the 164 elements, 16% were pure on-elements, 5% pure off-elements, and 79% on-off-elements. *Ibid.*, The on-sensitivity to blue (*B*-on) was taken as the fundamental sensitivity... For those elements which showed no on-effect the off-sensitivity to blue (*B*-off) was used. **1972** H. TAMAR *Princ. Sensory Physiol.* iv. 153/2 Some 5 per cent of all color-responsive ganglion cells seem really to have receptive fields with centers which are either 'on' or 'off' to one color.

D. *sb.* **3.** (Earlier and later examples.) Hence **off-drive** *v. trans.*, to drive (a ball) towards the off; also with the bowler as object; so *off-driver, off-driving*; **off-theory,** a theory that favours concentrating the fielders on the off side and bowling the ball at or outside the off stump.

1836 *New Sporting Mag.* XI. 193 Thus if the bat be brought forward in a straight line to meet the ball moving in the same line, the ball will be struck directly to the bowler. It is on this principle, that more to the on or off, so will it be returned, and according as it is bowled, more to his left or right. **1847** [see *BREAK *v.* 32 b]. **1867** *Australasian* 2 Feb. 140/2 He made a very good off drive for four. **1883** W. L. MURDOCH in *Longman's Mag.* Jan. 292 At the present time, when bowlers place their men on the off side and bowl on what I might term the 'off theory', batsmen should be very careful what ball they hit at. **1884** *J. Lillywhite's Cricketers' Ann.* 5 Leslie's 144 was an example of that player's very best style, his..off-driving being masterly. **1893** R. DAFT *Kings of Cricket* vi. 103 C. G. Lane..could, I think, 'off drive' Jackson better than any other player of the day. **1904** F. C. HOLLAND *Cricket* 10 Ernest Hayes of Surrey is as hard an off-driver as any. **1927** G. A. TERRILL *Out in Glare* v. 95 Clement played his first ball defensively;..off-drove the next for three. **1955** *Times* 13 July 8/5 Off the third ball of what might have been the penultimate over Waite off-drove Tyson over the top of Lock. **1960** H. S. ALTHAM in A. Ross *Cricketer's Compan.* 292 The off-theory was being to some extent abandoned. **1963** *Times* 13 Feb. 4/3 A slightly mistimed off-drive led to a fine catch by Knight, running around in front of the screen. **1975** *Cricketer* May 14/2 Max Walker showed his 'leg-cutter' that snapped back from the off. **1977** *Guardian* 3 Jan. 11/6 Greig began by off driving Chandra for four.

5. The start of a race (cf. sense A. 1 e above); also *transf.*, the start, the beginning; departure; a signal to start or depart. *colloq.*

1959 *Times* 14 Sept. 3/1 Matthews broke once and on the second 'off' knocked down the first hurdle. **1963** L. Meynell *Virgin Luck* vii. 174 The price shortened and just before the 'off' I noticed it was being offered at nine to two. **1966** J. PORTER *Sour Cream* xiv. 180 It was too late. The students nearest to him..thought this was the off. They began to move forward. **1968** 'H. CALVIN' *Miranda must Die* iii. 34 'Time for off,' he said... He was gone. **1973** T. ALLBEURY *Choice of Enemies* xiii. 62 Jock..waited for someone to give him the off, and James said, 'O.K. Jock, you just give us the general picture.' **1973** 'I. DRUMMOND' *Jaws of Watchdog* xviii. 240 How long before the off will they try to put the poison in? **1978** *Lancashire Life* Apr. 50 (*caption*) Tangle-wrangle: Stan Lyons waits on the slipway for the 'off', while helpers sort-out the lines from his harness.

off, *v.* Add: **2.** (Earlier and later examples.) Cf. OFF *adv.* 9. Also *to off it*, to depart; also (*slang*), to die.

1889 T. E. BROWN *Manx Witch* 18 'And will you go linkin with me?' says Jack... 'I'm thinkin I'd better,' says Nessy... And offs with him. **1890** *Punch* 28 June 310/2 He found out after they'd off'd it that they didn't own a white mouse among 'em! **1930** J. BUCHAN *Castle Gay* iv. 72 He has probably offed it abroad. **1930** BROPHY & PARTRIDGE *Songs & Slang 1914–18* 143 *Off it*, to die. **1965** *Listener* 27 May 797/2 He ups and offs from wife, job, kids.

6. To kill.

Recorded chiefly in Black English contexts in the U.S.

1968 N. GIOVANNI *Revolutionary Tale* in *Negro Digest* June 77/1 The only way we can ever justify offing a brother is if we have already offed twenty whiteys. **1970** *Time* 11 May 29 At the swamp, Alex was offed... Warren shot him first, Lonnie hit him a second time. **1970** *Time* 2 Nov. 25/1 The Panthers' rhetoric is inflammatory and irresponsible, and it is impossible to say how many people take their 'off the pig' injunctions seriously. **1971** *Black Scholar* Sept. 40/2 If they caught a bitch or dude fuckin' around with the honkies, they offed 'em. **1974** R. B. PARKER *Godwulf Manuscript* (U.S. ed.) iii. 18 There were various recommendations about pigs being offed scrawled on the sidewalk. **1977** *Time* 31 Jan. 52/1 There is a contract out on him and he will be offed as sure as next morning's sunrise.

off-, *prefix.* Add: **4. b.** With sbs. used *attrib.* or as *adj.*, as **off-course,** situated or taking place away from a race-course; **off-design,** that is not allowed for or expected; of or pertaining to such circumstances; **off-farm,** produced or sold away from a farm; **off-gold,** of a nation: not using the gold standard; **off-highway,** of or pertaining to travel that is not on highways; **off-ice,** of or pertaining to ice-hockey players when they are not engaged in a game; **off-pitch** *Mus.*, of a note: not of the correct pitch; **off-road,** used or taking place away from roads; **off-site,** occurring away from a site; removed from a site; **off-track,** (*a*) that is off one's intended route; (*b*) done away from a race-track (*spec.* of betting). See also main entries: OFF-COLOUR etc. in Dict., *OFF-AIR etc. in Suppl.

1963 *Times* 7 Mar. 3/2 Those who bet on racecourses and have off-course businesses as well must include the net profit of the racecourse business when determining their category. **1964** A. WYKES *Gambling* viii. 195 In France, bookmaking is illegal; and the law against off-course, non-totalizator gambling is strictly enforced. **1977** *Times* 2 Apr. 14/2 If it [*sc.* the Tote] had a monopoly of off-course betting..it could provide..£35m a year for racing. **1962** S. L. BRAGG *Rocket Engines* ii. 34 Its performance at off-design pressure ratios is better than that of a conventional nozzle. **1972** *Lebende Sprachen* XVII. 134/1 Motors designed for high altitude use are frequently tested under off-design conditions. **1962** *Economist* 24 Mar. 1098/2 Target prices for off-farm dairy products ..are pitched at a much lower level. **1963** *Times* 11 Jan. 9/3 In agriculture the slow progress of both total output and off-farm sales has meant that the income of the collective farm economy has not risen fast enough. **1935** *Economist* 20 Apr. 900/2 The bulk of their trade is done with off-gold countries, and in commodities whose prices are determined by conditions in those off-gold countries. **1961** *Engineering* 10 Nov. 626 The problem of off-highway mobility. **1968** *Globe Mag.* (Toronto) 17 Feb. 5 There are now lucrative possibilities in many parts of North America for Leafs who once sold their off-ice services, personal appearances and so on very cheap. **1945** Off-pitch [see *BLUE *a.* 3 d]. **1961** *Engineering* 10 Nov. 628 Spheres of off-road and industrial haulage. **1968** *Economist* 21 Sept. 82/2 The new engine..is more suited..to off-road vehicles (dump trucks and earth movers of all sorts). **1973** *Observer* (Colour Suppl.) 2 Sept. 51/3 Off-road racing started in California about seven years ago with the development of beach buggies and other fun cars. **1975** *Courier-Mail* (Brisbane) 11 Apr. 16/2 Off-road and recreational vehicles are becoming more and more popular. **1969** *Ibid.* 22 Feb. 14/2 Anybody involved in a fight is automatically 'off site' on the next plane. In other words all parties involved lose not only their jobs but their accommodation and have to find a new town. **1970** *Guardian* 22 Aug. 2/4 Underground nuclear explosions in Nevada..would have negligible off-site effects. **1956** WALLIS & BLAIR *Thunder Above* (1959) i. 7 He could have deviated up into Scotland for an off-track landing at Prestwick. **1964** A. WYKES *Gambling* 340 Whereas the on-track betting turnover was the equivalent of $64,680,000, off-track betting brought in $65,240,000. The only legal way to make an off-track bet is through the Totalization Agency Board. **1970** *Globe & Mail* (Toronto) 26 Sept. B1/1 Very little of the money bet through off-track messenger betting shops reaches the pari-mutuel machines. **1976** *Times* 20 Mar. 14/6 Many off-track activities including a *concours d'elegance* of classic road cars.

5. Prefixed to the names of colours to denote colours that are almost the same as the colour specified, as *off-black*, *-green*, *-yellow*; also *OFF-WHITE *sb.* and *a.*

1927, etc. [see *OFF-WHITE *sb.* and *a.*]. **1930** *Daily Express* 8 Sept. 5 One of the new off-black shades.., a sort of unripe blackberry colour, is used for the third model. **1958** J. BETJEMAN *Coll. Poems* 250 The walls are alternately painted Off-yellow and festival mauve. **1960** *Guardian* 9 Dec. 8/5 A feeling for the gentler blues and off-greens. **1978** *Detroit Free Press* 2 Apr. 10D (Advt.), Colors included..nocturne (off-black).

offa (ǫ·fă). Repr. U.S. colloq. pronunc. of *off of* (see OFF *adv.* 7 b in Dict. and Suppl.).

1935 Z. N. HURSTON *Mules & Men* II. i. 233 Ah keeps her offa me too. **1954** W. TUCKER *Wild Talent* (1955) iv. 43 Roll your tail offa there and come on! **1973** *Black World* Jan. 65/2 She just couldn't take her eyes offa me. **1976** G. V. HIGGINS *Judgement D. Hunter* xiii. 128 Get offa the pot, willya?

off-ai·r, *a.* and *adv.* [*OFF- 4 b, OFF *prep.* + AIR *sb.*[1]] **A.** *adj.* **a.** Operating on a closed circuit; not involving the broadcasting of programmes.

1961 *Times* 2 June 14/6 (Advt.), The ship of the year.. relies on Marconi Marine..for closed circuit television. A completely co-ordinated internal and 'off-air' television system—..providing passengers with closed circuit telecine and live television programmes.

b. Involving the transmission of programmes by broadcasting.

1971 *Morning Star* 10 Dec. 4/1 An attempt to prevent the allocation to ITV of Britain's last off-air television channel. **1975** *ITV Evidence to Annan Committee* i. 30 The cable companies are eager..to deliver programmes into homes by cable rather than from off-air transmission by the IBA and the BBC. **1977** *Rep. Comm. Future of Broadcasting* (Cmnd. 6753) xiv. 218 The Cable Television Association..saw no reason why those who currently contribute to off-air television should not also participate in programme making for cable television.

c. Carried out or done from received broadcast transmissions.

1973 *B.B.C. Handbk. 1974* 45/2 The off-air recording of educational programmes by educational institutions is another problem. **1980** *Amat. Photographer* 15 Mar. 119 (*caption*) Transferring film to video tape... Tuner/timer (for 'off-air' recording).

B. *adv.* From broadcast transmissions.

1974 *Author* Winter 149 A video cassette player/recorder ..will..record off-air (you can record BBC 1 while watching ITV or BBC 2). **1975** *ITV Evidence to Annan Committee* i. 31 The cable companies, if they are to offer anything more than is already available off-air, will be forced to provide a menu of feature films and big sporting occasions. **1977** *Gramophone* June 124/1 The BBC's Matrix H tapes (including one recorded 'off-air') were as good a compromise as I have heard.

off-a·xis, *a.* and *adv.* [f. *OFF- 4 b, OFF *prep.* + AXIS[1].] (Situated) away from an axis.

1939 *Sci. Amer.* Aug. 120/2 The 'off-axis' type..is exceedingly useful in practice because, with this arrangement. the photographic plate or film may be placed outside the light beam. **1962** A. NISBETT *Technique Sound Studio* ii. 36 Place the second person just the same amount off-axis in the other direction. **1971** J. H. RICHARDSON *Optical Microscopy for Materials Sci.* i. 47 Even though a lens may be spherically corrected for objects situated on the microscope axis, spherical aberration may exist for off-axis objects.

off base, off-base, *phr.* (*adv.*) and *a.* [OFF *prep.*, *OFF- 4 b.] **1.** Unawares, off one's guard, by surprise; mistaken. Cf. *BASE *sb.*[1] 15 d. *U.S.*

1936 J. STEINBECK *In Dubious Battle* vii. 109 If they can catch us off base, they'll bounce us. **1947** *Time* 20 Oct. 11/1 Your Latin American department was off base in its comparison of the Portillo Hotel in Chile with our famous Sun Valley. **1948** *Daily Ardmoreite* (Ardmore, Okla.) 26 May 6/4 There are more men caught off base at cocktail parties than ball games. **1955** W. C. GAULT *Ring around Rosa* vii. 88 You're way off base, Bobby, and I think this kind of talk is in poor taste. **1971** B. MALAMUD *Tenants* 141, I don't feel lovely. I feel off-base, off-key, dissatisfied. **1974** *Publishers Weekly* 18 Mar. 43/1 Off base with his moralizing, an innocent in economics, overshadowed by the Kennedys.

2. Situated elsewhere than on a military base (BASE *sb.*[1] 16 and *16 b).

1962 *Economist* 1 Dec. 921/2, 136 families live on the base, 220 in an off-base village. **1967** *Ibid.* 30 Sept. 1196/3 The defence establishment has often been a pioneer in ending the colour bar, both at its own installations and 'off-base'. *Ibid.*, To fight off-base discrimination against Negro Soldiers. **1977** R. GADNEY *Champagne Marxist* xiv. 92 'I'd like to speak with you.' 'Fine.' 'Off-base?' 'Of course, if that's what you want.'

off beam, off-beam, *phr.*, *a.*, and *adv. colloq.* Also **off the beam.** [f. OFF *prep.*, *OFF- 4 b + *BEAM *sb.*[1] 24 c.] On the wrong track; wrong, mistaken.

1951 'J. TEY' *Daughter of Time* ix. 121 'He's away off the beam. Away off.' 'I suspected as much. Let us have the facts.' **1958** *Woman* 20 Sept. 4/4 Funny how we all get off-beam ideas of each other, isn't it? **1960** *Spectator* 20 May 729 My thinking, which was quite off-beam, convinced me at that time that the man was a charlatan. **1973** *Guardian* 15 Feb. 14/4 Mr Patrick is far from off-beam in tracing connections between environment and the behaviour he describes. **1977** *Time Out* 17–23 June 10/3 'A Question of Ulster' was not only way off beam for explanation, it was also five years ago.

off-bearer. (Earlier and further examples.)

1866 *5th Rep. Children's Employment Commission* 142/1 in *Parl. Papers* XXIV. 1 The walk flatter is often a young woman, and the off-bearer a young man. **1887** A. A. BROWN *Lumbering on the Cumberland* 47 Caleb occupied the position of honor, and acted as 'sawyer'. Abe was 'setter', and Eph was 'off-bearer'. **1939** D. HARTLEY *Made in England* v. 170 In one shed there seemed to be about six workers, and their names indicated their share of the job; 'moulder', 'temperer', 'off-bearer', [etc.].

o·ff-beat, *sb.* and *a.* [f. OFF *prep.*, *OFF- 4 b + BEAT *sb.*[1]] **A.** *sb. Mus.* An unaccented beat; = UPBEAT *sb.* 1; *spec.* the second or fourth beat in common time; a heavy accent on these beats.

1928 *Grove's Dict. Mus.* (ed. 3) V. 424/2 It is therefore in the nature of things that much music should begin on the offbeat. *Ibid.*, It is convenient to confine 'upbeat' to the last of the bar, leaving 'offbeat' for any other note than the first. **1946** A. HUTCHINGS in A. L. Bacharach *Brit. Music* xvi. 205 A rhythmic figure..beginning on an off-beat so that its entry in another part will be effective and beget movement. **1958** C. WILFORD in P. Gammond *Decca Bk. Jazz* ii. 31 The pianist's left hand marks the beat firmly and unvaryingly, usually also with sharply staccato off-beats. **1973** J. WAINWRIGHT *Pride of Pigs* 175 The washboard player tapped the off-beats with the tips of his thimbles.

B. *adj.* **1.** *Mus.* Of, pertaining to, or comprising off-beats; having a marked rhythm on the off-beats. Also *transf.*

1927 *Melody Maker* Sept. 926/2 In a thirty-two bar passage the rhythm might appear thus: Six bars 'off-beat', two bars 'charleston', six bars 'four in a bar', [etc.]. **1936** *Metronome* Feb. 61/2 *Off beat cymbal*, sock cymbal. **1952** J. STEINBECK *East of Eden* xvi. 151 Samuel Hamilton rode back home... Doxology's loud off-beat hoofsteps silenced the night people until after he had passed. **1959** D. COOKE *Lang. Mus.* v. 263 Another 'oom-pah' bass without the 'oom' (the cheapest of jazz-rhythms, emphasized by off-beat side-drum taps). **1970** P. OLIVER *Savannah Syncopators* 15 Off-beat phrasing of melodic accents.

2. Unusual, unconventional; strange, eccentric. *colloq.* (orig. *U.S.*).

Occas. with even stress.

1938 D. BAKER *Young Man with Horn* I. iv. 35 He tried ..to teach him to sweep with a utilitarian slant, all the strokes going in the same direction in such a way that.. you inevitably have a pile of whatever it is, right there in front of your broom... But..Smoke would go right back into his off-beat swishing. **1951** *N.Y. Herald-Tribune* 13 Dec. 34 The author..has a highly individual wit, a fey and off-beat slant on the process of making people laugh. **1958** S. ELLIN *Eighth Circle* (1959) II. xiii. 140 One of those types who are a little offbeat when they talk to you. **1958** *Economist* 13 Dec. 993/1 The most important postwar development has been the enormous popularity of the 'off-beat' greeting card, which was first introduced seven or eight years ago. **1959** *Observer* 5 Apr. 11/4 It is the off-beat things, the eccentricities, that help give salerooms their perpetual appeal and surprise. **1960** P. CARSWELL (*title*) Offbeat spirituality. **1963** [see *FAR-OUT *a.* b]. **1967** *Daily Tel.* 16 Feb. 15/5 Suzanne Hywel, 23, looks off-beat but in fact has a yearning for the country that she left behind in Kent. **1976** *Times* 9 Aug. 10/1 One of London's oldest adult education institutions ran an off-beat course for reviewing the arts.

Hence **off-beatness,** the quality of being 'off-beat'; unconventionality.

1960 *Guardian* 11 Oct. 7/2 There is no deliberate off-beatness about her. **1962** J. M. BERNSTEIN tr. *Levi's Two-Fold Night* i. 7 There is..a hint of 'off-beatness' in their conformism, which is the city's tradition.

off-board, *a. U.S.* [f. *OFF- 4 b + *BOARD *sb.* 8 c.] Of stocks, bonds, etc.: dealt in or sold elsewhere than at the stock exchange; = *OVER THE COUNTER *adv.* (*a.*) a.

1950 in WEBSTER Add. **1968** *Economist* 6 Jan. 56/2 It is suspected in Wall Street that the agency's wily staff goes out of its way to prop up those offboard markets mainly to keep 'sassy' Wall Streeters off balance. **1977** *N.Y. Times* 14 Nov. 53/4 Most brokerage and investment banking firms, however, agree that the eventual elimination of what are called 'off-board trading restrictions' is inevitable.

off-break, *sb.* [OFF- 3.] **1.** The act or result of breaking off; a schism.

1866 W. GREGOR *Dial. Banffshire* 7 in *Trans. Philol. Soc.* The Free-kirk's an aff-brack fae the Aul' Kirk. **1892** [see OFF- 3]. **1934** *Discovery* Mar. 60/1 The line offering the most advantageous terrain must be carefully observed, glacier off-breaks noted, where and how often breaks occur.

2. *Cricket.* A ball bowled in such a way that, on pitching, it changes direction towards the leg side; such a change of direction. Also *attrib.*

1888 A. G. STEEL in Steel & Lyttleton *Cricket* iii. 117 The next spin or twist on the ball..is the rotary motion from left to right. This, in cricket phraseology, is termed the 'off' break. **1903** G. L. JESSOP in H. G. Hutchinson *Cricket* v. 134. On a bad wicket and with an off-break bowler the position of short leg is indispensable. **1927** G. A. TERRILL *Out in Glare* iv. 74 If the spin meant the usual off-break, the ball was straighter than Verlenden had intended. It would break right away to leg. **1955**, **1963** [see *CHINAMAN 4].

o·ff-break, *v.* [OFF- 1.] **1.** *trans.* To break off, rescind. *Sc. rare*[—1].

1872 M. MACLENNAN *Peasant Life* (Ser. 2) 47 She winna be ony speckillation tae the pairish by offbraikin' the banns.

2. *intr. Cricket.* Of a ball: to break towards the leg side. Usu. as **o·ff-brea:king** *ppl. a.*

1904 *Westm. Gaz.* 10 Aug. 3/1 Mr. Bosanquet..dismissed three batsmen lbw with his 'off-breaking leg-break'. **1907** *Ibid.* 18 July 4/2 The off-breaking leg-break of the Bosanquet school has exercised a great influence over South African cricket.

off-Broadway (ǫ:fbrǭ·dwē͝i), *a.* and *sb.* orig. *U.S.* [f. OFF *prep.* + *BROADWAY.] **A.** *adj.* Of a theatre, play, or performer: located in, appearing in, or associated with an area of New York other than the Broadway theatrical area; esp. with reference to experimental productions. Also *transf.*

1953 *Plays & Players* Dec. 24/3 There are still two other plays to consider... The former began life at an off-Broadway theatre and after some revisions was brought to the Vanderbilt on October 14. **1954** *New Yorker* 9 Oct. 38/1 Making a new translation of 'The Wild Duck' for an off-Broadway production. **1959** CORDELL & MATSON (*title*) The off-Broadway theatre. **1965** *Listener* 20 May 738/2 The Theatre of Drama and Comedy—a sort of off-Broadway Muscovite theatre. **1970** [see *FIT-UP]. **1971** B. MALAMUD *Tenants* 31 The black said his chick was an Off-Broadway actress.

B. *sb.* Off-Broadway theatres or productions collectively.

1958 *Observer* 14 Dec. 14/4 The small downtown play-houses generically known as 'off-Broadway'. **1960** L. KAUFFMANN *Waldo* (1962) vi. 69 What I say is, off-Broadway is going downhill. **1966** *Saturday Night* (Toronto) Oct. 25 Off-Broadway, basing itself in and around the [Greenwich] Village area, began to rock the American theatre with Albee's plays and the latest works from Europe. **1973** *Black World* Apr. 28/2 Many theater people went to Harlem and off-Broadway in hopes of improving their careers.

Hence **off-off-Broadway,** a collective term for theatres or theatrical productions away from 'off-Broadway', esp. those that are experimental or avant-garde; also *attrib.* and *ellipt.* as *off-off*.

1967 *National Observer* (U.S.) 10 Apr. 20/1 It had to happen and it did. The small, experimental theater circuit known as 'Off-Off Broadway'—more simply, just plain OOB—is changing. **1967** *Sat. Rev.* (U.S.) 10 June 20 These off-off Broadway playwrights are emerging in a period when no producer can expect to present their unconventional works except at a financial loss. **1967** *Listener* 31 Aug. 266/2 Off-Broadway and off-off Broadway are for those who genuinely love theatre. **1968** *Guardian* 8 Oct. 5/3 Off-off Broadway..never takes place in a 'real' theatre; instead, Off-off Broadway uses cafés, rooms, lofts, churches. **1971** 'T. COE' *Jade in Aries* (1973) vi. 63 He's had a couple of things produced. In coffee houses, you know. Off-Off-Broadway. **1973** *Guardian* 1 Mar. 20/3 Pierre..produces an off off-Broadway version of Peter Pan where all the characters are played by actors over sixty. **1975** *Times* 26 Apr. 7/6 The Off-Off-Broadway scene has changed... Off-Off has turned into either grant-oriented classical or imported productions, or showcases for Broadway.

off camera, off-camera, *phr.* and *adv.* [f. OFF *prep.* + CAMERA.] Outside the range of a film or television camera; when not being filmed or televised.

1960 *News Chron.* 15 July 4/5 He is certainly the most telegenic personality of our time—yet off camera he is shy. **1970** *Guardian* 14 Nov. 8/3 Off camera Garbo..would display a charming naïveté very different from the sophistication of the rôles she played. **1973** L. SNELLING *Heresy* I. iii. 20 If Frank thinks I'm going to let that pretentious little prick..keep me off-camera..he's crazy. **1976** *Scotsman* 25 Nov. 15/4 Information on..cuts is passed to Rippon by the director at a moment when she is off-camera.

off-campus, *a.* and *adv.* orig. *U.S.* [f. *OFF- 4 b, OFF *prep.* + *CAMPUS.] Outside a campus; existing or available away from a campus. Also *ellipt.* as *sb.*
1951 M. McCarthy in *Holiday* May 162/2 Today, 'off-campus' for the students is mainly represented by Alumnae House. *Ibid.*, There is no compulsion on the part of the college that off-campus social life should be conducted under these auspices. **1965** *Times Lit. Suppl.* 25 Nov. 1057/3 The available off-campus communities were relatively few. **1969** *Listener* 8 May 632/1 Amnesty is another favourite word, and it means that student rioters shall not be bound by the laws that apply off-campus. **1972** *Sat. Rev.* (U.S.) 4 Mar. 23/3 Off-campus housing is tight and expensive. **1975** *New Yorker* 21 Apr. 8/3 It's no wonder that this wood- and brick-walled beer-and-hamburger haunt serves as an extracurricular, off-campus student union. **1978** *N.Y. Times* 30 Mar. A1/6 Most of the off-campus programs operated in Westchester have been set up in the last decade.

off centre, off-centre, *phr.* (*adv.*) and *a.* Also (*U.S.*) **-center.** [f. OFF *prep.*, *OFF- 4 b + CENTRE *sb.* and *a.*] Not quite coinciding with a central position, awry; wrong, mistaken; eccentric.
1929 D. Hammett *Dain Curse* (1930) xii. 127 He had gone off center, was a dangerous maniac. **1932** *Kansas City* (Missouri) *Times* 30 May 12 This dear old country of ours can't be so terribly off center. **1934** Webster, *Off-center, Philately*, of a stamp, having margins of unequal width. **1947** J. Steinbeck *Wayward Bus* xviii. 291 The scar on his lip made the smile off-center. **1952** L. A. G. Strong *Darling Tom* 12 A round mahogany table with a doily a little off-centre. **1958** *Observer* 25 May 16/7 Miss Anna Kavan's weird, off-centre art. **1960** *Times* 23 June 15/2 The need to write..cannot be assuaged without tugging the character of its victim a little off-centre. **1971** *Listener* 25 Nov. 714/3 An out-of-date idea hung onto by slightly off-centre intellectuals. **1975** J. Wainwright *Square Dance* 196 The arrival of the Watfords had thrown little Thelma more than slightly off-centre.

off-centre, *v.* Also (*U.S.*) **-center.** [f. prec.] *trans.* To place or position off centre. So **off-centred** *ppl.a.*, not central; eccentric; **off-centring** *vbl. sb.*, displacement from a centre.
1947 R. H. Müller in J. S. Hall *Radar Aids to Navigation* vii. 273 A point 70 miles from the radar site has been designated by the intersection of two straight lines. This appears on the scope, with an off-centering of about 1·5 radii. **1947** Miller & McLaughlin in *Ibid.* ix. 351 The off-center PPI is, unfortunately, rather badly distorted as soon as it is off-centered by more than one tube diameter. **1958** *Proc. Inst. Electr. Engin.* CV. B. Suppl. No. 8. 355/1 Few radars are capable of off-centring the display by any appreciable amount. **1973** *Sci. Amer.* Dec. 87/2 When Copernicus introduced his heliocentric arrangement, the earth became one of the family of planets revolving in off-centered circles around the sun.

off colour, off-colour, *phr.* and *a.* Add: Also (*U.S.*) **off color. 1.** Also, not in good health, slightly unwell. (Earlier and further examples.)
1876 B. Harte *Gabriel Conroy* II. IV. iv. 90 Mr Hamlin had not been well, or, as he more happily expressed it, had been 'off colour'. **1898** G. Giffen *With Bat & Ball* xi. 195 The devil with which the ball..seemed to rise from the pitch..made him a nasty bowler when the wicket was off-colour. **1898** G. B. Shaw *Mrs. Warren's Profession* III. 200 *Frank*: Off colour? *Rev. S.*: (repudiating the expression) No sir: unwell this morning. **1931** A. J. Cronin *Hatter's Castle* I. iv. 80, I haven't been myself at all these last few days—quite off colour. **1955** *Times* 10 Aug. 3/3 Hampshire if slightly off colour at the end, duly won at Portsmouth yesterday. **1966** 'J. Hackston' *Father clears Out* 86 He did not sit in the shed for just a while, as a man does when he suddenly feels off-colour. **1974** A. Fowles *Pastime* ii. 12 'Where's Christine?' he said. 'Over her mum's. Her mum's off colour. She's staying..till she picks up.'
2. (Earlier example.)
1860 A. de Barrera *Gems & Jewels* 164 If the manufactured diamond is found to contain a flaw, or what is technically termed 'off-color', its value is proportionately diminished.
3. Of questionable taste, disreputable, improper, indecent; esp. of jokes; risqué; hinting at obscenity; = DIRTY *a.* 2.
1875 J. G. Holland *Sevenoaks* in *Scribner's Monthly* Mar. 582/1 Everybody invited her, and yet every body, without any definite reason, considered her a little 'off color'. **1883** *National Police Gaz.* (U.S.) 17 Mar. 3/1 A few choice specimens of the off color morals and hypocritical manners of the stage. **1915** *Sat. Even. Post* 23 Jan. 27/3 It is almost inevitable that sooner or later some one would be moved to tell an off-color story. **1932** *Kansas City* (Missouri) *Times* 25 Mar. 21 It seemed a bit strange for a minister to be so devoted a reader of such a (then) decidedly off-color publication. **1952** [see *FEST]. **1954** Koestler *Invis. Writing* 58 It was still possible among intimate friends to pass on a joke that was politically off colour. **1958** *Spectator* 20 June 803/2 Landladies with their slangy off-colour jokes. **1972** 'G. Black' *Bitter Tea* (1973) iv. 56 He had never played an off-colour commercial trick on me, possibly because I had never given him the chance.

off-coloured, *a.* (Further examples.)
1904 *Daily Chron.* 18 May 3/4 These were the 'off-coloured', the half-castes, the outcome of white supremacy in a black country. **1913** C. Pettman *Africanderisms* 317 *Mêlées*, the off-coloured diamonds from two carats down. **1936** *Times Lit. Suppl.* 12 Sept. 717/2 A rabble of races, white, black and off-coloured, thus inhabits the Southern Africa of to-day.

offcome. Add: **5.** An outsider, stranger; one who is not a native of the district. *north. dial.*
1859 J. S. Bigg *Alfred Staunton* i. 6 'Is this Morecambe Bay?'..'Eye! eye! Morkim Bay ye offcomes ca' t'; but we ca' 't t' Sands!' **1899** H. S. Cowper *Hawkshead* v. 298 The Burtons were 'offcomes', for the name does not occur in the older register. **1946** M. Lane *Tale of Beatrix Potter* v. 97 The north-country preference for distinguishing newcomers for at least a generation as 'off-comes', which can be..translated as 'rubbishing foreigners'. **1961** *Guardian* 18 Dec. 6/2 Farm workers cannot compete for cottages with..weekending 'off-comes' out of Lancashire.
So **o·ffcomed** *ppl.a.*, coming or having come from outside; **o·ffcomer**, an outsider.
1882 A. B. Taylor *Westmoreland Sketches* 27 Ise nivver fergit them two off-cumt chaps singin. **1895** *Leeds Mercury* (Weekly Suppl.) 28 Sept. 3/8 Yond's a off-comed un. **1898** B. Kirkby *Lakeland Words* 109 *Off-comer*, a stranger in the sense of not having been born in the locality. Ther's nin seea mich good i' some o' ther off-comers. **1958** *Listener* 26 June 1054/2 The educated people ..are almost entirely strangers, off-comers. **1971** *Country Life* 9 Sept. 630/2 'Ah'll wager 'twas yon.' 'Why?' 'He's an off-comer.' **1972** 'G. North' *Sgt. Cluff rings True* i. 10 Give them three years: they'll cotton on to you... In the old days you were still an off-comed-un after twenty.

offcut. Add: **1.** (Further examples.) *esp.* an odd or waste piece left after the sawing of timber.
1960 'N. Shute' *Trustee from Toolroom* 284 The offcuts were turned into pulpwood for newsprint. **1967** *Times Rev. Industry* July 44/2 On the building site..a litter of broken and unbroken bricks, torn cement bags,..and timber offcuts is commonplace. **1973** *Listener* 30 Aug. 291/1 There was another piece of filming about canals which looked like the off-cuts from some more ambitious documentary.

off-diagonal (ǫfdəi,æ·gǫnăl), *a.* (*sb.*) *Math.* [f. *OFF- 4 b, OFF *prep.* + DIAGONAL *sb.*] Applied to an element of a square matrix that is not on the principal diagonal (from top left to bottom right). Also as *sb.*, such an element.
1940 *Physical Rev.* LVIII. 108/2 The only approximation made..is the neglect of the off-diagonal elements. **1957** L. Fox *Numerical Solution Two-Point Boundary Probl.* iii. 59 In *U* the off-diagonal terms are identical with those in the corresponding positions of the original matrix *A*. **1972** *Jrnl. Social Psychol.* LXXXVI. 198 *All* possible comparisons are set out here—i.e., including the congruences in the off-diagonals. *Ibid.*, The off-diagonal entries are the congruences between one factor in the one study and every other factor in the other study.

off-drive: see OFF *sb.* 3 in Dict. and Suppl.

off duty, off-duty, *phr.* (*adv.*) and *a.* [f. OFF *prep.*, *OFF- 4 b + DUTY.] Of a person: not engaged or occupied with one's normal work; of things, actions, etc.: of, pertaining to, or suggestive of this state. Hence *ellipt.* as *sb.*, time spent off duty.
1852 [see DUTY 5 e]. **1903** 'G. Thorne' *When it was Dark* III. v. 352 The ship..wore a somewhat neglected, 'off-duty' aspect. **1904** *Daily Chron.* 23 Dec. 4/4 The off-duty policeman. **1937** D. L. Sayers *Busman's Honeymoon* vii. 153, I like to do a bit o' reading in my off-duty. **1946** *Nature* 9 Nov. 646/2 To provide facilities for adults to educate themselves in their off-duty hours. **1962** R. P. Jhabvala *Get Ready for Battle* iv. 173 Joginder yawned, the luxurious off-duty yawn of a hardworking man. **1968** K. O'Hara *Bird-Cage* xxii. 180 Maureen took her off-duty in the morning. **1973** W. J. Burley *Death in Salubrious Place* i. 14 As on other off-duty Sundays, at twelve o'clock Matthew went into the Seymour Arms.

offen (ǫ·fən), *prep. dial.* (also *U.S.*). Also **affn, offan, off'n.** [var. of *off of* (see OFF *adv.* 7), by substitution of *on* for *o'*: see O *prep.*[1] and *prep.*[2]] Off from; off.
1824 *Blackw. Mag.* Oct. 457/1 'Set down that bottle,' quoth I, wiping the saw-dust aff n't with my hand. **1871** E. Eggleston *Hoosier Schoolmaster* xxxi. 216 He told his wife that the master had jist knocked the hind-sights offen that air young lawyer from Lewisburg. **1871** S. Lanier *Wks.* (1945) I. 23 He picked all the rocks off'n the groun'. *Ibid.* 195, I got down off'n my load. **1903** 'O. Henry' in *Ainslee's* Feb. 60/2 He'd jest light off'n his bronco and hunt a place to camp. **1922** E. O'Neill *Hairy Ape* (1923) v. 45 Clean, ain't it? Yuh could eat a fried egg offen it. **1930** *Life & Work* Feb. 63 Lottie says A maun stop letting ye borrow offan me. **1938** M. K. Rawlings *Yearling* i. 14 You knock them plates offen the table..and you'll see who's riled. **1940** W. Faulkner *Hamlet* I. ii. 43 She was taking Ab's breakfast offen the stove, onto two plates. **1944** C. Himes *Black on Black* (1973) 198 That made me mad, them sendin' that jalopy for me. But I was so high off'n them dreams I let it pass. **1977** J. Cleary *Vortex* v. 121 Who took the gun off'n her, then?

Offenbachian (ǫ·fənbā:kiăn), *a.* [f. *Offenbach* + -IAN.] Of, pertaining to, or characteristic of the French composer Jacques Offenbach (1819–80), or his music.
1869 *Porcupine* 24 July 152/3 The Offenbachian piece which is now drawing all London to the theatre of the Brahams. **1888** G. B. Shaw *London Music 1888–89* (1937) 36 Its absurdly Offenbachian finale to the first act. **1937** *Scrutiny* Dec. 286 The peculiar poised vivacity of Offenbachian *opéra bouffe* is partly explained by Shaw. **1970** *Daily Tel.* 21 May 16/3 Poulenc's one-act opera..is an amusing piece in his most Offenbachian vein.

offence, offense, *sb.* Add: **5. c.** Colloq. phr. *no offence*: do not take offence; no offence is meant or taken.
1829 G. Griffin *Collegians* II. xvii. 37 'Is poor Dalton really dead?' 'He is, sir. I have already said it.' 'No offence my boy. I only asked, because if he be..it is a sign that he never will die again.' **1855** Mrs. Gaskell *North & South* II. iii. 32 I'd rather think yo' a fool than a knave. No offence, I hope, sir. **1973** R. Busby *Pattern of Violence* ii. 24 Be better when I'm out of this piss hole—no offence, gents.
9. (See quot. 1961.) *N. Amer.*
1928 G. H. Ruth *Babe Ruth's Own Bk. Baseball* ii. 19 A game of baseball is like a battle... It's a battle of defense against offense and the best organization wins. **1961** J. S. Salak *Dict. Amer. Sports* 303 *Offense*, the team, or a player of the team, on the attack, being at bat (as in baseball) or in possession of the ball (as in football). **1969** *Internat. Herald Tribune* 6 Nov. 13/4 The Leafs, with Dave Keon and Murray Oliver leading the offense.., whipped Oakland 5–2. **1970** *Toronto Daily Star* 24 Sept. 18/4 Knechtel can play offence if somebody gets hurt. **1974** *State* (Columbia, S. Carolina) 3 Mar. 3-D/4 The Bears had to look elsewhere for their offense, and it came in the person of Pat Edwards, who led the charge with 16. **1976** *Washington Post* 19 Apr. D1/6 The chief defect of the Washington Bullets has been made painfully obvious in their last two playoff games with the Cleveland Cavaliers—the team is suffering from a sick offense.

offenceful, *a.* For *rare*—[1] read *rare*, and add further example.
1970 V. Nabokov in *New Yorker* 23 May 44 With each year..That separation seems more offenseful. And the offense more absurd.

offender. See also *first offender* s.v. *FIRST *a.* (*sb.*) and *adv.* C. 2; *old offender* s.v. *OLD *a.* (*adv.*, *sb.*[1]) D. 4.

offensive, *a.* (*sb.*) Add: **7.** In sports, of or pertaining to the offence (*OFFENCE *sb.* 9). *N. Amer.*
1912 C. Mathewson *Pitching in a Pinch* vi. 124 Offensive coaching means the handling of base runners, and requires quick and accurate judgment. **1928** G. H. Ruth *Babe Ruth's Own Bk. Baseball* ii. 23 The change from defensive to offensive play came gradually. **1969** *Eugene* (Oregon) *Register-Guard* 3 Dec. 1D/2 They picked Oregon's Bob Moore as the outstanding sophomore offensive back, and he more than lived up to expectations. **1970** *Toronto Daily Star* 24 Sept. 18/6 Argos had to keep an extra offensive lineman right from the start. **1974** *Anderson* (S. Carolina) *Independent* 18 Apr. 6C/1 In 1972, Heard was voted most valuable defensive player and in '73 he was picked most valuable offensive player. **1978** *Detroit Free Press* 2 Apr. 6E/2 He mentions the offensive linemen simply because they caught such hell for past Lions failures.
B. *sb.* **2.** *fig.* Forceful action or movement directed towards a particular end; a sustained campaign or effort; esp. in *peace offensive.*
1918 in S. Sassoon *Siegfried's Journey* (1945) vii. 72 There are indications that the enemies' peace offensive is creating the danger which is its object. **1919** G. B. Shaw *Peace Conf. Hints* ii. 18 Even when Germany capitulated they [*sc.* the Jingos] were still under such a terror of peace that they called her collapse 'a peace offensive'. *Ibid.* 29 There was only one really valid word in England about peace; and that was that those who preached it were the enemies of their country. Peace proposals were called peace offensives. **1939** *War Illustr.* 21 Oct. 192/1 Mr. Chamberlain stated in the House of Commons that nothing in the German 'peace offensive' could modify the attitude which Great Britain had felt it right to take. **1943** J. D. Wilson *Fortunes of Falstaff* i. 1 An excursus on Falstaff published in 1927 is, for instance, one of the more powerful offensives in the perennial campaign which Professor Stoll wages against the romantic school of Shakespearian criticism. **1952** *Ann. Reg. 1951* 321 China.. publicly supported the various manifestations of the Soviet 'peace offensive'. **1970** R. Lowell *Notebk.* 189 You mean our National Peace Offensive?

offer, *sb.* Add: **1. b.** (Further examples.)
1847 A. Brontë *Agnes Grey* xiv. 219 The conceited wretch chose to interpret my amiability of temper his own way, and at length..he actually—made me an offer! **1971** G. Mitchell *Lament for Leto* iv. 121 Ronald Dick.. certainly would make me an offer if I were free. **1976** *Scottish Rev.* Spring 6 She had plenty of flames and several guid offers.
d. (Further examples.) In *Comm.* also, the fact of being offered for sale at a low price, as sales promotion.
1966 *Listener* 9 June 830/1 The cheaper and nastier Hollywood series, which are always on offer. **1967** *Ibid.* 1 June 704/1 Purchasing the most sophisticated weapons we have on offer. **1971** *Woman's Own* 27 Mar. 21 Next week..bargain vanity case offer.
2. c. An opportunity or 'opening'. *dial.* or *colloq.*
1831 S. Lover *Legends & Stories of Ireland* 9 The first offer afther I make her as good as new. **1877** *Coursing Calendar Autumn 1876* 302 Napoleon went past Countess in the race to the hare, and..never gave his antagonist an offer. **1925** *Dialect Notes* V. 337 *Offer*, a chance (at seals).

offer, *v.* **3. b.** Delete †*Obs.* and add later example.
1939 C. Morley *Kitty Foyle* 328, I offered him to go in the bathroom to wash.
g. *refl.* To present (oneself) to a person for acceptance or refusal; to put (oneself) forward, *spec.* as a suitor.

1765 H. Walpole *Castle of Otranto* i. 18 In short, Isabella, since I cannot give you my son [in marriage], I offer you myself. **1893** M. E. Mann *In Summer Shade* II. xi. 28, I have this evening offered myself to Mary Burne, and she has accepted me. **1903** *Eng. Dial. Dict.* IV. 332/2 He did nothing but offer himself for her for so long as she lived. **1930** G. B. Shaw *Apple Cart* II. 75 It is my intention to offer myself to the Royal Borough of Windsor as a candidate at the forthcoming General Election. **1978** I. Murdoch *The Sea, The Sea* 436 Charles, darling, tell me... When you came here today were you going to offer yourself to me?

† **h.** *intr.* To stand as a candidate for office. *Obs.*

1766 J. Wedgwood *Let.* 4 June (1965) 40 Some of our friends suspected a Candidate would offer who lived at too great a distance from the centre of the business. **1803** W. R. Davie *Let.* 20 Aug. in J. Steele *Papers* (1924) I. 405 The Gentlemen who prevailed upon me 'to offer' as they call it, consisted principally of the moderate men of both parties. **1835** A. B. Longstreet *Georgia Scenes* 234 Then lowering his voice to a confidential but distinctly audible tone, 'what you offering for?' continued he.

i. *trans.* With spoken words as object: to say tentatively or helpfully.

1881 M. Crommelin *Miss Daisy Dimity* I. ii. 32 'There are two hens to be set with Brahma eggs this morning, and a brood of young Cochins coming out,' offered Polly hesitatingly. **1894** 'R. Andom' *We Three & Troddles* iv. 21 'A coffee-mill,' suggested Wilks. 'Or a sewing machine,' I offered. **1973** J. Rossiter *Manipulators* v. 51 'Perhaps,' Bradley offered helpfully, 'you've been name-calling somebody. And they didn't like it.' **1974** 'E. Lathen' *Sweet & Low* v. 52 'Just like civil war in Nigeria,' offered Charlie sagely.

j. *Telephony.* To direct (a call) *to* a piece of apparatus.

1950 J. Atkinson *Herbert & Procter's Telephony* (new ed.) II. ii. 33/2 It is readily possible to read off the traffic offered to any particular contact for any value of total traffic. **1960** R. Syski *Introd. Congestion Theory Teleph. Syst.* v. 194 The *N* sources originate calls which are offered to *R* channels. **1960** *Post Office Electr. Engineers' Jrnl.* LIII. 76/2 This form of control will facilitate the provision of automatic alternative routing, which will permit traffic to be offered to a direct route and then, if all circuits are engaged, to overflow to the transit network.

7. b. To put (a part of a structure, etc.) in place to see how it looks or whether it fits properly; to hold up or display (something) to test its appearance or correctness. Usu. const. *up* (occas. *on*). orig. *dial.*

1854 A. E. Baker *Gloss. Northamptonshire Words* II. 73 One of his workmen said, 'Shall I offer up, or offer on, that frame, to see if it will fit the picture?' **1887** Parish & Shaw *Dict. Kentish Dial.* 110, I once heard a master paperhanger say to his assistant, when a customer was inspecting some wall-papers, 'Just offer this paper up for the lady to see.' **1903** *Eng. Dial. Dict.* IV. 332/2, I will offer the shrubs before planting them. **1952** Granville *Dict. Theatr. Terms* 125 *Offer up*, to show the producer the position of a picture or an ornament for approval before fixing it permanently, particularly mirrors which reflect the stage lighting. (2) Carpenters *offer up* doorways to fit into the door-frames, in fact they offer up anything before it is approved. The term is used by carpenters outside the theatre and is peculiar to their trade.

offerable, *a.* (Further example.)

1917 E. Pound *Let.* 26 Aug. (1971) 120 The minimum offerable arrangement would be six articles a year at 10 dollars each.

offered, *ppl. a.* Add: **1. b.** In the sense of *offer *v.* 3 j.

1960 R. Syski *Introd. Congestion Theory Teleph. Syst.* v. 194 If an offered call cannot be served immediately because at the instant of its arrival no free channel is available, the source which originated it nevertheless continues to demand service. **1974** Cox & Reudink in W. C. Jakes *Microwave Mobile Communic.* vii. 550 Sometimes estimates of offered traffic are made directly instead of estimating attempt rates and holding times separately.

offeree (ǫfəɹī·). [f. Offer *v.* + -ee[1].] A person to whom something is or has been offered. Also *attrib.*

1952 *All England Law Reports* I. 1092 Provided the offer is not one which for some reason the offeree is entitled to refuse. **1967** *Economist* 20 May 754/1 The now-familiar rise in the price of an offeree company's shares before the announcement of a bid. **1972** *Real Estate Rev.* Winter 56/2 The statutes define such offerings in terms of the number of buyers, or the number of offerees, or the total number of stockholders or security holders after completion of the offering, or combinations thereof.

offering, *vbl. sb.* Add: **2. c.** Something offered to the public for entertainment, patronage, purchase, etc.; *spec.* a theatrical production.

Quot. 1820 has connotations of sense 2 a in Dict.

1820 *Offering of Sunday-School Teacher* p. iv, The Book is really what its title imports,—'The Offering of a Sunday-School Teacher' etc.; and it is equally adapted to the Sunday Schools of every denomination of Christians. **1834** *Offering* p. i, The increased demand for works of this description, has induced the Editor of '*The Offering*' to usher into the world another of the class of books which, of all others, has met with the largest share of public patronage; and it is with peculiar pleasure that he again presents himself before his friends in the capacity of a compiler or gatherer. **1848** *Sporting Life* 29 Apr. 103/2 The Easter offerings at this house [*sc.* the Strand Theatre] are *Woman's Faith* and a new burlesque extravaganza. **1901** *Munsey's Mag.* July 587/1 There were so many offerings which critics and first night audiences liked,.. which the paying public regarded with indifference. **1903** *Boston Even. Transcript* 29 Aug. 8/2 On Saturday next the Transcript will print an unusually attractive line of real estate offerings. **1932** *New Yorker* 11 June 46/2 If Mme. Sylva can summon so many listeners for subsequent offerings, her company should thrive.

3. (Examples corresp. to *offer *v.* 3 j.)

1938 Herbert & Procter *Telephony* (ed. 2) II. ix. 371 The trunk offering selector and the trunk offering final selector together cater for a 4-digit numbering scheme. **1950** J. Atkinson *Herbert & Procter's Telephony* (new ed.) II. xxv. 778/1 The telephonist dials a special number over the trunk offering switching train to the exchange concerned. **1964** K. H. Brinkmann tr. *Trautmann's Design Automatic Teleph. Exch.* II. 63 An offering subgroup comprises the offering trunks which carry the traffic to such a subgroup.

offeror, var. Offerer; *spec.* one who offers something for sale, esp. shares.

1930 A. Palmer *Company Secretarial Pract.* vi. 46 Any document by which the offer for sale is made shall..be deemed to be a prospectus issued by the company, but without prejudice to the liability of the offerors in respect of the offer. **1955** *Times* 18 May 3/8 There was no binding contract until notice of the acceptance was received by the offeror. **1972** *Mod. Law Rev.* XXXV. 74 The offer was to remain open until May 14, 1970, with the usual right being reserved to the offeror to extend the time during which the offeree shareholders could tender their acceptances.

offertorial, *a.* For *rare*$^{-1}$ read *rare* and add earlier example.

1856 *Tracts on Increase of Episcopate in Eng. & Wales* II. 9 To meet the continual demands for Church extension by stated Offertorial collections.

off flavour, off-flavour. [Cf. *off *adv.* 1 g.] A stale, rancid, or unnatural flavour in food.

1947 *Richmond* (Va.) *News-Leader* 3 Apr. 36/1 There are several good reasons for what they term 'off-flavors' in milk. **1950** *N.Z. Jrnl. Agric.* Mar. 265/3 White clover, subterranean clover, red clover, silage, lucerne, and chou moellier all produce an off flavour [in the cows' milk]. **1952** *Chambers's Jrnl.* June 340/2 They found that meat put under this apparatus loses its red colour, goes brown, and has a definite off-flavour. **1958** [see *anti-oxidant]. **1971** *Guardian* 19 May 8/1 Yogurts..are made with a living culture... The process is strictly controlled throughout so that off-flavours cannot develop.

off form, off-form, *phr.* and *a.* [f. Off *prep.* + Form *sb.*] In poor condition; 'out of form' (see Form *sb.* 16).

1912 C. Mathewson *Pitching in a Pinch* 142 The Chicago pitchers were away off form in the series. **1961** *Times* 20 Feb. 6/2 Mr. Ferber sounded a little off-form. **1965** *Listener* 24 June 930/1 There is scarcely a topic in the history of science that has attracted more great men to it —yet found them so sadly off-form—than the question of whether his intelligence is inherited or due to his upbringing. **1972** H. A. Williams *True Resurrection* ii. 35 They don't say, 'He's not as good as he was,' but just, 'He's off-form today.' **1976** *Listener* 26 Feb. 250/2 The musicians may be tired, off-form.

off-gau·ge, *a.* [f. Off *prep.* + Gauge, gage *sb.*] Of steel strip: having a thickness outside the permitted tolerance. Freq. *absol.*

1940 *Sheet Metal Industries* XIV. 611/1 It is believed that the predominating cause for off gauge while at running speed is the variation in the incoming strip. **1947** *Jrnl. Iron & Steel Inst.* CLVI. 398/2 The phenomenon undoubtedly contributes to 'off-gauge' strip in wide-strip mills and other mills rolling thin-gauge material, during acceleration and deceleration. **1953** *Engineering* 9 Jan. 33/1 As the measuring head cannot be mounted close to the roll gap, there is a delay between the rolling of off-gauge strip and its indication. **1962** C. W. Starling *Theory & Pract. Flat Rolling* ix. 149 Probably the most common cause of rejections in cold rolled sheet is 'off gauge', and as the tendency is to decrease gauge tolerances, accurate gauge control is of the utmost importance.

o·ff-glide. *Phonetics.* [f. Off *a.* + Glide *sb.*] A glide that terminates the articulation of a speech-sound, when the vocal organs either return to a neutral position or adopt a position anticipating the formation of the next sound. Cf. *on-glide. Hence **off-gliding** *ppl. a.*

1879 [see Breath 10]. **1888** [see *on-glide]. **1927** J. J. Hogan *Eng. Lang. in Ireland* 71 An important difference between I. [*sc.* Irish] and E. [*sc.* English] is the greater value of the off-glides of the Irish consonants. **1934** [see *on-glide]. **1954** F. G. Cassidy *Robertson's Devel. Mod. Eng.* (ed. 2) v. 104 An on-glide is one preceding the vowel (or consonant) and therefore gliding on toward it; an off-glide follows the vowel. *Ibid.*, Diphthongs develop from the addition of either on-gliding or off-gliding elements. **1964** E. J. A. Henderson in D. Abercrombie et al. *Daniel Jones* 418 There is frequently still sufficient pressure of air behind it for a weak off-glide to be audible. **1972** *Language* XLVIII. 865 The backness and roundness values of the following off-gliding vowels.

off-grain, *adv.* and *a.* [f. Off *prep.*, *off- 4 b + Grain *sb.*[1]] Of a fabric: against the direction of the threads; having a grain that is not straight.

1964 *McCall's Sewing* iii. 38/2 Finishing or printing processes will often pull them [*sc.* fabrics] off-grain. In some cases a permanent finish may lock the threads in the off-grain position and the fabric can never be straightened. *Ibid.* vii. 97/1 There are several ways to straighten off-grain fabrics. **1968** J. Ironside *Fashion Alphabet* 88 Cheap fabrics are often printed 'off-grain' and one is faced with the decision of either having the grain right (so that the garment hangs properly) or the pattern straight!

off-hand, offhand, *adv.* and *adj. phr.* Add: **A.** *adv.* **2.** Delete *rare* and add earlier and later examples. *U.S.*

1833 *Sk. & Eccentr. D. Crockett* ix. 119 Forty yards off-hand, or sixty with a rest, is the distance generally chosen for a shooting match. **1970** *Amer. Speech 1968* XLIII. 217 The shot could be made with a single-shot muzzle-loading rifle or with a *two-shoot gun*, fired either *off-hand* or *with a rest.*

3. *to farm off-hand*, to own or hold a farm without residing on it. *dial.*

1879 *Norfolk Archaeol.* VIII. 171 A farmer having an occupation apart from his homestead is said to farm it off-hand. **1898** *Longman's Mag.* Sept. 408 The land had been farmed 'off-hand', that is to say, the tenant did not live on the farm, but put in a working bailiff.

B. *adj.* **2. b.** *Mining.* (See quots.)

1888 W. E. Nicholson *Gloss. Terms Coal Trade, Offhand-men*, a term applied to all colliery workmen except hewers and putters. **1921** *Dict. Occup. Terms* (1927) §047 *Odd worker, off hand man, wage man*, general terms for men or boys employed above or below ground and paid by the day. **1926** [see *face-worker* s.v. *face *sb.* 27].

3. Of a shot: fired from a gun held in the hand without other support. *U.S.*

1856 R. Glisan *Jrnl. Army Life* (1874) xxiv. 328, I surprised everybody by killing the duck at an off-hand shot.

4. Of a farm: owned or held by a person who does not reside there. *dial.*

1873 F. T. Chevallier *Let.* 6 May in Thirsk & Imray *Suffolk Farming in Nineteenth Cent.* (1958) 106 On the off-hand farm I shall have a good opportunity of seeing what will be required during the ensuing year. **1880** R. S. Charnock *Gloss. Essex Dial.* 33 Some who hold farms in different parishes call those farms where they do not reside 'off-hand farms'. **1898** *Longman's Mag.* Sept. 408 The labourer in charge of an off-hand farm. **1960** G. E. Evans *Horse in Furrow* vii. 99 The whole capital he had sunk in the farms (the *Bransons Land* referred to was an *off-hand* holding) was not giving him the return it would have done if invested elsewhere. *Ibid.* xvi. 209 We generally spent two days at a farm, and perhaps another day at an 'off-hand' farm belonging to it.

5. *Engin.* Carried out with the workpiece held in the hand. Of a machine: intended for off-hand operations.

1931 E. P. Van Leuven *Cold Metal Working* iv. 65 We refer to grinding as off-hand, semiprecision or precision grinding, depending on the type of machine and the degree of accuracy required. **1961** L. E. Doyle et al. *Manuf. Processes* xxviii. 643 Nonprecision grinding, common forms of which are snagging and off-hand grinding, is done primarily to remove stock that cannot be taken off as conveniently by other methods. **1966** G. H. Thomas *Metalwork Technol.* xiii. 150 'Off-hand' grinders..are of two types—bench models and pedestal (or floor) models. **1969** C. R. Shotbolt *Workshop Technol.* I. vi. 120 The author does not believe in any expensive cutting tool being ground by hand on an off-hand grinding machine.

6. Designating glass-ware made by hand, without a mould; also denoting such a process.

1941 C. J. Phillips *Glass* viii. 156 The glass employed in 'offhand' glass blowing is usually melted in pots. **1949** P. Davis *Devel. Amer. Glass Industry* iv. 49 The process of blowing in a mold was closely similar to the off-hand method. **1967** C. Gaskin *Edge of Glass* vi. 144 He..took up his empty wineglass. 'If you were making this by the "off-hand" method—that's entirely by hand—you'd start with heating your batch.' **1970** *Canad. Antiques Collector* July–Aug. 14/2 You can feel the intrinsic beauty of an off-hand glass chain.

off-handed, *a.* Add: **b.** *Mining.* = prec. B. 2 b. *dial.*

1846 W. E. Brockett *J. T. Brockett's Gloss. North Country Words* (ed. 3) II. 59 All workmen about a coal-pit are said to be *off-handed* who are not engaged in the business of hewing and putting the coal. **1906** *Daily Chron.* 16 Oct. 5/2 The 'off-handed' men..dispersed into the four seams of the pit.

off-handedly, *adv.* (Earlier and later examples.)

1886 *19th Cent.* Oct. 541 The newspaper moralisers speak off-handedly of the skilled workman earning his two or three pounds a week. **1905** G. B. Shaw *Let.* 3 Jan. (1972) II. 485 At my third meeting I was asked to take the chair. I consented as offhandedly as if I were the Speaker of the House of Commons. **1973** J. Wainwright *Pride of Pigs* 123 He could have felt sorry for Fuller..to be systematically, off-handedly squashed.

offhandish (ǫfhæ·ndiʃ), *a.* [f. Off-hand, offhand *adj. phr.* + -ish[1].] Somewhat off-hand; off-handed. Hence **offha·ndishly** *adv.*, off-handedly.

1886 in H. Baumann *Londinismen* 124/2. **1926** E. M. Roberts *Time of Man* i. 28 The brown colt came from the other side of the enclosure, nibbling offhandishly at the wilted grass and edging always a little nearer. **1952** *Ethics* LXIII. 66/1 Commitments acknowledged only in an offhandish way by Moore.

office, *sb.* Add: **8. c.** Also followed by defining phrase, as *Office of Works.*

1880 E. W. HAMILTON *Diary* 11 Sept. (1972) I. 49 His [*sc.* W. P. Adam's] place will have to be filled up at the Office of Works. **1935** *Discovery* Aug. 217/1 Mr J. H. Markham, F.R.I.B.A., of H.M. Office of Works, has made a notable addition to London's public monuments. **1936** *Ibid.* July 199/1 A change in the Office of Works which archaeologists cannot but view with regret.

e. *Aeronaut. slang.* The cockpit of an aircraft.

1917 'CONTACT' *Airman's Outings* 123, I strapped our baggage, some new gramophone records, and myself into the observer's office. *Ibid.* 161, I withdraw into 'the office', otherwise the observer's cockpit. **1918** *Blackw. Mag.* Oct. 526/2 'Wouf!'—a deafening crash, and the old bus shakes violently as I put my head into the office. **1934** V. M. YEATES *Winged Victory* iv. 34 He put his head in the office and flew by the instruments. **1941** [see *GREENHOUSE 3]. **1942** 'B. J. ELLAN' *Spitfire!* p. x, The cockpit is called the office. **1966** *New Statesman* 13 May 687/2 'Up in the office they too knew it.' 'The office? You mean the flight deck?' 'Just that. No more. No less. The office.'

9. b. Also in *pl.*; *spec.* in phr. *usual office(s*.

1938 N. MARSH *Artists in Crime* vi. 84, I imagine it was to pay a visit to the usual offices. **1948** J. CANNAN *Little I Understood* ix. 124 Mildred had been too shy when Adam, indicating a door, had said, '"The usual offices"..,' to open the door and look in. **1951** N. MARSH *Opening Night* ix. 220, I went to the usual office at the end of the passage. **1955** N. FITZGERALD *House is Falling* xi. 188 He was having the usual offices in his house duplicated. **1957** J. BRAINE *Room at Top* i. 13 The bathroom's to the right and the usual offices next to it. **1959** W. GOLDING *Free Fall* ii. 36 There are the usual offices indoors now. **1963** *Gloss. Gen. Building Terms* (*B.S.I.*) 10 '*Offices*' (deprecated), service rooms and W.C.s.

12. a. *office boy* (earlier and later examples; also in extended use), *building, chair* (later example), *copy* (various senses: earlier and later examples), *desk, door, duty* (later example), *equipment, expenses, furniture, girl* (earlier and later examples), *job, politics, routine, stool* (further examples), *work* (earlier and later examples); **b.** (sense 4) *office-holder* (earlier and later examples), *-holding* (further example; also as ppl. adj.), *-hunter* (earlier and later examples), *-hunting, -mongering, -seeker* (earlier and further examples); *office-seeking* adj. (earlier example; also as vbl. sb.); (sense 8) *office-cleaner* (later examples), *-keeper* (later examples), *worker*; *office-bound* adj.

1961 *Times* 12 Oct. 16/2 The bliss of an office-bound youngster. **1972** *Daily Tel.* 24 Apr. 25/1 'I couldn't bear being office-bound from nine to five each day' is the cry of many a sixth-former. **1846** *Knickerbocker* XXVII. 457 No songs for you, my sad street-sweeper!..Nor for you, melancholy office-boy! **1865** A. J. MUNBY *Diary* 15 June in D. Hudson *Munby* (1972) 209 She kept on writing, in a hand like an office-boy's. **1914** G. B. SHAW *Misalliance* p. lxv, An office boy of fifteen is often more of a man than a university student of twenty. *Ibid.* 7, I said, 'Make him the Office Boy.' **1944** J. S. HUXLEY *On Living in Revolution* 118 Quoting from a recent address of David Lilienthal... 'An overcentralized administration is always characterized by the fact that its field officers tend to become messengers and office boys.' **1973** A. BEHREND *Samarai Affair* i. 15 His first job had been that of office boy. **1975** *Times* 13 Oct. 13/1 Mr [Ian] Smith..has to demonstrate to his hard-liners that he is not Pretoria's office-boy. **1840** *Niles' Reg.* 23 May 182/1 The Free Trader office building has been crushed in and much shattered. **1924** R. GRAVES *Mock Beggar Hall* 62, I was aware that during the war Mock-Beggar Hall had been used as a Government office-building. **1942** *London Replanned* (R. Academy) 25/1 The Surrey bank of the River is developed with Embankment gardens and office buildings. **1874** 'H. CHURTON' *Toinette* xl. 404 The old surgeon laid down his pen..and turned his office-chair round toward his visitor. **1944** *Times* 7 June 2/2 Mr. E. Granville.. asked the Secretary to the Treasury if he would arrange that..the members of the Government Minor and Manipulative Grades Association of Office Cleaners were referred to as such, and not as charwomen or charladies, which term..was resented. **1971** J. AITKEN *Nightly Deadshade* vii. 79 Here I am, on the spot after the office cleaners have cleared off. **1974** *Times* 4 Jan. 12/3 There are practically no Hutu left in government or the civil service—not even at chauffeur or office-cleaner level. **1789** J. MORGAN *Essays Law of Evidence* I. 87 Of Office Copies. **1836** S. F. AUSTIN *Let.* 22 Nov. in *Ann. Rep. Amer. Hist. Assoc. 1907* (1908) II. 142 It contains your commission, a letter of credence to the secretary of the United States, and office copies of them. **1928** F. M. FORD *Let.* 16 Apr. (1965) 178, I don't know if you have..an office copy that you would care to sell. **1946** J. IRVING *Royal Navalese* 126 *Office copy, the,* the other half (of the drink in hand). **1957** CLARK & GOTTFRIED *University Dict. Business & Finance* 246/1 *Office copy*, in general, a copy or transcript of any document..retained for office use. In law, a copy of a document made by an officer of the court or other public officer. **1881** *Rep. Indian Affairs* (U.S.) 151 The articles manufactured by the carpenters..were as follows..one office-desk [etc.]. **1907** G. B. SHAW *John Bull's Other Island* I. 3 Against the right hand wall is a filing cabinet,..and, nearer, a tall office desk and stool for one person. **1954** T. S. ELIOT *Confid. Clerk* II. 69 It's an office desk. Sir Claude got it for me...You see, I shall do a good deal of my work here. **1715** *Boston News-Let.* 11 Apr. 2/2 A fair Alphabetical List..hung up at the Office Door, would soon resolve any Person. **1863** 'E. KIRKE' *My Southern Friends* xxiii. 235 A short rap came at the office door. *a* **1885** G. B. MCCLELLAN *Own Story* (1887) xxxii. 534 He said that he was so much occupied with office-duty that it was impossible for him to leave. **1942** D. POWELL *Time to be Born* (1943) ii. 44 The profits..had been.. put back into the business, new office equipment, printing, one thing and another. **1962** D. FRANCIS *Dead Cert* x. 115 It had once been an elegant room and even the office equipment could not entirely spoil its proportions. **1972** *Guardian* 7 June 9/6 There is really no reason why office equipment shouldn't be good looking enough to go into private houses too. **1869** *Bradshaw's Railway Manual* XXI. 161 *Expended*..Office expenses, &c—£438. **1887** 'MARK TWAIN' *Lett. to Publishers* (1967) 233 On first 10,000, we deduct $5,000 office expenses and $1750 for author. **1972** P. GRIFFIN *A-Z Office Guide* 86 They [*sc.* IOUs] should not be allowed to build up to a point when cash becomes short for office expenses. **1903** G. B. SHAW *Man & Superman* II. 66 If you were to marry the son of an English manufacturer of awffice furniture, your friends would consider it a misalliance. **1911** *Daily Colonist* (Victoria, B.C.) 4 Apr. 4/4 (Advt.), We are selling lots of office furniture these days. **1974** N. FREELING *Dressing of Diamond* 188 A dislike of metal office furniture. **1863** A. D. WHITNEY *Faith Gartney's Girlhood* xi. 97 Faith looked up, and remembered the poor office girl of three years since. **1972** J. MCCLURE *Caterpillar Cop* xii. 193 Ye Olde Englishe Tea Shoppe..was crowded with office girls, buying roast beef sandwiches with luncheon vouchers. **1818** H. B. FEARON *Sk. Amer.* 143 Those dangerous abuses in government, introduced by office-holders, which..threaten..to become inveterate. **1957** P. WORSLEY *Trumpet shall Sound* 269 The tendency of the office-holder to merge his personal interests with those of his office. **1970** R. LOWELL *Notebk.* 56 The communist committed to his commune, Artist and office-holder to a claque of less Than fifty souls. **1835** D. CROCKETT *Acct. Col. Crockett's Tour* 106 The office-holding gentry..will meet with their match in an indignant people. **1857** [see **office-seeking*]. **1936** *Discovery* Feb. 63/1 The burden of compulsory office-holding ruined the well-to-do. **1957** V. W. TURNER *Schism & Continuity in Afr. Society* iv. 93 Social Drama I illustrates the conflict that may arise ..when only a few men remain in the senior, office holding generation in a village. **1806** *Deb. Congress U.S.* 24 Feb. (1852) 506/2 It would be a struggle between office-hunters and the people. **1845** W. L. MACKENZIE *Lives Butler & Hoyt* 75 General Spicer was a keen office-hunter. **1824** *Niles' Reg.* 20 Mar. 37/2 (*heading*) Office hunting. **1889** FARMER *Americanisms* 397 Office-hunting is quite a business with the thousand-and-one 'hangers-on' to the skirts of political parties. **1923** H. CRANE *Let.* 26 Oct. (1965) 153 My mind is divided between them and an office job. **1937** M. HILLIS *Orchids on your Budget* (1938) iv. 68 We ourselves have run our one-woman ménage both with and without an office job. **1834** *Chambers's Edin. Jrnl.* III. 229/1 Has the office-keeper acquainted you with the particulars I require? **1938** *Times* 16 Feb. 8/7 A short time ago a telegram was delivered at my office.. after I had left for the day. The office keeper..had it re-telegraphed to my home address. *a* **1919** T. ROOSEVELT in Ld. Charnwood *Theodore Roosevelt* (1923) 250 These men have a gift at office-mongering, just as other men have a peculiar knack in picking pockets. **1917** H. GRANT *Two Sides of Atlantic* 45 This is known in the States as 'office-politics'. **1961** 'J. WYNDHAM' *Consider her Ways* 216 Office politics, very likely... Many a young man's gifts are stunted by them. **1907** G. B. SHAW *Major Barbara* III. 258 He could learn the office routine without understanding the business. **1911** W. OWEN *Let.* 25 Apr. (1967) 70, I am not too young to..turn to Office Routine, Customs, Revenues. **1925** H. CRANE *Let.* 7 May (1965) 204 A change from office routine for awhile. **1813** *Deb. Congress U.S.* 6 Jan. (1853) 582/2 It would augment the office-seekers, who, with the friends of the Administration, were continually haunting the Executive. **1845** *Knickerbocker* XXV. 374 A Friend writing from Washington..gives us this pleasant sketch of a 'Sucker' office-seeker. **1882–3** W. WHITMAN *Specimen Days* 259 The members..were..the meanest kind of bawling and blowing office-holders, office-seekers. **1977** *Listener* 11 Aug. 163/1 In 1881..James A. Garfield..was assassinated by a disappointed office-seeker from his own party ranks. **1857** W. R. ALGER *Genius & Posture of Amer.* 4 Office-holding partisans, office-seeking demagogues. **1860** H. GREELEY *Overland Journey* 68 If he will work right ahead,..keeping clear of speculation and office-seeking, he can hardly fail to do well. **1884** F. M. CRAWFORD *Amer. Politician* I. iv. 76 We are sick with the foul disease of office seeking. **1907** G. B. SHAW *John Bull's Other Island* I. 13 He seats himself on the office stool, and tilts it back. **1953** J. WAIN *Hurry on Down* v. 91 You couldn't rightly say whether a fella was a workman or an office stool percher or a manager. *a* **1678** J. WESTLEY in E. Calamy *Continuation of Acct. of Ministers Ejected* (1727) I. 441 They are not a People that are fit Subjects, for me to exercise Office-work among them. **1849** DICKENS *Dav. Copp.* (1850) xvi. 167, I am not doing office-work... I am improving my legal knowledge. **1886** C. M. YONGE *Chantry House* II. xiv. 136 He had spent an entire day on his hands and knees..—the office-work, as we declared. **1956** 'C. BLACKSTOCK' *Dewey Death* iv. 83, I cannot see why all the office work should be held up. **1936** *Discovery* May 146/2 The lowest value of natural illumination which an office worker requires. **1956** A. H. COMPTON *Atomic Quest* 333 Mechanics and office workers and laborers of many kinds. **1973** 'E. MCBAIN' *Hail to Chief* viii. 136 The homeward rush of office workers had already begun.

c. Special Combs., as **office block,** a block (sense *14 f) containing offices; also *attrib.* and *fig.*; **office hours,** (*a*) the hours of work at an office; (*b*) a disciplinary session *U.S. Forces' slang*; **office hymn** (see quot. 1938); **office junior,** the youngest or newest member of the staff of an office; **office party,** a party held for members of the staff of an office; **office piano** *slang,* a typewriter; **office wife,** a business man's female secretary.

1942 *London Replanned* (R. Academy) 26/2 The large octagonal building prominent in the drawing..is a suggested office block with garden court or car park. **1951** *Ann. Reg. 1950* 406 The architectural standard of most of these buildings..was very poor; most of them..resembled pre-war commercial office blocks at their most tasteless. **1963** *Listener* 10 Jan. 71/1 Harry Bertoia's beautiful but boring silvery puffball of wire is the apotheosis of what I once heard called 'office-block art'—the triumph of taste and craftsmanship over feeling. **1967** B. PATTEN *Little Johnny's Confession* 47 Maud, is that you I see Alone among the office blocks? **1972** M. GILBERT *Body of Girl* xxv. 211 If there is a covering party, I guess it'll be in the office block opposite. **1802** D. RAWN *Let.* 29 Oct. in J. Steele *Papers* (1924) I. 326 He receives in addition thereto, 300 Dollars for services *termed extra*, but wholly performed during the usual Office hour. **1841** THACKERAY *Gt. Hoggarty Diamond* (1849) ix. 100 Gus Hoskins and I, who hunted after office hours in couples. **1852** [in Dict., sense 12 a]. **1898** J. H. PARKER *Hist. Gatling Gun Detachment* 23, I don't want to hear anything about it... If you want to see me about this subject, come to me in office hours. **1903** G. B. SHAW *Man & Superman* III. 80 It is the custom ..always to put off business until to-morrow. In fact, you have arrived out of office hours. **1922** *Marine Corps Gaz.* June 212 One morning after *Office Hours* the C.O. was sitting at his desk grumbling to himself and holding his head in his hands. **1933** *Leatherneck* Apr. 14 No 'office hours' were held during the month of January for any 'A' Company Marines. **1967** A. DUBUS *Lieutenant* 41 He committed an offense, he was brought in to office hours. **1972** 'H. HOWARD' *Nice Day for Funeral* iii. 41 We only meet outside office hours. I never impose on social relationships. **1907** *New Office Hymn Bk.* II. p. v, The Office Hymns are the Hymns in the Divine Office. **1931** *N. & Q.* 19 Sept. 216/2 We are told that the best place for the Office Hymn both at Matins and Evensong is immediately before the Psalms. **1938** *Oxf. Compan. Mus.* 629/1 *Office hymn*, a liturgical hymn appointed for the Office, or Service of the day... The Office Hymns of the Roman Breviary were not transferred to the English Prayer Book. **1959** J. C. DENYER *Office Managem.* xi. 83 For office juniors, the appropriate official to approach is the Juvenile Employment Officer. **1970** J. COOPER *How to survive from Nine to Five* 81 The office junior has used hair lacquer under her arms instead of deodorant and is walking round like a penguin. **1974** R. GADNEY *Something Worth Fighting For* ix. 64 A young man, neatly dressed, the obvious clerk or what is sometimes known as an office junior. **1955** W. GADDIS *Recognitions* I. iii. 101 Who made the first one? Will somebody tell me that? said The Boss at an office party. **1967** E. MCGIRR *Here lies my Wife* iii. 105 Kellerman had been in New Orleans the previous Christmas and so had missed the..office party. **1972** G. BROMLEY *In Absence of Body* xii. 142 'You seem to have a lot of office parties.' 'Yes. People leaving or getting married, or entertaining clients.' **1942** BERREY & VAN DEN BARK *Amer. Thes. Slang* § 75/38 *Typewriter,* mill, office piano. **1945** L. SHELLY *Jive Talk Dict.* 29/2 *Office piano,* typewriter. **1970** C. MAJOR *Dict. Afro-Amer. Slang* 87 *Office piano*,..a typewriter. **1942** BERREY & VAN DEN BARK *Amer. Thes. Slang* § 542/19 *Girl Friday, office wife,* a female secretary. **1952** G. W. BRACE *Spire* (1953) xxvii. 268 I've been a pretty faithful office wife to him, and though he has never invited me to share a bed..he does hate to part with me. **1955** H. KURNITZ *Invasion of Privacy* (1956) vii. 52, I know all about American business executives and their secretaries. Office wives, isn't that what you call them? **1972** C. WESTON *Poor, Poor Ophelia* (1973) viii. 41 The secretary smiled sweetly... 'I'll do that, Mr. Farr. Get a good night's sleep now. 'Bye.' My office wife, he thought sourly.

office, *v.* Restrict † *Obs.* to senses 1–4 in Dict. and add: **5.** (Further examples.) Hence **o·fficing** *vbl. sb.*

1841 *Swell's Night Guide* (Gloss.) *Office,* giving warning. **1846** *Ibid.* 58 She eased him of his fawney,..officed her cullies, they pasted his nibs, and scarpered rumbo. **1859** G. W. MATSELL *Vocabulum* 60 *Officing,* signalizing; a preconcerted signal by a confederate. **1914** JACKSON & HELLYER *Vocab. Criminal Slang* 63 *Office,* noun,..a signal;..a warning... Used also as a verb in the same sense. **1926** J. BLACK *You can't Win* xiii. 182 Sanc closed the door..and 'officed' me to follow him out. **1949** PARTRIDGE *Dict. Underworld* 479/1 *Officing,* a preconcerted signal. **1955** *Publ. Amer. Dial. Soc.* XXIV. 73 The tool *offices* that they will *clip* him as he enters the ramp... The tool *offices* for a *left bridge* and a *left prat,* and the *frame* closes.

6. *intr.* To have or work in an office (sense 8 a); to share an office *with* someone. *U.S.*

1892 *Nation* (N.Y.) 21 Apr. 303/2 An attorney officing in the same building. **1917** *Dialect Notes* IV. 347 *Office with,*..to share an office with. **1936** *Atlantic Monthly* July (Contributors' Col., 4) A local newspaper has just carried two want ads containing this wording:—'Chance for public accountant to office with lawyer.' 'Chance for high grade realtor to office with lawyer.' **1973** *N.Y. Times* 11 Aug. 10/1 Mr. Mardian spoke of a man who 'officed in that same agency'.

officeful (ǫ·fisful). Also **office-full.** [f. OFFICE *sb.* + -FUL.] That amount or number of anything which would fill an office.

1963 'W. HAGGARD' *High Wire* vi. 63 He had an office-ful of paper. **1966** 'E. PETERS' *Piper on Mountain* ii. 26 Put him among an office-full of civil servants, and you could lose him in a moment. **1976** J. WAINWRIGHT *Who goes Next?* 66 'You'll have witnesses, of course, sir?'.. 'A whole office-full, officer.'

office-man. Restrict †*Obs.* and *Sc.* to sense in Dict. and add: **2.** A man who works in an office; *spec.* a detective who remains at headquarters.

1904 'No. 1500' *Life in Sing Sing* xiii. 256/2 *Office Man,* headquarters detective. **1908** J. M. SULLIVAN *Criminal Slang* 17 *Office man,* headquarters detective. **1921** *Daily Colonist* (Victoria, B.C.) 12 Oct. 16/2 (Advt.), Wanted—position as office man, watchman, warehouse, or place of trust. **1949** PARTRIDGE *Dict. Underworld* 479/1 *Office man,* a headquarters detective.

officer, *sb.* Add: **3. b.** Used as a mode of address to a police officer.

1899 J. S. Clouston *Lunatic at Large* II. v. 140 Keep your eye on that man, officer,..and put your plain-clothes' men on his track. **1926** Galsworthy *Silver Spoon* I. vii. 50 'Pardon me, officer,' he said, 'but where is Wren Street?' **1934** D. L. Sayers *Nine Tailors* 143 It is said..that the plain bobby considers 'officer' a more complimentary form of address than 'my man', or even 'constable'. **1946** E. O'Neill *Iceman Cometh* (1947) IV. 211 She knows I was insane. You've got me all wrong, Officer. I want to go to the Chair... God, you're a dumb dick! **1965** M. Allingham *Mind Readers* iii. 44 'Officer!' said the voice.., 'I wish to give this lady in charge.' **1976** [see *officeful].

4. Also used in the air force, and in women's branches of the forces. Also *attrib.*

1943 C. H. Ward-Jackson *Piece of Cake* 4 The Service experiences of all sorts of people—pilots,..old R.N.A.S. and R.F.C. officers, padres,..and the rest. **1948** Partridge *Dict. Forces' Slang* 148 R.A.F. officer term. **1952** *Oxf. Jun. Encycl.* X. 493 Members of the three [women's] services..are administered by their own officers. **1959** *Chambers's Encycl.* I. 184/2 If aircraft were used in attack and defence,..it could be argued that they were manned ..by officers and men who could claim to be members of a service which belonged neither to the navy nor to the army. **1973** K. Giles *File on Death* iii. 63 Miss Sloper.. had worked as an officer in the Second World War.

b. Phr. *(an) officer and (a) gentleman*, applied to a person embodying the civilized qualities expected of both, freq. used ironically, also (occas. with hyphens) *attrib.* or as *adj. phr.* Hence *officer-and-gentlemanly* adj.

1845 Mrs. Gaskell *North & South* (1855) I. xiv. 164, I will bear with all proper patience everything that one officer and gentleman can take from another. **1871** *Porcupine* 29 July 275/3 They want their purchase, their officer-and-gentleman hobby, their..agreeable club of an army left undisturbed. **1888** Kipling *Plain Tales from Hills* 123 Golightly spent..that summer trying to get the Corporal..tried by Court-Martial for arresting an 'officer and a gentleman'. **1926** —— *Debits & Credits* 334 Ignatius is one of the subtlest intellects we have, and an officer and a gentleman to boot. **1946** E. O'Neill *Iceman Cometh* (1947) I. 48, I give you my word of honour as an officer and a gentleman, you shall be paid tomorrow. **1962** I. Murdoch *Unofficial Rose* xxxi. 304 He was paying the penalty..for being an officer and a gentleman. **1966** A. Prior *Operators* iii. 28 Oh, coming the officer and gentleman touch, was he? **1969** K. Giles *Death cracks Bottle* x. 110 We will just be very nice to the police in an officer-and-gentlemanly way. **1971** 'H. Calvin' *Poison Chasers* ix. 135 ''Evening, Sergeant,' I said. Hard, officer-and-gentleman tone. **1974** 'J. Graham' *Bloody Passage* i. 11 There wasn't much I could do except put my head on the block like an officer and a gentleman.

c. *Officers Training Corps*, an organization set up in schools and universities for the preliminary training of boys and young men who may later become officers in the armed forces.

1907 *Interim Rep. War Office Comm. Provision of Officers* 10 (*heading*) in *Parl. Papers* (Cd. 3294) XLIX. 549 Proposals respecting the Officers Training Corps at Universities. **1908** *Oxford Univ. Officers Training Corps* (Misc. Paper) 1 The present Oxford University Volunteer Corps is about to be transformed into a unit of 'The Officers Training Corps'. **1925** *Officers Training Corps Gaz.* Nov. 1/1 Though our first number is devoted to the University of London Contingent,..it is proposed to include all University units of the Officers Training Corps. **1957** *Encycl. Brit.* XXII. 392/2 The Officers' Training corps (O.T.C.) was set up in 1909 under the Haldane scheme... The junior division..consisted of boys in public secondary schools..; the senior division of university contingents... After World War II the training corps was replaced by the Combined Cadet force.

6. *officer cadet* (also *fig.*), *-caste*, *-class* (also *attrib.* or as *adj.*), *-type*. Also *officer material*: see *material *sb.* 6*.

1925 *Officers Training Corps Gaz.* Nov. 1/1 Our object.. is to foster a spirit of Unity and Co-operation among Officer Cadets. **1955** T. H. Pear *Eng. Social Differences* iii. 101 When..the functions of Sandhurst were modified, 'officer'-cadets succeeded 'gentleman'-cadets. **1962** L. Deighton *Ipcress File* xiii. 74 [He] reminded me of those N.C.O.'s who drilled officer cadets. **1973** 'S. Harvester' *Corner of Playground* I. iv. 38 Officer cadets due to receive their commissions at the passing-out parade. **1976** *Listener* 5 Feb. 139/1 We were a grateful generation... The fittest had survived to become the officer-cadets of the intellect. **1937** 'G. Orwell' in *New English Weekly* 29 July 308/2 The Popular Army..modelled as far as possible on an ordinary bourgeois army, with a privileged officer-caste, immense differences of pay, etc., etc. **1936** 'N. Blake' *Thou Shell of Death* v. 78 His army training had given him a possibly misplaced belief in the superior wisdom of what he would never have thought of calling 'the officer class'. **1950** G. Greene *Third Man* ii. 25 'Be quiet, can't you, sir,' my driver said. He had an exaggerated sense of officer-class. **1954** 'N. Blake' *Whisper in Gloom* II. xiii. 173 He treated his church wardens with a certain officer-class brusqueness. **1958** P. Shore in N. Mackenzie *Conviction* 28 The managers are often described as an officer class and this is..an apt analogy. **1968** A. Laski *Keeper* i. 10 Ralph's turning to Colin and saying, in the same frankly brutal officer-class manner [etc.]. **1942** E. Waugh *Put out More Flags* i. 64 'What do you think is the right type of officer?' 'The officer-type.'.. 'Now three-quarters of your officer-type live in towns'.

officering, *vbl. sb.* (Later examples.)

1890 *Century Mag.* Dec. 207 The American system of officering..was superior to that of the English. **1907** *Daily Chron.* 15 Feb. 7/4 The preponderance of the Japanese forces;..their energetic and capable officering. **1933** Belloc *Charles I* 231 The army was still quite unfitted to meet the better training, the larger numbers and the superior officering of the enemy. **1977** *Listener* 16 June 779/4 It was..to the manning of the Empire, or rather the officering of it, that the best products of the classical 'classical education' were destined.

officery, *a.* [f. Officer *sb.* + -y[1].] Resembling an officer; having the character or nature of an officer.

1905 H. G. Wells *Kipps* III. i. 289 Saw a lot of young officery fellers coming along.

officese (ǫfisī·z). f. Offic(e *sb.* + -ese.] = *commercialese.

1935 A. P. Herbert in *Punch* 19 June 730/2 It is just the misplaced effort to 'write like a book', to be elegant and flowery, that yields the sickliest growths of 'officese' and Jungle English—all these 'inst.'s' and 'ult.'s' and 'in regard to's' and 'favours' and 'representatives'. **1942** Partridge *Usage & Abusage* 218/2 Commercialese or Business English (or, as A. P. Herbert calls it, *Officese*). **1960** —— *Charm of Words* i. 22 Commercialese..has also been called officese.

official, *a.* Add: **3. b.** *official secrets*, information the disclosure of which outside official circles would constitute a breach of national security; so *Official Secrets Act*.

1889 *Act* 52 & 53 *Vict.* c. 52 § 10 This Act may be cited as the Official Secrets Act, 1889. **1911** *Encycl. Brit.* XXIV. 571/1 By the Official Secrets Act 1889 it was made a misdemeanour for an official to communicate any information or documents concerning the military or naval affairs of Her Majesty, to any person to whom it ought not to be communicated. **1931** 'G. Trevor' *Murder at School* vi. 127 'I think once again I must plead the Official Secrets' Acts,' he answered, jocularly. **1931** *Economist* 28 Nov. 1001/1 The editor of a German Radical newspaper has been sentenced to 18 months' imprisonment on the ground that, in the course of an article on civil aviation, he revealed official secrets, whose disclosure endangered national security. **1966** A. Firth *Tall, Balding, Thirty-Five* v. 61 He pushed forward the buff paper. It was a shortened version of the form of submission to the Official Secrets Act of 1929. **1973** *Guardian* 29 June 14/3 Today the House of Commons debates the Franks report on the Official Secrets Acts. **1976** *Howard Jrnl.* XV. i. 24 The workings of the Official Secrets Act and the requirement of 'submission for prior approval' before a prison official can make a public statement do not encourage the development of penological expertise.

5. (Further examples.)

1957 J. Passmore *100 Yrs. Philos.* i. 28 The 'Scottish school'..lingered on..in the United States, where it became a sort of 'official philosophy' in the less adventurous Colleges. **1959** *Chambers's Encycl.* XII. 745 English and Afrikaans are treated on a footing of equality as official languages... Every child shall learn the second official language. **1970** *Cape Times* 28 Oct. 22/6 (Advt.), A knowledge of both official languages is required. **1976** *Scotsman* 27 Dec. 5/1 At Celtic Park, the official attendance was 47,000. **1977** *Belfast Tel.* 24 Jan. 9/4 Sinn Fein.. has failed to gain any significant support at the polls, mainly because it has been regarded as the 'front organisation' for the official IRA.

officialese. Delete *nonce-word* and add further examples.

1924 P. MacDonald *Rasp* vi. 84 My—what's the officialese for it?—'suppression of the truth' gave Boyd clue number one. **1932** *New Statesman* 2 Jan. 7/1 Drink to me only with thine i's, and I will cross the t's, But leave no kiss within this cup of crabb'd officialese. **1941** *Manch. Guardian Weekly* 14 Mar. 214/3 Let us be fair to the Civil Servant: the official is not the only dealer in officialese. **1953** E. Simon *Past Masters* IV. ii. 220 One was left to infer between the lines of officialese. **1960** S. Foot *Emergency Exit* xiii. 110 Constitutional English is such a splendid language..but this was constitutional officialese. **1973** *Listener* 15 Feb. 221/3 The vocabulary Don Haworth's characters use..embodies chunks of jolting officialese. **1975** B. Garfield *Hopscotch* iii. 50 'You've read the backgrounding.' It was phrased in dry officialese.

officialize, *v.* Add: Hence **officializa·tion**, the rendering official in form or character.

1907 *Daily Chron.* 9 Nov. 4/4 One fails to detect a craving for any such officialisation.

officially, *adv.* Add: Also, for official purposes; in official or public statements, reports, etc. (but not in actuality).

1938 E. Ambler *Cause for Alarm* x. 163 The price per machine will..be higher... Officially, this fact will be accounted for by the modifications. Actually, those modifications are purely nominal. **1964** L. Deighton *Funeral in Berlin* vii. 51 'Does anyone have phones going across..Berlin?' 'Officially one. It connects the Russian Command..with the Allied Command.'.. 'Unofficially?' 'There *have* to be lines.' **1976** 'B. Shelby' *Great Pebble Affair* i. 30 Officially, I had been renting my apartment for three months before I even saw it.

officina. Add: **b.** Phr. *officina gentium*, a country or area from the inhabitants of which several nations develop; also *officina gentis*, the place of origin of a nation or people.

[*c* **550** Jordanes *Getica* (1882) iv. 25 Scandza..quasi officina gentium aut certe velut vagina nationum.] **1821** De Quincey *Confess.* (1822) 169 Southern Asia is.. the great *officina gentium*. **1832** *Edin. Rev.* LV. 499 The New Englanders have been the *officina gentis* to the American people. **1877** D. M. Wallace *Russia* (ed. 2) II. xxiv. 106 As Scandinavia was formerly called *officina gentium*—a workshop in which new nations were made. **1904** W. P. Ker *Dark Ages* iii. 131 [Jordanes] has a lofty conception of the destiny and fortunes of the Gothic race, and his account of the origin of the warlike nations in the Northern island, Scanzia, *officina gentium*, corresponds in prose to the epic genealogies of the poets. **1961** L. F. Brosnahan *Sounds of Language* ix. 195 The *officina gentium* which was Scandinavia at this period.

offing. Add: **3.** *in the offing*: nearby, at hand, in prospect, likely to happen in the near future; (in quot. 1779, exceptionally, in the distant future).

1779 J. Wedgwood *Let.* 30 May (1965) 234, I hope soon to say as far as 30 inches, perhaps ultimately up to 36 inches by 24, but that is at present in the offing. **1914** T. Dreiser *Titan* xvii. 139 The possibility of another woman equally or possibly better suited to him was looming in the offing. **1942** D. Powell *Time to be Born* (1943) x. 239 Somehow it didn't seem like real love without a husband in the offing. **1949** N. Mitford *Love in Cold Climate* I. v. 57 That look of concentration which comes over French faces when a meal is in the offing. **1970** G. F. Newman *Sir, You Bastard* viii. 241 Number six could be afforded if he got promoted, but promotion wasn't in the offing.

offish, *a.* (Earlier and later examples.)

1834 C. A. Davis *Lett. J. Downing* 75 Others are a little offish. *a* **1963** S. Plath *Crossing Water* (1971) 31 She stopped fitting me so closely and seemed offish.

off-island, *adv.* (*phr.*), *sb.*, and *a.* [f. Off *prep.*, *off- 4 b + Island *sb.*] **A.** *adv.* (*phr.*) Away from an island; spec. *U.S.*, away from the island of Nantucket.

1917 *Dialect Notes* IV. 335 *Off island*, elsewhere than on the island (Nantucket). 'What would I want to go *off island* for?' **1971** *N.Y. Times* 27 June 3 One islander was heard to remark recently that he never carried more than 30 cents in his pocket unless he planned to go off-island.

B. *sb.* An island off the shore of a larger or central island.

1969 *Sunday Times* 23 Feb. 63 The off-islands may seem to be just across the nautical street but the journey can still be an experience on a rough day. **1973** W. J. Burley *Death in Salubrious Place* i. 14 The pleasure boats were on their various ways to the off-islands. **1973** *Publishers Weekly* 19 Nov. 61/1 Letty Ward lives with her parents on Innish, an Irish off-island. **1976** *London Calling* Apr. 2/1 The Isles of Scilly... The four inhabited 'off-islands', as they are always called, are Tresco,..St Martin's, St Agnes and Bryher.

C. *adj.* Visiting or temporarily residing on an island.

1965 *New Yorker* 13 Feb. 42 This upset afforded small comfort to off-island Republicans here..because while the Guamanians are American citizens, they cannot vote in our Presidential elections.

So **off-islander**, (*a*) a visitor or temporary resident on an island; spec. *U.S.*, in Nantucket; (*b*) an inhabitant of an off-shore island.

1882 J. G. Austin (*title*) Nantucket scraps: being the experiences of an off-islander, in season and out of season, among a passing people. **1935** [see *Nantucketer]. **1939** S. Chamberlain *Nantucket* 4 Artists and summer visitors have discovered its allure, and many fortunate 'off islanders' now live in old Nantucket houses. **1961** D. M. Douglass *Saba's Treasure* (1963) vi. 98 Off-islanders like other harbors better. **1967** *Daily Tel.* 17 May 21/1 Mr. John Knott, Conservative MP for St. Ives, Cornwall, is to meet representatives of the Duchy of Cornwall, the Scillies Council, the Steamship Co. and 'off-islanders' on Saturday. **1968** *Time* 26 July 67 Many 'off-islanders', the regular summer residents, are concerned lest their historic hideaway lose its charm.

off key, off-key, *adv.* (*phr.*) and *a.* [f. Off *prep.*, *off- 4 b + Key *sb.*[1]] Without tonal organization; out of tune; also *fig.*, wrong(ly), inappropriate(ly).

1929 M. Lief *Hangover* 235 Eulalia Duncan sang so off-key last night that she had great difficulty moving her vowels. **1943** R. Chandler *Lady in Lake* xxxi. 171 There's something a little off key about everything you do. **1952** *Sci. Amer.* May 65 Friends..who sing everything in a monotone or in the same off-key pattern. **1953** *N.Y. Times* 29 Jan. 25/2 Miss Davis' performance in this scene is foolishly false—a travesty of sexy movie acting, illogical and wholly off-key. **1965** G. McInnes *Road to Gundagai* iii. 53 A faintly off-key piano. **1971** [see *off base *phr.* (*adv.*) and *a.*]. **1973** J. Wainwright *Devil you Don't* 18 He had a peculiar, off-key voice.

offlap (ǫ·flæp). *Geol.* Also **off-lap.** [f. Off *adv.* + Lap *v.*[2], after Overlap *v.* 3.] A progressive diminution in the lateral extent of conformable strata in passing upwards from older to younger strata, so that each stratum leaves a portion of the underlying one exposed; a set of strata exhibiting this.

1913 A. W. Grabau *Princ. Stratigr.* xviii. 734 (*caption*) Diagram illustrating regressive overlap (off-lap) and the formation of a sandstone of emergence..into which the shore-ends of the successive members of the retreatal series..grade. **1948** *Jrnl. Geol.* LVI. 147/1 Marine blanket sands represent the horizontal welding of many parallel prismatic shore lines during a long, continuous period of over-lap or off-lap. **1969** Bennison & Wright *Geol. Hist. Brit. Isles* i. 14 The offlaps of marine sedimentation are accompanied, in this case, by lateral and vertical gradation into beds of continental facies. **1975** *Nature* 10 Jan. 107/1 The stratigraphic relationship of the Devensian

Tills of eastern England is therefore one of offlap..and not of overlap.

So **o·fflapping** *ppl. a.*

1906 A. W. GRABAU in *Bull. Geol. Soc. Amer.* XVII. 615 Examples of regressively overlapping or, better, offlapping formations are frequently met. **1921** —— *Textbk. Geol.* I. xvii. 559 If, after a retreatal movement of the sea and the formation of an offlapping series.., a transgressive movement with overlapping of formations should follow, the sandstone bed of emergence would be in part reworked. **1974** *Nature* 15 Nov. 200/1 The sealevel curve is based on the series of transgression-regression cycles identified from successions of offlapping coral reefs.

off licence, off-licence. [OFF *a.* 5.] A shop or other establishment where alcoholic liquors are sold for consumption off the premises; also, a licence permitting such sales. Also *attrib.* Hence **off-licensed** *ppl. a.*; **off-licensee.**

1891, 1897 [see OFF *a.* 5]. **1907** *Daily Chron.* 16 Apr. 3/6 The number of off-license [*sic*] premises at the beginning of 1906 was 25,281. **1959** J. BRAINE *Vodi* iv. 55 It was an off-licence, very cool and smelling both earthy and antiseptic, with overtones of stale beer and tobacco. **1961** E. A. POWDRILL *Vocab. Land Planning* iii. 42 To double the population is to increase considerably the range of shops that are required, for instance, cafes, off-licences, adies' shops, etc. **1971** *Oxford Times* 15 Oct. 9 (Advt.), From our off-licensed branches. Guinness—small cans. 9p. **1975** J. AIKEN *Voices in Empty House* iii. 105 The old lady tottering..to the off-licence on the corner. **1978** *Morecambe Guardian* 14 Mar. 4/1 (Advt.), We cordially invite all Hoteliers Restaurateurs Off-Licensees, etc. to visit our new Wines & Spirits department.

off limits, off-limits, *adv.* (*phr.*) and *a.* orig. *U.S.* [f. OFF *prep.* + *pl.* of LIMIT *sb.*] Of an area, place, etc.: outside the limits within which a particular group or class of people must remain; not to be frequented or patronized, esp. by military personnel; out of bounds. Also *transf.* and *fig.*

1952 R. CUTFORTH *Korean Reporter* xv. 137 Over the door an official army notice barked in iron-mouthed print: Strictly Off Limits. **1959** *Amer. Speech* XXXIV. 155 As long as the infatuation lasts, the man is said to be *attached* and strictly *off limits* to other girls. **1960** *Encounter* Feb. 38/1 The Negroes do not blame the residents but know that..the white G.I.'s in effect declare a town off-limits. **1968** A. DIMENT *Bang Bang Birds* v. 58 We ain't going to take them out because they're brothels. If it was just that we'd mark them Off Limits to service personnel. **1968** *Economist* 5 Oct. 46/3 The federation's leaders have declared the UAW-Teamsters group to be off-limits, describing it as 'a dual labour organisation, rival to the AFL-CIO'. **1971** 'S. RANSOME' *Trap* 6 (1972) xiii. 139, I didn't intrude into the investigators' office. So far as I'm concerned that's off limits. **1973** A. DUNDES *Mother Wit* 259 White females were off-limits to Negro males. **1975** *N.Y. Times* 15 Sept. 9/1 In this central highlands town, which houses the legion's Corsican command post, three bars are off limits.

off-line (stress variable), *a.* and *adv.* [f. OFF *prep.* + LINE *sb.*[2]] **A.** *adj.* **1.** Not situated or performed on a railway or by rail.

1926 HUEBNER & JOHNSON *Railroad Freight Service* xvii. 338 Many railroads maintain 'off-line' offices or agencies at important industrial and commercial centers which they reach via connecting lines. **1973** E. RATH *Container Systems* vii. 175 Bimodal containerization uses truck trailers or other highway vehicles or special containers... This service uses the rail network as the main artery and as prime source of railroad revenue. The off-line service is given as an accommodation to the freight market. **1973** *Sci. Amer.* Oct. 24/3 The achievement is made possible by off-line loading and automatic, positive control of all motions of the vehicle.

2. *Computers.* Not on-line; other than on-line.

1950 W. W. STIFLER *High-Speed Computing Devices* ii. 7 For other applications, off-line operation, involving automatic transcription of data in a form suitable for later introduction to the machine, may be tolerated. **1957** D. D. MCCRACKEN *Digital Computer Programming* xii. 157 The reel of tape may then be removed from the auxiliary ('off-line') tape unit, placed on a tape unit which is connected to the computer ('on-line'), and read in at high speeds. **1959** [see *IN-LINE *a.* 3 c]. **1967** C. BERNERS-LEE in Wills & Yearsley *Handbk. Managem. Technol.* 16 Off-line equipment is, typically, a keyboard device preparing a paper tape to be read into a computer later. An on-line keyboard, on the other hand, is one wired directly into the computer. **1969** *Sunday Times* (Colour Suppl.) 16 Feb. 22/3 The clearance and updating must be done when the computer is..'off-line', i.e. is uncoupled from any systems that the computer itself is controlling. **1972** *Accountant* 26 Oct. 530/2 Off-line operation at Hendon is through a Varian 620I computer and dual tape unit, transferring data to tape for processing later on the 370/145.

B. *adv. Computers.* With a delay between the production of data and its processing; not under direct computer control.

1950 W. W. STIFLER *High-Speed Computing Devices* ii. 7 Some teletype machines operate on line. Their operators are in instantaneous communication. Other teletype machines are operated off line, through the intervention of punched paper tape. **1959** J. K. BRIGDEN in E. M. Grabbe et al. *Handbk. Automation, Computation, & Control* II. xx. 4 Obviously all the equipment used for on-line purposes can also be used off-line. **1964** T. W. MCRAE *Impact of Computers on Accounting* i. 17 The tape is then.. transferred to a smaller computer and printed off-line on the output printer of that computer. **1967** D. WILSON in Wills & Yearsley *Handbk. Managem. Technol.* 43 Because removable media systems can store inactive data off-line, the total capacity of these systems..is virtually unlimited. **1970** *Computers & Humanities* V. 36 Although the plotter, when run 'off line', is relatively cheap, it is slow. **1971** *Sci. Amer.* Sept. 17/1 (Advt.), Until recently, the best solution was to use the complex mathematics of the Fourier transform and program a computer to do the complex signal analysis computations off-line.

off-load, *v.* Add: 'Also with stress on second syllable' and for *S. Africa* read 'orig. *S. Afr.*'. (Further examples.) Also *transf.* and *fig.*, to discard, get rid of, relieve oneself of (a person or thing). Hence **off-loa·ding** *vbl. sb.* and *ppl. a.*

1850 R. G. CUMMING *Five Yrs. Hunter's Life S. Afr.* II. xx. 82 Having off-loaded my waggon, I handed it over to Mr. Arnott, the resident blacksmith, to undergo repairs. **1903** KIPLING *Five Nations* 208 Ubique means 'Off-load your guns'—at midnight in the rain! **1916** *Chambers's Jrnl.* June 373/2 At railhead the train is off-loaded into the motor-lorries. **1942** W. S. CHURCHILL *Second World War* (1951) IV. I. ix. 146 It will..be necessary for the *Indomitable* squadrons to be off-loaded in Ceylon. **1949** *Sun* (Baltimore) 21 Feb. 4/3 The machinery was off-loaded and shipped on to Nottingham by railway. **1950** *Daily Progress* (Charlottesville, Va.) 30 Jan. 1/5 Salvage team personnel have completed offloading the Big Mo's ammunition and all beach gear has been placed. **1952** C. DAY LEWIS tr. *Virgil's Aeneid* v. 113 They enrolled the women for the colony, off-loaded the men who wanted To stay there. **1957** *Economist* 2 Nov. 429/1 The vehicle industry finds that it has to offload more of its rising production of cars and lorries on to the home market. **1958** *Times* 19 Mar. 14/2 Bales were off-loaded. *Ibid.*, Cotton was stolen from the Liverpool Docks in the off-loading of 12 different ships. **1968** M. WOODHOUSE *Rock Baby* v. 43 A Director who has to offload one of his staff and is embarrassed. **1971** C. BONINGTON *Annapurna South Face* iii. 30 This period being taken up with off-loading, Customs clearance and the journey across India. **1972** *Daily Tel.* 1 Apr. 3/2 It arrived at Heathrow as mishandled luggage, having been wrongly off-loaded in Rome from a flight from Australia to London. **1977** J. MCCLURE *Sunday Hangman* ii. 17 [He] side-stepped into the shadow of an off-loading Coke truck.

off microphone, off-microphone, *adv.* (*phr.*) and *a.* [f. OFF *prep.* + MICROPHONE.] Away from a microphone; that is distant from, or not facing, a microphone. Also colloq. abbrev. **off-mike.**

1937 *Printers' Ink Monthly* May 39/3 *Off mike*, a position away from a performer or performer's position away from the microphone. **1940** A. OBOLER *Fourteen Radio Plays* 201 Pa (*off mike*). Hangin' around with loafers in the gymnasiums! *Ibid.* 257 Dialogue or effect is off-microphone, in other words, not at full volume in relation to other speeches or effects. **1958** *Listener* 13 Nov. 799/1 Those who may have wondered what goes on in the studios before the red light comes on were given an amusing picture of off-mike life in Mr. Robert Kemp's comedy, 'Young Mother Hubbard'. **1959** *Ibid.* 30 Apr. 774/1 The story..forced Mr. Naughton to move his magnifying glass from the street and to take it, as it were, off-mike. **1962** *Times* 3 Apr. 15/2 Goonery is not the most evident attribute of his off-microphone personality. **1962** A. NISBETT *Technique Sound Studio* ii. 40 The pages should be turned well off-microphone. *Ibid.* 48 Off-microphone voices and spot effects could be blended with on-microphone voices. **1973** *Washington Post* 5 Apr. B. 2 Something electric goes on between the comedienne and her husband... There are off-mike private jokes. **1977** *Rolling Stone* 19 May 89/1 Coltrane is occasionally off-mike.

off'n, var. *OFFEN *prep.*

off-off, off-off-Broadway: see *OFF-BROADWAY *a.* and *sb.*

off-peak, *a.* [f. *OFF- 4 b + PEAK *sb.*[2]] That is not at the maximum; of or pertaining to a period of less than busiest use, consumption, business, etc.

1920 A. C. PIGOU *Econ. of Welfare* II. xv. 261 If it is impracticable to charge differential rates directly as between peak and off-peak service, this may sometimes be attempted indirectly by differentiation between continuous and intermittent services. **1924** *World Power* I. 4 (*heading*) Electric heating by off-peak load. *Ibid.*, The continental technical press..gives particulars of successful applications of off-peak power for night uses at low tariffs. **1930** *Engineering* 11 Apr. 493/2 Such systems are generally arranged for supply by off-peak current. **1933** *Discovery* Apr. 111/2 Power is sold in large quantities at a very cheap rate so long as it is used during 'off-peak' hours. **1958** *Oxf. Mag.* 6 Mar. 336/2 Televised religious discussions attract over a million viewers even at off-peak times. **1971** *Times* 2 Oct. 13/2 The new off-peak fares should actually increase carryings. **1973** *Times* 21 Nov. 19/5 To prohibit the use of off-peak electric storage heating will not help the overall fuel position. **1976** P. R. WHITE *Planning for Public Transport* v. 113 Operating costs incurred for specified service levels are related to the ratio of peak to off-peak demand.

offprint, *v.* Delete *rare* and add: Also with stress on first syllable. (Further examples.)

1951 *Catalogues MS. Collections Brit. Mus.* (verso rear cover) Offprinted from the Journal of Documentation Volume 7. **1952** M. MCCARTHY *Groves of Academe* (1953) i. 8 Maynard Hoar, author of a pamphlet, 'The Witch Hunt in Our Universities' (off-printed from the *American Scholar* and mailed out gratis by the bushel to a legion of 'prominent educators').

off-put. Add: (Further examples.) Also, one who puts off, procrastinates, or wastes time.

1866 S. GILPIN *Songs & Ballads of Cumberland* 57 It was just for an off-put. **1893–4** R. O. HESLOP *Northumb. Words* II. 509 *Off-put*, delay, one that puts off time. 'Ye'r jeest an off-put o' time, laddy.' **1923** G. WATSON *Roxburghshire Word-Bk.* 223 It was duist an offpit! A ken 'im owre weel!

Hence **off-put** *v. trans.*, to put off; to disconcert; to repel; **off-putting** *vbl. sb.* (further examples); **off-putting** *ppl. a.* (further examples); *spec.* creating an unfavourable impression, causing displeasure; **off-pu·ttingly** *adv.*, in an off-putting manner; so as to disconcert or repel.

1828 MRS. B. HALL *Let.* 25 June in *Aristocratic Journey* (1931) 295 Forgetting that we had exchanged dilatory off-putting habits of the South for the anticipation in appointments of the North. **1833** *Chambers's Edin. Jrnl.* II. 234/1 Weel, mistress,..this off-putting will do nae langer. **1866** W. GREGOR *Dial. Banffshire* 6 *Aff-pittan*, the act of procrastination. **1893–4** R. O. HESLOP *Northumb. Words* II. 509 *Offputtin*, putting off, procrastinating, dallying. 'He's varry offputtin.' **1935** 'A. BRIDGE' *Illyrian Spring* xvii. 221 Your face isn't in the least off-putting, except when you're cross. **1951** WALLACE & BAGNALL-OAKELEY *Norfolk* vi. 66 The approach from the station is very off-putting:..Victorian and later ribbon-development soon started along the station road. **1955** M. ALLINGHAM *Beckoning Lady* xii. 169 Very off-putting, homely finances. **1960** M. SPARK *Bachelors* viii. 120 'Shut up about Ronald,' Tim said. 'It's jolly off-putting.' **1961** *Times* 4 Nov. 9/4 There is something..off-puttingly impersonal about a typed letter. **1969** D. FRANCIS *Enquiry* ix. 122 Composed, cool, off-puttingly gracious, she looked ..flawless. **1970** *Guardian Weekly* 7 Nov. 15 The peculiarity of a faith that can..be so offput by the female of any species that not even a cow is allowed to pasteurise here. **1973** *Nature* 16 Mar. 212/3 The appearance of the book is a little off-putting. **1974** *Country Life* 18 July 174/1 All this may sound offputtingly sporty. **1977** *Verbatim* Dec. 10/1 In case the number of pages is off-putting, it should be mentioned that the page size is 8-1/2″ × 11″.

off-ramp. *U.S.* [OFF- 4.] A sloping one-way road leading off a main highway.

1954 HEWES & OGLESBY *Highway Engin.* viii. 160 Capacity of off-ramps is affected by the number of through vehicles using the right-hand expressway lane. **1966** M. & G. GORDON *Undercover Cat prowls Again* v. 40 He took the Hollywood Freeway... Turning right at the Balboa off-ramp, he passed a city golf-course. **1968** 'R. MACDONALD' *Instant Enemy* xxx. 192, I took the first off-ramp and drove to the Langstons' neighborhood. **1973** W. MCCARTHY *Detail* iii. 247 Stuart looked for an off ramp... The next turnoff was ten miles ahead.

offretite (ǫ·frĕtəit). *Min.* Also † **offrétite.** [ad. F. *offrétite* (F. Gonnard 1890, in *Compt. Rend.* CXI. 1002), f. the name of Albert *Offret* (b. 1857), French mineralogist: see -ITE[1].] A hydrated aluminosilicate of potassium and calcium, which belongs to the zeolite group and is found as colourless hexagonal crystals at Mont Semiol, France.

1891 *Jrnl. Chem. Soc.* LX. 407 Offrétite is a zeolite which occurs in very small quantity, associated with christianite and chabasite, in the basalt of Mount Simiose [*sic*], near Montbrison. **1892** E. S. DANA *Dana's Syst. Min.* (ed. 6) 1043 Offrétite. **1894** *Amer. Jrnl. Sci.* CXLVIII. 188 Offretite. **1967** *Nature* 3 June 1005/2 Offretite and erionite are evidently two distinct but closely related minerals, which can intergrow. **1970** *Trans. Faraday Soc.* LXVI. 1616 Synthetic unfaulted offretite can provide a wide pore molecular sieve which can sorb molecules up to ∼7·1 Å in critical dimension... This zeolite appears to have possibilities as a versatile molecular sieve. **1975** *Nature* 28 Aug. 718/2 Offretite is a rare natural zeolite whose synthetic equivalent, zeolite O, is commercially important as a molecular sieve.

off-rhyme. [OFF- 4.] A partial or near rhyme.

1938 L. MACNEICE *Mod. Poetry* vii. 131 One can use internal rhymes, off-rhymes, bad rhymes, 'pararhymes'. **1944** —— *Christopher Columbus* 8 Your significant variations of rhythm, your internal rhymes, your off-rhymes and assonances and technical surprises, will get in the composer's way. **1956** E. WILSON *Piece of My Mind* (1957) vii. 124 Many kinds of liberties are countenanced—in the way of off-rhymes and irregular rhythms—in the writing of modern poetry. **1972** *Computers & Humanities* VII. 19 Taylor is not as unsystematic as might have been thought in his use of off-rhymes. **1972** J. WAIN in Cox & Dyson *20th-Cent. Mind* I. xi. 405 These half-rhymes of Owen's (para-rhymes, off-rhymes, even meta-rhymes, as they have been variously dubbed). **1977** *N.Y. Rev. Bks.* 9 June 29/4 Internal rhymes (trunks, sunk), off-rhymes (salt, silt), a lyrical vocabulary (sweetness, enchanted)—all these things are here, but none of them is obtrusive.

o·ff-saddle, *sb.* [f. the vb.] A break or rest in a journey during which horses are unsaddled.

1900 *Pall Mall Gaz.* 4 Jan. 1/3 The Cape horse..can canter along steadily all day under a burning sun, with an occasional off-saddle. **1908** *Daily Chron.* 10 Nov. 3/5, I had him by the hip at 'off-saddle' time.

offsaddle, off-saddle, *v.* For *S. Africa* read: 'Chiefly *S. Afr.*' (Add earlier and later examples.) Hence **off-saddling** *vbl. sb.*

1837 F. OWEN *Diary* (1926) 78 We off-saddled and sat on the ground on the outside of the fence. **1850** R. G. CUMMING *Five Yrs. Hunter's Life S. Afr.* I. 119 Accordingly we off-saddled, and in a few minutes I was once more asleep. *Ibid.* 129 Having off-saddled our horses, we knee-haltered them. **1906** RIDER HAGGARD *Benita* ix. 120 Directions as to their herding, and the off-saddling of the horses. **1915** KIPLING *New Army* 22 The batteries off-saddled in silence. **1939** [see *KNEE-HALTER *v.*]. **1974** B. MATHER *White Dacoit* ii. 22 They halted and off-saddled and picqueted the horses half a mile downstream.

off-sale. [OFF *a.* 5.] The sale of alcoholic liquors for consumption elsewhere than at the place of sale.

1899 [see OFF *a.* 5]. **1933** *Sun* (Baltimore) 17 Apr. 4/4 The local act also holds up issuance of an 'off sale' of beer in packages by Dressman Bros., grocers. **1963** *Times* 23 Apr. 20/3 Sales of bottles to take home ('Off-Sales') have increased very considerably, and there has been a reduction of sales by the glass. **1970** *Times* 18 Aug. 20 M. & B. wants to stop off-sales in favour of the 23 Wine Sellers off-licences it has opened in Birmingham. **1977** 'J. FRASER' *Hearts Ease* ix. 104, I see you're licensed for off-sales... Does that mean you have any wines?

offscouring. 2. b. (Further examples.)

1835 J. P. KENNEDY *Horse-Shoe Robinson* I. xiv. 180 Why, you off-scouring,..it is enough to make Old Scratch laugh, to hear you talk about conscience! **1871** *Scribner's Monthly* II. 546 Every Protestant is counted but the off-scouring of decent society. **1928** H. W. SHOEMAKER in *Publ. Pennsylvania Folk-Lore Soc.* I. IV. 10 That dressy offscouring will not come back for her... I've known him and his kind too well for more than fifty years. **1972** F. W. LINDSAY *Cariboo Dream* 13/2 Thugs, gamblers and the off-scourings of the world.

off screen, off-screen, *adv.* (*phr.*) and *a.* [f. OFF *prep.* + SCREEN *sb.*[1]] Not appearing on a film or television screen; = *OFF CAMERA *phr.* and *adv.* Also *fig.*

1935 *Motion Picture* Nov. 15/1 In addition, of course, you are the perfect lady, off-screen. **1953** K. REISZ *Technique Film Editing* i. 62 A reaction shot is shown and held while the character off screen is speaking his lines. **1958** *New Statesman* 9 Aug. 168/1 There were, of course, a few minor, off-screen, political controversies. **1962** *Guardian* 14 Aug. 5/3 This disarmingly frank and articulate off-screen comedian. **1973** 'E. MCBAIN' *Let's hear It* xiv. 209 The actors made important plot points offscreen, their voices floating in over the picture. **1974** *Times* 10 Apr. 13/8 The off-screen audience, real or canned, goes into mad paroxysms.

off season, off-season. See OFF *a.* 4. Also, a time of year other than the busiest or most popular time for a particular activity. Also *attrib.* or as *adj.*

1848, 1868 [see OFF *a.* 4]. **1897** [see *HIGH *a.* 4 a]. **1902** *Chambers's Jrnl.* July 433/2 The collection was not one of those which bore an historic name..and the sale took place in the off-season. **1905** A. BENNETT *Let.* 5 Apr. (1966) I. 61, I have a great notion of books being issued in off-seasons. **1908** *Daily Chron.* 21 Apr. 3/5 A great part of Miss Elwin's off-season work consists in meeting girls on their way to and from school. **1930** *B.B.C. Year-bk. 1931* 25 During the summer period, normally regarded as an 'off season', the average number of new licences taken out each month..was in excess of 20,000. **1957** L. F. R. WILLIAMS *State of Israel* 44 The coaches..are primarily intended for tourists, but..carry domestic traffic in the off-season. **1959** [see *BUDGET *sb.* 4]. **1971** W. J. BURLEY *Guilt Edged* iii. 59 The newcomers..disturbed the off-season peace of the Treen Hotel. **1976** *Washington Post* 19 Apr. D 1/6 With the series clinched, the Caps looked as though they were running their motors down for the offseason that begins when they fly off for a week's vacation in Hawaii.

offset, *sb.* Add: **2.** (Earlier and later examples.)

1629 J. PARKINSON *Parad.* xi. 114 The root is..compassed with a number of small rootes, or of of-sets round about it. **1925** A. J. MACSELF *Bulb Gardening* xiv. 215 Almost all bulbs and corms throw what are termed offsets, which are first attached to the basal wing of the bulb, drawing nourishment from the parent bulb, but later developing an independent root system. **1970** *Sunday Tel.* 3 May 19/2 The striped pineapple plant..which I have known having to be guarded at Chelsea Show for fear of the offsets that slowly form the new plants getting missed.

3. e. *Naut.* A current flowing outwards from the shore. Also *attrib.*

1902 *Daily Chron.* 30 Aug. 5/6 There was..what maritime men call an offset at the time Holbein was swimming. *Ibid.* 2 Sept. 5/5 He had got the benefit of a good off-set current under him.

5. (Earlier and later examples.)

1769 *Conn. Col. Rec.* (1885) XIII. 207 A petition..setting forth that the petitioner and petitionee have executions against each other now in the hands of Ezekiel Williams,..upon which the petitioner prays for an off-set of the same. **1932** *Daily Progress* (Charlottesville, Va.) 13 Aug. 1/3 Mr. Minor's action is what is known as an offset. He is asking the difference between $5,000 and the amount he alleges is due to him, or slightly more than $21,000. **1973** *Times* 11 June 14/1 Instead of being 50p better off, she gained only 15p a week. The High Court ruled that this automatic offset, which was standard commission procedure, was unlawful.

7. b. (Further examples.)

1856 *Porter's Spirit of Times* 18 Oct. 106/3 The hearth-stone, garden, 'offsets',..and a thousand delicious memories..swarm before us now. **1873** J. H. BEADLE *Undevel. West* xxvi. 555 He then walked along a flat offset five or six feet below the house. **1878** —— *Western Wilds* x. 157 About half way up the cliff is a small offset, where grows a beautiful pine.

10. b. Used, freq. *attrib.*, of a printing process whereby an image is first impressed on a rubber-covered cylinder and thence transferred to the paper; also used *attrib.* of paper suitable for use in this process.

1906 *Brit. Printer* Oct. 283/2 The offset process—that is, working first on the blanket and offsetting from this on to the paper fed into the machine—is as the usual method. **1909** *Brit. Pat. 25,446* 4 Nov., For printing in lithographic machines by the so-called offset process, the lithographic design used as the basis of printing is generally the opposite or the reverse of that which would be used in ordinary direct lithographic printing... By our invention we provide a press..for conveniently reversing designs or pulling proofs from reversed designs, such works being carried out by the offset method. **1918** *Pall Mall Gaz.* 29 June 8/5 A Litho Offset Press. **1921** *Dict. Occup. Terms* (1927) § 526 *Offset-litho operator*, a photographer..who obtains a negative, not reversed in position, with or without using a screen. **1926** *Encycl. Brit.* III. 220/2 By the offset method any paper, whether smooth- or rough-surfaced, may be used... Offset seems to be particularly adapted to colour-work. **1928** *Penrose Ann.* 111 The faulty soluble coating in so many classes of so-called offset papers, engenders printing troubles. **1929** *Horse* I. 61 The process employed in reproducing this notable painting is that known as offset. **1931** *Times Lit. Suppl.* 25 June p. viii/3 The rollicking offset-lithographs of Elsa Moeschlin. **1937** *Discovery* Oct. 297 An offset—a print made in a non-greasy powdered chalk. **1958** J. R. BIGGS *Woodcuts* 91 Offset cartridge, that is, the paper made for printing offset lithography, has a kindly surface, and a firm feel which is suitable for some subjects. **1958** *Times Lit. Suppl.* 4 Apr. 188/3 Dr. Willoughby's book, printed by offset from type-written script. **1967** KARCH & BUBER *Offset Processes* Pref., Although growth for the entire [printing] industry has been great, offset-lithography has grown at twice the rate of the industry as a whole. *Ibid.* ii. 12 Letterpress printed halftones..can often be..rescreened for printing by the offset-lithographic process. **1970** [see *FLEXOGRAPHY]. **1976** *Sci. Amer.* Jan. 135/1 This work is unappealing typographically, dominated by crowded typewritten copy in grayish offset.

11. offset purchase *Econ.*, a purchase made abroad by agreement to counter-balance revenues spent in the buying country by the selling country; **offset well** (see quot. 1971); also *ellipt.* **offset.**

1966 *Economist* 20 Aug. 731/2 The Germans continue to be slow in making their military 'offset' purchases to counter the dollars which are drained away by the cost of keeping American troops in Germany. *a* **1974** R. CROSSMAN *Diaries* (1975) I. 550 There was an appalling incident in the House when he was caught out about our attempt to pay for the new American planes with offset purchases. **1922** *Petroleum Gloss.* (Pan Amer. Petroleum & Transport Co.) 32 *Offset well*, a well drilled opposite to a well on an adjoining property. **1924** *Amer. Review of Reviews* Mar. 231 Adjacent to one of the California reserves were oil lands that were under active development, with wells near enough to the boundary lines of the naval territory to cause a draining away of a certain amount of oil that lay beneath the navy's property. Under such circumstances, it is customary to sink what are known as 'offset wells'. **1932** *World Petroleum* III. 467/1 Production in the light oil zone at the discovery well in the center of the field..has since been considerably augmented by the completion of offset wells. **1971** WILLIAMS & MEYERS *Oil & Gas Terms* (ed. 3) 294 *Offset well*, a well drilled on one tract of land to prevent the drainage of oil or gas to an adjoining tract of land, on which a well is being drilled or is already in production. **1974** R. D. GRACE in P. L. Moore et al. *Drilling Practices Manual* 349 Deviation to 10 degrees was recorded in the north offset.

offset, *v.* Delete 'Chiefly *U.S.*' and add: **1.** Also, to set off against part of something else. (Further examples.)

1930 G. B. SHAW *Androcles & Lion* Pref. 58 The triumphant solution of the first by our inventors and chemists has been offset by the disastrous failure of our rulers to solve the other. **1936** *Discovery* Sept. 278/1 To have a large family, it is essential for the parents to start at an early stage, and this is offset by the tendency to postpone marriage. **1968** *Lebende Sprachen* XIII. 51/2 The customer can offset claims on the bank only against liabilities in the same currency. **1975** E. F. L. BRECH *Princ. & Pract. Managem.* (ed. 3) v. x. 813 Companies were required to deduct tax at the standard rate from all dividends paid... The only exception to this rule was if the company had itself received a dividend under deduction of tax from some other UK company... The tax on the latter could then be offset and only the net balance was remittable.

off-set (ǫ·fset), *ppl. a.* [f. OFF *adv.* + SET *ppl. a.*] Set at an angle; placed off-centre or out of line.

1950 H. L. LORIMER *Homer & Monuments* v. 169 It lacks the off-set rim characteristic of the hoplite shield. **1950** *N.Z. Jrnl. Agric.* June 538/1 Equipment was further improved by acquiring sets of both tandem and off-set discs. **1960** *Farmer & Stockbreeder* 29 Mar. 76/3 This new 43in-cut offset harvester, known as the Taarup Tiger, weighs only 9½cwt.

off-set, *adv.* [f. OFF- 2 + *SET *sb.*] Out of range of the cameras in a film or television set or studio.

1948 L. LEVY *Music for Movies* ii. 13 When we had decided on a piece of music to accompany any one scene, the band would play off set while the actor went through his actions or lines in time with the music. **1968** M. WOODHOUSE *Rock Baby* vii. 64 In the next shot he'd gone off-set, the camera had moved in.

offsetting, *vbl. sb.* and *ppl. a.* (Further examples.)

1857 DICKENS *Perils Eng. Prisoners* iii, in *Househ. Words* Extra Christmas No., 7 Dec. 30/2 The off-settings and point-currents of the stream. **1908** *Daily Chron.* 24 Aug. 9/7, I was swimming against a strong offsetting tide. **1946** E. HODGINS *Mr. Blandings builds his Dream House* (1947) xvi. 208 The Blandings saw their house..in all its gleaming whiteness, the delicate waving leaves..the perfect offsetting foils. **1970** P. OLIVER *Savannah Syncopators* 28 The offsetting of the rhythms of the different drums against the gongs and against each other, sets up an exhilarating tension. **1975** *Times* 10 July 4/8 Mr Callaghan..sees the release of Mr Hills as unconditional. No offsetting arrangement will be discussed.

off shore, off-shore. Add: **B.** *adj.* **b.** (Further examples.) Also, away from the mainland. Esp. in *off-shore island*, an island close to the mainland; *spec.* (*a*) any of a number of small islands off the coast of China, in the Formosa Strait; (*b*) Great Britain, jocularly regarded as an 'off-shore island' of Europe; hence *off-shore islander*.

1921 *Daily Colonist* (Victoria, B.C.) 5 Apr. 7/2 The seas were breaking so high over the bar here yesterday and today that some off-shore shipping was compelled to remain outside. **1946** *Sun* (Baltimore) 30 Jan. 11/3 Drastic measures should be taken to complete whatever trade negotiations and shipping are necessary to hasten receipt of raw sugars and off-shore refined sugars. **1958** *New Statesman* 30 Aug. 241/2 It is impossible to say whether it is intended merely to put a stop to the various patrol activities which Chiang's forces mount from the Quemoy and Matsu groups of islands; whether it is a prelude to the occupation of these off-shore islands; or whether, possibly, we are witnessing the first stage in the invasion of Formosa itself. **1959** M. LASKI (*title of play*) The offshore island. **1963** *Listener* 14 Feb. 310/2 Reflect (as often) on the advantages of being an off-shore islander living in an intellectual fog where there is no black and white. **1966** *Economist* 8 Jan. 119/3 British Petroleum is busily finding itself another offshore rig to replace the defunct 'Sea Gem'. **1968** *Listener* 29 Feb. 264/1 The Empire had gone: England was an offshore island in competition with the giants of the world. **1972** *Guardian* 16 Aug. 12 (*heading*) View from an offshore island. Linda Christmas on the Isle of Man. **1972** P. JOHNSON *Offshore Islanders* 79 William I's work in re-building the Old English monarchy was..continued by an Angevin who became a thorough offshore islander in his turn. **1973** *Guardian* 17 Jan. 10/1 The purpose of Mr Peter Walker's new Offshore Supplies Office is..to bring more work and wealth to Britain. *Ibid.* 11 Opportunities for British industry from offshore oil and gas developments. **1973** C. CALLOW *Power from Sea* iv. 89 All the big off-shore pipelines have been supplied by foreign groups. **1974** E. AMBLER *Dr. Frigo* I. 45 Off-shore oil? Is that what they were looking for? **1975** *Petroleum Rev.* XXIX. 397/3 With the North Sea rapidly becoming the area for the most intensive offshore diving activity in the world, the growing pains of this..profession are felt..in the UK. **1975** *Weekend Mag.* (Montreal) 15 Nov. 7/3 Jamaicans are luckier than most offshore workers. Because their government has a tax convention with Canada, they are exempt from paying income tax and Canada pension.

c. Of, pertaining to, or designating goods purchased with American dollars by and from countries other than the United States (see quots.). Also, designating the dollars used in this way.

1948 *Economist* 8 May 768/1 The 16 nations will be provided with 'off-shore' dollars for buying from Germany. **1949** *Times* 10 Sept. 5/7 *Off-shore purchases*, the name given to supplies to countries in receipt of Marshall aid, which are financed by Marshall aid but which do not come from the United States itself. **1952** *Economist* 13 Dec. 759 An off-shore purchase, as its name implies, is the buying of goods from countries other than the United States with dollars supplied by the United States. **1953** *Ann. Reg. 1952* 220 'Off-shore' orders for military equipment were placed with Italian industry. **1960** *New Left Rev.* July-Aug. 45/2 The buoyancy of the Japanese economy..has been..guaranteed by massive off-shore purchases of military equipment.

d. *offshore funds* (see quot. 1972).

1972 *Observer* 8 Oct. 18/1 Offshore funds, investment funds similar to unit trusts but registered abroad, usually in countries with advantageous tax situations. **1977** *Times* 29 Nov. 22/5 (*heading*) Authorized Units, Insurance & Offshore Funds.

off side, off-side, *phr.* Add: **b.** Also with stress on second syllable. (Further examples.) Also quasi-*sb.* An occasion on which a player is, or becomes, off side.

1887 in B. James *England v Scotland* (1969) ii. 50 Dewhurst shot the ball in, and Cobbold helped it past Macauley, an appeal for offside by Dewhurst being disallowed. **1899** A. H. QUINN *Pennsylvania Stories* 24 Claims of 'off-side' were freely made and repudiated by the captains. **1925** *Kansas City* (Missouri) *Star* 22 Nov. 16/4 The ball was called back, and Kansas was penalized five yards for off-side. **1972** G. GREEN *Great Moments in Sport: Soccer* i. 24 Menti..twice put the ball in the England net, but each time the 'goal' was disallowed for offside. **1976**

Wymondham & Attleborough Express 19 Nov. 24/4 Hempnall were not to be denied and hit back immediately, Borroughes beating the offside trap to convert a fine pass from Tweedale. **1976** *Norwich Mercury* 10 Dec. 8/5 However, their well-drilled off-side trap prevented Thurton from ever really getting to grips with the bone-hard ground and getting any rhythm into their game.

off-side, offside, *v. Austral. colloq.* [Back-formation from *OFF-SIDER.] *intr.* To act as an off-sider or assistant. So **off-siding** *vbl. sb.*

1883 in M. Durack *Kings in Grass Castles* (1959) xxvi. 256, I have put up a yard on Galway since Uncle Jerry left—Pumpkin and Kangaroo offsiding. **1917** R. D. BARTON *Reminisc. Austral. Pioneer* vii. 93, I met a black-fellow..who was offsiding for the horsedriver, and was called Archie. **1930** V. PALMER *Passage* I. v. 41 A boy like Hughie might as well climb into his coffin right away as go off-siding for old Kunkel. **1936** I. L. IDRIESS *Cattle King* iii. 18 I'll get you a job offsidin' for me. **1953** A. UPFIELD *Murder must Wait* iv. 30 He's up at Mitford, and has asked me to send you up to off-side for him. **1960** —— *Bony & Kelly Gang* 167 Bony was asked to offside for Joe Flanagan, the settlement's electrician.

o·ff-sider, offsider. [f. OFF SIDE *phr.* + -ER[1].] **1.** An animal on the off side (see OFF *a.* 2 a) of a team (see also quot. 1898); hence, an assistant, *spec.* a bullock-driver's assistant; a companion, deputy, partner. orig. and chiefly *Austral.* and *N.Z. colloq.*

1880 H. C. KENDALL *Songs from Mountains* 41 And, as to a team, over gully and hill He can travel with twelve on the breadth of a quill, And boss the unlucky 'offsides'. **1898** *Bulletin* (Sydney) 17 Dec. (Red page), In draught work the laziest or worst horse is on the off-side, under the whip; thus it is an inferior man or thing that is *a bit off, off color, or an offsider*. **1903** 'T. COLLINS' *Such is Life* 46 Jam him agen the off-sider, so's he can't shift. **1905** A. B. PATERSON *Old Bush Songs* 6 They say there's no delay To get an off-sider For the old bullock dray. *Ibid.* 8 An offsider is a bullock-driver's assistant. **1924** 'R. DALY' *Outpost* xx. 191 A high and mighty gentleman is Mr. Whelan nowadays! Seems to think I'm only an off-sider, and that miners are the only people who know anything about the country. **1929** W. SMYTH *Girl from Mason Creek* 206 The Maori boy who acted as the cook's offsider. **1931** V. PALMER *Separate Lives* 244 Shorty's advent as off-sider did nothing to help matters. He and the bullock-driver had long arguments on the way. **1934** T. WOOD *Cobbers* 19 Friends with everybody though, and an off-sider of the Governor, too. **1942** 'M. INNES' *Daffodil Affair* II. 46 Too right, Mr Wine. You couldn't have a better off-sider than Ron. **1952** A. GRIMBLE *Pattern of Islands* 243 There was nothing for it but to leave me hanging around at Ocean Island as offsider to anyone the High Commissioner might send up to take charge. **1962** *John o' London's* 19 July 64/2 Jill Dawson takes a job as an off-sider—'more than a secretary and different'. **1973** *Nation Rev.* (Melbourne) 31 Aug. 1451/1 'Would you wait outside,' 'Salisbury' now said to his offsider. 'I'd like a word with matron in private.' **1977** *National Times* (Austral.) 17 Jan. 5/5 He now works as a truckie's offsider.

2. In certain games: a player who is off side. *rare.*

1927 *Daily Tel.* 21 Feb. 14/1 Nor did the referee have an eagle eye for the offsider.

off spin, o·ff-spi·n. *Cricket.* [OFF *a.* 2 b.] Spin that causes the ball to turn from the off side towards the leg side; bowling with this spin. Also *attrib.* Hence **off-spinner,** (*a*) a bowler who causes the ball to turn in this way; (*b*) a ball bowled with this spin; **off-spinning** *ppl. a.*

1904 P. F. WARNER *How we recovered Ashes* ii. 42 Arnold..occasionally managed to get a little off-spin on the ball. **1924** N. CARDUS *Days in Sun* 52 It is not that bowling is deadlier nowadays than it was, say, in the days of conventional off-spinners like Hearne and Wainwright. **1955** MILLER & WHITINGTON *Cricket Typhoon* 189 The off-spinning Ian Johnson. **1955** *Times* 14 May 4/4 The latter..was now bowling his normal off-spinners. **1956** R. ALSTON *Test Commentary* vi. 41 A superb piece of accurate off-spin bowling. *Ibid.* 42 This happy-looking cricketer..bowls a species of slow-medium off-spinner. *Ibid.* 43 He set about Johnson as no self-respecting off-spinner ought to behave to another of his kind. **1963** *Times* 14 May 4/5 Miller, of Cambridge, produced an excellent bowling performance, taking six wickets for 64 runs with his off-spin. **1975** *Cricketer* May 9/1 The 6 ft 3 ins off-spinner's recent games against England were in his winter Test rubber. **1977** *South China Morning Post* (Hong Kong) 13 Apr. 15/8 Richard Austin, better known as an opening bat and an off-spin bowler, was brought on.

off stage, off-stage, *adv.* (*phr.*) and *a.* [f. OFF *prep.*, *OFF- 4 b + STAGE *sb.*] Away from the stage; that is not appearing or occurring on a stage (see also quot. 1952). Also *transf.* and *fig.*

1922 *Times Lit. Suppl.* 12 Oct. 647/1 It is of no relevance to the story whether the apathy is produced by cocaine or Buddhism; the cause, whatever it is, is 'off stage', as it were. **1933** ST. JOHN ERVINE *Theatre in My Time* vii. 43 A player with a distinctive and adenoidal voice..made his first speech off-stage. **1942** BERREY & VAN DEN BARK *Amer. Thes. Slang* § 585/1 *Offstage leading lady*, an actor's sweetheart. **1948** *Times* 17 Jan. 5/3 The off-stage noises of those who work to distract attention from what is really going on. **1952** GRANVILLE *Dict. Theatr. Terms* 125 *On-stage*. Like off-stage, this is a somatic adjective. The on-stage arm is the one nearest the centre of the stage when an artiste faces the audience. Thus, in position *stage left*, the right will be the on-stage arm, and the left the offstage one... The same applies to furniture and properties so positioned. 'Bring the settee a little more off-stage' (i.e. towards the side). **1959** J. WAIN *Travelling Woman* viii. 110 The philosopher emptied one final shovelful of ashes into the bucket, carried it off to some unknown destination offstage, came back. *Ibid.* ix. 128 You didn't know me. I was just a figure off-stage somewhere. **1961** J. MCCABE *Mr. Laurel & Mr. Hardy* (1962) i. 31 If any of America's millions had seen the off-stage Charles Spencer Chaplin of 1910, they might well [etc.]. **1967** M. ARGYLE *Psychol. Interpersonal Behaviour* vii. 125 People do not work at their image-projection all the time; there is a difference between being 'on-stage' and 'off-stage'; in the former, people feel under observation and are very concerned about the image they are projecting. **1975** *New Yorker* 21 Apr. 103/3 The climax is the obligatory offstage pistol shot.

off-street, *a.* [f. *OFF- 4 b + STREET *sb.*] That is not on a street; esp. of parking facilities: located away from main streets. Also, that does not take place on a street.

1929 *Amer. City* Sept. 133/1 Off-street loading facilities ..reducing traffic congestion. **1937** *Sun* (Baltimore) 4 Dec. 8/1 Provision for off-street parking..should help solve the parking problem in that vicinity. **1947** *Evening Sun* (Baltimore) 12 Sept. 2/5 Fringe parking on the perimeter of the business district would help relieve traffic congestion whereas providing more off-street space for automobiles in the heart of a city would actually aggravate the problem. **1958** *Times* 1 Aug. 5/5 The provision of authorized long-term street parking places in the vicinity of railway stations where there are insufficient off-street facilities. **1969** [see *FEED *v.* 7 b]. **1977** *Stornoway Gaz.* 27 Aug. 1/5 The Council say the proposals contain inadequate provision for the off-street servicing of the premises.

offtake. Add: **1.** (Further examples.) Also, the removal of oil from a reservoir or supply. Also *attrib.*

1955 *Times* 12 May 17/2 Producers have not been keen recently to tender metal for the stockpile because of the high rate of commercial off-take. *Ibid.* 25 June 9/1 A reduced offtake at home has ensued on top of a persistent decline in export sales. **1960** *Farmer & Stockbreeder* 19 Jan. 5/1 Only a moderate offtake is reported for English barley but offers remain generally small. **1969** *Hindu* (Madras) 3 Aug. 1/5 With the opening of free market shops, the off-take from the existing ration shops would go down. **1973** 'D. JORDAN' *Nile Green* iv. 23 We might work out some sort of guarantee based on the projected offtake of their new oil discoveries in the Western Desert. **1974** *Information Handbk. 1974–5* (Shell Internat. Petroleum Co.) 73 In Spain the Amposta field..started production in February 1973 and at the end of the year had averaged 16 800 b/d: owing to offtake difficulties, well below the scheduled 30 000 b/d. **1975** *Petroleum Rev.* XXIX. 317/1 Links with local supply systems are effected at small offtake stations, where the pipework and associated control valves appear above ground.

off target, off-target, *adv.* (*phr.*) and *a.* [f. OFF *prep.*, *OFF- 4 b + TARGET *sb.*[1]] So as to fail to reach a target; that misses a target (freq. *fig.*).

1959 J. L. AUSTIN *Sense & Sensibilia* (1962) ix. 89 The second example is ineffective, off-target, in a rather similar way. **1960** V. JENKINS *Lions Down Under* 112 His kicking, for once, was off-target. **1967** *N.Y. Herald Tribune Internat.* 11–12 Feb. 10/6 The 'Daily Mail' carried Philip's entire speech with the headline 'Never Before a Royal Speech as Outspoken as This' and said in an editorial it thought he was way off target. **1977** R. E. HARRINGTON *Quintain* vi. 54 Though it was off-target, and glancing, the blow rocked him back.

off-the-peg: see *PEG *sb.*[1] 1 e.

off time, off-time, *sb.* [OFF *a.* 4.] A time when one is off duty or free from work; a holiday; a time when normal activity is reduced or suspended.

1866 DICKENS *Mugby Junction* in *All Year Round* Extra Christmas No. 10 Dec. 6/1 The answer to his inquiry, 'Where's Lamps?' was..that it was his off-time. **1894** MRS. H. WARD *Marcella* II. III. iv. 323 In hospital.. every hour was full, and there were always orders to follow. And the 'off' times were no trouble—I never did anything else but walk up and down the Embankment.. or go to the National Gallery. **1902** *Westm. Gaz.* 26 Aug. 8/1 The York Meeting..marks the close of the 'off' time, which has been experienced since the Goodwood gathering. **1936** W. R. TITTERTON *G. K. Chesterton* II. iii. 139, I used the stage there at off times to advertise the plays that we ran. **1940** C. DAY LEWIS tr. *Georgics of Virgil* I. 24 Winter's an off-time for farmers. **1956** 'J. WYNDHAM' *Seeds of Time* 216 In his off times he occupied himself..in teaching Lellie. **1975** *BP Shield Internat.* May 1/3 We are insisting on their having their homes within 70 miles of Aberdeen because, should there be an emergency, then they can be easily called in during their off-time to deal with it.

off-time, *a. U.S. slang.* [f. *OFF 4 b + TIME *sb.*] Out of time; badly timed (see also quots.).

1942 BERREY & VAN DEN BARK *Amer. Thes. Slang* § 582 *Off-time jive*, a sorry excuse. **1946** MEZZROW & WOLFE *Really Blues* xiii. 237 If somebody passed a remark that wasn't in line, he'd start singing and beating on the offtime cat. *Ibid.* 377 *Offtime*, out of harmony, old-fashioned, corny, offensive. **1973** C. HIMES *Black on Black* 188, I can stop in front of a joint where the juke-box's playing and cut a step of off-time boogie.

off-white, *sb.* and *a.* [*OFF- 5.] **A.** *sb.* A colour very close to white, usu. with grey or yellow tinge. **B.** *adj.* Almost white. Also *fig.*, not standard; not socially acceptable; *off-white collar*: of a worker or occupation: not manual but not quite 'white collar'.

1927 *Daily Mirror* 10 Dec. 16/1 Jumper suits in white, yellow, or what the Paris dressmakers call 'off whites' will see you through. **1931** *Daily Express* 18 Mar. 5/3 Fashionable colours are all off-white shades such as palest blues, greys, pinks, and greyish-greens. **1937** F. STARK *Baghdad Sketches* 187 A voluminous nightdress very much 'off white'. **1951** H. NICOLSON *Diary* 29 Aug. (1968) 208, I go to the B.B.C. to listen to recordings of King George's broadcasts. His voice is so like the present King's...it is what the B.B.C. would call 'off-white', meaning slightly cockney. **1954** M. PROCTER *Hell is City* III. ix. 120 The interrogation room..had white-tiled walls and an off-white ceiling. **1962** *Guardian* 13 Apr. 1/7 Off-white-collar workers..are showing an unpatriotic reluctance to subsidise richer men's meals. **1962** A. G. FRANK in *Monthly Rev.* (N.Y.) Nov. 384 There is movement into white or off-white collar jobs. **1962** M. ALLINGHAM *China Governess* (1963) iii. 51, I can be as 'off-white' as I like. I've no code to live up to. **1965** —— *Mind Readers* ix. 94 'You're telling me!' The voice could produce an off-white accent. **1969** Y. CARTER *Mr. Campion's Farthing* ii. 9 A very slight off-white accent... A suggestion of the lower orders. **1971** *Nature* 15 Jan. 175/2 It yielded about 200 mg of pure wildfire toxin as a fluffy, off-white powder.

off-wring, *v. poet. rare*[—1]. [OFF- 1.] *trans.* To wring or wrench off.

a **1889** G. M. HOPKINS *Poems* (1918) 90 His twiny books Fast he opens, last he offwrings Till walk the world he can with bare his feet.

oficina. (Later examples.)

1942 *Econ. Geol.* XXXVII. 198 Fig. 9 shows an oficina that has derived its nitrate from one of the small 'islands' or 'peninsulas' rising above the playa. **1966** POHL & ZEPP *Latin Amer.* vii. 120 Most of the *oficinas* are in the north, where groundwater is available.

Oflag (ǫ·flag). [G., abbrev. of *offizier(s)lager* officers' camp.] In Nazi Germany: a prison-camp for captured enemy officers.

1941 [see *ILAG]. **1945** *News Chron.* 20 Apr. 1/6 Unlike the guards of the stalags and oflags, they never wait to give themselves up. **1958** P. KEMP *No Colours or Crest* xii. 265 Her husband..had been a prisoner of the Germans since 1939 in an Oflag in Posen. **1969** *Listener* 10 Apr. 503/3 Wing-Commander Wassler (who for practical purposes is still in his wartime Oflag). **1974** *Times* 12 Oct. 12/7 He found himself in Oflag IHA/H, a prisoner-of-war camp in Spannenburg.

oft, *adv., a.* **A.** *adv.* **c.** (Further examples.)

1906 P. E. MORE *Shelburne Ess.* (4th ser.) 198 There are single lines here and there, such as the oft-quoted 'White arms out in the breakers tirelessly tossing', which have a magical power of evoking an image or the memory of subtle sounds and odors. **1922** JOYCE *Ulysses* 269 Her first merciful lovesoft oftloved word. **1954** O. NASH *Face is Familiar* (rev. ed.) 115 The oft-quoted remark of the prominent and respectable dignitary. **1976** M. BUTTERWORTH *Remains to be Seen* i. 11 The wary air of an oft-disappointed augur reading entrails.

often, *adv.* and *a.* Add: Now also with pronunc. (ǫ̇·ftən). **A.** *adv.* **1. b.** In colloq. phrases: (*as*) *often as not, more often than not*, at least half the time; frequently; *every so often*: see *EVERY *a.* 1 f; *once too often*: see *ONCE *adv.* 8 d.

1911 G. B. SHAW *Getting Married* Pref. 149 Such a transaction..is as often as not the inauguration of a life-long squabble. **1919** E. O'NEILL *In Zone* in *Moon of Caribbees* (1923) 16 All them German spies they been catchin' in England has been livin' there for ten, often as not twenty years. **1960** *Observer* 25 Dec. 7/6 The driver often as not wore chauffeur's livery. **1962** M. DRABBLE *Summer Bird-Cage* xi. 185, I..use a small red plastic colander, and everything eels into the sink as often as not. **1977** F. ROSS *Dead Runner* I. 64 More often than not the only successful outcome of a dead-run operation was the runner's grave.

oftening (ǫ̇·f'niŋ), *vbl. sb. rare*[—1]. [f. OFTEN *adv.* and *a.* + -ING[1].] Frequent repetition.

a **1889** G. M. HOPKINS *Jrnls. & Papers* (1959) 289 Repetition, *oftening, over-and-overing, aftering* of the inscape must take place in order to detach it to the mind.

oftenness. (Later example.)

1977 'E. CRISPIN' *Glimpses of Moon* ii. 27 The Pisser's [*sc.* a pylon's] noise..had actually intensified both in volume and in oftenness.

† og, ogg (ǫg). *Obs. Austral. & N.Z. slang.* [Cf. HOG *sb.*[1] 8.] A shilling.

1937 PARTRIDGE *Dict. Slang* 580/2 *Ogg* or *og*, a shilling. ..A corruption of *hog* (a shilling). **1945** BAKER *Austral. Lang.* v. 109, 1s...*og* and *rogue* (probably a clipping of the English rhyming slang *rogue and villain*, a shilling). **1946** *Penguin New Writing* XXVIII. 125 Three quid and seven og.

‖ ogbanje (ǫgbæ·nʒi). [Ibo.] (See quots.) Also *attrib.*

1958 C. ACHEBE *Things fall Apart* ix. 68 The child was an *ogbanje*, one of those wicked children who, when they died, entered their mothers' wombs to be born again.

Ibid. 68 Okonkwo had called in another medicine-man who was famous in the clan for his great knowledge about *ogbanje* children. **1976** *CRC Jrnl.* July 18/1 His daughter Aku-nna is so thin and delicate that it is even suggested that she might be an 'ogbanje', a 'living dead', a child only on loan to this world who will be called back to the other world while still young.

ogee. In etym. delete sentence beginning 'The use of ogee as the name of a moulding and curve is exclusively English': see C. Brunel in *Romania* (1960) LXXXI. 293. Add: **3. a. ogee wing** *Aeronaut.*, a wing whose outline is an ogee (used on some supersonic aircraft).

1960 *Aeroplane* XCIX. 791/1 The ogee wing is one of the highly swept delta wings with very low aspect ratio which are being proposed for supersonic airliners. Slender wings of this type have subsonic leading-edges and supersonic trailing edges. **1970** *New Scientist* 23 Apr. 172/2 The HS 133 is an ogee wing (Concorde shape).

Ogen (ōu·gen). Also with lower-case initial. [Place-name (see below)]. The name of a kibbutz in Israel, used attrib. in **Ogen melon** to designate a small melon with pale orange flesh and brownish-orange skin ribbed with green, belonging to a variety first developed there.

1967 *Guardian* 14 June 6/7 The tiny Ogen melon... Paler-fleshed than its French antecedent, the Charentais, it has the same voluptuous flavour. **1969** *Oxf. Bk. Food Plants* 118/2 'Ogen Melon'. The name is derived from a kibbutz in Israel where it was bred and whence it has been exported during the last decade. It is said to belong to the cantaloupe group of varieties. **1973** *Observer* (Colour Suppl.) 1 July 39/1 The small ogen melon, orange ribbed with green..was first grown by Nathan Fuchs at the Ogen kibbutz, north of Tel Aviv. **1976** *Listener* 12 Feb. 171/3 This one place on the Dead Sea..is now the source of such fruits as the ogen melons we enjoy in London in mid-winter.

-ogen (ŏdʒen), a suffix f. -O + -GEN, q.v. In *Biochem.* appended to the names, usu. terminating in *-in*, of biologically active compounds, esp. proteins, to form the names of their inactive precursors: as *CHYMOTRYPSINOGEN, FIBRINOGEN, PEPSINOGEN, RENNINOGEN.

1961 *Rep. Comm. Enzymes Internat. Union Biochem.* ix. 49 The names of enzyme precursors should no longer be formed by the use of the suffix '-ogen'; the prefix 'pre-' should be used instead.

ogg, var. *OG.

oggin (ǫ·gin). *Naut. slang.* [A corruption of *hog-wash.*] The sea.

1946 J. IRVING *Royal Navalese* 126 Oggin, the sea; the Drink; the Ditch. The term descends to us aitch-less from an earlier abuse of the sea as the Hog-Wash. **1949** W. GRANVILLE *Sea Slang Twentieth Cent.* 100 *Floggin' the 'oggin*, sailing the high seas. (Naval lower-deck.) *'Oggin* is a form of *'ogwash. Ibid.* 168 *'oggin*, the sea or *ditch*. A perversion of *'ogwash* (*hogwash*). **1973** D. LEES *Rape of Quiet Town* x. 165 No one told the two gunners that the sub was about to crash-dive and they had to run like hell to avoid being left behind in the oggin.

Oghuz (ogu·z). [ad. Turk. *oğuz* (which is also the name of a legendary Turkish hero).] **1.** Also **Ghuzz** (via Arabic), **Oghus, Oğuz.** One of various Turkic tribes, now more usually included among the Turkmen, who originally inhabited Siberia and, later, Transoxiana but who crossed the Oxus in the 11th century and invaded Persia, Syria, and Asia Minor; also, a member of one of these tribes. Also *attrib.* or as *adj.*

1843 *Penny Cycl.* XXV. 395/2 For many centuries the Oghuzes were perpetually at war with the Persians. **1845** *Encycl. Metrop.* XXV. 868/2 They [*sc.* the Uz-beks] are called Ghuzz by the Arabs. **1854** G. LARPENT in J. Porter *Turkey* I. 155 The Turks divided themselves into the Uigurs or Eastern Turks..and into the Oghus or Western Turks. **1888** *Encycl. Brit.* XXIII. 660/2 The old name Ghuzz, originally, as it seems, the Turkish Oghuz (an eponymous hero of whom Turkish chronicles tell many fables) was wholly superseded by the new name Turkman. **1899** SKRINE & ROSS *Heart of Asia* I. xix. 142 The Ghuz laid waste the whole of Khorāsān. **1947** AUDEN *Age of Anxiety* (1948) v. 103 The Ghuzz, the Guptas, the gloomy Krimchaks. **1953** [see *KIPCHAK]. **1965** H. M. SMYSER in Bessinger & Creed *Medieval & Linguistic Stud.* 93 Ibn Faḍlān's descriptions of..Oghuz (Ghuzz Turks)..are fascinating. **1972** [see *KIPCHAK]. **1974** G. LEWIS tr. *Bk. of Dede Korkut* 10 It is known that the term 'Oghuz' was gradually supplanted among the Turks themselves by *Türkmen*, 'Turcoman', from the mid tenth century on... The Turcomans were those Turks, mostly but not exclusively Oghuz, who had embraced Islam and begun to lead a more sedentary life than their forefathers. *Ibid.*, The stock epithet of the Oghuz ladies is 'white-faced'.

2. The southern division of the Turkic languages. Usu. *attrib.* or as *adj.*

1959 J. BENZING in *Philologiae Turcicae Fundamenta* I. 2 In what follows a survey is given of the Turkic languages, in which the individual languages and dialects are set together as they seem to me, on grounds of linguistic history (phonetic and especially grammatic) to be especially closely connected... b) Southern Turkic (the Oghuz group). Here belong: 1. Osmanli... 2. Azarbaijani... 3. Turkmen. **1974** *Encycl. Brit. Micropædia* X. 198/1 Turkmen is a member of the southwestern, or Oghuz, division of the Turkic languages.

So **Oghu·zian** *a.* and *sb.*

1603 R. KNOLLES *Gen. Hist. Turkes* 128 For although he [*sc.* Othoman] were a Turke borne, yet was he not of the Selzuccian family, as were the rest, but of another house and tribe, and therefore not of them fauoured or thought to have so good right vnto any of the late Sultans prouinces or territories, as had they who being of his house and holpen with the prescription of time, enuied at the sudden rising of this Oguzian Turke, being vnto them as it were a meere stranger. **1621** HEYLIN *Microcosmus* 312 Solyman the chiefe of the Oguzian family and Prince of Machan, flying the fury of the Tartars, was drowned in Euphrates. **1880** A. H. SAYCE *Introd. Sci. of Lang.* II. ix. 263 The one-eyed giant..reappears among the Turkish Oghuzians. *Ibid.* 264 In the Oghuzian version the story is amplified.

ogival, *a.* (*sb.*). Add: **2.** Having the shape of an ogee.

1962 *Flight Internat.* LXXXI. 269/1 One of the two Fairey FD.2 research aircraft owned by the Ministry of Aviation is being converted..to flight-test an ogival wing. **1965** *Times* 11 Sept. 7/6 Instead of being an ordinary, straight-sided delta, the Concord wing is ogival. Each wing starts as a sharp point.., spreads outwards and then curves in again. **1976** *Jane's Pocket Bk. Res. & Exper. Aircraft* 19 Special design features: Slender ogival delta wings.

ogive. Add: **4. b.** (Something having) the profile of an ogive, esp. the head of a projectile.

1904 *Sci. Amer.* 16 Jan. 44/1 It [*sc.* an airship] is cylindrical in form, with an ogive nose and a nearly hemispherical stern. **1947** L. E. SIMON *German Research in World War II* 115 They studied the way in which the ogive (the tapering head of the projectile) broke up. **1950** E. A. BONNEY *Engin. Supersonic Aerodyn.* v. 183 For a given base diameter, therefore, the drag of an ogive will be less than that of a cone of the same length. **1966** D. STINTON *Anat. Aeroplane* vi. 89 The shapes of such aircraft are determined by the need to produce favourable interactions between the relatively high-pressure regions behind shock waves and the adjacent airframe surfaces. The simplest example is shown in Fig. 6.9, in which an ogive, shedding a complete ogival Mach-cone, is split longitudinally and fitted with wings.

4*. *Statistics.* A graph in which each ordinate represents the frequency with which a variate has a value less than or equal to that indicated by the corresponding abscissa, which for many unimodal frequency distributions has the form of an ogee. (In earlier use the ordinates and abscissas were interchanged.)

1875 F. GALTON in *Phil. Mag.* XLIX. 35 When the objects are marshalled in the order of their magnitude along a level base at equal distances apart, a line drawn freely through the tops of the ordinates which represent their several magnitudes will form a curve of double curvature... Such a curve is called, in the phraseology of architects, an 'ogive'. *Ibid.* 46 A law of frequency of error founded on a binominal ogive. **1930** R. PEARL *Introd. Med. Biometry & Statistics* vi. 119 The ogive and integral forms of plotting a frequency distribution are fundamentally the same. The only difference is that in the case of the ogive frequencies are plotted along the abscissal axis, and in the integral along the *y* axis as usual. **1937** YULE & KENDALL *Introd. Theory of Statistics* (ed. 11) viii. 150 The values of the percentiles may be used to draw what is known as Galton's ogive curve. **1939** J. F. KENNEY *Math. of Statistics* (1940) I. ii. 26 The graphs of cumulative frequencies are called ogives. **1962** A. BATTERSBY *Guide to Stock Control* iii. 31 This curve has been derived from sales figures with a Normal distribution... It is called the 'ogive' of the Normal curve. *Ibid.*, For Normal probability paper, the scale is drawn so as to turn the Normal ogive into a straight line.

4.** *Geol.* A stripe or band of dark material stretching from side to side across the surface of a glacier, usu. arched in the direction of flow and arranged in a parallel series of similar bands.

1947 *Jrnl. Glaciology* I. 16 Then there is the question of 'Ogives' or pressure arches. **1949** *Ibid.* I. 327 Vareschi's latest and most important researches were made upon various systems of banding which appear in the tongue of the Great Aletsch Glacier, in particular what are locally called *Ogiven*. These are curved bands visible on the glacier surface, often in regular longitudinal series... The ogive itself is generally darker block ice, whilst between one ogive and the next is paler and higher *Buckel* ice. **1951** *Ibid.* I. 498 The study of the formation of ogives which in English-speaking countries are referred to as Forbes's Bands. **1974** *Encycl. Brit. Macropædia* IX. 183/1 In plan view, the ogives are invariably distorted into arcs or curves convex downglacier; hence the name ogive.

Oglala (ǫglā·lă). Also **Ogalalla, Ogallalla(h), Oglalla.** [Native word.] The chief tribe of the Teton Sioux Indians; a member of this tribe; also, their language. Also *attrib.*

1837 *Missionary Herald* (Boston, Mass.) XXXIII. 369/2 Came to the village of the Ogallallah Indians, consisting of more than two thousand persons. **1838** S. PARKER *Jrnl. Exploring Tour beyond Rocky Mts.* 63 They were Ogallallahs, headed by eight of their chiefs. **1857** *Porter's Spirit of Times* 21 Mar. 34/1 They proved to be a hunting-party of Ogallallah Sioux. **1867** *Harper's Weekly* 5 Oct. 629/2 The Commission..on August 19 held a council on the steamer..with the head chiefs of the Oglallas. **1876** H. T. WILLIAMS *Pacific Tourist* 47/1 Red Cloud is chief of the Ogalalla Sioux. **1897** C. KING *Warrior Gap* (1898) 31 With him rode Baptiste,..whose mother was an Ogallala squaw. **1921** F. HEBERT *40 Years Prospecting* 6 It was there that I saw Pawnee Killer, a big Ogalala Chief. **1933** [see *DAKOTA *sb.* 2]. **1947** B. A. DE VOTO *Across Wide Missouri* 123 When Sublette & Campbell brought the Oglalas to the Platte in 1834 [etc.]. *Ibid.* 191 Fort Laramie..would draw all the wandering trappers,..the Oglala Sioux, and finally the United States Army. **1973** *Freedomways* XIII. 81 There is much emphasis on the dance and its symbolic meaning to the Oglala. **1974** *Black Panther* 19 Jan. 3/3 Both Mr. Means, an Oglala Sioux, and Mr. Banks, a Chippewa, have wove the right to make opening statements to the jury once they are seated.

ogling, *vbl. sb.* Add: **b. ogling-glass** *U.S. humorous*, a monocle.

1843 *Knickerbocker* XXII. 111 There he was promenading,..an ogling-glass lifted to his eye.

o'goblin: see *GOBLIN².

Ogopogo (ōu·gopōu·go). *Canad.* [Fanciful, said to be from a British music-hall song by C. Clark (see quot. 1974).] The name of a water monster alleged to live in Okanagan Lake, British Columbia. Also *transf.*

No contemporary (1924) copy of the song referred to in quot. 1974 has been traced.

1926 *Province* (Vancouver) 24 Aug. 7 (*heading*) 'Ogopogo' now official name of the famous Okanagan sea serpent. **1927** *Ibid.* 25 Sept. 24 Alberta claims to have an Ogopogo all its own. **1933** *Sun* (Baltimore) 24 June 14/1 He blamed the 'ogopogo', famed lake monster. **1936** A. F. CROSS *Cross Roads* 71 Ogopogo's head is slightly reminiscent of Henry VIII, he has a torso like an accordion, and a tail like a shillelagh. Ogopogo is, of course, a celibate, because he lost his wife in the Carboniferous Age, and after the customary dinosaurian 1,000-year period of mourning, was once more seen about again. **1955** *Daily Progress* (Charlottesville, Va.) 8 Feb. 12/6 The dispute arose when Ogopogo's name appeared on a new bridge across the South Saskatchewan. **1962** G. MACEWAN *Blazing Old Cattle Trail* vii. 46 The way was described as rough and mountainous but no Ogopogo lake serpents were reported. **1974** P. COSTELLO *In Search of Lake Monsters* x. 222 The old Indian name for the animal was Naitaka, or Nha'a'itk; the settlers name for it is now Ogopogo, which is far more recent in origin. It is not, as some seem to have thought, an Indian word. Back in 1924 the following music hall hit from London was sung one night in Vernon: His mother was an earwig, His father was a whale. A little bit of head, and hardly any tail, And Ogopogo was his name.

‖ **o-goshi, ogoshi** (ōu,gǫ·ʃi). [Jap., f. *o*(*u*) big, major + *koshi* the waist or hips.] A hip throw in Judo.

1954 E. DOMINY *Teach yourself Judo* 190 *Ogoshi*,.. Floating Hip Throw. **1957** TAKAGAKI & SHARP *Techniques Judo* II. iv. 47 *O-goshi*: major hip throw... Throw by a pulling and twisting motion over your right hip. **1966** *Daily Tel.* 15 Nov. 21/4 A ballet dancer..broke an arm.. while trying an O Goshi throw.

Ogpu (ǫ·gpu). Also O.G.P.U. [f. the initials of the Russ. *Ob"edinënnoe Gosudárstvennoe Politícheskoe Upravlénie* United State Political Directorate.] An organization for investigating and combating counter-revolutionary activities in Soviet Russia, which superseded the *CHEKA and the G.P.U. (*G. III. f) in 1923 and was replaced by the N.K.V.D. (*N. II. 1) in 1934.

1923 *Times* 24 Nov. 13/5 By special decree the Soviet Government has created a new Supreme International Cheka (State Political Department), which is called 'Ogpu' (Unified State Political Department). **1927** *Daily Tel.* 7 June 10/2 A report from Leningrad states that the Ogpu (Cheka) has officially announced the execution without trial of 'all the active members of a band of incendiaries'. **1927** *Glasgow Herald* 13 June 12/3 The fertile imagination of the Ogpu, or 'State Political Department'. **1927** *Daily News* 17 Nov. 7/4 Trotzky is under arrest..and is being watched by officials of the O.G.P.U. (Secret Police). **1928** *Sunday Times* 8 Jan. 11/1 The day has gone by when Ogpu sought to conceal itself. **1939** *Ann. Reg. 1938* 211 The new chief of the O.G.P.U., one Beria, appointed only in November, is stated to have dismissed 470 of the highest officers. **1940** [see *GESTAPO]. **1940** *War Illustr.* 12 Jan. 608/1 Reported that Russians have brought up picked Ogpu troops into Karelian Isthmus. **1949** [see *CHEKA]. **1958** C. COCKBURN *Crossing Line* vi. 97 Dedicated men..with pistols in their hands ready to blaze away in case this OGPU desperado should get up to any tricks. **1972** T. WITTLIN *Commissar* (1973) xxxiv. 248 For almost ten years an intensive chase after Agabekov was conducted by the men of the OGPU in Paris.

ogrillon. For *nonce-wd.* read *rare*⁻¹ and substitute for etymol.: [a. F. *ogrillon*, f. *ogre* OGRE + suff. *-illon* in *moinillon*, *négrillon*, *oisillon*, etc.]

ohelo (ohē·lo). [Hawaiian.] The red or yellow fruit of a blueberry native to Hawaii, *Vaccinium reticulatum.* Also *attrib.*

1843 J. J. JARVES *Hist. Hawaiian Islands* i. 9 The banana, yam, sweet potato,..*ohelo* (a berry),..are indigenous and plentiful. **1888** W. HILLEBRAND *Flora Hawaiian Islands* 272 The shining fleshy berry, the 'Ohelo',..is the principal food of the wild mountain goose. **1977** *Time* 17 Oct. 41/1 Native Hawaiians have long attempted to placate the fire goddess Pele by dropping offerings—ohelo berries, liquor and, once upon a time, an occasional human—into the crater of the 4,090-ft. volcano Kilauea.

ohia (ohī·ă). Also **ohia lehua.** [Hawaiian.] = *LEHUA. Also *attrib.*

1824 C. S. STEWART *Jrnl.* 15 June in *Jrnl. Residence Sandwich Islands* (1828) xi. 305 The only trees and plants known to us, which we saw..were the koa, *acacia*, a large and beautiful tree of dark, hard wood, the Ohia, *eugenia malaccensis*, bearing a beautiful tufted, crimson flower, and a fruit called by foreigners, the native apple. **1825** [see *KUKUI]. **1866** 'MARK TWAIN' *Lett. from Hawaii* (1967) xi. 99 Shady groves of forest trees..and, handsomest of all, the ohia, with its feathery tufts of splendid vermilion-tinted blossoms. **1888** [see *LEHUA]. **1917** *Nature* 20 Sept. 57/2 The ohia..also called ohia lehua and lehua, resembles..our white oak, but bears beautiful clusters of scarlet flowers with long, protruding stamens. **1937** D. & H. TEILHET *Feather Cloak Murders* x. 185 A few gnarled ohia trees..grew between the twisted rocks. **1970** S. CARLQUIST *Hawaii* xvi. 301 The ohia lehua lends a somber air to wet forests because of its dark green foliage, dark gray bark, and often gnarled branches. Roots are formed on the sides of trunks of ohia trees... Ohia forest can be very tall, exceeding fifty feet... The tallest ohias are on the island of Hawaii.

Ohian (ohəi·ăn), *sb.* and *a.* = *OHIOAN *sb.* and *a.*

1819 in J. Flint *Lett. from Amer.* (1822) 128 The Ohian is in many cases growing up to manhood. **1836** C. R. GILMAN *Life on Lakes* I. 54 He..is the very man..who should be called Buck Eye and not Ohian. **1963** *Guardian* 1 May 10/7 The average Ohian. **1977** *Financial Times* 18 Oct. 17/1 Ohians can with some justification claim to be a boilerhouse of U.S. manufacturing industry. *Ibid.* 17/7 Even those Ohian politicians who rose to national prominence rarely put their stamp on the country's affairs.

Ohio (ohəi·o), the name of a North American river, a tributary of the Mississippi, and one of the United States, used *attrib.* in *Ohio bluebell, buck-eye, sandstone*; **Ohio fever, spread** (see quots.).

1842 C. M. KIRKLAND *Forest Life* II. xxxix. 142 A beautiful perennial, here called the Ohio bluebell, a far larger plant than the one we know by that name. **1810** F. A. MICHAUX *Hist. Arbres Forestiers de l'Amérique Septentrionale* I. 38 Ohio buck eye.., nom donné par moi. **1832** D. J. BROWNE *Sylva Amer.* 227 It is called Buckeye by the inhabitants,..but..we have denominated it Ohio Buckeye, because it is more abundant on the banks of this river. **1948** *Chicago Sun-Times* 20 Apr. 32/2 The Ohio buckeye..is the first of all the big trees to burst forth with leaves. **1816** in T. W. Robinson *Hist. Morrill* (1944) 155 The 'Ohio Fever' took away many of our best farmers. **1831** T. BUTTRICK *Voyages* 57 The 'Ohio fever' became a well known expression for this desire to move West. **1835** *Knickerbocker* V. 274 Such..as some fifteen years since happened to reside in any part of New-England where what was called the 'Ohio fever' prevailed. **1881** *Harper's Mag.* Apr. 711/1 Lime stone..and gray Ohio sandstone are much used in construction. **1971** M. TAK *Truck Talk* 111 *Ohio spread*, a trailer with a separation of eight feet between the axles.

Ohioan (ohəi·oăn), *sb.* and *a.* [f. *OHIO + -AN.] **A.** *sb.* A native or inhabitant of Ohio in the United States. **B.** *adj.* Of or pertaining to Ohio.

1818 E. P. FORDHAM *Pers. Narr. Trav.* (1906) viii. 165, I do not choose the risk of being insulted by any vulgar Ohioans. *c* **1848** W. WHITMAN in *Amer. Speech* (1961) XXXVI. 297 Ohioans [are called] *Buckeyes*. **1906** A. B. HULBERT in B. A. Botkin *Treas. S. Folklore* (1949) III. i. 421 When exactly one half had passed on a long gallop the Ohioan leaped down. **1927** H. CRANE *Let.* 7 May (1965) 296 Under the benign influence of Ohioan pollens during the months of June, July, Sept. & October. **1929** G. L. ESKEW in B. A. Botkin *Treas. S. Folklore* (1949) I. i. 13 Daniel Decatur Emmett, an Ohioan by birth, a traveling minstrel and showman by persuasion, made a song about 'Dixie, the Land of Cotton'. **1948** [see *NEBRASKAN *sb.*]. **1973** *Time* 25 June 11/1 A fellow Ohioan and Wooster alumnus. **1978** *Amer. Speech* LIII. 42 A wave of Ohioans in the middle nineteenth century inundated northern Indiana and a large area of Illinois.

ohm[2]**.** Add: (Earlier and later examples.) Now incorporated in the International System of Units, and defined as the resistance that exists between two points when a potential difference between them of one volt produces a current of one ampere.

The word *ohma* was orig. proposed for the practical unit of 'tension' (voltage), along with *volt* for the unit of resistance (see quot. 1861, which also appears in *Electrician* (1861) 9 Nov. 4 and is from the paper read at the Sept. 1861 meeting of the British Association). The origin of the change in application of the word has not been traced in print.

1861 CLARK & BRIGHT in L. Clark *Exper. Investigation Laws Propagation Electr. Current* 49 Let us derive terms from the names of some of our most eminent philosophers... We shall then have the following table: A.—Tension. 1 Daniell's Element = 1 Ohma, or unit of tension... B.—Quantity. 1 Ohma, by 1 metre square at 1 milliometre [*sic*] distance = 1 Farad, or unit of quantity... D.—Resistance. 1 Farad per second = 1 Volt, or unit of resistance. *Ibid.*, The ohma, or unit of tension, is practically a very convenient one for all battery purposes. **1865** *Proc. R. Soc.* XIV. 159 It is proposed that the new standard [of resistance] shall not be..described as so many metre/seconds, but that it shall receive a distinctive name, such as the B.A. unit, or, as Mr. Latimer Clark suggests, the 'Ohmad'. **1867** W. H. PREECE in *Phil. Mag.* XXXIII. 397, I beg to suggest..to those physicists and electricians who have adopted the British-Association unit for electrical measurements, that in place of expressing this unit, as is variously done at present, by B.A. unit, Ohmad, Ohm, 10^7 metre/second, &c., it would be very convenient to apopt some universal symbol analogous to that used for degrees (°). The Greek letter ω appears to me very convenient. *Ibid.*, The conductivity of the Atlantic cable would be given by 7524^{ω}, and its insulation by 2349^{Ω} per knot, which may still be read Ohm and Megohm. **1867** R. S. CULLEY *Handbk. Pract. Telegr.* (ed. 2) ii. 30 The unit [of resistance] adopted by the electricians of this country is that determined by a Committee of the British Association, and is called the 'ohm'.., and sometimes the 'B.A. unit'. **1943** F. E. TERMAN *Radio Engineers' Handbk.* II. 40 Wire-wound variable resistors of these types are available up to about 100,000 ohms, and are capable of dissipating up to about 15 watts. **1973** D. ALDOUS in *Pye Bk. of Audio* vii. 75/2 Most transistor amplifiers offer a wide range of output impedances, usually from 4 to 16 ohms.

2. *attrib.* and *Comb.*, as **ohm-centimetre,** the unit of electrical resistivity in the C.G.S. system, being the resistivity of a substance of which a centimetre cube has a resistance of one ohm; **ohm-metre,** the corresponding unit in the International System of Units, equal to 100 ohm-centimetres.

1920 W. T. MACCALL *Continuous Current Electr. Engin.* (ed. 2) iii. 18 The resistance of a conductor 1 cm. long and 1 sq. cm. cross-section..is called the specific resistance per centimetre cube... A better name is ohm-centimetre (or microhm-cm.). **1957** H. COTTON *Electr. Technol.* (ed. 7) iii. 67 It is..logical to express ρ as so many ohms-centimetre..or ohm-metre [*sic*]... For example, for copper at normal room temperature $\rho = 1{\cdot}72 \times 10^{-6}$ Ω-cm $= 1{\cdot}72 \times 10^{-8}$ Ω-m. **1974** *Encycl. Brit. Micropædia* VIII. 524/1 If lengths are measured in centimetres, resistivity may be expressed in units of ohm-centimetre. *Ibid.*, The resistivity of an exceedingly good electrical conductor, such as hard-drawn copper, at 20° C (68° F) is $1{\cdot}77 \times 10^{-8}$ ohm-metre, $1{\cdot}77 \times 10^{-6}$ ohm-centimetre, or 10·7 ohm-circular mils per foot.

ohmic, *a.* (s.v. OHM[2]). Substitute for def.: That obeys Ohm's law, or exhibits behaviour consistent with it. (Add further examples.)

1904 *Electrician* Nov. 150/1 The energy dissipation due to ohmic resistance in the metal. **1926** R. W. LAWSON tr. *Hevesy & Paneth's Man. Radioactivity* i. 14 This proportionality between current and potential..only maintains for the initial part of the curve (the region of Ohmic current, cf. Fig. 3). **1949** *Bell Syst. Techn. Jrnl.* XXVIII. 471 (*heading*) Semi-conductor with two *p-n* junctions and ohmic metal contacts. **1967** *Electronics* 6 Mar. 136/2 Ohmic heating in the device induces diffusions that form p-n junctions.

Hence **oh·mically** *adv.*, by, or as a result of, ohmic resistance.

1919 *Radio Rev.* Dec. 144 A set of triodes arranged in an ohmically-coupled cascade. **1968** C. G. KUPER *Introd. Theory Superconductivity* i. 10 *Changes* in the field produce eddy currents, but they will decay Ohmically.

Ohm's law. [see OHM[2].] **1.** *Electr.* The law that the strength of a constant electric current in a circuit is proportional to the electromotive force divided by the resistance of the circuit, and that the potential difference between any two points of it is proportional to the resistance between them. (The name was formerly used of some related principles also.)

Propounded by Ohm in *Die galvanische Kette, mathematisch bearbeitet* (1827).

1850 *Phil. Mag.* XXXVII. 463 (*heading*) On a deduction of Ohm's laws, in connexion with the theory of electro-statics. **1863** *Rep. Brit. Assoc. Adv. Sci. 1862* I. 127 The first relation is a direct consequence of Ohm's Law. **1867** *Phil. Mag.* XXXIII. 321 (*heading*) On one of Ohm's laws relating to an insulated circuit. **1910** *Encycl. Brit.* IX. 182/2 This result..obtained by Cavendish in January 1781, that the current varies in direct proportion to the electromotive force, was really an anticipation of the fundamental law of electric flow, discovered independently by G. S. Ohm in 1827, and since known as Ohm's Law. **1921** W. S. IBBETSON *Motor & Dynamo Control* iv. 131 Generally speaking, A.C. circuits do not obey Ohm's law. **1973** J. W. GARDNER *New Frontiers in Electricity* vii. 138 Superconductors constitute a very dramatic violation of Ohm's law.

2. *Acoustics.* The law that a complex musical sound is heard as the sum of a number of distinct pure tones into which the sound can be analysed by Fourier's theorem.

Propounded by Ohm in *Ann. d. Physik* (1843) LIX. 513, and called *Ohm's Regel* by Helmholtz in *Die Lehre von den Tonempfindungen* (1863) ii. 54.

1875 A. J. ELLIS tr. *Helmholtz' On Sensations of Tone* ii. 51 Every motion of the air..which corresponds to a composite mass of musical tones, is, according to Ohm's law, capable of being analysed into a sum of simple pendular vibrations, and to each such single simple vibration corresponds a simple tone, sensible to the ear. **1924** WILKINSON & GRAY *Mechanism of Cochlea* i. 14 Ohm's Law is a generalisation from the results of experiment. **1974** S. E. GERBER *Introductory Hearing Sci.* vi. 134 Ohm's law has generated over a century of research, largely aimed at demonstrating its limitations. *Ibid.*, When tones of relatively low intensity which differ considerably in frequency are presented together, they are perceived as two distinct tones, in accordance with Ohm's law.

oho, *int.* (Further examples.)

c **1874** D. BOUCICAULT *Shaughraun* in M. R. Booth *Eng. Plays of 19th Cent.* (1969) II. 224 Oho! if that's Robert Ffolliott, I'd like to know who's this? **1898** G. B. SHAW *Arms & Man* III. 56 Four telegrams——a week old. (He opens one). Oho! Bad news!.. My father's dead. **1933** E. O'NEILL *Ah, Wilderness!* III. i. 93 'Oho,' they cried, 'the world is wide, But fettered limbs go lame!' **1976** P. DICKINSON *King & Joker* ii. 27 Oho. So something had happened.

oh, oh (ǫ, ǫ), *int.* Also **ohoh.** [See O *int.* (*sb.*, *v.*) and OH *int.* (*sb.*)] An exclamation of alarm or dismay in response to adverse circumstances.

1944 E. S. GARDNER *Case of Black-Eyed Blonde* xvi. 156 Two police cars were closing in on them.. 'Oh, oh!' Della said under her breath. **1947** M. LOWRY *Under Volcano* v. 141 'Oh...Oh.' The Consul groaned aloud... It came to him he was supposed to be getting ready to go to Tomalín. **1958** J. MORGAN *Expense Account* i. 11 They were on the parkway, and Pete was thinking about the children, when he snapped his fingers and said, 'Oh, oh!' He had forgotten to buy them anything in Chicago. **1960** A. WEST *Trend is Up* vi. 259 Oh, oh, he thought, Silky is going to pass out before this night is through, that's for sure. **1962** J. F. POWERS *Morte d'Urban* iii. 58 'Oh, oh, I was afraid of that,' Wilf said.

oh-so (ōusōu), *adv.* Also **oh, so.** [f. OH *int.* + SO *adv.* III.] Prefixed as an intensive (usu. with hyphen) to adjectives or adverbs, with the sense 'ever so', 'extremely' (usu. with sarcastic or ironical overtones).

1922 *Sketch* 29 Mar. 513/3 A big grey felt hat, which looked, oh, so Spanish! **1952** M. LASKI *Village* ii. 33 Her sweet but, oh, so uninteresting face. **1960** J. BETJEMAN *Summoned by Bells* vii. 66 That mawkish and oh-so-melodious book Holds one great truth. **1965** *Listener* 27 May 797/2 The book is worth a shelf-load of those fashionable intellectualities that oh-so-knowingly chart out the spirallings of psychotic zombies, incapable of feelings, incapable of contacts, their spiritual telephone-wires all cut. **1966** J. PORTER *Sour Cream* xiii. 166 It just never entered Azatov's curly head that his oh-so-upright wife was cuckolding him every time his back was turned. **1972** J. GORES *Dead Skip* xiv. 97 The mailboxes were set against the oh-so-rustic redwood slat fence. **1973** *Radio Times* 20 Dec. 18/2 Very suave thriller with Laurence Harvey being oh-so-smooth. **1977** *Gay News* 7–20 Apr. 22/1 Most people do feel oh-so-slightly apprehensive about meeting him.

oh yeah (ōu yēə), *int. colloq.* (orig. *U.S.*). Also **O yeah.** [f. OH *int.* + *YEAH.] An exclamation or interrogative suggesting incredulity, disbelief, or scepticism; 'really?', 'is that so?'. Also as quasi-*adj.*

1930 *Forum* Dec. 376/2 Only recently, that cultural masterpiece *O yeah!* sounded its death rattle. **1931** LOEB & SCHENKER *Please Stand By* xii. 138 'Oh, are you William Wishtell,' the girl from the Globe asked... 'I've been dying to meet you.' 'Oh, yeah? Well, here I am in the flesh.' **1933** F. SCOTT FITZGERALD *Let.* 19 Oct. (1964) 237 No exclamatory 'At last, the long awaited, etc.' This merely creates the 'Oh yeah' mood in people. **1933** P. GODFREY *Back-Stage* xv. 194 They smiled indulgently, and greeted me with such remarks as 'I should worry' and 'Oh, yeah!' **1934** *Daily Mirror* 28 June 13/1 (*heading*) 'Oh Yeah!'..Observe that when you say, 'Oh, yes,' it doesn't mean at all the same thing as 'Oh, yeah,' when..you say *that.* 'Oh, yeah' means, really, 'Oh, *no*'; or 'you think you know about that do you, you guy, but I don't think you do, I don't.' **1936** *Variety* 24 June 47/3 Oh, Yeah? Agency men claim they can guess within $250 of any quoted price on a picture name. **1937** H. G. WELLS *Star Begotten* vii. 120 Confronted with an idea the American says 'Oh yeah!' or 'Sez you'. **1943** *Amer. Speech* XVIII. 256 A representative group of Americanisms which have wide currency in Australia:..oh yeah. **1966** D. FRANCIS *Flying Finish* vi. 74 'You look out, pal, you mustn't go around admitting that sort of thing...' 'Oh yeah?' I said, laughing.

Oi, oi (oi), repr. dial. or vulgar pronunc. I *pers. pron.*

1901 M. FRANKLIN *My Brilliant Career* xvi. 132 Sure O'i can't plaze yez anyhows. **1930** J. B. PRIESTLEY *Angel Pavement* iv. 188 Now, where was Oi? Losing mi plice, wasn't Oi?.. Ow, Oi know... Whoi dew the Catholics eat Fish on Froiday? **1939** JOYCE *Finnegans Wake* III. 551 Oi polled ye many but my fews were chousen. **1962** M. GREEN *Art of Coarse Sailing* ii. 20 Oi couldn't 'elp overhearing... If your friend's wife's 'aving 'er confinement she oughter come ashore... A Broads boat ain't no place for a babby to be born in. Shall Oi phone for the doctor? **1975** J. DRUMMOND *Slowly the Poison* i. 36 Oi washed down the cobbles. **1976** *Guardian* 6 Aug. 9 (Advt.), An' we're much 'bliged ta Whitbread, thassall oi can say.

oi, *int.*[1]: see *OY, OI *int.*

oi (oi), *int.*[2], var. HOY *int.* (*sb.*[2])

1962 JACKSON & MARSDEN *Educ. & Working Class* I. iii. 57 Father said, 'Oi, you two—you're not doing anything. Get some paint and paint under there!'

-oic, ending of the names of organic acids containing a carboxyl group, esp. in place of a methyl group. [App. first used in CAPROIC *a.*]

1971 *Nomencl. Org. Chem.* (I.U.P.A.C.) (ed. 2) C. 182 Carboxyl groups COOH replacing CH_3 at the end of the main chain of an alicyclic hydrocarbon are denoted by adding '-oic acid' or '-dioic acid' to the name of this hydrocarbon.

oick, oik (oik). *slang*. [Etym. obscure.] Depreciatory schoolboy word for a member of another school; an unpopular or disliked fellow-pupil. Also *gen.*, an obnoxious or unpleasant person; in weakened senses, a 'nitwit', a 'clot'. Hence **oi·kish** *a.*, unpleasant, crude; **oi·ckman** (see quot. 1925).

1925 *Dict. Bootham Slang, Hoick,*..spit. *Oick,*..to spit; abbreviated form of 'oickman'. *Oickman,*..labourer, shopkeeper, etc.; also a disparaging term. **1933** A. G. MACDONELL *England, their England* vi. 95 Those privately educated oicks are a pretty grisly set of oicks. Grocers' sons and oicks and what not. **1935** 'N. BLAKE' *Question of Proof* x. 189 Smithers is such an oick. **1940** M. MARPLES *Public School Slang* 31 Oik, hoik: very widely used and of some age; at Cheltenham (1897) it meant simply a working man, but at Christ's Hospital (1885) it implied someone who spoke Cockney, and at Bootham (1925) someone who spoke with a Yorkshire accent. **1940** M. DICKENS *Mariana* iv. 109 The old Oik mentioned it over a couple of whiskeys. **1946** G. HACKFORTH-JONES *Sixteen Bells* 260 Come to think of it he must have been a bit of an oik when he worked at Bullingham & Messer. That crack about long hair was well merited. **1957** F. KING *Widow* I. v. 63 He and Cooper had fought a battle with three 'oiks'—this was apparently school slang for the boys of the town. **1958** B. GOOLDEN *Ships of Youth* vii. 162, I only need my cap on back to front to look the complete oick. **1959** W. CAMP *Ruling Passion* xvi. 126 Who's that incredibly uncouth and oikish man? **1966** 'K. NICHOLSON' *Hook, Line & Sinker* viii. 95 So glad you got here before the oicks. **1968** *Melody Maker* 30 Nov. 24/5 Old Stinks from the third stream said: 'I say you oik, the Beach Boys latest is fab gear.' **1975** *Listener* 16 Jan. 83/1 The rigmarole about the flat was patent set-dressing, just to impress us oiks. **1975** *Times* 7 Aug. 7/7 His [*sc.* Oswald Mosley's] angels, a gang of gullible and bloodthirsty oiks ..would come pretty far down the roster of hell's legions.

oidiomycosis (o,i:diomaikōu·sis). [f. OIDI(UM + -O + MYCOSIS.] Infection of an animal or person with a fungus formerly classified in the genus *Oidium*, esp. the thrush fungus *Oidium* (now *Candida*) *albicans*. Now usu. called *candidiasis*. Cf. *MONILIASIS.

1901 [see *blastomycosis* s.v. *BLASTO-]. **1917** *Boston Med. & Surg. Jrnl.* CLXXVI. 771 (*heading*) Systemic oidiomycosis: with manifestations in the central nervous system. **1933** *Jrnl. Agric. Res.* XLVI. 169 Van Heelsbergen calls the disease oidiomycosis, and describes it as an affection of the mucous membrane of the mouth, fauces, esophagus, crop, stomach, and small intestine of birds, mammals, and man. **1938** H. T. KARSNER *Human Path.* (ed. 5) x. 297 (*heading*) Blastomycosis or oïdiomycosis. **1951** T. G. HUNGERFORD *Diseases of Poultry* (ed. 2) viii. 259 Fungus infection of the digestive tract is also known as thrush, moniliasis, oidiomycosis,..and sour crop. **1975** ARNALL & KEYMER *Bird Diseases* viii. 139 Candidiasis, Moniliasis, Oidiomycosis, Sour Crop or Thrush (*Candida albicans* infection). Turkeys, parrots, gamebirds and pigeons are mainly affected.

oik: see *OICK.

oik(o)umene, var. *ŒCUMENE.

oil, *sb.*[1] Add: **1. a.** (Further examples in sense 'mineral oil, petroleum'.) Cf. *PETROLEUM.

1860 *Chem. News* 6 Oct. 204/2 The wells yield, by pumping, from ten to twenty-five barrels per day of the crude oil. **1862** *Ibid.* 20 Sept. 149/2 It is believed that the United States and Canada possess natural supplies of petroleum to furnish the rest of the world, for ages to come, with sufficient quantities of oil to yield all the artificial light required, and perhaps much of the fuel also. **1907** V. B. LEWES *Liquid & Gaseous Fuels* iv. 85 In these early wells the oil had to be pumped, but in 1861 a well drilled to a depth of 460 feet yielded oil at such pressure that it rose to the surface and overflowed. **1930** C. T. BRUNNER *Probl. of Oil* p. iii, To-day the industrial importance of oil is incalculable... Transport interests.. depend mainly on oil..as the source of their power, while even the roads..are surfaced with a derivative of oil, bitumen. **1964** J. P. GETTY *My Life & Fortunes* ii. 23 Today, oil is big business, probably the biggest of all businesses. Without oil, there would be—there could be—no civilization as we know it. **1976** *Daily Tel.* 17 June 6/5 Converting more power stations from oil to coal would push up electricity charges.

e. *midnight oil*: see MIDNIGHT *sb.* 5.

3. a. (Later examples.) Also with stronger implications: nonsense, falsehood.

1917 *Amer. Mag.* Nov. 39/2 'Why dearie!' I remarks, kissin' her; 'You know I—'. 'Easy with the oil!' she cuts me off. **1924** [see *BUSHWA, -WAH]. **1926** MAINES & GRANT *Wise-Crack Dict.* 14/2 *Throwing the oil*, telling glib falsehoods. **1940** M. MARPLES *Public School Slang* 130 At Winchester..oil = an evasion. **1940** WODEHOUSE *Eggs, Beans & Crumpets* 168 Coo to him, and give him the old oil. **1954** —— *Jeeves & Feudal Spirit* i. 7 It was imperative that they be given the old oil, because she was in the middle of a very tricky business deal with the male half of the sketch and at such times every little helps.

f. For *U.S.* read 'orig. *U.S.*' and add earlier and later examples.

1862 *Amer. Ann. Cycl. 1861* 580/1 The oil, when first struck, has..been known to burst forth with great violence. **1930** 'SAPPER' *Finger of Fate* 180 The general consensus of opinion was that if his cricket was up to the rest of his form, Bob had struck oil. **1936** W. S. MAUGHAM *Cosmopolitans* 266 He'd struck oil a year or two ago and now he's got all the money in the world. **1973** N. GRAHAM *Murder in Dark Room* xiii. 94 You stopped with Scherz. I went a little further back and struck oil. **1975** *Times* 7 Oct. 5/2 When oil is struck..the oilman needs samples for laboratory analysis.

h. *oil and vinegar*: *lit.* used together as condiments; *fig.* said of two elements or factors which do not agree or blend together, or of any two incongruous constituents, with reference to the incompatible characters of oil and vinegar when mixed.

1629 J. PARKINSON *Parad.* II. xxxvi. 503 The first shootes or heads of Asparagus..being boyled tender, and eaten with..oyle and vinegar. **1747** H. GLASSE *Art of Cookery* i. 11 The French eat Oil and Vinegar with it [*sc.* broccoli]. **1777** R. POTTER tr. *Æschylus' Agamemnon* in *Tragedies* 232 Pour thou oil In the same vase and vinegar, in vain Wou'dst thou persuade th' unsocial streams to mix. **1820** KEATS *Let.* June (1931) II. 537 Men get such different habits that they become as oil and vinegar to one another. **1845** THACKERAY *Legend of Rhine* ix, in *George Cruikshank's Table Bk.* Sept. 194 Oil and vinegar, which he took with cucumber to his salmon. **1910** *Blackw. Mag.* Oct. 562/2 We might as well try to blend vinegar and oil, as mix together these two elements in one chamber. **1930** A. P. HERBERT *Water Gipsies* x. 120 'Why shouldn't our class marry his class?' 'It's oil and vinegar. They don't mix.' **1977** D. CLARK *Gimmel Flask* iii. 58 Your double oil and vinegar bottle.

i. Money; *spec.* money given in order to bribe or corrupt; a bribe. *U.S. slang.*

1903 A. H. LEWIS *Boss* 121 The sooner we get th' oil, th' sooner we'll begin to light up. **1935** *Detective Fiction Weekly* 31 Aug. 118/1 She didn't take care of her protection directly, that is, she didn't slip the oil to the cops herself. **1970** C. MAJOR *Dict. Afro-Amer. Slang* 87 *Oil*, graft, pay-off to authorities.

j. *Austral.* and *N.Z. slang.* Information, news, the true facts, esp. in phr. *dinkum oil* (see *DINKUM *a.*).

1916, etc. [see *DINKUM *a.*]. **1919** W. H. DOWNING *Digger Dial.* 36 *Oil*—News; information. **1930** *Bulletin* (Sydney) 1 Jan. 50/1 On a prospect..Old bloke what died gave me the dinkum oil. **1930** L. W. LOWER *Here's Luck* x. 84 We get the dinkum oil off him. **1944** J. H. FULLARTON *Troop Target* ii. 18 'What's the oil, Noel?' 'Yes, spill it.' **1946** F. I. COOZE *Ten Bob Each Way* 22 I'll give you the oil according to Hoyle. **1946** J. D. WOODS in *Coast to Coast 1945* 33 You'd better play a hand or two ..and get the oil about the place. **1948** V. PALMER *Golconda* xvi. 133 If anything were afoot, he told himself, Mahony would be sure to have the real oil about it, and he himself had a right to any inside information that was going. **1965** *Telegraph* (Brisbane) 5 July 8 The good oil, the drum, the griff.

4. b. Delete '*colloq.*' and 'Chiefly in *pl.*' and add earlier and later examples in *sing.*

1852 W. H. OXBERRY in W. Davidge *Footlight Flashes* (1866) xii. 110 An original painting of my father, by Drummond, and a little oil, by W. Beverly. **1912** W. OWEN *Let.* 26 Jan. (1967) 111, I herewith send a representation of my outward man; I[t] does not please me; nothing will, unless it were an oil by Sargent. **1938** W. T. WALSH *Philip II* xxviii. 573 One of the artists he employed was..Domenico Theotocópuli, whom he engaged to do a large oil of the martyrdom of St. Maurice. **1967** N. FREELING *Strike Out* 27 Over the chimney-piece was a large oil of three splendid horses. **1977** D. MACKENZIE *Raren & Kamikaze* iii. 39 A blackframed oil of a Labrador.

6. a. *oil-broker, change, company, dilution, -feed, filter, immersion, impregnation, magnate, -patch, priming, reserve, revenue, -room, sheikh, storage, supply, tannage, -valve*; *oil bomb, bunker, -canakin, -car* (examples), *-cell* (example), *-drum, -ladle, -pan, shell, -sump, -tank* (examples); *oil depot, district, industry, platform, refinery, -region* (earlier example), *sheikdom, show* [SHOW *sb.*[1] 5 c], *state, terminal, -works*; *oil gas* (later example); *oil-cooker, -heater, -lamp* (earlier and later examples), *-stove* (earlier and later examples); *oil picture* (earlier example), *portrait, sketch, -work*. **b.** *oil-bearing* (later examples), *-producing* (later examples), *-retaining* adjs.; *oil-burning* ppl. a. and vbl. sb.; *oil-cracking, -drilling, -raising, -sinking, -throwing* vbl. sbs.; *oil-catcher, -cooler, -distributor* (examples), *-feeder, gusher, separator*. **c.** *oil cooling, -firing, quenching, tanning*; *oil-bathed, -bound, -cooled, -fed* (examples), *-filled, -fired* (examples), *-foul, -immersed, -impregnated, -lit* (examples), *-mixed, operated, -primed, -proof, -quenched, -related, -rich, -sleeked, -stained, tanned* adjs; *oil-harden* vb. Also parasynthetic, as *oil-bunkered, -engined, -tanked* adjs.

1932 *World Today* LIX. 262/2 The camshaft and valve-gear as a whole are oil-bathed. **1863** *Jrnl. Franklin Inst.* LXXV. 271 The out-croppings of the lowest members of the Oil-Bearing Strata. **1946** *Nature* 28 Dec. 932/1 In the search for similar oil-bearing structures, geophysical surveys have been extended over wide areas. **1977** *Times* 9 Sept. 7/3 Mao Tse-tung..wanted Peking's parks to grow fruit and oil-bearing plants. **1918** E. S. FARROW *Dict. Mil. Terms* 417 *Oil bomb*, in trench warfare, a large oil drum containing oil and a quantity of high explosive, which dissipates the burning oil in all directions. **1947** *Illustr. London News* 25 Jan. 117/1 The magnificent hammer-beam roof of Westminster Hall..was extensively damaged by an oil bomb in 1941. **1945** *Archit. Rev.* XCVII. 42 Apart from the roof the remainder of the external steel finish is oil-bound paint. **1963** *House & Garden* Feb. 77/2 Oil-bound distempers, in which the binding material is an emulsion of oil or varnish, are more correctly called water paints. **1863** *National Almanac & Ann. Rec.* 687/2 A leading Liverpool oil-broker. **1977** *Yellow Pages Classified Telephone Directory: London (North)* 250/2 Oil Brokers. **1958** *Engineering* 28 Mar. 395/3 The closing of the Canal resulted in a sharp increase in the prices of oil bunkers. **1909** *Times Lit. Suppl.* 3 June 205/2 A plutocrat..who could quell the North Sea with oil-bunkered Dreadnoughts. **1886** *Marine Engineer* VII. 283/2 The oil-burning apparatus has been fitted. **1898** *Railway Mag.* Sept. 246/1 If the atmospheric conditions of the tunnels serve as an excuse..why not use oil-burning locomotives? **1920** E. C. BOWDEN-SMITH *Oil Firing for Kitchen Ranges* iv. 89 With regard to filtering the oil, this depends a great deal on the oil-burning system and the class of burner. **1924** *Domestic Engineering* XLIV. 191/2 The development of oil burning for land purposes has been retarded by the fluctuations in the price of oil. **1960** G. J. GOLLIN in W. F. B. Shaw *Domestic Heating* viii. 134 (*caption*) A complete oil-burning boiler installation. **1961** V. C. MILES *Domestic Vapouriser Burner Pract.* vii. 83 The vapourising type burner is being used in increasing quantities for the conversion of solid fuel boilers to oil burning. **1843** L. M. CHILD *Lett. from N.Y.* xl. 273 Children are driving hither and yon, one with a..band-box, or oil-canakin. **1876** J. S. INGRAM *Centenn. Exposition* 336 The oil..was loaded by gravity upon oil cars. **1897** KIPLING *Day's Work* (1898) 222 There were oil-cars, and hay-cars and stock-cars full of lowing beasts. **1850** *Rep. Comm. Patents 1849* (U.S.) 331 The complete hanger or pillow-block, with or without the oil-catcher. **1884** *Rep. Comm. Agric.* (U.S. Dept. Agric.) 363 When the cellular structure of the rind has completely developed, and the oil-cells have begun to fill. **1959** *Motor Manual* (ed. 36) x. 239 A second oil-change should be made before many hundreds of miles have been run. **1976** H. MACINNES *Death Reel* xii. 105, I am putting my car in for an oil change. **1827** J. S. MILL in *Westm. Rev.* VII. 177 A prohibition of gas-lights might be called..protection to the oil-companies. **1951** in M. McLuhan *Mech. Bride* (1967) 116/2 It's an oil company spending more money to make a better motor oil. **1974** E. AMBLER *Dr. Frigo* I. 53 One oil company would be bad enough. A consortium of five..must be quite oppressive. **1932** E. BOWEN *To North* xxiv. 231 She went into the scullery; here the oil-cooker was potent; she opened the window. **1977** J. THOMSON *Case Closed* vi. 81 A leanto scullery..that contained the sink and an oil-cooker. **1904** A. F. BERRY in M. Maclean *Mod. Electr. Pract.* II. I. vii. 79 Those [manufacturers] who use a shell-type oil-cooled construction of transformer..keep the temperature of part of the coils as nearly as possible at the temperature of the oil by spreading out the coils. **1962** *Science Survey* III. 89 (*caption*) The magnet weighs 750 tons and is energised by oil-cooled copper windings. **1973** R. W. SILLARS *Electr. Insulating Materials* x. 205 Oil-cooled power equipment..requires a medium which is fluid at all climatic and operating temperatures. **1940** *Chambers's Techn. Dict.* 590/1 *Oil cooler*, a small air-cooled radiator, used in aircraft and racing cars, for cooling the lubricant after its return from the engine and before delivery to the oil tank. **1911** BOHLE & ROBERTSON *Transformers* iv. 61 Another disadvantage of oil-cooling is the fact that if a fault occurs necessitating the withdrawal of the oil and the removal of the transformer it is frequently necessary to rewind the coils. **1970** J. SHEPHERD et al. *Higher Electr. Engin.* (ed. 2) ix. 278 For larger transformers oil cooling is needed, especially where high voltages are in use. **1929** *Times* 31 May 9/3 Notable advances are being made in the technology of oil-cracking processes. **1954** *Encounter* Sept. 34/1 Workmen in an oil-cracking plant in Oklahoma ..got angry, because, in a collective bargaining session, the management had referred to them as semi-skilled. **1863** Oil depot [see *oil derrick*, sense *6 e]. **1970** W. G. ROBERTS *Quest for Oil* xiv. 141 Even the small barge which plies up and down a big river to supply a local oil depot will have to have a crew. **1949** *Gloss. Aeronaut. Terms (B.S.I.)* II. 6 *Oil-dilution system*, a system by which the oil can be diluted to assist cold starting. **1889** *Century Mag.* Mar. 714/2 For pilot-boats oil-distributers [*sic*] are valuable when boarding vessels in breaking seas. **1909** *Daily Chron.* 17 Sept. 1/3 M. Blériot..was really thinking of the oil-distributor and the gauge showing the consumption of petrol. **1862** *Sci. Amer.* 22 Feb. 122/1 This oil district is peculiar in many respects. **1910** *Chambers's Jrnl.* Nov. 752/1 The apparatus has..demonstrated its value to the oil-district. **1937** M. HUXLEY *Let.* 13 Oct. in A. Huxley *Lett.* (1969) 427 We have seen so much, including..oil drilling. **1974** *Evening News* (Edinburgh) 10 Apr. 13/7 The next generation of British oil-drilling experts will be trained and produced in Scotland. **1909** *Daily Chron.* 24 July 6/3 Two small oildrums will be fixed beneath the plank. **1975** *Times* 22 July 14/2 The white Anglo-Saxon bass oil drum player. **1913** *Chambers's Jrnl.* Jan. 31/1 Oil-engined ships are..being built. **1924** *Times Trade & Engin. Suppl.* 29 Nov. 250/3 The large oil-engined liner. **1870** A. S. EVANS *Our Sister Republic* ii. 50 The watchmen..with muskets in their hands, and great oil-fed lanterns by their sides. **1886** *Chambers's Jrnl.* 16 Jan. 47/2 A vessel..propelled entirely by oil-fed furnaces. **1905** *Westm. Gaz.* 15 Feb. 8/2 It has a horizontal engine,..forced oil-feed, automatic carburation, [etc.]. **1900** CONRAD *Ld. Jim* vi. 74 He set the log for me; he..put a drop of oil in it too. There was the oil-feeder where he left it nearby. **1904** A. F. BERRY in M. Maclean *Mod. Electr. Pract.* II. I. vii. 78 If a fire breaks out in the oil-filled tank itself, the latter may be run out into the air. **1930** *Engineering* 24 Jan. 100/3 Various special designs, including the 132-kv. single-core oil-filled cables, which..are shortly to make their appearance in this country. **1957** W. J. JOHN *Mod. Electr. Engin.* I. iv. 126/1 In order to overcome the fire risk in oil-filled equipment, some attention has been paid to the use of chlorinated diphenyls. **1907** *Yesterday's Shopping* (1969) 713/3 Oil Filters... For filtering oil that has been used and become dirty, thus rendering it available for use again. **1925** *Morris Owner's Manual* ii. 28 Unscrew the large plug at the bottom of the sump, when the oil filter, which is attached to it, may be withdrawn. **1977** *Belfast Tel.* 22 Feb. 26/8 (Advt.), Oil filters for all cars. **1900** *Engineer* 22 June 651/1 It is coke instead of oil-fired. **1932** *Discovery* Aug. 248/2 In the oil-fired..liner high-class labour can be employed in the stokehold. **1961** I. MURDOCH *Severed Head* xxi. 168 The famous oil-fired central heating seemed to be making little impression on the temperature of the room. **1970** V. CANNING *Great Affair* v. 74 Aga oil-fired stoves in the kitchen. **1903** *Work* 11 July 364/1 The two firemen to be carried for coal burning would probably be reduced to one, there being little labour in oil firing. **1963** *Times* 12 Feb. 1/7 (*heading*) Trouble-shooting in oil-firing. **1931** W. FAULKNER *Sanctuary* xvi. 112 The white men sitting in tilted chairs along the oil-foul wall of the garage. **1958** *Times Rev. Industry* June 70/2 To build a..catalytic oil-gas process plant. **1921** *Daily Colonist* (Victoria, B.C.) 12 Oct. 9/7 One oil gusher in the new Fort Norman field, Northern Canada, produces 1,500 barrels a day. **1973** C. CALLOW *Power from Sea* i. 13 The big oil gushers being found in the North Sea. **1904** *Electrochem. Industry* Feb. 51/1 The usual method [for producing sorbite in steel] has been to reheat and oil-harden. **1895** *Montgomery Ward Catal.* 424/1 Oil Heater..will comfortably warm a large room in very cold weather. **1972** P. RUELL *Red Christmas* i. 10 The presence inside [the vehicle] of a small oil-heater and a lot of travelling rugs cheered him up. **1930** *Engineering* 9 May 599/3 Both sets of transformers are of the oil-immersed type. **1955** *Gloss. Terms Radiology* (*B.S.I.*) 34 *Oil-immersed tube*, an X-ray tube designed for operation in oil. **1883** *Encycl. Brit.* XVI. 268/1 A given angle in a water or oil immersion objective represents a much larger aperture than does the same angle in an air-objective. **1964** M. HYNES *Med. Bacteriol.* (ed. 8) xiv. 232 Growth may be obvious under the oil-immersion lens within 24 hours. **1940** *Chambers's Techn. Dict.* 591/1 *Oil-impregnated paper*, used for low and high voltage cables; the oil has resin in it to increase viscosity at working temperatures. **1946** *Nature* 28 Dec. 931/2 Such indications include seepages, gas-escapes, oil-impregnations, elaterite veins, and bituminous coatings in fractures and joints. **1880** *Harper's Mag.* Dec. 65 The oil industry has lent a powerful hand to the iron industry of Pittsburgh. **1951** in M. MCLUHAN *Mech. Bride* (1967) 114 Competition is just as much a part of the oil industry as wells or refineries. **1851** MELVILLE *Moby Dick* I. xx. 155 This excellent hearted Quakeress.. with a long oil-ladle in one hand. **1813** E. WEETON *Jrnl. of Governess* (1969) II. 92 A painted glass cylinder..intended to contain within it, either an oil lamp or a candle. **1962** L. DAVIDSON *Rose of Tibet* iii. 56 A dark and malodorous shack, lit by oil lamps. **1872** GEO. ELIOT *Middlem.* I. xv. 264 A dim, oil-lit street. **1974** G. JENKINS *Bridge of Magpies* vii. 107, I went down..to the shabby oil-lit cabin. **1927** U. SINCLAIR *Oil!* 312 Mountains on every side, and the oil magnate owned everything in sight. **1912** *Chambers's Jrnl.* Apr. 287/2 Oil-mixed concrete is best made by mixing the cement, sand, and water to a mortar, adding the oil to the mixture, [etc.]. **1946** *Happy Landings* (Air Ministry) July 3/3 Oil operated propellers are liable to 'run away' if the oil congeals. **1908** *Westm. Gaz.* 16 Apr. 4/3 Special oil-pans are fitted on each end of the throw for scooping up the oil from the base-chamber. **1955** W. GADDIS *Recognitions* II. vii. 642 The paving hardpacked with that snow, its whiteness..spotted and streaked from leaking oil-pans. **1965** M. BRADBURY *Stepping Westward* viii. 399 A floor covered with oil-patches. **1973** C. CALLOW *Power from Sea* iii. 75 There was a conspiracy of silence among the oil companies working in the 'oil patch' at this time. **1786** J. WOODFORDE *Diary* 4 Mar. (1926) II. 229 Rec'd an oil Picture from my Nephew Saml. from London. **1973** *Glasgow Herald* 7 Aug. 11/7 The oil-platform proposals. **1974** *Evening News* (Edinburgh) 12 Apr. 7/4 The public inquiry into the proposal to build giant concrete oil platforms at Drumbuie, Loch Carron, has ended after 43 days of speeches and evidence. **1939** WYNDHAM LEWIS *Let.* 15 Dec. (1963) 268, 1 oil-portrait and half-a-dozen chalk or pencil portraits. **1934** H. HILER *Notes Technique Painting* iii. 157 The ordinary oil-primed canvases. *Ibid.* i. 67 May be primed with an oil priming. **1959** *Daily Tel.* 13 Mar. 1/6 The Arab oil-producing countries. **1974** *Times* 21 Sept. 2/6 Scottish oil..could easily be undercut if the oil-producing states chose to lower their posted price. **1880** *English Mechanic* 24 Sept. 75/2 (*heading*) Oil-proof cement. **1906** *Daily Chron.* 29 May 5/4 The licensing authority should require motor bus proprietors to provide an oil-proof receptacle under the bonnet of each omnibus. **1914** Oil-quenched [see *air-hardened* ppl. a. (*AIR *sb.*[1] II)]. **1943** *Gloss. Terms Electr. Engin.* (*B.S.I.*) 53 *Oil-quenched fuse*, a liquid-quenched fuse in which the liquid is oil. **1937** *Discovery* May 155/2 Oil quenching..offers a uniform rate of cooling, without requiring the exercise of unusual care. **1910** *Chambers's Jrnl.* Nov. 750/1 This engineer, who has made a deep study of oil-raising methods. **1863** Oil refinery [see *oil derrick*, sense *6 e]. **1977** *Times* 21 Nov. (Eastern Province Suppl.) p. ii/8 (*caption*) Ras Tannurah, the country's main oil refinery and port. **1862** *Prelim. Rep. 8th Census* (U.S. Census Office) 72 The Pennsylvania oil region. **1974** *Evening News* (Edinburgh) 12 Apr. 11/4 Minister of State at the Scottish Office, Mr Bruce Millan, will tour oil-related developments in the Northeast of Scotland and Shetland during a three-day visit next week. **1975** *Petroleum Economist* Aug. 288/1 The Department of Energy,..expects that oil-related employment will increase as more companies enter the offshore market. **1950** *Chambers's Encycl.* X. 619/2 Table III shows the distribution of ownership of oil reserves. **1966** P. O'DONNELL *Sabre-Tooth* iii. 58 Kuwait..holds a quarter of the world's known oil reserves. **1977** *Listener* 17 Mar. 335/3 Overseas companies..own around 60 per cent of the North Sea oil reserve in the British sector. **1907** *Westm. Gaz.* 5 Dec. 4/2 The spring is..connected to the gear-box by an oil-retaining universal coupling. **1962** *B.S.I. News* Feb. 37 Bronze oil-retaining brushes and thrust washers for aircraft. **1975** P. SOMERVILLE-LARGE *Couch of Earth* x. 184 We should be prepared to forego a week's oil revenues. **1977** *Sunday Times* 20 Nov. 53/4 Part of the oil revenue will have to be used to tackle some of Britain's deep-seated industrial problems. **1959** *Daily Tel.* 13 Mar. 1/6 The oil-rich sheikhdoms of the Persian Gulf are still under British protection. **1975** N. LUARD *Robespierre Serial* iv. 16 The profile might have fitted any oil-rich Arab. **1877** *Harper's Mag.* Dec. 34/2 The three boys in the oil-room have used, of all grades of oil, twenty gallons less. **1886** *Boy's Own Paper* 2 Oct. 11/3 Disagreeable smells, as if of a steamboat's lower regions, proved this to be the oil-room. **1934** *Discovery* Apr. 88/2 The cost of oil separators is less than it used to be, and some of the prominent shipping companies are willing to introduce them. **1969** *Gloss. Terms Vacuum Technol.* (*B.S.I.*) 20 *Oil separator*, a device which reduces the loss of pump oil as droplets at the outlet. **1960** *Spectator* 30 Sept. 493 Spiritual oil-sheikhs waiting for their oil to be discovered. **1974** *Times* 31 Jan. 18/5 The oil shaikhs put paid to that as club after club buckled before the fuel crisis. **1972** *Guardian* 23 Feb. 2/1 Qatar is one of the smaller oil sheikdoms. **1904** *Sci. Amer. Suppl.* 9 Apr. 23641/3 Oil shells, that is, shells containing oil, which should distribute their contents upon the waves wherever they might happen to fall, could, by means of a cannon, be projected some distance in advance of a moving ship. **1953** WILSON & METRE in *Sci. Petroleum* VI. I. 122/1 Despite the wide distribution of oil shows and much exploratory drilling, only two oilfields of commercial importance have been found. **1977** *Offshore Engineer* May 8/1 (Advt.), All exploratory wells drilled—designated as either dry well, gas show, oil show, oilwell, gaswell, oil and gas well. **1961** *Aeroplane* C. 127/2 A Cessna 180D has been specially fitted with equipment to keep holiday beaches clear of oil contamination... This process is known as 'oil sinking' and has been developed in Germany. **1856** D. G. ROSSETTI *Let.* 15 May (1965) I. 301 That oil-sketch of the Queen and Page. **1977** *Times* 14 May 16/5 Oil sketches by Landseer, as opposed to large finished paintings, were fetching £10,000 and more a year or two back. **1952** C. DAY LEWIS tr. *Virgil's Aeneid* IV. 78 His chin and oil-sleeked hair set off by a Phrygian bonnet. **1907** *Westm. Gaz.* 11 Apr. 4/2 'Hygiene,' the *Lancet* says, 'would condemn the highly seasoned and oil-stained meerschaum or briar pipe.' **1944** *R.A.F. Jrnl.* Aug. 291 His cap, battered flat and copiously oil-stained, stuck on the back of his head. **1976** E. WARD *Hanged Man* xiii. 72 Quentin..took Wallace's oil-stained shoes. **1973** *Listener* 22 Nov. 698/3 The oil states are rich. **1974** *Times* 18 Apr. 5/6 (*heading*) Few concessions from oil states at UN debate. **1906** CONRAD *Mirror of Sea* xxxi. 164 Petroleum ships discharge their dangerous cargoes and the oil-storage tanks low and round with slightly-domed roofs, peep over the edge of the foreshore. **1973** *Times* 1 Dec. 2/3 He lives in a cottage beside it, and spends his days servicing and maintaining his donkey and its four cylindrical oil storage tanks and logging the amount of oil. [**1865** *U.S. Pat.* 45,957 17 Jan., Coal-oil stove.] **1880** *Harper's Mag.* Aug. 400 Oil stoves are objectionable because of the unpleasant odor of the fuel. **1921** *Daily Colonist* (Victoria, B.C.) 21 Oct. 6/6 (Advt.), Optimus oil stoves—solid brass, regular $10. **1933** DYLAN THOMAS *Let.* 11 Nov. (1966) 58 The oil-stove shines like a parhelion. **1977** A. CLARKE *Let. from Dead* ii. 18 'Could we give him a bed, Angy?'..'Of course. It'll have to be the front attic... I'll take one of the oil stoves up.' **1923** W. DEEPING *Secret Sanct.* ix. 85 A man was bending over one of the wings, pouring oil into the oil-sump. **1909** *Q. Rev.* Oct. 575 Depôt ships for destroyers, mother-ships for submarines, and oil-supply vessels. **1974** *Evening News* (Edinburgh) 10 Apr. 1/5, 27-year-old Spanish seaman decided to entertain women aboard a North Sea oil supply ship berthed at Leith last night. **1862** *U.S. Pat.* 34,426 18 Feb., Oil tank. **1923** H. S. BELL *Amer. Petroleum Refining* 293 Corrosion in oil tanks occurs at three points. **1951** DYLAN THOMAS *Selected Lett.* (1966) 352 O evergreen..oil-tanked..cradle of Persian culture. **1903** H. R. PROCTER *Princ. Leather Manuf.* xxiv. 384 We may apply some of the ideas which we have formed with regard to oil-tannages to the action of fats upon tanned leather. **1948** M. P. BALFE in *Progress in Leather Sci. 1920–1945* III. xxiv. 496 The oil tannage gave a leather which absorbed water more rapidly and to a greater extent than the combination tannage, and showed a greater degree of separation of the fibres. **1950** L. K. MASON *Pipe Dreams about Leather & Saddles* 15 *Oil Tannage*, or 'shamoying', used mainly for wash-leather sheepskins ('chamois') and the like. **1903** L. A. FLEMMING *Pract. Tanning* 46 Sheep and lambskins oil-tanned. **1953** D. WOODROFFE *Leather Dressing* vii. 80 Chamois or oil tanned leather is usually yellow, clothy and porous. **1972** *Materials & Technol.* V. 411 Chamois or wash leather is the term applied to oil tanned products obtained from the flesh splits of sheepskins. **1903** L. A. FLEMMING *Pract. Tanning* 410 Oil tanning with Turkey-red oil. **1958** C. GOERTH tr. A. Kuntzel in F. O'Flaherty et al. *Chem. & Technol. Leather* II. xxviii. 426 Oil tanning produces a leather having characteristics quite different from all other types of tanning. **1975** *Petroleum Rev.* XXIX. 387/3 The location of the oil terminal was proposed by Orkney County Council. **1977** *Observer* 24 Apr. 1/6 The blow-out occurred..just over 200 miles from the British oil terminal at Teesport. **1963** BIRD & HUTTON-STOTT *Veteran Motor Car* 101 Inadequate cooling and excessive oil-throwing. **1901** *Sketch* 17 July 498/1 Sand dropped into the oil-valves. **1611** CORYAT *Crudities* 25 Many goodly pictures of some of the Kings and Queenes of France..drawen out very liuely in oyle workes. *Ibid.* 26 Pictures made in oyleworke vpon wainscot, wherein..the nine Muses are excellently painted. **1869** *Bradshaw's Railway Manual* XXI. App. 117 Oil refiners... Works: British Oil Works, Saltney, near Chester. Victoria Oil Works, Collyhurst Road.

e. oil age, an age in which oil is used extensively, esp. as a source of power; **oil baron** = *oil king* below; **oil-belt**, a zone containing oil-fields; **oil-berg** [after ICEBERG], a large body of oil floating in the sea; **oil-break** *a.* (see quot. 1943); **oil-butt**, a butt (BUTT *sb.*[2]) containing oil; also *fig.* (see quot. 1937); †**oil-can**, also (*slang*), a German trench-mortar shell (*obs.*); **oil circuit-breaker**, an oil-break circuit breaker; **oil coal**, coal from which oil is obtained; **oil-cup** (earlier U.S. example); **oil-derrick** (examples); also *fig.*; **oil-drop**, (*b*) a drop of oil; freq. *attrib.* with reference to an experimental method of measuring the electronic charge; **oil field**: see as main entry; **oil-filler**, (*a*) one who or that which fills a container with oil; (*b*) an aperture through which an engine is filled with oil; (*c*) a coat of oil-paint used to fill in areas of a painted surface; **oil-gilding** (earlier example); **oil-jacket**, a seaman's jacket made of oil-skin; **oil king**, a magnate in the oil-trade; **oil-painter**, a painter in oils; **oil-painting**, (*b*) also used in negative phrases to indicate an unprepossessing appearance; **oil-palm**, substitute for def.: a palm tree yielding fruit from which oil is pressed, esp. *Elæis guineensis*, which is native to West Africa but widely cultivated in tropical regions; (further examples); **oil pollution**, contamination with oil discharged from a ship; **oil pool**, an extent of rock in which oil is present throughout without interruption, forming a single reservoir; **oil province**, an extensive area containing a number of oil fields that are geologically related; **oil-resin**, used *attrib.* to designate a cooked varnish used on paintings, and in painting mediums; **oil rig**, a rig (RIG *sb.*[6] 3 a) employed in drilling for oil; **oil-sand** (later examples); also extended to any oil-bearing rock; **oil shale**, shale which contains kerogen and on distillation yields oil; **oil-ship**, a vessel carrying whale-oil or fuel oil as cargo; **oil-silk:** delete † and add later examples; **oil slick**, a film or layer of oil, esp. one floating on an expanse of water; so **oil-slicked** *a.*; **oil-smeller** (example); **oil-soluble** *a.*, soluble in oil; **oil spill**, an escape of oil into the sea; **oil-spot**, (*a*) a marking on Chinese porcelain caused by deposition of iron in firing, used chiefly *attrib.* of Honan ware so marked; (*b*) on industrial glass (see quot. 1962); **oil spring** (earlier examples); **oil-strike** orig. *U.S.*, a discovery of an oil-field by drilling; **oil string**, the innermost length of casing (tubing) in an oil well, extending down to the oil-producing rock; **oil switch**, an oil-break switch; **oil-tanker**, a vessel having special tanks for the conveyance of oil; a vehicle designed for carrying oil; **oil thrower** (see quot. 1964); **oil-tight** *a.* (later example); **oil trap** (see *TRAP *sb.*); **oil–water** *a.*, situated between or involving oil and water. Also *OIL BURNER.

1911 *Chambers's Jrnl.* July 465/1 That was the beginning of the great Oil Age. **1969** M. PEI *Words in Sheep's Clothing* (1970) xx. 206 This favors Texas oil barons, but not people who wear out their bodies and brains working for a living. **1974** N. MARSH *Black as he's Painted* iii. 75 From the oil barons at the top to ex-business men at the bottom. **1976** *Time* 27 Sept. 65/2 Since it was launched in 1973 by Reporter-turned-Lawyer Michael R. Levy, 30, *Texas Monthly* has taken on just about every sacred steer in the Lone Star State: college football, the Miss Texas Pageant, oil barons, the Texas Rangers, Dallas banks. **1865** *Harper's Mag.* Apr. 563/2 The Canadian wells now flowing hundreds of barrels of oil are located on the borders of Lake Erie, far to the west of the so-called oil belt. **1901** *Chambers's Jrnl.* Feb. 126/1 The exploitation of..the most prolific oil-belt of the world. **1904** *Dialect Notes* II. 385 *Oil-belt*, the district including the supposed course of subterranean rivers of oil. **1966** *Economist* 24 Sept. 1275/1 There are considerable areas of doubt about the performance in rough weather of ships over 300,000 tons... The danger of underwater damage to floating oil-bergs with nearly 100 feet of ship below the surface is considerable. **1977** *Time* 10 Jan. 53/3 No scientists are willing to forecast the effects of the oil now spreading seaward from the *Argo Merchant*. Most believe that if the globs of oil, called oilbergs because most of their mass is below the surface, continue to move east, the damage will be held to a minimum. **1904** W. E. WARRILOW in M. Maclean *Mod. Electr. Pract.* II. II. i. 230 Figs. 482, 483 illustrate an oil-break switch for large powers, this type being suitable for a working current of 500 amperes at a pressure of 2000 volts. **1943** *Gloss. Terms Electr. Engin.* (*B.S.I.*) 62 *Oil-break*, applied to a switch, circuit-breaker or similar apparatus to denote that the circuit is opened in oil. **1851** H. MELVILLE *Moby Dick* III. xxix. 184 The cabin mess dined off the broad head of an oil-but, lashed down to the floor for a centre-piece. **1937** PARTRIDGE *Dict. Slang* 581/1 *Oil-butt*, a black whale. *a* **1917** E. A. MACKINTOSH *War, the Liberator* (1918) 156 'Look out, sirr,..oil can coming over.' Instantly self-preservation reasserted itself. **1917** A. G. EMPEY *Over Top* 302 '*Oil Cans*', Tommy's term for a German trench mortar shell. **1924** W. A. COATES *Choice of Switchgear* v. 89 Only small, unimportant oil circuit-breakers are operated by a hand lever directly upon the breaker itself. **1964** E. A. REEVES *Installation & Maint. Industr. Switchgear* iii. 32 Medium-voltage oil circuit-breakers may be either incorporated in a cubicle or fitted on the outside of a metal-clad unit. **1873** C. ROBINSON *New South Wales* 52 Deposits of brown cannel oil coals and oil shales. **1850** *Rep. Comm. Patents 1849* (U.S.) 233 The combination of the tight oil cup with the axle. **1863** *Boston Herald* 16 Aug. 3/3 You see, in close proximity on every side, oil depots, oil refineries, oil derricks. **1902** 'MARK TWAIN' *Speeches* (1910) 367 That long, lank cadaver, old oil-derrick out of a job. 1948 *Ada* (Okla.) *Even. News* 2 July 1/3 The work scheduled for Friday called for the shooting of scenes at the oil derrick. 1976 *Scotsman* 24 Dec. 6/3 Aberdeen District planning and building control committee yesterday granted planning permission for a 96-ft steel oil derrick which is to be built above a 1000-ft deep test well..near their manufacturing site on the Bridge of Don estate. 1911 *Physical Rev.* XXXII. 393 Instead of using oil drops he sucks into the observing chamber the metallic dust arising from the volatilization produced in a metallic arc. 1913 *Ibid.* 2nd Ser. I. 218 Improvements which the 'oil drop method' introduced into the study of the Brownian movements. 1939 X. Herbert in B. James *Austral. Short Stories* (1963) 115 The first sight that caught his eye was a row of sparkling oil-drops hanging from the face of yet another outcrop. 1946 *Nature* 30 Nov. 786/1 Oil drops..entered the field and were illuminated by flashes of light. 1968 M. S. Livingston *Particle Physics* ii. 13 The first precise measurement of the electronic charge came with the results of Millikan's oil-drop experiment in 1909. 1860 *Harper's Mag.* June 8/1 New Bedford is the chief seat of the whaling interest... Here the gaugers, clerks, supercargoes, oil-fillers..ply their busy offices. 1927 [see *dip-stick, dipstick*]. 1937 [see *guide coat*]. 1972 D. Bloodworth *Any Number can Play* xvi. 152 He..unscrewed the radiator cap..and then glanced at the oil filler. 1847 J. C. Maitland *Historical Charades* xv. 193 A gilder living in the village..explained to him the nature of oil-gilding. 1851 H. Melville *Moby Dick* II. vii. 54 That worthy,..buttoned up in his oil-jacket. 1898 *Contemp. Rev.* Aug. 236 The Bill..might have suited the English oil dealers; it was too much for the American oil kings. 1765 T. H. Croker et al. *Compl. Dict. Arts & Sci.* II. s.v. *Enamel*, Blue is made of the azure or lapis lazuli used by oil-painters. 1842 *Ainsworth's Mag.* I. 232 There are difficulties in the way of even our first oil-painters. 1891 R. Fry *Let.* 4 Mar. (1972) I. 129 Raphael..is a fresco painter and not an oil painter. 1930 J. B. Priestley *Angel Pavement* ii. 64 ''Member him, Edna?—teeth sticking out a yard, and all cross-eyed.'..'Still, we can't all be oil paintings.' 1932 N. Mitford *Christmas Pudding* iii. 39 The poor girl's certainly no oil painting. 1955 L. P. Hartley *Perfect Woman* viii. 76, I may not be an oil-painting, but I'm all right in my way. 1966 'O. Mills' *Enemies of Bride* i. 10 She's no oil-painting, so she wouldn't be besieged with offers. 1973 *Listener* 23 Aug. 246/1 Mr Tillett was no oil painting, but was a gentle-manly sort of man. [1725 H. Sloane *Voy. Jamaica* II. 113 (*heading*) The Palm Oil-Tree. 1731 P. Miller *Gardeners Dict.* s.v. *Palma*, The Oily Palm grows in great Plenty on the Coast of Guiney..: But these Trees have been transplanted to Jamaica and Barbadoes, in both which Places they thrive very well... The Inhabitants make an Oil from the Pulp of the Fruit.] 1907 Freeman & Chandler *World's Commercial Products* 374 The well-known Oil Palm of the West Coast of Africa..furnishes two different oils. 1954 R. E. Holttum *Plant Life Malaya* vi. 81 Oil palms are the next most important oil crop [after coconut] in Malaya. 1966 E. J. H. Corner *Nat. Hist. Palms* xiii. 305 The fruit of the oil-palm is a drupe one and a half inches long, with pulpy, red or black wall or pericarp and a small, pointed stone. 1975 T. C. Whitmore *Trop. Rain Forests Far East* xvii. 219/2 Western man introduced plantation agriculture, initially to grow spices, later to grow the other cash crops, with coffee, tea, rubber, and oil palm predominating. 1922 *Times* 15 June 2 (*heading*) Oil pollution of the sea. 1973 V. Canning *Flight of Grey Goose* iv. 67 Two great black-headed gulls that were recovering from the effects of oil pollution. 1903 *Bull. U.S. Geol. Survey* No. 212. 68 The foregoing account of the Gulf Coastal Plain has been given in some detail in order that the geologic environment of the oil pools might be readily understood. 1938 *Sun* (Baltimore) 18 Jan. 1/3 Kilgore is in the heart of the vast east Texas oil pool, the world's largest. 1971 I. G. Gass et al. *Understanding Earth* ix. 139/1 The oil-water interface in a sub-surface abiogenic oil-pool. 1926 E. R. Lilley *Oil Industry* iii. 22 [The writer will use the term 'province' when referring to an area containing connected or related fields.] *Ibid.* 539/2 (Index), Oil province. 1940 *Bull. Amer. Assoc. Petroleum Geologists* XXIV. 1024 The Pure Oil Company's discovery in Marshall County, in what is virtually a new oil province, may encourage other operators to venture farther into the unknown. 1975 *North Sea Background Notes* (Brit. Petroleum Co.) 3 The North Sea ..has now become one of the world's major offshore oil provinces. 1934 H. Hiler *Notes Technique of Painting* iii. 163, I have used an oil-resin medium for fifteen years. 1951 R. Mayer *Artist's Handbk.* i. 31 Some of the earlier American uses of tempera and oil-resin glazes are mentioned on page 27. 1885 *Engineering* 26 June 708/2 As I have referred to the Pennsylvanian oil rig, a brief mention of its principle may not be out of place here. This machine is specially arranged for deep sinking. 1965 M. Bradbury *Stepping Westward* viii. 391 They reached the section where the oil-rigs stand up. 1973 *Scotsman* 12 Jan. (Tayside Suppl.) p. vii/2 (*caption*) Montrose from the air. A new quay and purpose-built base will service up to 12 oil rig supply ships. 1974 *BP Shield Internat.* Oct. 17/2 It's the morning rush-hour to the North Sea oil rigs. 1975 *Times* 16 Sept. 3 (*heading*) Puzzle of oil-rig divers' death from overheating. 1915 C. Schuchert *Text-bk. Geol.* II. xxvii. 713 The oil and gas are stored in coarse, open-textured sandstones and conglomerates, and because of this the term *oil-sand* has come to be applied by drillers to all horizons yielding these volatile hydrocarbons. 1921 G. H. Cox et al. *Field Methods Petroleum Geol.* 217 Because of the higher average porosity of sandstone, most 'oil sands' are true sandstones, but many are porous limestones. 1925 A. B. Thompson *Oil-Field Explor.* I. ix. 426 Twenty or more workable oil sands have been encountered to 2,500 ft [in the Bibi-Eibat oil-field]. 1974 *Globe & Mail* (Toronto) 23 May 8/3 Research is also progressing on development of a micro-organism that could be used in the reclamation of the Alberta oil sands, Dr. Kaneda said. 1873 Oil shale [see *oil coal* above]. 1919 [see *Boghead, boghead*]. 1956 *Nature* 4 Feb. 216/1 In 1858 Geikie was able to indicate to James Young, founder of the Scottish oil industry, the general distribution of West Lothian oil-shales. 1974 'E. Lathen' *Sweet & Low* xiv. 138 Yet another optimistic study of oil shale. 1975 *Petroleum Economist* Sept. 349/2 Morocco is preparing to exploit its large oil shale deposits at Timahdit in the Middle Atlas Mountains. 1851 H. Melville *Moby Dick* II. xxxix. 257 However curious it may seem for an oil-ship to be borrowing oil on the whale-ground. 1911 J. J. Abraham *Surgeon's Log* vi. 195 No one is allowed to smoke on board the oil ships. 1870 G. H. Lewes *Jrnl.* 14 Apr. in *Geo. Eliot Lett.* (1956) V. 90 Bought oil silk for compress. 1938 *Times* 20 May 21/4 Oilsilk, that daughter of oilskin, has been developed into many types of mackintosh. 1965 M. Thomas *Grannies' Remedies* 91 An envelope of wetted linen or cotton, oil-silk, and thick flannel. 1889 *Century Mag.* Mar. 710/2 It had..formed an oil-slick thirty feet to windward. 1918 *Sat. Even. Post* 12 Oct. 90 The submarine when running close beneath the surface leaves what is known as an 'oil slick'. That is, the oil that is discharged in the exhausts floats on the top of the water in tell-tale streaks... 'Oil Slick' is American terminology. The British Admiralty did not approve at first. 1950 G. Hackforth-Jones *Worst Enemy* ii. 171 Meanwhile, no doubt, an 'oil slick' would be rising from the crumpled ballast tanks which must have suffered damage. 1973 *Guardian* 19 May 12/3, 200,000-ton tankers..letting loose their oil slicks in some of the most profitable fishing grounds in the world. 1958 *Oxford Mail* 15 Aug. 1/5 Wreckage picked up from the oil-slicked section of the Atlantic by the searching ships. 1967 L. Deighton *Expensive Place* xxvii. 164 The oil-slicked highway dared children and divided neighbours. 1976 *Leicester Mercury* 14 Oct. 10/2 The grey waters of the Clyde closed slowly over the oil-slicked plates of the huge submarine. 1865 J. H. A. Bone *Petroleum & Petroleum Wells* 20 A new class of people has sprung into existence under the cognomen of oil smellers, who profess to be able to ascertain the proper spot for boring by smelling the earth. 1925 *Jrnl. Physical Chem.* XXIX. 1206 A water-soluble emulsifying agent opposes the action of an oil-soluble agent. 1935 A. J. Norton in P. H. Groggins *Unit Processes in Org. Synthesis* xiii. 636 Strictly speaking, the oil-soluble resins are a subdivision of the thermoplastic resins. 1971 *Jrnl. Econ. Entomol.* LXIV. 1399 (*heading*) Oil-soluble black dye in larval diet marks adults and eggs of tobacco budworm and pink bollworm. 1970 *Internat. & Compar. Law Q.* XIX. 343 Compensating governments and tanker owners for the costs incurred in cleaning oil spills. 1975 *Offshore* Aug. 112/1 The company has been blocked from drilling for six years, initially by the moratorium imposed by the state following the January, 1969 oil spill. 1976 *Globe & Mail* (Toronto) 16 Feb. 9/3 Adequate contingency plans to deal with oil spills, especially in the ecologically sensitive Mackenzie delta and Beaufort Sea areas, have not yet been developed. 1922 A. L. Hetherington *Early Ceramic Wares of China* xviii. 124 The markings may assume quite a different appearance and silvery spots or 'oil spots' may take the place of the golden-brown streaks. *Ibid.*, A specimen with a Northern grey body and 'oil spot' glaze is shown in colour on Plate 38. 1934 *Burlington Mag.* May 214/2 A black glaze diapered with silvery spots..the much-prized 'oil-spot temmoku'. 1960 H. Hayward *Antique Coll.* 203/1 'Oilspot' glaze: some of the Chinese wares bearing so-called Honan brown and black glazes of the Sung dynasty bear attractive silver spots, caused by precipitated iron crystals. 1962 *Gloss. Terms Glass Industry (B.S.I.)* 40 *Oil spot*, a mottled, circular mark caused by carbonization of oil on electric lamp bulb or valve forming equipment. 1971 L. A. Boger *Dict. World Pott. & Porc.* 154/2 Some Honan wares have a body of buff or buff-white, or of white or grey white... The rare oil spot temmoku generally belongs to this group. Occasionally a rare tea bowl is found that is covered with small silver spots which are actually a silver-like reflection caused by the metallic luster of the brown. This is referred to by the Chinese as the oil spot glaze. 1762 in *Pennsylvania Mag. Hist. & Biogr.* (1913) XXXVII. 174 Mullen brot me a Bottle of Oyle from ye Oyl Spring at Mooskingum. 1832 B. Davenport *New Gazetteer* 272/1 s.v. *Franklin*, The celebrated Oil Springs..rise from the bed of Oil creek [Pa.] and afford an inexhaustible supply of oil. 1839 Z. Leonard *Adventures* 73/2 An oil spring, rising out of the earth. 1864 *Harper's Mag.* Dec. 59/2 It is certain that great oil-strikes are no longer looked for. 1973 *Scotsman* 21 Feb. 1/5 Ultramar shares moved up 1p to 271½p on hopes of an oil strike. 1921 W. H. Jeffery *Deep Well Drilling* xii. 346 When the drilling conditions, depth to the producing formation, etc., are known, the perforated casing is sometimes added to the oil string before the well is drilled in. 1943 *Bull. Amer. Assoc. Petroleum Geologists* XXVII. 519 The usual range of oil-string lengths is from 4,500 feet to 5,000 feet where casing is set above the 'pay'. 1946 *Mod. Petroleum Technol.* (Inst. Petroleum) 85 In low-pressure wells the upper section of the smaller diameter casing, the 'oil string', is sometimes removed as a measure of economy, but in wells in which gas or oil under high pressure is expected, each string of casing extends to the surface. 1960 C. Gatlin *Petroleum Engin.* xiv. 269/1 The final appearance of a typical completed well is shown in Figure 14.1. Note that three separate casing sizes are indicated: the surface pipe, the intermediate string, and the oil string. 1904 *Trans. Amer. Inst. Electr. Engin.* XXIII. 215 The design of the oil-switch lends itself readily to operation by control from a distance. 1964 E. A. Reeves *Installation & Maint. Industr. Switchgear* iii. 57 The type of oil switch described is essentially a fault-making and load-breaking device. 1920 *Isle of Man Weekly Times* 21 Sept. 3 Kermode's supplied..installations..for..British Admiralty oil-tankers. 1926 *Brit. Gaz.* 12 May 4/3 Many vessels have been docked and undocked, including oil tankers. 1927 *Daily Express* 20 Sept. 2/4 The goods train consisted mainly of oil-tankers. 1965 W. Soyinka *Road* 21 Have you known any other driver take an oil-tanker from Port Harcourt to Kaduna non-stop? 1967 N. Freeling *Strike Out* 73 Dickie looks as poor as a rat on an oil-tanker. 1903 Oil thrower [see *creepage*]. 1964 Dorian & Osenton *Elsevier's Dict. Aeronautics* 428 *Oil thrower*, a disk fixed on a shaft, so as to prevent oil from creeping along it, the oil being thrown off centrifugally. 1972 *Practical Motorist* Oct. 168/2 As the nut is tightened the neoprene ring is squeezed out to give an oil-tight seal. 1946 *Nature* 26 Oct. 572/1 An interesting series of transparent 50 per cent oil–water systems was described. 1964 G. H. Haggis et al. *Introd. Molecular Biol.* iii. 70 The unfolding of protein molecules at air–water or oil–water interfaces must be briefly described at this point. 1971 Oil–water [see *oil pool* above].

oil, *v.* Add: **1. a.** (Later example.)

1851 H. Melville *Moby Dick* (U.S. ed.) xxv. 124 A king's head is solemnly oiled at his coronation, even as a head of salad.

b. (Further examples.) Also, to rub (a person) with oil as a protection against sunburn. Also *refl.*

1876 Geo. Eliot *Dan. Der.* II. iv. xxxiii. 332 There's a bad style of humbug, but there is also a good style—one that oils the wheels and makes progress possible. 1896 C. M. Sheldon *His Brother's Keeper* ii. 39 Have you been greasing your boots with it?.. Half a pint wouldn't oil more than one of 'em. 1909 *Daily Chron.* 6 Sept. 3/3 Her craze for the 'psychic'..oils the wheels of the plot. 1941 A. Christie *Evil under Sun* vi. 107, I oiled myself and sunbathed. 1945 E. Waugh *Brideshead Revisited* I. ii. 43 Anthony had helped oil fading beauties on sub-tropical sands. 1972 *Mainichi Daily News* (Japan) 6 Nov. 13/1 Advertisement [*sic*] is a powerful factor in boosting the economy in free countries and it is the strongest means of oiling the wheel of manufacturer-consumer relations. 1972 'G. Black' *Bitter Tea* (1973) ix. 137 A cousin came over and oiled Sally's back. 1973 A. Holden *Girl on Beach* 51 She changed into her swimsuit, oiled herself all over. 1976 D. Francis *In Frame* xvi. 232 Our passage had been oiled by telexes from above. When we arrived..we found ourselves whisked into a private room. 1977 'A. Stuart' *Snap Judgement* 178 He set the deal up... He was oiling the wheels for when Brigitte arrived with the secrets.

c. To cover the surface of (water) with a film of oil in order to kill mosquito larvæ.

1921 M. Watson *Prevention of Malaria* (ed. 2) xvii. 190 When a clear pool containing the ordinary floating alga is 'oiled', the alga dies. 1952 P. F. Russell *Malaria* 133 Water recently oiled is unfit for bathing. 1959 A. A. Sandosham *Malariology* vi. 252 When oiling a ravine the seepages in which the ravine stream begins should get most attention.

2. Also, *to oil the knocker*: to bribe or tip a doorman. *slang.*

1870 *Brewer's Dict. Phr. & Fable* 632/1 *To oil the knocker*, to fee the porter. The expression is from Racine, *On n'entre point chez lui sans graisser le marteau* (No one enters *his* house without oiling the knocker)—'*Les Plaideurs*'. 1901 Farmer & Henley *Slang* V. 93/1 *To oil the knocker*, to fee the porter. 1968 *Gloss. Brit. Argot* (Paramount Pictures), *Oil the knocker*, tip the porter or caretaker.

3. (Later example.)

1923 *Man. Seamanship* (Admiralty) II. 80 The pumps in the oiler should be started gradually, attempts should not be made to oil individual tanks too rapidly.

b. *intr.* To take in a supply of oil.

1914 H. H. Fyfe *Real Mexico* 201 Some day vessels will call here..to 'oil' just as they now 'coal'. 1922 *Glasgow Herald* 21 Oct. 11 After that the Renown only stopped to oil.

5. *colloq.* To move or go in a quiet or stealthy manner; (const. *in*) to enter, (*fig.*) to interfere; (const. *out*) to depart, (*fig.*) to extricate oneself. Also const. other advbs.

1925 Wodehouse *Carry on, Jeeves!* vi. 139 As man to man, do you want to oil out of this thing? 1929 —— *Mr. Mulliner Speaking* i. 28 It would be a simple task to oil in, insert the soap, and buzz back undetected. 1930 —— *Very Good, Jeeves!* iv. 110, I..oiled round to where Jeeves awaited me. 1945 'A. Gilbert' *Don't open Door* xix. 172 As soon as he was alone he'd oil out and they could think what they pleased. 1958 —— *Death against Clock* 119 She might oil in, and..clinch a bargain on the spot. 1963 —— *Ring for Noose* x. 119 He deserves to lose his licence, oiling off and leaving you on your tod. 1968 G. Mitchell *Three Quick & Five Dead* i. 35 Do you think the girl was pestering for marriage, but that James wanted to oil out? 1977 'J. Le Carré' *Hon. Schoolboy* xxii. 527 That twerp Enderby is oiling through the back door.

6. *intr. to oil up*: to clog up with oil.

[1925: see *oiled-up* s.v. *oiled *ppl. a.* 5.] 1960 [see *foul *v.*[1] 1b]. 1975 *Country Life* 5 June 1470/1 In traffic..plugs oil up. And pedals are hard pressed to keep the engine alive.

oil-bag. c. (Later examples.)

a 1889 in *Century Mag.* Mar. 710/1 [I] placed two oil-bags, filled with linseed oil, over the bows. 1961 F. H. Burgess *Dict. Sailing* 152 *Oil bag*, any container that permits oil to drip out slowly to help quell the sea.

oi·l bath. Also **oil-bath.** [f. Oil *sb.*[1] + Bath *sb.*[1]] **1.** A receptacle containing oil for cooling, heating, lubricating, or insulating apparatus immersed in it, or for other purposes.

1838 [in Dict. s.v. Oil *sb.*[1] 6 a]. 1885 *Marine Engineer* 1 Sept. 151/2 The crank shaft at the lowest point of its revolution constantly touches the surface of an oil bath in the closed motion chamber. 1927 Mellanby & Cooper tr. *Kieser's Materials & Design Turbo-Gen. Plant* 52 The sudden drop in temperature is obtained by quenching the wheels in an oil bath. 1968 K. Ball *B.M.C. Autobk.* 4 198/2 *Oil-bath*... In air filters, a special oil supply for wetting the wire-mesh element. 1970 —— *Fiat 600* 164/2 Oil bath Reservoir which lubricates parts by immersion. 1971 *Power Farming* Mar. 57/3 It forms an oil-bath for the drive, the oil being circulated by the gears to the outboard end and returned through piping.

2. *India.* (See quots.)

1909 *Westm. Gaz.* 28 Apr. 5/2 The term oil-bath is only a misnomer, inasmuch as the bath is not taken in oil. It is applied to a process involved in besmearing the body with oil and then bathing in a river or tank to remove the oil from the body. **1967** Singha & Massey *Indian Dancer* ix. 96 First, the entire body is given an 'oil-bath', that is, oil is rubbed into it.

oi·l burner. **1.** A device in which oil is atomized and burned to produce heat.

1900 *Engineer* 22 June 651/3 A new muffle furnace with two oil burners of the luminous lamp type, but arranged to give a blue flame. **1946** K. Steiner *Fuels & Fuel Burners* xiv. 279 Domestic oil burners usually operate intermittently.., starting when heat is required and stopping when the heat demand is satisfied. **1946** E. Hodgins *Mr. Blandings builds his Dream House* (1947) II. xv. 204 The oil burner, starting up in answer to the call of its thermostat. **1970** D. Kut *Warm Air Heating* xx. 338 The grade of oil fuel best suited for a particular installation depends on the type of oil burner and on the hourly through-put of oil.

2. a. A vehicle or ship burning oil as fuel.

1902 *Westm. Gaz.* 29 Sept. 5/2 Tank engines were the first to be fitted as oil-burners, and now some of the newest main line locomotives are to be fitted. **1911** *Daily Colonist* (Victoria, B.C.) 20 Apr. 14/3 The steamer will be practically a duplicate of the Princess Adelaide but will be constructed as an oil-burner. **1923** R. D. Paine *Comrades of Rolling Ocean* ix. 160 That ship of his..is an oil-burner. **1942** Berrey & Van den Bark *Amer. Thes. Slang* § 766/6 *Oil burner*, a diesel-powered truck. **1971** M. Tak *Truck Talk* 111 *Oil burner*, (1) a diesel truck, as opposed to a truck that runs on gasoline.

b. *slang.* A vehicle which, because of its poor condition, uses up great quantities of lubricating oil.

1938 *Amer. Speech* XIII. 307/2 *Oil burner*, a bus which uses excessive amounts of oil. **1975** B. Garfield *Hopscotch* xvii. 166 Even in an old oil-burner he could have gone three times as far in a day's drive if he'd wanted to.

oilcake. (Earlier and later examples.)

1743 W. Ellis *Mod. Husbandman* June iv. 36 Dressing Ground with Lime, Chalk,..Oil Cake Powder, Malt Dust [etc]. **1942** *Sun* (Baltimore) 26 Nov. 8/2 The ships, operating under a safe conduct agreement between Sweden and belligerent nations, were laden with grain, oilcake and piece goods. **1971** *Post* (S. Afr., Cape ed.) (Suppl.) 9 May 10/1 (*caption*) Easy oil cake..easy and cheap to make. **1975** *Nature* 13 Feb. 488/3 The importance of the poppy crop lies primarily in the seed, as the principle [*sic*] source.., after extraction, of oil-cake for cattle feed.

oilcloth. Add: **1. b.** (Earlier and later examples.)

1796 H. Walpole *Let.* 20 Nov. (1905) XV. 430, I mentioned *carpets* made from Mr. Lysons's mosaic pavements; I ought to have said *oil-cloths*, which cost a great deal less. **1903** Kipling *Five Nations* 114 Then the oilcloth with its numbers, as a banner fluttered free. **1904** G. Stratton-Porter *Freckles* 72 Freckles..covered the [book-]case with oil-cloth. **1974** *Country Life* 3 Jan. 33/3 Fortunately preserved under later oilcloth is decoration in the upper hall and several of the bedrooms.

2. (Later examples.)

1917 W. Owen *Let.* 8 Aug. (1967) 481 Thus I need at once... The Oil-cloth raincoat. **1954** M. Sharp *Gipsy in Parlour* xiii. 133 Oilcloth-covered tables and bentwood chairs. **1974** R. B. Parker *Godwulf Manuscript* xii. 96 The kitchen with its oilcloth-covered table.

oi·l-clothed, *a.* [f. Oilcloth + -ed[2].] Laid or covered with oilcloth. So **oi·lclothy** *a.*, suggestive of or resembling oilcloth.

1894 M. Dyan *All in Man's Keeping* II. x. 185 There came..the tap of light heels on the oil-clothed landing. **1915** Galsworthy *First & Last* in *Cosmopolitan* June 12/2 He was in a gas-lighted passage, with an oil-clothed floor. **1923** U. L. Silberrad *Lett. J. Armiter* ix. 202 Everything was slippery and oilclothy. **1974** L. Thomas *Tropic of Ruislip* ii. 41 She..followed Andrew into The Bombardier Café where he was sitting at one of the tables covered with decorated oilcloth depicting badges of Britain's fighting forces... She and her grandfather sat at the next oilclothed table staring directly at him.

oi·ldom. [f. Oil *sb.*[1] + -dom.] The petroleum-producing districts of a country; petroleum producers and marketers regarded as a group.

1865 J. H. A. Bone *Petroleum & Petroleum Wells* 42 If he would see anything at all of oildom he must make the passage, unpleasant as it may be. **1880** *Harper's Mag.* Dec. 63 Huge shops..send..iron tanks into the oil regions—to hold the surplus of Oildom. **1904** I. M. Tarbell *Hist. Standard Oil Co.* I. 71 The rise [in freight rates] which had been threatening had come... At the news all oildom rushed into the streets. **1926** J. Ise *U.S. Oil Policy* xiii. 135 The new order immediately precipitated a fresh quarrel in oildom.

oiled, *ppl. a.* Add: **1.** (Later examples.) Cf. *to oil the wheels* (Oil *v.* 1 b) and *oil *v.* 1 b.

1932 D. L. Sayers *Have his Carcase* xx. 263 It was.. surprising to find the identification..going like oiled clockwork. **1933** *Brit. Birds* XXVII. 45 Very little has been heard of 'oiled' birds during the two years. **1971** 'D. Halliday' *Dolly & Doctor Bird* i. 2 Lying oiled in the sun. **1972** *Daily Tel.* 9 Mar. 9/2 Oiled birds, mostly razorbills and guillemots, are coming ashore in north Cornwall. **1973** J. Burrows *Like an Evening Gone* i. 8 Greta was capable. ..Her unlikely scheme proceeded as on oiled wheels. **1976** M. Millar *Ask for me Tomorrow* (1977) xvii. 135 It was the only house on Camino de la Cima, an oiled dirt road.

c. (Further examples.)

1808 M. Wilmot *Russ. Jrnls.* (1934) 316 He *has* a suite of apartments in the Tartar taste with oil'd paper instead of Glass windows. **1957** *Textile Terms & Definitions* (Textile Inst.) (ed. 3) 70 *Oiled wool*, unscoured or undyed knitting wool or wool dyed before spinning and containing added oil not subsequently removed. **1962** L. Deighton *Ipcress File* i. 15 His oiled teak desk. **1974** D. Ramsay *No Cause to Kill* i. 28 The carpeting was a basket weave..effective against oiled walnut, the only wood present. **1977** J. R. L. Anderson *Death in City* viii. 119 A heavyweight oiled-wool pullover.

3. *slang.* Drunk; if unmodified (by *well*, etc.) only mildly drunk, tipsy.

1737 *Pennsylvania Gaz.* 6–13 Jan. 2 He's Oil'd. **1899** A. M. Binstead *Gal's Gossip* 169 He was certainly well 'oiled'. **1916** E. V. Lucas *Vermilion Box* 141 He was, as the slang phrase has it, 'oiled'; which is a condition of alcoholic comfort well on this side of inebriety. **1926** E. Wallace *More Educated Evans* ix. 218 He'll come out in a minute, oiled to the world. **1948** Wodehouse *Spring Fever* xvi. 162 Augustus Robb, if not actually plastered, was beyond a question oiled. **1976** J. Wainwright *Who goes Next?* 76 When they're nicely oiled, one of 'em sometimes trots around here, and buys something.

4. Executed in oil-colours.

1903 Ld. R. Gower *Rec. & Reminisc.* 246 To make an oiled copy of the framed 'Three Maries', by Carracci.

5. *Comb.*, as **oiled-down,** smoothed or plastered down with (hair) oil; **oiled-up,** fouled or choked with oil.

1907 M. A. von Arnim *Fräulein Schmidt & Mr. Anstruther* xiii. 49 Her long respectable face and oiled-down hair. **1956** H. Gold *Man who was not with It* (1965) xxviii. 264 A yellow-fleshed, oiled-down, slicked-up head. **1925** *Morris Owner's Manual* 81 Sooty or oiled-up plugs will cause erratic running, loss of power and..increased petrol consumption.

oiler. Add: **4.** For *U.S. colloq.* read *colloq.* (orig. *U.S.*) and add to def: and/or trousers. (Further examples.)

1899 'Q' *Ship of Stars* ix. 69 Taffy wore a suit of oilers of which he was mighty proud. **1924** R. J. Flaherty *My Eskimo Friends* i. i. 6 Old Puggie, donning oilers and sou'wester,..settled down to the helm. **1969** *Islander* (Victoria, B.C.) 22 June 2/2 You can always spot Dolfie in his favorite open boat, because he almost invariably wears yellow oilers.

6. b. A naval vessel carrying oil for the use of other ships.

1916 'Taffrail' *Pincher Martin* xiv. 255 Perhaps they would be going alongside an oiler at dead of night to replenish their fuel, and the wind would get on the wrong bow. **1923** [see *oiling *vbl. sb.* 3]. **1943** *Times* 8 Dec. 3/3 A flash was followed by a sheet of flame and the oiler was burning fiercely when our aircraft left. **1960** 'N. Shute' *Trustee from Toolroom* viii. 215 She was a Fleet oiler that had discharged her cargo at Christmas Island. **1973** *Times* 15 Mar. 5/4 Sightings included a Soviet F class diesel electric submarine together with..an oiler. **1974** *Union* (S. Carolina) *Daily Times* 22 Apr. 8/1 The carrier Kitty Hawk, several escorting destroyers and an oiler were expected to sail through the Strait of Malacca today.

c. A vehicle transporting oil.

1948 Mencken *Amer. Lang.* Suppl. II. 714 A tank-car is a car or oiler. **1975** I. K. Martin *Regan & Manhattan File* 54 That truck..was a General Mills sixteen-wheel oiler.

7. a. A vessel using fuel-oil.

1911 J. Barten *Compl. Nautical Pocket Dict.* 138/2 *Oiler*, Dampfschiff mit Oelfeuerung. **1915** *Chambers's Jrnl.* Oct. 664/1 The word 'oiler', like 'steamer', for oil-driven ships..is coming into use.

b. An oil-engine.

1926 *Chambers's Jrnl.* Dec. 843/1 She is a cold-starter, two stroke 'oiler'.

c. A vehicle using oil as its fuel.

1935 *Economist* 7 Dec. 1136/2 As far as goods traffic is concerned, the growth of the Diesel lorry or 'oiler' has been at the expense of the 'steamer' as much as of the petrol vehicle.

8. *U.S. slang.* A Mexican. (*derogatory*).

1907 S. E. White *Arizona Nights* i. iv. 82 A few oilers livin' near had water holes in the foothills. *Ibid.* iii. ii. 282 We're livin' like a lot of Oilers.

oi·l field. Also **oilfield, oil-field.** [f. Oil *sb.*[1] + Field *sb.*] An area or a tract of country underlain by oil-bearing strata, the oil usu. being present in amounts that justify commercial exploitation and occupying a number of distinct pools. Also *attrib.* Cf. *oil province* s.v. *oil *sb.*[1] 6e.

1894 [in Dict. s.v. Oil *sb.*[1] 6 e]. **1912** Tower & Roberts *Petroleum* i. 11 In most cases there is a comparatively large area which can be called an 'oil field'... Within the main field there are usually several distinct areas, or 'pools', from which the chief production comes. **1926** E. R. Lilley *Oil Industry* iii. 21 The expression 'oil field' may be used to indicate an individual area of small extent such as the Salt Creek field of Wyoming.., or a group of such areas as the Lima-Indiana field.., or even an area of as wide extent as the Mid-Continent field which includes parts of Kansas, Oklahoma, Texas, Arkansas, and Louisiana. **1930** C. T. Brunner *Probl. of Oil* i. 11 The bulk of the American output still comes from the mid-Continental and Californian oilfields. **1964** *Oceanogr. & Marine Biol.* II. 136 There is a decline of sulphate with depth in the interstitial water of cores, due to the activity of sulphate-reducing bacteria and the interstitial water eventually comes to resemble oil field brine. **1973** *Scotsman* 21 Feb. 1/4 Another oilfield has been discovered in the North Sea, just inside the British sector and about 170 miles east-north-east of Aberdeen. **1975** *Offshore Engineer* Oct. 61 (Advt.), We will be fully equipped for on the spot repair and maintenance work of all oil field tools.

oiling, *vbl. sb.* Add: **1.** Also, oil pollution; the discharge of oil from a ship.

1949 *Brit. Birds* XLII. 378 No signs of oiling were visible. **1970** *Nature* 9 May 573/2 A recent 'routine' winter oiling along the east coast of Scotland exacted a known toll of about 8,000 seabirds.

b. *spec.* The covering of the surface of water with oil. Cf. *oil *v.* 1 c.

1887 [see sense 1 in Dict.]. **1910** R. Ross et al. *Prevention of Malaria* vi. 270 (*heading*) Oiling. **1927** P. Hehir *Malaria in India* 313 Anopheles larvæ succumb to oiling more readily than Culex larvæ. **1949** F. C. Bishopp in M. F. Boyd *Malariology* II. lxi. 1340/1 Malaria cases have also been markedly reduced on estates where oiling has been practiced regularly. **1966** P. H. Manson-Bahr *Manson's Trop. Dis.* (ed. 16) iv. 70 Oiling kills mosquito larvæ probably in several ways.

3. The taking of oil on board, esp. for fuel.

1906 *Westm. Gaz.* 27 Feb. 2/1 The difficulties in the way of 'oiling', to coin a word to correspond to 'coaling', at foreign ports. **1923** *Man. Seamanship* (Admiralty) II. 79 (*heading*) Oiling from an oiler.

4. The action of *to oil out* (cf. Oil *v.* 1 b).

1859 [see Oil *v.* 1 b]. **1962** R. G. Haggar *Dict. Art Terms* 231/2 *Oiling out*, in oil painting, the process of bringing out passages which have sunk in; a drying oil is applied.., the excess is removed and the surface gently polished.

oilless, *a.* (Later examples.)

1922 [see *graphited *a.*]. **1940** *Chambers's Techn. Dict.* 591/1 *Oil-less circuit-breaker*, a circuit-breaker which does not use oil either as the quenching medium or for insulation purposes. **1972** H. Osborne *Pay-Day* i. 19 Panjeh had always been a poor relation on the Coast, an oil-less sheikhdom. **1974** *Economist* 21 Dec. 11/2 France.. has come back in from its oilless cold to work with its allies.

oilman. Add: **e.** A person in the oil industry; an employee of an oil company.

1865 *Atlantic Monthly* XV. 388 She was still considering her probable success in finding an oil-man to take her down the Creek. **1880** *Harper's Mag.* Dec. 65 There are engines and boilers and pumps to be built for the oil men. **1912** Tower & Roberts *Petroleum* v. 83 The flowing or gushing wells are always regarded as lucky strikes among oilmen. **1951** T. Sterling *House without Door* i. 6 She knew what Texas oil men looked like. **1972** *Times* 27 Sept. 21/7 The oilmen look longingly at the areas north of the 62nd Parallel. **1973** A. Price *October Men* viii. 113 The oilman Ian Howard, just back from a year..in Saudi Arabia. **1975** *Lamp* (Exxon Corporation) Winter 11/1 When they began to commit sizable sums to North Sea oil development three and four years ago, oilmen expected the investment to be a costly one.

oil-nut. b, c. (Earlier and later examples.)

1694 *Town Rec. Topsfield, Mass.* (1917) I. 86/2 From thence on a straight line to an oylenut tree which is Isaac Burtons tree marked. **1778** J. Carver *Trav. N.-Amer.* 500 The Butter or Oilnut... The tree grows in meadows, where the soil is rich and warm. **1813** H. Muhlenberg *Catal. Plantarum Americæ Septentrionalis* 96 Oil nut, (*Pyrularia* or *Hamiltonia oleifera*). **1832** D. J. Browne *Sylva Amer.* 173 In Massachusetts, New Hampshire and Vermont it [*sc.* the butternut] bears the name of Oil Nut. **1912** E. Seton *Forester's Manual* 41 White Walnut, Oil Nut, or Butternut (*Juglans cinerea*). **1933** J. K. Small *Man. S.E. Flora* 1250 P[yrularia] pubera... Buffalo-nut. Oil-nut. Mountain-coconut.

oilskinned, *a.* (Earlier example.)

1857 C. Kingsley *Two Yrs. Ago* I. iii. 80 Oil-skinned coast-guardsmen.

oilstone, *sb.* (Later examples.)

1853 [see *abrasive B. *sb.*]. **1885** [see *Arkansas 1]. **1947** J. C. Rich *Materials & Methods Sculpture* x. 300 Fine oilstones are generally used for sharpening flat chisels. **1966** A. W. Lewis *Gloss. Woodworking Terms* 63 *Oilstone slips* or *slipstones*, oilstones of a variety of shapes used to sharpen gouges, [etc.].

oi·l well. Also **oil-well, oilwell.** [f. Oil *sb.*[1] + Well *sb.*[1]] A shaft sunk to obtain oil or from which oil is obtained. Freq. *attrib.*

1847 L. Collins *Hist. Sk. Kentucky* 249 The American Oil well is situated three miles above Burksville. **1861** *Chem. News* 28 Sept. 164/2 He states that the yield from the wells has greatly decreased, and that the oil well region, for practical working, is of very limited extent. **1903** G. H. Montague *Rise & Progress Standard Oil Co.* i. 4 With the success of Drake's oil-well at Titusville, Pennsylvania, in 1859, refiners had been released from the necessity of distilling coal into petroleum before refining petroleum into kerosene. **1946** *Mod. Petroleum Technol.* (Inst. Petroleum) 86 There are two main systems employed in drilling oil-wells: (1) the rotary or mud-flush system, and (2) the cable-tool or percussion system. **1946** *Nature* 20 July 84/1 The oil industry uses large quantities of nitroglycerine explosives..in the so-called oil-well 'shooting', where the explosives are employed to shatter the underground formation and thus open up fissures through which the oil may flow freely to the well. **1976** *Globe & Mail* (Toronto) 4 Feb. 7/4 The study made conclusions similar to those of Dr. Pimlott, saying existing technology could not cope with an oilwell blowout in the Beaufort Sea.

oily, *a.* (*adv.*). Add: **2. c. oily wad,** (*a*) a torpedo boat burning fuel-oil (*disused*); (*b*) a seaman without a special skill (see also quot. 1961).

1925 Fraser & Gibbons *Soldier & Sailor Words* 213 *Oily wads*, a Navy nickname for a class of oil burning torpedo boat destroyers. **1929** F. C. BOWEN *Sea Slang* 97 *Oily Wads.* The name occasionally applied to seamen in the Navy who do not specialise in anything, from the amount of time they have to spend cleaning brass-work with oily wads. **1931** 'TAFFRAIL' *Endless Story* xxii. 344 Numbered from 1 to 36, they were generally known in the Service as the 'oily wads'. **1932** KIPLING *Limits & Renewals* 199 Some oily-wad of a *Bulleana* struck up about not having got his proper bird. **1961** F. H. BURGESS *Dict. Sailing* 152 *Oily wad*, a seaman with no ambition. **1963** *Times* 13 June 17/1 His first command, which he held from May 1908, to January 1910, was torpedo boat no. 14 in the Home Fleet, one of the first oil-burning ships in the Navy, known to those serving in them as 'oily wads'.

D. *sb.* An oilskin garment. Chiefly in *pl.*

1893–4 R. O. HESLOP *Northumb. Words* II. 510 *Oily*, an oilskin coat. **1898** G. A. RUSHTON in W. A. Morgan *'House' on Sport* I. 73 Still wind and rain the next day—but we..putting on our oilies went ashore and tramped for miles. **1933** E. A. ROBERTSON *Ordinary Families* iv. 69 Soaked to the skin in spite of their oilies, Sootie and Ronald came down into the cabin. **1959** 'A. FRASER' *High Tension* x. 106, I..ran upstairs to put on a thick jersey... That and an oily would do. **1973** J. R. L. ANDERSON *Death on Rocks* vii. 127 His own oilies were in the club.

oink (oiŋk), *v.* [Echoic.] **a.** *intr.* Of a pig: to utter its characteristic sound. **b.** *transf.* To make a similar sound; to imitate this sound; to grunt like a pig. Also as *sb.*

1969 *New Yorker* 11 Oct. 55/2 (*caption*) I'm warning you—don't start oinking. **1971** *It* 2–16 June 11/4 Seale called the fab philosopher 'a moral coward who oinks like a pig'. **1971** E. BULLINS *Hungered One* 143 The pitter-patter of the returning dog's feet came from the road, and the cricket music and an occasional pig's oink and a drowsy duck quacked at the dark. **1972** J. WAMBAUGH *Blue Knight* (1973) iv. 55 One young guy..leaned back in his chair and made a couple of oinks and said, 'I smell pig.' **1973** *Times* 11 Apr. 13/5 The spasmodic oink-oink of chalk on cue. **1977** C. MCFADDEN *Serial* (1978) v. 16/2 They oinked at him, in concert, just about every time he opened his mouth.

ointment. *a fly in the ointment*: see *FLY *sb.*[1] 1 e.

‖ **oiran** (oi·răn). [Jap.] A Japanese courtesan of high standing. Also *collect.*

1871 A. B. MITFORD *Tales Old Japan* I. 67 They are employed to wait upon the *Oiran*, or fashionable courtesans. **1904** R. J. FARRER *Garden of Asia* xix. 181 Of all glories in Japan, the richest is that of the Oiran, or established beauty of the Yoshiwara. **1970** J. KIRKUP *Japan behind Fan* 90 The boys..who are indistinguishable from the *oiran*, the geisha and other women. **1972** *Mainichi Daily News* (Japan) 6 Nov. 20/2 (Advt.), 'Oiran'—the glittering Yoshiwara courtesans—recreate the ceremonies attendant on greeting an honored patron.

‖ **Oireachtas** (e·rəχtəs). [Ir., = assembly, gathering, convocation.] **1.** The assembly and festival held annually by the Gaelic League of Ireland, a gathering similar in concept to the Welsh eisteddfod and Scottish mod. Also *attrib.*

1902 W. B. YEATS *Let.* 20 Jan. (1954) 364 Royalties..I shall ask A. P. Watt to send..to the Sec. of Gaelic League, Dublin. Do you think I should specify the purpose? Say an Oireachtas prize. **1910** *Encycl. Brit.* V. 616/1 In 1898 it was decided to hold a festival called the *Oireachtas* ('hosting, gathering') on the lines of the Welsh *Eisteddfod.* **1911** W. H. G. FLOOD *Story of Bagpipe* xx. 164 The *Mod* is somewhat analogous to the *Oireachtas* in Ireland. **1913** *Irishman* Feb. 4/1 The keynote of this Oireachtas must be that Irish shall be plainly and unmistakeably the dominant language. **1971** *Daily Tel.* 5 Aug. 10/3 Prominent among the tents on the field for the first time this year is one representing Eire's equivalent of the Eisteddfod—the Oireachtas, to be held in October.

2. The legislature or parliament of the Republic of Ireland, consisting of the president and two houses, a house of representatives (Dáil Éireann) the members of which are elected by proportional representation, and a partially nominated senate (Seanad Éireann).

In quot. 1947 *An t-Oireachtas* is the regular Irish form that includes the definite article.

1922 *Daily Mail* 4 Dec. 9 The Provisional Government will be out of office by Wednesday, and the Oireachtas, as the Free State Parliament will be known, will come into being, consisting of Seanad Eireann (Upper House), comprised of 60 senators, 30 of whom will be nominated by the Government, and the remainder by the elected deputies of the people, who will sit as a Lower House, under the name of Dail Eireann. **1923** W. B. YEATS *Senate Speeches* (1961) 53 A joint committee of both houses to consider how suitable accommodations for Oireachtas may be obtained. **1930** G. B. SHAW *John Bull's Other Island* Pref., in *Works* XI. 72 The Northern Parliament will not merge into the Oireachtas. **1938** *Ireland: Citizen's Manual* 27 The Oireachtas may not enact a law repugnant to the Constitution nor declare acts to be unlawful after their commission. **1947** S. MALONE *Notes Procedure Oireachtas* p. vii, The National Parliament (An tOireachtas) consisting of the President and two Houses. **1969** HENIG & PINDER *European Pol. Parties* xi. 447 To win an election was, and is, to win the right to a virtual monopoly of legislative and policy initiative and the power to manage and control the *Oireachtas* (Parliament). **1975** *Irish Times* 9 May 8/1 Mr. Lynch said that there had been a tradition among the staff of the Oireachtas that if there was to be any easement of Standing Orders, that easement would be given in favour of the Opposition. **1977** *Cork Examiner* 6 June 2/8 Ever since it has been bandied about both in accusation and refutation on the subsequent occasions of the passage of an electoral Bill through the Oireachtas.

oiticica (oitisi·kă). [Pg., f. Tupi *oitisica.*] A name used for several tropical South American trees, esp. *Licania rigida*, of the family Chrysobalanaceæ, whose crushed seeds yield an oil used in paints and varnishes. Also *attrib.*

1918 E. R. BOLTON in *Analyst* XLIII. 251 (*title*) Oiticica oil—a new drying oil. *Ibid.*, During the early part of 1917 we examined a new oilseed sent apparently for the first time from Brazil, bearing the native name of Oiticica or Oilizika. **1925** MORRELL & WOOD *Chem. Drying Oils* ii. 67 The oil is extracted from the kernels of oiticica (a name applied to several species of *Moquilea* and *Conepia*, belonging to the *Rosaceæ*). **1931** B. MIALL tr. *Guenther's Naturalist in Brazil* vii. 124 The handsomest tree of the Sertão is the Oiticica. A sturdy trunk, divided into many branches, lifts itself from roots which run high over the ground. From the dense green roof of foliage the older leaves hang like silver tassels. **1944** H. G. KIRSCHENBAUER *Fats & Oils* vi. 88 Oiticica seed oil owes its outstanding drying properties to the presence of licanic acid. **1944** S. PUTNAM tr. *E. da Cunha's Rebellion in Backlands* ii. 123 An old abandoned shack overgrown with oiticica boughs. **1951** R. MAYER *Artist's Handbk.* iii. 112 Oiticica Oil is a Brazilian product. **1967** *Times* 27 Apr. 27/3 The rather bewildering news yesterday that the Oiticica crop in the State of Ceara in South America has been almost a complete failure may well have sent some commodity men hurrying for their dictionaries.

Ojibwa(y (ǒudʒi·bwěi). Numerous varr. [Ojibwa, based on a root meaning 'puckered' (see quot. 1824); *CHIPPEWA is a corrupted form of *Ojibwa(y.*] **a.** A member of an Algonquian people of North American Indians, inhabiting the lands around Lake Superior and, in more recent times, certain adjacent areas from Saskatchewan to Lake Ontario. **b.** An Algonquian language spoken by this people. Also *attrib.* or as *adj.*

'Chippewa and *Ojibwa(y* are the same word. Of these the former was the common English form until well into the nineteenth century... *Chippewa* is now the common spelling in the U.S. and *Ojibwa(y* in Canada. Hence these forms tend to be used for somewhat different local groups, but the usage is not consistent. Ethnologists, and especially linguists, tend to use *Ojibwa(y* for all the groups in question.' (Dr. I. Goddard)

1700 in *Documents Colonial Hist. New-York* (1854) IV. 749 Upon the sides of [Lake Huron]..live several Nations, vizt. the Christinos, the Ochipoy [etc.]. **1783** in *Mass. Hist. Soc. Coll.* (1809) X. 123 Chactaws 600... Upichweys 3000. **1824** W. H. KEATING *Narr. Expedition St. Peter's River* II. 151 The term Chippewa, which is generally applied to this nation, is derived from that of O'chepe'wag, which..signifies plaited shoes, from the fashion among those Indians of puckering their moccasins. **1835** C. F. HOFFMAN *Winter in West* II. 15 The Chippewa, or Ojibboai..is generally considered the *court language* of our North-western tribes. **1853** DICKENS *Noble Savage* in *Househ. Words* 11 June 337/1 Mr. Catlin..with his Ojibbeway Indians. **1855** LONGFELLOW *Hiawatha* I. 13 From the great lakes of the Northland, From the land of the Ojibways. **1872** W. F. BUTLER *Great Lone Land* viii. 110 Little ones..jabbered the smallest amount of English or French, and a great deal of Ojibbeway, or Cree, or Assineboine. **1903** CHESTERTON *R. Browning* i. 7 If his great-aunt had been a Red Indian, should we not have said that only in the Ojibways and the Blackfeet do we find the Browning fantasticality combined with the Browning stoicism? **1916** [see *MONTAGNAIS *sb.* and *a.*]. **1921** E. SAPIR *Language* 53 In many, as in Italian or Swedish or Ojibwa, long consonants are recognized as distinct from short ones. **1937** R. H. LOWIE *Hist. Ethnol. Theory* ix. 133 Foremost among his earlier students was the part-Fox William Jones, who transcribed a superb series of Fox and Ojibwa texts. **1968** *Globe & Mail* (Toronto) 5 Feb. 6/3 A. E. Bigwin, an Ojibway who is a Toronto school principal, states [etc.]. **1972** W. B. LOCKWOOD *Panorama Indo-Europ. Lang.* vii. 117 The biggest languages in this [*sc.* the Algonquian] family are Chippewa (USA) or Ojibwa (Canada) with 35,000 speakers, [etc.]. **1974** *Sat. Rev. World* (U.S.) 2 Nov. 23/2 Armed Ojibwa militants had occupied a 14-acre park..in the resort town of Kenora, Ontario.

‖ **ojime** (ǭu·dʒime). [Jap., f. *o* string + *shime* fastening, fastener.] A bead or bead-like object, often very elaborate, used in Japan as a sliding fastening device on the strings of a bag or pouch, or of an inro.

1889 M. B. HUISH *Japan & its Art* xii. 167 Japanese Art metal-work..consists of the following branches:-.. 4. Articles for personal use, notably pipes.., beads (*ojime*), [etc.]. **1902** F. BRINKLEY *Oriental Series: Japan* VII. v. 173 There is reason to think that the *ōjime* was the first highly ornate appendage of both the *inro* and the *kinchaku.* **1960** *Times* 2 Jan. 9/4 The inro consisted of interlocking compartments that..were opened and closed by means of sliding beads termed ojimes. **1972** *Times* 15 June 21/2 Each [inro] was complete with a coral ojime and ivory netsuke.

O.K. (ǒukēi·), *a.*, *sb.*, and *v. colloq.* (orig. *U.S.*). Also **OK, o.k., ok.** [App. f. the initial letters of *oll* (or *orl*) *korrect*, jocular alteration or colloq. pronunc. of 'all correct': see A. W. Read in *Amer. Speech* XXXVIII (1963), XXXIX (1964), etc.

From the detailed evidence provided by A. W. Read it seems clear that *O.K.* first appeared as a jocular alteration of the initial letters of *all correct* (i.e. orl korrect) in 1839, and that in 1840 it was used as an election slogan for 'Old Kinderhook' (see sense A b). Thence by stages it made its way into general use. Other suggestions, e.g. that *O.K.* represents the Choctaw *oke* 'it is', or French *au quai*, or that it derives from a word in the West African language Wolof via slaves in the southern States of America, all lack any form of acceptable documentation.]

A. *adj.* **a.** Chiefly in predicative use or as *int.*: all correct, all right; satisfactory, good; well, in good health; also in phr. *O.K. by* (someone): acceptable to (that person); freq. used as an exclamation expressing agreement: 'yes', 'certainly', 'all right'; also appended to a statement or declaration as a strong form of challenge or appeal in which affirmation or agreement is expected. Also as *adv.*

1839 C. G. GREENE in *Boston Morning Post* 23 Mar. 2/2 He..would have the 'contribution box', et ceteras, *o.k.*—all correct—and cause the corks to fly, like *sparks*, upward. **1839** *Salem Gaz.* 12 Apr. 2/3 The house was O.K. at the last concert, and did credit to the musical taste of the young ladies and gents. **1839** *Evening Tattler* (N.Y.) 2 Sept. 2/2 These 'wise men from the East'..are right..to play at bowls with us as long as we are willing to set ourselves up, like skittles, to be knocked down for their amusement and emolument. O K! all correct! **1839** *Boston Even. Transcript* 11 Oct. 2/3 Our Bank Directors have not thought it worth their while to call a meeting, even for consultation, on the subject. It is O.K. (*all correct*) in this quarter. **1839** *Philadelphia Gaz.* 12 Nov. 2/1 Yes—that's good—O.K.—I.S.B.D. [*sc.* it shall be done]. **1840** *Morning Herald* (N.Y.) 30 Mar. 2/1 A few years ago, some person accused Amos Kendall to General Jackson of being no better than he should be. 'Let me examine the papers,' said the old hero... The General did so and found every thing right. 'Tie up them papers,' said the General... 'Mark on them, "O.K.",' continued the General. O.K. was marked upon them. 'By the eternal', said the good old General.., 'Amos is *Ole Kurrek* (all correct) and no mistake.' *Ibid.* 21 Apr. 2/4 The Brigadier ..reviewed his Brigade..and pronounced every thing O.K. **1840** *Boston* (Mass.) *Daily Times* 15 Dec. 2/3 What is't that ails the people, Joe? They're in a kurious way, For every where I chance to go, There's nothing but O.K. **1847**, etc. [see O 5 d]. **1853** F. TOWNSEND *Fun & Earnest* 14 To the earnest inquiries of another, he simply respondeth, O.K. **1864** *Boy's Own Mag.* Nov. 450/1 No thought of taking the trouble to find out whether the order was O.K., or 'orl korrect', as Sir William Curtis phrased it. **1865** W. H. RUSSELL *Atlantic Telegraph* 61 The communication with shore continued to improve, and was, in the language of telegraphers, O.K. **1866** *N. & Q.* 18 Aug. 128/2 The following telegram has been received from Mr. R. A. Glass..'O.K.', (all correct). **1874** E. S. WARD *Trotty's Wedding Tour* xiii. 133 We had an O.K. time till we went to bed. **1886** *Lantern* (New Orleans) 29 Sept. 3/2 Favetto umpired the game all O.K. **1894** C. H. DONOVAN *With Wilson in Matabeleland* xi. 253 As our American friends would say, we were still 'O.K.' **1918** [see WET *a.* 4 b]. **1922** D. H. LAWRENCE *England, my England* 101 At first Joe thought the job O.K. **1922** J. REITH *Diary* 14 Dec. (1975) ii. 128 He said..that if things went OK I should get a rise soon. **1932** H. NICOLSON *Public Faces* i. 8 'O.K.,' he had said, 'I'll remind old Peabottle.'.. The expression 'O.K.' was not one which should be used in the Foreign Office, and least of all by an Assistant Private Secretary. **1937** D. L. SAYERS *Busman's Honeymoon* viii. 148 'I say, Mr. Superintendent, are you going to want me any more? I've got to get back to Town.' 'That's O.K. We've got your address.' **1939** *Times* 24 Oct. 4/5 'O.K.' is an abbreviation of the expression 'Orl korrec'—all correct. It is English, I think Cockney—not an Americanism. I was born in the sixties and remember it when I was a boy. **1940** 'N. BLAKE' *Malice in Wonderland* I. ii. 20 Anything that was efficiently organised was O.K. by Paul Perry. **1941** *Coast to Coast 1941* 224 He'd have reckoned it was O.K. to have gone or to have done what I did. **1957** J. MONTGOMERY *Twenties* xviii. 262 By mid-1929, when sound films had spread across Britain, there was hardly a town or village without some child who was saying 'O.K.' when previously he would have said 'Yes'. **1968** *Encounter* Sept. 22/1 Direct transliterations from Yiddish or 'Yinglish' versions thereof... O.K. by me. **1973** *Railway World* Apr. 172/2 It seems OK now to refer to that bit of the Mae Khlaung as the 'River Kwai'. **1973** [see the verb, below]. **1976** *Publishers Weekly* 12 Jan. 52/2 The older dog asks if Pepper will allow him to go along for awhile and Pepper says ok. **1976** *Punch* 11 Feb. (recto front cover), Harold rules—OK? **1976** *Spectator* 15 May 3/1 George Davis was released by the Home Secretary, to the delight of headline writers, and the groans of others. The *Spectator* is bored by that line OK? **1976** *Sunday Times* 16 May 42 When George Davis stepped out of Parkhurst prison last week few headline writers could resist the temptation. *George Davis is free OK?* (the Sun), *George Davis is free—but is it OK?* (the Guardian). **1976** *Observer* 13 June 1/5 He added belligerently: 'I don't want to answer no more questions, OK? No disrespect to the court.' **1976** *Sunday Express* 4 July 6/3 He kept going on and on: '..there are certain standards to be maintained in first-class compartments.'.. And when he left the train..he gave..a look which said: 'First Class Rules—O.K.?' **1977** *Times* 26 Apr. 8/4 The popular graffiti—*Rules-OK*, which originated amongst the Glasgow razor gangs of the thirties. **1977** *Zigzag* June 31/1 We could have had a great album, rather than an OK album.

b. Used as a slogan by the Democrats in the American election campaign of 1840, influenced by the initials of *Old Kinderhook*, a nickname for Martin Van Buren (1782–1862), the Democratic candidate for the presidency, who was born at Kinderhook in New York

State. *O.K. Club*, a Democratic club of New York City in 1840. *Obs.* exc. *Hist.*

1840 *Democratic Republ. New Era* 23 Mar. 3/2 (Advt.), The Democratic O.K. Club are hereby ordered to meet at the House of Jacob Colvin. **1840** *Newark Daily Advertiser* 28 Mar. 2/4 The *war cry* of the locofocos was O.K., the two letters paraded at the head of an inflammatory article in the New Era of the morning. 'Down with the whigs, boys, O.K.' was the shout of these poor, deluded men. **1840** *National Intelligencer* (Washington) 7 Apr. 1/2 Already the Locofocos have got out their banners and procession, and 'the Butt-enders' and 'Point-enders' are marching at night through our streets, led by the so-called 'O.K.' club, which is just now a cant phrase in Tammany. **1840** *Democratic Republ. New Era* 27 May 2/6 We acknowledge the receipt of a very pretty gold Pin,..having upon it the (to the 'Whigs') very frightful letters O.K., significant of the birth-place of Martin Van Buren, old Kinderhook, as also the rallying word of the Democracy of the late election, 'all correct'... Those who wear them should bear in mind that it will require their most strenuous exertions..to make all things O.K. **1948** PARTRIDGE *World of Words* (ed. 3) 175 O.K. was in 1840 the watchword of the O.K. Club, that Democratic Club of New York City which took its name from *Old Kinderhook*, nickname of Martin van Buren (1782–1862), born at Kinderhook in New York State and in 1836–40 the President of the United States.

c. Socially or culturally acceptable; correct; fashionable, modish; having or showing prestige, high-class.

1869 *Henry De Marson's New Singer's Jrnl.* xxxv. 246 The Stilton, sir, the cheese, the O.K. thing to do, On Sunday afternoon, is to toddle in the Zoo. **1899** R. WHITEING *No. 5 John St.* xxiii. 233 She objected to the parting of the ass's mane as 'too O.K. for a moke'. **1950** S. POTTER *Some Notes Lifemanship* i. 30 The word 'diathesis'..is now on the O.K. list for conversationmen. *Ibid.* v. 78 Just as there are O.K.-words in conversationship, so there are O.K.-*people to mention* in Newsstatesmanship. **1957** *Observer* 22 Sept. 5/4 She left her campaign to save the theatre in the elegant hands of the Piccadilly and St. James's Association Ltd.—a very O.K. organisation of local shopkeepers and business, who like to keep the district nice. **1958** *Spectator* 19 Sept. 360/3 Mr. Macmillan ended his letter by saying we must treat this crisis 'calmly and constructively'. Both these are very OK words just now. **1960** *New Left Rev.* May–June 55/1 To give up his clerk's post in favour of a much better paid (but socially less OK) job in a factory. **1963** *Listener* 17 Jan. 140/3 In an eminently 'Third Programme' talk..he drew a comparison between this opera and his recent *King Priam* which was bedevilled by O.K. names and words. **1973** *Times Lit. Suppl.* 8 June 650/5 Handy quotations from such OK literary luminaries as Macaulay, Nietzsche, Strindberg, [etc.]

B. *sb.* **a.** A member of the O.K. Club (see A. b, above). *Obs.*

1840 *Morning Herald* (N.Y.) 30 Mar. 2/1 The O.K.'s are now the most original and learned locofoco club of the day. *Ibid.* 4 Apr. 2/1 All the clubs of Buttenders, O.K.'s, N.C.'s, [etc.]. **1840** *Boston Even. Transcript* 15 Apr. 2/1 The tail of the Democratic party, the roarers, buttenders, ringtails, O.K.'s (flat burglary this latter title) and indomitables.

b. The letters 'O.K.', esp. as written on a document or the like, to express approval of its contents; an endorsement, approval, or authorization.

1841 'Dow, Jr.' *Short Patent Sermons* 106 Fortitude.. infuses new life into his soul, while Hope adds an O.K. to his condition. **1896** *Congress. Rec.* 5 Mar. 2507/1 The deputy marshall..would send word to the prosecuting attorney asking for an 'O.K.' **1901** MERWIN & WEBSTER *Calumet 'K'* xiv. 273 A formal permit..signed by Porter himself, and bearing the O.K. of the general manager. **1910** S. E. WHITE in *Sunset* Sept. 311/1 The high official added his OK to the others. **1925** H. CRANE *Let.* 21 Oct. (1965) 218 My questionnaire..had won an OK sign in the upper right corner. **1930** *Liberty* 11 Oct. 30/3 Rube copped a sneak on the joint to find out if it was ready. In twenty minutes he gives us the O.K. **1956** *Rev. Eng. Stud.* VII. 440 It is Pound who is to give the O.K. to the gods (not to God). **1961** L. MUMFORD *City in Hist.* xvii. 535 The fifth vice-president whose name or O.K. sets the final seal of responsibility upon an action.

C. *v. trans.* To endorse by marking with the letters 'O.K.'; to approve, agree to, sanction, pass.

1888 *Missouri Republican* 25 Jan. 10/4 The expression, 'Please O.K. and hurry return of my account,' is grammatically correct. The noun account is governed by the preposition of, and is also the object of the active transitive verb O.K. **1891** *Congress. Rec.* 13 Feb. 2635/2 If those who were to go into the clerical service of the Government were to be 'O.K.'d' by any one except the Civil Service Commission. **1898** H. E. HAMBLEN *Gen. Manager's Story* 82 He hunted the hook over until he found the 227 's report signed, Grinnell, O.K'd., and signed by the man who had done the work. **1921** R. S. WOODWORTH *Psychol.* xix. 505 Not that Freud would OK our account of dreams up to this point. Far from it. **1923** GALSWORTHY *Captures* 192 He finished pencilling, O.K.'d the sheets,..and went back to his room. **1932** E. WILSON *Devil take Hindmost* xxi. 224 The company submits plans to us and we O.K. them... We've O.K.'d Boulder City. **1942** E. PAUL *Narrow St.* xxvii. 238 Of course, he [*sc.* Petain] had not counted on having the decrees he signed dictated by a German Führer, or at least O.K.'d when their hearts beat exactly as one. **1973** P. DICKINSON *Gift* v. 76 'OK, OK,' said Mr Venn soothingly... But you know quite well head office wouldn't OK it... I'm not going to risk it.' 'OK,' said Mr Palozzi. **1976** *Columbus* (Montana) *News* 27 May 3/4 Smith's report..was not officially OKed by the War Department for release until July 9.

oka, var. OCA in Dict. and Suppl.

okapi (okā·pi). [Native name.] A rare ungulate mammal, *Okapia johnstoni*, of the family Giraffidæ, about the size of a horse and reddish-brown in colour, with horizontal white stripes on the legs; native to forested regions of the Congo, where it was discovered in 1900 by Sir Harry Johnston (1858–1927), the English explorer.

1900 H. JOHNSTON in *Proc. Zool. Soc.* 775, I found the Bambuba natives dwelling alongside the dwarfs called it 'Okapi'. **1901** *Chambers's Jrnl.* July 493/1 The native name for this strange beast, which is quite inoffensive, is the *okapi*. **1930** *Punch* 24 Sept. 337/2 A photographer has succeeded in getting a 'close-up' of the shy okapi. **1958** *Listener* 23 Jan. 154/1 The Pygmies are excellent trappers and they are paid to catch various kinds of beasts including the rare okapi, the short-necked forest giraffe, which are sold to zoos. **1960** M. SPARK *Ballad of Peckham Rye* iii. 35 'You look to me like an Okapi,' he said. 'A what?' 'An Okapi is a rare beast from the Congo. It looks a little like a deer, but it tries to be a giraffe.' **1974** MOCHI & CARTER *Hoofed Mammals of World* i. 7 The only living relative of the giraffe is the okapi, a forest animal living in the great rain forest of the Congo.

okay (ōukēi·), *a.*, *sb.*, and *v. colloq.* (orig. *U.S.*). Also **okeh, okey.** [Repr. pronunc. of *O.K. *a.*, *sb.*, and *v.*] **A.** *adj.*

a. = *O.K. *adj.* a. Also as *adv.*

1919 MENCKEN *Amer. Lang.* 161 Dr. Woodrow Wilson is said..to use *okeh* in endorsing government papers. **1929** J. P. McEVOY *Hollywood Girl* ix. 147 *Jimmy* (*dashing out door*): I'll kill the son of a—*Girl* (*going back to kitchenette*): Okay, big boy. **1932** *Sunday Express* 3 July 9/6, I had given my hand to the comedian and heard him say: 'Hold on, baby... Hold on. It's okay. You're going to be fine.' **1934** N. SAINSBURY *Gridiron Grit* xii. 142 Okay by me. **1936** J. B. PRIESTLEY *They walk in City* viii. 237 The short one took the letter... He nodded. 'Righty-o. Seems okay.' **1939** E. B. WILSON *My Memoir* 174 Approval was designated by 'Okeh, W.W.' on the margin of a paper. Someone asked why he [*sc.* Woodrow Wilson] did not use the 'O.K.' 'Because it is wrong,' Mr. Wilson said. He suggested that the inquirer look up 'okeh' in a dictionary. This he did, discovering that it is a Choctaw word meaning 'It is so'. **1944** 'N. SHUTE' *Pastoral* i. 7 Okay. I'll tell the boys. **1945** E. WAUGH *Brideshead Revisited* 304 'Don't let on to anyone that we've made a nonsense of the morning.' 'Okey, Ryder.' **1953** J. Y. COUSTEAU *Silent World* 91 Tailliez came up and reported, 'Everything okay. They're playing chess.' **1966** D. M. THOMAS in *Listener* 17 Feb. 247/1 Okay, my starsick beauty!.. Where would you like to go? **1972** *Publishers Weekly* 6 Mar. 31/2 He says most of that magazine's ex-staffers have done 'okay' in re-adjusting. **1974** 'E. LATHEN' *Sweet & Low* xix. 185 He got through a third degree okay.

b. = *O.K. *adj.* c.

1958 *Observer* 7 Sept. 13/4 Being in fusion is the really okay thing now. **1966** *New Statesman* 11 Mar. 348/1 The writer's ideas are rooted deep in the soil of experience and have not been processed into pet ideas and okay-words before they have ripened. **1970** G. GREER *Female Eunuch* 159 His secretary had..moved out of Haight Ashbury when it ceased to be okay to live there. **1974** *Listener* 16 May 642/1 The current psychiatric okay-word is the cautious and benign 'disturbed'. **1976** *New Society* 1 Jan. 5/1 In spite of the levelling effect of package holidays, skiing is still an okay sport. A survey..showed that British skiers were more likely to be upper middle class ABS living in the prosperous southern counties.

B. *sb.* = *O.K. *sb.* b.

1925 ADE *Let.* 28 Mar. (1973) 104 If, while he was putting his okeh on this material, he privately disapproved of it and was sending word back east that the material was not what you wanted, of course he was putting me in a tough position. **1925** *Dollar Mag.* Dec. 207 To find new and more vivid forms of expression..in the hope that they will, in time, receive the okeh of the reading public. **1931** *North Amer. Rev.* Jan. 15/2 During the last two years Raskob has either put his okay on every major move that Jouett Shouse has made, or else suggested it himself in the first place. **1973** *Freedomways* XIII. 18 Nothing goes down without his okay. **1974** *Columbia* (S. Carolina) *Record* 25 Apr. 6-D/1 In the more than 14 years since the dam was first proposed, the estimated $75 million cost has more than doubled. Whether it will get an *okay* on environmental grounds has not been determined.

C. *v. trans.* = *O.K. *v.*

1930 *Amer. Speech* VI. 119 Parachute company stock sale okehed. **1938** *Times* 18 Jan. 13/4 The proposal to call this haunt of pleasure the 'Non-stop Journal Kino' was taken to the Supreme Court before being—as the delighted proprietor probably put it—okayed. **1945** H. I. PHILLIPS *Private Purkey's Private Peace* vii. 40 When they okayed me at that abduction center 'for the duration' I thought it meant just for the duration of the war. **1947** *People* 22 June 5/3 Micky and ex-light-weight champion Dave Crowley did the same fight 25 times before the final take was okayed. **1958** S. ELLIN *Eighth Circle* (1959) I. i. 18 Every place where you can okay it, you put down O.K. and your initials. **1968** *Listener* 5 Dec. 771/1 Okayed by Western governments, the Prague festival enjoyed a substantial dollar bonus in the form of the Illinois State University Jazz Band. **1974** *Times* 22 Feb. 19/4 Scripts Limited comes in after the screenwriter has been commissioned by a film company, has written his first draft and had it okayed.

Okazaki (ōukāzā·ki). *Biology.* The name of Reiji *Okazaki* (1930–75), Japanese molecular biologist, used *attrib.* to designate fragments formed during the replication of chromosomal DNA, first described by Okazaki et al. in 1968 (*Proc. Nat. Acad. Sci.* LIX. 598).

1969 *Proc. Nat. Acad. Sci.* LXIV. 1065 Some of the Okazaki fragments are present in a single-stranded state in cell lysates prepared under nondenaturing conditions. **1971** *Jrnl. Molecular Biol.* LVII. 351 The assembly of small fragments of newly synthesized DNA—the so-called Okazaki fragments..—to form a larger structure. **1975** *Nature* 4 Sept. 76/3 The synthesis of new DNA strands during the process of DNA duplication seems to occur in rather short sections (now known to everyone as 'Okazaki pieces').

oke (ōuk), *a. colloq.* (orig. *U.S.*). [Abbrev. of pronunc. of *O.K. *a.*, *sb.*, and *v.*] = *O.K. *adj.* a.

1929 D. HAMMETT *Dain Curse* (1930) v. 45 Try not breathing so hard. Everything will probably be oke. **1932** A. WOOLLCOTT *Let.* 31 Dec. (1946) 95 Dear Lady Cavendish..gets along famously with her mother-in-law, the Duchess of Devonshire. Has the Duchess saying 'Oke' already. **1933** DYLAN THOMAS *Let.* Oct. (1966) 38 Laleham arrangement, though in the air, is oke by me, and if there is any one expression worse than 'sez you' this is it. **1935** *Spectator* 15 Feb. 257/1 A child replied 'oke', to something I said. **1944** L. A. G. STRONG *Director* 93 'How was it, Votty?' 'Oke.' **1951** GREEN & LAURIE *Show Biz* 570/1 *Oke*, OK. **1960** S. H. COURTIER *Gently dust Corpse* xiv. 196 He's oke now. Get some brandy.

okeh, okey, varr. *OKAY *a.*, *sb.*, and *v.*

okey-doke (ōu:kidōu·k), *a. colloq.* (orig. *U.S.*). Also **oakie-doke, okay-doke, okee-doke, okey-dokey, okie-dokie, okle-dokle.** [Redupl. *O.K. *a.*] = *O.K. *adj.* a.

1932 *Amer. Speech* VII. 334 *Okey-dokey*, O.K. **1934** M. H. WESEEN *Dict. Amer. Slang* xiii. 190 *Okey dokey*, O.K. *Ibid.* xxi. 373 *Okay doke*, satisfactory; agreeable; all right. **1935** *Evening Sun* (Baltimore) 7 Feb. 7/1 An attorney asked Carl Bush, witness, to answer a 'yes or no' question. 'Oakie-Doke,' replied Bush. **1936** M. HARRISON *All Trees were Green* 305 Captain Sarsfield said: 'Everything okey-doke up at the mansion?' **1936** D. POWELL *Turn, Magic Wheel* I. 36 He saw that tiresome red-faced fellow.., the man who knew everybody and said 'okie-dokie' to everything. **1944** M. LASKI *Love on Supertax* iv. 53 Things are okey-doke for a lot of people now. **1947** B. SCHULBERG *Harder they Fall* vii. 121 'Hey, Killer, tell Jack to pick me up in front of the door right away.' 'Okle-dokle,' the Killer said. 'Where we goin'?' **1957** C. MACINNES *City of Spades* II. iii. 95 One Guinness stout, right, I thank you, okey-doke, here it is. **1968** C. BROWN in A. Dundes *Mother Wit* (1973) 236/1 There are certain classic soul terms... Among the classical expressions are: 'solid', 'cool',..'okee doke', [etc.]. **1977** J. FLEMING *Every Inch a Lady* I. i. 7 Light out, silence, everything okey dokey, she goes off to bed. **1977** *New Yorker* 16 May 33/1 Now, if for any reason you lose your paper clips, you're in big trouble. Okeydoke.

Okhrana (ǫχrā·nā). Also **Ochrana.** [a. Russ. *okhrána*, lit. 'guarding, protection'.] An organization of political police set up in 1881 in tsarist Russia after the assassination of Alexander II to maintain the security of the state and suppress revolutionary activities, and disbanded in 1917. Cf. *CHEKA.

1899 P. KROPOTKIN *Mem. of Revolutionist* II. vi. 246 A secret league for the protection of the Tsar [Alexander III] was started... This league still exists in a more official shape, under the name of Okhrána (Protection). **1906** *Cosmopolitan* Dec. 237/2 The exact number, local distribution, and cost of the 'okhrana'..are known to no single official. **1920** *Contemp. Rev.* June 861 The Soviet authorities were confronted with the task..of abrogating individual laws permeated by the spirit of the Tsarist Okhrana. **1928** *Illustr. Hist. Russ. Rev.* I. 65 The confidential reports of the police and the 'Okhrana' furnish convincing evidence of the political nature of the unrest in the capital. **1930** A. T. VASSILYEV (*title*) The Ochrana: the Russian secret police. **1949** I. DEUTSCHER *Stalin* ii. 36 *Okhrana*, or the Third Department, was the political police set up in 1881, after the assassination of Alexander II. **1974** T. P. WHITNEY tr. *Solzhenitsyn's Gulag Archipel.* I. I. ii. 67 Section 13, presumably long since out of date, had to do with service in the Tsarist secret police—the Okhrana.

Okie (ōu·ki). *colloq.* [f. *Ok*lahoma, one of the United States + -IE (see -Y[6]).] A migrant agricultural worker, *spec.* one from Oklahoma forced to leave his farm during the depression of the 1930s. Also, a native or inhabitant of Oklahoma. Also *attrib.* Cf. *OKLAHOMAN.

1938 *Forum & Century* Jan. 12 About a fifth of [the migratory workers in California] are Okies. **1939** J. STEINBECK *Grapes of Wrath* xviii. 280 Okie use' ta mean you was from Oklahoma. Now it means you're a dirty son-of-a-bitch. **1941** S. LONGSTREET *Last Man around World* 356 The hillbilly, the Okie..and people who once shook hands with Warren G. Harding..fill the land. **1948** *Daily Ardmoreite* (Ardmore, Okla.) 11 July 21/5 Sooners have less reason to be offended at being called 'Okies' than residents of other states have for their nicknames. **1957** J. KEROUAC *On Road* (1958) 167 This was an Okie from Bakersfield, California. **1964** *Amer. Folk Music Occasional* I. 87 The songs of the 'Okies', those modern Forty-niners from the depleted farm lands of the Southwest. **1964** E. A. NIDA *Toward Sci. Transl.* viii. 180 Procházka ..describes the problem of reproducing in Czech the Okie speech used by some of Steinbeck's characters. **1970** J. HANSEN *Fadeout* (1972) viii. 67 I'm a dirty, ignorant Okie to him. **1975** *New Society* 19 June 705/1 Oklahoma got most attention, but migrants drifted from other places across the Great Plains and rural south... As time passed, nearly all migrants came to be called Okies once they had reached California. **1978** *Chicago* June 40/2 Glenn Allen

Smith's new play about the zany misadventures of an Okie hero-type is not quite zany enough to carry its weight.

|| **okimono** (ōukimōu·no). [Jap., = 'put thing', f. *oku* to put + *mono* thing.] A standing ornament or figure, esp. one put in a guest room of a house.

1886 W. ANDERSON *Pict. Arts Japan* III. xi. 112 The ornament pure and simple, the *Okimono* of the Japanese, was..made by artists in metal from a very early period... The first of the modern *Okimono* school appeared to have been a woman named Kamé or Kamé-jo. **1890** *Artistic Japan* V. 348 It is important to distinguish between netsukés, articles made for a special purpose..and okimonos ..ornaments never intended either for use or wear. **1911** J. F. BLACKER *ABC of Jap. Art* vi. 116 Elephant's tusks.. were used chiefly for *okimonos*—alcove ornaments. **1916** JOLY & TOMITA *Jap. Art & Handicraft* 198 (*caption*) 22 *Okimono*, figure of Fukurokujiu with staff and *tama*. **1961** *Times* 7 Nov. 24/5 (Advt.), A collection of Japanese colour prints, netsuke, and works of art..including netsuke carved in wood and ivory, okimono and ivory carvings. **1962** F. A. TURK *Jap. Objets d'Art* II. 81 From the late figure-group Netsuke,..arose the *okimono* (i.e. a carving to stand in an alcove). **1975** *Times* 8 May 16/3 A mid-nineteenth century wood figure of a demon..is an okimono rather than a true netsuke, too elaborate and delicate to use as a button.

Okinawan (ōukinā·wăn, ǫk-), *sb.* and *a.* [f. the place-name *Okinawa*, f. Jap. *okinawa*, lit. 'rope on the sea': see -AN.] **A.** *sb.* A native or inhabitant of the Okinawa Islands, esp. of Okinawa, the largest of the Ryukyu (Nansei) group south-west of Japan; also, the dialect of Japanese spoken there. **B.** *adj.* Of or pertaining to Okinawa or the Okinawa Islands, to its people or its language.

1944 *Civil Affairs Handbk.: Ryukyu Islands* (U.S. Navy Dept.) xiv. 44 These phonetic differences impart a characteristic accent to Japanese as spoken by Okinawans. **1945** *N.Y. Times* 3 Apr. 3/1 Hundreds of kimono-clad Okinawans who fled to the hills with the first shells of the American pre-invasion bombardment are now streaming into our lines. **1945** *Ibid.* 5 Apr. 3/1 Dozens of enterprising GI's..saddled small, shaggy-maned Okinawan ponies with their gear. **1947** *Sci. Monthly* Mar. 235/2 Since the dawn of recorded history the Okinawans, although nominally independent, were influenced by both China and Japan and at times paid allegiance and tribute to both. At one time Okinawan sailing vessels carried on widespread commerce with the Asiatic mainland and the islands of the Western and Southwestern Pacific. **1955** C. J. GLACKEN *Great Loochoo* 3 The most significant characteristic of Okinawan culture is the family system. *Ibid.* viii. 166 This fish is caught with the aid of a home-made triangular wire device (*yamaguchi* in Okinawan). **1960** B. LEACH *Potter in Japan* iii. 72 About seventy relatives, Okinawans and members of the Japanese Craft Society assembled. *Ibid.* 73 Two Okinawan scholars spoke next. **1964** *Listener* 24 Sept. 473/1 Brando..has appeared in comedy before—as the Okinawan Sakini in *The Teahouse of the August Moon.* **1966** P. S. BUCK *People of Japan* (1968) xiv. 176 Okinawans wish once again to become part of Japan. **1973** C. L. HOGG *Okinawa* 13 Take the very name of the island... Okinawans have always called it Uchina, but no one else has ever paid the slightest attention to what Okinawans call their island... Okinawa, the name bestowed on Uchina by the Japanese, may be translated 'rope in the offing'. **1973** *Guardian* 24 May 4/4 More than half of Okinawans dislike Americans, because of their offensive behaviour. *Ibid.* 4/6 Two Okinawan women waiting at a bus stop were killed by a drunken American driver.

Oklahoma (ōuklahōu·mă). The name of a State in the south-west of the United States (see next), used *attrib.* and *absol.* to designate a kind of rummy orig. played in Oklahoma.

1945 A. A. OSTROW *Compl. Card Player* 578 *Oklahoma Rummy...* The cards rank in sequence as in standard rummy, but ace is high only and never low. Deuces are wild. **1948** [see *CANASTA]. **1949** J. SCARNE *On Cards* (1955) ix. 63 *Oklahoma Gin.* In this variation the twenty-first card..determines the maximum number of points in unmatched cards with which a player may knock. *Ibid.* 64 Oklahoma usually incorporates the Spades Double feature. *Ibid.* xiii. 163 *Oklahoma Rummy.* A variation of Fortune Rummy. Played for years throughout the Middle West. **1973** G. F. HERVEY *Hamlyn Illustr. Bk. Card Games* 110 Oklahoma may be played by any number of players from two to five, but is generally considered best when played by three.

Oklahoman (ōuklahōu·măn). [f. *Oklahoma*, one of the United States, f. Choctaw *okla* nation, people + *homma* red: see -AN.] A native or inhabitant of the State of Oklahoma.

In quot. 1894 as the name of a newspaper.

1894 (*title*) Evening Oklahoman (Oklahoma City, Okla.). **1901** *Outlook* (N.Y.) 2 Feb. 280/1 Many of the old Oklahomans who are selling out expect to secure new homes at the opening. **1934** L. GANNETT *Sweet Land* iv. 40 The Texans held that 'Pretty Boy' was no Oklahoman at all. Some held that he was a genuine West Texan. **1948** *Durant* (Okla.) *Daily Democrat* 4 July 2/5 Every Oklahoman appreciates an agency which seeks to protect our lives and property. **1959** C. OGBURN *Marauders* (1960) ii. 53 John P. McElmurray, a very tall, very spare, taciturn, profane Oklahoman. **1973** *Black Panther* 1 Sept. 16/1 'Those animals,' declared Mrs. Johnson, a typical racist Oklahoman.

O.K.-ness (ōukē̆i·nės). [f. *O.K. *a.*, *sb.*, and *v.* + -NESS.] The fact or quality of being O.K.; acceptability.

1935 E. GILL *Let.* 31 Jan. (1947) 321, I rejoice..to have your assurance as to orthodoxy, decency & general o.k.ness of the..'article'. **1950** S. POTTER *Some Notes Lifemanship* 76 The absolute O.K.-ness of French literature..cannot be too much emphasised. **1962** M. DRABBLE *Summer Bird-Cage* iv. 55, I carried an aura of vicarious theatrical OK-ness. **1969** *Punch* 19 Feb. 256/2 The rest of us..should be able to talk quite fluently about the varying OK-ness of split, one-piece, or cracked-edge construction.

okoume (okū·me). Also **okoumé.** [Native name.] = *GABOON, GABOON.

1922 C. T. CAMPION tr. *Schweitzer's On Edge of Primeval Forest* vi. 108 The chief sorts [of wood] dealt in are mahogany,..and okoume (*Aucoumea klaineana*), the so-called false mahogany. **1933** —— tr. *Schweitzer's My Life & Thought* xiii. 163 The trade in okoume wood..was just beginning to flourish in the Ogowe district. **1947** J. C. RICH *Materials & Methods Sculpture* x. 293 *Okoume* is another name for Gaboon Mahogany. The wood is soft and light-weight and is a light reddish-brown color. **1956** *Handbk. Hardwoods* (Forest Prod. Res. Lab.) 97 Gaboon is known as okoumé in France. The tree grows mainly in French Equatorial Africa.

okra, now the usual spelling of OKRO. (Further examples.)

1878 N. A. DONNELLEY *Lakeside Cook Bk.* 4/2 (*recipe*) Okra Gumbo. **1923** H. C. THOMPSON *Vegetable Crops* xxvii. 454 Okra is a tender plant and grows best in hot weather. **1949** *Caribbean Q.* I. I. 33 The little yellow cups of witchery known as Okra flowers. **1963** J. KIRKUP *Tropic Temper* 49 The chicken curry..is particularly good, with its rich, really hot sauce containing a curious, ribbed, tasteless vegetable called okras. **1964** E. HUXLEY *Back Street New Worlds* xiv. 141 The Shepherd's Bush market has a shop devoted wholly to West African foods ..like gbure and okra, tete and apan. **1967** *Guardian* 8 Dec. 6/4 Fresh bhindi (which some people know as ladies' fingers, others as okra). **1972** Y. LOVELOCK *Vegetable Bk.* 147 Perhaps the best known member [of the hibiscus family] is okra.., of African origin and said to have been cultivated in ancient Egypt. It is now grown widely in Africa, the Mediterranean region and the Americas. **1973** *News & Courier* (Charleston, S. Carolina) 4 Nov. 3-E/1 A lunch of sandwiches and okra soup will be served from noon to 1 p.m.

|| **okrug** (ǫ·krug). [a. Russ. and Bulg. *ókrug.*] In Russia and Bulgaria, a territorial division for administrative and other purposes. Also *attrib.* Cf. *OBLAST.

1886 *Encycl. Brit.* XXI. 69/2 Area and population of the Russian Empire... *Okrugs*, or *otdyels* (territories) under military government. **1902** *Ibid.* XXVI. 448/2 The country [*sc.* Bulgaria] is divided into twenty-two departments (*okrŭg*, pl. *okrŭzi*), each administered by a prefect. **1935** B. W. MAXWELL *Soviet State* I. i. 30 Russia, before the Revolution, was divided for purposes of administration into seventy-eight governments (*guberniya*), twenty-one regions (*oblast*), and one circuit (*okrug*). **1958** D. J. R. SCOTT *Russ. Polit. Institutions* ii. 74 The new administrative *okrugs*..completed in 1952, were the product of a new acute phase of the persistent concern over effective supervision of districts by higher authorities... Shortly after the death of Stalin..the *okrugs* began to be abolished again, and none of them is now in existence. **1971** J. S. RESHETAR *Soviet Polity* vii. 257 The least of the ethnic autonomous administrative units is the 'national area' (*okrug*). They have been established for the numerically small peoples of the Soviet Far North and Far East who inhabit large and sparsely populated areas. **1976** *Survey* Spring 65 There are [in the USSR] 14 union republic central committees, 10 *okrug* committees..and 4,243 city and *raion* committees.

okta (ǫ·ktă). *Meteorol.* [f. OCTA- by alteration.] (See quot. 1950.)

1950 *Meteorol. Gloss.* (Meteorol. Office) (ed. 3) Amendment List No. 4. 7 *Okta*, unit, equal to area of one eighth of the sky, used in specifying cloud amount. **1957** *Weather Map* (Meteorol. Office) (ed. 4) iv. 35 From January 1, 1949, cloud amount has been observed and reported in oktas or eighths of sky covered, code figure 0 representing a clear sky, 1 representing 1 okta (eighth) of sky covered or less, but not zero, 2 representing 2 oktas (eighths), and so on..8 representing 8 oktas (eighths) (sky completely covered), and 9 representing sky obscured or cloud amount cannot be estimated. **1960** *Handbk. Aviation Meteorol.* (Meteorol. Office) xii. 178 The number of oktas of sky covered by any particular cloud layer is estimated as if no other clouds were present. **1961** C. E. WALLINGTON *Meteorol. for Glider Pilots* iii. 38 Cloud amount is usually reported in eighths of the sky covered... Sometimes the internationally convened word 'oktas' is substituted for 'eighths'. **1977** 'J. LE CARRÉ' *Hon. Schoolboy* xviii. 455 Cloud is anticipated at six to seven okta... One okta is one eighth of sky area covered.

ol (ǫl). *Chem.* [a. G. *ol* (A. Werner 1907, in *Ber. d. Deut. Chem. Ges.* XL. 2113), f. the suffix *-ol* -OL.] Used *attrib.* and in *Comb.* to designate a complex containing a hydroxyl group of which the oxygen atom is bonded to two metal atoms; also applied to the group itself.

1907 *Chem. Abstr.* I. 2537 There is no simple or normal hydroxyl group in these compounds because they will not add HX to form an aquo salt. Hence they should not be designated 'hydroxy' compounds, but may be designated 'ol' compounds, to signify that the hydroxyl group is in the complex radical. **1929** J. A. WILSON *Chem. & Leather* 29 Bjerrum succeeded in preparing an ol-compound with a nucleus containing 12 chromium atoms. **1931** *Jrnl. Physical Chem.* XXXV. 46 With the conversion of hydroxo groups to ol groups to oxo groups there results increasing resistance to the action of acids. *Ibid.* 47 The authors hazard the guess that the oxolation of ol complexes would result in a loss of the reaction with neutral salts. **1962** J. R. LEACH tr. *Grinberg's Introd. Chem. Complex Compounds* ix. 266 The acid-base equilibria can.. be complicated by the formation of polynuclear complexes with 'ol' bridges, or with 'oxo' bridges. **1974** D. NICHOLLS *Inorganic Complexes* iii. 26 This species with the hydroxo or *ol* bridges can react in the presence of added base.

ol' (ōul). Also **ol.** A representation of a *colloq.* and Black English pronunc. of OLD *a.* Cf. *OLE[2].

1894 A. MORRISON *Tales of Mean Streets* 224 'That's all right, ol' cock,' roared Bill Napper. **1901** W. N. HARBEN *Westerfelt* iv. 44 How are you, ol' hoss... Glad to see you. **1915** C. JOHNSON *Battleground Adventures* liv. 418 Holt met the ol' man comin' from the barn as hard as he could run. *Ibid.* 420, I got a little ol' box to sit on. **1938** M. K. RAWLINGS *Yearling* iv. 34 He'll rip them leaves offen the stems and cram 'em in his ugly ol' mouth like a person. **1944** C. HIMES *Black on Black* (1973) 202 Just a li'l ol' knot at the bottom. **1971** *Jamaican Weekly Gleaner* 3 Nov. 32/2 'Sure hate to be back at that same old school.' 'Same ol' tests.' **1973** S. HENDERSON *Understanding New Black Poetry* 21 Thus in the spirituals we have..Tell ol Pharaoh to let my people go. **1977** *Washington Post* 7 Dec. B1/1 Some people will be carried away by NBC's Bette Midler special, 'Ol' Red Hair is Back', at 10 o'clock tonight on Channel 4.

-ol. 3. Add: see *-OLE, which is now the usual form.

-ola, *suffix.* Chiefly *U.S.* Prob. derived from the second element of PIANOLA and now found esp. in commercial use as a suffix to form nouns, as *MOVIOLA, *PAYOLA, *VICTROLA, etc.

See *Amer. Speech* (1961) XXXVI. 104–116.

olation (ǫlē̆i·ʃən). *Chem.* and *Tanning.* [f. *OL + -ATION.

Though often attributed to Bjerrum and to Stiasny the word has not been found in their publications.]

Conversion of a complex into an ol form; linking of metal atoms by hydroxyl ligands. Used esp. with reference to chromium compounds used in tanning.

1931 *Jrnl. Physical Chem.* XXXV. 27 Bjerrum..postulated that perhaps the hydroxo groups in the complex ions were becoming more firmly bound to form larger complexes... Bjerrum called this process 'olation'. **1931** *Chem. Abstr.* XXV. 2325 The basicity of the Cr salt in a one-bath Cr liquor is greater than that of the liquor as a whole because of 'olation'; the complex ol compds. react with the free acid only very slowly. **1941** D. WOODROFFE *Fund. Leather Sci.* viii. 107 This condensation is termed 'olation' and the larger complex compound obtained is described as an olated chromium salt. **1948** *Progress in Leather Sci. 1920–45* II. xxvi. 524 Stiasny..termed this process 'olation' and postulated that hydroxy groups react immediately with acid whereas 'ol-groups' only react after deolation. **1969** T. C. THORSTENSEN *Pract. Leather Technol.* viii. 120 At higher temperatures there is greater fixation of the chrome tanning compound by the hide protein and greater olation of the chrome complexes. **1974** D. NICHOLLS *Inorganic Complexes* iii. 26 The hydroxo–aquo complexes may combine together in a process known as *olation.*

Hence (as back-formations) **ola·te** *v. intr.*, to form an ol group or compound; **ola·ted** *ppl. a.*

1931 *Jrnl. Physical Chem.* XXXV. 45 The hydroxo groups then 'olated', resulting in the formation of large aggregates, eventually reaching colloidal size. *Ibid.*, It would be expected..that the greater the degree of olation, the more sluggish would be the reaction of the complex olated ion. **1936** E. W. MERRY *Chrome Tanning Process* i. 9 Chrome alum solutions prepared hot are green and contain strongly olated chromium compounds. *Ibid.*, It is not possible to forecast what will be the actual basicity of the chrome salts..or the extent to which they will olate. **1941** [see above]. **1945** MCLAUGHLIN & THEIS *Chem. Leather Manuf.* xiv. 416 A chrome compound is said to be 'olated' when one or more of its hydroxyl groups is held between two chromium atoms.

Olbers' paradox (ǫ·lbəɪz). *Astr.* [named after H. W. M. *Olbers* (1758–1840), German astronomer, who propounded it in *Astron. Jahrb.* (1826) 110.] The paradox that if stars were distributed evenly (in sufficient numbers) throughout an infinite static universe, the sky should be as bright at night as in the daytime, owing to the fact that whilst the apparent brightness of individual stars decreases with distance the number of stars increases in the same proportion.

1952 H. BONDI *Cosmol.* iii. 23 Olbers' paradox does not arise in a static universe in which, roughly speaking, the stars did not start to radiate until some moment which can be determined..to have been between 10^8 and 10^{10} years ago. **1969** ROSSER & MCCULLOCH *Relativity & High Energy Physics* vi. 131 Olbers' paradox can be resolved by the fact that the distant stars..are going away from the earth at high speeds (the expanding universe).

old, *a.* (*adv.*, *sb.*[1]) Add: **1. a.** *old folk*(*s*) (later examples), *old one*, *old un*, an elderly person, *esp.* one's father or mother; *any old*: see *ANY *a.* and *pron.* 1 e.

1836 DICKENS *Pickw.* (1837) xx. 204 'It's the old 'un.' 'Old one,' said Mr. Pickwick. 'What old one?' 'My father, Sir,' replied Mr. Weller. **1854** C. M. YONGE *Heartsease* I. II. xiv. 341 He is the great pride of the old folks at Worthbourne. **1868** *Haileyburian* I. 4/2 The Present won the toss, and completely 'penned' the 'old 'uns'. **1915** N. L. MCCLUNG *In Times like These* xix. 130 Did you ever visit an old folks' home and notice the different spirit shown by the men and women there? **1921** G. B. SHAW *Back to Methuselah* v. 253 There! What have you to say to that, old one? **1968** M. BRAGG *Without City Wall* xxvi. 237 In the Women's Institute the streamers, well hung.. were still taut, after the Old Folks' Tea. **1976** *National Observer* (U.S.) 21 Feb. 2/4 Many more old folks would pay an additional charge for the protection in any one year than would enjoy its benefits against large doctor and hospital bills. And that's not the best way to harvest votes among the elderly.

c. *old bag* (see *BAG *sb.* 16*); *old boy*, used of an old man (see also as main entry in Suppl.); *old geezer* (see GEEZER in Dict. and Suppl.); *old girl*: see GIRL *sb.* 2 a in Dict. and Suppl.; *old pot*, one's father (chiefly *Austral.*); *old trot* (see TROT *sb.*[2]); *old trout* [perh. var. of TROT *sb.*[2] infl. by TROUT *sb.*[1] 4], *colloq.* applied to an old woman.

1893 G. B. SHAW *Widowers' Houses* II. iv. 43 He wont have any news to break, poor old boy: she's read all the letters already. **1916** C. J. DENNIS *Songs Sentimental Bloke* 124 *The old pot*, the male parent (from 'Rhyming Slang', the 'old pot and pan'—the 'old man'). **1930** G. B. SHAW *Apple Cart* I. 3 When they found him he was melancholy mad, poor old boy; and he never got over it. *a* **1938** C. J. DENNIS in *Penguin Bk. Austral. Ballads* (1964) 234 Oh, w'erefore art you Romeo, young sir? Chuck yer ole pot, an' change yer moniker! **1938** N. MARSH *Artists in Crime* ix. 128 Miss Troy thought I was good enough to come here, even if my old pot did keep a bottle store. *Ibid.* 129 'What about Mr. Pilgrim?' 'Aw, he's different... I get on with him good-oh, even if his old pot is one of these lords. Him and me's cobbers.' **1956** B. GOOLDEN *Singing & Gold* viii. 172 Drives old ladies about the town and that... Wouldn't suit me though. Don't see yours truly rushing to carry the old trouts' shopping baskets. **1958** J. CANNAN *And be a Villain* vi. 140 The old trout wasn't exactly throwing her money about, he'd say. **1964** R. BRADDON *Year Angry Rabbit* x. 90 Too high and mighty for his old trout of a mum nowadays is young Gary. **1972** N. MARSH *Tied up in Tinsel* xviii. 197 'Er old pot was killed saving the colonel's life. **1974** L. THOMAS *Tropic of Ruislip* ii. 42 You could scare the old boy and he'll spill his tea. He spills things all the time.

3. c. *any old*: see *ANY *a.* and *pron.* 1 e.

5. b. *old coon.*

1835 A. B. LONGSTREET *Georgia Scenes* 216 To be sure I will, my old coon—take it—take it, and welcome. **1862** *Punch* 1 Feb. 42/2, I guess them saucy Britishers Won't easy get to leeward Of such an all-fired smart old 'coon As William H. Seward. **1877** BARTLETT *Dict. Amer.* (ed. 4) 436 'He's an old coon,' is said of one who is very shrewd; often applied to a political manager.

7. b. *old pal*: an old friend, freq. with reference to association or collusion in business, *spec.* in phr. *old pal's act* (and variants), favour or cooperation based on prior acquaintance.

a **1966** M. ALLINGHAM *Cargo of Eagles* (1968) ii. 26 The Old Pal's Act isn't confined to you public school types above stairs now. **1972** E. GRIERSON *Confessions of Country Magistrate* i. 7 What is this mysterious process by which the man in the street is suddenly transformed into the magistrate on the bench? How, if not by the Old Pals' Act or the Signs of the Zodiac, is the miracle accomplished? **1973** *Times* 23 May 2/3 All these favours given by the Post Office on the old pals network. **1975** T. HEALD *Deadline* ii. 18 The old pals act will operate as far as the press is concerned.

d. Phr. (*as*) *old as the hills*, exceedingly old; perh. in allusion to Job xv. 7 'Art thou the first man that was born? or wast thou made before the hills?'.

1819 *Metropolis* I. iii. 58, I thought he was going to make a die of it! Why he's as old as the Hills. **1820** SCOTT *Monastery* ix. 251 If you were as good a priest as the Pope, and as old as the hills to boot, you shall not carry away Mary's book without her leave. **1821** BYRON *Let.* 1 Oct. in *Works* (1901) V. 385 The Pulci Style, which the fools in England think was invented by Whistlecraft—it is as old as the hills in Italy. **1849** DICKENS *Dav. Copp.* (1850) xv. 156 All the angles and corners, and carvings and mouldings, and quaint little panes of glass, and quainter little windows, though as old as the hills, were as pure as any snow that ever fell upon the hills. **1898** [see sense 7 a in Dict.]. **1914** 'BARTIMEUS' *Naval Occasions* ix. 66 'Sides, she's as old as the hills. **1937** A. HUXLEY *Ends & Means* iv. 25 A violent revolution cannot achieve anything except the inevitable results of violence, which are as old as the hills. **1954** B. & R. NORTH tr. *Duverger's Pol. Parties* II. i. 255 Dictatorship is as old as the hills. **1956** A. WILSON *Anglo-Saxon Att.* I. i. 14 Fifty-five must seem as old as the hills to a girl like you.

e. *the old story* (and variants), a familiar tale or excuse (usu. with a connotation of implausibility).

1700 [see STORY *sb.*[1] 6 a]. **1859** GEO. ELIOT *Adam Bede* I. iv. 75 'What! father's forgot the coffin?' 'Ay, lad, th' old tale; but I shall get it done.' **1898** J. D. BRAYSHAW *Slum Silhouettes* 28 'What brought 'em to that?' Oh, the old story—liftin' their little finger. **1919** R. FROST *Let.* 4 Jan. (1964) 80 Pelle was good reading. But none of it was any news. Not a phrase but was old story. **1938** E. AMBLER *Cause for Alarm* xi. 184 Too much or too little—empty stomachs or overfed ones—the old, old story.

8. a. *old bean*: see *BEAN *sb.* 6 e; *old boy*: see also BOY *sb.*[1] 5; *old dear*: usu. of a woman (cf. DEAR *a.*[1] and *sb.*[2] B); *old fellow* (U.S.): an overseer or 'boss'; *old fruit*: see *FRUIT *sb.* 2 e; *old girl*: see GIRL *sb.* 2 a in Dict. and Suppl.; *old hen* (see HEN *sb.* 5 a); *old horse* (cf. HORSE *sb.* 4); *old hoss*: see HORSE *sb.* 4, *HOSS 2; *old lady*: a girl or woman, esp. one's wife or mother; also *transf.* of a man whose behaviour resembles that of an old lady; *old man* (earlier example); *old son* (cf. SON *sb.* 3 b); *old sport*: see *SPORT *sb.*[1]; *old thing*: see *THING *sb.*[2]; *old top* (cf. TOP *sb.*[2]).

1880 [see DEAR *a.*[1] and *sb.*[2] B]. **1955** J. THOMAS *No Banners* ii. 23 Remember the old dear at La Souterraine who fed us on bread and ham and cheese and a bottle of wine? **1901** S. E. WHITE *Blazed Trail* xxvii. 187 He was intensely loyal to his 'Old Fellows' [= 'bosses' of lumber camps]. **1906** WODEHOUSE *Love among Chickens* v. 63 Garney, old horse, you're a marvel. You think of everything. We'll buckle to right away. **1924** —— *Ukridge* i. 12 It's a wearing life, laddie. A wearing life, old horse. **1942** *R.A.F. Jrnl.* 3 Oct. 11 'Well, old horse,' I thought, 'You're going to be disappointed.' **1960** A. CHRISTIE *Adventure of Christmas Pudding* 209 He said with a remarkable lack of medical decorum: 'That you, Poirot, old horse?' **1976** 'A. HALL' *Kobra Manifesto* ii. 24, I wish someone had told me, old horse. **1836** DICKENS *Let.* 21 Mar. (1965) I. 141 Let me have particular word how your rheumatism is, old lady. **1859** MRS. GASKELL *Lett.* (1966) 545 You must not send us any more work to do, old lady, for Caroline is slow, & there is a great deal to do. **1871** E. EGGLESTON *Hoosier Schoolmaster* (1872) xvii. 134 Here's the old lady and Shocky. **1914** CONRAD *Chance* II. i. 244 The old lady's first-rate, sir, thank you. **1932** D. L. SAYERS *Have His Carcase* xii. 152 'There, there, Mother,' muttered Henry... 'Bit of a staggerer for the old lady, this.' **1938** H. NICOLSON *Diary* 10 Nov. (1966) 378 This memorandum was not at all liked by the old ladies of the Executive. **1967** C. HIMES *Blind Man with a Pistol* (1973) 133 A man called T-bone Smith sat..looking at television with his old lady, Tang. **1976** *New Yorker* 17 May 34/2 It is a sign that you wish to share your old lady. **1870** 'MARK TWAIN' *Let.* 22 Mar. (1917) I. 172, I can make the money without lecturing. Therefore, old man, count me out. **1916** 'TAFFRAIL' *Pincher Martin* viii. 142 'Ow are we, ole son? Feelin' a bit squeamish?' **1951** S. SPENDER *World within World* ii. 66 Do you know, old son, this is the first time you've ever talked with me that I haven't been completely bored? **1974** L. DEIGHTON *Spy Story* xx. 218 You're doing well, old son. **1974** N. FREELING *Dressing of Diamond* 41 Right then, old son. **1912** *Collier's* 28 Sept. 19/1 'Tough luck, old top,' he muttered. **1915** WODEHOUSE *Something Fresh* ii. 24, I say, Dickie, old top, I want to see you about something devilish important. **1932** A. J. WORRALL *Eng. Idioms* 56, I say, old top! Do you like these?

c. In trivial use with connotations of familiarity and in jocular and mildly disparaging senses of persons and things.

Quot. 1898 under sense 6 in Dict. belongs here.

1905 *Smart Set* Sept. 117/2 No one else is going to run off with your old car. **1913** F. H. BURNETT *T. Tembarom* xxxiv. 438 Whatever happens, you are both fixed all right... Whatever old thing happens. *a* **1917** E. A. MACKINTOSH *War, the Liberator* (1918) 91, I always wondered If our old barrage could Be half as bloody good As the Staff said it would. **1938** M. K. RAWLINGS *Yearling* i. 3 'There'll come a little old drizzly rain before night-fall,' he thought. **1942** Z. N. HURSTON in A. Dundes *Mother Wit* (1973) 28/2, I had done..cooked you a great big old cake. **1945** *Tee Emm* (Air Ministry) V. 38 Getting the 'general impression'..to register in the old brain-box. **1949** B. A. BOTKIN *Treas. S. Folklore* p. xx, It is a land where the word 'old'—the Old South,..Old Man So-and-So, little old this-and-that—are terms of affection and pride. **1965** J. BINGHAM *Fragment of Fear* iv. 49 'I have been successful.'.. 'Good old you!' **1971** P. O'DONNELL *Impossible Virgin* i. 12 When you look in poor old Tina's tum there's just a grotty old mish-mash of bits and pieces. **1971** D. FRANCIS *Bonecrack* viii. 101 'They didn't take my advice.' 'Silly old them.'

9. b. Also *the old boy* (see BOY *sb.*[1] 6 in Dict. and Suppl.).

11. a. See also *old light*(*s* LIGHT *sb.* 6 d), *old school* (SCHOOL *sb.* 5 b), *old tenor* (TENOR *sb.*[1] 1 c).

c. Prefixed to the name of a language, to denote an early period in its history, or the earliest of several periods, preceding that usu. called *middle* (see MIDDLE *a.* 4 b), as in *Old English* (see ENGLISH *sb.* 1 b in Dict. and Suppl.), *Old Norse* (see NORSE *sb.* 3), *Old Prussian* (see *OLD PRUSSIAN *sb.* b). Abbrev. O (see O 5 b in Dict. and Suppl.).

d. Prefixed to a sb. or adj. to denote a former member of a particular institution or society, esp. a public school.

1824 M. R. MITFORD *Our Village* I. 147 One meets with an old Etonian, who retains his boyish love for that game [*sc.* cricket]. **1848** C. H. NEWMARCH *Recollections of Rugby* i. 1 'Oh! mihi præteritos referat si Jupiter annos,' is an exclamation, in which, remembering..a duck hunt at Swift's, every old Rugbæan will, I hope, most heartily concur. **1857** *Manx Sun* 4 July in *Geo. Eliot Lett.* (1954) II. 337 The writer is a gentleman of our own acquaintance, an old Cantab. **1870** *Wellingtonian* May 152 The above Match proved a very exciting one..inasmuch as it was only won by two wickets by the old Wellingtonians. **1892** (*title*) Eton of old..by an Old Colleger. **1902** S. A. BARNETT in H. Barnett *Canon Barnett* (1918) II. xxxiv. 70 The 'Old Northeyites' has kept the educational side well in front. *Ibid.* 71 The 'Old Dalgleishers'—whose special feature is the Easter expedition—enjoyed it for the eighth year in succession. **1914** 'I. HAY' *Knight on Wheels* (ed. 2) xviii. 172 Each happened to be wearing an Old Studleian tie, so common ground was established at once. **1920** GALSWORTHY *In Chancery* I. iv. 42 He went out to dinner alone—an old Malburian [*sic*] dinner. **1936** G. M. YOUNG *Victorian England* xiv. 96 The Old Giggleswickian was not yet a named variety. **1964** C. MACKENZIE *My Life & Times* III. 52 Henry Cruft had been at Eton and then..sent to Shrewsbury. He still considered himself an Old Etonian. *Ibid.* 126 Cyril Bailey..was an Old Pauline who had left before I went to St Paul's in 1894. **1967** V. CANNING *Python Project* iii. 46 He..straightened his Old Etonian tie. **1970** P. DICKINSON *Seals* i. 11 His Old Etonian tie was knotted round a starched white collar. **1975** *Listener* 6 Feb. 164/1 The son of an Army officer and an Old Harrovian.

12. a. *Old Adam* (later, allusive examples).

1888 KIPLING *Wee Willie Winkie* (1889) 6 The idea that he shared a great secret..kept Wee Willie Winkie ..virtuous for three weeks. Then the Old Adam broke out, and he made..a 'camp-fire' at the bottom of the garden. **1976** *Listener* 26 Feb. 232/1 The best way to keep evil and the old Adam down was to flog the child.

b. *the old country* (earlier and later examples); also applied to a (person's) country of origin other than Great Britain, *spec.* (occas. in *pl.*) to the countries of Europe, the 'old world'; hence *old-countryman*; *Old Commonwealth*: Canada, Australia, and New Zealand (cf. *NEW COMMONWEALTH); *the Old Dominion*: see *DOMINION 2 b; *Old England* (further examples); *Old South*, the southern states of the U.S. before the civil war of 1861–5; *Old World* (earlier example).

c **1596** DONNE *Poems* (1912) I. 76 If you from spoyle of th'old worlds farthest end. **1782** 'J. H. ST. JOHN DE CRÈVECŒUR' *Lett. from Amer. Farmer* i. 3 A person who hath been to Paris,..and who hath seen so many fine things up and down the old countries. **1796** F. BAILY *Jrnl. Tour N. Amer.* 25 Dec. (1856) 172 The scenery..so very different from what we had been used to in the *old* country. **1828** *Amer. Q. Rev.* IV. 211 Even the illiterate in our country will distinguish an Englishman by his pronunciation, and will designate him as an 'old country-man'. **1840** *Southern Lit. Messenger* VI. 241/1 More of Old England is left in the hearts of the Old Dominion than in all the states beside, save [etc.]. **1848** BARTLETT *Dict. Amer.* 239 *Old Countryman*, a native of England, Scotland, Ireland, or Wales. **1873** *Harper's Mag.* July 271/1 Never in her most boastful days did the old South, under her cherished system of slave labor, produce better crops. **1884** *Boston Jrnl.* 30 Dec. 2/4 Our goods are crossing the water to keep alive old England. **1898** J. D. BRAYSHAW *Slum Silhouettes* 8 Loudly declaiming..about the injustice done to 'the ould counthry', and forcibly giving vent to his views upon 'Home Rule'. **1927** M. M. BENNETT *Christison* xiv. 133 In 1877, twenty-five years after he had sailed from Liverpool for Victoria, Christison left Australia to visit the Old Country. **1947** E. A. MCCOURT *Flaming Hour* vi. 32 In the old country..there would be spinach, brussels sprouts, artichokes. **1950** W. L. JAMES in A. Dundes *Mother Wit* (1973) 431/2 It was those cries which Negroes made famous in the Old South. **1965** *New Society* 26 Aug. 18/1 The 'old' Commonwealth consists of Canada, Australia and New Zealand; the 'new' Commonwealth includes all remaining Commonwealth countries. **1966** B. H. DEAL *Fancy's Knell* (1967) ii. 26 Bill was Old South and Mildred wasn't. **1973** *Guardian* 26 Jan. 1/2 The rules as drafted would lead to unacceptable treatment of people from the Old Commonwealth. **1973** *Sunday Bulletin* (Philadelphia) (Discovery Suppl.) 14 Oct. 17/2 People referred to Europe (or any nation therein) as 'the old country'. **1975** *Listener* 29 May 692/2 We now see not just the African Commonwealth, but also the Old Commonwealth and the Asian Commonwealth, beginning to make their own direct links with the Community. **1975** A. PRICE *Our Man in Camelot* i. 25 There was much more of the Old South in Shirley's voice.

c. *Old Christmas* (*Day*) (later examples); also *Old Christmas Eve*; *Old Lady Day*, *Old Michaelmas* (*Day*) (earlier example), *Old Midsummer*.

1783 W. OWEN *New Bk. of Fairs* 14 Friday before Old Michaelmas, meeting by custom for horned cattle. *Ibid.* 65 Monday before Old Midsummer July 5, for sheep and horned cattle. *Ibid.* 70 Monday before Old Lady Day, for broad and narrow cloths, and leather. **1931** *Sun* (Baltimore) 7 Jan. 7/2 In the church calendar the day is known as Epiphany and in England as Twelfth Night, but among the Colonists it was known as 'Little Christmas' or 'Old Christmas', deriving the name from the fact that when the calendar was changed centuries ago an error was made. **1935** *Evening Sun* (Baltimore) 5 Jan. 18/3 On Old Christmas Eve, tomorrow night, daffodils, hops and elders are supposed to shoot mysterious sprouts through snow and frozen ground. **1948** *Richmond* (Virginia) *Times-Dispatch* 8 Jan. 26/1 In Rodanthe, N.C., and probably in some other remote places, 'Old Christmas' is observed on January 5. **1956** *Sun* (Baltimore) 5 Jan. 3/2 Why residents of the Outer Banks celebrate Epiphany or Old Christmas, as well as December 25..is something lost in antiquity. **1969** in Halpert & Story *Christmas Mumming in Newfoundland* 176 From before Christmas till Old Christmas Day called Twelfth Day, they held high carnival.

d. *old days* (or *times*): past times; freq. in phr. *good* (or *bad*) *old days* (or *times*).

1828 *Oscotian* (ed. 2) I. 1 However glorious those '*good old times*' may have been, they still were destitute of one very important advantage. **1856** GEO. ELIOT in *Westm. Rev.* X. 55 The aristocratic dilettantism which attempts to restore the 'good old times' by a sort of idyllic masquerading. **1898** G. B. SHAW *Mrs. Warren's Profession* II.

197 Suppose we were both as poor as you were in those wretched old days. **1906** *Nature* 3 May (Suppl.) p. vii/2 In writing of times that are past and gone, while still within our recollection, we have all to be on our guard against a popular illusion as to the 'good old days'. **1911** G. B. Shaw *Getting Married* 261, I felt that I had left the follies and puerilities of the old days behind me for ever. **1932** H. E. Williams in N. Hodgins *Some Canadian Essays* 225 While museums exemplify the distances that we have travelled since 'the good old days', they are not the best place in which to extract the old-time flavour. **1935** *Discovery* Jan. 29/2 Even in the bad old days, however, there are some things on which Canada may well pride herself. **1950** E. H. Gombrich *Story of Art* xxv. 379 There was one thing to be said for the 'good old days'—no artist need ask himself why he had come into the world at all. **1958** A. Huxley *Brave New World Revisited* (1959) 27 In the bad old days children with considerable, or even with slight, hereditary defects rarely survived. **1973** *Archivum Linguisticum* IV. 90 Associated with 'the old days', that is with the Rana regime.

e. *old ice*: in polar regions, ice formed before the most recent winter; similarly *old snow* (see quots. 1952, 1966).

1856 E. K. Kane *Arctic Explorations* I. xii. 128 Fissures ..were beginning to break in every direction through the young ice... I therefore made for the old ice to seaward. **1885** *Encycl. Brit.* XIX. 328/1 Old ice is believed to become thicker in a second winter, and even to attain a thickness of 10 feet. **1935** *Handbk. Weather, Currents & Ice* (Meteorol. Office) vii. 102 The Arctic peak consists of old ice, which due to rafting and hummocking forms massive fields. **1952** *Jrnl. Glaciology* II. 150 The definition of *firn*, adopted by the Eidg. Institut für Schnee- und Lawinenforschung, and included in the latest 'Draft on an International Snow Classification' suggested by the Committee on Snow Classification of International Association of Scientific Hydrology, is as follows: 'old snow which has outlasted one summer at least (transformed into a dense heavy material as a result of frequent melting and freezing)'. **1966** T. Armstrong et al. *Illustr. Gloss. Snow & Ice* 30 *Old snow*, deposited snow whose transformation into *firn* is so far advanced that the original form of the ice crystals can no longer be recognized.

f. *old quantum theory*: see *QUANTUM THEORY; *Old Red Sandstone*: see SANDSTONE.

g. Of a coinage: designating a former monetary unit that has been replaced by a new one with the same name (see *NEW *a.* 4).

The French *old franc* was replaced in 1960; in Britain new' decimal currency was introduced in 1971.

1959 *Times* 10 Nov. 10/6 The new 'heavy franc', which is worth 100 old francs, is to become legal currency on January 1 next year. **1965** R. Ferguson *Woman with Secret* x. 76 She left me 40,000 francs. Old francs. **1969** *Times* 21 July (Decimal Currency Suppl.) p. 1/5 Below 5p the only old coin which will be an exact equivalent of the new will be sixpence ($2\frac{1}{2}$p). *Ibid.* 6 The $\frac{1}{2}$p coin being smaller than the old farthing..will be universally unpopular. **1972** D. Lees *Zodiac* 46 That's over four thousand dollars..more than two million old francs. **1974** L. Thomas *Tropic of Ruislip* ix. 178 'Blimey,' she said. There's one of the old pennies in here. That's not yours, is it?' 'No,' he answered. 'I cashed all my old ones in.' **1976** *Listener* 8 Apr. 430/2 Gary was born on 5 April 1966... In those pre-decimal days, you could buy a loaf of bread for 15 old pennies.

C. *sb.*[1] **3. b.** *sing.* A type of ale noted for its strength. Hence *old and mild*, a combination of old and mild ale in equal parts.

1904 A. Makins *Licensed Victuallers' Handbk.* xiv. 224 The number of different kinds of malt liquors now produced are not numerous...'Bitter', 'Stout', 'Mild', and 'Old' (usually called by the public 'Burton'). **1923** *Month* July 37 A glass of 'owd' (old ale) is his only inspiration. **1930** A. P. Herbert *Water Gipsies* xxiii. 341 The total price of two mild and bitters, one old and mild, two small ports. **1932** L. Golding *Magnolia St.* I. iii. 56 Two quarts of old, please! **1933** A. G. Macdonell *England, Their England* vii. 105 The row of gaffers on the rustic bench.. called for more pints of old-and-mild. **1957** J. Braine *Room at Top* xx. 177 I'd had two pints of old at the St. Clair. **1967** A. Bailey in L. Deighton *London Dossier* 66 Try Burton, sometimes called 'Old'...a strong, dark and sweet draught beer..often mixed in the glass with mild ale when it becomes..known as 'Old and Mild'. **1974** *Guardian* 19 Jan. 11/1 In the tap-room..I encountered.. a most impressive Old which is in effect a draught barley wine.

D. 1. a. *old-young* (examples). **b.** *old-established* (earlier and later examples).

1785 *Daily Universal Reg.* 1 Jan. 3/2 The following articles, in Silver, at the Old established Wholesale Prices. **1961** New Eng. Bible *Matt.* xv. 2 Why do your disciples break the old-established tradition? **1834** 'Nimrod' in *New Sporting Mag.* VIII. 82 There stood before me, a round-shouldered, decrepid, tottering *old-young* man. **1907** *Daily Chron.* 8 July 3/3 Liverpool..the old-young city. **1932** V. Woolf *Common Reader* 2nd Ser. 130 A 'round-shouldered, tottering old-young man bloated by drink'. **1951** Dylan Thomas *Lett.* (1966) 352 These old-young men are shipped back also, packed full with shame and penicillin. **1959** N. Mailer *Advts. for Myself* (1961) 21 The colourful old-young men of American letters. **1974** J. Mann *Sticking Place* v. 83 She was not a girl at all, on close inspection..but an old-young woman.

2. b. *old-boyishness, -fogydom, -fogyish* (earlier example), *-liner* (earlier and later examples), *-masterish, -masterishness, -masterly* (later example), *old soldierism* (the conduct of an 'old soldier').

1850 *Punch* 3 Aug. 52/1 There is a jolly-buckism or an old-boyishness about the concern. *c* **1905** F. Rolfe *Nicholas Crabbe* (1958) xxvii. 188 Exasperate and purulent oldfogeydom. **1920** T. P. Nunn *Education* xii. 147 At that age..old fogeydom already lays his hand on most of us, little as we may expect it. *a* **1877** in Bartlett *Dict. Amer.* (1877) (ed. 4) 437 He's slow and rather *old-fogyish.* **1855** *Richmond* (Virginia) *Whig* 15 Mar. 1/1 Endorsed thus by two 'old liners', he was most cordially received. **1903** *N.Y. Even. Post* 31 Oct. 5 The old-liners quietly backbite him for taking up a 'fanatic' like Johnson. **1908** R. W. Chambers *Firing Line* xxix. 493, I didn't expect any cordiality..but..they classed us with the old-liners. **1925** A. Huxley *Those Barren Leaves* I. ii. 14 One of those large, handsome, old-masterish women. **1961** *Listener* 16 Nov. 822/3 There are no 'properties', no old-masterish bits and pieces, to keep the thing going. **1937** *Burlington Mag.* Mar. 137/1 The same contempt for 'old masterishness' and its devotees. **1968** S. Hynes *Edwardian Turn of Mind* ix. 317 A taste in painting that was neither Old Masterly..nor academic. **1911** H. S. Harrison *Queed* xxii. 276, I think old-soldierism is the meanest profession the Lord ever suffered to thrive.

3. *old-home, -issue, -line* (examples), *Line State* (Maryland), *-master, -standard, -wave, -year.*

1928 Blunden *Undertones of War* xvii. 177 Flinging old-home repartee at your pal passing by. **1959** *Word* XV. 147 Langer gives a considerable number of examples of old-home expressions which were lost and replaced. **1879** A. W. Tourgée *Fool's Errand* xvii. 87 Robert..was..an 'old-issue free nigger' (freed before the war). **1899** C. W. Chesnutt *Wife of his Youth* 214 Wright came of an 'old issue' free colored family, in which though negro blood was present in an attenuated strain, a line of free ancestry could be traced beyond the Revolutionary War. **1856** *Congress. Globe* 9 Jan. 180/3 Have they offered us one of my colleagues, an old-line Whig? **1908** R. W. Chambers *Firing Line* xxi. 353 I'm in an old-line institution. **1928** F. Scott Fitzgerald *Let.* 1 Feb. (1964) 383, I rode.. with the president of a very prominent club, not my own, a Princetonian of the rather old-line, conservative, very gentlemanly type. **1949** *Sun* (Baltimore) 7 Sept. 12/4 Mr. Taft's mental and moral force has been a reservoir of strength to the old-line men. **1958** *Spectator* 20 June 791/3 In spite of his reputation as an old-line Stalinist, Suslov supported Khrushchev. **1962** R. Tyre *Douglas in Saskatchewan* v. 78 The Socialists had high hopes of winning the 1934 election but the farmers were not quite ready yet to abandon their traditional support of the old line parties. **1973** *Deb. Senate Canada* 28 Mar. 2710/1 The two old-line parties are afraid of treading on the toes of the financial institutions. **1872** Schele de Vere *Americanisms* xii. 660 Maryland bears the proud title of *Old-line State* from the *Old-Line* regiments which she contributed to the Continental Army in the War of the Revolution—the only State that had regular troops of 'the line'. **1948** Mencken *Amer. Lang.* Suppl. II. 604 *Maryland Free State*...has overshadowed all the old nicknames..including *Old Line State* and *Terrapin State.* **1950** D. Gascoyne *Vagrant* 56 Though that's what this old-master lute-master opines. **1959** *Times* 19 Mar. 4/3 Still-life studies combining an old-master flavour with a slightly surrealist inclination. **1838** J. F. Cooper *Home as Found* I. x. 163 That is the First Presbyterian, or the old standard [church]; a very good house. **1962** *Listener* 30 Aug. 315/1 This reaction has not come from Old Wave film makers. **1967** *Observer* 26 Feb. 21/3 All the addicts were middle-aged...typical old-wave addicts. But what of the new ones? **1897** R. M. Stuart *In Simpkinsville* i. 14 They got him to come to the old year party one year, jest for the fun of it.

4. old bach (see *BACH *sb.* 1); **Old Baptist, Old Christian (church)** *U.S.*, names of religious denominations; **Old Bill** *slang*, the police force; a policeman; **old-clothes-man, -shop,** (later examples); **old contemptible**: see *CONTEMPTIBLE *a.* 4; **old crock** (see *CROCK *sb.*[3] 4); **old firm,** a group of friends or associates (cf. *FIRM *sb.*[1] 2 c); **old gang** *colloq.*, a group or clique of friends or colleagues, esp. politicians, accustomed to supporting each other in matters of business or policy; **Old Glory** *U.S.*, the 'Stars and Stripes'; **old guard** (see GUARD *sb.* 9 b in Dict. and Suppl.); **old hand,** (*b*) (earlier and later examples); **old home week** *U.S.* (see quot. 1904); **Old Kingdom,** a name given collectively (*a*) to the Third, Fourth, Fifth, and Sixth Dynasties, which ruled Egypt from the 27th to the 22nd century B.C.; (*b*) to a period of Hittite history extending from the 18th to the 16th century B.C.; **old master** *U.S.*, the former master of a (Negro) slave; also **old mistress** (see also *OLE[2]); **old money,** old-established wealth; **old offender,** an habitual criminal; **old religion,** a religion or belief which is replaced or ousted by another, *spec.* (*a*) a pre-Christian religion; paganism; (*b*) witchcraft; (*c*) Roman Catholicism; **old-rich,** those whose wealth is old-established, opp. *new rich* (*NEW *a.* 8 d); also *attrib.* or as *adj.*; **Old Ritualist** [tr. Russ. *staroobryddets*], = *OLD BELIEVER; **old rope** *slang* (orig. *Naval*), rank tobacco; **old settler** [SETTLER 2 in Dict. and Suppl.], one of the earliest settlers in a community; **old ship** *Naval slang*, an old shipmate; **old sledge** (later examples); **old soldier** *sb. U.S. slang*, the remaining part of a smoked cigar or chewed quid; also, an empty liquor bottle (Webster 1909); **old-spelling,** the unstandardized early spelling of English; **old squaw,** the long-tailed duck, *Clangula hyemalis*; = LONG-TAIL 1 b (in Dict. and Suppl.), OLD WIFE 2; also *attrib.*; **old-standing** *a.* (further examples); **old style** *Typog.*, one of a group of type-faces first produced in the 19th century and modelled on the 18th-century old-face fount cast at the Caslon foundry; also *attrib.*; cf. *CASLON, *OLD-FACE; **old sweat** *slang*, an old soldier; **old thing** *Austral.* (see quots.); **old Thirteen** *U.S.*, the original thirteen American colonies, which declared their independence in 1776; also, the original 'Stars and Stripes', a flag with thirteen stars and thirteen stripes; **Old Tom** (earlier and later examples); **old witch,** a children's game; **old witch-grass,** a North American panic grass, *Panicum capillare.*

1845 A. Wiley in *Indiana Mag. Hist.* (1927) XXIII. 18, I see nothing awaiting the 'old Baptist' churches but utter annihilation. **1889** P. Butler *Personal Recoll.* 252 'Hardshell' Baptists..wish to be known as Old Baptists, or United Baptists. **1958** F. Norman *Bang to Rights* 138 Two Old Bill's came up to me and told me they had a warrant for my arrest. **1967** *Guardian* 14 Mar. 8/6 He observed a couple of men supping nearby who looked suspiciously like plainclothes men. Coulson asked the landlord. 'Oh no,' he said, 'they're drinking pints. Old Bills only drink halves.' **1970** G. F. Newman *Sir, You Bastard* viii. 272 Giving Old Bill a bung was still an offence, and there would have been no consideration for the information. **1973** K. Royce *Spider Underground* i. 19 It's me he's out to fix by bringing Old Bill about my ears. **1976** *New Statesman* 12 Mar. 322/3 If they were caught at it when the Old Bill (police) staged one of their frequent raids then we would all be up on a charge of 'maintaining a disorderly house'. **1849** E. Chamberlain *Indiana Gazetteer* (ed. 3) 175 Presbyterians, Methodists, United Brethren, Christian,..Old Christian, (or new Light) and Baptists. **1834** *Chambers's Edin. Jrnl.* III. 141/1, I feel convinced that these old-clothes-men only address persons of gentlemanly appearance. **1968** *N.Y. City* (Michelin Tire Corp.) 82 The dark smoke-filled bars which alternate with old-clothes dealers along the street..shopkeepers.. tailors and old-clothes men. **1851** A. O. Hall *Manhattaner* 6 Groups of old clo' shops, gaudily set forth with parti-colored handkerchiefs. **1930** A. P. Herbert *Water Gipsies* vii. 72 Five shillings each way... Don't desert the Old Firm! **1935** D. L. Sayers *Gaudy Night* iv. 64 If you ever want me, you will find the Old Firm at the usual stand. **1975** 'D. Jordan' *Black Account* xiii. 66 'Always happy to help the Old Firm,' he declared. **1885** J. Chamberlain in J. R. Ware *Passing Eng.* (1909) 187/1 In deference to his [*sc.* Lord Randolph Churchill's] opinion, there will no doubt be a clearance out of some of those whom the Fourth Party is in the habit of politely designating as the 'Old Gang'. **1889** *Judge* (N.Y.) XV. 368/1 Yankee Doodle came to town Astride his thoroughbred. He met the old gang going out With Grover at their head. **1891** G. B. Shaw *How to become Mus. Critic* (1960) 195 Mr Chappell has at last awakened to the fact that his stock players were becoming what vestry politicians call an old gang. **1900** —— *Let.* 4 Mar. (1972) II. 150 In excited times nominations are apt to be made freely; and what happens then is that though the old gang is pretty safe, the other seats go anyhow. **1901** *Punch* 3 Apr. 250/2 There is so much favoritism that only the Old Gang and Rank Outsiders get chosen. **1916** Mrs. Belloc Lowndes *Let.* 8 Dec. (1971) 78 Violet Markham thinks L.G. will last out a good while but that all 'the Old Gang' as people are beginning to call them, will gradually crystallise into a Peace Party. **1933** Wyndham Lewis *Old Gang & New Gang* 9 Every morning when Mr. Everyman opens his newspaper he reads about the doings of the 'Old Gang'—or rather about their non-doing and non-caring. **1934** G. G. Coulton in *S.P.E. Tract* XLIII. 103 Within six years he [*sc.* Hart] had gathered eleven colleagues whom, at a much later prize-giving, he affectionately described as 'the Old Gang', and of whom Fowler was one. **1940** H. Nicolson *Let.* 6 June (1967) 94 There is a growing feeling against what is called 'the old gang'... The men who have come back from the front feel that Kingsley Wood and Inskip let them down and must go. **1961** R. Hoggart *W. H. Auden: a Selection* 24 A feeling that 'the old gang' were always hopelessly out of touch and wrong. **1964** C. Barber *Ling. Change Present-Day Eng.* ii. 26 A rejection of Old Gang politics,..general resentment at the Establishment. **1862** W. Driver in *Salem* (Mass.) *Reg.* 10 Mar. 2, I carried my flag, 'Old Glory', as we have been used to call it, to the Capitol, presented it to the Ohio 6th. **1930** J. Dos Passos *42nd Parallel* II. 153 They wrapped me in the Stars and Stripes and brought me home on a frigate to be buried..I was wrapped in Old Glory. **1973** *Sat. Rev. World* (U.S.) 4 Dec. 16/2 The right to substitute the peace symbol for the stars in Old Glory. **1975** *Times* 15 Apr. 6/7 Come what may, the American Ambassador to Saigon..will be rescued by the Marines, with the 'Old Glory' flag rolled in his arms. **1845** C. Griffith *Present State of Port Philip* 76 The old hands are men, who, having been formerly convicts..have become free by the expiration of their sentences. **1857** R. B. Paul *Lett. from Canterbury, N.Z.* ii. 26 Only enter the dwelling of the roughest 'old hand' among us, and you will meet with.. much kindness. **1911** C. E. W. Bean *'Dreadnought' of Darling* xxxii. 283 Lots of these fellows near Bourke were 'old hands'. Some of them were decent, good fellows, and the rest—well, they were horrible—the blackest, unmitigated rascals, fearing neither God nor the devil, men who would stick at nothing. **1946** K. Tennant *Lost Heaven* (1947) 1 On one side is Limeburners', where the 'old hands' used to pound oyster shells for lime. **1904** *Boston Herald* 2 Aug. 6 In..Massachusetts this first week in August is being observed as Old Home Week, and preparations have been made for welcoming back..visitors who return to their native, or earlier, home to renew acquaintance with former scenes and companions. **1949** T. Rattigan *Harlequinade* 63 What with Mums in front and babies in the wings it's not so much a dress rehearsal as old home week. **1973** 'I. DRUMMOND' *Jaws of Watchdog* i. 11 He and Jenny embraced warmly. 'Old home week,' said the Princess sourly. **1905** J. H. BREASTED *Egypt through Stereoscope* 22 With the accession of the 3rd Dynasty..we see Egypt rising into her first great period of power and prosperity, which we call the Old Kingdom. *Ibid.* 143 The king who made the sphinx must have dismantled some Old Kingdom mastabas to clear the rock. **1910** *Encyl. Brit.* IX. 39/1 A valuable stele from Sakkara of the beginning of the Old Kingdom was presented to the Ashmolean Museum at Oxford in 1683. **1928** C. DAWSON *Age of Gods* vii. 151 We must be prepared to allow for a margin of error of more than 800 years in dealing with.. the Old Kingdom of Egypt. **1938** E. M. SANFORD *Mediterranean World in Anc. Times* I. 55 The foundation of the united Old Kingdom of the Hittites was delayed by the rivalry of individual states. **1952** O. GURNEY *Hittites* i. 25 Telipinus is usually regarded as the last king of the Old Kingdom. **1961** A. GARDINER *Egypt of Pharaohs* I. iv. 60 Our evidence for the Old Kingdom is purely archaeological. **1973** R. J. WILLIAMS in D. J. Wiseman *Peoples Old Testament Times* iv. 83 Great advances were made in medicine, which reached heights in the Old Kingdom never surpassed in ancient Egypt. **1974** *Encycl. Brit. Macropædia* VI. 465/1 There is good reason to regard this king [*sc.* Khasekhemui] as the founder of the Old Kingdom. **1872** S. POWERS *Afoot & Alone* 61 Negroes everywhere..seemed to think they were not free unless they left the old master. **1892** 'MARK TWAIN' *Amer. Claimant* viii. 81 When a bell ring..en old marster tell me to—. **1949** B. A. BOTKIN *Treas. S. Folklore* I. iii. 58 The chief protagonist and antagonist of master–slave folklore are Old Massa and Old John. **1859** D. D. EMMETT *Dixie's Land* (song) (1960), Old missus marry Will de Weaber... Here's a health to de next old missus. **1874** 'MARK TWAIN' in *Atlantic Monthly* Nov. 592/1 Well, bymeby my ole mistis say she's broke. **1963** *Times* 25 Feb. (Canada Suppl.) p. xv/3 Having noted that the Canadian rich, particularly the old-money rich, tend to dwell among exquisite eighteenth-century chattels, the poorer folk aspire to antiques themselves. **1966** 'D. SHANNON' *With a Vengeance* i. 22 There's a lot o' money—kind of substantial *old* money, you know—her husband was a banker. **1967** L. J. BRAUN *Cat who ate Danish Modern* ii. 18 People with Old Money always avoid publicity on their real estate. **1817** *2nd Rep. Comm. State of Police of Metrop.* 329 in *Parl. Papers* VII. 321 The greater part of these Juvenile Offenders,..are mixed indiscriminately with old offenders of all ages. **1890** W. BOOTH *In Darkest Eng.* II. v. 177 C.M. Old offender, and penal servitude case. **1970** P. LAURIE *Scotland Yard* x. 263 If he is an old offender, the threat failed to deter him. **1848** W. D. COOLEY tr. *Erman's Trav. in Siberia* II. xii. 306 The Bugoi of the Buraets of the old religion, maintain that they know..how to deal with certain mischievous spirits. **1934** A. HUXLEY *Beyond Mexique Bay* 159 The old religion came..boldly out into the open in 1745. **1964** *Listener* 12 Mar. 445/3, I am glad to see that the witch-religion is becoming so respectable... Jean Morris.. now proposes..that the Templars were of the 'old religion'. **1967** D. PINNER *Ritual* x. 106 If the Old Religion possessed this village, I probably would be too frightened to be anything but a warlock voyeur. **1972** P. DENNISON in N. Tiptaft *Religion in Birmingham* 140 Wherever a local squire remained Catholic there was a good chance for the survival of a small pocket of the old religion in his territory. **1973** J. WAINWRIGHT *High-Class Kill* 77 Some of 'em stumble against witchcraft. Sorcery. Demonology. The so-called 'old religion'. **1975** *Country Life* 6 Feb. 318/2 In Queen Mary's reign he was, as a reliable adherent of the old religion, put on the Council of the Welsh Marches. **1927** *Public Opinion* 18 Feb. 149/1 These mistakes..seem folly to an old-rich man. *Ibid.* 149/2 The old-rich know these things well enough, but the new-rich never discover them. **1976** T. ALLBEURY *Only Good German* xiv. 101 The kind of places that the old rich go to rather than the new rich. **1885** A. J. C. HARE *Studies in Russia* vi. 301 In later times the schismatics have divided into the Stároobriádtsi, or Old Ritualists..and the Bezpopoftsi, or priestless people. **1911** Old Ritualist [see *OLD BELIEVER]. **1954** G. VERNADSKY *Hist. Russia* (ed. 4) v. 132 Outstanding among the leaders of the Old Ritualists, as the anti-Nikonians eventually became known, was the archpriest Avvakum. *Ibid.* viii. 180 The movement of the Old Ritualists by 1800 ceased to be a unit and broke into several separate sects. **1974** R. PIPES *Russia under Old Regime* ix. 236 Russian dissenters are customarily divided in two basic groups: the Old Believers, known to themselves as 'Old Ritualists' (*Staroobriadtsy*) and to the official church as 'Splitters' (*Raskol'niki*), and the Sectarians. **1943** HUNT & PRINGLE *Service Slang* 48 *Old rope*, any tobacco which offends the nostrils of those present, and especially the finer varieties such as Egyptian. **1946** J. IRVING *Royal Navalese* 127 *Old Rope*, any offensive smelling tobacco. **1744** *Colonial Rec. Georgia* (1906) VI. 117 Thomas Ellis has been an old Settler in the Colony. **1815** Old settler [see SETTLER 2 b]. **1854** R. B. PAUL *Some Acct. Canterbury Settlemt.* 5 Having now resided more than two years in the Canterbury Settlement..[I] may almost call [myself] an 'old settler'. **1964** S. M. MILLER in I. L. Horowitz *New Sociol.* 293 'Old-settler' Protestant recruits largely from farm and rural areas. **1927** *Daily Express* 11 Oct. 3/4 He gave a vivid description of waiting for the train at Charing Cross, then he met an 'old ship', and they went to have a drink. **1948** PARTRIDGE *Dict. Forces' Slang* 131 *Old Ship*, a former messmate (Navy). **1884** 'C. E. CRADDOCK' *In Tennessee Mts.* II. 82 The mingled charms of Old Sledge and apple-jack had occasioned comment. **1950** R. P. WARREN *World Enough & Time* iii. 101 The groups of men who played 'Old Sledge' and 'Brag' on the sidewalk. **1834** W. A. CARUTHERS *Kentuckian in N.Y.* I. 12, I smokes the old sodgers what the gentlemen throws on the bar-room floor. **1869** 'MARK TWAIN' in *Buffalo Express* 4 Sept. 1/1 A wooden box of sand, sprinkled with cigar stubs and 'old soldiers'. *a* **1877** in Bartlett *Dict. Amer.* (1877) (ed. 4) 438 Ladies who swab our sidewalks,.. And.. Haul off old soldiers lying there at rest. **1936** *Amer. Speech* XI. 304/1 *Old soldier*, 'a partly-smoked cigar'... I have heard this more frequently as *dead soldier*, applied to empty beer or whiskey bottles but not to cigar butts. **1927** R. B. MCKERROW *Introd. Bibliogr.* III. i. 246 The composition rates for old spelling texts are some 10 per cent above the normal rate. **1960** *Studies in Bibliogr.* XIII. 49 (*heading*) The rationale of old-spelling editions of the plays of Shakespeare and his contemporaries. **1969** *N.Y. Rev. Bks.* 30 Jan. 32/2 In the first place the words aren't old-spelling [in an edition of Shakespeare]. **1838** J. J. AUDUBON *Ornith. Biogr.* IV. 105 They have various appellations, among others those of 'old wives' and 'old squaws'. **1884** etc. [see SQUAW *sb.* (and *a.*) 4]. **1892** B. TORREY *Foot-Path Way* 41 The cliffs..offer an excellent position from which to sweep the bay in search of loons, old-squaws, and other sea-fowl. **1963** *Kingston* (Ontario) *Whig-Standard* 8 Feb. 11/2 Large numbers of Old Squaw ducks were sighted during the survey. **1971** *Islander* (Victoria, B.C.) 10 Oct. 13/1 Oldsquaw is one of the few ducks with two complete annual plumage changes. **1975** *Globe & Mail* (Toronto) 9 Dec. 11/5 Almost all the affected ducks are oldsquaws, long-tailed Arctic ducks that winter by the thousand on the Great Lakes. **1927** A. BENNETT *Let.* 14 Apr. (1966) I. 365 The Beaverbrook papers, which have my stuff at 1/6d a word under an old-standing arrangement. **1962** A. SORSBY in A. PIRIE *Lens Metabolism Rel. Cataract* 298 The characteristic subepithelial opacities seen in this affection are an oldstanding observation. *c* **1869** (*title*) Specimens of old style types (Miller & Richard). **1884** BIGMORE & WYMAN *Bibliogr. Printing* II. 42 Perceiving the tendency to go back to a former taste in printing, this foundry [*sc.* Miller & Richard], about 1850, commenced to cut a series of what they termed 'old-style founts', the success of which has been unexampled in the annals of type-founding. **1913** J. H. QUINN *Library Cataloguing* xv. 222 'Old-style' in type does not mean old-fashioned, but the more artistic and readable type modelled on the lettering of the early printers, principally those of the Italian presses. **1966** H. WILLIAMSON *Methods Bk. Design* (ed. 2) viii. 101 In 1852 Miller and Richard..led the way to a new development by issuing specimens of a regularized old face which they named Old Style. The new class of old style types, of which this was the first, reverted to gradual shading and to oblique top-serifs, but retained vertical stress. **1919** *Athenæum* 8 Aug. 727/2 A 'gasper' is a cheap cigarette, an 'old sweat' an old soldier. **1924** A. J. SMALL *Frozen Gold* i. 38 You're a levelheaded old sweat, I know, or you wouldn't be carrying the button. *a* **1935** [see *EASY *a.* 13 b]. **1955** J. THOMAS *No Banners* ix. 80 These were followed by two lank British privates, old sweats of the Regular Army. **1973** *Guardian* 16 Mar. 12/5, I speak feelingly as an 'old sweat' who served in Ireland in an earlier time of 'troubles'. **1848** H. W. HAYGARTH *Recoll. Bush Life Austral.* i. 6 The Traveller's entertainment is confined to the 'old thing', as it is contemptuously called, that is to say, beef and 'damper'. **1945** BAKER *Austral. Lang.* iv. 80 It was what W. W. Dobie called the *muttonous* diet of the outback that produced the expression *the Old Thing* for a meal of mutton and damper. **1845** *Southern Lit. Messenger* XI. 584/2 Charleston..[was] the chief commercial city of the 'Old Thirteen'. **1854** B. F. TAYLOR *Jan. & June* 68 The 'Old Thirteen' were blazing bright—There were *only* thirteen then! **1904** *Hartford* (Connecticut) *Courant* 30 Aug. 10 We want to see the Old Thirteen draw closer and closer together. **1821** P. EGAN *Real Life in London* I. ix. 187 *Old Tom*—It is customary in public-houses and gin-shops in London and its vicinity to exhibit a cask inscribed with large letters—OLD TOM, intended to indicate the best gin in the house. **1971** R. DENTRY *Encounter at Kharmel* iv. 75 A bottle of Old Tom and two hot-glasses. **1881** *Harper's Mag.* Jan. 184/2 The young folks..played at 'prisoner's base' or 'old witch by the wayside'. **1906** *Dialect Notes* III. 148 *Old witch*,..an outdoor game. The players circle around one of their number, the old witch, to whom the following is addressed: 'Chickamy, chickamy, crany-crow... What time is it, old witch?' **1859** W. DARLINGTON *Amer. Weeds* 403 Old-witch grass... Sandy pastures, cultivated grounds; throughout the United States. **1894** J. M. COULTER *Bot. W. Texas* III. 508 Old witch grass... Annual... In cultivated land everywhere.

Old Aca·demy. Also **old Academy.** [ACADEMY 2.] The school of philosophy founded by Plato in the fourth century B.C., as distinguished from schools founded by later Heads of the Academy, the **Middle Academy* of Arcesilaus, and the *NEW ACADEMY of Carneades. So **Old Acade·mic** *sb.* and *a.*

1702 S. PARKER tr. *Tully's Five Bks. of De Finibus* v. 281, I am..well pleas'd that you've fallen upon so seasonable a Subject of Discourse, my Cousin being ambitious of a right Notion of that Hypothesis which the Old Academicks and Peripateticks you speak of, propagated about Moral Ends. **1744** W. GUTHRIE tr. *Cicero's Academical Treatises* in *Morals of Cicero* 304 If it were not too much Trouble, I should desire to hear anew, from your Mouth, both that and the whole System of the old Academy. *Ibid.* 316 The old Academics did not hold that all Virtue consisted in Reason. **1811** W. WARD *Acct. Writings, Relig. & Manners Hindoos* I. 357 This was the doctrine taught by Anaxagoras, and after him by Plato, and the whole Old Academy. **1874** J. S. REID *Cicero's Academica* p. xviii, It is a positive duty to discuss all aspects of every question, after the example of the Old Academy and Aristotle. **1876** ALLEYNE & GOODWIN tr. *Zeller's Plato & Older Acad.* xvi. 617 The Old Academy had even then, in many of its members, departed very far from genuine Platonism. **1885** J. S. REID *Cicero's Academica* (new ed.) 15 Varro evidently means that Cicero, having in earlier works copied the *writings* of 'Old Academic' philosophers, is about to draw on the literary stores of the New Academy. **1908** *Encycl. Relig. & Ethics* I. 59/2 The 'Old Academy' carried on the discussion of the problems which Plato had raised in his oral teaching. **1937** *Oxf. Compan. Classical Lit.* 2/1 The Academy under these leaders was known as the Old Academy. **1950** F. MAYER *Hist. Ancient & Medieval Philos.* xiv. 198 Conventionally, the Platonic school is divided into three periods. The first is the period of the Old Academy, which lasted from 347 B.C. to 250 B.C. **1974** A. A. LONG *Hellenistic Philos.* v. 224 Antiochus saw a very sharp distinction between the Old and the New Academy.

old age pension. [OLD *a.* 2.] A pension paid in certain countries by the state or, less frequently, by a private institution, to persons who have reached a specified age and are eligible for such assistance; also *ellipt.*, as *old age*. Used *attrib.* with *act*, *scheme*, etc. So **old age pensioner**, one who receives an old age pension.

1879 *19th Cent.* VI. 903 When the great clubs are able to mature the scheme which they are already entertaining for the payment of old age pensions. **1890** *Chambers's Jrnl.* 8 Feb. 88/1 To qualify..the worker must contribute ..for an old-age pension for fourteen hundred and ten weeks. **1892** *Q. Rev.* Apr. 507 Old age pensions commence at seventy years of age. **1895** W. S. COTTEW *Scheme for Old Age Pension Fund* 1/2 After all working and other expenses paid, interest, etc., to form an Old Age Pension Fund, and as a further addition to the fund, there shall be an Old Age Pension Rate, not to exceed one penny in the £. **1906** *Chambers's Jrnl.* 10 Mar. 239/1 There are two possible systems for an old-age pension scheme for this country. **1908** *Act* 8 *Edw. VII* c. 40 § 1 The sums required for the payment of old age pensions under this Act shall be paid out of moneys provided by Parliament. **1909** *Westm. Gaz.* 4 Jan. 3/3 We..believe that the Old-Age Pensions Act was almost universally intended to create a new social stratum. **1910** G. B. SHAW *Let.* 24 July (1972) II. 936 A list..which includes a choice collection of old-age-pensioners. **1931** *Times Lit. Suppl.* 4 June 441/2 The inspiration served its avowed purpose in providing him with 'an old-age pension'. **1936** *Act* 26 *Geo. V* & 1 *Edw. VIII* c. 31 § 4 Not more than one old age pension..shall be payable to any one person. **1945** A. HUXLEY *Let.* 30 Jan. (1969) 514 A nation like England..by 1975, will probably have declined to under forty millions, one quarter of whom will be drawing old age pensions. **1951** *Bull. Nat. Old People's Welfare Comm.* Feb. 10 In one London Borough on a given day each week old-age pensioners may attend the Municipal Baths at a cost of 1d. per bath. **1959** *Daily Tel.* 9 Apr. 1/7 Old age pensioners has much to gain from stability of prices. **1967** K. GILES *Death & Mr. Prettyman* viii. 160 'Not the old-age?'... 'The old-age for tax evaders? You're joking!' **1973** A. CHRISTIE *Postern of Fate* III. 127, I must go and talk to some old age pensioners at their club. **1976** *Sunday Tel.* 30 May 1/6 Sixteen old-age pensioners were injured..when a coach from Dundee crashed over an embankment.

Old Belie·ver. [tr. Russ. *starovér.*] A member of that section of the Russian Orthodox Church which refused to accept the liturgical reforms of the patriarch Nikon (1605–1681). Also called RASKOLNIK.

1814 R. PINKERTON tr. *Platon's Present State Greek Ch. in Russia* 293 On the death of the first leaders of the modern Raskolniks, some of the sects resolved to admit runaway priests into their communion, and to acknowledge their ordination on condition of their becoming Old Believers. **1879** L. B. LANG tr. *Rambaud's Hist. Russia* I. xxii. 433 She had arrested certain 'old believers'. **1911** *Encycl. Brit.* XIX. 692/1 This ruthlessness goes far to explain the unappeasable hatred with which the 'Old Ritualists' and the 'Old Believers', as they now began to be called, ever afterwards regarded Nikon and all his works. **1921** F. C. CONYBEARE *Russ. Dissenters* I. iii. 140 Court Kolovrat, the protector of the Old believers in Austria. **1931** *Times Lit. Suppl.* 12 Feb. 105/3 In Kiev, where he made the acquaintance of the community of Old Believers, who upheld the schism in the Orthodox Church. **1932** M. EASTMAN tr. *Trotsky's Hist. Russ. Revolution* I. i. 27 The struggle against the state church did not go farther than the creation of peasant sects, the faction of the Old Believers being the most powerful among them. **1957** *Oxf. Dict. Chr. Ch.* 960/2 His [*sc.* Nikon's] liturgical reforms were sanctioned..and the formation of the schismatical sect of the Old Believers followed. **1959** *Listener* 19 Feb. 338/3, I would put the number of practising Orthodox Christians (including Old Believers) [in the U.S.S.R.] somewhat lower than the figure..suggested by Mr. Kolarz. **1962** K. S. LATOURETTE *Christianity in Revolutionary Age* IV. xix. 508 In 1957 the Old Believers were known to have a church in Moscow. **1963** V. NABOKOV *Gift* ii. 122 In 1862, sixty Russian Old-Believers with their wives and children lived for half a year in these parts. **1963** N. V. RIASANOVSKY *Hist. Russia* xix. 221 Shchapov and numerous others have stressed the social composition of the Old Believers and the social and economic reasons for their rebellion. **1973** *Guardian* 5 Mar. 2/7 The Soviet magazine Science and Religion..was criticising small groups of Old Believers.. in Tuvinskaya province.

Old Bill. The name of a cartoon character created during the war of 1914–18 by the British cartoonist Bruce Bairnsfather (1888–1959) and portrayed as a grumbling veteran soldier with a large moustache. Freq. in allusive and *transf.* use.

1915 *Bystander* III. 4 Again, 'Old Bill' and 'Our Bert' and 'Alf', seriously comical and comically serious, fill the pages with their humour. **1925** FRASER & GIBBONS *Soldier & Sailor Words* 213 *Old Bill*, a veteran. Any old Soldier; in particular one with a heavy, drooping moustache. (From Captain Bairnsfather's celebrated creation 'Old Bill'). **1930** *Daily Express* 6 Oct. 4/4 An enormous mouth fringed all around with stiff hairy bristles, just like an 'Old Bill' moustache. **1933** B. BAIRNSFATHER *Laughing through Orient* i. 15 Old Bill who, for many years, has been so closely entwined with my existence. **1939** H. HODGE *Cab, Sir?* 54 Here comes Old Bill himself. **1942** P. V. BRADSHAW *They make us Smile* 9 The creation of Old Bill was never deliberate. Bill somehow created himself. **1946** *R.A.F. Jrnl.* May 163 During the last war, Bruce Bairnsfather created 'Old Bill', a lovable grumbler, typifying the foot-slogger of the British Army in Flanders. **1973** *Times* 2 Nov. 13/7 The Old Bill moustache starts twitching.

old boy. [f. OLD *a.* + BOY *sb.*[1]] A former pupil of a (particular) boys' school, esp. an English public school. Also as quasi-*adj.* Hence **old-boyish** *a.*, characteristic or suggestive of an old boy; **old-boyishness.** Also used *attrib.* (influenced by OLD *a.* 8 a), *spec.* in **old boy(s') net(work),** to designate comradeship or favouritism shown among old boys; also *transf.*; **old boys' tie,** phr. suggesting attitudes or activities typical of old boys. See also *old girl* s.v. *GIRL *sb.* 2 a.

1868 *Haileyburian* I. 4/2 On Nov. 30th, was played our first *Old Boys* football match. **1894** A. BEARDSLEY *Let.* 2–3 Oct. (1971) 76, I had hoped to be at the Old Boys' dinner next month but I fear it is out of the question. **1910** H. G. WELLS *New Machiavelli* (1911) I. iii. 92 (*heading*) The school chapel; and how it seems to an old boy. **1920** BEERBOHM *And Even Now* 297 The accounts given to me by 'old boys' of other schools. **1931** 'G. TREVOR' *Murder at School* i. 16 'It is always a pleasure for Oakington to receive her old boys.'.. A little old-boyishness in response seemed clearly indicated... Within five minutes Revell had ceased to be old-boyish. **1936** 'G. ORWELL' *Keep Aspidistra Flying* iii. 57 He..developed unorthodox opinions about the C. of E., patriotism and the Old Boys' tie. **1959** 'J. BYROM' *Take only as Directed* viii. 88 'Well, blow me down!' I chose a phrase that seemed suitably Old Boy. **1959** *Guardian* 10 Nov. 8/4 The party must show that the Old Boy network of the Left does not prevent its speaking out when necessary. **1960** *Observer* 26 June 27/2 They write, therefore they are—that is, are part of literary history or, if the anthology is contemporary, part of the Old Boy circuit. **1960** *Punch* 10 Aug. 208/1 His [*sc.* Shakespeare's] marvellous understanding of the old-boy net as it was operated in the upper echelons of the Greek and Trojan armies. **1961** *Guardian* 19 Jan. 20/7 The atmosphere of old-boyishness and good-chappery which is a deadly threat to our society. **1964** *New Scientist* 24 Sept. 793/1 Dr. Bertrand Goldschmidt..managed to obtain, on an 'old boy basis', about 3 microgrammes of plutonium. **1970** *Wall St. Jrnl.* 30 Mar. 1/1 Management experts here see a decline [in Britain] in the 'Old Boy Network'. *Ibid.*, The Old Boy Net is being replaced by professional managers who take perks for granted. **1971** J. R. L. ANDERSON *Reckoning in Ice* vii. 143 To hanker after reunions, Old Boys' gatherings and the like suggests that nothing in one's later life has ever quite matched school. **1972** *Daily Tel.* (Colour Suppl.) 1 Dec. 40/4 There is a clubbish sort of old boys' net in The Room [at Lloyd's]. **1973** A. PRICE *October Men* xii. 178 The Russians don't go much on the old boys' network. **1975** *Times* 27 Feb. 14/8 The [Central Intelligence] Agency..is a cosy gentleman's club whose members have a strict code of their own... They operate on an old boy net, extensive if exclusive.

old chum: see CHUM *sb.*[1] 1 b (in Dict. and Suppl.).

Old Dart. *Austral.* and *N.Z. colloq.* [Origin uncertain: cf. DART *sb.* 7 (in Dict. and Suppl.).] The 'old country'; Great Britain, *esp.* England.

1908 E. S. SORENSON *Quinton's Rouseabout* 206 Murty unexpectedly came in for something like £800 by the death of a distant and almost forgotten relative in the old dart. **1933** *Bulletin* (Sydney) 13 Dec. 58/4 He was a forward in the British team of 1904, led by Bedell Sievwright, about the best side from the Old Dart to visit these shores. **1935** 'J. GUTHRIE' *Little Country* i. 6 The present generation..still finds under its skin a queer, rooted, and sometimes flowering love for the Old Dart. **1945** BAKER *Austral. Lang.* x. 184 He would be less maudlinly sentimental over *Home, the old country, the old dart,* or *the old land* as Britain was known. **1950** K. S. PRITCHARD *Winged Seeds* 357 'It means,' Dinny said slowly, 'that Australia's backin' the Old Dart with $31,500,000 worth of gold a year.' **1952** J. CLEARY *Sundowners* 157, I married her when I was over in the Old Dart during the war. **1966** 'J. HACKSTON' *Father clears Out* 143 If you'd come from the Old Dart yourself you'd have been the first to start chucking snow. **1973** *Austral. Women's Weekly* 25 July 79/3 Fresh from the Old Dart, I was as willing as they came. I wanted to write that success letter home to England.

olde (ōuld, ōu·ldi), *a.* An affected form of OLD *a.*, supposed to be archaic and usu. employed to suggest (spurious) antiquity, *esp.* in collocations often also archaistically spelt, as *olde English(e), Englyshe, worlde, worldy.* Also as *sb.*

Also *oldie, oldy.*

1927 C. CONNOLLY *Let.* 7 Mar. in *Romantic Friendship* (1975) 281 There remain consolations, such as finding places that aren't spoilt and not being surprised by their destruction into the..oldie worldie type. **1929** —— *Let.* [undated] in *Romantic Friendship* (1975) 325 Oldy-worldy England is such a dreary opposite [to America]. **1930** E. POUND *XXX Cantos* viii. 31 Ye spirits who of olde were in this land. **1931** M. ALLINGHAM *Look to Lady* v. 61 There's something so Olde English about you, Val, that I expect a chorus of rustic maidens. **1932** N. MITFORD *Christmas Pudding* v. 74 You just made the mistake..of confusing old world with olde worlde. You should have been more careful to find out whether or not there was an 'e'; so much hangs on that one little letter. **1933** A. G. MACDONELL *England, their England* vii. 101 It was as if Mr. Cochran had..brought Ye Olde Englyshe Village straight down by special train from the London Pavilion. **1934** C. LAMBERT *Music Ho!* V. 280 We..pour our bootleg gin into cracked leather bottles with olde-worlde labels. **1939** JOYCE *Finnegans Wake* I. 7 A glass of Danu U'Dunnell's foamous olde Dobbelin ayle. **1939** O. LANCASTER *Homes Sweet Homes* 10 All over Europe the lights are going out, oil-lamps, gas-mantles, electroliers, olde Tudor lanthorns, standards and wall-brackets. **1950** M. J. C. HODGART *Ballads* v. 106 We don't know what Percy's corrections were, but the Olde Englishe of this stanza may be suspected: Lord Thomas he saw Fair Annet wex pale. **1956** E. POUND tr. *Sophocles' Women of Trachis* 25 E'en from fond eyes, olde flowers are cast away. **1958** B. NICHOLS *Sweet & Twenties* viii. 105 The oldy-worldy cafés. **1959** *Good Food Guide* 38 A lot of olde realle beames in Amersham and a lot of olde phonie cookynge too. **1967** 'D. SHANNON' *Rain with Violence* (1969) i. 9 A little coffee shop... Decorated in very pseudo Olde Englishe. **1970** P. GEDDES *November Wind* viii. 95 Bear... An olde Englishe, where-did-you-put-my-cricket-bat teddy bear. **1972** *Guardian* 4 Dec. 11/3 The interior is old but not olde worlde, the medieval oak beams have been left..without..horse brasses and warming pans. **1974** 'P. B. YUILL' *Bornless Keeper* vii. 65 Why did we have to come..to this quaint olde aleshoppe? **1976** *Rhyl Jrnl. & Advertiser* 9 Dec. 18/6 (Advt.), Gwaenysgor. Charming stone built olde worlde Cottage of immense character.

Old English, *sb.* and *a.* **A.** *sb.* **1.** See ENGLISH *sb.* 1 b in Dict. and Suppl.

2. *Typog.* (In Dict. s.v ENGLISH *sb.* 6 b.) Also *attrib.* (Examples.)

1701 M. BULL *Let.* 12 June in *Private Corr. Samuel Pepys* (1926) II. 230 There is no picture in it, nor any thing writt in capital or Roman letters, but all printed in the old english letter. **1849** MRS. GASKELL *Let.* 7 Dec. (1966) 94 Two birch-wood rocking chairs, with 'Mina' & 'Sam' carved in old English on the back of each. **1883** in A. Adburgham *Shops & Shopping* (1964) xix. 226 Woven ingrain red initial letters, old English style; whole names in old English or script. **1950** M. ALLINGHAM *Mr. Campion & Others* 191 The embossed address..in semi-Old English script. **1966** S. MARCUS *Other Victorians* ii. 34 In the index [of *Index Librorum Prohibitorum*], authors' names are in Small Capitals, titles are in Old English. **1967** E. CHAMBERS *Photolitho-Offset* ii. 13 Text type faces are of the style worked almost exclusively by Gutenberg and are sometimes known as 'Old English'. **1967** B. COPPER *No Flowers for General* vii. 85 [There] was a large white-painted board. In black Old English lettering it said: Fitzgoerge [*sic*] Country Club. **1974** *Listener* 24 Jan. 98 In those days..mortgage deeds were written out ('engrossed') and the word 'mortgage' appeared in Old English lettering on the back sheet.

3. Old English sheep-dog, a large, thick-set dog of the breed so called, with a long, blue-grey and white coat; also known as the bob-tail. Also *absol.*

1890 R. B. LEE *Hist. & Descr. Collie* v. 81 The old English sheep dog was at one time pretty equally distributed through various parts of the kingdom. **1928** F. T. BARTON *Kennel Encycl.* 313 The type of old English sheep-dog varies considerably in different counties. **1971** F. HAMILTON *World Encycl. Dogs* 77 The Old English Sheepdog has been known as a distinct variety in Britain for at least two hundred years. The Old English is quite unlike the Collie varieties of sheepdog.

B. *adj.* Made by English craftsmen of an earlier period, esp., of table silver, made to a pattern used from the mid-18th century, with plain shapes and flat stems spreading to the rounded ends.

1907 *Yesterday's Shopping* (1969) 215/1 Nickel Silver, Old English Pattern, Spoons and Forks. *a* **1910** 'MARK TWAIN' *Autobiogr.* (1924) II. 93 Her prized and precious old-English sugar bowl..was an heirloom in the family. **1973** *Country Life* 15 Feb. 389/3 William Bateman..was making Old English teaspoons as late as the 1820s, a decade after the fiddle pattern became fashionable.

oldest, *a.* Add: **3.** Phr. *oldest inhabitant*; freq. in joc. use.

1850 HAWTHORNE *Scarlet Letter* 13 The whereabouts of the Oldest Inhabitant was at once settled, when I looked at them. **1859** 'L.N.R.' *Missing Link* x. 130 No bedstead has been seen there in the 'memory of the oldest inhabitant'. **1914** 'I. HAY' *Lighter Side School Life* iv. 105 The Wag and the Oldest Inhabitant are usually permitted to offer observations. **1926** CHESTERTON *Incredulity of Father Brown* v. 160 A curse on the place, according to the guide-book or the parson or the oldest inhabitant or whoever is the authority. **1950** 'J. TEY' *To Love & be Wise* xv. 196 The Oldest Inhabitant..was a vain old party but he was the representative..of..Race Memory. *a* **1966** M. ALLINGHAM *Cargo of Eagles* (1968) xii. 141 'The ancient mariner in the corner of The Demon?' enquired Campion. 'The professional oldest inhabitant?' **1974** E. LEMARCHAND *Buried in Past* xi. 187 Good Lord, look at the Oldest Inhabitant stepping in front of a moving car... the chap's managed to pull up.

old-face. *Typog.* [See FACE *sb.* 22.] A type-face characterized by a pleasingly irregular appearance with little contrast between thick and thin strokes and with bracketed serifs, modelled on the roman and italic letters that were derived from classical inscriptions and early humanist hands and used by printers of the 15th to 18th centuries. Also *attrib.* Also **old-faced** *a.*

[**1824** J. JOHNSON *Typographia* II. xix. 647 Such letter..could not possibly last so long as that of the old cut.] **1863** G. UNWIN (*title*) Specimens of the old-faced series of type in use at the Gresham Steam-press. **1875** *Caslon's Circular* July 1/1 He [*sc.* Charles Whittingham] was supplied by Mr. Caslon with the complete series of original old-face founts. *Ibid.*, There appeared in the market a modern imitation of the old-face character called Old Style. *Ibid.* 1/2 There followed a demand for the old-face founts. **1888** C. T. JACOBI *Printers' Vocab.* 90 Old-cut type, founts similar to the Caslon old-faced type. **1922** D. B. UPDIKE *Printing Types* II. xxi. 201 In England Caslon types are called 'old face'. **1923** MORISON & JACKSON *Brief Survey Printing* ii. 16 The raw material of the revival was ready as far back as the year 1720, when Caslon set up his type foundry and began the casting of the now famous old face founts which have become classical. **1931** *Times Lit. Suppl.* 25 June (Suppl.) p. i/2 Bold woodcuts stencilled with bright colours on a large page need stronger support than can be furnished by a quiet old-face in readable eleven-point. **1951** S. JENNETT *Making of Bks.* xii. 198 Text faces can be divided into two clear categories, known to the printer as 'old faces' and 'modern faces'; such types as had appeared up to and including Caslon..are grouped under the term 'old face'... The chief characteristic of old-face types is the fundamental relation of the line to that made by the pen. The stress is tilted..and the accent diminishes gradually into the thin stroke without obvious junction; exaggeration and artificial emphasis are generally avoided. **1972** P. GASKELL *New Introd. Bibliogr.* 210 The demand for the old faces came to an abrupt end. *Ibid.* 212 From the 1840s there was a gradually quickening revival of interest in old-face romans.

old-fashioned, *a.* Add: **1. a.** Also *absol.*

1904 *Daily Chron.* 7 Jan. 3/3 She..does not hesitate to lean to the old-fashioned if occasion require.

b. Of a plant, belonging to an old-established variety no longer common in cultivation.

1920 'O. DOUGLAS' *Penny Plain* i. 8 A herbaceous border..blazed in a sweet disorder of old-fashioned blossoms. **1939** S. SITWELL *Old Fashioned Flowers* i. 21 There can be more than a mere sentimental fondness for these old flowers. It is not enough that they are old-fashioned and in danger of being classed as quaint. **1960** F. C. STERN *Chalk Garden* v. 53 There are a number of 'old-fashioned' primroses which are great fun in the garden. **1975** R. GENDERS *Growing Old-fashioned Flowers* 7 In most cottage gardens there may still grow at least a few of the old-fashioned plants.

3. (Further examples.)

1858 R. M. BALLANTYNE *Coral Island* i. 11, I overheard them [*sc.* shipmates] sometimes saying that Ralph Rover was a 'queer, old-fashioned fellow'. **1972** J. WILSON *Hide & Seek* iv. 76 She's not very happy at school... She can seem irritating and annoying at times—she has this quaint old-fashioned sort of knowing air, and she asks the teachers lots of questions.

4. Disapproving, tart, reproachful: used *spec.* of facial expression. Also as *adv.*, in a disapproving, reproachful or quizzical manner. Freq. in phr. *to give* (someone) *an old-fashioned look, to look old-fashioned at* (someone).

Quot. 1911 may belong in sense 3.

1911 F. H. BURNETT *Secret Garden* xvii. 181 She.. examined them with a solemn savage little face. She looked so sour and old-fashioned that the nurse turned her head aside to hide the twitching of her mouth. *a* **1922** T. S. ELIOT *Waste Land Drafts* (1971) 13 No, ma'am, you needn't look old-fashioned at me. **1926** S. JAMESON *Three Kingdoms* vi. 154 Laurence listened, said: 'Oh. Bring her up in two minutes,' and gave Macdougal what he mentally classified as an old-fashioned look. **1933** E. WILLIAMS *Late Christopher Bean* II. 51, I was wrong thinking wrong things, and acting so old fashioned with you. **1935** *Archit. Rev.* LXXVII. 270/3 He straightened his back and gave me an old-fashioned look as who should say 'And I dare you to laugh at me in your damn superior way, blast you.' **1935** N. MARSH *Enter Murderer* vii. 83 'Don't you act old-fashioned at me,' snarled the man. **1943** P. CHEYNEY *You can always Duck* i. 15 She looks at me sorta old-fashioned. **1948** 'N. SHUTE' *No Highway* vi. 149 They'll probably look a bit old-fashioned at me. **1951** M. KENNEDY *Lucy Carmichael* VII. iv. 379 I've tried to tell her twice..and all I get is an old-fashioned look. **1959** 'R. SIMONS' *Houseboat Killings* xiii. 133 The commissionaire gave them an old-fashioned look as they spun the revolving doors, but it was lost on Wace. **1974** *Blackw. Mag.* Sept. 197/2 Comrade Supervisor gave her an old-fashioned look and answered: 'Lidia died the moment she fell, the moment she touched the ground.'

5. Special collocations: **old-fashioned cocktail** *U.S.*, a cocktail consisting principally of whisky, bitters, and sugar, served with ice; also *ellipt.*, as *old-fashioned*; **old-fashioned rose** = *OLD ROSE a; **old-fashioned waltz,** a waltz played in quick time; **old-fashioned winter,** a winter marked by snow and hard frost.

1901 *Cocktail Bk.* 27 (*heading*) Whiskey Cocktail—Old-fashioned. **1930** H. CRADDOCK *Savoy Cocktail Bk.* I. 114 Old Fashioned Cocktail. 1 Lump Sugar. 2 Dashes Angostura Bitters. 1 Glass Rye or Canadian Club Whisky. **1942** D. POWELL *Time to be Born* (1943) x. 237 He charged ten cents more for old-fashioneds than Bill's did. **1958** G. GREENE *Our Man in Havana* v. iii. 212 A Scotch, sir? A sherry? An Old-Fashioned? **1963** E. CLARKE *Shaking in 60's* 95 Old fashioned cocktail. Use a small heavy tumbler glass... Place in 1 lump of sugar..add a lump of ice.. pour into the prepared glass 2 measures of Bourbon. **1975** 'M. DUKE' *Death of Holy Murderer* ix. 111 We're drinking old-fashioneds beside the swimming pool. **1888** J. W. RILEY (*title*) Old-fashioned roses. **1889** *Garden* 6 July 14/3 If this conference does no more than further the cultivation of the many climbing and other old-fashioned Roses, it will have achieved a great object. **1937** C. SPRY *Flowers in House & Garden* 75 Grass paths divide large irregularly-shaped beds filled with..old-fashioned roses. **1962** A. CHRISTIE *Mirror Crack'd* i. 17 Laycock had cut down the old-fashioned roses in a way more suitable to hybrid teas. **1971** J. RAVEN *Botanist's Garden* vi. 120 We grow..four others of the showiest of the old-fashioned roses. **1927**

Melody Maker Aug. 787/2 The old-fashioned tango is not so dissimilar to the modern, and there are still many sincere lovers of the old-fashioned waltz left. **1952** M. Laski *Village* ii. 41 The Rhythm Ragamuffins were starting off with an old-fashioned waltz. **1865** M. Eyre *Lady's Walks S. of France* xvi. 189, I like an old-fashioned English winter—hard frosts and deep snows in their season. **1939** L. M. Montgomery *Anne of Ingleside* xiii. 86 We never seem to have old-fashioned winters nowadays.

old-fashionedly (earlier and later examples.)

1813 M. Edgeworth *Let.* 16 May (1971) 60 She is now huge and very plainly dressed old fashionedly but she must have been beautiful and graceful formerly. **1967** V. Gielgud *Conduct of Member* iii. 27, I don't see that we can ask for Lestrange's resignation because he's old-fashionedly moral. **1968** *Economist* 9 Nov. p. iii/3 He could be, obsessively and old-fashionedly, wrong. **1976** 'M. Albrand' *Taste of Terror* vii. 46 Kent had reacted old-fashionedly. If he lived with a woman..he would feel compelled to marry her.

old field. Add: **a.** (Earlier and further examples.)

1635 in *Amer. Legal Rec.* (Amer. Hist. Soc.) (1954) VII. 31 Mr. John wilkins made suit..for a neck of land..boundeth..northerly on Cugleyes ould field. **1839** *Southern Lit. Messenger* V. 113/1 First..no such foreigner has the faintest idea of what an old-field is. **1859** *Trans. Illinois Agric. Soc.* III. 452 In 1840 I became possessed of the tract of land containing what was called the 'old field'. **1905** *Forestry Bureau Bull.* (U.S.) No. 63, 5 The life history of second-growth white pine on old fields and pastures in New England. **1938** G. H. Collingwood in *Amer. Forests* Sept. 417 Pure stands of young Virginia pine frequently follow on old fields when agriculture is abandoned.

b. old-field birch, substitute for def.: one of several North American birches, esp. the white birch, *Betula populifolia*; (examples); **old-field mouse,** a white-footed, pale brown mouse, *Peromyscus polionotus,* found in sandy regions of the south-eastern U.S.A.; **old-field pine,** substitute for def.: one of several North American pines, esp. the loblolly pine, *Pinus tæda*; (earlier and later examples).

1810 F. A. Michaux *Hist. Arbres Forestiers de l'Amérique Septentrionale* I. 26 White birch [ou] Old field birch (Bouleau des terreins secs.). **1832** D. J. Browne *Sylva Amer.* 123 In the state of Maine,..[the name] Old Field Birch is..employed to distinguish the white birch from the canoe birch. **1946** W. D. Brush in *Amer. Forests* Sept. 431 This accounts for the tree quickly taking possession of burned-over, cutover and abandoned land, which has given it the name 'oldfield birch'. **1921** A. H. Howell in *N. Amer. Fauna* XLV. 44 The little old-field mouse occurs rather commonly in suitable situations throughout the eastern, central, and northeastern parts of the State [of Alabama]. **1936** *Jrnl. Mammalogy* XVII. 420 A number of breeding stocks of old-field mice..were collected in parts of Alabama and Florida. **1971** *Nature* 12 Nov. 102/2 Crosses of *Peromyscus maniculatus,* the deermouse, and *P. polionotus,* the oldfield mouse,..showed that placental weights of foetuses..differed significantly from each other. **1797** B. Hawkins *Let.* 23 Feb. (1916) 89 The whole grown up with old field pine, some of them a foot and a half diameter. **1841** *Southern Lit. Messenger* VII. 452/1 The old-field pine had not intruded so largely on the domain of the ploughman and reaper. **1894** J. M. Coulter *Bot. W. Texas* III. 554 *Pinus Taeda*... Extending from the Gulf States to the valley of the Colorado. 'Loblolly pine.' 'Old-field pine.' **1967** N. T. Mirov *Genus Pinus* ii. 118 This tendency of pines to occupy newly exposed ground can be observed even now in abandoned fields ('old field pine' is the common name for *P. tæda*).

c. *old-field colt, ground, plum, preacher, school, school-master, scrub.*

1835 *Southern Lit. Messenger* I. 582, I could..only remember that every untrimmed old field colt was a regular descendant of Eclipse. **1772** in *Maryland Hist. Mag.* (1919) XIV. 278 Our corn..is very good at all the quarters, some of this old field ground..excepted. **1887** *Harper's Mag.* Sept. 588/2 She been goin' out..betewen times, and getherin' old-field plums. **1904** T. Watson *Bethany* II. iii. 168 The tremendous emphasis with which the old field preacher uttered the words. **1834** W. A. Caruthers *Kentuckian in N.Y.* I. 26 He sold his horse and cart too, and then turned into keepin an old-field school. **1853** J. G. Baldwin *Flush Times Alabama* 125 The master of the old field school was one of the regular faculty. **1948** E. N. Dick *Dixie Frontier* 172 Schools... located on worn-out cultivated areas, were called 'old field' schools. **1853** J. G. Baldwin *Flush Times Alabama* 106 He had been an old-field schoolmaster. **1834** W. A. Caruthers *Kentuckian in N.Y.* I. 12, I bet you my horse Talleyrand..against an old field scrub.

old girl: see Girl *sb.* 2a in Dict. and Suppl.

old gold: see Gold[1] 8b in Dict. and Suppl.

oldhamite. Substitute for etym.: [f. the name of Thomas *Oldham* (1816–1878), director of the Indian Geological Survey + -ite[1].] (Earlier example.)

1863 *Rep. Brit. Assoc. Adv. Sci. 1862* App. 11 In it [*sc.* an aërolite] Mr. Maskelyne has detected a mineral to which he gives the name of Oldhamite—a yellow transparent body of cubic crystallization.

old hat. *slang.* [Old *a.* + Hat *sb.*] Something considered to be old-fashioned, out of date, or unoriginal. Also *attrib.* or as *adj.*

1911 A. Quiller-Couch *Brother Copas* iv. 78 Men have ..put it, with like doctrines, silently aside in disgust. So it has happened with Satan and his fork: they have become 'old hat'. **1916** D. H. Lawrence *Let.* 19 Feb. (1962) I. 433 The whole of the consciousness and the conscious content is old hat—the millstone round your neck. **1920** ——*Touch & Go* I. i. 21 *Oliver.* What was the address about, to begin with? *Willie.* Oh, the same old hat—Freedom. **1932** G. B. Shaw *Platform & Pulpit* (1962) 250 If I mention that sort of thing I am told that is old hat, that I am a back number. **1940** R. Chandler *Farewell, my Lovely* xxi. 98 We curved..past the Georgian-Colonial vogue, now old hat, past the handsome modernistic buildings. **1944** W. Stevens *Let.* 12 Sept. (1967) 474 This is all growing to be old hat now, and I am eager..to go on to something else. **1959** N. Kneale *Quatermass Experiment* III. 82 All pious generalizations, plus old-hat background waffle. **1959** *Observer* 5 Apr. 18/3, I suppose we couldn't possibly revive 'The Nymph'? Too old hat. **1960** J. MacLaren-Ross *Until Day she Dies* ii. 30 This drammer ..that's sure going to make *A Hatful of Rain* look just like a handful of old hat. **1961** *Listener* 16 Nov. 826/1 Today's contemp'ry is tomorrow's old-hat. **1963** *Ibid.* 3 Jan. 45/2 The late-romantic style of performance is now regarded as 'ham' and 'old hat'. **1970** *New Scientist* 5 Mar. 476/2 Those who have been told that they belong to an 'old-hat' arts culture are now looking to climb on a 'new-hat' science-culture bandwagon. **1974** V. Gielgud *In Such a Night* xii. 110 She..had made all jokes on the subject of mothers-in-law not only 'old hat' but..meaningless.

old identity. *Austral.* and *N.Z.*: see *identity 7.

oldie (ōu·ldi). *colloq.* Also **oldy.** [f. Old *a.* + -ie (see -y[6]).] **1.** An old or elderly person; an adult; an 'old hand'. Freq. in ironical contexts.

1874 L. Troubridge *Life amongst Troubridges* (1966) 89 We scurried off pretty quick, leaving all the oldies buried in spiders' nests (not their bodies but their minds). *Ibid.* 97, I am now in my seventeenth year, isn't it sad? I shall soon be an 'oldy'. I shan't wear a cap. **1936** *Silver Screen* Feb. 64 Ruthie is..upset at the thought of her sister marrying such an oldie as Mr. Kruger. **1957** W. Camp *Prospects of Love* ix. 183 Of course Mrs. Lawrence must come too. She would keep the 'oldies' company. **1959** C. MacInnes *Absolute Beginners* 10 As for me, eighteen summers, rising nineteen, I'll very soon be out there among the oldies. **1959** *Encounter* Oct. 73/2 As for me, as an oldie and a taxpayer I dig this book. **1968** *Blues Unlimited* Dec. 26 The artists here are 'oldies, but goodies'. **1971** *Daily Tel.* 12 May 14/6 To oldies over 30, the mere phrase 'alternative society' is liable to be a cause for instant apoplexy. **1972** J. Brown *Chancer* xv. 199 We've got our rights, haven't we, same as the oldies.

2. Something old or familiar; an old song, tune, film, etc. Also, an old or well known idea or suggestion.

1940 *Amer. Speech* XV. 205/1 *Oldies,* old tunes or films. **1951** *Daily Progress* (Charlottesville, Va.) 17 Dec. 3/5 If your old jalopy is cranky and has been acting up under the stresses of urban life, maybe you ought to retire it to Prudence Island... Real oldies are just the thing on Prudence Island. **1955** W. Gaddis *Recognitions* II. iv. 475 Here's an oldie, friends, Rudy Vallee singing, *Love Made a Gypsy Out of Me.* **1959** 'O. Mills' *Stairway to Murder* xv. 157 'But fiddling with the clock-face—what an oldie!' ..'It's so well-worn, I don't think anyone'd still have the nerve to pull it.' **1962** *John o' London's* 4 Jan. 18/1 Then there is the slightly more dubious pleasure of watching goodish oldie films like *Rebecca.* **1970** E. Lee *Music of People* xiv. 236 These tunes..are frequently rehashed as new versions of 'good old oldies'. **1972** *Guardian* 22 May 11/1 The arguments against? To begin with, an oldie: do you punish an effect or cure the cause? **1972** *Practical Motorist* Oct. 162/1 On recirculatory heaters—used on the 'oldies'—a rheostat switch controls the speed of the fan. **1973** *Times* 29 Nov. (Christmas Bk. Suppl.) p. ii/5 Those two golden oldies, *Frenchman's Creek* and *Jamaica Inn.* **1975** *Listener* 9 Jan. 57/1 Dragging up old revue skits.. patter songs..golden oldies ('These Foolish Things'), one-liners and sketches. **1975** *Ibid.* 10 Apr. 486/1 There you are, sitting in your lovely home..watching a late-night oldie.

old land. a. *dial.* Also **olland, ollunt.** Land newly ploughed after having been uncultivated for some time; also, arable land sown with grass for a period of more than two years.

1674 J. Ray *Coll. Eng. Words* 73 Old land: ground that hath layn untilled long time and is new plowed up. Suff[olk]. **1788** *Ann. Agric.* IX. 429 The following is the former [crop rotation]: 1 and 2. Ollond, or lay of two years, 3. Wheat or oats on one earth, 4. Turnips, 5. Barley. **1882** in *N. & Q.* 18 Nov. 406/2 It was the land ploughed out of grass (out-land), which was known as olland. **1895** P. H. Emerson *Birds, Beasts, & Fishes Norf. Broadland* 8 Newlays and ollunts close by the marsh farmhouse. **1909** *Eastern Daily Press* (Norwich) 23 Jan. 8/1 Oats also do much better on an olland than on loose land.

b. *U.S.* Land that has been in cultivation for a long time, or land exhausted by a long period of cultivation.

1715 in *Amer. Speech* (1940) XV. 290/2 At the Corner of the said Jones's old land. **1748** J. Eliot *Essay Field-Husbandry New Eng.* 16 The third sort of Land I would speak of is our old Land which we have worn out. **1833** B. Silliman *Man. Sugar Cane* 10 Violet cane..prefers old land, and that which is rather dry. **1872** *Rep. Indian Affairs 1871* (U.S.) 230 It is my intention, during the coming season, to..summer-fallow as much of the old land as can be spared from cultivation. **1919** D. L. Cady *Rhymes Vermont Rural Life* 67, I learnt soon after I was born To never use 'old land' for corn.

c. *Geol.* Usu. as one word. Land which lies behind a coastal plain of more recent origin, esp. where the coastal plain has been built up from sedimentary material derived from that same land; also, an area of very ancient crystalline rocks, esp. when reduced to low relief. Also *attrib.*

1895 *Geogr. Jrnl.* V. 133 The old-land streams..are extended across the new coastal plain by the addition of consequent lower courses. **1897** *Ibid.* IX. 538 For convenience all the land back of this initial shoreline will be called the 'oldland', and all alluvial accumulation built in front of the oldland..will be called 'foreland'. **1903** *Jrnl. Geol.* XI. 617 The Canadian shield of Suess..marks the site of the oldland area from which the materials of the later sedimentary deposits were derived. **1937** [see *fall zone* s.v. *fall *sb.*[1] 29]. **1939** A. K. Lobeck *Geomorphol.* xiv. 447 It [*sc.* a coastal plain] may rest upon an oldland of simple structure or of complex structure. **1957** *Geogr. Jrnl.* CXXIII. 503 Observations carried out on the Dartmoor tract of the oldland of south-west England.

Old Left. [Old *a.* 12.] The name given to older liberal elements in the socialist movement, as distinct from the more radical *New Left. So **Old Leftist,** a member or supporter of the Old Left.

1960 *New Left Rev.* Sept.–Oct. 11/2 Side by side with the Old Left—and, at the present moment, 'objectively' reinforcing it—is a New Left, growing in strength. **1967** *Time* 21 Apr. 15 New York police on horseback—in contrast with the 'Cossack' image so many Old Leftists apply to them—kept the countermarchers from breaking up the parade. *Ibid.* 28 Apr. 14 The Old Left organized and proselyted, playing its part in bringing about the American welfare state. **1968** *Harper's Mag.* May 65 The New Left is, of course, an enormously diverse group, ranging from slightly disguised representatives of the Old Left to political fauna so bizarre as to defy classification. **1971** *N.Y. Times* 7 June 31 Daniel instead produces notes toward an autobiographical novel about his Old-Left parents.

oldly, *adv.* Delete '† *Obs.*' and substitute '*rare*'. Add later examples.

1910 W. de la Mare *Three Mulla-Mulgars* xviii. 241 'On his woman-hand stood no fourth finger.' 'Was the little woman-finger newly gone, or oldly gone?' **1922** Joyce *Ulysses* 34 He raised his forefinger and beat the air oldly before his voice spoke. **1960** 'A. Burgess' *Doctor is Sick* 244 He chuckled oldly.

old maid. Add: **3. b.** *U.S.* The velvet-leaf or Indian mallow, *Abutilon theophrasti,* or a zinnia, *Z. elegans.*

1839 *Southern Lit. Messenger* V. 751/2 A particular spot in his garden was appropriated to the culture of old maids. **1880** *Scribner's Monthly* May 101/2 In my section an annoying weed is *Abutilon,* or velvet-leaf, also called 'old maid'. **1888** *Century Mag.* XXXVI. 896/1 The flower-garden overrun with..four-o'clocks, old-maids, and sunflowers.

4. (Examples.)

1831 E. Leslie *Amer. Girl's Bk.* 144 *Old Maid*...When played by girls, three of the queens must be put away as useless. **1874** L. Troubridge *Life amongst Troubridges* (1966) ix. 89 After dinner..we had to begin a stodgy game of Old Maid, just us two. **1959** [see *heart *sb.* 24b].

Hence **old-mai·ddom** = *old maidhood*; **old-maidenhood** (earlier examples); **old-mai·dishly** *adv.*, in the manner of an old maid; **old-maidishness** (further examples); **old-mai·dy** *a.* = *old-maidish* adj.

1920 D. H. Lawrence *Lost Girl* vi. 93 She was withering towards old-maiddom. **1847** A. Brontë *Agnes Grey* ix. 144 Never marry at all, not even to escape the infamy of old-maidenhood. **1889** C. M. Yonge *Reputed Changeling* II. xxvii. 184 Old maidenhood came earlier then than in these days. **1975** 'P. Loraine' *Ask the Rattlesnake* II. viii. 239 Clifford tut-tutted old maidishly. **1907** G. B. Shaw *Major Barbara* Pref. 185 Here am I,..economically disposed to the limit of old-maidishness. **1950** M. Peake *Gormenghast* xviii. 112 In spite of his old-maidishness, his clipped and irritatingly academic delivery.., he had a strongly developed sense of the ridiculous. **1975** J. Symons *Three Pipe Problem* xvi. 152 With precise old-maidishness he took a small key from his watchchain. **1884** 'Mark Twain' *Huck. Finn* xxxv. 357 Whoever heard of getting a prisoner loose in such an old-maidy way as that? **1905** J. C. Lincoln *Partners of Tide* i. 8 The old maids are pretty conscientious, spite of their bein' so everlastin' 'old maidy'. **1923** U. L. Silberrad *Lett. J. Armiter* xiii. 253 She is much nicer and better really than I, in my old-maidy prejudice, used to think.

old man. Add: **1. a.** (Further examples.)

Also *U.S.* in *old man eloquent,* applied after Milton's phrase (see quot. *c*1645 in Dict.) to John Quincy Adams (1767–1848), sixth President of the United States.

1839 C. M. Kirkland *New Home* xii. 75 'I reckon you'd ha' done better to have waited till the old man got back.' 'What old man?' asked I... 'Why, *your* old man to be sure,' said he laughing. I had yet to learn that in Michigan, as soon as a man marries he becomes 'th'old man'. **1846** *Brackenridge's Mod. Chivalry* (rev. ed.) I. xxiii. 114 You are welcome, Sir, if you wish to stop..though since my old man's time, we don't take in strangers for common. **1846** *Quincy* (Illinois) *Whig* 3 Mar. 2/3 We should suppose that the 'old man eloquent', would pause in his career, and look about him. **1848** *Congress. Globe* 24 Feb. 388 Let not the grave of the old man eloquent be desecrated by unfriendly remembrances. **1871** E. Eggleston *Hoosier Schoolmaster* (1872) iii. 28 My ole man's purty well along in the world. **1900** *Congress. Rec.* 25 Jan. 1208/1

John Quincy Adams, the 'Old Man Eloquent', expressed very happily what we now..believe. **1901** S. E. White *Claim Jumpers* i. 4 He's been pestering the old man to send him West. Old man doesn't approve. **1914** 'Bartimeus' *Naval Occasions* xix. 171 Not bad work,..bagging your Old Man's ship. **1932** [see *kid *v.*[4]]. **1946** R. Allen *Home Made Banners* xiii. 163 My old man says Quebec or no Quebec they'll have to send the Zombies over. **1974** 'J. Le Carré' *Tinker, Tailor* vi. 47 She was a sight better qualified than her old man.

b. (Earlier and later examples.)

1835 N. Ames *Old Sailor's Yarns* 53 The commander of a merchantman, although perhaps under twenty years of age, is invariably called the 'old man', by all hands on board. **1840** R. H. Dana *Two Yrs. before Mast* xxxi. 374 The 'old man'..was determined to carry sail till the last minute. **1845** *Knickerbocker* XXVI. 206 I've known the Old Man come on deck at midnight. **1873** 'Mark Twain' & Warner *Gilded Age* iv. 44 The 'old man' was the captain—he is always so, on steamboats and ships. **1897** Kipling *Capt. Cour.* vii. 143 The *Jennie Cushman*..cut clean in half—graound up an' trompled on at that! Not a quarter of a mile away. Dad's got the old man. **1916** 'Taffrail' *Pincher Martin* v. 68 Having a sherry-and-bitters with 'the old man'. **1924** 'P. Blundell' *Confessions of Seaman* ii. 22 You'd better come along and see the 'old man' now. He's just off ashore. **1958** N. Marsh *Singing in Shrouds* (1959) ix. 184 Did you ever know such a *bloody* Old Man! **1968** *Daily Tel.* 14 Aug. 15/4 'It was just like a furnace,' said Mr. Martin Jones, deckhand, of Slough, Bucks. 'The old man was grand.'

b*. Hence applied in the other Services to a commanding officer.

1830 J. P. Martin *Narr. Adventures Rev. Soldier* viii. 190 They and some others of the men..were about to have some fun with 'the old man', as they generally called the Captain. **1890** Kipling *Life's Handicap* (1891) 41 An' whin I'm let off in ord'ly-room through some thrick of the tongue an' a ready answer an' the ould man's mercy, is ut smilin' I feel? **1917** A. G. Empey *Over Top* 311 '*The Old Man*', captain of a company. He is called 'the old man', because generally his age is about twenty-eight. **1942** *R.A.F. Jrnl.* 3 Oct. 24 It was preposterous to think of the Old Man on a bicycle... The idea of the Old Man riding a bicycle set us back a long way. **1948** Partridge *Dict. Forces' Slang* 131 *Old Man*, the Commanding Officer. The Air Force gets it from the Army, which gets it from the Navy, which gets it from the Merchant Service. **1967** *Everybody's Mag.* (Austral.) 18 Jan. 36/2 Today, in Vietnam, Australians are again catching up on American Army Slang... The Company Commanding Officer is a CCO or the Old Man—even if he's all of 23. **1977** 'D. MacNeil' *Wolf in Fold* xiii. 137 The Old Man had commanded longer than most lieutenant-colonels.

d. *old man of the mountain(s)* [tr. Arab. *šaiḵ-al-jibal*], (*a*) name applied to Hasan ibu-al-Sabbah, founder of the Assassins (see Assassin 1) and his successors; (*b*) applied allusively to other political murderers, and *fig.* to persons of ruthless ambition; (*c*) a rock formation resembling the face of an old man.

1579 J. Frampton tr. *Marco Polo's Travels* xvii. 27 That way,..could not be travelled to Crerima for the crueltie of the king of that countrie,..from whome fewe coulde scape, but eyther were robbed or slayne. And for this cause manye kings did paye him tribute, and hys name is as muche to saye, as the olde man of the mountayne. **1625** Purchas *Pilgrimes* III. i. iv. 72 Hauing spoken of the Countrey, the old man of the Mountayne shall bee spoken of, of whom Marco heard much from many. His name was Aloadine, and was a Mahumetan... Aloadine had certaine Youthes from twelve to twentie yeares of age,..other Lords and his Enemies were slaine by these his Assasines. **1773** W. Jones *Hist. Life Nader Shah* p. xiii, It may be worth while to remark in this place, that the Old man of the mountain, who is mentioned in our accounts of the Crusades, was no other than a Prince of the Ismaëlian family. **1777** J. Richardson *Dict. Persian, Arabic & Eng.* p. xvi/1 He was stabbed by a Batanist, one of the subjects of the Old Man of the Mountain; whilst he was reading a petition which the assassin had presented. **1792** H. Walpole *Let.* 4 Sept. (1905) XV. 138 A whole senate has assumed the accursed dignity of the 'Old Man of the Mountain', and spawned a legion of assassins. **1818** W. Marsden tr. *Trav. Marco Polo* I. xxi. 112 (*heading*) Of the old man of the mountain; of his palace and gardens; of his capture and his death. *Ibid.* 114 There was no person however powerful, who having become exposed to the enmity of the Old man of the mountain, could escape assassination. **1837** H. Martineau *Society in Amer.* I. ii. 220 Our party..was..struck with the romance of the domestic history of the old man of the mountain, as the guide is called. **1871** *N.Y. Herald* 6 Sept. 6/6 It seems as if 'the Old Man of the Mountains' [*sc.* Brigham Young] meant to fight every step of the federal government for the supremacy of Utah. **1888** Kipling *In Black & White* (1889) 67 He might have been the original Old Man of the Mountains. **1905** H. W. C. Davis *Eng. under Normans & Angevins* xi. 308 An Arab writer lays the blame on Saladin, affirming that he had offered the chief of the Assassins, the Old Man of the Mountain, a heavy bribe. **1934** A. Huxley *Beyond Mexique Bay* 80 The lessons of Loyola and the Old Man of the Mountain. **1936** J. Buchan *Island of Sheep* vi. 118 Desperadoes who had crushed their lives were in-spanned in Castor's sense... like the servants of the Old Man of the Mountain in the Crusades. **1939** G. B. Pickwell *Deserts* 48/2 The devil's garden is well named: with boulders and 'barrels' and 'Old Men of the Mountain' it is a grotesque feature of the land of sun and wind and freakish rain. **1957** *Encycl. Brit.* II. 554/1 Before long perfervid imaginations detected the hand of the Old Man of the Mountain in political murders and attempts even in Europe. **1965** J. Fleming *Nothing is Number* i. ii. 21 You are great *assassins*,..the word itself is your very own, it comes from the Arabic *hashshash*, dating from the Crusades when your old sheik, Old Man of the Mountains, sent out his Moslem fanatics to kill the Christian leaders. They filled themselves with *hashish* to get themselves in the right mood.

e. *old man of the sea*: in the story of Sinbad the Sailor in the *Arabian Nights*, the sea-god who forced Sinbad to carry him on his shoulders for many days and nights until he was thwarted by being made so drunk that he toppled off. Hence, allusively, a person of whose company one may not easily be rid; a heavy and encumbering burden, esp. in *fig.* use. Also *attrib.*

1712 tr. *Arabian Nights' Entertainments* (ed. 2) III. lxxxiv. 57 You fell say they into the Hands of the old Man of the Sea, and are the first that ever escap'd strangling by him. **1809** W. Scott *Let.* 7 Aug. in J. G. Lockhart *Scott* (1837) II. vii. 252 About three years ago I accepted the office I hold in the Court of Session, the revenue to accrue to me only on the death of the old incumbent. But my friend has since taken out a new lease of life... Such odious deceivers are these invalids. Mine reminds me of Sindbad's Old Man of the Sea, and will certainly throttle me if I can't somehow dismount him. **1850** C. M. Yonge *Henrietta's Wish* viii. 112 Uncle Roger has got hold of him, and he is as bad as the old man of the sea. **1856** G. Meredith *Let.* 15 Dec. (1970) I. 28 The *Dulness* is something frightful, and hangs on my shoulders like Sinbad's old Man of the Sea. **1874** M. Clarke *His Natural Life* (1875) I. 9 The old-man-of-the-sea burden of parsimony and avarice which he had voluntarily taken upon him was not to be shaken off. **1899** *Strand Mag.* Mar. 308/1 When a man once gets a Cavalanci and plays to it, it sticks to him like the Old Man of the Sea. **1904** G. Stratton-Porter *Freckles* iii. 54 Again Freckles' 'old man of the sea' sat sullen and heavy on his shoulders and weighed him down until his step lagged and his heart ached. **1927** *Times* 22 July 15/4 The bad habit into which we slip almost unconsciously fixes itself about our necks as firmly as any Old Man of the Sea. **1947** M. Lowry *Under Volcano* ix. 281 What could she do under the weight of such a heritage? How could she rid herself of this old man of the sea? **1957** C. F. MacIntyre *Stephane Mallarmé: Selected Poems* p. viii, Mallarmé has been like the Old Man of the Sea, like the Biblical poor. There's no getting rid of him! **1965** N. Freeling *Criminal Conversation* ii. xx. 186, I am tired. I find you like the Old Man of the Sea. **1971** A. Price *Alamut Ambush* xiv. 169 'He's a man who likes to use others to do his own work. He likes to ride on other people's backs.' The Old Man of the Sea, thought Roskill.

f. *Theatr.* An actor playing the role of an old man, *esp.* one who specializes in such roles. Also, the role itself. Cf. *old woman 1 c.

1747 T. Whincop *Scanderbeg* 243/1 An Actor of great Humour in low Comedy, especially in the Parts of Old Men. **1762** J. Love *Let.* 5 July in D. Garrick *Private Corr.* (1831) I. 144 His feeble old men, which he has only tried one season, will increase your hopes. **1775** T. Holcroft *Let.* 1 June in *Mem.* (1816) I. ii. iv. 236, I have succeeded best in low comedy and old men. **1794** C. Mathews *Let.* 3 Aug. in A. Mathews *Mem. Charles Mathews* (1838) I. 101 He is a very respectable performer in a general line, but mostly 'old men'. **1849** *Theatrical Mirror* 24 Sept. 31 Mr. Basil Baker..is engaged for the first old men at Drury Lane. **1901** C. Morris *Life on Stage* vii. 39 A company was generally made up of a leading man.., first old man, second old man, heavy man, first comedian, [etc.]. **1957** *Oxf. Compan. Theatre* (ed. 2) 772/1 The old stock company was formed of a group of actors each of whom undertook some special line of business... The Old Man played Sir Anthony Absolute and Sir Peter Teazle, and was a person of consequence.

g. A person set in authority over others: a master, overseer, or foreman; a superintendent or senior official; a 'boss'.

1837 *Southern Lit. Messenger* III. 86, I say, darkie, the old man keeps good liquor, and plenty of belly timber, don't he? **1844** *Knickerbocker* XXIII. 83 The 'old man' himself came to the door, and looking down at his apprentice, shook his head sorrowfully. **1845** E. J. Wakefield *Adventure N.Z.* I. xi. 331 Tommy Evans, the 'old man' who headed the principal station, started..to get on board. **1887** C. B. George *40 Yrs. on Rail* ix. 167 They feel that if they can only lay it before the 'old man' it will be properly dealt with. **1913** C. E. Mulford *Coming of Cassidy* xii. 197 'Is there any chance to get a job here?' he asked anxiously. 'You'll have to quiz th' Old Man.' **1921** H. G. Wells *Grisly Folk* in *Story-Teller* Apr. 14/1 There was no Old Man who was lord and master and father of this particular crowd. **1935** A. J. Pollock *Underworld Speaks* 82/2 *Old man*, the big underworld boss; boss politician. **1949** W. Hertrich *Huntington Bot. Gardens* 32, I declined to accept it, but suggested that he deduct this amount 'from the Old Man's bill'. **1958** 'Castle' & 'Hailey' *Flight into Danger* x. 137 Is that you, Dave? Harry. Surprise for you—the Old Man is on the line. **1967** E. & M. A. Radford *No Reason for Murder* xii. 80 The Old Man is the traditional police name for a Chief Constable. **1974** 'P. B. Yuill' *Bornless Keeper* xiii. 119 Has the old man been on? He'll be wanting to ask your old mates at the Yard for help. *Ibid.*, The old man wants to hear a progress report.

h. Substituted familiarly for 'old Mr.—'. orig. and chiefly *U.S.*

1843 'R. Carlton' *New Purchase* I. 92 It ain't more nor a mile to ole-man Sturgisses. **1859** Bartlett *Dict. Amer.* (ed. 2) 301 In the South and West, instead of saying.. 'Old Mr. Smith', it is customary to say, 'Old man Smith'. **1862** R. R. Butler *Let.* 8 Jan. in *Congress. Globe* (4 Mar. 1868) 1664/1, I send a few lines to you by old man Jesse Price. **1902** A. D. McFaul *Ike Glidden* xvii. 126 There is old man Spencer who had always been poor. **1930** *Chicago Daily Maroon* 28 Oct. 1/3 Old Man Stagg spoke a few words in commending..the students for their show of enthusiasm. **1949** [see *old *a.* 8 c]. **1961** 'E. Lathen' *Banking on Death* (1962) xv. 123 Old man Michaels didn't like him.

i. *slang.* The penis.

1902 Farmer & Henley *Slang* V. 99/1 *Old man*,..the penis. **1968** R. Lait *Chance to Kill* xxii. 139 There was David getting out of bed in his shirt, his old man hanging out. **1971** B. W. Aldiss *Soldier Erect* 23 She had been opening up her legs before the reprise. Those glorious mobile buttocks... I felt my old man perking up again at the memory.

j. *fig.* Applied to things; spec. *Old Man River*, the Mississippi (see also quot. 1932).

1910 W. M. Raine *Bucky O'Connor* iii. 37 When Old Man Trouble comes knocking at the door. **1919** C. P. Thompson *Cocktails* 252 Why, being officially booked to meet Old Man Death on ground, I had kept the appointment in the air. **1927** Kern & Hammerstein (*song-title*) Old man river. **1932** *Sun* (Baltimore) 24 Sept. 16/3 Old Man River Sinking... The north branch of the Susquehanna river is lower than it was 112 years ago. **1933** *Lit. Digest* 12 Aug. 28/2 (*heading*) Who Owns Old Man River? **1649** *Natural Hist.* Nov. 427/3 At last they have succeeded in vaulting the natural barriers between the Great Lakes and Old Man River. **1976** B. Bova *Multiple Man* v. 55 St. Louis is a dull town... Old Man River is wide and sluggish.

4. b. *Austral.* and *N.Z. slang.* Used *attrib.* to denote the largeness or significance of the thing specified; freq. of animals (see also sense 4a in Dict.).

1834 G. Bennett *Wanderings New South Wales* I. xv. 286 Many persons when alone are afraid to face a large 'old man' Kangaroo. **1845** R. Howitt *Impressions Australia Felix* 233, I stared at a man one day for saying that a certain allotment of land was 'an old man allotment': he meant a large allotment, the old-man kangaroo being the largest kangaroo. **1866** R. Henning *Let.* 18 July (1966) 226 Spring, a very fine kangaroo dog we have here, killed ..an old-man kangaroo about five feet high. **1888** D. Macdonald *Gum Boughs* 7 Who that has ridden across the Old Man Plain. **1902** Kipling *Just So Stories* 87 Still ran Kangaroo—Old Man Kangaroo... He ran till his hind legs ached. **1906** E. Dyson *Fact'ry 'Ands* xv. 199 Two 'underd ole-man rats that 'ad bin glued on t'Bunyip in mortil combat. **1930** J. Devanny *Bushman Burke* i. ii. 17 [He] had once taken an Old Man pig with a slasher. **1934** A. Russell *Tramp-Royal in Wild Austral.* xxix. 190 An 'Old Man' sand storm. Lashed up and hurried along by a forty-mile-an-hour gale..an inferno of swishing sand and gravel..in Central Australia. **1936** I. L. Idriess *Cattle King* xii. 107 The river-bed is indicated by wide flats, mostly lignum bush, by big old-man coolabahs, and big old gums in places. **1941** —— *Great Boomerang* xi. 82 Fifteen years may pass before an old man flood brings a miracle to the land. **1945** Baker *Austral. Lang.* xiv. 244 Especially heavy gales of this type are often called *old man southerlies* or *old man busters*. **1947** J. Stevenson-Hamilton *Wild Life S. Afr.* xxxi. 259, I was the owner of a large boarhound which killed a great many 'old men' baboons. **1953** A. Upfield *Murder must Wait* xviii. 157 An old-man red-gum growing close to the track. **1965** [see *dogger[4]]. **1972** P. Newton *Sheep Thief* ii. 17 The homestead..was fringed with a towering belt of real old-man pines. **1973** 'D. Shannon' *No Holiday for Crime* (1974) 78 You're going to be like Old Man Kangaroo, my girl. As per Mr. Kipling. Very truly sought after.

5. (Later examples.)

1920 E. Thomas *Collected Poems* 97 Old Man, or Lad's-love—in the name there's nothing To one that knows not Lad's-love, or Old Man, The hoar-green feathery herb. **1973** F. A. Boddy *Foliage Plants* iv. 62 Old world charm and sentimentality can be further satisfied with the grey, feathery, aromatic leaves of *Artemisia abrotanum*, commonly called southernwood, lad's love or old man.

7. old man salt-bush, an Australian shrub, *Atriplex nummularia*, of the family Chenopodiaceæ, used as food for sheep in dry areas.

1880 W. A. Dixon in *Jrnl. & Proc. R. Soc. New South Wales* XIV. 140 The order in which the salt-bushes proper are considered to stand from a grazier's point of view are 1st, *A. numularia* [*sic*], or old man salt-bush. **1903** 'T. Collins' *Such is Life* 16 He disappeared in the timber and old-man salt-bush. **1933** *Bulletin* (Sydney) 14 June 25/1 Old-man saltbush is a rapid grower and gives more fodder in drought-time than any other tree. **1954** B. Miles *Stars my Blanket* x. 58 A great valley, the floor..thickly covered with Old Man Saltbush. **1965** *Austral. Encycl.* VII. 541/2 The round-leaved *Atriplex nummularia* (old-man or cabbage saltbush) is one of the tallest species and may reach 10 feet in height.

8. old man's beard (earlier and later examples).

1742 W. Ellis *Mod. Husbandman* June vi. 67 In this Month [*sc.* June], be sure to cut..what we in Hertfordshire call the Old-Man's Beard. **1952** *Cape Argus Mag.* 30 Aug. 2/4 That soft yellowy-green parasite that festoons itself so theatrically over the tops of the trees, giving the forests that appearance of hoary old age, is known as 'old-man's-beard'. **1965** E. Richardson *Living Island* 10 Many standing trees are dead hosts to tattered Old Man's Beard and other lichens. **1972** R. & R. Wright *Cariboo Mileposts* 86 Old man's beard lichen, the small green plant often seen in trees. **1974** *Islander* (Victoria, B.C.) 3 Nov. 7/3 Across the path and up into the old man's beard hanging from the pines.

old-ma·nnish, *a.* [f. Old man + -ish.[1]] Characteristic or suggestive of an old man.

1865 J. A. Symonds *Let.* 15 Apr. (1967) I. 535 Ughtred grows even more noisy, patronizing, old mannish, & goodnatured than he used to be. **1898** *Tit-Bits* 30 Apr. 85/1 We are all more or less acquainted with the precocious child—the 'old-mannish' boy or the 'old-womanish' girl. **1927** W. Deeping *Kitty* vii. 91 His affection for that corner of the City of Westminster grew more deep and old-mannish.

old master. *Art.* See Master *sb.*[1] 15 in Dict. and Suppl.

Oldowan (ǫ·ldowăn), *a.* Also **Olduwan.** [f. the name of the *Oldoway* (or Olduvai) Gorge, Tanzania + -AN.] Belonging to an African culture of the early Pleistocene period, characterized by primitive stone tools.

1934 L. S. B. LEAKEY *Adam's Ancestors* v. 104 In the Kanam deposits we find examples of a culture which has been given the name of Oldowan. This name is derived from Oldoway, the site where this culture was first recognized. **1964** K. P. OAKLEY *Frameworks for dating Fossil Man* iv. 172 The oldest known artifacts in the world are the Oldowan pebble-tools which occur in.. South Africa, East Africa and North Africa. **1972** [see *NUT-CRACKER 5]. **1973** B. J. WILLIAMS *Evolution & Human Origins* xi. 189/2 Even among Olduwan materials (pre-handaxe) there are stone balls that have been rounded and smoothed to a far greater degree than can be explained by any possible functional requirement.

Old Prussian, *sb.* and *a.* [f. OLD *a.* + PRUSSIAN *a.* and *sb.*] **A.** *sb.* **a.** A member of a medieval people, related to the Lithuanians, who inhabited the shores of the Baltic sea east of the Vistula. **b.** The West Baltic language of this people, which ceased to be spoken in the 17th century. See also *BALTIC A. *adj.* 2. **B.** *adj.* Of or pertaining to this people or their language.

1872 [see LETTIC *a.* (*sb.*)]. **1891** [see *BALTIC *a.* 2]. **1917** *Encycl. Relig. & Ethics* IX. 487/1 Both the Este and the Old Prussians drank mare's milk and mead. *Ibid.* 488/1 References to Old Prussian religion occur in Lives of St. Adalbert. **1922** [see *BALTO-]. **1933** L. BLOOMFIELD *Language* i. 13 A similar relation, though less close, was found to exist between the Baltic languages (Lithuanian, Lettish, and Old Prussian) and the Slavic. **1946** T. G. CHASE *Story of Lithuania* i. 3 The Old Prussians..were annihilated by the Teutonic Knights. **1951** A. SPEKKE *Hist. Latvia* vi. 133 Christianus seems to have booked some success among the Old Prussian aristocracy. **1974** *Encycl. Brit. Micropædia* VII. 514/3 Old Prussian preserves many archaic Baltic features that do not occur in the related East Baltic languages.

old régime: see RÉGIME 2 b.

old rose. [f. OLD *a.* + ROSE *sb.* and *a.*] **a.** A shrub rose belonging to a species long in cultivation or a variety grown before the development of the hybrid tea rose about 1890, generally bearing fragrant, less formal flowers during a single mid-summer period.

1885 'E. V. B.' *Ros Rosarum* p. xx, In my own garden I gather together and fondly nurture every Old Rose that can be found. **1899** G. JEKYLL *Wood & Garden* vii. 78, I have also learnt from cottage gardens how pretty are some of the old Roses grown as standards. **1936** E. A. BUNYARD *Old Garden Roses* p. xi, The Old Roses are restrained and never garish. **1955** G. S. THOMAS *Old Shrub Roses* ii. 31 Many of the most shapely and sumptuous of our old roses were raised during the nineteenth century.

b. A shade of deep pink. Also *attrib.* or as *adj.*

1893 *Ladies' Home Jrnl.* Jan. 29/2 Old-rose and black.. is a specially fashionable combination. **1897** *Sears, Roebuck Catal.* 255/1, 36-inch all wool albatross, colors cream, pink, old rose, nile green. **1922** W. J. LOCKE *Tale of Triona* xxi. 241 Her mother's room, with the old rose curtains and Chippendale. **1923** W. DE LA MARE *Riddle* 290 The chest was empty, except that it was lined with silk of old-rose. **1932** G. ATHERTON *Adventures of Novelist* 349, I had brought with me an old-rose rug; I had the walls papered to match, and found an old-rose silken cover for the bed. **1948** 'J. TEY' *Franchise Affair* xi. 115 At the Alençon—cream paint and old-rose couches against the walls. **1973** *Harrods Christmas Catal.* 50 Cocktail bar with mahogany finish, and leather panels in old rose..£130.

old school. [f. OLD *a.* + SCHOOL *sb.*^{1} 5.] **a.** A group of people or a section of society noted for its conservative views or principles; members of a profession or a political party who adhere to its traditional views or methods. Freq. *attrib.* or as *adj.* Also, *in the old school*: according to traditional or old-fashioned methods.

1798, etc. [See SCHOOL *sb.*^{1} 5 b]. **1806** T. G. FESSENDEN *Democracy Unveiled* (ed. 3) II. 61 These bring grave old-school reflections. **1808** H. MORE *Lett.* (1925) 188 It was said more than twenty years ago, that I was the only one of the old school who strongly relished Cowper. **1815** *Niles' Reg.* IX. 120/2 The federal and 'old school' democratic candidate for congress. **1818** M. EDGEWORTH *Let.* 19 Sept. (1971) 101 Lord Bathurst is..an *agreeable* diplomatist..dry faced—of the old school. *c* **1830** [see OLD *a.* 12 a]. **1838** J. F. COOPER *Eve Effingham* II. iii. 81, I could just get a look of our clergyman's wig; for he was an old school man. **1842** F. A. KEMBLE *Let.* 2 Oct. in *Rec. Later Life* (1882) II. 268 Some old-school Whigs, sound politicians, and great friends of mine. **1911** G. B. SHAW *Doctor's Dilemma* I. 23 Did I hear from the fireside armchair the bow-wow of the old school defending its drugs? *a* **1963** S. PLATH *Crossing Water* (1971) 60 Bowing and truckling like an old-school oriental. **1972** 'E. PETERS' *Death to Landlords!* i. 20, I was trained in the old school.. and by hard work I built up the business. **1973** E. MCGIRR *Bardel's Murder* ii. 45 He saw Captain Joyningstowe doing the old-school act with a couple of stern dowagers. **1974** *Times* 18 Apr. 19/5 The Old School certainly accept the view that the rise in the price of oil is deflationary.

b. Used *attrib.* to designate conservative or traditional religious views, as *old school Baptist, old school Church, old school Presbyterian.*

1816, etc. [see *NEW SCHOOL a]. **1875** *Richmond* (Virginia) *Daily Whig* 3 Sept. 2/3 He should never have terminated his affiliation with the Old School Church. **1873** 'MARK TWAIN' & WARNER *Gilded Age* vii. 80 Grandmother..was an Old-School Baptist. **1878** J. H. BEADLE *Western Wilds* xii. 183 The Old School Baptisses never went nigh the Methodis' meetin' house. **1898** I. H. HARPER *Life S. B. Anthony* I. 218, I recommend that you form an acquaintance..with some well-settled Old-School-Presbyterian clergyman. **1933** *Sun* (Baltimore) 21 Oct. 6/8 More than one thousand members of the Old School Baptist Churches are meeting in a three-day session at Little Creek Church. **1949** *Pacific Northwest Q.* Apr. 124 In the period before the Civil War [they] generally preferred to be called Old School Baptists. **1961** K. S. LATOURETTE *Christianity in Revolutionary Age* III. vii. 166 We have seen the separation of the New School from the Old School Presbyterians.

old school tie. [f. OLD *a.* + SCHOOL *sb.*^{1} 1 + TIE *sb.* 4.] A tie of characteristic pattern worn by former members of a particular school, esp. an English public school; used *transf.* and *fig.* to denote the wearer of such a tie and the behaviour and attitudes usually associated with it, esp. conservatism and group loyalty. Also *attrib.* or as *adj.* Hence **old school tie·ism.**

1932 KIPLING *Limits & Renewals* 86, I was thinking over the moral significance of Old School ties and the British social fabric. **1936** S. SMITH *Novel on Yellow Paper* 140 Cynthia was..an old-school-tie acquaintance of mine. **1939** G. HOUSEHOLD *Rogue Male* 40 The only class-conscious people are..the suburban old-school-tie brigade and their wives. **1942** A. CHRISTIE *Body in Library* iii. 35 The Inspector was tacitly accusing him of favouring his own class—of shielding an 'old school tie'. **1943** J. B. PRIESTLEY *Daylight on Saturday* ix. 58 Now this Old School Tie stuff..is only a protest against inefficiency and nothing else. **1944** G. B. SHAW *Everybody's Pol. What's What?* i. 4 To the Old School Ties the dictators seem ignorant uneducated rebels. **1949** R. CHANDLER *Let.* 13 May in *R. Chandler Speaking* (1966) 139, I don't want to be revoltingly old-school-tie, but it does seem to me that a line has to be drawn. **1957** *Numbers* Mar. 17, I just met an old school-tie in the cloakroom. **1958** S. HYLAND *Who goes Hang?* xi. 54 He was an Etonian..and he made his jokes unsmilingly as a concession to the old school tie convention. **1960** T. HUGHES *Lupercal* 45 As soon Let the old school tie be rent Off their necks. **1965** *Listener* 22 July 125/1 One thing I have learned is to distrust a lot of the familiar chat about old school ties. **1969** *Ibid.* 9 Jan. 41/1 He wore an old-school tie and an air of off-hand insolence which he thought of as easy and confident. **1973** 'S. HARVESTER' *Corner of Playground* I. v. 55 Their being boys from adjoining villages, the African version of old school tieism.

Oldspeak (ōu·ldspīk). [f. OLD *a.* + SPEAK *v.*] The name used for Standard English, as opposed to the artificial language *NEWSPEAK, in G. Orwell's novel *Nineteen Eighty-Four*, applied to normal English usage, *spec.* as distinct from technical or propagandist language. Hence **Oldspeaker,** one who uses Oldspeak.

1949 'G. ORWELL' *Nineteen Eighty-Four* I. 54 You haven't a real appreciation of Newspeak... Even when you write it you're still thinking in Oldspeak. *Ibid.* 299 It was expected that Newspeak would have finally superseded Oldspeak (or Standard English, as we should call it) by about the year 2050. **1960** *Encounter* Nov. 10/1 The substitution of 'Newspeak' for 'Oldspeak' (or present-day English) is designed to effect nothing less than the destruction of human reason by linguistic means. **1974** *Daily Tel.* (Colour Suppl.) 20 Sept. 10/3 Sometimes they say that 'real' freedom, being quite different from the crude concept mistakenly used by Oldspeakers, can exist only in a socialist state.

oldster. Add: **1.** (Earlier example.)

1818 'A. BURTON' *Adventures J. Newcome* II. 77 An Oldster with a Gunter's scale Bestow'd his blows as fast as hail.

2. (Later examples.) Also *attrib.*

1938 [see *MARRIED *sb.*]. **1942** *Sun* (Baltimore) 10 Oct. 10/3 The oldsters, travelling salesmen and the like, have learned to tote their own satchel. **1957** *New Yorker* 21 Sept. 33/3 Last week, our interest in nimble oldsters led us to the twenty-fifth floor of the Whitehall Building. **1964** *Wall St. Jrnl.* 5 Feb. 16 'The youngsters are chafing at the bit and aren't willing to wait and see how the civil rights bill shapes up,' he adds, 'and we oldsters can't hold back any longer.' **1973** M. AMIS *Rachel Papers* 112 What was more, the producers could afford only middle-aged actors and actresses. I shifted in my seat as the camera inexpertly focused on a parade of oldster genitals. **1974** *Anderson* (S. Carolina) *Independent* 18 Apr. 4A/2 By getting married, two oldsters in a Portland, Ore., nursing home had their Social Security cut from $412 a month to $309.40 a month because the regulations assume two can live as cheaply as one.

old-time, *a.* Add: **2. a.** Pertaining to or characteristic of an earlier or former time.

1870 'MARK TWAIN' in *Buffalo Express* 1 Jan. 2/6 Conrad's color came back to his cheeks and his old-time vivacity to his eyes. **1936** F. CLUNE *Roaming round Darling* xiv. 120 Whitney, old-time driver for Cobb and Co.'s coaches (later a grazier), planted here a score of fig-trees. **1975** *Nature* 29 May 360/2 What they have is a lot of old-time researchers who are accustomed to pursuing their own interests.

b. In ballroom dancing, applied to styles of dance and music fashionable in the nineteenth and early twentieth centuries. Also in form *old(e) tyme.* Also *absol.* as *sb.*

1887 E. SCOTT *Grace & Folly* iv. 64 It may not be uninteresting to enquire a little into the nature of some of the old-time dances. **1929** *Radio Times* 8 Nov. 389/2 Other records were... *Old Time Favourites*, the London Orchestra. **1933** AUDEN *Dance of Death* 11 Select partners for an old-time waltz. **1947** J. R. GILLESPIE (*title*) Old tyme dancing. **1950** A. WILSON *Such Darling Dodos* 116 Derek's crazy to take up dancing in a big way again. He adores all this old-time dancing. **1952** [see *DRAG *v.* 1 e]. **1960** D. POTTER *Glittering Coffin* iii. 43 The primary school..is opened only for occasional old-time dances. **1967** O. NORTON *Now lying Dead* iii. 54 Tuesdays he stays at home because that's Her night for her Old Time. **1974** *Radio Times* 11 Apr. 52/3 9.2 Time for Old Time in Radio 2 Ballroom. **1975** R. BUTLER *Where all Girls are Sweeter* vi. 75 'It's kind of romantic, really.'.. 'Like Old Tyme dancing on BBC radio, you mean?'

old-timer, for 'chiefly *U.S.*' read 'orig. *U.S.*' and add later examples.

1888 *New Princeton Rev.* Jan. 122 Most of us 'old-timers'..are poor now. **1910** [see *FEST]. **1922** [see *ANIMAL A. 6]. **1928** *Daily Mail* 25 July 2/3 Many types are represented. There is..the old-timer, who knows more about Oxford than the inhabitants of the city themselves. **1928** D. H. LAWRENCE *Woman who rode Away* 60 But he was an old-timer miner. **1929** A. WOOLLCOTT in *New Yorker* 4 May 44/2 The big walnut tree that was an old-timer even in her day. **1939** *Sun* (Baltimore) 4 Apr. 12/7 Remarks about this type of vessel seem to have struck a responsive chord in the breasts of several old-timers. **1942** 'M. INNES' *Daffodil Affairs* II. ii. 46 You ought to meet some of the old-timers there, Mr Wine. **1962** *Coast to Coast 1961–62* 46 'Well thanks for the welcome, old-timer,'..Marlett said. **1966** *Listener* 10 Mar. 344/2, I am not sure..that some old-timers might not welcome a return to the traditional style of the Promenade Concerts. **1973** R. L. SIMON *Big Fix* (1974) xviii. 146, I raised the hoe... 'Sorry old timer,' I said and brought it down on the back of his neck. **1978** *Jrnl. R. Soc. Arts* CXXVI. 194/1 This may seem familiar stuff to some of you old-timers.

o·ld-timey, *a.* Also **old-timy.** [f. OLD-TIME *a.* + -Y^1.] Old-fashioned in character; (nostalgically or sentimentally) recalling the past.

1850 A. J. DOWNING in *Horticulturist* V. 265 The terraced garden, too, is quaint and 'old-timey'. **1879** F. R. STOCKTON *Rudder Grange* xvii. 206 Things that were apparently so 'old-timey'..that David Dutton did not care to take them with him. **1892** KIPLING & BALESTIER *Naulahka* ix. 94 The venerable..institution of matrimony is still in use here... The 'Doll's House' glanced right off this blessed old-timey country. **1921** O. W. HOLMES in *Holmes–Laski Lett.* (1953) I. 372, I must have mentioned Bryce's two nights with us I think—very pleasant and old timey. **1935** 'L. FORD' *Burn Forever* 28 They're real old-timey over at the Curriers. **1936** J. DOS PASSOS *Big Money* 221 Look how oldtimy the street looks. **1971** E. BULLINS in W. King *Black Short Story Anthol.* (1972) 62 Every year in August the Mary's Shore colored community gave an ole timey camp meetin'. **1973** —— *Theme is Blackness* 103 Well, man, I don't want to hear nothin' 'bout some fat ole-timey black bitch that I'm supposed to be like. **1974** *Columbia* (S. Carolina) *Record* 24 Apr. 14-B/4 Beds have old timey coverlets and primitive barn markings form popular wall plaques. **1975** *Publishers Weekly* 17 Nov. 98/3 Large format and illustration with old-timey black-and-white drawings.

old town. [f. OLD *a.* + TOWN *sb.* 4.] The older part of a city or town contained within its modern limits. Also *attrib.* Hence **old-towner,** an inhabitant of an old town.

1752 G. ELLIOT *Proposals Publ. Works Edin.* 32 In these cities, what is called the *new town*, consists of spacious streets and large buildings..while the *old town*..is more crouded than before these late additions were made. **1797** LADY NEWDIGATE *Let.* 16 July in A. E. Newdigate-Newdegate *Cheverels* (1898) xiii. 154, I am told that ye Steyne & everything beyond the Old Town has been built within ye last 30 years. **1842** QUEEN VICTORIA *Jrnl.* 3 Sept. in D. Duff *Victoria in Highlands* (1968) 32 We set off..for Edinburgh... The procession moved through the Old Town up the High Street. **1924** 'P. BLUNDELL' *Confessions of Seaman* xi. 147 There is not, of course, any real 'old town' in Hamburg. Most of the city was burnt down in 1842. **1966** G. LYALL *Shooting Script* xxvi. 208 They are staying at the Colombo, on the beach front near the old town. Jiminez will control the old town, whatever happens. **1968** M. TRIPP *One is One* ii. 15 The beautiful Old Town in Annecy where ancient houses were backed by wooden galleries. **1973** *Guardian* 30 May 7/1 The fears of the old-towners are certainly understandable. The population has declined. Runcorn new town..has been growing. **1973** R. PARKES *Guardians* viii. 137 The granite masses of old-town Helsinki.

old woman. Add: **1. a.** (Further examples of disparaging use.)

1852 C. M. YONGE *Two Guardians* xv. 294 What does she do but let me go muddling on with that old woman Wells! **1867** TROLLOPE *Claverings* I. xi. 141 Who is it says so? A parcel of old women. **1876** G. M. HOPKINS *Let.* 23 Sept. (1956) 142 The Pope, it is well known, is a very fine looking man but there are some smutty smirking old-woman presentments of him. **1911** *Chambers's Jrnl.* 46/1 The new commanding officer was, however, of the genus known in the service as 'old woman', and the regiment suffered accordingly. **1918** E. POUND *Pavannes & Divisions* 39 But surely the worst of your old-women are the male ones. **1953** E. SIMON *Past Masters* II. 74 Macphail is an old wooman [*sic*]... He thought it his duty to let me know. **1975** B. WOOD *Killing Gift* 177 He didn't want Marvin on guard against him... 'Give it some time, Marvin... Maybe I'm being a bit of an old woman.'

b. (Examples.)

a **1775** J. BOUCHER *Gloss. Archaic & Provinc. Words* (1832–3) p. l/1, Could my *old woman*, whilst I labour'd thus, At night reward me with a *smouch*, or buss. **1834** W. G. SIMMS *Guy Rivers* II. 97 The old woman, by whom we mean..to indicate the spouse of the wayfarer, and mother of the two youths, was busied about the fire. **1839** C. M. KIRKLAND *New Home* xv. 96 If my old woman was to stick up that fashion, I'd keep the house so blue she couldn't see to snuff the candle. **1869** MRS. STOWE *Oldtown Folks* xxxvii. 481 The old woman is just as choice of her boys as if [etc.]. **1916** 'TAFFRAIL' *Pincher Martin* xviii. 337 'Ow's Hemmeline an' Mrs Fig—yer ole woman? **1926** I. M. PEACOCKE *His Kid Brother* xiv. 216 His wife... a small round dumpling of a woman with rosy cheeks, whom the policeman addressed as 'Old woman'. **1976** J. O'CONNOR *Eleventh Commandment* xi. 143 If you went home and found someone indoors with your old woman, what would you do?

c. *Theatr.* An actress playing the role of an old woman, esp. one who specializes in such roles. Cf. *OLD MAN I f.

1838 A. MATHEWS *Mem. Charles Mathews* I. 101 Mrs. Davenport,..the inimitable 'Old Woman' of Covent Garden Theatre, having succeeded Mrs. Webb in that line soon after this period. **1901** C. MORRIS *Life on Stage* vii. 40 Then came the leading lady, the first old woman (who was sometimes the heavy woman)..and the ladies of the ballet. **1957** *Oxf. Compan. Theatre* (ed. 2) 772/1 The Old Woman took Juliet's Nurse.

d. old woman's tooth, a simple kind of wooden router plane used by cabinet makers.

1846 C. HOLTZAPFFEL *Turning & Mech. Manipulation* II. xxiii. 487 This plane..is generally called 'the old woman's tooth'. **1907** E. ROWE *Pract. Wood-Carving* 7 The router, very similar to the tool called by the joiner an 'old woman's tooth', may occasionally be used. **1969** E. H. PINTO *Treen* 389 Plate 417, *F*, is an 'old woman's tooth', a router plane of French walnut, probably 16th- or 17th-century.

Hence **old-wo·manishness,** behaviour characteristic of an old woman.

1941 B. SCHULBERG *What makes Sammy Run?* xi. 266 An old-womanishness that's won him the reputation of best-loved producer. **1977** *Listener* 28 Apr. 535/2 His mother's..puritanism and old-womanishness..seemed to hover over Owen's editorial shoulder.

old-world, *a.* Add: **2. a.** (Examples.)

1877 *Harper's Mag.* Dec. 91/2 This was..a beautiful garden kept in old-world order by a Scotch gardener. **1931** E. F. BENSON *Mapp & Lucia* i. 19 Seven bedrooms, four sitting-rooms h. & c., and an old-world garden. **1965** *Canad. Jrnl. Linguistics* X. 97 Consolidation with various Old-World stocks (Uralic, Indo-European) has been sought. **1967** *Boston Sunday Globe* 23 Apr. 23 (Advt.), Old world wood finish and antique polished bronze [lamp].. antique empire gold and black candelabra. **1977** *N.Y. Rev. Bks.* 13 Oct. 14/1 For most Americans political assassination was an Old World phenomenon of bomb-throwing Bolsheviks and Balkan fanatics.

b. Old World monkey, a catarrhine monkey belonging to the superfamily Cercopithecoidea or the family Cercopithecidæ, which includes the monkeys of Africa and Asia.

1863 H. W. BATES *Naturalist on River Amazons* II. v. 326 The Marmosets, have thirty-two teeth, like the Old World monkeys and man. **1894** H. O. FORBES *Hand-bk. Primates* I. 252 The family *Cercopithecidæ* includes all the Old World Monkeys except the Anthropoid or true Apes, and Man. **1936** E. G. BOULENGER *Apes & Monkeys* vi. 120 The old-world monkeys are very widely distributed. **1968** *Times* 15 Nov. 8/6 Two fossil monkeys of the primate group known as the Old World monkeys, or Cercopithecoidea. Living representatives of the group include baboons, mandrills and macaques. **1974** S. I. ROSEN *Introd. Primates* vi. 86 The Old World monkeys are biologically closer to man than the New World primates.

Hence **old-wo·rldliness** = *old-worldism*.

1934 *Archit. Rev.* LXXV. 178 The patron public was becoming patina-conscious, aware of texture, age-effects, old-worldliness, the charm of mellowness.

‖**ole**[1] (ōᵘ·le). [Sp. *ole* Andalusian dance.] The name of a Spanish folk-dance, which is accompanied by castanets and singing.

1846 R. FORD *Gatherings from Spain* xxiii. 328 The dance..is called the *Ole* by Spaniards, the *Romalis* by their gipsies... The whole person..trembles like an aspen leaf. **1950** L. ARMSTRONG *Dances of Spain* I. 9 *Olé*, Gaditanian (Cadiz) folk dance of apparently great antiquity. A solo with castanets. **1964** W. G. RAFFÉ *Dict. Dance* 360 *Ole* (Spain), a woman's solo dance with castanets... The dance is accompanied by rapid vocal acrobatics..to the syllables 'ay' or 'olé' (from which the dance may take its name).

ole[2], dial. and Black English var. of OLD *a.* Cf. *OL'.

1844 (*song-title*) Ole Bull and Ole Dan Tucker. **1874** [see *old mistress* s.v. *OLD *a.* (*adv.*, *sb.*[1]) D. 4]. **1880** J. C. HARRIS *Uncle Remus* i. 18, I speck de ole 'oman en de chilluns kin sorter scramble roun' en git up sump'n fer ter stay yo' stummuck. **1907** G. B. SHAW *Major Barbara* II. 217 Youre ony a jumped-up, jerked-off, orspittle-turned-out incurable of an ole workin man. **1935** Z. N. HURSTON *Mules & Men* I. iv. 101 It laid dere for thousands of years, then Ole Missus said to Ole Massa: 'Go pick up dat box.' **1936** M. MITCHELL *Gone with Wind* iv. 63 'Mammy gettin' ole,' said Dilcey, with a calmness that would have enraged Mammy. **1950** R. AMES in A. Dundes *Mother Wit* (1973) 488/1 The old time darky's.. love for 'ole marse' and 'ole mist'ess'. **1962** J. D. SALINGER *Franny & Zooey* 85 That's the spirit...That's putting the ole foot down. **1971** *Jamaican Weekly Gleaner* 3 Nov. 18/2 Long debt better dan ole grudge. **1972** G. BEARE *Bee Sting Deal* i. 12 'I work here,'..'But surely not at 5.30 a.m., ole gel.' **1973** [see *LIMER[3]]. **1973** *Black World* May 13/1 They succinctly and repeatedly lay the flaming blame at Ole Massa's front door. **1974** *Sunday Guardian* (Port-of-Spain) 28 July 12/2, I took a bus to Martin's Bay, and there was laughter and ole talking all the way. Down on the wharf I find gangs of limers giving jokes and ole talkin. **1977** *Time* 29 Aug. 31/1 'My God,' sighed Bell, 'I still wish we could get ole Frank Johnson to take it.'

‖**olé** (ōᵘle·), *int.* [Sp. *olé* bravo.] Bravo. Also as *sb.*, a cry of olé. Usu. assoc. with Spanish music and dance and with bullfighting.

1922 J. HERGESHEIMER *Bright Shawl* 55 An uproar of applause rose from the theatre, a confusion of cries, of Olé! Olé! Anda! Anda! Chiquella! **1940** E. HEMINGWAY *For whom Bell Tolls* v. 60 'Olé!' someone said. 'Go on, gipsy!' **1962** J. STEWART tr. *Cousseau's Death of Miss Cunningham* 44 The unheard *Olés* of the crowd..in Caracas. **1966** R. E. PICKERING *Himself Again* vi. 42, I.. picked up the little glass, and drained it. 'Olé,' said Charley. **1967** J. POTTER *Foul Play* i. 17 Freda and Basil had launched themselves into a perilous exhibition tango, to encouraging olés from the surrounding circle of boozers. **1973** *Sat. Rev.* (U.S.) 25 Sept. 29/1 The *plaza de toros* was packed; and..before I could even see the ring, I heard the *olés*.

-ole, *suffix* [partly f. L. *oleum* oil, partly a var. -OL], used to form chemical names. **1.** In the names of compounds containing five-membered, unsaturated rings with at least one hetero-atom, e.g. *carbazole, indazole, indole, pyrrole, thiazole, triazole*.

Although applicable to older words like *pyrrole* (1835), this systematic use of *-ole* is of more recent date.

1928 *Jrnl. Amer. Chem. Soc.* L. 3078 For five-membered rings proposals made by Widman, Bouveault and others have found their way into use. The ending *-ol* or *-ole* appears in such names as pyrrole, imidazole and even dioxole (which is non-nitrogenous). It conflicts with the ending *-ol* for alcohols and phenols (hence the modified spelling *-ole*), but its use to denote a five-membered ring is well known. **1971** *Nomencl. Org. Chem.* (I.U.P.A.C.) (ed. 3) B. 53 (*table*) No. of members in the ring..5. Rings containing nitrogen: unsaturation..-ole... Rings containing no nitrogen: unsaturation..-ole.

2. Unsystematically, in the names of aromatic ethers, e.g. *anisole, phenetole, safrole*, which were regarded as being derived from carboxylic acids in the same way as 'benzole' (benzene) is from benzoic acid.

1852 *Rep. Brit. Assoc. Adv. Sci. 1851* I. 136 The use of the analogous termination *ole* for those [bodies] formed by the abstraction of 2 atoms of carbonic acid from the same [*sc.* vegetable acids] may be apt to cause some ambiguity. Thus we use the terms benz*ole*, phen*ole*, and anis*ole*, as being derived respectively from the benzoic, salicylic, and anisic acids.

oleaginous, *a.* Add: **2.** (Later examples.)

1922 JOYCE *Ulysses* 406 The scent, the smile.., the dark eyes and oleaginous address. **1945** R. HARGREAVES *Enemy at Gate* 31 The shifty, oleaginous, power-greedy place-man Olympius. **1966** *Listener* 18 Aug. 244/3 Many of the other works have a rather nasty oleaginous inconsistency of texture. **1973** *Daily Tel.* 13 Oct. 11/2 A piped programme that included an oleaginous instrumental version of part of a Chopin nocturne. **1976** *National Observer* (U.S.) 17 July 5/1 For years, the conferences have been sponsored and paid for by big companies and their oleaginous lobbyists.

oleaginosity: delete † and add later examples; also **olea·ginously** *adv.*

1912 L. J. VANCE *Destroying Angel* x. 119 Three doors, in one of which a rotund Chinaman beamed oleaginously. **1912** W. DEEPING *Sincerity* xxxii. 247 His hands were fat, his neck full of red creases, his manner towards women oleaginously gallant. **1939** JOYCE *Finnegans Wake* 54 Whileas oleaginosity of ancestralolosis sgocciolated down the both pendencies of his mutsohito liptails.

oleander. (Later examples.)

1880 G. W. CABLE *Grandissimes* xxvi. 193 Their long, over-arched avenues of oleander. **1915** H. H. THOMAS *Greenhouse* vi. 57 Oleanders require the protection of a cool greenhouse in winter. **1956** *Railway Mag.* Mar. 165/1 A fertile valley, with magnificent oleanders. **1962** *Coast to Coast 1961–62* 13 In the shade of the giant oleander bush sat Brett's half-Persian she-cat, licking and preening herself with a too obvious absorption.

b. oleander hawk(-moth), a large moth, *Daphnis nerii*, of the family Sphingidæ whose caterpillars feed on oleander or periwinkle leaves.

1843 HUMPHREYS & WESTWOOD *Brit. Moths* I. 21 The Oleander Hawk-moth..measures about 4½ inches in the expansion of its fore wings, of which the ground colour is an olive-green. **1907** R. SOUTH *Moths Brit. Isles* 1st Ser. 45 (*heading*) The Oleander Hawk-moth. **1955** E. B. FORD *Moths* i. 6 The other form [of green colouring]..is found.. in some Sphingidae such as the Oleander Hawk. **1972** *Shooting Times & Country Mag.* 24 June 20/3 When they flew they reminded me of one of the hawk moths, the Oleander perhaps, or the Elephant Hawk moth.

oleandomycin (ōu:li,ændomai·sin). *Pharm.* [f. *oleand-rose*, a sugar of which a residue is present in the oleandomycin molecule (f. OLEANDR(INE + -OSE[2]) + -O + *-MYCIN.] (The phosphate of) a macrolide, $C_{35}H_{61}NO_{12}$, produced by a strain of the bacterium *Streptomyces antibioticus*, which is active against a wide range of Gram-positive bacteria and has been used in treating staphylococcal enteritis and skin infections.

1956 B. A. SOBIN et al. *U.S. Pat. 2,757,123* 31 July, This invention relates to a new and useful antibiotic called oleandomycin. **1967** [see *ERYTHROMYCIN]. **1968** [see *MACROLIDE]. **1974** D. PERLMAN in W. O. Foye *Princ. Med. Chem.* xxxi. 742/1 Oleandomycin, a macrolide bacterial antibiotic closely related to erythromycin, has been losing value as a therapeutic agent for infections caused by gram-positive bacteria because of high incidence of side effects.

olearia (ōuli,ēə·riă). [mod.L. (C. Moench *Suppl. Methodus Plantas Horti Botanici et Agri Marburgensis* (1802) 254), f. the name of Johann Gottfried *Olearius* (1635–1711), German theologian and horticulturist.] An evergreen shrub or tree of the Australasian genus so called, belonging to the family Compositæ and bearing clusters of white, yellow, or mauve flowers; = *daisy-tree* (*DAISY *sb.* 7).

1839 G. DON *Sweet's Hortus Britannicus* (ed. 3) 344 (*heading*) Olearia DC. [English name] Olearia. **1852** *Curtis's Bot. Mag.* LXXVIII. 4638 Mr. Gunn's Olearia ..is another interesting plant of Van Diemen's Land, which braves the cold of England. **1868** *Trans. N.Z. Inst.* I. III. 4 Along the shore there is a profusion of shrub Veronicas and Olearias. **1882** T. H. POTTS *Out in Open* 64 Soon to be lost beneath a covering screen of *veronicas, olearias*, gnarled and knotted *griselinias*. **1918** *Chambers's Jrnl.* Apr. 221/1 The trees, especially the rata and the olearia, grow for nearly half their length along the ground. **1959** *Listener* 22 Jan. 174/1 He sometimes tears at the bark of the ceanolthus and olearias. **1971** *Homes & Gardens* Sept. 127/2 Many olearias have grey under-sides to the foliage.

olefine. Add: Now usu. spelt **olefin**, in accordance with the practice of reserving -INE[5] for the naming of basic substances and heterocyclic compounds containing nitrogen. (Further examples.)

1923 T. G. PHILLIPS *Fundamentals Org. & Biol. Chem.* ix. 131 Similar series [of compounds] may be derived from the olefin hydrocarbons. **1949** R. F. GOLDSTEIN *Petroleum Chemicals Industry* vi. 124 The higher olefins are present in all fractions of the petrol range of thermally and catalytically cracked oils. **1968** R. O. C. NORMAN *Princ. Org. Synthesis* viii. 262 This discussion indicates the difficulties necessarily present in effecting the dimerization of an olefin.

Hence **olefi·nic** *a.*, of, having the nature of, or characteristic of an olefin; applied *spec.* to a double bond between two carbon atoms such as is characteristic of olefins (cf. *ETHYLENIC *a.*).

1898 J. WADE *Introd. Study Org. Chem.* lvi. 344 On gentle oxidation it [*sc.* linaloöl] yields an olefinic ketone. **1923** *Daily Mail* 15 Feb. 3 Those olefinic and empyreumatic substances which result from the distillation of coal or oil. **1968** R. O. C. NORMAN *Princ. Org. Synthesis* vii. 248 Although carbanions..do not react with simple olefins, they do so if the olefinic double bond is conjugated to a group of —*M* type. **1974** *Jrnl. Amer. Chem. Soc.* XCVI. 7934 (*heading*) Stereochemistry of olefinic cyclization.

olenellid (olənə·lid), *sb.* and *a.* [a. mod.L. family name *Olenellidæ*, f. generic name *Olenell(us* (E. Billings *Palæozoic Fossils* (1861) I. 11) + -ID[3].] A trilobite belonging to the family Olenellidæ; of or pertaining to this family.

1892 PEACH & HORNE in *Q. Jrnl. Geol. Soc.* XLVIII. 239 Among the *disjecta membra* of Olenellid trilobites from the dark shales..are certain portions of the carapaces of a much larger species. *Ibid.* 240 One word of speculation as to the systematic position of the Olenellids may be admissible here. **1937** *Jrnl. Paleont.* XI. 577/1 Olenellids present a most interesting association of primitive and specialized characters. *Ibid.* 578/2 The olenellid shell is for its size excessively thin. **1969** BENNISON & WRIGHT *Geol. Hist. Brit. Isles* iv. 87 The fauna of the Lower Cambrian chiefly comprises Olenellid trilobites. **1973** P. TASCH *Paleobiol. Invertebr.* xi. 518/1 The so-called abortive segments in..other olenellids might be evidence of the type of asexual budding that occurs in certain primitive polychaete worms.

oleo, *a.* Add: **3.** [f. OLEO-.] Applied to (a system containing) a telescopic strut, used esp. in aircraft undercarriages, which absorbs shocks by means of a hollow piston into which oil is forced through a small orifice on compression of the strut (see also quot. 1965).

1916 N. J. GILL *Flyer's Guide* iii. 39 The commonest form of shock absorber is the rubber type, but Oleo gear are [*sic*] now also used to a considerable extent. **1920** *Flight* XII. 14/1 The undercarriage is at present of the usual Vee type with stream-line steel tube struts and rubber shock absorbers, but later an oleo undercarriage will be fitted. **1935** C. G. Burge *Compl. Bk. Aviation* 596/1 The piston must return to the original position as quickly as possible after each impact, and to secure this the oleo leg frequently incorporates a compressed-air chamber. **1965** C. N. Van Deventer *Introd. Gen. Aeronaut.* vii. 149/2 The more usual method of absorbing the impact of landing is the through the use of oleo struts. Of the two general types, one has a moving piston..and the other has a fixed piston and uses a spring instead of air. **1977** D. Beaty *Excellency* i. 17 The searchlight began fingering the fuselage. The port oleo leg blossomed a brilliant silver.

B. *sb. Aeronaut.* An oleo strut or leg.

1929 F. H. & H. F. Colvin *Aircraft Handbk.* (ed. 4) iii. 64 To prepare oleo for use. 1. Pull piston out of cylinder and remove auxiliary piston. 2. Fill tube up to 6 inches from top with G.E. transformer oil No. 6. 3. Insert auxiliary piston with bolt head down. 4. Insert main piston. **1931** *Handbk. Aeronautics* (R. Aeronaut. Soc.) iii. 190 (*table*) 2 Large oleos... 2 Small oleos... 2 Front struts... 2 Rear struts. **1958** H. G. Conway *Landing Gear Design* ix. 184 The combination of tyre and oleo will thus have an efficiency well below 100 per cent. **1977** D. Beaty *Excellency* xx. 223 He felt the main wheels shake on their oleos.

oleo² (ōᵘ·lio). *rare.* Abbreviation of Oleograph.

1921 Galsworthy *Captures* (1923) 57 Taking up the oleos, he turned his back on the photographs. **1932** *Daily Express* 25 June 9/3 A little room hung with lace and oleos.

oleo-. Add: **a. oleophi·lic** *a.* [*-philic], having an affinity for oils or oily materials; readily absorbing oil; **oleopho·bic** *a.* [-phobic], tending to repel, or not to absorb, oils or oily materials; **oleo-pneuma·tic** *a.*, applied to a device or system which absorbs shocks by a combination of forcing oil through an orifice and compression of air or another gas; **oleotho·rax** *Med.* [ad. F. *oléothorax* (A. Bernou 1922, in *Bull. de l'Acad. de Méd.* LXXXVII. 457)], a method of treatment, now disused, in which oil is introduced into the pleural cavity; introduction of oil in this manner.

1957 *Brit. Jrnl. Appl. Physics* VIII. Suppl. 6. S23/2 For oils containing oleic acid, the behaviour is different. Zinc and copper behave initially as the other metals in becoming more oleophobic on continued contact with oil and water but this eventually gives place to a reverse trend to increasingly oleophilic behaviour. **1967** [see *hydrophobic *a.* (*sb.*) 2 a]. **1970** *Sci. Jrnl.* Feb. 21/3 Sawdust treated with appropriate silicones is water repellent but strongly oleophilic and will soak up many times its weight of oil. **1946** *Jrnl. Colloid Sci.* I. 513 The..conclusion was that the observed phenomenon was due to the adsorption of eicosyl alcohol from solution upon the interior walls of the flask, to form a film possessing the property of being oleophobic to (unwetted by) the oil solution. **1967** E. Chambers *Photolitho-Offset* xiv. 210 Others were unsuitable because of extreme low sensitivity to light, or the inherent oleophobic (ink rejecting) character of the tanned coatings. **1909** *Aëronaut. Jrnl.* Apr. 64/1 The front wheel is fitted with an oleo-pneumatic brake for safety purposes. **1930** *Engineering* 16 May 647/1 (*heading*) Oleo-pneumatic shock absorber for aeroplanes. **1960** *Times* 30 Aug. 4/5 All four wheels..are independently sprung by means of wishbones and Girling oleo-pneumatic spring and damper units. **1922** *Jrnl. Amer. Med. Assoc.* 24 June 1996/2 The normal pleura would not bear this direct treatment, but in such pathologic conditions the oleothorax answered the desired purpose. **1938** *Brit. Encycl. Med. Pract.* IX. 309 Oleothorax is a therapeutic method consisting in the introduction of a sterile oil or an oil containing an antiseptic into the pleural cavity. **1962** H. Spencer *Path. Lung* xii. 384 They [*sc.* liquid paraffin granulomas in the lung] have also been reported following oleothorax... This form of pulmonary oil granuloma has now largely disappeared following the cessation of this form of therapy.

oleograph. Add: (Earlier and later examples.) Also **oleolithograph.** Hence **oleogra·phically** *adv.*; **oleo·graphist.**

1873 *Young Englishwoman* Sept. 466/1 Oleographs are now very cheap, and, if well chosen, are most pleasing. **1897** W. Archer *Theatr. 'World' 1896* 173 Seems..incredible even in Germany, with the sacred *eikon* of the Kaiser oleographically lowering over the scene. **1907** R. Brooke *Let.* 23 Aug. (1968) 100 The book plate of one Frederick Leighton—the notable oleographist, I take it? **1922** Joyce *Ulysses* 698 Artistic oleograph on inner face of door. **1928** D. L. Sayers *Lord Peter views Body* 176 Lord Peter sat down on a red velvet arm-chair, fixed his eyes on a gilt-framed oleograph, and became wrapped in contemplation. **1939** J. Cary *Mr. Johnson* 45 He is the happy husband adoring and adored in a perpetual and rather solemn dignity like an oleolithograph of the Royal Family. **1974** N. Freeling *Dressing of Diamond* 57 It was only in books that kidnappers had a handy stammer or a gold tooth, and a flat with a large coloured oleograph on the wall of President Kennedy, or the Pope, or Marilyn Monroe.

olericulture. For *rare*⁻⁰ read *rare* and add later example.

1966 *McGraw-Hill Encycl. Sci. & Technol.* XIV. 286/1 The term olericulture, referring to vegetable production, is used occasionally.

oleum (ōᵘ·liəm). Pl. **oleums.** [L., = 'oil'.] An oily liquid which is produced by dissolving sulphur trioxide in concentrated sulphuric acid in the contact process and is used in sulphonation and nitration processes; fuming sulphuric acid.

1905 Blount & Bloxam *Chem. for Engineers & Manuf.* (ed. 2) II. i. 23 Ordinary vitriol is still called in Germany English sulphuric acid, in contradistinction to the fuming acid or 'oleum'. **1949** P. W. Vittum tr. *Fierz-David & Blangey's Fund. Proc. Dye Chem.* 83 When sulfonation is done with oleum, usually only the SO_3 is used up. **1954** *Thorpe's Dict. Appl. Chem.* (ed. 4) XI. 296/1 (*heading*) Boiling-points of oleums. **1973** *Times* 20 Jan. 3/1 It [*sc.* a tanker] was carrying a maximum load of 20 tons of oleum, a corrosive acid said to react violently when in contact with a small quantity of water.

O-level, see *O 5 d.

oleyl (ōᵘ·li,il, -əil). *Chem.* [f. Ole(ic *a.* + -yl.] The radical $CH_3(CH_2)_7CH{=}CH(CH_2)_7CH_2$—, which has the same carbon atom skeleton as oleic acid; **oleyl alcohol,** an oily liquid, $C_{18}H_{35}OH$, which occurs in fish oils and is used in the manufacture of surface-active agents; *cis*-9-octadecen-1-ol.

1903 *Jrnl. Chem. Soc.* LXXXIV. i. 730 Ethyl oleate gave oleyl alcohol, $C_{18}H_{36}O$, as a colourless liquid. **1951** Kirk & Othmer *Encycl. Chem. Technol.* VI. 271 The reaction of acetylene with oleyl alcohol gives vinyl oleyl ether, which is polymerizable and copolymerizable with other vinyl monomers. **1972** *Materials & Technol.* V. ix. 262 Oleyl alcohol can be epoxidised with peracids to yield polyhydroxy compounds. **1972** *Arch. Biochem. & Biophysics* CL. 199/2 Oleyl CoA inhibits the adenine nucleotide transport system..of rat liver mitochondria.

olfactometer (ǫlfæktǫ·mītəɹ). [f. as next + -ometer.] **a.** An instrument for measuring the sensitivity of a subject to odours or the intensity of odours.

1889 H. Zwaardemaker in *Lancet* 29 June 1301/1, I have lately constructed a small instrument which, I think, deserves the name of 'olfactometer'. Its component parts consist of two tubes fitting into each other. The outer one is lined with scented material, and made to glide up and down over the inner one, of which one end remains free and is bent to fit the nostril. **1922** G. H. Parker *Smell, Taste & Allied Senses* iii. 51 Two single olfactometers may be combined so that one current carrying an odorous material..may be introduced into one nostril and another carrying a second odorous substance..into the other nostril. **1969** J. R. Hughes et al. in C. Pfaffmann *Olfaction & Taste* 173 Stimuli have been presented by a portable two-channel olfactometer. **1969** *Daily Tel.* 9 Sept. 20/8 He has developed devices, known as olfactometers, which at present measure only the intensity of odours but do not differentiate between them.

b. A device for investigating the responses of animals to odours.

1926 *Jrnl. Econ. Entomol.* XIX. 552 Adult potato beetles were collected in potato patches and were tried in the insect olfactometer. **1969** *New Scientist* 17 Apr. 134/2 Some initial experiments using an olfactometer suggested that the sense of smell did not play any part in bringing the male and female spiders together.

olfactometry (ǫlfæktǫ·mětri). [f. L. *olfact-*, ppl. stem of *olfacere* to smell (see Olfacient) + -o + -metry.] The measurement of the sensitivity of the sense of smell, the use of an olfactometer; also, = *odorimetry.

1898 *Amer. Jrnl. Psychol.* X. 85 Olfactometry is that branch of psychophysics which is concerned with the measurement of the keenness of smell. **1898** [see *odorimeter]. **1935** [see *odorimetry]. **1967** J. W. Johnston in T. Hayashi *Olfaction & Taste II* 48 The characterization of a simple blend as a nonresinous woody odor by means of olfactometry and G-L chromatography has shown the way to the elusive correlation of the physical parameter, odorant intensity, and the psychological dimension, subjective (odorant) strength. **1968** W. McCartney *Olfaction & Odours* 151 When olfactometry is being practised, great care must be taken to avoid fatigue (adaptation) of the perceiving organ.

Hence **olfactome·tric** *a.*, of olfactometry.

1898 *Amer. Jrnl. Psychol.* X. 101 (*heading*) Control in Zwaardemaker's olfactometric method of the factors which determine the intensity of the stimulus. **1963** *Nature* 20 Apr. 272/2 As the syntheses were completed, the compounds were tested.., using advanced olfactometric techniques, for intensity and quality of odour. **1973** *Biol. Abstr.* LV. 2568/1 An olfactometric method is proposed for estimating the attractant properties of chemical compounds for insects.

olfactorily, *adv.* (s.v. Olfactory *a.*). (Further examples.)

1944 R. W. Moncrieff *Chemical Senses* ix. 187 Structurally, the esters bear the same relation to the acids as the ethers do to the alcohols... Olfactorily, however, there is a difference. **1969** *Psychol. Bull.* LXXI. 60/1 Olfactorily acting and oral pheromones.

olfactorium (ǫlfæktōᵊ·riəm). Pl. **-ia.** [f. as next + *-orium.] A large odour-proof enclosure in which olfactory experiments are conducted.

1950 D. Foster et al. in *Amer. Jrnl. Psychol.* LXIII. 433 The design was..made cubical and the apparatus finally devised and described here was called the olfactorium. **1968** W. McCartney *Olfaction & Odours* 148 The 'olfactoria' (capacity 500 cubic feet, for example) that have recently been constructed in the U.S.A...are essentially the same as was Fischer and Penzoldt's test room.

olfactronics (ǫlfæktrǫ·niks), *sb. pl.* (const. as *sing.*). [f. L. *olfact-*, ppl. stem of *olfacere* to smell (see Olfacient) + *(elec)tronics.] The detection, analysis, and measurement of vapours by means of instruments.

1964 *Aviation Week & Space Technol.* 16 Nov. 46/1 'Olfactronics.' Chicago—Combination of chemical analysis and electronic techniques appears to offer many interesting possibilities..beyond the detection of hidden explosives on aircraft, according to Dr. Andrew Dravnieks of the Illinois Institute of Technology. **1967** *N.Y. Times* 16 July iv. 8 Eventually olfactronics may be used to guard bank vaults against burglars. **1970** *Jrnl. Reproductive Med.* Apr. 69 (*heading*) Changes in vaginal odors... A study in applied olfactronics.

Hence **olfactro·nic** *a.*, of or pertaining to olfactronics; **olfactro·nically** *adv.*, by olfactronic means.

1966 *New Scientist* 15 Sept. 623/2 A human carries an olfactronic 'image' of his recent environment, provided that this environment contained some olfactronically distinguishable features. **1969** *Product Engineering* 10 Mar. 11 Acoustic or vibration sensors, heat-detection devices, and even olfactronic detectors might prove more effective. **1970** *Jrnl. Reproductive Med.* Apr. 70/1 The atmosphere around the study object..must be known and examined olfactronically.

oligæmia (ǫligī·miă). *Med.* Also (*U.S.*) **oligemia.** [mod.L., ad. F. *oligaimie* (A. N. Gendrin *Traité philos. de Méd. pract.* (1838) I. i. 37), ad. Gr. ὀλιγαιμία (Arist.), f. ὀλίγος (see Oligo-) + αἷμα blood.] = *hypovolæmia* s.v. *hypo-; now distinguished from *anæmia,* which is applied to a diminished concentration of blood cells.

1843 T. Watson *Lect. Princ. & Pract. Physic* I. iv. 49 The blood is scanty and poor—what Andral calls (though with questionable propriety) anæmia. Oligæmia is the cacophonous but more exact name assigned to it by Gendrin; but poverty of blood is the ordinary English phrase for it, and the best of the three. **1861** T. H. Tanner *Man. Practice Med.* (ed. 4) i. i. 7 Anæmia.—Deficiency of blood (poverty of blood, spanæmia, hydræmia, or oligæmia) arises generally..where there has been deprivation. **1866** [in Dict. s.v. Oligo-]. **1942** M. M. Wintrobe *Clin. Hematol.* vii. 243 Anemia, which..refers to the concentration of oxygen-carrying substance in a certain volume of blood, is to be distinguished from oligemia, which signifies a reduction of the total amount of blood in the body. **1974** Passmore & Robson *Compan. Med. Stud.* III. iii. 2/1 Rarely, oligaemia with shock arises from loss of plasma proteins in the urine in the course of the nephrotic syndrome.

Hence **oligæ·mic** *a.*

1848 C. D. Meigs *Females & their Diseases* xxxii. 421 Your thin, pale oligæmic patient cannot take up enough oxygen out of the air she breathes, to make her *strong.* **1947** *Amer. Heart Jrnl.* XXXIII. 645 The cardiodynamic alterations are characteristic of progressive and terminal stages of shock associated with low blood volumes; that is, oligemic shock. **1965** *Proc. Soc. Exper. Biol. & Med.* CXIX. 884/1 Experimental animals were maintained until death or sacrifice at an oligemic hypotension of about 30 mm Hg.

oligarchization (ǫligāɹkəizēⁱ·ʃən). [f. Oligarch(y + -ization.] Movement towards oligarchy.

1966 *Social Forces* XLIV. 328/1 Oligarchization may be defined as the concentration of power, in the Weberian sense, in the hands of a minority of the organization's members. **1974** tr. *Wertheim's Evolution & Revolution* 405 The Continued Revolution; China and the Iron Law of 'Oligarchization'.

oligo-. Add: **oligodynamic,** add: [ad. G. *oligodynamisch* (C. von Nägeli 1893, in *Neue Denkschriften d. allgem. schweiz. Ges. f. d. ges. Naturwiss.* XXXIII. i. ii. 8)]; substitute for def.: effected or exerted by minute quantities of metallic ions in solution; acting or being active at very low concentrations; (further examples); **oligoe·ster** *Chem.*, an oligomer in which adjacent monomeric units are linked together by an ester grouping, —CO·O—; **oligoha·line** *Oceanogr.* [ad. G. *oligohalin* (H. C. Redeke 1922, in *Bijdragen tot de Dierkunde* (Amsterdam) XXII. 330), f. Gr. ἅλιν-ος of salt], characterized by salinity in the range immediately above that of 'fresh' water (a division of the *mixohaline category); **oligole·ctic** *a.* [Gr. λεκτ-ός chosen], of bees, gathering pollen from only a few closely related plants; **oligomenorrhæa,** now written **oligomenorrhœa** or (*U.S.*) **-rrhea;** (further example); hence **o:ligomenorrhœ·al** **-rrhœ·ic** *adjs.*; **oligomy·cin** *Pharm.* [*-mycin], (any of) a group of antifungal antibiotics produced by the bacterium *Streptomyces diastatochromogenes*, which inhibit certain mitochondrial phosphorylation reactions; **oligonu·cleotide** *Biochem.* [ad G. *oligo-nucleotid* (F. G. Fischer et al. 1941, in *Jrnl. f. prakt. Chem.* CLVIII. 81)], any polynucleotide whose molecules are made up of a relatively small number of nucleotides; **oligope·ptide** *Biochem.* [ad. G. *oligopeptid* (Helferich & Grünert 1940, in *Naturwissenschaften* 28 June 411/2)], any peptide whose molecules are composed of a relatively small number of amino-acid residues; **oligo·phagous** *a. Zool.* [-PHAGOUS], of insects, feeding on a limited number of plants; so **oligo·phagy** (-ǫ·fădʒi); **oligophre·nia** [Gr. *φρήν* mind], feeble-mindedness; **o·ligopod** *a. Ent.* [ad. It. *oligopodo* (A. Berlese 1913, in *Redia* IX. 128) f. Gr. *πούς, ποδ-* foot], of an insect larva, having well-developed thoracic limbs; **oligosa·ccharide** *Biochem.* [ad. G. *oligosaccharid* (B. Helferich et al. 1930, in *Ber. d. Deut. Chem. Ges.* LXIII. 991)], any carbohydrate whose molecules are composed of a relatively small number of monosaccharide residues; **o:ligosapro·bic** *a. Ecology* [ad. G. *oligosaprob* (Kolkwitz & Marsson 1902, in *Mittheilungen aus der K. Prüfungsanstalt f. Wasserversorgung und Abwässerbeseitigung* I. 46): see *SAPROBE], of, being, or inhabiting an aquatic environment that is rich in dissolved oxygen and (relatively) free from decayed organic matter; so **oligosa·probe,** an oligosaprobic organism; **oligospe·rmia** *Med.* [Gr. *σπέρμα* seed], orig. the condition in which the amount of semen secreted is reduced; now usu. = *oligozoospermia* below; hence **oligospe·rmic** *a.*; **oligotro·pic** *a. Zool.* [ad. G. *oligotrope* (E. Loew 1884, in *Jahrb. Bot. Gartens Berlin* III. 256): see *-TROPIC], of bees, collecting nectar from only a few kinds of flower; **o:ligozoospe·rmia** *Med.* [*zoosperm* s.v. ZOO-], the condition of having the number of spermatozoa in the semen sufficiently reduced to affect fertility; **oliguria** (earlier and later examples); so **oligu·ric** *a.*, of, pertaining to, or involving oliguria; also as *sb.*, one who suffers from oliguria.

1941 *Jrnl. Marine Res.* IV. 186 Containers made of copper, zinc, tin or nickel alloys are not suitable for the collection of samples of sea water for bacteriological analysis due to the inimical oligodynamic action of the metals. **1965** B. E. Freeman tr. *Vandel's Biospeleol.* xix. 337 The Thiobacteria can synthesise oligodynamic substances (nicotinic acid..pyridoxine, vitamin B_{12}). **1973** *Times* 25 Apr. 19/5 The ability of minute amounts of these metals to exert a lethal effect upon micro-organisms is referred to as oligodynamic action. **1957** *Makromolekulare Chemie* XXIII. 31 Linear oligoesters of terephthalic acid and glycol form three polymer-homologous series: ester-diols, ester-dicarboxylic acids, and ester-hydroxyacids. **1968** *Encycl. Polymer Sci. & Technol.* IX. 491 For the synthesis of oligoesters and amides, the carboxyl group is usually activated by transformation into acid chloride or azide, as well as to a mixed anhydride or active ester. **1951** *Rep. Comm. Treatise Marine Ecol.* (National Research Council, U.S.) xI. 50 As originally proposed by Redeke, this classification was related to chlorinity rather than to the total salinity... This scheme, as set up by Redeke..is best presented in tabular form:..Cl, o/oo... Brackish water. 0·1–1·0. Oligohaline. **1971** *Nature* 24 Sept. 281/1 Next, there is a conglomerate which contains brackish oligohaline facies fauna. **1925** C. Robertson in *Ecology* VI. 413, I have used the term oligolectic for a bee collecting pollen from a species, genus or family, where the relationship of the flowers seems to determine the preference, and polylectic for one collecting pollen from unrelated plants. **1972** *Science* 12 May 601/2 There are very few oligolectic bees. **1973** Proctor & Yeo *Pollination of Flowers* v. 151 Bees that visit only one or a few species of flowers for food are described as oligotropic, while those showing a similar restriction for pollen supplies are called oligolectic. **1974** Passmore & Robson *Compan. Med. Stud.* III. xxviii. 6/1 Although there are important exceptions, in general those conditions which cause primary amenorrhoea are congenital, while those causing secondary amenorrhoea or oligomenorrhoea are acquired. **1963** Oligomenorrheal [see *POLYMENORRHŒAL *a.*]. **1955** *Obstetr. & Gynecol.* V. 661 Five of the 7 patients were amenorrheic at the time of the first visit, while 2 were oligomenorrheic with menses occurring once to three times a year. **1977** *Lancet* 15 Oct. 805/1 Bromocriptine restores normal gonadal function in some amenorrhœic or oligomenorrhœic patients who have normal serum-prolactin levels. **1954** R. M. Smith et al. in *Antibiotics & Chemotherapy* IV. 962 The purpose of this paper is to report a presumably new antifungal antibiotic, oligomycin. **1958** *Jrnl. Amer. Chem. Soc.* LXXX. 6093/1 The oligomycins are active against the fungi producing oak-wilt and Dutch elm diseases. **1964** *Ann. Rev. Biochem.* XXXIII. 737 In loosely coupled mitochondria, oligomycin abolishes phosphorylation, and the available evidence is consistent with the conclusion that oligomycin inhibits ATP formation from all three coupling sites of the respiratory chain. **1969** J. Dekker in D. C. Torgeson *Fungicides* II. xiii. 621 Oligomycin..is an antifungal antibiotic active against various fungal plant pathogens. The results, however, have not been good enough to warrant practical applications. **1942** *Chem. Abstr* XXXVI. 785 From a study of dialysis coeffs., the oligonucleotide has a mol. wt. 3·5–5·3 times that of a mononucleotide. **1961** *Lancet* 12 Aug. 377/2 Many oligonucleotides and polynucleotides stimulate the growth of protozoans. **1971** *Nature* 28 May 217/2 There were several oligonucleotides missing from the former RNA. **1941** *Chem. Abstr.* XXXV. 78 (*heading*) *N*-methanesulfonyl derivatives of amino acids and oligopeptides. **1955** *Nature* 9 July 72/2 The importance of the amino-acids and oligopeptides and the complexity of their mixtures often encountered stimulate a demand for more powerful analytical tools. **1968** *New Scientist* 22 Aug. 402/2 The first section, that on the posterior pituitary hormones, is mainly concerned with the fact that these oligopeptides do not occur free in the nerve cells. **1920** C. T. Brues in *Amer. Naturalist* LIV. 317 A distinction is made between vegetarian species with a single food-plant (Monophagous), those with several definitely fixed ones (Oligophagous) and those with quite indiscriminate food habits (Polyphagous). **1946** —— *Insect Dietary* iii. 145 (*heading*) Polyphagy, oligophagy and monophagy. **1969** R. F. Chapman *Insects* ii. 27 Other insects..feed on only a limited range of plants. They are called oligophagous. *Ibid.* 28 Oligophagy may also arise in this way [*sc.* the presence of particular chemical stimulants in certain plants]. **1899** *Allbutt's Syst. Med.* VIII. 196 *Oligophrenia*, enfeeblements of cerebral (psychical) development, with a parallel enfeeblement in the evolution of personality. **1932** *Brit. Jrnl. Psychol.* XXIII. 21 The oligophrenia, or 'small wittedness' as Continental writers call the condition, is due to an insufficiently developed brain. **1972** *Encycl. Psychol.* II. 345/2 *Oligophrenia*, synonymous with the term *amentia*..mental subnormality. [**1925** A. D. Imms *Gen. Textbk. Entomol.* II. 179 In the oligopod phase the embryo has reached an advanced condition.] **1934** R. A. Wardle *Folsom's Entomol.* (ed. 4) iii. 173 A less active type of oligopod larva..has a cylindrical fleshy body. **1957** T. W. Kirkpatrick *Insect Life in Tropics* iv. 64 Oligopod larvae usually have well-developed thoracic legs but no abdominal feet and are typical of most beetles and Neuroptera. **1969** R. F. Chapman *Insects* xx. 399 The least modified [larval form] with respect to the adult is the oligopod larva. **1930** *Chem. Abstr.* XXIV. 3762 The name *oligosaccharides* is suggested for the simpler cryst. sugars (intermediate between the monoses and the polysaccharides) which form 2 or more monoses on hydrolysis. **1957** *Sci. News* XLV. 87 Human breast milk..contains a number of oligosaccharides. **1968** Oligosaccharide [see *MONOSACCHARIDE]. **1925** *Bull. Illinois Nat. Hist. Survey* XV. 441 The part of a stream lying between the mesosaprobic lower limit and that of the cleanest zone normal to rivers has been called by Kolkwitz and Marsson oligosaprobic. **1933** *Water Pollution Res. Technical Paper* (D.S.I.R.) No. 3. 134 The classification of the organisms into poly-, meso-, and oligo-saprobic..is now generally in use in defining the ecological status of aquatic organisms. It is based on the conditions which result when sewage or similar polluting liquids flow into small streams or into series of lagoons; in such cases a characteristic succession of biological associations is found, beginning with the poly-saprobes living in the crude liquid and ending with the oligo-saprobes in the region where self-purification is complete. **1950** *Folia Limnologica Scand.* V. 77 The oligosaprobic zone is regarded chemically as the zone in which oxidation (mineralisation) is nearly completed. **1970** Oligo-saprobic [see *mesosaprobic* adj. s.v. *MESO-]. **1848** Dunglison *Dict. Med. Sci.* (ed. 7) 599/2 *Oligospermia*, paucity of spermatic secretion. **1897** White & Martin *Genito-Urinary Surg.* xxviii. 1027 Oligospermia, or a diminution in the quantity of semen ejaculated, may be due to deficiency in quantity or absence of any of the constituent parts of this fluid. **1936** H. Bailey *Dis. Testicle* xviii. 148 The causes of male sterility are:... 2. Oligospermia; spermatozoa are few and inactive. **1944** R. S. Hotchkiss *Fertility in Men* ix. 185 Defective spermatogenesis results in the failure to supply the full complement of spermatozoa to the ejaculate. This varies in degree from complete atrophy of the seminiferous tubule to a reduced number of spermatozoa in the seminal discharge. The former condition produces azoospermia, while the latter causes oligospermia. **1974** Passmore & Robson *Compan. Med. Stud.* III. xxviii. 21/1 A diminution of fertility can be demonstrated when sperm density falls below 20 M/ml, and values below this level on repeated counts constitute oligospermia. **1892** *Syd. Soc. Lex.*, Oligospermic. **1971** *Nature* 19 Feb. 534/2 In veterinary and medical practice artificial insemination facilitates the use of incapacitated or oligospermic males. **1899** C. Robertson in *Bot. Gaz.* XXVIII. 29 The difference between a monotropic and an oligotropic bee may depend merely upon the accident that only one species occurs in the neighbourhood. **1919** J. H. Lovell *Flower & Bee* 106 When a species of bee restricts its visits..to a few allied kinds of flowers [it is termed] an oligotropic bee. **1946** C. T. Brues *Insect Dietary* iii. 107 Some more specialized bees and other insects restrict their visits to a much more circumscribed assortment of plant species. With these oligotropic kinds the advantages to the plant are obviously greater. **1892** F. P. Foster *Med. Dict.* IV. 2447/1 *Oligozoospermia*, of De Sinety, a variety of sterility in the male in which the spermatozooids are diminished in number and activity. **1897** White & Martin *Genito-Urinary Surg.* xxviii. 1027 Oligozoöspermia indicates a condition in which the semen ejaculated contains few spermatozoa. **1962** *Lancet* 27 Jan. 218/1 There was nothing to suggest oligozoospermia due to external causes. **1876** Dunglison *Dict. Med. Sci.* (rev. ed.) 721/2 Oliguria. **1961** *Lancet* 22 July 187/2 The œdema, oliguria, albuminuria, and absence of an impressive cardiac murmur may result in the condition being mistaken for acute nephritis. **1907** *Amer. Jrnl. Med. Sci.* CXXXIV. 77 The oliguric urine..is of higher specific gravity and contains less indican. **1918** *Endocrinology* II. 95 In man it is common to observe diuresis, especially in oligurics. **1961** *Lancet* 16 Sept. 632/1 In mushroom poisoning hæmodialysis is obviously essential where..severe oliguric renal failure occurs.

oligodendrocyte (ǫligode·ndrosəit). *Histology.* [f. *OLIGODENDRO(GLIA + -CYTE.] A kind of neuroglial cell similar to an astrocyte (but with fewer processes), found characteristically round nerve cells in the central nervous system and concerned with the maintenance of myelin.

1932 [see *OLIGODENDROGLIA]. **1966** Wright & Symmers *Systemic Path.* II. xxxiv. 1243/2 The oligodendrocyte greatly outnumbers all other cells in the brain. **1974** J. A. G. Rhodin *Histol.* xv. 316/1 The primary function of the oligodendrocytes is the formation of the myelin sheath.

oligodendroglia (ǫ:ligodendrogləi·ă). *Histology.* [ad. Sp. *oligodendroglía* (P. del Rio-Hortega 1921, in *Bol. de la Real Soc. Española de Hist. Nat.* XXI. 63): see OLIGO-, DENDRO-, and NEURO)GLIA.] Oligodendrocytes. Usu. const. as *pl.*

1924 *Brain* XLVII. 430 (*heading*) Oligodendroglia and its relation to classical neuroglia. **1932** W. Penfield *Cytol. & Cellular Path. Nervous Syst.* II. ix. 437 Oligodendrocytes or oligodendroglia were first demonstrated by Robertson (1899, 1900 *a*) under the name of mesoglia by means of his platinum method. Del Rio-Hortega (1921 *b*) independently re-discovered the cells by means of a more reliable and complete staining method. He called them oligodendroglia..because, as compared with astrocytes or the astroglia, the branches of these cells were small and apparently few and he recognized them as one type of neuroglia. **1951** O. Larsell *Anat. Nervous Syst.* (ed. 2) iv. 127 The elements of oligodendroglia are related to the astrocytes but are smaller and have smaller nuclei. **1962** [see *MICROGLIA]. **1974** Bergman & Afifi *Atlas Microsc. Anat.* vi. 111 Oligodendroglia are smaller than astrocytes and have a denser nucleus and cytoplasm. **1974** J. A. G. Rhodin *Histol.* xv. 314/2 Oligodendroglia or oligodendrocytes are small, angular cells of neural ectodermal origin.

Hence **o:ligodendrogli·al** *a.*

1929 *Jrnl. Path. & Bacteriol.* XXXII. 736 An oligodendroglial cell contains a spherical nucleus which is smaller than the nucleus of a neuroglial cell. **1972** *Science* 19 May 801/3 These vacuoles..were found..in axons, astrocytes, and oligodendroglial cells.

oligodendroglioma (ǫ:ligodendrogləi,ōu·mă). *Path.* [f. *OLIGODENDROGLI(A + *-OMA.] A tumour derived from oligodendroglia.

1926 Bailey & Cushing *Classification Tumors of Glioma Group* 54 With few exceptions the true brain tumors may be classified under fourteen major categories as follows:..Medullo-epithelioma...Oligodendroglioma... Neuroblastoma. **1929** *Jrnl. Path. & Bacteriol.* XXXII. 735 (*heading*) Oligodendrogliomas of the brain. **1967** *Nursing Times* 27 Jan. 108/1 Some of these, such as the oligodendroglioma, grow very slowly and are compatible with normal life in many cases for 10 years or more. **1978** *Jrnl. R. Soc. Med.* LXXI. 419 Oligodendroglioma, a tumour which, in *in vitro* studies..has been shown to have a high oxygen consumption.

oligohydramnios (ǫ:ligohəidræ·mniǫs). *Obstetrics.* [f. OLIGO- + HYDR(O- + AMNIOS.] A deficiency in the amount of amniotic fluid.

1889 [see *POLYHYDRAMNIOS]. **1928** W. G. Lee *Childbirth* xv. 227 A 'dry uterus' and an oligohydramnios.. often result in either a constriction ring or a uterus closely molded to the fetal mass. **1962** D. E. Reid *Texbk. Obstetr.* xxiv. 630/2 in oligohydramnios, rather than the normal 1,000–2,000 ml., only 100–200 ml. is found. **1972** E. D. Morris in C. J. Dewhurst *Integrated Obstetr. & Gynaecol.* xxii. 381 Oligohydramnios is evident clinically in two particular circumstances: in association with a small-for-dates baby, and with severe renal anomalies of the foetus.

oligomer (ǫ̆li·gŏməɹ). *Chem.* [f. OLIGO- + *-MER.] Any polymer whose molecules consist of relatively few repeating units.

1952 van der Want & Staverman in *Rec. Trav. Chim. Pays-Bas* LXXI. 379 In the course of an investigation into the chemical and physical properties of polymers of different molecular weight it appeared desirable to us to have available condensation products of ε- amino-caproic acid: $H[NH(CH_2)_5CO]_nOH$ with low and exactly specified values of n ('linear oligomers') e.g. $n = 2$, 3, 4 and 5. **1967** [see *leucoanthocyanidin* s.v. *LEUCO-]. **1969** *Nature* 13 Sept. 1125/2, Table 1 shows the frequencies of monomers, dimers and higher oligomers of mitochondrial DNA. **1975** *Ibid.* 6 Mar. 83/2 The extent to which each of the characteristic oligomers (pentanucleotides and larger) of *Escherichia coli* 16S rRNA is conserved across phylogenetic lines.

Hence **oligome·ric** *a.*

1957 *Makromolekulare Chemie* XXIII. 32 The van der Wyk-rule, which permits calculation of the melting points of straight-chain paraffins, can be applied to the oligomeric esters of terephthalic acid and glycol after introduction of suitable constants. **1970** *Nature* 13 June 1004/2 A series of oligomeric substrates, up to twelve glucose units in length and labelled at the end-group, was prepared. **1974** *Sci. Amer.* Nov. 64/1 The *J* chain is present in oligomeric forms, and the dimer, when found in secretions such as saliva and tears, is bonded to yet another polypeptide.

oligomerization (ǫ̆li:gŏmĕrəizēi·ʃən). *Chem.* [f. prec. + -IZATION.] The formation or production of an oligomer from a monomer.

1958 *Jrnl. Chem. Soc.* 3563 (*heading*) The cationic oligomerisation of the stilbenes. **1972** *Jrnl. Amer. Chem. Soc.* XCIV. 6968 (*heading*) The mechanism of the oligomerization of hydrogen cyanide and its possible role in the origins of life. **1974** *Encycl. Brit. Macropædia* XIII. 716/2 Aluminum alkyls also cause dimerization, oligomerization, or polymerization of olefins.

So **oli·gomerize** *v. trans.*, to form an oligomer of.

1967 *Nature* 29 Apr. 480/1 Hydrogen cyanide could be oligomerized to the dimer, trimer, tetramer, etc., to form the parent skeletons of glycine, alanine and aspartic acid, and other organic compounds. **1972** *Proc. Nat. Acad. Sci.*

LXIX. 3389/1 Linear double-stranded molecules of simian virus (SV)40 DNA..are oligomerized by either ligase.

oligomictic (ǫligomi·ktik), *a.* [f. OLIGO- + Gr. μικτ-ός mixed + -IC.] **1.** *Petrol.* [ad. Russ. *oligomiktovyĭ* (M. S. Shvetsov *Petrografiya Osadochnȳkh Porod* (1934) viii. 155).] (See quot. 1935.)

1935 *Jrnl. Sedimentary Petrology* V. 106/2 Rocks consisting of one to two dominant minerals are termed oligomictic and those composed of several minerals polymictic... The book is written in Russian... The review is based on a typewritten summary in English. **1949** F. J. PETTIJOHN *Sedimentary Rocks* xiv. 438 Schwetzoff.. noted that oligomictic rocks are the characteristic deposits of epicontinental seas and are found rarely in geosynclinal depressions, whereas polymictic rocks are characteristic of geosynclinal regions. **1959** W. W. MOORHOUSE *Study of Rocks in Thin Section* xix. 337 The typical oligomictic conglomerate is composed predominantly of quartz. **1971** *Nature* 28 May 247/1 Structureless to planar cross-stratified, sheet-like bodies of oligomictic conglomerates and subarkoses are interbedded.

2. *Limnology.* Applied to a lake that exhibits a stable thermal stratification and only rarely undergoes an overturn.

1956 HUTCHINSON & LÖFFLER in *Proc. Nat. Acad. Sci.* XLII. 84 Although at low altitudes in the humid tropics small temperature gradients can maintain stable stratifications, no stable stratification develops at the low temperatures of high altitudes, where the density difference per degree centigrade is very small. The lack of seasonal variation, that permits almost perennial stratification at low altitudes in equatorial latitudes, thus permits perennial circulation at high altitudes in the same latitudes. We propose for these two types of equatorial lake the terms oligomictic and polymictic, respectively. **1968** R. W. FAIRBRIDGE *Encycl. Geomorphol.* 617/1 The lake water body is stratified, thus oligomictic.

oligopoly (ǫligǫ·pǒli). [f. OLIGO- + Gr. πωλ-εῖν to sell, after MONOPOLY.] A state of limited competition when a market is shared by a small number of producers or sellers.

1895 J. H. LUPTON *Utopia of Sir Thomas More* I. 55/2 More makes an antithesis between *monopolium* and *oligopolium*. We have 'monopoly' but not 'oligopoly' (the sale by a few), and so cannot preserve the point of the sentence. **1933** E. H. CHAMBERLIN *Theory Monopol. Competition* i. 8 The theory of value..has been treated..with particular reference to the problem of two sellers, or 'duopoly', and we may extend this terminology, adding 'oligopoly' for a few sellers. **1954** *Wall St. Jrnl.* 13 Dec. 3/3 'Oligopoly'—monopoly power in the hands of two or more companies. **1957** *Economist* 7 Sept. 769/2 The small but bustling textile industry is now giving a miniature demonstration of the oligopoly stage of capitalism as the big firms begin to mop up the smaller ones. **1959** [see *DUOPOLY b]. **1967** J. K. GALBRAITH *New Industrial State* xvi. 180 Under the cognomen of oligopoly it is assumed in its price-making to have some of the powers of a monopoly and some of the restraints of competition. **1970** *Daily Tel.* 23 Jan. 18 Deciding when monopoly or oligopoly is or is not..'against the public interest'. **1974** M. B. BROWN *Econ. of Imperialism* iii. 52 The driving force behind the extension of commodity production under capitalism is the competition of capitalists, even under conditions of oligopoly. **1977** *Dædalus* Fall 92 Oligopolies will tend to have excess physical capacity.

Hence **oligo·polist; oligo:poli·stic** *a.*

1939 J. A. SCHUMPETER *Business Cycles* I. ii. 60 The general statement that oligopolistic prices are indeterminate would be misleading. **1947** *Jrnl. Pol. Econ.* LV. 432/1 Observed price rigidities in oligopolistic industries. **1958** *Jrnl. of Business* (Chicago Univ.) XXXI. 198/1 Frequently, in the case of older products, some measure of oligopolistic uncertainty exists. **1959** *Economist* 28 Mar. 1175/1 Increases between 1953 and 1957 came about entirely from prices in the oligopolistic industries. **1959** DE CHAZEAU & KAHN *Integration & Competition in Petroleum Industry* xvii. 443 Having achieved the touchstone of crude oil production control, the leading firms and practically the industry as a whole behave like self-conscious oligopolists. **1967** *Spectator* 28 July 113/2 The big cleaning material manufacturers (I mean, of course, the soap and washing powder oligopolists) have all been making efforts to grab a slice of this easy market. **1971** K. HOPKINS *Hong Kong* 212 Oligopolistic industries dominated by large corporations do not exist in Hong Kong. **1975** *New Law Jrnl.* 11 Sept. 892/1 The provisions of article 86 of the EEC treaty are designed to proscribe monopolistic, oligopolistic or, in certain respects, a monopsonic position being exploited at the expense of other producers or of consumers in the European Common Market. **1977** *Dædalus* Fall 92 The world is not a two-person zero-sum game, and no oligopolist expects competitors to hold their prices or quantities fixed in response to his moves.

oligopsony (ǫligǫ·psǒni). *Econ.* [f. OLIGO- + Gr. ὀψων-εῖν to buy provisions; after *MONOPSONY; cf. OPSONY.] A marketing state in which only a small number of buyers exists for a product; also *attrib.* Hence **oligo·psonist, oligo:psoni·stic** *a.*

1943 E. R. WALKER *From Econ. Theory to Policy* iv. 61 It is surely only a matter of time before [market situation] No. 23 is christened 'oligopsony'. **1949** W. FELLNER *Competition among Few* i. 11 The problem is that of oligopoly, oligopsony, and bilateral monopoly, and, of course, also of markets which are oligopsonistic on the demand side and oligopolistic on the supply side...The oligopsonist..attempts to select a definite price to be paid for the materials and services he buys. **1961** N. F. KEISER *Introductory Econ.* v. 77 At one time the major cigarette manufacturers were oligopsonists in their purchases of tobacco. **1965** D. GREENWALD et al. *McGraw-Hill Dict. Mod. Econ.* 358 *Oligopsony*, a market structure with relatively few buyers... An oligopsonistic situation may lead to express or tacit collusion among the sellers. **1965** HAILSTONES & DODD *Econ.* (ed. 5) xi. 229 *Oligopsony* exists when a few buyers dominate the market... The author of a college textbook faces an oligopsonistic market in the publication of his manuscript. **1972** HUNT & SHERMAN *Econ.* xviii. 275 Some large firms have extra market power as large buyers of commodities (technically, oligopsony power). **1972** J. WINKLER *On Marketing Planning* xiii. 205 Companies operating in oligopsonistic markets find that great power flows to their salesmen.

oligotrophic (ǫligotrǭᵘ·fik), *a. Ecol.* [ad. G. *oligotroph* (A. Thienemann *Die Binnengewässer Mitteleuropas* (1925) iv. 198 (*-trophie* sb.), 200 (*-troph*)), f. Gr. ὀλίγος small, little + τροφή nourishment: see -IC.] Relatively poor in plant nutrients and (in the case of a lake) containing abundant oxygen in the deeper parts.

[**1928** *Proc. Linn. Soc.* CXL. 100 The typical oligotroph lakes are deep, with submerged beaches narrow or absent, inconsiderable or no littoral vegetation, and an indistinct littoral zonation.] **1931** R. N. CHAPMAN *Animal Ecol.* xvi. 304 The oligotrophic type of lake is rich in oxygen even to the bottom. It owes its characteristic partly to a geologic formation which permits relatively little inwash of organic material..; and partly to biotic conditions which do not favour rapid decomposition with the consequent oxygen consumption. **1943** G. K. FRASER *Peat Deposits of Scotland* I. 3 The remains of plants nourished on rich soils (technically termed eutrophic soils)..will be able to support a greater bacterial population than those of plants grown on poor or impoverished soils (oligotrophic soils). *Ibid.* 9 Acid ground waters are usually oligotrophic and can support only short herbage such as smaller sedges. **1955** *New Biol.* XVIII. 115 *N. alba* occupies a wide range of waters in the British Isles, from the oligotrophic, or nutrient-poor, peat-bottomed moorland lakes in Scotland and Ireland, to the eutrophic, or nutrient-rich, fen-lodes and broads of East Anglia. **1972** J. G. CRUICKSHANK *Soil Geogr.* vi. 186 Also acid and infertile is oligotrophic peat.

So **o·ligotrophy**, an oligotrophic condition.

1928 *Proc. Linn. Soc.* CXL. 109 Even if the natural course is from oligotrophy to eutrophy, the opposite process may also be found. **1957** G. E. HUTCHINSON *Treat. Limnol.* I. ix. 644 Hutchinson set limits [on oxygen loss] of 0.017 mg. cm.$^{-2}$ day^{-1} for oligotrophy. **1967** [see *EUTROPHY]. **1973** P. A. COLINVAUX *Introd. Ecol.* xviii. 258 It is the change from oligotrophy to eutrophy, simulating as it does the natural aging of a lake, which gives rise to the idea that polluted lakes are dying or actually dead.

olingo (ǫli·ŋo). [Amer. Sp., f. native name.] A small, nocturnal mammal of the genus *Bassaricyon*, belonging to the family Procyonidæ, native to forest regions of Central and South America, and distinguished from the kinkajou by a straight tail which is not prehensile.

1920 E. A. GOLDMAN in *Smithsonian Misc. Coll.* LXIX. No. 5. 155 (*heading*) *Bassaricyon gabbii gabbii* Allen. Bushy-tailed Olingo. **1964** L. S. CRANDALL *Managem. Wild Mammals in Captivity* 314 Closely allied to the kinkajou and apparently often confused with it is the olingo (*Bassaricyon gabbii*). *Ibid.* 315 The olingo is a grayer brown, over-all, than most kinkajous, with pale gray face and noticeably longer and more pointed muzzle. Its most obvious character is the long tail, which is very faintly ringed, somewhat bushy, and non-prehensile. **1965** D. MORRIS *Mammals* 278 Allen's Olingo bears a strong resemblance to the Kinkajou... Where the two species do differ, the Olingo is always the more primitive. **1975** *City Press* 4 Sept. 16/3 Who would suspect that the City has anything to do with 18,985 rats, 1,110 baboons, 10 anteaters and an olingo?

olio. Add: **2. b.** Further examples; *spec.* a variety act or show; also *attrib.*

1809 S. BRECK *Recoll.* (1877) App. 271 We..rode round to Mr. Brent's,..with whose family we took tea, and afterward accompanied them to an olio concert. **1928** *Amer. Speech* IV. 68 Behind these *drops*,..are the *oleos*, or *act-curtains*. These..are used for small vaudeville acts... Such acts.. are termed *oleo acts*, or *acts in one.* **1951** GREEN & LAURIE *Show Biz* 570/1 *Olio*, scenery, in front of which an act, generally a 'sidewalk comedy' team performs; also specialties performed between acts in burlesque. **1956** M. STEARNS *Story of Jazz* (1957) xi. 116 The second part, or olio (a word derived from the Spanish *olla*, meaning mixture), consisted of a series of solo acts that later evolved into variety or vaudeville. **1961** BOWMAN & BALL *Theatre Lang.* 237 *Olio*; *oleo*... A scene consisting of a specialty act..played..while another scene is being set. Also as *olio act* (or *scene*)... A backing, drop, or tableau curtain for a front scene... Also as *olio drop*... A medley of songs, dances, comic sketches and the like. **1961** A. BERKMAN *Singers' Gloss. Show Business* 64 *Oleo*, miscellaneous Vaudeville or Variety Acts presented between the acts or during the intermissions of a play. **1964** *Punch* 2 Dec. 852/1 The audience is invited to stay.. for the Olio,..which here means an Aftershow. **1976** *Publishers Weekly* 9 Feb. 96/3 It is a mixture of self-indulgent prose, sickening violence and unbelievable happenings. The whole olio is, clearly, a bid for Bicentennial attention.

olisbos (ǫ·lizbǫ̆s). [ad. Gr. ὄλισβος] = *DILDO[1].

1887 [see *GODEMICHE]. **1941** G. R. SCOTT *Phallic Worship* x. 178 Aristophanes speaks of the use, by Milesian females, of an *olisbos* made of leather. **1955** V. NABOKOV *Lolita* I. xxii. 126, I had blazed in her face an olisbos-like flashlight. **1967** CROSLAND & DAVENTRY tr. *de Becker's Other Face Love* plate 13 (*caption*) Two women together using a double olisbos.

olistolith (ǫli·stolip). *Geol.* [f. Gr. ὀλισθ-stem of ὀλίσθημα slip, slide + -LITH.] One of the discrete bodies contained within the matrix of an olistostrome.

1956 [see next]. **1974** *Nature* 26 Apr. 745/1 It is possible that these domes represent olistoliths transported over a long distance from the Turkish shelf.

olistostrome (ǫli·stostrǭᵘm). *Geol.* [f. as prec. + Gr. στρῶμα bed.] A sedimentary deposit composed of a heterogeneous mixture of materials and formed by the sliding or slumping of semi-fluid sediment.

1956 G. FLORES in *Proc. 4th World Petroleum Congr. 1955* I. 122/2 By Olistostromes we define those sedimentary deposits occurring within normal geologic sequences that are sufficiently continuous to be mappable, and that are characterized by lithologically and/or petrographically heterogeneous materials, more or less intimately admixed, that were accumulated as a semi-fluid body. In any Olistostrome we distinguish a 'binder' or 'matrix' represented by prevalently pelitic, heterogeneous material... The name '*Olistolith*'..is applied to the masses included as individual elements within the binder. **1972** *Nature* 8 Dec. 328/2 The mixture is now floating in a matrix of middle Miocene olistostrome.

oliva. 1. (Later example.)

1973 A. H. WHITEFORD *N. Amer. Indian Arts* 133 Trade routes from the Gulf of California and Mexico brought..oliva shells into the Southwest.

olive, *sb.*[1] Add: **1. b. American olive** (examples).

1785 H. MARSHALL *Arbustrum Amer.* 98 American Olive tree..grows naturally in Carolina and Florida, and is a beautiful ever-green tree. **1866** *Land We Love* (Charlotte, N. Carolina) May 78 American Olive..is a very fine evergreen, producing clusters of small white flowers. **1901** C. T. MOHR *Plant Life Alabama* 14 Their banks adorned with evergreen andromedas, American olive,.. sweet bay, and azaleas.

10. A greenish-brown moth, *Zenobia* (or *Ipomorpha*) *obtusa*, of the family Noctuidæ, found in Europe and northern Asia.

1832 J. RENNIE *Conspectus Butterflies & Moths Brit.* 83 The Olive..feeds on the poplar. **1908** R. SOUTH *Moths Brit. Isles* 2nd Ser. 9 The Olive..is somewhat similar in general appearance to the last mentioned [*sc.* the Double Kidney]. **1974** B. GOATER *Butterflies & Moths of Hampshire* 376 The Olive..widespread but associated with *Populus* species.

11. A mayfly with an olive-coloured body belonging to the genus *Baetis*, which includes species with transparent wings, or the genus *Ephemerella*, esp. *E. ignita*, which has blue wings.

1889 F. M. HALFORD *Dry-Fly Fishing* ix. 206 The blue-winged olive..is known to modern entomologists as *Ephemerella ignita*. **1911** —— *Mod. Devel. Dry Fly* iii. 18, I think the dark olive is, as a rule, not so well taken by the fish as the common olive. **1949** A. C. WILLIAMS *Dict. Trout Flies* II. 267 Whereas other insects are seasonal, the olive is more or less always with us. **1971** *Country Life* 21 Oct. 1084/1 Often there is a good hatch of olives in the morning or afternoon—sometimes both—which usually brings a response not only from the grayling but from the trout.

b. An artificial fly made in imitation of an insect of this type.

1895 *Montgomery Ward Catal.* Spring & Summer 495/2 Bass Flies, consisting of the following styles:.. Oak, Olive, Montreal, Professor, [etc.]. **1907** *Yesterday's Shopping* 674/2 Special Irish Salmon Flies... Golden Olive with Blue and Jay Shoulder. **1911** F. M. HALFORD *Mod. Devel. Dry Fly* iii. 18 No. 7 of the series of patterns is the olive dun male. **1921** G. E. M. SKUES *Way of Trout with Fly* II. ii. 109 The floating subimago I tried to imitate with a darkish variety of a stock pattern of olive. **1938** W. C. PLATTS *Mod. Trout Fishing* vii. 68 Among the wet flies in use may be mentioned..various Olives. **1968** C. F. WALKER *Art of Chalk Stream Fishing* xvii. 147 My own choice would be the Rough Olive, a most successful fly.

C. a. *olive crop, culture, -grove* (later examples), *industry, spray.* **d.** *olive-backed* (earlier and later examples), *-skinned* adjs.; also with reference to the shape of an olive, as *olive-shaped* adj. **e. olive-back,** substitute for def.: a North American forest thrush, *Hylocichla ustulata*, also known as Swainson's thrush; (earlier and later examples); **olive-backed thrush** = **olive-back*, **olive thrush*; **olive-berry** (later example); **olive crescent,** a pale greenish-brown European moth, *Trisateles emortualis*, of the family Noctuidæ; **olive drab,** of a brownish green colour, used *spec.* of the colour of U.S. Army uniform; also *ellipt.*; **olive-fly** (examples); also *olive fruit fly*; **olive thrush** = **olive-back*; **olive whistler,** an Australian bird, *Pachycephala olivacea.*

1845 S. JUDD *Margaret* I. xvi. 143 The olive-backs trolled and chanted among the trees. **1892** B. TORREY *Foot-Path Way* 19 The olive backs began to make themselves heard. **1945** *Mass. Audubon Soc. Bull.* Mar. 43 Two thrushes of annual interest to students are the migrant Olive-back and the Gray-cheek. **1844** J. E. DEKAY *Zool. N.Y.* II. 74 The Olive-backed Thrush is closely allied to the [hermit thrush]. **1892** B. TORREY *Foot-Path Way* 99 Two birds dashed by me—a blackpoll warbler in hot pursuit of an olive-backed thrush. **1946** T. M. STANWELL-FLETCHER *Driftwood Valley* 187 We spend the long bright evenings out on the lake, listening to the chorus of olive-backed thrushes. **1958** E. T. GILLIARD *Living Birds of World* 336/2 The Olive-backed Thrush..winters south to Argentina. **1869** MRS. STOWE *Oldtown Folks* xvi. 176, I guess our olive-berries are pretty well beaten off now. **1832** J. RENNIE *Conspectus Butterflies & Moths Brit.* 146 The Olive Crescent..resembles the Clay-Fan-Foot. **1908** R. SOUTH *Moths Brit. Isles* 2nd Ser. 88 The Olive Crescent..is exceedingly rare in England. **1974** B. GOATER *Butterflies & Moths of Hampshire* 411 Olive Crescent... One taken in bright sunlight..in late July, 1939. **1884** *Encycl. Brit.* XVII. 762/1 Apart from occasional damage by weather or organic foes, the olive crop is somewhat precarious even with the most careful cultivation. **1977** J. AIKEN *Last Movement* ii. 42 Local staff, who came and went when the orange or olive crop demanded their attention. **1893** K. A. SANBORN *Truthful Woman in S. California* xii. 155 Olive culture is just now the fad. **1957** *Encycl. Brit.* XVI. 774/1 Specialized olive culture is an important industry on hillsides throughout Greece. **1897** *Sears, Roebuck Catal.* 21/3 One gallon of this paint will cover (two coats) over 300 square feet of surface. Always order by color number as well as catalogue number... 214 Olive Drab. **1908** *Sears, Roebuck Catal.* 71/2 *Colors of..house paint...* Nile Green.. Olive Drab..Cream. **1917** A. WOOLLCOTT *Let.* Oct. (1946) 28, I was afflicted because I had signed, have been in olive drab for three months—been away from America for almost three months. **1942** —— in *Reader's Digest* Nov. 23/2 Wherefore, as he [*sc.* Irving Berlin] toils away at something for the boys in olive-drab to sing out with real emotion, he has only to listen to the bugle notes for a motif. **1948** W. J. STOKOE *Caterpillars Brit. Moths* I. 274 The caterpillar..is slaty-brown, inclining to olive-drab above. **1970** N. ARMSTRONG et al. *First on Moon* iii. 66 Check the olive-drab lap and shoulder strapping for each man. **1886** R. C. HALDANE *Subtropical Cultivations* 183 *Musca oleæ* (the olive-fly) lays its eggs in the young fruit, and is a most destructive insect. **1972** SWAN & PAPP *Common Insects N. Amer.* 627 The Olive Fruit Fly, *Docus oleae*, is a serious pest of olives in the Mediterranean area. **1878** O. WILDE *Ravenna* 6 Dark olive-groves and noble forest-pines. **1959** *Times* 29 Sept. 12/6 Vineyards and olive groves. **1893** K. A. SANBORN *Truthful Woman in S. California* xii. 155 Pomona is head-quarters for the olive industry. **1968** *Encycl. Brit.* XVI. 937/1 In South America and Australia, development of a commercial olive industry is..recent. **1908** *Practitioner* Sept. 360 The sounds which will best aid are those..having interchangeable olive-shaped metallic heads. **1930** T. S. ELIOT tr. *St.-J. Perse's Anabasis* 65 He who fashions a leather tunic, wooden shoes and olive-shaped buttons. **1904** W. H. HUDSON *Green Mansions* 4 The nervous olive-skinned Hispano-American of the tropics. **1970** H. M. DAVY *Caring for your Appearance* iii. 35 Some of your friends may have a very pale skin throughout all seasons... Some others, with the very darkest colouring, we may describe as olive skinned. **1864** J. R. LOWELL *Fireside Trav.* 222 Climbing the sides of the nearer Monticelli in a gray belt of olive-spray. **1957** *Encycl. Brit.* XVI. 773/2 The wild olive spray of the Olympic victor. **1904** S. E. WHITE *Silent Places* i. 4 The white-throats and olive thrushes called in a language hardly less intelligible. **1911** J. A. LEACH *Austral. Bird Bk.* 152 Olive Whistler, Olivaceous Thickhead... Olive brown; head dark-gray... Liquid, whistling note. **1933** *Bulletin* (Sydney) 20 Sept. 21/1 A curious example of vocal variation among birds..is found in the 'olive whistler'. **1944** A. RUSSELL *Bush Ways* xxii. 105 A recluse of the open scrubs of the dry south-eastern interior, as the olive whistler is to the mountain mists of the coast ranges. **1965** *Austral. Encycl.* IX. 292/1 The olive whistler, of eastern Australia and Tasmania, is probably one of the sweetest singers among the birds of Australia.

olive-branch. 1. b. (Further examples.)
1856 R. GLISAN *Jrnl. Army Life* (1874) xxiv. 324 The troops..moved up Rogue River..with the olive branch in one hand, and the sword in the other. **1936** WODEHOUSE *Laughing Gas* v. 60 He read his *National Geographic Magazine*. I read mine. And for some minutes matters proceeded along these lines. Then I thought to myself: 'Oh, well, dash it,' and decided to extend the olive branch. **1975** B. GARFIELD *Hopscotch* xxvii. 283 Abandoning the manuscript..could be an olive branch: Kendig's..assurance he was quitting.

olive-oil. Add: Also attrib.
1895 *Montgomery Ward Catal.* Spring & Summer 109/2 A pure, natural color olive oil soap made of the finest selected oil imported for this purpose. **1957** *Encycl. Brit.* XVI. 774/2 California olive oil output is normally less than 1% that of Spain. **1970** 'D. HALLIDAY' *Dolly & Cookie Bird* ii. 10 They have..vineyards and..three olive-oil factories. **1977** P. WAY *Super-Celeste* 52 The Mafia godfathers could..declare they were olive oil merchants.

2. A jocular mispronunciation of *au revoir*.
1906 *Dialect Notes* III. 148 *Olive oil, n. phr.*, au revoir. Facetious. **1909** J. R. WARE *Passing Eng.* 187/2 *Olive oil* (Music Hall, 1884). English pronunciation of *au revoir.* **1933** PARTRIDGE *Slang To-day & Yesterday* III. iii. 206 For 'good-bye', the boys at Dulwich already in 1906 used.. *olive oil* (au revoir). **1960** WENTWORTH & FLEXNER *Dict. Amer. Slang* 364/2 *Olive oil*, good-bye.

Oliver³ (ǫ·livəɹ). *slang.* Also **oliver.** [A male Christian name, perh. alluding to *Oliver* Cromwell (1599–1658), leader of the Parliamentary troops in the Civil War.] The moon.
1781 [see WHIDDLE *v.*]. **1834** W. H. AINSWORTH *Rookwood* II. v. 360 Now Oliver puts his black nightcap on, And every star its glim is hiding. *Ibid.* III. v. 284 Oliver whiddles!—who cares—who cares If down upon us he peers and stares? Mind him who will? with his great white face, Boldly *I'll* ride by his glim to the chase. **1870** R. F. BURTON *Vikram & Vampire* v. 171 But, look sharp, mind old Oliver, or the lamb-skin man will have the pull of us. **1882** *Sydney Slang Dict.* 6/2 *Oliver*, the moon. 'When Oliver looks pale,' when the moon is waning. **1895** *New Rev.* July 7 'There's a moon out.' 'The better for us to pick 'em off, Dan,' I returned, laughing at him. 'What —Oliver? damn Oliver!' said Zacchary. 'Let's push forward and come to quarters.' **1935** E. WEEKLEY *Something about Words* vi. 107 *Oliver*, thieves' cant for the moon, is not in the Oxford Dictionary.

Oliver⁴ (ǫ·livəɹ). [The name of William *Oliver* (1695–1764), a physician of Bath, who invented the recipe.] = *Bath Oliver* (s.v. *BATH *sb.*² 2 a). Also *attrib.*
1853 E. M. SEWELL *Experience of Life* ii. 18 The Oliver biscuits, in the small, deep, old china dessert plates, were to my belief then never bought at any shop in Carsdale. *Ibid.* vii. 64 She was sitting..at a table..on which stood ..a china basket with Oliver biscuits.

Olivetti (ǫlive·ti). [Name of the manufacturers.] The proprietary name of a range of typewriters.
1949 *Trade Marks Jrnl.* 23 Mar. 255/1 Olivetti...Typewriters. Ing. C. Olivetti & C., Società per Azioni .., Ivrea, Province of Turin, Italy; machine manufacturers. **1966** AUDEN *About House* 18 The Olivetti portable, The dictionaries (the very Best money can buy). **1968** *Listener* 28 Nov. 736/1 You can still go for a walk down Gloucester Crescent and below the chatter of a dozen Olivettis catch the soft murmur of extra-marital associations. **1977** G. FISHER *Villain of Piece* i. 3, I..glared at my Olivetti. There was a sheet of copy paper in it.

olivescent (ǫlive·sĕnt), *a.* [f. OLIVE + -ESCENT.] Of colour: bordering on or slightly olive.
1900 *Proc. Zool. Soc.* 506 *Kirontisa whiteheadi...* Upper-side deep olivescent brown. Fore wing with two paler olivescent marks within.

olive-yard. (Later examples.)
1880 J. H. SHORTHOUSE *John Inglesant* xxxvii. 523 He had come into the cool pastures and olive yards. **1911** *Encycl. Brit.* XX. 87/1 Many olive-yards now exist in Upper Egypt.

olivine. c. (Examples.)
1895 A. HARKER *Petrol.* 115 Numerous olivine-diabases are associated with the Carboniferous strata of the Midlands. *Ibid.* 68 The Tertiary gabbros of the western islands of Scotland..are in general olivine-gabbros. **1900** [see *KENTALLENITE]. **1936** J. S. FLETT in Wilson & Knox *Geol. Orkney* xvii. 180 They are the only olivine-basalt dykes that have been discovered in the Orkneys. **1956** W. EDWARDS in D. L. Linton *Sheffield* 15 Boreholes in the southeastern part of the coalfield have revealed thick, sill-like beds of olivine-dolerite and analcime-dolerite. **1965** E. L. P. MERCY in G. Y. Craig *Geol. of Scotland* vii. 243/2 Rhythmic banding in the olivine-gabbros and troctolites has been described.

olland, var. *OLD LAND.

Ollendorffian (ǫlĕndǭ·ɹfiăn), *a.* Also **Ollendorfian.** [f. the name of Heinrich Gottfried *Ollendorff*, German educator and grammarian (1803–65) + -IAN.] In the stilted language of foreign phrase-books.
[**1876** C. M. YONGE *Womankind* vi. 40 German [learnt] by the Ollendorf method.] [**1886** F. M. CRAWFORD in H. Norman *Broken Shaft* 18 The simple but instructive dialogues of Herr Ollendorff.] **1892** *New Rev.* Feb. 252 But the characters have as much individuality as the Ollendorffian prattlers about the gardener. **1900** *Sketch* 21 Feb. 191/2 She persisted in firing off Ollendorfian French at the waiters. **1905** *Westm. Gaz.* 8 July 2/3 'Views' which we snapshot, be they views of mountains or of men, and whether we use Kodak or Ollendorffian chitchat to produce them. **1918** L. HUXLEY *Life J. D. Hooker* II. xliii. 327 He started them also, and very successfully, with colloquial Latin from an Ollendorffian French handbook. **1934** H. G. WELLS *Exper. Autobiogr.* II. ix. 766 A sort of Ollendorfian French.

ollunt, var. *OLD LAND.

olm (ōulm). [G.] = PROTEUS 3 b.
1905 A. SEDGWICK *Student's Text-bk. Zool.* II. x. 307 *Proteus* Laur., the olm, 3 fingers, 2 toes, eyes hidden, Carniola subterranean waters. **1926** J. S. HUXLEY *Ess. Pop. Sci.* viii. 93 Three or four other species of animals, such as Proteus, the blind 'Olm' of Carniola, and Necturus, which..are not known in a land-form at all. **1955** W. LEY *Salamanders* i. 3 The olm's rather restricted habitat..is a mountainous area in southern Europe, at the northern end of the Balkan peninsula. *Ibid.* 4 The olm is blind, having no use for eyes in the cold dark caves where it normally lives. **1965** B. E. FREEMAN tr. *Vandel's Biospeleol.* iii. 22 It was *Proteus* which firstly, because of its size, attracted the attention of man, and [was] also the first to receive a vernacular name, the olm.

Olmec (ǫ·lmek). [ad. Nahuatl *Olmecatl*, pl. *Olmeca* lit. 'inhabitants of the rubber country'.] **1.** Also **Olmeca.** A native American people or peoples inhabiting the coast of southern Veracruz and western Tabasco during the 15th and 16th centuries, to where they probably migrated during the 12th century from the Mexican altiplano.
1787 C. CULLEN tr. *Clavigero's Hist. Mexico* I. II. 103 The Olmecas and the Xicallancas, whether one nation, or two distinct nations, but constantly allied and connected together, were so ancient in the country of Anahuac, that many authors account them prior to the Toltecas. **1883** P. J. J. VALENTINI in *Proc. Amer. Antiquarian Soc.* II. 193 (*heading*) The Olmecas and the Tultecas: a study in early Mexican ethnology and history. **1914** T. A. JOYCE *Mexican Archaeol.* v. 125 Though bows were found among the Olmec and Huaxtec, they must have been of quite late introduction. **1931** G. MASON *Columbus came Late* xi. 238 The Olmeca people that inhabited the damp country of southern Vera Cruz and western Tabasco. **1947** M. COVARRUBIAS *Mexico South* iv. 129 The builders of the cities of El Tajín and Teotihuacán..were the Olmecs proper. **1964** C. GIBSON *Aztecs under Spanish Rule* 9 The most important migrant peoples pertinent to Valley [of Mexico] history in the Post-Classic or late pre-colonial period were the Olmeca, Xicalanca, Tolteca, Chichimeca, Teochichimeca, Otomi. .. The first five of these were historically extinct, absorbed, or expelled by the time of the arrival of Europeans.

2. A prehistoric people inhabiting the same area *c* 1200–100 BC. Also *attrib.* or as *adj.*; *spec.* designating the culture of this people or its characteristic artistic style, also found elsewhere in southern Mexico. So **O·lmecan, O·lmecoid** *adjs.*
[**1927** H. BEYER in *El Mexico Antiguo* II. 306 (*caption*) Idolo Olmego di Piedra Verdosa.] **1929** *Indian Notes* (Mus. Amer. Indian, Heye Foundation) VI. 280 Beyer published a picture of what he calls 'an Olmecan idol' formerly in his possession and now in a private collection. *Ibid.* 285 This peculiar type of mask may be safely assigned to the ancient Olmecan culture, which apparently had its center in the San Andrés Tuxtla area around Lake Catemaco. **1932** *Natural Hist.* XXXII. 519/2 There is often described in the traditions a highly civilized people called the Olmec, who lived anciently as far north as Tlaxcala, but were later dispersed to southern Vera Cruz, Chiapas, southern Puebla, and eastern Oaxaca. They were famed for their work in jade and turquoise, and were credited with being the chief users of rubber in Central America. *Ibid.* 520/2 Perhaps investigations in the Olmec area would clarify the much discussed relationship between the Mexicans and the Mayas. **1943** M. W. STIRLING *Stone Monuments S. Mexico* 7 Two years later he released a study..of the giant head in which he emphasized its 'Ethiopian' features, features which have since been identified with the style of art called Olmec. *Ibid.* 54 The niche..represents the 'Olmec' open-jaguar-mouth motive. **1960** *Times* 6 Oct. 4/6 The Veracruz region, which is rich in..treasures of the Olmec..coastal cultures of ancient Mexico. **1962** G. ASHE *Land to West* viii. 222 A clay Fire-god of the prehistoric Olmecs on the Gulf coast. **1965** M. D. COE in R. Wauchope *Handbk. Middle Amer. Indians* III. II. 738 (*heading*) The Olmec style and its distributions. *Ibid.* 765 As one moves away from the core region and also into later time periods, many objects are encountered which are more or less Olmecoid, but these are not Olmec in our meaning. **1966** *Listener* 29 Dec. 957/1 The most ancient civilization of Mesoamerica is that of the Olmecs. **1967** L. DEUEL *Conquistadors without Swords* xxi. 287 (*caption*) Substructure of Pyramid E-VII with its Olmecoid stucco masks. **1973** *New Yorker* 24 Mar. 108/2 The Olmec civilization was not identified as such until the nineteen-forties. **1973** *Black World* July 13/1 The huge stone heads of Olmec deities, exhibited an unmistakably African physiognomy. **1973** *Times* 15 Oct. 11/8 The Olmec Forerunners, the archaic predecessors of the Maya though probably not themselves Maya. **1977** *Sci. Amer.* Mar. 116/1 The Olmec, one of the earliest of the complex societies in the region, built major ceremonial centres on the low-lying coastal plain of the Gulf of Mexico; examples are San Lorenzo and La Venta. *Ibid.*, At the same time the Olmec zone of cultural influence and Olmec trade extended into much of the high plateau.

ological. (Earlier example.)
1854 DICKENS *Hard T.* I. xv. 120, I hope you may now turn all your ological studies to good account.

-ology, ology, *suffix* and quasi-*sb.* Add: **2.** Also **'ology.** (Further examples.)
1854 DICKENS *Hard T.* II. ix. 236 Ologies of all kinds, from morning to night. If there is any Ology left..that has not been worn to rags in this house..I hope I shall never hear its name. **1886** KIPLING *Departmental Ditties* (ed. 2) 57 And after—ask the Yusufzaies What comes of all our 'ologies. **1927** G. D. H. & M. COLE *Murder at Crome House* iv. 42 'I don't think she's interested in anything except some 'ology—' 'Psychology, I think, sir,' said Johnson. **1972** C. L. COOPER in W. King *Black Short Story Anthol.* 237 With Famat's help,..I came to grasp an ology that was an intermixture of Ax, orthodox Islam, and theory. **1976** A. PRICE *War Game* I. ix. 172 One's doing a thesis on geology now, and the other's writing a book on meteorology. Ology is about the only thing they have in common.

ololiuqui (ōuloliū·ki). Also **ololiuhqui.** [ad. Amer. Sp. *ololiuque*, f. Nahuatl *ololiuhqui* 'one that covers'.] A Mexican climbing plant, *Rivea corymbosa* (*Ipomœa sidifolia*), of the family Convolvulaceæ; also, the narcotic drug prepared from its seeds. Also *attrib.*
1915 W. E. SAFFORD in *Jrnl. Heredity* VI. 311 It is very strange that Mexican botanists living in the country of the

Ololiuhqui have not solved the mystery of its identity. **1926** *Chambers's Jrnl.* Aug. 513/2 [He] bemused himself with the seeds of the ololiuhqui. **1941** R. E. SCHULTES (*title*) A contribution to our knowledge of *Rivea corymbosa*, the narcotic ololiuqui of the Aztecs. **1954** A. HUXLEY *Let.* 2 Mar. (1969) 699 Ololiuqu(i) is used by the Mexican and Cuban witch doctors to increase ESP faculties and relieve disease. **1962** —— *Island* xi. 171 He began to talk about the indoles recently isolated from the ololiuqui seeds that had been brought in from Mexico last year. **1966** *New Scientist* 21 Apr. 156/1 In Mexico, the seeds of climbing convulvulus plants known as 'morning glory' are made into a drug called 'ololiuqui'. **1973** *Sci. Amer.* Oct. 130/2 The seeds of certain Mexican morning glories, . . the source of a magic Aztec potion, ololiuqui, used to 'communicate with the gods and receive the secret things'.

Olonetsian (ǫlone·tsiăn). Also **Olonecian, Olonetzian.** [f. *Olonets*, the name of a town and former government in N.W. Russia.] A dialect of Karelian spoken to the north east of Lake Ladoga. Also **Olo·nets.**

1932 W. L. GRAFF *Lang.* xi. 405 Finno-Ugric . . dialects. These are . .: Carelian, Olonetsian, [etc.]. **1933, 1939** [see *LUDIAN]. **1946–47** *Slavonic & E. European Rev.* XXV. 436 Olonecian (Aunus), heard on the eastern shores of Lake Ladoga . ., and the Ingrian . . of Ingria . ., are dialectical varieties of Carelian. **1954** PEI & GAYNOR *Dict. Linguistics* 154 *Olonetzian*, a member of the Finnish group of the Finno-Ugric (or Uralic) sub-family of the Ural-Altaic family of languages. **1957** B. COLLINDER *Survey Uralic Lang.* p. v, The dialects spoken in the Karelian-Finnish Soviet Republic are called Karelian (kr, in the north) and Olonets (ol, in the south). **1965** —— *Introd. Uralic Lang.* i. 11 Olonets (Olonetsian) is a variant of Karelian, spoken in the former province of Olonets . . and strongly influenced by Russian. **1975** G. F. CUSHING tr. *Hajdu's Finno-Ugrian Lang. & Peoples* 199 Tver Carelian is spoken in the Upper Volga region, Aunus or Olonets to the north-east of Lake Ladoga.

oloroso (ǫlŏrōᵘ·so). [Sp. *oloroso* fragrant.] A type of dry or medium sherry; a glass of such sherry.

1876 H. VIZETELLY *Facts about Sherry* v. 46 The olorosos . . are deeper in colour than the amontillados. **1888** [see *FINO]. **1908** C. E. HAWKER *Chats about Wine* vii. 105 There are several varieties of Sherry . . the 'fino' . . and the 'Oloroso'. **1920** G. SAINTSBURY *Notes on Cellar-Bk.* ii. 20 One might jangle a long time on Montillas and Olorosos. **1935** 'R. HULL' *Keep it Quiet* iv. 34 It seemed best . . to let them try the proposed new Oloroso . . Both . . pronounced the new sherry to be disgusting. **1955** W. GADDIS *Recognitions* I. i. 59 He seemed prepared to sit over that dark oloroso sherry all evening. **1961** [see *AMONTILLADO a]. **1966** *Harper's Bazaar* Mar. 105 Oloroso, the darker, fuller style of sherry which, although dry in the natural state, is almost invariably sweetened for export. **1972** *Times* 20 Oct. 4/6 (Advt.), A very old, rich oloroso cream sherry. **1974** *Times* 23 Feb. 13/5 In Jerez, the producers like to start the day with a glass of natural dry oloroso. **1976** *Daily Tel.* 26 Oct. 17 [Yesterday] it [*sc.* the High Court] gave the sherry producers of the Jerez district of Spain what they had sued to obtain in 1970—exclusive right in Britain to use the descriptions *amontillado, oloroso* and *fino.*

olpe (ǫ·lpe). *Greek Antiq.* [ad. Gr. ὄλπη leather oil-flask, ewer, wine-jug.] **a.** A leather flask for oil or some other liquid. **b.** A kind of jug with a pear-shaped body and a handle.

1883 J. W. MOLLETT *Illustr. Dict. Art & Archæol.* 233/2 *Olpê* . . a kind of *aryballos* with a curved handle, but no spout (originally a leather oil-flask). **1937** *Times Lit. Suppl.* 6 Feb. 93/1 An interesting eye olpe. **1961** *Oxf. Univ. Gaz.* 10 Mar. 832/1 A small late (?) Corinthian olpe with waves, dots and wavy lines. **1969** R. MAYER *Dict. Art Terms & Techniques* 269/1 *Olpe*, in ancient Greek pottery, a short-necked jug tapering to a foot . . The word also denoted a leather flask used for carrying liquids. **1974** SAVAGE & NEWMAN *Illustr. Dict. Ceramics* 207 *Olpe* (Greek), a type of wine-jug resembling an *oenochoë.*

oly-cook, oly-koek. Add: Also **oliekoek, olycoek, -coke.** (Later examples.)

1881 *Harper's Mag.* Mar. 533/1 His favorite city has surpassed all others in . . olie koeks, and New Year cookies. **1889** R. T. COOKE *Steadfast* vi. 78 Refreshing him with hot flip, oly koek, or Indian preserves. **1895** *Dialect Notes* I. 387 In the Dutch-settled districts the word *olykoeks*, which Washington Irving has made classic, is used for some of the varieties [of doughnut]. **1947** R. BEROLZHEIMER et al. *U.S. Regional Cook Bk.* 138 The doughnut originated in Holland where it was called 'olie koeken'.

Olympia (oli·mpiă). The name of a town at the southern end of Puget Sound, the capital of the state of Washington, used *absol.* or *attrib.* in **Olympia oyster** to designate a small oyster, *Ostrea lurida*, native to the region.

[**1887** G. B. GOODE *Fisheries U.S.: Geogr. Rev.* 626 No fishing is done at Olympia, the harbor being nearly bare at low water and lined with oysters. The shipment of these oysters to San Francisco is the only fishing industry of the town. The first shipment of these oysters was made two or three years ago.] **1908** *Nat. Geogr. Mag.* Mar. 225/1 New beds will have to be planted, and it will be five years before the so-called 'Olympia oyster' will again be on the market. **1911** *Encycl. Brit.* XX. 97/1 Olympia oysters are widely known in the Pacific coast region; they are obtained chiefly from Oyster Bay, Skookum Bay, North Bay and South Bay, all near Olympia. **1953** R. FROMAN *One Million Islands* 180 The tiny Olympia oysters also have their own unique flavor. **1957** M. MCCARTHY *Memories Catholic Girlhood* viii. 203 Tiny Olympia oysters . . . Olympia oyster cocktail. **1961** *Spectator* 8 Dec. 879/1 American ingredients and American cooking . . have always to me seemed most mysterious . . . Olympia pan roast (olympia is an oyster) and Green Goddess dressing . . turn out to be entirely local [i.e. West Coast] inventions. **1965** M. TRACY *Shellfish Cookery* v. 99 Olympia oysters are tiny West Coast oysters . . . They are ambrosial, and fabulously expensive even near their home waters.

Olympiad. Add: **1. b.** A quadrennial celebration of the ancient Olympic Games.

a **1490** J. SKELTON tr. *Diodorus Siculus' Bibliotheca Historica* (1956) I. 382 Whiche maner of fayttis, thus ordeyned by his former instytucion, were callyd Olympiades. **1614** RALEGH *Hist. World* I. II. xxiii. 576 These Olympiads . . . To tell the great solemnitie of them, and with what exceeding great concourse of all Greece they were celebrated, I hold it a superfluous labour. **1728** I. NEWTON *Chronol. Anc. Kingdoms Amended* i. 47 This Breviary seems to have contained nothing more than a short account of the Victors in every Olympiad. **1852** G. GROTE *Hist. Greece* X. 439 They revenged themselves by pronouncing the 104th Olympiad to be no Olympiad at all. **1913** F. A. M. WEBSTER *Olympian Field Events* I. i. 7 We have certain proof that it [*sc.* javelin throwing] was a part of the Pentathlon in the Ancient Olympiads. **1960** A. R. BURN *Lyric Age Greece* ix. 177 He [*sc.* Pheidon of Argos] was said to have marched west to Olympia and presided over the Games of the eighth Olympiad (748). **1977** *Jrnl. Hellenic Stud.* XCVII. 16 This no doubt partly accounts for the well-known string of Spartan victories in running events at the early Olympiads.

2. A (quadrennial) celebration of the modern Olympic Games revived in 1896. Hence, an occurrence of other competitions held on a regular basis. Also *fig.*

1907 *Westm. Gaz.* 1 Aug. 10/3 When the last Olympiad was held at St. Louis, U.S.A., in 1904, it was decided to hold the next in Rome. **1923** *Glasgow Herald* 26 Mar. 11/4 But the Oxford supporters were clamant in their championing, and by the time the final preparations were made the element of discord, like the seed of the apple of the Olympiads, had entered into the multitudes. **1935** *Encycl. Sports* 440/2 The next Olympiad, as the games came to be called, was held at Stockholm [in 1912]. **1957** W. PERELMAN tr. *Flohr's Twelfth Chess Tournament of Nations* 5 The first Olympiad was held in London in 1927, . . when 16 countries took part. **1959** *Listener* 22 Oct. 706/3 There was no reason why a British team [of Bridge players] should not be successful in the first World Olympiad next spring. **1964** —— 29 Oct. 695/1 Next week the chess olympiad begins in Tel Aviv, Israel . . . Unlike the Olympic Games, this is a team event, held every two years. **1967** —— 17 Aug. 213/2 Sixth-form specialisation is indeed producing diminishing returns: is the flight from maths and science compensated for by the winning of a mathematical Olympiad? **1972** *Daily Tel.* 21 June 14/5 Britain scored 42 victory points out of 60 during Monday's play in the World Bridge Olympiad. *Ibid.* 30 Aug. 9/3 Miss Pauline Dukelow, 16, paralysed from the age of three, is to receive the Andrew and Booth Courage award for the 21st Olympiad of the Paralysed at Heidelberg this month. **1976** *Radio Times* 15 May 37/1 In the following six Olympiads the Soviet Union have won over 500 medals. **1977** *Daily Times* (Lagos) 25 Feb. 17/4 This great cultural Olympiad was a gigantic step towards pan-Africanism and the unity of the black man.

Olympian, *sb.* Add: **1. b.** A competitor in the modern Olympic Games.

1976 *Billings* (Montana) *Gaz.* 27 June 7-F/6 The games are part of a 12-game tour for the *Olympians*, coached by North Carolina's Dean Smith, in preparation for the Montreal Games in July. **1977** *Time* 13 June 21/1 To support themselves during the rigors of year-round training, many Olympians have accepted deals from manufacturers and fees for appearing in track and field meets, hiding their earnings from Olympic, Amateur Athletic Union and international sports federations officials.

Olympic. Add: **A.** *adj.* **2. b.** Of or pertaining to the modern *Olympic Games*, which were revived as a quadrennial international athletic meeting at Athens in 1896 and have been held in various places since then. Also *transf.*

1896 *Scribner's Mag.* Apr. 453/1 The revival of the Olympic Games. Restoring the Stadion at Athens. **1908** *Westm. Gaz.* 31 Mar. 8/3 There is now some confusion with regard to the International Olympic games. **1914** R. BROOKE *Let.* 5 Dec. (1968) 638 A New Zealand youth who was fighting in Mexico, heard the news in August, walked 300 miles to the coast, got a boat, and turned up here. He is also an Olympic Swimmer: and *knows* the *South Seas.* **1936** J. BUCHAN *Island of Sheep* iv. 60 It was not the Peter that you knew in the War, but Peter ten years younger, with no grey in his beard, and as trim and light and hard as an Olympic athlete. **1960** *Times* 5 Sept. 4/6 Hill . . was representing a Germany united for Olympic purposes. **1962** *Listener* 1 Feb. 234/1 A match [at Bridge] between Italy and the U.S.A. in the Olympic event two years ago. **1964** D. M. KUNZLE in G. C. Kunzle *Parallel Bars* 14 It was the whole conception of modern Olympic Gymnastics which was under fire. **1965** V. CANNING *Whip Hand* xii. 134 He's also first class with foils and sabre, Wimbledon standard tennis, Olympic standard swimming, and a double-first Oxford. **1968** MRS. L. B. JOHNSON *White House Diary* 10 Mar. (1970) 637 Lyndon . . can break an Olympic record for getting dressed . . . We were out the door in about eight minutes. **1972** G. LYALL *Blame the Dead* i. 7 He scuttled away, carrying the pencil and cartridge case in front like a little Olympic torch. **1972** *Guardian* 19 Aug. 1/4 It is very important that he doesn't bring any infection that could affect other athletes in the Olympic Village. **1974** *Times* 21 Jan. 4/3 The boys are encouraged to join in games with them, swim in the pool of Olympic dimensions and just talk to them during breaks between intelligence tests and interviews. **1976** *Scotsman* 20 Nov. (Weekend Suppl.) 2/6 She used 30 cameramen and shot more than a million feet of film glorifying the Olympic ideal.

c. *Comb.*, with reference to the modern Olympic Games, as *Olympic-size, -sized, -style* adjs.

1966 J. BALL *Cool Cottontail* (1967) 17 A beautifully decked Olympic-size swimming pool. **1970** 'E. LATHEN' *Pick up Sticks* (1971) iv. 36 The heart of Fiord Haven, where Havenites will enjoy an Olympic-size indoor swimming pool. **1969** *Guardian* 16 June 2/6 The 600-acre military 'city', 40 miles from Saigon . . contains . . an Olympic-sized swimming pool. **1966** *Times* 28 Feb. (Canada Suppl.) p. xiv/5 Canada's 1967 Pan-American Games, which includes Olympic-style amateur wrestling.

B. *sb.* Add to def.: Used esp. of the revived Olympic Games. Also *transf.*

1928 in *Funk's Stand. Dict.* **1948** KIERAN & DALEY *Story of Olympic Games* (rev. ed.) xiii. 327 The 'surest thing' in the Olympics never looked surer. **1948** *Official Rep. Olympic Games* (Brit. Olympic Assoc.) 41/1 No boxing competition of comparable size had been attempted anywhere in the world since the Berlin Olympics of 1936. **1949** W. M. HUGILL in *Phoenix* (Toronto) III. 31 One school of thought has repudiated any connection between culture and the modern Olympics. **1951** *European Bridge Rev.* June 5/1 The 1951 Australian Jubilee Year World Olympic for contract bridge pairs. **1974** *Encycl. Brit. Macropædia* II. 274/1 The development of the modern Olympics into the pre-eminent athletic events in the world. **1976** *New Scientist* 28 Oct. 203/2 Any competitor in the gravitational Olympics must be able to pass the three classical tests of relativity that Einstein proposed in 1916.

‖ **om** (ǭm), *int.* Also **o'm.** [Skr.] In Hinduism and Buddhism, an utterance of assent used in prayer and meditation. Also as *sb.*, an instance or example of this assent, and as *v. intr.*, to utter the assent. (See also quot. 1917.)

1788 W. JONES in *Asiatick Researches* I. 262, I am inclined, indeed, to believe, that not only *Crishna* or *Vishnu*, but even *Brahma'* and *Siva*, when united, and expressed by the mystical word *o'm*, were designed by the first idolaters to represent the Solar fire. **1810** E. MOOR *Hindu Pantheon* 410 The character, that, if uttered, would yield the sound of *o'm*; or, being triliteral, better, perhaps, written *aum. Ibid.* 412 A suppression of breath is thus explained by an ancient legislator to imply the following meditation: '*Om*! earth! sky! heaven!' **1899** R. WHITEING *No. 5 John St.* xv. 153 The Brahmin leads us gently to the outermost courts of Nirvana. In spite of the outward symbol, we look within, and there we may hope to find *om.* **1917** A. B. KEITH in *Encycl. Relig. & Ethics* IX. 490/2 The first evidence of this important position of the word is to be found in the *Aitareya Brāhmaṇa* (v. 32) in which it is declared that *om* is the world of heaven and the sun, and where it is resolved into the three letters *a, u,* and *m.* **1937** M. COVARRUBIAS *Island of Bali* (1972) ix. 318 Typical Brahmana are the speculations about the sacred syllable *ong*, the Om of India. **1956** E. WOOD *Yoga Dict.* 113/1 *Om*, the greatest *mantra* . . or word of power. *Ibid.* 114/1 *Om* is recited by devout Hindus at the beginning of all prayers, hymns and words of worship or aspiration. **1971** *Illustr. Weekly India* 4 Apr. 31/2 The note greets me, '*Hare Krishna.* Please accept my *Om* prayers for your eternal well being. I would like to see you for a few minutes.' **1972** P. HOLROYDE *Indian Music* ii. 58 The sound '*om*' . ., pronounced 'a-u-m', rings out like the tolling of a cathedral bell. **1976** B. JACKSON *Flameout* i. 17 He . . took deep yogic breaths, loudly hummed a long, resonant '*om—om—om—*' . . . 'It's sure good to hear you *om*-ing.'

-oma, terminal element repr. Gr. -ωμα, in which ω repr. ω (or ο) in the parent word (usu. a vb.) and -μα is a Gr. suffix forming neut. sbs., exemplified in Eng. words adopted from the Gr. such as CARCINOMA, COLOBOMA, DERMA, DIPLOMA, ECZEMA, GLAUCOMA, PHYMA, PLASMA, SARCOMA, TRACHOMA, and in words on Gr. analogy such as LIPOMA. In *Bot.* -*oma* has usu. been anglicized to *-OME. In *Med.* the examples of *sarcoma* (17th c. in English) and *carcinoma* (18th c.) have been taken as types on which to base new names of neoplasms and other localized swellings, -*oma* († -*ome*) being used as a suffix denoting 'tumour, growth' (cf. also Gr. ὄγκωμα swelling): e.g. FIBROMA († FIBROME), *CEMENTOMA, *OLIGODENDROGLIOMA, *TUBERCULOMA († TUBERCULOME).

Omaha (ōᵘ·mahā). Also **† Maha, † Omawhaw.** Pl. **Omaha, Omahas.** [ad. Omaha *umonhon* upstream people.] A Siouan people in north-eastern Nebraska, or their language; a member of this people. Also *attrib.* or as *adj.*

1804 W. CLARK in Lewis & Clark *Orig. Jrnls. Lewis & Clark Expedition* (1904) I. 34 As we were pushing off this morning two Canoos Loaded with fur &c came to from the Mahas nation. *Ibid.* 124 This Village was built by a Indian Chief of the Maha nation. **1814** H. M. BRACKENRIDGE *Views Louisiana* I. vi. 76 Mahas, (or Oo-ma-ha) Reside on the Maha creek. **1823** E. JAMES *Acct. Expedition Rocky Mts.* I. 190 Several of the Pawnee *caches* . . had been broken open and robbed of their corn by the Omawhaws. **1839** *Boston Weekly Mag.* 12 Jan. 145/2 The Omaha village was one of the most beautiful that can be imagined. **1854** W. G. Simms *Southward Ho!* 406 The Pawnees and the Omahas were neighboring but hostile nations. **1900** G. B. Grinnell *Indians of To-day* 12 He killed one more Omaha. **1920** [see *avunculate]. **1936** F. B. Streeter *Prairie Trails* iv. 190 He went with the Omaha Indians on a buffalo hunt. **1957** [see *Kansa]. **1964, 1968** [see *Crow *a.* 2]. **1972** W. B. Lockwood *Panorama Indo-Europ. Lang.* vii. 117 The plains between the Mississippi and the Missouri were occupied by the Siouan family [of languages], of which the most significant today are Dakota (45,000) and Omaha (10,000). **1974** *Encycl. Brit. Micropædia* VII. 528/3 *Omaha*, North American Indian people of the Dhegiha branch of the Siouan language stock. *Ibid.*, Omaha social organization was elaborate, with a class system of chiefs, priests, physicians and commoners.

omanhene (ōᵘ·manhene). [Ashanti f. *oman* council + *-hene* combining form of *ohene* chief.] Among the Ashanti people of West Africa, a paramount chief of a state or district, under whom are the lesser chiefs of villages.

1909 Moore & Guggisberg *We Two in W. Africa* xi. 146, I met my first *omanhin* at Tarkwa—'king' he would have been called some years ago but his title is not officially recognised now, the head chief of a tribe being known by the native equivalent of *omanhin*. **1923** R. S. Rattray *Ashanti* xxii. 264, I am greatly indebted to an Ashanti chief, Osai Bonsu, *Omanhene* of Mampon, for permitting his drummer to drum this complete history into a phonograph. **1955** D. E. Apter *Gold Coast in Transition* iv. 94 The chief became known as the *omanhene* or head of council, among the Ashanti. **1959** A. Abbs *Ashanti Boy* i. 17 That was nothing strange to a conscientious Omanhene to whom the family in its widest sense meant 'the tribe'. **1961** *Guardian* 10 Nov. 1/1 Chiefs and their retinues from all over the country..Nenes, Omanhenes, Nanas, Niis, Togbes, and..[the] Fiaga of Peki. **1962** C. G. Baëta *Prophetism in Ghana* iii. 61 The head of the Church is referred to as *Omanhene* or 'Paramount Chief'.

Omani (omā·ni), *sb.* and *a.* Also 9 **Omanee, Omany.** [Arab., f. *Oman* name of a coastal region in the south-east of the Arabian peninsula + *-i* adj. suffix.] **A.** *sb.* A native or inhabitant of Oman. **B.** *adj.* Also in form *Oman* (the place-name used *attrib.*). Of or pertaining to Oman or its inhabitants.

c **1819** F. Warden in *Sel. Rec. Bombay Govt.* (1856) No. 24, 433 It would give the Omanees sufficient time to unite and assemble for their general defence. **1819** —— in *Ibid.* 44 It is probable that the Oman Chiefs of the Hinavi tribe will..return to their former relations with the Imaum. **1838** J. R. Wellsted *Trav. Arabia* I. ii. 16 In consequence of the difference in their faith, the Omán Arabs and Persians seldom intermarry. *Ibid.* xix. 292 The Omány in all ages is celebrated in the songs of the Arabs as the fleetest. **1865** W. G. Palgrave *Narr. Journey through Arabia* II. xv. 256 The principal family whose chiefs headed the original settlement was, according to 'Omânee tradition, that of the Ya'aribah. *Ibid.* 262 These new hostilities on the part of Islam suggested to the sectarian 'Omânees the expediency of new measures. **1871** G. P. Badger *Hist. of Imâms & Seyyids of Omân* p. xvii, A battle was fought in which the 'Omânis were defeated with great loss. *Ibid.* p. xxxvii, In order to test the pluck of the 'Omâny sovereign..he sent him a viciously restive horse. **1928** A. T. Wilson *Persian Gulf* xii. 174 The inhabitants virtually deserted the island, by this means bringing the Omani occupation to an end. A year or two later..the Omanis seized certain islands off the Persian coast. **1931** E. Waugh *Remote People* 165 Instead of the cultured, rather decadent aristocracy of the Oman Arabs, we have given them [*sc.* the Zanzibar Islanders] a caste of just, soap-loving young men with public school blazers. **1973** *Nat. Geographic* Feb. 209/1 Omanis danced in the streets for days. **1973** *Times* 15 Feb. 7/1 He saw in Muscat an Omani whom he recognized as having served as a political commissar in..Dhufar in 1971. **1973** *Black Panther* 4 Aug. 11/2 The struggle of the Oman people has..had wide success in the building of institutions to insure the people's survival. **1974** *Times* 18 Jan. 15/4 The 'Red Line' is the name given by the Omani guerrillas to the road linking the town of Salalah..to the Omani capital Muscat.

Omaresque (ōᵘmăre·sk), *a. rare.* [f. as next + -esque.] Suggestive of Omar Khayyam or his poetry.

1892 *Academy* 5 Nov. 404/1 In shorter measures there is often an Omaresque effect of thought.

Omarian (omā·riăn), *a.* and *sb.* [f. the name of the Persian mathematician and epigrammatist, Ghiyāthuddīn Abulfath *'Omar* bin Ibrāhīm al-Khayyāmī (*c* 1100) + -ian.] **A.** *adj.* Of or pertaining to Omar Khayyam or his poetry; having the style or character of his poetry. **B.** *sb.* A student or admirer of Omar Khayyam; a member of the Omar Khayyam Club.

1898 *Daily News* 31 Jan. 6/3 To the devout Omarian a reproduction in black-and-white of this early MS. will carry something of the fragrance [etc.]. **1898** *Westm. Gaz.* 22 Feb. 3/4 The next service demanded of Omarian scholarship is an edition in the original Persian. **1901** *Ibid.* 8 Jan. 2/3 Marie's needs are almost Omarian in their simplicity. **1907** *Daily Chron.* 13 Feb. 3/3 Serious Omarians..are willing to do more for their master than merely turn down an empty glass. **1934** A. J. A. Symons *Quest for Corvo* xi. 154 An American Omarian..contributed an Introduction.

Hence **Oma·rianism, O·marism,** admiration or imitation of Omar Khayyam; the doctrines or cult of Omar Khayyam. So **O·marite** = *Omarian *a.*

1897 *Daily Chron.* 9 Dec. 7/2 All more or less imbued with the spirit of what is called 'Omarianism', and all..decorously convivial. **1898** J. H. McCarthy in *Westm. Gaz.* 22 Feb. 3/3 The protest against what may be called Omarism. **1900** *Academy* 21 July 55/2 Mr. Fawcett called Omarism a fad. *Ibid.*, The Omarite message was interpreted: 'Get drunk as often as you can, and stay so long as you can, for there's nothing in life half so profitable.' **1918** *Naval Intelligence* xxxix. 180 Stanza after stanza, which he reeled off in an ecstatic and maudlin manner with his eyes half closed and his head wagging—all Omarites do this, you may have noticed.

Omayyad, var. *Umayyad *a.* and *sb.*

‖**ombré** (ǫnbre), *sb.* and *a.* Also **ombre.** [Fr., pa. pple. of *ombrer* to shade.] **A.** *sb.* A fabric woven or dyed in a series of colour tones graduating from light to dark and usu. producing a striped effect. Also, such an effect or design.

1895 *Funk's Stand. Dict.* II. 1227/2 *Ombré*.., a cheap grade of silk prints. **1921** A. Ganswindt *Dyeing Silk* 147 *Ombres*. Shaded effects on hank silk can be obtained by binding the hanks firmly on rods, using only a small amount of dyestuff in the bath [etc.]. **1930** R. Cuthill tr. *Schober's Silk* iv. 271 *Ombré*, a fabric in a number of colours, one fading off into the other, this effect being obtained by the use of yarns printed before weaving. **1966** A. J. Bliss *Dict. Foreign Words & Phrases Current Eng.* 264 *Ombré*.., (a fabric) woven with variably dyed yarns so as to produce a shaded effect. **1975** *Country Life* 30 Oct. 1192/2 Degradé, a fabric that is shaded from light to dark and sometimes called ombré in the dress side of the trade.

B. *adj.* Shaded from light to dark in tints of one or more colours.

1918 S. Kline *Man. Processes Winding* iii. 61 Ombré warps. **1928** *Daily Express* 27 Feb. 5/5 Rainbow effects have been produced by the use of what are known as ombre yarns, in which cotton and artificial silk of different colours are admixed. **1963** *Times* 24 Jan. 12/4 He varies the plain colours with *ombré* effect and brilliant spots. **1969** *Daily Tel.* 21 Apr. 12/6 Other leather is speckly and *ombre* with tiny splatters of black on grey highlighted with *art nouveau* silver buckles. **1974** D. Ramsay *No Cause to Kill* i. 9 She was tempted by a blue silk *ombré* plaid.

‖ **ombre chevalier** (ǫnbrə ʃəvalie). Also **omble chevalier.** [Fr.] A freshwater race of the char, *Salvelinus alpinus*, of the family Salmonidæ, found in certain French and Swiss lakes, esp. the Lake of Geneva.

1884 G. B. Goode *Fisheries U.S.: Nat. Hist. Aquatic Animals* 501 The Saibling of Bavaria and Austria is one and the same thing with the 'Ombre Chevalier' of France and Switzerland,.. the 'Char' of England and Scotland. **1905** D. S. Jordan *Guide to Study of Fishes* II. iv. 108 The only really well-authenticated species of charr in European waters is the red charr, sälbling, or ombre chevalier. **1940** A. Simon *Conc. Encycl. Gastron.* II. 67/1 *Omble Chevalier*... The best fish of the Swiss and Savoy lakes; it never leaves the lakes for the running waters of rivers. **1960** E. David *French Provincial Cooking* 38 Some *ombres-chevaliers* from the lac du Bourget, cooked and left to get cold in white wine. **1968** V. Canning *Melting Man* iii. 58 Tonight I shall be in France, eating *omble chevalier*, straight from the lake. **1971** *Times* 29 Mar. (Switzerland Suppl.) p. iii/5 The *ombre chevalier*, a type of salmon trout, especially from the Lake of Geneva.

‖**ombrelle** (ǫnbrɛ·l). *poet.* [Fr.] A parasol or sunshade.

1925 E. Sitwell *Troy Park* 75 What hotels Hide their bustles and their gay ombrelles. **1942** —— *Street Songs* 13 All that I knew of shade Was the cloud, my ombrelle of rustling grey Sharp silk.

‖**ombrellino** (ǫmbrĕlī·no). [It.] (See quot. 1957.) Also, a parasol or sunshade.

1847 F. W. Faber *Let.* in R. Chapman *Father Faber* (1961) viii. 163 It was a dark still night, and the bell and lights and singing and the flashing *ombrellino* had a most touching effect among the trees. We deposited our Lord in His own tabernacle after receiving His Benediction. **1949** D. Attwater *Catholic Encycl. Dict.* (ed. 2) 354/1 *Ombrellino* (It., a little umbrella). A small flat canopy with one staff borne over the Blessed Sacrament when it is carried from its own altar to another for exposition, etc., and, in some countries, when it is taken to the sick. **1957** *Oxf. Dict. Chr. Ch.* 983/2 *Ombrellino*, in the W. Church the small umbrella-like canopy of white silk carried over the Blessed Sacrament when it is moved informally from one place to another. **1964** *Punch* 26 Feb. 326/3, I came round lying on the sand under an *ombrellino*.

‖**ombres chinoises** (ǫnbrə ʃinwāz). [Fr., Chinese shadows.] = Galanty show.

1785 Lady Newdigate *Let.* 25 May in A. E. Newdigate-Newdegate *Cheverels* (1898) iv. 61 We talk of having another representation of our *Ombres Chinoises* on Friday. **1802** *Monthly Mag.* Sept. 132/1 Besides the great theatre, there are..several smaller ones for..different exhibitions, such as ombres Chinoises. **1948** G. Speaight in M. Batchelder *Puppet Theatre Handbk.* p. xx, 'Ombres chinoises' were extremely popular in France and England during the eighteenth century, but later fell from favour. **1950** H. W. Whanslaw *Shadow Play* vi. 48 Tronchet describes the theatre of Francois-Dominique Seraphin, in the Palais Royale,.. where he exhibited his famous *Ombres Chinoises—Le Spectacle des Enfants de France.* **1960** O. Blackham *Shadow Puppets* 98 In March 1779 Astley re-opened his Amphitheatre near Westminster Bridge, and here the *ombres chinoises* continued to be advertised right up to the summer of 1790. **1974** *Encycl. Brit. Micropædia* VII. 530/2 *Ombres chinoises*.., European version of the Chinese shadow puppet show, introduced in Europe in the mid-18th century by returning travellers.

ombro-. Add: **ombro·genous** *a.*, of moorland or marsh, needing a high rainfall for its development; **ombro·philous** *a.* [a. G. *ombrophile* (J. Wiesner 1893, in *Sitzungsber. Akad. Wiss. Wien* Abth. I. CII. 503)], of a plant, able to flourish in conditions of excessive moisture; so **ombro·phily**; **ombro·phobous** *a.* [a. G. *ombrophobe* (J. Wiesner 1893, *loc. cit.*)], of a plant, not well adapted to very wet conditions; so **ombro·phoby.**

1939 A. G. Tansley *Brit. Islands & their Vegetation* xxxv. 718 Blanket moss or bog—ombrogenous. **1946** *Proc. Prehist. Soc.* XII. 3 The blanket-bog is termed an 'ombrogenous' mire, to indicate the fact that its existence is directly determined by the rainfall and evaporation to which it is subject. **1952** P. W. Richards *Trop. Rain Forest* ix. 215 The vegetation of the ombrogenous moors is tall evergreen forest. **1975** J. R. Etherington *Environment & Plant Ecol.* iii. 91 Some other peat soils are topogenous rather than ombrogenous. **1895** *Jrnl. R. Microsc. Soc.* 194 Plants which, on the one hand are uninjured (ombrophilous) and on the other hand are injured (ombrophobous) by excessive rainfall. *Ibid.*, Some species..growing in moist shady situations, are nevertheless ombrophobous. *Ibid.*, Xerophilous plants..are hardly ever ombrophilous. **1903** W. R. Fisher tr. *Schimper's Plant-Geogr.* I. i. 2 Xerophytes perish after two or three days of continuous rain; they are rain-avoiding, ombrophobous, whereas hygrophytes are, as a rule, ombrophilous... Ombrophilous foliage is capable of being wetted, ombrophobous foliage is unwettable. *Ibid.* III. i. 225 Reference may here be made to Wiesner's investigations regarding the ombrophily and ombrophoby of tropical vegetation. **1897** *Jrnl. R. Microsc. Soc.* 412 Ombrophoby of flowers.—By this term Prof. A. Hansgirg designates the phenomena of curvature by which many flowers protect themselves against injury from long-continued rain or other exposure to moisture.

ombú (ombu·). Also **ombu.** [Amer. Sp., f. Guarani *umbú*.] An evergreen tree, *Phytolacca dioica*, of the family Phytolaccaceæ, native to temperate regions of South America. Also *attrib.*

1871 R. O. Cunningham *Notes Nat. Hist. Strait of Magellan* xiv. 466 A variety of cottages, each shaded by the umbrageous foliage of the large Ombu. **1878** E. Clark *Visit S. Amer.* ix. 123 The gnarled ombus and willows, and poplars and peach trees, affording the welcome shade. **1902** W. H. Hudson *El Ombú* i. 1 In all this district..you will not find a tree as big as this ombú, standing solitary, where there is no house. *Ibid.* 2 They say..that those who sit much in the ombú shade become crazed. **1923** *Chambers's Jrnl.* Dec. 828/2 A huge, gnarled tree, tremendously thick and spreading like an *ombú*. **1931** B. Miall tr. *Guenther's Naturalist in Brazil* iv. 79 In the Argentine I have often admired the monumental character of one of the native trees, the Ombú. The roots rise from the ground like great brown bladders, lifting the trunk into the air, and from the trunk the branches spring like a tracery. **1941** E. Nash *I Liked Life I Lived* vi. 70 The humble dwelling was called the house of the twenty-five ombú trees. **1961** G. Durrell *Whispering Land* i. 30 Small, neat *estancias*, gleaming white in the shade of huge, carunculated *ombú* trees, that stood massively and grimly on their enormous squat trunks. **1969** T. H. Everett *Living Trees of World* 144/1 The ombú becomes 60 feet tall with a branch spread of more than 100 feet. From the bottom of its very thick trunk it develops extraordinary irregular outgrowths that look like fantastic and bulky roots. *Ibid.*, The elliptic or ovate leaves of the ombú are evergreen and male and female flowers are on separate trees; the fruits are small and berry-like. **1975** *New Yorker* 14 Apr. 36/1 They give shade from the bare sun to man and beast, and men mark their way on the endless plains by remembering this or that ombu tree.

Ombudsman (ǫ·mbudzmæn). Also with small initial. [Sw. (see below) f. *ombud* commissioner, agent, repr. ON. *umboð* charge, commission, *umboðsmaðr* commissary, manager.] An official appointed to investigate complaints by individuals against maladministration by public authorities; *spec.* in U.K., the Parliamentary Commissioner for Administration. (Corresp. to Sw. *justitieombudsmannen*.) Also *attrib.* and in extended and *fig.* uses.

In Sweden, an *ombudsman* is a deputy of a group, particularly a trade union or a business concern, appointed to handle the legal affairs of the group and protect its interests generally. With the definite suffix *-en* it normally denotes a particular office. The office of *justitieombudsmannen* (abbrev. *JO*), which was instituted in Sweden in 1809, is the one which is referred to in the following quotations, and it is this office which was established in New Zealand in 1962. In Sweden the office of *militieombudsmannen* (abbrev. *MO*) was also introduced in 1809 as a parliamentary commissioner appointed to supervise and enforce the observance of laws and statutes concerned with national defence. In 1968 the offices of *justitieombudsmannen* and *militieombudsmannen* were replaced by four independent officers under the joint name of *justitieombudsmännen*. The word *pressombudsman* connotes a public relations officer, and in its definite form *pressombudsmannen* an office instituted in 1969 to supervise and enforce ethical standards of the press.

The office of *ombudsman* was introduced in Finland in 1919, in Denmark in 1954, and in Norway in 1962.

[**1911** *Encycl. Brit.* XXVI. 195/2 By revisers elected annually the Riksdag controls the finances of the kingdom, and by an official (*justitieombudsman*) elected in the same way the administration of justice is controlled; he can indict any functionary of the state who has abused his power. **1914** J. GUINCHARD *Sweden* iii. 200 The Riksdag has yet another form of control over the High Court of Justice and the Supreme Administrative Court in that the 'Justitieombudsman' may in certain cases arraign a member of the Court before the Court of Impeachment. **1958** S. HURWITZ in *Public Law* Autumn 236 A precedent existed in Sweden, where a 'Justitieombudsman' and a 'Militieombudsman', appointed by Parliament, were introduced in 1809 and in 1915 respectively.] **1959** *Listener* 16 July 89/1 Sweden has been running the Ombudsman system for 150 years, and Denmark has a very active Ombudsman. **1963** *Times* 23 Apr. 13/6 The perfunctoriness with which the Government recently rejected the conclusions of the unofficial inquiry conducted by Justice into the Scandinavian *ombudsman* procedure was disappointing. **1966** *N.Z. News* 28 Sept. 3/2 Britain's Ombudsman, Sir Edmund Compton, is now in New Zealand consulting New Zealand's Ombudsman, Sir Guy Powles, about the workings of his office and the way in which he deals with complaints. **1966** S. OAKLEY *Story of Sweden* xiv. 164 The private citizen was protected from the bureaucracy by a so-called *ombudsman*, elected by the Estates to hear and investigate complaints against abuses of power by public servants. **1969** *Daily Tel.* 13 Dec. 1/5 Complaints from hospital patients and staff may shortly be dealt with by a special type of Ombudsman. **1970** MORRIS & HAWKINS *Honest Politician's Guide to Crime Control* 100 We do not doubt that the ombudsman system would work well here. **1970** *Harper's Mag.* Dec. 59/1 He had come to protest to the newspaper, his only ombudsman that day. **1971** *N.Y. Post* 15 Nov. 46 She was everywhere, doing everything—columnist, lecturer,..ombudsman for every injustice. **1972** *Daily Tel.* 23 Feb. 2 The Health Service is to have its own Ombudsman or Health Service Commissioner, who will be responsible for carrying out independent investigations into patients' complaints. **1973** *Daily Californian* 1 Feb. 2/1 A state ombudsman's office, sort of an official wailing wall. **1974** M. GILBERT *Flash Point* i. 12 He had approached..his own member of parliament..the Ombudsman and..the press. **1975** *Local Council Rev.* Autumn 95 A layman's guide to the complaints machinery set up under the 1974 Local Government Act. Explains what the ombudsmen can and cannot do, how complaints should be put to them. **1976** *Daily Tel.* 2 Dec. 2/5 He complained to the Department of Education and eventually to Baroness Serota, the Ombudsman for the area, who found Surrey education committee guilty of maladministration. **1978** *Times* 7 Mar. 4/8 The appointment of local ombudsmen has had a considerable impact on local authority procedures, in the view of the authors of the first critical appraisal of their work.

Hence *ombuds-committee*; **o·mbudsmanry,** the profession or practice of being an ombudsman; **o·mbudsmanship,** the office or function of an ombudsman; **o·mbudswoman,** a female ombudsman.

1961 *Observer* 12 Nov. 40/8, I suppose I have become a sort of ombudswoman on turnstiles. **1964** *Economist* 7 Mar. 875/2 A sort of Ombudscommittee for people who feel cheated. **1970** *Daily Tel.* 6 Aug. 2/4 A resolution calling for an inquiry into promotion procedures and for the setting up of an arbitration 'ombuds-committee' has been tabled. **1971** *New Society* 25 Mar. 489/3 It is obvious that local ombudsmanry on a national scale would mean setting up a new light industry. **1966** *Times* 5 July 13 The whole field of ombudsmanship and the scrutiny of administrative practice and legislative principle..at present goes largely unmarked. **1971** *New Scientist* 3 June 597/2 The loquacious ombudsmanship of Bernard Braden. **1965** *Manch. Guardian Weekly* 21 Oct. 6 The only answer is for more councillors to see themselves as Ombudsmen and Ombudswomen. **1972** *New Yorker* 30 Sept. 6/3 Mabel Mercer, ombudswoman to all who have ever played at love. **1973** *Maclean's Mag.* June 45/1 She had previously been ombudswoman for the Status of Women Council [etc.].

omdah, omdeh. Also **omda.** [ad. Arabic *ʿumdah* column, support, trustworthy authority, village-chief, f. root *ʿmd* to support.] The headman of a village in Arab countries.

1907 *Daily Chron.* 20 Aug. 3/7 Village omdehs to be elected by the whole mass of the villagers. **1922** *Q. Rev.* Apr. 428 Omdehs and others who may be tempted to revert to the old ways would do well to reflect. **1924** *Glasgow Herald* 23 Dec. 7 The numerous 'omdas', or village headmen, who were dismissed during the Zaghlulist regime. **1926** *Blackw. Mag.* Apr. 409/1, I was reluctantly compelled to accept the hospitality of the Omdah..for lunch. **1928** *Observer* 11 Mar. 19/3 The Omdas—representatives of the central authority in the villages. **1976** *Times* 31 July 10/2, I used to go from village to village, discussing their affairs with the omdas and shaikhs.

-ome, anglicized form of *-OMA (partly through influence of G. *-om*, F. *-ome*), occurring chiefly in *Bot.* in terms such as CAULOME, *HADROME, PHYLLOME, RHIZOME, and usu. signifying a structure or group of cells forming a normal part of the anatomy, in contrast with the abnormality implied by *-oma* (cf. *MYCETOME, an organ in insects, MYCETOMA, a fungal skin disease). It also occurs in a few obs. forms of words now written *-oma*, e.g. FIBROME, TUBERCULOME.

omee (ōu·mi). *slang.* Also **omer, omie.** [Corruption of It. *uomo*, man.] A man, esp. a landlord or itinerant actor.

1859 HOTTEN *Dict. Slang* 70 *Omee*, a master or landlord. **1893** P. H. EMERSON *Signor Lippo* xiii. 42 When I got back the cullies said, 'Well, cully, how did you get on with the omer?' **1928** *Sunday Express* 14 Oct. 5 Man [in slang of busking] is 'omey'. **1937** N. MARSH *Vintage Murder* vii. 82 'A lot of omies the others were then.'..'Ted means they were bad actors doing worse shows in one-eyed towns up and down the provinces.' **1962** L. KNIGHT (*title*) A proper circus omie.

omega. Add: **1.** (Earlier examples.)

c **1400** MANDEVILLE *Trav.* (1725) iii. 25 What Lettres thei ben..with the Names..α Alpha, β Betha..ω Omega. **1640** S. DAINES *Orthoepia Anglicana* (1908) 11 *Oa*, sounds generally after the Greeke *Omega. Ibid.* 12 *Oo* in *Poore* imitates in sound the Greek *Omega*.

2. a. Also *from Alpha to Omega*: from beginning to end; from top to toe.

1929 D. G. MACKAIL *How Amusing!* 307, I was a gentleman..from alpha to omega. **1978** D. QUINN *Fear of God* II. 161 Vast explosions of silence..marching..from Alpha to Omega and..beyond the infinite.

b. Omega point, in the work of P. Teilhard de Chardin (1881–1955) a hypothesized point of convergence, absorption, or transformation which is the divine end, or God, towards which the forces of evolution are moving (see quot. 1964).

1959 B. WALL tr. *Teilhard de Chardin's Phenomenon of Man* ii. 57 He goes on to add these words which my readers would do well to recall when I come to unveil (with all due reservations and corrections) the perspective of the 'Omega point'. *Ibid.* IV. ii. 259 Accordingly its enormous layers, followed in the right direction, must somewhere ahead become involuted to a point which we might call *Omega*, which fuses and consumes them integrally in itself. **1964** N. DENNY tr. *Teilhard de Chardin's Future of Man* vi. 122 Ahead of, or rather in the heart of, a universe prolonged along its axis of complexity, there exists a divine centre of convergence... In order to stress its synthesising and personalising function, let us call it the *point Omega*. **1965** *Listener* 3 June 817/2 The idea has something in common with Teilhard de Chardin's concept of the 'Omega Point'. **1977** *Time* 28 Feb. 45/1 Teilhard believed man would eventually transcend his individualism and converge at the 'Omega Point' with the Omega—God.

2*. *Nuclear Physics.* † **a.** (Written *Ω*.) A former designation of certain hyperons. *Obs.*

The decay schemes in quot. 1953 are those of the sigma (*Σ*) particles, whilst the mass specified in quot. 1954[2] (and elsewhere) is that of the xi minus. In quot. 1954[1] a lambda particle is referred to.

1953 *Nuovo Cimento* X. 1741 Two decay schemes have been proposed by analogy with the decay of V_1^0-particles. Adopting the nomenclature proposed at the Bagnères Conference these are: (*a*) $\Omega_{\pi}{}^{\pm} \rightarrow n + \pi^{\pm} + Q$, (*b*) $\Omega_p{}^{+} \rightarrow p + \pi^0 + Q$. **1954** *Sci. News* XXXI. 62 Ω^0-particle. Mass, 2,184±7 [≡1116 MeV]. Lifetime, $(3{\cdot}3 \pm 1) \times 10^{-10}$ seconds... Decay scheme: $\Omega^0 \rightarrow p^+ + \pi^-$. **1954** *Physical Rev.* XCVI. 543/1 The known hyperons, Λ^-, Ω^-, have masses equivalent to 1200 and 1320 Mev, respectively.

b. In full *omega meson.* A neutral meson with zero hypercharge, zero isospin, unit spin, and negative parity that is observed as a resonance (as when protons and antiprotons of sufficient energy collide), has a mass of 784 MeV (1534 times that of the electron), and on decaying usu. produces a positive, a negative, and a neutral pion. Freq. written as *ω*.

1961 B. C. MAGLIĆ et al. in *Physical Rev. Lett.* VII. 178/1 The existence of a heavy neutral meson with $T = 0$ and $J = 1^-$ was predicted by Nambu... Such a particle is also expected in the vector meson theory of Sakurai and.. according to the unitary symmetry theory; and for other reasons. We will refer to it as *ω*. *Ibid.* 181/1 We conclude that the data fit the qualitative criteria for an axial vector matrix element (*ω* meson). **1961** *New Scientist* 5 Oct. 48/1 Four physicists at the Lawrence Radiation Laboratory, Berkeley, have made observations..that appear to indicate unequivocally the presence, in a proton-antiproton reaction, of the omega-meson. **1971** *Sci. News* 10 Apr. 250 It appears that electromagnetic forces are mediated to leptons directly by photons and to hadrons by phi, rho or omega. **1971** *Sci. Amer.* July 100/2 Three vector mesons with zero strangeness are currently known: the rho, the omega and the phi. **1974** *Nature* 6 Dec. 438/2 The omega meson, which has all the same normal quantum numbers as the phi,..decays very rapidly to three pions.

c. *omega minus* (or *particle*): a negatively charged hyperon having hypercharge of −2, zero isospin, a spin of 3/2, positive parity, and a mass of 1672 MeV (3272 times that of the electron), and decaying via the weak interaction into either a xi particle and a pion or a lambda particle and a kaon. Freq. written as Ω^-.

1962 M. GELL-MANN in *Proc. Internat. Conf. High-Energy Physics* 805/2 Starting with the resonance at 1238 MeV, we may conjecture that the $Y_1{}^*$, at 1385 MeV and the Ξ^* at 1535 MeV might belong to this supermultiplet... If $J = 3/2^+$ is really right for these two cases, then our speculation might have some value and we should look for the last particle, called, say, Ω^- with $S = -3$, $I = 0$. At 1685 MeV, it would be metastable and should decay by the weak interactions into $K^- + \Lambda$, $\pi^- + \Xi^0$, or $\pi^0 + \Xi^-$. **1964** *Physical Rev. Lett.* XII. 204/1 The multitude of resonances which have been discovered recently..can be arranged as a decuplet with one member still missing... This particle (which we shall call Ω^-, following Gell-Mann) is predicted to be a negatively charged isotopic singlet with strangeness minus three. *Ibid.* 206/1 In view of the properties..established for particle 3, we feel justified in identifying it with the sought-for Ω^-. **1964** *Daily Tel.* 21 Feb. 25/2 Dr. Maurice Goldhaber, director of Brookhaven, said yesterday: 'The discovery of Omega Minus forms the capstone in a building which was so far held together only by the bold imagination of Dr. Gell-Mann and Dr. Ne'eman.' **1964** *Listener* 30 Apr. 711/1 The new theory [*sc.* that of unitary symmetry] has made one striking prediction which was subsequently found to be correct: the observation of the negatively charged Omega particle. **1972** *Daily Colonist* (Victoria, B.C.) 24 Feb. 5/2 The physicists hope to make the first observation of 'quarks'..by studying the activity of a rare and elusive sub-atomic particle called the omega-minus. **1974** FRAUENFELDER & HENLEY *Subatomic Physics* i. 6 The negative kaon..collides with a proton and produces a positive kaon, a neutral kaon, and an omega minus. The Ω^- decays into a Ξ^0 and a π^-.

3. Used *attrib.* (with capital initial) to designate a style of interior decoration and design associated with the Omega Workshops, a short-lived undertaking begun in London by the art critic Roger Fry in 1913 and influenced by the work of William Morris.

1922 D. H. LAWRENCE *Aaron's Rod* iii. 30 Into this reticence pieces of futurism, Omega cushions and Van-Gogh-like pictures exploded their colours. **1970** *Oxf. Compan. Art* 790/2 The Omega artists believed that the creative joy of the artist and craftsman should go into the making of articles for everyday use. **1973** *Guardian* 22 Jan. 8/1 Drawings and paintings of the Bloomsbury artists still crowd the walls... The dining-room's Omega chairs attend its round painted table.

omegatron (ōu·mĭgătrǫn). *Physics.* [f. OMEGA (*ω* being the symbol of angular frequency) + *-TRON.] A mass spectrometer that employs the principle of the cyclotron to identify and measure gases at very low pressures, a radio-frequency electric field being applied at right angles to a magnetic field so that charged particles having a certain charge-to-mass ratio impinge on a collecting electrode.

1949 J. A. HIPPLE et al. in *Physical Rev.* LXXVI. 1878/1 Since this device measures *ω*, it is suggested that it be called the omegatron. **1966** W. SUMMER tr. *E. von Angerer & H. Ebert's Physical Lab. Handbk.* x. 208 The omegatron..is useful as a gauge down to 10^{-12} torr. *Ibid.*, The ion-collecting efficiency of an omegatron is high and operation is satisfactory in the range 10^{-5} to 10^{-9} torr. Below 10^{-7} torr resolution up to $m = 30$ is very good... Resolution is less complete for $30 < m < 100$, but ions present can be identified. **1975** *Nature* 6 Feb. 408/2 Partial pressures were measured with an omegatron radio-frequency mass spectrometer which formed part of the UHV section.

omelet, omelette, *sb.* Add: **c.** *attrib.*, as *omelette (frying)-pan.*

1846 *Jewish Manual, or Pract. Information Jewish & Mod. Cookery* v. 99 A small omelette frying-pan is necessary for cooking it [*sc.* the omelette] well. **1879** A. D. WHITNEY *Just How* 292 Finish beating and mixing the omelette, setting on the omelette-pan when almost ready. **1948** *Good Housek. Cookery Bk.* II. 369 To season a new omelet pan. Heat the pan slowly, then melt a knob of butter in it and rub it well in with a piece of soft paper. **1977** T. HEALD *Just Desserts* vii. 174 Gabrielle won't go anywhere without her favourite omelette pan.

d. omelette (aux) fines herbes, a savoury omelette flavoured with herbs; **omelette soufflée,** an omelette made by folding the separately beaten egg whites into the mixture.

1845 E. ACTON *Mod. Cookery* xix. 489 Seasoned with minced herbs,..[it] is then called an '*Omlette aux fines herbes*'. **1846** [see *FINES HERBES]. **1928** A. CHRISTIE *Mystery of Blue Train* xix. 150 The Comte de la Roche had just finished *déjeuner*, consisting of an *omelette fines herbes*. **1845** E. ACTON *Mod. Cookery* xix. 491 (*heading*) An omelette soufflée. **1930** W. S. MAUGHAM *Cakes & Ale* xii. 145 No one could make a better *omelette soufflée* than she. **1968** *Radio Times* 28 Nov. 25/1 Colourful Cookery.. Puffed Onion Tart..Omelette Soufflée. **1975** HUME & DOWNES *Cordon Bleu Desserts* ii. 64 Omelet Soufflé with Strawberries... Omelet Soufflé 'en Surprise'. **1977** D. RAMSAY *You can't call it Murder* ii. 108 During lunch.. they disposed of..the most subtle of *omelettes fines herbes*.

o·melet, o·melette, *v.* [f. the sb.] *trans.* To make into an omelet. Also *transf.*

1872 E. EGGLESTON *End of World* xxiii. 155 The eggs.. were not poached, they were not scrambled, they were not omeletted. **1908** *Westm. Gaz.* 6 Oct. 3/1 (*caption*), I don't want to be omeletted!

omen, *sb.* Add: **c.** *omen-animal.*

1902 *Man* II. 61 The chapters on the omen-animals and the cult of skulls are of special value.

omeno·logy. [f. OMEN *sb.* + -OLOGY.] The study or science of omens.

1904 J. HASTINGS *Dict. Bible* V. 559/2 Such..occurrences as the lunar eclipse, would serve as a basis for lunar omenology.

omentopexy (ome·ntopeksi). *Surg.* [f. OMENT(UM + -O + *-PEXY.] Any operation in which the omentum is sutured to another structure, e.g. the abdominal wall.

1905 *Jrnl. Amer. Med. Assoc.* 25 Nov. 1700/2 Omentopexy was undertaken to provide collateral circulation for the portal vein. **1957** J. G. ALLEN et al. *Surgery* xxxiii. 795/2 Omentopexy was introduced by Morison, Talma and others about 1900. **1962** *Lancet* 13 Jan. 66/2 Subsequently 1 (case 12) had an omentopexy, which controlled hæmorrhage for two years.

omer, var. *OMEE.

‖ **omertà** (omerta·). [dial. form of It. *umiltà* humility, with reference to the Mafia code which enjoins submission of the group to the leader as well as silence on all Mafia concerns.] Refusal to give evidence by those concerned in the activities of the Mafia.

1909 *Evening Sun* (N.Y.) 13 May 8/1 There is..the belief that it is unmanly to tell anything about a fellow countryman which could get him into trouble. It is called 'Omerta' in the Sicilian tongue, which means manliness. **1963** R. I. MCDAVID *Mencken's Amer. Lang.* 720 *Omertà*, the very strict code of the Mafia. **1965** *Times Lit. Suppl.* 25 Nov. 1058/4 He could call on a good many witnesses more bound to *omertà* than to the truth. **1965** J. WAINWRIGHT *Death in Sleeping City* II. vii. 129 They [*sc.* the Mafia] have a law... It's called the Omerta. It's an unwritten law—a code of conduct, really. **1968** *Listener* 29 Feb. 268/3 An island [Sardinia] where omerta is stronger than democracy. **1969** *Sunday Truth* (Brisbane) 30 Nov. 25/2 He had broken the highest law of the Mafia—omerta, or silence. **1970** G. GREER *Female Eunuch* 222 *Vendetta* and *omertà*..are not significant until the familial, regional community is threatened by political authority. **1977** *Time* 12 Sept. 43/1 The protection program was formally established after passage of the Organized Crime Control Act of 1970 to hasten the breakdown of *omertà*, the underworld code of silence.

Omeyyad, var. *UMAYYAD *a.* and *sb.*

‖ **omi** (ō^u·mi). Also, with prefixed *ō-* 'great'. [Jap.] In early imperial Japan, a high-ranking administrative official claiming imperial ancestry (cf. *MURAJI); a title of members of a family upon which such an office was bestowed.

1901 [see *MURAJI]. **1931** G. B. SANSOM *Japan* I. ii. 37 We have the *ō-omi*, or great ministers, who were appointed from among the heads of clans closely related to the imperial family. *Ibid.*, The *omi* and *muraji* of lesser standing. **1964, 1970** [see *MURAJI].

omicron (ǫ·mikrǫn, ō^u mǝi·krǫn). [Gr. ὂ μικρόν, lit. 'little O'.] The fifteenth letter (*O*, *ο*) of the Greek alphabet, originally having the value of short *o*.

c **1400** MANDEVILLE *Trav.* (1725) iii. 25 What Lettres thei ben..with the Names..α Alpha, β Betha,..ο Omicron ..χ Chi, [etc.]. **1631** R. HARRIS *Arraignement Whole Creature* xiii. 208 The whole Globe..cannot fill this little triangulary heart: so many Omicrons, cannot fill one little Delta. **1727–41** [see OMEGA 1]. **1893** E. M. THOMPSON *Handbk. Gr. & Lat. Palæogr.* x. 135 The very small size of *theta* and *omikron*, may also be noticed. **1947** *Jrnl. Investigative Dermatol.* IX. 215 Where *-oma* occurs as the ending in words *properly* formed from the Greek, the stem always ends in omicron or omega (as a lengthening of omicron). *Ibid.* 213 Many such Greek verb stems, but by no means all, end in *o* represented by omicron when the pronunciation is short (ŏ) or by omega (ω) when it is long (ō). **1959** A. G. WOODHEAD *Study of Greek Inscriptions* ii. 18 This differentiation, like that between *omicron* and *omega*, gradually spread to the rest of the Greek world.

omie, var. *OMEE.

omissible, *a.* Add: Hence **omissibi·lity.**

1961 in WEBSTER. **1966** *Amer. Speech* XLI. 182 Certain self-explanatory terms have been examined with a view to their omissibility from *NID 3* (Webster's Third New International Dictionary). **1971** D. CRYSTAL *Linguistics* 202 The omissibility of *here tomorrow*. **1971** T. F. MITCHELL in *Archivum Linguisticum* II. 43 The omissibility of a following noun.

‖ **om mani padme hum** (ǭm mani padme hūm), *int.* [Skr., lit. 'Hail! Jewel in the Lotus!' See *OM *int.* and quot. 1848 below.] In Tibetan Buddhism, a mantra or mystic formula intoned in prayer and meditation. Also as *sb. phr.*

1774 G. BOGLE *Narr. Mission Tibet* (1876) iii. 29 Some old women..were counting their beads and repeating their *Om mani padmi hums!* **1836** B. H. HODGSON in *Jrnl. Asiatic Soc. of Bengal* V. 88 The celebrated *Shadakshari Mantra*, or six-lettered invocation of him, viz. *Om! Mane padme hom!* of which so many corrupt versions and more corrupt interpretations have appeared. **1848** J. D. HOOKER *Himalayan Jrnls.* (1854) I. x. 229, I..returned down the 'via sacra', a steep paved path flanked by..low stone dykes, into which were let rows of stone slabs, inscribed with the sacred 'Om Mani Padmi om'.—'Hail to him of the lotus and jewel'; an invocation of Sakkya, who is usually represented holding a lotus flower with a jewel in it. **1863** E. SCHLAGINTWEIT *Buddhism in Tibet* viii. 84 Amitâbha then blessed Padmapâni Bôdhisattva by laying his hands upon him, when, by virtue of this benediction, he brought forth the prayer 'Om mani padme hum'. **1895** L. A. WADDELL *Buddhism of Tibet* vi. 148 The commonest mystic formula in Lāmaism, the 'Om-ma-ṇi pad-me Hū-ṃ,'—which literally means '*Om!* The Jewel in the Lotus! *Hūṃ!*'—is addressed to the Bodhisat Padmapāni who is represented like Buddha seated or standing within a lotus-flower. He is the patron-god of Tibet. **1901** KIPLING *Kim* ii. 47 In the pauses of their talk they could hear the low droning—'*Om mane pudme hum! Om mane pudme hum!*'—and the thick click of the wooden rosary beads. *Ibid.* v. 111 He clicked the beads, and began the '*Om mane pudme hum*' of his devotion. **1924** A. HUXLEY *Little Mexican* 16 A mystic formula, a kind of *Om mani padme hum.* **1970** J. BLOFELD *Way of Power* I. i. 38 Old women twirling their prayer-wheels and intoning *Om Mani Padme Hum* while riding in buses.

† **ommateum** (ǫmătī·ǝ̆m). *Zool. Obs.* [mod. L., f. Gr. ὄμμα, ὀμματ- eye.] (See quots.) Hence **ommate·al** *a.*

1883 LANKESTER & BOURNE in *Q. Jrnl. Microsc. Sci.* XXIII. 182 This enlarged portion of the hypodermis is, in fact, the soft or living tissue of the eye [of the Scorpion], and may be distinguished from the lens in front of it by a special name. We propose to call it the ommatēum'. The ommateum and the lens together form the eye. *Ibid.*, A well-marked 'basement membrane', which in the region of the ommateum may be called the eye-capsule, or, better, the 'ommateal capsule'. **1884** [see next]. **1898** A. S. PACKARD *Text-bk. Entomol.* 250 (*heading*) The compound or facetted eye (ommateum).

ommatidium. Add: (Earlier and later examples.)

1884 J. CARRIÈRE in *Q. Jrnl. Microsc. Sci.* XXIV. 674 The whole set of eye-units (ommatidia) of Musca vomitoria are enclosed in a chitinous capsule. [*Note*] The term 'ommateum' was introduced by Lankester in his memoir on the eyes of Scorpions to signify the entire soft parts of the non-segregate (unicorneal) eye of Arachnida and Hexapoda... The similar term 'ommatidium' is introduced in this paper to signify the units consisting each of a retinula and a vitrella, together with their sheath of pigment cells, into which the ommateum of the multi-corneal (polymeniscous) eye of Arthropods, is segregated. **1925** A. D. IMMS *Gen. Textbk. Entomol.* I. 79 The distinctness of vision depends partly upon the number and size of the ommatidia. **1932** METCALF & FLINT *Fund. Insect Life* iv. 110 It is believed that each ommatidium does not form an image of the whole object, but only preserves the intensity, pattern, and color of the light coming from the particular small part of the object that is in line with its long axis. Indeed, the several ommatidia, or 'tubes', are usually so isolated from each other by pigment, that no light can pass from one to the other. **1973** *Sci. Amer.* Dec. 35/3 The compound eye of *Drosophila* is a remarkable structure consisting of about 800 ommatidia: unit eyes containing eight receptor cells each.

ommati·dial *a.* (examples).

1890 *Anatomischer Anzeiger* V. 356 This spine-bearing cornea is soon shed and a faceted one formed, each facet.. often containing in the centre the remnants of an ommatidial spine. **1925** A. D. IMMS *Gen. Textbk. Entomol.* I. 76 The hypodermis between the ommatidial pillars becomes transformed into the secondary pigment cells. **1975** *Nature* 10 Apr. 522/2 The axons from seven retinula cells of one ommatidium interweave with those of their four neighbouring facets in such a way that four bundles of three fibres, heterogeneous with regard to their ommatidial origin, plus one single axon are produced.

ommatin (ǫ·mătin). *Biochem.* Also **-ine.** [a. G. *ommatin* (E. Becker 1939, in *Biol. Zentralbl.* LIX. 622), f. Gr. ὄμμα, ὀμματ- eye: see -IN[1].] Any of the group of ommochromes characterized by weaker colours, less stability to alkalis, and lower molecular weights as compared with the ommins.

1940 *Biol. Abstr.* XIV. 1238/1 The 2 eye pigments [of *Ephestia*] are typical of those found among insects. The dark red or brown ommines occur in Lepidoptera, Hymenoptera, Coleoptera, Hemiptera Heteroptera, and in the nematocerous Diptera. The more weakly colored ommatines are found in the cyclorrhaphous Diptera, Odonata, and Orthoptera. **1965** [see *OMMOCHROME]. **1969** R. F. CHAPMAN *Insects* vii. 109 Tyndall blues are rare in insects, but the blue of dragonflies is produced in this way, the dark background being provided by a brown-violet ommatin. **1975** D. G. COCHRAN in Candy & Kilby *Insect Biochem.* iii. 237 Storage of large quantities of 3-hydroxykynurenine occurs in vesicles or dilations of the endoplasmic reticulum of tubule cells [of *Drosophila*], and, at least in certain mutants, it is converted into ommatins and ommins.

Ommiad(e, var. *UMAYYAD *a.* and *sb.*

ommin (ǫ·min). *Biochem.* Also **-ine.** [a. G. *ommin* (E. Becker 1939, in *Biol. Zentralbl.* LIX. 611), f. Gr. ὄμμ-α eye: see -IN[1].] Any of the group of ommochromes characterized by stronger colours, greater stability to alkalis, and higher molecular weights as compared with the ommatins.

1940, etc. [see *OMMATIN]. **1964** T. H. GOLDSMITH in M. Rockstein *Physiol. Insecta* I. x. 425 The principal ommin is widely distributed in arthropods and cephalopods. **1965** [see *OMMOCHROME].

ommochrome (ǫ·mǒkrō^um). *Biochem.* [ad. G. *ommochrom* (E. Becker 1942, in *Zeitschr. f. indukt. Abstammungs- und Vererbungslehre* LXXX. 179), f. Gr. ὄμμ-α eye + χρῶμ-α colour: see -O.] Any of a group of insect pigments derived by condensation reactions from kynurenine and giving yellow, red, and brown body colours and commonly also found in the accessory cells of the eyes of insects.

1945 *Biol. Abstr.* XIX. 450/1 The distribution of this new group of pigments, the ommochromes, among arthropods has been examined. **1965** B. E. FREEMAN tr. *Vandel's Biospeleol.* xxv. 405 In the arthropods, melanines are replaced by ommochromes (ommines and ommatines). **1965** V. B. WIGGLESWORTH *Princ. Insect Physiol.* (ed. 6) xiii. 556 The ommochromes fall into two groups: the non-dialysable 'ommines', with large molecules, and the dialysable 'ommatines' with small molecules. **1970** *Nature* 26 Dec. 1336/2 The integumental pigments of the isopod Crustacea are ommochromes. **1974** *Ibid.* 30 Aug. 799/2 An early effect of ecdysoids at metamorphosis in some caterpillars is conversion of tryptophane into red ommochrome pigments.

omni-. Add: **o·mni-antenna,** an omnidirectional antenna; **omnici·pient** *a.* = *omnipercipient*; **omnifo·cal** *a. Ophthalm.*, designating a lens whose power changes continuously from top to bottom; also as *sb.*, such a lens; **omni-fu·tuant, -fu·tuent** *adjs.* [L. *futuere* to have sexual relations with], practising or tolerant of both homosexual and heterosexual activity; **omnila·teral** *a.*, facing all directions; representing all points of view; so **omnila·terally** *adv.*; **omnipercipient** *a.* (later example); **omnipo·llent** *a.*, all-powerful; **omnipurpose** *a.*, serving all purposes; **o·mnirange** *Aeronaut.*, (part of) a navigation system in which short-range omnidirectional VHF transmitters serve as radio beacons; **omnise·ntient** *a.*, having universal feeling or sensation; **omni-su·bjugant** *a.* [cf. SUBJUGE *v.*], subjugating everything or everyone; **omnitemporal** (earlier and later examples); so **omnite·mporally** *adv.*; **omni-tooled** *a.*, possessing many tools; **omni-vica·rious** *a.*, taking the place of (anything).

1974 *New Scientist* 24 Jan. 191 (*caption*) Omni-antenna. **1976** *CB Mag.* June 110 (Advt.), Beam antennas vs. omni-antenna range. **1899** BEERBOHM *More* 162 Omnicipient in material, the master of many styles. **1962** *Jrnl. Amer. Med. Assoc.* 19 May 595 (*heading*) The omnifocal lens for presbyopia. **1962** *Arch. Ophthalm.* LXVIII. 777/1 (*heading*) Use of the omnifocal. *Ibid.*, Omnifocals are used binocularly but are effective monocularly in cases where only one eye can be used. **1965** *Maclean's Mag.* 20 Feb. 1 An optical company in Ohio offers to solve this problem with an 'omnifocal' lens which has power that's gradually increased from top to bottom with no blurred area or transition zone. **1974** *Year Bk. Ophthalm.* 38 Three types of lens included..Varilux, Zoom and Omnifocal. **1929** A. HUXLEY *Do What you Will* 132 The ancient Greeks were evidently, in Sir Richard Burton's expressive phrase, 'omnifutuent'. **1966** *Listener* 24 Mar. 445/1 Stephen learns to accept himself as a homosexual only by entering a society which is innocently omnifutuant. **1967** *Ibid.* 30 Mar. 433/1 Anthony Burgess..to whom, among others, I owe such words as *omnifutuant* and *futuancy.* **1936** *Times Lit. Suppl.* 2 May 378/2 The present eight hundred pages set forth the science of omnilateral aristology. **1953** *Essays in Crit.* III. II. 374 He [*sc.* Chaucer] sees life steadily, and if he is not omnilateral, he *is* manysided. **1936** *Times Lit. Suppl.* 2 May 378/2 Of old, man was omnilaterally oriented. **1932** H. H. PRICE *Perception* vii. 202 This could only be avoided if we had been *omni*percipient. **1922** JOYCE *Ulysses* 377 The certain sign of omnipollent nature's incorrupted benefaction. **1961** Omnipurpose [see *OMNICOMPETENT *a.*]. **1947** *Electronics* Oct. 95/2 There are also voice channels on both the runway localizer and the omnirange, which are used generally for traffic control and weather information. **1951** *Gloss. Aeronaut. Terms* (*B.S.I.*) III. 27 *V.H.F. Omni-range*, a short-range, very-high-frequency, omni-directional beacon which provides an indication in the aircraft of the bearing of the beacon, or left-right track indication. **1959** K. HENNEY *Radio Engin. Handbk.* (ed. 5) xxv. 27 As of June 30, 1955, there were 410 omniranges in operation. **1966** D. FRANCIS *Flying Finish* xvii. 199 The V. O. R.—Very high frequency Omni-range—by which one navigated from one radio beacon to the next. **1932** H. H. PRICE *Perception* iv. 72 If we were *omnisentient* beings,.. able to sense all at once all the sense-data which can ever be sensed by every sentient human or non-human. **1911** BEERBOHM *Zuleika D.* ii. 23 But would she ever meet whom, looking up to him, she could love—she, the omnisubjugant? **1956** P. FLEMING *My Aunt's Rhinoceros* 141 After the war the bureaucrats no longer held their omnisubjugant trump. **1883** B. F. WESTCOTT *Historic Faith* xi. 144 The 'eternal' does not in essence express the infinite extension of time but the absence of time, not the omni-temporal but the supra-temporal. **1970** P. A. BERTOCCI *Person God Is* xii. 223 It is..my concern to press the question on both Advaitin and Visishtadvaitin: Why not reconceive the perfection of God so that good and evil, truth and error, progress and decay, can affect the qualitative manner in which God experiences himself and the world, and in a way consistent with his omnitemporal unity and continuity? **1961** E. NAGEL *Struct. of Sci.* iv. 70 Suppose there are (omnitemporally) no physical objects that do not attract each other. **1964** *Philos. Rev.* LXXIII. 486 For something to qualify as being true omnitemporally. **1851** H. MELVILLE *Moby Dick* III. xxi.

146 This omni-tooled, open-and-shut carpenter, was,.. no mere machine of an automaton. **1967** V. NABOKOV *Speak, Memory* (ed. 2) ii. 42 The game in use was the regular 'draw poker', with, occasionally, the additional tingle of jackpots and an omnivicarious joker.

omni (ǫ·mni). Abbrev. *omnirange.
1949 *Proc. IRE* XXXVII. 832/1 The flag alarm of the course-deviation indicator is actuated by the omni receiver. **1950** *Time* 31 July 28/2 Each omni sends out a radio signal that is different for each direction from the station.

omnibus. Add: **A.** *sb.* ¶. *Omnibi*, representing a spurious 'plural' (in quot. 1889 genitive singular) form, occurs occasionally.
1840 W. HOWITT *Visits to Remarkable Places* (ser. 1) 200 Trains of omnibuses, or omnibi, are flying down to the Broomielaw every hour. **1889** E. DOWSON *Let.* 23 June (1967) 85, I trust you arrived chez toi—in all sobriety last night & accomplished the de[s]census Av—I should say omnibi with discretion. **1969** *Times* 18 Jan. 20/3 The portmanteau term 'reprint' evades definition. It covers series, 'evergreens', omnibi, disinterments, defrostings, definitive editions, [etc.].

2. a. (Earlier example.)
1844 C. G. F. GORE *Quid pro Quo* (ed. 3) 81 What if I.. swell the 'Bravos' of the Omnibus?

b. Short for *omnibus book* (see sense *B. 3).
The word 'omnibus' was also used in the sense 'omnibus journal', i.e. a newspaper comprising a variety of items, in two early 19th-century publications, *The National Omnibus; and General Advertiser* (1831), and *The Lancashire Omnibus, a Journal of Literature and Amusement* (1832).
1930 *Writer* Jan. 74/2 One of the recent omnibuses contained selected short stories. **1931** 'J. GROVE' (*title*) The omnibus of romance. **1937** 'A. ARMSTRONG' (*title*) The laughter omnibus. **1976** R. USBORNE *Wodehouse at Work* (rev. ed.) iii. 92 The Preface that Wodehouse wrote for the 1974 omnibus *World of Psmith*. **1978** *Bookseller* 8 Apr. 2196/3 When.. Charles Pick.. dreamed up those jumbo Heinemann Octopus omnibuses, it seemed.. only a matter of time before Collins put some.. authors into similar vehicles.

5. *omnibus-driver, -office, -riding, sleigh, -ticket, traffic* (earlier examples); **omnibus man** (earlier example).
1843 POE *Mystery of Marie Roget* in *Ladies' Compan.* (N.Y.) Feb. 166/1 The omnibus-driver, Valence. **1870** 'F. FERN' *Ginger-Snaps* 304 This honored name, shouted from lungs that would not have disgraced an omnibus-driver. **1857** *Christian Misc.* July 219/2 We know no class of men in this country who undergo a more severe life of toil.. than the omnibus-men and cabmen of London. **1854** M. CUMMINS *Lamplighter* xviii. 112 You know the way from the omnibus-office. **1844** *Knickerbocker* XXIV. 91 His opinions against the omnibus-riding of so many of our idle citizens. **1860** *Boston Auditor's Ann. Rep. 1859–60* 323 One covered omnibus sleigh. **1852** E. E. HALE *If, Yes, & Perhaps* (1868) 3 This [sum].. would buy the omnibus tickets. **1869** *Engineering* 26 Nov. 348/1 With some slight modifications of detail, Mr. Wright's doors might.. be advantageously applied to many railway carriages employed in working metropolitan, or as it is often called, 'omnibus' traffic. **1883** E. W. HAMILTON *Diary* 15 Dec. (1972) II. 525 Trains worked by electricity admit of any amount of subdivision, which is no small consideration as it facilitates *omnibus* traffic and dispenses with the necessity of constructing the permanent way as strong as it now is.

B. *adj.* **1.** (Earlier and further examples.)
1842 *Congress. Globe* 27th Congress 2 Sess. App. 661/1 These two articles.. were caught in the omnibus, or dragnet section, which is placed in the rear of the bill. **1850** *Ibid.* 31st Congress 1 Sess. App. 524/1, I am opposed to all omnibus bills, and all amalgamation projects. **1889** *Echo* 16 Nov. 2/3 Each man pays an 'omnibus' contribution of a shilling a week for benefits. **1968** *Globe & Mail* (Toronto) 3 Feb. 40/2 All organizations said, however, that changes in existing regulations are necessary and many of the Criminal Code amendments contained in an omnibus bill presented by Justice Minister Pierre Trudeau are good ones. **1972** *N.Y. Law Jrnl.* 10 Oct. 18/9 Defendant's omnibus motion is disposed of as hereinafter indicated. **1974** *Times* 30 Aug. 15/2 The plan.. is to work up some omnibus convention which most will sign.

2. *omnibus box* (later examples).
1902 *Chambers's Jrnl.* Dec. 823/2 On this level, where it touched the stage, we had an 'omnibus box', exactly after the pattern of the proverbial one at Her Majesty's, and occupied usually by the same distinguished noblemen. **1922** A. HADDON *Green Room Gossip* iv. 95 The passing of the green room reminds me of another effete institution of the English theatre—the omnibus box.

3. omnibus book, volume, etc., a book or volume having a large and occas. varied content, *spec.* one containing several reprinted works by a single author or works of the same kind and published at a price designed to place it within the reach of a wide public; **omnibus letter,** a letter intended for more than one recipient; **omnibus-sized** *a.*, of the size of an omnibus book; **omnibus ticket,** one admitting a number of persons.
1929 *Daily Tel.* 1 Jan. 6/2 It is a day of what the publishers call 'omnibus books', meaning works which carry many and varied passengers. **1933** *Mind* XLII. 525 Hume's omnibus letter addressed to Dr. Hugh Blair, and through Blair to Dr. Jardine. **1931** *Times Lit. Suppl.* 19 Nov. 918/1 This second instalment of his short stories, an almost omnibus-sized book. **1868** *Rep. Iowa Agric. Soc. 1867* 408 Some.. tender hearted friends would take in their settlement [= family] and then proceed to some hole .. in the fence and hand his 'omnibus ticket' to some other parent. **1928** *Times Lit. Suppl.* 12 July 514/4 The 'omnibus' volume of 'Great Short Stories of Detection, Mystery and Horror',.. runs to some 1,250 pages. **1928** *Observer* 22 July 8 The four novels together make one of the most desirable of 'omnibus' volumes. **1928** *Publishers' Circular* 14 July 39/2 (*heading*) The Omnibus Wells.

omnibus, *v.* Delete *nonce-wd.* and add: (*a*) (earlier example, in *absol.* use); (*c*) to convey by omnibus; (*d*) to publish an omnibus edition of (an author).
1833 W. C. MACREADY *Diary* 7 Nov. (1912) I. 76, I omnibused down to Drury Lane. **1863** 'G. HAMILTON' *Gala-Days* 121 We were quickly omnibused to the relics of Donegana. **1933** *Times Lit Suppl.* 5 Jan. 1/2 For the author the possibility of becoming popular enough in his lifetime to be omnibused or to omnibus himself with profit may be looked on as a new prize in the race for fame.

omnicompetent (ǫ:mnikǫ·mpĭtěnt), *a.* [f. OMNI- + COMPETENT *a.*] Competent to deal with everything; *spec.* possessing jurisdiction or authority to act in all matters. Hence **omnico·mpetence.**
1827, 1889 Omnicompetent [in Dict. s.v. OMNI-]. **1900** Omnicompetence [in Dict. s.v. OMNI-]. **1926** R. H. TAWNEY *Relig. & Rise of Capitalism* ii. 124 Recent political theory has been prolific in criticisms of the omnicompetent state. **1937** *Times Lit. Suppl.* 1 May 320 His omnicompetence dealt with the history of ideas as swiftly as with the measurement of the hide. **1943** C. S. LEWIS *Abolition of Man* iii. 30 The man-moulders of the new age will be armed with the powers of an omnicompetent state and an irresistible scientific technique. **1952** V. A. DEMANT *Relig. & Decline of Capitalism* ii. 57 The principle of the omnicompetent state and the myth of the self-sufficient individual. **1961** *Economist* 30 Dec. 1276/1 A sort of ghostly middleman between omnipurpose boroughs and omnicompetent Government departments. **1967** *Punch* 11 Oct. 541 She comes from a famous wine family.. so she is omnicompetent, bullying her *maître de chai*, [etc.]. **1971** *Mod. Law Rev.* XXXVI. 611 Parliament as an institution must be sovereign or omnicompetent at any given moment of time. **1973** *Times Lit. Suppl.* 28 Dec. 1588/2 The computers are no longer considered even by their supporters to be omnicompetent. **1975** *Times* 25 July 13/5 Deference to professional omnicompetence is, of course, gratifying.

o:mnidire·ctional, *a.* Also **omni-directional.** [f. OMNI- + DIRECTIONAL *a.*] Of equal sensitivity or power in all directions (usu., all horizontal directions).
1927 *Daily Tel.* 22 Mar. 13 The Marconi Company quoted £66,153 for the Beam system and £29,163 for a system of omni-directional communication. **1932** *Times Educ. Suppl.* 31 Dec. p. i/2 The other short-wave transmitter worked on 15,140 kc/s, using an omni-directional aerial. **1947** BUCK & PIERCE in J. S. Hall *Radar Aids to Navigation* ii. 51 The uhf omnidirectional beacons.. are based primarily on the low-frequency system used for marine navigation. **1952** E. A. LAPORT *Radio Antenna Engin.* ii. 94 Experience has been gained with vertical radiators at many hundreds of broadcast stations, each employing one or more for omnidirectional or directive radiation. **1959** H. HOBSON *Mission House Murder* xxi. 140 They.. fixed an omni-directional, remotely controlled microphone which transmitted on a closed circuit. **1969** R. B. FULLER *Operating Man. Spaceship Earth* vi. 88 Einstein formulated his famous equation E = M (matter's mass, explained in the terms of C²—speed of an omni-directional (radiant) surface wave's expansion, unfettered, in a vacuum). **1976** *CB Mag.* June 7/1 (Advt.), Electrical design of the long, 64 wavelength vertical radiating element plus full size radials guarantee.. highest signal radiation efficiency in the desired vertical plane and omnidirectional, full coverage transmitting and receiving pattern.

Hence **o:mnidirectiona·lity,** the property of being omnidirectional; **o:mnidire·ctionally** *adv.*, in all directions.
1950 *Jrnl. R. Aeronaut. Soc.* LIV. 279/2 By comparing the phase of the rotating radiation pattern with that of a reference signal radiated omni-directionally, the bearing of the aircraft from the beacon is determined. **1966** L. V. BLAKE *Antennas* vii. 330 In unstabilized-spacecraft applications three-dimensional omnidirectionality may be desired. **1972** *Science* 20 Oct. 273/1 In order to achieve omnidirectionality, a second array is envisaged, located at right angles to the first. **1976** *Wireless World* Mar. 44/3 Real antennas do not radiate omnidirectionally, but concentrate the power into a directional beam.

omni·ficence. [f. OMNIFIC *a.* + -ENCE.] The fact or quality of being omnific, or of making or doing everything.
1881 RUSKIN *Our Fathers have told Us* I. ii. 62 Unwearied in protective friendship, in meekly dextrous omnificence, in latent tutorship. **1941** *Mind* L. 297 He therefore devotes the rest of the chapter to divine 'omnificence', *i.e.* the doctrine that all that is in fact done is done by God.

omnificent, *a.* (Earlier and later examples.)
1677 LOCKE *Jrnl.* 8 Feb. in *Essay Draft A* (1936) 84 They who out of a great care not to admitt unintelligible things deny or question an eternall omnificent spirit run them selves into a greater difficulty by makeing an eternall and intelligent matter. **1929** R. BRIDGES *Testament of Beauty* iv. 177 Joyful obedience With reverence to'ard the omnificent Creator and First Cause.

omniscient, *a.* Add: **omnisci·entist,** one who purports to be, or is alleged to be, omniscient.
1932 R. A. KNOX *Broadcast Minds* ii. 20 (*heading*) The omniscientists. *Ibid.* 21 We are all omniscientists now, at least in ambition... It only remains that we should pride ourselves on knowing something about everything. **1948** A. O'RAHILLY *Relig. & Sci.* iv. 32 We stand.. opposed to the usurpations and truculent dogmatism of the omniscientists.

omnopon (ǫ·mnŏpǫn). *Pharm.* Also **Omnopon.** [f. L. *omn-is* all + OP(IUM *sb.* + *-on*, arbitrary ending.] A proprietary name in the U.K. for a mixture of the hydrochlorides of the opium alkaloids. Cf. *PANTOPON.
1909 *Trade Marks Jrnl.* 1 Dec. 1962 Omnopon... All goods included in class 3 [*i.e.* chemical substances prepared for use in medicine and pharmacy]. The firm of F. Hoffman La Roche & Co.,.. Bale, Switzerland; chemical manufacturers. **1910** *Lancet* 15 Oct. 1169/1 Pantopon is known in Great Britain as 'Omnopon'. **1922** C. T. CAMPION tr. *Schweitzer's On Edge of Primeval Forest* v. 92 He is given an injection of omnipon [*sic*]. **1957** I. MAGILL in Gillies & Millard *Princ. & Art Plastic Surg.* I. iii. 64 For premedication Omnopon and scopolamine are preferred, as their action is synergistic. **1970** *Sunday Mail* (Brisbane) 15 Mar. 4 Police took possession of a huge quantity of cannabis, opium, L.S.D., omnopon.. and cocaine. **1970** PASSMORE & ROBSON *Compan. Med. Stud.* II. v. 48/2 It is widely believed that there is no therapeutic advantage in using mixed alkaloid preparations from opium, such as papaveretum (omnopon).

omphalo-. Add: **omphali·tis** [-ITIS], inflammation of the umbilicus; **omphalo·scopy** [Gr. -σκοπία], contemplation of the navel.
1876 DUNGLISON *Dict. Med. Sci.* (rev. ed.) 722/2 Omphalitis. **1897** *Trans. Amer. Pediatric Soc.* IX. 208 Of the remaining cases.. one.. was due to pyæmia following omphalitis in the newly-born. **1974** PASSMORE & ROBSON *Compan. Med. Stud.* III. II. xlv. 22/1 The appearance [in the newborn] of non-specific signs of infection, whether or not there is liver enlargement, jaundice or evidence of omphalitis, is always an indication for culture of the umbilicus and the blood. **1931** T. H. PEAR *Voice & Personality* iv. 35 The psychologist, unless mental omphaloscopy contents him, must go and fetch his material. **1960** *Times* 30 Nov. 7/2 In particular he made fun of 'omphaloscopy'—gazing at the navel.

omphaloid, *a.* (Later example.)
1942 *Oxoniensia* VII. 47 Sandy, smoothed, dull black, well finished. Omphaloid base of medium-sized bowl.

omul (ōu·mul). [a. Russ. *omul'*.] A fish of the salmon family, *Coregonus autumnalis*, found in Lake Baikal and regions bordering the Arctic Ocean.
1884 *Encycl. Brit.* XVII. 605/2 Only two species of fish are of any importance [in Novaya Zembla]—the goltzy (*Salmo alpinus*) in the western rivers, and the omul (*Salmo omul*) in the eastern. **1955** *Bull. Amer. Mus. Nat. Hist.* CVI. 279/2 The salmon-herring, or omul, has a spawning run of 1500 kilometers (930 miles) in the Yenesei [*sic*] River. **1969** *Nature* 13 Sept. 1091/2 Lake Baikal is particularly noted for its reserves of omul'. **1970** G. V. NIKOLSKY et al. in Lindsey & Woods *Biol. Coregonid Fishes* 257 The omul is an anadromous fish, which lives in waters of higher salinity than other coregonid fishes... Lake Baikal omul forms a separate subspecies. **1976** 'S. HARVESTER' *Siberian Road* i. 18 The Cossacks.. went after sturgeon and omul, a white-fish.

on, *prep.* Add: **I. 1. d.** Also in reference to a means of communication, as *on the air* (see *AIR *sb.*¹ 1 c), *on the telephone*, etc. Hence, broadcast on a specified channel, frequency, or wavelength.
1917 R. FRY *Let.* 23 Nov. (1972) II. 420 London's just awful for me because of the millions of people that catch me on the telephone. *c* **1928** *Ibid.* 632 I've just been talking for the second time today with Vanessa on the 'phone. **1929** *Ibid.* 5 Feb. 636, I have still two 'talks' hanging over me—one at the Athenaeum Club and one on the wireless. **1944** *Sun* (Baltimore) 7 Jan. 8/3 Common usage is unerringly correct: one does not hear a program in or even by or through the radio. He hears it on the radio. **1966** *Listener* 11 Aug. 190 Viscount Dilhorne and Lord Shawcross, Q.C., interviewed by Robin Day on B.B.C.-1. *Ibid.* 8 Sept. 363/3 Earlier, on B.B.C.-2, Rozhdestvensky was back again with the Moscow Radio Orchestra and the young pianist Nicolai Petrov. **1969** D. E. WESTLAKE *Up your Banners* xviii. 124 The beautician hollered from the living room, 'Leona, come quick! You're on the TV!' **1973** P. O'DONNELL *Silver Mistress* iv. 73 Get on the phone and book three seats.. to Hong Kong. **1974** *Oxford Mail* 1 May 4/7 James Dalton, the Queen's College organist, can be heard on Radio Three on Monday. **1977** *Custom Car* Nov. 11/3 Anyone with that kind of money contact Richard on Berkhampstead 71619.

i. Indicating a musical instrument which is being played, = UPON *prep.* 25. Of a musician: playing (a specified musical instrument) *colloq.* (orig. *U.S.*).
c **1386** CHAUCER *Miller's Tale* (1885, Harl. MS. 7334) 3214 And al aboue þer lay a gay Sawtrye On which he made a nightes melodye. *c* **1400** [see PLAY *v.* 26 a]. *a* **1529** [see LUTE *sb.*¹ 1 a]. **1767, 1768** [see PIANOFORTE]. **1842, 1903** [see PERFORM *v.* 7 c]. **1926** WHITEMAN & MCBRIDE *Jazz* xii. 241 Gus Miller.. was wonderful on the clarinet and saxophone. **1934** *Down Beat* Aug. 4/2 Oscar Eiler remains on cello... Hunter Kahler replaced George Frewit on piano... Milt. Chalifoux is still on drums, as is Ralph Mazza on guitar and violin. **1955** SHAPIRO & HENTOFF *Hear me talkin' to Ya* xiii. 206 Our three pieces including Sonny, Sterling Conway on banjorine, and myself. *Ibid.* 251 We went into the Little Club—Gil Rodin, myself, and Benny Goodman on saxes, Glenn

Miller on trombone..; and Ben Pollack, of course, on drums. **1962** *Sunday Times* (Colour Suppl.) 10 June 3 A powerful and accomplished saxophonist—mainly on alto, originally rather too closely modelled on Charlie Parker. **1971** *Radio Times* 11 Nov. 3/4 Neither Cat Anderson on trumpet nor Lawrence Brown on trombone were able to make this tour.

j. *Math.* (Defined or expressed) in terms of (the elements of).

1934 *Ann. Math.* XXXV. 119 By an abstract ϵ p-simplex σ_p on A is meant a set of $p+1$ points of A whose sum is of diameter $<\epsilon$. **1937** R. D. CARMICHAEL *Introd. Theory Groups of Finite Order* viii. 240 Show how to form the most general group of linear homogeneous transformations on a given set of variables. **1953** BIRKHOFF & MACLANE *Survey Mod. Algebra* (rev. ed.) vi. 119 A function defined on the elements of the set S_1 with values in T. **1968** E. T. COPSON *Metric Spaces* i. 11 Suppose we have a relation $\sim$ defined on a set E. **1971** *Sci. Amer.* Aug. 94/3 The objects..will be real-valued functions f defined on some set S. In other words, f is a rule that assigns to each point s belonging to the set S a real number $f(s)$ belonging to the real-number set. **1971** *Nature* 31 Dec. 527/1 We define a pairwise dissimilarity matrix d on a set of objects P as a real-valued function on pairs of elements of P such that $d(a, b) \geqslant 0$ for all a, b in P [etc.].

k. Addicted to or regularly taking (a drug or drugs). Cf. *ON *adv.* 1 b. *colloq.* (orig. *U.S.*).

1936 *Amer. Speech* XI. 124/2 *On drugs*, addicted. **1955** SHAPIRO & HENTOFF *Hear me talkin' to Ya* xxi. 333 The habit is a false crutch. Don't get on the H. *Ibid.* 335, I don't think all musicians are on junk by any means. **1971** *Lancet* 30 Oct. 985/1 A woman aged 49 received lithium carbonate 900 mg. daily... She was also on tranylcypromine 30 mg. daily. **1972** M. J. BOSSE *Incident at Naha* i. 60 Linda..asked what I was on these days. 'Pot, and not much of that,' I told her. **1972** D. SELMAN *Sudden Death* iv. 96, I suppose he didn't *truly* rape me... I mean I'm on the pill and everything. **1973** BOYD & PARKES *Dark Number* vii. 82 Julia went through a pretty bad time.. after the accident—on the pills, seeing psychiatrists and what have you. **1976** P. HILL *Hunters* v. 59 He dropped his mouth to hers... 'Are you on the pill?' he asked.

l. Drinking (alcoholic liquor) in large quantities or to excess. *on the booze*: see *BOOZE *sb.* 2 b; *on it* (Austral. colloq.): drinking heavily, 'hitting the bottle'.

1938 E. LOWE *Salute to Freedom* 38 He knew how drink affected Brand, and he muttered to his wife, 'He's on it proper to day mother.' **1951** E. LAMBERT *Twenty Thousand and Thieves* ix. 140 'They reckon Groggy's on it again,' observed Tommy. **1955** P. WHITE *Tree of Man* (1956) 141 'It is him,' she said finally. 'It is that bastard. He is on it again.' **1962** A. SEYMOUR *One Day of Year* 12 And how long was you on it before the pubs shut? *a* **1966** 'M. NA GOPALEEN' *Best of Myles* (1968) 291 Easy seen you were on the beer last night. **1966** 'J. HACKSTON' *Father clears Out* 104 When he was on it, and wanted..another drink.. he never had to press the bell, but pressed the button with a bullet. **1967** H. STOREY in *Coast to Coast 1965–66* 203 One of the neighbours had ribbed him about 'being on the bottle'. **1976** *Daily Mirror* 18 Mar. 9/3 Watch that daily tipple, ladies. You could end up on the bottle.

6. a. Also used redundantly in *on tomorrow*, *on yesterday*, etc. *dial.* and *U.S.*

1829 *Virginia Lit. Museum* 30 Dec. 459/2 *On.* As '*on* tomorrow'; a mere expletive. Common. **1848** *Southern Lit. Messenger* XIV. 636/2 'On' yesterday, (another Southern emendation of the Queen's English, which is funny enough,) I was so unfortunate [etc.]. **1852** *N.Y. Tribune* 9 Jan. 6/1 It was the intention to send in the Treasury Report..on yesterday. **1880** W. H. PATTERSON *Gloss. Words Antrim & Down* 74 *On*..is sometimes prefixed to the words to-morrow and yesterday, thus—'I'll do it on to-morrow.' **1914** *Dialect Notes* IV. 160 On yesterday; on last week. **1922** H. C. LODGE in *Congress. Rec.* 27 Dec. 942, I took occasion to ask the Secretary of State on yesterday. **1922** JOYCE *Ulysses* 645 Lionel's air in *Martha, M'appari*, which..he heard, or overheard, to be more accurate, on yesterday. **1944** H. W. HORWILL *Dict. Mod. Amer. Usage* (ed. 2) 214/2 The expression *on yesterday* is an example of the Am. use of *on* where it would be considered superfluous in Eng. **1977** *Irish Press* 29 Sept. 2/1 (Advt.), Removal of remains to St. Bridget's Church, Kilcurry on today (Thursday) at 6.30 o'clock.

d. *on time*: see also TIME *sb.* 43.

10. c. *on it*: (*a*) *U.S. slang*, ready for, or skilled in, something; (*b*) *dial.*, preceded by an adverb or adjective: in a particular condition or situation, usu. one that is distressing.

1865 *Harper's Mag.* May 694/1 She's tolerable peert—the old 'oman is. Oh, she's on it, you bet. **1866** 'MARK TWAIN' in *Daily Union* (Sacramento) 22 May 3/4 In San Francisco sometimes, if you offend a man, he proposes to take his coat off, and inquires, 'Are you on it?' **1880** A. A. HAYES *New Colorado* (1881) v. 77 You bet he could cook. He was just *on it*. **1886** R. E. G. COLE *Gloss. Words S.-W. Lincs.* 103 Such phrases as 'Sorely on it', 'Sadly on it', for Sorely off, Sadly off; 'Two or three days ago I was strangely on it.' **1889** E. PEACOCK *Gloss. Words Manley & Corringham, Lincolnshire* (ed. 2) 886 He's sorely on it yit, 'cause his wife's runn'd awaay fra him. **1890** BARRÈRE & LELAND *Dict. Slang* II. 102/1 *On it* (American). This eccentric expression meant originally that a man was decidedly engaged in anything. It implied determination. 'I'm on it,' I understand it. **1946** F. SARGESON *That Summer* 96 He looked pretty crook on it.

II. 20. d. Of a joke, laugh, etc.: against or at the expense of (someone).

1866 *Harper's Mag.* July 271/2 There may be a joke about it; but if there is, it is on the Colonel, for he told me so. **1901** *Munsey's Mag.* XXV. 711/2 'It was Lanse—Lanse all the time,' he exploded. 'Oh, wasn't that one on me!' **1906** *Nation* (N.Y.) 6 Dec. 478 The people rejoiced that the laugh was on those whom they consider their natural enemies. **1933** [see *B.O.* s.v. *B. III]. **1936** N. COWARD *To-night at 8.30* 27 The joke is on us... We've never even been lovers. **1939** L. M. MONTGOMERY *Anne of Ingleside* vi. 33 The joke is on us... And a nice laugh he will have on me. **1967** *Listener* 11 May 634/1 The trouble is we enjoy a good laugh, especially if the joke's on us. **1977** P. HARCOURT *At High Risk* vi. 196 The joke was on me, and it left a sour taste.

e. Indicating a person, etc., who is to pay the bill, esp. for a treat of any kind. *colloq.*

1871 *Republican Rev.* (Albuquerque, New Mexico) 29 July 2/4 After the first round they said it was 'on me'. **1889**, etc. [see *HOUSE *sb.*[1] 2 c]. **1902** C. J. C. HYNE *Mr. Horrocks, Purser* 78 And now come and have a bit of cheap lunch. We'll consider we've tossed for it, and it's on me. **1919** 'I. HAY' *Last Million* vii. 85 'This is on us,' Al Thompson hastened to add. **1938** L. MACNEICE *Earth Compels* 22 Five minutes spent at a bar Watching the fish coming in, as you parry and shrug This is on me or this is on me. **1973** 'P. REID' *Harris in Wonderland* iii. 26 Arbuthnot wanted to drink... I explained my financial predicament but he waved it aside. 'On me, man.'

f. To the disadvantage or detriment of (a person); so as to affect or disturb. *colloq.*

1880 W. H. PATTERSON *Gloss. Words Antrim & Down* 74 'Don't break it on me,' *i.e.* don't break that thing of mine. **1892** E. LAWLESS *Grania* I. II. iv. 184 It was the devil's own abuse he got from his wife..for letting her fine spring chickens be drowned on her, which she had been months upon months of rearing. **1907**, etc. [see *DIE *v.*[1] 1 e]. **1907** J. M. SYNGE *Tinker's Wedding* II. 26 There she is waking up on us, and I thinking we'd have the job done before she'd know of it at all. **1946** K. TENNANT *Lost Haven* (1947) vii. 103, I never knew such a man for pickles——he must have eaten a bottle on me just over tea and breakfast. **1955** R. P. HOBSON *Nothing too Good for Cowboy* vii. 63 My lead cows bunched up on me and refused to face the storm. **1963, 1966** [see *GO *v.* 44 a]. **1971** M. SMITH *Gypsy in Amber* (1975) ii. 17 You're turning into a dilettante on me. **1974** M. BUTTERWORTH *Man in Sopwith Camel* iii. 34 He's passed out on me... Had some kind of seizure.

21. b. *to have a down on*: see *DOWN *sb.*[3] 5; *to have nothing* (or *something*) *on* (a person): see *HAVE *v.* 14 h.

III. 26. Restrict †*Obs.* to uses in Dict. and add: **b.** Used *colloq.* (chiefly *Austral.*) in locative senses, where 'at' would normally occur in standard use.

1853 *Bendigo* (Victoria) *Advertiser* 9 Dec. 1/1 We have for many months vainly endeavoured to procure suitable materials for publishing a Newspaper on Bendigo, to be devoted Exclusively to the Mining Interests. **1860** *Mining Surveyors' Rep.* (Mining Dept., Victoria) Aug. 198 This will be one of the richest claims on Ballarat. **1892** P. H. EMERSON *Son of Fens* xxv. 248 You grind my old Beccy [*sc.* scythe]; you're a better hand on it than I am. **1901** M. FRANKLIN *My Brilliant Career* iii. 17 Why, on Bruggabrong the women never had to do no outside work. **1966** BAKER *Austral. Lang.* (ed. 2) xvi. 348 A gold-seeker was never *at* a goldfield, but always *on* it. **1968** *Listener* 29 Aug. 267/2 The only reason she was on a bus stop at that un-Christian hour is that if she didn't catch that particular bus she would miss the only connection that would get her to the house in time to do a day's work. **1974** *Publishers Weekly* 5 Aug. 8/2 He began to put it all together, writing in the evenings and on weekends.

27. (Further examples.)

1829 D. JERROLD *Black-Eyed Susan* (1855) I. vi. 27 We found..three pilots' telescopes. This is one on 'em! **1848** THACKERAY *Van. Fair* li. 463 We're three on us—it's no use bolting. **1898** J. D. BRAYSHAW *Slum Silhouettes* 221 There was 'undreds on 'em, men, women, an' kids, an' most on 'em seemed ter be Total Obstinate Sons o' the Phoenix. **1916** 'TAFFRAIL' *Pincher Martin* xi. 204 'Ere's another on 'em! **1931** M. ALLINGHAM *Look to Lady* xvi. 170 Don't take no notice on 'im... 'E's as right as ever 'e was. **1937** —— *Case of Late Pig* xiv. 98, I don't know what he'll think on us—two on 'em instead of one. **1973** R. PARKES *Guardians* ix. 165 No doubt on it, mate. **1974** 'S. WOODS' *Done to Death* 41 Nobody as I knows on. .. It was nothing, really, to get hold on.

27*. In *dial.*, *N. Amer.*, and casual contexts, used where 'in' would normally occur in standard use.

1762 BOSWELL *London Jrnl.* 13 Dec. (1950) 82, I feel a surprising change to the better on myself since I came to London. **1787** J. ELPHINSTON *Propriety* II. II. 93 Dhe Scotch can see no incongruity in meeting a person *on* dhe street,..hwaraz dhe Inglish meet a person *in* dhe street. **1892** E. G. VINCENT *Newfoundland to Cochin China* iii. 45 The City Hall in this street, or 'on', as the Canadians would say. **1900** *Times* 6 Jan. 14/5 The genuine Dorset native always says, 'I see'd it on the paper', or 'I read it on the paper'. **1924** R. MASSON *Use & Abuse of Eng.* (ed. 4) iii. 42, I will likely know a great difference on her. **1938** J. STUART *Beyond Dark Hills* vi. 139 That took lifting and skill on flipping steel. *Ibid.* x. 396 They took 14 stitches on the other fellow. **1956** A. J. LERNER *My Fair Lady* (1958) I. viii. 86 Let the time go by, I won't care if I Can be here on the street where you live. **1972** *Scholarly Publishing* III. 181 My work as assistant editor is only a sideline. Since I do it largely on my own time, I avoid extra work and correspondence. **1972** *Time* 17 Apr. 37/2 An agreement..to help finance what is now called the Barsky Unit on the grounds of the Cho Ray Hospital. **1974** H. L. FOSTER *Ribbin'* iii. 109 Terror is waiting on line at 6:30 in the morning..for the Brooklyn Paramount to open for Alan Freed's rock and roll revue. **1974** *Melody Maker* 4 May 21/1 Hospitalized not long ago with a blood clot on his leg, he entered Beth Israel hospital again last week. **1977** *Irish Press* 29 Sept. 13/1 Michael Keane..is back on the Kerry team for Sunday's All-Ireland Under 21 Football final.

on, *adv.* (*a.*, *sb.*) Add: **1. b.** *to be on*: to be addicted to, or regularly taking, a drug or drugs; to be under the influence of drugs. Cf. *ON *prep.* 1 k. *U.S. slang.*

1938 *Amer. Speech* XIII. 188/2 *To be on*, to be addicted or actively indulging the [drugs] habit. **1955** W. GADDIS *Recognitions* I. v. 197 She's high right now, can't you see it? She's been on for three days. **1956** B. HOLIDAY *Lady sings Blues* (1973) xiv. 121 When I was on, I was on and nobody gave me any trouble. No cops, no treasury agents, nobody. I got into trouble when I tried to get off. **1968** *Sun Mag.* (Baltimore) 13 Oct. 19/3 When I took sets, I'd do it on the way to school... I'd always be on when I had to read in speech class.

11. b. Colloq. phrases: *to be on about*: to keep talking about, to harp on, to speak or write about (a subject); *to be on at*: to nag or scold (a person); *to go on about*: see *GO *v.* 84 g; *to go on at*: see GO *v.* 84 g; *to keep* (or *go*) *on and on*: to persist in speaking or questioning, to nag *at* a person.

1909 *Westm. Gaz.* 22 Sept. 8/2 Yesterday morning complainant was 'on' to him again about his religion. **1916** *Kelso Chron.* 24 Mar. 3 He was on about wa's that had ears. **1936** R. LEHMANN *Weather in Streets* viii. 348 Marda's always asking me why I don't get a divorce... Last year she was always on about it. **1938** N. MARSH *Artists in Crime* x. 145, I told him it would upset me but he went on and on. **1941** BAKER *Dict. Austral. Slang* 51 *On at* (*a person*), *to be*, to scold, reprove, nag at a person. **1952** A. BARON *With Hope, Farewell* 94 Well, now the second one's on at him to get married. **1958** N. F. SIMPSON *Resounding Tinkle* II. in *Observer Plays* 267 Fred was on at me to go up but I had my old coat on. **1966** *Listener* 22 Dec. 939/1 A reflection that brings us back to atmosphere and art forms, which I was on about some weeks ago. **1973** 'C. AIRD' *His Burial Too* iv. 40 The garage key that Ada Turvey was on about..that's still in the lock. **1974** G. BUTLER *Coffin for Canary* ii. 35 'You looked terrible yesterday,' he said. He kept on and on. He always did. **1974** 'J. MELVILLE' *Nun's Castle* ix. 214 He kept on and on at me till he got it out. I wouldn't have told him otherwise. **1975** K. BARCLAY tr. *P. Orum's Whipping-Boy* xxiii. 161 'He kept on and on at me.'.. 'I didn't do it.'.. 'Why can't you let me alone?'

13. b. (Further examples.) Also, of an event: arranged; going to happen. Of food or the like: placed on the stove, etc., to cook; cooking. Also *to have nothing on*: to have no engagements, business, etc.

1748, etc. [see PUT *v.*[1] 46 k]. *c* **1825** J. WALKER *Factory Lad* I. iii. 8 Interior of Allen's House—Fire place, with saucepan on. **1841** DICKENS *Barnaby Rudge* xvii. 31 Hurrah! Polly put the ket-tle on, we'll all have tea. **1841** MRS. GASKELL *Let.* 23 Dec. (1966) 46 Yesterday this plan seemed quite given up—today..it's *on* again—if all goes on well. **1883** W. AITKEN *Lays of Line* 135 The fire's black oot, and the parrich no on. **1908** R. W. CHAMBERS *Firing Line* iv. 46 If you and Virginia have nothing better on I'll dine with you tonight. **1915** R. FRY *Let.* 27 Feb. (1972) II. 383 I'm pushed away into any place and only wanted when there's nothing better on. **1938** D. RUNYON *Furthermore* vii. 129, I have nothing on of importance at the moment. **1955** M. ALLINGHAM *Beckoning Lady* ii. 21 It's still on, is it, the party? **1955** E. COXHEAD *Figure in Mist* ii. 69 'I left the potatoes on,' she muttered, and fled into the house. **1972** J. GILL *Tenant* I. iii. 25 I've nearly done, just putting the rice on. **1973** J. BURROWS *Like an Evening Gone* i. 11 Miss Limb, amazingly, had fallen in with Greta's plans. 'So it's on.' **1973** 'E. MCBAIN' *Hail to Chief* iv. 55 The television set was on, but the volume control was apparently broken. **1974** M. INGATE *Sound of Weir* xvii. 150 I'd better be getting the dinner on. We've only got sausages. **1974** *Times* 14 Mar. 16/3 It must have been the only diplomatic function on in London because many hundreds of the most notable people..were there.

c. Freq. in colloq. phr. *you are* (or *you're*) *on*: the bet or bargain is agreed.

1933 *Sun* (Baltimore) 25 Apr. 18/7 'I'll bet you a lobster dinner and all the champagne we can drink, if legal, that the dam will be filled by February 1,' said Mr. Smith... 'You're on,' said Mr. Crozier. **1961** J. SEYMOUR *Fat of Land* i. 19 'I'll let you have the two cottages..for ten pounds a year.' 'You are on,' I said. **1967** J. BURKE *Till Death us do Part* x. 153 'I'll give it [*sc.* smoking] up if you do.'.. 'All right,' snapped Alf. 'All right, you're on.' **1969** Y. CARTER *Mr. Campion's Farthing* xvi. 156 'Just to seal the bargain,' he said... 'You're on.' **1974** L. DEIGHTON *Spy Story* xviii. 194 'A quid,' I said. 'You're on,' said Ferdy.

d. *to be on*: to be in favour of, or willing to be a party to, something. *colloq.*

1888 'R. BOLDREWOOD' *Robbery under Arms* I. xi. 132 'What shall we do, Jim?..go or not?'.. 'I'm half a mind to tell Warrigal to..say we're not on.' *Ibid.* 138 Now we're here what's the play called, and when does the curtain rise? We're on. **1890** —— *Miner's Right* II. xiii. 23 'I'm on,' answered Joe, a ray of humour irradiating his honest countenance. **1898** 'H. S. MERRIMAN' *Roden's Corner* xiv. 145 If there is going to be fight..I'm on. **1916** 'TAFFRAIL' *Pincher Martin* xiv. 270 'What about a glass of sherry to celebrate the auspicious occasion?' 'I'm on, Peter,..but I really think it's up to me to pay for it.' **1923** WODEHOUSE *Inimitable Jeeves* xiv. 161 This jamboree is slated for Monday week. The question is, Are we on? **1939** K. TENNANT *Foveaux* IV. 350 'Are you on?' Herb asked impatiently as he began to remove his coat. 'I'll give it a go.' **1969** V. GIELGUD *Necessary End* i. 15 I'm on—if you want to play the equivalent of Twenty Questions.

e. In a state of knowledge or awareness regarding a person, state of affairs, etc. Cf. *ON TO *prep.* 2. *U.S. slang.*

1885 *Santa Fé Weekly New Mexican* 9 July 2/2 He hoped to sell the cavalry a large lot of supplies, but Major Van Horn was 'on'. **1900** ADE *Fables in Slang* 68 The

Preacher didn't know what all This meant,..but you can rest easy that the Pew-Holders were On in a minute. **1902** [see *NEXT *a.* 13c]. **1909** [see *DOPE *sb.* 3a]. **1934** J. M. CAIN *Postman always rings Twice* i. 10, I saw he was on, and quit talking about the guy in the Cadillac. **1973** R. STOUT *Please pass Guilt* (1974) xviii. 164 Wolfe, turning and seeing Saul, was on as quick as I had been. He said.. 'What?'

f. In negative contexts: acceptable, allowable; possible, likely; esp. in phr. *it's (just) not on. colloq.*

1935 in Partridge *Dict. Slang* (1937) 587/2 The majority of amateur [snooker] players..wildly attempt shots that are not 'on'. **1957** *Economist* 19 Oct. 200/1 This proposal is no longer 'on'. **1958** M. PUGH *Wilderness of Monkeys* 38 'I say, that's a bit much,' the military man said. 'Not on.' **1963** P. H. JOHNSON *Night & Silence* xxviii. 208 He could not conceivably go on believing in Matthew's guilt. It was just not on. **1963** *Times* 29 May 10/5 How can a ship fight effectively if a third of the crew is Portuguese, a third Belgian, and a third Danish? The thing is just not on. **1968** R. V. BESTE *Repeat Instructions* xvi. 174 'I'd like to dump the last two together next time.' 'That's not on,' King told him tersely. '..Stick to procedure.' **1973** 'M. INNES' *Appleby's Answer* ii. 23 How, I repeat, is a fellow to come by a cathedral? It just isn't on. **1975** *Guardian* 20 Jan. 4/3 Reductions in the standard of living were not on.

g. Of an item of food: on the menu; available. Cf. *OFF *adv.* 3e. *colloq.*

1949 'M. INNES' *Journeying Boy* xx. 248 Champ is off and eggs are on. **1953** R. FULLER *Second Curtain* ix. 131, I always have the curry when it's on. **1963** 'L. BRUCE' *Crack of Doom* vi. 53 Are you going to have lunch in the hotel? They've got sheeps' hearts on today.

h. *it was* (or *is*, etc.) *on* (*for young and old*): a description of complete disorder, a free-for-all. *Austral. colloq.*

1951 E. LAMBERT *Twenty Thousand Thieves* (1952) xvii. 258 Peter Dimmock bounded between the tents leaping into the air at every few paces and whooping: 'It's on! It's on for young and old!' **1955** J. MORRISON *Black Cargo* 77 A day come when some of our blokes in Sydney just put their coats on and walked off the job. It was on then for young and old. **1969** W. DICK *Naked Prodigal* 50 Just before closing time a brawl started when some bloke walking by spilt beer on Ackie so Ackie's young brother King hit him and the bloke's mate stepped in so Ackie hit him—and then it was on. **1971** D. MARTIN *Hughie* (1972) xi. 106 He almost forgot about it until the evening of Sunday when the party was due and when, in Harry's words, it was on for young and old.

B. *adj.* **1.** (Earlier and later examples.) Also of a ball or hit on this side.

1833 J. NYREN *Young Cricketer's Tutor* 34 The best way to play a ball, bowled as wide as your legs on the on side. **1836** [see *OFF *a.* 2b]. **1836** *New Sporting Mag.* July 196 On-balls have a greater tendency to turn in towards the wicket. **1854** J. PYCROFT *Cricket Field* (ed. 2) vii. 117 An angle sufficient to make Off or On hits. **1898** K. S. RANJITSINHJI *With Stoddart's Team* (ed. 4) i. 32 For..excellence of 'on side' play he can be compared with the best players. *Ibid.* vi. 112 Iredale..got out to Hearne in attempting a huge 'on' hit. **1903** *Westm. Gaz.* 23 June 3/1 In all those on-side strokes..Fry is a master. **1904** F. C. HOLLAND *Cricket* 16 The on strokes are not so often used as the off strokes. **1909** *Westm. Gaz.* 17 Apr. 16/2 A good back and on-side player ..may confidently expect to do well under these conditions. **1959** *Times* 11 June 3/5 Bold strokes, particularly on the onside.

b. *on-verse* [tr. G. *Anvers*]: the first half-line of a line of Old English verse. Also *attrib.* Cf. *off-verse* (*OFF *a.* 2c).

1935, 1953 [see *OFF *a.* 2c]. **1953** [see *ICTUS 1]. **1970** *Jrnl. Eng. & Gmc. Philol.* LXIX. 438 Rime forces all final lifts in on-verse or off-verse into prominence.

3. Corresponding to the state (of an electrical device) of being on (ON *adv.* 13b).

1899 J. PIGG *Railway 'Block' Signalling* vii. 364 When the arm is in the 'on' position, the mercury connects the two plates and completes the circuit. **1924** *Wireless World* 19 Mar. 772/2 This sort of switch is called a double-pole single-way switch, because it controls two circuits with one operation and has only one 'on' position. **1962** SIMPSON & RICHARDS *Physical Princ. Junction Transistors* vii. 142 Because the voltage across the transistor is a fraction of a volt losses in the 'on' state are small. **1962** E. G. DAVIES in G. A. T. Burdett *Automatic Control Handbk.* iii. 2 The isolator is hand operated and provided with distinct ON and OFF positions. **1967** *Electronics* 6 Mar. 133/1 With the modified circuit the relay's on-time is independent of input pulse characteristics.

4. *Physiol.* Of, pertaining to, or exhibiting the electrical activity that occurs briefly in some optic nerve fibres in vertebrates upon the commencement of illumination of the retina.

1903 F. GOTCH in *Jrnl. Physiol.* XXIX. 393 The first portion is the rise due to the sudden illumination; this I propose for brevity to term the ON effect. *Ibid.* 394 The upward movement of the image of the mercury indicates a positive (+) change in the eyeball in the ON, continuous and OFF reactions. *Ibid.* 398 The development of the ON change under these two conditions. **1937** *Brit. Jrnl. Psychol.* XXVII. 302 In the human eye the 'on effect' may occupy a time of the order of 0·1 sec. **1941** S. H. BARTLEY *Vision* xi. 286 The on-response is, in the main, duplex. **1948, 1972** [see *OFF *a.* 7].

C. *sb.*[1] (Earlier and later examples.) **on-theory,** a theory that favours concentrating the fielders on the on side and bowling the ball at or outside the on stump.

1862 *Baily's Monthly Mag.* Aug. 87 A on-drive from Jackson for 5. **1896** *Badminton Mag.* Sept. 280 A few bowlers have an 'on-theory'. **1900** W. J. FORD *Cricketer on Cricket* x. 118 George Giffen..could bowl 'off-theory' or 'on-theory'..with equal skill. **1963** *Times* 11 June 4/6 With a powerful on-drive Barker took his score to 49 and off the next ball completed a fine half century.

‖ **on** (ǫn), *sb.*[2] [Jap.] In feudal or prewar Japan, the sense of deep gratitude with an obligation or duty of service towards often highly formalized favours, as towards one's parents, teachers, lords, or the Emperor.

1946 R. BENEDICT *Chrysanthemum & Sword* (1947) v. 99 The word for 'obligations' which covers a person's indebtedness from greatest to least is *on*... *On* is in all its uses a load, an indebtedness, a burden, which one carries as best one may. *Ibid.* 101 *On* is always used in this sense of limitless devotion when it is used of one's first and greatest indebtedness, one's 'Imperial *on*'. This is one's debt to the Emperor, which one should receive with unfathomable gratitude... Every kamikaze pilot of a suicide plane was, they said, repaying his Imperial *on*. **1964** I. FLEMING *You only live Twice* iv. 56 He's acquired an ON with regard to me. That's an obligation—almost as important in the Japanese way of life as 'face'. When you have an ON, you're not very happy until you've discharged it honourably.

on (ǫn), *v.* [f. the adv.] **1.** *intr.* To go on; to move forward. Cf. ON *adv.* 9b. *U.S. dial.*

1840 C. F. HOFFMAN *Greyslaer* II. II. x. 27 I'll see the eend of it. So with that, I ups and ons.

2. *to on with*: to place or put on. Cf. ON *adv.* 4b. *dial.*

1843 'R. CARLTON' *New Purchase* I. xix. 170 She bethought as how she'd render off her fat; and so she ons with the grate pot. **1899** DICKINSON & PREVOST *Gloss. Words Cumberland* 231/2 Ah on's wi' my cwoat an' off teh wark. **1960** *Forfar Dispatch* 28 Jan. 8/5, I ons w'ee porridge pot.

on-, *prefix*[1]. Add: **4. onsurge,** an onward surge; **on-sweep** (earlier example).

1960 J. FINGLETON *Four Chukkas to Austral.* 16 His presence allowed the English bowlers to recover from O'Neill's onsurge. **1963** *Economist* 1 June 872/2 The real onsurge into the consumer durables revolution. **1866** *Dublin Rev.* Jan. 170 The rights of property alone.. formed the basis of resistance to the onsweep of revolution.

b. With sbs. used *attrib.* or as *adj.*, as **on-air,** while broadcasting; **on-axis,** situated or occurring on the axis; **on-course,** situated or taking place at a race-course; **on-demand,** done or available when demanded; **on-duty,** engaged or occupied with one's normal work; **on-farm,** occurring or used at a farm; **on-form,** that is in good form or condition; **on-street,** that is on a street; esp. of parking facilities; **on-track,** of betting: done at the race-track.

1972 *Guardian* 11 July 14/5 Parents shared what they thought about the programmes..by responding to on-air appeals to complete a questionaire. **1976** *Listener* 25 Mar. 362/1 The on-air behaviour of certain national and local disc-jockeys. **1962** A. NISBETT *Technique Sound Studio* 248 *Dead side* (of microphone), the angle within which the response of a microphone is low compared with the on-axis response. **1971** R. J. COLLIER et al. *Optical Holography* ii. 54 On-axis observation of either image is disturbed by the out-of-focus light from the other. **1964** A. WYKES *Gambling* viii. 195 These offices are in fact merely extensions of the on-course totalizators. **1973** *Times* 12 Apr. 12/4 The Tote, which does most of the on-course betting, earned a meagre profit of £100,000 last year. **1962** *Times* 9 Apr. (British Oxygen Co. Suppl.) p. v, Ready supply and on-demand delivery make sure your production goes smoothly. **1971** *Flying* (N.Y.) Apr. S5/3 Probably the most revolutionary innovation within this new system will be an on-demand capability. **1970** K. PLATT *Pushbutton Butterfly* (1971) xiv. 155 The on-duty cop outside the room. **1974** 'S. WOODS' *Done to Death* 184 His voice had..that wooden, on duty tone. **1969** *Times* 20 Jan. 2/1 There must be more integration with on-farm testing to select the bulls for central testing. **1970** *Daily Tel.* 26 Oct. 8/3 The economics of on-farm compounding with a mobile mill and mixer look fairly good. **1965** *Universe* 11 June 14/5 Mick Norman..last week..hit a convincing 70 against an on-form Sussex side. **1968** *Melody Maker* 23 Nov. 22/5 An on-form Phil Seamen is still one of the most exciting things to catch in a London jazz club or pub. **1959** *Manch. Guardian* 26 May 8 There might be strict prohibition of 'on-street parking' but 'not necessarily' of loading and unloading. **1973** D. WESTHEIMER *Going Public* iv. 64 A busy thoroughfare with no on-street parking. **1964** On-track [see *off-track* s.v. *OFF- 4b].

-on, *suffix*[1]. [f. the ending of ION (and *anion, cation*).] **1.** *Physics.* **a.** Used (first in *ELECTRON[2]) to form the names of sub-atomic particles, as *hyperon, meson, neutron, proton.*

The example of *electron* gave rise to a few particle names in *-TRON, q.v.; but *proton*, chronologically the second word of this group, has proved the dominant model.

b. Used to form the names of quanta, as *graviton, phonon.*

2. Used, esp. in molecular biology, to form the names of some entities conceived of as units, as *codon, muton, operon, pedon.*

-on, *suffix*[2]. [f. Gr. -ον, neut. of -ος, nom. masc. sing. ending of many adjs.] The ending of the names of the noble gases other than helium, as *argon* (the earliest named), *radon.*

on and off, *adv. phr.* (*sb.*). Add: **b.** (Further examples.) Now usu. with hyphens.

1904 *Westm. Gaz.* 13 Jan. 2/3 The buyer resented this on-and-off policy. **1936** *Discovery* July 222/1 His left hand works an 'on-and-off' key, sounding the note when it is pressed and killing it when released. **1965** T. CAPOTE *In Cold Blood* (1966) i. 4 She had been an on-and-off psychiatric patient the last half-dozen years. **1974** *Country Life* 21 Feb. 394/3 Grazed..on a rotational or 'on and off' system. **1977** *Time* 19 Sept. 30/1 The signing of a Panama Canal treaty that was initialed last month after 13 years of on-and-off efforts through the Administrations of four U.S. Presidents.

onanism. Add: (Further examples.) Also = **coitus interruptus.* Also *fig.*

1892 A. K. GARDNER *Conjugal Relationships* vii. 96 This man put into practice, to calm the fears of his wife,.. the best calculated refinements of conjugal onanism. **1900** L. B. SPERRY *Confidential Talks with Husband & Wife* x. 150 Another scheme for the prevention of conception is to withdraw the penis from the vagina just before the ejaculation of semen. This method is appropriately called 'Onanism'. **1939** R. CAMPBELL *Flowering Rifle* III. 96 Who sponsor Onanism and Divorce And let the birthrate flounder on its course. **1952** *Encycl. Sexual Knowl.* (ed. 2) I. 78 It is therefore not correct to attribute the practice of masturbation to Onan, though the word onanism is to-day widely accepted in this latter sense and it would be pedantic not to recognize this term. **1967** G. STEINER *Lang. & Silence* 98 The recent university experiment in which faculty wives agreed to practise onanism in front of the researchers' cameras. **1977** P. ROONEY in D. Marcus *Best Irish Short Stories* II. 141 The onanism of the language, a phrase masturbated without hope of final clear expression.

onanist, onanistic *a.* (examples).

1855 W. WHITMAN *Leaves of Grass* 70 The sick-gray faces of onanists. **1867** ROBERTSON & RUTHERFORD tr. *Griesinger's Mental Path. & Therapeutics* II. iii. 173 That hidden strife betwixt shame, repentance, good intentions, and irritation, which imperiously impels to the act, we consider, after not a little acquaintance with onanists, to be by far more important than the primary, direct physical effect. **1926** tr. *M. von Gruber's Hygiene of Sex* vii. 120 The disturbances, which the physician so frequently finds in onanists are the same as those found in persons who indulge in extreme excesses of intercourse. **1934** F. SCOTT FITZGERALD *Tender is Night* II. ix. 199 There was something wooden and onanistic about her. **1961** D. HOLBROOK *Eng. for Maturity* iv. 45 Our essential cultural experiences are not celebrative, they are, rather, onanistic. **1962** *Listener* 20 Sept. 438/2 Quilty's fundamental childishness, his self-regarding, onanistic posing sets the tone of the whole film. **1966** *Ibid.* 22 Dec. 937/3 An uneasy childhood..Wykehamist Schooldays from the bullying horrors of which he escapes into an onanistic fantasy-world. **1973** *Daily Tel.* 23 Mar. 15/1 The onanistic aspect of these brief encounters in public places.

Onazote (ǫ·năzǝᵘt). Also **onazote.** A proprietary name for a type of rubber which has been expanded to a cellular condition by causing it to absorb a neutral gas under pressure during vulcanization and which is used for making life-belts and floats.

1920 *Trade Marks Jrnl.* 29 Dec. 2470 Onazote... Raw, or partly-prepared, india-rubber, balata and gutta-percha for use in manufactures. Charles Lancaster Marshall,..London,..manufacturer. **1940** *Jrnl. R. Aeronaut. Soc.* XLIV. 30 Onazote has a cellular structure in which each air bubble is completely separated from its neighbours. **1960** E. L. DELMAR-MORGAN *Cruising Yacht Equipment & Navigation* ix. 108 Though cork or Onazote lifejackets are well established and approved by the M.O.T. they are bulky and not very easily stowed in a yacht. **1960** *House & Garden* Aug. 46/4 Red and white lifebelt, onazote, £3 11s.

on board, *adv. phr.* and *a.* [f. ON *prep.* + BOARD *sb.*] **A.** *adv. phr.* See BOARD *sb.* 12c and 14 in Dict. and Suppl.

B. *adj.* (Written *on-board, onboard.*) That is on board a ship, aircraft, spacecraft, or the like.

1966 *Electronics* 17 Oct. 35 In an operational launch vehicle, the signal would go to an onboard computer that would determine whether the problem was serious enough to shut down the rocket and eject the astronauts. **1967** *Technology Week* 20 Feb. 12/1 Persons who may discover the capsule are being advised that the on-board radiation source is sealed. **1969** *Jane's Freight Containers 1968–69* 433 An officially approved on-board cargo loader for Boeing 707 and 727 aircraft. **1972** *Nature* 24 Nov. 222/1 The synchronization was continuously monitored during the flight by checking the on-board clock one pulse per second against the station clock one pulse per second. **1974** HAWKEY & BINGHAM *Wild Card* xv. 128, I have to.. stand by to override the on-board computer in the event of a failure.

on-camera, *adv.* (*phr.*) and *a.* [f. ON *prep.* + CAMERA.] Within the range of a film or television camera; that is being filmed or televised.

1962 J. D. MACDONALD *Girl* xiii. 193 We are down here ..to do ten tropical commercials... We are surrounded by the Loyal Ones, on and off camera. Shrewd agency minds. **1971** R. PARKES *Line of Fire* ii. 26 To give chase, play the heroine. Maybe get interviewed on-camera afterwards. **1972** *Village Voice* (N.Y.) 1 June 26/3 Primo was an on-camera reporter for KDKA in Pittsburgh, went from there to Philly, then became director of local news here. **1974** *Keowee Courier* (Walhalla, S. Carolina) 24 Apr. 3/4 Peter Falk, star of the NBC-TV series 'Columbo', will serve as on-camera host. **1975** *Listener* 28 Aug. 258/2 Sheikh Mujib..has refused all on-camera interviews.

once, *adv.* Add: **A.** Forms. *γ.* 8— *dial.* and *U.S.* spellings **oncest, oncet, oncst, onct, onecest, onst.**

1789 Webster *Dissertations Eng. Lang.* 111 In the middle states also, many people [say]..*oncet* and *twicet*. This gross impropriety [has]..prevalence among a class of very well educated people; particularly in Philadelphia and Baltimore. **1840** C. F. Hoffman *Greyslaer* II. III. xiv. 255, I ups rifle at onct, and hand on trigger to cut the string with a bullet. **1847** E. Brontë *Wuthering Heights* I. xiii. 322 Couldn't ye uh said soa, at onst? **1851** Mayne Reid *Scalp-Hunters* I. xxi. 291 He *may* shoot well; he did onecest on a time—plum centre. **1867** A. D. Richardson *Beyond Mississippi* xi. 135 Even some graduates of leading universities habitually use 'oncet' and 'twicet'. **1875** W. D. Parish *Dict. Sussex Dial.* 105, I dunno but what you'd best shun him out of the fore-door at oncest. **1878** H. Alger *Joe's Luck* in *Street & Smith's N.Y. Weekly* 8 Apr. 2/5, I kin whip my weight in wild cats, am a match for a dozen Indians to onst, and kin tackle a lion without flinching. **1883** H. D. Rawnsley in *Trans. Wordsworth Soc.* VI. 164 He niver oncst said owt. Ye're well aware if he'd been fond of children he 'ud 'a spoke. **1898** J. D. Brayshaw *Slum Silhouettes* 1 We was born to it, an' never expec's nuffink better; but 'e's been a real toff onct, Satan 'as. **1906** E. Dyson *Fact'ry 'Ands* viii. 95 What led me on t' wish t' be er gentleman onst more. **1909** J. Masefield *Tragedy of Nan* I. 14 Why weren't I told to onst? **1913** C. E. Mulford *Coming of Cassidy* vii. 117, I saw you onct an' I wondered if I was right. **1921** [see *lamp *v.*[1] 4]. **1922** E. O'Neill *Hairy Ape* (1923) i. 16 But aw say, come up for air onct in a while, can't yuh? *Ibid.* v. 45, I useter go to choich onct—sure—when I was a kid. **1932** V. Randolph in B. A. Botkin *Treas. S. Folklore* (1949) III. i. 453 We seen a feller in town oncet a-wearin' a coat made out'n a piedy horse-hide. **1934** C. Carmer in *Ibid.* III. ii. 506 Chillun..think twict befo' yuh speak onct. **1967** in A. Dundes *Mother Wit* (1973) 270/2 Love me and hug me oncet..again.

δ. *dial.* and *U.S.* **wance, wancet, wanst, wonst, wunst.**

1840 *Crockett Almanac* 2 Davy Crockett got skeered wunst. *Ibid.* 14, I wonst had an old flame. **1890** Kipling *Soldiers Three* 12 Wanst upon a time, as the childer-books say, I was a recruity. **1898** J. D. Brayshaw *Slum Silhouettes* 20 The poor bhoy shall be a gintleman for wance in his life. **1904** E. Nesbit *Phoenix & Carpet* v. 94, I see at wunst 'e was wuth 'is weight in flimsies. **1923** 'B. M. Bower' *Parowan Bonanza* v. 52 Beans,..wancet they've been wrinkled wit' rain water and dried agin. **1972** L. Lamb *Picture Frame* xv. 139 Seen him wunst, I reckon. Spoke pleasant, like. **1977** *Transatlantic Rev.* LX. 152 'Lissn,' says Davey, 'Ah've been ower baurs duzzins a times an Ah've nivir wance goet feart anuff tae jum paff.'

B. 3. Delete *Obs.* and add: Now *U.S. dial.*

1903 S. Clapin *New Dict. Amer.* 294 *Once*,..in parts of Pennsylvania settled by Germans, used as an expletive: 'Sit down *once*,' i.e. once for all. **1917** *Dialect Notes* IV. 338 'Come here *once*'..among German settlers. **1948** *Amer. Speech* XXIII. 109 Give me the knife once. **1953** *Ibid.* XXVIII. 246 Will you hand me that hammer once?

4. *once upon a time* (earlier example); also as *sb. phr.* (sometimes hyphened) and *attrib.*

1595 G. Peele *Old Wives' Tale* sig. B1v, Once vppon a time there was a King or a Lord, or a Duke. **1876** R. E. Francillon in *Gentl. Mag.* Oct. 423 There is all the difference between 'Daniel Deronda' and 'The Mill on the Floss' that lies between Now and Once upon a Time. **1927** S. Southwold (*title*) Once upon a time stories. **1944** Blunden *Cricket Country* iv. 43 So runs this once-upon-a-time in my memory. **1959** *Listener* 22 Jan. 164/2 The horse-drawn chaises of once upon a time. **1974** J. Wainwright *Hard Hit* 173 The talk between two middle-aged has-beens about once-upon-a-time days.

7. (Further examples.)

1911 Kipling *Years Between* (1919) 7 Our ears still carry the sound Of our once Imperial seas. **1931** A. Huxley *Cicadas* 44 The pause and once-more fury of the gale. **1939** Dylan Thomas *Map of Love* 6 These once-blind eyes have breathed a wind of visions, The cauldron's root through this once-rindless hand. **1943** D. Gascoyne *Poems 1937–42* 52 The once-met And long remembered faces. **1946** *Nature* 20 July 86/1 The once-popular 'tiger nut'. **1949** S. Spender *Edge of Being* 56 That past greatness and that once-willed Future Beyond the storm. **1951** W. de la Mare *Winged Chariot* 38 Once-green skeleton leaf. *Ibid.* 39 The angelic hierarchies Dome with their glory the once-empty skies. **1974** *Country Life* 21 Mar. 643/1 Once-popular composers..drop out of favour. **1977** J. Cleary *Vortex* v. 135 The once-beautiful eyes, already dark with death.

b. *spec.* **once-fired** *a.*, of pottery: subjected only once to the process of firing. Also in Combs. with advs.: **once-off** *a.*, happening only once; hence as *sb.*; cf. *one off* s.v. *one *numeral a.* B. 29*b; **once-only** *a.*, occurring only once; **once-through** *a.*, being or employing water that enters a system, flows once through it, and then leaves it.

1952 V. Eley *Monk at Potter's Wheel* 19 *Once fired*, an expression relating to pottery that has been glazed and fired without having received a previous firing. Mediaeval English pottery was fired in this way. **1960** H. Powell *Beginner's Bk. Pott.* II. iv. 42 If you wish to make, decorate, and glaze in one operation, this is known as once fired. **1970** *Gloss. Industrial Furnace Terms* (*B.S.I.*) 19 *Once-fired kiln*, a kiln in which the body and the glaze thereon are fired at one and the same time, instead of in two separate firings. **1965** *Math. in Biol. & Med.* (Med. Res. Council) I. 8 But in a 'once-off' job where a standard program cannot be used..these advantages are lost. **1969** *Guardian* 1 Mar. 1/3 Steam turbines are built to a specification, often on a once-off basis or in pairs. **1973** *Times* 19 Jan. 12/1, 50 different juvenile weeklies, aside from the 'once-offs' that appear from time to time. **1976** *Gramophone* Oct. 670/3, I suppose that is the fault of once-off recordings. **1960** *Sunday Express* 28 Feb. 12/8 It is, alas, a once-only gratuity. **1963** *Listener* 7 Feb. 263/2 A 'once only' talker can never be as good as a hardened professional. **1965** M. Frayn *Tin Men* xxiii. 125 The open-endedness of a once-only job would require a computer so complex..that it would be cheaper to use a human being. **1971** A. Price *Alamut Ambush* ix. 115 They wouldn't like doing it... But for a once-only job they might stretch a point. **1940** *Chambers's Techn. Dict.* 87/1 *Benson boiler*, a high-pressure boiler of the once-through type in which water is pumped successively through the various elements of the heating surface. **1946** J. N. Williams *Steam Generation* vi. 126 Forced circulation boilers may be divided into two classes according to whether the water is in continual circulation or is pumped through at one end of the heating surface and, making a single or 'once through' passage, leaves at the other end in the form of steam. **1978** *Environmental Conservation: Chemicals* (Shell Internat. Petroleum Co.) 2 Where sufficient surface water—lakes or rivers, for example—is available, waste heat from chemical plants has traditionally been discharged in the form of once-through (as opposed to re-used) cooling water.

II. 8. c. *once for all* (further examples); now usu. *once and for all*; also as *sb.*, hence *once-for-allness*; *once in a way* (examples); *once in* (or irreg. *and*) *a while* (earlier and later examples); *once in a blue moon*, rarely, exceptionally.

1781 J. Witherspoon in *Pennsylvania Jrnl.* 23 May 1/3 He will *once in a while*, i.e. *sometimes*, get drunk. [Used in] the middle states. **1869** Mrs. Stowe *Oldtown Folks* x. 116 If he could come down here once and a while after work-hours. **1869** W. C. Hazlitt *Eng. Proverbs* 305 Once in a blue moon. **1876** Once in a blue moon [see *blue moon* s.v. Blue *a.* 13]. **1891** J. M. Dixon *Dict. Idiomatic Eng. Phrases* 230 *Once in a way*, sometimes; at long intervals; on rare occasions. **1895** Morris & Wyatt tr. *Beowulf* x. 23 E'en that in mind had I.., that for once and for all the will of your people would I set me to work. **1922** G. R. S. Mead in *Quest* XIII. 490 For the Jewish eschatologist it was a once for all event he expected, whereas for such men as the Stoical thinkers it was a perpetual recurrence. **1928** E. O'Neill *Strange Interlude* II. 76 Well, then, a little truth for once in a way! **1934** G. B. Shaw *On Rocks* I. 197, I really think, father, you might for once in a way take some slight interest in the family. **1949** *Scottish Jrnl. Theol.* II. 86 A radical misunderstanding of the New Testament teaching about eschatological once-for-allness and eschatological continuity. *Ibid.* 87 The only primitive wholeness that the Reformed Churches recognise is the once-and-for-all *wholeness* of Jesus Christ in whom God and man are at one. **1951** Auden *Nones* (1952) 14 The once-for-all that is not seen nor said. **1955** *Times* 26 Aug. 7/4 And when, by some mischance, once in a blue moon, the bell does ring, how startled we are. **1957** *Ann. Reg. 1956* 137 The 1956 Budget..had..included a 'once-for-all' item of $961,000 for the 'Atoms for Peace' conference at Geneva. **1960** *Times* 12 Aug. 13/6 But contractile tissue as such seems to have been a once-for-all invention. **1960** V. Nabokov *Invitation to Beheading* xvi. 159 Every once in a while he would jerk his flabby cheeks and his chin. **1963** *Times* 22 Feb. 16/7 Some absolute, once-and-for-all answer had to be found. **1970** T. Lupton *Managem. & Social Sci.* (ed. 2) iv. 101 Pose questions like this and then try to think up once-for-all answers. **1972** *Police Rev.* 17 Nov. 1487/3 A once-and-for-all deduction from pension. **1975** J. B. Harley *O.S. Maps* i. 1 Before World War II.. there was a tendency to regard the published large scale map as something of a 'once-and-for-all' record of fact. **1976** *National Skat & Sheepshead Q.* Mar. 18 How many of you readers 'blow' the big hand—the one that appears once in a blue moon? **1977** *Times* 12 Feb. 7/3 Try not to let the once-for-allness of the occasion tempt you to eat the whole menu.

d. *once in a lifetime*, such as occurs only once in a person's life; freq. (with hyphens) *attrib.* and often used hyperbolically; *once too often*, of a thing said or done: once more than necessary or tolerable; usu. implying unpleasant repercussions.

[**1854** C. Patmore *Angel in House: Betrothal* VIII. ii. 110 Love wakes men, once a life-time each.] **1908** Yeats & Gregory *Unicorn from Stars* III. 122 There is a fiery moment, perhaps once in a lifetime, and in that moment we see the only thing that matters. **1915** H. T. Webster *Our Boyhood Thrills* 7 (*heading*) The thrill that comes once in a lifetime. **1921** G. B. Shaw *Back to Methuselah* III. 131 Havnt you said that once too often already this morning? **1929** J. B. Priestley *Good Companions* II. v. 369 Don't be a scoffer... I've known people to scoff at these things once too often. **1932** R. Aldington *Soft Answers* 122 They had simply got drunk once too often and lost their money. **1934** E. O'Neill *Days without End* II. 68 But I warned him he'd humiliate me once too often—and he did! **1962** M. Summerton *Nightingale at Noon* (1963) xii. 174 Fate presented him with a once-in-a-lifetime opportunity to get rid of her. **1962** *Times* 20 June 14/6 That once-in-a-lifetime occasion. **1973** *Mad Mag.* Oct. 8/1 Now cool it and let me really ham up this once-in-a-lifetime role! **1975** P. Moyes *Black Widower* xiii. 155 I'm afraid this is a once-in-a-lifetime trip for us. **1977** *Washington Post* 18 May C 6 (Advt.), Singer. Once-in-a-lifetime sale.

e. Phr. *once over lightly*; also (hyphenated) as *sb.* and *attrib. phr.* (chiefly *U.S.*).

1941 *Time* 12 May 55/1 Her pretty posturing, pouts, stunned, exotic stares are meaningless when she tries to do them once over lightly. **1960** Wentworth & Flexner *Dict. Amer. Slang* 364/2 *Once over lightly*, cursorily; quickly; temporarily. **1961** S. Arne in Webster s.v. *n.*, Had given political problems the once-over-lightly. **1961** S. Hyman in *Ibid.* s.v. *adj.*, Gets the once-over-lightly treatment. **1967** M. Kenyon *Whole Hog* i. 16 The young man raised the egg... Was it sunny-side-up..or once-over-lightly?

III. 9. b. *for once in your* (or *his, my,* etc.) *life*, on this single occasion in your (etc.) life.

1801 M. Edgeworth *Belinda* I. iv. 144 She has succeeded for once in her life. **1846** [see *life *sb.* 3 c]. **1857** Trollope *Barchester T.* III. iv. 81 And so the signora resolved..to do a good natured act for once in her life. **1859** *Blackw. Mag.* Aug. 224/2 For once in my life I agreed with my wife. **1862** W. Collins *No Name* I. I. ix. 115 Magdalen was caught, for once in her life, at the end of all her resources. **1881** H. James *Portrait of Lady* III. xii. 189 Be a little wicked, feel a little wicked, for once in your life! **1964** 'S. Woods' *Trusted like Fox* viii. 79 Mr. Justice Conroy..for once in his life owned himself puzzled.

c. (Later examples of *the once*.)

1887 T. Darlington *Folk-Speech S. Cheshire* 282 'A thing for the once'..is an unusual or unprecedented thing. **1924** A. D. Sedgwick *Little French Girl* I. viii. 74 'He came twice afterwards.'.. 'I didn't know that. I thought it was only the once.' **1967** N. Freeling *Strike Out* 89 [He] thought he'd live for ever... He came the once for a checkup.

o·nce-born, *a.* [Once *adv.* 7.] Designating or pertaining to someone whose attitude to life has retained a child-like simplicity and straightforwardness. (See also quot. 1942.) Cf. Twice-born *a.* 3.

1849 [see Twice-born *a.* 3]. **1902** W. James *Var. Relig. Exper.* iv. 82 Another good expression of the 'once-born' type of consciousness, developing straight and natural, with no element of morbid compunction or crisis, is contained in the answer of Dr...Hale. **1942** Berrey & Van den Bark *Amer. Thes. Slang* § 325/5 *Once-born*, not regenerated or not believing in regeneration.

onceness (wɒ·nsnės). [f. Once *adv.* + -ness.] The fact or quality of happening only once, or all at once.

1866 R. & S. Redgrave *Century of Painters of Eng. School* I. iv. 108 [George] Barret's pictures are painted with the firm pencil and vigorous once-ness which characterize the works of the best painters of his time. **1917** E. Pound *Let.* 18 Apr. (1971) 109 H. Monroe seems to think that if her Chicago widows and spinsters will only shell out she can turn her gang of free-versers into geniuses all of a onceness. **1948** *Scottish Jrnl. Theol.* I. 141 In the Old Testament, he maintains, there is only one 'onceness' which is of theological significance, and that is the onceness of Christ. **1951** *Ibid.* IV. 3 That is to say, history is the field of relative uniqueness, but never of absolute once-ness.

once-over (wɒ·nsˌōuvəɹ). *colloq.* (orig. *U.S.*). [f. Once *adv.* + Over *prep.*] A glance; a rapid inspection (often with an implication of cursoriness); *to give the once-over*, to make a rapid assessment of; to give (a person) an appraising or inviting glance; to search someone (for weapons).

1915 *Recruiter's Bulletin* (U.S.) Jan. 7/2 After giving an applicant the 'once-over' the other day I told him that I was sorry but I could not take him. **1915** *Dialect Notes* IV. 234 *Once-over*,..a glance. **1916** *Daily Colonist* (Victoria, B.C.) 27 July 6/3 Individuals whose presence on the deserted thoroughfares around the midnight hour aroused suspicions to be given what, in police parlance, is known as the 'once over'. **1926** [see *jerry *a.*[2]]. **1927** *Daily Express* 31 Oct. 4/3 You require a couple of days, as distinct from the traditional American 'once over', to see Chelsea Old Church. **1938** E. Bowen *Death of Heart* II. ii. 190 Daphne gave the rest of the cakes a rather scornful once-over. **1948** M. Allingham *More Work for Undertaker* xix. 219 They had entered without invitation and were giving it what Luke called 'the old once-over'. **1949** *Sun* (Baltimore) 26 Aug. 10/3 Whenever travelers enter Baltimore from abroad by ship or air, they are given the onceover by Cap'n Jenks. **1951** J. D. Salinger *Catcher in Rye* x. 85 They probably thought I was too young to give anybody the once-over..—you'd've thought I wanted to *marry* them or something. **1953** E. Taylor *Sleeping Beauty* ix. 152 Len was curious about Betty..and wished to give her..what he called the once-over. **1954** *Encounter* Feb. 26/2, I could feel his eyes on me even more sharply than before. He was, so to speak, giving me a professional once-over. **1972** J. Philips *Vanishing Senator* (1973) III. iv. 171 Give Mr. Styles a quick once-over, Francine, but try to remember you're looking for a gun and not trying to excite him sexually. **1977** *New Yorker* 4 July 22/1 He gave his display of perfect strawberries the once-over.

oncer (wɒ·nsəɹ). *colloq.* Also **once-er.** [f. Once *adv.* + -er[1].] **1.** One who, or that which, does a particular thing only once; a thing that occurs only once; formerly *spec.* one who attends church once on a Sunday.

1892 *Review of Reviews* V. 41/2 He [*sc.* Gladstone] has a poor opinion of those whom he humorously terms 'oncers'. **1909** *Daily Chron.* 22 Apr. 4/7 A minister regretted an increasing disposition on the part of the people to become 'oncers'. **1917** *Dialect Notes* IV. 327 *Oncer*,..he who (or that which) does a thing but once, esp. a church member who attends service but once on Sunday. **1938** *Amer. Speech* XIII. 35 For an extremely rare word..there may be only one slip, a *oncer*. **1944** Auden *For Time Being*

(1945) 11 Could he but once see Nature as In truth she is for ever, What oncer would not fall in love? **1972** B. RODGERS *Queens' Vernacular* 143 *Oncer*, somebody who does it once, and never again with the same person; Mr. fuck 'em and forget 'em. **1973** *Shooting Times & Country Mag.* 7 July 13/3 Eventually a fish did move under an overhanging alder, but it was a 'oncer' and I had grave doubts about it rising again.

2. *slang.* A one pound note.

1931 *Police Jrnl.* IV. 502 They spieled [*sc.* played] first for stakes of a sprazey [*sc.* sixpence],..increasing it to half a tosh,..and eventually to a oncer. **1936** [see *GEE *v.*[2] 1 c]. **1953** K. TENNANT *Joyful Condemned* iii. 27 Sure he took your oncer. But..here's another quid in place of it. **1968** L. DEIGHTON *Only when I Larf* vi. 80 He'd pay in used oncers, no cheques. **1970** A. ROSS *Manchester Thing* 122, I got my wallet out and let him look at a pound note... I laid a second oncer on top of the other. **1978** M. KENYON *Deep Pocket* vii. 82 They gave you an 'undred quid in oncers to see things their way.

oncest, oncet, see *ONCE *adv.* A. *γ*.

onchocercal (ǫŋkosō·ɹkăl), *a.* [f. as next + -AL.] Belonging to the genus *Onchocerca* (see next); caused by worms of this genus.

1934 R. P. STRONG et al. *Onchocerciasis* I. ii. 6 Calderon ..published a monograph on the onchocercal *Filaria.* **1974** A. W. WOODRUFF *Med. in Tropics* xiv. 237/1 In the early stages of massive onchocercal infection in African adults a dark purplish-brown plaque-like skin reaction.. may..be seen.

onchocerciasis (ǫːŋkosəɹsəi·ăsis, -səɹkəi·ăsis). *Path.* Also **onco-**. [f. mod.L. *Onchocerca* (f. Gr. ὄγκος barb + κέρκος tail), name of a genus of parasitic filarioid worms + *-IASIS.] Infestation with or a disease caused by filarioid worms of the genus *Onchocerca*; in man *spec.* that caused by *O. volvulus* and transmitted by biting flies of the genus *Simulium*, common in tropical Africa and parts of Central America and marked by characteristic lesions of subcutaneous tissue and the eyes, often with blindness.

1911 R. T. LEIPER in *Rep. Local Govt. Board on Public Health & Med. Subjects* (Ministry of Health) No. 45. 6 The condition here termed Onchocerciasis is met with in frozen beef imported from Australia. **1911** STEDMAN *Med. Dict.* 604/2 *Oncocerciasis*, infestation of the ox with a species of *Oncocerca.* **1912** *Jrnl. Trop. Med. & Hygiene* XV. 232/1 (*heading*) Some notes and suggestions in connection with the etiology of bovine onchocerciasis. **1934** R. P. STRONG et al. *Onchocerciasis* I. iv. 19 The limitation of the centers of onchocerciasis in Guatemala to certain zones of territory..is very striking. **1967** A. W. JONES *Introd. Parasitol.* xiv. 184 In onchocerciasis of horses (and rarely of cattle), adult *Onchocerca* live in the tendons and ligaments of the back and neck region. **1971** *Nature* 21 May 151/3 In tropical and sub-tropical man-made lakes..explosive outgrowths of water weeds after filling had led to a very significant increase in the incidence of diseases carried by insects, such as malaria and onchocerciasis. **1974** *Daily Tel.* 9 Sept. 3/8 With him was.. a tropical eye disease expert from Swindon, who during the journey is to lead an investigation into onchocerciasis, a strange river blindness endemic in Central Africa. **1975** *Hansard Lords* 27 June 1706 To ask Her Majesty's Government what was the reason for the delay in presenting to Parliament the Onchocerciasis Fund Agreement 1974... Baroness Gaitskell: May I ask my noble friend to pronounce the name of the Fund? Lord Goronwy-Roberts: As if it were spelled 'Onkoserkiasis'.

onchocercosis (ǫːŋkosəɹkōᵘ·sis). *Path.* [f. as prec. + -OSIS.] = prec. Hence **oːnchocerco·tic** *a.* (*sb.*)

1918 P. LUNA in *Amer. Jrnl. Ophthalm.* I. 122/2 The visual disturbances which I have met with among the carriers of this filaria..and which I shall call onchocercosis. *Ibid.* 125/2 The lesions..appear in the onchocercotic, all of whom suffer disturbances of vision. **1931** *Ibid.* XIV. 518 (*heading*) Onchocercosis in Mexico. *Ibid.* 518/1 In.. Guatemala the onchocercotic infection had been demonstrated..next to the international boundary. **1972** *Biol. Abstr.* LIV. 5491/1 In none of these cases was the infestation localized to the orbital cavity as in other filarial infections (Loa-loa, onchocercosis).

onchosphere, var. *ONCOSPHERE.

onco-. Add: **oncofœ·tal** (*U.S.* **-fetal**) *a. Med.*, occurring in tumours and in the fœtus but not in the adult; **o·ncolite** *Petrol.* [-LITE], a small, rounded body found in sedimentary rocks that is composed of incomplete concentric layers of calcareous material and is believed to be of algal origin; hence **oncoli·tic** *a.*; **oncolo·gic** *a.* (chiefly *U.S.*) = *oncological* adj. s.v. ONCO-; **onco·logist**, an expert or specialist in oncology, now esp. one concerned with treatment by means of drugs rather than surgery or radiotherapy; **oncology** (examples).

1972 P. ALEXANDER in *Nature* 21 Jan. 137/2 Table 1 is an attempt to classify the different types of onco-foetal 'antigens' (OFAs). It seems necessary to coin this phrase because the more elegant description of carcino-embryonic antigen has been pre-empted to describe one class of these compounds. **1975** *Ibid.* 25 Dec. 734/2 In man the two best known oncofoetal antigens are the α-foetoprotein (AFP)..and the carcinoembryonic antigen (CEA) of the human digestive system. **1933** R. B. YOUNG in *Trans. Geol. Soc. S. Afr.* XXXV. 32 Professor Julius Pia, in Hirmer's *Handbuch der Paläobotanik*, places the stromatolites among the *Schizophyceae* and separates them into two groups, the *Stromatolithi* and the *Oncolithi*, the latter embracing the forms..that occur as separate or individual bodies. In this paper the term 'oncolite' will be employed in the same sense, but without any implication that the bodies..differ from the rest of the stromatolites in any respect other than that generally they have formed round detached nuclei. *Ibid.* 34 When they were for a time completely stationary, the oncolitic growth became continuous, spreading over the surface of the bed to form thin but fairly extensive stromatolitic layers. **1967** *Jrnl. Sedimentary Petrology* XXXVII. 1163/2 A carbonate rock of which oncolites form a significant part may be termed oncolitic. **1972** H. BLATT et al. *Origin Sedimentary Rocks* xii. 422 Oncolites..up to 3 in. in diameter, have been found. **1974** *Nature* 22 Feb. 522/2 *Facies E.* Concentrically stacked spheroid stromatolites (oncolites). **1906** *1st Ann. Rep. Amer. Oncologic Hospital, Philadelphia* 3 The name of the Corporation shall be The American Oncologic Hospital. **1952** A. NETTLESHIP *Basic Princ. Cancer Pract.* xix. 389 The need for a clinically useful oncologic science is clear. **1925** H. GILFORD *Tumors & Cancers* xxvi. 574 Oncologists in general still adhere to older methods of operative treatment, supplemented, it may be, by actinic and other remedies. **1968** BETHELL & BURG tr. *Solzhenitsyn's Cancer Ward* (1969) I. vii. 96 On top of this a society of oncologists had been started recently. **1971** *Lancet* 21 Aug. 419/2 Although the oncologist's clinical experience with malignant disease is often limited, his pharmacological background has enabled him to make a substantial contribution to the subject. **1857** R. G. MAYNE *Expos. Lex. Med. Sci.* (1860) 810 Oncology. **1915** F. L. HOFFMAN *Mortality from Cancer* i. 1 There are few more interesting subjects for statistical analysis than cancer, or what is, perhaps, more appropriately termed the science of oncology, which comprehends tumors of all kinds, whether malignant or benign or ill-defined. **1968** BETHELL & BURG tr. *Solzhenitsyn's Cancer Ward* (1969) I. i. 3 According to the arrangement with the head doctor of the oncology clinic, the matron was supposed to wait for them at two o'clock in the afternoon. **1971** *Nature* 19 Feb. 517/3 The Imperial Cancer Research Fund (ICRF) last week announced the establishment of.. a medical oncology unit.

oncocerciasis, var. *ONCHOCERCIASIS.

oncogene (ǫ·ŋkŏdʒīn). *Biol.* [f. ONCO- + *GENE.] A gene in a virus particle held to be responsible for transforming a host cell into a tumour cell.

1969 HUEBNER & TODARO in *Proc. Nat. Acad. Sci.* LXIV. 1087 It is postulated that the viral information (the virogene), including that portion responsible for transforming a normal cell into a tumor cell (the oncogene), is most commonly transmitted from animal to progeny animal and from cell to progeny cell in a covert form. **1970** *New Scientist* 3 Sept. 465/2 Occasionally, an 'oncogene' of the virus becomes switched on, and the host cell is transformed into a cancer cell. **1971** *Nature* 6 Aug. 373/2 Attempts to analyse genetically the oncogenes in adenovirus genomes, by the isolation of temperature sensitive mutants, seem most promising. **1975** *Ibid.* 7 Aug. 498/1 The oncogene theory contends that type C viruses possess oncogenic information and that malignancy is the result of activation of this genetic information.

oncogenesis (ǫŋkŏdʒe·nĕsis). *Biol.* [f. ONCO- + -GENESIS.] The formation or production of a tumour or tumours.

1932 in Dorland & Miller *Med. Dict.* (ed. 16) 891/1. **1944** *Jrnl. Exper. Med.* LXXX. 122 In these cases [of rapid growth of papillomas and carcinomatoids] actual oncogenesis must have been exceedingly swift, not the drawn out process it is generally held to be. **1961** *Proc. 4th Nat. Cancer Conf.* (U.S.) 41 (*heading*) Hormones and experimental oncogenesis; mammary and mammotropic tumors. **1977** *Proc. R. Soc. Med.* LXX. 393/2 It would seem plausible to think that the susceptibility to light-induced mutations..may favour viral oncogenesis in the presence of appropriate viral elements.

So **o·ncogen**, an agent that causes oncogenesis.

1969 *Jrnl. Biol. Chem.* CCXLIV. 4075/2 Present evidence does not favor 3-hydroxyuric acid as a proximate oncogen. **1971** *Nature* 5 Feb. 418/2 Hamster cells exposed to a dilute concentration of highly oncogenic compounds or to larger doses of weak oncogens can enter and pass through a complete mitotic cycle in spite of repair synthesis already in progress.

oncogenic (ǫŋkŏdʒe·nik), *a. Biol.* [f. ONCO- + *-GENIC.] Causing the development of a tumour or tumours; of or pertaining to this effect.

1949 *New Gould Med. Dict.* 696/2 Oncogenic. **1959** *Jrnl. Nat. Cancer Inst.* (U.S.) XXIII. 277 (*heading*) The oncogenic spectrum of two 'pure' strains of avian leukosis. **1970** *New Scientist* 3 Sept. 464/2 The discovery, and confirmation, of an enzyme carried by oncogenic RNA viruses. **1971** *Nature* 29 Jan. 296/2 Both the oncogenic and protovirus hypotheses postulate that tumour viruses are escaped cellular genetic elements.

So **oncogeni·city**, the property of being oncogenic.

1944 *Jrnl. Exper. Med.* LXXX. 119 Manifestly the real criterion is the time required to render the first cell neoplastic; for oncogenicity properly speaking is contained in that act. **1967** *Cancer Res.* XXVII. 929/2 No distinction can now be made between the oncogenicities of the 7-*N*-oxide derivatives of guanine and xanthine. **1971** *Nature* 5 Feb. 416/2 The data indicate a link between oncogenicity of a compound and its capacity to provoke DNA repair synthesis.

oncolysis (ǫŋkǫ·lĭsis). *Biol.* [f. ONCO- + *-LYSIS.] The absorption or destruction of a tumour. So **oncoly·tic** *a.*, of, pertaining to, or causing oncolysis.

1928 STEDMAN *Med. Dict.* (ed. 10) 712/2 Oncolysis. *Ibid.*, Oncolytic. **1933** *Brit. Jrnl. Ophthalm.* XVII. 754 He finds that in these animals the oncolytic power is *nil*, and thence concludes that the eye is specially susceptible to attack by new growths. **1952** *Ann. N.Y. Acad. Sci.* LIV. 945 (*heading*) Viruses with oncolytic properties and their adaptation to tumors. *Ibid.*, Oncolysis, by viral action, has not been studied very thoroughly until recently. **1972** *Nature* 30 June 486/2 (*heading*) Oncolytic viruses. **1972** *Nature New Biol.* 5 July 8/1 No oncolysis occurred when subcutaneous tumours were treated with BEV.

on-coming, *a.* Add: Also **oncoming. 2.** Ready to be sociable; friendly, welcoming, forthcoming, sympathetic.

1925 C. P. SLATER *Marget Pow* 183 He doesna seem to be very oncomin', for he's never been in the house yet. **1938** E. BOWEN *Death of Heart* II. iv. 248 If I were a more oncoming sort of fellow I should offer you a penny, and so on. **1942** N. BALCHIN *Darkness falls from Air* vi. 109, I think we might possibly get this through... The Secretary seemed quite oncoming. **1953** M. HOPKIRK *Queen over Water* v. 102 Some people were less oncoming. Ibid. x. 222 At Cambridge..he was welcomed effusively, but other places were less oncoming. **1967** N. MARSH *Death at Dolphin* v. 133 I'm not all that oncoming, even here.

oncornavirus (ǫŋkǭ·ɹnăvəiᵊrŭs). *Virology.* [f. ONCO- + *PICO)RNAVIRUS.] = *LEUKOVIRUS.

1970 R. C. NOWINSKI et al. in *Virology* XLII. 1152/1 We..propose the term 'oncornaviruses' to represent the oncogenic RNA viruses (following the style 'picornaviruses' for small RNA viruses). **1974** FRAENKEL-CONRAT & WAGNER *Comprehensive Virology* I. 34 Oncornavirus group. Not yet officially accepted term for leukoviruses or RNA tumor viruses, all equally imperfect names. Medium large (100 nm diameter) enveloped and ether-sensitive particles; studded in regular manner with projections and containing a dense eccentric nucleoid. **1975** *Nature* 3 Apr. 457/2 In several animal species, C-type oncogenic RNA viruses (oncornaviruses) cause malignant tumours of mesodermal origin, such as leukaemia.

Hence **onco·rnaviral** *a.*

1975 *Nature* 3 Apr. 458/1 Cultures were screened for the presence of different cytoplasmic C-type oncornaviral antigens.

oncosine (ǫ·ŋkŏsīn). *Min.* Also **onko-, -in.** [ad. G. *onkosin* (F. von Kobell 1834, in *Jrnl. f. prakt. Chem.* II. 296), f. Gr. ὄγκωσ-ις swelling (from its behaviour when heated in a blow-pipe flame): see -INE[5].] An aluminosilicate of potassium, other alkali metals, and magnesium, which is a variety of, or perhaps a mixture containing, muscovite.

1854 J. D. DANA *Syst. Min.* (ed. 4) II. 504 Onkosin... In roundish pieces, having an apple-green color; sometimes grayish or brownish. **1868** *Ibid.* (ed. 5) 480 Oncosin ..occurs in roundish masses imbedded in dolomite with mica, at Passecken near Tamsweg, in Salzburg. **1923** *Mineral. Abstr.* II. 112 Muscovite, the variety onkosine is plentiful in the salbands of the lodes. **1939** *Geol. Förening. Stockholm Förhand.* LX. 622 The vein material in the pollucite, where late muscovite occurs in the somewhat unusual form of deep mauve-coloured, compact, cryptocrystalline masses, mineralogically referred to the subspecies oncosine. **1962** *Mineral. Abstr.* XV. 393/2 Pegmatites with giant crystals of amblygonite, spodumene, and oncosine and aggregates of montebrasite.

oncosphere (ǫ·ŋkosfīᵊɹ). *Zool.* Also **oncho-**. [f. ONCO- + SPHERE *sb.*] An embryonic form of certain tapeworms. Also *attrib.*

1906 P. FALCKE tr. *Braun's Anim. Parasites Man* 202 The embryo enclosed within the embryonal shell, the oncosphere, is of spheroid or ovoid form, and is distinguished by the possession of three pairs of hooklets. **1929** H. A. BAYLIS *Man. Helminthology* 65 It [*sc.* the tapeworm embryo] is frequently referred to as a 'hexacanth embryo' or 'onchosphere'. **1949** *New Biol.* VII. 114 A ripe segment, ready to fall off the end of the worm [*sc.* the pork tapeworm]..contains 30,000–40,000 eggs, each already developed into a little six-hooked embryo (onchosphere) and protected by a shell. **1962** J. D. SMYTH *Introd. Animal Parasitol.* xx. 229 In the taenioids, the embryo develops to the oncosphere stage in the uterus of mature proglottids. **1969** A. M. DUNN *Vet. Helminthology* 112/2 The embryo is called the onchosphere. **1973** T. C. CHENG *Gen. Parasitol.* xiv. 485 The oncosphere..remains passive in the eggshell..until the embryo is ingested by a vertebrate or invertebrate intermediate host.

oncost. Add: **2.** (In general use.) Overhead expenses or costs. Also *attrib.*

1912 J. G. WILLIAMSON *Counting-House & Factory Organisation* 65 Oncost expenditure, such as wages of foremen, labourers, and general works supplies, etc...is dealt with in the same manner. *Ibid.* 71 Establishment Charges or Oncost is every expense in the Profit and Loss Account other than the prime cost of Productive work. **1924** J. STAMP *Stud. Current Probl. Finance & Govt.* 18 Such a tabulation..would enable us to..test its ratios of oncost and various kinds of unit efficiency. **1931** H. E. COLESWORTHY *Pract. Directorship* xii. 120 Overhead or running charges, such as salaries, office expenses, selling expenses, and so on, are termed 'oncost'. *Ibid.*, It is sometimes customary to divide oncost into two classes—'works oncost' and 'office oncost'. **1970** *Money Which?* Mar. 25/2 Another method is to take the figure arrived at by the first method, but add to it what is known as manufacturing 'on-cost'. This is a proportion of your manufacturing overheads, such as the rent, rates, lighting and heating of your factory or workshop. **1972** *Accountant* 23 Mar. 383/1 The problem becomes even more obscure when we look at oncost loadings—obviously the administrative backing is an essential part of running any business.

oncotic (ǫŋkǫ·tik), *a. Physiol.* [f. Onco- + -otic.] Applied to the osmotic pressure exerted by a colloid, esp. plasma protein.

1935 C. J. Wiggers *Physiol.* li. 802 Starling demonstrated that colloids in a sol state exert a small osmotic pressure, but this varies in uncontrollable fashion owing to the fact that colloidal molecules or aggregates called micellae vary considerably. This has tersely been called oncotic pressure. **1977** *Proc. R. Soc. Med.* LXX. 693/1 A reduction in oncotic pressure due to hypoproteinaemia.

ondatra. Add to etym.: [Adopted as a generic name in H. F. Link *Beyträge zur Naturgeschichte* (1795) I. ii. 52]. Substitute for def.: The North American musk-rat, *Ondatra zibethicus*; = Musk-rat 1. (Later example.)

1867 *Amer. Naturalist* I. 400 The Musk-rat, or Ondatra (*Fiber zibethicus*), so extensively diffused over North America.

‖ **Ondes Martenot** (ǫnd mãɹtəno). Also **Ondes, Ondes Musicales, Ondium Martenot.** [After F. *ondes musicales*, lit. musical waves; named by and after Maurice *Martenot* (b. 1898), its inventor.] An electronic keyboard musical instrument, capable of producing only one note at a time.

1936 E. S. Bensinger tr. *K. London's Film Music* iv. 177 Before all others, let us recommend the *Ondium Martenot*, the apparatus derived from Theremin's ether-wave music, but with the sound-scale anchored on a keyboard, so that no sound-fluctuations are possible. **1937** *Nature* 6 Feb. 215/1 The author's brief treatment of the comparatively new electro-musical instruments, the *Ondium Martenot*, the trautonium and the Neo-Bechstein piano, is also good. **1940** C. Sachs *Hist. Mus. Instrum.* (1942) 448 The most important monophonic instruments are Maurice Martenot's *Ondes musicales* (1928) [etc.]. **1954** *Grove's Dict Mus.* (ed. 5) V. 591/1 Martenot..is the inventor of a radio-electric instrument called Ondes Musicales (now usually called Ondes Martenot by composers who score for it), which he first brought out in 1928. *Ibid.* 591/2 In 1937 he organized concerts with a team of eight Ondes. **1957** Manvell & Huntley *Technique Film Music* ii. 37 Ondes Martenot: an electronic instrument of great versatility, first introduced in 1928. It combines the principle of the Thérémin with a keyboard, adding additional devices for vibrato and glissando effects. **1977** *Times Lit. Suppl.* 11 Mar. 277/2 As a music student he earned a living by playing the ondes martenot in pit orchestras.

‖ **ondol** (ǫ·ndǫl). [Korean, ad. Chinese *wên* hot, warm + *t'u* funnel, smoke tube.] A form of domestic heating by means of a flue running underfloor from a fire or furnace, commonly used in Korea. Also *attrib.*

1964 R. Rutt *Korean Works & Days* i. 21 The famous *ondol* or hot floor, built by making flues under a floor of stone or mud. **1969** *Korean Folklore & Classics* I. 8 He found the newly-laid ondol floor..pierced by a sharp drill in a thousand places... 'This ondol cost me a lot of money.' **1970** *Korea: its People & Culture* vii. 224/1 The people have held on to their traditional, radiant floor heating system, the *ondol*. **1972** P. M. Bartz *S. Korea* 32/2 About six o'clock the inhabitants get up, re-stoke their *ondol* furnaces, and start charcoal fires for breakfast.

on-drive, *v.* Add: (Further examples.)

1928 *Morning Post* 7 June 16/4 Holmes attacked the bowlers after a quiet start, twice on-driving Astill for 6. **1955** *Times* 19 May 5/1 In the next over Atkinson beautifully on-drove Johnson for his 152 in 198 minutes.

b. *absol.* or *intr.* To drive the ball to the on. Hence **on-driving** *vbl. sb.*

1930 *Morning Post* 7 Aug. 13/1 Bryan on-drove and hooked most effectively. **1961** *Times* 21 Aug. 3/3 His cutting and on-driving were a delight. **1963** *Times* 13 Feb. 4/3 Pulling and on-driving with remarkable acumen, he dispatched six successive balls for a six and five fours.

o·n-driving, *a.* [On *adv.*] That drives on.

1884 A. de Vere *Poetical Wks.* II. 435 And ever as she sang, the on-driving snow Choked the sweet strain. **1927** *Chambers's Jrnl.* Jan. 39/1 Because there was a check, there arose long on-driving shouts from the huntsmen.

one, *numeral a.*, *pron.*, etc. Add: **B. I. 1. c.** *like one o'clock* (further examples); also, splendidly, excellently; readily, enthusiastically.

1852 Dickens *Bleak Ho.* (1853) xx. 200 He has seen him through the shop-door, sitting in his back premises, sleeping 'like one o'clock'. **1889** E. Dowson *Let.* 31 July (1967) 97 If I can only shake off Cursitor St I will go to the oeuvre like one oclock. **1901** M. Franklin *My Brilliant Career* xix. 161 He had a taste for literature, and we got on together like one o'clock. **1924** Galsworthy *White Monkey* iii. xv. 321 Anything about the meeting, sir? Your speech must read like one o'clock! **1970** V. C. Clinton-Baddeley *No Case for Police* viii. 179 It's going to rain like one o'clock. **1973** *Guardian* 27 Oct. 11/6 Hedgehogs drink beer like one o'clock.

d. With ellipsis of *glass* or *drink*; *one for the road*, a final drink before departure. See also *quick one* (*Quick *a.* 25 b). *colloq.*

1925 R. J. B. Sellar *Sporting Yarns* 165 'Did I have one over the regulation number last night?' 'Not at all.. you were perfectly all right.' **1925, 1928** [see *eight *sb.* 4]. **1934** Wodehouse *Right Ho, Jeeves* xi. 126, I..put my feet up, sipping the mixture with carefree enjoyment, rather like Cæsar having one in his tent the day he overcame the Nervii. **1937** D. & H. Teilhet *Feather Cloak Murders* i. 20 You run off to bed like a good fellow. You've had one too many. **1943** J. Mercer (*song-title*) One for my baby (and one more for the road). **1948** 'E. Crispin' *Buried for Pleasure* vi. 47 How about one for the road? **1959** G. Greene *Complaisant Lover* i. i. 20 One for the road. I insist. While I call a taxi. **1968** J. Sangster *Touchfeather* xiii. 140 Didn't mean to be crude. Must have had one too many. **1972** J. Blackburn *For Fear of Little Men* xi. 119 'What about giving me one for the road, my dear.' He gulped down the remains of the sherry. **1976** *South Notts Echo* 16 Dec. 5/4 If you are driving do not have one for the road.

† **e.** Ellipt. for 'one horse' (to pull a carriage, etc.). Cf. Four *a.* 2 c. *Obs.*

1777 P. Thicknesse *Year's Journey* II. lv. 185 If you can find me out a sensible valetudinarian..who will travel as we do..in a landau and one. **1785** Cowper *Task* i. 5 Two citizens who take the air Close pack'd and smiling in a chaise and one.

f. A one-pound note or a one-dollar bill.

1846 *Illinois State Register* (Springfield) 2 Oct. 2/6 Independent of the older issues, and such as are described in the Detectors, Ones, on the Banks of 'Broome county' and 'Whitestown'..have made their appearance. **1948** *Savings & Loan News* Mar. 18/2 My billfold had a $10 bill in it, not ten ones. **1966** O. Norton *School of Liars* iii. 55 'Do you want this in ones, Mrs. Hetherington?' 'In ten-shillingses, dear boy.' **1967** 'A. Gilbert' *Visitor* iii. 45, I counted the notes, which took a ridiculously long time as they were mostly in ones. **1970** M. Kenyon *100,000 Welcomes* iii. 18 He counted out seven one-pound notes and a five..and selected three ones. **1976** J. Wainwright *Walther P. 38* 24 Drysdale started with five fives, followed by five ones, then he paused...he counted out five more singles.

g. One point or position on a scale, order, or the like; esp. in phr. *go up* (or *down*) *one*, expressing commendation (or disapprobation). *colloq.*

1909 J. R. Ware *Passing Eng.* 142/2 *Go down one*, to be vanquished. *Ibid.* 143/2 *Go up one*, applause. Derived from the school class—the scholar going one nearer the top as he goes up one. **1967** E. Lemarchand *Death of Old Girl* v. 59 'I was thinking maybe..the blood on that made the mark.' 'So was I,' said Pollard. 'Go up one.'

4. b. *murder one*: see *murder *sb.* 5.

5. b. *one in* (a specified number): designating a gradient in which the height increases or decreases by one foot (or other measure) vertically for the specified number of feet, etc., horizontally; also *ellipt.* as *sb.*

1830 M. Edgeworth *Let.* 18 Oct. (1971) 419 The inclined plane the rise of which was one in 36. **1869**, etc. [see *in *prep.* 4]. **1910** Kipling *Divers. Creatures* (1917) 322 It was all of a one in three gradient. **1968** N. Tranter *Cable from Kabul* iii. 37 Down at the foot of a one-in-three hill, I found myself in some sort of village. **1971** G. Household *Doom's Caravan* ii. 44 Its original builders had no objection to a slope of one in four. **1976** J. Wainwright *Bastard* i. 11, I slither and skid the car up the one-in-six.

6. d. See also Number *sb.* 5 b.

II. 7. c. Used as a more emphatic substitute for the indefinite article: (*a*) with adjs. in sense 'a very ——', 'an extremely ——'; (*b*) with sbs., esp. *hell* (see *hell *sb.* 4 d, *helluva). *colloq.*

1828 *Punch & Judy* i. i. 77 Toby, you're one nasty cross dog: get away with you! **1911** J. London *Let.* 7 Apr. (1966) 343 Let me tell you that you have given me one hell of a time. **1920** [see *hell *sb.* 4 d]. **1925** T. Dreiser *Amer. Trag.* (1926) i. xii. 82 He went out in the kitchen and blacked up an' put on a waiter's apron and coat and then comes back and serves us. That's one funny boy. **1934** [see *helluva]. **1948** E. Pound *Pisan Cantos* (1949) lxxviii. 66 Steele that is one awful name. **1967** 'T. Wells' *Dead by Light of Moon* (1968) xi. 111, I wondered what Mai Farmer was doing. She was one striking girl. **1967** [see *helluva]. **1972** A. Price *Col. Butler's Wolf* xii. 132 The last two, three weeks he was one worried young man. **1973** J. Di Mona *Last Man at Arlington* (1974) ii. xvi. 100 'Tell everyone I'm not Cuban,' said Medwick, hoping to get a rise out of the driver. But none came. This was one serious boy. **1976** *Publishers Weekly* 9 Feb. 85 (Advt.), Come spring, this [forthcoming book] is going to be One Hot Number.

IV. 15. b. *one of those*: a homosexual; *one of us*: a member of our group; *spec.* (*a*) a harlot (*obs.*); (*b*) a homosexual. *colloq.*; *one of these days*: see Day *sb.* 7 b; *one of those days*: see *day *sb.* 7 b.

1785 Grose *Dict. Vulgar T.*, *One of us*, one of my cousins, a woman of the town, a harlot. **1915** Conrad *Victory* i. ii. 9 Morrison was 'one of us'. He was owner and master of the *Capricorn*, trading brig, and was understood to be doing well with her. **1933** [see *nancy[3]]. **1956** [see *camp *a.* and *sb.*[5]]. **1961** Partridge *Dict. Slang* Suppl. 1207/1 *One of us, he's*, he is a homosexual. **1968** J. R. Ackerley *My Father & Myself* xvi. 185, I divined that he was homosexual, or as we put it, 'one of us'. **1976** *Times* 27 May 16/4 It would go a long way towards helping..to understand..if others would stop saying 'New Commonwealth' when they mean something like 'coffee-coloured' and 'Old Commonwealth' when they mean..'One of us'. **1977** *Gay News* 24 Mar. 18/2 Her husband..probably fits none of the stereotypes whereby she would normally identify 'one of those'.

c. *a one*: a person who is remarkable, extraordinary, outrageous, impudent, etc.; esp. in phr. *you are a one*; (*a*) *one for*: a person who likes, admires, practises, supports, etc. (something) to an outstanding degree; a devotee, champion, or admirer of (something); (*a*) *one to*: the sort of person who would (do a particular thing). *colloq.*

1880 C. M. Yonge *Bye-Words* 303 Tittering, and now and then, 'O Miss Annie, don't, pray!' 'O Miss Annie, you are a one!' **1888** —— *Our New Mistress* i. 3 Her daughters ..all married, except Lady Mary, who was always such a one for schools and poor people. **1894** S. Baring-Gould *Queen of Love* II. vi. 59, I am not one to fly in the face of Providence. **1906** E. Dyson *Fact'ry 'Ands* iii. 29 'Oh, Mr. Ellis, you are a one!' she said. **1927**, etc. [see *great *a.* 16 a]. **1932** N. Royde-Smith *Incredible Tale* 91 She was a one for football. **1934** N. Marsh *Man lay Dead* vii. 126 'The left-hand print on the stair knob is Mr. Wilde's,' said Bailey. 'Is it?' answered Alleyn without enthusiasm. 'Aren't you a one?' **1935** G. Heyer *Death in Stocks* iii. 22 Constable Dickenson had warned the Inspector that she was not one to talk. **1948** 'G. Orwell' *Let.* 10 July in *Coll. Ess.* (1968) IV. 438 Farm life seems to suit him, though I am pretty sure he is one for machines rather than animals. **1966** J. B. Priestley *Salt is Leaving* viii. 96 You're a bit of a one, aren't you, Dr Salt? **1973** J. Thomson *Death Cap* vi. 86 He's never been one for the women. I think he's a bit afraid of them.

17. c. *one thing*: something acceptable or satisfactory, contrasted with *another* (*thing*) that is unacceptable or unsatisfactory.

a **1678** H. Scougal *Life of God* (1726) 392, I do not condemn all chearfulness and freedom, nor the innocent exercises of wit: but it is one thing to make use of these now and then when they come in our way, and another to search and haunt after them. **1735** Berkeley *Defence Free-Thinking in Math.* xxxvii. 44 It is one thing when a Doctrine is placed in various lights: and another, when the principles and notions are shifted. **1828** Scott *Chron. Canongate* 2nd Ser. I. viii. 244 It is one thing to employ the revenues of the Church..in the suitable and dutiful reception of your royal Majesty, and another to have it wrenched from us by the hands of rude and violent men. **1904** H. James *Golden Bowl* (1905) v. 66 It was one thing to have met the girl casually at Mrs. Assingham's and another to arrange with her thus for a morning practically as private as their old mornings in Rome and practically not less intimate.

d. Ellipt. for 'one or the other'. *U.S. dial.*

1895 *Dialect Notes* I. 373 *One* seems to be superfluous or else 'or the other' is omitted. 'I will see you or send word, one.' **1926** E. M. Roberts *Time of Man* (1927) vii. 257, I met a parcel of travelers that owned a bear could read or tell fortunes—one, I forget which. *Ibid.* viii. 298 It was the road overseer's fault.., or the magistrate's, one. **1937** *Scribner's Mag.* Apr. 22/2 He's making it [*sc.* liquor] on my farm or your farm, one. **1938** M. K. Rawlings *Yearling* xv. 169 Now do things go wrong again, you or Buck, one ,ride back for me. So long.

V. 21. (Further examples specially meaning the speaker himself.)

1956 R. Henriques *Red over Green* iii. 60 He meant nothing... One can't even remember his face. **1959** E. H. Clements *High Tension* ii. 19 'Do you often have your fan-mail in person?'..'Not often. One isn't in the telephone book'.

23. b. *spec.* A story or anecdote; a joke; a lie. *colloq.*

1813, etc. [see *good *a.* 1 g]. **1925** Wodehouse *Carry On, Jeeves!* x. 254 Story? Story?.. I wonder if you've heard the one about the stockbroker and the chorus-girl? **1926** D. L. Sayers *Clouds of Witness* xiii. 240 Mr. Parker endured five stories with commendable patience, and then suddenly broke down. 'Hurray!' said Wimsey... 'I'll spare you the really outrageous one about the young housewife and the traveller in bicycle-pumps.' **1931** J. Betjeman *Mount Zion* 22 Each learning how to be a sinner And tell 'a good one' after dinner. **1961** 'F. O'Brien' *Hard Life* x. 71, I will tell you a funny one, Father, Mr Collopy said. **1967** Wodehouse *Company for Henry* x. 175 The low comedians of his musical comedy days who had called him 'laddie' and begged him to stop them if he had heard this one. **1977** *Listener* 24 Nov. 674/2 'Have you heard the one about the Queen Mother?' We had not heard it, and it was very funny.

VIII. Phrases.

29. c. *all one*: see also All *adv.* 5 b in Dict. and Suppl.

29*. With following adverb.

a. one down: one point behind one's opponent in a game; inferior in one respect; disadvantaged; also (with hyphen) *attrib.* or as *adj.* Hence **one-downmanship,** the art or practice of being 'one down'; **one-downness,** the fact or state of being 'one down'. Cf. sense 29* c below.

1907 [see *down *adv.* 14 b]. **1952** S. Potter *One-Upmanship* ii. 32 To increase the one-downness, bring in the washing-the-hands gambit immediately after touching hands with Patient. **1961** *Times* 8 Mar. 17 (*heading*) Handy guide to art of onedownmanship. *Ibid.* 22 Mar. 16/3 It is the Negroes who are educated, who 'talk posh', who go to university; the native English who are one-down, with less money and less culture. **1964** M. ARGYLE *Psychol. & Social Probl.* iii. 36 Stephen Potter has given an amusing list of techniques for making others feel 'one-down', together with counterplоys for dealing with such methods when used by others. **1967** *Punch* 4 Oct. 514/3 If he were to check his facts would he not find that on the contrary the majority of Fleet Street was indulging in a form of one-down-manship towards the British public? **1976** N. POSTMAN *Crazy Talk* 44 He will naturally be one-down in the situation, a 'child' to the government agent's 'adult'.

b. one off: a single example of a manufactured product; something not repeated; a prototype. Freq. (with hyphen) *attrib.* or as *adj.* Also *transf.* and *fig.* Cf. *OFF *adv.* 13, *once-off* adj. s.v. *ONCE *adv.* B. 7b.

1934 *Proc. Inst. Brit. Foundrymen* XXVI. 552 A splendid one-off pattern can be swept up in very little time. **1935** *Jrnl. R. Aeronaut. Soc.* XXXIX. 41 One off per machine does not give us much opportunity for reducing production costs. **1947** *Ibid.* LI. 308/1 With the lofting technique it is possible to cut down the time required to produce a prototype aircraft for..it is possible to reproduce full-scale layouts directly on to the material to be worked..thus cutting out what was originally the factor which absorbed the most production time in the freehand manufacture of 'one offs'. **1954** *Archit. Rev.* CXVI. 411/2 Hills built the first part of Cheshunt as a 'one off' job, with no guarantees of further business, though of course it was intended to be the first of a line. **1955** *Ibid.* CXVII. 226/2 None of the motor-cars illustrated is a standardized mass-produced model; all are expensive, specialized, handicraft one-offs which can justly be compared to the Parthenon because, like it, they are unique works of handmade art. **1958** *Listener* 25 Sept. 458/2 Both the estates of the speculative 'rush' builders and the architectural one-offs are unable to keep pace with the demand [for new houses]. **1961** *Times* 3 Oct. (Computer Suppl.) p. v/3 The centres are..even able to do a 'one-off' job, such as eliminating a production bottleneck, very cheaply. **1965** R. B. ORAM *Cargo Handling* iv. 70 Tailor made, or 'one-off', machines, may give great satisfaction. **1968** *Sunday Times* 29 Sept. 25 Jenkins has already made a crude stab at a wealth tax with his special charge on investment incomes... But this was a one-off effort. **1970** *Times* 28 Mar. 21 All these relationships involve money and are on a continuing basis rather than a one-off purchase. **1973** *Daily Tel.* 22 Oct. 12/4 When Barry Took's *Grub Street* (BBC-2) was screened as a one-off..I rashly predicted that it could make a series. **1974** F. WARNER *Meeting Ends* II. i. 35 But we find it much harder to shake a man off afterwards, and anyway, I don't like those 'one off' dates. I need companionship, an outing, warmth. **1976** *Scottish Rev.* Spring 33 For the most part they could only produce an endless stream of one-off building prototypes. **1977** *Hot Car* Oct. 97/1 There seems to be a good deal of misunderstanding about the way the Type Approval Regulations apply to 'one-offs' or cars built by private individuals.

c. one up: scoring one point more than an opponent; ahead of another person; (fig.) maintaining a psychological advantage; also (with hyphen) *attrib.* or as *adj.* Hence **one-u·pmanship,** the art or practice of being 'one up'; so **one-up** *v. trans.*, to do better than (someone); **one-upman,** an exponent of one-upmanship; **one-upness, -uppance,** the fact or state of being 'one up'.

1919 [see UP *adv.*[2] 13 e]. **1924** WODEHOUSE *Leave it to Psmith* i. 30 Which would make her pretty chirpy, as well as putting you one up. **1929** J. B. PRIESTLEY *Good Companions* II. vii. 449 He can give old Omar himself points in not believing in anything, for he has cut out the book of verse, most of the loaf, and the Houri stuff, and just sticks to the jug, though he has added a clay pipe and is one up on Omar there. **1952** S. POTTER (*title*) One-upmanship. *Ibid.* I. ii. 26 The establishment of one-up relations between doctor and doctor and doctor and patient and vice versa. *Ibid.* v. 64 The basic gambit is of course the achievement of the state of one-upness on the rest of the public. **1957** *Economist* 26 Oct. 295/1 This piece of applied relativity..may go down in the annals of international one-upmanship as the sputnik ploy. **1959** N. N. HOLLAND *First Mod. Comedies* 38 This was a perhaps pardonable attempt to retain 'one-upness' in the large eyes of a rather nasty little genius. **1959** *Times Lit. Suppl.* 6 Nov. 650/4 They are one-upmen, seen from the receiving end, and they give Mr. Gibb endless opportunities for recording sillier aspects of the contemporary social scene. **1960** *News Chron.* 14 Apr. 3/1 Will Granada deny there was an element of one-upness in its satisfaction? **1961** S. PRICE *Just for Record* v. 37 Stephen Potter was a square in nappies compared to these one-up graduates. **1963** *Canada Month* Mar. 10/1 John Wintermeyer..one-upped the socialists by endorsing the Saskatchewan plan. **1964** 'C. E. MAINE' *Never let Up* xvii. 172 It's a kind of one-upmanship. You thought you were smart, but he had to prove that he was even smarter. **1966** *Listener* 27 Oct. 622/1 Virginia Woolf can still show herself to be one up, in her literary judgements, on most current criticism. **1967** *Maclean's Mag.* Oct. 46 Another trap the psychiatrist must strive to avoid is the mistake of being one-up. The psychiatrist is in the perfect position to be the one-up man. **1969** D. S. DAVIS *Where Dark Streets Go* (1970) xviii. 162 You one-upped us there, Father. We came dead-end in a housing development. **1970** 'JENNER' & SEGAL *Men & Marriage* ii. 45 Marrying a doctor still gives a girl a bit of one-uppance amongst the neighbours. **1973** J. WAINWRIGHT *Touch of Malice* 87 Smithson's one-up-man-ship ploy of keeping a senior police officer waiting. **1975** *Times* 14 Mar. 14/5 There are one-upmanship entries. A power cruiser 'built for royalty' is offered. **1976** *Listener* 28 Oct. 544/4 The objects of human vituperation..seem to be pretty well limited to people who are one up on us, and other people's pleasures. **1977** *Time* 24 Jan. 37/1 His sweet, sporting spirit as he sits trying to absorb his defeat while graciously applauding a trickster's win is something with which any weekend athlete who has been one-upped by an allegedly friendly opponent can identify.

29**. Misc. phrases.

a. *one and the same*: used as a more emphatic form of 'the same'. Cf. L. *unus et idem.*

1869 *Bradshaw's Railway Manual* XXI. 365 This modification has..the effect of comprising in one and the same network the two lines from Paris to Lyons. **1941** H. L. MENCKEN *Newspaper Days* (1942) xvi. 245 His father had been, at one and the same time, a Confederate general, a French nobleman, and a graduate of both Oxford and Cambridge. **1960** C. P. SNOW *Affair* v. xxxix. 364 You'd obviously got to raise the dust about Nightingale and give them an escape-route at one and the same damned time. **1973** D. AARON *Unwritten War* IV. xi. 167 Abolitionism or Black Republicanism, to the South Carolinian, one and the same thing. **1976** G. BUTLER *Vesey Inheritance* iv. 117, I wonder..whether the King and Mr Koenig could be one and the same person?

b. *one man, one vote*: a slogan advocating that every adult man (or adult person) should have a vote; also formerly, that each voter should have only one vote; also *attrib.*

1884 A. PAUL *Hist. of Reform* ii. 19 'One man, one vote', a cry which may have had a novel sound to some in 1883 was one of Cartwright's political principles. **1889** W. E. GLADSTONE in *Times* 13 June 7/2 The important measure which is briefly designated under the well-known phrase—one man, one vote. **1891** [see sense 1 a in Dict.]. **1907** H. LAWSON in Murdoch & Drake-Brockman *Austral. Short Stories* (1951) 73 The One-Man-One-Vote Bill was passed. **1964** *Punch* 15 July 74/3 To ensure that one-man-one-vote democracy is swiftly introduced. **1971** 'G. BLACK' *Time for Pirates* ii. 32 The government..had declared martial law, suspending the constitution... 'So much for one man, one vote,' Russell said. **1975** D. BAGLEY *Snow Tiger* xiii. 115 Not so democratic as to be a one man, one vote system.

c. *one hand for oneself and one for the ship*: a nautical proverb referring to the practice of holding on to a rope, etc., with one hand while working with the other hand; also in similar phrases (see quots.).

1799 *Port Folio* (Philadelphia) 1812 VII. 130 Always keep one hand for the owners, and one for yourself. **1902** B. LUBBOCK *Round the Horn* 58 The old rule on a yard is, 'one hand for yourself and one for the ship', which means, hold on with one hand and work with the other. **1924** R. CLEMENTS *Gipsy of Horn* iii. 50 One hand for yourself and one for the owners. **1938** F. A. WORSLEY *First Voy. in Square-Rigged Ship* 119 One hand for the Queen and one for yerself. **1968** L. MORTON *Long Wake* i. 10, I did not know then the old adage 'one hand for oneself and one hand for the company'.

d. *one and only*: one's sweetheart; one's only child or love; also *transf.* Also (with hyphens) as *attrib. phr.*, unique, unrepeatable.

1906 E. DYSON *Fact'ry 'Ands* i. 4 She's er little *boshter* ..'n' I'm 'er one 'n' only. **1933** J. D. CARR *Mad Hatter Mystery* iv. 64 He'd met some girl at a dance who was the absolute One and Only. **1961** *Times* 13 May 11/3 Artur Schnabel thought that such a one and only performance was obtainable. **1966** *Harper's Bazaar* Sept. 64 A coat so versatile it could be the treasured one-and-only in your life. **1967** I. HAMILTON *Man with Brown Paper Face* vi. 83 Daddy wasn't too happy about his one-and-only's choice of companion. **1967** J. WAINWRIGHT *Worms must Wait* lxxvii. 201 He had the truncheon ready for what he knew was going to be a one-and-only chance. **1975** J. MCCLURE *Snake* xii. 159 She'd been with the family since their one-and-only was five. **1977** J. VAN DE WETERING *Japanese Corpse* (1978) xvii. 152 She had been unwilling to admit that she had ever slept with other men. Kikuji Nagai had been her one and only.

e. *one for the (end) book*: a notable, extraordinary, or incredible event, action, saying, etc. *U.S. colloq.*

1922 H. C. WITWER *Fighting Blood* (1923) 170 Gents, this was one for the book! **1946** *Amer. Speech* XXI. 69/1 When a friend approaches with an anecdote which is strange or incredible, he often prefaces it with the remark, 'Here's one for the book'. *Ibid.*, At racetracks where parimutuel betting machines are not used..it was customary for bookmakers to line up in a designated area... If a bettor asked unusually high odds, the bookie might comment, 'Here's one for the end book', implying that no one but a green newcomer..would accept those odds. **1955** *Publ. Amer. Dial. Soc.* xxiv. 179 There is always someone with one for the end book, or a story that is hard to believe.

f. (*just*) *one of those things*: something inevitable or inexplicable; a fact or happening that one cannot do anything about. *colloq.*

1934 J. O'HARA *Appointment in Samarra* i. 25 No, it was just one of those things. **1935** C. PORTER (*song-title*) Just one of those things. **1935** *Time* 4 Mar. 17/3 Said Comedian Durante: 'Aw, it's just one of those things.' **1936** R. LEHMANN *Weather in Streets* vii. 248 Oh, well... It can't be helped. It's just one of those things. **1941** C. MORGAN *Empty Room* i. 46 'What is it, Carey?' She smiled. 'Nothing. One of those things.' **1951** 'J. WYNDHAM' *Day of Triffids* ii. 28 My inability to make any column of figures reach the same total twice caused me to be something of a mystery as well as a disappointment to him [*sc.* my father]. Still, there it was: just one of those things. **1955** A. HUXLEY *Let.* 16 Dec. (1969) 778 Her daughter is going to have a baby—husband twenty-one and still at college, daughter supporting the household for the moment. Which is one of those things. **1971** *Daily Tel.* 19 Nov. 3/1, I know Mr Butler is a bit choked about it, but it's just one of those things. **1974** M. BABSON *Stalking Lamb* xviii. 136 The price was too high.. to be shrugged off as 'just one of those things'.

g. *one-of-a-kind* attrib. phr., (*a*) of only one kind; (*b*) unique.

1961 *Times* 25 Apr. 4/2 The one-of-a-kind series for racing catamarans organized last year. **1963** *New Yorker* 1 June 72 Among the one-of-a-kind mannerly materials are Paisley cotton prints. **1973** *Publishers Weekly* 23 July 66/3 A one-of-a-kind book that merits a place on the political science shelf. **1975** *New Yorker* 21 Apr. 17/3 *Children of Paradise* (1945)—A one-of-a-kind film. **1977** *Rolling Stone* 24 Mar. 48/4 Fleetwood Mac had this one-of-a-kind charm. They were gregarious, charming and cheeky onstage. *Very* cheeky.

30. d. in one. (*g*) At one stroke or attempt; esp. *to get it in one*: to succeed at the first attempt. Cf. sense (*e*) in Dict., and *hole in one* s.v. *HOLE *sb.* 4 a. *colloq.*

1938 J. PARISH *St. Michael comes to Shepherd's Bush* 11 As a matter of fact, that's just what I am. You've got there in one. **1942** 'A. BRIDGE' *Frontier Passage* vi. 91 'In fact, our old friend the Hidden Hand in Biarritz runs the sabotage as well as the rest—that the idea?' Crampaun enquired. 'Got it in one!' **1972** W. GARNER *Ditto, Brother Rat!* xv. 106 Got it in one, old son. **1975** 'C. AIRD' *Slight Mourning* iii. 26 'What we are checking on is whether someone tried to kill him...' 'Got it in one, Sloan.'

IX. 32. a. *one-child, -class, -clause* (examples), *-colour, -crop, -culture, -day* (later examples), *-deck, -digit, -drink, -electron, -family, -level, -light, -line, -member, -parent, -particle, -party, -person, -reel, -room, -sex, -star, -step, -storey* (also *-story*) (earlier, later, and *fig.* examples), *-string, -tap, -term, -volume, -word.*

1905 *Daily Chron.* 18 Nov. 6/3 It is desired to secure such a reform in the law as will bring one-child cases within the sphere of inspection. **1971** J. Z. YOUNG *Introd. Study Man* xxiv. 326 The effect has been an increase of 2 per cent in one-child families. **1908** *Daily Chron.* 21 Nov. 9/3 They are one-class, one-price machines. **1909** *Westm. Gaz.* 21 Oct. 1/3 For short-distance travelling Sir Albert is in favour of one-class carriages. **1931** *Times* 5 Nov. 8/3 The sooner the 'one class' party is abolished,..the better for the nation and Empire. **1960** WILLMOTT & YOUNG *Family & Class in London Suburb* viii. 97 Working Men's Clubs and other one-class organizations. **1973** A. BEHREND *Samarai Affair* ii. 24 A very small one-class passenger liner. **1898** *Daily News* 28 July 3/1 The Government are being pressed to introduce a one-clause Bill. **1965** *Language* XLI. 74 There are many one-clause sentences. **1946** *Happy Landings* (Air Ministry) July 11/3 We recall ..young pilots, chests aflame with so many medals that it made the Aurora Borealis look like a one-colour miniature. **1942** *E. Afr. Ann. 1941–2* 85/2 Kenya..has suffered from one-crop farming. **1970** *Guardian* 10 Apr. 3/5 The Prime Minister, Dr Fidel Castro, [is] bent on diversifying what has been a one-crop economy based on sugar. **1962** *Times* 10 May 17/3, I decided to be a one-culture man to make reading more enjoyable. **1974** *News & Press* (Darlington, S. Carolina) 25 Apr. 7/6 A one-day golf tournament..will be held at the Tifton Golf Club in Darlington. **1975** *Cricketer* May 4/1 MCC won both their one-day matches in Hong Kong. **1977** *Times* 25 Aug. 2/7 It will not be a couple of one-day strikes. It will be a case of weeks and maybe months, but we will force the rise. **1906** *Daily Chron.* 23 Feb. 2/2 They started with the old style one-deck buses. **1935** H. STRAUMANN *Newspaper Headlines* 150 They..occur in second decks or in one-deck crossheads. **1962** *Gloss. Terms Automatic Data Processing* (*B.S.I.*) 60 *One-digit adder*, a logic element with two outputs and two inputs to which may be applied signals representing a digit of a number and a single addend or carry digit. One output signal represents a digit of the sum, the other represents a digit to be carried forward. **1966** OGILVY & ANDERSON *Excursions in Number Theory* 156 What we have just said means that $q(n) = x - 1$ (not *x*, because in the first decade none of the one-digit numbers 2, 4, 8 qualify). **1906** *Westm. Gaz.* 13 Aug. 5/1 Most of them are 'one-drink' people, although they may have 'another'. **1909** J. WARE *Passing Eng.* 188/2 *One drink house*.., where only one serving is permitted. If the customer desire a second helping, he has to take a walk 'round the houses' after the first. **1955** H. B. G. CASIMIR in W. Pauli *Niels Bohr* 119, $n(\epsilon_0)$ is the density of one-electron states per energy-interval in the neighbourhood of this maximum energy. **1970** W. G. WOODGATE *Elem. Atomic Struct.* i. 1 Bohr's semi-classical theory was not general enough to describe more than the gross features of the simplest one-electron atom. **1968** *N.Y. City* (Michelin Tire Corp.) 47 There are 3000 one-family dwellings in Manhattan. **1972** *Country Life* 28 Dec. 1781/1 They were not originally one-family houses; rather was it a case of a family a floor. **1957** N. FRYE *Anat. Crit.* 71 The criticism of literature can hardly be a simple or one-level activity. **1908** A. L. FROTHINGHAM *Monuments Christian Rome* II. 192 The lower story or two had a one-light opening. **1945** G. B. GRUNDY *55 Yrs. at Oxf.* 148 The one-light system, i.e. shading from an imaginary perpendicular light. **1655** One-line [in Dict.]. **1901** G. B. SHAW *Admirable Bashville* Pref. 87, I like the melodious sing-song, the clear simple one-line and two-line sayings. **1952** M. RICHERT *Reconstr. Carmelite Missal* iii. 67 A small (one-line) blue, tan, and gold letter. **1965** B. MATES *Elem. Logic* vii. 110 A derivation can begin with a tautology, as in the following one-line derivation. **1965** HUGHES & LONDEY *Elem. Formal Logic* xxix. 218 We shall usually write one-line proofs in this abbreviated form. **1884** E. W. HAMILTON *Diary* 29 Oct. (1972) II. 720 The Tory scheme leans to the one-member principle. **1924** O. JESPERSEN *Philos. Gram.* 306 An old-fashioned grammarian will feel a certain repugnance to this theory of one-member sentences. **1963** J. LYONS *Structural Semantics* ii. 22 Some of the distributional classes will, of course, be one-member classes; but the majority will not. **1967** D. H. MONRO *Empiricism & Ethics* xvi. 201 It is not irrational to treat an individual as a one-member class. **1969** *Times* 7 Nov. 15/7 A committee to consider the problems of one-parent families in society. **1974** *Evening News* (Edinburgh) 12 Apr. 7/5 An Easter holiday play scheme for children from some of Edinburgh's one-parent families ended today on the slopes of Arthur's Seat. **1976** *Times* 21 May 1/6 That benefit..is paid to fewer than half the one-parent families in Britain. **1955** W. PAULI *Niels Bohr* 32 This method is essentially based on the assumption that the theory for free particles (without interactions) holds for the so-called one particle states. **1937** H. TINGSTEN *Political Behavior* v. 216 In certain American so-called one party states one can hardly speak of an election campaign. **1950** 'G. ORWELL' *Shooting an Elephant* 156 The appearance of one-party régimes based on police terrorism, faked plebiscites, etc. **1964** T. B. BOTTOMORE *Elites & Society* v. 95 The possible or probable concomitants of this kind of one-party rule, dictatorship and loss of personal liberty, persecution and widespread suffering. **1971** *Guardian* 11 Dec. 10/4 India..was a benign one-party state. **1975** *Times* 11 Apr. 6/5 Independent observers had little doubt that this would be the beginning of a one-party system in Portugal. **1956** J. M. MOGEY *Family & Neighbourhood* 14 One-person households. **1966** J. TUNSTALL *Old & Alone* xiv. 281 'Under-occupation' defined as one-person household in 4+ rooms or two-person household in 5+ rooms. **1977** G. SCOTT *Hot Pursuit* ii. 16 It's a one-person flat. **1920** I. P. GORE in *Stage Year Bk.* 53 Such tit-bits as..a one-reel comedy founded on the rollicking antics of a malignant tumour. **1961** GETLEIN & GARDINER *Movies, Morals & Art* iv. 51 *The Great Train Robbery* is a one-reel film. **1897** One-room [in Dict.]. **1934** *Archit. Rev.* LXXV. 41 (*heading*) The one-room flat. **1972** C. WESTON *Poor, Poor Ophelia* (1973) vi. 30 A hippie joint, you think? Anyhow, a bunch of one-room pads. **1949** M. MEAD *Male & Female* xviii. 368 A one-sex world would be an imperfect world. **1966** P. WILLMOTT *Adolescent Boys E. London* vii. 128 Younger boys more often belong to one-sex clubs. **1908** *Daily Chron.* 4 Nov. 3/3 In the meadows we did roam; And in the one-star night returned Together home. **1961** *Guardian* 24 Mar. 21/4 One-star restaurants, rather slightingly dismissed by M. Michelin as 'a good restaurant for its class'. **1975** tr. *Melchior's Sleeper Agent* (1976) III. 168 The French general..was scheduled to tap four officers for the Legion of Honor, two one-star generals and two bird colonels. **1977** 'R. ROSTAND' *Killing in Rome* i. 4 A small one-star hotel. **1964** D. B. FRY in D. Abercrombie et al. *Daniel Jones* 64 He answered correctly all the items involving a one-step difference between A and B. **1964** *English Studies* XLV. 383 The difference between a normal one-step process, beginning with Scandinavian forms and limited to names, and the multi-step process. **1833** B. SILLIMAN *Man. Sugar Cane* 64 The bagasse houses at Demerara are high one story buildings. **1858** [see ONE-HORSE *a.* 2]. **1970** J. HANSEN *Fadeout* (1972) i. 3 The house was one-story, rambling, sided with cedar shakes. **1938** *Oxf. Compan. Mus.* 591/1 The one-string principle is also applied to the *Tromba Marina*. **1970** *Islander* (Victoria, B.C.) 8 Feb. 10/1 Occasionally from some nearby window you caught the strains of the [Chinese] one-string fiddle blending with the sing-song street cries of the vendors of lottery tickets. **1976** LD. HOME *Way Wind Blows* vii. 112 Some three hundred of them were gathered round, and he began to teach them, accompanied by a one-string banjo. **1952** A. COHEN *Phonemes of Eng.* 29 These two sounds (one-tap and fricative *r*) are in no way opposed. **1845** *Congress. Globe* 28th Congress 2 Sess. 122/2 The North.. never had had any but one-term presidents, democratic or federal. **1961** Y. OLSSON *On Syntax Eng. Verb* ii. 34 A two-term sub-system commutable with the one-term sub-system. **1966** *Philos. Rev.* LXXV. 406 Plato confuses relations with one-term predicates. **1862** MRS. GASKELL *Let.* 30 Sept. (1966) 698, I am going to publish a one-volume story in 'All the Year Round', where..it will occupy from ten to twelve numbers. **1961** R. B. LONG *Sentence & its Parts* xix. 414 There is no possibility of doing it justice in a one-volume grammar. **1977** *Listener* 17 Nov. 651/2 The *Times* one-volume edition [of the Pentagon Papers]. **1924** R. M. OGDEN tr. *Koffka's Growth of Mind* v. 320 Single words have been spoken as one-word sentences. **1956** 'H. MACDIARMID' *Stony Limits* 141 The great one-word metaphors of the Enneads. **1960** W. V. QUINE *Word & Object* i. 10 'Red' as a one-word sentence usually needs a question for its elicitation. **1963** F. T. VISSER *Hist. Syntax Eng. Lang.* I. iv. 603 When a noun is the object of both a merged verb and a one-word verb.

d. *one-handled, -leafed, -leaved, -membered, -minded, -pointed* (so *-pointedness*), *-seeded* (earlier and later examples), *-storied* (earlier example), *-volumed, -winged, -worded.*

1922 JOYCE *Ulysses* 146 Settle down on their striped petticoats, peering up at the statue of the onehandled adulterer. *Ibid.* 564 Steel shark stone onehandled Nelson. **1952** A. G. L. HELLYER *Sanders' Encycl. Gardening* (ed. 22) 463 *Sophronitis...* Pseudo-bulbs usually small, one-leafed, stout, with one or few terminal flowers. **1875** *Amer. Naturalist* IX. 17 The singular one-leaved ash, *Fraxinus anomala.* **1946** DYLAN THOMAS *Deaths & Entrances* 29 Under the one leaved trees ran a scarecrow of snow. **1972** *Hilliers' Man. Trees & Shrubs* 507 [pinus cembroides] monophylla... 'One-leaved Nut Pine'. An unusual variety in which the..leaves occur singly. **1884** E. W. HAMILTON *Diary* 25 July (1972) II. 659 Mr. G... rather favours one-membered constituencies. **1877** A. DOBSON *Proverbs in Porcelain* 99 We, bound with him in common care, One-minded, celibate. **1941** L. MACNEICE *Poetry of Yeats* x. 218 If Lawrence is..an eclectic, he is.. a one-minded one. **1811** One-pointed [see *BLUE GRASS 2]. **1958** *Listener* 11 Sept. 374/2 They receive an incredibly tough kind of training, which..produces 75 per cent. completely one-pointed fanatics. **1960** J. HEWITT *Yoga* xi. 153 If the mind takes one thought and holds it, one-pointed and still, time is erased, it ceases—psychologically—to exist. **1923** *Contemp. Rev.* Feb. 223 He has an innate tendency to 'onepointedness'—as it is sometimes called—to concentration on unity. **1941** A. HUXLEY *Grey Eminence* v. 120 Complete consistency comes only with complete one-pointedness, complete absorption in ultimate reality. **1960** J. HEWITT *Yoga* ix. 135 In..another method to achieve withdrawal and onepointedness, the meditator imagines that he has a diamond in each ear, [etc.]. **1796** W. WITHERING *Brit. Plants* (ed. 3) I. 69 Monosperma, one-seeded. **1846** D. J. BROWNE *Trees Amer.* 215 *Gleditschia monosperma*, the One-seeded Gleditschia. **1964** E. J. H. CORNER *Life of Plants* xii. 208 Some normally one-seeded fruit, as acorns, avocado, palm fruits, or grass 'seed', will show considerable difference in the size of the true seed. **1821** W. WIRT *Let.* 29 Aug. in J. P. Kennedy *Mem. W. Wirt* (1849) II. 132 It is a small, red, hip-roofed, one-storied old house. **1880** GEO. ELIOT *Let.* 19 Apr. (1956) VII. 261, I prefer Muxon's one-volumed edition of Wordsworth to any selection. **1909** *Daily Chron.* 26 July 1/1 Away it went over the cliff, that monstrous one-winged bird. **1957** One-worded [see *many-worded* adj. s.v. *MANY *a.* 6 c].

e. *one-rater, -roomer.*

1896 *Rudder* VII. 245/1 Next year will see a one-rater craze; or, correctly speaking, an epidemic of 20-foot racing-length yachts. **1924** D. H. LAWRENCE *Let.* 16 May (1962) II. 789 There's a two-room cabin where Mabel can come when she likes, and a one-roomer for Brett.

33. one-bar *a.*, of an electric fire: having only one heating element; **one-base hit** *Baseball*, a hit that enables the batter to reach the first base; also *one-baser*; **one-book** *a.*, of an author: having written only one book, or only one good book; **one-catch-all** *dial.*, a children's outdoor chasing game; **one-cross** *a.*, denoting a type of tin-plate (see quot. 1890); **one-design** *a. Naut.*, designating a yacht built from a standard design, or a class of such ships which are almost identical; also *absol.* as *sb.*; hence **one-designer**, such a yacht; **one-dimensional** *a.*, having, or pertaining to, a single dimension; hence *one-dimensionality*; **one-directional** *a.*, having, or pertaining to, a single direction; **one-egg** *a.*, (*a*) characterized by a single egg; (*b*) = *MONOZYGOTIC *a.*; **one-for-one** *a.*, denoting a situation, arrangement, etc., in which one thing corresponds to, or is issued or exchanged for, each of a set of things; **one-inch** *a.*, measuring, or done at a distance of, one inch; *spec.* of a map: having a scale of one inch to the mile; also *ellipt.* as *sb.*; **one-liner** (chiefly *U.S.*), (*a*) a headline consisting of only one line of print; (*b*) a very short joke or witty remark; **one-lunger,** (*a*) a person with only one lung; (*b*) *slang*, an engine with a single cylinder; a vehicle or boat driven by such an engine; also *attrib.*; **one-man** *a.* (earlier and later examples); also in *comb.*; (*b*) loving, obedient, or attached to one man only; **one-man band,** a man who plays several musical instruments simultaneously; also *transf.* and *fig.*; **one-man show,** a show, entertainment etc., consisting of, or done by, one man only; *spec.* an exhibition of the work of one artist; **one–many** *a.*, applied to a correspondence or relation such that each member of one set is associated with or related to two or more members of a second set; **one-night** *a.*, lasting, residing, or used for a single night; **one-nighter,** (*a*) a person who stays at a place for a single night; (*b*) orig. *U.S.* = **one-night stand*; **one-night stand** [STAND *sb.*[1] 2 e] orig. *U.S.*, a single performance of a play, show, or the like at a particular place; esp. a performance given by a touring company, band, etc.; a town, theatre, etc., where such a performance or performances take place; also *transf.* and *fig.*, *spec.* a casual sexual encounter; **one-old-cat** *U.S.*, a form of baseball in which a batter runs to one base and home again, remaining as batter until the player who puts him out succeeds him; **one–one** *a.* = **one-to-one* adj. (see below); **one-one,** at Cambridge University, a degree in the first section of the first class; **one-on-one** *a.* (*U.S. slang*), designating or pertaining to a situation in which two opponents or the like come into conflict; **one-over-one** *a.*, in Bridge, denoting a bid of one in a suit, made in response to a preceding bid of one in a suit; also *ellipt.* as *sb.*; **one-piece** *a.*, made or designed in a single piece; consisting of a single piece; esp. of clothing: comprising a single garment; **one-pip** *Mil. slang* (see quot. 1919); also *one-pipper*; **one-place** *a. Logic*, of an assertion, etc., in which only one thing is postulated or involved; **one-plus-one** *a. Computers*, applied to (the use of) an instruction that contains the address of an operand and that of the next instruction to be performed; **one-pole** *a.*, (*a*) (see quot. 1892); (*b*) consisting of a single pole; (*c*) (see quot. 1940); **one-pounder,** (*a*) a gun that fires one-pound shells; (*b*) a one-pound note; **one-reeler,** a film lasting for one reel, usu. for ten minutes or less; **one-ring circus,** a small circus containing only one ring; also *transf.* and *fig.*; **one-stop** *a.* (orig. *U.S.*), denoting a shop or the like that can supply all a customer's needs within a particular range of goods or services; **one-stress** *a.*, of a line of Old English verse, having only one stress; **one-suiter** *U.S.*, a suitcase designed to hold one suit; **one-tail** *a. Statistics* = next; **one-tailed** *a. Statistics*, applied to a test that tests for deviation from the null hypothesis in one direction only; cf. **two-tailed* adj.; **one-time** *a.* (earlier and later examples); (*b*) pertaining to a single occasion; done or used only once; = *ONE-SHOT *a.*; **one time** *adv.* (*colloq.* and *dial.*), (*a*) simultaneously, at the same time; (*b*) on one occasion, once; (*c*) at once, immediately; **one-time cipher, system,** etc., a cipher in which the cipher representation of the alphabet is changed at random for each letter of the message, generating a key as long as the message; **one-time pad,** a pad of keys for a one-time cipher each page of which is destroyed after being used once, so that each message is sent using a different key; **one-to-many** *a.* = **one-many* adj. (see above); **one-to-one** *a.*, applied to a correspondence or relation such that each member of one set is associated with one member of a second set, and *vice versa*; also *adv.*, as, or by means of, a one-to-one relation; **one-track** *a.*, of a person's mind: that is concentrated on, or capable of, only one line of thought or action; obsessional; also *transf.*; **one-trip** *a.*, of a bottle or other container: that is used only once; **one-two,** (*b*) *Boxing*, two punches in quick succession with alternate hands; (*c*) *Football, Hockey*, etc., an interchange of the ball between two players; (*d*) also *transf.* and *fig.*; also *attrib.*; **one-up, one-down** *a.*, designating a house consisting of one main room upstairs and one downstairs; **one-valued** *a.*, having one value (for each component); chiefly *Math.*, = *SINGLE-VALUED *a.*; **one-while** *a.* or *adv.*, see also WHILE *sb.* 6 b in Dict. and Suppl.; **one-woman** *a.*, of, pertaining to, or by one woman only; *spec.* loving, obedient to, or attached to one woman only; **one-world** *a.*, of, pertaining to, or holding the view that there is only one world, or that the world's inhabitants are or should be united; hence *one-worlder.*

1962 L. DEIGHTON *Ipcress File* ix. 54 Dalby stood..in front of a puny one-bar electric fire. **1972** J. MCCLURE *Caterpillar Cop* 147 The gigantic fireplace..had a one-bar electric fire poised for winter in its grate. **1909** *Collier's* 5 June 11/1 The batter..would..score only a one-base hit, perhaps, instead of the home run. **1937** *Amer. Speech* XII. 244/1 *Bingle* is generic for a hit, but also indicates a one-base hit or single. **1880** *Chicago Tribune* 12 May 8/5 Clapp..was brought in by Anson's one-baser. **1949** *Los Angeles Times* 13 Mar. 25/8 Unser led off with a one-baser. **1887** *Graphic* 2 Apr. 355/1 That not uncommon literary phenomenon, the one-book man, whose endeavour to repeat a happy accident is the most imprudent thing he can do. **1890** One-book [see sense 32 in Dict.]. **1970** *Daily Tel.* 26 Sept. 8/6 The next book,..certainly a better novel than the second, enjoyed more success but the feeling began to grow that Remarque was a one-book author. **1854** One catch all [see *COWARDY *a.*]. **1876** J. BURROUGHS *Winter Sunshine* VIII. i. 210, I could not only walk upon the grass, but..play 'one catch all' with children, boys, dogs, or sheep upon it. **1898** A. B. GOMME *Traditional Games* II. 25 One Catch-all. The words 'Cowardy, cowardy custard' are repeated by children playing at this game when they advance towards the one who is selected to catch them. [**1818** S. PARKES *Let.* 20 Feb. in P. W. Flower *Hist. Trade in Tin* (1880) vii. 92 The following table will show the different sizes of tin plate which are made in Great Britain, and the marks by which each kind is known in commerce... Common No. 1 [size] 13¾ × 10..CI... Cross No. 1 13¾ × 10..XI.] **1890** *Cent. Dict.*, *One-cross*, a term applied to tin-plate..having the thickness of No. 30 Birmingham wire-gage, and having an average weight of 0·5 lb. per sheet. **1897** F. C. MOORE *How to build Home* viii. 120 He is to furnish all tin cellar heating-pipes of best (one cross) tin. **1902** *Encycl. Brit.* XXXIII. 906/2 What are called one-design, or restricted classes [of yachts] have latterly become popular. **1904** *Rudder* Nov. 609/2 A one-design boat is one of a fleet built from the same plans. **1928** *Daily Tel.* 11 Sept. 15/6 The East Coast one-design class to the number of nine, started at 10.30 a.m. to sail a course of a dozen sea miles. **1933** E. A. ROBERTSON *Ordinary Families* v. 76 My dinghy's in for the Orwell one-designs. *Ibid.*, The one-designs will be single-handed. **1949** *Sun* (Baltimore) 27 Aug. 8/8 Little Penguin Class dinghies, one of the most popular of the smaller one-design racing sailboats. **1928** *Daily Tel.* 11 Sept. 15/6 The second place on this occasion went to an Essex one-designer. **1883** One dimensional [see DIMENSIONAL *a.* 2]. **1909** W. M. URBAN *Valuation* iii. 57 All these differences are reducible to differences in intensity and duration of a one-dimensional continuum, pleasantness-unpleasantness. **1936** V. A. DEMANT

Christian Polity ix. 153 History was seen as a one-dimensional continuum. **1958** M. KENNEDY *Outlaws on Parnassus* ix. 141 Daniel..is as one-dimensional to her as Klesmer was. **1964** *Philos. Rev.* LXXIII. 497 A proposition is a linear or one-dimensional structure. **1970** G. K. WOODGATE *Elem. Atomic Struct.* ii. 19 Equation (2.50) is in the form of a one-dimensional equation of motion. **1975** *Nature* 22 May 279/2 Fairly recently however there has been a sharp switch of attention to 'one-dimensional materials' (composed of parallel long chain molecules). **1951** S. F. NADEL *Found. Social Anthropol.* v. 90 In the order of groupings we find no exactly equivalent instances of 'one-dimensionality'. **1976** *Sci. Amer.* Dec. 105/2 These purely genetic studies were followed by cytological and biochemical work showing that the one-dimensionality of linkage maps was associated with the linear arrangement of the genes along the chromosome. **1937** *Mind* XLVI. 87 There is a one-directional character to events, an irreversibility in their order. **1950** AUDEN *Enchafèd Flood* (1951) ii. 65 The determination to live in one-directional historical time rather than in cyclical natural time. **1953** N. TINBERGEN *Herring Gull's World* xvi. 132 In the one-egg phase the bird often stands a few feet away from the nest. **1959** *Listener* 29 Oct. 729/1 One-egg twins, being genetically identical, have exactly the same blood and tissue antigens. **1976** *Times* 23 Nov. 15/4 Siamese twins..are always one-egg twins. **1955** *Times* 1 July 15/1 The capital as doubled last year by the one-for-one capitalization issue. **1962** W. NOWOTTNY *Lang. Poets Use* i. 4 The equivalence is more complex than a simple one-for-one relation. **1975** *Listener* 6 Feb. 162/1 Arms are to be replaced only on a one-for-one basis. **1886** T. P. WHITE *Ordnance Survey of U.K.* vi. 102 On the one-inch map, also,..are shown the foot-paths as cross-cuts between roads. **1913** M. I. NEWBIGIN *Ordnance Survey Maps* ii. 17 The scale of the 1-inch map is too large for any rapid form of locomotion. **1929** W. E. COLLINSON *Spoken Eng.* 88 I've got a one-inch ordnance [survey]. **1948** *N.Y. Jrnl. American* (Sunday Mail ed.) 9 May 1/1 The Court packing plan was defeated by a one-inch punch. **1960** *Farmer & Stockbreeder* 1 Mar. 62/1 The one-inch-to-the-mile survey sheet of Carmarthenshire. **1974** G. MOFFAT *Corpse Road* vii. 108 'Have you got that one-inch?' he asked. Barber brought him the map. **1904** 'MARK TWAIN' in *Harper's Weekly* 2 Jan. 18/1 There were headings—one-liners and two-liners—and that was good. **1969** *Harper's Mag.* May 85/2 McCarthy had a one-liner for everyone in Washington, and the reporters who found favor were those who learned to leer and feed straight lines. **1975** *New Yorker* 19 May 23/3 Gail Parent's novel is in the form of a fat girl's jokey suicide note, full of one-liners. **1976** *Times Lit. Suppl.* 11 June 688/5 His dear cousins collapse in mirth at Berry's one-liners and monologues. **1908** S. FORD *Side-Stepping with Shorty* 90 Then me and Sadie in her bubble, towin' the busted one-lunger behind. **1911** H. QUICK *Yellowstone Nights* v. 124 The Old Man..was a one-lunger. **1943** 'T. DUDLEY-GORDON' *Coastal Command* xiii. 125 Angus, the local boatman, came alongside in his elderly 'one-lunger' motor-boat and took us ashore. **1963** BIRD & HUTTON-STOTT *Veteran Motor Car* 15 The 'Varsity' model, and a few of the old one-lungers. **1976** *Islander* (Victoria, B.C.) 11 Apr. 10/1 This engine, a one-lunger, as it was called, drove the Scud..at a speed of six knots. **1842** *Congress. Globe* 27th Congress 2 Sess. App. 812/3 Those whose clamors are so unceasing against what they are pleased to call the 'one-man power'. **1844** *Mechanics' Mag.* XLI. 370 A common road one-man carriage. **1929** D. H. LAWRENCE *Lovely Lady* (1933) 99 I'm afraid Virginia is a one-man woman. **1939** L. M. MONTGOMERY *Anne of Ingleside* xxiv. 161 There are dogs like that—one-man dogs. **1951** J. C. FENNESSY *Sonnet in Bottle* vii. i. 244 Goebbels is a one-man monkey—he doesn't like anybody but me. **1956** *Railway Mag.* May 301/2 The current practice appears to be dictated..by the economics and safety of one-man operation. **1967** *Economist* 9 Dec. 1031/2 Mr Frank Cousins is facing the Government once more—this time in an attempt to keep some thousands of unnecessary bus conductors riding around on routes that could become profitable with one-man bus operation. **1975** A. HUNTER *Gently with Love* xi. 32 Anne has been a one-man girl ever since she met Earle. **1976** *Dumfries & Galloway Standard* 25 Dec. 16/3 The way to make economies without too much cutting down of services is to..bring in one-man-operated buses. **1931** (*record-title*) The one-man band. **1938** PARTRIDGE *Dict. Slang* Suppl. 1018/2 *One-man band*, a person that takes rather too much on himself..; slightly ob., as is *l'homme orchestre* supplying the origin. **1958** *Listener* 23 Oct. 663/2 The versatility..was capitally sustained. The 'one-man band' was never 'off-beat'. **1962** *Sunday Times* (Colour Suppl.) 14 Oct. 9/1 There should also be remembered the great one-man bands of the museum world: men like Sandberg of the Stedelijk Museum in Amsterdam. **1965** *Listener* 10 June 877/1 That odd one-man-band, the three-hole pipe and tabor, which is now almost entirely confined to the border lands of France and Spain. **1974** N. BENTLEY *Inside Information* vi. 57 We're two mechanics short and the accountant's on holiday, so I'm a one-man band at the moment. **1977** *Listener* 7 Apr. 447/1 A young antiquarian ..did a one-man-band act..making lonesome horn noises with his mouth to accompany his own piano solo. **1896** G. B. SHAW *Our Theatres in Nineties* (1932) II. 287 The real objection to Cibber's version is that it is what we call a 'one man show'. **1905** *Today* 15 Mar. 211/1 One of the young artists..is now having his first 'one-man-show' in London. **1943** F. SCULLY *Rogue's Gallery* 132 He lectured on the drama at Columbia, and even took up painting in his middle age staging several one-man shows though he never had an art lesson in his life. **1955** *Ann. Reg. 1954* 373 The Beaux Arts Gallery..held..the first one-man show..of John Bratby. **1962** *Listener* 6 Sept. 358/3 Uncle Kweku..started singing 'Happy birthday' in English... It..became a one-man show. **1976** 'Z. STONE' *Modigliani Scandal* I. ii. 25 'Usher's one-man show has had it.' 'I'm afraid so..it won't harm him all that much. His talent will tell in the long run.' **1910**, etc. One-many [see *many-one* adj. s.v. *MANY *a.* 6 c]. **1945** R. G. COLLINGWOOD *Idea of Nature* I. ii. 71 The Platonic form is not a 'logical universal', and the things, in the natural world..to which it stands in a one-many relation are not instances but approximations of it. **1964** E. BACH *Introd. Transformational Gram.* iii. 35 Rules which replace a single symbol by one or more symbols (one-many rules). **1972** *Lect. R. Inst. Philos.* V. 77 Berkeley regarded the relation between the self and its ideas as a necessary one-many relation. **1900** H. LAWSON *On Track* 124 But for the one-night lodgers..I was pretty comfortable there. **1915** T. S. ELIOT *Prufrock* (1917) 9 Restless nights in one-night cheap hotels. **1943** D. GASCOYNE *Poems 1937–1942* 46 Dozens of one-night rooms. **1976** *New Yorker* 15 Nov. 56/3 A fund-raising one-night gala performance. **1923** U. L. SILBERRAD *Lett. J. Armiter* iii. 62 The people of the house follow a sort of 'sheep and goat' plan, keeping us separate; we, the maiden-lady-some-stay visitors, sit at the upper end of the table, the one-nighters at the other end. **1937** *Amer. Speech* XII. 184/2 *One nighter*, an engagement to play for a single night. **1959** H. HOBSON *Mission House Murder* iii. 22 Johnny hasn't quite become a national star yet, but he pulls in a stack of lolly doing one-nighters, mostly in the provinces. **1973** *Guardian* 28 June 15/5 Bloated, badly dressed, he was doing one-nighters with a zombie rhythm section. **1977** 'L. EGAN' *Blind Search* iv. 55 We don't get so many one-nighters like we used to. **1880** D. K. RANOUS *Diary of Daly Débutante* (1910) 189 This coming week..is to be what they call 'one-night stands'. **1883** *National Police Gaz.* (U.S.) 8 Dec. 3/3 One night stands are not going to be subject, if they can help it, to the experiments of one troupe of queer fakirs after another. **1896**, etc. [see STAND *sb.*[1] 2 e]. **1904** G. V. HOBART *Jim Hickey* i. 13 I'm too delicate for this one-night stand gag. I'm going to New York and build a theatre. **1912** WODEHOUSE *Prince & Betty* ii. 28 What's the use of a Republic in a place like this? For a little bit of a one-night stand like this you want something picturesque, something that'll advertise the place. **1916** G. B. SHAW *Let.* 14 May in *B. Shaw & Mrs. Campbell* (1952) 186, I told you not to do those one-night stands. **1937** *New Republic* 24 Nov. 70/2 The band plays a one-night stand in some town near. **1956** B. HOLIDAY *Lady sings Blues* (1973) i. 3 When he went on the road with that band it was the beginning of the end of our life as a family. Baltimore got to be just another one-night stand. **1959** 'F. NEWTON' *Jazz Scene* xi. 185 One of the worst kinds of professional life, that of the touring artist, often passing through a succession of one-night stands. **1963** A. HERON *Towards Quaker View of Sex* iii. 23 These affairs may still be very promiscuous—'one night stands'—or mainly emotional. **1972** J. WILSON *Hide & Seek* viii. 138 Nearly everyone else he knew had had at least a few casual affairs or one-night stands. **1860** *Harper's Mag.* July 195/1 Mrs. Tyler Todd caught the toss, like a skilful player at 'one old cat', on the edge of her..bonnet. **1929** *Sun* (Baltimore) 27 Mar. 10/3 Supervised play has taken the place of 'one old cat', and hockey has replaced shinney. **1949** *Chicago Daily News* 6 July 14/7 Juvenile pirates had their hang-outs and..one-old-cat and high-button-shoe football thrived. **1974** *Amer. Speech* 1971 XLVI. 84 Ball, puck, and tin-can games..one old cat baseball. **1903** B. RUSSELL *Princ. Math.* xi. 113 This requires that there should be some one–one relation whose domain is the one class and whose converse domain is the other class. **1922**, etc. One–one [see *many–many* adj. s.v. *MANY *a.* 6 c]. **1950** C. M. BOWRA *Romantic Imagination* 33 For him [*sc.* William Blake] allegory in the good sense is not the kind of 'one–one correspondence' which we find in *Pilgrim's Progress*. **1965** PATTERSON & RUTHERFORD *Elem. Abstr. Algebra* i. 3 If..f is a mapping of S_1 into S_2 such that $f(x_1) = f(x_2) \Rightarrow x_1 = x_2$, then f is called a one–one mapping or a one–one correspondence. **1972** *Lect. R. Inst. Philos.* V. 80 If there were ideas..in this sense 'simple' they would stand only in a one–one relation to minds. **1924** *Granta* 25 Apr. 361/2 Last but not least he took a 'one one' in the French Tripos last year. **1968** K. MARTIN *Editor* i. 3, I had taken a One-one in my Tripos at Magdalene. **1967** *Technology Week* 20 Feb. 3/1 In the one-on-one, relatively 'simple' intercepts run during the 1962–63 test series, the 'old' *Nike-Zeus* scored on 10 of 14 attempted live ICBM intercepts. **1972** J. GORES *Dead Skip* (1973) i. 7 He had started as a field agent..three years before, when he had realized he wasn't going to be middleweight champ of the world after all; it was the only profession he knew which could give him the same one-on-one excitement he'd found in the ring. **1974** 'E. LATHEN' *Sweet & Low* xi. 113 He was not in a one-on-one confrontation. There was a goodly array of..small fry present. **1932** D. BURNSTINE *Four Horsemen's One over One Method of Contract Bidding* i. 1 The One-Over-One system of bidding has achieved its present fame because of its use by players who have won the majority of contract tournaments. *Ibid.* 3 The One-Over-One offers leeway in arriving at the correct contract with ease. **1934** *Amer. Speech* IX. 10/1 There are..several varieties of one-over-one bids. **1959** *Listener* 19 Mar. 530/1 Many completely minimum hands..could be hamstrung by a simple one-over-one response on the first round. **1880** G. A. SALA *Amer. Revisited* (1882) II. 13 Slop-shops, or 'one-piece stores' overflowing with guernseys, pea jackets, sou'-wester hats. **1895** *Montgomery Ward Catal.* 501/2 Bathing suits. One-piece suits. **1912** *Woman's Weekly* 25 May 100/3 (*caption*) A One-Piece Dress, One-Piece Petticoat, One-Piece Drawers, and One-Piece Bodice. **1930** *Engineering* 7 Mar. 309/3 The housing and arm being also a one-piece casting. **1972** J. MOSEDALE *Football* ii. 21 The Van Buren uniform included a one-piece fiber crown replacing the sewn leather helmets of the pre-1940s. **1973** 'D. HALLIDAY' *Dolly & Starry Bird* xiv. 203 A gorgeous one-piece black bathing suit. **1974** F. WARNER *Meeting Ends* I. i. 2 Wrasse..in modern one-piece bathing costume. **1919** W. H. DOWNING *Digger Dial.* 37 *One-pip*, Second Lieutenant. **1937** PARTRIDGE *Dict. Slang* 589/1 One-pipper. **1956** D. M. DAVIN *Sullen Bell* 181 Whatever young one-pipper it was could get a night's leave. **1974** G. M. FRASER *McAuslan in Rough* 17 Keith was a mere pink-cheeked one-pipper of twenty years, whereas I had reached the grizzled maturity of twenty-one and my second star. **1938** *Jrnl. Symbolic Logic* III. 11. 83 Chapter 2 supplements the propositional calculus..with the Boolean algebra of one-place predicates. **1947** H. REICHENBACH *Elem. Symbolic Logic* § 17. 83 The term 'property'..is usually applied only to one-place situational functions. **1967** S. C. KLEENE *Math. Logic* § 27. 145 More essential use is made of the predicate calculus with quantification of one-place predicates in Example 19. **1974** *Canad. Jrnl. Linguistics* XIX. 151 But what I want to focus on here is the claim that *easy* is a one-place predicate with a sentential subject, while *eager* has a sentential object. **1959** J. W. CARR in E. M. Grabbe et al. *Handbk. Automation, Computation, & Control* II. ii. 58 In the one-plus-one addressing procedure, each instruction has a basic single-address format, but also includes a second address to be used to designate the location of the next instruction to be performed. **1969** P. B. JORDAIN *Condensed Computer Encycl.* 351 The one-plus-one address instruction has only the power (or flexibility) of a one-address instruction, because only one operand reference is included. **1892** J. A. EWING *Magn. Induction in Iron* ii. 40 We may distinguish this as the 'one-pole' method, seeing that the deflection of the magnetometer is mainly caused by one of the bar's poles. **1932** 'N. SHUTE' *Lonely Road* i. 15 From the set of her one pole mast she might have been a Thames bawley of about fifty tons. **1940** M. MILLER *Harbor of Sun* xxviii. 311 When a fisherman describes the size of a school as 'one-pole tuna', 'two-pole tuna' and sometimes 'three-pole tuna', he is but saying that the size of the tuna in that special school required one, two or three men to a team for hauling in each fish. **1845** C. M. KIRKLAND *Western Clearings* (1846) 27 Some scattered grains of coarse powder from near the touch-hole of the one-pounder that was fired all day by the opposition. **1893** 'MARK TWAIN' in *Century Mag.* Jan. 339/2 They find they've given a tramp a million-pound bill when they thought it was a one-pounder. **1916** 'B. M. BOWER' *Phantom Herd* v. 69 We've made quite a haul since you left. A bunch of one-reelers. **1976** *Listener* 23–30 Dec. 833/1 When you were making the one-reelers, did each have a lengthy script? **1922** WODEHOUSE *Clicking of Cuthbert* vi. 142 No human being could play golf against a one-ring circus like that without blowing up. **1972** *Village Voice* (N.Y.) 1 June 40/3 An opera house that is not a cultural force is only a one-ring circus made up of vocal acrobats who use music as a trampoline. **1934** *Amer. Speech* IX. 112/2 Plenty of one-stop service stations for washing, minor repairs, lubrication, etc. **1962** *Economist* 5 May 452/1 Commercial banks which are able to offer complete 'one stop' banking service—including current accounts, consumer loans and so on. **1971** *E. Afr. Jrnl.* Mar. 34 (Advt.), You will find Text Book Centre a one-stop warehouse for all your educational requirements. **1978** *Oxford Consumer* Mar. 5/1 The store will specialise in the provision of food lines at economic prices and will be backed up by a sufficient range of household goods to enable the shopping public to derive the maximum convenience from a 'one stop' shopping trip. **1958** A. J. BLISS *Metre of Beowulf* 62 We must, in fact, recognize the possibility of one-stress verses. Sievers himself in later life envisaged such one-stress verses; Pope, too, makes one-stress verses a mainstay of his new theory. **1965** *Eng. Stud.* XLVI. 419 As examples of light, one-stress verses he gives: hu ða æðelingas. **1961** WEBSTER, One-suiter. **1971** 'O. BLEECK' *Thief who painted Sunlight* (1972) xx. 181 He was carrying something that looked like a one-suiter. **1947** C. EISENHART et al. *Sel. Techniques Statistical Anal.* 459/2 (Index), One-sided or one-tail tests of statistical hypotheses. **1954** *Brit. Jrnl. Psychol.* XLV. 174 The difference between these means is..only just significant at the 5% level, using the one-tail test. **1950** M. H. QUENOUILLE *Introd. Statistics* v. 98 Here, since we are interested in deviations in one direction only, probabilities calculated using χ^2 must be halved. We are then said to be using a one-tailed test. **1969** R. H. KOLSTOE *Introd. Statistics Behav. Sci.* x. 203 In a few situations the research worker, *before collecting his data*, decides that he is interested in one specific directional hypothesis... In this case a one-tailed test of significance would be indicated. **1971** B. ERRICKER *Advanced Gen. Statistics* xiv. 206 If we were only interested in whether the tensile strengths of the components of the first manufacturer are greater than those from the second we would only need a one-tailed test. **1850** W. HOWITT *Year-bk. Country* vi. 179 Old Lodge, we salute thee for thy venerable antiquity; but we owe thee no respect as the one-time resort of the boasted virgin queen! **1870** *Appleton's Jrnl.* 5 Feb. 161/2 Then you would have one brought after the other, unless accompanied by the request, 'all at the same time', or, in their [*sc.* native Liberians'] own language, '*go fetch 'em come; both two; one time*'! **1873** C. J. G. RAMPINI *Lett. from Jamaica* 177 Man can't smoke an' whistle one time. **1886** F. T. ELWORTHY *West Somerset Word-bk.* 537 There used to be a public-house there one time, but he bin pulled down 'is gurt many years. **1899** C. J. C. HYNE *Further Adventures Capt. Kettle* ii. 31 He wouldn't stop for fighting-palaver. He'd be off for bush, one-time. **1924** *Time* 7 Jan. 30/2 Died. Richard Wittig, brother of Maximillian Harden, famed German publicist, onetime friend of the Kaiser, onetime Oberburgomaster of Posen. **1928** *Flynn's Weekly* 4 Feb. 436/1 Big Bill Douglas was enjoying a year's vacation from his usual haunts up at Sing Sing at the expense of the State. To his underworld associates he was doing a short bit in the Big House, or a one time loser. **1942** Z. N. HURSTON in A. Dundes *Mother Wit* (1973) 225/2 A Zigaboo..asked a woman that one time. **1950** 'S. RANSOME' *Deadly Miss Ashley* viii. 96 Duncan Westling's onetime confidential secretary was now the secretary of Duncan Westling's onetime mistress? **1959** *Listener* 10 Dec. 1023/1 The Soviet Union has lately placed some big orders with British industry... But we have a feeling that these are, or may be, one-time orders to enable the Soviet Union to progress towards self-sufficiency. **1967** *Ibid.* 2 Feb. 157/1 S. W. Johnson-Marshall, one-time chief architect at the Ministry of Education. **1973** *N.Y. Law Jrnl.* 27 Mar. 4/5 The tenant insisted that the only increase he was obliged to pay was a one-time increase. **1955** *Gloss. Soviet Military Terminol.* (U.S. Army Technical Manual 30–544) 228/1 One-time system. **1977** *Sci. Amer.* Aug. 120/3 It is easy to see why the one-time cipher is uncrackable even in principle. Since each symbol can be represented by any other symbol, and each choice of representation is completely random, there is no internal pattern. **1953** *N.Y. Times Mag.* 15 Mar. 62/2 The Russians are notorious for their reliance on a device known as the 'one-time-pad'. This means..that each message is sent in a completely different code. **1966** M. R. D. FOOT *SOE in France* iv. 105 By now [*sc.* 1944] the British were using a much safer..

cipher: one-time pad... The agent held a pad of silk slips, each printed with columns of random letters or figures from which any message could be enciphered or deciphered; he..was supposed to tear each slip off and burn it after use. **1977** *Sci. Amer.* Aug. 120/3 If the one-time pad provides absolute secrecy, why is it not used for all secret communication? The answer is that it is too impractical. Each time it is employed a key must be sent in advance, and the key must be at least as long as the anticipated message. **1959** One-to-many [see *CORRESPONDENCE 1 b]. **1976** P. R. WHITE *Planning for Public Transport* v. 112 In a one-to-many situation, passengers joining at the fixed point(s) request the driver to serve a destination, and no radio contact is necessary. **1873** *Proc. Lond. Math. Soc.* IV. 252 The equations..being supposed to establish a 'one-to-one' correspondence between the two integral spaces. **1882**, etc. One-to-one [see *CORRESPONDENCE 1 b]. **1903** B. RUSSELL *Princ. Math.* xi. 113 Two classes have the same number.. when their terms can be correlated one to one, so that any one term of either corresponds to one and one only term of the other. **1931** C. FOX *Mind & its Body* iii. 62 One of the most important assumptions of psychological physiology was this one-to-one correspondence between neural processes and mental processes. **1936** J. R. KANTOR *Objective Psychol. Gram.* xvii. 237 There is no clear-cut one-to-one relation between a grammatical form and a definite time point. **1963** J. LYONS *Structural Semantics* iii. 37 It is not so much that one language draws a greater or less number of semantic distinctions than another which prevents the matching of their vocabularies one-to-one. **1968** C. G. KUPER *Introd. Theory Superconductivity* xii. 193 There is a one-to-one correspondence between the states of a gas of non-interacting Bosons and those of a family of harmonic oscillators. **1973** One-to-one [see *NICOTINIC *a.* 2]. **1928** D. H. LAWRENCE *Lady Chatterley* xix. 363 They're all one-track minds nowadays. **1932** *Kansas City* (Missouri) *Times* 5 May 20 The persons with the one-track mind are the ones who usually have the most collisions. **1934** H. NICOLSON *Curzon: Last Phase* 18 He has been accused of possessing a 'one-track mind', of being deficient in creative, as opposed to emotional, imagination. **1935** B. MALINOWSKI in M. Black *Importance of Lang.* (1962) 78 The advertisements emanating from such one-track remedies. **1944** 'BRAHMS' & 'SIMON' *Titania has Mother* viii. 68 Her son..had launched himself onto a one-track conversation. **1957** P. FRANK *Seven Days to Never* ii. 48 The electronic machines..could distract a Russian missile's one-track mind. **1968** *National Observer* (U.S.) 3 June 15/1 It's not that I'm antisocial. It's just that I'm preoccupied. I have a very one-track mind. **1973** 'H. HOWARD' *Highway to Murder* vii. 77 I've got a one-track mind... All this started with a man getting shot and I keep thinking along those lines. **1967** *Times Rev. Industry* May 72/2 Most containers are 'one-trip' in the sense that the product is used and the container is thrown away. **1811** *Sporting Mag.* XXXVIII. 140/2 He..had no difficulty at getting at his man when he chose with a *one, two.* **1815** *Pancratia* (ed. 2) 359 He fought cautiously..and whenever he closed put in his *one two* with the greatest dexterity. **1910** G. W. E. RUSSELL *Sketches & Snapshots* xlvii. 445 A smart one-two on his smeller effectually tapped his claret. **1931** *Times Lit. Suppl.* 22 Oct. 819/1 The flawless stance and one-two punch of Peter Jackson. **1948** *Economist* 20 Mar. 454/1 His [*sc.* Stalin's] one-two play in Czechoslovakia and Finland. **1952** A. WILSON *Hemlock & After* III. i. 201 Even Ron was surprised that his 'old one two' was quite so compelling. **1960** *Times* 4 Oct. 13/4 'The old one-two', in the boxing slang of a more vulgarly robust age, indicated a quick follow-up with the right immediately after the left had landed, and the near synchronization of the two blows added immensely to their effect. **1970** *Times* 1 Oct. 10/3 Hinton came up from his position of centre back to play a one-two with Hutchinson and leave the wretched Christidis stranded. **1974** J. GARDNER *Corner Men* xi. 100 Let Hart and Harvey work them over, then we can go in and do the old routine... The old one two. **1978** *Sunday Times* (Colour Suppl.) 28 May 34/4 *One-two*, using a colleague for an immediate return pass, to run on to. **1933** A. SALTER in A. F. Brockway *Bermondsey Story* (1949) ii. 12 The house was one up, one down, with a small scullery. **1968** BUSBY & HOLTHAM *Main Line Kill* vi. 68 Some of the back to back terraces of poky little one-up, one-down houses had been pulled down. **1898** W. B. SMITH *Infinitesimal Analysis* i. 7 When to one value of the one variable there corresponds only one value of the other, this latter is called a one-valued or unique function of the former. **1913** *Trans. Amer. Math. Soc.* XIV. 481 None of the equivalent postulate-sets here referred to is in terms of its undefined entities one-valued ('categorical')—that is, each determines not a single algebra but a class of algebras. **1943** *Amer. Speech* XVIII. 220 The first stage of human development ..is that of the savage, prelogical mentality, with a one-valued semantics (or system of evaluations), in which, as Lucien Lévy-Bruhl has said, 'everything is everything else' by 'mystic participation'. **1968** E. T. COPSON *Metric Spaces* vii. 85 A function is, by definition, one-valued. **1894** HALL CAINE *Manxman* I. ix. 45 I'm a one-woman man, Kate; but loving one is giving me eyes for all. **1937** M. HILLIS *Orchids on your Budget* (1938) iv. 68 We ourselves have run our one-woman ménage both with and without an office job. **1960** P. TOMPKINS in G. B. Shaw *To a Young Actress* 151 Thirty-five paintings for a one-woman exhibition at the Leicester Galleries. **1962** I. MURDOCH *Unofficial Rose* ii. 32 He's a one-woman cat. **1974** J. CLEARY *Peter's Pence* v. 156 I'm a one-woman man. **1926** A. E. TAYLOR *Plato* viii. 198 The epiphenomenalist is tied by his theory to a 'one-world' interpretation of human experience; morality presupposes a 'two-world' interpretation. **1947** *Collier's* 7 June 12 (*title*) Dunkirk—the one-world town. **1948** *Sun* (Baltimore) 22 June 2/1 His selection of Stassen for Taft's running mate was new and was surprising, in view of his oft-repeated denunciation of Stassen as a 'one-worlder' who would be unsafe in high office. **1958** *Spectator* 15 Aug. 228/2 'Men live and die for a flag; it is indeed the only thing for which they are willing to die in masses..' is a statement of a truth which one-worlders ignore at their peril. **1965** *Social Crediter* 31 July 2/2 The *active* Socialists, Communists, and One-Worlders.

one, *v.* **1.** (Later example.)

1921 B. WILLIAMSON *Supernat. Mysticism* v. 45 The human race was so oned with Adam that all sinned in him.

one-act, *a.* [ONE *numeral a.* 32 a.] Denoting a short play or other production consisting of a single act. Hence as *sb.*, such a play. So **one-a·cter**, a one-act play; also *fig.*

1888 *Playgoers' Mag.* Feb. 45 The story of Carton's self-sacrifice would form a touching little one-act play. **1895** One-acter [in Dict. s.v. ONE *a.* 32]. **1905** *Athenæum* 7 Oct. 477/3 The one-act trifle which serves as *lever de rideau.* **1912** E. NESBIT *Let.* in D. L. Moore *E. Nesbit* (1933) xv. 269, I have had a one-act play accepted by a London manager. **1927** J. POLLOCK (*title*) Twelve one-acters. **1940** G. MARX *Let.* 5 Sept. (1967) 25 El Capitan..has done magnificently with the Coward one-acts. **1960** A. COREN in *Introduction: Stories by New Writers* 70 The sane guy is the one who realises that life is a short one-acter. **1967** *Oxf. Compan. Theatre* (ed. 3) 223/2 The one-act play survives mainly in the productions of the amateur theatre in England and America. **1967** *Wall St. Jrnl.* 24 Apr. 18/4 The play for the evening was Lanford Wilson's 'The Madness of Lady Bright', a 45-minute one-acter. **1973** *Guardian* 23 Mar. 12/3 Tchaikovsky's seventh and last opera is a one-acter. **1976** *Scottish Rev.* Spring 17 *The Stick-Up*, a one-acter from *Fifteen Poems and a Play* (Edinburgh, 1969). **1977** L. MEYNELL *Hooky gets Wooden Spoon* xiii. 157 She had written a one-act play for herself.

one argument. *Logic.* [f. ONE *numeral a.* + ARGUMENT *sb.* 3.] The variable of a function or operator of only one variable; also *attrib.*

1941 O. HELMER tr. *Tarski's Introd. Logic* 107 In order to differentiate between two-termed and three-termed functional relations, we speak, in the first case, of functions of one variable or of functions with one argument. **1951** J. ŁUKASIEWICZ in *Proc. R. Irish Acad.* LIV. A. 27 Such values are not only constant functors of one propositional argument, as *N*, negation, for example, but also complex expressions like a functor of one argument. **1955** H. LEBLANC *Introd. Deductive Logic* 191 We have studied..so-called one-argument functions like the functions square of, double of, and so on. **1957** A. N. PRIOR *Time & Modality* 2 A system must contain a pair of one-argument operators forming statements out of statements. **1965** HUGHES & LONDEY *Elem. Formal Logic* iii. 19 The following are *monadic operators*, (i.e. they take one argument). **1967** H. WEBER tr. J. Łukasiewicz in S. McCall *Polish Logic* iii. 47 Since this proposition is valid for all functors with one argument, it is also valid for the functor '*M*'.

one-arm (wɒ·n,ɑːm), *a.* [ONE *numeral a.* 32 a.] Having one arm; using only one arm; *spec.* **one-arm bandit** (orig. *U.S.*) = **one-armed bandit*; **one-arm joint** or **lunch** (**room**) *U.S.*, a cheap eating-house where customers sit in seats which have one arm wide enough to support plates of food, etc.; also *ellipt.* as *one-arm* sb.

1906 *Westm. Gaz.* 7 Sept. 3/2 Ordinarily I can do a one-arm press of 90 lb., but I must confess that I was almost beaten in getting hoisted some of these sheaves. **1912** M. NICHOLSON *Hoosier Chron.* 297 Everybody's saying 'Stop, Look, Listen!'..the white aprons in the one-arm lunch rooms say it now when you kick on the size of the buns. **1915** *N.Y. World Mag.* 9 May 14 *One arm joint*, a chair dairy lunch. **1926** *New Masses* May 9/4 Countermen in the one-arm lunches yell '*coffee-and*' not so fiercely. **1931** H. MUTSCHMANN *Gloss. Americanisms* 43/2 *One-arm driver*, man steering auto with one arm and necking his girl with the other. **1935** J. HARGAN *Gloss. Prison Lang.* 6 *One arm joint*, a cheap restaurant where one takes his food to a chair to eat. **1938** *Sun* (Baltimore) 6 Oct. 24/1 The Court of Appeals at Annapolis yesterday declared.. that the so-called 'one-arm bandit' type of slot machine is illegal. **1939** *Detective Fiction Weekly* 18 Feb. 36/2 A one-arm joint is a white-tiled place that suggests a clinic. Two long rows of armchairs line the walls. The right arm of each chair is expanded into china-topped slab. You park your food on it. **1940** J. O'HARA *Pal Joey* 57 She went with me to this one-arm where I eat. **1943** *Sun* (Baltimore) 27 Jan. 5/6 Three of the [slot] machines were described by police as the 'one-arm bandit' type. **1944** B. HOPE *I Never left Home* v. 63 He flew a plane back from a mission once holding his wounded copilot in his arms. That's one-arm driving that counts. **1951** E. KEFAUVER *Crime in Amer.* (1952) xiii. 151 The iniquitous 'one-arm bandit' slot machines sprang up in bars and cigar stores. **1956** S. HOPE *Diggers' Paradise* 156 In the exclusive clubs, with few exceptions, you may see an array of 'one-arm bandits' ranged against the walls. There fruit machines—or poker machines—are usually rigged to work with shilling discs bought from the bar steward. **1960** *Times* 2 Dec. 8/4 Six fruit machines, or 'one-arm bandits', were on display at Scotland Yard.

one-armed (wɒ·n,ɑːmd), *a.* [ONE *numeral a.* 32 d.] Having one arm; also *transf.*; *spec.* **one-armed bandit** (orig. *U.S.*) = *fruit machine* (see *FRUIT *sb.* 9).

1809 *Thespiad* 10 Every subsequent comedy would have contained a weather-beaten, one-armed sailor. **1818**, etc. [see ONE 32 d]. **1886** F. T. ELWORTHY *West Somerset Word-Bk.* 536 *One-arm'd landlord*, cant name for a pump. **1914** W. B. YEATS *Responsibilities* 26 A one-legged, one-armed, one-eyed man. **1938** *Time* 28 Feb. 33/1 Last fortnight, with her ax she demolished two more—as she called them—'one-armed bandits'. **1945** BAKER *Austral. Lang.* iv. 88 *Ned Kelly* is displacing *one-armed bandit* for a poker machine. **1948** *Richmond* (Virginia) *Times-Dispatch* 8 Apr. 5/1 He was convicted of a charge of having two slot machines, familiarly known as 'one-armed bandits', in his possession. **1959** *Times* 12 Feb. 10/7 To-day the Senators were ringed with juke-boxes, pinball tables, 'one-armed bandits', and other coin-operated devices. **1971** P. TOYNBEE *Working Life* iv. 60 You slip your card into the slot and pull down the lever which punches the time on it. 'Talk about a one-armed bandit', someone jokes... 'Trouble is, it's never been known to pay out.' **1972** D. FRANCIS *Smokescreen* vi. 70 There's more cars parked along the streets down there than one-armed bandits in Nevada.

one-berry. Add: **b.** *U.S.* = CHECKERBERRY, *Indian turnip* s.v. INDIAN *a.* 4 b, WINTERGREEN.

1877 BARTLETT *Dict. Amer.* (ed. 4) 319 Jack-in-the-Pulpit. (*Arisæna triphyllum*)... In Connecticut, it is called One-berry. **1892** *Jrnl. Amer. Folk-Lore* V. 100 *Gaultheria procumbens*, one-berry. **1931** M. GRIEVE *Mod. Herbal* II. 766 *Mitchella repens*... Partridgeberry, Checkerberry, Winter Clover, Deerberry, One-berry.

one-er, var. ONER *sb.*

one-eyed, *a.* Add: † **b.** *U.S. slang.* Dishonest. *Obs.*

1833 *Sk. & Eccentr. D. Crockett* i. 24 In the slang of the backwoods, one swore that he would never be '*one-eyed*'.

2. As a general term of disapproval or contempt: small, inferior, inadequate, unimportant; = ONE-HORSE *a.* 2, esp. of a town. *colloq.* (orig. *U.S.* or *dial.*).

1871 D. G. ROSSETTI *Let.* 28 Oct. (1967) III. 1021 A little hamlet called Kelmscott, the nearest town to which is Lechlade,—that being however but a 'one-eyed' town as the Yankees say. **1881** HARDY *Laodicean* III. 246, I shouldn't care for such a one-eyed benefit as that. **1887** PARISH & SHAW *Dict. Kentish Dial.* 111 'That's a middlin' one-eyed place.' 'I can't make nothin' of these here one-eyed new-fashioned tunes they've took-to in church; why they've a'most done afore I can make a start.' **1937** G. HEYER *They found him Dead* i. 19, I wasn't born to this humdrum life in a one-eyed town. **1947** *E. Afr. Ann. 1946–7* 101/2 Some had said it was a grand little town; others, a one-eyed hole! **1977** *Times* 14 May 8/7 In its somewhat one-eyed way, it [*sc.* Tobago] is among the loveliest..of all the Caribbean islands.

b. Narrow in outlook; prejudiced, narrow-minded. Hence *one-eyedness.*

1863 J. BROWN *Let.* Mar. (1912) 206, I do believe the man thinks he is doing God service and is honest in his way, though vain and one-eyed to ludicrosity, as you have most thoroughly and delightfully shown. **1874** SWINBURNE *Let.* July (1959) II. 302 With all his rhetorical power, he [*sc.* J. A. Froude] seems to me (even apart from his one-eyed prepossession and palpable special pleading) but a shallow reader of character. **1921** G. B. SHAW *Back to Methuselah* p. li, There is no reason to suspect Weismann of Sadism... It was a mere piece of one-eyedness; and it was Darwin who put out Weismann's humane and sensible eye. **1971** *Austral. Seacraft* June 4/2 It seems your correspondent is one-eyed so far as the southern part of Australia is concerned.

one-handed, *a.* Add: **B.** as *adv.* Using only one hand.

1962 J. D. MACDONALD *Girl* ix. 113 You can do it okay one-handed, just push down with your thumb. **1963** *Times* 12 June 5/2 He was caught at long on, finishing his stroke one-handed. **1974** R. ADAMS *Shardik* v. 43 He crouched upon his knees, fumbling one-handed along the undulating tree-trunk. **1975** J. MITCHELL *Smear Job* v. 37 Lonely drank one-handed.

Hence **one-ha·ndedly** *adv.*, with one hand; **one-ha·ndedness**, the state of being one-handed; (by back-formation) **one-ha·nd** *v. trans.*

1972 J. ROSSITER *Rope for General Dietz* xiii. 185, I lit a cigarette one-handedly. **1973** R. STOUT *Please pass Guilt* (1974) iv. 32 Jones stretched an arm and one-handed it [*sc.* the ball], and kept it. **1975** *Times* 12 Feb. 4/3 In spite of her one-handedness, [she] had followed hobbies of gardening, paper hanging, tennis. **1977** S. COULTER *Soyuz Affair* i. 9 He..onehandedly fingered a cigarette out of the packet.

one-horse, *a.* **2.** For *U.S. colloq.* read *colloq.* (orig. *U.S.*). Esp. *one-horse town*, a small or rural town; a town where nothing important or exciting happens. (Add further examples.)

1853 *Oregonian* (Portland) 19 Nov. 2/1 These *one-horse* meetings are got up by men whose capital consists in *brass.* **1855** *Knickerbocker* XLVI. 106 'In this "one-horse town",' writes a Mobile friend, 'as our New-Orleans neighbors designate it, [etc.].' **1884** *Liverpool Daily Post* 15 Oct. 5/1 The first thing it is to do is to take possession of that 'one-horsiest' of railways, from the Dock Cottages to West Kirby, and to make it into a channel of communication fit for civilised men. **1933** P. FLEMING *Brazilian Adventure* III. x. 378 Doctor Amyntas was the big noise; in this one horse town he might be said to own the horse. **1940** L. A. G. STRONG *Sun on Water* 161, I was sick with I don't know what early summer passion in that one-horse store. **1969** L. KENNEDY *Very Lovely People* i. 73 Their names were Homer and Arnold and they worked in a one-horse garage down a side street in Botafogo. **1973** 'D. JORDAN' *Nile Green* viii. 39, I said, 'It's a one-horse town.' **1977** *Zigzag* June 23/2 I've a new song..about a girl of sixteen trying to get out of a one horse town.

Oneida (onəi·dă). *N. Amer.* [ad. Oneida *onẽnyoteˀ* erected stone (the name of the main Oneida settlement at successive locations, near which, traditionally, a large syenite boulder always appeared).] One of the five (later six) tribes of the Iroquois Confederacy of North American Indians commonly called the Five Nations (Six Nations), originally inhabiting upper New York state; a member of this tribe; their language. Also *attrib.*

1666 J. ALLYN *Let.* 10 July in *Mass. Hist. Soc. Coll.* (1849) 3rd Ser. X. 63 Hereof the Mohawkes and the Oneiades have given assured notice. **1722** S. SEWALL *Diary* 19 Oct. in *Ibid.* (1882) 5th Ser. VII. 311 The Messenger of the Oneidas was buried in the South Burying place. **1760** in J. W. Lydekker *Faithful Mohawks* (1938) 102 Genl Amherst being at the Oneida Lake on the preceeding Sunday went up as far as the Oneida town. **1823, 1933** [see *CAYUGA]. **1959** [see *Five Nations* s.v. *FIVE *a.* and *sb.* C. 2]. **1965** *Canad. Jrnl. Linguistics* X. 105 The structure of Pawnee as compared with Oneida. **1969** *Observer* (Colour Suppl.) 25 May 53/3 West of them were the extraordinarily fierce Oneida. **1973** A. H. WHITEFORD *N. Amer. Indian Arts* 148 Lakes area silverwork probably began when the Oneida, an Iroquois tribe, moved to northeast Wisconsin.

one-ideaed, -idea'd, *a.* Also **one-idead.** Add: (Earlier example.) So **one-idea** *a.* Hence **one-idea(d)ness,** the fact or quality of being one-ideaed.

1842 *Lancet* 12 Mar. 830 The dead superstitions, and one-idead theories, of the middle ages. **1852** *Blackw. Mag.* Aug. 261/2 His absorbed one-ideadness. **1862** M. B. CHESNUT *Diary* 13 Mar. (1949) 199 He is a one-idea man. That idea is to get every possible man into the ranks. **1920** H. BEGBIE *Life W. Booth* I. xxii. 365 It was..this intense singleness of view, this consuming one-ideaness of soul, which made William Booth so successful. **1934** E. BOWEN *Cat Jumps* 252 She..was in fact a rather one-idea girl.

oneing (wʊ·niŋ), *vbl. sb.* Also **one-ing.** [f. ONE *v.* + -ING[1].] Union; fusion. Also *attrib.* or as *ppl. a.*

1919 D. H. LAWRENCE in *Eng. Rev.* June 488 There in the sexual passion the very blood surges into communion, in the terrible sensual oneing. **1921** B. WILLIAMSON *Supernat. Mysticism* vii. 68 Sanctity is the oneing of the soul with God. **1934** *Blackfriars* Mar. 184 Mother Julian..saw it [*sc.* pain] first and foremost as the blessed instrument of our one-ing with Christ. **1958** C. PEPLER *Eng. Relig. Heritage* IV. i. 224 In *The Cloud* the question of Christ's passion restoring all men to the oneing affection with God lost by Adam makes no reference to his sacrifice. *The Epistle*, on the other hand, speaks of this 'oneing' in terms of a continual offering of the sacrifice of a man's whole being.

oneiric, *a.* Delete *rare*⁻¹ and add further examples.

1953 *Scrutiny* XIX. 151 Their..dictation of the unconscious, oneiric delirium,..may be fragmentary..but they bear witness..to their determination to make all possible aspects of poetry incentives to life. **1963** T. PYNCHON *V.* xi. 335 The green light deepened, drowning the island of Malta and the island of Fausto and Elena hopelessly deeper in its oneiric chill. **1974** *Monthly Film Bull.* (Brit. Film Inst.) Apr. 84/2 Even though his film's philosophical focus may occasionally seem blurred, the images themselves..retain throughout a haunting and oneiric quality.

oneiro-. Add: **oneirocrisy,** delete † and add later example; **oneiromancer** (later example); **oneiromancy** (later examples).

1976 *Proc. Classical Assoc.* LXXIII. 20 Intellectual constructions such as onirocrisy and physiognomony readily degenerate into the collection of *paradoxa*, upon which the temperament of the age commonly puts a religious interpretation. **1952** G. SARTON *Hist. Sci.* I. xiv. 371 There are two kinds of dreams, those of divine origin, which concern oneiromancers, and those of physiologic origin. **1931** E. JONES *On the Nightmare* II. iii. 95 This cure for disease by Incubation—known as oneiromancy—was practised in Scotland and Ireland... Here the person slept in the skin of a sacrificed sheep, just as the worshippers of Ammon did in Thebes. **1935** J. S. LINCOLN *Dream in Primitive Cultures* I. 3 At Nineveh was a collection of books on oneiromancy or dream interpretation.

one-legged, *a.* **1.** (Earlier example.)

1872 V. LUSH *Jrnl.* 6 Nov. (1975) 130 In the evening Martin took Annette to the Theatre Royal to see Donato the one-legged dancer and Zuila perform on the trapeze, &c.

one-pi·pe, *a.* [f. ONE *numeral a.* + PIPE *sb.*[1]] **a.** Applied to a system of hot-water central heating in which radiators take water from and return it to the same pipe, which runs in a complete circuit from the boiler and back to it again.

1897 F. DYE *Hood's Pract. Treat. Warming Buildings* (ed. 3) xix. 352 It is not usual for the one-pipe system to extend to three floors above the boiler without modification. **1970** J. J. BARTON *Domestic Heating* viii. 127 Two basic circuits, the 'one-pipe' and the 'two-pipe' circuit.. are commonly used in small bore heating practice.

b. Applied to a system of plumbing in which waste from sinks and the like is conveyed to the sewer by the same pipe as that from water-closets and urinals.

1910 W. P. GERHARD *Water Supply, Sewerage & Plumbing* iii. 187, I am..convinced that the one-pipe system, as I have sometimes called it, is the coming system. **1933** *Archit. Rev.* LXXIV. 54/3 The drainage and sanitary installation throughout is on the one-pipe system. **1972** T. A. TOMPSON *Guide Sanitary Engin. Services* vii. 228 Repetitive planning at each floor level of a multi-storey building favours localised application of single-stack principles of sanitation... This has led to the development of the modified one-pipe system., achieving even greater economy than with the one-pipe system.

oner, *sb.* Add: **2.** (Further examples.) *spec.* One pound; one hundred pounds.

1950 *Austral. Police Jrnl.* Apr. 116 *One-r*, £1. **1962** PARKER & ALLERTON *Courage of his Convictions* IV. i. 154 A one-er for the Guv'nor, and fifty each for me and George here, that's cut price. Two hundred all told, how's that? **1969** I. & P. OPIE *Children's Games* vii. 229 When one conker breaks another into pieces so that nothing remains on the string, the winning conker becomes a 'one-er'. *Ibid.* viii. 251 He may shout a number like 'a oner', this means that the rest of the team have to jump over the person's back from the line, taking only one step. **1970** G. F. NEWMAN *Sir, You Bastard* viii. 225 Worth a oner to you. **1974** H. R. F. KEATING *Underside* xxii. 218 You'd pay me five sovereign?.. Five golden oners?

onery, onnery, o'n'ry, varr. *ORNERY *a.*

1849 J. J. HOOPER *Night at Ugly Man's* in *Spirit of Times* 24 Nov. 471/2 We had an old one-horned cow, mighty onnery (ordinary) lookin'. **1860** M. J. HOLMES *Maude* v. 63 She pronounced her 'not quite so *onery* a white woman as she at first took her to be.' **1887** E. CUSTER *Tenting on Plains* ix. 286 He's a good enough fellow, only he's an onery scamp of a Republican. **1905** *Dialect Notes* III. 63 The *onriest* critter. **1913** H. KEPHART *Our Southern Highlanders* viii. 169 'What sort of men are they?' 'Torn down scoundrels, every one.' 'Oh, come now!' 'Yes, they are; plumb onery.' **1939** *Nat. Geogr. Mag.* Aug. 144/1 Wild sweet williams in the wood lot were much more alluring than the 'o'n'ry' weeds. **1943** *Pocahontas Times* (Marlinton, W. Va.) 4 Mar. 2/1 That onery cuss of a jay bird. **1962** W. STEGNER *Wolf Willow* III. i. 135 No Canadian steer would ever be angry or stubborn; he would be o'nery or ringy or on the prod.

one-shot, *a.* and *sb.* [ONE *numeral a.* 32 a.] **A.** *adj.* Achieved or done with a single shot, stroke, attempt, etc.; consisting of a single shot or try; occurring, performed, produced, used, etc., only once; single, isolated.

1907 *Westm. Gaz.* 28 Mar. 9/1 The one-shot hole..gives good play its just reward... A hole which can just, and only just, be reached from the tee by a fine driver is, therefore, an excellent hole. **1927** *Sunday Pictorial* 28 Aug. 8/4 This includes such up-to-date owner-driver features as..one-shot oiling for all other chassis points. **1948** *Sun* (Baltimore) 31 May 8/2 For this he asked a force in being fully equipped and trained. He called this 'a stop-gap, one-shot army, a plug in the dike until we rallied sufficient and effective reserves'. **1950** *N.Y. Times* 28 Dec. 3/6 A 'one-shot' insecticide system that operates when the pilot pushes a button. **1953** POHL & KORNBLUTH *Space Merchants* (1955) ii. 16 Fowler Schocken was too big for one-shot accounts. What we wanted was the year-after-year reliability of a major industrial complex. **1954** K. W. GATLAND *Devel. Guided Missile* (ed. 2) 29 The latter method is of chief interest for 'one-shot' rockets as the target plate burns away during running unless low specific impulse propellants are used. **1959** E. FENWICK *Long Way Down* xx. 155 It was hard to get anybody for a one-shot cleaning job. **1962** A. NISBETT *Technique Sound Studio* ii. 43 A 'one-shot' technique was used, i.e. the whole programme was taken as a continuous sequence. *Ibid.* xiii. 232 It is essential that the basic 'message' of a piece should be understood in a single hearing—for sound is basically a 'one-shot' medium. **1966** *Listener* 18 Aug. 234/1 Not enough one-shot original plays are presented on television. **1968** M. WOODHOUSE *Rock Baby* xvii. 163 If it had been a one-shot thing, we might have been able to do it that way... But we couldn't afford any sort of mistake. **1972** D. E. WESTLAKE *Cops & Robbers* (1973) xvi. 251 We were pitting our one-shot plan against a normal company's normal routine. **1978** *Guardian Weekly* 7 May 15/4 Copper produces 90 per cent of Zambia's foreign exchange, and the percentage is also high for the other producing countries that have what some economists call 'one-shot economies'.

B. *sb.* An event, transaction, process, etc., that occurs only once; something that is used or intended for use only once; *esp.* a single appearance by a performer, production of a play, etc.; a story or article that has no sequel. Also *one-shotter*. orig. *U.S.*

1937 *Printers' Ink Monthly* May 40/1 *One shot*, a single program which is not one of a series. **1942** H. HAYCRAFT *Murder for Pleasure* xi. 267 Some..magazine editors have been experimenting with novelette-length condensations ('one-shots' as they are called in the trade). **1943** *Sat. Even. Post* 20 Nov. 28/3 A one shot..is usually a charity event sponsored by a political or social organization with no professional knowledge of selling tickets. **1947** *Jrnl. Brit. Interplanetary Soc.* VI. 113 The application for which a motor is designed also has a profound effect on its design. The major variables are, magnitude and duration of thrust; fixed or variable thrust; whether for repeated use or a 'one-shot', and in the former case its total operating life. **1967** A. ARENT *Gravedigger's Funeral* (1968) iv. 44 What was it going to be? A brush-off? A friendly hint that this was just a one-shotter? **1967** WODEHOUSE *Company for Henry* ix. 172 He..has actually sold it [*sc.* the book] as what he calls a one-shotter to a magazine. **1972** M. J. BOSSE *Incident at Naha* iii. 137 'But you'd give her *my* money?' 'Sure, because you're a one-shot. I'd never have any peace if the bread came from me.'

one-sided, *a.* **2. b.** (Earlier and later examples.)

1813 H. MUHLENBERG *Catal. Plantarum Americæ Septentrionalis* 49 One-sided Hawthorn. **1832** J. LINDLEY *Introd. Bot.* IV. 413 One-sided..; having all the parts by twists in their stalks turned one way; as the flowers of Antholyza. **1945** STEP & JACKSON *Wayside & Woodland Ferns* (ed. 2) 25 Wilson's Filmy-fern... Known also as the One-sided Filmy-fern.

one-sidedness. (Earlier and later examples.)

1831 J. S. MILL *Let.* 20–22 Oct. (1910) I. 11 The next thing that struck me was the extreme comprehensiveness and philosophic spirit which is in him [*sc.* Wordsworth]. By these expressions I mean the direct antithesis of what the Germans most expressively call one-sidedness. **1974** tr. *Wertheim's Evolution & Revolution* i. 20 Another factor contributing to a rather general rejection of 'evolutionism'..was connected with a certain one-sidedness in evolutionary views, as propagated about 1900. **1977** *South China Morning Post* (Hong Kong) 13 Apr. 13/6 To avoid accusations of one-sidedness and to round out the image of his subject, Dr Abrahamsen spoke to a number of Mr. Nixon's admirers.

one-step (wʊ·nstep), *sb.* Also **one step.** [f. ONE *numeral a.* + STEP *sb.*] A ballroom dance in quick time, in which the steps resemble simple walking. Hence as *v. intr.*, to dance the one-step.

1911 *Home Chat* 7 Oct. 108/1 Camilla is just mad about the 'One-step'. **1914** V. CASTLE *Mod. Dancing* 44 Simply *walk* as softly and smoothly as possible, taking a step to every count of the music. This is the One Step, and this is all there is to it. **1916** H. L. WILSON *Somewhere in Red Gap* iv. 172, I caught him..in the deserted library later, while the rest was one-stepping in the..ballroom. **1921** H. S. WALPOLE *Young Enchanted* III. i. 230 Bunny says I one-step better than anyone he's ever known. **1924** [see *HESITATION 3]. **1938** B. SCHÖNBERG tr. *Sachs' World Hist. of Dance* vii. 445 We have shortly after 1900 the *one-step* or *turkey trot.* **1956** G. P. KURATH in A. Dundes *Mother Wit* (1973) 106/1 The one-step or turkey-trot.. was little more than a smooth walk. **1969** F. RUST *Dance in Society* x. 84 After the one-step came the fishwalk and the horsetrot—of ephemeral interest only.

one-way, *a.* [f. ONE *numeral a.* + WAY *sb.*[1]]

† **1.** Of bread: see ONE *a.* 33. *Obs.*

2. Applied to a plough which can turn the furrows in one direction only. Also *ellipt.*

1884 [see ONE *a.* 33]. **1886** F. T. ELWORTHY *West Somerset Word-Bk.* 537 A two-way-zull, eens can plough vore and back in the same vore, is a handy thing like, but can't make such good work way un's can way a proper good one-way-zull. **1960** *Times* 15 Feb. 19/2 A one-way plough much lighter in weight. **1965** G. SHEPHERD *West of Yesterday* x. 77 We used a plough, for there was no 'one-way', as the modification of the disc plough was later named.

3. a. Leading, tending, pointing, thinking, or developing in one direction only.

1824 M. WILMOT *Let.* 5 Feb. (1935) 206 Our one way life, dearest Alicia, gives me so little to say. **1928** A. S. EDDINGTON *Nature Physical World* 295 The notion evidently implies that something may be born into the world at the instant Here-Now, which has an influence extending throughout the future cone but no corresponding linkage to the cone of absolute past. The primary laws of physics do not provide for any such one-way linkage. **1938** L. MACNEICE *Earth Compels* 61 Endurance of one-way thinking. **1951** KOESTLER *Age of Longing* i. 6 One-way pupils that took the light in, gave nothing out. *Ibid.* vii. 127 He put on the guarded, one-way gaze. **1953** J. S. HUXLEY *Evolution in Action* i. 12 All reality, in fact, *is* evolution, in the perfectly proper sense that it is a one-way process in time. **1960** PARTRIDGE *Charm of Words* 40 In a one-way dictionary, the explanations are made in the same language as that of the words defined. **1966** G. N. LEECH *Eng. in Advertising* v. 48 Many intonation contrasts in English signal personal attitudes and contextual presuppositions which can scarcely apply to one-way public communication. **1973** *Australian* 17 Dec. 16/7 Your child could be studying under a Miss Brooks at school and your spouse or boy-friend may well be a one-way baby (simply a term for self-centred emotional types). **1977** *Rep. Comm. Future of Broadcasting* iii. 19 Broadcasting..is a one-way communication; viewers and listeners cannot question or express approval or disapproval.

b. *spec.* Of a ticket: entitling the holder to a journey in one direction only; 'single'. Also *fig.*

1906 *Dialect Notes* III. 148 Over three hundred negroes left Springfield, purchasing oneway tickets to many different towns. **1949** L. HUGHES (*title*) One-way ticket. **1973** *Nation Rev.* (Melbourne) 31 Aug. 1464/2 One journalist..later earned himself further notoriety and a oneway ticket to Van Diemen's Land. **1976** J. LEE *Ninth Man* 258 You've bought yourself a one-way ticket to obscurity. **1977** *Times* 5 Oct. 17/8 On most days people are not having to queue to buy their one-way tickets to America at £59 a head.

c. Of a thoroughfare: along which traffic is permitted in only one direction; of traffic: passing only in one direction; also, of or pertaining to such traffic. Also *fig.*

1914 *World's Work* Aug. 302/1 Some little has already been done in the small streets off Piccadilly to *request* drivers to avoid some streets when going north and others when going south, thereby aiming at 'one-way' traffic, but there is no power to enforce the requests. *Ibid.* 304/1 Where streets are too narrow to permit of the rotary system the difficulty can be overcome by one-way streets. **1926** *Glasgow Herald* 11 Sept. 9 A complaint has been heard from shop-keepers against the one-way system in certain streets. **1933** [see *clover-leaf* s.v. *CLOVER *sb.* 4]. **1956** B. HOLIDAY *Lady sings Blues* (1973) xxi. 171 This is a one-way street. If someone plants something on you and you're innocent, you have no way in the world to prove it. **1959** *Daily Tel.* 8 May 12 One-way study for London. *Ibid.*, The pros and cons of proposals for one-way traffic. **1961** [see *DREAM *sb.*[2] 1 b]. **1961** L. VAN DER POST *Heart of Hunter* III. xv. 202 The European..tends to believe that the consequences are only for the primitive and that he..is immune from them. But actually there is no one-way traffic on these eventful occasions. **1963** *Traffic in Towns* (Ministry of Transport) ii. 40/2 One-way streets and the elimination of right-hand turns have been the main features that have caught public attention. **1970** P. LAURIE *Scotland Yard* iv. 96 They put up temporary one-way signs, controlled junctions. **1972** J. GORES *Dead Skip* (1973) xv. 105 Kearny entered town on one-way Howard Street. **1976** *Northumberland Gaz.* 26 Nov. 19/9 It was virtually one-way traffic in the second half as Berwick kept the visitors pinned in their own area. Heslop and Renwick added further tries and Dudgeon kicked a further three penalty goals.

d. *one-way pockets*: the pockets of a miserly person. *slang.*

1926 MAINES & GRANT *Wise-Crack Dict.* 11/2 *One-way pockets*, pockets of tightwad. **1961** WODEHOUSE *Service with Smile* (1962) ix. 143 His one-way pockets are a by-word all over England.

e. Of a window, mirror, or the like: that permits vision from one side; transparent from one side only.

a **1940** F. SCOTT FITZGERALD *Last Tycoon* (1949) ii. 31 Nowadays all chief executives have huge drawing rooms, but my father's was the first. It was also the first to have one-way glass in the big French windows. **1961** W. BROWN *Bedeviled* 40 Obscene exhibitions viewed through peepholes made of one-way glass. **1964** F. POHL in *Galaxy Mag.* Oct. 192/2 The cameras..that the studio people had activated for me behind every one-way mirror in the room. **1967** C. DRUMMOND *Death at Furlong Post* iii. 27 What looked like a dirty bit of glass was a one-way window. **1972** *Jrnl. Social Psychol.* LXXXVIII. 153 Further, Ss [*sc.* subjects] were observed during the experiment through the one-way mirror for any reactions. **1975** *Times Lit. Suppl.* 7 Mar. 241/2 Two of Dizzy's aristocratic sprigs jostle at a one-way mirror watching the most high-minded statesman of all trying to reclaim a tart.

4. *Electr.* Of a switch or the like: providing only one possible path for current.

1896 W. P. MAYCOCK *Electr. Lighting* (ed. 3) I. v. 113 Fig. 49 shows a simple or one-way switch. **1925** O. RANKIN *Switches in Wireless Circuits* 56 Two ordinary 'one-way', or 'bell switches', A and B, are used to effect the usual series-parallel switching of the A.T.C. **1965** P. HONEY *Planning Electricity in House* iii. 71 Wall switches are available in one-way and two-way types, the latter being used for the control of lights from two different points (e.g. on staircases).

onewhere, *adv.* (Further example.)

1887 G. M. HOPKINS *Poems* (1918) 65 Each limb's barrowy brawn, his thew That onewhere curded, onewhere sucked or sank.

onflowing, *vbl. sb.* and *ppl. a.* Add: (Further examples.) Also **on-flow** *v. intr.*, to flow on.

1861 A. DE VERE *Sisters* 17 No eye Finer pursued the on-flowing line: her wheel Murmur'd complacent joy. **1879** —— *Legends of Saxon Saints* ii. 23 Forward on-flowed in Apostolic might Augustine's strong discourse. **1905** R. DAVEY tr. *Serao's In Country of Jesus* VI. iv. 167 The rapidly on-flowing waters reflect the azure blue of the sky above. **1930** *Tablet* 26 July 107/2 The large and stately on-flowing of history.

on-glaze, *a.* (*sb.*) *Ceramics.* [f. ON *prep.* + GLAZE *sb.*] Of, pertaining to, or designating colour, a pattern, etc., applied on top of a glaze; = OVERGLAZE *a.* Also as *sb.*, colour, etc., applied on top of a glaze.

1897 SPARKES & GANDY *Potters* i. 56 The class of enamel colours... The name of *overglaze* or *onglaze* is borne by the whole group. **1913** J. C. WEDGWOOD *Staffordshire Pott.* viii. 131 There was something crude and hard about the effect of the on-glaze printing. *Ibid.* 133 In 1770 he [*sc.* Josiah Spode] leased Banks' works in the centre of Stoke, and began making printed cream colour. This was the old 'on-glaze', or 'black' printed ware, used to guide the enameller rather than as a decoration by itself. **1957** MANKOWITZ & HAGGAR *Conc. Encycl. Eng. Pott. & Porc.* 65/2 The development of on-glaze enamelling c.1760 by the Daniel family in Hot Lane. *Ibid.* 168/2 *On-glaze*, decoration applied after the ware has been glazed and fired. **1959** *Which?* Oct. 127/1 A good deal of decorated pottery has patterns applied on top of the glaze, because this allows a much wider range of colours to be used... With this type of decoration, known as on-glaze, the colours are directly exposed to the action of the detergent. **1961** M. JONES *Potbank* xxv. 108 On-glaze decoration, working on ware that has been glazed and then fired, is more usual [than under-glaze decoration]. **1969** *Canad. Antiques Collector* Feb. 10/1 After this glost firing the onglaze enamel paintings of birds and flowers are done. **1974** *Nature* 25 Jan. 197/2 Cadmium sulphide has been shown by x-ray diffraction to be present in the onglaze decoration.

o·n-glide. *Phonetics.* [f. ON *a.* + GLIDE *sb.*] A glide produced at the beginning of articulating a speech-sound. Cf. *OFF-GLIDE. Hence **on-gliding** *ppl. a.*

1888 H. SWEET *Hist. Eng. Sounds* 10 All consonants consist of three elements, (1) the consonant itself, (2) the on-glide, and (3) the off-glide. **1919** E. KRUISINGA *Handbk. Present-Day Eng.* (ed. 3) I. iv. 72 The chief difference between English and Dutch voiced stops is the difference between the on-glides of initial stops. **1934** *PMLA* XLIX. 1167 In the English pronunciation of parasitic (n) before (t) in *maintenant*, the (n) is an off-glide of the nasal vowel and an on-glide of the (t). **1934** PRIEBSCH & COLLINSON *German Lang.* 385 The intermission of the breath on-glide (so noticeable in English and German). **1950** D. JONES *Phoneme* 5 The on-glide and stop of this affricate resemble those of the English t. **1954** [see *OFF-GLIDE]. **1965** *Language* XLI. 478 The first allophone has a rapid palatal onglide, the second has a rapid onglide of central-vowel quality; both onglides are conditioned by the preceding consonants. **1976** *Ibid.* LII. 341 Under certain conditions of stress and sentence rhythm, syllable-final stops come to be preceded by vocalic onglides.

on-going, *sb.* **2.** Delete *rare*, and add earlier and later examples.

1860 F. W. FABER *Precious Blood* iii. 107 Not only is the continuous preservation of all things..an almost illimitable extension and ongoing of creation, but new souls of men are literally created out of nothing every moment of time. **1880** W. M. THOMSON *Land & Bk.* 2 The long ongoing and outworking of the Mosaic Economy. **1962** *Listener* 11 Oct. 559/1 Experiment must be analytical and predictive in its actual on-going. **1977** *Times* 11 Apr. 5/7 The logical conclusion of a process long in the ongoing.

on-going, *a.* Add: Also **ongoing.** Also, continuing, continuous; that is in progress; current; proceeding, or developing. (Earlier and later examples.) Hence **o·n-go:ingness.**

1877 J. BLACKWOOD *Let.* 15 Oct. in *Geo. Eliot Lett.* (1956) VI. 405 This edition..will be a steady on-going thing, a capital leading franchise in the business. **1937** [see *INTEGRATION 1 b]. **1949** M. MEAD *Male & Female* xvi. 336 American women have become..less willing to be merely part of some on-going operation. **1951** V. BARCLAY *Challenge to Darwinians* vi. 60 Bergson..held that an ongoing movement issued from that creative act. **1951** E. C. TOLMAN in Parsons & Shils *Toward Gen. Theory Action* III. 352 What..would be the necessary conditions for the non-disintegration, the on-goingness, of a personality system? **1953** *Scottish Jrnl. Theol.* VI. 211 Within the time of this on-going age there would be a thousand years of political triumph for the Jews. **1954** D. RIESMAN *Individualism Reconsidered* (1955) xxii. 334 Sufficient time has elapsed since Freud built his system..to permit..critical re-examination of the sort undertaken here... Its aim is..to contribute to the sociology of knowledge and to the ongoing effort. **1957** P. LAFITTE *Person in Psychol.* 59 Life..is tense,..as an inescapable consequence of its being rich, varied, ongoing, and creative. **1959** P. WHEELWRIGHT *Heraclitus* iii. 38 For Heraclitus the most basic ontological fact is the ongoingness of things. **1960** in L. Pincus *Marriage* 8 The worker's capacity to learn from his on-going cases. *Ibid.* I. 16 This pattern of interaction can be understood only in the context of an on-going process. **1961** R. KEE *Refugee World* vii. 73 The refugee problem in our time is an on-going problem. **1967** G. WILLS in Wills & Yearsley *Handbk. Managem. Technol.* 179 Time, in an on-going marketing situation, costs money. **1972** P. LASLETT *Household & Family in Past Time* 68 The danger of mistaking a set of coincidences for an ongoing institution. **1973** *Guardian* 13 Oct. 2/3 We have an on-going military relationship which we are continuing. **1974** *Times* 1 May 6/8 The President assigned the responsibility for the on-going investigation to Mr Petersen. **1976** *Publishers Weekly* 16 Feb. 85/1 The ongoing polemic about the role of the atelier artist versus his university-based colleague. **1977** *Gay News* 24 Mar. 13/1 Dozens of other special relationships hold the potential of working well and of maintaining the symbiosis of ongoingness.

ongon (ǫ·ngǫn). [Russ.] In the Shamanist religion of the Buriats of Mongolia, an image of a god or spirit supposed to be endowed with the power of the force it represents; a fetish.

1901 D. BANTZAROFF tr. J. Stadling in *Contemp. Rev.* LXXIX. 89 The dim idea of the immortality of the soul and a future life gave rise to the *Ongones*, the deified spirits of the ancestors. **1910** *Encycl. Relig. & Ethics* III. 12/1 The Turks of Yenisei call the ongon *tyus*, whereas among the Altaians it is named *Kurmes*. On the one hand, it is an image of God, and, on the other, God himself, a fetish possessed of his own power. The tyus, or ongon, reminds us of the rôle which among some Christian peoples is filled by the images of saints. **1936** V. A. DEMANT *Christian Polity* xi. 191 The Ongons of the Mongolic Buriats are effigies of dead heroes, and so are the images of Indo-China. **1950** *Funk's Stand. Dict. Folklore* II. 823/1 *Ongon*, in Buriat religion, an image embodying a god and therefore possessing the power of the god: among the Altai called *kurmes*, among certain Turks, *tyus*. **1970** *New Society* 5 Mar. 393/1 The word, 'ongon', means both a spirit and the material representation of a spirit. Drawings are made only of known spirits, each of which has particular magical powers. Since the representation *is* the spirit, the drawings themselves become magical: according to the spirit, an ongon can cure smallpox, keep young lambs healthy, give protection to fishermen and so on.

Oni (ǭu·ni). Also with lower-case initial. [Yoruba.] The title given to the ruler of Ife, a large town now in the Western State of Nigeria.

1900 *Niger & Yoruba Notes* Sept. 19/1 The Oni of Ile Ife..granted..a desirable plot of ground for the Mission premises. **1904** *Jrnl. Afr. Soc.* July 472 The Oni of Ife..has had very little political power during the present generation. **1911** *Encycl. Brit.* XXVIII. 937/1 The chief of Ife bears the title of *oni* (a term indicating spiritual supremacy). To the oni of Ife or the alafin of Oyo all the other great chiefs announce their succession. **1937** *Nigeria* xii. 4 The earliest Onis of Ife were reputed to have reigned each for as long as 200 or more years. **1974** J. R. BAKER *Race* xxi. 412 Most of the Ife bronzes are in the Oni's palace. **1967** F. WILLETT *Ife in Hist. W. Afr. Sculpture* 22 The fact that three of the heads were crowned,..suggests that these are representations of Onis or divine kings of Ife... During this century, the Oni has appeared increasingly in public, but even the Oni Ademiluyi, who died in 1931, used to cover his mouth with a fan when he as much as took kola in public. **1976** *Daily Times* (Lagos) 8 July 11/6 Hundreds of traditional rulers including the Oni of Ife..are attending the meeting.

-onic, *suffix. Chem.* [f. -ON(E + -IC, prob. after *LACTONIC *a.* 1.] An ending used in forming the names of acids, esp. of carboxylic acids obtained by oxidation of aldoses, as *GALACTONIC, *GLUCONIC, *URONIC *adjs.*, etc. (Cf. also ARSONIC *a.* (f. ARSONIUM), PHOSPHONIC *a.* (f. PHOSPHONIUM), SULPHONIC *a.* (f. SULPHONE).)

onion, *sb.* Add: Forms: *β.* Also 9 *U.S. dial.* **ineon, ingyon.**

1825 J. NEAL *Bro. Jonathan* II. 84 Ingyons are proper good, when ye're sick.

2. b. bog onion, substitute for def.: one of several plants with roots resembling an onion, esp. the royal fern, *Osmunda regalis*; (earlier and later examples).

1832 W. D. WILLIAMSON *Hist. State Maine* I. 120 The Brake, of which there are several varieties, the root of which is sometimes called the 'bog-onion'. **1878** W. DICKINSON *Cumberland Gloss.* (ed. 2) 9/1 *Bog onion*, the *Osmunda Regalis* or flowering fern. **1892** *Jrnl. Amer. Folk-Lore* V. 104 *Arisæma triphyllum*, bog onion. Worcester Co.

5. b. *slang.* Head; esp. in phr. *off one's onion*, mad.

1890 BARRÈRE & LELAND *Dict. Slang* II. 94/2 *Off his onion* (costermongers), imbecile, cracked. **1909** H. G. WELLS *Tono-Bungay* II. ii. 176 He come home one day saying Tono-Bungay till I thought he was clean off his onion. **1922** WODEHOUSE *Girl on Boat* xii. 202 When..she informed him one day that she was engaged.., he went right off his onion. **1928** *Daily Express* 11 Dec. 7/4 After four drops of beer I am properly off my onion. **1971** WODEHOUSE *Much Obliged, Jeeves* vi. 52 What on earth was the idea of inviting a fiend in human shape like that here?.. You must have been off your onion, old ancestor.

c. *to know one's onions*, to be experienced or knowledgeable in the subject, etc., on hand; (only P. G. Wodehouse) (*not*) *the only onion in the stew*, (not) the only person or thing to be taken into consideration.

1922 *Harper's Mag.* Mar. 530/1 Mr. Roberts knows his onions, all right. **1934** WODEHOUSE *Right Ho, Jeeves* vii. 75, I claim the right to have a pop at these problems..without having everybody behave as if Jeeves was the only onion in the hash. **1952** 'E. C. R. LORAC' *Murder in Mill-Race* v. 52 If I know my onions the woman's death has been an almighty relief to the lot of them. **1956** S. ERTZ *Charmed Circle* v. 86 'That old man,' he said, 'doesn't know his onions, luckily for you.' **1958** J. CANNAN *And be a Villain* ix. 200 Shakespeare knew his onions, didn't he? **1958** *Times* 16 June 9/4 A man 'who knows his onions' is a man wise in the ways of the world, shrewd in affairs, a tough bargainer, by no means born yesterday. **1972** WODEHOUSE *Pearls, Girls & Monty Bodkin* vii. 109 She wanted to stimulate competition. By showing you you weren't the only onion in the stew she would get your attention. **1974** J. WAINWRIGHT *Evidence I shall Give* xxxii. 166 They know their onions... They are old in wisdom and experience.

6. b. *Naut.* A fraction of a knot.

1916 'TAFFRAIL' *Pincher Martin* v. 73 We got about six and an onion out of the old bus,..and reached there about noon. **1938** F. A. WORSLEY *First Voy. in Square-Rigged Ship* iv. 71 The speed..was 13 knots or, as Stringer put it: 'Thirteen and an onion in the squalls.' **1958** F. H. SHAW *Seas of Memory* ii. 48 'Fifteen, sir, fifteen and an onion!' called the second mate. 'That's the way I like her to move,' said Fegan.

c. = *flaming onion* (*FLAMING *ppl. a.* 1 c).

1917 *Blackw. Mag.* Apr. 560/1 A line of fiery rectangles shot up... These were 'onions', the flaming rockets which the Boche keeps for..hostile aircraft. **1918** in *Amer. Speech* 1972 (1975) XLVII. 84 The airmen's pest is the 'onion', or large flaming anti-aircraft shell. **1936** 'McSCOTCH' *Fighter Pilot* vi. 122 On heading south for the other balloon the 'onion' battery had another shot at me.

8. *onion bed* (later examples), *crop*, *-green* (also as adj.), *roll*, *salt*, *sauce*, *-seller* (later examples) (so *-selling*), *soup*, *spire*, *steeple*; *onion-loving*, *-shaped*, *-spired*, *-towered* adjs.; **onion dome,** a dome on a church, palace, etc., shaped like an onion; so **onion-domed** *a.*; **onion-fly,** for '*Anthomyia ceparum*' substitute '*Delia cepetorum*'; (earlier and later examples); **onion ring,** a circular segment of an onion; **onion set** (see quots.); **onion-skin** (*b*) (examples); also (see quot. 1879) a ballot paper of very fine paper; also *attrib.*

1857 *Quinland* I. I. xiii. 184, I spaded up the onion-bed after supper. **1874** *Rep. Vermont Board Agric.* II. 551

Raked as smooth as an onion bed. **1975** D. GREEN *Food & Drink from your Garden* 91 They..no longer need the special onion beds which took so many years to perfect. **1879** *Congress Rec.* 46th Congress 1 Sess. App. 120/1 The onion crop of South Carolina. **1956** R. MACAULAY *Towers of Trebizond* ii. 20, I dreamed too of the Crimea, of crumbling palaces decaying among orchards by the sea, of onion domes. **1960** N. MITFORD *Don't tell Alfred* xxiv. 245 The French papers were full of lines and sidelines on Russia, no photograph without its onion dome. **1973** J. M. WHITE *Garden Game* 54 The exotic onion-dome of a church looming through the veiled whiteness. **1959** *Manch. Guardian* 26 Feb. 9/4 The Kremlin, with its three onion-domed cathedrals. **1974** *Aiken* (S. Carolina) *Standard* 22 Apr. 6-A/1 Entering through Persian onion-domed archways, guests saw the Fermata Club in Aiken transformed into a festive pavillion of purple and orange. **1840** J. & M. LOUDON tr. *Kollar's Treat. Insects* II. 159 The larva very much resembles that of the onion fly. **1966** *Punch* 6 Apr. 510/2 Sets..will grow onions..without onion fly risk. **1975** D. GREEN *Food & Drink from your Garden* 92 The main pest is the onion fly, which lays its eggs in May and June. **1906** S. W. BUSHELL *Chinese Art* II. viii. 23 The brilliant grass-greens of the Lung-ch'üan porcelain, called *ts'ung-lü*, or 'onion-green' by the Chinese. **1925** W. DE LA MARE *Two Tales* 71 The very ferocious onion-green dragon. **1811** SHELLEY *Let.* 17 May (1964) I. 76 How gets on your onion-loving Deist. **1952** M. NORTON *Borrowers* iii. 24 She [*sc.* a midget] took the onion ring from Homily and slung it lightly round her shoulders. **1974** *Times* 21 Feb. 10 Thinly sliced onion rings. **1967** C. POTOK *Chosen* v. 100 Lunch turned out to be a massive affair, with a thick soup, fresh rye bread, onion rolls, bagels. **1972** *New Yorker* 15 Apr. 35/3 Most of the women buy some kind of bread (a loaf of rye bread ..or a few onion rolls). **1938** E. WAUGH *Scoop* III. ii. 287 A little store of seasonings..onion salt, Bombay duck, gherkins. **1958** Onion salt [see *garlic salt]. **1723** J. NOTT *Cook's & Confectioner's Dict.* sig. X5 (*heading*) To make onion sauce. Cut..Onions into slices, put them into a Sauce-pan with some Veal-gravy,..simmer. **1787** J. WOODFORDE *Diary* 4 Dec. (1926) II. 356, I gave them for Dinner..a couple of Rabbitts boiled and Onion Sauce. **1877** E. S. DALLAS *Kettner's Bk. of Table* 320 (*heading*) Onion sauce.—See the Soubise sauce, the Breton sauce, and the Sauce Robert. **1939** T. S. ELIOT *Old Possum's Pract. Cats* 45 And when he's finished, licks his paws So's not to waste the onion sauce. **1914** W. B. YEATS *Responsibilities* 15 What th' onion-sellers thought or did. **1970** V. CANNING *Great Affair* xvi. 300 Troops.. strung with hand grenades..like French onion sellers. **1915** *Daily Chron.* 23 Nov. 5/3 Onion-selling parties in England. **1886** *Harper's Mag.* Oct. 708/2 'Onion sets'.. are produced by sowing the ordinary black seed very thickly on light poor land. **1951** *Dict. Gardening* (R. Hort. Soc.) III. 1424/2 Small bulbs grown in the previous autumn and known as 'onion sets' may..be planted in spring for the raising of dry bulbs. **1975** D. & T. HOOBLER *Vegetable Gardening & Cooking* 77 Growing onions from seeds takes up to four or five months, so most home gardeners buy onion 'sets', which are the baby onion bulbs, ready to be buried in early spring, 2 inches deep, 4 inches apart, in rows 12 inches apart. **1949** R. HARVEY *Curtain Time* 97 And a brand-new wooden church, bright blue with a yellow onion-shaped dome. **1959** J. BRAINE *Vodi* vi. 87 The chapel..was a compact red-brick building with large round-headed windows, topped rather incongruously by a tower with an onion-shaped dome. **1879** C. G. WILLIAMS in *Congress. Rec.* 9 Apr. 167/2 From that time to the wee small hours of the morning onion-skin ballots went in unchallenged but not uncounted. *Ibid.* 23 June App. 120/1 The term 'onion skin' or 'tissue ballots' has obtained a generic and well-defined meaning synonymous with the 'stuffing' of ballot-boxes. **1892** *Paper & Press* July, facing p. 49 (Advt.), The Highest Grades of Typewriter Paper a Specialty. Onion Skin. Manifold Linen. **1922** *Handbk. Quality-Standard Papers* (Amer. Writing Paper Co.) 360 Onion Skin. A thin, transparent, highly glazed paper made of rag and sulphite. **1923** H. A. MADDOX *Dict. Stationery* 56 *Onion skin*, an American paper trade expression..applied to very thin and crisp typewriting or bank paper, which in texture, tear and crackle has some-of the nature which characterizes the skin of an onion. **1956** S. BELLOW *Seize the Day* (1957) iv. 99 He took out a substantial bundle of onion-skin papers and said, 'These are the receipts of the transactions. Duplicates.' **1970** *New Yorker* 20 June 25/2 The shredding of a quarto of onionskin stationery, to simulate the tearing up of a billion dollars. **1973** R. THOMAS *If you can't be Good* (1974) xxii. 191 He handed me some folded sheets of onion skin.. I unfolded the onion-skin sheets. **1747** H. GLASSE *Art of Cookery* ix. 77 An Onion Soop. **1861** MRS. BEETON *Bk. Househ. Managem.* vi. 73 Onion Soup... 6 large onions,.. ½ pint of cream. **1942** E. PAUL *Narrow St.* xxv. 223 Most of us missed our lunch but ate onion soup and sausage with sauerkraut in midafternoon. **1966** J. B. PRIESTLEY *Salt is Leaving* xiii. 179 He..opened a tin, French and good, of onion soup. **1977** P. HARCOURT *At High Risk* i. 31 We settled for onion soup, a *filet* with a wine sauce, salad. **1966** *New Statesman* 17 June 893/1 The onion spires of Alaska. **1959** *Times* 25 Apr. 9/5 A baroque, onion-spired church. **1868** G. M. HOPKINS *Jrnls. & Papers* (1959) 179 The churches here have those onion steeples nearly all. **1960** *Times* 11 June 11/6 A Church with Baroque 'onion' steeple. **1959** *Listener* 15 Jan. 131/1 Almost every little South Swabian and Bavarian village has its delightful onion-towered church.

oniony, *a.* (Later examples.)

1922 JOYCE *Ulysses* 233 Armpits' oniony sweat. **1971** *Guardian* 5 May 9/4 Onions always smell oniony. **1975** L. LEE *I can't stay Long* 31 Garlic sprawls rank and oniony in the woods. **1977** *Times* 10 Dec. 9/6 An oniony omelette.

-onium, *suffix. Chem.* [abstracted from AMMONIUM.] Used in forming the names of complex cations that contain a more or less electronegative central atom, usu. bonded to a number of protons (or to other species that are regarded as substituents), as ARSONIUM, *CARBONIUM, *HYDRAZONIUM, *NITRONIUM, *OXONIUM, PHOSPHONIUM, *tetrachlorophosphonium*, etc.

1971 *Nomencl. Inorg. Chem.* (I.U.P.A.C.) (ed. 2) 20 Names for polyatomic cations derived by addition of more protons than required to give a neutral unit to monatomic anions, are formed by adding the ending -onium to the root name of the anion element.

onium (ōᵘ·niŏm), *a. Chem.* Also **'onium.** [f. prec.] Applied to (compounds containing) ions of the kind named in *-onium*.

1905 *Jrnl. Chem. Soc.* LXXXVIII. I. 281 Carbon differs from other elements, which form 'onium' bases, in that it forms salts only. **1923** G. N. LEWIS *Valence* ix. 108 The formation of the typical 'onium' ion is a process which differs in no essential respect from the other processes in which hydrogen or other radicals become attached to lone pairs. **1952** KIRK & OTHMER *Encycl. Chem. Technol.* IX. 596 Several important classes of dyes, for example the cyanine dyes.., the azine dyes.., and the amino-substituted triphenylmethane dyes.., are onium compounds. **1953** C. K. INGOLD *Struct. & Mech. Org. Chem.* v. 208 It is not necessary that the anion of the 'onium salt should be the substituting agent. **1973** J. F. WILLEMS in R. J. COX *Proc. Symposium Photogr. Processing Univ. Sussex* 227 Various onium compounds considerably accelerate the bleaching out of the silver.

onkosine, var. *ONCOSINE.

onlap (ǫ·nlæp). *Geol.* [f. ON *adv.* + LAP *v.*[2], after *OFFLAP.] A progressive increase in the lateral extent of conformable strata in passing upwards from older to younger strata, so that each stratum is hidden by the one above; a set of strata exhibiting this.

1947 F. A. MELTON in *Bull. Amer. Assoc. Petroleum Geologists* XXXI. 1869 The writer proposes that the simpler name *marine-onlap*, which has already been used by various authors, be substituted for the more cumbersome term used by Grabau. Marine-onlap is thus used to describe the regular progressive pinching-out of marine strata above an unconformity..in such a way that the younger beds extend farther landward than do the older beds which lie beneath... The term terrestrial-onlap can be used in connection with terrestrial formations. **1955** *Sci. Amer.* Mar. 84/2 When the sea advanced, under the simplest conditions the new deposits overlapped the older in a shoreward direction—a process called onlap. **1968** R. W. FAIRBRIDGE *Encycl. Geomorphol.* 340/1 The 'Schooley Peneplain' of the Appalachians..dips unmistakably under the mid-Tertiary transgressive onlap of the Atlantic Coastal Plain.

onlay, *v.* For † *Obs.* read '*Obs.* exc. as *ppl. adj.*' and add later examples.

1880 L. HIGGINS *Handbk. Embroidery* v. 54 '*Onlaid appliqué*' is done by cutting out the pattern in one or many coloured materials, and laying it down on an intact ground of another material. **1971** *Bodl. Libr. Rec.* VIII. 264 The covers are decorated with onlaid straw, a wide outer band of large stylized flowers..with doublures bearing similar straw onlays. **1976** *Times Lit. Suppl.* 25 June 805/4 Thomas Fassam's *An Herbarium for the Fair*, 1949, onlaid with butterflies and woodruff by a new-comer, Angela James.

onlay, *sb.* Add: (Further examples.)

1959 L. M. HARROD *Librarians' Gloss.* (ed. 2) 194 *Onlay*, a decorative panel of paper or other material glued to the cover of a book without preparing the cover to receive it. **1961** J. CARTER *ABC for Bk. Collectors* (ed. 3) 139 The technique was occasionally adapted to publisher's cloth between 1840 and 1860, when the onlays were sometimes of paper. **1971** [see prec.]. **1976** *Times Lit. Suppl.* 25 June 805/1 Technical innovations since the Second World War have greatly extended the binder's decorative range. Before then decoration was limited to gold or blind-tooling and coloured onlays.

b. *Dentistry.* An occlusal rest extended so as to cover the whole occlusal surface of a tooth.

1906 J. A. LENTZ *U.S. Pat. 833,883* 23 Oct., My objects are, first, to facilitate and expedite the reproduction or duplication in gold, gold alloy, or similar substance of a variety of forms, such as inlays, onlays, cusps, [etc.]. **1935** G. M. ANDERSON *Dewey's Pract. Orthodontia* (ed. 5) xxii. 427 If the tooth is sufficiently exposed so that one need not cut into it, an onlay may be used in conjunction with the auxiliary spring. **1973** L. BAUM *Advanced Restorative Dentistry* xi. 169 Onlays are generally more acceptable than inlays in middle-aged and older patients because the design of onlay preparations provides for a casting which will bond together the remaining tooth structure.

c. onlay graft *Surg.*: a bone graft in which a piece of bone is fixed over a fracture.

1927 *Southern Med. Jrnl.* (Nashville, Tennessee) XX. 114/2 Of the thirty-eight bones in which the onlay graft was employed, three failed to induce osseous union. **1957** ROB & SMITH *Operative Surg.* V. IX. i. 12 Fixation by onlay graft. The technique is the same as for fixation by a metal plate except that a cortical slab graft..is used instead of the metal plate.

on-licence: see ON *a.* 2.

onlie, var. ONLY *a.* (in Dict. and Suppl.).

on-line (stress variable), *a.*, *adv.*, and *phr.* Also **online.** [f. ON *prep.* + LINE *sb.*[2]] **A.** *adj.* (Usu. stressed o·n-line.) **1.** *Computers.* Directly connected, so that a computer receives an input from or sends an output to a peripheral device, process, etc., as soon as it is produced; carried out while so connected or under direct computer control.

1950 W. W. STIFLER *High-Speed Computing Devices* ii. 7 For some applications, of which the most prominent are those in which the reduced data are used to control the process being measured, the input must be developed for on-line operation. In on-line operation the input is communicated directly..to the data-reduction device. **1957** [see *OFF-LINE *a.* 2]. **1959** [see *IN-LINE *a.* 3c]. **1964** T. W. MCRAE *Impact of Computers on Accounting* i. 17 If we are processing..a payroll,..and the output printer is directly hooked up to the computer store so that each payslip is printed immediately after it is calculated, we use the term on-line processing. **1965** *Math. in Biol. & Med.* (Med. Res. Council) VI. 295 Without time-sharing, the 'on-line' use of a fast modern machine would be unthinkably costly. **1968** *Times* 26 Oct. 4/4 It was found..by radio astronomers using the 250 ft. dish telescope connected to an on-line computer. **1971** *Computers & Humanities* V. 192 The SHOEBOX is an automatic text-processing and retrieval system implemented for on-line operation on an IBM 360/50 computer. **1972** *Accountant* 27 Apr. 549/1 A completely integrated computer data system which..through a built-in system of analysis and recording enables managers at any level to have immediate 'on-line' access to that part of the information which is relevant.

2. Occurring or effected on the current authorized routes of an airline.

1969 *Jane's Freight Containers 1968–69* 429/2 Online and interline use [*sc.* of air cargo pallets] by JAL. **1973** E. RATH *Container Systems* x. 285 Those airlines who had purchased both the 747 and either the DC-10 or the L-1011 realized that standardization of lower-deck containers would permit them to effect on-line and interline transfers of complete containers between these different types of aircraft.

3. = *IN-LINE *a.* 2.

1972 *Physics Bull.* Jan. 29/3 Dr K. A. Andrews.. described the progress which was being made with the problem of on-line ultrasonic testing of hot steel. **1976** *Gramophone* Aug. 354/2 Mass production calls for high speed working, sophisticated on-line testing and..a high degree of automation.

B. *adv.* (Usu. stressed *on-li·ne.*) With processing of data carried out simultaneously with its production; while connected to a computer, or under direct computer control.

1950 [see *OFF-LINE *adv.*]. **1964** *Ann. N.Y. Acad. Sci.* CXV. 654 The goal of the development has been a machine which..is fast enough for simple data-processing 'on-line' while the experiment is in progress. **1966** *Economist* 23 July 382/3 Information will be available 'on-line'..to 100 BOAC centres throughout the world. **1966** *New Scientist* 27 Oct. 161/2 All the files of the users of the system are put on-line—that is, made directly accessible to the central processor. **1968** *Amer. Documentation* Jan. 72/1 Editing will be done on-line with a display scope and keyboard. **1977** *Catalogue & Index* XLVI. 8 Those who want to work on-line will be able to work in a format designed to reflect..the way the data is stored in the computer.

C. *phr.* (Written as two words.) = *ON STREAM *adv. phr.* a.

1968 *Daily Colonist* (Victoria, B.C.) 28 Nov. 13/6 The Skookumchuck mill recently came on line, but none of the B.C.-produced pulp destined for Japan is in the present cardboard packages. **1975** *Nature* 9 Oct. 435/3 Domestic uranium reserves will be totally committed to those nuclear reactors which are brought on line in the next 20 years.

only, *a.* Add: **2. b.** *only child*: so *only-childish* adj., characteristic or suggestive of an only child; *only-childishness*, *only-childism*, the fact or state of being an only child.

1927 *Times* 29 Dec. 7/3 They might come to speak, not of drink, but of 'only-childism', as the greatest curse of this country. **1928** *Daily Tel.* 11 Sept. 11/6 Dr. Gillespie alluded to 'Only childishness'... It had been suggested that only children were peculiarly liable to become neurotic. **1938** E. BOWEN *Death of Heart* III. ii. 341 A face at a window for no reason is a face that should have a thumb in its mouth: there is something only-childish about it. **1949** —— *Heat of Day* iii. 57 Anything that savoured of only-childishness.

5. *onlie begetter* [f. BEGETTER 2, quot. 1606], the sole originator; *onliest* (later examples).

1907 *Yesterday's Shopping* (1969) 1136/2 Comic and humorous songs... Ma Onliest One. **1929** H. W. ODUM in A. Dundes *Mother Wit* (1973) 190 Onliest way could git him. **1937** N. MARSH *Vintage Murder* vii. 81 The Firm..was founded and built up by Mr Meyer... He was..the onlie begetter. **1969** *Australasian Post* 19 June 40/3 Isadora Duncan was..the onlie begetter of all the trends in 'free dance' which are now so familiar to us. **1971** *Black World* Oct. 62/1 The onliest time I had to say something bout it was when he was playin checkers on the stoop one time and he commenst to hummin. **1972** *Daily Tel.* 30 Mar. 6/7 Stalin's onlie begetter and mentor in murder—Lenin. **1973** *Times Lit. Suppl.* 2 Mar. 228/1 The enigmatic personality of [*Citizen*] *Kane*'s onlie begetter. **1975** *Times* 14 July 13/3 William Robson, Professor Emeritus of Public Administration, University of London, and 'the onlie begetter' of *The Political Quarterly*.

only, *adv.*, *conj.* (*prep.*) **B. 2. a.** Delete 'Now only *dial.*' and add later examples.

1899 T. WATTS-DUNTON *Aylwin* vii. 238 I've been a-listenin' to a v'ice as nobody can't hear on'y me. **1914**

JOYCE *Dubliners* 44 And say what he would do to her only for her dead mother's sake. **1922** E. O'NEILL *Anna Christie* II. 140 And only for me,..we'd be being scoffed by the fishes this minute! **1934** S. O'CASEY *Pound on Demand* in *Windfalls* 195 Who else could he be, only Mr. Adams? **1939** *New Yorker* 13 May 23/1 Her boy friend was working his way thru the Illinois U. and didn't get to Chi only two or three times a year. **1961** W. G. POLLARD *Physicist & Christian* (1962) 57 Yet are not we of the mid-twentieth century..just as bad off as they—only in a different way?

b. Delete † *Obs.* and add later examples.

1901 M. FRANKLIN *My Brilliant Career* iii. 16 Only I promised to stick to the missus a while I'd scoot tomorrer. **1914** JOYCE *Dubliners* 146 Only I'm an old man now I'd change his tune for him.

only (ōu·nli), *sb.* [f. the adj.] **1.** Used *absol.* for 'the only chance'.

1878 J. H. BEADLE *Western Wilds* xxvi. 417, I seed it was my first, last and only, and I sot old Sally at a gallop for that pint.

2. An only child.

1931 J. CANNAN *High Table* ii. 17 But poor little Theodore was 'an only', said Lady Oliver. **1963** *Guardian* 22 Feb. 8/7 The 'only', on the other hand..envies her friends with brothers and sisters. **1975** C. STORR *Chinese Egg* xviii. 121 If you're an only, you're sort of a target. Everything your parents think or feel has to be worked out on you.

3. In *redupl.* form. The state of being alone. *nonce-wd.*

1946 J. B. PRIESTLEY *Bright Day* vi. 199 Left on my only-only today. Wife's had to dash over to Leeds.

onmun (ǫ·nmun). [Korean, ad. Chinese *yên* say(ing) + *wên* letter, language.] = *HANGUL[2].

1948 D. DIRINGER *Alphabet* 443 The Christian missionaries, who were the first to realise that Ŏn-mun was better adapted to their use than the cumbersome Chinese characters. **1950** G. M. MCCUNE *Korea Today* vi. 94 Fifteen million textbooks written in the native *Onmun* alphabet for use in the elementary schools. **1951** [see *HANGUL[2]].

‖**onnagata** (ǫnaga·ta). [Jap., f. *onna* woman + *kata* figure.] In Japanese Kabuki drama and related forms, a man who plays female roles. Commonly also called *oyama*.

1901 O. EDWARDS *Jap. Plays & Playfellows* iii. 92 Peculiar attention is given to the training and discipline of *onnagata*, or impersonators of female parts. **1928** F. A. LOMBARD *Outl. Hist. Jap. Drama* xi. 294 In the earlier *Kabuki* men had often played the part of women; but now, when it had become necessary that they should do so on all occasions, a professional class of womenfolk (*onnagata*) grew into prominence. **1955** A. C. SCOTT *Kabuki Theatre of Japan* viii. 169 The good *onnagata* must symbolize feminine qualities in a way that no actress can do. **1972** *Nat. Geographic* Sept. 378 Greatest of today's *onnagata*, or male players of female roles, Utaemon Nakamura has spent a lifetime developing the charm and grace of a leading lady.

onnery: see *ONERY.

on-off, *a.* [f. ON *adv.* + OFF *adv.*] **1.** Of a switch or the like: that turns something on or off.

1946 *Nature* 12 Oct. 501/1 In the counting and control circuits, all valves are used entirely as on-off elements, not as amplitude-sensitive elements. **1958** *Times Rev. Industry* Oct. 92/3 Photoelectric equipment designed to perform on-off switching operations. **1960** *Times* 15 Mar. 18/4 The overdrive operation is therefore more complicated than the simple on-off switch. **1973** D. FRANCIS *Slay-Ride* viii. 96 Behind me..stood my portable television... I..found the on-off switch, and turned the volume up to maximum.

2. = OFF AND ON *a.*

1953 [see *HUNT *v.* 7 b]. **1962** *John o' London's* 19 July 66/2 Forget the hoo-ha, the on-off engagements. **1965** H. I. ANSOFF *Corporate Strategy* (1968) vii. 108 Concern with strategy had followed an 'on-off' cycle attuned to the appearance of major strategic opportunities. **1974** J. WAINWRIGHT *Evidence I shall Give* xxxvii. 209 The on-off pulse of the lighthouse beam. **1976** W. GREATOREX *Cassover* 119 Over the roast lamb Amberley had made fun of Galina's on-off vegetarianism.

onolatry (ǫnǫ·lătri). [f. Gr. ὄνο-ς ass + λατρεία -LATRY.] Worship of the ass. Also *fig.*

1903 *Jrnl. Amer. Folk-Lore* July–Sept. 203 *Onolatry*. Reinach, S.: Le culte de l'âne... Treats of the charges of worshipping a donkey made by the pagans against the Jews and early Christians. **1953** E. SITWELL *Gardeners & Astronomers* 28 The crowd's onolatries Echo that laughter.

onomasiology (ǫnomēˈsiǫ·lŏdʒi, -ziǫ·lŏdʒi). [f. Gr. ὀνομάσι-α name + -OLOGY.] The study of the principles of nomenclature, esp. with regard to regional, social, or occupational variation. Hence **onomasiolo·gic, onomasiolo·gical** *adjs.*, **onomasio·logist.**

1931 G. STERN *Meaning & Change of Meaning* 2 The referents..are the basis of research in onomasiology. **1937** J. ORR tr. *Iordan's Introd. Romance Ling.* iii. 248 The study of a map is..a study of the nomenclature applied to such and such an object. Studies of this kind are termed onomasiological. *Ibid.*, It should not be thought.. that we a reclaiming onomasiology as a child of linguistic geography. **1954** *Archivum Linguisticum* VI. I. 57 Onomasiological investigation of Latin words for 'head'. **1962** Y. MALKIEL in Householder & Saporta *Probl. Lexicogr.* 18 Array of regional or temporal counterparts of each basic entry—an arrangement sometimes called 'onomasiologic' in the Central European tradition of modern-language scholarship. **1969** *Word 1967* XXIII. 578 The functional principle is useful not only in the sphere of syntax but also in the sphere of onomasiology. **1973** *Archivum Linguisticum* IV. 113 The onomasiological or semantic bases of the taxonomic principles. **1974** *Language Sciences* Aug. 28/3 Eventually the onomasiologist may be able to decide whether what we call conceptual structure is something strange of a shape we can scarcely probe by introspection. **1975** *Amer. Speech 1972* XLVII. 166 These are valid onomasiological statements (that is, statements about the relationship of extralinguistic objects to linguistic expressions), but not structural ones.

onomastic, *a.* and *sb.* Add: **B.** *sb.* **3.** *pl.* The study of the origin and formation of proper names, esp. of persons.

The *sing.* in quot. 1930 is unusual.

1930 T. S. ELIOT tr. *St.-J. Perse's Anabasis* x. 67 The man learned in sciences, in onomastic. **1936** *New Yorker* 8 Feb. 54 (*heading*) The advance of municipal onomastics. **1957** M. AUROUSSEAU *Rendering of Geogr. Names* i. 1 The scientific study of names as names, that is, of the human habit of naming things, is the science of onomastics. **1972** J. L. DILLARD *Black English* iii. 135 The subject has not yet been investigated, but it seems possible that the West African influence on Southern onomastics has been very great indeed. **1973** *Amer. Speech 1969* XLIV. 221 This collection of essays..covers the nature of language, cognition, onomastics, [etc.].

onomatology. Add: (Examples.) Hence **onomatolo·gical** *a.*

1919 W. DE MORGAN *Old Madhouse* 324 He therefore endeavoured to bring back the discussion from the onomatologies into which it had strayed. **1931** *Times Lit. Suppl.* 1 Oct. 747/2 'Onomatology', the ugly name which Mr. Ewen gives to this kind of research, is not an exact science. **1961** *Brno Studies in English* III. 10 Their conception of the opposition of analysis *vs.* synthesis is so wide as to include differences of lexical (more specifically onomatological) order.

onomatomania. [See ONOMATO-.] Add: Now usu. with secondary stress on first syllable. **b.** A morbid preoccupation with words; a mania for word-making.

1895 tr. *M. Nordau's Degeneration* III. i. 242 Trichophobia (fear of hair), onomatomania (folly of words or names), pyromania (incendiary madness). **1919** W. OSLER in *Proc. Classical Assoc.* 28 Within the narrow compass of the primitive cell..onomatomania runs riot.

onomatopœics (onǫ:mătopī·iks). [a. Gr. ὀνοματοποίησις the making of a name + -IC 2.] = ONOMATOPOËSIS.

1934 *Times Lit. Suppl.* 1 Feb. 73/2 It is obviously a *tour de force* in onomatopœics not quite so obvious as all the R sounds in Meredith's 'The Lark Ascending'. **1934** C. LAMBERT *Music Ho!* IV. 243 The mechanically picturesque onomatopœics of the piece [*sc. Pacific 231*]. **1978** *Language* LIV. 204 My 1969 paper on onomatopoeics in the Indian linguistic area.

onomatopoietical (ǫno:mătopoiˌe·tikăl), *a.* Also **onomatopoietic.** [f. ONOMATO- + ποιητικός creative (see POIETIC) + -AL.] = ONOMATOPŒIC *a.*

1709 W. KING *Useful Transactions in Philos.* II. 29 An Onomatopoietical Formation. **1883** [see ONOMATOPOETIC *a.*].

onomatopy. Delete † *Obs.* and add later examples.

a **1913** F. ROLFE *Desire & Pursuit of Whole* (1934) 133 'Launchchchchch' was a lovely new onomatopy for the motor-boats. **1946** *Word* Aug. 124 *Synchronic* semasiology ..deals with..polysemantism, affective-value, onomatopy and congeners. **1947** *Ibid.* III. 9 The element of onomatopy in language is too slight to invalidate the general principle.

Onondaga (ǫnǫndā·gă). [Onondaga *onōntáˀke* on the hill (the name of the main Onondaga settlement).] One of the five (later six) tribes of the Iroquois Confederacy of North American Indians commonly called the Five Nations (Six Nations), traditionally living near Syracuse, New York; a member of this tribe; their language. Also *attrib.* or as *adj.*

1684 in *Mass. Hist. Soc. Coll.* (1871) 4th Ser. IX. 187, I haue perswaded all the considerable Indians, the Maquas, Sineques, Onondages..to give up their lands. **1765** in *Documents Colonial Hist. New-York* (1856) VII. 719 The Onondaga Speaker Tyawarunt spoke as follows. **1823** [see *CAYUGA]. **1826** J. F. COOPER *Last of Mohicans* I. xii. 181 The Mohawks, with their Tuscarora and Onondaga brethren. **1874** B. F. TAYLOR *World on Wheels* I. 31 The painted Senecas and the smoky Onondagas went gliding about like vanishing shadows. **1933** [see *CAYUGA]. **1959** [see *Five Nations* s.v. *FIVE *a.* and *sb.* C. 2]. **1971** D. HEFFRON *Nice Fire & Some Moonpennies* vii. 59 My mother is an Onondaga and my father was a Mohawk. **1974** H. WOODBURY in *Papers in Linguistics, Conf. Iroquoian Res. 1972* 2 One way of characterizing Onondaga noun incorporation is to describe its appearance in the surface structure of this language. *Ibid.* 5 In Onondaga, complex sentences are subject to special rules with respect to noun incorporation. *Ibid.* 15 Onondaga does not have relative clauses in the same sense that English does.

onru·sh, *v. poet.* [f. ON-[1] + RUSH *v.*[2]] *intr.* To rush on. So **onrushing** *vbl. sb.*

1861 A. T. DE VERE *Sisters* 71 One through deserts drear On rushing in that race distraught. **1875** W. MORRIS tr. *Virgil's Aeneids* XII. 652 Saces on his foaming steed.. onrusheth to the place. **1882** A. T. DE VERE *Foray of Queen Meave* 169, I hear the on-rushing of the car! **1887** W. MORRIS tr. *Homer's Odyssey* II. xv. 276 Grey-eyed Athene sent them a wind that blew aright through the lift on-rushing fiercely.

Onsager (unsa·gər, ǫ·nsāgəɹ). *Physics.* The name of Lars *Onsager* (1903–76), Norwegian chemist, used *attrib.* and in the possessive with reference to a theorem orig. obtained for the thermodynamics of irreversible processes, but of wide applicability in physics and biophysics, as **Onsager coefficient,** a tensor coefficient expressing the degree of interference between two irreversible processes; **Onsager('s) law** or **principle,** a statement of the reciprocal nature of the interference between two irreversible processes occurring simultaneously, *spec.* that the Onsager coefficients for each direction of flow between the two processes are equal; cf. **reciprocity theorem*; **Onsager (reciprocal** or **reciprocity) relation,** a mathematical statement of the Onsager principle.

1945 *Rev. Mod. Physics* XVII. 343 (*heading*) On Onsager's principle of microscopic reversibility. **1952** *Physica* XVIII. 182 Verschaffelt has given an example of a linear transformation of flux and force variables which leaves the entropy production invariant and yet which destroys the Onsager relations. **1955** I. PRIGOGINE *Introd. Thermodynamics Irreversible Processes* iv. 46 These Onsager reciprocity relations express that when the flux, corresponding to the irreversible processes *i*, is influenced by the affinity X_k of the irreversible process *k*, then the flux *k* is also influenced by the affinity X_i through the same interference coefficient L_{ik}. **1965** W. C. REYNOLDS *Thermodynamics* xiv. 381 Some restrictions on the signs of the Onsager coefficients are provided by the requirement that the entropy-production rate be positive. **1965** KATCHALSKY & CURRAN *Nonequilibrium Thermodynamics in Biophysics* x. 120 Onsager's law provides a quantitative relation between the phenomena of ultrafiltration and osmotic flow. **1968** *Times* 31 Oct. 5/4 In the simplest terms possible, the Onsager principle or 'reciprocity theorem', as it is sometimes called, asserts that where two or more kinds of flow affect each other the equations describing them will be reciprocally related in a specific way. **1977** S. H. CHUE *Thermodynamics* ii. 248 In the Onsager coefficients the subscript *i* refers to the flux and the subscript *j* to the driving force. **1978** B. H. LAVENDA *Thermodynamics Irreversible Processes* ii. 29 The derivation of the Onsager reciprocal relations was based on an apparent analogy between the conditions of chemical equilibrium and the 'principle of detailed balance at equilibrium'.

‖**onsen** (ǫ·nsen). [Jap., ad. Chinese *wên-chüan* hot-spring.] In Japan, a thermal spring, esp. one thought to have medicinal properties; a hot-spring resort.

1933 *Discovery* June 189/1 The *onsen*, the native 'spa' or hot spring so dear to the heart of the folk of the *inaka*, the true countryside of this extraordinary land. **1959** R. KIRKBRIDE *Tamiko* xv. 118 At the Onsen he asked for Richi. **1965** W. SWAAN *Jap. Lantern* xvii. 197 Its *onsen* or hot-spring resorts more than came up to expectations.

onset, *sb.*[1] Add: **2. b.** *Phonetics.* (*a*) The movement of the speech-organs preparatory to, or at the start of, the articulation of a speech sound. (*b*) The initial part of a syllable; the consonant or consonants at the beginning of a syllable. Also *attrib.*

1933 L. BLOOMFIELD *Language* vii. 118 In passing from silence to a stressed vowel, we usually make a gradual onset of the voice. **1948** J. R. FIRTH *Papers in Linguistics 1934–51* (1957) ix. 131 These are the weak, neutral, or 'minimal' vowel, the glottal stop or 'maximum' consonant, aitch, or the pulmonic onset—all of which deserve the general name of laryngals. **1951** TRAGER & SMITH *Outl. Eng. Struct.* 15 Turning to the quality of the vocalic nuclei here, we find that there is an onset in raised lower high front position. **1955** C. F. HOCKETT *Man. Phonol.* 56 Onsets are *simple*, consisting of one or another of some eighteen or twenty *consonants*.., or *complex*, consisting of certain clusters of some of these consonants. **1962** [see *CENTRALIZATION 3]. **1963** *Amer. Speech* XXXVIII. 57 Even if one were to agree that /h/ as an onset consonant 'is a voiceless anticipation of the following peak nucleus' [etc.]. **1966** J. C. POPE *Rhythm of Beowulf* (ed. 2) p. xix, These crests occur at or soon after the onset of the vowel. **1971** T. M. LIGHTNER in W. O. Dingwall *Survey Linguistic Sci.* 501 Word-initial voiced consonants in English begin with voiceless onset. **1973** *Canad. Jrnl. Linguistics* XVIII. 115 The onset of the back-gliding diphthong is typically slightly higher and slightly backer than the onset of the front diphthong.

on shore, on-shore, *adv. phr.* (*adj.*) Add: **2.** (Further examples.)

1932 BELLOC *Napoleon* III. 175 The..torrid day, whose heat was barely mitigated by an on-shore wind from the west. **1961** B. FERGUSSON *Watery Maze* xiv. 342 The strong onshore wind had caused the tide to rise as much as half the hour ahead of almanac time.

b. Existing or occurring on the shore or on land.

1959 *Listener* 5 Mar. 432/3 Glances at the on-shore life. **1973** C. CALLOW *Power from Sea* ii. 67 There is a steadily growing interest in Britain's on-shore oil potential. **1974** *Daily Tel.* 5 Jan. 19/2 By comparison with some of the 20 million tons a year North Sea finds it is a drop in the ocean but encouraging when measured against other onshore finds. **1975** *Offshore* Sept. 97/1 The discovery of oil seeps along the western shore of Cook Inlet led to the drilling of several shallow onshore wells between 1900 and 1906.

on site, on-site, *adv.* (*phr.*) and *a.* [f. ON *prep.* + SITE *sb.*[2]] On a particular site; occurring or situated at a site.

1959 *New Statesman* 17 Jan. 57/3 Russia now accepts.. on-site inspection to identify suspicious phenomena. **1960** *Farmer & Stockbreeder* 19 Jan. (Suppl.) 36/1 Calor Propane is delivered in cylinders or to bulk storage tanks on-site. **1967** A. BATTERSBY *Network Analysis* (ed. 2) xv. 271 On-site management may appear to save time and trouble through less paper work. **1968** *Sci.-Tech. News* Fall 61/1 The librarian..may have to visit personally a large library..and reproduce the material on site. **1975** M. RUSSELL *Murder by Mile* viii. 84 On-site moulding..had been thought preferable... 'But pre-casting might have been quicker?' *Ibid.* 85 He lives on site too.

on stage, on-stage, *adv.* (*phr.*) and *a.* [f. ON *prep.* + STAGE *sb.*] On the stage; that is appearing or occurring on a stage. Also *transf.* and *fig.*

1927 T. S. ELIOT in *Newton's Seneca* I. p. xi, It is not at all clear whether he [*sc.* Hercules] destroys his family on-stage or off. **1944** *New Yorker* 24 June 32/1 Part of Duke's character goes well enough with the onstage Ellington who periodically throws back his head and emits a long-drawn-out 'Ah-h-h!' **1949** *Theatre Arts* XXXIII. 100/3 She might not have taken to sitting dangerously close to the onstage edge of the wings. **1952,** etc. [see *OFF STAGE, OFF-STAGE *adv.* (*phr.*) and *a.*]. **1966** D. F. GALOUYE *Lost Perception* v. 52 Radcliff strode on-stage, supervised a pair of attendants as they positioned the recording camera. **1975** *New Yorker* 5 May 51/2 Everything that he did onstage was done with an excruciating and highly theatrical intensity. **1976** *Country Life* 12 Feb. 346/2 The orchestra..are as well matched.. as the on-stage cast. **1977** *Broadcast* 7 Nov. 13/2 Dickens is very skilled at keeping mechanical dolls waiting in the wings, ready to be wound up and come on-stage.

on stream (stress variable), *adv. phr.* and *a.* Also as one word (see below). [f. ON *prep.* + STREAM *sb.*] **A.** *adv. phr.* (Usu. as two words.) **a.** Of industrial plant and resources, etc.: in or into productive or useful operation.

1930 *Refiner* IX. I. 58/1 The problem which has been most annoying has been one of keeping the unit on stream. **1945** H. S. BELL *Amer. Petroleum Refining* (ed. 3) xvii. 262 For operating on a charge stock which produces more coke a four-case cycle may be used, with ten minutes on stream, ten minutes for purging and valve changes, and twenty minutes for regeneration of the catalyst. **1952** *Economist* 6 Sept. 584/2 The Vacuum Company's refinery..is expected to come on stream this autumn. **1958** *Times Rev. Industry* May 52/2 This material..will be manufactured at Grangemouth where the plant..is due to come on stream in 1959. **1974** *Daily Tel.* 9 Feb. 15/3 Another eight large brickmaking factories are due on stream this year raising capacity to 8,000 million. **1977** *N.Z. Jrnl. Agric.* Jan. 5/2 The dairy came on stream early in August last year.

b. *fig.*

1965 *Economist* 30 Oct. 495/1 The responsiveness of Congress to the evolution of public opinion on various questions of social, economic and fiscal change had been retarded unnaturally until 1965 and then suddenly came on stream. **1972** *Times* 14 Mar. (Hotels Suppl.) p. i/8, London had become enormously attractive to young people all over the world..because 'le mini', Carnaby Street and the swinging set had come on stream all at more or less the same time.

B. *adj.* (Written *on-stream, onstream.*) Productive; done or occurring in the course of normal production.

1938 *Proc. Amer. Petroleum Inst.* XIX. III. 145/1 The catalyst activity decreases during the on-stream period of the cycle due to the accumulation of carbonaceous deposits. **1945** H. S. BELL *Amer. Petroleum Refining* (ed. 3) xvii. 260 A reduction of on-stream time per cycle has the same effect on a fixed-bed unit as an increase in catalyst-to-oil ratio on a continuous catalytic unit. **1971** *Physics Bull.* June 358/1 The main advantage of on-stream analysis is that it obviates the need for tedious sampling and separate analysis of each sample. **1975** *Petroleum Rev.* XXIX. 324/1 Among the advantages claimed for this system are..earlier onstream production when compared with conventional offshore field developments.

ontal (ǫ·ntăl), *a.* [f. Gr. ὄν, ὀντ- being: see ONTO- + -AL.] Relating to reality; comprising reality, not mere phenomena; also *absol.*

1902 J. WARD in *Encycl. Brit.* XXXII. 67/1 The former we may call the phenomenal, and the latter the ontal, meaning of 'aspect'. **1930** F. R. TENNANT *Philos. Theol.* II. i. 20 Further investigation of the regularity of Nature..must wait on inquiry as to what the ontal things which underlie phenomena may be. **1935** *Theology* XXX. 320 A conception of experimental religion which is capable of being held in organic relation with the ontal and axiological arguments. **1970** P. BERTOCCI *Person God Is* 164 Data..provident of fresh knowledge-contact with the ontal.

Ontarian (ǫntē̆ə·riăn), *sb.* and *a.* [f. *Ontari(o,* a lake and a province of Canada + -AN.] **A.** *sb.* A native or inhabitant of Ontario. **B.** *adj.* Of or pertaining to Ontario.

1888 [see SEIGNEUR]. **1936** *Times Educ. Suppl.* 18 Apr. p. iv/2 Proposals..that the Ontarian Government should acquire the house. **1967** *Economist* 30 Sept. p. v/1 A Maritimer earning three-quarters of the average income of all Canadians and only two-thirds of the average Ontarian, has a different perspective from a Quebecois. **1970** *Globe & Mail* (Toronto) 26 Sept. 5/2 After three years' striving to bring the Toronto Franco-Ontarian community together, La Chasse Galerie, a Toronto cultural organization, received official recognition from Secretary of State Gerald Pelletier yesterday. **1975** *Times Lit. Suppl.* 10 Oct. 1188/1 A majoritarian and imperialist view of the Canadian nation that was typically Ontarian. *Ibid.* 1188/5 To Ontarians especially..it seemed to point the direction of Canada's future.

o:n-the-ma·keness. *rare.* [f. phr. *on the make* (MAKE *sb.*[2] 8) + -NESS.] The fact or state of being *on the make.*

1923 GALSWORTHY *Captures* 5 In talking with Steer one never lost consciousness of his keen 'on-the-make-ness'.

o:n-the-spo·t, *a.* [SPOT *sb.*[1] 9.] Done, occurring, or located at the very place in question; observed or made by an eye-witness; immediate, instantaneous.

1886 G. M. HOPKINS *Let.* 11 Feb. (1956) 257 Some on-the-spot account of the late riots, as witnessed by yourself or friends and informants. **1955** *Astounding Sci. Fiction* Dec. 8 You'll..maybe do some on-the-spot generalling. **1955** *Times* 5 July p. iv/1 In these 'on-the-spot' laboratories routine tests are made continuously while the machines are running. **1956** *B.B.C. Handbk. 1957* 90 'On-the-spot' recordings. *Ibid.* 121 On-the-spot reports in sound and television. **1957** [see *CONVECTIONAL *a.*]. **1960** *Guardian* 11 Apr. 8/1 The use of traffic wardens and on-the-spot fines. **1960** [see *CASTROISM]. **1972** *Listener* 3 Feb. 159/2 The increasing use of 'voice pieces' by on-the-spot correspondents. **1977** *Herald* (Melbourne) 18 Jan. 1/1 Surgeons performed on-the-spot amputations.

ontic (ǫ·ntik), *a.* [f. Gr. ὄν, ὀντ- being (see ONTO-) + -IC.] Of or pertaining to knowledge of the existence or structure of being in a given entity (but see quots.). Hence **o·ntical** *a.*, **o·ntically** *adv.*

1949 W. BROCK *Heidegger's Existence & Being* 31 One important difference between science and learning on the one hand and philosophy on the other seems to him [*sc.* Heidegger] to consist in the fact that every kind of scientific and scholarly knowledge was concerned with a limited set of objects, of what he called 'ontic'. **1952** *Mind* LXI. 131 The final outcome of ontically objective values. **1954** *Scottish Jrnl. Theol.* VII. 47 We have to recognise the ontic basis of our faith and obedience. **1957** M. FEAGINS tr. H. Kunz in P. A. Schilpp *Philos. K. Jaspers* II. xiii. 509 It is unavoidable to use the empirical, objectifiable data of knowledge (biological or psychological, for example) as guides to an explication of the ontic character of man as an active, experiencing and self-understanding being. **1960** W. V. QUINE *Word & Object* iii. 120 Of the three evident advantages of 'ontic' over 'ontological', in the special sense of 'as to what there is', brevity is the least. **1962** MACQUARRIE & ROBINSON tr. *Heidegger's Being & Time* i. 31 Ontological inquiry is concerned primarily with *Being*; ontical inquiry is concerned primarily with *entities* and the facts about them. *Ibid.*, The ontical inquiry of the positive sciences. **1969** A. RICHARDSON *Dict. Christian Theol.* 241/2 R. Bultmann..argues that what is ontologically a human possibility, i.e. something which it is possible for men to know, is ontically actualised in Christian faith... It is much discussed today whether religious language.. possesses ontic significance. **1970** J. W. YOLTON *Locke & Compass of Hum. Und.* i. 30 The more typical passages find Locke denying any ontic sense of 'kinds'. **1975** *Times Lit. Suppl.* 25 July 848/2 Before you can elicit the ontic commitment of a statement, you must indulge in what R. G. Collingwood contemptuously described as the scholastic pedantry of reducing to logical form. **1976** D. E. LINGE tr. *Gadamer's Philos. Hermeneutics* xi. 203 Anonymous intentionalities, that is, conceptual intentions in which something is intended and posited as ontically valid.

on to, onto, *prep.* Add: β (Earlier and later examples.)

1715 *Duxbury* (Mass.) *Rec.* (1893) 105 [A] place gutted away by the rain down onto Mr. Wiswells land. **1758** R. PUTNAM *Jrnl.* 3 June (1886) 62 Capt. Nixon's men..fell a tree onto some men as they were in another camp. **1788** J. MAY *Jrnl.* 30 June (1873) 75, I put powder-horn and shot-bag onto him, and a gun in his hand. **1938** L. BEMELMANS *Life Class* II. iii. 142 Everything..can be rushed at a moment's notice onto the tables. **1954** C. S. LEWIS *Horse & his Boy* vi. 76 He jumped down onto the rubbish. **1963** *New Statesman* 24 May 781/3 Russia..has heaved itself onto the plateau of the advanced industrial powers. **1973** G. GREENE *Honorary Consul* III. iii. 132 The man was telling him to get back onto the so-called bed. **1973** [see *LEAD *sb.*[2] 1 f]. **1976** D. HEFFRON *Crusty Crossed* xxviii. 175 He was hanging onto Dot as though they both might collapse to the ground if he let go.

2. Aware of or knowledgeable about (a person, state of affairs, etc.); 'wise to' (something). Cf. *ON *adv.* 13 e. *colloq.* (orig. *U.S.*).

1877 *Chicago Street Gaz.* 20 Oct. 1/2 May Willard, why don't you take a tumble to yourself and not be trying to put on so much style around the St. Mark's Hotel, for very near all of the boys are on to you. **1887** *Lantern* (New Orleans) 9 July 4/3 Who is onto the rag racket. **1888** *New York Mercury* 21 July 3/3 A wife poisoner..ought to have for his wife a woman who is on to him, and who can meet his poison advances with a kerosene bath. **1899** A. H. QUINN *Pennsylvania Stories* 115 The class is about on to us, anyway, and if they find out about this deal [etc.]. **1911** J. C. LINCOLN *Cap'n Warren's Wards* xvi. 254 Everybody has been on to that for some time. **1919** WODEHOUSE *Damsel in Distress* xxi. 248 'So you're on to him, too?' said Billie. 'When did *you* get wise?' **1959** J. OSBORNE *World of Paul Slickey* I. v. 50, I can't help feeling that he's on to us... That he knows about us. **1973** G. MITCHELL *Murder of Busy Lizzie* xiii. 151 'Won't you even tell Gavin that we may be on to something?'.. 'You may say that I have certain suspicions, if you like.'

2. *Math.* (Written **onto.**) Used (in place of *into*) to express the relation of a set to its image under a mapping when every element of the image set has an inverse image in the first set.

1940 C. C. MACDUFFEE *Introd. Abstract Algebra* ii. 54 If a homomorphism of *A* onto *B* exists, we write $A \sim B$. **1962** B. H. ARNOLD *Intuitive Concepts Elem. Topology* vii. 113 Each of the sets *X* and *Y* is the set of all real numbers; $f(x) = 2x$. The transformation $f: X \to Y$ is onto *Y*. **1965** PATTERSON & RUTHERFORD *Elem. Abstract Algebra* i. 3 We shall denote a mapping *f* of S_1 into S_2 by $f: S_1 \to S_2$... If every element *y* of S_2 is of the form $f(x)$ for some $x \in S_1$, we call *f* a mapping of S_1 onto S_2. **1971** E. C. DADE in Powell & Higman *Finite Simple Groups* viii. 307 λ is an epimorphism of *A* onto a field $\bar{F}$.

B. *adj. Math.* Used to designate a mapping of one set 'onto' another.

1942 S. LEFSCHETZ *Algebraic Topology* i. 7 If a transformation is 'onto', the inverse image of the complement of a set is the complement of the inverse image of that set. **1949** —— *Introd. Topology* 216 (Index), Onto transformation. **1951** N. JACOBSON *Lect. Abstract Algebra* I. 4 If α is a mapping of *S* into *T*, and β is a mapping of *T* into *S* such that $\alpha\beta = 1_S$ and $\beta\alpha = 1_T$, then α and β are 1–1, onto mappings and $\beta = \alpha^{-1}$. **1968** [see *INTO *a.*]. **1971** E. C. DADE in Powell & Higman *Finite Simple Groups* viii. 285 By Lemma 9.5 the map is onto.

onto-. Add: **ontotheo·logy** (see quots.); so **ontotheolo·gical** *a.*

1798 A. F. M. WILLICH *Elem. Critical Philos.* 171 Onto-theology is the cognition of a Supreme Being from bare conceptions. **1854** GEO. ELIOT tr. *Feuerbach's Essence Christianity* ii. 38 The *ens realissimum*, the most real being of the old onto-theology. *Ibid.* 40 The onto-theological predicates are merely predicates of the understanding.

ontogenetical, *a.* For *rare*—[0] read *rare* and add example.

1965 *Sci. World* IX. iv. 4/2, I propose to classify the processes which concern biologists as molecular, physiological, ontogenetical, historical and evolutionary.

ontogenic (ǫntodʒe·nik), *a.* [f. ONTOGENY + -IC.] Pertaining to or distinguished by ontogeny; = ONTOGENETIC *a.*

1893 *Proc. Boston Soc. Nat. Hist.* XXVI. 98 The product of the evolution of an ancestor into a phylum through successive independent forms or ontogenic cycles. **1944** B. MALINOWSKI *Sci. Theory of Culture* viii. 78 A new organism comes into being..starting a partly independent career of ontogenic development. **1965** B. E. FREEMAN tr. *Vandel's Biospeleol.* xxii. 367 The information available on ontogenic evolution in the Trechinae will be given.

ontologist. (Later example.)

1856 MILL *Logic* (ed. 4) I. I. iii. 65 Refutation of the Ontologists from their own premises and in their own language, which he [*sc.* Sir Wm. Hamilton] has furnished in the first paper of his *Discussions.*

ontologize, *v.* Add: Hence **onto·logizing** *vbl. sb.* and *ppl. a.*

1878 S. H. HODGSON *Philos. of Reflection* I. 138 The 'too much' of ontologising philosophers. **1897** W. M. URBAN *Hist. Princ. Sufficient Reason* iv. 34 The ontologizing of this fundamental law is the Transcendental Logic of the Kantian *Kritik.* **1940** *Mind* XLIX. 118 Some categories ..are 'ontological or ontologising', *i.e.*, have metaphysical import.

onwards, *adv.* **1. b.** (Later examples.)

1916 G. B. SHAW *Androcles & Lion* I. 9 You may be called on to appear in the Imperial Circus at any time from tomorrow onwards. **1961** NEW ENG. BIBLE *Acts* iii. 24 So said all the prophets, from Samuel onwards. *a* **1976** A. CHRISTIE *Autobiogr.* (1977) VII. ii. 330 From then onwards I should have first-class advice.

onychogryphosis (ǫ:nikogrifō̆u·sis). *Med.* Also **-gryposis.** [f. Gr. ὀνυχο-, comb. form of ὄνυξ nail + γρύπωσις hooking of the nails.] The condition of having overgrowth, accompanied by thickening and curvature, of one or more nails (usu. of the toes).

1833 DUNGLISON *Dict. Med. Sci.* II. 104/1 Onychogryphosis, onychogryposis. **1887** *Boston Med. & Surg. Jrnl.* CXVII. 301/1 When the whole nail is affected, its free border has a tendency to curve downwards. It may occur in various directions, according as it is disturbed in the vertical or transverse way (onychogryphosis). **1901** *Encycl. Medica* VIII. 220 The subject of onychogryposis was first fully investigated by Virchow. **1972** A. ROOK et al. *Textbk. Dermatol.* (ed. 2) II. 1662/1 Nail hypertrophy implies thickening and increase in length, whilst onychogryphosis implies curvature also.

onychomycosis (ǫ:nikomaikō^u·sis). *Med.* Pl. **-mycoses.** [f. as prec. + MYCOSIS.] Fungal infection of a finger- or toe-nail, causing brittleness and discoloration.

1865 *Dublin Q. Jrnl. Med. Sci.* XL. 353 (*heading*) Two cases of onychomycosis. **1887** *Buck's Handbk. Med. Sci.* V. 104/2 The onychomycoses are..of only two kinds, that due to favus, and tinea tricophytina. **1954** A. C. ALLEN *Skin* xiii. 460/2 Onychomycosis is caused by many species of *Trichophyton* as well as by *Epidermophyton floccosum*, several species of *Aspergillus*, and *Candida albicans.* **1975** *Daily Colonist* (Victoria, B.C.) 5 Mar. 2/1 Onychomycosis (also called ringworm of the nails) is caused by a fungus infection.

onychophagist (ǫnikǫ·făd3ist). [See ONYGOPHAGIST.] One who bites his nails. So **onychopha·gia, onycho·phagy,** the habit of biting one's nails.

[**1834**: see ONYGOPHAGIST.] **1900** DORLAND *Med. Dict.* 456/1 Onychophagy. **1900** *Daily Chron.* 10 July 5/2 'Onychophagia' is far more frequent in Parisian than in provincial schools. **1903** Onychophagist [in etym. of ONYGOPHAGIST]. **1907** *Daily News* 4 July 6/7 Dr. Didsbury..suggests that onycophagists [*sic*] should wear his new dental apparatus, which is fastened to the lower molars and just prevents the upper and lower teeth from meeting. **1956** D. M. PILLSBURY et al. *Dermatol.* xlv. 1017 Onychophagia denotes biting of the free edge of the nail. **1977** *Woman's Jrnl.* Apr. 10 Are you an onychophagist? ..This rather long name simply means that you bite your nails.

onymously (ǫ·nimǝsli), *adv. rare.* [f. ONYMOUS *a.* + -LY², after ANONYMOUSLY *adv.*] With the writer's name given or attached.

1889 V. HORSLEY in S. Paget *Sir Victor Horsley* (1919) 86 He anonymously or onymously is not worth powder and shot.

o'nyong-nyong (onyǫ·ŋnyǫŋ). *Med.* Also **onyongnyong.** [See quot. 1960.] A mosquito-borne virus disease in East Africa, similar to dengue, which is caused by an arborvirus and carried by anopheles.

1960 A. J. HADDOW et al. in *Trans. R. Soc. Trop. Med. & Hygiene* LIV. 517 (*heading*) O'nyong-nyong fever: an epidemic virus disease. *Ibid.*, The epithet 'o'nyong-nyong' originated among the Acholi, one of the first tribes to be affected, and, being the first recorded, has been selected as the definitive name of the disease. *Ibid.* 518 The Map.. shows the approximate dates at which o'nyong-nyong appeared in the various affected areas in Uganda. **1966** *Guardian* 8 Sept. 2/8 It has recently been established in Africa that a fever virus called onyongnyong is transmitted by the anopheline mosquito. **1974** A. W. WOODRUFF *Med. in Tropics* xxii. 322/1 O'nyong-nyong has caused one very major epidemic which started in Uganda in 1959 and spread to Kenya, Tanzania and Malawi involving an estimated 2 million people.

oo², 'oo² (ū), a representation of a child-like pronunciation of *you.*

1713 SWIFT *Jrnl. to Stella* (1948) II. 644, I allow oo Six. **1900** M. CORELLI *Boy* i. 8 Oh, Poo Sing! Does 'oo feels ill? Does 'oo feels bad? **1965** *Listener* 1 July 12/2 There is now an enormous gap between a tiny avant-garde and the vast mass of viewers and listeners, between people who are happy with a painting entitled 'Won't Oo Kiss Doggie?' and the few who can accept 'sculpture' made out of old motorbikes and dustbin lids.

oo³, 'oo³ (ū), a representation of a colloq. (orig. Cockney) or vulgar pronunciation of *who.* So **'oom,** whom.

c **1870** A. LLOYD in W. Matthews *Cockney Past & Present* (1938) 91 Then left me for a feller 'oom she thought was much more grand. **1883** *Kaukneigh Awlminek* 7 People 'oo down't profit by experience is medder then moust loonatics. *Ibid.* 15 There's more then fifty thousan' pussons in Lendin oo can't write. I 'ear thet sem uv 'em is editors. **1901** G. B. SHAW *Capt. Brassbound's Conversion* II. 244 Oo a you orderin abaht, ih? **1903** KIPLING *Five Nations* 199 What *is* the sense of 'atin' those 'Oom you are paid to kill? **1950** C. S. FORESTER *Mr. Midshipman Hornblower* 232, I was wonderin' 'oo'd come to my rescue. **1970** M. MOORCOCK *Chinese Agent* x. 71 Oo's gonna pay for all me lovely china! **1973** J. LEASOR *Host of Extras* viii. 147 'Oo're you?' he asked belligerently.

oo⁴ (o,o). Also **o-o.** [Hawaiian.] Also *oo bird.* A black and yellow bird, *Moho braccatus*, belonging to the family Meliphagidæ or honeyeaters and now believed to be extinct.

1890 S. WILSON in *Ibis* II. 179 Large numbers of the O-o must have been taken in old days. **1902** H. W. HENSHAW *Birds Hawaiian Islands* 70 The brilliant shining black body feathers of the o-o were..in great demand for making cloaks. **1937** D. & H. TEILHET *Feather Cloak Murders* x. 181 The little Oo and Mamo birds..from which they plucked..the coloured feathers to make the cloaks. **1944** G. C. MUNRO *Birds Hawaii* 84 If it still exists no effort should be spared to save what would be the last of the famous Hawaiian oos. **1960** *Guardian* 3 Nov. 10/3 Robes made from the tufted feathers of the o-o bird. **1970** S. CARLQUIST *Hawaii* xi. 214 Oos were black, with tufts of yellow feathers extracted to make the yellow feather cloaks. This may well have helped to extinguish the oo. **1977** *Nat. Geographic* Nov. 588/1 (*caption*) Biologist John Sincock..of the U.S. Fish and Wildlife Service sloshes through Alakai Swamp in hope of spying the yellow-thighed oo..one of the world's rarest birds.

oo-. Add: **oogenesis** (later examples); **oogenetic** (example).

1925 R. E. SNODGRASS *Anat. & Physiol. Honeybee* xii. 270 The process [of development] in the case of the egg cells involves oogenesis and maturation. **1960** *New Biol.* XXXI. 94 The process of oogenesis must not predetermine the post-fertilization history of the egg. **1974** L. B. AREY *Developmental Anat.* (ed. 7 rev.) iii. 31 The word 'egg' or 'ovum' is often used when referring to any stage in the course of differentiation of the female sex cell during oögenesis. **1895** D. SHARP in *Cambr. Nat. Hist.* V. xxii. 500 Some hypothetic rudiments they [*sc.* Weismann and others] consider to exist at the very earliest stage of the embryonic, or oogenetic process.

oo, *v.*: see *OOH *v.*

oocyte (ōu·ŏsǝit). *Biol.* [f. OO- + -CYTE, as ad. G. *ovocyte* (now *oozyte*) (T. Boveri 1892, in *Anat. Hefte* Abt. II. I. 446): see OVO-.] An egg mother-cell, which gives rise to a mature ovum by meiosis; the *primary oocyte* gives rise in meiosis I to the *secondary oocyte* and a small polar body; the secondary oocyte gives rise to the mature ovum and another polar body in meiosis II. Also (with some writers), a polar body so produced. Cf. *OVOCYTE.

1895 *Jrnl. R. Microsc. Soc.* 511 (*heading*) Peculiar mitosis in young oocytes of salamander. **1927** [see *OOTID]. **1945** W. J. HAMILTON et al. *Human Embryol.* ii. 12 The formation of the first polar spindle..initiates the first maturation, or reduction, division, the oocyte dividing into a larger cell, the secondary oocyte, and a much smaller cell, the first polar body. **1946** B. M. PATTEN *Human Embryol.* ii. 31 The primary oöcyte divides to form two secondary oöcytes. One of these receives little cytoplasm and is called the first polar body. **1968** PASSMORE & ROBSON *Compan. Med. Stud.* I. xxxvii. 10/2 All the primary oocytes so formed begin their first meiotic division before birth, but the completion of prophase is arrested until after puberty... Meiosis restarts in individual oocytes when their follicles undergo maturation in subsequent ovarian cycles... The remainder of the first meiotic division is completed by the time of ovulation, at which time a secondary oocyte is released into the tube. The second meiotic division follows immediately and.. is not normally completed until the oocyte is penetrated by a spermatozoon. **1970** AMBROSE & EASTY *Cell Biol.* xii. 390 Only one ovum is formed from each oöcyte in contradistinction to the four sperm formed from each spermatocyte.

ood, var. *OUD.

oodle (ū·d'l). Also **-lin** (in sense 1). [Of uncertain origin.] **1.** In *pl.*, large or unlimited quantities; abundance, 'heaps'. *colloq.*

1869 *Overland Monthly* III. 131 A Texan never has a great quantity of any thing, but he has 'scads' of it, or 'oodles', or 'dead oodles', or 'scadoodles', or 'swads'. **1887** J. C. HARRIS in *Century Mag.* Apr. 846/2 All you lack 's the feathers, and we've got oodles of 'em right here. **1892** J. BARLOW *Irish Idylls* iii. 57 A grand young pig, they'll be gettin' oodles o' money on at the fair afore Lent. **1900** ADE *Fables in Slang* 80 Jethro..had learned Oodles of slang up in Chicago. **1904** W. N. HARBEN *Georgians* 115 An' now *you*, a man with oodlin's an' oodlin's o' pore blood kin..are a helpin' at the job. **1919** H. L. WILSON *Ma Pettengill* iii. 78 It snowed hard. Just oodles of the most perfectly dazzling snow. **1928** *Daily Sketch* 7 Aug. 6/2 With oodles of 'Och Ayes', more Scots than ever bled with Wallace have flooded the office with caustic correspondence. **1929** D. G. MACKAIL *How Amusing!* 409 You wouldn't catch *me* coming down to the City every day, if I'd got oodles of boodle like that. **1940** O. NASH *Face is Familiar* 7 And he had one object all sublime, Which was to save simply oodles of time. **1957** *Sunday Times* 14 Apr. 13/3 Oodles for the rich, and practically nothing for the poor. **1967** *She* Dec. 95/1 The cover assures me that there are 'oodles of prizes', which indeed there are. **1975** *New Yorker* 19 May 95/2 (Advt.), Front and back yokes and oodles of shirring for fullness.

2. *Austral.* and *N.Z. slang.* Money in general. *rare.*

1941 in BAKER *Dict. Austral. Slang* 51.

oo-er (ū,ō·ɹ), *int.* Also **ooo-er.** An exclamation expressing surprise, wonder, etc.

1912 C. MACKENZIE *Carnival* ix. 104 'Oo-er!' cried Jenny. 'We aren't going to sleep in the dark?' **1926** C. BEATON *Diary* 18 Oct. in *Wandering Yrs.* (1961) 143 Everyone 'talked common'—the smart thing to do at the moment: 'That 's a bit of all right; I don't mind if I do; oo-er!' **1933** D. L. SAYERS *Murder must Advertise* x. 169 When told what he had missed he merely remarked 'Oo-er!' **1934** R. FERGUSON *Celebrated Sequels* 246 Those who saunter, cry 'oo-er', bathe, knit. **1955** M. ALLINGHAM *Beckoning Lady* xvi. 223 'Oo-er.' Tonker bristled. **1958** S. HYLAND *Who goes Hang?* xvi. 73 'Oo-er,' said Alec Beasley, vulgarly. **1961** *Guardian* 20 Jan. 7/4 The reader will either dutifully say 'Oo-er!' or..'Come off it!' **1977** J. SAVAGE *Nemesis Club* vi. 76 Ian's mouth fell open. 'Ooo-er!'

oof. Add: **oo·finess,** wealth; **oo·fless** (examples); **oo·flessness,** lack of cash.

1888 *Bird o' Freedom* 10 Oct. 5/2 When Jack is on the spree His love may be termed free, And the tarts will oofless be Till his ship comes back. **1889** E. DOWSON *Let.* 18 Jan. (1967) 26, I shall be very oofless tho' & must I fear be a Pinolitic pittite on the occasion. *Ibid.* 17 Mar. (1967) 50, I foresee great—great—oofessness—as the result of this week—much dissipation. **1935** WODEHOUSE *Luck of Bodkins* xvii. 211 His amazing oofiness had a tendency to slip from the mind.

oof, var. OUF, OUFF *int.* in Dict. and Suppl.

1934 in WEBSTER. **1966** L. COHEN *Beautiful Losers* (1970) I. 116 You wanted sock! pow! slam! ugg! oof! yulp! written in the air between you and all the world. **1976** 'R. B. DOMINIC' *Murder out of Commission* iii. 27 'Oof! What a night!' he grunted.

oogamy. (Examples.)

1894 S. H. VINES *Students' Text-bk. Bot.* 225 Oogamy: the female organ is an oogonium. **1933** G. M. SMITH *Fresh-Water Algae U.S.* 288 The evolution from isogamy to oögamy may be independent of any evolution in thallus structure. **1971** P. H. B. TALBOT *Princ. Fungal Taxon.* vii. 91 Oogamy, such as occurs in some of the lower fungi, is but a specialized form of gametangial contact.

oogonial (ōu,ŏgōu·niăl), *a.* [f. OOGONIUM + -AL.] Of or pertaining to an oogonium.

1902 *Science* 21 Mar. 457/1 The protoplasm in contact with the oogonial wall. **1938** G. M. SMITH *Cryptogamic Bot.* I. ii. 74 An oögonial mother cell..may be terminal or intercalary in position. **1970** J. WEBSTER *Introd. Fungi* 73 The oogonial initial is multinucleate.

oogonium. Add: Pl. **oogonia.** **2.** *Biol.* [coined in Ger. as *ovogonium* (T. Boveri 1892, in *Anat. Hefte* Abt. II. I. 446): see OVO-.] A primordial female reproductive cell that gives rise to primary oocytes by mitosis.

1895 *Jrnl. R. Microsc. Soc.* 511 The oogonia show a nucleus with few chromatin fragments and a very delicate, but dense linin-framework. **1920** L. DONCASTER *Introd. Study Cytol.* v. 61 After a number of divisions..the spermatogonia and oogonia cease to divide and begin to increase considerably in size. At this stage they are called primary spermatocytes..and oocytes. **1940** G. A. BAITSELL *Human Biol.* xii. 319 The immature egg or oögonium. **1970** AMBROSE & EASTY *Cell Biol.* x. 330 In the female the oögonia, corresponding to spermatogonia, give rise to oöcytes.

ooh (ū), *int.* Also **oo, ooohh,** etc. [var. OH *int.* (*sb.*)] An exclamation of pain, surprise, wonder, disapprobation, etc. Hence as *sb.*; also **ooh-a(a)h, ooh and ah.**

1916 E. O'NEILL *Bound East for Cardiff* in *Provincetown Plays* 1st Ser. 16 It hurts like hell—here... I guess my old pump's busted. Ooohh! **1919** G. B. SHAW *Great Catherine* iv. 152 Agh!! (*She has again applied her toe*). Oh! Oo! *Ibid.* 154 Agh! Ooh! Stop! Oh Lord! **1939** JOYCE *Finnegans Wake* I. 149 Wee skillmustered shoul with his ooh, hoodoodoo! **1957** R. HOGGART *Uses of Literacy* vi. 165 A world so complex that even those who are immersed in the business of tending its more important machines can only hope to understand a little of it, is daily reduced to a local and spuriously manageable 'ooh-aah', when the paper drops on the mat. **1964** L. DEIGHTON *Funeral in Berlin* xlviii. 301 There was a great 'Ooohh' and 'Aaahh' as the rocket burst. **1975** *Times* 19 Feb. 14/1 The oohs and ahs of a 13-year-old schoolgirl contemplating the Osmonds. **1976** *New Musical Express* 12 Feb. 24/2 All that mopery and Ooooh, it's so hard and lonely at the top. **1977** F. PARRISH *Fire in Barley* ii. 19 Ooh, she's a powerful snob.

ooh (ū), *v.* Also **oo.** [var. OH *v.*] *intr.* To say 'ooh'; also *trans.*, to express with the sound 'ooh'. Freq. in conjunction with *AH *v.* Also in reduplicated form *ooh-ooh.*

1953 POHL & KORNBLUTH *Space Merchants* (1955) x. 102 Above me the respectable Costa Rican consumers oohed and ahed at the view from the prism windows. **1957** 'P. QUENTIN' *Suspicious Circ.* i. 7 Monique was oohing and aahing about 'bone structure' and 'divinity of movement'. **1960** [see *AH *v.*]. **1961** W. SANSOM *Last Hours of Sandra Lee* 112 Mouths ooed and nummed noises of appreciation. **1963** *Times* 8 May 5/6 Vociferous idiots who 'ooh' and 'ah' every time their favourites..set two feet off the stage. **1964** W. MARKFIELD *To Early Grave* (1965) iv. 75 Where do you come off with..that moaning and groaning, that ooh-ing and aah-ing? **1965** J. B. PRIESTLEY *Lost Empires* III. x. 273 People laughed and clapped and Oo'd and Ah'd. **1971** A. MORICE *Death of Gay Dog* xiii. 141 He.. oohed and ahed his way through the column in quite the proper spirit. **1977** *New Musical Express* 12 Feb. 14/5 Pumping their arms in unison, pirouetting and ooh-oohing like crazy, they're very slick, very infectious and warmly humorous.

ooh-la-la (ū·lālā), *int.* Also **oo-la-la, oolala,** etc. [ad. F. *ô là! là!*] An exclamation of surprise, appreciation, etc. Hence as *sb.*, (*a*) the interjection 'ooh-la-la'; (*b*) *slang*, the 'naughtiness' popularly associated with the French; 'spiciness'; (*c*) an attractive or provocative girl. Also *attrib.* or as *adj.*, and as *v. intr.*

1924 *Dialect Notes* V. 274 Exclamations in American English (*title*)..oo(h):..—la la. **1940** E. A. ROBERTSON *Summer's Lease* xx. 269 He went to France..believing that French girls were all 'Oo la la and snatch my garter'. **1943** HUNT & PRINGLE *Service Slang* 49 *Oolala*, Army French meaning O.K. or 'hot stuff'. **1950** BROOKS & WARREN *Fund. Good Writing* xii. 402 Bug-eyed young matrons oo-la-la-ing over the purchase of sheets or toothbrushes. **1952** 'J. TEY' *Singing Sands* xiii. 215 'I like my iniquity with some ooh-la-la in it.' 'Hasn't Daphne got any ooh-la-la?' 'No. Daphne's very la-di-da.' **1952** S. J. PERELMAN *Ill-Tempered Clavichord* (1953) 72 Their silken ankles a target for the ardent glances of gendarmes twirling spiked mustaches and muttering appreciative ooh-la-las. **1959** *Spectator* 24 July 102/3 The ooh-la-la French maid. **1960** I. CROSS *Backward Sex* 72 If this red-haired oo-la-la gets out of hand, I'll fix her for you. **1961** *Sunday Express* 7 May 17/2 The Swiss rely on precision..and the French on oo-la-la. **1970** S. J. PERELMAN *Baby, it's Cold Inside* 161 The playful slaps and oo-la-la's that rang through the valley reassured us that they were still alive. **1973** *Times* 10 Apr. 7/6 Those two great standbys of French fashion, quality and a little bit of ooh-la-la. **1973** A. HUNTER *Gently French* viii. 75 He gave a dirty laugh. 'I've heard about her [*sc.* a French-woman]. When do you get to the ooh la la?' **1975** J. F. BURKE *Death Trick* (1976) vii. 89 'I'll have a French Seventy-five,' she said. Cathleen said, '*Oo! La-la!*' and started a split of bubbly.

ooid (ōu·oid). *Petrol.* [a. G. *ooid* (E. Kalkowsky 1908, in *Zeitschr. f. deutsch. geol. Ges.* LX. 72), f. Gr. ᾠοειδής egg-shaped.] = *OOLITH.

[**1918** *Jrnl. Geol.* XXVI. 593 For an individual grain of an oölite the term 'ovulite'..appears to be preferable to Kalkowsky's 'oöid'.] **1945** *Univ. Texas Publ.* No. 4301. 136/1 *Oöid*, the individual tiny spheroid in an oölitic rock. **1949** H. W. FAIRBAIRN *Struct. Petrol. Deformed Rocks* (ed. 2) iii. 49 Early structural studies of ooids include those of Albert Heim and Loretz. **1965** J. T. GREENSMITH *Hatch & Rastall's Petrol. Sedimentary Rocks* (ed. 4) viii. 199 A normal oolitic limestone or oolitic calcarenite is made up of an aggregate of spherical allochems called ooliths or ooids, usually about 1 mm. or less in diameter. **1974** *Nature* 15 Feb. 452/1 The formation is mainly dolomitic. .. It contains desiccation cracks,..oöids and algal stromatolites.

oojah (ū·dʒā). *slang.* Also **oojar, ujah.** [Of uncertain origin.] A substitute expression used to indicate vaguely a thing of which the speaker cannot at the moment recall the name, or which he does not care to specify precisely; a 'what-you-may-call it', gadget. So in extended forms **ooja-ka-piv** (ū·dʒākā-piv), (**ujah-ka-piv**), **oojah-capiff** (ū·dʒākāpif), **ooja-ka-pivi** (ū·dʒākāpivi), (**ooja-ka-pivvy, oojah capivvy**). See also next word. So **oojah-cum-spiff** *a.*, all right, 'O.K.'.

1917 W. MUIR *Observations of Orderly* xiv. 229 'Oojah', anything. **1925** FRASER & GIBBONS *Soldier & Sailor Words* 215 *Oojah* (*also Ooja-ka-pivi*), a substitute expression for anything the name of which a speaker cannot momentarily think of, *e.g.* 'Pass me that h-m, h-m, oojah-ka-pivi, will you?' **1930** WODEHOUSE *Very Good, Jeeves!* i. 25 'All you have to do,' I said, 'is to carry on here for a few weeks more, and everything will be oojah-cum-spiff.' **1931** J. VAN DRUTEN *London Wall* II. ii. 73 There's a whole lot in the Oojah Capivvy now. **1933** PARTRIDGE *Words, Words, Words!* III. 192 For *thingummy*, Tommy says *oojah*, with variants *oojah-ka-piv, oojah-cum-pivvy*, and *oojiboo*. **1935** D. L. SAYERS *Gaudy Night* viii. 178 Oh, look! your bag's opened itself wide and all the little oojahs have gone down the steps. **1941** P. KENDALL *Gone with Draft* 118 An oojah..a gadget. **1943** HUNT & PRINGLE *Service Slang* 49 *Oojah*, sauce or custard. **1951** *Landfall* V. 89 For Pete's sake, boy, don't lose that little oojah. **1962** *Sunday Times* 4 Feb. 31/6 This was the catch-phrase in a music-hall song in use during the first world war... I remember the line and the tune: 'You cannot eat it, or see it, or hear it—you just ask for Ujah-ka-piv. *Ibid.*, 'Ujah'..was used as widely and as indiscriminately as 'gimmick' and 'gadget' are used now. **1966** 'L. LANE' *ABZ of Scouse* 78 *Whur's ther oojah-capiff?*, where is the hammer, spanner or whatever it might be? **1971** B. W. ALDISS *Soldier Erect* 94 I've seen blokes in hot countries go clean round the oojar because of the perverted practices of native women.

oojiboo (ū:dʒĭbū·). *Soldiers' slang.* [Arbitrary extension of *OOJ(AH, with meaningless suffix.] = prec. So (by metathesis) **oobyjiver** (ū:bĭdʒəi·vəɪ).

1918 *Daily Express* 2 Oct. 2/5 The oojiboo may be a hammer, a saw, a spanner, but Jimmy, or anyone else, knows exactly what is wanted. *Ibid.*, A laundry van bumped into me and carried away my oojiboo [*sc.* a tail lamp]. *Ibid.*, I dropped the old oojiboo [*sc.* kitbag] on the platform and nipped into the refreshment-room. Wasn't gone two minutes, but d—n me if somebody hadn't won the oojiboo [stolen the kitbag]. **1925** FRASER & GIBBONS *Soldier & Sailor Words* 215 *Oojiboo*, much the same as Oojah. **1933** [see *OOJAH]. **1963** *New Society* 22 Aug. 5/2 Colourful words like 'oobyjiver', meaning 'whatsis' pop up regularly.

ook (uk). *slang.* [Origin unknown.] Something slimy, sticky, or otherwise unpleasant. Hence **oo·ky** *a.*, slimy, viscous, repellent; also *fig.*

1964 S. BELLOW *Herzog* (1965) 277 He writes poems and reads them to Mama... He looks ooky when he says them. **1969** DISCH & SLADEK *Black Alice* viii. 81 She had been ..glad..to be here, to be anywhere so long as it marked an end, so long as she could..take a shower to wash off all this brown ook. *Ibid.* 85 'Ain't no shower,' Clara declared flatly. 'A bath, then? I want to wash this ook off of me.' *Ibid.* xiv. 158 The milk was so warm and ooky it was like yogurt.

oolakan. Add: Also **eulachon, olachen, oolaghan, oolichan, ulichan.** Substitute for etym.: [f. Chinook *ûlakân*.] (Earlier and later examples.)

1834 W. F. TOLMIE *Jrnl.* 16 Apr. (1963) 275 The canoes were laden with..dried herring spawn which they are to barter for Oolaghans. **1849** A. ROSS *Adventures First Settlers Oregon River* vi. 97 There is a small fish resembling the smelt or herring, known by the name of ulichan, which enters the river in immense shoals, in the spring of the year. **1911** J. G. FRAZER *Golden Bough: Magic Art* (ed. 3) I. v. 262 The Tsimshian Indians of British Columbia believe that twins..can..call the salmon and the olachen or candle-fish. **1926** B. A. MCKELVIE *Huldowget* 2 They came today for the oolichan fishing. **1953** *Beaver* Mar. 40/2 Oolikan, olachan, eulachon, uthlecan, hollikan and hoolican—spell it as you wish. *Ibid.* 43/1 Exchange value of a large box of olachen grease equalled one caribou skin.. or $1.50 in cash, a century ago. **1965** *Fisherman* (Vancouver) 19 Mar. 2/5 Robichaud said commercial exploitation of eulachons was banned by regulation. **1972** *Evening Telegram* (St. Johns, Newfoundland) 15 July 34/4 Fried and steamed clams, oysters, halibut and oolichans. **1975** H. WHITE *Raincoast Chron.* (1976) 176/2 There were oolachen oil street lamps on cross beams in front of each house.

oo-la-la, oolala, varr. *OOH-LA-LA *int.*

oolite. Add: **4.** = *OOLITH.

1851 H. T. DE LA BECHE *Geol. Observer* viii. 123 The little grains termed oolites, formed of concentric coatings of calcareous matter. **1907** E. H. ADYE *Mod. Lithology* xii. 60 The oolites..formed in shallow waters are cemented together by calcareous material. **1955** E. E. WAHLSTROM *Petrographic Mineral.* x. 335 Most oolites in clastic rocks contain a nucleus of organic matter, a fragment of shell, or a more or less rounded silicate or carbonate particle. **1961** J. H. JOHNSON *Limestone-Building Algae* 256 Algal pisolites are composed of more or less spherical masses ranging in size from that of a large oolite to spherules having a diameter as much as an inch across.

oolith (ōu·ŏliþ). *Petrol.* [f. Gr. ᾠόν egg + λίθος stone (see -LITH).

Mod.L. *oolithus* occurs in this sense in 1721 (F. E. Brückmann *Specimen Physicum Exhibens Historiam Naturalem Oolithi seu Ovariorum Piscium et Concharum in Saxa Mutatorum* 5) and may be the source of both this word and OOLITE (= ad. F *oölithe*).]

Each of the small rounded granules of which oolite is composed.

1788 J. H. DE MAGELLAN *A. F. Cronstedt's Ess. Syst. Mineral.* (ed. 2 rev.) I. 76 The Stalagmites..get a mammillary form, whilst the Stalactites acquire a conic figure: the Oolithes and Pisolites belong to the same species. **1892** *Jrnl. R. Microsc. Soc.* 839 These ooliths are undoubtedly the product of a lime-separating Schizophyte; and the author believes this to be the case with the greater number of the marine calcareous ooliths with a regular zoned and radial structure. **1926** G. W. TYRRELL *Princ. Petrol.* xiii. 227 The grains are called ooliths and the rock containing them oolite or oolitic limestone. Ooliths generally show a series of concentric coats of calcareous material in which a radiating crystalline structure can often be made out. **1938** M. BLACK *Hatch & Rastall's Petrol. Sedimentary Rocks* (ed. 3) viii. 175 A normal oolite is made up of an aggregate of spherical bodies, called ooliths, usually about 1 mm. or less in diameter, cemented by some interstitial material, usually calcite. **1971** I. G. GASS et al. *Understanding Earth* i. 31/2 Ooliths are formed in environments where calcite is being precipitated and there is strong and continuous wave action.

‖ **oom** (ōm). *S. Afr.* [Afrikaans, = Du. *oom*, G. *oheim*, OE. *ēam* EME.] Uncle: often used as a respectful appellation when referring to or addressing an older or elderly man.

1822 W. J. BURCHELL *Trav. S. Afr.* I. xvii. 433 Old Lucas, or as he was more familiarly called, *Oom Hans* (Uncle Hans), now turned back with us. **1883** 'R. IRON' *Story Afr. Farm* II. xii. 227 At the farmhouses where he stopped the 'ooms' and 'tantes' remembered clearly the spider with its four grey horses. **1885** J. NIXON *Compl. Story Transvaal* vi. 116 Sir Theophilus Shepstone, by direction of the High Commissioner, applied to Paul Kruger, inviting him to help with a Boer force; but 'Oom' (uncle) Paul, as he was familiarly termed, declined. **1889** H. A. BRYDEN *Kloof & Karroo* i. 42 Mr. Pieter Maynier, familiarly called by Graaff Reinetters, 'Oom Piet' (Oom, or uncle, being a term of affection in South Africa). **1913** C. PETTMAN *Africanderisms* 349 *Oom* Paul, the ordinary designation of the President of the late Transvaal Republic. **1923** *Radio Times* 28 Sept. 8/2 'Oom Jannie', as he [*sc.* Smuts] is known among his own people. **1951** L. G. GREEN *Grow Lovely* i. 17 That lean old man..—Oom Cappy van der Westhuysen is his name. **1971** *Rand Daily Mail* 27 Mar. 5/5 Mr. Sneech, still active and still running his business, is known to almost every citizen as 'Oom Harry'. **1974** *State* (Columbia, S. Carolina) 28 Mar. 15-B/5 Why is it that man has to remain constantly at war with himself, oom Paul?

'oom: see *OO³.

oompah, oom-pah (ū·mpā). Also **oompa, umpah.** [Imitative.] A repetitive monotonous sound characteristic of a bass brass-instrument; hence, an instrument that makes such a sound. Also in reduplicated forms *oompah-oompah, oomp-pah-pah*. Also *attrib.* and as *v. trans.*

1877 *Brooklyn Monthly* Oct. 21/2 If a young lady takes her place at the piano to sing, it is your duty as a gentleman to accompany her with a very bass 'oom-pah, oom-pah, bum, bum, bum'. **1896** *Scribner's Mag.* July 16/2 And some, near the elephant, have set aside money sufficient for a day within sound of Seidl's orchestra, yet they prefer the oom-pah bands of rusted brass. **1904** ADE *True Bills* 86 He practised until he was able to crawl inside of a big Oom-pah and eat all of the Low Notes in the Blue Book. **1919** *Red Cross Mag.* Mar. 4/2 But the bands still bang and *oom-pah*. **1924** P. ROSENFELD *Port of N.Y.* 72 And the sheer noise..the 'rhythmic oompa of brasses'..saturate him, thrill grim, rough sardonic joy up in him. **1926** *Scribner's Mag.* Sept. 303/2 A genuine, imported, inimitable oompah, a horn among horns, grotesque, gigantic, inescapable. **1927** R. HUGHES *Patent Leather Kid* 224 That's the ole oompah-oompah horn... I nachelly gotta git that oompah. **1929** W. THURMAN *Blacker the Berry* 122 A brutal sliding trumpet call on the trombone..an umpah, umpah by the bass horn..and the orchestra was playing another dance tune. **1930** I. GOLDBERG *Tin Pan Alley* 272 It was an oom-pah, oom-pah in quick tempo. **1951** AUDEN *Nones* (1952) 65 As a trombone the clerk will bravely Go oompah-oompah to his minor grave. **1958** *Spectator* 31 Jan. 135/1 A bombastic crescendo of the utmost thematic poverty and vulgarity, complete with oom-pah off-beat chords. **1959** D. COOKE *Lang. Mus.* v. 257 A grotesquely galumphing 6/8 rhythm of the 'oom-pah' kind is set up, featuring the lewd tenor saxophone. **1961** *Listener* 30 Mar. 950/3 The last movement, an erratic oom-pah of ninth chords, over which the violin sings a hymn. **1966** *Ibid.* 8 Sept. 354/1 The other night the clear air of New York City was heavy with the beat of drums and the oom-pah of brass bands. **1969** M. GILBERT *Etruscan Net* I. v. 71 They had a band..with trombones, and cornets. And a huge instrument that went oompah-oompah. **1971** *Guardian* 4 June 10/6 It was like watching a one-man band. You appreciate his oompah versatility but you don't want to hear what he's playing. **1972** J. WAIN in Cox & Dyson *20th-Cent. Mind* I. xi. 395 These newer poets favoured the woodwinds of the orchestra rather than the brass section so vigorously oompah'd by their seniors. **1974** *N.Y. Times* 23 Dec. 1/1 (*caption*) Holiday Oomp-pah-pah. **1975** *New Yorker* 3 Nov. 127/1 In place of oompah figures or tenths or clusters of offbeat chords in the left hand, he plays on-the-beat guitar chords—rump rump rump rump.

oomph (ūmf). *slang.* (orig. *U.S.*). Also **umph, umphh, oomf.** [Of imitative origin.] Sex appeal, glamour, attractiveness; vitality, enthusiasm. Also *attrib.*, esp. *oomph girl.*

1937 *Sat. Even. Post* 10 Apr. 55/2 With actors, the 'it' quality has to do with their visual personality—sex appeal, magnetism, or whatever you care to call it. Back of the camera, we refer to the ingredient as 'umphh'. **1937** W. WINCHELL in *San Francisco Examiner* 12 Sept. 25/6 Jolson's energy gave the show most of its umph too, that gave the Gershwin memorial program its pace. **1939** *Sun* (Baltimore) 29 Apr. 10/3 The modern [girl] knows she'll make the grade if she has plenty of oomph. **1939** *Life* 31 July 2 Three cheers for the Oomph Girl—yours, *Look's* and *Collier's*—all in one week!.. This Ann Sheridan certainly must have oomph to win the attention of three such important magazines in issues which hit the newsstands at the same time. **1939** W. C. & H. S. PRYOR *Let's go to Movies* 52 'Look, Alice'—to the heroine—'try to put a little more 'umph' into your lovemaking.' **1942** 'W. B. JOHNSON' *Widening Stain* 30 Lucie Coindreau, you know, is the oomph-girl of the Romance Language Department. **1943** P. CHEYNEY *You can always Duck* xii. 192 She has such allure, sex appeal, *oomph* an' what-have-you-got generally. **1951** *New Yorker* 6 Oct. 34/1 Q—What else does it [*sc.* the plot of the play] lack? A—Substance, drive, authority, emotional power, and oomph. **1960** *Guardian* 19 May 9/3 A Lhasa belle, complete with high heels, lipstick, and 'oomph'. **1970** *Daily Tel.* 20 Jan. 15/2 This strictly-tailored suit has more oomph than any see-through ever had. **1973** *Philadelphia Inquirer* (Today Suppl.) 7 Oct. 41/1 If it's on plain black and white paper it doesn't have the *oomf*. Especially to children, it just doesn't have the *oomf*. **1974** *She* Jan. 80/4 We were going to need..a fantasy element to generate enough excitement..in the children to give them the necessary *oomph*. **1974** *San Francisco Examiner* 1 May 35/1 He says I ought to use my 'oomph' to help get BART [*sc.* Bay Area Rapid Transit] finished. What 'oomph' is the man talking about? *Ibid.* 35/2 All old World War II types will remember when Annie S. was 'the oomph girl'. **1977** *Church Times* 28 Oct. 9/3 This prayer may take the form of thanks—for the fact that I am alive with enough energy and oomph to my personality to hate and lust.

oonchook (ū·nʃuk, ōu·n-). Also **eunchuck, owenshook, ownshuck,** etc. [ad. Ir. *óinseach*, Gael. *òinnseach* foolish woman, clown.] † **1.** *Newfoundland.* One of the men dressed as women who participated in a mummers' parade. *Obs.*

1885 W. WHITTLE in *Evening Telegram* (St. John's, Newfoundland) 21 Dec. (1962) 22 'Munn' Carter..was always a conspicuous 'fool'... Davey Foley was always the owner of a stylish rig, while his friend, Masey Murphy, appeared, I think, as an 'Owenshook'. The 'Owenshook' was always a terror to encounter, for he rarely was merciful to any one who made him draw upon his wind, and woe to the man who disputed his right of giving a sound castigation for the trouble incurred. **1895** D. W. PROWSE *Hist. Newfoundland* xiii. 402 Some were dressed as women, with long garments, known as 'eunchucks'. They were all masked, and ran at passengers with an Indian yell, and spoke in a falsetto voice. *a* **1930** G. J. BOND in J. R. Smallwood *Bk. Newfoundland* (1937) II. 259/1 Joined with these gaily bedecked Fools were a smaller number of veiled men in women's garments. They bore the appellation of Oonchooks, and were perhaps more persistent and punishing in their thrashing of people than their more spectacular companions. **1969** in Halpert & Story *Christmas Mumming in Newfoundland* 49 The Newfoundland eyewitnesses draw particular attention..to both the fools who belaboured the bystanders with whips and inflated bladders, and the 'oonchooks'.

2. *Newfoundland* and *Ireland.* (Also in form **oonshick** (-ʃik).) A person who acts foolishly, a noodle. *colloq.*

1937 P. K. DEVINE *Folklore of Newfoundland* 35 *Ownshook*, an ignorant stupid fellow. **1955** *Historic Newfoundland* (Newfoundland Tourist Devel. Office) 35 *Oonshick*, a person of low intelligence. **1961** 'F. O'BRIEN' *Hard Life* x. 83 The divil himself is in the hearts of that Corporation ownshucks. *a* **1966** 'M. Na Gopaleen' *Best of Myles* (1968) 152 Begob if I used the word ownshuck you might take my meaning! **1975** *Globe & Mail* (Toronto) 1 Mar. 27/4 Moreover, all those jokes depicting Newfoundlanders as oonshicks—the vernacular for persons of low intelligence—are..ill-considered comment on the disintegration of 478 years of community loyalty and individual fortitude.

oont (ūnt). *Indian* and *Austral. colloq.* Also **unt.** [ad. Hindi (and Urdu) *ūnṭ* camel.] A camel. *Comb.* **oont-wallah,** a camel-driver.

1862 Mrs. J. B. Speid *Our Last Yrs. in India* ix. 214 The Oont-wallah or camel-man. **1892** Kipling *Barrack-room Ballads* 27 O the oont, O the oont, O the commissariat oont! With 'is silly neck a-bobbin' like a basket full o' snakes. **1894** A. G. Leonard *Camel* 101 The baggage [camel], known as 'Gamal' and 'Unt' respectively in Egypt and India. **1900** *Pall Mall Gaz.* 1 Jan. 1/3 A mule..requires more experience in handling than the bubbling oont of India. **1902** *Chambers's Jrnl.* July 431/1 To judge from the selection of pillage, some one conversant with the interior economy of the caravan was involved, and it was significant that a number of the *oont-wallahs* (camel-drivers) were missing. **1933** *Bulletin* (Sydney) 26 Apr. 33/2 Hell! what a lot of calculation had to go into piloting a couple of smelly oonts! **1945** [see *humpy *sb.*[2]]. **1961** Partridge *Dict. Slang* Suppl. 1207/2 *Oont,*..a camel: Australian.

oophorectomy. Add: Hence o:ophore·ctomize *v. trans.* = *ovariectomize, *ovariotomize *vbs.*; o:ophore·ctomized *ppl. a.*

1955 *Jrnl. Amer. Med. Assoc.* 31 Dec. 1701/2 Of 38 women with metastatic breast cancer, all of whom had previously been oophorectomized, bilateral adrenalectomy produced objective remissions in 45%. **1961** *Lancet* 7 Oct. 793/1 In one case it was found that a woman who had been oophorectomised and adrenalectomised still appeared to be excreting large amounts of œstrogens. **1972** *Jrnl. Endocrinol.* LIV. 115 Oestrogens have been shown to stimulate glycolytic activity in the uteri of oophorectomized rats.

ooplasm (ōu·ŏplæz'm). *Biol.* [f. Oo- + Plasm.] The cytoplasm of an egg (see also quot. 1956).

1899 *Bot. Gaz.* XXVIII. 237 There is a stage called zonation in which the nuclei, usually in metaphase, are lined up around the ooplasm. **1939** P. Weiss *Princ. Devel.* I. 78 Only that part of the egg which consists of true oöplasm is broken up into cells, while those portions which consist mainly of yolk remain either unsegmented or cleave with considerable delay. **1956** C. H. Waddington *Princ. Embryol.* i. 16 The different regions of the cytoplasm of the egg may have specific properties, so that a particular region can only develop in one way. Such regions are spoken of as ooplasms; an older name was 'organ-forming substances'. **1974** *Acta Anat.* LXXXIX. 616 A granular or flocculent material, presumed to consist of blood proteins, in the intercellular spaces outside the oocyte, in the pinocytotic vesicles inside the oocyte, and in the ooplasm itself.

Hence **oopla·smic** *a.*

1905 *Jrnl. Exper. Zool.* II. 147 The third cleavage is equatorial... The ectoplasm is now completely segregated in the four ventral cells but the other oöplasmic substances are not as yet located in separate cells. **1925** E. B. Wilson *Cell* (ed. 3) iv. 338 The enormous increase in the cytoplasmic or oöplasmic substance during the growth of the oöcyte leads to the production of the largest known forms of cells. **1961** N. J. Berrill *Growth* xix. 483 Some insight into the ooplasmic specialization of the primitive chordate egg may be gained by a comparison among the embryonic developments in the ascidian *Styela*, the larvacean tunicate *Oikopleura*, and *Amphioxus*. **1968** F. G. Gilchrist *Survey of Embryol.* iv. 65/2 A considerable rearrangement of the materials of the cytoplasm also takes place during meiosis... The rearrangement is termed ooplasmic segregation.

oops (ūps, ups), *int.* Also **o-o-o-ps, ooops, oooops.** [A natural exclamation.] An exclamation expressing apology, dismay, or surprise, used esp. after making an obvious mistake.

1933 'R. James' *Worth Remembering* xiii. 423 Slap fighting—smiting one's opponent with the open hand—a method even Babe would scurn. Oops! Oops! Oops! **1937** L. B. Murphy *Social Behavior & Child Personality* I. i. 45 Julius picked up Gregory, carried him into the bathroom and dropped him on the floor, said 'Oops!' picked him up again, then let him walk. **1939** L. M. Montgomery *Anne of Ingleside* xliii. 334 She caught her foot in a croquet hoop... Gilbert only said 'O-o-o-ps!' and steadied her. **1939** D. Parker *Here Lies* 70 Oops, I'm sorry I joggled the bed. **1944** 'P. Quentin' *Puzzle for Puppets* i. 5 Iris..said: 'Oops' as she ran into headlong collision with a Marine sergeant. **1960** V. Nabokov *Invitation to Beheading* xii. 119 She..knocked the pencil off, did not catch it in time, and said 'oops!' **1961** J. Heller *Catch-22* (1962) x. 108 'Ooops, there it goes again.' The rain began falling again. **1972** J. Burmeister *Running Scared* v. 80 If something went wrong you went Oops and called an expert. **1974** *Sunday Post* (Glasgow) 5 May 32/3 The 'keeper gave the ball the wet soap treatment—Oops, butter fingers! **1975** *Daily Mirror* 29 Apr. 16 Now, I'm all for new faces—oops, sorry, Hughie—appearing on talent shows on TV.

oo·ps-a-dai:sy, phonet. var. *upsidaisy.

1953 C. S. Forester *Hornblower & Atropos* 76 'There, baby', said the landlady. 'Daddy's going to play with you. Oops-a-daisy, then.' **1967** Partridge *Dict. Slang* Suppl. 1277/2 *Oops-a-daisy!*, a c.p. [*sc.* catch phrase] of consolation as one picks up a child that has fallen. **1970** K. Giles *Death in Church* viii. 190 'Ooops a-daisy,' said the gunman and the Inspector was hurled to the twelve-feet-high ceiling. **1974** N. Freeling *Dressing of Diamond* 173 He..smacked Colette lightly on the bottom, and said, 'Oops-a-daisy, girl: half-time.' **1976** *South Notts Echo* 16 Dec. 6/5 Only a series of oops-a-daisy mishaps, however, persuaded him to slim down in time.

oorial. [a. Punjabi *ūrīal.*] Substitute for def.: A wild sheep, a subspecies of *Ovis orientalis,* having a reddish coat and long, curved horns, found in northern India and other parts of central Asia. (Earlier and later examples.)

1860 P. L. Sclater in *Proc. Zool. Soc.* XXVIII. 127 The Koch, or Oorial of the Sulimani Range, has already been well described. **1898** R. Lydekker *Wild Oxen* 172 The urial, as this sheep is termed in the Salt Range and other districts of the Punjab, is not entitled to specific separation from the sha of Astor and Ladak. **1928** V. G. Childe *Most Anc. East* ix. 201 The foot-hills to the north and west are still the haunts of urial sheep. **1969** J. Fisher et al. *Red Bk.* 168/1 The group of sheep known as Asiatic mouflon, red sheep, and urial are all forms of *Ovis orientalis.*

Oort (ɔːt). *Astr.* The name of Jan Hendrik *Oort* (b. 1900), Dutch astronomer, used *attrib.* and in the possessive to designate concepts proposed by him or arising out of his work, as **Oort('s) (comet) cloud,** a cloud of small bodies that Oort proposed orbited the sun well beyond the orbit of Pluto and acted as a cometary reservoir; **Oort('s) constant,** either of two constants in the equation relating the radial velocity of a star in the galaxy to its distance from the sun (see quot. 1977).

1941 B. J. & P. F. Bok *Milky Way* v. 106 The 'Oort' constant..measures the maximum effect [of differential rotation] at a standard distance. *Ibid.* 108 The best value of Oort's constant *A* is between five and six kilometers per second for a distance of one thousand light years. **1966** *McGraw-Hill Encycl. Sci. & Technol.* VI. 12/1 The radial velocities may be closely represented by the equation Radial velocity $= rA \sin 2l$ where r is the distance to the object from the Sun, l its galactic longitude, and *A*, known as Oort's constant, depends on many factors including the mass of the galaxy and the distance of the Sun from the galactic center. Its value is approximately 18 km/(sec) (1000 parsecs). **1968** D. C. Knight *Comets* 38 The American astronomer Fred L. Whipple recently proposed that a yet-to-be-seen comet belt, distinct from Oort's 'comet cloud', lies near the orbit of Pluto. **1976** *Nature* 29 Jan. 290/1 Some theories go even further and predict that, in addition to these comets in the Oort cloud, the remains of a primaeval comet belt may still exist at a distance of ~50 AU. **1976** *National Observer* (U.S.) 24 Apr. 6/1 Van Flandern's work also casts doubt on 'Oort's Cloud', one of the more cherished concepts of comet studies. **1977** J. Narlikar *Struct. Universe* iii. 62 Oort expressed the transverse velocity of the star in the following form $T = r\{B + A \cos 2(l - l_0)\}$. Here r is the distance of the star from the Sun, l its galactic longitude, and l_0 is the galactic longitude of the galactic centre. *A* and *B* are constants called Oort's constants.

oosi, var. *oozi.

ootid (ōu·ŏtid). *Biol.* [f. Oo- after *spermatid.*] A haploid cell formed by the division of a secondary oocyte; by some writers restricted to the ovum, as contrasted with the polar body.

1908 F. R. Lillie *Devel. of Chick* 14 The mature ovum (oötid) and the polar bodies are the precise equivalent of the four spermatids, but..only the ovum on the female side is functional. **1927** W. Shumway *Vert. Embryol.* ii. 34 In this way four (or three, if the smaller secondary oöcyte fails to divide) oötids are produced, of which the single large cell is the ovum, while the smaller ones are known as polocytes. **1946** B. M. Patten *Human Embryol.* ii. 31 The secondary oöcyte..divides again, and in this division..the bulk of the cytoplasm goes to one of the two resulting oötids, which is then commonly called the 'matured ovum'. **1964** N. S. Cohn *Elem. Cytol.* II. xiii. 206 The secondary oöcyte undergoes a second meiotic division, producing one large cell, the oötid, and a small second polar body. *Ibid.*, The oötid..matures into the egg or ovum. **1972** *Nature* 28 Jan. 213 It must be recalled that the sea urchin egg is an ootid whose maturation divisions ..have been completed.

ooze, *sb.*[1] Add: **2. b.** Short for *ooze leather* (see sense 4 below). Also *attrib.*

1916 *Daily Colonist* (Victoria, B.C.) 18 July 14/1 (Advt.), Ladies' 8-Inch High Laced White Ivory Ooze Boot, blind eyelets, small perforations, full Louis heel. **1922** M. B. Houston *Witch Man* vi. 78 A 'gift' volume of Shakespeare, bound in dark blue ooze.

4. ooze (or **oozed**) **leather** = *ooze-calf.*

1890 in *American Mail Order Fashions* (1961) 27 Boys' Eton Caps in ooze leather. Price, $1. **1897** *Sears, Roebuck Catal.* 324/3 A Very Good Oozed Leather Tobacco or Coin Pouch. **1928** *Publishers' Weekly* 9 June 2348 In four styles of binding..ooze leather, two colors, green or brown, $2·50. **1937** S. V. Benét *Thirteen O'Clock* 71, I could stomach Jeremy Jason, the homespun philosopher, whose small green ooze-leather booklets..produced much the same sensation in me as running a torn fingernail over heavy plush. **1960** G. A. Glaister *Gloss. Bk.* 286/2 Ooze leather, calfskins or split sheepskins prepared to give them a suede or velvet finish on the flesh side.

ooze, *sb.*[2] Add: **2.** (Earlier examples.)

1858 J. Dayman *Deep Sea Soundings* 7 The sinker was detached, and the valve..full of soft oaze. *Ibid.* 9 Between the 15th and 45th degrees of west longitude lies the deepest part of the ocean, the bottom of which is almost wholly composed of the same kind of soft mealy substance, which, for want of a better name, I have called oaze.

b. A deposit or layer of ooze on the ocean floor.

1876 *Proc. R. Soc.* XXIV. 532 In the *Globigerina*, Radiolarian, and Diatom oozes we have found..only one or two shark's teeth. **1926** G. W. Tyrrell *Princ. Petrol.* xiv. 236 The oozes which cover great areas of the ocean floor are mainly calcareous and foraminiferal. **1971** *Nature* 3 Sept. 46/1 The ophiolites in those deep-sea troughs were overlain by Upper Jurassic and Lower Cretaceous radiolarian and nannofossil oozes.

ooze (ūz), *sb.*[4] [prob. f. *ooze, oos(e)*, plur. of *oo*, Sc. form of Wool *sb.*] The nap or short fibres that project from yarn.

1892 J. Nasmith *Students' Cotton Spinning* 373 When thread is intended for lace purposes..it is passed several times through a gas flame at a high speed, so as to burn off the filaments or 'ooze' on its surface and leave it bare. **1909** *Engineer* 1 Oct. 352/1 The term 'gassing' is applied to the process of burning off the ends of fibres or 'ooze' on the different kinds of yarn.

ooze, *v.*[1] Add: **2. c.** Of persons, objects. Often with *out, up, off,* etc.

1929 D. G. Mackail *How Amusing!* 350 Whenever I came oozing along the street, he sort of edged away. **1929** Wodehouse *Mr. Mulliner Speaking* ix. 313 She had planned to lure him into the thing and then ooze off and land him with these septic kids. **1930** —— *Very Good, Jeeves!* v. 122 He oozed out, leaving me to play the sparkling host. **1935** D. L. Sayers *Gaudy Night* xi. 232 Thought I must just ooze over and pass the time of day. ? **1953** [see *eel *v.*]. **1956** N. Marsh *Off with his Head* (1957) viii. 176, I believe I oozed off before they got going. **1963** C. D. Simak *They walked like Men* x. 57, I oozed into the place and shut the door behind me, then slid along the wall and stood there..with my back against the wall. **1966** D. Francis *Flying Finish* ii. 19 He oozed on to a bar stool, his bulk drooping around him. **1971** *Daily Tel.* 15 Sept. 9/4, 18ft 10in of gleaming black Daimler Limousine oozed up the drive and stopped outside. **1971** D. E. Westlake *I gave at the Office* (1972) 127 Decrepit people..sort of oozed out of doorways. **1977** M. Russell *Dial Death* I. iii. 27 The absence of briefcase and umbrella told her that Mr Trenchard had oozed away for the night.

3. (Further examples of *fig.* use.)

1925 E. J. P. Benn *Confessions of Capitalist* i. 21 Women over- or under-dressed, oozing money, and giving from their conversation no trace of education or of finer feeling. **1959** *Listener* 29 Jan. 228/1 The amount of charm oozed at us from the television screen. **1971** *Daily Tel.* 13 Apr. 10/7 The way he oozes bonhomie over everything from day-old chicks to old-age pensioners I find grating. **1975** B. Garfield *Death Sentence* (1976) xxix. 138 The car radio oozed wallpaper music as viscous as syrup.

‖ **oozi** (ū·zi). Also **oozie, oosi.** [ad. Burmese *ù-zì* one seated at the head of an elephant or at the prow of a boat, f. *ù* head + *sì* to mount, ride on.] An elephant-driver; a mahout.

1901 G. H. Evans *Treatise on Elephants* ii. 18 Every domesticated elephant necessarily has its own particular attendant ..*oo-si*(the man who rides in front), or *mahout. Ibid.*, The *oo-si* should have experience of the most approved methods of fettering, catching, subduing, and approaching unruly animals. **1905** R. T. Kelly *Burma* v. 84 It is interesting to watch the elephants at work; their sagacity is remarkable, and they hardly seem to require the direction of the 'oozis' who sit astride their necks. **1930** Mitton & Yoe *Life Story of Elephant* xiii. 205 The *oozi* who had come with me from Mandalay for some reason left me, and a new man altogether took me in hand. **1960** *News Chron.* 12 July 6/1 Working with oozies (elephant drivers) who believed in magic and nats (spirits) and every form of what we call superstition, I kept a very close hold upon myself. *Ibid.*, The drinks flowed..because they knew that very soon they would be out on trek again, alone, except for their dogs, their servants, the oozies and the elephants.

oozle (ū·z'l), *v. Austral.* and *N.Z.* (*rare*). [f. Ooze *v.*[1] + -le.] *trans.* and *intr.* To undulate; to move slowly.

1934 T. Wood *Cobbers* xii. 153 The octopus..goggled his eyes and oozled his slimy, restless-writhing arms. **1958** *Tararua* XII. 29 The critics will no doubt note that *to oozle* and *to trickle*, which denoted much slower modes of locomotion, were comparatively little used.

oozlum bird (ū·zlɒm). [Fanciful.] A mythical or unrecognized bird (see quots.).

1899 W. T. Goodge *Hits, Skits, & Jingles* 6 It's a curious bird, the Oozlum, And a bird that 's mighty wise, For it always flies tail-first to Keep the dust out of its eyes! **1951** Partridge *Dict. Slang* (ed. 4) 1126/1 *Oozlum bird*, 'a bird whose species you cannot recognise on sight', ..: Naval. **1974** P. Cave *Dirtiest Picture Postcard* xvii. 113 The fabulous oozlum bird, which flies round in ever-decreasing circles until it disappears up its own arsehole in a puff of blue smoke.

op[2] (ǫp). *Mus.* Pl. **opp, ops.** Abbrev. Opus 1 (rarely *opus *v.*).

In some early uses the abbreviation may be of the Italian *opera.*

1784 (*title*) A Favorite Concerto for the Harpsichord or Piano Forte with Accompanyments: Composed by Giuseppe Haydn. Op. 37. *a* **1865** MRS. GASKELL *Let.* (1966) 817 Violet: 'Have you brought any music down Miss Gaskell?' Meta: 'No.' Violet: 'Oh—but I've brought *Op.* 7 down with me.' **1880** [see OPUS 1]. **1885** W. S. GILBERT *Mikado* II. 36 The music hall singer attends a series Of masses and fugues and 'ops' By Bach, interwoven With Spohr and Beethoven, At classical Monday Pops. **1901** *Punch* 1 May 325/2 (*caption*) Lady (referring to programme, to friend). '"Schumann, Op. 2". What's the meaning of "Op. 2"?' 'Arry (who thinks he is being addressed, and always ready to oblige with information). 'Oh, Op. 2. Second dance; second 'op, yer know. May I 'ave the pleasure?' **1921** [see *OPUS *v.*]. **1924** *Public Opinion* 12 Sept. 258/2 No longer does light and irresponsible music suffice as it did in days that are gone. The inclination of the public is towards the classical. The programmes that give the 'symphonies and ops' prove the most attractive. **1933** *Radio Times* 14 Apr. 108/2 The famous violinist, Rode, for whom Beethoven..composed this sonata for violin and pianoforte, Op. 96. **1968** *Listener* 11 July 56/2 These waltzes..differ considerably in style from the fine set of six waltzes for piano duet, Op. 22, of only a little later. **1974** *Times* 19 Oct. 9/6 Ashkenazy chooses..slow tempo for the fugues..in Op. 110. **1975** *Gramophone* July 205/1 Dvorak. Slavonic Dances, Opp. 46 and 72.

op³ (ǫp). **1.** Colloq. abbrev. OPERATION. **a.** = OPERATION 6.

1925 W. DEEPING *Sorrell & Son* xviii. 273 Motor-bus ran over her..pretty hopeless. Winter has seen her,—but thought she wouldn't stand an op. **1932** A. CHRISTIE *Peril at End House* iii. 50 Just before my op... Operation. For appendicitis. **1933** JOYCE *Let.* 30 May (1966) III. 281 Dangerous for operated eye which may go blind during op. because of loss of vitreous. **1934** *Punch* 11 Apr. 397/1 No need for immediate op.; right eye untouched, but he fears left may be permanently damaged. **1953** C. DAY LEWIS *Italian Visit* v. 59 I'd not advise you to believe There's a slick op. to end your grief. **1964** G. L. COHEN *What's Wrong with Hospitals?* iv. 74 The probationers agreed that minor ops gave the most trouble. **1973** *Guardian* 26 May 1/5 Ops on rates. Free vasectomy operations..were available in Birmingham from yesterday. **1974** O. MANNING *Rain Forest* II. i. 139 'I was so tired the evening we reached Al-Bustan, I forgot to take that damn pill.' 'If it was as long ago as that, it *is* too late, dear, unless you want a major op.'

b. Freq. pl. = OPERATION 7. Also *attrib.* and *transf.*

In quots. 1941¹, 1942¹ short for *Operations Room.*

1925 FRASER & GIBBONS *Soldier & Sailor Words* 215 *Ops.*, operations. **1941** *Jrnl. Aeronaut. Sci.* (Aeronaut. Rev. sect.) Jan. 32/3 The atmosphere of the room is recreated, even to the introduction of some of the new aeronautical colloquialisms, such as 'Ops' for the operations room. **1941** *Illustr. London News* CXCVIII. 434/1 The bomber pilot is aware that his squadron is scheduled for what the Service calls 'Ops' (Operations) when his batman wakes him with an early-morning cup of tea. **1942** T. RATTIGAN *Flare Path* I. 112, I went up to ops. at five-thirty. **1942** *R.A.F. Jrnl.* 30 May 33 The..officer..delved into his brief-case and produced the ops log. **1942** *Tee Emm* (Air Ministry) II. 89 Make certain before going out on ops. that you have your whistle. **1944** 'N. SHUTE' *Pastoral* iii. 57 Each day we practise some new thing that we have learnt from the last op. **1949** *Radio Times* 15 July 38/3 Ann Scott,..gets into conversation..with an American girl who met a boy in the R.A.F. three months ago... 'Now he's starting Ops and he wants us to get married right away—he's like that!' **1967** O. WYND *Walk Softly* xi. 171 'This is the ops room.' The place had one door and was about thirty feet square. **1970** *Daily Tel.* 16 June 7/1 A seasoned campaigner watched the campaign in awe. 'It is like a military op,' he said. **1973** 'A. HALL' *Tango Briefing* x. 120 They'd been forced to set up the op... The decision-making had been at Prime Minister level. **1973** D. MILLER *Chinese Jade Affair* xviii. 173, I looked in some awe at the maps spread out in true 'Ops Room' fashion.

2. Colloq. abbrev. OPERATIVE *sb.*, OPERATOR. **a.** A (private) detective (see *OPERATIVE *sb.* 3b).

1926 *Clues* Nov. 162/1 *Op*, a private detective agency operator. **1927** D. HAMMETT in *Black Mask* May 24/1 He says in all his fifty years of gum-shoeing he's never seen such a handsome op, besides being a fashion plate and a social butterfly and the heir to millions. **1929** —— *Dain Curse* (1930) xx. 224 'Can you spare me another op?' I asked. 'MacMan is available.' **1975** J. GORES *Hammett* viii. 60 Watching the stocky two-hundred-pound op.. Hammett felt a little ill... 'You going to take over the investigation of the police department?'

b. A radio or telegraph operator (see OPERATOR 5 in Dict. and Suppl.). (See also quot. 1970.)

1931 G. IRWIN *Amer. Tramp & Underworld Slang* 138 *Op*, a telegraph operator. **1942** T. RATTIGAN *Flare Path* I. 94 Two bumped off—tail gunner and wireless op. **1970** *Amer. Speech 1968* XLIII. 288 *Op*, a telephone, telegraph, or teletype operator. **1973** A. ROSS *Dunfermline Affair* 13 He had been a Radio Op in the R.A.F.

op⁴ (ǫp), colloq. abbrev. *OPTICAL *a.* 2c. *op art*, =*optical art* s.v. *OPTICAL *a.* 2c. orig. *U.S.* Also *attrib.*

1964 *Time* 23 Oct. 78/1 No less a break from abstract expressionism than pop art, op art is made tantalizing, eye-teasing, even eye-smarting by visual researchers using all the ingredients of an optometrist's nightmare. *Ibid.*, The Museum of Modern Art is planning an op show titled 'The Responsive Eye' early next year. **1964, 1965** [see *OPTICAL *a.* 2c]. **1965** *Observer* 28 Feb. 2/6 'Op Art'—as it is known among the smart set—has taken America's contemporary art enthusiasts by storm, and made its predecessor, 'Pop Art', seem *passé*. *Ibid.* (Colour Suppl.) 23 May 23/2 Op(tical) dresses are dazzling—literally. They jar the eye with geometric billboard colour... Trad dresses are gentle and demure. Op. dresses are stark and simple. **1965** *Sun* 24 May 5/7 Then you get a blasting of Op art—that's the optical illusion art that the young artists are raving about. **1966** *Time* 28 Jan. 44 Hard on the heels of op artists, who address their work to the retina, has come a widespread number of 'kinetic' artists, who try to combine mechanics and art. **1966** *Punch* 2 Feb. 158/1 (*caption*) Or there's this op-art bowler, sir, for more formal occasions. *Ibid.* 15 June 876/3 Knee-length skirts, non-plastic fabrics, non-Op shoes; also short-haired men and neat girls in plain stockings. **1967** J. SYMONS *Man who killed Himself* II. vi. 184 She was dressed now in a black and white op art dress. **1967** *Punch* 21 June 906/1 Infinite trouble is taken by op artists to produce an illusion of movement. **1967** *Spectator* 18 Aug. 194/3 With bright Op patternings, primary Pop colours and uninhibited use of synthetic materials, these designers..parallel our painters and sculptors in inventing new shapes and forms through the use of new materials. **1970** M. DE SAUSMAREZ *Bridget Riley* i. 15 Its decorative potential..has been..widely exploited commercially in 'Op' dresses, 'Op' advertising, and 'Op' packaging. **1970** W. J. BURLEY *To kill Cat* i. 12 A sleeveless frock in gay op-art material. **1974** *Encycl. Brit. Micropædia* VII. 545/1 The effects of Op art can be based either on perspective illusion or on chromatic tension; in painting, the dominant medium of Op art, the surface tension is usually maximized to the point at which an actual flickering is perceived by the human eye. **1974** *Listener* 24 Jan. 108/2 Artists (especially Op-artists and the like) can impose an unjustifiable authority on the observer. **1976** 'Z. STONE' *Modigliani Scandal* I. iii. 35 He..looked at the desk... The grain..flowed like an op-art painting.

opacification (opæ:sifikē·ʃən). [f. as next + -IFICATION.] The process of rendering or becoming opaque.

1903 *Med. Rec.* (N.Y.) LXIII. 333/2 Hyperplasia, degeneration—these are results of malnutrition and the essentials of opacification [of the lens]. **1947** *Jrnl. Soc. Glass Technol.* XXXI. Abstr. Sect. 29 A boron-free enamel might be fired to a certain degree, after which opacification decreased because the TiO_2 was dissolved. **1953** *Radiology* LX. 366/1 (*caption*) The poor opacification [to X-rays] of the liver and of the portal vein is typical of cirrhosis. **1970** *Nature* 24 Oct. 363/1 Opacification of the lens began as an increase in sheen posteriorly.

opacifier (opæ·sifəiˌəɹ). [f. next + -ER¹.] A substance which renders something opaque.

1911 *Chem. Abstr.* V. 168 Cast Iron Enamels... SnO_2 and cryolite are the best opacifiers. **1959** *Which?* Nov. 152/1 Opacifiers (which make it look opaque and creamy) make the shampoos look more attractive. **1973** *Daily Tel.* (Colour Suppl.) 12 Oct. 72/4 The developer then gets to work on the negative and the opacifier which gradually clears to reveal the dyes, now released from the negative and visible above the white pigment. *a* **1977** *Harrison Mayer Ltd. Catal.* 23/2 Tin oxide is widely used as a glaze opacifier.

opacify (opæ·sifəi), *v.* [f. OPAC(ITY + -IFY; cf. F. (*s'*)*opacifier*.] **a.** *trans.* To render opaque.

1940 *Chem. Abstr.* XXIV. 4268 (*heading*) Paper opacified with calcium carbonate. **1955** P. D. TREVOR-ROPER *Ophthalm.* xxiii. 413 Post-operative uveitis may opacify the posterior corneal layers. **1957** S. D. GERSHON et al. in E. Sagarin *Cosmetics* xxiv. 615 Initially, cold-waving lotions were marketed as transparent liquids. Shortly thereafter, the advantage of marketing an opaque liquid, the milkiness connoting richness and gentleness, became evident. As a result, practically all marketed waving lotions were opacified. **1971** *Country Life* 6 May 1084/1 Milk-white glass opacified with arsenic displays a fiery opalescence if held to the light.

b. *intr.* To become opaque.

1954 S. DUKE-ELDER *Parson's Dis. Eye* (ed. 12) ii. 24 If either of these membranes [of the cornea] is disrupted, fluid is absorbed and the tissue opacifies. **1967** *Amer. Jrnl. Roentgenology* C. 410/2 The fluid-filled fundus of the stomach..opacifies during abdominal aortography. **1971** *Nature* 12 Mar. 120/2 Corneas rapidly opacified and swelled with the first enzyme digestion after the initial irradiation.

So **opa·cified** *ppl. a.*, **opa·cifying** *ppl. a.* and *vbl. sb.*

1914 *Chem. Abstr.* VIII. 224 The opacifying effect of the metallic oxides of Sn, Zr, Ti and Al..utilizable for white enamels. **1947** *Endeavour* VI. 117 The opacifying agent dissolves, leaving the glass transparent while molten, but causing it to become opaque upon cooling. **1954** *Amer. Jrnl. Roentgenology* LXXII. 592/1 In the later films the liver seems to be more opacified..than the spleen. **1963** *Times* 25 May 11/4 These enamels were produced by fusing what amounted to opacified glass on to wafer-thin copper. **1973** *Sci. Amer.* Oct. 128/1 A talc base will often be augmented with an opacifying pigment such as zinc oxide or titanium dioxide.

opacimeter (opæsi·mĭtəɹ). [f. OPACI(TY + -METER.] An instrument for measuring opacity, esp. by reflection.

1919 *Chem. Abstr.* XIII. 2892 (*heading*) Opacimeter designed for the estimation of the quantity of bacteria. **1944** *Paper Trade Jrnl.* 26 Oct. 27/2 The white body consists of a white standard protected by a cover glass, as is the case in the Bausch and Lomb opacimeter. **1967** *TAPPI* Feb. 59A/1 The B & L Opacimeter reads either printing opacity (as defined by Davis) or contrast ratio (as defined by TAPPI official methods).

opacious, *a.* Delete *Obs.* and add later example (prob. used as a conscious archaism).

1953 S. BECKETT *Watt* III. 158, I was very fond of fences, of wire fences,..; not of walls, nor palisades, nor opacious hedges, no.

opacity. Add: **2.** *spec.* the ratio of the intensity of the light incident on a sample or object to that of the light transmitted by it.

1890 HURTER & DRIFFIELD in *Jrnl. Soc. Chem. Industry* 31 May 455/2 The inverse of that fraction, or $I/I_x = e^{kA}$ measures the opacity of the substance. **1926** J. W. T. WALSH *Photometry* xiii. 392 The opacity is then measured by placing the exposed area of the plate between a source of light and a photometer. **1939** *Q. Jrnl. R. Meteorol. Soc.* LXV. 417 In the case of five stations..the summer values of opacity are higher than the winter values, owing to the prevalence of sea fogs in summer. **1966** R. J. ROSS *Television Film Engin.* iv. 169 The silver deposit and the opacity are so related that the logarithm of the opacity is directly proportional to the mass of silver.

b. Also used with reference to other forms of radiation. (Further examples.)

1928 [see *LIPIODOL]. **1971** *Jrnl. Electron. Microsc.* XX. 124/1 The pronounced electron opacity was localized especially..on the outer membrane.

3. c. With reference to a rule in *Phonology*: the state or quality of being opaque (sense *3 c).

1971 [see *OPAQUE *a.* 3 c]. **1975** *Trans. Philol. Soc. 1974* 113, I have myself argued..that for French the elegance of such a solution is outweighed by its disadvantages and that restructuring occurred when generalization of the loss of word-final [ə] made for opacity: the conditioning of denasalization before an intervocalic nasal was no longer discernible from surface phonetic shapes. **1977** *Language* LIII. 19 In each instance of opacity, a phonological rule which relates a large number of surface lexical items is obscured by the presence of other items in which the rule appears to fail.

opal. Add: **1. c.** The colour of an opal.

1890 O. WILDE *Pict. Dorian Gray* v, in *Lippincott's Monthly Mag.* July 41 The sky was pure opal now. **1897** *Sears, Roebuck Catal.* 212/1 Dainty colorings.. baby blue, rose pink, opal, [etc.]. **1901** [see *ASH *sb.*² 1 e]. **1914** R. BROOKE in E. Marsh *Rupert Brooke* (1918) vii. 142 Like an Italian town in silver-point..with a sea and sky of opal and pearl and faint gold around. **1966** G. W. TURNER *Eng. Lang. Austral. & N.Z.* iv. 83 The sky turned into an unlucky opal.

2. (Earlier and later examples.) Also with reference to the opalescence of the glass (rather than the colour). Also *attrib.*

1885 *List of Subscribers, Classified* (United Telephone Co.) (ed. 6) 229 (Advt.), Crystal and Demi-Crystal Table Services and Ornaments..Opal, Flint, and Coloured Goods. **1949** W. A. THORPE *Eng. Glass* (ed. 2) ix. 226 It [*sc.* a 'nine-pin' bottle] belonged in the main to Bristol and Stourbridge manufacturers, and in..white opal it lasted well into the nineteenth century. **1970** F. & L. SCHULER *Glassforming* vi. 50 To the commercial decorators the term 'glass color'..means any fusible coating for glass, including both the transparent colors and the opal colors.

3. b. *spec.* Applied to an electric light bulb made of translucent white glass.

[**1901** F. B. CROCKER *Electr. Lighting* II. xvii. 423 Lamps are made in many colors, such as red, blue, green, amber, opal, frosted, etc., besides the ordinary clear glass bulbs.] **1904** *Electr. Rev.* 19 Feb. (Suppl.) p. ix (Advt.), The 'Ideal' half opal lamp. **1926** *Gloss. Terms Electr. Engin.* (*B.S.I.*) 148 *Opal lamp*, a filament lamp, the bulb of which is made of opalescent glassware so as to enlarge the source of light with a consequent reduction in surface brightness [etc.]. **1934** *Discovery* Aug. 229/2 A hole in a screen in front of an opal lamp. **1938** [see *PEARL *sb.*¹ 16 b]. **1976** *Daily Tel.* (Colour Suppl.) 25 June 15/2 Opal light bulbs are primarily suitable for use where the bulb is clearly visible, for their coating hides the filament.

4. *opal-buyer, -field, -seeker; opal-black, -green, -grey, -hued* (earlier example), *-pale, -shelled* adjs.; **opal dirt** *Austral.*, the type of earth in which opal is found; **opal glass** (earlier and later examples); also *attrib.*; **opal gouger** *Austral.*, one who digs for opal; cf. *GOUGER c; **opal ware,** ware made of opal glass, *spec.* a type of heat-resistant opalescent ware (now, with capital initial and as one word, a proprietary name in the U.K.).

a **1963** J. LUSBY in B. James *Austral. Short Stories* (1963) 225 The eyes opal-black in wrinkled slits of skin. **1911** C. E. W. BEAN *'Dreadnought' of Darling* xxv. 222 The most precious colour, the opal-buyers told us, was 'fire'—the rich glow as of a red-hot horseshoe, which you find in the heart of the best opal. **1925** *Ann. Rep. Dept. Mines New South Wales 1924* 85/2 The 'Opal Dirt' is picking ground, being simply a layer of clay or sandy clay overlain by sandstone. **1963** Opal-dirt [see *BOTTOM *v.* 5]. **1965** *Ann. Rep. Dept. Mines New South Wales 1963* 51/2 Using air compressor and jack spade on the softer opal dirt. **1902** *Chambers's Jrnl.* Aug. 496/2 There are few men on the opal-fields who do not average five pounds per week. **1866** 'J. EASEL' in *Queen* 11 Aug. 93/2 The opal glass, which transmits a rich and lovely iridescent light, exactly like the precious stone from which it is named. **1923** *Vogue* Oct. 47/1 A pair of feathered bird pictures and French opal glass bottles. **1956** L. M. ANGUS-BUTTERWORTH *Brit. Table & Ornamental Glass* iii. 10 The handle in opal glass. **1931** V. PALMER *Separate Lives* 200 The bleary-eyed opal-gougers, who spoke as if the hot winds had dried up the fountains of their speech. **1936** A. RUSSELL *Gone Nomad* vii. 57 Lured on by the uncertainty of what the next stroke of his pick will reveal, the opal-gouger never abandons hope, until, with his funds and credit exhausted, he may hope no longer. **1955** S. SPENDER *Coll. Poems 1928–53* 113 The eye is carried by the choppy tide To a shore opposite of opal-green spaces. **1867** A. J. MUNBY *Diary* 7 June in D. Hudson *Munby* (1972) 239 All things were cool and charming, and opal-grey, in the cool sweet morning. **1881** O. WILDE *Poems*

126 Tremulous opal-hued anemones. **1946** W. de la Mare *Traveller* 25 Opal-pale..A strange and deepening lustre tinged the air. **1902** *Chambers's Jrnl.* Aug. 496/1 At that hour the opal-seeker must cease his daily toil. **1922** V. Woolf *Jacob's Room* i. 11 Out pushes an opal-shelled crab. **1894** *Montgomery Ward Catal.* 520/3 Blue Opal Ware. A new pattern, just out, made in fancy colored glass in blue opal. *Ibid.* 521/1 Opal Ware. **1929** *Encycl. Brit.* X. 412/1 In 1927 the United States had..23 manufacturers making opal ware. **1958** *Mixed Batch* (J. A. Jobling & Co.) July 47 This new glass..was a delicate pearly white; and it was given the name Opal-ware. **1964** *Trade Marks Jrnl.* 29 Apr. 688/2 Jobling Opalware... Tableware..made of opal glass. James A. Jobling & Company Limited,..Sunderland, manufacturers.

opaline, *a.* and *sb.* Add: **A.** *adj.* Also, resembling opal other than in colour. (Further example.)

1962 C. Frondel *Dana's Syst. Min.* (ed. 7) III. 296 Common opal. In general, opal without a play of colour. .. Includes..rock-forming opaline silica.

B. *sb.* **2.** (Later examples.) Also, translucent glass of a colour other than white.

1964 [see *make-up mirror* s.v. *make-up 6]. **1970** G. Savage *Dict. Antiques* 296/1 The manufacture of opaline was at its most popular between 1840 and 1870, after which it declined in popularity.

opalite (ōᵘ·păləit). Also **Opalite.** [f. Opal + -ite¹.] Opal glass made in the form of tiles or bricks suitable for building purposes. (Formerly a proprietary name.)

1903 *Science* 13 Feb. 266/2 The feature of this building is the treatment of the interior of the cages with light-green opalite tile. **1940** *Archit. Rev.* LXXXVII. 19 The walls and counter fronts are faced with black and white opalite glass. **1975** Huntington & Mickadeit *Building Construction* (ed. 4) x. 520 Structural glass is available in the form of tile or slabs..for use as a finish on exterior and interior wall surfaces. It is known by various trade names such as *Carrara Glass*, *Vitrolite*, and *Opalite*.

opaque, *a.* (*sb.*) Add: **2. a.** *spec.* of glass which is not translucent.

1836 E. W. Lane *Acct. Manners & Customs Mod. Egyptians* II. 368 There is a very common kind [of bracelet]..of opaque, coloured glass, generally blue or green. **1878** A. Nesbitt *Descr. Catal. Glass Vessels S. Kensington Mus.* p. ii, It can be produced either wholly devoid of colour or tinted with any hue, and either opaque or transparent, without loss of brilliancy. **1907** E. Dillon *Glass* xvii. 291 Much opaque white glass was made in Germany.. in the first years of the eighteenth century... At South Kensington may be seen a covered beaker of this *milch-glas* elaborately painted. **1926** W. Buckley *European Glass* ii. 11 The Venetians in the 14th century made an opaque red glass resembling jaspar. **1961** E. M. Elville *Collector's Dict. Glass* 145/1 Nine out of every ten glasses with opaque-twist stems will show an unknopped stem.

b. (Further examples.)

1903 Pusey & Caldwell *Pract. Application Röntgen Rays* vi. 133 It will be a great help to the radiographer if the dressings are of a material which is not opaque to the ray. **1937** I. C. C. Tchaperoff *Man. Radiol. Diagnosis* iv. 167 The emphysematous area remains transparent in the radiograph of full expiration, whereas the normal areas become more opaque on expiration. **1972** *Jrnl. Ultrastruct. Res.* XXXIX. 580 The transverse..tubules and sarcoplasmic reticulum..of *Limulus* myocardium have been examined by infusing hearts with materials which either produce electron-opaque reaction products.. or which are inherently electron opaque.

3. c. *Phonology.* Of a rule: that cannot be extrapolated from every occurrence of the phenomenon; in which not every context implies the rule.

1971 P. Kiparsky in W. O. Dingwall *Survey Linguistic Sci.* 621 Define the concept *opacity of a rule* as follows:.. A rule A→B/C—D is opaque to the extent that there are surface representations of the form (i) A in environment C—D or (ii) B in environment other than C—D... Let us refer to the converse of opacity as *transparency*. **1974** S. R. Anderson *Organization of Phonol.* xii. 209 Kiparsky gives examples..in which historical change can be seen to operate on nontransparent (or *opaque*) rules so as to make them more transparent or to eliminate them from the grammar. *Ibid.* xiii. 250 If we disregard the second possible application instead, we derive *djalum + ba: + daŋ + be:*, which is not opaque because the long vowels are not adjacent. **1977** *Language* LIII. 18 Palatalization is opaque to the extent that there are, on the surface, some palatalized consonants not in the environment of a following *i*.

B. *sb.* **a.** (Later examples.)

1903 *Westm. Gaz.* 20 Aug. 4/1 A red batiste of voile or open canvas is more lovable than a red face-cloth or serge or tweed or linen; and, again, it is to be noted how of these red opaques the linen is better than the others. **1969** *Earth & Planetary Sci. Lett.* VII. 237/1 All the samples showed some effects—oxidation of the opaques and reddening of the silicates. **1976** *Nature* 22 Jan. 196/1 The Santiago lavas contain up to 10% phenocrysts of olivine and plagioclase in a matrix of plagioclase laths, clinopyroxene, olivine and opaques.

2. *Photogr.* **a.** A water colour or other substance for producing opaque areas on negatives, as in retouching.

1908 Schriever & Cummings *Compl. Self-Instructing Libr. Pract. Photogr.* IV. xl. 322 To make the opaque, add one ounce of No. 1 to four ounces of No. 2. **1943** *Chem. Abstr.* XXXVII. 1946 (*heading*) Removing opaque from photographic negatives. **1953** A. Sussman *Amat. Photographer's Handbk.* (ed. 4) xiv. 254 To spot a negative you can use a little India ink or you can buy a cake of opaque.

b. A print made on opaque paper.

1959 *Recomm. for Density & Contrast Range of Monochrome Films* (*B.S.I.*) 5 Prints of black-and-white photographic opaques should be made in such a way that a middle tone..will have a reflection density within the range 0·5 to 0·7. **1969** *Focal Encycl. Film & Television Techniques* 518/1 *Opaque*, term contrasting with transparency, such as a lantern slide, to denote a printed picture on opaque paper.

opaque, *v.* Add: Hence **opa·qu(e)ing** *ppl. a.* and *vbl. sb.*

1912 E. Heilmann *Brit. Pat. 26,498*, Materials which cannot be used alone as opaquing substances for enamel, yield good opaquing effects when heated so highly as to form spinels. **1913** *Chem. Abstr.* VII. 2460 Opaqueing agents for white enamels. **1967** E. Chambers *Photolitho-Offset* v. 52 Opaquing is used for spotting out pinholes, edge lines and other undesirable marking on the negatives. **1967** Karch & Buber *Offset Processes* v. 195 Paint out these holes and scratches..with an opaquing solution.

op art: see *op⁴.

op. cit. (ǫp sit). Abbrev. of L. *opus citatum*, the work quoted, or *opere citato*, in the work quoted.

1883 *Nineteenth Century* Feb. 213 *Op. cit.* vol. ii pp. 200, 201. **1966** *Listener* 1 Sept. 305/1 Van Bath (*op. cit.*) has drawn attention to the relation between urban prosperity and agricultural improvement in the Netherlands. **1970** J. Needleman *New Religions* 233 J. G. Bennett, op. cit., p. 53.

Op-Ed (ǫpˌe·d). *U.S.* [Abbrev. *op*posite *ed*itorial.] In full *Op-Ed page*. A page of a newspaper, opposite the editorial page, devoted to personal comment, feature articles, etc.

1970 *Time* 10 Aug. 32 The Op-Ed page—so named because it runs opposite a newspaper's editorial page—became a journalistic tradition with the rise of the personal column. Pioneered by the Pulitzers in the old New York morning *World*, the Op-Ed provides a variety of viewpoints in dozens of major metropolitan dailies. **1970** *N.Y. Times* 21 Sept. 42/2 Through the new page opposite the Editorial Page that we inaugurate today, we hope that a contribution may be made toward stimulating new thought and provoking new discussion on public problems... The two pages together—Editorial and Op. Ed.—are designed to create an intellectual forum. **1974** *Verbatim* Dec. 6/1 The Op-Ed Page of *The New York Times*. **1977** G. V. Higgins *Dreamland* i. 8 If you don't get a regular fix of the stuff that goes on the front page, you're not going to have anything to be insightful about on the Op Ed page.

open, *sb.* Add: **4. a.** (*e*) public knowledge or view, *spec.* in phrs. *to come* (*out*) *into the open*: to reveal one's plans, acts, thoughts, etc.; *to bring* (something) (*out*) *into the open*, to bring into public notice or view.

1942 T. Bailey *Pink Camellia* v. 35 We may as well come into the open, Miss Merryman. **1965** *New Statesman* 30 Apr. 670/2 The Tory Party statement which last year brought immigration into the open as a Birmingham election issue. **1965** *Listener* 16 Sept. 399/2 The Peking *People's Daily* came out into the open, supporting Pakistan's version of events. **1976** K. Royce *Bustillo* iv. 45 They both had something to hide... It would be better out in the open.

b. (Further examples.)

1846 J. W. Webb *Altowan* I. ii. 42 All openings or natural clearings are called 'opens' by the half-breeds of the Indian country. *Ibid.* viii. 201 They cautiously entered where there seemed no indication of an open. **1880** *Encycl. Brit.* XIII. 603/1 Living in herds of from fifty to one hundred in the grassy 'opens'. **1958** *Edmonton* (Alberta) *Jrnl.* 28 July 4/3 The animal seemed to distrust the bald opens of the marsh.

5. b. *Electr.* An accidental break in the conducting path for a current.

1913 T. Croft *Amer. Electricians' Handbk.* i. 55 Open circuits in multiple wiring installations are usually readily located... The lamps on the generator side of the 'open' will..burn while those on the far side will not. **1933** F. F. Fowle *Stand. Handbk. Electr. Engineers* (ed. 6) iii. 193 Open-circuit faults or 'opens' are produced by breaks in the conductors. **1967** *Electronics* 6 Mar. 320/2 The D200's..identify shorts or opens and the polarity of diodes. **1977** *Sci. Amer.* Feb. 88/1 (Advt.), That's the beauty of the TDR, it's not limited to identifying shorts or opens—it points out any disturbances.

c. An open competition, tournament, or the like; cf. Open *a.* 14.

1926 Wodehouse *Heart of Goof* iv. 128 'After all, there is always golf.' He nodded. 'Yes... Who knows?.. The Amateur Championship—' 'The Open!' I cried... 'The American Amateur,' said Chester, flushing. 'The American Open,' I chorused. **1930** *Daily Express* 8 Sept. 11/4 Miss Brazier also has played in 'opens'. **1972** *Country Life* 7 Dec. 1600/3 Jack White who, in 1904, was the first man to break 300 in the Open. **1973** *Guardian* 28 June 13/3 The World Open is a ten-round [chess] championship open to all-comers.

d. *the Open*: the Open University. *colloq.*

1970 *Guardian* 29 Aug. 9/6 Along with Jennie Lee, Mrs Thatcher has a right to be seen as the saviour of the Open. **1972** *Ibid.* 15 June 9/5 Pupils in schools..had to wait until 21 to qualify for the Open or 23 to enter other universities as 'mature' students.

open, *a.* (*adv.*) Add: **2. c.** Of a shop, public house, etc.: accessible to use by customers (at a particular time); available for business; *they are open*: the public houses are open.

1824 E. Weeton *Let.* 8 June in *Jrnl. of Governess* (1969) II. 287 As I go to any place of Worship, fruit stalls are in the road, and confectioners shops open, as on any other day. **1836** Dickens *Sunday under Three Heads* i. 5 In streets like Holborn and Tottenham Court Road, which form the central market of a large neighbourhood, inhabited by a vast number of mechanics and poor people, a few shops are open at an early hour of the morning. **1942** 'S. Campion' *Bonanza* 19 It was eleven—'they' were open. **1952** E. O'Neill *Moon for Misbegotten* iii. 152 There'll be a speak open, and some drunk laughing. *Ibid.* iv. 173 The bar at the Inn won't be open for hours. **1961** 'E. Fenwick' *Friend of Mary Rose* (1962) i. 16, I was talking to Mrs. Rudd... I wanted to be sure she was open. **1965** J. Porter *Dover Three* ii. 30 Just one question, laddie... Are they open yet? **1973** A. Mann *Tiara* xiii. 118 Piccoli's will still be open. Shall I nip down and get pictures of all these types?

d. Designating a prison, borstal, or the like where the inmates are seldom or never locked up.

1946 *Rep. Commissioners of Prisons 1939–41* 47 in *Parl. Papers 1945–6* (Cmd. 6820) XIV. 281 All were now required to pass straight from the restraint of a prison wall to associated life in buildings designed as a perfectly open Borstal. **1950** *Prisons & Borstals* (Home Office) 20 The first prison camp in England was started in connection with the training prison at Wakefield in 1933... The open prison is therefore beyond the stage of experiment: it is a well-established feature of this as of many other prison systems. **1957** *Economist* 2 Nov. 397/3 Miss Size's last job was as Governor of the first open prison for women, at Askham Grange, near York, a pleasant Victorian mansion where there are neither high walls nor keys. **1964** M. Argyle *Psychol. & Social Probl.* v. 69 Open borstals had a higher success rate than closed borstals, at all levels of expected failure. **1972** P. D. James *Unsuitable Job* vii. 210 Perhaps they would send her to an open prison. Open. It was a contradiction in terms.

e. *open heart*, a practically bloodless heart that has been temporarily by-passed and cut open for examination or surgery; usu. *attrib.*

1950 *Surgery* XXVIII. 474 Recent rapid strides in the field of vascular surgery are leading inevitably to the point where a direct surgical attack on the open heart is possible. **1960** *Sci. Amer.* Feb. 84/1 The cardiac surgery group at Minnesota has now performed nearly 1,000 open-heart operations with the aid of the heart-lung machine or other methods of by-pass. **1977** *Private Eye* 1 Apr. 5/3 As he recovers from open-heart surgery (new valves) Sir Christopher Soames is confident of an early return to Parliament.

4. a. *open carriage* (earlier examples), *open car*.

1797 Lady Newdigate *Let.* 30 July in A. E. Newdigate-Newdegate *Cheverels* (1898) xiv. 200, I have never felt yᵉ Downs too hot for my open Carriage till yesterday, when I was forced to put up yᵉ Head to shade me from yᵉ Sun. **1803** M. Wilmot *Let.* 6 Aug. in *Russ. Jrnls.* (1934) i. 36 We drove about in an open Carriage, the night was lovely. **1948** M. Laski *Tory Heaven* ix. 123 An open car..ceases to be a source of pure pleasure after a certain age. **1976** *Times* 1 Mar. 13/6 Having read the correspondence for and against..seat belts, it seems that no one has put forward the case for the driver of the open car. **1977** G. V. Higgins *Dreamland* xii. 139 A small four-passenger open car with a canvas roof.

b. Of a fire: that is not enclosed in a stove or the like; also of a fireplace.

1876 [in Dict., sense 22 a]. **1886** [see *flue-curing* s.v. *flue *sb.*³ 6]. **1894** *Country Gentlemen's Catal.* 117/1 The Nautilus dog grate... A cheerful open fire. **1926** *Daily Colonist* (Victoria, B.C.) 24 Jan. 20/1 He used to be heard singing..at night, beside his open fire. **1931** E. O'Neill *Homecoming* ii, in *Mourning becomes Electra* (1932) 51 At rear, centre, is an open fireplace. **1949** M. Laski *Little Boy Lost* x. 150 'How nice to see an open fire,' he said tritely. Madame Mercatel laughed... 'One finds open fireplaces in many old French houses.' **1965** in P. Jennings *Living Village* (1968) 122 It looks as if open coal fires are on the way out in England at last. **1976** 'Trevanian' *Main* xiii. 249 He enjoys fiddling with open fires... The bark has begun to crackle and flutter with blue flame.

5. a. (Further examples.) See also *wide open* s.v. Wide *adv.* 3 b. *open jet*: see sense *22 c.

1962 *Newnes Conc. Encycl. Electr. Engin.* 728/2 The majority of switchgear manufactured up to 11 kV is of the metal-enclosed type and above this the trend is towards outdoor open type switchgear. **1968** *Gloss. Terms Offset Lithogr. Printing* (*B.S.I.*) 12 *Open arc*, an arc lamp in which the electrodes burn in free air.

c. Of a telephone line or other transmission line: above ground.

1876 [in Dict., sense 5]. **1909** *Trans. Amer. Inst. Electr. Engin.* XXVIII. 1079 Even the best cable circuit is much less efficient than an open-wire circuit. **1925** *Bell Syst. Techn. Jrnl.* IV. 524 Practically all long toll circuits were in open wire construction; that is, individual wires mounted..on poles. **1966** *McGraw-Hill Encycl. Sci. & Technol.* XIV. 48/1 Open-wire construction is used for communication or power transmission wherever practical and permitted, as in open country.

d. *Med.* Communicating with or exposed to the air; involving the deliberate exposure of an interior part of the body, esp. a fracture, so as to make it directly accessible.

1894 J. C. Da Costa *Man. Mod. Surg.* xviii. 307 Compound fracture is an open fracture, or one in which an open wound admits air to the seat of bone-injury. **1897**

STIMSON & ROGERS *Man. Operative Surg.* (ed. 3) v. 257 (*heading*) Suture of the patella. I. Open Method. **1944** C. A. PANNETT *Surg.* xliii. 541 Union of the fracture after open operation always takes longer than if a closed method has been employed. **1949** P. KIELY *Text-bk. Surg.* xxvi. 700 Injuries to the Bowel. These may be subcutaneous or open. **1969** F. T. HOAGLAND in S. I. Schwartz *Princ. Surg.* xlvi. 1658/2 Open reduction [of a fracture] carries the risk of local infection. **1975** *Nature* 10 Apr. 529/1 Human liver obtained by open biopsy.

e. *Med.* Of (a case of) tuberculosis: accompanied by the discharge of infectious material from the body.

1930 J. A. MYERS *Tuberculosis among Children* ii. 9 The source of infection is found to be cases of open tuberculosis in the homes. **1939** *Brit. Encycl. Med. Pract.* XII. 288 The rapid decline in the number of open cases of tuberculosis..have reduced the sources of infection. **1961** *Times* 30 June 15/3 Infectious (or 'open') tuberculosis. **1974** PASSMORE & ROBSON *Compan. Med. Stud.* III. I. xiv. 2/2 Occasionally outbreaks have occurred in young tuberculin-negative adults who have been heavily exposed to open cases [of tuberculosis].

7. b. *Chem.* and *Metallurgy*. (See quot. 1938).

1938 HUME-ROTHERY & RAYNOR in *Phil. Mag.* XXVI. 130 A rough indication of the nature of a metal or alloy may be obtained by comparing the interatomic distances in the crystal with the suitably defined ionic radii of the atoms concerned. In brief, if the ionic radius is small compared with the interatomic distance, we shall have a metal of what may be called the 'open' type, whilst if the ionic radii are nearly equal to the interatomic distances we shall have a metal of the 'full' type, with many different properties. **1967** A. H. COTTRELL *Introd. Metall.* xix. 322 In open metals we need consider only the valency electrons, for the electrons in the ionic shells are negligibly disturbed by the metallic binding.

8. a. Esp. in *open space*; *spec.* an area without buildings in a city or town; a small park or the like for public recreation; also *great* (or *wide*) *open spaces*: large tracts of open country.

1827 J. S. BUCKINGHAM *Trav. Mesopotamia* I. xi. 375 Attached to it are extensive stables, and a Maidan, or open space, where the horses are kept in the air. **1850** *Household Words* 3 Aug. 451/2 Suburban open spaces are being entombed in brick-and-mortar mausoleums. **1869** A. MACKENZIE (*title*) The parks, open spaces and thoroughfares of London. **1896** [in Dict.]. **1910** H. G. WELLS *New Machiavelli* (1911) I. iv. 131, I recall as if I had been there the wide open spaces, the ragged hillsides [of South Africa]. **1913** C. B. PURDOM *Garden City* viii. 112 An open space in a city has come to mean..even a disused churchyard... In the Garden City the characteristics of the open space belong to the town as a whole. **1924** WODEHOUSE *Leave it to Psmith* viii. 138 You will find me somewhere out there in the great open spaces where men are men. **1942** *Ann. Reg. 1941* 286 Mr. G. E. Hatfield..bequeathed to the National Trust Marden Hall estate,..for preservation as an open space. **1943** *Our Towns* (Women's Group on Public Welfare) p. xvi, The special town conditions of overcrowding, lack of open spaces, smoke and noise. **1944** [see *closed book* s.v. *CLOSED *ppl. a.* 3]. **1965** K. GILES *Some Beasts no More* i. 12 A phony passport, maybe, and life anew in the great open spaces. **1969** S. COULTER *Embassy* xiv. 159 The big huskies, the boys from the wide open spaces. **1971** *Daily Tel.* 13 July 2/8 The Wimbledon centre court was not an open space within the meaning of the 1936 Public Order Act. **1974** *Guardian* 28 Mar. 19/3 What do people want today—apart from open space? **1975** *Times* 8 Feb. 10/4 If you seek clean fresh air and the wide open spaces (cliche though it is, that phrase is exactly right), this is the place.

11. a. Of a brass instrument: not muted. Of a cymbal: left free to vibrate.

1926 *Melody Maker* Mar. 30 Nothing is better suited to obtain a highly successful result than the beautiful, sweet full tone of the open instrument, and I advise all artistes to try a few 'open' solos. **1927** *Ibid.* June 609/3 The cymbal must be 'open' when it is struck and must remain 'open' for practically the full length of the beat being played, only being choked out just before the next beat. **1955** KEEPNEWS & GRAUER *Pict. Hist. Jazz* xiii. 141 Cootie Williams, ..strictly an open-horn stylist until he took over Bubber Miley's chair and produced a fine, muted 'jungle' sound. **1956** B. EDWARDS in S. Traill *Play that Music* vi. 60 Short-damped cymbal beats or loud and frequently aimless open ones. **1967** *Crescendo* Apr. 7/2 The Les Brown trick of trumpets in tin mutes playing above open trombones. **1972** *Jazz & Blues* Nov. 11/3 Razor-sharp riffs, and sweeping, open-horn statements.

e. (Earlier example.)

1845 W. E. JELF *Gram. Greek Lang.* I. iii. 30 When a syllable ends with a vowel it is called an open, when with a consonant, a close syllable.

f. *Electr.* Having a break in the conducting path for an electric current; esp. in *open circuit* (see sense *22 c).

1827, etc. [see **open circuit*]. **1869** *Phil. Mag.* XXVIII. 2 When the shunt is open the battery is unable to send a steady current through the voltameter. **1884** S. P. THOMPSON *Dynamo-Electr. Machinery* vii. 133 Dynamos.. which leave the circuits of some of the armature coils open during part of the rotation, are sometimes termed 'open-circuit' dynamos. **1901** *Chambers's Jrnl.* Sept. 617/2 If a new machine, the switches should be left open, the brushes lifted, and the machine allowed to run without load for a little time. **1962** J. P. GREGORY in G. A. T. Burdett *Automatic Control Handbk.* ii. 21 With the initiating switch open, the timing capacitor..is charged to the peak value of the a.c. voltage. **1975** I. CLUCAS *Reed's Electr. for Deck Officers* vii. 212 The inductance in the circuit..tries to maintain the current once the switch is open.

g. Of a game of chess: developed either by gambits or by opening up the files. Cf. *CLOSE *a.* 2 c.

1856 C. TOMLINSON *Chess-Player's Ann.* 75 He was a very accomplished player, and generally preferred open games, gambits, &c. **1890** R. F. GREEN *Chess* v. 14 An Open Game is one in which the development is effected chiefly in advance of the pawns. P to K4 as a first move on both sides, leads generally to an open game; and formerly all games begun in this way were called open—other openings being treated as close. **1917** J. DU MONT tr. *Lasker's Chess Strategy* (ed. 2) iv. 43 We find an early break-up of the centre, and concurrently the opening of the Ks or Qs file for the Rooks. That is why games opened in this fashion have been classed very generally as 'open', whilst all the other openings are called 'close games'. **1936** W. WINTER *Chess for Match Players* ii. 24 In the category of Open games come the vast majority of the King's side openings. **1959** H. GOLOMBEK *Mod. Opening Chess Strategy* 11 Certain openings suit certain people—some like an open type of game, others prefer a close.

h. *Med.* Applied to methods of administering anæsthetics in which the patient's respiratory tract is in communication with the air so that exhaled air is not rebreathed.

1888 D. W. BUXTON *Anæsthetics* v. 78 The open method. .. A common towel is arranged so as to form a square of six folds, and enough choloroform is poured upon it to wet an area the size of a hand's palm. **1922** *Encycl. Brit.* XXX. 137/2 The induction of anaesthesia by the open method is liable to be somewhat prolonged. **1972** J. C. SNOW *Anesthesia* v. 39 The Ayre T-tube system is another example of an open or semi-open system.

i. *Math.* Of a set of points: not containing any of its boundary points. Of an interval in the real line: not containing either of its end points.

1902 *Proc. Lond. Math. Soc.* XXXIV. 289 Open sets of points. **1939** M. H. A. NEWMAN *Elem. Topology of Plane Sets of Points* ii. 25 The sum of any set of open sets is an open set. **1956** E. M. PATTERSON *Topology* ii. 23 An example of a set which is not open is the set defined by $0 \leq x < 1$; no ϵ-neighbourhood of $x = 0$ lies entirely in the set, for every ϵ-neighbourhood of $x = 0$ contains a point whose coordinate is negative. **1968** P. A. P. MORAN *Introd. Probability Theory* iv. 185 An open interval in R_n is defined to be a set of points whose coordinates satisfy the inequalities $a_i < x_i < b_i$..where the a_i may be $-\infty$ and the b_i, $+\infty$. An open interval is clearly an open set.

j. *Logic* and *Math.* Of a statement or equation: containing at least one free variable or undetermined quantity.

1937 A. SMEATON tr. *Carnap's Logical Syntax of Lang.* I. 21 If a variable which is free in $\mathfrak{A}_1$ occurs in $\mathfrak{A}_1$, then $\mathfrak{A}_1$ is called open; otherwise it is called closed. *Ibid.*, Our classification into closed and open sentences corresponds to the usual classification into sentences and sentential functions. **1952** S. C. KLEENE *Introd. Metamath.* vii. 151 Let A be a formula containing free exactly the distinct variables $x_1, \ldots, x_n$ in order of first occurrence. According as $n > 0$ or $n = 0$, we call A open or closed. **1963** W. V. QUINE *Set Theory* 1 Imagine a sentence about something. Put a blank or variable where the thing is referred to. You have no longer a sentence..but an open sentence, so called, that may hold true of each of various things and be false of others. **1967** M. L. TOMBER *Introd. Contemporary Algebra* ii. 63, $5 \cdot 3^{-1} = \frac{5}{3}$ is a solution of the open equation $3x = 5$. **1971** *Sci. Amer.* Mar. 55 The technique of long division represents a decision procedure for the predicate 'x is divisible by y', where x and y can be any natural numbers. (A predicate is an open sentence: one that can be completed by assigning names to its variables.)

k. *Astr.* Of the universe: having a negative or zero radius of curvature; spatially infinite and always expanding.

1937 E. HUBBLE *Observational Approach Cosmol.* iii. 55 The radius [of curvature] in our universe might be positive, negative, or zero, and might be large or small... A negative curvature implies open space, an infinite universe. **1965** J. D. NORTH *Measure of Universe* vi. 135 The logical advantages of an open model were generally thought to be fewer than those of a model with positive curvature. **1976** *New Scientist* 2 Dec. 514/1 Indirect evidence for a low-density (or 'open') Universe—one which will expand for ever—comes from the recent discovery that deuterium (heavy hydrogen) exists in interstellar space. **1978** *Daily Tel.* 27 Mar. 7/2 This question of whether the universe will prove to be 'open' or 'closed' raises an important philosophical question about the existence of God. If the cosmos is going to expand for ever,.. for countless thousands of millions of years of its future history, life anywhere will be impossible.

13. *spec.* Designating administration or government in which the public is kept well-informed and is invited to participate.

1968 R. M. NIXON in *N.Y. Times* 20 Sept. 33/2 It's time we once again had an open administration—open to ideas from the people, and open in its communication with the people—an administration of open doors, open eyes, and open minds. **1971** J. AITKEN *Officially Secret* xv. 211 The absence of effective checks and controls on the activities of the contemporary Civil Service has recently led to demands for 'more open government'. **1973** *Public Administration* LI. 428 'Open government' and 'greater public participation' were becoming increasingly fashionable political slogans at this time. **1975** *Times* 11 Jan. 12/2 The need for 'open government', in which people are informed about what is being decided and have a chance to make their own suggestions. **1976** LD. HOME *Way Wind Blows* vii. 115 That this crisis was averted was in the greatest part due to the instinct for fair play and open government practised by the Tunku Abdul Rahman. **1977** *Time* (Overseas ed.) 17 Jan. 13/1 The coalition's goal, explained Dowiyogo in an interview with the *Australian*: to replace DeRobert's increasingly personal rule with 'open government—that is, to tell the people what we plan to do and why'. **1978** *Times* 17 Mar. 6/5 The Civil Service Department has refused a formal request from *The Times*, arising from the Prime Minister's open-government policy announced last July, that background material used in the preparation of the White Paper on the Civil Service published on Wednesday should be disclosed.

b. Of a place of work: in which both union and non-union workers are employed, esp. *open-shop* (cf. **closed shop*); also *attrib.* orig. *U.S.*

1896 *Typogr. Jrnl.* IX. 445 Our next efforts were directed to the Morning Leader, also an 'open' office. **1901** *World's Work* (N.Y.) July 914/2 The shop had previously been an 'open' one—that is, union and non-union men were employed without distinction. **1904** *N.Y. Even. Post* 15 Aug. 2 The Exposition is conducted along the lines of an 'open shop', by permitting the employment of both union and non-union labor. **1906** *Daily Colonist* (Victoria, B.C.) 1 Jan. 133 What is all this talk that's in the papers about the open shop? **1909** *Daily Chron.* 3 May 1/5 The strike has originated in the intention..to enforce an 'open shop' on the lake boats. **1939** *Sun* (Baltimore) 18 Apr. 22/7 As a direct result of the shutting down of union mines.., 'open-shop' mines in Garret county..were working at maximum capacity. **1964** E. H. POWELL in I. L. Horowitz *New Sociol.* 333 The open-shop crusade of the 'twenties was known as the 'American plan'.

15. b. *to lay* (one) *open to*: to render (one) liable to (something), to expose (one) to.

1853 C. BRONTË *Villette* I. viii. 149, I shall make blunders that will lay me open to the scorn of the most ignorant. *Ibid.* x. 183 There was something in it that pleased, but something too that brought surging up into the mind all one's foibles and weak points: all that could lay one open to a laugh. **1931** T. R. G. LYELL *Slang* 455 Judging by the people he knows and the books he reads and recommends, he certainly lays himself open to the suspicion of being one [*sc.* a Communist].

20. *open mind*, a mind accessible to all arguments or points of view, esp. in phr. *to keep an open mind*. See also *open-minded* adj. (sense 22 c in Dict. and Suppl.).

1841 [in Dict.]. **1911** G. B. SHAW *Doctor's Dilemma* I. 6 *Schutzmacher*. Oh, in my case the secret was simple enough... I'm afraid youll think it rather infra dig. *Ridgeon*. Oh, I have an open mind. What was the secret? **1914** —— *Misalliance* 29 *Lord Summerhays*. Giving the show away is a method like any other method... I should keep an open mind about it. *Johnny*. Has it ever occurred to you that a man with an open mind must be a bit of a scoundrel? **1974** 'M. ALLEN' *Super Tour* vi. 210 We'd rather you go into all this with an open mind. **1976** *Star* (Sheffield) 29 Oct. 1/3 Senior detectives said they were keeping an open mind whether the attacker is the same man who has committed several rapes in the Barnsley area.

21. *open book*, a person or thing that can be readily understood; a person who conceals nothing; also in phr. *to read* (someone) *like an open book* (cf. READ *v.* 5 d); *open house*, welcome or hospitality for all visitors; also *attrib.* (see also HOUSE *sb.*[1] 17 b); *open letter*, a letter, esp. one written in protest against something, addressed to a particular person or persons but made public by being printed, e.g. in a newspaper.

1853 G. H. BOKER *Bankrupt* IV. ii, in *Amer. Lost Plays* (1940) 105, I read your black heart like an open book. **1919** WODEHOUSE *Damsel in Distress* iv. 53 There's no mystery about me. I'm an open book. **1934** A. G. STREET *Endless Furrow* xv. 254 Talk about old Nicholas Crawford's art and mystery in grocerin', why, that's an open book compared to farmin'. **1944** Open book [see *closed book* s.v. *CLOSED *ppl. a.* 3]. **1973** 'S. WOODS' *Enter Corpse* 60 'You haven't tried to shake them off?' 'What would be the good?.. My life is an open book.' **1824** BYRON *Don Juan* XVI. lxviii. 98 Though not exactly what's called 'open house'. **1836** T. POWER *Impressions Amer.* II. 71 Mr. Oliver was one of a class of excellent open-house men, of which class there are specimens to be found in every part of this Union. **1907** *Westm. Gaz.* 30 Dec. 8/1 On the seventieth anniversary there was an 'open-house' reception. **1921** *Daily Colonist* (Victoria, B.C.) 23 Oct. 15/1 Victoria's three great laundries will hold 'open house' daily from 9 a.m. to 4.30 p.m. **1971** *Daily Tel.* 11 Oct. 15/2 Clarksons has an 'open house' hospitality suite at the Majestic where free liquor is flowing almost round the clock. **1878** (*title*) Open letter to the English nation from Berlin. **1890** R. L. STEVENSON (*title*) Father Damien. An open letter to the Reverend Doctor Hyde of Honolulu. **1917** *Fortn. Rev.* Nov. 748 (*heading*) Problems of finance: an open letter to Lord Milner. **1966** *Listener* 6 Oct. 506/1 There are three open letters in the memorial volume. **1977** *Time* 21 Mar. 49/1 In 1972 he attacked the Black Muslims in an open letter, an act that is thought to have led to the execution of his family.

22. a. *open-cell, -class, -deck, -face, -frame, -seam, -web.*

1933 *Amer. Speech* VIII. III. 30 *Open-cell wing*, division of the main prison building in which there were no bars on the front of the cells. **1957** *N.Z. Timber Jrnl.* Dec. 59/2 *Open-cell process*, a means of impregnating wood under pressure. The preservative is retained in the cell walls only, and the cells left empty. **1971** C. BONINGTON *Annapurna South Face* App. B. 243 A thin layer of open-cell foam in the sleeves. *Ibid.* 249 Open-cell foam mattresses. **1949** R. K. MERTON *Social Theory* II. iv. 136 Despite our persisting open-class-ideology, advance toward the success-goal is relatively rare..for those armed with little formal education. **1954** F. C. AVIS *Boxing Reference Dict.* 79 *Open class contest*, an amateur contest consisting of four 3-minute rounds, with 1-minute intervals. **1974** *Times* 26 Oct. 12/3 P & O..the last [line] to operate two-class cruises, decided..to..revert to 'open-class' cruising. **1886** *Harper's Mag.* June 18/2 In vessels of this class it is usual to have an open-deck battery. **1906** 'H. McHugh' *Skiddoo!* v. 75 The Human Hog was invented long before the open-face street car began to stop for him. **1931** *Amer. Speech* VII. 51 Custard [in lumberjack lingo] is 'open face pie'. **1942** Berrey & Van den Bark *Amer. Thes. Slang* § 91/27 *Open-face pie*, pie without an upper crust. **1946** *Sun* (Baltimore) 13 Mar. 22/7 The proposed serving of 'open-face' pies and sandwiches. **1940** *Chambers's Techn. Dict.* 595/2 *Open-frame girder*, a girder consisting of upper and lower booms connected at intervals by (usually) vertical members, and not braced by any diagonal members. **1969** *Jane's Freight Containers 1968–69* 477/2 Tilt covered open-frame containers are available. **1910** *Installation News* Jan. 4/1 The much abused open-seam conduit and the socket joint conduit. **1968** E. McCourt *Saskatchewan* iii. 36 The most fascinating by-products of open-seam mining are the miniature mountain ranges formed of the clay stripped away to expose the coal seams. **1871** T. Cargill *Strains Bridge Girders* 63 The lattice, or open web girder.

b. *open-collared, -throated, -topped.*

1945 Dylan Thomas *Let.* 30 July (1966) 277 Such lovely ladies and gentlemen.., open-collared and wild-haired in the photographers' wind. **1966** R. Ellmann *Lett. of J. Joyce* II. p. liii, The open-collared eloquence of D. H. Lawrence. **1891** 'L. Malet' *Wages of Sin* II. iv. iii. 81 The north wind blew piercing, strong and tonic... Colthurst drank it down open-throated. **1962** K. Orvis *Damned & Destroyed* 111 A loud, open-throated sports-shirt. **1904** *Westm. Gaz.* 9 Dec. 7/2 The sight should be adjustable with open-topped hood. **1964** W. L. Goodman *Hist. Woodworking Tools* 93 It is in effect an open-topped steel box.

c. open access, a system whereby users of a library have direct access to the bookshelves; also *attrib.*; **open admission** *U.S.* = **open enrolment*; **open-and-shut** *a.* (orig. *U.S.*), (*a*) simple, straightforward; esp. of a legal case in which there is no doubt as to the outcome; (*b*) of weather: characterized by alternating sunny and cloudy conditions; hence as *sb.*, (*a*) a simple or straightforward operation, case, etc.; also in phr. *as* (or *like*) *open or shut*: easily, straightforwardly; (*b*) alternately sunny and cloudy conditions; **open back** (see quot. 1923); **open bite** *Dentistry*, lack of occlusion of the front teeth when the jaw is normally closed; **Open Board** *U.S.*, an association formed in cities of the U.S. to transact dealings in options on a small scale not permitted by the local board of trade; **Open Brethren,** a branch of the Plymouth Brethren which does not practise extreme separatism; **open-cast** (earlier and later examples); also, a method of mining coal, ore, etc., by removing surface layers and working from above, not from shafts; hence as *adj.*, of, pertaining to, or designating this method of mining; also quasi-*advb.*; **open-casting,** open-cast mining; **open chain** *Chem.* (see *chain *sb.* 5 g); freq. *attrib.*; **open cheque,** (*a*) an uncrossed cheque (see Cross *v.* 7 c); (*b*) a cheque for an unstated amount; also *fig.*; **open circuit,** a circuit, esp. an electric circuit, that is incomplete; freq. *attrib.*; applied to breathing apparatus in which air is exhaled into the atmosphere and so lost; hence **open-circuited** *a.*, consisting of or containing an open circuit; (as a back-formation) **open circuit** *v. trans.*; **open city,** an undefended city; *spec.* a city declared to be unfortified and undefended, and hence, under international law, exempt from enemy bombardment; **open classroom,** a classroom in which instruction is informal, individual, and free-ranging; **open community** *Ecology*, an area in which the plant cover is not dense; **open compound** *Linguistics*, a compound in which there is a space (i.e. no hyphen) between the component elements; **open cover,** marine insurance that covers all the shipments made by a person or firm without specification in advance of the details of each shipment; **open credit** *Finance*, a credit free from restrictions; **open cycle,** a cycle of operations in which a working fluid, coolant, etc., is used only once (cf. **closed cycle*); **open day,** a day when a place, e.g. a school, which is normally closed to the public is made accessible to visitors (in quot. 1892, a day kept as a holiday at Durham University); **open end** *a.* = **open-ended* adj.; *spec.* (*a*) of an investment trust (see quot. 1940); (*b*) *Spinning* (see quot. 1975); **open-ended** *a.*, having an open end; freq. *fig.*, having no predetermined limit or boundary as to time, extent, size, etc.; *spec.* of a question or test: to which the respondent frames his own answer, as opp. to selecting one or two or more pre-phrased answers; hence **open-endedness; open enrolment** *U.S.*, the unrestricted enrolment of students at schools, colleges, etc., of their choice; **open-faced** *a.*, *N. Amer.*, also of a sandwich, pie, etc.: without an upper layer of bread or pastry; **open floor** (see quot. 1932); **open go** *Austral. colloq.*, an unimpeded opportunity; a 'fair go' (see *go *sb.*[1] 4 d); **open housing** *U.S.*, property that can be rented or bought without restriction on racial grounds; also *attrib.*; **open jet,** a stream of air in a wind-tunnel which is not bounded by rigid walls in the working section; **open juncture** *Linguistics*, the type of juncture (sense *2 c) found at word boundaries or marked syllable division within the word; **open line,** (*a*) a telephone line on which conversations can be overheard or intercepted by others; (*b*) used *attrib.* to denote a radio or television programme in which the public can participate by telephone; **open loop,** a control loop (*loop *sb.*[1] 4 l) without feedback, each operation or activity being affected only by those earlier in the sequence; **open market,** a market in which any buyer or seller may trade freely and where prices are determined by supply and demand; also *attrib.*; **open-minded** *a.* (examples); hence **open-mindedly** *adv.*, in an open-minded manner; **open-mindedness** (earlier and later examples); **open-neck,** a collar of a kind that leaves the neck unrestricted; *spec.* as *adj.*, of a shirt, that is worn with the collar unbuttoned, without a tie; also *fig.*; hence **open-necked** *a.*; **open occupancy** *U.S.*, occupancy of housing available to persons of any race; **open-pit** *a.* chiefly *N. Amer.*, = **open-cast* adj.; **open plan,** an architectural style allowing for no (or few) internal walls or partitions within a building, esp. an office or a school; freq. *attrib.*; hence **open-planned** *adj.*, **open-planning; open question,** a matter on which differences of opinion are legitimate; **open range,** (*a*) *N. Amer.*, a range or tract of land that is not intersected with fences; also *attrib.*; (*b*) used *attrib.* or as *adj.* = *free range* (*b*) s.v. *free *a.* D. 2; also *fig.*; **open-reel** *a.*, employing or having tape reels of such a kind that they and the tape they carry are accessible (in contrast to cassettes and cartridges); **open road,** (*a*) *U.S.*, a road that is not private; (*b*) a country road or a main road outside urban areas; (somewhat sentimentally) a road or route along which one can travel without care or hindrance; also *attrib.*; **open roof** (see quot. 1932); **open sandwich,** a sandwich without a top slice of bread; **open score** *Mus.* (see quot. 1899); **open season,** the season when hunting or fishing is allowed; also *transf.* and *fig.*, a time when something, esp. criticism, is unrestricted; **open shed** *N.Z.* (see quots.); **open shelf,** a bookshelf that is not enclosed behind a door or the like; in a library: one of any number of shelves from which the readers can take books themselves; freq. *attrib.* or as *adj.*; **open-side,** in *Rugby Football*, the side of the scrum on which the main line of the backs is ranged; opp. *blind side* (*blind *a.* and *adv.* 2 c); also *attrib.*; **open skies,** used, chiefly *attrib.*, to designate a system whereby aircraft of any nation are allowed to fly over a particular territory; *spec.* of a system whereby two or more nations permit surveillance of one another from the air; also *open sky*; **open society,** a society characterized by its flexible structure and beliefs; one having much contact with other peoples or tolerant of change or of diversity in its existing order and traditions; opp. *closed society* (*closed *ppl. a.* 3); **open stage** (see quots.); also *attrib.*; **open-stock** (*N. Amer.*), goods that are always kept in stock by a shop, etc.; esp. a crockery set for which items can be bought separately at any time; also *attrib.*; **open subroutine** *Computers*, a routine that is written, in full, directly into a program wherever it occurs; **open system,** a material system in which the total mass or energy fluctuates; an incomplete or alterable system (of ideas, doctrines, things, etc.); **open texture** *Philos.* (see quots.); hence **open-textured** *adj.*; **open-texturedness; open toe(d)** *a.*, designating a shoe that is open at the front to reveal the toes; **open-top** *a.*, having an open top; also as *sb.* (*U.S. colloq.*), a vehicle, trailer, or the like with an open top; hence **open-topped** *a.*; **open town,** (*a*) *U.S.*, a town characterized by a lack of restrictions on drinking and gambling places and the like; (*b*) = **open city*; **open tread** *a.*, of a staircase: having no risers; **open university,** a university having few if any restrictions on admission, *spec.* (with capital initials) a university founded in Great Britain in 1969 to provide courses for adult working people based on correspondence and radio and television broadcasts; also *fig.*; **open vegetation** = **open community*; **open ward,** a hospital ward designed to accommodate several patients; also *attrib.*; **open water** (chiefly *Canad.*), the melting of the ice on rivers and lakes in spring, or the time when this happens or has occurred; a stretch of water in which there is little or no ice; **open window unit** *Acoustics* (see quot. 1968[1]); **open wood, woodland** (see quot. 1889); **open woods** *N. Amer.*, a patch of woodland in which there is no undergrowth; cf. Opening *vbl. sb.* 3.

1894 *Library* VI. 344 There is absolutely no novelty about the principle of open-access. **1899** (*title*) Account of the safe-guarded open-access system in public lending libraries. **1934** *Archit. Rev.* LXXVI. 168/1 The new library has one important feature that distinguishes it from most large libraries in this country and elsewhere; I refer to the system of 'open access'. *a* **1956** A. Esdaile in D. Lodge *Brit. Mus. is falling Down* (1965) vi. 96 Free or open access can hardly be practised in so large a library as this. **1977** *Times Lit. Suppl.* 30 Dec. 1532/2 The long-standing fight about open access..is won now... Behind lay a deep-seated fear..in some librarians..of anyone from the outside world actually having the run of the shelves. **1969** *Sat. Rev.* (U.S.) 20 Dec. 54/1 (*heading*) The challenge of open admissions. Will Everyman destroy the university? **1970** *Time* 28 Sept. 36 Under its new 'open admissions' policy, CUNY [*sc.* the City University of New York] was taking such students despite their academic shortcomings. **1973** E. Taylor *Serpent under It* (1974) xii. 176 The kinds of things that stir them [*sc.* students] up these days are parietal hours and open admissions and black studies. **1976** *Times* 13 Jan. 7/4 There were three basic principles at [New York's] City University: quality education, free tuition and open admission. **1977** *Time* 28 Mar. 13/2 The country's enduring recession and unlimited open-admissions policies have turned Italian universities into what students call 'unemployment factories' or 'jobless parking lots'. **1841** *Picayune* (New Orleans) 11 Mar. 2/3 The contest between *Humming Bird* and *Maria Collier* was considered all but a 'dead open and shut game'. **1848** G. P. Burnham in F. A. Durivage *Stray Subjects* 128 That chap's snoring beat *all* the high-pressures he *ever* heerd—jest as easy as open and shet! **1890** *Dialect Notes* I. 19 The common New England maxim is 'Open and shet's a sign of wet'. **1893** *Harper's Mag.* May 975/2 The case was a dead open-and-shut one. **1904** W. H. Smith *Promoters* x. 162 It seems as if it was a dead open and shut that we've got to stay with 'em. **1930** Kipling *Limits & Renewals* (1932) 262 Like broken water, with the sun tipping it. Like Portland Race in open-and-shut weather. **1936** M. Allingham *Flowers for Judge* ix. 139 They [*sc.* the police] feel they've got an open-and-shut case. **1966** T. H. Raddall *Hangman's Beach* III. xv. 230 It was what fishermen call an open-and-shut day, with patches of black cloud, and occasional showers of rain. **1971** 'D. Shannon' *Ringer* (1972) ix. 163 This was such an open-and-shut thing. **1974** A. Morice *Death of Heavenly Twin* xiii. 138 What's the hurry if it's as open and shut as you make out? **1975** 'E. Lathen' *By Hook or by Crook* iii. 28 It's an open-and-shut case. There's no doubt. **1976** *Encounter* June 12/2 'No sweat, Mr Dennie,' said the police chief... 'It's an open and shut. The lady must have fell asleep smoking a cigarette.' **1923** H. A. Maddox *Dict. Stationery* 56 *Open back*, a bookbinding term alternatively described as hollow back, spring back, or extra... Letterpress books are either 'fast back' (in which case the leather is pasted directly on the folded sections) or 'open back' (in which case the book has a false back or is actually cased). **1961** Open back [see *loose back* s.v. *loose *a.* 9]. **1893** Smale & Colyer *Dis. & Injuries Teeth* ii. 14 Lack of anterior occlusion, or open bite may be caused in several ways—by thumb, finger, lip or tongue sucking [etc.]. **1975** W. J. B. Houston *Orthodontic Diagnosis* iv. 36 A skeletal open bite can not be satisfactorily treated by attempting to extrude the anterior teeth which have already grown as much as possible. Nor should posterior teeth be ground or extracted. **1870** J. K. Medbery *Men & Mysteries Wall St.* 16 The consolidation of the Government and the Open Boards with the old historic Stock Exchange. **1902** G. H. Lorimer *Lett. Merchant* ix. 113 If she is the daughter of old Job Dashkam, on the open Board, I should say..that she was a fine girl to let some other fellow marry. **1879** A. Miller *Brethren* v. 66 The new motto on the standard of the Open Brethren was, 'The blood of the Lamb is the union of the saints'. **1883** J. S. Teulon *Hist. & Teaching of Plymouth Brethren* ii. 18 Henceforth the Brethren parted into two hostile camps. The followers of Messrs. Müller and Craik, under the name of Open Brethren, adhered to the principles which had animated the movement in its earliest days. **1909** *Encycl. Relig. & Ethics* II. 845/2 The 'Open' Brethren.. fraternize freely with other Christians. **1968** F. R. Coad *Hist. Brethren Movement* x. 159 Those who refused to apply his decree against Bethesda... Commonly called 'Open Brethren', but in this book referred to hereafter by the more accurate name of independent Brethren. **1713** in *Sc. Nat. Dict.* (1965) VI. 487/3, 33½ fadoms wrought of closs Mynding besyds what is wrought of a flagged Mynd, and oppen cast. **1789** J. Williams *Nat. Hist. Mineral Kingdom* I. ii. 272 This open-cast has been worked to a great length upon the bearing and the old works now exhibit a horrid and frightful gulph of great length. **1802** J. Mawe *Mineral. of Derbyshire* 207 *Opencast*, when a vein is worked open from the day. **1811** [see *open-work 2]. **1903** *Copper Handbk.* III. 260 Veins are stripped and worked open-cast. **1944** *Times* 8 Apr. 2/4 The movement of opencast coal has been increased by 80,000 tons a week. **1955** *Times* 27 May 19/1 We are in process of pumping the water out of this opencast. *Ibid.* 1 July 17/3 Your company has taken a leading part in the operations of open-cast mining and has dug, during the year under review, over a quarter of a million tons of coal. **1974** *Country Life* 14 Feb. 284/2 Development and exploitation, ranging from housing estates to open-cast mining. **1886** J. Barrowman *Gloss. Scotch Mining Terms* 48 *Open-casting*, holing above the seam: working as a quarry. **1976** *Ilkeston Advertiser* 10 Dec. 11/1 Mr Alex Eadie, Parliamentary Under-Secretary of State for Energy, praised the council for its 'exceptional foresight' by co-operating with the Coal Board in planning and restoring land after opencasting. **1884** M. M. P. Muir *Treat Princ. Chem.* ii. 164 In an open chain molecule the action does not return to the carbon atom at which it started. **1928** [see *chain *sb.* 5 g]. **1968** O. R. C. Norman *Princ. Org. Synthesis* i. 23 Organic reactions frequently lead to the formation of cyclic compounds from open-chain (alicyclic) compounds. **1882** R. Bithell *Counting-House Dict.* 212 *Open cheque*, an uncrossed cheque, payable to Bearer or to Order on presentation. **1977** J. Wainwright *Nest of Rats* I. iii. 17 'I'll pay... Just name it.'..'An open cheque. That makes it very big.' **1827** J. Cumming *Man. Electro-Dynamics* iv. 164 In all cases of continued rotation, one of the conductors forms an open circuit. **1876** Preece & Sivewright *Telegraphy* iv. 105 Where many intermediate stations are fixed on one wire worked on the Morse principle, the closed circuit system offers considerable advantages over the open circuit system. **1893** S. R. Bottone *How to manage Dynamo* 42 This line of conductors is said to form an open circuit when there is any gap in the way; and then no current can flow. **1904** *Electrician* 13 May 139/2 If the field winding on one of the limbs of a Manchester-type dynamo is open-circuited, this limb will magnetically short-circuit the remaining limb. **1907** J. Erskine-Murray *Handbk. Wireless Telegr.* 5 Modern wireless telegraphy is, in general, open circuit telegraphy. **1927** A. E. Claxton *Performance & Design D.C. Machines* xii. 269 An open-circuited coil prevents the passage of current in its circuit. **1939** *Jrnl. Exper. Zool.* LXXXII. 420 The method employed for measuring the rate of metabolism was an open-circuit respiration system modified from the system originally developed by Haldane. **1953** [see *closed circuit* s.v. *closed *ppl. a.* 3]. **1954** *Induction Motor* (Brook Motors Ltd.) xii. 184 If one phase is open-circuited, the motor will make a humming noise when switched on. **1956** C. Evans *Kanchenjunga* ix. 92, I planned that every European going above Camp 3 should..climb with an open-circuit oxygen set. **1957** *Practical Wireless* XXXIII. 539/1 The input resistance with open-circuited output, and output resistance with short-circuited input, remain the same. **1962** J. P. Gregory in G. A. T. Burdett *Automatic Control Handbk.* ii. 7 The timing of the relay is brought about by delaying the decay of the flux in its magnetic circuit after switching off the supply to the coil, either by short-circuiting or open circuiting it. **1977** G. V. Higgins *Dreamland* vi. 59 If I don't touch an open circuit..it'll be a cave-in, or a blast. **1914** Duchess of Sutherland *Six Weeks at the War* p. xii, Unfortunately Namur is not an open city so she suffered for a short time from horrors worse than 'moral effect'. **1938** *Newsweek* 4 July 9/3 A pact restricting bombing of 'open' cities. **1944** *Ann. Reg. 1943* 57 The Government had been urged in Parliament to treat Rome as an open city. **1965** H. Kahn *On Escalation* ix. 178 Military disengagement on the open-city model. **1971** *N.Y. Times* 8 June 39 An open classroom means nothing to me unless it means that a child learns in that classroom that learning is not dependent at every level on the presence of a teacher. **1973** *Britannica Bk. of Year 1972* 732/3 *Open classroom*, a system of education in which activities involving multidisciplinary skills replace traditional subject courses. [**1909** Groom & Balfour tr. *Warming's Oecol. Plants* xxxv. 137 In some communities the soil is densely covered,..but in others the vegetable covering is so open that the colour of the soil imparts to the landscape its hue.] **1923** A. G. Tansley *Pract. Plant Ecol.* ix. 126 We get an open community in stable equilibrium with its habitat. **1929** Weaver & Clements *Plant Ecol.* vii. 142 Open communities are invaded readily. **1975** O. Rackham *Hayley Wood: Hist. & Ecol.* iii. 124 It is an open community: these plants do not form a carpet, and there is plenty of bare ground. **1961** Webster, Open compound. **1965** *Amer. Speech* XL. 41 An enterable open compound like *threshing machine*. **1884** D. Owen *Marine Insurance* (ed. 2) 56 (*heading*) Agreement to execute policies. (Off open cover.) **1895** W. Gow *Marine Insurance* xiv. 229 In every case with which the writer is acquainted the open cover is a mere document of honour. **1928** F. W. S. Poole *Marine Insurance of Goods* iv. 59 Open covers provide the merchant with continuous protection, enabling him to calculate the insurance charges for shipments ahead. **1960** *Times* 24 Oct. (Finance. Rev.) p. xiii/2 It was to meet this convenience that the 'open cover' type of policy was developed. **1903** *Pitman's Business Man's Guide* 326 *Open credit*. This is the name given to a letter of credit which contains an unconditional request to pay money to another person. **1920** J. Stephenson *Princ. & Pract. Commerc. Corr.* III. iv. 186, I..now beg to inquire whether you would be inclined to open an Account Current with me, granting me an open credit of £875. **1950** *Nucleonics* Mar. 47/1 The open cycle system is generally practical only with a plentiful and inexpensive coolant like air or water, except in the case of a rocket drive. **1957** *Gloss. Terms Nuclear Sci.* (Nat. Res. Council, U.S.) 114 *Open cycle*, cycle of operation of a heat engine in which the power fluid is used only once... Also applicable to a cooling system in which the coolant is used once and the discarded. **1958** M. J. Zucrow *Aircraft & Missile Propulsion* II. vi. 13 An open-cycle power plant is a continuous-flow prime mover using atmospheric air as the working fluid. **1971** M. M. El-Wakil *Nuclear Energy Conversion* vii. 200 In designing open cycles, the extent of induced radioactivity in the coolant and its effects on plant and surroundings should be carefully evaluated. **1973** Kettani & Hoyaux *Plasma Engin.* viii. 243 In the open cycle system, fuel is burned with the oxidiser to which -eed is added without preheating. **1892** *Durham Univ. Calendar* 6 February 22..M. Open Day. **1941** H. G. Stead *Mod. School Organisation* xv. 261 Open Days..let parents and other interested friends have an opportunity of seeing the school in action. **1953** A. K. C. Ottaway *Educ. & Soc.* vi. 117 Whenever 'open days' for visitors are possible these are appreciated by parents. **1971** *Guardian* 23 Aug. 4/1 Tours or 'open days' are being held..on sites within the Roman 'colonia' at Lincoln. *Ibid.* 12 Nov. 7/3 It was like most school open days. The women questioned the staff about how the teaching would help John's or Simon's career. **1975** B. Meyrick *Behind the Light* xi. 143 Open Days on local Trinity service vessels were an annual event. **1908** *Daily Chron.* 13 Feb. 6/2 The open-end garden-seated light car..might be trailed as a relief car. **1940** *Sun* (Baltimore) 26 Apr. 23/9 Open-end trusts are those in which shares are redeemable at their asset value at any given time. **1945** Webster Add., *Open-end*, of a contract calling for the filling by a particular contractor of all government needs for a specific product during a specified period. **1952** W. J. H. Sprott *Social Psychol.* vi. 102 The questions..may be 'open-end' questions which allow of a more elaborate answer. **1953** *Economist* 21 Feb. 500/1 An open-end trust is in all major respects similar to a flexible unit trust. It holds a portfolio of securities and cash, against which units are issued to the public, and the managers have a wide discretion in their investment policy. *Ibid.* 500/2 The principle of the open-end fund is sound. **1954** [see *closed-end* s.v. *closed *ppl. a.* 3]. **1955** T. H. Pear *Eng. Social Differences* iii. 110 Questionnaires, 'closed or open-end', might lead to interviews and written personal and private communications. **1966** *Listener* 23 June 926/1 This was what happened in the open-end discussion. **1972** *Guardian* 21 July 16/1 There was a considerable debate in financial quarters about the wisdom of open-end funds, or unit trusts, which invest in property. **1972** *Sci. Amer.* Dec. 55/1 Open-end spinning has been the subject of intense development during the past five years. Commercial frames of Czechoslovakian and Japanese design have recently become available. **1974** *Times* 22 Mar. 21/1. The demand background is there and with its lead in 'open end' and 'self twist' machines Stone should be able to exploit it whilst it lasts. **1975** A. J. Hall *Stand. Handbk. Textiles* (ed. 8) iii. 170 In an open-end spinning a sliver of, say, cotton is fed into a relatively small device.. in which the fibres under air pressure are impelled by centrifugal action and an existing air vortex on to the internal surface of a high speed (up to 40000 rev/min) rotating cylinder and are therefore carried forward with their twisting together to an exit point from which they are drawn in the form of yarn having an appropriate degree of twist. **1976** *National Observer* (U.S.) 13 Mar. 10/6 (Advt.), A managed diversified Open-end Investment Trust. **1825** Open-ended (in Dict., sense 22 b]. **1935** [see *hydraulic gradient* s.v. *hydraulic *a.* 1]. **1940** M. Mead *Male & Female* ii. 47 The problem will be whether ..those who read can keep such words as 'men', 'women', and 'children' open-ended words. **1952** *Newsweek* 26 May 39/2 This program..is bound to fail if it is looked upon as a final step. Like the original Union of our States, it should be 'open-ended'. **1952** *Sat. Even. Post* 25 Oct. 150/3 Unlike the atomic bomb, the hydrogen bomb is an 'open-ended' weapon. In theory, if you want to make it more powerful, you just shovel in more of the heavy-hydrogen mixture. **1953** E. G. Williamson in *Ann. Rev. Psychol.* IV. 344 The open-ended interviews were concerned with the manner in which an individual was currently dealing with his problem of occupational choice. **1953** K. Cobb in *Ibid.* 367 A study of visually handicapped school children, tested with an open-ended adjustment inventory printed in large print or Braille. **1957** R. K. Merton *Student-Physician* 314 Questions marked with an asterisk were initially asked in open-ended form. **1964** *Ann. Reg. 1963* 401 This at least was suggested by their answers to questions in standard intelligence tests, which tended to an alarming degree to be of the closed rather than open-ended type. **1967** M. Argyle *Psychol. Interpersonal Behaviour* ii. 39 Questions vary in the extent to which they are open or closed—an open-ended question requires a lengthy explanation rather than a choice between alternatives; the best way to get someone to talk is to ask this kind of question. **1970** D. Goldrich et al. in I. L. Horowitz *Masses in Lat. Amer.* v. 177 It seemed desirable to use mainly open-ended interviewing techniques. **1973** *Daily Tel.* 2 Mar. 2/5 Powers of punishment for contempt are open ended as no maximum prison sentence or fine is laid down. **1953** W. H. McNeill *Amer., Brit., & Russia* I. i. 63 It was almost irresistible to look at the war-time history in the light of what had come after, to search for signs and portents of the strained situation which had prevailed since 1946 or 1947, and to forget or minimize the 'open-endedness' of Allied relationships during the war years. **1973** *Amer. Speech 1969* XLIV. 289 The seeming 'open-endedness' of the set of sentences of a language presents a challenge to transformational theory. **1974** G. F. Newman *Price* vii. 218 The open-endedness of the situation worked as well for her. She was as free as Sneed to quit. **1964** *N.Y. Times* 12 Jan. E11/1 The New York system in 1960 inaugurated a policy of 'open enrollment' which permitted youngsters from designated predominantly non-white schools to apply for transfer to designated predominantly white schools. **1970** *Ibid.* 7 Jan. 42 The open enrollment policy for the city universities will be a mistake. **1974** *Florida FL Reporter* XIII. 80/3 If indeed the phrase is not to become a meaningless slogan as many people regard the term 'open enrollment' in the City University of New York. **1934** Webster, *Open-faced*.. Of pies, etc., without top crust. **1946** *Sun* (Baltimore) 26 Apr. 6/1 A spokesman for the Case-Moody Pie Corporation..said it expected to realize a one fourth savings in flour by bringing out an 'open-faced' pie in which the top crust is eliminated. **1970** *Islander* (Victoria, B.C.) 22 Feb. 14/2 This little book tells you exactly how to make.. toppings for world famous and eye-appealing Open-Faced Sandwiches. **1976** *National Observer* (U.S.) 14 Feb. 7/2 They can be fried and covered with goodies, thus becoming a pre-Columbian open-faced sandwich. **1932** T. Corkhill *Conc. Building Encycl.* 146 *Open floor*, one with exposed joists, not covered by a ceiling. **1919** W. H. Downing *Digger Dial.* 36 *Open go*, see *fair go*. **1959** H. P. Tritton *Time means Tucker* ii. 15/1 The sergeant said we were putting on a better show than the professionals. He said we could have an open go the following night. **1973** *Bulletin* (Sydney) 25 Aug. 24/1 This intimidatory behavior, the company charges, contrasts with the 'open go' policy being afforded two other major prawning operators in the region. **1966** *Guardian* 29 Aug. 7/2 The agreement provides for stronger enforcement of open-housing regulations. *Ibid.*, Labour leaders agree to support open housing. **1971** *N.Y. Times* 1 June 28 The Suburban Citizens for Open Housing, an organization pushing for integration of the outer city. **1976** *National Observer* (U.S.) 8 May 6/2 The Rev. James E. Groppi, the Roman Catholic priest who led open-housing marches in the '60s. **1932** *Jrnl. R. Aeronaut. Soc.* XXXVI. 999 In a tunnel of any sort the provision of an open jet calls for rather more power than a walled-in jet would need. **1947** A. Pope *Wind-Tunnel Testing* ii. 34 For propeller and rotor tests..the open jet offers considerable advantage. **1971** D. C. Bain et al. *Wind Tunnels* ii. 1/2 Open jet tunnels are mainly used for air flow observations and have the advantage of easy access to the model for modifications and an unobstructed view for observation and photography. **1941** Open juncture [see *juncture 2 c]. **1942** Bloch & Trager *Outl. Ling. Analysis* iii. 47 In a phonemic transcription, external open juncture is marked by leaving a space between symbols, internal open juncture by a hyphen. **1966** [see *junctural *a.*]. **1973** D. Rockey *Phonetic Lexicon* 43 Spanish permits no clusters before final pause and open juncture. **1974** *Amer. Speech 1969* XLIV. 57 The liquids occur only immediately before open juncture. **1963** 'W. Haggard' *High Wire* xiv. 151 He..booked a call to London. It would be an open line, but he didn't have access to another. **1966** 'G. Black' *You want to die, Johnny?* iii. 47 Perhaps I should tell you, even on an open line, that I've just had a summons, from Ministerial level. **1970** *New York* 16 Nov. 5/2 Her over-involvement with the Renaissance Project and the Open-Line Program present an unbalanced image. **1972** *Guardian* 25 Sept. 4 Open-line radio shows, during which the visitor sits in..a radio studio and answers questions in amplified telephone conversations with local people. **1973** 'D. Jordan' *Nile Green* xliv. 223 They had also given me an open line to London. **1947** *Jrnl. Inst. Electr. Engin.* XCIV. IIA 5/3 (*heading*) Examples of open-loop and closed-loop control. **1954, 1962** [see *loop *sb.*[1] 4 l]. **1966** *New Scientist* 30 June 830 Almost all skilled muscular activities seem to exhibit many 'open-loop', pre-programmed characteristics. An open-loop system (one that draws little or no information from the thing it governs) can always be operated more effectively than a closed-loop one, provided that its task is well defined and not subject to major disturbances. **1967** *Electronics* 6 Mar. 306/2 Typical open-loop voltage gain is greater than 200,000. **1766** Blackstone *Comm.* II. xxx. 449 Our Saxon ancestors prohibited the sale of any thing above the value of twenty pence, unless in open market. **1838** W. Bell *Dict. Law Scotl.* 627 The law of Scotland differs from that of England as to the legal effect of a sale in open market. **1870** J. K. Medbery *Men & Mysteries Wall St.* 18 The stock which has occasioned the default is sold or bought in the open market under the rule. **1930** *Economist* 22 Mar. 630/1 The failure of the Reserve Bank's buying rate to go down as fast as the open-market rate. **1933** R. McKenna *Speech Midland Bank* 10 During the period of open market buying bank deposits continued to decline, though only slightly. **1934** [see *berry *sb.*[1] 1 c]. **1961** *Wall St. Jrnl.* 24 Mar. 26 This was a departure from its open market activities in the previous four weeks, in which the System extended these operations to securities in the medium-term range, with maturities up to ten years. **1972** *Times* 26 Jan. 6/2 To have the said rent reviewed at the said time by reference to the open market rental value of the demised premises. **1828** Carlyle in *Foreign Rev.* II. 115 To open-minded, truth-seeking men, the deliberate words of an open-minded, truth-seeking man can in no case be wholly unintelligible. **1861** T. Hughes *Tom Brown at Oxf.* III. xii. 223 In fact, he is a wonderfully open-minded man for his age, if you only put things to him the right way. **1903** G. B. Shaw *Let.* 6 Mar. (1972) II. 316 You can't feel at home with anything that is strange, no matter how open-minded you may be. **1969** *Jane's Freight Containers 1968–69* 31/3 CN will be open-minded about participating. **1976** P. Donovan *Relig. Lang.* iv. 43 The words..would appear to have little relevance to testing which stems from belief and faith, or even from openminded enquiry. **1909** H. G. Wells *Tono-Bungay* II. iv. 230 'Your aunt makes Game of people,' was Marion's verdict, and, open-mindedly; 'I suppose it's all right..for her.' **1832** Carlyle in *Fraser's Mag.* V. 386/1 Boswell wrote a good Book..because of his free insight, his lively talent, above all, of his Love and childlike Open-mindedness. **1914** *Jrnl. Iron & Steel Inst.* LXXXIX. 184 Whilst he could not but admire the authors' eloquence and open-mindedness, he certainly considered that they had not proved the theory which they had set out to expound. **1972** *Science* 16 June 1209/2 Much conventional scientific training..tends to produce rigidity and avoidance of personal involvement with subject matter, rather than open-mindedness and flexibility. **1939–40** *Army & Navy Stores Catal.* 656/3 All-Wool Sweaters... V-shape open neck, plain or cable stitch. **1949** *Penguin New Writing* XXXVIII. 14 The sleeves of his open-neck shirt were rolled up. **1971** D. Bagley *Freedom Trap* vii. 152 She looked too damned fetching in stretch pants, open-neck shirt and short jacket. **1976** *Daily Mirror* 16 July 13/1 An elaborately casual outfit of trousers and jacket, in man-made fibre and worn with an open-neck shirt. **1959** E. H. Clements *High Tension* v. 83 His step-cousin's [neck] rose, long and boyish-looking, from an open-necked shirt. **1973** P. Moyes *Curious Affair of Third Dog* iii. 32 A slim, fair-haired girl in corduroy trousers and an open-necked shirt. **1975** N. Luard *Robespierre Serial* xv. 131 The burly men in open-necked shirts. **1976** *Listener* 10 June 751/1 Australia?..A free-and-easy, no-nonsense, open-necked continent. **1953** *Open Occupancy in Public Housing* (U.S. Housing & Home Finance Agency) i. 3/1 When a shifting is made from a policy of enforced segregation to one of open occupancy, clear-cut policy..is found to be mandatory. **1966** *Economist* 28 May 962/2 The landlords' association, which Core blames in part for the persistent refusal of the City Council to pass an open-occupancy law. **1968** M. Harrington *Toward Democratic Left* x. 289 And study after study documents a correlation between high educational attainment and libertarian views on civil liberties, capital punishment, open occupancy—and the war in Vietnam. **1913** *Amer. Year Bk. 1912* 421/2 The eight-hour day in Arizona..has been extended to all open-cut workings and open-pit workings. **1959** *Times* 12 June 17/4 It [*sc.* British capital] has pioneered in the new technique of open-pit borate mining. **1971** *Daily Colonist* (Victoria, B.C.) 19 Feb. 11/3 H. M. Wright..says open-pit mines in British Columbia are 'a beautiful sight'. **1975** *New Yorker* 3 Mar. 74/2 Copper was hardly worth taking out of the ground, and times were hard in Bisbee. In 1951, Phelps Dodge began a new open-pit mine—the Lavender Pit. **1938** *Archit. Rev.* LXXXIII. 90/2 The open plan is almost universal but perhaps less easy to work than it looks. **1954** *Ibid.* CXV. 213 A few are more experimental, influenced either by the pre-war work of Arne Jacobsen and Mogens Lassen or, more recently, by the open-plan American house. **1960** M. Spark *Ballad of Peckham Rye* iii. 38 We used to have an open-plan... So that you could see everyone in the office without the glass. **1973** 'R. MacLeod' *Burial in Portugal* ii. 41 An open-plan stairway curved..towards the upper floor. **1975** in Cox & Boyson *Black Paper 1975* 30/2 The education hierarchy.. doubt the wisdom of having an open-plan school in a difficult area. *Ibid.* 31/1 For children from a less fortunate environment open plan is disaster. **1958** *Washington Post* 16 Aug. B 10/1 Open-planned kitchens have been described by designers as 'one of the most desirable areas in the home'. **1960** *Guardian* 24 Feb. 12/5 Comparatively few people have really lived in modern, open-planned houses. **1976** *Ilkeston Advertiser* 10 Dec. 12/5 (Advt.), Front shop (ideal lounge), open-planned living kitchen. **1958** *Washington Post* 16 Aug. B 10/1 The welcome theme of this architect-designed House of The Week is 'open planning'. **1958** *Listener* 25 Sept. 459/1 The trend towards open planning favours development of this method. **1859, 1983** Open question [in Dict., sense 18]. **1972** *Guardian* 2 Feb. 7/4 A sixth-form general studies unit..was designed to promote discussion of 'open' questions, to which there may be no known or agreed answers. **1976** *Howard Jrnl.* XV. I. 17 What brought about this change is an open question. **1890** *Stock Grower & Farmer* 15 Mar. 6/3 The cow men of the open ranges will make money. **1905** *Bull. Bureau of Forestry* (U.S. Dept. Agric.) No. 62, 9 The great bulk of the western stockmen are definitely in favor of the Government control of the open range. *Ibid.* 52 Under the open-range system the honest and law-abiding cattleman was at a great disadvantage. **1958** *Spectator* 11 July 60/1 Occasionally they [*sc.* the chickens] have been a little flavourless, probably because these were not open-range birds. **1959** *Times Lit. Suppl.* 6 Nov. 639/1 After the..novels laid by American and western European novelists in their batteries or deep litter, it is pleasant to discover a Greek novel as tasty as an open range egg. **1962** W. Stegner *Wolf Willow* (1963) II. ii. 45 Last survival of the open-range cattle industry, booby prize in a belated homestead rush, this country saved each stage of the Plains frontier long past its appointed time. **1970** *High Fidelity* Nov. 77/1 Here we encounter what may well be a very significant parting of the ways between cassettes and open-reel tapes. **1971** *Gramophone* Dec. 1125/1 An 8-track cartridge machine capable of recording and reproducing and a sophisticated recorder covering open-reel, cassette and cartridge recording and reproducing. **1977** *Rolling Stone* 7 Apr. 6/1 (Advt.), A cassette, unlike its open-reel counterpart, actually becomes an integral part of your system the instant you put it in your cassette deck. **1817** E. P. Fordham *Jrnl.* 31 July in *Pers. Narr. Trav.* (1906) vi. 100 This state [*sc.* Indiana] is one vast forest, intersected by a few Blaze roads and two or three open roads. **1856** W. Whitman *Leaves of Grass* (ed. 2) 223 Afoot and lighthearted I take to the open road! **1920** E. O'Neill *Beyond Horizon* III. ii. 162 So I thought I'd try to end as I might have—if I'd had the courage to live my dream. Alone—in a ditch by the open road—watching the sun rise. *a* **1930** D. H. Lawrence *Phoenix II* (1968) 220 Some of these sonnets are very fine: they stand apart in an age of 'open road' and Empire thumping verse. **1968** L. Deighton *Only when I Larf* i. 16 I'm for the open road, the jet routes, Cannes, Nice, Monte; where the pickings are rich and the living is easy. **1975** *Country Life* 16 Oct. 1007/1 Open-road motoring is inhibited by ever-lower speed limits. **1976** *Southern Even. Echo* (Southampton) 2 Nov. 15/2 Yet on the open road a new virtue is revealed, and the VX becomes an admirable companion for covering long distance in comfort. **1932** T. Corkhill *Conc. Building Encycl.* 146 *Open roof*, one in which the principals are on view. No ceiling. **1946** *Sun* (Baltimore) 13 Aug. 2/8 Some lunch counters were serving 'the open sandwich', a single slice affair. **1959** *Listener* 15 Jan. 136/2 The simplest open sandwich or even everyday platter of roast meat. **1973** D. Bagley *Tightrope Men* xxv. 172 The open sandwiches of Scandinavia. **1899** Bridge & Sawyer *Course Harmony* ii. 8 There are two methods of writing harmony—viz., in open score and short score. In open score each voice is written on a separate staff. **1979** *Early Music* Oct. 531/1 The..music examples..are offered in open score to avoid the congestion inevitable with reduction to short score. **1896** *Outing* Sept. 596/2 The first day of September marks the beginning of the open season on pheasants, grouse, and quail in Oregon. **1914** 'High Jinks, Jr.' *Choice Slang* 16 *Open season*, time when a person may expect no mercy or protection. **1918** [see *bee[1] 5 b]. **1948** *Chesterton* (Indiana) *Tribune* 28 Oct. 6/4 A brief open season on pheasants will enhance this autumn's pleasure for Hoosier sportsmen. **1958** *Listener* 18 Sept. 416/1 The open season for tropical storms is declared in the last week in August. **1969** 'J. Morris' *Fever Grass* i. 10 He remembered those thirty years, before the island became independent and open season on its security tacitly declared. **1974** *Times* 18 Feb. 14/7 Any appearance of open season for pay could spark off an explosion. **1977** D. Anthony *Stud Game* xxviii. 189 It happened to be a year the state allowed open season on does, to thin out the herd. **1872** M. A. Barker in D. M. Davin *N.Z. Short Stories* (1953) 37 Brown and Wetherby's was an 'open shed', where any shearers that came were taken on until there were hands enough. *a* **1948** L. G. D. Acland *Early Canterbury Runs* (1951) vii. 169 Clayton was an 'open shed', that is, the shearers were not engaged beforehand, but turned up and took their chance of a pen on the advertised starting day. **1821** M. Edgeworth *Let.* 12 Dec. (1971) 290 They live in the library—open shelves—mixture of half bound and bound books. **1897** *Library Jrnl.* Jan. 44/1 The adoption of the open-shelf system. **1910** A. E. Bostwick *Amer. Publ. Library* 38 Practically all small and moderate sized American libraries are now 'open-shelf', which means that the user is allowed to go personally to the shelves and select his book. **1906** Gallaher & Stead *Compl. Rugby Footballer* xi. 145 (*heading*) Tactics—combined attack on the open side. **1960** E. S. & W. J. Higham *High Speed Rugby* vii. 71 Break to the openside and close to the scrum if the openside flank is going straight for your fly-half. **1945** *Richmond* (Virginia) *Times Dispatch* 10 Feb. 12 (*heading*) U.S. accepts agreements on aviation pact. Will exchange 'open skies' rights. *Ibid.*, Today's action confirmed the position taken by the United States delegation in favor of 'open skies' or virtually unlimited freedom of the air. **1956** *Friends Jrnl.* 18 Feb. 103/2 The United States position is that until the scientists have solved the problem of detecting stocks, priority should be given to the Eisenhower 'open skies' plan and other measures designed to create confidence rather than to affect disarmament. **1957** *Daily Mail* 7 Oct. 6/2 The day when the Communists gave an ironic answer to President Eisenhower's plea for 'Open Skies'—by creating just that. **1965** D. D. Eisenhower *White House Yrs.* (1966) II. v. xx. 470 The Open Skies proposal was criticized by the Soviets because, they said, it covered only the territories of our two homelands and would fail to cover territory where United States forces were stationed overseas. **1973** *Times* 31 Jan. (Mediterranean Suppl.) p. iv/3 To attain their ambitious targets the Greek authorities proclaimed an 'open skies' policy for charter flights. **1944** *Sun* (Baltimore) 30 Nov. 7/2 The British apparently now have the choice of going along with the 'open sky' program or facing the development of a large bloc of nations which want something along the lines of the United States. **1955** *Ibid.* 11 Nov. 1/7 Vyacheslav M. Molotov buried President Eisenhower's 'open-sky' plan for disarmament under a five-point indictment here tonight. **1935** R. Audra at al. tr. *Bergson's Two Sources Morality & Relig.* iv. 230 Never shall we pass from the closed society to the open society, from the city to humanity, by any mere broadening out. **1940** *Mind* XLIX. 116 Bergson's distinction of 'open' and 'closed' societies, when applied to the society of all mankind, leads to the conclusion that this all-inclusive society will be 'quantitatively closed'. **1945** K. Popper (*title*) The open society and its enemies. **1954** P. Mason *Ess. Racial Tension* xvii. 119 The painful transition from a society based on status to an open society in which contract and competition play a part. **1973** *Listener* 17 May 635/1 Mill's..overriding goal of maintaining an open society..in which might be realised..the flowering of human individuality in all its diversity. **1953** R. Southern *Open Stage* 41 The name 'open stage' cannot be given merely on the grounds of there being a platform free on three sides... Those three sides must be occupied by audience. **1960** *Times* 15 July 16/4 A cynic might regard the crude..Riviera settings as a powerful argument in favour of open-stage methods. **1962** *Listener* 8 Nov. 771/3 It is I think now widely accepted that the term 'open stage' is conveniently used to include not only the three-sided open stage of which Dr Southern was primarily writing in his book, but all forms of theatre where the acting area is in the same room as the audience. **1897** *Sears, Roebuck Catal.* 681 Decorated dinner-ware. Patterns sold in open stock. **1911** *Daily Colonist* (Victoria, B.C.) 23 Apr. 4/4 We are in receipt of the latest open stock pattern in Limoges China... You can always replace a broken piece at any time. **1970** *Globe & Mail* (Toronto) 26 Sept. 13/1 (Advt.), 30% off makers' suggested retail prices on open stock dinnerware patterns. **1976** *Columbus* (Montana) *News* (Joliet Suppl.) 17 June 2/4 'Open stock' is the term for piece-by-piece sales instead of sales by the place setting category. The theory behind open stock sales is that you can buy just the pieces you need as you wish them, and you can replace items as you need. **1951** M. V. Wilkes et al. *Preparation of Programs for Electronic Digital Computer* 22 The simplest form of subroutine consists of a sequence of orders which can be incorporated as it stands in a program... This type of subroutine is called an 'open' subroutine. **1958** [see *inline *a.* 3 a]. **1969** P. B. Jordain *Condensed Computer Encycl.* 353 Typically, an open subroutine will convert floating-point numbers to fixed-point numbers or fixed-point to floating-point (four to six instructions), find the next larger integer value, or find the absolute magnitude. The advantages of open subroutine [*sic*] consist of simple usage.., faster execution, and if used sparingly, conservation of memory. **1939** F. H. MacDougall *Thermodynamics & Chem.* (ed. 3) x. 134 When a transfer of matter to or from a system is also possible, the system may be called an open system. **1962** P. Strevens *Papers in Lang.* (1965) xii. 152 The study of closed-system items is what we conventionally call 'grammar', while the open systems constitute 'lexis'. **1963** A. K. Rice *Enterprise & its Environment* IV. xx. 184 Open systems exist and can only exist by the exchange of materials with their environment... An open system can achieve a time-independent steady state. **1971** J. Z. Young *Introd. Study Man* ii. 26 Organisms are not stable systems..but 'open' systems maintained in a steady state by continual expenditure of energy. **1945** F. Waismann in *Aristotelian Soc. Suppl. Vol.* XIX. 121 The failure of the phenomenalist to translate a material object statement into terms of sense data..is due to..the 'open texture' of most of our empirical concepts... I owe this term to Mr. [W. C.] Kneale who suggested it to me as a translation of *Porosität der Begriffe*, a term coined by me in German. *Ibid.* 123 It is not possible to define a concept like gold with absolute precision, *i.e.* in such a way that every nook and cranny is blocked against entry of doubt. That is what is meant by the open texture of a concept. **1956** J. Holloway in A. Pryce-Jones *New Outl. Mod. Knowl.* 35 Waismann's term for this pervasive quality of language [*sc.* its ineradicable fluidity] was 'open texture'... The view is that the meanings of most words and expressions in common use are not precisely and exhaustively fixed, and ..that it would be very inconvenient if they were. **1965** *Amer. Philos. Q.* II. 112/2 There are *practical* reasons independent of vagueness, open-texture and the like for refusing to equate names with descriptions. **1966** *Ibid.* III. 116/2 There is a certain 'open texture' about Christian beliefs. **1950** *Mind* LIX. 159 Straightway we have a case of a vague and open textured criterion. **1965** *Amer. Philos. Q.* II. 120/1 The concepts they express are open-textured. **1974** T. E. Wilkerson *Minds, Brains & People* 7 A concept is too open-textured, so we tighten it up a little. **1966** *Jrnl. Linguistics* II. 243. The ordinary language philosopher..emphasizing the intricacy, variety and 'open-texturedness' of language. **1938** *Chatelaine* Mar. 32/3 Open-toe shoes will be more popular than ever. **1942** *Sun* (Baltimore) 12 Aug. 10/7, I don't understand window dressing, but it looks to me that some of the 'girls' displaying fur coats in Charles street windows are standing in the snow with open-toe shoes on. **1942** R. Chandler *High Window* (1943) v. 43 She wore..blue and white open-toed sandals. **1965** 'M. Neville' *Ladies in Dark* viii. 80 The shoe was none too new, open-toed and with a strap round the heel. **1973** 'R. MacLeod' *Burial in Portugal* iv. 91 She had simple open-toed sandals. **1771** Open top [in Dict., sense 22 a]. **1856** *Trans. Mich. Agric. Soc.* VII. 61 John Patton..[exhibited an] open top buggy. **1935** *Discovery* June 163/1 The tin can has gradually developed into the present day open top or 'sanitary' can, with the ends rolled on by machine, and made airtight by a rubber gasket. **1955** *Amer. Speech* XXX. 92 *Open top*, a rig with sides but no permanent top. **1972** D. E. Westlake *Bank Shot* ii. 17 Open-top cartons full of paperback books. **1974** 'J. Ross' *Burning of Billy Toober* ix. 89 A veteran open-top Bentley in racing dark-green. **1964** L. Deighton *Funeral in Berlin* xix. 111 The open-topped Mercedes that drove lazily past. **1977** L. Gordon *Eliot's Early Years* v. 99 He walked across London Bridge amidst horse-drawn carts, open-topped buses. [**1901** 'J. Flynt' *World of Graft* 11 The City Hall gang went into office on the promise that the town was to be open, an' they've kept it open.] **1915** *Amer. Mag.* Sept. 51/2 On an 'open town' platform Gill was elected mayor in March, 1910. **1938** H. Nicolson *Diary* 22 Sept. (1966) 364 It may mean surrender..in return for such quite valueless concessions as..'no bombing of open towns'. **1939** R. Campbell *Flowering Rifle* vi. 148 Keep safe his bomb-dump while our patience lasts While from its store our open towns he blasts. **1946** *Reader's Digest* July 96/2 Amarillo is the most open-town in the country. **1975** J. Gores *Hammett* vi. 43 They form a Committee to clean up San Francisco, and as chairman they take the man who's been running it as an open town for sixteen years. **1960** *Guardian* 11 Mar. 8/7 Modern architects are known to favour open-tread stairs. **1972** *Daily Tel.* 29 Nov. 24/3 A circular, opentread hardwood stairway gives on to a galleried landing **1966** *New Statesmen* 14 Oct. 548/3 The Open University..is the latest and most impressive offspring of the founders of ACE (Advisory Centre for Education). **1968** *Listener* 12 Dec. 806/1 (Advt.), January 1971 is the starting date for the transmission of the BBC radio and television programmes which form part of the Open University foundation year courses. **1969** *Radio Times* 27 Nov. 12 Originally named 'the University of the Air', the Open University offers an exciting new opportunity for adults throughout the country to study for degree qualifications through the media of integrated television, radio and specially-designed correspondence courses. **1973** *Listener* 17 May 634/1 [John Stuart] Mill.. set out to be a public thinker, a one-man Open University. **1977** *R.A.F. News* 11–24 May 2/3 Gp Capt Frank Rice (Retd)..played a major part..in setting up the Cyprus Open University scheme. **1960** N. Polunin *Introd. Plant Geogr.* xiv. 447 Cacti in the New World and cactus-like Euphorbias in the Old World frequently form a characteristic feature of the usually open vegetation [in semi-deserts]. **1971** D. W. Shimwell *Descr. & Classification of Vegetation* ii. 106 Where there is space between individuals which can be colonized.., the term open vegetation is applied. **1960** A. Huxley *Let.* 27 Dec. (1969) 901 Maxwell Jones..pioneered the Open Ward system in English mental hospitals. **1965** *Nursing Times* 5 Feb. 183/2 The staff kept her under as close observation as was possible in an open ward. **1922** *Beaver* Jan. 33/1 We remained at Mountain House until open water in the spring. *Ibid.* Sept. 9/1 When the open water came, I got one hundred and thirty-two beaver. **1930** L. Munday *Mounty's Wife* iii. 50 We had to keep him at Cumberland until he could be taken to Prince Albert at open water. **1956** H. S. M. Kemp *Northern Trader* (1957) x. 130 When open-water came..we were able to pitch-off to our private trapping grounds. **1956** *Polar Record* Jan. 8 *Open water*, a relatively large area of water free of ice. **1971** T. Boulanger *Indian Remembers* 4 The people came home after open water at Oxford House. **1900** W. C. Sabine in *Amer. Architect* LXVIII. 22/1 [Hereafter all results..will be expressed in terms of the absorbing power of open windows.] *Ibid.*, The absorbing power was found to be ·73 of open-window units. **1957** D. H. Fender *Gen. Physics & Sound* xii. 398 The area of material multiplied by its absorption coefficient measures its total absorption in 'open window units'. **1968** *Punch* 11 Sept. 364/2 An Open Window Unit (o.w.u.) is a unit of sound absorption... It is equal to the absorption by an open window of one square foot in area. **1968** R. C. Stanley *Light & Sound for Engineers* xvi. 308 If the area of the surface is expressed in square feet, then the absorption is expressed in open window units or sabins. **1889** W. Schlich *Man. Forestry* I. 9 Thin Wood, or open wood, means a wood in which the crowns of the trees do not interlace. **1926** Tansley & Chipp *Study of Vegetation* x. 210 Open woodland consists of open woodland without a closed and thickly interlaced canopy. **1790** J. Armstrong *Jrnl.* in *Ohio Archaeol. & Hist. Q.* (1911) XX. 82 A course a little to the N. of W., passing through several small prairies and open woods. **1799** J. Smith *Acct. Remarkable Occurrences* 13 About the lick was clear, open woods, and thin white-oak land. **1823** C. Vignoles *Obs. Floridas* 77 Instead of the clear open woods generally seen, masses of young pine saplings are thickly spread over the rocky ground. **1824** D. E. Burch *Let.* 30 Oct. in *Florida Hist. Q.* XIV. 105 In the open woods, especially in the pine barrens, these [*sc.* fallen trees] can always be avoided by turning out. **1939** *Canad. Hist. Rev.* XX. 282 The general results..would seem at first sight to point to the 'groves', 'open woods', 'oak openings', parklands, or whatever name one may give them, being more pronounced on the western borders of this huge territory than on the Atlantic slope.

B. *adv.* (Later examples.)

1780 J. Woodforde *Diary* 24 Oct. (1924) I. 293 He.. spoke very open and ingenuous about it. **1921** E. O'Neill *Diff'rent* II, in *Emperor Jones* 252 Tell me all about 'em. You needn't be scared—to talk open with me.

open, *v.* Add: **2. d.** (Earlier example.)

1865 W. Howitt *Hist. Discovery in Austral.* I. xiii. 207 Measures were..instituted to construct a high road through the whole distance already gone... It was then, in modern phraseology, opened by the governor, attended by Mrs. Macquarie, and an escort on horseback.

6. c. *Electr.* To break or interrupt (an electric circuit); to put (a switch or the like) into a condition in which there is no path through it for an electric current.

In quot. 1834 the meaning is the opposite, viz. 'to create, close' (Close *v.* 10 e).

[**1834** M. Faraday in *Phil. Trans. R. Soc.* CXXIV. 429 The presence of a piece of platina touching both the zinc and the fluid to be decomposed, opens the path required for the electricity.] **1836** *Ann. Electr., Magn., & Chem.* I. 71 The shock is never produced only at the moment of opening the voltaic circuit. **1876** Preece & Sivewright *Telegraphy* iv. 103 If B wishes to communicate with A he ..opens the switch. **1924** Wedmore & Trencham *Switchgear for Electr. Power Control* xxiii. 252 A smart operator can open a medium-voltage circuit safely with a plain lever switch. **1962** *Newnes Conc. Encycl. Electr. Engin.* 735/1 The circuit-breaker contacts are held closed by springs and the contacts are opened in the event of a fault by the overcurrent in a series solenoid coil. **1975** M. Mandl *Basics of Electr.* vi. 123 When voltage is applied to the coil, the flexible section is pulled down.., opening the switch.

13. b. *Bridge.* To commence (the bidding); to offer (a particular bid).

1958 *Listener* 6 Nov. 753/1 What should West open, assuming that he is playing a Two Club system? **1964** N. Squire *Bidding at Bridge* ii. 17 When you open the bidding with a *suit* your strength may be absolutely minimum. *Ibid.* 21 You should open One Diamond, as your hand is unsuitable for you to be declarer in no-trumps. **1977** *Times* 10 Dec. 13/5 North has opened One Spade at game and 30. **1977** *Harpers & Queen* Dec. 26/2 West opened the bidding with one of those..artificial Two Diamond calls.

16. (Further examples.)

1864 E. A. Parkes *Man. Pract. Hygiene* 107 The windows should open at the top, and in case the wind has a high velocity, means should be taken to distribute it. **1871** L. W. M. Lockhart *Fair to See* I. iii. 103 'A Cameron of Aberlorna!' exclaimed the host, in a tone of unaccountable astonishment, his eyes opening wide upon Bertrand. **1893** M. E. Mann *In Summer Shade* I. x. 238 Claude's eyes opened slowly upon his brother's face. **1912** *Chambers's Jrnl.* Feb. 82/1 Suddenly the great eye of the lighthouse opened. **1952** M. Allingham *Tiger in Smoke* iv. 68 It was just when we were opening... I was just getting my keys for the spirits.

d. *Electr.* Of a circuit or device: to become open (*open *a.* 11 f); to suffer a break in its conducting path.

1836 *Ann. Electr., Magn., & Chem.* I. 71 If there is a spark..it is..feeble when compared to that seen when the circuit is opening. **1924** Wedmore & Trencham *Switchgear for Electr. Power Control* ii. 14 The circuit breaker.. is designed to open freely and quickly. **1975** I. Clucas *Reed's Electr. for Deck Officers* vii. 215 A second pair of contacts..are the first to close and the last to open... They take the full brunt of the spark when opening. *Ibid.* 224 When the main switch is closed the buzzer should sound..and the individual circuits open.

22. (Further examples.) Also, to begin to speak (occas. with the quoted words as quasi-obj.).

1851 C. Cist *Sk. Cincinnati in 1851* 296 They [*sc.* strawberries] usually open at 20 to 30 cents per quart. *c* **1871** J. Albery *Apple Blossoms* I, in *Dramatic Wks.* (1939) I. 244 Come and see me open to-night. **1926** A. Bennett *Lord Raingo* I. xiii. 63 'I quite agree with you, Clews,' Sam opened immediately. **1972** *Time* 17 Apr. 28/1 Joey and Sina, whose young daughter opened in the Broadway play *Voices* last week, soon became a part of the theater-going, nightclubbing celebrity set. **1976** B. Freemantle *November Man* iv. 47 'Jocelyn is still the big tycoon,' he opened predictably. **1977** A. Morice *Murder in Mimicry* I. i. 11 Gilbert is our new lead... His name alone ensures a sell-out for the entire run..before we even open.

23. open out. f. *trans.* and *intr.* To open the throttle of (an engine); to accelerate. *colloq.* Cf. sense 24 e below.

1906 *Punch* 19 Sept. 200/1 'Open her out!' my host had said; And on the instant word The mobile monster flew ahead Like a prodigious bird. **1918** 'Q' *Foe-Farrell* 105 There was a certain amount of outcry in the rear. But I opened-out down the slope and soon had it well astern. **1922** *Encycl. Brit.* XXX. 41/1 Such a 'light' engine would not withstand being opened out fully near the ground.

24. open up. a. Also *absol.*; *spec.* to open a door or the like.

1935 M. M. Atwater *Murder in Midsummer* xxii. 210 Why didn't you open up when I knocked? **1976** 'H. Carmichael' *False Evidence* i. 14 Someone knocked at the door... 'Open up, Miss Crawford.'

c. *trans.* and *intr.* To shear wool from (a particular area, esp. the neck, of a sheep). *Austral.* and *N.Z.*

1882 Armstrong & Campbell *Austral. Sheep Husbandry* xiv. 167 The fleece should be opened up the neck, commencing at the brisket. **1904** 'G. B. Lancaster' *Sons o' Men* 81 A big Maori was making the [shearing] pace; opening up in a scientific fashion with a clean-run cut over the ear-root. **1914** H. B. Smith *Sheep & Wool Industry Australasia* vi. 37 The machine is then driven up the front of the neck several times till the neck wool is well opened up. **1956** G. Bowen *Wool Away!* (ed. 2) iii. 32 Three short sharp blows are essential here to open up the neck for clean shearing.

d. *intr.* To talk; to speak openly; to cease to be secretive.

1921 *Sat. Even. Post* 12 Feb. 61/4 We had a drink and we had another and a couple more. Finally he opened up... It took him two hours to tell his story. **1949** B. Wolfe in A. Dundes *Mother Wit* (1973) 534 How much did the Negroes tell him when they 'opened up'? Just how far did they really open up? **1952** 'N. Shute' *Far Country* 244 It's just possible she might open up with me. *a* **1953** E. O'Neill *Hughie* (1959) 23 At first, he wouldn't open up. Not that he was cagy about gabbin' too much. But like he couldn't think of nothin' about himself worth saying. **1970** M. Braithwaite *Never sleep Three in a Bed* xvi. 197 Although he never answered—or perhaps because of it—I opened up to him completely, telling him things I'd never told anyone. **1976** J. Crosby *Nightfall* xii. 66 You're not being very helpful... You must have a few ideas. Open up!

e. *trans.* and *intr.* To open the throttle of (an engine); to accelerate. Cf. sense 23 f above.

1922 *Encycl. Brit.* XXX. 41/1 At height, however, it [*sc.* an aircraft engine] could be fully opened up, and the increased power..taken advantage of. **1926** T. E. Lawrence *Let.* 27 Sept. (1938) 500 It's my great game on a really pot-holed road to open up to 70 m.p.h. or so and feel the machine gallop. **1942** *Tee Emm* (Air Ministry) II. 95 On no account..should the engine be opened up during the final stages of ditching. **1970** K. Benton *Sole Agent* vii. 78 She's a nice car, the Chevvy. She'd do ninety if I opened her up. **1973** 'D. Halliday' *Dolly & Starry Bird* ix. 131 As soon as he's got a clear stretch of road, he'll open up and you'll lose him.

f. *intr.* To start shooting (*at* or *on* someone). Also *fig.*

1939 H. L. Ickes *Diary* 30 July (1954) II. 688 Two or three days ago John L. Lewis, before the Labor Committee of the House, opened up savagely on Garner. **1974** *Black Panther* 16 Mar. 16/4 Frelimo guerrillas opened up on the train from both sides 'creating panic among the passengers', according to the report. **1974** J. Cleary *Peter's Pence* i. 25 Someone had fired a shot at the Tans and the latter had opened up as if on a duck shoot.

open air, open-air. Add: **2.** (Earlier and later examples.) Also *transf.* and *fig.*

1830 *New Baptist Misc.* Aug. 331/1 (*heading*) Open air preaching in the villages. **1842** W. Howitt *Rural & Dom. Life Germany* xvii. 237 Those open-air concerts, walks and other amusements. **1926** C. Connolly *Let.* Jan. in *Romantic Friendship* (1975) 111 It is nice being able to sit out or go..to open air cinemas full of fireflies. **1949** Koestler *Promise & Fulfilment* III. i. 296 A people living underground must be single-minded..; but these qualities when carried over into open-air politics, become a grave handicap. **1958** *Times* 25 Oct. 10/7 His editorial influence was always exerted towards purity and strength [in music]. .. His songs..are animated by the same open-air kind of ideals. **1960** C. Day Lewis *Buried Day* x. 219 It was decided we should hold an open-air meeting. **1973** 'R. MacLeod' *Burial in Portugal* ii. 36 Brightly lit open-air cafés. **1975** J. Rathbone *Kill Cure* I. ii. 17 This hotel.. overlooked..an open air cinema.

open door. Add: **1. b.** (Later examples.)

1927 *New Republic* 21 Sept. 108/1 There is some merit in the general plea for 'most-favored nation' treatment, if only under the open-door policy. **1964** *Listener* 1 Oct. 492/2 Not only Americans, but almost everyone else thinks of the 'open-door' doctrine as American. **1974** *Times* 14 Dec. 13/5 Israel's open door policy to Jewish refugees from all parts of the world. **1976** *Listener* 9 Sept. 302/3 The Americans stood by their own open door policy—that China, just like every other part of the world except the United States, should be wide open to everybody's trade.

3. b. Designating a mental hospital in which patients are allowed the maximum freedom of movement and communication.

1958 *Spectator* 11 July 49/1 All over the country mental hospitals have been converting to the 'Open Door' system. **1969** *Daily Tel.* 1 Nov. 2 The modern vogue for open-door mental hospitals, far from improving conditions for some patients, has led to reprehensible methods of restraining them. *Ibid.*, Plain common sense ..required that such patients be managed in a secure environment and not in an open-door system. **1977** *Lancet* 18 June 1302/1 A total open-door policy is considered to be progressive; but in practice it means that mentally ill people who lack insight and are troublesome ..cannot be contained there for treatment.

opener. Add: **1. a.** Also *opener-up*.

1911 *Chambers's Jrnl.* Mar. 149/2 Carl Mauch, another German opener-up of South Africa. **1946** *Mind* LV. 102 The great philosopher is an opener-up of *new* paths for the mind of man.

b. Delete † *Obs.* and add later examples. Now *U.S. slang.*

1931 G. Irwin *Amer. Tramp & Underworld Slang* 139 *Openers*, cathartic pills. **1942** Berrey & Van den Bark *Amer. Thes. Slang* §91/5 Laxative food, *loosener, opener. Ibid.* §874/14 *Openers*, cathartic compound pills.

c. An implement or device for opening tins, cases, etc. See also **bottle-opener, *can-opener, tin-opener*.

1906 *Daily Chron.* 15 Aug. 5/2 An ordinary packing-case opener had been used to force the door of the case. *Ibid.*, When the robbery was discovered the iron opener was found lying on the floor. **1912** *Chambers's Jrnl.* Feb. 144/1 The man who invented an opener for tins did well. **1942** Berrey & Van den Bark *Amer. Thes. Slang* §75/6 *Opener*.., a jimmy. *Ibid.* §259/2 Key, *opener*. **1951** T. Sterling *House without Door* x. 113 She turned the bright red handle of her opener and the squat tin spun around under the knife. **1964** G. Lyall *Most Dangerous Game* i. 13 He had a bottle in one hand and an opener in the other. **1970** *Which?* Jan. 27/2 The tin which the openers found hardest to manage was the squared one. **1977** S. Coulter *Soyuz Affair* x. 110 You have a cold beer, Jim?.. There an opener someplace?

d. The first of a series of events, etc.; *spec.* in *U.S.*, the first game in a baseball match. Also *opener-upper*. orig. *U.S.*

1941 in Wentworth & Flexner *Dict. Amer. Slang* (1960) 368/2 A patriotic opener-upper, 'Under the Double Eagle'. **1942** Berrey & Van den Bark *Amer. Thes. Slang* §9/1 *Opener, starter-offer*, that which comes first. *Ibid.* §9/2 *Opener*, an opening remark. *Ibid.* §590/16 First act,.. *opener*. *Ibid.* §675/5 First game of a 'double-header' [at baseball],..*opener*. **1949** *Down Beat* 11 Mar. 15 *Frost* is a simple but fairly bright arrangement with a good opener. **1962** *John o' London's* 19 Apr. 388/4 *Measure for Measure* ..is a little lacking in lustre for a Stratford opener. **1967** [see *double-header c]. **1967** *Crescendo* June 10/3 The opener, Lennie's composition 'Morning Stroll', should please all stride piano fans. **1970** *Globe & Mail* (Toronto) 28 Sept. 23/3 Queen's Golden Gails and the..Mustangs struggled through three quarters of the Ontario–Quebec Athletic Association football opener here. **1974** *Cleveland* (Ohio) *Plain Dealer* 26 Oct. 5–D/3 Vaclav Nedomansky, the hulking center iceman from Czechoslovakia who will do his skating for the Toronto Toros, in town for the Coliseum opener Sunday night. **1976** *Daily Tel.* 21 June 8 The opener of the present trilogy from Granada's 'The State of the Nation'..did little to allay worries about the unaccountable power exercised by Whitehall over Westminster. **1977** A. C. H. Smith *Jericho Gun* vi. 80 I'll tell you what's going to win the opener. You see that bay gelding? **1978** *Rugby World* Apr. 25/2 It was draftsman Bertranne's tackle, after half-an-hour in Paris, in the championship opener on January 21, that put Maxwell out of the game.

e. *Cricket.* One of the two batsmen who open an innings.

1950 R. G. Strutt *Schoolboy Cricket* vi. 81 No. 3..can get on better with his brilliant scoring strokes if the openers have taken the shine off the ball. **1959** *Listener* 19 Mar. 517/1 The breakdown of our batting, chiefly of the openers. **1974** *Observer* 9 June 24/6 The other opener, Geoff Greenidge, had just flicked Lever for two fours round his legs. **1976** Dexter & Makins *Test Kill* 83 The Australian batting had collapsed on a wicket that the England openers found tolerably easy.

f. Colloq. phr. *for* (or *as*) *openers*: to begin with; for a start.

1967 *Boston Sunday Herald* 2 Apr. (T.V. Mag.) 6/2 Joey hosts Danny Thomas for openers. **1970** K. Platt *Pushbutton Butterfly* (1971) xvi. 176 'Didn't they tell you at the plant? I quit.' That was good enough for openers. **1970** E. Tidyman *Shaft* (1971) xi. 152 Shaft decided to tear the trap apart. He killed Caroli as openers, then went plunging through the door. **1971** J. Sangster *Your Friendly Neighbourhood Death Pedlar* viii. 106 It was Walpole calling from London. 'I thought you were being hanged,' he said for openers. **1974** P. Erdman *Silver Bears* iv. 54 I'd like to ask you a few simple questions.. for openers, what's with this place here? **1976** *Word 1971* XXVII. 58 These suggestions and observations call for professional reconsideration, not only of a fundamental definition of Speech per se, but of phonology, idiolect, lexicon, and Child Language as well, just for openers.

3. *Poker.* (*pl.*) Cards on which a player can open the betting. Also *fig.*

1902 *Out West* Mar. 291 'I got openers, this pot,' says he, tapping the rifle. **1909** R. A. Wason *Happy Hawkins* 114, I didn't hold openers, an' yet if I didn't draw some cards an' see it out, I stood to lose entirely. **1920** C. E. Mulford *Johnny Nelson* ii. 25 A round or two had been played when Big Tom drew his first openers. **1946** Morehead & Mott-Smith *Penguin Hoyle* 122 If the opener cannot prove to the satisfaction of other players that he held openers, his hand is dead and cannot win the pot.

opening, *vbl. sb.* Add: **1. c.** (See quots.)

1888 C. P. Brooks *Cotton Manuf.* i. 17 *Opening* or passing the matted pieces of the bales through a series of armed beaters..separating the material into small flakes and removing the heavier impurities. **1901** T. Thornley *Cotton Spinning* I. iii. 64 *Q.* Give a statement of the objects aimed at in the operation of opening... *A.* This process first opens out the matted masses of fibres to a very fleecy, soft condition; secondly, it extracts the major portion of the impurities present in the cotton..and also much seed that has escaped the ginning process; thirdly it almost now always makes a lap. **1963** A. F. W. Coulson et al. *Man. Cotton Spinning* II. II. vi. 129 Better opening and cleaning will be obtained if the machines can be kept working and operating on the cotton continuously in a rather small quantity.

2. d. Two pages of a book, etc., that face one another.

1906 E. Johnston *Writing & Illuminating* vi. 110 Parchment sheets should have their smooth sides so placed together that each 'opening' of the book has both its pages rough or both smooth. **1914** *Trans. Bibliogr. Soc.* XII. 239 A line of type at the top of a page, above the text, is called a 'head-line'; or, if it consists of the title of the book (or of the section of the book) on every page or every 'opening' (*i.e.*, two pages facing one another), sometimes a 'running-title' or 'running-head'. **1963** *Listener* 21 Mar. 522/1 A good example of his elaborate book-production is *The Book of Ruth*, with alternate openings in full colour and in golds and greys.

4. c. (Earlier and later examples.)

1825 P. Egan *Life of Actor* vii. 264 To get up splendid Spectacles; write openings for Pantomimes. **1894** J. A.

CAVE *Jubilee Dramatic Life* (ed. 2) xix. 177 For the openings of my pantomimes I was able, as opportunity occurred, to secure the services of such inimitable burlesque performers as the Vokes family.

e. *Theatr.* The first performance of a play or entertainment; a première. *U.S.*

1855 W. B. WOOD *Pers. Recoll. Stage* ix. 191 The loss we sustained was less important in a pecuniary view..than in rendering our opening still more embarrassing. **1916** *Variety* 27 Oct. 12/1 Openings here next week include Marie Tempest in 'A Lady's Name' (Plymouth); 'Sybil' (Colonial); [etc.]. **1923** H. RUBY *Let.* 16 Aug. in G. Marx *Groucho Lett.* (1967) 183 The out-of-town opening.. occurred in Fairmont, West Virginia. **1959** J. THURBER *Years with Ross* xv. 247 I'm having dinner with Aleck and he's taking me to an opening. **1977** J. AIKEN *Last Movement* i. 37 'What about your opening?'..'Big success. I'll show you our press notices.'

f. The start of an art exhibition, fashion show, or the like.

1905 E. WHARTON *House of Mirth* II. ix. 428 Beings without definite pursuits or permanent relations, who drifted on a languid tide of curiosity from restaurant to concert-hall, from palm-garden to music-room, from 'art exhibit' to dress-maker's opening. **1952** D. AMES *Murder, Maestro, Please* xxxv. 255 Geoffrey insists on taking me to Paris for the autumn dress openings. **1969** D. S. DAVIS *Where Dark Streets Go* (1970) ix. 89 There was a showing of Tchelitchew drawings at the Burns Gallery... 'Not everybody who goes to an opening signs in. Especially when it's not new work.' **1972** P. MARKS *Collector's Choice* ii. 62 He never went to museums except for openings.

6. opening night, the first night of a theatrical play, entertainment, etc.; **opening-time**, (*a*) the time at which a place, esp. a public house, is opened; (*b*) the time that a device takes to open.

c **1814** (*play-title*) The opening night; or, the manager hoax'd. **1828** J. EBERS *Seven Yrs. King's Theatre* 210 The interest felt by the public in the arrival of the gran maestro, on the opening night. **1929** Opening night [see *DOODAH I]. **1975** P. G. WINSLOW *Death of Angel* 9 The milkman finds a body dressed up for opening night. **1927** D. L. SAYERS *Unnatural Death* xii. 136 Within, a cheerful bustle in the bar announced the near arrival of opening time. **1943** *Gloss. Terms Electr. Engin.* (*B.S.I.*) 66 *Opening time*, applied to a circuit-breaker: the time interval from the instant of application of the tripping power when in the closed position to the instant of separation of the arcing contacts. **1971** 'H. CALVIN' *Poison Chasers* i. 7 We got back around opening time... I said to Dai, 'I'll get drinks while you're telephoning.'

opening, *ppl. a.* Add: **1. a.** (Further examples.)

1783 [see *CHELTENHAM I]. **1912** *More Secret Remedies* (B.M.A.) x. 157 Do the bowels act regularly without opening medicine? **1965** A. NICOL *Truly Married Woman* 72 Magnesium sulphate for opening-medicine.

b. Esp. in *Cricket*, designating or pertaining to the batsmen who open the innings, or the bowlers who open the attack.

1929 P. G. H. FENDER *Turn of Wheel* iii. 92 Hendry.. had a habit of..retreating when facing Larwood, and that would never do, especially in an opening batsman. **1952** J. H. MORGAN *Glamorgan County Cricket* facing p. 64 (*caption*) Arnold Dyston, a stylish opening bat. **1955** A. E. R. GILLIGAN *Urn Returns* 36 The pace attack of Statham and Tyson keeps Rutherford and Sawle, the opening pair, strictly on the defensive. **1971** *Times* 15 Feb. 8/2 Their opening partnerships for the seven Test matches have averaged as much as 75. **1976** J. SNOW *Cricket Rebel* 25 Tony Buss, his opening partner, was far more dangerous to face than he looked from the ringside. **1977** *Times* 29 Nov. 12/5 Geoffrey Arnold's two for 95 were the best figures by a recognized opening bowler in three Tests.

open-work. Add: **1.** (Earlier examples.)

1598 FLORIO *Worlde of Wordes* 460/2 *Zegandlla*, such small fine net worke or open worke as gentlewomen use to make and weare vpon their heads in caules. **1782** T. PENNANT *Journey Chester to London* 264 The fronts are of most elegant gothic open work. **1819** SHELLEY *Cenci* Pref. p. xiv, With balcony over balcony of open work.

2. (Earlier example.)

1811 J. FAREY *Gen. View Agric. & Minerals Derbyshire* I. 359 The sinking was further continued, and the heaps on the sides of these *open-works*, or open-casts, increased.

opepe (ǫpī·pi). Also **epepe.** [Yoruba.] A West African tree, *Sarcocephalus diderrichii*, of the family Rubiaceæ, or its hard yellowish-brown wood; also (see quot. 1908) occasionally used for an evergreen tree of the genus *Terminalia*.

1891 *Kew Bull.* 43 Names of Yoruba Timbers... 4. Opepe. **1908** *Ibid.* 193 An unnamed species of Terminalia..is also likely to furnish timber suitable for the home markets... The Yoruba name of the tree is 'Epepe'. **1920** *Nature* 29 July 692/1 Other heavy constructional woods [in the Empire Timber Exhibition] ..are..the gamboge-coloured Opepe..and Apa. **1936** J. D. KENNEDY *Forest Flora S. Nigeria* 217 The accepted trade name for this timber in England is Opepe. **1956** *Archit. Rev.* CXX. 229 The board room [has] an opepe wood block floor. **1972** *Timber Trades Jrnl.* 13 May 40/2 Opepe, an early substitute for greenheart, was originally thought to be a bottomless pit, but..the bottom of the pit had been reached about two years ago. So they were already interested in a substitute for a substitute.

opera. Add: **3.** *horse opera*: see *HORSE *sb.* 27a; *soap opera*: see as main entry in Suppl.; *opéra comique* (earlier and later examples); *opéra bouffe, opera buffa* (earlier and later examples); also *attrib.* or as *adj.*; *opera-bouffer* (earlier example); *opera magica* (*rare*), opera with a fantastic or supernatural subject; *opera semiseria*, seriocomic opera; *opera seria*, serious or tragic opera, *spec.* a type of Italian opera flourishing in the 18th century, usually with a classical or mythological subject.

1801 F. BURNEY *Jrnls. & Lett.* 22–24 Apr. (1975) V. 267 Made d'henin made a party for us all to meet again the next day, & go to the Opera Buffa. **1870** D. J. KIRWAN *Palace & Hovel* xvi. 235 Mademoiselle Helena Schneider, the opera bouffe singer. **1895** G. B. SHAW *Let.* 31 Aug. (1965) I. 553 Such are the opera bouffe depths to which I have descended. **1937** *New Statesman* 25 Dec. 1102/2 The *opéra-bouffe* Jupiter who attempts to cuckold him [*sc.* Amphitryon] by assuming his form. **1970** W. APEL *Harvard Dict. Mus.* (ed. 2) 187/2 A special type of comic opera is represented by the *opéras bouffes* of Offenbach. **1882** J. J. JENNINGS *Theatr. & Circus Life* 76 There is something so indescribably funny in the costumes, in the facial make-up, and all that, of the happy opera-bouffer or festive burlesquer. **1802** C. WILMOT *Let.* 31 Jan. in *Irish Peer* (1920) 39 We have been to the Opera Buffa or the Italian Opera. **1842** *Ainsworth's Mag.* II. 78 It is satisfactory to see the Italian Opera..returning to the opera buffa of Fioravanti. **1963** AUDEN *Dyer's Hand* 184 For Falstaff, time does not exist, since he belongs to the *opera buffa* world of play and mock action. **1965** C. HIBBERT *Garibaldi & his Enemies* I. i. 13 He [*sc.* Mazzini] joined the Carbonari..but the *opera buffa* ceremony of the ritualistic initiation, in which he was required to swear allegiance to unknown leaders on a bared dagger.. struck him as absurd. **1968** S. TOWNELEY in *New Oxf. Hist. Music* IV. xv. 837 Cavalieri divides the work into three acts. And he suggests the *intermedii* should intersperse them—a practice which a century later helped in the creation of *opera buffa*. **1744** H. WALPOLE *Let.* 22 July (1903) II. 40 Young Churchill has got a daughter by the Frasi; Mr. Winnington calls it the *opéra comique*; the mother is an opera girl; the grandmother was Mrs. Oldfield. **1866** G. H. LEWES *Jrnl.* 30 Dec. in *Geo. Eliot Lett.* (1956) IV. 328 A wretched opera comique—*Cartouche*. **1955** *Times* 6 May 14/7 It was doubtful whether, had it not been for Grétry, we should have had some of the striking later developments of *opéra comique*. **1976** *New Yorker* 16 Feb. 110/3 In 1870, Verdi was toying with the idea of writing an opéra comique. **1956** AUDEN & KALLMAN *Magic Flute* Pref. p. xiv, We have written the dialogue in verse, because it seemed to us the right medium for the spoken word in an *opera magica*. **1963** AUDEN *Dyer's Hand* 484 *Die Zauberflöte*..stylistically, an *opera magica*. **1947** A. EINSTEIN *Mus. Romantic Era* xvi. 290 The stereotyped insipidity of the Italian *opera semiseria* since Rossini. **1959** *Times* 21 Aug. 13/2 The world première of Heimo Erbse's *Julietta*, an *opera semiseria*. **1970** W. APEL *Harvard Dict. Mus.* (ed. 2) 601/2 *Opera semiseria* is a serious opera including comic elements, e.g., Mozart's *Le Nozze di Figaro*. **1876** STAINER & BARRETT *Dict. Mus. Terms* 392/2 *Seria* (*It.*), serious, grave, tragic, as, *Opera seria*, a tragic opera. **1880** GROVE *Dict. Mus.* II. 513/2 The gradual development of the Opera Buffa from the Interludes which were formerly presented between the Acts of an Opera Seria, or Spoken Drama. **1892** G. B. SHAW *How to become Mus. Critic* (1960) 211 The public had been educated by Gluck to expect at least a show of seriousness in an *opera seria*. **1911** *Encycl. Brit.* XX. 124/2 *Opera seria* is classical Italian opera with secco-recitative; almost always..on a Greek or Roman subject, and,..with a happy ending... The only great classic in *opera seria* is Mozart's *Idomeneo*. **1951** M. COOPER *Russian Opera* i. 14 The Empress Catherine,..favoured the opéra comique—the opera of social comment and ideas—rather than the more exclusively musical opera seria. **1975** *New Yorker* 31 Mar. 82/1 Sometime in mid-1780, Mozart was commissioned to write the principal work, an *opera seria*, for the Munich carnival season.

4. a. *opera ballet* (later examples), *band, -box* (earlier and later examples), *chorus, company* (earlier example), *-goer* (earlier and later examples), *-going, hero, -night* (earlier example), *repertory, stage, ticket* (earlier example); *opera-going* adj. (later example).

1955 *Times* 1 July 7/4 In the production at the Louvre on Tuesday the piece was given in the form of an 'opera-ballet'. **1964** *Conc. Oxf. Dict. Opera* 23/1 So popular did the opera ballet become in Paris that Wagner had to rewrite and develop the opening scene of *Tannhäuser*..to meet the demands of the Parisians. **1798** T. HOLCROFT *Diary* 14 Oct. in *Mem.* (1816) III. 48 Gave young Watts the letters of recommendation for the opera band. **1814** J. MAYNE *Jrnl.* 2 Sept. (1909) 30 The orchestra consists of nearly sixty performers, whereas our opera band seldom musters forty. **1811** *Times* 21 Jan. 3/2 You have permitted an anonymous paragraph to appear in your columns, reflecting on a noble young lady, and accusing her of..authorising an act of..injustice, by the improper disposal of an Opera Box... It is a gross..falsehood; neither is it true that this was the cause that induced Mr. Taylor to deprive the Portland family of their Opera box. **1828** J. EBERS *Seven Yrs. King's Theatre* iv. 82 It had been customary with my predecessors to publish, at the commencement of every season, a little book, specifying what boxes were taken for the season by the different subscribers—a sort of Opera-box directory. **1865** D. G. ROSSETTI *Let.* 28 June (1965) II. 560 Couldn't you work up the Opera-box design? **1840** H. COCKTON *Life Valentine Vox* xi. 72 His real name is Growlaway. He's in the Opera chorus, and a regular trump he is too. **1947** A. EINSTEIN *Mus. Romantic Era* xvi. 275 It is an Italian opera chorus; one ought not to think of Handel in connection with it. **1827** W. CLARKE *Every Night Bk.* 146 There are several persons in the opera-company besides those we have mentioned. **1850** 'J. TIMON' *Lorgnette* (ed. 2) i. 21 A prim clergyman, who, though he is not an Opera-goer, has yet a good ear for a fiddle. **1854** H. MORLEY *Jrnl.* 15 July (1866) 91 The opera-goer who enjoyed that musical farce..now finds the enjoyment of it trebled by the addition of Ronconi's..drolleries. **1947** A. EINSTEIN *Mus. Romantic Era* xix. 358 The bourgeois opera-goer of 1880 had not only the opportunity of hearing an international repertory. **1955** P. VINCENT in H. Van Thal *Fanfare for E. Newman* 177 It appears that each opera-goer has his own preference for a particular 'school' of opera. **1975** *Country Life* 13 Nov. 1312/1 For Russian audiences, memories of the book [*sc.* War and Peace] may perhaps give the opera a sort of unity which it lacks for most English opera-goers. **1876** GEO. ELIOT *Dan. Der.* I. II. xviii. 359 It was enough for them to go on in their old way, only having a grand treat of opera-going (to the gallery) when Hans came home on a visit. **1947** A. EINSTEIN *Mus. Romantic Era* xvi. 239 In it the most intimate experience of the soul is made into an *opera* and presented to the opera-going public, to the mass. **1949** *Penguin Music Mag.* VIII. 16 The beginning of my opera-going was marked by outstanding failure. **1955** P. VINCENT in H. Van Thal *Fanfare for E. Newman* 175 The first years of opera-going are among our most satisfying. **1834** J. R. PLANCHÉ *Deep, Deep Sea* in *Extravaganzas* (1879) I. 164 To sing a song—As Opera heroes choose Always to do, when they've no time to lose. **1855** W. B. WOOD *Pers. Recoll. Stage* v. 113 As the representative of opera heroes..he had no superior. **1776** J. WALLACE in D. Garrick *Private Corr.* (1832) II. 140 She had objections to both: Saturday was Opera-night; Monday degraded her. **1898** STAINER & BARRETT *Dict. Mus. Terms* (rev. ed.) 329/2 Their works are still part of every Opera repertory. **1763** D. GARRICK *Let.* in R. B. Peake *Mem. Colman Family* (1841) I. 90 The famous Gabrielli pleased me much; she has a good person, is the best actress I ever saw on an opera stage, and has the most agreeable voice I ever heard. **1948** *Penguin Mus. Mag.* VII. 58 Wagner..in the end..had to sell out to the commercial opera-stage. **1755** LADY W. W. MONTAGUE in *Poems by Eminent Ladies* II. 170 There was a time (oh! that I could forget!) When opera-tickets pour'd before my feet.

b. opera-cloak (earlier example); **opera-hat** (earlier example); **opera-house** (later example).

1835 DICKENS *Sk. Boz* (1836) 1st Ser. II. 47 There..was the young lady, wrapped up in a hopera-cloak. **1810** *Irish Mag.* III. 226 Strutting as gentlemen, by aid of.. silk stockings, opera hats. **1976** *New Yorker* 9 Feb. 81/1 The decision to present this production in the large opera house of the Academy instead of in the pleasant new theatre downstairs did it no good.

c. Applied to styles of women's underclothing suitable for wearing with evening dress, characterized by low tops and narrow shoulder-straps, as *opera combinations, shape, top*.

1923 *Weekly Dispatch* 18 Feb. 14 (Advt.), Pure Wool Opera Combinations... Ribbon shoulder straps. **1928** *Daily Mail* 31 July 1/1 (Advt.), Artificial silk vest..opera shape. **1921** *Daily Colonist* (Victoria, B.C.) 18 Oct. 19/1 (Advt.), Women's 'Turnbull's' Mixture Combinations, with low neck, short or no sleeves, with opera tops and ankle length. **1923** *Daily Mail* 17 Feb. 4 (Advt.), Ladies' Pure Wool Combinations,..opera tops, ribbon straps. **1968** J. IRONSIDE *Fashion Alphabet* 72 Vest..sometimes with shoulder-straps, and known as 'Opera top'.

operability (ǫpĕrăbi·lĭti). [f. next + *-BILITY.] The state of being operable; *spec.* in *Med.*, suitability for surgical treatment.

1905 *Jrnl. Nerv. & Mental Dis.* XXXII. 481 (*heading*) Brain tumors: a study of clinical and post-mortem records bearing on their operability. **1910** *Practitioner* Jan. 84 The question of operability or otherwise is a matter in which surgeons differ considerably. **1922** *Ann. Surg.* LXXVI. 396 In estimating the final value of any operative 2rocedure for the cure of cancer, the operability rate is the crux of the situation. **1952** *Sci. Amer.* Sept. 104/2 The gun parts could be interchanged among all 10 without affecting the guns' operability. **1972** *Brit. Jrnl. Dis. Chest* LXVI. 162 (*heading*) The value of mediastinoscopy in assessing operability in carcinoma of the lung. **1975** J. HOWLETT *Christmas Spy* III. vi. 96 Zürich had been correct about the operability of two-way traffic.

operable, *a.* and *sb.* For **a, b** read **A, B,** restrict † *Obs.* to sense B, and add: **A.** *adj.* **1.** (Later examples.)

1911 H. S. HARRISON *Queed* xiii. 160 How could this principle be..reduced to an operable law? **1961** *Medicine in Nat. Defense* (Final Rep. Office of U.S. Asst. Secretary of Defense) vi. 69 Visual and operable training aids..were used in support of Army Medical Service mass casualty exercises.

2. *Med.* Capable of being treated by an operation.

1904 *Arch. Middlesex Hosp.* III. 163 Patients..are admitted in practically all cases for operable cancer. **1925** W. DEEPING *Sorrell & Son* xxxviii. 381 'But, my dear sir, if the thing is operable—' 'No, thank you. Besides, it is only a question of a few days. If you can help me to fight the pain.' **1925** H. GILFORD *Tumours & Cancers* xxvi. 580 Of operable uterine cancers as large a number can be destroyed by the [radium and X-]rays as by surgical operation. **1973** *Cancer* XXXI. 180/2 Patients with carcinoma of the cervix are admitted ..only if..the tumor is considered operable and the patient potentially curable by surgery.

operand. (Further examples.)

1956 BERKELEY & WAINWRIGHT *Computers* II. 37 The first two registers receive the operands, or numbers operated on. **1965** *Language* XLI. 377 There is also a zero (and affix) causative in which the *W* contains no new verb, but the *N* and *V* of the operand sentence are permuted: *The children sat→He seated the children.* **1969** P. B. JORDAIN *Condensed Computer Encycl.* 354 In the mathematical operation of division, the dividend and divisor are two operands. *Ibid.*, Most digital computer instructions have one or more operands, each indicated by a field within the instruction. **1973** D. U. WILDE *Introd. Computing Probl.* v. 106 The *or* operation is said to be true if either or both of its operands are true; otherwise, it is false. The *and* operation is true if both operands are true; otherwise, it is false.

operant, *a.* and *sb.* Add: **A.** *adj.* **b.** *Psychol.* Involving the modification of behaviour by the reinforcing or inhibiting effect of its consequences; opp. *respondent.* Cf. *INSTRUMENTAL *a.* 7.

1937 [see B. 1 b below]. **1938** B. F. SKINNER *Behavior of Organisms* xiii. 439 Comparing conditioning of Type S (which is largely, if not wholly, respondent) with Type R (which is apparently wholly operant). **1941** *Amer. Jrnl. Psychol.* LIV. 568 (*heading*) An automatic device for providing motivation and reinforcement in operant conditioning. **1959** *Jrnl. Exper. Analysis of Behavior* II. 57 Young and Boycott (1955) describe behavior in the octopus which is almost certainly operant in nature, i.e., not elicited, but maintained by its consequences. **1963** P. SWARTZ *Psychol.* x. 208/2 In contrast to respondent conditioning, in which the reinforcing agent is coupled with the conditioned stimulus, in operant learning the appearance of the reinforcer is dependent upon the occurrence of the response. **1964** RATNER & DENNY *Compar. Psychol.* xi. 566 A common distinction between instrumental and operant learning, at least in the laboratory, is that the animal is free to respond at any time in the operant situation but is usually given discrete trials when the learning is labeled instrumental. **1968** *Listener* 29 Aug. 265/2 The sickest man in the hospital was selected to be..the first experiment in 'operant conditioning' therapy on a severely regressed and catatonic schizophrenic in Britain. **1970** HINSIE & CAMPBELL *Psychiatric Dict.* (ed. 4) 150/2 It has been suggested that many forms of psychotherapy are applications of operant conditioning... The patient learns what the therapist expects or wants to hear, and he modifies his own speech and behavior accordingly. **1975** *Nature* 20 Mar. 219/1 Behaviourism..puts us in a position to alter and improve the condition of mankind if only we will apply its commanding insights..into the agency of such cardinal notions as reinforcement and operant behaviour.

B. *sb.* **1. b.** *Psychol.* An item of behaviour that is held to be not a response to a prior stimulus but something which is initially spontaneous on the part of the organism, 'operating on' or affecting the environment so as to produce consequences which may reinforce or inhibit its recurrence.

1937 B. F. SKINNER in *Jrnl. Gen. Psychol.* XVI. 274 There is also a kind of response which occurs spontaneously in the absence of any stimulation with which it may be specifically correlated... It does not mean that we cannot find a stimulus that will elicit such behaviour but that none is operative at the time the behaviour is observed. It is the nature of this kind of behaviour that it should occur without an eliciting stimulus, although discriminative stimuli are practically inevitable after conditioning... I shall call such a unit an operant and the behavior in general, operant behavior. **1938** —— *Behavior of Organisms* i. 21 If the occurrence of an operant is followed by presentation of a reinforcing stimulus, the strength is increased. **1941** *Amer. Jrnl. Psychol.* LIV. 568 Aversion drives..offer certain advantages which other drives, *e.g.* hunger and thirst, do not... Reinforcement can follow immediately the emission of the operant; under hunger motivation several responses may intervene between the operant that is measured and its subsequent reënforcement. **1967** KOESTLER *Ghost in Machine* i. 8 Operant strength is usually measured, for technical reasons, by the 'rate of extinction'—how long the rat will persist in pressing the lever after the supply of pellets has been stopped. **1972** *Jrnl. Social Psychol.* LXXXVI. 11 Recent analyses have conceived of conforming behavior as an instrumental response directed toward the attainment of functional goals... It can be considered a kind of social operant, which should change..with changes in the characteristics of reinforcement.

o·pera:table, *a. rare.* [f. OPERAT(E *v.* + -ABLE.] Capable of being operated (on); operable.

1895 *Funk's Stand. Dict.*, *Operatable*, that can be operated or worked; operable. **1932** JOYCE *Let.* 12 July (1966) III. 248 The right eye was still operatable 20 months ago. Now the cataract is total.

operate, *v.* Add: **4. c.** Also *transf.*, of a gambler, criminal, etc.

1883 SWEET & KNOX *On Mexican Mustang through Texas* (1884) i. 16 This high-toned and honorable desperado 'operated' in one of the inland cities of Texas two years ago. **1901** 'J. FLYNT' *World of Graft* 19 The West Side grafters..who have 'operated' in Chicago. **1955** D. W. MAURER in *Publ. Amer. Dial. Soc.* XXIV. 30 There are the *lone wolves*, who are professionals, but who operate predominantly alone, without the support of a mob,..for example, jewel thieves of some types, swindlers, expert forgers. **1975** T. ALLBEURY *Special Collection* xi. 73, I set up a network for him dealing with industrial espionage. It operated into West Germany.

d. (Later examples.)

1889 *Harper's Mag.* Aug. 448/1 Do you think all men who are what you call operating around are like that? **1961** in WEBSTER.

e. To function, to fulfil a function, to act. (Closely related to sense 4 a.)

1931 J. T. ADAMS *Epic of Amer.* viii. 221 There were..a thousand boats operating regularly on the Mississippi. **1932** [see *CYLINDER *sb.* 6]. **1932** N. M. BUTLER *Looking Forward* xi. 117 Government officials operating in all parts of the country. **1971** *Gloss. Electrotechnical, Power Terms* (*B.S.I.*) I. iii. 13 A relay operates when it completes its designed function in a specified output circuit(s). **1972** *Daily Tel.* 16 Nov. 7/1 Extra buses and Underground trains will operate on most routes. **1976** *National Observer* (U.S.) 2 Oct. 18/3 Rudderless and without a keel, the 195-foot craft operates similar to a flat-bottomed fishing boat.

7. For chiefly *U.S.* read orig. *U.S.* and add later examples.

1948 'N. SHUTE' *No Highway* i. 19 C.A.T.O. are operating five or six of them [*sc.* aircraft] on the Atlantic route. **1971** D. POTTER *Brit. Eliz. Stamps* xii. 130 Cambrian Airways..took over the operation of some internal routes previously operated only by BEA. **1974** *Anderson* (S. Carolina) *Independent* 20 Apr. 2A/1 Joe King, who operates a hardware store 13 miles south of Greenville on S.C. 25, fired four bullets into their car as they fled.

8. *Surg.* To operate on. (See sense 4 b.)

1908 *Practitioner* Sept. 423, I know of two cases of pyelitis which were operated in mistake for appendicitis. **1915** W. OWEN *Let.* 1 Mar. (1967) 324 Dr Denucé (who operated Sarah Bernhardt—and Charlie). **1925** SIMMONS & FISHBEIN *Art & Pract. Medical Writing* v. 43 'Operate' means, and is generally synonymous with, 'to work': the terms nearly always may be used interchangeably. The surgeon who would hesitate to say 'I worked this patient' says, without a blush, 'I operated this patient.' **1930** *Amer. Speech* V. 289 Of those questioned 26½ per cent used 'operated him', 40 per cent used 'operated on', and 33⅓ per cent used 'operated upon him'.

operatic, *a.*[1] Add: **b.** as *sb. pl.* The production or performance of operas.

1907 N. MUNRO *Daft Days* xvi. 142 He says he could never die a Christian death if he had to listen to them at their operatics through the wall. **1920** *Punch* 10 Mar. 197/1 Operatics. It has been suggested before now that Opera might be improved if the singing were done behind the scenes and the performance on the stage were carried out in dumb show by competent actors. **1928** *Daily Express* 6 Nov. 9/3 This is a real event in London's amateur operatics.

operating, *vbl. sb.* Add: **a.** (Later example.)

1913 ROBERTS & SMITH (*title*) Practical locomotive operating.

b. *operating altitude, box, control, costs, expenses, height, revenue*; **operating crew** (see quot.); **operating system** *Computers*, a set of programs for organizing the resources and activities of a computer.

1956 D. E. CHARLWOOD *No Moon Tonight* 15 Where the planes were circling, climbing steadily to operating altitude. **1918** 'Q' *Foe-Farrell* 117, I..found..the operating box and the gallery, switched on the lights, and shinned down a pillar to the stalls. **1930** *Daily Express* 6 Sept. 5/5 The 'operating control' can be readily grasped from the sketch. **1913** ROBERTS & SMITH *Pract. Locomotive Operating* 26 Operating costs. **1972** *Lebende Sprachen* XVII. 34/1 US *operating costs, operating expenses*—BE working expenses. **1975** 'D. JORDAN' *Black Account* xi. 54 Condon said, 'Let's settle the totals like this, then,' and wrote... Initial operating costs and interest: $85 million. **1965** Operating crew [see *flight crew* s.v. *FLIGHT *sb.*[1] 15]. **1869** *Bradshaw's Railway Manual* XXI. 417 The operating expenses are about 51 per cent. of the gross earnings. **1909** *Daily Chron.* 25 Feb. 3/5 At the same time the operating expenses had gone down from 67·9 per cent. of gross receipts in 1907 to 54·5 in 1908. **1948** 'N. SHUTE' *No Highway* iv. 111 I'm prepared to shut down the inboard engines after climbing up to operating height. **1930** *Daily Express* 9 Sept. 10/2 Operating revenues show a gain of about 40 per cent. at £556,936, compared with £389,518, and while profit on sales of securities is lower, the gross earnings have expanded by nearly £80,000 to £740,582. **1961** *Computer Jrnl.* IV. 222 (*heading*) The Manchester University Atlas operating system. **1963** GREGORY & VAN HORN *Automatic Data-Processing Syst.* (ed. 2) xii. 477 Operating Systems are programs that increase machine operating efficiency by controlling the compilation and execution of programs, supervising input and output operations, converting data from one medium to another, testing programs to debug them, and simulating the operation of one processor on another. **1973** D. U. WILDE *Introd. Computing* ii. 43 When a computer system is under the control of a monitor or operating system, the computer operator loads programs into the card reader, mounts tape reels onto tape drives, and removes results from the printer while the monitor schedules the work flow and keeps the CPU busy.

operating, *ppl. a.* (Further example.)

1904 *Daily Chron.* 16 July 7/3 The operating company is to take over the tunnel before the end of the month.

operation. Add: **4. b.** *Psychol.* A mental activity whereby the effect of actions or ideas is logically understood or predicted, esp. with reference to the supposed stages of a child's development; also *concrete operations, formal operations* (see esp. quots. 1960, 1963). Cf. *PREOPERATIONAL *a.*

1930 M. GABAIN tr. *Piaget's Child's Concept. Phys. Causality* IV. 301 At each stage of intellectual development we can distinguish roughly two groups of operations. **1953** MAYS & WHITEHEAD tr. *Piaget's Logic & Psychol.* ii. 8 Psychologically, operations are actions which are internalizable, reversible, and coordinated into systems characterized by laws which apply to the system as a whole. **1960** J. S. BRUNER *Beyond Information Given* (1974) xxiii. 415 Concrete operations, though they are guided by the logic of classes..are means for structuring only immediately present reality. **1963** J. H. FLAVELL *Developmental Psychol. J. Piaget* iii. 86 The period of formal operations (11–15)... The adolescent can deal effectively not only with the reality before him..but also with the world of pure possibility. **1975** J. W. BRUNK *Child & Adolesc. Devel.* vi. 252 In the period of concrete operations (approximate ages 7–11), the child becomes capable of logical thought processes that can be applied to concrete problems.

5. a. (Further examples.)

1927 P. W. BRIDGMAN *Logic Mod. Physics* i. 5 To find the length of an object, we have to perform certain physical operations. The concept of length is therefore fixed when the operations by which length is measured are fixed. **1935** *Psychol. Rev.* XLII. 517 Only those constructs based upon operations which are public and repeatable are admitted to the body of science. **1967** *Encycl. Philos.* V. 544/1 By the end of the nineteenth century, however, scientists had accepted the view that if we cannot devise operations which would disclose whether or not space was Euclidean, then no definite geometrical properties can be assigned to space.

b. (Earlier and later examples.) Also more generally, a business activity or enterprise. Also *transf.*

1832 *Reg. Deb. Congress U.S.* 22nd Congress 2 Sess. App. 107/1 The liability to be called upon for large advances, for the above operation,..makes it absolutely necessary that the limit should be strictly attended to. **1848** W. ARMSTRONG *Stocks* 11 We conceive that this operation [*sc.* betting] is too well understood to need any particular explanation. **1851** C. CIST *Sk. Cincinnati in 1851* 236 Such is the extent of the operations of this firm. **1889** *Harper's Mag.* Aug. 448/1 One is an operation, and the other is embezzlement. **1911** J. C. LINCOLN *Cap'n Warren's Wards* xi. 178, I judged..that you were well enough acquainted with Wall Street to know that queer operations take place there. **1928** F. A. BRADFORD *Money* xv. 283 The open market operations of the reserve banks. **1938** J. B. WILLIAMS *Theory of Investment Value* ii. 10 The rate of operations never precedes stock prices. **1960** 'E. MCBAIN' *Give Boys Great Big Hand* iv. 30 A photo of the bag on the front pages..might not be bad for our operation... You can't buy that sort of advertising space, now can you? **1977** 'J. LE CARRÉ' *Hon. Schoolboy* xviii. 442 The spearhead of the operation will be handled by ourselves.

7. (Further examples.) Also, the strategic movement of troops, ships, etc.; the people concerned with such movements. Freq. *attrib.* See also **combined operation*.

1915 R. W. CAMPBELL *Private Spud Tamson* xiii. 167 Any chapter on training must also refer to night operations, generally called Night Attacks. These operations are never popular in times of training. They interfere with social engagements. **1939** *War Pictorial* 22 Dec. 9 (*caption*) The gallery above is the Operations Section of the R.A.F. Fighter Command. **1941** N. MACMILLAN *Air Strategy* iv. 30 We must perforce ignore..the layout of an Operations Room which functions as the brain to the body, the body in this case being the operational aircraft. **1943** J. S. HUXLEY *TVA* 108 The operations crew..get their orders from the control room. **1946** *R.A.F. Jrnl.* May 170 Now, in a world at peace, operations are but a faint memory for the men. **1968** R. L. ACKOFF in *Internat. Encycl. Social Sci.* XI. 291/1 British military executives turned to scientists for aid when the German air attack on Britain began... These teams of scientists were usually assigned to the executive in charge of operations. **1975** A. BEEVOR *Violent Brink* vii. 167 In the Operations Room.. two members of the Security Committee had advocated that the two sides should be left to fight it out.

b. Used as first element of the code-name for a military or civil campaign.

1938 'TAFFRAIL' *Operation 'M.O.'* iii. 58 It's stuffed full of secret papers that I was going to work on at home! Operation 'M.O.' **1941** *New Statesman* 26 Apr. 443/2 In this brief workmanlike account of the Evacuation from Dunkirk, Mr. Masefield... brings back a plain exact narrative of The Operation Dynamo (as the lifting was officially called). **1945** *News Chron.* 1 June 1/4 This is the first picture to be released of Operation 'Fido'. **1946** T. DRIBERG in *Reynolds News* 28 Apr. 4 Note to sub-editors and others: please cooperate in killing..the most overworked of current clichés—the whimsical application to a variety of topics of the military locution 'Operation —'. **1950** *Nat. Geographic Mag.* Sept. 367/1 'Operation Link', they call the project because when completed, the 4-mile bridge will link Maryland's eastern and western shores. **1968** *Listener* 23 May 656/2 Between Tet and the 'second wave', General Westmoreland launched 'Operation Final Vietcong' to sweep the enemy from the surroundings of Saigon. But this enterprise, nicknamed 'Operation Final Solution', failed. **1973** *Guardian* 25 Jan. 2/1 The operation to return the..prisoners of war..Operation Homecoming, as the Pentagon has called it.

8. a. (Further examples.) In connection with *Computers* freq. identical with sense 5; also = *FUNCTION *sb.* 3 d.

1885, etc. [see *logical operation* s.v. *LOGICAL *a.* (and *sb.*) 7]. **1946** *Ann. Computation Lab. Harvard Univ.* I. 50 Since the control tapes deal with operations only, they represent the solution of a mathematical situation independent of the values of the parameters involved. **1947** *Math. Tables & Other Aids to Computation* II. 356 Provision is planned for squaring, taking the reciprocal, and the maximum or minimum of two quantities, but these operations are not yet available. **1953** A. D. & K. H. V. BOOTH *Automatic Digital Calculators* vi. 35 It is customary, in *all* existing computers, to have circuits which will perform the operations of addition and subtraction. *Ibid.* 37 The left shift operation is more complex. **1956** BERKELEY & WAINWRIGHT *Computers* ii. 38 The arithmetical operations of a computer..include addition, counting, subtraction,..truncating, rounding off, [etc.]. **1969** P. B. JORDAIN *Condensed Computer Encycl.* 358 In general, an operation is a single irreducible step in the performance of a computer program... In some higher-level languages, an operation is a single higher-level step (such as finding a square root). **1972** GROSS & BRAINERD *Fund.*

Programming Concepts ix. 248 The first hexadecimal digit is called the operation code and specifies which operation is to be performed, such as add, subtract, print, etc.

b. In the numerical solution of simultaneous linear equations by relaxation, the process of changing the trial value of one of the unknowns in order to reduce the magnitude of one of the residuals.

[**1935** R. V. Southwell in *Proc. R. Soc.* A. CLI. 65 In the operation considered, B is held fixed and A is moved.] **1940** —— *Relaxation Methods in Engin. Sci.* i. 1 The Relaxation Method takes it farther by devising methods of systematic adjustment: we apply a series of operations, each one an indirect solution of a particularly simple kind, and in this way we 'tune up' a trial solution..until it conforms with some imposed standard of accuracy. **1957** L. Fox *Numerical Solution Two-Point Boundary Probl.* iii. 38 The computations are embodied in Tables 1 and 2, showing respectively the possible operations and details of the relaxation process. **1969** W. A. Watson et al. *Numerical Anal.* I. vi. 160 Usually the operation which reduces the magnitude of the largest residual is used at any stage of the working.

11. operation code *Computers*, a character or set of characters that when put into the operation part of an instruction specifies the operation that is performed; **operation part** *Computers*, the part of an instruction that receives the operation code; **operations research** *U.S.* = *operational research* (*Operational *a.* 1 b); so *operations researcher*; **operations table** *Math.*, in the numerical solution of simultaneous linear equations by relaxation, a table showing the changes in the values of the residuals that result when each unknown in turn is increased by one.

1949 E. C. Berkley *Giant Brains* vi. 103 Division has the code 76 and multiplication the code 761, and so the difference is essentially an operation code not in the third or *C* field. **1972** C. B. Germain *PL/1 for IBM 360* ii. 14/2 The general format of 360 instructions is an operation code..specifying the operation to be performed followed by two addresses to specify the data, or operands, involved in the operation. **1957** D. D. McCracken *Digital Computer Programming* ii. 14 Instruction Format... The first two digits..are called the operation part, and tell the machine what to do. The next four digits are termed the address part. **1969** P. B. Jordain *Condensed Computer Encycl.* 359 The operation part is usually at the left end of the instruction, and is of fixed length. **1945** E. J. King in G. C. Marshall et al. *War Rep.* (1947) 719 The application, by qualified scientists, of the scientific method to the improvement of naval operating techniques and material, has come to be called operations research. **1956** Berkeley & Wainwright *Computers* vii. 281 Much operations research can be carried out with pencil, paper, and a desk calculating machine. **1969** J. Argenti *Managem. Techniques* 81 The same problem occurs in Operations Research, i.e. in those management techniques that depend largely upon mathematics. **1970** P. M. Morse in G. J. Kelleher *Challenge to Syst. Analysis* iii. 23 Operations research has emerged as a unified area of applied science.. designed to influence policy. **1953** *Operational Research Q.* IV. 51 The operations researcher's competence stops. **1940** R. V. Southwell *Relaxation Methods in Engin. Sci.* i. 8 Having completed the calculations we can present their results in an operations table. **1957** L. Fox *Numerical Solution Two-Point Boundary Probl.* iii. 40 The full number of figures is used for the calculation of residuals, but the coefficients can be rounded-off to convenient numbers for use in the operations table. **1969** W. A. Watson et al. *Numerical Anal.* I. vi. 159 For ease of reference during the working it is convenient to summarise the effects on the residuals of unit changes in the unknowns in a table, usually referred to as the operations table.

operational (ǫpĕrēi·ʃənăl), *a.* [f. Operation + -al.] **1. a.** Of or pertaining to operation or operations; *spec.* engaged in or connected with active military operations as distinct from being under training, in reserve, etc.

1922 *Edin. Rev.* Oct. 212 The development of..air communications..ensuring the maintenance of a large and flourishing constructional and operational aircraft industry. **1928** C. F. S. Gamble *Story N. Sea Air Station* x. 146 They were placed in various groups for disciplinary and operational purposes. **1940** *War Illustr.* 5 Jan. 568/2 Each balloon can be raised to its operational ceiling in a very few minutes. **1941** *Economist* 19 Apr. 521/2 The new status is not intended merely to prevent wastage. There are operational reasons. The range of women's duties in the Army and the Air Force is extending. **1943** B. J. Hurren *Eastern Med.* xii. 129 The air forces moved up their advanced aerodromes (technically known as Operational Landing Grounds). **1962** A. Nisbett *Technique Sound Studio* 246 The soundproof room equipped with control desk, gramophone and tape reproducers and high quality loudspeaker, which is occupied by production and operational staff. *a* **1963** J. Lusby in B. James *Austral. Short Stories* (1963) 222 They were young, quiet, and looked tired. Operational men, instructing for a 'rest'. **1963** C. W. Bary (*title*) Operational economics of electric utilities. **1964** *Ann. N.Y. Acad. Sci.* CXV. 683 The problems of achieving adequate operational flexibility..underline the need for more appropriate computer systems. **1974** M. Babson *Stalking Lamb* ii. xvii. 127 He intended to make the mews house his operational headquarters... It would be safe, quiet, unsuspected. **1977** *R.A.F. News* 11–24 May 3/4 The real test lies in our operational efficiency.

b. *operational research*: a method of mathematically based investigation for providing a quantitative basis for management decisions (orig. for military planning); abbrev. O.R., OR (*O 5 d); so *operational researcher*.

1941 P. M. S. Blackett in *Advancement of Sci.* (1948) V. 27/1 The work of an Operational Research Section should be carried out at Command, Groups, Stations or Squadrons as circumstances dictate. *Ibid.* 29/1 One of the tasks of an Operational Research Section is to make possible..a numerical estimate of the merits of a change over from one device to another. **1945** *World Rev.* June 49 The Operational Research Section..is a new element in the organisation of the Royal Air Force which has been evolved during the war. **1948** *Nature* 13 Mar. 377/1 In war, operational research was applied to the use of weapons, to tactics, and to strategy. In the peace-time applications of operational research, studies are directed, for example, to the use of equipment and man-power, to operating procedures, and to the solution of those many problems faced by management..or by Government authorities. **1948** *Advancement of Sci.* IV. 320/1 The operational researcher was visualised as requiring dual ranges of knowledge; on the one hand a wide and fairly detailed knowledge of technical possibilities..; on the other..a close personal knowledge of the working conditions. **1953** *Economist* 15 Aug. 465/1 This technique is called 'operational research'; and under it, teams that may include engineers, mathematicians, statisticians, economists and sociologists combine together. **1959** *Birmingham Mail* 11 Mar. 1/5 London Transport has set up an operational research team to investigate the desirability of increasing the non-smoking accommodation in Tube coaches. **1964** M. Argyle *Psychol. & Social Probl.* xvi. 194 The kind of research done by social scientists working for organizations can be divided into trend analysis, operational research and experiments. **1967** R. Whitehead in Wills & Yearsley *Handbk. Managem. Technol.* 70 The operational researcher seeks to control the situation by making a model of the outside factors from which he can to some extent predict and form a plan of production. **1967** E. Duckworth in *Ibid.* 99 The purpose of operational research is..to assist a manager to take decisions and to help him to take fewer decisions. **1971** D. C. Hague *Managerial Econ.* (rev. ed.) 6 Managerial economics is a background subject which both the line manager and the operational researcher must understand if they are to be successful.

c. In a condition of readiness to perform some intended (esp. military) function.

1944 H. St. G. Saunders *Per Ardua* xvii. 270 Only the Martinsyde F.4, not then operational, was superior to them. **1948** 'N. Shute' *No Highway* i. 19 'Could you.. find out how many hours flying these machines have done?'.. 'They can't have done much. They've only been operational for about a month.' **1963** R. M. Hare *Freedom & Reason* iii. 46 We are to make morality again (as the military writers say) 'operational'. **1965** *New Statesman* 14 May 758/1 The new Russian weapon is clearly operational. **1974** *Nature* 22 Nov. 279/2 The Cambridge group operates the majority of operational catenary instruments.

d. Of, or pertaining to, mental operations (see *Operation 4 b).

1953 Mays & Whitehead tr. *Piaget's Logic & Psychol.* p. xviii, The structures which emerge in the analysis of the operational mechanisms of thought. **1963** J. H. Flavell *Developmental Psychol. J. Piaget* v. 168 The operational systems of middle childhood have certain definable properties. **1975** M. D. Smith *Educ. Psychol.* ii. 40 When a learner becomes able to deal with things that are not actually present..and to relate images and memories to predict and control the future, then he is in the formal operational stage of thought.

2. a. *Math.* Of, involving, or employing operators.

1927 H. Jeffreys (*title*) Operational methods in mathematical physics. **1937** E. Stephens (*title*) The elementary theory of operational mathematics. **1957** L. Fox *Numerical Solution Two-Point Boundary Probl.* ii. 8 We easily produce the operational equivalents $E = e^{hD}$, $E - 1 = \Delta$... With few restrictions these operators can be manipulated according to the rules of ordinary algebra. **1973** L. E. Edwards *PL/1 for Business Applications* ii. 55 An expression may consist of a single variable or a single constant or a combination of these using operators, and is then referred to as an operational expression.

b. Electronics. *operational amplifier*: an amplifier with a very high open-loop gain and a very low output impedance that is used (usu. with negative feedback) as the basis of a circuit for performing a particular mathematical operation on an input voltage with high accuracy, the relation of output to input being effectively determined solely by the arrangement and magnitude of the other, passive, circuit elements.

1947 J. R. Ragazzini et al. in *Proc. IRE* XXXV. 444/2 As an amplifier so connected can perform the mathematical operations of arithmetic and calculus on the voltages applied to its input, it is hereafter termed an 'operational amplifier'. **1962** Simpson & Richards *Physical Princ. Junction Transistors* xiii. 309 The operational amplifier is also valuable as a linear adder. Because the input and output resistances are very low, the base voltage may be made accurately proportional to the sum of a number of separate input voltages each 'weighted' by its own summing resistor. **1963** B. Fozard *Instrumentation Nucl. Reactors* xii. 152 The basic unit of an electronic analogue computer is the operational amplifier. **1972** Vassos & Ewing *Analog & Digital Electronics* v. 139 Deviations from ideality in operational amplifiers are very often negligible. For this reason the input–output relation is independent of the characteristics of the particular amplifier. This property brings about a unique simplicity of design, which is the key to the extensive use of operational amplifiers in instrumentation and control systems.

3. Of, pertaining to, or in accordance with operationalism.

1927 P. W. Bridgman *Logic Mod. Physics* i. 8 Einstein, in thus analyzing what is involved in making a judgment of simultaneity..is actually adopting a new point of view as to what the concepts of physics should be, namely, the operational view. **1935** *Psychol. Rev.* XLII. 517 Operational doctrine makes explicit recognition of the fact that a concept, or proposition, has empirical meaning only if it stands for definite, concrete operations capable of execution by normal human beings. **1937** *Harper's Mag.* Dec. 51/1 Some deductions may still be sound, but all are suspect pending operational check in modern America. **1941** A. Huxley *Grey Eminence* iii. 48 That 'operational philosophy' which contemporary scientific thinkers have begun to apply in the natural sciences. **1952** G. Sarton *Hist. Sci.* I. xvi. 404 It [*sc.* the Platonic method] is sterile because it is unworkable, or, to use our modern terminology, it is not 'operational'. **1955** A. Huxley *Genius & Goddess* 21 'Wouldn't he have lived to eighty-seven without the pills?'.. 'We can never know how his self-medication was related to his longevity. And where there's no possible operational answer, there's no conceivable sense in the question.' **1971** *Brit. Med. Bull.* XXVII. 37/2 The operational definition of hypertension in the population should be flexible.

operationalism (ǫpĕrēi·ʃənăliz'm). [f. prec. + -ism.] A theory or system which accepts only such concepts as can be described in terms of the operations necessary to determine or prove them.

1931 *Jrnl. Philos.* XXVIII. 545 Operationalism must be understood to state that a concept has no meaning unless its definition formulates performable operations. **1941** P. Frank *Between Physics & Philos.* 5 Professor Bridgman's views have..been labelled 'operationalism', although he himself is not pleased by this name. **1950** *Mind* LIX. 571 Pragmatism and its modern offspring operationalism. **1965** N. Chomsky *Aspects of Theory of Syntax* 194 Perhaps this loss of interest in theory..was fostered by certain ideas (i.e., strict operationalism or strict verificationism) that were considered briefly in positivist philosophy of science..in the early nineteen-thirties. **1965** [see *operationally *adv.*]. **1968** M. Black *Labyrinth of Lang.* vi. 142 Operationalism may rank with Freudianism as one of the major intellectual forces in the Western world between the first two World Wars. **1972** *Language* XLVIII. 418 It would appear that the appeal of various forms of operationalism, positivism, and behaviourism,.. had a great deal to do with the emergence of a new professional identification on the part of a small group of young men.

Hence **opera·tionalist** *sb.* and *a.*

1931 *Jrnl. Philos.* XXVIII. 545 When the operationalist defines a concept in terms of operations, the meaning of the concept thus defined is not restricted to performed operations or to operations which are actually going to be performed. **1934** *Mind* XLIII. 201 This Mead wants to prove by following the operationalist argument about the concepts of physics. **1941** A. Huxley *Grey Eminence* iii. 48 Buddha was not a consistent operationalist. **1965** J. D. North *Measure of Universe* xv. 335 One of the biggest objections to the operationalist philosophy is that it appears to deny meaning even to such apparently harmless dispositional words as 'imperceptible', 'movable', and so on. *Ibid.* 336 But (runs the operationalist's argument) even where D_1 and D_2 turn out to be more or less the same and even where, as a matter of convenience, one assimilates the two concepts, in any careful or philosophical account they must always be distinguished. **1977** *Language* LIII. 170 In the period when a strictly behaviorist and operationalist philosophy dominated American linguistics, constraining the linguist to discount any data beyond the 'physical' record, Hoijer delivered a paper at the 8th International Congress of Linguists on the importance of 'Native reaction as a criterion in linguistic analysis'.

operationality (ǫ:pĕrēiʃənæ·lĭti). [f. *Operational *a.* + -ity.] The property of being operational.

1972 *Computers & Humanities* VII. 81 First, how well have the available [computer] programs served the current generation..? Second, considering basic design tensions—flexibility and uniformity, elegance and operationality—what directions should future design and dissemination efforts take? **1973** *Nature* 21/28 Dec. 532/1 Piaget's insistence on 'operationality' makes his experiments indirect and complicated.

operationalizable (ǫpĕrē:ʃənăləi·zăb'l), *a.* [f. next + -able.] Capable of being operationalized.

1975 *Cooperation & Conflict* (Oslo) X. 35/1 As it consists of transactions, the transactor profile characteristic is more easily operationalizable. **1976** *Brit. Jrnl. Sociol.* XXVII. 35 However, my goal is to develop a single, broad operationalizable interpretation from the philosophical sources and to test the contemporary usages against that standard.

operationalize (ǫpĕrēi·ʃənăləiz), *v.* [f. *Operational *a.* + -ize.] *trans.* To express or determine in operational terms. Hence **opera·tionalizing** *vbl. sb.*

1954 *Jrnl. Abnormal Psychol.* XLIX. 460 Once the codability variable..had been operationalized, it remained to relate this variable to some nonlinguistic behavior. **1964** [see *codability]. **1966** Hughes & Pinney in E. L. Pinney *Compar. Politics & Polit. Theory* 67 Most of these interpretations are exercises in conceptualization, rather than efforts to operationalize the concept. **1972** *Jrnl. Social Psychol.* LXXXVII. 30 Previous studies have operationalized panic in terms of average time of group escape. **1975** *Gen. Systems* XX.

116/2 By accommodating evolution, class exploitation, and industrialism, cultural materialism helps operationalize anthropology.

Hence **o:perationaliza·tion**, the process of operationalizing.

1966 Hughes & Pinney in E. L. Pinney *Compar. Politics & Polit. Theory* 67 The problem which must be solved in order to exploit the usefulness of the concept is basically one of operationalization. **1969** P. Worsley in Ionescu & Gellner *Populism* 235 The formulation and operationalization of policy..is thus a function of many other things than simply adhesion to some kind of ideology. **1973** *Sociol. Rev.* XXI. 419 The term 'operationalisation' is usually reserved for the process of trying to turn hypotheses into testable postulates, and for the problems of selecting or creating techniques to test them. **1975** *Political Stud.* XXIII. 75 That Deutsch himself is aware of the limitations of his operationalization is indicated by his calling a 'politicized people' a 'nationality', and not inhabitants of a society featuring a large public sector.

operationally (ǫpĕrēi·ʃənăli), *adv.* [f. as prec. + -LY[2].] In terms of, or as regards, operation(s), esp. the operations required to define a concept or term (cf. *OPERATIONALISM).

1927 *Jrnl. Philos.* XXIV. 663 Every concept must henceforth be defined operationally, i.e., we know what a concept means when we know what operations must be performed in order to produce an instance of that concept. **1934** *Times* 26 June (Air Suppl.) p. xvii/2 It was decided, therefore, shortly after the War ended that the third Service, the Royal Air Force, should be operationally responsible for the units..engaged in the air defence of the country. **1948** *Jrnl. Abnormal Psychol.* XLIII. 143/1 There remains the evanescent residual category of 'personality', at once too broad to be operationally useful.. and too ubiquitous to be neglected. **1951** [see *OPERATIONIST *a.* and *sb.*]. **1965** J. D. North *Measure of Universe* viii. 152 The belief that any theory must be provided with a 'sound conceptual foundation' is..often closely allied to the doctrine of operationalism, coinciding with that variant form according to which *every* concept must be explicitly 'operationally defined', even if only hypothetically so. **1972** *Science* 5 May 545/3 It is operationally impossible to distinguish between selection at a single locus and selection for closely linked genes. **1975** *Daily Tel.* 30 May 2/3 Operationally, the occasion on which the drop of a complete parachute brigade would be required and feasible has for long seemed remote.

operationism (ǫpĕrēi·ʃəniz'm). [f. OPERATION + -ISM.] = *OPERATIONALISM.

1935 *Psychol. Rev.* XLII. 517 The principles of operationism provide a procedure by which the concepts of psychology can be cast in rigorous form. **1942** D. D. Runes *Dict. Philos.* 219/2 Operationism makes explicit the distinction between *formal* and *empirical* sentences. **1970** *Jrnl. Gen. Psychol.* LXXXII. 113 About 25 years ago, during the period that I may call rampant operationism, a great many psychologists were misled into believing that here at last..was the long-needed panacea for guaranteeing useful scientific terms. **1975** *New Left Rev.* Nov.–Dec. 53 Baihelard's concept of the transitive dimension of science is flawed by operationism and an unrelenting hostility to the role of the imagination in science.

Hence **opera·tionist** *a.* and *sb.* = *OPERATIONALIST *sb.* and *a.*

1950 *Brit. Jrnl. Psychol.* XL. 112 An unwarranted assumption is..that a person who is frustrated in a behaviourist or operationist sense, necessarily feels frustrated. **1951** *Mind* LX. 46 The operationist school in psychology. *Ibid.* 53 All operationists are rationalistic in the sense that they maintain that unless scientists define their terms operationally they will not uncover Nature's secrets. **1956** E. H. Hutten *Lang. Mod. Physics* ii. 62 The operationist theory of meaning..is not acceptable.

operative, *a.* and *sb.* Add: **A.** *adj.* **1. a.** *spec.* in legal use, applied to those words in a document which express the intention to effect the transaction concerned.

1792 [in Dict.]. **1872** in J. Russell *Rep. Cases High Court of Chancery* V. 344 If the operative part of a deed be doubtfully expressed, there the recital may safely be referred to as a key to the intention of the parties; but where the operative part of the deed uses language which admits of no doubt, it cannot be controlled by the recital. **1925** G. C. Cheshire *Mod. Law Real Property* 601 We will now turn to the operative words of the conveyance. **1951** *Times* 27 Nov. 7/4 Something to prevent that should be put into the operative part of the treaty.

b. Of words, sentences, etc.: containing the main point or key, essential to the meaning of the whole.

1926 *Sat. Rev* .3 July 12/1 Every English sentence has an operative word. **1954** Koestler *Invis. Writing* ii. 28 The tendency of the novel had to be 'operative', that is, didactic; each work of art must convey a social message. **1963** N. Marsh *Dead Water* (1964) ii. 43 'It was nice getting your occasional letters,' Patrick said, presently. 'Operative word "occasional".' **1973** O. Lancaster *Littlehampton Bequest* 24 He was known..to have trailed a pike in the Low Countries when there were those..who loudly proclaimed that in his case 'trailed' was the operative word.

c. Of political ideas or principles: (*a*) capable of being put into effect; likely to be beneficial; (*b*) (see quot. 1954).

1938 H. G. Wells *Brothers* iii. 46 Are you lot over there really giving it an operative form? That's one of my phrases, brother—*operative form*... *Competent receiver* and *operative form*; two phrases for two problems that Socialism and Communism ought to have tackled forty years ago. **1954** Koestler *Invis. Writing* xx. 224 It is called the 'operative principle'. It means that you cannot write about the strategy of Communism without having worked in a factory, or Party cell, or underground organisation.

d. In weakened sense (without reference to specific activity or production): significant, important.

1955 J. L. Austin *How to do Things with Words* (1962) i. 7 But 'operative'..is often used nowadays to mean little more than 'important'. **1977** 'D. Cory' *Bennett* ii. 74 After all, she *didn't* bring the boy on that operative Saturday.

B. *sb.* **3. b.** A detective or agent employed by a detective agency; a secret-service agent.

1905 *N.Y. Press* 23 Oct. 6/4 The word 'detective' became so offensive..that it was dropped by some successful [detective] agencies. The word chosen by the Pinkertons to take its place was 'operative'. **1930** *Sat. Even. Post* 26 July 142/2 Riding on the train with him was another operative who had spent that day following Castagara. **1934** A. Christie *Murder on Orient Express* ii. ix. 137 That's not to say he'll remember me from a crowd of other operatives. **1937** *N.Y. Times* 22 Dec. 22/5 *Operative*, a spy employed by an agency. Usually has a secret designation. An operative may be a hooked man or a professional spy. **1954** W. Tucker *Wild Talent* (1955) xiv. 184 Paul wondered if this new woman in the adjoining apartment would be a plant... Slater might be playing it doubly safe and ringing in another operative on him. **1966** J. Porter *Sour Cream* iii. 36, I thought..you might just care to make your will. I advise all my operatives to do it. **1977** J. Crosby *Company of Friends* viii. 56 Sascha looked at her, pierced with reluctant admiration. What an operative!

operator. Add: **2.** *spec.* A secret-service agent. Cf. *OPERATIVE *sb.* 3b.

1966 J. Porter *Sour Cream* iii. 36, I'm sure you won't find any snags. She's a most experienced operator. *Ibid.* viii. 101 I'll know by mid-morning if Feodorov's side of the operation has been successful... He's a very experienced operator. **1977** S. Coulter *Soyuz Affair* vii. 73 He keeps a close watch on his things... He's a trained operator.

4. (Later examples.) Also now freq. with a stronger implication of speculativeness or shrewdness; one who acts in an underhand manner.

1895 *Daily News* 30 Dec. 7/5 The market declined early on large receipts, but eventually improved, due to local operators covering. **1951** [see *HOLE *sb.* 11]. **1955** D. W. Maurer in *Publ. Amer. Dial. Soc.* XXIV. 35 Also, unlike many if not most other types of underworld operator, he tends to take his woman on the road with him. **1959** N. Mailer *Advts. for Myself* (1961) 399 He spent years hobnobbing with gentlemanly shits and half-ass operators. **1964** A. W. Gouldner in I. L. Horowitz *New Sociol.* 209 The whole world may be seen as one of marks and operators. **1970** *New Yorker* 6 June 132/3 He is what we call nowadays an 'operator', and completely unscrupulous and unashamed. **1971** D. Potter *Brit. Eliz. Stamps* i. 15 Stamps were solemnly discussed in the financial columns,..and get-rich-quick operators joined in the *mêlée*. **1974** *Times* 4 Feb. 12/6 One almost expects him to say, with J. K. Galbraith, that modesty is a much overrated virtue, but he is far too smooth an operator to be trapped into such an admission.

5. a. (Earlier and later examples.) *spec.* One who works at the switchboard of a telephone exchange (now the usual sense). Also in *Comb.*

1847 *Commerc. Rev. of South & West* Nov. 138 Its receipt [was] acknowledged by the Montreal operator in 30 minutes. **1858** E. E. Hale *If, Yes, & Perhaps* (1868) 119 It is not the business simply of 'operators' in telegraphic dens to know this Morse alphabet. **1865** *Harper's Mag.* July 169/2 Here they gathered a new force.., a telegraph operator, and workmen. **1884** *List of Subscribers* (London & Globe Telephone Co.) 2 The Special Telephone Exchange Switchboard is so constructed, that the operators ..do not overhear the conversation between Subscribers. **1921** [see *DIAL *v.* 4]. **1927** Haldane & Huxley *Animal Biol.* vi. 140 The human cerebrum contains more than a thousand million nerve-cells each connected by fibres with scores or hundreds of others,..so we can get some idea of its complexity by imagining a telephone exchange in which the whole human race were acting as operators. **1972** B. F. Conners *Don't embarrass Bureau* (1973) ii. 201 Operator, I'd like to call person to person to Officer Dolan. **1976** *Norwich Mercury* 10 Dec. 10/2 Bookings for operator-connected international telephone calls over Christmas will be accepted by the Post Office from Monday. **1977** G. Markstein *Chance Awakening* xix. 55 He dialled 100. He gave the operator the number. 'What seems to be the trouble?' asked the operator.

b. *U.S.* One who is licensed to drive a motor vehicle.

1967 *Boston Sunday Herald* 7 May iii. 1/1 Several witnesses to the accident have supplied police pieces of information, which, when put together, revealed the involvement of this other car—and male operator, who stopped at this point, without knowing his car—and he —had actually been involved in the tragedy. **1972** *N.Y. Law Jrnl.* 24 Oct. 18/6 At the time involved defendant was a resident of the State of New Jersey and the holder of a New Jersey operator's license. It also appears from a Motor Vehicle Bureau exhibit..that defendant's New York license had been cancelled.

6. (Earlier examples.) Also in wider use, of companies, corporations, etc.

1838 *Niles' Reg.* 13 Oct. 112/2 Our trade..is brought nearly to a stand again, by a collision between the dealers, operators and boatmen, as regards the price of freight. **1851** C. Cist *Sk. Cincinnati in 1851* 170 The largest operators in this line [manufacturing alcohol], are Lowell Fletcher & Co. **1857** *Harper's Mag.* Sept. 459/1 The leases of the operators usually covered a 'run' upon the out-crop ..of from fifty to seventy yards. **1875** *Chicago Tribune* 30 Sept. 2/4 The operators on the Pan-Handle Railroad have been paying 2½ cents per bushel for mining over 1½ inch screen. **1953** *Manch. Guardian Weekly* 19 Nov. 9 The State, through a new sort of BBC is to own the new system and will hire it out to commercial 'operators'. **1962** *Listener* 8 Mar. 401/1 Though they [*sc.* the nationalized industries] were to be regarded partly as commercial operators, partly as public services, the relation between these two functions was not defined in the legislation that set them up. **1972** *Lebende Sprachen* XVII. 134/1 The official body representing the majority of independent operators is the British Independent Air Transport Association. **1977** *Times* 23 Mar. 14/3 Exporters have turned increasingly to road haulage for cargoes... This traffic..has attracted a large number of operators who are not equipped for the job. **1977** *Offshore Engineer* May 42/1 The results of the four wells are being closely studied by the operator Elf Aquitaine and partners ETAP and STEG.

7. (Further examples.) Also, a sign or symbol which effects other types of operation, as logical, phonological, syntactic, etc.

1925 Bryant & Correll *Alternating-Current Circuits* iii. 74 The operator, $j = \sqrt{(-1)}$, turns the vector through 90 degrees in a counterclockwise direction each time it is used. **1936** *Jrnl. Symbolic Logic* I. 60 The formal system.. employs material implication, propositional negation, universal quantification, and operators analogous to the combinatory operators *I*, *B*, and *C*. **1937** A. Smeaton tr. *Carnap's Logical Syntax of Lang.* i. §6. 21 The expressions which occur at the beginning of the sentences above ..are called the *unlimited* universal operator, the *unlimited* existential operator, the *limited* universal operator, and the *limited* existential operator respectively. **1952** *Eng. & Gmc. Stud.* IV. 12 We may regard Modern English *stone* as the result of operating with an operator that I shall write {AS. ā > MnE. [ou]} on Anglo-Saxon *stān*. **1952** S. C. Kleene *Introd. Metamath.* iv. 73 Let us call an expression of one of these ten forms an operator. In particular, ⊃, &, v, ⌐ are *propositional connectives*, and operators of the forms ∀x and ∃x are *quantifiers*..; these six are *logical operators*. **1957** L. Fox *Numerical Solution Two-Point Boundary Probl.* ii. 8 In the theory of finite differences we carry this farther, introducing first the operator *E*, the effect of change of position, and defined by the equation $y(x+ph)=E^p y(x)$. **1964** E. Bach *Introd. Transformational Gram.* v. 113 The concatenation operator +. **1965** Phillips & Williams *Inorg. Chem.* I. i. 12 Wave mechanics sets up, as postulates, equations of the type $H\psi = X\psi$, where ψ is the wave function, and *X* some observed property such as the energy, momentum, etc. *H* is a mathematical instruction (e.g. differentiate with respect to *x*) or set of instructions..called an operator. **1966** A. Koutsoudas *Writing Transformational Gram.* i. 6 The rules of a transformational grammar consist of three types of symbols: (1) vocabulary symbols, (2) operators, and (3) abbreviators. Vocabulary symbols are symbols used to represent syntactic classes and other linguistic units; operators, as their name indicates, symbolize certain operations; and abbreviators are devices used to conflate the listing of rules. **1968** Corlett & Tinsley *Pract. Programming* ii. 14 Numbers and variables may be combined by the arithmetic operators + − × ÷ / ↑ to form an arithmetic expression. **1969** V. J. Calderbank *Course on Programming in FORTRAN IV* iii. 28 Another very common form of logical expression..is the relational expression. This has the general form $e_1\ r\ e_2$ where e_1 and e_2 are arithmetic expressions..being compared by one of the following relational operators, *r*: .EQ. Equal to (=); .LT. Less than (<); [etc.]. **1969** P. A. M. Seuren *Operators & Nucleus* iv. 116 Our hypothesis of operators as a deep structure category in grammar thus has a philosophical pedigree leading back to both the theory of quantifiers and the logic of modalities. **1976** A. R. Lacey *Dict. Philos.* 148 A logical operator is any expression whose function is to affect in a specific way the logical properties (e.g. the entailments) of an expression or expressions to which it is attached, e.g. 'and' operates on two propositions by joining them into a whole, which has entailments neither of them has separately.

8. a. In 'Basic English', an article, particle, preposition, etc., or one of certain words used as substitutes for verbs; a 'superverb'.

1929 C. K. Ogden in *Psyche* IX. iii. 1 The number of necessary names is 400, of qualifiers (adjectives) 100, of operators, particles, etc., 100. **1930** —— *Basic English* iii. 60 In conversation, the operators are frequently shortened to more convenient forms. Thus *I will* becomes *I'll*. **1946** H. Jacob *On Choice of Common Lang.* iii. 104 Three analogical extras, *say*, *see*, and *send*..provide a useful link between the operators and the verb-system proper. **1966** M. Pei *Gloss. Ling. Terminol.* 188 *Operator*, one of the verbal forms, prepositions, articles, etc. (about one hundred in number) in Basic English.

b. *Linguistics.* = *form-word* s.v. *FORM *sb.* 22, *function word* s.v. *FUNCTION *sb.* 3c.

1938 B. L. Whorf *Lang. Thought & Reality* (1956) 128 Predication..operators (words specialized for predication, otherwise lexical meaning blank ('be, become, cause, do') or vague ('make, turn, get,' etc.)). auxiliary verbs. **1957** S. Potter *Mod. Linguistics* vii. 143 Operators are.. forms like articles, prepositions, conjunctions and conjunction adverbs..which perform syntactic functions. **1967** [see *FUNCTOR 2].

9. *Biol.* [tr. F. *opérateur* (Jacob & Monod 1959, in *Compt. Rend.* CCXLIX. 1284).] A segment of chromosomal DNA which is thought to control the activity of the structural gene(s) of an operon, protein synthesis occurring when it is uncombined with a repressor (or is absent altogether).

1961 *Cold Spring Harbor Symp. Quant. Biol.* XXVI. 194/1 The synthesis of messenger RNA is supposed to be a sequential and oriented process which can be initiated only at certain regions, or operators, on the DNA strands. **1969** *New Scientist* 28 Aug. 416/1 In the presence of substrate, the repressor is altered, so that it can no longer bind to the operator, and enzymes are synthesized freely. **1971** D. J. Cove *Genetics* xi. 165 A mutation in the operator gene prevents the recognition of the structural genes by the repressor. **1973** *Nature* 16 Nov. 133/1 The sites on DNA to which repressors bind are called operators.

operculate, *a.* (Further examples of botanical use.)

1879 W. Phillips tr. E. Boudier in *Grevillea* VIII. 46, I would call the first section [of Discomycetes] by the name of *Operculate Discomycetes*, or simply *Operculæ*, because in this section the opening of the asci takes place by the elevation of a little lid at its summit. **1913** *Trans. Brit. Mycol. Soc.* IV. 402 The asci in the operculate series are generally larger. **1929** *Ibid.* XIV. 275 The material for this study has been gathered in great part from the accounts which have already been given by other investigators, chiefly on operculate species. **1971** P. H. B. Talbot *Princ. Fungal Taxon.* xi. 160 The dehiscent types [of ascus], both operculate and inoperculate, become turgid and discharge their ascospores forcibly.

operculum. 2. b. The lid of the ascus or sporangium of certain fungi.

1879 W. Phillips tr. E. Boudier in *Grevillea* VIII. 46 After the examination of a considerable number of Discomycetes, I am able to call the attention of mycologists to the necessity of separating this family into two very natural sections, according as to whether the mode of dehiscence is with or without an operculum. **1887, 1888** [see *astropyle]. **1971** P. H. B. Talbot *Princ. Fungal Taxon.* xi. 160 Operculate asci have an operculum at the apex: a hinged lid-like opening.

operette (ǫpĕre·t). Also ‖ **opérette** (ǫpere·t). English (with accent, French) form of Operetta. Also *transf.*

1890 E. Dowson *Let.* 19 May (1967) 149 Playing snatches of opérette—Gilbert & Sullivan, Sultan of Mocha etc. **1928** *Observer* 15 Apr. 21/2 Few operettes launched on the public nowadays can compare with the delicious music of Pongrác Kacsoh. **1935** *Discovery* July 211/2 The Estonians have some charming 'operettes', too, which..without being heavy have much more in them than our average musical comedies. **1938** N. Coward (*title*) Operette. **1961** *Times* 7 Mar. 8/4 On the borderline between *opera bouffe* and *opérette*. **1977** *Listener* 30 June 867/1 Joan Aiken's *Lost Movement*, an entirely enjoyable story, offers..a pretty and melodramatic operette.

operettist (ǫpĕre·tist). [f. Operetta + -ist.] A writer or composer of operettas.

1922 *Blackw. Mag.* June 717/2 There are a mass of Hungarian operettists.

operon (ǫ·pĕrǫn). *Biol.* [ad. F. *opéron* (F. Jacob et al. 1960, in *Compt. Rend.* CCL. 1729), f. *opér-* (in *opérer* to effect, work, *opération* Operation, etc.): see *-on[1].] A unit of coordinated gene activity which is believed to account for inducible and repressible enzymes in bacteria and hence for the regulation of protein synthesis, and is usu. conceived as a linear sequence of genetic material comprising an operator, a promoter, and one or more structural genes.

1961 Jacob & Monod in *Jrnl. Molecular Biol.* III. 344 This genetic unit of co-ordinate expression we shall call the 'operon'. **1969** *Nature* 18 Jan. 219/2 Essentially, Grodzicker and Zipser's experiment was to take strongly polar nonsense mutants of the lactose operon of *E. coli.* **1969** A. M. Campbell *Episomes* ix. 116 The genes of one operon are all transcribed onto the same messenger molecule. **1971** J. Z. Young *Introd. Study Man* iii. 59 Each operon is controlled by one or more regulator genes. **1973** B. J. Williams *Evolution & Human Origins* vi. 91/1 The model of genetic control receiving the most attention today is that of the operon.

operose, *a.* **1.** (Earlier and later examples.)

1678 Cudworth *Intell. Syst.* 884 An Operose, Cumbersom, and Moliminous Business. **1855** Geo. Eliot *Let.* 25 June (1954) II. 206 Such sentences..make a style seem operose and unwieldy. **1959** *New Scientist* 19 Nov. 983 Operose and scholarly collected editions.

ope-tide. For †*Obs.* read *arch.* and add later example.

1911 Beerbohm *Zuleika D.* iii. 28 Her soul was as a flower in its opetide. She was in love.

Ophelian (ǫfī·liăn), *a.* [f. the name of the heroine of Shakespeare's play *Hamlet*: see -an.] Resembling or characteristic of Ophelia.

1903 'Marjoribanks' *Fluff-Hunters* 101 Some time ago I felt so moody and sad that I sought out a pretty pool, with an Ophelian resolution. **1928** *Observer* 18 Mar. 15/3 One can hardly fail to hear this play's Shakespearean echoes... The Gaoler's Daughter is of pure Ophelian stock. **1929** D. H. Lawrence *Pansies* 6 Its transience, its breath, its maybe mephistophelian, maybe palely ophelian face. **1962** *John o' London's* 25 Jan. 91/4 Miss Maclaine would be well advised to drop her Ophelian aspirations.

ophelimity (ǫfēli·miti). *Econ.* [f. F. *ophélimité* (also used), ad. Gr. ὠφέλιμος useful, serviceable.] (See quots.)

1896 V. Pareto *Cours d'Économie Politique* I. 3 Nous emploierons le terme *ophélimité*, du grec ὠφέλιμος, pour exprimer le rapport de convenance qui fait qu'une chose satisfait un besoin ou un désir, légitime ou non.] **1896** *Political Sci. Q.* XI. 750 The term utility, for example, has its ambiguities; and Professor Pareto substitutes the word ophélimité, meaning capacity to satisfy any want, whether rational or irrational. **1920** A. C. Pigou *Econ. of Welfare* ii. 23 Several writers have endeavoured to get rid of the confusion..by substituting for 'utility'..some other term such, for example, as Professor Pareto's 'ophelimity'. **1935** Bongiorno & Livingston tr. *Pareto's Mind & Society* I. i. 29 In pure economics my hypothesis of 'ophelimity'..remains experimental so long as inferences from it are held subject to verification on the facts. **1966** D. Mirfin tr. *Pareto's Sociol. Writings* 99 We shall employ the term *ophelimity*..to designate the relationship of convenience which makes a thing satisfy a need or desire, whether legitimate or not... *Utility* will be required for use in its ordinary accepted sense as the property which makes a thing favourable to the development and well-being of an individual, a community or the whole human species.

opherion (ofī·riǫn). Used by T. S. Eliot, perhaps in error for Orpharion.

a **1922** T. S. Eliot *Waste Land Drafts* (1971) 99 (*title*) Song. For the opherion.

ophidian, *a.* **1.** (Later example.)

1939 T. S. Eliot *Family Reunion* i. ii. 56 The dead stone is seen to be batrachian, The aphyllous branch ophidian.

ophiolite. Add: **b.** *Geol.* Any of a group of basic and ultrabasic igneous rocks, including serpentinite and serpentinized peridotite, gabbro, and diabase, which occur associated with pillow lava and radiolarian chert in a characteristic pattern of layers in the Alps and certain other regions and are thought to have been formed as a result of the submarine eruption of oceanic crustal and upper mantle material; so **ophiolite suite** or **association,** the assemblage of ophiolites, pillow lava, and radiolarian chert.

This use originated in Ger. with the recognition of the association by G. Steinmann (*Ber. d. naturforsch. Ges. zu Freiburg i. Br.* (1906) XVI. 18–49).

1937 A. L. Du Toit *Our Wandering Continents* viii. 168 There is a wide development in Morocco, Spain and the Alpine region of the so-called greenstones or 'ophiolites'. **1963** *Spec. Papers Geol. Soc. Amer.* No. 73. 204 Throughout the Alpine–Himalayan system extensive lavas occur in close association with coarse mafic and ultramafic rocks... This assemblage is the ophiolite suite of Alpine writers. It seems to represent long pre-orogenic extrusion of ultramafic magma. **1970** J. C. Maxwell in Johnson & Smith *Megatectonics of Continents & Oceans* viii. 181 The assemblage of igneous rocks which Europeans call ophiolites seems incompatible with the dominantly sedimentary melange in which it typically occurs. **1971** I. G. Gass et al. *Understanding Earth* iv. 132/2 The former is dominantly volcanic (a thick sequence of ophiolites with subsidiary cherts, carbonates and pelites). **1972** *Sci. Amer.* May 65/3 Within the Alpine–Himalayan mountain belt are narrow zones characterized by a distinctive assemblage of rocks, known as the ophiolite suite. *Ibid.* 66/3 The Ural and Appalachian-Caledonian mountain belts..have narrow zones where ophiolites are found... This implies that the Urals, for example, were created by the collision of two continental masses and that the ophiolites were generated by sea-floor spreading at a ridge axis before the continents were brought together. **1977** A. Hallam *Planet Earth* 166 The whole assemblage of sea-floor basalts and associated upper-mantle peridotites is known as the ophiolite association.

ophiolitic *a.* (Examples.)

1909 H. B. C. & W. J. Sollas tr. *Suess's Face of Earth* IV. v. 153 The sheet of the green-rocks (Ophiolitic, Rhaetic, Vindelician sheet; Steinmann). **1911** *Geol. Mag.* Decade V. VIII. 243 The constant association of dialase (spilite), serpentine, and gabbro in the northern Alps with radiolarian cherts has led Steinmann..to regard these 'ophiolitic eruptives' as the typical volcanic rocks of abysmal depressions. **1963** D. W. & E. E. Humphries tr. *Termier's Erosion & Sedimentation* xvii. 341 Radiolarites associated with the rocks of the ophiolitic suite (of geosynclines), demonstrate the subordinate role of living organisms in comparison to that played by transported material. **1971** *Nature* 3 Sept. 46/2 One of the most significant drilling results..was the discovery of a Lower Cretaceous and Upper Jurassic pelagic sequence above an ophiolitic oceanic basement, almost identical to the coeval Alpine sequences.

ophiology. (Earlier example.)

1817 *Blackw. Mag.* May 187/1 Reserving the history of the serpent tribes for the article *Ophiology.*

ophiomorphic, *a.* (Example.)

1909 Ld. Balcarres *Ital. Sculpture* i. 16 In the Celtic art of the North..these ophiomorphic meanderings of line bewilder the eye by their complexity.

ophitic, *a.*[1] Add: By some writers restricted to textures in which augite predominates and the feldspar laths do not in general touch each other. (Earlier and later examples.)

1875 G. H. Kinahan in *Proc. R. Irish Acad.* II. 118 The passage-rock..may be called ophitic hornblende-rock or amphibolic-ophyte, according to the mineral predominating. **1881** *Jrnl. Chem. Soc.* XL. 697 The ophitic rocks of the Pyrenees are characterised by the development of microliths of triclinic felspar embedded in elongated layers of pyroxene. *Ibid.*, The labradoric ophite.. showed the passage from trachytoidal to ophitic structure. **1970** K. C. Jackson *Textbk. Lithology* v. 300 Diabasic texture... Composed of tabular plagioclase with smaller interstitial granular pyroxene crystals. Ophitic texture... Small tabular plagioclase embedded in larger anhedral pyroxene crystals. **1973** G. J. H. McCall *Meteorites* xiii. 174 (*heading*) Eucrite showing ophitic intergrowth of narrow plagioclase laths.

Hence **ophi·tically** *adv.*, with an ophitic texture.

1908 *Q. Jrnl. Geol. Soc.* LXIV. 491 [The biotite] is moulded ophitically on these minerals. **1971** *Nature* 3 Dec. 265/1 The plagioclase-phyric basalts contain abundant pyroxene..,most of which has crystallized ophitically with the small calcic plagioclase laths.

ophthalmic, *a.* and *sb.* Add: **A.** *adj.* **4.** *ophthalmic acid*, a tripeptide found in the lenses of various mammals (see quot. 1958).

1956 S. G. Waley in *Biochem. Jrnl.* LXIV. 715/1 The work..deals only with acidic peptides. One such peptide (for which the name ophthalmic acid is proposed) is particularly abundant. **1958** *Ibid.* LXVIII. 192/1 The electrophoretic mobility of ophthalmic acid, a tripeptide isolated from calf lens, shows that the glutamic acid residue is γ-linked, and hence that ophthalmic acid is γ-glutamyl-α-amino-*n*-butyrylglycine. **1962** R. van Heyningen in H. Davson *Eye* I. v. 237 Although liver contains but little ophthalmic acid, extracts of liver will synthesize ophthalmic acid from the amino-acids. **1970** J. F. R. Kuck in C. N. Graymore *Biochem. Eye* iii. 206 An interesting feature of the relationship between glutathione and ophthalmic acid is that the former is a specific coenzyme for glyoxalase while ophthalmic acid is a potent inhibitor of this same enzyme.

ophthalmologic, *a.* Delete *rare* and add: Chiefly *U.S.* (Examples.)

1901 [see *homatropine]. **1972** Aronson & Elliott *Ocular Inflammation* xiv. 314/2 Ophthalmologic examination was requested because she complained of intermittent blurring of vision in her right eye.

ophthalmophorous, *a.* (Example.)

1896 *Natural Sci.* VIII. 340 [G. A. Boulenger] has, too, for the first time, utilized the development or want of an ophthalmophorous shelf to the second suborbital as a family character.

-opia, formative element [a. Gr. -ωπία, f. ὤψ, ὠπ- eye, face: see -ia[1].] of terms denoting visual disorders and abnormalities, as Amblyopia, Myopia, Polyopia. Occas. anglicized as **-opy** [cf. -y[3]].

opiate, *a.* and *sb.* Add: **B.** *sb.* **1. a.** (Further example.)

1948 *Arch. Internal Med.* LXXXII. 387 These men were..again offered the choice of either an opiate or methadon.

b. *fig.* (Further examples.) See also *opium *sb.* 1 b.

1927 C. Connolly *Let.* 4 Mar. in *Romantic Friendship* (1975) 276, I find covering ground rather an opiate. **1942** *R.A.F. Jrnl.* 30 May 24 There's no more beautiful feeling than the opiate of unguarded sleep on a sunny boat deck. **1960** D. Eisenhower in W. Safire *New Lang. Politics* (1968) 309/1 Hundreds of millions behind the Iron Curtain are daily drilled in the slogan: 'There is no God, and religion is an opiate'. But not all the people within the Soviet accept this fallacy; and some day they will educate their rulers, or change them. **1968** tr. M. de Unamuno in *Bartlett's Familiar Quotations* (ed. 14) 870/1 One of those leaders of what they call the social revolution has said that religion is the opiate of the people. **1975** *Gen. Systems* XX. 109/1 The European revolutionary found religion an opiate to be abolished. **1976** C. Dexter *Last seen Wearing* xxi. 158 The heady, heavy opiate of the gambling game.

2. Any drug having similar addictive effects to those of the opium alkaloids morphine and cocaine. Freq. *attrib.*

1954 *Ann. Rev. Med.* V. 318 Another interesting field of usefulness for nalorphine is in the detection of opiate addiction. Administration of 5 mg. nalorphine to individuals addicted to morphine or methadon induces abstinence symptoms within 15 min. **1960** *Federal Register* (U.S.) 5 Aug. 7351/2 The word 'opiate'..shall mean any drug..found by the Secretary or his delegate..to have an addiction-forming or addiction-sustaining liability similar to morphine or cocaine. **1961** *Jrnl. Pharmacol. & Exper. Therap.* CXXXIII. 371/1 Codeine accounts for at least 80% of the natural opiates sold on prescription. **1970** *Nature* 14 Apr. 323/1 Methadone itself is an addictive opiate. **1974** M. C. Gerald *Pharmacol.* xiii. 242 In 1973 evidence was presented demonstrating the existence of an opiate receptor in the brain. *Ibid.* 251 Although acute opiate withdrawal is thought to be a very dangerous and often fatal process, there is no evidence to support this belief.

opihi (opī·hi). [Hawaiian.] A limpet belonging to the genus *Helcioniscus*, or its shallow shell. Also *attrib.*

1915 W. A. Bryan *Nat. Hist. Hawaii* xxxv. 466 To the old-world limpets belongs the opihi of the natives. It is a favorite food with the Hawaiians... This knee-cap or umbrella shell is roughly though evenly ribbed without and pearly white within. **1976** *National Observer* (U.S.) 10 Apr. 17/2 Legend has it that when the highly prized Opihi Shell is given to one's sweetheart, the love between them becomes eternal. Thus, wearing the Opihi around the neck assures that the shell—and their love—is preserved forevermore!

opinion, *sb.* Add: **1. b.** *public opinion* (earlier and later examples); also *attrib.*, as *public opinion investigation, poll* [*POLL *sb.*¹ 7 d], *polling, survey* (see *opinion poll, survey*, sense 9 below), etc.

1735 BOLINGBROKE *On Parties* (ed. 2) p. xxxi, Let them stand, or fall in the publick Opinion, according to their Merit. **1751** tr. *Rousseau's Discourse Arts & Sci.* 36 They only hate all publick opinions. **1763** CHESTERFIELD *Duke of Newcastle* in *Lett.* (1845) II. 463 The public opinion put him below his level: for though he had no..eminent talents, he had a most indefatigable industry, a perseverance. **1769** BURKE *Let.* 30 July (1844) I. 181 We must strengthen the hands of the minority within doors, by the accession of the public opinion, strongly declared to the court. **1939** G. GALLUP (*title*) Public opinion in a democracy. **1952** W. J. H. SPROTT *Social Psychol.* 87 It is difficult to put into exact terms what is meant by 'public opinion'... We might, of course, define 'public opinion' on any particular issue..in terms of the people who actually have an 'opinion' on that issue. **1961** L. VAN DER POST *Heart of Hunter* I. v. 88 Tom refused to let public opinion create a sense of shame in him. **1964** GOULD & KOLB *Dict. Social Sci.* 477/2 *Public opinion* is a nebulous concept; it is not the simple aggregate of the opinions of the members of a public, but depends on the society's power structure, the mass media, channels of influence, etc.

attrib.

1936 L. DENNING *Coming Amer. Fascism* 299 A score of great corporations can raise ten million dollars for anti-social purposes of price-fixing or public-opinion manipulation. **1937** *Sociometry* I. I. II. 155 (*title*) Public opinion polls. **1939** G. GALLUP *Public Opinion in Democracy* 3 The development during the last few years of the public-opinion survey or unofficial poll has raised..a host of new and far-reaching questions. **1940** GRAVES & HODGE *Long Weekend* xxiii. 401 From the United States came public opinion investigation. *Ibid.*, Public opinion investigation was first started on a large and permanent scale by the American Dr. Gallup. **1941** J. S. HUXLEY *Uniqueness of Man* xi. 231 The modern scientific public opinion poll, indeed, is developing such uncanny accuracy that it is infringing upon practical politics. **1944** G. GALLUP *Guide to Public Opinion Polls* lxix. 91 The chief function of public opinion polls, and their chief value, is to report the *trend* of opinion. **1958** *Listener* 20 Nov. 813/1 Public-opinion polls... Public-opinion surveys. **1963** *Rep. Comm. Inquiry Decimal Currency* 5, in *Parl. Papers* 1962–3 (Cmnd. 2145) XI. 195 We considered going to further than this by commissioning a public opinion survey. **1964** *Ann. Reg. 1963* 5 His dominance of the parliamentary party was soon apparent in the major debates of the next five months, assisted, no doubt, by Labour's soaring lead in the public opinion polls. **1967** M. ARGYLE *Psychol. Interpersonal Behaviour* ix. 153 Public opinion polls are more closed questions, research surveys make more use of open-ended ones. **1972** *Jrnl. Social Psychol.* LXXXVII. 136 The sealing methodology employed was discussed and suggested as a possibly new public opinion polling device.

4. Phr. *a second* (or *another*) *opinion*, the opinion of a second medical adviser. Also in *transf.* and extended uses.

1885 C. M. YONGE *Nuttie's Father* II. xvii. 201 Dr. Brownlow became very grave over the injury. He said it was a surgical case, and he should like to have another opinion. **1924** J. BUCHAN *Three Hostages* xvi. 237 There's no cause to worry about Peter John... But if you want another opinion, why not get it? *Ibid.* 238, I think a second opinion would please Dr. Greenslade, for he too looked rather anxious. **1954** M. SHARP *Gipsy in Parlour* xxiv. 228 So my father and Miss Jones agreed... I didn't think my father would be quite so pleased to know of this second opinion, so to speak. **1966** J. B. PRIESTLEY *Salt is Leaving* xvi. 213, I have quite a competent doctor... He's never suggested a second opinion. **1970** P. LOVESEY *Wobble to Death* v. 52 Herriot sought for words to influence the doctor... 'Perhaps—another opinion. Your colleague..may see the possibility of a faster recovery.' **1971** A. PRICE *Alamut Ambush* x. 124 So he..wanted a second opinion on what he had seen—that made sense. **1972** J. WAINWRIGHT *Night is Time to Die* 121 You're not here *as* a solicitor... Therefore, you're entitled to call some other solicitor... You might need advice—a second opinion.

9. *opinion-former, leader, maker*; *opinion-forming, -tapping* ppl. adjs.; *opinion-making* ppl. adj. and vbl. sb.; **opinion poll**, the assessment of the opinion of all, or of a section of, the general public by questioning a random or representative sample; hence *opinion polling, pollster*; (see also sense 1 b above); **opinion survey** = **opinion poll.*

1906 G. W. E. RUSSELL *Social Silhouettes* xiii. 90 A Journalist of this type once said to me, with all imaginable gravity, 'I should, I confess, resent any change which interfered with my position as chief opinion-former in the neighbourhood of'—Leeds or Plymouth, or whatever was the name of his town. **1962** *Times Lit. Suppl.* 24 Aug. 633/4 To hear well over half the electors of Britain talk, or read or listen to their favourite opinion-formers, one would conclude that it would be best..if no profits were made by any business. **1967** *Economist* 22 Apr. 338/1 The opinion-formers have begun their debunking. **1977** *Private Eye* 13 May 14/2 He has a fine independence of outlook and a contemptuous disregard for whatever is smart or fashionable among opinion-formers. **1959** *Encounter* Nov. 66 Literary parties..the opinion-forming fringe of the United States. **1969** *Guardian* 28 Aug. 11/6 One section of Oxfam has argued that the organisation should abandon direct aid and devote itself wholly to an opinion-forming rôle. **1974** *Broadcast* 9 Dec. 17/1 The advertising industry has few friends in the educational and opinion-forming strata. **1949** LAZARSFELD & STANTON *Communications Res.* II. vii. 217 The opinion-leaders are not identical with the socially prominent people in the community. **1968** *Internat. Encycl. Soc. Sci.* III. 51 The hard-core noncommissioned officers constituted a cadre of 'opinion leaders' who supported the control structure. **1975** *Times* 25 Feb. 14/1 His audience of nearly 200 were predominantly..people whom the Wessex area office staff would describe only as opinion leaders. **1952** *Time* 27 Oct. 20/1 To intellectuals and other 'opinion makers', Eisenhower was infinitely preferable to the other two. **1957** *Economist* 28 Sept. 1005/1 The reactions of..professional opinion makers were more precise, but just as personal. **1975** S. RANGANATHAN in H. M. Patel et al. *Say not the Struggle Nought Availeth* 297 There are limits to growth as world opinion-makers are trying to explain. **1909** *Westm. Gaz.* 16 June 1/3 The Conference at the Foreign Office..exceeded expectations. The question that out-shadowed all others at this council of 'opinion-making power' was..Imperial Defence. **1956** C. W. HILLS *Power Elite* xiii. 310 The means of opinion-making..have paralleled in range and efficiency the other institutions of greater scale. **1937** Opinion poll [implied in *public opinion poll*, sense 1 b above.] **1946** *Vogue* Aug. 2/2 Try a little opinion-poll for yourself. Ask a representative sample of Englishmen the following question: [etc.]. **1951** M. MCLUHAN *Mech. Bride* (1967) 46/2 Opinion polls function as educational rather than fact-finding agencies. **1965** *New Statesman* 30 Apr. 670/3 The substantial pro-Labour swing indicated by the opinion polls. **1971** *Guardian* 10 July 11/8 Mr Heath..interprets every unfavourable opinion poll as a clear signal that the public is one hundred per cent behind him. **1976** *Times* 27 Feb. 14/4 It is clear from opinion polls that the very large majority of people in Scotland wish to remain part of Britain. **1963** *Economist* 7 Dec. 1094/1 Opinion-polling is still a young..art in Spain. **1970** *Times* 2 June 1/2 The increase has no statistical significance when allowance is made for the tolerance limits of opinion polling. **1977** *Times* 18 Oct. 16/4 One of the weaknesses of much opinion-polling is that..it must exclude..extended questioning. **1951** M. MCLUHAN *Mech. Bride* (1967) 47/1 The cabdriver tends to be the opinion-pollster hero. **1970** *Times* 19 June 1/6 (*heading*) Opinion pollsters admit to wide margin of error. **1977** *News of World* 17 Apr. 1/1 Its existence is unknown to two out of every three women in the country, according to opinion pollsters. **1939** G. GALLUP *Public Opinion in Democracy* 12 If elections themselves do not impose clôture on debate, is it likely that opinion surveys will? **1958** *New Statesman* 23 Aug. 213/3 The first would entail many interviews with people by the well-tried opinion-survey methods. **1948** J. TOWSTER *Political Power in U.S.S.R.* vii. 153 The Party conference..is primarily..an opinion-tapping and effort-mobilizing agency.

opinionation (ǫpiːnyǒnēⁱ·ʃən). [f. OPINION *sb.* + -ATION.] The state or condition of persisting in holding a dogmatic opinion or opinions.

1925 *Inner Life* x. 184 Self-expression in the immature stages may become mere self-opinionation, with an unwillingness to heed advice or guidance. **1957** R. HOGGART *Uses of Literacy* vi. 167 It can be said, with some justice, that this is an age of 'opinionation', that though few people take the trouble thoroughly to understand any problem, a great many assume that their opinions on almost every general issue will have weight. **1960** *Times Lit. Suppl.* 27 May 339/1 What is expected of him is to..advise and comment on public affairs—..to add his mite to the flood of opinionation which is slopping over the world, obscuring the inner world of values.

opinionator. Delete †*Obs. rare* and add later examples.

1930 *New Statesman* 8 Nov. 147/1, I can only regret that Mr. West devotes so much of his space to Mr. Wells the opinionator instead of to Mr. Wells the artist. **1960** *Times Lit. Suppl.* 27 May 339/1 The opinionators..are quite ready to sign petitions and organize meetings, and to these the artist is supposed to contribute his ration of right-feeling and right-thinking. **1973** *Ibid.* 16 Mar. 294/2 A pleasure that ought never to be tasted by the professional opinionator. **1974** *Ibid.* 7 June 610/2 The age demands superstars, intellectual acrobatics, personality cults, instant opinionators.

opinionnaire (ǫpiːnyǒnēə·ɹ). Also **opinionaire.** [f. OPINION *sb.* + *-aire*, after *QUESTIONNAIRE.] A series of questions designed to gauge (public) opinion on a specific issue; a questionnaire.

A word of doubtful usefulness.—Ed.

1949 R. K. MERTON *Social Theory* II. 207 Interview techniques in all their numerous variety..questionnaires, opinionnaires and attitude tests. **1955** M. REIFER *Dict. New Words* 148 *Opinionaire*, a questionnaire to be filled in by various persons, for polling public opinion. **1964** P. MEADOWS in I. L. Horowitz *New Sociol.* 450 Researchers, equipped with pencils, pads, and opinionnaires, sought to throw on the screen of national attention the bright beams of percentages and averages of mass opinions. **1973** *Jrnl. Genetic Psychology* Mar. 56 Compliance was defined as correspondence between the child's report on an opinionnaire and the parent's report. **1975** *Bull. Canad. Assoc. Univ. Teachers* Feb. 7/3 The report..admonishes its reader not to rely on student opinionnaires in the evaluation of university teaching.

opioid (ōᵘ·pioid). [f. OPI(UM *sb.* + -OID.] = *OPIATE *sb.* 2.

1957 *Pharmaceutical Jrnl.* CLXXIX. 321/1 Acheson has suggested that the morphinans and other synthetic morphine substitutes should be called opioids. **1972** R. D. DRIPPS et al. *Introd. Anesthesia* (ed. 4) xxv. 347 Opioids administered intravenously..may be followed by hypotension. **1974** M. C. GERALD *Pharmacol.* xiii. 237 Synthetic narcotic agents or opioids, which bear only highly subtle similarities to the structure of morphine. **1974** *Nature* 20 Dec. 708/2 Antiserum obtained after immunisation with morphine-6-hemisuccinyl-bovine serum albumin..has highest and approximately equal affinity for morphine and heroin and progressively less for opioids of decreasing structural similarity.

O. Pip: see *O 5 d.

opisthe (ǫpi·sþi, ǫpī·st). *Biol.* [a. F. *opisthe* (Chatton & Lwoff 1936, in *Arch. de Zool. expér. et gén.* LXXVIII. 85), f. Gr. ὄπισθεν behind.] In ciliate protozoa, the posterior of the two organisms formed by transverse fission. Cf. *PROTER.

1950 A. LWOFF *Probl. Morphogenesis Ciliates* xi. 74 (*caption*) The peristome of the opisthe is formed from one kinetosome. **1961** MACKINNON & HAWES *Introd. Study Protozoa* iv. 214 At fission the organism [*sc.* a ciliate] divides to produce 2 daughters, an anterior proter and a posterior opisthe. **1977** *Jrnl. Protozool.* XXIV. 23/2 There is a need for enlargement or formation of oral parts such as..enlargement of oral structures in young opisthes.

opisthion (ǫpi·sþiǫn). *Anat.* [a. F. *opisthion* (P. Broca 1875, in *Bull. de la Soc. d'Anthrop. de Paris* X. 345), f. Gr. ὀπίσθιον hinder part.] (See quot. 1878.)

1878 R. T. H. BARTLEY *G. Topinard's Anthropol.* II. ii. 234 *Opisthion*, the posterior border of the occipital foramen at the median line. **1933** *Jrnl. R. Anthrop. Inst.* LXIII. 403 The remainder, which includes the opisthion, is missing. **1971** *Nature* 20 Aug. 568/1 Of the seven available specimens of *Homo erectus*, the positions of opisthion were uncertain in Java 1 and 6 and have been estimated in the literature.

opisthoglyph (ǫpi·sþoglif), *sb.* (*a.*) *Zool.* [a. F. *opisthoglyphe*, mod.L. *Opisthoglypha* (A. H. A. Dumeril 1853, in *Mém. Acad. Sci.* XXIII. 412) f. OPISTHO- + Gr. γλυφή carving.] A snake belonging to a group characterized by grooves in the upper back teeth. Also *attrib.* or as *adj.* So **opistho·glyphous** *a.*

1895 Opisthoglyphous [in Dict. s.v. OPISTHO-]. **1896** *Proc. Zool. Soc.* 615 The grooved teeth in the Opisthoglyphs vary in number from one to three. **1923** *Nature* 14 Apr. 579/1 A comparative study of the buccal glands and teeth of opisthoglyph snakes, and a discussion of the evolution of the order from Aglypha. **1965** R. & D. MORRIS *Men & Snakes* viii. 177 The aglyphs and the opisthoglyphs do not release their prey, once they have bitten it. **1968** R. D. MARTIN tr. *Wickler's Mimicry in Plants & Animals* xii. 112 The fangs may possess a groove that connects with the outlet of a poison gland. If the hind teeth in the upper jaws are grooved, they are called opisthoglyph. Snakes with grooved hind teeth are weakly to moderately poisonous. **1969** A. BELLAIRS *Life of Reptiles* I. v. 186 Each of the big teeth generally has a groove down its anterior face for carrying the venom into the prey. Snakes showing this condition are called 'back-fanged' or opisthoglyphous.

†**opitulation.** (Later example.)

1724 R. SUTTON *Let. to Sir T. Parkyns* (1726) 4, I received such Opitulation from your Dicæology.

opium, *sb.* Add: **1. b.** (Later examples.) Freq. referring to religion, esp. in phr. *the opium of the people* (see quot. 1844); also in *transf.* and allusive uses.

[**1840** HEINE *Ludwig Börne* IV. 287 Für Menschen, denen die Erde nichts mehr bietet, ward der Himmel erfunden... Heil dieser Erfindung! Heil einer Religion, die dem leidenden Menschengeschlecht in den bittern Kelch einige süsse, einschläfernde Tropfen goss, geistiges Opium. **1844** MARX 'Zur Kritik der Hegel'schen Rechts-Philosophie' in *Deutsch-Französische Jahrbücher* Feb. 72 Die Religion ist der Seufzer der bedrängten Kreatur, das Gemüth einer herzlosen Welt, wie sie der Geist geistloser Zustände ist. Sie ist das *Opium* des Volks.] **1848** *Politics for People* 27 May 58 We have used the Bible as if it was a mere special constable's handbook—an opium-dose for keeping beasts of burden patient while they were being overloaded—a mere book to keep the poor in order. **1860** GEO. ELIOT *Let.* 26 Dec. in J. W. Cross *George Eliot's Life* (1885) II. xi. 283, I have faith in the working out of higher possibilities than the Catholic or any other Church has presented... The 'highest calling and election' is to *do without opium*, and live through all our pain with conscious, clear-eyed endurance. **1881** T. S. EGAN tr. *Heine's Ludwig Börne* IV. 169 For these people, to whom this world had nothing more to offer, Heaven was invented... Hail to this invention! Hail to that religion which could pour a few sweet soporific drops into the bitter cup of the suffering human race, spiritual opium. **1926** H. J. STENNING tr. *Marx's Selected Ess.* 12 Religion is the moan of the oppressed creature, the sentiment of a heartless world, as it is the spirit of spiritless conditions. It is the opium of the people. **1939** G. B. SHAW *Geneva* I. 28 Karl Marx—Antichrist—said that the sweet and ennobling consolations of our faith are opium given to the poor to enable them to endure the hardships of that state of life to which it has pleased God to call them. **1951** N. ANNAN *Leslie Stephen* vii. 201 Kingsley might protest that religion was being used as opium for the people. **1957** tr. *M. de Unamuno's San Manuel Bueno* 39 One of those leaders of what they call the social revolution has said that religion is the opium of the people. Opium...opium... opium, yes. Let us give them opium and let them sleep and dream. **1968** *Daily Tel.* (Colour Suppl.) 13 Dec. 43/4

Drink, in other words, is becoming the opium of the people. **1971** G. Steiner *In Bluebeard's Castle* iv. 93 A good deal of classical music is, today, the opium of the good citizen. **1974** *Times Lit. Suppl.* 28 June 692/5 A revue like *Here is the News* only shows politics becoming the opium of the people.

3. b. *opium addict, cellar, cigarette, -dealer, haul, house, -pipe, -smoker* (examples), *-smoking* (later example), *-smuggler, -taking* (earlier examples). **c. opium den** (earlier and later examples); **opium dream,** a dream during an opium-induced sleep; also in extended use; **opium joint** (earlier and later examples); **opium poppy,** substitute for def.: the white poppy, *Papaver somniferum*; (examples); **opium war,** a war waged by Britain against China (1839–42) following China's attempt to prohibit the importation of opium into China; also, a later war (1856–60) against China by Britain and France.

1974 *Times* 2 Dec. 8/7 Charles was a charming opium addict and rural clergyman. **1911** O. Onions *Widdershins* 278 He took me into an opium-cellar within a stone's throw of Oxford Street. **1920** Opium cigarette [see *heroin]. **1841** J. Sturge *Let.* 30 Sept. in *Visit to U.S. in 1841* (1842) p. lxiv, Waging a murderous war to compel them to make restitution to the contraband opium dealers. **1977** 'J. Le Carré' *Hon. Schoolboy* xviii. 451 By afternoon he was airborne, and..chatting merrily to a couple of friendly opium dealers. **1882** J. D. McCabe *New York* 590 Here are the headquarters of the Mongolians, their..opium dens. **1921** *Daily Colonist* (Victoria, B.C.) 25 Mar. 6/4 Lee Fong was charged in the City Police Court yesterday with being the keeper of an opium den at 536 Cormorant Street; and also with being in unlawful possession of opium. **1969** Opium-den [see *Chinatown]. **1821** Byron *Don Juan* iv. xix. 201 This is in others a fictitious state, An opium dream of too much youth and reading. **1922** W. S. Maugham *Writer's Notebk.* (1949) 202 Singapore: Opium Dream. I saw a road lined on each side with tall poplars. **1974** J. Philips *Power Killers* (1975) i. ii. 18 What about his theory? It sounds like an opium dream. **1975** *Listener* 11 Sept. 343/2 *Who Am I Now?*, a fantasy based..on the opium dreams of George Crabbe. **1974** *Evening News* 27 June 1/7 (*headline*) £250,000 opium haul. **1888** Kipling *Plain Tales from Hills* 233 It was a *pukka*, respectable opium-house, and not one of those stifling, sweltering *chardoo-khanas*. **1966** 'A. Hall' *9th Directive* vi. 54 The opium house at the Phra Chao. **1882** H. H. Kane *Opium-Smoking* 5 The principal places, known as 'opium joints', are in Mott, Pell, and Park streets. **1926** *Daily Colonist* (Victoria, B.C.) 4 July 6/2 Charged with being inmates of an opium joint in Theatre Alley, Lee and Jim, Chinese, were each fined $15. **1890** Kipling *City of Dreadful Night* (1891) vi. 40 The lamp for the opium-pipe is the only one in the room. **1976** M. Butterworth *Festival!* i. 12 A crude photo print of a naked youth.. carrying an opium pipe. **1863** Opium poppy [see Poppy *sb.* 3]. **1880** Bentley & Trimen *Medicinal Plants* I. 18 It cannot be said that the opium poppy is known anywhere in a thoroughly wild condition. **1921** A. Huxley *Crome Yellow* xxii. 247 They passed a bed of opium poppies, dispetaled now. **1931** M. Grieve *Mod. Herbal* II. 651 The Opium Poppy..is indigenous to Asia Minor, and is cultivated largely in European and Asiatic Turkey, Persia, India and China for the production of Opium. **1975** *Times* 31 May 5/3 (*caption*) Peasant women tilling an opium poppy field in Turkey. **1860** H. Greeley *Overland Journey* 259 [The Chinaman] is..an opium-smoker. **1921** *Daily Colonist* (Victoria, B.C.) 1 Apr. 6/4 The magistrate said that the accused had admitted ownership of the opium smoking paraphernalia, and to being an opium smoker himself. **1971** *Listener* 11 Nov. 644/1 A large existing market of opium-smokers. **1938** N. Marsh *Artists in Crime* (U.S.) xiii. 202 Fox had found Malmsley's opium-smoking impedimenta. **1976** *Times* 4 Sept. 7/4 What are the pros and cons of opium smoking? **1841** J. Sturge *Let.* 30 Sept. in *Visit to U.S. in 1841* (1842) p. lxii, To take under his protection one of the most extensive opium smugglers. **1966** J. Cleary *High Commissioner* iii. 50 The Chinese opium smugglers he had met before he had gone on to the Murder Squad. **1975** M. Stern in L. M. Alcott *Behind Mask* p. xxi, William Henry Thomes..had sailed aboard an opium smuggler that plied between China and California, and was himself a mine of suggestions for authors whose thrilling romances he would publish. **1821** De Quincey *Confess.* (1822) ii. 90 The whole art and mystery of opium-taking. **1836** H. C. Robinson *Diary* 29 Aug. (1967) 161 A letter written by Coleridge..in which he gives an account of his sad habit of opium-taking. **1841** J. Sturge *Let.* 30 Sept. in *Visit to U.S. in 1841* (1842) p. lxi, Opium War with China. **1917** *Encycl. Sinica* 406/1 The action which forced the foreign merchants at Canton to deliver up their stocks of opium, which was destroyed by the Commissioner, and the subsequent events which led to war with Great Britain. This has been called the 'Opium War'. **1969** V. G. Kiernan *Lords of Human Kind* v. 148 The West resorted to force, and the Opium Wars of 1840–42 and 1856–60..inducted China into..the comity of nations. **1974** *Listener* 8 Aug. 175/1 The Opium War totally destroyed Chinese confidence.

opopanax. 2. (Earlier and later examples.)

1867 *Gardeners' Chron.* 29 June 690/1 New Perfumes.—Opoponax. **1913** [see *mignonette 1 d]. **1924** Galsworthy *White Monkey* i. vii. 55 A profiteer who dropped his aitches and reeked of opoponax.

opossum. Add: **2.** (Further examples.)

Now normally replaced in Australian usage by *possum* but still the more usual form in New Zealand.

1911 C. E. W. Bean *'Dreadnought' of Darling* xvii. 162 Australia, at one time, along with its harmless marsupial kangaroos, opossums..and the rest, had its own beasts of prey. **1911** E. M. Clowes *On Wallaby* ii. 19 The only possible chance visitor is an occasional opossum on the roof. **1944** *Living off Land* iii. 57 To improvise a water container, copy the blacks, who used the skins of opossums. **1968** *Wanganui* (N.Z.) *Chron.* 15 Nov. 10/6 (Advt.), Opossum skins. Good prices, wanted immediately for overseas contract. **1973** *Massey Ferguson Rev.* (N.Z.) Mar.–Apr. 8/3 Intensive control measures around the farms by the New Zealand Forest Service and local pest destruction boards have reduced opossum numbers with the aim that this will break the cattle infection cycle and stop Tb-tested cattle from becoming re-infected.

opo·ssuming, *vbl. sb.* [-ing[1].] Opossum-hunting.

1917 'H. H. Richardson' *Fortunes R. Mahony* iii. iv. 211 There is to be opossuming and a moonlight picnic to-night.

opotherapy (ǫpǒþe·răpi). *Med.* [f. Gr. ὀπός juice + Therapy.] = *organotherapy.

1897 *Index Medicus* XIX. 899/2 Opotherapy. **1899** *Ann. Rep. Board of Regents Smithsonian Inst. 1897–98* 696 An entire new method, designated under the name of opotherapy, or treatment by organic extracts. **1902** *Brit. Med. Jrnl.* 12 Apr. 909/1 (*heading*) Placentophagy and placental opotherapy. **1908** *Practitioner* Mar. 412 The many different substances recently utilised in opotherapy. **1915** [see *ketogenetic* adj. s.v. *keto- a].

oppo (ǫ·po). *slang* (orig. Forces'). Abbrev. of **opposite number*.

1939 *Airman's Gaz.* Dec., Get an oppo to relieve you for 'break'. **1942** *Gen* 1 Sept. 13/2 A sweetheart or companion in the navy is an 'oppo'. **1948** Partridge *Dict. Forces' Slang* 133 *Oppo*,... In the Navy and Air Force; a companion..or even one's wife. **1955** P. Wildeblood *Against Law* 99 Me and my oppo was in the Royal Navy. **1961** F. H. Burgess *Dict. Sailing* 154 *Opposite number, oppo*, one of two hands who perform similar duties alternately; he may be on another ship or station. **1962** K. Dobbs *Running to Paradise* 49 My oppo, my best friend in the mess, was a former Sussex poacher. **1967** D. Reeman *Deep Silence* iii. 48 Me an' the kid is oppos, see? **1971** B. W. Aldiss *Soldier Erect* 101 He's dotty on them Wog gods, aren't you, Stubby, me old oppo? **1973** *Times* 24 May 18/4 He was Mr Justice Lawson,..and what is more he was accompanied by his oppo, Mr Justice Mais.

opponens (ǒpōu·nĕnz), *a. Anat.* [L., pr. pple. of *opponere* to set against.] Used, ellipt. as sb. (L. *musculus* being usu. omitted), in the names of four pairs of small muscles of the hands and feet: the *opponens pollicis*, which helps to draw the thumb across the palm; the *opponens digiti minimi*, which helps to raise the little finger when the palm is stretched out flat; the *opponens digiti minimi*, of the foot; and (seldom distinguished) the *opponens hallucis* of the foot. Cf. Opponent *a.* 3.

1797 J. Bell *Anat. Bones* ii. iii. 280 The opponens pollicis, is often called the metacarpal of the thumb. **1836–9** R. B. Todd *Cycl. Anat. & Physiol.* II. 519/2 Flexor ossis metacarpi, or opponens pollicis..of a rhomboidal form. *Ibid.* 521/1 Adductor ossis metacarpi or opponens minimi digiti. **1902** D. J. Cunningham *Text-bk. Anat.* 329 The opponens minimi digiti..arises from the anterior annular ligament and the hook of the unciform bone. **1967** G. M. Wyburn et al. *Conc. Anat.* ii. 68/2 The opponens..is inserted into the shaft of the 1st metacarpal bone. **1973** *Gray's Anat.* (ed. 35) 582/2 Part of the muscle [*sc.* the adductor hallucis] may be attached to the first metatarsal, constituting an opponens hallucis.

opportunism. Add: **1. b.** *Socialism* and *Communism.* A policy of concessions to bourgeois elements of society in the development towards socialism.

1902 *Social-Democrat* Aug. 232 Bernstein's position leads him straight to opportunism, the denial of the class war, reform-politics, classes working together for the common good.., &c. **1903** [see *Marxism[1]]. **1921** in J. Degras *Communist Internat. Documents* (1956) I. 247 The parties of the Communist International will become revolutionary mass parties only if they overcome opportunism, its survivals and traditions, in their own ranks. **1930** M. J. Olgin tr. *Lenin's Conference of Foreign Sect. of R.S.-D.L.P.* in *Coll. Wks.* XVIII. 148 The collapse of the Second International is the collapse of Socialist opportunism. *Ibid.*, The crisis created by the war has exposed the real substance of opportunism, revealing it in the role of a direct aid to the bourgeoisie against the proletariat. **1934** tr. Lenin in *Lenin on Britain* iv. i. 149 To explain to the masses the inevitability and the necessity of breaking with opportunism, to educate them for revolution by a merciless struggle against opportunism,..is the only Marxian line to be followed in the world labour movement.—*Autumn* 1916. **1942** M. J. Olgin tr. *Lenin's Imperialism* in *Coll. Wks.* XIX. 194 That bond between imperialism and opportunism, which revealed itself first and most clearly in England. **1957** R. N. C. Hunt *Guide to Communist Jargon* 101 Opportunism stood for that disposition of mind which rejected Marx's revolutionary teaching, with its insistence upon the total destruction of the capitalist system, in favour of concessions made by the bourgeoisie within its framework. **1974** tr. *Sniečkus's Soviet Lithuania* 26 In its relentless struggle against reformism, opportunism and Trotskyism, it [*sc.* the Lithuanian Communist Party] became even more Bolshevik in character.

2. Opportunistic state or activity. **a.** *Med.* (See *opportunistic *a.* 3.)

1962 *Laboratory Investigation* XI. 1073/1 The concept of microbial opportunism as an important occasional factor in the etiology of infectious disease has been generally recognized and its validity has been accepted.

b. *Ecol.* (See *opportunistic *a.* 2.)

1967 G. E. Hutchinson *Treat. Limnol.* II. xxii. 366 There is reason to believe that the same sort of lognormal distribution may arise by a process of evolutionary opportunism among competitive species. **1973** P. A. Colinvaux *Introd. Ecol.* xxvii. 392 If you are small and short-lived, opportunism is probably the only satisfactory strategy for life in unstable places, but if you are big, and with a low metabolic rate,..you may just sit tight through the bad times, living on your reserves and reducing your life processes to the minimum.

opportunist. Add: **1. a.** *spec.* in Socialism and Communism, an advocate of opportunism (sense *1 b).

1902 *Fortn. Rev.* Jan. 128 The mountain of the [German Social Democratic] party joined hands with the Opportunists. **1903** *Social-Democrat* VII. 87 It is constantly being brought as a reproach against the German Party that they were more severe with the revolutionary dissenters from the party theory than they have been with the opportunists. **1909** M. Epstein tr. *Sombart's Socialism & Social Movement* ii. iii. 217 All authoritative Revisionists, Opportunists, Reformers..stand firm for the class war, and..desire the total abolition of the capitalist system, and not merely its reformation. **1919** Trotsky in J. Degras *Communist Internat. Documents* (1956) I. 41 The opportunists, who before the world war appealed to the workers to practise moderation for the sake of the gradual transition to socialism. **1930** M. J. Olgin tr. *Lenin's Conference of Foreign Sect. of R.S.-D.L.P.* in *Coll. Wks.* XVIII. 149 It would be a harmful illusion to hope to restore a real Socialist International without drawing a clear line of organisational demarcation between real Socialists and opportunists. **1934** tr. Lenin in *Lenin on Britain* iv. i. 142 The *opportunists* (social-chauvinists) are working together with the imperialist bourgeoisie..in the direction of creating an imperialist Europe on the backs of Asia and Africa;..the *opportunists* are a section of the petty bourgeoisie [etc.]... *Autumn* 1916.

b. (Examples in Socialist and Communist sense.)

1902 *Fortn. Rev.* Jan. 129 Where Marx is fatalistic, Bernstein is opportunist. **1903** *Social-Democrat* VII. 86 To turn..to the German Party, the opportunist tendency has naturally always existed. **1929** J. Fineberg tr. *Selections from Lenin* I. 177 Axelrod and Martov..have dropped into the opportunist wing of our Party... They have to repeat opportunist phrases..to seek..some kind of justification for their position. **1934** tr. Lenin in *Lenin on Britain* v. iv. 212 The victory of the revolutionary proletariat is impossible..unless the opportunist social-traitor leaders are exposed, disgraced and driven out... *April–May* 1920. **1974** tr. *Sniečkus's Soviet Lithuania* 12 A reformist opportunist trend..had developed on the basis of the petty-bourgeois nationalistic ideology. **1974** J. White tr. *Poulantzas's Fascism & Dictatorship* iv. i. 147 The 'left opportunist' elements bore a very grave responsibility in the advent of fascism.

2. *Med.* An opportunistic fungus or micro-organism (see *opportunistic *a.* 3). Also *attrib.* or as *adj.*

1937 M. Frobisher *Fund. Bacteriol.* xiv. 138 These organisms..do not initiate the rot. They are opportunists. **1967** *Jrnl. Hygiene* LXV. 575 (*heading*) Classification of *Mycobacterium avium* and related opportunist mycobacteria met in England and Wales. *Ibid.*, Overt opportunist infection. **1973** *Amer. Jrnl. Med.* LV. 862/1 As an opportunist, its ability to produce human disease depends not on its intrinsic virulence but on abnormalities of host defenses. **1976** *Lancet* 27 Nov. 1169/1 There was no evidence of opportunist infection.

3. *Ecol.* An opportunistic species (see *opportunistic *a.* 2). Also *attrib.* or as *adj.*

1970 *Lethaia* III. 70 Even in habitats of low physicochemical stress and great stability, opportunists may participate in occasional invasions of an otherwise stable fauna. **1973** P. A. Colinvaux *Introd. Ecol.* xvii. 392 It is opportunist animals..which, exposed to hazard of weather in their normal lives, are most likely to have their numbers curbed by accident of weather. *Ibid.* 393 Opportunists, being specialists at dispersion, are likely to get there first but, since the fresh bare ground may be in a place of generally stable climate, the equilibrium species will not be far behind. The opportunists enjoy the new land only briefly, after which they are eliminated by competition. **1975** *Nature* 20 Nov. 197/1 These data suggest that birch is behaving as an opportunist in the composition of the forest.

opportunistic, *a.* Add: **1.** (Further examples.)

1958 J. Baldwin in W. King *Black Short Story Anthol.* (1972) 284 Their religion was strongly mixed with an opportunistic respectability and with ambitions to better society and their own place in it. **1976** *Brit. Jrnl. Sociol.* XXVII. 89 The common man is portrayed as the innocent and helpless victim of opportunistic and self-serving politicians who must be replaced by enlightened and benign rulers. **1976** *Publishers Weekly* 15 Mar. 118/3 An opportunistic TV programmer brings him to New York and takes an exploitation piece. **1977** *Listener* 20 Oct. 515 The ebullient..Furnivall comes out of it badly (vain, unprincipled,..opportunistic, unscholarly—though no one contributed more quotations for the dictionary).

2. *Ecol.* Of a species: especially suited to unexploited or newly formed habitats and occurring in populations whose size is not determined primarily by their density, being characterized by poor competitiveness in relation to other species and an ability to increase rapidly in numbers and to disperse readily.

1960 R. MacArthur in *Amer. Naturalist* XCIV. 33 A distinction is made between opportunistic and equilibrium species. **1974** *Jrnl. Marine Res.* XXXII. 267 *Capitella capitella* and the other relatively opportunistic species discussed may be continuously present if the environment is unpredictable or may disappear as in the case of recovery following the oil spill.

3. *Med.* Of a fungus or micro-organism: not normally pathogenic but becoming so in certain circumstances, as when the body is rendered vulnerable by other agencies. Of an infection: caused by such an organism.

[**1955** *Sci. Amer.* May 31/2 Was it not possible, they argued, that the bacteria were only the secondary cause of disease—opportunistic invaders of tissues already weakened by crumbling defenses?] **1962** *Ann. N.Y. Acad. Sci.* XCVIII. 617 (*heading*) Experiences with and diagnosis of diseases due to opportunistic fungi. **1962** *Laboratory Investigation* XI. 1073/1 Opportunistic infections by bacteria, viruses, and protozoa are known. **1970** C. W. Emmons et al. *Med. Mycol.* (ed. 2) 3 The fungi which cause systemic and subcutaneous mycoses have been called 'opportunistic fungi' to emphasize the aspect of a normally saprobic fungus which can suddenly become parasitic and pathogenic when it is introduced by inhalation or traumatic implantation into the human body... It has also been used to designate fungi which cause disease only in a patient with a concurrent disease which increases his susceptibility, or in one whose innate immunity has been otherwise impaired. **1973** *Chest* LXIII. 4/1 Even more striking is the rise of opportunistic fungal infections accompanying: transplantation, immunosuppression, heart surgery and intravenous hyperalimentation. Today one can no longer accept a culture report of 'nonpathogenic fungus isolated', for indeed there may be no truly nonpathogenic fungus.

Hence **o:pportuni·stically** *adv.*, in an opportunist manner.

1958 *Times* 27 Dec. 2/4 In one brief interlude Phillips nearly scored opportunistically at the other end. **1960** W. V. Quine *Word & Object* v. 188 We can vacillate between two, opportunistically enjoying their incompatible advantages. **1972** *Maclean's Mag.* Sept. 10/1 He will act with expediency but not often, I think, opportunistically. **1976** *Sci. Amer.* Apr. 117/2 At the same time the adults will feed opportunistically on lesser prey: frogs, crabs and small fish.

opportunity. Add: **2. c.** *equality of opportunity*: equal chance and right to seek success in one's chosen sphere regardless of social factors such as class, race, religion, and sex.

1891 *Econ. Rev.* I. 474 It will possibly, however, be contended that here the ideal is equality of Opportunity. **1920** M. Beer *Hist. Brit. Socialism* II. xiv. 295 By 'equality of opportunity' Fabian women do not necessarily mean 'similarity of opportunity'. **1920** H. G. Wells *Outl. Hist.* II. ix. xli. 754/2 A sufficient measure of social justice, to ensure health, education, and a rough equality of opportunity. **1930** W. K. Hancock *Australia* ix. 183 Equality of opportunity implies free scope for natural talent, which must create new inequalities; whereas what Australian democracy desires is equality of enjoyment. **1950** G. B. Shaw *Farfetched Fables* 67 Democratic civilization is impossible, because equality of opportunity is impossible. **1973** R. R. Palmer in P. P. Wiener *Dict. Hist. Ideas* II. 146/2 The key words are fair competition, equality of opportunity, reward for merit, and careers open to talent. **1976** R. Williams *Keywords* 102 *Equality of opportunity*..can be glossed as 'equal opportunity to become unequal'.

7. Phr. *opportunity knocks* (*but once*): an opportunity presents itself (but once).

1942 Wodehouse *Money in Bank* (1946) xv. 134 Opportunity knocks but once, and he had allowed it to knock in vain. **1946** *Calif. Folklore Q.* July 241 A number of sayings surely not peculiar to Oregon; rather, trite and obvious, but still effective:..Opportunity knocks but once. **1970** *Computers & Humanities* V. 16 From the earliest English settlements to the closing of the frontier and the advent of industrialism, opportunity knocked for young men of high and low social status at fairly regular alternate intervals. **1970** *Globe & Mail* (Toronto) 28 Sept. 29/4 (Advt.), Opportunity knocks for a fluently bilingual representative over 25 with a B.Sc. **1972** *Accountant* 21 Sept. p. xvii/1 (Advt.), Opportunity knocks for an experienced qualified man.

8. *attrib.* and *Comb.* **opportunity cost** *Econ.* (see quots.); **opportunity state,** a country which offers many opportunities for advancement.

1911 H. J. Davenport in *Amer. Econ. Rev.* Dec. 725 These displacements of possible products, these foregoings of alternative openings, these sacrifices of some second thing in the process of getting some particular thing, are perhaps best indicated under the term *opportunity cost.* To go without fish to get game..may be taken as illustrative of one of the simplest aspects of the doctrine. **1926** L. D. Edie *Econ.* III. viii. 121 The opportunity cost is the sacrifice of foregoing some alternative utility. **1936** Ault & Eberling *Princ. & Probl. Econ.* xiii. 217 Opportunity or alternative costs play a very important part in determining the nature and direction of industrial development... The principle of opportunity cost is effective in bringing about great changes in the field of production. **1951** J. R. Winton *Dict. Econ. Terms* (ed. 3) 63 *Opportunity cost.* In economic life, decisions are constantly being made which involve a choice between alternatives... One particular alternative must be chosen, ..the 'opportunity-cost' of which is represented by the alternatives foregone. **1964** Gould & Kolb *Dict. Social Sci.* 143/2 The determination of implicit cost, as well as other managerial decisions, must be based on the concept of alternative or opportunity costs, which measures cost in terms of alternatives or opportunities that are foregone. **1965** Seldon & Pennance *Everyman's Dict. Econ.* 312 To answer the question, 'Should good agricultural land be built over?' requires a comparison of the opportunity costs for society of the various alternatives. **1971** D. C. Hague *Managerial Econ.* (rev. ed.) II. v. 121 A very useful concept is that of 'opportunity cost'... If the businessman would have invested the money at 10 per cent interest, had he not put it into the business, then the 'opportunity cost' of investing in his own business is the 10 per cent interest he has foregone. **1974** *Guardian* 27 Aug. 14/7 Couples in the United States..are well aware of the opportunity cost of having children. **1957** Opportunity state [see *contract *v.* 2 d]. **1958** *Listener* 26 June 1068/3 The mental distance between himself and his appalling younger daughters, products of the opportunity state, is brilliantly suggested.

opposed, *ppl. a.* Add: **1. b.** *Mech.* (Having pistons) arranged in pairs moving in opposite directions along the same straight line.

1910 W. A. Tookey tr. *Mathot's Construction & Working Internal Combustion Eng.* v. 71 In Europe, the two-cylinder 'twin' engine soon displaced the type with opposed or *vis-à-vis* cylinders, because the latter gave a great deal of trouble in practical work. **1925** A. W. Judge *Automobile Engines* iii. 87 Although the balance and torque of the opposed two-cylinder engine are excellent, the overall length and the cylinder dimensions limit it to power units of about 12 to 15 H.P. (maximum) for car use. **1932** A. F. Evans *Hist. Oil Engine* ii. 71 In the 'seventies we had engines with opposed pistons in one cylinder. **1966** G. F. Allen *Brit. Rail after Beeching* iv. 115 English Electric took an intricate but compact 18-cylinder opposed-piston engine originally applied to fast, small naval craft..and with it achieved a six-axle 3,300 h.p. diesel-electric unit. **1977** *Lancashire Life* Jan. 79/1 The horizontally opposed engine is air cooled.

opposer. Add: **1. b.** (Usu. with capital initial.) One of two examiners formerly appointed to carry out at Winchester College the elections to New College, Oxford. Cf. Poser[1] I.

Rarely used, in preference to *poser*, even before 1901 (P. Yeats-Edwards, Fellows' librarian, Winchester College, private communication 28 Jan. 1977).

1891 R. G. K. Wrench *Winchester Word-bk.* 32 *Poser*, an examiner. A very old word: also still used at Eton. *Apposer* and *opposer* are other old forms of it. **1901** Rashdall & Rait *New College* vi. 132 The Warden and Opposers are not to take bribes.

opposite, *a.*, *sb.* (*adv.*, *prep.*). Add: **A.** *adj.* **5.** *opposite number*, a person or thing similarly placed in another set, etc., to the given one; a partner, a counterpart; an opponent.

1906 Kipling *Actions & Reactions* (1909) 202 'And your Opposite Number?' Penfentenyou described him. **1915** 'Bartimeus' *Tall Ship* iv. 84 We were 'opposite numbers' at your brother's wedding. **1917** *Times* 7 May 6/2 The establishment of personal contact between Sir William Robertson and his opposite number, General Pétain. **1917** E. Wallace *Kate plus Ten* (1919) vi. 107 Pick up Mr. Fretherston and don't lose him—you may choose your own opposite number. **1927** *Observer* 24 July 4/6 The 'A.A.'s' opposite number..the Automobile Association of America..has issued a very interesting map of the United States. **1969** *Times* 13 Mar. 25/2 (*caption*) The model bison the papermakers' association got from its Polish opposite numbers. **1973** J. Rossiter *Manipulators* xiii. 134 Before leaving for B Division he should have telephoned his opposite number there, clearing his proposed incursion on to another's territory.

B. *sb.* **3.** (Later example.)

1874 Swinburne *Bothwell* IV. v. 397 The task was hard with Knox for opposite To bend the council.

C. quasi-*adv.* **3.** *to play opposite*: to have (a specified actor or actress) as one's leading man or lady. Also in similar phrases.

1926 J. Agate in *Sunday Times* 7 Feb. 6/1 'Opposite him,' as they say, was Miss Ilise Marvenga, who..made Kathie into a semblance of one of those expensive mechanical dolls with a staccato utterance. **1931** P. MacDonald *Crime Conductor* II. iv. 178 Mary Wheelwright—England's Première Leading Lady—was not to play 'opposite' Kristania in *Harlequin's Holiday.* **1936** *Times Lit. Suppl.* 31 Oct. 894/3 He was to play 'opposite to' Anna Kenney, a very famous figure on the stage.

oppositely, *adv.* Add: **1.** (Later examples.)

c **1864** E. Dickinson *Poems* (1955) II. 695 A Suspicion.. That I am looking oppositely For the site of the Kingdom of Heaven—. **1929** R. Bridges *Testament Beauty* iii. 129 Thatt other hath the arm bent down and oppositely nerved.

2. b. (Later examples.)

1909 *Bodleian* Mar. 3/1 'You can have a dead rat,.. but not a dead artist.' But oppositely, and appositely, a dead rat has no signification. **1972** *Science* 27 Oct. 425/1 Or, oppositely, should we encourage economic growth.

opposition. Add: **4. e.** *Semantics.* The state or condition of being opposite in meaning; the relationship between antonyms.

1870 [see Antonym]. **1925** P. Radin tr. *J. Vendryès's Language* III. iii. 218 Among animal names the same opposition is frequent. Latin had *equus* and *equa*... In English *horse* is apposed to *mare.* **1932** C. K. Ogden *Opposition* i. 8 The theory of opposition offers a new method of approach not only in the case of all those words which can best be defined in terms of their opposites..but also to *any* word whose use may give rise to controversy. **1963** J. Lyons *Structural Semantics* iv. 68 The polarity of a term is a function of its opposition to its antonym, and not vice versa. **1967** R. A. Waldron *Sense & Sense Devel.* v. 107 *Black* and *white* are often two ends of a scale but in 'people are inclined to see things in black and white'..the pair is taken as the type of all 'either/or' antonymic opposition. **1976** F. R. Palmer *Semantics* iv. 82 A quite different kind of 'opposite' is found with pairs of words which exhibit the reversal of a relationship between items... Lyons suggests the term *converseness* for these, but I am more concerned to point out their essentially relational characteristics, and would thus prefer *relational opposition.*

f. *Linguistics.* A functional, or potentially functional, contrast between partially similar linguistic elements.

[**1931** *Travaux Cercle Ling. Prague* IV. 311 *Opposition phonologique*..—Différence phonique susceptible de servir, dans une langue donnée, à la différenciation des significations intellectuelles.] **1936** *Amer. Speech* XI. 110 A 'phonological system' is defined as the ensemble of phonological oppositions proper to a given language. **1953** [see *binary *a.* k]. **1963** J. Lyons *Structural Semantics* iv. 68 In Russian or German..there is an opposition to be recognized, in word-initial and word-medial position, between the voiced and the voiceless plosives. **1970** G. C. Lepschy *Survey Struct. Ling.* iii. 58 In order to have distinctive function, speech sounds must be opposed to each other (distinction presupposes opposition). An opposition can be either *distinctive* (or *phonological*), or non-distinctive. Only sounds which may occur in the same context (i.e. that are permutable) can be in opposition. **1972** M. L. Samuels *Ling. Evol.* viii. 171 In the fifteenth and sixteenth centuries there are signs that the opposition /ɛ∼ɑ/ in class III verbs is no longer adequate. **1978** *Jrnl. Lancs. Dial. Soc.* Jan. 20 The opposition between the reflex of ME ui/oi and ME *i* is preserved.

8. *opposition bench*(*es*) (examples), *party*, *spokesman.*

1815 N. W. Wraxall *Hist. Mem.* II. 167 The Treasury Bench, as well as the Places behind it, had been for so many years occupied by Lord North and his friends, that it became difficult to recognize them again in their new Seats, dispersed over the Opposition Benches, in great coats, frocks, and boots. **1819** Keats *Cap & Bells* in R. M. Milnes *Life, Lett., & Lit. Remains J. Keats* (1848) II. 221 I'll make the opposition-benches wince. **1976** *Hansard Commons* 7 Dec. 252 The Government..cannot accept views expressed from the Opposition Benches... I object strongly to that. *Ibid.* 8 Dec. 570, I am far more concerned about the measures that would be enacted by the rabble sitting on the Opposition Benches if they were in Government. **1795** tr. *C. P. Moritz's Trav.* 60 They tell me, that at these elections when there is a strong opposition-party, there is often bloody work. **1824** J. S. Mill in *Westm. Rev.* I. 505 The Edinburgh Review..has really exhibited the vices, which we described as likely to characterize a periodical publication attached to the Opposition party. **1930** G. B. Shaw *Apple Cart* p. xxiii, Nothing has any sense or reality in it except the vituperation of the opposition party. **1974** *Times* 12 June 2/5 Mr Heseltine, Opposition spokesman on trade, said..yesterday [etc.].

oppositionary (ǫpǒzi·ʃənări), *a. rare.* [f. Opposition + -ary[1].] = Oppositional *a.* 2.

1926 *Contemp. Rev.* Sept. 276 Petrograd ('Leningrad') became the centre of Zinoviev's oppositionary activity.

oppositionist, *sb.* and *adj.* (Later examples.)

1962 S. E. Finer *Man on Horseback* xii. 231 The members of the nationalist movement have been reared in an oppositionist mentality. **1963** *Cambr. Rev.* 4 May 405/2 An individual perception of reality—as distinguished from a conformist perception, whether it be 'official' or 'oppositionist'—is of value and interest. **1965** A. Nove in B. Pearce tr. *Preobrazhensky's New Economics* p. xiv, Like other former oppositionists he came to the Congress to apologize for past misdeeds and to denounce Trotsky. **1971** I. Deutscher *Marxism in our Time* (1972) vi. 113 In June 1957, exactly twenty-five years will have elapsed since I was expelled from the Party as an oppositionist. **1973** *Sunday Advocate-News* (Barbados) 16 Dec. 4/3 The Consul-General attributed the rumours to be the work of 'oppositionists' who he said are trying to embarrass the Government.

oppositious (ǫpǒzi·ʃəs), *a. rare.* [f. Oppos(ite *a.* + -itious[2].] Inclined to oppose; recalcitrant.

1923 *Blackw. Mag.* Aug. 176/2 He became oppositious on leaving truly delectable posadas to left and right.

opposive, *a.* Delete †*Obs.*—[1] and add later example. *rare.*

1911 W. De Morgan *Likely Story* 107 He had an opposive or lazy disposition.

oppre·ssingly, *adv. rare.* [-ly[2].] So as to oppress or be oppressive; oppressively.

1925 *Glasgow Herald* 17 May 7/1 That it [*sc.* the cost] is oppressingly large no one will deny.

oppressive, *a.* Add: **2.** Also with *of.*

1972 *Times* 10 Mar. 9/1 The art world is so international today that it is not oppressive of a world-renowned art dealer living in France to have an action against him tried in England.

opry (ǫ·pri), representation of a U.S. dial. pronunc. of Opera; also *attrib. Grand Ole Opry*: a concert of country music broadcast on radio from Nashville, Tennessee; the type of music performed there.

Grand Ole Opry is registered as a proprietary name in the U.S.

1914 R. Grau *Theatre of Science* 23 The local manager could not see any future in exhibiting films, so he went back to the town where he had his 'op'ry house'. **1950** *Official Gaz.* (U.S. Patent Office) 18 Apr. 723/1 WSM, Incorporated, Nashville, Tenn. Grand Ole Opry. For radio program broadcasting services. **1957** *Time* 15 Apr. 49/1 Donegan..often..sounds like *Grand Ole Opry* cornball recorded at 33⅓ r.p.m. played at 78. **1961** A. Berkman *Singers' Gloss. Show Business* 64 *Opry*,..opera. **1968** *Rolling Stone* 24 Aug. 17/3 Roy Acuff tried unsuccessfully to give the audience a taste of Grand Ole Opry. He was too corny for most people's taste. **1974** *New Yorker* 6 May 46/1 They asked me where I was going. I said, To Nashville to see the Grand Ole Opry. Friday is the last show..before the Opry moves out to Opryland U.S.A. **1976** *Time* 27 Sept. 98/1 For the mass market, cruder Southern products flooded the land: hillbilly music, gospel music, the Grand Ole Opry. **1977** *Parade* (*Washington Post*) 9 Oct. 12/3 Grand Ole Opry began in 1925 almost incidentally, when Nashville station WSM put on an hour-long program featuring a country fiddler named Uncle Jimmy Thompson. The show happened to follow a broadcast of Walter Damrosch's music appreciation hour from New York, so announcer George D. Hay started out by saying: 'For the past hour you've listened to grand opera, now you're going to hear some grand *ole* opry.'

ops. (= military operations): see *op³ 1 b.

opsin (ǫ·psin). *Biochem.* [Back-formation from *rhodopsin* s.v. Rhodo-.] A protein liberated from rhodopsin by the action of light.

1951 G. Wald in *Science* 15 Mar. 287/2 Rhodopsin and porphyropsin are carotenoid-proteins—proteins bearing carotenoid prosthenic groups to which they owe their color and sensitivity to light... The protein probably varies from one animal to another; it may be called *opsin*, and named for the animal of origin. **1956** *Nature* 28 Jan. 174/1 When opsin is in excess.., the synthesis of rhodopsin removes neo-*b* retinene almost entirely from solution. **1970** R. W. McGilvery *Biochem.* xxvi. 644 The interaction of the conjugated hydrocarbon chain with the opsins creates the particular absorption spectrum of the visual pigments, and therefore the spectral sensitivity of the eye.

‖ **opsit** (ǫ·psit), *v. S. Afr.* [f. Du. *opzitten* to sit up.] (See quot. 1955.)

1887 Rider Haggard *Jess* viii. 72 How often do you 'opsit' (sit up at night) with Uncle Croft's pretty girl, eh? **1899** —— *Swallow* i. 6 After we had 'opsited' together several times according to our customs, and burnt many very long candles, we were married. **1900** H. A. Bryden *From Veldt Camp Fires* 195 Tobias meant to make a bit of a splash today,..although he was not prepared for the solemnity of an 'opsitting' (that all-night form of courtship, dear to the heart of the Boer). **1913** C. Pettman *Africanderisms* 351 *Opsit*.., in Cape Dutch this word is descriptive of the peculiar method of courting which in earlier days was in vogue among the Dutch farming population. **1939** S. Cloete *Watch for Dawn* 377 Why, if you wanted to court her, could you not opsit like a Burger in the sit-Kamer with a candle between you? **1955** W. Robertson *Blue Wagon* xix. 181 'In my young days I had to *opsit* for weeks.' He referred to the Boer custom of two young people sitting up by the light of a candle after the elders had gone to bed. When the candle burned out it was time for the young man to go, and if the girl did not favour him she would produce a candle-end instead of a long one as a hint she preferred his going to his company.

opsonic (ǫpsǫ·nik), *a. Bacteriology.* [f. as next + -ic.] Of or pertaining to opsonins; produced by or involving opsonins.

1903 [see next]. **1906** *Practitioner* Dec. 750 A doubling of the opsonic index means that the quantity of opsonin present has been increased in a far greater proportion. **1911** G. B. Shaw *Doctor's Dilemma* Pref. p. xxxviii, A few doctors have now learnt the danger of inoculating without any reference to the patient's 'opsonic index' at the moment of inoculation. **1929** Topley & Wilson *Princ. Bacteriol. & Immunity* I. vi. 175 Normal serum loses almost all its opsonic action when diluted 15 times with saline. **1950** C. J. Witton *Microbiol.* xxii. 297 Opsonic test. If the patient's white blood cells show unusual ability to engulf the bacteria, it indicates the presence of specific opsonins. **1969** H. I. Winner *Microbiol. in Mod. Nursing* xiii. 154 Yet another serological test, not much used today, is that to determine the opsonic index of a serum. **1972** *Pediatrics* XLIX. 225 (*heading*) Fatal familial Leiner's disease: a deficiency of the opsonic activity of serum complement.

opsonin (ǫ·psǒnin). *Bacteriology.* Formerly also **-ine.** [f. L. *obs-, opsōn-āre* to buy provisions, cater (f. Gr. ὀψωνεῖν) + -in¹.] A substance (usu. an antibody) in blood serum which combines with bacteria or other foreign cells and renders them more susceptible to phagocytosis.

1903 Wright & Douglas in *Proc. R. Soc.* LXXII. 366 We may speak of this as an 'opsonic' effect (opsono—I cater for; I prepare victuals for), and we may employ the term 'opsonins' to designate the elements in the body fluids which produce this effect. **1904** [see *saturation experiment* s.v. Saturation 5]. **1906** *Practitioner* Dec. 750 We know..that the presence of opsonins is necessary for phagocytosis. **1911** G. B. Shaw *Doctor's Dilemma* 10 Opsonin is what you butter the disease germs with to make your white corpuscles eat them. **1937** R. W. Fairbrother *Text-bk. Med. Bacteriol.* ix. 116 There seems to be little doubt that opsonins are quite distinct from complement. **1950** [see prec.]. **1970** W. H. Parker *Health & Dis. in Farm Animals* ix. 116 Polymorphs.. will consume many times more bacteria of a particular species if the right opsonin is present, i.e. if the animal concerned is immunised against that species.

Hence **o·psonist** (*nonce-word*), an advocate of the therapeutic use of opsonins; **opsoniza·tion,** the process of opsonizing; **o·psonize** *v. trans.*, to render (a bacterium or other particle) more susceptible to phagocytosis.

1906 G. B. Shaw *Let.* 18 Nov. (1972) II. 661 A vaccine opsinises [*sic*] your disease germs—to opsinize = à rendre friande—so that the white blood corpuscles pitch into them with an appetite. **1907** *Practitioner* Apr. 581 The hungry phagocyte is supposed to have its diet daintily opsonized for it. **1907** *Science* 13 Sept. 346/1 An alkalinity ..prevented opsonization. **1911** G. B. Shaw *Doctor's Dilemma* Pref. p. xci, Add to the newly triumphant homeopathist and the opsonist that other remarkable innovator, the Swedish masseur. **1936** *Med. Rec.* (N.Y.) CXLIII. 16/1 It seems wise..to divide the reactions occurring with antigen and antibody into three groups: A. Protective. These include neutralization.., lysis.., killing..and opsonization. **1970** Harris & Sinkovics *Immunol. Malignant Dis.* i. 6 Antibody may have opsonized the antigen before it reaches the lymph node. **1973** *Sci. Amer.* Nov. 64/3 Antibody and complement render bacteria susceptible to phagocytosis, a process called opsonization.

opsonocytophagic (ǫ:psǫ̆nosəitofæ·dʒik), *a. Bacteriology.* [f. *opson(in + -o + Cyto- + Gr. -φαγία eating (sb.) + -ic.] = *opsonic *a.*

1910 Glynn & Cox in *Jrnl. Path. & Bacteriol.* XIV. 92 We have expressed the result of comparing the combined action of leucocytes plus serum of two persons by the term Opsono-cytophagic Index. Such an index denotes.. the total phagocytic power of any blood. **1940** Schaub & Foley *Methods Diagnostic Bacteriol.* viii. 219 The opsonocytophagic test in brucellosis determines the immunity status of the individual toward Brucella. **1950** C. J. Witton *Microbiol.* xxii. 297 This figure is called the opsonic index, or opsonocytophagic index. *Ibid.* xxv. 338 The presence of antibrucella antibodies..may be tested by agglutination tests and by opsonocytophagic tests. **1969** Wilson & Mizer *Microbiol. in Nursing Pract.* xix. 447/2 Opsonins also develop, as recognized by tests that demonstrate increased phagocytosis of brucellae in the presence of the patient's serum (opsonocytophagic test).

opster (ǫ·pstəɹ). *U.S.* [f. *op⁴ + -ster.] A practitioner of op art. *Temporary.*

1965 *Sat. Rev.* (U.S.) 29 May 29/3 It would seem that two older artists have been curiously misunderstood—Albers by the 'opsters' and Duchamp by the 'popsters'. **1967** *N.Y. Times* 18 Mar. 25 The intricate light-and-shadow wall reliefs of the opster Ben Cunningham.

opt, *v.* Add: **2.** Phr. *to opt out of*: to choose not to do or participate in (something); also *absol.* So, **opter-out,** one who opts out (of something). Hence phr. *to opt into*: to choose to do or participate in something; also *absol.* as *to opt in.* See also *opting *vbl. sb.*

1922 [see *opting *vbl. sb.*]. **1951** *Ann. Reg. 1950* 82 It became clear that many of the older and larger schools.. were likely to opt out [of the Education Act]. **1966** 'A. Hall' *9th Directive* i. 12 A man wants to opt out; they have to give him an incentive that will make him opt in again. **1966** *Maclean's Mag.* 20 Aug. 43 Morgan has no cures for society so he opts out, even if his Mum does call him a class traitor. **1968** *Globe & Mail* (Toronto) 17 Feb. 1/1 Pierre Trudeau opted into the Liberal leadership race yesterday. **1968** *Listener* 20 June 790/3 But the problem is compounded if one section of the affluent majority now decides to avert its eyes from the whole sordid business of material betterment. The opters-out may not realise it, but they will make it harder to remove the remaining pockets of real poverty. **1970** *New Scientist* 30 Apr. 226/1 It is clearly impossible for the UK to opt out of the microelectronics race. **1971** 'G. Black' *Time for Pirates* v. 85, I looked at the princely opter-out conscious of how much I liked him. **1973** C. Bonington *Next Horizon* xii. 174, I did not intend to go to the top, having already opted out on grounds of risk. **1976** *Country Life* 26 Feb. 496/3 Her group of rather dim students..are all determined pre-adolescents. Neither drop-outs, nor opter-outs, they have simply refused to opt in. **1977** *Church Times* 29 Apr. 2/4 The OCU said that mercy-killing extended to cases in which there was no dissent from the victim was even more permissive than the recommendations of voluntary euthanasia Bills—'in these at least the victim has to 'opt in' to be killed. Should these recommendations become law it will not easily be possible to 'opt out' of being killed.'

Optacon (ǫ·ptăkǫn). Also **optacon.** [f. Op(tical *a.* + Ta(ctile *a.* + Con(verter.] A device for enabling a blind person to recognize printed characters by touch, the fingertip being placed on an array of many tiny rods certain of which vibrate in accordance with the pattern of light from the characters.

1970 *N.Y. Times* 24 July 33/2 Another technique—that of turning symbols and letters into touch—has also become a practical reality recently because of a lightweight, portable transistor device developed by Prof. John Linvill..and Prof. James Bliss... This device, called the Optacon, consists of a tactile stimulator and an optical scanner, connected together electronically. **1973** *Times* 26 May 16/5 Mr Richard Dufton, director of research for St Dunstan's, said..that the Optacon imposed a severe learning task because the reader's right hand had to track the camera accurately across the page, picking up the print letter by letter. **1975** *Telegraph* (Brisbane) 18 May 22/3 The optacon is being used successfully in Washington, U.S., by a blind radio announcer.

optant (ǫ·ptănt). [G. and Da. *optant*, f. L. *optant-, optans*, pr. pple. of *optāre* to choose.] A person who, when the territory of which he is a citizen changes its sovereignty, has a choice between retaining his former citizenship, and accepting a new one.

1914 W. R. Prior *North Sleswick under Prussian Rule* 9 Nearly 40,000 of the Sleswick Danes had become optants... The peril to which their optant relatives and neighbours were exposed. **1927** *Daily Tel.* 8 Mar. 11/5 This arbitral tribunal pronounced in favour of the Hungarian optants. **1930** *New Statesman* 10 May 138/2 Both sides have made considerable concessions, especially with regard to the difficult problem of the dispossessed Hungarian optants. **1937** V. Bartlett *This is my Life* x. 143 The Hungarian optants—Hungarians in Transylvania who had the right to choose between Hungarian and Roumanian nationality after the territory had been transferred to Roumanian rule.

optation. Add: (Later example.)

1922 E. Pound *Let.* 4 May (1971) 177 As you have been so explicit in yr. optation of undisturbed solitude I hesitate to offer to prolong my sojourn in Italy.

optic, *sb.* Add: **2. b.** *pl.* The optical components of an instrument or apparatus.

1942 J. Mitchell *Ilford Man. Photogr.* xiv. 297 (*heading*) Optics of the condenser enlarger. **1948** *Rev. Sci. Instruments* XIX. 153/2 Now that better optics and energy detectors are more generally available..polarization work will undoubtedly increase. **1962** *Analyt. Chem.* XXXIV. 242/2 A double-beam infrared microspectrophotometer employing a double-beam-in-time system and reflecting optics having 8× magnification. **1972** *Physics Bull.* Mar. 155/2 It is easy to arrange the x ray optics so that the diffracted beams from a selected set of parallel crystal planes form an image of the crystal.

5. (Properly with capital initial.) The proprietary name of a device fastened to the neck of a bottle for measuring out spirits, etc.; also *optic measure.*

1926 *Trade Marks Jrnl.* 22 Sept. 2158 *Optic*, an apparatus included in Class 8, for delivering a measured quantity of Spirits or other Liquids. Gaskell & Chambers Limited. **1953** *Word for Word: Encycl. Beer* (Whitbread & Co.) 27/2 *Optic*, a measuring and dispensing device widely used for spirits. It is usually inserted into the neck of an inverted bottle. **1967** *Guardian* 18 Feb. 3/1 Overnight, with the drop in temperature, a small amount of the alcohol in optics is lost... Now the Licensed Victuallers Association has told the landlords to take the bottles down each morning and allow the liquor in the optics to flow back into the bottle. **1968** 'P. Barrington' *Accessory to Murder* i. 16 Joe, the landlord, was surprised to see him...'Going to a sale somewhere, then?' he asked genially, holding a small glass under the optic measure. **1968** 'A. Haig' *Sign on for Tokyo* 58 Joe could see his face reflected in the glass behind the bar, between the spirits bottles on their optic measures. **1970** V. Canning *Great Affair* xii. 215 A row of shining optics under the whisky and gin bottles. **1974** P. Cave *Dirtiest Picture Postcard* xiii. 85 She swung at her empty glass, sending it flying across the smooth bar-top to smash against a row of optics.

optical, *a.* Add: **1.** (Further examples.) Also *fig.*

c **1806** D. Wordsworth *Jrnl.* (1941) I. 253 Right before us..were several small single trees..but some optical delusion had detached them from the land on which they stood, and they had the appearance of..little vessels sailing along the coast of it. **1859** *Rep. Brit. Assoc. Adv. Sci. 1858* II. 14 (*heading*) On an apparatus for exhibiting optical illusions of spectral phenomena. **1911** *Rep. Labour & Social Conditions in Germany* (Tariff Reform League) III. 193 It may have been an optical illusion, but it certainly did seem to me that Germany was in a state of abounding prosperity. **1922** Joyce *Ulysses* 370 Looks like a phantom ship. No. Wait. Trees are they? An optical illusion. Mirage. **1937** K. Blixen *Out of Africa* v. 386 Between.. the mellow English landscape and the African mountain ridge, ran the path of his life: it is an optical illusion that it seemed to..swerve—the surroundings swerved. **1961** C. Greenberg *Art & Culture* 77 Flatness may now monopolize everything, but it is a flatness become so ambiguous and expanded as to turn into illusion itself—at least an optical if not, properly speaking, a pictorial illusion. **1971** D. Francis *Bonecrack* xiii. 169 Don't be tempted by the optical illusion that the winning post is much nearer than it really is. **1976** *Times* 20 Feb. 14/4 But it will be said, surely the growth of public spending has..been arrested... Not, alas, so. This is an optical illusion.

2. a. (Further examples.) Also used with specific reference to visible light as contrasted with other electromagnetic radiation: *spec.* operating in or employing the visible part of the spectrum.

optical density, (*b*) the logarithm to the base 10 of the opacity.

1891 W. Abney in *Jrnl. Soc. Chem. Industry* 31 Jan. 20/1 From the colour of the negatives..the photographic and optical densities were very nearly alike. **1953** J. W. T. Walsh *Photometry* (ed. 2) v. 161 The reciprocal of the transmission factor of a plate is sometimes termed the opacity of the plate and the logarithm to base 10 of the opacity is often known as the optical density of the plate. **1958**, etc. [see *maser]. **1960** [see *laser² 1]. **1966** S. D. Rockoff in G. D. Whedon et al. *Progress in Devel. of Methods in Bone Densitometry* 7/1 The mean optical density of the bone, obtained from densitometric scanning of the radiographic image of the bone is expressed in terms of thickness of calibration wedge material which gives the same optical density. **1967** *Listener* 27 Apr. 544/2 Before the radio telescope made its impact..the optical telescopes were able to photograph galaxies. **1970** *Sci. Jrnl.* Mar. 14 The first machine to automate completely one of the important processes of optical astronomy. **1974** *McGraw-Hill Yearbk. Sci. & Technol.* 11/2 The VLA will allow scientists to see, study, and map the radio sky at wavelengths of 1 cm or greater, with detail even greater than that possible for earthbound optical telescopes.

b. Used with reference to electromagnetic radiation other than light, and to beams of particles analogous to light: relating to the transmission of such radiation.

1933 [see *electron-optical* adj. s.v. *ELECTRON[2] 2 b]. **1938** MALOFF & EPSTEIN *Electron Optics in Television* i. 38 The electron optical problem of the electron microscope is to obtain electrostatic or magnetostatic lenses of short focal lengths capable of producing high magnifications with low image distortions. **1944** R. A. SAWYER *Exper. Spectroscopy* xi. 277 Infrared spectroradiometers differ from those used in the ultraviolet, or visible, regions chiefly because of the optical characteristics of the infrared region. **1964** *Jrnl. Optical Soc. Amer.* LIV. 15/2 A recent study of optical properties in the extreme ultraviolet.

c. Designating a form of abstract art and visual decoration in which optical effects are used to provide illusions of movement in the patterns produced. Chiefly as *optical art, artist, painting*, etc. Abbrev. *OP[4]. orig. *U.S.*

1964 *Time* 23 Oct. 78/1 Preying and playing on the fallibility in vision is the new movement of 'optical art' that has sprung up across the Western world. **1964** *Life* 11 Dec. 133 Op-art is short for 'optical art', a paradoxical movement dedicated to the practice of fascinating deceptions. **1965** *Reporter* (N.Y.) 14 Jan. 46/3 They [*sc.* Israeli artists] do have the beginnings of Pop Art and Op Art (Optical Art). **1965** *Listener* 4 Feb. 196/3 To pass..to the American optical painter Edward Avedisian, and thence to the British Patrick Caulfield, is to realize the impossibility of trying to apply consistent standards to modern art. **1965** *Observer* 28 Feb. 2/6 The occasion was the private viewing of the most important show of the New York art season—an exhibition called 'The Responsive Eye', which has gathered together, for the first time, a comprehensive international collection of optical art. **1965** *New Scientist* 20 May 491 Leaving aside the question of the contemporary fashion for 'optical' painting, Vasarely's work shows—indeed it largely created—two important trends in abstract art today. **1968** N. WESTON *Kaleidoscope of Mod. Art* xv. 220 The public has taken to Optical art in a big way, and it has spread rapidly from the art galleries to the Press. **1969** *Time* 7 Feb. 4 The Manhattan optical artist [*sc.* Josef Levi] has devised several new dizzying exercises with illuminated shadow boxes superimposed on black and white perforated metal screens. **1969** *New Yorker* 1 Nov. 12/3 Optical paintings by a leading Latin-American artist. **1970** C. BARRETT *Op Art* i. 7/1 The evolution of abstract art was a preliminary step towards the development of optical painting. **1973** J. LANCASTER *Introducing Op Art* ii. 28 Optical art is a method of painting concerning the interaction between illusion and picture plane, between understanding and seeing.

4. (Earlier examples.)

1610 H. WOTTON *Let.* 13 Mar. in L. P. Smith *Life & Lett. Sir H. Wotton* (1907) I. 486 The Mathematical Professor at Padua, who by help of an optical instrument.. hath discovered four new planets. *a* **1666** EVELYN *Diary* an. 1641 (1955) II. 64 Those spotts in the Moone, attributed to the seas there &c according to our new Philosophy & the Phænomenas by optical Glasses.

5. *optical bleach, brightener, white*: a substance applied to textiles which produces a whitening effect by absorbing ultraviolet light and re-emitting it as blue light; so *optical bleaching, brightening, whitening*.

1947 *Jrnl. Textile Inst.* XXXVIII. A 521 'Optical bleaching' is defined as the physical alteration of a white fabric in such a way as to make it reflect, in addition to white light, a certain amount of blue light, and thereby producing a much 'bluer' and also brighter white than before. **1948** *Amer. Dyestuff Reporter* XXXVII. 432/3 Whereas 'bluings' improve the appearance of white products by absorbing red light, and 'bleaches' improve their appearance by destroying the yellow color, 'optical bleaches' operate on the entirely different principle of transforming ultra-violet and violet radiation into visible blue light. **1959** *Which?* Sept. 107/2 If a detergent with optical white is used on a white fabric too generously or too often, the fabric can get a blue or mauve tint which is not particularly pleasing. **1961** COHEN & LINTON *Chem. & Textiles for Laundry Industry* v. 79 Optical bleaches will give blue by light emission and consequently improve brightness both psychologically and actually—that is, a 'whiter' white is obtained. **1964** KIRK & OTHMER *Encycl. Chem. Technol.* (ed. 2) III. 739 The principle of optical bleaching was described in 1929 by Krais, but the industrial use of optical brightening began about ten years later. **1964** *Ibid.* XIX. 13 The majority of optical brighteners that are commercially available are based on stilbene derivatives. **1971** A. K. SARKAR *Fluorescent Whitening Agents* i. 1 Fluorescent whitening agents are known under various names, e.g. optical whitening agents, optical bleaching agents or optical bleaches, fluorescent bleaching agents, whiteners, brighteners, etc. **1974** *Encycl. Brit. Macropædia* XVI. 916/2 Now an integral part of all washing powders, optical brighteners are dyestuffs absorbed by textile fibres from solution but not subsequently removed in rinsing. *Ibid.*, The chemical structures of optical brightening agents are complicated.

6. Special collocations: **optical activity,** the ability of a substance to produce optical rotation; **optical axis, centre**: see sense 2 in Dict.; **optical bench,** a straight, rigid bar, usu. graduated, along which supports for lenses, light sources, and the like can be slid and to which they can be clamped; **optical character reader,** a device which performs optical character recognition and produces coded signals corresponding to the characters identified; **optical character recognition,** identification of printed characters using photoelectric devices; **optical comparator,** an instrument for facilitating comparisons of two objects by projecting shadows or transparencies of them on to a screen; **optical fibre,** a fibre that will act as a light guide in fibre optics; **optical flat** (see *FLAT *sb.*[3] 2 f); **optical glass,** glass of specially high homogeneity manufactured for use in optical components (see also sense 4); **optical isomer,** each of two isomeric compounds whose molecules are enantiomorphs and which are distinguishable by their equal but opposite optical rotations; so **optical isomerism;** † **optical length** = *optical path* below; **optical model** *Nuclear Physics*, a model of the atomic nucleus in which it is treated as having a potential well with an additional negative imaginary component, so that its behaviour with respect to incident particles is somewhat analogous to that of a partially absorbing body with respect to incident light waves; **optical path,** the distance which in a vacuum would contain the same number of wavelengths as the actual path followed by a ray of light, equal to the product of the actual path-length and the refractive index of the medium if the latter is homogeneous; **optical printer** = *projection printer* s.v. *PROJECTION 10; **optical pumping** [tr. F. *pompage optique* (A. Kastler 1950, in *Jrnl. de Physique et la Radium* XI. 257/2)], the production of an inversion in the population of certain energy levels in the atoms of a gas by the absorption of optical (visible) resonance radiation of suitable polarization; **optical pyrometer,** a device for measuring the temperature of an incandescent body by comparing its brightness with that of a heated filament in the instrument; **optical rotation,** the rotation of the plane of polarization of plane-polarized light by a substance through which it passes; *spec.* = **specific rotation*; **optical scanner** = *optical character reader* above; **optical scanning,** scanning in which the light reflected or transmitted by the area being scanned is detected, esp. as used in optical character recognition; **optical sound** *Cinemat.*, sound recorded by optical (photographic) means on a film.

1877 *Chem. News* 23 Nov. 230/1 The optical activity disappears in those derivatives of active bodies, by the formation of which the so-called asymoetry [*sic*] of the carbon atoms ceases. **1883** Optical activity [in Dict., sense 2]. **1967** K. B. KRAUSKOPF *Introd. Geochem.* xi. 295 If a natural material containing carbon compounds can be shown to possess optical activity, the conclusion seems inescapable that living organisms played a role in its formation. **1883** R. T. GLAZEBROOK *Physical Optics* v. 113 The experiment is usually made on an optical bench. **1974** *Sci. Amer.* Apr. 28/3 An optical laboratory needs a large optical bench that is typically 20 feet long. **1962** *Proc. Symposium Optical Character Recognition* 1. 133 The IBM 1418 Optical Character Reader..provides an example of the maximum tolerance for several of these variables that can be obtained in today's commercially available character readers. **1968** *Amer. Documentation* Jan. 74/2 Typed pages are transferred to magnetic tape by an optical character reader. **1974** *Encycl. Brit. Macropædia* XIV. 892/1 The U.S. Post Office has had an alphanumeric optical character reader in operation on live mail since 1965. **1962** *Proc. Symposium Optical Character Recognition* 1. 93 A research and development program was initiated..to create a wide-tolerance optical character recognition system. **1970** O. DOPPING *Computers & Data Processing* iii. 64 In optical character recognition (OCR), the reader responds to the darkness of the ink, just as the human eye does. **1935** O. W. BOSTON *Engin. Shop Pract.* II. ix. 452 An optical comparator or Optimeter is a gage used for comparing the size of various parts with that of master gages. **1967** *Economist* 14 Oct. 4 (Advt. suppl. following p. 176), The image of the gauge, magnified to 50 times its size, is projected on the screen of the Optical Comparator so that the finest details of the thread can be examined and checked. **1976** M. MAGUIRE *Scratchproof* iii. 40 Perhaps the boys at forensic had made a gaff. Perhaps the optical comparator was malfunctioning. **1970** *Sci. Jrnl.* Dec. 68 Nobody has yet produced glass which meets all the challenging requirements of optical fibres. **1974** *McGraw-Hill Yearbk. Sci. & Technol.* 27/1 Optical fibers that act as 'light pipes' have been around for some years, serving in a variety of ways—in medical instruments, in photocopying machines, in automobile instrument panels. **1840** *Mem. R. Astron. Soc.* XI. 165 (*heading*) On the optical glass prepared by the late Dr. Ritchie. **1879** *Encycl. Brit.* X. 665/1 Optical glass is of two principal kinds—flint and crown. **1922** L. BELL *Telescope* iii. 60 The fundamental difference between the making of optical glass and the ordinary commercial varieties lies in the individual treatment of each charge necessary to secure uniformity and regularity. **1973** D. G. HOLLOWAY *Physical Prop. Glass* iv. 107 The characteristics of optical glasses are customarily represented by quoting the refractive index for one of the sodium D lines and the constringence. **1892** Optical isomer [see *ENANTIOMORPH]. **1974** *Encycl. Brit. Macropædia* V. 138/2 Optical isomers differ from the other isomeric coordination compounds in that their physical and chemical properties are identical. **1894** *Jrnl. Chem. Soc.* LXVI. 1. 422 (*heading*) Optical isomerism of closed chain compounds. **1968** R. O. C. NORMAN *Princ. Org. Synthesis* v. 156 Optical isomerism in biphenyls is possible because the conformation..which possesses a plane of symmetry is strained with respect to non-coplanar conformations. **1894** *Phil. Mag.* XXXVII. 515 The time it takes for an impulse at G to pass completely through F will be that required by light to go over a space equal to the difference in optical length of the extreme rays GBF and GAF. **1934** W. H. A. FINCHAM *Optics* ii. 26, *nl* is termed the optical length of a path *l* in medium of refractive index *n*. **1952** LE LEVIER & SAXON in *Physical Rev.* LXXXVII. 40/1 There is an energy range for which the problem of nucleon-nuclei scattering is somewhat analogous to the scattering of light by a conducting glass sphere... Such a medium is conventionally described by introducing a complex index of refraction... We have investigated an optical model for nucleon-nuclei scattering in which a complex square well potential is used, this being equivalent to a complex index of refraction. **1963** P. E. HODGSON *Optical Model Elast. Scattering* i. 3 The initial development of the optical model was due to Fernbach, Serber, and Taylor (1949). **1970** I. E. MCCARTHY *Nuclear Reactions* i. iii. 70 A mechanistic description of a non-elastic reaction..involves an optical model description of the system while it is in the entrance channel and another one while it is in the exit channel. The transition between these channels is described by a model which includes details of nuclear structure. **1893** *Phil. Mag.* XXXV. 471 The phenomenon is due to the interference of two parallel gratings... Their distance, which is virtually constant, is the optical path, $2ne$, e being the thickness, and n the index of the gelatine. **1923** GLAZEBROOK *Dict. Applied Physics* IV. 216/1 The differences of optical paths are a direct measure of the distortion from true spherical form of the waves emerging from a lens system. **1957** G. E. HUTCHINSON *Treat. Limnol.* I. vi. 391 Poole and Atkins computed *b*, the mean optical path per meter, as 1·19. **1944** *Jrnl. Soc. Motion Pict. Engin.* XLII. 204 The use of the optical printer to enhance the value of the modern motion picture is demanded increasingly by studios with foresight enough to give a free hand to the man in charge of the optical department. **1953** L. J. WHEELER *Princ. Cinematogr.* v. 144 Figure 61 shows in outline the layout of the intermittent or 'stop' optical printer. **1974** L. LIPTON *Independent Filmmaking* i. 39 Optical printers are used to make dissolves, special effects, frame line corrections, freeze-frame printing and so on. The optical printer is also ideal for the preparation of master printing material printed from original camera film. **1952** *Physical Rev.* LXXXV. 1051/2 The net result is an optical 'pumping' as Kastler suggests, from $m = -\frac{1}{2}$ to $m = +\frac{1}{2}$, or a tendency in the direction of nuclear orientation. This is in competition with a disorienting tendency caused by collisions. **1959** [see *MULTILEVEL *a.*]. **1970** G. K. WOODGATE *Elem. Atomic Struct.* ix. 191 Recently..the methods of optical pumping, double resonance, and level-crossing spectroscopy have begun to provide data on the hyperfine structure of excited states. **1901** G. K. BURGESS tr. *Le Chatelier & Boudouard's High-Temperature Measurements* viii. 155 The optical pyrometer, by reason of the uncertainty of emissive powers.., cannot give as accurate results as other pyrometric methods. **1922** GLAZEBROOK *Dict. Appl. Physics* I. 649/1 It is possible to calibrate optical pyrometers by direct observations of freezing- or melting-points. **1958** BUSSARD & DELAUER *Nuclear Rocket Propulsion* viii. 303 The optical pyrometer has been built around the frequency-response characteristics of the human eye. **1895** C. S. PALMER tr. *Nernst's Theoret. Chem.* II. v. 288 The connection with constitution is shown in no other physical property so clearly as it is in this of optical rotation. **1929** R. A. GORTNER *Outl. Biochem.* xxi. 473 Naturally-occurring tartaric acid is the *d* form, and its purity is usually determined by the optical rotation of a solution of the acid. **1967** *Oceanogr. & Marine Biol.* V. 190 Suzuki and Suzuki..have demonstrated that ovalbumin has an optical rotation of $-27{\cdot}6°$ in the native state. **1962** *Proc. Symposium Optical Character Recognition* 1. 16 (*caption*) An example of the actual printed output which optical scanners are required to read. **1975** *McGraw-Hill Yearbk. Sci. & Technol.* 201/1 An optical scanner..reads a symbol printed on the product as it is passed over a slit in the checkout counter. **1958** J. MOIR *High Quality Sound Reproduction* xviii. 540 Optical scanning of the sound track takes place while the film is held in contact with the drum and rotating with it. **1971** *Computers & Humanities* V. 282 Optical scanning of printed texts (avoiding the need for keypunching the material). [**1933** B. BROWN *Amat. Talking Pict.* vii. 146 The optical sound system of the R.C.A. portable is shown diagrammatically.] **1960** *McGraw-Hill Encycl. Sci. & Technol.* III. 124/2 The magnetic sound track is..26 frames ahead [of the picture] on 16-mm film, the same as optical sound. **1970** *New Yorker* 29 Aug. 22/1 Here we have to use optical sound—printed down the side of the film.

B. *sb.* **1.** *Cinematogr.* and *Television.* (See quots.)

1953 K. REISZ *Technique Film Editing* 281 *Optical*, any device carried out by the optical department of a laboratory requiring the use of the optical printer, e.g., dissolve, fade, wipe. **1959** HALAS & MANVELL *Technique Film Animation* 340 *Opticals*, mixes, fades, wipes, etc., which are made by the processing laboratories on an optical printing machine after the scenes have been photographed, instead of in the camera during photography. **1959** *Punch* 28 Oct. 366/2 Many amateurs are clearly of the opinion that this [*sc.* the subject matter] is of minor importance, their chief concern being to demonstrate their skill at devising star-burst wipes and other trick opticals. **1969** C. O. RASPOR in W. R. R. Park *Plastics Film Technol.* iv. 94 It has become customary to distinguish three properties of films which are generally categorized as 'opticals': gloss, haze, and transparency. **1970** A. FOWLES *Dupe Negative* xiv. 192 'I've got four hundred feet of 35 mm. ECO original here,' I said, 'how long will it take to strike a master positive?'.. 'You can have it by five this evening,' he said, 'but wouldn't you rather have an optical?' **1974** L. LIPTON *Independent Filmmaking* vi. 273 When printed with an optical printer, the image can have the same orientation as it had on the camera film. If we used a contact printer to make the fades and dissolves, and then cut them into the master, we'd wind up with release prints with flopped opticals.

2. An example of optical art.

1966 *New Statesman* 5 Aug. 208/2 A sizzling red-blue optical by Ellsworth Kelly.

optician. Add: **2.** *spec.* One who makes up and dispenses spectacles and corrective lenses (sometimes also testing the eyes and providing a prescription).

1892 *Keystone* (Philadelphia) June 578/2 Some persons are unkind..enough, after the optician has spent a great deal of time testing their eyes, to ascertain from him the proper number of the glasses they need, and then..go around the corner to some street peddler of spectacles. **1897** *Sears, Roebuck Catal.* 462/1 Opticians make a practice of imposing on their customer..and give as an excuse for the prices charged, 'that the lenses were ground to order'. **1912** L. LAURANCE *Visual Optics* p. vii, I have endeavoured to cover..all that is essential for the sight-testing optician. *Ibid.*, No apologies are needed for mentioning some indications of pathological conditions, since a person with defective sight may go to the optician when he should go to the oculist. **1928** S. DUKE-ELDER *Practice of Refraction* xxiii. 333 The ophthalmologist has no more valuable and essential asset than a reliable optician with whom to co-operate. **1951** R. L. STIMSON *Ophthalmic Dispensing* vi. 140 An ophthalmic dispenser's First Commandment is, an optician shall never express an opinion pertaining to a patient's vision or eye health. **1969** *Which?* Feb. 43/1 Ophthalmologist. He is a qualified doctor who has had a further training in eye disease... He will give you a prescription for your spectacles... He will not make up the spectacles... Ophthalmic Opticians are opticians who do sight tests... After giving you a prescription for your spectacles, an Ophthalmic Optician will usually expect to make them up herself. *Ibid.*, A Dispensing Optician does not do sight tests but makes up your spectacles to your prescription, wherever you have got it. **1975** *Nature* 8 May 151/1 It has sometimes been noted by opticians involved in the fitting of contact lenses that the sensitivity of the cornea seems to vary, depending on whether the patient has blue or brown eyes.

opticity (ǫpti·sĭti). [ad. F. *opticité* optical quality: see OPTIC *a.* and *sb.* and -ITY.] In the brewing and food industries, the degree of optical activity of a solution, as a measure of its concentration.

1900 *Jrnl. Federated Inst. Brewing* VI. 219 The pyridine solutions of osazones are..very suitable for determinations of opticity. **1924** J. GRANT *Chem. of Breadmaking* (ed. 4) xiii. 197 Two instruments in common use for the determination of the opticity of sugars and other optically active carbohydrates are the Laurent..and the Schmidt-Haensch.

optico-. Add: **o:pticokine·tic** *a.* = *OPTOKINETIC *a.*

1950 F. H. ADLER *Physiol. Eye* x. 372 Opticokinetic nystagmus is induced in a subject using wide alternating stripes on a rotating drum. **1965** F. W. NEWELL *Ophthalm.* xxvi. 442/2 Opticokinetic nystagmus arises from looking at constantly moving objects, such as telegraph poles, from a moving automobile or train.

optimal, *a.* Delete *Biol. rare* and add further examples. Add to def.: most satisfactory.

1900 A. L. LOEB tr. *J. Loeb's Compar. Physiol. Brain* xv. 223 The greatest happiness in life can be obtained only if all the instincts—that of workmanship included—can be maintained at a certain optimal intensity. **1935** ADAMS & ZENER tr. *Lewin's Dynamic Theory of Personality* iii. 110 Optimal environmental conditions..vary considerably with different individuals. **1935** *Mind* XLIV. 359 There might be *optimal* sense-data, such as the one which a man senses when he observes a penny head on, from a short distance, in a good light, with a normal eye, etc. **1956** AMOS & BIRKINSHAW *Television Engin.* II. xv. 222 The constants of a feedback circuit can be proportioned to give an optimally-flat response, i.e., one with an equation having no terms in frequency. Such feedback is termed optimal and gives the widest possible frequency coverage. **1961** *Atlantic Monthly* Apr. 42/2 Students.. have often told me that it doesn't pay to be too interested in anything, because then one is tempted to spend too much time on it, at the expense of that optimal distribution of effort which will produce the best grades. **1970** *Sci. Jrnl.* Jan. 25/1 A controller..automatically adjusts the speed and feedrates of the drill so as to maintain optimal performance as the drill wears. **1971** D. C. HAGUE *Managerial Econ.* (rev. ed.) i. 11 An optimal decision is the one which comes as close as possible to achieving a given objective.

Hence **o·ptimally** *adv.*, in the best or most advantageous way.

1933 *Proc. R. Soc.* B. CXII. 505 The animal's tissues were not optimally hydrated. **1950** D. HALLIDAY *Introd. Nucl. Physics* ix. 340 Phase-defocused atoms are not optimally accelerated and do not contribute to the useful beam. **1956** [see above]. **1972** *Sci. Amer.* Sept. 148/3 The time of physicians is not always optimally employed. **1976** *Lancet* 13 Nov. 1039/1 In the absence of bacteria the nitrosation reaction proceeds optimally at an acid pH.

ptimality (ǫptimæ·lĭti). [f. OPTIMAL *a.* + -ITY.] The state or quality of being optimal.

1944 VON NEUMANN & MORGENSTERN *Theory of Games* iii. 162 (*heading*) Mistakes and their consequences. Permanent optimality. **1961** W. J. BAUMOL *Econ. Theory & Operations Analysis* ix. 184 Our condition..is a geometric representation of the following basic optimality rule. **1964** GOULD & KOLB *Dict. Social Sci.* 573/2 The rational consumer of formal economic theory maximizes his expected utility, and the rational entrepreneur maximizes his expected profit. If a distinction is wanted between this very strict species of rationality and more general forms, the former may be termed optimality, the latter adaptiveness or functionality. **1970** P. A. SAMUELSON *Economics* (ed. 8) IV. xxxii. 609 Graduate treatises call this a case of 'Pareto optimality', named after Pareto's work at the turn of the century. **1971** *Nature* 31 Dec. 527/2 Jardine and Sibson showed that the single-link method is the only hierarchic cluster method which satisfies certain invariance and optimality conditions. **1974** *Times Lit. Suppl.* 22 Feb. 172/3 A model of the city which achieves Pareto optimality (i e, a condition in which no one can get richer through moving without making someone else poorer).

optimalization (ǫ:ptimăləizēⁱ·ʃən). [f. OPTIMAL *a.* + -IZATION.] = *OPTIMIZATION.

1965 *Economist* 31 July 446/3 A mechanistic commentary on optimalisation theory and resource allocation. **1971** *Nature* 15 Jan. 150/3 The council pulled its punch, and decided to 'limit itself to searching for optimalization within the possibilities existing in the present constitutional situation'. **1975** *Gen. Systems* XX. 108/2 Allen Johnson..found that legends of agricultural affinity well befitted ecological optimalization in northeastern Brazil. **1977** *Language* LIII. 327 We have seen that 'optimalization of phonotactic structure' (i.e. the *C + *h* constraint) wins out over 'paradigm coherence' (i.e. the invariable prefixation of pronouns) in Hua.

optimate, *sb.* **1.** (Later examples.)

1954 I. MURDOCH *Under Net* xvii. 234 The editor was calling on the *optimates* to exercise..strong measures. **1966** AUDEN *About House* 20 As Nietzsche said they would, the *plebs* have got steadily Denser, the *optimates* Quicker still on the uptake.

optimific (ǫptimi·fik), *a.* *Philos.* [f. L. *optim-us* best + -FIC.] Producing the maximum good consequences.

1930 W. D. ROSS *Right & Good* 34 No one *means* by 'right' just 'productive of the best possible consequences', or 'optimific'. **1933** *Mind* XLII. 181 The 'Maximalist' Theory (this designation suggests quantity better than 'Optimific'). **1940** ——XLIX. 230 The first half of Universalistic Ethical Hedonism, to wit the theory that being optimific is the one and only right-making characteristic.

optimization (s.v. OPTIMIZE *v.*). Add to def.: The action or process of rendering optimal; the state or condition of being optimal. (Further examples.) Freq. *attrib.*

1951 PARSONS & SHILS *Toward Gen. Theory Action* II. ii. 123 An important superordinate problem concerning mechanisms which depend entirely on the learning–performance distinction (when this is taken as relevant to the over-all problem of the system—the optimization of gratification). **1959** *Times Rev. Industry* June 39/2 Optimization problems (e.g. minimization of costs or maximization of profits). **1961** *Aeroplane* CI. 725/1 These desiderata were then used in what the Americans delight in calling 'optimization' studies, to find the best of some 300 helicopter configurations. **1966** S. BEER *Decision & Control* x. 211 Given this framework, the process of reaching the best decision is known as optimization. **1968** *Brit. Med. Bull.* XXIV. 242/1 This resulted in a major advance known as optimization of treatment..which in essence is for the computer to give the radiotherapist a number of alternative plans, and for the radiotherapist to decide which he considers to be the most suitable. **1974** COOPER & STEINBERG *Methods & Appl. Linear Programming* i. 1 In an optimization problem we seek values of the..variables which do not violate the several constraints imposed on them, but which lead to an optimal (maximal or minimal) value of the function which is to be optimized. **1976** *Daily Times* (Lagos) 22 Sept. 3/3 The socio-economic development of any nation depended on the optimisation and maximisation of land use.

optimize, *v.* Add: **2. b.** To render optimal.

1946 [see *BEAM *sb.*[1] 24]. **1958** *New Scientist* 17 July 410/1 They could optimise the designs to be submitted.. for the first three nuclear power stations to be built in Britain. **1965** *Economist* 15 May 788 The shape of the aircraft, i.e. its geometry, can be optimised for what ever it happens to be doing. **1966** T. LUPTON *Managem. & Social Sci.* II. 44 To optimize any one of these elements does not necessarily result in a set of conditions optimal for the system as a whole. **1974** [see prec.]. **1975** *Nature* 10 Apr. 498/2 If the expected signal wavelength is known there are specialised methods which can optimise the sensitivity of such an experiment. **1978** *N.Y. Times* 30 Mar. C 11/4 As a small businessman, you never really understand the importance of optimizing time and effort.

3. *intr.* To become optimal.

1971 *Nature* 23 July 251/1 The eight radii model quoted cannot optimize to the two layer model above. **1972** *Physics Bull.* Feb. 91/3 The bonding of p electrons in the broadside on (π) arrangement optimizes at shorter distances than that in the end on (σ) position.

optimum, *sb.* (*a.*) Delete ‖ and *Biol.* and add to def.: The best, or the most favourable or advantageous, condition, situation, etc.

1955 SCHULTZ & CLEAVES *Geol. in Engin.* xvii. 416 It can be seen from the shape of the curves near optimum that moisture content is extremely critical in the compaction of soils. **1970** O. DOPPING *Computers & Data Processing* xxii. 340 In many planning programs..time limitations make it impossible to reach the optimum and provide proof that this has been reached. **1971** *Marriage, Divorce & Church* iii. 50 In principle the State need not encourage more children when population growth appears to be reaching, or to have passed, an optimum.

B. *adj.* (Further examples.) Cf. *OPTIMAL *a.*

1926 RIDEAL & TAYLOR *Catalysis* (ed. 2) v. 113 Most of the statements concerning promoter action by added substances have no information which would indicate what the optimum concentration of promoter is for the given reaction. **1929** S. LESLIE *Anglo-Catholic* iii. 34 How shall we strike the so-called optimum density, which is best for both the health and the soul of London, and keep the population there? **1930** *Economist* 1 Nov. (Russ. Suppl.) 13/1 The question of the optimum size of such a farm is not quite settled. **1935** *Planning* 18 June 8 It is a problem of maintaining the numbers and balance of population in such a manner as to enable optimum social and economic activity. **1949** E. W. KIMBARK *Electr. Transmission* xiii. 279 Another matching device is used at the sending end of the line..in order to obtain optimum power output from the transmitter. 'Optimum' signifies a compromise between maximum output and other considerations. **1950** G. B. SHAW *Farfetched Fables* Pref. 98 While the time lag lasts the future remains threatening. The problem of optimum wealth distribution..will not yield to the well-intentioned Utopian amateurs. **1954** H. M. CORLEY *Successful Commerc. Chem. Devel.* ix. 152 The question of the optimum production rate for a new plant is not easy to answer. **1967** E. DUCKWORTH in Wills & Yearsley *Handbk. Managem. Technol.* 110 When the optimum order quantities have been decided, problems may occur in scheduling these through factories in the optimum manner. **1975** *New Yorker* 21 Apr. 92/2 These drivers are deviant only in that they depart from ideal or optimum behavior.

o·pting, *vbl. sb.* [f. OPT *v.* + -ING[1].] The action of the verb OPT. Freq. const. *out.* So **opting-in** *vbl. sb.*, **opting-out** *vbl. sb.*

1922 *Glasgow Herald* 13 Apr. 6 The opting of Australia out of the chain..does..impair the symmetry of the Imperial chain plan. **1958** [see *APOLITICAL *a.*]. **1966** *Guardian* 17 Oct. 1/5 An opting out of the Church's duty. **1969** *Daily Tel.* 19 Aug. 20/1 On the crucial question of when doctors should be allowed to use the hearts of accident victims, the weight of opinion is that an 'opting in' principle should apply—only people who have signed a legal document stating that this can be done should be used as heart donors. **1970** *Globe & Mail* (Toronto) 28 Sept. 1/6 The provincial cabinet will study a proposal from Dr. Robillard for an entirely new opting-out scheme for the plan. **1973** D. AARON *Unwritten War* III. viii. 125 Howells neither extenuated nor deprecated his opting out in his reminiscences. **1977** *Jrnl. R. Soc. Arts* CXXV. 639/2 'Alienation'..too often..is used as an alibi for inaction, lack of imagination or a sort of 'opting out' (another dangerous expression).

option, *sb.* **1.** Add to second part of def.: an alternative, a choice. (Further examples.) *soft option*: a choice which entails no difficult or strenuous actions or decisions; also (with hyphen) *attrib.*

1923 *Granta* 2 Mar. 315/1 It follows that our Tripos must be difficult; that we have little use for 'duds', for Tutors who misconceive it as being a soft option. **1953** R. LEHMANN *Echoing Grove* II. 42 The lifelong consequences of a choice that, once made, is made to be adhered to with no soft option. **1957** M. K. JOSEPH *I'll soldier no More* (1958) xiii. 238 Odd bods from various HQs and soft-option types with vague jobs. **1967** *Technology Week* 23 Jan. 11/1 (Advt.), Everything is modular—memory, input/output processors, peripherals, central processor options, software. **1967** *Listener* 6 July 5/2 There is a tendency for many prospective students to regard social studies as a soft option. **1969** *Guardian* 14 May 1/2 Mr. Callaghan..is understood to have reserved his decision—or, in the current jargon, 'kept his options open'. **1971** J. B. CARROLL et al. *Word Frequency Bk.* p. xv, This decision was guided by the results of a pilot test undertaken to try out various procedural options for the eventual work on the AHI Corpus. **1972** D. DELMAN *Week to Kill* 139 This cut down my options. **1973** 'M. INNES' *Appleby's Answer* xxi. 183 You've been most fiendishly clever... You've kept your options open. **1976** K. THACKERAY *Crownbird* v. 94 Gould had tremendous self-assurance, the ability to cope when all the options were running out. **1977** *Times* 22 Apr. 18/8 The British electorate have a powerful instinct for the soft option and a quiet life.

b. *spec.* in *Amer. Football*, a play in which a quarter- or half-back chooses whether to pass or to run with the ball; also *attrib.*

1954 *Sun* (Baltimore) 25 Nov. 15/4 We couldn't pass enough from it and our quarterbacks couldn't take the pounding on the option play as a steady diet. **1966** ROTE & WINTER *Lang. Pro Football* III. 127/2 *Option*, play where ball carrier has choice of running or passing; option pass play. **1974** *Cleveland* (Ohio) *Plain Dealer* 13 Oct. 1-c/3 He baffled the Badgers with the option run, gaining 146 yards and scoring on runs of 11 and six yards. **1976** *Webster's Sports Dict.* 291/2 When a halfback is running the option play, it is commonly called the *halfback option*.

2. b. Alternative; esp. in phr. *with* (or *without*) *the option* (*of a fine*).

1901 *Chambers's Jrnl.* Sept. 582/2 A third [conviction] should result in imprisonment without the option of a fine. **1903** 'T. COLLINS' *Such is Life* (1944) iii. 106 Yet he has thoughts that glow, and words that burn, albeit with such sulphurous fumes that, when uttered in a public place, they frequently render him liable to fourteen days without the option. **1908** *Daily Chron.* 16 Sept. 4/6 A Suffragette who has been offered the option of a fine. **1914** E. PANKHURST *My Own Story* 71 They were given the option of a fine. **1925** WODEHOUSE *Carry on, Jeeves!* vii. 159 He will serve a sentence of thirty days in the Second Division without the option of a fine.

4. (Further examples.)

1857 *Hunt's Merchant's Mag.* XXXVII. 134 A purchase of stocks at the brokers' board, buyers' option, thirty, sixty, or ninety days, can call for the stock any day within that time... He pays interest at the rate of 6 per cent up to the time he calls. *Ibid.*, *Seller's option.* This gives the seller the option to deliver any time within the time of his contract, or at its maturity... The buyer..pays interest up to delivery. **1909** D. LLOYD GEORGE in *Hansard Commons* 29 Apr. 519 'Option notes' will be charged at similar rates, calculated upon the value of the securities to which the option relates. **1928** *Daily Mail* 25 July 18/5 None of the shares of the Company are under option. **1976** *Listener* 29 Apr. 533/3 You had bought the option for a book that they hadn't yet written. **1976** L. ST. CLAIR *Fortune in Death* iii. 25 'And the stocks you are interested in?' 'Just one. Aglia Petroleum. Thought I might pick up some calls on it.' '"Options" is our term.' **1977** *Gay News* 7–20 Apr. 22/1 WH Allen, who have the option on it here, are wary of libel suits. **1977** A. MORICE *Scared to Death* i. 7 One condition of this guarantee is an option on each of the plays.

6. *option market, note, plan, price, time*; also *options exchange*.

1865 *Shareholders' Guardian* 8 Nov. 847/2 If at the expiration of the 'option' time the price be the same as the 'option' price, the person who paid the money has the right to buy, sell, or neither, as he thinks proper. **1909** Option note [see prec. sense]. **1930** *Daily Express* 30 July 10/3 (*heading*) The option market. **1961** 'E. LATHEN' *Banking on Death* (1962) xv. 123 He had 10 per cent of the stock already as part of an option plan. **1973** *N.Y. Law Jrnl.* 4 Sept. 7/5 (Advt.), The Chicago Board Options Exchange opened in late April.

b. (gen.) **option mortgage** (see quots.).

1966 *New Statesman* 4 Mar. 312/1 People will be free in future to choose between taking an ordinary mortgage and an 'option' mortgage. **1971** *Reader's Digest Family Guide to Law* 61/1 The Option Mortgage Scheme..gives the borrower the choice of foregoing tax relief in return for a Government subsidy which reduces the interest on his mortgage loan. *Ibid.* 61/2 The Option Mortgage Scheme was devised to lower the cost of home ownership to people who do not pay enough tax to obtain full advantage from tax relief on mortgage repayments. **1975** in R. Crossman *Diaries* I. 343 The Minister had announced the new option-mortgage scheme, providing subsidies on mortgages whatever the ruling interest rate if mortgagors would forgo tax relief at the standard rate. **1976** *Star* (Sheffield) 3 Dec. 6/4 Our mortgage is an Option Mortgage, therefore we get no tax relief.

o·ption, *v.* Chiefly *U.S.* [f. the sb.] *trans.* To buy or sell under option; also, to have an option on.

1934 in WEBSTER. **1947** *Sun* (Baltimore) 3 Apr. 20/1 It was necessary for the Flock to purchase him inasmuch as Cleveland could not option him out again. **1966** E. V. RICKENBACKER *Rickenbacker* (1968) viii. 127, I also optioned the land around the company for future expansion. **1968** R. LOCKRIDGE *Murder in False Face* (1969) v. 68 A friend of his had had a musical optioned a dozen times. 'Lived on options for years,' he said. **1973** *Publishers Weekly* 26 Feb. 121/2 She has written a first novel and had it optioned for films. **1975** *Bookseller* 11 Oct. 2038/3 With [the book] *Saladin* already optioned by the film makers for 150,000 dollars. **1977** *Ottawa Citizen* 8 Feb. 17/2 Irwin Meyer and Stephen R. Friedman..heard the score for Annie. They liked it; they optioned it.

optional, *a.* Add: **1.** (Further examples.)

1934 *Language* X. 120 Occasionally one finds free variants, that is, non-conditional or optional variants. **1964** E. PALMER tr. *Martinet's Elem. Gen. Linguistics* iii. 68 In the case of the actor who 'rolls' his r's on the stage but uses the 'throaty' pronunciation elsewhere, we may rather speak of 'optional' variants. **1971** *Good Motoring* Sept. 18/2 Rubber mats are standard; carpets are an optional extra at £10·88. **1972** BERMAN & SZAMOSI in *Language* XLVIII. 313 In the above examples, the phenomenon of 'optional' stress placement does not seem to correlate with significant differences in meaning or sense.

2. (Later examples.)

1930 [see *ARTIFICIAL *a.* 3 b]. **1962** *Gloss. Terms Automatic Data Processing* (*B.S.I.*) 39 *Optional stop instruction*, an instruction which includes the possibility of stopping the operation of the program immediately before or after the instruction is obeyed, there being some means of permitting or inhibiting this facility as required. **1967** *Technology Week* 23 Jan. 11/1 (Advt.), Input/output is managed independently by one built-in and five optional I/O processors, with up to 160 automatic I/O channels. **1970** D. DODGE *Hatchetman* i. 17 'Underwriters..are being tapped for U.S. dollar payoffs under an airtight optional-money clause.' 'What's an optional-money clause?'.. 'Most major insurers in international trade write it... You put a clause in your insurance policy giving you an option to take payment in another money of your choice.'

o·ptional, *sb.* orig. *U.S.* [f. the adj.] An optional subject or course of study; a group of students constituting a class devoted to an optional subject.

1855 *Songs Biennial Jubilee Class of '57* (Yale Univ.) 3/2 For optionals will come our way. **1857** *Yale Lit. Mag.* XXII. 291 What was never known before, since the establishment of optionals, the number pursuing the study of Hebrew is nine. **1900** *Dialect Notes* II. 47 *Optional.* 1. An optional course selected by a student in addition to his regular work. 2. A student who elects only optional or special courses. **1930** *Times Educ. Suppl.* 12 Apr. 167/3 The advanced mathematics paper set as an 'optional' by London University. **1934** *Times Lit. Suppl.* 8 Mar. 162/2 *Optional.*—An optional subject of study. One example, of 1857, is given from Yale. For over 40 years at St. Paul's School the word has meant the class studying such a subject—e.g., the Spanish optional.

optiona·lity. [f. OPTIONAL *a.* + -ITY.] Optional quality; opportunity or freedom of choice.

1880 *Scotsman* 24 Jan. 6/3 How much optionality there may be in an option which is allowed to opt only in one direction may yet be a question for the learned. **1972** *Language* XLVIII. 337 (*heading*) Stress Optionality and the Global Alternative. *Ibid.* 340 The second case of optionality concerns questions. **1975** *Amer. Speech 1973* XLVIII. 39 Even so, the number of implicational relationships remains huge, suggesting..that at least some optionalities are '*not* learned by the child, but [are] predictable from exactly the kinds of substantive constraints..[and] general functional considerations..as those discussed' in Kiparsky's article and suggested to him on quite independent grounds. **1975** *Language* LI. 1015 Generative grammar has no way of formalizing optionality.

o·ptionalize, *v.* [f. OPTIONAL *a.* + -IZE.] *trans.* To make optional.

1921 *Proc. Classical Assoc.* XVIII. 43 Scotland, where the disastrous results of optionalising Greek in the Universities..have had time to manifest themselves.

o·ptionless, *a. poet.* [-LESS.] Without choice, without an option.

1908 HARDY *Dynasts* III. I. i. 328 The hunger for embranglement That gnaws this man, has left us optionless, And haled us recklessly to horrid war.

optoacoustic (ǫ·ptoˌăkū·stik), *a.* Also **opto-acoustic.** [f. OPTO- + ACOUSTIC *a.*] Involving or being the effect whereby a light beam periodically interrupted at an audio frequency produces an audible sound when made to irradiate an enclosed body of gas.

[**1959** *Science Progress* XLVII. 459 (*heading*) The optic-acoustic effect in gases.] **1971** *Jrnl. Appl. Physics* XLII. 2934/1 This technique uses the optoacoustic effect which was discovered by Bell, Tyndall, and Röntgen. **1976** *Nature* 19 Aug. 681/2 Opto-acoustic detection was discovered by Bell nearly a century ago, but was recently revived as a means of monitoring low concentrations of pollutant molecules.

optochin (ǫ·ptotʃin). Also **optoquine.** *Pharm.* [ad. mod.L. *optochinum* (coined in Ger. by M. Goldschmidt 1913, in *Klin. Monatsbl. f. Augenheilkunde* LI. II. 449), f. OPTO- (from its use in treating eye infections) + G. *chin-in* QUININE.] = *ethylhydrocuprein*(*e* s.v. *ETHYL.

1914 *Chem. Abstr.* VIII. 3692 (*heading*) Chemotherapy of the pneumococci infections of the eye, particularly of the ulcus serpens by means of optochin ointment (ethylhydrocuprein). **1925** [see *ethylhydrocuprein*(*e* s.v. *ETHYL]. **1957** J. H. BURN *Princ. Therapeutics* xxvii. 225 When by 1918 it was agreed that, clinically, optochin was dangerous, hope of treating bacterial infections seemed to fade away. **1959** *Acta Path. et Microbiol. Scand.* XLVII. 315 The optochin test is more reliable than the bile test in differentiating between pneumococci and streptococci. **1970** *Jrnl. Gen. Microbiol.* LXI. 138 Assays were made.. for the single transformant, to erythromycin, streptomycin, and optochin resistances.

optoelectronic (ǫ:ptoˌĭlektrǫ·nik), *a.* Also **opto-electronic.** [f. OPTO- + *ELECTRONIC *a.*] Involving or pertaining to the interconversion or interaction of light and electronic signals.

1955 *Proc. IRE* XLIII. 1906/1 The opto-electronic characteristics of electroluminescent and photoconductive transducers make them suitable for..devices and functional networks capable of light amplification, light switching, and light storage. **1959** *RCA Rev.* XX. 742 The simplest class of optoelectronic devices consists of converters. One of the earliest optoelectronic converters is the photovoltaic cell. **1969** *Sci. Jrnl.* Jan. 72/1 The integration of the semiconductor lamp into a microcircuit is a logical step towards opto-electronic applications. **1976** *Pract. Electronics* Oct. 838 (Advt.), This catalogue..offers items from advanced opto-electronic components to humble (but essential) washers.

optoelectronics (ǫ:ptoˌĭlektrǫ·niks). *sb. pl.* (const. as *sing.*). Also **opto-electronics.** [f. OPTO- + *ELECTRONICS.] The study and application of optoelectronic effects.

1959 *RCA Rev.* XX. 742 Solid-state optoelectronics concerns the use and control of numerous relations among optical and electronic phenomena in solids. **1963** T. E. BRAY in D. K. Pollock et al. *Optical Processing of Information* xvi. 216 Much of the interest in optoelectronics stems from its low cost potential. **1968** *Brit. Universities Ann.* 20 Courses in Man–Machine Systems Engineering and Opto-Electronics. **1973** *Electronics & Power* 5 Apr. 117/4 The use of an optoelectronics transmitter as a means of transmitting quantity and price data from self-service petrol pumps to garage cash desks. **1976** *Pract. Electronics* Oct. 803/3 With over 150 pages the catalogue is broken down into seven sections; Transistors; Integrated Circuits; Diodes and Rectifiers; Opto Electronics; Resistors; Capacitors and Accessories.

optokinetic (ǫptokine·tic, -kəine·tik), *a.* [f. OPTO- + KINETIC *a.*] Pertaining to or designating a form of nystagmus produced by attempting to fixate objects which are rapidly traversing the visual field; also, more widely, = *OPTOMOTOR *a.*

1925 H. W. STENVERS in *Acta Otolaryngologica* VIII. 545 (*heading*) On the optic (opto-kinetic, optic-motorial) nystagmus. **1947** *Jrnl. Neurol., Neurosurg. & Psychiatry* X. 110/1 When the patient watched a revolving drum the direction of which was reversed, the optokinetic nystagmus obtained to the left side was greater than that obtained to the right. *Ibid.* 116/2 The optokinetic responses ..suggest an epileptogenic zone in the left temporal zone. **1966** *New Scientist* 2 June 598/1 Many animals move their eyes or their head if they see something move, and this 'optokinetic' response is often useful as an indication.. that an animal has perceived a movement. **1974** *Nature* 8 Feb. 403/1 Newborn infants showed optokinetic nystagmus to a 4 cycles per degree pattern. **1975** *Ibid.* 22 May 330/2 If the visual surround of a walking animal is rotated, the animal turns in a characteristic way. With arthropods, this optomotor (optokinetic) response has usually been described in terms of the angular velocity of the body or eyestalks.

Hence **optokine·tically** *adv.*

1959 *Experientia* XV. 443/2 The question..seems to be whether the nystagmic movements observed..are optokinetically released by the movements of images along the photosensitive surface of the eye. **1965** *Proc. R. Soc. B.* CLXI. 243 The seeing eye is brought artificially instead of optokinetically to the same position.

optometry (s.v. OPTOMETER). Add: (Examples); also, the occupation concerned with the measurement of the refractive power of the eyes and the prescription of corrective lenses.

1886 C. M. CULVER tr. *Landolt's Refraction & Accomm. of Eye* iii. 259 One important matter to consider is the point of the retina to be chosen in optometry. **1903** *Optical Jrnl.* Nov. 658 Kindly let me know..if there is any law in New York State governing 'optometry'. **1923** GLAZEBROOK *Dict. Appl. Physics* IV. 287/1 Optometry is a term sometimes applied to all ocular methods of estimating the refraction of the eye. We confine the application here to that generally accepted in Europe, *i.e.* to instruments where an adjustment of lenses is made by the patient in order to obtain the image of an object. **1948** H. W. HOFSTETTER (*title*) Optometry: professional, economic and legal aspects. **1971** *Optometry Today* (Amer. Optometric Assoc.) 15 One such program, which the profession of optometry has encouraged..is the Model Reporting Area for Blindness.

Hence **optome·tric, -ical** *adjs.*, of or pertaining to optometry; **optome·trically** *adv.*, by means of optometry; **opto·metrist** (chiefly *U.S.*), one who practises optometry; an ophthalmic optician.

1864 W. D. MOORE tr. *Donders' Anomalies Accomm. & Refraction of Eye* i. 71 It was extremely important to see how far these results of measurement and calculation agreed with those of the simple optometrical investigation in the same persons. *Ibid.* (*heading*) Comparison of R and P, deduced from measurements on the eye and optometrically determined. **1886** C. M. CULVER tr. *Landolt's Refraction & Accomm. of Eye* iii. 252 To determine this degree of the ametropia, we may use all the above-mentioned optometric methods. **1903** *Optical Jrnl.* Oct. 558/2 The word 'optometrist'..coined by Mr. Eberhardt [President of the American Association of Opticians], is a popular one, and likely to be adopted by the American Association at its Milwaukee Convention in 1904. **1923** GLAZEBROOK *Dict. Appl. Physics* IV. 287/2 This optometric system is the best if one can rely upon the accurate judgment of comparison by the patient. **1945** *Amer. Jrnl. Ophthalm.* XXVIII. 669/1 It seems obvious that optometrists will continue to perform a large percentage of the refractions in America and will always be interested in matters that concern ophthalmologists also. **1957** A. HUXLEY *Let.* 12 Jan. (1969) 815 The medical and optometrical lobby has gone to work in the various state legislatures. *Ibid.*, What is happening in the US is that optometrists—a breed superior to opticians, in as much as they get a long training, but not fool [*sic*] blown oculists.. are steadily adopting..Batesian procedures. **1965** *Amer. Jrnl. Optometry* XLII. 50 Optometry has taken on a brighter public image in those areas where optometric educational institutions exist. **1971** 'D. SHANNON' *Murder with Love* (1972) v. 79 Nearly every tenant..was a professional of some kind: doctors, dentists, optometrists. **1976** *Casper* (Wyoming) *Star-Tribune* 29 June 6/1 Members voted to assist Dr. James Lane, an optometrist, with the Vision Day program on July 19. Children who will attend first grade in the fall are given a free eye examination to rule out serious problems with their vision.

optomotor (ǫ·ptŏmōᵘtəɪ), *a.* [f. OPTO- + MOTOR *a.*] Pertaining to or characterized by turning of the eyes or body in response to the visual perception of a moving object.

1926 *Brain* XLIX. 333 This nystagmus has been termed 'railway nystagmus', 'optomotor nystagmus' or simply 'optic nystagmus'. **1932** *Arch. Neurol. & Psychiatry* (Chicago) XXVIII. 1024 Interruption of the optomotor pathway at any point in its course would disturb the ocular adaptation to a certain direction of movement of the visual field. **1961** H. SCHÖNE in T. H. Waterman *Physiol. Crustacea* II. xiii. 492 The fine adjustment of turning movements in locomotion is checked by optomotor mechanisms. **1971** *Nature* 9 July 128/1 In the classical optomotor experiment an animal is placed inside a rotating striped drum. **1975** [see *OPTOKINETIC *a.*].

optophone (ǫ·ptŏfōᵘn). Also **Optophone.** [ad. G. *optophon* (E. E. F. d'Albe 1912, in *Physikal. Zeitschr.* XIII. 942/2), f. *opto-* OPTO- + Gr. φωνή voice, sound.] An instrument designed to enable blind persons to read, in which a photoelectric cell is employed to scan a text and produce electrical signals that are converted into audible ones corresponding to the different characters.

1913 E. E. F. D'ALBE in *Electrician* 24 Oct. 103/1 The reading optophone consists essentially of a selenium preparation illuminated by a line of light broken up into dots. **1923** *Glasgow Herald* 3 Oct. 6 Messrs Barr and Stroud..by the invention and manufacture of their 'Optophone' have supplied the blind with a practical means of reading almost any printed type. Every letter sounds a tiny musical-motive up in the treble region. **1960** *Daily Tel.* 18 Oct. 15/1 She used an optophone, an experimental instrument developed from an invention of the late Dr Fournier d'Albe. **1973** *Nature* 27 Apr. 591/1 A device for converting letters into auditory signals, the 'Optophone' of E. F. d'Albe, allowed a trained blind person to read ordinary print.., but never met the ultimate criterion of success because reading..was slow, and learning to do it was very difficult.

optoquine, var. *OPTOCHIN.

optotype. Add: [first formed as mod.L. *optotypus* (H. Snellen 1875, in *Klin. Monatsbl. f. Augenheilkunde* XIII. 479).] (Examples.)

[**1886** C. M. CULVER tr. *Landolt's Refraction & Accomm. of Eye* iii. 229 These tables of type figures, 'optotypi', as Snellen calls them, are what we use in optometry.] **1905** *Trans. Amer. Ophthalm. Soc.* X. 648 Attempts have been made..to construct special optotypes adapted to the limited capacity and observing powers of young children and illiterates. **1963** *Arch. Ophthalm.* LXX. 113/2 Amblyopic eyes required more light to read optotypes than did normal eyes. **1970** A. H. KEENEY *Ocular Exam.* iii. 29/1 Letters and numbers in the patient's own language most closely relate to his daily seeing requirements and therefore are the most practical optotypes.

o·pt-out, *sb.* [f. *to opt out* (*OPT *v.* 2).] A radio or television programme broadcast by a regional station for local consumption (in preference to one distributed nationally). Also *attrib.* or as *adj.*

1962 *B.B.C. Handbk.* 27 The regions have concentrated on providing themselves with facilities for putting out television programmes which have either been fed into the national programme or have provided special programmes for local consumption on an 'opt out' basis. *Ibid.* 38, I think it would probably be convenient and sensible to place most of the regional programmes, the opt-outs as we call them, in one channel. **1964** *Listener* 31 Dec. 1049 An 'opt-out' programme is one broadcast only on a regional wavelength. **1970** *Daily Tel.* 9 Nov. 6/5 At present in Birmingham there is one weekly opt-out time slot. **1972** P. BLACK *Biggest Aspidistra* I. ii. 24 The regional listeners preferred London to their local station, though..you could sometimes tune in to the local opt-out as well as the net-worked programme. **1975** *Listener* 6 Feb. 166/3 The BBC in the North-East has to divide its ration of opt-out time. **1977** *Private Eye* 1 Apr. 4/2 Moreover, a mere 250,000 viewers watch *Tonight* at the best of times and it's only a regional opt-out programme anyway.

opus. Add: **3.** Applied to slighter productions, compositions, etc.

1957 J. D. SALINGER *Zooey* in *New Yorker* XXXIII. 93/1 The most courageous goddam offbeat television opus you ever read. **1959** P. BULL *I know Face* ix. 147 'B' films and other ghastly opuses. **1967** *Crescendo* May 8/2 'When Lights Are Low' is the old Benny Carter opus—one of my favourites. **1967** *Telegraph* (Brisbane) 30 June 12 Nine young couples are determined to go ahead with New York's latest open air opus—a 'wed-in'. **1976** *Publishers Weekly* 15 Mar. 49/3 A spooky chiller of a first novel, this will have readers waiting impatiently for the next Ryder Brady opus to come along.

opus (ǫ·pŏs, ōᵘ·pŏs), *v.* [f. the sb.] *trans.* To include and number among the works of a composer of music. Abbreviated *Op.*

1900 W. A. ELLIS *Life Wagner* I. 376 This negligence in 'opus-ing' his musical works. **1921** A. B. SMITH in *Music & Lett.* II. 364 A large class of composers..write pieces solely for the pleasure of opusing them. *Ibid.*, Every piece of his [Gurlitt] is Op.-ed.

‖ **opus alexandrinum** (ǫ·pŏs æ:leksandrī·nŏm). Also with capital initials. [med.L., lit. 'Alexandrian work'.] A type of pavement mosaic work consisting of coloured stone, glass, and semiprecious stones arranged in intricate geometric patterns. It was much used in Byzantium in the 9th century and is later found in Italy.

1852 *Murray's Handbk. N. Italy* (ed. 4) 546/1 A mosaic..of that kind which is called 'opus Alexandrinum'. **1854** WYATT & WARING *Byzantine & Romanesque Court in Crystal Palace* 38 The *Opus Alexandrinum*——we may describe it generally as tessellated marble-work..an arrangement of small cubes, usually of porphyry or serpentine. **1875** F. E. HULME *Princ. Ornamental Art* i. 10 The *opus Alexandrinum* was a marble tessellation generally composed of porphyry..and serpentine..arranged into geometric patterns that were cut into the white marble slabs that composed the groundwork of the pavement. **1897** J. WARD *Historic Ornament* vii. 345 Another kind of mosaic used in pavement is that known as *opus Alexandrinum.* **1904** L. F. DAY *Ornament* v. 122 But for the economic instinct prompting men always to find use for a waste product, nothing like Opus Alexandrinum might ever have been done. **1955** *Times* 18 May 12/4 The sacristy lost the whole of its contents, but still retains part of the ancient pavement of *opus alexandrinum.* **1974** *Encycl. Brit. Micropædia* I. 228/3 In the 12th century several variations of *opus Alexandrinum* evolved at local centres in Italy, including the well-known Cosmati work..of Rome.

‖ **opus anglicanum** (ǫ·pŏs æŋglikā·nŏm). Also with capital initials. [med.L., lit. 'English work'; see ANGLICAN *a.* and *sb.*] The name given to the fine pictorial embroidery produced in England in the Middle Ages, esp. between *c* 1250 and *c* 1350, and used esp. for ecclesiastical vestments.

[**1277–81** in A. G. I. CHRISTIE *Eng. Medieval Embroidery* (1938) 2 Unum pretiosissimum pluviale ad ymagines Sanctorum contextum de opere Anglicano. *c* **1840** LADY WILTON *Art of Needlework* vii. 66 So celebrated was the English work, the Opus Anglicum, that other nations eagerly desired to possess it.] **1848** C. H. HARTSHORNE *Eng. Medieval Embroidery* 11 English embroidery has consistently enough been called the *opus Anglicanum*, from being a manufacture extensively and skilfully pursued in our own country. **1870** D. ROCK *Textile Fabrics* 281 This invaluable and matchless specimen of the far-famed 'Opus Anglicanum', or English needlework. **1909** L. DE FARCY in *Embroidery* VI. 168/2, I hope that..soon I may applaud their [*sc.* that of the English] success in the revival of their *opus Anglicanum.* **1922** *Daily Tel.* 12 June 20/6 (Advt.), The collection of XV Century vestments from Whalley Abbey, including some magnificent examples of 'Opus Anglicanum', the property of the Right Hon. Lord O'Hagan. **1936** *Burlington Mag.* Oct. 182/1 The rich collection of *Opus Anglicanum* at the Victoria and Albert Museum. **1954** M. RICKERT *Painting in Brit.: Middle Ages* v. 128 The fineness of quality which is to give to English embroidery, the so-called *opus anglicanum*, its wide reputation during the late thirteenth and early fourteenth centuries. **1960** D. M. WILSON *Anglo-Saxons* v. 155 In the twelfth century, embroideries of 'English work' (*opus anglicanum*) were to become famous throughout Europe. **1964** tr. *A. Geijer's Textile Treasures of Uppsala Cathedral* 23 Technical similarities to recognized examples of *opus anglicanum*, the famous English art of the High Middle Ages, have caused some scholars..to attribute this work to England. **1974** *Encycl. Brit. Micropædia* VII. 557/1 Opus anglicanum has..survived all over Europe wherever historic vestments are treasured.

‖ **opus anglicum** (ǫ·pŏs æ·ŋglikŏm). Now *rare.* [med.L., lit. 'English work'; see ANGLIC *a.* and cf. prec.] A type of manuscript illumination regarded as characteristically English (see quot. 1860).

1860 F. DELAMOTTE *Primer of Art of Illumination* 11 When the graceful and luxuriant curves of foliage begin to steal into the pages of the MS. they are to be found also forming the capital of the column,..a style of illumination generally known as the *opus Anglicum.* **1901** J. W. BRADLEY *Hist. Introd. Coll. Illum. Lett. & Borders V. & A. Mus.* vi. 81 So excellent is the work and so famous did it become that it was considered on the Continent as typical of our national art and received the appellation of 'opus Anglicum'.

‖ **opus araneum** (ǫ·pŏs ærā·niŏm). [med.L., lit. 'spider's work'.] Darned netting; a type of delicate embroidery done on a ground of net. Also called *spiderwork* (SPIDER *sb.* 10).

1865 F. B. PALLISER *Hist. Lace* ii. 17 Distinct from all these geometric combinations was the Lacis of the sixteenth century, done on a network ground (réseau), identical with the 'opus araneum', or spider-work of continental writers. **1870** D. ROCK *Textile Fabrics* 162 This is a good specimen of a kind of cobweb weaving, or 'opus araneum', for which Lombardy..earned such a reputation at one time. **1874** [see *spiderwork* s.v. SPIDER *sb.* 10]. **1882** CAULFEILD & SAWARD *Dict. Needlework* 233/1 During the Middle Ages this Network was called Opus Araneum, Ouvrages Masches, Punto a Maglia, Lacis, and Point Conté. **1900** F. N. JACKSON *Hist. Hand-Made Lace* 185 *Opus araneum*, Spider Work. The ancient name for Cluny Guipure Lace and Darned Netting.

‖ **opus consutum** (ǫ·pŏs kǫnsū·tŏm). [med.L., lit. 'work sewn together'.] = APPLIQUÉ *sb.*

1870 D. ROCK *Textile Fabrics* p. cii, *Our old English opus consutum, or cut work,* in French, 'appliqué', is a term of rather wide meaning, as it takes in several sorts of decorative accompaniments to needlework. **1882** CAULFEILD & SAWARD *Dict. Needlework* 7/2 This work was anciently known as *Opus Consutum* or cut work. **1899** E. T. MASTERS *Bk. of Stitches* i. 1 The average woman feels no interest in knowing that when she is working an *appliqué* panel..she is executing the classical *opus consutum.* **1972** *Country Life* 6 Jan. 24/1 Pieced work, or the sewing together of different materials for ornamentation—the *opus consutum* of the convents—was a common form of fabric adornment in the Middle Ages.

‖ **opus Dei** (ǫ·pŏs de·ī). [med.L. (attributed to St. Benedict).] **1.** *Eccl.* The work of God, *spec.* the Divine Office, or liturgical worship in general, seen as man's primary duty to God.

[*c* **530–540** *Rule of St. Benedict* (1952) xliii. 102 Ad horam divini Officii mox auditum fuerit signum, relictis omnibus quaelibet fuerint in manibus, summa cum festinatione curratur... Ergo nihil operi Dei praeponatur.] **1887** F. C. DOYLE *Teaching of St. Benedict* xix. 141 An 'opus Dei'—namely, the 'care of souls', which, according to the teaching of theologians, is even more the 'work of God' than psalmody. **1896** F. A. GASQUET in C. F. De Montalembert *Monks of West* I. p. xiii, The Divine Office was the daily service and formal homage rendered to the Divine Majesty. This, the *opus Dei*, was the crown of the whole structure of the monastic edifice. **1907** *Cath. Encycl.* II. 469/2 This public worship of God, the *opus Dei*, was to form the chief work of his monks. **1921** J. MCCANN tr. *Delatte's Commentary on Rule of St. Benedict* viii. 133 Our Holy Father and other ancient writers are well inspired when they call the liturgy in its totality the *Opus Dei* (Work of God). **1929** R. EATON *Benedictines of Colwich* iv. 47 The nuns were desolate of all spiritual help ..their one consolation being to continue the 'Opus Dei' as best they could in the dismantled chapel. **1939** J. CHAPMAN *St. Benedict & Sixth Cent.* v. 86 St. Gregory the Great follows St. Benedict in the habitual use of *opus Dei.* **1969** R. GODDEN *In this House of Brede* ii. 71 'Everything we do..,' said Dame Clare, 'our work, our reading, our private prayer, even our meals..are simply pauses, meant to prepare ourselves for real work, the Opus Dei.' **1977** *Church Times* 5 Aug. 10/4 The complete *Opus Dei*—Mattins, Solemn Eucharist and Evensong—is sung at Edington Priory Church..from Sunday evening, August 21, until the following Sunday morning by cathedral and collegiate choristers.

2. (With capital initials.) The name of a Roman Catholic organization of laymen and priests founded in Spain in 1928 with the purpose of re-establishing Christian ideals in society through the implementation of them in the lives of its members. So **Opusdei·sta,** a member of this organization.

1954 V. S. PRITCHETT *Spanish Temper* v. 99 The infiltrations of the members of Opus Dei who work, exactly in communist fashion, to frustrate professional groups. **1960** *Spectator* 25 Nov. 803 The organisation..is known as *Opus Dei*; the Jesuits call it 'The White Freemasonry'. **1961** *Ibid.* 9 June 830 A group of *Opus Dei* economists within the Spanish Government. **1967** G. HILLS *Franco* xv. 432 Ullastres and Navarro Rubio were known to be.. members of a religious society, *Opus Dei*, men pledged by a solemn vow to the dedication to God of all their professional talents. **1968** K. BIRD *Smash Glass Image* vi. 79 Hostile to the Government..were monarchists, liberals, Christian Democrats, Communists, anarchists, the Opus Dei. **1970** J. W. D. TRYTHALL *Franco* ix. 226 Members of Opus Dei, like freemasons, form the sort of semi-secret, loosely organised body that everybody who is not a member regards as a conspiracy. **1973** L. MACKENZIE in *Govt. & Opposition* VIII. 72 The Opus Dei was founded as a religious organization in 1928 by Father Escrivá de Balaguer in Spain. **1974** *Encycl. Brit. Micropædia* VII. 557/2 The two economic ministries were entrusted to Opusdeistas, and since that time [*sc.* 1956] other members of Opus Dei have held ministerial posts and other positions in government.

‖ **opus filatorium** (ǫ·pŏs filatōᵊ·riŏm). [med.L., lit. 'work of threads'.] An early name for darned netting or spiderwork. Cf. *OPUS ARANEUM above.

1882 CAULFEILD & SAWARD *Dict. Needlework* 233/1 In this lace [*sc.* Guipure d'Art]..we have the modern revival of the Opus Filatorium, or Darned Netting, or Spiderwork, so much used in the fourteenth century. **1883** J. W. MOLLETT *Illustr. Dict. Art. & Archæol.* 235/2 *Opus filatorium*, a kind of embroidery, 14th century; modern 'filet brodé'.

‖ **opus sectile** (ǫ·pŏs se·ktile). [L., lit. 'cut work'.] A form of floor decoration dating from Roman times and made up of pieces shaped individually to fit the pattern or design, in which respect it differs from mosaic which is an arrangement of regularly shaped pieces.

1852 *Murray's Handbk. N. Italy* (ed. 4) 491/1 This Florentine mosaic seems to be the 'opus sectile' of the Romans. **1854** WYATT & WARING *Byzantine & Romanesque Court in Crystal Palace* 39 'Opera di commesso'—that is, a mosaic formed by slices of marble, arranged somewhat on the principle of the ancient 'opus sectile', the projections of one piece being so cut as to enter into the recesses of another. **1935** E. W. ANTHONY *Hist. Mosaics* iii.48 The work which the Romans designated as *opus sectile* does not come under the head of mosaic, although it has sometimes been thus classified. **1948** *Antiquity* XXII. 77 Opus sectile floors at the major sites of Cyrene and Tolmeita. **1950** O. DEMUS *Mosaics of N. Sicily* III. i. 369 There existed..a technique of decoration somewhat akin to mosaic, the Saracenic *opus sectile.* **1971** P. FISCHER *Mosaic* 80 Earthenware pieces are specially cut to the individual shapes required by the design..rather in the manner of the second type of Roman *opus sectile.* **1978** *Sci. Amer.* Jan. 116/2 This kind of pavement is known as *opus sectile* (the Latin phrase for cut work), and the example in our house is the first Byzantine *opus sectile* floor found in a private house in Carthage that can be confidently dated.

‖ **opus signinum** (ǫ·pŏs signī·nŏm). [L. *opus* work + *signinum* Signian, of or pertaining to Signia.] A flooring material used by the Romans and consisting of broken tiles and other fragments mixed with lime mortar, being named after Signia (modern Segni), a town in Latium which was famous for its tiles.

References to *opus signinum* occur in the works of Columella, Vitruvius, and Pliny: see Lewis and Short *Lat. Dict. s.v.* Signinus. A description of the making of *opus signinum* is found in Vitruvius *De Architectura* VII. vi. §14.

1745 *Columella's Husbandry* I. vi. 34 They, it seems, contrived a plaister or flooring made with bruised tiles, or sheards of earthen vessels, and lime, tempered together. With this composition they made very durable floors, &c. and this they called *opus Signinum.* **1899** R. GLAZIER *Man. Hist. Ornament* 75 *Opus Signinum*, small pieces of tile. **1937** *Discovery* July 208/1 A [Roman] floor of bits of stone and tile bound together with cement (*opus signinum*). **1967** *Antiquaries Jrnl.* XLVII. 269 The two northern cells retained their floors of *opus signinum* which, in both cells, had been once renewed. **1971** P. FISCHER *Mosaic* 45 The humblest mosaic-type floor decoration, *opus signinum* (named after Signia, a town in Latium), is a levelled surface made up from odd fragments of stone or pottery of different colours, set at random in lime mortar rather like raisins in a cake. **1974** *Encycl. Brit. Micropædia* VII. 557/3 *Opus signinum* was the prevalent form of pavement in Roman houses from the 1st century BC to about the 2nd century AD when it was rapidly replaced in main rooms by patterned pavement mosaics of the tessellated variety.

Oquassa. Substitute for def.: The name of one of the Rangeley Lakes in western Maine, used *attrib.* or *absol.* to designate a small trout, the blue-back trout, *Salvelinus oquassa*, found in these lakes. (Examples.)

1883 J. J. LALOR *Cycl. Polit. Sci.* II. 215/2 The oquassa, or blue-backed trout (*Salvelinus oquassa*) of the lakes of Maine is a noteworthy American form. **1884** *Bull. U.S. Nat. Mus.* No. 27. 427 Oquassa Trout; Blue-Back Trout. Lakes in western Maine. **1888** G. B. GOODE *Amer. Fishes* 93 Tautog, chogset,..oquassa and namaycush are among the best of them [*sc.* aboriginal American fish names]. **1902** JORDAN & EVERMANN *Amer. Food & Game Fishes* 217 Oquassa Trout; Blueback Trout... The blueback trout is the smallest and one of the most handsome of the charrs... Formerly this fish was very abundant.

or, *conj.*² (*adv.*³) Add: **1.** *or otherwise*: see *OTHERWISE *sb. phr., adv., adj.* A. c; *or something*: see *SOMETHING *sb.*, (*adj.*), and *adv.* **c.** In modern colloq. use *or* can introduce an emphatic repetition of a rhetorical question.

1939 P. CHEYNEY *Poison Ivy* vii. 122 Just then Mirabelle comes through [on the telephone]. Has that dame gotta a swell voice or has she? *Ibid.* xii. 198, I blew in here a coupla hours ago on the *Minnetonka*, an' directly I read the papers an' saw that you was stuck here, did I run here or did I? **1946** 'BRAHMS' & 'SIMON' *Trottie True* vii. 201 'Well,' said Bradford, torn between pride and regret, 'she may be going to marry a Lord, but can I pick 'em or can I pick 'em?'

5. *or else*: see also *ELSE *adv.* 4 b.

7. *or* introduces questions which, in the character of an afterthought, cast doubt on a preceding assertion or on the presuppositions behind a preceding statement or question.

c **1907** W. B. YEATS *Let.* 4 July (1954) 483, I suppose the matter is technically your concern as well as mine, or is it? **1924** R. MACAULAY *Orphan Island* xvi. 212 Matilda had the laugh of the bees after all. Or did she? I'm not so sure! **1930** E. WAUGH *Vile Bodies* iv. 59 It really would serve him right if..he lost his job, don't you think so, Sir James..or don't you? *Ibid.* x. 203 They shouldn't put up symbols like that in the middle of the road, should they, or should they? **1935** V. MARKHAM *Deadly Jest* xi. 138 They couldn't have come from the servants' quarters or you'd have heard. Or would you? You were dropping off. **1937** W. FAULKNER *Monk* in *Scribner's Mag.* May 22/2 You force me to do what, for all you know, may be against my own principles too—or do you grant me principles? **1937** D. SAYERS *Busman's Honeymoon* xii. 251 These spiky cactus-affairs didn't like too much damp. Or did they? **1950** A. WHITE *Lost Traveller* IV. iv. 186 'Don't let's speak of falling in love, even as a joke.' 'Ah, but I want to speak of it,' he said... 'Or do I? I was certain I did when I ran into you this afternoon. Now I'm not so sure.' **1954** 'H. CECIL' *According to Evidence* i. 16 But you didn't need any help, did you? Or *did* you? **1956** H. MCCLOY *Two-Thirds of Ghost* (1957) i. 8 Vera must know how everyone who cared for Amos felt about her. Or did she? Probably not. **1962** I. MURDOCH *Unofficial Rose* I. 12 She must surely, he reminded himself, be fourteen now. Or was she? **1971** *Times* 20 Oct. (Motoring Suppl.) p. ii/7 The connoisseur needs taste, a limitless cheque book and the ability to differentiate at the level of an expert. Or does he? He can be impulsive, illogical and tasteless. Or can he?

II. 8. As *sb.*² or *adj.* A Boolean function of two or more variables that has the value unity if at least one of them is unity, and is otherwise zero; also called *inclusive or* (= L. *vel*); also (*exclusive or*), a function that has the value unity if at least one, but not all, of the variables are unity; (= L. *aut*). Usu. *attrib.* and in capitals, esp. designating devices for realizing this function.

[**1938** C. E. SHANNON in *Trans. Amer. Inst. Electr. Engin.* LVII. 718/1 There are many special types of relays and switches... The operation of all these types may be described with the words 'or', 'and', 'if', 'operated', and 'not operated'. **1940** W. V. QUINE *Math. Logic* i. 12 When 'or' is used in the inclusive sense..joint truth of the components verifies the compound. An 'or'-compound in this sense can be expressed more clearly by adding the words 'or both'. *Ibid.* 13 The exclusive use of 'or' is not frequent enough in technical developments to warrant a special name and symbol.] **1947** *Proc. IRE* XXXV. 758/1 The 'or' operation is performed by a 'buffing' circuit. **1949** E. C. BERKELEY *Giant Brains* ix. 149 The 'or' (as in statement 7) that is defined in the truth table is often called the inclusive 'or' and means 'and/or'. Statement 7, '1 or 2', is considered to be the same as '1 or 2 or both'. There is another 'or' in common use, often called the exclusive 'or', meaning 'or else'. **1950** [see *NOT *adv.* and *sb.* 13*]. **1959** *Electronic Engin.* XXXI. 591/2 The two input lines are fed into an 'or' circuit,.. which gives out a pulse whenever a pulse is received on one or both inputs. **1969** J. J. SPARKES *Transistor Switching* iv. 100 OR gates in one logic system are AND gates in the other. **1970** O. DOPPING *Computers & Data Processing* i. 25 Several functions can be combined in one and the same equation... The order in which different operations are taken is important. The normal order is NOT, AND, OR in decreasing order of priority. **1971** J. H. SMITH *Digital Logic* iv. 45 OR units are not extensively employed because they are usually constructed with components such as diodes, which have no amplification. **1972** [see *NOT *adv.* and *sb.* 13*].

ora². Add: **3. ora serrata** *Anat.* [L. *serrātus* SERRATE *a.*], the serrated edge of the retina, just behind the ciliary body.

1839 K. GRANT *Hooper's Lexicon Medicum* (ed. 7) 963/2 *Ora serrata*, the posterior serrated edge of the ciliary processes is so called. **1849** S. G. MORTON *Illustr. Syst. Human Anat.* 606 The retina..terminates behind the ciliary body in an irregular border, ora serrata. **1908** L. LAURANCE *Eye* i. 17 The sensibility of the retina to light diminishes rapidly from the macula ring to the ora serrata. **1973** *Brain Res.* LXIII. 285 Such new cells as are added after this period are added at the margin of the *ora serrata*.

oracle, *sb.*¹ Add: **9*.** (With capital initial.) The proprietary name of a type of teletext system. [See quot. 1976².]

1973 *IBA Technical Rev.* III. 61 Oracle—broadcasting the written word. Engineers of the IBA have recently developed and demonstrated an experimental data system, Oracle, capable of providing a continuous public information service on conventional television transmitting networks. With this system the public could receive up to 50 different 'pages' of information 'written' on their television screens, each page containing up to 880 characters, or roughly 120 words. These messages can be displayed or superimposed on the screen of a domestic television receiver without in any way affecting the reception of normal television programmes. *Ibid.* 62/1 Experimental Oracle transmissions are being made on the IBA's London television stations. *Ibid.* 63/2 The domestic television set requires adaptation for Oracle either by means of an independent add-on unit or,..by an internal modification. **1974** *Trade Marks Jrnl.* 17 July 1295/2 Oracle... Apparatus for the transmission or reception of television signals and apparatus for the transmission of, processing of, or visual display of alphanumeric characters and/or characters for defining parts of diagrams. Independent Broadcasting Authority.., London,..; manufacturers and merchants. **1975** *Spectator* 19 July 86/3 Within a year or two..'teletext'—the generic term for the system used by both Ceefax and Oracle—will take its place in the ordinary person's vocabulary. **1976** *Times* 19 May 1/8 At present experimental Teletext services are being broadcast by both the BBC and the Independent Broadcasting Authority, under the names Ceefax and Oracle respectively. **1976** P. R. HUTT in *IBA Technical Rev.* IX. 4/2 The author hit on the idea of the name 'ORACLE' one Sunday while lunching with friends. Being a classical source of advice and information the name seemed to be very apposite, and it was not long before it was made into an acronym for 'Optional Reception of Announcements by Coded Line Electronics'.

10. oracle bones, bones used in ancient China for divination (see quot. 1970).

1915 *Encycl. Relig. & Ethics* VIII. 262/1 During recent years a very interesting discovery of 'oracle bones' and tortoise-shell fragments was made in the province of Honan. **1934** K. S. LATOURETTE *Chinese* I. ii. 40 Inscriptions on the 'oracle bones', used for divination. **1970** BRAY & TRUMP *Dict. Archaeol.* 167/2 *Oracle bones.* Animal bones, particularly ox shoulder-blades and tortoise shells, were employed by the ancient Chinese for divination purposes. A groove was cut in the bone, after which a hot point was applied nearby, and the shape of the resulting cracks determined the answer. **1977** G. W. HEWES in D. M. Rumbaugh *Lang. Learning by Chimpanzee* i. 31 He found evidence for this theory in ancient Egyptian hieroglyphs, and in the most ancient form of Chinese writing, on the Shang oracle-bones and bronzes.

oracle, *v.* Add: **1.** (Later examples.)

1922 JOYCE *Ulysses* 183 All these questions are purely academic, Russell oracled out of his shadow. **1952** C. DAY LEWIS tr. *Virgil's Aeneid* III. 58 This is not the land which Delian Apollo Oracled for you.

ora·culate, *v. rare.* [f. L. *ōrācul-um* (see ORACLE *sb.*) + -ATE³.] *trans.* and *intr.* To say or speak oracularly.

1822 E. NATHAN *Langreath* II. 315, I think I behold you shaking your wise head..as you would oraculate, 'the simple Madelina little suspects' [etc.]. **1919** J. BUCHAN *Mr. Standfast* I. i. 32 He boomed and oraculated and the Misses Wymondham prattled. **1930** —— *Castle Gay* viii. 134 The Professor oraculated on letters, with an elephantine deference to his hearers' opinions.

oracy (ǭᵊ·rasi). [f. L. *ōs, ōr-* mouth + -ACY, after LITERACY.] The capacity or ability to express oneself fluently in speech. Also, oral transmission of poetry, etc.

1965 A. WILKINSON *Spoken Eng.* 14 The term we suggest for general ability in the oral skills is *oracy*; one who has those skills is *orate*, one without them *inorate*. **1965** *New Society* 12 Aug. 4/2 A new qualification has been proclaimed: oracy, 'general ability in the oral skills'. The coiner of word and concept is Andrew Wilkinson, lecturer in education at Birmingham. **1967** *Daily Mirror* 16 Oct. 18 The team is making a three-year investigation into oracy ..with a £15,000 grant from the Schools Council. **1971** *Daily Tel.* 20 Apr. 14 An additional year..of the schooling ..will not..benefit them unless it has been preceded by ..a successful learning of literacy and of oracy. **1972** T. A. SHIPPEY *Old Eng. Verse* iv. 89 Though literacy and the fixed text may have killed 'oracy' in the long run, the change need not have happened as quickly as in the present century.

‖**oraison funèbre** (orẹzoṅ fünẹ̄br'). [Fr.] A funeral oration.

1874 H. L. FARRER *Bossuet* vii. 313 [On] the occasion of the Queen's death,..Louis XIV requested him [*sc.* Bossuet] to preach her Oraison Funèbre. This was in 1683. **1876** *Encycl. Brit.* IV. 70/2 In the *Oraisons Funèbres* Bossuet is unapproachable... Nowhere does his genius take such wing as at the grave's mouth. **1907** G. MEREDITH *Let.* 22 Dec. (1970) III. 1620 You will not care for an *oraison funèbre.* **1953** W. STEVENS *Let.* 16 Nov. (1967) 802 An *oraison funebre* is not in my line. **1957** N. FRYE *Anat. Crit.* 296 The corresponding form in oratorical prose is the *oraison funèbre*, which survives in some forms of modern obituary.

oral, *a.* (*sb.*) Add: **1.** *oral history*: (the collection or study of) tape-recorded historical information concerning matters from the personal knowledge of the speaker; such a taped record; *Oral Law, oral law*: the part of Jewish religious law passed down by oral tradition before being collected in the Mishnah.

1733 tr. *B. Picart's Ceremonies & Relig. Customs* I. 46 A Man who hath made the Oral Law his principal Study.. is looked upon by the Generality amongst them as a Doctor. **1797** *Encycl. Brit.* XVIII. 303/2 The Mishna is divided into six parts... In the fourth..are named those by whom the oral law was received and preserved. **1879** Oral Law [in Dict.]. **1907** Oral law [used s.v. MISHNAH, MISHNA]. **1962** *New Jewish Encycl.* 362/1 At present, most Jews, though they may deviate from certain of its practices, believe the Oral Law to be divinely inspired. **1971** WEBSTER Add., Oral history. **1976** C. BERMANT *Coming Home* I. vii. 93 The Talmud incorporates the Oral Law, and..the Oral Law was dictated with the written Law by God to Moses on Sinai, and..the Oral Law was received intact by the Rabbis. **1977** *Times* 16 May 7/7 Oral history..enables the historian to put the questions he wants. **1977** *Program Announcement 1977–78* (U.S. Nat. Endowment for Humanities) 11 (*caption*) Oral history taping sessions, and a more informal jam session took place as part of..an NEH Division of Research Grants project that brought together these St. Louis jazz musicians to recount their experiences... Taping sessions..produced an oral history which will be made available to music historians and centers of research through the University's Learning Resources Center. **1978** P. THOMPSON *Voices of Past* ii. 19 The term 'oral history' is new, like the tape recorder; and it has radical implications for the future.

b. (Of poetry, etc.) delivered or transmitted orally; of or pertaining to such poetry. Also *transf.* So **oral-formulaic** *a.*, of or pertaining to (usu. early) poetry belonging to a spoken tradition which is characterized by the use of poetic formulae as an aid to memory.

1628 [see sense 1 in Dict.]. **1767** PERCY *Ess. Anc. Eng. Minstrels* (Notes) 44 He [*sc.* Asser] has however particularly recorded Alfred's fondness for the oral Anglo-Saxon poems and songs. **1774** T. WARTON *Hist. Eng. Poetry* I. Diss. 1 p. l, That scalds were common in the Danish armies when they invaded England, appears from a stratagem of Alfred; who, availing himself of his skill in oral poetry and playing on the harp, entered the Danish camp habited in that character, and procured a hospitable reception. **1777** J. BRAND *Observations Pop. Antiq.* p. iv, These [ceremonies],..though erazed by public Authority from the *written Word*, were committed as a venerable Deposit to the keeping of *oral Tradition*. **1892** J. EARLE *Deeds of Beowulf* p. xlvi, Müllenhoff had discovered six different authors, of which the first two were oral poets, but the third had a written copy of the rudimentary work as it then existed. *Ibid.* p. xlviii, The oral Epic was simple in outline and plain in style, and therefore the contradictions, irregularities, inversions..and intolerable repetitions..can only be explained by the gradual accretion of heterogeneous elements in the process of transmission. **1898** S. A. BROOKE *Eng. Lit. fr. Beginning to Norman Conquest* ii. 42 This was the origin of the early unhistoric sagas, like that of Beowulf, and such a saga was the highest form of the oral literature of the German tribes. **1906** G. P. KRAPP *Andreas* 75 The poem opens with the conventional epic formula, citing the authority of oral tradition for the story. **1928** W. W. LAWRENCE *Beowulf & Epic Trad.* 289 A written version of *Beowulf* might conceivably have served as a guide for oral recitation. **1929** W. E. LEONARD in Malone & Ruud *Stud. Eng. Philol.* 1 The intrinsic nature..of oral or chanted verse as inevitably emphasizing an organic metrical pattern. **1953** S. A. BROWN in A. Dundes *Mother Wit* (1973) 40/1 The Negro was contributing..through what we call oral literature—folk literature. **1953** F. P. MAGOUN in *Speculum* XXVIII. 446 (*heading*) Oral-formulaic character of Anglo-Saxon narrative poetry. **1970** *Jrnl. Eng. & Gmc. Philol.* LXIX. 72 Even contemporary criticism has tended to damn with faint praise by suggesting that Old English poems were largely collections of formulae indicative of oral composition... The conclusion that the presence of formulae is an indication of oral composition has been attacked as illogical. *Ibid.* 439 It would have been possible to use [in the OE *Riming Poem*] some of the oral formulae of other elegies and add a second half-line that rimed. **1972** T. A. SHIPPEY *Old Eng. Verse* iv. 89 The theory claims that much classical and modern poetry has been composed by an 'oral-formulaic' process. **1973** *Black World* Nov. 10/2 Black music..as a basically oral-tradition music, is lacking in the kind of documentation that..would clarify these aspects.

3. b. Involving or being sexual activity in which the genitals of one partner are stimulated by the mouth of the other; freq. in

Comb., as *oral-genital* adj. Cf. *CUNNILINGUS, *FELLATIO.

1948 A. C. KINSEY et al. *Sexual Behavior Human Male* II. x. 373 Most prostitutes are from the lower social levels, and consequently..few of them engage freely in oral activities. **1953** —— et al. *Sexual Behavior Human Female* vii. 257 Oral stimulation of the male genitalia by the female occurs somewhat less frequently. **1958** G. S. SPRAGUE et al. in C. Berg *Homosexuality* II. i. 213 At one end..would stand the most primitive oral pattern, fellatio. **1961** *Encounter* XVI. v. 77 His short paragraph on oral-genital techniques. **1969** 'J' *Sensuous Woman* 1970) xi. 79 A few minutes of oral-genital play was a small price to pay. **1973** S. FISHER *Female Orgasm* vii. 209 Most of the women..received manual and often oral stimulation of the clitoral region. **1973** *Sunday Times* (Colour Suppl.) 11 Mar. 20 Her main discovery is that oral sex is fun. **1977** *Time Out* 17–23 June 45/3 There's more erotic charge from two seconds of Damiano's close-up oral sequences than in Ms Richmond's entire oeuvre.

4. b. Administered or taken through the mouth; involving such administration.

1957 *Amer. Jrnl. Med. Sci.* CCXXXIV. 28/1 The purpose of this study was to evaluate the efficacy of an oral alcohol-water solution of theophylline in terminating acute asthmatic attacks. **1959** *Science* 10 July 81/1 This property..led to the experimental testing of a norethynodrel-estrogen combination as an oral contraceptive. **1959** K. H. BEYER in Waife & Shapiro *Clin. Eval. New Drugs* ii. 18 Oral efficacy..is certainly a limiting factor in the acceptance of a new drug for systemic use. **1962** *Lancet* 22 Dec. 1315/2 Oral contraception is now a matter of practical politics. **1967** *Proc. Soc. Exper. Biol. & Med.* CXXIV. 483/1 The acute oral toxicity of sodium selenite in the rat does not seem to have been investigated. **1970** W. J. BURLEY *To kill Cat* i. 24 A sachet of oral contraceptives. **1974** PASSMORE & ROBSON *Compan. Med. Stud.* III. I. xxviii. 34/1 A number of women..experience amenorrhoea after discontinuing oral contraception.

5. *Psychol.* In psychoanalysis, characterized by having the mouth as the main focus of infantile sexual energy and feeling.

[**1910** *Amer. Jrnl. Psychol.* XXI. 316 In infantile sexuality the oral and anal-urethral erogeneous zones..as well as sadistic and masochistic impulses rule.] **1925** J. RIVIERE tr. *Freud's Infantile Neurosis* in *Coll. Papers* III. v. 587, I have been driven to regard as the earliest recognizable sexual organization the so-called 'cannibalistic' or 'oral' phase. **1954** R. W. PICKFORD *Analysis of Obsessional* iii. 68 In general the oral stages are concerned with taking in of objects and ideas, or introjection. **1972** ROSEN & GREGORY *Abnormal Psychol.* (ed. 2) 53/2 The child's relationship with his parents as established during the oral period.

6. *Phonetics.* Of a sound: that is articulated with the velum raised, so that there is no nasal resonance. Cf. NASAL *a.* 2. So *oral-nasal* adj.

1919 E. KRUISINGA *Handbk. Present-Day Eng.* (ed. 3) I. I. i. 14 We see therefore that sounds can be produced..with the nose-passage shut: *oral* sounds. **1924** J. S. KENYON *Amer. Pronunc.* 36 (*heading*) Oral and nasal consonants. **1933** L. BLOOMFIELD *Language* vi. 96 Most sounds of speech are purely *oral*; the velum is completely raised and no breath escapes through the nose. **1955** P. STREVENS *Papers in Lang. & Lang. Teaching* (1965) ix. 114 In rapid speech the consonant may be omitted, leaving a nasalized vowel where Received Pronunciation would have an oral vowel followed by a nasal consonant. **1961** H. A. GLEASON *Introd. Descriptive Linguistics* (ed. 2) xv. 250 If only the mouth is open, the sound is an oral resonant. **1962** *Amer. Speech* XXXVII. 228 Differences between oral and nasal vowels. **1965** *Language* XLI. 478 The oral-nasal contrast is neutralized after a nasal; such vowels are written in this paper as oral. **1970** *Ibid.* XLVI. 81 There are eight consonants in Maxakalí, comprising an oral-nasal pair at each of four points of articulation. **1975** P. LADEFOGED *Course in Phonetics* i. 3 Note that the air passages that make up the vocal tract may be divided into the oral tract within the mouth and the pharynx and the nasal tract within the nose.

B. *sb.* **b.** Short for *oral examination.*

1876 G. H. TRIPP *Student-Life Harvard* 18 Do something splendid on the mathematics and the 'orals', and I will wage any thing you will pass clear. **1927** W. E. COLLINSON *Contemp. Eng.* 124 In regard to teaching within the University the only terms worthy of notice are the use of Oral (where some universities use Viva for Viva Voce)..and tutorials. **1973** D. MAY *Laughter in Djakarta* xii. 194 Examiners told candidates their marks immediately at the end of the oral. **1974** B. JOHNSTON *It's been a Lot of Fun* vi. 45 One of the dons pointed this out to me during my oral.

orality. Delete *rare*—[1] and add: Also, preference for or tendency to use spoken forms of language.

1946 *Hansard Commons* 17 Oct. 1055 Does the right hon. Gentleman not appreciate that it is the uncertainty about the date when written Questions will be answered which promotes orality? **1967** A. L. LLOYD *Folk Song in England* i. 25 Orality is a most important characteristic..and we have every right to speak of the grandeurs of oral tradition. **1973** *Times Lit. Suppl.* 26 Oct. 1323/2 A synthesis of Black orality with White literacy and technocracy. *Ibid.* 1323/3 The Black man enslaved took his African orality with him.

2. In sense of *ORAL *a.* 5.

1934 LEWIN & ZILBOORG tr. *Fenichel's Outline Clin. Psychoanal.* x. 372 Our findings then are:—ambivalence, turning against the ego, orality. **1951** W. & J. MCCORD in *Jrnl. Mental Sci.* XCVII. 765 (*title*) The problem of 'orality' and of its origin in early childhood.

3. *Phonetics.* With reference to a sound: the quality or state of being oral (see *ORAL *a.* 6 above).

1949 *Word* V. 158 Nasality vs. Orality. **1952** A. COHEN *Phonemes of Eng.* ii. 36 Features that are not actually relevant in distinguishing two phonemes, e.g. alveolarity, plosion, orality..must be taken into account all the same as contributing to the existence of both phonemes. **1964** R. H. ROBINS *Gen. Linguistics* iv. 155 Orality and voicelessness being regarded as the absence of a feature, nasality and voice, respectively.

orally, *adv.* Add: **2.** Also in *Comb.*

1957 R. HOGGART *Uses of Literacy* iv. 86 These views usually prove to be a bundle of largely unexamined and orally-transmitted tags. **1966** C. M. SIMPSON *Brit. Broadside Ballad* p. ix, The orally circulating ballad of tradition. **1967** A. L. LLOYD *Folk Song in England* iii. 144 Orally-diffused amateur composition. *Ibid.* v. 368 There is the anonymous, orally-spread, firmly traditional kind of song. *Ibid.* v. 381 The text is from a broadside... The orally-transmitted versions are not so complete.

3. With the mouth, as a means of sexual stimulation. Cf. *ORAL *a.* 3 b.

1951 FORD & BEACH *Patterns Sexual Behaviour* (1952) iii. 54 Alorese men occasionally stimulate the woman's genitals orally. **1953** A. C. KINSEY et al. *Sexual Behavior Human Female* vii. 258, 16 per cent had stimulated the male genitalia orally.

-orama, -(r)ama, *suffix.* [a. Gk. ὅραμα view, as in the second element of CYCLORAMA, PANORAMA.] As a suffix suggestive of considerable size or expanse, in commercial use to form nouns the nature of which is indicated by the first element. Cf. DIORAMA in Dict. and Suppl., *CINERAMA.

1824 E. WEETON *Jrnl.* 17 July (1969) II. 306 Visited the Cosmorama... I had now seen many of the -ramas in London, Ignoramus' and all. **1896** E. MARRIAGE tr. *Balzac's Old Goriot* 54 The diorama, a recent invention,..had given rise to a mania among art students for ending every word with *rama*.. 'Well, Monsieur-r-r Poiret,..how is your health-orama?' *Ibid.* 'There is an uncommon *frozerama* outside!'... 'Why do you say *frozerama*?..it should be *frozenrama*.' **1954** *Amer. Speech* XXIX. 157 Audiorama, a display of acoustic instruments;..*striporama*, a burlesque movie. **1962** *Word Study* Dec. 6/2 An exhibition of automobiles known as Motorama,..a Launderama (coin-operated automatic washers with dryers). **1963** *Guardian* 24 Aug. 6/3, I observe from your London Letter..that a fresh verbal monstrosity is to be inflicted on the defenceless English population—something called a 'scent-a-rama'. **1973** *Advocate-News* (Barbados) 15 Dec. 6/1 With all the 'ramas' like cyclerama, brassorama, musicrama and laugharama, why can't we call this one ugly-o-rama? Doesn't it sound great? **1977** *Radio Times* 29 Oct. 20/3 *Swaporama* with Keith Chegwin.

orange, *sb.*[1], *a.* Add: **A.** *sb.* **1. c.** *Oranges and lemons* (earlier and later examples).

1873 *Young Englishwoman* Mar. 154/2 Could you..give me the words in full of 'Oranges and Lemons'; 'I wrote a Letter to my Love'; 'Kiss in the Ring'; and any other of the old games? **1939** [see *London bridge]. **1969** I. & P. OPIE *Children's Games* viii. 236 Players..are invited to be an 'orange' or a 'lemon' in the game of 'Oranges and Lemons'.

d. *absol.* = Orange squash, orange juice.

1950 [see *GIN *sb.*[2] 2 a]. **1968** T. KINSELLA *Nightwalker* 45 A small jug of orange. **1972** *Guardian* 20 June 4/6 And so, back to fizzy orange and the ritual conference. **1977** N. SLATER *Crossfire* iii. 60 'What can I get you?' 'Fresh orange. At least I can..set you an example.'

7. a. *orange-juice* (examples), *leaf, salad, -wood*; *orange-crate* (also fig.), *-girl* (further examples), *-man* (example); *orange bitters, cream, crush, Curaçao, gravy, sauce, squash.* **b.** *orange squeezer.*

c **1870** in H. W. Allen *Number Three St. James's St.* (1950) vii. 186/2 Orange bitters. **1877** E. S. DALLAS *Kettner's Bk. of Table* 328 Parfait Amour is made of the bitter zest of limes,..syrup,..spirit of roses, and..spicy odours. It is in fact a kind of orange bitters spoilt. **1958** A. L. SIMON *Dict. Wines* 121/1 *Orange bitters*, the most popular form of bitters used for flavouring cocktails and other mixed drinks. It is made from the bitter Seville orange. **1977** *Sunday Times* (Colour Suppl.) 6 June 63/2 (Advt.), Sherry..with a dash of orange bitters. **1968** 'J. LE CARRÉ' *Small Town in Germany* xiv. 229 An old lady dropped a two-Mark piece into an orange-crate. **1972** L. ANDERSON *Let.* 20 June in *Amer. Speech 1972* (1975) XLVII. 38 In pilots training, we called the planes..'orange crates'. **1977** M. KENYON *Rapist* ix. 107 [He] sat on an orange crate in the storeroom. **1723** J. NOTT *Cook's & Confectioner's Dict.* sig. L5 *Orange Cream.* Take..Oranges, grate the Peels into..Water; beat..Eggs..sweeten..set it on the Fire, stir till it is as thick as Cream. **1861** MRS. BEETON *Bk. Househ. Managem.* 736 Orange cream... 1 oz of isinglass, 6 large oranges, 1 lemon, sugar to taste, water, ½ pint of good cream... Squeeze the juice from the oranges and lemon; [etc.]. **1939–40** *Army & Navy Stores Catal.* 31/2 Kia-Ora Orange Crush—bot. 1/6. **1952** [see *CRUSH *sb.* 4 e]. **1973** D. MAY *Laughter in Djakarta* iii. 54 What was almost the national drink of the Indonesian middle classes, orange crush. **1907** *Yesterday's Shopping* (1969) 100/2 Curaçao..Orange..3/6. **1951** E. DAVID *French Country Cooking* 27 Grand Marnier, Mirabelle and Orange Curaçao are particularly good for soufflés and for omelettes. **1965** *House & Garden* Dec. 90/2 *Bols.* This old-established Dutch firm covers almost every liqueur—best known for Kummel, Apricot and Orange Curaçao. **1977** *Times* 9 July 10/7 A little brandy..or orange curaçao may be added. **1842** *Knickerbocker* XX. 472 The orange-girl is generally allowed to enter [an auction-store], for auctioneers are mortal, and sometimes eat oranges. **1939** G. B. SHAW *In Good King Charles's Golden Days* I. 60, I never was an orange girl; but I have the gutter in my blood all right. **1963** M. FRAYN in Sissons & French *Age of Austerity* 336 The orange-girls, dressed up as replica Nell Gwyns. **1845** E. ACTON *Mod. Cookery* iii. 109 *Orange Gravy, For Wild Fowl.* Boil.., in..Espagnole, half the rind of a Seville orange,..and a small strip of lemon-rind... Strain it off, add to it..port or claret. **1877** Orange gravy [see *BIGARADE]. **1877** E. S. DALLAS *Kettner's Bk. of Table* 340 The present practice over the Continent is to stew them [*sc.* perch] in vinegar, fresh grape, orange-juice, or other sour sauce. *a* **1901** C. M. YONGE *Autobiogr.* in C. Coleridge *C. M. Yonge* (1903) iii. 85, I did not like to eat orange juice out of a pewter spoon. **1960** F. RAPHAEL *Limits of Love* I. i. 10 Think I'll have an orange juice. **1977** J. ARCHER *Shall we tell President?* x. 130 'An orange juice for me. I'm watching my weight.' Doesn't he know that orange juice is the last thing to drink if you're dieting? **1838** C. GILMAN *Recoll. Southern Matron* iii. 25 An orange leaf..was laid on every finger bowl. **1877** E. S. WARD *Story of Avis* 408 The splendor slept..upon the green pulses of the orange-leaves. **1880** G. W. CABLE *Grandissimes* ii. 15 Perfumed ad nauseam with orange-leaf tea. **1858** *Punch* 13 Mar. 103/1 There have bawled..in his street, sweeps, orangemen, dustmen. **1845** E. ACTON *Mod. Cookery* xxv. 629 *Orange Salad.* Take off the outer rinds,..from some fine China oranges; slice them thin,..strew over them..white sifted sugar, and pour on them a glass or more of brandy. **1973** 'I. DRUMMOND' *Jaws of Watchdog* ix. 123 Elaborate spreads of cold duck and orange salad. **1867** *Common Sense Cook Bk.* 28 Orange Sauce for Game. **1977** *Vogue* Feb. 114/3 Scallops in orange sauce. **1926–7** *Army & Navy Stores Catal.* 34/1 Orange squash..Kia Ora..Schweppes'. **1936** *Discovery* June 192/1 Fruit Squashes..were analogous to the well-known orange and lemon squashes. **1975** J. MCCLURE *Snake* iii. 42 A uniformed sergeant..was drinking orange squash..because he was on duty. **1949** M. MEAD *Male & Female* xii. 247 Idly turning the pages of a catalogue that shows the best type of orange-squeezer. **1962** L. DEIGHTON *Ipcress File* ii. 21 Stainless steel orange squeezers. **1884** G. W. CABLE *Dr. Sevier* lvii. 437 He moved his orange-wood staff an inch. **1889** *Harper's Mag.* Dec. 106/2 Strangers..were detained by eager vendors of flowers and orange-wood walking-sticks. **1910** *Daily Chron.* 23 Apr. 7/3 Dilute peroxide with one-half water and apply under nails with cotton on an orangewood stick.

d. orange skin food, a type of moisturizer for the skin; **orange stick,** a short stick, usu. of orange-wood, used for manicuring the nails.

1926–7 *Army & Navy Stores Catal.* 492 An Elizabeth Arden treatment is based on..Cleansing..Toning..Nourishing, with *Orange Skin Food* or the delicate *Velva Cream.* **1939–40** *Ibid.* 438/3 Seymour[,] Jane..Orange Skin Food—2/9. **1944** M. LASKI *Love on Supertax* iii. 36 She slapped the Orange Skin Food on to her face. **1974** D. GRAY *Dead Give Away* xv. 144 She now patted Elizabeth Arden's Orange Skin Food into her face. **1911** H. S. HARRISON *Queed* vii. 89 Orange-stick in mouth, he went around like a museum guide. **1922** F. COURTENAY *Physical Beauty* 46 You may use an orange stick..to push back the cuticle from the nails. **1966** [see *CUTICLE 1 d].

B. *adj.* **1. b.** *spec.* Applied to a variety of opal.

1902 *Chambers's Jrnl.* Aug. 494/1 The miners..say, one stroke of the pick may lay bare a seam of 'pin-fire' opal or break in two a rich band of 'orange'. **1971** J. S. GUNN *Opal Terminol.* 32 *Orange*, name given to opal with this distinctive colour.

2. a. *orange-fiery, -pink, vermilion* adjs. (sbs.). **b.** *orange-keyed* adj.

1922 JOYCE *Ulysses* 296 The orangefiery and scarlet rays. *Ibid.* 715 Orangekeyed ware..consisting of basin, soapdish and brushtray.., pitcher and night article. **1956** D. BARNHAM *One Man's Window* vi. 67, I am enveloped in a world of luminous orange-pink. **1967** O. RUHEN in *Coast to Coast 1965–6* 189 The orange-pink of its desert sand. **1895** *Montgomery Ward Catal.* 253/1 Special colors...Orange Vermilion. **1951** R. MAYER *Artist's Handbk.* ii. 56 *Orange vermilion*, a variety of real vermilion.

c. orange book, a report of the Ministry of Agriculture and Fisheries dealing with marketing questions and published in orange covers; **orange grass,** (*b*) *U.S.* = *NIT-WEED; **orange pekoe,** a type of black tea.

1928 *Daily Express* 30 Apr. 7/4 The report is one of the Ministry's famous 'orange' books—those scientific farming pamphlets for the education of English farmers. **1932** *N. & Q.* 30 Jan. 73/2 We were glad to have a note of the reception of the Orange Books on Marketing which the Ministry of Agriculture has been putting forth. **1837** W. DARLINGTON *Flora cestrica* (ed. 2) 324 Ground Pine. Nit-Weed. Orange-grass. **1882** E. K. GODFREY *Island of Nantucket* 36 The orange grass with its fragrance now greeting us at every turn. **1907** Orange-grass [see *NIT-WEED]. **1877** *Cassell's Dict. Cookery* 961/1 One pound of Moning Congo, a quarter of a pound of Assam, and a quarter of a pound of Orange Pekoe. **1911** *Encycl. Brit.* XXVI. 480/2 They [*sc.* the leaves] are now broken apart and sorted by mechanical sifters into the various grades or qualities, which are described as Orange Pekoe, [etc.]. **1960** A. E. BENDER *Dict. Nutrition* 123 Orange Pekoe [is made] from the first opened leaf.

Orange, *sb.*[2]. Add: **2.** *Orange Order.*

1940 L. MACNEICE *Last Ditch* 28 A framed Certificate of admission Into the Orange Order. **1975** *Irish Times* 10 May 9/3 Mr. Thomas Passmore, grand master of the Orange Order in Belfast, said yesterday that while Britain would be simply a small member in an exclusive club if she remained in Europe, outside it she could once again earn the title of Great Britain. **1977** P. CARTER *Under Goliath* i. 5 To make sure that the Protestant religion stays on top of the league in Northern Ireland, is what the Orange Order is all about.

orange-blossom. Add: **1. a.** (Later example.)

1971 K. WHEELER *Epitaph for Mr. Wynn* (1972) xxvii. 355 Orange blossoms and murder trials don't mix.

2. A cocktail flavoured with orange juice. Also *attrib.*

1930 *Savoy Cocktail Bk.* 117 Orange Blossom Cocktail. ½ Orange Juice. ½ Dry Gin. Shake well. **1938** L. BEMELMANS *Life Class* (1939) II. ii. 134 Waiters stand about with trays of cocktails, the favourite being Orange Blossoms, a mixture of gin and orange juice. **1960** B. KEATON *Wonderful World of Slapstick* (1967) 158 After taking a couple of orange blossoms, a cocktail made of orange juice and gin, Virginia got sick. **1963** I. FLEMING *On H.M. Secret Service* x. 105 A sprinkling of feminine cocktails—Orange Blossoms, Daiquiris. **1965** T. CAPOTE *In Cold Blood* (1966) iv. 223 We'd bought a bottle of ready-mix Orange Blossoms—that's Orange pop and vodka.

orange-flower. Add: **4. orange flower skin food** = **orange skin food*.

1908 *Sears, Roebuck Catal.* 798/1 Orange Flower Skin Food..acts as skin nourisher and wrinkle remover.

Orangeman. (Further examples.)

1844 MACAULAY *Let.* 4 July (1977) IV. 202 If the letters were opened, it was not by any authority from the late government, but by some rascally Orangemen in the Post Office. **1894** W. B. YEATS *Let.* 16 Dec. (1954) 242, I lectured..on Fairy lore to an audience of Orangemen. **1921** *Daily Colonist* (Victoria, B.C.) 12 Mar. 2/4 Orangemen from all over the world will convene in Winnipeg in 1923, according to an announcement made today. **1975** *Irish Times* 24 May 9/4 Mr. William Douglas, Official Unionist (U.U.U.C.) Convention member for Derry said that as an Orangeman, Unionist and Loyalist he was convinced that all Ulster people who loved their country should say no to the Common Market. **1976** *Daily Record* (Glasgow) 29 Nov. 17/4 Orangeman [*name given*], from Edinburgh, will face 400 delegates from Scottish lodges at Govan next Saturday over remarks on TV about leading the Ulster Defence Association in Scotland.

orange-peel. Add: **2.** Used, usu. *attrib.*, to designate a suspended bucket or grab composed of a number of curved, pointed segments that are hinged at the top and come together to form a container.

1905 C. PRELINI *Earth & Rock Excavation* x. 129 Excavator-buckets are usually either clam-shell or orange-peel buckets. **1912** C. G. ELLIOTT *Engin. for Land Drainage* (ed. 2) xiv. 209 The orange-peel is particularly useful in building levees. **1922** POWERS & TEETER *Land Drainage* xvi. 170 (*caption*) A small dry land excavating outfit with orange-peel bucket. **1959** *Micropaleontol.* V. 218/1 Two sampling devices were used, the Hayward standard orange-peel grab and a snapper sampler. **1967** *Oceanogr. & Marine Biol.* V. 527 The samples were taken with an orange-peel bottom sampler. **1975** B. FELL *Introd. Marine Biol.* iii. 21 An orange-peel grab..has four valves that appear to form the four segments of an orange when cut along its meridians.

orange-tip. For '*Euchloë Cardamines*' substitute '*Anthocharis cardamines*'. (Later examples.)

Only the male has orange tips on the wings.

1906 R. SOUTH *Butterflies Brit. Isles* 43 The Orange-tip ..has a large patch of orange colour on the outer third of its white, or creamy white, fore wings. **1930** *Times Educ. Suppl.* 4 Oct. p. iv/4 The little orange-tip flickering along the hedgeside. **1973** T. G. HOWARTH *South's Brit. Butterflies* 58 The Orange-tip is essentially a butterfly of lanes, hedgerows and rough fields. **1973** *Shooting Times & Country Mag.* 7 July 20/2 An orange-tip butterfly went fluttering by.

orangey, *a.* Delete *rare* and add: Also **orangy.** (Later examples.) Also, covered in orange; suggestive of oranges.

1913 H. S. WALPOLE *Fortitude* I. xii. 165 My fingers are all over orange... I always have an orange before dinner. .. I am orangy, but then I was late and couldn't finish it. **1919** C. ORR *Glorious Thing* xx. 245 A delicious, warm, orangy smell hung about the kitchen walls. **1966** *New Statesman* 6 May 663/1 Olivier's blue-black face and frame, Maggie Smith's pink-pallid Desdemona move for too much of the time against a dreadful orangey backcloth. **1974** N. GORDIMER *Conservationist* 199 A sun as pale as last night's..moon was orangey, is stiffening the topmost leaves of that tree. **1977** C. FREMLIN *Spider-Orchid* iv. 32 The orangy glow of the standard lamp.

b. *Comb.*, as *orangey-blue, -brown, -buff, -red, -yellow* adjs.

1977 A. SCHOLEFIELD *Venom* III. 118 Eyes weeping, knuckles orangey-blue. **1968** H. R. F. KEATING *Inspector Ghote hunts Peacock* i. 8 Its hideous orangey-brown colour, masquerading as the tan of leather. *a* **1973** 'G. ASHE' *Herald of Doom* (1974) v. 49 An orangey-brown kilted suit. **1976** H. R. F. KEATING *Filmi, Filmi* xiii. 123 A sportingly cut orangey-buff suit. **1977** E. W. HILDICK *Loop* iv. 17 Fashionable orangey-red blush make-up. **1974** *Times* 2 May 8/7 This year's recommended colour..is a warm orangey-yellow.

orans (ō·rănz). = ORANT. Also *attrib.*

1900 [see ORANT]. **1937** *Burlington Mag.* July 25/2 Though the Trecento type, the seated Virgin with clasped hands, persists in the Quattrocento, it is the Virgin derived from the old 'orans' type, of which the Antwerp *Assumption* is the earliest Italian example. **1949** O. DEMUS *Mosaics Norman Sicily* 309 The Orans was seen 'spreading out her pure hands to ensure the Emperor's triumph over his enemies'.

Oraon (orā·ǫn). [Indian name, of undetermined origin.

The following are among numerous explanations of the meaning of the name: **1900** F. HAHN *Kurukh Gram.* p. iii, The Hindus, who are supposed having invented the name *Urāõ* or *Orāõ* for the *Kurukh* people, might have concluded that the whole nation was called by the name of this sept, *i.e. Orgorā*; this word means hawk or cunny bird, and educated Urāõs believe that the foreign designation *Orāõ* or *Orā* is derived from this totemistic word. **1906** G. A. GRIERSON *Linguistic Survey India* IV. II. 406 Hindūs say that the word 'Orāõ' is simply the Indo-Aryan *urāū*, spendthrift, the name being an allusion to the alleged thriftless character of the people to whom it is applied. **1915** S. C. ROY *Orāons of Chōtā Nāgpur* i. 14 The name [of a monster-king] Rāwan, pronounced, as some people do, with an arrested 'O' sound at the beginning gave us the present form 'O-rāwan' or Orāon.]

(A member of) an aboriginal tribe, which calls itself *Kurukh*, dwelling in the state of Bihar in northern India; the Dravidian language of this tribe. Also *attrib.* or as *adj.*

1872 E. T. DALTON *Descriptive Ethnol. Bengal* VIII. i. 245 The Khurñkh or Orāons of Chútiá Nágpúr are the people best known in many parts of India as 'Dhángars', a word that from its apparent derivation (*dang* or *dhang*, a hill) may mean any hillmen... According to the traditions I have received from the most venerable and learned of my Oráon acquaintances, the tribe has gradually migrated from the western coast of India... Oráon appears to have been assigned to them as a nickname, possibly with reference to their many migrations and proneness to roam. **1892** H. H. RISLEY *Tribes & Castes Bengal: Ethnogr. Gloss.* II. 138 *Oráon, Uráon, Kunokh, Kunrukh*, a Dravidian cultivating tribe of Chota Nagpur, classed on linguistic grounds as Dravidian, and supposed to be closely akin to the Málés of the Rájmahál hills. **1908** [see *KORKU]. **1915**, etc. [see *MALER *sb.* and *a.*]. **1917** *Encycl. Relig. & Ethics* IX. 501/2 The Orāons..call themselves Khuṛñk or Kūṛukh, a Dravidian term of uncertain origin, connected by some with the word *horo*, 'man', or with *kuruk*, 'a crier', or one capable of speaking, in contradistinction to the other races, whose language is not intelligible to them... This word *horo* is probably the origin of the name Orāon. **1939** L. H. GRAY *Foundations of Lang.* 386 Kurukh, consisting of Kurukh or Orāõn in the western part of the Bengal Presidency and the neighbouring parts of the Central Provinces, and Malto in the Rajmahal Mountains of Bengal. **1972** W. B. LOCKWOOD *Panorama Indo-European Lang.* 224 Kurukh and Malto. The former, also termed Oraon, is used by 150,000 persons in the western ranges of the Chota Nagpur Hills, in the districts of Raigarh and Sambalpur. **1974** *Encycl. Brit. Micropædia* VII. 563/1 Speakers of Oraon number about 1,140,000, but in urban areas, and particularly among Christians, many Oraon speak Hindi as their mother tongue.

orarion (orē·ə·riǫn). *Eccl.* [late Gr. ὠράριον, ad. L. *orarium* ORARIUM.] = ORARIUM.

1772 J. G. KING *Rites & Cerem. Gk. Ch. in Russia* 36 Plate III. represents a deacon officiating in his..Orarion which is a sort of tippet thrown over his left shoulder. **1850** J. M. NEALE *Hist. Holy Eastern Ch.* I. 310 The stole was frequently called the orarion in the Western Church. **1907** A. FORTESCUE *Orthod. Eastern Ch.* 408 Other clerks wear a shorter sticharion and an orarion wound around them.

ora serrata: see *ORA[2] 3.

‖ **oratio** (orē¹·ʃiǫ). [L. *ōrātiō, ōrātion-em*: see ORATION *sb.*] Speech, language. Only in phrases: **oratio obliqua** [L. fem. of *oblīqu-us*: see OBLIQUE *a.* 5 b], indirect speech; **oratio recta** [L. fem. of *rect-us* straight, direct], direct speech.

1842 W. E. JELF *Gram. Greek Lang.* II. iv. 508 The infin. and acc. follows the verb in the *oratio obliqua*, and then follows a dependent clause in which the verb stands in the *oratio recta*. **1876** Oratio obliqua, oratio recta [see ORATION *sb.* 3]. **1929** R. HUGHES *High Wind in Jamaica* i. 35 Then she put it into Oratio Recta, told it as a story, beginning with that magic phrase, 'Once I was in an Earthquake.' **1968** *Listener* 25 July 120/2 The stilted *oratio obliqua* of court reportage. **1962** *Times Lit. Suppl.* 26 Oct. 826/2 This involves questions of phraseology, idiom, *oratio obliqua*, and the adjustment of dialogue to the pace and mood of the narrative. **1957** R. SPEAIGHT *Life H. Belloc* ix. 175 Belloc would have been on safer ground if he had covered his quotation by making it clear that he was only giving the sense of Robespierre's words, or if he had abridged them in *oratio obliqua*.

oratist (ǫ·rătist). *rare.* [f. ORATE *v.* + -IST.] One given to orating.

1887 SWINBURNE in *Fortn. Rev.* XLII. 173 The orotund oratist of Manhattan.

oratorial, *a.* **2.** (Later example.)

1923 *Daily Mail* 8 Aug. 8/1 The very front rank of our oratorial singers.

Oratorianism. (Earlier examples.)

1847 J. H. NEWMAN *Let.* 31 Dec. (1962) XII. 140, I am anxious you should [try] if you have fully mastered *what* Oratorianism is. **1848** F. W. FABER in R. Chapman *Father Faber* (1961) viii. 172 There is nothing in what you say about oratorianism which takes any of us by surprise.

oratorianize, *v.* (Earlier example.)

1848 F. W. FABER in R. Chapman *Father Faber* (1961) ix. 182 It seems you have not captivated him, and he won't Oratorianize.

oratorship. (Examples.)

1592 G. HARVEY *Foure Letters* (1969) iii. 17, I was supposed not vnmeet for the Oratorship of the vniuersity. **1869** R. C. JEBB *Let.* 3 Nov. (1907) 98, I was standing for the Public Oratorship.

orb, *sb.*[1] Add: **13.** *orb-like* (later examples); **orb-weaver,** (read:) a spider of the family Argiopidæ, which builds an orb-web; **orb-web,** a web formed of lines radiating from a central point, produced by a spider of the family Argiopidæ; also *attrib.*; so **orb-webbed** *a.*

1925 T. DREISER *Amer. Trag.* I. II. xxxi. 367 Her eyes, which were now fixed on him in round orblike solemnity. **1935** W. DE LA MARE *Poems, 1919 to 1934* 335 The white dews drip untrembling down, From bough to bough, orb-like, unblown. **1889** H. C. MCCOOK *Amer. Spiders* I. iii. 53 The round web of the Orbweaver probably deserves the distinction of having given the popular name cobweb to the whole spinningwork of spiders. **1941** W. S. BRISTOWE *Comity of Spiders* II. 244 Most orb-weavers renew their webs, other than the framework, daily. **1889** H. C. MCCOOK *Amer. Spiders* I. iii. 53, I define an orbweb as a snare constructed of right lines radiating from a common centre. **1971** *Oxf. Bk. Invertebr.* 150/1 *Meta* is a common orb-web spinner. **1958** W. S. BRISTOWE *World of Spiders* xix. 256 A series of papers..is opening the door to clearer understanding of the unhesitating route pursued by the orb-webbed spiders in the course of completing their webs.

orbicular, *a.* (*sb.*) Add: **A.** *adj.* **6.** *Petrol.* Containing orbicules.

1824 H. T. DE LA BECHE tr. *Sel. Geol. Mem. in Annales des Mines* p. ix. Diabase... Orbicular D. Spheres with concentric zones of hornblende and compact felspar in a diabase of moderately sized grains. (Orbicular granite of Corsica.) **1857** J. B. JUKES *Student's Man. Geol.* iii. 73 (*heading*) Globular diorite, orbicular greenstone, Corsican granite. **1873** *Proc. Geol. Assoc.* II. 267 The so-called 'orbicular silica'. **1954** H. WILLIAMS et al. *Petrogr.* vii. 132 A few granites have an orbicular texture. **1970** K. C. JACKSON *Textbk. Lithology* v. 280 Orbicular granite... Very commonly, the orbicules show abnormal concentration of the ferromagnesium minerals.

orbicularis (ǭɹbi:kiŭlā·ris), *a.* (*sb.*) *Anat.* Pl. **orbiculares.** [L., = ORBICULAR *a.*] **a.** In full (*musculus*) *orbicularis oris* [L. *ōs, ōr-* mouth]. A muscle surrounding the lips that is partly responsible for moving the lips and the mouth.

1681 J. BROWNE *Compl. Treat. Muscles* 31 There is also another Constrictive Muscle, which hath gotten the name of orbicularis common to the upper lip. **1733** G. DOUGLAS tr. *Winslow's Anat. Expos. Struct. Human Body* II. x. 136 The Semi-Orbiculares are commonly looked upon as one Muscle, surrounding both Lips, from whence it is called Orbicularis. **1797** J. BELL *Anat. Human Body* (ed. 2) I. II. i. 200 The orbicularis oris, or muscle round the mouth, is often named constrictor oris, sphincter, or osculator. **1906** *Practitioner* Dec. 726 The muscles..which..soon become implicated by the disease when cancer begins in this region [*sc.* the angle of the mouth] are: the orbicularis oris, risorius, buccinator, [etc.]. **1970** *Language* XLVI. 315 Electromyographic data were obtained from the cricothyroid and orbicularis muscles of a female speaker of American-English.

b. In full (*musculus*) *orbicularis palpebrarum* [L. *palpebra* eyelid] or (now more commonly) *oculi* [L. *oculus* eye]. A flat muscle that surrounds the orbit and occupies the upper and lower eyelids, responsible for closing the lids (voluntarily or involuntarily).

In quot. 1967 *palpebræ* is the gen. sing. rather than the more usual gen. pl. of *palpebra*.

1681 J. BROWNE *Compl. Treat. Muscles* 14 There is held a Dispute whether that these two Muscles be not properly one, and that *Orbicularis* being so generally received; though the one doth depress, and the other..lift up..to make a perfect close over the eye. **1733** G. DOUGLAS tr. *Winslow's Anat. Expos. Struct. Human Body* II. x. 89 The Muscles of the Palpebræ are commonly reckoned to be two, one peculiar to the upper Eye-Lid, named Levator Palpebræ Superioris; the other common to both, called Musculus Orbicularis Palpebrarum. *Ibid.* 91 The Supercilia..may be moved..downward by the Orbiculares. **1797** J. BELL *Anat. Human Body* (ed. 2) I. II. i. 194 Orbicularis oculi, or palpebrarum, is a neat and regular muscle, surrounding the eye. **1887** J. TOMES *Syst. Dental Surg.* (ed. 3) 573 The spasm of the orbicularis was so great that the right eye could only be opened by great effort. **1902** D. J. CUNNINGHAM *Text-bk. Anat.* 376 The orbicularis palpebrarum (m. orbicularis oculi) is a transversely oval muscle surrounding and occupying the eyelids. **1967** G. M. WYBURN et al. *Conc. Anat.* v. 131/1 Incise the fibres of the orbicularis palpebrae and expose the tarsal plates. **1968** PASSMORE & ROBSON *Compan. Med. Stud.* I. xxi. 17/1 Paralysis of the orbicularis oculi abolishes the blinking response, so that the affected eye is totally unprotected from direct injury.

orbicule (ǭ·ɹbikiŭl). *Petrol.* [back-formation from ORBICULAR *a.*; cf. L. *orbiculus* (see ORBICLE).] A spheroidal inclusion, esp. one composed of a number of concentric layers.

1931 A. JOHANNSEN *Descr. Petrogr. Igneous Rocks* I. ii. 17 In many glassy rocks there are found certain more or less spherical bodies varying in size from pellets visible only under the microscope..to huge spheres ten feet or more in diameter. These rounded bodies are called spherulites when the constituents are arranged radially..and orbicules when these constituents are in concentric shells. **1956** L. E. SPOCK *Guide to Study of Rocks* iii. 26 A few gneous rocks contain orbicules. These are close spherical concentrations of amphibole arranged radially or of biotite in concentric-tangential pattern. **1970** [see *ORBICULAR *a.* 6].

orbit, *sb.* Add: **2.** (Examples referring to artificial satellites and spacecraft generally.) Also, one complete passage around the orbited body.)

1951 *Jrnl. Brit. Interplanetary Soc.* X. 219 He predicted the establishment of 'Earth satellite vehicle' rockets in orbits 25,000 miles from the Earth within about 10 years. **1951** A. C. CLARKE *Sands of Mars* vii. 82 They were now floating round Mars in a free orbit. **1962** J. GLENN in *Into Orbit* 144 Al would also give me the exact times at which the retro-rockets would have to be fired to start bringing the capsule home at the end of one, two and three orbits. **1974** *Sci. Amer.* Jan. 115/1 In its polar orbit it swings close to the North Pole, then moves south across the Equator and finally, having traversed Antarctica, returns north for the next orbit. **1977** J. SCOTT *Hot Pursuit* x. 90 Tracking stations..spotted it straight away when the orbit altered.

d. In extended use: An approximately circular or elliptical path traced by something in motion (e.g. round an atomic nucleus, in a surface wave in a liquid, or in a particle accelerator).

1827 [see *planet-wheel* s.v. *PLANET *sb.*[1] 4]. **1864** W. J. M RANKINE in *Phil. Trans. R. Soc.* CLIII. 131 The centres of the orbits of the particles in a given surface of equal pressure stand at a higher level than the same particles do when the liquid is still. **1891** *Sci. Trans. R. Dublin Soc.* IV. 599 The dominant orbit of the electron..as affected during the subsequent flight of the molecule by an apsidal perturbation. **1904** *Phil. Mag.* VII. 454 If the spectra of the elements be due to the motion of electrons revolving in circular orbits, as above supposed, several rings of orbits must exist where there are different series of spectra. **1913** BOHR in *Ibid.* XXV. 11 The forces which keep the electrons in their position—or their orbits—inside the atom. **1942** J. D. STRANATHAN *'Particles' of Mod. Physics* xi. 426 A magnetic field between two peculiarly shaped pole faces serves to guide the electron repeatedly around an orbit in this field. **1962** *Newnes Conc. Encycl. Nucl. Energy* 169/1 As the particle energy rises the radius of curvature of the path in the magnetic field increases and so the particles execute approximately spiral orbits. **1962** I. R. & M. W. WILLIAMS *Basic Nucl. Physics* i. 15 The physical significance of ψ..means that the exact position of electrons in an atomic orbit or indeed the exact location of the orbit cannot be precisely defined. **1972** M. G. GROSS *Oceanography* ix. 243 In deep water..the water parcels move in nearly stationary circular orbits... The diameter of these orbits at the surface is approximately equal to the wave height.

e. The state of being or moving in an orbit; also *fig.*; chiefly in *in, into orbit* (also with intervening qualifier).

1958 *Spectator* 22 Aug. 263/2 The US satellite now in orbit. **1959** *Economist* 21 Feb. 706/2 One observer.. describes the stock market as being 'in orbit', released from the gravitational pull of the bond market. **1959** *Daily Tel.* 21 Nov. 1/2 The United States put a satellite into orbit from Vandenberg Air Force base in California today. *Ibid.*, Recovery from orbit has never been accomplished by us or Russia. **1961** L. MUMFORD *City in Hist.* (1966) xvi. 580 Our descendants will perhaps understand our curious willingness to expend billions of dollars to shoot a sacrificial victim into planetary orbit. **1967** W. R. HINDMARSH *Atomic Spectra* ii. 9 If an ion..has, like hydrogen, a single electron in orbit about the nucleus. **1969** R. AIRTH *Snatch!* x. 99 Morland..said they were great, which sent Giorgio approximately into orbit. **1971** *Nature* 17 Sept. 160/3 A Salyut spacecraft is already in Earth orbit. **1973** R. BUSBY *Pattern of Violence* v. 81 So Charlie's an acid head... He's probably in orbit by now.

orbit (ǭ·ɹbit), *v.* [f. the sb.] **1.** *trans.* To revolve round in an orbit; to travel round.

1946 *R.A.F. Jrnl.* May 169 Orbiting the target at low level, Pathfinders' Master Bomber assessed the T.I. markers. **1949** *Jrnl. Brit. Interplanetary Soc.* VIII. 3 The way to overcome this difficulty is to have the object circle the earth at a greater distance. It might, in fact, be convenient to have it orbit the earth at a distance of 22,200 miles up. **1951** A. C. CLARKE *Sands of Mars* xi. 141 Orbiting Saturn was Titan, the largest satellite in the Solar System. **1954** *N.Y. Times* 29 Aug. 39/1 If there are satellites orbiting the earth fairly close to it, the Army Office of Ordnance Research will locate them. **1959** D. BEATY *Cone of Silence* xiv. 154 He had been slowly cruising round Mayfair in the car, orbiting huge squares. **1960** *Daily Tel.* 22 Aug. 1/6 (*caption*) Television pictures received from space by the Russians of their dogs.. as they orbited the earth in a 4½-ton space ship. **1963** *Ann. Reg. 1962* 399 Orbiting the moon, and finally landing from a parking orbit round the earth. **1973** *Sci. Amer.* Dec. 47/1 One cannot be sure that real galaxy pairs orbit each other in the parabolas or elongated ellipses demanded by our models. **1975** *Times* 11 Aug. 10/5 In 1971 and 1972, the next Mariner spacecraft to orbit the planet revealed a new..face of Mars.

2. *intr.* **a.** To move in an orbit. Const. various preps.

1951 [see *ORBITAL *a.* 2]. **1955** *Time* 14 Feb. 112/3 When Allingham sketched a sun with planets orbiting round it on a pad, he says, the visitor smiled and pointed to the fourth planet and then to his own space-suited figure. **1957** *Times* 7 Oct. 9/2 The satellite..is orbiting too high to be of maximum value for observations. **1962** F. I. ORDWAY et al. *Basic Astronautics* i. 3 Manned space capsules have orbited several hundred miles above the Earth. **1970** *Nature* 3 Oct. 11/1 American spy satellites orbiting over the Soviet Union have spotted 18 new sites. **1972** *Sci. Amer.* Nov. 105/3 Earlier investigations..showed.. how muonic atoms behave when the muons orbit within the nucleus.

b. To fly in a circle.

1952 *Sat. Even. Post* 27 Dec. 26/3 Clapp broke off and flew south to drop a flare. I orbited just north of the bridge. **1957** R. WATSON-WATT *Three Steps to Victory* 315 Dive-bombers and fighters were to orbit as required till they were joined by the slower torpedo-bombers. **1969** I. KEMP *Brit. G.I. in Vietnam* iii. 68 We had been orbiting in our helicopter for about forty-five minutes.

c. To go into orbit. Also *fig.*

1958 *Times* 30 Aug. 6/1 The Vanguard satellite which failed to orbit on May 27 probably travelled 7,500 miles into the south Atlantic. **1970** *Daily Tel.* 8 June 16/1 The company suspended dealings in March..and they should be resumed by the end of July. The shares should orbit in next to no time. **1970** *Toronto Daily Star* 24 Sept. 22/1 There is no velocity test on the British ball. So, in effect, the manufacturers could improve it to the point where it orbits.

3. *trans.* To put, send, or place in orbit.

1958 *Spectator* 14 Feb. 192/1 Soon after Explorer was orbited the air below it was filled by television stations with five-minute talks. **1961** *Listener* 20 Apr. 684/1 The news of the first man to be orbited and brought to earth. **1962** F. I. ORDWAY et al. *Basic Astronautics* ii. 25 By 1962 the two countries had orbited over a hundred objects into space. **1970** *Nature* 13 June 1011/1 France has been orbiting modest satellites with her own launcher. **1973** *Sci. Amer.* Oct. 75/3 Coronagraphs orbited in space can be constructed differently from their ground-based counterparts.

Hence **o·rbited** *ppl. a.*, **o·rbiting** *vbl. sb.* See also *ORBITING *ppl. a.*

1956 *Spaceflight* I. 6/2 Whether we can land on all of them is improbable, but orbiting trips will be made to get a closer look. **1958** *Engineering* 28 Feb. 270/1 A vehicle weighing 2,000 lb. would expend only a further 70 lb. of propellent in accelerating from an orbiting speed of 18,000 m.p.h. to the escape speed of 25,000 m.p.h. **1966** *Aviation Week & Space Technol.* 5 Dec. 22/3 The separately orbited satellite modules could be mothballed in space—fully equipped with all experiments, however—until ready for use.

orbital, *a.* Add: **1. b.** Anthrop. *orbital index* [tr. F. *indice orbitaire* (P. Broca 1875, in *Mém. de la Soc. d'Anthrop. de Paris* II. 172)], one hundred times the ratio of the height of an orbit to its width.

1879 A. DE QUATREFAGES *Human Species* xxx. 388 The smallest orbital index known is that of the old man of Cro-Magnon, which we have seen to be 61·36. **1904** W. L. H. DUCKWORTH *Stud. from Anthrop. Lab. Anat. Sch. Cambridge* xvii. 104 The mean orbital index of thirty-one skulls is 82·6: that of twenty-four males 81·2; of three females 87·4. **1955** *Chambers's Encycl.* I. 460/2 Similar conventional divisions of the orbital index..are: chamaeconchic ('low orbits') *x*–75·9, mesoconchic ('medium orbits') 76·0–84·9, and hypsiconchic ('high orbits') 85·0–*x*.

2. Delete *Astron.* and add: moving in an orbit; pertaining to such motion. (Further examples.)

1932 [see sense B below]. **1949** W. LEY *Conquest of Space* (1950) 48 Probably the manned moonship will have to be postponed until there is an orbital station. **1951** A. C. CLARKE *Exploration of Space* 47 'Orbital refuelling'..is the key to interplanetary flight. It depends simply on the fact that once a spaceship had reached circular velocity outside the atmosphere, it would continue to orbit indefinitely without the use of power. **1961** *Guardian* 6 May 1/4 The Mercury programme itself could be used as a means of sending men into substantially protracted orbital flights. **1961** *New Scientist* 27 July 203 The advent of *Midas* in orbit raises the whole question of orbital warfare. Either manned or unmanned orbital bombers are an obvious starting point for such conceptions. **1962** I. R. & M. W. WILLIAMS *Basic Nucl. Physics* i. 9 The innermost orbital electrons are the most tightly bound to the atom. **1970** G. K. WOODGATE *Elem. Atomic Struct.* iv. 55 A single-electron atom has a magnetic moment associated with the orbital motion of the electron. **1972** M. G. GROSS *Oceanography* ix. 243 (*caption*) Orbital motion and displacement of a water particle during the passage of a wave.

3. Designating a road, railway, or rail or road system encircling a large town; cf. *RING-ROAD. Also *ellipt.* as quasi-*sb.*, an orbital road.

1933 *Archit. Rev.* LXXIV. 166/2 Orbital road system around London. **1937** *Times* 13 Apr. (British Motor Suppl.) p. x/2 The plan may provide for orbital and radial roads, parkways, viaducts and tunnels, communications to aerodromes, railway stations, and docks. **1939** *N. & Q.* 1 July 1/2 The proposal to thrust an orbital road through land belonging to the National Trust. **1967** *Times Rev. Industry* Apr. 50/2 Essential features are good car parking space..and good communications. Orbital roads, motorways and similar positions are popular. **1970** *Times* 3 Feb. 2 First priority for roads, after the orbitals outside Greater London, is Ringway 2 (North and South Circular Roads). **1975** *Country Life* 16 Oct. 970 (*caption*) Near Great Warley. The London Orbital will pass across the fields in the middle distance. *Ibid.*, The London Outer Orbital Route—a far-flung bypass..running around London. **1976** *Conservation News* Nov./Dec. 7/2 Conservationists..are already presently split on their views of the proposed extension of the M25, London Outer Orbital Motorway. **1977** *Modern Railways* Dec. 459/3 This would effectively establish one of the north orbital routes discussed in the Barran Committee's *London Rail Study* three years ago.

B. *sb. Physics* and *Chem.* A possible pattern of electron density in space which can be realized by two electrons at the most in an atom or molecule; the wave function of a single electron corresponding to any such pattern.

1932 R. S. MULLIKEN in *Physical Rev.* XLI. 50 From here on, one-electron orbital wave functions will be referred to for brevity as orbitals. The method followed here will be to describe unshared electrons always in terms of atomic orbitals but to use molecular orbitals for shared electrons. **1956** *Nature* 11 Feb. 275/1 The resultant *g* values..will yield details on the orbitals involved in the chemical binding of the central iron atom. **1964** J. W. LINNETT *Electronic Struct. Molecules* i. 6 In quantum mechanics the orbits of the Bohr-Sommerfeld semi-classical methods are replaced by orbitals. *Ibid.* 9 Since each spatial orbital is defined by the three quantum numbers *n*, *l* and *m*, this [*sc.* the Pauli Principle] is equivalent to saying that each orbital can accommodate two electrons. **1970** *Sci. Amer.* Apr. 54/2 Each orbital is characterized by a set of 'quantum numbers', denoting various properties of the electrons in that orbital (for instance their spin, angular momentum and the probability of finding the electrons in various regions of space). **1971** J. Z. YOUNG *Introd. Study Man* ii. 26 They are atoms able to receive electrons in the orbitals of their outer shell.

orbitale (ǭɹbitēi·li, -ā·li). [neut. of med.L. *orbitālis* cyclic, f. L. *orbita* ORBIT.] The lowest point on the lower edge of the orbit.

1920 H. H. WILDER *Lab. Man. Anthropometry* I. i. 47 *Orbitale*, the lowest point in the margin of the orbit; one of the points used in defining the Frankfort Horizontal. **1933** *Jrnl. R. Anthrop. Inst.* LXIII. 30 The orbitales..are found, with the aid of the scriber, by rotating the cranium round its auricular axis until the lowest point on the inferior margin of whichever orbit is being considered is at the same height above the drawing-board supporting the instruments as is the auricular axis. **1974** *Nature* 8 Mar. 165/1 Six bilateral and four single roentgenographic landmarks were delineated... The bilateral landmarks were: orbitale; centre of condylar shadow; [etc.].

orbiter (ǭ·ɹbitəɹ). *Astronautics.* [f. *ORBIT *v.* + -ER[1].] A spacecraft in orbit or intended to go into orbit, esp. one that does not subsequently land.

1958 C. C. ADAMS et al. *Space Flight* 140 It is not inconceivable that variations of Project Farside, or Kurt Stehling's proposal Saloon (balloon-launched satellite) may hold the key to economy-type orbiters. **1961** *Life* 3 Mar. 33 The Russians will follow their manned orbiter.. with a multi-manned moon orbiter..and space station. **1969** *Times* 4 Feb. 13/4 Maps drawn from orbiter photographs can differ by nearly two km., depending on the position assumed for the satellite when the photographs were taken. **1971** *Daily Tel.* (Colour Suppl.) 12 Nov. 12/4 While the Viking orbiter continues to survey Mars from space, the lander will start a robot examination of its surroundings. **1976** *Times* 4 Sept. 4/3 He explained that the failure occurred just after the lander separated from the orbiter and prepared to fire a crucial rocket blast that would knock it out of orbit towards Mars.

orbiting (ǭ·ɹbitiŋ), *ppl. a.* [f. *ORBIT *v.* + -ING[2].] That is moving in or into an orbit.

1957 *Observer* 20 Oct. 14/4 Such tricky problems as traffic regulations for orbiting satellites. **1960** *Eng. Lang. Teaching* XIV. 85 The orbiting prices also smooth the road to merger. **1962** *Newnes Conc. Encycl. Nucl. Energy* 37/2 The number *Z* of orbiting electrons equals the number of protons. **1965** *Newsweek* 20 Dec. 57 After weeks inside an orbiting laboratory, the physiological changes may be so profound that Earth becomes the alien environment. **1969** *Guardian* 17 Jan. 1 Russia yesterday created the first orbiting space station. **1971** *Nature* 23 Apr. 494/2 The orbiting Explorer 42 satellite is beginning to oust rocket and balloon borne X-ray experiments from their position of prime importance. **1976** *Field* 18 Nov. 979/1 Orbiting satellites..can tell quickly and comprehensively what is happening on earth at the present, particularly in the matter of temperatures and wind.

orbivirus (ǭ·ɹbivəiᵊrǝ̆s). *Biol.* [f. L. *orbis* ring, circle (see quot. 1971) + VIRUS.] Any of a group of arthropod-borne RNA viruses which cause disease chiefly in higher animals and are similar to reoviruses.

1971 E. C. BORDEN et al. in *Jrnl. Gen. Virol.* XIII. 269 The authors suggest as a name for the distinctive group of viruses described, *orbiviruses* (from *orbis*, (L.), ring or circle). This name reflects the especially large, doughnut-shaped capsomeres seen on the surface of virus particles in negative contrast preparations. It is proposed as a 'genus' name, equal in hierarchy to *reoviruses*. **1974** W. K. JOKLIK in Fraenkel-Conrat & Wagner *Comprehensive Virology* II. v. 236 Since very few orbiviruses have yet been characterized with respect to the structure of their RNA or the polypeptide constitution of their capsids, and since they are serologically very diverse.., the principal criterion for admission to this genus is morphology. *Ibid.*, Although only few orbiviruses have been isolated from vertebrates, antibodies to them are widely distributed. **1976** FENNER & WHITE *Med. Virol.* (ed. 2) xxii. 407 Colorado tick fever virus is the only orbivirus so far recognized as a human pathogen.

orc. Add: **2.** Used by J. R. R. Tolkien (1892–1973) in his tales: one of an imaginary war-like people in whom are combined human and ogreish characteristics. Also *attrib.* and *Comb.*

1937 J. R. R. TOLKIEN *Hobbit* vii. 149 Before you could get round Mirkwood in the North you would be right among the slopes of the Grey Mountains, and they are simply stiff with goblins, hobgoblins, and orcs of the worst description. **1954** —— *Fellowship of Ring* 15 The last battle..was beyond living memory: the Battle of Greenfields, S.R. 1147, in which Bandobras Took routed an invasion of Orcs. *Ibid.* 23 With the help of the ring he escaped from the orc-guards at the gate and rejoined his fellows. *Ibid.* 339 The orcs were dismayed by the fierceness of the defence. *Ibid.* 346 There was a guard of orcs crouching in the shadows behind the great door-posts towering on either side. *Ibid.* 350 The cut is not poisoned, as the wounds of orc-blades too often are. **1954** —— *Two Towers* 48 Orc-speech sounded at all times full of hate and anger. *Ibid.* 138 There the hugest Orcs were mustered, and the wild men of the Dunland fells. *Ibid.* 171 He was not so obviously orc-like as most of these were. **1955** —— *Return of King* 279 No welcome, no beer, no smoke, and a lot of rules and orc-talk instead. *Ibid.* 412 But Orcs and Trolls spoke as they would, without love of words or things; and their language was actually more degraded and filthy than I have shown it. *a* **1973** —— *Silmarillion* (1977) x. 96 And when Thingol came again to Menegnoth he learned that the Orc-host in the west was victorious.

orca (ǭ·ɹkă). [a. L. *orca* a kind of whale, adopted as a generic name by J. E. Gray in Richardson & Gray *Zool. Voy. Erebus & Terror* (1846) I. 33.] The killer whale, *Orcinus orca* (formerly *Orca gladiator*); cf. ORC, ORK 1.

1866 tr. D. F. ESCHRICHT in W. H. Flower *Recent Mem. Cetacea* ii. 172 The teeth of the Orcas are of quite a different kind from those of the cachalots. **1906** *Windsor Mag.* Sept. 469/2 A school of killers or orcas had quietly come up. **1964** E. P. WALKER et al. *Mammals of World* II. 1121/1 Killer Whales; Orcas. **1977** *N.Y. Rev. Bks.* 14 July 26/1, I was called out on deck by excited voices to gaze on a pod of orcas, or killer whales, that flanked and followed our boat as if in escort.

Orcagnesque (ǭɹkănye·sk), *a.* [f. the nickname *Orcagna* Archangel, of Andrea di Cione (active *c* 1308–*c* 1368): see -ESQUE.] Resembling in subject-matter, style, or quality the work or manner of Andrea di Cione, Florentine painter, sculptor, and architect.

1910 W. J. LOCKE *Simon* xix. 261 Call it the Valley of the Shadow, if you like. But don't you think the attendant circumstances were rather mediæval, gargoyley, Orcagnesque? **1933** *Burlington Mag.* Oct. 173/1 He builds upon the remnants of the Orcagnesque tradition and upon Gothic sculpture. **1938** *Ibid.* Dec. 238/1 Lorenzo [Monaco]..may..have been impressed by the decorative style and the pretty colours of Jacopo [di Cione]..because of the very Sienese features which, together with the Orcagnesque basis of the forms, produce a pleasant effect.

orcelite (ōɹse·ləit). *Min.* [ad. F. *orcélite* (also used) (S. Caillère et al. 1959, in *Compt. Rend.* CCXLIX. 1773), f. the name of Jean *Orcel* (b. 1896), French mineralogist: see -ITE[1].] An arsenide of nickel, Ni_2As, found as bronze-coloured hexagonal crystals.

1960 *Amer. Mineralogist* XLV. 753 Orcelite... The mineral has a rose bronze color, browner than that of niccolite. **1962** *Mineral. Abstr.* XV. 352/1 Orcélite.. occurs as a bronze mineral making up a large part of a vein in serpentinized harzburgite in the Trebaghi massif, New Caledonia.

orch, var. *ORK.

orchard. Add: **2.** *orchard-close, -land; orchard-circled, -fresh* adjs.

1889 W. B. YEATS *Wanderings of Oisin* 90 They will lead her home again To the orchard-circled farm. **1844** E. B. BROWNING *Lost Bower* in *Poems* II. 100 In the pleasant orchard closes, 'God bless all our gains,' say we. **1881** O. WILDE *Poems* 116 Past sombre homestead and wet orchard-close. **1922** E. K. CHAMBERS in *Poems of Today* 2nd Ser. 101, I like to think how Shakespeare..ate his pippin in his orchard close. **1971** *Countryman* Autumn 201/2 (Advt.), Direct delivery in own transport to most areas (south of and incl. Glasgow) to reach you in orchard-fresh condition. **1687** *Southampton Rec.* (1877) II. 55 One acre for his orchard land. **1903** *Daily Chron.* 4 Mar. 7/1 In the orchard-land of Normandy the privately distilled liquor is..a recognized medium of exchange. **1938** [see *grain-land* s.v. *GRAIN *sb.*[1] 18 a]. **1977** P. G. WINSLOW *Witch Hill Murder* ii. 126 The Brewster land was orchard land.

orcharded, *a.* Delete *rare* and add later examples.

1791 J. BYNG *Torrington Diaries* (1935) II. 350 Most religious houses have the same kind of low sequester'd situation; and were well orcharded, and well supplied with ponds. **1968** G. JONES *Hist. Vikings* III. iii. 231 Its one perdurable asset was its rich and orcharded soil.

orcharding. **2.** (Earlier and later examples.)

1654 in C. W. Manwaring *Digest of Early Connecticut Probate Rec.* (1904) I. 155 One halfe of all my howsing, Barnes and orcharding. **1818** *Massachusetts Spy* 25 Feb. 1/2 [A farm] is well proportioned into Mowing, Pasturing, Ploughland, Woodland and Orcharding. **1863** *Rep. Maine Board Agric.* 142 One acre of orcharding on suitable soil.. will produce three times the amount in value of any other crop.

orchestra. Add: **1. c.** In modern use, a section of the auditorium of a theatre, now usually the forward part or all of the main floor. Chiefly *U.S.*

1768 STERNE *Sentimental Journey* I. 192 At the end of the orchestra..there is a small esplanade... Though you stand, as in the parterre, you pay the same price as in the orchestra. **1786** *Independent Jrnl.* (N.Y.) 5 Aug. 2 The Pit is very large, and the Theatrum and Orchestra elegant and commodious. **1872** *Chicago Tribune* 28 Mar. 5/4 The interior will contain an orchestra and three circles. **1911** *World's Work* (N.Y.) Sept. 14840/1 They were accustomed, when they went to the theatre, to pay an extra half dollar for seats in the front rows of the orchestra. **1924** D. LAWRENCE *True Story Woodrow Wilson* 117 A President.. cannot sit in the orchestra or in the balcony. **1927** *Amer. Speech* Oct. 23 In the early days of the English theatre what we know as the 'orchestra' or parquet floor of the house, was called the 'pit'. **1961** BOWMAN & BALL *Theatre Lang.* 242 *Orchestra* 1. The seating area on the main level of an auditorium.

3. *fig.* (Later examples.)

1927 CHESTERTON *Coll. Poems* 40, I salute your three violinists... They play my accompaniment; but I shall take no notice of any accompaniment; I myself am a complete orchestra. **1958** M. KENNEDY *Outlaws on Parnassus* v. 77 Writers using an orchestra of minds to tell their story for them were obliged to consider..the variety of language, as used by different minds.

4. (Further examples.) Also, **orchestra pit,** the space in front of, and below, the stage, where the orchestra plays; **orchestra seat** (*U.S.*), **stall,** a seat in a theatre in the orchestra; also, a seat in a theatre next to the orchestra and stage.

1849 *Theatrical Programme* 11 June 22 New Strand Theatre... In order to add to the convenience of the Audience, the Orchestra Stalls have been made more commodious. **1856** *Porter's Spirit of Times* 20 Dec. 262 Laura Keene's Theatre..Reserved Orchestra Seats, 75 cents... Seats in orchestra stalls, $1 each. **1872** *Chicago Jrnl.* 18 July 3/1 The house is divided into an orchestra circle, which includes the entire main floor, Mr. McVicker having decided to discard the names parquet and parquet circle, orchestra and orchestra chairs, and dress circles of first and second balcony circle. **1874** W. LENNOX *My Recoll.* II. 108, I was ensconced in a snug orchestra stall. **1895** *N.Y. Dramatic News* 19 Oct. 3/4 You wouldn't know the orchestra seats were $1,..the scale 75, 50, 25 being displayed everywhere. **1901** Orchestra stall [see STALL *sb.*[1] 5 c]. **1903** *Smart Set* IX. 57/1 There would be a modest little dinner at a quiet French restaurant..and an orchestra-chair at the Metropolitan. **1923** G. SELDES in *Vanity Fair* (N.Y.) Jan. 57/2 It [*sc.* the revue] corresponds to those de luxe railway trains which are always exactly on time..; jazz or symphony may sound from the orchestra pit, but underneath is the real tone of the revue, the steady, incorruptible purr of the dynamo. **1932** *Times Lit. Suppl.* 24 Nov. 888/3 The only other playbill reference.. is a King's Theatre bill for July 13 [1831], which advertised stalls and orchestra places at a guinea each for a concert. **1940** M. DE LA ROCHE *Whiteoak Chron.* II. vii. 241 He had got orchestra chairs for a Russian vaudeville. **1952** GRANVILLE *Dict. Theatr. Terms* 128 *Orchestra stalls,* the seats nearest the orchestra. **1956** G. DURRELL *My Family* viii. 109 Two of them were thrown into the orchestra pit before someone had the sense to lower the curtain. **1977** R. BARNARD *Death on High C's* xv. 155 The opening chords of *Rigoletto* were sounding from the orchestra pit. **1977** *Times* 24 Sept. 12/7 Two sweeping shell-like roofs..cover all but 10 rows of orchestra seats... The opera house sits on a hillside.

orchestral, *a.* Add: Also *transf.* in *orchestral effects.*

1888 KIPLING *In Black & White* 66 It [*sc.* the Religion] added an air-line postal *dak,* and orchestral effects. **1918** *Sphere* 9 Feb. 125/1 The orchestral effects of Monday night's raid.

orchestralist (ǭɹke·strălist). [f. ORCHESTRAL *a.* + -IST.] A writer of orchestral music; an orchestrator.

1899 F. J. CROWEST *Beethoven* 221 The enharmonic change in the first movement..again illustrates the wonderful resources of this king of orchestralists.

orchestrate, *v.* Add: **b.** *fig.* (Further examples.)

1956 H. WHITEHALL in *Kenyon Rev.* XVIII. 418 The traditional 'ideal' metrical patterns..have been 'orchestrated' since Marlowe. **1957** *Times Lit. Suppl.* 6 Dec. 789/2 *Nostromo,* greatest and most splendidly orchestrated of all his fictions. **1967** C. L. WRENN *Word & Symbol* 11 Swinburne's poem *Dolores.* Here there is a kind of orchestrated language which conveys a mood of meaning but no clearly describable sense. **1969** *Daily Tel.* 25 Nov. 30 Russia and America yesterday ratified the treaty banning the spread of nuclear weapons. They chose the same day by a diplomatic agreement typical of the way the two super-Powers are 'orchestrating' their moves in this front. **1974** *Guardian* 23 Jan. 2/8 The White House deployed its heavy artillery today... The counter-attack was well orchestrated. **1975** *N.Y. Times* 31 Oct. 11/6 Planning and organization were particularly striking today, when three busloads of foreign journalists were brought to the staging camps on an officially sponsored visit. The enthusiasm that greeted them was as carefully orchestrated as is the march itself. **1977** *Time* 7 Mar. 8/2 Owen helped to orchestrate the European Community's fishing agreement with the Soviet Union.

orchestration. Add: **b.** (Further examples.)

1905 *Smart Set* Sept. 113/1 Suddenly there was developed a terrific orchestration of chromatic odors. **1936** *Essays & Stud.* XXI. 150 *The Wreck of the Deutschland* has a completeness, an intellectual and emotional unity, a subtlety and variety of verbal orchestration which are unique not only in English but in the literature of the world. **1953** J. S. HUXLEY *Evolution in Action* vi. 138 The world community which we envisage and hope to bring to the birth is a variety-in-unity. In the useful phrase of the American writer, L. K. Frank, it involves an orchestration of cultures. **1956** H. WHITEHALL in *Kenyon Rev.* XVIII. 418 Yet 'orchestration' is affected by another feature of English. **1959** [see *BUILD-UP c]. **1966** *Economist* 2 Apr. 17/2 What is required is the orchestration of the western countries' common interest in reaching an arrangement with Russia. **1975** *Country Life* 16 Jan. 139/2 Braque..achieved a marvellous orchestration of colours and forms. **1975** *New Yorker* 5 May 132/2 Each night, the great orchestration of the evening news went on. **1977** *Time* 17 Oct. 22/1 A conference that collapsed because of poor orchestration was even worse than no conference at all.

c. An overcoat. *U.S. slang.*

1940 *Music Makers* May 37/3 *Orchestration,* an overcoat. **1970** in C. MAJOR *Dict. Afro-Amer. Slang.*

orchestrator (ǭ·ɹkėstrēⁱtəɹ). [f. ORCHESTRATE *v.* + -OR.] One who composes or arranges music for an orchestra, band, etc. Also *fig.*

1907 E. WALKER *Hist. Mus. Eng.* 306 As an orchestrator he [*sc.* Elgar] is among the very greatest in musical history. **1927** *Observer* 20 Nov. 14/4 Liszt, as an orchestrator, seems to overtop the other. **1954** *Grove's Dict. Mus.* (ed. 5) VII. 56/2 Although he [*sc.* Ravel] is a born orchestrator and his command of the medium is unsurpassed, hardly any of his works were originally conceived for the orchestra. **1974** *Times Lit. Suppl.* 1 Nov. 1226/3 An effort was made..to smooth away the more absurd elements of 'crusade' historiography... The orchestrator of this campaign was to be Ricardo de la Cierva, a dynamic and prolific historian. **1976** *Gramophone* May 1750/2, I had no idea what a superb orchestrator he was before I heard that record.

orchestrelle (ǭɹkėstre:l). [f. ORCHESTR(A + Fr. dim. suffix *-elle.*] (See quot. 1961.)

a **1910** 'MARK TWAIN' in *Harper's Mag.* (1911) Jan. 215/1 Paine began playing on the orchestrelle Schubert's *Impromptu.* **1912** A. B. PAINE *Mark Twain* III. 1227 He added..a great Æolian Orchestrelle, with a variety of music. **1925** T. DREISER *Amer. Tragedy* (1926) I. II. xviii. 288 Fox-trots and one-steps were being supplied by an orchestrelle of considerable size. **1961** E. AMES *Daughter of House* (1963) I. vi. 95 The orchestrelle..was a kind of organ which could either be played manually, or—by switching to electrical controls—could be made to play perforated rolls like a player piano.

orchid. Add: **b.** (Further examples.)

1852 B. S. WILLIAMS (*title*) The orchid-grower's manual. **1884** *Encycl. Brit.* XVII. 818/1 Orchid-lovers have better reasons to support their fancy than had the speculative growers and barterers of tulips. **1903** *Daily Chron.* 9 Nov. 3/5 One can never tell what the orchid-seed of enterprise may blossom into. **1908** *Westm. Gaz.* 28 May 12/1 The dangers of orchid-hunting. **1909** *Chambers's Jrnl.* July 430/2 Many an orchid-hunter has sacrificed his life to his daring. **1935** N. MITCHISON *We have been Warned* I. ii. 24 Joyce's dress was long and diaphanous, orchid-coloured. **1974** *Country Life* 18 Apr. 950/4 Already my alpine house and orchid house have been shaded and humidity increased in the latter. **1974** *Encycl. Brit. Macropædia* XIII. 648/1 Discussions about orchids, whether among professional botanists or amateur orchid enthusiasts, often leave the impression that orchids are 'somehow different' from other plants. **1977** A. WILSON *Strange Ride R. Kipling* iii. 136 Singapore's orchid garden.

2. A purplish colour or tint.

1923 *Daily Mail* 15 Jan. 1 Shades are Navy, Bisque, Rust, Champagne, Orchid, Flesh, Silver, Nattier Blue, Black, Jade & Ivory. **1936** *Times* 6 Jan. 11/3 A model Court gown in orchid morganza. **1971** *Guardian* 28 Sept. 11/2 Quilted raincoat... In sand, orchid, or damson. **1975** D. RAMSAY *Descent into Dark* ii. 78 He wore orchid pyjamas of real silk.

orchidacity (ǭɹkidæ·sĭti). [f. ORCHID + -ACITY.] The quality of being 'orchidaceous' (sense 2).

1897 *Sat. Rev.* 13 Feb. 169, I have power and passion, orchidacity and flamboyancy. **1933** *Times Lit. Suppl.* 2 Nov. 747/3 He [*sc.* Kenneth Grahame].., sheltered within the sinister orchidacity of the *Yellow Book,* wrote 'pagan' papers full of the fresh air.

orchidean. Add: Also **orchidian.**

1914 C. A. MERCIER *Astrol. in Med.* 4 One eminent physician discovered..the elixir of life in orchidian extract.

orchidectomy. Add: (Earlier and later examples.) For 'the testicles' read 'one or both of the testicles'. Cf. *ORCHIECTOMY.

1870 *Austral. Med. Jrnl.* XV. 277 Dr. [D. J.] Thomas said, 'I look upon it as a case of strumous sarcocele, requiring operation, which I have taken upon myself to call Orchidectomy. Notices appearing in the daily papers of the operations to take place at this hospital, I thought, that excision of the testicle, or the word castration, would not look well.' **1947** *Nature* 4 Jan. 15/1 Cancers of the male breast yield to orchidectomy. **1967** *Med. Ann.* LXXXV. 217 In cases of male pseudohermaphroditism with testicular feminization, orchidectomy is carried out after puberty..and oestrogen therapy given. **1977** BLACK & BISHOP *Sisterhood* viii. 74 An orchidectomy involves the removal of the testicles.

Hence **orchide·ctomize** *v. trans.,* to perform orchidectomy on; to castrate; **orchide·ctomized** *ppl. a.*

1942 *Amer. Jrnl. Anat.* LXXI. 456 One castrate member..had been orchidectomized when 12 years of age. **1965** *Endocrinology* LXXVI. 1220/1 An intact group and an orchidectomized group were given ·9% saline. *Ibid.* 1222 (*heading*) Orchidectomized rat given saline.

orchidize (ǭ·ɹkidəiz), *v.* [f. ORCHID + -IZE.] *trans.* To make like an orchid. (In quots. *fig.*)

1918 A. Bennett *Pretty Lady* xxxi. 222 In the right environment she would become another being, that was to say, the same being, but orchidised. 1922 Joyce *Ulysses* 418 Jesified orchidised polycimical jesuit!

orchid-like (ǭ·ɹkid,ləik), *a.* [f. Orchid + -like.] Like or resembling an orchid.

1881 W. Robinson *Wild Garden* xii. 93 The German Irises, with their great Orchid-like blossom. 1918 C. W. Beebe *Jungle Peace* (1919) viii. 180 And later, orchid-like, violet, butterfly peas which at first flowered among the ashes on the ground, but climbed as soon as they found support. 1923 D. H. Lawrence *Birds, Beasts & Flowers* 39 What would I not give To bring back the rare and orchid-like Evil-yclept Etruscan?

orchido-. Add: **o·rchidopexy.** *Surg.* [*-pexy], fixation of a testicle, esp. of an undescended testicle in the scrotum.

1893 W. H. A. Jacobson *Dis. Male Organs* i. ii. 83 (*heading*) Transplantation of a retained or misplaced testicle into the scrotum.—Orchidopexy. 1974 Passmore & Robson *Compan. Med. Stud.* III. i. xxvii. 8/1 The operation of choice [for imperfect descent of the testis] before puberty is orchidopexy, and after puberty orchidectomy.

orchiectomy (ǭɹki,e·ktŏmi). *Surg.* [See Orchidectomy.] = Orchidectomy in Dict. and Suppl.

1894 in Gould *Dict. Med.* 938/1. 1948 Bailey & Love *Short Pract. Surg.* (ed. 8) III. xxxiii. 602 Orchiectomy is indicated when the other testis is normal, and the cord too short to allow replacement of the maldescended organ in the scrotum. 1963 *Lancet* 5 Jan. 21/1 In four cases where the testicle was regarded as non-viable the operation was orchiectomy. Orchiopexy was carried out in the rest though it was not always thought that the organ would function. 1974 *Acta Endocrinol.* LXXVI. 237 A progressive decrease in the pituitary FSH level was observed up to 72 h after orchiectomy.

orchiopexy (ǭ·ɹki,ŏpeksi). *Surg.* [f. Gr. ὄρχι-ς testicle + -o + *-pexy.] = *orchidopexy* s.v. *orchido-.

[1909 F. Torek in *N.Y. Med. Jrnl.* XC. 952/2, I had to present one of my cases of orcheopexy before this section of the Academy.] 1931 —— in *Ann. Surg.* XCIV. 97 My original spelling, orcheopexy, should therefore be changed to orchiopexy. 1938 Bailey & Love *Short Pract. Surg.* (ed. 4) xxix. 544 If this treatment fails, orchiopexy should be advised. 1963 [see *orchiectomy]. 1974 *Investigative Urol.* XI. 303 Nephropexy and orchiopexy using tissue adhesives were performed on rats and rabbits.

orcinol. Add: Now the usual name for the substance (which gives a purple colour with ribose and is used in estimating nucleic acids). (Earlier and later examples.)

1880 *Jrnl. Chem. Soc.* XXXVIII. 113 (*heading*) Resorcinol and orcinol derivatives. 1921 W. T. K. Braunholtz tr. *Moureu's Fund. Princ. Org. Chem.* vii. 372 An ammoniacal solution of orcinol undergoes oxidation in the air, giving orceïn,..which is a red dyestuff. 1922 *Chem. Age* VII. 709/1 The various orders of *Variolaria*.., *Rocella* and *Lecanora* all contain orcinol in the free state, and these lichens are now used for the production of the two substitution products, litmus and archil. 1969 *Phytochem.* VIII. 2223 Orcinol (5-methylresorcinol) has been detected for the first time in higher plants, in ten species of the Ericaceae. 1973 N. C. Mishra et al. in Niu & Segal *Role of Ribonucleic Acid* 261 DNA and RNA were determined chemically by diphenylamine and orcinol reactions respectively.

orciprenaline (ǭɹsipre·nălīn). *Pharm.* [f. Orci(nol + *iso)prenaline.] A sympathomimetic amine, $C_6H_3(OH)_2CH(OH)CH_2NHCH(CH_3)_2$, that is closely related to isoprenaline in structure and is taken (usu. as the sulphate, a white, bitter-tasting powder) for the relief of bronchitis and asthma, usu. in an inhaler or as tablets or a syrup.

1963 *Med. Digest* VIII. 95/1 Alupent (orciprenaline) is a recently introduced synthetic drug, 1-(3,5-dihydroxyphenyl)-2-isopropylamino-ethanol sulphate. 1964 *Brit. Med. Jrnl.* 18 Apr. 1017/2 Orciprenaline ('alupent'), an analogue of isoprenaline was..effective in the relief of airways obstruction..whether taken by mouth or by inhalation. 1971 *Brit. Med. Bull.* XXVII. 27/1 Death might be caused by the excessive use of aerosol inhalers containing..orciprenaline. 1974 *Times* 12 Jan. 1/3 Her pregnancy..lasted 37 weeks aided by a muscle-relaxant drug called Orciprinaline [*sic*].

order, *sb.* Add: **I. 1. c.** *Physics.* Each of a successive series of spectra formed by the interference or diffraction of light; hence, a positive number characterizing a particular spectrum or interference fringe, now recognized as equal to the number of wavelengths by which the optical paths of successive contributing rays differ.

1704 Newton *Opticks* ii. 6 The third Circuit or Order was purple, blue, green, yellow, and red. 1722 *Phil. Trans. R. Soc.* XXXI. 244 We had here four Orders of Colours, and perhaps the beginning of a fifth, for what..I call the Purple, is a Mixture of the Purple of each of the upper Series with the Red of the next below it. 1831 [see sense 1 a]. 1874 *Phil. Mag.* XLVII. 194 In considering the influence of the number of lines (n) and the order of the spectrum (m), we will suppose that the ruling [of the diffraction grating] is accurate. 1953 Spink & Feigl tr. *Pinsker's Electron Diffraction* ii. 26 We obtain..$n\lambda = 2d \sin \theta$, n being the order of the reflection [*sc.* of electrons from a crystal]. This gives the number of whole wavelengths corresponding to the path difference for waves scattered by two neighbouring parallel planes of the direct lattice. 1967 W. H. Steel *Interferometry* viii. 139 Observation of the interference fringes yields only the excess fraction ϵ of the order of interference, the amount by which the order exceeds some unknown integer.

II. 6. a. In the Roman Catholic Church, the orders of subdeacon, exorcist, and *ostiarius* were suppressed in 1972.

c. (Later examples of *sing.*)

1873 E. E. Estcourt *Question of Anglican Ordinations* i. 4 Holy Order is a Sacrament, requiring a certain matter and form. 1977 *Christian* IV. 31 There are two priesthoods... One is conferred on all, in baptism; the other on some, in the sacrament of holy order. *Ibid.* 34 The sacrament of order is a direct participation in the mystery of Pentecost.

8. *Order of Merit*; hence *Order-of-Merited* adj. (*nonce*).

1799 *Public Characters of 1799–1800* II. 164 The King of Poland..also conferred on him the honours of knighthood of the Order of Merit. 1842 T. Campbell *Frederick the Great* II. xv. 71 If the order of the Black Eagle was conferred on any of the members of the order of Merit, he had to send back the latter to the king. 1880 Disraeli *Endymion* II. xv. 150 Now you tell your master..that if he wants to strengthen the institutions of this country, the government should establish an order of merit. 1902 *Pall Mall Gaz.* XXVIII. 71/1 The King's new Order of Merit would have attracted more attention if the list had appeared alone, and not at the tail of the honours bestowed at the Coronation. 1912 G. W. E. Russell *Afterthoughts* xxxix. 325 An 'Order of Merit'—as far as History goes, *the* Order of Merit—was founded by Frederick the Great in 1740; and the name was copied in turn by Hesse Cassel, Baden, Bavaria, Saxony, Oldenburg, Würtemberg, and Belgium. 1929 A. Huxley *Swift* in *Holy Face & Other Ess.* 64 If Swift were alive to-day, he would be the adored..the Order-of-Merited author, not of *Gulliver*..but of *A Kiss for Cinderella* and *Peter Pan.* 1959 *Chambers's Encycl.* X. 228/2 The Order of Merit (O.M.) was instituted in 1902 and is awarded to officers of the fighting services and civilians for conspicuous service. 1970 C. L. Cline *Lett. George Meredith* I. p. xxix, In 1905 came official recognition: he became the twelfth member of the recently founded Order of Merit.

b. (Earlier example of *pl.*)

1818 Keats *Let.* 14 Oct. (1958) I. 396 No sensation is created by Greatness but by the number of orders a Man has at his Button holes.

c. *order of the boot*: see *boot *sb.*³ 1 c.

10. (Further examples.) *of the same order*, said of two variables whose ratio tends to a finite number as they both tend to zero or to infinity; *to the first* (or *second*, etc.) *order*, neglecting quantities of higher order than the first (or second, etc.). Also in *Comb.* with preceding ordinal number.

1838 *Penny Cycl.* XII. 472/2 A succession of infinitely small quantities, each of which is infinitely smaller than the preceding, is said to be a series of infinitesimals of different orders. Such a series is x, x^2, x^3, &c. 1843 *Scientific Mem.* III. 172 It follows..that for an infinitely small ρ, a/ρ must itself be infinitely small; but the two values will be of the same order only if there is a finite radius of curvature. *Ibid.*, If we assume a/ρ to be of the same order as ρ^u,..then $a/(\rho^{1+u})$ represents a finite quantity varying continuously. 1880 *Encycl. Brit.* XIII. 14/1 Two infinitesimals α, β are said to be of the same order if the fraction β/α tends to a finite limit. If β/α^n tends to a finite limit, β is called an infinitesimal of the nth order in comparison with α. 1908 G. H. Hardy *Course Pure Math.* v. 169 We shall say that $\phi(x)$ is of the kth order of greatness when x is small if $\phi(x)/x^{-k} = x^k\phi(x)$ tends to a limit different from zero as x tends to 0. 1922 *Phil. Mag.* XLIII. 945 Both Sommerfeld and Epstein have obtained the value of W..by slightly different methods to the first order in F... We shall proceed to a second approximation. 1937 E. C. Kemble *Fund. Princ. Quantum Mech.* xi. 384 In order to get the second-order corrections to E_k and Ψ_k we differentiate Eq. (47·2) twice with respect to λ and then set λ equal to zero. *Ibid.* 386 These second-order formulas are so complicated that they are seldom used and the corrections of the third and higher order [*sic*] are still more complex. 1952 D. R. Hartree *Numerical Anal.* ix. 192 If $a_1 \neq 0$..the number of additional correct significant figures obtained from each repetition of such a process (or..the number of repetitions required to obtain each new correct significant figure) is the same, however many figures have been obtained. Such a process is called 'first-order'. But if $a_1 = 0$, $a_2 \neq 0$..the successive errors ξ_n are ultimately related by $\xi_{n+1} = a_2\xi_n^2$... The number of correct significant figures is approximately doubled for each repetition of the iterative process... Such a process is called 'second-order'. 1962 Simpson & Richards *Physical Princ. Junction Transistors* vi. 110 This discussion shows that h_{rb} and h_{ob} arise in such an indirect manner that they might almost be regarded as second-order effects. Their magnitudes confirm this impression. 1971 *Nature* 19 Feb. 522/2 Talk of the eclipse being an unusual strain to the Earth is idle nonsense when eclipse type conditions prevail to first order twice every lunar month.

b. *of the order of*: (*a*) *Math.* (also *of order*), having a ratio to (the quantity specified) that tends in the limit to a finite number, or that is neither a large number nor a small fraction; (*b*) *gen.* (also *in* or *on the order of*), in the region of; somewhere about.

1903 O. Lodge *Mod. Views Matter* 7 Their mass is of the order one-thousandth of the atomic mass of hydrogen. 1913 *Rep. Brit. Assoc. Adv. Sci. 1912* 398 The change of weight..should have been of the order of 1 in 10^7 per 1°C. 1927 N. V. Sidgwick *Electronic Theory of Valency* ii. 20 The accuracy of spectroscopic measurements (of the order of one in a million). 1937 Michell & Belz *Elem. Math. Analysis* I. i. 94 A number is said to be of order 10^n if its ratio to 10^n is neither large nor small. *Ibid.*, The function $f(x)$ is said to be of the order of x^n as x converges to zero, or to be of the nth order with respect to x, if the ratio $f(x)/x^n$ has two focal bounds of the same sign. *Ibid.* 95 The notation $f(x) = O(x^n)$ is sometimes used to express that the function $f(x)$ is of the order of x^n, that is, of the nth order, when x converges to zero. 1947 R. L. Wakeman *Chem. Commercial Plastics* xxvi. 786 Concentrations of catalyst in the order of 1 per cent. 1955 D. A. Quadling *Math. Analysis* xi. 178 We may write..$|E/h^n| \leq K$, where K is independent of h. In such a case we say that E is 'of order h^n', or 'of the nth order of small quantities'. 1958 *Times* 10 Dec. 10/4 Their radioactivity was of the order of tens of millicuries. 1962 F. I. Ordway et al. *Basic Astronautics* x. 422 Specific impulses on the order of 3000 lb-sec/lb are possible. 1963 R. A. Rankin *Introd. Math. Analysis* vii. 455 The statement $f(n) = O\{\phi(n)\}$ as $n \to \infty$, or for large n, means that there exist real numbers $K \geq 0$ and $X \geq X_0$, which are independent of n, and are such that $|f(n)| \leq K\phi(n)$ for all $n > X$... The statement.. may be read as '$f(n)$ is a quantity of the order of $\phi(n)$'. 1970 *Daily Tel.* 3 Dec. 21/1 (Advt.), A salary in the order of £1,500 is envisaged. 1971 *Sci. Amer.* June 24/1 Pulses lasting on the order of a nanosecond or longer can be reliably produced. 1975 *Nature* 10 Apr. 478/1 The average flow through the gorge is of the order of 2,000–3,000 cubic metres per second.

c. *order of magnitude*: approximate number or magnitude in a scale in which equal steps correspond to a fixed multiplying factor (usu. taken as 10); a range between one power of 10 and the next; also, the order (Order *sb.* 10) of an infinitesimal or an infinite number. Also *attrib.* (with hyphens).

1875 *Jrnl. Anthrop. Inst.* IV. 143 The number of surnames extinguished becomes a number of the same order of magnitude as the total number at first starting in N. 1891 *Phil. Mag.* XXXII. 296 The electrochemical equivalent of gas atoms is of the same order of magnitude as that of the same atoms in electrolytes. 1903 D. A. Murray *First Course Infinitesimal Calculus* iii. 31 When the limiting value of the ratio m/n is a finite number, m and n are said..to be of the same order of magnitude. *Ibid.* 32 Infinite numbers, being reciprocals of infinitesimals, also have different orders of magnitude. 1909 J. P. Iddings *Igneous Rocks* I. vi. 193 The grains..are not all of the same order of magnitude, since one may be nine or ten times larger than another. 1937 Michell & Belz *Elem. Math. Analysis* I. i. 94 Two numbers (or quantities) are of the same order of magnitude when their ratio is neither a large number nor a small fraction... It is often convenient to make a comparison of a number with a power of 10. 1941 Courant & Robbins *What is Math.?* viii. 469 We shall say that b_n tends to infinity faster than a_n, or has a higher order of magnitude than a_n, if the ratio a_n/b_n (numerator and denominator of which both tend to infinity) tends to zero as n increases. 1968 R. A. Lyttleton *Mysteries Solar Syst.* v. 157 The general size..would be expected to be of the order of the width of the stream. An order-of-magnitude estimate of this can be made in the following way. 1971 I. G. Gass et al. *Understanding Earth* iv. 78/2 The dynamo theory seems natural and unforced, and order-of-magnitude arguments are encouraging. 1971 *Physics Bull.* Oct. 586/1 The width of the second line of the hydrogen Balmer series, Hβ, is now considered to be a reliable measure of electron density to better than 10% over four orders of magnitude (say 10^{14}–10^{18} cm^{-3}). 1974 *Sci. Amer.* June 27/1 These processes multiply the power per unit area by 14 orders of magnitude from 10^5 watts per square centimeter..to 10^{19} watts per square centimeter.

d. *Math.* (i) The number of elements in a group.

1878 A. Cayley in *Amer. Jrnl. Math.* I. 51 A set of symbols α, β, γ..such that the product $\alpha\beta$ of each two of them..is a symbol of the set, is a group... When the number of the symbols (or terms) is $= n$, then the group is of the nth order. 1941 [see next sense]. 1965 Patterson & Rutherford *Elem. Abstr. Algebra* ii. 36 The set of all permutations of 1, 2, 3,..., n forms a group with respect to multiplication... It is a finite group of order $n!$ and it plays an important part in the theory of finite groups.

(ii) The smallest positive integer m for which g^m is equal to the identity element of a group, g being any given element.

1897 W. Burnside *Theory of Groups of Finite Order* ii. 14 Let S be an operation of a group of finite order N... If S^{m+1} is the first of the series [*sc.* $S, S^2, S^3, \ldots$] which is the same as S,..then..$S^m = 1$... The integer m is called the order of the operation S. 1941 Birkhoff & MacLane *Survey Mod. Algebra* vi. 147 Every element of a finite group G has as order a divisor of the order of G. 1968 I. D. Macdonald *Theory of Groups* iii. 45 A periodic group is a group in which every element has finite order.

e. Each of the ranks or levels in a (non-mathematical) hierarchy in which every member save those in the lowest rank is a function of members of the next lower rank; *spec.* in *Logic* (see quot. 1908) and *Psychol.* (see quot. 1947). Freq. in *Comb.* with preceding ordinal number.

In *Math.* this sense is identical with 10 in Dict.

1908 B. Russell in *Amer. Jrnl. Math.* XXX. 238 A proposition containing no apparent variable we will call an elementary proposition... Elementary propositions together with such as contain only individuals as apparent variables we will call first-order propositions... We can thus form new propositions in which first-order propositions occur as apparent variables. These we will call second-order propositions... Thus, *e.g.*, if Epimenides asserts 'all first-order propositions affirmed by me are false', he asserts a second-order proposition. *Ibid.*, Propositions of order *n*..will be such as contain propositions of order *n*−1, but of no higher order, as apparent variables. **1929** A. W. WHITEHEAD *Process & Reality* II. ix. 285 We must provide a reason..why one 'ground' is selected rather than another... We are thus driven back to a second-order 'ground' of probability. **1936** *Mind* XLV. 170 Necessary propositions are, thus, second-order propositions, which implicitly define 'proposition' by stating the properties of anything that is a proposition. **1941** J. S. HUXLEY *Uniqueness of Man* xi. 245 Cells are first-order individuals, bodies second-order ones, and human societies (like hydroid colonies or beehives) third-order ones. **1947** L. L. THURSTONE *Multiple-Factor Analysis* xviii. 411 Factors that are obtained from the test correlations will be called first-order factors... Factors that are obtained from the correlations of the first-order factors will be called second-order factors. **1954** I. M. COPE *Symbolic Logic* 336 The hierarchy of orders prevents us from speaking about all functions or properties of a given type, permitting us to speak only about all first order functions of a given type, or all second order functions of a given type, etc. *Ibid.* 337 A proposition is of order $n+1$ if it contains a quantifier on a propositional variable of order *n* but contains no quantifier on any propositional variable of order *m* where $m \geq n$. **1961** J. B. WILSON *Reason & Morals* i. 4 Philosophers themselves are accustomed to speak of philosophical statements as being 'second-order' statements. **1971** *Sci. Amer.* Aug. 98/1 All the axioms of a complete ordered field are first-order sentences except for the completion axiom.., which talks about a property of *all* subsets. **1977** A. HALLAM *Planet Earth* 75/3 In this system, fingertip tributaries are described as first-order; when two first-order streams combine the result is a second-order stream. Two second-orders give a third-order, and so on.

f. *Chem.* The sum of the exponents of the concentrations of reactants, or the exponent of any particular reactant, in the expression for the rate of a chemical reaction. Freq. in *Comb.* with preceding ordinal number.

1902 H. C. JONES *Elem. Physical Chem.* ix. 465 Although there are only two substances, there are three molecules involved in the reaction, and we would expect it to be a reaction of the third order. **1933** E. A. MOELWYN-HUGHES *Kinetics of Reactions in Solution* vii. 219 Ionic reactions have occasionally been found to be of a higher kinetic order than is now regarded as possible. **1950** W. J. MOORE *Physical Chem.* xvii. 514 This is also a second-order reaction. It is said to be *first-order with respect to* C_2H_5Br, *first-order with respect to* $(C_2H_5)_3N$, and *second-order over-all*. **1968** R. O. C. NORMAN *Princ. Org. Synthesis* iii. 78 The decarbonylation of acetaldehyde is of non-integral order but contains both unimolecular and bimolecular steps.

g. *Physics* and *Chem.* An integer (usually 1 or 2) characterizing a change of phase of a substance, equal to the order of the lowest-order derivatives of the free energy that exhibit a discontinuity at the change. [After the similar use of G. *ordnung* introduced by P. Ehrenfest 1933 (see quot. 1933).]

1933 *Proc. Sect. Sci. Kon. Akad. Wetensch. Amsterdam* XXXVI. 152 *G* may be a function of *p* and *T* which suffers along a λ-curve (Fig. 3) a discontinuity of the second order[1], so that along that curve..$\Delta G = 0$, whereas the differential coefficients of *G* make a jump. [[1]*Note*] Cf. P. Ehrenfest. Proceedings of this meeting. [i.e. *Ibid.* 153–7 (in Ger.)]. **1946** *Nature* 28 Dec. 924/2 At low temperatures both crystalline and amorphous states [of rubber] give place to the glass-hard condition. The transition to the glassy state—the so-called second-order transition—is discussed. **1948** *Jrnl. Chem. Physics* XVI. 665 (*heading*) Note on a relation between the order of a phase transition and discontinuities in the distribution functions of molecules. **1967** A. H. COTTRELL *Introd. Metall.* xiv. 220 First-order changes such as melting and polymorphic changes of crystal structure. **1968** C. G. KUPER *Introd. Theory Superconductivity* ii. 23 The superconducting transition in the absence of a magnetic field is of second order (Ehrenfest 1933). In other words, the specific heat is discontinuous but there is no latent heat.

III. 12. b. *order of battle*, the arrangement or disposition of sections of an army or naval force; now *spec.* the organization, movements, weaponry, etc., of an enemy force; the discovery of this; a tabular record of this; also *attrib.*

1769 [see BATTLE *sb.* 12]. **1797** *Encycl. Brit.* III. 81/1 A Roman legion, ranged in order of battle, consisted of *hastati*, placed in the front; of *principes*, who were all old experienced soldiers, placed behind the former; and of *triarii*, heavy armed with large bucklers, behind the *principes*. **1889** H. R. GALL *Mod. Tactics* ii. 11 A practical and experienced soldier, seeing his enemy get under arms and form up in order of battle, will rapidly gather a lot of valuable information regarding his numbers, artillery positions [etc.]. **1924** W. C. SWEENEY *Military Intelligence* viii. 172 Enemy Order of Battle. This section is charged with maintaining the battle order of the enemy located within the area of responsibility of the commander. **1928** H. M. D. PARKER *Roman Legions* ix. 251 Arrian, in his order of battle against the Alani, shows that the legions were drawn up as a phalanx eight deep. **1934** WEBSTER s.v., *Order of battle*.., a tabular compilation by unit showing organization, commanders, movements, etc. over an extended time. **1946** CHANDLER & ROBB *Front-Line Intelligence* xii. 137 O/B (Order of battle) is a military science whose mission is to determine: (1) How strong the enemy is. (2) How he is organized. (3) What kind of weapons he has. (4) Experience of his troops. (5) Leadership of his troops. (6) Where his units are located. **1948** F. R. COWELL *Cicero & Roman Republic* ii. 36 The Greeks..were the first to invent an order of battle in which drilled men acting together as a unit.. were able to overcome unorganised enemies many times more numerous. **1950** *Tactics & Techniques Infantry* (U.S.) II. ii. 312 When a new enemy unit is identified, order of battle records will indicate its last known strength and special equipment such as tanks, armored cars, and artillery; its combat record; or any quirks of its commander. A new operation is contemplated; order of battle data will provide information as to the strength, equipment, location, mobility, and combat efficiency of the specific units the enemy can employ. *Ibid.* 313 Strategic order of battle deals with all enemy military units, regardless of location. **1966** D. G. CHANDLER *Campaigns of Napoleon* (1967) 1099 Order of battle of the Army of Italy, April 12, 1796. **1971** *Combat Intelligence* (U.S. Dept. of Army, Field Manual 30-5) vii. 7-1 In determining enemy capabilities and probable courses of action, commanders must consider order of battle intelligence together with other intelligence pertaining to the enemy, weather, and terrain. **1975** T. ALLBEURY *Special Collection* ii. 11 There were daily situation reports from both the west and east fronts including Wehrmacht orders-of-battle. **1977** S. COULTER *Soyuz Affair* v. 42 The spy..who brought you the cypher table or the enemy order of battle.

13. d. Equipment, uniform, etc., for some purpose, as *drill order, field-day order, review order*; *marching order*: see MARCHING *vbl. sb.* d in Dict. and Suppl. Also with sbs. descriptive of appearance, as *shirt-sleeve order*. (Orig. and chiefly *Mil.*)

1852 R. BURN *Naval & Milit. Techn. Dict. French Lang.* (ed. 2) II. 176/2 *Drill order*, tenue d'exercise, petite tenue. **1874** *Queen's Regulations Army 1873* 162 Review-order; to be worn when the Sovereign is present, for Royal escorts and guards of honour. *Ibid.* 163 Field-day-order; to be used generally for summer field-days, divisional and brigade drills,..[etc.]. *Ibid.*, Drill-order; to be used at ordinary drills and in riding-schools. **1876** Review order [see REVIEW *sb.* 3]. **1968** J. LOCK *Lady Policeman* viii. 60 My serge skirt feels heavy, my feet feel hot and sticky. Still, we are lucky to have shirt-sleeve order—the PCs haven't and look as if they are about to expire. **1973** R. HILL *Ruling Passion* II. vii. 138 The warm weather..had returned..it would be shirt-sleeve order before the day was out. **1977** 'D. MACNEIL' *Wolf in Fold* v. 49 Behind them, dressed in review order, marched the infantry of the British Army.

18. (Earlier examples.)

a **1751** in *Camden Miscellany* (1969) XXIII. 170 His vanity will make him constantly puzzling our Speaker and our Chairmen of Committees, in points of order, which in reality he will know better than they. **1781** *Parl. Reg.* 27 Nov. 46 After some debate on the point of order, respecting the right of reply, claimed by those who had made a motion.

20. *spec.* of tobacco. Cf. *CASE *sb.*[1] 5 b.

1897 M. WHITNEY in *U.S. Dept. Agric. Farmers' Bull.* No. 60. 4 'Order' or 'case' in tobacco curing means a mint condition in which the tissue will not break. **1966** *Pubn. Amer. Dial. Soc.* XLV. 18 The tobacco has to be in order before it can be properly stripped.

21. (Further example.)

1938 J. CARY *Castle Corner* 435 The sentry threw his gun to the order and shouted in one word, 'alt-oo-go dar. Pass, friend'.

IV. 23. a. (Earlier and later examples of *under orders*.) Cf. *under starter's orders* s.v. *STARTER.

1835 DICKENS *Let.* *c* 29 Dec. (1965) I. 113, I regret to say that my being under orders from The Chronicle will prevent my enjoying the pleasure of seeing you tomorrow. **1969** H. R. F. KEATING *Inspector Ghote plays Joker* iii. 55 This authoritative figure took the microphone..and made an announcement that the horses were under orders. **1977** A. C. H. SMITH *Jericho Gun* iv. 52 The PA commentary told him when they were under orders, and off.

b. *Order in Council*: an order issued by the British sovereign († or the governor of a British colony) on the advice of his or her privy council; also, an order issued by a government department under powers bestowed by Act of Parliament.

[**1674–5** (*title*) His Majesties Declaration for enforcing a late Order made in Council.] **1746** in *New Jersey Archives* (1882) 1st Ser. VI. 369 An Embargo on all Vessels in this Province for the Space of one Month unless his [*sc.* the president's] Order in Council shall be first Obtained for the Sailing of any Vessel. **1785** [see COUNCIL *sb.* 6 a]. **1809** *Ann. Reg. 1807* xii. 227/2 English commerce..was not only greatly cramped, but lay prostrated on the ground, and motionless, before a protecting and self-defensive system was interposed by our orders in council. **1867** A. TODD *On Parl. Govt. in Eng.* I. v. 287 The crown has no right, by a mere Order in Council,..to sanction a departure from the requirements of an existing law. **1892** W. R. ANSON *Law & Custom of Constitution* II. i. 47 An Order in Council is practically a resolution passed by the Queen in Council, communicated by publication or otherwise to those whom it may concern. **1911** *Encycl. Brit.* XX. 187/2 At the present day orders in council are extensively used by the various administrative departments of the government, who act on the strength of powers conferred upon them by some act of parliament. **1928** A. FITZROY *Hist. Privy Council* iv. 85 The Orders in Council in reply to Napoleon's Milan and Berlin decrees. **1961** *Halsbury's Laws Eng.* (ed. 3) XXXVI. 477 Proclamations and Orders in Council are instruments made by the Crown, the latter, by which the great majority of powers conferred on the Crown are required to be exercised, being orders expressed to be made by and with the advice of the Privy Council. **1964** *Mod. Law Rev.* XXVIII. III. 335 His Majesty could by Order in Council provide..that the registers of a particular country..should be deemed to be 'a public register'. **1973** *Trinidad & Tobago Overseas Express* 28 May 4/2 If the initiative came from Britain then the Order-in-Council method would be applied. **1977** *Gay News* 24 Mar. 1/3 Mr. Mason is expected to draw up an Order in Council.

c. *doctor's orders*: instructions from one's physician; *fig.*, any injunctions which cannot be evaded.

1841 DICKENS *Let.* 18 Jan. (1969) II. 189, I have been obliged to make up my mind—on the doctor's orders—to stay at home this evening. **1886** H. MUNBY *Let.* 12 Mar. in D. Hudson *Munby* (1972) 410 Oh the miserable & false step you took when you separated me from you, by the doctor's orders. **1932** A. CHRISTIE *Peril at End House* ix. 104 No one..will be admitted... 'Doctor's orders,' they will be told. A phrase very convenient and one not to be gainsayed. **1940** W. FAULKNER *Hamlet* 73 He returned to the gallery offering his candy about. 'Doctor's orders,' he said. 'He'll probably send me another bill now for ten cents for advising me to eat a nickel's worth of candy.' **1970** *Guardian* 26 Nov. 3/4 The absence of East German leader, Herr Ulbricht, whose official explanation of 'doctor's orders' failed to convince a Communist journalist. **1976** *Sci. Amer.* Mar. 127/2 'Doctor's orders' excuse almost any behaviour, yet they are mere advice.

d. Phr. *orders are* (also vulg. or joc. *is*) *orders*: commands must be obeyed.

1852 H. MELVILLE *Pierre* XVI. ii. 323, I am sorry, sir, but orders are orders:..I can't disobey him. **1933** 'HAY' & 'ARMSTRONG' (title of play) Orders are orders. **1939** A. RANSOME *Secret Water* i. 18 I'm awfully sorry, you people. It just can't be helped. Orders is orders. **1973** *Times* 2 June 12/3 The delicious ridiculousness of the telegram perhaps has to be explained... But orders were orders.

e. *Computers.* = *INSTRUCTION 4 c, *COMMAND *sb.* 1 d; *esp.* one in machine language or another low-level language.

1946 GOLDSTINE & VON NEUMANN in J. von Neumann *Coll. Wks.* (1961) V. 26 In performing a multiplication one usually performs about 3 or 4 associated additions or subtractions or comparisons; hence at least 4–5 orders must be given and at least that many numbers transferred—it is assumed that an order specifies only one basic operation, together with its transfers. *Ibid.*, We agree to store our orders in the same place as our numbers. **1948** [see *INPUT *sb.* 2 d]. **1958** [see *INSTRUCTION 4 c]. **1967** KLERER & KORN *Digital Computer User's Handbk.* I. i. 10 Machine-language coding uses the machine order code, which is directly interpreted by the instruction register. **1970** O. DOPPING *Computers & Data Processing* vi. 98 The detailed information sent to the input/output units from the local control units can be called orders.

24. b. (Examples with sense 'postal order'.)

1891 YEATS *Let.* Dec. (1954) 186, I had intended to return the £1 at once... Some days passed by..the order which I enclose being all the time on my table awaiting posting. **1913** W. OWEN *Let.* 16 Dec. (1967) 221, I have cashed the Order long ago.

c. *a large order* (further examples). Also, *a big order, a strong order*; *a tall order*: see TALL *a.* 8 d in Dict. and Suppl.

1880 TROLLOPE *Duke's Children* I. xxiv. 284 In her opinion it would be best that the Duke should..give them money enough to live upon. 'Is not that a strong order?' asked the Earl. **1907** G. B. SHAW *Major Barbara* I. 210 *Barbara.* Yes. Give us Onward, Christian Soldiers. *Lomax.* Well, thats rather a strong order to begin with, dont you know. **1919** V. WOOLF *Night & Day* xxiv. 340 Well, Greek may be rather a large order. I was thinking chiefly of English. **1923** H. G. WELLS *Men like Gods* II. ii. 174 'You mean to jump this entire Utopian planet?' said Mr. Hunter. 'Big order,' said Lord Barralonga. **1927** *Sunday Times* 6 Mar. 23/3 There is no technical necessity now for the spark system, but it would be a rather big order to ask that all ships should abolish it. **1958** 'A. BRIDGE' *Portuguese Escape* viii. 125 This is quite a large order, isn't it? Suppose you tell me a bit more.

e. *colloq.* A request for refreshments or food, e.g. in a restaurant or public house; a portion or helping of a dish or article of food or drink served in a restaurant, snack-bar, etc.

1836 DICKENS in *Bell's Life in London* 17 Jan. 1/1 'Pray give me your orders gen'lm'n—pray give me your orders'..and demands for 'goes' of gin, and 'goes' of brandy, and pints of stout, and cigars of peculiar mildness, are vociferously made. *c* **1863** T. TAYLOR in M. R. Booth *Eng. Plays of 19th Cent.* (1969) II. 90 Now then James! Jackson, take orders. Interval of ten minutes allowed for refreshment. Give your orders, gents. **1898** A. BENNETT *Man from North* v. 29 A waitress, who approached and listened condescendingly to his order. **1904** 'O. HENRY' in *N.Y. World Mag.* 27 Mar. 10/4 And all this while she [*sc.* the waitress] would be performing astounding feats with orders of pork and beans, pot roasts, [etc.]. **1905** —— in *N.Y. World* 16 July (Oregon Fair Suppl.) 3/2 The screaming of 'short orders'..and all the horrid tumult of feeding man. **1934** G. B. SHAW *Village Wooing* 120 *Z*... Will you take a string bag? *A.* Yes. *Z.* Thanks very much. Shall I put the rest of the order into it? *A.* Of course. What else do you suppose I am buying it for? **1934** *Punch* 8 Aug. 158/3 The publican wanted to call on his clients with orders. 'What orders?'..'Beer.' **1949** *Crisis* (N.Y.) Nov. 305/2 They looked like the best tasting flapjacks in the world. They went inside and had an order. **1963** V. NABOKOV *Gift* v. 302 One could already hear the energetic '*psst, psst*' of Shahmatov, who had been served the wrong order. **1973** J. SHUB *Moscow by Nightmare* xiv. 165 Two orders of stuffed vine leaves, please. **1978** K. O'HARA *Ghost of T. Penry* xiii. 112 The pub sign was swinging furiously in the wind..inside.. they were taking last orders.

f. *order to view*: a requisition from a house or estate agent to an occupier to allow a client to inspect his premises.

1911 W. J. LOCKE *Glory of Clementina Wing* xxiii. 337 A caretaker took the order-to-view given by the estate agents and conducted the party over the place. **1922** E. H. Young *Bridge Dividing* III. xi. 301 It's to let. I've got an order to view. **1940** L. MacNeice (*title of poem*) Order to view. **1967** C. Drummond *Death at Furlong Post* iv. 36 Vacant these fourteen years... There have been many orders to view. **1971** M. Tripp *Five Minutes with Stranger* II. v. 125 I'll call in personally tomorrow and get an order to view.

V. See also *10, *23, *24, etc. **25. a.** (Earlier examples.) **c.** (Later examples.)

1698 *House of Commons Jrnl.* 8 Apr. (1742–62) XII. 198/2 The House, according to the Order of the Day, resolved itself into a Committee of the whole House to consider further of Ways and Means for raising the Supply granted to his Majesty. **1729** E. Knatchbull *Parliamentary Diary* (1963) 95 The orders of the day were moved for and so this day's debate ended. **1779** *Parl. Reg.* 5 May 401 The order of the day was read for the House to resolve itself into a committee of supply. **1959** *Times* 19 Sept. 7/7 The restorers are at work: *anastylosis* is the order of the day. **1976** *Abingdon Herald* 9 Dec. 5/2 The removal of ice from the moving parts and sheets was the order of the day. The light air and bright cold conditions required a high degree of concentration.

27. in order. c. Appropriate to or befitting the occasion; suitable; called for; also, in fashion, current, correct. orig. *U.S.*

a **1861** T. Winthrop *John Brent* (1862) viii. 85 If the gent has made a remark what teches you, apologies is in order. **1878** J. H. Beadle *Western Wilds* xxv. 399 One week sufficed to conclude my business in Oregon, but before leaving a few general notes are in order. **1903** *N.Y. Times* 4 Sept. 2/3 Good byes were in order on the Erin last night. **1931** G. T. Clark *Leland Stanford* xiv. 457 It was quite in order..that when this bill was before the Senate, he should express himself upon it. **1973** 'M. Innes' *Appleby's Answer* xv. 128 A confidential and man-to-man note will be in order. **1977** N. Marsh *Last Ditch* vi. 151 Is it in order for us to ring up your father and ask him to dine?

d. *in* (or *at, on*) *short* (or *quick*) *order*: without delay, immediately, summarily. orig. *U.S.*

1834 W. G. Simms *Guy Rivers* I. 204 Be off now in a hurry, or I shall fire upon you in short order. *a* **1852** F. M. Whitcher *Widow Bedott Papers* (1856) xxv. 307 If ever you dew it agin you'll git your walkin'-ticket on short order. **1892** *Outing* Apr. 19/1, I was so thoroughly comfortable that I went to sleep in short order. *a* **1916** H. James *Ivory Tower* (1917) III. iv. 198 Your solution, is marriage to a wife at short order. **1932** N. Hodgkins *Some Canad. Ess.* 202 We had made a sailor of him in short order. **1973** E. Berckman *Victorian Album* 180 The woman checked... This doesn't mean she failed to tally, because she did in short order—and all the more savagely. **1976** *Publishers Weekly* 24 May 58/3 Linda descends on twenties London to become, in short order, a model, the toast of lords [etc.].

30. out of order: (Later examples of mechanical or electrical devices.) Also (sometimes hyphenated) *attrib.*

1926 E. O'Neill *Great God Brown* III. i. 70, I forgot to tell him something important this morning and our phone's out of order. **1928** D. L. Sayers *Unpleasantness at Bellona Club* xii. 141 The telephone cabinet..was so annoyingly labelled 'Out of Order'. **1950** T. Walsh *Nightmare in Manhattan* III. 82 A phone booth behind the news-stand—it has an out-of-order sign on it. **1971** R. Thomas *Backup Men* xxii. 190 The two elevators wore *out of order* signs. **1977** A. Scholefield *Venom* IV. 172 She had also telephoned the house..and had received an out-of-order tone.

31. *order-maker, -making* vbl. sb. and ppl. adj.; *order–disorder* adj.; **order form** (examples); **order man, orderman,** a man who takes or makes out orders; **order mark** (see quot. 1963); **order pad,** a pad (Pad *sb.*[3] 4) of order forms; **order-paper,** (*b*) in the House of Lords, a publication of questions, etc., for the remainder of the session; **order wire** *Teleph.*, a wire used to communicate verbal information about the setting up of a connection for a customer, or between operators at different manual exchanges, or between a customer and an operator in establishing a data link.

1938 *Nature* 9 Apr. 643/1 Fröhlich has tried to interpret the λ-phenomenon of liquid helium as an order-disorder transition. **1964** *Discovery* Oct. 65/2 The theory of order–disorder transformations in alloys. **1894** *Country Gentlemen's Catal.* 3 We hope..that subscribers..will use our Enquiry and Order Forms. **1929** *Radio Times* 8 Nov. 114/2 Note in Order Form below the extra saving made by ordering 500 or 1000 [cigarettes] at a time. **1972** *Accountant* 26 Oct. 504/1 The phrase 'order forms' is to be understood to mean forms which the company makes available for other persons to order goods or services from the company. **1906** W. James *Mem. & Stud.* (1911) ix. 222 Not only in the great city, but in the outlying towns, these natural ordermakers, whether amateurs or officials, came to the front immediately. **1902** —— *Var. Relig. Exper.* viii. 170 Unhappiness is apt to characterize the period of order-making and struggle. **1963** *Times* 22 Feb. The order-making machinery in the Bill. *a* **1951** A. C. Headley in Murdoch & Drake-Brockman *Austral. Short Stories* (1951) 367 It was the rent and the order man, and a new pair of shoes. **1977** *N.Z. Herald* 5 Jan. 2-11/5 (Advt.), An experienced timber orderman is required for timber yard in western suburbs. **1912** A. Brazil *New Girl at St. Chad's* vi. 99 By general custom all pencils ..or other stray possessions were put into what was known as the forfeit tray, whence their owners might reclaim them by paying the penalty of the loss of an order mark. **1963** Barnard & Lauwerys *Handbk. Brit. Educ. Terms* 141 *Order mark*, a punishment (usually confined to girls' schools) for offences of a comparatively trivial kind. **1936** L. C. Douglas *White Banners* x. 226 She pushed the order-pad and pencil towards him. **1972** M. Kaye *Lively Game of Death* (1974) i. 4 Manufacturers..whip out order pads and hope to sell enough merchandise. **1946** *May's Treat. Parliament* (ed. 14) II. xii. 245 Together with the Minutes of Proceedings is printed the Order Paper, consisting of a programme of future business so far as appointed. **1912** Thiess & Joy *Toll Telephone Pract.* xiv. 214 (*caption*) Phantom circuit used as an order wire. **1948** J. Atkinson *Herbert & Procter's Telephony* (new ed.) I. xvii. 345/1 The out-going order-wires are multiplied throughout all positions at the originating exchange. **1973** R. N. Renton *Data Telecommunication* ix. 211/1 Communication with the customer for setting up and clearing connections is effected over telephone circuits (order wires) via the normal telephone exchange.

order, *v.* Add: **6.** Also with ellipsis of *to be*. Chiefly *U.S.*

1781 J. Witherspoon in *Pennsylvania Jrnl.* 9 May 1/2 These things were ordered delivered to the army. **1794** [in Dict.] **1799** in *Essex Inst. Hist. Coll.* (1877) XIII. 61 But the wind growing faint, I ordered the signal taken in. **1873** J. H. Beadle *Undevel. West* xi. 191 My bill was introduced by Senator Williams of Oregon, read by title, and ordered printed. **1875** J. G. Holland *Sevenoaks* in *Scribner's Monthly* Sept. 599/1 He went out,..jumped into Mr. Talbot's waiting coupe, and ordered himself driven home. **1938** W. T. Walsh *Philip II* xxi. 423 The Duchess ordered ships fitted out to meet and escort him. **1972** *Sci. Amer.* July 76/1 Frederick ordered the children raised in silence, so that they would not hear one spoken word. **1976** M. Machlin *Pipeline* l. 510 Coutts ordered the ship's speed reduced to six knots. **1977** *Time* 19 Dec. 9/2 When the local military commander was ordered removed after having congratulated the throng on its patriotic singing, Lagoa angrily summoned the marchers back on the pavement.

7. b. (Earlier and later examples of *to order about.*)

1853 C. Brontë *Villette* I. iv. 74, I refused to be ordered about and thrust from him. **1942** R. G. Collingwood *New Leviathan* 201 For a man of weak or undeveloped will nothing is so pleasant as being ordered about.

c. *to order up*, in the game of euchre: to order (the suit of the card turned up by an opponent who is dealing) to be adopted as trumps; also *absol.*

1847 J. S. Robb *Streaks of Squatter Life* 129 His antagonist ordered the king up. **1878** [see *assist *v.* 7 c]. **1950** *Hoyle's Games Modernized* (ed. 20) 88 If the non-dealer thinks his hand good enough, with the suit of the turn-up card as trumps, to make three tricks, he says..'I order it up'. **1963** G. F. Hervey *Handbk. Card Games* 184 The elder hand (non-dealer) may either order up or pass. If he orders up, the suit of the exposed card becomes the trump suit, and the dealer must take up the exposed card and discard..a card.

8. Also const. *up* and *absol.*

1763 J. Woodforde *Diary* 3 Sept. (1924) I. 31 Mrs. Bacon pressed me to drive with her, but I had ordered in Hall, and I could not. **1895** *Montgomery Ward Catal.* Spring & Summer 1 Please read remarks and rules before ordering. *Ibid.*, How to order. Commence your order similar to the sample heading on page 2. **1930** A. Bennett *Imperial Palace* II. liv. 400 The waiter wrote and vanished. When Gracie returned, Evelyn said: 'I've ordered.' **1946** D. Stivens *Courtship Uncle Henry* 197 We all drank together and ordered again. **1967** 'L. Egan' *Nameless Ones* xvi. 212 'Would you like to order, sir?' Obsequious waiter. **1973** J. Gores *Final Notice* (1974) xxvi. 166 We'll have some more sparkling burgundy and then we can order. **1976** B. Lecomber *Dead Weight* vi. 72, I.. ordered up two toasted ham sandwiches. **1976** J. M. Brownjohn tr. *Kirst's Time for Payment* vi. 134 Order up, ladies and gentlemen, and don't worry about the breath test.

orderable, *a.* Add: **b.** That may be arranged in series. **c.** That may be ordered (at a snack bar, etc.).

1949 *Mind* LVIII. 194 Recently it was realised that it was not necessary to regard satisfactions as additive; all previous conclusions about economic behaviour could still be deduced if they were merely regarded as orderable. **1962** C. O. Frake in J. A. Fishman *Readings Sociol. of Lang.* (1968) 438 Some, but apparently not all, orderable items at a lunch counter are distinguished by the term *something to eat.*

order-book. Add: **c.** (Examples.)

1844 Erskine May *Law of Parl.* viii. 168 Each member ..rises and reads the notice he is desirous of giving, and afterwards..delivers it..to the second clerk assistant, who enters it in the Order Book. **1929** G. F. M. Campion *Introd. Proc. House of Commons* ii. 65 The Order Book, which is also coloured white, is issued each day before the meeting of the House. **1964** Abraham & Hawtrey *Parl. Dict.* (ed. 2) 128 The Order Book of the House of Commons is published in the afternoon of each sitting day. It contains a complete list of all the orders, notices and questions for the following and subsequent days up till the end of the session.

d. (Earlier and later examples.) Also *transf.*, the amount of orders to be fulfilled; also *fig.*

1771 J. Wedgwood *Let.* 10 Apr. (1965) 105, I had immediate recourse to the order book where I did not doubt of finding some of the Vases we had ordered unmade. **1856** *National Rev.* III. 354 Passions are contending; life is a discipline; there is a reference every moment to the directory of the discipline—the order-book of the passions. **1910** A. Bennett *Clayhanger* II. i. 161 I've shown him he's wrong by our order-book, but he wouldn't see it. **1955** *Times* 13 May 19/2 The order book at the year-end was satisfactory, comparing very favourably with the position at the end of 1953. **1958** *Times Rev. Industry* Sept. 79/1 Order-book position is patchy. **1971** *Daily Tel.* 4 Aug. 13/3 Much of the industry remains pessimistic, with many companies still facing stagnant or declining order books. **1974** *Listener* 24 Oct. 531/3 You would think there was a boom on, from our order book.

ordered, *ppl. a.* Add: **2. c.** *Math.* Of a set: having the property that there is a transitive binary relation, >, such that for any elements *a, b* of the set $a>b$, $b>a$, or $b=a$; *ordered pair*, a pair of elements (a, b) such that $(a, b) = (u, v)$ if and only if $a=u$ and $b=v$; similarly *ordered triple*, *n-tuple.*

1901 *Bull. Amer. Math. Soc.* VII. 225 Consider the ordered assemblage $1, 2, \ldots, n', \ldots, n, \ldots n''$, where n', n and n'' are definite and subject to the condition that, in (*S*), n' comes before n and the latter before n''. **1906** W. H. & G. C. Young *Theory of Sets of Points* vi. 121 A set in given order will be called an ordered set... Its components..may be distinguished as ordered components. **1941** Birkhoff & MacLane *Survey Mod. Algebra* ii. 55 There are many other ordered fields: the field of real numbers, the field..of numbers $a+b\sqrt{2}$.., and other subfields of the real number field. **1953** *Mind* LXII. 541 A notion so little abstruse as that of an ordered pair. **1963** H. J. Ryser *Combinatorial Math.* i. 5 Let *S* be a set and let $(a_1, a_2, \ldots, a_r)$ be an ordered *r*-tuple of not necessarily distinct elements of *S*. **1966** Meyer & Hanlon *Fun with New Math* vii. 90 To each point in 'the Cartesian Plane'..there corresponds a unique ordered pair of real numbers. **1968** E. T. Copson *Metric Spaces* i. 5 The set of all ordered triples (x, y, z) of real numbers.

orderedness. (Later examples.)

1935 *Jrnl. Theol. Stud.* XXXVI. 314 The belief that the world's orderedness or knowability is an expression of mind. **1974** *Sci. Amer.* Mar. 43/1 (Advt.), In liquid-crystal work, one deals with the different forms and degrees of orderedness among molecules.

orderly, *a.* and *sb.* Add: **A.** *adj.* **4.** *orderly buff* (slang) = **orderly sergeant* (*b*); (see also quot. 1948); *orderly corporal*, (*a*) a corporal who attends upon an officer to carry orders or messages; (*b*) a corporal whose turn it is to attend to the domestic affairs of his corps or regiment; *orderly dog* (slang) = **orderly corporal* (*b*); (see also quot. 1948); *orderly officer* (*b*) (examples); *orderly pig* (slang) = *orderly officer* (*b*); (see also quot. 1948); *orderly room* (earlier and later examples); *orderly sergeant* (further examples); (*b*) a sergeant whose turn it is to act as officer of the day.

1757 Loudoun & Lyman *Gen. Orders of 1757* (1899) 126 Each Corp is to have an Orderly Searj[ean]t Ready. **1802** C. James *New Mil. Dict.* s.v., *Orderly Officer.* See Officer of the Day. *Ibid.*, Orderly serjeants when they go for orders are sashed. Orderly corporals and orderly men wear their side arms. **1806** H. Burrard *Let.* 26 Mar. in *Circumstantial Rep. Charges against Duke of York* (1809) 269 Your messenger knows where to find me, as I am at this Orderly Room for two or three hours most days. **1833** *Mirror of Parliament* 11 June 2216/2 They (often from connexion or friendship with the Orderly-room clerks) got their ages entered as eighteen. **1867** J. M. Crawford *Mosby* 121 Horace Johnson of Warrenton..was appointed orderly sergeant. **1917** A. G. Empey *Over Top* 302 *Orderly-corporal*, a non-commissioned officer who takes the names of the sick every morning. **1918** E. S. Farrow *Dict. Mil. Terms* 420 *Orderly Officer*, the officer of the day, or that officer of a corps or regiment whose turn it is to supervise for the day the arrangements for food, cleanliness etc. **1925** Fraser & Gibbons *Soldier & Sailor Words* 216 *Orderly buff*, orderly sergeant. *Ibid.*, *Orderly dog*, orderly corporal. **1934** V. M. Yeates *Winged Victory* 224 Grey..was censoring the men's letters, being orderly dog for the day. **1943** C. H. Ward-Jackson *Piece of Cake* 45 *Orderly buff*, orderly corporal. *Ibid.*, *Orderly dog*, orderly sergeant. *Ibid.*, *Orderly pig*, orderly officer. **1948** Partridge *Dict. Forces' Slang* 132 *Orderly buff, dog, pig.* Strictly speaking, *dog* seems to have been officer or corporal, *buff* sergeant, and *pig* corporal. The non-regular Army, however,..used all three phrases indiscriminately. **1953** K. Tennant *Joyful Condemned* xviii. 163 David.. was signed into the care of an orderly sergeant. **1964** A. Powell *Valley of Bones* i. 31 Tell the Orderly Corporal Mr Bithel is reporting sick this morning. **1971** S. Milligan *Adolf Hitler* III. 51 Oh those military meals!.. Visits from orderly officers did little to help. **1974** G. M. Fraser *McAuslan in Rough* 39 When I was..doing my recruit training..there was a villainous orderly sergeant who used to get us up in the mornings. **1977** J. Tarrant *Rommel Plot* xviii. 187 He asked the operator to put him through to the Orderly Room.

5. Also *orderly box.*

1904 *Daily Chron.* 18 Mar. 6/3 They had..been seen bearing up documents and throwing them into orderly boxes.

B. *sb.* **1.** (Earlier and later examples.)

1781 *Calendar Virginia State Papers* (1875) I. 452 The orderly, his wife and negro woman at York..have never received one single shilling. **1966** [see *batman[2]].

‖**ordinaire** (ǫrdinẹ̄r), *sb.* [Fr.] Short for *vin ordinaire. Also as *adj.*

1861 Thackeray *Roundabout Papers* xiv, in *Cornh. Mag.* July 123 A sound genuine ordinaire, at 18*s.* per doz. let us say. **1888** Mrs. H. Ward *R. Elsmere* II. III. xxii. 215 He ate his boiled mutton and drank his *ordinaire* like a man. **1906** *Daily Chron.* 24 July 6/5 What is 'ordinaire' as applied to wine?.. That is a local term which has existed for two centuries in France. **1920** [see *BOURGEOIS *a.* 4]. **1936** H. G. WELLS *Croquet Player* ii. 11 He.. ordered another half litre of wine. Either out of ignorance or preference he was drinking red ordinaire. **1959** *Good Food Guide* 32 Spanish ordinaires at 1/6 a glass. **1960** *House & Garden* July 13/1 Two decent, slightly better than *ordinaire* wines. **1972** *Ibid.* Feb. 100/4 Roodeberg is an honest wine, distinctly better than an *ordinaire.*

ordinary, *sb.* Add: **10.** Add to def.: usu. with capital initial, in the Roman Catholic rite, those parts of a service, esp. the mass, which do not vary from day to day; *spec.*, those unvarying parts which form the mass as a musical setting (Kyrie, Gloria, Credo, Sanctus, Benedictus and Agnus Dei). Also *transf.*, of other rites. (Later examples.)

1905 PROCTOR & FRERE *New Hist. Bk. Common Prayer* (rev. ed.) i. 12 In the Liturgy, the 'Canon' or central prayer..was the Roman canon, and in fact the rest of the invariable framework of the public service (or 'Ordinary') was that adopted from Rome. **1929** E. C. THOMAS *Lay Folks' Hist. Liturgy* I. v. 22 These Nestorian Liturgies differ in the Anaphora, but the Ordinary of the Mass is the same in all. **1944** W. APEL *Harvard Dict. Mus.* 427/2 Around 500, the Mass consisted only of the chants of the Proper, alternating with lections from the Epistles, etc. Gradually, the chants of the Ordinary were introduced, probably in the following chronological order: Sanctus, Kyrie, Gloria, Agnus Dei, Credo. *Ibid.* 523/2 Other services [than the Mass]..also comprise invariable and variable portions. For instance, the Magnificat forms a part of the Ordinary of Vespers. **1974** *Daily Tel.* 20 July 7/8 Surely the way Haydn in his 70s appears tormented by sudden doubts at the word 'mortuorum' belies the confidence of the preceding 'Et expecto resurrectionem', uniquely so in any setting of the Ordinary. **1976** *Gramophone* Apr. 1653/3 It is found in ninth-century manuscripts and may well be connected with two well-known items of the Ordinary, Sanctus I and Sanctus XI.

14. a. (Later examples.)

1908 G. B. SHAW *Lett. to Granville Barker* (1956) 114 Charlotte at a farmers' ordinary at Towcester was immense. **1928** *Daily Chron.* 9 Aug. 4/4 Lord Beaconfield [*sic*] was accustomed to make some of his most important pronouncements at the farmers' ordinary at Aylesbury. **1976** N. ROBERTS *Face of France* xv. 157 The establishment in an English market town which still does a good farmers' ordinary.

c. (Earlier examples.)

1637 in *Essex Inst. Hist. Coll.* (1869) IX. 55 Mr. John Holgraue..hath undertaken to keep an ordinary for the entertainment of strangers. **1650** *Archives of Maryland* (1883) I. 294 Wine or other Provisions to bee expended in any Ordinaries within this Province. **1680** in *New Hampsh. Hist. Soc. Coll.* (1866) VIII. 15 What person soever..shall profane ye Lord's Day..by Dining at ordinarys in time of publique worship..shall forfeite 10s.

16. a. (Later examples.)

1909 *Times Lit. Suppl.* 20 May 185/2 Shakespeare introduces the ordinary, whether in characters or in events, only as a foil to the extraordinary. **1977** 'D. CORY' *Bennett* iv. 121 The case I'm engaged on..is rather out of the ordinary. **1978** *Atlanta Jrnl. & Constitution* 14 Jan. 23T (Advt.), Tapas. When you're fed up with the ordinary... Our European chef proudly presents over 40 delightfully different hot and cold appetizer treats.

c. One of a class of inmates in a poor-house.

1910 *Daily Chron.* 14 Jan. 8/5 The 'ordinaries' (whom we should call able-bodied) were able to roam all over the building.

17. c. (Later example.)

1964 *Financial Times* 23 Mar. 12/3 Plans are being considered to fund back indebtedness through..a 1-for-1 rights issue of 5s Ordinary at par.

18. b. (Later examples.)

1934 *Burlington Mag.* Oct. 182/2 In this very year, January 1431, the King's painter to Charles IX of France was Henry Mellein, and his painter-in-ordinary was Conrad de Vulcop. **1944** *Ibid.* Dec. 307/1 Jacques d'Arthois, painter-in-ordinary of the Forêt de Soignes, is one of the leading figures of the Brussels landscape school of the seventeenth century.

19. a. *ordinary-keeper* (earlier examples).

1645 in *Essex Inst. Hist. Coll.* (1869) IX. 136 To provide for a ordinarie keeper. **1662** *Archives of Maryland* (1883) I. 447 All Ordinary Keepers debts either upon bill or accompt..shall be allowed due.

ordinary, *a.* Add: **3. d.** Of language, usage, discourse, etc.: that most commonly found or attested, *spec.* as contrasted with logical symbolism or a specialized terminology.

1685 tr. *Arnauld & Nicole's Logic* II. x. 221 As when I say, *All Men have two Arms.* This Proposition ought to pass for true, according to ordinary use. *Ibid.* III. xv. 70 Whereas it is the method of the Schools to propound the Argument entire, and afterwards to prove the Proposition which receives the difficulty, that which is usual in ordinary discourse, is to join to doubtful propositions the Proofs that confirm 'em. **1690** LOCKE *Essay Hum. Und.* II. xxi. 121 Philosophy it self,..must have so much Complacency, as to be cloathed in the ordinary Fashion and Language of the Country. **1828** J. S. MILL in *Westm. Rev.* IX. 145 Arranging all these propositions in that *order*, which (so strongly does ordinary language corroborate our view of the case) is termed their *logical* order. **1843** —— *Logic* I. I. i. 25 We must begin by recognising the distinctions made by ordinary language. *Ibid.* II. IV. v. 268 These changes, by which words in ordinary use become more and more generalized. **1874** W. WALLACE tr. *Hegel's Logic* 43 The deeper and philosophical meaning of truth can be partially traced even in the expressions of ordinary language. **1892** —— *Ibid.* (ed. 2) 52 The deeper and philosophical meaning of truth can be partially traced even in the ordinary usage of language. **1902** W. JAMES *Var. Relig. Exper.* ii. 36 Trifling, sneering attitudes even towards the whole of life... It would strain the ordinary use of language too much to call such attitudes religious. **1906** B. RUSSELL in *Mind* XV. 256 One of the objects to be aimed at in using symbols is that they should be free from the ambiguities of ordinary language. **1909** W. M. URBAN *Valuation* ii. 33 Our ordinary usage, at least, makes a clear distinction between feeling and will. **1932** H. H. PRICE *Perception* viii. 256 We also stick to common sense and the ordinary usage of language. **1939** *Mind* XLVIII. 62 While it is true that a formal calculus frequently assists in detecting errors which are unnoticed in ordinary language, each formal calculus carries with it new sources of confusion. **1949** *Mind* LVIII. 147 The redefinitions which are implicit in philosophical paradoxes do quite often..receive a certain backing from ordinary usage. **1951** J. HOLLOWAY *Lang. & Intelligence* viii. 123 Ordinary language is the language of persons unacquainted even with the idea of conforming to a dictionary. **1957** J. PASSMORE *100 Yrs. Philos.* xviii. 438 Not all ex-students of Wittgenstein look with kindness on the 'ordinary language' philosophies which have latterly dominated the philosophical scene at Oxford. **1977** *Oxford Times* 9 Dec. 5/3 He is the leading exponent of ordinary language philosophy, and became a fellow of the British Academy in 1960.

5. b. *ordinary wine* (Fr. *vin ordinaire*). Cf. *ORDINAIRE *sb.*

1814 M. BIRKBECK *Notes Journey through France* 102 Such is the habitual temperance..that the inns..seldom have any liquor stronger than their ordinary wine. If you call for brandy, they are obliged to send for it to the Caffé. **1860** DICKENS *Uncomm. Trav.* (1861) vii. 92, I was in the dear old France of my affections. I should have known it, without the well-remembered bottle of rough ordinary wine.

c. *Comm.* Of shares, stock, etc.: forming part of the common stock and without 'preference'; also applied to shareholders holding such stock.

1869 *Bradshaw's Railway Manual* XXI. 10 No dividend was declared in March on the ordinary stock. *Ibid.* 42 An obligation..to pay to the ordinary shareholders a dividend..at the rate of 2 per cent. **1878** [see PREFERENCE 8]. **1891** [see SHARE *sb.*[2] 2]. **1955** *Times* 12 May 17/7 The issue of three shares to Ordinary shareholders for every five which they hold at present. *Ibid.* 1 July 16/5 The balance-sheet shows the increase in ordinary share capital arising from this capitalization and the manner in which the reserves have been applied. **1974** *Terminol. Managem. & Financial Accountancy* (Inst. Cost & Managem. Accountants) 60 *Ordinary shares*, shares which entitle the holders to the remaining divisible profits (and, in a liquidation, the assets) remaining after prior interests (e.g. preference shareholders) have been satisfied. **1977** *Times* 1 Dec. 20/7 Earning per Ordinary Share 4.44p... Ordinary Dividend 3.4914p.

d. Of people: typical of a particular group; average; without exceptional experience or expert knowledge.

1855 GEO. ELIOT *Let.* 12 May (1954) II. 201, I really think a taste for descriptive writing is the rarest of all tastes among ordinary people. **1902** G. B. SHAW *Mrs. Warren's Profession* Pref. p. xvii, The ordinary Briton thinks that if every other Briton is not under some form of tutelage..he will abuse his freedom viciously. **1903** —— *Man & Superman* III. 76 But I am well aware that the ordinary man—even the ordinary brigand, who can scarcely be called an ordinary man (Hear, hear!)—is not a philosopher. **1922** M. A. VON ARNIM *Enchanted April* iii. 50, I don't think references are nice things at all.. between ordinary decent women. **1952** A. CHRISTIE *Mrs McGinty's Dead* ii. 21 It's not the sort of thing that an ordinary man—or a jury—can believe. **1971** *Listener* 28 Oct. 566/1 The language of everyday speech is used in verse..because the role of the poet is an ordinary-man role. **1974** *Times* 11 Oct. 14/8 A government claiming that it wants to involve ordinary people in decision-making. **1975** T. HEALD *Deadline* ii. 19 The *Globe*..made its appeal to 'the man in the street'. Leader writers were instructed..to spice their texts with frequent references to 'ordinary folk'.

e. *ordinary level*, the lowest of the three levels of the General Certificate of Education; abbrev. *O level* (*O 5 d).

1947 *Examinations Secondary Schools* (Secondary Schools Exam. Council) 8 An examination at 'Ordinary', 'Advanced' and 'Scholarship' levels should be available each year to candidates who are at least sixteen on Sept. 1st. **1959** *Listener* 29 Jan. 195/2 The arts sixth former who has perhaps 'done' a little science to 'ordinary level'. **1960–1** *Where* Winter 14/1 Ordinary (O) level is normally taken at 16 after a 5-year course. **1963** BARNARD & LAUWERYS *Handbk. Brit. Educ. Terms* 99 In 1951 the *School* and *Higher School Certificate* examinations in secondary schools were replaced by a General Certificate of Education..examination at three levels—ordinary, advanced, and scholarship. **1978** *Nature* 27 Apr. 784/1 Asimov carefully explains the inverse-square law of force in a manner that should be comprehensible to a pupil considered incapable of taking ordinary level school physics.

6. (Later U.S. example; cf. *ORNERY *a.*)

1800 *Aurora* (Philadelphia) 1 May 2/3 This ordinary drunken wretch is supposed to be the perpetrator.

ordinate, *sb.* **b.** Add: In mod. use, the distance of a point from the left-to-right (x) axis measured parallel to the other (y) axis; the y co-ordinate of a point. (Further examples.)

1855 I. TODHUNTER *Treat. Plane Co-ordinate Geom.* i. 2 OM is called the abscissa of the point P; and ON, or its equal MP, is called the ordinate of P. **1880** *Proc. R. Soc* XXX. 511 The horizontal ordinates give the stress.., the vertical ordinates give the elongation. **1896** *Min. Proc. Inst. Civil Engin.* CXXVI. 233 The area of the loop, with the magnetizing force as abscissas, and the magnetization as ordinates, represents the energy dissipated. **1948** *Electronic Engin.* XX. 10/1 This apparatus was constructed to produce a trace on a cathode ray tube in which the ordinates were proportional to shutter opening and the abscissa to time. **1951** R. M. GARRELS *Textbk. Geol.* 470 In order to graph these changes, it is customary to begin by drawing two lines at right angles to each other. One is usually drawn horizontally (the X axis or abscissa), the other vertically (the Y axis or ordinate). **1971** NILES & HABORAK *Calculus with Analytic Geom.* i. 14 The directed distance OM is the x-coordinate or abscissa of point P and is denoted by x. The directed distance ON is the y-coordinate or ordinate of point P and is denoted by y.

ordinate, *v.* Add: **5.** *Statistics* and *Ecology.* To subject to the mathematical operation of ordination (sense *1 c).

1962 *Ecol. Monogr.* XXXII. 137 (*heading*) Ordinating forest communities by means of environmental scalars and phytosociological indices. **1969** E. C. PIELOU *Introd. Math. Ecol.* xx. 255 When we wish to ordinate vegetation by means of a principal components analysis, there are four decisions to make.

ordination. Add: **I. 1. c.** *Statistics* and *Ecology.* [tr. G. *ordnung.*] The arrangement of a set of points, given as in a multidimensional space, into a space of fewer dimensions with minimal distortion.

1954 D. W. GOODALL in *Austral. Jrnl. Bot.* II. 323 Factor analysis does not result in a classification of vegetation in the ordinary sense, but in an arrangement of the vegetational data in a multi-dimensional series. For such an arrangement, there appears to be no word in English which one can use as an antonym to classification; I would like to propose the term 'ordination'. **1969** E. C. PIELOU *Introd. Math. Ecol.* xx. 250 As a method of summarizing the results of a survey, ordination has two great advantages over classification: it obviates the need for setting up arbitrary criteria for defining the classes and there is no need to assume that distinct classes (if there are any) are hierarchically related. **1971** BLACKITH & REYMENT *Multivariate Morphometrics* xvi. 229 Proctor..found that ordinations of some British liverworts gave readily interpretable polarities.

ordinator. 1. (Later examples.)

1929 R. BRIDGES *Testament of Beauty* i. 134 And wouldst thou play Creator and Ordinator of things. **1952** G. SARTON *Hist. Sci.* I. xvi. 421 The world artificer (*dēmiurges*) is not a creator but, like the *nus* of Anaxagoras, an ordinator.

ordnance. Add: **5. ordnance datum** (examples); **ordnance map** (earlier example); **ordnance survey** (earlier and later examples); also *fig.*

1833 W. DYOTT *Diary* Nov. (1907) II. 170 On the 17th Captain Gosset, who had been employed last year stationed at Lichfield on the ordnance survey service called. **1839** C. FOX *Jrnl.* 8 Oct. (1972) 59 Sir H. Vivian was chuckling over the admirable Ordnance map. **1886** T. P. WHITE *Ordnance Survey of U.K.* vi. 106 The Ordnance datum for Ireland is not the same as for Great Britain. **1889** G. W. USILL *Pract. Surveying* ix. 177 The ordnance datum of this country was determined by the ordnance authorities to be 'the approximate mean water at Liverpool'. **1934** C. LAMBERT *Music Ho!* 11 This book makes no attempt to be an ordnance survey of modern music. **1956** Ordnance datum [see O.D. s.v. *O 5 d]. **1972** L. ALCOCK *By South Cadbury* ii. 24 The summit is a little over five hundred feet above Ordnance Datum, with the hill itself standing about two hundred and fifty feet above the surrounding countryside. **1973** *Times* 13 Aug. 4/1 Mounting pressure from country walkers..may save the popular 2½ in. Ordnance Survey map.

ordoñezite (ǭɹdǫ̆nyē·zəit). *Min.* [f. the name of Ezequiel *Ordoñez* (1867–1950), Mexican geologist + -ITE[1].] An antimonate of zinc, $ZnSb_2O_6$, which is found as brown tetragonal crystals at Guanajuato, Mexico.

1954 *Mineral. Abstr.* XII. 303 (*heading*) Ordoñezite, zinc antimonate, a new mineral from Guanajuato, Mexico. **1955** *Amer. Mineralogist* XL. 66 Ordoñezite occurs as drusy or stalactitic masses of repeatedly twinned tetragonal crystals having a maximum size of 2 mm. **1968** I. KOSTOV *Mineral.* II. iv. 264 To this [byströmite] group are referred the following oxides, which are isostructural with rutile and tapiolite. ($P4_2/mnm$): byströmite.., ordoñezite.., and tripuhyite.

Ordovician, *a.* Substitute for def.: Of, pertaining to, or designating the second earliest period of the Palæozoic era, following the Cambrian and preceding the Silurian. Also *absol.*, the Ordovician period or its rocks. Add earlier and later examples.

1879 C. LAPWORTH in *Geol. Mag.* Decade II. VI. 14 The whole of the great Bala district where Sedgwick first worked out the physical succession among the rocks of the intermediates or so-called Upper Cambrian or Lower Silurian system..lay within the territory of the *Ordovices*; a tribe as undaunted in its resistance to the Romans as the Silures... Here, then, we have the hint for the appropriate title for the central system of the Lower Palæozoics. It should be called the Ordovician System. **1902** A. J. JUKES-BROWNE *Student's Handbk. Stratigr.*

Geol. viii. 118 In Ayrshire..the Ordovician has the ordinary facies of a formation accumulated at no great distance from a continental coast-line. **1955** *Times* 4 June 8/5 It is a site of great geological interest for its variety of Ordovician volcanic lavas, with intrusive igneous rocks interbedded with fossiliferous mudstones and slates. **1967** D. H. RAYNER *Stratigr. Brit. Isles* iv. 80 In the British Isles the first fragmental remains of vertebrates are known from the Silurian beds, although bony plates have been found in the Ordovician of the United States.

ore[2]. Add: **1.** (Further examples.) Also applied to minerals mined for their content of non-metals.

1910 J. F. KEMP in *Jrnl. Canadian Mining Inst.* XII. 357 Sometimes..in the mining of the non-metallic substance sulphur, the output of the mine is called 'sulphur-ore', although no metal is involved at all. Yet while we may not especially controvert this usage, it cannot be said to seriously affect the general and large conception of ore as limited to the metalliferous minerals. **1913** W. LINDGREN *Mineral Deposits* i. 4 The use of the term 'ore' is not quite consistent. Ordinarily it implies a metal, but the expression 'sulphur ore', meaning pyrite, is sometimes seen, and occasionally such terms as 'sapphire ore' are found. **1939** G. A. ROUSH *Strategic Mineral Supplies* xiv. 401 The deposits of ore, or caliche, are highly irregular. **1951** A. F. TAGGART *Elem. Ore Dressing* i. 2 The miner was principally responsible for making ore of the low-grade California gravels by discovering ways to mine them that are..cheap. **1970** *Materials & Technol.* III. ii. 97 There are no fundamental differences between the treatment of metalliferous ores and other types of ore.

3. a. *ore bin, -bucket, -pass, -vein* (example). **b.** *ore-carrier, -carrying, dresser, -dressing* (further examples). **c. ore body** (examples as one word); **ore-shoot** = SHOOT *sb.*[1] 7.

1935 *Economist* 8 June 1334/1 It will be necessary..to sink the shaft..below the reef and to cut stations and ore bins. **1962** R. B. FULLER *Epic Poem on Industrialization* 197 The magnificent horizontal and vertical lines of its highways,..ore bins, and skyscrapers. **1955** *Times* 12 July 15/6 Difficulties being met are the poor bearing quality of the ground..and the presence of unconsolidated footwall beds associated with considerable volumes of water in No. 1 shaft area—which is holding up the advance towards the orebody. **1971** *Wall St. Jrnl.* 19 Feb. 20/5 Bad weather during the past three weeks delayed stripping of the overburden of the Black Cub orebody. **1977** *Bulletin* (Sydney) 22 Jan. 42/1 But a mineral deposit doesn't become an orebody unless the mineral concerned can be extracted and sold at a profit. **1912** *Chambers's Jrnl.* Dec. 784/2 The men..had begun to send the ore-buckets down empty. **1936** *Atlantic Monthly* CLVII. 164/2 Our great..ore-carriers..are no exception, because their existence is due to the State's primary intervention in granting monopoly rights to the rental value of the.. ore-fields they tap. **1975** 'D. JORDAN' *Black Account* viii. 46 Ore shipping studies comparing the capacity of Japanese ore carriers with the proposed berthing and loading facilities. **1909** *Westm. Gaz.* 29 Nov. 8/2 During the storm three ore-carrying steamers were beached near the entrance to the harbour. **1974** *Encycl. Brit. Micropædia* IV. 194/2 This ability of the ore dresser to modify the flotability of minerals made possible many seemingly magical separations. **1909** H. LOUIS *Dressing of Minerals* i. 4 It appears better to treat coal-washing and ore-dressing as one and the same subject. **1914** S. J. TRUSCOTT tr. *Beyschlag's Deposits Useful Minerals* I. 72 There should be at least sufficient iron present..to cover the costs of ore-dressing and of metallurgical treatment. **1946** *Nature* 27 July 140/1 To provide an information service dealing with publications concerning all branches of geology, mineralogy,..ore-dressing and production metallurgy. **1878** *Encycl. Brit.* XVI. 453/2 E the main lode, H permanent levels, and K ore-pass reserved amidst the rubbish (*deads*) D. **1884** J. A. PHILLIPS *Treat. Ore Deposits* 50 As a general rule, all the ore-shoots in a given vein dip in the same direction. **1944** *Q. Jrnl. Geol. Soc.* C. 251 A mineral vein may carry several ore-shoots, separated by barren stretches. **1906** *Chambers's Jrnl.* Feb. 159/2 A few digs with the shovel laid bare the outcropping of the ore-vein.

orectic, *a.* **a.** *Philos.* Delete *rare* and add later examples. Hence **orecti·vity.**

1906 S. S. LAURIE *Synthetica* I. 161 Let us rather call it Orectivity or Conation. **1947** [see *AFFECTIVE *a.* 7 b]. **1952** C. P. BLACKER *Eugenics* 216 We may perhaps be on the threshold of a period when similar advances will be made in tests of the so-called 'orectic' functions; these comprise the qualities which make up what is commonly called character. **1970** G. GREER *Female Eunuch* 67 For, no matter which theory of the energy of personality we accept, it is inseparable from sexuality... Flügel called it orectic energy.

oregano (ǫrẽgā·no, ǫre·găno). [Sp. and Amer. Sp. var. of ORIGANUM.] The dried leaves of wild marjoram, *Origanum vulgare*, or, esp. in North and Central America, the dried leaves of a shrub of the genus *Lippia*, esp. *L. graveolens*; both are used as seasonings for food, the latter having a stronger flavour.

1771 J. R. FORSTER tr. *Osbeck's Voy. to China* I. 33 *Origanum Creticum*, Spanish *Oregano*, known by the name of Spanish hops, is used to make anchovies and other meats more palatable. **1889** S. WATSON in *Proc. Amer. Acad. Arts & Sci.* XXIV. 67 *Lippia* (*Zapania*) *Palmeri*... 'Origano'; with a strong sage-like odor and used as a pot-herb. **1899** *Contrib. U.S. Nat. Herbarium* V. 226 Lippia spp. Oregano. The leaves of oregano are very much used to flavor food. *Ibid.* 227 The name 'oregano' seems to be a generic term applied to the leaves thus used of several species of Lippia. **1959** *Listener* 2 Apr. 601/2 The hallway smelled of herbs, of oregano and basil. **1969** F. ROSENGARTEN *Bk. Spices* 276 The pungent Mexican oregano, indigenous to the warmer areas of the Western Hemisphere, is of the genus *Lippia*... The milder European oregano..is of one of several species of *Origanum* native to the Mediterranean region, principally *Origanum vulgare* L. The perplexing confusion between marjoram and oregano, and between the two types of oregano, is not limited to botanists. **1972** M. J. BOSSE *Incident at Naha* i. 17, I rolled some grass from the oregano jar where we keep ours and smoked the joint. **1976** *National Observer* (U.S.) 2 Oct. 11/4 Cook the meat loaf for 15 minutes, and then sprinkle the top with seasoning mixture of oregano, cinnamon, and sugar.

Oregon (ǫ·rigǫn). The name of one of the United States of America, situated on the Pacific coast, used *attrib.* to designate plants and animals found in the region, as **Oregon ash,** a species of ash, *Fraxinus oregana*, or its wood; **Oregon cedar** = *Lawson cypress* (*LAWSON); **Oregon fir** = *Douglas fir* (*DOUGLAS[1]); **Oregon grape,** an evergreen shrub, *Mahonia aquifolium*, bearing racemes of yellow flowers followed by dark berries resembling grapes; also, the berry itself; **Oregon junco,** a small black, brown, and white bunting, *Junco oreganus*; **Oregon lily,** one of the hybrid lilies produced by Jan de Graaff at the Oregon Bulb Farms; **Oregon pine** = *Oregon fir*.

1869 *Amer. Naturalist* III. 407 Oregon Ash... This first appears at the Dalles. **1969** T. H. EVERETT *Living Trees of World* 287/1 Other American ashes worthy of note include the Oregon ash..most important of Western species, which grows to a height of 80 feet and may have a trunk 4 feet in diameter. **1872** F. F. VICTOR *All over Oregon & Washington* xxvii. 279 The Oregon cedar..grows very abundantly near the coast. **1971** F. H. TITMUSS *Commercial Timbers of World* (ed. 4) 94 Alternative names for the timber [of Lawson cypress] include Oregon Cedar and White Cedar. **1904** E. O. WOOTON *Native Ornamental Plants of New Mexico* 15 The Douglas Spruce or Oregon Fir..and the Bull Pine..would well repay the care necessary to getting them established. **1851** *Oregon Statesman* (Oregon City) 27 June 3/1 Oregon Grape, so called, is not a grape, but resembles the grape in size and appearance. **1873** G. M. GRANT *Ocean to Ocean* 283 A dark green prickly-leaved bush like English holly, called the Oregon grape. **1949** *Jrnl. N.Y. Bot. Gdn.* July 153/1 In one bed is Oregon grape and beauty-berry. **1971** *Daily Colonist* (Victoria, B.C.) 27 May 53/3 The meat is then placed in the pit and covered with kelp, seaweed, Oregon grape and other wild plants. **1974** J. E. UNDERHILL *Wild Berries* 69 Still other people are devotees of Oregon Grape wine. **1917** T. G. PEARSON *Birds Amer.* III. 47 Maybe the handsomest is the Oregon Junco..with a black head and breast sharply defined against a mahogany-brown back, white under parts, and pinkish-brown sides. **1964** A. WETMORE *Song & Garden Birds N. Amer.* 364/2 In winter flocks of Oregon juncos roam western foothills, canyons, and suburbs. **1971** *Islander* (Victoria, B.C.) 13 June 13/3 Oregon junco..come from the north during winter. **1964** *Horticulture* Dec. 49/1 (Advt.), *World Famous Oregon Lilies*, Higo Iris, Hardy Cyclamen and Exbury Azaleas. Send for free catalog. Rex Bulb Farms..Newburg, Oregon. **1967** J. DE GRAAFF *Lilies* 31 Those [lilies]..are becoming known as the Oregon lilies because they are bred and raised in Oregon. **1845** *N. Amer. Rev.* LX. 166 One of those gigantic Oregon Pines..whose prostrate trunk Douglas found to be two hundred and fifty feet in length. **1888** *Encycl. Brit.* XXIV. 386/2 The principal timber is yellow and red fir, ordinarily known as 'Oregon pine', which constitutes the bulk of the forests. **1889** [see *Nootka fir* s.v. *NOOTKA B. *adj.* 2]. **1947** R. PEATTIE *Sierra Nevada* 148 Douglas fir..is known in the trade as Oregon pine. **1964** *House & Garden* Oct. 95/1 Her kitchen units, in Oregon pine.

Hence **Oregone·se,** the people of Oregon; **Orego·nian** *a.*, belonging to Oregon; as *sb.*, a native or inhabitant of Oregon; **O·regonly** *adv.*, after the manner of an Oregonian.

1848 E. BRYANT *California* xv. 197, I think the Oregonese had a little the advantage of us in this respect. *a* **1861** T. WINTHROP *John Brent* (1862) xxii. 243 Armstrong's opinion was only my own, expressed Oregonly. **1863** *Harper's Mag.* Sept. 570/2 If one does not know the 'lingo', he will often be troubled in conversing with the Oregonians. **1873** J. H. BEADLE *Undevel. West* xxxv. 762 There is a distinctively Oregonian look about all the natives and old residents. *Ibid.* xxxvi. 772 No Oregonians will eat of salmon caught above the mouth of the Willamette. **1974** *New Yorker* 25 Feb. 88/3 Oregonians, in whatever part of the state they reside, tend to be small-town-ish.

oregonite (ǫ·rigǫ̆nəit). *Min.* [ad. G. *oregonit* (Ramdohr & Schmitt 1959, in *Neues Jahrb. f. Min. Monatshefte* 247), f. prec.: see -ITE[1].] An arsenide of nickel and iron, Ni_2FeAs_2, which occurs as white hexagonal crystals with a metallic lustre in Oregon and has been made artificially.

1960 *Mineral. Abstr.* XIV. 500/1 A new nickel-iron arsenide from Josephine Creek, Josephine County, Oregon, is named *oregonite*. **1968** *Ibid.* XIX. 285/2 By heating at 470°C under a pressure of 1600 kg/cm² mixtures of arsenic ground with iron and nickel or with Fe–Ni alloys (36, 50, and 77% Ni) oregonite,..was obtained.

orenda (ore·ndă). [Iroquoian.] (See quots.).

1902 J. N. B. HEWITT in *Amer. Anthropologist* IV. 33 (*title*) Orenda and a definition of religion. *Ibid.* 37 This subsumed magic power is called..*manitowi* by the Algonquian, *pokunt* by the Shoshonean, and *orenda* by the Iroquoian tribes. And it is suggested that the Iroquoian name for the potence in question, *orenda*, be adopted to designate it. **1911** *Encycl. Brit.* XVII. 306/2 Everything in nature, and particularly all animate objects, have their *orenda*; so have gods and spirits... *Orenda* is above all the power of the medicine man. **1917** *Encycl. Relig. & Ethics* IX. 556/1 The term *orenda* is, in fact, only one of a large group of terms, members of which are found in most, if not all, Indian languages, which have the same general meaning—invisible power or energy. **1920** [see *MANA]. **1947** C. S. LEWIS *Miracles* xi. 100 It [*sc.* pantheism] may even be the most primitive of all religions, and the *orenda* of a savage tribe has been interpreted by some to be an 'all-pervasive spirit'.

Oreo (ōə·rio). *U.S. slang.* Also **oreo.** [See quot. 1973.] A derogatory term for an American Black who is seen (esp. by other Blacks) as part of the white establishment.

1968–70 *Current Slang* (Univ. S. Dakota) III–IV. 89 *Oreo, n.*, a black who thinks like a white or tries to join white society. (Blacks on the outside but whites on the inside). **1969** *Harper's Mag.* Mar. 61 Trouble is Negroes been programmed by white folks to believe their products are inferior. We've developed into a generation of Oreos—black on the outside, white on the inside. **1970** H. E. ROBERTS *Third Ear* 11/1 *Oreo*, a black person with white-oriented attitudes. **1971** *Black World* June 31/1 Every Black man or woman who refers to his Black brother or sister by a derogatory label such as *Tom*, *nigger*, or *oreo*.. is deliberately walking into the enemy's trap. **1973** A. DUNDES *Mother Wit* 596 One term of derision is 'oreo' for such an individual [*sc.* a Negro with 'white' mentality]. The term comes from a standard commercially prepared cookie which has two disc-shaped chocolate wafers separated by sugar cream filling. An 'oreo' is thus brown outside but white inside, hence, a Negro who has internalized white values. **1975** *Amer. Speech 1972* XLVII. 151 Black educators are sometimes included in this hostile cosmos, for they are labeled *Oreos*.

‖ **ore rotundo** (ōə·ri rotɒ·ndo), *adv. phr.* [L. abl. of *ōs* mouth + abl. of *rotundus* round.] Lit. 'with round mouth'; with round, well-turned speech. Cf. OROTUND *a.* (*sb.*).

[HORACE *Ars Poetica*, Grais ingenium, Grais dedit ore rotundo Musa loqui]. **1720** SWIFT *Let.* 1 Dec. in *Works* (1859) II. 300/1 Is taught there to mouth it gracefully, and to swear, as he reads French, *ore rotundo*. **1845** R. FORD *Hand-bk. for Travellers Spain* I. 82 The Castilian speaks with a grave distinct pronunciation, *ore rotundo*; he enunciates every letter and syllable. **1922** BLUNDEN *Bonadventure* 144 Replying You. Big. Stiff *ore rotundo*. **1931** M. SUMMERS *Supernatural Omnibus* 7 In his fine stage voice *ore rotundo* he would declaim some half a dozen wilting lines and demand applause.

orf[2] (ǭɹf). [Var. of dial. *hurf*, prob. f. ON. *hrufa* crust or scab on boil; cf. dial. *reef* skin eruption, dandruff.] A virus disease of sheep, cattle, and goats, characterized by a secondary infection with the bacillus *Fusiformis necrophorus*, which causes ulcers and scabs in and around the mouth and on the feet or other parts of the body; also called scabby mouth, contagious ecthyma, or contagious pustular dermatitis.

1868 J. C. ATKINSON *Gloss. Cleveland Dial.* 362 Orf... Scurf on an animal's skin. **1876** C. C. ROBINSON *Gloss. Mid-Yorks.* 95/1 Orf.., applied to a running sore on cattle. **1948** *Brit. Jrnl. Dermatol.* LX. 405 The virus of orf could produce lesions in man. **1959** *News Chron.* 9 July 5/5 Live sheep..have been found to be suffering from orf, a skin disease. **1972** *Country Life* 30 Mar. 812/3 The flock is then dipped, vaccinated against orf and allowed to scavenge.

orf (ǭɹf), *prep.* and *adv.* Representing a 'phonetic' spelling of a vulgar or affected pronunciation of OFF *adv.*, *prep.*, *adj.*, and *sb.*[1]

1889 [see *GREEN *a.* 1 j]. **1901** B. PAIN *De Omnibus* i. 2 Pressintly a gint calls 'im an' orf 'e goes. **1916** [see *COBBER *sb.*[2]]. **1937** N. MARSH *Vintage Murder* xx. 226 She tells 'im orf a treat. **1955** M. ALLINGHAM *Beckoning Lady* iv. 55 Just then orf come 'is 'at, and lord luvaduck! **1976** M. BUTTERWORTH *Remains to be Seen* v. 82 Do you mind awfully if I push orf? There's a point-to-point. **1978** A. PRICE *'44 Vintage* xxiii. 260 Everyone had scarpered—cleared orf.

orful (ǭ·ɹful), *a.* Representing a 'phonetic' spelling of an affected or emphatic pronunciation of AWFUL *a.*

1890 KIPLING *Courting of D. Shadd* (ed. 2) 166 'Got any money?' 'On'y a little—orful little.' **1901** A. H. RICE *Mrs. Wiggs of Cabbage Patch* ix. 123 He coughs all the time... Other day he had an orful spell. **1946** A. CHRISTIE *Hollow* iv. 34 'Feel pretty bad, don't you?'.. 'Orful, I feel.'

Orford (ǭ·ɹfǒɹd). The name of the *Orford* Copper Company of New Jersey, U.S.A., used *attrib.* to designate a process it developed for separating nickel from copper by making use of the difference in the solubilities of their sulphides in molten sodium sulphide.

1895 *Mineral Industry* III. 458 The Orford Copper Company was employed some time ago by the United States Navy Department to separate copper from nickel in a large quantity of Canadian matte purchased by the department, and to deliver nickel in the form of an oxide for use in alloying steel. In order to do this the company employed a new process, which may fairly be called the Orford process, and this has been from time to time improved until there is now produced from the Canadian mattes by a fire process metallic nickel which is from 99% to 99·3% pure. **1923** U. R. EVANS *Metals & Metallic Compounds* III. 183 Copper sulphide is soluble in fused sodium sulphide; nickel sulphide is not (the principle of the Orford process). **1967** J. R. BOLDT *Winning of Nickel* 276 Inco completed replacement of the Orford method by the matte separation process at the Copper Cliff smelter in 1948.

org (ǭɹg). *colloq.* abbrev. of ORGANIZATION. Also in *Comb.*

1936 *Esquire* Sept. 160/3 The Joe Breen (Hays org) influence on pix. **1951** GREEN & LAURIE *Show Biz* 570/2 *Org*, organization. **1970** *Harper's Mag.* Apr. 86 They [*sc.* White Anglo-Saxon Protestants] drew the institutions around themselves, moved to the suburbs, and became org-men. **1973** R. HAYES *Hungarian Game* xxi. 129 A private C and D org? **1976** *Times Lit. Suppl.* 5 Mar. 273/5 Systems theorists wish, unlike biologists, to 'explain' the brain..in cybernetic terms of the global properties of organizations ('orgs' as Mr Serebriakoff calls them). **1977** *Time* 6 June 48/2 Many are anti-org types and hard to count.

organ, *sb.*[1] Add: **5. d.** *Jacobson's organ:* see also *JACOBSON.

8. (sense 2) *organ-music* (fig. examples), *-note* (later fig. examples), *recital*, *-stop* (fig: cf. *STOP *sb.*[2]), *-tone* (earlier examples); *organ-toned* adj.; (sense 5) *organ regeneration*, *transplant*, *transplantation*; **organ-cactus**, substitute for def.: the giant cactus or saguaro, *Carnegiea gigantea*, found in south-western North America and so called from its resemblance to the pipes of an organ; (later example); **organ clock** (see quot. 1962); **organ specificity** *Biol.*, specificity towards a particular organ, esp. as exhibited by an antigen, so **organ-specific** *a.*

1947 *Time* 10 Mar. 18/2 The two Presidents rode between rows of organ cacti. **1956** G. H. BAILLIE et al. *Britten's Old Clocks & Watches* (ed. 7) 155 Musical and organ-clocks became more popular during the last half of the eighteenth century. **1962** E. BRUTON *Dict. Clocks & Watches* 126 *Organ clock*, clock playing a small pipe organ every three hours. Popular in the second half of the eighteenth century. **1973** *Times* 2 Jan. (Europe Suppl.) p. xii/2 The centrepiece of the show will be an organ clock by Charles Clay. **1869** G. MEREDITH *Let.* 25 June (1970) I. 382 He [*sc.* Poe] gave the idea shape in a fine roll of organ music. **1934** Organ music [see *MIMSEY *a.*]. **1921** A. HUXLEY *Let.* 8 Sept. (1969) 204 Papini..one can read with much pleasure... Great sharpness and clarity and wit combined with melody and organ notes and sweeping gesture. **1942** *R.A.F. Jrnl.* 3 Oct. 26 The organ-note of four engines hoisting the flying boat into the air. **1958** WODEHOUSE *Cocktail Time* iii. 29 A good bishop, denouncing from the pulpit with the right organ note in his voice. **1881** *Harper's Mag.* May 814/1 Piano and organ recitals have long been fashionable. **1923** *Radio Times* 28 Sept. 9/1 3.0.—Organ recital at Steinway Hall, London. **1974** *Times* 12 Nov. 15/2 No one would be happier than I to have Sunday afternoon organ recitals once again at the Palace. **1927** HALDANE & HUXLEY *Animal Biol.* ix. 174 Among reptilia, lizards are the only animals which possess even the power of organ-regeneration. **1972** L. V. POLEZHAEV *Organ Regeneration in Animals* i. 3 It is conventional to divide all animals into..those which are capable of organ regeneration and those which are not. **1936** K. LANDSTEINER *Specificity Serol. Reactions* iii. 64 Upon injection of the organ specific substances. **1971** J. Z. YOUNG *Introd. Study Man* xvii. 210 Organ-specific inhibitors are known from many tissues. **1911** *Jrnl. Exper. Med.* XIV. 48 Absolutely no organ specificity is demonstrable as regards the agglutination experiments. **1968** H. HARRIS *Nucleus & Cytoplasm* iv. 78 It has been contended that the pattern of puffing shows organ specificity but the evidence for this does not seem to be at all conclusive. **1955** A. L. ROWSE *Expansion Eliz. Eng.* 27 The Queen..was furious... At once all the organ-stops are out. **1971** P. WORSTHORNE *Socialist Myth* iii. 37 The Tory Party has..a liking for the language of togetherness, and real patriotic fervour. These are the organ-stops it can pull out with genuine faith and zest. **1819** KEATS *Hyperion* I, in *Lamia & other Poems* (1820) 148 She spake In solemn tenour and deep organ tone. **1894** 'MARK TWAIN' in *Century Mag.* Mar. 773 There was nothing weak in the deep organ tones that responded. **1895** *New Age* 12 Sept. 372/2 An organ-toned voice of prodigious depth. **1922** JOYCE *Ulysses* 454 The strains of the organtoned melodeon. **1968** *Listener* 18 July 90/2 Idea-transplants are as difficult as organ-transplants: in both cases human beings have a built-in mechanism for rejection. **1970** *Memorandum Organtranspl.* (Netherlands Red Cross) § 5c Should an organ transplant be considered..it will be desirable not to have the diagnosis of the donor's death made by one physician only. **1971** *Essentials from Rep. Organtranspl.* (Netherlands Red Cross) 3 It was considered necessary, in the context of organtransplantations, to establish a precise..criterion of..death.

organal, *a.* **3.** Of or pertaining to the medieval style of part-singing known as organum. (Cf. ORGANUM[1] in Dict. and Suppl.)

1916 STANFORD & FORSYTH *Hist. Mus.* 128 At this time the organal voice had..become finally fixed in its position above the plain-song. **1932** *Music & Lett.* XIII. 190 The melody has a long reciting note on b, which, as he [*sc.* Otker] says, 'has no proper organal response.' **1977** *Early Music* July 337/1 The upper voice seems rather like an ornamented organal voice.

organelle (ǭɹgăne·l). *Biol.* Formerly also **organella.** [mod.L. *organella* (see ORGAN *sb.*[1] and -EL[2]), after earlier *organulum* (K. Möbius 1884, in *Biol. Centralbl.* IV. 392; O. Bütschli *H. G. Bronn's Klassen und Ordnungen des Thier-Reichs* (1888) I. III. 1412), dim. of ORGANUM[1] (see -ULE).] Any of various specialized structures of an individual cell, analogous to the organs of multicellular organisms.

1909 H. M. WOODCOCK in E. R. Lankester *Treat. Zool.* I. I. 212 A Trypanosome was merely described as possessing an unmistakable nucleus, and also a small deeply-staining element..situated at the root of the flagellum, and termed variously 'blepharoplast', centrosome, or micronucleus. It is to Schandinn that we are indebted for the revelation of the essential nuclear nature of the latter organella. **1912** E. A. MINCHIN *Introd. Study Protozoa* i. 1. However complex the structure and functions of the body [of Protozoa], the organs that it possesses are parts of a cell ('organellæ'), and are never made up of distinct cells. **1924** HEGNER & TALIAFERRO *Human Protozool.* vi. 233 Division of the trophozoite is by longitudinal fission, the posterior end of the animal splitting before the anterior organelles are completely divided. **1926** L. W. SHARP *Introd. Cytol.* (ed. 2) iii. 59 It is also frequently urged that 'organelle' rather than 'organ' should be used for intracellular differentiations. **1955** *New Biol.* XIX. 27 Essentially similar organelles, cilia, cover many membranes..of animals. **1969** F. E. ROUND *Introd. Lower Plants* ii. 19 Within the outer cytoplasmic membrane occur all the normal organelles—chloroplast, nucleus, dictyosome(s) (Golgi body), endoplasmic reticulum, granules, and vacuoles. **1974** *Sci. Amer.* Oct. 45/1 Bacteria also have flagella, but these are an entirely different organelle.

Hence **organe·llar** *a.*

1970 *Genetics* LXVI. 305 (*heading*) Organellar damage and revision as a possible basis for intraclonal variation in *Paramecium.* **1975** *Nature* 13 Mar. 160/2 If this were the case in my wild carrot protoplasts, about 20% (the approximate proportion of organellar DNA in these cells) of the dimers would have remained after maximum excision.

organetto (ǭɹgăne·to). [It.] A small portative organ used in the Middle Ages.

1876 STAINER & BARRETT *Dict. Mus. Terms* 340/2 *Organetto* (*It.*), a little organ. **1952** W. L. SUMNER *Organ* iii. 58 Francesco Landini..was an excellent player on several instruments, but he preferred the portative or organetto. **1959** *Collins Mus. Encycl.* 474/1 *Organetto*.., small portative organ of the Middle Ages. **1960** D. J. GROUT *Hist. Western Mus.* (1962) iv. 129 In addition to the portative organ or organetto, there were positive organs. **1976** D. MUNROW *Instruments Middle Ages & Renaissance* ii. 16/1 The *organetto*, usually known today as the portative organ, was one of the most popular instruments, regularly illustrated from the thirteenth to the sixteenth centuries.

organic, *a.* Add: **4. b.** (ii) Of an element: contained in an organic compound.

1868 *Jrnl. Chem. Soc.* XXI. 87 Estimation of the carbon and nitrogen contained in the organic portion of the solid constituents (organic carbon and nitrogen). **1900** [see *NITRIFYING *ppl. a.*]. **1924** L. DONCASTER *Introd. Study Cytol.* (ed. 2) ii. 20 Practically the whole of the organic phosphorus in the nucleus is contained in..nucleic acid. **1957** G. E. HUTCHINSON *Treat. Limnol.* I. xii. 735 There is no information available as to the fraction constituting the soluble or colloidal organic phosphorus of lake waters. **1972** *Limnol. & Oceanogr.* XVII. 349/2 Dissolved organic carbon.., particulate organic carbon.., and particulate nitrogen.. were measured to determine the distribution of organic matter.

d. Of a fertilizer or manure: produced from natural substances, usually without the addition of chemicals.

1869 S. R. HOLE *Bk. about Roses* vi. 76, I made anxious experiment of a multiplicity of manures—organic and inorganic, animal and vegetable. **1942** *Organic Farming & Gardening* I. 3/2 Compost fertilizer is a purely organic material as distinguished from mineral fertilizers (chemicals). **1952** C. E. L. PHILLIPS *Small Garden* iii. 18 Compared with the chemical fertilizers, the organic ones are slow in action but enduring in effect. *Ibid.* 19 Of other forms of organic manure, the following are valuable. **1960** *Times* 27 Feb. 9/2 A good organic-based general fertilizer. **1975** D. GREEN *Food & Drink from your Garden* v. 38 There is probably something in the theory that vegetables have their quality improved by the use of organic fertilizers.

e. *organic soil*: (see quot. 1928).

1928 *Bull. Amer. Soil Survey Assoc.* IX. 33 *Organic soils*, soils composed mainly of organic material; the organic content being sufficient to dominate the soil characteristics. **1943** MILLAR & TURK *Fund. Soil Sci.* ii. 63 Deposits of organic soils are of common occurrence in the northern border states of Minnesota eastward. **1966** *McGraw-Hill Encycl. Sci. & Technol.* XII. 423/1 Organic soils such as peats and mucks may contain as much as 95% carbonaceous material.

f. Of farming or gardening: growing plants without the use of chemical fertilizers, pesticides, etc., adding only organic fertilizers to the soil.

1942 J. I. RODALE in *Organic Farming & Gardening* I. 3/1 What is claimed roughly for these organic methods of farming is that they increase the fertility of the soil, produce much better tasting crops,..reduce weeds, do away with the necessity of using poisonous sprays, improve the mechanical structure of the soil. **1948** *Sci. Monthly* June 482/1 Considerable success is claimed in the humid tropics with 'organic farming' where labor is plentiful..and where fertilizers are very expensive or difficult to obtain. *Ibid.*, The organic devotees are primarily interested in production. *Ibid.* 482/2 Great claims have been made for soil improvement by earthworms, usually as a special phase of 'organic' gardening. **1971** *Islander* (Victoria, B.C.) 13 June 14/2 An organic gardener uses natural mineral and organic fertilizers to build his soil. **1973** *Country Life* 6 Dec. 1986/4 Organic farming community. Six professional couples with children wish to purchase..large country residence with small-holding acreage. **1975** *Listener* 14 Aug. 203/2 The great thing about organic farming is that you..build up life in the soil, using natural organic manures such as compost and farmyard manure.

g. Of food: produced without the use of chemical fertilizers, pesticides, etc.

1972 *Daily Tel.* 12 Feb. 6/7 The organic food market is booming. *Ibid.*, 'Ninety per cent of the "organic" apple juice being sold in California is not made from organically grown apples,' said a spokesman for one of the country's biggest organic food wholesalers. **1972** R. BLOCH *Night-World* (1974) xiv. 93 Past the organic-food hangouts for the health freaks. **1975** *Times* 5 Sept. 14/8 Another great interest was the growing of food organically, which resulted in a number of books on organic food..in the late 1940s and early 1950s.

5. a. (Further examples.)

1895 E. B. TITCHENER tr. *Külpe's Outl. Psychol.* I. ii. 140 By 'organic sensations' we mean the sensations adequately stimulated by changes in the condition of the bodily organs,—muscles, joints, etc. **1901** W. JAMES *Let.* 10 July (1920) II. 158 What I *crave* most is some wild American country. It is a curious organic-feeling need. **1933** G. MURPHY *Gen. Psychol.* viii. 124 From what has been said about hunger and thirst it seems reasonable to believe that these organic sensations depend partly upon the compounding of simple sense qualities.

d. *organic selection* (see quot. 1942).

1896 J. M. BALDWIN in *Amer. Naturalist* XXX. 444 We may simply..apply the phrase, 'Organic Selection', to the organism's behavior in acquiring new modes or modifications of adaptive function. **1942** J. S. HUXLEY *Evolution* vi. 304 We have here a beautiful special case of the principle of organic selection,..according to which modifications repeated for a number of generations may serve as the first step in evolutionary change. **1970** T. DOBZHANSKY *Genetics Evol. Process* ix. 303 The term organic selection has been coined to describe the parallelism between racial genotypic and environmental phenotypic variability.

6. a. (Further examples.)

1817 COLERIDGE *Biog. Lit.* I. xii. 237 The fairest part of the most beautiful body will appear deformed and monstrous, if dissevered from its place in the organic whole. **1847** W. SMITH tr. *Fichte's Characteristics Present Age* 94 What this organic unity of a work of Art..really is,—will be asked by no one to whom it is not already known. **1870** S. H. HODGSON *Theory of Practice* II. 166 Rome..was unequal to..incorporating into an organic whole the nations included in her empire. **1874** W. WALLACE tr. *Hegel's Logic* 19 The truths of philosophy are valueless, apart from their interdependence and organic union. **1923** *Psychol. Rev.* XXX. 371 Thinking is not an isolated fact... It is the final step in an organic learning process. *a* **1943** R. G. COLLINGWOOD *Idea of Hist.* (1946) 123 Marx..conceived this unity not as an organic unity.

b. (Earlier and later examples.)

1849 *Congress. Globe* 30th Congress 1 Sess. App. 47 [The origin of a Territorial Government] is not from *such people*, but from the law of Congress, usually styled the 'organic law', establishing it. **1857** in Bartlett *Dict. Amer.* (1860) 304 The powers of the corporation of Washington are only those which are conferred by the organic law, the charter. **1963** M. KHADDURI *Mod. Libya* vii. 184 Both the Tripolitanian and Fazzanese organic laws permit the amendment of any provision during the first session of the legislative assemblies by a simple majority of all the members.

c. Phr. *organic composition of capital* (Econ.): see esp. quot. 1887.

1887 MOORE & AVELING tr. *Marx's Capital* II. xxv. 625 The composition of capital is to be understood in a twofold sense. On the side of value, it is determined by the proportion in which it is divided into constant capital or value of the means of production, and variable capital or value of labour-power, the sum total of wages. On the side of material, as it functions in the process of production, all capital is divided into means of production and living labour-power... I call the former the *value-composition*, the latter the *technical composition* of capital. Between the two there is a strict correlation. To express this, I call the value-composition of capital, in so far as it is determined by its technical composition and mirrors the changes of the latter, the *organic composition* of capital. Wherever I refer to the composition of capital, without further qualification, its organic composition is always understood. **1937** M. DOBB *Pol. Econ. & Capitalism* i. 14 The important simplifying assumption that the ratio of labour to capital employed in different lines of production was everywhere equal: what Marx termed equality in the 'organic composition of capital' or what later economists would have called uniformity of the 'technical coefficients'. **1966** J. ROBINSON *Essay Marxian Econ.* ii. 7 We can avoid ambiguity, without falsifying Marx's meaning, if we use symbols *c*, *v* and *s* only for rates per unit of time of depreciation and raw material lost, wages and profit, and speak of the organic composition of capital, not as *c*/*v* but as capital per man employed. **1972** G. C. HARCOURT *Some Cambr. Controv. Theory Capital* 8 The assumption..is akin to that of Marx.., namely, a uniform organic composition of capital for the processes..of each technique. **1974** M. B. BROWN *Econ. of Imperialism* iii. 54 With the increasing application of machinery to production the organic composition of capital would rise. **1975** *Chinese Econ. Studies* VIII. iv. 84 Capital accumulation and capital concentration inevitably increase the organic composition of capital.

B. *sb.* An organic compound. Usu. *pl.*

1953 R. E. GRIM *Clay Mineral.* iv. 62 Studies of the methylation of certain organics during their adsorption by montmorillonite. **1970** *Nature* 11 July 149/1 Small samples..of the meteorite..were ground with a small chisel previously heated to a dull red to remove organics. **1974** *Sci. Amer.* May 75/1 The biological material in Dean's recipe..represents 2,000 times the amount of organics normally present in seawater.

organically, *adv.* Add: **1. e.** Without the use of chemical fertilizers, pesticides, etc.

1971 *Countryman* Autumn 203/1 (Advt.), Homely atmosphere, quality food, organically grown vegetables, log fires. **1972** *Guardian* 3 Apr. 7/3 Apple pie... Wash apples (don't peel if organically grown). **1975** *Listener* 14 Aug. 204/2 Their last crop of the season, hand-grown, organically-manured leeks.

organicism. Add: **1. b.** The doctrine that everything in nature has an organic basis or explanation; that everything in nature is part of an organic whole (in sense of ORGANIC *a.* 6 a).

1912 A. TRIDON tr. *Delage & Goldsmith's Theories Evol.* 163 In that respect, organicism is the perfect antithesis of Weismannism. **1928** *Jrnl. Philos. Stud.* Jan. 39 This is the reason why modern organicism, the organic theory of nature, seems so important for modern biology. **1945** [see *HOLISM]. **1960** *Encounter* XV. II. 73 Mr. Tate and his friends..were accused of sentimental organicism, of naïvely hoping to revive the virtues of the antique world by restoring its economic forms. **1969** *Times Lit. Suppl.* 20 Nov. 1341 Organicism..holds that some organic properties are not reducible to those of smaller parts. **1976** *Nature* 3 June 439/1 Reductionism rests on the belief that the whole can be fully explained in terms of the parts whereas organicism (biological holism) asserts that the whole cannot be fully explained in this way.

organicist, (*b*) one who holds the organic theory of nature; also *attrib.* or as *adj.* So **organici·stic** *a.*

1912 A. TRIDON tr. *Delage & Goldsmith's Theories Evol.* 164 Roux and the other organicists lay special stress on the factors of individual evolution. **1928** *Jrnl. Philos. Stud.* Jan. 29 That which was common to the organicists, said Delage, was that they regarded..life, the form of the body..as resulting from the reciprocal play or struggle of all its elements. *Ibid.* 39 The organicistic schema formerly covered the living world, and now covers also the world of the non-living. **1941** J. NEEDHAM in P. A. Schilpp *Philos. A. N. Whitehead* 251 About the historical origins of the organicistic viewpoint in biology a great deal could be said. **1941** W. M. URBAN in *Ibid.* 304 Bergson from whom..the organicist philosophy has got its main insights. **1954** D. RIESMAN *Individualism Reconsidered* vi. 401 All such 'organicistic' analogies are..dangerous. **1969** P. A. ROBINSON *Freudian Left* 164 He [*sc.* Marcuse] argued that the Fascist conception of the state was in fact heir to the organicist tradition in political theory. **1971** *Nature* 24 Dec. 490/1 These factors are added to a resurgence of organicist philosophy and a revulsion against Jensenism. **1974** D. L. HULL *Philos. Biol. Sci.* 125 Exchanges between the so-called mechanists and organicists, materialists and vitalists, reductionists and holists, to mention but a few of the terms used to characterize the two sides of this perennial dispute. **1976** *Times Lit. Suppl.* 15 Oct. 1301/1 Extending the organicist thinking of his 'master', the Scottish planner and regionalist Patrick Geddes.

organicity (ǭɹgăni·siti). [f. ORGANIC *a.* + -ITY.] The quality or state of being organic.

1936 V. A. DEMANT *Christian Polity* ix. 161 Instead of a return to true organicity, we have Collectivism, both in the patchwork of decaying Capitalism and in Russian Communism. **1945** *Mind* LIV. 53 This fourth and last of the distinctively mental properties..might be called 'organicity' as well as 'integration'. **1970** *Jrnl. Gen. Psychol.* July 110 Concepts relating to organicity and psychosis were excluded in order to limit the population of concepts. **1977** A. SHERIDAN tr. *J. Lacan's Écrits* vi. 213 Freud first threw light on the evolution itself of the process, thus making it possible to illuminate its own determination, by which I mean the only organicity that is essentially relevant to this process.

organification (ǭɹgæ:nifikē^i·ʃən). [f. ORGANI(C *a.* + -IFICATION.] Incorporation into an organic compound.

1937 *Nature* 15 May 836/1 (*heading*) Rate of 'organification' of phosphorus in animal tissues. **1966** WRIGHT & SYMMERS *Systemic Path.* II. xxxi. 1099/1 Thiocarbamide and aniline derivatives..impair organification of iodine in the thyroid. **1976** *Lancet* 27 Nov. 1191/2 Congenital goitres and hypothyroidism have been caused by maternal ingestion of iodides, presumably because the iodides had blocked the organification of iodine and induced pituitary-dependent thyroid hyperplasia.

organigram (ǫɹgæ·nigræm). Also **organogram.** [f. ORGANI(ZATION + -GRAM.] = *organization chart* (*ORGANIZATION 4).

1962 A. SAMPSON *Anat. Brit.* xxvii. 437 (*caption*) The organogram of Shell October 1959. *Ibid.* xxx. 490 The aircraft companies, built up by brilliant pioneers like de Havilland or Sopwith, are passing painfully into an era of accountants and organograms. **1967** *Economist* 22 Apr. 392/2 A current joke is that Montedison is drawing up, not an organigram, but a 'baronigram'. **1975** A. BEEVOR *Violent Brink* iii. 64 Many notes had been taken..and doodles drawn. The CGS had a complicated organigram sketched in front of him. **1977** *Official Jrnl.* (Patent Office) 23 Nov. 3791 The first issue of the Official Journal of the European Patent Office will appear in December 1977. The contents will include..an organigram of the European Patent Organisation.

organism. Add: **2. b.** *Philos.* The theory that in science everything is eventually an organic part of an integrated whole.

1925 A. N. WHITEHEAD *Sci. & Mod. World* (1926) 112 This doctrine involves the abandonment of the traditional scientific materialism, and the substitution of an alternative doctrine of organism. **1928** *Jrnl. Philos. Stud.* III. 33 He [*sc.* Lloyd Morgan] saw no reason why the term organism should not be applied to all those 'natural entities', as he called them, existing throughout the universe in emergent degrees of complexity. **1959** A. W. LEVI *Philos. & Mod. World* xii. 486 The 'philosophy of organism'..suggests the synthesis of incompatibles. **1965** E. E. HARRIS *Foundations of Metaphys. in Sci.* xiv. 282 The appropriate philosophy for contemporary science must be..a philosophy of organism.

4. organism-environment, designating the relationship between an animal and its surroundings.

1946 C. MORRIS *Signs, Lang. & Behavior* iii. 84 One action rather than another..is 'required' by the organism-environment situation. **1958** *New Biol.* XXVI. 84 His [*sc.* man's] social, mental, and technological achievements do not make his 'organism-environment' relationship less important than that of other animals. **1969** *Listener* 13 Nov. 655/1 What lemmings are supposed to do when they get too many has become almost apocryphal and the simile has been used often enough to prophesy courses of human behaviour by people who have no understanding of lemmings or their environment or of the organism-environment relation.

organismic (ǭɹgăni·zmik), *a.* [f. ORGANISM + -IC.] Of or pertaining to an organism; applied esp. to theories, etc., relating to interdependence or organic unity. Hence **organi·smically** *adv.*

1886 J. C. BURNETT (*title*) Diseases of the skin, from the organismic standpoint. **1921** C. M. CHILD *Origin & Devel. Nervous Syst.* i. 3 The problem..is the problem of the nature and origin of the pattern which constitutes the organism as a whole, whether it consists of one cell or many, in short, the problem of organismic pattern. [*Note*] In view of the fact that the word 'organism', which implies the existence of a unity and order in the entity so designated, is universally accepted and employed, the word 'organismic' is not only biologically and etymologically justified but fills a need which is becoming more and more apparent. **1923** *Psychol. Bull.* XX. 684 (*heading*) The organismic vs. the mentalistic attitude toward the nervous system. **1934** *Jrnl. Philos. Sci.* I. 474 Having thus given, in organismic terms, a brief over-view of the nature and content of thought, we may now consider for a moment its logical aspect. **1943** C. L. HULL *Princ. Behavior* ii. 28 The basic principles of organismic behavior are to be viewed against a background of organic evolution. **1948** M. SHERIF *Outl. Social Psychol.* I. ii. 29 The perfectly defensible organismic position..holds that typical reactions of the organism are not fragmentary and that the conceptual or abstract level of psychological functioning is the level of human functioning in the normal conditions of civilized life. **1951** E. E. EVANS-PRITCHARD *Social Anthropol.* iii. 54 Professor Radcliffe-Brown has..clearly and consistently stated the functional, or organismic theory of society. **1961** WEBSTER, Organismically. **1967** *Encycl. Philos.* V. 549/1 The term 'organismalism' was coined by the zoologist W. E. Ritter in 1919 to describe the theory that..'the organism in its totality is as essential to an explanation of its elements as its elements are to an explanation of the organism'. Subsequent writers have largely replaced 'organismal' with..'organismic' as a title for this theory. **1971** *Jrnl. Gen. Psychol.* LXXXV. 230 This finding suggests that cognitive style is organismically based. **1975** *Nature* 27 Mar. 370/2 Luria emphasises molecular aspects of biology, but not to the exclusion of organismic aspects.

organistic, *a.* Add: **b.** Of or pertaining to an organism; based on organisms.

1910 *Fabian News* XXI. 16/1 He adopts the organistic view of society—that society is a being. **1953** *Essays in Crit.* III. 429 Is it speech about individual things..or speech about their feeling of being related, a Whiteheadian organistic 'feeling'?

organistrum (ǭɹgăni·strɒ̆m). [a. med.L. *organistrum*, f. *organum* organ.] A name for the earliest form of hurdy-gurdy (see quots. 1954, 1974.)

[*c* **1350** *Nova Legenda Anglie* (1901) II. 310 Tundalus..uidit quasi castrum et papiliones plurimas..in quibus chordas et organa, timpana et citharas cum organistris et cymbalis canentes..audierat.] **1870** C. ENGEL *Descr. Catal. Mus. Instrum. S. Kensington Mus.* 38 The *organistrum* had three strings, producing three different tones, which appear to have consisted of the tonic, fifth, and octave. **1940** C. SACHS *Hist. Mus. Instruments* (1942) xiv. 272 The hurdy-gurdy then [*sc.* in the 13th century] was no longer called *organistrum*, but *symphonia* in Latin (or rather Greek), *chifonie* in French and *cinfonia* in Spanish. **1954** *Grove's Dict. Mus.* (ed. 5) IV. 416/1 In the 12th century the organistrum was about five feet in length, and two executants were required, one of them to turn the handle which moves the wheel (*rotulus*) and the other to manipulate the key-mechanism (*plectra*). There were three strings, the outer tuned in octaves, the middle one a fourth or fifth below the highest string. **1960** *Times* 10 June 4/5 The New York performers [of the *Ludus Danielis*], however, have added an orchestra consisting of a trumpet, soprano recorder, oboe, carillon, handbells, viola, hurdy-gurdy (organistrum), [etc.]. **1974** *Encycl. Brit. Macropædia* X. 437/1 The organistrum, a large medieval hurdy-gurdy operated by two players: one turned a crank rotating a wheel that rubbed against one or more strings to make them sound, while the other produced different notes by turning the key-shaped levers that stopped the strings at various points.

organistry (ǭ·ɹgănistri). *rare.* [f. ORGANIST + -RY.] The post of organist.

1890 *Peel City Guardian* 19 July 4/1 He..held the local town hall organistry.

organity. Restrict † *Obs.* to sense in Dict. and add: **2.** An organized whole or organism.

1929 R. BRIDGES *Testament of Beauty* iv. 801 These perfected unify'd organities..all act in response to external stimulants.

organization. Add: **2. c.** Esp. as *social organization* in *Sociol.* and *Anthropol.*

1829 J. S. MILL *Let.* 7 Nov. in *Wks.* (1963) XII. 40 Several great steps should be taken in the improvement of the social organisation. **1865** —— *Auguste Comte* 88 In constructing..a theory of society, all the different aspects of the social organization must be taken into consideration at once. **1873** [in Dict.]. **1882** L. STEPHEN *Sci. of Ethics* iii. 109 This vast social organization is the work of a vast series of generations unconsciously fashioning the order which they transmit to their descendants. **1914** W. H. RIVERS *Kinship & Social Organisation* 1 The aim of these lectures is to demonstrate the close connection which exists between methods of denoting relationship or kinship and forms of social organisation. **1937** R. H. LOWIE *Hist. Ethnol. Theory* xii. 225 Most important of all..is Radcliffe-Brown's contribution to Australian social organization. **1944** *Mind* LIII. 352 Social organisation should be designed to encourage change in desirable directions. **1951** E. E. EVANS-PRITCHARD *Social Anthropol.* i. 12 The social organization of the Yao of southern Nyasaland. **1952** GERTH & MARTINDALE tr. *Weber's Anc. Judaism* I. i. 15 In Israelite antiquity, social organization is usually articulated in terms of father houses. **1967** M. ARGYLE *Psychol. Interpersonal Behaviour* iv. 73 A great deal of social behaviour takes place against a background of social organization—in families, industry, hospitals, and elsewhere. 'Social organization' means the existence of a series of ranks, positions or offices—such as father, foreman, hospital sister, etc. which persist regardless of particular occupants. **1974** R. J. SMITH (*title*) Social organization and the applications of anthropology.

d. Phr. *organization and methods* (see quot. 1968).

1959 *Listener* 10 Dec. 1020/1 Organization and Methods may indeed prove that the central principles of local government are irrational. **1963** *Ibid.* 28 Feb. 389/2 The Old English state was a ramshackle..affair, lying in 1066 wide open to a take-over bid from William the Conqueror and certain to benefit both spiritually and materially from the brisk and ruthless operations of his Organization-and-Methods men. **1968** JOHANNSEN & ROBERTSON *Managem. Gloss* 97 *Organisation and Methods (O & M)*, 1. An advisory service for management specifically designed to assist in obtaining maximum efficiency and accuracy in organisation and procedures. 2. The application of work study and other management techniques to administration procedures and systems within a company. **1969** J. ARGENTI *Managem. Techniques* 189 Organisation and Methods is a group of techniques rather similar to Work Study but applied usually to office work. **1971** K. GOTTSCHALK in B. de Ferranti *Living with Computer* v. 46 Groups concerned with efficiency in the office are sometimes called organization and methods (O & M) groups.

4. Special comb.: **organization centre** *Embryol.* [tr. G. *organisationszentrum* (H. Spemann 1921, in *Arch. f. Entwicklungsmech. d. Organismen* XLVIII. 568)], a region of an embryo that acts as an inductor (*INDUCTOR 5); **organization chart,** a graphic representation of the structure of an organization showing the relationships of the positions or jobs within it; **organization man** orig. *U.S.*, a man who subordinates his individuality and his personal life to the organization he serves.

[**1927** H. SPEMANN in *Proc. R. Soc.* B. CII. 180 The region of the early gastrula where these organizers lie may be called for the present a 'centre of organization'.] **1928** *Biol. Abstr.* II. 1320/2 Experiments..confirm the assumption that the organization centers are localized in the 2 cell stage. **1935** *Discovery* May 136/2 If..an organisation centre is grafted out of its usual place..it will cause these new surroundings to develop into a complete embryo or complete organ. **1956** C. H. WADDINGTON *Princ. Embryol.* x. 177 The extent of the organisation centre was examined by inserting small fragments of one gastrula into the blastocoel cavity of another. **1941** P. E. HOLDEN et al. *Top-Managem. Organization* 5 A good organization chart for the company as a whole, with auxiliary charts for each major division, is an essential first step in the analysis, clarification, and understanding of any organization plan. **1958** L. A. ALLEN *Managem. & Organization* III. xiii. 289 The organization chart is a graphic means of showing organization data. **1967** *Harper's Mag.* Jan. 38 (*title*) How to Read an Organization Chart for Fun and Survival. **1970** *Time* 10 Aug. 8 According to the tidy White House organization charts, the key influence on presidential decisions in all but foreign affairs ought to be the Domestic Affairs Council, headed by John Ehrlichman. **1956** W. H. WHYTE (*title*) The organisation man. **1958** J. K. GALBRAITH *Affluent Society* xviii. 208 Our liberties are now menaced by the conformity exacted by the large corporation and its impulse to create..the organization man. **1958** A. HUXLEY *Let.* 16 Feb. (1969) 847 It justifies the Organization Men and the dictators in satisfying their urge for tidiness. **1958** *Economist* 4 Oct. 27/1 Are we gradually getting our equivalents of the 'organisation man', smooth, able, well-adjusted, unexceptionable—and unexceptional? **1960** KOESTLER *Lotus & Robot* 277, I loathe crooners and swooners..the Organization Man and the *Reader's Digest*. **1966** N. FREELING *King of Rainy Country* 27 Canisius is just an accountant, an organisation man. A nobody. **1972** 'J. QUARTERMAIN' *Rock of Diamond* xiii. 74 He's expendable, an organisation man and a useful commodity in America.

organizational, *a.* Add: (Later examples.)

1938 I. KUHN *Assigned to Adventure* xxx. 315 Fox itself went through three complete organizational changes in less than two years. **1960** *Guardian* 12 July 1/7 The high noon of the twentieth century 'organisational man'. **1962** A. BATTERSBY *Guide to Stock Control* vii. 62 Such organizational problems are combined with investigations of the nervous systems of animals and the design of servo-mechanisms in the new studies called cybernetics. **1964** M. ARGYLE *Psychol. & Social Probl.* xiv. 171 *Organizational pathology* refers to the tendency for organizations to become ineffective in several characteristic ways. The most familiar trouble is the over-elaboration of formal rules and procedures, seen by the outsider as 'red-tape'. **1965** *New Society* 22 Apr. 14/3 Industry has its problems. Can organisational psychology help? **1969** J. ARGENTI *Managem. Techniques* v. 22 *All* organisations..have organisational problems. **1970** T. LUPTON *Managem. & Social Sci.* (ed. 2) iii. 71 The organizational environment for maximum performance and human satisfaction. **1973** A. DUNDES *Mother Wit* p. xiii, Having explained the organizational plan of the book, I should like to add a final word about the title.

Hence **organiza·tionally** *adv.*

1933 *Times Lit. Suppl.* 15 June 415/3 This is a moment for fresh, organizationally detached and sympathetically cooperative thinking. **1959** *Internat. Jrnl. Appl. Radiation & Isotopes* VI. 305/1 Even were technical feasibility successfully achieved, the firms organizationally capable of using the process and exploiting its marginal advantages are few. **1962** *B.B.C. Handbk.* 94 Organizationally, the External Services are an integral part of the BBC. **1976** *Nature* 8 July 88/3 'Organisationally,' it says, 'OTA lacks the minimum of orderly structure.'

organizator (ǭ·ɹgănəizēi·təɹ). *Embryol.* [ad. G. *organisator* organizer (given this sense by H. Spemann 1921, in *Arch. f. Entwicklungsmech. d. Organismen* XLVIII. 568).] = *ORGANIZER 2, *INDUCTOR 5.

1924 *Nature* 23 Feb. 276/2 Spemann has proved that the dorsal-lip region is a differentiator (or 'organisator' as he styled it). **1928** *Biol. Abstr.* II. 1320/2 Embryos with 1 axis are harmonically built, developing from germs in which 'organizators' lie close beside each other. **1939** E. E. JUST *Biol. Cell Surface* xi. 290 By experiment it is possible to analyze the factors which set up the conditions for differentiations in a more normal or natural manner than..in experiments with transplantations involving conceptions of 'organizators' and the like.

o:rganiza·tory, *a.* [f. med.L. *organizat-*, ppl. stem of *organizāre*, see ORGANIZE *v.* + -ORY^2.] Of or pertaining to organization.

1921 *Public Opinion* 17 June 560/1 The merely organisatory work of delivering wooden houses and materials to France. **1926** *Ibid.* 2 July 15/3 If the question of women's professions was a theoretical and ethical problem in the beginning, it must be regarded as an intellectual and organisatory one nowadays.

organize, *v.* Add: **2. b.** (Further examples.)

1904 'MARK TWAIN' *$30,000 Bequest* (1906) 7 When we organize, we'll get three shares for one. **1966** *McGraw-Hill Encycl. Sci. & Technol.* II. 614/2 They may organize into complex structures such as plastids. **1976** *Spare Rib* Nov. 26/4 This is not the first time women have organised for peace.

c. *trans.* With a person as obj.: to provide for; to make (special) arrangements for. Also *refl.*

1892 'MARK TWAIN' *Amer. Claimant* ii. 35 I'll get you organized in no time. **1952** M. TRIPP *Faith is Windsock* iv. 72 'Where's Arthur?' asked Bergen. 'Gone off with a Waaf, I think. Jake's organised too.' **1959** 'M. CRONIN' *Dead & Done With* viii. 122 There were going to be official complaints reaching the office in the morning about his activities... He felt he could organize himself out of most of it. **1977** B. PYM *Quartet in Autumn* v. 46 She was the kind of person who liked to keep herself to herself and must not be organized in any way.

d. *trans.* To arrange (personally); to take responsibility for providing (something); to 'fix up'. *colloq.*

1952 M. LASKI *Village* ix. 141 Martha organized a scratch meal. **1972** G. DURRELL *Catch me a Colobus* ix. 179 We spent the rest of the day organizing a car to take us to Mexico City the following morning. **1976** P. HILL *Hunters* v. 55 Got a big job fer you, son... Organize some sandwiches from the pub.

4. *trans.* To acquire deviously or illicitly; to obtain cleverly (orig. *Mil. slang*). Cf. G. *organisieren* Mil. slang in same senses.

1941 *New Statesman* 30 Aug. 218/3 *Organise*, to acquire illicitly. (A new R.A.F. equivalent for the last-war word 'win', meaning to 'scrounge'). **1942** *R.A.F. Jrnl.* 16 May 12 Even the plugs in the washbasins are replaced. Why do people like to 'organize' those plugs? They just fade away..and have to be replaced; but what use they are to the lads who make them souvenirs, few know. **1957** H. ROOSENBURG *Walls came tumbling Down* ii. 53 The verb 'to organize' had been widely in use in the [Nazi] prisons and camps and simply meant to acquire what one needed by stealing, bamboozling, or any other means at one's disposal. *Ibid.* iii. 73 Those Frenchwomen..were busy organizing some sausages from a reluctant butcher.

organized, *ppl. a.* Add: **2. b.** Acquired deviously, illicitly, or cleverly. (Cf. *ORGANIZE *v.* 4.) *slang.*

1957 H. ROOSENBURG *Walls came tumbling Down* v. 127 They had moved in..with a few organized mules and removed all the stores.

4. Of or pertaining to a coordinated criminal organization directing operations on a large or widespread scale, esp. in phr. *organized crime.*

1929 J. LANDESCO *Organized Crime in Chicago* ii. 25 Organized crime is not, as many think, a recent phenomenon in Chicago. *Ibid.* ix. 205 Newspaper writers,.. interested in establishing the national and international ramifications of organized criminals. **1931** F. D. PASLEY *Muscling In* iii. 94 Next to beer and booze, organized prostitution yielded the heaviest profits. **1941** H. ASBURY *Underworld of Chicago* ix. 299 During the last few months of Mayor Harrison's final term Chicago was probably as free from organized vice as at any time in its history. **1952** TURKUS & FEDER *Murder, Inc.* i. 9 In all the history of crime, there has never been an example of organized lawlessness to equal the Syndicate. **1973** *Black Panther* 5 May 2/2 It is widely known that Inman is himself a kingpin in the city's organized crime and racket rings, as is Atlanta Mayor Sam Massell. **1975** *Globe & Mail* (Toronto) 3 June 1/9 He was named in police evidence before the Quebec organized crime inquiry as one of the four top lieutenants of the Godfather of organized crime in Montreal.

5. Special combs.: **organized games,** athletics or sports as organized in a school, college, etc.; **organized labour,** workers affiliated by membership in trade or labour unions.

1933 D. L. SAYERS *Murder must Advertise* xviii. 304 In Brotherhood's régime of bread and circuses, organised games naturally played a large part. **1944** L. P. HARTLEY *Shrimp & Anemone* i. 16 The world of day-schools and organized games. **1974** *Times* 5 Jan. 10/3 At modern Oxbridge there has been a decline in the participation by undergraduates in organized games. **1885** in C. Evans *Hist. United Mine Workers of Amer.* (1918) I. 131 To organized labor..and to the generous and sympathetic public..we return our sincere and heartfelt thanks. **1924** L. WOLMAN *Growth of Amer. Trade Unions* 82 The number of wage earners..would not be considered by some a thoroughly fair base for measuring the achievement in size of an organized labor movement. **1926** *Brit. Worker* 10 May 2/4 The fight to maintain the workers' standard of living will be won by the united forces of organised labour. **1948** *Time* 15 Mar. 27/2 He thought of himself as the leader of all the people, not just of organized labor. **1975** *Times* 7 Jan. 12/8 The rise of both organized labour and high management around the turn of the century.

organizer. Add: **1. a.** Also, one who 'organizes' criminal activity (cf. *ORGANIZE *v.* 4).

1945 C. BURNEY *Dungeon Democracy* I. 19 He was an admirable 'organiser' at worst,..and succeeded in building up a private stock of those luxuries which did not come on the standard lists of the canteen. **1976** E. WARD *Hanged Man* iii. 15 Gold was now an organizer—setting up criminal work on commission.

2. *Embryol.* [tr. G. *organisator* (see *ORGANIZATOR).] = *INDUCTOR 5.

1925 H. SPEMANN in *Brit. Jrnl. Exper. Biol.* II. 500, I have given the name of 'organisers' to cells capable of inducing the formation of new anlagen. **1927** —— in *Proc. R. Soc.* B. CII. 177 (*heading*) Organizers in animal development. **1934** [see *EVOCATOR b]. **1946** [see *INDUCTOR 5]. **1970** A. M. WINCHESTER *Concepts Zool.* xviii. 474/1 The transplanted dorsal lip acted as an organizer. **1975** *Nature* 13 Nov. 129/2 The organiser for the axial pattern of the whole body [of *Xenopus*] during amphibian development is a small group of cells at the dorsal lip of the blastopore.

organo-. Add: In many compounds a secondary stress may be given as *o:rgano-* or *orga:no-*, and is not indicated in the individual words listed below. **organoleptic** *a.*, also, involving the use of the senses; (examples); hence **organole·ptically,** *adv.*, as regards organoleptic properties; **organometallic** *a.* (earlier example); also *absol.*, an organometallic compound; **organosedime·ntary** *a. Geol.*, produced by or involving sedimentation as affected by living organisms.

1852 T. R. BETTON tr. *Regnault's Elem. Chem.* I. 13 (*heading*) Of the different physical and organoleptic characters by which bodies are distinguished. *Ibid.*, The organoleptic characters are those impressions produced on the organs of taste, smell, and touch. **1940** *Nature* 21 Dec. 796/1. Unimpeachable organoleptic evidence exists for the statement that even under modern conditions cheese-making is not by any means a fully controlled industrial process. **1963** W. SUMMER *Methods Air Deodorization* iii. 228 Science has failed, so far, to conceive of an instrument which might be called an artificial nose and which would allow comparisons..between organoleptic sensations and instrumental measurements. **1970** *Daily Tel.* (Colour Suppl.) 25 Sept. 32/2 Each morning he must check the contents of the 50 vats to ensure they are suitable for bottling. His responsibilities there are organoleptic, that is, he is concerned with the qualities of the senses—sight, taste and smell. **1976** *Daily Colonist* (Victoria, B.C.) 30 May 4/7 The U.S. Food and Drug Administration would be crippled without its organoleptic analysts. **1959** *Proc. Florida State Hort. Soc.* LXXII. 145/1 Celery air-expressed from California was compared with freshly harvested Florida celery in April and May of 1957. The samples were rated organoleptically and analyzed chemically for several constituents. **1970** H. E. NURSTEN in A. C. Hulme *Biochem. Fruits & Products* I. x. 246 (*heading*) Organoleptically significant components of specific fruits. **1852** *Phil. Trans. R. Soc.* CXLII. 417, I have continued my researches upon the organo-metallic bodies. **1938** H. GILMAN *Org. Chem.* I. iv. 463 They [*sc.* organomercurials] are the only organometallics in the first two groups which can be manipulated in water. **1965** *New Scientist* 2 Dec. 658/1 Organometallics have already amply proved their worth as catalysts. **1974** *Encycl. Brit. Macropædia* XIII. 716/1 The syntheses of many specific organometallics are dictated by the particular properties or reactions of a single compound or group of compounds. **1976** *Nature* 4 Mar. 11/1 Thus, so far as σ-bonded transition metal organometallics are concerned, the realisation of the difference between their kinetics and thermodynamic stabilities has led several research groups to design stable molecules. **1964** *Jrnl. Geol.* LXXII. 81/2 Algal stromatolites are laminated organosedimentary structures formed by the activity of algal mats in binding fine particulate sediment. **1972** *Ibid.* LXXX. 592/1 'Molar tooth' structure..most likely resulted from organosedimentary processes similar to those forming algal stromatolites.

2. *Chem.* **a.** Prefixed to the names of elements to form adjs. designating compounds in which an atom of the element is bound to an organic radical; as *organochlorine, -lead, -lithium, -magnesium, -mercury, -phosphorus, -silicon, -tin, -zinc.* These may also be used *absol.*

1961 *Jrnl. Econ. Entomol.* LIV. 636/1 The..effectiveness of six organochlorine insecticides applied to soil were determined in the field against *Hippelates* gnats. **1970** *Motor Boat & Yachting* 16 Oct. 25/2 Two serious disadvantages about the early organochlorines such as D.D.T. were that they were..concentrated in certain tissues of the bodies of successive predators. **1974** *Country Life* 26 Dec. 1984/2 The gradual decline in the use of organochlorine pesticides has allowed predatory birds.. to re-establish themselves. **1861** *Q. Jrnl. Chem. Soc.* XIII. 228 Organo-lead compounds are arranged under the types of sesquioxide and peroxide of lead. **1974** *Physics Bull.* May 180/1 Lead alkyl petrol additives provide virtually the only source of organolead compounds in the environment. **1932** *Jrnl. Amer. Chem. Soc.* LIV. 1957 It is possible to prepare many organolithium compounds by the direct interaction of lithium with an RX compound in ether or benzene. **1974** *Chem. & Pharm. Bull.* XXII. 1711 Many reports have been published so far on the reactions between organolithiums and open chain compounds. **1901** *Jrnl. Chem. Soc.* LXXX. I. 263 The organo-magnesium compound produced crystallises in colourless, flattened needles. **1968** R. O. C. NORMAN *Princ. Org. Synthesis* vi. 202 Organomagnesium compounds, known as Grignard reagents after their discoverer, are the most widely used of organometallic reagents. **1860** *Chem. News* 30 June 26/1 At present the representatives of the organo-mercury series all belong to the mercuric type. **1963** A. J. HALL *Textile Sci.* v. 263 Shirlan is also much used for protecting cotton against mildew attack. A number of complex organo-mercury compounds are also effective for this purpose. **1974** *Nature* 20 Sept. 236/2 The ability of organomercury compounds, particularly methylmercury, to concentrate in tissues of fish and other animals at levels which are toxic for human consumption, is of increasing environmental concern. **1950** G. M. KOSOLAPOFF *Organophosphorus Compounds* i. 7 In many classes of organophosphorus compounds we find mixtures that are inseparable by fractional distillation. **1962** *Brit. Birds* LV. 431 Certain organophosphorus sprays were used on Brussels sprouts. **1971** *Homes & Gardens* Aug. 89/3 A servicing company can apply a long-lasting organo-phosphorus insecticide to pendant fittings. **1941** *Jrnl. Amer. Chem. Soc.* LXIII. 1194/1 The lack of a clear understanding of the behavior of the substituted organo-silicon compounds and the possibility of producing useful resinous polymers for them led to an investigation of some of the disubstituted compounds. **1955** BROWN & DEY *India's Mineral Wealth* (ed. 3) x. 391 The resultant organosilicon chlorides are hydrolised [*sic*] to silanols which condense into the polysiloxanes or silicones. **1974** *Encycl. Brit. Macropædia* XIII. 716/1 The organosilicon halides..are prepared by a special reaction using copper as catalyst. **1866** WATTS *Dict. Chem.* IV. 220 No organo-tin compounds containing only one equivalent of positive radicle, have hitherto been produced. **1960** *Times Rev. Industry* Apr. 83/3 Among the new chemicals are..organotin compounds of germicidal.. nature. **1860** *Chem. News* 30 June 26/1 Organo-zinc compounds are decomposed by water, oxide of the metal and hydride of the radical being produced. **1966** *McGraw-Hill Encycl. Sci. & Technol.* IX. 403/1 For many years organozinc compounds were used for synthetic purposes.

b. Prefixed to the names of various types of compounds to form sbs., indicating the presence of an organic radical in the molecule, as *organoalkali, -borane, -mercurial, -metal, -phosphate, -siloxane*; these may also be used *attrib.* Also **organocompound,** an organometallic compound.

1932 *Jrnl. Amer. Chem. Soc.* LIV. 1958 A corresponding simpler technique might be used with organoalkali compounds like phenyl-lithium. **1968** G. E. COATES et al. *Princ. Organometallic Chem.* iii. 34 A large class of charge-delocalized organoalkali compounds consists of the addition compounds between alkali metals and bi- or polynuclear aromatic hydrocarbons. **1957** Organoborane [see *HYDROBORATION]. **1971** J. D. ROBERTS et al. *Org. Chem.* xix. 536 The boron halides and the organoboranes (BR_3) are Lewis acids. **1976** *Nature* 15 Jan. 163/2 Chapters 4–6 .., on four-coordinate organoboranes, organodiboranes, and other polyboranes, are particularly welcome. **1866** WATTS *Dict. Chem.* IV. 224 Aluminium series. — The only known organo-compounds of this series are aluminic methide, $Al'''(CH^3)^3$, and aluminic ethide, $Al'''(C^2H^5)^3$. **1974** *Nature* 13 Dec. p. x (Advt.), Each chapter provides a complete review of all aspects of the organocompound in question. **1972** *Ibid.* 25 Feb. 414/3 The dumping of substances likely to find their way into the food chains is completely prohibited—these include organohalogen and organosilicon compounds. **1977** *Offshore Engineer* May 29/1 The real villains on the 'blacklist' are certain organohalogens (for example the extremely toxic and readily absorbed printing by-product PCB), mercury and cadmium. **1866** WATTS *Dict. Chem.* IV. 221 A brisk action with considerable elevation of temperature attends the formation of the organo-mercurial compound. **1938** H.

GILMAN *Org. Chem.* I. iv. 463 Organomercurials are the least active organometallic compounds of the first two groups. **1961** *Times* 27 Mar. 5/3 It is comparable with the organo-mercurials against apple scab. **1971** *Nature* 23 July 222/1 Only inhaled elemental mercury vapour is comparable with the above organo-mercurials in inducing intoxication. **1866** WATTS *Dict. Chem.* IV. 230 Arsenic Series.—This series..contains the first discovered organo-metal, cacodyl. **1971** *Nature* 31 Dec. 518/1 The use of metal complexes as organo-metal catalysts for the synthesis of industrially important organic intermediates and polymers. **1958** *Jrnl. Econ. Entomol.* LI. 714 (*heading*) New organophosphate insecticides developed on rational principles. **1974** M. C. GERALD *Pharmacol.* vii. 133 Medically, organophosphate compounds are used for the treatment of glaucoma. **1946** E. G. ROCHOW *Introd. Chem. Silicones* i. 2 The period since 1940 has seen rapid development of the organosiloxanes or silicone polymers. **1970** *Sci. Jrnl.* Feb. 21/3 Cement and plaster can be made water repellent by incorporating into the mix small uantities of organosiloxanes which have a large propor-o n of silicon bonded hydroxyl groups.

organogenic, *a.* (s.v. ORGANOGENY). Add: (*b*) *Petrol.* = *ORGANOGENOUS *a.* Hence **organoge·nically** *adv.*

1934 WEBSTER, *Organogenic* Petrog., derived from organic substances. **1949** F. J. PETTIJOHN *Sedimentary Rocks* x. 301 These crinoidal limestones may be termed 'organogenic conglomerates'. **1967** *Oceanogr. & Marine Biol.* V. 550 The coralligenous biocoenosis..is particularly well developed..on rocky as well as on organogenically fixed bottoms.

organogenous (ǭɹgănǫdʒe·nəs), *a. Petrol.* [f. ORGANO- + *-GENOUS.] Of a rock: formed from organic materials.

1881 E. RENEVIER in *Proc. Geol. Assoc.* VI. 426 (*table*) Organogenous.—Sedimentary by organic means. **1967** *Oceanogr. & Marine Biol.* V. 503 The soft substrata of the circalittoral zone are made up of terrigenous sediments.. and organogenous remnants.

organoid, *a.* Add: **B.** *sb. Biol.* = *ORGANELLE.

1930 MAXIMOW & BLOOM *Text-bk. Histol.* i. 5 The constituents of the cytoplasm..may be classified as the organoids and the inclusions. The organoids are structures ..which are probably endowed with the ability to divide ..in contrast to the inclusions which are passive, lifeless, temporary constitutents of the cell. The organoids comprise the mitochondria, the Golgi apparatus, the centrioles, and fibrils. [*Changed to* organelle *in ed.* 7 (1957).] **1956** *Anatomical Rec.* CXXV. 481 The presence of mitochondria in smooth muscle was described by Cowdry ('34), long after these organoids had been studied in other tissues. **1957** H. S. D. GARVEN *Student's Histol.* i. 19 The centrosome... Not infrequently this organoid is found lying embedded in the skein of the Golgi body.

organology. Add: **4.** The study of the history of musical instruments.

1959 *Times Lit. Suppl.* 17 July 428/4 More specialized aspects of 'organology' (to use the term proper to the study of old instruments) formed the topics of the fifteen papers read by members of the Galpin Society. **1960** *Times* 18 Mar. 4/6 Organology..pursues one branch of ethnomusicology, the comparative study of instruments as they are found in the various communities. **1971** *Times Lit. Suppl.* 19 Nov. 1453/5 (Advt.), Studies in keyboard organology. **1977** *Early Music* July 405/2 Only one thing is lacking to help the student of organology: a photograph of each instrument.

organolical *a.*, **organologist** (later examples, in sense *4).

1976 *Early Music* July 293/1 Munrow's emphasis on the musical use of instruments reflects a refreshing and welcome new departure in organological studies. **1976** *Jrnl. Amer. Mus. Instrument Soc.* II. 120 He must be counted among the finest organologists of our generation.

organosol (ǭɹgæ·nǫ̆sǫl). [a. G. *organosol* (E. A. Schneider 1892, in *Ber. d. Deut. Chem. Ges.* XXV. 1164): see ORGANO- and *SOL *sb.*[6]] A dispersion in which the dispersion medium is an organic liquid; *spec.* one of particles of a synthetic resin in a liquid consisting of plasticizer and volatile components, which can be converted into a solid plastic simply by heating (cf. *PLASTISOL).

1892 *Jrnl. Chem. Soc.* LXII. 775 Organosol Ag ([in] ethyl alcohol) is formed by the dialysis of the hydrosol in absolute alcohol. **1931** E. S. HEDGES *Colloids* xiv. 192 When the organosols are treated with a liquid which is soluble in the dispersion medium, but does not dissolve the disperse phase, the latter is precipitated. **1946** *Mod. Packaging* Mar. 262/2 Conversion..from solution coating to an organosol dispersion more than doubled the unit output of one modern coating plant. **1960** *Times Rev. Industry* May 23/2 The best known of the organosol coatings are the vinyl synthetic resin types. **1963** H. R. CLAUSER *Encycl. Engin. Materials* 454/2 Several plants are using spread coaters for the application of organosols and plastisols to strip steel to provide materials competitive with the light metals and plastics. **1972** *Materials & Technol.* V. xi. 338 Organosols are easier to spray in conventional equipment, and give thinner films with a greater range of flexibility and hardness.

organotherapy (ǭːɹgănoþe·răpi). *Med.* [f. ORGANO- + THERAPY.] Treatment by the administration of preparations made from animal organs, esp. glands.

1896 *Med. Times & Hosp. Gaz.* XXIV. 545/2 The belief..that diseases arising from a lack of the normal secretion of a certain gland, may at times be treated with benefit by administering the secretion of that gland from lower animals..forms the basis of modern organotherapy. **1915** [see *KETONE 2]. **1939** M. A. GOLDZIEHER *Endocrine Glands* i. 1 Organotherapy is as old as mankind and is used by primitive peoples to-day. **1958** *Internat. Jrnl. Fertility* III. 315 It is difficult to determine the incidence of endocrine disorders in studies of sterility. It is largely for this reason that organotherapy is either neglected or applied empirically. **1968** *Guardian* 27 Apr. 7/6 Organotherapy—the use of organs, animal or human, as a form of treatment.

Hence **o:rganotherapeu·tic, -the·rapic** *adjs.*, of or pertaining to organotherapy; **o:rganotherapeu·tics** *sb. pl.* = *ORGANOTHERAPY.

1900 *Lancet* 25 Aug. 610/2 Dr. J. G. Soutar..regarded the subject of organo-therapeutics as one of great importance. **1905** *Ibid.* 19 Aug. 554/2 Tests whereby organo-therapeutic substances might be recognized. **1908** *Practitioner* Sept. 428 All forms of medical treatment of this affection, whether hygienic, dietetic, medicinal, organotherapic, or electrical in nature, are unsatisfactory. **1911** *Encycl. Brit.* XXVI. 798/2 The success which has been achieved has led to the use of many other organs in a raw or compressed form, or as extracts, in other diseases... To this method of treatment the name of organo-therapeutics or opo-therapy has been given. **1923** H. R. HARROWER *Index of Organotherapy* 26 Measures that I know have been unusually effective..are not necessarily organotherapeutic. **1928** F. W. BRODERICK *Dental Med.* xi. 223 There may exist..certain definitely recognisable conditions in which appropriate organotherapeutic and other measures will be extremely useful. **1934** *Q. Cumulative Index Med.* XV. 934/2 Action of certain organotherapeutic preparations on coronary vessels of isolated heart of animals and of man.

organ-pipe. Add: **2. d.** = *organ-cactus* (ORGAN *sb.*[1] 8 in Dict. and Suppl.).

1854 *Colburn's United Service Jrnl.* Feb. 274 A specimen of [cactus]..which from its shape is commonly called 'the organ pipe' rose to the height of about twenty feet. **1957** J. KEROUAC *On Road* (1958) IV. v. 276 We began to see the ghostly shapes of yucca cactus and organ-pipe on all sides.

3. organ-pipe cactus = sense 2 d above.

1908 W. T. HORNADAY *Camp-Fires on Desert* 352 The mines are quite the northern limit of the organ-pipe cactus. **1977** *Times* 21 Apr. 16/8 Organ-pipe cacti still grow alongside..golf course greens [in Arizona].

organum[1]. Add: **2.** (Later examples.) Also *attrib.*

1884 W. H. FRERE *Winchester Troper* p. xxi, He [*sc.* Notker] first tried his hand with the melody known as Organa. *Ibid.* p. xxxix, The Organum became not a mere mechanical repetition of the principalis, but another part more or less independent of it. **1932** *Music & Lett.* XIII. 185 This singing in two parts..was also popularly called 'Organum'. *Ibid.* 189 The alto and bass have the melody, the others the organum. **1965** *Listener* 20 May 756/3, I specially liked the alternating plainchant and two-part polyphony in *organa* style of the Kyrie. **1977** *New Yorker* 23 May 126/3 The 'Hymn for a New Age' is an antiphonal chant given out by the children in organum fourths, accompanied by oboes and English horn.

organza (ǭɹgæ·nză). [ad. F. *organsin*, It. *organzino*: see ORGANZINE.] A thin stiff transparent dress-fabric of silk or synthetic fibre.

1820 M. EDGEWORTH *Let.* 4 June in C. Colvin *M. Edgeworth in France & Switz.* (1979) 144 The distinguishing characteristic is a silk organza handkerchief. **1934** *Times* 22 June 17/4 The latter in checked organza in red, white and black colourings. **1956** 'R. CROMPTON' *Matty & Dearingroydes* x. 93 The dress was egg-shell blue organza. **1964** D. FRANCIS *Nerve* xvi. 210 Alice front-view in spotted organza at a Hunt Ball. **1973** *Country Life* 19 Apr. 1114/2 The pink and green flowers used for the cap sleeves..are cut from the exquisite organza fabric.

orgasm. Add: Also *attrib.*

1936 H. M. & A STONE *Marriage Manual* viii. 276 Orgasm incapacity is more frequent. **1949** *Orgone Energy Bull.* Apr. 94 *Orgasm reflex*, the unitary involuntary contraction and expansion of the total organism in the acme of the sexual embrace. **1965** P. & E. KRONHAUSEN *Sexual Response in Women* II. i. 64 The kind of 'orgasm anxiety' to which our informant referred is very common among women. **1967** P. S. CATLING *Experiment* xxxvi. 228 You might have expected higher I.Q. levels to mean ..an enhanced orgasm yield. **1968** R. KYLE *Love Lab.* xxiv. 322 With his help, she had broken through into orgasm country. **1973** S. FISHER *Female Orgasm* i. 31 The amount of time spent by the husband stimulating his wife does not correlate with her orgasm frequency.

Hence **orga·smal** *a.* = *ORGASMIC *a.*

1964 *Brit. Jrnl. Med. Psychol.* XXXVII. 63 Failure to achieve normal adult heterosexual adjustment was shown ..by frigidity, and sometimes promiscuity with orgasmal disappointment. **1969** C. ALLEN *Textbk. Psychosexual Disorders* (ed. 2) iv. 71 Castration seems to have little effect on the desire or orgasmal capacity of the woman.

o·rgasm, *v.* [f. the sb.] To experience a sexual orgasm.

1973 S. FISHER *Female Orgasm* vii. 207 It often takes me as much as 15 minutes of stimulation before I can orgasm. **1974** *New Direction* IV. IV. 5/3 He stroked my clitoris until I orgasmed. **1977** *Observer* 25 Sept. 23/7 Approved wisdom has it that women should orgasm from that which achieves male orgasm and reproduction —penile thrusting; not from direct clitoral stimulation.

orgasmic (ǭɹgæ·zmik), *a.* [f. ORGASM + -IC.] Of or pertaining to sexual orgasm; in a state of sexual orgasm. Also *transf.* and *fig.*

1935 R. V. STORER *Sexual Technique* xxi. 278 The orgasmic contractions of the uterus act as a kind of suction pump. **1946** M. PEAKE *Titus Groan* 368 What had gone wrong? The orgasmic moment [of murder] he had so long awaited was over. **1947** J. STEINBECK *Wayward Bus* xiv. 197 Back in the bus he had felt, in anticipation, a bursting, orgasmic delight of freedom. **1953** A. C. KINSEY et al. *Sexual Behavior Human Female* ix. 390 It had acquainted the girl with the nature of an orgasmic response. **1966** MASTERS & JOHNSON *Human Sexual Response* ix. 131 The female is capable of rapid return to orgasm immediately following an orgasmic experience. **1968** *New Statesman* 16 Aug. 208/1 The Trojans meet the Greeks like lovers, almost naked, agog for the dark orgasmic flutter of killing or being killed. **1969** *Daily Tel.* (Colour Suppl.) 7 Mar. 7/2 She lay naked on the floor doing the standard orgasmic heaving. **1971** *Daily Tel.* 3 Apr. 14 Television commercials are often blatantly erotic, so that even the simple act of eating a chocolate bar is turned into an orgasmic experience. **1971** 'V. X. SCOTT' *Surrogate Wife* 13 Women do *not* ejaculate any sort of fluid.., but they *do* have an orgasmic reaction that is physiological, not just mental. **1976** L. DEIGHTON *Twinkle, twinkle Little Spy* xviii. 186 From Katerina came a long orgasmic whimper.

Hence **orga·smically** *adv.*

1972 D. F. BARBER *Pornography & Society* iii. 93 The orgasmically satisfied man or woman is unlikely to throw a bomb. **1974** *Forum* VII. 30/2 While she is still glowing orgasmically, he should enter her.

orgasmist (ǭɹgæ·z'mist). *rare*[—1]. [f. ORGASM + -IST.] One who delights in sexual excitement.

1938 DYLAN THOMAS *Let.* 6 July (1966) 205 It's a crack at young Georgians, not at New-Versers, intellectual muckpots leaning on a theory, post-surrealists and orgasmists, tit-in-the-night whistlers, [etc.].

orgastic, *a.* Add: (Later examples.)

1930 *Internat. Jrnl. Psycho-Anal.* XI. 439 In many cases the trauma of punishment falls upon children in the midst of some erotic activity, and the result may be a permanent disturbance of what Reich calls 'orgastic potency'. **1942** T. P. WOLFE tr. W. Reich in *Internat. Jrnl. Sex-Econ. & Orgone Res.* Mar. 33/2 Psychic as well as somatic disturbances are due to the *stasis* (damming-up) of energy in the organism. This stasis is due to *orgastic impotence*; only *orgastic potency*, i.e. biologically correct discharge of sexual energy, guarantees a normal energy household (sex-economy). **1963** H. I. SCHNEER *Asthmatic Child* vi. 78 She said that it was often impossible to have an orgastic response with her husband. **1969** P. A. ROBINSON *Freudian Left* 17 Orgastic potency was *defined* in economic terms; it was 'the capacity for complete discharge of all dammed-up sexual excitation through involuntary pleasurable contractions of the body'.

Hence **orga·stically** *adv.*

1941 *Internat. Jrnl. Psycho-Anal.* XXII. 215 The patient was also orgastically potent in Reich's sense of the term. **1953** W. REICH *Murder of Christ* 189 Orgastically impotent physicians in the realm of medical orgonomy will mess up the medical techniques to establish the orgonotic streaming in sick organisms or will forget them. **1973** S. FISHER *Female Orgasm* i. 32 The more a woman is capable of responding orgastically to her spouse,..the happier their marriage will be.

Orgatron (ǭ·ɹgătrǫn). [f. ORGA(N *sb.*[1] + *ELEC)TRON(IC *a.*] A kind of electronic organ.

Registered as a trade mark in the U.S. in 1935 but this mark was later cancelled. It was re-registered as a trade-mark in 1975.

1935 *Official Gaz.* (U.S. Patent Office) 16 July 518/2 Everett Piano Company, Chicago, Ill... Orgatron..For Musical instruments—Namely, Key-Board Instruments for Producing Pipe Organ Tones through Electronic Means. Claims use since Apr. 12, 1935. **1935** *Piano Trade Mag.* May 8 The Everett Piano Co., South Haven, Mich., this month announces its new musical instrument, the Orgatron, an electronic instrument with the tone of a fine pipe organ. **1937** *Sun* (Baltimore) 12 Nov. 19/4 The feature of the entertainment program will be a recital each afternoon and evening on 'The Orgatron', one of the latest developments of the electric organ. **1940** *Chambers's Techn. Dict.* 599/1 *Orgatron* (*Acous.*), an electronic musical instrument using the pneumatic action of a reed organ. The electrical current for the operation of radiating loudspeakers is obtained by electrostatic pick-ups operated by the motion of the languids of the air-operated reeds, using adequate amplifiers. **1959** *Collins Mus. Encycl.* 218/1 The Everett Orgatron..amplifies the vibration of harmonium reeds. **1975** *Official Gaz.* (U.S. Patent Office) 1 Apr. TM 23/1 GTR Products, Inc., Cranford, N.J... Orgatron. For Electronic Organs.. First use Oct. 29, 1973.

orgiast. Delete *rare* and add later examples.

1939 JOYCE *Finnegans Wake* 254 Orion of the Orgiasts. **1957** M. SPARK *Comforters* iv. 87 'He's an orgiast on the quiet.' 'A what?' 'Goes in for the Black Mass.' **1967** *Punch* 8 Nov. 723/2 That's why orgiasts have to be slightly tight And orgiate in the middle of the night. **1975** R. H. RIMMER *Premar Experiments* (1976) ii. 194 Sorry, love bug. I'm not an orgiast.

orgiastical, *a.* Add: (Further example.)

1930 *Observer* 26 Jan. 10 The Greek Tragedy up to date includes a number of ballads, revolutionary songs, and orgiastical dances.

Hence **orgia·stically** *adv.*

1930 A. BENNETT *Imperial Palace* xliii. 310 A grand climacteric of display designed orgiastically to receive the New Year into the infinite succession of years. **1934** [see

*COLOURISTIC *a.*]. **1961** J. HELLER *Catch-22* (1962) xxiii. 238 Yossarian and Dunbar were busy in a far corner pawing orgiastically at four or five frolicsome girls and six bottles of red wine. **1965** *Eng. Stud.* Feb. 28 We may get nearer the truth by seeing Venus..as having fused orgiastically with Adonis.

orgone (ǭ·ɹgōun). [f. ORG(ANISM, ORG(ASTIC *a.* + *-one* as in *HORMONE.] In the psycho-analytical theory of Wilhelm Reich (1897–1957), a vital energy or life force which supposedly informs the universe and can be collected and stored in an *orgone accumulator* or *box* for subsequent use in the treatment of mental and physical illnesses. Also *attrib.*

1942 T. P. WOLFE tr. *Reich's Discovery of Orgone* I. ix. 341 This energy, which is capable of charging non-conducting substance, I termed *orgone*. *Ibid.*, The orgone energy can be demonstrated visually, thermically and electroscopically in the soil, the atmosphere and in plant and animal organisms. **1942** —— tr. W. Reich in *Internat. Jrnl. Sex-Econ. & Orgone Res.* July 138/2 Our orgone therapy experiments with cancer patients consist in their sitting in an orgone accumulator. *Ibid.* 143/2 The patient left the orgone box. **1948** —— tr. *Reich's Discovery of Orgone* II. iv. 95 The orgone accumulator consists of an outer wall of organic material such as wood or celotex and an inner wall of sheet metal. **1949** *Orgone Energy Bull.* Apr. 95 *Physical orgone therapy*, application of physical orgone energy concentrated in an orgone accumulator to increase the natural bio-energetic defenses of the organism against disease. *Ibid.*, *Psychiatric orgone therapy*, mobilization of the orgone energy in the organism, i.e., the liberation of biophysical emotions from muscular and character armorings and the establishment of orgastic potency. **1952** M. MCCARTHY *Groves of Academe* (1953) ii. 24 A senior girl's voice, plaintive, 'Dr. Mulcahy, really, do we have to believe in orgones?' **1955** W. GADDIS *Recognitions* I. v. 194 Max was discussing orgone boxes as though he had lived in one all of his life. **1957** J. KEROUAC *On Road* (1958) 152 Why don't you fellows try my orgone accumulator? **1959** N. MAILER *Advts. for Myself* (1961) 295 God who is It, who is energy, life, sex, force, the Yoga's *prana*, the Reichian's orgone. **1973** A. S. NEILL *Neill! Neill! Orange Peel!* II. 141, I could not understand Reich's theory of Orgone Energy... He had a small motor which was charged by an orgone accumulator. **1973** *Sat. Rev. World* (U.S.) 6 Nov. 4/1 Reichian orgone therapy.

orgonity (ǭɹgǭ·niti). [f. *ORGON(E + -ITY.] (See quot. 1949.) So **orgono·tic** *a.*, **orgono·tically** *adv.*

1942 T. P. WOLFE tr. *Reich's Discovery of Orgone* I. ix. 342 Many biologists..have observed the blue coloration of frogs in sexual excitation, or a bluish light emanating from flowers; we are dealing here with the biological (orgonotic) excitation of the organism. **1942** —— tr. W. Reich in *Internat. Jrnl. Sex-Econ. & Orgone Res.* Nov. 205/2 Mix on a microscopic slide biologically (i.e., orgonotically) weak blood with rot bacteria or T-bacilli. **1945** —— in *Ibid.* Apr. 19/2 Protozoa form in the organism only in the case of orgonotic weakness in the respective organs, and that they disappear with strong orgonity. **1949** *Orgone Energy Bull.* Apr. 95 *Orgonity*, the condition of containing orgone; the quantity of orgone contained. **1953** W. REICH *Murder of Christ* ii. 17 The qualities of the freely functioning orgonotic living system..bear out this mystified religious inkling of a basic truth.

orgonomy (ǭɹgǭ·nŏmi). [f. as prec. + -NOMY.] The study or investigation of 'orgone'. Hence **orgono·mic** *a.*, pertaining or relating to orgonomy; **orgo·nomist**, one who practises orgonomy.

1949 *Orgone Energy Bull.* Jan. 23 (*heading*) The First Orgonomic Conference at Orgonon, August 30 to September 3, 1948. *Ibid.*, On Sunday evening, Aug. 29, 1948, 35 physicians, educators, and laboratory workers gathered in the laboratory at Orgonon, Rangeley, Maine, for a 4-day conference in the field of orgonomy. *Ibid.* 27 Reich concluded by saying..orgonomy represented a new way of thinking and a new science. **1950** *Ibid.* Apr. 93 It happens again and again that a physician who has not finished his training in medical orgonomy, or has never even entered training, poses as a trained medical orgonomist. **1953** W. REICH *Murder of Christ* 200 Orgonomy.. is the factual comprehension of the universal 'Cosmic Orgone Energy'. **1964** *Parade* (Austral.) Mar. 47/2 Indeed they came in such numbers that the Austrian [*sc.* Wilhelm Reich] was forced to put on a staff of orgonomists—regular doctors who saw quick profits in this new branch of medicine. **1969** P. A. ROBINSON *Freudian Left* 59 The student who has immersed himself in Reich's early work will find the science of Orgonomy curiously familiar.

orgulous, *a.* (Add examples in modern literary use.)

1922 JOYCE *Ulysses* 383 Then spoke young Stephen orgulous of mother Church that would cast him out of her bosom. **1928** V. WOOLF *Orlando* i. 46 There was an orgulous credulity about him which was pleasant enough. *Ibid.* iv. 151 A covey of swans floated, orgulous, undulant, superb. **1929** WYNDHAM LEWIS *King Spider* (1930) iv. 227 Charles, baffled here, turns his eyes elsewhere, filled with orgulous dreams. His imagination and his early successes have turned his head. **1941** AUDEN *New Year Let.* 187 That the orgulous spirit may while it can Conform to its temporal focus with praise. **1946** E. LINKLATER *Dark of Summer* 60 Coloured prints..all were bright, fantastic, orgulous—and serenely defiant of war and the cold Atlantic. **1976** M. SPARK *Takeover* x. 147 This confidence ..frequently over-rides with an orgulous scorn any small blatant contradictory facts.

oribatid (ǭri·bătid), *sb.* and *a.* [f. mod.L. family name *Oribatidæ*, f. generic name *Oribata* (P. A. Latreille in C. N. S. Sonnini *Buffon's Hist. Nat. Insectes* (1802) III. 65), perh. f. Gr. ὀρειβάτης mountain-ranging: see -ID.[3]] **A.** *sb.* A small, oval, dark-coloured mite belonging to the family Oribatidæ or the order Oribatoidea, which includes non-parasitic mites with a thickened integument, giving them a leathery appearance. **B.** *adj.* Of or pertaining to this group of mites.

1875 *Encycl. Brit.* II. 276/1 The Oribatides in general live on vegetable matter. **1914** *Brit. Mus. Return* 170 in *Parl. Papers* LXXI. 193 Thirty-three Oribatid Mites from Hawaii. **1924** *Glasgow Herald* 12 Jan. 4/2 The hard-shelled 'beetle-mites', or Oribatids feed on decaying vegetable matter. **1967** M. E. HALE *Biol. Lichens* vii. 101 The lichens..are in turn infested with oribatid mites that appear to be lichenivorous. **1972** J. BALOGH *Oribatid Genera of World* 9 The Oribatid mites are one of the richest soil Arthropodan groups. *Ibid.* 14 Permanent mounts with framing are wholly unsuitable for the study and conservation of Oribatids. *Ibid.* 15 The Oribatid specimen to be studied is carefully lifted from the lactic acid.

o·rielled, *a. rare.* [f. ORIEL + -ED[2].] Provided with oriels (sense 2).

1905 *Westm. Gaz.* 4 Nov. 6/2 Tawny sunlight works bright wizardries In orielled cloisters.

oriency. Add: Also **orience.** *poet.*

c **1865** G. M. HOPKINS *Poems* (1967) 120 Once it was scarce perceivèd Lent For orience of the daffodil. *Ibid.* 139 The heightening dawn with milky orience Rounds its still-purpling centreings of cloud.

orient, *sb.* Add: **6. Orient Express,** the name of a train which ran (from 1883 to 1961) between Paris and Istanbul and other Balkan cities, via Vienna, and of its successors (see quots. 1961, 1977). Also *attrib.* in *fig.* sense, in allusion to its association with espionage and intrigue.

1883 *Times* 2 Nov. 10/1 A small folded card,..the back giving the timetable of the journey up to Constantinople, ..and the front, under the heading 'Orient Express', the direction 'M. — is requested to take his seat, in carriage —, bed No. —'. **1904** A. E. HOUSMAN *Let.* 23 Sept. (1971) 75, I *can* pay the sum they ask, but I very much object to, as Constantinople and the Orient Express are both pretty expensive. **1920** *Cornh. Mag.* Jan. 23 From Paris onwards, my three days journey was happily in the diplomatic train, the one-time Orient Express. **1925** C. CONNOLLY *Let.* May in *Romantic Friendship* (1975) 81, I was thinking of..vanishing on the orient express. **1937** E. AMBLER *Uncommon Danger* i. 24 He could see a destination board on..one of the sleeping cars—Wien, Buda-Pesth, Belgrade, Sofia, Istanbul. The Orient Express looked warm and luxurious inside. **1960** O. MANNING *Great Fortune* i. 5 The day before had been spent on familiar territory, even if the Orient Express had kept to no schedule. **1961** *Guardian* 29 May 11/3 The Orient Express is no more. After 78 years of existence the train..is today [May 28] on its last journey from the Gare de l'Est station here [Paris] to Bucharest. **1965** *Observer* 16 May 9/1 Amateurish-sounding Orient Express techniques..are widely used... Master agent Lonsdale passed messages via drawing pins stuck..in a Lyons Corner House. **1977** *Daily Tel.* 2 May 6 (Advt.), Thursday, 19th May, 1977, will mark the death of a legend... On that day..*The Orient Express*..will begin its final run... On 22nd May the great train comes to rest in Istanbul's Sirkeci Station. **1977** *Ibid.* 19 May 10/8 The train, known since 1969 as the 'Direct-Orient', goes..to Belgrade, where first- and second-class coaches, including sleepers, separate. One section then heads for Athens and the other for Istanbul. After tonight there will be no through coaches to Athens or the Bosphorus... All that will be left..will be the Simplon Express from Paris Gare de Lyon to..Belgrade. The sole survivor of the original northern route, still wistfully and only symbolically labelled 'Orient Express', will run from the Gare de l'Est in Paris to Budapest and Bucharest.

orient, *v.* Add: **1. b.** (Further examples.)

1896 *Science* 3 July 11 We are now at a loss to orient the several parts of the cranium. **1926** C. E. MULFORD *Cassidy's Protégé* xiii. 170 Hesitating for a moment while he oriented the report, he started toward the edge of the hill-top. **1953** E. LYNAM *Mapmakers' Art* ii. 48 All early maps were oriented with the East at the top (whence our words 'to orient'). **1965** *Orienteering* ('Know the Game' series) 31 Once a map has been 'set' or oriented an orienteer should be aware of his position at all times by relating the map to the ground over which he is moving. **1972** N. J. W. THROWER *Maps & Man* vii. 102 A network of fundamental survey lines oriented predominantly in cardinal directions.

2. (Further examples.) Also, to assign or give a specific direction or tendency to.

1940 W. FAULKNER *Hamlet* 223 So he held himself still .., trying to orient himself by looking back up the slope, to establish whether he was above or below the tree, to the right or left of it. **1952** G. SARTON *Hist. Sci.* I. xxii. 579 The orator's art consist[s] in shaping and orienting the passions of the people who listen to him. **1972** *Sci. Amer.* Dec. 6/2 The program is oriented toward the long-range goal of providing small power sources, automobiles included, with nonpolluting synthetic fuels. **1977** D. BENNETT *Jigsaw Man* iv. 88 He had recognised the lie of the land... He was fully oriented.

4. *Chem.* **a.** *intr.* Of a substituent in a ring: to direct atoms and groups to a specified position in the ring when they enter it as substituents.

1924, 1937 [implied in *ORIENTING below]. **1949** ENGLISH & CASSIDY *Princ. Org. Chem.* vi. 106 Why should one group orient predominantly ortho and para, and another predominantly meta? **1971** [see *ORTHO *a.* (*adv.*) 1].

b. *trans.* To ascertain the relative positions of the substituents in (a ring or a cyclic compound).

1941 F. E. RAY *Org. Chem.* xv. 375 To prove the structure (orient the ring) of an unknown di-substituted compound. **1958** READ & GUNSTONE *Text-bk. Org. Chem.* xxiv. 419 After sound methods of orienting substituted benzenes had been devised it became possible to study more satisfactorily the substitution reactions concerned.

5. *trans.* To cause the molecules of (a plastic or other material) to assume a position in which their axes are parallel.

1958 W. D. PAIST *Cellulosics* xi. 252 Considerable enhancement of the physical properties of many resin films has been realized on biaxially orienting the formed film. **1969** W. R. R. PARK *Plastics Film Technol.* ii. 26 Virtually any thermoplastic material can be oriented.

Hence **o·rienting** *vbl. sb.* and *ppl. a.*; *spec.* in *Chem.* (cf. sense *4 a).

1727–41 [in Dict. s.v. ORIENT *v.* 1 a]. **1924** *Jrnl. Chem. Soc.* CXXV. 1377 (*heading*) The orienting influence of the thiocyano-group in aromatic compounds. **1937** F. C. WHITMORE *Org. Chem.* III. 723 Benzotrichloride and other meta orienting compounds. **1962** F. I. ORDWAY et al. *Basic Astronautics* iv. 159 (*caption*) Magnetic field measuring devices carried by Soviet Sputniks, showing orienting apparatus. **1965** *Orienteering* ('Know the Game' Series) 32 The engraved arrow inside the compass housing points to the top of the map and the orienting lines lie parallel to the grid lines. **1977** 'A. STUART' *Snap Judgement* 167, I did some orienting..by looking out of the [helicopter] window.

orientable (ōə·riĕntăb'l), *a.* [f. ORIENT *v.* + -ABLE.] Capable of being oriented; in *Math.* [tr. G. *orientierbar*], applied to a surface for which it is possible, if each point is regarded as surrounded by a small closed curve, to assign a sense (clockwise or anticlockwise) to each curve so that they are the same for all points sufficiently close together; not non-orientable; also used analogously of spaces of higher dimension.

1935 A. P. HERBERT *What a Word!* iii. 85 One of our great motor-manufacturers advertises 'A very neat orientable anti-glare visor.' **1949** S. LEFSCHETZ *Introd. Topology* ii. 82 Two orientable connected closed surfaces are homeomorphic if they have the same genus. **1952** P. NEMENYI tr. *Hilbert & Cohn-Vossen's Geom. & Imagination* vi. 306 It can be demonstrated that all two-sided surfaces are orientable. **1960** L. PICKEN *Organization of Cells* vii. 265 Cleveland's material suggests only that in hypermastigine flagellates the centrioles utilize all orientable material. **1965** tr. *Lietzmann's Visual Topology* 120 A one-sided surface is not orientable. **1968** A. H. WALLACE *Differential Topology* vi. 79 The sphere is orientable but the projective plane is not. **1975** W. M. BOOTHBY *Introd. Differentiable Manifolds* v. 215 A manifold M is orientable if and only if it has a covering..of coherently oriented coordinate neighborhoods.

Hence **o:rientabi·lity**, the property of being orientable.

1949 S. LEFSCHETZ *Introd. Topology* ii. 76 Orientability implies that the triangles of K may be 'oriented' (in an intuitive sense) so that adjacent triangles always have their orientations disposed as in Fig. 37. **1956** E. M. PATTERSON *Topology* i. 9 The idea of orientability is derived from the physical idea of two-sidedness. **1972** *Nature* 13 Oct. 387/1 Within general relativity it is necessary to impose time orientability on the E_4 manifold such that the arrows placed on timelike world lines agree in sign.

oriental, *a.* and *sb.* Add: **A.** *adj.* **3. b. oriental poppy,** a perennial poppy, *Papaver orientale*, with large scarlet flowers, native to western Asia; (earlier and later examples).

1731 P. MILLER *Gardeners Dict.* s.v. Papaver. *Papaver; Orientale*... Very rough Oriental Poppy, with a large Flower. **1963** W. BLUNT *Of Flowers & Village* 139, I think the oriental poppy..is the most exciting of them all.

c. *Oriental stitch*, substitute for def.: a long straight stitch tied down with a short diagonal stitch in the centre. (Further example.)

1900 DAY & BUCKLE *Art in Needlework* 66 Oriental-stitch, sometimes called 'Antique-stitch', is a stitch in three strokes, just as feather-stitch is a stitch in four.

d. Other Special Combs.: *Oriental carpet, rug*: a hand-knotted carpet or rug made to one of various designs in the Orient; a carpet or rug made to a similar design elsewhere; *Oriental Jew*, a Jewish person from the Middle or Far East, esp. from Yemen, Ethiopia, Iraq, or India; *Oriental Languages*, Eastern languages; these as a subject of university study; *oriental-looking* ppl. adj.; *Oriental Lowestoft*: name given to Oriental porcelain erron. thought to have been made or decorated at Lowestoft, England; see sense *B. 4.

1868 C. L. EASTLAKE *Hints Household Taste* 267/2 Oriental carpets. **1894** *Country Gentlemen's Catal.* 114 *Oriental carpets and rugs.* In Selected Designs and Colourings, Imported direct. **1972** *Guardian* 8 Sept. 11/5

You'll find an Aladdin's cave crammed full of authentic, handmade Oriental and Persian carpets. **1938** R. T. FEIWEL *No Ease in Zion* xxi. 298 One-fifth of Tel Aviv consists of Oriental Jews. **1961** L. FINKELSTEIN *Jews* II. xxv. 1179 Shakespeare's *Comedy of Errors*,..appealed greatly to the imagination of the Oriental Jew. **1968** MRS. L. B. JOHNSON *White House Diary* 7 Feb. (1970) 628 Some interesting excerpts: Between 60 and 65 percent of the people of Israel are 'Oriental' Jews. **1822** M. EDGEWORTH *Let.* 23 Jan. (1971) 334 We have just walked to see Hertford College... There are eight professors—two for classical literature—three Oriental languages, [etc.]. **1970** M. KELLY *Spinifex* i. 23, I went up to Cambridge, doing Oriental Languages. **1972** 'J. BELL' *Death of Poison-Tongue* i. 8, I have come to Polford to do Oriental languages. **1869** 'MARK TWAIN' *Innoc. Abr.* viii. 79 A ragged, oriental-looking negro. **1964** P. F. ANSON *Bishops at Large* viii. 281 This long-bearded, oriental-looking prelate. [**1866** W. CHAFFERS *Marks Pott. & Porc.* (ed. 2) 317 There is such a peculiarity in the form and quality of the Lowestoft porcelain that we are surprised any one at all conversant with..collections of china, could ever mistake it for Oriental.] **1949** G. SAVAGE *Ceramics for Collector* ii. 41 The former belongs to the 'Oriental Lowestoft' or 'East Indian China' group. **1971** L. A. BOGER *Dict. World Pott. & Porc.* 67/1 It [*sc.* Chinese Lowestoft] is also called Chinese Export Porcelain and Oriental Lowestoft. **1974** SAVAGE & NEWMAN *Illustr. Dict. Ceramics* 208 *Oriental Lowestoft*, an erroneous term, first given currency by W. Chaffers.., for the enormous quantity of porcelain made in the 18th century in China for export to Europe. **1881** C. C. HARRISON *Woman's Handiwork* III. 138 Oriental rugs are so generally used. **1931** A. U. DILLEY (*title*) Oriental rugs and carpets. **1966** M. G. EBERHART *Witness at Large* (1967) vii. 95 The wide hall upstairs had faded oriental rugs placed at spots almost sure to trip anybody. **1976** J. VAN DE WETERING *Corpse on Dike* ii. 20 A table, covered with a thick oriental rug.

B. *sb.* **4.** Denoting a variety of porcelain imported from China by European countries from *c* 1700 to *c* 1835; also known as *Oriental Lowestoft, Chinese Lowestoft, Chinese Export Porcelain.* Also *attrib.*

1863 W. CHAFFERS *Marks Pott. & Porc.* 134 Brameld. This mark is in red, on porcelain vases, in imitation of Oriental. **1873** C. SCHREIBER *Jrnl.* (1911) I. 201 A collection of choice specimens of Oriental. **1926** [see *MINTON].

5. Used *ellipt.* for *Oriental carpet, pattern, rug*, etc.

1897 *Sears, Roebuck Catal.* 220/2 *Extra Fine Lace Back Suspenders...* A magnificent assortment of patterns. Persians, Orientals, Dresdens. **1938** I. GOLDBERG *Wonder of Words* v. 91 The noun *oriental* has ceased, or half-ceased, to mean a rug woven in the Orient; it has come to mean a rug of a certain design and coloring. **1969** M. G. EBERHART *Message from Hong Kong* xvii. 152 The rugs in the hall were old Orientals, worn thin too, but still glowing in reds and blues. **1972** E. BERCKMAN *Fourth Man on Rope* i. 19 On its polished floor-boards lay a thin faded Oriental, once a very good one. **1977** C. MCFADDEN *Serial* (1978) xxx. 67/2 Martha..began to pull Kate unsteadily across the Oriental.

Orientalia (ōᵊriˌentēⁱ·liă), *sb. pl.* Also **orientalia.** [mod.L., neut. pl. of L. *orientālis* oriental.] Things, esp. books, relating to or characteristic of the Orient.

1916 *Asiatic Rev.* VIII. p. iii, (*Index*) Orientalia. **1928** H. CRANE *Let.* 28 Mar. (1965) 322, I enjoyed your historical notes and orientalia. **1932** *N. & Q.* 16 Jan. 35 (Advt.), *Books, prints, autographs...* No. 534. Orientalia. **1973** *Country Life* 20 Sept. (Suppl.) 73 19th Century Orientalia. **1975** *Sat. Rev.* (U.S.) 22 Mar. 57/2 Gumps, San Francisco—celebrated for *objets d'art*, orientalia, china, glass, jade.

orientalizing, *vbl. sb.* and *ppl. a.* (In Dict. s.v. ORIENTALIZE *v.*) Add: *spec.* designating a style of Greek art, or the period to which it is dated (*c* 750–*c* 650 B.C.), in which influences from the art of the Near East are discernible.

1902 *Encycl. Brit.* XXV. 574/2 From Ionia the style of vase-painting which,..may best be termed the 'orientalizing', spread to Greece proper. **1939** J. D. S. PENDLEBURY *Archaeol. Crete* vi. 335 Courby, in his study of such vases, divides them into three groups... Orientalizing, which he dates from 750 to 650. *Ibid.* 336 In the Orientalizing Period a number of important works of art in bronze was produced in Crete. **1948** [see *black-figure* s.v. *BLACK *a.* 19]. **1950** H. L. LORIMER *Homer & Monuments* ii. 74 Late Geometric and Early Orientalizing graves. **1960** T. BURTON-BROWN *Early Mediterranean Migrations* iii. 74 There was a group which..knew the same kinds of procedure in architecture and sculpture, as the Greeks used from the Orientalizing Period. **1973** P. GREEN *Conc. Hist. Anc. Greece* 55 (*caption*) The domestication of mythical and other beasts was typical of 'Orientalizing' art.

orientate, *v.* Add: **3.** *trans.* (*Chem.*) = *ORIENT *v.* 4 b.

1924 E. J. HOLMYARD *Outl. Org. Chem.* xix. 368 When several compounds have been orientated in this way, the constitution of other substances may be ascertained by converting them into substances of known constitution. **1926** J. READ *Text-bk. Org. Chem.* xxiv. 550 Such multitudes of benzene derivatives have been orientated that it is a comparatively simple matter to apply this method.

o·rientated, *ppl. a.* [f. ORIENTATE *v.* + -ED¹.] **1.** = *ORIENTED *ppl. a.* 1.

1886, 1900 [see ORIENTATE *v.* 1].

2. = *ORIENTED *ppl. a.* 3 (and similarly hyphenated).

1967 *Indexer* V. 162/2 We must, as far as possible, be customer- or user-orientated. **1968** *Listener* 1 Aug. 153/1 Stravinsky's Webern-orientated style. **1971** *Guardian* 18 Oct. 8/1 Polytechnics..are too big, too static, too institutional, too degree-orientated. **1972** C. JONES *Introd. Middle English* 4 Earlier works on the subject of medieval English language..have tended to be performance-orientated. **1974** *Cape Times* 1 Aug. 1/8 The highest percentage of votes appeared to be recorded at the Progressive Party-orientated..polling districts. **1975** *Daily Tel.* 26 July 11/3 His attitude..has been condemned as 'irresponsible and politically orientated'.

o·rientating, *ppl. a.* [f. as prec. + -ING².] That orientates or orients; *spec.* in *Chem.* (cf. *ORIENT *v.* 4 a).

1876 *Jrnl. Chem. Soc.* XXIX. 240 The author closes this section with some remarks on the value of the 'orientating' influence exercised by various radicles. **1920** *Christian World* 19 Aug. 7/1 Upon these young men and women the lecture must have had a great orientating effect. **1921** E. HERMAN *Creative Prayer* 104 For that world of reality ..is..Love, and its highway—the great orientating path that gives it coherence—is Christ. **1952** *Mind* LXI. 484 The use of warning, priming or orientating signals. **1966** G. P. ELLIS *Mod. Textbk. Org. Chem.* v. 101 The substituent A possesses a specific directing or orientating effect on the incoming group.

orientation. Add: **2. c.** Also, = ORIENTALIZATION.

1914 G. K. CHESTERTON *Flying Inn* viii. 81 He also wants to drive a tunnel—between East and West—to make the British Empire more Indian; to effect what he calls the orientation of England and I call the ruin of Christendom.

4. b. *Chem.* The process of ascertaining the relative positions of the substituents in a ring.

1891 *Jrnl. Chem. Soc.* LX. 1199 The method employed by Claus and Runschke..for the orientation of 4:6-dichlorometaxylene. **1903** WALKER & MOTT tr. *Holleman's Text-bk. Org. Chem.* II. 473 Oxidation is another important aid in their orientation, and is employed to determine whether the substituents are attached to the same or to different rings. **1953** ASTLE & SHELTON *Org. Chem.* xxii. 420 (*heading*) Korner's absolute method of orientation.

5. b. An introduction to some subject or particular situation; a briefing. Also *attrib.*, as (U.S.) *orientation course, program* (see quots.).

1942 in Partridge *Usage & Abusage* 226/2 *Orientation course*, American pedagoguese for an introductory, general or historical study, usually of the social sciences, designed for college freshmen or sophomores. **1953** K. REISZ *Technique Film Editing* II. viii. 140 Had we, for instance, opened the sequence with the long continuous scene of the bearded forest (as an *orientation* scene of the locale in which the tale was set) we would have no preparation to understand and appreciate its charms and mysteries. **1968** *Globe & Mail* (Toronto) 17 Feb. B6 (Advt.), Selected applicants will be offered a comprehensive orientation program in branch banking. **1968** *N.Y. Times* 23 July 41/1 Mr. Mailer was giving an 'orientation' (or was it a sophisticated party game?) for nearly 100 participants in his third film venture. **1970** *Toronto Daily Star* 24 Sept. 2/2 A student orientation program at the University of British Columbia. **1972** D. DELMAN *Sudden Death* (1973) iii. 73 'I needed..an insight into the way you tennis cats think.' 'In other words I've just delivered what amounts to an orientation lecture.' **1976** *Columbus* (Montana) *News* 10 June 4/2 Four prospective LABO host families met Sunday evening at the home of Mr. and Mrs. Bill Wright to go over an orientation program and participate in a Japanese style dinner. **1976** J. CROSBY *Nightfall* xxxviii. 231 Hawkins had read Wittgenstein only because Theresa had. Her books were his orientation course.

6. *Chem.* The orienting effect of a substituent in a ring on other atoms or groups (see *ORIENT *v.* 4 a).

In quot. 1890 the word could be interpreted in sense 2 b.

1890 *Jrnl. Chem. Soc.* LVIII. 484 The study of substitution phenomena, especially in the aromatic series, shows that the so-called orientation rules are dependent on the atomic or molecular weight of the atom or radicle which dominates or directs the position taken up by the substituting-group. **1946** A. A. MORTON *Chem. Heterocyclic Compounds* ii. 33 Replacement reactions are unique in that the position of the entering group is largely determined by the nature of the reactant, not by any orientation by groups. **1971** J. D. ROBERTS et al. *Org. Chem.* xx. 574 When the two substitutents have opposed orientation effects, it is not always easy to predict what products will be obtained.

7. Special Comb.: **orientation triad** (see quot. 1962).

1953 H. HABER *Man in Space* 155 If all three components of the orientation triad are intact, the human body is fully equipped to reckon with the force of gravity, to keep its balance and to remain properly aligned relative to the vertical. **1962** F. I. ORDWAY et al. *Basic Astronautics* xii. 475 The center of the body's orientation system is located in the inner ear; the system, however, consists of three elements, often called the orientation triad. The first component is sight, and the second is the system of mechanoreceptors or nerve endings..that are sensitive to pressure. But the vestibular apparatus of the inner ear is the heart of the system since it contains the mechanism that senses acceleration.

orientational (ōᵊriˌĕntēⁱ·ʃənăl), *a.* [f. ORIENTATION + -AL.] Pertaining to or involving orientation, esp. of variable elements in a specified context.

1952 [see *COGNITIVE *a.*]. **1962** CORSON & LORRAIN *Introd. Electromagn. Fields* iii. 113 We then considered orientational polarization in which molecules with a permanent dipole moment tend to be aligned by an external field. **1968** J. LYONS *Introd. Theoret. Linguistics* vii. 275 The notion of *deixis*..is introduced to handle the 'orientational' features of language which are relative to the time and place of utterance. **1974** R. JESSOP *Traditionalism, Conservatism & Brit. Pol. Culture* i. 17 Most political scientists employ 'political culture' as a mere catchword.. for all sorts of influences..that include both structural and orientational factors. **1976** *Nature* 23 Sept. 353/2 An extraordinary orientational relationship between the rhombohedral green rust..and magnetite..has been reported.

Hence **orienta·tionally** *adv.*

1975 *Nature* 31 Jan. 310/2 The molecules are positionally ordered but orientationally disordered and mobile.

oriented (ōᵊ·riˌented), *ppl. a.* [f. ORIENT *v.* + -ED¹.] **1.** Having a definite or specified orientation; *spec.* in *Math.*

1918 O. VEBLEN *Projective Geom.* II. ix. 426 If two oriented points are similarly oriented with respect to a line *l*, they are similarly oriented with respect to a line *m* if and only if *l* and *m* do not separate the two points. **1950** D. J. STRUIK *Lect. Classical Differential Geom.* i. 6 The sense of increasing arc length is called the positive sense on the curve; a curve with a sense on it is called an oriented curve. **1951** C. PALACHE et al. *Dana's Syst. Min.* (ed. 7) II. 181 From Tsumeb..as a secondary mineral associated with smithsonite (in part as oriented growths thereon). **1960** L. PICKEN *Organization of Cells* vii. 265 Once we admit..that the centromeres..are 'sticky' to oriented proteins, we may have conceded all that is necessary for them to figure as centres of orientation. **1970** A. GOETZ *Introd. Differential Geom.* i. 6 The space with a chosen ordered triple $\mathbf{e}_1$, $\mathbf{e}_2$, $\mathbf{e}_3$ of independent vectors is called an oriented space. **1975** *Nature* 29 May 389/1 A shipboard palaeomagnetic reconnaissance of 295 vertically oriented basement samples.

2. Of a plastic or other material: having the constituent molecules oriented with their axes parallel to one another.

1947 R. NAUTH *Chem. & Technol. Plastics* viii. 195 Table 32..indicates the qualities of 'oriented' and 'unoriented' vinylidene chloride plastics. **1950** V. STANNETT *Cellulose Acetate Plastics* i. 17 If a poorly oriented fibre is loaded only those chains lying parallel to the axis take the load. **1969** L. S. MOUNTS in W. R. R. Park *Plastics Film Technol.* v. 139 Oriented polystyrene films have excellent clarity, sparkle, and gloss.

3. Having an emphasis, bias, or interest indicated by a preceding sb. (usu. joined by a hyphen) or advb.

1950 *Psychiatry* XIII. 181 Our language patterns..are adult-oriented. **1957** *Jrnl. Nervous & Mental Dis.* CXXV. 459/2 The 'disease-oriented' physician and his 'person-oriented' fellow commonly encounter difficulties in agreeing. **1960** R. K. WEBB *Harriet Martineau* x. 295 Our psychologically oriented, relativistic age. **1968** *Globe & Mail* (Toronto) 17 Feb. B7 (Advt.), Multi-faceted and expansion oriented company with operations in Eastern Canada and United States. **1971** *Computers & Humanities* VI. 30 SIMS will provide a user-oriented language, making it easy for the user to define, validate, interrogate, and analyze the data. **1971** M. MCCARTHY *Birds of America* 269 Why are you so art-oriented, all of a sudden? **1972** *Lebende Sprachen* XVII. 134/1 Environmentally oriented research. **1974** *Times* 12 Feb. 11/5 We simply must produce managers in the future who are design oriented. **1978** *Jrnl. R. Soc. Arts* CXXVI. 744/2 To move away from performance-oriented drama towards more reflective drama.

orienteering (ōᵊriˌĕntīᵊ·riŋ). [ad. Sw. *orientering* orienteering; cf. ORIENT *v.*] The competitive sport of finding one's way on foot across rough country with the aid of map and compass; this sport as undertaken on horse-back or by car, canoe, etc. Also *attrib.* So **orientee·r,** one who engages in orienteering; also as *v. intr.* and *fig.*

1948 *Amer. Ski Ann. 1949* 146/1 Senior Scouts representing 15 Boy Scout Councils from New York and New Jersey met at Snow Ridge Ski Center last winter to compete in the first official Ski Orienteering race to be held in America. **1949** *Univ. Mass. Executive Bull.* 8 Dec., Dr. Bjorn Kjellstrom, from Sweden, and instigator of the new sport of Orienteering will show a new colored film on training for Cross-Country and Touring Skiing. **1954** *Time* 1 Nov. 58 Known officially as 'orienteering', the sport dates back to 1918 when the first Swedish club was formed to hold formal competitions. **1956** *Official Gaz.* (U.S. Patent Office) 10 Apr. TM92/2 Bjorn Kjellstrom, d.b.a. American Orienteering Service, New York, N.Y... *Orienteering.* For Instructing in Map and Compass Reading Through Lectures Delivered in Person With or Without Illustrations by Means of Film. Use since August 1946. **1965** *Orienteering* ('Know the Game' series) 10 The orienteer must remember that peat hags can be very rough pasture. *Ibid.* 36 Ankle support is very important in rough orienteering country. *Ibid.* 40 There are fascinating opportunities to orienteer by canoe, cycle, pony or ski. **1971** 'D. HALLIDAY' *Dolly & Doctor Bird* v. 60 You were supposed to be treating my blisters, not orienteering all over my torso. **1971** *Sunday Times* 10 Oct. 30 Furthermore, Swedish orienteers bled their way into medical history a few years ago following an epidemic of the disease. **1973** *Whole Earth Catal.* 23/1 Within recent years, Orienteering as a sport, in the form of 'Orienteering Races' has swept Europe... Orienteering events have become regular features in many athletic and outdoor clubs. **1976** *Observer* 26 Sept. 16/3 Egil Johansen, asked to single out the most compelling attraction of orienteering, says simply: 'It is the fellowship of the other orienteers.'

orientite (ǭəri͵e·ntəit). *Min.* [f. *Orient-e*, the name of the province in Cuba where it was first found + -ITE¹.] A hydrated silicate of calcium and manganese, $Ca_4Mn^{III}{}_4Si_5O_{20}\cdot 4H_2O$, found as light brown or pink orthorhombic crystals.

1921 HEWETT & SHANNON in *Amer. Jrnl. Sci.* CCI. 491 As the mineral is known to occur in two localities in Oriente Province, where many manganese deposits are found, and it may be widespread in the region, it is appropriate that the geographic relation be perpetuated in the name *orientite*. **1961** *Amer. Mineralogist* XLVI. 227 The largest known crystals of orientite do not exceed 1 mm. in length.

orificial, *a.* Restrict †*Obs. rare*⁻¹ to sense in Dict. and add: **2.** Of or pertaining to an orifice or orifices; in *Med.* used *spec.* with reference to a theory that many pathological conditions arise from irritation of the orifices of the rectum and urogenital system and can be relieved by surgery or other treatment of these areas.

1887 E. H. PRATT *Orificial Surg.* i. 14, I believe that all forms of chronic diseases have one common predisposing cause, and that cause is a nerve-waste occasioned by orificial irritation at the lower openings of the body. **1926** *Spectator* 25 Sept. 473/1 With a fine inconsistency, they belong to societies of so-called 'orificial surgery' and follow strange cults of electrical healing. **1960** [see *CLITORIDECTOMY]. **1973** *Biol. Abstr.* LV. 6287/1 This..revealed an orificial pulmonary stenosis which clinical investigation had failed to detect.

origami (ǫrigā·mi). Also **origame.** [Jap., f. *ori* fold + *kami* paper.] The Japanese art of folding paper into intricate designs. Also *attrib.*

[**1922** F. STARR in *Japan* (San Francisco) Oct. 43/1 Their book on paper-folding in schools compares favorably with any we have. It is entitled *shikaka origami dzukai*, paper-folding explained with figures.] **1956** 'R. HARBIN' *Paper Magic* 14 The art of *origami* has been handed down from father to son through countless generations. **1959** R. CONDON *Manchurian Candidate* (1960) ii. 56 While they had light he..amused them or startled them or flabbergasted them with the extent of his skill at *origami*. **1961** E. KALLOP in S. Randlett *Art of Origami* (1963) 16 Apart from origami as an art in the sense of the individually unique, folded paper has a role in the ceremonial etiquette of Japanese life. **1963** 'R. HARBIN' *Secrets of Origami* 11 If you can obtain a supply of Japanese Origami paper, so much the better. **1968** R. V. BESTE *Repeat Instructions* vii. 67 You should try origame..Paper-folding. It's a Jap word. **1972** C. FREMLIN *Appointment with Yesterday* xi. 83 The Origami cut-outs they'd had such a craze for over Christmas, they were on the bed too. **1973** M. CROWELL *Greener Pastures* 101 There are..paper stars and origami birds.

Origenian, *a.* (Earlier and later examples.)

1661 G. RUST *Origen* 19 A perfect explication of the Trinity after the Origenian way. **1879** R. ORNSBY in *Dubl. Rev.* July 64 A fourth branch of the Origenian evidence is prophecy and its fulfilment.

Origenism. (Later examples.)

1903 W. BRIGHT *Age of Fathers* II. xxix. 54 Anastasius ..condemned Origenism in a Roman synod. **1908** L. B. RADFORD (*title*) Three Teachers of Alexandria: Theognostus, Pierius and Peter. A Study in the Early History of Origenism and Anti-Origenism. **1960** H. C. GRAEF tr. *Altaner's Patrology* v. 242 He [*sc.* Methodius] is important principally as a successful opponent of Origenism. **1966** H. CHADWICK *Early Christian Thought & Classical Tradition* iv. 120 In judging the system of Origen as a whole it is important to remember that some of the most characteristic features of 'Origenism' are not his personal invention.

original, *a.* and *sb.* Add: **A.** *adj.* **4. c.** *original print*, a print made directly from a master image on wood, stone, metal, etc., which is executed by the artist himself, printed by him or under his supervision and, in recent times, usually signed by him.

1961 *What is an Original Print?* (Print Council of Amer.) 9 An *original print* is a work of graphic art, the general requirements of which are: 1. The artist alone has made the image in or upon the plate, stone, wood block or other material, for the purpose of creating a work of graphic art. 2. The impression is made directly from that original material, by the artist or pursuant to his directions. 3. The finished print is approved by the artist. *Ibid.* 12 The difference in the price commanded by an original print and a reproduction acknowledged as such is largely a reflection of the difference in their aesthetic qualities. **1965** ZIGROSSER & GAEHDE *Guide to Collecting Original Prints* ii. 14 When we speak of an *original* print, we mean that the artist both conceived and executed it. **1970** P. GILMORE *Mod. Prints* 7 Several committees between 1960 and 1965 tried variously to define, protect, and elevate the 'original' print, always equating it with artist handwork. **1970** *Studio Internat.* June 283/3 These [assemblage] prints look just as individual as most original prints. **1972** J. HELLER *Printmaking Today* (ed. 2) p. v, The 'original' print has become a significant feature of contemporary life.

B. *sb.* **3. e.** An image or impression produced during an actual photographing or recording session from which copies may subsequently be made.

1918 H. SEYMOUR *Reprod. Sound* 16 At first, every record sold to the public was an original, or what is technically described as a 'master', but means were soon found by which copies could be secured from the master. **1949** FRAYNE & WOLFE *Elem. Sound Recording* xiv. 266 Making the master from the original is a process involving several operations. **1970** A FOWLES *Dupe Negative* xiv. 196 This type of film doesn't have a negative... The piece of film that actually runs through the camera is called the original..from which all subsequent prints are struck. **1971** L. B. HAPPÉ *Basic Motion Picture Technol.* ix. 277 (*caption*) Duplicates from reversal originals.

4. b. *spec.* in Fashion and *haute couture*, a garment specially designed by a couture house for exhibition in a collection, or a copy of such a garment made to order. Also *Mus.*, (usu. jazz), a piece written by the performer(s).

1946 B. G. CHAMBERS *Keys to Fashion Career* x. 86 Partner and designer of the firm of Young Originals. **1957** M. B. PICKEN *Fashion Dict.* 238 *Original*, a garment designed in and produced by a couture house, bearing the label of the house. It is usually a duplication made to order of the model shown in the collection. Each order is called a 'repeat' by the couture house. **1966** *Crescendo* Oct. 22/3 The Monk Quartet was playing originals—'Hackensack', 'Rhythm-A-Ning' and 'Epistrophy'. **1967** *Melody Maker* 28 Jan. 15/5 The material is a nice mixture of originals, blues and ballads. **1975** R. H. RIMMER *Premar Experiments* (1976) ii. 195 My sister, wearing Pucci originals. **1976** *Observer* 22 Feb. 32/5 (Advt.), Anna Belinda announce that until February 28th they will continue to add a further distinction to their hand-made originals in silks, velvets and Liberty prints.

originality. Add: **1.** (Earlier example.)

1742 H. WALPOLE *Let.* 14 July (1903) I. 256 It is one of the most engaging pictures I ever saw. I have no qualms about its originality.

3. (Earlier example.)

1742 T. GRAY *Let.* 24 May (1935) I. 206 My Lady of Queensbury is come out against my Lady of Marlborough; & she has her Spirit too, & her Originality, but more of the Woman, I think, than t'other; as to the Facts it don't signify two pence, who's in the right.

‖ **orihon** (ǫ·rihǫn). [Jap., f. *ori* fold + *hon* book.] A book formed by folding a printed roll alternately backwards and forwards between the columns, and usu. fastening it with cord down one side.

1907 C. DAVENPORT *Book* ii. 28 The Chinese and Japanese..by help of the ancient device of 'stabbing' the flattened roll along one of its sides,..produce a form called an 'Orihon', easy to consult, strong. **1910** *Encycl. Brit.* IV. 216/2 A roll [of vellum, paper, etc.] of this kind can be folded up, backwards and forwards, the bend coming in the vacant spaces between the columns of writing. When this is done it..becomes a book, and takes the Chinese and Japanese form known as *orihon*—all the writing on one side of the roll or strip of paper and all the other side blank... The earliest fastening of such books consists of a lacing with some cord or fibre run through holes stabbed right through the substance of the roll, near the edge. Now the *orihon* is complete, and it is the link between the roll and the book. **1951** S. JENNETT *Making of Bks.* xi. 155 This form of book was much used throughout the East, and was known as an orihon. **1960** G. A. GLAISTER *Gloss. Bk.* 287 *Orihon*, a manuscript roll on which the writing was done in columns running the short way of the paper with margins between each. The roll was then folded, the margins having the effect of a closed fan. **1968** E. G. TURNER *Greek Papyri* 173 It has been suggested that the codex evolved out of an intermediate form of leather or skin roll in which stitches were inserted in the spaces between every second column, the skin being folded on itself at the intervening column, so that the whole roll was folded concertina-fashion. Books of this kind (termed *orihon*) are still in everyday use in China and Japan.

orinasal, *a.* (*sb.*) Add: The form **oronasal** is now usual. (Further examples.)

1882 *Brit. Med. Jrnl.* 1 July 13/1 Metal Respirators. 1. The principal forms made by Jeffries..are three: one for the mouth only..; a second.., for the mouth, with a scarf; and a third, for the mouth and nose (ori-nasal). **1888** MARTINDALE *Extra Pharmacopœia* (ed. 5) 163 (*heading*) Oro-nasal inhalations. **1926** JORDAN & KINDRED *Textbk. Embryol.* xx. 407 The oronasal groove is obliterated by the fusion of the median nasal and maxillary processes to form the upper lip. **1938** *Jrnl. Aviation Med.* IX. 184/2 Since most aviators breathe through the nose, it would be necessary to use an oronasal type of mask only in the presence of nasal obstruction. **1960** J. J. SHARRY in W. L. McCracken *Partial Denture Construction* xxi. 468 The palatal repair itself may look adequate, and yet we find that there may be an oronasal perforation in the labial mucobuccal fold. **1970** *Jrnl. Physiol.* CCVI. 22P (*heading*) Oronasal distribution of inspiratory flow during various activities.

Hence **orona·sally** *adv.*, by means of the mouth and nose.

1970 *Science* 15 May 858/2 In the course of previous experiments, more than 100,000 newborn..mice received reovirus 3 oronasally.

O-ring: see *O 6.

Orisha (ori·ʃă). [Etym. obscure (see quot. 1926).] A name given to a number of native deities of Southern Nigeria. Also *attrib.*

1926 P. A. TALBOT *Peoples S. Nigeria* II. iii. 29 A hierarchy of Orisha (derived perhaps from 'ri', see, and 'sha', select—or from the Edo word Oyisa). **1929** A. C. M. BURNS *Hist. Nigeria* ii. 39 A number of minor deities (Orishas) who are more directly interested in mundane matters. **1937** M. PERHAM *Native Admin. Nigeria* II. xii. 189 The House of the Orishas or sacred images stands in the market outside the official residence of the Ataoga. *Ibid.*, The visits to Orisha-houses and consultations of oracles. **1949** G. PARRINDER *West Afr. Relig.* ii. 16 The chief divinities, generally non-human spirits, often associated with natural forces (called *abosom, vodŭ, orisha*). **1961** J. JAHN in A. Dundes *Mother Wit* (1973) 97/1 Without the drums it was impossible to call the orishas. *Ibid.* 98/2 The procedure which in the African orisha cult evokes ecstatic immobility..produces, in the Negro churches, 'mass ecstasy'. **1974** *Afr. Encycl.* 548/3 Many Yoruba people are Christians or Muslims, but still follow the traditional religion, which has several powerful Gods ..and many less important ones called 'orisha'. **1976** *Wilson Q.* Autumn 77 The African deities (*orishas*) became identified with various Christian saints.

Orissi (ori·si). *India.* [f. *Orissa* a state of eastern India.] = *ODISSI.

1960 C. FABRI in *Mārg* (Bombay) XIII. II. 5 Orissi.. bears great resemblance not only to Bharata Natya, but also to Kuchipudi, in Andhra, which may be described as 'next door'. **1962** B. GARGI *Theatre in India* 51 Orissi dance, practised in Orissa in South-East India, is recognised by scholars as an authentic classical dance... This dance style..claims to be over two thousand years old. **1965** E. BHAVNANI *Dance in India* vi. 50 The Orissi dance has its roots in devotional ritual. **1971** *Femina* (Bombay) 2 Apr. 9/1 The first part of the programme was in Bharat Natyam, the second and third in the Kuchipudi and Orissi styles of dancing. **1974** *Encycl. Brit. Macropædia* XIII. 741/1 The classical dance of Orissa, known as the *orissi* dance, has survived for more than 700 years.

-orium, *suffix.* Add: Now used, esp. in America, in many, often hybrid, formations, as *barbatorium, bobatorium, healthatorium*, etc.

1925 *Amer. Speech* I. 38/2 *Barbatorium*, a barber shop. *Bobatorium*, a place where hair is bobbed. *Healthatorium*, synonymous for *sanatorium*. *Infantorium*, a sanatorium for infants... *Motortorium*, an automobile repair shop... *Suitatorium*, a place where suits are cleaned and pressed. [etc.]. **1943** *Ibid.* XVIII. 71/1 Perhaps the following forms on the *-orium* ending have not previously been noted: *furnitorium* (a furniture store), *hairitorium* (a store dealing in wigs and hair goods), and *puritorium* (a Hebrew ritual bath). **1957** *Journal des Traducteurs* II. 49 In recent decades advertisers intent on catching the public eye have freely exploited such suffixes as *-orium*..to form *hairorium, meatorium, sportorium*. **1959** *Times* 28 Oct. 13/4 A market gardener in New South Wales..keeps a lonely stall bearing the notice 'Potatorium'. *Ibid.* 31 Oct. 7/7 Lubritorium (United States) is, inevitably, not Latin. *Ibid.* 2 Nov. 13/4 Thirty years ago there was a 'pantatorium' in Cambridge (Mass.), which pressed pants.. rapidly. **1963** R. I. McDAVID *Mencken's Amer. Lang.* 221 The former [*-orium*] has given *lubritorium* (the lubricating rack in a filling station), *printorium, corsetorium, hotdogatorium, parentorium* (a parent guidance center), *puritorium* (a Jewish ritual bath) and *eatatorium*.

Oriya (orī·yă), *a.* and *sb.* Also **Ooreah, Ooriya, Uriya,** etc. [f. Skr. *Odra* name of a region of India.] **A.** *adj.* **a.** Of or pertaining to Odra, an ancient region of India corresponding to the State of Orissa. **b.** Of or pertaining to the State of Orissa, which takes its name from Odra. **B.** *sb.* **a.** A native of Odra. **b.** The Indo-European language of Odra, which is spoken widely in Orissa.

1801 *Asiatick Researches* VII. 225 Utcala or Ódradésa is co-extensive with the Subá of Órésá... The language of this province, and the character in which it is written, are both called Uríya... the Bráhmens of this province use the Uríya character in writing the Sanscrit language. **1831** A. SUTTON *Introd. Gram. Oriya Lang.* p. vii, The Oriyas speak every word with the bold rusticity of an English countryman... A Bengallee can scarcely be met with who speaks Oriya, but he may instantly be detected by his peculiar mode of pronunciation. **1848** J. H. STOCQUELER *Oriental Interpreter* 177/2 The *Ooreahs* are, in some respects, excellent servants; they are very careful of furniture. *Ibid.* 179/1 The language of the Ooreah nation is a dialect of the Sanscrit, much resembling the Bengalee, and called the Ooreah. **1855** H. H. WILSON *Gloss. Indian Terms* p. xxii, The Telugu..meeting on the north with Uriya, on the west with Maráthí and Karnáta. **1866** G. CAMPBELL in *Jrnl. Asiatic Soc. Bengal* XXXV. II. (Suppl.) 52 They [*sc.* the 'Bhooyas']..speak Oorya on the Ooriah borders..and Hindee farther north. *Ibid.* A resemblance in appearance to the Ooryahs, among whom high cheek bones seem to prevail. **1872** W. W. HUNTER *Orissa* I. v. 171 The Uriyá language held its own for centuries, almost to the walls of Kalingapatnam itself. **1873** E. BALFOUR *Cycl. India* (ed. 2) IV. 266/1 A monster snake..was worshipped by the Ooryah as a deity. *Ibid.* 267/1 In Vizianagram, Telugu is only spoken in the open country, and Urya in the mountains. **1903** G. A. GRIERSON *Linguistic Survey India* V. II. 367 It is called Oṛiyā, Ōḍrī, or Utkalī, that is to say the language of Ōḍra or Utkala, both of which are ancient names of the country now known as Orissa. *Ibid.* 368 The Oṛiyā verbal system is at once simple and complete. **1930** R. D. BANERJI *Hist. Orissa* I. x. 136 The average Oriya..is usually dwarfish in stature and brownish black in complexion. **1954** PEI & GAYNOR *Dict. Linguistics* 155 *Oriya*, an Indic language (also called *Odri*) spoken in Orissa, Bihar, Bengal, the eastern regions of the Central Provinces and in the northern part of the Madras Presidency, by a total of about 13,000,000 native speakers. **1971** *Femina* (Bombay) 30 Apr. 29/1 A student of Hindustani classical music, she knows many Oriya songs. **1972** W. B. LOCKWOOD *Panorama Indo-European Lang.* 206 Oriya is the state language of Orissa, where it is the native medium of sixteen and a half millions. *Ibid.*, The Oriyas reached their present seats after advancing from the west.

ork (ǭɹk). *slang.* (orig. and chiefly *U.S.*). Also **orch.** [abbrev. of ORCHESTRA.] An orchestra, *spec.* a jazz or dance band.

1936 *Metronome* Feb. 61/3 Orville Knapp and ork back in town... Curly Riggs and ork home from the Santa Rita Hotel, Tucson engagement. **1937** in *Variety* 10 Nov. 58/3 Philly Orch on Thursday (11) night will preem..'Mystic Pool'. **1950** *Down Beat* 1 Dec. 13 (*title*) Ina Ray Ork looks good on TV; plays well, too. **1959** C. MACINNES *Absolute Beginners* 136 The Dickie Hodfodder ork, led by Richard H. in person, playing away merrily. **1977** *Zigzag* June 41/4 'Weeping Willow'—recorded in London backed..by Georgie Fame, Colin Green and the Norrie Paramour Ork!

Orkney (ǭ·ɹkni). The name of a group of islands off the north coast of Scotland, applied *attrib.* to various local animals and products; **Orkney sheep,** a small feral sheep distinguished by horns curving backwards and a brown, white, or speckled fleece; **Orkney vole,** a larger subspecies of the European vole, *Microtus arvalis orcadensis,* found only in the Orkney Islands.

[**1805** G. BARRY *Hist. Orkney Islands* III. i. 319 The Sheep (*ovis aries*, Lin. Syst.) here is a peculiar breed, and, from some features in its character, seems to have sprung from the same stock with those of Iceland, the Ferroes, and Shetland.] **1861** MRS. BEETON *Bk. Househ. Managem.* 320 The Leicestershire breed [of sheep] is the best example of this lymphatic and contented animal, and the active Orkney, who is half goat in his habits, of the restless and unprofitable. **1905** J. G. MILLAIS *Mammals Gt. Brit. & Ireland* II. 279, I have noticed that both the Orkney and the Water Voles often possess a white tip to the end of the tail. **1912** H. J. ELWES in *Scottish Naturalist* 6 Orkney Sheep. Sheep never seem to have been as important here as in Shetland. **1926** *Daily Colonist* (Victoria, B.C.) 7 Jan. 5/3 A group of smartly designed coats of the popular Orkney cloth in half a dozen beautiful shades. **1935** *Discovery* June 168/2 All our voles, including the Orkney and Skomer voles, seem as numerous as they have ever been. **1952** L. H. MATTHEWS *Brit. Mammals* vi. 155 In captivity the Orkney vole is noticeable for its pugnacious disposition and its readiness to bite. **1965** T. FITZGIBBON *Art Brit. Cooking* 133 Orkney cheese is a creamy Cheddar type cheese made in the Orkney Islands, but exported to England. **1971** [see *inverted pleat* s.v. *INVERTED *ppl. a.* 9]. **1972** *Country Life* 3 Aug. 273/2, I shall be grateful if you can give me any information regarding Orkney chairs... As the name suggests, this is a traditional Orkney kind of furniture. **1973** *Scotsman* 21 Feb. 10/1 Cheese straws made from Orkney cheese. **1974** J. M. DONEY et al. in P. A. Jewell et al. *Island Survivors* iv. 124 The litter size of these [Soay] lambs was 1·28, which is the same as..the Orkney sheep on North Ronaldshay. **1978** *Vole* No. 6. 54/2 Orkney is distinguished in having its own special vole, the Orkney vole, larger than its mainland cousin.

Orkneyman (ǭ·ɹknimæn). = ORCADIAN *sb.* A native or inhabitant of the Orkney Islands.

1775 HEARNE & TURNOR *Jrnls.* (1934) 191, I have interfered so far as to ask what encouragement they required to which the Orkneymen seem'd to intermate that 12L per annum would enduce them to be active & useful. **1842** *Trans. Lit. & Hist. Soc. Quebec* iv. 1333 The animals frequenting this country [include]..the Common Hare of Canada, called Rabbits, by the Orkney men in the service of the Hudson's Bay Company. **1936** *Beaver* (Winnipeg) Dec. 4/1 In the year 1799 about five hundred and thirty persons were employed by the Hudson's Bay Company, at their fur trade posts in North America, of whom four hundred and sixteen..were Orkneymen. **1956** V. FISHER *Pemmican* 30 He had heard that..there were..a few red-faced Orkneymen, a few Moravian sisters and brothers. **1961** J. W. ANDERSON *Fur Trader's Story* i. 1 For nearly two hundred years Orkneymen played a prominent part in the fur trade of Canada. **1969** G. M. BROWN *Orkney Tapestry* 26 Hardly a thing is known about these first Orkneymen..apart from the monuments they left behind them.

orl (ǭɹl), *a.* and *adv.* Representing a 'phonetic' spelling of a vulgar pronunciation of ALL *a.* and *adv.*

1864 [see *O.K. *a.* a]. **1898** J. D. BRAYSHAW *Slum Silhouettes* 14, I could 'ear the plates abreakin' pretty nigh orl night. **1923** 'R. CROMPTON' *William Again* xiv. 240 That..looks a bit of orl *right.* **1939** [see *O.K. *a.* a]. **1955** M. ALLINGHAM *Beckoning Lady* ii. 31 Orl right, orl right, I'll go. **1971** *Listener* 9 Sept. 342/2 To use her own quaint phraseology *May bien*, she was a bit of orlright. **1972** *Buster & Jet* 15 Jan. 33 Orl right, you ol' Scrooge! I'm meetin' some real tightwads today, it seems!

Orleanian (ǭɹlī·ăniăn). [f. *Orlean(s* + -IAN.] An inhabitant of New Orleans in the United States.

1946 *New Orleans Times-Picayune* 23 Mar. 17/4 (*heading*) Orleanian tells of Jap tortures. **1947** in B. A. Botkin *Treas. S. Folklore* (1949) III. ii. 535 Perhaps the most famous of romantic Mardi Gras stories that Orleanians tell is that one concerning the 'ghost dinners' served each Shrove Tuesday. **1948** *Highway Traveler* Dec. 18/1 Because Orleanians at one time depended upon the duel as a means of settling disputes, the extensive display of dueling pistols and swords on the second floor has special interest. **1952** B. ULANOV *Hist. Jazz in Amer.* (1958) v. 46 The dance-music instrumentation familiar to most Orleanians.

Orleanist. (Earlier and later examples.)

1834 tr. *C. M. Catherinet de Villemarest's Life Prince Talleyrand* II. ix. 184 The letter of the Abbé Maurice [*sc.* Talleyrand]..proves to me, that after having been an anarchist, an Orleanist, and not having been able to become a Robespierrist..he has now become a Directorist. **1976** W. GÉRIN *E. Gaskell* xiv. 155 Mary Anne Clarke..an Orleanist to the backbone..had the good fortune to charm Chateaubriand.

Orlon (ǭ·ɹlǫn). Also **orlon.** A proprietary name of a man-made polyacrylonitrile fibre which makes a soft, warm yarn for textiles and knitwear. Freq. *attrib.*

1948 *N.Y. Times* 25 Aug. 43/3 The DuPont Company announced today it had adopted the trade mark 'Orlon' for a synthetic textile fiber on which it has been conducting research for several years and which previously has been known as Fiber A. **1950** *Official Gaz.* (U.S. Patent Office) 17 Oct. 677/1 E. I. DuPont de Nemours and Company... *Orlon.* For yarns of synthetic fibers. Claims use since Aug. 3, 1948. **1952** *Trade Marks Jrnl.* 9 Jan. 31/1 *Orlon...* Raw or partly prepared synthetic textile fibres. E. I. DuPont De Nemours and Company..Wilmington, State of Delaware, United States of America; manufacturers. **1952** [see *ACRILAN]. **1956** A. HUXLEY *Let.* 17 Nov. (1969) 811 It is interesting to find ruffles coming back—in orlon and nylon, no ironing, no starch. **1957** P. WILDEBLOOD *Main Chance* 36 His smiling teeth looked as expensively synthetic as his orlon shirt and dacron suit and nylon socks. **1969** 'J. MUNRO' *Innocent Bystanders* vii. 98 The journey was a gruelling one, and by the end of it the yellow Orlon dress had lost its glitter. **1973** *Materials & Technol.* VI. 327 Polyacrylonitrile, best known under the trade names of 'Courtelle', 'Acrilan' and 'Orlon'.

o·rmer, *v. Channel Islands.* [f. the sb.] To collect ormers. Chiefly as **o·rmering** *vbl. sb.*; also *attrib.*

1903 *Eng. Dial. Dict.* IV. 359/2 He's gone ormering. **1953** W. D. HOOKE *Channel Islands* iv. 110 Ormering is another important amusement. A very low tide is always referred to in the Islands as 'an Ormering tide'. **1953** S. P. B. MAIS *Channel Islands* 67 It was a full moon and a spring tide, 'ormering' time. **1953** M. PEAKE *Mr. Pye* x. 71 'Where are you going, Tintagieu?' 'Ormering.'.. 'I d-didn't know there was an ormer tide.' **1965** 'J. CHRISTOPHER' *Wrinkle in Skin* vi. 77 Matthew had walked out occasionally, on an ormering tide. **1968** R. M. LOCKLEY *Channel Islands* 74 Even hard-hearted employers have forgiven employees absent from work over a low tide when the excuse has been 'ormering'. **1976** W. RUTHERFORD *Jersey* iii. 40 The land and the sea were exploited to the utmost for the islanders' subsistence, and from them came the traditional customs: the ormering parties, held when the *oreille-de-mer* were gathered.

orming (ǭ·ɹmiŋ), *a. dial.* [The same word as HAWM *v.*] Ungainly and clumsy in movement, tall and awkward; (quot. 1913) (standing about) gawping and staring.

E.D.D. Hawm v.[1] cites from 'Sc., Yks., Chs., Der., Not., and Lin.'.

1903 *Eng. Dial. Dict.* IV. 359/2 *Orming*, ppl. adj... Notts. Tall and awkward. **1913** D. H. LAWRENCE *Love Poems* 52 Niver a baby had eyes As sulky an' ormin' as thine. **1922** —— *England, my England* 261 Mrs. Goodall.. fairly hated the sound of correct English. She *thee'd* and *tha'd* her prospective daughter-in-law, and said: 'I'm none as ormin' as I look, seest ta.' Fanny did not think her prospective mother-in-law looked at all orming.

ornament, *sb.* Add: **2. d.** *Mus.* A grace note; a decorative figure used to embellish a melodic line.

1664 J. PLAYFORD *Introd. Skill of Musick* (ed. 4) I. 58 There is made now adayes an indifferent and confused use of those Excellent Graces and Ornaments to the good manner of Singing, which we call Trills, Grapps, [etc.]. *c* **1779** W. WARING tr. *Rousseau's Dict. Mus.* 185 *Graces in Singing.* By this term are called, in the French music, certain turns and shakes in the throat, and other ornaments joined to the notes, which are in such or such a position, according to the rules prescribed by a taste in singing. **1801** BUSBY *Dict. Mus.* p. xxx, Of the graces in music... To these ornaments may be added the *Slur*,..the *Staccato.* **1885** G. B. SHAW *How to become Mus. Critic* (1960) 67 Her voice is not yet quite solid, and..she appended a dreadful 'ornament' to Hark, those Chimes. **1962** *Listener* 17 May 885/2 The important indications of Rameau's ornaments were either unnecessarily simplified or omitted, regrettably since ornaments are not optional embellishments in music of this period; they form an integral part of the harmony, frequently devised to prepare or resolve dissonance. **1969** *Ibid.* 26 June 904/3 The ornaments are not frequent, and only come on emotional words.

ornamental, *a.* Add: **b.** *ornamental-leaved* adj.

1870 B. S. WILLIAMS (*title*) Choice stove and greenhouse ornamental-leaved plants. **1952** A. G. L. HELLYER *Sanders' Encycl. Gardening* (ed. 22) 122 Ornamental-leaved kinds [of coleus] require to have points of their shoots pinched off in early stage of their growth to ensure dwarf or well-shaped plants.

B. *sb.* **2.** A tree or shrub grown for the sake of its attractive appearance.

1903 *Pop. Sci. Monthly* Jan. 277 It could be done more easily with strawberries, or with some of the common ornamentals that do not reproduce true to seed. **1972** *House & Garden* Feb. 24/2 When planting ornamentals, plant fruit trees and bushes too.

ornamentalist. (Further examples.)

1868 C. C. PERKINS *Italian Sculptors* vi. 234 After his [*sc.* Piero Giacomo Illario's] day Mantuan sculptors are few, and are generally ornamentalists in marble or stucco. **1925** *Daily Tel.* 13 May 20/6 Pastrycooks.—First hand required. Must be first-class decorator and ornamentalist.

ornamentation. Add: **3.** *Mus.* The use of grace notes to provide embellishment of a melodic line.

1879 [see *ARABESQUE *sb.* 5]. **1938** *Oxf. Compan. Mus.* 675/1 Ornamentation in the old Italian vocal style had become so much second nature with them that nothing he could say would induce them to keep to the copies before them. **1947** A. EINSTEIN *Mus. Romantic Era* xvii. 310 The ornamentation of the Russo-Oriental folk song. **1962** *Listener* 2 Aug. 189/3 Her ornamentation is always designed to stress dissonances at crucial points. **1963** *Ibid.* 3 Jan. 45/3 Should we not consider carefully whether, say, spread piano chords are not as obligatory in playing Ravel as correct ornamentation in playing Bach?

orné, *a.* Add: (Earlier and later examples.) Also, decorated, ornate.

1781 J. BYNG *Torrington Diaries* (1934) I. 48 The place ..[*sc.* a garden bower] is not sufficiently ornée. **1781**, etc. [see *COTTAGE 4 a]. **1864** TROLLOPE *Small House at Allington* I. i. 9 A solitude in the centre of a wide park is now the only site that can be recognized as eligible. No cottage must be seen, unless the cottage orné of the gardener. **1951** N. MITFORD *Blessing* I. ii. 22 If she could propose an 18th-century mausoleum..or cottage orné as the object for a walk, he would accompany her.

orneriness (ǭ·ɹnərinės). Chiefly *U.S.* [f. *ORNERY *a.* + -NESS.] Meanness, cussedness, contrariness.

1899 B. TARKINGTON *Gentleman from Indiana* iv. 45 They..let loose their deviltries just for pure orneriness. **1927** W. R. JAMES *Cow Country* 229 The bronk's orneriness had come to the top, and that pony..begin to get sort of desperate and to looking for a way out. **1957** *Economist* 9 Nov. 469/2 Some of these groups are based on geography, like Indonesia's island dissidents, some on tribal differences, like Ghana's Ashantis, and some arise out of pure political orneriness. **1959** J. THURBER *Years with Ross* v. 75 Some orneriness of mood aggravated by.. peptic ulcers. **1973** W. H. AUDEN in *Listener* 22 Feb. 238/2, I out of sheer orneriness said: 'I'll drive cars for the TUC.'

ornery (ǭ·ɹnəri), *a. dial.* and *colloq.* Also **ornary.** [dial. var. of ORDINARY *a.* 5.] Commonplace, of poor quality, coarse, unpleasant; low, mean, cantankerous. (Now chiefly *U.S.*)

1816 U. BROWN *Jrnl.* in *Maryland Hist. Mag.* (1915) X. 369 The Land is old, completely worn out, the farming extremely ornary in general. *a* **1861** T. WINTHROP *John Brent* (1862) vii. 71 Good company betters the orneriest sort er weather. **1875** C. M. YONGE *My Young Alcides* II. ix. 261 If I refused, he should think..that I couldn't take that 'ornary object', as he had overheard himself described that day. **1924** GALSWORTHY *White Monkey* II. ix. 196 A low-down thought—mean and ornery. **1937** P. K. DEVINE *Folklore of Newfoundland* 35 *Ornery*, ugly or plain; no good. **1938** I. KUHN *Assigned to Adventure* xiv. 128 If he had not mentioned the clothes I should not have become ornery. But these clothes were a sore point with me. I was on the defensive at once. **1938** *Sun* (Baltimore) 28 Jan. 10/3 We are forced to spend all this money solely because mankind up to now is too ornery to organize international life on some more sensible basis. **1941** J. FAULKNER *Men Working* 201 Mules is the orneriest critters. **1944** T. D. CLARK *Pills, Petticoats & Plows* xvi. 28 Not a thing, you ornery cuss do you have to do. **1958** M. SAKEL *Epilepsy* (1959) 40 He may, contrary to his usual behavior, become argumentative, pugnacious or 'ornery' in behavior. **1962** G. MACEWAN *Blazing Old Cattle Trail* xxi. 143 There the sheep were in one of their orneriest moods, determined not to get their nice Merino wool wet. **1972** *Newsweek* 10 Jan. 18/3 The public as a whole might turn ornery if some semblance of prosperity were not found just around the corner.

ornithischian (ǭɹniþi·skiăn), *a.* and *sb.* [f. mod.L. order name *Ornithischia* (H. G. Seeley 1887, in *Proc. R. Soc.* XLIII. 170), f. ORNITH(O- + ISCHIUM: see -IA[2], -IAN.] **A.** *adj.* Of, pertaining to, or designating an ornithischian. **B.** *sb.* A herbivorous dinosaur of the order Ornithischia, which includes forms having a pelvic structure resembling that of birds.

1901 H. G. SEELEY *Dragons of Air* xvii. 199 In some at least of the..Ornithischian Dinosaurs, there is no antorbital vacuity. **1933** A. S. ROMER *Vertebrate Paleontol.* ix. 195 It is probable that few ornithischians were entirely bipedal in habits. **1965** E. H. COLBERT *Age of Reptiles* i. 19 The ornithischian dinosaurs, in which the rod-like pubic bone of the pelvis had rotated backwardly to run parallel to the ischium,..were..of late Triassic origin. **1967** *New Scientist* 16 Mar. 534/2 [In Lesotho] they also found a fair proportion of ornithischians, a group with an elongated bird-like pelvis. **1971** *Nature* 12 Nov. 75/1 Before 1962 the genus *Geranosaurus*, which is represented by a single jaw, was the only undisputed Triassic ornithischian on record, but since that date knowledge of the earliest ornithischian dinosaurs has increased considerably. **1977** *Radio Times* 17 Dec. 45 One of the liveliest of these disputes concerns the two great groups of dinosaurs, the saurischians (with hip-bones like those of lizards) and the ornithischians (in which they were more bird-like).

ornitho-. Add: **o:rnithocopro·philous** *a.* [cf. *coprophilous* (s.v. COPRO-)] (see quot. 1928).

1928 B. D. JACKSON *Gloss. Bot. Terms* (ed. 4) 454/1 Ornithocoprophilous.., applied to lichens, which benefit by the excreta of birds. **1958** J. J. BARKMAN *Phytosociol. & Ecol. Cryptogamic Epiphytes* ii. 104 *Xanthoria candelaria* is highly ornithocoprophilous on rocks in Sweden. **1967** [see *NITROPHILOUS *a.*].

ornithogalum (ǭɪniþǫ·gălǒm). [mod.L., ad. L. *ornithogalē*, Gr. ὀρνιθόγαλον, f. ὀρνιθο- bird + γάλα milk, adopted as the name of a genus by Linnæus (*Hortus Cliffortianus* (1737) 124) and earlier botanists.] A bulbous plant of the genus so called, belonging to the family Liliaceæ, native to Europe, Asia, or Africa, and usually bearing racemes of white flowers; = ORNITHOGAL, *Star of Bethlehem* (STAR *sb.*[1] 22 c).

1664 [see ORNITHOGAL]. **1755** [see *Star of Bethlehem* s.v. STAR *sb.*[1] 22 c]. **1792** *Curtis's Bot. Mag.* VI. 190 (*heading*) Golden ornithogalum. **1825** [see ORNITHOGAL]. **1901** L. H. BAILEY *Cycl. Amer. Hort.* III. 1174/2 Ornithogalums may be divided into hardy and tender groups, and each of these may be subdivided into dwarf and tall. **1931** M. GRIEVE *Mod. Herbal* II. 770/1 Only one [species] is truly native to Great Britain, the spiked Ornithogalum, *O. pyrenaicum* (Linn.), and is not common, being a local plant, found only in a few counties. **1966** E. PALMER *Plains of Camdeboo* xvii. 284 Milk-white Ornithogalums of various species grew here and there, Chinkerinchees to us all.

ornithologically, *adv.* (Examples.)

1862 *Ibis* 87 The country..is rather poor ornithologically. **1970** *Daily Tel.* 2 May 11/4 This month is quite the best for the ornithologically minded. **1977** *Listener* 30 June 867/1 A superb setting, a marshy bird reserve in Southern Spain where..the..narrator's ornithologically outrageous mania which traps him into seeing too much, forces him into flight among sordid tourist development.

ornithologize, *v.* (Earlier example.)

1872 *Amer. Naturalist* VI. 268 At Topeka..we also tarried for ten days, devoting the time almost exclusively to ornithologizing.

ornithophile (ǭ·ɪniþofəil). [f. ORNITHO- + -PHILE.] **1.** = ORNITHOPHILIST.

1963 *Punch* 10 July 69/3 Irresistible to ornithophiles.

2. *Bot.* A plant pollinated by birds.

1970 *Watsonia* VIII. 67 Mountain regions..are..also regions where ornithophiles from diverse plant genera congregate.

ornithophilous, *a.* (Later examples of *Bot.* use.)

1890 G. F. SCOTT-ELLIOTT in *Ann. Bot.* IV. 265 (*title*) Ornithophilous flowers in South Africa. **1906** J. R. A. DAVIS tr. *Knuth's Handbk. Flower Pollination* I. 76 The following Cape plants are ornithophilous. **1975** *New Phytologist* LXXIV. 366 There are species [of giant lobelia] which are ornithophilous.

ornithophily. Add: **2.** *Bot.* [cf. mod.L. *Ornithophilæ*, name of a group of plants pollinated by birds (F. Delpino in H. Müller *Die Befruchtung der Blumen* (1873) 15).] Pollination by birds.

1903 W. R. FISHER tr. *Schimper's Plant-Geogr.* I. vi. 121 The ornithophily of a species of Erythrina was also established by Belt. **1970** *Watsonia* VIII. 67 The plates (75 colour photographs, mainly of birds visiting flowers) are..illustrative of the importance of ornithophily in the U.S.A. **1975** *New Phytologist* LXXIV. 368 Ornithophily is replaceable by autogamy.

ornithopod, *a.* and *sb.* [Add to etym. after *Ornithopoda*: (O. C. Marsh 1881, in *Amer. Jrnl. Sci.* 3rd Ser. XXI. 423).] Substitute 'sub-order' for 'order' in def. and add examples.

1933 A. S. ROMER *Vertebrate Paleontol.* ix. 196 (*caption*) Dorsal and lateral views of the ornithopod dinosaur *Camptosaurus*. *Ibid.* 197 The arch of the back was stiffened in ornithopods by a latticework of tendons. **1975** *Nature* 23 Oct. 668/1 We describe here ornithopod dinosaur remains from the Lower Cretaceous of western North America. **1977** A. HALLAM *Planet Earth* 275 Larger ornithischians, known as ornithopods, had appeared in the middle Jurassic.

ornithopter (ǭ·ɪniþǫptəɪ, ǭɪniþǫ·ptəɪ). *Aeronaut.* Also † **-ptere.** [ad. F. *ornithoptère* (P. Renard 1908, in *L'Aérophile* 15 Jan. 35), coined to replace *orthoptère* (*ORTHOPTER 2) because of the latter's etymological inappropriateness and its entomological meaning; see ORNITHO-.] A machine designed to achieve flight by means of flapping wings.

1908 *Aeronautics* I. 86/1 *Orthinoptere* denotes a machine in which the means of sustentation and propulsion consist of beating-wings. **1909** *Flight* I. 99/2 There are many who watch most anxiously for the success of artificial flapping flight by the aid of machines which have been variously named 'orthopters' and 'ornithopters'. **1933** *Jrnl. R. Aeronaut. Soc.* XXXVII. 205 This gentleman.. produced a machine of the ornithopter type for military observation. **1957** *Listener* 19 Dec. 1021/2 Where the aeroplane was concerned, Leonardo gave most of his attention almost obsessionally to the flapping wing ornithopter. **1960** *Observer* 17 Apr. 17/1 A Tass announcement said that the ornithopter—apparently powered by a motor-cycle engine—was flown 'for several yards' in Moscow. **1973** *Nature* 16 Nov. 173/3 A book largely concerned with a theoretical synthesis of man-powered ornithopters. **1976** *Globe & Mail* (Toronto) 4 Aug. 2/6 Mr. Newell, 64, has built five of his airplanes, called ornithopters, in the past 12 years.

ornithosaur. (Examples.)

1887 H. G. SEELEY in *Phil. Trans. R. Soc.* B. CLXXVIII. 191 This osseous condition approximates to that which characterises the bones of Ornithosaurs and Birds. **1913** *Q. Jrnl. Geol. Soc.* LXIX. 372 An Ornithosaur from the Wealden Shales of Atherfield (Isle of Wight).

ornithosaurian, *a.* (*sb.*) (Examples.)

1888 R. LYDEKKER *Catal. Fossil Reptilia Brit. Mus.* I. 24 Considerable portion of the skeleton of a large Ornithosaurian..from the Wealden of Brook, Isle of Wight. **1901** H. G. SEELEY *Dragons of Air* xvi. 187 In many ways the Ornithosaurian animals are like Birds. **1913** *Q. Jrnl. Geol. Soc.* LXIX. 372 The late Rev. W. D. Fox..discovered..many associated ornithosaurian bones.

ornithosis (ǭɪniþōᵘ·sis). [f. ORNITHO- + -OSIS.] A disease affecting birds, certain small mammals, and man, caused by a micro-organism belonging to the genus *Chlamydia*, and producing severe, sometimes fatal, pneumonitis in man and respiratory or generalized infection in birds and other animals. Cf. PSITTACOSIS in Dict. and Suppl. Hence **ornitho·tic** *a.*

1939 K. F. MEYER et al. in *Proc. Soc. Exper. Biol. & Med.* XLI. 173 (*title*) Complement-fixation test..as aid in recognizing latent avian psittacosis (ornithosis). **1947** W. P. BLOUNT *Dis. Poultry* xliii. 388 There are, however, other allied virus infections of birds, such as that under investigation..in the pigeon, which is equally ornithotic. **1951** *Lancet* 29 Sept. 572/2 This monograph is essentially a review of present knowledge of the clinical features [etc.]..and treatment of psittacosis and ornithosis. **1959** *Times* 25 Mar. 8/6 A generalized virus infection known as psittacosis or ornithosis. **1966** *Daily Tel.* 4 Nov. 13/4 A much bigger danger..is the wood pigeon, which..suffers from ornithosis, more usually associated with budgerigars, that can give man a form of pneumonia. **1973** *Observer* 4 Nov. 5/3 A steadily increasing number of people..catch psittacosis—or ornithosis, as it is known in humans—from imported parrot-like birds.

oro-, formative element repr. Gr. ὄρος mountain (as in *orometric* (1774), *orology* (1781)). For the var. **oreo-** see etym. of OROGRAPHY.

orobus. Delete *Obs.* and substitute for second part of etym.: [adopted by Linnæus (*Genera Plantarum* (1737) 325) and earlier botanists as the name of a genus.] Substitute for def.: A herb of the genus so called, belonging to the family Leguminosæ and now usually included in the genus *Lathyrus*; = *bitter-vetch* (BITTER- *a.* 2). (Later examples.)

1703 tr. *van Oosten's Dutch Gardener* II. cv. 135 Of the Orobus. This is a small blue purplish Flower, bears plentifully; it is a sort of Vetches. **1801** *Curtis's Bot. Mag.* XV. 521 (*heading*) Early-flowering Orobus. **1894** W. ROBINSON *Wild Garden* (ed. 4) vi. 53 Among the plants that are suitable for hedgerows and lanes, &c. are..May Apple, Orobus in variety, many Narcissi. **1903** *Flora & Sylva* I. 202/1 The name 'Orobus' is useful, for it expresses a race of plants..distinct from the climbers to which the name 'Lathyrus' was formerly exclusively applied. These Orobi..supply some of the most beautiful of spring and early summer flowers.

orocline (ǫ·rokləin). *Geol.* [f. *ORO- + κλίνειν to bend.] (See quot. 1955.)

1955 S. W. CAREY in *Papers & Proc. R. Soc. Tasmania* LXXXIX. 257 For an orogenic system which has been flexed in plan to a horse-shoe or elbow shape, the name *orocline* is proposed. **1970** LINTON & MOSELEY in *Cambr. Anc. Hist.* (ed. 3) I. I. i. 21 Carey recognizes six oroclines in the orogenic belt in Europe. **1972** *Nature* 13 Oct. 389/2 The orocline concept is incompatible with strong plates and offers no reason why arcs should be circular.

orocratic (ǫrokræ·tik), *a.* *Geol.* [f. *ORO- + κράτ-ος strength + -IC.] Characterized by an increase in the roughness of relief as a result of crustal upheaval.

1924 W. RAMSAY in *Geol. Mag.* LXI. 155 Only after the orogenic phases was the relief comparable to that of the present day, or still higher and more broken. For such a condition I will use the term *orocratic*. **1929** L. J. WILLS *Physiogr. Evol. Brit.* vi. 71 The Carbo-Permian times witnessed..one of the greatest orocratic phases that is known. **1961** *Times* 28 Aug. 9/4 A 'pediocratic period' is a relatively quiet one between two 'orocratic periods'.

orogen (ǫ·rǒdʒěn). *Geol.* Also **orogene.** [a. G. *orogen* (L. Kober *Der Bau der Erde* (1921) i. 21): see *ORO- and -GEN.] An orogenic belt.

1923 *Bull. Geol. Soc. Amer.* XXXIV. 167 Geanticlines and orogens may remain as dry lands or may sink into the depths of the oceans. **1934** *Geogr. Jrnl.* LXXXIII. 517 The orogen on the west North American Cordillera. **1953** [see *mountain system* s.v. *MOUNTAIN 9 a]. **1964** L. V. DE SITTER *Struct. Geol.* (ed. 2) xxxi. 424 The Pyrenees are essentially a Hercynian orogene reactivated in the Alpine Period. **1970** *Nature* 28 Nov. 838/2 The width of the orogen is anomalously great in the region of the central United States. **1975** *Ibid.* 20 Feb. 599/2 The effects are restricted to the western seaboard of Scandinavia and within overthrust masses on the respective sides of the Caledonian orogene.

orogenesis. (Further examples.)

1925 [see *EPEIROGENESIS]. **1970** *Nature* 9 May 498/1 Basaltic dykes have been used to separate chronologically two principal periods of orogenesis.

orogenetic (ǫrodʒěne·tik), *a.* *Geol.* [f. ORO(GENESIS + -GENETIC.] = OROGENIC *a.*

1888 J. J. H. TEALL *Brit. Petrogr.* 441 *Orogenetic*, that which relates to the formation of mountains. **1925** J. JOLY *Surface-Hist. Earth* i. 24 The orogenetic movements which developed the Appalachians. **1956** *Nature* 28 Jan. 156/2 The rate of cooling [of the earth] was greater in the past.., and this suggests that orogenetic activity may have decreased. **1970** R. J. SMALL *Study of Landforms* iii. 89 Over much of the earth compressive forces in the crust, stemming mainly from orogenetic movements of diverse age, have produced folding of sedimentary strata.

Hence **orogene·tically** *adv.*

1923 *Bull. Geol. Soc. Amer.* XXXIV. 158 There must have been another crustal element orogenetically connected with it. **1949** *Ibid.* LX. 1756/2 He is..strongly convinced..that the anorogenetic periods were of long duration, as against the short orogenetically active phases.

orogenic, *a.* Add: *orogenic belt*, a strip of the earth's surface which has been subjected to folding or other deformation during an orogeny.

1942 M. P. BILLINGS *Structural Geol.* v. 95 Some geologists, however, believe that entire orogenic belts are due to gigantic terrestrial couples. **1944** A. HOLMES *Princ. Physical Geol.* xviii. 378 It is..essential to discriminate carefully between the geographical concept of a mountain range or system and the geological concept of an orogenic belt: the one refers to the height and relief of the land; the other to the structure of the rocks, whether the region be high, low, or submerged. **1969** *Sci. Jrnl.* Feb. 52/2 The entire orogenic belt bordering the eastern margin of the Pacific may have been caused by sea floor spreading and the consequent underthrusting along the eastern Pacific margin.

Hence **oroge·nically** *adv.*, by orogenesis.

1935 *Geogr. Jrnl.* LXXXVI. 76 Neither in the orogenically nor in the isostatically affected areas. **1971** I. G. GASS et al. *Understanding Earth* xxii. 323/2 The ancient diamondiferous sediments of the Ivory Coast were orogenically deformed some 2000 million years ago.

orogenital (ōᵊ:rodʒe·nitǎl), *a.* [irreg. for *origenital*, f. L. *ōs*, *ōr-* mouth + GENITAL *a.*] = *ORAL *a.* 3 b.

1963 A. HERON *Towards Quaker View of Sex* 56 In the U.S.A. (and probably in this country) orogenital contact seems much less common in what are often called the lower social classes. **1971** *Nature* 16 Apr. 433/1 Human sex play has a large, though tabooed, orogenital component. **1974** E. ROSEN et al. *Abnormal Psychol.* (ed. 2) xv. 277/2 The technical terms for oro-genital activity are cunnilingus..and fellatio.

orogeny (s.v. OROGENESIS). Add: **a.** = OROGENESIS.

1890 [see *EPEIROGENY]. **1950** F. E. ZEUNER *Dating Past* (ed. 2) xi. 349 The periods of regression and orogeny result in intensified erosion on the continent. **1972** *McGraw-Hill Yearbk. Sci. & Technol.* 305/1 Orogeny results from interactions of this global, continuously evolving system of oceanic ridges and trenches, according to the concepts of..lithosphere plate tectonics.

b. A geological period of mountain-building.

1914 *Jrnl. Geol.* XXII. 647 Throughout its range the Laramide orogeny was marked by great volcanic activity. **1940** *Geogr. Jrnl.* XCVI. 51 The conception of the orogenic cycle..gets little support from a study of the Variscan orogeny of Central Europe. **1974** *Nature* 5 Apr. 471/2 Is it generally correct to associate all previous Chinese orogenies with times of rapid seafloor spreading?

orographic, *a.* Add: **b.** *Meteorol.* Applied to precipitation which results from moist air being forced upwards by mountains, and to the action of mountains in producing such precipitation.

1915 *Q. Jrnl. R. Meteorol. Soc.* XLI. 41 These considerations at once brought into prominence the distinction between orographic and cyclonic rainfall, which was perhaps one of the most puzzling features in British meteorology. **1938** E. G. BILHAM *Climate Brit. Isles* v. 101 Thunderstorm rains..do not often produce total amounts of rainfall..of the same order of magnitude as are observed when intense cyclonic rains are augmented by orographic action. **1955** W. J. SAUCIER *Princ. Meteorol. Analysis* x. 324/2 To the windward of the Appalachians..orographic lifting of the moist and turbulent air is sufficient to produce precipitation without needing convergence in surface flow. **1968** *Jrnl. Appl. Meteorol.* VII. 857/1 Orographic precipitation has long been considered to be an attractive target for cloud seeding. **1976** B. LECOMBER *Dead Weight* iii. 41 It's the same pattern on all the West Indian Islands:..on the high ground, where the orographic clouds form and double or treble the rainfall, you find the jungles.

orographical, *a.* Add: **b.** *Meteorol.* = prec.

1909 H. R. MILL in *Geogr. Teacher* V. 75 Placing this established fact of the dependence of the annual rainfall on the height or the configuration of the land side by side with the equally established fact of the complete independence of heavy cyclonic or thunderstorm rains on terrestrial conditions, we are obliged to divide rain into two classes; one greater in intensity but shorter in duration, and, in aggregate, trifling in amount, which we may call meteorological rain (in thunderstorms and cyclones), and the other kind of rain, of less intensity but greater frequency and duration, we may call orographical rain. **1921** *Geofysiske Publikationer* II. III. 9 The effects of orographical rain are strongly restricted by the tendency of all stable air currents to curve round the mountains horizontally. **1947** *Q. Jrnl. R. Meteorol. Soc.* LXXIII. 16 The orographical rain was well developed over North Wales and the English Lake District.

Hence **orogra·phically** *adv.*, in accordance with, or by, orography; by the action of mountains.

1873 *Q. Jrnl. Geol. Soc.* XXIX. 389 These two lakes.. are separated by a prolongation of the parallel ridges of the Schaffberg massif, so that orographically the Wolfganger See lies in a synclinal trough which may be traced along a line of lakeless valleys, and is separated from the head of the Foschelsee by a narrow ridge. **1877** *Ibid.* XXXIII. 143 The part of North Greenland here described can be geologically and orographically divided into three districts. **1902** D. G. HOGARTH *Nearer East* 14 Here is a continuous parting of waters, but not, orographically, a continuous mountain range. **1947** *Q. Jrnl. R. Meteorol. Soc.* LXXIII. 13 Warm front rain is intensified orographically, but not so much as warm sector rain. **1971** *Nature* 23 Apr. 504/1 The development of ice fog in relatively still, orographically protected areas.

orography. Add: (Further examples.) Also, the orographical features of a region.

1853 E. HITCHCOCK *Outl. Geol. Globe* 10 A knowledge of the Hydrography of a country aids as much in determining its geology as does its Orography,—that is, a description of its mountains. **1873** *Q. Jrnl. Geol. Soc.* XXIX. 382 As the general circumstances of climate and orography are fairly similar throughout the great Alpine chain, it may reasonably be expected that any explanation suggested for the lake-basins of one district should apply also to another. **1904** *Geogr. Jrnl.* XXIII. 183 How the system of orography of Eastern Siberia accords with the orography of Asia altogether, such as it now appears from the recent explorations in Central Asia. **1923** *Q. Jrnl. R. Meteorol. Soc.* XLIX. 226 The 'normal' orographical distribution of rainfall depends of course not only on the orography of the country but on the constancy of the prevailing wind. **1955** W. J. SAUCIER *Princ. Meteorol. Analysis* x. 304/1 Local circulations due to convection or orography may..cause discrepancy between local winds and the flow pattern of the surroundings. **1975** *Weather* XXX. 141 Orography has the main influence in mountainous regions while the latitude effect is most important in regions with smooth orographies.

orohydrography (ǫːrohəidrǫ·grăfi). [f. *ORO- + HYDROGRAPHY.] (See quot. 1967.) Hence **oːrohydrogra·phic, -gra·phical** *adjs.*

1892 *Syd. Soc. Lex.*, *Orohydrography*, a description of the water sheds of mountains. **1900** *Geogr. Jrnl.* XVI. 35 The oro-hydrographic conformation of the Andine region extending southwards of Mount Tronador is extremely complex. **1908** C. R. ENOCK *Peru* i. 2 A glance at the map will show the remarkable series of parallel topographical—or rather oro-hydrographical—features which exist, due to this agency. **1936** *Geogr. Jrnl.* LXXXVIII. 268 There are..maps, geological and orohydrographical, covering the whole region. **1967** E. VOLLMER *Encycl. Hydraulics* 208 *Orohydrography*, the branch of hydrography which deals with the relation of mountains to drainage. **1970** *Soviet Hydrology: Selected Papers* No. 1. 19 As an example of one of the most ancient orohydrographic discrepancies we can mention the crossing of the Penzhina Range by the Talovka River.

orometric, *a.* (Later example.)

1945 *Q. Jrnl. R. Meteorol. Soc.* LXXI. 44 At the other end of the orometric scale it seems pretty evident that the British mountains which only exceptionally reach an altitude of even 4,000 feet are neither high enough nor compact enough to produce the maximum amount of orographic rainfall.

orometry (orǫ·mĕtri). *Geogr.* [f. *ORO- + -METRY.] The measurement of forms of relief.

1898 *Geogr. Jrnl.* XI. 205 As the geoid is treated in geodesy, he treats the *oroid* in orometry. **1972** P. TILLEY tr. *Hettner's Surface Features of Land* 160 Ideas used in analytical geometry to express geometrical figures arithmetically have been copied in orometry.

oronasal: see also *ORINASAL *a.* (*sb.*).

oropendola (ǫrope·ndolă). [a. Sp. *oropendola* golden oriole.] Any of several birds belonging to one of the species of the family Icteridæ, found in tropical regions of south and central America. Also *attrib.*

1898 *Auk* XV. 327 (*heading*) Cassin's Oropendola. **1912** BRABOURNE & CHUBB *Birds S. Amer.* I. 431 Swainson's Oropendola. **1955** *Sci. News Let.* 23 July 64/3 Nests of the oropendola, or 'giant oriole', are narrow bags two to three feet long, woven of straws and weeds. **1968** *Sci. Jrnl.* Nov. 11/3 Nests of oropendolas—a bird found in the Republic of Panama—containing also one or two young of the cowbird..often produce more oropendola fledglings than 'unparasitized' ones. **1970** R. MEYER DE SCHAUENSEE *Guide Birds S. Amer.* 352 This family [*sc.* Icteridæ] comprises an assortment of birds ranging from forest-inhabiting oropendolas and caciques to the more familiar grackles, cowbirds and meadowlarks. **1974** *Nat. Geographic* Nov. 687 Oriole-like oropendolas were building their hanging nests in nearby trees.

Oropesa (ǫropī·ză). The name of the vessel first used to test the apparatus, used *attrib.* to designate a minesweeping device first developed during the war of 1914–18.

1939 *War Illustr.* 9 Dec. 399/2 Minesweepers work in pairs, with each unit 300 to 500 yards apart. Between them, sometimes suspended from two sets of apparatus called Oropesa floats, is drawn the sweep wire, which has a series of steel cutters. Should this come into contact with a mooring cable, the mine will rise to the surface and it can then be destroyed by gunfire. *Ibid.* 29 Dec. 538/1 *Oropesa*, a type of minesweeping float. The name originated from that of a trawler in which the newly-invented gear was first tested. **1940** *Manch. Guardian Weekly* 12 Apr. 297 A little farther on a minesweeper was being reconditioned, grim-looking with bristling gun, and oropesa sweeps. **1949** J. S. COWIE *Mines, Minelayers & Minelaying* vi. 105 The spread of an Oropesa type of sweep. **1965** K. LANGMAID *Approaches are Mined!* II. vii. 138 The introduction of..the Oropesa Float made it possible for a *single* vessel to sweep a wide area in a reasonably short time.

oro-pharyngeal, *a.* (Earlier and later examples.)

1885 *N.Y. Med. Jrnl.* XLII. 376/1, I experimented with regard to the isolation of the temperature sense in the nasal and oro-pharyngeal cavities. **1967** *Nursing Times* 8 Sept. 1196/2 An oropharyngeal airway will help, but the proper position of the attendant's fingers is far more important.

oropharynx. (Examples.)

1887 L. BROWNE *Throat & its Dis.* (ed. 2) iii. 53 (*heading*) Inspection of the mouth, fauces, and oro-pharynx. **1894** P. W. WILLIAMS *Dis. Upper Respiratory Tract* ii. 12 For clinical purposes the pharynx is divided into three regions, the naso-pharynx, the oro-pharynx and the laryngo-pharynx. **1935** R. S. STEVENSON *Rec. Adv. Laryngol. & Otol.* ii. 38 Norman Patterson is of opinion that at the present time a combination of diathermy and radiation is usually best in the treatment of malignant disease of the oro-pharynx. **1976** *Lancet* 4 Dec. 1248/1 There was diffuse ulceration in the oropharynx.

orosomucoid (ǒrōᵘ·somiū·koid). *Biochem.* [f. Gr. ὀρός serum + -O + *MUCOID *sb.*] A glycoprotein which forms the major component of seromucoid.

1955 R. J. WINZLER in *Methods Biochem. Analysis* II. 281 The major component in human seromucoid is an electrophoretically and ultracentrifugally distinct acidic glycoprotein which has been crystallized and quite well characterized by chemical, physical, and immunological methods... It is appropriate to assign to this protein the name orosomucoid..to indicate its source and nature. **1965** *Biochim. & Biophys. Acta* CI. 336 The human and bovine orosomucoids had molecular weights of 41 600 and 37 300 respectively by the sedimentation diffusion method. **1972** *Res. Communications Chem. Path. & Pharmacol.* III. 663 Important increases in the level of orosomucoid accompany exudative inflammatory processes.

orotic (orǫ·tik), *a.* *Chem.* [ad. It. *orotico* (Biscaro & Belloni 1905, in *Ann. della Soc. Chim. di Milano* XI. 18), f. Gr. ὀρό-ς serum, whey + It. *-otico* -OTIC.] *orotic acid*, a colourless crystalline heterocyclic acid, $C_4HN_2(OH)_2$-COOH, which is found in milk and is a growth factor for some micro-organisms.

1905 *Jrnl. Chem. Soc.* LXXXVIII. I. 672 The occurrence of small crystals of an organic compound in the mother liquor of lactose has led to the discovery of a new acid, orotic acid, which has been found to be a normal constituent of milk. **1944** *Nature* 26 Feb. 251/2 Four out of five of the strains of Group *C* streptococci of various types which were tested also needed uracil or orotic acid for optimal growth. **1965** T. L. V. ULBRICHT *Introd. Nucleic Acids* vi. 70 Studies with bacterial mutants showed that orotic acid..was an effective precursor of both DNA and RNA pyrimidines.

Hence **oro·tate** [-ATE[1] c], the anion, or an ester or salt, of orotic acid; **oro·tidine** [*-IDINE d], a nucleoside containing an orotic acid residue, the phosphate of which is a precursor of pyrimidine nucleotides.

1905 *Jrnl. Chem. Soc.* LXXXVIII. I. 672 Methyl orotate,..a white, crystalline powder with a somewhat bitter taste, melts at 248–250° and dissolves in water or alcohol, forming faintly acid solutions. **1973** HENDERSON & PATERSON *Nucleotide Metabolism* xi. 182 Under certain circumstances, the carbamyl phosphate product from the liver enzyme may be diverted..into the orotate pathway. **1951** A. M. MICHELSON et al. in *Proc. Nat. Acad. Sci.* XXXVII. 396 (*heading*) A new ribose nucleoside from Neurospora: 'orotidine'. **1963** A. M. MICHELSON *Chem. Nucleosides & Nucleotides* ii. 44 Periodate oxidation and enzymatic synthesis..and conversion into uridine show that orotidine is 3-β-D-ribofuranosylorotic acid. **1973** J. R. BRONK *Chemical Biol.* xii. 465 The resulting orotidine 5′-phosphate is then decarboxylated to give..uridine 5′-phosphate.

orotic aciduria (orǫːtik æsidiū·riă). *Path.* Also as one word. [f. *orotic acid* (see prec.) + -URIA.] A rare genetic disorder in which an enzyme deficiency impairs the metabolism of orotic acid, resulting in anæmia and excessive amounts of the acid in the blood and urine. Hence **oroːtic acidu·ric** *a.*

1959 SMITH & BAKER in *Jrnl. Clin. Invest.* XXXVIII. 798/1 Only recently has a 'pyrimidine disease', orotic aciduria, been described. **1961** *Ibid.* XL. 662/2 No large survey has..been undertaken to document the true incidence of the orotic aciduric defect. **1962** *Jrnl. Laboratory & Clin. Med.* LIX. 852 The family of an infant with congenital oroticaciduria excreted normal amounts of pseudouridine. **1972** F. NOUR-ELDIN *Haematol.* xxi. 218/2 Hereditary orotic aciduria is a rare disorder of the pyrimidine metabolism with megaloblastic anaemia, refractory to vitamin B_{12} but responding to uridine.

orotundity. (Examples.)

1909 in *Cent. Dict.* Suppl. **1922** J. M. MURRY *Probl. Style* 20 Wordsworthians were there to discover the hallmark of genius on his most insignificant orotundities. **1936** 'M. INNES' *Death at President's Lodging* ix. 167 D.C. was absorbed in his narrative now: the self-consciousness, the orotundity were gone. **1960** *Spectator* 2 Sept. 347 Those thudding clichés, those meaningless orotundities. **1963** *Punch* 16 Jan. 105/3 An orotundity which isn't meant to be funny.

Oroya fever (oroiːă fī·vəɹ). *Path.* [f. La *Oroya*, the name of a town in central Peru + FEVER *sb.*[1]] An acute, frequently fatal, febrile and hæmolytic disease which occurs in Peru as the first stage of infection with the bacterium *Bartonella bacilliformis*, the second, chronic, stage being verruga peruana.

1873 T. J. HUTCHINSON *Two Yrs. in Peru* II. xx. 61 The 'Oroya fever', as it was called, from the simple circumstance of its having occurred on this line [*sc.* the Callao–Lima–Oroya railway line] (although more than a hundred miles distant from the terminus at the little town of Oroya), caused a dreadful mortality here during the years of 1870 and 1871. **1903** *Encycl. Medica* XIII. 326 Death ensues without any appearance of eruption, constituting the grave form or Oroya fever. **1949** M. A. JENNINGS in H. W. Florey et al. *Antibiotics* II. xxxi. 1033 *Bartonella bacilliformis*, the organism of Carrion's disease —known also in its acute stage as Oroya fever, and in its chronic stage as verruga peruana—is highly sensitive to penicillin. **1962** GORDON & LAVOIPIERRE *Entomol. for Students of Med.* xx. 138 In addition to being a severe biting nuisance, sandflies are responsible for the transmission to man of several forms of leishmaniasis, a sandfly fever and Oroya fever or Carrion's disease. **1974** PASSMORE & ROBSON *Compan. Med. Stud.* III. I. xii. 86/2 In those who survive Oroya fever, after an interval..the dermal lesions of verruga peruana develop.

orphan, *sb.* and *a.* Add: **A.** *sb.* **2. b.** *slang.* A discontinued model of a motor vehicle.

1942 BERREY & VAN DEN BARK *Amer. Thes. Slang* § 81/7 *Orphan*, a discontinued make. **1948** MENCKEN *Amer. Lang.* Suppl. II. 724 *Orphan, or off-breed*, an obsolete model. **1967** W. & M. MORRIS *Dict. Word & Phr. Origins* II. 280 *Load, orphan, pig*,..and *iron* all designate poor cars.

3. orphan asylum (examples).

1811 *Freemason's Mag.* (Philadelphia) Nov. 97 The other proclaims its benevolent character in its name, 'The Orphan Asylum Society'. **1833** J. B. PURCELL in *Catholic Hist. Rev.* (Washington) (1919) V. 241 There was a benefit at the L. [Louisville] Theatre for the Orphan-Asylum, at this time. **1921** E. O'NEILL *Diff'rent* II, in *Emperor Jones* 281 He'll go and leave all he's got to some lousey orphan asylum. **1964** D. OWEN *Eng. Philanthropy* (1965) II. v. 159 This London Orphan Asylum at Clapton, opened in 1825... Again..a movement was launched which, by the early 1840's, had established the Infant Orphan Asylum at Wanstead. **1978** E. HEALEY *Lady Unknown* ii. 60 Faraday's earliest letters to her..were..mostly requests for proxy votes for his protégés at the Orphan Asylum of which they were both patrons.

B. *adj.* **b.** *Orphan Annie*: see *little Orphan(t) Annie* (*LITTLE *a.* 13).

2. *Path.* **orphan virus**, any virus that is not known to be the cause of a disease.

1954 J. L. MELNICK in *Amer. Jrnl. Publ. Health* XLIV. 572/1 The remainder of this report is concerned with... 3. The detection of new viruses, provisionally called 'orphan viruses' (as we know so little to what diseases they belong) from patients suspected of having nonparalytic poliomyelitis. **1955** [see *ECHO VIRUS]. **1961** P. L. CARPENTER *Microbiol.* ix. 110 A considerable number of viruses recently isolated from the feces of healthy as well as ill individuals are not known to produce disease... These viruses..are called orphan viruses, and those isolated from humans are known as ECHO viruses.

orphaned, *a.* Add: **3.** *slang.* Of a motor vehicle: discontinued as a model. Cf. *ORPHAN *sb.* 2b.

1920 F. B. SCHOLL *Automobile Owner's Guide* 3 Orphaned cars may run as well..as anybody could ask for, but when a company fails or discontinues to manufacture a model, the car immediately loses from one-third to one-half of its natural value.

orphenadrine (ǭɹfe·nădrīn). *Pharm.* [f. OR(THO- + *-phenadrine* (contraction of *DI)PHENHYDRAMINE).] A bitter-tasting ortho-methyl derivative of diphenhydramine used (as its white crystalline citrate or hydrochloride) as an antispasmodic, esp. in the treatment of Parkinsonism; $(CH_3C_6H_4)$-$CH(C_6H_5){\cdot}O{\cdot}CH_2CH_2N(CH_3)_2$.

1957 *Jrnl. Amer. Med. Assoc.* 13 Apr. 1352/1 The new drug, orphenadrine (Disipal) hydrochloride..has proved exceptionally beneficial in the control of..symptoms of Parkinsonism, without increasing tremor. **1963** *Practitioner* Nov. 646 Two cases are recorded in which the distressing symptoms of persistent hiccup were relieved by orphenadrine citrate. **1977** *Lancet* 16 Apr. 858/2 He was put on orphenadrine but because of progressive extrapyramidal disability levodopa with benserazide ('Madopar') was prescribed.

Orphic, *a.* (*sb.*) Add: **A.** *adj.* **3.** Of, pertaining to, or characteristic of Orphism (*ORPHISM 2).

[**1913** G. APOLLINAIRE *Méditations Esthétiques* vii. 25 *Le cubisme orphique* est l'autre grande tendance de la peinture moderne. C'est l'art de peindre des ensembles nouveaux avec des éléments empruntés non à la réalité visuelle, mais entièrement créés par l'artiste. **1914** A. J. EDDY *Cubists & Post-Impressionism* (1915) v. 69 *Cubism Orphique* is created entirely by the artist; it takes nothing from visual, objective realities, but is derived wholly from the painter's imagination; it is pure art.] **1950** D. COOPER tr. *Raynal's Hist. Mod. Painting* III. 52 Apollinaire used to distinguish between 'scientific Cubism', 'physical Cubism', 'instinctive Cubism' and 'Orphic Cubism'. **1959** *Listener* 19 Nov. 869/1 He [*sc.* Apollinaire] distinguished two kinds of pure Cubism—scientific and Orphic... Orphic Cubism..dealt with the universe of mind and imagination, the inner world. **1974** *Encycl. Brit. Micropædia* VII. 594/3 Apollinaire's use of the word 'Orphic' recalls both the Symbolist painters' use of the term 'Orphic Art'..and the poetry of Orpheus.

Orphism. Add: **2.** A movement within Cubism, identified by Guillaume Apollinaire (1880–1918) and pioneered by a group of French painters calling themselves *Le Section d'Or*, which emphasized the lyrical use of colour in pure abstract designs.

1914 A. J. EDDY *Cubists & Post-Impressionism* (1915) xiv. 207 Superficial Impressionism leads naturally to the painting of pure color effect—*color music, orphism, compositional* painting. **1915** *Forum* (N.Y.) Dec. 663, I have always held that Orphism and Simultaneism are merely extended Impressionism. **1959** H. READ *Conc. Hist. Mod. Painting* III. 91 Robert Delaunay..was responsible for another deviation from orthodox Cubism... This deviation Apollinaire christened Orphism. **1959** BROWN & SLATER tr. *Pasternak's Safe Conduct* xi. 259 In its symbolism, that is to say, in everything in the imagery verging on orphism,..the romantic view of life is devastatingly vivid and it is incontrovertible. **1971** J. WILLETT in A. Bullock *20th Cent.* x. 235/1 Expressionism..was an all-absorbent force which sucked up every other new tendency since Fauvism (Cubism, Futurism and Delaunay's near-abstract Orphism). **1976** *Telegraph* (Brisbane) 20 Oct. 2/3 Apart from orphism, futurism and several other arty isms, the doc is an expert on early Australian painters.

Hence **Orphist** (less commonly **Orphiste**) *sb.* and *a.*

1914 A. J. EDDY *Cubists & Post-Impressionism* (1915) v. 60 Today we have the 'Neo-Impressionists',..the 'Futurists', the 'Orphists', [etc.]. *Ibid.* 64 A form of dramatic representation that is essentially Cubist, Futurist, and Orphist in its expression. **1915** *Blast* July 41 Less interesting..is the Orphiste movement. Delaunay is the most conspicuous Orphiste. **1959** J. GOLDING *Cubism* i. 39 Léger,..whose art was now becoming more obviously divergent, is also sometimes referred to as an Orphist. **1959** *Listener* 13 Aug. 253/2 After 1911..he [*sc.* Chagall] begins to place his figures among arbitrary arcs of colour which are like caricatures of *Orphist* forms. **1970** C. BARRETT *Op Art* i. 9/2 Delaunay..and..other Orphists were familiar with Chevreut's theory of simultaneous contrast.

orpiment. (Later example.)

1969 R. L. S. BRUCE-MITFORD *Art of Codex Amiatinus* 3 The third leaf, a purple-stained folio with text written in yellow orpiment (not gold), carried on its recto and verso respectively a prologue and a table of contents.

orra, *a.* Add: *orra man* (also *orraman*) (earlier and later examples.)

1802 J. SIBBALD *Chron. Scot. Poetry* IV. (Gloss.), *Orrow man*, a day labourer. *a* **1867** E. SMITH *Mem. Highland Lady* (1898) ix. 161 Orraman means the jobber or Jack-of-all trades. **1937** F. NIVEN *Staff at Simson's* xxv. 243 Of his return the cashier was made aware by the arrival in his office of the odd-job man—the 'orra man'. **1955** in *Sc. Nat. Dict.* (1965) VI. 494/2 (Advt.), Orraman (married) or Orrawoman required for Hillhead, attend some cattle in winter. **1973** *Courier & Advertiser* (Dundee) 14 Feb. 1/3 (Advt.), Tractor-Orraman wanted for intensive livestock and cropping.

Orrefors (ǫ·rėfǭɹz). The name of the town in Sweden where glass is manufactured, used to designate glassware produced there and the style of decoration characteristic of it.

1928 T. PALM tr. *Wettergren's Mod. Decorative Arts Sweden* 23 The relation between the figures of the Orrefors glasses and these daughters of the Renaissance and of the baroque style proves to be a result of the material..and of the technique. **1929** *Encycl. Brit.* X. facing p. 404 (*caption*), Modern cut and engraved European glass. 1. 'Fashion' vase of engraved Orrefors glass designed by Edvard Hald. **1931** G. JANNEAU *Mod. Glass* ii. 21 The Orrefors production is not entirely limited to this style. **1935** N. MITCHISON *We have been Warned* IV. 427 The Orrefors mirror and the linen sheets on the bed. **1961** E. M. ELVILLE *Collector's Dict. Glass* 174/2 The examples ..are illustrative of the vigorous, muscular figures which have established the Orrefors tradition. **1970** *House & Garden* May 41/1 Scandinavian elegance of design..is, literally, crystallized in Orrefors glass. **1970** W. WAGER *Sledgehammer* (1971) iii. 13 He put down the Orrefors pitcher.

orright (ǭrəi·t), repr. a vulgar or colloq. pronunciation of *all right* s.v. RIGHT *a.* 15 c.

1941 M. TREADGOLD *We couldn't leave Dinah* iii. 58 Thomas gave a little sigh of relief. 'Orright,' he said. **1969** E. MCGIRR *Entry of Death* v. 89 It's orright, yer money's on. **1971** J. WAINWRIGHT *Dig Grave* 54 'Here, have another toffee, Billy.' 'Orright. Ta.' **1971** 'J. RIPLEY' *Davis doesn't live Here* 18 'You wanna say summat?'.. 'Orright. Say it.' **1978** J. WAINWRIGHT *Jury People* xxiii. 68 'I'll do orright.' 'On social security?' 'Aye.'

orsell, os(s)el, ossil, oz(z)el, etc. varr. NORSEL *sb.*

1750 in *Sc. Nat. Dict.* (1965) VI. 495/3 The Ossels..each 18 inches long..are fixed to two Mashes at one End by an Eye. **1881** *Proc. Soc. Antiquaries Scotl.* III. 150 The nets ..are attached to a strong..rope by means of thinner cords known as 'ozzels'. **1921** [see *NORSELLER]. **1972** M. F. WAKELIN *Patterns Folk Speech Brit. Isles* 18 Figure 2 shows the *sole-rope* as made fast to the net by the *ossils*. *Ibid.* 24 There are four fairly well-defined usages. *Ossil* extends, with one or two breaks, from Burnmouth as far as Lossiemouth. **1973** W. ELMER *Terminol. Fishing* ii. 54 The bait..is put on a *skewer*..or hung on an *orsle*..(a short piece of line), and the whole is weighted with stones.

orseller, var. *NORSELLER.

ort. (Later examples.)

1913 D. H. LAWRENCE *Love Poems* 50 Then what art colleyfoglin' for?—I'm not havin' your orts and slarts. **1917** —— *Look! We have come Through!* 60 To me it seems the seed is just left over From the red rose-flowers' fiery transience; Just orts and slarts. **1922** BLUNDEN *Shepherd* 44 With hungry hubbub begging crusts and orts. **1940** V. WOOLF *Writer's Diary* 30 May (1953) 334 Scraps, orts and fragments. **1946** K. TENNANT *Lost Haven* (1947) xi. 169 'Orts and leavings, that's what pigs eat.' The idea of a set of pigs fattening on what Bee-Bonnet left from his scanty meal amused the loungers. **1950** R. MOORE *Candlemas Bay* 223 Neal took the orts out to the hens and hurled them, dish and all, over the henyard wall. *Ibid.* 224 Neal started back to the house, kicking the orts dish along the gravel walk in front of him. **1972** J. METCALF *Going Down Slow* iv. 61 When you've eaten every last ort and scrap, would you like dessert? Coffee? Brandy? **1976** 'M. INNES' *Gay Phoenix* iv. 54 A waiter..wheeled up a trolley of elaborately bedized scraps, orts and broken meats.

ortanique (ǭɹtǎnī·k). [f. OR(ANGE *sb.*[1] + TAN(GERINE *sb.* 2 + UN)IQUE *a.*] A citrus fruit resembling a slightly flattened orange, produced by crossing an orange and a tangerine and cultivated in the West Indies. Also *attrib.*

1937 *Times* 16 Feb. 11/2 Jamaica shows ortaniques, a cross between the usual orange and a tangerine. **1961** *Spectator* 9 June 857 The West Indian experimental ortaniques, a cross between a tangerine and an orange. **1969** 'J. MORRIS' *Fever Grass* viii. 72 I've got to risk turning fifty acres of certain sugar into avocadoes, ortaniques and Bombay mangoes. **1969** *Harrod's Summer Food News* 6/2 Canadian Ortanique Juice 19 oz. tin 3/3.

‖ **orteguina** (ǭɹtegī·nă). [Sp., f. the name of Domingo *Orteg(a* (born 1906), Spanish bullfighter, who practised it + *-uina*.] In bullfighting, a decorative pass made with the muleta; = *MANOLETINA.

The more usual term is *manoletina.*

1957 A. MACNAB *Bulls of Iberia* viii. 86 Domingo Ortega introduced a variant in which the man..passes his left arm behind his back and grips the lower edge of the cloth with his left hand. This was called the *orteguina* but is now generally called *manoletina* owing to its having been popularised by the late Manolete. **1959** [see *MANOLETINA]. **1962** B. CONRAD *Encycl. Bullfighting* 174/1 *Orteguina*, a cape pass attributed to Domingo Ortega in Spain... Also may refer to a *muleta* pass similar to the *manoletina*. **1967** MCCORMICK & MASCAREÑAS *Compl. Aficionado* iv. 147 The manoletina is another embellishment... Formerly, it was called the *orteguina*, after Domingo Ortega, who took it from the nineteenth-century repertoire and refurbished it. Manolete picked it up and further refined (i.e. vulgarized) it.

orter (ǭ·ɹtəɹ), a representation of a colloquial or vulgar pronunciation of *ought to*. Cf. *OUGHTA, OUGHTER.

1864 HOTTEN *Slang Dict.* 196 Where's the party as 'ad a orter be lookin' arter this 'ere 'oss? **1886** F. H. BURNETT *Little Lord Fauntleroy* xiii. 243 'Seems like somethin' orter be done,' said Mr. Hobbs. **1897** KIPLING *Capt. Cour.* iv. 88, I orter ha' warned you. **1917** E. O'NEILL *Long Voyage Home* in *Smart Set* Oct. 84/2 Orter wear a muzzle, you ort! **1931** *Amer. Speech* VII. 91 Ater Maud's death he orter do better'n' he use' to. *a* **1966** M. ALLINGHAM *Cargo of Eagles* (1968) v. 73 His regular mate..wasn't there to 'elp 'im..like wot 'e orter 'ave bin.

‖ **orterde** (ǭ·ɹtēəɹdə). *Soil Sci.* [G.] (See quot. 1939.)

1930 *Bull. Wisconsin Geol. & Nat. Hist. Surv.* LXXVIIA. 86 Dark rusty brown sandy loam containing coffee-brown cemented lumps (the orterde of the Podsol). **1936** J. S. JOFFE *Pedology* vi. 132 These chemical compounds are responsible for the condition of ortstein and orterde (hardpan). **1939** *U.S. Dept. Agric. Yearbk. 1938* 1173 *Ortstein*, hard irregularly cemented, dark-yellow to nearly black sandy material formed by soil-forming processes in the lower part of the solum. Similar material not firmly cemented is known as orterde. **1965** B. T. BUNTING *Geogr. Soil* xiii. 152 Modal iron podsols are the true forest podzol, usually under spruce, with deep F1, 2, 3 layers, and deep orterde rather than pan.

orthaxial, *a.* (Example.)

1886 J. A. RYDER in *Rep. U.S. Comm. Fisheries 1884* 985 The word orthaxial is used to designate the archaic straight type of vertebrate axis which is not bent upwards at its posterior extremity.

orthesis (ǭɹþī·sis). *Med.* [f. Gr. ὀρθ-ός straight, right + *-esis*, after PROSTHESIS.] = *ORTHOSIS.

1956 R. L. BENNETT in *Physical Therapy Rev.* XXXVI. 721/1 To my knowledge, the words, 'orthesis', 'orthetics', and 'orthetic devices', have not been used before... The word 'orthesis' may be defined as a medically prescribed device applied to or around a weakened bodily segment to give support and increased function. **1963** *Med. Electronics & Biol. Engin.* I. 511/1 Prehensile motion of the hand..is to be performed by an externally powered orthesis, but is not to be preprogrammed and is to be completely controlled by the patient. **1971** *Rand Daily Mail* 4 Sept. 14/1 He has developed various aids for the disabled. The most useful, perhaps, is the motorised orthesis or hand splint which can be connected to a blow-and-suck pipe or any other control system.

orthicon (ǭ·ɹþikǫn). [abbrev. of next.] A kind of television camera tube similar to the iconoscope but having a transparent target plate, so that the scanning beam can be made to strike normally the opposite side to that on which the image is projected, and employing low-speed electrons for the beam, resulting in increased sensitivity and an absence of the spurious signals associated with the iconoscope. See also *image orthicon* (*IMAGE *sb.* 8).

The term was registered in the U.S.A. as a proprietary name in 1940, but it is now a generic term in the public domain.

1939 [see next]. **1942** *Electronic Engin.* XV. 127 Because of the greater light sensitivity of the orthicon it is expected that the equipment will fill a need for lightweight equipment to be used under adverse light conditions. **1955** G. M. GLASFORD *Fund. Television Engin.* iv. 98 The disadvantages of the orthicon have encouraged the search for better tubes in spite of the improvement over the iconoscope in the matter of increased sensitivity. The orthicon suffers from a very poor contrast scale with a very small range of intermediate grays as compared with the iconoscope. **1968** *Brit. Med. Bull.* XXIV. 261/2 Tubes such as..orthicons integrate the light energy incident upon each part of the tube over the entire frame-scanning interval.

orthiconoscope (ǭɹþəikǫ·nǒskōᵘp). Now *rare* or *Obs.* [f. ORTH(O- + *ICONOSCOPE; see quot. 1939.] = prec.

1939 *Electronics* July 11/1 On June 7th Albert Rose and Harley Iams of the RCA Manufacturing Company Research Laboratories at Harrison, revealed..the details of a new developmental television pick-up tube which..is one of the most significant advances in television electronics since the advent of the iconoscope itself. The new tube's formal name is 'Orthiconoscope' ('Orthicon' for short) from the Greek root ortho meaning 'straight' and iconoscope for 'image-viewer'. The name derives from the fact that the curve between input light and output current is a straight line, in contrast to the similar curve of the iconoscope which is not linear. **1940** D. G. FINK *Princ. Television Engin.* iii. 111 The orthiconoscope displays no spurious signal, and there is accordingly no background shading defect to be compensated. **1953** AMOS & BIRKINSHAW *Television Engin.* I. 81 The orthicon (orthiconoscope in full) was developed by Rose and Iams in America and used in that country immediately before the Second World War for outside broadcasts.

ortho-. Add: **1.** **o·rthocone**, the conical shell of certain fossil nautiloid cephalopods or a fossil characterized by a shell of this shape; hence **orthoco·nic** *a.*, of or pertaining to a fossil or a shell of this type; **o·rtho-cousin**, one of cousins whose related parents are of the same sex (cf. *cross-cousin* s.v. *CROSS- B); **orthodi·gita** (see quot. 1939); hence **orthodi·gital** *a.*; **orthofe·rrite**, any of the compounds with the formula $AFeO_3$, where A is a trivalent metal ion (usu. a rare earth), which have an orthorhombic crystal structure and exhibit weak ferromagnetism at room temperature; **o·rthoform** *Pharm.* [after CHLOROFORM *sb.*], methyl *m*-amino-*p*-hydroxybenzoate, $C_8H_9NO_3$, a crystalline compound with anæsthetic properties which has been used as a dusting powder for wounds and ulcers and in dentistry; **o:rthogeosy·ncline** *Geol.* [ad. G. *orthogeosynklinale* (H. Stille 1935, in *Sitzungsber. d. preuss. Akad. d. Wissensch.* (*Phys.-mat. Kl.*) 182)], a linear geosyncline between a continental and an oceanic kratogen (craton), typically comprising a miogeosyncline and an adjacent eugeosyncline; hence **o:rthogeosyncli·nal** *a.*; **o·rthogneiss** *Petrogr.* [a. G. *orthogneiss* (H. Rosenbusch *Elem. d. Gesteinlehre* (1898) 467)], gneiss derived from igneous rocks; **orthokine·sis** *Zool.* [*KINESIS 2], a kinesis in which linear movement is shown; hence **orthokine·tic** *a.*; **o:rthopercu·ssion** *Med.*, very light diagnostic percussion of the chest by means of one finger striking the knuckles of another bent at right angles and with its tip resting in an intercostal space; **orthophony** (further examples); hence **orthopho·nic** *a.*, pertaining to orthophony; reproducing sounds correctly; **orthopho·ria** *Ophthalm.* [Gr. φορός bearing], the state of perfect oculomotor balance, in which the visual axes tend towards being parallel in the absence of a fusion stimulus; hence **orthopho·ric** *a.*; **o·rthopho:to, orthopho·tograph,** an image produced optically or electronically from aerial photographs by eliminating distortions of angles and scales so as to give a result corresponding to a planimetric map; **orthopho·tomap,** a map made up from an assembly of orthophotographs on which relief has been indicated by contours or shading; **o·rthophyre** *Petrogr.* [a. F. *orthophyre* (H. Coquand 1856, in *Mém. de la Soc. d'Émulation du Dép. du Doubs* I. 64)], porphyry in which the phenocrysts are chiefly of orthoclase; **orthophy·ric** *a. Petrogr.* [ad. G. *orthophyrisch* (H. Rosenbusch *Mikrosk. Physiogr.* (ed. 2, 1887) II. 594)], (of the groundmass of porphyritic rocks) containing short, stout feldspar crystals of rectangular or quadratic cross-section; **o·rthoploid** *a. Cytology* [a. G. *orthoploid* (H. Winkler 1916, in *Zeitschr. Bot.* VIII. 422)], having a complete or balanced set of chromosomes: with most authors = *EUPLOID *a.*; **orthopyro·xene** *Min.* [ad. G. *orthopyroxen* (E. Düll, at the suggestion of F. Rinne, in *Zeitschr. f. Krystallogr. und Mineral.* (1902) XXXVI. 654)], any orthorhombic pyroxene; **ortho·(r)rhaphous** *a. Ent.* [f. mod.L. *Orthorhapha* (later *Orthorrhapha*) (F. Brauer *Monographie der Oestriden* (1863) 33), f. Gr. ῥαφή seam], belonging or pertaining to the suborder Orthorrhapha, a group of dipterous insects in which the adult emerges from the puparium through a straight or T-shaped split; cf. *cyclorrhaphous* adj. (*CYCLO-); **orthotecto·nic** *a. Geol.* [ad. G. *orthotektonik* sb. (H. Stille *Einführung in den Bau Amerikas* (1940) i. 9)] formed by, or of the nature of, a deformation which produces complicated and crowded systems of fold belts such as the Alps and is characterized by much magmatism and lateral thrusting (believed to be characteristic of orthogeosynclines); cf. *paratectonic* adj. (*b*) s.v. *PARA-¹ 1; **orthoto·pic** *a. Med.* and *Biol.* [Gr. τοπικ-ός of place], involving transplantation of a structure to the same site in the recipient as it occupied in the donor; also said of the transplanted structure; hence **orthoto·pically** *adv.*; **o·rthovoltage** *Med.*, a voltage (in an X-ray tube) of the size used in conventional deep therapy (200–400 kilovolts); usu. *attrib.*; **o·rthowater** = *POLYWATER.

1900 A. Hyatt in C. R. Eastman tr. *von Zittel's Text-bk. Paleont.* I. 573 An orthocone is the young of the straight as well as many of the coiled forms [of fossil cephalopod]. **1935** Twenhofel & Shrock *Invertbr. Paleontol.* ix. 368 Early cephalopod shells were dominantly straight or but slightly coiled... Among the Nautiloidea this type of shell is known as an orthocone. **1969** Bennison & Wright *Geol. Hist. Brit. Isles* iv. 88 In the Durness sequence..the commonest fossils are gastropods..together with orthocone cephalopods. **1970** R. M. Black *Elements Palaeont.* viii. 78 *Orthoceras* and similar orthocones range in length from about 3 cm to possibly 460 cm. **1926** A. F. Foerste in *Jrnl. Sci. Lab. Denison Univ.* XXI. v. 304 (*heading*) Orthoconic genera. *Ibid.* 310 The specimen is figured as having its ventral side ribbed and fluted vertically in a manner very similar to that of *Kionoceras*, a form of ornamentation unknown in any other orthoconic triangular cephalopod. **1935** Twenhofel & Shrock *Invertbr. Paleontol.* ix. 367 (*caption*) Idealized diagram of an orthoconic cephalopod. **1974** *Nature* 8 Feb. 396/1 Glaciomarine beds..in South West Africa have yielded..an orthoconic nautiloid. **1918** J. G. Frazer *Folk-Lore in Old Testament* II. II. vi. 98 It has become customary to call the marriageable cousins *cross-cousins*, because..the related parents are of opposite or cross sexes. There has hitherto been no special name for the unmarriageable cousins, the children of two brothers or of two sisters, but for convenience I propose to call them *ortho-cousins* to distinguish them from cross-cousins. In the case of ortho-cousins the related parents are of the same sex. **1932** [see *cross-cousin* s.v. *CROSS- B.]. **1937** R. Stout *Red Box* iii. 38 Ortho-cousins are..the children of two brothers or of two sisters. **1972** D. Davies *Dict. Anthropol.* 141 *Ortho-Cousin*, a term little used now,..can be a synonym for parallel cousin..or for a parallel cousin of the same unilineal descent..group as the person concerned. **1937** *Fiopian Footprints* VIII. 3/2 Let us hope that the history of orthodigita will in time be replete with names of those who will..have illuminated Podiatry. **1939** H. A. Budin in *Jrnl. Exper. Podiatry* I. 19 (*heading*) New and improved orthodigital appliances in the non-surgical correction of deformities of the..toes. *Ibid.*, In his first lecture on this subject, delivered at a local society meeting in February 1934, the writer introduced some of the appliances and the technic which he had devised... For the purpose of designation of this newer phase of therapeusis, the author..chose the term Orthodigita... Orthodigita may be defined as the amelioration or correction, by non-surgical means, of toe deformities or malalignments. **1968** Fisher & Whitney in F. Weinstein *Princ. & Pract. Podiatry* xii. 265/1 Although permanent orthodigital correction is sought in adults also,..the patient may need to wear the appliance continually in order to keep the toes in proper alignment. **1978** *Chiropodist* XXXIII. 105 Although I personally favour the qualities (for most orthodigita) of KE 20 silicone rubber, I have found that Otoform provides..an inexpensive and effective method of introducing removable silicone appliances to patients. **1956** *Jrnl. Chem. Physics* XXIV. 1239 (*heading*) Magnetic properties of a gadolinium orthoferrite, $GdFeO_3$, crystal. **1966** *McGraw-Hill Encycl. Sci. & Technol.* V. 219/2 Many of the orthoferrites are strongly ferromagnetic at liquid helium temperatures. **1971** *Sci. Amer.* June 83/2 The first magnetic materials found to have the desired properties for studying the new bubble technology were orthoferrites, a special class of ferrites with the chemical formula $RFeO_3$, where R represents yttrium or one or more rare-earth elements. Samarium terbium orthoferrite is a good example. **1897** *Lancet* 18 Sept. 738/1 It has been found by Dr. Einhorn and Dr. Heintz, of Munich, that the compound methylic ether of amidoxybenzoic acid is possessed of remarkable anæsthetic, or rather analgesic, properties when locally applied. To this substance the name of 'orthoform' has been given. **1940** F. R. Davison *Synopsis Materia Medica* xi. 383 Orthoform..has also been used in dentistry, nasal catarrh, hay fever, and in similar conditions. **1965** Faulconer & Keys *Foundations Anesthesiol.* II. iv. 806 In the light of these considerations it is understandable that the Orthoform group anesthetizes better than the corresponding benzoyl combinations. **1941** Orthogeosynclinal [see *parageosyncline* s.v. *PARA-¹ 1]. **1945** *Bull. Geol. Soc. Amer.* LVI. 1172 Marginal geosynclines gaining principal detritus from uplifts in orthogeosynclinal belts. **1975** *McGraw-Hill Yearbk. Sci. & Technol.* 223/1 The orthogeosynclinal belts of Stille and Kay have come to be understood as an assemblage of crustal features related to continental shelf subsidence. **1936** tr. H. Stille in *Bull. Amer. Assoc. Petroleum Geologists* XX. 853 Although the orogenic movements took place at the same time in different areas, they were strong (Alpine type) only in certain mobile belts which had developed as orthogeosynclines. **1951** *Mem. Geol. Soc. Amer.* XLVIII. 88 The later Devonian and Carboniferous are of argillite and graywacke when detritus could reach the subsiding structural basin from distant highlands of rocks laid in orthogeosynclines. **1968** Orthogeosyncline [see *foredeep* s.v. *FORE- 5]. **1902** Orthogneiss [see *paragneiss* s.v. *PARA-¹ 1]. **1932** A. Harker *Metamorphism* xvii. 271 The more or less distinctly banded crystalline rocks which are conveniently styled orthogneisses (in contradistinction to paragneisses, which are highly metamorphosed sediments) attain in some countries a vast development. **1962** *Mineral. Abstr.* XV. 553/2 Alkaline syenitic orthogneisses form a lenticular body 5 km in length in biotite gneisses in the Cevadais area, near Ouguela, Alto Alentejo, Portugal. **1937** D. L. Gunn et al. in *Nature* 18 Dec. 1064/2 Variations in generalized, undirected, random locomotory activity..are kineses... We propose to divide kineses into (*a*) ortho-kineses..variations in linear velocity (previously called simply kineses), [etc.]. **1940** Fraenkel & Gunn *Orientation of Animals* II. ii. 17 Woodlice aggregate in moist air.. by means of an ortho-kinesis. **1971** J. D. Carthy in J. E. Smith et al. *Invertebr. Panorama* xii. 251 This behaviour, consisting of changing rates of movement with different levels of stimulation, is known as an orthokinesis. **1958** —— *Introd. Behaviour Invertebr.* xii. 317 When the stones are beneath the surface..they [*sc.* chitons] do not tend to congregate by a simpleorthokinetic response. **1973** *Nature* 16 Nov. 168/1 An orthokinetic effect may serve to influence adult movements, as their rate of progress over the reefs is almost certainly affected by the ease with which they can find adequate food and shelter from daylight. **1907** *Practitioner* Apr. 530 The chief disadvantage of Goldscheider's ortho-percussion is that it requires an absolutely silent room. **1916** L. F. Barker *Monographic Med.* II. 499 In orthopercussion, the force of the blow is directed exactly perpendicular to the surface. **1966** *Lancet* 31 Dec. 1469/1 The technique of percussion (orthopercussion) of the patient's abdomen in order to recognise peritoneal irritation is shown. **1926** *Daily Colonist* (Victoria, B.C.) 2 July 6/6 (Advt.), The genuine His Master's Voice Victrola is the only true orthophonic. **1927** *Gramophone* V. 309/2 The gramophone part of it contains an improved form of orthophonic horn. **1954** Pei & Gaynor *Dict. Linguistics* 155 *Orthophonic*, relating to orthophony..; conformable with the standard or accepted rules of pronunciation. **1969** *John Edwards Mem. Foundation Q.* V. II. 81 This valuable discographic aid lists all Victor Recordings..starting with the introduction of the electrical 'orthophonic' recording system in February, 1925. **1845** W. Russell *Orthophony* p. xiii, The term orthophony is used to designate the art of cultivating the voice. The systematic cultivation of the vocal organs..is a branch of education for which our own language furnishes no appropriate designation. The compiler of this manual has ventured to adopt, as a term convenient for this purpose, the word *orthophony*—a modification of the corresponding French word '*orthophonie*', used to designate the art of training the vocal organs. **1954** Pei & Gaynor *Dict. Linguistics* 155 *Orthophony*, Correct pronunciation or articulation. **1886** Orthophoria [see *exophoria* s.v. *EXO-]. **1907** J. H. Parsons *Dis. Eye* xxviii. 563 In cases of latent squint the position of rest is not orthophoria, with the visual axes parallel, but heterophoria, with some deviation of the axes. **1950** F. H. Alder *Physiol. Eye* x. 386 It is unfortunate that the implication is frequently made that orthophoria is the normal condition and heterophoria an abnormal one. This is not true. **1888** *Arch. Ophthalm.* XVII. 159 In the orthophoric state the eyes are able to unite images when a prism of 2° to 3° is introduced with its base up or down before one of the eyes. **1954** S. Duke-Elder *Parsons' Dis. Eye* (ed. 12) xxix. 483 Since the position of rest is usually one of slight divergence, few people are orthophoric and some degree of heterophoria is almost universal. **1965** *Photogrammetric Engin.* XXXI. 223/1 Several stereo aerial models from test areas were successfully compiled into contour maps and orthophotos. **1972** *McGraw-Hill Yearbk. Sci. & Technol.* 245 The orthophoto, like any good map, allows the engineer to lay out a proposed highway with accurate scale, direction, and curvature. **1955** *Photogrammetric Engin.* XXI. 529/2 Given an orthophotograph, the engineer, surveyor, forester, geologist,..can correlate points imaged on the orthophotograph with points observed on the ground, and..can make direct measurements on the orthophotograph to determine distances between points. **1970** J. A. Howard *Aerial Photo-Ecol.* xii. 136 No doubt orthophotographs will have a wide application in natural resource studies not requiring a stereoscopic examination. **1967** *Photogrammetric Engin.* XXXIII. 274/1 The altitude contours derived from the height measured can then be added, along with any desired annotations, to form an accurate 'orthophotomap' of the area of interest. **1974** *Geo Abstr.* G. 520 The Topographic Division of the U.S. Geological Survey produces a series of orthophoto products ranging from separate photos for in-house use..to the multicoloured orthophotomap. **1890** *Cent. Dict.*, Orthophyre. **1895** A. Harker *Petrol.* viii. 102 The most usual type of orthoclase-porphyry (orthophyre of Rosenbusch) is exemplified by dykes and sills in the Carboniferous of Thuringia. **1930** Peach & Horne *Geol. Scotl.* iv. 108 Examples of dykes of orthophyre occur on Sgonnan Mòr. **1947** E. E. Wahlstrom *Igneous Minerals & Rocks* x. 301 Orthophyre is a porphyritic trachite consisting largely of orthoclase. **1895** A. Harker *Petrol.* viii. 102 Other porphyrites have the 'orthophyric' type of groundmass (with short felspar-prisms), as in the porphyries. **1964** G. A. Joplin *Petrogr. Austral. Igneous Rocks* v. 65 Most trachytes are porphyritic with phenocrysts of anorthoclase in an orthophyric and/or trachytic groundmass. [**1920** *Svensk Bot. Tidskr.* XIV. 301, I have in my material found the following numbers: 14, 21, 28, 35 and 42. Further, in some specimens, I met with numbers not being a multiple of 7 (anorthoploid forms).] **1932** *Proc. 6th Internat. Congr. Genetics* II. 63 The ratios between orthoploid and aneuploid gametes in the cases studied were found to be 1·4:1. **1937** T. Dobzhansky *Genetics & Origin of Species* ix. 268 In a translocation heterozygote at least six classes of sex cells can be produced... Classes 1 and 2 carry normal gene complements..; 1 and 2 are termed regular or orthoploid. **1963** *Portugaliae Acta Biol.* A. VII. 8 The unfortunate terms orthoploid and anorthoploid have been used in various senses also by more recent writers. *Ibid.* 9 There is no doubt that euploid and aneuploid should be maintained and orthoploid and anorthoploid definitely dropped. **1903** *Mineral. Mag.* XIII. 374 Following Rinne, E. Düll..proposes the terms ortho-pyroxene and klinopyroxene. **1940** *Amer. Mineralogist* XXV. 282 Orthopyroxenes of plutonic igneous rocks normally show well developed diopsidic lamellae. **1963** W. A. Deer et al. *Rock-Forming Min.* II. 33 Many orthopyroxenes can be distinguished from clinopyroxenes by their characteristic pink to green pleochroism. **1970** *Science* 28 Aug. 866/2 (*heading*) Orthopyroxene-plagioclase fragments in the lunar soil from Apollo 12. **1890** *Cent. Dict.*, Orthorhaphous. **1899** D. Sharp in *Cambr. Nat. Hist.* VI. vii. 458 In the Mesozoic epoch the Order [*sc.* Diptera] is found as early as the Lias, the forms being exclusively Orthorrhaphous. **1946** *Nature* 2 Nov. 636/2 Against the orthorrhaphous Diptera, 'Gammexane' shows a high degree of activity. **1961** Orthorrhaphous [see *cyclorrhaphous* adj. s.v. *CYCLO- 1]. **1956** L. V. de Sitter *Struct. Geol.* i. 16 A later uplift, separated from the last orogenic paroxysmal phase by a period of erosion, is typical of orthotectonic regions. **1969** *Earth & Planetary Sci. Lett.* VI. 189 The orthotectonic orogens forming island arcs such as Japan lie entirely within ocean basins. **1969** J. F. Dewey in M. Kay *N. Atlantic* xxiv. 309/1 Strata ranging in age from late Precambrian through early Ordovician constitute a northern orthotectonic belt, characterized by complex recumbent and commonly triclinic fold geometry and high-grade metamorphism. **1921** *Jrnl. Exper. Zool.* XXXII. 7 Limb bud placed in natural location—orthotopic transplantation. **1958** *Immunology* I. 46 The survival times of successive sets of orthotopic scale (skin) homografts revealed that increasing systematic immunity develops rapidly in stepwise fashion. **1968** *National Observer* (U.S.) 29 Jan. 4/4 Dr. Starzl performed the first orthotopic liver transplant, in which the diseased liver is removed and another implanted, in 1963. **1921** *Jrnl. Exper. Zool.* XXXII. 61 The shoulder-girdle in orthotopically grafted limbs is derived in part from the host and in part from the transplanted tissue. **1974** *Nature* 11 Oct. 553/1 When solid tissue allografts are transplanted orthotopically to alien hosts they are rejected with a characteristic tempo and vigour that depends primarily on the immunogenetic disparity between donor and host. **1976** *Ibid.* 22 Jan. 209/1 We used a standardised H-test procedure in which tail-skin grafts were orthotopically exchanged in a 'reciprocal circle' among syngeneic mice. **1967** M. E. J. Young *Radiological Physics* (ed. 2) xi. 372 Superficial therapy..60–120 kVp. Medium voltage therapy... 120–140 kVp. Deep therapy or orthovoltage therapy..200–400 kVp. Megavoltage therapy... Above 1 MV. **1972** Barnes & Rees *Conc. Textbk. Radiotherapy* iii. 63 In recent years there has been a tendency for deep X-ray therapy (orthovoltage radiation) to be largely superseded by megavoltage therapy as the advantages of the higher energy radiation become more generally appreciated. **1976** *Lancet* 6 Nov. 1031/2 All patients received induction treatment..for 4 weeks followed by 2400 rad of orthovoltage cranial irradiation plus five intrathecal injections of methotrexate. **1966** B. V. Derjaguin in *Discussions Faraday Soc.* XLII. 118 The usual state of water and certain other liquids is thermodynamically metastable... It would be convenient to call 'usual water' metawater, and the anomalous columns—orthowater. **1969** *Nature* 27 Dec. 1293/1 Water condensed into glass or quartz capillaries has unusual properties, which have been ascribed to the formation of a new polymer termed 'orthowater', 'anomalous' water or 'polywater'. **1970** *Compton Yearbk.* 176/2 The substance, variously called orthowater, anomalous water, polywater, and superwater, differs radically from ordinary water.

2. b. orthoxy·lene, an isomer of xylene that is a colourless mobile liquid and is now obtained from petroleum naphtha for use esp. as a source of phthalic anhydride.

1872 *Jrnl. Chem. Soc.* XXV. 893 (*heading*) Preparation of orthoxylene from liquid bromotoluene. **1968** *Economist* 14 Dec. 63/3 Both BP Chemicals and ICI have existing plants for phthalic anhydride. ICI's 20,000 ton plant at Wilton manufactures from naphthalene, an older method being replaced by the ortho-xylene method as oil supersedes coal tar as a source of raw materials for the chemical industry.

3. *Physics* and *Chem.* Of, pertaining to, or designating the form of some homonuclear diatomic molecules in which (as in orthohydrogen) the two nuclei have parallel spins (see also quot. 1940[2]); also more widely, characterized by the presence of parallel spins. Also as an independent word.

1927 T. Verschoyle tr. *Haas's Atomic Theory* v. 182 No spectroscopic transition between the normal para-term and the lowest (two-quantum) ortho-term is possible. **1939** J. W. T. Spinks tr. *Herzberg's Molecular Spectra* I. iii. 150 The modification with the *greater* statistical weight is usually called the ortho modification and that with the smaller weight the para modification. **1940** Glasstone *Text-bk. Physical Chem.* i. 79 From the spectrum of helium it is known that the ortho-levels have less energy than the par-levels with the same values of the quantum numbers *n* and *l*. *Ibid.* 96 Symmetrical polyatomic molecules, such as water, deuterium oxide, cyanogen and acetylene, exist in ortho- and para-forms; they behave in a manner similar to hydrogen, deuterium and nitrogen molecules, since the other atoms, viz., carbon and oxygen, have no nuclear spins. **1966** D. H. Whiffen *Spectroscopy* ix. 114 The best-known example is hydrogen where the ortho states with odd *J* have three times the degeneracy of the even *J* or para states. **1970** P. J. Wheatley *Chem. Consequences Nucl. Spin* xi. 50 The hydrogen molecule, $^1H_2$... The rotational levels with *J* odd are associated with symmetric nuclear states, that is with ortho states, and..the rotational levels with *J* even are associated with antisymmetric nuclear states, that is with para states. *Ibid.* 51 The deuterium molecule, $^2D_2$... Ortho-D_2 will be associated with rotational levels having even values of *J*, and para-D_2 with those having odd values of *J*. **1977** *Sci. Amer.* Oct. 66/3 The parallel quark spins combine to give each meson one unit of spin. This arrangement of spins is known in atomic physics as the 'ortho' configuration.

ortho (ǭ·ɹþo), *a.* (*adv.*) [f. Ortho-.] **1.** *Chem.* (Now usu. italicized.) Characterized by or relating to (substitution at) two adjacent carbon atoms in a benzene ring; at a position adjacent *to* some (specified) substituent in a benzene ring. Also as *adv.*

1876 *Jrnl. Chem. Soc.* I. 240 An influence is exercised by the NO_2-group in favouring the displacement of Cl, Br,.. &c., *only* when it is in the ortho (1:2) or para (1:4) position relatively to one or other of these radicles. **1903** Walker & Mott tr. *Holleman's Text-bk. Org. Chem.* II. 347, 1:2 = 1:6 substitution-products are called *ortho*-compounds. **1920** *Conquest* Apr. 260/3 The ortho acid is the one of use to the Saccharin manufacturer, the para form producing a compound of very slight sweetening power. **1924** [see *meta *a.*]. **1938** L. F. Fieser in H. Gilman *Org. Chem.* I. ii. 73 The ortho coupling and ortho bromination of phenols involve substitution at the carbon atom connected to that carrying the hydroxyl group by a double linkage. **1949** [see *orient *v.* 4 a]. **1968** G. E. Coates et al. *Princ. Organometallic Chem.* ii. 26 Contrast the effect of heat on mercuric benzoate, when substitution of the aromatic ring *ortho* to the carboxyl group occurs. **1971** J. D. Roberts et al. *Org. Chem.* xx. 573 Halogen substituents..strongly orient *ortho* and *para* through conjugation of the unshared electron pairs.

2. *Photogr.* [f. Ortho(chromatic *a.*] Orthochromatic. Also *ellipt.*, an orthochromatic plate.

1904 G. B. Shaw *Let.* 26 July (1972) II. 435, I have..a box of half-plate extra-rapid Ortho plates which I got 6 months ago. **1906** *Westm. Gaz.* 17 May 14/2 The Barnet medium ortho is about half the speed of the well-known extra-rapid Barnet ortho-plate... For the best results the Barnet ortho screen is recommended. **1921** *Glasgow Herald* 27 Apr. 9, I have said something in previous articles about ortho plates. **1956** E. Mytum *Introd. Photogr. Materials* iii. 58 If the emulsion is optically sensitized by a dye which absorbs green and yellow light, it is said to be orthochromatic, often abbreviated to 'ortho'.

3. See *ortho- 3.

orthochoanite (ǭɹþokōu·ănəit). *Palæont.* Also Ortho-. [f. Ortho- + Gr. χοάν-η funnel + -ite[1] 2 a.] A nautiloid cephalopod having a straight, very short septal neck; also, a member of the obsolete sub-order Orthochoanites, of which such necks were characteristic.

1898 A. Hyatt in *Proc. Amer. Assoc. Adv. Sci.* XLVII. 364 The suborders..are as follows:..IV. Orthochoanites. The siphuncles small except in primitive forms and without deposits, or, if present, these are irregular and are gathered around the funnels. No endosiphuncles. The funnels are straight and the siphuncle is apt to be tubular. **1944** E. O. Ulrich et al. *Ozarkian & Canad. Cephalopods III* (Geol. Soc. Amer. Spec. Papers, No. 58) 27 Some of the Canadian nautilicones have lamellar deposits within the camerae... Apparently they are not present in the holochoanites, but they are being found in many orthochoanites and cyrtochoanites of the Paleozoic and the Triassic. **1952** R. C. Moore et al. *Invertebr. Fossils* ix. 342/1 The Cyrtochoanites have been found to include a very diverse assemblage of which some are closely related to 'Holochoanites' and others to 'Orthochoanites'.

Hence **orthochoani·tic** *a.*

1905 [see *holochoanitic *a.*]. **1944** E. O. Ulrich et al. *Ozarkian & Canad. Cephalopods III* (Geol. Soc. Amer. Spec. Papers, No. 58) 26 In all the coiled Canadian cephalopods, the siphuncle is orthochoanitic in structure, the septal necks being short and straight. **1964** C. Teichert in R. C. Moore *Treat. Invertebr. Paleont.* K. 95/2 Kuhn.. separated the straight, orthochoanitic nautiloids as a new 'suborder' termed Orthoceracea. *Ibid.* 174/2 Siphuncle large..; septal necks very short, orthochoanitic.

orthochromatic, *a.* Add: In mod. use, having a sensitivity which is more nearly uniform throughout the visible range than that of silver halide used alone, but which is relatively low in the red and high in the blue part of the spectrum (cf. *panchromatic *a.*). (Further examples.)

The emulsions, etc., orig. called 'orthochromatic' were in fact orthochromatic in the foregoing sense.

1903 A. Payne *Pract. Orthochromatic Photogr.* vi. 88 Orthochromatic plates possessing additional sensitiveness to the yellow and green rays only may be handled in a red light possessing abrupt absorption... Plates.. sensitive to the whole of the spectrum..require to be treated in darkness. Such plates are occasionally termed panchromatic. **1919** *Conquest* Nov. 24/1 Plates known as 'orthochromatic' or 'isochromatic' are sensitive to some of the greens and yellows... Nevertheless, even with these plates, the delicate greens of springtime, the yellow of the gorse, and many other colours in nature, are rendered unsatisfactorily, while the red leaves of autumn photograph as black [*sic*]. **1920** *Jrnl. Franklin Inst.* CLXXXIX. 25 In the commercial orthochromatic (sensitive to green and yellow) and panchromatic (sensitive to all colors) plates, the dyes are incorporated in the emulsion and the mixture flowed over the glass plate. **1944** *Electronic Engin.* XVI. 326/1 It is essential to use either an orthochromatic or panchromatic emulsion. **1970** *Amat. Photographer* 11 Mar. 60/1 As positive film is orthochromatic (that is, it is not sensitive to the red component of the visible spectrum), it can be handled under a red photographic safelight.

2. *Biol.* Exhibiting or characterized by the same colour as that of the stain used.

1899 *Jrnl. R. Microsc. Soc.* 379 Orthochromatic macrocytes which are without nuclei and appear late in embryonic life and in anæmia. **1930** Maximow & Bloom *Text-bk. Histol.* v. 114 In this way erythroblasts arise in which the protoplasm is purely acidophil, and stains a bright pink with the Romanowsky mixture. These cells are called orthochromatic erythroblasts or normoblasts. **1971** *Cancer Res.* XXXI. 505/1 This behavior was paralleled by a shift in the pH of the transition from orthochromatic to metachromatic staining of the nucleus after methanol fixation.

So **orthochro·matized** *ppl. a.*, **orthochro·matizing** *vbl. sb.*

1902 P. H. Mell *Biol. Lab. Methods* xii. 175 M. Monpillard says that, for scientific purposes, he prefers ready orthochromatized plates. **1903** A. Payne *Pract. Orthochromatic Photogr.* iv. 46 This process is termed orthochromatising, and plates so treated are known as orthochromatic or isochromatic plates. **1956** E. Mytum *Introd. Photogr. Materials* iii. 59 Sometimes the word *isochromatic*..was applied to the earlier orthochromatised emulsions.

† **orthodiagraphy** (ǭɹþodəi,æ·grăfi). *Med. Obs.* [ad. G. *orthodiagraphie* (F. Moritz 1900, in *Münch. med. Wochenschr.* 17 July 992/2): see Ortho-, Dia-[1], and -graphy.] A technique for producing sketches showing the exact sizes of organs by projecting the shadow formed by a narrow beam of X-rays on to a fluorescent screen perpendicular to the beam and drawing round the shadow.

1904 C. Beck *Röntgen Ray Diagnosis* iii. 44 (*heading*) Orthoradiography. **1907** *Practitioner* Apr. 524 By means of orthodiagraphy..the exact size and shape of an organ or tumour can be ascertained. **1930** D. A. Rhinehart *Roentgenographic Technique* 382/1 (Index), Orthodiagraphy of heart.

Hence **orthodi·agram**, a sketch produced by orthodiagraphy; **orthodi·agraph**, an instrument for orthodiagraphy; **orthodiagra·phic** *a.*, of or pertaining to orthodiagraphy; performed by means of orthodiagraphy; **o:rthodiagra·phically** *adv.*

1904 C. Beck *Röntgen Ray Diagnosis* iii. 44 The orthodiagraph made by Hirschmann permits direct tracing by the aid of a movable screen. *Ibid.*, The fact that the size of all skiagraphs is larger than that of the objects they represent, led to the construction of orthodiagraphic apparatus, by the aid of which the exact size of a body is determined. **1907** *Practitioner* Apr. 526 Changes in the size of the heart..can be determined by the system..of measuring orthodiagrams which have been taken direct on paper. **1930** D. A. Rhinehart *Roentgenographic Technique* xvii. 305 With certain types of fluoroscopes or with special attachments that may be fastened to other kinds, orthodiagraphic tracings of the cardiac outlines, giving nearly the exact dimensions of the heart shadow, can be made. **1931** P. Kerley *Rec. Adv. Radiol.* iv. 76 When screening the heart at 2 metres' distance, it takes only twenty seconds for the operator to map out an outline with a pencil, and this measurement is as accurate as that of an orthodiagram. **1938** K. C. Clark *Positioning in Radiogr.* xviii. 290/2 As an alternative to teleradiography,..the orthodiagraph may be used to record the size of the heart, a short anode-film distance being employed. **1938** *Jrnl. Amer. Med. Assoc.* 14 May 1718/1 Trimani found the parapericardial triangular shadow at the left lower arch of the roentgen silhouette of the heart in fifty-seven of 3,568 teleoentgenograms and 400 orthodiagrams which he studied. **1938** *Brain* LXI. 118 Measured Orthodiagraphically, the transverse diameter of his chest was 26 cm.

orthodontia (ǭɹþodǫ·ntiă). *Dentistry.* [f. as next + -ia[1].] Orthodontics.

1849 C. A. Harris *Dict. Dent. Sci.* 554/2 Orthodontia. **1850** —— *Princ. & Pract. Dental Surg.* (ed. 4) I. xi. 149 Fauchard and Bourdet were among the first who turned their attention to orthodontia. **1908** *Practitioner* Dec. 858 A case showing the importance of moving the roots of the teeth in orthodontia. **1939** S. J. Bregstein *Dentist & his Control of Pract.* v. 155 Preventive orthodontia, however, is regarded..as more commendable than corrective realignment of teeth and jaws. **1970** *Biol. Abstr.* LI. 3601/2 Surgery and orthodontia in 'retained teeth'.

orthodontic (ǭɹþodǫ·ntik), *a.* and *sb.* *Dentistry.* [f. Ortho- + Gr. ὀδοντ-, ὀδούς tooth + -ic.] **A.** *adj.* Serving to correct the positions of the teeth; of or pertaining to orthodontics.

1905 *Brit. Dental Jrnl.* XXVI. 993 (*heading*) Where extraction is justifiable in connection with orthodontic operations. **1939** S. J. Bregstein *Dentist & his Control of Pract.* v. 155 Speech defects, psychiatric disturbances, personality changes, rhinological pathoses all are correctable through orthodontic measures. **1962** Blake & Trott *Periodontology* xiv. 148 More permanent and more satisfactory immobilization can be obtained by fitting stainless steel orthodontic bands to each individual tooth. **1974** *Trans. European Orthodontic Soc. 1973* 403 A practitioner undertakes treatment in co-operation with the fully-trained orthodontic specialist.

B. *sb. pl.* The branch of dentistry concerned with the treatment and prevention of irregularities of the teeth and jaws. Usu. const. as *sing.*

1909 *Trans. Brit. Soc. Study Orthodontics* II. 86 The President..said that it was decided..that some change should take place in the name of the society. The council ..thought it desirable..the name of the society should be 'The British Society for the Study of Orthodontics'. He said..they had had the opinion of Dr. Murray the great philologist, of Oxford, to guide them. Mr. [C.] Schelling, as the originator of the suggested new title, here explained why he introduced the word Orthodontics. Mr. Schelling proposed..that the title of the society should be changed to the above, and..the motion was carried. **1939** L. B. Higley in Higley & Boyd *Dentistry for Children* ix. 218 Many difficult problems confronting the general dentist and orthodontist could be eliminated if preventative orthodontics were more thoroughly understood and practiced by all dentists who do work for children. **1941** J. D. McCoy *Appl. Orthodontics* (ed. 5) 6 Orthodontics has an abundant literature. **1955** G. M. Anderson *Dewey's Pract. Orthodontics* (ed. 8) ii. 89 Does orthodontics today differ from the practice of forty..years ago? **1971** *Daily Tel.* 24 Sept. 11/5 Unknown to many mothers, orthodontics (correction of irregularities in teeth) are available on the National Health Service.

Hence **orthodo·ntically** *adv.*, with regard to orthodontics.

1935 G. M. Anderson *Dewey's Pract. Orthodontia* (ed. 5) xxii. 458 Cases which though completed orthodontically were never satisfactory esthetically. **1940** M. G. Swenson *Complete Dentures* xxvi. 436 Orthodontically any movement of a tooth or teeth..will cause a change in the relationship of the inclines of the moved teeth to the remainder of the teeth. **1972** *Biol. Abstr.* LIV. 4614/2 An orthodontically interesting pair of twins.

orthodontist (ǭɹþodǫ·ntist). *Dentistry.* [f. *orthodont(ic *a.* and *sb.* + -ist.] One who practises orthodontics.

1903 *Dental Ann.* 130 Orthodontist, a newly-coined word, already considerably used in the United States to signify one who studies and practises orthodontia, or the treatment of irregularity, malposition, or malocclusion of the teeth. **1939** [see *orthodontic *sb.*]. **1969** *Daily Tel.* 7 Feb. 22 (*caption*) Mr. Lewis, an Australian orthodontist, is returning to Sydney as he is dissatisfied with working under the National Health Service.

orthodox, *a.* and *sb.* Add: **A.** *adj.* **5.** Also Orthodox. Of Judaism or Jews: adhering to the rabbinical interpretation of Biblical law and its traditional observances.

1853 *Jewish Chron.* 15 July 326/2 In all affairs of this kind, concessions are expected only on the orthodox side. **1858** *Manch. Guardian* 26 Mar. 3/4 He would not limit himself to a mere apology for their position, but confidently proclaim their right to the title of 'The truly orthodox Manchester Hebrew congregation'. **1876** Geo. Eliot *Dan. Der.* III. vi. xlvi. 308 He is not a strictly orthodox Jew, and is full of allowances for others. **1898** W. J. Locke *Idols* iv. 38 An elderly..Jewess of the most orthodox faith. **1904** *Jewish Encycl.* VII. 368/1 The stability and the immutability of the Law remained from the Orthodox standpoint one of the cardinal principles of Judaism. **1938** *Time & Tide* 12 Mar. 343/1 Peggy Simon, who was Jewish too, didn't have to bother about prayers.. because Peggy's father and mother weren't Orthodox. **1960** 'E. McBain' *Give Boys Great Big Hand* iv. 31 The family was..practising Orthodox Judaism. **1966** *Guardian* 28 July 6/5 The traditionalist right flank of Orthodox Judaism. **1973** *Jewish Chron.* 19 Jan. 22/2 It is ..unlikely that he would have been allowed to speak in an Orthodox pulpit in this country. **1974** *Encycl. Brit. Macropædia* X. 301/1 For many, the foreign designation 'orthodox' (used by Reform Jews for traditionalist Jews) makes little if any sense. **1973** J. Ryder *Trevayne*

(1974) xxxii. 247 It is the Hebrew Sabbath... This house is Orthodox. **1975** *Nature* 6 Nov. 9/2 For an Orthodox woman, sexual intercourse is only permitted during a limited period each month. **1977** *Rolling Stone* 21 Apr. 72/2 Conversation among Orthodox Jews never strays far from questions of ethics, points of law, one's religious activities.

6. Applied to sleep characterized by the absence of rapid eye-movements and probably of dreams and by lesser physiological activity as compared with 'paradoxical' or REM sleep.

1967 W. P. Koella *Sleep* II. i. 16 Subjects after being aroused from..'orthodox' sleep stages rarely recalled dreams. **1971** U. J. Jovanović *Normal Sleep in Man* ii. 75 We shall..use the Kleitman (1963) and Jouvet classification (1961, 1965, 1968), and divide up the entire polygraphic period of sleep in man into normal (orthodox) sleep and paradoxical sleep (periods of dream phases). *Ibid.* vii. 259 A phase of orthodox sleep lasts for about one-and-a-half hours.

B. *sb.* **1. c.** An orthodox Jew (see sense *A. 5).

1889 I. Zangwill in *Jewish Q. Rev.* I. 391 With the 'unintelligently orthodox', this mental attitude is generally associated with ignorance of our history and of the fluidity of ceremonial forms. **1892** I. Zangwill *Childr. Ghetto* II. 296 Now at last we poor orthodox will have a voice. **1914** *Encycl. Relig. & Ethics* VII. 608/2 The choice of method, unpleasing though it be to the orthodox, must be left to the conscience and judgment of the liberals themselves. **1927** E. O'Neill *Lazarus Laughed* I. ii. 35 Their former distinctions of Nazarenes and Orthodox are now entirely forgotten. *Ibid.* 42 The Nazarenes and the Orthodox separate and slink guiltily apart. **1964** E. E. Klein in W. Berkowitz *Ten Vital Jewish Issues* 48 The Conservative Jew always keeps one [*sc.* a yarmulke] in his pocket, and the Orthodox wears it on his head.

orthodoxy. Add: **d.** The orthodox practice of Judaism; the body of orthodox Jews.

1888 *Jewish Q. Rev.* I. 55 The Rabbis..would have either suspected the man's orthodoxy, or would have denied that his views were really what he professed them to be. **1892** *Ibid.* IV. 215 Let us..hope that Dr. Friedländer's conception is by no means Orthodoxy's last word. **1899** B. Drachman *Nineteen Lett. Ben Uziel* p. xvii, Hirsch set up that view of Judaism called in Germany 'Denkgläubigkeit', which we may translate as 'intellectual or enlightened Orthodoxy'. **1955** M. Sklare *Conservative Judaism* i. 25 It would be desirable to conclude this historical introduction with some statistics about the growth or decline of Orthodoxy, Conservatism and Reform. **1966** H. Kemelman *Saturday the Rabbi went Hungry* (1967) viii. 51 Some of the older congregants brought up in Orthodoxy. **1975** *Times* 13 Aug. 12/4 The mayor of Hackney..says: 'I never travel by car on Saturdays or Jewish festivals.'.. Now the mayor aims to combine his orthodoxy with a little money-making by getting people to sponsor his walks.

orthodromic, *a.* Delete *rare* and add: Also, representing great circles as straight lines. (Examples.) Also **o·rthodrome,** a great circle or a route forming part of one.

1855 J. Pryde *Treat. Pract. Math.* 455 The arc of a great circle, which is the shortest distance between two places, is called the orthodrome. **1922** R. Keen *Direction & Position Finding by Wireless* iv. 103 A chart on which all Great Circles are represented as straight lines is known as orthodromic. **1928** L. S. Palmer *Wireless Princ. & Pract.* xii. 487 This type of projection is the orthodromic projection and the map of the district surrounding the tangent point is termed a Gnomonic chart. **1935** *Geogr. Jrnl.* LXXXV. 466 The equation of the orthodrome (geodesic line). **1956** *McGraw-Hill Yearbk. Sci. & Technol.* VI. 267/2 The longer the distance, the greater the deviation between loxodromes and orthodromes.

2. *Physiol.* Being or involving a nerve impulse that is propagated in the normal direction.

1943 *Jrnl. Neurophysiol.* VI. 143 (*heading*) The interaction of antidromic and orthodromic volleys in a segmental spinal motor nucleus. **1954** *Jrnl. Physiol.* CXXVI. 501 (*heading*) Interaction between direct current and orthodromic stimulation. **1972** *Science* 2 June 1043/1 The prolonged inhibition of the monographic excitation of motoneurons by orthodromic volleys in muscle and cutaneous afferent fibers.

Hence **orthodro·mically** *adv.*

1954 Penfield & Jasper *Epilepsy & Functional Anat. Human Brain* v. 203 Distant projection of the impulses from a local after-discharge has been shown to be conducted only orthodromically (not antidromically) over transcortical bundles of fibers. **1976** *Nature* 4 Mar. 56/2 When the interval between the two spikes was reduced progressively, the antidromic response eventually disappeared because it collided with the direct spike travelling orthodromically along the same nerve fibre.

orthoepic, *a.* Add: (Later example); **orthoepically** *adv.* (later example).

1969 *Computers & Humanities* III. 259 The authors aimed at producing a broad phonetic transcription similar to the phonetic transcription already established for orthoepic French. **1975** *Amer. Speech 1973* XLVIII. 113 Being perhaps abnormally tenacious orthoepically and considerably past middle age, I use [æ] in all these words, but scholars and laymen alike have been seen to wince at the crudity of my speech.

orthoepist. Add to def.: used esp. of those 16th- and 17th-century writers whose aim was to describe a 'correct' pronunciation of English, to reform the spelling system to make it reflect such a pronunciation more accurately, etc. (Earlier and later examples.) Also *attrib.* or as *adj.*

1791 J. Walker *Crit. Pronouncing Dict.* s.v., *Orthoepist*, ..one who is skilled in Orthöepy. **1909** O. Jespersen *Mod. Eng. Gram.* I. ix. 248 Up to quite recent times, most orthoepists have disregarded natural pronunciation. **1917** J. M. Clark *Vocab. Anglo-Irish* 18 It is a well-known fact that in Tudor English a much more open *ō* was pronounced than is the case today. Apart from the testimony of orthoepists, the proof is to be found in contemporary American and Irish usage. **1920** H. C. Wyld *Hist. Mod. Colloq. Eng.* iv. 115 Hitherto writers upon the history of Modern English have relied mainly upon the Orthoepists. **1927** R. E. Zachrisson *Eng. Pronunc. at Shakespeare's Time* p. x, The old-fashioned types of pronunciation were, as a rule, taught by English orthoepists. **1957** E. J. Dobson *Eng. Pronunc. 1500–1700* I. ii. 193 The tendency to regard the spelling reformers as primarily interested in teaching 'correct pronunciation'..may be due to the difficulty of finding a term to cover all the sixteenth- and seventeenth-century writers on pronunciation; 'grammarians' is clearly inexact except in a few cases, and so the term 'orthoepists' has been widely accepted. **1969** A. C. Partridge *Tudor to Augustan English* viii. 173 On their own admission, orthoepists were students of language who sought to establish the principles of correctness in speech. **1972** M. L. Samuels *Linguistic Evol.* vii. 144 For Early Modern English, there is much orthoepist, phonetic and other evidence. **1975** *Language* LI. 747 It would be of great value if a presumably accurate report of upper-class speech of the period [*sc.* Early Modern English] could be carefully analysed and related to witnesses such as Hunt and the other orthoepists.

orthoepistic *a.* (later example); hence also **orthoepi·stical** *a.*

1913 R. E. Zachrisson *Pronunc. Eng. Vowels 1400–1700* 3 Statements in early grammars and spelling-books (= the orthoepistical evidence). **1957** E. J. Dobson *Eng. Pronunc. 1500–1700* I. i. 36 There is no other orthoepistical evidence for this pronunciation. **1972** *Eng. Studies* LIII. 506 This type of pronunciation was vulgar or dialectal..but at least in some words it must have infiltrated educated speech, as is shown by its frequent occurrence in orthoepistic works. **1972** P. M. Wolfe *Linguistic Change* iii. 31, I have in general limited myself to English orthoepistical works.

orthoepy. Add: Also, the study of the relationship between pronunciation and a writing system. (Later examples.)

1915 D. Agate in H. C. O'Neill *Guide to Eng. Lang.* I. v. 74/1 To these four divisions of grammar many grammarians have added Orthoëpy, which treats of pronunciation generally. **1957** E. J. Dobson *Eng. Pronunc. 1500–1700* I. ii. 193 In spite of his title *Orthoepia Anglicana*.. what he [*sc.* Daines] sets out to teach is orthography, not orthoepy. **1969** A. C. Partridge *Tudor to Augustan English* viii. 181 Though his was not the last shot fired in the hundred years' war of English orthoepy, Cooper's *Grammar* established that the criterion of correct Standard English rests firmly on its pronunciation. **1976** *Visible Language* X. 20 Phonetization of the alphabet and other writing systems is a province of orthoepy.

orthogenesis (ǭɹþodʒe·nĭsis). *Biol.* [a. G. *orthogenesis* (W. Haacke *Gestaltung und Vererbung* (1893) ii. 31), f. Ortho- + -genesis.] A series of similar variations in successive generations, leading to evolutionary change produced by these mutations. Also **orthogene·tics** *sb. pl.*

1895 *Nature* 3 Oct. 554/2 Prof. Eimer, of Tübingen, spoke..on the subject of orthogenesis. **1897** *Jrnl. R. Microsc. Soc.* 108 The causes of orthogenesis are to be found in the action of environment upon the constitution of the organism. **1911** *Encycl. Brit.* XXVII. 912/1 Many successful series,..as they have survived, must inevitably display orthogenesis to some extent. **1930** G. R. de Beer *Embryol. & Evolution* iv. 32 This incorrigible tendency to produce larger and larger horns, to vary continuously in the same direction, has been given the name of orthogenesis. **1937** A. Huxley *Ends & Means* xiv. 261 Neither Lamarckism nor the orthogenetics theory seems to be compatible with the fact that most mutations are demonstrably deleterious. **1956** *Nature* 18 Feb. 309/1 His [*sc.* Arthur Trueman's] contributions to the more philosophical aspects of palæontology ranged..from lineage and orthogenesis, to a reconsideration of the species concept. **1965** R. Howard tr. *de Beauvoir's Force of Circumstance* x. 500 They talked, not about birth control but about the joys of maternity, not about contraception but about orthogenesis. **1970** *Watsonia* VIII. 178 A telling argument in favour of mutation pressure (orthogenesis) rather than natural selection. **1973** *Nature* 10 Aug. 375/1 A non-Darwinian orthogenesis had sealed the fate of *Megaloceros* under the oppressive weight of its own enlarging antlers.

orthogenetic (ǭːɹþodʒene·tik), *a.* [f. prec.; see -genetic.] Of, pertaining to, or characterized by orthogenesis. Also *transf.* Hence **orthogene·tically** *adv.*

1899 H. Gadow in *Proc. Cambr. Philos. Soc.* X. 35 (*title*) Orthogenetic variation in the shells of Chelonia. *Ibid.* 37 Since these variations all lie in the direct line of descent..I call this kind of atavistic variation orthogenetic. **1911** J. Ward *Realm of Ends* xvii. 383 Can we conceive this world evolving orthogenetically, as a biologist would say? **1927** Haldane & Huxley *Animal Biol.* xi. 253 The orthogenetic series can be perfectly well explained by natural selection. *Ibid.*, The extinct cephalopod molluscs ..often evolved orthogenetically into the most bizarre forms. **1930** W. R. Inge *Christian Ethics & Mod. Probl.* i. 13, I shall not maintain that the evolution of Christianity has been..orthogenetic. **1965** B. E. Freeman tr. *Vandel's Biospeleol.* xiii. 198 Biospeologists..are more interested in orthogenetic evolution which proceeds in a parallel manner, in different phyletic lines. **1973** *Jrnl. Genetic Psychol.* CXXIII. 231 In its most general sense, Werner's theory of development centers on his orthogenetic principle.

orthogonal, *a.* Add: **2.** *Math.* **a.** Of a linear transformation: preserving lengths and angles; leaving unchanged quantities of the form ${x_1}^2+{x_2}^2+\ldots+{x_n}^2$ and the inner product of any two vectors.

1859 G. Salmon *Lessons Introd. Mod. Higher Algebra* xv. 125 What we may call the orthogonal transformation is to transform simultaneously a given quadratic function, and $x^2+y^2+z^2+w^2+$ &., so that the latter remaining of the same form, the former may become $Ax^2+By^2+Cz^2+Dw^2+$ &. **1893** L. G. Weld *Short Course Theory Determinants* ix. 227 The transformation, in analytical geometry, from one set of axes to another, without changing the origin, is orthogonal. **1941** Birkhoff & MacLane *Survey Mod. Algebra* ix. 222 A linear transformation T is orthogonal if it preserves the absolute value of every vector ξ, so that $|\xi T| = |\xi|$. **1972** F. E. Hohn *Introd. Linear Algebra* viii. 237 An orthogonal transformation of $\mathscr{E}^n$ maps orthogonal vectors onto orthogonal vectors and nonorthogonal vectors onto nonorthogonal vectors.

b. Applied to the group of all orthogonal matrices of a given order.

1898 *Bull. Amer. Math. Soc.* IV. 196 A linear substitution S on the marks of a Galois Field of order p^n..will be called orthogonal if it leaves absolutely invariant ${\xi_1}^2+{\xi_2}^2+\ldots+{\xi_m}^2\ldots$ The order of the orthogonal group G on m indices in the $GF[2^n]$ is thus [etc.]. **1941** Birkhoff & MacLane *Survey Mod. Algebra* ix. 225 This subgroup of the full linear group..is called the orthogonal group O_n; it is isomorphic to the group of all orthogonal transformations of the given Euclidean space. **1972** F. E. Hohn *Introd. Linear Algebra* viii. 252 Show that the set of all linear operators on $\mathscr{E}_n$ of the form $Y=UX$, where U is orthogonal, constitute a group (the orthogonal group).

c. Of a square matrix: representing an orthogonal transformation; such that the rows (and likewise the columns) are orthonormal when considered as vectors; equal to the inverse of its transpose; (these three properties are equivalent).

1907 M. Bôcher *Introd. Higher Algebra* xi. 154 An orthogonal transformation. [*Note*] The matrix of such a transformation is called an orthogonal matrix. **1964** N. N. Hancock *Matrix Anal. Electr. Machinery* ii. 18 The value of the determinant of an orthogonal matrix is necessarily ± 1, but the converse is not true.

d. Of two vectors or functions: perpendicular; having an inner product equal to zero. Of a set of vectors or functions: such that the inner product of any two is zero if and only if the two are distinct.

1913 *Proc. London Math. Soc.* XII. 297 The theory of Fourier series and of other series of orthogonal functions. **1926** E. W. Hobson *Theory of Functions of Real Variable* (ed. 2) II. x. 754 If $\{\psi_n(x)\}$ be a complete sequence of linearly independent functions for the interval (a, b), a normal orthogonal and complete system of functions $\{\phi_n(x)\}$ can be so determined that $\phi_n(x)$ is a linear function of $\psi_1(x), \psi_2(x), \ldots \psi_n(x)$. **1941** R. V. Churchill *Fourier Series* iii. 45 The functions $e^{inx}=\cos nx+i\sin nx$ $(n=0, \pm 1, \pm 2,\ldots)$ form a system which is orthogonal on the interval $(-\pi, \pi)$. **1967** A. A. Goldstein *Constructive Real Analysis* iii. 112 We define an inner product space $I[a, b]$ by introducing an inner product.. defined by $[f, g]=\int_a^b f(t)g(t)dt$. Two functions f and g in $I[a, b]$ are said to be orthogonal if $[f, g]=0$. *Ibid.* 115 Two points x and y of [a Hilbert space] H are orthogonal if $[x, y]=0$. Similarly, two subspaces M and N of H are said to be orthogonal if $[M, N]=0$. **1968** C. G. Kuper *Introd. Theory Superconductivity* i. 3 Bardeen, Cooper and Schrieffer (1957) constructed a variational wave function for a ground state with complete electron pairing, and orthogonal functions for low-lying excited states having only a few such pairs broken.

3. *Statistics.* Of a set of variates: statistically independent. Of an experimental design: such that the variates under investigation can be treated as statistically independent.

1933 *Jrnl. Agric. Sci.* XXIII. 110 In an ordinary replicated field experiment of the randomised block or Latin square type the differences of the means of plots receiving the same treatments are taken without hesitation to be true measures of treatment differences, but this is only so because the experiment has been specially arranged so as to be orthogonal. **1950** M. H. Quenouille *Introd. Statistics* iv. 59 If we are comparing a series of..measurements on people to determine the effect of age, these comparisons may be complicated by the effect of sex... The only manner in which we can assume that sex does not enter into the comparison is to choose the same proportion of each sex in each age group. The effect of sex is then said to be 'orthogonal' to the effect of age. **1967** *Word* XXIII. 219 Another model which provides a relevant comparison to phonological distinctive features is the mathematical method of factor analysis... The various mathematical methods employed lead to the positing of a number of independent 'orthogonal' factors and each test or other set of responses is described in terms of positive or negative loadings on each factor. **1973** *Jrnl. Genetic Psychology* CXXII. 45 Implicit in the work..is the concept that creativity and intelligence are relatively orthogonal (i.e., unrelated statistically) at high levels of intelligence.

orthogonality (ǭɹþǫgǒnæ·lĭti). [f. Orthogonal *a.* + -ity.] The property of being orthogonal. Freq. *attrib.*

1892 O. HEAVISIDE *Electr. Papers* II. 583/2 (Index), Orthogonality of electric and magnetic forces. **1930** P. A. M. DIRAC *Princ. Quantum Mech.* iii. 50 The orthogonality theorem. **1933** *Jrnl. Agric. Sci.* XXIII. 108 Orthogonality is that property of the design which ensures that the different classes of effects to which the experimental material is subject shall be capable of direct and separate estimation without any entanglement. **1935** PAULING & WILSON *Introd. Quantum Mech.* 441 (*heading*) Proof of orthogonality of wave functions corresponding to different energy levels. **1962** CORSON & LORRAIN *Introd. Electromagn. Fields* iv. 158 This property of orthogonality of the Legendre polynomials is important in evaluating the coefficients of Eq. 4-139. **1970** G. K. WOODGATE *Elem. Atomic Struct.* ii. 17 The spherical harmonics have the orthogonality property. **1972** A. W. F. EDWARDS *Likelihood* vi. 106 Such cases may be expected to be rather rare ..and the most important application of the concept of orthogonality is to the quadratic support surface. **1973** *Jrnl. Genetic Psychol.* CXXII. 202 The correlations between the E and N dimensions are low enough to justify the assumption of orthogonality of these two dimensions of personality.

ortho:gonaliza·tion. *Math.* [f. as prec. + -IZATION.] The procedure of constructing an orthogonal set of functions or vectors from ones that are linearly independent but not orthogonal.

1922 *Proc. London Math. Soc.* XXI. 97 We have now only to derive from $\{\chi_n(t)\}$ a new set $\{\psi_n(t)\}$ by the 'orthogonalisation method' of Mr. E. Schmidt to get a complete, orthogonal, and normalised set possessing the property (3). **1966** G. ARFKEN *Math. Methods for Physicists* ix. 342 Consider two (nonparallel) vectors **A** and **B** in the *xy*-plane. We may normalize **A** to unit magnitude and then form $\mathbf{B}' = a\mathbf{A} + \mathbf{B}$ so that **B′** is perpendicular to **A**. By normalizing **B′** we have completed the Schmidt orthogonalization for two vectors.

So **ortho·gonalize** *v. trans.*, to render orthogonal (and, often, to normalize); **ortho·gonalized** *ppl. a.*

1930 RUARK & UREY *Atoms, Molecules & Quanta* 747 Other systems of polynomials often used in wave mechanics are obtained by orthogonalizing the system, $p^{1/2}$, $xp^{1/2}$, $x^2p^{1/2}$,.. where $p(x)$ is a so-called 'weight function'. **1937** MICHELL & BELZ *Elem. Math. Analysis* II. xvii. 914 If the set of functions $\phi_k(x)$..is orthogonalized by means of the function $\psi(x)$. **1939** C. H. GOULDEN *Methods Statistical Analysis* xii. 192 If the number of varieties is 21, the numbers would be written out as below..and we would have to use a completely orthogonalized 4 × 4 square..to which the remaining numbers would be added as described above. **1948** BROWN & CAMPBELL *Princ. Servomech.* iii. 66 After the initial transformation, certain manipulations enable us to orthogonalize the mathematical forms. **1966** *McGraw-Hill Encycl. Sci. & Technol.* II. 93/1 Several techniques exist for solving the wave equation, at least for certain states, notably the Wigner-Seitz method and the orthogonalized-plane-wave method.

orthograde (ǭ·ɹþogrēⁱd), *a.* [irreg. f. ORTHO- + L. *-gradus* walking: see GRADE *sb.*] Holding the body upright.

1902 A. KEITH in *Jrnl. Anat. & Physiol.* XXXVII. 18 He [*sc.* the author] regards the primates as divided into two very distinct groups—those which carry the axis of the body in a horizontal position—the Pronograde Primates..; and those which carry the axis of the body in an upright position—the Orthograde Primates, into which group fall the gibbon, orang, chimpanzee, gorilla, and man. *Ibid.* 19 It is now generally recognised that the anthropoids, in their natural habitat, carry their bodies in an upright position, i.e. are orthograde. **1925** J. LAIRD *Our Minds & their Bodies* 46 An orthograde (or erect) animal, like man. **1940** *Nature* 6 July 27/1, I regarded the Gibbon as a representative of the pioneers of the orthograde stock. **1973** B. J. WILLIAMS *Evol. & Human Origins* viii. 112/2 Many features of this arboreal primate life..predisposed primates to a more orthograde, upright posture. *Ibid.* 114/1 Man being completely orthograde has a recurved spine that bends back sharply in the lumbar region.

orthography. 1. b. (Earlier example.)

1588 W. KEMPE *Educ. Children* sig. F 3ᵛ Orthographie ..teacheth with what letters euery syllable and word must be written, and with what points the sentence and parts thereof must be distinguished... Which expressing and skill of the hand, belongeth properly to the Arte of Painting, and not vnto Grammar.

orthohelium (stress variable). [f. ORTHO- + HELIUM, as an antonym of the earlier *par(a)-helium.*] The form of helium whose spectrum exhibits a fine structure of triplets owing to the spins of the two orbital electrons being parallel.

1922 A. D. UDDEN tr. *Bohr's Theory of Spectra* III. iii. 86 Helium was at first assumed to be a mixture of two different gases, 'orthohelium' and 'parhelium', but now we know that the two spectra simply mean that the binding of the second electron can occur in two different ways. *Ibid.* 87 The metastable state..is the final stage of the process giving the orthohelium spectrum. **1961** POWELL & CRASEMANN *Quantum Mech.* xii. 458 Spectroscopically, the singlet and triplet systems are independent of one another, and have been given the names *parahelium* (singlets) and *orthohelium* (triplets). The ground state of the orthohelium system..is therefore stable with respect to optical transitions of the usual kind, and has a correspondingly long lifetime.

orthohydrogen (stress variable). Also **ortho hydrogen** and with hyphen. [f. ORTHO- + HYDROGEN as tr. G. *orthowasserstoff* (Bonhoeffer & Harteck 1929, in *Naturwissenschaften* XVII. 182/1), coined on the analogy of *orthohelium* (see quot. 1935).] The form of molecular hydrogen in which the two nuclei in the molecule have parallel spins, so that the spectrum exhibits a hyperfine structure of triplets; it differs slightly in physical properties from the other form (*PARAHYDROGEN) and forms 75 per cent of hydrogen in equilibrium at room temperature.

1929 *Chem. Abstr.* XXIII. 2614 (*heading*) Experiments on para- and ortho-hydrogen. **1935** A. FARKAS *Orthohydrogen, Parahydrogen & Heavy Hydrogen* ii. 4 The parahydrogen molecules have antiparallel nuclear spins and even rotational quantum numbers, while the orthohydrogen molecules possess parallel nuclear spins and odd rotational quantum numbers. *Ibid.*, The names orthohydrogen and parahydrogen were chosen by Bonhoeffer and Harteck on analogy with the nomenclature for the helium atom (orthohelium and parahelium), but it must be emphasized that the distinction between the hydrogen modifications is based on the different orientations of the nuclear spins, while in the case of helium it depends on the orientation of the electron spins. **1962** P. J. & B. DURRANT *Introd. Adv. Inorg. Chem.* xiii. 368 Ordinary hydrogen gas is a tautomeric mixture of orthohydrogen and parahydrogen. **1966** D. H. WHIFFEN *Spectroscopy* ix. 114 In the absence of magnetic materials non-equilibrium mixtures of ortho and para hydrogen are stable for many months. **1969** H. T. EVANS tr. *Hägg's Gen. & Inorg. Chem.* xviii. 452 At 0°K..only parahydrogen exists at equilibrium.

orthometric, *a.* Add: (Examples.)

1854 J. D. DANA *Syst. Min.* (ed. 4) I. 23 In Crystallography there are three axes employed,..and these axes are either at right angles with one another, producing orthometric forms, or oblique, producing clinometric forms. **1883** *Encycl. Brit.* XVI. 349/2 All crystals may be divided into 'orthometric' or erect forms and 'clinometric' or inclined forms.

2. *Surveying.* Of, pertaining to, or being a height measured from the geoid.

1919 G. L. HOSMER *Geodesy* x. 254 The United States Coast Survey has adopted the method of applying to ordinary elevations the correction for convergence, called Orthometric Correction. **1923** D. CLARK *Plane & Geodetic Surveying* II. v. 205 A line of constant orthometric elevation is parallel to the mean sea level surface. **1967** HEISKANEN & MORITZ *Physical Geodesy* iv. 172 Orthometric heights are the natural 'heights above sea level', that is, heights above the geoid. **1974** *Encycl. Brit. Macropædia* XVII. 832/2 To correct these distortions, orthometric corrections..must be applied to long lines of levels at high altitudes that have a north–south trend.

Hence **orthome·trically** *adv.*

1952 G. BOMFORD *Geodesy* iv. 155 If no error of observation is made, Bb and aA will be measured orthometrically.

orthomolecular (ǭːɹþomole·kiŭlăɹ), *a. Psychol.* [f. ORTHO- + MOLECULAR *a.*] (See quot. 1968.)

1968 L. PAULING in *Science* 19 Apr. 265/1, I have reached the conclusion..that another general method of treatment, which may be called orthomolecular therapy, may be found to be of great value... Orthomolecular psychiatric therapy is the treatment of mental disease by the provision of the optimum molecular environment for the mind, especially the optimum concentrations of substances normally present in the human body. **1970** [see *megavitamins* s.v. *MEGA- a]. **1971** *Nature* 15 Oct. 452/2 The term 'orthomolecular psychiatry' introduced by Professor L. Pauling in 1968 has taught American psychiatrists to appreciate a principle well known to scientists. **1972** *Daily Colonist* (Victoria, B.C.) 16 July 25/3 Heavy doses of certain vitamins..correct biochemical imbalances. It's called the orthomolecular approach. **1977** *National Observer* (U.S.) 22 Jan. 11/5 Megavitamin, or orthomolecular therapy, is sometimes used to treat mental retardation, psychoses, hyperactivity, autism, dyslexia, and other learning disorders.

orthomorphic, *a.* Restrict *rare* to sense 1 and add further examples of sense 2.

1910 [see *CONFORMAL *a.* 2]. **1937** *Jrnl. Optical Soc. Amer.* XXVII. 338/2 The only telescope with orthomorphic object and image spaces is the unit power telescope. **1938, 1957** [see *CONFORMAL *a.* 2]. **1971** *Jrnl. Photographic Sci.* XIX. 24/2 A slit width of ¼ in. was used for orthomorphic copying.

Hence **orthomo·rphism,** the property of being orthomorphic.

1919 *Wireless World* May 69/2 Orthomorphism..may be possessed by many different types of graticule. **1940** *Geogr. Jrnl.* XCV. 381 It is well to preserve orthomorphism, if only for its help in solving great circle problems. **1975** J. B. HARLEY *O.S. Maps* ii. 19 The projection stretched the topography equally in all directions, rather than only in a north–south direction, and this gave it the property of conformality or orthomorphism, in which there is a minimal distortion of shape over small areas and the scale..is likewise equal in all directions at any one point.

orthonormal (ǭɹþonǭ·ɹmăl), *a. Math.* [f. ORTHO(GONAL *a.* + NORMAL *a.*] Both orthogonal and normalized.

1932 M. H. STONE *Linear Transformations in Hilbert Space* i. 7 Two elements *f*, *g* of $\mathfrak{h}$ are said to be orthogonal if (f, g) vanishes... A subset $\mathfrak{G}$ of $\mathfrak{H}$ is said to be an orthonormal set if, when *f* and *g* are elements of $\mathfrak{G}$,

$$(f, g) = \begin{cases} 1, f = g \\ 0, f \neq g \end{cases}.$$

1941 R. V. CHURCHILL *Fourier Series* iii. 35 The symbol $\{\phi_r\}$ will be used to denote an orthonormal set whose vectors are ϕ_1, ϕ_2, and ϕ_3. The simplest example of such a set is that consisting of the unit vectors along the three coordinate axes. **1965** PATTERSON & RUTHERFORD *Elem. Abstr. Algebra* v. 173 It is frequently desirable to choose an orthonormal basis: that is, a basis of which each vector is of unit length..and such that any two basic vectors are orthogonal. **1968** G. LUDWIG *Wave Mech.* I. iii. 33 The degree of such a complete orthonormal system can be called the dimension of a Hilbert space.

Hence **orthonorma·lity,** the property of being orthonormal.

1949 L. I. SCHIFF *Quantum Mech.* 401 (Index), Orthonormality. **1959** G. TROUP *Masers* ii. 16 This orthonormality is an expression of the independence of the stationary states. **1971** *Amer. Jrnl. Physics* XXXIX. 498/1 The $\{c_n{}^r\}$ must satisfy the orthonormality relation.

orthonormalize (ǭːɹþonǭ·ɹmălǝiz), *v. Math.* [f. prec. + -IZE.] *trans.* To make (a set of vectors or functions) orthonormal by orthogonalizing them and then multiplying each by an appropriate factor. Hence **o:rthonormali·zation.**

1935 *Trans. Amer. Math. Soc.* XXXVII. 309 When we orthonormalize $\{T^{*-1}\chi_i\}$ we obtain $\{\phi_i\}$. **1968** B. KRIPKE *Introd. Anal.* iii. 57 Orthonormalize the functions 1, *x*, x^2 with respect to the inner product $[f, g] = \int_0^1 f(x)g(x)dx$ on $\mathscr{C}([0, 1])$. **1972** A. KYRALA *Appl. Functions Complex Variable* xiii. 318 Establish the orthonormalization relations..for the associated Legendre functions. **1974** ADBY & DEMPSTER *Introd. Optimization Methods* iv. 89 Rosenbrock's method with linear search does not exhibit quadratic termination, due to the orthonormalization of the search directions in the second part of each iteration and the alignment of one of them towards the minimum.

orthopædic, -pedic, *a.* Add: *orthopædic bed,* a bed in an orthopædic ward; normally one individually designed to relieve specific skeletal symptoms; *more generally,* a bed with a very firm mattress or board; also *orthopædic bedding, divan,* etc.; *orthopædic shoe,* a shoe designed to ease or correct deformities of the feet (cf. quot. 1842 s.v. ORTHOPÆDICAL *a.*); also *orthopædic boot, footwear.*

1943 FUNSTEN & CALDERWOOD *Orthopedic Nursing* iv. 90 Orthopedic beds may be made with top linen placed over the end of the bed, rather than by tucking it in at the end of the mattress. **1971** B. MALAMUD *Tenants* 214 The tall mother..wears a plain white dress, orthopedic shoes, and a blue cloche hat that hides her eyes. **1974** N. GORDIMER *Conservationist* 241 She..turns a foot on the heel of one of those clogs, like orthopaedic shoes, the women are wearing these days. **1976** *P.O. Teleph. Directory: London Postal Area* June, Orthopaedic Bedding Centre. **1976** P. VAN RJNDT *Tetramachus Collection* (1977) i. 11 A cripple, obliged to wear a heavy orthopedic boot on his right foot. **1977** *Evening Post* (Nottingham) 27 Jan. 19/1 (Advt.), Modern single bed with mattress £15. Single bed base £10. Single orthopædic mattress as new £30. *Ibid.*, Orthopædic 4ft divan complete. As new. £130. **1977** *Daily Express* 1 Feb. 29 (Advt.), OBC orthopædic beds..look like any good quality bed... The big difference is this: They are designed with medical help and hand-assembled in thousands of different versions to give correct individual support to back sufferers whatever their weight or type of build. **1977** *Observer* 13 Feb. 18/6 (Advt.), Beds, soft, firm, extra firm, orthopædic. **1977** *Times* 14 May 25/7 (Advt.), Orthopaedic footwear our speciality.

orthopantomography (ǭːɹþopæntǒmǫ·grăfi). *Med.* [f. ORTHO- + *PANTOMOGRAPHY.] A modification of pantomography in which the X-rays are made to be more nearly normal to the line of the jaws, so that a radiograph can be obtained showing all the teeth and adjacent tissue in a straight line.

1959 Y. V. PAATERO in *Acta Radiologica* LI. 449 Since stereoscopy has been successfully adapted to ordinary pantomography..theoretical and experimental investigations into the possibility of obtaining equally good stereoscopic effects with the new pantomographic method 'orthoradial pantomography' (or orthopantomography for short), were considered to be justified. **1961** *Oral Surgery* XIV. 947 (*heading*) Pantomography and orthopantomography. **1968** *Brit. Jrnl. Radiol.* XLI. 872/2 They reported that during orthopantomography the exposure at the eccentric axis was 1·5 R and at the skin surface it varied from 0·3 R to 0·9 R.

Hence **orthopanto·mogram,** a radiograph obtained by orthopantomography; **ortho-panto·mograph,** an instrument for performing orthopantomography.

1959 Y. V. PAATERO in *Annales Medicinae Internae Fenniae* XLVIII. Suppl. 28. 223 As no 'orthopantomograph' suitable for clinical use was yet available, the accompanying pictures were taken of a dry skull with a hand-rotated miniature apparatus. **1959** —— in *Acta Radiologica* LI. 452 The jaws appear flat in orthopantomograms and not curved as in ordinary pantomograms. **1967** L. M. ENNIS et al. *Dental Roentgenol.* (ed. 6) x. 283 In operation of the Orthopantomograph, the patient remains stationary while the x-ray tubehead circulates from his right side around behind his neck to the left side, while the film rotates about an axis and at the same time, revolves from the left side of the patient's face, around the front and to the right side of the face. **1971** *Brit. Dental Jrnl.* CXXX. 429/2 There are two image layers in the orthopantomograph, one on either side of the rotational centre, the object further from the film presenting reversed images. *Ibid.* 433/2 This delicate spur of bone is not visible on the orthopantomogram.

orthopod (ǭ·ɹþopǫd). *slang.* [Alteration of ORTHOPAEDIC *a.*] An orthopædic surgeon.

1960 'R. GORDON' *Doctor in Clover* ix. 76 We were interrupted by the surgeon himself, a big, red-faced, jolly Irishman. Most orthopods are, when you come to think of it. **1966** I. JEFFERIES *House-Surgeon* vii. 131 We had two male beds and one female, and the orthopods had two spare beds. **1969** D. FRANCIS *Enquiry* xii. 164, I telephoned to the orthopod who regularly patched me up after falls. **1978** *New Yorker* 13 Mar. 82 The problem now was to persuade the orthopod to go in and remove the screws.

orthopraxy. Add: **1.** (Further examples.) Also **orthopraxis.**

1951 *Jrnl. Theol. Stud.* II. 98 The complete obedience of Jesus must be taken to be a complete vindication of the Law, and therefore the champions of legal orthodoxy (and orthopraxis), such as James and Peter, are the heroes of Jewish Christianity. **1960** J. PARKES *Foundations Judaism & Christianity* vi. 297 We cannot..imagine an orthopraxy, which made a mizwah of reciting a special blessing over a fruit tree in bloom, attached to a Puritan theology which was quick to threaten Hell-fire for any slight disobedience. *Ibid.*, Historically however, rabbinic orthopraxy was lived with an entirely different background. *Ibid.* 311 There does not appear to have been any single system, nor was any particular method of choice a matter of 'orthopraxis'. **1971** *Clergy Review* LVI. 218 The orthodoxy of faith in the coming universal kingdom must constantly be made true in the ortho-praxy of creative flight forward with the world. **1976** E. MACLAREN *Nature of Belief* vii. 73 No amount of impeccable ortho*doxy* is belief. Belief is ortho*praxis*, commitment to certain action.

orthopsychiatry (ǭɹþosəikəi·ătri). [f. ORTHO- + PSYCHIATRY.] A branch of psychiatry concerned especially with the prevention of mental or behavioural disorders. Hence **orthopsychia·tric** *a.*, **orthopsychi·atrist.**

1924 *Survey* (N.Y.) 15 Aug. 536/1 'Straightness of Spirit'—interpreting this title literally—is the goal toward which the recently organized Association of American Orthopsychiatrists will bend their efforts. **1930** (*title*) American journal of orthopsychiatry. A journal of human behavior (American Orthopsychiatric Association). **1956** O. POLLAK *Integrating Sociol. & Psychoanal. Concepts* iii. ix. 221 A field as energetic and imbued with the spirit of experimentation in practice as orthopsychiatry. **1971** E. M. BOWER *Orthopsychiatry & Educ.* 17 (*heading*) The challenge to education and orthopsychiatry.

orthopter. Add: (Later example.)

1935 *Discovery* July 199/1 Another orthopter, *Ephippigera vitium* Latr...lives in the Pacific and west Mediterranean areas, and in some places in Central Europe as a 'Pontic relic'.

† **2.** *Aeronaut.* Also **-ptere.** [ad. F. *orthoptère* (de Ponton d'Amécourt 1862: see S. Stubelius *Balloon, Flying-Machine, Helicopter* (1960) 90); so called because of the 'straight' (vertical) motion of the wings.] = *ORNITHOPTER. *Obs.*

App. misinterpreted at first in Eng. as referring to a clockwork flying model. The word was superseded *c* 1909 by *ornithopter*, and for a time attempts were made (chiefly in dicts. and glossaries) to differentiate the meanings of the two words on etymological grounds. (See S. Stubelius *Balloon, Flying-Machine, Helicopter* (1960) 93–7.)

1868 *Catal. First Exhib. Aeronaut. Soc. Gt. Brit.* 11 (*heading*) Working models. 12 Orthoptere. Viscount de Ponton d'Amecourt,..Paris. **1873** J. B. PETTIGREW *Animal Locomotion* 217 MM. Nadar, Pontin [*sic*] d'Amécourt, and de la Landelle have constructed clockwork models (*orthopteres*), which..raise themselves into the air. **1887** tr. *J. Verne's Clipper of Clouds* vii. 65 If the orthopter—striking like the wings of a bird—raised itself by beating the air, the helicopter raised itself by striking the air obliquely with the fins of the screw as it mounted on an inclined plane. **1906** *Sci. Amer.* 18 Aug. 115/3 'Aéronef', or 'appareil d'aviation' (aviation apparatus) means an apparatus heavier than air, of which there are several kinds, such as..(3) L'Orthoptère (orthopter) or mechanical bird, i.e., an aëronef sustained and propelled by beating wings. **1909** [see *ORNITHOPTER]. **1909** *Westm. Gaz.* 23 Mar. 4/2 The Lamplough orthopter is not dependent for its sustentation in the air on rapid motion. **1910** *Flight* II. 58/1 All types of helicopters [*sic*] and orthopters. **1917** *Jane's All World's Aircraft* A. 10/2 *Orthopter*, an intended-to-fly machine in which the wings are flapped mechanically in a manner which the designer believes would be the right way for a bird to flap its wings if its Creator had known more about aero-dynamics.

orthopteran, *a.* (Examples.)

1900 *Proc. U.S. Nat. Museum* XXIII. 393 The Orthopteran genus *Trimerotropis.* **1956** *Nature* 10 Mar. 490/1 This is a preliminary report of an investigation in progress dealing with cytogenetics of orthopteran insects of the southern hemisphere.

orthopteroid (ǫɹþǫ·ptĕroid), *a.* and *sb. Ent.* [f. ORTHOPTERA *sb. pl.* (P. A. Latreille in C. S. Sonnini *Buffon's Hist. Nat. Crustacés & Insectes* (1802) III. 267) + -OID.] **A.** *adj.* Belonging or pertaining to a group of insect orders closely related to the Orthoptera. **B.** *sb.* An insect included in this group.

1887 A. HEILPRIN *Geogr. & Geol. Distribution Animals* 146 The discovery..of an apparent orthopteroid (Palæoblattina) in the most nearly equivalent deposits of Calvados, France. **1889** NICHOLSON & LYDEKKER *Man. Palæont.* (ed. 3) I. 593 The Orthopteroid section of the *Palæodictyoptera* includes a group of forms representing the modern Cockroaches. **1910** *Encycl. Brit.* XIII. 432/1 Orthopteroid wing-neuration. **1942** E. O. ESSIG *College Entomol.* ii. 15 Frons—a single sclerite between and below the branches of the epicranial suture; carries the single frontal ocellus of orthopteroid insects. **1973** W. S. ROMOSER *Sci. of Entomol.* xi. 323 Like the paleopterous forms, orthopteroid insects are hemimetabolous.

orthopterous, *a.* (Later examples.)

1895 D. SHARP in *Cambr. Nat. Hist.* V. viii. 198 Three millimetres is the least length known for an Orthopterous insect. **1920** W. J. LUCAS *Monogr. Brit. Orthoptera* p. v, One or two new ones [*sc.* species] may fairly be looked for, when those naturalists who investigate our orthopterous fauna have become more numerous. **1965** D. R. RAGGE *Grasshoppers, Crickets & Cockroaches Brit. Isles* 2 The various types of Orthopterous insect have little in common.

orthoptic *a.* (*sb.*) Add: **3.** Substitute for def.: Employing the principles of orthoptics; of or pertaining to orthoptics. (Earlier and later examples.)

1886 C. M. CULVER tr. *Landolt's Refraction & Accomm. of Eye* v. 407 We may hope to effect a cure of the strabismus by means of orthoptic treatment, with the aid of stereoscopic exercise. **1907** J. H. PARSONS *Dis. Eye* xxviii. 559 If there is any evidence of some degree of binocular vision it may be advisable to attempt to cultivate this by orthoptic treatment. **1932** *Brit. Med. Jrnl.* 14 May 918/2 The Royal Westminster Ophthalmic Hospital established an orthoptic department..in January, 1930. **1968** KATZIN & WILSON *Strabismus in Childhood* viii. 65 In most patients with crossed eyes orthoptic exercises play a prominent role in treatment.

B. *sb. pl.* **orthoptics** (const. as *sing.*). The treatment (esp. by means of eye exercises) of defects in the action of the eye muscles, esp. those causing defective binocular vision.

1934 *Brit. Jrnl. Ophthalm.* XVIII. 429 The first examination in Orthoptics to be held in London will take place on July 3rd and 4th, at the Royal Westminster Ophthalmic Hospital. **1957** *New Scientist* 9 May 38/2 Many opticians nowadays have specialised in orthoptics..and it is now included in the training of all ophthalmic students. **1957** A. HUXLEY *Let.* 12 Jan. (1969) 815 Optometrists..are steadily adopting more and more the Batesian procedures into their system of 'orthoptics'. **1963** [see *orthoptically* below].

Hence **ortho·ptically** *adv.*, by means of or with regard to orthoptics. Also **ortho·ptist,** one who practises orthoptics.

1937 LYLE & JACKSON *Pract. Orthoptics in Treatment of Squint* i. 3 The orthoptist must remember that most squinting children who are old enough to have experienced the taunts of their schoolfellows suffer considerably from self-consciousness and inferiority. **1945** *Brit. Jrnl. Ophthalm.* XXIX. 420 (*heading*) An analysis of one hundred cases of strabismus treated orthoptically. **1963** *Arch. Ophthalm.* LXX. 117/1, 177 cases of accommodative strabismus..had been discharged as orthoptically satisfactory after treatment with glasses or miotics alone, or in combination with orthoptics and surgery. **1969** H. A. KNOLL in R. Kingslake *Appl. Optics* V. x. 282 The orthoptist is trained to diagnose and treat by nonmedical means binocular muscle anomalies. **1972** *Daily Tel.* (Colour Suppl.) 28 Apr. 10/1 On the staff at Ryegate..are a physiotherapist, an occupational therapist, an orthoptist (a therapist for the eyes), [etc.].

orthoroentgenography (ǭ:ɹþoröntgĕnǫ·grăfi, *etc.*). *Med.* [f. ORTHO- + *roentgenography* s.v. *ROENTGEN-.] A technique for producing radiographs showing the exact sizes of organs or bones by using a narrow beam of X rays perpendicular to the plate or film.

There are other pronuncs. of this word and its derivs. analogous to those of *ROENTGENOGRAPHY, -GRAM, etc.

1946 W. T. GREEN et al. in *Jrnl. Bone & Joint Surg.* XLIV. 60 In a study of growth by the Havard Infantile Paralysis Commission, it was found necessary to develop a method of measuring the lower extremities which would meet the following requirements... The method to be described has been designated 'orthoroentgenography'. **1972** M. O. TACHDJIAN *Pediatric Orthopedics* II. vii. 1486/2 The advantages of orthoroentgenography are that the true length of each bone can be measured, because magnification due to divergence of rays is eliminated by directing only perpendicular rays at the ends of the long bones.

Hence **orthoroe·ntgenogram,** a radiograph produced by orthoroentgenography; **o:rthoroentgenogra·phic** *a.*, (done by means) of orthoroentgenography.

1946 *Jrnl. Bone & Joint Surg.* XLIV. 63 The true length of each bone can be measured directly from orthoroentgenograms without computation. *Ibid.* 65 Orthoroentgenographic measurement of a dissected adult femur, 45·7 centimeters long, gave a length of 45·5 centimeters. **1951** L. A. W. KEMP *Students' Radiol. Math.* v. 62 In the second orthoroentgenographic technique, a narrow slit..in a sheet of metal opaque to X-rays, is arranged to be vertically below the source S, so that at any instant there is only a narrow line of X-rays..across the patient, the plane containing the rays being vertical. **1972** M. O. TACHDJIAN *Pediatric Orthopedics* II. vii. 1486/1 The technique [*sc.* teleoroentgenography] is not satisfactory for serial mensurations and bone detail is much less than that seen on spot orthoroentgenograms.

orthoscopic, *a.* Add to def.: *spec.* of binocular vision: without the reversal of convexity and concavity produced by pseudoscopic instruments. (Earlier and later examples.)

1853 *Q. Jrnl. Microsc. Sci.* I. 305 To produce orthoscopic binocular vision, simple, not erecting eye-pieces, are required. **1881** *Jrnl. R. Microsc. Soc.* I. 204 Orthoscopic vision is always obtained, when the right half of the right pupil and the left half of the left pupil only are employed—pseudoscopic vision in the opposite case. **1937** *Jrnl. Optical Soc. Amer.* XXVII. 333/1 The imagery should be as nearly orthoscopic as possible.

orthosis (ǭɹþōu·sis). *Med.* Pl. **-oses.** [f. Gr. ὄρθωσις making straight (f. ὀρθοῦν to set straight: see -OSIS.)] An artificial external device, as a brace or splint, which may be powered or unpowered and which prevents or assists relative movement in the limbs or the spine.

1958 H. A. RUSK *Rehabilitation Med.* ix. 196 Above all it is necessary for doctor, orthotist, and therapist to be fully aware of the tremendous physical and emotional impact of the orthosis on the total rehabilitation of the patient. **1966** *3rd Ann. Rocky Mountain Bioengin. Symposium* 79/1 The Rancho Electric Arm is the outgrowth of seven years of experimental work in upper extremity external power orthoses. **1970** J. KJØLBYE in G. Murdoch *Prosthetic & Orthotic Pract.* xi. 459 Orthoses used in conjunction with physiotherapy are of greatest use in the prevention of deformity by protecting the weaker group of muscles from the overactivity of their antagonists.

So **ortho·tic** *a.*, serving as an orthosis; of or employing an orthosis or orthoses; **ortho·tics,** the application of orthoses; **ortho·tist,** one who practises orthotics.

1951 *Jrnl. of OALMA* May 34/1 Skilled technicians now called Certified Orthotists or Prosthetists. **1955** *Artificial Limbs* May 99/1 On March 12 and 13, a two-day session dealing with prosthetic and orthotic devices brought together at the Statler Hotel in Los Angeles a record attendance of prosthetists, orthotists, and orthopedic surgeons. **1957** *Ibid.* Spring 116/1 Approximately 60 percent of the class time in orthotics was used for actual laboratory practice. **1968** *Math. Biosciences* III. 156 Essential problems in prosthetics, orthotics, remote handling, and robot design have a common theoretical background. **1970** R. D. MUCKART in G. Murdoch *Prosthetic & Orthotic Pract.* xi. 481 The orthotist would thus be able to devote his time more profitably to the solution of the splintage problems of the severely disabled patient. **1975** *Observer* 8 June 1/7 A critical report of the orthotic industry..is now circulating among orthopaedic surgeons. **1976** *Alyn & Deeside Observer* 10 Dec. 22/3 (Advt.), The post also offers experience in Plaster Work and Orthotics.

orthostat (ǭ·ɹþostæt). *Archæol.* Also **-state** (-stēit). [ad. Gr. ὀρθοστάτ-ης upright shaft, pillar, building stone laid with the longest edge vertical.] An upright stone or slab, either forming part of a building or set in the ground as a monument.

[**1909** A. MARQUAND *Greek Archit.* ii. 67 Walls of temples and other buildings were usually provided with both base and crown. The orthostatai were set off from the vertical face of the wall.., and, even when the entire wall was covered with stucco, formed a more or less visible base.] **1926** D. G. HOGARTH *Kings of Hittites* ii. 26 (*caption*) Orthostats of south gateway. **1933** *Antiquity* VII. 222 The orthostates rest against pairs of jambs kept apart by sills rising to about half the height of the chambers. **1950** G. E. DANIEL *Prehist. Chamber Tombs Eng. & Wales* iii. 34 Megaliths used as orthostats, i.e. set in the ground and standing upright. **1950** H. L. LORIMER *Homer & Monuments* 419 The actual remains of Geometric temples would lead us to expect a few courses of undressed stones (possibly with an outer facing of orthostats) supporting a wall of crude brick. **1970** *Encycl. Brit.* XVIII. 454/1 The practice of setting a series of stone slabs, called orthostates, at the bottom of a wall below the mud-brick upper parts became common in the Assyrian period and was seen again in Hittite architecture. **1972** Y. YADIN *Hazor* ii. vii. 72 The most important of these is a small orthostat of a lion... The lion is clearly an entrance-jamb orthostat. **1974** F. EMERY *Oxfordshire Landscape* i. 36 They, or their close followers the Beaker people, also built circles of standing stones..and orthostats.

orthostatic (ǭɹþostæ·tik), *a.* [f. ORTHO- + STATIC *a.*; in sense 1 coined as F. *orthostatique* (J. Teissier 1899, in *Semaine Medicale* 425/1).]

1. *Med.* Caused by, or resulting from, an upright posture; manifested or occurring while a person is standing up.

1902 *Med. Ann.* XX. 90 The condition..variously called intermittent or cyclical albuminuria, is perhaps best defined by the term orthostatic albuminuria, for..position is the factor which determines the appearance and disappearance of the albumin. **1927** *Physiol. Rev.* VII. 466 Disturbed vascular conditions, such as orthostatic albuminuria. **1961** *Lancet* 26 Aug. 475/1 The unusual disorder known as orthostatic hypotension of unknown origin. **1971** *New Scientist* 29 July 249/1 The cosmonauts of Soyuz 9 suffered from severe orthostatic hypotension and for several days were unable to assume the erect posture unaided.

2. *Archæol.* Set on end; constructed of stones or slabs set on end.

1912 T. E. PEET *Rough Stone Monuments* p. iv, The first and most important principle, that on which the whole of the megalithic construction may be said to be based, is the use of the orthostatic block, i.e. the block set up on its edge. *Ibid.*, The orthostatic slabs were often deeply sunk into the ground where this consisted of earth or soft rock. **1926** D. G. HOGARTH *Kings of Hittites* ii. 29 Ground-courses of orthostatic slabs. **1941** *Proc. Prehist. Soc.* VII. 1 The use of large stones for orthostatic walling. **1950** G. E. DANIEL *Prehist. Chamber Tombs Eng. & Wales* iii. 34 In almost all the chambers with orthostatic walls there is also intercalary walling to fill up the spaces.

Hence **orthosta·tically** *adv.*

1950 *Chambers's Encycl.* IX. 234/1 The burial chamber or chamber tomb, a vault or chamber walled with megaliths set orthostatically side by side.

o:rthostereosco·pic, *a.* [f. ORTHO- + STEREOSCOPIC *a.*] Showing solid objects with their true proportions and perspective, *spec.* without the reversal of convexity and concavity produced in pseudoscopic instruments.

1892 *Jrnl. Quekett Microsc. Club* V. 46 If orthostereoscopic vision is required the transposition must be corrected. **1937** *Jrnl. Optical Soc. Amer.* XXVII. 339/2 In the x-ray clinic, orthostereoscopic radiographs help to reduce error in diagnoses. **1941** R. M. ALLEN *Photomicrogr.* v. 236 It is not essential, especially for higher-power work with single objectives, that true orthostereoscopic effects be obtained. **1966** H. ASHER tr. *Valyus's Stereoscopy* ii. 94 Observation of these conditions ensures that an orthostereoscopic image is produced, i.e. one which shows a correct proportion in depth and undistorted perspective, and allows the visual fusion of the two stereograms into a single spatial percept.

Hence **orthoste·reoscope**, a binocular microscope giving orthostereoscopic images; **o:rthostereosco·pically** *adv.*, in an orthostereoscopic manner; **o:rthostereo·scopy**, the production of orthostereoscopic images.

1892 *Jrnl. Quekett Microsc. Club* V. 52 If the two prisms were joined into one, it would..make a very efficient orthostereoscope. **1928** B. J. LEGGETT *Theory & Pract. Radiol.* III. ix. 430 This process of ortho-stereoscopy has important practical bearings. **1937** *Jrnl. Optical Soc. Amer.* XXVII. 333/2 A Greenough type microscope, if the magnification is not too high, may be built to operate orthostereoscopically for related combinations of objective and eyepiece pairs. *Ibid.* 339/2 Accuracy in the making of contour maps by aerial stereophotography depends upon the complete achievement of orthostereoscopy. **1966** H. ASHER tr. *Valyus's Stereoscopy* ix. 380 Only when all these conditions are observed will the primary image system 'see' the object orthostereoscopically. *Ibid.* 409 To reproduce a natural relief the conditions of orthostereoscopy must be observed.

orthotropic, *a.* Add: **2.** Having three mutually perpendicular planes of elastic symmetry at each point.

1943 *Q. Appl. Math.* I. 128 Another important special case is that of an orthotropic elliptic plate bent by a linear load, for which the solution is new. **1963** P. FERN tr. *Lekhnitskii's Theory Elasticity of Anisotropic Elastic Body* i. 21 Delta-wood and plywood can be considered as homogeneous and orthotropic in the first approximation. **1971** P. J. DOWLING in K. C. Rockey et al. *Devel. in Bridge Design & Constr.* 557 After the war the orthotropic deck bridge was developed and this form of bridge has now become a common form of construction..where saving in weight or depth of construction are important parameters. **1975** CUSENS & PAMA *Bridge Deck Anal.* i. 18 For long-span steel bridges, the deck is frequently a plate with longitudinal stiffeners (stringers). This form of construction is known to steel designers as an orthotropic plate.

orthotropy. Add: **2.** The condition of being orthotropic.

1966 F. J. PLANTEMA *Sandwich Construction* v. 118 Numerical results have been computed only for a few typical cases of orthotropy corresponding to corrugated-core sandwich plates and sandwich plates having standard glass-fabric laminate faces. **1974** R. SZILARD *Theory & Anal. Plates* iii. 375 If we assume that the principal directions of orthotropy coincide with the *X* and *Y* coordinate axes, it becomes evident that four elastic constants..are required for the description of the orthotropic stress-strain relationships.

orticant (ǭ·ɹtikănt), *a.* (*sb.*) [ad. It. *orticante* stinging, URTICANT *a.*] Irritating to the skin. Hence as *sb.*, an orticant agent.

1939 L. W. MARRISON tr. *Sartori's War Gases* xiv. 217 The introduction of one or more sulphur atoms..between the chloroethyl groups..confers orticant properties. **1944** R. W. MONCRIEFF *Chem. Senses* vi. 140 In addition to the lachrymatories..there are the skin irritants or 'orticants'. *Ibid.* 141 Sym-dichloroacetone..has an 'orticant' action on the skin as well as being lachrymatory. **1965** *Economist* 27 Mar. 1361/3 Orticants are related to these [*sc.* vesicants like mustard gas] and cause itching. **1970** *Daily Tel.* (Colour Suppl.) 20 Feb. 19 Harassing agents..come in a profusion of varieties. There are..lachrymators..; orticants, which irritate the skin, and vomiting gases.

Ortolani's sign (ǭ·ɹtǒlāni). *Med.* [named after Marino *Ortolani*, Italian who described it (*La Lussazione congenita dell' Anca* 1948)).] A click which can be obtained from and is diagnostic of congenital dislocation of the hip in the newborn.

1965 RAINS & CAPPER *Bailey & Love's Short Pract. Surg.* (ed. 13) xvii. 346 The Ortolani test takes precedence over radiography. **1974** A. HENRY in R. M. Kirk et al. *Surgery* xv. 322 Diagnosis of the unstable or 'dislocatable' hip should be made in the newborn, and all midwives and doctors who participate in the care of the newborn child should be familiar with the examination of the baby's hip—Ortolani's sign.

‖**ortstein** (ǭ·ɹtʃtəin). *Soil Sci.* [G.] A hard-pan, esp. one in the B horizon of a podzol that is cemented with iron and organic matter.

1906 E. W. HILGARD *Soils* x. 184 The latter class of hardpans is especially conspicuous in the case of swampy ground and damp forests, where 'moorbedpan' and red-dish 'ortstein' are characteristic. **1932** G. W. ROBINSON *Soils* iii. 57 The most widely spread type of pan is that formed by deposition of hydrated ferric oxide, the so-called iron pan or 'ortstein'. **1972** C. B. HUNT *Geol. Soils* x. 234 Some hardpans are formed by accumulations of organic matter..as in the well cemented, lower layers (ortstein) of a Ground Water Podzol Soil.

Ortygian (ǫɹti·dʒiăn). [f. L. *Ortygi-us* (f. Gr. Ὀρτυγία (ὄρτυξ a quail) Quail-island) + -AN.] **1.** Of or pertaining to Ortygia, the ancient name of the island of Delos, held to be the birthplace of Apollo and Artemis.

1640 J. GOWER tr. *Ovid's Fasti* v. 120 These prayers make Mercury in heaven to smile, Remembring his Ortygian cheat yerwhile. **1729** G. ADAMS tr. *Sophocles' Tragedies* II. 180 And his [Apollo's] Ortygian Sister like-wise..Fire-bearing Diana. **1866** J. B. ROSE tr. *Ovid's Metamorphoses* I. 27 A votress of the power Ortygian. **1956** E. POUND tr. *Sophocles' Women of Trachis* 12 Sylvan Artemis, torch-lit Artemis With thy Ortygian girls.

2. Of or pertaining to Ortygia, an island which forms part of the city of Syracuse in Sicily. *rare.*

1820 SHELLEY *Arethusa* in *Posthumous Poems* (1824) 160 And at night they sleep In the rocking deep Beneath the Ortygian shore.

Orvieto. Add: (Earlier and later examples.) Also *attrib.*

[**1673** J. RAY *Observations Journey Low-Countries* 363 Heer [*sc.* in Rome] is great variety of Wines..as Greco, Lagrime of Naples..Orvietano.] **1846** DICKENS *Pictures from Italy* 159 Such wine in flasks, as the Orvieto. **1849** THACKERAY *Pendennis* I. xxxv. 344 We had some Orvieto wine for dinner. **1926** P. M. SHAND *Bk. Wine* viii. 225 Umbria is chiefly noted for its white wines, of which the most famous name is Orvieto. **1940** M. HEALY *Stay me with Flagons* 70 Orvieto, now sweet, now dry, offers varied charms. **1967** A. LICHINE *Encycl. Wines* 535 Orvieto is white, and one of Italy's most consistently delightful wines, some of it semi-sweet, some of it dry... The market for Orvieto *amabile* or *abboccato*..has fallen off... Sweet Orvieto has a particular charm and special delicacy... Dry Orvieto is usually considerably higher in alcohol. **1974** N. MARSH *Black as he's Painted* ii. 39 Bottles of dry Orvieto..and other Italian wines.

b. Used *attrib.* to designate a type of majolica ware manufactured there.

1925 B. RACKHAM tr. *E. Hannover's Pott. & Porc.* I. III. ii. 96 It requires a practised eye to distinguish between a genuine and a spurious Orvieto jug. **1959** G. SAVAGE *Antique Collector's Handbk.* 70 The earliest *maiolica* was a series of wares painted in green and manganese purple at Orvieto and elsewhere, and most are loosely called 'Orvieto ware'. **1960** R. G. HAGGAR *Conc. Encycl. Cont. Pott. & Porc.* 338/2 *Orvieto*, a distinctive class of early Italian maiolica painted in coppergreen and manganese-purple with decorations and shapes of a distinctly 'Gothic' type. **1973** *Times* 3 Nov. 2/2 A Parke Bernet expert called in to look over what was there found the Medici bowl in a cupboard under a broken Orvieto dish.

Orwellian (ǫɹwe·liăn), *a.* [f. the name of 'George *Orwell*', the nom-de-plume of the English writer Eric Blair (1903–50) + -IAN.] Characteristic or suggestive of the writings of 'George Orwell', esp. in his satirical novel *1984* which portrays a form of totalitarian state seen by him as arising naturally out of the political circumstances of his time. Hence as *sb.*, an admirer of the ideas of Orwell. So **Orwe·llianism, O·rwellism.**

1950 M. MCCARTHY *On Contrary* (1962) 187 A leap into the Orwellian future. **1952** *Time* 1 Sept. 19/2 Under the new rules, the Politburo and the Orgburo will be merged and the two ugly Orwellian names replaced by the stern old Latin 'Presidium'. **1958** *Times* 20 Feb. 11/3 In Orwellian language, 'imperious'. **1959** N. MAILER *Advts. for Myself* (1961) 309 Virtually perfect Orwellian ambivalences—(War is Peace, Love is Hate, Ignorance is Knowledge). **1961** [see *HUXLEYAN, HUXLEIAN *a.* b]. **1963** *Observer* 3 Nov. 33/1 There is an Orwellian grimness about the naming of the Abolition of Passes Act in South Africa, which ensured that an African had to carry 27 papers combined into one booklet. **1967** *Listener* 2 Nov. 583/2 It is Orwellianism transferred to the world of the commercial, in which machines work beautifully, everybody is on a kind of holiday and wears a blazer and a redcoat number, the daily flavour of the ice-cream is announced on the morning radio, [etc.]. **1970** *Guardian* 30 Nov. 11/2 His election night insistence that the blood on his face was nothing less than the blush of victory can now be seen as a triumph of public relations.., an interesting example of the progress of Orwellism in national politics. **1971** *Ibid.* 14 Jan. 7/1 McLuhanites and Orwellians are likely to block our view of their masters' arguments. **1972** *Ibid.* 17 Feb. 14/5 The Orwellian Newspeak style. **1974** *Daily Tel.* (Colour Suppl.) 20 Sept. 27/4 One sees a future Robin Day as an Orwellian Official Moderator of the Ministry of Received Truth. **1976** *Time* 5 Apr. 22/2 In foreign affairs, says Moynihan, there is something almost Orwellian about the transformation of the word liberal to mean the opposite of what it meant a decade or so ago.

orygine (ǫ·ridʒəin), *a. Zool.* [f. L. *oryg-*, stem of *oryx* (see ORYX) + -INE[1].] Resembling an antelope of the genus *Oryx*, esp. belonging to an African group including the addax, gemsbuck, roan, and sable antelopes, which share certain characteristics with the oryx, such as long horns, tufted tails, and large, square teeth.

1898 *Proc. Zool. Soc.* 352 The Addax, I think, is on the whole more an orygine type than a hippotragine. **1947** J. STEVENSON-HAMILTON *Wild Life S. Afr.* xi. 75 (*heading*) The orygine antelopes.

oryzenin (orəi·zěnin). *Biochem.* [f. L. *orȳz-a* (Gr. ὄρυζα) rice + *-enin*, prob. after *GLUTENIN.] A glutelin that is the chief protein in rice.

1908 ROSENHEIM & KAJIURA in *Jrnl. Physiol.* XXXVI. p. lv, These three proteins appear to be the only ones present in rice and we propose to call them respectively: Rice-globulin, Rice-albumin, and Oryzenin. **1926** *Jrnl. College of Agric. Hokkaido Imperial Univ.* XVI. 76 The differences between the common and the glutinous rice oryzenins are marked by their physico-chemical properties. **1952** *Chem. Abstr.* XLVI. 2747 As tested by fermenting each constituent of rice by *Aspergillus oryzae*, the odor of sake was found to be due mainly to the oryzenin. **1972** B. O. JULIANO in D. F. HOUSTON *Rice* ii. 41 Glutelin or oryzenin is the major protein fraction of brown and milled rice.

‖ **osaekomi waza** (ōsaˌekōmi waza). *Judo.* Also **osae waza.** [Jap., lit. 'art of holding', f. *osae* to press upon or against + *komi* to be packed up + *waza* art.] (See quot. 1932.)

1932 E. J. HARRISON *Art of Ju-Jitsu* v. 64 '*Osaekomi-waza*', otherwise methods of holding down one's opponent on the mats for a longer or shorter interval. *Ibid.* 65 The first trick of *osaekomi-waza*..is the so-called Locking of the Upper Four Quarters. **1941** M. FELDENKRAIS *Judo* 173 Immobilizing or holding down (osae-waza). **1956** K. TOMIKI *Judo* iii. 90 Practice in *katame-waza* (art of grappling) had better be based on that in *osae-waza* (art of holding, or hold-down). **1962** LEBELL & COUGHRAN *Handbk. Judo* vi. 103 (*heading*) Osaekomiwaza—hold on there! Hold down techniques. **1970** A. P. HARRINGTON *Judo Guide* i. 31 Methods of holding the opponent with his back largely on the ground with one or both arms under restrictive control are known as Hold-downs (Osaekomi-waza).

Osage (ōu·sēidʒ), *sb.* and *a.* [ad. Osage self-designation *wazhazhe.*] **A.** *sb.* A member of a Siouan Indian people coming originally from the Osage river valley, Missouri. Also, their language. **B.** *adj.* Of or pertaining to this people.

1698 tr. *Hennepin's New Discovery* I. 141 Several Savages of the Nations of the Osages, Cikaga, and Akansa, came to see us. **1722** D. COXE *Descr. Carolana* 16 The Yellow [River] is called the River of the Massorites, from a great Nation inhabiting in many Towns near its juncture with the River of the Osages. **1804** [see *FIX *v.* 14 b]. **1832** [see *HEAP *sb.* 4 d]. **1835** W. IRVING *Tour on Prairies* i. 7 He spoke a Babylonish jargon of mingled French-English, and Osage. **1906** *Indian Affairs: Laws & Treaties* (U.S.) (1913) III. 253 All lands belonging to the Osage tribe of Indians..shall be divided among the members of said tribe. **1931** C. TURNER tr. *von Schmidt-Pauli's We Indians* xiii. 132 The long-drawn-out and piercing war-cry of the Osages. **1933** L. BLOOMFIELD *Language* iv. 72 The Siouan family includes..Dakota,..Omaha, Osage, [etc.]. **1945** J. J. MATHEWS *Talking to Moon* 87 She..said in Osage to the chief, 'I want to tell my son about the way we did things.' **1973** A. H. WHITEFORD *N. Amer. Indian Arts* 90 Oto and Osage also wove hat and neck bands of horsehair. **1974** *Encycl. Brit. Micropædia* VII. 602/3 The discovery of oil on the Osage reservation in the late 19th century.. made the Osage a uniquely prosperous people.

Osage orange. [f. prec. + ORANGE *sb.*[1]] = *MACLURA, a tree native to Arkansas and neighbouring regions formerly occupied by the Osage tribe; also, the fruit of this tree. Also *attrib.*

1817 [see ORANGE *sb.*[1] 3 a]. **1838** H. W. ELLSWORTH *Valley Upper Wabash* v. 52 These fences, whose tops are covered with a luxuriant growth of the wild locust hawthorn, or Osage Orange. **1846** D. J. BROWNE *Trees Amer.* 465 The Osage Orange-tree. **1857** *Trans. Illinois Agric. Soc.* II. 23 The practicability of successfully cultivating the Osage Orange plant into a protective hedge. **1859** [see ORANGE *sb.*[1] 3 a]. **1891** *Harper's Mag.* Sept. 579/2 There was a hedge of Osage Orange on one side of the yard. **1940** E. FERGUSSON *Our Southwest* ix. 157 Mrs. Hayden found a stately adobe house with water piped in, an osage orange hedge around an orchard. **1970** *New Yorker* 28 Feb. 41/2 When we were little..we could bowl the Osage oranges down. **1974** A. DILLARD *Pilgrim at Tinker Creek* vi. 100 Beneath the overarching limbs of tulip, walnut, and Osage orange, I see the creek pour down.

Osagyefo (ōusagye·fo). [Fante]. Redeemer: a name given to Kwame Nkrumah (1909–72), first prime minister of Ghana (1952–60), president of the Republic (1960–66).

1961 *Guardian* 29 Sept. 10/1 The Osagyefo (or Redeemer, as he is called by his press). **1964** *Economist* 14 Mar. 983/3 The Osagyefo offered a careful welcome. **1965** *Ibid.* 24 Apr. 389/1 Everyone's suspicions of the Osagyefo (it means redeemer) were discussed. **1975** H. R. ISAACS in H. M. Patel et al. *Say not the Struggle Nought Availeth* 265 He found it impossible to follow Nkrumah on the way to becoming the Osagyefo, the Messiah, the Savior of the People.

osazone (ǭu·săzǭun). *Chem.* [f. the suffix -*osazone*, ad. G. -*osazon* (E. Fischer 1884, in *Ber. d. Deut. Chem. Ges.* XVII. 580): see -OSE², AZO-, and -ONE.] Any of the yellow crystalline solids whose molecules contain two adjacent hydrazone groups, which are obtained by treating compounds containing the groups —CO·CHOH— or —CO·CO— with phenylhydrazine and are used for characterizing sugars.

1888 *Jrnl. Chem. Soc.* LIV. 1267 The osazones of all saccharoses dissolve in cold, fuming hydrochloric acid with a dark-red coloration. **1938** M. L. WOLFROM in H. Gilman *Org. Chem.* II. xvi. 1404 The three fundamental procedures used by Fischer..in his great feat of elucidating the configuration of the sugars were osazone formation, oxidation to *meso* acids.., and the methods for building up or degrading the members of the sugar series. **1972** J. W. SUTTIE *Introd. Biochem.* iii. 28 Sugars which differ in configuration only at carbons 1 or 2, such as glucose, mannose, and fructose, will give the same osazone.

Osborne (ǫ·zbǭəɹn). The name of a former royal residence on the Isle of Wight used *attrib.* and *absol.* to designate a type of sweetish plain biscuit.

Said by the manufacturers (private communication 14 March 1977) to have been first made in 1860. It was originally intended to name them after Queen Victoria, but she asked that the biscuit should be named after her favourite home—Osborne—on the Isle of Wight.

1876 *Official Guide Cunard Steamship Co.* 158 (Advt.), Huntley & Palmers..List of Biscuits..Osborne Biscuits. **1888** *Mrs. Beeton's Bk. Househ. Managem.* ii. 31/2 Biscuits..Osborne..1*s.* 6*d.* per tin. **1911** A. BENNETT *Hilda Lessways* VI. vi. 402, I should like another biscuit. But I don't want the Osbornes—the others. **1926** W. DE LA MARE *Connoisseur* 49 My stranger in the tea shop had been refreshing himself with Osborne biscuits. **1938** S. BECKETT *Murphy* v. 96 The biscuits..were the same as always, a Ginger, an Osborne, a Digestive, a Petit Beurre. **1960** R. COLLIER *House called Memory* ii. 28 My mother's first memory..was of sitting on the steps..and being given some Osborne biscuits. **1972** D. BLOODWORTH *Any Number can Play* x. 77 The gibbon..grabbed three Osborne biscuits from a tin on the low, marble table.

osbornite (ǫ·zbǭəɹnəit). *Min.* [f. the name of George *Osborn-e* (see quot. 1870) + -ITE¹.] Titanium nitride, TiN, found as small yellow octahedra in oldhamite in the meteorite which fell at Bustee, India.

1870 N. S. MASKELYNE in *Phil. Trans. R. Soc.* CLX. 198 This microscopic mineral I wish to name Osbornite in honour of Mr. Osborne, and in order to commemorate the important service that gentleman rendered to science in preserving and transmitting to London in its entirety the stone which his zeal saved at the time of its fall, and in recording all he could collect about the circumstances associated with that fall. **1941** *Mineral. Mag.* XXVI. 36 The minute octahedra of osbornite are easily visible with a lens in the meteorite itself. **1962** B. MASON *Meteorites* x. 156 The only nitrogen mineral recorded from meteorites is osbornite, TiN, a rare accessory known only from Bustee (an enstatite achondrite).

Oscan (ǫ·skăn), *a.* and *sb.* Also 6–8 **Oscian.** [f. L. *Osc-us* (pl. *Osci*) Oscan + -AN.] **A.** *adj.* **a.** Of or pertaining to the Osci (also called Opsci, Opici), a pre-Sabellian people centred on Campania in southern Italy. **b.** Of or pertaining to the Italic language called Oscan (see sense b of the sb.).

1598 R. GRENEWEY tr. *Tacitus' Annals* IV. 95 The Oscian play, a light sport pleasing the peoples humor. **1600** HOLLAND tr. *Livy's Romane Hist.* x. 365 Such as were well seene in the Oscian toung. **1649** J. OGILBY tr. *Virgil's Aeneid* VII. 24 Saticulus with them And Oscian bands. **1728** T. GORDON tr. *Tacitus' Annals* IV, in *Works* I. 164 The Oscan Farce, formerly only the contemptible delight of the vulgar. **1731** J. TRAPP tr. *Virgil's Aeneid* VII, in *Works* III. 92 And the Oscian Band. **1797** G. BAKER tr. *Livy's Hist. Rome* II. x. 356 He..sent persons, who understood the Oscan language. **1845** [see UMBRIAN *a.* 1]. **1948** D. DIRINGER *Alphabet* II. ix. 503 The Oscan script..was an offshoot of the Etruscan alphabet in its southern Campano-Etruscan sub-species. **1958** E. PULGRAM *Tongues of Italy* xvii. 229, I do not believe in the existence of Umbrian, Oscan, and Latinian types of dialects outside of Italy. **1958** E. BADIAN *Foreign Clientelae* ix. 195 Of other patrons of Marius we know of the Herennii,..themselves of Oscan origin. **1969** E. T. SALMON *Roman Colonization* v. 88 Atella and Calatia, also joined Hannibal, as did a number of the Oscan and Greek allies of Rome in southern Italy. **1974** *Encycl. Brit. Macropædia* XIV. 789/2 The Oscan village of Pompeii..soon came under the influence of the cultured Greeks..across the bay.

B. *sb.* **a.** A member of the Osci. **b.** A name given to the Italic dialects of central and southern Italy, used by the Sabellian peoples who displaced or absorbed the Osci. See *OSCO-UMBRIAN *a.* and *sb.*

1753 C. PITT tr. *Virgil's Aeneid* VII, in *Works* III. 355 The rough Saticulan and Oscan stood. **1813** J. C. EUSTACE *Tour through Italy* II. x. 258 Oscan was not unknown even in the age of Cicero and Augustus. **1835** [see *LIGURIAN *sb.*]. **1882** [see UMBRIAN *sb.* 2]. **1897** R. S. CONWAY *Italic Dial.* II. 472 In some few cases in Oscan the final -*s* of the Nom. and Gen. is still wanting. **1934** S. ROBERTSON *Devel. Mod. Eng.* (1936) ii. 21 Of the latter [*sc.* non-Latin Italic dialects], the Oscan and the Umbrian..are to be distinguished. **1939** [see *MARSIAN *sb.* and *a.*]. **1948** D. DIRINGER *Alphabet* II. ix. 501 The Oscans..or Osci, in Greek, Oskoi or Opikoi, from Opsci or Opici..were Italic tribes who inhabited southern Italy in the second half of the first millennium B.C. **1969** H. V. MORTON *Traveller in S. Italy* vii. 272 We encountered a workman, still apparently speaking Oscan. **1969** E. T. SALMON *Roman Colonization* ii. 44 In 354, Rome signed an alliance with the Samnites, an Oscan-speaking people of the south. *Ibid.* ix. 149 Sulla's colonies in the north and south had helped to bring the use of Etruscan and Oscan to an end. **1974** *Encycl. Brit. Macropædia* XIV. 789/2 It seems certain that Pompeii, Herculaneum, and Stabiae were first settled by the Oscans. **1976** *Archivum Linguisticum* VII. 62 Latin shares a number of lexical items with Oscan.

Oscar¹ (ǫ·skăɹ). Also with small initial. *Austral.* and *N.Z.* [Rhyming slang on *Oscar Asche* (an Australian actor, 1871–1936).] Cash, money.

1919 W. H. DOWNING *Digger Dial.* 36 *Oscar*, money. **1931** W. HATFIELD *Sheepmates* xix. 161 Sit in, some o' yous that aint flyblown—.., an' their IOU's is good, if there's no real Oscar about the joint. **1942** L. MANN *Go-Getter* ii. 16 Get the oscar off Tom soon's I see him. He's honest. **1945** E. G. WEBBER *Johnny Enzed in Middle East* 20 'Well, me lending you my balance to get you out of the cart,' said the bloke, 'and them sending me the oscar so that you can pay it back.' **1949** *Newsweek* 31 Oct. 60/2 He would have been glad to buy me a pail of suds if he'd had any Oscar. **1959** D. NILAND *Big Smoke* i. 21 If you'd been fighting all those blokes in the ring you'd have more oscar in your kick now than the Prime Minister himself. **1969** [see *DINKUM B. *adj.*].

Oscar². [Said to be an arbitrary use of the Christian name of *Oscar* Pierce, 20th-c. American wheat and fruit grower (see below).] One of the statuettes awarded by the Academy of Motion Picture Arts and Sciences, Hollywood, U.S.A., for excellence in film acting, directing, etc. These awards have been made annually since 1928. So *Oscar-winner*, *-winning*.

A former secretary of the Academy of Motion Picture Arts and Sciences is said to have remarked in 1931 that the statuette reminded her of her 'Uncle Oscar', namely Oscar Pierce.

1936 *Time* 16 Mar. 56/2 Neither Director Ford nor Screenwriter Nichols appeared to claim their prizes—small gold statuettes which Hollywood calls 'Oscars'. **1949** [see *EMMY]. **1958** *Punch* 25 June 838/3 A quiet scene, with the camera in close-up, every word counting, and the actors playing for an Oscar. **1962** *Times* 30 Oct. 16/1 The Oscar-winning Fellini pictures. **1968** B. FOSTER *Changing Eng. Lang.* i. 45 The Oscar statuette is..gold-plated. **1974** *Times* 1 Mar. 13/4 Luis Buñuel's eminence as..1973 Oscar-winner. **1975** C. NESBITT *Little Love & Good Company* xix. 246 If I were to start thanking the Lunts for all the gifts..that I have received from them I should sound like an Oscar-winning starlet. **1976** *Southern Even. Echo* (Southampton) 6 Nov. (Advt. Suppl.) 5/1 Ed Begley (he got an Oscar) as a vicious town boss whose daughter (Shirley Knight) gets ruined by Newman.

b. In *transf.* use applied to any award for an outstanding performance or achievement.

1941 *Time* 2 June 82/2 That these trials..did not keep Producer Gabriel Pascal from turning out a polished and distinguished product is a transcendent Oscar in the one-time cavalryman's lap. **1947** *Sun* (Baltimore) 1 July 7/6 René Clair's 'Silence Est D'Or' (Silence Is Golden) won the grand prize of Brussels' world film competition today and was awarded the Belgian 'Oscar', a small statuette of Brussels' patron saint, St. Michael. **1949** *Natural Hist.* Nov. 417/3 If there are any 'Oscars' to be awarded in the world of animal acting, the vote of many naturalists will..go to the hognose snake. **1954** *Economist* 29 May 739/2 The first British 'Oscar' for a company report, represented by a pair of silver wall sconces, has been given to Thomas W. Ward. **1959** *Times Lit. Suppl.* 13 Nov. 662/3 Once a year it publishes an annual which is in effect a kind of collection of Oscars for design in these fields. **1963** *Guardian* 8 Feb. 8/2 An ensemble for spring..which won an export Oscar last year. **1971** *Daily Tel.* 18 Dec. 10 A local artist is being commissioned to make an 'Oscar' which will be presented annually to the publishing house which..has made the most distinctive contribution to literature. **1973** J. WAINWRIGHT *Pride of Pigs* 215 An Oscar-winning performance, lad. **1978** *Guardian* 27 Feb. 16/5 QPR had been given their first goal when an Oscar-winning dive in the penalty area by Shanks brought an unbelievable penalty decision from the referee.

oscillate, *v.* Add: **1. c.** *Electronics.* Of a circuit or device: to cause oscillations in an electric current flowing in it.

1917 R. D. BANGAY *Elem. Princ. Wireless Telegr.* I. 84 The methods employed for causing an aerial to oscillate, and thus radiate electric waves, fall under two headings. **1928** *Times* 23 Mar. 20/1 If too much retroaction is employed the circuit resistance may become negative, when the whole system will begin to oscillate. **1948** A. L. ALBERT *Radio Fund.* x. 370 If some of the output signal voltage is fed back into the control-grid in the proper manner, a vacuum tube will oscillate. **1971** L. T. AGGER *Introd. Electr.* xxiv. 432 A circuit containing inductance and capacitance will oscillate at its own natural frequency, provided it is left undisturbed after the oscillation has been started.

d. Of a radio or (*transf.*) its user: to transmit radio waves owing to faulty operation.

1921 *Wireless World* 29 Oct. 481/1 For a set to 'react' or 'oscillate' it is necessary that the main inductance and the reaction coil should be so connected that the direction of windings bear a certain relation to one another. **1926** *Westm. Gaz.* 3 Feb. 3/1 Listeners-in who oscillate may find themselves deprived of their licences. **1933** 'R. STRANGER' *Elem. Wireless* xxxvi. 181 A good way of telling when a receiver is oscillating is to have a milliammeter connected in the anode circuit of the detector... Without the milliammeter you may oscillate and not even know it. **1943** C. L. BOLTZ *Basic Radio* xiv. 222 An interesting effect is observable if the tuning condenser is used when the receiver is oscillating.

3. (Further examples.)

1883 *Phil. Trans. R. Soc.* CLXXIII. 663 The ring (with wire circuit open) was oscillated backwards and forwards. **1905** PREECE & SIVEWRIGHT *Telegraphy* (new ed.) 462 The spark gap which oscillates the energy.

4. *intr. Math.* To increase and decrease alternately as successive terms are taken (in the case of a series) or as the variable tends to infinity (in the case of a function).

1898 HARKNESS & MORLEY *Introd. Theory Analytic Functions* viii. 102 In the series $(1-1)+(1-1)+(1-1)+\ldots$, each term is 0 and the limit is 0, but the series $1-1+1-1+\ldots$ oscillates. **1940** C. A. STEWART *Adv. Calculus* i. 7 $n^2 \cos n\pi$, $n+(-1)^n n^3$ oscillate infinitely. **1973** D. G. BALL *Introd. Real Anal.* iii. 43 A sequence which has no limit at all is said to oscillate.

oscillating, *ppl. a.* Add: **2.** *Math.* Of a series or function (see *OSCILLATE *v.* 4).

1898 HARKNESS & MORLEY *Introd. Theory Analytic Functions* viii. 102 Most English text-books regard oscillating series as not divergent. **1973** D. G. BALL *Introd. Real Anal.* iii. 59 Consider the sequence $2\frac{1}{2}, -1\frac{1}{2}, 2\frac{1}{4}, -1\frac{1}{4}, 2\frac{1}{8}, -1\frac{1}{8}, 2\frac{1}{16}, -1\frac{1}{16}, \ldots$ This sequence is bounded and oscillating.

3. *Electronics.* Of an electric current or the like: undergoing rapid periodic reversals in direction. Of a circuit or device: characterized by such a current (cf. *OSCILLATE *v.* 1 c).

Oscillating as used of a current implies a much higher frequency than *alternating* and also a different origin (see *OSCILLATOR 2 a).

1906 A. E. KENNELLY *Wireless Telegr.* viii. 94 (*heading*) Energy of electric oscillations, or oscillating currents, set up in a vertical receiver. **1920** E. W. STONE *Elem. Radiotelegr.* xi. 44 If two oscillating circuits containing inductance and capacity be..coupled together, they act very differently than when they are allowed to oscillate by themselves. **1948** A. L. ALBERT *Radio Fund.* x. 386 Variations in the plate output circuit will not be reflected back into the control-grid oscillating circuit. **1974** 'I. DRUMMOND' *Power of Bug* xi. 166 The tiny transmitter..emitted a high, oscillating signal on ultra short wave.

oscillation. Add: **2. b.** *Psychol.* Fluctuation of attention or mental efficiency.

1895 *Amer. Jrnl. Psychol.* VII. 84 *Schwankungen der Aufsmerksamkeit*, oscillations *or* fluctuations of the attention. **1927** C. S. SPEARMAN *Abilities of Man* xix. 319 We may now conveniently turn to a phenomenon which may be described as oscillation of cognitive efficiency, and which probably has an intimate connection with..fatigue. *Ibid.* 326 Here in oscillation, then, we have come upon a new single and universal factor, a third in addition to *g* and perseveration. **1943** C. L. HULL *Princ. Behavior* xvii. 306 One may reasonably conjecture that it was produced by some factor in the experimental situation other than the primitive oscillation tendency. **1950** P. E. VERNON *Struct. Human Abilities* viii. 89 An Oscillation factor in rate of fluctuation of reversible perspective figures.

3. *Electronics.* A rapid alternation in the direction of flow of a current; the state of a circuit in which this is occurring; also, a rapidly varying electromagnetic field produced by such a current.

1853 tr. H. Helmholtz in *Sci. Mem. Trans. Foreign Acad.* (*Nat. Philos.*) 143 It is easy to explain this law if we assume that the discharge of a battery is not a simple motion of the electricity in one direction, but a backward and forward motion between the coatings, in oscillations which become continually smaller until the entire *vis viva* is destroyed by the sum of the resistances. **1885** *Electrician* 18 Dec. 106/1 It shows that if the resistance be reduced to nothing, whilst the coefficient of self-induction of the circuit is finite..the oscillations continue for ever undiminished in strength. **1911** *Encycl. Brit.* XXVI. 532/2 The transmitting antenna wire is alternately charged to a high potential and discharged with the production of high frequency oscillations in it. **1932** E. V. APPLETON *Thermionic Vacuum Tubes* 102 Since the applied anode potential is negative no anode current flows unless oscillations are present. **1951** A. SHEINGOLD *Fund. Radio Communication* xii. 254 The desirable operational properties of an oscillator may include the property of being self-starting, the ability to maintain continuous oscillation, [etc.]. **1959** R. L. SHRADER *Electronic Communication* xii. 307 If it is desired to prevent a radio circuit from going into oscillation, it may be necessary to introduce degeneration in it, or neutralize it. **1975** BARRON & JOYCE *Electricity* xv. 450 The electrical oscillations of a capacitor-inductor loop can be used to transmit oscillations of radio frequency.

4. *Math.* **a.** The difference between the greatest and the least values of a function in any given interval.

1893 HARKNESS & MORLEY *Treat. Theory of Functions* ii. 49 If $f(x)$ be a discontinuous function of x, which is always finite between a and b, its values within an interval δ will have an upper and a lower limit. The difference between these upper and lower limits is named the oscillation of the function. **1937** MICHELL & BELZ *Elem. Math. Analysis* I. i. 73 If the focal bounds are unequal, the sequence is said to be divergent and to have a finite oscillation. *Ibid.* 91 The functions sin *x*, (sin *x*)/*x*. The former function has a finite oscillation −1 to +1 at $x = +\infty$. **1973** G. KLAMBAUER *Real Analysis* iii. 75 The oscillation is a monotone mapping in the sense that if J_1 and J_2 are bounded open intervals and $J_1 \subset J_2$, then $\omega(f; J_1) \leqslant \omega(f; J_2)$.

b. Variation consisting of alternate increase and decrease (cf. *OSCILLATE *v.* 4).

1908 T. J. I'A. BROMWICH *Introd. Theory Infinite Series* ii. 22 If all the terms..of the series are positive, the sequence..steadily increases; and so..the series Σa_n must be either convergent or divergent; that is, oscillation is impossible. **1968** FOX & MAYERS *Computing Methods for Scientists & Engineers* vii. 129 A characteristic of a good approximation is a type of oscillation property, effectively produced by the presence of $n+2$ alternating maxima and minima of the error.

5. *attrib.*, as † *oscillation circuit* (now called *oscillator circuit*), *detector*, † *valve*; **oscillation constant** (see quot. 1940); † **oscillation transformer** = *JIGGER *sb.*[1] 5 p.

1906 A. F. COLLINS *Man. Wireless Telegr.* ii. 32 The resistance of an oscillation circuit is practically negligible. **1923** —— *Everybody's Wireless Bk.* xii. 198 The resistance of an oscillation circuit, whether it is a closed circuit or the aerial, must be made as low as possible in order to let the high frequency currents oscillate in it freely. **1908** C. C. F. MONCKTON *Radio-Telegr.* ii. 36 For different circuits, as long as the oscillation constants are the same the natural periods of vibration are the same. **1940** *Chambers's Techn. Dict.* 601/1 *Oscillation constant*, the square root of the product of the inductance (in henries) and the capacitance (in farads) of a resonant circuit. **1908** J. A. FLEMING *Elem. Man. Radiotelegr.* ix. 324 It is necessary to employ in the receiving circuit an oscillation detector which is..not merely affected by oscillations, but affected to some extent proportionately to their amplitude. **1906** Oscillation transformer [see *JIGGER *sb.*[1] 5 p]. **1923** A. F. COLLINS *Everybody's Wireless Bk.* viii. 130 There are two distinct types of tuning coils used for continuous wave sending sets, and these are (1) the helix, or close-coupled coil, and (2) the oscillation transformer, or loose-coupled coil. The former gives much better results. **1906** *Proc. Physical Soc.* XX. 177 (*heading*) The construction and use of oscillation valves for rectifying high-frequency electric currents. **1908** J. A. FLEMING *Elem. Man. Radiotelegr.* vi. 205 A very simple but effective form of oscillation valve was invented by the author in 1904.

oscillator. 2. a. Substitute for def.: an apparatus for generating oscillatory electric currents by non-mechanical means. (Add earlier and later examples.)

1889 *Electrician* 9 Aug. 359/1 A practical application is to the theory of a Hertzian oscillator. **1907, 1908** [see *HERTZIAN *a.*]. **1933** *Geogr. Jrnl.* LXXXII. 327 In the shoal range the sound producer is a Type 399 oscillator mounted inside the ship. **1951** A. SHEINGOLD *Fund. Radio Communication* xii. 263 Special oscillators, viz., the klystron and the magnetron, have been designed for operation in the very-high-frequency range. **1962** A. NISBETT *Technique Sound Studio* xii. 202 An oscillator is a valid 'concrete' sound source. **1970** B. ZEINES *Electronic Communication Syst.* viii. 327 Essentially, a feedback oscillator is an amplifier deriving its input signal from its own output. **1977** N. FREELING *Gadget* v. 222 The oscillator is a multi-vibrator affair using a couple of integrated circuit chips.

b. A person who causes or allows a radio to transmit radio waves (cf. *OSCILLATE *v.* 1 d).

1927 *Daily Tel.* 1 Mar. 6 Cases where engineers..have succeeded in tracking down oscillators. **1927** *Glasgow Herald* 20 Sept. 8/2 The running-to-earth of offending oscillators.

3. Something that moves to and fro.

1911 *Sci. Abstr.* A. XIV. 402 In the theory referred to [of 1901] the emission of the elements of energy is assumed to be excited by the continuous steady absorption of energy from the radiation incident upon one of the assumed oscillators. This the author [*sc.* Planck] now replaces by the assumption that the emission and absorption are entirely independent. **1936** P. M. MORSE *Vibration & Sound* ii. 27 Every driven oscillator is mass controlled in the frequency range well above its natural frequency ν_0, is resistance controlled near ν_0.., and is stiffness controlled for frequencies much smaller than ν_0. **1970** G. K. WOODGATE *Elem. Atomic Struct.* iii. 45 In trying to make a model of a one-electron atom out of three classical oscillators (one for each direction of polarization) we do not take account of the fact that the atom can emit many frequencies..whereas the classical oscillators emit only one frequency. **1973** *Country Life* 19 July 151/2 The best oscillators have a device which enables the degree of oscillation to be varied from a wide to a narrow throw.

4. *attrib.*, as *oscillator circuit*.

1931 MOYER & WOSTREL *Radio Handbk.* VII. 390 (*heading*) Typical oscillator circuits. **1970** B. ZEINES *Electronic Communications Syst.* viii. 326 Oscillator circuits are commonly used in communication systems.

oscillatory, *a.* Add: Now also with pronunc. (ǫsi·lătəri). **2.** *Electronics.* Of a current: = *OSCILLATING *ppl. a.* 3. Of a circuit or device: capable of sustaining oscillations (*OSCILLATION 3).

1853 *Phil. Mag.* V. 399 It is probable that many remarkable phenomena which have been observed in connexion with electrical discharges are due to the oscillatory character which we have found to be possessed when the condition..$C < 4A/k^2$ is fulfilled. **1878** *Jrnl. Soc. Telegr. Engin.* VII. 319 The discharge is oscillatory if R is less than 40,000 ohms, and continuous if it is greater than that amount. **1905** *Electrician* Feb. 614/1 The effect on the rate of radiation, of varying the length of that portion of the air wire included in the coupled oscillatory circuit. **1948** SLURZBERG & OSTERHELD *Essent. Radio* x. 449 The essential parts of a vacuum-tube oscillator are (1) the oscillatory or tank circuit,..(2) a vacuum-tube amplifier, (3) a feedback circuit. **1971** L. T. AGGER *Introd. Electr.* 442 Calculate the natural frequency of an oscillatory circuit in which the inductance is 0·1 H and the capacitance is 10 μF. **1973** J. YARWOOD *Electr. & Magnetism* xi. 428 The oscillatory current obtained by the discharge of a capacitor through an inductance decays in amplitude with a logarithmic decrement of $RT/2L$.

3. *Math.* = *OSCILLATING *ppl. a.* 2.

1908 T. J. I'A. BROMWICH *Introd. Theory Infinite Series* i. 16 Since an oscillatory sequence always contains at least two convergent sub-sequences (those giving the extreme limits),..an oscillatory series can always be made to converge by grouping the terms in brackets. **1968** H. M. LIEBERSTEIN *Course in Numerical Anal.* (1969) vii. 126 The error term is oscillatory and unbounded... In computation with small *h* one will see for small *n* very good answers being produced, but eventually as *n*..becomes larger, a 'flowering' will take place as the oscillatory error term takes over.

oscillogram (ǫ̆si·lŏgræm). [f. as prec.: see -GRAM.] A record obtained by means of an oscillograph.

1903 *Jrnl. Inst. Electr. Engin.* XXXII. 43 (*heading*) A study of the phenomenon of resonance in electric circuits by the aid of oscillograms. **1917** G. D. SHEPARDSON *Telephone Apparatus* iii. 32 As illustrative of the original oscillograms Fig. 7 shows the record of the sound *d* in *day*. **1938** *Amer. Speech* XIII. 69/1 Simultaneous oscillograms of accented vowels taken from above and below the vocal cords reveal no measurable difference in time for the beginning of the voice vibrations. **1950** *Ann. Reg. 1949* 428 There had been brought back..more than 400 oscillograms from explosions in depths between 300 and 3,500 fathoms. **1976** *Word 1971* XXVII. 57 No matter how phonemically obvious certain vocalized continua may appear to be, the differing articulations producing these phonemic samenesses will not produce phonetically same oscillograms or sound spectrograms, the only reliable measuring artifacts in such assessments. **1976** *Gramophone* Mar. 1530/3 The accompanying oscillograms (Fig. 4) show the distortion at 40Hz for power levels of 1 and 5 watts.

oscillograph (ǫ̆si·lŏgrɑf), *sb.* [f. L. *oscill-āre* to swing + -O + -GRAPH.] **1.** An instrument for detecting and measuring the motion of a ship or of the sea.

1874 E. BERTIN *Notes on Waves & Rolling* 118 We may ..hope for favourable results from the employment of the oscillograph with two pendulums which Mr. Froude has invented; the French Admiralty has caused a similar instrument to be constructed. **1896** *Trans. Inst. Naval Archit.* XXXVII. 322 The graphic tracing of the movements of the sea with the help of the 'oscillograph' was undertaken. **1904** C. H. PEABODY *Naval Archit.* 344 Investigations of the rolling of ships in quiet water and among waves have been made..by aid of instruments known as oscillographs which have slow and quick pendulums, and registering devices.

2. [ad. F. *oscillographe* (A. Blondel 1893, in *Compt. Rend.* CXVI. 502).] Any instrument for displaying as a continuous curve the form of a varying voltage (e.g. that associated with an oscillatory or alternating current, or one derived from a bodily or non-electrical phenomenon); properly restricted to recording instruments, but freq. also used (esp. formerly) to denote the cathode-ray oscilloscope even without the camera needed for recording the display.

1893 A. BLONDEL in *Electrician* 17 Mar. 571/1 The object of this communication is to describe some new galvanometric apparatus or oscillographs allowing one to determine by direct observation..the periodic curves of alternating currents. **1910** G. W. PIERCE *Princ. Wireless Telegr.* xviii. 181 The necessary sensitiveness..was finally obtained with a Braun's cathode tube oscillograph. **1913** *Electrician* 7 Nov. 172/1 For many purposes, particularly in the teaching of alternating currents to elementary students and in the elucidation of certain problems in the higher branches of alternating-current engineering, the kathode-ray oscillograph is convenient and practical. **1925** *Lit. Digest* 11 July 25/1 The stethoscope makes the heart-beat audible, and the oscillograph gives graphic presentation of its action. **1927**, etc. [see *OSCILLOSCOPE d]. **1932** *News Chron.* 23 Sept. 10/6 In one of the wooden huts at Slough I watched lightning flashes from thousands of miles away being recorded on the glass face of an oscillograph some 9in. in diameter. **1933** E. W. GOLDING *Electr. Measurements* xv. 526 In some forms of cathode-ray oscillograph special provision is made for photographing the wave-form under observation. **1968** M. WOODHOUSE *Rock Baby* ix. 93 The single hooded eye of an oscillograph peered from the shadows. **1974** *Sci. Amer.* Mar. 94/3 In the electromechanical oscillograph..a tiny mirror is attached to the moving coil of a galvanometer, which oscillates in sympathy with the applied voltage.

3. = *OSCILLOGRAM.

1936 *Discovery* June 197/2 Some excellent oscillographs are shown..of damped and undamped waves. **1957** *Electronics* 1 May 163/2 The same tube inserted in a tapered S-band waveguide circuit produces an oscillograph as shown in Fig. 1B. **1957** *New Biol.* XXIII. 35 Plate 11..shows some oscillographs (records made with the oscilloscope) of the songs of two species of insects. **1975** *Nature* 5 June 514/3 The photographic and line illustrations are adequate, but the oscillographs and sonograms have reproduced poorly.

oscillograph (ǫ̆si·lŏgrɑf), *v.* [f. prec. sb.] *trans.* To record or display by means of an oscillograph.

1910 G. W. PIERCE *Princ. Wireless Telegr.* xviii. 182 The drum must be driven synchronously with the alternating current which is being oscillographed. **1926** *Physical Rev.* XXVIII. 554 The signal is detected, amplified, and oscillographed.

oscillographic (ǫsi:logræ·fik), *a.* [f. *OSCILLOGRAPH *sb.* + -IC.] Of, pertaining to, or employing an oscillograph.

1908 J. ERSKINE-MURRAY tr. *Ruhmer's Wireless Teleph.* II. xiii. 145 Two oscillographic records from a singing arc. **1934** *Amer. Speech* XIV. 311/2 From an oscillographic investigation the author concludes that loudness depends on frequency. **1957** MANVELL & HUNTLEY *Technique Film Music* iii. 171 Soon afterwards Scholpo and Rimsky-Korsakoff began the oscillographic analysis of natural sounds. **1972** C. N. HERRICK *Instruments & Measurements for Electronics* xv. 356 (*heading*) Oscillographic camera equipment.

Hence **osci:llogra·phically** *adv.*, by means of or as an oscillograph. Also **oscillo·graphy,** the use of oscillographs.

1925 *Jrnl. Inst. Electr. Engin.* LXIII. 1091/1 After Braun (1897) had produced the first two-dimensional electron-jet instrument.., Zenneck (1899) proceeded to work it oscillographically. **1931** *Proc. Physical Soc.* XLIII. 502 (*heading*) A time base for the cathode-ray oscillography of irregularly recurring phenomena. **1938** *Physical Rev.* LIV. 34/2 Average heights of oscillographically recorded pulses. **1964** *Times Rev. Industry* Apr. 5/3 (Advt.), The workshop..will feature demonstrations of industrial and scientific applications of instant photography including: Photomicrography, Oscillography, [etc.]. **1974** *Nature* 8 Nov. 122/1 Each utterance was analysed oscillographically.

oscillometer (ǫsilǫ·mĭtəɹ). [f. as prec. + -METER.] **1.** A gyroscopic form of oscillograph (sense *1).

1899 *Sci. Amer.* 29 July 71/2 An interesting gyroscopic device termed the 'oscillometer', has been put on the market by a Milanese firm.

2. *Med.* [ad. F. *oscillomètre* (V. Pachon 1909, in *Compt. Rend. hebd. des Séances et Mém. de la Soc. de Biol.* 735).] An instrument for indicating or recording the magnitude and rhythm of the pulse.

1910 *Brit. Med. Jrnl.* 3 Dec. 1765/2 With the oscillometer..the disappearance or reappearance of the pulse is indicated by the needle. **1934** C. J. WIGGERS *Physiol. Health & Dis.* (1935) xl. 606 Some blood pressure instruments are equipped with a form of oscillometer by means of which the magnitude of the pressure fluctuations created within the bag can be read or recorded. **1974** PASSMORE & ROBSON *Compan. Med. Stud.* III. I. xvii. 3/2 The oscillometer measures the amplitude of pulsation at different levels of the limb and provides an index of pulsatile blood flow.

Hence **osci·llometric** *a.*; **oscillo·metry,** the use of an oscillometer.

1933 *Amer. Heart Jrnl.* VIII. 398 Oscillometric studies carried out on 214 patients revealed that the maximal oscillometric phase..did not occur at the point of disappearance of the systolic tone. **1934** WEBSTER, Oscillometry. **1961** *Neurology* XI. 25/2 Carotid oscillometry is easy to manage and is harmless as blood pressure determination. **1974** J. D. MAYNARD in R. M. Kirk et al. *Surgery* xi. 234 Oscillometry, skin temperature measurements, and plethysmography at present are only research investigations. **1974** J. R. MARSHALL in Lichtiger & Moya *Introd. Pract. Anesthesia* ix. 93 The oscillometric method of measuring blood pressure requires a wide cuff containing two narrow inflatable bags.

oscilloscope (ǫ̆si·lŏskōup). [f. as prec. + -SCOPE.] † **a.** (See quot.) *Obs.* exc. as in d.

1909 WEBSTER, *Oscilloscope*, an instrument for showing visually the changes in a varying current; an oscillograph.

† **b.** (See quots.) *Obs.*

1915 R. KNOX *Radiogr.* I. 53 The best method of detecting reverse current is by the use of an oscilloscope tube... Two aluminium wires, separated by a small gap, are enclosed in an oblong glass tube, and the wire connected with the negative pole becomes, when the current passes, surrounded by a violet fluorescence, but if each wire is alternately negative and positive both wires become fluorescent and the length of the fluorescent band indicates the intensity of the current. **1926** *Gloss. Terms Electr. Engin.* (Brit. Engin. Stand. Assoc.) 206 *Oscilloscope*, an auxiliary discharge tube in which the length of the negative glow affords an indication of the amount of current passing.

† **c.** An apparatus in which the principle of the stroboscope is employed to render visible irregularities in the motion of rapidly rotating or oscillating machinery. *Obs.*

1922 *Glasgow Herald* 10 Oct. 6 The Elverson oscilloscope ..is an apparatus for slowing down to the eye..any high-speed machinery. **1924** A. J. H. ELVERSON in *Jrnl. Sci. Instrum.* I. 116 The 'Elverson Oscilloscope' is an opto-mechanical device which has been designed to facilitate the examination of the behaviour of high speed movements *under working conditions.* This is effected by presenting, in rapid succession, accurate pictures of the movement at predetermined intervals of angular displacement in such a way that, owing to persistence of vision, the eye of an observer sees a true representation of the movement at a speed which is a fraction of the true speed. **1927** *Trans. Amer. Inst. Electr. Engin.* May 550/1 There was a device produced in England a few years ago by a Mr. Elverson, designed for visualizing the movements of rapidly oscillating mechanisms. It is purely mechanical and optical in its nature and is now generally known as the Elverson oscilloscope.

d. More fully cathode-ray oscilloscope. An electronic instrument in which a moving spot on the screen of a cathode-ray tube represents by its position the relationship between two variables, usu. a steady or varying signal voltage (vertically) and time (horizontally), and which is capable of displaying a periodic variation in voltage as a stationary trace.

1927 Bedell & Reich in *Trans. Amer. Inst. Electr. Engin.* May 546 These limitations..may be removed and the field of usefulness of the cathode-ray oscillograph so widened that it becomes practically a new instrument. As the instrument developed for this purpose..is primarily intended for visual observation, we have given it the name 'oscilloscope'. Permanent record may be obtained.. by a photograph in the usual way. On the other hand, an *oscillograph* of the Blondel or Duddell type, both in name and in fact, is primarily for graphical record. **1936** Karapetoff & Dennison *Electr. Lab. Exper.* xix. 451 The need exists for an oscillograph possessing negligible inertia. Such an instrument is the cathode-ray oscillograph, or oscilloscope. **1953** A. C. Clarke *Prelude to Space* xxiii. 121 Clifton seemed to be hypnotised by a cathode-ray oscilloscope, the screen of which was filled with fantastic geometrical figures, continually shifting. **1967** G. F. Fiennes *I tried to run a Railway* viii. 99 One weekend the oscilloscope at one depot, Liara, found seven axles flawed. **1972** C. N. Herrick *Instruments & Measurements for Electronics* xv. 350 A conventional oscilloscope can be converted into an oscillograph by mounting a camera in front of its crt screen. **1976** *Word 1971* XXVII. 522 A small computer generated displays of letter-like elements on an oscilloscope screen.

Hence **osci:llosco·pic** *a.*, **osci:llosco·pically** *adv.*

1949 *Jrnl. Appl. Physics* XX. 1105/1 In all of the oscilloscopic records at 200 volts there are 10 examples of the ends of transient opens. **1961** *Trans. Symposium Electrode Processes 1959* 186 All measurements were made oscilloscopically. **1962** *Trans. Faraday Soc.* LVIII. 389 The potential changes were generally recorded oscilloscopically. **1965** *Math. in Biol. & Med.* (Med. Res. Council) iv. 136 Few, if any, systematic studies have been made to assess an experimenter's information-handling capacity as applied to his ability to view oscilloscopic traces or examine film records.

Oscotian (ǫskōu·ʃən), *sb.* [f. *Oscot(t)* + -ian.] A member or former member of the Roman Catholic college and seminary called St. Mary's at Oscott, near Birmingham. Also as *adj.*

The date of the original foundation, at Old Oscott, was 1794, and the college was transferred to New Oscott in 1838.

1828 (*title*) The Oscotian or Literary Gazette of St. Mary's..edited by the students of Oscott College. **1828** *Oscotian* I. 45, I met a body of youngsters escorted by a gowned superior: these I concluded to be Oscotians. **1853** J. Morris in J. H. Pollen *Life J. Morris* (1896) iv. 88 An Oscotian, thoughtful, gentlemanly, having a turn for philosophy. **1860** F. C. Husenbeth *Life Mgr. Weedall* iii. 43 Every Oscotian knows the favourite Oscott game of 'Bandy'. **1908** *Catholic Times* 22 May 8/2 No man was ever more of an Oscotian than he. **1956** *Oscotian* 83 Oscott has now acquired a tape-recorder... The 'sounds off' have not yet managed to convince any Oscotian that he is a budding Peter Ustinov. **1968** *Ibid.* 42 Allowing for the time it takes Oscotian cricketers to warm up—..we managed about ten days sporadic cricket.

Osco-Umbrian (ǫ·sko,ʋ·mbriăn), *a.* and *sb.* Also **Oscan-Umbrian**. [f. L. *Osc-us* *Oscan *a.* and *sb.* + -o + Umbrian *sb.* and *a.*] **A.** *adj.* Of or pertaining to a group of Italic languages including Oscan and Umbrian and related dialects. **B.** *sb.* This language-group. Also, a member of the peoples who spoke languages of this group.

1894 J. Rhys in *Trans. Philol. Soc. 1891–4* 117 The Romans used *qu* just as the ancient Irish did..for the Osco-Umbrian dialects replaced *qu* by *p*. *Ibid.* 119 The Siculo-Latin race had already settled down when the Osco-Umbrians arrived. **1895** C. D. Buck (*title*) The Oscan-Umbrian verb-system. *Ibid.* 135 The plural and passive forms have developed independently and on different lines in Oscan-Umbrian and in Latin. **1897** R. S. Conway *Italic Dial.* II. 469 (*heading*) Accidence of the Osco-Umbrian dialects. **1904** C. D. Buck *Gram. Oscan & Umbrian* p. iv, This grammar is called a Grammar of Oscan and Umbrian, not of the Oscan-Umbrian dialects, for it does not pretend to treat systematically the minor dialects included under the name Oscan-Umbrian. **1939** [see *Latino-Faliscan* s.v. *Latino-]. **1948** D. Diringer *Alphabet* ii. ix. 501 'Italic' is mainly used..to indicate the Osco-Umbrian sub-branch of the Italic branch of the Indo-European family. **1958** E. Pulgram *Tongues of Italy* xvii. 228 Beeler..explains the agreements of Latin with Oscan-Umbrian by their existing in close vicinity over several..centuries. *Ibid.* xviii. 232 The chronologies suggested for all these invasions are hopelessly..irreconcilable, going as low as..2300 b.c. for the Osco-Umbrians. **1971** *Archivum Linguisticum* II. 99 The *sē*-stem is..an imperfect subjunctive in Latin as well as in Osco-Umbrian. *Ibid.* 100 The complex system of Latin and Osco-Umbrian subjunctives..is also an innovation of the Italic group. **1974** A. Watson *Legal Transplants* iv. 26 It is not absolutely certain that *poena* is a direct borrowing from Greek: it is possible, though unlikely, that it was borrowed at second hand, first passing through some intermediate language like Osco-Umbrian. **1976** *Archivum Linguisticum* VII. 60 Comparison of the above types with their Oscan-Umbrian counterparts reveals separate historical origins.

-ose[2]. Add to def.: Now extended to carbohydrates which are not isomers of glucose, saccharose, or cellulose, as *arabinose, rhamnose, ribose, xylose*, etc., and to classes of sugars, as *aldose, furanose, hexose, pentose, pyranose*, etc.

-ose[3], a suffix corresponding to -osis, used to form the names of fungal diseases of plants, as *erinose.

Osgood–Schlatter (ǫ·zgud ʃlæ·təɹ). *Med.* The names of Robert Bayley *Osgood* (1873–1956), U.S. surgeon, and Carl *Schlatter* (1864–1934), Swiss surgeon, used *attrib.* and in the possessive to denote a disease described independently by them in 1903, viz. epiphysitis of the tibial tubercle.

[**1909** *Edin. Med. Jrnl.* II. 249 The name of Schlatter's Disease has been given to this lesion since it was described by that surgeon in 1903, though Müller had published an account of it in 1887.] **1912** *Amer. Jrnl. Orthopedic Surg.* IX. 317 Some have suggested Osgood-Schlatter disease, but it is my own opinion that the condition was recognized..many years previous to the work of these two gentlemen. **1921** *Ann. Surg.* LXXIII. 77 This condition is usually referred to as Osgood-Schlatter's Disease, but should really be classed as an injury and not a true disease. **1932** W. Mercer *Orthopædic Surg.* ix. 32 The true Osgood-Schlatter disease shows..characteristic bony changes which stamp it as a definite disease entity. **1961** R. D. Baker *Essent. Path.* xxi. 559 Names of men designate the disease in its various locations. For example, Osgood-Schlatter's disease is idiopathic aseptic necrosis of the tibial tubercle.

‖ **oshibori** (ǭ·ʃibōəri). [Jap., f. *o-* deferential prefix + *shibori* that which has been wrung out.] A towel which has been wrung out, usually in hot, but sometimes in cold, water; used in Japan to wash the hands and face before a meal. Also *oshibori towel*, etc.

1959 R. Kirkbride *Tamiko* vii. 47 They..wiped their hands upon first the hot and then the cold oshibori brought to them in bamboo baskets. **1963** *New Yorker* 22 June 14 A fragrant o-shibori hot towel to refresh you. **1970** *Guardian* 12 Dec. 6/6 The little thoughtfulness of the oshibori hot towel to begin a meal. **1974** *New Yorker* 22 Apr. 131 (Advt.), Hot *oshibori* towels. Or, how to freshen up without getting up.

-oside (osəid), *suffix. Chem.* [f. -ose[2] + -ide, after Glucoside, *glycoside.] Used to form the names of glycosides and classes of glycosides, as *furanoside, ganglioside, glucuronoside, pyranoside*, etc.

Osirian, *a.* Add: (Later examples.) Hence **Osi·rism**, the cult or ritual associated with Osiris.

1906 W. M. F. Petrie *Relig. Anc. Egypt* v. 38 The earliest phase of Osirism that we can identify is in portions of the Book of the Dead. **1968** *New Larousse Encycl. Mythol.* (new ed.) 19/1 Isis, in the Osirian myth, represents the rich plains of Egypt. **1971** E. Iversen in J. R. Harris *Legacy of Egypt* (ed. 2) vii. 183 Annius of Viterbo ..used Diodorus' version of the myth as a background to his curious efforts to establish a heroic genealogy for his papal patron Alexander VI Borgia, identifying the bull of the papal coat of arms with the Osirian Apis, and making the Pope a descendant of the god himself. **1972** P. M. Fraser *Ptolemaic Alexandria* I. v. 256 This identification [of Sarapis with the powers of the Underworld], which also proceeds from the Osirian character of Sarapis, is not attested by dedications.

Osirify (osəiə·rifəi), *v.* [f. the name *Osiris* (see Osirian *a.*): see -fy.] *trans.* To identify (a man or god) with Osiris. Hence **Osi:rifica·tion**, identification with Osiris.

1890 *Cent. Dict.*, Osirify. **1906** W. M. F. Petrie *Relig. Anc. Egypt* iv. 23 The most renowned was the *Hapi* or Apis bull of Memphis..who was Osirified and became the Osir-hapi. **1912** *Encycl. Relig. & Ethics* V. 238/1 In the earliest royal monuments the dance of men in the festival of Osirification of the King is represented.

Oslo (ǫ·zlo). The name of the capital of Norway, used *attrib.* in phr. *Oslo breakfast*: a type of meal for children planned to supply nutritional deficiencies in their diets and introduced into Norwegian schools by Dr. Carl Schiotz. So *Oslo meal*, etc.

1937 *Bull. Health Organisation* (League of Nations) VI. 197 Certain schools [in Norway] introduced the 'Oslo breakfast', whilst other schools continued the older practice of giving a hot lunch. The quality of this hot meal was less good than that of the 'Oslo breakfast', which consists of protective foods (milk, Kneipp rusks and Kneipp bread, cheese, butter, orange, apple or raw carrot). **1938** *Rep. School Medical Officer* (*London County Council*) 47 Considerable attention has of late been directed to the method of giving school meals to necessitous school children and others in the schools of Norway and other northern countries. This method is generally referred to as 'the Oslo breakfast'... It has attracted the attention of dieticians in other countries..and suggestions have been made that it should be introduced into London schools in substitution for the present provision of hot mid-day meals. *Ibid.* 49 It may be held that the Oslo meal would have the same effect if given at midday as if given first thing in the morning. **1949** D. Macardle *Children of Europe* vii. 123 The Oslo breakfast was planned by Professor Schiotz to give the child calories..vitamins..and to..strengthen their jaws by chewing. It consists of.. pasteurized milk, two biscuits made of wholemeal wheaten flour,..margarine..cheese made of goat's milk,..rye bread.., a raw carrot.., or half a banana..orange or.. apple. **1952** J. J. Morel *Progressive Catering* I. ii. 34 An Oslo breakfast, or a health dinner as it is known in England. **1958** R. Stow *To Islands* i. 19 Feed him on..free milk and Oslo lunches. **1962** *Guardian* 26 Oct. 5/2 'The Oslo breakfast'..consisted of..milk, half an orange, wholemeal bread, and goat's milk cheese.

osmanthus (ǫzmæ·nþʊ̆s). [mod.L. (J. de Loureiro *Flora Cochinchinensis* (1790) 28), f. Gr. ὀσμή scent + ἄνθος flower.] An evergreen shrub of the genus so called, belonging to the family Oleaceæ, usually native to eastern Asia or North America, and bearing clusters of small white or cream, usually fragrant, flowers.

1877 *Gardeners' Chron.* 24 Feb. 239/2 (*heading*) Note on Osmanthus. **1912** *Curtis's Bot. Mag.* CXXXVIII. 8459 The *Osmanthus* which is here figured is one of the most pleasing of new evergreen shrubs. **1976** *Country Life* 26 Feb. 478/1, I am advocating..lighter, altogether less domineering shrubs like..phormiums, variegated osmanthus, [etc.].

osmate. Substitute for def.: A salt or ester of osmic acid (H_2OsO_4) in which osmium has an oxidation state of 6, and in the case of alkali metals having the formula $M_2[OsO_2(OH)_4]$ and obtainable by the action of a reducing agent such as alcohol on an alkaline solution of osmium tetroxide. (Add examples.)

1852 G. Fownes *Man. Elem. Chem.* (ed. 4) ii. 368 Osmate of potassa is produced when the metal is fused with nitre. **1868** J. P. Cooke *First Princ. Chem. Philos.* (1870) xix. 420 Osmic anhydride..is unknown, but potassic osmate..can easily be obtained. **1909** L. Kahlenberg *Outl. Chem.* xxxi. 525 The chlorides $OsCl_2$, Os_2Cl_6, and $OsCl_4$ are known, as are also osmates like $K_2OsO_4.2H_2O$. **1950** N. V. Sidgwick *Chem. Elements* II. 1501 The tetroxide reacts with potassium or caesium hydroxide in methyl alcohol to give the tetramethyl osmate $(MO)_2Os^{VI}(O{\cdot}CH_3)_4$. **1973** S. E. Livingstone in J. C. Bailar et al. *Comprehensive Inorg. Chem.* III. xliii. 1230 Potassium osmate, originally formulated as $K_2OsO_4{\cdot}2H_2O$, has the octahedral structure $K_2[OsO_2(OH)_4]$.

osmatic (ǫzmæ·tik), *a.* [ad. F. *osmatique* (P. Broca 1878, in *Revue d'Anthropologie* VII. 397), f. Gr. ὀσμή smell + -atic.] Having well-developed olfactory organs and a good sense of smell; cf. *macrosmatic *a.*, *microsmatic *a.* So **o·smatism**, the degree of development of the olfactory organs.

1890 W. Turner in *Jrnl. Anat. & Physiol.* XXV. 106 He [*sc.* Broca] has classified the Mammalia, in relation to the magnitude of their olfactory apparatus, into two groups: osmatic mammals, which possess a well-developed rhinencephalon with a keen sense of smell, and anosmatic mammals, in which the rhinencephalon and olfactory sense are either feeble or not developed at all. **1903** *Amer. Anthropologist* V. 638 The related doctrines that the olfactory organs are large in osmatic, small or absent in anosmatic animals. **1903** *Trans. Linn. Soc.* (*Zool.*) VIII. 369 The size of the hippocampal formation does not seem to vary directly..with the degree of osmatism.

osmiate. Add to def.: = *perosmate. Now *Obs.* (Earlier and later examples.)

The passage in ed. 8 (1895) of *C. Bloxam's Chem.* corresponding to quot. 1890 occurs s.v. *perosmate.

1844 *Phil. Mag.* XXIV. 394 A solution of osmiate of potash. **1852** [see *osmite]. **1854** *Chem. Gaz.* 1 July 242 The air..which is still saturated with vapour of osmic acid, passes into a solution of potash, and finally to the aspirator; the osmiate of potash thus produced is treated with a few drops of alcohol, and collected in the form of crystallized osmite of potash. **1890** Thomson & Bloxam *C. Bloxam's Chem.* (ed. 7) 428 By dissolving osmic anhydride in potash and adding alcohol, the latter is oxidised at the expense of the potassium osmiate, and rose-coloured octahedral crystals of potassium osmite ($K_2OsO_4.2Aq$) are obtained.

b. = *osmate.

1905 Gooch & Walker *Outl. Inorg. Chem.* ii. xviii. 490 By fusing osmium compounds with potassium hydroxide and potassium nitrate, potassium osmiate, K_2OsO_4, is formed. **1962** P. J. & B. Durrant *Introd. Adv. Inorg. Chem.* xxiv. 1033 All three elements in the Group, iron, ruthenium, and osmium, are present in the oxidation state VI in the ferrates, the ruthenates, and the osmiates; the general formula is K_2MO_4.

osmic, *a.* Add: *osmic acid*, (*b*) the acid H_2OsO_4, known chiefly in the form of its salts (osmates).

1879 ROSCOE & SCHORLEMMER *Treat. Chem.* II. II. 458 In addition to these the salts of osmic acid, H_2OsO_4, are known, but neither the acid nor the corresponding oxide, OsO_3, have been prepared. **1936** J. W. MELLOR *Comprehensive Treat. Inorg. & Theoret. Chem.* XV. lxxii. 705 H. Moraht and C. Wischin obtained a black substance by the action of heat on a mixture of potassium osmate and nitric acid... [They] found that when dried over phosphorus pentoxide, in vacuo, its composition corresponds with the hydrate, $OsO_3.H_2O$, or osmic acid, H_2OsO_4. O. Ruff and K. Bornemann could not confirm the analysis. **1950** N. V. SIDGWICK *Chem. Elements* II. 1499 Hexavalent osmium... There are two binary compounds..and a considerable number of complex salts, all of which are in some sense derivatives of osmic acid H_2OsO_4.

osmic (ǫ·zmik), *a.*[2] [f. Gr. ὀσμή smell, odour + -IC.] Of or pertaining to odours or the sense of smell. Hence **o·smically** *adv.* Cf. *OSMICS *sb. pl.*

1938 G. M. DYSON in *Chem. & Industry* XVI. 647/1 When the mucus linings are inflamed and covered with thickened mucus..the ability to smell will be considerably diminished..by reason of the osmic sensory processes being cut off from access to the air. *Ibid.* 648/1 Certain chemical groups and configurations..lead to the development of intra-molecular frequencies capable of affecting the osmic sensory processes. These are referred to, subsequently, as the osmic frequencies. **1964** *Ann. N.Y. Acad. Sci.* CXVI. 557 If this can be confirmed, it will help to define a lower limit to the range of 'osmic frequencies'. **1966** *Nature* 5 Feb. 551/1 The osmic properties that have been identified are the non-specific ones. They do not correlate with particular odours such as those of rose..or peppermint. The fact is that the osmically specific properties of odorous substances have still not been securely identified.

osmicate (ǫ·zmikēit), *v. Biol.* [f. OSMIC *a.* + -ATE[3].] *trans.* To stain or treat with osmic acid (osmium tetroxide). So **o·smicated** *ppl. a.*

1914 STEDMAN *Med. Dict.* (ed. 3) 658/1 *Osmicate*, to stain with osmic acid. **1943** *Proc. Nat. Acad. Sci.* XXIX. 228 The classical Golgi apparatus of the fixed and osmicated cell. **1971** *Nature* 2 Apr. 334/2 Random pieces of grossly normal thyroid tissue..were diced.., fixed in 1·5% glutaraldehyde..post-osmicated, dehydrated and embedded in 'Araldite 502'. *Ibid.* 17 Sept. 199/1 Teased preparations of osmicated nerves from paralysed rabbits revealed focal, segmental myelin loss characteristic of EAN.

So **osmica·tion**, treatment with osmic acid.

1899 *Jrnl. Morphol.* XV. Suppl. 73 A curious effect of osmication was noted in some peripherally lying cells..in a preparation of *Spelerpes ruber*, which had been fixed in Flemming's chromo-aceto-osmic mixture. **1928** *Biol. Rev.* III. 337 Nassonow..has made a..study of *Paramecium* and some other protozoa by methods of fixation (osmication) and by study *in vivo*. **1934** L. W. SHARP *Introd. Cytol.* (ed. 3) iv. 69 After osmication or silver impregnation they may appear like hollow structures with a blackened periphery. **1972** B. M. WAGNER in I. Mandl *Collagenase* II. 68 Fixation in glutaraldehyde in the presence of 3% basic fuchsin, followed by osmication, resulted in increased stainability of collagen with phosphotungstic acid (PTA).

osmics (ǫ·zmiks), *sb. pl.* (const. as *sing.*). [f. Gr. ὀσμή smell, odour: see -IC 2.] The branch of science concerned with odours and the sense of smell.

1922 J. H. KENNETH *Osmics* 3 Osmics..is a convenient term to connote that area of the field of science which is concerned with smell... Briefly, osmics is the science of the stimuli, organs, and the sense of smell. **1965** *Cold Spring Harbor Symp. Quant. Biol.* XXX. 635/1 It must surely be conceded that the science of osmics has come of age with the recognition of its modulating psychophysical principle as being related to the sizes and shapes of volatile molecules.

osmio-. Add: Also used in other words, as *OSMIOPHILIC *a.*

osmiophilic (ǫzmiofi·lik), *a. Biol.* [f. OSMIO- + *-PHILIC.] Having an affinity for, or staining readily with, osmium tetroxide.

1927 *Biol. Bull.* LIII. 182, I am..of the opinion that these fatty granules of Guilliermond..have nothing to do with the osmiophilic platelets here described. **1942** *Nature* 10 Jan. 52/1 Granules..which at some stages produce osmiophilic substances. **1971** *Ibid.* 25 June 535/1 In OsO_4-fixed ultrathin sections of the costo-chondral junctions of 1 month old guinea-pigs, Bonucci has found osmiophilic bodies with mean diameters of 500–2,500 Å.

osmiridium. Add: Now usu. distinguished from *iridosmine* (see quots. 1968, 1973). (Further examples.) [For references to G. *osmiridium* (1828, 1831), *osm-iridium* (1824), and *osmium-iridium* (1821) see *Mineral. Mag.* (1963) XXXIII. 716.]

1938 *Mineral. Abstr.* VII. 162 Osmiridium (nevyanskite) from Bolshaya Victorievka mine, Kusuetsky Alatau, West Siberia..gave Os 40·3, Ir 41·6, Ru 4·2, Pt 1·1, Au 1·8, Fe 8·5. **1963** [see *NEVYANSKITE]. **1966** PHILLIPS & WILLIAMS *Inorg. Chem.* II. xxxiv. 609 The platinum metals occur native in the alloy osmiridium. **1968** I. KOSTOV *Mineral.* II. i. 90 Iridosmine (Ir, Os) with Os > 35%, and osmiridium (Os, Ir) with Os < 35%; hexagonal... Occurs as small triangular or hexagonal plates. **1973** *Canad. Mineralogist* XII. 105/1 Iridosmine occurs with osmiridium in two grains (samples 10120, gr. 2 and M12339, gr. 1). *Ibid.* 110 An excellent historical review on the nomenclature of natural Os-Ir alloys was made by Hey (1963)... He suggested that the most suitable nomenclature..be the following: For the *cubic* alloys: *osmiridium* with Os < 32 at. %. For the *hexagonal* alloys: *iridosmine* with 32 < Os < 80 at. %. Native *osmium* for Os > 80 at. %... Our proposals for alloys in the Os-Ir-Ru system are that:.. e) *Iridosmine* of Hey (1963) be redefined as *hexagonal* (Os, Ir) alloys with no single other element > 10 at. % of total, and where Os < 80 at.% of (Os + Ir)... f) *Osmiridium* of Hey (1963) be redefined as *cubic* (Ir, Os) alloys with no single other element > 10 at. % of total, and where Ir < 80 at. % of (Ir + Os).

osmite. Add: = *OSMATE. Now *Obs.* [first formed as F. *osmite* (E. Frémy 1844, in *Jrnl. de Pharm. et de Chim.* V. 189).]

1844 *Phil. Mag.* XXIV. 394 The liquor..deposits a crystalline powder of osmite of potash. **1852** tr. *Regnault's Elem. Chem.* II. III. 352 Osmite of potassa is obtained by pouring a few drops of alcohol into a solution of osmiate of potassa. *Ibid.*, No osmite of ammonia is known. **1891** W. RAMSAY *Syst. Inorg. Chem.* xxix. 483 Potassium osmite, $K_2OsO_4.2H_2O$, is prepared by dissolving the tetroxide in potassium hydroxide, and adding alcohol.

osmium. Add: **b.** Special comb.: **osmium lamp,** a filament lamp in which the filament is made of osmium; **osmium tetroxide,** OsO_4, a poisonous, pale yellow solid that has a distinctive pungent and harmful vapour and is used in solution as a biological stain, esp. for lipids, and a fixative; also called *osmic acid.*

1907 *Westm. Gaz.* 16 Feb. 14/2 The osmium lamp..was expensive to start with, and could be used only in the pendent position. **1952** H. HEWITT *Mod. Lighting Technique* iv. 34 Whilst further developments such as the Nernst lamp, the osmium lamp and the tantalum lamp were all of technical interest, it was not until the adoption of the tungsten filament by Coolidge in 1909 that there was any considerable advance towards more efficient electric lamps. **1876** *Encycl. Brit.* V. 537/2 Osmium tetroxide is reduced at red heat. **1920** *Jrnl. R. Microsc. Soc.* 133 The Golgi apparatus has the following reactions: ..2. Black in Kopsch's or Mann-Kopsch's osmium tetroxide methods. **1954** H. W. DEANE in R. O. Greep *Histol.* iii. 43 Many lipid substances will also blacken with osmic acid (osmium tetroxide). In most instances..this blackening apparently depends on the fact that unsaturated fatty acids reduce the colorless osmic acid to black osmium dioxide. However, many nonfatty protoplasmic constituents..may also be blackened with osmic acid. **1968** J. MARCH *Adv. Org. Chem.* xv. 616 There are many reagents which add two OH groups to a double bond. OsO_4 and alkaline $KMnO_4$ give cis addition, from the less hindered side of the double bond. Osmium tetroxide adds rather slowly, but almost quantitatively. **1974** *Nature* 18 Jan. 145/1 White Leghorn chicken embryos..were fixed in glutaraldehyde and osmium tetroxide.

osmo-[1]. Add: Also used to repr. OSMIUM (cf. OSMIO-), as in **osmophi·lic** *a.*[1] = *OSMIOPHILIC *a.*

1961 in WEBSTER. **1961** *Lancet* 16 Sept. 656/1 The appearance of osmophilic densities in the zones of lamellar discontinuity at the nodes of Ranvier. **1972** *Jrnl. Electron Microsc.* XXI. 85/1 In order to check the nature of the osmophilic granules..in enlarged axons, the distribution, origin and properties in the area postrema were studied in a morphological comparison..with neurosecretory granules in the hypothalamus.

osmo-[2]. Add: **osmometer**[2], also, an instrument for the measurement of osmotic pressures; (further examples); **osmometry**[2], **-metric** *a.*[2] (examples); hence **osmome·trically** *adv.*; **osmophi·lic** *a.*[2] *Biol.* [ad. G. *osmophil* (A. A. von Richter 1912, in *Mycolog. Centralbl.* I. 74)] tolerating or thriving in a medium which exerts a high osmotic pressure; so **o·smophile,** an osmophilic organism; **o·smoreceptor** *Biol.*, any sensory organ which reacts to changes in osmotic pressure (concentration) in the body fluids.

1903 M. H. FISCHER tr. *Cohen's Physical Chem.* ix. 139 Pfeffer measured the osmotic pressure of sugar solutions of various concentrations with a mercury manometer, and obtained with such an osmometer the following results. **1974** TOMBS & PEACOCKE *Osmotic Pressure Biol. Macromolecules* iii. 86 Claesson and Jacobsson..have made an osmometer with a very precise optical method for determining the difference in height of two menisci. **1976** *Nature* 12 Aug. 578/1 The total osmolality of the fluid was obtained with a Clifton nanolitre osmometer. **1913** *Chem. Abstr.* IV. 298 In a series of expts. in an 'osmometric vessel'..the following mol. wts. are obtained by balancing the pressure of the salt against a sugar soln. on the other side of the membrane. **1964** J. ELIASSAF tr. *Rafikov's Determination Molecular Weights* vi. 169 The osmometric measurement of molecular weight is based on the fact that the osmotic pressure..is proportional to the number..of gram-molecules of dissolved material in a definite volume of solution. **1943** *Jrnl. Physical Chem.* XLVII. 69 The molecular weight of a carefully fractionated sample determined osmometrically checks the value obtained for the same polymer by means of the ultracentrifuge. **1964** J. ELIASSAF tr. *Rafikov's Determination Molecular Weights* vi. 223 It was found that for molecular weights of less than 75,000 a difference begins to appear between the molecular weight determined osmometrically and the molecular weight computed by the Mark-Houwink equation. **1913** *Chem. Abstr.* VII. 297 (*heading*) Osmometry of saline solutions and the theory of Arrhenius. **1973** *Nature* 27 Apr. p. xv (Advt.), It also shows how osmometry, ultracentrifugation, light scattering,..and gel filtration are used to analyze polydisperse systems. **1961** P. L. CARPENTER *Microbiol.* xiii. 201/1 Microorganisms that have become adapted to high osmotic pressure are called osmophiles. **1969** L. DO CARMO-SOUSA in Rose & Harrison *Yeasts* I. iii. 88 She also suggested the possibility of finding obligate osmophiles..in Antarctic soils which have a high content of soluble salts. **1920** F. W. TANNER tr. *A. Guilliermond's Yeasts* iv. 120 The maximum concentration for spore formation in a yeast depends upon the species. For an osmophilic species like *Zygosaccharomyces Mandshuricus* the concentration is high. **1960** L. E. HAWKER et al. *Introd. Biol. Micro-Organisms* xvi. 380 Sugar concentrations of 50 to 70 per cent effectively prevent the growth of most micro-organisms... A few osmophilic yeasts and bacteria may grow slowly. **1972** *Sci. Amer.* Apr. 95/2 Because of the high osmotic pressure of honey, they are yeasts of the type called osmophilic, meaning that they live or thrive in a medium that has a high osmotic pressure. **1946** E. B. VERNEY in *Lancet* 30 Nov. 782/1 The osmoreceptors, wherever they may be, do not accommodate during short-period exposure to a rise in the osmotic pressure of the carotid plasma produced by NaCl. **1947** —— in *Proc. R. Soc.* B. CXXXV. 68 It becomes justified, therefore, to introduce the term 'osmoreceptors' as descriptive of the autonomic receptive elements with which the neurohypophysis is functionally linked, and through whose activation the pituitary antidiuretic substance is released. **1970** A. J. VANDER et al. *Human Physiol.* xii. 354/2 Receptors must exist which are sensitive to extracellular osmolarity. These osmoreceptors are located in the hypothalamus. **1973** *Nature* 14 Dec. 383/1 The osmoreceptors which control the salt glands in marine birds are located in or near the heart.

osmoceptor (ǫ·zmoseptǫɹ). *Physiol.* [a. G. *osmoceptor* (L. Ruzicka 1920, in *Chem.-Zeitung* XLIV. 94/2), f. Gr. ὀσμο- OSMO-[1] + G. *re)ceptor* (now *rezeptor*) RECEPTOR.] A sensory receptor for the sense of smell.

1944 R. W. MONCRIEFF *Chem. Senses* xii. 314 (*table*) Author... Ruzicka... Date... 1920... General class... Chemical... Salient features... Osmophore and osmoceptor. **1952** PIRENNE & ABBOTT tr. *H. Piéron's Sensations* II. v. 105 Such a correspondence between osmoceptors and osmophores may be important in the explanation of the qualitative differentiation between smells. **1968** W. MCCARTNEY *Olfaction & Odours* 159 If a substance reacts with the primary but not with the secondary osmoceptors, odourlessness (fatigue) follows saturation of the primary osmoceptors.

osmol (ǫ·zmǫl). Also **osmole** (-mōul). [Blend of OSMOTIC *a.* and *MOLE *sb.*[7]] A thousand milliosmols.

1942 J. L. GAMBLE *Chem. Anat., Physiol. & Path. Extracellular Fluid* (ed. 4) Notes to chart 17-B, 0·64 osmoles per liter. Solute concentration. **1956** A. C. GUYTON *Textbk. Med. Physiol.* xxvi. 302/2 If each molecule ionizes into two ions each of which is osmotically active, then 1 mol of solute equals 2 osmols. **1964** L. MARTIN *Clin. Endocrinol.* (ed. 4) i. 51 In *normal* subjects they found that the initial serum osmolality was 285 ± 4·4 m-osmoles/kg. of water. **1971** W. S. BECK *Human Design* vii. 207/2 The numerical unit in which osmotic pressure is expressed is the osmol. We speak of osmols or milliosmols per liter.

osmolal (ǫzmōu·lăl), *a.* [Blend of OSMOTIC *a.* and *MOLAL *a.*] Of the concentration of a solution: expressed as an osmolality.

1939 [see *milliosmol* s.v. *MILLI-]. **1971** W. S. BECK *Human Design* x. 348/2 The osmotic concentration measured by freezing point depression is properly termed an *osmolal* concentration—milliosmols of solute per kilogram of solvent—in contrast to an osmolar concentration—milliosmols of solute per liter of solution. The two values differ only slightly in ordinary dilute solutions, however.

Hence **osmola·lity,** the number of osmotically effective dissolved particles per unit quantity of a solution, esp. when expressed as (milli)osmols per kilogramme of solvent. Cf. *OSMOLARITY.

1959 *Q. Jrnl. Med.* LII. 237 The blood was centrifuged, and the plasma osmolality (m-osmoles per kg.) estimated from the freezing-point depression. **1963** *Jrnl. Amer. Med. Assoc.* 31 Aug. 699/1 Normal subjects are characterized by an initial serum osmolality between 273 and 293 milliosmoles (mOsm) per kilogram. **1968** PASSMORE & ROBSON *Compan. Med. Stud.* I. v. 29/1 Sweat..is essentially a weak solution of sodium chloride. The osmolality lies between 100 and 200 mOsm/l. **1972** [see *milliosmole* s.v. *MILLI-]. **1974** *Nature* 12 Apr. 605/1 Controls of the osmotic pressure of the solutions of inorganic ions..showed that their osmolalities were practically independent of temperature. **1976** *Lancet* 25 Dec. 1414/1 A man of 61 was admitted to the neurology unit in stupor, which proved to be hyponatræmic (serum osmolality 236 mos-mol/kg).

osmolar (ǫzmōu·lăɹ), *a.*, [Blend of OSMOTIC *a.* and *MOLAR *a.*[3]] Of the concentration of a solution: expressed as an osmolarity.

1942 J. L. GAMBLE *Chem. Anat., Physiol. & Path. Extracellular Fluid* (ed. 4) Notes to chart 17–B, Multiplying osmolar concentration by cubic centimeters of urine produces a measurement of total solutes as milliosmoles. **1944** *Proc. Amer. Philos. Soc.* LXXXVIII. 152/1 If we divide degrees of freezing point depression by 1·86 we obtain osmolar concentration. Multiplying osmolar concentration by cubic centimeters of urine, defines the total output of solutes as milliosmoles. **1963** *Jrnl. Amer. Med. Assoc.* 31 Aug. 700/2 The serum osmolar concentration of 25 normal subjects..was 285 ± 4·4..milliosmoles (mOsm) per kilogram of water. **1971** [see *OSMOLAL *a.*].

Hence **osmola·rity**, the number of osmotically effective dissolved particles per unit quantity of a solution, esp. when expressed as (milli)osmols per litre of solution. Cf. *OSMOLALITY.

1953 *Lancet* 12 Sept. 540/2 An assumed plasma osmolarity of 310 milliosmols per litre. **1962** J. H. KINOSHITA et al. in A. Pirie *Lens Metabolism Rel. Cataract* 406 The final glucose concentration..was 5 μmoles/ml. The total osmolarity was calculated as 307 μosmoles/ml. **1965** *New Scientist* 24 June 868/1 The most important functions of the kidney are to keep constant the volume, osmolarity and composition of the fluid which surrounds the cells of the body. **1973** *Jrnl. Biol. Chem.* CCXLVIII. 4172/1 Solutions of low osmolarity.

osmophore (ǫ·zmofōəɹ). [f. OSMO-¹ + -PHORE; in sense 1 a back-formation from *OSMOPHORIC *a.*] **1.** A chemical group whose presence in the molecules of a substance causes it to have a smell.

1919 *Perfumery & Essent. Oil Rec.* 21 May 105/1 Both Rupe and Majewski and Cohn point out that one osmophore can often replace another without distinctly changing the odour. **1944** R. W. MONCRIEFF *Chem. Senses* ix. 185 The ether group is only a weak osmophore and is easily overpowered by other features of the molecule. **1963** W. SUMMER *Methods Air Deodorization* i. 66 One and the same osmophore appearing with different molecules usually causes different odours.

2. [ad. It. *osmoforo* (G. Arcangeli 1883, in *Nuovo Giornale Bot. Ital.* XV. 75).] A scent gland found in the flowers of certain plants belonging to the families Orchidaceæ, Araceæ, Aristolochiaceæ, and Asclepiadaceæ.

1966 S. VOGEL in *Proc. 5th World Orchid Conf.* 254/1 We could find such glands, called osmophores, in many different orchidaceous groups... A genuine scent organ or osmophore..may be defined as a glandular, multicellular and clearly differentiated tissue within the floral region, which is well exposed to the atmosphere. **1967** *New Scientist* 22 June 725/2 Several orchids and a few other flowers have..developed glands (osmophores) producing scent substances (terpenes) in liquid form. **1974** C. L. WITHNER et al. in C. L. Withner *Orchids* vi. 305 The scent tissue is ultimately organized into scent glands, or osmophores.

So **osmopho·ric** *a.* [ad. G. *osmophor* (Rupe & Majewski 1900, in *Ber. d. Deut. Chem. Ges.* XXXIII. 3402)], of, pertaining to, or being an osmophore (in either sense).

1901 *Jrnl. Chem. Soc.* LXXX. I. 103 (*heading*) Osmophoric groups. **1922** G. H. PARKER *Smell, Taste, & Allied Senses* iii. 79 Osmophoric groups are such as the hydroxyl, aldehyde, keton, ester, nitro, and nitril groups. None of these..is associated with a particular odor, but any one may be the occasion of odor, if it occupies an appropriate place on a benzene ring. **1968** W. McCARTNEY *Olfaction & Odours* 133 These investigations suggest that the quality of the odour of a compound depends largely on the steric structure and is modified..by the presence of osmophoric groups. **1974** C. L. WITHNER et al. in C. L. Withner *Orchids: Sci. Stud.* vi. 305 The richness of the osmophoric cells in reserve materials relates to their production of fragrant terpene oils.

osmoregulation (ǫ:zmoregiŭlēi·ʃən). *Physiol.* [a. G. *osmoregulation* (used, prob. for the first time, by R. Höber 1906, in *Physik. Chem. der Zelle und der Gewebe* (ed. 2) ii. 31): see OSMO-² and REGULATION.] The maintenance of a more or less constant osmotic pressure in the body fluids of an organism.

1931 *Q. Cumulative Index Med.* IX. 870/2 (*heading*). Disturbances of osmoregulation in experimental uremia. **1932** *Sci. Rep. Tôhoku Imperial Univ.* VII. 229 (*heading*) On the osmoregulation of the blood of several marine and fresh water molluscs. **1964** *Oceanogr. & Marine Biol.* II 306 Osmo-regulation is known in all bony fishes. **1971** *Nature* 16 Apr. 469/2 The role of the amphibian urinary bladder in osmoregulation is well documented.

Hence **osmore·gulate** *v. intr.*, to maintain the osmotic pressure of the body fluids at a constant level; **osmore·gulating** *vbl. sb.*; **osmore·gulator**, an organ or part of the body concerned in osmoregulation; an organism capable of osmoregulation; **o:smoregula·tory** *a.* [ad. G. *osmoregulatorisch* (Höber *loc. cit.*)], of, pertaining to, or effecting osmoregulation.

1911 STEDMAN *Med. Dict.* 616/2 *Osmoregulatory*, influencing the degree and rapidity of osmosis. **1927** *Biol. Abstr.* I. 238/2 Parallel experiments with sucrose instead of urea showed that the more rapid recovery from plasmolysis in etherized solutions was due to more rapid penetration of urea, not to any osmoregulatory or ether stimulus to the production of new cell solutes. **1935** *Biol. Rev.* X. 357 The excretory organs of numerous freshwater animals act as osmoregulators. **1958** *Jrnl. Exper. Biol.* XXXV. 234 The very great osmo-regulating ability of *Artemia* has been described. *Ibid.* 241 Animals whose branchial epithelium has been damaged by a brief exposure to saturated $KMnO_4$ solution have lost the ability to osmo-regulate. **1959** SOUTHWOOD & LESTON *Land & Water Bugs Brit. Isles* xiv. 395 Its osmo-regulatory mechanism enables the bug to live in waters with from 5 to about 18 parts per thousand of salt in solution. **1960** *Biol. Abstr.* XXXV. 2729/2 The degree of activity of their osmoregulating mechanisms. **1963** R. P. DALES *Annelids* v. 109 In view of the lack of evidence that the nephridia do more than act as drains as far as nitrogenous wastes are concerned, we can but incline to the view that they are primarily osmoregulators. **1964** *Oceanogr. & Marine Biol.* II. 307 Holeurysaline osmo-regulators can regulate in salinities ranging from that of pure fresh water to that of full strength sea water or higher. **1969** *New Scientist* 30 Jan. 243/1 Herring embryos could osmoregulate even before chloride cells had developed. **1970** *Nature* 24 Oct. 378/1 A primary osmoregulatory function of prolactin is the reduction of extrarenal sodium outflux.

osmosis. Add: This, rather than *osmose*, is now the usual term.

2. *fig.* Any process by which something is acquired by absorption.

1900 [in Dict., sense 1]. **1930** E. POUND *XXX Cantos* xxix. 137 Languor has cried unto languor about the marshmallow-roast (Let us speak of the osmosis of persons). **1968** *Times Lit. Suppl.* 26 Sept. 1079/1 A director born (like Godard) in 1930 is in a position to know, by a sort of unconscious osmosis, more than a director born in 1898 (like René Clair) can hope to learn, however conscientiously he may try. **1970** *Author* LXXXI. 113 It is not a question how much you teach them but how much they learn, perhaps largely by osmosis. **1977** P. D. JAMES *Death of Expert Witness* III. 128 News percolated through a village community by a process of verbal osmosis.

osmotic, *a.* Add: *osmotic pressure*, the excess pressure that must be applied to a solution to prevent the entry into it of pure solvent when they are separated by a semipermeable membrane, or the excess pressure that develops in the solution when osmosis is allowed to occur in such circumstances; *osmotic shock*, rupture of a cell following a sudden drop in the osmotic pressure of the surrounding liquid, owing to the inflow of liquid that occurs.

1888 *Jrnl. Chem. Soc.* LIV. 778 (*heading*) Osmotic pressure in the analogy between solutions and gases. **1950** T. F. ANDERSON in *Jrnl. Appl. Physics* XXI. 70/1 The similar viruses, T2, T4, and T6 which appear in the electron microscope to have membranes surrounding the internal structures of the heads can be disintegrated by what might be termed 'osmotic shock'... Presumably, the virus heads swell when the osmotic pressure is suddenly reduced, and actually burst if the reduction is sufficiently large and sudden. **1970** AMBROSE & EASTY *Cell Biol.* ii. 83 A solution containing one gramme-molecule of non-ionizable solute in 22·4 litres exerts an osmotic pressure of 1 atmosphere at 0°C. The use of a delicate manometer by Adair and Adair enabled them to determine the molecular weight of proteins by comparing their osmotic properties with those of known solutes. **1973** D. A. ANDERSON *Introd. Microbiol.* x. 110/1 The cells of many bacteria ..are likely to burst when placed in distilled water. This method (osmotic shock) is often used to release components from inside the cell for biochemical analysis. **1973** R. KRUEGER et al. *Introd. Microbiol.* v. 201/2 The cytoplasmic water contains a tremendous variety of small organic and inorganic molecules and numerous ions and soluble enzymes... Gram-positive bacteria have an osmotic pressure of 22 atm (atmospheres).

2. In *fig.* senses. Cf. *OSMOSIS 2.

1952 W. D. JACOBS *William Barnes* i. 10 There is also the strong and numberless clan which utilizes all the latinic iridescence at its command..to rejoice that the language had such osmotic good fortune. **1965** *Economist* 24 Apr. 451/2 In the osmotic way these things happen, virtually all of them [*sc.* workers] were absorbed by other local industries. **1975** B. GARFIELD *Hopscotch* xxii. 236 The joy she took from flying..in some profound osmotic way.. had communicated itself to him.

osmotically, *adv.* Add: Also *fig.*

1974 *Times Lit. Suppl.* 20 Dec. 1437/5 A reminder of how much royal legend is osmotically absorbed by even the most reluctant reader of royal biography. **1976** *Times* 20 Jan. 11/6 The chic of the actresses was absorbed, osmotically, into his ranges [of clothes].

osmunda (ǫzmʋ·ndă). [med.L. (see OSMUND²), adopted as a generic name by J. Petiver in *Musei Petiveriani centuria VI & VII* (1699) 53.] A fern of the genus so called, esp. the royal fern, *Osmunda regalis.*

1789 E. DARWIN *Bot. Garden* II. 11 The fair Osmunda seeks the silent dell. **1818** [see *cinnamon fern*]. **1858** J. A. SYMONDS *Let.* 6 June (1967) I. 144 Is the Osmunda yet in flower? **1865** M. EYRE *Lady's Walks S. of France* xxv. 272 The *Osmunda* grew at the other end of the lake. **1894** W. BROCKBANK in W. Robinson *Wild Garden* (ed. 4) xiii. 143 The brooklet was..fringed with marsh plants.. together with Osmundas, Hart's-tongues, and other Ferns. **1974** R. GROUNDS *Ferns* v. 57 This method [*sc.* container-growing] is ideal if one wants to use a stronggrowing osmunda, for example, as a specimen plant.

2. In full, *osmunda fibre.* A fibre generally made from the roots of *Osmunda cinnamomea* or *O. claytoniana*, used as a potting medium for orchids.

1910 *Gardeners' Chron.* 5 Nov. 329/3 He [*sc.* H. G. Alexander] decided that Osmunda fibre was the best material procurable. **1932** *Bull. Amer. Orchid Soc.* Dec. 87/2 Osmunda fibre taken from swampy land should not be used. **1942** LAURIE & RIES *Floriculture* xix. 460 Osmunda peat makes the best medium for this group [of epiphytic orchids]. **1942** C. L. WITHNER *Orchids: Sci. Survey* viii. 349 Its [*sc.* tree fern's] water-retention and drying capacities are very similar to osmunda. **1951** *Dict. Gardening* (R. Hort. Soc.) III. 1440/2 Osmunda is at present the best material for general use [in potting orchids] but in fact several other fibres are in use to eke out and modify Osmunda fibre. **1959** *Listener* 17 Dec. 1094/3 A piece of osmunda fibre, or wire netting filled with moss and fastened round a cane, can be driven into the pot and kept moist with spraying. **1966** T. B. MORRIS *Orchids with Murder* i. 7 The pleasantly familiar smell of damp loam and sphagnum and osmunda fibre. **1974** C. L. WITHNER *Orchids: Sci. Stud.* iii. 154 Osmunda fiber plus water provided adequate fertility for orchids.

osmundine (ǫ·zmʋndīn). *N. Amer.* [f. *OSMUNDA + -INE⁴.] = *OSMUNDA 2.

1932 *Bull. Amer. Orchid Soc.* Sept. 52/2 The best compost to use for growing Cattleyas should consist of good fibrous brown fern root, osmundine as it is called. **1934** R. STOUT *Fer-de-Lance* vii. 101 Supplies—pots, sand, sphagnum..osmundine.

Osnaburg. Delete †*Obs.* and add later examples. Also with small initial.

1917 J. HERGESHEIMER *Three Black Pennys* (1918) 38 Tobacco and shoes, ozenbrigs and molasses and rum. **1938** M. K. RAWLINGS *Yearling* xi. 110 Beyond the utensils were the dress goods; calico and Osnaburg, denim and shoddy, domestic and homespun. **1949** *Caribbean Q.* I. 1. 12 Every October cloth was issued, at the rate of seven yards of osnaburgs. **1959** POTTER & CORBMAN *Fiber to Fabric* (ed. 3) ix. 153 When made of waste mixed with low-grade cotton it is known as part-waste osnaburg.

b. *attrib.*, made of Osnaburg linen.

1681 *Rec. Court. of New Castle on Delaware* (1904) 493 Twoo Remnants of Osnabriggs Linnen. **1758** in *Essex Inst. Hist. Coll.* (1874) XII. 145 Others very much soaked in their Osombrige Tents. **1774** in *Maryland Hist. Mag.* (1911) VI. 41 John Johnson..had on..a pair of leather breeches and osnabrig trousers. **1813** J. TAYLOR *Arator* 137 A regular supply of a winter's coat,..two oznaburg shirts, a good hat and blanket. **1841** *Southern Lit. Messenger* VII. 775/2 Our slaves in the South-West are annually supplied with two cotton Oznaburg shirts. **1863** 'E. KIRKE' *My Southern Friends* vii. 99 The thin Osnaburg gown.

osone (ōu·sōun). *Chem.* [ad. G. *oson* (E. Fischer 1889, in *Ber. d. Deut. Chem. Ges.* XXII. 87), f. *-ose* -OSE² + *-on* -ONE.] Any compound containing two adjacent carbonyl groups, obtained by hydrolysing an osazone.

1889 [see *glucosone* s.v. *GLUCO-]. **1938** PRESCOTT & RIDGE *Org. Chem.* xx. 353 The osone, which may be isolated as the lead compound, is reduced with zinc dust and acetic acid to a ketose. **1957** J. W. GREEN in W. Pigman *Carbohydrates* vi. 334 The osones exist only as amorphous or sirupy materials.

‖ **O-soto-gari** (ǭsōᵘtogāri). Also **Osotogari, o-.** [Jap., f. *o* grand + *soto* outside + *gari* f. *kari* to mow, to reap.] The name of a throw in Judo.

1941 M. FELDENKRAIS *Judo* 45 Pull the opponent's sleeve and attack by the first leg throw (*O-Soto-Gari*). **1956** E. J. HARRISON tr. *H. Aida's Kodokan Judo* iii. 58 Should you anticipate your opponent's attempted Osotogari then just at the moment when he is contemplating the reaping action with his right leg swiftly pull him near you to counter. **1963** P. BUTLER *Judo Complete* iii. 59 The *osotogari* is my own favourite throw and many variations are possible upon the basic method. **1970** A. P. HARRINGTON *Judo Guide to Black Belt* i. 28 Now..try the O-sotogari against your opponent.

Ossetian (ǫsī·ʃăn), *sb.* and *a.* Also **Ossetan** (-ī·tăn), **Osset(e)** (ǫ·set, -īt), **Ossetic** (ǫse·tik). [f. Russ. *osetin*, f. Georgian *os*, *oset'i* Ossetia (place-name) + -IAN.] **A.** *sb.* **a.** A member of a people of the Central Caucasus, inhabiting North Ossetia (the North Ossetian Autonomous Soviet Socialist Republic) and South Ossetia (an Autonomous Oblast of the Georgian Soviet Socialist Republic). **b.** The language of this people, one of the Eastern Iranian group.

1814 [see *CHECHEN]. **1841** [see *MEDIAN *sb.*² 2]. **1869** C. ENGEL *Examples of Art Workmanship* 4 The Ossetes, or Ossetines, are an Indo-Germanic race dwelling in Central Caucasus. They call themselves Irôn; Oseti is the name given to them by the Georgians and other neighbouring nations. **1888** J. WRIGHT tr. *Brugmann's Elem. Compar. Gram. Indo-Gmc. Lang.* I. 5 Ossetian (spoken in the neighbourhood of the Caucasus). **1902** [see *INGUSH]. **1913** [see *ALAN²]. **1925** P. RADIN tr. *Vendryès's Language* ii. 38 This phenomenon [*sc.* sound-shifting] is found in other languages besides the Germanic: in Armenian, for example, and in Ossetic. **1933** C. D. BUCK *Compar. Gram. Greek & Latin* 8 Modern Iranian is represented by..the isolated Ossetan in the Caucasus. **1933** L. BLOOMFIELD *Language* iv. 62 An isolated offshoot [of Iranian], far to the west is Ossete, in the Caucasus, spoken by some 225,000 persons. **1933** *N. & Q.* CLXIV. 192/1 Ossetian is a modern Iranian vernacular, spoken by the Ossetes, a tribe in central Caucasus. **1944** G. A. NEBOLSINE tr. *Vernadsky's Hist. Russia* (rev. ed.) i. 16 The Caucasian Alans were called *As* or *Os*—a name which their descendants, the Ossetians, still bear. **1959** B. GEIGER et al. *Peoples & Lang. Caucasus* 47 Ossetian has the status of a literary language. **1964** R. H. ROBINS *Gen. Linguistics* viii. 328 Georgian, Armenian, and Ossetic, languages spoken in contiguous regions, but belonging to different families, Armenian and Ossetic being I-E languages, and Georgian one of the members of the Caucasian family. **1965** G. Y. SHEVELOV *Prehist. of Slavic* 615 Ossetian, the language which to a certain degree continues the Ir[anian] dialects north of the Black Sea, is known only in its modern form. **1970** D. A. RUSTOW in *Cambr. Hist. Islam* I. IV. vi. 691 The neighbouring Circassians, Chechens and Ossetians proved almost equally tenacious. **1971** L. ZGUSTA et al

Man. Lexicogr. vii. 300 The glosses would probably be given in Ossetic, the dictionary being determined for the Ossetes.

B. *adj.* Of or pertaining to this people or their language.

1877 A. H. Keane tr. *Hovelacque's Sci. of Lang.* v. 207 The Ossetian declension is fuller than the Persian. **1910** *Encycl. Brit.* V. 552/2 The Mamison Pass, over which runs the Ossetic military road (made passable for vehicles in 1889)..lies at an altitude of 9270 ft. **1932** *Times Lit. Suppl.* 2 June 398/4 Joseph..Jugashvili (otherwise Koba, otherwise Stalin) was the son of a Georgian father and an Ossetian mother. **1953** R. G. Kent *Old Persian* (ed. 2) 7 The Ossetic dialects, in the general region of the Caucasus; derived from the Scythian of Southern Russia. **1962** D. M. Lang *Mod. Hist. Georgia* i. 9 The Ossetian Military Road runs northward from Kutaisi towards the Mamison Pass. *Ibid.* iii. 49 The Ossete mountaineers and the villagers of Mtiuleti were forced to toil without payment. **1974** *Country Life* 24 Jan. 146/4 An Ossete folk-ballad, adapted by the poet Kosta Khetagurov (the Caucasian equivalent of Robert Burns), begins: The fox has been whetting her teeth for the badger.

‖ **ossia** (ǫsī·ă, ǫ·syā), *conj.* [It., f. *o sia*, or maybe.] In musical directions: or rather, or alternatively.

1876 Stainer & Barrett *Dict. Mus. Terms* 340/2 *Ossia*.., or else, as *ossia più facile*, or else in this more easy way. **1959** *Collins Music Encycl.* 476/2 *Ossia*, 'or'. Used to indicate an alternative, usually simplified, to a passage in a composition.

ossiculectomy (ǫsi:kiŭle·ktŏmi). *Surg.* [f. L. *ossicul-um*, dim. of *os*, *ossi-* bone + *-ectomy.] Excision of the auditory ossicles.

1900 *Lancet* 10 Mar. 702/2 An uncomplicated otorrhoea which has resisted all forms of treatment for six months is certainly a case for ossiculectomy. **1959** G. E. Shambaugh *Surg. Ear* xix. 515 (*heading*) Partial ossiculectomy.

ossified, *ppl. a.* Add: Also *fig.*

1901 *Yale Fun* 55/2 'Did you hear about the row over in Peabody Museum?' 'What was the trouble?' 'A lot of the exhibits got ossified.' **1922** S. Lewis *Babbitt* xxix. 337 Oh, but wasn't T. D. stewed! Say, he was simply ossified! **1934** Webster s.v., *Ossified*..2. Figuratively, fixed; hardened; set in a conventional form; ultraconservative. *a* **1953** E. O'Neill *Long Day's Journey* (1956) iv. 156 What's the matter with the Old Man tonight? Must be ossified to forget he left this out. **1961** in Webster s.v., Bitterly criticized the organization for being ossified. **1976** *Times* 5 Nov. 14/8 That lack of any spirit of initiative..that is normally the hallmark..of ossified totalitarianisms.

‖ **osso bucco** (ǫ:so bu·ko). Also **ossobuco.** [It., lit. 'marrowbone'.] Shin of veal stewed in wine with vegetables.

1935 M. Morphy *Recipes of All Nations* 144 *L'osso buco* (veal stew). This is one of the most famous Italian dishes. **1961** *Guardian* 21 Apr. 8/7 *Florentine Veal Stew* is reminiscent of the Osso Bucco most of us approve of. **1961** A. Wilson *Old Men at Zoo* ii. 97 She..had arranged with Grazia my favourite meal—ossobuco, a light red chianti, zabaglione. **1963** E. Humphreys *Gift* ii. i. 209, I ordered *osso bucco* and half a litre of Chianti. **1966** *Daily Tel.* 9 Nov. 13/4 There is a super snack bar..where you can fortify yourself with Osso Bucco, Beef Stroganoff or roast lamb. **1974** *Times* 2 Nov. 11/5 Prepared beef olives and osso bucco.

ostatki (ǫstæ·tki), var. *astatki.

1913 V. B. Lewes *Oil Fuel* 71 The oil remaining in the retort, called 'Ostatki' in the Russian distilleries and 'Residuum' in America, is used for fuel.

ostectomy (ǫste·ktŏmi). *Surg.* Also †**osteectomy** (ǫsti,e·ktŏmi). [f. Ost(eo- or Oste(o- + *-ectomy.] (See quots.)

1894 Gould *Dict. Med.* 946/1 *Osteectomy*, excision of a portion of bony tissue. **1900** Dorland *Med. Dict.* 465/2 *Ostectomy, osteectomy*, the excision of a bone. **1969** *Gloss. Terms Dentistry* (*B.S.I.*) 36 *Ostectomy*, the division of a bone at two points with removal of the intervening portion of bone. This procedure is, in effect, similar to a resection..but the term 'ostectomy' is reserved for operations designed to correct some structural deformity of a congenital, developmental, or acquired nature whereas 'resection' applies to the removal of diseased bone. **1977** *Proc. R. Soc. Med.* LXX. 432/1 Bell & Dann (1973) found no changes in the surgically repositioned bone and only small changes in incisor overbite and overjet in 25 patients following anterior maxillary ostectomies and lower labial segmental procedures.

ostension. Add: **1. b.** Logic. = **ostensive definition* (see next).

1950 W. V. Quine in *Jrnl. Philos.* XLVII. 629 The ostensions which introduce a general term differ from those which introduce a singular term. **1960** —— *Word & Object* 115 Our explorer learns each of the names by ostension on the part of the natives. **1963** J. Lyons *Structural Semantics* iv. 54, I accept that ostension plays a necessary part in the normal process of learning a language. **1968** —— *Introd. Theoret. Linguistics* ix. 409 The difficulty of explaining the meaning of any word without using others to limit and make more explicit the 'scope' of 'ostension'.

ostensive, *a.* Add: **2. b.** *ostensive definition* (Philos.), the explanation of a word by pointing at or otherwise indicating, or by presenting, one or more objects to which it applies.

1921 W. E. Johnson *Logic* I. vi. 94 We may now introduce the technical term 'ostensive' which will suggest as its opposite the familiar term 'intensive'... Imposing a name in the act of indicating, presenting or introducing the object to which the name is to apply,..this it is that constitutes ostensive definition. **1940** A. J. Ayer *Found. Empirical Knowl.* ii. 88 This is effected by the method of ostensive definition. **1950** R. Robinson *Definition* ii. 15 'Ostensive definition' is the name of a method, the method that makes use of pointing or physical introduction. **1953** I. M. Copi *Introd. Logic* iv. 108 An ostensive definition refers to the examples by means of pointing or some other gesture. **1960** K. Amis *New Maps of Hell* (1961) i. 21 One might under adverse conditions learn a human language, by ostensive definition and the like. **1968** J. Lyons *Introd. Theoret. Linguistics* ix. 409 Ostensive definition, of itself, is never sufficient.

Hence **oste·nsiveness,** the state or quality of being ostensive.

1933 *Mind* XLII. 190 (*heading*) Tests for ostensiveness. **1971** T. F. Mitchell in *Archivum Linguisticum* II. 40 Ostensive meaning. 'Specification' as a category of linguistic experience may encompass such varied grammatical classes as articles, ordinal numerals, and deictics... It is perhaps particularly to the area of deixis that 'ostensiveness' belongs.

ostensively. Add: **c.** By pointing, gesture, or presentation.

1921 W. E. Johnson *Logic* I. vi. 94 A simple adjective-name—such as red—cannot be defined analytically but only ostensively. **1948** B. Russell *Human Knowl.* 83 Most children learn the word 'dog' ostensively. **1953** W. V. Quine *From Logical Point of View* iv. 78 Once a fund of ostensively acquired terms is at hand there is no difficulty in explaining additional terms discursively.

osteo-. Add: **osteoarthri·tic** *a.*, of, pertaining to, or affected by osteoarthritis; **osteoarthritis,** substitute for def.: degeneration of the joints of the body, which occurs to a greater or lesser extent from the third decade of life, is manifested as pain, discomfort, and stiffness in the joints, and results from progressive deterioration of articular cartilage until finally bone is rubbing directly against bone; **o:steoarthro·pathy** [*arthropathy* s.v. Arthro-], any disease which affects both the bones and the joints; *spec.* a syndrome (pulmonary osteoarthropathy) marked by broadening and thickening of the fingers, painful swollen joints, and enlarged distal ends of long bones, and seen chiefly as a complication of various chest diseases; hence **o:steoarthropa·thic** *a.*; **osteoarthro·sis** [-osis] = **osteoarthritis*; hence **osteoarthro·tic** *a.*; **o·steocyte** [-cyte], an osteoblast that has ceased its bone-forming activity and is enclosed within a lacuna in the bone matrix; **o:steodo:ntokera·tic** *a.* *Anthrop.* [Odonto- + Kerat(o- + -ic], (of a culture) based on the use of bone, tooth, and horn implements; **osteola·thyrism** *Med.* [Lathyrism], an experimental skeletal disease of animals produced by the ingestion of seeds of some plants of the genus *Lathyrus* or certain chemicals; **osteo·lysis** [*-lysis], the pathological destruction or disappearance of bone tissue; so **osteoly·tic** *a.*, causing or characterized by osteolysis.

1902 *Amer. Jrnl. Med. Sci.* CXXIV. 808 The frequency with which osteo-arthritic changes are found in Paget's disease has not received the attention which they invite. **1962** *Lancet* 8 Dec. 1233/1 Mr. Philip Newman and Mr. Harry Piggott described a ten-year follow-up of osteo-arthritic knees. **1972** Hollander & McCarty *Arthritis* (ed. 8) lv. 1009 Osteoarthritis is a non-inflammatory disorder of movable joints characterized by deterioration and abrasion of articular cartilage, and also by formation of new bone at the joint surfaces. **1903** *Med. Rec.* (N.Y.) 21 Feb. 312/1 Walter Berent reports a case which shows the intimate relations which exist between nerve lesions and osteoarthropathic changes. **1972** Hollander & McCarty *Arthritis* (ed. 8) lxxiv. 1369/1 The data failed to demonstrate any factor in the blood of the donor (osteoarthropathic) dog that would produce peripheral vascular effects. **1893** *Brit. Med. Jrnl.* 3 June 1155/2 (*heading*) Three cases of 'hypertrophic pulmonary osteo-arthropathy', with remarks. **1901** *Encycl. Medica* IX. 4 In leprosy osteo-arthropathies have been described by Heiberg which have many of the characteristics of the osteo-arthropathies of tabes. **1958** *Jrnl. Bone & Joint Surg.* XL. B. 538 (*heading*) Familial osteoarthropathy of the fingers. **1974** J. D. Maynard in R. M. Kirk et al. *Surgery* x. 216 Polyneuritis and pulmonary osteoarthropathy..are sinister clinical findings. **1932** W. Boyd *Text-bk. Path.* xxxii. 898 Osteoarthrosis.—This is commonly called osteoarthritis, but as the condition is essentially degenerative with no suggestion of inflammation it would appear preferable to speak of osteoarthrosis. **1970** *New Scientist* 4 June 487/1 One, rheumatoid arthritis, is an inflammatory condition of unknown cause, starting in the synovial lining... The second, osteoarthrosis, is essentially a disorder of cartilage. **1974** Passmore & Robson *Compan. Med. Stud.* III. i. xxv. 37/1 Osteoarthrosis (osteoarthritis) is a common disease of diathrodial joints in both men and animals. **1964** W. S. C. Copeman *Textbk. Rheumatic Dis.* (ed. 3) xiii. 276 Restriction of the use of a joint may protect it from developing osteo-arthrotic changes. **1974** Passmore & Robson *Compan. Med. Stud.* III. i. xxv. 37/1 There are biochemical differences between senescent and osteoarthrotic cartilage. **1943** *Q. Jrnl. Exper. Physiol.* XXXII. 9 Superficially placed osteocytes. **1965** M. C. Hall *Locomotor Syst.: Funct. Histol.* vi. 87 Once it has formed the matrix around itself this cell, the osteoblast, becomes an inhabitant of its own secretions. Its function changes from a bone forming cell to a bone maintaining cell and it is then known as an osteocyte. **1957** R. A. Dart in *Transvaal Mus. Mem.* No. 10. 1 The purpose of this paper..is to show that..the essential culture of *Australopithecus prometheus* was osteodontokeratic... This long name indicating literally 'bone-tooth-horn' may appear unduly ponderous. **1963** J. W. Kitching (*title*) Bone, tooth & horn tools of palaeolithic man: an account of the osteodontokeratic discoveries in Pin Hole Cave, Derbyshire. **1967** *New Scientist* 27 Apr. 202/1 This has been published by Dr Dart under the jaw-cracking title of the osteodontokeratic (literally bone, tooth and horn) culture of the Australopithecines. **1957** H. Selye in *Revue Canad. de Biol.* XVI. 1 An apparently quite unrelated skeletal disease, 'osteolathyrism', can be induced experimentally in laboratory animals by feeding them the seeds of other types of Lathyrus plants, especially *L. odoratus*. The active principle of the latter is aminopropionitrile. **1971** *Sci. Amer.* June 51/1 One form of this disease, called osteolathyrism, can be produced experimentally in animals by administering aminonitriles and related compounds. In osteolathyrism the inhibition of cross-links in elastin and collagen brings about structural abnormalities in the connective tissues, particularly those of blood vessels and bone. [**1859** S. Wilks *Lect. Path. Anat.* i. 34 There is a third form of cancer,..to which Lobstein has given the name of osteolyosis, or cancerous erosion.] **1875** —— & Moxon *Ibid.* (ed. 2) 63 These formations appear to be of the same nature as those called osteolysis by Lobstein. **1926** *Surg., Gynecol. & Obstetr.* XLIII. 308/2 There is regression of bone (osteolysis). **1969** B. S. Epstein *Spine* (ed. 3) ix. 692/2 As a result of the infiltration of the marrow with Gaucher's cells minimal, moderate or extensive osteolysis may occur. **1875** Wilks & Moxon *Lect. Path. Anat.* (ed. 2) 63 (*heading*) Osteolytic cancer. **1935** *Jrnl. Bone & Joint Surg.* XXXIII. 840 (*caption*) Osteolytic osteogenic sarcoma in the femur of a child. **1974** Passmore & Robson *Compan. Med. Stud.* III. i. xxvi. 31/1 Giant cell tumour (osteoclastoma)... Commonly a thin shell of bone covers the lesion, which is osteolytic.

osteoclastoma (ǫ:stioklæstōᵘ·mă). *Path.* Pl. **-omas, -omata.** [f. *osteoclast* s.v. Osteo- + *-oma.] A giant-cell tumour of bone characterized by the presence of numerous osteoclast-like cells; orig. applied to a variety of mostly benign tumours, but now restricted to a type that is often malignant.

1926 *Jrnl. Path. & Bacteriol.* XXIX. 399 (*heading*) A case of osteoclastoma (myeloid sarcoma, benign giant-cell tumour) with pulmonary metastasis. **1931** *Brit. Jrnl. Surg.* XIX. 242 Generalized osteitis fibrosa with multiple osteoclastomata. **1948** [see *myeloma]. **1961** *Lancet* 30 Sept. 751/2 Osteoclastomas respond well to irradiation. **1974** Passmore & Robson *Compan. Med. Stud.* III. i. xxvi. 31/1 Giant cell tumour (osteoclastoma)... The nature of the cells is not definitely known, but the possibility that the giant cells are osteoclasts has led to the alternative name, osteoclastoma.

osteoderm (ǫ·stiodǝɹm). *Zool.* [Back-formation from *osteodermal* adj. s.v. Osteo-.] A bony plate in the skin, esp. in reptiles.

1898 H. Gadow *Classification of Vertebrata* 27 Body scaly without osteoderms. **1902** *Proc. Zool. Soc.* I. 208 Exquisite examples of true dermal bones are those ossifications 'within the skin' which in Amphibia and Reptiles are now generally called osteoderms. **1969** A. Bellairs *Life of Reptiles* II. vii. 319 Many reptiles have an armour of bony scutes or osteoderms in the dermal layers of the skin.

osteodystrophy (ǫstiodi·strŏfi). *Med.* Also as mod.L. **-dystrophia.** [f. (in Ger.) as mod.L. *osteodystrophia* (J. von Mikulicz 1905, in *Verhandl. d. Ges. deutsch. Naturforscher und Ärzte* LXXVI. ii. Med. Abt. 108), f. Osteo- + *dystrophia* s.v. Dys-: see -y³.] Any of several disorders affecting the whole skeleton in which there is defective bone development owing to a badly balanced diet or faulty metabolism; *spec.* one in which there is increased resorption of bone and its replacement by fibrous and poorly mineralized tissue, producing skeletal pain and brittle bones, which are often enlarged and deformed in the young; it occurs in animals, esp. horses, as a result of too high a ratio of dietary phosphorus to calcium (*osteodystrophia fibrosa* [coined in Ger. by T. Stenholm in *Pathologisch-anat. Studien über die Osteodystrophia Fibrosa* (1924) 90]), and in man in association with chronic renal insufficiency and hyperparathyroidism (*renal osteodystrophy*).

1930 *Jrnl. Exper. Med.* LII. 669 (*heading*) Experimental fibrous osteodystrophy (ostitis fibrosa) in hyperparathyroid dogs. *Ibid.* 690 The hypostotic-porotic form of osteodystrophia fibrosa. **1932** W. Boyd *Text-bk. Path.* xxxi. 883 Among these..osteitis fibrosa, osteitis deformans, osteomalacia, rickets,..hereditary chondrodysplasia, and marble bones may be mentioned. As they are disorders of the growth of bone they may be considered together under the heading of the osteodystrophies. **1953** *Jrnl. Path. & Bacteriol.* LXV. 302 In severe renal osteodystrophy the local upheaval in bone formation may result in the development of lesions resembling either osteopetrosis or Paget's disease. **1963** JUBB & KENNEDY *Path. Domestic Animals* I. i. 8/1 The classical osteodystrophies are rickets, osteomalacia, and osteodystrophia fibrosa. *Ibid.* 25/1 (*heading*) The osteodystrophy of fluorine poisoning. **1966** WRIGHT & SYMMERS *Systemic Path.* II. xxxvii. 1384/2 Renal osteodystrophy is..one of the commonest metabolic diseases of bone. The bone changes consist of fibrous replacement of bone..together with rickets or osteomalacia. **1970** A. R. JENNINGS *Animal Path.* xii. 233 Equine osteodystrophia fibrosa arises if horses are fed on a diet containing large quantities of bran which is rich in phosphorus. The same situation is sometimes seen in pigs... In dogs, however, the prime cause is renal insufficiency with secondary hyperparathyroidism. **1974** PASSMORE & ROBSON *Compan. Med. Stud.* III. I. xxii. 10/2 The clinical features of renal osteodystrophy are most marked in children, in whom there is growth retardation.

So **o:steodystro·phic** *a.*

1925 *Physiol. Abstr.* IX. 529 Osteodystrophic factors in different animals. **1960** *Proc. Zool. Soc.* CXXXIV. 307 Osteo-dystrophic conditions have been recognized in New World monkeys for many years.

osteofibrosis (ǫ:stiofəibrōᵘ·sis). *Vet. Sci.* [f. OSTEO- + *FIBROSIS; perh. ad. F. *ostéofibrose* (Achard & Thiers 1925, in *Gaz. des Hôpitaux civils et militaires* XCVIII. 917/1).] Osteodystrophia fibrosa of animals.

1936 *Vet. Rec.* XLVIII. 1400/1 The third osteodystrophic disease in animals is one which has only come to be recognised within recent years. It is osteodystrophia fibrosa, also known as osteofibrosis. Although by no means uncommon.., it has most often been described as osteomalacia or osteoporosis, conditions which we now know to have a different pathology. **1961** J. O. L. KING *Vet. Dietetics* viii. 99 Osteofibrosis is a bone disease, commonly known as bran or millers' disease, which is found in horses fed on rations which are very low in calcium, especially when there is an excess of phosphorus.

Hence **o:steofibrotic** *a.*

1938 J. R. GREIG et al. *Hutyra's Special Path. & Therapeutics* (ed. 4) III. 224 Osteofibrotic pigs with thickening of the cranial bones (snuffles).

osteogenesis. (Further examples.)

1950 A. W. HAM *Histol.* xvi. 192/2 The formation of bone is usually spoken of as ossification or osteogenesis. **1963** JUBB & KENNEDY *Path. Domestic Animals* I. i. 9/2 Alkaline phosphatase..is very active in osteogenesis.

b. osteogenesis imperfecta [mod.L. (W. Vrolik *Tabulæ Illustrandam Embryogenesin Hominis et Mammalium* (1849) tab. 91)], an inherited disease characterized by extreme weakness of the bones, which break frequently even before birth.

1903 *Amer. Jrnl. Med. Sci.* CXXV. 762 The disease called by Vrolik and by Stilling osteogenesis imperfecta, which previously in all probability was classed under fœtal rickets, is a definite, intrauterine process, the chief characteristics of which are great brittleness and softness of the bones, numerous fractures, and resulting deformities, due to as yet obscure disturbances of myelogenic and periosteal bone formation. **1923** *Brit. Jrnl. Surg.* XI. 737 Osteogenesis imperfecta is the name given to a disease which is characterized by a congenital defect in the evolution of the osteoblast, and recognized clinically by defective ossification of the cranium and a multiplicity of fractures resulting from trivial causes. **1974** PASSMORE & ROBSON *Compan. Med. Stud.* III. II. xlv. 47/1 Osteogenesis imperfecta congenita is easily distinguished from achondroplasia but unnaturally short limbs, the result of prenatal fractures, create a superficial resemblance.

osteogenetic, -genic, -genous *adjs.* (examples).

Osteogenic is the usual adj.; *osteogenous* is *rare.*

1867 *Quain's Elem. Anat.* (ed. 7) I. p. cv, This soft transparent matter, which becomes ossified, may.. be distinguished by the name of 'osteogenic substance', as proposed by H. Müller, or simply of 'osteogen'. **1874** A. E. J. BARKER tr. *Frey's Histol. & Histochem. of Man* 258 It is easy to recognise here..the similarity of the osteogenetic process to that in other parts of the system. **1905** J. S. FERGUSON *Normal Histol.* xi. 177 The osteogenous tissue of this layer, containing osteoblasts, osteoclasts, and developing blood vessels, grows into the cartilage. **1931** M. SINCLAIR *Fractures* xv. 180 Certain forms of ununited fractures may be stimulated towards union by the presence of actual osteogenetic tissue in a bone graft. **1947** *Radiology* XLIX. 310/2 Similar osteogenic sarcomas were described in persons poisoned with radium for eight to ten years. **1951** S. GILDER tr. *Lacroix's Organization Bones* xv. 204 Autoplastic grafts of marrow are osteogenic in adult animals as well as in young animals. **1975** *Nature* 29 May 373/3 It was felt that statistical analysis could be based only on that bone tumour type for which solid prognostic data exist, agreed by all to be classical osteogenic sarcoma.

osteoid, *a.* Add: *spec.* consisting of or being the uncalcified amorphous matrix that is the organic constituent of bone. (Earlier and additional examples.)

osteoid osteoma, a characteristic kind of benign tumour of bone, small and usu. painful.

1840 C. WEST tr. *Müller's Nature of Cancer* I. II. i. 136 The osteoid tumor of the bones..is a growth composed entirely of osseous substance. **1859** *Proc. R. Soc.* IX. 662 It seems to follow that the peculiar distribution of real osseous tissue and of the 'osteoid' structure, as the osseous tissue without [bone-]corpuscles may be called, has a deeper signification. **1859** S. WILKS *Lect. Path. Anat.* I. 31 There is encephaloid and scirrhous cancer of bone,..if the latter is wholly ossified, we have osteoid cancer. **1875** —— & MOXON *Ibid.* (ed. 2) 54 The microscope shows a structure which can best be compared to those plates of osteoid cartilage which are so common on the spinal pia mater after middle life, *i.e.* it closely resembles bone which has been decalcified by acids. **1916** E. H. KETTLE *Path. Tumours* II. 96 A tumour may form osteoid tissue consisting of trabeculæ, almost typical in every respect except that there is no deposition of calcium salts in the matrix. **1935** H. L. JAFFE in *Arch. Surg.* XXXI. 724 One feels forced to conclude that one is dealing here with a benign bone neoplasm the distinctiveness of which has not hitherto been recognized and which I am designating 'osteoid-osteoma'. **1950** A. W. HAM *Histol.* xvi. 190/2 Under normal conditions..newly formed bone exists in an uncalcified or osteoid state for only a transitory period. **1966** WRIGHT & SYMMERS *Systemic Path.* I. xxxvii. 1400 An osteoid osteoma takes the form of a rounded mass of gritty, reddish-grey tissue... Histologically.., the lesion consists of vascular osteoblastic tissue, containing much osteoid matrix and some calcified bone. **1969** W. A. BERESFORD *Lect. Notes Histol.* vii. 49 The osteoid seam is a very poorly mineralized zone of matrix, 1–3 μ wide, seen with light microscopy between the true bone and the active osteoblasts.

B. *sb.* † **a.** A kind of malignant tumour composed of osteoid tissue. [The original sense, after G. *osteoid* sb. (J. Müller *Ueber den feinern Bau und die Formen der krankhaften Geschwülste* (1838) 44), and that in quot. 1847–9 in Dict. (given more fully below).] *Obs.*

1847–9 R. B. TODD *Cycl. Anat. & Physiol.* IV. I. 135/2 Osteoid.—Under the names of osteoid or ossifying fungous tumour, Müller describes a growth..composed of a greyish white, vascular, nodulated substance, of the consistence of fibro-cartilage. **1854** W. E. SWAINE tr. *Rokitansky's Man. Path. Anat.* I. ix. 181 This series [of new-growths]..separates into the osteoid, and into the bony concretion. *Ibid.* 185 Müller's osteoid is a bone-formation which enters redundantly into the parenchyma of cancer.

b. Osteoid tissue, uncalcified bone. Also *attrib.*

1934 *Vet. Jrnl.* XC. 157 They were not considered to be genuinely rachitic, because the pathognomic osteoid formation was absent, or the amount of osteoid was not considered sufficient. **1943** *Bull. Johns Hopkins Hosp.* LXXII. 236 Osteoid in the normal adult individual is usually absent or very scanty. **1963** JUBB & KENNEDY *Path. Domestic Animals* I. i. 9/2 Osteoid consists of fibrillar protein (collagen) in a non-fibrillar medium which is probably largely of mucopolysaccharides. **1972** H. L. JAFFE *Metabolic Dis. Bones* xv. 387 It is the presence of abundant osteoid that characterizes the histologic picture of both rickets and osteomalacia. **1972** *Science* 2 June 1032/3 Light microscopic observations indicated no obvious differences between treated and control cultures with respect to proliferation of boneforming cells or degree of osteoid formation.

osteologically, *adv.* (Examples.)

1891 *Proc. Zool. Soc.* 196 It will at once be seen that, osteologically, *Starnœnas* is quite different from any of our other pigeons. **1946** F. E. ZEUNER *Dating Past* vii. 206 This form is osteologically quite distinct from *Lynx pardina* Temminck.

osteon (ǫ·stiˌǫn). *Histology.* Also **osteone.** [a. G. *osteon* (W. Biedermann 1914, in H. Winterstein *Handb. d. vergleich. Physiol.* III. I. 1150), f. Gr. ὀστέον bone.] = *Haversian system.*

1928 MOORE & KEY tr. *Leriche & Policard's Normal & Path. Physiol. Bone* i. 24 Recently, several histologists have tried to make the Haversian systems the structural units of bone, and have given them the name of osteons. This neologism is useless. **1958** *Jrnl. Bone & Joint Surg.* XL. A. 419 Haversian systems or osteons course primarily longitudinally in the long bones. **1968** PASSMORE & ROBSON *Compan. Med. Stud.* I. xvi. 12/1 The osteones branch and interweave one with another. **1971** *Nature* 30 July 335/1 The osteons were orientated along the length of the femur, and tangentially to the surface of the frontal bone of the skull.

osteopetrosis (ǫstiopetrōᵘ·sis). *Path.* [f. OSTEO- + L. *petra*, Gr. πέτρα rock + -OSIS.] A rare hereditary disease in man in which there is excessive formation of dense trabecular bone with resulting brittleness; also, any similar disease of animals.

1926 R. G. KARSHNER in *Amer. Jrnl. Roentgenol.* XVI. 405/1 Osteopetrosis is an hereditary disease. *Ibid.* 405/2 The term osteopetrosis (stony bones) is chosen because in one word it describes the primary pathological condition, bone petrification. **1947**, etc. [see *marble bone* s.v. *MARBLE *sb.* 9]. **1948** *Jrnl. Exper. Med.* LXXXVIII. 579 (*heading*) Hereditary osteopetrosis of the rabbit. **1974** PASSMORE & ROBSON *Compan. Med. Stud.* III. I. xxvi. 20/2 (*caption*) In osteopetrosis the bone texture is uniformly dense and no medullary cavity is present.

Hence **osteopetro·tic** *a.*

1951 *Jrnl. Bone & Joint Surg.* XXXIII. A. 937 The transverse lines in the metaphyses of osteopetrotic bones are fractures in various stages of healing. **1965** *Ibid.* XLVII. A. 1365 (*heading*) Avian osteopetrotic bone.

osteoporotic, *a.* (s.v. OSTEOPOROSIS). (Examples.)

1910 *Brit. Jrnl. Dental Sci.* LIII. 482 The bone itself presenting a sclerosed rather than an osteoporotic condition. **1970** *Sci. Jrnl.* Aug. 72/3 All individuals, whether normal or osteoporotic, therefore lose a small amount of bone mineral at night which is made up during the day.

Osterizer (ǫ·stərəizəɹ). Also with lower-case initial. [f. the name *Oster* (see quot. 1949) + -IZE + -ER[1].] The proprietary name of a type of electric food mixer.

1949 *Official Gaz.* (U.S. Patent Office) 5 Apr. 39 John Oster Manufacturing Company..Osterizer. For electric food mixers. **1967** E. B. NICKERSON *Kayaks to Arctic* xv. 142 Back in the days before osterizers, when celluloid was virtually the only plastic known. **1977** *Rolling Stone* 30 June 73/2 Her kitchen is very white—walls, doors, floors, white appliances, Braun coffee grinder and Osterizer, white salt and pepper shakers, [etc.].

Ostiak, var. *OSTYAK.

ostial (ǫ·stiăl), *a. Anat.* [f. OSTI(UM + -AL.] Of, pertaining to, or having an ostium or ostia; of the nature of an ostium (in an insect's heart).

1900 MIALL & HAMMOND *Struct. & Life Hist. Harlequin Fly* 76 All the valves found in the heart of any Chironomus, whether cellular, ostial, or aortic, appear to be derived from the semicircular muscle-cells. **1910** *Practitioner* Jan. 51 The ostial end of the tube dilates to allow of the passage of the mole. **1969** R. F. CHAPMAN *Insects* xxxii. 662 (*caption*) Incurrent ostial valves in the larva of *Chaoborus* at different phases of the heartbeat. **1969** *Jrnl. Thoracic & Cardiovasc. Surg.* LVII. 792/2 At autopsy all showed varying degrees of coronary ostial sclerosis with stenosis.

ostiate (ǫ·stiˌēⁱt), *a. rare.* [f. OSTI(UM + -ATE[2].] = *OSTIAL *a.*

1897 *Natural Sci.* Apr. 266 The parapodial jaws and the ostiate heart cannot be supposed to have been *both* developed independently in each group of arthropods.

‖ **ostinato** (ǫstinā·to), *a.* and *sb. Mus.* [It., obstinate, persistent.] **A.** *adj.* Recurring, frequently repeated. **B.** *sb.* Pl. **ostinati, ostinatos.** A musical figure which recurs unchanged and at the same pitch. Also *transf.* Cf. *basso ostinato* s.v. *BASSO.

1876 STAINER & BARRETT *Dict. Mus. Terms* 340/2 *Ostinato* (*It.*) *Lit.* obstinate, used in the sense of 'frequently repeated', as *basso ostinato*, a ground-bass. **1928** *Daily Express* 27 Aug. 3/2 It is clear that there are three principal themes, the *ostinato* on page three obtruding itself against a version of the second theme. **1934** C. LAMBERT *Music Ho!* II. 126 We find the juxtaposition of short lyrical phrases..with ostinatos of extreme and deliberate bareness. **1946** G. ABRAHAM in A. L. Bacharach *Brit. Music* iii. 62 Neuritis..had exaggerated his [*sc.* Holst's] mannerism of *ostinato* bass-figures through the ease with which they could be indicated by repeat-signs. **1947** A. EINSTEIN *Mus. Romantic Era* xi. 143 The combination of *doloroso* and *agitato*, of *cantabile* and rhythmic *ostinati*, is typical. **1959** R. FULLER *Ruined Boys* II. ix. 131 He became aware of the noises of summer—of insects, larks, leaves—that provide the normally unidentified *ostinato* that nevertheless enriches the obvious themes of colour, sun and cloud. **1971** *Times Lit. Suppl.* 1 Oct. 1180/2 In *Erwartung*..the Way becomes an ostinato figure that marks the beginning of Schoenbergian serialism. **1973** E.-J. BAHR *Nice Neighbourhood* ix. 98 The kids were performing an ostinato of whining. **1974** *Early Music* II. 227 A series of fanfare-like ostinati alternating between the lower two voices. **1975** *Countr Life* 2 Oct. 846/1 Mime's forge is equipped with a..mechanical hammer which superimposes its own *ostinato* on Wagner's music. **1976** *Gramophone* May 1766/3 The only place which sounds like a slip-up to me comes three bars before fig. 139, in the 'Action rituelle', where the tam-tam suddenly sticks out of the percussion ostinato of which it forms a part.

ostium. Add: **2.** Also, a slit-like valve in an insect's heart. Also in combs. with mod.L. adjs. (Earlier and later examples.)

1828 J. QUAIN *Elem. Anat.* viii. 537 The fimbriated border presents a fissure or opening, (ostium abdominale) into which the impregnated ovum is received at the moment of its liberation from the ovarium, and thence conveyed along the tube, which opens into the uterus by another aperture, (ostium uterinum). **1874** J. HINTON tr. *von Tröltsch's Surg. Dis. Ear* v. 36 The tympanic opening of the [Eustachian] tube (ostium tympanicum) lies directly opposite the irregularly shaped entrances to the mastoid cells. **1909** BAILEY & MILLER *Text-bk. Embryol.* x. 232 The valves between the atrium and ventricle.. develop for the most part from the walls of the triangular atrio-ventricular opening (ostium atrio-ventriculare). **1925** A. D. IMMS *Gen. Textbk. Entomol.* 123 The blood enters the heart through lateral inlets or ostia, a pair of which is situated at each constriction between adjacent chambers. **1951** C. K. WEICHERT *Anat. Chordates* viii. 321 The ovum then passes through the ostium tubae into the Fallopian tube. **1962** W. H. HOLLINSHEAD *Textbk. Anat.* xix. 581/1 The atrium opens into the right ventricle by way of the right atrioventricular ostium. **1969** R. F. CHAPMAN *Insects* xxxii. 661 The anterior and posterior lips of each ostium are reflexed into the heart so that they form a valve permitting the flow of blood into the heart.., but preventing its outward passage. *Ibid.* 663 There are unpaired excurrent ostia in the heart of Plecoptera and Embioptera.

Ostmark (ǫ·stmāɹk). [G., f. *Ost* east + *mark* MARK *sb.*[2] 2c.] The name sometimes given in western countries to the currency of the German Democratic Republic, usu. to distinguish it from the West German Mark.

1948 *Times* 9 July 5/6 In the Soviet sector [of Berlin],.. only the *Ostmark*, the temporary currency of the Soviet zone, circulates legally. *Ibid.*, There was no intention that the *Deutschemark* [*sic*] should rival the *Ostmark* as a currency in the western sectors. [**1950** *Britannica Bk. of Year* 300/2 According to a report of the Deutsche Notenbank the note circulation in Eastern Germany was estimated in Feb. 1949 at Deutsche Mark (Ost) 4,112 million.] **1959** *Times* 18 Feb. 14/4 West German demand for Ostmarks is relatively weak. *Ibid.* 14/5 The 'real' value of the Ostmark is about ·50 west mark. **1972** R. W. LAST tr. *Freund's From Cold War to Ostpolitik* 28 The commandants of the western sectors declared that the Soviet orders relating to the introduction of the Ostmark into Greater Berlin were null and void.

ostomy (ǫ·stǒmi). orig. *U.S.* [f. *COL)OSTOMY and similar words.] An operation such as colostomy or ileostomy that involves making a permanent artificial opening in the body.

1957 *Ileostomy Q.* July 62/2 (Advt.), 'Ostomy' Skin Cream... United Surgical Supply Co. **1961** *Ibid.* Summer 65/2 Mr. Reynolds... doesn't look on his 'ostomy' as a handicap or hindrance to work or play. **1963** (*title of periodical*) Ostomy quarterly. **1964** *Hospitals* XXXVIII. 88 At present 35 ostomy clubs..in this country [*sc.* the U.S.A.] provide a means for persons with ileostomy, colostomy, ureterostomy, and ileal bladder to meet together and learn more about the management of their condition. *Ibid.* 90 Diet need not be a major problem to those with an ostomy. **1975** *Globe & Mail* (Toronto) 22 Aug. 25/8 There are three main types of ostomy: urostomy or urinary diversion, mostly due to cancer or birth defects; ileostomy or diversion of the small intestine due mostly to ulcerative colitis and Crohn's disease; and colostomy or diversion of the large intestine, due mostly to cancer and birth defects.

Hence **o·stomate** [cf. -ATE[1]], a person who has had an ostomy.

1966 *Ostomy Q.* Spring 15/2 What can be more rewarding than the feeling you have after visiting a new ostomate and knowing you have helped them? **1973** *Daily Colonist* (Victoria, B.C.) 2 Mar. 17/7 The ostomate faces a life of carrying the plastic bag outside the body. **1975** *Globe & Mail* (Toronto) 22 Aug. 25/8 Whether or not you are one of the 100,000 or more ostomates in Canada you should be interested in the current convention of the United Ostomy Association going on in Toronto. **1977** *Telegraph* (Brisbane) 2 Aug. 2/1 Ostomates are people who have had operations to by-pass bowel or urinary tracts, and who have to wear bags attached to their body to collect their body wastes.

Ostpolitik (ǫ·stpǫliti:k). [G., f. *Ost* east + *Politik* policy.] German policy towards Eastern Europe, associated mainly with the Federal Republic of Germany's cultivation of good relations with the Communist block during the 1960s, but applied also, by extension, to the policies of other western countries regarding the East as a whole.

1961 T. PRITTIE *Germany Divided* vi. 155 They will scarcely overlook Hitler's statement,..'The goal of *Ostpolitik* is to open up an area of settlement for one hundred million Germans.' **1967** *Economist* 6 May 558/3 Herr Kiesinger..promised that the government would not pursue its Ostpolitik 'behind the backs of the expellees'. **1968** *Ann. Reg. 1967* 253 Immediately the East German Government, supported by Moscow, took steps to hamper further progress by Bonn's *Ostpolitik.* **1970** *Atlantic Monthly* July 26 In the west, the big change was Willy Brandt's narrow victory in the West German elections last October, and the formation of a new Bonn coalition government dominated by the Social Democrats, prepared to abandon the rigidities of the Adenauer foreign policy of the last twenty years and embark on an entirely new and dynamic course of Ostpolitik. **1971** *Times Lit. Suppl.* 15 Oct. 1246/2 The politicians of Bonn are rather unhappy at the widespread use of the term 'Ostpolitik' by their Western allies. In the history of twentieth-century Germany, this term has signified a whole range of activities, from Hindenburg's humiliation of Russia at Brest-Litovsk to the East-West balancing act of Rapallo, and back to the domination of the East by Schacht's financial diplomacy and Hitler's armies. **1971** *New Yorker* 23 Oct. 156 Nixon as a risk-taker is something of a surprise... But his *Ostpolitik* is daring. It is a repudiation of his entire past. **1972** R. W. LAST tr. *Freund's From Cold War to Ostpolitik* 75 Brandt knows better than anyone else that Berlin is the real test of the new Ostpolitik.

ostracod. Now the usual spelling of OSTRACODE *a.* and *sb.* (but see quots. 1953 and 1974[2]). Substitute for etym.: [a. mod.L. *Ostracoda* and Fr. *ostracode* (P. A. Latreille *Genera Crustaceorum et Insectorum* (1806) I. 17), formerly *Ostrachoda, ostrachode* (P. A. Latreille in C. S. Sonnini *Buffon's Hist. Nat. Crustacés & Insectes* (1802) II. 361), f. Gr. ὀστρακώδης testaceous.] (Later examples.)

1935 TWENHOFEL & SHROCK *Invertebr. Paleontol.* x. 436 Ostracods are small, bivalved Crustacea which are found inhabiting all waters but are most abundant in marine habitats. **1953** *Ibid.* (ed. 2) xiii. 548 Ostracodes are minute, lentil-shaped crustaceans having a bivalve carapace that completely encloses the indistinctly segmented body. **1956** [see *MYSID]. **1957** *New Biol.* XXIV. 70 Some of the ostracods..possess haemoglobin. **1965** B. E. FREEMAN tr. *Vandel's Biospeleol.* ix. 112 Hypogeous ostracods are known from Europe, North America and Japan. **1969** BENNISON & WRIGHT *Geol. Hist. Brit. Isles* viii. 164 Ostracod shales were laid down contemporaneously in deeper waters in the Torquay area. **1974** A. DILLARD *Pilgrim at Tinker Creek* viii. 132 An ostracod, a common fresh-water crustacean of the sort I crunch on by the thousands every time I set foot in Tinker Creek. **1974** *Smithsonian Contrib. Earth Sci.* No. 13. 22/1 Constituents were counted and grouped in the following classes: terrigenous (mica and other, including quartz), bioclastic remains (pelagic forams, benthonic forams, pteropods, and other), plant fragments, and other (including ostracode valves, sponge spicules, unidentifiable fragments, etc.).

ostracoderm (ǫ·străkodəɹm), *sb.* and *a.* [a. mod.L. sub-class name *Ostracodermi* (E. D. Cope 1889, in *Amer. Naturalist* XXIII. 852), f. Gr. ὀστρακόδερμος hard-shelled.] **A.** *sb.* A small, primitive, fossil fish belonging to the group formerly designated the sub-class Ostracodermi. **B.** *adj.* Of or pertaining to this group of fossils.

1891 A. S. WOODWARD *Catal. Fossil Fishes in Brit. Mus.* (*Nat. Hist.*) II. p. xvii, The Arachnid theory is based upon a complete misapprehension of the most fundamental points in Ostracoderm skeletal anatomy. **1898** [see OSTRACO-]. **1933** A. S. ROMER *Vertebr. Paleont.* ii. 24 Almost all are covered with various types of armor, a feature to which the name 'ostracoderms' ('shell-skinned') is due. **1935** *Amer. Jrnl. Sci.* CCXXIX. 323 (*title*) The ostracoderm genus *Dartmuthia* Patten. **1968** A. S. ROMER *Procession of Life* viii. 148 By that time [*sc.* early Devonian] higher fish types descended from the ostracoderm stock were already evolving. **1969** BENNISON & WRIGHT *Geol. Hist. Brit. Isles* viii. 182 The jawless Ostracoderms with dorsal shield and granular armour..had made their appearance in the Upper Ludlow Beds.

ostrakon (ǫ·străkǫn). Also **ostracon.** Pl. **ostraka, -ca.** [ad. Gr. ὄστρακον potsherd.] A sherd of pottery or (more rarely) limestone used in antiquity as a surface for writing or inscribing, often, at Athens and in other Greek cities, to cast a vote (see OSTRACISM 1), or as a common writing material. Used (freq. in *pl.*) of archæological finds of this kind in the Middle East.

1883 *Proc. Soc. Biblical Archaeol.* V. 84 The British Museum has lately acquired..a considerable number of ostraka or potsherds discovered at Elephantine, Thebes, and other places. *Ibid.* 119 Two ostraka or slices of limestone formed for the purpose, inscribed with hieratic inscriptions. **1900** *Athenæum* 23 June 783/1 The study of Greek ostraca is a comparatively new one. **1921** G. A. F. KNIGHT *Nile & Jordan* 251 The name Bata has been recovered in a hieratic ostrakon. **1934** *Discovery* Apr. 90/2 The smaller finds include..actual *ostraca* from the voting of 483 B.C. when 'Aristides the Just' was banished. **1952** G. SARTON *Hist. Sci.* I. iv. 114 Two late mathematical papyri,..as well as Coptic ostraca from Wādī Sarga (near Asyūt)..contain unmistakable examples of Egyptian computation. **1960** [see *FIND *sb.* 4]. **1968** V. EHRENBERG *From Solon to Socrates* Notes 414 The number of ostraca found by archaeologists gives little evidence as to the actual results of the voting. **1972** *Times* 18 May (Egypt Suppl.) p. iv/4 During the excavation of the temple terrace, many fragments of stone stelae and *ostraca* (inscriptions on potsherds) were found bearing dedications to Isis. **1978** *N.Y. Times Bk. Rev.* 21 May 39/1 Demotic is known today from papyri and ostraca—broken bits of pot that have been scribbled on.

ostrich[1]. Add: **1. c.** Short for 'ostrich skin'.

1939 R. STOUT *Some Buried Caesar* xiii. 161 The brown ostrich card-case, gold-tooled. **1973** J. DRUMMOND *Bang! Bang! You're Dead!* iii. 6 She walked from the room, carrying the jewel-case and a matching ostrich purse.

2. a. (Further examples.)

1598 J. MARSTON *Pigmalion* Sat. I. 34 Fie that his Ostridge stomack should digest His Ostridge feather. **1844** E. B. BROWNING *Let.* 11 Jan. (1954) 212 But the squeamishness of this Age,..this Ostrich age..which exposes its own eggs, and then hides its head in the sand,..is really to me quite monstrous. **1952** DYLAN THOMAS *Let.* 6 Nov. (1966) 380 These ostrich griefs were always with me. **1976** *Listener* 6 May 585/2 The typical ostrich-Briton of today.

b. *ostrich-like* (later examples), *-skin*; **ostrich-egg cup**, a decorated cup made from an ostrich-egg; **ostrich-farm** (earlier and later examples); **ostrich-farming** (later examples).

1937 *Burlington Mag.* Apr. p. xxiv/2 The Leipzig *Ostrich Egg Cup* called thus because of the egg being decorated with the figures of birds. **1960** H. HAYWARD *Antique Coll.* 205/2 *Ostrich egg cup*, sometime supposed to be the eggs of griffins or phoenixes, ostrich eggs were often mounted as cups (and occasionally made into flasks) in the 16th cent. and later. Many surviving specimens are German. **1876** C. M. YONGE *Three Brides* II. i. 10 He has been acting as manager on an ostrich farm. **1926** *Daily Colonist* (Victoria, B.C.) 18 July 21/5 The White and Gold Room at Buckingham Palace, in which ladies sit in rows before passing into the Throne Room to curtsy to Their Majesties, is irreverently referred to on court-nights by junior members of the household as 'the ostrich farm'. **1927** CHESTERTON *Coll. Poems* 180 Old Noah he had an ostrich farm and fowls on the largest scale. **1974** *Encycl. Brit. Micropædia* VII. 618/1 This demand [for plumes] led to the establishment of ostrich farms in South Africa, the southern U.S., Australia, and elsewhere. **1902** *Chambers's Jrnl.* Jan. 53/2 His unconscious host,..prosed on concerning himself chiefly with..the future of ostrich-farming. **1957** *Encycl. Brit.* XVI. 959/2 Ostrich farming is carried on in Cape Colony, Egypt, Algeria, the French Riviera, Southern U.S. and elsewhere. **1944** *Sci. Jrnl. R. Coll. Sci.* XIV. 64 Profound influences are continually at work causing changes in the general constitution of man, and no amount of ostrich-like behaviour will prevent their action. **1966** *Guardian* 30 July 3/5 Britain is more ostrichlike in its approach to the problem than America. **1976** *Times* 5 Apr. 3/2 It would be an ostrich-like attitude on the part of the executive if this chance was turned down. **1926–7** *Army & Navy Stores Catal.* 84/3 Ostrich skin Cigar Case..each 8/6. **1971** P. DRISCOLL *White Lie Assignment* ii. 17 Transferring the cigarettes..into an ostrich-skin case. **1976** J. MCCLURE *Rogue Eagle* xiii. 222 He was loading his pipe from an ostrich-skin pouch.

ostrich-feather. Add: **1.** (Later examples.) Also *fig.*

1932 D. GASCOYNE *Roman Balcony* 12 The ostrich feathers Of the waves That flap against the shore. **1957** M. B. PICKEN *Fashion Dict.* 238/2 *Ostrich feathers*, wing and tail feathers from an ostrich. Often several feathers are carefully glued together as one to give abundant appearance. Dyed in all colors and beautifully curled. **1977** *Listener* 15 Dec. 794/1 Before I graduated to ostrich feathers..I had absorbed..[a] vital principle: that diplomatic privilege exists mainly not to be made use of.

Comb. (Later examples.)

1884 *List of Subscribers* (London & Globe Telephone Co.) Henry, C. S. & Co... Ostrich Feather Merchants, 12, Jewin Crescent. **1908** *Westm. Gaz.* 27 June 13/1 This suit was worn with a hat and ostrich-feather ruffle of a very charming soft grey tone. **1966** J. LAVER *Victoriana* 131 Towards the end of the [19th] century large ostrich feather fans became fashionable.

ostrichism. (In Dict. s.v. OSTRICH[1].) Delete (*nonce-wd.*) and add later examples in allusive and extended uses.

1944 J. S. HUXLEY *On Living in Revolution* 3 The fact that a world war existed and the ostrichism of our reactions to it were most obvious in the case of Spain. **1945** R. HARGREAVES *Enemy at Gate* 285 A departure into Maginot Line ostrichism which had ended..in the rigid chain of defence works being 'turned'. **1958** *New Statesman* 1 Mar. 260/2 Geoffrey Dawson's calculated ostrichism towards the Fascist dictators..during the Thirties. **1960** *Spectator* 15 July 106 A new wave of ostrichism in regard to defence is sweeping the country.

ostrobogulous (ǫstrobǫ·giŭləs). *slang.* [Etym. obscure; see quot. 1973.] A word associated with the writer Victor B. Neuburg (1883–1940), used with various shades of meaning to describe the bizarre, unusual, or interesting (see quots.). Hence **ostrobo·gulatory** *a.*; **ostrobogula·tion, ostrobogulo·sity,** *sbs.*

1951 A. CALDER-MARSHALL *Magic of My Youth* i. 31 'Ostrobogulous' was Vickybird's favourite word. It stood for anything from the bawdy to the slightly off-colour. Any *double entendre* that might otherwise have escaped his audience was prefaced by, 'if you will pardon the ostrobogulosity.' **1952** A. GRAVES *Ostrobogulous Pigs* 7 Once upon a time there were..five ostrobogulous skipperty flipperty filthy grubby muddy little pigs. *Ibid.* 10, I can no longer endure this ostrobogulatory behaviour. *Ibid.* 11 'I can no longer endure the odorous and objectionable ostrobogulations of those creatures,' said Angelina Boghurst-Fisher. **1963** *Sunday Times* 29 Dec. 19/2 (*heading*), An ostrobogulous year for the toy men. *Ibid.* 19/6 Minnie King works full time for Ostrobogulous—which is a word, they say, used by children and means 'mischievous but gorgeous'. **1965** J. O. FULLER *Magical Dilemma V. Neuburg* I. iv. 58 Some of the entries were not printed because they were ostrobogulous. This was a wonderful word of Vicky's. It was used in the place of indecent or pornographic, and had the advantage..that it implied no moral attitude. *Ibid.* 59 He would speak of an ostrobogulous tale... He took Morton's opinion as ostrobogulosity. **1968** *Times Lit. Suppl.* 24 Oct. 1196/3 There has been no developing tradition of the ribald, raw and ostrobogulous (to use the word Victor Neuburg applied to this work) merely because there have been no similar collections. **1972** *Ibid.* 30 June 757/4 His career, fabulous, prestigious, sordid, sinister, and in the word of Victor Neuburg ostrobogulous. **1973** *Ibid.* 27 July 871/2 It was sick, dirty, or more precisely, 'ostrobogulous', which according to Victor Neuburg..meant etymologically full of (Latin, *ulus*) rich (Greek, *ostro*) dirt (schoolboy, *bog*).

Ostrogoth. Add: (Earlier example.)

1605 J. SYLVESTER tr. *Du Bartas's Devine Weekes* 456 Normans, Allains, Ostrogothes.

c. as *adj.* = OSTROGOTHIC *a.*

1920 H. G. WELLS *Outl. Hist.* 350/1 The adventurous wanderings that ended at last in the Ostrogoth Kingdom in Italy. **1954** ARNOLD-BAKER & DENT *Everyman's Dict. Dates* 275/1 Theodoric..became a figure of Germanic legend, and founded an Ostrogoth kingdom in Italy *c.* 500.

Ostwald (ǫ·stwăld). The name of Wilhelm *Ostwald* (1853–1932), Russian chemist, used *attrib.* and in the possessive to denote apparatus invented and principles enunciated by him, as **Ostwald('s) dilution law,** the law that for dilute solutions of a binary electrolyte the square of the degree of dissociation of the solute, multiplied by its concentration, and divided by one minus the degree of dissociation, is a constant for the solute; **Ostwald pycnometer,** a pycnometer in the form of a bulb joined at the top to a horizontal capillary tube and at the bottom to a U-tube bearing a graduation at the level of the capillary; **Ostwald('s) viscometer,** an instrument in which the viscosity of a liquid is determined by the time taken for a measured volume to pass through a capillary bore in a U-tube.

[**1899** J. WALKER *Introd. Physical Chem.* xxi. 227 Certain empirical relations have..been found connecting the degree of dissociation and the dilution, and these have a form similar to that of Ostwald's dilution formula.] **1902** H. C. JONES *Elem. Physical Chem.* vii. 354 (*heading*) Testing the Ostwald dilution law. **1930** C. W. DAVIES *Conductivity of Solutions* i. 12 Ostwald's dilution law breaks down completely when it is applied to solutions of the common salts. **1973** A. W. ADAMSON *Textbk. Physical Chem.* xii. 538 Weak electrolytes obey the Ostwald dilution law well, and their behavior is thus determined primarily by a dissociation equilibrium. **1910** A. EWELL *Text-bk. Physical Chem.* 25 An Ostwald pyknometer is very convenient as a weighing pipette. **1962** PERRY & KOENIG in A. Pirie *Lens Metabolism Rel. Cataract* 306 For viscosity measurements, Ostwald viscometers were used to measure flow rates at 25°C. Densities were measured with Ostwald pycnometers. **1924** *Abstr. Bacteriol.* VIII. 2 Direct inoculation of the sterilized gelatin culture media in Ostwald's viscometer was tried for a period of 3 months. **1967** MARGERISON & EAST *Introd. Polymer Chem.* ii. 103 The usual method employed to measure the solution and solvent viscosities utilizes an Ostwald viscometer.

Ostyak (ǫ·stiak). Also **Ostiac, Ostiack, Ostiak,** etc. [Russ. *ostyák.*] **a.** (A member of) a Finno-Ugric people, also called *Khantý*, living in the Ob River basin in Western Siberia. **b.** The language of this people, belonging to the *OB-UGRIAN group. Also *attrib.* or as *adj.*

1722 tr. *Muller's Manners & Customs of Ostiaks* in tr. *F. C. Weber's Present State of Russia* II. 56 The Ostiacks and Samoiedes often venture over those high Rocks into the Country, where they kill Elks and Rain-Deer. **1757** J. DYER *Fleece* IV. 143 Land of the lazy Ostiacs, thin dispers'd. **1841** *Penny Cycl.* XXI. 467/1 South of the Samoyedes are the Ostiaks, who occupy both banks of the river Obi. **1859** G. W. DASENT *Pop. Tales from Norse* p. lxvii, The Ostjaks, a tribe akin to the Lapps. **1870** J. LUBBOCK *Origin of Civilisation* iii. 96 The Ostiaks regard it as a crime to marry a woman of the same family or even of the same name. **1880** A. H. SAYCE *Introd. Sci. of Lang.* II. viii. 204 It is difficult..to distinguish the Ostiak forms ..from the persons of the Sanskrit verb. **1889** T. DUKA *Essay Ugor Lang.* 32 Klaproth..makes mention of five Finn dialects, but describes..the Ostjak around the river Ob, and the Magyar. **1911** J. G. FRAZER *Golden Bough: Magic Art* (ed. 3) II. ix. 11 The Ostyaks and Woguls, two peoples of the Finnish-Ugrian stock in Siberia. **1933,** etc. [see *OB-UGRIAN]. **1938** *N. & Q.* 23 Apr. 291/1 The Ostyaks of the Tobolsk region have a spirit of death whom they call *xeina.* **1944** [see *NENETS]. **1959** *Chambers's Encycl.* XI. 432/2 The Uralics, so termed by Bunak, are perhaps best represented by the western Siberian Voguls and Khuntu or Ostyaks, between the Urals and the Ob basin, in reality a single people who call themselves 'Mansi'. **1966** T. BURROW *Sanskrit Lang.* (ed. 2) 23 Vogul and Ostyak are now found to the East of the Urals, but are considered to have moved there from the West. **1971** [see *MORDVIN]. **1972** W. B. LOCKWOOD *Panorama Indo-European Lang.* 152 East of the Zyryene-speaking area, in Siberia, lie Ostyak and Vogul which with Hungarian form the Ugric division of Uralic. **1974** T. P. WHITNEY tr. *Solzhenitsyn's Gulag Archipel.* I. I. i. 6 From Karger they took his archive of the Yenisei Ostyaks. **1975** G. F. CUSHING tr. *Hajdu's Finno-Ugrian Lang. & Peoples* iii. 123 Anthropologically the Voguls and Ostyaks..are classed by anthropologists as Europo-Sibirid or Uralic.

‖**osu** (ǫ·su). *W. Afr.* [Igbo.] An outcast, an 'untouchable'.

1958 C. ACHEBE *Things fall Apart* xviii. 140 These outcasts, or *osu*, seeing that the new religion welcomed twins and such abominations, thought that it was possible that they would also be received. **1960** —— *No Longer at Ease* vii. 71 'I am an *osu*,' she wept... 'So you see we cannot get married,' she said, quite firmly, almost gaily—a terrible kind of gaiety. *Ibid.* 75 Obi knew better than anyone else that his family would violently oppose the idea of marrying an *osu*. *Ibid.* xiv. 133 Our fathers in their darkness and ignorance called an innocent man an *osu*, a thing given to idols, and thereafter he became an outcast, and his children, and his children's children for ever. *Ibid.* 134 Obi repeated his points again. What made an *osu* different from other men and women? Nothing but the ignorance of their forefathers. **1960** *Spectator* 21 Oct. 616 He falls in love with Clara, an *osu* or 'untouchable'. **1973** *Black World* June 39/2 This..explains the violent objection of the clansmen to Obi marrying an *osu* (a cult-slave; for this reason ostracized from the normal life of the village).

Oswego (ǫzwī·go). [The name of a river and a town in the northern part of the state of New York.] **1. a.** = **Oswego bass.*

1857 [see *LUNGE *sb.*[3]].

b. A proprietary name for a type of cornflour.

1881 J. T. GILL *Compl. Bread, Cake & Cracker Baker* I. v. 75 Maizena..is maize deprived of all its albuminoid or flesh-forming constituents..and is, therefore, simply pure starch... Corn flour and Oswego are only other names for the same substance. **1907** *Official Gaz.* (U.S. Patent Office) 29 Jan. 1758/2 National Starch Co., Jersey City, N.J. and Oswego, N.Y. Filed Dec. 17, 1906. Used ten years. Oswego. Particular description of goods.—Corn-starch. **1911** *Encycl. Brit.* XVII. 449/1 When deprived of the gluten it [*sc.* maize] constitutes oswego, maizena or corn flour.

c. = **Oswego biscuit.*

c **1900** in A. Davis *Package & Print* (1967) (*frontispiece*) Peek, Frean & Co. Biscuits. Oswego. **1907** *Yester-day's Shopping* (1969) 8 Biscuits..Oswego..

2. *attrib.* **Oswego bass** = *large-mouth* (*bass*) s.v. LARGE *a.* 15 a in Dict. and Suppl.; **Oswego biscuit, cake,** a biscuit or cake made with **Oswego flour** (= sense *1 b); **Oswego tea,** a herbaceous perennial plant, *Monarda didyma*, belonging to the family Labiatæ and native to eastern North America; its leaves were formerly used to make a medicinal tea.

1758 C. REA *Jrnl.* 20 July in *Essex Inst. Hist. Coll.* (1881) XVIII. 112 The Lake affords plenty of a Fish call'd Oswego Bass. **1840** J. F. COOPER *Pathfinder* I. ix. 130 Even the Major himself..will sometimes swear that an oat-meal cake is better fare than the Oswego bass. **1884** [see **large-mouth* (*bass*)]. **1965** A. J. MCCLANE *Standard Fishing Encycl.* 473/1 The largemouth bass is regionally known as green bass, green trout, Oswego bass, and black bass. **1936** CHESTERTON *Autobiogr.* 324 Do let me offer you an oswego biscuit. **1963** C. MACKENZIE *My Life & Times* II. 94 However well Huntley and Palmer may have made Oswego and Osborne biscuits..they could not reproduce the authentic flavour of real Petit Beurres. **1907** M. I. RIVERS *Tips for Tea* vii. 50 Oswego cakes... Cream the butter and sugar together until they are white; add the eggs one at a time, and stir in lightly the oswego. **1949** A. R. DANIEL *Baker's Dict.* Oswego flour. A particular type of flour obtained from maize, but not just pure cornflour. **1752** P. MILLER *Gardeners Dict.* (ed. 6) s.v. *Monarda*, The inhabitants drink an infusion of this Herb as Tea, and call it Ozweega Tea. **1759** —— (ed. 7) s.v. *Monarda*, It [*sc.* Monarda with Flowers collected in Heads] is commonly called Oswego Tea, by which title it was brought to England. **1760** [see TEA *sb.* 6]. **1789** [see *MONARDA]. **1850** S. F. COOPER *Rural Hours* 117 Humming-birds..are partial to the bee larkspur also, with the wild bergamot or Oswego tea. **1947** *Nat. Geogr. Mag.* July 62/1 Among the many useful plants they found ..were two of this same Mint Family, Oswego Tea (*Monarda didyma*), and Wild Bergamot (*Monarda fistulosa*). **1954** C. HYLANDER *Macmillan Wild Flower Bk.* 344 Oswego Tea, also known as Bee-balm, has a natural range from New York to Michigan..; it is frequently cultivated as an ornamental. **1970** B. MILES *Bluebells & Bittersweet* vii. 113/3 *M*[*onarda*] *didyma* (Oswego-tea) is usually red, raising round heads of lipped flowers 4 feet in midsummer.

Otaheitean (ōutāhī·tiăn), *a.* and *sb. Obs.* Also **Otahitean, Otaheite, Otaheitan.** [f. *Otaheite* early name of the Pacific island of Tahiti.] = *TAHITIAN *a.* and *sb.*

Cf. OTAHEITE APPLE in Dict.

1773 W. WALES *Jrnl.* 31 Aug. in Cook *Jrnls.* (1961) II. 796 With regard to the Personal Beauties of the Otahitean Ladies, I believe it would be most prudent to remain entirely silent. **1792** W. BLIGH *Voy. to South Sea* vi. 81 Among people so free from ostentation as the Otaheiteans ..the strictness with which the punctilios of rank are observed, is surprising. *Ibid.* xii. 147 In a small vocabulary, that I made..only four words, out of twenty-four, differed from the Otaheite. **1793** F. BURNEY *Jrnl.* 3 May (1972) II. 104, I saw nothing of this *Tio*:—I accept your otaheité epithet, & like it much. **1799** *Sporting Mag.* XIV. 203/1 Our Otaheitean girl, who was tolerably fair, and had a comely person. **1817** T. COGAN *Ethical Questions* v. 233 The good-natured Otaheite *feels* it to be an obligation of hospitality, to present his wife or daughter to a stranger. **1819** SHELLEY *Let.* 3 Nov. (1964) II. 140 A North American Indian, or an Otaheitan. **1851** *Illustr. Catal. Gt. Exhib.* IV. 980/1 All the above-mentioned sugars are the produce of the Otaheite or Tahiti cane. **1861** R. BENTLEY *Man. Bot.* 674 The starch known as Tacca starch, Tahiti Arrow-root, or Otaheite Salep.

otavite (otā·vəit). *Min.* [ad. G. *otavit* (O. Schneider 1906, in *Centralbl. f. Mineral., Geol. und Paläont.* 389), f. *Otavi*, name of a town in northern South West Africa: see -ITE[1].] Naturally occurring cadmium carbonate, $CdCO_3$, occurring as crusts of minute rhombohedral crystals usu. white or greyish white in colour.

1906 *Jrnl. Chem. Soc.* XC. II. 620 A new mineral which is named otavite, after the locality. **1943** *Mineral. Abstr.* VIII. 366 Otavite, previously described as a basic carbonate of cadmium from Tsumeb, South-West Africa, forms thin crusts of minute rhombohedra often in parallel growth on smithsonite. X-ray powder photographs agree with Zachariasen's (1928) determination for artificial $CdCO_3$. **1967** *Soviet Physics: Crystallogr.* XII. 417 Artificial otavite, $CdCO_3$, crystals were obtained, which were activated by Co^{+2} so that EPR spectra of the magnetic Co^{+2} ion were observed at varying orientations of the external magnetic field at 4·2°K.

other, *adj. pron.* (*sb.*). Add: **A.** *adj.* **2. c.** *the other half*: (*a*) the other half of the world; people of a different class or those enjoying a different (usu. more affluent) way of life, *spec.* in phr. *how the other half live*(*s*); (*b*) orig. *Naval slang*: a second drink; a drink bought in return for another.

(*a*) [**1532** RABELAIS *Pantagruel* (1547) II. xxxi. 206 La moitié du monde ne sçayt comment l'aultre vit. **1607** J. HALL *Holy Observations* xvii. 26 One half of the world knowes not how the other liues.] **1640** G. HERBERT *Outlandish Proverbs* No. 907, in *Witts Recreations* sig. D7[v] Halfe the world knowes not how the other halfe lies [*sic*]. **1830** MARRYAT *King's Own* I. x. 141 It is an old proverb that 'one half the world do not know *how* the other half live.' Add to it, nor *where* they live. **1890** J. A. RIIS *How Other Half Lives* 1 Long ago it was said that 'one half of the world does not know how the other half lives'. *Ibid.* 3 The sufferings and sins of the 'other half'..are but..a just punishment upon the community that gave it no other choice. **1945** N. L. MCCLUNG *Stream runs Fast* xiii. 106 We were only amateurs but we did find out a few things about how the 'other half' lived. **1965** E. O'BRIEN *Aug. is Wicked Month* xiii. 141 'Why not, see how the other half live...' she said... They would have the pool and servants to wait on them. **1968** J. SANGSTER *Touchfeather* xiii. 140 He said if I was ever in Los Angeles to look him up. Glad I did. Talk about how the other half lives! **1970** 'D. SHANNON' *Unexpected Death* (1971) ix. 141 'My God,' said Higgins. 'How the other half lives.' **1975** *Times* 15 Jan. 15/4 In the interests of national unity, may I support your plea to the other half (and if they do not know they are in it, that is half the trouble) to accept that the shocking conditions of the London comprehensives as reported by you are really good for their children, and for society.

(*b*) **1922** W. S. MAUGHAM *On Chinese Screen* lii. 211 No sooner was your glass empty than he was prompt with the China phrase: 'Ready for the other half?' **1931** C. LITHGOW *Simple Sailor* xv. 184 You won't have the other half? Sure? **1936** 'G. ORWELL' *Keep Aspidistra Flying* v. 117 Drink up!..It's time we had the other half of that. **1965** R. JEFFRIES *Dead against Lawyers* vii. 69 You'll have the other half, Inspector? Two whiskies under the belt are better than one. **1966** A. PRIOR *Operators* ii. 16 'The other half please, George.' 'Yessir, Mr. Barclay.'.. The barman turned to him. **1975** E. BERCKMAN *Indecent Exposure* viii. 101 'Have to be shoving off now, sorry—.' 'The other half,' Dennison objected. 'What were you drinking, whisky—?'

d. *the other side*: (*a*) the world to come, the world beyond the grave, esp. as inhabited by the spirits of the dead; (*b*) *Austral.* and *N.Z. slang* (see quots.); (*c*) an opponent or an opposing side; one regarded as such.

(*a*) **1684** BUNYAN *Pilgrim's Progress* II. 220 So he passed over, and the Trumpets sounded for him on the other side. **1819** [see SIDE *sb.*[1] 12a *fig.*]. **1926** A. CONAN DOYLE *Hist. Spiritualism* I. viii. 187 The sharp detail which we receive from the Other Side is incompatible with any vague grandiose idea of the sort. **1941** AUDEN *New Year Let.* 38 It is Utopian to be dead, For only on the Other Side Are Absolutes all satisfied. **1945** A. HUXLEY *Time must have Stop* vi. 66 Are they still obese on the other side? I'd like to ask next time you have a séance. **1960** M. SPARK *Bachelors* ii. 22 When Patrick's under the control I shouldn't think he could help saying what comes to him from the other side. **1973** *Listener* 8 Mar. 306/2 Max [Aitken]..is devoted to the memory of his father [*sc.* Beaverbrook] and..allows his father to edit the paper from the Other Side. **1974** 'D. SHANNON' *Crime File* xii. 185 They went to Katie May Blaine's funeral... 'You don't want to worry,' she told Mrs. Blaine simply. 'She's being looked after, the other side.'

(*b*) **1855** W. HOWITT *Land, Labour & Gold* ii. 362 Scenery precisely like hundreds of miles which I have seen 'on the other side', as they call Victoria, and as the Victorians call Van Diemen's Land. **1884** A. COX *Recollections* 125, I ax your pardon, zur, but were you ever at the Yan Yean works over the other side? *a* **1948** L. G. D. ACLAND *Early Canterbury Runs* (1951) 389 *Other side*,..Australia. **1963** X. HERBERT *Disturbing Element* 2 My parents..were what were called T'othersiders, meaning people who had come to West Australia from the other side of the continent.

(*c*) **1916** 'TAFFRAIL' *Pincher Martin* xiv. 259 Their expeditions to that region known as 'the other side', for the express purpose of discomforting the Hun. **1939** 'N. BLAKE' *Smiler with Knife* iii. 57 They've youth and independence and courage. They're England. And you know what the other side says—'Woman is for the recreation of the warrior'. **1966** I. ASIMOV *Fantastic Voyage* i. 19 I've met him several times at scientific conferences on the other side. **1967** B. NORMAN *Matter of Mandrake* xxv. 211 There was a change of plan... The Other Side was becoming too worried. **1972** *Sat. Rev. Society* (U.S.) Dec. 33/2 The way is far more open..to similar wars of 'aggression' or 'national liberation' or whatever the Vietnam War has been. The 'other side' can now engage in such activities with the understanding that the United States will be very reluctant to intervene. **1976** B. FREEMANTLE *November Man* iv. 45 Hugo will know it was an attempt on his life... If he runs to the other side, everything is going to be easy for us.

e. *the other place*: one place regarded from the point of view of or with reference to another place; *euphem.*, Hell (as opp. Heaven). Also in depreciatory senses; *spec.* Oxford as regarded in Cambridge (and vice versa).

1841 F. A. KEMBLE *Let.* 29 Dec. in *Rec. Later Life* (1882) II. 156, I conclude that letters will occasionally come *to* heaven, and always be written in—the other place. **1874** 'MARK TWAIN' *Gilded Age* xi. 108 Washington was alternately in paradise or the other place just as it happened that Louise was gracious to him or seemingly indifferent. **1880** TROLLOPE *Duke's Children* I. xx. 245 Shall I go to heaven for doing that?.. Or mayn't I rather go to the other place? **1920** 'O. DOUGLAS' *Penny Plain* i. 13, I wouldn't much care to go to heaven myself, for all my friends are in..the Other Place. **1944** A. THIRKELL *Headmistress* ix. 204 Sir Hosea Weaver..a Cambridge man..had..taken the highest kind of degree that the other place can give in Political Economy. **1958** *Listener* 14 Aug. 232/1 Cambridge has always tried to be more typical and less exotic than the other place. **1967** V. GIELGUD *Conduct of Member* ii. 15 There were Oxford men who persisted in speaking of Cambridge as 'the other place'. **1970** *Guardian* 22 Apr. 24/2 In the *other place*, it had been the rule to have sponsors since 1688 and Stormont had the same rule. **1972** 'M. INNES' *Open House* xi. 101 There being neither youth or age, sir, in the 'avenly mansions—no, nor in the other place either. **1973** *Deb. Senate S. Afr.* 17 May 2807, I am thinking..of the important task of industrial decentralization about which so much has been said in this House and in the Other Place. **1973** 'M. YORKE' *Grave Matters* v. ii. 84, I don't know Oxford at all well... I know the other place better. Isn't that what you call it? **1974** *Oxford Times* 5 July 1/4 (*heading*) By punt to the other place. **1976** *Gramophone* Oct. 552/2 In the old days, 'the other place' never seemed to me to compete at all, but it is very different now with several excellent offerings from Magdalen under Bernard Rose.

f. *the other thing* (colloq.): the contrary, opposite, or reverse; something quite different. *euphem.* sexual activity; the penis. Phr. *to do the other thing*: to do as one pleases (usu. as an expression of contemptuous dismissal).

1846 *Swell's Night Guide* 89 The wealthy voluptuary cannot choose but be gratified, as far as feasting, drinking, and the other thing goes. **1848** TROLLOPE *Kellys & O'Kellys* I. vii. 172 They'd ax him to come and see his sister married, and av' he didn't like it, he might do the other thing. **1885** C. M. YONGE *Nuttie's Father* II. xix. 224 It's the sort of thing that one only laughs at because otherwise one would have to do the other thing! **1913** A. BENNETT *Regent* I. vi. 165 You mean you won't!.. Well, you can do the other thing! **1922** JOYCE *Ulysses* 359 Besides there was absolution so long as you didn't do the other thing before being married. **1923** E. P. MATHERS tr. *Mardrus's Bk. of Thousand Nights & One Night* VII. 55 His heart is hard, his other thing is soft. **1929** J. VAN DRUTEN *Young Woodley* xii. 241 'You don't believe me?' 'I do not.'.. 'Then you must do the other thing.' **1953** H. CLEVELY *Public Enemy* xxii. 165, I couldn't have a better home.., and anybody who doesn't like it can do the other thing. **1977** 'D. CORY' *Bennett* iv. 127 The C.D.I. wouldn't like it, no. But, then, he could always do the other thing.

g. *the other man* (and varr.): a man with whom a woman already in an amatory relationship forms a new attachment; a lover. Similarly *the other woman*: a woman with whom a man forms a new attachment in such circumstances; a mistress.

Quot. 1867 may not have the overtones of the other examples.

1855 BROWNING *Men & Women* 88 Why must I..Put any kiss of pardon on thy brow? Why need the other women know so much? **1867** TROLLOPE *Last Chron. Barset* I. xxxviii. 331 A woman, when she is jealous, is apt to attribute to the other woman with whom her jealousy is concerned, both weakness and timidity. **1886** KIPLING *The Other Man* in *Plain Tales from Hills* (1888) 80 They married her when she..had given all her poor little heart to another man... We will call him the Other Man. **1909** F. BARCLAY *Rosary* xxiii. 242 The 'other man' is always a problem. **1912** T. DREISER *Financier* xxxvii. 418 Curiously, the other woman did not seem so vastly important—that is, who she was. **1920** *Ladies' Home Jrnl.* Apr. 36 The cast includes Thomas Meighan as the husband, Gloria Swanson as the wife he changed, and Bebe Daniels as the other woman. **1927** E. GLYN *'It'* xiv. 137 What if being in the corner should make Ava go for help to the *other man*? **1935** *Mademoiselle* Aug. 3/2 Mr. Montgomery is the erring husband and Mr. Tone the 'other man'. **1946** G. MILLAR *Horned Pigeon* xxi. 360 She told me that her engagement had been broken, in fact her fiancé..was already married to 'the other woman'. **1953** K. TENNANT *Joyful Condemned* xxxix. 391 'Who's the other guy?' 'There isn't any other guy.' **1966** 'S. RANSOME' *Hidden Hour* ii. 20 She had been here before. With the 'other man'? **1973** G. MOFFAT *Deviant Death* i. 15, I had to sit in the corner and keep quiet. I knew how the other woman feels at the posh family funeral of her lover. **1975** *Daily Mirror* 29 Apr. 9/5 They married in 1967 after Miss Smith was named as the 'other woman' by Mr. Stephens' first wife.

h. *the other end*: the person (or his location) with whom one is communicating by telephone.

1941 B. SCHULBERG *What makes Sammy Run?* vi. 121 Julian managed to get Sammy on the other end of a telephone. **1974** R. B. PARKER *Godwulf Manuscript* iii. 17 The phone rang... The girl's voice at the other end was thick and very slow. **1978** T. ALLBEURY *Lantern Network* xi. 160 The fruity voice on the other end of the line.

5. f. *other ranks*: in the armed forces, non-commissioned officers and ordinary soldiers, seamen, etc. Occas. in *sing.*, a member of the other ranks. Also *transf.* and (in form *other-rank*) *attrib.* Cf. RANK *sb.*^{1} 5 b.

1925 FRASER & GIBBONS *Soldier & Sailor Words* 216 *Other ranks*, the usual official designation for N.C.O.'s and privates in orders, etc., as distinguished from Commissioned Officers. **1926** F. M. FORD *Man could stand Up* II. ii. 106 There were all these inscrutable beings; the Other Ranks, a brownish mass, spreading underground, like clay strata in the gravel. **1929** T. E. LAWRENCE *Let.* 18 Apr. (1938) 652 M.B. is an amateur of the R.A.F., like me: but he doesn't know the other ranks in it, and won't like their dirt and brutality. **1931** —— *Let.* 20 Aug. (1938) 733 A book written by an 'other rank' would not mention the officers. **1946** *R.A.F. Jrnl.* May 150 The Sussex Square Club and Hostel..has been opened for male other ranks. **1959** *Encounter* July 85/1 Before the war the young officer really believed that the social circumstances of his upbringing and birth entitled him to give orders to 'other ranks'; and the 'other ranks' were on the whole quite satisfied. **1960** J. MACLAREN-ROSS *Until Day she Dies* vi. 94 There was a mob of other ranks sitting around on their kitbags. **1960** A. WAUGH *Foxglove Saga* vi. 107 The other ranks of the Pigs were mostly recruited from the criminal and the stupid. **1965** G. MCINNES *Road to Gundagai* ii. 26 The promenade deck was abruptly curtailed by a wooden grille..with the sign 'Other Ranks Only. No Entry. Military Police.' **1966** *Times* 9 July 9/6 The Army have given the expression 'other ranks' its marching orders. Commands have been told the term 'soldier' is preferred. **1968** R. WEST *Sk. Vietnam* ii. 46 Many marine other-ranks have college degrees. **1971** S. HILL *Strange Meeting* iii. 169, B Company has lost 2 officers and 3 wounded, and about 30 of other ranks. **1973** *Listener* 5 July 22/1 They, like their other-rank colleagues, knew well enough what it was all about. **1974** K. ROYCE *Trap Spider* i. 8 'Good man,' he said, as if he'd invited an 'other rank' to the officers' mess for a special treat. **1976** *Daily Tel.* 20 July 4/3 The withdrawal of British regular units from Oman will not affect..the secondment of British officers and other ranks of all three services to the Sultan's forces.

B. 10. as *sb.* Sexual activity; sexual intercourse. Also occas., homosexual practices. *slang.*

1922 JOYCE *Ulysses* 358 They would be just good friends like a big brother and sister without all that other. *Ibid.* 429 Bit light in the head. Monthly or effect of the other. **1928** D. H. LAWRENCE *Lady Chatterley* xiv. 241 She loved me to talk to her and kiss her... But the other, she just didn't want. **1936** J. CURTIS *Gilt Kid* 135 'Doing half I was.' 'What for? The other?' 'Yes.' The pansy simpered. *Ibid.*, He gets a stretch for screwing and another stretch on top of that for the other. **1969** F. NORMAN *Banana Boy* 127, I..usually managed to get Mary behind a haystack for a 'bit of the other'. **1974** *Spectator* 22 June 764/2 I've got to be noticed by any guy who's on the prowl away from home and looking for a bit of the other.

D. 1. *other-dimensional* (of or from another dimension); *other-mindedness.*

1926 *Public Opinion* 30 Apr. 436/3 The habit of..other-mindedness. **1940** J. BETJEMAN *Old Lights for New Chancels* 50 Coffee and Ulysses, Tennyson, Joyce, Alpha-minded and other dimensional, Freud or Calvary? Take your choice. **1961** *John o'London's* 25 May 592/2 His humour is so naturally other-dimensional.

2. *other-centred* (centred in others); *other-directed* Sociol. (applied to persons whose behaviour and goals are directed by standards they feel acceptable to others, esp. some kind of peer group; cf. *inner-directed* (*INNER *a.* (*sb.*^{2}) 1 n), **tradition-directed*; hence as *sb.*; also *other-directedness, -direction*); *other-regard* (regard for others); *other-regarding* (further examples); *other-regardingness* (further examples).

1925 *Inner Life* (Ser. 2) 219 Love of the large room is characteristic of souls that are other-centred. **1950** D. RIESMAN et al. *Lonely Crowd* i. 9 The society of incipient population decline develops in its typical members a social character whose conformity is insured by their tendency to be sensitized to the expectations and preferences of others. These I shall term other-directed people. *Ibid.* 20 It is also my impression that the conditions I believe responsible for other-direction are affecting increasing numbers of people in the metropolitan centers of the advanced industrial countries. *Ibid.* 23 What is common to all other-directeds is that their contemporaries are the source of direction for the individual. **1953** *Brit. Jrnl. Psychol.* XLIV. 187 From having been in the nineteenth century inner-directed..most Americans have now become 'other-directed', taking standards and guidance mainly from their contemporaries at each stage in their lives. **1957** V. PACKARD *Hidden Persuaders* xvi. 168 The increasing desire of Americans to make a good impression on their peer group, as a part of the trend to other-directedness. **1959**, etc. [see *INNER *a.* (*sb.*^{2}) 1 n]. **1966** D. JENKINS *Educated Society* i. 27 Dangers..of excessive 'other-directedness' and the production of 'organization men'. **1973** *Listener* 17 May 635/1 [J. S.] Mill's fears were those of post-war American sociologists like David Riesman, who saw American society as full of 'other-directed' men. **1975** R. H. RIMMER *Premar Experiments* (1976) i. 48 The deep joy and satisfaction he discovers in other-directedness and his love for people-involvement. **1938** *Times Lit. Suppl.* 8 Oct. 635/2 When we come..to the consideration of the two major types of Sentiment, Self-regard and Other-regard (or Love), we are on firmer ground. **1923** J. S. HUXLEY *Ess. Biologist* vii. 273 The instincts that are self-regarding and those that are other-regarding. **1947** *Mind* LVI. 277 If the common good is our principle, we should expect a preference to be given to other-regarding ends over self-regarding ones. **1952** V. GOLLANCZ *My Dear Timothy* xx. 274 At the bottom of it..was an element of something other-regarding. A sense of public service should have taken its place. **1969** *Listener* 6 Feb. 164/1 And protest in our society seems to be of these two kinds also—self-regarding and other-regarding—in rather comparable proportions. **1958** *Times Lit. Suppl.* 31 Jan. 54/5 Reason, objectivity, tolerance, charity, other-regardingness—these are not natural gifts of men.

otherliness (*ɒ·ðəɹlinės*). *rare.* [f. OTHER *a.* + -NESS; cf. -LY^1.] The quality of being different or apart in some way.

1949 KOESTLER *Promise & Fulfilment* II. i. 194 That eery odour of otherliness, of vagrancy and jugglery which surrounds Mr. Abramowitz. **1967** E. GRIERSON *Crime of one's Own* x. 86 It was another fault of the romantic spirit to imagine that..agents..[had] some special quality of 'otherliness', whereas their very profession must demand the opposite. **1976** A. KOESTLER in D. Villiers *Next Year in Jerusalem* 101 Do I really consider myself a member of a chosen race... If not, what right have I to go on.. inflicting on my children the stigma of otherliness?

otherwise, *sb. phr., adv., adj.* Add: **A. c.** Phr. *or* (occas. *and*) *otherwise*, following a noun, adjective, adverb, or verb, to signify a corresponding word of opposite or different meaning.

1886 *Rep. Brit. Assoc. Adv. Sci. 1885* 872 The index number..is 1 or 100, according to the use or otherwise of the decimal point. **1892** [see *playing week* s.v. PLAYING *vbl. sb.* 2]. **1895** *Pall Mall Mag.* Jan. 35 The most amusing feature of the case was the conflict of professional evidence as to the merits, or otherwise, of Mr. Whistler's paintings. **1910** *Practitioner* Jan. 84 The question of operability or otherwise is a matter in which surgeons differ considerably. **1911** E. C. WORDEN *Nitrocellulose Industry* II. xiv. 697 These enamels may be closely imitated..by taking a given pattern, enlarging it pantographically or otherwise, [etc.]. **1922** C. MACKENZIE *Altar Steps* vii. 56 Mrs. Lidderdale's dread..was that her son would acquire a West country burr, and it was considered more prudent, economically and otherwise, to let him go on learning with his grandfather and herself. **1966** *Listener* 22 Sept. 427/2, I do not question the eruption at Santorin,..but the supposed connection of the underwater survey with the historicity or otherwise of the Atlantis myth. **1972** W. A. PANTIN *Oxf. Life* iv. 52 Professor Southern gave us some stimulating reflections about the aims, development, and achievements (or otherwise) of the Honour School of Modern History. **1972** *Times Lit. Suppl.* 13 Oct. 1233/1 The circumstances of the publication of the Penguin Books version of D. H. Lawrence's *Lady Chatterley's Lover* in November 1960 led to much public discussion of the desirability or otherwise of printing these long-banned sexual words. **1973** *Oxford Times* 30 Nov. 10, 12,000 Cowley workers enjoyed (or otherwise) an enforced holiday because of a strike by plant attendants at the car assembly factory.

other world, other-world, *sb.* and *a.* Also o·therworld. Add: **1.** (Earlier and later examples.) Also (in sense c) more *gen.*, a range of experiences conceived in imagination or fantasy as lying outside the world as normally known.

c **1200, 1611** [see WORLD *sb.* 1 d]. **1612** W. STRACHEY *Trav. Virginia* (1849) I. iv. 60 The liuetenant..with his dagger, sent him to accompanye his master in the other world. **1679** [see GUARANTEE *sb.* 1]. **1762** STERNE *Tr. Shandy* V. xlii. 141 Baldus..entered upon the law so late in life, that every body imagined he intended to be an advocate in the other world. **1804** M. WILMOT *Let.* 29 June in *Russ. Jrnls.* (1934) I. 107 What think you..the place is like?..to let you at once into the secrets of Other Worlds, know that Kattova is very like a wooden village. **1880** G. M. HOPKINS *Let.* 22 Dec. in Hopkins & Dixon *Corr.* (1935) 37 The other-world of imagination. **1887** G. B. SHAW *Short Stories, Scraps & Shavings* in *Works* (1932) VI. 101 With gho—with people from—with ladies and gentlemen from the other world. **1920** D. H. LAWRENCE *Women in Love* iv. 46 The whole otherworld, wet and remote, he had to himself. **1953** A. HUXLEY *Let.* 21 June (1969) 678 His [*sc.* the schizo phrenic's] commonest experiences are of an Other World, not heavenly but infernal and purgatorial. **1960** S. PLATH *Colossus* 39 These..sheets..Speak in sign language of a lost otherworld, A world we lose by merely waking up. **1968** T. WOLFE *Electric Kool-Aid Acid Test* v. 60 The whole *other world* that LSD opened your mind to. **1975** *Times Lit. Suppl.* 25 Apr. 445/3 Mr McCarthy sets his saga of Servier County in the strange otherworld of a Tennessee winter.

2. (Further examples.)

1892 J. S. STUART-GLENNIE in *Proc. Internat. Folk-Lore Congr. 1891* 225 Myths which..I would name..the Sacerdotal. By these I mean especially all the Otherworld Myths. **1917** [see *IMMRAM]. **1957** G. ASHE *King Arthur's Avalon* i. 28 A Lake Villagers' burial ground on Ynyswitrin, with a resulting Ghosts' High Noon presided over by other-world deities.

otherworldly, *a.* Add: **1.** (Further examples.)

1955 A. HUXLEY *Let.* 10 Jan. (1969) 720, I took mescalin yesterday, for the second time... The experience had a human content, which the earlier, solitary experience, with its Other Worldly quality..did not possess. **1957** G. ASHE *King Arthur's Avalon* iii. 107 The poem entangles Arthur in a network of other-worldly themes, a network which takes in Glastonbury and the quest for a miraculous vessel. **1972** *Where* Oct. 275/3 Other..readers..may find the results almost as other-worldly as might a non-literate home in the East End.

3. Also, of or pertaining to the world to come. Also *absol.* as *sb.*

1920 E. I. WATKIN in C. Hess *God & Supernatural* 141 Nor have these souls merely desired sufferings as the unavoidable price of an other-worldly reward. **1932** C. P. CURRAN in F. J. Sheed *Irish Way* 134 The other-worldly man must put on the man of affairs, the monk-bishop become a politician. **1950** 'G. ORWELL' *Shooting Elephant* 106 The other-worldly, anti-humanist tendency of his [*sc.* Gandhi's] doctrines. **1961** NEW ENG. BIBLE *Luke* xvi. 8 For the worldly are more astute than the other-worldly in dealing with their own kind.

other-worldness (*ɒːðəɹwɒ̄·ɹldnės*). [f. OTHER WORLD *sb.* and *a.* + -NESS.] = OTHERWORLDLINESS.

1915 J. LONDON *Jacket* i. 1 These child glimpses are of other-worldness, of other-lifeness, of things that you had never seen in this particular world of your particular life. **1956** I. BROMIGE *Enchanted Garden* II. ii. 87 It was an expressive face. In repose, it had an appealing wistfulness, an other-worldness. **1961** P. DOUGHERTY *Mother Mary Potter* iii. 35 In the Portsea–Southsea district..Mary's persevering and unobtrusive other-worldness was inevitably discussed.

otitis. Add: **b.** In mod.L. collocations: *otitis externa* [tr. F. *otite externe* (J. M. G. Itard *Traité des Maladies de l'Oreille* (1821) I. i. 164)], inflammation of the external ear; *otitis interna* [tr. F. *otite interne* (loc. cit. 170)], inflammation of the inner ear († or the middle ear); = *LABYRINTHITIS; *otitis media*, inflammation of the middle ear.

1864 D. B. ST. J. ROOSA tr. *von Tröltsch's Dis. Ear* vi. 60 By Otitis interna I understand the purulent catarrh of the middle ear, or cavity of the tympanum. *Ibid.*, Otitis externa, or diffuse inflammation. **1874** J. HINTON tr. *von Tröltsch's Surg. Dis. Ear* viii. 56 (*heading*) Acute suppurative catarrh of the middle ear, or acute otitis media. **1883** J. P. CASSELLS tr. *Politzer's Text-bk. Dis. Ear* 711 (*heading*) Inflammation of the labyrinth (otitis interna). **1959** *Woman* 16 May 31/1 She has all the signs of a really bad acute otitis media—or infection of the middle ear. **1974** PASSMORE & ROBSON *Compan. Med. Stud.* III. II. xxxii. 5/1 If there is no time to soften the wax in this way, a proprietary wax solvent may be used, but these are more likely to cause otitis externa than the simpler substances. **1976** M. Machlin *Pipeline* iii. 36 Diseases that could be easily treated, such as chronic *otitis media*,..were let to run their courses for lack of doctors.

oto-. Add: **ototo·xic** *a.*, having a toxic effect on the ear or its nerve supply; so **o:totoxi·city**, the property of being ototoxic.

1951 *Trans. 10th Conf. Chemotherapy of Tuberculosis* 224 The growing list of tuberculostatic antibiotics which have an ototoxic action..suggests that still other substances derived from Streptomyces may be expected to show a similar toxicity. **1967** Busch & Lane *Chemotherapy* v. 86/2 The ototoxic effect is exerted primarily on the cochlear division of the 8th nerve. **1974** *Arch. Path.* XCVI. 304/1 Methyl mercury is a unique ototoxic agent. **1951** *Trans. 10th Conf. Chemotherapy of Tuberculosis* 224 (*heading*) Ototoxicity of hydroxystreptomycin. **1975** *Nature* 3 Jan. 45/1 Kanamycin ototoxicity yields such cochlear lesions that histological and audiometric measures are well correlated.

otolaryngology (ǫ:tolæriŋgǫ·lŏdʒi). *Med.* [f. Oto- + *laryngology* s.v. Laryngo-.] The branch of medicine concerned with the ear and the larynx; also often used to include the nose (avoiding the cumbersome *otorhinolaryngology).

1897 *Jrnl. Laryngol., Rhinol., & Otol.* XII. 554 (*heading*) Holocaine [*printed* holoraine] in oto-laryngology. **1945** *Electronic Engin.* XVII. 555 A book which embodies the experience of twenty five years of research and teaching..in otolaryngology. **1955** *Sci. News Let.* 13 Aug. 109/1 The cat's hearing span was measured by Drs. William D. Neff and Joseph E. Hind of the University of Chicago's Laboratories of Physiological Psychology and Otolaryngology. **1973** Paparella & Shumrick *Otolaryngology* I. p. ix/1 We, the editors, felt both honored and challenged when the Saunders Company invited us to prepare a new and definitive reference source in otolaryngology. The new book was to replace the classic Jackson work, *Diseases of the Nose, Throat and Ear.* **1975** Felton & Fowler *Best, Worst & Most Unusual* 250 Dr. Eugene M. Batza of Cleveland Clinic's Department of Otolaryngology, examined a five-member rock combo and found that all of them suffered from..laryngitis.

Hence **o:tolaryngolo·gic** (chiefly *U.S.*), **-lo·gical** *adjs.*, of or pertaining to otolaryngology, or to the ear, (nose) and throat; **o:tolaryngo·logist**, one who specializes in otolaryngology.

1898 (*title*) Transactions of the Ophthalmologic Division of the Western Ophthalmological and Oto-Laryngological Association. **1898** *Laryngoscope* May 311 One of the most practical factors of the organization was the division into two sections, one the ophthalmologic, the other the otolaryngologic. **1911** *Jrnl. Laryngol., Rhinol., & Otol.* XXVI. 661 The moral responsibility..rests upon oto-laryngologists as teachers. **1961** *Lancet* 30 Sept. 782/1 A meeting of the North of England Otolaryngological Society is to be held on Saturday, Oct. 7. **1964** D. A. Dolowitz *Basic Otolaryngol.* p. vii, These gains have lengthened the otolaryngologic resident training period to four years after internship. **1973** *Sci. Amer.* Sept. 92/1 Gynecologists, urologists, ophthalmologists, otolaryngologists and others each operate on their respective organs and tissues. **1974** *Encycl. Brit. Macropædia* XVII. 822/2 Otolaryngologic surgery is performed in the area of the ear, nose, and throat. *Ibid.*, Benign and malignant tumours of the upper air passages..are currently dealt with by the otolaryngological surgeons.

Otomi (ōᵘtŏmi·). Pl. **Otomi, Otomies.** [Sp., f. Nahuatl *Otomí.*] An Indian people inhabiting parts of central Mexico; a member of this tribe. Also, the language of the Otomi. Also *attrib.* or as *adj.*

1787 C. Cullen tr. *Clavigero's Hist. Mexico* I. ii. 105 The Mazahuas were once a part of the nation of the Otomies, as the languages of both nations are but different dialects of the same tongue. **1845** [see *Huastec]. **1877** L. H. Morgan *Anc. Society* ii. vii. 194 The confederacy was confronted by hostile..tribes..the Mechoacans on the west, the Otomies on the northwest. **1883** *Encycl. Brit.* XVI. 207/1 The languages of the Nahua nations..show no connexion of origin with the language of the Otomi tribes. **1891** D. G. Brinton *Amer. Race* 338 The Otomi presents so many sounds unfamiliar to the European ear that the attempt to represent it by our alphabets can be only remotely accurate. **1948** D. Diringer *Alphabet* vii. 124 They [*sc.* Chichimeca]..are considered by some experts as of Otomi origin. **1954** *Bible Translator* V. 61 Otomi people suffer from considerable cultural insecurity. **1964** *Language* XL. 81 A great variety of person-tense-aspect prefixes are available to the speaker of Otomi. **1972** *Ibid.* XLVIII. 847, 6b is given by Hockett for..Otomi nasal vowels. **1972** [see *Mixtec].

otorhinolaryngology (ǫ:torəi:nolæriŋgǫ·lŏdʒi). *Med.* [f. Oto- + Rhino- + *laryngology* s.v. Laryngo-.] The branch of medicine concerned with the ear, nose, and throat. Cf. *otolaryngology, E.N.T. s.v. *E III.

1900 Dorland *Med. Dict.* 468/1 Otorhinolaryngology. **1902** *Nature* 2 Oct. 554/1 The congress will be divided into the following sections:—..oto-rhino-laryngology, [etc.]. **1962** *Lancet* 27 Jan. 195/2 No special techniques need to be learnt, as in neuro-surgery, urology, or otorhinolaryngology. **1968** W. McCartney *Olfaction & Odours* 235 Author of 'Essai d'Olfactique Physiologique' (1919) and of many papers on oto-rhino-laryngology.

Hence **o:torhi:nolary:ngolo·gical** *a.*; **o:torhi:nolaryngo·logist**, one who specializes in otorhinolaryngology.

1938 W. H. C. Romanis in Rolleston & Moncrieff *Mod. Anæsthetic Pract.* x. 185 Local anæsthesia..its use in ophthalmic or oto-rhinolaryngological operations. **1948** *Brit. Dental Jrnl.* LXXXV. 223/1 He had..no history of oto-rhino-laryngological trouble. **1960** *Times* 3 Mar. 5/2 Then there is 'otorhinolaryngologist'. No one would wish to charge large fees if he called himself an ear, nose and throat specialist. **1962** *Listener* 10 May 809/1 Oto-rhinolaryngologists, botanists or X-ray crystallographers.

otosclerosis (ōᵘtosklĕrōᵘ·sis, -sklīərōᵘ·sis). *Path.* [mod.L., ad. G. *otosclerose* (A. Politzer *Lehrb. der Ohrenheilkunde* (ed. 4, 1901) 263): see Oto- and Sclerosis.] A disease of the ear in which the normal tissue of the temporal bone is replaced by spongy bone, with the result that movement of the stapes becomes impeded and deafness ensues. Hence **otosclero·tic** *a.*, of, pertaining to, or affected by otosclerosis; also as *sb.*, one who suffers from otosclerosis.

1901 *Arch. Otology* XXX. 279 Otosclerosis, so frequent, distressing, and little amenable to treatment, receives 12 pages. **1904** *Jrnl. Laryngol., Rhinol., & Otol.* XIX. 518 It was especially difficult to differentiate between true otosclerosis and fixation of the stapes following tympanic inflammations. **1933** M. Yearsley *Otosclerosis* iii. 7 Körner..recorded the marriage of two otosclerotics. *Ibid.*, The marriage of an otosclerotic male with his otosclerotic niece resulted in seven otosclerotic children. **1933** *Punch* 20 Dec. 700/1 He..exhibits Swift with much pathos as the sufferer from the particularly cruel disease which now bears the ugly name of otosclerosis. **1974** I. Friedmann *Path. Ear* v. 247 Otosclerosis is very common in Indians and whites. *Ibid.*, Every tenth adult person has otosclerotic foci within his temporal bone.

‖**otriad** (ǫtrya·d). [a. Russ. *otryád* a detachment.] In Russia: a detachment, group of soldiers (see also quot. 1916).

1916 *Yorkshire Post* 23 Feb. 4/4 An Englishman who works with a volunteer ambulance or otriad, behind the Russian lines. **1919** H. S. Walpole *Secret City* i. xvii. 117 Zinaida Fyodorovna had just come back from her Otriad on the Galician front. **1933** —— *Vanessa* iv. i. 672 The Retreat had begun and with the rest of the Otriad he had been flung into the little town of O——.

Otshi-herero (ōᵘ:tʃiherēə·ro). Also **Otjiherero, Otyi-.** The name used by the Hereros for their language, generally called *Herero.

1859 H. Hall *Man. S. Afr. Geogr.* xviii. 73 Damara and Orampoland, or the land of the Otjiherero, present a belt of sandy country between the coast and the high inhabited table lands. **1871** J. Mackenzie *Ten Yrs. North of Orange River* 494 Otyiherero (Damara). **1880** *Encycl. Brit.* XI. 732/2 By their language (Otyiherero) the Herero belong to the great Bantu family. **1910** *Ibid.* XIII. 358/1 They call themselves Ovaherero and their language Otshi-herero. **1919** H. H. Johnston *Compar. Study Bantu & Semi-Bantu Lang.* I. 350 Ꞷci-hererꞷ.

Ottawa (ǫ·tăwă). [a. Canad. F. *Outaouais*, f. Ojibwa tribal name *otāwā.*] A North American Indian people of the Algonquian family first encountered on the shores of Lake Huron; a member of this tribe. Also *attrib.* or as *adj.*

1687 in *Documents Colonial Hist. New-York* (1853) III. 442 A party of Sinnekes and Onnondages have plundered some French..and have also taken some Ottawa Indians prisoners. **1754** [see *Chippewa]. **1768** J. Lees *Jrnl.* Aug. (1911) 39 On the Miami River, the greatest part of the nation of the Ottawas inhabit, they..are spread about it..cheifly on the North side of Lake Huron..and towards the North West. These, the Pous and Chipewas have almost the same language, and is [*sic*] called the Ottawa-Tongue. **1833** A. Jackson in *Messages & Papers of Presidents* (1896) III. 38, I transmit..a treaty concluded between the commissioners on the part of the United States and the united nation of Chippewas, Ottawas, and Potawatamies, at Chicago. **1835** [see *Kickapoo]. **1865** [see *Algonquin, -kin *sb.* and *a*]. **1890** J. G. Frazer *Golden Bough* II. iii. 113 When men of the Bear clan in the Otawa tribe killed a bear, they made him a feast of his own flesh. **1910** F. W. Hodge *Handbk. Amer. Indians* II. 171/1 There were 197 Ottawa under the Seneca School, Okla. **1962** D. H. Hymes in J. A. Fishman *Readings Sociol. of Lang.* (1968) 129 The Ottawa believed the cries of infants to be meaningful. **1967** D. Jenness *Indians of Canada* (ed. 7) xviii. 282 The Iroquois turned their arms against the Ottawa and drove them from Georgian bay. Some fled west towards lake Superior; others took refuge with their Potawatomi kinsmen in the United States... Many of these refugees returned to..the north shore of lake Huron. **1977** *Detroit Free Press* 11 Dec. 16–C/1 'It's a hidden attack by commercial interests on native Americans,' said Mrs. Waunetta Dominic, chairwoman of the Northern Michigan Ottawa Association in Petoskey.

otter, *sb.* Add: **4. c.** A type of paravane, used esp. by merchant vessels. Later, any paravane.

[**1910** *Blackw. Mag.* June 899/1 We might adapt to naval use those poaching expedients, the 'cross-line' and the 'otter'.] **1920** *Nature* 8 Jan. 487/1 The paravane or otter..proved a very effective weapon against both mines and submarines. **1920** *Rep. Brit. Assoc. Adv. Sci. 1919* 273 The Protector Paravanes, or Otters, carry a form of cutter, but no explosive charge whatever. **1954** Bradford & Quill *Gloss. Sea Terms* 138/2 The mooring of a mine coming in contact with this taut tow-line slides along to the otter where it enters a pair of cutting jaws and is cut adrift.

7. *otter-skin* (later examples); **otter-board,** (*a*) a fishing-tackle consisting of a board with several hooks attached; (*b*) = *door 4 b; **otter-man,** a fisher who uses an otter-line or otter-board; †**otter-sheep** *U.S.*, a variety of sheep with short, crooked legs; cf. Otter *sb.* 6; **otter tail** (see quot. 1932); **otter-trawl** (examples).

1901 *Field* 5 Jan. 19/2 The otter-board was only employed..upon those lakes where the trout were indifferent to the angler's flies. **1904** *Daily Chron.* 21 Nov. 5/7 He lost his otter-board and had to put a new trawl on next morning. **1936** J. Buchan *Island of Sheep* xiii. 247 Look at the trawl. It's absurd. It has no otter-boards... There's something wrong with this ship. **1971** *Daily Tel.* (Colour Suppl.) 21 May 21/3 The net flops into the water and sinks away sideways. When it is some way out it is followed by the shuddering crash of the two otter-boards, ton-weight doors, that are towed at an angle to keep the net open on the bottom. **1901** *Field* 5 Jan. 19/2 The otterman must chuckle inwardly when he sees a perspiring and jaded angler..with one or two fish in his basket. **1809** E. A. Kendall *Trav. Northern Parts U.S.* I. 309 Some of the farmers [in Connecticut] are partial to a remarkable variety of sheep, which they call the otter-sheep. **1863** H. S. Randall *Pract. Shepherd* (ed. 7) v. 42 A family of them, the Otter Sheep—so termed from their short, crooked, rickety legs. **1873** *Amer. Naturalist* VII. 742 The otter sheep..originated on the farm of Seth Wright, near Charles River, Mass. **1884** *Century Mag.* Feb. 516/1 There were also the Otter sheep, said to have originated on some island on our eastern coast. **1849** F. Parkman *Calif. & Oregon Trail* x. 144 The dandy carried a bow and arrows in an otter-skin quiver at his back. **1971** *Country Life* 28 Oct. 1128/3 Red chokers about sun-burned necks, and more than one round hat of otter-skin. **1932** Lady Howe in A. C. Smith et al. *Hounds & Dogs* viii. 69 The tail..should be very thick towards the base gradually tapering towards the tip, of medium length, should be practically free from any feathering, but should be clothed thickly all round with the Labrador's short, thick, dense coat, thus giving that peculiar rounded appearance which has been described as the 'otter' tail. **1948** B. Vesey-Fitzgerald *Bk. Dog* 1000 Otter tail: A thick tapering tail similar to that of an otter, much desired in the Labrador Retriever. **1973** P. R. A. Moxon *Gundogs* (ed. 9) iv. 71 The Labrador Retriever..is undoubtedly ideal for water, the sleek water-resisting coat and 'otter' tail seeming almost designed for the job. **1899** W. C. McIntosh *Resources of Sea* 93 The new otter-trawls capture more round than flat fishes. **1936** Russell & Yonge *Seas* (ed. 2) 275 In the case of the otter-trawl two 'otters' or 'doors' are used. To these the sides of the net's mouth are attached, and they are set at such angles that as they are drawn over the sea bottom they diverge farther and farther from the centre of the net's mouth until an equilibrium point is reached and the mouth of the net is stretched agape. **1973** W. Elmer *Terminol. Fishing* ii. 71 In many places the otter trawl has ousted the beam trawl. **1973** *Fisheries Fact Sheet* (Environment Canada Fisheries & Marine Service) No. 1. 2/3 The former two [*sc.* the trawler and dragger]..catch fish by dragging an otter-trawl or similar device. This is a large baglike arrangement of nets which captures fish as the vessel tows it through the water.

o·ttered, *ppl. a.* [f. Otter *v.* + -ed[1].] That has been fished with otter tackle. So **o·tterer;** **o·ttering** *vbl. sb.*

1901 *Field* 5 Jan. 19/2 An observant gamekeeper..tells me that he knows well the signs of an ottered lake. *Ibid.* 19/3 Very gradually, may be, the otterers will learn that they are ruining many fine waters by their malpractices. **1907** *Westm. Gaz.* 24 Jan. 2/1 Trout..obtained by the unsportsmanlike method of netting or 'ottering'.

otto[1]. a. (Later examples.)

1908 *Westm. Gaz.* 30 Mar. 10/3 As a scent otto of violets has become increasingly popular each year. **1919** S. Kaye-Smith *Tamarisk Town* i. ii. 48 There was a drift of faint perfumes: flowers, macassar oil, otto of roses, lavender and peau d'espagne. **1939–40** *Army & Navy Stores Catal.* 431/1 Cold cream, 'Otto of Rose' jar, 1/3.

Otto[3] (ǫ·to). The name of Nikolaus August *Otto* (1832–1891), German engineer, used *attrib.* to designate (*a*) the four-stroke cycle employed in most petrol and gas engines (cf. *four-stroke *a.*), idealized as adiabatic compression followed by heat addition at constant volume, adiabatic expansion, and heat rejection at constant volume; and (*b*) an engine employing this cycle.

The cycle was orig. proposed by A. Beau de Rochas in 1862, but Otto was the first to build an engine employing it (in 1876) after conceiving the idea independently.

1878 *Sci. Amer.* 30 Mar. 195/1 The new Otto horizontal gas engine..closely resembles the ordinary horizontal steam engine. **1885** W. Macgregor *Gas Engines* ii. 81 The original and classic type of the Otto engine has received improvements at the hands of both its German and English manufacturers. **1886** D. Clerk *Gas Engine* vii. 183 The indicator diagrams prove the very efficient nature of the Otto cycle. **1930** *Engineering* 7 Feb. 186/1 Theoretically, the Otto cycle..promised higher efficiencies than the constant-pressure Diesel cycle. **1966** *McGraw-Hill Encycl. Sci. & Technol.* VII. 201/1 For an Otto engine, an increase in either the air temperature or density increases the tendency of the engine to knock. **1975** *Sci. Amer.* Jan. 34/3 According to the DOT-EPA report, the

40 percent improvement by 1980 should be attainable with the present Otto-cycle (four-stroke) gasoline engine, in combination with improved transmissions, reduced weight and aerodynamic drag and improved accessories.

† **b.** Used *ellipt.* for *Otto engine*. *Obs.*

1886 D. CLERK *Gas Engine* vi. 106 The Otto is only half single acting. **1903** *Work* XXV. 18/2 Petrol car engines are of the vertical single-acting Otto type, any variations consisting chiefly of horizontal Ottos.

ottoman, *sb.*^{2} **2.** (Later examples.)

1922 BARKER & MIDGLEY *Analysis Woven Fabrics* (ed. 2) xv. 301 *Ottoman cloth*, a dress fabric of a warp-rib structure, usually made from hard, crisp yarns. **1948** G. L. FRASER *Textiles by Britain* Gloss., *Ottoman*, dress material in either silk or rayon with a broken rib face and plain-weave back. It is produced in various sizes of rib. **1951** A. T. C. ROBINSON *Rayon Fabric Construction* viii. 79 A high-class Ottoman suitable for dressy coats. **1968** MRS. L. B. JOHNSON *White House Diary* 9 Apr. (1970) 659, I had worn my yellow ottoman cotton with an easy skirt. **1972** M. L. JOSEPH *Introductory Textile Sci.* (ed. 2) xxii. 239 Many rib-weave fabrics have heavy yarns inserted as picks. Examples of this construction include poplin, faille, bengaline, and ottoman.

Ottomanism (ǫ·tǒmăniz'm). [f. OTTOMAN *a.* and *sb.*^{1} + -ISM.] The culture (or aspects of it) of the Ottoman Turks; Ottoman civilization.

1911 *Q. Rev.* July 261 On behalf of an Ottomanism honestly applied to all the Ottoman nationalities. **1930** *Times Lit. Suppl.* 7 Aug. 635/1 Her leaders had been experimenting with Ottomanism. **1930** [see *LEVANTINIZE *v.*]. **1974** C. E. DAWN (*title*) From Ottomanism to Arabism.

ottomanize, *v.* (in Dict. s.v. OTTOMAN *a.* and *sb.*^{1}). (Later example.) So **O:ttomaniza·tion,** the fact or process of enforcing Ottoman ideals or Ottomanism. **O·ttomanizing** *ppl. a.*

1912 *Chambers's Jrnl.* Dec. 817/2 If the Young Turks.. had tried fraternisation instead of persisting in Ottomanisation, Turkey's credit would have risen immediately. **1920** *Glasgow Herald* 17 Mar. 10 The inhabitants were anticipating enforced Ottomanisation when the Italian fleet arrived at Astypalea. *Ibid.* 15 July 4 His liberalism earned him the utter hatred of the ottomanising Committee of Union and Progress. **1936** R. C. K. ENSOR *England, 1870–1914* xiii. 436 Turkey..had alienated the liberal Powers by reverting to policies of Ottomanization and massacre. *Ibid.* 463 They were united by the Ottomanizing policy of the Young Turks. **1972** D. DAKIN *Unification of Greece* xii. 178 The new policy was to ottomanise the empire, to abolish the nationalist organisations, and to disarm the warring factions.

Ottonian (ǫtōu·niăn), *a.* [ad. late L. *Ottoniān-us*, f. the name of *Otto* I (cf. NERONIAN *a.*): see -IAN.] **a.** Of or pertaining to the East Frankish dynasty of the Holy Roman Empire founded by Otto I (912–73), which ruled from 962 to 1002. Also (*rare*) as *sb.*, a member of this dynasty. **b.** Pertaining to or characteristic of the art of this period, in part a revival of Carolingian art and extending into the 11th century.

1898 H. FISHER *Medieval Empire* I. iii. 95 The dominion of the Ottonian house was one thing in Saxony and another thing outside the Saxon borders. **1928** E. F. JACOB *Holy Roman Empire* v. 73 Yet the theory of the Empire reached its finest and truest form when the days of the Hohenstaufen were over and it was obvious that the unity of the Ottonian Reich could never be restored. **1936** A. W. CLAPHAM *Romanesque Archit.* viii. 179 The splendours of the Ottonian revival in painting, miniature, ivory, and metal work. **1938** *Times Lit. Suppl.* 12 Nov. 732/2 A group of over seventy Carolingian and Ottonian bindings. **1939** *Archit. Rev.* LXXXVI. 130/3 It is no service to German art to maintain that it is best when purest; its real triumphs are those happy marriages of Teutonic exuberance and Latin elegance which bear their first fruit in Ottonian miniatures. **1943** *Burlington Mag.* Sept. 228/2 The style of the work is 'Ottonian', an early phase of Romanesque. **1951** A. R. LEWIS *Naval Power & Trade Mediterranean, 500–1100* vi. 223 The increase of Byzantine gold coins in Germany, the luxury of the Ottonian court, the influence of Byzantine art motifs in German Romanesque architecture. **1958** *Times Lit. Suppl.* 3 Jan. 4/4 Paintings of the Rheims school in Carolingian times are shown to herald the transcendental outlook of Ottonian miniatures. **1967** *Cambr. Hist. Later Greek & Early Medieval Philos.* 587 After 950 the Ottonian dynasty were capable of re-establishing monarchical power. *Ibid.* 590 Bishop Adalbold of Utrecht..was a man of many-sided activities in his diocese, his territory and at court, representing a type not infrequent under the Ottonians. **1968** *Eng. Hist. Rev.* LXXXIII. 24 It is impossible even to suggest a figure for the size of Saxon contingents during the decades when the Ottonians acquired their *imperium*. **1970** *Oxf. Compan. Art* 799/2 The Byzantine strand, always present in Ottonian art, was particularly strong in the School of Regensburg. **1976** *Times Lit. Suppl.* 19 Nov. 1463/3 Ottonian art (as this art of the Saxon and Salian dynasties is generally called).

Otyiherero, var. *OTSHI-HERERO.

ou (*o·ū*). [Hawaiian.] A green and yellow bird, *Psittirostra psittacea*, belonging to the subfamily Coerebinæ, or honeycreepers.

1887 L. STEJNEGER in *Proc. U.S. Nat. Mus.* X. 93 The Ou, feeds on bugs and sings on the wing. **1890** *Ibis* II. 194 The constant twittering the Ou almost invariably makes while feeding at once betrays its identity. **1903** [see *IEIE]. **1944** G. C. MUNRO *Birds of Hawaii* 123 With its yellow head and bright green body in varying shades on different parts the ou is a beautiful bird. **1970** S. CARLQUIST *Hawaii* xi. 191 The ou eats fruits, seeds, leaves, and caterpillars.

ouad, var. *OUED.

ouananiche. For *'Salmo salar* var.' substitute *'Salmo saler ouananiche'*. (Add earlier and later examples.)

1873 *Forest & Stream* 4 Sept. 53/2 When you have had a surfeit of fresh water salmon *ouinanish*—retrace your steps to Chicoutimi. **1907** J. G. MILLAIS *Newfoundland* i. 2 Newfoundland is a most attractive place, with its thousands of lakes and pools; picturesque streams teeming with salmon, trout, and ouananiche. **1966** *Globe & Mail* (Toronto) 15 Jan. 29/5, I..tied into my first ouananiche with him on Trout Lake near North Bay. **1969** H. HORWOOD *Newfoundland* xvi. 128 All [*sc.* North Harbour, Rocky, Colinet, and Back Rivers] have exceptional fishing for sea trout, brook trout, or ouananiche.

oubaas (ōu·bās). *S. Afr.* Also **ou baas, oud baas.** [Afrikaans, f. *ou(d)* old + *BAAS.] Elderly head of a family; elderly man, old gentleman. Also used as a form of address and prefixed to a surname or a Christian name.

1869 T. BAINES *Diary* 2 July (1946) I. 59 They recognised at once and were rather pleased with the likeness of 'Oud Baas', Mr. Hartley. **1914** L. H. BRINKMAN *Breath of Karroo* ii. 24 The master of the house is addressed as 'Ou baas' and a young man, 'Klein baas'. **1942** 'B. KNIGHT' *Sun climbs Slowly* IV. xxx. 286 No, it was not the *Oubaas*, she said, but someone she had not seen before. **1946** V. POHL *Land of Distant Horizons* 50 They were so incredulous that the Hottentot exclaimed indignantly: 'Oubaas, if I have never told the truth, I am telling it now'. **1947** *Forum* (Johannesburg) 19 Apr. 1/1 The problems which faced the Oubaas this week ranged from the spreading boycott of Indian traders in the Transvaal..to the need for separate trade unions for Africans. **1952** E. H. BURROWS *Overberg Outspan* vi. 161 These were the people who congregated on Sundays with the family to hear the *oubaas* read a chapter of the Bible. **1959** *Cape Times* 14 Feb. 3/4 Joe told him that he and Moyisi had hit the *oubaas* with kieries. *Ibid.* 5 June 13/5, I..recognized him as *oubaas* De Greef. **1973** *Deb. Senate S. Afr.* 17 May 2807 Old Koos..said: 'Oubaas,..I don't know why you should start so late.'

oublietje, var. *OBLIETJIE.

ouch, *int.*^{1} Add: (Earlier and later examples.) Also as *sb.*^{2}

1838 J. C. NEAL *Charcoal Sk.* 38 'Ouch!' shrieked Dabbs; 'my eye, how it hurts!' **1843** 'R. CARLTON' *New Purchase* I. ii. 9 The tiers becoming all vocal with 'bless my soul's'—'my goodnesses!'—and vulgar 'ouches!' **1918** GALSWORTHY *Five Tales* 235 Freda gurgled: 'Ouch! You *are* a beast!' **1958** R. GODDEN *Greengage Summer* v. 56 'Ouch!' said Joss and looked as if she would be sick again. **1972** D. DELMAN *Sudden Death* (1973) iv. 110 'Ouch,' she said, grinning. 'Ouchie-wowchie. Well, that tears that, doesn't it?'

Ouchterlony (ǫχ-, ǫktərlōu·ni). *Immunol.* The name of O. T. G. *Ouchterlony* (b. 1914), Swedish microbiologist and immunologist, used *attrib.* and in the possessive with reference to a standard precipitin test devised by him, which normally involves placing antigen and antibody in separate wells sunk into a layer of agar on a plate and observing the line of precipitation which develops as the substances meet after diffusing through the agar.

1952 *Methods Med. Res.* V. 368 Ouchterlony's technique deviates from the ideal particularly with respect to points (1) and (2). **1954** *Jrnl. Immunol.* LXXIII. 232/1 We undertook an experimental evaluation of Ouchterlony's test. **1955** *Ibid.* LXXV. 460 (*heading*) Interpretation of the Ouchterlony precipitin test. **1962** LUNTZ & WRIGHT in A. Pirie *Lens Metabolism Rel. Cataract* 319 Serum from each patient was put on Ouchterlony plates and tested against..human lens protein. **1975** *Nature* 21 Aug. 656/1 This antiserum gave a single line on Ouchterlony gel diffusion with MAF.

‖ **oud** (ūd). Also **ood, oude, ʿūd.** [ad. Arab. *ʿūd*, lit. 'wood'.] A form of lute or mandolin played principally in Arab countries.

1738 T. SHAW *Trav. Barbary & Levant* 270 They [*sc.* the Moors] have the *Rebebb*, a Violin of two Strings, which is played upon with a Bow: the A-Oude, a Bass double stringed Lute, bigger than our Viol, which is touched with a Plectrum. **1836** E. W. LANE *Acct. Manners & Customs Mod. Egyptians* II. v. 69 The *'oo'd* is a species of guitar, which is played with a plectrum. **1870** C. ENGEL *Descr. Catal. Musical Instruments S. Kensington Museum* 8 The *Oud*..was brought by the Moors to Spain, where it is still known as the *laud*. *Ibid.*, The Oud is generally provided with frets made of cords of gut. **1883** *Encycl. Brit.* XV. 70/1 The modern Egyptian 'ʿûd' is the direct descendant of the Arabic lute. **1931** H. G. FARMER *Stud. Oriental Mus. Instruments* (Ser. 1) viii. 92 That the *mizhar* and the *'ūd* were distinct types of lute we know from several authorities. **1950** P. BOWLES in *Penguin New Writing* XXXIX. 10 As he passed over into the unlighted district he heard a few languid notes being strummed on an oud. **1957** H. G. FARMER in *New Oxf. Hist. Music* I. 446 The greatest of all the instruments of Islamic peoples was the *ʿūd* or lute. **1960** *New Yorker* 16 July 86 A couple of Near Eastern love songs performed..on the oud, a large Egyptian stringed instrument that resembles a gourd sliced in half and that emits an urgent nasal, tinging sound. **1972** J. WAMBAUGH *Blue Knight* (1973) xiv. 252 He plucked and stroked those *oud* strings with the quill of an eagle feather. It's a lute-like instrument and has no frets like a guitar. **1976** D. MUNROW *Instruments Middle Ages & Renaissance* 25/2 The earliest tuning employed [for the lute] is thought to have been a series of fourths, adopted from the *'ūd* and still used by Arab players today.

Ouds (audz). = O.U.D.S. (*O. 5 d).

1914 C. MACKENZIE *Sinister St.* II. iv. 567 Are you running the Ouds as well as The Oxford Looking-Glass? **1967** E. COXHEAD *Thankless Muse* vii. 135 Presently the Ouds producer appropriated her.

‖ **oud-stryder** (ōu·tstrēi:dər). *S. Afr.* [Afrikaans, = ex-soldier.] A veteran of the South African War (1899–1902) who fought on the side of the Boer republics. Also *gen.*, an ex-soldier.

1947 *Cape Argus* 29 Mar. 1 More than 1,600 Oudstryders to-day waited to give the Royal Family their own special welcome. **1947** *Cape Times* 31 Mar. 6/5 One of the happiest features of the visit of the Royal Family to Pretoria was the sincere welcome they received from the Oudstryders. **1948** *Ibid.* 21 Sept. 4/3 Calculating the means limit of *oudstryders*. **1954** *Sunday Times* (Johannesburg) 26 Sept. 1 Many oudstryders and ex-servicemen of both World Wars will attend. **1957** *Cape Argus* 12 Apr. 6/8 Legislation..had provided for oudstryders' pensions. **1975** *Eastern Province Herald* (S. Afr.) 13 Oct. 11 The uncompromising Boer oudstryder..told the Queen that he could never forgive the British for fighting against the Boers. The Queen was all sympathy; as a Scot, she said, she understood his feelings perfectly.

‖ **oued** (wed). Also **ouad.** [Fr. rendering of Arabic *wādī* WADI, WADY.] = WADI, WADY.

Usu. used only in contexts relating to those territories in N. Africa which were formerly under French control.

1854 J. R. MORELL *Algeria* vii. 121 The Ouad-Foddah, or river of silver, has its rise in a high rugged mountain. **1874** *Q. Jrnl. Geol. Soc.* XXX. 117 Lignite occurs..at El Kheicha on the banks of the Oued M'Zi, a branch of the L'Aghouat river. **1883** *Encycl. Brit.* XV. 608/1 Mascara, a fortified town of Algeria..occupies two small hills separated by the Oued Toudman. **1920** *Glasgow Herald* 27 Nov. 4 For an hour we followed the course of the oued (or river). **1965** MOUNTJOY & EMBLETON *Africa* iv. 180 A large number of small oueds descend from the mountains and water this immediate piedmont zone.

ouf, ouff, *int.* Add: (Also with pronunc. uf, *ŭf*.) **1. a.** (Earlier and later examples.) Also, expressing a sense of alarm or annoyance.

1851 LONGFELLOW *Jrnl.* 9 Feb. in S. Longfellow *Life H. W. Longfellow* (1886) II. 189 There was no violent discussion; so that the Count did not, so often as usual, clasp his round head with both hands and say, 'Ouf!' **1913** G. B. SHAW *Let.* 9 July in *B. Shaw & Mrs. Campbell* (1952) 130 You shut the door on me..and said 'Ouf!' when it slammed. **1951** R. SENHOUSE tr. *Colette's Chéri* 33 Back in Paris again—ouf!—I'll pack him off to his precious studies. **1958** L. DURRELL *Balthazar* iv. 237 Ouf! I fled. **1967** A. LASKI *Seven Other Years* iv. 59 'Ouf!' he said... 'This is not my dance.'

b. As an expression of resignation or relief.

1909 MRS. H. WARD *Daphne* iii. 56 Daphne, with an 'Ouf!' of fatigue, took off her hat. **1921** G. B. SHAW *Back to Methuselah* v. 261 *All.* Ouf! (*A great sigh of relief.*) **1964** V. NABOKOV *Defence* xiii. 220 'Ouf,' sighed Mrs. Luzhin, 'we're finally rid of them.' **1976** N. FREELING *Lake Isle* xiv. 109 'Ouf,' said Sophie, sitting down and kicking her shoes off.

2. Cf. WUFF *sb.*

ought, *sb.*^{2} (Examples of *pl.*)

1908 A. BENNETT *Human Machine* 43 You have a special apparatus within you for dealing with a universe where *oughts* are flagrantly disregarded. **1933** W. DE LA MARE *Lord Fish* 269 His master had told him little about his oughts. **1941** *Daily Progress* (Charlottesville, Va.) 3 July 10/7 (Advt.), Oughts for a great vacation. Bathing, boardwalk and 'loaf-life' specials. Mens & Boys Swim Trunks.

ought, *v.* Add: **IV. 8.** With periphrastic auxiliary *did*, corresponding to uses under sense 5. *dial.*, *colloq.*, and *vulgar*.

1854 C. M. YONGE *Heartsease* II. III. ix. 236, I..told him he didn't ought to go. **1867** R. YOUNG *Rabin Hill's Excursion to Weston-super-Mare* 12 That's jist how things did ought to be. **1876, 1888** [see next]. **1932** D. L. SAYERS *Have his Carcase* xxvii. 356, I did ought to have spoke up at the time. **1942** 'M. INNES' *Daffodil Affair* I. 17 And I hope that none here will say I did anything I didn't ought. For I only done my duty.

oughta, oughter (ǭ·tə), a representation of a colloq. or vulgar pronunciation of *ought to* (see OUGHT *v.* 5, 7 c and *8). Cf. *ORTER.

1876 C. M. YONGE *Three Brides* II. i. 7 They ought to be ashamed of themselves, they did oughter. **1888** RIDER HAGGARD *Col. Quaritch* III. v. 79 You are my lawful husband, and I calls on you to cease living as you didn't oughter and to take me back. **1901** M. FRANKLIN *My Brilliant Career* iii. 16 You oughter go out more. **1926** F. M. FORD *Man could stand Up* I. ii. 34 'He hadn't ought'er done it!' He hadn't really oughter. **1935** 'R. WEST' *Harsh Voice* ii. 151 He reckoned I oughta see London and Paris and Rome. **1943** K. TENNANT *Ride on Stranger* iii. 24 She didn't oughter do it. **1945** A. KOBER *Parm Me* 180 No joking, Mac, you oughta take it easy. **1959** N. MAILER *Advts. for Myself* (1961) 54 He could see the other house. It had oughta be away from the town. **1963** [see *DADDY-O]. **1967** E. GRIERSON *Crime of one's Own* ii. 22 'I expect 'e buys 'er things.' 'So 'e oughter.' **1971** D. HEFFRON *Nice Fire & Some Moonpennies* i. 11 Indian huh? Well she oughta go for this then. **1974** W. GARNER *Big enough Wreath* i. 8 You didn't oughter've done that, Mr Smith. You know the regs. **1976** M. MAGUIRE *Scratchproof* iii. 45 Somebody oughta lock you away.

oughtness. Delete '*rare*' and add later examples.

1918 [see *GOOD *a.* 14 c]. **1931** W. M. URBAN *Fund. Ethics* i. 9 The forms of conduct or behavior which have this character of *oughtness* are then called standards or norms. **1948** A. O'RAHILLY *Moral Princ.* iv. 21 On the occasion of experience we see the oughtness of certain acts, we have an intuitive appreciation of an objective moral order. **1958** R. C. ANGELL *Free Society & Moral Crisis* ii. 16 The peculiar power of our moral lenses is to pick out and see clearly all the elements in society that reveal 'how oughtness is organized'. **1967** D. VON HILDEBRAND *Trojan Horse in City of God* xxv. 190 The victory of truth and value is the fulfillment of an oughtness.

Ouidaesque (wīdā͵e·sk), *a.* [f. *Ouida*, the nom-de-plume of the English novelist Marie Louise de la Ramée (1839–1908) + -ESQUE.] Characteristic or suggestive of the novels of 'Ouida'; marked by extravagance or lack of restraint.

1909 *Westm. Gaz.* 6 Apr. 4/2 It is the case of the 'Ouida-esque' young man with the big cigar of the motor shows over again. **1915** W. J. LOCKE *Jaffery* xxi. 287 Like the Ouidaesque hero, who could ride a Derby Winner with one hand, and stroke a University Crew to victory with the other. **1929** *Sunday Express* 20 Jan. 9 The 'dark Odyssey of Gilbert Stroud' is almost Ouidaesque. **1930** *Times Lit. Suppl.* 17 Apr. 338/3 A hero of almost Ouida-esque impressiveness. **1971** E. MAVOR *Ladies of Llangollen* xii. 201 In Mr Penruddock's final Ouida-esque version, the successful elopement occurs on the night of a grand ball.

Ouija (wī·dʒa). [f. F. *oui* yes + G. *ja* yes.] A proprietary name for a board having the letters of the alphabet and other signs used for obtaining messages and answers in spiritualistic séances and in the practice of telepathy. Also (with lower-case initial) applied generally to spiritualistic spelling devices. Also *ouija-board*.

1891 *Official Gaz.* (U.S. Patent Office) 3 Feb. 510/2 Toys known as Talking Boards.—Kennard Novelty Company, Baltimore, Md... Used since July 1, 1890. The word 'Ouija'. **1895** *Montgomery Ward Catal.* 236/2 Ouija, or Egyptian Luck Board. **1895** I. M. RITTENHOUSE *Maud* (1939) 590 Once or twice he had referred to something a Ouija-board in Chicago had said, and how it had spelled my name in full. **1904** *Pop. Sci. Monthly* Jan. 195 The various alphabet-using forms of amateur mediumship, such as table tipping, the 'Ouija-board', and certain other devices for making our muscles leaky. **1909** H. CARRINGTON *Physical Phenom. Spiritualism* 67 The phenomena of table-tipping, of ouija and planchette writing. **1922** O. LODGE *Raymond Revised* 45 By the use of instruments known as 'planchette' and 'ouija', often employed by beginners. **1931** *Times Lit. Suppl.* 24 Dec. 1036/4 When receiving communications Ingeborg..is all the while writing, or moving swiftly with the pointer of the ouija board. **1944** AUDEN *For Time Being* (1945) 114, I have prohibited the sale of crystals and ouija-boards. **1949** *Official Gaz.* (U.S. Patent Office) 20 Sept. 638/2 William Fuld, Baltimore, Md. Ouija..for Gameboard, utilizing a Planchette and sometimes known as a Talking Board. Claims use since July 1, 1890. **1968** *Trade Marks Jrnl.* 22 May 835/2 *Ouija*... Board games, being parlour games providing answers to questions. Parker Brothers, Inc. (a Corporation organised and existing under the laws of the State of Maine, United States of America), 190, Bridge Street, Salem, State of Massachusetts, United States of America; Manufacturers. **1968** *Daily Tel.* 10 Sept. 20/6 A television advertising campaign to promote Ouijas as games at Christmas. **1973** *Listener* 20 Sept. 386/2 Professor [John] Taylor's schedule of talks to a medium, a ouija-board operator, a scientist and a hard-line theologian. **1974** *Sci. Amer.* Jan. 108/1 Tens of thousands of young people in the U.S. (particularly in California), caught up in the current occult explosion and eager to know more about Eastern mysticism and early Chinese history, are now consulting the *I Ching* as seriously as they consult the Ouija board or the tarot cards.

ouklip (ōu·klip). *S. Afr.* [Afrikaans, f. Afrikaans, Du. *oud* OLD *a.* + *klip* (see *KLIP *sb.*).] A kind of lateritic conglomerate found in southern Africa.

1892 *Graham's Town* (Cape Province) *Jrnl.* 20 Sept. 2 A few months ago it was discovered..that large beds of Ou Klip (honeycomb gravel rock) on the farm were literally saturated with mercury. **1940** *Min. Resources Union S. Afr.* (Dept. of Mines) (ed. 3) IV. 458 There are many types of laterite or 'ouklip' in this country. The harder types of conglomerate ouklip generally form a very good basecourse for bitumen... Some types of soft conglomerate ouklip which contain an appreciable quantity of sandy soil binder generally yield satisfactory sand-clay bases... The pebble type ouklip..consists mostly of fairly hard lateritic pebbles and soil binder. **1950** *Cape Times Week-end Mag.* 8 Apr. 4/7 This was an outcrop of granite and ouklip. **1955** J. H. WELLINGTON *S. Afr.* I. II. x. 289 In the western highlands of Natal, Peutz recognizes a third grassveld type..in which the infertile sandy soils, underlain by 'ouklip' (i.e. pirolitic ironstone) produce a poor type of veld. **1961** M. M. COLE *S. Afr.* iv. 87 The weathering processes..result in the formation of soils comprising an A horizon of some 12 to 24 inches of friable sand.. overlying a B horizon of mottled clayey-sand containing many ferruginous concretions which in the lower part are cemented to form a hardpan called 'ouklip'.

ould (auld), a representation of an Ir. pronunciation of OLD *a.*

c **1675** *Purgatorium Hibernicum* (MS. 470, Nat. Libr. Ireland) 100 Singing 'Ould Rose' and 'Tory Rory'. **1803** G. COLMAN *John Bull* II. ii. 17 I'm as aisy as an ould glove. **1829** G. GRIFFIN *Collegians* I. vii. 153 O, wirra, Eily! this is the black day to your ould father. *c* **1874** D. BOUCICAULT in M. R. Booth *Eng. Plays of 19th Cent.* (1969) II. 174 This cabin where the remains of the 'ould family', two lonely girls, live. **1898** J. D. BRAYSHAW *Slum Silhouettes* 8 The ould counthry. **1936** 'N. BLAKE' *Thou Shell of Death* iii. 46 She's a bit of an ould stick, but there's no harm in her. **1970** S. J. PERELMAN *Baby, it's Cold Inside* 152 From the moment I had first set foot on the Ould Sod I had yearned to pick up a typical sample of the local crafts. **1977** *Time* 12 Dec. 30/1 Overseas Chinese may not want to go back to live in the People's Republic any more than a U.S. enthusiast for Ireland wants to live on the Ould Sod.

‖ **Ouled Nail** (ū·lėd nā·il, -nəil, -nēil). [Fr., f. *Ouled Naïl*, ad. Arab., lit. 'sons of Nail'.] A group of Arab peoples of Algeria; *spec.* in North African cities: an Arab professional dancing girl belonging to these peoples.

1881 A. A. KNOX *New Playground* xiii. 324 Perhaps the less said the better about the dancing women, who are, if I remember right, called 'oulad nail'. They inhabit a street apart at Biskra, and come from some distant part of the desert. **1906** M. W. HILTON-SIMPSON *Algiers & Beyond* iv. 77 One of the most interesting features..is the *cafés maures*, in which the Ouled Naïl girls dance. *Ibid.* 82 The Ouled Naïls will speak to anyone... Their morality will not bear close investigation. **1914** M. D. STOTT *Real Algeria* ii. 20 Khadava admitted with the most sweet of cynical smiles that it was only to English and Germans that she confessed to being an Ouled Nail—it was found to be more profitable. **1956** L. MORGAN *Flute of Sand* v. 82 'The psychology of an Ouled Naïl dancing girl,' a French administrator had told me, 'is very difficult to understand.' **1973** WODEHOUSE *Bachelors Anonymous* ix. 122 'Oh dear. Are you hurt?' she wailed, and ran to where Mr Trout was pirouetting like an Ouled Nail dancer with his hand to his mouth. **1975** 'P. LORAINE' *Ask Rattlesnake* I. ii. 53 The Ouled Nails, the North African tribe which trains its women to become whores in the dissolute coastal cities.

ouma (ōu·mă). *S. Afr.* [Afrikaans = grandmother, f. *ou* old + *ma* mother.] A name used in addressing or referring to one's grandmother or to an elderly woman.

1910 D. FAIRBRIDGE *That which hath Been* 42 A coloured person, mevrouw;—'Ou'ma Jannetje' she calls herself. **1929** P. SMITH *Little Karoo* (rev. ed.) 181 Was it but three days ago..that Ou-ma had buried her son? **1937** S. CLOETE *Turning Wheels* xxvii. 423 'I am sorry, Ouma,' he said, 'to find you like this.' **1952** *Cape Times* 2 Sept. 14/3 Three drunk *skollies* approached her and asked whether *ouma* had no one to take her home. **1953** J. PACKER *Apes & Ivory* iii. 28 Sybella Margaretha Krige, known to her friends as 'Isie' until the Second World War when the Springbok soldiers she helped so devotedly christened her 'Ouma' (Grannie). **1971** *Cape Herald* 15 May 2/9 But how does Ouma busy herself besides sweeping?

ounce, *sb.*[1] Add: **4. b. ounce force,** a unit of force equal to the weight of a mass of 1 ounce, esp. under standard gravity (cf. *GRAMME and **gramme force*).

1961 *B.S.I. News* Oct. 26/2 A similar distinction is made between..ounce (oz) and ounce-force (ozf). **1966** [see *gramme force* s.v. *GRAMME b].

‖**oung** (auŋ), *v.* Also **aung.** [Burmese.] *trans.* In Burma of an elephant: to push, roll, or drag logs from one place to another or down a stream.

1900 M. & B. FERRARS *Burma* v. 118 (*caption*) Pushing the logs off the shoals (aung). **1901** G. H. EVANS *Treatise on Elephants* i. 9 A well-trained tusker always commands a good price; he is so much more useful both in the yards and forests, as with his tusks he can '*oung*'.., stack timber, assist in getting logs over obstacles, &c. *Ibid.* xvi. 191 It is advisable for some time after such an accident [to the loins] that the animal be loaded lightly; it is also as well not to put him to any heavy work such as *aunging* heavy timber. **1935** R. CAMPBELL *Teak-Wallah* iv. 44 Is there any spectacle, I wonder, that can surpass in magnificence the sight of twenty or thirty elephants, all in the prime of condition, 'ounging' timber down a swollen jungle stream? *Ibid.* xiv. 208 Mounted on a tusker, I spent all day riding up and down the river, superintending the work of the 'ounging' elephants and seeing that they did not allow stacks to form. **1974** *Encycl. Brit. Macropædia* V. 971/2 In India, Sri Lanka..and Burma, their chief use now is in lumbering—they drag logs through the jungle and push floating logs around bends and off sandbanks ('aunging').

oupa (ōu·pă). *S. Afr.* [Afrikaans = grandfather, f. *ou* old + *pa* father.] A name used in addressing or referring to one's grandfather or to an elderly man.

1920 R. Y. STORMBERG *Mrs. Pieter de Bruyn* 40, I had secret misgivings that the Nooitgedacht sheep wouldn't pass the test, even though Oupa Cloete is nearly stone blind. **1934** 'N. GILES' *Ridge of White Waters* I. xiii. 165 Ou'pa Wessels, although well over seventy, insisted on accompanying the commando. **1939** S. CLOETE *Watch for Dawn* 161 What is it? Tell me, oupa. **1951** P. ABRAHAMS *Wild Conquest* 88 But Oupa Johannes didn't kill us and we didn't kill him. **1953** U. KRIGE *Dream & Desert* I. 13 When his father had told him of Oupa's death, Jannie had been very sad since he had loved Oupa. **1976** J. MCCLURE *Rogue Eagle* xii. 204 Wolraad grinned... 'Where's Pa gone, *oupa*?' he asked.

our, *pron.* Add: **B. 1. e.** Used familiarly with a Christian name to denote a relative (esp. a child) or acquaintance of the speaker. Also, with surname, an employee of a company, and, in joc. address to a patient, the diseased or injured part of the body.

1847 A. BRONTË *Agnes Grey* xi. 163, I sent our Bill to beg Maister Hatfield to be so kind as look in on me some day. **1856** DICKENS *Dorrit* (1857) I. xiii. 118 Now, let's see whether there's anything else the matter, and how our ribs are? **1864** —— *Mut. Fr.* (1865) I. II. ix. 246 Sloppy explained..that the Orphan (of whom he made mention as Our Johnny) had been ailing. **1911** F. H. BURNETT *Secret Garden* xxvii. 298 He..took a golden sovereign from his pocket and gave it to 'our 'Lizabeth Ellen', who was the oldest. **1932** N. ROYDE-SMITH *Incredible Tale* ix. 131, I sent up our Mr. Wilkinson, who has lived in Russia. **1936** 'G. ORWELL' *Diary* 11 Feb. in *Coll. Ess.* (1968) I. 175 The son 'our Joe', just turned 15. **1952** 'W. COOPER' *Struggles of Albert Woods* I. ii. 23 'What do you think of it, our Albert?' his mother cried. **1968** 'J. FRASER' *Evergreen Death* v. 40 'What are you doing out here then, our Arnold?' his sister asked. **1977** G. MARKSTEIN *Chance Awakening* xxii. 70 'He's a swinger,' said Chance. 'Our Mike gets around.'

f. *our hero*: used familiarly of the hero by the writer of a work of fiction, biography, etc.

1804 J. BISSET *Crit. Ess. Young Roscius* p. x, Our little Hero caught the first theatric spark. **1854** RAWDON BROWN *Let.* 6 May in M. Lutyens *Millais & Ruskins* (1967) 205 He..said that he had amused him more than anyone since Robinson Crusoe! A greater compliment could certainly not have been paid our hero. **1905** H. A. VACHELL *Hill* v. 110 Much of our hero's time was spent in the company of the Duffer. **1961** *Mind* LXX. 104 And so our hero escapes from his appalling predicament: with one bound, Jack was free. **1975** *Radio Times* 29 May 13/1 Most of the books have a fair amount of physical violence which leaves Our Hero battered almost to pulp.

Ouranian (auərēi·niăn), *a.* [f. Gr. οὐράνι-ος heavenly + -AN.] Of or pertaining to heaven or the upper regions. (Cf. URANIAN *a.*[1])

1908 G. G. A. MURRAY in R. R. Marett *Anthropol. & Classics* 68 A great proportion of our anthropological material is already to be found in prehistoric Crete..the stones, the beasts, the pillars, and the ouranian birds.

ouroboros, var. *UROBOROS.

ours, *poss. pron.* Add: *spec.* = our regiment, chiefly in phr. 'of ours'. Also in *transf.* and extended uses.

1787 W. DYOTT *Diary* Nov. (1907) I. 38 The company at dinner was..Captain Gladstanes, 57th regiment; Captain Dalrymple, 42nd; Hodgson of ours, and myself. **1823** *Spirit of Public Jrnls. M.DCCC. XXIII* (1825) I What is't attracts the optic pow'rs Of Ensign gay, when fortune show'rs Down prospects of 'a step' in 'ours'? **1847** DICKENS *Dombey* (1848) xxi. 206 Edith Skewton, Sir,.. married (at eighteen) Granger of Ours. **1847** THACKERAY *Van. Fair* (1848) xxvii. 235 Run Simple (Ensign Simple, of Ours, my dear Amelia). **1877** G. M. HOPKINS *Let.* 6 Jan. (1938) 94 Lancashire..from where a good many of Ours come. **1894** 'MRS. ALEXANDER' *Choice of Evils* II. ii. 47 We have a young fellow..in 'ours', who has just saved the Colonel's life by a lucky shot. **1922** W. CATHER (*title*) One of ours. **1975** *Listener* 25 Dec. 893/3 A short, highly professional story of a competent war time spy of Ours who goes back to the game. **1977** T. HEALD *Just Desserts* i. 10 You know he was one of ours?.. Provided us with information, tip-offs, odds and ends.

‖**oursin** (ūərsæn). [Fr.] = SEA-URCHIN I.

1928 R. HALL *Well of Loneliness* xl. 376 Many loved Prunier's..because of its galaxy of sea-monsters. A whole counter there was of incredible creatures—Oursins, black armoured and covered with prickles; Bigorneaux; serpent-like Anguilles Fumées. **1931** *Daily Express* 21 Sept. 3/4 There are..other strange fish known as oursins, literally 'little bears'. **1950** E. DAVID *Bk. Mediterranean Food* 142 *Oursins* (those spiny sea-urchins cut in half from which you scoop out the coral with a piece of bread). **1966** P. V. PRICE *France: Food & Wine Guide* 274 There are also *oursins* (sea-urchins), which look just like prickly chestnuts, and taste rather like a snail that has been taken to the sea. **1972** *Guardian* 1 Jan. 11/4 Men bring nets full of *oursins* to quayside cafés. **1973** D. MILLER *Chinese Jade Affair* xvii. 156 A basket of shell-fish..belons, oursins, moules, crevettes and Marennes.

Ouspenskyist (ūspe·nski͵ist). [f. the name of Peter Demianovich *Ouspensky* (1878–1947), Russian philosopher + -IST.] A follower of Ouspensky or his teaching. Also **Ouspe·nskian, Ouspe·nskyite** *adjs.*

1958 L. DURRELL *Balthazar* ii. 29 Alexandria is a city of sects..Steinerites..Ouspenskyists, Adventists. **1968** T. WOLFE *Electric Kool-Aid Acid Test* iv. 54 Alpert soars in Ouspenskian loop-the-loops. **1975** M. BRADBURY *History Man* v. 81 A radical Catholic priest and his Ouspenskyite mistress.

ouster[1]. Delete 'now implying a wrongful dispossession' and add: Also, eviction (from office, etc.) by judicial process or as a result of revolution or political upheaval. **b.** In lay use: dismissal, expulsion; the action of manœuvring out of (a place or position). Now chiefly *U.S.*

1961 P. HOLMES *Sheppard Murder Case* ix. 82 Mr. Y, who had been asked no questions about a possible criminal record, had answered in the negative when asked if he had ever been a witness in any court. If it could be shown that Mr. Y had testified at his 1943 trial this answer could be made the basis for his ouster. **1967** K. GILES *Death in Diamonds* ix. 164 Mary Smith had to leave because of her bad influence on the other girls. She was fifteen when she got the ouster. **1968** *Telegraph* (Brisbane) 3 May 11/1 Mr. Cecil Harmsworth King lost his job as chairman of the International Publishing Corporation in a 'palace revolution' by his own directors. The ouster came three weeks after..a critical article. **1972** *Newsweek* 10 Jan. 25/3 When the court ouster came, the vets..marched out, clenched fists raised. **1973** *Listener* 20 Dec. 842/1 It is the hope..that enough damning evidence would be found to force the ouster of the President overnight—to make him resign. **1974** *Spartanburg* (S. Carolina) *Herald* 22 Apr. A1/2–3 The report..forced the resignation of Lt. Gen. David Elazar, the military chief of staff, and fueled demands for the ouster of Defense Minister Moshe Dayan. **1975** *N.Y. Times* 12 Sept. 6/1 The Communists appeared eager not to be isolated from power as a result of the recent ouster from the premiership and the High Council of the Revolution of Gen. Vasco Gonçalves, whom they had backed. **1976** *Honolulu Star-Bull.* 21 Dec. A-2/2 Hay said one problem still open in Chile concerns persons missing since Allende's ouster and death. **1977** *Time* 9 May 17/2 He was especially anxious to court the Kremlin in view of the rapid cooling of the U.S.'s interest in Ethiopia following the junta's ouster of the Emperor.

oustiti (ū·stiti). [ad. F. *ouistiti* (used in same sense) (see WISTITI).] = OUTSIDER 4.

¶ Properly spelt *ouistiti*.

1941 G. HEYER *Envious Casca* x. 178 'Which would lead one to suppose that the murderer found the door locked, and turned the key from the outside.' 'With an *oustiti*,' nodded the Sergeant. **1962** 'D. BETTERIDGE' *Package Holiday Spy Case* ii. 19 An essential item of a burglar's tool kit is..an *oustiti*. It resembles a long pair of pliers, but..has two semi-circular metal tongues. Inserted into a keyhole, it will grip firmly a key on the other side, and gentle but powerful wrist-work will turn it in the lock.

out, *adv.* Add: **I. 3. c.** *from this out*: henceforth, from now on; also *from here* (*on*) *out*, *from that out*. *colloq.* (chiefly *U.S.* and *Anglo-Irish*).

1867 F. A. BUCK *Lett.* (1930) 214 Now, I am going to try to be a Jew from this out. **1882** W. D. HOWELLS *Mod. Instance* in *Century Mag.* Apr. 925/1 I'll take a back seat from this out. **1899** W. B. YEATS *Let.* 28 Nov. (1954) 330, I imagine I am about the only person who belongs to the orderly world she is likely to meet from this out. She seems to be perfectly mad. **1905** H. CORKRAN *Lucie & I* 36 From this out I will think of you as a young *diablesse*. **1907** J. J. HORGAN *Great Catholic Laymen* (ed. 2) i. 37 Napoleon was then at the height of his power. From that out his Empire began to decline. **1922** JOYCE *Ulysses* 432 Mrs Marion from this out, my dear man, when you speak to me. **1941** in H. WENTWORTH *Amer. Dial. Dict.* (1944) 434/1 He has run the race and is fairly entitled to sit on the sidelines from here out. **1942** *Ibid.*, Bob Maslow's at the controls from here on out. **1972** A. FRIEDMAN in Cox & Dyson *20th-Cent. Mind* I. xii. 420 There are symbolic signs everywhere that Charlotte's and Adam's lives from here on out will be lives of protracted emptiness and captive anguish.

7. b. *to have it out*, add to def.: also with other objects; also, to discuss fully or reveal (a matter); to settle (a dispute or misunderstanding) *with* someone; (earlier and further examples).

1811 JANE AUSTEN *Sense & Sens.* II. viii. 129 She had better have her cry out at once and have done with it. **1825** H. WILSON *Mem.* I. 77 O let us have it all out now, and have done with it. **1839** DICKENS *Nickleby* xxxi. 305, I shall double-lock myself in with him and have it out before I die. **1847** J. A. FROUDE *Shadows of Clouds* iv. 52 The result was the advice which best harmonized with the suggestion of his own heart, to go off at once to Morlands, have it all out with Emma, and put his father's letter into Mr. Hardinge's hands. **1880** TROLLOPE *Duke's Children* II. xi. 126 Let us have this out, Mabel, before we go. **1932** E. BOWEN *To North* xxvi. 385 You must have this out with Emmeline, find how she stands with this young man and..*strongly* discourage the whole affair. **1959** H. HAMILTON *Answer in Negative* x. 118, I was trying to decide whether I ought to leave it alone or have it out with him. **1971** *Where* Dec. 361/1 We eventually went to the LEA and saw an assistant education officer who agreed that we should meet the head and the doctor and have the whole thing out.

13. a. (Later examples.) From the 1960s frequently used as a chant (preceded by the name of a politician or by a word signifying something unwanted) by political demonstrators. Also used in written political slogans.

1968 *Times* 8 July 1/7 More than 100 Pakistani students took over the Pakistan High Commission in Lowndes Square, S.W., last night... Demonstrators lined the balcony chanting and waving placards saying: 'This building is occupied' and 'Ayub out'. **1970** B. LEVIN *Pendulum Years* xv. 259 The streets of Britain continued [in the 1960s] to echo to cries of 'Americans out of Vietnam!' and the ritual chanting of 'Ho-ho-ho Chi Minh!' **1970** D. NEVILLE-ROLFE *Power without Glory* II. 244 Even the stone-throwing rioters displayed their own brand of charm when they paraded in front of the Embassy their very home-made banners boldly declaring '*out—perfide albino*'. **1970** (*recorded from oral evidence*) Wilson *out*! **1973** *Times* 21 Nov. 18/4 'Anti-abortion—*out out out*; Free Abortion on Demand—*in in in*,' they chanted. **1976** *New Society* 26 Aug. 435/2 (*heading*) Hashish, out. **1977** *Woman's Own* 26 Mar. 31/3 Then you notice the blackened buildings, boarded up houses and the painted slogans in the housing estates: 'Brits out.' 'Join the IRA.'

b. *out with it*: an exhortation to a speaker to admit or assert something over which he is hesitating.

1709 [in Dict.]. **1924** GALSWORTHY *Forest* I. i. 11 Out with it, Mr. Farrell. **1974** 'S. WOODS' *Done to Death* 35 Come on, Dick, out with it. What do you know about them?

II. 15. b. (Further examples.) So *school is out* (chiefly *U.S.*): school is at an end. See also *day out* (*DAY *sb.* 19), *night out* (NIGHT *sb.* 5a in Dict. and Suppl.). *out to lunch*: see *LUNCH *sb.*[2] 2b.

1827 W. TAYLOR *Poems* (ed. 2) 91 In that whimp'ling burn when the school was out. **1843** MRS. STOWE *Mayflower* 172 But, when 'school was out', James's spirits foamed over as naturally as a tumbler of soda-water. **1870** [see EVENING *sb.*[1] 3]. **1911** in *Sc. Nat. Dict.* (1965) VI. *s.v.*, Word went through the toon like lichtenin, for the school wis out. **1925** WODEHOUSE *Carry On, Jeeves!* v. 108, I have already visited some of New York's places of interest on my evening out. **1948** 'J. TEY' *Franchise Affair* ix. 94 'Shouldn't leave your car. Take it with you. .. It's Saturday.' 'Saturday?' 'School's out.' 'Oh, I see. But there's nothing in it..that's movable.' **1956** B. HOLIDAY *Lady sings Blues* (1973) ii. 17, I finished up the fifth grade, and as soon as school was out Grandpop put one those big tags around my neck, saying who I was and where I was going. **1965** *Times Lit. Suppl.* 22 Apr. 317/1 In a recent road safety cartoon on B.B.C. television, I was surprised to hear the Americanism 'when school is out'. **1974** 'R. TATE' *Birds of Bloodied Feather* vi. 127 'I trust I'm not disturbing you?' 'What's the time?' 'Four.' 'School's out'... 'Come on in'. **1974** *Times* 8 Apr. 14/7 A retired bricklayer..spoke to me in the owlishly conspiratorial tones of one who has been cheered by his evening out.

c. (Further examples of sense 'on strike'.) Cf. sense *19b. *out there*, in the war of 1914–18: at the Western Front; in France. *colloq.*

1917 A. G. EMPEY *Over Top* 302 *Out there*, a term used in Blighty which means 'in France'. Conscientious objectors object to going 'out there'. **1920** W. J. LOCKE *House of Baltazar* xii. 150, I want to kick myself for sitting here in luxury when there's so much to be done out there. I had got my platoon—I was acting first lieutenant—like a high-class orchestra. **1929** *Papers Mich. Acad. Sci., Arts & Lett.* X. 312/2 *Out there*, England's equivalent for 'Over there'. **1974** *Times* 27 Feb. 14/3 The miners are still out; world prices are still rising. **1977** 'J. LE CARRE' *Hon. Schoolboy* vi. 121 Pound's in the soup again... Electricians out. Railways out.

i. *to be out for*: to have one's interests or energies directed to, to be intent on (something); also *to be out to* (do something). Cf. *ALL OUT *adv. phr.* 4. orig. *U.S.*

1901 MERWIN & WEBSTER *Calumet 'K'* i. 13 They're mostly out for results up at the office. Let's see the bill for it. **1901** S. E. WHITE *Westerners* xxix. 272 When they are out to have a good time,..they want somebody they can have their sort of fun with. **1907** BEERBOHM in *Sat. Rev.* 13 Apr. 457/1 She is not 'out for' fun. She is an ardent suffragist. **1912** *Humanitarian* Oct. 76, I am sure that no person in this country, save him who is out for personal gain, wishes us to lag behind in this movement. **1913** H. WALPOLE *Fortitude* III. x. 388 She's out for happiness at any cost and you're out for freedom. *Ibid.* IV. iii. 474 He was 'out' to defend his whole life. **1926** A. L. MAYCOCK *Inquisition* v. 116 All the Inquisitors..were out to convert and reconcile, not to condemn. **1956** A. L. ROWSE *Early Churchills* xii. 236 The Dutch vetoed a battle... Marlborough was exceedingly disappointed: he was out for decision. **1959** N. MAILER *Advts. for Myself* (1961) 42 They kept actin' like they was out to get him first.

19. b. (Further example.) Also, out of work, unemployed. Cf. sense 15c in Dict. and Suppl.

1878 T. WOOD in J. Burnett *Useful Toil* (1974) III. 309, I..was regarded as an enthusiast in some places for seeking work when so many were out who were known to the masters. **1890** W. BOOTH *In Darkest England* I. iv. 38, I would often be out of work a fortnight to three weeks at a time. Once earned £3 in a week, working day and night, but then had a fortnight out directly after. **1920** J. FERGUSON in *Northern Numbers* 98 She had been 'out' since May, Her 'panto' savings now were well-nigh spent. **1935** N. MITCHISON *We have been Warned* I. 74 He's a riveter. He came..when there was work going at the docks... Now he's out. **1968** J. BINGHAM *I Love, I Kill* viii. 95 When I told him I was 'out', he bought me a pint instead. And he gave me two tickets for the show he was in. **1973** *Listener* 29 Nov. 736/1 A British prime minister discovered as having been implicated in the same kind of depths as Nixon would be out. **1977** *Times* 6 Dec. 6/6 Because my husband's out of work he's not a man to take anything off us... Since the time he has been out they've never gone short of shoes.

c. For 'IN *adv.* 5c' read 'IN *adv.* 6d'. (Earlier example.) Freq. *not out* (cf. NOT-OUT *a.* in Dict. and Suppl.); also *transf.* and *fig.*

1609 R. ARMIN *Hist. Two Maids of More-clacke* D2[v] *Tutch.* What doe you call it when the ball sir hits the stoole? *Filbon.* Why out. **1746** in J. Nyren *Young Cricketer's Tutor* (1833) 111 England, 1st Innings... Newland 18—not out. **1881** *Sportsman's Year-Bk.* 137 He..has been in 36 times, and 'not out' four times. **1906** E. DYSON *Fact'ry 'Ands* vi. 62 The..thermometer.. registered 103°, not out. **1937** PARTRIDGE *Dict. Slang* 424/2 *Not out* (96), 96 and still alive. **1955** *Times* 11 July 4/2 Waite, when he had made 61 and with the total at 314, was given not out caught behind the wicket off Lock.

d. (Further examples.)

1930 E. WALLACE *Lady of Ascot* i. 13 'How long have you been out?'.. 'I don't know what you mean,' he said. 'How long have you been out of gaol?' **1934** D. L. SAYERS *Nine Tailors* 279 Well, as you know, I wasn't out. I was inside again, owing to a regrettable misunderstanding. **1967** M. PROCTOR *Exercise Hoodwink* xiii. 91 He was a hardened criminal... The days 'out' were great days, a life of affluence and excitement. The days 'in' were the price he paid. **1976** 'B. GRAEME' *Snatch* v. 56 It was Reg Abbott who got two [years], wasn't it? Reg should be out by now.

e. Unconscious; *spec.* in *Boxing*, defeated through failing to rise within the ten seconds allowed after being knocked down; so *out on one's feet*: dazed or barely conscious, although still in a standing position; *out like a light*: see *LIGHT *sb.* 5f; *out to it* (*Austral. slang*): dead drunk; fast asleep.

1898 B. J. ANGLE in W. A. Morgan *'House' on Sport* I. 45 A competitor stopped by a blow on the mark is as much 'out' as though rendered helpless by a hit on the point. **1901** R. FITZSIMMONS *Phys. Cult. & Self-Defense* 159 Time was up. The champion was out. **1918** *War Birds* (1927) 150 She responded..by hitting him playfully over the head with an empty port bottle... It was a terrific crack and he was out for some time. **1941** BAKER *Dict. Austral. Slang* 52 *Out to it*, dead drunk. **1947** 'N. SHUTE' *Chequer Board* 3, I..fell down..on the floor, clean out. **1946** K. TENNANT *Lost Haven* (1947) xi. 171 He was properly out to it that night. We made speeches about how sorry we was to see him go. **1952** M. ALLINGHAM *Tiger in Smoke* xix. 270 You're ill... You may not know it, but you're out on your feet. **1955** E. HILLARY *High Adventure* 175 For God's sake, Charles, keep an eye on John! He's out on his feet but doesn't realise it! **1963** N. MARSH *Dead Water* (1964) ix. 246 When he opened his eyes he thought with astonishment: 'I was out.' **1973** 'H. HOWARD' *Highway to Murder* vii. 85 He was still out cold but he began coming round just before the ambulance got there.

22. b. (Further examples.)

1936 M. MITCHELL *Gone with Wind* xii. 227 He had seen no pantalets on the streets, so he imagined they were 'out'. **1954** [see *IN *adv.* 6i]. **1959** *Encounter* Dec. 16/1 It is becoming steadily easier for newspaper or television programmes to dictate what is *out*, what is *in*. **1972** *Daily Tel.* 15 Mar. 14 Creativity is 'in', while spelling, punctuation and well-formed handwriting..are 'out'.

c. Out of the question, impossible, not to be considered; unwanted, unacceptable, prohibited; out of place, irrelevant.

1936 W. STEVENS *Let.* 27 Jan. (1967) 307 Any form of hell raising is simply out. **1938** *Topeka* (Kansas) *Capital* 15 June 10/1 (*headline*) Rail legislation out? **1940** 'M. INNES' *There came both Mist & Snow* ii. 26 The revolver-shooting fad to which I had been so unexpectedly introduced appeared to me childish in itself and oddly 'out' in the sort of house-party characteristic of Belrive. **1945** *Tee Emm* (Air Ministry) V. 33 Unauthorised low-flying should be out, repeat *out*. **1956** I. BROMIGE *Enchanted Garden* II. ii. 91 Fiona left her velvet coat and tulle dress in the back of the car, tied the raincoat tightly round her waist and rolled up the sleeves... Glamour was out that evening. **1973** 'H. HOWARD' *Highway to Murder* i. 16 'Tell your boss to have a quiet word with the law.'.. 'No, that's out.'

23. Also, having exhausted one's supply of a particular thing; out of stock of a specified article.

1885 *List of Subscribers* (United Telephone Co.) p. xv, The hotel cellarman came up... 'Sir,' said he, 'we have had a run upon minerals, and are nearly out.' **1935** J. STEINBECK *Tortilla Flat* iii. 36 Run down and get four bottles of ginger-ale. The hotel is out. **1942** 'A. BRIDGE' *Frontier Passage* xi. 194 You haven't got a gasper, have you? We're out. **1972** J. MCCLURE *Caterpillar Cop* iii. 30 Got a smoke? I'm out.

b. Used in radio communication to indicate that the speaker has finished speaking and expects no reply. *over and out*: see *OVER *adv.* 6b.

1950 'D. DIVINE' *King of Fassarai* xi. 73 He called the signaller. 'Take this down... "No signs occupation. Out."' **1955** E. WAUGH *Officers & Gentlemen* I. ix. 108 He took the instrument. 'Headquarters to D Troop. Where are you? Over... You can't be... Damn. Out.' **1958** 'CASTLE' & 'HAILEY' *Flight into Danger* i. 23 The acknowledgement came on the air. 'Flight 714. This is Winnipeg Control. Roger. Out.' **1966** D. HOLBROOK *Flesh Wounds* 218 'Hallo Roger Baker, Hallo Roger Baker. Able Zebra asks for hornet support. Roger Baker over.' 'Roger Baker O.K. Out.' **1971** J. WAINWRIGHT *Dig Grave* 16 At County Headquarters Wireless Operations Room they used the more powerful, country-wide air waves... 'Purple Fifteen to Control. Understood and out.' **1976** L. DILLS *CB Slanguage Dict.* (rev. ed.) 51 *Out*, through transmitting.

26. b. (Earlier examples.)

c **1792** JANE AUSTEN *Minor Wks.* (1954) 151 This mighty affair is now happily over, and my Girls *are out*. **1813** —— *Pride & Prej.* II. vi. 72 Are any of your younger sisters out, Miss Bennet? *Ibid.* 73 The younger ones out before the elder are married!

c. (Further examples.)

1872 B. JERROLD *London* xv. 127 The ginger-beer merchant..gesticulating and pattering one sultry morning... 'The Best Drink Out!' was his perpetual cry. **1973** *Times*

15 Oct. 22/8 A Triumph is still the best bike out, as a Norton represents a compromise between design criteria and production costs.

IV. 32. out and return. = sense 30 a.

1963 *Times* 31 May 16/2 The lengths of the out-and-return paths to the ionosphere. **1966** A. BATTERSBY *Math. in Managem.* vi. 157 Each unit represents 1,000 tons making an out-and-return journey of 2 miles.

out, *sb.* Add: **1. b.** *slang.* (See quots.) So *three-out*, a glass holding a third of some measure of liquor.

1835 [see *GIN *sb.*² 2 a]. **1903** *Daily Chron.* 24 June 7/2 'Two Bass's and three outs' is an order which seems to be instantly comprehended by a barmaid who distributes the contents of two bottles among three glasses. **1908** *Ibid.* 6 Feb. 4/7 In a gin palace an 'out' is a dram glass.

3. c. (Earlier examples.)

1823 M. R. MITFORD *Our Village* (1824) I. 209 He.. thinks nothing of contending with both sides, the ins and the outs, secure of out-talking the whole field. **1853** F. GALE *Public School Matches* 13 The 'Outs' are pleased at the steady pace, and the 'Ins' are equally pleased with the steady batting.

d. *colloq.* An out-patient at a hospital. So *outs*, the out-patient department.

1933 PARTRIDGE *Slang To-day & Yesterday* III. iii. 192 *Outs*, out-patient department. **1964** G. L. COHEN *What's Wrong with Hospitals?* iv. 76 Distinction between the 'ins' and the 'outs' is inevitably fading.

4. d. An attempt, undertaking; the achievement of a particular result; progress, success; usu. in phr. *to make an out. colloq.* and *dial.*

1843 H. Y. WEBB *Diary* 4 May in *Amer. Speech* (1951) XXVI. 183/1 A man..that made half as many good resolutions as I have or made a worse out in sticking to them. **1845** M. M. NOAH *Gleanings* 148 He slipped the fatal jack of diamonds from the bottom of the pack, and claimed the money then in stake... I at first thought him in jest, and laughed at him for making so bungling an out. **1853** J. G. BALDWIN *Flush Times Alabama* 31, I might have made a pretty good *out* of it, if I had thrown myself upon the merits of my case. **1854** A. E. BAKER *Gloss. Northamptonshire Words* II. 82 'He made a good out of that speculation.' 'He made a poor out of his speech.' **1893** J. SALISBURY *Gloss. Words SE. Worcestershire* 27 'Making a goodish out' or 'a poorish out', are terms applied to any undertaking when successful or the reverse. **1904** W. N. HARBEN *Georgians* xix. 176 Warren got down on his knees then and actually tried to pray; but he made a pore out. **1938** M. K. RAWLINGS *Yearling* xxvi. 347, I often figger I made a sorry out of it, not encouragin' you. **1951** H. E. GILES *Harbin's Ridge* xv. 125 Let the woman of a house get sick, and it just goes to pieces. In the city, now, a man can make out very well... But in the country he makes a poor out of it when the hub of the house comes down.

e. *Baseball.* The act of getting a player out. *U.S.*

1860 in *Amer. Speech* (1947) XXII. 204/1 Three 'outs' and one 'run'. **1886** H. CHADWICK *Art of Pitching & Fielding* 15 Mere speed costs more in wild pitches, and called and passed balls than it yields in outs or strikes. **1973** *N.Y. Herald Tribune Internat.* 15 June 15/4 Evans, whose only out in 17 straight appearances was a sacrifice fly, wiped out a 3-2 Pirate lead with his 14th homer. **1974** *Index-Jrnl.* (Greenwood, S. Carolina) 18 Apr. 10/1 After two outs in the second, winning pitcher Jack Davenport singled and scored when the next three batters walked.

f. A way out, means of escape; an excuse, defence, alibi. *slang* (orig. *U.S.*).

1919 R. LARDNER *Real Dope* iii. 79, I am not one of the kind that are looking for an out and trying to hide behind a desk..because I am afraid to go into the trenches. **1926** J. BLACK *You can't Win* vi. 69 If a copper grabs you you've got an out. You ain't exactly beggin'. **1934** R. STOUT *Fer-de-Lance* xvii. 287 There are times when I would welcome..an escape from life's meaner responsibilities—what Mr. Goodwin would call an out. **1953** P. FRANKAU *Winged Horse* I. i. 4 You like thumbing your nose at common sense... And it gives you an Out from me. **1970** G. F. NEWMAN *Sir, You Bastard* 12 He wanted an out, a plausible story that would extricate his head from the chopping block. **1974** *New Yorker* 22 Apr. 130/2 Ardent pro-Europeans on Mr. Wilson's team would stand firm..against those ministers who will probably be for rejection of any terms and a quick out.

5. b. A defect, disadvantage, blemish. *colloq.* and *dial.* (chiefly *U.S.*).

1886 E. S. WARD *Burglars in Paradise* 48 Sound as sense! Hadn't an out about him. **1893** K. SANBORN *Truthful Woman in S. California* 69 Are there no 'outs', no defects in this Pasadena? **1917** H. GARLAND *Son of Middle Border* xiii. 129 Even hostling had its 'outs', especially in spring when the horses were shedding their hair. **1955** W. W. DENLINGER *Compl. Boston* 167 A perfection in one part cannot make up for serious 'outs' elsewhere in the whole dog.

7. Phr. *at* (or *at the, on the*) *outs*: at variance or enmity (*with* someone or something). *colloq.* and *dial.*

1824 W. CARR *Horæ Momenta Cravenæ* 97 'To be at outs,' is to be at variance. **1877** E. PEACOCK *Gloss. Words Manley & Corringham, Lincolnshire* 185/2 They fell at outs last Brigg fair was three year, an' hev nivver hed a good wod for one another sin'. **1884** *Congress. Rec.* 23 Apr. 3326/1 His church and the Unitarians [were] very much at outs. **1915** D. H. LAWRENCE *Rainbow* iv. 90 She was always at outs with authority. **1917** G. B. McCUTCHEON *Green Fancy* 87 My daughter and I are..what you might say 'on the outs' at present. **1928** A. WAUGH *Nor Many Waters* ii. 84 We were at outs pretty badly about that time. And when you're at outs it doesn't take much to send you off. **1936** M. DE LA ROCHE *Whiteoak Harvest* ix. 113 You could scarcely have done a worse thing. Renny and Alayne are at the outs. **1955** W. GADDIS *Recognitions* III. i. 732 It's all right, don't explain. I'm on the outs with them too. **1973** J. PORTER *It's Murder with Dover* vii. 67 Soon as he [*sc.* a cat] gets at outs with one of the guests the old devil's off upstairs making a convenience of the chap's bed.

out, *a.* Add: **2. b.** *out island*, also (often with capital initials) *spec.* any of the outlying islands of the Bahamas (see quot. 1957). Hence *out islander.* (Often hyphened.)

1875 *Encycl. Brit.* III. 238/1 The inhabitants of the out-islands were reduced to indigence and want. **1957** *Ibid.* II. 928/1 New Providence.., although not one of the larger islands, is the most important..; the others are known collectively as the Out Islands. **1971** 'D. HALLIDAY' *Dolly & Doctor Bird* i. 6 A former minor Ambassador ..living on one of the Bahamian out-islands. **1971** *Bahamas* XXIII. III. 20 Bahamian Out Islanders are among the world's friendliest people. **1973** *Whitaker's Almanack 1974* 775/1 There are a General Post Office in Nassau, 4 branch offices in New Providence and 109 sub-offices in the Out Islands.

7. Unfashionable; opp. *IN *a.* 2.

1966 *Punch* 29 June 946/1 Nowhere have I come across a word of guidance for the 'out' crowd—the vast, non-swinging, switched-off, palateless, utterly without-it lot who dominate the community. **1969** *Daily Tel.* 24 July 17/6 They [*sc.* children] want to eat savoury things most of all; but there are certain 'in' sweet-stuffs and a very great many 'out' ones.

out, *v.* **1.** Delete 'now *Obs.* exc. *dial.*' and add later examples.

1927 H. A. VACHELL *Dew of Sea* 269 I'll out 'em both, even if it breaks the contract. **1941** E. R. EDDISON *Fish Dinner* vii. 103 Should a been unlorded long since, outed of all his hopes, for's misgovernment. **1942** E. WAUGH *Put Out More Flags* ii. 137 It was just a question of outing those fellows in the government. Sir Joseph had seen many governments outed... He'd soon out Hitler if he were alive and a German. **1968** *Daily Mirror* 27 Aug. 7/3 No one throws things away any more. They 'out' them.

b. Delete '*Obs.* exc. *dial.*' and add later examples. So *out pipes* (Naut.), to cease smoking pipes; also as *sb.* (see quots.).

1899 *Daily News* 30 Jan. 6/4 The water flooded high the stoke-holes, outing the fires. **1900** *Black & White Budget* 1 Sept. 684/1 The times set apart for smoking are generally from noon till about 1.15, when the marine drummer beats a long roll on his drum as a signal to 'Out-pipes'. **1916** 'TAFFRAIL' *Pincher Martin* ii. 25 At one-ten the bugle sounded 'Out pipes', and the decks were cleared up. **1950** *Publ. Amer. Dial. Soc.* XIV. 50 *Out*,..to extinguish, as a lamp, a fire. **1961** F. H. BURGESS *Dict. Sailing* 154 *Out pipes*, the order to stop smoking.

c. (Further examples.) Also, to murder.

1900 G. R. SIMS *In London's Heart* xlviii. 294 He glanced contemptuously at the prostrate form of his accomplice. 'Looks like I've outed him,' he said. 'Good job if I have—he'll never blab again.' **1913** E. C. BENTLEY *Trent's Last Case* ii. 27 The body not being robbed looks interesting, but he may have been outed by some wretched tramp. **1915** E. CORRI *30 Yrs. Boxing Ref.* 221 Lewis.. promptly hit him a terrific punch on the point. 'Outed' by bluff! **1927** E. WALLACE *Feathered Serpent* xviii. 229 I've heard fellers in Dartmoor say that if ever they got the chance they'd 'out' him.

d. In a ball game, esp. lawn tennis: to send (the ball) outside the court or playing area.

1865 W. S. BANKS *List Provincial Words Wakefield* 3 *Ahted*, put out. 'Ahted t'first ball.' **1927** *Daily Express* 22 June 2/2 Raymond, striving for extra speed, netted and outed a succession of returns. **1928** *Ibid.* 5 July 11/4 He outed and netted two drives.

e. In cricket: to put or declare (a batsman) out. ? *Obs.*

1899 *Captain* I. 517/1 Never forget that there are other ways of outing a man besides clean bowling him. **1906** *Daily Tel.* 23 Aug. 9/7 Myers went in, but was almost immediately 'outed' under singular circumstances.

4. b. (Further examples.)

1896 G. B. SHAW *Let.* 11 Feb. (1965) I. 596 There is something fundamentally unfriendly in having a grievance and not outing with it. **1942** W. FAULKNER *Go Down, Moses* 167 The negro he was shooting at outed with a dollar-and-a-half mail-order pistol..only it never went off. **1975** *Bookseller* 17 May 2540/1, I was just getting ready to say that as sometime chief solo-boy at Exeter College, Oxford, I was as good as Ernest Lough, when McCarry outed with: 'My *Hear My Prayer* was *very* sweet.'

c. Of information, news, etc.: to become known. *dial.*

1893–4 R. O. HESLOP *Northumb. Words* II. 515 It suin *outed*'—became commonly known. **1905** E. PHILLPOTTS *Secret Woman* I. ix. 87 Yet it outed as she'd said 'no' to him.

out, *prep.* **1.** Delete '*Obs.* or *arch.* exc. in *from out*' and add later examples.

Not current in Received Standard in the U.K. but common in dial., and in various regions abroad. Several of the examples are U.S., Austral., and N.Z.

1926 A. G. McADIE *Man & Weather* 19 The ship would make easier weather by proceeding out the western entrance. **1958** *Otago Daily Times* 24 Feb. 5/2 He flew out the side of the cloud to warmer air. **1960** M. SPARK *Ballad of Peckham Rye* (1960) x. 150 You should of pushed him out the nest long ago. **1961** *Coast to Coast 1959–60* 34 During this time he had tried to throw everything movable out the wardroom window. **1962** *Amer. Speech* XXXVII. 269 To drive with the left arm out the window. **1967** *Southerly* XXVII. 75 She looked out the window..at all the other houses. **1968** K. WEATHERLY *Roo Shooter* 111 Sam was really crook, leaning out the window spewing. **1969** *Listener* 31 July 162/2 Schoenberg kept the 12 notes we ended up with but threw the hierarchy out the window. **1969** *Eugene* (Oregon) *Register-Guard* 3 Dec. 1D/1 'And,' continued Belko, 'that's when our whole plan went out the window.' **1972** D. E. WESTLAKE *Cops & Robbers* (1973) iii. 46 He looked out the windshield. **1973** *Black World* Aug. 55/2 He slid on back out the kitchen door. **1975** *New Yorker* 29 Sept. 43/2 Mrs. Santana and her children contribute to the refuse by throwing their trash and garbage out their windows.

out-. Add: **A. I. 1.** *out-district* (examples), *-school, -shed.*

1849 in *Worcester* (Mass.) *City Documents* No. 1, 33 Most of the schools in the out-Districts, have been conducted.. under the new order. **1858** J. MORGAN *Let.* 9 June in *Richmond-Atkinson Papers* (1960) I. 408 The sale of spirits on the two-gallon system..I consider to be the chief curse of the out districts. **1927** *Scots Observer* 8 Oct. 11/4 Back this summer from six months in the district in charge of out-schools. **1957** V. W. TURNER *Schism & Continuity in Afr. Society* v. 154 Chikimbu was the problem child of the local Mission out-school. **1895** J. ROBERTS *Diary* 6 This led into someone's outshed.

2. *out-nurse, -porter, -pupil* (earlier example), *-sister* (later examples).

1909 *Englishwoman* Apr. 269 If she has a baby, it has to be dragged from bed and carried to some out-nurse. **1902** *Chambers's Jrnl.* Nov. 717/2 'Boots' will select for him that out-porter who will most briskly wheel his colossal pile of cases. **1927** *Daily Express* 14 July 9/2 Both men were out-porters at Snow Hill Railway Station. **1853** MRS. GASKELL *Ruth* II. vii. 183 I'm a sort of out-pupil of yours. **1877** G. M. HOPKINS *Let.* 6 Jan. (1938) 93 The eldest, Milicent, is given to Puseyism: she is what is called an out-sister of the Margaret Street Home. **1939** M. PHILIP *Companions of Mary Ward* I. i. 6 Her entrance.. into the Convent of Poor Clares as an out-sister.

4. *out-party* (later examples).

1949 *Manch. Guardian Weekly* 11 Aug. 3 The Opposition is an 'out' party in the brawling 18th century sense. **1965** *N.Y. Times* 18 July IV. 8 For a minority out-party, any position except 'me too' almost inevitably is going to become simple opposition. **1976** *Guardian Weekly* 26 Sept. 7/3 Whichever party does not control the White House—the 'out-party'—does not even have a leader.

6. *out-path* (earlier and later examples).

1573 T. CARTWRIGHT *Replye to Whitegift* 27 It is our partes to walke in the broade and beaten way, as it were the common caussie of the commaundement, rather then an outpathe of the example. **1897** G. MACDONALD tr. Schiller in *Rampolli* 64 Could I but the outpath follow—Ah, how were my spirit blest!

II. 7. *outstress.*

1881 G. M. HOPKINS *Sermons & Devotional Writings* (1959) 197 The first intention then of God outside himself or, as they say, *ad extra*, outwards, the first outstress of God's power, was Christ; and we must believe that the next was the Blessed Virgin.

B. 10. *outflooding, -hanging.*

1909 R. KANE *Sermon of Sea* xix. 306 Its eager essence is roused, directed, loosened, and flung forward in the out-flooding force of a soul's quest, in the torrent-like tide of love. **1850** W. HOWITT *Year-bk. Country* ix. 313 In the lower, out-hanging towers are dungeons. **1851** H. MELVILLE *Moby Dick* I. ii. 13, I at last came to a dim sort of outhanging light not far from the docks. **1972** D. HASTON *In High Places* iii. 38 A few words of explanation and 1,500 feet of long, out-hanging, body-burning abseils.

11. *out-flung* (later examples), *out-fought* ppl. adjs.

1940 W. FAULKNER *Hamlet* III. i. 159 This time his outflung hands touched the farther bank. **1955** V. CRONIN *Wise Man from West* xiii. 243 They heaved themselves up by hand and foot over outflung eaves of the plateau. **1892** STEVENSON & OSBOURNE *Wrecker* xii. 189 Our out-fought enemy [*sc.* a squall] only a blot upon the leeward sea.

12. Also, away from the thing named, as *out-shore.*

1947 [see *KICK-BACK, KICKBACK c]. **1961** *Times* 2 Aug. 4/1 Meanwhile, the outshore current looked more attractive to three other good starters.

C. I. 14. *outflood, -lean* (later example).

1920 D. H. LAWRENCE *Women in Love* xxiii. 349 The marvellous fulness of immediate gratification, overwhelming, out-flooding from the source of the deepest life-force. **1900** HARDY *Poems of Past & Present* (1902) 170 The land's sharp features seemed to be The Century's corpse outleant.

15. a. *outfan, outheave* vbs.

1930 R. C. CAMPBELL *Adamastor* 87 Victory-vanned, with her feathers out-fanned, The palm tree alighting my journey delayed. **1957** —— *Coll. Poems* II. 253 The Spring with rosy spinnaker outfanned Comes curling silver fleeces through the land. **1850** W. B. ULLATHORNE *Remarks on Proposed Education Bill* 14 A momentum with which to outheave from the soul of youth both the principle of authority and the positive doctrines of religion together. **1908** HARDY *Dynasts* III. III. iii. 104 Till dawn began outheaving this huge day, Pallidly—as if scared by its own bringing.

b. *out-tire* (later examples).

a **1877** SWINBURNE *Lesbia Brandon* (1952) xvi. 165 Her limbs shuddered now and then..as if cold or out-tired. **1905** 'Q' *Shining Ferry* I. vii. 91 And so, out-tired with their long day,..they came at nightfall..to the palace of enchantment.

16. *out-elbow* vb. (*poet.*).

1936 DYLAN THOMAS *Twenty-Five Poems* 9 Now that my symbols have outelbowed space.

II. 18. *out-achieve, -bat, -bowl, -break, -cook, -field, -hustle, -skate, -sprint, -wait* (later examples).

1960 V. PACKARD *Waste Makers* (1961) xxiv. 295 The Russians outachieved the United States in launching earth satellites. **1970** *Time* 17 Aug. 39 Getting along with parents has never been easy in the U.S. America has almost begged for trouble by expecting children to out-achieve their parents. **1773** J. DUNCOMBE in R. Freeman *Kentish Poets* (1821) II. 364 To see the Surry cricketers Out-bat them and out-bowl. **1873** *Chicago Tribune* 4 June 1/7 The Mutuals outbatted their opponents. **1970** Outbat [see *outbowl* below]. **1773** Outbowl [see *outbat* above]. **1823** *Lady's Mag.* July 388/1 There was no doubt that Andrews could, if he chose, out-bowl Samuel Long, and out-bat Tom Coper. **1970** *Sunday Tel.* 20 Dec. 21/7 This weakened M.C.C. side..have been outbatted, outbowled and outfielded by South Australia. **1944** *Sun* (Baltimore) 15 Jan. 9/3 Outbreaking her rivals, the light-coated filly opened up a length advantage in the run to the turn. **1955** *Ibid.* 19 May 20/4 Aeschylus outbroke the opposition but could not keep pace. **1839** DICKENS *Let.* 9 Sept. (1965) I. 578 A woman..who..far out-cooked the cook of Petersham! **1970** N. ARMSTRONG et al. *First on Moon* ii. 34 Mike Collins, who had become fond of dishes like coq au vin.., definitely could outcook Lew Hartzell. **1976** *S. Wales Echo* 23 Nov., He proved it last night when he out-cooked five girls to win the South Glamorgan round of the Wales Gas schools cookery competition. **1875** *Chicago Tribune* 17 Aug. 5/6 The Browns were outbatted and outfielded. **1960** *Times* 19 May 21/2 They had been out-batted, out-bowled, and out-fielded. **1970** Outfield [see *outbowl* above]. **1961** in WEBSTER, It is one thing to be beaten and quite another to be out-hustled. **1966** *Daily Progress* (Charlottesville, Va.) 8 June 30/2 We out-hustle them, out-position them, and in all but two games have actually out-rebounded them. **1975** *New Yorker* 7 Apr. 116/2 The other Knicks,..out-hustling the Lakers, double-teamed them all over the court. **1963** *Times* 4 Mar. 3/7 M. Schnelldorfer..had some bad falls and was outskated by his fellow Bavarian, the ebullient S. Schönmetzler. **1968** *Globe & Mail* (Toronto) 15 Jan. 19/1 Detroit Red Wings outskated, outhustled and outshot Chicago Black Hawks Saturday night. **1938** *Times* 25 July 5/1 Pender had struck two even shrewder blows for his side by out-sprinting A. Pennington twice. **1963** *Times* 11 Feb. 3/3 Snell was outsprinted in a mile. **1929** D. H. LAWRENCE *Pansies* 95 Still a man can be A meeting place for sun and rain, Wonder outwaiting pain As in a wintry tree. **1957** T. HUGHES *Hawk in Rain* 28 Where the insects couple as they murder each other, Where the fish outwait the water. **1977** J. B. HILTON *Dead-Nettle* i. 9 She had..succeeded in out-waiting her antagonists. Her patience..had become too much for their nerves.

20. *out-game, -modern* vbs.

1940 *Sun* (Baltimore) 14 June 20/1 The Greentree filly outgamed Rosetown in a thrilling battle to the wire. **1957** *Ibid.* 1 Feb. 22/1 Careless Miss..caught Miss Erlen inside the sixteenth pole and then outgamed that filly, thanks to Brooks's superior handling. **1922** *19th Cent.* Apr. 654 The old dog could in truth out-modern the best of them. **1935** Out-modern [see sense *23 a].

21. *out-feature, -figure* (example), *-gambit, -luck, -machine, -monster, -poll* (later examples), *-rebound* vbs.

1929 R. BRIDGES *Testament of Beauty* I. 714 True beauty of manhood outfeatureth childish charm. **1866** HARDY *Time's Laughingstocks* (1909) 54 Intently busied with a vast array Of epithets that should outfigure thee. **1962** L. DEIGHTON *Ipcress File* v. 34, I felt tired and out-gambited. **1916** H. TITUS *I Conquered* ix. 119 The hind legs straightened, that mighty force bore on his footing—and the stone slipped. The Captain [*sc.* a horse] was out-lucked. **1928** *Daily Express* 9 July 13/1, I ran into Charles Kingsley there, who..was just outlucked as [*sic*] Wimbledon. 'I drew Patterson in the third round... What do you think of that for bad luck?' **1942** *Ann. Reg. 1941* 39 General Wavell had to conduct simultaneously a number of campaigns in each of which he was outnumbered and outmachined. **1955** E. BOWEN *World of Love* iv. 74 See, today, how even Antonia had been out-monstered. **1968** *Economist* 11 May 21/1 A list of delegates pledged to support Mr. Kennedy at the Democratic nominating convention in August..outpolled by a margin of two to one a list pledged to Mr. Humphrey. **1973** *Guardian* 19 Apr. 4/5 In Oakland, California, incumbent Republican John Reading outpolled Black Panther party chairman Bobby Seale by more than 34,000 votes in an eight-man race for Mayor. **1976** *Time* 27 Dec. 8/2 Soares..had hinted he might resign if his party was heavily out-polled. **1966** Out-rebound [see *out-hustle* s.v. sense *18]. **1974** *State* (Columbia, S. Carolina) 8 Mar. 4-B/5 Maryland badly out-rebounded us when they beat us by 11 points at College Park. They are a great board team. **1977** *Detroit Free Press* 11 Dec. 5-D/2 This is the first time we've been outrebounded all year.

23. a. *to out-fiend fiends, outfish fish, out-modern the moderns, outmonster the monstrosities, outrainbow the rainbow.*

a **1918** W. OWEN *Coll. Poems* (1963) 53 The few who rushed in the body to enter hell, And there out-fiending all its fiends and flames With superhuman inhumanities. **1930** E. BLUNDEN in *Time & Tide* 3 Jan. 16 The new painters, with their endeavours to outmonster the monstrosities of uninspired futurists. **1935** *Amer. Speech* X. 192/2 She *out-moderns* the moderns in a frock that is made for *cocktailing*. **1956** 'H. MACDIARMID' *Stony Limits* 33 The range of the tartans outrainbowing the rainbow. **1960** T. HUGHES *Lupercal* 46 Four-legged yet water-gifted, to outfish fish.

outa (au·tă), a representation of a colloq. or vulgar pronunciation of OUT OF *prep. phr.* orig. *U.S.* Cf. *OUTER, *OUTTA.

1896 [see *OUT-OF-SIGHT *adj. phr.* 2]. **1906** H. GREEN *At Actors' Boarding House* 42 Outa twelve hundred a week yuh kin pay it back an' have ten-fifty left. **1931** E. LINKLATER *Juan in Amer.* III. ii. 215 My act's *different*. Outa the ordinary, see? **1952** B. MALAMUD *Natural* (1963) 93 Yeah..but we're outa the cellar now and who done that—the wind? **1963** [see *BEEZER 1]. **1966** 'J. HACKSTON' *Father clears Out* 51 We must've taken close on a 'undred an' fifty thousan' pounds' worth of gold outa that mine. **1970** R. D. ABRAHAMS *Positively Black* iii. 73 The white man's rooster would then just beat the goddamned shit outa that son-a-bitch. **1973** *Black World* July 56/2 They all looked high outa it. **1976** *New Musical Express* 12 Feb. 28/6, I felt like it might sometimes have got a bit outa hand. The rhythm got lost.

out-act, *v.* (Later examples.)

1906 *Westm. Gaz.* 2 June 6/3 The best of Hamlets [is sometimes] outacted by the worst of gravediggers. **1975** D. GRAY *Ride on Tiger* viii. 62 She knew she could out-act Anna any day.

outage (au·tėdʒ), *sb.* orig. and chiefly *U.S.* [f. OUT *adv.* + -AGE.] A period or state in which (esp. electrical) apparatus is not operating as a result of disconnection or failure; *spec.* a power cut.

1903 *Electr. World & Engin.* 18 Apr. 653/1 The lamp hours were 54,187; percentage of lamp outage, 6–10; globes broken, 23. **1951** *Engineering* 5 Jan. 28/2 Outages will occur for about 50 per cent. of the flashovers so that trouble due to lightning can be expected once per annum per 500 miles. **1955** *Tweed* (Ontario) *News* 14 Apr. 10/6 Defective lamps will be replaced on Friday of each week. To report outage phone 207 before Friday each week. **1958** J. G. BROWN *Hydro-Electric Engin. Pract.* III. vi. 118 The outage which is to be expected with hydro plant is less than with steam turbo-generators. **1963** K. NEVILLE in D. Knight *100 Yrs. Sci. Fiction* (1969) 73 There's an outage in the Silver Lake Area. The brakes on a bus failed and took out an overhead section. **1974** *Indian Express* 26 Dec. 1/7 An inspection of the pipelines in all the reactors in America had been ordered... It had been decided that the first unit would have an outage for refuelling from January 13. **1976** *Washington Post* 19 Apr. A8/3 The outages were caused by overheating of the fuses that sit atop the power lines' poles. **1976** *Cody* (Wyoming) *Enterprise* 23 June 16/7 Mr. Royale has lived in Wapiti Valley since 1921, has had electric power since 1947, and remarked that this was the longest power outage he could remember.

outarm (autā·ɹm), *v.* [OUT- 18 a.] *trans.* To exceed in possession or acquisition of weapons of war. Also *refl.*, to provide (oneself) with more arms than a competitor.

1930 H. BELLOC in *G. K.'s Weekly* 25 Jan. 309/1 Those [governments] who have the less money seek for a pledge from those who have the more not to outbuild them and not to outarm themselves against their power competitors. **1950** *N.Y. Times* 31 Dec. 22/1 We shall not only out-arm our foes but 'out-sacrifice' them. **1955** V. CRONIN *Wise Man from West* xiii. 243 Outnumbered and outarmed, he had recourse to a trick. **1966** *Listener* 8 Sept. 355/3 A country..which is accustomed to..out-arming everybody.

outasight (au·tăsəi·t), *a.* Also **out-a-sight, outasite.** Colloq. contraction of *OUT-OF-SIGHT *adj. phr.*

1893 S. CRANE *Maggie* xviii. 150 You're the kind of man we like, Pete. You're outa sight! **1968** *Surf International* (Austral.) I. VII. 44 Sydney's got a lot of girls, but Cape Town has an unbelievably high standard, I reckon. We check them out at lunch time—outasight! Too much! **1969** *Observer* 16 Feb. 40/6 Pendennis boogaloos, falls by cats into numbers, and lays down heavy outasight rappings. Translation: Pendennis arranges events, calls on people in the money, and produces a lot of fantastic gossip. **1971** *Oz* May 5, I gave this guy nearly £30 and he rented a room for me in some outasite neighbourhood. *Ibid.* 7 On they trotted. 'Outasite, outasite,' yelled Lee after them. **1973** *Black World* June 63 This Sistuh here sho give some out-a-sight sets.

ou·t-at-elbow(s. 1. See ELBOW 4 c. **2.** Of a dog (see quots.). Used predicatively (usually without hyphens) and *attrib.*

1922 F. T. BARTON *How to choose a Dog* 155 The elbows turn outwards from the chest wall, so plainly seen in the Bulldog, but in other dogs to be out at elbows is a serious fault. **1943** H. N. BEILBY *Staffordshire Bull Terrier* vii. 34 A dog that is out of condition..is just as unsound as one which is out-at-elbow due to incorrect placement of the shoulder-blades. **1954** C. L. B. HUBBARD *Compl. Dog Breeders' Man.* 225 Out at Elbows. Having the elbow joints noticeably turned away from the body due to faulty front formation. **1975** T. GRAY *Beagle* (ed. 3) 196 Out at Elbow. Elbows turned away from the chest, uneven in appearance, loose.

out-back, *adv.* Add: Also **out back, outback.** (Earlier and later examples.)

1878 'R. BOLDREWOOD' *Ups & Downs* iii. 31 There was not a streak of crimson in the pearly dawnlight, as the whole party..rode silently along the indistinct trail which led 'out back'. **1893** H. LAWSON *Coll. Verse* (1967) I. 447 Scenery outback isn't like Illawarra. **1901** M. FRANKLIN *My Brilliant Career* iii. 12 The boys, as they attained manhood, drifted Out Back to shear, drove, or to take up land. *Ibid.* xxxiv. 289 George Melvyn had a large station Out Back. **1909** *Daily Chron.* 29 Jan. 4/7 Under the title of 'The Church Outback', Dr. G. H. Frodsham, Bishop of Northern Queensland..has published in an Australian paper a lively account of his experiences in..his enormous diocese. **1936** I. L. IDRIESS *Cattle King* i. 2 Fascinating stories..of the big mobs outback. **1942** C. BARRETT *On Wallaby* i. 13 Out Back I have met honest sundowners. **1944** *Living off Land* iii. 49 Anyone who has been out-back..will know..how every waterhole becomes alive with frogs.

2. (As two words.) Outside at the back of a house or other building; in or into the back garden or back yard. *U.S.*

1892 'MARK TWAIN' *Amer. Claimant* iii. 36 There was a message, now, from out back, and Colonel Sellers went out there in answer to it. **1964** T. WOLFE in *Esquire* Feb. 97 If this wasn't such a high-class joint we would take wiseacres like you out back and beat you into jellied madrilene.

B. *adj.* Of, pertaining to, or characteristic of the Australian interior or back-country.

1900 H. LAWSON *Darling River* in *Prose Wks.* (1948) 269 'The Queenslan' rains'..seem to be held responsible.. for most of the out-back trouble. **1906** A. B. PATERSON (*title*) An outback marriage. **1913** W. K. HARRIS *Outback in Australia* i. 2 Of course, you get various opinions of Outback hospitality. **1931** *Times Lit. Suppl.* 1 Oct. 738/1 Sydney was the natural centre of outback adventurers. **1957** *Times* 11 May 7/6 In its own way the project is as brave as any bit of outback pioneering for metals or minerals. **1971** *Southerly* XXXI. 27 We've already rejected the proposition that wallabies are too shamingly outback to be possible material for poetry. **1977** A. WILSON *Strange Ride R. Kipling* iii. 157 'Men only' bars are disappearing even in outback Australia.

C. *sb.* **1.** The Australian interior or back-country.

1907 *Gentl. Mag.* July 78 These young dwellers in the Out Back have often no educational opportunities. **1911** in E. M. Clowes *On Wallaby* iv. 115 The Outback can still breed some true mates. **1920** B. CRONIN *Timber Wolves* 9 In the seclusion of the outback they are at liberty to revert to grossness unspeakable. *Ibid.* ii. 40 Such men are not uncommon in the outback. **1930** *Times Lit. Suppl.* 10 July 577/2 Its travesty of the essentially peaceable 'out-back' is no worse than the scenario writer would think permissible. **1955** *Times* 6 July 17/3 The Duke of Edinburgh..cited, and discussed in detail, the scope for aircraft in the outback. **1971** *Sunday Australian* 8 Aug. 17/3 Australia's tourist future lies in the outback. **1977** *Hongkong Standard* 12 Apr. 9/6 It still has not as yet agreed to finance the cost of building a prototype solar-energy collection and storage plant in the Australian outback.

2. *transf.* Applied to other regions or countries with allusion to the Australian interior. Also *fig.*

1959 *Listener* 15 Jan. 140/3 Tramp your way through Wales's 'outback'. **1963** *Times* 20 Apr. 9/7 The recent wave of village school and mosque building in this hitherto neglected outback [in Turkey]. **1972** *Guardian* 3 Apr. 2/5 Senator Humphrey's statement came after a 14-hour swing around the Wisconsin outback. **1975** *Times* 5 Dec. 1/4 Mr Wilson's statement..provided a field day for.. skinheads of the parliamentary outback. **1976** J. VAN DE WETERING *Tumbleweed* x. 91 Cunucu, that's the out-back, the outback of Curaçao. **1978** *Globe & Mail* (Toronto) 4 Mar. 8/3 A B.C. government plan to use television and radio to bring higher learning to the out-back has thrown academia into a tizzy.

Hence **ou·tbacker,** a native or inhabitant of the out-back; **ou·tbackery,** the cultivation of attitudes and values characteristic of the out-back.

1913 W. K. HARRIS *Outback in Australia* i. 3 Another feature in the character of the Outbacker..is his honesty. **1918** R. H. KNYVETT *Over There* iii. 28 In their enthusiasm the people of the capital city practically mobbed these 'outbackers', loading them..with cigarettes and candy. **1927** *Blackw. Mag.* Oct. 461 A grove of giant Tasmanian tree-ferns,..the 'old man' fern of outbackers. **1933** *Bulletin* (Sydney) 18 Jan. 11 Paddy Whelan is far from being the first outbacker to do a perish for water. **1966** T. RONAN *Once there was Bagman* 124 The phase of life, now sneered at by our pharisaical, suburban, scholarship-nurtured intelligentsia—'Outbackery', they call it—has its intervals of excellence. **1971** *Southerly* XXXI. 22 We began to dismiss the image of the explorer, the bush-ranger, the whole outbackery. **1971** *Bulletin* (Sydney) 14 Aug. 49 No violence, no sex, no self-conscious outbackery; the only complaint, the book is too short.

ou·t-basket. [f. OUT *a.*, OUT- 6 + BASKET *sb.*] In an office, etc.: a basket or tray for outgoing correspondence or other documents. Cf. *OUT-TRAY.

Sometimes written as two separate words with *out* regarded adjectivally.

1940 *Amer. Speech* XV. 247 His incoming mail is put in an in-basket and his outgoing mail in an out-basket. **1944** 'N. SHUTE' *Pastoral* v. 115 He sealed the letter... He tossed it into the OUT basket. **1952** *Chambers's Jrnl.* Aug. 493/2 The phones stood primly, the in and out baskets were in their places, and he was in charge of it all. **1968** MRS. L. B. JOHNSON *White House Diary* 20 Aug. (1970) 704 It looks as if the Russians have emptied their out-basket to us. They have answered *all* of the President's correspondence. **1970** [see *IN-BASKET].

out-blo·ssoming, *vbl. sb.* [OUT- 9.] The act of blossoming out or forth; a flowering; usu. *fig.*

1907 *Daily Chron.* 31 July 4/4 'Sunday out' has become a well-nigh universal out-blossoming. **1924** W. B. SELBIE *Psychol. Relig.* 178 The religious awakening of adolescence ..is..generally an outblossoming of the whole nature into a larger and more wonderful world. **1932** M. JOYNT tr. *Gougaud's Christianity in Celtic Lands* ii. 45 The wonderful out-blossoming of Christianity which distinguished Ireland in the following ages.

ou·tblowing, *vbl. sb.* [OUT- 9.] A blowing out or outwards. Also **ou·tblowing** *ppl. a.*, that blows out.

1900 *Geogr. Jrnl.* XVI. 406 Blowing towards and in upon the polar regions to make good the drain caused by the surface outblowing south-easterly winds. **1909** *Daily Chron.* 31 May 4/4 An intaking and outblowing of the breath between the teeth. **1928** PEAKE & FLEURE *Steppe & Sown* 14 The borders..had acquired their characteristic loess soil..through the outblowing of the winds from the ice sheets over the loose detritus.

outboard, *a.*, *adv.* Add: **A.** *adj.* **2.** Of a motor: attached to the outside of a boat, at the stern; also of a motor-boat propelled by such an engine. Also *ellipt.* as *sb.*, such a motor or boat. Hence *outboard motor-boating, -motoring, -motorist(e)*.

1909 *National Sportsman* Mar. 488/1 (Advt.), Make a motor boat of any boat in 5 minutes..with the Waterman Outboard Motors. **1914** *Yachting Monthly* XVI. 408 The demand for the outboard motor steadily increases. **1926** S. LEWIS *Mantrap* i. 14 When we don't use the out-board motor, they [*sc.* the Indians] do the paddling, not us. **1928** *Daily Express* 21 Apr. 10/3 The racing 'outboard' boat has given us a fascinating pastime. **1928** *Daily Tel.* 10 July 17/5 Miss Joan Spicer..is one of the best-known of 'out-board-motoristes'. **1928** *Daily Mail* 25 July 17/4 The new pastime of outboard motor-boating. **1928** *Ibid.* 7 Aug. 19/6 One of the big appeals of outboard motoring is the ease with which the boat and engine can be handled. **1935** *Discovery* Mar. 77/1 The journey will be made in the semi-decked whale boat which will be fitted with a 'Seagull' outboard engine. *Ibid.* Aug. 225/1 There are four outboards, with a speed of twenty-five knots. **1943** J. W. DAY *Farming Adventure* iii. 41 In peace-time you would find..the creek noisy with outboards. **1959** P. CAPON *Amongst those Missing* 165 It's probably a canoe with an outboard motor. **1972** D. BLOODWORTH *Any Number can Play* xxi. 214 There's a man looking after the outboard I came in. **1973** J. LEASOR *Host of Extras* v. 66 The roar of an outboard engine splintered my dreams. **1974** *State* (Columbia, S. Carolina) 8 Mar. 4-B/1 (Advt.), Meet the 1974 Mercs. The most advanced outboards in boating. **1977** *Daily Tel.* 24 Feb. 19/7 The water was like glass as the Royal barge came in, chased by..outboards.

3. (See quot. 1956.)

1928 V. W. PAGÉ *Mod. Aircraft* vii. 267 The parasitic resistance..can be greatly reduced by properly streamlining the engine supports, especially those of the outboard engines as properly housing the engine mounted in the fuselage offers no particular difficulty. **1956** W. A. HEFLIN *U.S. Air Force Dict.* 365/1 *Outboard.* Of aircraft components: Out toward an airfoil tip; away from the fuselage or hull... *Outboard engine*, on an airplane having four or more engines, an engine farthest from the fuselage or hull.

outbreathed, *ppl. a.*[1] (Later example.)

1914 R. M. JONES *Spiritual Reformers 16th & 17th Cent.* 177 This entire manifested or out-breathed universe is, he says, the expression of the divine desire for holy sport and play.

ou·tbred, *ppl. a.* [OUT- 11.] Bred from parents not closely related.

1903 *Biometrika* II. 171 Waltzing mice must be crossed with in-bred and out-bred pure-bred albinos and in-bred and out-bred cross-bred albinos. **1955** *New Biol.* XVIII. 38 In an outbred population..things are very different. **1959** C. D. DARLINGTON *Darwin's Place in Hist.* x. 56 All the 'plasticity' (or variability) is due to the inbreeding of outbred plants and animals, or to the outbreeding of inbred plants and animals. **1977** *Times* 14 Apr. 14/4 There were consistent differences [in I.Q.] between the outbred children and the children of first cousins.

outbreed, *v.* [OUT- 14, 18.] **1.** (Stress even or on first syllable.) *trans.* and *intr.* To breed from parents not closely related.

1919 EAST & JONES *Inbreeding & Outbreeding* xi. 214 Whether plants are inbred or outbred is a matter which is left to regulate itself. **1968** *Times* 23 May 17/4 In the wild it is usually an advantage for plants to outbreed—to reproduce by fertilization with other individuals not themselves.

2. (Stress on second syllable.) *trans.* To be quicker or more prolific in breeding than.

1903 [listed s.v. OUT- 18]. **1926** BELLOC *Compan. Wells's Outl. Hist.* ii. 24/2 A slightly faster minority of swallows always outlive and outbreed their slower rivals. **1976** K. BONFIGLIOLI *Something Nasty in Woodshed* i. 10 Only the sparrow..can outbreed magpies by diddling his mate all the year round.

ou·tbreeder. [OUT- 8 + BREEDER 1.] A plant which is not self-fertile, or an animal in which breeding pairs are not closely related.

1963 E. MAYR *Animal Species & Evolution* xiv. 421 The entire breeding system of outbreeders is so organized as to accumulate and preserve genetic variation. **1963** DAVIS & HEYWOOD *Princ. Angiosperm Taxon.* xiii. 424 In many forest trees which are outbreeders, pollen may disperse for long distances. **1975** S. K. JAIN in Frankel & Hawkes *Crop Genetic Resources* ii. 22 We speak of..outbreeders, inbreeders, and apomicts.

ou·tbreeding, *vbl. sb.* [f. *OUTBREED *v.*] Breeding from parents not closely related.

1901 *Bull. U.S. Dept. Agric. Div. Veg. Physiol.* XXIX. 38 'In-and-in breeding', 'outbreeding' and other expressions relating to the close or distant relationship of parents have been prominent subjects among animal breeders. **1902** *Encycl. Brit.* XXV. 372/2 The tribes practised far more in-breeding than outbreeding. **1919** EAST & JONES *Inbreeding & Outbreeding* i. 13 Interest in the effects of inbreeding and of outbreeding is not confined to the professional biologist. **1940** *Nature* 30 Mar. 485/2 If we are to regard unisexuality simply as one of a number of outbreeding mechanisms, it is necessary to account for the fact that it is frequently found in some groups..but rare in others. **1959** C. D. DARLINGTON *Darwin's Place in Hist.* xii. 70 Outbreeding is necessary for the recombination of differences. **1964** E. J. H. CORNER *Life of Plants* xi. 197 Flowers have devices..to carry pollen from one flower to another, and, preferably, from one plant to another, to secure outbreeding. **1967** *Economist* 16 Dec. 1108/2 There is no evidence..that dairy stock are suffering from too close breeding through artificial insemination. Too much out-breeding..would be a more valid criticism. **1975** S. K. JAIN in Frankel & Hawkes *Crop Genetic Resources* ii. 22 Many specific genetic factors are known which regulate the degree of outbreeding.

outburst, *sb.* Add: **1. b.** *Astr.* A solar radio emission of great intensity and several minutes' duration which occurs in conjunction with a solar flare.

1947 C. W. ALLEN in *Monthly Notices R. Astron. Soc.* CVII. 387 Besides steady noise and bursts, one can detect, rather rarely, sudden outbursts of radio noise, which last for a few minutes, fluctuating violently, and then disappear. *Ibid.* 394 It is this correlation between flares and outbursts that shows that an outburst has a particular physical significance. **1955** *Sci. Amer.* June 42/3 The more common type of burst is a brief surge of intensity lasting only a few seconds; we call this a 'radio flash'. During a week of intense activity on the sun, there may be 100 flashes. The second type, far less frequent, is a burst lasting several minutes; this is called an 'outburst'. The outbursts..come only during a solar flare. **1971** J. S. HEY *Radio Universe* v. 104 Large flares are often accompanied by very intense outbursts of radiation on metre wavelengths lasting between about 5 and 30 min. In a classification of radio bursts according to their characteristic properties, these outbursts have been designated as Type II radio bursts. *Ibid.* 108 The microwave outbursts, often called microwave Type IV, sometimes accompany large flares and are particularly interesting because of their association with solar cosmic rays.

ou·t-camp. Chiefly *N. Amer.* [OUT- 1.] A camp at some distance from the main camp.

1844 *Knickerbocker* XXIII. 116 The Sioux..would not fail to attack, according to their custom, the out-camps. **1944** T. ONRAET *Sixty Below* ix. 96, I had a little rice and bacon in one of my out-camps. *a* **1951** E. HILL in Murdoch & Drake-Brockman *Austral. Short Stories* (1951) 292 The lone little cavalcade..passed a deserted out-camp. **1970** *Islander* (Victoria, B.C.) 1 Nov. 12/2 From his main cabin, Sam had four outcamps along his trapline.

outcaste, *v.* Add: Also *reflex.*

1915 KIPLING *New Army in Training* 64 What will be the position..of the young man who has deliberately elected to outcaste himself from this all-embracing brotherhood?

ou·t-city, *a.* [OUT- 12.] Situated outside a city; suburban.

1939 J. STEINBECK *Grapes of Wrath* xiii. 118 Then the buildings grew smaller... The wrecking yards and hot-dog stands, the out-city dance halls. **1963** *Economist* 9 Nov. 571/1 Those [rents] to be paid in out-city areas.

outclass, *v.* Add: (Further examples.) Also *transf.* (with connotations of *CLASS *sb.* 5 b).

1909 *Chambers's Jrnl.* Jan. 61/1 In the process of production..the Americans soon found themselves outclassed. **1911** *Ibid.* Oct. 702/2 It [*sc.* the aeroplane] can even outclass the telegraph upon short journeys. **1955** *Times* 20 June 13/3 The Ferrari team..was quite outclassed and the chief opposition to the German cars came from the Maseratis. **1966** M. WOODHOUSE *Tree Frog* xii. 105 He was practised in these techniques..and..I was outclassed. **1977** R. L. WOOLF *Gains & Losses* i. 35 A bumbling Church of England rector..hopelessly outclassed in argument by three chief Catholic spokesmen.

out-countenance, *v.* For *Obs.* read *Obs.* exc. in *arch.* use and add later example.

a **1945** E. R. EDDISON *Mezentian Gate* (1958) xxxix. 222 In him..burned..that same recklessness and superfluity which, when he..went on..into known instant peril of death at Middlemead, had outcountenanced the great lamp of heaven.

ou·t-country, *a.* [OUT- 1, 12.] **a.** Associated with or suggestive of the country (as opp. a town). **b.** Situated or coming from a particular country.

1943 *Time* 22 Feb. 53/2 With his clear, healthy, out-country look..baggy, tweedy clothes..Will White had strolled into his office. **1963** [see *IN-COUNTRY].

ou·t-county, *a.* [OUT- 12.] Situated, or coming from, outside a particular county.

1961 *Observer* 26 Mar. 12/6 A..version of this scheme..was shown..to representatives of the L.C.C.'s expanding 'out-county' towns. **1963** *Times* 16 Feb. 12/3 This is one of the oldest of the 15 'out-county' estates of the L.C.C. and contains altogether 9,584 dwellings. **1972** *Where?* Feb. 62/2 If the neighbouring borough is the only reasonable alternative then they are pretty well duty bound under Section 8 of the 1944 Act to approach that borough for a place, *but Section 8 in no way binds the out-county borough to offer one. Ibid.* 63/2 She could opt to go to another college outside the area, so long as she was prepared to pay the higher fees which generally apply to out-county students.

ou·t-cri:cket. [f. OUT- 3 + CRICKET *sb.*[2]] In cricket: bowling and fielding, as opposed to batting.

1884 *J. Lillywhite's Cricketer's Ann.* 63 Kent's first victory of the season, the result mainly of creditable out cricket. **1904** *Westm. Gaz.* 22 Feb. 3/1 Bad batting lost us the game, for our out-cricket in both innings was up to a very high standard. **1927** M. A. NOBLE *Those 'Ashes'* 206 Larwood's fast bowling was the feature of England's out-cricket. **1963** *Times* 25 Feb. 4/1 Between luncheon and tea, New Zealand's courage made for such splendid out-cricket that Barrington and Cowdrey were compelled to display most of their resources. **1975** *Sunday Tel.* 27 Apr. 32/3 Lancashire's out-cricket was far too positive for their total of 215 for six to be more than a pious dream for Yorkshire, whose innings closed at 137 for seven. **1977** *Guardian* 3 Jan. 11/5 India, who won the toss, were dismissed by some brilliant English outcricket for 155.

outcrier. a. (Later examples.)

1902 BEERBOHM *Around Theatres* (1924) I. 344 If..any of our outcriers harbour the delusion that a School would inculcate something more than technical tricks [etc.]. **1931** *Tablet* 23 May 673/1 Once more the outcriers have cried out before they are hurt. **1942** BEERBOHM in *Listener* 24 Sept. 389/1 One is taught to believe that the outcriers are entirely altruistic men.

ou·tcropper. [f. OUTCROP *sb.* + -ER[1].] One who takes coal from an outcropping seam or vein.

1926 *Glasgow Herald* 7 Oct. 8/3 The outcroppers are doing good business for themselves. *Ibid.* 5 Nov. 7 Prosecutions which revealed extensive damage being committed by coal outcroppers..were brought in the Airdrie J.P. Court yesterday.

outcross, *sb.* Add: (Further examples.) Also *attrib.*

1918 *Genetics* III. 475 When double-throwing Matthiola is used as egg parent in an outcross to ordinary singles, half the offspring receive a factor for doubleness. **1949** R. B. KELLEY *Sheep Dogs* (ed. 3) iv. 62 It is not necessary to purchase such out-cross dogs. **1971** *Farmer & Stock-breeder* 16 Feb. 49/1 An unplanned out-cross with an unknown wheat took place and this brought much improved fertility. **1975** *Times* 25 Aug. 8/5 Original out-crosses were Northumberland-bred Scottish Blackfaces. **1977** *Horse & Hound* 14 Jan. 15/3 Malacate stands out as a potential outcross for the majority of high-class European mares.

outcross, *v.* (Stress even.) [f. the sb.] *trans.* To cross (an animal or plant) with one not closely related. Also *absol.*

1918 *Genetics* III. 437 Each [beaded fly] was outcrossed separately to a fly from some non-beaded stock. **1931** E. B. FORD *Mendelism & Evolution* ii. 40 If the now highly inbred stock be outcrossed to ordinary wild-type flies, it is found that the extracted recessives..have returned to the original condition. **1949** R. B. KELLEY *Sheep Dogs* (ed. 3) iv. 62 It will be necessary continually to out-cross by introducing dogs unrelated to the favoured animal, so that close-breeding is avoided.

ou·tcrossing, *vbl. sb.* [f. *OUTCROSS *v.*] The crossing of an animal or plant with one not closely related to it.

1950 *Brit. Jrnl. Psychol.* XL. 132 Vigour is restored by out-crossing. **1973** PROCTOR & YEO *Pollination of Flowers* xii. 382 It is seldom easy to establish the amount of out-crossing which takes place under natural conditions. **1973** B. J. WILLIAMS *Evolution & Human Origins* xiv. 249/2 Heterosis can occur as a result of outcrossing, or mating between breeding isolates.

outcry, *sb.* Add: **2.** Also *U.S.*

1931 *Amer. Speech.* VII. 20 *Public outcry*, an auction sale. **1961** in WEBSTER, *Southeastern Reporter*. The executor's duty to sell it at public outcry. **1974** *News & Reporter* (Chester, S. Carolina) 15-A/6 (Advt.), I, the undersigned Special Referee will sell at public outcry to the highest bidder..the following described real estate.

outcry, *v.* **1. a.** (Later example.)

1849 THACKERAY *Pendennis* I. xxii. 204 She at once took side with Helen against Doctor Portman, when he outcried at the enormity of Pen's transgressions.

ou·t-cue:. *Broadcasting.* [OUT- 7.] A cue (*CUE *sb.*[2] 1 c) that indicates when a particular recording or transmission is about to end.

1962 A. NISBETT *Technique Sound Studio* viii. 139 The main things to mark on the script are as follows:..(iv) Duration (or other means of noting in advance when the outcue is coming up). (v) Type of fade out. **1969** S. HYLAND *Top Bloody Secret* i. 81 The BBC's duty director..waited for the Presentation announcer's out-cue. **1972** D. LEES *Zodiac* 119 It was Zodiac's television experience that led him to leave on a good 'out cue'.

ou·t-curl. *Curling.* [OUT- 7.] = *OUT-TURN.

1903 [see *IN-CURL].

ou·tcurve. [OUT- 7.] **1.** *Baseball.* The bending or curving of a ball outwards (i.e. away from the batter); the course of such a ball; a ball pitched so as to curve in this way.

1881 *N.Y. Herald* 29 July 6/5 Reipslaugher,..not being used to the difficult delivery of Bond, found great difficulty in handling the in-shoots and out-curves. **1886** [see *INCURVE *sb.*]. **1897** [see *INSHOOT]. **1910** *Encycl. Brit.* III. 459/2 The commonest of these swerving deliveries, and the first invented, is the out-curve, the ball coming straight towards the batsman until almost within reach of his bat, when it suddenly swerves away from him towards the right. if he be right-handed. **1943** *Amer. Speech* XVIII. 106 Various types of curve ball are the sinker.., the in-curve, the out-curve,..and the screwball.

2. *gen.* An outward curve or prominence.

1902 *Encycl. Brit.* XXVIII. 622/2 It is convenient to employ a specific name for a projection of a coast-line less pronounced than a peninsula, and for an inlet less pronounced than a bay or bight; outcurve and incurve may serve the turn. **1912** GALSWORTHY *Inn of Tranquility* 68 The sharp outcurve of his dark head. **1945** *Sun* (Baltimore) 19 July 7-O/5 This designer bows to the new round-shouldered vogue, but builds hers in an 'outcurve', to avoid the drooping look apparent in many of the new styles.

ou·tcurved, *a.* [OUT- 11.] Of the bow of a violin or other stringed instrument: having a curve in the direction away from the hair.

1954 *Grove's Dict. Mus.* (ed. 5) I. 855/2 The mechanics of a bow with slight positive curve (away from the hair; out-curved) necessarily differ somewhat from those of an incurved bow. **1970** *Daily Tel.* 5 May 16/2 She had used an archaic 'outcurved' bow to play gamba sonatas by J. S. and W. F. Bach on a modern viola. **1976** *Early Music* Oct. 513/1 The baroque cello..was strong in gut... The lower pitch, combined with the out-curved bow, which was in current use until the end of the 18th century, help maintain the correct style of playing.

outdated, *ppl. a.* Add: (Later examples.) Hence **outda·tedness.**

1909 BELLOC *Marie Antoinette* vi. 106 His outworn, out-dated ambition. **1937** 'C. CAUDWELL' *Illusion & Reality* vi. 115 The development of capitalist production remorselessly turns the craftsman into a labourer... Eventually, employed as a factory hand, he may still cherish his outdated skill by making models. **1960** *20th Cent.* Mar. 259 By his lofty and elusive outdatedness, he has outwitted the practically minded, the men of action and the men of defeat. **1967** KARCH & BUBER *Offset Processes* v. 187 Causes of fog: 1. Poor storage of film. 2. Outdated film. **1976** R. LEWIS *Witness my Death* i. 35 For you, it's a matter of protecting a professional reputation, going by an out-dated rulebook drawn up by old men.

out-door, outdoor, *a.* (*adv.*) Add: **1.** (Earlier example.)

1748 RICHARDSON *Clarissa* III. 208 In other words, to employ itself rather in the *out-door* search, than in the *in-door* examination.

5. Special collocations: *outdoor department*, that section of a public house that sells liquor for consumption off the premises; also *ellipt.* as *sb.*; *outdoor girl*, a girl or young woman who likes an open-air life; *outdoor things*, clothes that are worn out of doors.

1958 *Times* 29 Apr. (Beer in Britain Suppl.) p. ix/6 *Jug-and-Bottle*. For the purchase of drinks for 'consumption off the premises'. Term now obsolescent. *Off-Licence, Off-Sales, Outdoor Departments*: the modern equivalent. **1961** M. JONES *Potbank* i. 6 Every pub has its off-licence department, known as the Outdoor. **1971** R. ROBERTS *Classic Slum* vi. 94 A great deal of beer bought in jugs from the 'Outdoor Department' was drunk at home... Lower-class women..stood crushed together drinking in the 'Outdoor'. **1907** J. WEBSTER *Jerry Junior* xiii. 198 Nannie was a big wholesome outdoor girl of a purely American type. **1947** M. LOWRY *Under Volcano* ix. 275 The Hawaiian Islands gave us this real outdoor girl who is fond of swimming, golf, dancing. **1969** D. THOMAS *Honey Bk. Beauty* 31/2 Outdoor girls who swear by hair spray must be careful in their choice. **1847** E. BRONTË *Wuthering Heights* II. xiv. 280, I snatched my outdoor things... the way was free. **1904** E. NESBIT *Phoenix & Carpet* x. 185 Every one put on its outdoor things..and all was ready. **1927** E. GLYN *'It'* xiv. 136 Ava..put on her outdoor things and left. **1960** B. COBB *Don't lie to Police* xi. 187 You told me Miss Cart was there when you returned. In her outdoor things?

outdoors, *adv.* Substitute for entry: **ou:t-doo·rs,** *adv.* (*sb.*) [OUT *prep.*] **A.** *adv.* Out of doors; in the open air.

1817 S. R. BROWN *Western Gazetteer* 113 The chimney is sure to be placed out doors. **1846, 1882** [in Dict.]. **1913** G. STRATTON-PORTER *Laddie* xiii. 404 What you learn there [*sc.* at school] doesn't amount to a hill of beans compared with what you can find out for yourself outdoors. **1937** C. MARSTON *Bible comes Alive* vi. 149 At Jericho..the people mostly lived outdoors.

b. Phr. *all outdoors* (*U.S. colloq.*), the whole world; everybody; freq. in comparisons alluding to the immensity of the areas out of doors.

[**1825** J. NEAL *Bro. Jonathan* I. 111 Stuffy feller (that bear) as ever you see'd; big as all out o' doors.] **1830** S. SMITH *Life & Writings J. Downing* (1833) 64, I had a letter from him..as long as all out doors. **1844** [in Dict.]. **1846** *Quincy* (Illinois) *Whig* 17 Feb. 2/2, I was going to speak of the President's message—Jimmy K's statement to all out-doors, and some parts of Ashey. **1861** [in Dict.]. **1940** W. FAULKNER *Hamlet* III. 213 The hot sun of July falling through the shadeless and even curtainless windows open to all outdoors. **1948** *Chicago Tribune* 28 Mar. 6/3 Its spirit is literally 'as big as all out-doors'.

B. *sb.* = OUT-OF-DOOR, -DOORS *sb. phr.* Freq. in phr. *the great outdoors*, the 'great open spaces' (see *OPEN *a.* 8a).

1857 N. P. WILLIS *Convalescent* (1859) 121 The 'down party'..were enjoying the river from the uncommon outdoors of Mr. Grinnell's broad prairies. **1932** *Ann. Reg.* *1931* II. 47 The 'great outdoors' was represented most elaborately in 'Cimarron', which starred Richard Dix in a fine dramatisation of the opening up of Oklahoma, and 'Trader Horn', a picture of wild life in Africa. **1940** [see *CLIFF-HANGER]. **1949** *Skyline Trail* Mar. 14/2 Trail Hikers, like all lovers of the outdoors, are by nature animal lovers as well. **1968** *Globe & Mail* (Toronto) 17 Feb. 44 During the 30 years (good heavens, is it that long?) that I have been writing about the outdoors, changes have been great. **1968** *Listener* 30 May 713/1 The Victorians worked hard to get the great outdoors inside a theatre. **1977** *Times* 23 Apr. 12/7 Ideal for anyone who wants that taste of the great outdoors without straying too far from..civilization.

Hence **outdoo·rsman,** one who likes outdoor activities; **outdoo·rsy** *a.*, associated with or characteristic of the outdoors; fond of an outdoor life; hence **outdoo·rsiness.**

1952 BERG & SAMUELS *Lady on Beach* vi. 184 In my attempts to be a truly outdoorsy woman at all times I had a ludicrous crab-hunting misadventure of my own. **1958** *Globe & Mail* (Toronto) 24 July 8/6 He's kept busy coping with appetites of outdoorsmen. **1960** I. WALLACH *Absence of Cello* (1961) 105 It was hardly an outdoorsy vacation. **1961** *Guardian* 4 Mar. 4/7 These new-style outdoorsmen. **1967** E. B. NICKERSON *Kayaks to Arctic* xii. 112, I..find no personal satisfaction in..showing an obnoxious out-doorsiness in a dozen..ways. **1973** J. GORES *Final Notice* (1974) vii. 43 Larry Ballard, good-looking in a wind blown, outdoorsy way. **1974** *Publishers Weekly* 18 Mar. 42/1 A poor boy who..became a prodigious outdoorsman and mountain climber. **1976** *Ibid.* 11 Oct. 91/2 His interviews read like scenes out of a good outdoorsy novel. **1976** *Parliamentarian* July p. viii, The hazards of translation in the European Parliament have given Mr Michael Stewart an undeserved reputation as an outdoorsman of unusual dexterity. He had spoken of his job as being like 'paddling a canoe shooting rapids', but the German interpreter thought he had said '..shooting rabbits' and translated accordingly. Mr Stewart was promptly wished good hunting by two German Members. **1976** *National Observer* (U.S.) 18 Sept. 1/4 They're the sort of out-doorsy fellows we usually associate with television shows about tagging grizzlies and spying on beavers in Wyoming.

outdra·wn, *ppl. a.* [OUT- 11.] Extended, drawn out.

1905 E. F. BENSON *Image in Sand* i. 8 Bank after bank of out-drawn stops and keyboard coupled to keyboard makes the air thick with tumultuous melody.

outdrive, *v.* Add: **2. b.** *Golf.* To drive farther than; = *OVERDRIVE *v.* 5.

1906 *Daily Chron.* 22 May 9/4 MacFarlane, after being outdriven from the tee, played a perfect approach to within a yard of the hole. **1923** *Weekly Dispatch* 13 May 1 He seemed to set out not to out-drive his opponent..but to steer a straight course. **1952** B. DARWIN *James Braid* ii. 29 James in a state of bliss straightway outdrove all those who but lately had had the audacity to outdrive him.

outed, *ppl. a.* Add: (Further examples.) Also *slang*, killed.

1919 W. H. DOWNING *Digger Dialects* 37 *Outed*, killed. *a* **1945** E. R. EDDISON *Mezentian Gate* (1958) ii. 23 Put case I had fallen in with your fine design to match me to yonder outed Prince of Akkama. **1950** PARTRIDGE *Here, There & Everywhere* 73 The English synonyms for death.. are less numerous than the French... *Wiped out*, whether of one's person or one's military unit;..*outed*, from boxing.

outen, *adv.*, *prep.* (*a.*) Add: **B.** *prep.* **1. b.** Out of; out from. *dial.* and *colloq.* (chiefly *U.S.* and *Sc.*)

1854 *Laird of Logan* 441, I cud get as gweed a yane onyday out'n a hedge at the road-side. **1867** 'MARK TWAIN' *Celebr. Jumping Frog* 38 He'd yank a sinner outen (Hades), And land him with the blest. **1895** *Horse Rev.* 31 Dec. 1840/3, I hearn Marse Henry cum outen de house lak he did in de days ob old. **1898** R. BLAKEBOROUGH *Wit, Folklore of North Riding* 425 Sha tumm'l'd outen t' winder. **1926** [see *FEISTY *a.*]. **1944** C. HIMES *Black on Black* (1973) 197 They done left me outen it altogether. **1945** in *Sc. Nat. Dict.* (1965) VI. 511/1 Ye're aye tryin tae mak an auld wumman ooten me. **1976** T. GIFFORD *Cavanaugh Quest* i. 16, I come outen the elevator and I'm heading through the delivery hallway.

outen (au·tən), *v. U.S. dial.* [perh. f. OUT *adv.* 22a, 23: see -EN[5].] **1.** To extinguish, put out, erase.

1916 *Dialect Notes* IV. 338 Be sure to outen the light when you go to bed. **1933** M. K. RAWLINGS *South Moon Under* 331 Outen that light. **1937** *Amer. Speech* XII. 205 The average [Pennsylvania German] speaker will employ in speech, and often in writing, all the forms ascribed above to the educated person, and in addition..such forms as 'outen the light', [etc.]. **1950** *Publ. Amer. Dial. Soc.* XIV. 50 *Outen*: *v. t.*, to extinguish, as a fire. To erase, as writing on a slate. **1961** in WEBSTER, You might outen the candles there.

2. To come out with, utter, tell.

1951 L. CRAIG *Singing Hills* viii. 68 Finally Maje said, 'Outen it, fellow. Give out what you know.' *Ibid.* xiii. 126 There are words we want to outen and we can't.

outer, *a.* (*sb.*[1]). Add: **1. b.** *Printing.* In sheet work, designating the forme containing the type pages from which the outer side of the sheet is printed and including the type page for the first page of the printed sheet.

1755 J. SMITH *Printer's Gram.* x. 262 They [*sc.* compositors] lay one extremity thereof against the hind side of the Fifteenth page, if it is an Inner Form; or against the hind side of the Thirteenth page if it is an Outer Form. **1808** C. STOWER *Printer's Gram.* vii. 171 A sheet in Folio. Outer Form. Inner Form. **1841,** etc. [see *INNER *a.* (*sb.*[2]) 1 e].

c. *Phonetics.* Denoting an articulation in a part of the mouth nearer the lips than that designated by the term qualified by 'inner'.

1867 [see *CLOSURE 5c]. **1888** [see *INNER *a.* (*sb.*[2]) 1g]. **1972** HARTMANN & STORK *Dict. Lang. & Ling.* 39/2 The outer closure may occur at the lips, the teeth, the alveolar ridge, the palate, velum, pharynx, or glottis or any intermediate point.

3. Outer Circle, the road running round the perimeter of Regent's Park, London; **outer form,** (*a*) (see sense 1 b above); (*b*) *Linguistics* (see quot. 1972); also *outer speech form*; **outer multiplication** *Math.*, the formation of an outer product; **outer product** *Math.* [tr. G. *äusseres produkt* (H. Grassmann *Die lineale Ausdehnungslehre* (1844) p. xi)], a vector product (*rare*); more commonly, a related product of two vectors or tensors that yields a tensor of higher rank than either of them; **outer space,** the region beyond the earth's atmosphere or beyond the solar system; *from outer space*, a colloq. phr. implying outlandishness and frightfulness as of creatures described in some science fiction; **outer suburb,** one of the more remote suburbs of a city or town; so *outer-suburban* adj.; **outerwear,** clothing designed to be worn outside other garments; opp. *underwear*.

1829 *Picturesque Guide to Regent's Park* 29 The outer circle or Ring consists of a fine level drive, planted with trees on each side; within this is another circle or pathway. **1867** H. LARGE *Large's Way about London* 336/2 *Outer Circle, Regent's Park, N.W.*, from the Marble Arch along Oxford st..through Orchard st, Portman sq, Baker st, Upper Baker st and Clarence gt to the Outer circle. **1938** E. BOWEN *Death of Heart* I. i. 28 Cars slid lights all round the Outer Circle. **1974** *Kelly's Post Office London Directory* 667/4 Regent's Park..Outer Circle. Hanover Lodge..Zoological Society's Gardens. **1972** HARTMANN & STORK *Dict. Lang. & Ling.* 113/2 The grammatical and semantic structure of a particular language is unique to that language (*inner form*), however susceptible its sound system (*outer form*) may be to influences from other languages. **1898** A. N. WHITEHEAD *Treat. Universal Algebra* I. iii. 207 Progressive and Regressive Multiplication are called Outer Multiplication. **1959** M. R. SPIEGEL *Schaum's Outl. Theory & Probl. Vector Analysis* viii. 169 Inner and outer multiplication of tensors is commutative and associative. **1929** H. W. TURNBULL *Theory of Determinants* xi. 183 It involves a determinantal factor ($\alpha\beta\gamma$) which is an outer product of the symbolic linear sets α, β, γ. **1959** M. R. SPIEGEL *Schaum's Outl. Theory & Probl. Vector Analysis* viii. 169 The product of two tensors is a tensor whose rank is the sum of the ranks of the given tensors. This product which involves ordinary multiplication of the components of the tensor is called the outer product. **1965** J. ABRAM *Tensor Calculus* iii. 27 We could have written eqn. (3.14) as $a^j(b_ic_j - b_jc_i)$ in which the bracket is an anti-symmetric tensor of order two. It is known as the outer product of the two vectors b_i and c_i. Only in three dimensions can the outer product be replaced by the vector product. **1970** BEDFORD & DWIVEDI *Vector Calculus* iv. 168 Since the outer product of two vectors is not commutative, we stress again the fact that the order of the two factors in the outer product is important. **1901** H. G. WELLS *First Men in Moon* iii. 45 After all, to go into outer space is not so much worse, if at all, than a polar expedition. **1935** *Discovery* Apr. 105/1 In America it was proposed to explore Mars or Venus or even the very realms of outer space. **1958** *Observer* 16 Mar. 1/2 The Soviet Union yesterday put forward a plan for banning the military use of outer space. **1961** WODEHOUSE *Ice in Bedroom* xxiii. 191 Every time I see this little horror from outer space, I want to sock him. **1964** *Ann. Reg. 1963* 31 On 25 July the treaty banning nuclear tests in the atmosphere, in outer space, and under water was initialled. **1972** 'H. CALVIN' *Take Two Popes* xii. 135 If your job says expend somebody, you expend... Do you think I'm an inhuman thing from outer space? **1973** *Times* 4 Dec. 8/4 Pioneer should be able..to send pictures of Jupiter..as it goes past it before flying away into outer space. **1901** Outer speech form [see *INNER *a.* 2b]. **1937** Outer suburb [see *ASPIRIN]. **1974** P. HEYWOOD *Planning & Human Need* vi. 104 The crisis of the ghetto must be met, at least in part, in the outer suburbs. **1937** Outer-suburban [see *CREEPING *ppl. a.* 2b]. **1964** P. F. ANSON *Bishops at Large* vi. 202 Ethelbert Lodge..had been both the archi-episcopal curia and outer-suburban country estate of the Landaffs for several years. **1928** *Daily Express* 7 May 4 (Advt.), Seven guineas and three guineas are probably the two most popular prices for outerwear garments. **1946** *Daily Tel.* 27 Mar. 5/8 From April 1 elastic can be used without restriction in the manufacture of underwear, ..outerwear,..and miscellaneous articles. **1963** [see *LEISURE *sb.* 6 a and c]. **1971** 'E. LATHEN' *Ashes to Ashes* ix. 91 They wore hairy outerwear and came from socially aware suburbs. **1977** *Times* 24 Dec. 17/1 In the six months to October 31, Forminster, which makes ladies' and children's outerwear clothing, turned in a pre-tax profit of £564,000.

B. *sb.* **2.** *Electr. Engin.* In a three-wire distribution system, either of the two conductors whose potentials are respectively above and below that of the earth or neutral by equal amounts.

1900 [see *NEUTRAL *a.* and *sb.* B. 4]. **1932** R. RAWLINSON in E. Molloy *Pract. Electr. Engin.* V. 1590/2 The potential difference between the outers is still 500 volts, and..they may therefore be used for power supply, while lighting load may be taken on a circuit between either outer and the mid-wire. **1970** H. FERRY *Electr. Supply* I. ii. 35 The cancellation of the two currents flowing in opposite directions in the middle wire..enabled the section to be safely reduced to one-half that of the outers.

3. (*a*) *pl.* Outdoor clothing. (*b*) An outer garment or the outer part of a garment.

1904 E. NESBIT *Phoenix & Carpet* vi. 111 'We'd best put on our outers in case—.' 'We might rescue a traveller buried in the snow.' **1971** C. BONINGTON *Annapurna South Face* xi. 129 It needed a distinct effort of will..to force on frozen boots. I kept the felt inners inside the sleeping-bag, but the outers were too bulky and I used these as a pillow; even so, each morning they were frozen solid. T. FROST in *Ibid.* xviii. 222, I put on my..proofed nylon outers. **1976** *Horse & Hound* 3 Dec. 18/2 (Advt.), The Husky Riding Waistcoat, with its strong nylon outer, filled with polyester for thermo-insulated warmth, will keep those biting winter winds at bay.

4. *Austral. slang.* The part of a racecourse outside the enclosure; also *transf.* Hence in phr. *on the outer*: penniless; out of favour, excluded.

1924 *Truth* (Sydney) 27 Apr. 6 *Outer, on the*, to be poor; to be outside. **1926** 'J. DOONE' *Timely Tips for New Australians* Gloss., *Outer*, a slang word denoting a betting ground overlooking a race-course. **1928** A. WRIGHT *Good Recovery* 157 You told me yourself that you were the cause of my being on the outer. **1953** T. A. G. HUNGERFORD *Riverslake* 174 And you're on the outer for sticking up for him? **1963** A. ROSS *Australia 63* iii. 86 Fine drizzle delayed things for half an hour, then shirts were ripped off again in the Outer, the beer cans were set up, and play proceeded. **1970** I. SOUTHALL *Bread & Honey* 54 Warren had always been on the outer, like a stray dog, always getting pushed.

5. An outer container into which one or several objects already enclosed in their own containers are packed for transport or display.

1920 J. STEPHENSON *Princ. & Pract. Commerc. Corr.* II. xii. 129 Size and description of outer. **1950** J. G. DAVIS *Dict. Dairying* 356 Packing of freshly frozen and packaged ice cream into 'outers' containing dozens of units..considerably slows the rate of hardening. **1955** *Sales Appeal* Jan.–Feb. 37/2 Display outers, cut-outs and showcards. **1967** *Times Rev. Industry* May 83/3 An instrument..provided with a carrying case was packed in a corrugated outer for transit. **1971** *Guider* Nov. 407 (Advt.), Your Net Profit per [chocolate] bar: 5p. Your Net Profit per outer (18 bars per outer): 90p.

outer, colloq. var. OUT OF *prep. phr.* Cf. *OUTA, *OUTTA.

1856 [see *GEEWHILLIKINS *int.*]. **1898** J. D. BRAYSHAW *Slum Silhouettes* 221 ''Ave a cigar,' an' 'e pulls a 'andful outer 'is skyrocket. **1926** *Opportunity* Mar. 83/2 The devil often assumes an importance entirely unbecoming to one who has been summarily 'kicked outer heaven'. **1954** M. PROCTER *Hell is City* II. iv. 53 If I could get outer 'ere I could be 'ome in less nor an hour.

outfall. 3. b. (Further example.)

1933 *Catholic Bulletin* Mar. 182 In *The Commonweal*, Padraic Colum..now finds a suitable outfall for his anti-Irish spate.

outfield, out-field, *sb.* Add: **3. a.** (Earlier and later examples.) Also *transf.* and *fig.*

1851 W. CLARK in W. Bolland *Cricket Notes* 136 If you are in the out field, and the batsman is on the alert, he will steal a run. **1868** H. CHADWICK *Game of Base Ball* 73 The Irvingtons..placed the substitute in the out-field. **1948** *Denison* (Texas) *Herald* 2 July 12/3 Have you ever played the outfield? **1971** *Times* 16 Feb. 7/6 The groundsman at the cricket ground here has been mowing the outfield. **1975** *Cricketer* May 19/1 When they batted the opening pair put on 85 in the first 20 overs, a splendid rate on an extremely wet outfield. **1976** *Billings* (Montana) *Gaz.* 16 June 1-C/3 Playing both first base and the outfield, Rudi was regarded as one of the most valuable players in the league every season from 1970–75. **1976** P. HARCOURT *Dance for Diplomats* ii. 15 We taxied around the runways..and came to a stop somewhere in the out-field. **1977** J. LE CARRÉ *Hon. Schoolboy* iii. 58 Martindale..in the Whitehall outfield lived in a state of primaeval innocence about the reality of Smiley's world.

b. (Earlier and later examples.) Also, the out-fielders collectively.

1867 *J. Lillywhite's Cricketers' Compan.* 160 [He is] a fine out-field. **1867** H. CHADWICK *Base Ball Player's Bk. Reference* 138 The Out-Field—The out-fielders are the left[,] centre and right-field positions. **1868** —— *Game of Base Ball* 17 The out-field being neither active in their movements, or sure catchers. **1910** *Blackw. Mag.* Jan. 93/2 Tyldesly..ten years ago was one of the finest outfields imaginable. **1948** *Daily Ardmoreite* (Ardmore, Okla.) 30 Mar. 6/4 If the Boston Braves win.., they will do it without an outfield which is particularly strong defensively. **1956** *People* 13 May 13/3 Cliff is an attractive all-round cricketer and an especially good long-throwing fast-moving outfield.

out-field, *v. Cricket* and *Baseball.* **1.** *intr.* [f. the sb.] To field in the out-field. *rare.*

1862 *Baily's Monthly Mag.* Aug. 85 The Surrey people ..selecting..an F. Lee, a Daniel, and an E. B. Rowley to out-field.

2. *trans.* (See *OUT- 18.)

out-fielder. (Earlier and later examples.)

1868 H. CHADWICK *Game of Base Ball* 73 The Irvingtons..took an out-fielder from his regular position. **1942** *Sun* (Baltimore) 3 Apr. 18 Estel Crabtree, Cardinal outfielder, attributed his greatly improved batting in 1941 to constant work with the machine. **1972** *Village Voice* (N.Y.) 1 June 69/2 He'd lyricize an outfielder's grace and then demean baseball as a little boy's game. **1974** *Anderson* (S. Carolina) *Independent* 19 Apr. 4B/3 The A's used Allan Lewis, an outfielder with little hitting ability, as a pinch running specialist the last two World Series.

out-fielding, *vbl. sb.* (Earlier and later examples.)

1860 in *Ball Players' Chron.* (1867) 12 Dec. 3/1 The out-fielding was only so-so. **1861** *Times* 25 May 9/4 Notwithstanding the truly fine bowling and general good out-fielding, Mr. Burbidge and Griffith defended their wickets in a masterly manner. **1973** B. RICHARDS *On Cricket* x. 98 Outfielding, too, requires concentration.

ou·t-fighting, *vbl. sb.* [OUT- 2.] Fighting that is not at close quarters.

1848 *Sporting Life* 5 Feb. 297/2 At out-fighting, Bateman was decidedly the quickest and the best. **1905** *Times* 6 Mar. 4/2 It is probable that this outfighting, before the adversaries close, will be fruitful in important lessons relating to the art of naval war.

outfit, *sb.* Add: **2. a.** (Further examples.) Also, equipment of any kind; a set of articles for a particular purpose.

1867 J. F. MELINE *Two Thousand Miles on Horseback* 74 The saddler who sold me my saddle assured me it was the best outfit he had furnished for some time. Bought a hat, and was told, 'Well, Sir, I call that a good outfit.' **1869** A. K. MCCLURE *3,000 Miles through Rocky Mts.* 211 Everything is an 'outfit', from a train..to a pocket-knife. **1873** E. B. TUTTLE *Boy's Bk. Indians* 45 Friday had a beautiful set of arrows, bow and quiver, which I desired to purchase... Friday would not sell his 'outfit', as it is called, for money. **1924** T. E. LAWRENCE *Home Lett.* (1954) 359 A solo isn't as secure on a wet road as a side-car outfit. **1958** *Amer. Speech* XXXIII. 271 *Outfit*, a man's equipment.

c. A person's clothes; a set of garments.

1852 [in Dict., sense 2 a]. **1875** *Scribner's Monthly* Dec. 286/1 The comfortable dress for the mother or flannel outfit for the baby, can be sent. **1946** *Chicago Daily News* 10 Aug. 12/3 Elaborate ceremonial outfits are fashioned by the women of the tribe. **1968** J. IRONSIDE *Fashion Alphabet* 104 Accessories..really can change the whole feeling of an outfit and turn a last year's garment into something swinging or chic. **1976** C. BERMANT *Coming Home* I. vii. 105 She did not wear the same outfit two days running.

d. The apparatus used by a drug addict for taking drugs.

[**1935** A. J. POLLOCK *Underworld Speaks* 84/2 *Outfitted*, to get a supply of dope.] **1951** *N.Y. Times* 14 June 22/2 'John' went into a drugstore on upper Park Avenue, asked for an 'outfit', and for 45 cents got an envelope containing a medicinal dropper and a hypodermic needle, such as used by 'mainliners' for heroin injections. **1953** W. BURROUGHS *Junkie* (1972) ix. 86, I asked him to come back to my apartment to take a shot. We went back to my room, and I got out my outfit that hadn't been used in five months. *Ibid.* xii. 121 She keeps outfits in glasses of alcohol so the junkies can fix in the joint and walk out clean. **1960** *Times Lit. Suppl.* 16 Sept. 589/4 Anyone who has snorted or used the outfit and then kicked would find it [*sc.* a book] of absorbing interest.

3. (Earlier examples.)

1867 *Harper's Mag.* July 137/2 Their 'outfit' (in the language of the plains this word signifies the conveyance, its contents, and the team) consisted of a Concord coach [etc.]. **1869** S. BOWLES *Our New West* viii. 163 With a mounted escort of about twenty gallant young miners.. we made up a grand 'outfit'.

b. A group of people; an organization; a business firm or concern.

1883 'MARK TWAIN' *Life on Mississippi* ii. 31 In that day, all explorers travelled with an outfit of priests. De Soto had twenty-four with him... The expeditions were often out of meat, and scant of clothes, but they always had the furniture and other requisites for the mass. **1925** *Amer. Speech* I. 149/2 The big cattle companies or 'outfits'. **1926** J. BLACK *You can't Win* iv. 37, I was left on the bench with the two drunks... The desk man pointed to us. 'What will I do with this outfit, Hayes?' **1927** [see *LAY-OUT 2 c]. **1930** D. L. SAYERS *Strong Poison* iv. 48 You must get me passed in as part of your outfit. **1935** WODEHOUSE *Blandings Castle* xii. 310 'Come and join my little outfit,' he said heartily. 'I've always room for a personal friend.' **1939** F. W. CROFTS *Fatal Venture* xi. 154 He's carrying this entire outfit on his shoulders. Only for Stott your job and mine might go phut. **1943** H. L. MENCKEN *Heathen Days* vii. 89, I was presently playing trios and quartettes with an outfit that devoted four hours of every week to the job. **1951** C. W. MILLS *White Collar* I. ii. 23 The great bulk of businesses are small outfits, which do not last long. **1958** S. ELLIN *Eighth Circle* (1959) II. i. 33 There's a couple of other agencies—Inter-American, Fleischer—pretty good outfits that might do just the job you want. **1962** *Observer* 25 Nov. 12/8 Aldermaston is 'less stuffy than Harwell' and usually beats the other nuclear outfits at rugger. **1975** *New Yorker* 21 Apr. 69/2 Investigators working not only for Retail Credit but for other large consumer-investigation outfits confirm this. **1977** J. WAINWRIGHT *Do Nothin'* v. 67 Some of the modern outfits don't have brass. Just a four-piece sax line-up.

c. *spec. Services' colloq.* A group of servicemen; a regiment, squadron, or the like.

1916 [see *anti-tank* s.v. *ANTI-[1] 4 (iii)]. **1922** C. E. MONTAGUE *Disenchantment* ii. 18 A man is wanted for Post Corporal... 'Cushiest job in the 'ole outfit!' **1930** F. A. POTTLE *Stretchers* 28 The bowlegged officer flew into a disciplinary rage and addressed the boy as follows: 'What outfit do you belong to? How long have you been in the army?' **1951** H. HASTINGS *Seagulls over Sorrento* I. i, in J. Trewin *Plays of Year* IV. 52 Incidentally, wot are you doing in an outfit like this? **1959** *Times Lit. Suppl.* 30 Jan. 57/3 The sergeant, though a war hero and the only soldier in a slack outfit, is a psychopathic bully and a pathetically lonely man. **1966** *Inland* (Inland Steel Co., Chicago) Autumn 13/1 Recruits from all over the United States are assigned to the same military outfit. **1978** A. PRICE *'44 Vintage* xix. 220 France in '40, then the Middle East... And finally Yugoslavia as a weapons adviser to a big Partisan outfit.

4. *Canad.* The name given to the fiscal year of the Hudson's Bay Company; hence, a year.

1791 in *Beaver* (1947) Dec. 11/2 The difficiency in the order for the carrot tobacco arises from the great overplus we have for the ensuing outfit. **1833** J. G. MCTAVISH *Let.* 18 Dec. in G. de T. Glazebrook *Hargrave Corr.* (1938) 124, I had thought, of getting away in one or two outfits. **1841** G. SIMPSON *London Corr.* (1973) 9 The lease..will expire..with the close of Outfit 1841/2. **1874** in *Alberta Hist. Rev.* (1956) Spring 16 The Athabasca accounts for the Outfit were closed and the Packet given over to the care of Mr. Moberly. **1913** I. COWIE *Company of Adventurers* 280 The end of each business year—called 'Outfit'—was May 31, upon which date the inventory of everything belonging to the Company at the fort was taken. **1935** in D. Jenness *Eskimo Admin.* (1964) II. 51 Altogether sixteen deaths occurred during the outfit and only four births that I know of. **1973** W. R. SAMPSON *J. McLoughlin's Business Corr. 1847–48* p. xix, He was to be made a wintering partner with a share in the profits of the concern for Outfit 1814.

5. A person (usu. pejorative). *slang* (chiefly *U.S.*).

1867 J. F. MELINE *Two Thousand Miles on Horseback* 74 To cross the plains, or go to the mountains, every one must get an outfit; and having outfitted, you become yourself an outfit. **1924** C. E. MULFORD *Rustlers' Valley* xi. 130 You ain't believin' everythin' *this* outfit tells you, are you? **1925** *Ladies' Home Jrnl.* May 26/2 'But that young outfit will drive me wild,' protested Mrs. Denmeade. **1942** BERREY & VAN DEN BARK *Amer. Thes. Slang* § 379/2 *Person*,..outfit.

outfit, *v.* Add: **a.** (Further examples.) Also simply, to provide or supply (a person or thing) *with.*

1924 W. M. RAINE *Troubled Waters* xvi. 167, I outfitted some of the boys with guns. **1928** *T. Eaton & Co. Catal.* Spring & Summer 219/4 Two or three suits like this would outfit him for the Summer. **1935** A. SQUIRE *Sing Sing Doctor* xiv. 205 The condemned man is outfitted with new clothing. **1953** K. TENNANT *Joyful Condemned* xxxix. 381 She was smartly outfitted: white shoes, white hat.. and a black-and-white striped dress. **1971** *Sci. Amer.* Aug. 24/1 When the slim merchantman was ready for launching, its owner must have visited a ship chandler to buy the gear needed to outfit the vessel. **1972** P. H. KOCHER *Master of Middle-Earth* (1973) ii. 23 They helped to outfit the dwarf expedition when it was penniless. **1973** 'D. HALLIDAY' *Dolly & Starry Bird* iv. 55 Enough polo necks to outfit the entire British Raj. **1975** *Nature* 10 July 150/3 Such cameras are intrinsically sensitive to the near ultraviolet band, and to be used for ultraviolet viewing need only be outfitted with an ultraviolet-transmitting lens and filter. **1976** *National Observer* (U.S.) 19 June 8/6 And began to practice out of the van that he and several seabee friends had outfitted.

b. (Earlier and later examples.)

1881 *N.Y. Times* 18 Dec. 4/3 To 'outfit' is to fit out for any purpose whatever. 'We outfitted at St. Paul.' **1902** S. E. WHITE *Blazed Trail* xxv. 168 It's a good place to outfit from because we can probably get freight rates direct by boat. **1919** H. L. WILSON *Ma Pettengill* iv. 129 He outfitted at the Chicago Store in Tucson, getting the best all-wool ready-made suit in Arizona. **1924** C. E. MULFORD *Rustlers' Valley* x. 115 Yestiddy was pay-day, an' if they don't outfit now, some of 'em won't have no money after to-night. **1976** H. & G. GORDON *Ordeal* xv. 108 A party of four went down the trail... Three males and a female. Ring up the Big Rock Trading Post... Get the trader up and find out if they outfitted there.

Hence **ou·tfitted** *ppl. a.*

1975 *Offshore Progress: Technol. & Costs* (Shell Internat. Petroleum Co.) 5 Several semi-submersibles delivered early in 1975 have hulls 300 ft long, and a total outfitted weight of up to 16,500 tons. **1977** *Time* 19 Dec. 31/1 Outfitted in quilted parkas, they can be seen roaming the snow-covered hills and hollows of Appalachia in search of game to keep down meat bills.

outfitting, *vbl. sb.* and *ppl. a.* (Further examples.) Also *ellipt.*

1908 *Westm. Gaz.* 24 Apr. 7/4 Until the cold weather and overcoats finally disappear there will be no improvement in outfitting. **1932** D. L. SAYERS *Have his Carcase* xxxi. 409, I went to the men's outfitting and asked for collars. **1964** A. ADBURGHAM *Shops & Shopping* xii. 130 Outfitting was the euphemism employed for both men's and women's underclothes. **1976** *Cody* (Wyoming) *Enterprise* 23 June 1/1 Many of the complaints about the grizzly bear's critical habitat center around the effect such a definition would have on the outfitting business. A confrontation between outfitting camps and grizzlies within a critical habitat area would result in the relocation of the camp rather than the grizzly. **1977** *Times* 30 Nov. 2/4 The decision by more than 1,600 angry outfitting trades at Swan Hunter's [shipbuilding] yard to continue their over-time ban.

outfla·nker. [-ER[1].] One who outflanks.

1920 *Q. Rev.* Jan. 107 As fast as Joffre created a new Army to prolong his left..so fast did the Germans cover their threatened right and seek to outflank their would-be outflankers.

outflash, *v.* **a.** (Earlier and later examples.)

1833 BROWNING *Pauline* 59 Do I not..burn to see thy calm, pure truths out-flash The brightest gleams of earth's philosophy. **1939** JOYCE *Finnegans Wake* 210 A pretty box of Pettyfib's Powder for Eileen Aruna to whiten her teeth and outflash Helen Arhone.

outfling, *v.* Add: (Further examples.) Hence **outfli·nging** *vbl. sb.*

1894 A. S. WAY tr. *Euripides' Tragedies* I. 135 What speech in thy frenzy outflingest thou? **1896** *Ibid.* II. 186 Through Hades' hall to thee I call, Day after day my cries outflinging. **1922** JOYCE *Ulysses* 415 Outflings my lord Stephen, giving the cry. **1932** S. GIBBONS *Cold Comfort Farm* v. 73 Judith thrust the words aside with a heavy movement of her hand, like the blind outflinging of a tortured beast. **1950** R. BRADBURY *Martian Chronicles* 86 If art was no more than a frustrated outflinging of desire, ..what good was life?

outflow, *v.* (Later example.)

1909 *Daily Chron.* 3 Mar. 5/7 Then outflowed a stream of facts and figures whose accumulated force swept the critics off their feet.

outflowing, *vbl. sb.* (Further examples.)

1884 H. B. MACKEY tr. *St. Francis de Sales' Treat. Love of God* VI. xii. 267 The outflowing of a soul into her God is a true ecstasy. **1932** F. J. SHEED *Irish Way* 332 Work itself was..an outflowing or a special directing of the steady fixedness of the soul in God. **1953** R. C. JOHNSON *Imprisoned Splendour* i. 31 Mystical experiences..are, an out-flowing into awareness of something from a higher level of the self even than the buddhic.

outflowing, *ppl. a.* (Later example.)

1975 *Sci. Amer.* Mar. 33/3 The compact star in its orbit plows through this outflowing wind and captures only a tiny part of its matter.

outflux. Add: In mod. use, *spec.* the outward movement of ions through a cell membrane.

1949 *Physiol. Rev.* XXIX. 132 If the high K concentration in muscle and nerve cells as compared with the K concentration of the surroundings is due to a Donnan equilibrium then the K influx and the K outflux through the cell membranes must be the same. **1974** *Nature* 11 Jan. 96/1 The..rate of sodium outflux (15 min) in turkey erythrocytes was not modified.

outfly, *v.* Add: **2.** *spec.* of aircraft and their pilots: to surpass in terms of skill or speed in flying.

1908 H. G. WELLS *War in Air* viii. 253 Light as this armament was.., it was sufficient for them to outfight as well as outfly the German monster airships. **1942** *Tee Emm* (Air Ministry) II. 94 It's no good outflying the Hun if you can't shoot him down. **1975** *Listener* 17 July 77/1 It could outfly the Focke Wulf Condor and..that sort of German bomber. **1976** *Globe & Mail* (Toronto) 28 Jan. 29/2 Capt. Stinson..flatly states that the computer can 'out-land a human pilot three to one. I'll admit it can outfly me.'

outfox (autfǫ·ks), *v.* [f. OUT- 18 b + FOX *v.* 2 c.] *trans.* To outdo in deception or cunning; to outwit.

1962 K. ORVIS *Damned & Destroyed* xii. 81 He finally out-foxed himself. **1965** C. D. EBY *Siege of Alcázar* (1966) ii. 54 Pozas was no fool. Perhaps he had even outfoxed them. **1965** R. SHECKLEY *Game of X* (1966) xix. 133 We have outfoxed Forster at every turn, and we shall outfox him now for the final time. **1973** J. JONES *Touch of Danger* lvi. 320, I guess you've got the drop on me... You outfoxed me. **1976** *National Observer* (U.S.) 19 June 6/5 As one Republican National Committee official put it: 'The Ford people have no right to be bitter. They were just out-foxed, outmaneuvered, and out-organized.'

out front, *advb.* and *adj. phr.* Chiefly *U.S.* [f. OUT *adv.* + FRONT *sb.*] At or to the front; in front; *spec.* (*a*) at or to the battle-front; (*b*) *Theatr.*, in front of the stage; in the auditorium; (*c*) *fig.*, in the forefront (of a political or intellectual movement); progressive. Also (with hyphen) *attrib.*

1916 'BOYD CABLE' *Action Front* 200 These average good men who had 'joined up' freely, who had longed for the end of home training and the transfer 'out Front'. **1934** J. M. CAIN *Postman always rings Twice* vi. 57 She went out front with an order, and me and the Greek sat down. **1937** C. HIMES *Black on Black* (1973) 129 This little white lain pulled up out front in a big Lincoln touring a block long. **1962** *Listener* 11 Oct. 570/1 Obsolete accommodation, backstage and out-front. **1963** AUDEN *Dyer's Hand* 186 There is no difference for Falstaff between those on stage and those out front. **1968** T. WOLFE *Electric Kool-Aid Acid Test* iv. 53 A community of intelligent, very open, out-front people—out front was a term everybody was using. **1973** *Black World* Mar. 36 His behind-the-scenes rather than vigorous outfront leadership. **1976** L. ALTHER *Kinflicks* ii. 22 'Have you seen the new fishburger franchise?' Mrs Yancy asked, pointing out the window at a red and silver building with a sign out front featuring in neon a one-legged pirate tangoing with a laughing swordfish. **1977** *New Yorker* 10 Oct. 156/3 Powell himself was said to be deeply bothered by that, and to have realized that he had been too 'out front' on the issue.

outgas (autgæ·s), *v.* [OUT- 26.] **1.** *trans.* **a.** To drive off sorbed gas or vapour from (a solid), esp. by heating in a vacuum.

1921 [implied in *OUTGASSED *ppl. a.*]. **1925** *Physical Rev.* XXVI. 658 When the surface layer of gas is removed from a fresh specimen the increase in the photo-electric current is greater than the decrease from the maximum value as the specimen is outgassed. **1953** *Electronic Engin.* XXV. 19 The cathodes were out-gassed by eddy-current heating. **1965** C. M. VAN ATTA *Vacuum Sci. & Engin.* iii. 101 After the gauge tube and elements have been thoroughly outgassed, an opposite effect becomes noticeable.

b. To release (sorbed or dissolved gas or vapour).

1971 I. G. GASS et al. *Understanding Earth* ix. 137/2 Only gradually, as volcanoes continued to outgas volatile products still trapped in the mantle, will a secondary atmosphere and ocean have replaced the primary envelope. **1974** *Nature* 31 May 438/1 If NH_3 is outgassed from the Martian crust it would be photolysed.

2. *intr.* To give off sorbed gas or vapour.

1962 [implied in *OUTGASSING *vbl. sb.*]. **1965** C. M. VAN ATTA *Vacuum Sci. & Engin.* ix. 365 Untreated metal samples outgas at the rate of about 10^{-7} torr liter/sec cm^2 after 1 hr of vacuum pumping at room temperature. **1975** *Sci. Amer.* Feb. 110/3 Any polymer surface will outgas (a 'virtual leak' into your clean volume) two orders of magnitude more than steel.

So **outga·ssed** *ppl. a.*, **outga·ssing** *vbl. sb.*

1921 *Proc. Nat. Acad. Sci.* VII. 115 The coarsely granular sample of the thoroughly outgassed material is weighed and placed in a steel pressure bomb which is then evacuated until all adsorbed gases are removed. **1925** *Physical Rev.* XXVI. 657 His thermionic measurements show that the value of *A* in the Richardson equation.. decreases from $4{\cdot}76 \times 10^{27}$ for the slightly outgassed position to $1{\cdot}7 \times 10^{26}$ for continued outgassing. **1952** *Trans. Faraday Soc.* XLVIII. 739 The vessel F was 'protected' by a series of traps in liquid air, some of which..contained carefully outgassed granulated charcoal. **1962** F. I. ORDWAY et al. *Basic Astronautics* iii. 49 Whatever outgassing that may occur from the surface would expectedly give rise to a more substantial, albeit tenuous, atmosphere. **1971** I. G. GASS et al. *Understanding Earth* ii. 43/2 This so-called 'excess' argon is probably produced by heating and outgassing of ancient, potassium-bearing rocks. **1973** *Nature* 3 Aug. 272/2 The relative abundances of these gases will depend critically on the subsequent history of the outgassed methane. **1973** B. J. WILLIAMS *Evolution & Human Origins* vii. 97/2 If these dates are correct then the evolution of life must have begun, as we would expect, almost immediately after the earth's crust melted and the outgassing of the early atmospheric gases ceased.

outgeneral, *v.* Add: **b.** *transf.* and *fig.*

1859 J. S. MILL in *Fraser's Mag.* LX. 767/1 A nation which thinks of nothing but of outwitting and outgeneralling its neighbours. **1910** J. DRISCOLL *Ringcraft* 14 He was the better boxer and the stronger man, but was outgeneralled during two-thirds of the bout. **1940** W. FAULKNER *Hamlet* III. ii. 184 At last he outgeneralled himself with his own strategy:..even his father admitted that there was nothing else about the farm for him to learn. **1973** WODEHOUSE *Bachelors Anonymous* x. 128 However confident he may be that he has outgeneralled a woman, a man likes to have reassurance on the point from a knowledgeable third party. **1976** *Billings* (Montana) *Gaz.* 26 June 1-B/6 Tanner has played better tennis —little Kirmayr out-generalled him time and again—but always in reserve was his 140 m.p.h. cannonball service.

outgiving (au·tgiviŋ), *ppl. a.* [OUT- 10.] That gives out; open-hearted, generous. Hence **outgi·vingness.**

1942 J. LEES-MILNE *Ancestral Voices* (1975) 31 K. as outgiving as ever. **1961** *Spectator* 26 May 763/2 [Brendan] Behan is still..a talker and singer for talking and singing's own sake, spontaneous and out-giving. **1963** *London Mag.* Sept. 11 Her face was round and pleasantly fleshed, her eyes cool and outgiving when she was not anguished or perturbed. **1968** *Listener* 10 Oct. 458/2 She had lost a great deal, I think, of her out-givingness in that way and the novels perhaps reflect this. **1972** *Times* 3 July 16/7 There can rarely have been such an outgiving man who was less of an extrovert.

outgo, *sb.* **4.** (Earlier example.)

1869 S. BOWLES *Our New West* i. 26 The great Salt Lake of Utah..has no visible outgo, though richly fed from various quarters.

outgo, *v.* **1.** For *Obs.* read '*Obs.* except *poetic*' and add later examples.

1899 P. H. WICKSTEED tr. *Dante's Paradiso* xiii. 161 That living Light which so outgoeth from its Source that it departeth not therefrom. **1905** *Outlook* 4 Nov. 629/1 So you, dear Frank, were last of those To whom a tender thought outgoes.

outgoing, *vbl. sb.* **2.** Delete † *Obs.* and add later *literary* examples.

1864 G. M. HOPKINS *Poems* (1967) 130 The hill Which with its lined and creased flank The outgoings of the vale does block. **1918** D. H. LAWRENCE *New Poems* 49 Each door, each mystic port Of egress from you I will seal and steep in perfect chrism..So you shall feel Ensheathed invulnerable with me, with seven Great seals upon your outgoings.

outgoing, *ppl. a.* Add: **c.** Suitable for wearing when one goes out.

1867 QUEEN VICTORIA *Let.* 19 Nov. in R. Fulford *Your Dear Letter* (1971) I have just returned from a drive with dear Marie F... I can't judge of the figure in her out-going dress. **1909** 'O. HENRY' *Roads of Destiny* x. 162 Take him back..and fix him up with outgoing clothes. Unlock him at seven in the morning.

d. Extrovert, sociable, open-hearted, friendly.

1950 *Brit. Jrnl. Psychol.* XXII. 107 Out-going primary or secondary need-determined behaviour may be thwarted and aggressiveness may result. **1955** in D. Tidyman *Dummy* (1974) iii. 40 He is a rather attractive, out-going child. **1964** J. PHILIPS *Laughter Trap* (1965) III. iii. 132 She was a warm, outgoing girl. **1966** *Tablet* 22 Oct. 1185/1 The..poem, whose outgoing, solicitous concern is for the whole of man's relation to the world around him. **1973** C. BONINGTON *Next Horizon* ix. 138 He appeared outgoing, frank, and immensely enthusiastic. **1978** E. HEALEY *Lady Unknown* ii. 62 Gregarious and out-going, he brought a brilliance and radiance to every gathering.

outgoingness (further examples).

1960 G. ASHE *From Caesar to Arthur* vi. 160 For the moment we may leave him in Ireland, fitly typifying the outgoingness of the British saints. **1967** C. FREMLIN *Prisoner's Base* ii. 22 Claudia's gifts..tolerance—outgoingness—sympathy. **1971** *New Scientist* 1 Apr. 44/2 Bondi's natural eloquence and outgoingness could be usefully harnessed to his new job.

outgrabe (autgrēⁱ·b), *v.* A factitious word introduced by 'Lewis Carroll' (see quot. 1855[2]). (In quot. 1903 used for 'outdo', after the style of *out-Herod*, etc.)

Quot. 1855[1] also occurs in the first verse of 'Jabberwocky' in *Through the Looking-Glass* (1871) i. 21.

1855 'L. CARROLL' *Rectory Umbrella & Mischmasch* (1932) 139 All mimsy were the borogoves; And the mome raths outgrabe. *Ibid.* 140 *Outgrabe*, past tense of the verb to *outgribe*. (It is connected with the old verb to *grike* or *shrike*, from which are derived 'shriek' and 'creak'.) 'Squeaked.' **1876** —— *Hunting of Snark* v. 50 The Beaver had counted with scrupulous care, Attending to every word: But it fairly lost heart, and outgrabe in despair, When the third repetition occurred. **1903** *Sat. Rev.* 7 Feb. 164/1 Deadmanship! wrote..Dr. Shrapnel..; and the word is fit to stir the jealous admiration of Carlyle or even Lewis Carroll. Indeed Dr. Shrapnel 'outgrabed' them both.

ou·t-group. [Cf. OUT *a.* 1.] Those people not necessarily forming a group themselves, who are excluded from or do not belong to a specific in-group; also *attrib.* Hence **out-grou·per,** an individual who does not belong to a specific in-group.

1907 [see *IN-GROUP]. **1934** K. YOUNG *Introd. Sociol.* I. i. 13 One is prejudiced against the members of the out-group. **1949** R. K. MERTON *Social Theory* II. vii. 186 The systematic condemnation of the out-grouper continues largely irrespective of what he does. **1952** M. MCCARTHY *Groves of Academe* (1953) vi. 119 Where discrimination exists, protection of the out-group is mandatory. **1967** M. ARGYLE *Psychol. Interpersonal Behaviour* iv. 71 Two people from different groups are apt to treat each other as 'outsiders', members of the out-group, and to reject one another through their failure to conform to the norms of the in-group. **1970** *Jrnl. Gen. Psychol.* Oct. 259 An error was considered..outgroup intrusion if a word paired with a dissimilar stimulus was elicited. **1970** C. T. RESTREPO in I. L. Horowitz *Masses in Lat. Amer.* xiv. 516 Violence developed the conflict with respect to the out-group and institutionalized it. **1976** *Times Lit. Suppl.* 2 Jan. 2/4 Gypsy legends..provide a charter for the in-group rather than the out-group reference of their morality.

outgrow, *v.* Add: **1.** Also *refl.*

1878 HARDY *Ret. Native* I. I. iii. 54 His mother cried for scores of hours when 'a was a boy, for fear he should outgrow himself and go for a soldier.

outguess (autge·s), *v.* [f. OUT- 18 b + GUESS *v.*] *trans.* To outwit (someone) by guessing more cleverly or shrewdly.

1913 *Jrnl. Animal Behaviour* III. 90 It was clearly a case of the chick 'outguessing' the experimenter. **1921** E. O'NEILL *Emperor Jones* i. 163, I kin outguess, outrun, outfight, an' outplay de whole lot o' dem all ovah de board. **1936** M. MITCHELL *Gone with Wind* I. v. 78 Mammy sighed resignedly, beholding herself outguessed. **1956** 'J. WYNDHAM' *Seeds of Time* 187, I don't know whether he outguessed me or whether he was just lucky. **1972** P. H. KOCHER *Master of Middle-Earth* iii. 44 Her function in the story is to warn them, and herself, to tend to the duty in hand and not rashly to presume that finite minds can outguess the supreme architect who plans the whole. **1975** *Publishers Weekly* 6 Jan. 52/3 Murders and cover-ups follow, with the reader trying to outguess the author all the way.

out-gun, *v.* Add: (Further examples.) Also, to surpass in gunnery; to outshoot. Also *fig.* Hence **outgu·nned** *ppl. a.*

1942 *R.A.F. Jrnl.* 13 June 12 The wolf—helpless, outranged and outgunned so far as the *Devonshire* was concerned. **1945** *Sun* (Baltimore) 17 Mar. 9–0/1 We're just out-tanked and out-gunned, that's all. **1960** *Observer* 28 Aug. 25/6 The Corporation has shown that it can outgun its rival. **1973** *Daily Tel.* 28 Nov. 15 The Battle of the River Plate, in which three outgunned cruisers took on the German pocket battleship Admiral Graf Spee. **1977** *Times* 5 May 1/8 Mr Callaghan, Dr Owen..and Mr Rees.. could well be outgunned by a majority of ministers.

outgush, *sb.* Add: Also *fig.*

1871 BROWNING *Balaustion's Adventure* 170 Frank outgush of the human gratitude Which saved our ship and me. **1919** [see *LA, LA].

ou·thalf, out-half. *Rugby Football.* [f. OUT- + HALF *sb.* 6 d.] = *fly-half* (*FLY *sb.*[2] 8). Cf. *outside half* s.v. *OUTSIDE *a.* 6.

Fly-half is the more usual term in the U.K.

1961 in WEBSTER. **1973** *Irish Times* 2 Mar. 3/7 At their heels was scrum-half Early.., while Spring is a cool outhalf. **1976** *Sunday Tel.* 23 May 39/8 'Oh my,' said Mike Quinn, the outhalf, 'if the New Zealand centres are as quick as that what are their wings like?' **1977** *Belfast Tel.* 27 Jan. 25/8 No sooner had he settled into the side than out-half Keith Gilpin was sidelined.

outhouse. Add: **b.** A privy. Chiefly *U.S.*

1819 W. Sewall *Diary* 14 June (1930) 53/1 Near the paddles or wheels which propel the vessel forward are two outhouses, which is a very great convenience. **1832** W. Irving *Jrnl.* Nov. (1919) III. 185 Old Spanish wooden building, with piazza—out houses—French buildings, with casement. **1912** *Dialect Notes* III. 584 *Out-house*,..a privy. **1921** H. Kephart *Camping & Woodcraft* (1928) I. xii. 210 If the well is near a stable or outhouse, or if dish-water is thrown near it, let it alone. **1968** C. Helmericks *Down Wild River North* I. xviii. 286 They still clung steadfastly to the old outhouse. **1973** *N.Y. Law Jrnl.* 26 July 16/7 (Advt.), Executive hideaway, L.I. Rustic appointments throughout..attractive 2 seater outhouse.

c. At a school, a house (see House *sb.*[1] 4 c) separate from, or subsidiary to, the main or central house.

1900 Farmer *Public School Word-Bk.* 144 *Out-houses* (Charterhouse),—all the boarding houses except Sanderites, Verites, and Gownboys. The names of the eight out-houses are Girdlestonites, Lockites, [etc.]. **1933** L. A. G. Strong *Sea Wall* 187 A tall, genial boy named Adams, belonging to another of the out-houses.

outing, *vbl. sb.* Add: **3.** (Earlier example.)

1849 *Bell's Life in London* 30 Sept. 6/2, I Zingari averages, 1849. Results with bat and ball... Innings... Runs... Outings... Bowled.

4. b. An appearance in an athletic contest, race, etc.

1943 *Sun* (Baltimore) 22 Apr. 18/1 Benefitting from a previous outing at the meeting, Mrs. Ray Feinberg's Charge, ridden by Danny Scocca, closed fast. **1976** J. Snow *Cricket Rebel* 29 Any young cricketer brought into the traditional twelve for his first Test outing could expect a back page headline in the national newspapers. **1976** *Evening Times* (Glasgow) 30 Nov., Bula, although only once successful in three outings so far this season, is my confident choice to register a repeat victory at Haydock Park.

7. (Further examples.) **outing flannel** *U.S.*, a type of flannelette; also *attrib.*

1890 *Advt.* (Schairer & Millen, Ann Arbor), 15 pieces new stripe outing flannels, 15 cent quality, now 10 cents. **1897** *Sears, Roebuck Catal.* 258/3 Outing flannel. This flannel is suitable for ladies' wrappers, waists, night robes, childrens' cloaks, also men's and boys' shirts and night shirts. **1916** *Daily Colonist* (Victoria, B.C.) 9 July 3/6 (Advt.), New awning stripe outing skirts. *Ibid.* 22 July 2/1 (Advt.), Take a Camera Wherever You Go. What is more delightful than having pictures of outing parties, picnics, scenery, etc.? **1925** T. Dreiser *Amer. Tragedy* (1926) I. II. xv. 262 He was pleased by the..summery appearance he made in an outing shirt and canvas shoes. **1938** M. K. Rawlings *Yearling* v. 51 The gray fur was as soft as his mother's outing flannel nightgown. **1967** *Boston Sunday Herald* 14 May II. 17/2 Every summer its members provide rafts and guides for vacationing families, outing groups, and student expeditions.

outland, *sb.* and *a.* **A.** *sb.* **3. a.** Delete † *Obs.* and add later examples. Also *transf.*

1931 *Sun* (Baltimore) 21 Oct. 14/6 Were it [*sc.* the weasel] the size of a bear or lion..the outlands would be unsafe for man unless he carried a gun. **1961** in Webster, In the outlands, the Yankees had been strangers. **1970** R. Lowell *Notebk.* 190 Someone comes here from the outlands, Trinidad.

outlander. Delete '(Now *poetic*, or a literary revival, or a mannerism of translation.)' and add earlier and later examples.

1598 Florio *Worlde of Wordes* 265/1 Pellegrino..a stranger, an alien, an outlander, an outlandish man. **1909** W. Tuckwell *Pre-Tractarian Oxford* iii. 59 Unfortunate outlanders whose digestion of the dinner and relish of the port wine were spoiled by these animated dialectics, went away complaining that Oriel Common Room *stunk* of Logic. **1930** *Time & Tide* 20 Sept. 1167, I think, if it is not an impertinence for an outlander to make a suggestion, that England does need [etc.]. **1938** *Englische Studien* LXXII. 323 The printed page marks the outlander by the use of italics and preservation of the French accents. **1952** G. Wilson *Julien Ware* 117 But, having admitted this outlander to his home and table, Mr. Craig felt it necessary to talk for his education and profit. **1964** *Listener* 24 Sept. 453/2 Mr [Robert] Kennedy is of course Boston Irish... He lives in Virginia... He saw the beguiling prospect of a Senate seat in New York. This State now echoes..with the cry of 'carpet-bagger' and 'outlander'. **1976** *Ibid.* 15 July 38/2 He tried to go to New York to the big law firms and they turned him down—he was an outlander from California. **1976** *Verbatim* Sept. 8/a In three essays on the phonology of Georgia place-names, Goff discusses local designations, recording divided usage,..and clarifying accentuation when needed. Outlanders are given the preferred native pronunciations of *Albany* ('All' benny'), *Aragon* ('Arrow'gun' or 'Arrer'gun'), *Schley* ('Sly''), and *Taliaferro/Bolivar* (which make a perfect rhyme in Georgia).

outlandish, *a.* Add: **2.** Also, immoderate, exceeding proper limits. (Partly arising from sense 3.)

1955 *Times* 6 June 7/4 One or two [people]..will shatter the monotonous efficiency of the [refreshment drinks] machine with some outlandish demand for a highly individual brew. **1977** *Time* 10 Jan. 46/1 The outlandish cost of armaments—$25 million for an F-15 today, v. $4 million for a Phantom jet in 1970—along with the rising prices of other imports, pushed the inflation rate into the stratosphere.

3. (Earlier examples.)

1792 J. Byng *Torrington Diaries* (1936) III. 53 So in an *outlandish* place I must creep to bed and pray for summer. **1842** Dickens *Let.* 16 Apr. (1974) III. 202 The inns in these outlandish corners of the world would astonish you by their goodness.

outlaugh, *v.* **2.** (Later example.)

1908 Swinburne *Duke of Gandia* i. 32 Her..Whose eyes outlaugh the splendour of the sea.

outlaw, *sb.* Add: **3.** Also *attrib.* or quasi-*adj.*, esp. in **outlaw strike,** a withdrawal of labour without the authority of a trade union, an unofficial strike.

1903 *Wide World Mag.* Mar. 546/2 The whole Western country was scoured for the wildest and most vicious 'outlaw' bronchos that could be found. **1912** C. A. Siringo *Cowboy Detective* v. 87, I told him to trot out his outlaw horse. **1920** *Harvey's Weekly* 17 Apr. 5/2 The 'outlaw' railroad strikes..are unjustifiable. **1931** *Economist* 6 June 1215/2 Arbitration would consume a good many months at best, and would probably be followed by 'outlaw' strikes. **1937** *Times* 22 Nov. 21/3 On top of this disappointment came a fresh outbreak of 'outlaw' strikes in the motor industry. **1949** *N.Y. Times Bk. Rev.* 13 Mar. 22/4 His brother Billy was thrown by an outlaw bronco. **1977** *New Yorker* 6 June 90/2, I did bring in fifty of them outlaw steers that way once.

outlawed, *ppl. a.* Add: **b.** That has been allowed to run wild. *U.S.*

1907 C. E. Mulford *Bar-20* xx. 197 Yu has got about as much show catchin' one of them as a tenderfoot has of bustin' an outlawed cayuse.

outlawry. 1. (Further *fig.* examples.)

1924 Kellor & Hatvany (*title*) Security against war... Vol. II. Arbitration. Disarmament. Outlawry. **1946** *Rep. Internat. Control Atomic Energy* (U.S. Dept. of State) I. 4 We..studied..the factors..involved in an international inspection system supposed to determine whether the activities of individual nations constituted evasions or violations of international outlawry of atomic weapons. **1964** *New Statesman* 1 May 682/2 When Baldwin writes about homosexuals he writes with a Negro's sense of another 'outlawry'.

outlet, *sb.* Add: **1.** *spec.* a shop, a retail store; an institution disposing of the produce of a manufacturer; a market (for goods).

1919 *Brit. Manufacturer* Nov. 28/1 India..is the most important outlet for British goods. **1933** [see *consumer 2 c]. **1962** *Daily Tel.* 29 May 12/2 The Six are reluctant to guarantee 'comparable outlets' in advance. **1964** *New Society* 27 Feb. 20/2 The shopper..has a choice between self-service and counter-service, and..between the supermarket and smaller self-service... Given this rather bewildering variety of 'outlets' for groceries it is of interest to consider why any housewife should choose one shop rather than another. **1966** *Listener* 17 Mar. 376/1 One may hope that the stimulus given by National Library Week will..lead to a permanent improvement in the outlets for the distribution of reading matter. **1975** *Sci. Amer.* Oct. 122/3 Both the motor and its companion controller are available from W. W. Grainger, Inc., an electrical-supply firm with retail outlets in all major U.S. cities. **1976** *National Observer* (U.S.) 27 Nov. 8/2 Yet Moldafsky and Bird are outlet experts. Each has more than 10 years' experience in outlet shopping, and both have researched and written guide books to outlet stores.

b. (Further examples.)

1916 Joyce *Portrait of Artist* (1969) ii. 64 The ambition which he felt astir at times in the darkness of his soul sought no outlet. **1928** E. O'Neill *Strange Interlude* I. ii. 67 She's got to find normal outlets for her craving for sacrifice. **1938** 'G. Graham' *Swiss Sonata* 260 You think Mlle Lemaitre and the average wife are doing the same thing; in different ways each one is seeking an outlet. **1978** E. Healey *Lady Unknown* iv. 138 Dickens..needed ..an outlet for that driving energy.

c. *Anat.* The opening of a cavity of the body formed by the skeleton; used orig. of the pelvis and later of the thorax. Opp. *inlet *sb.* 4*.

1797 J. Bell *Anat. Bones, Muscles & Joints* I. v. 140 The outlet of the pelvis is the lower circle again, composed by the arch of the pubis and by the sciatic ligaments. **1828, 1906** [see *inlet *sb.* 4*]. **1960** E. Gardner et al. *Anat.* xxix. 339/1 The thoracic cavity communicates with the abdomen by the inferior thoracic aperture, or thoracic outlet, which is closed by the diaphragm. **1974** Passmore & Robson *Compan. Med. Stud.* III. II. xliii. 2/1 There are two areas which present the greatest potential mechanical obstruction to descent of the fetus, the pelvic brim and the effective bony outlet at the level of the ischial spines.

d. = *point *sb.*[1] A. 19 e.

1892 E. A. Merrill *Electr. Lighting Specifications* 77 The building shall be wired to —— lamp outlets, —— switch outlets... At each outlet the loose wire shall be neatly coiled and the ends carefully taped. **1917** A. L. Cook *Interior Wiring* III. 213 Wherever there is an outlet, such as a lighting fixture or a switch. **1925** G. A. Willoughby *House Wiring* i. 68 Some local ordinances require the number of watts to be counted for each type of outlet in various rooms. **1958** M. Dickens *Man Overboard* iv. 54 There was only one electric outlet from which a multiple plug sent fraying wires in all directions. **1968** Paschkis & Ryder *Direct Analog Computers* xxvi. 377 A second board is provided having male plugs fitting the female outlets on the board. **1972** C. L. Cooper in W. King *Black Short Story Anthol.* 221 He set it [*sc.* a tape recorder] down next to an..easy chair, unlatched the top, and plugged the cord into one of the wall outlets.

5. (sense 1 b) *outlet mechanism*; (sense 1 d) **outlet box,** a box used to contain connections to wires where they are led out of conduits.

1906 N. Harrison *Electric Wiring* vi. 133 With all metallic conduits whether flexible or not there are employed junction and outlet boxes. **1971** W. N. Alerich *Electr. Construction Wiring* v. 92/1 An outlet box or the equivalent must be inserted at every point in the system where access to enclosed wires is necessary. **1949** Koestler *Insight & Outlook* v. 69 In the gradually emerging sense of humour, we have a further outlet mechanism.

outlier. Add: **1. c.** (Later examples.)

1939 Joyce *Finnegans Wake* 97 From his holt..the outlier, a white noelan.., led bayers the run. **1976** *Abingdon Herald* 25 Nov. 7/2 Another outlier found near Sparsholt went through Sparsholt Copse, across to the Spinneys again, and back to Westcot. **1977** *Field* 13 Jan. 52/1 Hounds found an outlier at the back of Alexton village and hunted him past the hall.

2. a. (Later examples.)

1955 A. Thom in *Jrnl. R. Statistical Soc.* A. CXVIII. 275 Many of the circles have one or more outliers, i.e. single upright stones outside the ring. *Ibid.* 283 Why not also include *Little Meg* as an outlier to the circle at *Long Meg and her Daughters*?

c. (Further examples.) Also *attrib.*

1885 R. F. Burton tr. *Arabian Nights' Entertainments* V. 177 They took leave of him and departing to the outliers of the city, flew..to their several abodes. **1926** [see *Hattic *a.*]. **1928** *Library Assoc. Rec.* Dec. 244 The Central Library has wisely recruited several of the larger public libraries..to act as outlier libraries. **1961** T. Landau *Encycl. Librarianship* (ed. 2) 259/2 Its 'Outlier' libraries, which lend their specialized books and periodicals on the N.C.L.'s request when other resources fail, now number 281. **1973** *Computers & Humanities* VII. 136 What..differentiates 'La Comtesse d'Escarbagnas', at the top of the diagram, from the remaining plays? What is special about an outlier such as 'Dom Garcie'? **1977** *Jrnl. R. Soc. Arts* CXXV. 269/2 The Library is an 'outlier' library of the British Library.

outline, *sb.* Add: **2. c.** The representation of a word in shorthand.

1850 *Phonography, or, Phonetic Shorthand* 1/2 It [*sc.* Phonography] is..as intelligible as speech itself;..and as used in verbatim reporting, a perfect and intelligible outline. **1886** *Encycl. Brit.* XXI. 839/2 By this method the number of possible readings of an unvocalized outline is greatly reduced. **1898** [see *Pitman's]. **1933** D. L. Sayers *Murder must Advertise* i. 14 He..went on dictating and my hand was so shaky I could hardly make my outlines. **1969** G. Charlesworth *Effective Teaching Techniques in Commercial Subjects* 9 The difficulty of outlines should be very gradually increased and only one point of theory at a time should be so revised. **1973** E. M. Arlett *So You want to be a Shorthand Typist* ii. 18 The pen races smoothly over the pages, filling them with neat outlines that presently will be read back with practised ease.

d. *Typogr.* A display type-face in which the letters are drawn only in outline, perhaps with added shading. Also *attrib.*

1878 *Specimens of Newspaper, Book & Ornamental Founts* (Sir Charles Reed & Sons), Grotesque Outline... Clarendon Outline... English Black Outline. **1970** W. P. Jaspert et al. *Encycl. Type Faces* (ed. 4) 243 Zephyr... An accentuated outline titling, giving a somewhat three-dimensional effect.

3. Also, a précis of a proposed article, novel, scenario, etc.

1928 E. O'Neill *Strange Interlude* I. iv. 123 Charlie's coming to bring his suggestions on my outline for Gordon's biography. **1967** H. Van Siller *Biltmore Call* 164 You know the way he worked. A short outline first, then the first draft. **1968** D. Francis *Forfeit* i. 9 And when you've thought out how you'd like to present it, send us an outline. **1969** L. Hellman *Unfinished Woman* vi. 66 It was..too hard to write a shooting script, or even an outline, about a war I did not know. **1976** D. Quinn *Limbo Connection* xi. 189 It is a good story... I just delivered a few pages of outline to my agent... So let nobody forget, I own the film rights.

6. outline plan, a draft or sketch lacking many details; **outline planning permission,** permission sought by or from an authority, for building, demolition, or industrial development; so *outline planning application*; **outline stitch** (further examples).

1972 *Guardian* 5 Aug. 11/2 Westminster City Council are sitting on outline plans to knock down..a tenement of 89 flats. **1968** *Act* 16 & 17 *Eliz. II.* c. 72 § 66 'Outline planning permission' means planning permission granted, in accordance with the provisions of a development order, with the reservation for subsequent approval by the local planning authority or the Minister of matters..not particularised in the application. **1971** *Reader's Digest Family Guide to Law* 100/1 If the householder does not wish to spend a lot of money on detailed plans and drawings, he can submit brief details and ask for approval of the building work in principle. If this outline planning permission is granted, it will justify further expenditure on more detailed plans. **1973** *Guardian* 25 Apr. 8/7 A meeting has been called..to protest against an outline planning application..for underground mining in the parish. **1908** M. H. Morgan *How to Dress Doll* iii. 34 Fill in with the chain or outline stitch and work with the embroidery buttonhole stitch. **1960** B. Snook *Eng. Hist. Embroidery* 14 Couching, laid-work and outline stitch are used.

ou·t-lot, outlot. *U.S. Obs.* exc. *Hist.* [Out- I.] A lot or piece of ground situated outside a town or other area.

1643 *Rec. Colony & Plantation New Haven* (1857) I. 94 Mris Eldreds out lotts. **1774** in *Amer. Archives* (1837) (ser. 4) I. 278 An out lot, of ten acres, contiguous to the town, shall be laid off for such as desire the same at an easy rent. **1779** [see *in-lot 2]. **1837** W. Jenkins *Ohio Gazetteer* 148

A tract of land on the east side of the town has like-wise been divided into 23 outlots of five acres each. **1886** Z. F. Smith *Hist. Kentucky* 29 [They gave] to each man a half-acre lot and a ten-acre outlot. **1948** [see *in-lot 2].

ou·t-migrant. [Out- 8.] One who leaves one country or place to settle in another. Cf. *in-migrant *sb.* and *a.*

1953 *Caribbean Q.* II. iv. 53 This year, the number of out-migrants may outstrip even 1951's record figure. **1971** *Sci. Amer.* July 18/3 The state of New York for the first time had more out-migrants than in-migrants.

ou·t-migrate, *v.* [Out- 14.] *intr.* To leave one country or place to make one's home in another. Hence **ou·tmigra:tion.** Cf. *in-migration.

1953 *Caribbean Q.* II. iv. 53 This January, twice as many net-out-migrated as in January of 1949, 1950, 1951. *Ibid.*, Out-migration grows like snowballs running down hill. **1970** S. L. Barraclough in I. L. Horowitz *Masses in Lat. Amer.* iv. 157 Without greater agricultural production and accelerated out-migration, however, incomes resulting from reform would be dissipated by population increase within a generation or so. **1971** [see *in-migration]. **1975** *N.Y. Times* 17 Nov. 24/3 The problem for cities that are victims of outmigration is that population decline correlates with at least a relative fall in average income. **1976** *Time* 27 Sept. 55/3 Meanwhile, the out-migration of young blacks and whites has been reversed. **1977** *Jrnl. R. Soc. Arts* CXXV. 551/1 High rise flats.. proved to be particularly unsuitable for families with young children, with the result that out-migration of such families was accelerated.

outmode (autmōu·d), *v.* [Out- 21; cf. F. *démoder.*] *trans.* To put out of fashion. (Chiefly in pa. pple.) So **out-moded** *ppl. a.*, no longer in fashion, out-of-date.

1903 *Academy* 17 Jan. 71/1 Jesse Berridge is a poet, not a poetess, to use a somewhat outmoded word. **1906** R. S. Hichens *Call of Blood* ii. 15 He was not wholly emancipated from la petite femme tradition, which will never be outmoded in Paris. **1906** *Westm. Gaz.* 26 May 2/3 Even the out-moded globe-trotter will find that his sport may be maddeningly slow. **1915** T. Burke *Nights in Town* 392 The poor laddie is sadly outmoded, but he doesn't know it. **1926** W. J. Locke *Stories Near & Far* 133 The joined fragments showed an old photograph of a young man, in out-moded raiment. **1927** *Daily Express* 24 Sept. 8/4 George Ade has been out-moded by Will Rogers, whose jests die as soon as they are born. **1942** *Amer. Speech* XVII. (Reprints & Monogr. No. 4) 4 The people of this region might also have preserved out-moded features of speech. **1952** R. Neill *Moon in Scorpio* xi. 96 It's new Penny—and you're outmoding all Whitehall. **1971** *Sci. Amer.* Oct. 27/1 He believes such a union would outmode the present broadcast networks. **1978** E. Healey *Lady Unknown* vi. 149 Mrs Livingstone in a queer out-moded bonnet.

outmost, *a.* Add: **1.** Also *fig.*

1866 Ruskin *Crown Wild Olive* ii. 108 The outmost and superficial spheres of knowledge.

b. (Later examples.)

1887 W. Morris tr. *Homer's Odyssey* I. i. 2 Thə far-dwellers outmost of menfolk. **1927** E. S. Rae *Hansel fae Hame* 1 The hert rugs hame fae outmaist eyens o' earth.

c. (Later example.)

1887 W. Morris tr. *Homer's Odyssey* I. ix. 166 And but little it lacked, but the outmost of the helm it lighted on.

out of, *prep. phr.* Add: **I. 5. e.** From a base in; using (a place) as a centre of operations.

1960 'E. McBain' *Give Boys Great Big Hand* xii. 146 We were going to run away together... I could always get work out of Miami. **1974** *Publishers Weekly* 24 June 56/2 Working out of Bozeman, Montana, Jack Folsom has enjoyed the help of some 60 'friends'. **1975** *Listener* 27 Nov. 712/2 Marshall McLuhan still works out of a ramshackle office in a converted coach-house on the edge of the University of Toronto. **1975** B. Garfield *Hopscotch* xv. 145 He was the District Director out of Atlanta. **1976** *Times Lit. Suppl.* 25 June 784/4 The miscellaneous radio amateurs and visionaries who worked out of shacks and garages. **1976** *Church Times* 26 Nov. 7/4 Mrs. Briant now works out of Vancouver's Christ Church Cathedral, where she has set up a ministry for shut-ins.

II. 8. e. *out of this world*: see *world *sb.*

9. (Further examples.) *out of one's head*: out of one's mind or memory (see also Head *sb.* 36 in Dict. and Suppl.).

1814 Jane Austen *Mansf. Park* I. i. 6 She could not get her poor sister and her family out of her head. **1901** 'L. Malet' *Hist. R. Calmady* v. x. 469 Obviously it was impossible to go back. He must go on rather—out of sight, out of mind. **1912** F. M. Hueffer *Panel* I. iv. 109 You meant to get her out of your head. **1935** M. de la Roche *Young Renny* iv. 32 Lord, what a waist he has! Do you suppose he can put a solid meal out of sight? **1938** W. de la Mare *Memory* 40 So gaily resigned To out-of-sight being out-of-mind.

10. d. *out of it* (earlier and later examples.)

1830 M. Edgeworth *Let.* 8 Dec. (1971) 442 Poor Davies Gilbert to whom the place was in every way unsuited is well out of it. I hope he thinks so. **1880** *Punch* 25 Dec. 299/1, I was out of it, jolly clean out of it. **1904** H. James *Golden Bowl* I. I. xxi. 344 He..moved her by..taking pity ..on her just discernible depression... He guessed that she felt herself, as the slang was, out of it. **1916** Galsworthy *Sheaf* i. 15 She is simply too 'out of it' to know anything. **1955** *Times* 13 Aug. 8/7 Feeling not a little out of it, we nevertheless took tea with the ladies of the parish. **1959** *News Chron.* 10 July 3/4 Bungalow dwellers ..may well have felt out of it. **1973** R. Lewis *Of Singular Purpose* vii. 157 You're well out of it, Harry. Believe me, you're well out of it.

e. (See quots.)

1963 *Amer. Speech* XXXVIII. 174 Drunk: soused, out of it, stoned, bombed. **1967** Wentworth & Flexner *Dict. Amer. Slang* Add. 698/1 *Out of it*... 3. Not concerned with mundane things, as when under the influence of a drug, obsession, all-consuming idea, etc.; in a state of euphoria. 4. Not 'with it'; stupid; 'square'. **1973** *To our Returned Prisoners of War* (Office of U.S. Secretary of Defense) 8 *Out of it*, to be out of touch with reality when under the influence of a drug, especially hallucinogens. To lack understanding and awareness, especially in a subculture. **1973** *Black Panther* 27 Oct. 12/3 James Jenkins ..describes several inmates on 'F' block, who were once 'sharp dudes' as being 'completely out of it' following 'therapeutic sedation'.

11. b. *out of work, out-of-work*: see Work *sb.* 27 in Dict. and Suppl.

12. (Further examples.)

1858 Geo. Eliot *Scenes Clerical Life* II. 189 Furnishing sugar or vinegar to..families that found themselves unexpectedly 'out of' those indispensable commodities. **1973** 'D. Halliday' *Dolly & Starry Bird* iii. 36, I hadn't a light for his cigar; Charles and I were out of matches.

13. In current use, both in the *spec.* sense, and as a *fig.* development of this.

1892 A. W. Pinero *Magistrate* I. 24 You nominated yourself for the Matrimonial Stakes. Mr. Farringdon's The Widow, by Bereavement, out of Mourning. **1924** Galsworthy *White Monkey* III. xii. 295 The room seemed to him to have been got by a concert-hall out of a station waiting-room. **1950** 'P. Woodruff' *Island of Chamba* vii. 110 Their [*sc.* Muslims'] thought has the same pedigree as ours: by Greece out of Palestine. **1956** N. Marsh *Off with his Head* (1957) viii. 177 Teutonic Dancer by Subsidise out of Substiteuton. **1968** *Listener* 3 Oct. 452/2 If there were a radio stud-book, it could contain some such entry as 'Any Questions? by After-Dinner Speaker out of Group Therapy'. **1973** 'I. Drummond' *Jaws of Watchdog* xvi. 210 Humblebee was bred..by an imported French champion out of a mare by an Argentine quadruple-crown winner.

14. Used with *balance, *phase, *register: see the sbs.

III. *out-of-awareness* (also as *sb.*), *out-of-balance* (also as *sb.* and *vb.*), *out-of-bounds* (earlier example; also as *sb.*), *out-of-breath*, *out-of-condition*, *out-of-context*, *out-of-control* (also *ellipt.*), *out-of-focus* (later examples; also as *sb.*), *out-of-form*, *out-of-hours*, *out-of-key*, *out-of-office*, *out-of-phase*, *out-of-place* (later example), *out-of-pocket* (further and *ellipt.* examples), *out-of-school* (further examples), *out-of-season* (further examples), *out-of-sync*, *out-of-the-body*, *out-of-the-ordinary*, *out-of-the-season*, *out-of-tune* (examples; also *ellipt.*); *out-of-wedlock*.

out-of-round: see *round *sb.*; *out-of-true*: see *true *sb.*; *out-of-truth* see *truth *sb.*

Further derivatives, as *out-of-breathness*, *out-of-the-worldness*, *out-of-touchness*, *out-of-trueness*.

1965 *Canad. Jrnl. Linguistics* Fall 36 When one hears the paralanguage of a speaker, one first, rapidly and out-of-awareness, establishes the base line of the speaker. **1974** *Florida FL Reporter* XIII. 11/2 Children work on language in an out-of-awareness situation. **1921** W. S. Ibbetson *Motor & Dynamo Control* vi. 194 It would not be correct to balance an out-of-balance pulley by fixing a counter-weight on the armature core. **1932** R. Rawlinson in E. Molloy *Pract. Electr. Engin.* V. 1590/2 The function of voltage balancing on the two sides is done by a '3-wire balancer set', which is designed with regard to the maximum out of balance current which the supply company considers it necessary to legislate for. **1958** *Listener* 13 Nov. 780/1 Friction..and the slightest out-of-balance of the motor cause the axis of the gyroscope to deviate. **1967** L. Holmes *Odhams New Motor Manual* viii. 189/2 Out-of-balance can be caused by wheel damage or brake drum eccentricity. **1968** Burdett & Ellis *Motor Vehicle Mechanics' Course* II. xii. 284 Any 'out-of-balance' weight on the wheel..may give rise to a tendency to 'throw' the wheel up from the road and back down on to it once in every revolution of the wheel. **1974** Harvey & Bohlman *Stereo F.M. Radio Handbk.* v. 119 In this type of detector ..the setting of R_4 is arranged to out-of-balance the signal currents in Q_{19} and Q_{22}. **1857** T. Hughes *Tom Brown's School Days* I. ix. 219 Many of the old wild out-of-bounds habits stuck to them as firmly as ever. **1947** M. Lowry *Let.* 24 July (1967) 150 Into what roughs, out-of-bounds and quagmires we shall get ere the book be finished..one knows not. **1973** *Guardian* 21 May 22/3 The long sixteenth, a treacherous hole into the wind with an out-of-bounds lurking on left. **1939** G. Greene *19 Stories* (1947) 156 Low out-of-breath tones. **1900** E. Glyn *Visits of Elizabeth* 98 His snorts of out-of-breathness could be heard for miles. **1972** C. Fremlin *Appointment with Yesterday* xi. 85 She should have realised that her middle-aged, out-of-condition body would..rebel. **1977** F. Branston *Up & Coming Man* xiii. 133 A puffy, out-of-condition young man. **1951** *Mind* LX. 91 The unused, out-of-context sentence specifies no speaker. **1973** R. Ludlum *Matlock Paper* ii. 16 Rumor; out-of-context statements..; constructed evidence. **1961** *Daily Mail* 20 July 9/8 His out-of-control tractor plunged 20 ft. into the River Nar. **1974** H. L. Foster *Ribbin'* vii. 321 Most workers have strong feelings against intervening physically with a child's out-of-control behavior. **1974** G. Jenkins *Bridge of Magpies* vii. 104 Finally the out-of-control twisting of the boat eased. **1977** *O.D.* No. 3. 9/1 The circumstances of our interview with Schmidt were curious, weird, if not verging on the out-of-control. **1946** *Nature* 30 Nov. 786/1 Thus any error in magnification due to slight out-of-focus in one camera was compensated by the other. **1962** L. S. Sasieni *Princ. & Pract. Optical Dispensing* xii. 303 From this we see the extent of the out-of-focus region. **1966** D. G. Brandon *Mod. Techniques Metallogr.* 29 The out-of-focus image of the specimen surface. **1967** E. Chambers *Photolitho-Offset* xi. 160 Slight out-of-focus and gentle vibration of the front of the camera during exposure are 'dodges' also used. **1961** *Times* 27 Dec. 4/1 Parfitt..must now have a chance of gaining his first Test cap in place of the out-of-form M. J. K. Smith. **1977** *South China Morning Post* (Hong Kong) 22 July 18/5 Rick McCosker, Australia's out-of-form opener, boosted his chances of retaining his place for the third cricket Test against England next week with a fighting 77 against Warwickshire yesterday. **1967** *Guardian* 3 Aug. 3/7 A scheme for out-of-hours deliveries in Greater London. **1977** *Times* 9 Sept. 2/3 An out-of-hours repair service for customers. **1962** *Times* 17 Jan. 13/1 The..slightly out-of-key episode with the travelling salesman. **1976** 'J. Fraser' *Who steals my Name?* vii. 89 A tiny little oddness, one of those strange out-of-key facts a policeman is trained to spot. **1961** *Times* 4 Sept. 5/1 His out-of-office activities as a dosshouse owner. **1973** 'W. Haggard' *Old Masters* i. 11 An out-of-office politician. **1938** L. F. Blume *Transformer Engin.* xiv. 369 It would be of no advantage to introduce a circulating current having an out-of-phase component. **1968** C. G. Kuper *Introd. Theory Superconductivity* iv. 65 The real part and the imaginary part of the dielectric constant respectively relate the in-phase and out-of-phase parts of the displacement to the electric field. **1974** *Country Life* 26 Dec. 1997/3 A smaller telescope..would still be an out-of-place intrusion on the landscape. **1902** G. B. Shaw *Let.* 22 Oct. (1972) II. 284 Actual out-of-pocket loss. **1971** D. C. Hague *Managerial Econ.* iii. 67 It is unlikely that prices will be cut below out-of-pocket costs. **1972** G. Durrell *Catch me a Colobus* ix. 182, I said that..I would be willing to cover his out-of-pocket expenses if he'd join the expedition to help us with our work. **1973** 'I. Drummond' *Jaws of Watchdog* vii. 92 He was to be paid £15,000 in used notes, for his own pay-off and his out-of-pocket. **1930** *Times Educ. Suppl.* 26 July 329/3 Organizational activities are relegated to out-of-school hours. **1959** *Times* 20 Jan. 9/3 The result is to be seen in those out-of-school activities which may land them in the juvenile courts. **1970** G. E. Evans *Where Beards wag All* xix. 217 One of Mrs. Jay's out-of-school jobs was keeping pigs. **1944** M. Laski *Love on Supertax* ii. 12 Lack of..out-of-season fruits. **1960** *Farmer & Stockbreeder* 12 Jan. 41 (Advt.), Details of the January out-of-season discounts are now available from your New Holland Dealer. **1966** *Listener* 24 Nov. 783/3 A boy, bored and neglected, at an out-of-season hotel. **1948** *Proc. IRE* XXXVI. 904/1 The effect would be to prolong excessively the out-of-sync condition whenever a discontinuity occurred in the transmitted sync signal. **1956** M. Stearns *Story of Jazz* (1957) xxiv. 301 The hectic, 'out-of-sync' short, *The Jazz Dance*, was filmed in one evening. **1967** *Listener* 21 Sept. 380/1, I rather miss the deliciously ludicrous sight of a singer trying to catch up with his own voice, like an out-of-sync film. **1977** *New Yorker* 25 July 19/3 Rumbles of thunder interspersed the lightning flashes in belated, out-of-sync fashion. **1946** G. N. M. Tyrrell *Personality of Man* vii. xxii. 199 These out-of-the-body cases are of exceptional interest. It is worth pointing out that in two such cases.. the percipients describe the process of getting out of their bodies in almost identical terms. **1969** *New Scientist* 3 July 33/2 Old wives tales..such as spontaneous telepathy, out-of-the-body experiences or poltergeists. **1931** *Times Lit. Suppl.* 15 Oct. 788/1 A disturbing..absolutely out-of-the ordinary life-story. **1974** *Times* 9 Nov. 12/5 Andorra.. has caught the imagination of many skiers looking for an out-of-the-ordinary holiday. **1955** *Times* 3 May 4/2 Permission has been given by the Rugby Union for the Coventry team to play an out-of-the-season game. **1876** H. Sidgwick *Let.* 24 Aug. in A. & E. Sidgwick *Henry Sidgwick* (1906) 323 There is a great charm in this scenery and in the feeling of out-of-the-world-ness. **1916** D. H. Lawrence *Let.* 9 Jan. (1932) 306 But come and see us here, because of the sea and the silence and peace and the out-of-the-worldness of it all. **1957** M. Stewart *Thunder on Right* iii. 38 The out-of-the-worldness of the place pressed heavily upon her. **1952** M. Lowry *Let.* May (1967) 317 The essential..points are too often clouded as a result of the technical out-of-touchness of the writing. **1960** *Guardian* 21 July 8/4 'Out-of-touchness' has produced a fervent desire for recognition. **1921** *Spectator* 26 Feb. 268/2 When you start your wall there seems by eye very little or nothing wrong with it, but when you have got it up some thirty or forty feet the out-of-trueness is appalling. **1803** H. Wynne *Diary* 6 July (1940) III. 83 A beautifull out of tune Symphony, consisting of hair-dressers, butchers, &c. opened the play. **1917** T. S. Eliot *Prufrock* 20 The voice returns like the insistent out-of-tune Of a broken violin. **1930** J. Dos Passos *42nd Parallel* I. 129 A little out of tune orchestra was playing. **1977** J. Wainwright *Day of Peppercorn Kill* 125 Somebody was whistling an out-of-tune version of *Sleepy-Time Gal.* **1961** M. Beadle *These Ruins are Inhabited* (1963) ix. 129 Some Irish girls emigrate briefly to give birth to out-of-wedlock babies. **1972** *Guardian* 22 July 5/7 A single woman experiencing an out-of-wedlock pregnancy.

out-of-date, *adj. phr.* Add: Also *absol.*

1928 *Manch. Guardian Weekly* 17 Aug. 132/1 This column..is apt to specialise in the out-of-date. **1938** *Times* 27 Aug. 3/5 There is to the comparatively unmodern and out of date something indefinably comforting in a winning score of 300.

ou:t-of-da·teness. [f. Out-of-date *adj. phr.* + -ness.] The state or condition of being out-of-date; obsoleteness.

1915 E. Carpenter *Healing of Nations* xvii. 208 Finally..one realizes the monstrosity and absurdity of the present conflict—its anachronism and out-of-dateness in the existing age of human thought and feeling. **1928** *Sunday Dispatch* 30 Dec. 10/5 Consider the rich opportunity to tell the good man of his stuffiness, his out-of-dateness. **1930** A. HUXLEY *Vulgarity in Lit.* i. 3 It took several centuries to reduce Dante's guide-book to out-of-dateness. **1940** 'G. ORWELL' *Inside Whale* 103 They continue to be read in spite of their obvious out-of-dateness.

out-of-door, -doors. Add: **B.** *sb.* (Earlier and later examples.)

1819 KEATS *Let.* 4 Feb. (1958) II. 37 One not ill enough to forget out-of-doors. **1970** D. MATHEW *Courtiers of Henry VIII* III. vi. 206 Henry VIII had been a great King of the out-of-doors. **1975** R. V. REDINGER *Geo. Eliot* (1976) vi. 377 The many scenes which take place in the unhampered out-of-doors.

ou:t-of-doo·rness *nonce wd.*, the state or condition of being out-of-doors.

1929 W. DEEPING *Roper's Row* xxiii. 255 Hazzard liked..the play of the wind through his aggressive hair. It gave him a feeling of out-of-doorness and of freedom.

out of print, *adj. phr.* [See OUT OF *prep. phr.* 14, III and PRINT *sb.* 7 b.] Of a book: no longer available from the publisher; also used with reference to gramophone records. Also as *sb.*

Written with hyphens when used *attrib.*

1674 [see PRINT *sb.* 7 b]. **1800** C. LOFFT in R. Bloomfield *Farmer's Boy* (ed. 3) 128 (*Appendix*), I am happy to be stopt here, by so good a cause as the urgency of the Publishers to complete a Third Edition; they informing me that the second is entirely out of print. **1895** [see PRINT *sb.* 7 b]. **1896** [see OUT OF *prep. phr.* III]. **1927** R. B. MCKERROW *Introd. Bibliogr.* p. vi, I have..been repeatedly asked to reissue the pamphlet (now out of print). **1938** *New Statesman* 13 Aug. 262/1 There are two admirable lieder records. Karl Schmitt-Walker..sings..two of the very best of Hugo Wolf's songs..the latter only available in the out-of-print Gerhardt album of Wolf. **1950** *John o' London's Weekly* 7 July 398/3 Every reader has got his own favourites among the out-of-print. **1965** *Amer. N. & Q.* Oct. 24/1 *New Variorum Edition of Shakespeare*—What is the status of in- and out-of-print volumes in the set? **1973** L. SNELLING *Heresy* I. 12 Some out-of-print unknown... Why, by the way, is he unknown and out of print? **1975** *Times Lit. Suppl.* 22 Aug. 956/6 (Advt.), Any American books, new or out-of-print. **1977** *Gramophone* Sept. 448/2 (Advt.), We still have second-hand LP and 78 Departments where many unusual and out of print records may be found.

out of series, *adj. phr.* [f. OUT OF *prep. phr.* 8, III + SERIES.] (See quot. 1952.)

Written with hyphens when used *attrib.*

1952 J. CARTER *ABC for Bk. Collectors* 128 Of an edition specifically limited in number, there will usually be printed some extra copies... Such copies are understood not to invalidate the certificate of limitation; and their status is sometimes indicated by the words out of series, instead of a number. **1977** *Q. Jrnl. Library of Congress* July 233/2 The copy acquired by the Library is an out-of-series, unnumbered example on Arches paper.

ou:t-of-si·ght, *adj. phr.* (*sb.*) [f. OUT OF *prep. phr.* 9, III + SIGHT *sb.*[1] 10 b.] **A.** *adj. phr.* **1.** Outside the range of sight; distant.

1876 GEO. ELIOT *Dan. Der.* II. IV. xxxi. 280 She was really getting somewhat febrile in her excitement... Was it at the novelty simply, or the almost incredible fulfilment about to be given to her girlish dreams of being 'somebody'—walking through her own furlongs of corridor and under her own ceilings of an out-of-sight loftiness.

2. Excellent, incomparable, superior; delightful, exciting, surprising. *slang* (orig. *U.S.*).

1896 S. CRANE *Maggie* (rev. ed.) v. 43 D'way I plunked dat blokie was outa sight. **1896** ADE *Artie* xi. 94 She looked out o' sight! Some of 'em have got their sealskins and their sparklers, but this little girl, with that new make-up and the flowers, beat the best of 'em. **1897** C. W. CHESNUTT *Let.* 24 Sept. in H. M. Chesnutt *Charles Waddell Chesnutt* (1952) x. 81, I saw the Shaw Memorial and the new Public Library Building, which are 'out of sight'. **1902** J. D. CORROTHERS *Black Cat Club* i. 26 'Out o' sight!' yelled a dozen voices as the poem was concluded. **1927** C. SANDBURG *Amer. Songbag* 279 The corn we raise is our delight, The melons, too, are out of sight. **1961** *Down Beat* 5 Jan. 23, I find some of the musicians I've encountered on the road rather ridiculous... It seems everything is 'something else' these days. Or is it 'out of sight'? **1966** *Surfer* VII. IV. 11 The waves are a perfection 10 to 15 feet and straight over. Really up tight and out of sight! **1970** *Times* 6 July 8/5 Whenever possible he liked to make a point of talking to drug users on their own ground... An action that led one girl student to remark 'for an official person he's absolutely out of sight.' **1973** *Ottawa Jrnl.* 14 July 24/2, I met this groovy dude at the bowling alley. He is out of sight.

B. *sb.* One who or that which is unseen. *rare.*

1930 AUDEN *Poems* 18 Better where no one feels, The out-of-sight, buried too deep for shafts.

ou:t-of-sta·te, *adj. phr.* [f. OUT OF *prep. phr.* 8, III + STATE *sb.* 31 c.] Originating from outside a state of the United States. Also *ellipt.* as *sb.*, the area outside a particular state. Hence **ou:t-of-sta·ter,** a person originating from outside a particular state.

1935 *Amer. Mercury* July 290/2, I was also faced with their prejudice against out-of-town and out-of-state teachers. **1938** *Amer. Speech* XIII. 178 The larger southern part [of Idaho]..since the days of the Oregon trail has received a greater percentage of 'out-of-staters'. **1943** *Sun* (Baltimore) 28 Apr. 28/3 Dealers in a poultry black market on the Eastern Shore, including..live-chicken buyers from out-of-State and Baltimore wholesalers. **1948** *Herald-Press* (St. Joseph, Mich.) 14 Aug. 1/1 Many a speeding out-of-state motorist is of the opinion that the St. Joseph policemen are a lot of meanies. **1964** J. MASTERS *Trial at Monomoy* i. 11 Bunch of crackpots, long-hairs, foreigners, out-of-staters. **1973** *N.Y. Law Jrnl.* 26 July 1/6 The law students interviewed, most of them from out-of-state, made these observations. **1973** D. BARNES *See Woman* (1974) 90 A Buick. It had out-of-state plates on it. **1974** *Columbia* (S. Carolina) *Record* 25 Apr. 18-C/5 Many out-of-staters are showing a lot of interest in purchasing real estate in the Santee-Cooper complex. **1976** *CB Mag.* June 23/1 (Advt.), Special Bonding Service—protects you from being arrested if you ever get caught speeding out-of-state without enough money to pay the fine.

out-of-the-way, *adj. phr.* Add: **B.** as *adv.* Oddly; exceptionally, extraordinarily.

1717 [in Dict., sense 4]. **1901** 'M. FRANKLIN' *My Brilliant Career* x. 80, I really believe that on that night I did not look out of the way ugly. **1928** E. M. FORSTER in *Life to Come* (1972) 105 He was completely sincere when he told the Trevor Donaldsons that he had had an out-of-the-way pleasant weekend. **1939** —— in *Ibid.* 118 If only he wasn't so handsome, so out-of-the-way handsome.

C. as *sb.* A remote spot, an out-of-the-way place.

1971 *Islander* (Victoria, B.C.) 7 Nov. 13/4 Colorful people who lived at these out-of-the-ways on the west.. coast.

out-of-the-wayness. (Further examples.)

1899 KIPLING *From Sea to Sea* I. xii. 307 It [*sc.* Kobé, in Japan] lives among hills, but the hills are all scalped, and the general impression is of out-of-the-wayness. **1926** S. T. WARNER *Lolly Willowes* II. 129 There's not such another village in Buckinghamshire for out-of-the-wayness.

out-of-time, *adj. phr.* Delete † *Obs.* and add later example.

1909 *Westm. Gaz.* 4 Sept. 13/2 He is so full of admiration for James III.—the 'Old Pretender', in common language —that he casts an out-of-time vote for him.

ou:t-of-tow·n, *adj. phr.* (*sb.*) [OUT OF *prep. phr.* 8, III.] **A.** *adj.* Situated, originating from, or occurring outside a town. Also, unsophisticated.

1825, 1891 [in Dict. s.v. OUT OF *prep. phr.* III]. **1903** R. BEDFORD *True Eyes* 198 The two walked down the rise on its out-of-town side. **1930** E. WAUGH *Vile Bodies* x. 174 There were a great number of journalists making the best of an 'out-of-town' job. **1937** M. HILLIS *Orchids on your Budget* iv. 71 When an out-of-town cousin turns up, you undoubtedly entertain her more lavishly. **1957** H. ROOSENBERG *Walls came tumbling Down* ix. 209 She was going..to make some out-of-town phone calls. **1959** *Manch. Guardian* 10 Aug. 3/1 Scotland's 'Theatre in the Hills' is a model for out-of-town theatres. **1971** *Daily Hampshire Gaz.* (Northampton, Mass.) 9 Nov. 1/3 Servicemen based in Northampton led groups of out-of-town based gas men to various sections of the town. **1973** J. MANN *Only Security* vii. 81 I've never seen anything so horrible as one of those out-of-town shopping centres I saw in the Midlands. **1977** *New Yorker* 9 May 35/1 Most of them [*sc.* students] were so nice and out-of-town that they were not completely comfortable with escalators and revolving doors.

B. *sb.* A person originating from outside a particular town. Also **ou:t-of-to·wner.**

a **1911** D. G. PHILLIPS *Susan Lenox* (1917) II. vi. 162 Except for 'out-of-towners', the married men were the chief support of their profession. **1941** *Reader's Digest* May 29/1 Sometimes out-of-towners leave no tip at all. **1958** *Manch. Guardian* 7 June 4/6 The out of towners swarm in and laugh in the wrong places. **1966** 'W. HAGGARD' *Power House* xiii. 136 The driver..[had] mistaken him for an out-of-town and he'd cruise him through Regent's Park and..claim the full fare. **1973** J. DRUMMOND *Bang! Bang! You're Dead!* xxv. 84 Out-of-towners or won't-works agitate at so much the hour, never mind what about. **1976** *New Yorker* 15 Nov. 162/2 It had found that many of the out-of-towners in charge of choosing convention sites..had had to be talked out of changing their plans at the last minute.

out-party: see OUT- 4 in Dict. and Suppl.

outpass, *v.* Add: **1.** (Later examples.)

1928 J. H. MOZLEY tr. *Statius* I. 47 Mayst thou outpass the limits of old Nestor's age. **1929** R. BRIDGES *Testament of Beauty* IV. 150 That fadeth only as it outpasseth mortal sight.

2. (Later example.)

1930 *New Statesman* 28 June 360/1 Parties which have historically played their part..but now find themselves outpassed by newer parties.

out-patient. Add: **b.** *pl.* The out-patient department of a hospital.

1910 *Practitioner* July 87 After death..she was recognised as the woman who had previously attended at out-patients. **1968** 'L. BLACK' *Outbreak* i. 8 There's a smallpox suspect in the Outpatients at St Swithin's. **1977** B. PYM *Quartet in Autumn* v. 47 A visit to out-patients at the hospital.

ou·t-peeping, *ppl. a.* [OUT-10.] That peeps out.

1908 A. AUSTIN *Sacr. & Prof. Love* 72 And on out-peeping roots the sun-god shoots The shafts of his golden quiver.

outperform (ɑutpəɹfǭ·ɹm). [f. OUT- 18 + PERFORM *v.*] *trans.* To perform better than; to surpass in a specified activity or function.

1960 *Farmer & Stockbreeder* 9 Feb. 92 It has been out-performing other light tractors ever since it was introduced and using less fuel in doing it. **1966** *Economist* 26 Mar. 1239/2 The fund..will be expected to outperform other mutual funds. **1972** *Times* 30 Sept. 9/5 Salzburg's cast, in voice and temperament, outperform their studio rivals. **1973** M. WOODHOUSE *Blue Bone* xii. 122 It out-performs structural steel by a factor of ten times. **1975** *Publishers Weekly* 30 June 22/1 In the sweeping stock market recovery of 1975, book publishing companies—after years in the Wall Street doghouse—have sharply outperformed the general market. **1978** R. V. JONES *Most Secret War* xli. 390 The Mustang could outperform all the standard German day fighters.

out-place. Delete †*Obs.* and add later examples.

1838 F. OWEN *Diary* 8 Jan. (1926) 94 Most of the inhabitants were absent at the out places or villages. **1911** *Chambers's Jrnl.* Apr. 221/1 It is this longing..that sends the sportsman into the out-places. **1956** W. R. BIRD *Off-trail in Nova Scotia* vi. 176 But that reminds me of my scrap book. You know we in these out places keep such things.

outplace, *v.* [OUT- 18, 15.] *trans.* **a.** To displace or oust. **b.** (see quot. 1970.)

1928 *Daily Express* 16 Jan. 5/3 Skirts dipping at one side will outplace in many houses the skirt dipping at the back that was so popular during the winter. **1970** *Time* 14 Sept. 83 Instead of simply bouncing a subordinate, the boss can send him to a firm that specializes in helping unwanted executives to find new jobs. The practitioners have even coined a euphemistic description for the process: 'outplacing' executives who have been 'dehired'.

outplay, *v.* (Further examples.)

1938 L. BEMELMANS *Life Class* II. iii. 144 The bands always tried to outplay each other, waging a musical warfare. **1972** G. GREEN *Great Moments in Sport: Soccer* ii. 35 England has been outplayed..in a number of ways. **1977** J. WAINWRIGHT *Do Nothin'* v. 67 Krupa on tom-toms and James on the horn..two of the best in the business trying to out-play each other.

out-po·cketing, *vbl. sb. Biol.* [OUT- 9.] The outward movement of part of a surface so as to form a pocket- or sac-like cavity.

1924 L. B. AREY *Developmental Anat.* i. 8 Circumscribed folds..produce (*a*) evaginations, or out-pocketings, and (*b*) invaginations, or in-pocketings. **1968** *Progress in Brain Res.* XXIX. 55 Portions of the outer nuclear envelope..could project into the cytoplasm and pinch off... Out-pocketings of the outer nuclear envelope are frequently seen in early neuroepithelial cells. **1971** *Nature* 16 Apr. 472/2 The glands arise as an outpocketing of the vagina.

outpoint, *v.* Add: **3.** In various sports and games, esp. boxing: to score more points than; to defeat on points. Also *transf.* and *fig.*

1903 *Westm. Gaz.* 19 Feb. 7/3 In the second [coursing] ties, Priestlaw, notwithstanding his speed, was out-pointed cleverly by Handsome Creole. **1909** *Ibid.* 2 Feb. 12/2 With Aiken unable to settle down [in a billiards match] and failing to make any material use of some nice openings, he continued to be outpointed. **1909** *Ibid.* 20 Feb. 16/3 Driscoll outpointed the American featherweight champion. **1922** *Weekly Dispatch* 12 Nov. 11 In a ten-rounds boxing contest here to-night Bermondsey Billy Wells (England) outpointed Johnny Tillman. **1949** *Sun* (Baltimore) 16 July 9/6 Barfly regularly outpoints and out-foots all who sail against her. **1955** *Times* 12 May 4/3 Eddington, the coloured American, had been outpointed in Ireland. **1959** *Economist* 11 Apr. 159/1 BOAC happens to have been outpointed in the never-ending game of poker that the airlines play with traffic rights for chips. **1970** *Globe & Mail* (Toronto) 28 Sept. 21/3 Scot Ken Buchanan won the world lightweight boxing title Saturday in San Juan, Puerto Rico, when he outpointed champion Ismael Laguna of Panama under a blazing sun. **1976** *Daily Record* (Glasgow) 4 Dec. 30/5 The Baillieston man outpointed Irish champion John McLoughlin after both had been floored in an amazing second round.

outport[1]. Add: **1. b.** Chiefly in Labrador and Newfoundland, a small remote fishing village. Also *attrib.* Hence **ou·tporter,** an inhabitant of an outport.

1820 in C. R. Fay *Life & Labour in Newfoundland* (1956) viii. 138 Almost every fifth fisherman is what is termed a 'Planter', particularly in the outports of the Island. **1904** *Westm. Gaz.* 6 May 10/1 The Newfoundland outporters are hardy, courageous, boldly adventurous, simple-lived. **1907** J. G. MILLAIS *Newfoundland* p. xv, I have tried to enter into the life of the true Newfoundlander—the man of the outports. **1949** [see *NEW LIGHT 3 a]. **1964** L. E. F. ENGLISH *Historic Newfoundland* 6 Visit the fishing villages, the so-called outports of the Province of Newfoundland. **1966** A. R. SCAMMELL *My Newfoundland* 17 Environment and circumstance..developed in the young outport lad initiative, and a sense of responsibility. **1973** B. BROADFOOT *Ten Lost Years* xix. 214 Mallory and Derek, pretty fancy names for a couple of outporters, eh? **1974** *Nat. Geographic* Jan. 116 Most islanders cling to the seaside in isolated villages called outports. **1978** *Globe & Mail* (Toronto) 14 Jan. 8/2 Trudeau's Government.. killed a subsidy that keeps a useful ferry service going between the mainland and outer islands in the Queen Charlottes and between the Vancouver supply area and the tiny outports of the northern coast.

c. A small port, located to support the commerce of a main port.

1935 J. A. Fraser *Spain & W. Country* x. 108 It was from Seville and its little out-port Sanlucar de Barrameda ..that nearly all the early Spanish voyages of discovery went forth. **1952** F. W. Morgan *Ports & Harbours* 76 In order to prevent a loss of trade the port undertakes the development of an 'outport' nearer the sea, which can attract the larger vessels. **1956** *Sun* (Baltimore) 3 Sept. 4/5 It just wouldn't work to have a New York contract cover each of the outports.

out-posi·tion, *v.* [f. Out- 21 + Position *sb.*] *trans.* In various sports and games, to secure an advantage over (an opponent) in terms of position; to defeat in a contest for a particular position.

1928 *Sunday Express* 24 June 21 Tilden got to everything with that long, easy stride of his, and Hunter was often outpositioned by shots that he did not expect would be returned. **1960** E. S. & W. J. Higham *High Speed Rugby* xi. 131 The further he progresses, the more necessary it will become to out-position and out-think the opposition. **1966** *Daily Progress* (Charlottesville, Va.) 8 June 30/2 We out-hustle them, out-position them, and in all but two games have actually out-rebounded them.

outpost, *sb.* Add: **b.** (Further examples.)

1881 D. G. Rossetti *Ballads & Sonnets* 196 Shall my sense pierce love,—the last relay And ultimate outpost of eternity? **1917** E. V. Lucas (*title*) Outposts of mercy.

c. (Further examples.)

1776 *Battle of Brooklyn* II. i. 19 We are the remains of the out post guard. **1870** De B. R. Keim *Sheridan's Troopers* 206 This simple means is also resorted to by the troops on outpost duty. **1923** Kipling *Irish Guards in Great War* I. 226 The blockhouse..was absorbed into our outpost-line. **1946** *R.A.F. Jrnl.* May 175 In Berlin and Hamburg..and on airfields and outpost stations, the R.A.F. has taken root. *Ibid.* 176 Then, these outpost men are busy.

2. A trading settlement situated near a frontier or at a remote place in order to facilitate the commercial contacts of a larger and more centrally situated town or settlement. Also, by extension, any of various other kinds of remote settlements and institutions (see examples). Also *attrib.*

1802 in E. Coues *New Light on Early Hist. Greater Northwest* (1897) I. 204 [I] made up the assortment of goods for the outposts, equipped the summer men, clerks, etc. **1911** A. K. Chignell (*title*) An outpost in Papua. **1955** W. G. Hardy *Alberta Golden Jubilee Anthol.* 212 In Alberta, after World War I, it set up 'outpost hospitals' for the brides and families of soldier-settlers in the outlying reaches of the province. **1956** H. S. M. Kemp *Northern Trader* 17 The red [thumbtacks] represent the Company's permanent, year-round establishments; the blue ones, the winter posts and outposts. **1961** L. van der Post *Heart of Hunter* I. v. 80 Tsane had once possessed a district commissioner, but had declined into a remote police outpost. **1970** *Islander* (Victoria, B.C.) 22 Feb. 5/3 The post here [*sc.* Cambridge Bay] is what is called an Outpost where goods are landed to be drawn on by other posts that may run short.

3. The furthest territory of an empire, esp. in the phr. *outpost of* [*the British*] *Empire*, common since the end of the nineteenth century, and now occasionally used in a nostalgic or ironic sense. Also *attrib.*

1912 Kipling *Songs from Bks.* 94 There he shall blaze a nation's ways with hatchet and with brand, Till on his last-won wilderness an Empire's outposts stand. **1924** E. M. Forster *Passage to India* xx. 182 His simple words had reminded them that they were an outpost of Empire. **1924** *Granta* 25 Apr. 361/1 Attock Fort, in the Punjab... An outpost of Empire, where the Cabul and the Indus meet. **1929** J. B. Priestley *Good Companions* II. vii. 448 May she marry the outpost-of-Empire lad in the Sudan. **1934** Dylan Thomas *Let.* 25 Apr. (1966) 111 Then I shall walk back..covering up a..weakness with a look of fierce & even Outpost-of-the-Empire determination. **1937** 'G. Orwell' *Road to Wigan Pier* ix. 173 In an 'outpost of Empire' like Burma the class-question appeared at first sight to have been shelved. **1970** R. Johnston *Black Camels* ii. 26 You've sure got an impressive outpost of empire here. **1971** R. Roberts *Classic Slum* vi. 81 Some families..had male members..who had soldiered in the outposts of empire.

outpromise, *v.* (Later example.)

1938 *Sun* (Baltimore) 9 July 6/1 Many more experienced statesmen have thought that they had outpromised the field, only to find themselves sadly in arrears at election time.

outpunch (aʊtpʌ·nʃ), *v.* [f. Out- 18 + Punch *v.*[1] 3.] *trans.* In boxing, to surpass (an opponent) in punching ability.

1950 F. Mills *Twenty Years* xiii. 168 For the next few rounds.., he was gradually coming back..and for the seventh, eighth and ninth, I think he outboxed and outpunched me. **1956** —— *Forward the Light-Heavies* ix. 99 Delaney made a bad start in 1927 by being out-punched by Jim Maloney over 10 rounds at the new Garden. **1960** *Times* 26 Apr. 17/3 He was outthought, outboxed and.. outpunched by the Mexican. **1961** *Times* 6 June 5/4 J. Malcolm was outpunched and outpointed.

output, *sb.* Add: **1.** (Further examples.)

1942 *R.A.F. Jrnl.* 30 May 34 Dislocation of other factories depending on the Billancourt output. **1959** C. Singer *Short Hist. Sci. Ideas* iv. 116 This drug book [of Pliny's] is the prototype of the medical output of the next fifteen hundred years. **1965** Seldon & Pennance *Everyman's Dict. Econ.* 315 Output is normally understood to be gross output; but..the most useful definition..relates to gross output less the goods and services used in production; this amount is called net output. **1971** *Cabinet Maker & Retail Furnisher* 24 Sept. 524/1 The United Kingdom is the planned market for 80% of the output. **1972** *Value Added Tax: Gen. Guide* (H.M. Customs) 16 The goods and services he [*sc.* the taxable person] supplies are called his outputs and the tax he charges is his output tax. **1976** *Times* 21 May 4/1 *Manpower Paper No. 8*... estimated the output of graduates to 1981.

c. Energy produced by a device or system; *spec.* an electrical signal delivered by, or available from, an electronic device.

1884 S. P. Thompson *Dynamo-Electr. Machinery* vii. 113 The result is an extraordinary increase in the 'output', or, as Sir William Thomson terms it, 'activity' (i.e. amount of work done per second) of the machine. **1902, 1933** [see *input *sb.* 2 b]. **1956** *B.B.C. Handbk. 1957* 57 The equipment used in studio control cubicles for selecting and mixing the outputs of the various microphones. **1962** A. Nisbett *Technique Sound Studio* i. 17 The output of individual studios is fed in 'live', and linked together by station identification and continuity announcements. **1969** *Times* 7 Mar. 15/1 A television camera scans the object to be viewed, and output from the camera controls whether the pad vibrates. **1975** *Which?* Sept. 258/1 For the same output of heat, one of the gas fires..might land you with a bill of £26 a year, another with one of only £16. **1976** *Gramophone* June 116/3 Using the Bruel and Kjaer wave analyser to measure separate harmonics, rather than distortion factor including noise, suggested even lower figures: 0.048% at full output, 0.038% at −20dB and 0.074% at −30dB.

d. *Computers.* Data or results produced by a computer; also, the physical medium on which these are represented.

1948 *Math. Tables & Other Aids to Computation* III. 7 The 'output' or result of computation consists of numbers only. It has been proposed..to build a 'thinking' machine whose output would be orders rather than numbers. **1949** [see *input *sb.* 2 d]. **1959** E. M. McCormick *Digital Computer Printer* ix. 133 The output punch could be activated and would punch the output into the card. **1964** F. L. Westwater *Electronic Computers* vi. 105 Quite sophisticated computers use punched cards as a supplementary output. **1967** D. Wilson in Wills & Yearsley *Handbk. Managem. Technol.* iii. 44 Figure 3.1 outlines the basic steps for validating (editing), processing (sorting and calculating, etc.), and recording the output (writing the data on magnetic tape or disk, printing out, etc.). **1971** P. Harvey *Computer Sci.* vii. 102 If a decimal print out is required for visual inspection the binary output must be converted to a form suitable for operating a printer.

e. *Linguistics.* A structure resulting from the application of a lexical, grammatical, or phonological rule. Cf. *input *sb.* 2 f.

1961, etc. [see *input *sb.* 2 f]. **1968** P. M. Postal *Aspects Phonol. Theory* iii. 34 The phonetic representations are the final output of the entire set of phonological rules. **1970** *Language* XLVI. 261 The use of transformational rules applied to the output of structure-free grammars. **1971** *Archivum Linguisticum* II. 139 We can represent the output of the realization rules in the conventional way, partly by orthographic forms and partly by generalized morpheme-symbols such as *-s.*

2. A place where, or device through which, an output is delivered by a system, esp. an electronic device.

1933, 1946 [see *input *sb.* 3]. **1958** *Electronic Engin.* XXX. 1/2 The weakest part of a computer installation is, in general, the input and output which is usually slow compared with the speed of the machine itself. **1962** D. S. Halacy *Computers* iii. 66 (*caption*) A high-speed printer is the output of this computer. **1973** N. H. Crowhurst *Basic Audio Syst.* (1974) ix. 169 The essential ingredients of a feedback loop..are: an amplifier of some sort and feedback from output to input.

3. The action or process of supplying an output.

1947 [see *input *sb.* 4]. **1947** D. R. Hartree *Calculating Machines* 12 Functions of calculating machine components... (iii) Input (reception of data from the outside world). (iv) Output (supply of results to the outside world). (v) Transfer. (vi) Control. **1960** Gregory & Van Horn *Automatic Data-Processing Syst.* ii. 64 Output of results is the fourth stage in the flow of data. **1967** D. Wilson in Wills & Yearsley *Handbk. Managem. Technol.* iii. 46 In the early types of machine, input, computing, and output occurred serially so that large areas of expensive hardware were unused for much of the time. **1970** O. Dopping *Computers & Data Processing* xi. 154 When a computer is used for process control, the input and output is largely effected via..devices which convert analogue to digital information and vice versa.

4. *attrib.* and *Comb.* **a.** simple attributive, as *output circuit, device, impedance, punch, routine, stage, transformer, tube, unit, valve.* **b.** constituting output, as *output current, power, voltage.*

1920 H. J. Van der Bijl *Thermionic Vacuum Tube* vii. 178 Distortionless amplification is obtained if the amplified current in the output circuit is..an exact enlarged reproduction of the input current. **1973** N. H. Crowhurst *Basic Audio Syst.* (1974) vi. 118 The input circuit requires a fixed component of voltage or current to insure that the device operates at the correct combination of voltage and current in its output circuit. **1920** H. J. Van der Bijl *Thermionic Vacuum Tube* vii. 168 This would produce distortion since the output current is not an exact reproduction of the input. **1962** Simpson & Richards *Junction Transistors* ix. 219 The shift due to the rise in ambient temperature is thus relatively small and can be tolerated for peak-to-peak output–current swings of about 7mA. **1929** K. Henney *Princ. Radio* xii. 281 Output devices are used to (1) Keep d.c. current from the loud speaker winding; (2) Prevent serious loss in plate voltage; [etc.]. **1948, 1968** Output device [see *input device* s.v. *input *sb.* 5]. **1930** Moyer & Wostrel *Pract. Radio Construction & Repairing* (ed. 2) iv. 54 The plate resistance..in the case of audio-frequency amplification may be considered as the output impedance. **1962** J. H. & P. J. Reyner *Radio Communication* x. 409 (*heading*) Effect of feedback on output impedance. **1920** H. J. Van der Bijl *Thermionic Vacuum Tube* vii. 237 If the tube is used to amplify modulated high-frequency oscillations.. it must obviously be capable of giving a much larger output power. **1972** *IEEE Trans. Geoscience Electronics* X. 13/1 A CW output power of 1 W with a power efficiency of 70 percent has been achieved. **1959** Output punch [see sense *2 d]. **1962** *Gloss. Terms Automatic Data Processing (B.S.I.)* 96 *Automatic tape punch, output punch* [deprecated], a tape punch which automatically transcribes coded electrical signals into rows of holes in a paper tape and moves the tape as necessary. *Ibid.* 43 *Output routine*, a routine which organizes the output process of a computer, e.g. starts the output equipment, presents data to it at suitable intervals of time, and specifies format. **1926** *Wireless World* 1 Sept. 317/2 If, however, we are *not* within five miles of a B.B.C. station, the value of extra low impedance in the output stage is unnecessary. **1962** J. H. & P. J. Reyner *Radio Communication* x. 409 Voltage feedback..has the effect of reducing the effective internal impedance of the output stage. **1929** K. Henney *Princ. Radio* xii. 281 An output transformer is necessary to provide maximum energy transfer from the tube to the speaker. **1968** L. G. Sands *Easy Way to service Radio Receivers* (1973) ii. 52 Between points 1 and 3 you should get a higher resistance reading... If not, the output transformer may be grounded. **1929** J. H. Morecroft *Elem. Radio Communication* vii. 242 If the speaker is to use 100 milliwatts on the average,..the output tube should be drawing from its battery at least 10 watts. **1959** M. H. Wrubel *Primer of Programming* i. 9 In some cases the output unit can produce a printed sheet of answers directly; in other cases..the cards or tapes produced by the computer must be fed into an auxiliary machine. **1940** *Chambers's Techn. Dict.* 603/2 Output valve. **1942** *Electronic Engin.* XIV. 726 The stages in the receiver are covered in sequence from R.F. amplifiers to L.F. output valves. **1937** W. G. Dow *Fund. Engin. Electronics* 267 The useful output voltage..is the alternating component of the voltage across R_L. **1962** A. Nisbett *Technique Sound Studio* 259 Where a microphone impedance is strongly capacitative..its output voltage is fed to the grid of a valve.

output, *v.* **4.** (Further examples.)

1946 *Nature* 12 Oct. 504/1 Results are output in the form of punched cards. **1965** K. Nicol *Elem. Programming* vii. 31 A comparable output device is the graphical plotter which can directly output the results of a calculation as curves or points on a paper chart. **1972** P. B. Gove in H. D. Weinbrot *New Aspects Lexicogr.* 153 The *Seventh Collegiate*..has been completely programmed so that most of the relationships seen by the eye on a printed page can be output by the computer. **1976** *Physics Bull.* July 298/2 The most common device for inputting and outputting information is still the venerable teletype.

outputter[2].

For *Mod. Newspr.* read **1902** *Spectator* 22 Nov. 784/1.

out-quencher. For † read '*Obs.* exc. *hist.*' and add later example.

1959 L. Gross *Housewives' Guide to Antiques* viii. 84 Similar in appearance are the 'douters' or out-quenchers, which were used to extinguish candle flames...these had two discs between which the burning wick was nipped.

outrage, *sb.* Add: **3. d.** A person of strange or wild appearance, or one who is extravagant in behaviour.

1869 'Mark Twain' *Innoc. Abr.* 35 Who is that smooth-faced, animated outrage yonder in the fine clothes? **1884** —— *Huck. Finn* 236 Blamed if he warn't the horriblest-looking outrage I ever see. **1909** 'O. Henry' *Roads of Destiny* 351 This old medical outrage floated down to my shack when I sent for him.

out-rai·l, *v.*[2] *nonce-wd.* [f. Out- 21 + Rail *sb.*[2] 2 b.] *trans.* To surpass in respect of a railing.

1866 Ruskin *Crown Wild Olive* p. xii, The publichouse-keeper on the other side of the way presently buys another railing, to out-rail him with.

outrake[2]. Restrict † *Obs.* to sense a in Dict. and add: **b.** (Later example.)

1976 G. Moffat *Short Time to Live* v. 49 This lady at Burblethwaite... I saw her walking up the outrake.

outrance. b. (Further examples.)

1837, 1860 [see * à l'outrance]. **1955** *Times* 19 May 10/2 Powerful Mau Mau 'generals'..are in favour of continuing the struggle *à outrance.* **1959** *Listener* 8 Oct. 589/1 The destruction of her fragile world and the war *à outrance* to keep something of it intact.

outrange, *v.* Add: **1. b.** *transf.* In certain ball games, to have a greater command of the field of play than (an opponent).

1930 *Times* 15 Mar. 6/1 At fullback, Scotland will have ..R. C. Warren, but he may be outranged by J. C. Hubbard.

3. c. *Aeronaut.* Of an aircraft: to have a greater range than (another aircraft).

1942 [see *out-gun *v.*].

outrank, *v.* Add: (Earlier and later examples.) Hence **outra·nked** *ppl. a.*

1842 *Spirit of Times* (Philad.) 1 Sept. (Th.), It won't be long before he fills the place of some one of the drones and cakes who now outrank him. **1903** *Westm. Gaz.* 26 Aug. 4/1 Barr did not outrank Wringe here as he had done at the start. **1948** K. ANTHONY *Lambs* i. 11 She laid some strange claim to a gentility outranking her husband's. **1973** J. WAINWRIGHT *Pride of Pigs* 179 You haven't a leg to stand on.. You don't even out-rank me. **1974** S. GULLIVER *Vulcan Bulletins* 21 The luckless, outranked, beautifully-spoken captain of shooting.

outré, *a.* (Further examples.)
1883 C. M. YONGE *Stray Pearls* I. iv. 42 Madame de Port Royal..is..suspected of being outrée in her devotion. **1934** C. LAMBERT *Music Ho!* v. 304 He will adopt a more eclectic and less outré manner. **1961** J. MCCABE *Mr. Laurel & Mr. Hardy* (1962) vii. 139 Physical humour was becoming outré. **1975** L. FARAGO *Aftermath* xix. 320 The prosecution of criminal Nazis is coming to be widely regarded as a kind of séance in which the spirits of another era are conjured up by some *outré* hocus-pocus. **1975** *Times* 20 Sept. 6/2 Poirot..was the Englishman's notion of the comic foreigner, *outré* as everybody knew foreigners to be.

outreach, *sb.* Add: Also, the extent or length of reaching out; *spec.* the fact or extent of an organization's involvement in the community. (Further examples.) Also *attrib.*
1941 F. MATTHIESSEN *Amer. Renaissance* III. ii. 114 That has caught Browne's ability to take the familiar and to give it an unexpected outreach. **1950** *Theology* LIII. 417 The spiritual outreach of the body politic. **1965** R. B. ORAM *Cargo Handling* i. 15 The management should have, ready for hire, cranes that may provide an outreach of 38 metres, as are to be found in Rotterdam. **1967** *Times* 27 Jan. 17/1 (*caption*) Each lantern is attached to 12ft. long outreach brackets on..tapered steel columns. **1967** *Gleaner* (Jamaica) 12 Nov. 9 Means and methods of furthering the outreach of the Jamaican church. **1972** *Evening Telegram* (St. Johns, Newfoundland) 24 June 35/5 Real preaching instead of the kind that people grow fat on; real outreach concern, whether it's over the back fence or overseas. **1974** *Times Lit. Suppl.* 18 Jan. 50/3 That was how he came to think of the Church, in its 'outreach' into the complex social whole. **1977** M. WILES in J. Hick *Myth of God Incarnate* viii. 162 In his attitudes towards other men his life was a parable of the loving outreach of God to the world. **1978** *Amer. Libraries* IX. 67 As assistant deputy director of Buffalo and Erie County (N.Y.) Public Library, William Miles..oversees such special services as library outreach for community centers.

outreaching, *vbl. sb.* and *ppl. a.* (Further examples.)
1875 H. E. MANNING *Internal Mission of Holy Ghost* xiv. 405 The symmetry and outlines of the Tree of Life, with its outreaching branches. **1902** A. T. MAHAN *Retrospect & Prospect* iv. 111 This outreaching of an imperialistic arm by all the greater nations..constitutes..the motive to a closer union. **1905** *Daily Chron.* 14 Dec. 3/4 Such entire absence of out-reachings towards 'virility', 'grip', and 'tenseness'. **1972** *Science* 26 May 855/1 Certainly strong, outreaching, and complete fertility-control programs are desirable.

out-reckon, *v.* Restrict † *Obs.* to sense in Dict. and add: **b.** To overestimate. *rare.*
1898 HARDY *Wessex Poems* 154 But though, your powers outreckoning, You hold you dead and dumb.

out-relief. Add: **a.** Also *fig.*
1973 G. E. AYLMER *State's Servants* ii. 51 Ireland was still regarded as an out-relief centre for the less hopeful and worse-qualified members of the English governing class.
† **b.** *concr.* A person receiving out-door relief. *Obs.*
1904 *Westm. Gaz.* 22 Apr. 3/2 Still worse is the case of the aged 'out-relief', with his 3*s*. a week.

outride, *sb.* Add: **3.** In the writings of Gerard Manley Hopkins: (see quots.).
1880 G. M. HOPKINS *Let.* 22 Dec. (1935) 41 By means of the 'outrides' or looped half-feet..I secure a strong effect of double rhythm, of a second movement in the verse besides the primary and essential one. *c* **1883** —— *Poems* (1918) 5 Two licences are natural to Sprung Rhythm. The one is rests, as in music... The other is *hangers* or *outrides*, that is one, two, or three slack syllables added to a foot and not counting in the nominal scanning. **1934** C. DAY LEWIS *Hope for Poetry* ii. 10 What Hopkins called 'outrides', unstressed syllables occasionally placed before the stressed ones at the beginning of the foot. **1973** *Studies Eng. Lit.: Eng. Number* (Tokyo) 24 In certain of the poems written in sprung rhythm..'outrides' appear to be extensively used, and these Hopkins has taken great pains to indicate... Without the help of these signals, there is little chance of the reader being able to distinguish between an 'outriding' and an ordinary foot.

outride, *v.* Add: **2. c.** To ride out of or beyond.
1903 J. L. WESTON tr. *Sir Gawain at the Grail Castle* I. 15 In that one night had he outridden Britain and all that country.
4. (Example in Canad. use.)
1964 *Albertan* (Calgary) July 15/6 He's driving two chuckwaggon outfits [and] will probably outride for a couple more.
5. *trans.* To keep cattle from going beyond (a tract of land) by riding along the boundaries of it. *U.S.* (? *Obs.*).
1874 J. G. MCCOY *Hist. Sk. Cattle Trade* 375 He does not herd his cattle but designates certain bounds within which the employees permit the stock to range at will. This manner of holding stock is termed 'out riding' the country.

outrider. Add: **2. b.** *spec.* A fellow of New College, Oxford, accompanying the Warden on an official visitation of the estates of the college. Hence **outri·dership.**
1901 RASHDALL & RAIT *New College, Oxf.* 187 The outridership..was claimed by two Fellows,..who both wanted to accompany the Warden on progress. *Ibid.* 251 The Warden (or Sub-warden) accompanied by a Fellow known as 'Out-rider'..and the Steward, visit the farms on some part of the College estates. **1952** A. H. SMITH *New College, Oxf.* iii. 47 An out-rider is still appointed each year to go with the warden on his summer progress around the estates.
5. (Further examples in *fig.* use.) *spec.* An escort mounted on a motor-cycle.
1851 H. MELVILLE *Moby Dick* II. 164 Sharks also are the invariable outriders of all slave ships crossing the Atlantic. **1939** *Sun* (Baltimore) 25 Aug. 6/4 A motorcycle out rider was killed in Vermont while escorting a troop train. **1957** *Economist* 21 Sept. 912/2 The panoply of police cars, blue lights and motorised outriders with which the Chancellor chooses to move about. **1971** *Daily Tel.* 9 Aug. 11/4 We were given the full VIP treatment, including an escort of police motor-cycle outriders all the way from Boulogne to Le Touquet. **1975** T. ALLBEURY *Special Collection* xiii. 86 Under his chin were the telltale outriders of a dewlap. **1977** *Belfast Tel.* 22 Feb. 5/5 The Belfast councillors were driven through Dublin's streets in a convoy, with Gardai motorcycle outriders halting traffic so the entourage could travel speedily.
6. *U.S.* A mounted herdsman who prevents cattle from straying beyond a certain limit (see also quot. 1872).
1872 *Kansas Magazine* 319/2 Where the grower does not drive his own stock to market, the buying and driving is done by a class of speculators known in Texas as 'outriders'. **1874** J. G. MCCOY *Hist. Sk. Cattle Trade* 348 [The] trail escapes the vigilant eye and Indian cunning and proficiency of the herdsman or outrider. **1907** S. E. WHITE *Arizona Nights* I. vi. 117 We saw..the whole herd and the outriders and the mesas far away. **1939** P. A. ROLLINS *Gone Haywire* 230 Cowboys, patrolling as 'outriders' and 'line riders', had always to keep an eye on them. **1968** R. F. ADAMS *Western Words* (rev. ed.) 214/2 *Outrider*, a cowboy who rides about the range to keep a sharp lookout for anything that might happen to the detriment of his employer; also called *range rider*.
7. *U.S.* A mounted official who escorts racehorses to the starting post.
1947 *Sun* (Baltimore) 8 Nov. 11/4 Them outriders ought to get extra pay for steeplechases. **1961** ATKINSON & FREEMAN *All the Way!* iv. 50 The outriders in their red hunting coats also accompany the field. Years ago there was only one..but today there are three at several of the major tracks. *Ibid.*, One outrider stands just to the outside in front of the gate, one takes a position outside the gap, three-sixteenths down the track, and the third remains behind the gate. **1968** M. T. MALLOY *Racing Today* 42/1 A couple of other horses meanwhile may be running away with their jockeys hanging on for dear life, and with the track's red-coated outriders in hot pursuit.
8. *Canad.* 'In a chuckwagon race,..one of the four riders who load the wagon, direct the horses during the starting turns, and gallop with the outfit to the finish line' (*Dict. Canad.*).
1955 W. G. HARDY *Alberta Golden Jubilee Anthol.* 169 There are four outriders to each of the four outfits in every heat. When the starting-horn blows, one outrider holds back the team of horses fighting to be on its way. Another throws the stove in the rear of the chuckwagon. The remaining two pitch the flies and poles into the covered wagon. **1958** *Encycl. Canadiana* IX. 393 A new feature introduced in the 1923 [Calgary] stampede was the chuckwagon race... Each wagon is pulled by a four-horse team..and each has its outriders. **1964** *Albertan* (Calgary) 7 July 1/2 Three crack-ups..saw all drivers, outriders and horses come out unscathed.

outriding, *vbl. sb.* Add to def.: Also, *U.S.*, the work of an outrider (sense *6); a spell of executing this.
1907 C. E. MULFORD *Bar-20* 6 Skinny Thompson took his turn at outriding one morning after the season's round-up. **1926** D. BRANCH *Cowboy & his Interpreters* 94 Groups of cowboys rode on inspection trips, 'out-ridings', to locate the scattered groups of cattle, to note the condition of grass and water [etc.]. **1968** R. F. ADAMS *Western Words* (rev. ed.) 214/2 *Outriding*, performing the duties of an *outrider*..; also called *range riding*.

outriding, *ppl. a.* Add: Applied to a syllable in the poetry of Gerard Manley Hopkins: see *OUTRIDE *sb.* 3.
1877 G. M. HOPKINS *Let.* 21 Aug. (1935) 45 There are no outriding feet in the *Deutschland*. An outriding foot is.. a recognized extra-metrical effect; it is and it is not part of the metre..not being counted... Outriding feet belong to counterpointed verse. *c* **1883** —— *Poems* (1918) 5 These outriding half feet or hangers are marked by a loop underneath. **1953** W. H. GARDNER in G. M. Hopkins *Sel. Poems & Prose* 224 The rhythm is sprung and outriding. **1973** [see *OUTRIDE *sb.* 3].

outrigger. Add: **4. b.** An addition to a trailer to increase its carrying capacity.
1971 M. TAK *Truck Talk* 113 *Outriggers*, the short brackets that extend, if needed, from the sides of a lowboy trailer. **1973** *Amer. Speech 1969* XLIV. 207 *Outrigger*, device used for increasing the width of a trailer.
5. b. *Aeronaut.* A supporting structure that projects outwards from the main part of an aircraft or spacecraft.
1909 *Flight* 27 Mar. 176/2 One of the most characteristic features of the machine is that derived from the appearance of the outrigger framework which carries the biplane elevator in front and the rigid biplane tail behind. **1922** *Encycl. Brit.* XXX. 20/2 In the pusher..the controlling surfaces are carried on an open frame ('outriggers') in front, at the rear, or in both positions. **1928** CHATFIELD & TAYLOR *Airplane & its Engine* xiii. 235 The tail surfaces of the flying boat are usually carried on the stern of the hull, but sometimes..they are supported on outriggers, or booms. **1969** *Times* 3 June (Moon Suppl.) p. iii/7 The clusters were mounted on outriggers 90° apart on the ascent stage. **1978** *Aeroplane Monthly* Jan. 6/1 The new W.11 [helicopter] used the same engine and transmission as the original design, but married them to a skeletal fuselage and outriggers with three three-bladed rotors.
8. *outrigger canoe.*
1908 E. J. BANFIELD *Confessions of Beachcomber* II. i. 238 The grandfathers of the blacks of Hinchinbrook Island..have been popularly credited with the art of making out-rigger canoes, such as were common a few miles to the north. **1967** J. SEVERSON *Great Surfing* 155 *Outrigger canoe*, a canoe employing the use of an outrigger. **1974** 'M. ALLEN' *Super Tour* (1975) ix. 322 The [Fijian] natives..rode in outrigger canoes.

ou·tright, *v.* *U.S. Sports slang.* [f. OUTRIGHT *adv.* (*adj.*).] *trans.* To give (a baseball player) a free transfer.
1975 *Cleveland* (Ohio) *Plain Dealer* 6 Apr. 9-C/1 It was very difficult when Joe was outrighted to Oklahoma City on Saturday. **1975** *New Yorker* 23 June 46/1 The Pirates had finally released him late in March ('outrighted' him, in baseball parlance).

outroar, *sb.* Delete *rare* and add examples.
1845 *Dublin Rev.* June 314 'God strike you, Satan' was the Reformer's outroar. **1891** G. MEREDITH *One of our Conq.* II. ii. 28 As it were, the towering wood-work of the cathedral organ in quake under emission of its multitudinous outroar. **1955** V. CRONIN *Wise Man from West* vii. 139 On the day of a solar eclipse..all the inhabitants of China were assembled by townships, prostrate on the ground, to frighten away with cymbals, drums and an outroar of yelling the monster that would otherwise swallow the sun.

out-room. Delete † *Obs.* and add examples in N. Amer. use. Also *attrib.*
1865 A. D. WHITNEY *Gayworthys* ii. 21 Gersham..ran up and down the out-room staircase. *Ibid.* 28 As she came into the out-room again. **1929** J. SHELTON *Salt-Box House* xii. 88 The floors were..sprinkled with white sea sand, that on the 'out-rooms' being swept lightly in fanciful patterns by brooms. **1971** *Islander* (Victoria, B.C.) 22 Aug. 5/2 He has a basement and an outroom full of bottles waiting to receive attention.

out-run, *sb.* Add: **3.** *spec.* The outward run of a sheepdog.
1938 [see *FETCH *sb.*[1] 1]. **1955** [see *LIFT *sb.*[2] 5 i]. **1973** *Country Life* 25 Oct. 1292/1 The collie's gathering outrun follows a wide curving natural cast..and ends behind the sheep.
4. [G. *auslauf*.] In *Skiing*: see quots.
1913 F. H. HARRIS *Dartmouth out o' Doors* 101 The 'outrun'—the level stretch at the foot of the hill on which the jumpers check their speed. **1957** *Encycl. Brit.* XX. 749/2 He leans far forward over the points of his skis with arms outstretched, planing his body to increase his distance, lands with a slight give to his knees and speeds onto the outrun. **1963** *Amer. Speech* XXXVIII. 206 *Out run*, in general, the bottom end of a ski run. In ski-jumping, the distance between the take-off and the landing point. **1974** *Encycl. Brit. Macropædia* XVI. 836/2 After the slope levels off, the jumper stops by turning on the outrun.

outscape, *sb.* Add: **2.** *rare.* [SCAPE *sb.*[3]] The outward appearance of a region. Cf. *INSCAPE *sb.*
1868 G. M. HOPKINS *Jrnls. & Papers* (1959) 184 In the afternoon we took the train for Paris and passed through a country of pale grey rocky hills of a strong and simple outscape.

outsco·re, *v.* [OUT- 18.] *trans.* In various sports and games: to score more than; to surpass in scoring.
1958 *Times* 17 Oct. 20/1 Keenan..then settled down to outscore the Canadian consistently. **1960** E. W. SWANTON *W. Indies Revisited* ii. 24 Nurse..actually out-scored Sobers, who found himself humorously slow-clapped. **1968** *Globe & Mail* (Toronto) 5 Feb. 17/2 In other games yesterday, Brampton Rockets outscored Aurora Tigers 8–7 and league-leading Dixie Beehives edged North York Rangers 3–2. **1968** [see *PACE *v.* 5]. **1977** *Daily Mirror* 16 Mar. 30/4, I thought Mo outscored Dagge by at least five punches to one throughout most of the fight.

outseg (autse·g), *v.* *U.S. colloq.* [f. OUT- 18 + *SEG, abbrev. of *SEGREGATIONIST.] *trans.* To support or advocate a more segregationist policy than (someone else).
1967 *Time* 13 Oct. 19 Governors Spiro Agnew of Maryland and Winthrop Rockefeller of Arkansas won office even though their Democratic opponents 'outsegged' them. **1970** *Manch. Guardian Weekly* 4 Apr. 14 Brewer.. acquired a reputation as an effective administrator, and, most important, he has no intention of being 'Out-segged' by Wallace. **1970** M. PEI *Words in Sheep's Clothing* xvii. 166 'Segregation', a word that has given rise to such slang abbreviations as 'seg' and 'to outseg'. (Someone was once described as 'outsegging' Wallace.)

outsell, *v.* **2.** (Later examples.)
1961 Webster s.v., Nonfiction..continues to outsell fiction in the bookstores—*Publishers' Weekly.* **1968** *Globe & Mail* (Toronto) 17 Feb. 40 (Advt.), Again in 1967, Islington Plymouth outsold every metro Plymouth dealer. **1976** *National Observer* (U.S.) 10 Apr. 3/1 Washington outsold the Soviet Union, its nearest rival in the arms business, by almost two to one in 1974. **1977** *Times* 29 Dec. 17/1 A fine car found itself being outsold on its home ground by Continental competitors.

outsetting, *vbl. sb.* Add: **1.** (Later examples.)
1903 W. B. Yeats *In Seven Woods* 42 It's time to build up Emain that was burned At the outsetting of these wars. **1909** *Tablet* 17 Apr. 606/1 The start was made from Blois a few days later, as strange an outsetting as ever was made by a fighting army.
3. What is outside the self. *rare.*
1880 G. M. Hopkins *Sermons & Devotional Writings* (1959) 127 This applies to the universal mind or being too; it will have its inset and its outsetting; only that the outsetting includes all things, with all of which it is in some way..identified.

outshoot, *sb.* Add: **4.** *Baseball.* = *Outcurve 1.
1887 *Courier-Jrnl.* (Louisville, Kentucky) 5 May 6/3 He has a queer drop and out-shoot on which McQuaid failed to give him strikes. **1903** R. H. Barbour *Weatherby's Inning* 230 Then followed an out-shoot and a drop, neither of which did Joe take to. **1911** W. Patten *Bk. Baseball* 63/1 The plain horizontal outshoot, by the way, is no more in fashion. **1972** B. Shaw *Pitching* v. 86 Years ago, terms like 'drops', 'downer', 'out-shoot' were used to describe the curve ball.

outshot, *sb.* Add: **1.** (Later examples.)
1957 E. E. Evans *Irish Folk Ways* v. 69 In the traditional house of the north-west..a small bed-wing—the outshot or *cailleach*—projects out from one of the side-walls at the chimney end of the kitchen. **1961** M. W. Barley *Eng. Farmhouse & Cottage* II. iii. 88 Sometimes the third room is called 'the room below the entry'; in other cases it is a 'backend', like the backhouse in East Anglia. In two cases it is an 'outend', presumably an outshot. **1975** *New Society* 14 Aug. 363/2 The rubble-walled, barrel-roofed, thatched cottage [in rural Ireland] with end chimney and no division, but with a projection or 'outshot' for the bed—a feature of the western and northern fringes.
3. b. (Examples.)
1880 J. Dunbar *Pract. Papermaker* 13 Fines, Seconds, Thirds, Cords both dark and light, Outshots, Prints, and the various qualities of Hemp and Jute Bagging. **1883** R. Haldane *Workshop Receipts* (Ser. 2) 389/1 Fines consist of fine white cottons; seconds, soiled white cottons;..outshots, good, strong, and sound rags. **1937** E. J. Labarre *Dict. Paper* 171/2 *Outshots*, a class of canvas or low white cottons found among rags.

outshout, *v.* Add: (Later examples.) Also *fig.*
1934 T. N. Wilder *Heaven's my Destination* ix. 165 The hold-up man finally outshouted them: 'Say, shut up, you two! What's the idea?.. I'm not fooling.' **1962** R. P. Jhabvala *Get Ready for Battle* ii. 105 But Mala outshouted them both and..shut the door behind them. **1962** *Spectator* 24 Aug. 272/3 Ronald Fraser..outshouts the rest of the cast. **1971** *Daily Tel.* (Colour Suppl.) 8 Jan. 15/4 It is still too early to say whether the voices calling for a new airways system will outshout those in favour of improving the present set up. **1976** *New Yorker* 15 Nov. 131/1 The story of Demosthenes, who learned to speak clearly by out-shouting the surf through a mouthful of pebbles.

outsho·ve, *v.* [Out- 18.] *trans.* To outdo or surpass in shoving; to shove harder than.
1938 D. Runyon *Furthermore* vii. 142 Then the next thing anybody knows, the Yales outshove the Harvards, and now the game is over. **1960** *Times* 29 Feb. 3/3 Often they outshoved the French pack. **1963** *Times* 11 Mar. 3/5 With the Irish forwards outshoving Wales in the tight and felling all in their path in the loose, Wales were unable to free themselves of anxiety of some sort.

ou·tshut, var. Outshot *sb.* 1.
1624 in S. O. Addy *Gloss. Words Sheffield* (1888) 167 Richard Staniforth 2 out shutts in lease, iiijs. **1637** *Ibid.*, Sisley Bagshaw widow holdeth at will the chiefe dwelling house belonging to Aslopp Farme with the barnes and out shuts one parcell of the demesnes by the yearly rent of £6. 8s. 4d. **1943** H. J. Massingham *Men of Earth* iii. 26 A limestone village..with stone-slats to the roofs and even the byres, outshuts and barns. **1945** —— *Wisdom of Fields* v. 94 We were in his outshut, and I sat, half-frozen and half-choked by the fog, watching him [*sc.* a basketer].

outside. Add: **A.** *sb.* **3. b.** In isolated regions of Northern Canada and Alaska: the world outside these regions, esp. as an area of settlement and civilization.
1827 in *Beaver* (Winnipeg) (1927) Dec. 141 He was to bring in the last letters from outside which we could expect until next spring. **1898** *Yukon Midnight Sun* (Dawson, Yukon Territory) 11 June 5/2 Many of these are men who have just arrived from the outside. **1904** J. Lynch *Three Yrs. Klondike* 54 On September 22 the last boat left for the 'outside' *viâ* the Lakes and Skagway. **1941** G. de M. Poncins *Kabloona* 13 Only the Arctic existed for them; and everything that lay below the Mackenzie River, was to them the remote, the virtually non-existent 'Outside'. **1968** R. M. Patterson *Finlay's River* 108 From there the survey party travelled with the horses, passing over the Wolverines in the first snow, headed for Fort St. James and 'the outside'. **1972** *Globe & Mail* (Toronto) 5 Dec. 35/1 He believes the story of Old Crow is valuable because it also shows how little people in The Outside—the rest of Canada in Yukon language—understand of the situation inside the territory.
c. *Austral.* The unsettled areas in the interior or bush.
1888 'R. Boldrewood' *Robbery under Arms* I. vii. 95 Dick Dawson came in from outside, and he said things are shocking bad; all the frontage bare already, and the water drying up. **1949** *Geogr. Mag.* Feb. 371 Rural life offers you such terms as *backblocks, outback* and *outside*, meaning remote, inland country. **1959** Baker *Drum* 132 *Outside*, unsettled districts in the interior or bush.
d. *slang.* The world out of prison; also the world out of the Army, civilian life.
1903 'J. Flynt' *Rise of R. Clowd* ii. 80 A boy in a Reform School with a 'plant' on the 'outside' takes a high place among his companions. **1919** D. G. Rowse *Doughboy Dope* 9 A is the Army at that stage of your young life when you were on what the Army calls 'the outside'. **1933** *Amer. Speech* VIII. III. 26/2 'Whitey', who escaped three times from solitary confinement clear to the outside, was an acknowledged eel. **1965** C. D. B. Bryan *P. S. Wilkinson* 369, I never asked..what you did on the outside. **1972** C. Drummond *Death at Bar* ii. 56 Kath hasn't been having it so good, what with a couple of worthless sons who haven't the sense to keep on the outside.
e. In Surfing: see quots.
1963 *Surfing Yearbk.* 42/2 *Outside*, surfing area past the breaking surf. **1963** *Pix* 28 Sept. 62/3 *Outside*, the surfing area outside the breaking wave.
6. (Earlier and later examples.)
1789 J. Woodforde *Diary* 13 June (1927) III. 114 For the remaining part of our fare paid..for 1 outside 12/0. *a* **1800** in *Norfolk Fair* (1970) Nov. 31/7 This Coach from Norwich to London by Newmarket every Day Convey 8 Insides..and 6 Outsides in the most Pleasant And Agreeable Stile. **1902** *Chambers's Jrnl.* Nov. 715/1 The 'George' at Grantham is still..one of the best inns in England, as it was when these two prudent 'outsides' left the Yorkshire coach and 'turned in' there. **1914** 'I. Hay' *Lighter Side School Life* vi. 152 He was called at half-past two..and by three o'clock was off as an 'outside' upon the Tally-Ho Coach.
b. = Outsider 2.
1898 [see *behind *sb.* 2 b]. **1899** *Captain* II. 186/1, I headed out to the right, [and] saw our outside get it. **1906** *Field* 13 Oct. 610/1 Their outsides showed so crude a conception of passing that [etc.]. **1927** *Observer* 21 Aug. 18/3 The team are young and play attractive football, with a clever set of outsides who combine well. **1963** *Times* 23 Feb. 3/1 Although their forwards were playing such a solid game the Westminster outsides were too slow to beat their opposite numbers.
8. Short for *outside paddle-wheel* on a river steamboat.
1876 'Mark Twain' *Tom Sawyer* 29 Come ahead on the stabboard! Stop her! Let your outside turn over slow. **1894** —— in *Century Mag.* May 19 Set her back on de outside... Come ahead on de inside.
B. *adj.* **1.** *outside (jaunting) car* (earlier examples); *outside passenger*, one who travels on the outside of a conveyance.
c **1810** W. Hickey *Mem.* (1960) 326 One of the stage-coaches, with a number of outside passengers..frightened our horse. **1815** Outside passenger [in Dict.]. **1829** [see Jaunting-car]. **1849** W. Allingham *Diary* 30 June (1907) 49 Our party took leave and mounted a back outside-car in Gloucester Street. **1849** Dickens *Dav. Copp.* (1850) v. 51 The story of my supposed appetite getting wind among the outside passengers, they were merry upon it. **1874** 'G. Ramsay' *Thomas Grant* i. 23 They drove up on an outside car to the quays.
2. a. (Earlier and later examples of *outside world.*)
In some uses indistinguishable from sense 3.
a **1902** S. Butler *Way of all Flesh* (1903) lxxx. 366 Days before those in which he had begun to bruise himself against the great outside world. **1926** Galsworthy *Silver Spoon* I. iii. 22 Our trade-unionists despise the outside world. They've never seen it. **1947** E. F. Russell in Aldiss & Harrison *Decade 1940s* (1975) 168 He..looked out through the dome... The outside world slumbered. **1969** *Times* 9 Jan. 4/5 They [*sc.* the Hutterites]..live in almost complete isolation from their neighbours and the outside world. **1976** *Listener* 29 July 104/2 All of us [blacks] will want to see blacks on television. The outside world will be astonished at the talent we have. **1976** *Norwich Mercury* 19 Nov. 2 Mr Sims finished his comments with a reference to the outside world's contact with the school—the wide range of evening classes available, [etc.].
c. *spec.* of a water closet: situated outside the house, building, etc.
1939 M. Spring Rice *Working-Class Wives* iv. 73 Mrs. P. of Glasgow... Under the drawbacks of her house she says 'Outside lavatory, (used by six families.) Public house at close which is objectionable [etc.].' **1943** *Our Towns* (Women's Group on Public Welfare) iii. 88 The outside closets are generally much less well kept than the inside ones...The majority of houses have outside W.C.'s only. **1959** B. J. Farmer *Murder Next Year* ii. 7 The keys of the house had been left in the outside w.c. **1960** P. Hastings *Sandals for my Feet* I. i. 13 I'm tired of..the smell of damp and that filthy outside loo. **1974** P. Highsmith *Ripley's Game* ii. 11 The little brick structure, formerly an outside toilet, that served as a tool shed.
3. b. In Northern Canada and Alaska: belonging to or obtained from another part of the world, esp. from the settled or urbanized parts.
1896 C. Whitney *On Snow-Shoes to Barren Grounds* 40 Gairdner had annoyed me a great deal, and no doubt we had worried him not a little, breaking in upon the even and lethargic tenor of his monotonous life with our 'outside' (as the great world is called by the denizens of this lone land) hustling ways. **1904** J. Lynch *Three Yrs. Klondike* 141 The leader is always a small 'outside' dog, usually of the Scotch collie breed. **1922** H. Footner *Huntress* 189 No bannock and sow-belly; no sir! Real raised outside bread and genuine cow-butter from the mission. **1958** P. Berton *Klondike Fever* ix. 307 Expense!.. Don't show your ignorance by using that cheap Outside word. **1977** *Globe & Mail* (Toronto) 8 Jan. 11/7 By special arrangement, one outside reporter will attend the dance.
6. Special collocations: **outside broadcast** (see quot. 1941); **outside broadcaster,** (*a*) one who makes or supervises an outside broadcast; (*b*) an outside contributor to broadcasting; **outside broadcasting,** the action of making an outside broadcast; **outside cabin,** a cabin with a window or porthole on the side of the ship; **outside chance,** a very unlikely chance; **outside forward,** in association football and hockey, either of the two players, called the outside left or right (see below), of the forward line; **outside half** = *fly-half* (*Fly *sb.*[2] 8); **outside interest,** an interest not directly or necessarily connected with one's everyday life or interests; **outside job** *slang*, a crime committed in a house, etc., by a person not connected or associated with the household or building concerned; **outside leaf,** an outer leaf on a vegetable, esp. cabbage; **outside left, right,** in association football and hockey, a player playing on the extreme left or right of the forward line; **outside line,** a telephonic connection with an external exchange (cf. *Line *sb.*[2] 1 e); **outside man** *U.S. slang*, one involved in any of various special roles in a confidence trick or robbery; **outside right** (see *outside left* above).
1927 *B.B.C. Handbk. 1928* 274 *Outside broadcast*, a broadcast item taking place at some point other than the studio. **1937** *Discovery* Nov. 331/1 Outside broadcasts of entertainments and public events can be readily arranged. **1941** *B.B.C. Gloss. Broadcasting Terms* 22 *Outside broadcast* (*abbrev.* O.B.), programme originating elsewhere than in the studio of a broadcasting organization; (specifically broadcast description of an event in progress. **1953** *News Chron.* 2 June 3/5 It is a long way from 1937, when B.B.C) television mounted its first outside broadcast from Hyde Park Corner on another Coronation day. **1972** I. Hamilton *Thrill Machine* xv. 63 He had brought the outside broadcast truck. **1971** R. Lewis *Error of Judgment* i. 10 The technicians were already bundling out of the van, unloading..mysterious television equipment. Outside broadcasters. **1972** P. Black *Biggest Aspidistra* III. ii. 164 Gilbert Harding..began on the entertainment side of radio as an outside broadcaster. **1929** *Melody Maker* Apr. 363/2 Outside broadcasting is now not so much worth your while. **1937** *Discovery* Feb. 43/2 Much of the popularity of television will be linked up with the development of outside broadcasting. **1972** P. Black *Biggest Aspidistra* I. iii. 27 In the early days the bands played mostly in clubs and hotels, and so were part of outside broadcasting. **1963** Outside cabin [see *inside *adj.* a]. **1966** *Guardian* 29 Oct. 5/5 Two-berth outside cabins with private shower and w.c. **1971** 'A. Garve' *Late Bill Smith* i. 33 The Greek motor vessel *Circe* specially built as a luxury yacht for a limited number of privileged passengers; fully air-conditioned and stabilised; swimming pool and two bars; all outside cabins. **1909** *Daily Chron.* 11 Jan. 4/6 The chance that the right marriage of poetry and music should come is an outside one. **1928** R. A. Knox *Footsteps at Lock* xiv. 135 By an outside chance you might find it lying about somewhere. **1930** A. P. Herbert *Water Gipsies* xx. 300 Here she was, risking everything..going all out for an outside chance. **1973** 'D. Rutherford' *Kick Start* viii. 169 He had an outside chance of lifting the moon stones from under Hadim's nose. **1897** *Encycl. Sport* I. 517/1 (*Hockey*) Of the two outside forwards, he on the right has much the easier position in which to play. **1898** J. Goodall *Assoc. Football* 18, I would not tell the outside forward that it is his duty to centre the ball. **1935** *Encycl. Sports* 289/1 (*Association Football*) The throw-in is usually done by a half-back or by an outside forward. **1949** *Rugby League Football* ('Know the Game' Series) 8 Stand off half back or outside half. **1969** *Programme* (Llanelli *v.* Swansea 1 Apr.) 6 Gwyn Ashby. Maswr. Outside-half. **1971** *Guardian* 22 Feb. 16/5 Dick Cowman ..gave a superb exhibition of outside-half play. **1860** J. W. Palmer tr. *Michelet's Love* IV. vii. 235 It is the fault of the labor, the business, the outside interests and the cases with which I have been occupied. **1925** R. Hall *Saturday Life* xxix. 301 Could two deeply-loving and devoted people tolerate outside interests? **1974** R. Rendell *Face of Trespass* ii. 26 What you need..is some outside interest, something to take you out of yourself. **1925** A. Christie *Secret of Chimneys* xii. 120 Either he was killed by someone in the house, and that someone unlatched the window after I had gone to make it look like an outside job..or else..I'm lying. **1928** Wodehouse *Money for Nothing* v. 104 It's got to look like an outside job. **1931** A. Christie *Sittaford Mystery* xi. 92 The police are quite certain that this is not what they call an 'outside job'—I mean, it wasn't a burglar. The broken open window was faked. **1972** Outside job [see *inside job* s.v. *inside *a.* e]. **1739** E. Smith *Compl. Housewife* (ed. 9) 37 Take a well-shap'd Cabbage, peel off some of the outside leaves. **1747** H. Glasse *Art of Cookery* iv. 57 Take a fine White-heart Cabbage..half boil it..take great Care not to break off any of the the outside Leaves. **1861** Mrs. Beeton *Bk. Househ. Managem.* 560 *Boiled cabbage*... Pick off all the dead outside leaves. **1960** *Good Housek. Cookery Bk.* (rev. ed.) 217/1 Wash the chicory and remove the outside leaves. *Ibid.* 218/1 *Leeks*... Remove the coarse outside leaves. **1900** *Football Who's Who* 134 Cassidy, Joseph, Manchester City (outside left). **1905**

GIBSON & PICKFORD *Assoc. Football* I. 161 Every one knows Alec Smith. He's the outside left of the Rangers. **1960** B. LIDDELL *My Soccer Story* xvi. 102 To get down to my final choice at outside-left, I vote for Peter McParland, an unorthodox type of winger with a wonderful turn of speed. **1965** *Men's Hockey* ('Know the Game' Series) (rev. ed.) 24/2 The outside right when about to pass to his left will find it more convenient to have the ball a little in front of his left foot. The outside left, however, must make a half turn to the right when passing right [etc.]. **1975** *Liverpool Echo* (Football ed.) 1 Feb. 3/1 There seems to have been some debate as to who was the Liverpool outside left before Billy Liddell. **1944** Outside line [see *LINE *sb.*[2] 1 e]. **1962** E. S. GARDNER *Case of Blonde Bonanza* (1967) x. 117 You can't get an outside line on these phones unless they connect you. **1972** D. BLOODWORTH *Any Number can Play* xx. 203 Ivansong seized the telephone (which..was automatically switched to an outside line). **1926** J. BLACK *You can't Win* ix. 111 He..made his living serving as 'target' or outside man, for the yegg mobs that preyed on country banks. **1937** *N.Y. Times* 22 Dec. 22 *Outside man*, a spy under a cover, but not masquerading as an employe of a plant. **1938** F. D. SHARPE *Sharpe of Flying Squad* xiv. 151 She was acting as look out or 'outside man' for two expert safe breakers. **1947** *Amer. Speech* XXII. 169/1 *Outside-man*, the member of a *shell-mob* who locates promising suckers on the lot, steers them to the game, and assists in the play. **1890** C. W. ALCOCK *Football: Assoc. Game* 48 The outside-right should not be more than eight or ten yards beyond him. **1974** *Sunday Mail* 14 Apr. 39/1 Both goals..were scored by the outside rights.

C. *adv.* **1. b.** In Northern Canada and Alaska: in the settled or urbanized areas outside these regions; abroad.

1898 F. RUSSELL *Explor. Far North* 80 To 'go in', by the way, is to descend the Athabasca; to return to civilization is to 'go outside'. **1923** F. WALDO *Down Mackenzie through Gt. Lone Land* 246, I had thought that life beyond the 65th parallel or so was life beyond the pale; but I was now to learn that the Arctic Circle is the inner circle, and the real outsider is—of course—the one who lives 'Outside'. **1945** R. W. SERVICE *Ploughman of Moon* 321 If I had been Outside it would have taken me five years to save a thousand dollars. **1955** *Whitehorse* (Yukon Territory) *Star* 24 Feb. 2/1 One of the outstanding characteristics of the Yukon is the general indifference to what is going on Outside. **1970** *Islander* (Victoria, B.C.) 1 Nov. 13/3 Sam Otto spent 14 years in the Barren Lands and Northwest Territories, without going outside once.

c. *Austral.* In the interior or bush. *rare.*

1911 C. E. W. BEAN '*Dreadnought' of Darling* xxxv. 317 But, be the 'inside' country never so tame and densely populated, there will always be a huge stretch of country 'outside' which cannot by any known means be closely settled.

d. *slang.* Out of prison; in civilian life.

1919 W. LANG *Sea-Lawyer's Log* ix. 108 You *got* to 'ave some bloody religion in the Navy. Now, wot church did you go to outside? **1937** *Research Stud.* (Washington State Coll., Pullman) V. 19 A boy entering this institution [*sc.* a reformatory] learns more bad habits than he would ever think of learning out side. **1961** PARTRIDGE *Dict. Slang* Suppl. 1210/1, I don't care what you were 'outside'; you're in the Andrew now, so don't forget it, or you'll be in the rattle.

e. In Surfing: see quots.

1962 T. MASTERS *Surfing made Easy* 65 *Outside*, out past the breaking waves, or at the furthest break. **1962** *Austral. Women's Weekly* 24 Oct. (Suppl.) 3/3 *Outside* or *out the back*, a long way out at sea, beyond the first line of breakers.

3. a. (Further examples.)

1869 *Galaxy* June 831 Don't let's get outside of more'n a bottle apiece, and that plain whiskey. **1886** [see *GET *v.* 40*]. **1915** J. WEBSTER *Dear Enemy* 174 He likes to dine outside of the family vault. **1943** G. GREENE *Ministry of Fear* I. ii. 29 Murderers..are very, very seldom..gentlemen. Outside of story-books. **1975** *Nature* 20 Mar. p. xx (Advt.), These books are..distributed outside of the U.S.A. and Canada by Academic Press. **1976** *Gramophone* Nov. 903/2, I was able to spend some time in their CD-4 four-channel disc cutting room—the most important such facility outside of Japan.

b. For *U.S. colloq.* read *colloq.* (orig. *U.S.*). Add earlier and later examples.

1859 A. L. ELWYN *Gloss. Supposed Americanisms* 82 *Outside*, this word is frequently used by writers in newspapers in a sense not known to the language. In a *Ledger* of a late date, there is a phrase..'*outside* of the Secretary of War', for 'no one but that official'. **1913** R. FRY *Let.* 5 Apr. (1972) II. 367 I'm very much interested by what you said about the need of some big belief outside of art. **1968** *Listener* 22 Aug. 234/1 The only power we have is to expel a union for corruption or for following a communist or a fascist policy. Outside of that the unions pretty much take care of their own business. **1972** *New York* 8 May 62/2 Outside of a slightly annoying tendency to call all female customers 'Hon', everything about Mr. Blume inspires confidence.

ou·tside-i:nside, *a. rare.* [f. OUTSIDE *a.* + INSIDE *a.*] Of or pertaining to both the outside and the inside.

1930 R. GRAVES *Ten Poems More* 11 Neat outside-inside, neat below-above Hermaphrodising love. **1951** M. MCLUHAN *Mech. Bride* (1967) 35/2 It can be picture-framed by a Pond's ad for the 'special outside-inside face treatment'.

outsider. Add: **1.** (Further examples, with varying degrees of specificness.) Also *attrib.*

1897 J. MCCARTHY *Gladstone's Life* xxvii. 90/2 The outsider class..quarreled with Mr. Gladstone because he was always giving them a surprise. **1912** T. E. LAWRENCE *Let.* 10 Feb. (1938) 136 About the Jerablus seals:—I can't give you those, only the five outsiders: the Jerablus ones were bought [etc.]. **1935** *Amer. Speech* X. 271/2 *Outsiders*, buyers who ship special kinds of livestock to other markets. **1944** F. BROWN in B. W. Aldiss *Introd. SF* (1964) 69 No one knew who the Outsiders were..or from what far galaxy they came. **1958** *Amer. Speech* XXXIII. 167 (*Australian Cattle Lingo*) *Outsider*,..a stray. **1974** *Nat. Geographic* Jan. 114/2 The fishermen talked shyly in the presence of an outsider from upalong. (An 'outsider' is any off-islander, including even other Canadians.) **1977** *Globe & Mail* (Toronto) 5 July 8/3 So far, he says, the inquiry has been lucky enough to be seen as a unit, not as two Yukoners—one for whites and one for Indians led by an outsider.

b. (Earlier examples.) Also *transf.*, a person who fails to gain admission to the 'ring'; a person who habitually backs outsiders in a race; *rank outsider*, (*a*) an outsider at very long odds; (*b*) a person who is considered socially inferior (cf. sense 1 c below).

1836 R. S. SURTEES *Let.* in A. Mathews *Mem. Charles Mathews* (1839) IV. ix. 185 An unfortunate outsider, called Astracan. **1836** *Spirit of Times* 5 Mar. 20/1 The Brother to Maria, the Babel colt, and Taishteer, are a shade worse, owing, no doubt, to the money laid out upon Brother to Nell Gwynne. No change amongst the outsiders. **1845** *Ibid.* 31 May 158 The 'outsiders' won 'smartly' on both races, and the staunch friends of Fashion, who have backed her 'all through', have 'got hunk' and a good deal over. **1855** J. R. PLANCHÉ *New Haymarket Spring Meeting* in *Extravaganzas* (1879) V. 1. 94 Which are the favourites, and which outsiders? **1871** R. A. PROCTOR *Light Sci.* (Ser. 1) 288 The success of a rank outsider will be described as 'a misfortune to backers'. **1890** BARRÈRE & LELAND *Dict. Slang* II. 170 *Rank outsider* (common), a vulgar fellow, a cad. From a racing term applied to a horse outside the rank. **1902** FARMER & HENLEY *Slang* V. 116/1 *Outsider*,..(racing), a person who fails to gain admission to the 'ring' from pecuniary or other causes. **1908** *Magnet* I. 1. 8/2, I ask you if you ever saw such a rank outsider in all your natural?

c. A person who is isolated from or does not 'fit' into conventional society either through choice or on account of some social, intellectual, etc., reason. Often deprecating. *spec.* In literary criticism: the archetypal artist or intellectual seen as a person isolated from the rest of society. Also *attrib.*

1907 'I. HAY' *Pip* x. 322 'I didn't think you ought to play [golf] with him,' said Pip coolly. 'He's an utter outsider.' **1908** *Magnet* I. 1. 7/1 'You rotten outsider!' said Bulstrode, in tones of concentrated rage. 'You're not fit to be at a decent school.' **1913** H. KEPHART *Our Southern Highlanders* xiii. 294 A bastard is a woods-colt or an outsider. **1946** S. GILBERT tr. *Camus's L'Étranger* (*title*) The Outsider. **1956** C. WILSON *Outsider* i. 14 Many great artists have none of the characteristics of the Outsider. Shakespeare, Dante, Keats were all apparently normal and socially well-adjusted. **1957** *Times Lit. Suppl.* 25 Oct. 640/1 His [*sc.* C. Wilson's] original contribution was simply the Outsider gimmick. **1958** [see *DOWN AND OUT *adj. phr.*]. **1958** J. RAYMOND *England's on Anvil!* 40 Like Proust the Jew, Pope the Roman Catholic son of a linen-draper was an outsider. **1959** *Times Lit. Suppl.* 1 May 261/4 It throws light on two generations of 'outsider' philosophers grappling with their own sudden emergence into the world of letters and art. **1963** *Spectator* 4 Oct. 430/1 *The City of Dreadful Night*..is Outsider poetry. **1966** C. SWEENEY *Scurrying Bush* xiv. 201, I remember an odd fellow when I was in Nigeria. Bit of an outsider, really, but do anything with snakes.

Hence **outsi·derdom, outsi·derhood,** the condition or state of being an outsider (in sense 1 c, above); **outsi·derish** *a.*, of the nature or character of an outsider; so **outsi·derishness; outsi·derism,** the theory or practice of being an outsider; **outsi·derliness,** the quality or fact of being an outsider (in sense 1 c); **outsi·derly** *a.*, characteristic of an outsider or of outsiderliness.

1956 C. WILSON *Outsider* viii. 216 He had accepted his 'Outsider-ishness', not as a symptom of some strange disease, but as a sign that his healthy soul was being suffocated in a world of trivial, shallow, corrupted fools. **1957** *Times Lit. Suppl.* 25 Oct. 640/4 That the seeds of outsiderliness are found in us all may well account for Mr. Wilson's success. **1958** *Ibid.* 28 Mar. 165/3 A final view of Mr Freund..might be that he is a sort of Colin Wilson without a theory of Outsiderdom, searching for the religious viewpoint that will include the complexities of modern science. **1958** *Listener* 26 June 1070/1 Genuine outsiderhood, as experienced by delinquents, psychotics, alcoholics, unmarried mothers, and a whole host of people who..find themselves the wrong side of the law. *Ibid.* 10 July 63/3 His 'outsiderism' made him enjoy shocking the professional scientists. **1959** *Times Lit. Suppl.* 23 Jan. 44/1 His account of that heredity is wry, humorous, and outsider-ish. His Jewish ancestry has its roots in Poland and Slovakia. *Ibid.* 4 Sept. 503/3 The outsiderly novel by Henri Barbusse, *L'Enfer*, which was the starting point of Mr. Wilson's first book. **1960** *Ibid.* 8 Apr. 221/1 Poetic abstraction and 'outsiderish' philosophical terminology. **1961** *Guardian* 23 June 9/6 The jigging of today's young is their alternative to 'outsiderism'. **1961** *John o' London's* 16 Nov. 548/2 The trouble with Outsiderdom as a philosophy is the squalid assortment of fellow-travellers it attracts. **1962** *Times Lit. Suppl.* 21 Sept. 710/2 Accompanying such pieces of outsiderly narcissism is a certain amount of fashionable philosophizing. **1966** *New Statesman* 8 July 61/1 An outsiderly Old Etonian whose rebellion against the ethics of his upbringing has driven him mad.

ou·tsize, *sb.* and *a.* [f. OUT *a.* + SIZE *sb.*[1]] **A.** *sb.* **a.** A person or thing larger than the normal or the majority; esp. a ready-made garment larger than the standard sizes. Also *transf.*

b. Greater size than normal.

1845 *Ainsworth's Mag.* VII. 213 The borrowed child being *ra*-ther an out-size..rendered Cora's carrying him a matter of difficulty. **1883, 1894** [see OUT *a.* 5]. **1902** E. NESBIT *Five Children & It* viii. 211 Robert was indeed what a draper would call an 'out-size' in boys. **1924** *Mod. Draper* II. 69 With regard to all ladies' underclothing it is necessary to keep a good assortment of outsizes. **1924** A. CHRISTIE *Man in Brown Suit* xii. 96 'I don't think he'll have any out sizes,' murmured Pagett, measuring my figure with his eye. **1933** CHESTERTON *St. Thomas Aquinas* i. 14 In the present case the outline is rather an outsize. The gown that could contain that colossal friar is not kept in stock. **1957** M. B. PICKEN *Fashion Dict.* 238/2 *Outsize*, size larger than the regular sizes; generally used for sizes larger than 46 bust. Also applied to hosiery having a top larger than average. **1970** V. GIELGUD *Candle-Holders* I. iv. 34 This impression of massive outsize was only exaggerated by the sight of George Eltham standing at the top of the flight of shallow steps which linked the drive with the great front doors.

B. *adj.* Larger than the average, usual, or stock size. Also *transf.* Also **o·utsized** *ppl. a.* Hence **outsi·zeness,** the fact or quality of being outsize.

1880 *Good Words* 46/1 He was what is sometimes called an 'outsized man'..imposing in appearance. *c* **1890** in *American Mail Order Fashions* (1961) 12 Ladies' outsize plated silk hose. **1895** *Westm. Gaz.* 20 July 2/1 She was a great outsized woman. **1904** H. G. WELLS *Food of Gods* I. ii. 19 He conceived a picture of coops and runs, outsize and still more outsize coops, and runs progressively larger. **1906** *Westm. Gaz.* 5 May 5/1 'An out-sized cat, I call him,' remarked the cook soon after his arrival. **1922** JOYCE *Ulysses* 715 A pair of outsize ladies' drawers of India mull, cut on generous lines. **1928** *Blackw. Mag.* May 709/1 A valley of utter desolation,..with an outsize snow mountain..at either end of it. **1937** AUDEN & MACNEICE *Lett. from Iceland* xii. 173 She wears an amazing woollen helmet with earflaps which combined with her goggles and general outsizeness makes her look like a piece of Archaic Greek sculptuary. **1952** *Manch. Guardian Weekly* 9 Oct. 3/4 The Republicans are undoubtedly united in an outsize bed where there is room for everybody except the few liberals who got the General [*sc.* Eisenhower] his nomination. **1958** *Times* 31 Oct. 3/5 Her voice is of a rich mezzo-soprano quality, not outsize, but certainly amply big enough for most lieder. **1974** A. WILLIAMS *Gentleman Traitor* v. 86 He..dressed in an outsize suit of white slub-silk. **1976** *Publishers Weekly* 26 Apr. 3/3 (Advt.), A massive, out-sized book of more than 800 pages.

outskirt, *sb.* **1.** For 'Now only in *pl.*' read 'Now usu. in *pl.*' and add further *sing.* examples.

1891 HARDY *Tess* I. xix. 245 The outskirt of the garden in which Tess found herself had been left uncultivated for some years. **1943** J. BETJEMAN *Eng. Cities & Small Towns* 14, I am reminded of that moving passage about a provincial suburb in Gissing's story *Fate and the Apothecary* describing, I think it must be, an outskirt of Exeter.

2. (Later example.)

a **1930** D. H. LAWRENCE *Last Poems* (1932) 46 Corpse-eaters They dwell in the outskirt fringes of nowhere.

outsmart (autsmā·ɹt), *v.* [f. OUT- 20 + SMART *a.*] *trans.* To get the better of or overcome by superior craft or ingenuity; to prove too clever for; to outwit. Also *refl.*

1926 H. C. WITWER *Roughly Speaking* iii. 95 Young Farrell seemed to have more than recovered from Ben's terrible right hand blow, for he was now doing what Pete told me was 'outsmarting' Ben. **1948** E. WAUGH *Loved One* 105 'All his stories are about the same thing—American innocence and European experience.' 'Thinks he can outsmart us, does he?' **1954** J. STEINBECK *Sweet Thursday* xxi. 131 It is such fun to outsmart a smart guy. **1957** P. FRANK *Seven Days to Never* 48 It takes a machine to outsmart a machine. **1961** 'B. WELLS' *Day Earth caught Fire* viii. 128 Hell, we're all so bloody clever at outsmarting nature. Anything you can split I can split better. **1974** J. HELLER *Something Happened* 296 'I'm going to sock you one, Daddy,' he squeals in frustration, as he feels himself outsmarted. **1975** J. F. BURKE *Death Trick* (1976) xii. 156 Like all smart crooks, he outsmarted himself. **1977** *R.A.F. News* 8–21 June 4/2 While the authorities dither and disagree on a plan of action, the beast continues his rampage of death, outsmarting every move to trap him.

outspan, *sb.*[1] (Earlier examples.)

1822 W. J. BURCHELL *Trav. S. Afr.* I. iv. 92 These *uitspan*, or *outspan places*, are, in fact, the caravanserays of the Cape. **1844** *Colburn's United Service Mag.* May 23 *Outspan*,..place of rest, where the oxen are unyoked and turned out to graze.

ou·tspeech. *rare.* [OUT- 7.] Frank or candid words; plain language or terms; outspeaking.

1919 W. DE MORGAN *Old Madhouse* 439 Outspeech would be the safest course as well as the easiest, with this girl. **1921** —— *Old Man's Youth* xxvii. 267, I was sorry a moment after for my own outspeech.

outspeed, *v.* (Later examples.)

1911 *Chambers's Jrnl.* Jan. 57/1 If the black, whirling maelstrom of a cyclone looms up before him, he will make a detour or even outspeed it. **1930** R. CAMPBELL *Adamastor* 31 Bold is he..And swift—outspeeding as he runs The corposants of Leda's sons. **1962** *Times* 28 Mar. 4/2 He had outspeeded Spinks in the early rounds. **1977** 'O. JACKS' *Autumn Heroes* viii. 112 It became clear that the truck would survive once it outsped the fire line.

outspread, *v.* Add: **3.** *intr.* To spread out, extend itself.

1906 *Westm. Gaz.* 26 June 2/3 Each young branch, outspreading in the sun, Reflects in shadow on the sod below. **1925** [see *ASILE].

outsta·ndingly, *adv.* [f. OUTSTANDING *ppl. a.* + -LY[2].] In a notable or outstanding manner; in or to an exceptional degree; remarkably or conspicuously.

1909 *Westm. Gaz.* 18 Jan. 12/2, I don't mean to say that he is an outstandingly good putter. **1922** A. S. M. HUTCHINSON *This Freedom* II. ix. 150 There was outstandingly one such day of absorption in delight..for Rosalie. **1928** *Observer* 18 Mar. 23/3 Her Wagner songs are outstandingly fine. **1961** R. J. CORSINI et al. *Role-playing in Business* ix. 142 A district manager who had been recently appointed to his position after being outstandingly successful as a store manager, found that in supervising other managers he was having a difficult time.

ou·tstate, out-state, *a. U.S.* [f. OUT- + STATE *sb.* 31 c.] **a.** Of or pertaining to a part of a state away from the largest population centre (see also quot. 1931). **b.** Coming from or living in another state; = *OUT-OF-STATE *adj. phr.*

1931 *Amer. Speech* VI. 310 'Out-state' is a compound word not yet recognized by the dictionaries but frequently used by Nebraskans, Iowans, Coloradans, and Wyomingites. University students from these states reported two meanings: out in the state away from the main city, and out in the state away from the speaker's home. **1934** *Sun* (Baltimore) 2 Nov. 2/1 The vote which Mr. Picard would have to pile up there to overcome his opponent's out-State lead. **1961** in WEBSTER, Lost the governorship because the outstate vote went against him. *Ibid.*, A gorge of unusual natural beauty which few outstate visitors see—M. W. Fishwick. **1967** *National Observer* (U.S.) 12 June 5/1 The pattern of an all-too-familiar Western movie, the one about the clever outstate cattle barons displacing the local nesters.

out-station. Add: (Further examples.) Esp. in *Austral.* and *N.Z.* use (cf. STATION *sb.* 14).

1844 *Port Phillip Patriot* 11 July 1/3 (Morris), There are four out-stations with huts, hurdles..and every convenience. **1859** F. FULLER *Five Years' Residence N.Z.* viii. 157 Out-stations are started for the shepherds, who watch separate flocks, to live in. **1862** R. HENNING *Let.* 29 Sept. (1966) 107 Another bedroom wherein reside any other members of the 'staff' who happen to be at home—more than half are always at the out-stations. **1911** C. E. W. BEAN *'Dreadnought' of Darling* xxxv. 311 When the out-station was reached, she rang up. **1944** F. CLUNE *Red Heart* 64 Southwards he trudged, came to the outstation of the Darling Downs. **1947** P. NEWTON *Wayleggo* (1949) 154 Some high country districts are so extensive that it is necessary to have a second homestead situated in some distant part of the property. Such a place is termed an 'out-station'. **1954** G. DURRELL *Three Singles to Adventure* v. 122, I prefer not to remember the ride to the outstation.

b. A subordinate branch of a business or other enterprise. Also *attrib.*

Some examples not clearly distinguishable from those in sense a.

1872 W. F. BUTLER *Great Lone Land* (ed. 2) xi. 161 About five miles from the mouth of Rainy River there was a small out-station of the Hudson Bay Company kept by a man named Morrisseau. **1962** *Housewife* (Ceylon) Feb. 8 For the benefit of our outstation members, who have borne with us for so long, we will be opening branch Associations in Kandy and Galle very shortly. **1968** D. LAMPE *Last Ditch* xii. 135 Underground broadcasting from fixed stations is untenable. The out-station operators would have been in great danger. **1970** *Guardian* 24 Aug. 14/1 Small outstations dealing with separate processes in the manufacturing cycle have been established in towns up to 20 miles from the city. **1973** *Sunday Advocate-News* (Barbados) 21 Jan. 2/5 He first appeared in uniform on normal patrol work attached to Central Station. He next underwent a short spell of duty at 'outstations' before returning to the Bridgetown Division office to take up clerical duties. **1975** *Times* 9 June 13/8 (Advt.), National Railway Museum..York..an outstation of the Science Museum London.

outstay, *v.* Add: **2. b.** To surpass in endurance.

1877 *Coursing Calendar Autumn 1876* 5 Laughter made the early points with Lady Don, but the latter fairly outstayed the dog. **1951** *Publ. Amer. Dial. Soc.* XVI. 48 *Outstay*, to be able to equal the speed of one's nearest competitors long enough to defeat them... *Outstay the field: phr.*, of a horse: to take the lead and hold it until the finish.

outstep, *sb.* Restrict *rare* to sense in Dict. and add: **2.** In full *outstep well.* An oil well drilled beyond an area already drilled in order to extend the productive area or ascertain its limits.

1947 *Economist* 5 July 40/1 Some of these wells were considerable outsteps to test the possibilities of outlying areas, thereby extending the limits of the proven producing area to the west and north. **1955** *Bull. Amer. Assoc. Petroleum Geologists* XXXIX. 1353 In the latter part of the year a contract National 80 B rig began drilling a program of outsteps to evaluate the oil find at Alcata-I. **1973** R. E. CHAPMAN *Petroleum Geol.* xii. 256 More problems arise when planning an 'out-step' well, to prove an extension to the accumulation, or to define its limits.

outstretch, *sb.* **2.** (Later example.)

1918 A. SYMONS *Cities & Sea-Coasts* iii. 312 Grass, or any soil, was but a rare interval between a broken and distracted outstretch of grey rock.

outstride, *v.* (Further examples.)

1798 JANE AUSTEN *Let.* 17 Nov. (1952) 27 Though she does not gain strength very rapidly, my expectations are humble enough not to outstride her improvements. **1972** *Times* 11 Sept. 3/1 The department outstrides those of many universities in equipment and reputation.

outstrip (autstri·p), *v.*[2] [f. OUT- 18 + STRIP *v.*[1]] *trans.* To surpass in stripping; to wear less clothing than. (With punning reference to OUTSTRIP *v.* in Dict.)

1887 *Daily News* 29 Dec. 5/3 'Yes,' replied his cynical friend, after a glance at the young lady, 'I admit that she out-strips them all.' **1897** W. C. HAZLITT *Four Generations Lit. Family* II. 155 The abridged petticoats of the ladies proceeded to an intolerable pitch; and many tried, as Byron said, to outstrip one another. **1938** H. M. ALEXANDER *Strip Tease* 19 'Then it was competition that was responsible for the peeling.' 'Yeah.' Garns laughs. 'They tried to outstrip each other.'

outswinger (au·tswi:ŋəɹ). [f. OUT- 7 + SWING *v.*[1]] **1.** *Cricket.* A ball bowled with a swerve or swing from the leg to the off in its flight; also, the bowler of such a ball. So **ou·tswing,** the swerve or swing imparted to such a ball. Also **ou·tswi:nging** *ppl. a.*

1920 E. R. WILSON in P. F. Warner *Cricket* 67 Mr. E. W. Clark bowled 'out-swingers'. **1925** *Country Life* 18 July 93/2 To make a ball swerve in the air from the leg stump into the slips (the out-swinger, it is called). **1953** MILLER & WHITINGTON *Cricket Typhoon* 144 It was perfectly controlled late out-swing. **1955** A. ROSS *Australia 55* 211 He drove the out-swinging ball. **1958** P. RICHARDSON *Tackle Cricket this Way* iii. 50 Trueman, also, is primarily an outswinger. **1963** A. ROSS *Australia 63* iii. 82 Barrington, reaching out, played an out-swinger beautifully wide of mid-off. **1968** N. CARDUS in J. Arlott *Cricket: Great Bowlers* 21 He told me that he obtained his out-swing by spin. **1975** *Cricketer* May 9/1 His lifting outswing is more difficult and his pace changes more skilful.

2. (*Assoc.*) *Football.* A pass, usu. across the mouth of the goal, in which the flight of the ball curves away from the centre of the goal.

1959 *Times* 19 Mar. 18/3 Riley lost his man and sent over an out-swinger. **1961** F. C. AVIS *Sportsman's Gloss.* 37/1 *Outswinger*, a centre pass, particularly from a corner kick, that moves in its flight to goal in a slight arc away from the centre of the goal.

outta (au·tă), colloq. contraction of OUT OF *prep. phr.* orig. and chiefly *U.S.* Cf. *OUTA.

1937 C. HIMES *Black on Black* (1973) 142 You keep outta dis, yellow niggah. **1958** KEITH & BERGMAN (*song-title*) Outta my mind. *Ibid.*, And I came out-ta my spin, That dizzy spin I was in, Don't ask me, 'Where have I been?' Been out-ta my mind! **1967** *Boston Sunday Herald* 14 May (Comic Section), Outta the way, Barrey boy. **1971** B. BRANDON (*title*) Outta sight, Luther. **1973** *Black World* Jan. 65/1 Tears was dripping down the Grand Worthy Matron's face, making a mess outta all her powder and rouge. **1977** *Ripped & Torn* VI. 2/2 Is this a last ditch attempt by me to make some money outta this thing?

out-take (au·t,tēik), *sb.* [f. OUT- 7 + TAKE *sb.*] A length of film or tape rejected in editing.

1960 O. SKILBECK *ABC of Film & TV* 92 *Out takes*, takes rejected in the cutting room. **1970** *Guardian* 27 Jan. 1/3 Unused film, what in the industry are called 'the out-takes'. **1972** I. HAMILTON *Thrill Machine* xxxii. 147, I got the original neg. all the out-takes, and seven prints.. and the film was out of circulation. **1973** T. CHASTAIN *Pandora's Box* (1975) xv. 149 We're going to show you.. all the film we shot yesterday..including the out-takes—that is, the stuff we won't be using on the air after we've finished editing. **1977** *Zigzag* Mar. 29/3 Both the album's opener, Gene's 'Home Run King', and the traditional 'In The Pines' could have easily been outtakes from either D & C album. **1977** *Time* 24 Oct. 54/3 *Looking for Mr. Goodbar* has narrative lapses, jerky editing and confusing fantasy sequences that look like Ken Russell outtakes.

out-think, *v.* Add: **2.** (Later examples.)

1934 *Sun* (Baltimore) 10 Jan. 1/1 The farmers..outthought the railway officials. They telephoned back to Burlington and appraised the pickets there of the train's approach. **1941** STEINBECK & RICKETTS *Sea of Cortez* xvi. 161 The mule..knows he can out-think a horse and he is pretty sure he can out-think a human. **1954** D. DODGE *Lights of Skaro* ii. 50 They could outrun us, outfight us, or overwhelm us, but they couldn't out-think us. **1962** L. DEIGHTON *Ipcress File* xiii. 78 What chance did I stand.. they were both out-thinking me at every move. **1972** 'H. CALVIN' *Take Two Popes* vi. 48 His quarry had outthought him, and fled into the unexpected area on the other side of the road.

out-thrown, *ppl. a.* (Further examples.)

1927 *Month* May 398 The sides of the outthrown headland are too steep to be rushed. **1978** *Nature* 26 Jan. 318/2 The 'grid', however, may result principally from the overlapping of outthrown debris produced by the giant basin forming collisions.

out-thrust, *sb.* Add: (Later examples.) Also *transf.* and *fig.*

1950 J. JENKS *From Ground Up* xxi. 215 It was social and economic self-reliance at home that made possible an out-thrust of such vigour, that we became for a time not only the workshop of the world, but its merchant, carrier, and banker as well. **1955** J. R. R. TOLKIEN *Return of King* 162 An out-thrust of the eastward hills. **1973** *Baptist Federation of Canada Prayer Calendar* 16 Aug., Pray that the out-thrust of the Gospel by individual Christians will be unobstructed by timidity, busyness and fear.

out-thrust, *v.* Delete *rare* and add later examples.

1887 W. MORRIS tr. *Homer's Odyssey* I. x. 89 Sheer outthrusting nesses each other hold in face. **1892** G. MEREDITH *Poems: Empty Purse* 40 From him are the brutal and vain, The vile, the excessive, out-thrust. **1907** *Daily Mail* 7 Dec. 6/4 He sat his horse as if he were a part of it, the reins dangling carelessly, his feet out-thrust in the huge Moorish stirrups. **1963** C. D. SIMAK *They walked like Men* iii. 17 He lay back in the chair, with..his long legs outthrust into the shadow underneath the radio console.

out-tray (au·t,trēi). [f. OUT- 3 + TRAY *sb.*[2]] In an office, etc.: a tray for outgoing and completed correspondence and other papers. Cf. *IN-TRAY, *OUT-BASKET.

Sometimes written as two separate words with *out* regarded adjectivally.

1943 [see *IN-TRAY]. **1943** G. GREENE *Ministry of Fear* I. ii. 25 There were two trays on his desk marked In and Out, but the Out tray was empty. **1947** L. HASTINGS *Dragons are Extra* ix. 198 Invariably they were removed to the 'out' tray, probably with the tongs. **1959** *Punch* 30 Sept. 249/1, I looked around at the dusty chaos and saw how orderly it all could be..files here, records there, in-trays, out-trays. **1969** J. ARGENTI *Managem. Techniques* 247 Put this piece of paper in the Out-tray. **1976** DEAKIN & WILLIS *Johnny go Home* vi. 90 His desk is adorned with..wire In and Out trays.

out-turn. Add: (Further examples.) spec. *Econ.*, an amount or result attained, as distinct from an estimate.

1928 R. S. TROUP *Silvicultural Syst.* ix. 115 Both [the farmer and the gardener] take such measures as they can to improve the quality and increase the outturn of their field or garden crops. **1930** *Economist* 5 July 19/2 The wheat harvest has begun in the south-west... The out-turn promises to be about as large as last year. **1932** *Times* 29 Sept. 15/3 The Budget had been balanced on paper, but it remained to be seen what the actual result would be at the end of the financial year. The outturn proved the soundness of the balancing. **1957** *Times* 18 Nov. (Ann. Financial & Commerc. Rev.) p. xxxii/1 Barring frosts or other calamities, the out-turn delivered to the market can be reduced only by the action of growers or of some intermediary agency in withholding stocks. **1963** *Guardian* 15 Mar. 3/2 The figures for the outturn of defence expenditure in 1961–62 are provisional. **1972** *Accountant* 21 Sept. 350/1 Some indication of the outturn for the current year. **1976** *Daily Tel.* 3 Apr. 17 There is little point in the Government producing White Papers on public expenditure since the outturn has been so consistently different from official projections.

b. *gen.* A result, outcome.

1881 W. PAUL *Past & Present of Aberdeenshire* 19 Rahab, spoken of in the Bible, made a bad beginning, but she had a fine out-turn,—she had a fine out-turn, she married Salmon. **1961** *Atom* Feb. 12/2 Any statement on the future cost of power involves a complicated judgment of the out-turn of many factors.

2. *Curling.* A turning motion given to a stone which causes it to curve to the left.

1890 J. KERR *Hist. Curling* 411 No curler is..entitled to be reckoned a graduate of arts in curling until he has mastered the knowledge of the *in-turn* and the *out-turn.* **1900** —— in A. E. T. Watson *Young Sportsman* 200 The in-turn is made when the curl is to be toward the right, the outturn when it is to the left. **1969** R. WELSH *Beginner's Guide Curling* xi. 82 The..'in-turn' and 'out-turn', are activated in different ways.

ou·t-vote, *sb. rare.* [OUT- 2.] The vote of an out-voter; such votes collectively.

1790 E. SHERIDAN *Let.* June in T. Moore *Mem. Life R. B. Sheridan* (1825) 465, I suppose you have sent for the out-votes; but, if they are not good, what a terrible expense will that be! **1945** G. B. GRUNDY *55 Yrs. at Oxf.* 121 Rosebery was defeated on the out-vote.

out-voter. Add: (Further examples.) Also *transf.*

1931 *Birmingham Post* 24 Oct. 8/1 (*headline*) Aeroplane to bring up out-voters. **1965** W. R. WARD *Victorian Oxford* v. 96 Out-voters were told that a scheme designed by the heads to keep dissenters out on respectable grounds was a plan to let them in. **1967** *Economist* 6 May 575/1 Some distinguish between freeman electors and ten-pound householders, and between resident voters and out-voters.

outwall. Add: **b.** Used by Edmund Blunden in the sense 'outward appearance'.

1933 E. BLUNDEN *Charles Lamb* v. 131 He [*sc.* Wordsworth] does express the *altitudo* of Lamb's personality and influence far more thoughtfully than a host of subsequent writers to whom Lamb's outwall with its Punch and Judy shows and all the fun of the fair has been the principal thing to report. **1937** —— in *Essays & Stud.* XXII. 60 Acquaintances who did not always separate the man from his outwall. *Ibid.*, The candour and keenness of the first period, when the outwall had not yet become necessary.

outwander, *v.* Delete *Obs. rare* and add later *literary* example. Hence **outwa·ndering**

vbl. sb., a wandering out or outwards (in quot. *fig.*).

1880 H. COLLINS *Heaven Opened* II. xiv. 215 God does not mind the out-wanderings of our vagabond imaginations. **1922** JOYCE *Ulysses* 379 On her stow he ere was living with dear wife and lovesome daughter that then over land and seafloor nine years had long outwandered.

outward, *adv.* Add: **4.** *outward-looking, -steeled, -turning* adjs.

1890 W. JAMES *Princ. Psychol.* I. x. 296 Our considering the spiritual self at all is a reflective process, is the result of our abandoning the outward-looking point of view. **1927** A. HUXLEY *Proper Stud.* 52 How repulsive, how incomprehensible I find the philosophy which is the rationalization of these people's outward-looking passion for their fellows! **1975** *Times* 5 Apr. 3/3 Teachers try to capture the interests of these pupils with vocationally oriented, outward-looking courses. **1888** G. M. HOPKINS *Poems* (1918) 69 The heroic breast not outward-steeled. **1930** *Times Lit. Suppl.* 30 Oct. 888/4 As in a maze, the outward-turning paths lead back to the centre. **1976** *Listener* 12 Aug. 176/3 This bodily prosperity, this outward-turning energy.

outward-bound, *a.* Add examples relating to travel other than by sea.

1777 P. THICKNESSE *Year's Journey* II. xlvi. 110 My entertainment at this house, *outward-bound*, was half a second-hand roasted turkey. **1832** *Chambers's Edin. Jrnl.* I. 86/3 He would find himself on the top of one of the outward-bound coaches of the metropolis.

2. (With capital initials.) The name of a sea school founded by Kurt Hahn at Aberdovey in 1941, on the basis of which an Outward Bound Trust was formed in 1946 with the aim of establishing further residential schools for the training of boys and girls in mountaineering as well as naval and other outdoor activities. Also *transf.* Hence **Outward-Bound course, scheme, school,** etc. (see quots.).

1943 *Times* 28 June 2/4 Dr. G. M. Trevelyan..at Aberdovey on Saturday gave the name of Garibaldi to a sea-going ketch presented by the partners of Alfred Holt and Co., shipowners, to the Outward Bound Sea School. **1947** *Times* 23 Sept. 2/5 To-day the experiment begun in war-time is firmly established as a permanent undertaking operated by the Outward Bound Trust. **1950** *Times Educ. Suppl.* 16 June 474/1 Variety is the spice of the Outward Bound life. **1957** K. HAHN in D. James *Outward Bound* 10 In July 1941..Lawrence Holt, the shipowner.. secured the financial support of his firm, the Blue Funnel Line, for the foundation of the first Short-Term School at Aberdovey. The name Outward Bound Sea School was his invention. **1958** *Listener* 12 June 976/1 Sir Richard Livingstone and 'Outward Bound' enthusiasts both saw in the training of character a panacea for a world adrift. **1961** VISCT. MONTGOMERY *Path to Leadership* xi. 173 In my opinion the best character training given to boys in Britain is that provided by the Outward Bound Trust, through their sea and mountain schools... Outward Bound can take only some 4,000 boys a year. **1965** M. MORSE *Unattached* v. 159 He had been sent on the Outward Bound course by his firm. **1973** C. BONINGTON *Next Horizon* xiv. 213 Sebastian in the mist, looking like a bedraggled outward-bound schoolboy in the mists of Wales or the Lakes. **1977** P. THEROUX *Consul's File* 42 He was the local magistrate. An Outward Bound type..dead keen to go camping.

outward-bounder. Add: (Earlier example.)

1851 H. MELVILLE *Moby Dick* II. xi. 72 The long absent ship, the outward-bounder, perhaps, has letters on board.

2. (With capital initials.) A pupil at an 'Outward Bound' school; an advocate of such schools and their methods.

1961 *Sunday Times* 19 Feb. 34/2 Knowing how to tie reef-knots,..with all the other indispensable appurtenances of the Outward Bounder. *Ibid.* 26 Feb. 39/3 We 'intelligent' talkers have to thank the 'Outward Bounders' for the liberty and freedom to be so.

ou·twash. *Geol.* [OUT- 7.] Material (chiefly sand and gravel, or further away silt and clay) carried out from a glacier by melt-water and deposited beyond the terminal moraine. Freq. *attrib.*

1894 T. C. CHAMBERLIN in *Jrnl. Geol.* II. 533 There were, however, tracts of assorted material formed by waters outflowing from the ice where no definite terminal ridging took place. Such forms may be designated *outwash* aprons in distinction from *overwash* aprons. **1905** *Ibid.* XIII. 245 One of the pronounced features of the outwash is the pitted-plain development. **1908** *Amer. Jrnl. Sci.* CLXXV. 108 The river terraces of outwash gravel. **1934** *Antiquity* VIII. 306 The retreat of the ice and the formation of the outwash plain in front of the moraine. **1947** AUDEN *Age of Anxiety* v. 116 And you, bright Prince,..O stiffly stand, a staid monadnock, On her peneplain; placidly graze On her outwash apron, her own steed. **1957** [see *OVERWASH *sb.*]. **1963** D. W. & E. E. HUMPHRIES tr. *Termier's Erosion & Sedimentation* vii. 163 During the recession of the Quaternary ice sheets, detrital accumulations were left behind, either in the form of outwash fans deposited at the snouts of glaciers by subglacial streams.., or as fluvio-glacial ridges often filling in lakes (eskers). **1971** R. F. FLINT *Glacial & Quaternary Geol.* vii. 187 In the downstream direction, outwash is diluted by an ever-increasing proportion of nonglacial alluvium derived through tributary streams that did not originate in glaciers. **1972** J. G. CRUICKSHANK *Soil Geogr.* ii. 59 Outwash alluvium is usually similar in texture, but may include some fine debris where the melt water has spread over a large area.

out west (aut we·st), *sb.* and *adv. phr.* [f. OUT *adv.* 2, 16 + WEST *adv.* 2 c.] **A.** *sb.* Orig., the territory to the west of the early American settlements; by extension, the distant West of the U.S. as regarded by inhabitants of the East (cf. WEST *sb.* 3 b). Also *attrib.* **B.** *adv. phr.* In or to this region. Also *transf.* in or to the western parts of Canada or Australia.

1835 C. F. HOFFMAN *Winter in West* II. 119 Old Kaintuck..whips all 'Out-West' in prettiness. **1848** R. W. GRISWOLD *Passages from Corr.* (1898) 243 The 'out West Editor' would inform her..as to who he is. *Ibid.* 244 Why is it your new volume is not out West? **1857** *Lawrence* (Kansas) *Republican* 4 June 2 Any one who has spent any time in farming 'out west', will see that this is a mistake. **1887** C. B. GEORGE *40 Yrs. on Rail* 62 New York State was considered 'out West' then. **1890** S. M. ST. MAUR *Impressions Tenderfoot* xiii. 173 All ponies and dogs 'out West' seem shy of women. **1898** P. L. FORD *Tattle-Tales of Cupid* 205 As they say out West, it's come to stay and grow up with the country. **1944** *Living off Land* iv. 81 The country out-west is full of dead men's bones. **1952** *Manch. Guardian Weekly* 17 July 15 He worked as a section hand out west on the Union Pacific railroad. **1961** *Maclean's Mag.* 29 July 36/1 I've worked freights that have carried more passengers than the passenger runs did, especially out west in the Depression.

outwinter (au·t,wintəɹ), *v.* Also **out-winter.** [OUT- 15.] *trans.* To keep (animals) in the open during the winter. So **ou·twintered** *ppl. a.*, **ou·twintering** *vbl. sb.* Cf. *IN-WINTER *v.*

1959 *Times* 2 Nov. 21/1 Our first decision was to have our own acclimatized breeding outwintered cattle. **1960** *Farmer & Stockbreeder* 8 Mar. 109/3 Gimmer hoggs that are outwintered well in North-East Cheshire have yielded fleeces up to 11 lb. *Ibid.* 15 Mar. 81/3 An average of 35s for outwintering. **1965** COOPER & THOMAS *Profitable Sheep Farming* viii. 75 Grazing obtained by outwintered ewes in a more normal season is not appreciable.

outwith, *prep.* and *adv.* For 'Chiefly *north.*; now only *Sc.*' read: 'Chiefly *north.* and *Sc.*'

A. *prep.* **1.** (Later examples.)

1927 W. D. SIMPSON *Historical St. Columba* 17 Of the four peoples..who struggled for mastery in what is now Scotland, the Angles alone were entirely outwith the pale of Christianity. **1947** H. FARMER *Hist. Music Scotl.* 216 In music, there was but one name, John Abell (d. 1724), and he gained his fame *outwith* Scotland, to use the appropriate Scots word. **1970** 'E. FERRARS' *Seven Sleepers* iv. 46 I'm moving into a small bungalow outwith the town. **1972** G. HENDERSON *Early Medieval* vi. 232 Outwith history painting the image of the crucified Christ, as an evocation of the Passion and redemption, was slow to make itself felt. **1975** C. N. MANLOVE *Mod. Fantasy* iv. 99 What he came to demand was 'rational' friendship, the bond of a common interest in something outwith the self. **1978** *Dumfries & Galloway Standard* 21 Oct. 1/8 Attempts might be made..to promote the greater use of existing static caravan sites outwith the July/August period.

b. (Later examples.)

1705 in *Aberdeen Jrnl. N. & Q.* (1909) II. 309/1 It shall be leisum to them..to take themselves outwith the family. **1958** *Times* 5 Dec. 8/7 Their value may also extend outwith the narrow sphere of medicine.

outworking, *vbl. sb.* Add: (Further examples.)

1881 W. M. THOMSON *Land & Bk.* 2 The long ongoing and outworkings of the Mosaic Economy. **1958** *Church Times* 5 Dec. 1/3 If the outworking of *apartheid* policies meant such cruelty and callousness, then even the Slightest Smell of a *Compulsory apartheid* must be removed from our Churches. **1961** B. R. WILSON *Sects & Society* III. xiv. 288 Christadelphians do take a keen interest in political events, as out-workings of biblical prophecy. **1976** M. WILES *What is Theology?* iv. 108 Philosophical assumptions implicit in these [Freudian] ideas and their practical outworking in therapy.

2. The work of an out-worker.

1970 G. GREER *Female Eunuch* 131 As an alternative to nursing or outworking, waitressing..is not conspicuously preferable. **1974** *Daily Tel.* 12 Jan. 2/6 There are..areas of the country where 'out-working' has been traditional, as with lace at Nottingham.

outworldish, *a.* (Later example.)

1880 G. MACDONALD *Bk. Strife* 73 A strange auroral bliss, an Arctic awe, A new, outworldish joy awoke intense.

outy (au·ti). *colloq.* [f. OUT *adv.* + -Y[6].] The act of letting a dog or other pet out of the house, or taking it for a walk; 'walkies'. Freq. in *pl.*

1949 C. H. B. KITCHIN *Cornish Fox* xi. 167 He was Mrs. Ropford's dog, and Mrs. Steele was giving him his evening 'outy'. **1962** N. MARSH *Hand in Glove* vii. 230, I was going to bed and he asked for outies. **1967** B. WHITAKER *Chained Crocodile* iii. 37, I must see to Skipper first, 'e wants outies rather bad.

outyield (autyī·ld), *v.* [f. OUT- 18 + YIELD *v.* 8.] *trans.* To surpass in terms of yield; to produce more than.

1927 *Daily Tel.* 15 Nov. 12/1 The Danish swede crop outyields ours by about six tons per acre. **1957** *Times* 2 July (Agric. Suppl.) p. i/1 Wheat after sugar beet will almost invariably outyield wheat taken after a one-year mixed ley.

ouvala, var. *UVALA.

ouvarovite, var. UVAROVITE.

‖ **ouvert** (uvɛ̄r). *Ballet.* [Fr., = open.] (See quots.)

1914 *Techn. Encycl. Theory & Pract. Art of Dancing* 110 *Ouvert*,..any movement in which the legs are open sideways to right or left. **1952** KERSLEY & SINCLAIR *Dict. Ballet Terms* 72 *Ouvert(e)*,..a position of the feet in which the feet do not touch. **1968** J. WINEARLS *Mod. Dance* (ed. 2) iv. 103 The name given to all opening and closing movements of this type is Ouvert.

‖ **ouvreuse** (uvrȫz). [Fr.] In France, a woman who 'opens' theatre boxes; an usherette in a French theatre or cinema.

1892 G. B. SHAW *Let.* 21 Apr. (1965) I. 338 It took the united strength of my three companions, the *ouvreuse*, the acting manager, the fireman, and a commissionaire to hold me down and restrain me from hurling an opera glass at her head. **1944** H. CROOME *You've gone Astray* i. 11 A disgruntled old *ouvreuse* in a Paris theatre. **1968** *Guardian* 27 Apr. 9/8 An ouvreuse in a theatre or cinema. **1972** *Ibid.* 5 Feb. 3/8 An inescapable one franc for the cloakroom and another for the *ouvreuse*.

‖ **ouvrier** (uvrie). [Fr.] A workman. Also *fem.* **ouvrière,** a working woman.

1848 J. ARNOLD *Let.* 28 Mar. in J. Bertram *N.Z. Lett. T. Arnold* (1966) 36 France has been absorbed into the great cities, the cities into Paris, Paris into the middle and lower classes—these into the 'ouvriers', the Ouvriers into the clubs. *a* **1855** C. BRONTË *Professor* (1857) II. xxiv. 205 You, a scion of Seacombe, have proved your disdain of social distinctions by taking up with an *ouvrière*. **1857** C. M. YONGE *Dynevor Terr.* I. xx. 334 She..had seen him ..preceded by a brave and faithful *ouvrier*. **1904** A. BENNETT *Great Man* xxiv. 267, I come from the *ouvriers*, ..the working peoples. **1972** R. COBB *Reactions to French Rev.* iv. 142 All that the *ouvrière* might know of the Revolution was that it appeared to be..oppressive and interfering. **1975** —— *Paris & its Provinces* v. 199 An extended family group..Marie-Anne Deloutre, *tricoteuse*; Ludovine Deloutre, *ouvrière*; and Constance Deloutre, *ouvrière*.

Hence **ouvrierism, -isme, ouvrierist** (see quots.).

1969 G. STEDMAN JONES in Cockburn & Blackburn *Student Power* 29 Such ouvrierism—the belief that the traditional working class has a monopoly of socialist potential—is a mystification. **1974** J. WHITE tr. *Poulantzas's Fascism & Dictatorship* IV. i. 166 The fascist and national socialist *leaders* are extremely cautious in the use of this double-edged weapon, the 'ouvrierist' use of corporatist themes. **1976** F. ZWEIG *New Acquisitive Society* II. x. 134 Ouvrierism implies that the worker can never be the wrongdoer, he can be wronged but he cannot wrong others. **1977** *Foreign Affairs* LV. 805 There has been little of the *ouvrièrisme* in this party that has marked the French.

ouwarovite, ouwarowite, varr. UVAROVITE.

ouzo (ū·zo). Also **ouso.** [mod.Gr. οὖζο.] A Greek spirituous drink flavoured with aniseed; a glass of this.

The etymology of the Greek name οὖζο is disputed. A popular etymology derives it from the Italian designation *uso Massalia* 'for the (commercial) use of Marseilles' stamped on packages of selected silkworm cocoons exported in the 19th century via Volos from the Thessalian town of Tyrnavos. The designation came to stand for 'superior quality', which the spirit distilled as *ouzo* was thought to possess: see A. Tzartzanos in *Indogermanische Forschungen* (1932) LII. 217–20.

1898 H. N. BRAILSFORD *Broom of War-God* 4 The Prefect had placed a chair beside him and had pledged his in *ouso*. **1935** *Chem. Abstr.* 880 (*heading*) Method for controlling the purity of alcohol used in the preparation of 'ouzo'... The beverage known as 'ouzo' in Greece has an alc. content of 35–45%. **1957** L. DURRELL *Bitter Lemons* 25 The excellent *ouzo* and his general affability transformed the journey. **1957** F. KING *Man on Rock* ii. 61, I devoured a whole tin of American bully-beef, washed down with ouzo. **1965** O. MANNING *Friends & Heroes* xx. 202 Alan had a bottle of ouzo on his table and he started filling the glasses. **1973** D. LANG *Freaks* 8 Stavros downed another ouzo. **1975** *Daily Colonist* (Victoria, B.C.) 18 May 4/6 Constantine, late of Greece, could..take to peddling ouzo.

ovablastic (ōuvăblæ·stik), *a. rare*—[1]. [f. L. *ova*, pl. of OVUM egg + Gr. βλαστικ-ός sprinting forth.] Making eggs burst open (in the womb).

1922 JOYCE *Ulysses* 397 Mr Dixon..took on to ask Mr Mulligan himself whether his incipient ventripotence.. betokened an ovablastic gestation in the prostatic utricle.

Ovaherero (ōu:văherīə·ro) = *HERERO; also a tribe of the Hereros.

1855 F. N. KOLBE in W. Holden *Hist. Natal* 436 Damara-land is inhabited by a nation divided into two principal tribes, the Ovaherero and Ovampantera. **1856** C. J. ANDERSSON *Lake Ngami* iv. 52 The Damaras are divided into two large tribes, the *Ovaherero* and the *Ovapantiereu*. **1880** *Encycl. Brit.* XI. 731/2, 110,000 are Herero (80,000 Ova Herero and 30,000 Ova-mbanderu). **1884** A. LANG *Custom & Myth* 20 The Ovahereroes in

South Africa..appease with a black sheep the spirits of the departed. **1910** *Encycl. Brit.* XIII. 358/1 Herero or Ovaherero.

oval, *a.*[1] and *sb.*[1] Add: **A.** *adj.* **2.** *Oval office* the office of the President of the United States in the White House.

[**1962** *N.Y. Times Mag.* 8 Apr. 38 (*caption*) New look—The oval office in the White House's west wing reflects increasingly the interests and personality of the man who spends upwards of seven hours of his long working day in it.] **1965** L. P. Jones *First Bk. White House* 30 In 1909, seven years after the President's offices had been moved into the West Wing, the President's Oval Office was added. **1966** P. B. Fay *Pleasure of his Company* xxiv. 259 One Saturday morning in the Oval Office I asked the President, 'Is there any truth to the rumor that you intend to dump Lyndon in '64?' **1972** W. McGivern *Caprifoil* viii. 133 This is the first time I've ever interrupted the President... Mary Donovan..walked to the door that connected her office to the Oval Office. **1973** *Times* 18 June 1/6 Mr Krogh told him that the order for the break-in came 'from the Oval Office'. **1973** *Time* 13 Aug. 20/1 The President rarely appears in testimony. The word comes from 'the Oval Office'. **1974** *Times* 9 Aug. 8/5 The President of the United States will address the nation on radio and television from his Oval Office. **1977** *Time* 17 Jan. 16/1 With Carter in the Oval Office, the Democrats chose in Byrd a man well equipped to push the Administration's programs.

5. a. *oval-faced* (examples).

1886 Ruskin *Praeterita* I. 326 A graceful oval-faced blonde of fifteen. **1976** J. Drummond *Funeral Urn* xxi. 109 They..looked alike, oval-faced, straight-nosed, small-mouthed.

B. *sb.* **2.** (Further examples.)

1910 *Blackw. Mag.* Jan. 89/1 On the Oval, Surrey..had snatched a victory by five runs. **1927** *Daily Express* 26 Mar. 9/2 The Prince of Wales..will..open a games oval. **1928** M. Arlen *Lily Christine* (1929) iii. 42 Her father..liked nothing so much as spending long afternoons at Lords' or the Oval. **1973** *Sun-Herald* (Sydney) 26 Aug. 15/4 Police were searching late tonight for two girls, who disappeared from the crowded Adelaide Oval while attending a football match with parents and friends. **1977** C. Storr *Tales Psychiatrist's Couch* 118 I'll be back to take her off to the Oval... She's a cricket fan.

oval (ōᵘ·văl), *v.* [f. Oval *a.*[1] and *sb.*[1]] **a.** *trans.* To make oval, to give an oval shape to. **b.** *intr.* To move in oval-shaped curves. Hence **o·valling** *ppl. a.*

1665 Hooke *Micrographia* 218 The more the limb is flatted or ovalled, the more red does the body appear. **1874** M. Clarke *His Natural Life* ii. viii. 121 The rings were too strong to be 'ovalled', or he would have been free long ago. *Ibid.*, 'To oval', is a term in use among convicts, and means to so bend the round ring of the ankle fetter that the *heel* can be drawn up through it. **1922** Joyce *Ulysses* 444 The odour of the sicksweet weed floats towards him in slow round ovalling wreaths. **1969** 'R. Stark' *Blackbird* iv. 26 Grofield's plane ovaled between massed gray clouds and the grubby sprawl of New York City.

ovalbumen, -in. Add: In mod. use written **ovalbumin** and applied to the albumin that is the principal protein of egg-white. (Further examples.)

1905 C. E. Simon *Text-bk. Physiol. Chem.* (ed. 2) xxi. 457 According to Gautier and some of the older observers, white of egg (albumen) contains a number of different albumins, which in part seem to belong to the true albumins and in part to the globulins. They have been designated as α-, β-, and γ-ovalbumin, and α- and β-ovoglobulin. **1934** W. R. Fearon *Introd. Biochem.* vi. 86 Ovalbumin makes up the greater part (10–13 per cent.) of egg-white. **1959** [see *ovoglobulin]. **1970** R. W. McGilvery *Biochem.* viii. 150 The principal protein of egg whites, ovalbumin, is especially susceptible to denaturation in this way.

ovality (ōᵘvæ·lĭti). [f. Oval *a.*[1] and *sb.*[1] + -ity.] = Ovalness.

1937 *Times* 13 Apr. p. xv/1 Some idea of the precision to which this one operation alone is worked can be appreciated from the fact that the tolerance of error allowed is only one ten-thousandth part of an inch combined taper and ovality. **1947** *Times* 30 Sept. 3/2 The gauge is used to check the internal diameter of the bore in the body of the injector, and reveals any ovality, taper, barrel-shape, or bell-mouth inaccuracies. **1962** *Gloss. Terms Glass Industry* (*B.S.I.*) 42 *Ovality*, deviation of a glass article from a circular towards an elliptical cross section. **1976** *Drive* Nov.–Dec. 61/2 A rake-adjustable steering column and slight steering wheel ovality.

Ovaltine (ōᵘ·văltīn). Also with small initial. [Prob. a fanciful extension of Oval *a.*[1] 3.] The proprietary name of a powder composed principally of malt extract, milk, and eggs; a drink made from this.

1906 *Trade Marks Jrnl.* 13 June 820 Ovaltine... Alimentary products..Albert Wander,..Berne, Switzerland; manufacturer of alimentary products. **1907** *Yesterday's Shopping* (1969) 516/2 Ovaltine—tin, 1/4½. **1912** R. Brooke *Let.* 26 Jan. (1968) 354 These things go on round,..Mrs Digby on India, and Mrs Fox at Bridge, and Ovaltine. **1930** J. Cannan *No Walls of Jasper* 64 The parlourmaid..set down a cup of Ovaltine on the corner of the writing table. **1937** J. Betjeman *Continual Dew* 22 He gives his Ovaltine a stir And nibbles at a 'petit beurre'. **1940** F. Stark *Winter in Arabia* xv. 290 Qasim woke me with hot ovaltine at one-thirty. **1960** S. Plath *Colossus* 58 You fed My brother and me cookies and ovaltine. **1969** *Trade Marks Jrnl.* 19 Feb. 306/2 Ovaltine... Food preparations (not medicated) in powder or tablet form composed principally of malt, milk and eggs, the malt predominating; and rusks. A. Wander, Limited,..London,..manufacturing chemists. *Ibid.* 29 Oct. 1802/2 Ovaltine... Preparations of milk, malt and eggs, flavoured with cocoa, the malt predominating, for use in making food beverages; biscuits (other than biscuits for animals), cakes, rusks, chocolate and non-medicated confectionery. A. Wander, Limited,..London,..manufacturing chemists. **1973** 'P. Loraine' *Voices in Empty Room* ii. iv. 115 Lulu Jenkins..lay slumped up on the pillows of her large bed, sipping Ovaltine.

Ovambo (ovæ·mbo), *sb.* and *a.* Also **Ambo, Avamba, Ovampo.** [f. Bantu *ova-* pl. prefix + *ambo* man of leisure.] **A.** *sb.* **a.** A member of a Bantu people living in the northern part of South-West Africa; this people collectively. **b.** The language of the Ovambos. **B.** *adj.* Of or pertaining to the Ovambos.

1853 F. Galton *Narr. Explorer Trop. S. Afr.* vi. 179 The Ovampo were twenty-four in number with a tall enterprising-looking young man as captain. **1856** C. J. Andersson *Lake Ngami* xiv. 163 At a considerable distance to the north, there lived a nation called Ovambo. **1864** T. Baines *Explor. S.-W. Afr.* ii. 40 The Damaras..could not even make an assegai, but bought their weapons of the Ovampo. **1884** *Encycl. Brit.* XVII. 318/2 Many..of the Bantu-speaking southern races..[including] Ovambos of the south-west coast..are also variously affected by foreign elements. **1897** J. Bryce *Impressions S. Afr.* v. 42 On the higher grounds and generally in the far northern parts [of German South West Africa], where the Ovampo tribe dwell, grass is abundant. **1902** *Encycl. Brit.* XXXII. 736/2 The Ovambo or Ambo, in the northern part of the protectorate, are agriculturists. **1909** *Daily Chron.* 28 July 4/4 Three and a-half days' work with a mere handful of Ovambo 'boys'. **1911** J. G. Frazer *Golden Bough: Magic Art* (ed. 3) I. iii. 63 The Ovambo of South-western Africa believe that some people have the power of bewitching an absent person by gazing into a vessel full of water till his image appears to them in the water. **1953** L. G. Green *Lords of Last Frontier* ii. 18 Battels deserted and lived for sixteen months among the Ovambos. *Ibid.* xvi. 235 Finnish missionaries learn Ovambo before they leave Finland. **1959** *Chambers's Encycl.* X. 277/2 The Ovambo people are the largest community of South-west Africa. **1967** *Courier-Mail* (Brisbane) 20 Apr. 18/6 It was interesting to find the tall, slim, gentle houseboy employed by my host and hostess was an Ovambo. **1973** *Daily Tel.* 21 Nov. 4/6 They were familiar with Ovambo tribal customs. **1974** *Encycl. Brit. Micropædia* I. 295/3 Ambo, also known as Ovambo or Avamba, people located in the dry grassland country of northern South West Africa and southern Angola... They speak a language of the Bantu group. **1974** *Times* 14 Oct. 7/2 Oshakati, the Ovambo capital near the Angolan border.

ovariectomy. Add: (Further examples.)

1932 S. Zuckerman *Social Life Monkeys* v. 77 If the ovaries of any mature mammal are experimentally removed (the operation of ovariectomy), all cyclic activity in the accessory reproductive organs ceases. **1958** *Sci. News* XLVII. 85 Removal of the ovary (ovariectomy) from a young hen results in the growth of cock-like spurs, a large comb, and male plumage. **1969** J. H. Green *Basic Clin. Physiol.* xviii. 104/2 Once the placenta has developed, the corpus luteum of pregnancy in the ovary is no longer essential for the maintenance of pregnancy and an ovariectomy (oophorectomy) could be carried out.

Hence **ovarie·ctomize** *v. trans.*, to deprive of one or both ovaries; **ovarie·ctomized** *ppl. a.*

1924 *Physiol. Abstr.* IX. 33 In two ovariectomised hens ..a testis was found. **1928** *Proc. Soc. Exper. Biol. & Med.* XXV. 490 Guinea pigs..on the fourth day after œstrum were ovariectomized. **1958** *Sci. News* XLVII. 85 The antlers of young stags do not develop after castration, and ovariectomized female deer may produce horns. **1974** *Nature* 5 Apr. 525/1 All rats were ovariectomised and thyroidectomised on day 1 of the experiment.

ovariole. (Later examples.)

1925 A. D. Imms *Gen. Textbk. Entomol.* 147 Each organ [*sc.* ovary] is composed of a variable number of separate egg-tubes or ovarioles which open into the oviduct. **1965** B. E. Freeman tr. *Vandel's Biospeleol.* xxii. 364 The female of *Aphaenops*..has a single ovariole on each side of the body. **1976** *Nature* 17 June 614/2 Cells which display the highest levels are those which have been assumed to be the most active and specialised, such as..the trophocytes of insect ovarioles.

ovariotomy. Add: (Earlier example.) Hence **ovario·tomize** *v. trans.* = *ovariectomize *v.*; **ovario·tomized** *ppl. a.*

1844 *Lond. & Edin. Monthly Jrnl. Med. Sci.* IV. 58 Her case..is believed only by the few who have lately come into the field as the champions of Ovariotomy. **1916** *Biol. Bull.* XXX. 293 The ovariotomized duck may or may not undergo a change in plumage, corresponding to that of the male. **1927** *Jrnl. Physiol.* LXII. 312 Does a lactating ovariotomised mouse require more œstrin to produce œstrous symptoms than a non-suckling ovariotomised mouse? To answer this question a number of mice were ovariotomised soon after parturition. **1964** *Biol. Abstr.* XLV. 7553/1 Ovariotomized rats..were starved for 20–22 hours.

ovate, *a.* Add: **1. c.** *absol.* as *sb. Archæol.*, an implement having an oval blade.

1946 F. E. Zeuner *Dating Past* ix. 283 It is clear, however, that by the end of this interglacial the Acheulian had acquired all its characteristic attributes, like ovates and the S-twist. **1956** A. L. Armstrong in D. L. Linton *Sheffield* 91 Three more hand-axes, all ovates of middle Acheulean type and refined technique, are recorded from our area. **1959** J. D. Clark *Prehist. Southern Afr.* vi. 157 The same assemblage of wood-working tools occurs—small, nearly parallel-sided picks, small flat ovates, miniature 'tea cosies', [etc.].

ovational, *a.* Add: (Later example.) Also, resembling or in the nature of an ovation.

1928 *Music & Lett.* July 235 The ovational ecstasy is not essentially connected with the musical impression.

oven, *sb.* Add: **2. c.** *transf.* A small oven-like tomb built at ground level.

1851 E. S. Wortley *Trav. U.S.* I. xxi. 237 The graves are also elevated. The dead are buried in sepulchral houses, which are termed here 'ovens'. **1879** *Cassell's Techn. Educ.* IV. 267/2 Owing to the damp nature of the ground..there are no graves in the cemeteries, the coffins with the dead being deposited in tombs or 'ovens' erected above the soil. **1921** *Chambers's Jrnl.* Aug. 511/1 There was no system in the arrangement of the 'ovens'.

d. A cremation chamber; *spec.* one of the chambers used by the Germans during the war of 1939–45 for the cremation of Jewish corpses.

1945 [see *gas oven]. **1962** M. Procter *Body to Spare* xxi. 158 The two incinerators, invariably called ovens by local undertakers. **1964** L. Deighton *Funeral in Berlin* xxiii. 129 He couldn't eat his lunch for the stink of the cremation ovens. **1967** C. Potok *Chosen* xiii. 228 Where else [but Palestine] could the remnant of Jewry that had escaped Hitler's ovens go? **1976** L. Sanders *Hamlet Warning* (1977) ix. 75 This beats those Nazi ovens.

f. *fig.* A woman's womb; chiefly in colloq. phr. *to have something in the oven* (and variants), to be pregnant. See also *bun *sb.*[2] 1a, *pudding *sb.* 5c.

1962 'B. Graeme' *Undetective* ii. 19 Good lord! You mean there's something in the oven? **1967** H. W. Sutherland *Magnie* ii. 24 She knew definitely she had one in the oven. **1976** 'D. Fletcher' *Accomplices* v. 143 She's in the club, you know. Got one in the oven, eh?

4. *oven-dry, -hot, -ready* adjs.; **oven-bottom(ed)** *a.*, designating cake or bread baked at the bottom of the oven; **oven-cloth,** a heat resistant cloth used for handling dishes in an oven; **oven-cook** *v.*, to cook in an oven; **oven-glass,** glass ware suitable for use in an oven; **oven glove,** an oven cloth made in the form of a glove; **oven mit(t)** = *oven glove* above; **ovenproof** [Proof *a.* (*adv.*) 1 b], suitable for use in an oven; **oven timer** (see quot. 1961); **oven-to-table** *a.*, designating ovenware designed also for use at the table for serving; **ovenware,** dishes that can be used for cooking in an oven; **oven wood** (later examples).

1956 G. Mann *Good Food from Old England* 185 A piece of dough was always reserved for Leather Cake, or Oven Bottom Cake. The name Oven Bottom Cake naturally came from the fact that the cake was baked on the bottom of the oven where the heat was. **1957** J. Kirkup *Only Child* ix. 121 We..ate warm, freshly-baked 'oven-bottom cake'. **1959** *Times* 9 Mar. (Britain's Food Suppl.) p. xii/5 Many..in the over-40 age group..look back with nostalgia to the crusty oven-bottomed bread of their youth. **1967** 'S. Woods' *And shame Devil* 74 [She] did her own baking and ate oven-bottom cake and treacle every day for tea. *c* **1909** D. H. Lawrence *Collier's Friday Night* (1934) ii. 38 *Ernest* (rising and going to the oven, picking up the oven-cloth from the hearth). **1977** *Limerick's Catal.* Spring 5 Oven cloth... To protect the hands. Mitten type. Each 68 p. **1957** J. Kirkup *Only Child* ii. 44 Whenever she opened the oven door she used an 'oven-cloth'. **1969** D. Clark *Death after Evensong* v. 133 Maria carried in a pizza... She slid it off the glove oven-cloth. **1953** *Britannica Bk. of Year* 639/1 Compounds like oven-cook (verb)..also occurred. **1974** *Times* 7 Mar. 13/7 If your frying pan is on the small side, there's no reason why you should not oven-cook the chicken halves. **1966** A. W. Lewis *Gloss. Woodworking Terms* 63 *Oven dry*, wood which has been baked in an oven at 100°C (212°F), until it ceases to lose weight, i.e. until all the moisture has been removed. **1971** *Gloss. Soil Sci. Terms* (Soil Sci. Soc. Amer.) 12/1 *Oven-dry soil*, soil which has been dried at 105C until it reaches constant weight. **1939–40** *Army & Navy Stores Catal.* p. xlviii/1 Oven Glass, Phoenix. **1961** *Guardian* 12 June 6/7 Phoenix oven glass..[is] one of the reliable heat-proof glasses. **1965** *Sun* 3 Nov. 40/4 Oven gloves help to cheer up a kitchen on a dull morning. **1968** 'E. Peters' *Grass Widow's Tale* vi. 84 Her nursery towelling oven gloves. **1976** *Oadby & Wigston Advertiser* 26 Nov. 9/2 Oven gloves..make very welcome gifts. **1922** Blunden *Shepherd* 30 The night drooped oven-hot. **1962** [see *Jaffa]. **1976** E. Ward *Hanged Man* xx. 118 Parma ham and oven-hot bread. **1969** *Guardian* 10 Feb. 9/4 Trendy gifts like oven mits. **1973** 'D. Halliday' *Dolly & Starry Bird* ii. 21 He put both hands around the handle like oven mitts. **1939–40** *Army & Navy Stores Catal.* 714 *Phoenix* is the latest oven proof glass-ware. **1957** *Housewife* Sept. 89/2 Scandinavian saucepan in oven-proof pottery. **1961** *Harper's Bazaar* Feb. 29/2 Two casserole dishes..are flame-proof and oven-proof. **1974** *Country Life* 5 Dec. 1735/3 Ramekins..in ovenproof pottery. **1960** A. E. Bender *Dict. Nutrition* 90/2 *Oven ready*, term applied to poultry that have been plucked, neck, legs and entrails removed,..and finally sealed into heat-shrinkable Cryo-vac wrapping—ready for oven without any further handling. **1960** *Farmer & Stockbreeder* 23 Feb. 64/3 A new firm..has been formed with the aim of becoming one of the largest producers of oven-ready turkeys and ducklings in the country. **1962**

[see *fish finger* s.v. *FISH *sb.*[1] 7]. **1973** *Times* 16 Nov. 4 Wholesale prices of oven-ready turkey and chicken have fallen slightly in the past week. **1961** *Which?* Oct. 250/1 One cooker..had an automatic *oven timer*. This, like the ringers had a clockwork mechanism, which turned the oven on and off after a pre-set time. **1977** *Transatlantic Rev.* LX. 87 Then he [mimes] a man shaving and showering in a flurry of interruptions: the phone, the doorbell, the oven timer. **1979** *House & Garden* Mar. 78/3 (Advt.), Oval casserole from versatile range of oven-to-table ware. **1977** *Jrnl. R. Soc. Arts* CXXV. 215/2 A wide range of ceramic items from the early beginnings to the latest oven-to-table ware. **1926–7** *Army & Navy Stores Catal.* 785 Pyrex transparent 'glass' oven ware. **1933** *Archit. Rev.* LXXIV. 26 (*caption*) Some very well shaped Vitreosel quartz ovenware. **1959** *Listener* 5 Feb. 267/1 Bake fillets of cod or haddock in an ovenware dish. **1973** *Guardian* 23 May 9/5 Prestige's second eleven price range, Skyline, for their ovenware passes on many of the blessings of their first team's design.

ovenette (ɒv'ne·t). [f. OVEN *sb.* 2 + -ETTE.] A small or subsidiary oven.

1919 [see *KITCHENETTE]. **1976** *Southern Even. Echo* (Southampton) 11 Nov. 7/2 (Advt.), Eye-level grill-rotisserie-ovenett [*sic*], plus roomy autotimed warming drawer.

over, *adv.* Add: **2. b.** *to be* (someone) *all over*: to be very characteristic of (that person); to be exactly what one might expect of (someone specified). Also *transf.*

1721 R. PALMER *Let.* 31 Aug. in M. M. Verney *Verney Lett.* (1930) II. xxiv. 90 [Mr. Churchill is] Vulponi all over. **1799** C. LAMB *Let.* 20 Mar. (1935) I. 153 The last stanza hath nothing striking in it, if I except the two concluding lines, which are Burns all over. **1821** SCOTT *Pirate* II. v. 114, I see where you would be—this is Sebastian and Dorax all over. **1852** [see *ALL OVER *advb. phr.* 1a]. **1863** J. S. MILL *Let.* 22 Nov. (1910) I. 310 This is Spencer all over; he throws himself with a certain deliberate impetuosity into the last new theory. **1898** J. D. BRAYSHAW *Slum Silhouettes* 14 Ah! gal, that's married life all over—fight and agree, fight and agree! **1906** GALSWORTHY *Man of Property* II. xii. 257 That's Phil all over—he was always like that. **1913** A. BENNETT *Regent* II. viii. 249 He's his father all over, that lad is! **1945** H. CLOSS *High are Mountains* 56 It was old Longshanks all over to send one off on some futile errand. **1973** A. HOLDEN *Girl on Beach* 37, I could have killed Dick when he..said he'd asked these two men to dinner, but that's Dick all over of course, just expects me to cope.

6. a. (See also *GET *v.* 66e.)

b. Used in radio communication to indicate that the speaker has finished speaking and intends his communicator to reply. *Over and out*: used to indicate that the communication is at an end. Cf. *OUT *adv.* 23 b. Also *transf.*, esp. in *over to you*: it is your turn (to speak, act, etc.).

1926 J. L. PRITCHARD *Bk. Aeroplane* viii. 144 'Hullo, Croydon,..now passing Biggin Hill. Over!'..The final word 'Over' tells the Croydon operator that the pilot is switching his transmitting apparatus over to receiving so that he can hear what Croydon has to say. **1940** 'GUN BUSTER' *Return via Dunkirk* II. iv. 117 X calling Robert Eddy...I can hear you...remain on receive...over to you over. **1955, 1966** [see *OUT *adv.* 23b]. **1967** 'R. FOLEY' *Fear of Stranger* (1968) x. 105 Over to you, pal, Kay thought in amusement. **1969** *Guardian* 22 July 11/1 Thank you Peter, thank you Paul, to name but two. Over, like, and out. **1972** N. MARSH *Tied up in Tinsel* v. 123 'Well, ta for the tip anyway. Over and out.' Alleyn hung up. **1973** G. MITCHELL *Murder of Busy Lizzie* xv. 175 'But, for the moment, we are concerning ourselves with the Lovelaine family, I thought.' 'Sorry! Over to you, then.' **1974** P. WRIGHT *Lang. Brit. Industry* xiv. 135 It [*sc.* language repetition] occurs particularly where.. actions and accompanying words amount to a drill, as in the radio operator's *Over and out*. **1976** L. DILLS *CB Slanguage Dict.* (rev. ed.) 51 *Over*, through transmitting but listening.

9. b. Until a later time or period; till the next season; overnight.

1861 *Trans. Illinois Agric. Soc.* IV. 317 Old bugs live over, and produce eggs the following season. **1884** J. HAY *Bread-Winners* xi. 172, I am so glad you resolved to stay over. **1899** A. NICHOLAS *Idyl of Wabash* 53 We don't want to winter them steers over. **1953** N. GORDIMER *Lying Days* II. xx. 168, I was going to sleep over at the house of an old friend of my mother's. **1968** J. SANGSTER *Touchfeather* xiv. 149 'You're staying over.'..'But I haven't brought any clothes.' **1973** 'D. SHANNON' *No Holiday for Crime* (1974) vi. 91 He..put a second shirt and a razor in a briefcase in case he had to stay over.

14. Phr. *over* (*and done*) *with*: completed, finished; dispensed with.

1938 R. D. FINLAYSON *Brown Man's Burden* 53 The others..were glad when they were free to go, for..the salutations were over and done with. **1970** AUDEN in *New Yorker* 21 Feb. 118/1, I have one slight criticism.. which I will get over with at once. **1977** S. WOODS *Thief or Two* 136, I thought, if I was going to do it, I'd get it over with.

over, *prep.* Add: **1. c.** (Earlier and later examples.)

1805 in *Spirit of Public Jrnls.* (1806) 96 A writer over the signature of Zanga, is another buckram expression. **1826** *New Harmony* (Indiana) *Gaz.* 22 Mar. 207/2 A writer over the signature of 'A Farmer'..states that he has been completely successful..in saving his wheat [from weevils]. **1934** H. G. WELLS *Exper. Autobiogr.* II. viii. 626 Bennett ..wrote much of the little weekly paper, *Woman*, he was editing..over the signature..of 'Aunt Ellen'. **1946** *Sunshine Mag.* Apr. (front cover), New preface over the author's own signature.

7. a. (See also *ALL OVER *advb. phr.* 1 c).

d. (Further examples.)

1916 T. MACDONAGH *Lit. in Ireland* 120 The characteristic qualities of the ancient Irish lyrics are those of good lyric poetry the world over. **1930** *Publishers' Weekly* 23 Aug. 675/2 There are many more like me, the country over, really anxious to feed their fanaticism. **1971** *Guardian* 14 Jan. 11/8 Policemen love one another the world over.

e. *Math.* (Defined or expressed) in terms of (the elements of); *esp.* having coefficients or co-ordinates in, or having elements with coefficients or co-ordinates in.

1932 *Trans. Amer. Math. Soc.* XXXIV. 171 (*heading*) Theory of cyclic algebras over an algebraic number field. **1938** A. A. ALBERT *Mod. Higher Algebra* ii. 40 The most interesting and important linear sets for our purposes are those of finite order n over a field $\mathscr{F}$...Their elements may be thought of as points in an n-dimensional space with coordinates in $\mathscr{F}$. **1965** J. J. ROTMAN *Theory of Groups* vi. 103 A number $\alpha \in C$ is algebraic over F in case $F(\alpha)$ is a finite-dimensional vector space over F (otherwise α is transcendental over F). **1972** A. G. HOWSON *Handbk. Terms Algebra & Analysis* xi. 55 The polynomials form a subring..called the ring of polynomials over K.

12. b. *over the wicket*: see *BOWL *v.*[1] 4 b.

13. Add to def.: by means of (a telephone, radio communication, or the like); = *ON *prep.* 1 d.

1899 [in Dict.]. **1928** BLUNDEN *Overtones of War* iv. 43 Persons who, speaking over the field telephones, gave away any information at all..would be court-martialled. **1929** *Radio Times* 8 Nov. 387 'Pickwick', and other such novels, should be read serially over the microphone. *Ibid.*, Over the wireless a reading can be listened to without.. irrelevant disturbances. **1946** *Ibid.* 8 Feb. 3/3 His boys and girls who had been heard over All-India Radio. **1966** *Listener* 17 Nov. 725/1 He is asking you over the telephone, so you cannot point or use gestures. **1969** *N.Y. Rev. Books* 2 Jan. 5/1 In his Security Gap speech over CBS on October 25, Nixon said one of his major aims would be to 'correct its (the Pentagon's) over-centralization'.

15. b. Having recovered from (an illness, disease, or the like). Cf. GET *v.* 41 b.

1929 'S.N.D.' *Sir W. Howard, Visct. Stafford* iii. 29 He was in England, just over an illness, and straitened for lack of money in the autumn of 1646. **1942** D. POWELL *Time to be Born* (1943) vi. 139 You're over it, aren't you, Vicky? That's wonderful. **1964** L. DEIGHTON *Funeral in Berlin* xviii. 109 Finally there is not being in love and liking that—you are over it then—cured. **1975** J. GRADY *Shadow of Condor* (1976) i. 18 My wife just got over the flu..she's over it now. **1977** P. SMALLEY *Trove* ii. 78 He had guessed about the alcoholism as soon as Daley said he had been in hospital... He probably was over it, but you never knew for sure.

over, *sb.*[2] **2. b.** *pl. Printing.* Copies printed in excess of the number ordered, to allow for wastage.

1888 C. T. JACOBI *Printers' Vocab.* 92 *Overs*, the 'plus' copies beyond a certain number. **1901** D. COCKERELL *Bookbinding* I. ii. 36 The printers usually keep a number of 'overs' in order to make good such imperfections. **1946** J. A. EISLER in H. Whetton *Pract. Printing & Binding* xxvii. 328/2 Finding the net amount of paper entailed in the production of a job (exclusive of overs) should present few difficulties to the man familiar with ordinary paper usage. **1961** T. LANDAU *Encycl. Librarianship* (ed. 2) 269/2 Overs. The number of sound copies over after the printing of the net number of copies ordered.

4. Add to def.: Since 1900, an 'over' has normally consisted of 6 balls, except in Australia, and recently occas. elsewhere, where it is 8. (Earlier and later examples.) Also *attrib.* Cf. MAIDEN *a.* 4 b in Dict. and Suppl.

1833 *New Sporting Mag.* V. 325 The Anglesea are in the field, And Floyer bowls the over. **1921** LD. HARRIS *Few Short Runs* xi. 284 Under such circumstances how we welcome the umpire's 'Last over, gentlemen.' **1955** *Times* 9 May 15/1 When one says that only one hook was aimed at Tayfield in 37 overs the reader will get some idea of the fullness of his length. Before each over he stands over his stumps and performs a kind of ritual. **1960** E. W. SWANTON *W. Indies Revisited* 282 The over-rate during the First Test was higher than in any subsequent one. **1974** B. JOHNSTON *It's been a lot of Fun* xvi. 116 'Stick to the play, Percy, and keep that sort of chat for between the overs,' said the producer. **1977** *Times* 18 Jan. 9/8 The fact that the ball had to be replaced three times,..and that the sightscreens are not easily shifted, all helped to bring down the Indian over rate..to just under 11 to the hour.

5. *Mil.* (chiefly *pl.*). A bullet, shell, or other missile that passes beyond its target. *colloq.*

1915 W. H. L. WATSON *Adventures Despatch Rider* v. 66 He believes the Uhlans were North Irish Horse and the bullets 'overs'. **1928** BLUNDEN *Undertones of War* iv. 43 A familiar place far enough from the Brickstack which we held to receive the 'overs'. **1944** A. JACOB *Traveller's War* 238 Men on the fringe of the battle area..receive the 'overs' and keep ducking flat as they hear the hissing approach of tank ammo, that has missed its mark. **1969** I. KEMP *Brit. G.I. in Vietnam* vi. 140, I..laid them behind a tree..; they should be moderately safe there from 'overs'.

over, *v.* **4.** (Further examples.)

1847 A. BRONTË *Agnes Grey* xi. 163, I was sore distressed Miss Grey—thank God it's owered now. *Ibid.* xii. 185 You'll *both* stay while this shower gets owered. **1933** L. A. G. STRONG *Sea Wall* II. xiv. 219 He done an operation on a woman and she never overed it. **1936** 'N. BLAKE' *Thou Shell of Death* xiii. 231 Master Dermot was killed in France, the year of the Easter Rising. His da never overed it. **1949** *Amer. Speech* XXIV. 111 *Over*, to recover from, as a disease or an injury.

over-. Add: **I. 8.** Also with the sense 'upon the surface so as to cover in part', as in *OVERPAINT *sb.*, *OVERPRINT *v.* II. **a.** *overscreen, -stamp* vbs.

1906 HARDY *Dynasts* II. I. ii. 17 Draw down the curtain, then, and overscreen This too-protracted verbal fencing-scene. **1935** *Burlington Mag.* June 288/1 Over-stamping on Sheffield-made candlesticks the London date-letter 1775–6. **1963** *Times* 23 May 9/6 She would inquire about what they were suffering from 'and they would tell me nerves, flu, bronchitis, or gastritis and so on, and I just wrote out the certificate and signed "T. G. Boyle", and overstamped'. **1977** *Belfast Tel.* 22 Feb. 3/1 Your book will be overstamped to include an extra £1 a week for your first child from 4th April, 1977, and posted back to you.

c. *over-bolster, -boot, -cover, -gaiter* (further example), *-jumper, -mitt, -shirt* (earlier and later examples), *-sock, -stocking, -trousers.*

1917 D. H. LAWRENCE *Phoenix II* (1968) 64 A single bed, opened for the night, the white over-bolster piled back. **1939–40** *Army & Navy Stores Catal.* 607/2 Motoring Overboots, in Brown Sheepskin. **1959** *Times* 2 Oct. 14/6 Her..macintosh, rain hood, and over-boots testified to a careful preparation for the realities of the English climate. **1971** C. BONINGTON *Annapurna South Face* xiii. 143 Mick got ready for the next pitch, removing crampons and overboots in readiness for what was obviously going to be a hard piece of free rock climbing. **1915** F. M. FORD *Good Soldier* IV. ii. 224 Fishing-rods in green baize over-covers. **1963** *Times* 23 Feb. 11/3 Plentiful over-cover induced the deer to stay. **1908** 'O. HENRY' *Voice of City* 233 It was Rosalie, in..gray walking suit, and tan oxfords with lavender overgaiters. **1975** *Times* 7 Oct. 11/4 Over-jumper with wide sleeves..and a square neck. **1971** Overmit [see *LINER[1] 3]. **1971** C. BONINGTON *Annapurna South Face* 298, Gloves with waterproof over-mitts are standard. **1805** LEWIS & CLARK *Orig. Jrnls. Expedition* (1905) II. 159 The weather being warm I had left my leather over shirt and had woarn only a yellow flannin one. **1974** *Country Life* 2 May 1096/2 The man wears a cotton..striped overshirt, denim shorts and pull-on hat. **1911** WEBSTER, Over-sock. **1929** *Footwear Organiser* Jan. 31 (*heading*) The Oversock vogue spreads throughout the country. **1971** 'D. HALLIDAY' *Dolly & Doctor Bird* iii. 29 For golf, I have always worn..oversocks with good shoes. **1892** KIPLING *Lett. of Travel* (1920) 6 The driver with red mittens on his hands, felt overstockings that come up to his knees, and, perhaps, a silvery-gray coon-skin coat on his back, walks beside me. **1852** *Harper's Mag.* Apr. 707/1 My duck over-trousers..were beginning to be rather tender in certain places. **1968** *Daily Tel.* 28 Sept. 9/4 Come rain or snow the lot would be covered by over-trousers or over-skirts and waterproof jackets. **1976** *Good Motoring* Nov. 24/1 Coats, jackets and overtrousers.

13. b. Prefixed to a plural number (or occas. a singular number used *attrib.*) to denote persons who are older than that particular age.

1940 GRAVES & HODGE *Long Week-End* xvii. 303 The *Evening News*..throwing open its columns to the over-forties. **1959** *Manch. Guardian* 19 Aug. 3/6 Sir Compton Mackenzie and Miss Ruby Miller, for the over-70s, sparring with youthful zest. **1960** *Guardian* 13 Apr. 6/6 There seems to be no place for the over-fifties. **1960** C. WATSON *Bump in Night* ii. 25 We shall want to take a closer look.. without being trampled to death by the Over-Sixty clubs. **1972** M. J. BOSSE *Incident at Naha* 47 They had their hair done in an over-thirty style. **1973** M. AMIS *Rachel Papers* 22 The over-twenties, I grant you, must see it [*sc.* sex] largely as a matter of obligation, too: but obligation to the partner, not to oneself, like us. **1975** B. MEYRICK *Behind Light* xiv. 183 After the boys' competitions, where I came in second in the over-twelves, came..community hymn singing. **1977** *New Wave* No. 7. 8 The only night spots, right, are an over-25's place and Mecca.

19. *over-matter* (further examples).

1928 *Daily Express* 7 Feb. 3/6 Early buyers of lingerie had all the advantages, for most of the real bargains.. belonged to ranges that..were 'overmatter' that had to be cast out of stock. **1967** *Economist* 2 Dec. p. iii/2 This one book is only a bit of overmatter from all his earlier over-writings. **1972** *Observer* 12 Mar. 16/8 Large quantities of titanium overmatter..were just thrown into the dustbin. **1977** *Oxf. Diocesan Mag.* Oct. 4/1 The carry-forward of over-matter means that no issue can be planned as 'an island, entire of itself'.

II. 23. *over-bowl* (earlier and later examples). Cf. also sense *27 a.

1844 *W. Lillywhite's Illustr. Hand-bk. Cricket* 18 Do not over bowl yourself by random bowling. **1962** *Punch* 1 Aug. 152/3 A Cowdrey who would certainly not overbowl himself.

27. a. *over-accentuate, -bowl, -commit, -complicate, -condense, -control, -cook, -deflate, -dramatize, -elaborate, -emphasize* (examples), *-enrich* (example), *-express* (examples), *-ink, -interpret, -invest, -linger* (later example), *-order, -prove* (examples), *-rank, -regulate, -rev* (trans. and intr.), *-secrete, -stress* vbs.

1885 A. BRERETON *Dramatic Notes* 31 She slightly over-accentuated certain passages. **1977** *Gramophone* Jan. 1160/1 If anything the conductor over-accentuates at the expense of broader phrasing. **1962** *Times* 15 May 4/2 It must be a temptation for his captain to overbowl him. **1976** J. SNOW *Cricket Rebel* 41 In his first full championship season in 1974 Andy [Roberts] was overbowled consistently throughout the summer while Hampshire tried to retain the county title. **1964** Y. Malkiel in *Archivum Linguisticum* XVI. 15 W. J. Entwistle may have over-committed himself. **1973** *Guardian* 11 Apr. 8/7 A few [families] were found to have overcommitted themselves with hire purchase. **1966** A. Battersby *Math. in Managem.* v. 130 One can easily over-complicate a model, and the manager and mathematician must collaborate closely to decide not only what is relevant, but what is significant. **1976** H. Tracy *Death in Reserve* xiv. 113 You're over-complicating the whole thing. **1933** *Mind* XLII. 391 The actual statement of the theory is, in view of its importance, somewhat over-condensed, and ought perhaps to have been expanded. **1962** A. Nisbett *Technique Sound Studio* xiii. 232 Pace is not achieved by over-condensing vital information. **1941** *Sun* (Baltimore) 28 June 1/5 He simply overcontrolled the ship. **1904** *Daily Chron.* 30 May 8/3 So you can over-cook even a sauce. **1963** R. Carrier *Great Dishes of World* xiii. 225 Be careful not to overcook *pasta*. **1975** I. Daly in D. Marcus *Best Irish Short Stories* (1977) II. 32, I want the steak medium-rare... All you Irish overcook meat. **1977** *Harpers & Queen* Sept. 28/1 The salmon was overcooked. **1962** *Daily Tel.* 15 June 14/2 The reported trends are signs ..that the economy has been over-deflated and that confidence in future expansion needs fostering. **1974** *Times* 28 Feb. 19/2 A Labour Government would be tempted to overdeflate in the Budget in order to make itself more attractive to foreign lenders. **1955** S. Spender *Making of Poem* iv. 63 Perhaps I over-dramatize the affair. **1976** M. Butterworth *Remains to be Seen* vii. 111 The flat..he now saw as a fortress... He hoped he was over-dramatizing his situation. **1905** *Daily Chron.* 2 Sept. 3/1 Mr. Phillpotts has resisted the temptation..to over-elaborate his descriptions of natural scenery. **1933** W. E. Orchard *From Faith to Faith* ix. 206 These [dogmas] were over-elaborated during the early controversies, and have only obscured His personal power by theories about Him. **1905** *Outlook* 7 Oct. 485/1 He over-emphasises when he suggests that Hungary is a solid State and Austria but a bundle of provinces. **1926** J. S. Huxley *Ess. Pop. Sci.* 153 This..we must discount unless we are to over-emphasize the antinomy between the microcosm and the macrocosm. **1968** H. Harris *Nucleus & Cytoplasm* i. 12 It cannot be over-emphasized that actinomycin D is an extremely toxic compounds. **1852** Mill *Pol. Econ.* (ed. 3) I. II. ii. 276 Wealth which could no longer be employed in over-enriching a few. **1883** 'Mark Twain' *Life on Mississippi* 399 Terms which did not over-express the admiration with which the people viewed him. **1959** N. Mailer *Advts. for Myself* (1961) 17, I am not suited for this sort of confrontation despite..a bloody season of overexpressed personal opinions as a newspaper columnist. **1927** *Observer* 12 June 9 The literary man..is apt to over-ink his pictures of contemporary morals. **1939** T. S. Eliot *Family Reunion* II. i. 77 You overinterpret. I am sure that your mother always loved him; There was never the slightest suspicion of scandal. **1963** *Times* 9 May 16/4 She..sometimes fell into the opposite trap of overinterpreting detail. **1975** *Nature* 18 Dec. 562/3 There is a danger, however, that such a negative result could be over-interpreted as suggesting that recombinant experiments are inherently safe. **1934** Webster, Overinvest. **1958** *New Statesman* 25 Jan. 94/3 The trouble about Poland today..is that we are rather like a furniture manufacturer who has plenty of table legs but no table tops. We have over-invested in legs and now we want more capital for the tops. **1895** W. B. Yeats *Poems* 23 He has over-lingered his welcome. **1950** *Times* 20 Feb. 7/7 It was not surprising that, when steel was most scarce, the distribution scheme worked least well: firms over-ordered and accumulated stocks and there was nothing to encourage them to use as little steel as possible. **1977** D. Bennett *Jigsaw Man* v. 106 'You aren't liking your good grub.' 'I think I over-ordered.' **1912** A. Lang *Shakespeare, Bacon & Great Unknown* iv. 81 Mr. Collins, 'a violent Stratfordian', overproved his case. **1929** R. Graves *Poems* 31 Now is a sheet of paper, A not blank expectation,..A being, over-proved, A report of happiness. **1958** *New Statesman* 23 Aug. 222/3 In answering poll-questionnaires..'we tend to over-rank ourselves'. **1972** *Korea Times* 17 Nov. 2/3, I am no longer willing to remain patient with the parade of overranked non-entities whose actions reflect their own ignorance. **1938** *Sun* (Baltimore) 16 Apr. 8 Mr. Roosevelt is equally muddled in his general attitude toward trade and industry. For five years he has overregulated trade and industry. **1973** *Sci. Amer.* Sept. 165/1 Some observers believe that the pharmaceutical industry is now overregulated and that bureaucratic interference with the industry has reached such a level that the American public is being denied certain drugs available overseas. **1935** C. G. Burge *Compl. Bk. Aviation* 87/1 The control stick is pushed forward to give the diving position and the throttle eased slightly back to avoid over-revving the engine. **1978** *Daily Tel.* 26 July 3/2 Mr Wheatcroft adjusted the accelerator, but..he noticed that the coach seemed to be 'over-revving', as though the driver was not using the brakes to slow it down. **1927** Haldane & Huxley *Animal Biol.* viii. 164 If the pituitary begins to over-secrete before the epiphyses have been joined by bone to the shafts, the patient becomes a giant. **1916** T. MacDonagh *Lit. in Ireland* 66 An Irish reader would be content to pronounce the words as they come,..not overstressing 'in' and 'up'. **1933** *Mind* XLII. 238 It is also admitted that children have to be taught cleanliness (which parents often over-stress from snobbishness!). **1970** *Daily Tel.* 26 Sept. 9/7 It would however be wrong to overstress the importance of colour in lithography. **1977** *Bitumen* (Shell Internat. Petroleum Co.) 7 Knowledge of such properties has made it possible to design roads and airfield runways on sound engineering principles, ensuring that no part is over-stressed even under the heaviest loads.

b. *over-blessed, -characterized, -concentrated, -concerned, -involved, -preoccupied, -recovered, -rehearsed, -represented* (further examples), *-technicized* pa. pples.

c **1804** Wordsworth *Vaudracour & Julia* in *Misc. Poems* (1820) I. 283 His spirit sank, Surcharged, within him,—overblest to move Beneath a sun that wakes a weary world. **1918** *Nation* (N.Y.) 7 Feb. 130/1 Not by any means a leader even in a body that has not of late been overblessed with outstanding personages. **1977** D. Clark *Gimmel Flask* iii. 58 Green wasn't over-blessed with good manners. **1959** *Times* 9 Nov. 6/1 To begin with they [*sc.* the figures] are heavily over-characterized (by the dangerous means of self-description). **1957** K. G. Wittfogel *Oriental Despotism* 24 On-the-spot rains create additional dangers when they are overconcentrated. **1934** Webster *s.v.* Over- 6, Overconcerned. **1941** *Mind* L. 2 You are under-concerned about the cases which don't trouble you at the moment, and over-concerned about the one that is striking you at the moment. **1976** P. Hill *Hunters* vi. 67 Was he then weak..over-concerned with what others thought of him. **1965** M. Morse *Unattached* iii. 90 Even the most..skilled of workers can..become over-involved with the..situation at hand. **1975** *Times Lit. Suppl.* 13 June 669/1 Historians ..had been overpreoccupied with what was done to the slaves and had slighted what slaves had done for themselves. **1962** *Which?* (Car Suppl.) Jan. 11/2 Where there is a minus figure, it means that the braking system had over-recovered and needed less pressure than usual; this may make control difficult. **1967** D. Goch in Wills & Yearsley *Handbk. Managem. Technol.* 147 Fixed overheads, being relatively unaffected by fluctuations in the number of units produced during the period, will be either under- or over-recovered to the extent that output varies from that which was assumed to be normal when the standards were set. **1976** *Gramophone* May 1732/1 Most concerts are under-rehearsed and rely too much on the inspiration of the moment, or are over-rehearsed and so dead. **1965** J. Hajnal in Glass & Eversley *Population in Hist.* vi. 121 The deaths of young women are very probably over-represented. **1974** *Howard Jrnl.* XIV. 39 ESN schools, where West Indian youths are significantly over-represented, mainly because they have been wrongly placed there. **1953** *Mind* LXII. 424 It is a joy to go back to the beginnings of a subject which has since become over-technicised.

28. a. *over-articulate, over-clean* (examples), *-complimentary, -concise, -conscious* (example), *-controversial, -dependent, -elaborate, -fast, -friendly, -fussy, -ingenious, -insistent, -keen, -logical* (later examples), *-mellow* (later example), *-mighty* (later examples), *-nimble* (example), *-obvious, -optimistic, -patient* (example), *-pessimistic, -picturesque, -plump, -prolific, -prone* (later example), *-rapid, -ready* (earlier and later examples), *-sensational, -shy, -susceptible* adjs.

1975 *Christmas Greeting* (Rhodes House, Oxford) 6 When dons behave badly, they behave very badly: it is partly the fault of being over-articulate, though early rearing probably has something to do with it too. *c* **1806** D. Wordsworth *Jrnl.* (1941) I. 327 Two beds, with not over-clean bedclothes. **1818** 'A. Burton' *Adventures J. Newcome* I. 32 The Bed-cloaths, when by daylight seen, They did not fancy over-clean. **1867** Mill *Exam. Hamilton's Philos.* (ed. 3) p. vii, Some of the writers are.. even over-complimentary. **1940** W. Stevens *Let.* 30 Aug. (1967) 374 The trouble here is that the lines are over-concise. **1965** *Language* XLI. 142 In his desire to be complete..and informative, Kukenheim is over-concise. **1851** H. Melville *Moby Dick* I. i. 5 Whenever I begin to..be over conscious of my lungs. **1862** H. Sidgwick *Let.* 28 Jan. in A. & E. M. Sidgwick *Henry Sidgwick* (1906) 74 It seems smashing, but he loses by being over-controversial. **1975** *New Yorker* 21 Apr. 127/2 We fought the war for them and made them overdependent on air support. **1931** A. Esdaile *Student's Man. Bibliogr.* vi. 198 Incised bindings..also became over-elaborate, especially in Germany. **1934** Webster, Overfast. **1949** R. Blesh *Shining Trumpets* ii. 41 Overfast tempos did not appear in Afro-American music until very recently. **1939** R. Campbell *Flowering Rifle* vi. 142 In their own tanks they ha ve to be locked up As in a box an over-friendly pup. **1962** E. Godfrey *Retail Selling & Organization* xii. 131 Personal comments and an over-friendly manner also amount to discourtesy. **1974** N. Freeling *Dressing of Diamond* 135 Richard asked..whether I'd perhaps let myself get over-friendly with Colette. **1962** *Times* 16 Feb. 15/2 The ballet-boyish treatment of the pirate chorus is new, and inclined to look over-fussy. **1858** Bagehot *Coll. Works* (1965) II. 70 It would be over-ingenious to argue..that he had no peculiar interest in young ladies in general. **1977** A. Wilson *Strange Ride R. Kipling* iv. 208 The over-ingenious method of Kipling's narration. **1915** D. H. Lawrence *Let.* 26 Feb. (1962) I. 323, I wish you'd tell me when I am foolish and overinsistent. **1977** *N.Y. Rev. Bks.* 13 Oct. 35/2 The slightly overinsistent Ciceronianisms here draw attention to themselves. **1934** Webster *s.v.* Over- 6, Overkeen. **1959** I. & P. Opie *Lore & Lang. Schoolch.* x. 181 The word 'sap'..at Eton is primarily used to castigate someone who is over-keen on his work. **1977** J. Bingham *Marriage Bureau Murders* x. 130 A girl in trouble with an over-keen lover. **1920** W. R. Inge *Truth & Falsehood in Relig.* 19 Exclusive intellectualism in religion..commits us to an over-logical scheme. **1966** *Eng. Stud.* XLVII. 299 Occasionally Williams seems to make Shakespeare over-logical. **1930** Wyndham Lewis *Let.* 30 July (1963) 190 Joyce is like an over-mellow hot-house pear. **1887** W. Morris tr. *Homer's Odyssey* I. x. 188 There was one Elpenor, the youngest;.. In war not over-mighty. **1920** G. Robinson *David Urquhart* 11 The ephemeral predominance of an over-mighty subject. **1950** *Catholic Times* 17 Feb. 6/3 Some will perceive first the dangers of the Overmighty State. **1966** *Economist* 15 Jan. 170/3 Officialdom is also angry with the overmighty bishops for taking a political initiative without consulting the government. **1978** *Jrnl. R. Soc. Arts* CXXVI. 212/2 Monopolistic bodies have a tendency to become over-mighty. **1885** W. B. Yeats in *Dublin Univ. Rev.* June 111/2 Cease! no more! Thou hast an over-nimble tongue. **1925** I. A. Richards *Princ. Lit. Crit.* xxxv. 287 If to some readers parts of it appear unnecessary—either *irrelevant*, in the one case; or *over-obvious* in the other—I have nothing to add. **1951** Koestler *Age of Longing* II. iv. 243 Not to mention such over-obvious facts as the disparity in the number of divisions. **1953** *Encounter* July 48/1 If *The Tempest* is over-pessimistic and manichean, *The Magic Flute* is over-optimistic and pelagian. **1976** *Broadcast* 29 Mar. 4/1 Over-optimistic predictions of BBC income in the coming year. **1881** 'Mark Twain' *Prince & Pauper* 137, I like not much bandying of words, being not overpatient in my nature. **1934** Webster, Overpessimistic. **1953** Over-pessimistic [see *over-optimistic* above]. **1938** L. MacNeice *Mod. Poetry* 10 His [*sc.* Housman's hanged man, his soldiers, are over-picturesque. **1932** W. Faulkner *Light in August* xiii. 300 Hightower leans there..in the August heat, oblivious of the odor in which he lives—..that odor of overplump desiccation and stale linen as though a precursor of the tomb. **1923** D. H. Lawrence *Birds, Beasts & Flowers* 179 Those over-prolific white mice. **1976** N. Freeling *Lake Isle* viii. 51 His ma..was overprone, maybe, to well-meant advice about bringing up the children and such. **1848** Mill *Pol. Econ.* I. II. xi. 413 Where a labouring class..refrain from over-rapid multiplication, the cause..has always hitherto been, either actual legal restraint, or a custom of some sort [etc.]. **1964** *Ann. Reg. 1963* 263 Credit also became tighter, and full employment created the conditions for an over-rapid rise in wages and salaries. **1628** O. Feltham *Resolves* (ed. 3) xcvii. 283 And yet there are, that are over-ready in the wayes of pleasing, and labour. **1859** Bagehot *Coll. Works* (1965) II. 114 We may seem to make unusual criticisms, and to be over-ready with depreciation or objection. **1906** *Westm. Gaz.* 24 Mar. 2/3 They may be gazing on the..over-ready-to-burst chestnut-buds. **1959** *Times* 3 Sept. 13/2 He is sometimes oversensational and has tried to stuff too much into one book. **1939** L. MacNeice *Autumn Jrnl.* xi. 46 Over-shy at times, morose, defeatist. **1934** Webster, Oversusceptible. **1966** *Eng. Stud.* XLVII. 286 The connection..is made by the over-susceptible sensibility of Emily.

b. *over-demanding, -pressing, -refining* ppl. adjs.

1949 M. Mead *Male & Female* iii. 74 Too much emphasis upon the assertive demanding aspects of the mouth may build a female picture that is over-active, over-demanding, and threatening. **1893** *Harper's Mag.* Aug. 335/1 The finding..such a palpable motive as revenge against an overpressing and clamorous creditor tipped the balance. **1940** Dylan Thomas *Portrait of Artist as Young Dog* 122 And I never felt more a part of the remote and overpressing world, or more full of love and arrogance and pity and humility. **1855** Bagehot *Coll. Works* (1965) I. 322 The sceptical, over-refining Toryism of Hume and Montaigne.

c. *over-arranged, -controlled, -cultivated, -emotionalized, -expanded, -inflated, -inked, -mechanized, -nourished, -oiled* (example), *-padded, -perfumed, -polished, -qualified, -schematized, -sensitized* (also as sb.), *-sophisticated, -speculated, -spiritualized, -structured, -sugared* ppl. adjs.

1924 R. H. Mottram *Spanish Farm* 148 She was after all only saying the same thing in French, when a frail, fair, over-arranged lady kept her waiting in the glove department of the Bon Marché. **1956** G. Coulter in M. T. Williams *Art of Jazz* (1960) 167 Most of these bad performances take place in an over-arranged, be-violined setting. **1977** *New Musical Express* 12 Feb. 10/5 We hated over-arranged stage acts and gimmicks constructed just to go with one particular piece of music. **1964** M. Argyle *Psychol. & Social Probl.* ix. 123 Anxiety neurosis is an extreme case of the over-controlled personality resulting from a strict upbringing. **1968** J. S. & B. M. Bruner in *Internat. Jrnl. Psychol.* III. 239 In early human growth, the initially well-organized systems seem to be predominantly of the automatic or 'overcontrolled' type, as with breathing, swallowing, and initial sucking. **1868** W. James *Let.* 5 Apr. in R. B. Perry *Tht. & Char. W. James* (1935) I. 268 The cool acceptance by the bloody old heathens of everything that happened around them [etc.]..would all make their society perfectly hateful to these overcultivated and vaguely sick complainers. **1970** S. L. Barraclough in I. L. Horowitz *Masses in Lat. Amer.* iv. 138 Erosion of overcultivated hillsides is prevalent. **1938** R. G. Collingwood *Princ. Art* iii. 52 Plato..thinks that the new art of the decadence is the art of an over-excited, over-emotionalized world. **1965** H. J. Habbakuk in Glass & Eversley *Population in Hist.* vii. 157 These epidemics..cannot have been a Malthusian punishment inflicted on an overexpanded population. **1934** E. Pound *Eleven New Cantos* xxxiii. 14 The meeting decided we were over-inflated. **1964** W. G. Smith *Allergy & Tissue Metabolism* i. 3 The post mortem picture shows over-inflated lungs. *a* **1974** R. Crossman *Diaries* (1975) I. 585 The economy was over-inflated now, we needed to take some of the heat out and to drive a little of the employment out of it. **1978** *New York* 3 Apr. 71/2 His reputation is overshadowed..by that of Sir Edward Elgar, on whose inflated scores a grossly overinflated revival is now being perpetrated. **1967** Karch & Buber *Offset Processes* viii. 281 A heavy flow of ink will cause over-inked copy resulting in scum. **1960** *Farmer & Stockbreeder* 1 Mar. 135 (Advt.), If you haven't got a Lundell today, you're overmechanised. **1977** *Listener* 20 Oct. 517/2 It provides..a record..of what happens when a lumpish, over-mechanised and wrongly-trained army..meets a lightweight but adept Asian guerilla force in its own country. **1931** H. Read *Meaning of Art* II. 94 'Barock' with its dark and loaded sound implying well the heavy, swollen, over-nourished forms that must be urged into movement to make their impression. **1957** E. Pound tr. *Rimbaud* 13 A woman's head with brown over-oiled hair. **1938** L. MacNeice *Mod. Poetry* i. 4 Reaction from this poetry, which they felt to be priggish or pontifical or merely dull and overpadded. **1857** Bagehot *Coll. Works* (1965) II. 28 An over-perfumed softness pervades the poetry of society. **1938** H. Nicholson *Let.* 22 Apr. (1966) 337 An ex-diplomatist with those overpolished manners, that *boulevard extérieur* elegance, which always faintly annoys me. **1957** Manvell & Huntley *Film Music* iv. 180 The lighting cameraman may be concerned with a range of problems, from the over-polished console of an electric organ to the number of arcs required to illuminate the Royal Albert Hall. **1968** *N.Y. Times* 3 Feb. 19/5 It is often hard to get the message across to personnel men 'who make points hiring over qualified people for less than they're worth'. **1969** *Time* 28 Mar. 41 Applications are flooding colleges across the country. The problem is how to cull the lucky few from the over-qualified many. **1977** *Times* 19 Aug. 6/3 The unemployed PhD.., the over qualified school-leaver, have already brought home..the consequences of..rising unemployment and rising qualifications. **1962** U. Weinreich in Householder & Saporta *Probl. Lexicogr.* 35 Over-schematized though it may be, ad hoc intralinguistic considerations suggest [etc.]. **1965** *Language* XLI. 504 Rigid, overschematized synchronic analysis. **1926** E. Hemingway *Sun also Rises* xiv. 154, I read the Turgenieff..in the oversensitized state of my mind after much too much brandy. **1965** *Punch* 17 Mar. 397/2 This double disability may at first sight seem hard on the over-sensitised. **1975** *New Yorker* 26 May 18/2 *Blow-up*..An over-sensitized and wildly misaccented account of the mod, mad world of London, 1966. **1918** Oversophisticated [see *film fan* s.v. *film *sb.* 7 c]. **1971** *Guardian Weekly* 10 Apr. 14/4 An overdeveloped oversophisticated country. **1971** D. Potter *Brit. Eliz. Stamps* xv. 163 Prices began to rise on all sides. Only the overspeculated commemoratives failed to make progress. **1951** S. Spender *World within World* iii. 118 With him I escaped to some extent from the over-spiritualized, puritan, competitive atmosphere in which I had been brought up. **1959** N. Mailer *Advts. for Myself* (1961) 18, I find to my perhaps over-structured horror that I rather enjoy the high-pressured rubber of bridge. **1971** *Nature* 27 Aug. 591/1 The organization that has resulted from all the wrangles and compromises is over-structured. **1906** *Westm. Gaz.* 15 Aug. 4/2 No better corrective of their over-sugared literature, with its artistic embellishment, could be suggested than Mary Wollstonecraft's unflattering plain-dealing. **1968** *Daily Tel.* 17 Dec. 13/7 Much of this [Amontillado] sold here tends to be rather flat and over-sugared.

d. *over-banked, -muscled* adjs.

1930 *Times* 27 Mar. 21/2 The Port of Karachi..is considerably over-banked. **1966** *Economist* 18 June p. xxxiii/1 It has reduced its branches in Scotland, which is more overbanked than England. **1956** H. Gold *Man who was not with It* (1965) ix. 74 His weary overmuscled body. **1977** *Gay News* 7–20 Apr. 23/1 No, I don't like that, over-muscled... I do like people who keep their bodies in shape though.

29. a. *over-caring, -drugging, -farming, -meddling* (example), *-packaging, -packing, -padding, -planning, -revving, -soiling* vbl. sbs.

1938 Belloc *Sonnets & Verse* 39 Believe in none and die of over-caring. **1868** A. B. Garrod *Materia Medica* (ed. 3) 375 Much discredit has been thrown upon the whole subject of the medicinal treatment of disease by the practice of indiscriminate prescribing and over-drugging. **1946** *Nature* 23 Nov. 733/1 In his keen observation, in his reflexion and deductions, and in his dislike of over-drugging, More had all the endowments of a wise physician. **1943** J. S. Huxley *TVA* vi. 33 Over-farming was not the only exploitation. **1861** Mill *Repr. Govt.* iv. 82 A government..required to hold its hands from over-meddling..is not to the taste of such a people. **1972** *Computers & Humanities* VII. 81 Rarely has the sociology of knowledge provided such an obvious example of technology shaping the formulation of research conception as in the over-packaging of most social science statistical analysis. **1967** Karch & Buber *Offset Processes* vii. 262 Repeat until satisfactory, but avoid overpacking. **1962** *Economist* 8 Sept. 925/1 Wasteful overpadding of junior executive posts. **1974** T. P. Whitney tr. *Solzhenitsyn's Gulag Archipel.* I. i. x. 393 To defend *quality*..amid the general uproar about *quantity*, planning, and overplanning. **1977** *Times* 16 Feb. 15/5 The country has suffered from intensive over-planning. **1976** F. Greenland *Misericordia Drop* i. v. 39 After some predictable over-revving with the clutch out, they were off. **1959** *Times* 12 Jan. 11/3 It is advisable to avoid over-soiling and consequent hard rubbing.

b. *over-accentuation, -aspiration, -blame, -classification, -commitment, -consumption* (examples), *-control, -dramatization, -expansion, -expression, -influence, -insistence* (examples), *-interpretation, -involvement, -moralization, -multiplication, -nutrition, -organization, -ornamentation, -recovery, -regulation* (examples), *-reliance* (examples), *-secretion, -sophistication, -speculation* (earlier and later examples), *-stress, -tension* (examples).

1907 R. Fry *Let.* 11 Jan. (1972) I. 280, I find even in Dürer's portrait of himself here a certain over-accentuation, a self-consciousness. **1928** I. C. Ward *Phonetics of Eng.* xiii. 115 In order to cure over-aspiration, it is necessary to tell the pupil to make the contact firm and the release vigorous. **1964** Crystal & Quirk *Syst. Prosodic & Paralinguistic Features Eng.* iii. 38 Voice qualities... Over-aspiration (excessive pressure being released as compared with normal articulation) particularly noticeable on vowels, and on those consonants where there is normally little aspiration. **1874** Tennyson *Merlin & Vivien* in *Wks.* VI. 12 Of overpraise and overblame We choose the last. **1955** *Bull. Atomic Sci.* Apr. 127/3 In other defense activities it is undoubtedly true that overclassification is the rule. **1961** *Lancet* 26 Aug. 497/1 He was..a little bit impatient with the fussy overclassification that was coming into vogue in his specialty. **1964** Y. Malkiel in *Archivum Linguisticum* XVI. 14 Undercommitment versus overcommitment. **1934** Webster, Overconsumption. **1974** *Daily Colonist* (Victoria, B.C.) 15 Nov. 1/6 The Norwegian delegation is pushing a conference resolution stating that overconsumption impairs the health of the affluent. **1941** O. E. Patton *Aircraft Instruments* vii. 114 A follow-up mechanism is a necessary part of an automatic control, in order to prevent overcontrol, which gives rise to oscillations, or hunting, of the aircraft. **1957** J. S. Bruner in *Psychological Rev.* Mar. 144/2 George Klein's work..suggests that, in general, people who are not able to shift categorization under gradually changing conditions of stimulation tend also to show what he describes as 'overcontrol' on other cognitive and motivational tasks. **1973** *Sociometry* XXXVI. 135 A false fire-alarm went off precisely as the stimulus-subject in a severe condition was screaming from the electrical shock, providing an extremely amusing overdramatization of an already impactful event. **1976** R. Hill *Another Death in Venice* i. i. 21 Out there was a young *mafioso*... No, that was an absurd over-dramatization. **1935** *Planning* III. liii. 5 The legacy of war-time over-expansion, often in uneconomic locations, and of post-war over-capitalisation is a second [factor]. **1964** E. H. Powell in I. L. Horowitz *New Sociol.* xx. 332 The drive for profit produced a disastrous fluctuation of the business cycle, with periods of over-expansion and prosperity followed by bleak times of contraction and business failure. **1899** W. James *Talks to Teachers* viii. 75 This ceaseless over-tension, over-motion, and over-expression are working on us grievous national harm. **1908** *Edin. Rev.* July 71 That greatest snare of Faber's unquestionable eloquence: over-expression. **1966** 'H. MacDiarmid' *Company I've Kept* iii. 85 The Scottish public has been..debauched and distorted by English over-influence. **1934** Webster, Over-insistence. **1953** K. Reisz *Technique Film Editing* ii. 114 An over-insistence on one aspect of the theme..may..divert the spectator's attention from the main theme. **1965** W. S. Allen *Vox Latina* Appendix B. 109 His [Erasmus'] conclusions appear to arise partly out of an over-interpretation of Marius Victorinus. **1968** F. G. Lounsbury in J. A. Fishman *Readings Sociol. of Lang.* 53 The above..is possibly also an overinterpretation of the facts. **1964** P. Worsley in I. L. Horowitz *New Sociol.* 385 Their problem would not be separateness..but over-involvement. **1976** *Times* 20 May 18/7 [Jerry] Brown.. has reportedly made himself a pain in the neck by over-involvement in detail and incapacity to delegate. **1933** A. N. Whitehead *Adventures of Ideas* xii. 201 The forgetfulness of this doctrine leads to an over-moralization in the view of the nature of things. **1931** J. S Huxley *What dare I Think?* i. 28 Can he [*sc.* the biologist], by studying the pest in its original home, discover what are the other species that normally act as checks on its over-multiplication? **1899** Overnutrition [see *undernutrition* s.v. Under-[1] 10 b]. **1936** *Discovery* Apr. 98/2 While diseases associated with under-nutrition (tuberculosis, etc.) are steadily decreasing here, those associated with good nutrition—not to say over-nutrition —(diabetes, etc.) are on the increase. **1971** *New Scientist* 25 Feb. 407/1 Enormous problems of malnutrition and overnutrition remain unsolved and untackled. **1976** *Sci. Amer.* Sept. 40/2 Malnutrition may come about in one of four ways. A person..may be taking in too many calories or consuming an excess of one component or more of a reasonable diet; this condition is overnutrition. **1946** *Nature* 21 Sept. 392/2 There was no disposition on the part of the delegates to encourage the over-organisation of such interchange or movement of scientific workers. **1968** C. A. Doxiadis *Betw. Dystopia & Utopia* 18 In 1959, Aldous Huxley..explains what disasters we should expect because of over-population, over-organization, and brain-washing. **1933** R. Tuve *Seasons & Months* iv. 188 Poets had come to take delight in over-ornamentation. **1967** D. Goch in Wills & Yearsley *Handbk. Managem. Technol.* 148 At an output level of 510,000 there is an over-recovery of 10,000 × 1*s.* 0*d.* = £500. **1875** *Encycl. Brit.* II. 575/1 Appointments..were made under the purchase system... Every regimental commission had a fixed regulation price..in addition to which an over-regulation price, which sometimes even exceeded the regulation price, had sprung up. **1950** A. L. Rowse *England of Elizabeth* iv. 113 The natural energy, inventiveness, enterprise of the people, that was..not discouraged, thwarted and stifled by over-regulation. **1976** *National Observer* (U.S.) 4 Dec. 10/2 What is really wrong with government overregulation is not that business people find it burdensome and costly, but that its principal victim is the consumer. **1833** J. S. Mill in *Monthly Repos.* VII. 663 Over-reliance on our own judgment is one thing, over-reliance on the judgment of the world when in unison with our own, is another. **1961** L. F. Brosnahan *Sounds of Language* iii. 50 An apparent over-reliance on the spelling as a means of identification of dental fricatives. **1948** Martin & Hynes *Clin. Endocrinol.* i. 20 Acromegaly... A disease due to over-secretion of the hormones of the acidophil cells of the pars anterior in adult life. **1934** C. Lambert *Music Ho!* i. 44 That modern craving—essentially a product of over-sophistication—for the dark and instinctive that we find in D. H. Lawrence. **1857** J. S. Mill in *Coll. Wks.* (1967) V. 502 To prevent the Bank, at times when there is a tendency to overspeculation, from encouraging that tendency. **1940** *Times* 27 Feb. 14/4 The Spanish Council of Ministers has approved the reopening of the stock exchanges at Madrid, Barcelona, and Bilbao on March 1... The reopening is subject to various restrictions aimed at curbing over-speculation. **1965** G. J. Williams *Econ. Geol. N.Z.* iii. 23/1 A period of depression resulted from over-speculation. **1923** J. S. Huxley *Ess. Biologist* i. 55 Whatever overstress and maladjustment the complexity of modern civilization has brought with it, [etc.]. **1971** *Daily Tel.* 26 July 11/1 The effect of overstress is cumulative, causing structural weaknesses over a period of time. **1899** Over-tension [see *over-expression* above].

c. *over-capacity, -consciousness, -dominance, -exactness* (example), *-expressiveness, -intensity* (examples), *-lusciousness, -optimism, -susceptibility* (example).

1934 Webster, Overcapacity. **1960** *New Left Rev.* May–June 20/1 Under-capacity use of the railways..and over-capacity use of the roads. **1971** *New Scientist* 8 Apr. 96/1 Industry is currently suffering from some over-capacity following the cutback in the aerospace effort. **1911** J. Ward *Realm of Ends* xv. 337 *Only* to differentiate this 'Over-consciousness' from all such consciousness as we can conceive is the term 'the Unconscious'..applied to it. **1960** *Farmer & Stockbreeder* 1 Mar. 65/1 From a geneticist's point of view in-breeding deterioration is explained by a decrease in those combinations showing overdominance. **1976** *Nature* 15 July 227/2 Population geneticists have never agreed on the extent to which over-dominance of fitness—that is, the situation in which the fitness of the heterozygote exceeds the fitness of both homozygotes—is responsible for the maintenance of genetic variability in populations. *a* **1866** J. Grote *Treat. Moral Ideals* (1876) 169 In danger of erring on the side of..over-exactness. **1976** *Gramophone* Apr. 1598/3, I found a trace of over-expressiveness in such movements as the second of the *Norwegian Melodies* and the Sarabande from the *Holberg Suite*. **1858** Bagehot *Coll. Works* (1965) II. 101 We endure the over-intensity..of the surrounding misery. **1899** W. James *Talks to Teachers* viii. 74 Our faces, all contracted as they are with the habitual American over-intensity and anxiety of expression. **1978** *N.Y. Rev. Bks.* 23 Feb. 30/1 TB was understood, like insanity, to be a kind of one-sidedness: a failure of will or an overintensity. **1898** G. Saintsbury *Short Hist. Eng. Lit.* x. i. 671 A certain over-lusciousness traceable in his [*sc.* Keats's] earlier work. **1963** *Times* 25 Apr. 12/7 If the facts are as stated this is the biggest step towards the controlled release of the energy obtainable from the fusion of heavy hydrogen nuclei since the phase of early overoptimism represented in Britain by Zeta (Zero Energy Thermonuclear Apparatus). **1976** B. Freemantle *November Man* ii. 14 Dennison had an aptitude for over-optimism. **1843** J. S. Mill *Let.* 21 Oct. in *Coll. Wks.* (1963) XIII. 600, I cannot charge myself with any oversusceptibility in the matter.

d. *over-ambition, -elaboration, -emphasis* (further examples), *-precision*.

1929 A. N. Whitehead *Process & Reality* p. xi, Speculative philosophy and overambition. **1973** *Times* 18 Oct. 15/3 His career was blighted by over-ambition. **1901** *Chambers's Encycl.* VII. 141/2 A frequent over-elaboration of style and strainedness of wit that fatigues rather than exhilarates. **1940** *Mind* XLIX. 69 Many readers may feel that there is a danger in mathematical over-elaboration. **1974** tr. *Wertheim's Evolution & Revolution* i. 72 Phonetic spelling could not be realized in Egypt precisely because of the over-elaboration of the cumbersome hieroglyphic system. **1912** J. S. Huxley *Individual in Animal Kingdom* i. 24 By an over-emphasis of the species-individuality of which we are the parts, it is often said that our bodies are only 'cradles for our germ cells'. **1935** *Planning* III. xlix. 1 Many of these arguments..are based on a more or less crude over-emphasis of certain aspects at the expense of the whole. **1949** M. Mead *Male & Female* x. 215 Human children..will make well-balanced but individual selections [of food], compensating one day for an over-emphasis of the day before. **1926** Fowler *Mod. Eng. Usage* 684/1 That is the logical arrangement, which..is free from any taint of over-precision. **1952** C. P. Blacker *Eugenics* 112 It is difficult..to steer a course that shall keep clear of the mudflats of platitude on the one hand, and not come to grief against the rocks of over-precision on the other.

30. *over-often* adv. (later example); *over-cheerily, -closely, -diligently* (example), advbs.

1947 Dylan Thomas *Let.* 20 May (1966) 307 Did you receive the postcard, overcheerily scribbled with messages? **1909** *Westm. Gaz.* 15 Apr. 12/2 The loving parent does well not to examine overclosely into the reasons for this regret. **1690** Locke *Essay Hum. Und.* iii. vii. 228 This part of Grammar has been, perhaps, as much neglected, as some others over-diligently cultivated. **1976** R. Barnard *Little Local Murder* iii. 38 His sports jackets did not go over-often to the dry cleaner's.

III. 31. *overpage* adv.

1870 D. G. Rossetti *Let.* 29 July (1965) II. 893, I send another correction overpage. **1932** R. A. Cram in *Newsletter Mediaeval Acad. Amer.* 15 Nov. 3 Over page is a list of a few books recently issued by these publishers. **1970** *Daily Tel.* 5 Sept. 15 Money-go-round is continued overpage.

32. *over-centre, -life-size, -ocean, -shoulder* adjs.

1975 *Sunday Times* 23 Feb. 17/4 McDonnell Douglas designed a rear-cargo door with four electrically-driven 'over-centre latches'. They were to close over spools in the aircraft body and pull the door shut against its seal. **1937** *Burlington Mag.* Mar. 133/2 The little terra-cottas are to the finished, often over-life-size, sculptures what the drawings are to the big pictures of the same period. *Ibid.*, A finely executed sketch for the over life-size bronze statue of *Innocent X*. **1955** S. Spender *Making of Poem* 40 Over-life-size people seen through the eyes of his childhood. **1967** E. Short *Embroidery & Fabric Collage* iii. 64 A round rug could be worked with one giant over-life-size sunflower as its basis. **1906** *Daily Chron.* 22 Feb. 3/2 Mr. Raleigh is at some pains to show how those over-ocean discoveries and adventures acted on the poetry and imagination of their own times. **1946** R. A. McFarland *Human Factors Air Transport Design* x. 420 In the early stages of overocean flying, an extra station for the navigator has received little criticism. *Ibid.* 410 (*caption*) The flight deck of the B-314 flying boat. The photograph shows a typical layout of stations for multiple flight crews employed in long-range overocean flying. **1957** *Economist* 21 Dec. 1021/2 On the flight deck other qualified Clipper pilots (at least four are on every overocean flight) relieve him. **1955** W. Gaddis *Recognitions* ii. viii. 674 Some of the guests were leaving, with over-shoulder looks of last-minute anticipation. **1959** *Daily Tel.* 22 July 7/1 Air attack 'over-shoulder' bombing... There was a spectacular demonstration of 'over-the-shoulder' bombing, when projectiles..climb thousands of feet before plunging into the sea while the delivery aircraft flies off at top speed.

over-abundance. (Later example.)

1971 *Nature* 19 Feb. 548/1 The large overabundances of Li, Be and B are probably due to spallation.

overabundant, *a.* (Later examples.)

1964 *Ann. Reg. 1963* 249 And though wine, wheat, and beef production were well below the previous year's exceptionally high figures, milk, fruit and vegetables were over-abundant. **1971** *Nature* 19 Feb. 548/1 The element F is undetected in several energy ranges, but may be over-abundant in the 50–200 meV/nucleon range.

over-achie·ver. *Psychol.* [f. OVER- 22 + ACHIEVER.] One who achieves more, as a result of environmental or personality factors, than tests based only on intelligence predict; someone who achieves more than is expected.

1953 *Jrnl. Abnormal Psychol.* XLVIII. 533/1 Ambitious students regularly achieve beyond their predicted 'aptitude' by dint of hard work; such 'overachievers' will not usually fail. *Ibid.* 534/2 Overachievers among public school boys who are most frequently and fiercely driven by ambition. **1964** M. ARGYLE *Psychol. & Social Probl.* ii. 26 There is evidence that people who produce a lot of achievement imagery tend to be over-achievers at school work. **1973** *Times* 17 Nov. 12/2 Mr Kirstein turned out to be one of nature's over-achievers. He founded a great American school of ballet. **1975** *Listener* 13 Mar. 331/2, I would never have been an over-achiever if it hadn't been for that unhappy love-affair with my mother. **1976** *Kingston* (Ontario) *Whig-Standard* 10 Jan. 6/3 It is even more boring than all those grabbers about the man of the year, the women of the year, and grannies, do-gooders, athletes, tots, and other over achievers of the year.

So **over-achie·ve** *v. trans.* and *intr.*; **over-achie·vement; overachie·ving** *vbl. sb.* and *ppl. a.*

1953 *Jrnl. Abnormal Psychol.* XLVIII. 533/2 Academic overachieving and underachieving were measured by the difference between a man's Predictive Rank List..and his attained Rank List. *Ibid.* 536/1 Academically acceptable groups who are over- and underachieving. **1961** J. S. BRUNER in *Harvard Educ. Rev.* XXXI. 26 Our tests on such children show them to be lower in analytic ability than those who are not conspicuous in overachievement. **1967** *Economist* 2 Sept. 788/2 Mr Funston has..over-achieved his goal of selling America on the delights of investing. **1968** *N.Y. Times* 2 May 58 This succinct yet passionate ballet overachieves its immediate purpose by choreographically summing up the Dumas story with a series of brilliantly visualized cinematic-style vignettes. **1971** *Time* 15 Feb. 33 When the 'morning after' rolls around, many an overachieving boozer prays for a hang-over cure. **1972** *Accountant* 6 Apr. 444/1 Where budgetary control is employed..the sales variance analyses would explain the reasons for over- or under-achievement. **1973** *Jrnl. Genetic Psychol.* CXXIII. 252 Overachieving high school males tend to rely less on RV. **1976** *Woman's Day* (N.Y.) Nov. 54/2 David continued to 'overachieve' all through high school, college and a distinguished law school.

over against: see OVER *adv.* 7 b.

overage (ōu·vəɹėdʒ), *sb.*[2] [f. OVER *a.* 3 + -AGE.] A surplus, an excess; an additional amount; *spec.* an actual amount (of goods, money, etc.) greater than that estimated.

1945 MENCKEN *Amer. Lang.* Suppl. I. 366 *Overage* (a bank term: the opposite of a *shortage*). **1949** *Richmond* (Virginia) *Times-Dispatch* 30 Aug. 2/2 The warehousemen agreed to the..sales plan with an 'overage schedule' which is intended to assure Danville the sale each day of 8,800 baskets of tobacco. **1957** *Britannica Bk. of Year* 512/1 *Overage*, costs in excess of estimated or contracted price. **1965** *Economist* 11 Dec. 1235/1 Those export earnings..have not been offset by earlier unforeseen *increases* in export proceeds, inelegantly christened 'overages'. **1968** *Punch* 27 Mar. 447/1 A barman who doesn't show a regular ten per cent 'overage' in favour of his employers will be dismissed because he either gives the customers too much (or too little ice) or he fiddles on his own behalf beyond the customary limits tolerated by the management. **1971** *Daily Colonist* (Victoria, B.C.) 26 Nov. 39/2 His normal welfare allowance would be only $95 a month. However..the man was eligible for overages, which would make his total monthly allowance $120.50. **1973** *Times* 10 May 25/5 A good average for overages is about 6 per cent on monthly sales, minus the minimum rent. In other words, if a store does $50,000 of business in a month and pays a minimum rent of $1,000 a month it has to pay an additional $2,000 in overages. **1975** *Budget* (Sugarcreek, Ohio) 20 Mar. 8/2 Every shortage, or overage, has to be accounted for.

over-aged, *a.* Add: **2.** *Metallurgy.* Subjected to over-ageing.

1953 *Jrnl. Inst. Metals* LXXXII. 265/2 The normal-purity alloys gave ductile fractures when tested in the overaged condition. **1967** A. H. COTTRELL *Introd. Metallurgy* xxi. 405 After plastic working, the over-aged structure gives the stronger alloy.

over-a·geing, *vbl. sb. Metallurgy.* Also **over-aging.** [OVER- 29 a.] Prolonged artificial ageing of metal so that its hardness begins to decrease.

1954 *Gloss. Terms Iron & Steel* (*B.S.I.*) 21 Overageing. **1955** *Jrnl. Inst. Metals* LXXXIII. 529/1 This work provides direct evidence for the supposition that over-ageing during fatigue has a controlling influence on the fatigue strength of precipitation-hardening aluminium alloys. **1970** *Materials & Technol.* III. i. 32 This 'over-aging' effect is due to the increased diffusion giving rise to precipitation and agglomeration into more massive particles.

overall, *sb.* Add: **2. b.** Also, close-fitting trousers worn as a part of army uniform. Also *overall trousers*.

1900 *Dress Regulations Officers of Army* 76 Units may decide to wear either white waistcoat, kamarband instead of waistcoat, white mess dress with kamarband, or white jacket with kamarband and cloth overalls or trousers. **1938** J. CARY *Castle Corner* 152 Some sticky substance on the General's chair had glued him to his seat. His overalls were ruined. **1942** E. WAUGH *Put out More Flags* iii. 177 He looked very elegant and old-fashioned in his blue patrol jacket and tight overall trousers. **1960** A. WAUGH *Foxglove Saga* xii. 223 Martin had donned the Pig's Full Dress Mess Kit..and in its smart red monkey-jacket, narrow blue overalls with a broad red stripe..he really did look most striking. **1967** *National Observer* (U.S.) 3 July 12/3 France entered the war and started uniforming the American troops: Blue regimental coats, waistcoats, breeches or overalls, and black cocked hats.

d. Now often made with a bib and strap top, and sometimes worn by themselves or with a shirt and not over trousers.

1897 *Sears, Roebuck Catal.* 178/2 Painters' white drill overalls, made with apron and shoulder straps. **1926–7** *Army & Navy Stores Catal.* 748/1 Bib and brace overall. Blue and Brown Dungaree. Price, 8/6. **1949** 'G. ORWELL' *Nineteen Eighty-Four* I. 6 A smallish, frail figure, the meagreness of his body merely emphasized by the blue overalls which were the uniform of the Party. **1969** R. T. WILCOX *Dict. Costume* (1970) 253/2 *Overalls*, loose-fitting overtrousers with a front bib held by a strap around the neck.

Hence **o·veralled** *a.*, wearing overalls.

1908 *Smart Set* June 94/1 The familiar spectacle of half-grown boys and overalled and unshaven men. **1916** C. H. STAGG *High Speed* i. 2 He saw an overalled boy jump into the air and crack his heels together. **1928** *Sunday Express* 12 Feb. 9 Plainly there was something seriously amiss with the engine... The overalled mechanic gave an impatient stamp of his foot. **1972** *Guardian* 23 Oct. 11/1 White-overalled, stethoscoped Napoleons. **1974** N. FREELING *Dressing of Diamond* 53 Two overalled characters.. on the garbage-collection round.

overall, over-all, *adv.* Restrict † *Obs.* to senses in Dict. and add: **1. c.** Taking all aspects into consideration; generally.

1958 *Spectator* 6 June 753/2 Overall, the profits from trading for the year..were somewhat less than in 1956. **1959** *Wall St. Jrnl.* 30 June 2/3 'Over-all our line is up,' J. D. Bassett, Jr., of Bassett Furniture Industries,..said. **1967** *Autocar* 5 Oct. 50/3 In the up to 1,300 cc race, John Fitzpatrick..was mopping up the opposition to win the up to 1,000 cc class easily and also came fourth overall. **1974** *Cape Times* 1 Aug. 1/6 The United Party was thought to have the edge overall through having a commanding lead in the postal and special votes. **1975** *Physics Bull.* Aug. 365/3 Overall, an excellent and stimulating book. **1976** *Church Times* 16 July 6/5 'Sylvia's Lovers' is the most tantalising of Mrs. Gaskell's books: a failure overall, maybe, but embodying some exceptionally brilliant scenes. **1976** *Oxford Mail* 6 Mar. 1 All these figures are up. So is crime overall. **1976** *Nature* 25 Mar. 376/3 There are some strange omissions too, in what is overall a very comprehensive text. **1976** *Gramophone* Mar. 1525/2 The latter was virtually flat overall.

over-all, *adj. phr.* Add: Now usu. written **overall** (stressed *o·verall*) and treated as a fully developed adj. Also with wider meaning: Considered over the whole range of components, features, or aspects. (Further examples.)

1904 R. M. WALMSLEY *Mod. Pract. Electr.* IV. iv. 984 (*caption*) Overall dimensions of tramcar motors. **1927** R. T. NICHOLSON *Austin Seven Bk.* iii. 6 Overall length, 9 ft. 2 ins. Overall width, 3 ft. 10 ins. **1930** *Daily Express* 6 Sept. 3 The New B P has 'high overall volatility'. All of it evaporates quickly. **1940** *Economist* 20 July 83/1 The recent fall in the over-all rate of net interest..has been due..to higher taxation on all investment income. **1941** *B.B.C. Gloss. Broadcasting Terms* 22 *Over-all merit*, technical rating of a radio channel, expressed in numerals ranging from nought to five to represent the combined effect on reception of signal strength, fading, interference, depth of modulation, and distortion. **1956** A. L. ROWSE *Early Churchills* viii. 139 We must add an appreciation of the importance of sea-power in the conduct of over-all military operations. **1958** *Oxf. Univ. Gaz.* 7 Mar. 679/2 Approximately equal in its overall area to the Weldon Room it differs from the latter in design in that it is not a single room covering the entire space available, but has been subdivided into three. **1958** *Engineering* 11 Apr. 455/2 The estimated overall efficiency of the rectifier is 94·2 per cent. **1967** M. ARGYLE *Psychol. Interpersonal Behaviour* x. 195 In some studies there has been an overall decline in effectiveness, possibly due to unskilled trainers. **1972** P. OLYSLAGER *Handbk. Ford Cortina Mk. III* 3 The overall length is the same as on the Mk II Cortina. **1974** *Country Life* 26 Dec. 2019/1 It is the overall balance of trade that is important. **1976** *Daily Tel.* 30 June 4/6 They had taken a 'significant step forward in cooperation' aimed at seeing that the current overall recovery. .does not touch off a new round of inflation.

o·ver-and-u·nder, *a.* [OVER *adv.* 1.] Designating a kind of shotgun in which the barrels are mounted not side by side as is usual but one above the other. Also *ellipt.* as *sb.*

1930 G. BURRARD *In Gunroom* 30, I have ordered a pair of Over and Under guns as I prefer the grip on this type of gun. **1961** C. WILLOCK *Death in Covert* iv. 89 Under his arm he carried a beautiful Churchill over-and-under gun. **1968** *Globe & Mail* (Toronto) 17 Feb. 44 Most of the over-and-unders have only one trigger, to be pulled once for each shot, the fastest two shots in the sport. **1973** *Country Life* 28 July 268/2 Over and under shotguns. **1973** D. LEES *Rape of Quiet Town* vii. 118 He was carrying an over-and-under that must have set him back the thick end of a thousand quid, and, behind that much gun, even plus-fours..couldn't make him look silly. **1976** *Field* 30 Dec. 1272 (Advt.), These superb over-and-unders meet the growing demand from the modern sportsman for a genuine dual purpose gun, combining the advantage of the over-and-under for clay shooting with balance and handling qualities of the game gun.

over-anxiety. (Earlier and later examples.)

1826 J. S. MILL in *Parl. Hist. & Rev. 1826* 658/1 The discredit into which the small notes had fallen through their over-anxiety to get rid of them in a hurry. **1829** —— *Autobiogr.* (1924) 302 They did not consider it very dignified to evince an over-anxiety to stand forth in defence of themselves on slight occasions. **1955** *Times* 13 July 3/4 The issue hung in the balance for the last two hours and both sides made mistakes through over-anxiety. **1976** J. WAINWRIGHT *Who goes Next?* 145 He'd have to watch his step..not to make a hash of things, because of over-anxiety.

overarching, *ppl. a.* Add: (Further examples.) Also *fig.*

1913 [see *lamp-shine* s.v. *LAMP *sb.*[1] 4 a]. **1926** J. S. HUXLEY *Ess. Pop. Sci.* 192 The great biological invention, the amnion, came into existence—an overarching membrane grown by the embryo for its own protection. **1929** V. WOOLF *Granite & Rainbow* (1958) 98 Some over-arching conception, something which we may call 'a reading of life.' **1938** E. BEVAN *Symbolism & Belief* iii. 62 The wholly separate world he sees overhead..gives, as nothing else can give, the vision of overarching immensity. **1972** *Listener* 9 Mar. 301/3 There is a hunger for sociological theory—but there is no over-arching Newtonian scheme..by which the differences can be resolved. **1976** *Brit. Jrnl. Sociol.* XXVII. 348 The 'world economy'..is a *world*-system like the world-empire—but which has no overarching political structure.

overarm, *a.* Add: **1.** (Further examples.) Also as *adv.*

1897 K. S. RANJITSINHJI *Jubilee Bk. Cricket* iii. 85 All bowling—fast, medium, or slow—may be delivered either over-arm, round-arm, or under-arm. *Ibid.* 92 Over-arm bowling..is the kind most generally adopted now. **1907** *Westm. Gaz.* 22 Aug. 20/1 The earliest over-arm bowlers were very fast, and..when Brighton Browne and Mynn were in rapid mood, nine of the ten fieldsmen were placed behind the wicket. **1934** W. J. LEWIS *Lang. Cricket* 30 *Over-arm* or *over-hand bowling*, that in which the hand is raised above the level of the shoulder in delivery, the ball being delivered with a downward swing of the arm. **1970** R. BOWEN *Cricket* viii. 127 The Demon bowler, F. R. Spofforth, who is generally credited with introducing true over-arm bowling to England. **1975** *Oxf. Compan. Sports & Games* 195/1 Virtually all bowling nowadays is over-arm. *Ibid.* 200/2 Over-arm—as distinct from the lower bowling actions (under-arm and round-arm)—had a profound effect upon the character of the game.

2. *Swimming.* Applied to a stroke in which one or both arms are lifted out of the water before being advanced; also of a swimmer, that employs an over-arm stroke.

1887 *Encycl. Brit.* XXII. 770/1 Harry Gardener..used the overhand or overarm stroke. **1893** SINCLAIR & HENRY *Swimming* iii. 79 The old-fashioned over-arm swimmer lay on the water, with his shoulder blades at right angles to the surface. **1908** [see *BACK-STROKE c]. **1912** F. SACHS *Compl. Swimmer* 133 Until the last few years a swimmer who desired to race, first endeavoured to master the over-arm side stroke. **1933** [see *BACK-STROKE c]. **1968** W. ANDERSON *Teaching Physically Handicapped to Swim* iii. 37 In the prone position he can cultivate a side stroke and an alternative over-arm stroke with bi-lateral breathing. **1975** *Oxf. Compan. Sports & Games* 1015/1 From breast-stroke came side stroke, then English overarm, or side overarm stroke.

3. *Lawn tennis.* Of a style of service, in which the racket is swung above the shoulder to hit the ball.

1929 W. E. COLLINSON *Spoken Eng.* 90 Last time some of your overarm serves were unplayable. **1978** J. SYMONS *Blackheath Poisonings* II. 111 I'm better than George, because..his horizontal service..can never really compare with an overarm service in strength.

o·vera:rm, *sb.* [OVER- 1 d.] An overhanging arm, esp. that which extends over the work-table of a milling machine.

[**1903** W. H. VAN DERVOORT *Mod. Machine Shop Tools* xxiii. 321 Suitable ties are now furnished with most makes of milling machines connecting the outer end of the over-hanging arm with the knee.] **1922** H. D. BURGHARDT *Machine Tool Operation* II. viii. 169 Braces for tying the overarm, outer arbor support and knee together. **1964** S. CRAWFORD *Basic Engin. Processes* vi. 148 The overarm is accurately located on the top face of the column, providing support and correct alignment for the cutter arbor. **1976** *Gramophone* Oct. 695/1 The British-made Collaro B610..is a record changer for up to six records, or its overarm can be removed and a stub spindle can be substituted for single record use.

o:ver-arti·culate, *v.* [OVER- 27.] *trans.* To articulate or pronounce too carefully. Hence **o:ver-arti·culated** *ppl. a.*; **o:ver-articula·tion.**

1921 H. E. PALMER *Princ. Lang. Study* 72 The teacher may have considered it his duty to over-articulate his words. **1935** A. L. JAMES *Broadcast Word* iii. 103 Is he pedantic? (i.e. over-articulating sounds); is he clerical? **1935** G. K. ZIPF *Psycho-Biol. of Language* (1936) 217 It [*sc.* the speech of the obsessed speaker] offends the auditor because it is over-articulated in meaning. *Ibid.* 218 The normal stream of speech steers between the Scylla of over-articulation and the Charybdis of under-articulation. **1975** *Time Out* 9 May 13/2 To overarticulate is a mistake because making a film is an attempt to express the unconscious.

o·ver-award. [OVER- 19.] In Australia, used *attrib.* to designate a sum paid by an employer in addition to an agreed minimum wage or salary award.

1950 A. W. FOSTER in Copland & Barback *Conflict of Expansion & Stability* (1957) ix. 677 The Court..has no power to fix maximum rates nor to impose any sanction upon an employer who pays over award rates. **1963** G. PALMER *Guide Austral. Econ. Statistics* v. 101 The wages referred to..are simply the minimum wages as prescribed in specific awards. They do not include overtime, over-award payments, bonuses, etc. **1965** *Economist* 14 Aug. 583/1 Australian arbitration awards are minima only and a major problem of the post war period has been the growth of 'over-award' payments (i.e. wage drift). **1969** *West Australian* 5 July 2/2 A sub-contractor on the S.E.C. power house site..could increase his contract price to cover an award rise of $5 a week. However, his contract would not allow him to pass on over-award rises.

overbank, *v.* Add: **2.** *Aeronaut.* [OVER- 27.] **a.** *trans.* To bank (an aircraft) too much when making a turn; also with the turn as obj.

1915 *Tech. Rep. Advisory Comm. Aeronaut. 1914–15* 307 If a turn be overbanked it will bring into play a lateral component of gravity which produces sideslip. **1919** W. G. ASTON *Aeronaut. made Easy* xvii. 160 If on the turn the machine is overbanked, it will side-slip inwards. **1936** *Discovery* Mar. 72/2 It is essential that the machine is not overbanked on a turn, since there are no ailerons to correct this.

b. *intr.* Of an aircraft: to bank too much. Also said of the pilot.

1929 F. A. SWOFFER *Learning to Fly* iv. 38 (*heading*) Why an aeroplane overbanks. **1932** D. GARNETT *Rabbit in Air* I. 17, I overbanked and didn't use enough rudder. **1952** A. Y. BRAMBLE *Air-plane Flight* xii. 181 During the turn..there is a greater tendency to overbank in a climb than in level flight.

Hence **overba·nking** *vbl. sb.*

1915 *Tech. Rep. Advisory Comm. Aeronaut. 1914–15* 307 (*heading*) Objections to extreme overbanking. **1921** *Sci. Amer.* 15 Oct. 275/3 The side-slip—a lateral movement of a plane caused by overbanking or by underbanking—is measured.

o·verbank, *sb. Aeronaut.* [OVER- 29.] The action of overbanking (*OVERBANK *v.* 2).

1919 A. W. JUDGE *Handbk. Mod. Aeronaut.* xiii. 676 Inward slip..results from an overbank, which causes the machine to turn inwards, and slip down sideways. **1955** M. ROYCE *Studies for Student Pilots* II. 94 The inner mainplane now experiences the greater A[ngle of] A[ttack] and the increment of lift it obtains tends to neutralize the overbank tendency.

over-bark. [f. OVER- 8c + BARK *sb.*[1] I.] Used *attrib.* to designate measurements of logs taken before the bark has been removed.

1953 H. L. EDLIN *Forester's Handbk.* xiv. 214 As a rule, logs are measured..while they still have their bark on. This is over-bark measure, and is of course greater than the volume of actual timber. **1967** SCOTT & PALMER *Hiley's Woodland Managem.* (ed. 2) ix. 131 (*caption*) Percentage of bark in the over-bark volume.

overbear, *v.* Add: **4.** *intr.* To produce too much fruit, thereby affecting the quality of it.

1863 *Horticulturalist* XVIII. 295/2 You can now point out every tree that was allowed to overbear. **1872** *Rep. Vermont Bd. Agric.* I. 118 The Bartlett and Louise Bonne de Jersey commence bearing young, and are inclined to over bear. **1901** *U.S. Dept. Agric. Yearbk. 1900* 387 It is a great mistake to allow pear trees to overbear.

overbelief. [OVER- 1 e, 18, 29 c.] **a.** A belief which determines other beliefs. **b.** A belief surviving from the past. **c.** Belief in more than is warranted by the evidence or in what cannot be verified; also, such belief beyond that which is customary among adherents of a particular faith or sect.

1897 W. JAMES *Will to Believe* p. xiii, The most interesting and valuable things about a man are his ideals and over-beliefs. **1900** J. MORLEY *Oliver Cromwell* I. iii. 51 Faith in the literal construction of the word was pushed to an excess..resembling a true superstition or over-belief. **1901** [see OVER- 18]. **1920** 'W. S. PALMER' *Christianity & Christ* 153 We have these 'over-beliefs'; and we even count men poor who are without them. **1930** *Times Lit. Suppl.* 27 Nov. 1011/1 All is well, or will be well, when the new over-beliefs dominate. **1961** M. LASKI *Ecstasy* xxviii. 295 Whatever may be the ultimate source of these beliefs, which I shall call primary overbeliefs, it is generally accepted that their expression must at least partially be a temporal, local and natural matter. **1971** E. CARPENTER *Cantuar* VI. iv. 340 He [*sc.* Archbishop Tait] was sensitive to the contemporary agnosticism of such as Tennyson, and was convinced that this could not be combated by insisting on the 'over-belief' characteristic of the protagonists of the Oxford Movement. **1973** M. PAFFARD *Inglorious Wordsworths* II. xii. 162 Their overbeliefs—their own assumptions or conclusions about the significance (if any) of the experiences they described.

overbend, *v.* **1.** Delete '(Only in *pples.*)' and add further example of sense b.

c **1886** G. M. HOPKINS *Poems* (1967) 97 Her earliest stars, earlstars, stárs principal, overbend us.

o·verbend, *sb.* [OVER- 5 b.] The curved stretch of pipe above the point of inflexion in the S-shaped length of pipeline being lowered on to the sea bed from a barge. Cf. *SAGBEND.

1969 *Preprints 1st Ann. Offshore Technol. Conf.* II. 38/1 As the lay barge proceeds into deep water the articulated stinger curves downward and the suspended pipe span acquires a distinct S-shaped curve. The upper part of this curve, called the over-bend, is supported by the stinger. **1976** *Offshore Platforms & Pipelining* 130/1 The overbend is supported by rollers on the barge and stinger.

overbid, *v.* Add: **2. c.** *trans.* and *intr.* In Bridge = *OVERCALL *v.* Also *fig.*

1908 R. F. FOSTER *Auction Bridge* 51 If the hand is overbid, the suit named may be a guide as to the advisability of changing to no-trumps. **1908** [see *BID *sb.* 2]. **1917** E. BERGHOLT *Royal Auction Bridge* 87 It is imperative to overbid with Two Clubs, as a warning—colloquially known as a 'rescue'. **1918** R. F. FOSTER *On Auction* (1919) 169 Overbidding a suit just because there are four honours in it is quite unnecessary. **1923** *Daily Mail* 6 Oct. 6/4 The partner of the under-bidder..cannot make any further bid unless the opponents double or overbid. **1936** A. HUXLEY *Eyeless in Gaza* iv. 35 'Poor child!' his father said to himself; and then, overbidding as it were, 'Poor motherless child!' he added deliberately. **1947** S. HARRIS *Fund. Princ. Contract Bridge* I. i. 17 If one of the adversaries did overbid him, North would almost certainly make a sacrifice bid of four Spades. **1952** I. MACLEOD *Bridge* vii. 82 Be chary of overbidding a suit bid with one No Trump. **1952** PHILLIPS & REESE *Bridge with Mr. Playbetter* xxviii. 118 Mrs. Portly raised to Two Spades; an aggressive player, at the score, might have risked a shut-out bid of Three Spades, but Mrs. Portly knew better than to overbid when playing with Hurry. **1973** *Bridge Mag.* Feb. 123/2 Let us not forget that partner might have overbid slightly in this position. **1974** *Times* 15 June 9/1 They scrape up a bid whenever they can, convinced that by overbidding him they make the declarer work harder for his contract. **1975** *Times* 5 Dec. 14/6 Some European leaders, in overbidding the Brussels game, had seriously misled the public.

Hence **o·verbidder**, one who makes an overbid (see next); **o·verbidding** *vbl. sb.*, the action of one who overbids.

1912 F. IRWIN *Fine Pts. Auction Bridge* 85 There is no fault as common in Auction as overbidding. **1929** M. C. WORK *Compl. Contract Bridge* iii. 15 This artificial system is apt to cause overbidding. **1936** E. CULBERTSON *Contract Bridge Complete* II. xxix. 345 When the overbidder is vulnerable, the extent of the overbid should be less than two tricks. **1964** *Official Encycl. Bridge* 404/1 The overbidder must not be allowed to think that he is playing with an underbidder, or worse will follow. **1974** *Country Life* 17 Jan. 98/1 It is rewarding to study hands..and see what caused a poor result... Here is the tragedy of *Overbidding*.

o·verbid, *sb. Bridge.* [f. the vb.] A bid that is higher than is justified by one's cards; also = *OVERCALL *sb.*

1917 [see *flag-flying* s.v. *FLAG *sb.*[4] 7]. **1947** S. HARRIS *Fund. Princ. Contract Bridge* I. i. 15 If one of the adversaries then makes an overbid of Diamonds or Clubs,.. North can then bid his Spades. **1952** I. MACLEOD *Bridge* iv. 46 When I use the term 'bid suit' that means a suit bid as a genuine suit—it does not include cue-bids or overbids in the opponent's suit. **1967** P. ANDERTON *Play Bridge* v. 40 The number of points lost when you go down on the overbid should represent a considerable saving on what you would lose if the opponents obtained game and rubber. **1969** *Bridge Mag.* Oct. 219/2 North made a slight overbid of three hearts, but ensured the right strain. **1972** *Ibid.* June 386/2 He bid three clubs. Scared of..the overbid of three spades or the underbid of two spades.

o·verbite. *Dentistry.* [OVER- 8(?).] The overlapping of the lower teeth, esp. the incisors, by the corresponding upper teeth; now usu. confined to overlap in a vertical direction. Cf. *OVERJET.

1887 W. G. A. BONWILL in W. F. Litch *Amer. Syst. Dentistry* II. 487 It will be found in 95 per cent. of cases that the upper teeth project over the lower, and that the depth of overbite varies as the depth of the cusps of the bicuspids are deep or shallow. **1924** T. GOODHUGH *Art of Prosthetic Dentistry* x. 246 The least amount of overbite occurs with the wisdom teeth, and the greatest amount at the incisors. **1947** E. HYAMS *William Medium* vii. 137 An immensely long upper lip rising from a prominent overbite and barely covering a number of long, yellow horse-teeth. **1971** R. M. & F. M. KEESING *New Perspectives in Cultural Anthropol.* 55 The 'overbite' in the mouths of most of today's readers is apparently an adaptation in the maturation process to eating soft foods.

over-bitter, *a.* (Examples.)

1600 R. PERSONS in *Publ. Catholic Rec. Soc.* (1906) II. 120 But the rest for that it was longe and over bitter against some particular men, I thought good to leave it out. **1927** H. CRANE *Lett.* (1965) 283 A good dig at certain people, but I think the sarcasm is over-bitter. **1943** *Pope & People* (Catholic Truth Soc.) ix. 171 There is now commonly much dispute, and sometimes over-bitter dispute, on this topic.

overblea·ch, *v.* [OVER- 27.] *trans.* To bleach excessively so that the material bleached deteriorates. Hence **overblea·ched** *ppl. a.*, **overblea·ching** *vbl. sb.*

1921 S. H. HIGGINS *Bleaching* xiii. 111 The 'copper value' standardised by Schwalbe is the most definite measure available for the diagnosis of chemical modification in celluloses, particularly by overbleaching. *Ibid.*, The copper value of strongly overbleached cottons may rise as high as 16. **1946** L. E. WISE *Wood Chem.* vi. 150 In pulp manufacture, overbleaching gives a paper with lowered strength, due to oxycellulose formation. **1950** B. E. HARTSUCH *Introd. Textile Chem.* vii. 188 If the specific viscosity of the cotton is greater than 1, the cloth has been overbleached. **1963** A. J. HALL *Textile Sci.* ii. 25 Overbleached cotton containing oxycellulose resists dyeing with direct cotton dyes, so that if this overbleaching is not even, the bleached yarn or fabric is liable to dye unevenly. **1972** L. PALLADINO *Princ. & Pract. Hairdressing* xi. 153/1 Overbleached hair when wet is almost like chewing gum.

o·ver-blouse. [OVER- 8 c.] A blouse worn over another outer garment.

1921 *Daily Colonist* (Victoria, B.C.) 2 Apr. 20/1 (Advt.), A new style Over-Blouse of Silk Crepe de Chine, in shades of white, flesh, navy and black, effectively embroidered with silk floss in contrasting shades. **1923** *Daily Mail* 13 Feb. 15 In usefulness no similar garment can compete with the over-blouse. **1960** *Times* 20 Jan. 8/4 Suits were generally accompanied by sleeveless silk overblouses. **1963** *New Yorker* 23 Nov. 189 Our double-knit 2-piece dress with slender skirt and scalloped overblouse. **1974** *Country Life* 28 Feb. 456/3 Full overblouse with..a matching full-length skirt.

overblow, *v.*[1] Add: **6.** (Further examples.) Also *intr.* for *refl.*

1938 *Oxf. Compan. Mus.* 228/1 The cornet is horrible when overblown. **1946** MEZZROW & WOLFE *Really Blues* (1957) 363 They have to overblow their instruments, fighting to be heard. **1956** M. STEARNS *Story of Jazz* (1957) xvii. 214 Benny Goodman reacted differently: 'This is the first time..that I've ever heard a tenor sax played the way it should be and not overblown.' **1976** *Early Music* Oct. 511/1 Then Jacob Denner (1732) developed an instrument, which, by means of a key, overblew into the higher register, at an interval of an octave plus a tritone (the modern clarinet overblows at an interval of a twelfth).

7. *Metallurgy.* To subject (a charge) to an excessive length of blast. Cf. OVERBLOWN *ppl. a.*[1] 3.

1869 *Chem. News* 9 Apr. 170/2 If a charge is 'overblown'—that is, if it be subjected to the action of the air for too long a period,..the steel will be found to be defective in proportion to its unskilful treatment. **1932** E. GREGSON *Metall.* ii. 32 Great experience is necessary at this point, since if the metal is 'over-blown' for only 15 seconds, steels containing a large proportion of iron oxide are obtained. **1951** G. R. BASHFORTH *Manuf. Iron & Steel* II. ii. 26 Frequently a heat that has been overblown may be dirty.

overblow (ōu·vəɹblōu), *sb. Metallurgy.* [f. prec. vb.] A period or instance of overblowing.

1879 *Jrnl. Iron & Steel Inst.* 158 One minute overblow and the phosphorus came down to ·75 per cent. **1946** *Ibid.* CLII. 12P This rather long overblow only caused a reduction of about 0·03% in the blown-metal carbon content.

overblow·ing, *vbl. sb.* [f. OVERBLOW *v.*[1] + -ING[1].] **1.** *Metallurgy.* Subjection to an excessive length of blast.

1879 *Jrnl. Iron & Steel Inst.* 121 The removal of phosphorus was assisted by slight over-blowing. **1890** W. M. WILLIAMS *Chem. Iron & Steel Making* xvi. 301 An experimentally overblown sample..in spite of overblowing, produced a high quality of mild steel after the addition of spiegeleisen. **1932** E. GREGORY *Metall.* ii. 35 Over-blowing results in the production of over-oxidised and 'wild' metal. **1949** *Jrnl. Metals* Dec. 27/2 One of the most important features of end-point control is the elimination of overblowing.

2. *Mus.* In the playing of a pipe or wind instrument: production of a harmonic or overtone instead of the fundamental note through extra force of air.

1879 *Organ Voicing & Tuning* 17 *Overblowing, or speaking the octave.* Causes:—(*a*), languid too low; (*b*), excessive wind-hole. **1898** [see OVERBLOW *v.*[1] 6]. **1938** *Oxf. Compan. Mus.* 59/1 Other wood-wind instruments..obtain their second octave by overblowing. **1954** *Grove's Dict. Mus.* (ed. 5) VI. 468/2 Overblowing greatly increases the natural compass of wind instruments. **1977** *Times* 13 Apr. 11/1 Michel Portal, a splendid clarinettist, was playing ill-toned microtones and strident chords (faked by overblowing in a manner now common in new music). **1977** *Early Music* July 351/1 A minute hole in the crook, especially on lower shawms, aids overblowing into the second octave.

overblown, *ppl. a.*[1] Add: **2.** (Later examples.)

1929 R. BRIDGES *Testament of Beauty* III. 55 The empty mind may float lightly in the full moonshine of o'erblown affluence. **1971** *New Yorker* 30 Oct. 25/2 This overblown, frolicsome Western [film].

3. (Examples.)

1879 *Jrnl. Iron & Steel Inst.* 156 The paper admitted that ferrous oxide was employed in the process, and he should wish to ask..how much of it was produced by oxidation in an overblown charge. **1946** *Ibid.* CLII. 9P A later shut-off results in overblown metal. **1951** G. R. BASHFORTH *Manuf. Iron & Steel* II. ii. 21 It is claimed that this application has reduced the likelihood of overblown heats and considerably improved the control of quality. **1958** A. D. MERRIMAN *Dict. Metallurgy* 222/2 If the blast is allowed to continue after this, oxidation of part of the iron occurs and the charge is then overblown.

overblown, *ppl. a.*[2] (Further examples.)

1844 E. B. BROWNING *Poems* II. 121 From those overblown faint roses, Not a leaf appeareth shed. **1916** JOYCE *Portrait of Artist* v. 260 The great overblown scarlet flowers of the tattered wallpaper. **1933** *Jrnl. R. Hort. Soc.* LVIII. 232 No useful purpose is served by leaving the flowers until they are in the overblown condition. **1960** P. GALLICO *Mrs. Harris goes to N.Y.* 178 Tired greens, dispirited cabbages and overblown sprouts. **1976** 'J. Ross' *I know what it's like to Die* v. 39 A creamy, overblown peach blonde.

overboard, *adv.* Add: **2.** Also, excessively, beyond one's means; esp. in phr. *to go overboard*, to behave immoderately; to go too far; to display excessive enthusiasm.

1931 D. RUNYON in *Collier's* 26 Sept. 8/2 We go overboard today. We are washed out. We owe every bookmaker.., and now we are out trying to raise some scratch to pay off. *Ibid.* 9/4 We do not have anything to bet on these races, or any way of betting on them, because we are overboard with every bookmaker we know. **1945** [see *BUST *v.*² f]. **1951** J. P. MARQUAND *Melville Goodwin* (1952) viii. 113 Did you ever hear about General Goodwin going overboard over an American girl in Paris..? **1953** 'S. RANSOME' *Hear no Evil* (1954) xv. 140 The man went overboard in a big way morally—he made himself a thief, deserted his family. **1960** *N.Z. Listener* 30 Sept. 11/1, I cannot admire 'abstract' interpretations any more than I can go overboard about sculpture rigged up out of bicycle parts. **1968** *Wall St. Jrnl.* 28 Feb. 16/2 It is easy to go overboard on the new techniques, for all their virtues. **1971** *Jrnl. Gen. Psychol.* Jan. 153 Many psychologists..have gone overboard in hypothetical and speculative associations of this sort. **1978** *Times* 9 Jan. 8/6 Lord Allen.. has been convinced of the importance of money..without going overboard in defence of it.

o·verboil, *sb. rare.* [f. the vb.] phr. *on the overboil*: in an overboiling condition, a state of ebullience.

1883 RUSKIN *Let.* 30 Oct. in *Igdrasil* (1890) June 218 And my brains always on the overboil, if I don't mind.

overbook (ōuvəɹbu·k), *v.* [f. OVER- 27 + BOOK *v.*] *trans.* To make more bookings for (a theatre, hotel, aircraft, etc.) than there are places or seats available; to book an excessive number of (customers, passengers, etc.). Also *intr.* Hence **overboo·ked** *ppl. a.*; **overboo·king** *vbl. sb.*

1903 *Daily Chron.* 10 Nov. 9/1 The booking clerks had by some oversight overbooked the theatre. **1964** G. L. COHEN *What's Wrong with Hospitals?* v. 104 A Ministry report on waiting time [at hospital clinics] pointed to the same causes of delay: over-booking and arbitrary appointment intervals. **1967** N. BUXTON *Travel '67* 674 The traveller is told..that the flight has been over-booked and that he must wait for the next plane. *Ibid.* 675 Over-booking may sometimes happen even in the most competently run organization. **1971** *Guardian* 28 July 7/8 An approach to end overbooking at some Spanish holiday hotels will begin in Madrid. **1972** J. POTTER *Going West* 77 All airlines overbooked by fourteen per cent as a matter of policy. **1973** *Daily Tel.* 5 Sept. 6/7 If we did not overbook our flights the jumbos would be flying with a mass of empty seats. *Ibid.*, We overbooked 31 passengers on a flight to Canada today. **1975** *Times* 24 June 19/5 Over-booking—the practice of selling seats twice over, followed by almost every airline in the world. **1976** *Times* 26 Jan. 19/4 The over-booked passenger, despite his protests, finds himself 'bumped' off the flight. **1978** *TV Times* 28 Jan. 65 (Advt.) Want a really carefree holiday this year? Like to stay overnight where and when you like, and not bother about over-booked hotels?

overborne, *ppl. a.* (Later examples.)

1901 G. B. SHAW *Devil's Disciple* I. 19 Uncle Titus, overborne, resumes his seat on the sofa. **1961** in WEBSTER *s.v.*, Art, industry, and commerce, so long crushed and overborne. **1977** *Navy News* Sept. 7/1, I seem to remember reading in Navy News a while ago that the Navy was so overborne with cooks that some could expect to be drafted to non-cooking billets.

overbought, *ppl. a.* [f. OVERBUY *v.*] (See quot. 1957.)

1957 CLARK & GOTTFRIED *University Dict. Business & Finance* 252/2 *Overbought.* 1. The condition of having purchased more than is needed to meet requirements. However, as used, the condition does not necessarily result from excessive buying, but may be the result of shrinking needs or resale volume. 2. In securities trade usage, a condition in which the demand for securities at existing prices has been filled, so that prices tend to drop. **1961** *Spectator* 26 May 774 When a market becomes..overbought, prices are extra sensitive to bad news. **1962** E. GODFREY *Retail Selling & Organization* xx. 199 If a buyer is overbought, he is informed of this fact immediately by stock control office. **1968** *Economist* 16 Mar. 86/2 One of the Americans' hopes would be that, after an initial soaring, the free market price of gold could come down again; partly because hoarders and speculators are now so overbought. **1974** S. MARCUS *Minding Store* iv. 61 They.. would never pass a desirable garment, however overbought they might be.

overbound, *v.*¹ For *Obs. rare*⁻¹ read *rare* and add later example.

1956 T. DRIBERG *Guy Burgess* iii. 45 Churchill seemed a little pleased. 'My eloquence!' he said. 'Ah, yes, that.. Herr Beans can rely on in full and indeed..some would say, in overbounding measure.'

over-bow, *v.* Add: **1.** Also *refl.*, to adopt too strong a bow.

1939 P. H. GORDON *New Archery* 72 Beginners should be most careful not to overbow themselves. **1976** *St. Louis* (Missouri) *Globe-Democrat* 17 Sept. 5 B A bow with a draw weight of 40 pounds or more is adequate for the taking of many deer. Many beginners 'overbow' themselves and sacrifice accuracy for unnecessary power.

over-breathe, *v.* Add: **3.** [OVER- 26.] *intr. Physiol.* = *HYPERVENTILATE *v.* a.

1928 F. W. BRODERICK *Dental Med.* xi. 221, I..advise the parent to see that the child is sitting or lying down at the time they are over-breathing. **1961** *Lancet* 5 Aug. 304/2 All divers should therefore be instructed not to overbreathe before diving.

overbreathing *vbl. sb.* (examples in the sense of *OVER-BREATHE *v.* 3).

1920 *Jrnl. Biol. Chem.* XLIII. 9 A continuation..of overbreathing and blowing off of CO_2 results in a compensatory disappearance of alkali from the blood. **1954** W. MAYER-GROSS et al. *Clin. Psychiatry* iv. 131 A prolonged period of over-breathing, causing alkalinity of the blood. **1968** *Brit. Med. Bull.* XXIV. 202/1 On overbreathing there are a few bilateral episodes of delta activity, maximal posteriorly.

over-bridge, *sb.* Add: (Earlier and later examples.) Also, a bridge across a road. Also as *adj.*, travelling or placed across bridges.

1876 [see UNDER-BRIDGE]. **1905** *Daily Chron.* 3 Feb. 6/6 Who..were the people who objected to the over-bridge trams? *Ibid.* 1 June 4/3 The Select Committee on the over-bridge tramways. **1959** *Manch. Guardian* 11 Aug. 6/5 More pedestrian overbridges and underpasses. **1962** *Engineering* 14 Dec. 775 The works will include..four overbridges. **1973** *Inverness Courier* 31 July 6/5 Because of the single track and few overbridges, this would be a relatively cheap route to electrify.

overbuild, *v.* Add: **2.** (Later examples.) Also *fig.*

1909 *Daily Chron.* 17 July 3/2 This is an enjoyable book. .. It has faults of plot—it is over-built—and of character-drawing [etc.]. **1946** *Sun* (Baltimore) 4 June 11/7 France also has some merit in his charge of 'overbuilding' players. **1946** 'R. WEST' *Train of Powder* (1955) 9 The German tendency to overbuild which has done much to get them into..recurring financial troubles. **1977** *Time* 8 Aug. 43/1 As a result of the slowdown in the growth of petroleum consumption and some reckless overbuilding by shipyards in the early 1970s, the tanker business is in the worst depression in memory.

3. (Further examples.) Also *fig.*

1865 W. WHITE *Eastern England* II. xxi. 283 To me.. its especial charm is that it is not overbuilt or cockneyfied. **1870** A. T. DE VERE *May Carols* (ed. 2) 12 That, wholly over-built by grace, Nature might vanish, like some isle In great towers lost. **1893** A. JESSOPP *Studies by Recluse* (ed. 2) iii. 97 It was one of the many religious houses that started in a very ambitious way, and early overbuilt themselves. **1939** *Sun* (Baltimore) 11 Apr. 3/3 'It seems a paradox,' he added, 'that in order to revive building operations and furnish employment for a class of workmen it must be carried on in places already overbuilt and becomes the real cause of the idleness of this class of workers.' **1961** *Wall St. Jrnl.* 24 Mar. 1/1 'I don't think the lower interest rates are going to have the slightest effect on housing demand,' says Henry Bubb, president of Capitol Federal Savings & Loan Association of Topeka, 'We're just overbuilt.' **1977** *Sat. Rev.* (U.S.) 17 Sept. 54/2 Is little New Orleans overbuilt? Perhaps not. By early summer the Hilton had already booked one million room-nights.

over-bu·ll, *v.* [f. OVER- 27 + BULL *v.*¹ 2.] *trans.* To raise the price of (stocks, etc.) excessively. Hence **over-bu·lled** *ppl. a.*; **over-bu·llishness.**

1905 *Daily Report* 14 Oct. 2/4 Readings were heavy, having apparently been over-bulled. **1938** *New Statesman* 16 July 132/1 Happily Wall Street has gone through a corrective period and over-bullishness has given way to more restrained optimism. **1965** *Economist* 23 Oct. 436/1 The market ignores the sad fate of so many American wonder electronic stocks: over-bulled, then crashing at the first set-back.

o·ver-bump, *v.* [f. OVER- 14 + BUMP *v.*¹ 3.] In bumping-races, to catch and bump (a boat ahead of a pair of other boats that have withdrawn after a bump), thus going up three places. So **o·ver-bump** *sb.*

1905 *Daily Chron.* 2 Mar. 7/3 One boat (Corpus) overbumped Selwyn and ascended three places. **1920** 'Two OF 'EM' *Guide Cambr. Univ. Life* 10 If three or more boats bump simultaneously the rear boat goes to the front of those boats, and is said to have made an 'over-bump'. **1930** *Magdalene Boat Club 1828–1928* v. 19 The year 1868 is notable as providing the only occasion upon which the first boat ever made an overbump. **1963** *Times* 31 May 5/3 Merton II also attempted a big task in going for an overbump on Queen's II and it was only by one foot that they failed to make it.

overburden, -burthen, *sb.* Add: (The spelling *-burthen* is no longer current.) **2. b.** The material lying over any particular point underground, esp. over a tunnel or pipeline; also, the pressure due to the weight of this material.

1948 TERZAGHI & PECK *Soil Mech. in Engin. Pract.* ii. 68 With respect to the present overburden, the clay on the right-hand side is a precompressed soft clay, and that on the left-hand side is a normally loaded soft clay. **1968** G. N. SMITH *Elem. Soil. Mech.* iv. 88 The overburden pressure at a point in a soil mass is simply the weight of the material above it. The effective overburden is the pressure from this material less the pore water pressure. **1970** *Daily Tel.* 27 June 2/5 The pipeline was laid in December 1967..but the unexpectedly heavy scouring action of the bottom waves in the shallow North Sea soon removed the two foot overburden.

c. Loose, unconsolidated material lying above bedrock.

1955 *Proc. Colorado Sci. Soc.* XVI. 102/1 *Overburden*,.. a term used by geologists and engineers in several different senses. By some it is used to designate material of any nature, consolidated or unconsolidated, that overlies a deposit of useful materials, ores, or coal, especially those deposits that are mined from the surface by open cuts. As employed by others *overburden* designates only loose soil, sand, gravel, etc., that lies above the bedrock. The term should not be used without specific definition. **1969** *Civil Engineering* (U.S.) June 43/2 A more detailed soil investigation of the upper 50 ft or so of the overburden.. showed that the allowable bearing capacity was only about 200 to 300 psf, much too low for the proposed bridge foundations.

overbuy, *v.* Add: **1. b.** To buy goods at a (wholesale) price beyond the means of (a competitor).

1886 HARDY *Mayor Casterbr.* II. iii. 36 We'll under-sell him, and over-buy him, and so snuff him out.

2. (Later examples.) Also, of a wholesaler or retailer: to buy goods, materials, etc., in excess of those needed; to accumulate surplus stock. See also *OVERBOUGHT *ppl. a.*

1938 *Sun* (Baltimore) 26 Feb. 18/8 The high level of delinquencies in Maryland results from several conditions —business recession, unemployment, 'overbuying'. **1950** *Times* 11 Mar. 9/7 Last year the Government overbought imported frozen fish and now fresh fish was being sold at a very low price. **1966** J. M. SHEWAN in *Proc. Internat. Symp. Food Irrad.* (Internat. Atomic Energy Agency) 496 Merchants, both wholesalers and retailers, frequently 'over-buy', particularly when supplies are plentiful and prices cheap.

overcall (ōuvəɹkǭ·l), *v. Bridge.* [OVER- 22, 26.] **a.** *trans.* and *intr.* To make a bid higher than (a previous bid or another player).

1908 R. F. FOSTER *Auction Bridge* 54 Neither should he bid a number of tricks which is more than necessary to overcall the previous declaration. **1916** F. IRWIN *Compl. Auction Player* 66 There is also a perfectly good suit with which to over-call. **1917** E. BERGHOLT *Royal Auction Bridge* 85 Here Y...is justified in over-calling with One Spade. **1918** R. F. FOSTER *On Auction* (1919) 183 The partner may be called upon to assist..when the second hand overcalls the dealer. **1929** M. C. WORK *Compl. Contract Bridge* ii. 9 He may overcall a No Trump with a suit-bid, or overcall a suit-bid with another suit or No Trump. **1974** *Country Life* 17 Jan. 98 To overcall One Club with One Spade on a modest hand is worthwhile.

b. To bid more on (one's hand) than it is worth. Also *fig.*

1927 A. H. POLLEN in 'Neon' *Gt. Delusion* p. xvi, The bright young conjurers of Kingsway have been overcalling their hands. **1930** *Time & Tide* 11 Apr. 463 His partner had been overcalling. **1934** L. H. DAWSON *Hoyle's Games Modernized* 31 Sometimes a forced bid is also a forcing bid, in that the inten tion is to make the opponents over call.

overcall (ōu·vəɹkǭl), *sb. Bridge.* [f. the vb.] A bid which is higher than a previous bid (see also quot. 1959). Cf. *OVERBID *sb.*

1916 F. IRWIN *Compl. Auction Player* 65 To bid against your partner, when no one else has bid, is to use the overcall. **1917** E. BERGHOLT *Royal Auction Bridge* 85 Third hand should not carry on the contest further, unless he has some additional reason which his first overcall was not sufficient to proclaim. **1959** REESE & DORMER *Bridge Player's Dict.* 159 An overcall is a bid made after an opponent has opened the bidding. **1973** *Country Life* 10 May 1331/1, I had to take West's One Spade overcall into account. He was likely to have both missing Kings.

over-care. (Further examples.)

1693 DRYDEN tr. *Persius' Satires* II. 81 The very overcare, And nauseous pomp, wou'd hinder half the Pray'r. **1833** C. LAMB *Last Essays* 103 Sunday itself—that unfortunate failure of a holyday..with my sense of its fugitiveness, and over-care to get the greatest quantity of pleasure out of it—is melted down into a week day. **1937** V. MCNABB *God's Way of Mercy* xii. 103 There is no over-care about tomorrow; just a love of God.

overcarefully, *adv.* (Examples.)

1865 DICKENS *Mut. Fr.* I. II. xiv. 296 'The sister,' said Bradley, separating his words over-carefully, and speaking as if he were repeating them from a book, 'suffers under no reproach.' **1870** —— *Edwin Drood* ii. 9 Life, for *you*, is a plum with the natural bloom on; it hasn't been over-carefully wiped off for *you*. **1939** JOYCE *Finnegans Wake* 122 Three *basia* or shorter and smaller *oscula* have been overcarefully scraped away.

overcarry, *v.* Add: **1. b.** (Later example.)

1972 M. MEAD *Blackberry Winter* xi. 148 The National Research Council had insisted on mailing my checks to me, and the next boat overcarried the mail. This meant that for six weeks I had no money.

Hence **overcarried** *ppl. a.*

1897 [see sense 1 b in Dict.]. **1903** KIPLING *Five Nations* 25 The galloping breakers stride, And their overcarried spray is a sea—a sea on the landward side.

overcast, *sb.* Add: **2.** (Further examples.) *spec.* in *Aeronautics*: cloud-cover which restricts visibility and necessitates reliance on instruments for navigation.

1938 [see *contact flying* s.v. *CONTACT *sb.* 6]. **1942** *Tee Emm* (Air Ministry) II. 69 In the past you scraped above the undergrowth, now, through the overcast. **1946** *Happy Landings* (Air Ministry) July 5/1 The aircraft..was seen emerging from the overcast. **1946** R. A. MCFARLAND *Human Factors Air Transport Design* ix. 396 The flight was progressing normally at an altitude of 10,000 ft until it entered a rapidly forming thunderstorm. Shortly thereafter, parts of the plane began to fall from the overcast. **1967** S. BLANC *Rose Window* (1968) xix. 183 It was only mid-morning and a high overcast that obscured the sun had not yet burned away. **1972** B. F. CONNERS *Don't embarrass Bureau* (1973) I. 6 He felt the sun starting to burn through the overcast as he climbed the ladder.

5. (Earlier examples.)

c **1840** LADY WILTON *Art of Needlework* xx. 317 There is back stitch—overcast—and seam stitch. **1867** C. AUSTEN *My Aunt Jane Austen* (1952) 7 She was a great adept at overcast and satin stitch—the peculiar delight of that day.

overcast, *v.* Add: **7.** Also in *Bookbinding* (see quot. 1956).

1880 J. W. ZAEHNSDORF *Art of Bookbinding* iii. 13 Each section is then overcast or oversewn along its whole length. **1901** [see *OVERCAST *ppl. a.* 3]. **1951** L. TOWN *Bookbinding by Hand* xx. 244 At this point the book must be marked up for sewing, as this cannot be done after the sections have been overcast. **1956** *Bookman's Conc. Dict.* 209/1 *Overcast*, to sew leaves, especially single leaves, in bookbinding, with a long hem-stitch style of sewing; also known as Whip Stitch. **1963** B. C. MIDDLETON *Hist. Eng. Craft Bookbinding Technique* iii. 25 The usual method.. involves overcasting separately a series of groups of leaves.

overcast, *ppl. a.* Add: **3.** Also in *Bookbinding* (see *OVERCAST *v.* 7) and in *Lace-making*.

1865 F. B. PALLISER *Hist. Lace* xiii. 181 It is only 'bride ordinaire';..very different from the clear 'over-cast' hexagon of the last century. **1901** D. COCKERELL *Bookbinding* v. 81 To 'overcast' the first and last sections..fails in the object aimed at by merely transferring the strain to the back of the overcast sections.

overcasting, *vbl. sb.* Add: **4.** Also in *Bookbinding*: see *OVERCAST *v.* 7.

1885 W. J. E. CRANE *Bookbinding for Amateurs* vi. 54 There is another way of overcasting more used in London. **1901** D. COCKERELL *Bookbinding* 316 Overcasting, over-sewing the back edges of single leaves or weak sections. **1931** A. ESDAILE *Student's Man. Bibliogr.* vi. 182 Overcasting, a more respectable form of stabbing, by which the folds are sewn together beyond, and enclosing, the ordinary sewing.

overcasting, *ppl. a.* (Further examples.)

1901 D. COCKERELL *Bookbinding* ii. 51 The custom with binders is to overcast the backs of the leaves in sections, and to sew through the overcasting thread. **1964** *McCall's Sewing* 134/2 A row of machine-stitching close to the raw edge serves as a guide for keeping overcasting stitches even.

o:ver-centraliza·tion. [OVER- 29 b.] Excessive centralization of administrative functions, leading to inefficiency. So **overce·ntralized** *a.*

1882 E. W. HAMILTON *Diary* 20 June (1972) I. 290 He spoke strongly of the dreadful 'administrative chaos' and over-centralisation which existed in Dublin Castle. **1896** L. T. HOBHOUSE *Theory of Knowl.* 276 The over-centralisation of the imperial government. **1944** J. S. HUXLEY *On Living in Revolution* xi. 118 An overcentralized administration is always characterized by the fact that its field officers tend to become messengers and office boys. **1949** I. DEUTSCHER *Stalin* vii. 241 Stalin obviously erred in the direction of over-centralization. **1962** *Punch* 7 Feb. 261/3 Jellicoe..had to fight with a machine encrusted with over-centralisation. **1971** *Time* 29 Mar. 36/3 Now the country [*sc.* Poland] is tense but quiet, as [Edward] Gierek attempts to consolidate his position and cope with an appalling economic mess caused by years of overconcentration on heavy industry, overcentralization and postponement of reforms. **1977** *Times* 7 Nov. 14/6 The [Soviet] economy is still an overcentralized shambles.

o·vercheck, *sb.*[2] [OVER- 8.] On cloth: a check pattern superimposed on a pattern of smaller check.

1906 *Daily Chron.* 25 Apr. 8/5 There will be a few very neat stripes,..while the finely-traced overchecks will be much in evidence. **1923** [see *GLENURQUHART, GLEN URQUHART]. **1959** [see *HOUNDSTOOTH]. **1967** N. FREELING *Strike Out* 27 The suit was..mohair in a large complicated overcheck of fuchsia, havana and off-white. **1974** *Daily Tel.* 6 Mar. 15 Tweedy, sporty men should be in their element as checks..get bigger, plaids get bolder and overchecks more aggressive.

So **overche·cked** *ppl. a.*

1925 *Eaton's News Weekly* 2 May 10 A fine brown and blue tweed, overchecked in rust. **1960** *Harper's Bazaar* Aug. 56/2 Predominantly bright red, it [*sc.* a coat] is overchecked in yellow and black. **1969** *Times* 30 Sept. 14/5 (Advt.), Stunning dresscoat in bold overchecked..wool. **1970** *Vogue* May 21/2 A willow green tweed jacket..overchecked in brown and navy.

over-cho·sen, *a. Sociology.* [OVER- 28 c.] Denoting those who, in a sociometric group study, are chosen by others well above the average number of times; the 'stars' of a sociometric group; also *ellipt.* as *sb.* Cf. *UNDER-CHOSEN *a.*

1943 H. H. JENNINGS *Leadership & Isolation* iv. 66 The test of whether or not this is true might be made by examining the choice behavior of the 'over-chosen' as compared with the 'under-chosen'. *Ibid.* 68 In Group A_{11} in which 16 percent are over-chosen..the number by whom they are chosen extends from 16 to 24 individuals, while the under-chosen who comprise 17 percent..are chosen by from zero to 3 individuals. **1956** J. KLEIN *Study of Groups* 91 The fact that certain people are over-chosen or under-chosen implies that members share certain standards which the over-chosen exemplify and the under-chosen fall short of. **1958** W. J. H. SPROTT *Human Groups* ix. 150 On work and living—with choice.. there was considerable overlap among what she calls the 'over-chosens'.

overclimb, *v.* (Later example.)

1882 'OUIDA' *Bimbi* v. 149 A loggia..all overclimbed by hardy rose-trees.

overclo·sure. *Dentistry.* [OVER- 29.] A condition in which the lower jaw is raised more than normal in relation to the upper jaw when put into the rest position.

1934 *Ann. Otol., Rhinol. & Laryngol.* XLIII. 7 (*caption*) Broken lines spheno-mandibular ligaments and pterygoid muscles further relaxed by marked overclosure of edentulous mouth. **1948** *Brit. Dental Jrnl.* LXXXV. 225/1 Men with severe recently acquired malocclusion (extreme voluntary overclosure after removal of their full dentures). **1975** H. THOMSON *Occlusion* iv. 51 A vertical extension of mandibular displacement where the IOD [*sc.* interocclusal distance] is in excess of 4 mm. is referred to as mandibular overclosure.

overcoat. Add: (Earlier and later examples.) Also *attrib.* Also *fig. spec.* with ref. to means of disposing of a body; *wooden overcoat*, a coffin. *slang.*

1802 *Monthly Mag.* XIV. 325/1 [He] presented to the king of Spain a very light and thin over-coat, which rain could not penetrate. **1807** *Salmagundi* 31 Dec. 395 Observing it to be dressed in a man's hat, a cloth overcoat, and spatterdashes, I framed my apology accordingly. **1857** P. CARTWRIGHT *Autobiogr.* 201 My pistol.. was in my overcoat pocket. **1860** MAYNE REID *Odd People* 136 Not contented with being tatooed, these also *paint* their bodies, by way of 'overcoat'. *c* **1864** E. DICKINSON *Poems* (1955) II. 705 The Spirit turns away Just laying off for evidence An Overcoat of Clay. **1903** FARMER & HENLEY *Slang* VII. 362/2 *Wooden-overcoat* (or *-surtout*),..a coffin. **1909** *Dialect Notes* III. 389 *Wooden-overcoat*, coffin. **1940** H. W. THOMPSON *Body, Boots & Britches* xix. 486 Your wooden overcoat won't have any pockets. **1942** [see *MEASURE *v.* 2 c]. **1958** M. KELLY *Christmas Egg* I. 9 He put his hands in his overcoat pockets. **1969** *Times* 15 Nov. p. vi/7 Felco secateurs are exceedingly popular... Their model..has one handle with a plastic 'overcoat' which rotates as you squeeze the handles together. **1971** *Guardian* 12 Aug. 11/2 The paratroops were edgy and the one who let me through the barricade reckoned I would come out in a wooden overcoat. **1972** K. BONFIGLIOLI *Don't Point that Thing at Me* xvii. 147 He..had to get us to ground of his own choosing before he could fit us for cement overcoats. **1974** *Times* 14 Dec. 1/7 The Foreign Office..asked Miami police searching for Mr John Stonehouse, the missing British MP..for a special report of..a Mafia style 'concrete overcoat' known to have contained a body. **1976** *Publishers' Weekly* 19 Apr. 80/1 The neighborhood gossips about a most unlikely overcoat flasher.

overcoating. (Further examples.)

c **1900** in *American Mail Order Fashions* (1961) 25 The fabric is a regular overcoating Vicuna... A firm but soft finished overcoating in one of the new shades. **1948** *Hansard Commons* 16 Mar. Written Answers 224 We have stipulated that half of the Italian supplies should be in men's suitings and overcoatings. **1967** *Times Rev. Industry* Apr. 53/3 J. and J. Crombie is to make 96,000 yards of overcoating, worth more than £250,000, for the Soviet Union.

o·vercoatless, *a.* [f. OVERCOAT + -LESS.] Not having, or not wearing, an overcoat.

1908 L. A. HARKER *His First Leave* vi. 60 An old gentleman, overcoatless, umbrellaless. **1929** J. B. PRIESTLEY *Good Companions* II. v. 389 Her hatless and overcoatless companion. **1936** E. SITWELL *Victoria of Eng.* xii. 149 So, overcoatless, since his threadbare overcoat was in pawn, he went out into the rainy streets.

overcome, *v.* Add: **2. c.** Phr. *we shall overcome*, used as a slogan by minority groups, with allusion to the text of a Negro Gospel song.

[**1901** C. A. TINDLEY in Miles & Clifton *New Songs of Gospel* No. 27 (*title*) I'll overcome some day.] **1948** *People's Songs* Sept. 8 We will overcome, We will overcome, We will overcome some day. Oh Down in my heart, I do believe, We'll overcome some day. **1961** *Jet* 14 Dec. 53 That the Freedom Riders left their imprint on the prison was evident from the songs and slogans they scribbled on the walls. A favorite was the crusaders' theme *We Shall Overcome.* **1963** *N.Y. Times* 23 July 21/1 The theme song of the integration movement, 'We Shall Overcome', has had its own history of integration, passing from Negro singers to white and back again to Negro. **1968** 'EBON' *Revolution* 15 'We shall overcome' And black Truth bombs Explode In the back, Alleys, Of Newark's Asshole. **1973** *Black World* Sept. 8/1 The Christian strains of 'We shall Overcome' gave way to the more Garrisonian 'We Shall be heard!' as the Sixties progressed.

7. (Further examples.)

1835 A. B. LONGSTREET *Georgia Scenes* 7, I had overcome about half the space which separated it from me. **1875** W. MORRIS tr. *Virgil's Aeneids* XII. 907 And e'en the hero-gathered stone..O'ercame not all the space betwixt.

o:ver-co·mpensate, *v.* Also as one word. [OVER- 24.] *trans.* and *intr.* To compensate excessively for (something); spec. in *Psychol.*, to exhibit over-compensation (see next). Hence **o:ver-co·mpensated** *ppl. a.*; **o:ver-compensa·tory** *a.*

1768–74 [see OVER- 24 a]. **1917** *Psychol. Bull.* XIV. 207 By psychological investigation and analysis, one may disclose the psychic phase of these compensatory and over-compensatory processes. **1934** H. C. WARREN *Dict. Psychol.* 190/1 *Overcompensate*, to make more than the necessary amount of allowance or adjustment. **1937** 'M. INNES' *Hamlet, Revenge!* II. viii. 194 One builds on the over-compensated Oedipus—Dad Advises Sonny-boy. **1947** *Partisan Rev.* XIV. 476 As a result he..over-compensates by consciously immersing himself in parochial attitudes shared by the folk. **1949** M. MEAD *Male & Female* iv. 88 Their sons again grow up similarly focussed on women, similarly in need of over-compensatory ceremonial to rescue them. **1958** 'E. CRISPIN' *Best SF Three* 11 As to human intellect, science fiction has emphasised its inadequacy over and over again. The *genre* 'overcompensates', no doubt, in showing the man animal so often defeated, or all but defeated, by the Other Thing, and this over-compensation is the origin of the accusations of pessimism that are so often levelled against it. **1962** SIMPSON & RICHARDS *Physical Princ. Junction Transistors* xii. 280 In case (b) (perfect compensation), the dashed curve coincides with the extrapolated linear sections of the transfer characteristics, and in the overcompensated case (c) it lies between the two linear sections. **1968** L. DURRELL *Tunc* i. 17 We sparred gracefully in the fashion of well-educated Englishmen overcompensating. **1973** 'D. HALLIDAY' *Dolly & Starry Bird* xviii. 277 Innes..will shortly give you a brandy because he is overcompensating. He thought you were guilty and is now ashamed. **1973** C. MULLARD *Black Brit.* II. iv. 44 In others [*sc.* classrooms] the teachers overcompensated and patronized their new pupils.

o:ver-compensa·tion. Also as one word. [OVER- 29 b. Cf. G. *überkompensation.*] A term used in psychological analysis by A. Adler to denote the exaggerated striving for power, etc., that can activate someone suffering from a severe sense of inferiority; an exaggerated response of making allowance or amends for something; more than equitable compensation.

1917 *Psychol. Bull.* XIV. 207 Adler thought he had discovered 'a remarkable relationship between somatic inferiority and somatic psychic over-compensation'. **1917** GLUECK & LIND tr. *Adler's Neurotic Constitution* (1921) I. i. 4 This fetal character..furnishes the increased possibility for compensation and over-compensation. **1932** *Brit. Jrnl. Psychol.* Apr. 347 Occasionally, over-compensation for this error [in colour memory] seems to be taking place. **1941** J. S. HUXLEY *Uniqueness of Man* xi. 228 Bias of this type has the additional danger that those who make an effort to discount it may readily swing into over-compensation—a bias of opposite sign. **1955** T. H. PEAR *Eng. Social Differences* vi. 138 Theories of compensation and over-compensation for inferiority-complexes. **1969** V. H. VROOM in Lindzey & Aronson *Handbk. Social Psychol.* (ed. 2) V. 220 The evidence reported concerning overcompensation and undercompensation pertains to its short-term effects on performance. **1977** D. CLARK *Gimmel Flask* vi. 106 Her over-compensation in over-spending may be due to her disappointment.

o:verco·mpound, *a. Electr. Engin.* [f. OVER- 24 b + COMPOUND *a.*] = next.

1931 G. C. BLALOCK *Princ. Electr. Engin.* ix. 95 The overcompound generator is adapted to more remote loads, since its rising characteristic will compensate for linedrop. **1972** I. L. KOSOW *Electr. Machinery & Transformers* iii. 99 Most commercial compound dc dynamos..are normally supplied by the manufacturer as overcompound machines.

o:vercompou·nded, *ppl. a. Electr. Engin.* [f. OVER- 24 b + COMPOUND *v.* + -ED[1].] Of a dynamo: compounded in such a way that the voltage increases with load.

1892 S. P. THOMPSON *Dynamo-Electr. Machinery* (ed. 4) xi. 295 For such work as supplying current to an electric tramway, an over-compounded dynamo with laminated field-magnets is the best generator. **1927** A. E. CLAYTON *Performance & Design D.C. Machines* viii. 181 With an over-compounded machine the value of the current in the shunt winding actually increases with increasing load. **1971** L. T. AGGER *Introd. Electr.* xvi. 299 If..the load has to be supplied over a considerable distance, the rising characteristic of the over-compounded generator..may be desirable.

So **overco·mpounding** *vbl. sb.*; also (as a back-formation) **overco·mpound** *v. trans.*

1892 S. P. THOMPSON *Dynamo-Electr. Machinery* (ed. 4) xi. 295 The same process suits for over-compounding, the excitation at full load being raised until the volts at terminals rise to the higher number of volts that will allow for the drop in the leads. **1914** A. GRAY *Princ. & Pract. Electr. Engin.* xiii. 75 For railway service the generators are overcompounded so as to maintain the trolley voltage at some distance from the power house. **1937** H. E. STAFFORD *Troubles of Electr. Equipment* iii. 46 To overcompound a generator not provided with diverters, the only permanent way is to increase the strength of the series and interpole fields. **1966** J. MEISEL *Princ. Electro-mechanical-Energy Conversion* ix. 394 Making $G_{as}\omega_0{}^r$ greater than $Ra + Rs$, or overcompounding the machine, gives an increasing output voltage with increasing load current. *Ibid.*, By a slight overcompounding the droop can be taken into account and the output voltage at no load..can be made equal to the output voltage at full-load current.

o:verconso·lidated, *ppl. a.* [OVER- 24 b.] Of soil or clay: consolidated to a greater degree than could have been produced by the present pressure of overburden.

1936 *Proc. Internat. Conf. Soil Mech. & Foundation Engin.* III. 52 Tests with strongly overconsolidated soils. **1957** BISHOP & HENKEL *Measurement of Soil Properties in Triaxial Test* 115 A series of tests on an over-consolidated clay. **1969** C. R. SCOTT *Introd. Soil Mech. & Foundations* vi. 139 Dense sands and over-consolidated clays increase in volume when sheared, if they are free to do so.

So **o:verconsolida·tion.**

Quot. 1960 represents a simple non-technical use.

1936 *Proc. Internat. Conf. Soil Mech. & Foundation Engin.* III. 51 In order to investigate the influence of the voids ratio on the shearing resistance, the test specimens were reconsolidated in three different ways, so that they at the start of the shearing test would be in a state of either natural consolidation, simple overconsolidation, or cyclic overconsolidation. **1960** *Farmer & Stockbreeder* 1 Mar. 94/3 There is no danger of over-consolidation with tractors in the silo. **1969** LAMBE & WHITMAN *Soil Mech.* xxix. 452/2 The natural water content considered in relation to the liquid and plastic limits gives some idea of the degree of overconsolidation.

over-correct, *v.* Add: **1.** Also, to correct (a lens) so that there is an aberration opposite to that of the uncorrected lens. (Earlier and later examples.)

1829 H. CODDINGTON *Treat. Reflexion & Refraction of Light* vi. 253 If a concave flint glass lens..be too powerful for a convex crown glass one when placed in contact, so as to over-correct the colour, as it is said, the achromatism may be made more perfect by separating them a little. **1885** T. LONGMORE *Illustr. Optical Manual* (ed. 3) ii. 43 It should be ascertained if the M[yopia] has not been over-corrected by the lenses supplied, and the eyes brought into a condition of H[ypermetropia]. **1975** M. RUBEN *Contact Lens Pract.* ii. 19/2 In hypermetropia..one eye (the non-dominant) can..be overcorrected by as much as 1·5 D so as to give the best binocular acuity for distance.

2. *trans.* and *intr.* To make an excessive correction to or in (something); to correct (someone) too frequently.

1956 *Publ. Amer. Dial. Soc.* XXVI. 45 But he may still have trouble remembering which sound belongs in which words, and in his anxiety he will overcorrect and hear *sung* for *sun* or *some.* **1966** J. DERRICK *Teaching Eng. to Immigrants* iii. 117 In this, as in all questions of pronunciation teaching, the greatest care and tact is necessary, so that the nervous pupil, from being over-corrected, does not become more nervous and inhibited. **1966** *Publ. Amer. Dial. Soc. 1964* XLII. 5 To overcorrect a slide, causing rear of car to waggle like a fishtail. **1966** *Rep. Com. Inquiry Univ. Oxf.* II. 325 This calculation almost certainly over-corrects for any error. **1967** J. RATHBONE *Diamonds Bid* iv. 39 The car..slewed towards the right. I over-corrected and the on-side fender hit a low wall. **1974** L. DEIGHTON *Spy Story* xx. 215 The machine tottered into the air, swinging as the nervous pilot over-corrected. **1976** *Columbus* (Montana) *News* 10 June 4/3 The driver overcorrected, causing the vehicle to go into a skid, overturning in the median after crossing the road.

over-corre·ction. [OVER- 29 b.] An excessive correction; a correction which results in error in the opposite direction; *spec.* (*a*) *Optics,* correction of a lens to such a degree as to produce the opposite aberration; (*b*) *Linguistics* = *HYPERCORRECTION.

1885 T. LONGMORE *Illustr. Optical Manual* (ed. 3) ii. 43 If there be no over-correction, but the concave lenses ordered are found to be only equivalent to the excess of refraction, or, in other words, to the degree of M[yopia] which they have been calculated to neutralise, [etc.]. **1947** E. H. STURTEVANT *Introd. Linguistic Sci.* viii. 80 Sometimes..he has caught himself creating such forms as [dju·, tju·] for *do* and *two.* Such 'over-corrections' have been observed very often in many languages. **1957** F. & R. LOCKRIDGE *Practise to Deceive* (1959) x. 137 That was prejudice, to be corrected. But, then, there was the danger of over-correction. **1961** F. G. CASSIDY *Jamaica Talk* iii. 46 All too easily this attempt leads to what is called 'over-correction', for he puts sounds into places where they do not belong in Standard. **1966** A. BATTERSBY *Math. in Managem.* vii. 185 Fifteen weeks after the sales increased, the rate of production at the factory had surged up to an increase of 45%; forty weeks later it had swung back in an over-correction. **1975** M. RUBEN *Contact Lens Pract.* ii. 19/1 In hypermetropia associated with convergence,.. overcorrection with a contact lens can be just as effective as spectacle lenses.

over-credulous, *a.* (Later example.)

1936 L. MACNEICE tr. *Aeschylus' Agamemnon* 29 The over-credulous passion of woman expands In swift conflagration.

over-critical, *a.* (Earlier and later examples.)

1851 MRS. GASKELL *Let.* 1 Sept. (1966) 161 She..is inclined to be *over*-critical & fastidious with everybody & everything. **1946** *Nature* 28 Sept. 457/1 The points of inflexion of various thermodynamical functions in the overcritical region. **1976** J. WILSON *Let's Pretend* v. 57 Lately she'd been over-critical of Margaret, finding her exasperating instead of endearing.

overcroft (ōu·vəɹkrɒft). [f. OVER- 8 c + CROFT *sb.*[2]] In early church architecture, a series of small rooms below the roof (see quot. 1925).

1925 P. POWER *Early Christian Ireland* ii. 22 On the inside the little building is roofed, or ceiled, by a barrel vault, between which and the outer stone roof there is an overcroft, or series of very small rooms, lighted by opes in the gable. **1964** B. WHELPTON *Unknown Ireland* xi. 149 The thirteenth-century Church of St. Doulough with its steep stone roof and overcroft.

overcrop, *v.* Add: **II. 3.** (Later examples.) Also *transf.*

1946 *Nature* 2 Nov. 606/2 Sometimes his [*sc.* man's] responsibility is brought home to him by physical disaster, ..as in the effects of deforestation, over-cropping or overgrazing. **1960** *Farmer & Stockbreeder* 9 Feb. 97/1 Many instances of 'soil sickness'..in the past would have been put down to thin or hungry soil, overcropping or bad drainage. **1974** *Times* 25 Apr. 12/6 He worries..about the over-cropping of the sea.

overcrowded, *ppl. a.* Add: (Earlier and later examples.) Hence **overcrow·dedness.**

1836 J. S. MILL in *London & Westm. Rev.* Apr. 18 In every overcrowded department there will arise a tendency among individuals..to unite their labours or their capitals. **1902** *Daily Chron.* 29 Sept. 3/3 It is here that the over-crowdedness of his pages comes most into evidence. **1911** G. B. SHAW *Doctor's Dilemma* p. lxxxiv, He is struggling for life in an overcrowded profession. **1950** T. S. ELIOT *Cocktail Party* II. 126 But they can't *all* stay there! I mean, it would make the place so over-crowded. **1960** *Encounter* Mar. 56/1 The spiritual effects of over-crowdedness. **1976** H. NIELSEN *Brink of Murder* ix. 81 Small businessmen, seeking relief from overcrowded cities.. gravitated seaward to create new forms of overcrowding. **1977** *Listener* 17 Mar. 339/1 A cell which..would beggar description in terms of coldness, smallness, over-crowdedness.

overcrowding, *vbl. sb.* (Earlier and later examples.)

1848 MILL *Pol. Econ.* I. II. xiv. 472 A sufficient degree of overcrowding may depress the wages of women to a much lower minimum than those of men. **1865** J. SIMON in E. R. Pike *Human Doc. Victorian Golden Age* (1967) vi. 292 Where 'overcrowding' exists in its sanitary sense, almost always it exists even more perniciously in certain moral senses. **1932** J. S. HUXLEY *Probl. Relative Growth* vii. 207 With overcrowding and less favourable food conditions 'degeneration' set in. **1955** M. GILBERT *Sky High* ii. 22 Every time we meet he's got a fresh reason for it. Overcrowding, parking offences, congestion of pavements. **1976** *Language* LII. 30 The unit in relation to which overcrowding must be described is the syntactic configuration, and not just the simplex S.

o·vercure, *sb.* [OVER- 29.] The process or result of overcuring; overvulcanization.

1915 *Jrnl. Soc. Chem. Industry* 15 Oct. 990/1 The load at breaking point was found to increase with the time of cure to a certain point and then to collapse, the rubber becoming very brittle at an overcure. **1952** J. DELMONTE *Plastics Molding* ix. 265 Translucent urea molded parts are the first to show the effects of overcure—by dullness or chalkiness in finished products. **1964** [see *OVERCURING *vbl. sb.*].

overcure (stress variable), *v.* [OVER- 27.] **a.** *trans.* To cure (plastic or rubber) for longer than the optimal period; to overvulcanize. Also *absol.* **b.** *intr.* To undergo overcuring.

1916 *Jrnl. Soc. Chem. Industry* 31 Aug. 872/1 It is.. common in the case of many goods for manufacturers when vulcanising to undercure rather than overcure the rubber so as to avoid the danger of over-vulcanising and consequent deterioration. **1949** B. L. DAVIES *Technol. Plastics* xxi. 405 The whole board is cured in the usual manner in the press, care being taken not to overcure. **1952** J. DELMONTE *Plastics Molding* viii. 211 Before the advent of thorough internal heating by high frequency, thick-molded parts would overcure on outside surfaces before the interior reached molding temperature. **1972** *Materials & Technol.* V. xiv. 523 The outside of a thick rubber article has to be cured longer than the optimum curing time (overcured) in order to ensure an optimum cure within the article.

So **o·vercured** *ppl. a.*; **overcu·ring** *vbl. sb.*

1912 *Jrnl. Soc. Chem. Industry* 16 Dec. 1100/1 It is important to note that (3) was almost fully cured at 35 lb. and over-cured at 45 lb. *Ibid.* 1101/2 Beyond this point it was probable that a decrease merely indicated overcuring. **1952** J. DELMONTE *Plastics Molding* ix. 265 An overcured plastics part is even more difficult to recognize than an undercured piece, primarily because most plastics are not critical in their time of cure. **1964** A. E. JUVE in Alliger & Sjothun *Vulcanization of Elastomers* ii. 30 Vulcanization occurs in three stages; (1) an induction period, (2) a curing or cross-linking stage, and (3) a reversion or overcure stage... Some systems..have little or no tendency toward reversion or increased tightness of cure as the result of overcuring.

o·vercurrent. *Electr.* [OVER- 29.] A current in excess of that which is normal, safe, or allowed for.

1931 H. W. BROWN *Electr. Equipment* (ed. 2) i. 19 (*heading*) Automatic protection against ground, short circuit, and overcurrent. **1971** MOORE & ELONKA *Electr. Syst. & Equipment for Industry* ii. 31 Direct-acting overcurrent trips are generally used on low-voltage circuit breakers.

overcut, *sb.* Add: **c.** *Mining.* A cut at or near roof level in a seam.

1940 *Trans. Inst. Mining Engin.* XCIX. 55 When the undercut is in coal, the importance of effective shovelling may be less, but it must always remain to give freedom of working to the machine, and it is only when an intermediate or overcut is taken that it is unnecessary. **1960** J. SINCLAIR *Winning Coal* vi. 170 When overcuts at a greater height are required..a hydraulic turret machine.. is generally most satisfactory.

d. In electrochemical machining, the distance between the outside surface of the cathode and the side of the cut in the part being machined.

1965 *New Scientist* 5 Aug. 336/2 If the voltage is allowed to fluctuate, the size of the overcut will fluctuate, and it becomes impossible to machine parts to close tolerances. **1974** J. A. MCGEOUGH *Princ. Electrochem. Machining* v. 146 The amount of overcut can be diminished by several devices, including insulation along the external side walls of the cathode.

over-cut, *v.* **1.** [OVER- 27.] *trans.* To fell too many trees in (a forest) at once, upsetting the regular supply of trees suitable for cutting.

1906 W. SCHLICH *Man. Forestry* (ed. 3) I. v. 75 Private owners are inclined to favour their own monetary interests to the disadvantage of future generations by overcutting ..their forests. **1913** *Q. Rev.* Oct. 446 In the case of private ownership, there is always a danger of the forests being overcut to obtain quick returns.

2. *Mining.* [OVER- 1.] *trans.* (See quot. 1967.) Also *absol.*

1907 *Trans. Inst. Mining Engin.* XXXI. 387 So far as the machine is concerned, it will overcut as well as under-cut. **1947** *Ibid.* CVI. 18 The first seam to be overcut with a machine designed specially for roof-forming was the Cockshead Seam in North Staffordshire. **1967** *Gloss. Mining Terms* (*B.S.I.*) VIII. 20 *Overcut,* to cut by machine at or near roof level in a seam.

3. [OVER- 27.] *intr.* To cut or produce a groove in a gramophone record with such amplitude as to run into an adjacent groove.

1935 H. C. BRYSON *Gramophone Record* iv. 73 For sounds of constant absolute intensity over the frequency range of 30–250, all the sounds have an equal tendency to over-cut. **1962** W. R. WELLMAN *High Fidelity Home Music Syst.* (ed. 2) viii. 175 When a recording is made, it is possible for the recording stylus to 'overcut', or run into an adjacent groove. **1976** *Gramophone* Sept. 514/3 The audible improvements over the transformer are subtle but very real, totally abolishing my previous reservations about slight sibilance on overcut records with the SL15/Mk. II.

Hence **o:vercu·tting** *ppl. a.* and *vbl. sb.* Also **o·vercu:tter,** a machine for overcutting.

1923 *M. & C. Machine Mining* II. 283 (*caption*) A repeat order for overcutting turbine driven universal machines for heading and longwall service. **1928** M. D. WILLIAMS *Pract. Machine Mining* iv. 45 The 'Samson' chain machine when adapted for overcutting is fitted with a jacking device which permits the raising or lowering of the machine in case of variation in the position of the band to be cut. **1928** *Daily Tel.* 9 Oct. 9/7 Wasteful over-cutting, forest fire, fungi, insects, and wind combined are rapidly wiping out Canada's available trees. **1935** H. L. BRYSON *Gramophone Record* iv. 83 If overcutting seems likely to occur, the electrical input of the recorder is cut down to the safety line, i.e., the amplitude is reduced. **1944** J. S. HUXLEY *On Living in Revolution* xi. 117 Over-cutting of the forests resulted in the closing of its [*sc.* Elma's] one big mill. **1946** *Trans. Inst. Mining Engin.* CVI. 20 (*caption*) Overcutting coal-cutter arranged to cut at 7 ft. *Ibid.* 21 An overcutter was required to cut at 4 ft. **1962** W. R. WELLMAN *High Fidelity Home Music Syst.* (ed. 2) viii. 175 Overcutting is prevented, during recording, by limiting the swing of the cutting stylus on low frequencies. **1966** S. D. WOODRUFF *Methods of Working Coal & Metal Mines* III. A. iv. 158 (*caption*) Hydraulic turret overcutter with down-curved jib for roof cutting. *Ibid.* 173 The cutting unit consists of a special long-wall coal cutter which is equipped with two horizontal jibs—one for undercutting and the other for overcutting.

overda·mped, *a.* [OVER- 24.] Of a physical system: damped to a greater extent than the minimum needed to prevent oscillations. So **overda·mp** *v. trans.*

1922 GLAZEBROOK *Dict. Appl. Physics* II. 373/1 The galvanometer system is non-oscillatory and overdamped. **1936** *Jrnl. Sci. Instruments* XIII. 101 Even with a resistance which overdamps the movement the rapidity of indication is said to compare favourably with that obtainable with pivoted instruments of a similar type. **1939** *Amateur Radio Handbk.* v. 79/2 The aerial should damp the network to flat resonance, though if it overdamps it, it may not be possible to draw any power from the anode circuit. **1962** SIMPSON & RICHARDS *Physical Princ. Junction Transistors* xv. 374 If the reverse is true the response will be overdamped and the output voltage will rise exponentially. **1975** *Nature* 10 July 121/1 If large, complex systems have the property that their linear connectivity is low, then they are more likely to be stable, and if stable, are more likely to be over-damped than to oscillate.

o·verday, *a.* [OVER- 32]. Designating a herring that is not freshly caught. Also *absol.*

1883 [see OVER- 32]. **1889** *Tit-Bits* 17 Aug. 298 About 24 hours after capture the herring is liable to the pouring out of extravasation of blood about his gills and fins, which..bruised appearance is quaintly called in the fish trade *over-day tarts.* **1927** *Sunday Express* 23 Oct. 5/1 Some of the herrings caught to-day are what is known as 'overdays'. A herring becomes an 'overday' if not sold within twelve hours of leaving the water, and its price drops precipitately. **1958** *New Statesman* 23 Aug. 218/1 'Overdays' herring, not completely fresh, can still make oil and meal, though 'sludge' needs fresh fish.

overdee·pen, *v. Geol.* [OVER- 22; *overdeepening* is tr. G. *übertiefung* (A. Penck 1899, in *Verhandl. des 7en Internat. Geographen-Kongr.* (1901) II. 232).] *trans.* To deepen further, to make even deeper. So **overdee·pened** *ppl. a.*, **-dee·pening** *vbl. sb.*

1900 *Proc. Boston Soc. Nat. Hist.* XXIX. 308 Penck has suggested that glaciated valleys of the Alpine kind should be called 'overdeepened'. **1902** *Q. Jrnl. Geol. Soc.* LVIII. 703 The hanging valleys in the lower part of the Val Ticino are attributed to the overdeepening of the main valley by ice. **1905** *Jrnl. Geol.* XIII. 392 As soon as a shallow wind-blown hollow is formed, that part of the integrated drainage system which leads to the hollow will supply waste to it whenever rain falls there;..the coarser waste will accumulate, and thus the tendency of the winds to overdeepen local hollows will be..counteracted. **1913** *Bull. Geol. Soc. Amer.* XXIV. 214 Similarly, a valley glacier, while actively overdeepening its trough, might develop a more or less abrupt step in the trough floor. **1968** R. W. FAIRBRIDGE *Encycl. Geomorphol.* 327/1 Regardless of whether the overdeepening of the river mouth is primarily due to eustatic rise of sea level or tectonic subsidence, it is said to be a drowned valley. *Ibid.* 743/2 The rock floors of overdeepened troughs remain bare in parts. *Ibid.*, Overdeepening is responsible for the production of numerous lakes, some of very large size. **1970** C. A. LEWIS *Glaciations Wales* ii. 25 The major through-valleys of Snowdonia were overdeepened and straightened at this time by lowering of the watersheds by ice moving radially outwards from a centre near Llyn Tegid.

overdesi·gn, *v.* [OVER- 26.] *trans.* To design to a standard of reliability or safety higher than the usual or minimum standard.

1964 M. GOWING *Britain & Atomic Energy, 1939–1945* x. 278 The team in fact decided to 'over-design' the pile. **1969** *Word Study* Apr. 4/2 Rocket boosters must contain.. hundreds of redundant systems to preclude failure and to provide reliability; they are overdesigned, well beyond what is necessary for normal function. The same overdesign appears in much of the prose. **1970** *Nature* 18 July 218/2 Once a tower has been shown to live up to its specification, the designer likes to see by how much he has overdesigned it, and about fifty per cent of the towers are eventually tested to destruction.

Hence as *sb.*, the action of overdesigning; an instance of this.

1969 [see above]. **1972** *Lebende Sprachen* XVII. 134/2 Greater reliability, without penalties caused by overdesign, are expected to be achieved through use of a simulator.

o:verdetermina·tion. [f. next.] The existence of more than one cause or contributory factor; *spec.* in *Psychol.*, the expression in one symptom of two or more needs or desires.

1917 C. R. PAYNE tr. *Pfister's Psychoanal. Method* 143 We have often had opportunity..to show these overdeterminations. **1925** A. & J. STRACHEY tr. *Freud's Analysis of Case of Hysteria* in *Coll. Papers* III. 73 In the world of reality..a complication of motives, an accumulation and conjunction of mental activities—in a word, overdetermination—is the rule. **1940** *Mind* XLIX. 370 A doubt such as 'I can never really know what another person is feeling' may arise from more than one of these sources. This over-determination of sceptical symptoms complicates their cure. **1955** J. STRACHEY tr. *Freud's Infantile Neurosis* in *Compl. Psychol. Wks.* XVII. 56 The contradiction is easily resolved if we regard it as a case of overdetermination. **1967** *Philos.* XLII. 374 There is a special kind of plurality, namely overdetermination. **1970** B. BREWSTER tr. *Althusser & Balibar's Reading Capital* (1975) 315 The overdetermination of a contradiction is the reflection in it of its conditions of existence within the complex whole, that is, of the other contradictions in the complex whole, in other words its uneven development. **1973** S. HEATH in *Screen* Spring/Summer 111 Underground cinema..has attempted to break through..the particular ideological overdetermination of the camera. **1975** *New Left Rev.* Nov.-Dec. 14 The ideological overdetermination is itself a forced response, and what forces it is a material dilemma.

overdete·rmine, *v.* [OVER- 24.] *trans.* To determine, account for, or cause in more than one way, or with more conditions than are necessary. So **overdete·rmined** *ppl. a.*, having more determining factors than the minimum necessary; having more than one cause; *spec.* in *Psychol.*, giving expression to more than one need or desire; **overdete·rmining** *vbl. sb.*

1879 *Encycl. Brit.* X. 377/2 The definitions which have not been mentioned are all 'nominal definitions', that is to say, they fix a name for the thing described. Many of them overdetermine a figure. **1917** C. R. PAYNE tr. *Pfister's Psychoanal. Method* 143 The neurotic symptom has several determining factors, at least two. Therefore, it is called over-determined. **1924** C. M. BAINES tr. *Freud's Ætiology of Hysteria* in *Coll. Papers* I. x. 213 The idea chosen as the basis of a symptom will be one which various factors combine to arouse and which is stirred up from several directions simultaneously;—a state of affairs I have elsewhere tried to formulate by saying that hysterical symptoms are over-determined. **1950** *Mind* LIX. 199 My large-scale map of the small area occupied by θ will show that its display of Q is over-determined. **1959** I. POOL in Saporta & Bastian *Psycholinguistics* (1961) 308/1 The third of the overdetermining influences in the development of contingency analysis was structural linguistics. **1969** G. STEDMAN JONES in Cockburn & Blackburn *Student Power* 30 Mass student insurgency is *par excellence* an 'overdetermined' phenomenon. **1974** J. WHITE tr. *Poulantzas's Fascism & Dictatorship* I. iii. 40 The economic process is overdetermined by the class struggle, which has primacy.

over-develop, *v.* Add: Hence **o:ver-deve·loped** *ppl. a.*

1974 *Environmental Conservation* I. 17/2 The kind of agricultural system that now predominates in the over-developed countries. **1974** B. PEARCE tr. *Amin's Accumulation on World Scale* I. ii. 157 In the overdeveloped economies,..the tendency to (relative) underconsumption weighs heavily upon investment. **1977** G. FISHER *Villain of Piece* ii. 14 Majorca's over-developed coastline.

over-development. (Later examples.)

1974 B. PEARCE tr. *Amin's Accumulation on World Scale* II. iv. 507 A favourable trade balance has beneficial effects only if saving tends to be superabundant, in a context of overdevelopment. **1976** *Survey* Summer-Autumn 156 The recognition of the planet's economic unity springs from a justifiable alarm at overdevelopment.

o:ver-differentia·tion. *Philol.* [OVER- 29 b.] The unnecessary differentiation of elements in a phonemic, graphemic, or grammatical system, or in its analysis. So **o:ver-differe·ntiated** *a.* Cf. *DIFFERENTIATION 1 b.

1933 L. BLOOMFIELD *Language* 223 Some irregular paradigms are *over-differentiated*. Thus, corresponding to a single form of an ordinary paradigm like *play* (*to play, I play, we play*), the paradigm of *be* has three forms (*to be, I am, we are*). *Ibid.* 269 Among the substantives are some pronoun-forms which, by over-differentiation, do not serve as actors: *me, us, him,* [etc.]. **1955** H. A. GLEASON *Introd. Descriptive Linguistics* xvii. 174 Over-differentiation can be discovered and corrected from the record alone by rigorous procedures. **1962** *Canadian Jrnl. Linguistics* VII. 105 The choice of an under- as against an over-differentiated graphemic system must be made by comparing the practical difficulties of each in relation to reading and writing. **1965** *Language* XLI. 67 This grammar is characterized by functional overdifferentiation... I mean the distinguishing of constructions that are functionally identical. **1965** *Amer. Speech* XL. 108 Overdifferentiation of phonemes involves the imposition of phonemic distinctions from English into the phonemic system of Texas German, where they are not required.

over-dispersion (ōu:vəɹdispə̄·ɹʃən). *Ecology.* [f. OVER- 29 b + DISPERSION.] A greater unevenness in the distribution of individuals than would be the case if the existence and position of each were independent of the rest, so that there is an increased proportion of the area with a large or a small concentration of individuals. Hence **o:ver-dispe·rsed** *a.*, distributed in this manner.

1936 *Jrnl. Ecol.* XXIV. 234 If in a set of counts of numbers of individuals per sample area the relative variance is greater than unity, this indicates that the dispersion is greater than would be expected on the assumption of random (Poisson) distribution... [This] first condition, over-dispersion, implies that individuals are scattered less evenly than would be expected. *Ibid.* 250 Over-dispersion shows itself in an excess of quadrats containing no 'individuals' or a large number of 'individuals', there being a corresponding deficit in central classes. **1946** *Ecology* XXVII. 329/2 The writer [*sc.* L. C. Cole] prefers the terms 'contagious' and 'negatively contagious' to 'overdispersion' and 'underdispersion' both of which have suffered reversals of meaning in the hands of different authors. **1948** *Bot. Rev.* XIV. 226 The study of overdispersion is of major importance in statistical ecology. *Ibid.*, Over-dispersion is the rule rather than the exception among animals. *Ibid.* 227 Cole applied this technique to the analysis of various over-dispersed populations. **1957** P. GREIG-SMITH *Quantitative Plant Ecol.* iii. 56 The former has been termed overdispersed (referring to the distribution curve obtained) and the latter underdispersed. Unfortunately these terms have sometimes been used in the reverse sense (referring to the pattern of individuals on the ground)..and are better avoided. **1964** V. J. CHAPMAN *Coastal Vegetation* ii. 24 The plants are over-dispersed or aggregated into clumps.

overdo, *v.* Add: **5.** (Further examples.) Also in phr. *to overdo it*, to do too much for one's health; to overtax one's strength.

1817 M. WHALLEY *Let.* 23 Apr. in J. Constable *Corr.* (1962) I. 164, I trust however that your Darling is better than when you wrote, & was not overdone with company yesterday. **1853** J. RUSKIN *Let.* 18 Aug. in M. Lutyens *Millais & Ruskins* (1967) 85 He overdid it last winter and now evidently stands in need of rest. **1866** GEO. ELIOT *Let.* 5 June (1956) IV. 267, I..have been a new creature ever since, though a little over-done with visits from friends and attention (miserabile dictu!) to petticoats etc. **1901** M. FRANKLIN *My Brilliant Career* v. 31 We were too overdone to make more than one-worded utterances, so waited silently in the blazing sun, closing our eyes against the dust. **1920** N. COWARD *I'll leave it to You* II. 24 You work terribly hard. I only hope you won't overdo it. **1924** A. HUXLEY *Let.* 3 Dec. (1969) 237 We must be careful not to make him overdo it, unless we want him laid up. **1973** N. MEYER *Target Practice* (1975) xv. 185, I worked at being normal. Perhaps I overdid it.

o·verdog. [OVER- 2 b.] A superior dog; usu. *fig.*, a dominant or victorious person. (Opp. UNDERDOG; cf. *top dog* s.v. TOP *sb.*[1] 32.) Hence **o·verdoggery.**

1908 *Westm. Gaz.* 17 Oct. 5/1 But the smart terrier was an Overdog, And knew a trick worth two of that. **1938** *Richmond* (Virginia) *Times-Dispatch* 6 Apr. 8/4 It's contrary to all instinct, yet, as one looks over the world today, one has to feel sorry for the overdogs. **1957** T. GUNN *Sense of Movement* 30, I praise the overdogs from Alexander To those who would not play with Stephen Spender. **1962** T. ZINKIN *Caste Today* 40 When the underdog begins to feel that he is as good as his neighbour, the result depends largely upon whether the overdog has stopped believing in his own over-doggery. **1966** *New Statesman* 28 Oct. 638/3 Underdogs abandoned by or abandoning inadequate male overdogs..revisit old haunts, look up old lovers, drift unsatisfactorily through a hostile world. **1970** R. LOWELL *Notebk.* 204 Dear Mary, with her usual motherly Solicitude for the lost overdog.

overdone, *ppl. a.* (Examples in sense 'overcooked'.)

1781 J. WOODFORDE *Diary* 24 Sept. (1924) I. 322 It was a shabby dinner and overdone. **1853** DICKENS *Child's Hist. Eng.* II. xvi. 25 All the sandy prospect lay beneath the blazing sun burnt up like a great overdone biscuit. **1964** L. DEIGHTON *Funeral in Berlin* xx. 117 A finger like a Lyons sausage—slightly overdone. **1975** B. WOOD *Killing Gift* (1976) II. iv. 75 The waiter..brought two plates of the overdone roast beef. **1977** P. G. WINSLOW *Witch Hill Murder* I. 20 She was not fond of overdone hamburger.

over-door, *sb.* (Further examples.)

1873 C. SCHREIBER *Jrnl.* 25 Oct. (1911) I. 236 Went on to Dirksen's, bought an over-door, also Watteau, for Ivor. **1967** A. EELES *Canaletto* 9/2 Smith also commissioned a group of 'over-doors', obviously intended to be part of a decorative scheme.

overdo·sage. [OVER- 29 b.] The administering or taking of too large a dose (of medicine, drugs, etc.).

1922 *Encycl. Brit.* XXX. 137/2 To find a method of preventing these chloroform deaths, by enquiring into the conditions of overdosage. **1929** *Irish Jrnl. Med. Sci.* Apr. 183 Such symptoms were obviously due to overdosage. **1964** L. MARTIN *Clin. Endocrinol.* (ed. 4) i. 12 The excessive secretion of, or therapeutic overdosage with ACTH produces the clinical picture of Cushing's syndrome. **1976** *Times* 11 Mar. 2/3 The recommendations on aspirin and similar pain killers reflect growing concern about overdosage.

overdose, *sb.* For quot. 1690 in Dict. substitute quot. 1700 below and add further examples.

1700 LOCKE *Essay Hum. Und.* (ed. 4) II. xxxiii. 223 Had this happen'd to him, by an overdose of Honey, when a Child, all the same Effects would have followed. **1916** [see *COBBER *sb.*[2]]. **1931** H. CRANE *Let.* 22 June (1965) 375, I have to leave most of this to your judgment of the potency and malfeasance of an overdose of tequila. **1952** M. LASKI *Village* ix. 147 An overdose of Miss Beltram produced the inevitable effect..you couldn't help taking the other point of view. *a* **1953** E. O'NEILL *Long Day's Journey* (1956) III. 105, I hope, sometime, without meaning it, I will take an overdose. **1965** *New Statesman* 7 May 729/3 Rosetti's..wife died after only two years of marriage, of an overdose of drugs. **1971** *Black Scholar* June 53/2 There are brothers..who have been singled out for overdoses of the atrocities that we are being subjected to. **1973** *Times* 16 July 14/7 Others were either seeking immediate emotional release or were trying to produce a dramatic effect on friends or relatives—and in both such cases an overdose achieved the desired result.

overdose, *v.* Add: **3.** *intr.* To take an overdose of drugs. Hence **o·verdosing** *vbl. sb.*

1973 R. LUDLUM *Matlock Paper* xxx. 261 The doctor told me that he'd prescribe heavier 'medication' but warned me not to overdose. **1974** G. MCDONALD *Fletch* (1976) xvii. 100 She was dead... He guessed she had overdosed. **1977** *Times* 19 Jan. 14/2 Heroin smoking.. throws overdosing figures into doubt. **1977** WOOD & GEASLAND *Twins* 21 You don't take a full bottle of an anticonvulsant if you mean to overdose on Seconal.

overdraw, *sb.* **2.** (Examples.)

1902 A. D. MCFAUL *Ike Glidden* xvi. 122 He was prancin' ..until he got him hitched inter this new bitin' gear an' overdraw. **1905** *Springfield* (Mass.) *Weekly Republ.* 8 Sept. 5 Much has been accomplished to abolish the pernicious practice of docking horses, but it is just as important that the abuse of the overdraw check should be corrected.

overdraw, *v.* Add: **II. 6.** (Earlier and later examples.)

a **1817** JANE AUSTEN *Northanger Abbey* (1818) II. vii. 140 Characters, which Mr Allen had been used to call unnatural and overdrawn. **1912** *Chambers's Jrnl.* June 359/1 Perhaps it will be said that the above statements are overdrawn.

7. *intr.* In card-games: to exceed the maximum permissible score by drawing too many cards. Also *refl.*

c **1805** JANE AUSTEN *Watsons* in J. E. Austen Leigh *Mem. J. Austen* (1871) 358 Vingt-un is the game at Osborne Castle... Lord Osborne enjoys it famously... I wish you could see him over-draw himself on both his own cards. *c* **1863** T. TAYLOR in M. R. Booth *Eng. Plays of 19th Cent.* (1969) II. 150 (*Draws card.*) Thirty-four—overdrawn—confound it! Now let's see your hand. **1950** *Hoyle's Games Modernized* (ed. 20) 158 Many players habitually stand at fifteen, and if the dealer is a reckless player, with a tendency to overdraw, it may be good policy to stand upon an even smaller figure.

Hence **overdra·wer**, one who overdraws a bank account, or has an overdraft.

1906 W. De Morgan *Joseph Vance* xxxvii. 378 Among the overdrawers, C. Vance & Co. was a conspicuous instance, figuring for a good round sum among the Debtors.

overdrawn, *ppl. a.* Add: *spec.* Of tea: infused too long.

1847 A. Brontë *Agnes Grey* xii. 189 Other thoughts assisted to..impart a relish to the cup of cold, overdrawn tea. **1969** V. C. Clinton-Baddeley *Only Matter of Time* 94 Cigarettes and cups of overdrawn tea.

overdress, *sb.* **1. a.** (Later examples.)

1975 *Country Life* 6 Feb. 346/1 The chemise has now become universally known as the overdress..because.. we have been pulling it over sweaters and shirts. **1976** *Ibid.* 19 Feb. 442 The beautiful, bright-green suede overdress by Jean Muir.

overdress, *v.* Add: **2.** (Later example.)

1947 *Sat. Rev. Lit.* (U.S.) 1 Mar. 23/2 There are times, too, when Mr. Miller overdresses the phrasing of his dialogue.

Hence **o:verdre·ssed** *ppl. a.*; **o:verdre·ssiness**; **o:ver-dre·ssing** *vbl. sb.*

1820 M. Edgeworth *Let.* 10 Aug. in C. Colvin *M. Edgeworth in France & Switz.* (1979) 209 Enter 3 English ladies overdressed in silks blonde and flowers! **1836** Dickens *Sunday under Three Heads* i. 2 There is a great deal of very unnecessary cant about the over-dressing of the common people. **1874** J. Brown *Let.* 4 Sept. (1907) 240 We saw the Duke with his eagle's feather, the Duchess in purple and lace, petite and overdressed. **1891** O. Wilde *Pict. Dorian Gray* i. 9 After I had been in the room about ten minutes, talking to huge overdressed dowagers and tedious Academicians, I suddenly became conscious that some one was looking at me. **1927** *Daily Express* 26 Aug. 1 What would look indecent in a London hotel becomes overdressiness here. **1932** W. W. Jacobs *Night-Watchman* iv. 680 Nothing looks worse than an over-dressed woman. **1939** Joyce *Finnegans Wake* 441 What's overdressed if underclothed? **1962** J. D. MacDonald *Girl* ix. 113, I got maybe forty [girls] stripped entire... Compared to them sixty broads, I was *overdressed.* **1975** J. F. Burke *Death Trick* (1976) ix. 132 An overdressed old mama.

overdrink, *v.* Add: (Further examples of *intr.* use.)

1904 'J. O. Hobbes' *Vineyard* iv. 55 They over-eat and over-drink, and they try to forget what they really want. **1932** Kipling *Limits & Renewals* 79, I steadily overdrank for a fortnight out of pure hunger. **1952** H. Waugh *Last seen Wearing* (1953) 53 She..says he's a show-off and over-drinks. **1967** N. Freeling *Strike Out* 29 Typical Bavarian, overate, overdrank, no exercise. **1976** *Times* 20 Oct. 14/3 Many of us over-eat, over-drink, and over-smoke.

overdrink *sb.*, delete †*Obs.* and add later examples; **o:ver-dri·nking** *vbl. sb.*

a **1902** S. Butler *Way of all Flesh* (1903) vi. 23 Even his excellent constitution was not proof against..over-feeding and what we should now consider overdrinking. **1906** *Westm. Gaz.* 19 Sept. 2/3 The Bishop of Oxford, in the protest..against the over-drinking of healths, appears to think that little was done in the way of similar protest between the far-off days of King Ahasuerus..and those of Queen Victoria. **1907** *Ibid.* 29 Oct. 12/1 The publicans are held responsible for the over-drinking of their customers. **1928** J. J. Walsh *Catholic Church & Healing* vi. 66 Bartholomew was aware, moreover, that insanity may come from overeating as well as from the overdrinking of strong wine. **1951** T. Sterling *House without Door* vii. 89 Her hands..had that luminous, slightly puffy look which comes from overdrinking. **1974** E. Brawley *Rap* (1975) 7 And her mother..had followed him two years later of love end overdrink. **1977** *Times* 7 Sept. 7/6 A first line of recovery from over-drink.

overdrip, *v.* (Later examples.)

1897 F. Thompson *New Poems* 176 Shake the lilies till their scent Over-drip their rims. **1898** A. S. Way tr. *Tragedies of Euripides* III. 198 'The altar, overdripped with Hellene blood?'.. 'Blood-russet are its rims in any wise.'

o·verdrive, *sb.* [Over- 26.] **1. a.** In a motor vehicle, a speed-increasing gear which may be brought into operation in addition to the ordinary (reducing) gears, so providing a gear higher than direct drive (the usual top gear), and in some cases correspondingly raising other gears, and thereby enabling engine speed to be reduced for a given road speed.

1929 *Trans. Soc. Automotive Engineers* XXIV. 335/1 The functioning of a transmission with either an overdrive or an underdrive through a double-internal-gear set in combination with a suitable clutch is exactly equivalent to that of a two-speed axle. **1932** Elliott & Consoliver *Gasoline Automobile* (ed. 4) xviii. 479 As a general thing, the high gear [on heavy trucks and buses] is a direct drive, although in some cases the high gear ratio is an overdrive, that is, the engine crankshaft turns at a slower speed than the propeller shaft. **1938** *Times* 23 Aug. 8/5 The overdrive is engaged by merely pushing in a lever just below the instrument board. **1958** *Times* 1 Oct. 8/3 To this can be added at extra cost a Laycock de Normanville overdrive operating on second and top gear. **1959** [see *gear ratio* s.v. *Gear *sb.* IV]. **1959** C. Campbell *Sports Car* (ed. 2) ix. 174 Some designers prefer to use the overdrive on top gear only, giving in effect a 5-speed gearbox. Others prefer to make it operative on both top and third, so that overdrive third gear is an intermediate step between direct third and direct top. **1970** *Motoring Which?* July 83/1 The 3-litre was comfortable up to about 95 mph (helped by its overdrive on 3rd and top). **1973** J. Wainwright *Devil you Don't* 5 It was a great car—a Jag. Mark II—well capable of three-figure speeds at the flick of the overdrive switch.

b. *fig.*

1962 L. Deighton *Ipcress File* i. 18 Dalby's voice trailed off as he slipped his mind into over-drive. **1967** *Times* 28 Oct. 20/2 Always the narrative is in smooth overdrive, even when it whisks you in successive paragraphs through Haiti..or the Preseli. **1969** *Times* 13 Dec. p. iv/7 The Websters knew everyone... Here, too, are Lilian Baylis and Sybil Thorndike, in overdrive as ever. **1970** G. Greer *Female Eunuch* 44 If women find that the clitoris has become the only site of their pleasure instead of acting as a kind of sexual overdrive in a more general response, they will find themselves dominated by the performance ethic. **1977** *Rolling Stone* 30 June 101/1 He shifts into overdrive on the first track, a fiery and propulsive Clarke composition entitled 'The Heat of the Battle', and never looks back for the whole album.

2. *Science Fiction.* = *hyperdrive.

1953 [see *interstellar *a.*].

overdrive, *v.* Add: **5.** *Golf.* To drive farther than (an opponent); to outdrive.

1900 *Gentl. Mag.* Feb. 126 If the opponent is a longer driver one is spared the temptation..of pressing to avoid being overdriven.

Hence **o:verdri·ving** *vbl. sb.*

1837 De Quincey *Revolt of Tartars* in *Blackw. Mag.* July 101/2 The cattle suffered greatly from over-driving. **1909** *Chambers's Jrnl.* Mar. 203/1 The electrical equipment is provided with suitable automatic devices to prevent over-driving. **1972** *Science* 16 June 1236/2 Control of the intensity is necessary to prevent overdriving by strong signals.

over-dry, *a.* Add: (Later examples.)

1891 W. Schlich *Man. Forestry* II. 32 *Dry Mould*..is formed by the decomposition of certain lichens on over-dry soil. **1959** A. H. Nissan *Textile Engin. Processes* xi. 293 It is then necessary to bring up the water content of the overdry parts by re-moistening them to a uniform and acceptable value. **1962** J. T. Marsh *Self-Smoothing Fabrics* xiii. 199 If the fabric is not sufficiently dry, then the subsequent mechanical operation is adversely affected; if the fabric is over-dry, then the durability of the finish, but not the initial effect, is adversely affected.

over-dryness (later example.)

1879 *Encycl. Brit.* X. 753/2 In extremely frosty weather ..they acquire so little moisture that then a difficulty arises from their over-dryness.

overdry, *v.* Add: **b.** (Later examples.) Hence **over-dry·ing** *vbl. sb.*

1867 K. H. Digby *Day on Muses' Hill* 146 The subsoil may be overdried. **1888** *Encycl. Brit.* XXIV. 657/1 Over-drying of wool has to be specially guarded against. *Ibid.* 657/2 Unless the wool is spread with great evenness..at points where the hot air escapes freely it may be much over-dried. **1959** A. H. Nissan *Textile Engin. Processes* xi. 293 It has already been demonstrated that overdrying the material before it is allowed to leave the drier consumes disproportionately longer time than drying it to the water content required in use. *Ibid.*, Unless there is close control, manual or automatic, on the uniformity of the final moisture content of the material in all directions, it is necessary to overdry the material so that its wettest part is within drying specification. **1962** J. T. Marsh *Self-Smoothing Fabrics* iii. 24 For many years the effect of drying has been recognised by the practical dyer in a qualitative manner, and there has been much warning as to the dangers of 'over-drying'. **1966** A. W. Lewis *Gloss. Woodworking Terms* 14 *Check*,..also called 'honeycombing'; due to over-drying too rapidly in the kiln.

overdu·b, *v.* [f. Over- 8 + *dub *v.*[5]] *intr.* and *trans.* To impose (additional sounds) on to an existing recording. So **overdu·bbing** *vbl. sb.*

1962 *John o' London's* 16 Aug. 162/4 His particular interest lies in multi-taping, or 'overdubbing'. **1969** *Rolling Stone* 28 June 19/1 On rhythm dates I only do bass, drums, guitar, overdub the guitar, overdub whatever,..and then Al overdubs the strings, the horns, or whatever. **1970** *Times* 18 July 7 Apparently Crosby, Stills and Nash went back to the studios to overdub their vocals on 'Suite: Judy Blue Eyes', but the rest are left as originally played. **1971** *Times* 5 Jan. 9 She also prefers to use her own voice, overdubbed several times, as a backing choir. **1973** *Sci. Amer.* Apr. 2/2 (Advt.), Overdubbing has become a familiar term to every knowledgeable musician. .. To overdub properly, the artist recording on the second track has to listen to the material recorded on the first track while performing in perfect synchronization to it. **1977** *New Yorker* 8 Aug. 66/3 The singing actors..then overdubbed the lyrics.

Hence **o·verdub** *sb.*, an act or instance of imposing additional sounds on to an existing recording.

1976 in *6,000 Words* 146 The last big album it took them eight months of overdubs to produce *Ibid.*, Vocal overdubs. **1976** *Gramophone* Aug. 353/2 By means of numerous synchronized re-recordings or 'overdubs', a typical pop recording is now built up over a period of days or weeks. **1977** McKnight & Tobler *Bob Marley* vi. 83 Wayne Perkins..is supposed to have added some overdubs.

overdue, *a.* Add: **c.** Of a library book: that has been retained by the borrower or reader longer than the period allowed; *overdue notice*, a notification sent to a reader requesting the return of an overdue book. Hence as *sb.*, an overdue book.

1890 T. Greenwood *Public Libraries* xxiii. 376 With this, as with other indicators,..books are shown in or out instantaneously,..and overdue books can be detected with little trouble. *Ibid.* 378 The borrowers' cards if arranged in a series of dated compartments, can be made to show the overdues. **1903** J. D. Brown *Man. Library Economy* xxix. 384 Overdue books could easily be detected by a register of this kind, on simply scanning the column of returns, filled up by the librarian. *Ibid.* 387 This personal form of ledger..makes the detection of overdues difficult. **1938** L. M. Harrod *Librarians' Gloss.* 109 *Overdue notice*, a request to a reader asking for the return of books which have been kept out beyond the time allowed. **1965** Smith & Baxter *College Library Administration* vii. 133 Whether the incidence of seriously overdue books is significantly reduced by charging fines is a matter for conjecture. **1966** E. V. Corbett *Introd. Librarianship* (ed. 2) I. xviii. 205 (*heading*) Fines and overdues. *Ibid.* 206 Other libraries may find that it is more economical to send out the first overdue notice not earlier than two months after the date due for return. **1970** *Times* 19 Nov. 15/6 He smiled only when he had returned them, like library books both overdue and unread, to the safety of the house. **1978** T. Allbeury *Lantern Network* xiii. 199 A library reminder for two overdue books.

d. Of a woman: not having had a menstrual period at the expected time. *colloq.*

1970 M. Tripp *Man without Friends* iii. 28 She placed her hand on mine, tenderly, 'I'm not overdue,' she said. **1972** F. Warner *Maquettes* 16 He doesn't even know I'm overdue. And he hasn't had it for a week. **1976** D. Francis *In Frame* viii. 115 She's feeling sick... I don't want a kid yet. She isn't overdue or anything.

overdye·, *v.* [Over- 8.] *trans.* To dye (something already dyed) with a second dye. Hence **overdye·ing** *vbl. sb.*

1946 Horsfall & Lawrie *Dyeing of Textile Fibres* (ed. 2) iv. 71 The question of overdyeing particularly concerns the production of shirtings or dress materials which are woven from grey unmercerised cotton, together with grey cotton dyed with fast-to-bleaching dyestuffs, and either undyed or dyed immunised cotton. These goods are piece bleached and overdyed with dyestuffs fast to light and washing in such a manner that the immunised and dyed cotton effects are unaffected. **1952** *Dyeing of Nylon Textiles* (I.C.I.) xi. 124 A two-bath process is necessary, the Vat dyestuff first being applied and oxidized and the union material then being overdyed with the acid dyestuff.

over-early, *adv.* and *a.* (Later examples.)

1871 C. Kingsley *At Last* II. x. 49 This over-early marriage among the Coolies is a very serious evil. **1922** M. E. Christie *Henry VI* iv. 119 The young Henry..now found the responsibilities of government over-early thrust upon him.

over-easily, *adv.* (Later example.)

1977 A. Wilson *Strange Ride R. Kipling* iii. 153 Trix's view of Violet Garrard has been..over-easily accepted.

overeat, *v.* **1. a.** *intr.* Delete (Now *rare*) and add further examples. **b.** *refl.* Delete (The usual construction) and add later example.

1879 [see *most *a.* II. 5 e]. **1888** Nye & Riley *Railway Guide* 8 My appetite is four sizes too large for a man of my height and every little while I over-eat. **1904** [see *overdrink *v.*]. **1944** L. P. Hartley *Shrimp & Anemone* iii. 33 You must see that he doesn't..over-eat himself. **1946** M. C. Self *Horseman's Encycl.* 291 A horse that from illness or some other cause is not being exercised will overeat. **1967** [see *overdrink *v.*]. **1972** D. S. McLaren *Nutrition & its Disorders* viii. 158 The view, commonly held, that all obese people overeat has not been substantiated by several surveys.

over-e·ducate, *v.* [Over- 27.] *trans.* To educate to excess or for too long. So **over-e·ducated** *ppl. a.*; **o:ver-educat·edness.**

1845 J. S. Mill in *Edin. Rev.* LXXXI. 510 The fears of the patrons and managers lest the poor should be 'over-educated'. **1899** W. James *Talks to Teachers* 257 To be imprisoned or shipwrecked or forced into the army would permanently show the good of life to many an over-educated pessimist. **1922** N. Coward *Coll. Sketches & Lyrics* (1931) 24 I've over-educated myself in all the things I shouldn't have known about at all. **1935** D. L. Sayers *Gaudy Night* xvii. 364 How many women care..about anybody's intellectual integrity? Only over-educated women like us. **1970** *Time* 19 Oct. 66 Critics contend that..new students are being 'over-educated' for non-existent jobs. **1970** *Worship* Oct. 491, I distinctly recall how self-conscious I felt of my over-educatedness the moment I sat down with him. **1977** *N.Y. Rev. Bks.* 14 Apr. 43/1 (Advt.), Seattle Professional Man, 36, newly settled, witty, travelled, over-educated, gentle, 5'9", seeks attractive woman counterpart.

over-egg, *v.* [Over- 27 a.] *fig.*, in phr. *to over-egg the pudding*, to argue a point with disproportionate force; to exaggerate.

1892 *Review of Reviews* Jan. 8/2 It is possible to over-egg your pudding and M. Stambuloff is doing it. **1961** *Daily Tel.* 9 Feb. 24/3 Mr Foot seems to have been ill served by his seconder, Mr Will Griffiths.., who is reported to have made the mistake of 'over-egging the pudding'. **1976** *Times* 2 Nov. 4/5 Mr Page, though remaining confident, wonders whether some of the recent [election] forecasts may have over-egged his pudding.

over-employ·ment. [Over- 29 b.] A situation in which vacancies for jobs, esp. skilled

jobs, exceed the number of unemployed, producing a labour shortage; a state of insufficient unemployment.
1944 *Times* 9 Nov. 5/3 Sir William Beveridge believes that..'Full employment'..'should mean a floating balance of not more than about three per cent unemployed'... The dangers of inflation implicit in an attempt to secure 'over-employment' are real enough in any full employment policy. **1958** *Times* 11 June 11/5 The contraction of demand has been felt in the United States in the form of unemployment, and in Great Britain in a relaxation of the state of over-employment.

o:ver-enginee·r, *v.* [OVER- 26, 27.] *trans.* To engineer to a standard higher than is technically necessary, or to an extent greater than is technically desirable. Hence **over-enginee·ring** *vbl. sb.*
1964 M. GOWING *Britain & Atomic Energy 1939–1945* ix. 259 Certain units were very much 'over-engineered' which in itself led to complications. **1967** *Gramophone* Dec. 317/1 Walter gives the warmest reading, though..the recording is certainly over-engineered. **1971** *Flying* Apr. 89/2 (Advt.), The brakes have been purposely over-engineered by twenty percent. **1977** *Gramophone* June 113/2 Some over-engineering seemed to have taken place, however, at the expense of complete fidelity.

over-enthu·siasm. [OVER- 29 d.] An excess of enthusiasm. So **o:ver-enthusia·stic** *a.*
1927 *Melody Maker* Aug. 781/2 Some of my readers.. have said that I am over-enthusiastic about Harry Richman. **1962** A. NISBETT *Technique Sound Studio* viii. 148 Over-enthusiasm has..resulted in the operator flicking the disc completely free from the turntable and skimming it across the room! **1962** A. BATTERSBY *Guide to Stock Control* viii. 77 There is also the over-enthusiastic salesman who offers to provide non-standard varieties of his company's products. **1970** *Nature* 24 Oct. 303/1 An over-enthusiasm for classifying projects of very marginal secrecy may have hampered progress. **1976** M. DRABBLE *Genius of T. Hardy* 166 The dog that destroys Gabriel Oak's sheep is over-enthusiastic, not malicious.

over-eru·ption. *Dentistry.* [OVER- 29.] Excessive extension of a tooth in the direction of the opposing teeth.
1961 H. R. B. FENN et al. *Clin. Dental Prosthetics* (ed. 2) xxiii. 628 Consideration must be given..to the extraction of the offending tooth..if the over-eruption is gross. **1975** H. THOMSON *Occlusion* viii. 130 Over-eruption of unopposed teeth..can be prevented by the muscle forces of tongue or cheek.
So **over-eru·pt** *v. intr.*, to undergo or exhibit over-eruption; **over-eru·pted** *ppl. a.*
1961 H. R. B. FENN et al. *Clin. Dental Prosthetics* (ed. 2) xxiii. 628 (*heading*) Over-erupted teeth. **1963** C. R. CROWELL et al. *Inlays, Crowns & Bridges* vii. 79 This wear may proceed to such an extent that the opposing teeth gradually overerupt. **1974** E. M. BARNETT *Pediatric Occlusal Therapy* vi. 161/1 The twin-wire arch is set so that the anterior wires lie slightly apical to where they should lie if the teeth were not overerupted.

over-estimate, *v.* (Earlier examples.)
1823 J. S. MILL in *Bermondsey Bk.* (1929) VI. 16, I may be told..that I over-estimate the effect of these motives on bad men. **1825** —— in *Westm. Rev.* Apr. 297 The habitual propensity of mankind to over-estimate advantages which they do not possess.

over-estimate, *sb.* (Earlier and later examples.)
1854 C. M. YONGE *Heartsease* I. II. xv. 357 A very good child, but spoilt..by John's over-estimate of her. **1895** *Geogr. Jrnl.* VI. 184 The liability..to an over-estimate of density [of population]. **1977** *Listener* 17 Mar. 327/1 The real membership of the Labour Party..is now 445,000..and..even this figure is probably an overestimate.

over-excitement. (Earlier example.)
1822 M. EDGEWORTH *Let.* 7 Jan. (1971) 313, I shall so arrange and *limit* our goings out..that Fannys health shall not suffer by over excitement.

over-exploi·t, *v.* [OVER- 27.] *trans.* To exploit excessively. So **o:ver-exploita·tion; over-exploi·ted** *ppl. a.*
1922 W. SCHLICH *Man. Forestry* (ed. 4) I. 273 The more accessible areas of the merchantable forests have been considerably over-exploited in the past. **1952** G. SARTON *Hist. Sci.* I. xi. 296 The mines were overexploited in the fifth century. By the middle of the following century only old workings were open. **1957** MANVELL & HUNTLEY *Film Music* iv. 191 Like all good ideas, they tend to be over-exploited to their own detriment. **1961** *Carolina Q.* Spring 18 It seems that only in today's Southern fiction does Tobacco Road..continue to live—but only as a weary, overexploited phantom. *Ibid.* 21 This legend.. well deserves a rest after the overexploitation of the past century. **1963** *Times* 6 Feb. 8/7 U. P. Gerasimov and E. K. Fedorov, commenting on over-exploitation of fisheries, alleged that trawlers..'are ploughing the seas near African and Asian shores in search of fish'. **1964** V. J. CHAPMAN *Coastal Vegetation* vi. 137 The question has been asked whether such dunes are the result of man's negligence or over-exploitation. **1970** *New Scientist* 3 Dec. 374/1 Improved international cooperation should limit overexploitation of important [fish] stocks. **1977** *Sci. Amer.* May 26/1 The floods of 1969 in Tunisia replenished all the reservoirs that up to then had been described as overexploited.

over-expose, *v.* Add: (Further examples.) Also *absol.*
1894 B. POTTER *Jrnl.* 12 Sept. (1966) 338 Went to Berwick again with papa who had over-exposed on Monday. We got out at Tweedmouth and he photographed from the same side at first and afterwards amongst the boats. **1925** B. BEETHAM in E. F. Norton *Fight for Everest, 1924* 325 We were all inclined to under-expose in tropical Sikkim and to over-expose in arctic Tibet. **1937** AUDEN & MACNEICE *Lett. from Iceland* iv. 45 In Iceland, even if you are using a meter, there is a tendency to over-expose. *a* **1963** S. PLATH *Ariel* (1965), 46, I could draw no breath, Dead and moneyless, Over-exposed, like an X-ray. **1971** *Radio Times* 23 Sept. 62 They hope that by not being over-exposed they'll be able to last longer, keep their standard higher. **1976** *Gramophone* Dec. 978/2 Nobody could say that this much maligned instrument [*sc.* the saxophone] is over-exposed now that it has faded from the pop scene.
over-exposure (further examples); *spec.* an excessive number of public appearances by an entertainer, actor, or the like.
1947 *Radiology* XLIX. 364/2 Is the peripheral blood picture as reliable an indicator of over-exposure as radiologists have considered it to be? **1969** *Guardian* 15 July 18/4 The company's general manager said that 'over-exposure' of records inhibited sales. **1971** *Ibid.* 6 Feb. 6/6 Future plans? A repeat of the 'Basil Brush Show' on the BBC, but careful avoidance of overexposure. **1974** *Times* 1 Feb. 19/6 We are all for exposure [on television], but we are against over-exposure. As anyone knows who handles films and photographs, you get unwanted results from over-exposure. **1974** *Physics Bull.* May 179/1 CO is not cumulative either in man or the environment but although moderate overexposure seems to cause no permanent damage to health, concern has been expressed about possible effects on the foetus following exposure of the pregnant mother. **1978** *Times* 5 Jan. 5/5 Perhaps renaissance is only the flip-side of over exposure.

over-exte·nd, *v.* [OVER- 27.] *trans.* **a.** To extend or reach further than (something). *rare.* **b.** To extend (a thing) too far. **c.** To take on (oneself) or impose on (another) an excessive burden of work, commitments, etc.; to attempt more than is practicable. Hence **over-exte·nded** *ppl. a.*; **over-exte·nsion.**
1937 R. ERSKINE *Stout Adventure M. Stewart* iii. 62 A culture and a civilization,..which, reckoned in the gross, outweighed and over-extended by a deal feudal, that is to say, English culture, manners and customs. **1938** *Sun* (Baltimore) 6 May 3/5 We are no longer over-extended in new construction or in capital equipment. **1962** L. DAVIDSON *Rose of Tibet* ii. 46 The arrangement was for a car to pick him up..but when..no car appeared, he realized he must have overextended Mr. Mukherjee, and took a bus instead. **1963** C. R. COWELL et al. *Inlays, Crowns & Bridges* iii. 25 The air-turbine instrument is usually less unpleasant for the patient, but there is risk of overextension. *Ibid.* vi. 64 If a temporary crown is overextended cervically the gingivae may be forced back. **1966** *Economist* 5 Mar. 898/2 Mr McNamara has defended himself vigorously, calling it 'absolutely false to say that we are over-extended.' **1968** *Blues Unlimited* Dec. 12 He never overextended himself and impressed with his command of the idiom. **1970** F. C. WEFFORT in I. L. Horowitz *Masses in Lat. Amer.* xi. 386 The sociological analysis..often considers what is merely possible, thus overextending the limits which the Brazilian historical situation allows for in the way of planned social change. **1973** *Daily Tel.* 7 Feb. 16 They have over-extended themselves in the purchase of jumbo jets and do not wish to make further capital commitments at this time. **1976** *National Observer* (U.S.) 3 July 9/4 In much the same way..it's easy to overextend yourself on vacations by scheduling too much sight-seeing and other activity.

overface, *v.* Add: **1. a.** (Further examples.) Also in non-*dial.* use, *esp.* to alarm or intimidate (a person, animal, etc.) by presenting too great a task or obstacle. Hence **overfa·ced** *ppl. a.*
1926 A. BENNETT *Lord Raingo* I. xliv. 196 There she stood, over-faced and dumb and apologetic in her plain brown dress. *Ibid.* lvii. 254 He scorned them, but in their collectivity they still over-faced him. **1944** *R.A.F. Jrnl.* Aug. 261 You cannot imagine any situation which would over-face them. **1950** W. A. RILEY in C. R. Acton *Dog Ann. 1951* 94 Personally, I think it is a great mistake to over-face them [*sc.* dachshunds], they are so game and will 'have a go', but they are not killers. **1958** *Times* 13 Dec. 9/4 Undoubtedly one of the most important points to remember is not to 'overface' the pony or its enthusiastic rider. **1971** R. ROBERTS *Classic Slum* vi. 94 Lower-class women, bold enough to enter a pub but too 'overfaced' to sit,..stood crushed together drinking in the 'Outdoor'. *Ibid.* vii. 109 Social intimidation..confused and 'overfaced' the simple. **1976** *Horse & Hound* 10 Dec. 69/3 (Advt.), This horse has been brought on slowly, never being overfaced.

overfall, *sb.* Add: **1.** (Further examples.) Also *transf.* and *fig.*
1947 A. C. DOUGLAS *Gliding & Advanced Soaring* i. 32 The cloud currents, the heat turbulence, high winds and mountain overfalls, which the aeroplane pilot finds so unpleasant or even dangerous, are regarded by the sail-plane pilot as friends, not as enemies. **1961** B. FERGUSSON *Watery Maze* iv. 89 Radiating in every direction from C.O.H.Q. were heavy overfalls, as they are called in seaman's parlance, or troubled waters, in landsmen's, needing more than a modicum of oil. **1970** *Motor Boat & Yachting* 16 Oct. 35/1 We didn't bother to avoid an area marked on the large scale chart with those squiggly lines that denote dangerous overfalls. **1975** J. R. L. ANDERSON *Death in North Sea* viii. 139 There were two main tidal streams... They might run up to about two knots, with a somewhat faster rate by some overfalls off Spurn Head.
3. Delete † *Obs.* and add later examples.
1811 D. BUCHAN in K. Winter *Shananditti* (1975) ii. 24 This day's distance is estimated at eleven miles allowing seven from the island..up to the overfall. **1921** H. GUTHRIE-SMITH *Tutira* i. 5 A meandering serpentine creek..which..breaks into a series of overfalls.

over-familiar, *a.* (Later examples.)
1936 R. W. CHAPMAN *S.P.E. Tract* XLVII. 237 'Your wife' may be over familiar, if I do not know Jones very well. **1955** H. KUTTNER in Aldiss & Harrison *Decade 1950s* (1976) 173 He saw the reflection of the over-familiar scene. **1976** B. BALL *Keegan: One-Way Deal* 16 Holmyard frowned. Ross was over-familiar. There was a time and a place for such things.

over-feeding, *vbl. sb.* Add: (Further example.) Also as *ppl. a.*
1621 H. WOTTON *Let.* 26 Nov. in L. P. Smith *Life & Lett. Sir H. Wotton* (1907) II. 219 As may excuse the English, whom otherwise they think an overfeeding nation. **1902** G. B. SHAW *Let.* 18 Nov. (1972) II. 289 Who is Doctor Buzzi? Is it starvation cure, or overfeeding cure, or water cure, or faith healing, or what?

overfill, *v.* Add: **1.** (Further examples: cf. next.) Hence **overfi·lling** *vbl. sb.*
1908 B. STOUGHTON *Metall. Iron & Steel* viii. 200 With open passes, the collars cannot be made to quite touch.. and the pressure may squeeze some metal between them, forming a 'fin' along the side of the piece. This is known as 'overfilling the pass'. **1953** D. J. O. BRANDT *Manuf. Iron & Steel* xxxii. 239 When the first portion of the rod enters the stands, there is no tension and the passes are overfilled but if there is tension when all the stands are rolling this will cause underfilling which will go on until the back end of the rod leaves the first stands, and the tension is relaxed, then overfilling will take place again. **1968** R. N. PARKINS *Mech. Treatm. Metals* iii. 135 The method adopted in this latter work was to determine the filling characteristic of a pass sequence, since this may be used to determine whether a given ingoing bar will under- or over-fill the pass. *Ibid.* ii. 78 Overfilling will cause the excess metal to spread into the roll joints..giving fins.

o·verfill, *sb. Metallurgy.* [f. the vb.] A projection on rolled metal due to the metal being too large for the aperture through which it was forced in rolling, so that the excess spread between the junction of the rolls; also, a bar or the like that is too large for the rolling it is to undergo.
1924 F. W. DENCER *Detailing & fabricating Struct. Steel* xxvii, 355 Material with overfills is not necessarily defective. **1929** *Rolling Mill Jrnl.* Jan. 15/1 If a bar when passing through a pass does not fill the groove, it is spoken of as an underfill. If it more than fills the groove and squeezes out at the sides, it is spoken of as an overfill and the material squeezing out at the sides is known as a fin or a flash. **1957** *Making, Shaping & Treating of Steel* (U.S. Steel) (ed. 7) xxx. 556/2 Overfills are broad and less sharp than fins. As a rule, overfills occur more frequently than fins and in many cases are associated on the same bar with underfills. **1964** N. WEINSTEIN tr. *Polukhin's Rolling Mill Pract.* xvii. 286 Fills and overfills obtained in rolling section steel are illustrated.

over-fish, *v.* Add: Now used esp. in reference to marine fishing grounds and the types of fish or shellfish caught there. (Later examples.) **over-fishing** *vbl. sb.* (Later examples).
1925 J. T. JENKINS *Fishes Brit. Isles* 137 All this statistical information has an important bearing on the vexed question of over-fishing [of cod]. **1941** *Sun* (Baltimore) 29 Nov. 6/3 Next year we won't have any oysters, and then, no doubt, we will be told that we overfished the beds this year. **1946** *Nature* 10 Aug. 189/2 Russell and Graham, discussing the overfishing problem, have recently emphasized that sea fisheries under present conditions have reached, if not over-reached, the limits of profitable yield. **1958** *New Statesman* 23 Aug. 218/1 Everybody who knows anything about fish..is anxious about over-fishing. **1973** *Daily Colonist* (Victoria, B.C.) 21 June 3/3 Industry spokesmen..have been pressing for action by Ottawa to halt alleged overfishing by foreign fleets. **1975** *Nature* 24 Jan. 290/3 Some [species], notably the European hake.. have been heavily overfished.

overfit (ōu·vəɹfit), *a. Physical Geogr.* [f. OVER- 28, after *misfit.*] Pertaining to or designating a stream which, if its average flow in the past was at present-day levels, would be expected to have eroded a larger valley than it has done.
1913 *Ann. Assoc. Amer. Geogr.* III. 18 Conversely, the capturing branch, AB, and its river, BD, below the entrance of the capturing branch, being increased in volume, should exhibit for a time an overfit relation to their valley curves, in the sense of actively enlarging them. **1954** W. D. THORNBURY *Princ. Geomorphol.* vi. 156 It is difficult to cite examples of overfit rivers, or streams with floodplains too small for the size of the stream. Hence there may well be a question whether overfit streams exist. The reason.. may be that a stream cannot long remain overfit, for an increase in volume will be accompanied by increased erosive power and rapid adjustment of valley size. **1968** R. W. FAIRBRIDGE *Encycl. Geomorphol.* 706/2 Davis..also recognizes overfit streams.

overflight (ōu·vəɹflait). [f. OVER- 4 + FLIGHT *sb.*[1]] The flight of an aircraft over specified territory without landing. Formerly also used of birds. Also *transf.*

1598 Florio *Worlde of Wordes* 383/1 *Soruólo*, an ouer-flight, a surflight. **1883** J. S. Stallybrass tr. *Grimm's Teutonic Mythol.* III. xxxv. 1133 Our early ages appear also to have seen a meaning in the *overflight* of certain birds. **1958** *Times* 8 Aug. 7/2 United States aircraft have now been given permission to fly over, but it was not clear yesterday whether British aircraft had permission. The question of overflights has been given much prominence. **1960** *N.Y. Times* 12 June 6E/2 The U-2 reconnaissance 'overflights' provided, by aerial photography and tape recording of Soviet radio and radar emissions, the most important intelligence gathered by the C.I.A. **1966** T. Pynchon *Crying of Lot 49* ii. 37 The can [of hair spray] hit the floor, something broke,..propelling the can swiftly about the bathroom. She looked up,..her field of vision cut across by wild, flashing overflights of the can, whose pressure seemed inexhaustible. **1970** C. Duerden *Noise Abatement* v. 88 Overflights are the problem. Once they are experienced, the reaction of the general public will be the deciding factor and supersonic flights may be prohibited over this country. **1970** *New Scientist* 1 Oct. 37/2 A single supersonic overflight cracked 95 per cent of the eggs of the terns breeding on the Dry Tortugas in Florida. **1973** *Sci. Amer.* Feb. 17/3 When Francis Gary Powers was shot down in May, 1960, the U-2 overflights ended, except for certain minor incursions. **1976** *Daily Tel.* 21 Jan. 2/6 It was bewildering that Britain and France, builders of the plane [*sc.* Concorde], did not allow supersonic overflights.

overflood, *v.* Add: (Further example.) Hence **overfloo·ded** *ppl. a.*; **overfloo·ding** *vbl. sb.* and *ppl. a.*

1881 E. W. Hamilton *Diary* 3 Nov. (1972) I. 182 The danger for the moment in Ireland seems to be the over-flooding of the Land Court. **1921** W. de la Mare *Veil* 47 Then silence, and o'er-flooding noon. **1955** E. Pound *Classic Anthol.* I. 16 At the over-flooded ford. **1973** *Nature* 21/28 Dec. 450/2 The whole is cut by a dyke swarm which is especially dense at the contact between the layered plutonic rocks and the other components of the formation, and was subsequently overflooded by three different basalt series.

overflow, *sb.* Add: **2. c.** *Telephony.* A situation in which more calls are directed to a group of switches or lines than they are able to handle; a call so directed. Usu. *attrib.*

1924 J. G. Mitchell *Mech. Manual Switching* i. 27 When the traffic reaches a peak so high as to prevent the prompt dispatch of calls by the operators on duty, those lines which are not receiving service will display a continuous signal on the overflow section. **1934** G. S. Berkeley *Traffic & Trunking Princ. Automatic Telephony* vii. 146 The overflow meter..records the number of calls lost due to the insufficiency of the plant. *Ibid.* 147 One overflow meter is provided to record the number of overflows occurring on the two levels. **1962** J. Riordan *Stochastic Service Syst.* iii. 39 Turn now to the size of overflow traffic, and write $P_n(t; r)$ for the stationary probability that in an interval of length *t*, whose initial point is an arbitrarily chosen point, there are *n* overflow calls from the first *r* servers. **1972** *Guardian* 19 Feb. 8/6 The BBC.. recorded 4,300 overflow calls. **1974** R. N. Renton *Internat. Telex Service* x. 383/2 Calls failing to find a free outlet in the level will hunt to the 11th bank contact, receive the appropriate service signal and operate the overflow meter. *Ibid.*, Tables of critical overflow are published.

d. *Computers.* The generation of a number having more digits than the capacity of the device holding it; also, the excess digit(s). Freq. *attrib.*

1951 *Proc. IRE* XXXIX. 275/1 *Overflow.* (1) The condition which arises when the result of an arithmetic operation exceeds the capacity of the number representation in a digital computer. (2) The carry digit arising from this condition. **1959** J. Jeenel *Programming for Digital Computers* iv. 187 The instruction..will cause program execution to proceed from 0104 to 0105 regardless of whether the overflow indicator is on or off. **1965** Swallow & Price *Elem. Computer Programming* xv. 279 The arithmetic operations of addition and subtraction are slightly more complex in the IBM 1401 than in the 141. One difference is in the handling of overflows. *Ibid.* 287 Whenever an overflow bit is carried into the zone of the high-order digit during an add or subtract operation, this indicator is turned on. **1969** P. B. Jordain *Condensed Computer Encycl.* 364 The most significant digit(s) are considered to be overflow. **1973** C. W. Gear *Introd. Computer Sci.* vi. 241 Most systems provide monitor subroutines that can be called to specify what is to happen in the case of overflow or underflow.

4. b. *Geol.* A natural notch or channel formed by water overflowing from a lake.

1902 *Q. Jrnl. Geol. Soc.* LVIII. 481 When the watershed is very uniform in height, and the ice has at one stage actually surmounted it, then several parallel overflows may be developed out of the gutters which are trenched in the outer slope by water flowing off the ice itself. The overflows..which cut through the Northern Cleveland watershed above the village of Egton are typical of this arrangement. **1973** R. J. Price *Glacial & Fluvioglacial Landforms* v. 128 So long as evidence for the existence of the ice-dammed lakes does not simply consist of the meltwater channels themselves, the interpretation of such meltwater channels as overflows cannot be disputed.

5. *overflow meeting* (further examples); **overflow channel** *Geol.* = sense 4 b above; **overflow table,** a table used to accommodate extra people attending a dinner, meeting, etc.

1902 *Q. Jrnl. Geol. Soc.* LVIII. 473 The criteria by which ancient extra-morainic lakes can be recognized are mainly four:—(1) beaches; (2) deltas; (3) floor-deposits; and (4) overflow-channels. **1969** Bennison & Wright *Geol. Hist. Brit. Isles* xvi. 356 Associated water-cut channels (called overflow channels) from ice-dammed lakes generally thought to result from water flowing marginally along ice sheets may, in many cases, also be a product of subglacial drainage. **1923** *Radio Times* 28 Sept. 2/1 The voice of a public man has been..made to operate loud-speakers of overflow meetings. **1974** *Times* 20 Feb. 1/1 Two eggs were hurled at Mr Wilson as he struggled through a crowd to enter Oxford Town Hall last night to address an overflow meeting of more than 1,000 people. The eggs went wide. **1973** A. Behrend *Samarai Affair* i. 14 There was a smaller overflow table where the members of the Pilotage Committee..liked to congregate.

overflow, *v.* Add: **I. 3. a.** (Later examples.) Also *fig.*

1890 *Forum* (N.Y.) VIII. vi. 700 The fiery lava of passion overflowing the appointed bounds. **1916** G. B. Shaw *Androcles & Lion* p. cviii, The causes which have produced this sudden clearing of the air include the transformation of many modern States, notably..the tight little Island of Britain, into empires which overflow the frontiers of all the Churches. **1973** R. J. Williams in D. J. Wiseman *Peoples of Old Testament Times* iv. 80 Fed by the yearly rains in the Abyssinian highlands, the river [*sc.* the Nile] rose steadily and overflowed its banks.

overflowing, *vbl. sb.* Add: **2.** Esp. in phr. (*full* or *to fill*) *to overflowing*: more than full, so as to overflow.

1879 R. A. Sterndale *Afghan Knife* II. vii. 69 In the meantime fugitives kept pouring into the house, which was full to overflowing. **1898** Skeel & Brearley *King Washington* (1899) xii. 75 The boys..were filled to overflowing with the excitement of the hour. **1920** H. M. Pim *Short Hist. Celtic Philos.* v. 62 They might have produced a Tartarus, and filled it to overflowing. **1961** *Washington Post* 1 June A24 The jails were filled to overflowing with political prisoners who had incurred his displeasure.

overflowingness. (Further example.)

1883 G. Meredith *Let.* 30 Oct. (1970) II. 718, I have been hearing from Will of your radiant overflowingness.

overfly, *v.* Add: **1. d.** Of an aircraft or its passengers: to fly over (a specified point, area, etc.). Also *absol.* Hence **o·verflying** *vbl. sb.* and *ppl. a.*

1944 L. L. Sell *Eng.-Spanish Techn. Dict.* 861 Overfly the field, to. **1946** *Happy Landings* (Air Ministry) July 7/1 Istres was planned as our first stop, but a 'mistral' put that airfield out of action and we had to overfly to Elmas (Sardinia). **1948** *Shell Aviation News* No. 120. 8/3 Following winds enabled us to overfly Marseilles, which we had intended as our first stop. **1957** *Times* 19 Sept. 8 A proposal by South Africa that she should be granted certain over-flying rights in the High Commission Territories has been accepted in principle by the British Government. **1958** 'N. Shute' *Rainbow & Rose* vi. 228 With the greater range of these aircraft we could overfly Canton and go direct to Fiji. **1965** *Listener* 2 Sept. 338/1 Any society will have..its quota of nuclear installations where overflying is prohibited. **1966** *New Scientist* 22 Dec. 669/2 The aircraft overflown by the supersonic liners, will 'take a fine old walloping'. **1973** *Daily Tel.* 17 Mar. 7/1 Mr Josefsson has been fighting for years to get rid of the Nato base at Keflavik, a vital link in tracking overflying Russian aircraft. **1973** 'A. Hall' *Tango Briefing* ii. 22 Did you get official overflying permission?.. Did you get official permission from the Algerian government to overfly their territory? **1977** *R.A.F. News* 5–18 Jan. 2/4 By remarkable coincidence, the golf course was overflown by two Phantom aircraft on a local low-level route.

2. (Further example.)

1954 D. A. Bannerman *Birds Brit. Isles* III. 278 It is of interest to note that the northern birds in general arrive somewhat earlier in the south of the Iberian Peninsula and so 'over-fly' their relatives from more southerly breeding places.

4. To exceed (the maximum flying-time allowed by regulations).

1966 *Daily Tel.* 1 Nov. 12/3 One or two of the pilots had 'overflown' their regulation number of hours and had to present themselves for 'medicals'.

overfulfil, *v.* Restrict † *Obs.* to sense in Dict. and add: Also (*U.S.*) **overfulfill. 2.** To achieve more than the mere fulfilment of (a plan, goal, etc.); to reach (a target) before the expected time. So **o:verfulfi·lment,** (*U.S.*) **-fulfillment.**

1950 *Sun* (Baltimore) 2 June 14/7 When the Russian whalers returned to their home port of Odessa on the Black Sea they had overfulfilled their production plan by 29·9 per cent. *Ibid.* 7 Aug. 10/2 If present rates [of Soviet production] are continued to December 31, a massive overfulfillment of the 1950 goals will result. **1952** Koestler *Arrow in Blue* 70 To omit a single one [*sc.* slogan]—say 'the strengthening of the production-offensive for the over-fulfilment of the light metal industry's revised counter-plan'..would have laid the lecturer open to the accusation [etc.]. **1964** K. G. Lockyer *Introd. Critical Path Analysis* vii. 61 Bars to the *left* of the observation line represent under-fulfillment, whilst those to the *right* represent over-fulfillment. **1966** J. Porter *Sour Cream* iv. 51 Even the waitresses had something to take their minds off their feet and the difficulties of over-fulfilling the latest five-year-plan. *Ibid.* v. 68 The current ten-year plan was going to be over-fulfilled. **1971** *New Society* 25 Mar. 475/2 Factories have undertaken commitments to overfulfil production targets in honour of the congress. **1975** *Nature* 16 Oct. 527/2 Soviet planners see agriculture as being essentially one more branch of industrial production, amenable to the same system of fulfilment and overfulfilment of plans. **1976** *Chinese Law & Govt.* IX. 101 We should fulfill or overfulfill the Fourth Five-Year Plan in 1975.

o·verfur. [Over- 8.] The outer layer of an animal's fur.

1913 [see *guard hair* s.v. *Guard *sb.* 18.] **1968** J. Ironside *Fashion Alphabet* 153 *Top fur.* This refers to the guard hairs or overfur; it is stiffer, coarser and usually darker than the underfur.

overgaze, *v.* **2.** (Later example.)

1879 A. T. de Vere *Legends Saxon Saints* 41 Meadow banks, Not yet o'er-gazed by Windsor's crested steep Or Reading's tower.

over-ge·neralize, *v.* [Over- 27.] *intr.* To draw general conclusions from inadequate data; to argue more widely than is justified by the available evidence, by circumstances, etc. Also *trans.*, to draw an over-general conclusion from (data, circumstances, etc.). Hence **o:ver-generaliza·tion; over-ge·neralized** *ppl. a.*

1904 [listed in Dict. s.v. Over- 27 a]. **1937** *Mind* XLVI. 243 He over-generalises. For example, he claims that implicit is superior to explicit comparison. **1947** J. G. Weightman *On Language & Writing* 87 In trying to think with precision we oscillate between two extremes, over-generalization and over-particularization. **1956** *Nature* 10 Mar. 478/2 The properties of larval blow-fly carbohydrases do not completely exemplify Weidenhagen's hypothesis of bond specificity, the over-generalized nature of which has been criticized more recently. **1957** K. A. Wittfogel *Oriental Despotism* 370 Overgeneralizing the experience of a rapidly changing Western world, they naively postulated a simple, unilinear, and progressive course of societal growth. **1970** S. L. Barraclough in I. L. Horowitz *Masses in Lat. Amer.* iv. 97 To avoid falling into the more obvious errors of overgeneralization about Latin America as a whole. **1971** *Sci. Amer.* Aug. 75/3 Although Sherrington was careful not to overgeneralize from his findings, less circumspect workers soon adopted the extreme position that most animal behavior consists of reflexes. **1975** R. V. Redinger *Geo. Eliot* (1976) v. 245 Slanted and overgeneralized as are many of its discussions, this book fulfilled a real need.

overget, *v.* Add: **4.** To prevail upon; to take possession of (a person).

1904 *Tradesman's Price-List* (Herbert Morris & Bastert) 11 Similarity of appearance so far overgets a customer as to induce him to pass us. **1928** *Sunday Dispatch* 16 Sept. 2/3 The thought to marry Fanny overgot the man, and he set out to see if it could be done. **1953** D. D. C. P. Mould *Rock of Truth* xi. 193 When I had been a Catholic some time and perhaps begun to grasp some idea of what God was really like, then the fear of hell did overget me.

overglaze, *sb.* Add: (Earlier and later examples.) Also in *Painting.*

1880 *Harper's Mag.* Nov. 904/1 The work most familiar to us as taught in America during the last three or four years has all been on the over-glaze. **1947** J. C. Rich *Materials & Methods Sculpture* ii. 49 Overglazes can be applied in several ways, the most frequent of which are direct painting with a soft brush, and fine spraying. **1948** F. A. Staples *Water-Color Painting* x. 116 Now that the first tone..is dry, the second, an overglaze, is painted. **1974** Savage & Newman *Illustr. Dict. Ceramics* 208 Overglaze..is by means of colours termed enamels.

overglaze, *a.* (Earlier and later examples.)

1879 J. C. L. Sparkes *Handbk. Pract. Pottery Painting* 28 Oil mediums may be used for over-glaze and for under-glaze work. *Ibid.* 31 In painting on china, earthenware and all 'over-glaze' ware with enamel colours the procedure is as follows. **1881** *Harper's Mag.* May 835/1 It was ..the most extensive and satisfactory exhibit of amateur overglaze decoration made up to that time. **1936** *Burlington Mag.* Oct. 145/2 Figural designs in polychrome over-glaze painting. **1970** *Ashmolean Mus. Rep. Visitors 1969* 46 Ginger jar with underglaze blue landscape decoration and later added dragons and flowers in overglaze colours. **1973** *Country Life* 7 June 1591/3 By the early 1770s..the head colourman, Constantine Smith, had invented a dark, semi-matt, over-glaze blue enamel of exceptional brilliance.

overglaze, *v.* Add: Hence **o:vergla·zing** *vbl. sb.*

1947 J. C. Rich *Materials & Methods Sculpture* ii. 49 Overglazing is a process in which color or overglazes are applied over glazes for decorative effects; they require an additional exposure to heat. *a* **1977** *Harrison Mayer Ltd. Catal.* 18/2 Over-glazing. This usually occurs on very porous or easy fired ware. Over-glazing can frequently lead to stuck ware and can cause underglaze colours to run.

overgo, *v.* Add: **4.** (Later examples.)

1917 *Ampleforth Jrnl.* Jan. 127 He resolves to emulate, perhaps even to overgo, the 'Orlando Furioso'. **1923** W. Renwick *Spenser Selections* p. ix, Ronsard's *Franciade*.. *Orlando Furioso.* Spenser would overgo both.

5. (Later example.)

1924 [see *Feather *sb.* 1 b].

overgoing, *vbl. sb.* (Later example in sense 'transgression'.)

1903 J. K. Jerome *Tea-Table Talk* v. 95, I was very severe upon both the shortcomings and the overgoings of man.

over-govern, *v.* Add: **2.** (Later examples.)

1938 *Sun* (Baltimore) 16 Apr. 8 For five years he [*sc.* F. D. Roosevelt] has overgoverned. It was not enough to have specific reform of specific evils, say, stock market practices. **1976** *Daily Record* (Glasgow) 29 Nov. 14/2 Another sign of distrust is shown by the fact that nine out of ten replies believe that Scotland is in danger of being over-governed.

So **over-go·verned** *ppl. a.*; **over-go·verning** *vbl. sb.*; **over-government** (further examples).

1847 J. S. Mill *Lett.* (1910) I. 131 The habitual over-governing by which power and importance are too exclusively concentrated upon the Government and its functionaries. **1848** —— *Pol. Econ.* II. v. xi. 529 The inferior capacity for political life which has hitherto characterized the over-governed countries of the Continent. **1861** —— *Repr. Govt.* iv. 83 The more popular the institutions,..the more monstrous the overgovernment exercised by all over each, and by the executive over all. **1976** *Times* 13 May 4/2 Scotland is over-governed, over-taxed and over-subsidized. **1976** *Scotsman* 15 Dec. 12/3 The Tories may have added to 'over government' by their reform of local government.

overgrazed (ōu·vəɪgrēi:zd), *ppl. a.* [Over- 27.] Of grassland: made susceptible to erosion by the destruction of vegetation through excessive grazing. Also *fig.*

1929 Weaver & Clements *Plant Ecol.* vii. 142 The latter [*sc.* dominant species] are handicapped..in overgrazed mixed prairie. **1949** *Pacific Discovery* July–Aug. 2/1 In the South I have seen cattle tracks in overgrazed land become gullies ten feet deep. **1972** 'G. North' *Sgt. Cluff rings True* i. 10 Thin, patchy grass, overgrazed, badly in need of lime. **1977** *Times Lit. Suppl.* 1 Apr. 402/2 He [*sc.* Christopher Isherwood] may cover ground.. that no doubt will be covered until there is not a blade of grass left on it when the PhD herd have moved on from the overgrazed 1920s.

overgra·zing, *vbl. sb.* [Over- 29 a.] Damage to vegetation, esp. grassland, by excessive grazing.

1935 *Discovery* Aug. 232/2 Overgrazing has removed most of the nutritious native grasses. **1943** J. S. Huxley *TVA* vi. 33 The method of row cropping allowed the top-soil to be washed away. Overgrazing followed, and now the land is completely useless. **1946** *Nature* 2 Nov. 606/2 There is also the risk of over-grazing, especially where the natural vegetation consists rather of shrubs and bushes than of turf. **1956** *Ibid.* 3 Mar. 417/1 Failure of natural regeneration in juniper forests in Somaliland is now attributed to micro-climatic changes following over-grazing. **1964** E. J. H. Corner *Life of Plants* xv. 268 We can form no idea of the destructive power..of over-grazing where trees, for lack of rain, are disappearing. **1971** *Country Life* 12 Aug. 390/2 Examination of the intensively grazed patches showed no overgrazing such as occurs when hill sheep become concentrated on heather. **1976** *Conservation News* Sept./Oct. 4/1 Over-grazing..has led to the whole vast area becoming degraded.

overground, *sb.* Restrict † *Obs.* to sense in Dict. and add later examples (see quots.: in most modern senses used in deliberate antithesis to *underground*).

1931 *N. & Q.* 11 Apr. 267/2 There has been for some long time past a line of motor-omnibuses running from Hadley Woods and Barnet to Victoria Station on the sides of which..is the word 'Overground'. **1966** *Evening Standard* 24 Feb. 16/2 The overground is an aerial railway with completely automatic operation. *Ibid.*, Buses would run through the suburbs to the edge of the city's centre... Passengers would change on to one or other of the overgrounds, a series of independent, six-mile rail loops. **1969** *Gandalf's Garden* vi. 11/1 *Overground*, like the Underground, from which it grew, it exists in the spirits of those who are living it, in the act of seeking a deeper understanding of life, in the expression of an aspirational lifestyle working in harmony with natural and mystical laws.

overground, *a.* Add: **b.** *fig.* Overt; unconcealed; publicly acknowledged. Opp. Underground *a.* 4.

1943 *Ann. Reg. 1942* 244 'Overground' resistance to the Germans was as strong as ever. **1961** *Times* 14 Jan. 7/7 But wherever they went the journalists were approached by 'overground' sympathizers with the independence fighters. **1970** *New York* 16 Nov. 50/2 They have been.. whipped around in the over- and underground press. **1971** *Times* 15 Jan. 12/8 Now even overground publishers are jumping on the revolutionary bandwagon. **1971** *Guardian* 27 Sept. 14/6 Overground media generally treat sex, drugs, and violence in a misguided matronly tone.

o:vergrou·nd, *adv.* [Over- 31.] Above the ground; into the open; opp. *underground.*

1930 *Sat. Even. Post* 22 Mar. 15/2 There was a rumbling as of a subway train heard over-ground. **1944** F. Clune *Red Heart* 6 After descending a few feet underground to have a look at the lode, I felt a desire to fly a few thousand overground to get a different angle of view. **1951** E. D. M. *St. Philomena the Wonder-Worker* (ed. 6) i. 16 The Christians could not safely perform the burial services in the presence of their heathen enemies over ground. **1963** *Times* 22 Apr. 11/1 Thought has been given to procedures by which rebels would 'come overground' and give up their weapons. **1968** *Economist* 3 Feb. 15/2 This seemed likely to mean that commercial gaming would continue underground in the pre-1960 manner..; but instead gaming popped overground into open places. **1973** *Times Lit. Suppl.* 23 Nov. 1455/4 Douglas Hayes has had an underground reputation... It is time for that reputation to appear overground.

overgrown, *ppl. a.* Add: **1.** (Later examples.) Also *fig.*

1804–20 W. Blake *Jerusalem* iv, in *Compl. Writings* (1972) 732 Of blood thro' all my nervous limbs; soon overgrown in roots I shall be closed from thy sight. **1907** R. Brooke *Let.* Dec. in E. Marsh *Rupert Brooke* (1918) 26, I have already..got some faith in the real, sometimes overgrown, goodness of all men. **1938** E. Ambler *Cause for Alarm* xvi. 273 There's an old disused road... It's overgrown by trees now. **1975** A. Dillard *Pilgrim at Tinker Creek* xii. 213 The forested cliffs..gave way to overgrown terraces.

overgrowth. **2.** (Earlier and later examples, in *lit.* sense.)

1879 *Jrnl. Chem. Soc.* XXXVI. 769 Those substances only should be considered as isomorphous which are capable of forming mixed crystals or which are capable of forming 'overgrowths' (*Ueberwachsen*), *i.e.*, when a crystal of the one is suspended in a solution of the other, the crystal increases in size, owing to the deposition on it of the substance in solution. **1896** G. B. Shaw *Let.* 14 Jan. (1965) I. 586 Those auburn tresses..concealed a grey—nay, a *white*—undergrowth, which is now an overgrowth. **1940** Glasstone *Text-bk. Physical Chem.* (1941) v. 342 Many instances of the production of overgrowths, e.g.,.. alums, monoclinic double sulfates, etc., are known. **1971** I. G. Gass et al. *Understanding Earth* xiii. 170/2 Silica can be deposited as overgrowths around detrital quartz grains.

overhand, *adv.* and *a.* Add: **A.** *adv.* **3. b.** *Archery.* (See quots.)

1875 *Encycl. Brit.* II. 378/2 Shooting over-hand is to shoot at the mark over the bow-hand. **1939** P. H. Gordon *New Archery* 404 *Overhand*, of shooting, same as ..*Forehand.*

B. *adj.* **1.** Delete † *Obs.* and add later example.

1888 Kipling *Barrack-Room Ballads* (1892) 122 The overhand stabbing-cut silenced the yell.

2. (Earlier and later examples.)

1828 in W. Denison *Cricket: Sk. Players* (1846) 44 It is the over-hand delivery to which I principally object,..it has all the qualities of a throw, except the force. **1975** *New Yorker* 17 Nov. 154/2 The Oakland scouting report on him warned he had six pitches..all of which he could serve up from the sidearm, three-quarters, or overhand sectors, and points in between.

b. *Swimming.* Applied to a variety of the side-stroke in the performance of which one hand is raised above the water and carried forward. Also *ellipt.* as *sb.*

c **1881** 'Capt. Crawley' *Swimming* 38 There are two styles of Side Swimming, severally known as the side-stroke and the over-hand. **1886** J. Finney *Hints on Swimming* 5 Taking into consideration the high rate of speed attainable by its means, the overhand stroke, when exhibited by a first-class swimmer, far exceeds any other style. **1905** 'Natator' *Swimming* 13 Overhand stroke. To change from the ordinary side stroke to the Overhand is simple. When the upper arm has finished its stroke, advance it *above* water, beyond the head, where it again enters, with the palm of the hand facing out. **1931** J. Buchan *Blanket of Dark* xiv. 260 Peter's long arms in an overhand stroke devoured the waters.

c. *Lawn Tennis.* Of a stroke: made with the racket above the arm or shoulder.

1889 H. W. W. Wilberforce *Lawn Tennis* 30 The form of service almost universally used is the overhand service. **1900** A. E. T. Watson *Young Sportsman* 379 For the ordinary overhand service the ball should be thrown up in line with the right ear and slightly backwards. **1911** *Encycl. Brit.* XVI. 301/2 High overhand service, by which alone any great pace can be obtained, was first perfected by the brothers Renshaw between 1880 and 1890. **1978** J. Symons *Blackheath Poisonings* ii. 105 For..ladies an overhand service was a great waste of strength.

overhand, *v.* Delete *arch.* and add further examples. So **overhanding** *vbl. sb.*

1908 M. H. Morgan *How to dress Doll* ii. 20 Overhanding is the real sewing of the seam... simply sewing over-and-over, close to the edge, with very small stitches. *Ibid.* v. 51 Overhand the neck and armholes with lace. **1964** *McCall's Sewing* ii. 31/1 *Overhanding*, a straight stitch used to hold finished edges together when a strong, flat, invisible seam is needed, as in table linen, undergarments, sewing on lace or patching.

over-handed, *a.* Add: **2. b.** *overhanded knot* = *overhand knot* (Overhand *a.* 4).

1883 *Man. Seamanship for Boys' Training Ships R. Navy* (Admiralty) (1886) 91 *Q.* How do you make a reef-knot..? *A.* ..First make an over-handed knot round the foot of the sail, [etc.].

overhang, *sb.* **a.** Delete 'Chiefly *Naut.*' and add further examples.

1908 H. G. Wells *War in Air* v. 158 The overhang of the gas-chambers intervened. **1919** T. K. Holmes *Man from Tall Timber* ix. 101 The two women..lived alone on Paradise Knoll, just under the overhang of its crown. **1924** J. Buchan *Three Hostages* xxi. 306 The corrie face.. seemed nothing but slabs and rotten rocks, while the few chimneys had ugly overhangs. **1940** W. Faulkner *Hamlet* i. i. 19 Once more Varner looked down into the cold impenetrable agate eyes beneath the writhen overhang of brows. **1957** *Brit. Commonwealth Forestry Terminol.* ii. 89 *Hang*, the forward lean given to the blades in a vertical frame saw so that the teeth engage with the wood in succession and not simultaneously (the *lead-in*). Syn. *Overhang. Ibid.* 127 *Overhang*, the forward slope given to the front of a stack of converted timber for protection against weathering. **1960** *Times* 22 Oct. 9/4 One lone perch will take up residence in a deep undercut or an overhang of bushes in much the same manner as a big trout. **1973** C. Bonington *Next Horizon* v. 81 The rock juts steeply above, in a series of bristling overhangs, cut by a broken crack. **1975** *New Yorker* 21 Apr. 34/2 She retreated only after high winds began to shred the plastic overhang that had been keeping the stage dry.

b. *Electr. Engin.* The part of an armature winding which projects beyond the armature core.

1915 M. Walker *Specification & Design Dynamo-Electr. Machinery* vii. 172 (*caption*) Dimensions of the overhang of concentric coils. **1936** Say & Pink *Performance & Design A.C. Machines* x. 193 The problem of the estimation of eddy current losses in overhang conductors is very difficult.

c. *Aeronaut.* (*a*) (The length of) the part of a wing beyond its outermost point of support; (*b*) in a biplane or multiplane, (the length of) the part of a wing that extends beyond the tip of an adjacent wing.

1915 *Flight* 9 Apr. 248/2 In plan form the main planes, of which the upper one has a slight overhang, have a pronounced taper towards the tips. **1919** Pippard & Pritchard *Aeroplane Struct.* iv. 17 The position of the top plane extending beyond the outermost inter-plane strut is called the extension plane or the overhang. **1928** V. W. Page *Mod. Aircraft* v. 180 A typical training biplane which has both a pronounced forward stagger and an overhang as well. **1933** W. Munro *Marine Aircraft Design* vi. 91 In older types of biplanes the upper wing used to be built with a much longer span and overhang than the lower wing. **1953** J. H. Stevens *Shape of Aeroplane* i. 29 The weight of the overhang when on the ground was taken by wires attached to kingposts protruding from the top plane above the outer pair of interplane struts. *Ibid.*, It was common practice on early aeroplanes to make the upper wing of larger span than the lower. This extra length was called the overhang. **1977** *Aeroplane Monthly* May 274/2 The B.E.2e was..distinguished by the large overhang of the upper wing extensions.

d. In a turntable unit, the distance between the stylus point and the centre of the turntable when the pickup arm is placed so that these two points and the pivot of the pickup are in line and the turntable centre is between the other two points.

1937 *Radio Engin.* Mar. 17/1 The curves in Fig. 3 have been calculated to show the initial tracking angle which occurs with a conventional pickup arm as a function of the radius R of the playing circle, the length of the arm L, and the overhang D, which is the distance between the center of the turntable and the needle point when the needle point is in line with the centers of the base and turntable. **1945** *Electronics* Mar. 111/2 If the needle point overhang *D* is 13/16 inch..the tracking angle varies from 32 deg at 6 inches through 27 deg at 3·3 inches back to 32 deg at the 2-inch radius. **1953** G. A. Briggs *Sound Reproduction* (ed. 3) xxvi. 330 The calculations for best offset angle and overhang..were made on the basis of zero tracking error at the inside groove of a standard 12″ record. **1958** S. Kelly in E. Molloy *High Fidelity Sound Reproduction* viii. 139 With a 7½ in. arm, this [*sc.* minimum distortion] requires an offset angle of 24½° and an overhang of 0·56 in. **1976** *Gramophone* Feb. 1406/1 The headshell has..a slot screw fitting to permit accurate setting of the effective pivot-to-stylus distance (overhang).

e. *Econ.* An excess of (estimated) expenditure over available or budgeted funds.

1953 *Sun* (Baltimore) 13 May 4/2 Humphrey pointed out that no revenue has been provided to cover the $81,000,000,000 'overhang' of appropriations which will be outstanding at the close of this fiscal year. **1954** *Britannica Bk. of Year* 638/1 Economic policy produced *Overhang*, an appropriation in excess of actual funds. **1974** *Financial Times* 19 July 22/8 The dollar overhang has disappeared, the Middle East war has ended. **1976** *Washington Post* 13 Mar. A19/3 That [*sc.* a big increase in the outflow of U.S. capital] meant a sizeable addition to the existing 'overhang' of dollars, amounting to nearly $200 billion held outside of the United States.

f. In sound recording and reproduction, the (usu. undesired) continued oscillation of a system after the cessation of the signal causing it; *spec.* that of a loudspeaker, esp. in the bass when the cone is insufficiently damped near its resonant frequency. Cf. *Hang-over, hangover 3, quots. 1961, 1967.

1971 J. Earl *How to choose Pickups & Loudspeakers* v. 126 When the cone oscillates at resonance it vibrates quite violently unless well damped. This can cause 'overhang' effects at the bass end. **1975** G. J. King *Audio Handbk.* ii. 34 A very low R_s in parallel with the loudspeaker inhibits overshoot and rings on transient type signal, and this is particularly desirable at the loudspeaker's bass resonance frequency where, without such damping, the cone can oscillate vigorously when triggered by a transient, an effect which is responsible for 'overhang' and 'boomy' bass. **1976** *Gramophone* Dec. 1028/3 The sound has warmth and resonance (the long overhang of the King's acoustic is expertly handled without the slightest muddying of the textures). **1977** *Ibid.* May 1774/3 Square wave response of all the cartridges showed virtually no overhang and an adequate rise time with little ringing.

overhaul, *v.* **3.** (Further *transf.* examples.)

1933 D. L. Sayers *Hangman's Holiday* 187 He..drove on, overhauling the police car. **1955** *Times* 12 May 4/3 (*heading*) American boxers overhauled. **1976** *Horse & Hound* 3 Dec. 53/2 Their pilot..circling left-handed.. doubled back to Loscar Common Plantation again and was overhauled in some kale after a good 35 min.

overhead, *adv., sb., a.* Add: **B.** *sb.* **2.** That which is above; the firmament.

1865 G. M. Hopkins *Poems* (1967) 151 The grass was red And long, the trees were colour'd, but the o'er-head, Milky and dark, with an attuning stress Controll'd them to a grey-green temperateness. **1911** *Chambers's Jrnl.* Jan. 79/1 It forms a handy guide, philosopher, and friend to the vast unfathomable overhead. **1959** E. Collier *Three against Wilderness* i. 8 Live sparks rocketed up into the smoky overhead.

3. (Freq. *pl.*) Ellipt. for *overhead charges, expenses*, etc.

1914 *Automobile Topics* XXXIV. 31/2 One of the numerous fallacies of business..is the argument that the small organization is in a position to serve the customer to better advantage for the reason that its 'overheads' are small. **1915** *Lit. Digest* 21 Aug. 360/1 (Advt.), Her typewriter is standing idle and adding to 'overhead'. **1922** *Public Opinion* 29 Dec. 629/2 We are able to reduce overheads through the employment of far more automatic machinery. **1930** J. B. Priestley *Angel Pavement* i. 36 The first thing, the very first thing, we've got to do is to reduce the overheads in this business. **1954** *Encounter* Dec. 79/1 The two million families..are the enemies of the workers in the modern sectors of the French economy. Their overhead is more than the traffic will bear, and the worker feels, if he does not understand, this. **1972** *Accountant* 17 Aug. 215/1 Work in progress to be stated at cost including overhead. **1972** *Computer Jrnl.* XV. 199/1 A possible objection to the use of streams might be that the overheads associated with their structure make them excessively inefficient. **1974** *Terminol. Managem. & Financial Accountancy* (Inst. Cost and Managem. Accountants) 19 *Overhead*, the total cost of indirect materials, wages and expenses.

4. *Lawn Tennis.* An overhead stroke.

1969 *New Yorker* 14 June 46/3 His overhead is hit with his whole arm—no mere flick of the wrist. **1972** D. Delman *Sudden Death* vi. 145 I'll hit lobs to you so you can work the kinks out of your overhead. **1977** *Transatlantic Rev.* LX. 108 He slashes, he wheels, he whaps an easy overhead into the net.

C. *adj.* **1. a.** (Further examples.)

1917 'Contact' *Airman's Outings* 36, I awoke to the roar of engines, followed by an overhead drone as a party of bombers circled round until they were ready to start. **1921** *Times Lit. Suppl.* 8 Sept. 574/3 Stress is laid on the complete clearance of overhead cover [from teak plantations]. **1949** P. Latham in Aldiss & Harrison *Decade 1940s* (1975) 204 Stoddard turned off the overhead light. **1959** *Chambers's Encycl.* V. 97/2 With A.C. systems difficulties may arise due to the inductance of overhead lines and the capacitance of underground cables. **1976** *Billings* (Montana) *Gaz.* 16 June 10-C/4 (Advt.), Comm. Warehouse Space 300, 400, 600 and 1000 sq. ft., paved, lighted, security fence, overhead door, cold storage.

b. *overhead cam-shaft*, a cam-shaft mounted above the cylinder block of an internal-combustion engine; *overhead valve*, a valve in an internal-combustion engine which has its seat in the top of the combustion chamber, in the surface opposite the piston.

1912 R. W. A. Brewer *Motor Car Construction* iii. 42 One of the principal objections to overhead valves in the past was the difficulty of driving an overhead camshaft... With the introduction of silent chain drives for camshafts these difficulties no longer exist. **1921** A. W. Judge *Automobile & Aircraft Engines* viii. 316 Another reason for the better volumetric efficiency of the overhead valve lies in the fact that in the case of the side-by-side valves the charge has to pass over a larger combustion chamber area before it arrives in the cylinder. **1958** *Times* 1 July 6/6 Instead of having a side valve engine of 1,265 c.c., the new model has the overhead valve 1,390 c.c. engine. **1966** *McGraw-Hill Encycl. Sci. & Technol.* XIV. 263/2 In overhead valve engines, the cam shaft may be mounted on the cylinder head near the valves. **1974** *Country Life* 21 Nov. 1579/1 The engine with its twin overhead cam-shafts is buzzy at high revs.

3. *Lawn Tennis.* Of a stroke: made with the racket above one's head.

1904 J. P. Paret et al. *Lawn Tennis* 345 *Overhead*, with the racket above the head. **1919** C. Hierons *Lawn Tennis* xiv. 61 In overhead volleying there is far too much pat ball. **1925** K. McKane *Lawn Tennis* vi. 98 The most important of all overhead strokes—the service. **1951** Harman & Monroe *Use your Head in Tennis* v. 45 For the overhead slice serve, take hold of your racket handle in the eastern grip.

4. Of costs or expenses: incurred in the production of a batch of articles apart from the prime cost of each (cf. Oncost), or in the upkeep of plant and premises.

1909 J. L. Nicholson *Factory Organization & Costs* i. 7 The distribution of manufacturing expenses, sometimes called overhead charges, and in other instances, indirect expense or burden. **1911** F. E. Webner *Factory Costs* xvii. 212 Under such a system most of the usual overhead expenses become direct. **1922** *Westm. Gaz.* 8 Dec. 6/2 The overhead cost of every factory that is gas-lighted will go up. **1930** A. H. Church *Overhead Expense* i. i. 1 Overhead expense in manufacturing is defined usually as consisting of the so-called 'fixed' charges (such as rent, interest, depreciation, insurance, taxes, etc.) plus all that large class of expenditure on labor and materials which cannot be charged definitely to any given job or lot of product. **1958** J. F. Magee *Production Planning & Inventory Control* iii. 26 Under absorption costing, the value includes not only direct costs but also allocated overhead charges (usually only factory overhead). **1970** *Encycl. Brit.* XVI. 1167/2 Overhead costs are various business expenses that cannot be readily identified with specific products or services produced or sold. **1974** *Terminol. Managem. & Financial Accountancy* (Inst. Cost and Managem. Accountants) 42 *Overhead distribution sheet*, a columnar form used for the purpose of distribution of overhead expenditure over cost centres, and for the apportionment of the accumulated expenses of service cost centres over others.

overhear, *v.* Add: **3.** Also *absol.*

1706 Swift *Baucis & Philemon* in *Poems* (1958) I. 92 The Strangers overheard, and said [etc.]. **1913** *Cassell's Mag.* June 2/1 Glancing over his shoulder to make certain that the nurse hadn't overheard. **1922** Joyce *Ulysses* 114 Mr Bloom, chapfallen, drew behind a few paces so as not to overhear. **1929** E. O'Neill *Dynamo* III. i. 132 He lowers his voice carefully as if he didn't want the dynamo to overhear. **1976** M. Millar *Ask for me Tomorrow* (1977) ii. 19, I couldn't talk to you freely this morning because I didn't want..that witch in his office to overhear.

overheat, *v.* Add: **2.** *intr.* To become too hot.

1902 C. S. Rolls in A. C. Harmsworth et al. *Motors & Motor-driving* 172 How to tell when a Motor is Overheating. **1908** *Westm. Gaz.* 27 Oct. 4/1 The engine overheated twice,..but this was when the car was taken out without any water in the radiator. **1950** *Sci. News* XV. 81 It may be found that the rocket overheats in spite of this cooling. **1971** *Sci. Amer.* Aug. 108/3 The compressors developed the required low pressure but overheated after several hours of continuous use. **1974** *Country Life* 21 Mar. 654/3 The mill overspeed, the stones overheated, and the mill caught fire.

3. (Usu. as *pa. pple.* or as *ppl. a.*) Of a national economy: to bring about a condition of marked inflation by placing excessive pressure on resources during a period of expansion in demand. Also **overheating** *vbl. sb.*, the inflationary consequences of such a state or condition.

1956 *Ann. Reg. 1955* 227 Heavy industry had..been 'over-heated', but there was no strain on producers of consumer goods, and retail prices in this field had hardly risen. **1962** *Daily Tel.* 16 July 10/2 Most people would accept that an economy must not become 'overheated'. **1962** *Economist* 1 Sept. 800/2 Its [*sc.* Japan's] balance of payments crises and periods of 'overheating'. **1965** *Ibid.* 16 Oct. 269/1 The money and securities markets in New York have allowed themselves in the past month a nice frenzy of fear about the economy's 'overheating'. **1971** *Observer* 14 Mar. 8/4 It was argued in the 1960s that a faster rate of growth produced so-called 'overheating'—the situation in which demand exceeds resources, whether of labour or plant. **1973** *Times* 16 May 27/3 The danger of an over-heated economy was 'reasonably small'. **1974** *Times* 23 Mar. 13/2 The second layer of trouble was the progressive overheating of the economy last year. *Ibid.* 9 Oct. 5/2 Successive governments..had overheated the economy by increasing public spending and boosting demand, consequently pushing up inflation. **1976** F. Zweig *New Acquisitive Society* II. ii. 94 No labour legislation can replace..general economic policy based on the discipline of the market system and avoidance of overheating of the economy.

overheating, *vbl. sb.* Add: (Further examples.) Cf. also prec. sense 3.

1961 *Family Handyman* Oct., Too light a feed..causes overheating of the tool and burning of the cutting edge. **1969** *Gloss. for Landscape Work* (*B.S.I.*) v. 13 *Overheating*, an undesirable spontaneous temperature rise, due to the action of bacteria during the decomposition of vegetable matter. **1973** J. Leasor *Host of Extras* i. 13 Early models..beset by unlucky snags like over-heating, and gears that jumped out on the over-run. **1977** M. Sokolinsky tr. *R. Merle's Virility Factor* xvi. 314 The rumors had appeared spontaneously among the blacks due to the overheating caused by the tense period.

over-hit, *v.* **b.** (Further example.)

1919 C. Hierons *Lawn Tennis* xiii. 57 The beginner should take care that he does not over-hit the ball.

over-housed, *ppl. a.* Add: (Further examples.) Hence (as a back-formation) **overhouse** *v. refl.*, to have house accommodation in excess of one's requirements or means.

1863 W. M. Thackeray *Let.* 23 Sept. in J. Brown *Lett.* (1907) 332 If I don't mistake there was a man who lived at Abbotsford [*sc.* Sir W. Scott] overhoused himself. **1921** *Spectator* 26 Feb. 261/1 Young people marrying on little and determined not to 'overhouse' themselves. **1963** *Guardian* 8 Mar. 4/4 Many of the chronic invalids were overhoused in that they were not able to make full use of their accommodation. **1970** *Times* 14 Mar. 3 In 1965 they found themselves over-housed and decided to sublet the fourth floor.

overhung, *ppl. a.* Add: **1. b.** = Overhanging *ppl. a.*

1923 H. G. Wells *Men like Gods* II. iii. 206 The gully was..difficult, he thought, to ascend, but quite practicable downward. It was completely overhung.

3. (Later example.)

1928 C. F. S. Gamble *Story N. Sea Air Station* 8 Somewhat similar to a Blériot monoplane, except for..the 'overhung' system of mounting the engine.

4. = *hung-over* (*Hung *ppl. a.* 4).

1964 I. Fleming *You only live Twice* v. 60 He was considerably overhung. The hard blue eyes were veined with blood. **1974** *Times* 4 Apr. 20/6 A young man hurried in at about 10, looking overslept and overhung. **1977** K. Benton *Red Hen Conspiracy* xiv. 115 Juan arrived..looking rather overhung.

over-hu·nt, *v.* [Over- 27.] *trans.* To hunt (an animal) to such an extent that an excessive number is killed; to hunt (a country) too much or to depletion. Also *fig.*

1862 *Q. Rev.* III. 229 That enthusiastic temper which leads men to overhunt a beaten enemy. **1936** *Discovery* Sept. 293/1 From time to time the moose is over-hunted in some districts, but after a few years' protection they come back again. **1968** C. Helmericks *Down Wild River North* II. xxiv. 385 The whole North has been overtrapped and overhunted.

o:verhydra·tion. *Med.* [Over- 29 b.] An excessive amount of water in the body or a part of it.

1943 *Jrnl. Clin. Investigation* XXII. 471 (*heading*) The relationship of dehydration and overhydration of the blood plasma to collapse in the management of artificial fever therapy. **1956** *Circulation* XIV. 1029/1 The physiologic and clinical consequences of an absolute excess of water consist of cellular overhydration, pulmonary edema ..and convulsions. **1974** Passmore & Robson *Compan. Med. Stud.* III. II. xlix. 6/2 While the physiological defences against the naturally occurring hazard of dehydration are extremely effective, those against the iatrogenic hazard of overhydration are much less efficient.

So **o:verhydra·ted** *ppl. a.*

1943 *Jrnl. Clin. Investigation* XXII. 482/1 Although definitely overhydrated..the patient did not become edematous. **1974** Passmore & Robson *Compan. Med. Stud.* III. II. xlix. 7/2 Patients with acute renal failure or oliguria may readily become overhydrated since water can be lost only by extrarenal routes.

o:verinclu·sion. *Psychol.* [Over- 29 b.] The indiscriminate inclusion of irrelevant responses to a stimulus, observed in some cases of severe mental illness. Hence **o:verinclu·sive** *a.*

1939 *Jrnl. Mental Sci.* LXXXV. 1019 The inability to select and to restrict, and to eliminate the less closely related elements from the conceptual structure, means that the psychological boundaries are functionally insufficient. The result of this situation is *over-inclusion.* **1942** Hanfmann & Kasanin *Conceptual Thinking in Schizophrenia* vii. 95 Some of the examples that Cameron brings as illustrating overinclusion can be also seen as examples of extreme primitivisation of thinking. **1951** Cameron & Magaret *Behavior Pathol.* xv. 457 The concept of overinclusion was first developed operationally, in connection with the sorting of behavior of schizophrenic patients. But its use since then has been expanded to cover a wide range of behavioral disorganization, both normal and abnormal. *Ibid.* 458 Excitement of any kind can lead to overinclusive behavior. **1974** *Psychiatric Q.* XLVIII. 109 (*title*) Investigation of factors related to stimulus overinclusion.

over-indulgence. (Earlier example.)

1754 Richardson *Grandison* II. xxxvi. 354 The Lady having, by her early over-indulgence, ruined the morals of her child.

o:verinhi·bited, *a.* *Psychol.* [Over- 28 c.] Applied to a person whose reactions, esp. in a social context, are abnormally inhibited. So **o:verinhibi·tion**, the state or fact of being overinhibited.

1899 W. James *Talks to Teachers* xv. 179 Certain melancholiacs furnish the extreme example of the over-inhibited type. **1942** Partridge *Usage & Abusage* (1947) 353/2 Thanks to the Freudians, we have..heard almost too much about the over-inhibited person. **1946** Hewitt & Jenkins *Fund. Patterns Maladjustment* 31 The..syndrome pattern of overinhibited behavior is of unquestionable familiarity to clinicians and mental hygienists. **1970** *Jrnl. Gen. Psychol.* LXXXII. 162 The apparent over-inhibition by schizophrenic Ss.

o:ver-insu·rance. [Over- 29 b.] Insurance (of goods, property, etc.) in excess of their real value.

1755 N. Magens *Ess. Insurances* I. 92 The Law of Spain ..ordains, 'That the Insurers who signed last in Date should return the Premium, in case of an Over-Insurance.' **1802** S. Marshall *Treat. Insurance* I. I. iv. 118 In the case of an over-insurance..the first underwriters on the policy were formerly holden to be answerable, to the extent of the loss, and the subsequent ones discharged. **1880** *Encycl. Brit.* XIII. 185/1 When the value proved under an open policy falls short of the sum originally insured, the difference..is technically termed an over-insurance. **1965** 'W. Haggard' *Hard Sell* xii. 136 Suspicion, the over-insurance of risks which were seldom worth the premium. **1970** M. Greener *Penguin Dict. Commerce* 232 *Over-insurance.* Property is over-insured if insured for more than it is worth. **1977** *Times* 5 May 4/3 If cover were provided for a longer period an element of over-insurance would lead to unnecessarily high subscription rates.

o:ver-insu·re, *v.* [Over- 27.] *trans.* To insure for more than the real value; to insure excessively. (Chiefly as pa. pple.)

1904 [listed in Dict. s.v. Over- 27 a]. **1910** *Times* 28 June 6/1 An old vessel, trading at a loss, over-insured. **1922** *Blackw. Mag.* Sept. 318/2 Ship and cargo are over-insured about ten times, I suppose? **1970** [see *over-insurance]. **1976** D. Francis *In Frame* iv. 68 If it was over-insured it was to allow for inflation.

o:ver-intelle·ctual, *a.* [Over- 28 a.] Excessively intellectual; concerned too much with reason or mental processes.

1854 Bagehot *Coll. Works* (1965) I. 219 It had no feverish excitement, nor over-intellectual introspection. **1944** J. S. Huxley *On Living in Revol.* xv. 184 Over-intellectual and over-specialized.

So o:ver-intellectualiza·tion; o:ver-intelle·ctualize *v. trans.*; o:ver-intelle·ctualized *ppl. a.*
1924 P. C. BUCK *Scope of Music* 72 Preaching the over-intellectualization of their art until the red blood has gone out of it. **1929** A. N. WHITEHEAD *Process & Reality* 263 The interest in logic, dominating overintellectualized philosophers, has obscured the main function of propositions. **1933** —— *Adventures of Ideas* iii. 53 Even here we must not over-intellectualize the various types of human experience. **1975** R. L. SIMON *Wild Turkey* (1976) xii. 86 The sauna of some over-intellectualized exhibitionists. **1975** *Verbatim* Sept. 7/1 Over-intellectualization is rampant: if the Old Believers in Russia avoided the use of the future tense, the only effect would have been to create a new future of some kind, to refer to tomorrow's planting of potatoes, with the old future relegated to taboo—no deep change in speech habits would have resulted. **1977** *Early Music* July 308/2 We must avoid the temptation to over-intellectualize the artists' procedure.

o·verjet. *Dentistry.* [OVER- 13(?).] The extent to which the upper teeth, esp. the incisors, project forward in a horizontal direction beyond the corresponding lower teeth. Cf. *OVERBITE.
1930 I. G. NICHOLS *Prosthetic Dentistry* vi. 149 A greater overjet or projection forward of the maxillary teeth is required in cases of deep overbite than in cases of shallow overbite. **1940** M. G. SWENSON *Compl. Dentures* xxvi. 445 The incisal guidance is governed mostly by the operator's choice of the desired inclination. This inclination may be changed by the amount of overbite (vertical overbite) and overjet (horizontal overbite). **1962** BLAKE & TROTT *Periodontology* xv. 155 In patients with abnormal overbite or overjet an habitual rest position may be established which assists the patient to form an efficient lip seal. **1977** *Proc. R. Soc. Med.* LXX. 432/1 Bell & Dann (1973) found..only small changes in incisor overbite and overjet in 25 patients following anterior maxillary ostectomies.

o·verki·ll (stress var.), *v.* orig. *U.S.* [OVER-27.] *trans.* and *intr.* To kill or destroy to a greater extent than is necessary. Also *fig.*
1946 *Sun* (Baltimore) 17 Jan. 4/5 It pointed all, or a great majority, of the guns at a single object. This method resulted in missing most of the in-coming attackers and of over-killing those which could be hit. **1958** *Lincoln* (Nebraska) *Evening Jrnl.* 8 Aug. 4/4 The argument that you do not need the power to 'overkill', if you already have H-bombs [etc.]. **1965** *New Statesman* 30 Apr. 690/3 His magnanimity towards those who ordained that Dresden should be overkilled. **1967** *Economist* 23 Dec. 1227/3 Mr Humphrey's oratory.. overkilled the McCarthy ridicule of what the Senator assails as an immoral and, equally unforgiveably, an irrational war. **1968** *Punch* 27 Nov. 751 We maintained armed forces to defend a non-existent Empire and spent uselessly and prodigally in a vain attempt to keep abreast of the titans in capacity to kill and overkill. **1971** B. CALLISON *Plague of Sailors* iv. 157 When you intend to decimate a whole nation, why get puritanical about over-killing a few dozen more?

o·verkill, *sb.* orig. *U.S.* [OVER- 29.] **a.** The capacity, esp. of nuclear weapons, to kill and effect destruction in excess of strategic requirements. Also *attrib.*
1958 *Time* 17 Mar. 25/2 A word coming more and more into Pentagon usage is 'overkill'—a blunt but descriptive term implying a power to destroy a military target not once but many times more than necessary. **1959** *Times* 18 May 7/2 The Chiefs of Staff of the Navy and the Army..told Congress..that this 'over-kill' capacity is unnecessary. **1962** *Economist* 30 June 1307/1 It is military nonsense for Britain and France to produce nuclear weapons, when the United States has an 'overkill' of those weapons coming out of both its ears. **1965** H. KAHN *On Escalation* 280 Overkill by a factor of ten or more, so that even the blind..would understand the situation. **1968** W. ASH *Ride Paper Tiger* xii. 191 There's no point in plastering a target which has already been demolished. Anyone carrying the weapons you do has to be a bit careful about the problem of overkill. **1971** *Guardian* 27 Sept. 13/3 The nuclear club reached the point of H-bomb overkill. **1976** J. COX *On Warpath* 7/1 A mere pin-head of a man-made poison could kill everyone alive today. Military strategists talk of 'Doomsday' and 'Overkill'.
b. *transf.* and *fig.*
1965 *New Scientist* 24 June 841/1 There is only a limited number of whales in the sea and the delegates must decide between an irrational short-term overkill or long-term conservation. **1967** *New Yorker* 1 Apr. 94 Its producer.. is a misguided champion of cinematic overkill: twice as large is twice as good, twice as loud is twice as convincing. **1968** *Guardian* 20 Mar. 10/1 Just how much Mr Jenkins ought to cut consumption is arguable. The world monetary crisis provides a strong psychological reason for going for 'overkill'. **1970** *Globe & Mail* (Toronto) 26 Sept. 7/5 The..social and economic consequences.. ascribed to 'advertising overkill'. **1973** *Times Lit. Suppl.* 21 Dec. 1555/3 It is astonishing, in these days of critical overkill, that Peter Wolfe's little book is the only one yet written on Rebecca West. **1975** *Listener* 3 July 22/3, I have only the smallest objection to the [Wimbledon] coverage, apart from the serious danger of overkill (three hours daily on BBC 1, over six on BBC 2). **1976** *Times* 30 Jan. 17/2 What point is there in producing things if over-kill taxation means that nobody will buy them?

overland, *a.* (Further examples.) Also *ellipt.* as *sb.*
1841 *Niles' Reg.* 6 Feb. 353/2 The news from China and India we have received by the overland mail. **1848** *Alfred in India* 158 Passengers went..across the desert to Alexandria, and from thence in another steamer... This is called the 'overland route'. **1861** B. I. HAYES *Let.* 11 Feb. in *Pioneer Notes from Diaries* (1929) vii. 253 By the Overland Stage arriving here on the 8th inst., I received your valued favor of the 12th ult. **1862** MRS. J. B. SPEID *Our Last Yrs. in India* iv. 79 Her Majesty's mail! What would England..say, could they witness the bi-monthly arrival of the overland here! **1901** *Daily Colonist* (Victoria, B.C.) 24 Oct. 1/5 The northbound Southern Pacific overland express..was held up by robbers..but the robbers secured little booty. **1977** C. ALLEN *Raj* 20 Before the opening of the canal the fastest means of getting to and from India was by taking the overland route..from Alexandria to Suez.

overland, *v.* Add: (Further examples.) So **overla·nding** *vbl. sb.* and *ppl. a.*
1871 M. CLARKE *Old Tales of Young Country* 163 'Overlanding' was a profitable and, withal, romantic occupation. Young men of spirit, wearied of the capital, and prompted by love of gain and adventure, purchased cattle and sheep in New South Wales, and drove them 'overland' to the 'New Orleans' of Colonel Torrens. **1916** *Chambers's Jrnl.* Nov. 729/1 Men live in the saddle..when 'overlanding' cattle. **1925** *Ibid.* Dec. 810/1 Overlanding drovers who were opening up new country passed by. **1933** *Bulletin* (Sydney) 16 Aug. 20/2 Overlanding from the N.T. to Queensland. **1941** I. L. IDRIESS *Great Boomerang* xviii. 128 Any of the great overlanding or exploring treks would have been more instructive to remember. **1965** *Sunday Truth* (Brisbane) 17 Oct. 32/4 In 1839 the entire Wills establishment..overlanded to..western Victoria. *Ibid.* 32/5 Heading an overlanding expedition of 25 men and women and 10,000 sheep Wills led his party slowly north to a destination in central Queensland. **1975** *Australasian Express* (London) 10 Oct. 24/2 Overlanding is a wonderful way of travelling.

overlander[2]. Add: **1. a.** Also *N.Z.* (Earlier and further examples.) Also *slang*, a sundowner, a tramp.
1841 G. GREY *Jrnls. Two Expeditions of Discovery* ii. 183 The Overlanders are nearly all men in the pride of youth, whose occupation is to convey large herds of stock from market to market and from colony to colony. **1852** *Lyttleton Times* (N.Z.) 27 Mar., Mr. A. Clifford has succeeded in driving about 1500 ewes from the Wairau district. .. Two other parties of 'over-landers' are reported to be close on his heels. **1898** MORRIS *Austral. Eng.* 333/1 *Overlander*... (2) A slang name for a *Sundowner.* **1907** A. SEARCY *In Austral. Tropics* 125 If a crowd of overlanders and backblockers happened to be present, things would be made lively. **1933** L. G. D. ACLAND in *Press* (Christchurch, N.Z.) 11 Nov. 15/7 *Overlander*, an Australian word for a man driving sheep or cattle a long distance. It was sometimes used in Canterbury in the early days. **1941** BAKER *Dict. Austral. Slang* 52 *Overlander*, a traveller. (2) One who makes long expeditions from one State to another with stock. (3) A settler from another State. (4) A drover. (5) A sundowner. **1967** *Woman's Day* (Austral.) 27 Feb. 10/3 Now in her early sixties, she still lives her life with all the zest of her overlander days.
b. *N. Amer.* One who moves from one part of the country to another; a migrant. *Obs.* exc. *Hist.*
1857 *Hutching's Mag.* Mar. 398/1 Reader, if you have never been an *over-lander*, I will tell you a little about camp life. **1916** A. C. LAUT *Cariboo Trail* 55 Some of the Overlanders had narrowly escaped a massacre. **1950** B. HUTCHINSON *Fraser* 88 The most remarkable immigrants of all deserve to be remembered—the Overlanders of '62, the men..who walked to Cariboo across the Rocky Mountains. **1963** *Canad. Geogr. Jrnl.* Oct. 112/3 Among those who heard the call of 'Gold in the Cariboo!' were the Overlanders. **1968** E. RUSSENHOLT *Heart of Continent* III. vii. 116 This summer [*sc.* 1859], three parties of 'Overlanders', some 60 in all, leave from Assiniboia for the Cariboo.
2. In general use: one who travels overland to a country which can also be reached by sea or air; one who travels a long distance overland.
1953 J. PACKER *Apes & Ivory* xxiii. 240 There were many 'overlanders' after the war, when it was impossible to get a sea-passage to Southern Africa. **1960** *Guardian* 22 Nov. 7/5 Everywhere beyond Austria the overlander will attract..the attentions of the idle bystander. **1974** *Country Life* 26 Dec. 2008/1 The intrepid long-distance overlander of today.

overlap, *sb.* Add: **1. a.** Also *transf.* and *fig.*
1880 [in Dict.]. **1931** A. KEITH *Place of Prejudice* 19 Head and heart are never quite separated; there is a large overlap in their fields of action. **1955** *Bull. Atomic Sci.* June 205/3 Perhaps outside help with parts of the investigation should be arranged, with some of the 'second laboratory' type of overlap providing the spur of competition. **1960** *Times* 31 Oct. 4/4 Later Glover scored a good try after Willcox had made the overlap in a set-piece movement. **1962** L. DEIGHTON *Ipcress File* xxiv. 156 That camera went out of action..but luckily we have overlap on the camera fields. **1970** K. BALL *Fiat 600, 600D Autobook* 164/2 *Overlap*, period during which inlet and exhaust valves are open together. **1970** *Times* 1 Oct. 10/3 Hollins again at the 29th minute..joined in an overlap with Mulligan. **1974** *Country Life* 3/10 Jan. 25/3 For the Garvan Gallery the William and Mary style runs from 1685 to 1730, Queen Anne from 1715 to 1765, Chippendale from 1750 to 1790 and Federal from 1788 to 1830. The overlaps are perfectly acceptable. **1974** *Times* 19 Dec. 6/8 There is a considerable overlap between the committee's membership and that of the Council for..Arab–British understanding. **1975** *Times* 11 Jan. 12/4 Allowing for duplications and overlaps..the CIA..'spies on 100,000,000 Americans'. **1976** *Sunday Post* (Glasgow) 26 Dec. 36/2 Better goal-kicking did the trick, since the try count was three-all, but Gala could have popped the result into their Christmas stockings a lot earlier if they had not so persistently kicked away overlaps.
b. overlap fault, an overthrust fault.
1883 W. S. GRESLEY *Gloss. Terms Coal Mining* 180 *Overlap fault*, a peculiar kind of fault where a seam is reversed or doubled back over itself. **1886** J. PRESTWICH *Geol.* I. xv. 257 (*caption*) Great slide or overlap fault in the Radstock coalfield.
c. In yacht-racing, a position in which a yacht overtaking another is debarred by the rules from passing one side, or in which the yachts concerned cannot turn toward each other without risking a collision.
1898 *Encycl. Sport* II. 585/2 If in rounding any mark in a race, or any obstruction, an inside yacht has an overlap, the outside yacht or yachts must give her sufficient room. **1935** *Encycl. Sports* 760/2 Provided that the overtaking yacht makes her overlap on the side opposite to that on which the overtaken yacht then carries her main boom, the latter may luff as she pleases [etc.]. **1958** *Times* 23 Sept. 14/2 The American yacht then went smoothly forwards to establish an overlap.
d. *Phonetics.* Concurrence of the concluding sound of one phoneme with the opening of the next, as represented spectrographically; homonymy (as French /sañ/, *cent* and *sans*).
1942 *Amer. Speech* XVII. 42 There is no over-lap between the length of this vowel when full grade..and its length when reduced grade. **1964** *Language* XL. 62 It is possible to raise the question of phonemic overlap... This instance of overlapping phonetic values..need not be regarded as a violation of phonemic principles.
e. *Linguistics.* (See quot. 1948).
1948 E. A. NIDA in *Language* XXIV. 431 Instances of 'overlap', i.e. forms which are in complementary distribution except at certain points where there is a contrast resulting from fluctuation of forms. **1973** *Archivum Linguisticum* IV. 12 /de/ and /bi/ and /bi/ and /na/ do have areas of overlap.
2. *Geol.* The extension of a stratum beyond or over the edges of younger underlying strata; also, the upper stratum; esp. = *ONLAP (a *transgressive overlap*); also = *OFFLAP (a *regressive overlap*); less commonly = *OVERSTEP *sb.* 2.
1846 H. T. DE LA BECHE in *Mem. Geol. Survey Gt. Brit.* I. 24 Proceeding westward..the overlap of the Old Red Sandstone becomes such that from Middleton Hall to the vicinity of Caermarthen, it rests on the lower Silurian rocks, covering up the higher Silurian beds. A. C. RAMSAY in *Ibid.* 319 This..shows a tendency to a certain amount of contemporary depression of coast and sea bottom on the south to admit of an overlap during the formation of these deposits. **1857** [in Dict.]. **1876** *Q. Jrnl. Geol. Soc.* XXXII. 377 By the term *overlap* no unconformity is here meant, but the concealment of lower beds by the extension, through a progressive subsidence, of those next in time upon the old rocks. **1883** [see *OVERSTEP *sb.* 2]. **1906** A. W. GRABAU in *Bull. Geol. Soc. Amer.* XVII. 569 The types of overlap of sedimentary strata may be classified as follows: A. Irregular or discontinuous overlap. B. Regular continuous or progressive overlap. 1. Marine. *a.* Transgressive. *b.* Regressive. 2. Non-marine. *c.* Fluviatile. **1913**, etc. [see *OFFLAP]. **1947** *Bull. Amer. Assoc. Petroleum Geol.* XXXI. 1868 There is much confusion in the uses of the word 'overlap' in geological literature. In recent years it has often been used to describe..: (1) the regular and progressive pinching-out of sediments above unconformities, and (2) the regular truncation of sediments below unconformities. **1962** READ & WATSON *Introd. Geol.* xii. 616 Stratigraphical traps are the result of unconformities, lensing, overlap and reflected buried hills. **1972** B. B. BROCK *Global Approach to Geol.* xvii. 224 The Lower Division forms remnants of a regressive overlap left by a contracting and retreating inland basin.
3. *Railways.* The distance beyond a signal that must be unoccupied before an engine is allowed to approach it past the previous signal.
1925 TWEEDIE & LASCELLES *Mod. Railway Signalling* x. 145 To work without overlaps it would be necessary to have some system of positive speed control which would bring a train to a stand at a stop signal independently of the driver. **1956** *Railway Mag.* Mar. 351/2 The standard British block telegraph overlap of 440 yd. beyond the home..signal can be modified by special instructions. **1969** H. R. BROADBENT *Introd. Railway Braking* i. 6 The overlap beyond the stop signal is therefore a form of margin on the distance between the warning and stop signals to cover for contingencies.
4. *Computers.* The strictly simultaneous performance of two or more operations during the execution of a program.
1963 L. SCHULTZ *Digital Processing* xi. 239 In a machine with a modular memory..the execution of a program might be significantly speeded by locating variables in one module and instructions in another, and by providing an overlap in the time needed for executing one instruction and fetching the next. **1969** P. B. JORDAIN *Condensed Computer Encycl.* 365 I/O overlap is a great improvement over strictly sequential operations, but it still leaves the electronics waiting for the slower main memory.

overlap, *v.* Add: **1. b.** (Later examples.)
1911 R. BROOKE *Let.* 13 Dec. (1968) 325 Ka appears some days later. James for a weekend... But some (e.g. Ka and Margery) will not overlap; so there'll not be too much of a crowd. **1971** *Nature* 22 Oct. 509/2 The Roths child inquiry and the Dainton inquiry overlap only at the edges. **1977** K. O'HARA *Ghost of T. Penry* viii. 65 The generations overlapped because the Binns were an enormous family.

overla·pped, *ppl. a.* [-ED[1].] That overlaps or is overlapped (in various senses).

1839 [see *double coal* s.v. *DOUBLE *a.* A. 6]. **1898** G. Saintsbury *Short Hist. Eng. Lit.* VIII. ii. 498 The constant preference of overlapped or enjambed lines for the strict couplet. **1926** J. Adams *Christian Good of Scotland* viii. 126 To neglect or overlook the nobler ideals of the Church, because of its presently divided and overlapped system, is neither politic nor wise. **1962** A. Nisbett *Technique Sound Studio* 263 *Permanent joint*, cemented joint in slightly overlapped tape.

overlapping, *ppl. a.* (Further examples.)
1926–7 *Army & Navy Stores Catal.* 854/3 Golfing requisites..Harry Varden's own overlapping grip. Each 4/6. **1958** *Jrnl. Social Issues* XIV. I. 39 A major research question in changing attitudes and behavior is involved in this issue of overlapping situations. **1964** *Language* XL. 62 This instance of overlapping phonetic values therefore need not be regarded as a violation of phonemic principles. **1971** *Brit. Med. Bull.* XXVII. 7/1 According to the theory of overlapping population distribution, the population screened is comprised of a diseased and a non-diseased group, both of whom possess the attribute being measured, though with different frequencies at various test levels. **1977** *New Yorker* 10 Oct. 124/2 A certain touring professional golfer barely missed equalling the record for fewest putts in a tournament round by a man using the ordinary overlapping (as opposed to the more popular reverse overlapping) grip. **1978** A. Price *'44 Vintage* ix. 103 The flick-knife was held, for the upwards [blow]..which came in under the overlapping ribs.

overlapping, *vbl. sb.* (Further examples.)
1896 [see *COALESCENCE 3]. **1935** *Discovery* Sept. 278/1 Room within this waveband..to accommodate several independent high-definition sound and picture channels without overlapping or interference. **1942** *Amer. Speech* XVII. 46 'Coarticulation' and 'overlapping'. **1956** Jakobson & Halle *Fund. of Lang.* ii. 14 The so-called overlapping of phonemes confirms the manifestly relational character of the distinctive features... The same sound [e] in one position implements the diffuse, and in another, the compact term of the same opposition. **1963** B. Fozard *Instrumentation Nucl. Reactors* x. 112 Overlapping, i.e. failure to resolve the pulses, may cause errors of measurement in three main ways.

over-late, *a.* and *adv.* Add: **a.** *adj.* (Later example.)
1958 T. Stanwell-Fletcher *Clear Lands* 245 The diminishing supply of native animals..despite overlate measures of restocking and conservation.
b. *adv.* (Later example.)
1875 W. Morris tr. *Virgil's Aeneids* VII. 597 And overlate the Gods thou shalt adore.

overlay, *v.* Add: **2. b.** (Examples.)
1888 C. T. Jacobi *Printer's Vocab.* 93 *Overlay*, to make ready by overlaying—the reverse of underlaying. **1894** *Amer. Dict. Printing & Bookmaking* 413/1 *Overlay*,..to secure proper effects in printing by means of graduated impression between the impressing surface and the sheet, using different thicknesses of paper. **1940** *Chambers's Techn. Dict.* 604/2 *Overlay*.., to adjust the impression surface of a machine by cutting and patching.

overlay, *sb.* Add: **2. a.** (Later examples.)
1888 Wilson & Grey *Pract. Treat. Mod. Printing Machinery* xxi. 337 The object of an overlay is not to equalise the impression, but to intensify the pressure upon the dark parts or solids, that they may be firm and bright, and to lessen the impression upon the lighter shades, in order to give them that degree of delicacy and cleanliness that would be altogether wanting if the pressure exerted were uniform. **1946** V. S. Ganderton in H. Whetton *Pract. Printing & Binding* xi. 132/2 In letterpress the gradation in tone of a half-tone plate corresponds to a gradation in resistance to pressure... The object of an interlay or overlay is to balance the variation in resistance by varying the pressure on the different areas. **1970** E. A. D. Hutchings *Survey of Printing Processes* iv. 57 Many of these operations [in make-ready] can be carried out..in the pre-press department, using..register tables..and other precision equipment such as mechanical overlay systems.
b. In offset lithographic printing: (see quot. 1974).
1967 Karch & Buber *Offset Processes* 548 *Overlay*, in offset, the transparent..covering on the copy on which directions..are placed in conjunction with the original. **1974** J. Craig *Production for Graphic Designer* 172/1 The copy for each additional color is pasted on acetate overlays, each one representing a color. *Ibid.* 190/2 Overlay. Transparent paper or film flap placed over artwork for the purpose of (1) protecting it from dirt or damage, (2) indicating instructions to the platemaker or printer, or (3) showing the breakdown of color in mechanical color separations.
3. a. (Further special senses.) Also *attrib.*, as *overlay mattress*.
1886 J. Barrowman *Gloss. Scotch Mining Terms* 48 *Overlay*, the material above the rock in a quarry. **1926–7** *Army & Navy Stores Catal.* 1076 Overlay mattresses for children's bedsteads and cots. **1930** *Daily Tel.* 9 Apr. 6/3 (Advt.), No bumps, no lumps, no sag in the 'Vi-Spring', the overlay mattress. **1949** H. M. Cautley *Norfolk Churches* 38 Another feature came into perfection, namely the overlay, with its imposed and crocketted hood-moulds on the face of tracery, giving such depth and solidity to the whole, as at Scarning..and Bedingham. **1953** *B.U. Encycl. Handbk.* (Bedding Publications Ltd.) App. 198 Upholstered overlay mattresses with spring or cellular rubber interior. **1962** A. McIntosh in Davis & Wrenn *Eng. & Medieval Stud.* 234 Just as we concluded earlier that Thornton transcribed B_1 and M_1 without very much tampering, so must we now conclude that S transcribed M_2 with sufficient fidelity for his own overlay not to have obliterated strong traces of an underlying language. **1968** *Lebende Sprachen* XIII. 104/2 *Overlay*, the action accomplished in the interfacing technique wherein linking events are meshed into a single event. **1972** H. Kurath *Studies Area Linguistics* viii. 124 The replaced language was an overlay (superstratum), as French in England or Frankish in northern France.
b. A transparent sheet bearing additional information, which is laid over a map or diagram.
1938 E. Raisz *Gen. Cartogr.* xv. 172 Transparent tracing papers are made of straw and cornstalk base and are used in map work for sketching, for copying, and for tissue overlays which indicate various colors and tints. **1952** V. Canning *House of Seven Flies* viii. 128 He put the overlay on the chart so that the cross..fell on the position of the house. **1964** G. Lyall *Most Dangerous Game* vi. 45, I did the real work using a celluloid overlay with wax-pencil marks. **1973** J. S. Keates *Cartogr. Design & Production* xx. 200/2 It is more satisfactory to produce the pattern stick-up on a separate overlay, and then combine this with the line image in a separate processing stage. **1974** *Sci. Amer.* May 126/1 The plastic overlay rotates around the pin. The track on the earth's surface over which the satellite passes during any orbit is plotted as a curved line on the overlay.
c. A layer of coloured glass added on top of clear glass in decorative glass-ware; usu. *attrib.* in *overlay glass, overlay paper-weight, overlay weight*; hence *ellipt.* for *overlay paperweight*.
1940 E. H. Bergstrom *Old Glass Paperweights* ii. 12 In an encrusted overlay weight, the color overlays and faceting were apparently followed by a final dip into clear crystal to complete the weight. **1954** E. M. Elville *Paperweights & Other Glass Curiosities* i. 16 Also highly prized by connoisseurs are the overlay paperweights. Overlays were usually made with the millefiori mushroom in a crystal globe..given..a final casing of a colour such as red, blue or green. **1958** G. B. Hughes *Eng. Glass for Collector 1660–1860* xx. 220 Those who toured the Continent in the early nineteenth century enthusiastically adorned their dining-tables and dressing rooms on their return with specimens of colourful Bohemian work known as cased or overlay glass. **1967** Wodehouse *Company for Henry* iii. 45 A French eighteenth-century paperweight alluded to as follows:..Clichy double overlay weight. **1968** *Canad. Antiques Collector* Aug. 9/1 We know that Burlington produced many sophisticated types of glass including overlay glass. **1973** J. Mackay *Glass Paperweights* viii. 54 The majority of these overlay weights are doubles with an inner overlay of white and an outer overlay in shades of red, green or blue.
d. *Med.* A gelling layer spread on top of a layer of cells in culture and containing an indicator of the presence or absence of some cell product.
1954 *Jrnl. Exper. Med.* XCIX. 168 The agar overlay, used to overlay the cultures after infection, consisted of 12 parts of 2·7 per cent agar (*A*), 12 parts of neutral red solution (*B*), 8 parts of fourfold Earle's saline (*C*), and 5 parts of embryo extract (*D*). **1960** *Virology* X. 377 The difference in diameter of plaques grown under agar overlay with and without viral antibodies serves as a measure of antigenic difference. **1974** *Nature* 20 Dec. 745/2 Virus pools were grown in Vero cells and titrated by plaque assay with a methylcellulose overlay as before.
4. *Dentistry.* A structure intended to improve the occlusal surface of the tooth or teeth over which it fits.
1935 G. M. Anderson *Dewey's Pract. Orthodontia* (ed. 5) xxi. 443 To stabilize the canine anchorage, the canine overlays are connected on the lingual surface with a clasp metal wire. **1954** *Brit. Dental Jrnl.* XCVII. 268/1 An upper acrylic bite overlay, sliding the mandible forward at the same time as opening the bite, gave complete relief in three days by preventing the condyles from being forced back in the fossæ. **1973** Anderson & Storer *Immediate & Replacement Dentures* (ed. 2) iv. 33 The retentive type of the overlay prosthesis should be considered where the residual ridges are almost non-existent and in cases where for reasons of speech, retching or excessive salivation, a palateless type of upper denture is necessary.
5. In betting, odds which are unjustifiably high. *U.S.*
1944 *Sun* (Baltimore) 21 Sept. 17/4 There is always a section that keeps in keen pursuit of the 'overlay', which means a horse rated, say, at 4 to 1 which closes at 10 to 1 or 12 to 1, well above his 'morning line' price. **1944** D. Runyon *Runyon à la Carte* (1946) 102 Everybody around is saying The Sky makes a terrible over-lay of the natural price in giving Brandy Bottle a G against his soul. **1955** *Amer. Speech* XXX. 27 The term *overlay* originally described the situation which existed if a bookmaker laid odds which, viewed objectively, were too high. At the present time *overlay* is used to describe odds meeting this test which appear in the pari-mutuel machine. Most often odds are considered an overlay if they are higher than the odds quoted in the so-called *morning line*.
6. *Computers.* The process of transferring a block of instructions or data to internal storage in place of what is already there, esp. in order to utilize a limited high-speed memory for those parts of a program that are in active use; also, a section of program so transferred.
1963 *Automatic Data Processing Gloss.* (U.S. Bureau of Budget) 38/1 *Overlay*, a technique for bringing routines into high-speed storage during processing, so that several routines will occupy the same storage location at different times. **1965** Swallow & Price *Elem. Computer Programming* xiv. 273 Once the new table is determined for a given run, the original table and the program for calculating the new one can be discarded, so the main program may be loaded over the previous one... This is frequently called an overlay. **1969** P. B. Jordain *Condensed Computer Encycl.* 367 When a program and its data are too large for the computer, the program must be divided into segments and so constructed that only the active segments (or overlays) need be in core. **1970** O. Dopping *Computers & Data Processing* xiv. 219 We can have a special memory area for overlay, or we can let a part of the program normally used—the main program, be overwritten. **1972** J.-L. Baer in A. F. Cardenas et al. *Computer Sci.* v. 170 If subroutines A and B will never call each other, then they can occupy the same positions in memory. If, at run-time, B is called while A is present, an overlay will be performed replacing A by B, and vice versa.

overlayer. (Later example.)
1917 *19th Cent.* Jan. 132 Faith in God and in a hereafter has been accompanied in history by an overlayer of superstition.

overlaying, *vbl. sb.* (Earlier and later examples of *Typogr.* sense.)
1839 T. C. Hansard *Treat. Printing & Type-Founding* (1841) 117 Anciently, the artist in wood contented himself with producing his lights and shades by cutting his lines.. upon a plane, leaving to the printer the task of producing the required effects by a tedious process of overlaying. **1967** V. Strauss *Printing Industry* vii. 428/2 Overlaying serves two purposes: one is to level the impression and the other to provide varying pressure.

overlea·rn, *v.* [Over- 27a.] *trans.* To learn excessively; *spec.* in *Psychol.*, to learn (something) beyond the stage of initially successful performance. Hence **overlea·rned** *ppl. a.*; **overlea·rning** *vbl. sb.*
1874 [see Over- 27a]. **1918** E. C. Tolman in *Psychol. Monogr.* XXV. I. 48 The first hypothesis would assume that this longer time corresponded to relatively more just supraliminal and relatively fewer 'over-learned' associations. **1929** R. S. Woodworth *Psychol.* (1930) iii. 94 Material that has been 'over-learned', i.e., studied beyond beyond the point where it can barely be recited without error, is forgotten more slowly. **1939** —— *Experimental Psychol.* ii. 30 Nagel went further; he pushed the original learning to the point of great overlearning. **1948** E. R. Hilgard *Theories of Learning* xii. 339 The most evident effect of overlearning is this one upon recall. It provides the explanation for the long retention of overlearned skills like swimming or bicycle riding. **1953** H. Schuell *Aphasia Theory* (1974) x. 203 Using some of the highly over-learned automaticisms of speech often produces this result quickly. **1963** W. B. Kolesnik *Educ. Psychol.* x. 248 She wants him to overlearn the material. **1972** J. L. Dillard *Black English* vii. 269 The technique consists of intensive practice to the point of overlearning.

over-length. Add: Also as quasi-*adj.*
1959 Halas & Manvell *Technique Film Animation* xviii. 170 If a film..becomes overlength through the addition of essential sound, it is usually better to consider cutting out a complete sequence. **1962** A. Nisbett *Technique Sound Studio* vii. 117 A programme..turns out to be seriously overlength. **1977** *Times Lit. Suppl.* 29 Apr. 537/1 *Middlemarch*, an over-length novel even by the generous Victorian reckoning.

over-light, *a.* (Later example.)
1908 *Daily Chron.* 21 Apr. 4/4 Now and then he was a trifle..over-light in his treatment of opponents.

overline, *v.*[1] Add: (Further example.) Hence **overli·ned** *ppl. a.*, having a line above it (usu. said of a printed character or number).
1879 *Proc. Lond. Math. Soc.* X. 21 The terms underlined and over-lined may both be omitted. **1963** *Amer. Jrnl. Physics* XXXI. 339/1 The overlined quantities are suitably taken average values of the specific heats in. dicated. **1967** A. Battersby *Network Analysis* (ed. 2) xii. 200 An overlined duration, e.g. $\overline{12}$, means that the present method calls for one man, but two men could be put on the job and would do it in half the time.

overling. Delete †*Obs.* and add later examples.
1917 [see *IDLE *a.* 8a]. **1976** *New Yorker* 22 Nov. 109/2 In Pinter's world, servants and other underlings are always filled with menace; the ominous likelihood is that they will prove to be overlings.

overlip (ōuvəɹli·p), *v. literary.* [Over- 1.] *trans.* To overflow the lip or brim of.
1868 G. M. Hopkins *Jrnls. & Papers* (1959) 181 The Jumeaux and..the Breithorn, both over-lipped with heavy cowls of snow. **1872** S. Butler *Erewhon* v. 38 The clouds rolled up to the very summit of the pass, though they did not overlip it.

overlive, *v.* Add: **a.** (Further examples.) Also, to live beyond (one's income).
1749 J. Cleland *Mem. Woman Pleasure* I. 124 He was the only son of a father, who..rather over-liv'd his income. **1842** Tennyson *Poems* II. 102 Perish in thy self-contempt! Overlive it—..be happy! wherefore should I care? *a* **1877** Swinburne *Lesbia Brandon* (1952) iii. 36 His clear, wary, untameable eyes which had seen many dangers through, had overlived and overcome much trouble. **1881** S. Evans *Evans's Leicestershire Words* (new ed.) 207 *Overlive*,..to out-live; survive.
c. Also, to live too intensely, or too actively.
1921 Galsworthy *To Let* II. ii. 126 He had only just relapsed, from having overworked, or overlived, himself again.
Hence **overliving** *vbl. sb.*
1817 Scott *Let.* 11 Aug. (1933) IV. 496 The task of maintaining a poor renderd effeminate and vicious by over wages and over-living and necessarily cast loose upon society.

overload, *sb.* Add: (Further examples.)

1937 J. ORR tr. *Iordan's Introd. Romance Linguistics* iii. 166 Semantic hypertrophy, or semantic overload, as it has been called. **1938** *Sun* (Baltimore) 11 July 2/6 The cabin behind the cockpit was crowded with..elaborate radio and navigation equipment. The plane weighs 25,000 pounds —an overload of 7,500 pounds. **1969** *Advancement of Sci.* XXVI. 72/1 Much the same applies to officials..who are responsible for the continuity of policy. They frequently live in a state of perpetual overload from which there is no obvious escape. **1974** *Gen. Systems* XIX. 62/2 A confused oldster may easily be maneuvered to sign a contract accepting the machine's uncompensible expensiveness. She thereby converts her overload into culturally-encouraged 'pathways to madness'.

b. *spec.* A current or voltage in excess of that which is normal or allowed for. Freq. *attrib.*, esp. designating devices for protecting against overloads.

1904 *Westm. Gaz.* 1 Dec. 8/1 A representative..was conducted through the mighty power-house... 'This is the biggest thing of its kind running in England. It is designed for 20,000 horse-power; at a pinch it could stand a 50 per cent. overload.' **1908** *Installation News* II. 38 There is always some novel addition to our Conduit System,..in addition to various side issues such as overload cut-outs. **1930** *Engineering* 3 Jan. 32/2 The overload trips are operated through a relay. **1962** A. NISBETT *Technique Sound Studio* 10 Striking a reasonable balance between noise levels, on the one hand, and overload or peak distortion, on the other, may take so much time and effort that the best part of the programme is lost. **1974** *Sci. Amer.* Nov. 34/1 The blackout was traced to the tripping of a circuit breaker in Ontario during a momentary overload. **1975** *Hi-Fi Answers* Feb. 38/1 The disc input has a fixed sensitivity of 2.5mV with an overload margin of 100mV. **1975** G. J. KING *Audio Handbk.* v. 112 A stereo amplifier switched to the mono mode may have an overload value which differs from that in the stereo mode.

overload, *v.* (Further examples.) Also *absol.*

1962 A. NISBETT *Technique Sound Studio* 254 Frequency modulation... Limiters are not needed to avoid overloading transmitter valves. **1973** *Times* 30 Nov. 6/7 He thought some circuits were overloaded by as much as four kilowatts. **1976** G. A. BROWNE *Slide* (1977) 8 The woman ..hoped she wouldn't overload again... Anyway, today she was prepared with eight extra fuses.

b. *intr.* To become overloaded.

1961 *Jrnl. Water Pollution Control Federation* XXXIII. 1280/1 Ice caused the aerator to overload, straining the drive belts. **1977** *Times* 16 July 5/8 The safety devices to stop them [*sc.* power lines] overloading came into action.

overloaded *ppl. a.* (further examples); **overloading** *vbl. sb.* (earlier and later examples).

1889 R. FRY *Let.* 2 Aug. (1972) I. 123 Ashbee..got hold of..*Atalanta in Calydon*, and read it with such overloading of sentiment as is usual with him. **1907** *Daily Chron.* 3 Oct. 2/2 The rapid increase in the number of companies not being admired by the somewhat overloaded bulls. **1958** *Spectator* 11 July 68/3 It is essential to retain its [*sc.* the Government's] legislative apparatus of control of borrowing. Overloading will never be prevented without it. **1962** A. NISBETT *Technique Sound Studio* iii. 67 There should be no trouble with this except where the output of a close balance on heavy brass is fed through pre-amplifiers of fixed gain; this can result in overloading and consequent distortion. **1962** R. H. SMYTHE *Anat. Dog Breeding* 70 These are the muscles which when well developed cause 'overloading' of the shoulders. *Ibid.* 77 What judges term, 'overloaded shoulders'. **1974** *Times* 9 Jan. 3/3 Surplus, damaged and overloaded goods were sold to people in the trade.

overlock, *v.* Add: **c.** *trans.* and *intr.* To secure (the edge of cloth) so as to strengthen it and to prevent fraying; also, to oversew (by machine). Usu. as **o·verlocking** *vbl. sb.*

1901–2 *T. Eaton & Co. Catal.* Fall & Winter 64/2 Men's fine imported natural wool night robes, made with collar attached,..overlocked seams, [etc.]. **1909** *Public Ledger* (Philadelphia) 24 June 5/2 Fishnet Lace Curtains, overlocked edge. **1921** *Dict. Occup. Terms* (1927) § 376 *Overlocking machinist*,..stitches round scolloped edge of finished lace curtain with overlocking machine. **1960** *Textile Terms & Definitions* (Textile Inst.) (ed. 4) 106 *Overlocking*,..effecting the joining of two or more pieces of fabric by means of an double or treble chain stitch... This operation is performed on overseaming machines. **1973** *Guardian* 12 Mar. 9/4 Most of the women work in..linking, cutting, and overlocking. **1976** *Leicester Trader* 24 Nov. 17/2 (Advt.), Klynton Davis require experienced employees with the following skills: lockstitching, overlocking, welting, [etc.]. **1978** *People's Friend* 13 May 24/2 (Advt.), Every detail is perfect—like the needle overlocking technique that ensures incredible strength at the seams.

overlocker (ōᵘ·vəɹlǫkəɹ). [f. *OVERLOCK *v.* c + -ER¹.] (See quot. 1921.)

1921 *Dict. Occup. Terms* (1927) § 419 *Overlocker*.., guides cut edges and seams of knitted fabrics under needles of power-driven overlock machine, thereby joining them together..with an overlock stitch. **1964** *Age* (Melbourne) 15 Aug. 62 (Advt.), Experienced overlockers and plain sewing machine operators and juniors to be trained are required for our making-up rooms. **1975** *Evening Herald* (Dublin) 8 May 12/5 (Advt.), Experienced overlockers, button machine operators and flat machinists. This staff is required for our slacks factory. **1976** *Leicester Mercury* 16 July (Advt.), Leta Knitwear Ltd., outerwear and underwear manufacturers require very urgently overlockers, binders, and designer.

overlooker. 2. (Later examples.)

1963 *Times* 25 May 9/7 'But t'brig isn't t'world', a sewing-shop overlooker says over his gill of mild. **1973** *Guardian* 12 Mar. 9/1 She has worked as an overlooker at Mansfield Hosiery for five years. **1974** *Times* 5 Dec. 5/2 A mill in the Preston area [where]..the first Asian overlooker was recently promoted. **1976** T. JEAL *Until Colours Fade* ix. 111 A group of all but naked men, working under an overlooker, raking out white-hot coke.

overlord, *sb.* Add: **1. b.** *transf.* A person (occas. an animal) in a position of superiority, authority, or power; *spec.* in British politics, a member of the House of Lords given charge of one or more government ministries; hence in the politics of other countries, and in industry.

1932 S. ZUCKERMAN *Social Life Monkeys* xiv. 228 Baboons are not promiscuous. Very few observations have been made of females having sexual relations with males other than their overlords. **1939** JOYCE *Finnegan's Wake* I. 97 To ongoad and unhume the great shipping mogul and underlinen overlord. **1951** *Economist* 8 Dec. 1394/2 Departmental ministers subject to an overlord would, under arrangements of this kind, rarely have direct access to the cabinet. **1953** *Ann. Reg. 1952* 36 The Opposition had long been critical of Mr. Churchill's 'overlords'—super-departmental Ministers screened from cross-examination by their membership of 'another place'. **1954** *Economist* 31 July 355/1 General Perón..did reduce the nominal number of ministries..; but this was accompanied by the appointment of four..'overlords'..concerned with defence, economic, technical, and political affairs. **1957** *Observer* 13 Oct. 1/4 Instead of appointing a missile overlord, as is being urged, the President has referred the whole problem..to yet another committee. **1969** *Daily Tel.* 20 Nov. 3/1 Lord Beeching..is being tipped for the job of 'overlord' to run BOAC and BEA. **1970** *Guardian* 11 May 10/1 The old problem of the Overlord Minister which re-emerged from the Churchillian past after Mr Wilson's last big reshuffle. **1970** *Daily Tel.* 11 Sept. 6/5 Under the reorganisation Vauxhall will become part of a European division of General Motors... Mr L. Ralph Mason..will become the European 'overlord'. **1977** *Time* 21 Feb. 24/2 In Mexico the destruction of planted fields and the arrests of several overlords,..have led to fierce internecine battles for control of the business.

2. (With capital initial.) The code-name for the allied invasion of German-occupied Normandy in June 1944.

1943 J. REITH *Diary* 18 Sept. (1975) vi. 310 Meeting.. about a ridiculous Churchill demand for a twenty-five per cent increase in Overlord (invasion of Europe) force. **1947** J. R. DEANE *Strange Alliance* I. ii. 22, I emphasized our commitments to Overlord, the Mediterranean, the Pacific. **1948** C. FALLS *Second World War* xxiv. 219 The title given to the plan for the invasion of the European Continent from the west, Operation Overlord, possessed a special significance. It was the over-riding operation. **1950** W. S. CHURCHILL *Second World War* III. II. xxxiv. 585 It was my earnest desire that the crossing of the Channel and the liberation of France (the operation then called 'Round-up', which was subsequently changed to 'Overlord') should take place in the summer of 1943. **1961** E. WAUGH *Unconditional Surrender* III. ii. 239 'Overlord', that one huge hazardous offensive operation on which, it seemed, the fate of the world depended. **1974** G. MARKSTEIN *Cooler* lxvi. 230 We've been working very hard to sell them the idea that the Pas de Calais is the objective of Overlord.

overlord, *v.* Delete *rare* and add later examples. Hence **overlo·rded, overlo·rding** *ppl. adjs.*

1910 GALSWORTHY *Sheaf* (1916) 132 Our dim consciousness of this serene and overlording principle of Equity. **1959** *Catholic Herald* 27 Nov. 5/3 The Ukrainians of Kiev ..resisted the attempts of the Moscow Orthodox Patriarchate to overlord them. **1961** B. VAWTER *Conscience of Israel* vi. 139 A fact that can help account for its economic expansion in a world overlorded by the Great King. **1966** *Economist* 24 Sept. 1234/3 They were feeling too overlorded. **1970** *Daily Tel.* 11 May 16/5 The appointment of a single executive to overlord the Dutch and British ends of the business would represent a major switch. *Ibid.* 16 Oct. 19/5 (*heading*) David Barran to 'overlord' Shell.

overly, *a.* Add: **2.** (Later example.)

1833 *Chambers's Edin. Jrnl.* 27 Apr. 97/1 Some day, your wife mentions to you, quite in what Mrs Pringle called an overly way, that she happened to meet her old friend Mrs Nicholson on the street that day.

overly, *adv.* Add: **1.** Now more widespread but still regarded as an Americanism in the U.K. (Further examples.)

1854 [see *DOGAN]. **1903** KIPLING *Five Nations* 21 Yet, caring so, not overly we care To brace and trim for every foolish blast. **1924** B. G. ELLIOTT *Automobile Repairing* x. 131 An overly rich mixture may be caused by the fuel nozzle valve being open too wide. **1926** J. A. MULLER *Stephen Gardiner* ii. 11 The intense, overly conscientious Thomas Bilney. **1929** M. C. WORK *Compl. Contract Bridge* v. 111 Overly sanguine or 'bad break' slam tries. **1942** *Sun* (Baltimore) 10 Oct. 10/2 A panting, frantic lady..is..not overly generous after she has stood for a while..shouting for an invisible porter. **1956** D. KARP *All Honourable Men* 50 She took one with an overly feline movement of her body and looked into his face as she accepted his light. **1963** *Wall St. Jrnl.* 25 Jan., As for the future, however, even the most annoyed American official seems not to be overly alarmed. **1968** *Globe & Mail* (Toronto) 17 Feb. 8/1 The Manitoba Minister of Agriculture is not overly impressed with the horsemen's woes. **1970** *Nature* 17 Jan. 213/1 Scientists are not going to be overly interested in the 'sociology of the sociology of science' if nothing is forthcoming except internal disagreement. **1970** G. F. NEWMAN *Sir, You Bastard* i. 27 Whoever had covered them hadn't been overly careful about the tubes. **1972** *Times Lit. Suppl.* 2 June 624/4 Those overly rationalistic readers who demand to see in her work plentiful evidence of a higher or deeper 'sanity'. **1977** *Dædalus* Summer 157 This is the methodological point lying behind Popper's overly propositional thesis about the eternal falsifiability of scientific truths.

overman, *sb.* Add: **4.** [tr. G. *übermensch.*] = SUPERMAN.

1895 tr. *M. Nordau's Degeneration* III. v. 470 The 'bullies' gratefully recognise themselves in Nietzsche's 'overman'. **1900** *Q. Rev.* July 116 In such old religion he discovers no prophecy of the man that is to be; he reaches forward to some 'overman' beyond it. **1908** H. G. WELLS *War in Air* xi. 365 His mind ran to 'improving the race' and producing the Over-Man. **1915** *Lond. Q. Rev.* Jan. 59 Such a process of superabstraction would involve either an overman or a *deus ex machina*. **1928** A. HUXLEY *Point Counter Point* vi. 108 If you were a little less of an overman,..what good novels you'd write! **1932** [see *NIETZSCHEAN *sb.* and *a.*]. **1971** *Black Scholar* June 50/1 The 'magnificent savage', 'the mindless overman', is even dying with the deficiency. **1976** M. & G. GORDON *Ordeal* xi. 69 He would overlook Charlie's shortcomings. An overman had to... Vince had read as much of Nietzsche as necessary to learn about the overmen—the supermen—and the inferiors, the masses.

overman, *v.* Add: **1.** (Further example.)

1851 H. MELVILLE *Moby Dick* I. xxxvii. 270 My soul is more than matched; she's overmanned—and by a madman!

Hence (in sense 2) **over-ma·nning** *vbl. sb.*

1971 *New Scientist* 9 Sept. 553/1 Output has reflected this over-manning. **1975** *Broadcast* 28 July 4/1 The ACTT does not consider overmanning..to be a central issue in the financial problems confronting ITV. **1975** *Times Lit. Suppl.* 12 Sept. 1028/4 During the winter overmanning was enforced—one labourer per fifteen acres. **1975** *Daily Tel.* 19 Sept. 3/3 (*heading*) Sir Keith urges TUC to curb overmanning. **1978** *Jrnl. R. Soc. Arts* CXXVI. 656/1 The overmanning in all the factories that I visited was very considerable.

overmark, *v.* Add: **4.** [OVER- 27a.] To award too many marks to (a candidate in an examination, competition, etc.)

1947 C. S. LEWIS *Miracles* xvii. 198 Some examiners tend to overmark any candidate whose opinions and character, as revealed by his work, are revolting to them. **1970** *Times* 5 Mar. 13 One judge admitted that she had overmarked Wood, for no good reason that I could discover other than sympathy for a champion in distress.

overmast, *v.* Add: (Later examples.) Hence **overma·sting** *vbl. sb.*

1902 CONRAD *Youth* 40 She was certainly over-masted. **1906** —— *Mirror of Sea* xi. 58 It was a fine period in ship-building, and also..a period of over-masting. **1930** J. MASEFIELD *Wanderer of Liverpool* 27 Mr. Potter was inclined to think that the *Wanderer* had been over-masted.

overmastering, *ppl. a.* (Later examples.)

1860 GEO. ELIOT *Mill on Floss* III. 209 He had been tortured by scruples, he had fought fiercely with overmastering inclination. **1903** *Camb. Mod. Hist.* II. xviii. 644 He [*sc.* Paul III] was not a zealot, possessed with one overmastering idea. **1915** F. S. OLIVER *Ordeal by Battle* iv. 120 Nietzsche is not concerned to evolve a sovereign and omnipotent state, but a high overmastering type of man. **1942** *R.A.F. Jrnl.* 13 June 2 What a blockade by sea can do..an overmastering force of bombers can most certainly do. **1957** J. S HUXLEY *Relig. without Revelation* (rev. ed.) v. 110 Some have this in an overmastering degree.

overmastery, *sb.* Restrict † *Obs.* to sense in Dict. and add: **b.** Supreme authority, sovereignty.

1901 T. SHAW *Patriotism & Empire* (Young Scots Soc. Publ. No. 1) 4 We are free..to think with a lifting of the heart of the struggle for Scottish independence against the overmastery of England. **1971** J. F. WATHEN *Great Sacrilege* ii. 28 God Himself..would prevent such a thing from happening, either directly or through His ordinary overmastery of all creatural actions.

over-measure, *v.* **a.** (Later example.)

1877 TENNYSON *Harold* IV. iii. 119 By St. Edmund I over-measure him.

overmod, *sb.* Delete quot. *c* 1200, which illustrates a different word (see *Medium Ævum* (1952) XXI. 38–9).

o:vermodula·tion. *Electronics.* [OVER- 29b.] Amplitude modulation that is so great as to result in unacceptable distortion; *spec.* modulation that causes the amplitude of the carrier to become zero for a significant part of each cycle of the modulating wave.

1927 *Exper. Wireless & Wireless Engin.* IV. 3/1 The strengths of..undesired harmonics relative to the desired fundamental decrease as the modulation ratio *a*/*a* is decreased. This is the ground for the term 'over-modulation' as a fault at the transmitter. Over-modulation shows, of course, only during the relatively loud passages. **1937** *Wireless World* 2 Dec. 563/1 Over-modulation of broadcast transmitters has been a serious problem. **1962** A. NISBETT *Technique Sound Studio* vii. 132 One of the problems which may arise when tape is re-used is a background 'chatter' from the previous recording. This can be due.. to overmodulation of the previous recording. **1968** *Radio Communication Handbk.* (ed. 4) ix. 4/2 In frequency modulation there is no condition equivalent to over-modulation.

So **overmo·dulate** *v. trans.*, to subject to overmodulation; *intr.*, to cause or suffer overmodulation.

1928 L. S. PALMER *Wireless Princ. & Pract.* xi. 418 As long as the modulator be not overworked, the oscillatory current cannot be over-modulated. **1937** *Wireless World* 2 Dec. 563/1 Automatically graduated compression, or limiting,..makes it almost impossible to overload or overmodulate the transmitter. **1962** A. NISBETT *Technique Sound Studio* ii. 48 Completely dead sound is difficult to balance: the transient peaks tend to over-modulate.

overname, *v.* (Later example.)

1902 J. H. SKRINE *Pastor Agnorum* 31 Twenty faces in three ranks, and, though no face is like another, we could have safely overnamed the varieties before we fronted them.

overner (ōᵘ·vəɹnəɹ). *local.* [? f. OVER *adv.* + -ER[1], after *northerner, southerner*, etc.] In the Isle of Wight, a visitor or immigrant from the mainland; = OVERER *sb.*[2] Cf. *OVERUN *a.* and *sb.*

1886 W. H. LONG *Dict. Isle of Wight Dial.* 46 *Overner*, or *overun feller*, a person whose home is over the water, on the main land; not a native of the Island. West countrymen, who come to work in the Island, are always 'overun fellers'.. 'I wish it had capsized they there overners, comen across.' **1951** B. VESEY-FITZGERALD in E. Molony *Portraits of Islands* 65 You may still find in the interior men who speak of people from the mainland as 'overners' (foreigners). **1965** L. WILSON *Portrait of Isle of Wight* i. 15 As well as a strong feeling of security it confers on the inhabitants a sense of identity which 'overners', as they call them, people from over the water, do not possess. **1974** *Isle of Wight County Press* 12 Oct. 19/6 Now there's myself (an Overner, surely) shedding a tear for a scene that had to go.

over-nicety. (Earlier example.)

1754 RICHARDSON *Grandison* VI. xxvii. 165 A little overnicety at setting out, will carry them into a road they never intended to amble in.

overnight, over night, *adv. phr.* (*sb.*, *a.*) Add: **A.** *adv. phr.* **3.** In the course of a single night; hence, rapidly, instantaneously; without any perceptible or significant passage of time.

1939 JOYCE *Finnegans Wake* II. 378 The unnamed nonirishblooder that becomes a Greenislander overnight! **1942** E. WAUGH *Put out More Flags* 246 Alastair's battalion found itself overnight converted from a unit in the early stages of training into first line troops. **1955** H. ROTH *Sleeper* viii. 60 Adults don't change—rarely, at any rate, and not overnight. **1955** 'A. GILBERT' *Is she Dead Too?* ii. 30 She'd been there two years when Alice Poulden died. It all seemed to happen overnight as you might say. **1957** F. & R. LOCKRIDGE *Practise to Deceive* (1959) vi. 90 Lane..was already 'the' polo player. A handicap justifying such phrasing is not acquired overnight. **1963** *Cambr. Rev.* 4 May 400/1 An article which overnight catapulted him to fame. **1966** *Word Study* Dec. 5/2 Overnight the vernacular of space became a popular idiom. **1972** P. GREEN *Shadow of Parthenon* 15 The classics have nearly half a century of revolutionary critical development to catch up on: the thing cannot be achieved overnight. **1972** *Observer* 12 Nov. 36/7 The great original thinker, the noble if flawed human being, the entranced and hallowed poet-sage—all these have virtually been blown away overnight. **1973** [see *OUSTER[1]].

B. *sb.* **2.** A stop or halt lasting for one night; also, a person who stops at a place for a single night (see quots.).; something that arrived during the night.

1959 *Times Lit. Suppl.* 9 Oct. 573/4 A highly convincing background of aviation and suburbia, dinettes, lounges (domestic, not airport), overnights and rosters. **1964** *Economist* 11 Jan. 114/2 The YHA..had a record number of..'overnights' (the total number of nights that beds were occupied). **1968** J. LOCK *Lady Policeman* xiii. 117 The gaoler brings the 'overnights' from the cells. **1974** *Guardian* 23 Mar. 14/3 With two overnights in Interlaken ..it sounded..soothing enough. **1976** C. WESTON *Rouse Demon* (1977) i. 4 Ten minutes to spare, pounding up the stairs to the Detective Bureau. ..Time to skim through the overnights before the morning rundown.

C. *attrib.* or *adj.* **2. a.** Designating a price or value as at the end of business on a particular day. **b.** Applied to money lent or borrowed, or otherwise made available, from one day to the next.

1909 *Westm. Gaz.* 7 Aug. 12/1 Finishing on the other side very strongly, the overnight prices were well above those ruling in the 'House' at the close of yesterday afternoon. **1928** *Daily Mail* 9 Aug. 18/6 Borrowers occasionally paid up to 4½ per cent. for fresh overnight money. **1930** M. CLARK *Home Trade* xxix. 233 Sometimes the loan is merely one from one day to the next—often termed 'overnight loans'; at other times it is for a short period of say seven days ('weekly loans'). **1973** *Times* 2 Feb. 14/7 New York money men have been known to quake in the knowledge that they have on deposit $1,000m of overnight money—money which can be withdrawn the next morning.

3. Of a person: transient, staying overnight; *fig.*, instantaneously esteemed or popular. Of a thing: achieved or accomplished rapidly.

1934 [see *air hostess* s.v. *AIR *sb.*[1] III. 4]. **1960** *News Chron.* 18 Mar. 6/6 He has become an over-night hero to countless people. **1961** *Sunday Express* 7 May 15/5 One really eye-catching picture in a top magazine, and she is an overnight star. **1974** S. SHELDON *Other Side of Midnight* iv. 86 The war, like all wars, had created overnight millionaires. **1974** HAWKEY & BINGHAM *Wild Card* xv. 127 His novel advances in the field of biodegradable materials..had brought him an overnight reputation.

4. Special collocations, as *overnight bag, case*, a light case or holdall carried by a traveller; *overnight telegram*, a telegram intended for delivery the following morning.

1925 *New Yorker* 17 Oct. 32/2 This is simply wonderful for travelers, though, as an overnight bag, it has the disadvantage of having no room in the bag for anything except, perhaps, a French nightie. **1955** 'N. SHUTE' *Requiem for Wren* i. 2 He took the overnight bag from me. **1972** M. CRICHTON *Terminal Man* I. v. 43 She lifted a small blue overnight bag. **1934** WEBSTER, Overnight case. **1935** *Montgomery Ward Catal.* 582 Wards finest—tray fitted overnight case. **1952** 'J. TEY' *Singing Sands* xiv. 238, I indicated my small overnight case which was lying..on the bunk. **1970** G. F. NEWMAN *Sir, You Bastard* 265 The overnight case belonged to Sneed. **1955** *P.O. Guide* July 309 Overnight telegrams are accepted between the hours of 8 a.m. and 10 p.m. daily for delivery next day..normally by the first post. **1974** *Ibid.* Nov. 367 An Overnight telegram may be sent between 8 a.m. and 10.30 p.m. for delivery, normally by first post, the following morning... The charge is 40p for 10 words or less and 2p for each extra word.

overni·ght, *v.* [f. the adv. phr.; cf. G. *übernachten.*] *intr.* To pass the night (*at* or *in*); to lodge for the night.

[**1876** GEO. ELIOT *Let.* 2 Sept. (1956) VI. 275 We saw no English or American visitors, except such as 'übernachten' there and pass on.] **1891** M. M. DOWIE *Girl in Karpathians* xiii. 177 He invites us to over-night at his house. Will you go? **1962** *Daily Progress* (Charlottesville, Va.) 2 Nov. 6/6 When a stewardess 'overnights' she spends the night in the city where the flight terminates. **1965** *Harper's Bazaar* Dec. 80/1 Anyone who has over-nighted in pre-Hilton Istanbul. **1971** R. FALKIRK *Chill Factor* v. 47 Her Icelandic philosophy was immensely popular.. wherever Icelandair overnighted. **1971** *Advocate-News* (Barbados) 20 Mar. 1/2 At the conclusion of his South American visits the President and party will again over night in Barbados on March 31 and leave for home on April 1. **1972** *Drive* Spring 49/2 With the horses provided you could trek deep into the forest, overnighting in a bivouac. **1976** J. B. HILTON *Gamekeeper's Gallows* xviii. 182 Fletcher over-nighted at Derby.

Hence **overni·ghting** *vbl. sb.* (also *attrib.*).

1948 K. ANTHONY *Lambs* vi. 132 The clambering in and out of stage-coaches, the overnighting in strange taverns. **1966** *Guardian* 19 Mar. 1/3 Overnighting facilities for climbers have been cut off, and visitors generally discouraged. **1969** 'J. MORRIS' *Fever Grass* x. 95 D'you have a spare shirt for this big man here? He didn't plan on overnighting.

o:verni·ghter. [f. OVERNIGHT *adv. phr.* + -ER[1].] **a.** = *overnight bag* (see *OVERNIGHT C. 4).

1959 *Sears, Roebuck Catal.* Spring–Summer 865/1 Easier Packing... 18-inch Overniter. **1967** 'S. MARLOWE' *Second Longest Night* vi. 58 Armed with two overnighters and the necessary toilet articles. **1967** K. GILES *Death in Diamonds* iv. 75 One suitcase..and a little overnighter with electric razor and stuff. **1972** M. CRICHTON *Terminal Man* I. v. 45 Benson placed the screwdrivers into the overnighter.

b. A person who stops at a place overnight (cf. *OVERNIGHT *sb.* 2).

1961 F. & R. LOCKRIDGE *Murder has its Points* (1962) ix. 96 At the Hotel Dumont there had, at the time in issue, been twenty-three overnighters. **1977** *Daily Tel.* 7 June 1/1 The area approaching St Paul's Cathedral was also becoming filled with overnighters.

o·ver-note. [OVER- 1 e.] A note heard through or above other sounds; an overtone.

1917 CONRAD *Shadow-Line* 204 He..burst into..a loud laugh... It was a provoking, mocking peal, with a hair-raising, screeching over-note of defiance.

over-old, *a.* (Later examples.)

1875 W. MORRIS tr. *Virgil's Aeneids* VIII. 509 My body over-old for deeds begrudged such government. **1883** LD. R. GOWER *My Reminisc.* II. 140 Their children..have a delicate over-old look for their age.

overpaint (ōᵘ·vəɹpēint), *sb.* [OVER- 8 c.] A second or further layer of paint; a paint used for overpainting.

1958 *Times* 1 July 5/4 The overpaint has now been cleaned off, revealing not only the skull which Petty holds but also two other skulls engraved on the page of the book to which the left hand is pointing. **1973** *Canad. Antiques Collector* Jan.–Feb. 17/1 This cupboard, when found, was over-painted; the over-paint was carefully removed to expose the original red on the cupboard proper, and the blue-green on the cornice and decorative mouldings. **1973** F. TAUBES *Painter's Dict.* 168 The evidence or absence of brushstrokes in the underpainting should be considered, for these may interfere with the overpaints.

o:verpai·nted, *ppl. a.* [OVER- 8 b.] That has been painted over another painted surface.

1967 J. N. BARRON *Lang. of Painting* 195 The painter plans the underpainting to obtain the variety of effects and optical mixtures he wishes in combination with, or in contrast to, the subsequent overpainted layers of paint. **1973** *Guardian* 16 Mar. 13/5 The National Portrait Gallery is..showing again..the family portrait of Sir Thomas More... The overpainted nineteenth century brown background has been removed.

overpai·nting, *vbl. sb.* [OVER- 8 b.] The action of the verb OVERPAINT (sense 1); a layer of paint applied over another.

1928 *Daily Express* 20 Dec. 1/3 The explanation of the over-painting is simple. The sitter..decided to have his sheriff's robes painted over the clothes in Holbein's picture. **1935** E. NEUHAUS tr. *Doerner's Materials of Artist* iv. 203 The overpainting must be applied somewhat more liquidly—at least in the first layer—than the underpainting. **1954** M. RICKERT *Painting in Brit.: Middle Ages* i. 23 The overpainting in thick white and yellow pigment. **1958** tr. *K. Herberts's Artists' Techniques* 140 Overpainting must be done with great care, since the lower layers of paint remain effaceable. **1973** *Guardian* 16 Mar. 26/1 Restoration..has removed the overpainting which had made the picture look unnaturally flat.

overpa·rk, *v. U.S.* [OVER- 27.] *intr.* To park a motor vehicle for longer than the permitted period. So **overpa·rked** *ppl. a.*, **overpa·rking** *vbl. sb.*

1938 *Daily Progress* (Charlottesville, Va.) 3 Mar. 1/8 The case of Clyde Anable, charged with overparking. **1957** *Times* (Seattle) 12 Sept. 38 The City Council today authorized the Police Department to hire ten 'meter maids', uniformed women who will patrol the streets and write tickets for overparking. **1974** *Keowee Courier* (Walhalla, S. Carolina) 24 Apr. 7/1 Gaillard also reported that the police are now issuing 'courtesy tickets' to people who overpark. These tickets provide only a friendly warning, and no fine, unless a person accumulates two in one day or three within a week. **1976** 'J. ROSS' *I know what it's like to Die* xxviii. 177 His Renault car had..been there all day... It had incurred fines for overparking. **1977** 'L. EGAN' *Blind Search* iv. 53 Officious meter maids checking overparked cars.

overparted, *a.* Add: (Further examples.) Also *transf.*

In quot. 1975[2] the sense is 'having a voice too strong for the part'.

1896 G. B. SHAW *How to become Mus. Critic* (1960) 240 As Siegmund the Unlucky he was quite overparted. *Ibid.* 244 He was overparted in Siegfried. **1959** *Times* 19 Nov. 16/2 Mr. William McAlpine seemed vocally over-parted as Boris. **1966** *New Statesman* 25 Mar. 437/3 Overparted Mr Constantine is persuaded to deliver himself of some grand lines, among which '*Je crois aux données immédiates de la conscience*' is probably as ludicrous as any. **1975** *Bookseller* 26 July 315/1 Seemed rather over-parted as the *Sunday Telegraph* lead reviewer. **1975** *Gramophone* Sept. 505/1 For some, Fischer-Dieskau is considerably overparted. **1977** *Listener* 5 May 592/2 The baritone and tenor soloists..rather seized the attention from the sadly overparted soprano.

overpass, *v.* Add: **3.** (Later example.)

1938 *Times* 16 Aug. 15/4 The stream..swelled uproariously. It did not anywhere overpass its deeply engraved channel, but raced helter-skelter and bank high to the road and the beach.

7. b. (Later examples.)

1905 *Daily Chron.* 24 Oct. 1 The Russian and Austrian agents in Uskub overpass their duties. *a* **1973** J. R. R. TOLKIEN *Silmarillion* (1977) 262 But the design of Manwë was that the Númenóreans should not..desire to overpass the limits set to their bliss.

8. (Later example.)

1872 G. M. HOPKINS *Let.* 5 Mar. (1956) 118, I cannot tell how I have overpassed your birthday and only been recalled to it now too late by seeing the date March 3 on a letter.

overpassing *vbl. sb.* (further example).

1865 MILL *Auguste Comte* 14 He deemed all real knowledge of a commencement inaccessible to us, and the inquiry into it an overpassing of the essential limits of our mental faculties.

o·verpass, *sb.* orig. *U.S.* Also **over-pass.** [OVER- 1 d.] A raised stretch of road or railway line that passes over another road or railway line; = *FLY-OVER 1. Also *attrib.*

1929 *Amer. City* Oct. 104/2 In certain cases where the construction of under- or over-passes cannot be avoided.. my system simplifies them to an astonishing extent. **1933** [see *clover-leaf* s.v. *CLOVER *sb.* 4]. **1938** *Sun* (Baltimore) 31 Aug. 7/3 Overpasses were built in both communities after years of agitation and numbers of serious crossing accidents. **1952** [see *EXPRESSWAY]. **1959** *Daily Tel.* 9 Nov. 1/1 But they refused to allow a car, scooter or even a bicycle to be pushed on these overpass roads. **1964** L. DEIGHTON *Funeral in Berlin* li. 313 Dominating the whole scene is the gleaming stone pillar of the Cenotaph like the freshly-built leg of a new overpass. **1969** *New Scientist* 17 Apr. 105/1 A major earthquake would..cause the overpasses into the city to collapse. **1973** H. NIELSEN *Severed Key* i. 11 The traffic lanes leading away from the airport were packed. Once over the overpass, Keith made a sharp right turn. **1974** *Anderson* (S. Carolina) *Independent* 23 Apr. 3A/5 A 180-foot overpass over Clinchfield railroad tracks on secondary road 126 in Spartanburg went to Dickerson, Inc., of Monroe N. C., which entered a low bid of $335,360. **1976** *National Observer* (U.S.) 5 June 1/1 As you top an overpass, your eyes are drawn to a red, white, and blue water tower on the horizon.

over-pe·dal, *v.* [OVER- 27.] *intr.* and *trans.* To over-use a piano's sustaining pedal; to play using the sustaining pedal too much. Hence **over-pe·dalled** *ppl. a.*, **over-pe·dalling** *vbl. sb.*

1961 *Times* 12 Apr. 6/1 He [*sc.* the pianist] was liable to force his tone, over-pedal. **1968** *Daily Tel.* 1 Nov. 21/3 The tempestuous coda to the Ballade, for instance, was smudged through over-pedalling. **1976** *Gramophone* June

69/1 Berman himself often overpedals in an over-resonant studio so that bigger climaxes are just a confused noise. **1976** *Ibid.* Sept. 421/3 The cadenza..is over-pedalled. **1976** *Daily Tel.* 29 Nov. 11/1 More control of rubato and over-pedalling is needed, but she has all the musical and technical talent to be an important pianist.

over-persuasion. (Later example.)

a **1817** JANE AUSTEN *Persuasion* (1818) III. vii. 142 It had been the effect of over-persuasion.

overpitch, *v.* **1.** (Earlier and later examples.) Also *absol.*

1851 [see *BOWL *v.*[1] 4 b]. **1958** D. BRADMAN *Art of Cricket* 104/1 If one's length is faulty, over-pitch rather than under-pitch that new ball. **1963** *Times* 28 May 4/5 On a perfect pitch, he played each good length ball with care, but those overpitched he punished severely and his 100 included four sixes and 10 fours.

2. (Later examples.)

1976 N. ROBERTS *Face of France* vi. 69 He is non-descript and correct, she high-coloured and over-pitched. **1977** *Church Times* 28 Jan. 6/4 The tone of much of Kingsley's writing..now seems overpitched to an almost hysterical degree.

Hence **overpi·tched** *ppl. a.*, of a ball: that is pitched too far.

1855 [see *BREAK *sb.*[1] 5]. **1897** [in Dict.]. **1900** A. E. T. WATSON *Young Sportsman* 147 He has lunged out as far as he can reach, hoping to 'smother' a somewhat over-pitched ball. **1958** D. BRADMAN *Art of Cricket* 101/2 Learn to bowl the yorker if you can but be prepared to get hit for some fours off the overpitched balls in the process.

over-play, *v.* Add: **1. b.** *fig.* To emphasize too much; to attach too great an importance to; *spec.* in phr. *to overplay one's hand,* to spoil a good case by exaggerating its value.

1930 *Times* 27 Mar. 15/3 Conditions are clearly more favourable to agreement..provided only that *Nahas Pasha* does not over-play his hand. **1933** *Sun* (Baltimore) 16 Aug. 10/7 American newspaper headline writers.. 'overplay' the news for which they write captions. **1952** *Essays in Crit.* II. 325 He [*sc.* Empson] thinks Tillyard and Dover Wilson..overplayed their hands in attending too exclusively to the 'official' explanations of Shakespeare's history plays. **1956** A. L. ROWSE *Early Churchills* 269 Here was the one chance of the Allies..thrown away by overplaying their hand. **1960** I. PEEBLES *Bowler's Turn* 190 Dexter over-played his luck and ran himself out. **1965** *New Statesman* 20 Apr. 673/3 One building society told me that the 'crisis' had been 'very much overplayed' and that there were already signs of the investment situation easing. **1968** *Globe & Mail* (Toronto) 13 Jan. 29/2 The problem has been overplayed, he said. The recent slump doesn't indicate a trend. **1977** F. DURBRIDGE *Passenger* iii. 146 Judy may have over-played her hand and tried to cut herself in on one of Andy's little rackets.

overplus, *sb.* (*adv., a.*) Add: **A.** *sb.* **c.** (Earlier and later examples.)

1721 M. W. MONTAGU *Let.* May (1966) II. 5, I beleive [I] shall take care another time not to involve my selfe in difficulties by an overplus of Heroic Generosity. **1794** D. O'CONNELL *Let.* 22 Apr. (1972) I. 17, I could spend three months at home in my native air free from all cost; which would compensate for the overplus of travelling charges. *a* **1817** JANE AUSTEN *Two Chapters of Persuasion* (1926) 27 To..pay for the overplus of Bliss, by Headake & Fatigue. **1934** E. POUND *Eleven New Cantos* xxxvi. 28 Cometh he to be when the will From overplus Twisteth out of natural measure. **1969** *Worship* XLIII. 394 In origin, the sacred is an overplus of meaning expressed with such power that it overwhelms everyone who perceives it. This overplus is beyond analysis.

over-pole, *v.* Add: Hence **overpo·led** *ppl. a.*, **overpol·ing** *vbl. sb.*

1742 W. ELLIS *Mod. Husbandman* Aug. xx. 98 Over-poling [of hops] is worse than Under-poling. **1758, 1861** Overpoled [in Dict.] **1890** Overpoling [in Dict., sense 2]. **1910** *Jrnl. Inst. Metals* IV. 207 In the case of 'overpoled' copper the gases were released in such a quantity as to not only neutralise the effect of shrinkage, but to elevate the surface of the ingot. *Ibid.* 230 'Poling' could be pushed further, before the stage of 'overpoling' was reached, than could be done in the case of pure copper. **1930** *Ibid.* XLIII. 121 Hence a very slight further poling beyond the point *A* will cause a marked increase in the porosity of the ingot; the surface will rise and all the defects of overpoling will appear. **1937** ARCHBUTT & PRYTHERCH *Effect of Impurities in Copper* iii. 34 Overpoled metal is not in a satisfactory condition to withstand rolling and fabrication for two reasons. **1949** J. E. GARSIDE *Process & Physical Metall.* xxii. 378 If poling has been too prolonged the cuprous oxide content is very low. This gives rise to the evolution of considerable quantities of water vapour on solidification and the metal expands in the mould, forming a ridge. Such material, too brittle for many purposes, is termed 'overpoled copper'.

over-population. (Earlier and later examples.)

1823 J. S. MILL in *Black Dwarf* XI. 754 Not only the master manufacturer but the landowner also, has an interest in over population. **1826** MALTHUS *Diary* 10 July (1966) 265 Landlord at Kenmore complained of the drought, the fall in the price of cattle, and the overpopulation of the country. **1959** A. HUXLEY *Let.* 26 Nov. (1969) 880 It may turn out to be hideously tragic when their efforts to modernize the country break down under the combined pressures of inefficiency and over-population. **1971** *Daily Tel.* (Colour Suppl.) 3 Dec. 24/3 Forrester has designed a model of the world system to try to discover the long term effects of pollution and overpopulation. **1977** *Times* 31 May 5/4 Mexico..is exporting its over-population.

overpotential (ōu·vəɹpŏtenʃăl). [OVER- 19, 29.] = *OVERVOLTAGE 1, 2.

1920 *Jrnl. Amer. Chem. Soc.* XLII. 94 Overpotential varies with the nature of the electrode. **1961** A. C. WHISH in G. F. Tagg *Pract. Electr. Engin.* II. 292 For the over-potential tests the transformer is excited in the normal way on one winding to twice or more than twice the value of its rated voltage. **1974** *Encycl. Brit. Macropædia* VI. 644/1 The overpotential can be considered as logarithmically dependent on the current density.

o:verprescri·be, *v.* [OVER- 27.] *trans.* and *intr.* To prescribe an excessive amount of (a drug). Hence **o:verprescri·bing** *vbl. sb.*; **o:ver-prescri·ption.**

1953 *Times* 31 Oct. 4/3 Many doctors admitted that since the introduction of the shilling prescription they often tended to over-prescribe to save the patient coming back for an extra shilling's worth. **1967** N. LUCAS *C.I.D.* x. 138 The over-prescribing of drugs by a small number of doctors. **1968** *New Scientist* 28 Mar. 679/2 There is the agricultural merchant who bends the regulations, there is the veterinary surgeon who over-prescribes, and finally there is the unscrupulous retail pharmacist. **1969** *Observer* 9 Nov. 3/5 Doctors could exercise greater control by restraining themselves from over-prescribing drugs. **1970** *Times* 4 Nov. 6 Dr. Hindmarch blames overprescription by doctors as the main source of illicit amphetamines. **1972** *Science* 26 May 883/2 Yet physicians themselves have a sense that they, as a group, over-prescribe and overuse psychoactive drugs. **1974** M. C. GERALD *Pharmacol.* xi. 205 In a recent survey of 55 physicians in the Boston area, 37 felt that their fellow physicians were overprescribing sedatives.

overpressure. Add to def.: pressure (of a fluid) in excess of that which is normal or allowed for. (Further examples.)

1936 B. JONES *Elem. Pract. Aerodynamics* xviii. 290 The pressure gages should be watched closely, especially before take-off. Overpressure indicates a stoppage in the line. **1941** O. E. PATTON *Aircraft Instruments* x. 153 The suction and overpressure tests are given to find out what will happen to the gauge if it is subjected to pressures below atmospheric or exceeding their normal range. **1962** *Trans. Faraday Soc.* LVIII. 194 A quantitative hydrogenation of a solution of the polymer in benzene was attempted using..an over-pressure of hydrogen (*ca.* 700 mm). **1963** *Ann. Med. Internae Fenniae* LII. 212 The idea of employment of over-pressure directed into the human organism may be questioned in principle. **1977** *Sci. Amer.* Mar. 82/1 Just above the vocal folds are the two 'false' vocal folds, which are engaged when someone holds his breath with an over-pressure of air in the lungs.

b. *spec.* The difference between the (highest) instantaneous pressure at a point subjected to a shock wave and the ambient atmospheric pressure.

1955 *Communications Pure & Appl. Maths.* VIII. 340 We evaluated the *D* corresponding to the shock over-pressure of 5°. **1961** *Shell Aviation News* No. 278. 9/2 It's quite conceivable that a ground overpressure of only 0·1 lb per square foot may be decidedly unacceptable to the farmer... and 0·04 lb per square foot to those who value peace and quiet. **1967** *Guardian* 5 July 1/8 Overpressures will vary from 1 to 1·5 lb a sq. ft. which is less than the maximum Concord bang. **1975** *Sci. Amer.* July 15/3 Overpressure is proportional to the energy released by a nuclear charge and is inversely proportional to the cube of the distance from the point of explosion.

overpri·ce, *v.* [OVER- 22, 27.] *trans.* To price (something) more highly or excessively highly; to price a commodity beyond the means of (someone). Also *absol.* Hence **overpri·cing** *vbl. sb.*

1605 P. ERONDELLE *French Garden* sig. K[v], Buye for me yonder waistcoate..for if I cheapen it, they will ouer price it me by the halfe, As for you, they knowe you haue better skill in it. **1972** K. BONFIGLIOLI *Don't point that Thing at Me* i. 5 He was the second greatest art-dealer of the century: he poisoned his life trying to over-price Duveen out of the field. **1976** 'Z. STONE' *Modigliani Scandal* i. iii. 29 My view is that you have been over-priced for some time... At present few of your canvases deserve to fetch more than £325. **1977** D. CLARK *Gimmel Flask* iii. 49 The antique world offers tremendous scope for faking,..underselling, overpricing and so on.

over-priced, *a.* Add: (Later examples.) Also, of a commodity: priced too highly.

1977 T. HEALD *Just Desserts* vii. 153 Rubbery prawns with over-priced vinegary Mexican wine. **1978** M. KENYON *Deep Pocket* i. 5 The vendors of over-priced ice-cream at Marble Arch.

overprint, *sb.* Add: **2.** [OVER- 8 c.] **a.** Overprinted matter, esp. on a postage stamp (see quot. 1913). **b.** The action or result of over-printing.

1876 *Let.* 6 Sept. in J. Easton *De La Rue Hist. Brit. & Foreign Postage Stamps, 1855–1901* (1958) xxiv. 710 We should be furnished with the duties which are to fall in the stamps clearly written or printed, so that we might avoid mistakes in making the overprint. **1899** *Captain* I. 421/2 The correct over-print should have been 'Z.C. de peso'. **1912** KNECHT & FOTHERGILL *Princ. & Pract. Textile Printing* VII. 319 Its darker colour will mask the paler tint of the over-print. **1913** E. B. EVANS *Stamps* (ed. 4) 58 *Overprint*, some addition to the design or inscriptions, printed or written upon a stamp which was already complete and fit for use without any such addition. **1928** *Daily Mail* 7 Aug. 18/4 On three values of this printing some sheets received the overprint upside down. **1938** KNOPF & INGERSON *Struct. Petrology* xiv. 197 Upon this earlier movement there was stamped an oblique overprint of a later deformation, now recorded in the quartz fabric. **1938** E. RAISZ *Gen. Cartography* xvi. 188 Each drawing must have register marks for perfect overprint. **1965** *Jrnl. Neurosurg.* XIII. 346 The pulses received by the scaler may be recorded by statistical overprint with a telegraphic printer. **1971** *Nature* 18 June 463/1 (*caption*) At top, 3 weeks raw data in °F with overprint of best fit cosine ware. **1973** *Daily Tel.* 23 June 25/6 The 10F on 90c exists with inverted overprint and makes about £1,500 in this condition.

over-print, *v.* Add: **2.** To print too many copies of (a book, etc.). Also *absol.*

1909 in WEBSTER. **1931** H. G. WELLS *Work, Wealth & Happiness of Mankind* (1932) ix. 353 The belligerent governments withdrew gold from internal circulation and resorted to the printing press to replace it. Each in its own measure overprinted. **1962** *Which?* Sept. 274/2 We always overprint and there are a few copies of this available if you should want it.

II. [OVER- 8.] **3.** *trans.* **a.** To print additional matter on (a surface already bearing print); to mark by a subsequent printing process. Also *transf.*

1863 in J. Easton *De La Rue Hist. Brit. & For. Postage Stamps, 1855–1901* (1958) xii. 263 Printed first from the Sixpenny plate and afterwards overprinted one penny & fourpence. **1876** *Let.* 6 Sept. in *Ibid.* xxiv. 710 As it is impossible to overprint the full sheet at one operation, and at the same time ensure the overprinted matter falling truly in the panels left blank for it, we could only overprint half the sheet at a time. **1899** *Captain* I. 187/1 The current stamps of Great Britain were overprinted with the company's name. **1912** KNECHT & FOTHERGILL *Princ. & Pract. Textile Printing* VII. 319 Dry the goods well and then—(2) Over-print them with either a cover or pad roller in steam Alizarin red or pink. **1912** *Chambers's Jrnl.* Nov. 750/2 In 1903 permission was again granted to firms to overprint the backs of stamps. **1950** *Chambers's Encycl.* II. 788/1 A white spot on a coloured ground will be obtained by first printing the fabric with a paste containing a reserve chemical and then over-printing with a thickened solution of a dye which will be destroyed or its fixation be prevented by the reserve chemical. **1967** *Q. Jrnl. Geol. Soc.* CXXIII. 274 In the north-west corner of Sheet 10/iii at Lepeidere the *A* and *B* domains come together and both are 'overprinted' and partly obliterated by *C* tectonism. **1974** *B.S.I. News* Jan. 14 BSI is prepared to accept bulk orders for copies of any one standard and have the covers overprinted to the purchaser's requirements. **1974** *Nature* 27 Sept. 296/2 Granite was part of a widespread event which overprinted any isotopic record of the early history of the gneisses in the area.

b. To print (additional matter) on a surface already bearing printing; to add by a subsequent printing process. Also *transf.*

1926 C. F. D. MARSHALL *Brit. Post Office* I. vi. 54 On the 1st of January, 1883, the 3d...and 6d...made their appearance in lilac, with the value overprinted in carmine. **1937** *Q. Jrnl. Geol. Soc.* XCIII. 583 There may be complete obliteration of the earlier fabric.., but frequently a second fabric is 'overprinted' on the earlier.. without complete loss of the latter's characteristics. **1938** E. RAISZ *Gen. Cartography* xvii. 199 The French overprinted a network of even kilometer squares upon their maps. **1975** J. B. HARLEY *O.S. Maps* ii. 21 This grid..was overprinted on War Office editions of Ordnance Survey maps.

So **o:verpri·nted** *ppl. a.*, **o:verpri·nting** *vbl. sb.*

1876 Overprinted [see sense 3 a above]. **1912** KNECHT & FOTHERGILL *Princ. & Pract. Textile Printing* VII. 320 The ground will be plain or 'patterned' according as the roller used in the second- or over-printing was a 'pad' or a cover. **1931** H. G. WELLS *Work, Wealth & Happiness of Mankind* (1932) ix. 353 The overprinting of paper money continued. **1962** *Collier's Encycl.* XVIII. 679/2 *Surcharged and overprinted*, stamps on which a new value or name has been printed; 'surcharge' is used when over-printing involves change in value. **1971** I. G. GASS et al. *Understanding Earth* ii. 51/1 Overprinted age patterns may span the entire interval between two (or more) thermal events. **1975** J. B. HARLEY *O.S. Maps* ix. 143 In addition to the coloured administrative diagrams, 1:100 000 scale base maps printed in grey are available without overprinting.

over-pri·vileged, *a.* [OVER- 28 d.] Possessing or enjoying too many privileges. Also *absol.*

1934 *Word Study* Mar. 6/2 If this country has an over-privileged class, it is the railroad phoneticians. **1941** *Times Educ. Suppl.* 6 Dec. 581/1 The over-privileged classes..and in general what is crudely described as the 'old school tie' influence in Government, business, and the professions, see their privileges threatened. **1956** C. W. MILLS *Power Elite* i. 14 The moral conception of the elite, however, is not always merely an ideology of the over-privileged. **1971** P. WORSTHORNE *Socialist Myth* viii. 192 Today..the majority..is not only overprivileged politically; it is overprivileged economically. **1973** *Nature* 16 Mar. 210/2 The weak and the poor are under-privileged because we are over-privileged.

over-production. Add: (Later examples.) Also *attrib.*

1934 C. LAMBERT *Music Ho!* IV. 233 The present age is one of overproduction. **1948** G. CROWTHER *Outl. Money* (rev. ed.) v. 151 'Over-production' and a slump result. *Ibid.* 153 The 'over-production' theory, then, like the 'under-consumption' theory, is, in a sense, sometimes right, but for the wrong reasons. **1960** *Farmer & Stockbreeder* 19 Jan. (Suppl.) 50/3 Over-production of Eggs sank prices to rock-bottom in 1959. **1974** M. B. BROWN *Econ. of Imperialism* viii. 199 The general opinion held in Germany in the mid 1880s was that colonies were needed to solve the problem of overproduction. **1974** *Country Life* 26 Dec. 2019/1 In America there has been overproduction resulting in shutdowns. **1975** *New Yorker* 21 Apr. 7/2 She is most effective as a live performer of her own material—projecting a loose, direct, unpretentious, spontaneous style that, unfortunately, is lacking on her records, which suffer from overproduction.

over-proof, *a.* (*sb.*) Add: (Later examples.) Also *fig.*

1906 *Daily Chron.* 11 May 9/2 The appeal to the Government..asking them to prohibit the importation of over-proof spirits into British territory. **1967** N. Marsh *Death at Dolphin* iv. 94 She really *is*..the original overproof *femme fatale.* **1973** J. Wood *North Beat* x. 131 'Try a punch at the brew,' the sergeant suggested. Collins tried a punch. He coughed..'What is it—some of the overproof stuff?'

o:verprote·ction. *Psychol.* [Over- 29 b.] The condition or act of protecting (someone, esp. a child) to an undue or unhealthy extent.

1930 *Smith Coll. Stud. Social Work* I. 42 Such over-protection would be increased if the child were sickly or handicapped in any way. **1938** D. M. Levy in *Psychiatry* I. 569/2 We would thus succeed in isolating those personality factors..that would be..a result of maternal overprotection. **1949** S. A. Stouffer et al. *Amer. Soldier* iv. 135 A theory currently of considerable interest in psychiatry seeks to trace some types of neurotic behavior to overprotection by the mother. **1964** M. Argyle *Psychol. & Social Probl.* ix. 123 Hysteria and psychosomatic complaints, especially in women, are related to a history of overprotection by the mother. **1970** H. Edelston *Foundations & Growth of Character* iii. i. 96 Just as maternal deprivation can be harmful in its effects, so can maternal overprotection. **1977** A. Wilson *Strange Ride R. Kipling* vi. 275 Much of her over-protection may have come from her sense of his strain.

So **overprote·ctive** *a.*, that protects to an undue or unhealthy extent; **overprote·ctiveness**, the state or condition of being over-protective. Also **overprote·ct** *v. trans.*; **overprote·cted, -prote·cting** *ppl. adjs.*

1930 *Smith Coll. Stud. Social Work* I. 58 One or both parents over-protective, rejecting, or were overambitious, as the category indicates. **1938** D. M. Levy in *Psychiatry* I. 569/2 How their personality traits resulting from growth in the medium of the overprotecting mother have shaped their destinies. **1949** M. Mead *Male & Female* xv. 310 He is often..over-protective towards his son. **1957** R. B. Cattell *Personality & Motivation* iv. 135 It is a sociological pattern, varying from family to family of 'Overprotectiveness—vs—Tough Neglect'. **1961** Webster s.v. *Overprotect*, Overprotected children. **1964** M. Argyle *Psychol. & Social Probl.* vi. 80 Women are prone to hysteria, especially when they have had a dominating mother who has over-protected them, thus concentrating attention on bodily complaints. *Ibid.* ix. 120 Several investigators reported that schizophrenics have mothers who are over-protecting, but when control groups have been used no such difference is found. **1969** M. D. Vernon *Human Motivation* x. 161 Even over-protectiveness..tends to create anxiety. **1973** R. Lewis *Blood Money* v. 60 She hadn't wanted him to talk to her daughter... She was over-protective. **1976** *Times* 1 Sept. 14/1 A warning against over-protecting elderly people. **1977** R. Barnard *Blood Brotherhood* xiv. 150 Over-protected and over-driven, Philip had drifted through.. life.

o:ver-pu·blicize, *v.* [Over- 27 a.] *trans.* To publicize too much or to excess; to give undue importance to by publicizing. So **o:ver-pu·blicized** *ppl. a.*

1939 *War Illustr.* 4 Nov. p. ii/1, I regard Lindbergh's pronouncement on the War as a piece of gratuitous impertinence... One of the most grossly over-publicised personalities of our age he expects too much if he thinks his words must carry weight just because he once flew the Atlantic. **1957** L. Feather *Bk. of Jazz* (1959) xv. 132 Admittedly the drummer today is over-publicized, over-featured and over-praised in proportion to the role he should play as a member of an ensemble. **1964** E. A. Nida *Toward Sci. Transl.* xii. 252 It is unfortunate that MT (standard abbreviation for machine translation) has been over-publicized. **1965** 'W. Haggard' *Hard Sell* i. 1 Over-publicized world beaters which mysteriously disintegrated.

o·verpunch, *sb. Computers.* [Over- 1 d.] A hole or hole position in the upper portion of a punched card.

1969 Maisel & Wright *Introd. Electronic Digital Computers* xiii. 325 If the overpunch is a 12, the number is positive, and if it is an 11 punch, the number is negative. **1970** O. Dopping *Computers & Data Processing* ii. 44 The two top rows are called zone punches or overpunches. The uppermost row is called 12 or Y, the second from the top, 11 or X. In addition, the uppermost numerical row, the 0 row, is used as a third overpunch. **1973** Murrill & Smith *Introd. Computer Sci.* vi. 219 When programs written in programming languages such as Cobol read numerical data, the sign does not normally occupy a separate column. Instead, it is entered as an overpunch in the rightmost digit.

So **o·verpunch** *v. trans.*, to represent by means of an overpunch; **o·verpu:nching** *vbl. sb.*

1962 *Gloss. Terms Automatic Data Processing* (*B.S.I.*) 90 *Over-punching*, the use of the upper curtate to represent a digit independently of the use of the lower curtate. **1973** Murrill & Smith *Introd. Computer Sci.* vi. 220 Figure 6·6 also illustrates the situation when the & symbol is overpunched in the same column as the 3.

overrange (ōu·vəɹ,rēɪndʒ), *sb. Electr.* [Over- 5, 13.] **a.** A signal larger or condition stronger than an instrument is designed to accept or measure. Freq. *attrib.* **b.** An extension of the nominal range of an instrument.

1941 T. J. Rhodes *Industr. Instruments for Measurement & Control* iii. 73 This may result in dangerously high pressures if the instrument is subjected to temperatures much higher than those for which it was designed. Usually these overrange temperatures are accidents which can be avoided. *Ibid.* 74 Where the instrument is subject to periodic overrange..it is necessary to provide a means of overrange protection. **1974** *Nature* 15 Nov. p. ix/2 (Advt.), 4-digit electronic display read-out, with 100% over-range, i.e. up to 19999. **1976** *Physics Bull.* Mar. 131/3 This instrument also has a digital voltmeter output and meter overrange protection.

overrate, *v.* Add: **2.** *Rowing.* [Over- 22.] To row at a faster rate than (an opponent).

1960 *Times* 4 Apr. 14/1 They [*sc.* Oxford] were still overrating Cambridge. **1961** *Times* 10 July 4/6 Lady Margaret made no mistakes in the Ladies' Plate, snatched an early lead, and, always overrating Eton, came home by a length and a third.

overreach, *sb.* Add: **1. b.** (Later examples.)

1961 B. Fergusson *Watery Maze* xv. 370 In Burma the Japs made their classic over-reach between March and June of 1944, when..they attempted to surround and defeat the British and Indian forces in Manipur. **1977** *Time* 10 Jan. 55/3 Felker's personal grandeur may match his managerial overreach. Since last spring he has asked for: 1) a 25% increase in his 1975 salary of $120,461, 2) the wherewithal to buy a house in Long Island's ducal Hamptons, and 3) company purchase of his super-duplex.

2. (Later examples.) Also *attrib.*

1932 J. Buchan *Gap in Curtain* iv. 193 Verona's mare got an overreach in a bog. **1949** 'J. Tey' *Brat Farrar* xxviii. 250 All the horses were safely back and all well except that Buster had an overreach. **1963** E. H. Edwards *Saddlery* xx. 151 A common injury sustained when jumping is caused by an over-reach and, in show jumpers, this often occurs low down on the heel or just above it. A rubber over-reach boot is usually the answer. **1976** *Horse & Hound* 10 Dec. 5/1 You would still have to change your clothes before riding and again when you returned, in order to remove muddy over-reach boots and turn your horse out.

overreaching, *vbl. sb.* (Further examples.)

1802 [see *dicker *v.*]. **1933** H. Belloc *William the Conqueror* 55 At that moment appeared the go-between who settled the whole affair, earning thereby the permanent gratitude and protection of Godwin and his sons. But it was an overreaching. They had better have kept away from such an ally! **1971** *New York Law Jrnl.* 23 Nov. 18/5 The 1955 amendment..was adopted..to protect such tenants from overreaching by landlords who authorized commercial and busines sleases upon tenants. **1977** A. Wilson *Strange Ride R. Kipling* iv. 202 His apprehensions of disaster brought on by overreaching and vainglory.

over-react (ōu:vəɹ,rɪ,æ·kt), *v.* [Over- 27.] *intr.* To respond with excessive force or emotion to a given situation. Hence **o:ver-rea·cting** *vbl. sb.*; **o:ver-rea·ction.**

1961 L. Mumford *City in Hist.* i. 26 At the same time, the male over-reacted against the feminine side of his own nature. **1962** *Times* 21 Aug. 5/6 The more emotional.. person tended to over-react to stress. **1965** *Economist* 13 Nov. 705/3 Some critics do think that the United States is in danger of getting its priorities wrong, by over-reacting to the threat of China and under-reacting to the possibilities of easing the Soviet dominance of east-central Europe. **1967** C. Cockburn *I Claud* xxxiv. 424 This 'over-reaction' to what were..reasonable queries and doubts, was psychologically very revealing. **1968** *Listener* 26 Sept. 410/1 This was the first escalation, triggered off when the militants goaded the authorities into over-reacting, closing the faculties and calling in the police. **1971** J. Osborne *West of Suez* i. 22, I just hope he..gets some innocent pleasure out of it, which he's entitled to without censorious philistines like me over-reacting. **1973** E.-J. Bahr *Nice Neighbourhood* x. 106 Jack cried despairingly. He always over-reacted. **1973** *Times* 16 Nov. 7/2 A number of Government members believed that the espionage charges levelled against the editors constituted an over-reaction to the articles published in the magazine. **1974** M. C. Gerald *Pharmacol.* i. 12 Whether this was an over-reaction to questionable laboratory results or a sound scientific decision destined to rescue mankind remains to be seen at a future, less emotionally charged time. **1976** *Times Lit. Suppl.* 22 Oct. 1324/4 The hostility to the medium which he encountered in the early days led Strand (like some other major photographers) to over-react, to overcompensate by being rather too serious, too ponderous, too unbending.

over-read, *v.* **2.** Delete †*Obs.* and add later example.

1925 W. de la Mare *Two Tales* 14 He was merely over-reading what he had read.

over-reave (ōuvəɹ,rī·v), *v.* [Etym. uncertain; perhaps f. Over- 16 + a confusion of Reeve *v.*[1] and Weave *v.*[1]] *trans.* A term used of the metre of his poetry by G. M. Hopkins, to denote scansion continued for a complete stanza, as distinct from that confined to individual lines (see quots.). So **over-rea·ving** *vbl. sb.*

1879 G. M. Hopkins *Lett. to R. Bridges* (1935) 86 These little graces help the 'over-reaving' of the verse at which I so much aim, make it flow in one long strain to the end of the stanza and so forth. **1880** —— *Let.* 22 Dec. in Hopkins & Dixon *Corr.* (1935) 40 In lyric verse I like sprung rhythm also to be *over-rove*, that is the scanning to run on from line to line to the end of the stanza. **1881** —— *Lett. to R. Bridges* (1935) 120 In my lyrics in sprung rhythm I am strict in overreaving the lines when the measure has four feet, so that if one line has a heavy ending the next must have a sprung head. **1973** *Studies in Eng. Lit.: Eng. Number* (Tokyo) 25 'Over-reaving', or the scanning of verse without break from line to line, is a structural necessity following upon the method of scansion Hopkins proposes for sprung rhythm.

over-record, *v.* [Over- 27.] *trans.* **a.** To record using too large a signal, so that distortion occurs. **b.** To make too many recordings of (a work or performer). So **over-reco·rded** *ppl. a.*, **over-reco·rding** *vbl. sb.*

1961 E. N. Bradley *Records & Gramophone Equipment* i. 23 Inter-groove modulation is caused by over-recording, or by too small a spacing between grooves. **1976** *Gramophone* Sept. 432/2 The comparatively little-recorded *Hamlet*..is linked with the vastly over-recorded *Serenade* for strings. **1977** *Ibid.* Mar. 1467/1 They might well buy the disc for Sabicas, who is not over-recorded these days. **1977** *Rolling Stone* 24 Mar. 79/3 The expanded 'louds' would cause overrecording or tape saturation.

override, *v.* Add: **3. b.** (Further example.)

1932 *Amer. Jrnl. Physiol.* C. 116 There is a significant difference between the amounts of theelin needed to blot out the normal progestational picture as compared to the amount it takes to over-ride a rabbit unit of injected corporin.

c. To cause the operation of (an automatic device) to be suspended, esp. in favour of manual control.

1946 [implied in *overriding* ppl. adj. below]. **1949** *Gloss. Aeronaut. Terms* (*B.S.I.*) ii. 11 *Boost control override*, a device to override the boost control so that a pressure higher than the normal controlled pressure can be obtained. **1967** *Instrumentation Technol.* Aug. 38/1 (*caption*) Differential pressure across column overrides temperature control. **1971** *Daily Tel.* 20 Oct. 2/2 It has four forward gears and reverse controlled by a speed-sensing governor which can be overridden by the driver using a gear lever. **1975** *Nature* 20 Mar. 193/1 An interactive computer display system using manual intervention where necessary to override automatic procedures has proved adequate.

o·verride, *sb.* [f. prec. vb.] The action or process of suspending an automatic function; a device for performing this. Freq. *attrib.*

1946 *Aircraft Engin.* XVIII. 112/1 A manual over-ride for landing operation would be necessary. **1949** [see *override *v.* 3 c]. **1952** A. Y. Bramble *Air-Plane Flight* x. 154 There is an 'over-ride' control introduced, by which the automatic limitation of boost can be exceeded at the will of the pilot in particular circumstances. **1957** *Practical Wireless* XXXIII. 697/1 The only connections yet to be made are those coupling up the override switch to the appropriate part in the circuit. **1963** *Amat. Photographer* 7 Aug. 43/1 (Advt.), Fully automatic [camera] with manual over-ride. **1968** *Instrumentation Technol.* Aug. 53/1 Overrides can be designed to provide gradual, rather than abrupt, corrective action and they can function in both directions so that manual reset is not required. **1974** 'A. Haig' *Peruvian Printout* 39 He pressed the override switch and the computer came instantly to life. **1976** *Offshore Platforms & Pipelining* 203/1 Mechanical overrides are provided should any of the automatic equipment fail.

overrider (ōu·vəɹ,rəi:dəɹ). Also **over-rider.** [f. Over- 8 c + Rider 12.] One of a pair of projecting pieces attached to the bumper of a car, affording added protection to the bodywork.

1937 *Times* 18 Oct. 20/3 The bumpers have over-riders. **1959** *Times* 6 Jan. 12/1 The overriders on bumpers must not have dangerous protuberances. **1963** J. T. Story *Something for Nothing* iii. 83 The Jaguar with its big overriders had suffered not at all. **1963** [see *mud flap* s.v. *mud *sb.*[1] 5]. **1974** 'A. Haig' *Peruvian Printout* 123 The bastard was ramming her back bumper. Thank God she had overriders fitted. **1975** J. Pidgeon *Flame* ii. 32 The charging Chevy's [*sc.* Chevrolet's] chrome overriders gored the big red and white arrow that pointed diagonally across the carriageway and tossed it high over the roof.

overriding, *vbl. sb.* and *ppl. a.* Add: (Further examples.) *spec.* **overriding commission,** an extra or additional commission. Also **o:verri·dingly** *adv.*

1894 Over-riding commission [in Dict.]. **1906** *Westm. Gaz.* 15 Feb. 11/1 As a rule, the terms of commission, both underwriting and 'over-riding', are very literal. **1930** W. S. Churchill *My Early Life* xiii. 184, I had not heard a word in Cairo of how Sir Herbert Kitchener had received the over-riding by the War Office of his wishes upon my appointment. **1930** A. Palmer *Company Secretarial Pract.* 47 Companies frequently pay 'over-riding' commission also. This is a commission paid to persons for procuring other persons who are willing to underwrite blocks of shares. **1946** R. A. McFarland *Human Factors Air Transport Design* x. 148 Many pilots feel..that in the event of an emergency they must have immediate access to engine instruments. Overriding throttle controls for the pilot may be advisable. **1956** A. H. Compton *Atomic Quest* ii. 126 If Oppenheimer has an 'Achilles' heel, it is his overriding loyalty to his friends. **1957** J. S. Huxley *Relig. without Revelation* (rev. ed.) ix. 232 If the full development of human individuals and the fulfilment of human possibilities is the over-riding aim of our evolution, then any over-population which brings malnutrition and misery, or which erodes the world's material resources.., is evil. **1968** *Lebende Sprachen* XIII. 5/1 All diverse organizations must be harnessed together into a single team directed towards the single overriding objective. **1969** W. K. Roots *Fund. Temperature Control* v. 118 An inexpensive overriding command system provides both the 'night shut down' and 'vacant-room shut down', features that can significantly reduce the heating cost of public buildings. **1973** A. Quinton *Nature of Things* 378 He cannot..maintain that morality is overridingly authoritative in this sense.

over-ripeness. Add: (Later examples.) Also *fig.*

1876 G. Meredith *Beauch. Career* III. x. 183 Immense wealth and native obtuseness combine to disfigure us with the aspect of over-ripeness, not to say monstrosity. **1904** [see *hypermaturity* s.v. *hyper- IV.]. **1976** *Listener* 12 Aug. 172/1 Henry James appraised Warwickshire... He felt a ripeness, he hints at an over-ripeness.

overroof, *v.* (Earlier example.)

a **1828** D. Wordsworth *Jrnl.* (1941) II. 272 The track ..was..over-roofed, like an outside staircase of a Castle.

over-ru·ff, *v.* [Over- 22.] *trans.* To over-trump. Also *absol.* and (with stress on first syllable) as *sb.*, an act or instance of over-ruffing.

1813 *Hoyle's Games of Whist & Quadrille* 50 *Ruff*, and *over-ruff*, to trump a suit led, second or third hand. *c* **1890** *Up to Date Games of Cards* 37 Ruff means to trump a suit second or third hand, when you are rid of that suit: *over-ruff* means to trump above. **1906** *Westm. Gaz.* 13 Oct. 14/1 Had A held neither of these cards he would have surely led a diamond.., instead of putting his partner to an over-ruff in the spade. **1926** M. C. Work *Auction Bridge Complete* ii. ii. 331 He should lead trumps before taking the ruff and so avoid any chance of an over-ruff... Dummy's ruff of the losing Club might be over-ruffed. **1974** *Oxford Times* 12 July 10/8 North can ruff in whenever he likes, but dummy overruffs and plays a diamond. **1975** *Times* 16 Aug. 7/4 East was end-played, whether or not he over-ruffed. **1976** *Country Life* 26 Feb. 498/1 When you see the chance of an easy overruff, don't be in too much of a hurry to take it.

overrun, *sb.* Add: **2. b.** An excess of expenditure over that estimated or budgeted for.

1956 *Wall St. Jrnl.* 10 Oct. 12/3 Some of our government officials get carried away with the thought of spending $156 million plus the over-run beyond the estimate. **1960** *Times* 21 Nov. (Canada Suppl.) p. xiii/2 Among these were cases of capital overruns and operating returns poorer than expected. **1973** *Nature* 23 Mar. 224/3 If there are cost overruns on the first two missions, the third may be scrapped. **1974** *Times* 26 Oct. 15/1 Britain's own advanced gas cooled reactor programme is hopelessly compromised by massive cost overruns brought about by.. constructional delays. **1976** *Sci. Amer.* July 122/1 The total cost had been $8 million, an overrun of some 40 percent. **1978** *Daily Tel.* 13 Apr. 21 This sum..is just under half what remains in the contingency reserve for overruns on public expenditure.

c. An excess of production.

1958 T. Landau *Encycl. Librarianship* 230/2 *Overrun*, copies surplus to the number ordered. **1962** J. N. Winburne *Dict. Agric.* 539/2 *Overrun*,..the excess amount of lumber actually sawed from logs over the estimated volume or log scale, usually expressed as a percentage of log scale. **1970** *Toronto Daily Star* 24 Sept. 27/1 (Advt.), Our huge purchase includes many carloads of the top lines of merchandise, plus close-outs, over-runs, sample bales.

3. (Examples.)

1898 J. Southward *Mod. Printing* I. xxxiv. 210 When there is a long over-run, the matter should be placed upon a small galley, which should be turned, so that the last line rests against its head. **1902** T. L. De Vinne *Pract. Typogr.: Correct Composition* (ed. 2) xvi. 309 Every paragraph containing an alteration that compels one or more overruns should be re-read. **1935** B. Perry *And gladly Teach* vii. 169 When the forms were made up, there was an over-run of three lines. **1977** *New Yorker* 26 Sept. 64/3 The *Times*..ran a front-page story, with a four-column overrun on a rear page.

4. The proportional increase in bulk that occurs when butter fat is made into butter or an ice-cream mix is made into ice-cream.

1906 H. Snyder *Dairy Chem.* vii. 71 During the process of butter making, the slight loss of fat in the skim milk and buttermilk is more than compensated for by the added water, casein, and salt in the butter. The additional butter made from a pound of butter fat is called the overrun. **1922** Mojonnier & Troy *Techn. Control Dairy Products* xv. 443 Insufficient overrun greatly increases the cost of the ice cream, and yields a product that is immediately detected by its heavy and soggy appearance. **1958** *Sunday Times* 22 June 23/6 Overrun is the aeration or amount any given mix [for ice-cream] will swell in volume when subjected to the freezing process. **1972** *New York* 15 May 4/1 (Advt.), The best coffee ice cream in New York... Sixteen per cent butterfat, 50 per cent overrun; one pint weighs 12¾ ounces.

5. Motion of a vehicle at a speed greater than that being imparted by the engine; freq. in phr. *on the overrun*. Also *attrib.*, designating a system of braking in a towed vehicle (see quot. 1967).

1928 *Observer* 8 Jan. 21/4 The engine runs smoothly and quietly throughout most of its range. There is a certain drumming noise, rather difficult to define and trace, on the over-run, but it is comparatively trifling. **1959** *Motor Manual* (ed. 36) v. 141 This..is at a maximum when the engine is on the over-run. *Ibid.* xiii. 273 When the car brakes are applied, or the car slows down against a closed throttle, the caravan tends to overrun, thus causing the bar to move back against the spring, push back the operating lever and thus apply the caravan brakes. This is known as the 'over-run' method. **1962** *Which? Car Suppl.* Oct. 131/2 The washers..would only operate properly when the engine was on the overrun, i.e. when the foot was taken off the accelerator. **1967** *Gloss. Caravan Terms (B.S.I.)* 2 *Overrun braking*, a system of braking in which the caravan brakes are automatically operated by the momentum of the caravan when the towing vehicle is braked. Normally this is achieved by mounting the coupling head on a shaft moving on the drawbar and restrained by a compression spring or a damper. **1969** J. G. Giles *Gears & Transmissions* i. 23 On down gradients heavy vehicles will drive the engine... On these over-run conditions, the transmission torques are reversed. **1977** *Good Motoring* May 3/1 A trailer with over-run brakes can weigh more than the kerb weight of the car, providing a limit of 40 mph is observed.

overrun, *v.* Add: **6.** (Further examples.)

1907 A. T. Ritchie *Let.* 4 July (1924) xii. 273 It [*sc.* Norway] is like Switzerland, but softer and bigger and not over-run. **1914** G. B. Shaw *Misalliance* p. li, We are over-run with Popes.

9. a. For 'Now *rare*' read 'Now chiefly *Mech.*'; *spec.* to rotate faster than.

1932 J. A. Moyer *Gasoline Automobiles* (ed. 4) viii. 382 The free-wheeling unit or overrunning clutch *G* is given this name because in this arrangement the driven member may overrun the driving member. **1955** W. H. Crouse *Automotive Transmissions* v. 123 The inner race drives, the outer race is driven. Also, the outer race can overrun, or turn faster than, the inner race. **1959** *Motor Manual* (ed. 36) xiii. 274 As the caravan over-runs the car, the shaft moves backwards against the spring and operates the brake-actuating lever. **1966** *McGraw-Hill Encycl. Sci. & Technol.* IX. 455/2 The second function [of an over-drive] is to permit the output shaft to overrun the transmission shaft.

10. a. (Further examples.)

1867 *Ball Players' Chron.* 14 Nov. 4/3 He fell over Murtha, who was in his way, and overran his base. **1889** E. Dowson *Let.* 24 Mar. (1967) 54 This appears to be an *extra* special [letter]: it is overrunning [*sic*] all limits. **1948** *News-Palladium* (Bluton Harbor, Mich.) 14 Aug. 6/3 Hazel, going down to second, overran the base as Joe Mack rifled the ball to McCoy. **1973** *Guardian* 1 Sept. 3 When he whispered to her she had overrun the schedule. **1974** M. S. Ehrich *Reincarnation of Peter Proud* xiv. 117 Daley stopped the Movieola... 'I overran it a little..I'll reverse the film.' **1977** *Times* 7 Feb. 7/2 In the opening three minutes Macdonald put Ross clean through, only for the wing half to overrun the ball after dribbling past the goalkeeper.

d. (Examples.) *spec.* in *Broadcasting*, to exceed the allotted time.

1959 *Sunday Express* 30 Aug. 17/3 Last time Borge overran by 15 minutes—and was kept on the air. **1962** A. Nisbett *Technique Sound Studio* i. 17 The announcer on duty in the continuity studio..must intervene if any contribution under-runs, over-runs, breaks down in the middle, or completely fails to materialize. **1962** *Rep. Comm. Broadcasting 1960* 95 in *Parl. Papers 1961–2* (Cmnd. 1753) IX. 259 The BBC bulletin is free to over-run when the service requires it. **1974** *Listener* 14 Feb. 209/1 Arthur Henderson, leader of the Labour rump, lost his head halfway through, thinking he was going to over-run, and ended in a gabble.

III. 12. [Over- 27.] To run (something) excessively; *spec.* (see quot. 1899).

1899 W. P. Maycock *Electr. Wiring* i. 48 If ordinary lamps..marked for 100 volts..be put on a circuit at, say, 105 volts, the light given will be increased by about 25 per cent., and the watts absorbed per candle-power diminished. This is called over-running lamps, and their life will..be short. **1926** T. T. Baker *Wireless Pict.* v. 67 It has been found convenient to use a 4·5 volt lamp over-run by a 6, 8 or even 10-volt battery. *Ibid.* 68 When a lamp is over-run it..becomes highly incandescent instantaneously. **1938** G. H. Sewell *Amateur Film-Making* iii. 35 The Photoflood is essentially a tungsten lamp of normal type which is 'overrun' by having a much higher pressure (voltage) of current passed through it than is normal for domestic burning. **1962** *Which?* Oct. 297/1 It is possible that many people over-run their [water-softening] units—that is, they are not aware of the moment when the water starts running hard, and go on using the hard water for a time.

overrunning, *vbl. sb.* (Further examples.)

1884 G. B. Shaw *Let.* 29 Aug. (1965) I. 95 The proofs.. ought not to be paged, as the insertion of additional slips would cause over-running. **1908** *Westm. Gaz.* 3 Apr. 12/1 Over-running in the cricket-field had..brought the doctors ..several youthful cases of a rather severe type. **1970** J. Seymour *Compan. Guide E. Anglia* ix. 166 The fishermen haul the shanks by hand using the technique known as 'overrunning'—or letting the boat drive down over the shank carried by the swift tide.

overrunning, *ppl. a.* Add: **2.** *overrunning clutch*: a clutch in which the normally driven member is able to rotate faster than the normally driving member.

1921 J. A. Moyer *Gasoline Automobiles* vii. 172 The engine is prevented from driving the [starting] motor by the use of an over-running clutch, which slips when the engine tends to drive the motor. **1930** [see *free wheel, free-wheel]. **1966** *McGraw-Hill Encycl. Sci. & Technol.* III. 224/1 The driven shaft can run faster than the driving shaft with an overrunning clutch. This action permits freewheeling as the driving shaft slows down or another source of power is applied.

over-sail, *v.*[1] Add: **3.** To sail beyond.

1851 H. Melville *Moby Dick* III. xlix. 295 I've over-sailed him [*sc.* Moby Dick]... Aye, he's chasing *me* now; not I *him*.

oversail, *v.*[3] Add: **2. a.** (Later examples.)

1960 N. Scarfe *Suffolk* 97/2 Columbine Hall..is an ancient moated manor house of beauty, standing straight out of the moat, its upper storey oversailing. **1978** A. & G. Ritchie *Anc. Monuments Orkney* 31 The lower parts of the walls are vertical, but the upper courses oversail slightly as they rise.

c. To project beyond or overhang (a base).

1912 C. E. Power *Eng. Mediaeval Archit.* ii. 483 In the Decorated period the triple roll base..begins to rise in height, often oversailing the plinth with flat under-side. **1931** *Antiquity* V. 48 The successive courses of the inner wall begin to oversail one another. **1938** *Proc. Prehistoric Soc.* IV. 199 The lowest layer was laid horizontally and each succeeding course was laid at an angle, each stone oversailing the other.

So **oversai·ling** *ppl. a.*

1833 J. C. Loudon *Encycl. Cottage, Farm & Villa Archit.* 227 These walls..should have what is called a. Welsh cornice (two or three oversailing (protruding) courses of brickwork). **1880** R. Blackmore *Mary Anerley* I. xvii. 278 Strong sunshine glared upon the over-saling [*sic*] tiles, and white buckled walls, and cracky lintels. **1954** N. Pevsner *Essex* 291 It has very heavy timbers and brackets to carry an oversailing upper storey. **1972** J. Fleming et al. *Penguin Dict. Archit.* (ed. 2) 209/2 *Oversailing courses*, a series of stone or brick courses, each one projecting beyond the one below it. **1976** *National Trust Newsletter* Autumn 12/1 A striking black and white timbered building with high oversailing gables.

oversalt, *v.* (Further examples.)

1816 Jane Austen *Emma* II. iii. 41 They must not over-salt the leg. **1939** S. Spender tr. *Toller's Pastor Hall* i. 14 Julie, tell cook not to oversalt the roast.

oversa·turated, *ppl. a.* [Over- 24 b.] Supersaturated; chiefly in *Petrol.*, applied to a rock or magma in which there is free silica (or some other specified oxide). Hence **o:versatura·tion,** the property of being oversaturated.

1913 S. J. Shand in *Geol. Mag.* Decade V. X. 510 Any rock which contains free quartz or tridymite of magmatic origin will be termed oversaturated. *Ibid.* 513 The connexion between mineral and chemical composition need not be obscured thereby, but rather the reverse, especially if..the relative degrees of oversaturation or undersaturation were introduced..in the classification. **1946** *Nature* 19 Oct. 549/1 We would rather expect such condensations to show no more rotation than the water droplets in a fog formed from oversaturated vapour. **1947** E. E. Wahlstrom *Igneous Minerals & Rocks* ix. 253 Rocks may be oversaturated, saturated, or undersaturated with respect to alumina or other oxides as well as with respect to silica. *Ibid.*, Free silica, which indicates oversaturation, is not present in rocks containing undersaturated minerals such as leucite and nephelite. **1974** A. D. Edgar in H. Sørensen *Alkaline Rocks* v. i. 357/1 The genesis of oversaturated alkaline rocks. **1974** W. C. Luth in *Ibid.* vi. vi. 506/2 Since the liquid is always silica oversaturated the crystalline assemblage must be silica undersaturated when a liquid is present.

oversay, *v.* Restrict †*Obs.* to senses in Dict. and add later example of sense b.

1874 [see Unswear *v.*].

c. To exaggerate, overstate.

1900 *Scribner's Mag.* Sept. 368/2 This is oversaying it, of course, but the truth is in what I say. **1933** *G.K.'s Weekly* 21 Sept. 41/2, I assure you that if what I say runs towards superlatives it does not oversay what I still think and feel.

Hence **oversay·ing** *vbl. sb.*

1916 T. MacDonagh *Lit. in Ireland* 46 Latin dispenses with the redundancies, the over-sayings, compressing a phrase into a verb.

overscore, *v.* Add: **b.** (Later examples.) Also *fig.*

1901 E. F. Benson *Luck of Vails* III. xii. 115 The gentle hum of the warm afternoon came languidly in. Suddenly a fuller note began to overscore these noises in gradual crescendo. *Ibid.* xx. 233 The boon of the doctor's arrival quite overscored that sinister impression he had formed of him.

c. [Over- 27.] To score (music) with excessively elaborate orchestration. Also *absol.*

1947 N. Cardus *Autobiogr.* iii. 263 There is a fine sensibility moving darkly in the symphonies of Arnold Bax, but he tends to let his texture become congested; he over-scores. **1947** C. Gray *Contingencies* i. 37 The characteristic vice of overscoring is significant [in music of the Edwardian era]. **1977** *Gramophone* Feb. 1249/1 It is all too easy to dismiss his post-war orchestral works as garrulous, repetitive and over-scored.

overscraw·l, *v.* [Over- 8.] *trans.* To scrawl over or on. Hence **overscraw·led** *ppl. a.*

1871 Browning *Prince Hohenstiel-Schwangau* 28 Why keep each fool's bequeathment, scratch and blur Which overscrawl and underscore the piece? **1879** G. Meredith *Egoist* II. xi. 220 A yet more instructive passage than the over-scrawled Seventieth, or French Section.

over-scrupulous, *a.* (Later examples.)

1908 *Westm. Gaz.* 17 Aug. 2/1 Mr. Bryan's over-scrupulous attitude towards advertisements. **1952** E. Grierson *Reputation for Song* xxi. 173 She was..a giver, if he'd ever seen one, and not over-scrupulous in conscience or other things.

oversea, *a.* and *adv.* Add: **A.** *adj.* **3.** (Later examples.)

1931 *Times* 17 Feb. 9/1 The competition of our rivals in the home and oversea markets. **1953** [see *DOMINION *sb.* 2 b]. **1955** P. TOWNSEND *China Phoenix* 9 He was Fukienese by birth, from a province of China from which came many oversea Chinese. **1959** *Times* 30 July 6/6 (*heading*) Council formed for oversea research. **1969** *IEEE Trans. Antennas & Propagation* XVII. 254/1 In ship-to-ship detectability studies it is important to have a method of estimating oversea radar range distribution.

B. *adv.* (Further examples.)

1903 W. B. YEATS *In Seven Woods* 15 And you are more high of heart than she For all her wanderings over-sea. **1955** *Times* 9 May 11/2 Private investment oversea. **1974** *Black World* Jan. 55/2 He have to go leave that Ford car when he go oversea from Fort Benning, and it stay in our front yard.

over-seas, *adv.* Add: **b.** quasi-*sb.* Foreign parts; abroad.

1919 *Empire Rev.*, Munition workers who have come from overseas. **1926** A. BENNETT *Lord Raingo* I. lix. 264 Every traveller from overseas was knocked silly by the spectacle. *Ibid.*, Britons whose secret conceit, compared to the ingenuous self-complacency of overseas, was as Mount Everest to Snowdon. **1966** *Listener* 8 Sept. 335/1 In the years before the war our financial income from overseas provided finance to pay for more than a third of our imports.

oversea·s, *a.* [f. the adv.] = OVERSEA *a.*; *overseas Chinese*, a native of China residing in another country.

Overseas is now more frequently used than *oversea*.

1892 KIPLING *Lett. of Travel* (1920) 47 Some day a man will bethink himself and write a book..called 'The Book of The Overseas Club'. **1905** *Daily Chron.* 29 Mar. 3/2 The political liberties of these islands were..deeply endangered by the overseas dominion..of Spain. **1908** *Westm. Gaz.* 26 June 9/3 The magnitude of the overseas possessions which we had to defend. **1912** *Chambers's Jrnl.* Nov. 754/1 In athletic prowess we are now far inferior to those overseas descendants of our race. **1918** P. S. ALLEN *Let.* 9 June (1939) 146 At Merton we are hoping to have some 'overseas' undergraduates next term. **1920** *Act* 10 & 11 *Geo. V* c. 29 (*title*) An Act to authorise the granting of credits and the undertaking of insurances for the purpose of re-establishing overseas trade. **1933** A. THIRKELL *High Rising* xi. 195 She'll be able to vamp the overseas students and have a splendid time. **1942** 'G. ORWELL' *Diary* 21 June in *Coll. Ess.* (1968) II. 433 The BBC simply isn't listened to overseas, a fact known to everyone concerned with overseas broadcasting. **1947** *Sun* (Baltimore) 22 Aug. 6/4 'Overseas' Chinese will participate in the elections not only as voters but as candidates as well. **1961** S. CHANDRASEKHAR *Communist China Today* viii. 155, I learned that Communist China was anxious to attract the savings of the overseas Chinese who would like to return to their homeland. **1966** [see *HOME *a.* 3 b]. **1968** D. TORR *Treason Line* 16 He was tall for an Overseas Chinese. **1970** V. CANNING *Great Affair* xii. 205 That..was in the overseas edition of *The Times*. **1972** J. BALL *Five Pieces Jade* viii. 96, I consider myself a Chinese-American, in other words an American citizen of Chinese descent. So do almost all of us. But to the Chinese in China—Taiwan or the mainland—either way, we are overseas Chinese. **1974** *Guardian* 27 Mar. 1/1 Tax to be charged on 90 per cent of overseas earnings whether remitted to UK or not. **1975** *Encounter* Feb. 43/2 My wife, phoning Chicago from London, asked, 'Is this the overseas operator?' A pitying male voice replied, 'This is *one* of them, madam.' **1977** 'J. LE CARRÉ' *Hon. Schoolboy* iv. 81 It was an overseas Chinese outfit.

overseer, *sb.* Add: **1. d.** *U.S.* A member of a board of officials which manages the affairs of a college, esp. Harvard College, Massachusetts.

1643 *New Englands First Fruits* 13 Over the Colledge are twelve Overseers chosen by the generall Court. **1812** in *Proc. Mass. Hist. Soc.* (1890) 2nd Ser. V. 176 [Harvard Commencement] The Corporation and Overseers arrived at 20 minutes past ten. **1832** W. D. WILLIAMSON *Hist. State Maine* II. 563 Its government was committed to a board of 13 Trustees, including the President, and a supervisory body of 45 Overseers. **1900** *Dialect Notes* II. 47 *Overseers, board of*, a special governing board of Harvard, chosen by the alumni from their own number. **1946** *Sat. Rev. Lit.* (U.S.) 14 Sept. 5 Then he too retired, but was promptly elected to a seat on the Board of Harvard Overseers. **1973** *Amer. Universities & Colleges* (ed. 11) 729/1 *Harvard University... Governing Board.* President and Fellows of Harvard College: self-perpetuating board of 7 members; life terms. Many board actions subject to consent of Board of Overseers, which is composed of 30 members elected by alumni for 6-year terms.

e. A Friend (FRIEND *sb.* 7) chosen for the pastoral supervision of the congregation to which he belongs.

1785 *Bk. of Discipline New England Yearly Meeting Soc. of Friends* 39 That each monthly meeting choose two or more sober and judicious men friends, and two or more women friends, to be overseers in each preparative-meeting, which overseers are to render account of their service to the monthly meeting at least once a quarter, and to be annually appointed or re-chosen. **1832** W. D. WILLIAMSON *Hist. State Maine* II. 699 Each society [of Quakers] has at least four Overseers, two males and two females. **1921** R. M. JONES *Later Periods Quakerism* I. iv. 131 These Overseers..were in the course of time charged with responsibility for the moral life of the membership. *Ibid.* 132 Like the Elders, they had no absolute rules to guide them, but there slowly accumulated..a body of Advices and Queries which furnished the Overseers with a pretty clear line of procedure. **1963** A. HERON *Towards Quaker View of Sex* i. 7 Particularly does this apply to elders and overseers in the Society of Friends. **1974** G. HUBBARD *Quaker by Convincement* iv. iii. 209 The responsibilities of Overseers are to encourage attendance at Meetings for Worship and for business, to exercise a care over younger members and children and those in need of assistance, [etc.].

o·ver-self. [OVER- 2 b.] The finer, stronger, or more assertive part of one's nature (see also quot. 1960).

1888 E. CLODD *Story of Creation* xi. 223 The terrible mass of wrong-doing can only be lessened and finally removed by suppression of the over-self. **1908** *Daily Chron.* 30 Apr. 3/1 It is the Shakespeare that projected his over-self into two score of masterpieces of poetry and drama that is Shakespeare for us. **1960** J. HEWITT *Yoga* 7 The Yogi believes that there is a universal Overself with whom he can make contact and identify himself in moments of higher consciousness. *Ibid.* xi. 155 To the Yogi Samadhi is the merging of the individual Soul or Self with the universal Soul or Overself.

oversell, over-sell, *v.* Add: **1. b.** To make excessive or unrealistic claims for (goods advertised or offered for sale, etc.); to give (someone) an exaggerated idea of the value or worth of something. Also *absol.*, *transf.* and *fig.*

1928 *Publishers' Weekly* 10 Nov. 1978/2 We remember—how perfectly!—the names and the publishers of books on which we were oversold last season, and had, subsequently, to send the way of all deadwood. **1957** *Technology* July 174/1 The word 'syndicate' and the syndicate method in management training has been over-sold for some time. **1960** *20th Cent.* Sept. 234 Mr Wesker's enemies dismiss him as a mere brand-name oversold by the theatrical Left. **1970** A. TOFFLER *Future Shock* (1974) xx. 463 It would be foolish to oversell the ability of science, as yet, to forecast complex events accurately. **1971** P. DICKINSON *Sleep & his Brother* iii. 56 'Why does he want to see me?' 'Aha! I fear I may have oversold you. We are his hobby, and he is not a patient man.' **1971** *Nature* 19 Nov. 118/3 The current disenchantment with science arises because science was oversold in the postwar years. **1973** E. LEMARCHAND *Let or Hindrance* xi. 132 Chap oversells himself..but he knows his way round in business. **1977** R. E. HARRINGTON *Quintain* iv. 34 'They believe they're safe.' Diamond..knew he was over-selling to Felix, and he damned himself for it.

Hence **overselling** *vbl. sb.* (later example); **oversold** *ppl. a.* (further examples).

1934 *Sun* (Baltimore) 5 Apr. 27/1 Word of this amendment..caught the wheat market in apparently an oversold condition. **1968** L. SELLERS *Doing it in Style* 206 If a reporter writes a story too hard it may get into the paper unqueried and result in trouble. If he oversells in advance he will only infuriate the executives... Overselling is the way to trouble. **1971** *Daily Tel.* 28 Oct. 19/4 The market is in a heavily oversold condition.

oversell (ōu·vəɹsel), *sb.* [f. the vb.] Excessive or ambitious claims for, or promotion of, goods offered for sale; also *transf.* and *fig.*

1969 *Computers & Humanities* IV. 53 No doubt we are partly the victims of oversell by our IBM salesmen and computer directors, who promised us the computer would do things it is quite unsuited for. **1970** G. GREER *Female Eunuch* 13 Perhaps the sexual sell was oversell. **1974** 'G. BLACK' *Golden Cockatrice* i. 17 It was another case of oversell, like that soap powder campaign..which drove irritated women to buy the brands which didn't promise.. a ten per cent whiter wash.

over-sensitive, *a.* Add: (Further examples.) So **over-sensiti·vity.**

1953 K. REISZ *Technique Film Editing* III. xv. 266 He becomes over-sensitive to his surroundings and suspicious of casual passers-by. **1965** HOUSE & STOREY *Lett. of Dickens* I. 146 Seymour..seems to have suffered from over-sensitivity. **1977** H. INNES *Big Footprints* II. ii. 137 The over-sensitivity of a boy who has lost his natural parents. **1978** E. HEALEY *Lady Unknown* i. 43 An over-sensitive skin that broke out in a rash when she was under strain.

oversew, *v.* Add: Also *transf.*

1938 L. M. HARROD *Librarians' Gloss.* 109 *Oversewing*, the act or process of sewing over and over the leaves of a book. **1969** R. MAINGOT *Abdominal Operations* (ed. 5) I. xxv. 428/2 The duodenal stump is next oversewn, securely closed, and inverted with sutures of fine silk.

over-sexed (ōuvəɹse·kst), *a.* [OVER- 28 d.] Having sexual propensities or qualities in an excessive degree; inordinately desirous of sexual gratification. Also *fig.* Hence **over-se·xedness.**

1898 C. P. STETSON *Women & Econ.* iii. 43 The male.. is a far more normal animal than the female of his species, —far less over-sexed. *Ibid.* 44 The secretion of milk is a maternal function,—a sex function. The cow is over-sexed. **1901** G. B. SHAW *Three Plays for Puritans* p. xi, I did not find that matters were improved by the lady pretending to be 'a woman with a past', violently over-sexed. **1908** A. NOYES *William Morris* 98 A creature so gluttonously over-sexed and selfishly serpentine as Gudrun. **1923** C. MACKENZIE *Parson's Progress* viii. 95 Nobody questions the ethical value of Christianity except a few oversexed egomaniacs. **1923** *Daily Mail* 5 Feb. 5 His..terra-cotta-coloured nudes..are repulsive and over-sexed. **1937** G. FRANKAU *More of Us* x. 112 Fearful lest one more line of such o'er-sexed stuff Leave us no energy to do our next stuff. **1941** AUDEN *New Year Let.* III. 54 Hearing how circumstance has vexed A broker who is over-sexed. **1953** *Encounter* Nov. 31/1 Y. is the political equivalent of a *nymphomaniac*... This kind of neurosis..flourishes chiefly in the climate of the Left—for, generally speaking, the Left is politically over-sexed. *Ibid.* 31/2 The unfulfilled urge 'to belong' may lead to 'political oversexedness', expressing itself in blind, self-sacrificing devotion to some unholy cause. **1973** 'D. HALLIDAY' *Dolly & Starry Bird* xv. 229 You've laid your oversexed little claws on my girl. **1977** 'H. CARMICHAEL' *Grave for Two* ix. 111 To put it mildly she was inclined to be over-sexed.

over-sharpness. (Examples.)

1858 BAGEHOT *Coll. Works* (1965) II. 84 'Over-sharpness' in the student is the most unpromising symptom of the logical jurist. **1955** J. L. AUSTIN *How to do Things with Words* (1962) vii. 90 Alice-in-Wonderland over-sharpness. **1970** *Nature* 19 Dec. 1218/1 The quality of supra-threshold vision in the fovea results from a balance between optical unsharpness..and neural 'oversharpness' (lateral inhibition).

overshoot, *v.* Add: **1. d.** *trans.* and *intr.* To fly beyond (a designated landing-point) while attempting to land an aircraft. Also *transf.*

1920 *Flight* XII. 368 (*caption*) Pilot heads..for aerodrome, knowing for certain he will overshoot. **1928** *Lit. Digest* 12 May 73/1 To 'put her on hot' is to land fast, usually resulting in 'overshooting' the field. **1932** D. GARNETT *Rabbit in Air* I. 35 In my first attempt I thought I had overshot for some reason when I had undershot hopelessly. **1958** 'CASTLE' & 'HAILEY' *Flight into Danger* vi. 79, I can't guarantee at all that this plane will get down on the field. She's just as likely to pan down short or overshoot. **1973** C. BONINGTON *Next Horizon* xviii. 248 We over-shot the runway once. **1974** P. ERDMAN *Silver Bears* iii. 54 The MG suddenly swung off the road... Doc was caught by surprise and overshot. Slowly he backed up.

overshoot (ōu·vəɹʃūt), *sb.* [f. the vb.] The action or result of OVERSHOOT *v.*; *spec.* in *Electronics* (see quot. 1971).

1944 *Flight* 1 June 584/1 Uncorrected over-shoot generally means a write-off. **1945** *Electronic Industries* Sept. 214 *Overshoot*, an excessive potential attained by a portion of the main body of a pulse. **1947** R. LEE *Electronic Transformers & Circuits* ix. 249 Added to this is a slight oscillation overshoot. **1956** AMOS & BIRKINSHAW *Television Engin.* II. i. 25 The consequent disturbance of the phase relationships frequently causes the phenomenon of overshoot illustrated in Fig. 11. This is an effect which can be compared with that of inertia in mechanical systems and causes the voltage, after executing the transient, to exceed momentarily the final steady value. **1963** R. P. DALES *Annelids* viii. 156 They have found that with posterior pieces there is often an 'overshoot', the new thoracic region having more segments than it should. **1969** J. J. SPARKES *Transistor Switching* iv. 113 Overshoot or undershoot of the output waveforms will result. **1970** *New Scientist* 17 Dec. 515/2 He sees the market economy as a system with high gain and strong feedback, possessing self-regulation, but troubled by overshoots. **1971** *Gloss. Electrotechnical, Power Terms* (*B.S.I.*) III. i. 37 *Overshoot*, transient exaggeration of the magnitude of the leading or trailing edge of a steep-sided signal. **1977** *Gramophone* Oct. 744/3 The square wave showed one sharp overshoot and was then well damped.

overshot, *a.* **1.** (Further examples.)

1880 [see *HIGH *a.* 4 c]. **1904** KIPLING *Traffics & Discov* 389 Mechanically, an overshot wheel with this head of water is about as efficient as a turbine. **1914** *Chambers's Jrnl.* Mar. 205/1 The sewage passes over a wheel of overshot or undershot type. **1968** J. ARNOLD *Shell Book of Country Crafts* xii. 175 The overshot wheel was used where there was a higher fall of water and was intended to turn by the *weight* of the descending water against the buckets or floats. **1978** J. B. HILTON *Some run Crooked* iii. 22 The Powder Mill..was a mid-nineteenth-century ruin..an overshot water-wheel, now crippled over a leaking weir.

overshot, *ppl. a.* Add: **3.** (Later examples.)

1931 T. R. G. LYELL *Slang* 668 There are innumerable synonyms applicable to different degrees of intoxication. Those most in general use are..*muddled, overcome, overshot*, [etc.]. **1942** BERREY & VAN DEN BARK *Amer. Thes. Slang* § 106/7 Drunk,..*overshot*.

7. Of a pattern or weave: that is characterized by uninterrupted lines of weft where the yarn has been made to pass over two or more warp threads before re-entering the fabric.

1952 H. J. BROWN *Hand Weaving* vi. 102 Any design that can be arranged on a formation of squares may be reproduced in overshot weaving... Many of the fine old American colonial coverlets that have been handed down as heirlooms were made in overshot design. **1965** E. TUNIS *Colonial Craftsmen* iv. 102 Such were the 'overshot' coverlets in wide variety which are prized examples of old weaving. **1970** E. REGENSTEINER *Art of Weaving* v. 77/1 In the weaver's language, patterns produced by this system are called 'overshot', because when the harnesses are raised, the weft threads skip or 'float' over the groups of warp threads.

overshroud, *v.* (Later example.)

1916 A. S. WAY tr. *Virgil's Aeneid* I. III. 113 A night of rain overshrouds The sky.

oversight, *sb.* Add: **1. a.** (Further examples.)

1931 H. J. ROSE tr. *W. Schmidt's Orig. & Growth Relig.* xvi. 275 The Supreme Being, thus exercising oversight on the doings of men, is likewise able to reward..and punish. *Ibid.* 277 His oversight of what men do and leave undone in the moral sphere. **1935** F. H. HAYWARD *Alfred the Great* xii. 81 There was no centralised mint and probably little centralised oversight. **1971** *Nature* 4 June 292/1 The need to continue investigations on a broad front to keep an ecological oversight of the biogeodynamics of each metal. **1977** *Time* 21 Feb. 38/1 Congressional oversight has proliferated.

c. A survey, view. *rare.*

1889 F. E. Gretton *Memory's Harkback* 291 You have a closer and more direct oversight of the home, or Herefordshire, view.

2. a. (Later examples.)

1927 *Public Opinion* 8 Apr. 329/2 The generous-hearted demand that we accord to China the recognition due to a modern nation is sometimes made in oversight of the fundamental elements in the problem. **1959** J. L. Austin *Sense & Sensibilia* (1962) ii. 13 These are the quite common cases of misreadings, mishearings, Freudian oversights, &c. **1976** *Washington Post* 19 Apr. A4/5 The backroom view in the White House is that there should be a single oversight committee on Capitol Hill to answer the clamor for corrective action.

b. Also, a person who is passed over.

1955 T. H. Pear *Eng. Social Differences* 241 When one studies the failures among those who were selected for grammar schools and the oversights among those who were not selected, not a few mistakes..might have been avoided had the child's social environment been taken into account.

Hence **oversi·ghted** *ppl. a.*, overlooked.

1857 J. Hyde *Mormonism* (ed. 2) ix. 215 There is one oversighted contradiction that stares us in the face.

o:versimplifica·tion. [Over- 29 b.] The action or process of simplifying to excess; the result of this; a simplistic style or procedure.

1930 R. A. Fisher *Genetical Theory Nat. Selection* 42 It is a patent oversimplification to assert that the environment determines the numbers of each sort of organism that it will support. **1934** *Discovery* Dec. 339/2 The danger of over-simplification of exceedingly complex problems. **1958** 'P. Bryant' *Two Hours to Doom* 91 'Since the war a dozen countries have gone Communist.'.. 'I realise that. But I think it's an over-simplification of the issue.' **1968** M. S. Livingston *Particle Physics* p. vi, The author accepts responsibility for any shortcomings or oversimplifications in these descriptions. **1975** *Listener* 4 Dec. 734/3 When the cars are there, they sell... This, of course, is an over-simplification.

oversi·mplify, *v.* [Over- 27.] *trans.* To render excessively or delusively simple; to explain in simplistic terms. Also *absol.* Hence **oversi·mplified** *ppl. a.*; **oversi·mplifying** *vbl. sb.* and *ppl. a.* Also **oversi·mplifier,** one who oversimplifies.

1934 Webster, Oversimplify. **1936** *Mind* XLV. 222 Preformation..errs by over-simplifying the problem. **1940** *Amer. Speech* XV. 67 The old fallacy of the over-simplifiers, searching for 'the' cause where there usually is a complex of causes, has also bedeviled philology. **1942** *Scrutiny* X. iv. 360 The difference cannot be explained simply by saying that the comic parts of *Chuzzlewit* are good and the 'serious' or 'sentimental' parts bad, because that is an over-simplifying of the case. **1946** *Sun* (Baltimore) 11 Mar. 10/3 (*heading*) It is easy to oversimplify about the Russians. **1946** J. S. Huxley *Unesco* ii. 47 In somewhat over-simplified terms. **1953** D. F. Pocock tr. *Durkheim's Sociol. & Philos.* iii. 74 This..would be preferable in our schools to the over-simplified..explanations with which we too often deceive the curiosity of youth. **1963** *Times* 21 Jan. 9/2 These two stubborn, over-simplifying old men. **1965** C. Walsh in J. Gibb *Light on C. S. Lewis* 114 He berated Lewis as an oversimplifier. **1975** R. Browning *Emperor Julian* i. 27 An over-simplified summary of results must suffice. **1976** *Listener* 28 Oct. 550/1 Magnus Pyke..has been accused..of 'popularising' his subject, of oversimplifying.

oversize, *sb.* Add: **1.** (Further examples.)

1920 E. Sitwell *Wooden Pegasus* 88 Neutralize The overtint and oversize. **1920** *New Yorker* 12 Sept. 90/1 (Advt.), This most unusual watch,..shown here in its actual over-size.

2. That which is above a certain size.

1902 *Encycl. Brit.* XXXI. 374/1 It then goes to a screen with eleven holes to the linear inch, and yields a granular undersize and oversize. **1905** *Electrochem. Industry* Mar. 124/2 The oversize, which contains no slime whatever, is delivered directly to four Wilfley concentrating tables.

oversize, *v.*[1] Delete †*Obs.* and add later U.S. examples of both senses.

1879 'Mark Twain' *Lett. to Publishers* (1967) 114, I say $1100 instead of $1042 to cover little possible mistakes in over-sizing the plates. **1904** —— in *Harper's Weekly* 2 Jan. 19/1 The whole of that is intelligible to me ..except..[one] remark... That one oversizes my hand. Gimme five cards. **1930** *Flight* 25 Apr. (Suppl.) 460e/1 With various wheel forms, the effect of oversizing tyres and the use of smooth or safety treads. **1957** R. Lister *Decorative Wrought Ironwork* 230 *Oversizing.* Iron oxidizes while being worked, and it is therefore sometimes necessary to work it slightly larger than its intended final size, or oversize it, in order to counteract any loss by this.

o·versize, *a.* [f. the sb.] = *outsize *a.*

1909 *Cent. Dict.* Suppl., *Oversize..*, of excessive size; specifically, noting material which is too large to pass through the meshes of a given screen or size. **1924** *T. Eaton & Co. Catal.* Spring & Summer 292/2 Oversize cord tires need special cord size inner tubes. **1936** W. Faulkner *Absalom! Absalom!* vi. 195 A new oversize overall jumper coat. **1960** I. Cross *Backward Sex* i. 12 That bald head, like an over-size tennis ball, the worse for much wear. **1973** *Publishers Weekly* 25 June 16 (Advt.), A magnificently illustrated, oversize book. 10″ × 11⅞″. **1976** *Billings* (Montana) *Gaz.* 1 July 2-D/5 (Advt.), Nearly new three bedroom split entry home featuring large bedrooms, a fully equipped oversize kitchen with lots of cabinets.

overskirt. (Earlier examples.)

1870 *Harper's Bazaar* 22 Oct. 675 Over-skirts are elaborate, and show great variety in design. **1873** *Young Englishwoman* Mar. 131/2 An over-skirt of tulle looped up with a scarf sash.

overslee·ping, *vbl. sb.* [-ing[1].] The action of the verb Oversleep.

1908 *Westm. Gaz.* 31 Oct. 3/2 What with your smashings, and your over-sleepings, and burning the dinner on Sunday, and all. **1912** R. Brooke *Let.* 25 Feb. in E. Marsh *Rupert Brooke* (1918) iv. 70 My cure consists in perpetual overeating and oversleeping. **1977** J. Aiken *Last Movement* vii. 136 Over-sleeping is as bad as over-eating.

o·verslung, *a.* [Over- 1 c.] Supported above the main part, or some particular part, of an apparatus.

1960 Shepherd & Withers *Mech. Cutting & Loading of Coal* v. 78 A number of low-type cutters provide for a range of appropriate adjustable positions between the underslung and overslung position of the reversible turret. **1971** B. Scharf *Engin. & its Lang.* xvi. 228 Overhead travelling cranes consist of (1) a load girder with a roller mounted carriage at each end running on top (overslung gantry type), or along the bottom flanges of gantry rails (underslung gantry type); (2) a trolley..; and (3) a hoist. **1971** J. M. Paxton *Man. Civil Engin. Plant* (ed. 2) I. 190/2 Both rear axles are driven via double reduction hubs with an over-slung worm and wheel from a 12-speed gearbox, giving 12 forward and 3 reverse speeds.

oversold: see Oversell *v.* in Dict. and Suppl.

over-soon, *adv.* (Later example.)

1878 Hardy *Ret. Native* II. ii. vi. 10, I told him 'twas barely decent to come so oversoon; but words be wind.

over-soul, *sb.* Add: Also, = Superman.

1908 [see *beyond *adv.* and *prep.* D].

o·ver-soul, *v.* [f. the sb.] *trans.* In passive, to be ruled or dominated in respect of the soul. Hence **over-sou·ling** *vbl. sb.*

1916 'A.E.' *National Being* ii. 13 None of our modern States create in us such an impression of being spiritually oversouled by an ideal as the great States of the ancient world. **1925** D. H. Lawrence *Refl. Death Porcupine* 168 A primrose has its own peculiar primrosy identity, and all the oversouling in the world won't melt it into a Williamish oneness.

o:ver-specializa·tion. [Over- 29 b.] Too much specialization, esp. in education or evolution.

1931 J. S. Huxley *What dare I Think?* iv. 144 Over-specialization produces..individuals with scientific hypertrophy and religious atrophy. **1936** *Discovery* Oct. 328/2 The author emphasises the importance of correlation between laboratory and clinical observation and deplores the over-specialisation which has gradually crept in and checked many valuable conclusions in medical science. **1957** *Technology* Mar. 3/4 The evils of over-specialization at school are never easily wiped out. **1958** *Spectator* 22 Aug. 258/2 Two extant species [of elephant] alone survive from 352 branches. Mr. Carrington suggests that the elephant declined more from this over-specialization than from unscrupulous Romans or Asiatics. **1974** tr. *Wertheim's Evolution & Revolution* i. 75 As soon as the dead end produced by over-specialization is reached, only a forceful..breakthrough can produce a reversal of the involutionary trends.

o:ver-spe·cialize, *v.* [Over- 27.] *intr.* To specialize too much (in a particular endeavour). So **o:ver-spe·cialized** *ppl. a.*

1926 J. S. Huxley *Ess. Pop. Sci.* p. vi, Science herself is over-specialised. **1930** G. R. de Beer *Embryol. & Evolution* xiii. 95 If a race has become excessively over-specialized, even the younger stages of the ontogenies of its individuals may have lost their plasticity. **1944** J. S. Huxley *On Living in Revolution* xv. 184 To overwork and over-specialize. **1953** N. Tinbergen *Herring Gull's World* ii. 5 They [*sc.* gulls] are not over-specialised gliding fliers like the shearwaters. **1960** *Farmer & Stockbreeder* 16 Feb. (Suppl.) 8/2 The emphasis must be changed from the over-specialized Wiltshire baconer.

o:ver-spe·cify, *v.* [Over- 27.] *trans.* To specify too narrowly; to limit excessively in scope; to specify in excessive detail. So **o:ver-speci·fic** *a.*; **o:verspecifica·tion.**

1957 R. K. Merton *Social Theory* (rev. ed.) x. 389 The practical problem had been overspecified in its initial formulation. *Ibid.*, This overspecification for a time diverted our attention from salient alternatives of investigation. **1962** U. Weinreich in Householder & Saporta *Probl. Lexicogr.* 32 A definition like *triangle* 'a figure that has three sides and three angles, the sum of which is 180°' is avoided as overspecific, since *triangle* is sufficiently defined by the number of sides. **1965** *Language* XLI. 234 Using it..might risk being overspecific in this instance, but this is preferable to a less unified system of description in which several concepts are used with less general application. **1968** M. S. Livingston *Particle Physics* ix. 167 The relationships between isotopic spin, multiplicity of charge states,..and baryon number for hadrons are overspecified. **1975** N. Chomsky *Logical Struct. Linguistic Theory* vii. 200 It is at once clear that the grammar 26 provides an overspecification since the following simpler grammar corresponds to 26.

o·ver-speech. [Over- 29 b.] Loquacity; indiscretion.

1865 see Over- 29 b]. **1920** E. Pound *Umbra* 115 Arnaut loves, and ne'er will fret Love with o'er-speech. **1922** E. R. Eddison *Worm Ouroboros* iv. 48 'Keep thou thy lips from overspeech,' said the King. 'These be mysteries whereon but to think may snatch thee into peril.'

o·verspeed, *sb.* [Over- 29 b.] (An instance of) overspeeding.

1914 H. Pender *Amer. Handbk. Electr. Engineers* 1315 Over-Speeds.—All types of rotating machines shall be so constructed that they will safely withstand an over-speed of 25 per cent. **1926** J. Kirsopp *Use of Power in Colliery Working* ii. 156 The entire device prevents overspeed of any description. **1950** *Sun* (Baltimore) 12 Apr. 32/1 The plane, flying at a speed of 135 miles per hour, developed 'a structural failure due to overspeed'. **1969** *Power System Protection* (Electr. Council) II. ix. 250 The governing system which requires an actual overspeed to produce a response and take corrective action.

overspee·d, *v.* [Over- 27.] *intr.* To drive or operate faster than is permitted or allowed for. So **overspee·ding** *ppl. a.* and *vbl. sb.*

1906 *Westm. Gaz.* 24 Apr. 4/2 The police had been.. engaged elsewhere to look out for over-speeding drivers. **1913** *Collier's* 11 Jan. ii. 50/2 There were but three convictions for overspeeding. **1950** W. W. Lewis *Protection Transmission Syst. against Lightning* xi. 367 It is believed that generator overspeeding and loss of load as single factors without solid faults will seldom give rise to dangerous overvoltages. **1971** M. Tak *Truck Talk* 114 *Overspeed,* to run an engine at an excessive number of revolutions per minute for the gear being used. **1972** *Lebende Sprachen* XVII. 134/2 A turbine undergoing tests at Calder Hall 'B' atomic power-station in Cumberland overspeeded last night and exploded. **1974** [see *overheat *v.* 2].

overspend, *v.* Add: **1. b.** (Later example.)

1951 L. MacNeice tr. *Goethe's Faust* 39 He backs away, gives way, the day is overspent.

2. c. (Later examples.)

1946 L. P. Hartley *Sixth Heaven* v. 107, I doubt if it's even wise to offer to pay half... You mustn't overspend yourself. **1953** E. Simon *Past Masters* iii. 159 From the outset [you] overspent... The money has all gone on inessentials. **1959** M. Summerton *Small Wilderness* xiii. 159 Money? Overspent yourselves in this place?

Hence **overspe·nding** *vbl. sb.* (in sense 2 of the vb.).

1932 *Ann. Reg. 1931* 300 The country [*sc.* the U.S.A.] regrets the over-spending of the past few years. **1963** *Times* 9 Jan. 9/2 They cover underspending less comprehensively than overspending, and without knowledge of both it is impossible to make an accurate interim assessment of trends in Government expenditure. **1976** *Times* 20 Oct. 14/3 The borrowing requirement (a euphemism for government overspending).

overspill, *sb.* Add: **a.** (Further examples.) Now usu. the movement of surplus population from a city to a less heavily populated area of the same country; this surplus population or the housing or new area occupied by it. Also *transf.*

1930 *Times* 22 Apr. 6/7 On the south lie the famous South Downs, within range of the overspill from the seaside towns. **1940** J. Buchan *Memory Hold-the-Door* vi. 145 Emigration undertaken as a reasoned policy..and not as a mere overspill of population. **1944** *Daily Tel.* 12 July 4/4 When one member objected to Mr. Morrison's use in connection with population of the word 'overspill', the Minister admitted that it was ugly, though convenient. **1946** *Nature* 13 July 39/1 Public interest has been stimulated equally by the controversies over the proposals for dealing with Manchester's overspill in a new town at Mobberley, or the even larger overspill problem of Liverpool. **1947** *Daily Mail* 22 May 1/1 We are apt to be too much concerned with the new satellites and 'overspills'. We should first reconstruct the other cities. **1955** *Times* 12 May 15/2 Since 1951 Socialist power there has been improved by an overspill of families of men and women who work in the factories and machine shops of Swindon. **1958** *Times* 3 Oct. 14/5 Although an overspill has been necessary to accommodate them all comfortably..most of the paintings look very handsome. **1959** *Economist* 3 July 42/1 Diversification may thus proceed from an overspill of strength in one department or another. **1965** A. Garner *Elidor* xv. 111 'That's what you must expect when you have overspill in a decent area,' said Mrs. Watson. 'They shouldn't be allowed to build out in the country. People aren't going to change when they move from the city.' **1972** F. Warner *Lying Figures* ii. 15 Epigyne is lit by the overspill from the two spots. **1972** *Times* 21 Dec. 4/4 *Overspill,* the planned movement of people who do not want to go to towns that do not want to have them. **1976** 'D. Halliday' *Dolly & Nanny Bird* xvi. 212 The next wave..struck us..and the two men huddled on the floor of the cockpit received the first overspill..from the lee side. **1976** T. Stoppard *Dirty Linen* 9 An overspill meeting room for House of Commons business in the tower of Big Ben.

b. *attrib.*

1945 *Ann. Reg. 1944* 63 The Bill for the purchase of so-called 'overspill' areas where those who were crowded out could be accommodated. **1946** [see sense a above]. **1952** *Economist* 21 June 799/2 No less than 28 of these [district councils] are intended under the plan to absorb 'overspill' population coming from Wolverhampton, Walsall,..and other congested towns... Over a quarter of the new houses ..would form part of 'overspill' schemes. **1958** *Spectator* 30 May 710/1 Recent 'overspill' housing policies. **1966** *New Statesman* 28 Jan. 140/2 Nor are we likely to get any transitional or 'overspill' benefit because of the restrictive provisos. **1972** *Guardian* 8 Sept. 6/5 Official overspill schemes and the movement to the suburbs..account for only half the population drift: the rest are leaving the country. **1975** Cox & Boyson *Black Paper 1975* 30/1 The school is built on the edge of a city overspill estate. *Ibid.* 31/2 There will be difficulties in any overspill area where people are moved away from family and familiar surroundings.

overspill, *v.* Add: (Further examples.) Also, to cause (something) to spill over; *spec.* to remove (surplus population) from a city. Also *intr.*, to spill over; to overflow. Hence **over-spi·lling** *ppl. a.*

1958 *Times Rev. Industry* Feb. 24/1 Some 70,000 people are to be 'overspilled' from Glasgow City..into the new towns of East Kilbride and Cumbernauld. **1961** *Times Lit. Suppl.* 27 Jan. 51/2 We overspill our savings..onto the backward nations. **1962** *Times* 7 Mar. 11/4 The process of being over-spilled in a familiar country-side..is bound to be at least slightly deterrent to the true Cockney. **1963** *Listener* 21 Mar. 516/1 The need to re-house ever more overspilling Londoners. **1970** G. F. Newman *Sir, You Bastard* vii. 196 The eighteen prisoners who finally stood charged over-spilled the dock at the committal proceedings. **1972** *Accountant* 28 Sept. 392/2 It is an illusion..for internal auditors to think that, by over-spilling into management functions and systems design, they will enhance the status..of their profession. **1977** *Daily Tel.* 14 Feb. 6/7, 30,000 homes were bulldozed inside 10 years and the occupants 'overspilled' beyond the city boundaries in the new or expanded towns of Runcorn, Skelmersdale, [etc.].

overspin, *v.* Restrict †*Obs.* to sense in Dict. and add: **2.** To confuse (an opponent) with overspin (see next).

1940 G. Marx *Let.* 5 Sept. (1967) 25 He's a left-hander and slashes and cuts and overspins his opponent dizzy.

o·verspin, *sb.* [Over- 6.] In *Cricket* and other ball games: a rotating motion imparted to a ball in which the upper part turns in the direction of flight, or is struck with upward inclination. Also (in full *overspin ball*), such a delivery. Now usu. called *topspin*. So **o·ver-spi:nner,** a ball delivered with overspin.

1904 F. C. Holland *Cricket* 54 The over spin gives to the ball the same over-and-over motion that is seen in a ball that has been topped at golf or billiards. **1908** A. W. Myers *Compl. Lawn Tennis Player* 109 A strong forward or over-spin is thus imparted to the ball. **1925** *Country Life* 18 July 93/1 The over-spin ball is the logical outcome of the googlie, inasmuch as..the hand turns over more than in the leg-break, but not so much as in the googlie. **1927** M. A. Noble *Those 'Ashes'* 178 Hendren was bowled by a faster overspin, which he mistook for a leg break. **1930** C. V. Grimmett *Getting Wickets* iii. 57 It would..have what is called 'overspin', and, after striking the pitch, gather pace as the spin took effect. *Ibid.* 60 An over-spinner will be produced if the back of the hand is outwards, and the hand pointing horizontally to the demonstrator's left. **1961** F. C. Avis *Sportsman's Gloss.* 130/1 *Overspin*, a forward rotating movement of the ball in flight, causing an acceleration off the pitch. *Ibid.* 259/1 (Lawn Tennis), *Overspin*, top spin imparted to the ball, to give power and unexpected movement off the court. **1970** H. Taylor *Golf Dict.* 150 *Overspin*, a word sometimes used for topspin.

o·verspray. [Over- 19.] Sprayed liquid that does not adhere to the object or area being sprayed.

1948 L. W. Lammiman in W. von Fischer *Paint & Varnish Technol.* xxvi. 453 Arcing the gun on a surface causes overspray to bounce obliquely off the surface. **1955** Edwards & Wray *Aluminium Paint & Powder* (ed. 3) iv. 95 The amount of paint sprayed is greatly reduced as most of the overspray is eliminated. **1972** *Materials & Technol.* V. xi. 371 Spraying is normally carried out in spraybooths..and overspray is removed by an efficient exhaust system. **1977** *Hot Car* Oct. 50/4 For a single pin stripe you must of course mask either side of the tapes to stop overspray going on to the base colour.

over-spru·ng, *ppl. a.* [Over- 27 b.] Fitted with too many or too flexible springs.

1923 *Daily Mail* 12 July 12 The saddle for my weight was over-sprung, and over pot-holes was inclined to bounce on to the frame. **1937** *Daily Herald* 16 Apr. 18/2, I have no very high opinion of the rather flashy high-powered over-sprung American car. **1962** L. Deighton *Ipcress File* xxi. 146, I..pulled the big oversprung Lincoln Continental on to the road.

oversquare (stress variable), *a.* [Over- 28.] Of an internal-combustion engine or its cylinders: having a bore greater than the stroke.

1959 *Times* 23 Sept. 5/4 The new engine is 'over-square' and has a cubic capacity of 6¼ litres. **1966** *Economist* 9 July p. xxv/1, If exaggerated, the over-square cylinder tends to have a wafer-thin combustion chamber with limited compression turbulence, and to suffer from indifferent combustion at low operating speeds. **1967** *Ibid.* 8 July p. xxix/1, Hauliers also fear wear on the fast (up to 3,300 rpm) V-engines: these are often oversquare, with neat chunky cylinders. **1971** *Motor* 16 June 26/1 The new 1971 cc engine in the 504 is a four-cylinder in-line over-square unit.

over-stai·n, *v.* [Over- 8, 27.] **1.** (In Dict. s.v. Over- 8 a.)

2. *Biol. trans.* To stain (tissue) excessively, usu. in order that certain parts may be differentiated by selective removal of some of the stain; also *absol.*

1885 C. O. Whitman *Methods of Research in Microsc. Anat.* ii. 39 If by any chance the sections are over-stained, the superfluous color may be extracted by a brief sojourn in very dilute ammonia. *Ibid.* 48 Diffuse staining may generally be avoided by first overstaining and then withdrawing the color to any desired extent by means of alcohol. **1935** Kingsbury & Johannsen *Histol. Technique* 38 In regressive staining the tissue is over-stained and the excess of stain removed by the application of a differentiator. *Ibid.* 40 The rule is to over-stain and watch the differentiation carefully with the microscope. **1971** A. Lamela *Introd. Med. Lab. Methods* xxiii. 238 The tissue is over-stained and then decolorized until the correct depth of color is obtained.

Hence **over-stai·ning** *vbl. sb.*

1885 C. O. Whitman *Methods of Research in Microsc. Anat.* ii. 42 Minot's picric-acid carmine..gives a stronger differential coloring than Ranvier's picro-carmine; but over-staining must be most carefully avoided. **1929** C. E. McClung *Handbk. Microsc. Technique* i. 23 Regressive stains..are allowed to act until overstaining is accomplished, after which the desired degree of differentiation is brought about by removal of the excess coloration.

overstand, *v.* Restrict †*Obs.* to sense 2 and add later examples of sense 1.

1888 G. M. Hopkins *Poems* (1967) 198 Fairyland; silk-beech, scrolled ash, packed sycamore, wild wychelm, hornbeam fretty overstood By. **1938** *Venerabile* Oct. 61 The lofty roof o'erstands the graceful shrine.

3. To pass over; to cross.

1949 *Sun* (Baltimore) 27 Aug. 8/8 But Colie outguessed him, for while Reckord was watching the Jersey boat, he overstood the mark. Colie whipped about and Scanty was second before the Baltimore sailor realized what had happened. **1976** *Yachts & Yachting* 20 Aug. 372/1 Colin Evans overstood the line, thus losing the much-disputed 3rd place to Geoff Tindale.

4. *to be overstanding for honours*: in the University of Oxford, to be incapable of obtaining honours in an examination because of the lapse of more than the permitted number of terms (normally twelve) since matriculation.

The phrase 'disqualified for Honours by standing' is preferred in the O.U. *Examination Decrees and Regulations.*

1933 V. Brittain *Testament of Youth* iii. x. 476 They had undertaken, since I was so excessively 'over-standing' for Honours, a special procedure on my behalf. **1965** N. Coghill in J. Gibb *Light on C. S. Lewis* 52 Had we taken two [years] we would have been overstanding for Honours.

o·verstayer. *N.Z. colloq.* [f. Overstay *v.* + -er[1].] A Polynesian or other immigrant who stays beyond the time permitted by a work permit.

1977 *N.Z. Herald* 5 Jan. 1-4/4 While expressing sympathy for the plight of overstayers, the Maori leader said the laws of the nation had to apply to everyone, regardless of race. **1977** *N.Z. Woman's Weekly* 10 Jan. 38/4 We have heard so much lately about the overstayers and while agreeing wholeheartedly that the law must be held in regard and obeyed, I have been wondering if we realize just how much we depend on some of these Island people. **1978** *Guardian Weekly* 22 Jan. 9/2 In October, 1975, the Auckland police suddenly cracked down on 'overstayers'—those Pacific Islanders who had stayed beyond the length of their work permits.

overstee·pened, *ppl. a. Physical Geogr.* [Over- 22.] Steepened further; *esp.* (of a valley) having a greater steepness than running water would have caused owing to the predominantly downward erosive action of a glacier. So **overstee·pening** *vbl. sb.*

1900 W. M. Davis in *Proc. Boston Soc. Nat. Hist.* XXIX. 308 In the same way, the waterfalls from the hanging valleys, the showering waste that forms the falls, and the landslides from the basal cliffs, all show that the banks of the glacial channel—the lower walls of the existing valleys—are too steep; and they may be therefore called 'oversteepened'. **1922** *Bull. U.S. Geol. Survey* No. 730. 13 In the Black Canyon..the broad floor of the valley and the steep cliffs that rise precipitously 2,000 feet at its side suggest oversteepening of the walls by ice. **1942** O. D. von Engeln *Geomorphol.* xix. 462 That side of a valley reach against which the glacier current impinges is regularly oversteepened. **1964** *Amer. Jrnl. Sci.* CCLXII. 783 Over the bar itself the steepened profile increases velocity and tends to erode the obstruction. This enhancement of erosion in the over-steepened reach and deposition in the flat area will..tend to eliminate the original bar. **1970** R. J. Small *Study of Landforms* iv. 131 Each stream profile displays several apparent knick-points or oversteepened sections coincident with the gorges.

o·versteer, *sb.* [Over- 29 b.] A tendency in a motor vehicle to increase the sharpness of the turn when made to deviate from the straight.

1936 *Proc. Inst. Automobile Engin.* XXX. 759 This proportion of the total roll couple carried by the front and rear tyres is found to have a very marked effect on steering, and has to be proportioned by trial to avoid excessive effects in the direction either of 'oversteer' or 'understeer'. **1957** *Which?* Autumn 25/2 Slight oversteer is noticeable if the boot is well loaded, but this is easily compensated by a slight increase of pressure on the rear tyres. **1972** *Sci. Amer. Aug.* 20/2 In a vehicle with oversteer the driver must turn the steering wheel away from the center of the turn as speed increases. **1977** *Hot Car* Oct. 23/2 The average driver can handle understeer more safely than oversteer.

overstee·r, *v.* [Over- 27.] *intr.* To exhibit oversteer. So **overstee·ring** *vbl. sb.* and *ppl. a.*

1936 *Proc. Inst. Automobile Engin.* XXX. 730 Parallel-motion rear springing would give excessive over-steering because of the slip angle of the rear tyres. *Ibid.*, Almost every car over-steers to a certain extent. **1948** R. Dean-Averns *Automobile Chassis Design* ii. 49 An oversteering vehicle when negotiating a bend above the certain critical speed of the vehicle for straight running will tend to run into its turn. **1959** *Motor Manual* (ed. 36) v. 147 When the slip angle is greater at the rear, the car over-steers (i.e. turns more sharply than the driver intends). **1962** *Times* 10 Apr. 6/5 Does this Volkswagen oversteer? **1962** *Which? Car Suppl.* Oct. 117/2 The car changed from having a strong understeering characteristic to the opposite oversteering one—that is, the rear wheels tended to turn the car more than the driver wanted. **1971** C. Williams *Car Conversions* ii. 29 An oversteering car..does not slow down appreciably when the steering correction is applied. **1972** S. Abbey *Bk. of Marina* xii. 110 If the rear tyre pressures are too low, the car will 'oversteer'.

overstep, *v.* Add: *to overstep the mark*: see *mark *sb.*[1] 12 e; also *ellipt.*

1931 W. Faulkner *Sanctuary* xvi. 118, I made a fire in the stove. I guess I over-stepped.

2. *Geol.* Of the upper strata of an unconformity: to extend over (underlying strata) in such a way as to form an overstep. Also *intr.* with *on to*. Chiefly *British*.

1883 J. G. Goodchild in *Geol. Mag.* Decade II. X. 227, I have found it convenient..to speak of this stratigraphical relation of unconformable beds to the various rocks immediately beneath as Overstepping. For example, I should say that the Roman Fell Beds in the neighbourhood of Melmerby overlap the Upper Old Red, while the Carboniferous formation..oversteps the older rocks there. **1937** *Q. Jrnl. Geol. Soc.* XCIII. 107 Some of the older records..seem to suggest that the Gault in East Sussex oversteps the Folkestone Sands within a short distance of their outcrop. **1938** A. K. Wells *Outl. Hist. Geol.* ii. 12 In the diagram section the Cambrian rocks overstep the Pre-Cambrian, and higher divisions overlap lower ones. **1969** [see *overstep *sb.* 2]. **1972** *Gloss. Geol.* (Amer. Geol. Inst.) 507/1 An unconformable stratum that truncates the upturned edges of the underlying older rocks is said to 'overstep' each of them in turn (except where the stratum and the underlying beds have the same strike).

So **overste·pping** *vbl. sb.*, *spec.* in *Cricket*, the action of bowling with either foot illegally positioned in relation to the creases.

1869 Mill *Subj. Women* i. 32 An overstepping of the proper bounds of authority. **1959** *Oxford Mail* 2 Feb. 8/7 Rorke..lost a lot of his fearsomeness after being rightly no-balled because of his long drag, called over-stepping in Australia. **1976** J. Snow *Cricket Rebel* 98 Rowan reports remarks I am alleged to have made..after I had been no-balled for overstepping.

overstep, *sb.* (s.v. Overstep *v.*). Add: **2.** *Geol.* In an unconformity, the structural relationship between the lowest stratum of the upper series and the truncated ends of the underlying strata when, as is often the case, these have a different dip from the upper series. Chiefly *British*.

1883 A. J. J. Browne in *Geol. Mag.* Decade II. X. 336 Both cases involve an unconformity, and..the difference between them is really this: in overlap the basement member of the upper series has a limited extension, while in overstep the basement bed has a continuous extension. .. The unconformity between the two series will generally be much greater in the case of overlap than in the case of overstep, for in the latter the beds all dip in the same direction, and the existence of an unconformity is usually only made patent by the fact of overstep. **1937** *Q. Jrnl. Geol. Soc.* XCIII. 120 In the two marginal parts of the Wealden trough..there is a definite overstep, due to the fact that while the freshwater Wealden beds were being deposited in the central subsiding area the margins of the trough were being gently uptilted. **1948** *Bull. Amer. Assoc. Petroleum Geologists* XXXII. 2297 The word *overstep*..in more than 60 years of existence..has not succeeded in gaining any recognition among American geologists and very little in England. **1969** Bennison & Wright *Geol. Hist. Brit. Isles* i. 10 In the case of any angular unconformity the lowest bed of a series of strata is seen to rest on beds of differing ages. Such a phenomenon is known as overstep, and the post-unconformity bed is said to overstep onto successively older beds.

over-stimulate, *v.* (Example of *absol.* use.)

1928 A. B. Callow *Food & Health* 24 Condiments.. have the effect of stimulating gastric secretion, but..they tend to over-stimulate.

overstock, *sb.* **2.** (Later examples.)

1976 *Author* Summer 51 The remainder merchants, who prefer to be called overstock dealers. *Ibid.*, A firm called B.S.C. Remainders—founded 12 years ago as an overstock wholesaler. **1976** *Billings* (Montana) *Gaz.* 18 June 4-B (Advt.), Powell's furniture outlets buy factory overstock.

overstocked, *ppl. a.* (Earlier example.)

1844 Mill *Ess. Pol. Econ.* ii. 71 An overstocked state of the market is always temporary.

o·verstorey. [Over- 1 d.] = *over-wood.

1959 *Ecology* XL. 478 The survival and average total height growth of loblolly pine seedlings in Arkansas were best under overstory openings of 43 feet in diameter and larger. **1962** A. Fry *Ranch on Cariboo* xv. 155 A rolling country where the cattle browsed under an overstorey of open timber. **1976** *Nature* 22 Jan. 207/2 It [*sc.* the cocoa crop] is thus in intimate contact with an overstorey of forest trees and an understorey of ground vegetation.

overstrain, *sb.* Add: *spec.* the condition of having been strained beyond the yield point.
1895 [see *FATIGUE *sb.* 1 d]. **1931** H. J. TAPSELL *Creep of Metals* iii. 32 The raising of the yield point at air temperature of mild steel was even more marked if the stress producing the overstrain were continued for a time. **1941** H. GILKEY et al. *Materials Testing* 132 The general nature of cold-working, of whatever sort, is simply overstrain.

overstrain, *v.* Add: **3. a.** *spec.* to strain (a substance) beyond the yield point.
1899 J. A. EWING *Strength of Materials* iii. 40 This operation was carried far enough to overstrain the piece a second time, and curve *D* then shows that a very imperfectly elastic condition has reappeared. **1931** H. J. TAPSELL *Creep of Metals* iii. 33 The effect of a period of rest on iron and steel overstrained at air temperature is to produce a recovery of elasticity and an increase in hardness. **1962** R. E. SMALLMAN *Mod. Physical Metall.* vii. 242 If a specimen which has been overstrained to remove the yield point is allowed to rest.., the yield point returns as shown.

overstrained *ppl. a.*, **overstraining** *vbl. sb.* and *ppl. a.* (further examples).
1895 *Proc. R. Soc.* LVIII. 131 The tendency to creeping is found..to be much reduced in consequence of the hardening and recovery of elasticity which the overstrained material undergoes. **1900** *Phil. Trans. R. Soc.* A. CXCIII. 15 Curve No. 2 illustrates the semi-plastic condition of the material immediately after the removal of the overstraining load. **1931** H. J. TAPSELL *Creep of Metals* iii. 32 An overstrained material does not resemble its former state: it is physically a new material. **1962** R. E. SMALLMAN *Mod. Physical Metall.* vii. 242 The absence of a yield point at the beginning of plastic flow is characteristic of a specimen in an overstrained condition. **1962** P. G. FORREST *Fatigue of Metals* vi. 191 The beneficial effect of tensile overstraining on the fatigue strength of a notched bar. **1971** *Afr. Wildlife* XXV. 51/1 During the past few years an increasing number of wild animal species has been found to be prone to the development of a disease complex for which the new name, overstraining disease, is suggested. *Ibid.*, It is characterized by muscular degeneration, paralysis especially of the hind limbs and the passage of dark red-brown urine. The course is variable and affected horses may die from acute heart failure or the accumulation of toxic amounts of excretory products, resulting from kidney damage. Overstraining disease in game..may result from various capturing techniques. **1974** *Nature* 22 Feb. 577/1 Capture myopathy (so-called overstraining disease) in wild animals has gained increasing prominence.

overstretch, *sb.* (Later examples.)
1964 *Listener* 3 Sept. 335/2 Her overstretch was made fatal by this by-passing strategy. **1974** *Daily Tel.* 7 Feb. 2/6 Reasons for this are said to be the considerable 'overstretch' in the Navy's resources caused by shortage of ships and manpower.

overstride, *v.* **2.** (Later example.)
1925 *Glasgow Herald* 5 Nov. 11/2 In conception and in achievement it [*sc.* The British Empire Exhibition] overstrode the confines of mere commercial partisanship.

overstrike, *v.* Add: **3.** [tr. F. *surfrapper*: see OVER- 8.] *trans.* To strike (a coin) with a new die, imposing a second design on the original; to strike (a new design) on a coin. Hence **o·verstrike** *sb.*, an overstruck coin; **overstru·ck** *ppl. a.*
[**1884** *Encycl. Brit.* XVII. 630/2 A coin is said to be *surfrappé* when it has been struck on an older coin, of which the types are not altogether obliterated.] **1905** *Numismatic Chron.* V. 110 Supposing a sufficient number of overstruck pennies of the same type are available. *Ibid.*, A well-known instance of overstriking coins in modern times occurred in 1804, when..two million Spanish dollars..were overstruck with new dies in the Boulton presses at Soho, and issued as British currency. **1911** *Encycl. Brit.* XIX. 871/1 A coin is said to be 'over-struck' or 're-struck' when it has been struck on an older coin, of which the types are not altogether obliterated. **1914** *Brit. Mus. Return* 114 in *Parl. Papers* LXXI. 193 Another [penny] of the same reign showing the ninth type..overstruck on the seventh. **1932** *Proc. Brit. Acad.* XVIII. 212 Sextantes, with mint-marks C and MA, of the same class as certain early denarii, are commonly found in Sardinia overstruck on Sardinian bronze. We cannot assign such overstrikes to any date earlier than 237 B.C. **1936** *Proc. Prehist. Soc.* II. 144 The Whaddon Chase type coins have been heavily overstruck. **1955** C. SELTMAN *Greek Coins* (ed. 2) 24 The coiners in a particular mint saved themselves the trouble of preparing metal blanks, and employed instead the actual coins of some other city, heating them first in the furnace and then striking them between their own punch- and anvil-dies... Such coins, technically known as overstruck coins, [etc.]. **1970** *Ashmolean Mus. Rep. Visitors 1969* 33 Fifth century overstrikes at Rhegium and Messana.

o·verstroke. [OVER- 6.] An overarm stroke in swimming.
1902 *Encycl. Brit.* XXV. 696/4 Over-stroke. **1934** E. POUND *Eleven New Cantos* xxxix. 44 Came Mara swimming with light hand lifted in overstroke. **1948** —— *Pisan Cantos* (1949) lxxvi. 44 No overstroke No dolphin faster in moving Nor the flying azure of the wing'd fish under Zongli.

o:verstu·ffed, *ppl. a.* [OVER- 8 b, 27 b, 28 c.] **1.** Of furniture: completely covered with a thick layer of stuffing.
1925 T. DREISER *Amer. Trag.* (1926) I. II. xxi. 302 An old, faded and somewhat decrepit overstuffed chair. **1928** S. LEWIS *Man who knew Coolidge* i. 46 You sit at home in the ole over-stuffed chair. **1930** U. PARROTT *Strangers may Kiss* 28 The two armchairs were guaranteed by the landlady to be overstuffed. **1931** *Times* 16 Mar. 22/6 (Advt.), Overstuffed Chesterfield suites in tapestry. **1962** M. DUCKWORTH in C. K. Stead *N.Z. Short Stories* (1966) 362 He passed a..man seated on an overstuffed couch. **1973** W. M. DUNCAN *Big Timer* x. 66 There were three over-stuffed armchairs.
2. *fig.* Inflated, exaggerated; obese, fat.
1936 L. C. DOUGLAS *White Banners* xi. 233 Hannah's fears that an overstuffed optimism might involve them all in a financial disaster were gradually allayed. **1946** E. LINKLATER *Private Angelo* xviii. 230 Some great overstuffed history of the world's calamities. **1972** *Daily Tel.* 15 Jan. 9/2 The vulgar antics of the overstuffed striptease dancers.

over-sum, *v.* Delete † *Obs.* and add later example.
1929 R. BRIDGES *Testament of Beauty* IV. 108 The imperativ obligation cannot be over-summ'd.

over-supply, *sb.* Add: (Later examples.) Also *attrib.*
1932 *New Yorker* 14 May 42/2 You will write things.. that will get the public interested in that oversupply of pongee somebody is trying to unload. **1964** *Times Rev. Industry* Apr. 3/2 Until the oversupply position improves, there will not be enough work for Britain's shipyards. **1971** *New Scientist* 2 Sept. 510/2 Even in these days of apparent oversupply of scientists it is clear there are never enough really creative minds on the genius level to go around. **1975** *Physics Bull.* Nov. 477/1 In Britain, despite the oversupply of staff and the shortage of money, every department is well equipped. **1977** *Living with Tanker Surplus* (Shell Internat. Petroleum Co.) 2 An impressive amount of new capacity will continue to add to the over-supply.

over-supply, *v.* (Earlier and later examples.)
1865 M. EYRE *Lady's Walks S. of France* ii. 18 The markets at Bordeaux and Pau and Tarbes were *over-supplied* with fruit, butter, poultry, and eggs. **1960** *Farmer & Stockbreeder* 15 Mar. 74/3 The market becomes over-supplied.

over-sweet, *a.* (Later examples.)
1935 [see *ICKY, IKKY *a.* and *sb.*]. **1951** S. SPENDER *World within World* v. 267 At the end of a lecture on the effect of gases.., I hid for half an hour in a telephone box, overwhelmed by the vision of human beings asphyxiating one another in poisonous over-sweet scents. **1976** *Times* 20 Oct. 14/7 The 2½-lb Christmas puddings..taste fine, if a bit over-sweet.

o·verswing. [OVER- 29 b.] **1.** An excessive swing.
1921 *Studies* Sept. 385 The overswing of a pendulum slipping from benevolent despotism of the priest into confiscation of church property. **1926** *Amer. Speech* I. 632 *Overswing*, a common fault [in golf]. **1971** I. G. GASS et al. *Understanding Earth* x. 148/2 We can speculate that such an overswing would eventually correct itself.
2. [OVER- 6.] In gymnastics, a movement in which the body swings or turns over.
1955 *Simple Gymnastics* ('Know the Game' Series) 22 *Overswing vault*—Take off both feet and spring high above the apparatus. Drop into the angle position with bent arms and head well back beyond the far edge of the apparatus. Keep the legs down while the hips fall forward. Then extend the hips and push hard with the hands. **1964** G. C. KUNZLE *Parallel Bars* ii. 63 You can also do this overswing off one bar outwards. **1965** *Trampolining* ('Know the Game' Series) 43/2 A simple dismount is to walk to the end of the bed, drop into a knee bounce, place the hands on the end rail and perform an overswing on to the feet, in the same way as you would do an overswing over a box horse.

overtake, *v.* Add: **1. a.** Now esp. of a motorist: to drive a vehicle past (another vehicle travelling in the same direction). Also *absol.*, and with the vehicle as subj.
1936 J. PRIOLEAU *Motorist's Compan.* xxix. 418 The commoner examples of dangerous driving are..cutting-in and overtaking another car travelling at any but an obviously lower speed [etc.]. **1938** M. CAMPBELL *Key to Motoring* ix. 107 One of the greatest dangers of fog-driving lies in overtaking or in passing stationary vehicles. **1959** [see *CHEESED *a.*] **1959** E. H. CLEMENTS *High Tension* vi. 100 'The journey back was worth it... West overtook me.'.. 'Where did he overtake you?' 'Rannoch.' **1973** R. HILL *Ruling Passion* II. iv. 114 A slow lorry suddenly appeared ahead... He swung out sharply to overtake. **1976** *Southern Even. Echo* (Southampton) 12 Nov. 5/2 Marshall was riding a motorcycle on dual carriageway..when a car in front pulled out to overtake.
10. *Bridge. intr.* To take with a higher card a trick already taken by one's partner. Also *trans.*, to play a higher card than (the card played by one's partner).
1904 J. B. ELWELL *Advanced Bridge* 164 With no re-entry in a hand, overtaking is often the only means of making a suit. **1939** N. DE V. HART *Bridge Players' Bedside Bk.* xviii. 73 Declarer ducked in dummy, but Herr von Bludhorn overtook. *Ibid.* xxxviii. 118 Declarer played out the King, Knave, and Ten of Trumps, overtaking the Ten with dummy's Queen. **1959** REESE & DORMER *Bridge Players' Dict.* 161 South..leads the jack of spades and, depending on which suit West unguards, overtakes or not with dummy's queen of spades. **1974** *Country Life* 17 Jan. 98/3 East should have overtaken the Spade King and switched to Diamonds.

overtaking *vbl. sb.* and *ppl. a.* (further examples).
1880 R. G. MARSDEN *Treat. Law Collisions at Sea* vi. 187 Article 20 is express as to the duty of an overtaking sailing-ship to keep out of the way. **1928** R. TOWNSEND *Motoring made Easy* v. 74 No attempt should be made at overtaking on a curve in the road or at a corner. **1960** [see *CUTTING *vbl. sb.* 9 c]. **1961** F. H. BURGESS *Dict. Sailing* 155 *Overtaking light*, a fixed white light, screened so as to be visible 12 points, i.e. from right astern to 2 points abaft the beam each side, and from two miles away; carried by all ships under way. **1966** [see *fast lane* s.v. *FAST *a.* 11]. **1970** *Motoring Which?* July 116/1 Five mirrors specifically designed for door-mounting (often called 'overtaking mirrors'). **1975** J. CLEARY *Safe House* ii. 100 He saw the beam of the overtaking vehicle's headlamps.

overtalk, *v.* **b.** (Further example.)
1903 E. M. FORSTER in *Temple Bar* Dec. 682 They shook him and tried to overtalk him, but he still went on.

overtasked, *ppl. a.* (Earlier U.S. example.)
1869 'MARK TWAIN' *Innoc. Abr.* 289 Relief for overtasked eyes and brain from study and sightseeing.

overtaxation. (Earlier example.)
1823 J. S. MILL in *Black Dwarf* XI. 749 Over-taxation cannot lower wages.

overtaxing, *vbl. sb.* (Example.)
1877 TENNYSON *Harold* I. i. 6 Nay, there be murmurs for thy brother breaks us With over-taxing.

over-the-board, *a.* [OVER *prep.* 12.] Of chess competition: with the participants actually present, as opp. to correspondence play; with opponents facing each other across the chess-board.
1932 E. LASKER *Manual of Chess* IV. 228/2 His talent for over-the-board play was not considerable. **1954** H. GOLOMBEK *World Chess Championship 1954* 54 He has retired from over-the-board play and has devoted himself to writing about and teaching the game. **1974** C. H. O'D. ALEXANDER *On Chess* III. ix. 214 For various reasons—no chess club in the locality, lack of time, finding over-the-board play too much nervous strain—a number of people don't play it.

over the counter, *adv.* (*a.*). [OVER *prep.* 12.] **a.** See COUNTER *sb.*³ 4. **b.** *N. Amer.* With reference to the selling of stocks and shares: as a direct transaction, (business concluded) outside the system of a recognized stock exchange. **c.** Hence of purchase and selling generally: (transacted) directly between seller and buyer; openly, legitimately. (Cf. *under the counter* s.v. *COUNTER *sb.*³ 4 b.) Also *transf.* and (usu. with hyphens) as *adj. phr.*
1875, 1889 [see COUNTER *sb.*³ 4]. **1921** *Mag. of Wall St.* 10 Dec. 179/2 There is another field which readers have expressed the desire to see us cover. That is the great field comprising unlisted securities, which are dealt in over-the-counter... In response to this demand, we are inaugurating, beginning with this issue, a new department to appear under the caption, 'Over-the-Counter'. *Ibid.*, It will be our effort to confine our analysis of over-the-counter stocks to as brief a space as possible. **1925** A. M. SAKOLSKI *Princ. Investment* x. 108 'Over-the-counter' transactions (i.e., those which occur privately, whether consummated directly by negotiation between buyer and seller or through dealers and brokers) generally, in the absence of special agreements, follow the common practices of the exchanges. **1929** WILLIS & BOGEN *Investment Banking* iii. 50 This market is referred to as the unlisted or over-the-counter market, because business is transacted..'over the counter' of the individual broker or dealer, rather than at..an exchange. **1934** *Sun* (Baltimore) 27 Apr. 2/3 The committee has heard evidence of extensive manipulation in certain New York bank stocks after their withdrawal from the New York Stock Exchange and while they were being sold 'over the counter'. **1936** WODEHOUSE *Laughing Gas* xv. 165 'You think this tooth could be sold?' 'Over the counter, sir, over the counter.' **1944** *Amer. N. & Q.* July 64/1 A North Carolinian illustration of this futile neologistic tendency found in high places is 'over-the-counter salesperson', for the simple..*clerk*. **1957** CLARK & GOTTFRIED *University Dict. Business & Finance* 253/2 The securities are traded on a face-to-face, or over-the-counter basis. In the actual operation of over-the-counter trading, a trader who specializes in a particular security arranges for all transactions, either by bringing buyers and sellers together, or by buying and selling the security for his own account. **1958** *Spectator* 11 July 58/3 The over-the-counter service of spit-roasted chicken is a development in the catering trade. *Ibid.* 60/1 The over-the-counter charge for the spit-roasted bird is 12s. 6d. **1963** *Times* 23 Apr. 20/3 Sales of bottles to take home ('Off-Sales') have increased very considerably, and there has been a reduction of sales by the glass—'Over the counter'—with a consequent reduction in profit. **1965** *McGraw-Hill Dict. Mod. Econ.* 367 In addition to common and preferred stocks, almost all U.S. government securities and municipal and corporate bonds are traded over the counter. **1968** *Globe & Mail* (Toronto) 17 Feb. B 2/1 An over-the-counter speculative issue that rose from 25 cents a share to $4.50 in the past six months. **1969** *Guardia* 25 July 6/6 If 'over the counter' pregnancy

testing is to come to Britain, the tests should be carried out by the pharmacist. **1972** *Times* 16 May (Wall Street Suppl.) p. iv/7 For 25 years he was a broker and then from 1964 to 1967 headed the National Association of Securities Dealers which regulates over-the-counter deals. **1974** M. C. GERALD *Pharmacol.* ii. 20 Nonprescription (over-the-counter, OTC) sleep-facilitating products..have capitalized on the drowsiness induced by methapyrilene. **1974** *Guardian* 22 Mar. 11/5 The retailers wanted to simplify the collection of air fuel surcharges on package holidays by including the sum on the over-the-counter invoice presented to the customer.

over the moon: see *MOON *sb.* 3 b.

over-the-road, *a.* [OVER *prep.* 13.] Of, pertaining to, or used in long-distance road transportation.

1945 *Sun* (Baltimore) 24 Oct. 14-0/8 Approximately 1500 members of Local 557, Freight Drivers and Helpers ..yesterday went on strike which threatens to halt about 50 per cent of trucking operations in the city and practically all over-the-road, inter-city hauling into and out of Baltimore. **1967** *Jane's Surface Skimmer Systems 1967–68* 63 Movement of shipment in cages installed on air-in-floor pallets eliminates rehandling between city pick-up trailers, terminal site, over-the-road trailers, second city terminal site and final delivery unit. **1969** *Jane's Freight Containers 1968–69* 407/3 Both the 20 ft and 40 ft units are designed to be used as over-the-road trailers. **1971** M. TAK *Truck Talk* 114 *Over-the-road driver*, a driver who hauls goods long distances. **1977** *Time* 13 June 36/2 Last week's decision ended a long and hard-fought case against..a trucking company based in Lubbock, Texas, which the Government accused of discriminating against blacks and Hispanics in deciding who would get over-the-road driving jobs.

overthought, *sb.* Add: **b.** [OVER- 2 b.] Conscious thought; an explicit concept; = OVER-SOUL.

1883 G. M. HOPKINS *Let.* 14 Jan. (1938) 105 Two strains of thought..the overthought that which everybody, editors, see..which might for instance be abridged or paraphrased..the other, the underthought, conveyed chiefly in the choice of metaphors etc used and often only half realised by the poet himself. **1884** W. JAMES in R. B. Perry *Tht. & Char. W. James* (1935) I. 583 Those who must answer this question negatively are forced to the notion of an Over-thought behind the phenomenal real.

overthrow, *sb.* Add: **1. d.** The state of being overthrown.

1903 *Daily Chron.* 12 Sept. 5/1 Half a dozen great trees were torn up by the roots, and lay in disorderly overthrow ready for the saws. **1906** F. THOMPSON *Ode Eng. Martyrs* in *Wks.* (1913) II. 136 Till she shall know This lesson in her overthrow: Hardest servitude has he That's jailed in arrogant liberty.

4. *Cricket* (earlier and later examples). *Baseball* (examples).

1748 in H. T. Waghorn *Dawn of Cricket* (1906) 21 To play or pay, bye balls, and overthrows to count. **1856** *Spirit of Times* 8 Nov. 165/1 Gessner [made]..three homes in succession, one of them being helped by an overthrow. **1949** *Telephone-Reg.* (McMinnville, Oregon) 4 Aug. 1/2 There is no sliding and a player cannot run on overthrows. **1955** *Times* 13 July 3/4 The Middlesex fielding was uncertain and Warwickshire were helped by indiscriminate throwing, which led to many over-throws.

5. *Archit.* A panel of decorated wrought-iron work forming the architrave of a gateway or arch.

1911 J. S. GARDNER *English Ironwork 17th & 18th Centuries* 26 The base of the overthrow took the form of a latticed girder, or two bars braced together by scrolls. **1932** *Times Lit. Suppl.* 10 Nov. 835/2 Making artistic ironwork—gates simple or elaborate, with or without 'overthrows'. **1957** R. LISTER *Decorative Wrought Ironwork Gt. Brit.* iii. 89 The overthrow, a composition built up from sixteen simple scrolls, reaches up symmetrically in the centre of the stretcher..terminating into a large disc bearing a garter and shield, and crested by a coronet. **1971** *Illustr. London News* Oct. 54/1 A good quality 18th century Italian Istrian marble wellhead with wrought iron overthrow. **1975** *Oxf. Compan. Decorative Arts* 481/2 The overthrows of the gates, swollen to gigantic size, plainly prefigure the Rococo.

overthrow, *v.* Add: **6.** *trans.* [OVER- 27.] To throw farther than is necessary or desired; to throw too far; *spec.* in *Cricket,* to throw (the ball) beyond or wide of the wicket, so as to concede overthrows.

1833 *Field Bk.* 141/1 The batters may take the advantage of running when a ball has been over-thrown. **1862** *Chambers's Encycl.* III. 320/1 Misconception of this [distance] may lead to overthrowing the ball, or throwing it short. **1875** *Baily's Mag.* Apr. 403 A ball..overthrown, on the ground where he learnt his cricket, means the loss of four, five, or even six or seven runs.

overthrowal (ōuvəɹþrōu·ăl). [f. OVERTHROW *v.* + -AL II.] The act of overthrowing; subversion, defeat.

1916 W. J. LOCKE *Wonderful Year* xxiii. 333 Thus came the overthrowal of all Corinna's scheme of values. **1920** —— *House of Baltazar* xxi. 257 The ultimate object of this gathering was the overthrowal of the Government. **1941** 'R. WEST' *Black Lamb* II. 196 The upsetting of kings and the overthrowal of empires. **1949** *Tablet* 3 Sept. 147/1 The overthrowal of the Second Reich of the Hohenzollerns. **1968** *Progressive* Nov. 10/3 Spiro Agnew..had coined at least two new words by early October: 'overthrowal' and 'uprisal'.

overthrust, *sb.* Add: In mod. use (also *overthrust fault*), a reverse fault in which the fault plane makes a relatively small angle with the horizontal; formerly, any reverse fault. (Further examples.)

1903 A. GEIKIE *Text-bk. Geol.* (ed. 4) I. 690, 1. Normal Faults... 2. Reversed Faults or Overthrusts. **1944** A. HOLMES *Princ. Physical Geol.* vi. 80 Reverse or Thrust Faults... When the resulting fracture is inclined at an angle between 45° and the horizontal..the corresponding fault is described as an overthrust. **1957** *Bull. Geol. Soc. Amer.* LXVIII. 168/1 The Medicine Lodge overthrust, a low-angle fault with a displacement of many miles. **1969** *Ibid.* LXXX. 953 Overthrust fault surfaces are actually undulatory rather than plane.

overthrust *v.* (examples); hence **o·verthrust** *ppl. a.*

1900 [see *CRUST *sb.* 13 b]. **1901** *Nature* 3 Jan. 234/1 Huge masses of country have been overfolded, fractured, and overthrust, the older being pushed over the newer. **1942** M. P. BILLINGS *Structural Geol.* x. 184 The thrusts dip north, and the overthrust sheets have traveled northward relative to the underlying formations. **1956** W. J. ARKELL *Jurassic Geol. World* ix. 225 The Jurassic and Cretaceous systems were strongly folded and overthrust in the post-Oligocene, pre-Miocene orogeny. **1968** [see *FORELAND 4*].

overthwart, *v.* **2.** (Later example.)

1937 *John o' London's* 5 Feb. 761/2 My parents were for ever overthwarting me, both on 'em. Always to school I had to go till I was twelve, and to church I had to go regular as clockwork.

overthwarting, *vbl. sb.* (Later example in sense 1 c of the verb.)

1942 W. ROSE *Good Neighbours* iii. 20 A field was first evenly ploughed all over, after which cross ploughing—called *over-a-thurting*—often followed, severing the furrows and leaving the soil thoroughly exposed to the air.

overtilt, *v.* Delete †*Obs.* and add later example.

1905 *Westm. Gaz.* 1 Feb. 2/3 Our house tottereth To ruin; because this people with the breath Of pity would overtilt it.

overtime, *sb., adv.* Add: **A.** *sb.* **a.** (Earlier and later examples.) Also, payment for work performed in excess of normal hours. *overtime ban,* industrial action in which the working of overtime is suspended.

1846 *Swell's Night Guide* 42 There are instances of the awful enemy lodging itself here, through some private tailing in overtime. **1911** *Daily Colonist* (Victoria, B.C.) 26 Apr. 14/5 A conference is to be held..with regard to the demand being made by the seamen for overtime pay. **1916** 'BOYD CABLE' *Doing their Bit* iv. 63 Their haggling over 8*d.* or 8½*d.* an hour pay, or Saturday half-holidays, or double overtime for Sunday. **1928** F. B. YOUNG *My Brother Jonathan* III. iii. 446 Joe Matthews..'picking up' six pounds a week, to say nothing of overtime, in Higgins's shell factory. **1952** *Times* 1 Dec. 2/5 (*heading*) Miners' overtime ban ended. **1968** *R. Comm. Trade Unions & Employers' Associations Res. Papers* No. 9, 82 The negotiations broke down during 1964 and the unions imposed an overtime ban and a work to rule. **1972** *Times* 15 May 17/3 Workers at another Ferranti factory are due to impose the restrictions—an overtime ban, work to rule and boycott of piecework—from today. **1973** C. D. GARRATT *Masterpieces in Steam* 128 My visit to Brynlliw was during the overtime ban prior to the miners' strike. **1973** *Times* 4 Dec. 3/6 The miners' overtime ban yesterday went into its fourth week.

b. In sporting contests: extra time added in the event of a draw. *N. Amer.*

1921 *Daily Colonist* (Victoria B.C.) 15 Mar. 11/1 Overtime game goes in favor of Towers. The Towers Club.. defeated the Senators..by 8 goals to 7, the game having to go into overtime to decide the match. **1946** *Richmond* (Virginia) *Times-Dispatch* 20 Mar. 17/3 His keen floor generalship..built up to a terrific climax—his 55-foot shot in the last two seconds that tied the score at 74–74 and led to the Ram's 82–79 overtime triumph. **1961** J. S. SALAK *Dict. Amer. Sports* 315 *Overtime*, continuance of play after the regulation time for a contest has expired when the score is tied. **1970** *Washington Post* 30 Sept. D 1/7 The Senators..lost two overtime games to the Baltimore Orioles. **1974** *State* (Columbia, S. Carolina) 3 Mar. 2-D/5 Freshman Walter Davis banked in a 35-foot jump shot at the end of regulation time to cap an incredible North Carolina comeback Saturday as the fourth-ranked Tar Heels nipped arch rival Duke, 96-92 in overtime.

B. *adv.* Also *fig.*

1938 E. AMBLER *Cause for Alarm* xvi. 262 In that moment my brain worked overtime. **1953** A. HUXLEY *Let.* 25 Sept. (1969) 685 They are pork manufacturers, with a farm where five thousand sows work overtime eating the garbage of the city of Long Beach and producing fifty thousand piglets per annum. **1971** *Nature* 26 Nov. 179/1 Washington's science policy machinery has been working overtime on plans that could significantly alter relationships between science and government. **1974** G. BUTLER *Coffin for Canary* i. 9 My tongue had worked overtime at the week-end..talking with my sister.

o·ver-ti:mer. [f. OVERTIME *sb.* + -ER¹.] One who works overtime.

1926 S. BALDWIN *On England* 99 The just and the unjust, the half-timers, the whole-timers and the overtimers.

overti·p, *v.* [f. OVER- 27 + TIP *v.*⁴] *trans.* To give an excessive gratuity to (one who has been of service). Also *absol.* Hence **o:verti·pping** *vbl. sb.*

1926 E. HEMINGWAY *Fiesta* (1927) III. xix. 269 The waiter seemed a little offended..so I overtipped him. **1928** A. HUXLEY *Point Counter Point* xxi. 388 The fare was three-and-six. Philip gave the driver two half-crowns... He made a habit of over-tipping. **1938** L. MACNEICE *Earth Compels* 38 And there are the men who appear to be men of sense,..For fear of opinion over-tipping in bars, For fear of thought studying stupefaction. **1941** *Penguin New Writing* VIII. 62 The guests in the guest-house, they were charmed with him too. They over-tipped him. **1965** *New Statesman* 7 May 729/3 If we had reason to believe that he once overtipped a cab-driver, it would be recorded here. **1976** E. WARD *Hanged Man* xvii. 98 He stopped the taxi..paid and overtipped. *Ibid.* xxxiii. 214 A taxi-driver collected the message for him. Anonymity is worth over-tipping.

overtone, *sb.* Add: **1.** Also, an analogous component of any non-acoustic oscillation, having a frequency that is an integral multiple of the fundamental frequency.

1922 A. D. UDDEN tr. *Bohr's Theory of Spectra* III. ii. 83 This apparent difficulty is explained by the occurrence in the motion of the hydrogen atom..of harmonic components corresponding to values of *r*, which are different from 1; or using a terminology well known from acoustics, there appear overtones in the motion of the hydrogen atom. **1937** JENKINS & WHITE *Fund. Physical Optics* xii. 283 If the charged oscillator is bound by a force which does not obey Hooke's law,..it will be capable of re-radiating not only the impressed frequency, but also various combinations of this frequency with the fundamental and overtone frequencies of the oscillator. **1973** *Physics Bull.* July 421/2 The first overtone spectrum of HBr near 4·95 μm has been obtained in this way.

2. *fig.* (Freq. in *pl.*) Applied to literature, esp. poetry: what is suggested or implied by the sound or meaning of the words. More generally, a connotation or subtle implication in thought, language, or action.

1890 W. JAMES *Princ. Psychol.* I. ix. 258 Let us use the words psychic overtone, suffusion, or fringe, to designate the influence of a faint brain-process upon our thought. *Ibid.* 281 The total idea..is the overtone, halo, or fringe of the word, as spoken in that sentence. **1904** J. G. HUNEKER (*title*) Overtones, a book of temperaments. **1911** BRERETON & ROTHWELL tr. *Bergson's Laughter* ii. 96 There would be nothing amusing in the saying, 'It serves you right, George Dandin', were it not for the comic overtones that take up and re-echo it. **1922** H. CRANE *Let.* 2 Apr. (1965) 83 The very effective literary device of under-accentuation in just the right place to produce 'overtones' of overwhelming effect. **1940** *Mind* XLIX. 209 Stripped of these mental overtones, his definition is quite close to the etymological meaning of the word *infinite*. **1952** *Jrnl. Theol. Stud.* III. 64 Once Israel had again fallen under the 'yoke of the heathen', the festival of dedication would have reminded the Jews of the exploits of Judas and could easily have taken on nationalistic overtones. **1957** *Economist* 21 Sept. 953/1 Seven per cent would have been a stronger gesture of resolve, if it had not been left so late as to suggest some overtones of desperation. **1965** *Listener* 25 Nov. 869/1 There are overtones of Aldous Huxley and Norman Douglas, and echoes of Firbank. **1976** 'D. HALLIDAY' *Dolly & Nanny Bird* xix. 258 The kidnapping and holding to ransom of an American child, in order to raise money for the self-styled Croatian Liberation Army. A simple crime with political overtones which the militia would work out for themselves.

overtone, *v.* Add: **2.** (Earlier example.)

1868 [see TONE *v.* 5].

3. To give an overtone or implication to. *rare.*

1871 G. MEREDITH *H. Richmond* II. xvii. 269 She threw a kindly-comical look, not overtoned, at the miniature ships on the mantelpiece, and the picture of Joseph leading Mary with her babe on the ass.

overtop, *adv.* (Later Austral. example.)

1921 'J. O'BRIEN' *Around Boree Log* (1937) 82 And every creek a banker ran, And dams filled overtop.

overtopped, *ppl. a.* Add: Of a small tree: growing beneath the canopy formed by larger trees and receiving no direct light. (Later examples.)

1917 *Jrnl. Forestry* XV. 74 The crown classes usually distinguished are: Dominant... Co-dominant... Intermediate... Overtopped. Trees with crowns entirely below the general forest canopy and receiving no direct light. **1948** *Ibid.* XLVI. 833/2 Seedlings overtopped but with considerable side light survive and grow just about as well as seedlings in small openings. **1976** G. W. SHARPE et al. *Introd. Forestry* (ed. 4) ix. 187 Suppressed. Pertaining to trees with small crowns that are entirely below the level of the canopy receiving no direct light from above or from the sides. Also called overtopped.

overtopping, *vbl. sb.* and *ppl. a.* (Later examples.)

1903 W. B. YEATS *In Seven Woods* 39 And he, The one over-topping man that's in the world, Keeps far away. **1959** *Times* 2 Nov. 21/1 Undertopping in no case exceeded 5 lb. to the hundredweight and overtopping with three machines did not exceed 3·4 lb. **1976** M. GREEN *Children of Sun* vi. 234 America's overtopping of England —England's overshadowing and diminution.

overtower, *v.* (Later examples.)

1928 E. Blom *Limitations of Music* 18 As an artist..he [*sc.* Mozart] overtowers every other figure in musical history. **1954** N. Pevsner *Essex* 385 The church is..cut off by the railway from the village and now overtowered by a modern factory.

over-train, *v.* **a.** (Later examples.)
1910 *Blackw. Mag.* Jan. 135/1, I was as hard as nails..; but was over-trained, and after a time did the walking, and even the shooting, with some loss of the keenness with which I began it. **1971** *Nature* 10 Sept. 126/2 Here rats are overtrained (by means of foot shock) to avoid entering a black box. **1976** A. Grey *Bulgarian Exclusive* v. 35 They're over-training the Olympic squad.

over-tra·p, *v.* [Over- 27.] *trans.* To trap (a region) too much in such a way as to deplete the fauna. So **over-tra·pped** *ppl. a.*
1964 P. Worsley in I. L. Horowitz *New Sociol.* 381 Over-trapped areas around the settlements. **1968** [see *over-hunt *v.*].

overtravel, *sb.* Add: **b.** Movement of part of a machine beyond the desired point; an allowance made for such travel. Freq. *attrib.*
1923 R. Grierson *Electr. Lift Equipment* xiii. 87 Over-travel spaces at both the top and the bottom of the shaft are essential, as the brake is subject to wear. **1939** R. S. Phillips *Electr. Lifts* xii. 177 The top overtravel is defined as the distance provided for the car floor to travel above the level of the top terminal landing before the car is stopped by the ultimate limit switch. **1962** E. G. Davies in G. A. T. Burdett *Automatic Control Handbk.* iii. 21 Series limit switches..are generally employed as emergency over-travel switches not called upon to operate except after the failure of the normal stopping or reversing pilot limit switch. **1977** *Economist* 3 Sept. 50/3 (Advt.), Overflow valves. Overtravel switches. Oxide magnets.
overtravel *v.* (*b*) (see quot. 1909).
1909 *Cent. Dict.* Suppl., *Overtravel*... In *mech.*, to travel farther than is necessary to do a certain act or perform a definite function. **1955** *Archit. Rev.* CXVII. 143/4 At top and bottom of the well there are Limit Switches which automatically cut off the lift motor in the event of the car overtravelling in either direction.

over-traw·l, *v.* [Over- 27.] *trans.* To trawl (a fishing-ground) too much or to depletion. So **over-traw·ling** *vbl. sb.*
1913 *Q. Rev.* Apr. 444 In 1892 the Trawlers' Society.. again protested against over-trawling.

o·vertrick. *Bridge.* Also with hyphen. [Over- 19.] A trick taken in excess of the number contracted for. Also *attrib.*
1921 F. Irwin *Compl. Auction Player* 15 Each over-trick is worth twice its value below the line. **1927** *Observer* 5 June 19/2 All over-trick bonuses gained by a vulnerable side..count double. **1929** M. C. Work *Compl. Contract Bridge* i. 2 A trick-score of 20 or 30 plus two over-tricks each worth 50. **1947** S. Harris *Fund. Princ. Contract Bridge* 88 This play may cost West an overtrick. **1966** *Listener* 16 June 891/3 One overtrick is a small premium with which to insure a hazardous contract. **1973** *Times* 10 Feb. 12/8 If he had kept three spades, declarer would have made an overtrick by putting him on play with a club or a heart.

overtrim, over-trim, *v.* **2.** (Earlier example.)
1816 Jane Austen *Emma* II. xvii. 328, I have the greatest dislike to the idea of being overtrimmed.

overturn, *sb.* Add: **6.** *Limnology.* The mixing or circulation of the water in a thermally stratified lake that usu. occurs once or twice each year as a result of the cooling or warming of the epilimnion.
[**1898** G. C. Whipple in *Amer. Naturalist* XXXII. 27 Soon the surface and bottom layers come to have substantially the same temperature, and vertical currents extend from top to bottom. This is the 'period of spring circulation', or the 'spring overturning'.] **1911** Birge & Juday in *Bull. Wisconsin Geol. & Nat. Hist. Survey* xxii. p. xi, The stratum of circulating water becomes increasingly thinner until..the permanent summer conditions are established. Thenceforward, until the overturn, only the water of the epilimnion can have direct contact with the air. **1935** P. S. Welch *Limnology* iv. 38 During the spring and fall overturns.., when the water is of uniform density from top to bottom, return currents may extend even to the bottom of relatively deep inland lakes. **1972** *Ann. Rep. Freshwater Biol. Assoc.* XL. 42 Before the overturn, the epilimnetic population of both Grasmere and Blelham Tarn went through the whole [nitrate] reduction process. **1974** *Encycl. Brit. Macropædia* X. 607/1 Mixing due to cooling or warming processes that increase the density of surface waters sufficiently to cause them to sink results in what is termed circulation, or overturn, of lake water.

overturn, *v.* Add: **3. b.** To reverse (a judicial decision).
1969 *Morning Star* 8 Aug. 1/3 Last month, the US circuit court of appeals in Boston overturned the verdict. **1973** *Observer* 22 July 10/1 The House of Lords unanimously overturned this decision.

overturned, *ppl. a.* Add: *spec.* in *Geol.* applied to a fold or the limb of a fold that is tilted beyond the vertical (cf. Overfold *sb.*).
1861 *Amer. Jrnl. Sci.* LXXXI. 218 Sometimes it may overlie the overturned Utica formation. **1896** [see Overfold *v.* 2]. **1907, 1970** [see *foreland 4*].

overun (ōu·vərən), *a.* and *sb. local.* Also **overrun(ner.** [f. Over *adv.* or *a.* + Un².] **A.** *adj.* In the Isle of Wight, coming from the mainland; not native to the Island. **B.** *sb.* = *overner.
1881 H. & C. R. Smith *Isle of Wight Words* 48 *Overun*, coming from 'across the water', from the mainland of the county. **1886** [see *overner]. **1889** F. Cowper *Captain of Wight* x. 130 There'll have to be some overrunners asked over. *Ibid.* xiv. 176 That's what I call a hardy knight... 'Tis a pity he's an overrun.

overve·ntilate, *v.* *Physiol.* [Over- 26.] **a.** *trans.* = *hyperventilate *v.* b.
1917 J. S. Haldane *Organism & Environment* i. 13 The very rapid and shallow breathing of a dog in hot weather does not over-ventilate its lungs. **1931** *Amer. Jrnl. Physiol.* XCVIII. 202 A dog with a low Ca of 6·05..was overventilated..with the corresponding precipitation of violent convulsions. **1963** Spalding & Smith *Clin. Pract. & Physiol. Artific. Respiration* iii. 43 A patient who has been overventilated during artificial respiration.
b. *intr.* = *hyperventilate *v.* a.
1927 *Jrnl. Physiol.* LXIV. p. xxiv, Nahun showed that there is a decrease in limb volume when a normal man over-ventilates. **1961** *Ibid.* CLVI. 240 The subject was instructed to overventilate from a 100 l. Douglas bag containing 4% carbon dioxide in air.

o:verventila·tion. *Physiol.* [Over- 26.] = *hyperventilation.
1911 *Amer. Jrnl. Physiol.* XXVIII. 387 Over-ventilation of the lungs..is at once suggested as an explanation. **1927** *Jrnl. Physiol.* LXIV. p. xxiv, The vessels of the skin play some part in maintaining the blood-pressure during over-ventilation in man. **1963** Spalding & Smith *Clin. Pract. & Physiol. Artific. Respiration* v. 76 Artificial overventilation may alter the response to CO_2 of the mechanism controlling respiration and may induce a volume-dependent type of respiration.

overview, *v.* Delete † *Obs.* and add later examples.
Quot. 1864 is in sense 1, quots. 1935, 1977 in sense 2. The use in quot. 1977 is influenced by *overview *sb.* 2.
1864 S. Warner *Old Helmet* I. xii. 247 Mrs. Powle's fair face would overview a moral desolation more hopeless and more cheerless [etc.]. **1935** E. R. Eddison *Mistress of Mistresses* xi. 197 From the sweep of eagles' wings it becometh us overview the matter, and what's just and allowable of our greatness, choose that. *Ibid.* xii. 225, I would have you, as a politic prince.., refer the whole estate you are in to your highness' deliberate overviewing again. **1977** *Canad. Jrnl. Linguistics 1976* XXI. 1. 17 The interplay of physiological-cognitive factors with respect to early speech perception and production has been critically overviewed by Gilbert (1975).

overview, *sb.* Restrict † *Obs.* to sense in Dict. and add: **2.** orig. *U.S.* A survey, summary, or comprehensive review of facts or ideas; a concise statement or outline of a subject. Hence **o·verviewer,** one who formulates an overview.
1934 *Amer. Speech* IX. 318/2 Editors testify that the new noun *overview* is now being worked as hard by educationists as 'purposeful', 'challenge', 'objective', 'motivation', *et al.*, have been in the past. **1944** *Mind* LIII. 276 According to the jacket..the purpose of this book is to present 'an overview of present-day philosophical trends'. **1958** *Times Lit. Suppl.* 28 Mar. 173/4 Her 'overview' of psycho-analytical thought is therefore followed by detailed expositions of the views of the principal dissidents. **1967** *Wall St. Jrnl.* 4 May 4/3 The first step is to take an 'overview' of the problem. **1969** M. Crichton *Andromeda Strain* v. 44 A scientist with a conscience, an overview, an appreciation of the significance of events. **1969** M. Scriven in N. R. Hanson *Perception & Discovery* p. vii, There is a..tension between the demands of exact historical scholarship and the more free-ranging interests of the overviewer. **1973** *Nature* 6 July 59/3 The chief drawback of this volume is that it lacks a chapter devoted to a critical overview of the comparative relevance of particular models as they relate to particular experimental ends. **1974** *Florida FL Reporter* XIII. 31/2 With presumably Ms. Hess as overviewer making some critical commentary on which of the arguments were stronger and why. **1975** A. S. Miskimin *Renaissance Chaucer* viii. 230 In an overview such as this, many questions will be begged. **1975** *Sci. Amer.* May 119/2 The first 50 pages of overview include a neat account of the logical architecture of possible machines. **1975** *Listener* 31 July 130/2 In its latest policy 'overview', the State Department ponders [etc.].

o·vervo:ltage. [f. Over- 19, 20 + Voltage², as tr. G. *überspannung* (W. A. Caspari 1899, in *Zeitschr. f. physikal. Chem.* XXX. 91).] **1.** The difference between the electrode potential for a reaction (as the liberation of a gas) in practical, irreversible conditions and the theoretical, reversible value.
1907 Whitney & Brown tr. *Le Blanc's Text-bk. Electro-Chem.* viii. 299 Not only in the case of hydrogen, but also in that of oxygen, an over-voltage which varies with the nature of the electrode..is produced by the separation of the gas. **1922** Glazebrook *Dict. Appl. Physics* II. 60/1 Platinised platinum as a cathode has the lowest overvoltage among the elements commonly available. **1965** Phillips & Williams *Inorg. Chem.* I. xi. 421 Using a mercury electrode the over-voltage of hydrogen is so great that the sodium is discharged and taken into the mercury as an amalgam.

2. A voltage in excess of that which is normal, safe, or allowed for.
1921 S. Q. Hayes *Switching Equipment for Power Control* v. 157 Relays are built to furnish protection on A.C. or D.C. circuits against overvoltage, no voltage, overload, no load, reverse load and reverse phase. **1963** B. Fozard *Instrumentation Nucl. Reactors* v. 56 It may sometimes occur that a tube must be used with an insensitive scaling equipment, in which case a high overvoltage may be necessary to give satisfactory operation.

o:vervulcaniza·tion. [Over- 29 b.] Vulcanization for longer than is necessary to achieve the maximum modulus of elasticity.
1900 W. T. Brannt *India Rubber, Gutta-Percha & Balata* iii. 111 If the articles are allowed to remain too long in the solution, over-vulcanization may take place, that is, the surface of the article becomes hard and brittle. **1967** tr. *W. Hofmann's Vulcanization & Vulcanizing Agents* i. 24 Its symptoms [*sc.* those of postvulcanization] are thus very similar to the rising characteristic of tensile stress at a given elongation which is associated with overvulcanization.

overvu·lcanize, *v.* [Over- 27.] *trans.* To subject (rubber) to overvulcanization; to make hard or brittle by vulcanizing. Hence **overvu·lcanizing** *vbl. sb.*
1911 P. Schidrowitz *Rubber* xi. 172 Bysow..found that with a total sulphur of from 3·44 per cent. to 8·91 per cent. equilibrium was not produced until the samples were over-vulcanized. **1916** [see *overcure *v.*]. **1922** *Encycl. Brit.* XXX. 35/1 In 1916 some resistance to petrol was introduced by using pure para heavily loaded with mineral matter and rather over-vulcanized. **1967** tr. *W. Hofmann's Vulcanization & Vulcanizing Agents* i. 24 When an article is wholly or partly overvulcanized (thick-sectioned articles, for example, are sometimes overvulcanized at the surface), efficient protection against ageing is always necessary.

o·ver-walker. *rare.* [-er¹.] One who walks too much or too far.
1876 R. L. Stevenson in *Cornhill Mag.* XXXIII. 685 It is here that your over-walker fails of comprehension.

overwash, *sb.* (Further examples.)
1894 [see *outwash]. **1909** *Jrnl. Geol.* XVII. 375 Locally overwash plains are conspicuous topographic features. **1957** J. K. Charlesworth *Quaternary Era* I. xxii. 442 Thus outwash may occur with or without moraines; the two types constitute respectively Chamberlin's overwash aprons and outwash plains or aprons.

o:ver-wa·ter, *a.* [Over- 32.] **a.** Performed or proceeding across water (in quot. 1900 = 'foreign'). **b.** Situated on or located over water.
1900 W. C. Murray *Week's Rambling with 'Bra Quamin'* 11 De talkin' tree is a ober water duppy tree. **1933** *Sun* (Baltimore) 7 Dec. 1/7 It was the longest over-water flight of their aerial survey tour. **1942** *R.A.F. Jrnl.* 16 May 16 It has a long range..which renders it suitable for over-water operation from shore bases. **1946** *Sun* (Baltimore) 30 July 8/2 If geophysical reports are favorable, over-water rigs will be erected later for drilling tests. **1960** *Washington Post* 20 Mar. B8/4 Air Guard spokesmen emphasized that missions..are routed over nonpopulated areas to an over-water course to the Buck Target Range in North Carolina. **1967** *Jane's Surface Skimmer Systems 1967–68* 2/1 Research and development programmes are dedicated in the main to the task of speeding up over-water transport. **1976** B. Lecomber *Dead Weight* ii. vii. 82 All aero-engines immediately go into auto-rough whenever you think about them on the over-water flight.

overweight, *sb.* Add: **1.** (Later examples.)
1886 J. Barrowman *Gloss. Scotch Mining Terms* 48 *Overweight*, excess weight of disposals over outputs. **1888** W. E. Nicholson *Gloss. Terms Coal Trade Northumb. & Durham* 62 *Overweight*, the difference between the standard weight and the average weight for a fortnight when over the standard.
3. b. Applied to a person: obesity, excess of weight.
1917 *Med. Times* (N.Y.) Aug. 217/2 (*heading*) Reduction cures for overweight. **1918** J. Broadhurst *Home & Community Hygiene* xviii. 298 (*heading*) The relation of overweight to death rates. **1923** J. W. Barton *That Body of Yours* 102 There are two kinds of overweight. First.. the kind you inherit. You have always been a little overweight. Then there is the kind that is acquired at the age of 27 to 37. **1925** Mrs. Belloc Lowndes *Diary* 10 Jan. (1971) 102 Lord Northcliffe was..distressed at what he regarded as my overweight. He told me that he and his wife weighed each other constantly. **1951** I. B. Allen *Youth after Forty* vi. 53 Raw fruits do not induce overweight. **1973** M. Senechal *Guarding your Family's Health* iv. 56/1 One of the commonest of all health problems revealed by a checkup is overweight. **1975** *Times* 20 Dec. 12/5 She needs to lose weight..an overweight caused by a careless diet.
5. *Pros.* An instance of overweighting (see quot.).
1940 J. R. R. Tolkien in Clark Hall & Wrenn *Beowulf & Finnesburg Fragment* p. xxxi, An example with double overweight would be *wéllmāde wárgeār.*

over-weight, *a.* Add: (Now usu. written as one word.) *spec.* of a person: too heavy for one's height and build; obese. Also *absol.*
1899 G. R. Shepherd in *Med. Examiner* July 211/2 From our mortality records the overweights are clearly

less desirable than the underweights. *Ibid.* 212/1 Are people who are overweight likely to live longer than those who are..underweight? **1910** A. Bryce *Laws of Life & Health* vii. 247 No 'over-weight' dies of old age or senility. **1925** C. E. Turner *Personal & Community Health* ii. 52 The tendency to become overweight is no doubt constitutional. **1935** H. Roberts *Everyman in Health & Sickness* II. iv. 152 Insurance companies find that 'overweights' are bad lives. **1941** F. Silver *Foods & Nutrition* iv. 117 A child..is considered overweight if he is 20 per cent above the average for his age and height. **1951** I. B. Allen *Youth after Forty* vi. 50 'She is an obese person' sounds right down [*sic*] unattractive—but if she is pounds overweight, that's just what she is. **1958** *Which?* Autumn 20/1 Overweight people can reduce their weight by reducing their food intake. **1974** *Times* 4 Jan. 5/3 The overweight have become America's largest, least protected minority group. **1976** 'L. Black' *Healthy Way to Die* ii. 12 How often must he have heard every possible comic remark about overweight women!

overweight, *v.* Add: **3.** *Pros.* To stress as in overweighting.

1940 J. R. R. Tolkien in Clark Hall & Wrenn *Beowulf & Finnesburg Fragment* p. xxxi, The second dip of B, C and the dip of D, E may not be overweighted.

overweighted, *ppl. a.* (Later examples.)

1927 Bowley & Stamp *Nat. Income 1924* 23 When we pass from the accidental grouping in the returns, overweighted by banks, to the whole numbers according to the census, the averages are brought up again to the medians. **1948** *Mod. Philology* XLVI. 86 Besides these.. light or weak verses there are, of course, many which are extra-heavy, 'overweighted', and many which seem overlong. **1949** *Penguin Music Mag.* Feb. 85 Such a combination provides a monotonous tone colour and the bass seems turgid and overweighted.

o:verwei·ghting, *vbl. sb.* [-ing[1].] The act or fact of giving or having too much weight; overloading, overload (see also quot. 1940).

1905 *Westm. Gaz.* 1 Sept. 2/3 The frightful overweighting of the postman because of the flood of pictorial postcards. **1914** R. M. Jones *Spiritual Reformers 16th & 17th Cent.* xv. 289 Their gravest difficulty being an overweighting of learning which they sometimes failed to fuse with their spiritual vision. **1940** J. R. R. Tolkien in Clark Hall & Wrenn *Beowulf & Finnesburg Fragment* p. xxxi, Overweighting and extension..are a means of including certain common but slightly excessive patterns in the metre; also of adding weight to the line where required, and of packing much significant word-material into a small space... It consists in replacing the dip by a long (subordinate) stress.

overwhe·lmment. [f. Overwhelm *v.* + -ment.] = Overwhelmedness; Overwhelmingness.

1866 W. M. Thomas tr. *Hugo's Toilers of Sea* II. vii. i. 90 There is a degree of overwhelmment which abstracts the mind entirely from its fellowship with man. **1960** *Angling Times* 9 Sept. 6/2 Our river may cause love at first sight, a sudden instantaneous overwhelmment with its manifest beauty.

o·verwind (-waind), *sb. Mining.* [Over- 29.] An instance of overwinding.

1892 *Trans. Fed. Inst. Mining Engin.* I. 58 With 'The Visor' applied to prevent a fast overwind, the arrangement in headgear to prevent the engines being started the wrong way, and good detaching hooks, disastrous overwinding seems an impossibility. **1929** H. Cotton *Electr. applied to Mining* x. 531 In the case of an overwind the pressure cylinder of the brake engine is opened to exhaust. **1958** I. C. F. Statham *Coal Mining Pract.* II. iv. 347 To protect against the aggravation of an overwind by starting the engine in the wrong direction, the overwind switches are connected through directional contacts in the master controller for the motor. **1973** *Daily Tel.* 31 July 1 An 'overwind' could have caused the descending cage, which works on the same winding system, to run out of control.

overwinder (s.v. Over-wind *v.*). Add def.: A device which guards against overwinding. (Further examples).

1912 McCulloch & Futers *Winding Engines* xv. 328 On overwinders working in pits in which double or treble decking takes place, a 'fourth attachment' is added. **1935** G. Poole *Haulage & Winding* xiii. 309 If..the cage is exceeding the predetermined speed at a particular point, the speed hook engages with the winged nut moving on the screw, and the overwinder comes into action. **1958** I. C. F. Statham *Coal Mining Pract.* II. iv. 343 The Whitmore overwinder is shown in Fig. 59, from which it may be seen that there is a separate swinging overspeed arm and travelling nut for each cage or skip.

over-winter, *v.* Add: **3.** *intr.* To live through the winter: said esp. of insects and fungi.

1933 *Jrnl. R. Hort. Soc.* LVIII. 227 The larvae [of apple sawfly] overwinter in cocoons in the soil. **1946** *Nature* 28 Sept. 454/2 The most probable causes of the disease [*sc.* tomato stem and fruit rot] are spores in propagating soil and spores which have overwintered in cracks of old cases. **1953** D. A. Bannerman *Birds Brit. Isles* I. 138 Either the Greenland or Hornemann's redpoll 'overwinters' in north-east Greenland. **1959** *New Biol.* XIX. 60 Temperate species [of midge] must normally overwinter as larvae. **1960** *Times* 9 July 9/2 Black spot overwinters on pieces of rose foliage. **1967** *Times* 23 Nov. 4/8 Two species of ticks and four of fleas..overwinter on the island [*sc.* Macquarie Island]. **1972** Swan & Papp *Common Insects N. Amer.* xxii. 589 *Culex* mosquitoes overwinter as fertilized females. **1977** J. L. Harper *Population Biol. Plants* xiii. 431 The butterfly lays its eggs in batches of 20–400 on the leaves of *Aster*, the larvae feed gregariously until the third instar when they disperse, over-winter and then start feeding again as solitary feeders.

4. *trans.* To keep (animals or plants) alive through the winter.

1945 *Scythe* Mar. 10 Primitive farming with low yields and no fodder crops on which to over-winter more than a minimum of domestic cattle. **1961** *Listener* 7 Dec. 992/3 The Chabaud and Nice types [of carnation] raised from August sowings would be safer if over-wintered in frames or under cloches. **1970** *Jrnl. R. Hort. Soc.* XCV. 358 The glaucous-leaved *Eucalyptus globulus*, sown in the previous July or August and overwintered under glass. **1976** *Evening Chron.* (Newcastle) 26 Nov., In this case the plants can be potted up into fairly large pots and overwintered in a cold frame until they can be planted out when the better weather comes along.

Hence **overwi·ntered** *ppl. a.*, **overwi·ntering** *vbl. sb.* and *ppl. a.*

1901 *U.S. Dept. Agric. Yearbk.* 1900 90 The overwintering crop. **1916** J. P. Lotsy *Evolution by Means of Hybridization* vii. 90 This experiment is yet in progress with the overwintered F_1 plants. **1923** *Glasgow Herald* 17 July 7 Preparations [are to be] made for a probable overwintering there next year. **1925** *Jrnl. Agric. Res.* XXXI. 1 (*title*) Further studies on the overwintering and dissemination of cucurbit mosaic. **1936** *Amer. Bee Jrnl.* LXXVI. 452 (*title*) Influence of pollen reserves on the surviving population of over-wintered colonies. **1958** *New Biol.* XXVI. 33 A lateral bud grows out from the corm [of the bulbous buttercup] in the autumn and gives rise to an overwintering rosette of foliage leaves. **1963** *Field Archaeol.* (Ordnance Survey) (ed. 4) 120 Overwintering sites may not have had very strong defences since they made use of natural obstacles and did not look far beyond the needs of a season. **1967** *Oceanogr. & Marine Biol.* V. 417 The spawning and over-wintering concentrations of Bank herring. **1971** *Farmer & Stockbreeder* 23 Feb. 45 (Advt.), Dose your overwintered cattle with 'Helmatac' now, and remove the winter worm burden. **1973** *Times* 18 June 16/2 The overwintered wild oat can produce at least twice as much seed to cause future trouble as those that start their lives in the spring. **1974** A. Dillard *Pilgrim at Tinker Creek* viii. 135 Look at an overwintering ball of buzzing bees.

o·ver-wood. [Over- 1 d.] The layer of vegetation formed by the tallest trees in a forest. Cf. *overstorey.

1889 W. Schlich *Man. Forestry* I. iii. 202 In fertile low lands Oak appears as overwood and underwood. **1928** R. S. Troup *Silvicultural Syst.* iv. 39 Silviculture may require the overwood to be retained for seeding purposes or for the protection of the young crop. **1969** *Gloss. Landscape Work* (*B.S.I.*) v. 34 *Overwood.* 1. Large free-growing trees growing above coppice. 2. The upper layer of a two-storeyed forest.

overwork, *v.* Add: **II. 3. a.** Also *transf.* and *fig.*

c **1878** G. M. Hopkins *Loss of Eurydice* in *Poems* (1967) 72 No Atlantic squall overwrought her. **1922** *Times Lit. Suppl.* 12 Oct. 642/2 Gobineau has carefully avoided any such threadbare device as that of the missing heir so overworked by Scott. **1951** T. Sterling *House without Door* iii. 35 Wall Street—you know that phrase is overworked. **1963** P. Phillips in Sissons & French *Age of Austerity* vi. 148 There was a New Look in daffodils.. in housing..in furniture... The phrase was disastrously over-worked. **1977** *Times* 7 Apr. 20/4 The episode is characteristic (the one word he overworks in this book).

overworked *ppl. a.* (earlier example); also *transf.* and *fig.*

1854 C. M. Yonge *Heartsease* II. iii. xiii. 292 Violet.. weak, anxious, and overworked. **1959** M. Summerton *Small Wilderness* i. 5 That over-worked truism about the wife being the last to know. **1978** *Times* 14 Jan. 14/1 The phrase 'low profile'..an over-worked image almost evacuated of meaning.

o·verworld. [Over- 1 d.] **1.** The celestial or immaterial world.

1858 [see Over- 1 d]. **1905** V. McNabb *Oxf. Conf. on Faith* 33 We would then represent our agnostic as saying ..'We are quite certain that there are natural forces and a great world of nature, of which we are a part. But we cannot get beyond this world. There may be an overworld, or an immanent world.' **1966** *Punch* 1 June 803/1 Since West Indies cricket was baptised..in 1928, it has produced players fit..to play in some overworld a representative company of cricket immortals. **1973** *Times Lit. Suppl.* 2 Mar. 249/2 Krishnamurti at thirteen found himself translated..into the theosophical over-world or under-world inhabited by the Lords Maitreya and Koot Hoomi on the astral..plane.

2. The terrestrial world, the earth, land, viewed from beneath water.

1911 Beerbohm *Zuleika D.* xix. 290 He floated up. There was air in that over-world. **1958** L. Durrell *Mountolive* i. 15 Water-tortoises and frogs and sliding fish—a whole population disturbed by this intrusion from the overworld.

3. The community of conventional, law-abiding citizens, as opposed to the 'underworld'.

1938 F. D. Sharpe *Sharpe of Flying Squad* i. 13 The difference between the Underworld and the Overworld folk is that one lot works for a living; the other 'acquires' wealth and regards toil as sin. **1950** [see *Mr. Fix* s.v. *Mr. 2 e]. **1959** *Encounter* May 29/2 The counter-society or underworld is, like the society or overworld which has expressed it from its own body, class-ridden.

overwrap, *v.* Add: (Further examples.) Hence **overwra·pping** *vbl. sb.*

1959 *Times* 12 Aug. 15/6 Rigidity is essential for a material intended for overwrapping. **1967** C. R. Oswin in F. A. Paine *Packaging Materials* xix. 262 This is particularly helpful when bulk overwrapping blocks of small packets. **1972** *Daily Tel.* (Colour Suppl.) 12 May 13/2 Overwrap anything large like poultry with mutton cloth for extra protection [in the freezer]. **1972** Briston & Neill *Packaging Managem.* ix. 180 Regenerated cellulose film, commonly known as 'Cellophane'..is the traditional material used for the overwrapping of products such as biscuits, cigarettes and chocolate.

overwrap (ōu·vəɹræp), *sb.* [Over- 8 c.] A flexible wrapping fitted over packaged goods.

1956 *Visible Packaging of Flour Confectionery* (British Cellophane Ltd.) 3 Pastries should not be included in packs which have an overwrap of fully-moistureproof film. **1969** L. S. Mounts in W. R. R. Park *Plastics Film Technol.* v. 122 The greater stiffness [of medium density polyethylene films] improves the machinability for overwrap applications.

overwrite, *v.* Add: **1. c.** *Computers.* To place new data in a section of memory and destroy what is already there: used with the old data or the location as obj.

1959 [implied in overwriting *vbl. sb.* below]. **1962** *Gloss. Terms Automatic Data Processing* (*B.S.I.*) 25 The previous data is said to be overwritten in this process. **1970** [see *overlay *sb.* 6]. **1972** *Computer Jrnl.* XV. 200/2 Only one field, which contains an entry stating who is allowed to overwrite the file, may be altered by the programmer. **1973** C. W. Gear *Introd. Computer Sci.* vi. 245 Storing into a data area will overwrite another piece of data.

3. (Further example.)

1933 W. E. Orchard *From Faith to Faith* v. 67 It did not seem to me to matter much whether the Book of Isaiah had one or more authors, or the Pentateuch had been overwritten by different hands much later than Moses.

4. a. (Further example.) **b.** (Earlier example.)

1815 Jane Austen *Let.* 31 Dec. (1952) 449 It encourages me..to believe that I have not yet..overwritten myself. *a* **1889** Browning *Let.* in F. L. Lucas *Tennyson* (1957) iii. 21, I have written too much, my dear Mr. Gosse; I have over-written; I have written myself out.

d. *trans.* (freq. in *ppl. adj.* and *vbl. sb.*). To write too elaborately or ornately; to write in a high-coloured, over-rich style.

1923 F. M. Ford *Let.* 15 Oct. (1965) 155, I have by me a story of his that I don't like *much.* I *might* print it—but it is extremely over-written and..the extravagance I least like is over-writing. **1931** *Daily Express* 31 Jan. 8/2 A fortnight ago an over-written but under-nourished play called 'Colonel Satan' broke the Haymarket record for brevity of life. **1937** C. S. Lewis *Let.* 8 Mar. (1966) 158 Have you read F. L. Lucas' *Decline and Fall of the Romantic Ideal?* Hideously over-written in parts, but well worth reading. **1947** —— in *Ess. presented to Charles Williams* p. vii, In the earlier stories..there was a good deal of over-writing, of excess in the descriptions and, in dialogue, of a false brilliance. **1968** [see *Nabokovian *a.*]. **1977** *Times* 28 Apr. 22/3 This book..is..so over-written at times it irritated me.

Hence **overwri·ting** *vbl. sb.*, **overwri·tten** *ppl. a.*

1850 J. Miley *Hist. Papal States* I. 8 This palimpsest, or multifariously over-written document, which we have thus discovered the superficies of the Papal territory to be. **1939** H. J. Massingham *Eng. Countryside* iv. 73 These are the legitimate South Downs, the over-written and exploited range. **1949** W. G. Hoskins *Midland England* i. 3 Stone that gives to not a few Midland towns and villages a beauty unsurpassed by the most over-written Cotswold places. **1956** N. R. Ker *Pastoral Care* 23 Besides additions, the text contains erasures, some with and many without overwriting... Overwriting where it occurs is mostly in the main hand. **1959** M. H. Wrubel *Primer of Programming* v. 113 A common error made by beginners is to erase program steps by storing data in the same location. An error of this kind, called 'overwriting', is easily detected.

overwrou·ghtness. *rare.* [-ness.] An overwrought condition.

1923 W. Deeping *Secret Sanct.* xxii. 229 He..poured out a glass of white wine for Stretton, sensing the man's overwroughtness, and noticing the tense mouth and the troubled eyes.

ovibos (ōu·vibǫs). [mod.L. (H. de Blainville 1816, in *Bull. Sci. Soc. Philomatique Paris* 76), f. L. *ovis* sheep + *bōs* ox, as the animal was considered to represent a type intermediate between the sheep and the ox.] A small, stocky ruminant of the monotypic genus so called, bearing long, shaggy, dark brown fur and native to Arctic regions of North America and Greenland; = Musk-ox.

1903 R. Lydekker *Mostly Mammals* 287 No objection can be taken to the prefix 'musk'..yet the English title 'ox' is in the highest degree misleading, while the technical 'Ovibos', which suggests characters intermediate between the oxen and the sheep, is equally unsatisfactory. **1921** V. Stefánsson *Friendly Arctic* 342 We found the ancient and far-decayed skull of a female ovibos. *Ibid.* 582, I shot two ovibos as all we needed out of the fifteen or twenty seen. **1925** *Chambers's Jrnl.* 14 Feb. 167/1 Here ..will roam large herds of the domesticated musk-ox or ovibos. **1929** *Encycl. Brit.* II. 306/1 With the ovibos domesticated, the potentialities of the Arctic will be greater. *Ibid.* Ovibos beef is indistinguishable from ordinary domestic beef.

ovicide². [f. Ovi-¹ + -cide.] An agent that kills eggs, esp. those of insects. Hence **ovi·ci·dal** *a.*²

1930 *Jrnl. South-Eastern Agric. College, Wye* XXVII. 147 Ovicides, contact insecticides and grease-banding.. having been tried. **1932** *Ibid.* XXX. 63 (*heading*) Studies on the ovicidal action of winter washes. **1961** *Lancet* 12 Aug. 371/1 AzUR given orally is an effective ovicide in the mouse, terminating early pregnancy at dosage levels which produce no detectable toxic effect in the mother. *Ibid.*, Different batches vary somewhat in activity, and their ovicidal activity and their toxicity are not necessarily related. **1967** *New Scientist* 20 Apr. 154/2 The experiments dramatically illustrate the effectiveness of juvenile hormone as an ovicide, as well as an insecticide.

ovigenetic (ōu:vidʒėne·tik), *a.* [f. Ovi-¹ + -genetic.] = Ovogenetic *a.*

1908 *Lancet* 23 May 1495/2 The spermatogenic and ovigenetic cells of the sexual glands in higher animals.

oviposition. Add: (Later examples.) So **ovi-posi·tional** *a.*, of or pertaining to oviposition.

1931 *Jrnl. Morphol.* LI. 22 The females [of Orthoptera] usually abandon them [*sc.* the eggs] as soon as oviposition is complete. **1965** Lee & Knowles *Animal Hormones* ii. 28 There is evidence that LTH is important for oviposition in some of the fishes. **1971** *Nature* 13 Aug. 484/1 Work is in progress..making use of the parasites' ovipositional response as a bioassay for the kairomone. **1973** *Ibid.* 30 Nov. 270/1 After oviposition these juveniles [of the nematode, *Deladenus siricidicola*] escape from the egg and enter a free living phase.

ovocyte (ōu·vosəit). *Biol.* [a. G. *ovocyte*: see *oocyte.] = *oocyte.

1905 *Jrnl. Acad. Nat. Sci. Philadelphia* XIII. 9 In a young [ascidian] ovocyte..there is no trace of yolk. **1941** J. F. Nonidez *Histol. & Embryol.* 83 After synapsis the female germ cells are known as primary ovocytes. **1967** *Nature* 30 Dec. 1315/2 *Xenopus* ovocytes have hundreds of nucleoli and *Asterias* ovocytes only one.

ovoflavin (ōuvoflēi·vin). *Biochem.* [a. G. *ovoflavin* (R. Kuhn et al. 1933, in *Ber. d. Deut. Chem. Ges.* LXVI. 318): see Ovo- and *flavin 2.] Riboflavin found in egg-white.

1933 *Chem. Abstr.* XXVII. 3480 The ovoflavin crystallizes from 2*N* AcOH in brown-orange needles. **1943** [see *hepatoflavin* s.v. *hepato-].

ovoglobulin (ōuvoglǫ·biŭlin). *Biochem.* Also † **ovi-.** [ad. F. *ovoglobuline* (Corin & Berard 1889, in *Arch. de Biol.* IX. 12): see Ovo- and Globulin.] A globulin present in egg-white.

1889 *Jrnl. Chem. Soc.* LVI. 1075 Their coagulation temperatures are:—oviglobulin α at 57·5°; oviglobulin β at 67°. **1905** [see *ovalbumen, -in]. **1959** *New Biol.* XXX. 16 Although the white of the egg contains both albumin and globulin these are chemically different from the blood proteins of the same name and they are usually distinguished by means of a prefix: ovalbumin and ovoglobulin.

ovomucin (ōuvomiū·sin). *Biochem.* [f. Ovo- + Mucin.] A water-insoluble mucoprotein in egg-white. Cf. *ovomucoid.

1898 A. Eichholz in *Jrnl. Physiol.* XXIII. 163 A new constituent of egg-white—ovomucin. I have to call attention to another constituent which has so far not been definitely described as a constituent of white of egg. This substance possesses all the properties assigned generally to mucin, and differs from the mucoids in being insoluble in distilled water. **1936** *Poultry Sci.* XV. 350/2 This change, which involves a decrease in the water insoluble fraction (ovomucin)..accompanies the loss of viscosity in the egg white. **1972** *Agric. & Biol. Chem.* XXXVI. 947 The carbohydrate content of ovomucin gel (B) obtained from the eggs stored in an atmosphere of carbon dioxide was higher than that of ovomucin gel (B) obtained from the eggs stored in air.

ovomucoid (ōuvomiū·koid). *Biochem.* [ad. G. *ovomukoïd* (C. Th. Mörner 1894, in *Zeitschr. f. physiol. Chem.* XVIII. 526): see Ovo- and Mucoid *a.*] A water-soluble mucoprotein in egg-white (also called *ovomucoid* α); also (*ovomucoid* β) = *ovomucin.

1894 *Jrnl. Chem. Soc.* LXVI. i. 264 Ovomucoid... This s the name given to a proteïd-like substance which can be obtained from white of egg, after boiling, acidifying, and filtering to separate albumin and globulin. **1938** K. Meyer in *Cold Spring Harbor Symp. Quant. Biol.* VI. 91 A logical classification of the hexosamine-containing compounds should be based on the nature of the carbohydrate radical... Table I shows the classification which we propose...A. Mucopolysaccharides...B. Glycoproteins, containing neutral mucopolysaccharides of unknown composition. a. ovomucoid-α (formerly called ovomucoid). b. ovomucoid-β (formerly called ovomucin). c. serum mucoid, serum glycoid. d. globulins... e. pregnancy urine hormone. *Ibid.* 100 A very viscous fraction precipitating out by dilution of egg white with water has been called 'ovomucin'. In order to avoid the term 'mucin' we propose the name ovomucoid-β. **1954** A. White et al. *Princ. Biochem.* viii. 142 Well-defined soluble mucoproteins have been obtained from egg white (ovomucoid α), from serum .., and from human pregnancy urine. *Ibid.* 143 Insoluble mucoids have been obtained from egg white (ovomucoid β), chalazae, submaxillary glands, and vitreous humor. **1972** *Jrnl. Biol. Chem.* CCXLVII. 6450/2 The four proteins studied in this paper, ovalbumin, conalbumin, ovomucoid, and lysozyme,..together account for 85 to 90% of the egg white proteins.

ovonic (ovǫ·nik), *a.* *Electronics.* Also **Ovonic.** [f. *ov-* (in the name of Stanford R. *Ovshinsky* (b. 1922), the U.S. physicist and industrialist who discovered the property) + *-onic* (in *electronic*).] Pertaining to, involving, or utilizing the property of certain amorphous semiconductors of making a rapid, reversible transition from a non-conducting to a conducting state on the application of an electric field stronger than some minimum value.

1966 *Electronics* 19 Sept. 191/2 This month, Ovshinsky ..was able to let the cat out of the bag. His company.. calls the device by its trade name, Ovonic. **1968** S. R. Ovshinsky in *Proc. Electronic Components Conf.* (Washington) 313 The Ovonic Threshold Switch (OTS) and the Ovonic Memory Switch (OMS) are described. **1968** *Daily Tel.* 12 Nov. 22/6 A company founded by Mr. Ovshinsky to develop glass semi-conductors is producing 150,000 'ovonic' devices a day. These are in the form of glass film a twentieth of the thickness of a human hair. **1968** *Economist* 30 Nov. 45/1 The big electronics research laboratories have been sceptical and even a bit cross that Mr Ovshinsky has put his name on to the 'ovonic devices' and the 'Ovshinsky effect'. Bell Telephone Laboratories declared that one of its scientists presented the first paper describing glass semi-conductors six years ago. **1970** S. R. Ovshinsky in *McGraw-Hill Yearbk. Sci. & Technol.* 359/1 Since ovonic switches have a number of unique characteristics, they are applicable to a wide range of uses. **1971** R. G. Neale et al. in W. B. Riley *Electronic Computer Memory Technol.* vii. 192/2 Each cell in the memory consists of an Ovonic amorphous semiconductor device and an isolating diode in series on a silicon substrate. **1973** *IEEE Trans. Electron Devices* XX. 190/1 A very high-speed electrically alterable read-only memory using Ovonic memory cells..has been designed and tested for use in the terminal multiplexor.

Hence **ovo·nics** *sb. pl.* (const. as *sing.*) [-ic 2], the study and application of ovonic effects and devices.

1968 *Economist* 30 Nov. 45/2 There are problems on the ovonics side too. The reliability of the glass semi-conductors is still suspect. **1969** *Sci. Jrnl.* Aug. 78/3 Other fields of application for Ovonics lie in a.c. control where the bidirectionality of Ovonic switches will be of prime importance.

ovovitellin (ōuvo,vite·lin). *Biochem.* Also **-ine.** [f. Ovo- + Vitellin.] The vitellin of egg-yolk.

1906 *Westm. Gaz.* 29 Aug. 2/2 The hæmoglobin of the blood of the chick is formed by certain cyanic ferruginous compounds which are found associated with ovovitelline. **1950** Sumner & Myrbäck *Enzymes* I. i. 20 It is likely that such food proteins as casein and ovovitellin are elaborated to serve as sources of amino acids for the suckling mammal or for the incubating embryo.

ovoviviparity. (Later examples.)

1931 H. R. Hagan in *Jrnl. Morphol.* LI. 18 Ovoviviparity. That type of viviparity in which the egg contains sufficient yolk to nourish the embryo until hatching. **1965** Lee & Knowles *Animal Hormones* iii. 62 The term ovoviviparity, in preference to viviparity, is sometimes applied to the birth of live young in reptiles, as it is claimed that the nutrition of the foetus in this class depends on the egg-yolk and not on the placenta. **1973** *Nature* 27 Apr. 617/1 Morphological adaptations to ovoviviparity would..include some means of internal fertilization.

Ovshinsky (ǫvʃi·nski). *Electronics.* The name of S. R. *Ovshinsky* (see *ovonic *a.*), used *attrib.* in the sense 'ovonic'.

1966 *Electronics* 19 Sept. 192/3 The potential versatility of the 'Ovshinsky effect' was his reason for secrecy. **1968** *Daily Tel.* 12 Nov. 22/6 Mr. Stanford Ovshinsky, 45, a scientist, from Troy, Michigan, explains in the journal the theory behind his discovery of 'The Ovshinsky Effect', which is that amorphous glasses have qualities similar to those of semi-conductors. **1971** *New Scientist* 1 Apr. 29/2 Amorphous semiconductors—the well-known 'Ovshinsky devices'—are being produced and used in the United States..in a 256-bit 'read-mostly' computer memory.

ovulate, *v.* Add to def.: Said of an organism and of a Graafian follicle. Hence of an ovum: to be discharged. (Examples.)

1888 H. N. Martin in B. C. Hirst *Syst. Obstetr.* I. 92 Women who have never menstruated have borne children: they must have ovulated without menstruating. **1928** *Q. Jrnl. Exper. Physiol.* XVIII. 197 The group of follicles which will ovulate at an œstrus period undergo nearly their whole maturation growth after the time when the œstrus stimulus becomes operative. **1959** *New Biol.* XXX. 21 The ovary at the time of ovulation looks like a bunch of grapes, but with the difference that all the grapes, or follicles, are of different size. The largest will ovulate first. **1968** D. W. Wood *Animal Physiol.* xiii. 303 Many [mammals] ovulate spontaneously as part of the oestrus cycle, but others require the stimulus of copulation before they will ovulate. Such induced ovulators include the ferret, the cat and the rabbit. **1974** *Biol. of Reproduction* X. 199/1 Amphibia are good subjects for *in vitro* studies of ovulation, for mature ovaries can be maintained in simple salt solutions at room temperature and can be induced to ovulate by the addition of crude extracts of..pituitary glands.

b. *trans.* To discharge (an ovum).

1924 *Amer. Jrnl. Physiol.* LXIX. 587 The periodic formation of new ova in the adult ovary makes it unnecessary to consider that ova in the immature ovary lie dormant until they either degenerate or are ovulated. **1934** *Science* 16 Nov. 462/1 Our observations would indicate that it is not necessary for the egg to be ovulated directly into the infundibulum. **1973** *Nature* 13 July 72/1 One species, the plains viscacha (*Lagostomus maximus*), has a bizarre reproductive habit in that it ovulates between 200 and 800 eggs from ovaries that look more like those of a fish than a mammal.

Hence **o·vulated** *ppl. a.*, **o·vulating** *vbl. sb.*

1910 F. H. A. Marshall *Physiol. Reproduction* iv. 133 The second spindle is formed at about the ovulating stage, and the second polar body is discharged into the interior of the Fallopian tube. **1940** *Record of Proc. Amer. Soc. Animal Production* 302 (*heading*) Potential fertility of artificially matured and ovulated ova in cattle. **1959** *New Biol.* XXX. 21 The ovulating hormone..causes the follicle to split along the line of the stigma, thus releasing the mature yolk from the ovary. **1970** *Sci. Jrnl.* June 94/1 This can be righted by supplying the hormone artificially and the ovulated eggs can then be fertilized. **1972** *Amer. Jrnl. Veterinary Res.* XXXIII. 1589, 25 ewes were given estradiol to induce release of endogenous ovulating hormone.

ovulation. (Earlier example.)

1848 C. D. Meigs *Females & their Diseases* xxxi. 403 The ovulation is marked by a natural return of the mensual hemorrhage.

ovulator (ōu·viulēitəɹ). *Physiol.* [f. Ovulat(e *v.* + -or.] An animal that ovulates (in a specified way).

1961 *Recent Progress Hormone Res.* XVII. 120 Both the cat and the rabbit are induced ovulators. **1968** [see *ovulate *v.* a]. **1971** J. Z. Young *Introd. Study Man* xv. 194 In the doe rabbit and domestic cat ovulation occurs only after copulation... Such animals are..said to be reflex ovulators. It has recently been shown that the rat, long considered to be a spontaneous ovulator, can be stimulated by coitus..to ovulate earlier than it would do otherwise.

ovulatory (ōuviulēi·təri), *a.* [f. as prec. + -ory².] Of or pertaining to ovulation.

1931 *Jrnl. Mammalogy* XII. 139 The sterility of the animals is due to the absence of an ovulatory cycle. **1972** *Endocrinology* XCI. 1253/1 The administration of various drugs on the afternoon of proestrus blocks the ovulatory surge of pituitary ovulating hormone. **1977** *Daily Mirror* 15 Mar. 7/4 In some cases when women come off the Pill, we can stimulate the return of periods with an ovulatory drug.

ow (au), *int.*² [A natural exclamation: cf. O *int.*, Oh *int.* and varr., Ow, ou *int.*, and Ouch *int.*¹] An exclamation expressing sudden pain.

1919 G. B. Shaw *Great Catherine* iii. 146 (*Claire twists herself loose; turns on him; and cuffs him furiously*) Yow—ow! Have mercy, Little Mother. *Ibid.* iv. 155 Ow! Youve nearly pulled my teeth out. **1926** —— *Translations & Tomfooleries* 239 *Reginald.* Oh! Oh! Oh! The crocodiles! Stop! Ow! Oh! **1969** D. E. Westlake *Up your Banners* (1970) xviii. 121 She threw another hammerlock on me. 'Ow,' I said. **1976** R. B. Parker *Promised Land* (1977) xi. 60, I..hugged her. 'Ow,' she said. I eased up a little on the hug.

owdacious (audēi·ʃəs), *a.* *colloq.* (orig. *U.S.*) [? A 'portmanteau' blending of Audacious *a.* and Outrageous *a.*] Impertinent, mischievous, bold. Hence **owda·ciously** *adv.*, outrageously.

1846 in Bartlett *Dict. Amer.* (1848) 243 He had a daughter Molly, that was the most enticin', heart-distressin' creature that ever made a feller get owdacious. **1847** in *Ibid.* 243, I was never so owdaciously put out with the abominable abolitionists before. **1857** C. M. Yonge *Dynevor Terr.* I. vi. 81, I wonder you aren't ashamed of yourselves, and the family in such trouble! Downright owdacious! **1947** W. de la Mare *Coll. Stories for Children* 98 Some crabbed old woman said they were owdacious, or imperent, or mischeevious.

owe, *v.* Add: **2.** *Sports.* To be under an obligation to give one's opponent in a match (a number of strokes or points) as a handicap.

1904 J. P. Paret *Lawn Tennis* 345 *Owe-fifteen* (*thirty or forty*), a term used in handicap play to indicate that one player must make one (fifteen), two (thirty), or three (forty) points in each game before he begins to score. **1908** *Daily Chron.* 24 Aug. 9/3 Mr. F. Scarf..owing one stroke, beat Mr. R. C. Oppenheimer,..(handicap 15), by 7 holes up and 5 to play.

2. b. (Later examples.)

1970 'E. Queen' *Last Woman* II. 135 'She'll come', Newly said grimly. 'After that yarn of hers, she owes me.' **1972** D. Anthony *Blood on Harvest Moon* i. 17 'Another job.'.. 'I couldn't turn this one down,' I said. 'I owe the lady.'

Owen² (ōu·ən). The name of E. E. *Owen* (1915–49), Australian inventor, used *attrib.* or alone to designate a sub-machine-gun invented by him.

1958 D. P. MELLOR *Role of Sci. & Industry* xv. 329 The Owen gun was an Automatic firearm of the usual recoiling breech bolt type, with a fire control member cooperating directly with the trigger. **1961** D. DEXTER *New Guinea Offensives* ii. 51 All sections testing the Owen preferred it to the Tommy-gun. **1965** *Austral. Encycl.* VII. 34/1 In the field of military inventions, one of the best-known is the Owen sub-machine gun, patented in 1941 by its inventor, E. E. Owen. **1967** 'E. LINDALL' *Time too Soon* iii. 32 An Owen gun slung across his body. **1970** M. KELLY *Spinifex* viii. 132 The Owen gun best and only friend.

Owenism. (Earlier examples.)
1830 *Mechanic's Press* (Utica, N.Y.) 10 June 254/2 What a precious compound of almost all that is unprincipled, is here presented:—Agrarianism, Owenism. **1833** J. S. MILL in *Tait's Edin. Mag.* III. 352 This doctrine..might easily have misled a less expanded mind..into the vagaries of Spenceanism and Owenism.

Owenite. Add: (Earlier and later examples.) Also *attrib.*
1829 SOUTHEY *Sir Thomas More* I. vi. 144 But wherefore do you think that the Owenite scheme is likely to be carried into effect only by sectarian agency? **1831** E. G. WAKEFIELD *Householders in Danger from Populace* 9/2 The desperadoes..may be divided into two classes, which I shall designate as *Huntites* and *Owenites*. *Ibid.* 10/1 The Owenites..are bent on the overthrow of all existing laws. **1836** 'BRONTERRE' tr. *Buonarroti's Hist. Babeuf's Conspiracy* II. 363 My readers of the Owenite or co-operative school will be forcibly reminded..of the many doubts.. addressed to Robert Owen, touching the possibility of reducing his system to practice. **1843** MILL *Logic* II. vi. ii. 485 If the Owenite stops here, he is in a position from which nothing can expel him. **1919** M. BEER *Hist. Brit. Socialism* I. II. ii. 131 George Mudie, an Owenite and journalist. **1950** G. B. SHAW *Farfetched Fables* Pref. 81, I am not stigmatizing all Owenites, Marxists, and Darwinists as immoral. **1956** W. H. G. ARMYTAGE in D. L. Linton *Sheffield* 205 This was an Owenite centre (Robert Owen had first visited the town on 30 December 1833), where a considerable amount of adult education was undertaken. **1975** V. CUNNINGHAM *Everywhere spoken Against* vii. 186 William Taunton..was a physical-force Chartist, an Owenite Socialist, manager of Coventry's first Co-operative Store.

owl, *sb.* Add: **2. b.** *Brown Owl*, the name given to the adult leader of a Brownie Guides pack; *Tawny Owl*, a Brown Owl's assistant.
1918 R. S. S. BADEN-POWELL *Girl Guiding* I. ii. 17 The Brown Owl (that is, the leader of the Pack) takes her place by the toadstool. *Ibid.* 21 Each Pack is under the charge of a grown-up leader—the Brown Owl. **1921** in —— *Brownies* (ed. 2) 60 A Brownie Pack consists of not less than two Sixes..under a Brownie Guider, who is called the Brown Owl, and her assistant the Tawny Owl. **1932** [see *PACK *sb.*[1] 3 d]. **1950** *Oxf. Jun. Encycl.* IX. 254/1 Brownies are divided into 'Packs' of 18–24 children, under the leadership of two adult leaders, known to the Brownies as 'Brown Owl' and 'Tawny Owl'. **1968** M. FINCH *Eye with Mascara* xiv. 149 She sounded like Brown Owl chivvying her Brownies. **1973** *Brownie* 10 Jan. 7/1 Our Pack has a membership of 20 keen Brownies... Our meetings are held at Brown Owl's house... Tawny Owl is a Sister at Hetune and walks all the way to our meetings. **1977** *Guider* July 331/2 She was a Guider in this Company, a Brown Owl of the 1st Teignmouth Pack, a Sea Ranger Skipper and a District Commissioner.

7. *owl-cote, -down, -hoot, -light, -time*; parasynthetic and similative, as *owl-dark, -dusk, -dusked, -eyed* (later example), *-headed* (later examples), *-soft, -wise* adjs.; also *owl-wise* adv.; **owl bus** *N. Amer.*, a bus running during the night; **owl car** *N. Amer.*, a tramcar running during the night; **owl jug**, a porcelain jug shaped like an owl; **owl-train** (earlier and later examples); **owl trolley** = **owl car*.
1947 *Sun* (Baltimore) 24 June 10/2 Operators of all other all-night busses and trolleys have been directed to connect with the owl bus, just as they did with the..owl trolley. **1975** *Washington Post* 26 Dec. A 22/3 Chances are the owl bus riders will..simply fade away.., just another segment of the population abandoned by the Metro system. **1889** FARMER *Americanisms* 405/2 *Owl-Car*, a tram-car plying late into the night. **1904** *N.Y. Even. Post* 7 May 1 The driver of an 'owl car' that rattled eastward on Spring street. **1911** *Daily Colonist* (Victoria, B.C.) 21 Apr. 12/7 An 'owl car' service has been inaugurated by the B.C.E.R. Company at Vancouver. **1947** *Sun* (Baltimore) 24 June 10/2 The No. 17 owl or all-night car has been supplanted by a No. 28 bus. **1863** 'G. HAMILTON' *Gala-Days* 107 For the substantial stone city..turns out to be a miserable little dirty, hutty, smutty, stagnant owl-cote. **1920** E. SITWELL *Wooden Pegasus* 41 In owl-dark garments goes the Rain. **1924** —— *Sleeping Beauty* ii. 18 Smoothing the dusky dawn's owl-down. **1928** —— *Five Poems* 18 That sang sweet country songs in owl-dusked leaves:..but time drifts owl-dusk o'er the brightest eyes. **1925** F. SCOTT FITZGERALD *Great Gatsby* iii. 45 A..man, with enormous owl-eyed spectacles. **1960** AUDEN *Homage to Clio* 55 Steatopygous, sow-dugged and owl-headed. **1968** *Listener* 11 July 59/2 A Chou Dynasty bronze bell with tiger-handle and an owl-headed drinking vessel. **1938** W. DE LA MARE *Memory* 11 Came owl-hoot From the thicket. **1925** B. RACKHAM tr. *E. Hannover's Pott. & Porc.* I. 554 The origin of the faïence owls..is fully discussed..by Walter Stengel..in the *Jahrbuch für Kunstwissenschaft* for 1924, p. 26. He gives good reason for regarding these owl-jugs,..as being of Nuremberg origin. **1936** [see *DOUBLE EAGLE 2]. **1960** R. G. HAGGAR *Conc. Encycl. Cont. Pott. & Porc.* 339/1 Faience owl jugs were made at Nuremberg in Germany... Specimens dating between 1540 and 1560 are recorded by Rackham. **1934** Owl light [see *moth-light* s.v. *MOTH *sb.*[1] 3]. **1936** DYLAN THOMAS *Twenty-Five Poems* 42 Altarwise by owl-light in the halfway-house The gentleman lay graveward with his furies. **1924** E. SITWELL *Sleeping Beauty* xvi. 59 An owl-soft shadow falling over folly. **1953** W. DE LA MARE *O Lovely England* 32 Owl-soft his wings. **1972** R. ADAMS *Watership Down* xxiii. 159 By owl-time Bigwig and his helpers had scratched out a kind of lobby inside the entrance to one of the runs leading down from the wood. **1856** *N.Y. Herald* 8 Jan. 1/2 The 'Owl Train', due at Jersey City at five o'clock yesterday morning, did not arrive until afternoon. **1876** S. & A. WARNER *Gold of Chickaree* 248 Must take the morning train. It's not quite an 'owl train'—but comes along, I believe, by eight o'clock. **1910** *N.Y. Even. Post* 22 Dec. 3 The engine of the 'owl train'—for by this term the one leaving New York after midnight is called..went off the track. **1947** *Los Angeles Times* 18 Jan. 1/1 (*heading*) 7 killed and 86 hurt in wreck of owl train. **1947** Owl trolley [see *owl bus* above]. **1906** KIPLING in *Tribune* 16 Jan. 4/3 Jimmy..rolled his congested eye-balls, owl-wise. **1912** W. DEEPING *Sincerity* xxxviii. 276 His round, lard-coloured, mildly owl-wise face. **1939** JOYCE *Finnegans Wake* I. 78 The eternals were owlwise on their side every time.

b. owl fly (*b*) = **owl midge*; **owl midge** = *moth-fly* (MOTH *sb.* 3).
1932 RILEY & JOHANNSEN *Med. Entomol.* xiv. 195 The *Psychodidae*, popularly known as moth flies, owl flies, sand flies, or papataci, are minute dark-coloured insects whose body and wings are densely covered with hairs. **1951** COLYER & HAMMOND *Flies Brit. Isles* 84 The Owl Midges or Hairy Moth-flies are easily recognisable; they may often be seen on windows, where they either run actively with a curious, jerky gait or remain perfectly still. **1962** GORDON & LAVOIPIERRE *Entomol. for Students of Med.* xx. 131 Flies belonging to the other three subfamilies [of Psychodidae]..are known as moth flies or owl midges.

owly, *a.* Delete †*Obs.* and add later examples.
1864 O. W. NORTON *Army Lett.* (1903) 203 Last night I was out all night in the rain..and I feel owly to-day. **1873** C. G. LELAND *Egyptian Sketch-bk.* 33 Up started a little, dark, old, owly, goblin, night-ghoul of a creature. **1978** R. HOLLES *Spawn* vii. 61 The round, slightly owly features of the woman in nursing uniform.

b. owly-eyed *a.* Also (*U.S. dial.*), intoxicated.
1900 *Dial. Notes* II. 47 *Owly-eyed*, intoxicated... Wise.

own, *a.* Add: **1.** (Further examples.) Phr. *to do one's own thing*: see *THING *sb.*[1]
1841 THACKERAY *Gt. Hoggarty Diamond* (1849) viii. 91, I would not have taken the lord mayor's own daughter in place of Mary with a plum for her fortune. **1931** M. ALLINGHAM *Police at Funeral* xiv. 200, I wonder if you would tell me in your own words how you came to have such a wound? **1962** L. DEIGHTON *Ipcress File* 7 'Just tell me the whole story in your own words, old chap..' I was wondering whose words he thought I might have used. **1974** G. BUTLER *Coffin for Canary* ii. 47 If we were every man his own Hitchcock, we wouldn't need to go and see the films.

b. *ownest* (later examples).
1907 G. B. SHAW *Major Barbara* I. 253 *Lomax*: How is my ownest today? *Ibid.* 272 My ownest, there is no danger. **1922** JOYCE *Ulysses* 352 Then mayhap he would embrace her gently..and love her, his ownest girlie, for herself alone. **1939** G. B. SHAW *Geneva* III. 53 My ownest and bestest, you are a Dame of the British Empire.

c. (Later examples.) Also, *to be one's own woman*.
c **1374** CHAUCER *Troylus* II. 750, I am myn owene woman wel at ese. **1966** J. POTTS *Footsteps on Stairs* (1967) i. 14 This final encounter with Vic was a necessary part of the ritual of release. With it behind her,..she was once more her own woman. **1969** *Guardian* 17 Feb. 2/7 He freely admitted that he had learned something from all the early masters... But..he was determined to be his own man. **1972** P. DICKINSON *Lizard in Cup* xi. 164 His own personal desire..to be his own man, to act and conquer outside Caesar's provinces. **1974** *Times* 2 Nov. 4/8 Mr Brown insists he is not a liberal... In truth, Mr Brown is his own man. **1975** D. BAGLEY *Snow Tiger* xvi. 138 There'll be no strings. I'm my own woman, I am.

2. c. *own goal*: a goal (see GOAL *sb.* 3) scored against one's own side. Also *fig.* (see quots.).
1947 *Sporting Mirror* 7 Nov. 10/3 Huddersfield were extremely unlucky to go under by an own-goal score to Charlton. **1952** *Times* 27 Dec. 8/1 Yesterday the Albion, with the help of two 'own goals', won a great game. **1962** *Punch* 11 Apr. 569/4 Mal holds the record for equalising own-goals. **1976** *Guardian* 11 Aug. 10/8 Two youngsters of Provisional IRA blown up by premature explosion of own bomb while crossing peace line... described as own goals by smiling Army press officers. **1976** *Norwich Mercury* 10 Dec. 8/6 With no one taking control J. Purling eventually left M. Warman stranded with a back header that lopped just under the crossbar for an own-goal. **1977** *Observer* (Colour Suppl.) 2 Jan. 12/2 The two men who had blown themselves up—'own goals' in the army's gruesome parlance. **1978** *Guardian* 30 Nov. 1/6 The Parliamentary scene was set last week for one of those gentlemanly arrangements which allows the opposition to have its say without actually scuppering the Government. Unfortunately, the Government scored an own goal.

3. *absol.* (Further example.)
1854 THACKERAY *Newcomes* I. xxiv. 233 Her teeth [were] as regular and bright as Lady Kew's own.

c. *to call* (a thing) *one's own*: cf. CALL *v.* 17 d; *to come into one's own*: to get possession of one's rightful property; to be properly esteemed; *to get one's own back*: see *GET *v.* 55 b (quots. 1910–22); *on one's own*: delete (*slang* or *colloq.*) and add later examples.
1613–1857 To call a thing one's own [in Dict. s.v. CALL v. 17 d]. **1902** J. MILNE *Epistles of Atkins* iv. 63 His one thought how to 'get his own back'. **1912** T. DREISER *Financier* vii. 71 The ready-made shoe—machine-made to a certain extent—was just coming into its own. **1917** A. G. EMPEY *Over Top* 302 *On your own*, another famous or infamous phrase which means Tommy is allowed to do as he pleases. An officer generally puts Tommy 'on his own' when he gets Tommy into a dangerous position and sees no way to extricate him. **1925** D. H. LAWRENCE *Phoenix II* (1968) 482 At night, when the silence of the moon, and the stars, and the spaces between the stars, is the silence of me too, then I am come into my own by night. **1929** —— *Ibid.* 580 For what does goodness mean? It means, in the end, being like everybody else, and not having a soul to call your own. **1930** A. HUXLEY *Let.* 18 Oct. (1969) 343 I've really had very little time to call my own. **1931** *Week-End Rev.* 24 Oct. 515/1 It looks as if the music of Jean Sibelius were at last coming into its own this winter. **1936** *Discovery* July 222 Electrical instruments will not come into their own until a large repertory of music has been composed specially for them. **1946** R. ALLEN *Home Made Banners* x. 115 But in these last moments each of them was on his own. **1969** *Listener* 24 July 109/1 At this point, alas, the Art Nouveau comes into its own. **1976** *National Observer* (U.S.) 18 Dec. 1/1 'Nixon spurred interest in this type of prosecution, but since he left we're more or less on our own,' says a lawyer who works part time on obscenity matters.

4. a. own brand, a class of goods marked with the name of the retailer instead of the manufacturer; also *attrib.*; **own category** *Psychol.*, a type of attitude test in which the subject is asked to select suitable categories into which to grade controversial statements and thereby reveals his own emotional involvement; also *attrib.*; **own-label** *attrib.*, of merchandise marked with a label showing the name of the retailer instead of the manufacturer; occas. (without hyphen) in non-*attrib.* position; **b. own-rooted** *a.* = *own-root*.
1970 *Times* 5 Feb. (Pedigree Dogs Suppl.) p. iii/6 A range of 23, some of which were 'own brands'. **1970** *Times* 16 Feb. (Food in Britain Suppl.) p. ix (*heading*) Own brands are money-savers. *Ibid.*, The principles of own-brand groceries date back to the turn of the century when stores such as Lipton and Home & Colonial did much of their own packaging. [**1953** SHERIF & HOVLAND in *Jrnl. Abnormal Psychol.* XLVIII. 135/2 Ultimately it may provide a means of utilizing the individual's own categorization of statements as a behavioral index of his stand on an issue.] **1961** —— & —— *Social Judgment* v. 118 (*heading*) Judgment of items with individual choice of categories—'own' categories. *Ibid.* 126 If future investigations bear out the promise of our results, it may prove feasible to order the stands of individuals on a controversial social issue through their placement of relevant items within their 'own' categories. **1970** *Jrnl. Gen. Psychol.* LXXXII. 147 The basic task for the Ss was that frequently used in cognitive complexity research, the free-sorting or own-categories technique. **1972** *Jrnl. Social Psychol.* LXXXVIII. 84 In the present study, the Q-sort variant known as the own-categories technique was used to investigate some effects of redundancy and congruence on judgement scales. **1973** N. LEMON *Attitudes & their Measurement* vii. 199 The development of the own categories procedure as a method of measuring involvement. **1961** *Economist* 11 Mar. 983/2 In the grocery and provisions trade, the larger multiples were almost all engaged in some food manufacture between the wars, supplemented by agreements for 'own-label' products from other manufacturers. **1969** *Times* 13 Mar. 23/3 Tesco and Woolworths have withdrawn supplies of 'Tuf' shoes and launched 'own label' brands. **1972** *Sunday Times* 31 Dec. 63/3 Lyons is particularly a supplier of supermarket own-label items and catering foods. **1975** *Times* 16 May 8/3 'Own label'..is the trade term for shops that sell groceries made by well-known companies but with the name of the shop, not of the maker, prominent on the packet. **1977** *Daily Tel.* 14 Jan. 1/6 Sainsbury's said most of its London shops were without supplies of its own-label bread, which it was still selling at 17p, but had normal supplies of proprietary loaves selling at 19p. **1915** M. E. KING *Gothic Ruin & Reconstruction* 12 Let the renascent art blunder at first, as it must if it be own-rooted and not parasitic.

own, *v.* Add: **2. c.** Of hounds: to show recognition of (the scent of the quarry).
1781 P. BECKFORD *Thoughts on Hunting* xx. 255 Foxes will run the roads at..times, and hounds cannot always own the scent. **1838** T. SMITH *Extracts Diary of Huntsman* v. 126 *Owning a scent*, when hounds throw their tongues on the scent. **1893** W. C. A. BLEW *Radcliffe's Noble Sci. Fox-Hunting* ix. 161 A couple or two, or a single hound, may have come across and struck upon the scent of a fox which has shifted, unseen, across a ride. The scent in the stuff is too stale for them freely to own. **1954** J. I. LLOYD *Beagling* 142 Hounds *own* a scent when it is strong enough for them to *speak* to it. **1971** G. WHEELER *Year Round* 21 Now the kale comes really alive as hounds drive through it converging on Ladybird's corner. One after another they own her line.

5. c. *to own up* (earlier and later examples.)
1853 J. A. BENTON *California Pilgrim* 55 However, you 'own up', and confess. **1858** S. A. HAMMETT *Piney Woods Tavern* 28 I'm willin' to own up that I'm ginerally considered to rather have a gift that way myself. **1861** *Harper's Mag.* Mar. 463/2 The English have long since resigned even the name of competitors,..as far as fishing on the Grand Bank is concerned... They have quit the field, 'owned up beat'. **1951** *People* 3 June 7/1 It will be difficult to find many regular backers who could truthfully own up to a good week at Epsom. **1966** *Listener* 10 Mar. 342/1 It is the usual thing to address the class sternly and demand that the culprit should 'own up'.

owner. Add: (Examples with sense 'a race-horse owner'.) *Slang.* The captain of a war-ship, barge, or other boat; also of an aircraft. So **ownere·ss,** the captain's wife.

1863 *Chambers's Encycl.* V. 428/2 The income of a jockey..is often very large: £1000 has frequently been given by a grateful owner. **1898** A. E. T. WATSON *Turf* v. 124 The winner of a selling race has..to be sold by auction; the owner receives no more than the entered selling price. **1903** KIPLING *Traffics & Discoveries* (1904) 49 I'm goin' to deviate to the owner's comfortable cabin direct. **1914** 'BARTIMEUS' *Naval Occasions* iii. 21 That there launch precious near fouled the mark-buoy... Their owner sailing 'er too. **1916** G. TAYLOR *With Scott* 213 Scott was invariably known as The Owner, a naval term always applied to the captain of a warship. **1923** *Blackw. Mag.* Apr. 445/2 The Owner and Owneress have a very jolly little cabin. **1930** in C. Allen *Raj* (1977) ix. 123 Cricket. Owners, Trainers and Jockeys, Vs. Patrons, Stewards and Officials. **1943** C. H. WARD-JACKSON *Piece of Cake* 45 *Owner,* the Commanding Officer, the captain of an aircraft. **1971** 'D. HALLIDAY' *Dolly & Doctor Bird* xiii. 192 Johnson slept for an hour. I left the wheel to go into the owner's cabin to rouse him. **1977** D. FRANCIS *Risk* ii. 14 Binny, Tapestry's trainer, didn't want me on the horse. 'Not in the Gold Cup,' he'd said..when the owner had proposed it.

b. appositive, as *owner-breeder, -driver, -manager, -occupant, -occupier, -operator;* also *owner-occupation, -occupiership; owner-driven, -managed, -occupied* adjs.

1937 E. RICKMAN *On & off Racecourse* i. 4 The most successful owner-breeders are in the game because they have a genuine love of the thoroughbred and of the sport. **1971** *Daily Tel.* 20 Oct. 17/4 Sir Humphrey, the fourth baronet, owner-breeder of Parthia, the 1959 Derby winner. **1919** *Honey Pot* I. III. 4 (Advt.), For immediate delivery. Daimler 57-hp special..owner driven. **1960** *Amer. Speech* XXXV. 240 In truckers' language a 'gypsy' is an owner-driven truck. **1918** A. BENNETT *Pretty Lady* xxxi. 214 The interior of the cab,..was ornate with toy-curtains..to indicate to the world that he was an owner-driver. **1924** *Morris Owner* Mar. 20/1 A sympathetic understanding of his car and of road-craft by an owner-driver..makes for more pleasurable motoring. **1963** *Times* 23 May 8/3 Last year there were 7,000 cabs in London, and 10,400 drivers, of whom 2,919 were owner-drivers. **1972** *Police Rev.* 17 Nov. 1484/1 In the case of haulage firms, and in particular the owner-driver..it pays to overload. **1972** *Accountant* 5 Oct. 411/3 Independent 'owner-managed' business as distinct from the large multi-national corporations. **1965** H. I. ANSOFF *Corporate Strategy* iv. 62 During the high-growth phase of the electronics industry many new firms were started by owner-managers. **1967** C. MARGERISON in Wills & Yearsley *Handbk. Managem. Technol.* 18 While they were never entirely a law unto themselves, the owner-managers of the nineteenth century were largely role-determining actors—they were able to control their factories and affairs very much in the manner that they wished. **1970** *Globe & Mail* (Toronto) 26 Sept. B2/3 Residual lending activities of CMHC in the owner-occupant market appear to have increased. **1958** *Ann. Reg. 1957* 71 The slowing up of the property market, especially in the sale of houses for owner-occupation. **1970** *Daily Tel.* 16 Mar. 11/1 The change-over to owner-occupation really began to show about 1920, when some 20 per cent. of the land was in the hands of those who farmed it. **1952** *Time* 9 June 66 (Advt.), Here in Philadelphia, the percentage of owner-occupied homes is greater than in any other large city in America..greater than the national average. **1960** *Times* 23 May 3/5 Northern Ireland is a country of small farms, mainly owner-occupied. **1961** E. A. POWDRILL *Vocab. Land Planning* iii. 44 This recognition is evolved from a study of the age and condition of buildings, densities, incidence of owner-occupied properties, and rateable values. **1972** M. JONES *Life on Dole* xi. 84 The old houses are, in general, owner-occupied. **1935** *Planning* II. XLIII. 2 There are for example the approaches of State ownership at the one extreme, and of sub-division among many thousands of small owner-occupiers at the other extreme. **1958** *New Statesman* 4 Jan. 7/3 Here and there an enterprising tenant, owner-occupier or determined landlord has repaired and repainted and the contrast is startling. **1971** *Reader's Digest Family Guide to Law* 460/1 An owner-occupier..does not pay capital gains tax on the sale of his home. **1974** *Times* 8 Aug. 18/7 It is questionable whether any public interest is served by requiring owner-occupiers to let commercial and factory premises where they have ceased to use them for their own purposes. **1924** *Glasgow Herald* 28 Nov. 9 As to owner-occupiership, the figures were..encouraging. **1957** E. BOTT *Family & Social Network* 161 Owner-operator of a small tobacco and sweet shop. **1971** M. TAK *Truck Talk* 114 *Owner-operator,* a trucker who both owns and drives his rig. **1976** *Woman's Day* (N.Y.) Nov. 50/2 'You can do damage if you don't replace a radiator cap..correctly,' warns Jim Gottfredsen, longtime owner-operator of Gup's West Side Service in Racine, Wisconsin.

ownership. (Further examples.)

1899 T. VEBLEN *Theory of Leisure Class* ii. 23 The practice of seizing women from the enemy as trophies, gave rise to a form of ownership-marriage. **1906** *Westm. Gaz.* 20 June 7/1 These were the 'ownership' voters, which were a scandal of the franchise. The speaker knows of a case where one man had sixty-seven ownership votes. *Ibid.,* As an instance of this plural voting by ownership, Wimbledon had 3,350 non-resident voters who owned property in the borough. **1910** *Ibid.* 10 Jan. 2/1 What..are the advantages which are claimed for the ownership system? **1944** W. TEMPLE *Church looks Forward* xxii. 158 At an earlier date Ownership and Management were very closely connected. **1956** H. GAITSKELL in Gould & Kolb *Dict. Social Sci.* (1964) 457/2 Nationalization..is generally understood to mean the taking over by the State of a complete industry so that it is owned by and managed and controlled for the Community, and public ownership..strictly speaking means the ownership by the community of any property whether individual or not, whether embracing the whole of an industry or only part of it. **1975** *Chinese Econ. Stud.* VIII. iv. 6 The ownership pattern refers to who owns the means of production (including means of labor, such as machines, plants, land, and objects of labor, such as raw materials).

owney-oh (ōᵘ:ni,ōᵘ). *joc.* Also **owneo, ownio, ownie-o, owny-oh.** [f. a popular song (1907) *Antonio & his Ice-Cream Cart.*] Phr. *on one's owney-oh,* on one's own; alone. (Cf. OWN *a.* 3 c.)

1922 JOYCE *Ulysses* 96 He's as bad as old Antonio. He left me on my ownio. **1956** A. WILSON *Anglo-Saxon Att.* I. iv. 117 As I see it, when you haven't anything more to give a person, well, then you're on your ownio. **1963** 'A. GILBERT' *Ring for Noose* xi. 132 'On your owney-oh?' she said. **1967** J. SYMONS *Man who killed Himself* I. vi. 54 Soon I shall be able to go shopping without worrying, all on my owneo. **1969** F. SARGESON *Joy of Worm* iii. 75 For that matter how in Hades have I managed with the job? Solo. All on my ownie-o. **1976** 'W. TREVOR' *Children of Dynmouth* xi. 200 She was crying and moaning in the wind, sir, up there on her owny-oh with nobody giving a blue damn about her.

owning (ōᵘ·niŋ), *ppl. a.* [-ING².] That owns property, plant, business interests, etc.

1904 *Electrical Investments* 7 Dec. 773/1 A set-off against any advantage the owning company may be said to secure in extra traffic by the connection. **1909** *Westm. Gaz.* 19 Jan. 2/1 Of the five owning companies three at least have other routes which are more profitable to them. **1923** M. SADLEIR *Desolate Splendour* 80 Morvane and the literal appellation of its owning family.

ownsome (ōᵘ·nsŏm). [f. after LONESOME *a.*] Phr. *on one's ownsome,* alone.

1939 M. HARRISON *What are we waiting For?* 130 You tucked up for bye-byes all on your little ownsome. **1948** D. BALLANTYNE *Cunninghams* 248 We'll call at the cottage..and dance on our ownsome. **1961** J. MACLAREN-ROSS *Doomsday Book* 103 I'm absolutely on my ownsome, old feller. **1967** R. PETRIE *Foreign Bodies* xi. 163 Oh, snap out of it. You'll pull through on your ownsome. **1976** G. SEYMOUR *Glory Boys* xii. 149 He's been left on his ownsome, and doesn't like it.

ownty-downty (ōᵘ·nti,dōᵘ·nti), *a.* Also **ownty-donty, owny-towny.** [A rhyming jingle.] A familiar or nursery extension of OWN *a.*

1815 D. HUMPHREYS *Yankey in Eng.* 19 My owny, towny, Lydy Lovett. **1871** L. M. ALCOTT *Little Men* v. 68 How nice it is to do it all my ownty donty self! **1882** O. W. HOLMES *Let.* 18 Mar. in J. Brown *Lett.* (1912) 449 It is told, the story, without any affectation, but so lovingly that the blessed little creature becomes our own child, our 'ownty-downty', as New England nursery small talk has it.

owt (aut). Repr. dial. pronunc. AUGHT *sb.*² Esp. in phr. *owt for nowt,* anything for nothing.

1847 E. BRONTË *Wuthering Heights* II. xviii. 344 'All well at the Heights?' I inquired of the woman. 'Eea, f'r owt Ee knaw!' she answered. **1895** J. T. CLEGG *Works* I. 238 There's olez tuthri cliverdicks to smile At owt they thinken rayther eaut-o'th'-road. **1913** D. H. LAWRENCE *Let.* 1 Feb. (1962) I. 183, I should think you've forgotten the Yorkshire proverb, 'An' if tha does owt for nowt, do it for thysen'. **1935** 'L. LUARD' *Conquering Seas* 128 He's got tongue that would fair make one think owt to nowt. **1963** [see *NOWT]. **1977** E. W. HILDICK *Loop* xviii. 123 Owt's possible, any bloody thing.

ox. Add: **4. a.** Delete † *Obs.* and add later examples. *dumb ox:* see *DUMB *a.* 7 b.

1906 E. DYSON *Fact'ry 'Ands* x. 126 You don't see 'em buckin' up, or playin' ther frivolous ox. **1922** JOYCE *Ulysses* 9 Don't you play the giddy ox with me! **1923** *Brewer's Dict. Phr. & Fable* (new ed.) 809/2 *To play the giddy ox,* to act the fool generally; to behave in an irresponsible or over-hilarious manner.

ox. Add: **5. a.** *ox-chain, -gad, -goad* (later examples), *-mill, -sawmill, -sled* (earlier and later examples), *-team* (later examples), *-train, -wagon* (earlier and later examples). **b.** *ox-driver* (earlier and later examples); *ox-broad* adj.

1953 DYLAN THOMAS *Under Milk Wood* (1954) 28 P.C. Attila Rees, ox-broad, barge-booted, stamping out of Handcuff House in a heavy beef-red huff. **1785** G. WASHINGTON *Diaries* (1925) II. 441 [1] Oxe Chain. **1817** J. K. PAULDING *Lett. from South* I. 128 Next came three men,..chained together with an ox-chain. **1842** [see *goose-yoke* s.v. *GOOSE *sb.* 8]. **1866** *Rep. Indian Affairs* (U.S.) 292, I also repaired 20 wagons, 15 ox chains, 15 grain cradles. **1828** A. ROYALL *Black Bk.* II. 114 He was one of your right down flat footed ox-drivers. **1843** *Yale Lit. Mag.* VIII. 332 'Gee Bright!' shouted the stentorian voice of an ox-driver. **1916** G. B. SHAW *Androcles & Lion* I. 23 *The ox driver.* The menagerie service is the Emperor's personal retinue. **1937** K. BLIXEN *Out of Africa* IV. 269 One strong young animal gave..his Native ox-drivers endless trouble. **1836** *Knickerbocker* VIII. 681 His father kept a long ox-gad to whip him with. **1843** *Ibid.* XXI. 125 The ladies requested the loan of Mr. Diddlemas's ox-goad to knock down chestnut burrs. **1848** E. BRYANT *California* iii. 32 The crack of the ox-goad, the 'whoa-haws',..create a most Babel-like and exciting confusion. **1916** G. B. SHAW *Androcles & Lion* I. 23 A man with an ox goad comes running through the central arch. **1826** T. FLINT *Recoll.* 211 Steam-mills arose in St. Louis, and ox-mills on the principle of the..tread-mill. **1837** J. M. PECK *Gazetteer Illinois* (ed. 2) I. 33 Ox mills on the inclined plane and horse mills by draught, are common throughout ..the state. **1817** in *Trans. Illinois State Hist. Soc. 1910* (1912) 150 An inclined Wheel ox Saw Mill with two saws. **1842** in *Kansas State Hist. Soc. Coll.* (1918) XIV. 755, I made also an oxsled. **1844** *Knickerbocker* XXIII. 445 Let us ride..home on the ox-sled. **1863** H. S. RANDALL *Pract. Shepherd* (ed. 7) xix. 228 The old-fashioned, lively and merry scene of hauling out hay on an ox-sled. **1904** M. E. WALLER *Wood-Carver of 'Lympus* 82 Uncle Shim is driving the ox-sled down the Pent Road. **1776** in *Huntington* (N.Y.) *Town Rec.* (1889) III. 17 Carting Genll Tryons Baggage from Huntington to Jamaica with an Ox team. **1848** E. BRYANT *California* i. 14 Ox-teams seem to be esteemed as preferable. **1913** J. LONDON *Valley of Moon* 297 The chest of drawers..had crossed the Atlantic by sailing ship and the Plains by ox team. **1974** M. FIDO *R. Kipling* 77/1 Hiring labourers and ox-teams. **1849** in E. Page *Wagons West* (1930) 120 We will now push off for good and any ox train that gets ahead of us will have to travele. **1850** L. H. GARRARD *Wah-to-Yah* 72 Overtaking a United States ox-train, with which I traveled and stayed all night. **1869** *Bradshaw's Railway Manual* XXI. 433 Four years ago the only way of traversing these 1,721 miles between the Missouri and the Pacific was by mail coaches, or by mule or ox trains. **1887** E. CUSTER *Tenting on Plains* 357 There is no picture that represents the weariness and laggard progress of life like an ox-train. **1968** E. MCCOURT *Saskatchewan* x. 112 Some settlers arrived..by ox train and Red River cart. **1831** J. M. PECK *Guide for Emigrants* II. 135 From twelve to fifteen large ox waggons are employed..in hauling it [*sc.* coal] to market. **1857** D. E. E. BRAMAN *Information Texas* iii. 56 The ox-wagons, the 'peculiar institution' of this country, are hauling away cotton. **1878** T. J. LUCAS *Camp Life & Sport S. Afr.* iii. 42 The Cape ox-waggon is quite an institution, and has been called, like the camel, the 'ship of the plains'. **1946** E. O'NEILL *Iceman Cometh* (1947) I. 44, I vas so tough and strong I grab axle of ox wagon mit full load. **1960** [see *BACKVELD]. **1971** *Sunday Express* (Johannesburg) 28 Mar. 11/1 Students to whom I spoke described the move as 'archaic and back to the ox-wagon'.

6. ox-beef (later example); **ox-chip,** a piece of dry ox-dung; **ox-frame,** a frame for holding oxen while they are being shod; also **ox-shoeing frame; ox-yard,** also, a yard where oxen are kept.

1878 *Amer. Home Cook Bk.* 5 Ox-beef, when it is young, will have a fine open grain, and a good red colour. **1857** E. BANDEL *Frontier Life in Army* (1932) 178 No timber to be seen yet, and our wood is gone. We must get along on what few buffalo or ox chips we can gather. **1857** W. CHANDLESS *Visit to Salt Lake* I. vii. 122 Some one pitched on an old camping-place studded with 'ox-chips'. **1844** *Knickerbocker* XXIII. 155 A little slab-roofed smithy... An ox-frame standing by the door, and at one side a shed. **1890** N. P. LANGFORD *Vigilante Days* I. xxvi. 384 We sat down upon the ox-shoeing frame, and talked over the whole matter. **1885** W. MORRIS in *Commonweal* I. 12/1 The straw from the ox-yard is blowing about. **1910** J. MASEFIELD *Ballads & Poems* 42 The red cock in the ox-yard crows.

b. ox-balm (examples).

1854 *Trans. Michigan Agric. Soc.* V. 130 The plants were very numerous, among which were oxbalm..and marsh grass. **1931** W. N. CLUTE *Common Names of Plants* 97 The ox-balm (*Collinsonia*) is merely a larger balm.

ox-. Add: **3.** Form of *OXA- before a vowel.

oxa-. Also before vowels **ox-.** Combining element in systematic chemical names used to denote the presence of an oxygen atom (regarded as replacing a —CH_2— group), as in *6-oxa-3-thiadecanenitrile, 1H-2-oxapyrene, oxirane, oxolane.*

1928 *Jrnl. Amer. Chem. Soc.* L. 3075 In order to avoid confusion with the ordinary meanings of oxy-, thio-, azo-, etc., it is recommended that the forms *oxa-, thia-, aza-,* etc., be employed to indicate the presence of hetero atoms in a ring (the *a* being dropped before a vowel). **1971** *Nomencl. Org. Chem.* (I.U.P.A.C.) (ed. 3) B. 53 (*table*) *Element* Oxygen..*Prefix* Oxa.

oxacillin (ǫksăsi·lin). *Pharm.* [f. *is*)*oxa*(*zole* (s.v. *ISO- b) + *PENI(CILLIN.] A semisynthetic penicillin, $C_{19}H_{18}N_3O_5NaS.H_2O$, that is used as an alternative to methicillin, having the same resistance to penicillinase and being in addition resistant to acid so that it can be taken orally; (5-methyl-3-phenyl-4-isoxazolyl)-penicillin sodium. Also called *oxacillin sodium* and *sodium oxacillin* (in the British and U.S. pharmacopœias respectively).

1962 *Proc. Mayo Clinic* XXXVII. 137, 5-Methyl-3-phenyl-4-isoxazolyl penicillin (Prostaphlin*). [*Note*] *Trade name of Bristol Laboratories, Inc... Since this paper was prepared for publication, 'oxacillin' has been adopted as the generic name of this drug. **1963** *New & Non-Official Drugs* 148 Sodium oxacillin is a semisynthetic penicillin salt for oral administration. **1967** *Martindale's Extra Pharmacopoeia* (ed. 25) 994/1 Oxacillin sodium is more resistant to destruction by the acid gastric secretion than benzylpenicillin or methicillin sodium. **1970** *Atlantic Monthly* Mar. 50 He was also given heavy doses of antibiotics, including a gram of chloramphenicol, a gram of oxacillin, [etc.].

oxal-. Add: **oxalace·tic acid,** a dicarboxylic acid, HOOC·CO·CH_2·COOH, which crystallizes as an enol form and is produced *in vivo* by transamination from aspartic acid and in the Krebs cycle by oxidation of malic acid; so **oxala·cetate**, the anion, or an ester or salt of, oxalacetic acid.

1891 *Jrnl. Chem. Soc.* LX. 1333 On mixing..a benzene solution of carbon oxychloride with copper oxalacetate.. the copper salt takes up an appreciable quantity of chlorine. **1969** Oxalacetate [see *GLYOXYLATE]. **1896** *Jrnl. Chem. Soc.* LXX. I. 599 Nef's ethylic ethoxyfumarate..when hydrolysed with hydrochloric acid, gives oxalacetic acid. **1939** *Ann. Reg. 1938* 375 In the biological fixation of nitrogen by root nodule bacteria the formation of aspartic acid via the oxime of oxalacetic acid was confirmed. **1972** *Arch. Biochem. & Biophysics* CLIII. 226/1 Oxalacetic acid..functions as a key substrate in metabolism as the keto form; however, the pure compound crystallizes as the *cis* enol of hydroxymaleic acid.

oxalate (ǫ·ksălēit), *v. Med.* [f. the sb.] *trans.* To add an oxalate to, esp. so as to prevent coagulation of blood.

1911 *Amer. Jrnl. Physiol.* XXIX. 204 The tissue extract was itself oxalated to remove any calcium that may have been present. **1934** *Brit. Med. Jrnl.* 7 July 10/2 Blood collected under paraffin was oxalated and centrifuged and the plasma examined spectroscopically. **1954** *Blood* IX. 610 The serum was decanted and 2·8 ml. were oxalated by adding 0·5 ml. of 0·1 M. potassium oxalate.

So **o·xalated** *ppl. a.*, containing added oxalate.

1893 *Jrnl. Path. & Bacteriol.* I. 443 (*heading*) Effect of graduated additions of calcium chloride to oxalated blood. **1946** *Nature* 16 Nov. 708/2 The prothrombin concentration in normal human oxalated plasma averaged approximately 2 mgm. per 100 ml. when expressed as protein nitrogen. **1964** W. G. SMITH *Allergy & Tissue Metabolism* vi. 69 Oxalated blood samples were collected both before and for several minutes after shock.

oxalo-. Delete 'used before consonants' and add: **oxaloa·cetate** = *oxalacetate* s.v. *OXAL-; **oxaloace·tic acid** = *oxalacetic acid* s.v. *OXAL-; **oxalo·sis** *Path.* [-OSIS], a rare disorder of metabolism in which crystals and stones of calcium oxalate are deposited in the kidneys and elsewhere, often causing death during childhood as a result of renal failure; **oxalosu·ccinate**, the anion, or an ester or salt, of oxalosuccinic acid; **o:xalosucci·nic acid,** a tricarboxylic acid, HOOC·CO·CH(COOH)·CH_2·COOH, which is an intermediate in the formation of α-ketoglutaric acid from isocitric acid in the Krebs cycle.

1943 SUMNER & SOMERS *Chem. & Methods of Enzymes* xviii. 324 Malate, oxaloacetate, or succinate could replace fumarate in reaction (c). **1962** S. G. WALEY in A. Pirie *Lens Metabolism Rel. Cataract* 356 Another γ-keto acid that undergoes enzymatic decarboxylation is oxaloacetate. **1937** *Nature* 18 Sept. 503/2 α-Ketoacids other than pyruvic, for example..oxaloacetic or phenylpyruvic acid, may equally serve as acceptors for the amino group of glutamic acid. **1940** [see *α-ketoglutarate* s.v. *KETO- a]. **1968** PASSMORE & ROBSON *Compan. Med. Stud.* I. ix. 14/2 Acetyl-CoA reacts with oxaloacetic acid to produce citric acid. **1952** YING CHOU & DONOHUE in *Pediatrics* X. 660 (*heading*) Oxalosis. Possible 'inborn error of metabolism' with nephrolithiasis and nephrocalcinosis due to calcium oxalate as the predominating features. **1973** N. M. R. BUIST et al. in Forfar & Arneil *Textbk. Pediatrics* xix. 1171/2 Treatment of oxalosis includes alkalinization of the urine, dietary restriction of calcium and a large fluid intake. **1911** *Chem. Abstr.* V. 3240 Tri-Et oxalosuccinate.. is best prepared by means of EtOK. **1962** S. G. WALEY in A. Pirie *Lens Metabolism Rel. Cataract* 355 In the citric acid cycle..two molecules of CO_2 are formed per turn of the cycle; one comes from oxalosuccinate, a β-keto acid. **1925** *Chem. Abstr.* XIX. 4423 (Index), Oxalosuccinic acid, triethyl ester. **1948** *Jrnl. Biochem.* CLXXIV. 144 The instability of oxalosuccinic acid makes an accurate estimation of this constant rather difficult. **1966** F. A. ROBINSON *Vitamin Co-Factors of Enzyme Syst.* viii. 541 In this organism [sc. *E. coli*], biotin appears to function in the conversion of oxalosuccinic acid into α-ketoglutaric acid.

oxamide. Add: [first formed as F. *oxamide* (J. Dumas 1830, in *Ann. de Chim. et de Physique* XLIV. 130).]

oxazepam (ǫksē·zĭpæm). *Pharm.* [f. OX- I + AZ(O- + *-ep*(*ine* (suffix designating an unsaturated seven-membered ring containing nitrogen) + AM(IDE.] A tricyclic, creamy-white powder, $C_{15}H_{11}ClN_2O_2$, which is a tranquillizer given to relieve anxiety states and to control the withdrawal symptoms of alcoholism.

1964 *Jrnl. Pharmaceutical Sci.* LIII. 1181/1 Oxazepam, 7-chloro-1,3-dihydro-3-hydroxy-5-phenyl-*2H*-1,4-benzodiazepine-2-one, has been characterized pharmacologically in our laboratories as an anticonvulsant and mild central depressant and is currently under clinical investigation as an antianxiety agent. **1966** *Jrnl. Amer. Med. Assoc.* 21 Nov. 952/1 Six days after oxazepam was stopped completely, her husband reported she had been up all night, was talking irrationally, and was having visual hallucinations. **1974** *Brit. Jrnl. Clin. Pract.* XXVIII. 65/1 Oxazepam, one of the benzodiazepine group, has an anxiolytic action with very little sedative potential.

oxazole (ǫ·ksăzōul). *Chem.* [ad. G. *oxazol* (Hantzsch & Weber 1887, in *Ber. d. Deut. Chem. Ges.* XX. 3119): see OX- I, AZO-, and *-OLE.] **a.** A weakly basic, heterocyclic compound, O·CH:N·CH:CH, which is a volatile liquid. **b.** Any of the derivatives of this compound obtained by substituting for hydrogen.

1888 *Jrnl. Chem. Soc.* LIV. 574 Oxazoles are obtained by the condensation of α-halogen-ketones with amides. **1892** [see *IMIDAZOLE]. **1929** R. A. GORTNER *Outl. Biochem.* xiv. 350 Polypeptides may be considered to enolize ..yielding substituted imidazoles or substituted oxazoles. **1966** *McGraw-Hill Encycl. Sci. & Technol.* IX. 461/1 Oxazole is miscible with water and organic solvents. **1968** A. ALBERT *Heterocyclic Chem.* (ed. 2) vi. 289 Oxazole alkaloids have been isolated from flowering plants in the Rutaceae and Graminae, and oxazolidines (their reduced analogues) occur in cabbages.

oxazolidine (ǫksăzǫ·lidīn). *Chem.* [f. prec. + *-IDINE.] Any of the compounds obtained by substituting for hydrogen in the hypothetical parent compound $CH_2CH_2NHCH_2O$ (which is the fully hydrogenated form of oxazole), some of which are anticonvulsants and are used in treating petit mal.

1902 *Jrnl. Chem. Soc.* LXXXII. I. 56 (*heading*) Synthesis of oxazolidines by the action of aldehydes on hydramines. **1953** *Chem. Rev.* LIII. 315 The oxazolidines are liquids or solids of basic character; their stability to hydrolysis is generally low. **1961** A. GOTH *Med. Pharmacol.* xix. 229 In the clinical use of the oxazolidine derivatives, the following toxic effects have been reported: drowsiness and ataxia, photophobia, and a strange visual disturbance.

oxazolone (ǫksæ·zǫ̆lōun). *Chem.* [f. as prec. + -ONE.] Any compound containing the nucleus obtained by hydrogenating one of the double bonds of oxazole and replacing a methylene group by a carbonyl group; = *AZLACTONE.

1899 JAPP & FINDLAY in *Jrnl. Chem. Soc.* LXXV. I. 1027 It occurred to us that, by substituting an α-hydroxy-acid for the α-keto-alcohol in the foregoing reaction, it might be possible to prepare oxazolones (ketodihydro-oxazoles). **1947** *Sci. News* IV. 70 The synthesis of penicillin G starts with a benzyl oxazolone and with penicillinamine, and attempts to recombine them. **1968** A. ALBERT *Heterocyclic Chem.* (ed. 2) vi. 290 Of the oxazolones, the 5-isomer..and its derivatives are the best known. **1968** R. O. C. NORMAN *Princ. Org. Synthesis* xviii. 604 The oxazolones or azlactones, prepared by the dehydration of *N*-acyl-α-amino-acids, are employed in Erlenmeyer's synthesis of α-amino-acids. **1975** *Nature* 13 Nov. 149/2 We have examined..the production of anti-parasite antibodies and parameters of T-cell function (the response to phytohaemagglutinin (PHA) and oxazolone).

ox-blood (ǫ·ks,blʊd). [f. OX + BLOOD.] The blood of the ox; a colour resembling this; also used *attrib.* or as *adj.*, *spec.* of a colour of opals, of porcelain, and of leather.

1705 *Whole Art of Dying* II. 53 *Ox-blood Colour.* First Tinge the Stuffs Yellow,..and work them till they are sufficiently beautiful, then..put into the Kettle a Tub of stale Urine, and boil it again till they take the Dye. **1707** [in Dict. s.v. Ox 5a]. **1897** *Sears, Roebuck Catal.* 194b/3 Men's Hard Cash Lace, best Russia Calf, latest Ox Blood (dark wine) color. **1936** *Burlington Mag.* Jan. 10/2 The splendid ox-blood and peach bloom reds of the Ch'ing dynasty. **1937** D. JONES *In Parenthesis* 118 You feel the pack of the Ox-blood Kid—it's as light as the Reg'mentals —there's a whole lot of them that work it. **1941** 'BRAHMS' & 'SIMON' *No Bed for Bacon* ii. 37 It was Elizabeth of England in ivory and ox blood. **1950** H. MCCLOY *Through Glass, Darkly* i. 5 A bowl of ox blood porcelain. **1950** C. FRY *Venus Observed* II. i. 34 Umber, bronze and brass, ox-blood, damson, Crimson, scalding scarlet. **1967** S. LLOYD *Lightning Ridge Bk.* 24 In the reds, miners describe colour as 'ox blood', 'pidgeon's blood', 'port wine red', and so on. **1968** *Listener* 27 June 825/1 One of the occupants..was wearing 'ski pants and ox-blood-coloured shoes'. **1968** D. TORR *Treason Line* 69 He..walked over to the Chinese vases in the window. He put one vase with an ox-blood glaze..into the window on the left. **1971** J. S. GUNN *Opal Terminol.* 32 *Ox blood,*..name given to the deepest of the red-coloured opals. **1974** 'G. BLACK' *Golden Cockatrice* x. 163, I got another vase..imitation ox blood. **1975** T. STOPPARD *Travesties* I. 27, I think to match the carnation, oxblood shot-silk cravat.

ox-bow. Add: **1.** (Further U.S. examples.)

1833 S. SMITH *Life & Writings J. Downing* 106 A farmer ort to stick to his ox bows and goard sticks. **1846** R. B. SAGE *Scenes Rocky Mts.* iii. 26 An extra quantity of ox bows, axle-trees..in case of accidents or breakage. **1881** *Rep. Indian Affairs* (U.S.) 398 Ox-bows, 2-inch..doz. 51.

2. b. More fully *ox-bow lake.* A curved lake left in a former meander of an adjacent river after the river has changed its course and cut through the narrow neck of the meander.

1898 W. M. DAVIS *Physical Geogr.* ix. 245 An abandoned meander is occupied by nearly stagnant water... In time it becomes an ox-bow lake. **1902** [see *MORTLAKE]. **1937** [see *CUT-OFF *sb.* 2]. **1944** A. HOLMES *Princ. Physical Geol.* x. 165 If a flood occurs when only a narrow neck of lands is left between adjoining loops, the momentum of the increased flow is likely to carry the stream across the neck... A deserted channel is left, forming an ox-bow lake which soon degenerates into a swamp. **1957** L. EISELEY *Immense Journey* 22 Fishes of this type who get themselves immured in oxygenless ponds or in cut-off oxbows buried in winter drifts. **1961** *Listener* 19 Oct. 614/1 In his lifetime the river flowed through his ox-bow. **1962** [see *MORTLAKE].

3. *Comb.* (in sense 1) **ox-bow key,** a key for fastening the end of an ox-bow; **ox-bow stirrup,** a stirrup resembling an ox-bow in shape; also *ellipt.*

1882 *Rep. Indian Affairs* (U.S.) 480 Ox-bow keys, 2 inch. *a* **1918** J. BRATT *Trails of Yesterday* (1921) xiii. 52 In the morning I was set to work..making ox-bow keys and fitting bows to yokes. **1907** S. E. WHITE *Arizona Nights* I. i. 5 Uncle Jim sat placidly on his white horse, his thin knees bent to the ox-bow stirrups, smoking. **1942** BERREY & VAN DEN BARK *Amer. Thes. Slang* §915/5 *Ox bows,*..wide old-fashioned wooden stirrups.

Oxbridge (ǫ·ksbridʒ). [Short for '*Ox*ford and Cam*bridge*'.] A name used to designate the universities of Oxford and of Cambridge; the characteristics common to both, esp. as distinct from other universities in the British Isles. Also *attrib.* Cf. *CAMFORD.

1849 THACKERAY *Pendennis* I. xxix. 286 'Rough and ready, your chum seems,' the Major said. 'Somewhat different from your dandy friends at Oxbridge.' **1906** V. WOOLF in Q. Bell *Virginia Woolf* (1972) I. 205 You see a pink cheeked boy whose only talk is of cricket..enter upon his first term at Oxbridge. **1907** G. W. E. RUSSELL *Seeing & Hearing* v. 35 We ran a neck-and-neck race at the University... In those days I little thought of settling down in Oxbridge. **1912** H. G. WELLS *Marriage* i. §1. 5 A ..meretricious dressing-bag of imitation morocco, which had been one of her chief financial errors at Oxbridge. **1924** E. F. BENSON *David of King's* i. 5 Useless..to delude the intelligent reader into believing that it was Queen's Parade at Oxbridge or Prince's Parade at Camford. **1955** T. H. PEAR *Eng. Social Differences* i. 20 He would often wish his sons to go to a public (boarding) school and to Oxbridge. **1958** *New Statesman* 30 Aug. 244/1 Whatever its merits or demerits, Oxbridge remains first choice for a majority of university applicants. **1960** AUDEN *Homage to Clio* 88 Oxbridge philosophers, to be cursory, Are products of a middle-class nursery. **1960** *Times* 14 Mar. 13/4 The University 'Rag'..is now more closely identified with what the jargon calls 'Redbrick' rather than 'Oxbridge', with the world of Kingsley Amis rather than that of the young Compton Mackenzie. **1964** S. BRITTAN *Treasury under Tories* i. 21 One characteristic that Whitehall does have in common with other *élite* groups is its overwhelmingly Oxbridge character. **1967** *New Scientist* 6 Apr. 39/2 Father is very likely public school and 'Oxbridge'. Son is 'redbrick'. **1973** D. ROBINSON *Rotten with Honour* 9 We'll have—Hale... Twenty-six, Oxbridge, degree in languages. **1975** *Sunday Tel.* 4 May 30/2 (*heading*) Fine win by Oxbridge. The Universities beat Worcestershire by 66 runs at Fenners. **1976** *Globe & Mail* (Toronto) 1 July 35/8 And as if to make the thing complete the prayer was often offered by a clergyman who read the liturgy with an Oxbridge accent even though he was a product of southern Ontario.

Hence **Oxbri·dgean, -ian** *a.* and *sb.*

1959 *Cambr. Rev.* 7 Feb. 315/1 They [*sc.* the Americans] are so polite, so ready to believe that the visiting Oxbridgean must find Yale or Harvard an anti-climax. **1959** *Guardian* 14 Dec. 6/4 'The mere fact,' you fretted, that such Oxbridgean institutions 'have refused the student loan money may make their actions suspect'. **1960** *Mind* LXIX. 419, I have wished I was reading one of those Oxbridgean philosophers who, had they taken the right turning early in life, would long ago have brought the filing and card-indexing systems of the British Civil Service up to a new peak of perfection. **1970** *Atlantic Monthly* May 132 As apt as an eighteenth-century Oxbridgean with the Latin tag. **1971** *New Scientist* 17 June 706 The ivy-covered, Oxbridgian atmosphere of Yale.

ox cart. [OX 5.] A cart drawn by an ox. Also *transf.*

1749 J. HEMPSTEAD *Diary* 6 July (1901) 526 No ox Carts in these parts & very few Horse Carts. **1877** [see OX 5]. **1918** E. S. FARROW *Dict. Mil. Terms* 427 *Ox Cart.* —A slang name for a heavy French shell which moves with a moderate velocity. **1973** *Country Life* 29 Nov. 1802/3 Continuously exploring..deeper into veldt and jungle, leading, on his Arab pony, a train of ox carts. **1975** *Times Lit. Suppl.* 5 Dec. 1462/1 Crane's noble and well-loved print 'The Triumph of Labour' with its procession of garlanded oxcarts and rejoicing workers.

Oxfam, OXFAM (ǫ·ksfæm). [Short for *Ox*ford Committee for *Fam*ine Relief.] An organization for the distribution of food, funds, etc., in disaster areas and to poor countries.

1963 D. MITCHELL in *Oxfam Ann. Rep. 1962/63*, At first the Oxford Committee for Famine Relief—Oxfam, as it is now known all over the world—was one of many similar groups with a temporary mission: the emergency relief of war suffering in Europe. **1968** *Listener* 8 Aug. 162/1 A grim, obsessed Oxfam worker, struggling to get a few scraps and leavings to millions of starving children. **1969** N. W. PIRIE *Food Resources* 15 Oxfam posters used to read 'Oxfam hates hungry babies' and went on to suggest ways of getting rid of the hunger. **1974** I. MURDOCH *Sacred & Profane Love Machine* 304 Her few inexpensive jewels had gone to Oxfam. **1975** J. BLACKBURN *Mister Brown's Bodies* i. 10 Those disgusting pictures of famine victims you see in the Oxfam shops.

Oxford. Add: **Oxford accent,** a style of pronouncing English popularly supposed to be particularly characteristic of members of the University of Oxford and (esp. before 1939) to be marked by affected utterance; **Oxford bags** [BAG *sb.* 16], a style of trousers very wide at the ankles; so **Oxford-bagged** *a.*; **Oxford blue,** a dark shade of blue, adopted as the colour of the university; **Oxford Blues:** see Blue *sb.* 7a; **Oxford clay,** add to def.: earlier called *clunch clay* (Clunch *sb.* 6), *plastic clay* (Plastic *a.* 5b); (earlier and later examples); **Oxford cloth** (see quots.); **Oxford(shire) Down,** a sheep of the breed so called, produced by crossing Cotswold and Hampshire Down sheep and developed by Samuel Druce at Eynsham about 1830; **Oxford English,** English spoken with an Oxford accent; the speech popularly supposed to be characteristic of a member of the University of Oxford; **Oxford frame** (later examples); **Oxford grey** (see *Oxford mixture*) (examples); also, the colour of such cloth; **Oxford Group:** see *group *sb.* 3d; **Oxford hollow,** in *Bookbinding,* a flattened paper tube inserted between the spine of the book and its cover, to strengthen the spine and allow the book to be opened flat more easily; **Oxford John,** a dish of sauced and stewed mutton with other ingredients; **Oxford marmalade,** a kind of coarse-cut marmalade originally manufactured in Oxford (registered as a trade-mark by Frank Cooper in 1908 and 1931); also *attrib.* and *fig.*; **Oxford plant** = **Oxford weed*; **Oxford punch** [Punch *sb.*[3]] (see quots.); **Oxford ragwort,** an annual herb, *Senecio squalidus,* belonging to the family Compositæ and bearing heads of yellow flowers (a native of southern Italy now naturalized in Britain, after having escaped from the Oxford Botanic Garden); **Oxford sausage,** a kind of sausage; also *fig.*; **Oxford scholar** *slang,* a crown; five shillings; a dollar; **Oxford shirt,** a shirt made from Oxford cloth; **Oxford shirting** = **Oxford cloth*; **Oxford trousers** = **Oxford bags*; **Oxford unit** *Pharm.,* a unit of penicillin originally adopted at the Sir William Dunn School of Pathology in the University of Oxford, being the amount which when dissolved in 1 c.c. of water gave the same inhibition as a certain partly purified standard solution; cf. **penicillin unit*; **Oxford voice** = **Oxford accent*; **Oxford weed,** the ivy-leaved toadflax, *Cymbalaria muralis.*

1904 J. K. Jerome *Tommy & Co.* v. 174 Somerville's Oxford accent is wasted here. **1924** Galsworthy *On Expression* 8 And dare we condemn cockney—a lingo whose waters, in Southern England, seem fast flooding in over the dykes of the so-called Oxford accent, and such other rural dialects as are left? **1934** *S.P.E. Tract* xxxix. 616 It might be said perhaps that the 'Oxford Accent' conveys an impression of a precise and rather foppish elegance, and of deliberate artificiality. **1940** G. Arthur *Concerning Winston Spencer Churchill* 194 Lacking the 'Oxford accent' he spoke as a Briton to Britons. **1959** J. Braine *Vodi* vi. 93 Dick assumed an Oxford accent. 'It's *naht* old-fashioned, dear brethren, to think of Hell in the language of fire and brimstone.' **1974** P. Dickinson *Poison Oracle* ii. 45 The Sultan's manner is very deceptive. .. His Oxford accent and his slang..are all a sort of parody of our civilisation. **1961** *Times* 18 May 16/6 Eton-cropped maidens sporting decorously with Oxford-bagged partners. **1927** *Dancing Times* Jan. 573/2 Oxford bags, plus fours, in fact, any old thing. **1933** P. Balfour *Society Racket* ii. 61 We wore high-necked jumpers and 'Oxford bags'. **1938** J. Betjeman *Oxf. Univ. Chest* i. 9 The pale-faced mechanics in Oxford bags and tweed coats, walk down the Cornmarket. **1948** H. Acton *Mem. Aesthete* vi. 119 Instead of the wasp-waisted suits with pagoda shoulders and tight trousers affected by the dandies, I wore jackets with broad lapels and broad pleated trousers. The latter got broader and broader. Eventually they were imitated elsewhere and were generally referred to as 'Oxford bags'. **1971** *Daily Tel.* 2 Aug. 9/5 By night you're either..Dietrich in a velvet blazer and Oxford bags, or Carole Lombard in a halter-neck satin top..and a long satin kilt. **1973** *Country Life* 19 Apr. 1115/1 A single-breasted striped suit for the bridegroom, which has Oxford bags and patch pockets. **1866** Mrs. H. Wood *Elster's Folly* I. viii. 191 'Strike your colours, ladies, you that sport the crimson and purple!' called out a laughing voice from one of the skiffs. 'Oxford blue wins.' **1875** *All Year Round* 20 Feb. 444/2 The hues peculiar to the best period of Sèvres were gros-blue, a dark heavy Oxford blue. **1923** Joyce *Let.* 26 Feb. (1966) III. 72 The smaller Oxford blue volume. **1959** M. Gilbert *Blood & Judgement* xvii. 176 He picked up a thin, Oxford-blue folder. **1973** R. Ludlum *Matlock Paper* xi. 101 A half-unbuttoned, oxford-blue shirt. **1818** W. Phillips *Selection of Facts Geol. Eng. & Wales* 66 In these ..are included the three strata..namely, the Forest marble, the Cornbrash limestone, and the clunch clay (Oxford Clay). **1967** D. H. Rayner *Stratigr. Brit. Isles* ix. 298 Around Peterborough, vast pits have been dug in the Oxford Clay for brick-making. **1964** *McCall's Sewing* iv. 58/2 *Oxford cloth,* plain-, basket- or twill-weave cotton, often used for shirting. It is fairly heavy cloth in which two yarns travel as one in the warp, and one filling yarn is equal in size to the two-warp yarns. **1968** J. Ironside *Fashion Alphabet* 243 *Oxford cloth,* a heavy cotton cloth used for shirts and sometimes jackets or summer suits. **1969** *Sears Catal.* Spring/Summer 24 Rajah shirt with soil release. Oxford cloth of polyester and cotton. **1976** *National Observer* (U.S.) 17 Jan. 10/3 (Advt.), Our fine quality, breathable, pure cotton oxford cloth pyjamas are unbeatable for wear all year 'round. [**1849** *Jrnl. R. Agric. Soc.* X. 436 The Cotswold is a large breed of sheep, and is the stock from which the class called new Oxford is sprung.] **1859** *Ibid.* XX. 345 Amongst the 'other short-woolled sheep' exhibited, we have Hampshire Downs, Oxfordshire Downs, [etc.]. *Ibid.,* The Oxford Downs date from the year 1833..when a neat, well-made Cotswold ram was used with Hampshire ewes. **1912** R. Lydekker *Sheep* v. 106 The formation of the Oxford down was commenced about the year 1833. **1970** *Observer* (Colour Suppl.) 26 Apr. 36/1 All six Down breeds..are shortwools, Oxford Down..being heaviest... Bold-looking sheep with top-knot of wool above dark face. **1926** D. H. Lawrence *Plumed Serp.* ii. 31 An odd, detached, yet cocky little man, a true little Indian, speaking Oxford English in a rapid, low, musical voice. **1932** *S.P.E. Tract* xxxvii. (*title*) 'Oxford' English. **1952** M. Steen *Phoenix Rising* iv. 72 Americans come over and proceed to acquire what they think is Oxford English. **1969** 'H. Pentecost' *Girl Watcher's Funeral* (1970) ii. ii. 100 It was Oxford English with a slight accent which I took to be French. **1975** *ITV Evidence to Annan Committee* 15 In the spoken word the traditional currency was, till recently, Oxford English. **1939** 'N. Shute' *What happened to Corbetts* iii. 88 He laid her on the ornate, gilded iron bed beneath a picture of the 'Stag at Bay' and a text in a wood Oxford frame that told them 'God is love'. **1973** J. Thomson *Death Cap* xiii. 177 The pictures on the walls were..pre-Raphaelite prints in Oxford frames. **1836** W. F. Tolmie *Diary* 28 Oct. in *Jrnls.* (1963) 322, 1 pr Extra S. fine dark Oxford grey trousers. **1864** J. S. Le Fanu *Uncle Silas* II. xii. 191 An old Oxford gray surtout that showed his lank length to advantage. **1903–4** Oxford grey [see *Donegal]. **1964** S. Bellow *Herzog* 237 A stylish oxford gray summer suit. **1973** R. Hayes *Hungarian Game* xxxix. 235 Urkowitz' face was turning a shade of fine Oxford gray. **1956** H. Williamson *Methods Bk. Design* xix. 308 Another method is to fix on the spine of the section a tube of paper, or Oxford hollow, and to fix the cover to this. **1960** G. A. Glaister *Gloss. Bk.* 289/1 Oxford hollow: a flattened paper tube which is attached to the back of a book..so that when the book is opened the back opens up independently of the spine... The O[xford] U[niversity] P[ress], who have supplied this note, state 'presumably the word Oxford was used to describe this kind of binding because undoubtedly the old Oxford bindery was the first to use it, particularly for leather-bound Bibles. It is properly applied only to a leather-bound book and is a style which is now used by most leather binders.' **1965** L. S. Darley *Introd. Bookbinding* 30 Another way of lining the spine, after the mull has been glued in place, is by making a tubular hollow—sometimes called an Oxford hollow—a device which provides a lining for the spine, a hollow for the cover and an additional point of union between the book and its case. **1892** *Encycl. Pract. Cookery* II. 68/2 Oxford John. **1952** F. White *Good Eng. Food* ii. iv. 136 *Oxford John.* Take a well hung leg of mutton [etc.]. **1907** *Yesterday's Shopping* (1969) 24 *Marmalade*..Oxford (Frank Cooper's). **1942** C. Morley *Thorofare* lxx. 459 There was Cooper's bitter Oxford marmalade—the only Oxonian product to which Uncle Dan would grant supremacy. **1962** *Sunday Express* 25 Feb. 6/3 Wyatt's thick-cut Oxford marmalade voice. **1973** 'S. Harvester' *Corner of Playground* i. viii. 74 A new jar of Oxford lime marmalade. **1856** Hawthorne *Jrnl.* 31 Aug. in *Passages from Eng. Note-Bks.* (1870) II. 150 We looked also at the outside of the wall [of New College], and Mr. Parker.. showed us a weed growing..hanging plentifully downward from a shallow root. It is called the Oxford plant, being found only here, and not easily, if at all, introduced anywhere else. **1845** E. Acton *Mod. Cookery* xxvi. 637 Oxford punch... Lemons..oranges..calf's foot jelly..white wine ..French brandy..Jamaica rum [etc.]. **1877** E. S. Dallas *Kettner's Bk. of Table* 322 Oxford punch.—The great characteristic of this punch is its having a quantity of calf's foot jelly dissolved in it. **1892** *Encycl. Pract. Cookery* II. 69/1 Oxford punch. **1884** W. Miller *Dict. Eng. Names Plants* 249/2 *Senecio...squalidus.* Oxford Rag-wort. **1886** G. C. Druce *Flora Oxfordshire* 158 Oxford Ragwort... Very plentiful in and around Oxford, where it was first noticed by Sir Joseph Banks. Dillenius sent seeds to Linnæus but whether he gathered them from the Oxford Garden or the wall of the town no memorandum exists. **1926** *Nat. Hist. Oxford District* 72 A few brave adventitious plants may be seen on the walls, including the ubiquitous Oxford Ragwort. **1948** Prime & Deacock *Shorter Brit. Flora* 149 Oxford Ragwort..; waste places, greatly on the increase. (This plant is very common on bombed sites in London.) **1969** *Nature* 27 Sept. 1303/2 Oxford ragwort (*Senecio squalidus*) spread throughout the railway system after seeds had been dispersed from the Botanic Garden to Oxford station. **1973** Gilmour & Walters *Wild Flowers* (ed. 5) xiii. 198 The Oxford ragwort..has achieved..an astonishing recent spread. **1764** (*title*) The Oxford sausage. **1877** E. S. Dallas *Kettner's Bk. of Table* 100 The Oxford sausage is a crêpinette, can be made at home. **1926** *Daily Colonist* (Victoria, B.C.) 5 Jan. 6/2 (Advt.), Fresh Made Oxford Sausage, 3 lbs. for 32 c. **1937** Partridge *Dict. Slang* 596/1 *Oxford Scholar,* five shillings (piece or sum): New Zealanders' rhyming s. on *dollar*: C. 20. Also from ca. 1870, in the S.W. of England. **1938** F. D. Sharpe *Sharpe of Flying Squad* 332 *Oxford Scholar,* dollar. **1960, 1965** Oxford scholar [see sense *2]. **1967** Oxford scholar [see *caser[2]]. **1926–7** *Army & Navy Stores Catal.* 717/1 Oxford shirts—With stiff cuffs, soft turnover cuff or small wristband to link and button—each 12/9. **1959** *Listener* 4 June 982/1 The cloth cap and the collarless Oxford shirt. **1971** *New Yorker* 9 Oct. 29/2 (Advt.), Our own make long staple cotton oxford shirt. [**1907** *Yesterday's Shopping* (1969) 742/2 Fancy cotton shirting... Oxford mat, best quality.] **1926–7** *Army & Navy Stores Catal.* 697/2 Oxford shirting (soft finish) 29 in. wide.. 1/1 Per yd. **1940** *Chambers's Techn. Dict.* 606/1 *Oxford shirting,* a plain-weave cotton fabric, generally striped, used for shirting. **1948** G. L. Fraser *Textiles by Britain* 165 *Oxford shirting,* plain or fancy woven striped shirting cloth. **1925** *Punch* 4 Mar. 244 (*caption*) Perils of the Dance. The terror of the Oxford trousers. **1937** J. Laver *Taste & Fashion* xvii. 241 The advent of Oxford trousers in the middle twenties. **1942** Florey & Jennings in *Brit. Jrnl. Exper. Path.* XXIII. 122 For those using the dilution method it may be stated that the 'Oxford unit' is that amount of penicillin which when dissolved in 50 ml. of meat extract broth just inhibits completely the growth of the test strain of *Staphylococcus aureus.* **1948** Wright & Montag *Textbk. Pharmacol. & Therap.* (ed. 4) xxxiii. 548 For the treatment of mild to moderately severe infections daily dosages of 80,000 to 120,000 Oxford units are sufficient. **1952** W. T. Salter *Textbk. Pharmacol.* xlix. 1084/1 The new international unit and the old Oxford unit are very close. **1920** A. Huxley *Limbo* 85 When the Military Representative spoke, he could hear again that wretched Nut's rendering of the Eton and Oxford voice. **1924** E. M. Forster *Passage to India* xxiv. 221 'We object to the presence of so many European ladies and gentlemen upon the platform,' he said in an Oxford voice. **1931** *Atlantic Monthly* Feb. 149/1 The pronunciation of the common people left its impress indelibly on the so-called best people, with a few languid drawls, terminal *aws,* clipped *g*s and feeble *h*s thrown in.., which..acquired the name of the Oxford voice. **1834** W. Baxter *Brit. Phænogamous Bot.* I. 23 This very pretty plant is a native of Italy, and is said to have been originally introduced into England by means of its seeds having been brought in some marble sculptures from that country to Oxford, where it has long established itself on the walls of the Colleges, gardens, &c. in such abundance as to have obtained the name of 'Oxford-weed'. **1976** C. Oman *Oxford Childhood* vii. 133 Mrs Pember was a qualified botanist and I was soon flattered by being sent up to the top of a crumbling wall..to get her specimens of Oxford Weed.

b. Used *attrib.* or as *adj.* to denote the characteristic manner, speech, behaviour, etc., of a present or former member of the University of Oxford; freq. = **Oxford accent.*

1877 H. James *Let.* 28 Feb. in R. B. Perry *Tht. & Char. W. James* (1935) I. 375, I lunched the other day with Andrew Lang to meet J. Addington Symonds,—a mild, cultured man, with the Oxford perfume. **1897** G. B. Shaw *Our Theatres in Nineties* (1932) III. 108 Stage smart speech, which, like the got-up Oxford mince and drawl of a foolish curate, is the mark of a snob. **1909** P. Gibbs *Street of Adventure* iii. 37 'Because I tell you so,' said Luttrell, with a touch of his Oxford manner. **1913** A. Lunn *Harrovians* ii. 27 Mr. Lee had neither a double chin nor an Oxford manner. **1919** J. B. Morton *Barber of Putney* ii. 24 Up and down one heard the Oxford drawl. **1922** Joyce *Ulysses* 6 He thinks you're not a gentleman... Because he comes from Oxford. You know, Dedalus, you have the real Oxford manner. *Ibid.* 431 In youth's smart blue Oxford suit with white vestslips. **1926** A. S. L. Farquharson in J. C. Wilson *Statement & Inference* I. p. xxv, 'The trouble is that one feels life is so short, *ars longa* but philosophy seems very much longer.' This is the scholar's last lesson, the clue perhaps to what is sometimes called Oxford irony. **1928** D. H. Lawrence *Woman who rode Away* 152 But, in a voice more expostulatingly Oxford than ever, he said [etc.]. *Ibid.* 153 Jimmy got up, with a bit of an Oxford wriggle, and held out his hand. **1934** *Spectator* 5 Jan. 18/2 Surely it is permissible to suggest..the Oxford Bleat by writing down the directions given me the other day as 'past a whaite house, between the water-tah and the pah station'. **1937** *N. & Q.* 12 June 428/1 What we term Oxford pronunciation, and wrongly so call it. **1938** F. D. Sharpe *Sharpe of Flying Squad* xvii. 189 A gentleman with an Oxford drawl..in darkest Hoxton. **1957** G. Avery *Warden's Niece* viii. 153 A young man..clumsily trying to propel his punt from the stern instead of the conventional Oxford position in front. **1958** B. Nichols *Sweet & Twenties* v. 74 If the worst came to the worst I could 'rely on the Oxford manner'. **1960** W. B. Gallie *New University* vi. 115 They were delighted by the fact that he so often appeared to be joking—for so they described Lindsay's elaborate Oxford irony.

2. *ellipt.* for Oxford English Dictionary, Oxford grey, marmalade, mixture, scholar, shirt, shoe, trousers, etc.

c **1890** in *Amer. Mail Order Fashions* (1961) 28/2 Women's tan Dongola Kid, square or pointed toe, fox heel Oxfords. French stay. **1890** *Illustr. London News* 24 May in L. de Vries *Victorian Advts.* (1968) 51/3 New Range of Coloured Oxfords, Cambrics, and Calcuttas for Shirts and Pyjamas. **1902** Farmer & Henley *Slang* V. 119/1 *Oxford,* a crown piece. **1903** in S. Nowell-Smith *Edwardian England* (1964) facing p. 180 (Advt.), The 'Oxford'. Blacking leather or glacé kid. **1914** *Glasgow Herald* 7 Sept. 10/2 Glasgow firms manufacture..zephyrs, Oxfords, shirtings, and dress goods. **1926** *Daily Colonist* (Victoria, B.C.) 21 July 16/4 (Advt.), A 4-ply worsted wool in shades of pink... Oxford. **1929** G. Mitchell *Mystery of Butcher's Shop* xi. 120 He fell down, and tore chunks out of his Oxfords on the brambles. **1932** *New Yorker* 11 June 45 Waterproof leather oxfords or ghillies..; suede oxfords at Brooks and Rogers Peet... Golf oxfords at Spalding [etc.]. **1945** M. D. Potter *Fiber to Fabric* viii. 155 *Oxford,* a plain weave of medium and heavy weights. **1950** W. Stevens *Let.* 21 Nov. (1967) 699, I look it up either at the office, where we have a Webster, or have someone look it up for me in the State library, where there is an Oxford. **1957** V. Nabokov *Pnin* i. 8 His conservative black oxfords had cost him about as much as all the rest of his clothing. **1958** [see *beetle-crusher* s.v. *beetle *sb.*[2] 5]. **1960** 'A. Burgess' *Doctor is Sick* 103 'We'll say a quid deposit, returnable on return of the hat, and a straight charge of an Oxford for the loan. Right?' 'Right.' The young man handed over his Oxford scholar. **1962** L. Deighton *Ipcress File* i. 13 He rocked on his hand-lasted Oxfords. **1964** J. Symons *End of Solomon Grundy* i. ii. 29 The routine of breakfast..Cooper's Oxford, the electric percolator. **1965** *Australasian Post* 4 Mar. 46 From 'dollar' we have the rhyming slang 'Oxford scholar', which eventually became shortened to an 'Oxford'. **1970** *Catal. L. L. Bean* (Freeport, Maine) Fall 32 Heavy duty nylon oxford outside is waterproof. **1971** D. E. Westlake *I gave at the Office* (1972) 139 Dressed in..new clothes—down to expensive black oxfords. **1972** 'I. Drummond' *Frog in Moonflower* 10 The Master..spread a piece of toast with Cooper's Oxford. **1976** *New Yorker* 26 Jan. 52/3 It is like seeing a pair of oxfords suspended from an ornate chandelier. **1978** *Spectator* (New Canaan High School, Connecticut) 66 Then I..pulled out four shirts: a turtleneck, a Lacoste 'alligator' shirt, a flannel shirt, and a wrinkled, white button-down Oxford.

b. The University of Oxford; *collect.*, the members of the University; quasi-adj., belonging to or supporting the University. With specific adj., any of various school examinations conducted under the auspices of the University.

a **1697** AUBREY *Wiltshire : Topogr. Coll.* (1862) 17 At Oxford, (and I believe at Cambridge) the rod was frequently used by the Tutors and Deans. **1886** H. BAUMANN *Londinismen* 129/2 Are you Oxford or Cambridge? **1899** BEERBOHM *More* 155, I was a modest, good-humoured boy. It is Oxford that has made me insufferable. **1916** W. OWEN *Let.* Apr. (1967) 389, I hear you are applying yourself to some solid study for the J[unior] Oxford. **1930** *Times Lit. Suppl.* 25 Dec. 1103/1 There is encouraging evidence elsewhere that young Oxford is beginning to recognize that mere cleverness is poetically sterile. **1966** *Rep. Comm. Inquiry Univ. Oxford* I. 17 Members of Oxford.

Oxfordian, *a.* Substitute for def. (s.v. OXFORD): Of, pertaining to, or designating a division of the Upper Jurassic in Britain lying below the Kimeridgian and above the Callovian (in continental Europe restricted to the lower part of this division). Also *absol.*, the Oxfordian stage or period. [In this sense ad. F. *oxfordien* (J. Thurmann 1830, in *Mém. de la Soc. d'Hist. nat. de Strasbourg* I. 22).] Add earlier and later examples.

1849 *Q. Jrnl. Geol. Soc.* V. 179 The clear definition of an equivalent of the Oxfordian group..had not been defined in the Southern Alps until M. von Buch demonstrated to the Italian geologists..that their 'Ammonitico rosso' was of Oxfordian age. *Ibid.* 182 The overlying stage..is therefore a good representative of the Oxfordian of the Alps. **1885, 1946** [see *CALLOVIAN *a.*]. **1967** D. H. RAYNER *Stratigr. Brit. Isles* ix. 275 The base of the Upper Jurassic is sometimes taken at the base of the Oxfordian stage. **1975** A. HALLAM *Jurassic Environments* ii. 16 The problem of correlation becomes much more serious from Upper Oxfordian times onwards. *Ibid.*, The increased difficulty of correlating the Upper Oxfordian is a consequence of northwards retreat of the boreal cardioceratid faunas which had ranged widely into southern Europe during the Lower Oxfordian.

2. [f. the title of Edward de Vere, Earl of *Oxford* (1550–1604) + -IAN.] Used with reference to the theory that the Earl of Oxford wrote the plays attributed to Shakespeare. Also as *sb.*

1930 P. ALLEN *Case for Edward de Vere* 20 These poems of Chapman..are, in my judgment, enough..to prove the Oxfordian authorship of 'Shakespeare'. **1930** *Times Lit. Suppl.* 11 Sept. 712/2 Oxfordians seem to start from the basic assumption that the association of the work of Shakespeare with the Stratford player needs explanation. **1932** *Ibid.* 23 June 462/4 For the ordinary reader, and especially for the reader unfamiliar with the Oxfordian theory, Mr. Allen's book is not wholly satisfactory. **1958** *Listener* 17 July 100/3 Baconians, Oxfordians, Rutlandians, Derbyites. **1970** S. SCHOENBAUM *Shakespeare's Lives* VI. ix. 609 Freud read the Looney book. It converted him to the Oxfordian faith. *Ibid.* 610 The contempt felt by reputable scholars for the Oxfordians.

Oxfordish (ǫ·ksfǒɹdiʃ), *sb.* and *a.* [f. OXFORD + -ISH[1].] **A.** *sb.* Oxford jargon or slang. **B.** *adj.* Of, pertaining to, or suggestive of the University of Oxford.

1863 C. READE *Hard Cash* I. 16 Ploughed is the new Oxfordish for plucked. **1921** R. MACAULAY *Dangerous Ages* iv. 74 A pleasant, Oxfordish room, with the brown paper and plain green curtains of..college days. **1931** W. HOLTBY *Poor Caroline* v. 196 'Ah, a very opportune arrival, sergeant,' he began in his formal Oxfordish voice. **1962** J. D. SALINGER *Franny & Zooey* 127, I can never bring myself to smile back at him when he's being charming and Oxfordish. He's on lend-*lease* or something from Oxford.

O·xfordy, *a.* [f. OXFORD + -Y[1].] Oxfordish, Oxonian.

1924 D. H. LAWRENCE in *Criterion* Oct. 27 It was his manner, his rather Oxfordy manner, more than anything else, that went beyond her. **1927** in *Lett. Gertrude Bell* I. i. 12 My sister..begged me to send Gertrude to stay with them for the winter..opining that frequenting foreign diplomatic Society might be a help for Gertrude 'to get rid of her Oxfordy manner'. *a* **1935** T. E. LAWRENCE *Mint* (1955) II. iii. 108 The rough end of the hut tries to copy the accent he displays when he reads our nominal roll. It's an Oxfordy drawl. **1959** *Encounter* Aug. 74/1 This deliciously fat Oxfordy volume.

oxic (ǫ·ksik), *a.* [f. OX(IDE *sb.*, OX(YGEN + -IC.] **1.** *Soil Science.* Applied to a subsurface mineral soil horizon more than 30 cm. thick that is characterized by the virtual absence of any weatherable materials and the presence of hydrated oxides of iron and aluminium, highly insoluble minerals such as quartz, and clays of the type in which single sheets of silica tetrahedra alternate with single sheets of alumina octahedra. Cf. *OXISOL.

1960 *Soil Classification: 7th Approximation* (U.S. Dept. Agric.) v. 53/1 The concept of the oxic horizon presented here is very tentative, as it has had little testing... The oxic horizon is one from which weathering has..removed or altered a large part of the silica that is combined with iron and aluminium, but not necessarily the quartz or 1:1 lattice clays. **1970** P. M. AHN *W. African Soils* (1974) vii. 221 The boundaries of the oxic horizon are usually gradual and diffuse, and the horizon shows no rock structure or very little. **1972** FOTH & TURK *Fund. Soil Sci.* (ed. 5) x. 262 All soils with oxic horizons belong to the Oxisol order. **1976** D. STEILA *Geogr. Soils* xi. 151 It is believed that the most extensive areal development of the oxic horizon may have taken place under paleo-climates of much higher rainfal.

2. [Back-formation from *ANOXIC *a.*] Involving, characterized by, or related to the presence of oxygen.

1970 *Acta Radiologica: Therapy, Physics, Biol.* IX. 257 The investigations..were conducted with the aim of comparing the reactions of different cell lines to oxic and anoxic roentgen radiation. **1972** *Radiation Bot.* XII. 151 The damage produced by anoxic irradiation can be enhanced by O_2, after irradiation, to give oxic damage. **1975** *Nature* 26 June 740/2 We have measured in oxic and anoxic cells the yield of strand breakage on bacteriophage λ DNA superinfecting lysogenic bacteria. **1975** *Ibid.* 4 Dec. 415/1 It is formed from phytol thermocatalytically in oxic conditions.

Hence **oxi·city**, oxic condition.

1978 *Nature* 16 Mar. 216/2 The available data suggest that the oxicity/anoxicity of the sediment and the water column affects the amount and nature of the organic matter incorporated into the sediment during deposition.

oxidant. Delete *rare* and add to def.: = OXIDIZER 1 in Dict. and Suppl. (Further examples.)

1930 M. STEPHENSON *Bacterial Metabolism* iii. 49 The position of a system..is determined by the Eh when [the concentration of] oxidant equals [that of] reductant. **1950** *Engineering* 29 Dec. 575/3 Fuels can be burned..with fluorine when no oxygen is present at all—although a fluorine compound would still be known as the 'oxidant'. **1961** *New Scientist* 12 Oct. 110/1 Oxidants may include oxygen, air, chlorine,..and so on, and many combinations of fuels and oxidants are possible for fuel cell development. **1972** *Daily Tel.* 27 Nov. 3/2 Engineers pumped more than a million gallons of fuel and oxidant in the fuel tanks in a count-down rehearsal.

oxidase (ǫ·ksidēiz, -s). *Biochem.* Also †OXYDASE in Dict. and Suppl. [ad. F. *oxydase* (G. Bertrand 1896, in *Compt. Rend.* CXXII. 1217), f. *oxyde* OXIDE *sb.*: see *-ASE.] Orig., any enzyme which brings about oxidation (now called an *OXIDOREDUCTASE); now used only of such enzymes that react with molecular oxygen, esp. those that catalyse the transfer of hydrogen from a substrate to oxygen so as to form water or hydrogen peroxide (cf. *OXYGENASE).

1896 *Chem. News* 19 June 293/2 (*heading*) A new oxidase, or oxidising soluble ferment of vegetable origin. **1935** *Times Lit. Suppl.* 28 Feb. 127 Xanthine oxidase is unable to attack nucleosides. **1946** P. H. MITCHELL *Textbk. Biochem.* xii. 340 Cytochrome Oxidase.—This enzyme specifically catalyzes the oxidation of cytochromes by molecular oxygen. **1956** *Sci. News* XL. 43 When fresh or withered [tea] leaf is damaged it absorbs oxygen from the air with the aid of an enzyme, an oxidase, occurring in the leaf cells. **1964** *Rep. Internat. Union Biochem. Comm. on Enzymes* in Florkin & Stotz *Comprehensive Biochem.* XIII. vi. 33 All enzymes catalysing oxido-reductions will be named 'oxidoreductases' in the systematic nomenclature... [In the trivial nomenclature] the terms 'dehydrogenase' or 'reductase' will be used much as hitherto... 'Oxidase' will be used only for cases where O_2 acts as an acceptor, and 'oxygenase' only for those cases where the O_2 molecule is directly incorporated into the substrate. **1970** R. W. MCGILVERY *Biochem.* xvii. 407 Aromatic rings may be opened by oxidations utilizing a complete molecule of oxygen. Examples:..the oxidation of hydroxyanthranilate by hydroxyanthranilate oxidase.

oxidation. a. (Further examples.) Add to def.: Also, the removal of hydrogen from a compound.

1866 [see *DEHYDROGENATION]. **1900** *Jrnl. Chem. Soc.* LXXVIII. I. 301 (*heading*) Oxidation of the nature of dehydrogenation by means of ferricyanides. **1959** CRAM & HAMMOND *Org. Chem.* vi. 73 In organic chemistry, oxidation involves the removal of hydrogen and (or) the addition of oxygen or some other hetero atom to a compound.

b. Add to def.: The partial or complete removal of an electron from an atom or molecule; an increase in the proportion of electronegative constituents in a molecule or compound. (Further examples.)

1907 WHITNEY & BROWN tr. *Le Blanc's Text-bk. Electro-Chem.* vii. 256 There must be, in every galvanic cell, an oxidation at one electrode and a reduction at the other. **1928** H. L. HIND tr. *Schoen's Probl. Fermentation* xiv. 167 There is a change from divalent iron to iron at a higher degree of oxidation. **1968** PASSMORE & ROBSON *Compan. Med. Stud.* I. viii. 5/2 It is also characteristic of biological oxidations that they are often linked together to form a chain along which the electrons flow.

2. Special combs.: **oxidation number,** the charge (expressed in units of the negative of the electron charge) which is assigned to an atom on the assumption that the bonding in the substance or radical in which it exists is completely ionic; the average formal charge so assigned to atoms of a particular element in a compound or radical; **oxidation potential,** the electrode potential required to bring about a particular oxidation reaction at the electrode; **oxidation–reduction** = *REDOX; freq. *attrib.*; **oxidation state,** oxidation number; the state of having a particular oxidation number.

1948 *Jrnl. Chem. Educ.* XXV. 278/2 The O_2 molecule..is made up of two neutral atoms..; the oxidation number of the O atom is coneequently zero. **1964** CRAM & HAMMOND *Org. Chem.* (ed. 2) vi. 98 The system described is similar to the inorganic system if effective oxidation numbers, ranging from −4 (in CH_4) to +4 (CCl_4 or CO_2), are assigned to *individual carbon atoms* within organic molecules. **1968** J. MARCH *Adv. Org. Chem.* xix. 853 Carbon in propane has an oxidation number of −2·67 and in butane of −2·5, though organic chemists seldom think of these two compounds as being in different oxidation states. **1900** *Jrnl. Chem. Soc.* LXXVIII. II. 642 An attempt was made to measure a number of oxidation potentials. **1942** C. E. K. MEES *Theory Photogr. Process* viii. 308 When a silver salt solution is added to a reducing solution, there is an adjustment of the oxidation potentials of each to a common value intermediate between the two. **1966** C. R. TOTTLE *Sci. Engin. Materials* x. 225 The readiness to ionize by losing electrons in the presence of an ionizing solvent is called the oxidation potential. **1909** *Chem. Abstr.* III. 2648 It is therefore unnecessary to assume..that the e.m.f. in an oxidation-reduction cell is due to H_2 or O_2 at definite pressure in the electrode. **1951** *New Biol.* XI. 29 The over-all reaction in photosynthesis is of a type, extremely important in living organisms, known as an oxidation-reduction, in which one compound becomes oxidized at the expense of another which is reduced. **1974** *Sci. Amer.* Dec. 65/2 Chemical processes of this kind, in which electrons are transferred from one molecule to another, are called oxidation-reduction reactions. **1975** *Jrnl. Biol. Chem.* CCL. 3929 The oxidation-reduction equilibrium of the γ chains of human fetal hemoglobin. **1942** SNEED & MAYNARD *Gen. Inorg. Chem.* vi. 120 In many cases an element in its oxide or chloride is not reduced to the free state [by hydrogen] but to a lower oxidation state. **1973** J. G. DICK *Analytical Chem.* ii. 15 The hydrogen atom is assigned an oxidation state of +1, except in hydrides where the oxidation state is generally −1.

oxidative, *a.* Substitute for def.: Involving, pertaining to, or characterized by oxidation. (Further examples.)

1923 *Q. Jrnl. Med.* XVI. 145 (*heading*) The rate of oxidative recovery from exercise in man. **1935** C. F. & G. T. CORI in Harrow & Sherwin *Textbk. Biochem.* xx. 567 This so-called 'oxidative quotient' was found to be between 3 and 6 for all tissues examined. **1962** DARDENNE & KIRSTEN in A. Pirie *Lens Metabolism Rel. Cataract* 419 Oxidative deaminations are of greater importance for the degradation of amino acids. **1972** *Daily Colonist* (Victoria, B.C.) 13 Feb. 27/5 It may be that the human need for Vitamin E is increasing due to the oxidative atmosphere man is creating around the world.

Hence **o·xidatively** *adv.*, by an oxidative process.

1964 *Oceanogr. & Marine Biol.* II. 152 The reineckate ion is removed with silver nitrate, and interfering substances (basic amino acids) are oxidatively deaminated by boiling with silver oxide. **1972** COTTON & WILKINSON *Adv. Inorg. Chem.* (ed. 3) xxiv. 773 Molecules that contain multiple bonds may be added oxidatively without cleavage to form new complexes which have 3-membered rings. **1976** *Lancet* 11 Dec. 1312/2 *Pseudomonas* metabolises carbohydrates oxidatively.

oxide. Add: **b.** *attrib.* and *Comb.*, as *oxide-coated* adj., *oxide coating.*

1933 J. H. MORECROFT *Electron Tubes* ii. 23 In making the modern oxide-coated filament the coating is applied in the form of a white carbonate. *Ibid.*, The amount of CO_2 released from the oxide coating of an ordinary rectifier tube.., when the carbonate is being reduced to the oxide, is sufficient to fill the bulb to about 10 mm Hg pressure. **1964** F. ROSEBURY *Handbk. Electron Tube & Vacuum Techniques* (1965) 95 Experimental tubes often do not require their oxide-coated cathodes to have exceptionally long life. **1966** *McGraw-Hill Encycl. Sci. & Technol.* XIV. 246/2 Oxide coatings commonly have a work function of the order of 1·1 ev.

oxidize, *v.* **1.** Add to def.: More widely, to cause to undergo oxidation; to remove an electron from, completely or partly. (Further examples.)

1894 PERKIN & KIPPING *Org. Chem.* I. vi. 95 Alcohol is readily oxidised by chromic acid, yielding acetaldehyde. **1913** MCPHERSON & HENDERSON *Course in Gen. Chem.* xxxiv. 471 Ferrous chloride is said to be oxidized to ferric chloride. **1942** SNEED & MAYNARD *Gen. Inorg. Chem.* xviii. 438 Chlorine oxidizes bromide ions and iodide ions to free bromine and iodine respectively. **1968** R. O. C. NORMAN *Princ. Org. Synthesis* iv. 143 The methyl group is oxidized when methane is converted by bromine into methyl bromide, because the electron-pair in the C—Br bond is less under the control of the carbon atom than the pair in the original C—H bond.

oxidizer. Add: **1.** *spec.* one used to support the combustion of fuel in a rocket engine or fuel cell. (Further examples.)

1950 *Sci. News* XV. 78 Liquid fluorine could be used as an 'oxidiser' with suitable fuels, but great care is needed when handling this liquid. **1952**, etc. [see *FUEL *sb.* 2* c]. **1973** *Daily Tel.* 3 Aug. 34/3 Like all rocket engines they use a fuel, monomethyl hydroazine, and an oxydiser, nitrogen tetroxide.

oxidoreductase (ǫ:xidorī·dʊ·ktē̆iz, -s). *Biochem.* Also †**oxydo-**. [ad. F. *oxydo-réducase* (Battelli & Stern 1921, in *Arch. internat. de Physiol.* XVIII. 413), f. *oxyde* OXIDE *sb.* + *réduc-tion* REDUCTION: see *-ASE.] Any enzyme that catalyses oxidoreduction.

1922 [see *HYDRATASE]. **1922** [see *HYDROLASE]. **1928** *Physiol. Abstr.* XIII. 141 The oxydoreductase of yeast, unlike that from milk, acts on methyl glyoxal almost as strongly as on acetaldehyde. **1958** *Nature* 15 Feb. 452/2 Enzymes catalysing oxido-reductions would be named oxidoreductases in the systematic nomenclature, according to the scheme 'donor–acceptor reductase'. **1964** [see *OXIDASE]. **1974** *Encycl. Brit. Macropædia* VI. 897/2 Oxidoreductases and transferases account for about 50 percent of the approximately 1,000 enzymes recognized thus far.

oxidoreduction (ǫ:ksidorī·dʊ·kʃən). *Biochem.* [f. OXID(ATION + -O + REDUCTION.] A process in which one substance is oxidized and electrons from it reduce another substance.

1934 *Jrnl. Faculty Sci. Hokkaido Univ.* II. (Ser. 3) 18 In animal and in plant cells, oxidoreduction occurs in parallel with the formation of peroxide. **1958** [see *OXIDOREDUCTASE]. **1971** *Ital. Jrnl. Biochem.* XX. 129 Crystalline lactate dehydrogenase..catalyzes the dismutation of glyoxylate to glycolate and oxalate producing the oxido-reduction system of NAD coenzymes illustrated in Figure 1.

So **o:xidoredu·ctive** *a.*, involving oxidoreduction.

1951 WHITBY & HYNES *Med. Bacteriol.* (ed. 5) xx. 314 Others obtain energy from amino-acids, probably by paired oxido-reductive deaminations. **1971** J. Z. YOUNG *Introd. Study Man* xxvi. 376 Oxido-reductive reactions are linked with phosphorylation to produce ATP.

oximeter (ǫksi·mǐtəɹ). *Med.* [f. OXI- + -METER.] A device for measuring the proportion of hæmoglobin in the blood which is in the oxidized form.

1942 G. A. MILLIKAN in *Rev. Sci. Instruments* XIII. 434 (*heading*) The oximeter, an instrument for measuring continuously the oxygen saturation of arterial blood in man. **1951** *Anesthesiology* XII. 549 With the oximeter it is possible to show how the anesthetist in his manipulations may induce trends which often lead to severe anoxemia. **1966** *McGraw-Hill Encycl. Sci. & Technol.* IX. 469/2 A second type of oximeter is designed to measure the oxygen saturation of blood outside the body during or shortly after withdrawal of the blood from various sites in the vascular system. **1975** *Sci. Amer.* Feb. 69/1 (Advt.), With the ear oximeter, the physician can make the measurement simply by attaching an optoelectronic device to the patient's ear and reading percent oxygen saturation on the display.

Hence **oxime·tric** *a.*, employing an oximeter; **oxi·metry**, the use of an oximeter.

1944 G. A. MILLIKAN in O. Glasser *Med. Physics* I. 900/1 (*heading*) Oximetry: continuous measurement of blood oxygen. **1948** *Federation Proc.* VII. 104/2 (*heading*) Oximetric determination of cardiac output in man. **1955** *Canad. Jrnl. Psychol.* IX. 67 (*heading*) Studies on the physiology of awareness: An oximetrically monitored controlled stress test. **1966** *McGraw-Hill Encycl. Sci. & Technol.* IX. 469/2 The physical basis of oximetry stems from the difference in absorption by oxygenated and reduced hemoglobin of red light of wavelengths in the region of 640 mμ. **1971** *Biol. Abstr.* LII. 9988 (*heading*) Cerebral venous oxygen saturation during rapid changes in the arterial blood pressure: an oximetric study in dogs.

oxine (ǫ·ksīn). *Chem.* [ad. G. *oxin* (Hahn & Vieweg 1927, in *Zeitschr. f. anal. Chem.* LXXI. 123), f. *ox*ychinol*in*, hydroxyquinoline.] 8-Hydroxyquinoline, C_9H_7NO, a crystalline phenol which forms water-insoluble complexes with many metal ions and is used in analysis and as a deodorant and antibacterial agent.

1927 *Chem. Abstr.* XXI. 2444 Oxine itself is difficultly sol. in water..but is more sol. in AcOH. **1947** [see *HYDROXYQUINOLINE]. **1956** R. G. W. HOLLINGSHEAD *Oxine & Its Derivatives* IV. xxxiv. 1167 The growth of athlete's foot is prevented by the use of an absorbent powder, such as talc or starch, containing oxine and finely divided boric acid. **1973** T. MOHÁCSY tr. *Burger's Organic Reagents in Metal Analysis* ii. 97 Oxine complexes are usually intensely coloured in chloroform. This renders possible the spectrophotometric determination of many metal ions.

Oxisol (ǫ·ksisǫl). *Soil Science.* [f. *OXI(C *a.* + *-SOL.] A type of stable, highly weathered mineral soil found in tropical regions (see quots. 1960, 1971). Cf. *OXIC *a.* 1.

1960 *Soil Classification: 7th Approximation* (U.S. Dept. Agric.) xvi. 238/1 The Oxisols include the soils that, in recent years, have been called Latosols, and many, if not most, of those that have been called Ground-Water Laterite soils... All soils that have oxic horizons are included in the order. **1970** P. M. AHN *W. African Soils* (1974) vii. 221 The Oxisol order probably includes only the oldest and most highly weathered of West African soils. **1971** *Gloss. Soil Sci. Terms* (Soil Sci. Soc. Amer.) 26/1 *Oxisols*, mineral soils that have an oxic horizon within 2 m of the surface or plinthite as a continuous phase within 30 cm of the surface, and that do not have a spodic or argillic horizon above the oxic horizon. (An order in the USDA soil taxonomy.) **1972** [see *OXIC *a.* 1]. **1976** D. STEILA *Geogr. Soils* xi. 150 There are two main regions of Oxisol concentration: in South America surrounding the alluvial soils of the Amazon and in equatorial Africa.

Oxo (ǫ·ksǫ). Also **oxo.** [f. OX + -O.] The proprietary name of an extract of beef, orig. a liquid, later in solid tablets, used as the basis of drinks and soups; also, the drink made from such tablets.

1899 *Trade Marks Jrnl.* 24 May 626 Oxo... Fluid beef. Liebig's Extract of Meat Company, Limited,..London,..and..Antwerp; manufacturers of Liebig Company's extract of meat, and manufacturers, shippers, and importers of South American produce. **1904** C. L. NEIL *Mod. Physical Culture* 15 Perhaps the handiest and best form in which to take this [*sc.* beef tea] is Oxo, made by Liebig's Extract of Meat Company. **1905** *Car* 24 May p. viii/1 A 4 oz. bottle of Oxo, and a few biscuits. **1907** *Yesterday's Shopping* (1969) 5/2 (*heading*) Liebig Co.'s Oxo Fluid Beef. **1914** D. O. BARNETT *Let.* 6 Nov. (1915) 4 Chocolate would be very welcome, also Oxo tablets. **1922** *Glasgow Herald* 13 Apr. 2 We shall carry..a thermos flask for Oxo. **1936** E. M. ANDERSON *Pract. Camp Cookery* 84 Brown sauce... 1 or 2 Oxo cubes. *Ibid.*, Use Oxo, relish, etc., if required, and season to taste. **1963** B. NILSON *Bk. Meat Cookery* 14/2 Pour over the Oxo stock. **1975** C. FREMLIN *Long Shadow* i. 10 Popping in with cups of tepid Oxo. **1976** A. HILL *Summer's End* i. 6 It smelled like a ton of flowers pressed into the space of an oxo-cube.

oxo(-) (ǫ·ksǫ), *prefix* and *a.* *Chem.* [f. OX(YGEN + -O.] **1.** As a word-forming element in the names of organic compounds used to denote the presence of a carbonyl group, as in *oxodecanoic acid*, *3-oxovaleric acid*, *OXOSTEROID.

1971 *Nomencl. Org. Chem.* (I.U.P.A.C.) (ed. 3) C. 176 In the presence of a group having priority over carbonyl for citation as principal group, or when all the carbonyl groups cannot be included in the ketone functional class name, the presence of carbonyl-oxygen atoms is indicated by the prefixes 'oxo-', 'dioxo-', *etc.*

2. With a hyphen, as quasi-*adj.* without a hyphen, or joined, as one word, to a sb. **a.** Applied to an oxygen atom linking two other atoms, and to compounds containing such a grouping. Now *rare.*

1921 *Jrnl. Chem. Soc.* CXIX. 1657 This is the value of the factor for the oxo-linking, —O—. **1922** *Ibid.* CXXI. 1811 In the oxo-compound the molecule is in one straight line. **1934** *Jrnl. Amer. Chem. Soc.* LVI. 795/1 Ol compounds readily change to oxo compounds upon heating their solutions. **1962** [see *OL].

b. Applied to compounds, ions or groups containing one or more oxygen atoms bonded to another atom (*spec.* in *Org. Chem.* indicating the presence of a carbonyl group; cf. 1 above), as *oxo acid, anion, group, ion.*

1935 H. J. LUCAS *Org. Chem.* xxxix. 514 If the oxo group is on the end of a carbon chain, the compound is an aldehyde acid. **1958** *Jrnl. Physiol.* CXL. 154 The normal metabolism of the intestinal cells overshadows or compensates for any changes in the oxo acid concentrations in the blood. **1959** *Nomencl. Inorg. Chem.* (I.U.P.A.C.) v. 44 Most of the common acids are oxoacids, *i.e.*, they contain only oxygen atoms bound to the characteristic atom. **1965** PHILLIPS & WILLIAMS *Inorg. Chem.* I. xiv. 523 Oxyacids are sometimes called oxo-acids to stress the fact that they contain XO groups in their structures. **1969** H. T. EVANS tr. *Hägg's Gen. & Inorg. Chem.* xxi. 500 Charged oxide molecules, that is oxo ions, should also be considered as oxides. The particular descriptions of these..and the corresponding oxo acids, are given under the respective central-atom element. **1971** *Nomencl. Org. Chem.* (I.U.P.A.C.) (ed. 3) C. 120 Trivial names for oxo carboxylic acids..may be used for the acyclic component. **1972** COTTON & WILKINSON *Adv. Inorg. Chem.* (ed. 3) v. 170 The second main class of acid behavior is shown by compounds with X—OH groups; these are called oxo acids, and generally have a formula of the type H_nXO_m, for example H_3PO_4. *Ibid.* xxi. 639 Many of the most important ligands having oxygen donor atoms are oxo anions, such as NO_2^-, NO_3^-, SO_4^{2-} and ClO_4^-. *Ibid.* xiv. 408 Tetrahedral oxo ions such as PO_4^{3-}, ClO_4^-, MnO_4^-.

c. Also **OXO, Oxo.** Applied to the hydroformylation process or reaction.

1947 *Chem. & Industry* 1 Feb. 73/2 The OXO reaction is one of general applicability to compounds containing the ethylenic double bond. **1949** R. F. GOLDSTEIN *Petroleum Chem. Industry* x. 187 The Oxo reaction is exothermic, 35k. cal. being liberated per mol of olefin reacted. **1966** *McGraw-Hill Encycl. Sci. & Technol.* VI. 543/1 Cobalt catalysts are universally used for the Oxo reaction. **1969** [see *hydroformylation* s.v. *HYDRO-]. **1971** *Nature* 20 Aug. 537/1 Roden..discovered the oxo or hydroformylation reaction which generates aldehydes and alcohols from olefins, carbon monoxide, and hydrogen in the presence of cobalt catalysts.

Oxonian. Add: **B.** *sb.* Also, used of residents of Oxford who are not members of the University.

1966 *Oxford Mail* 16 Mar. 8/3 We real Oxonians do still exist.

Oxonolatry (later example).

1932 A. QUILLER-COUCH in *Fifty Years* 46 What we, the lighter-hearted, did not renounce was the charm of the place, that 'Oxonolatry', if you will, which Swinburne had scoffed at.

oxonium (ǫksōᵘ·niə̆m). *Chem.* [f. OX- 1 + *-ONIUM.] The hydroxonium ion, H_3O^+, or any derivative of this in which one or more of the hydrogen atoms are replaced by organic radicals. Usu. *attrib.*

1899 COLLIE & TICKLE in *Jrnl. Chem. Soc.* LXXV. 717 If oxygen can replace phosphorus, nitrogen, or sulphur in bases, then these oxygen compounds can be viewed as derivatives of the hypothetical base, oxonium hydroxide, OH_3OH. **1929** R. A. GORTNER *Outl. Biochem.* xxx. 621 The anthocyanin compounds readily add acids to form oxonium salts. **1959**, **1966** [see *HYDRONIUM]. **1974** *Nature* 31 May 474/2 By dynamic reversal of the H_2O binding step before pseudorotation, the two oxygens in the pair of oxoniums could equilibrate with the H_2O oxygens of the medium.

oxosteroid (ǫksostīᵊ·roid, -ste·roid). *Biochem.* [f. *OXO- 1 + *STEROID.] = *ketosteroid* s.v. *KETO- a.

1956 *Biochem. Jrnl.* LXII. 1P Urinary 17-oxosteroid conjugates consist of a mixture of glucuronides and sulphates. **1968** PASSMORE & ROBSON *Compan. Med. Stud.* I. xxxi. 13/1 (*caption*) 17-Oxosteroids are derived mainly from androgens and are excreted in urine principally as their 3-sulphate derivatives.

oxotremorine (ǫksotre·mǒrīn). *Pharm.* [f. *OXO- + *TREMORINE.] A crystalline compound, 1-(2-oxopyrrolidino)-4-pyrrolidino-2-butyne, $C_{12}H_{18}N_2O$, a metabolite of tremorine, which is capable of inducing the symptoms of Parkinsonism and is used in research into this disease.

1961 A. K. CHO et al. in *Biochem. & Biophys. Res. Communications* V. 276 For purposes of rough measurement, a unit was defined as the dose per Kg. which on intravenous injection in mice gave this threshold effect. It proved to be equal to approximately 15 μg. of 2-oxotremorine base. **1970** PASSMORE & ROBSON *Compan. Med. Stud.* II. v. 560/2 Another method [of inducing symptoms of Parkinsonism] involves the use of the drug tremorine..or its active metabolite oxotremorine which induce tremor, rigidity, akinesia, analgesia and signs of peripheral cholinergic stimulation in many animal species. **1972** BRIMBLECOMBE & PINDER *Tremors* iv. 96 Leslie & Maxwell (1964) first suggested that oxotremorine is a more desirable tool in screening compounds for anti-Parkinson activity than is tremorine.

oxprenolol (ǫkspre·nǒlǫl). *Pharm.* [f. OX- 1 + *pren-* (f. *ISOPRENALINE) + reduplicated -OL (after *PROPRANOLOL).] The compound 1-(*o*-allyloxyphenoxy)-3-isopropylamino-2-propanol, $C_{15}H_{23}NO_3$, which is an adrenergic blocking agent used mainly (in the form of the white crystalline hydrochloride) in the treatment of cardiac arrhythmia, angina and hypertension.

1968 *Jrnl. Amer. Med. Assoc.* 29 July 292/1 The following nonproprietary names..have been adopted by the United States Adopted Names (USAN) Council... Oxprenolol hydrochloride. **1969** *Jrnl. Appl. Physiol.* XXVII. 366/1 Oxprenolol, a specific beta-receptor blocking agent, diminished effort tachycardia by 15·0% and emotional tachycardia by 34·2%. **1977** *Lancet* 5 Nov. 954/1 Players receiving oxprenolol feel calmer before performing and happier with their recital.

ox-tail. *ox-tail soup* (examples).

1834 H. W. BRAND *Simpson's Cookery* v. 64 Ox-tail soup. Blanch two ox-tails, cut into pieces of a size suited to be served at table. **1841** THACKERAY *Gt. Hoggarty Diamond* (1849) xi. 142 Three silver tureens of soup: viz. mock-turtle soup, ox-tail soup, and giblet soup. **1865** C. M. YONGE *Clever Woman* II. iv. 53 The whole party were in a little den at the pastrycook's; the boys consuming mutton pies, and the ladies ox-tail soup. **1868** M. JEWRY *Warne's Model Cookery* 172/2 (*heading*) Ox-Tail Soup. **1939** JOYCE *Finnegans Wake* I. 133 Can rant as grave as oxtail soup and chat as gay as a porto flippant. **1970** SIMON & HOWE *Dict. Gastron.* 286/1 It is said the first ox-tail soup was made by a starving French nobleman during the Reign of Terror.

oxter, *sb.* (Further examples in Irish, and occas. wider, use.)

1901 G. B. SHAW *Admirable Bashville* II. 304 But many felt that Byron shewed bad taste In taking old Ned Skene upon his back, And, with Bob Mellish tucked beneath his oxter, Sprinting a hundred yards to show the crowd The perfect pink of his condition. **1914** JOYCE *Dubliners* 206 Many a good man went to the penny-a-week school with a sod of turf under his oxter. **1932** AUDEN *Orators* II. 70 The madman keeper crawls through brushwood, Axe under oxter. **1956** H. SUTHERLAND *Irish Journey* iii. 25 Each carrying a loaf under his 'oxster'. **1964** *Listener* 19 Mar. 494/3 Alan Whicker..stood..on that bubbling pitch lake of Trinidad..and let us hear a calypso from a man who'd fallen into it up to his oxters. **1977** D. BAGLEY *Enemy* ix. 63 Benson's carrying a gun in his oxter. **1978** *Jrnl. Lancs. Dial. Soc.* Jan. 15/1 [Durham] *Oxter*, armpit.

c. *Comb.* **oxter-plate** (see quot. 1904).

1885 H. PAASCH *From Keel to Truck* 46 Plate,..oxter—Tôle de voûte contre l'étambot. Achselgrube-Platte.

1904 A. C. Holms *Pract. Shipbuilding* I. 526 The oxter plates are those which take the sternpost, immediately below, or partly on, the transom. 1927 G. F. Leechman *Theory & Pract. Steering* 51 The rotary current applies considerable pressure upon the hull in the vicinity of the oxter plate. 1948 R. de Kerchove *Internat. Maritime Dict.* 511/1 *Oxter plate*, a shell plate riveted to the stern frame in way of the rudderpost head.

oxy, *a.* For *rare*—¹ read *rare* and add: **b.** Resembling an ox.

In quot. with pun on *Oxford.*

1922 Joyce *Ulysses* 9 Tell that to the oxy chap downstairs and touch him for a guinea.

oxy (ǫ·ksi), *a.*² *Chem.* The prefix Oxy- (in sense 2) used without a hyphen as a quasi-*adj.*

1910 *Encycl. Brit.* VI. 51/1 Oxyaldehydes and oxyketones (viz. compounds containing an oxy in addition to an aldehydic or ketonic group) undergo both condensation and oxidation when treated with phenylhydrazine. 1923 W. M. Cumming et al. *Systematic Org. Chem.* v. 74 In the following section are discussed the more important of those condensations which give rise to oxy compounds—aldehydes, ketones, and quinones. 1962 Cotton & Wilkinson *Adv. Inorg. Chem.* v. 136 Many metal ions whose solutions are acidic may be regarded as oxy acids. 1975 *Inorg. Chem.* XIV. 1232/1 These chloroaluminate solvents are known to be effective chlorinating agents for a number of oxides and oxy anions.

oxy-. Add: **2.** Further examples of the use of *oxy-* to denote a combination or mixture of oxygen with a fuel gas, as *oxy-acetylene, -fuel, -gas, -propane*; all usu. *attrib.*; **oxy-helium,** a mixture of oxygen and helium, used as a breathing mixture in deep-sea diving.

1909 *Westm. Gaz.* 19 Jan. 4/2 A special weldless steel tubing brazed together by an oxy-acetylene process. 1939 L. Tibbenham *Welding Cast Iron* iii. 29 The temperature of an air-acetylene flame is about three-quarters that of oxy-acetylene. 1959 *Listener* 8 Oct. 583/3 Before the days of oxy-acetylene. 1961 C. Willock *Death in Covert* iii. 56 A desk which had been designed by a modern sculptor whose chosen tool was the oxy-acetylene welder's torch. 1975 R. C. Jain tr. *Castro & de Cadenet's Welding Metall.* iii. 20 The oxy-acetylene process is being largely replaced by the electric-arc methods since it has a number of disadvantages in the welding of stainless steels. 1969 *New Scientist* 8 May 284/2 The oxy-fuel burner was then lit and the charge melted with the burner operating under reducing conditions. 1951 E. G. West *Welding Non-Ferrous Metals* iii. 48 The oxy-gas cutting of ferrous metals, except stainless steels, depends on the rapid oxidation of the iron by the oxygen stream. 1974 *Nature* 4 Jan. 53/2 In this operation, in which oxy-gas torches have been used at the work face, temperatures are in the region of 3,000–3,500° C. 1966 A. B. Cameron in P. Hepple *Petroleum Supply & Demand* 38 The use of oxyhelium equipment now enables them [*sc.* divers] to remain as deep as 525 ft for periods up to 30 minutes. 1969 *Physics Bull.* Feb. 51/2 There is a problem of speech communication between divers breathing oxy-helium and the men on the surface. 1976 *Offshore Engineer* Apr. 23/1 Comex physiologists first described the High Pressure Nervous Syndrome (HPNS) during oxy-helium dives as long ago as 1968. 1963 A. C. Davies *Sci. & Pract. Welding* (ed. 5) vi. 371 Iron and steel can be cut by the oxy-hydrogen, oxy-propane, oxy-coal gas and oxy-acetylene cutting blow-pipes with ease, speed and a cleanness of cut. 1970 *Daily Tel.* 24 Sept. 2/2 On the morning of the explosion two workmen were using oxy-propane cutting tools.

oxyanion (ǫ:ksi͵æ·naiǝn). *Chem.* Also **oxy-anion** (with hyphen). [f. Oxy- 2 + Anion.] An anion containing one or more atoms of another element each linked to one or more oxygen atoms.

1940 *Jrnl. Chem. Soc.* 131 (*heading*) The interchange of heavy oxygen between water and inorganic oxy-anions. 1952 *Chem. Rev.* L. 456 Since oxyanions have a large amount of resonance stabilization, it is necessary to overcome this stability in order that a chemical reaction take place. 1972 W. R. Kneen et al. *Chemistry* xvii. 427 The phosphorus acids and oxyanions all contain approximately tetrahedral four-co-ordinate phosphorus.

oxy-arc (ǫ·ksi͵ɑ̄ɹk). Also **oxyarc.** [f. Oxy- 2 + Arc.] An arc struck in an atmosphere of oxygen between a work-piece and a hollow electrode through which the oxygen is supplied. Usu. *attrib.*

1956 A. C. Davies *Sci. & Pract. Welding* (ed. 4) vi. 349 (*heading*) Oxyarc cutting process. 1962 J. Bell *Crime in our Time* I. 15 They..attempted to burn the safe open with oxy-arc equipment. 1974 *Petroleum Rev.* XXVIII. 676/1 Oxy-arc, at present widely used, may be replaced by the technique of arc-plasma. 1976 *Offshore Platforms & Pipelining* 155/3 This entails..cutting the pipe with an oxy-arc tool.

oxycellulose (ǫksise·liulōᵘs). [f. Oxy- 2 + Cellulose *sb.*] Any of various substances obtained by the oxidation of cellulose, some of which are used as gauze or lint in cases of hæmorrhage.

1893 Cross & Bevan in *Jrnl. Chem. Soc.* XLIII. 22 A portion of the mass [of cellulose]..yields but slowly to the action of the nitric acid, in consequence, we find, of its conversion into an oxidised derivative, to which we have provisionally given the name *oxycellulose.* 1938 *Ann. Rev. Biochem.* VII. 58 When oxycelluloses are boiled with dilute alkalis, the fluidity is virtually unaffected and there is only a slight decrease in tensile strength. 1954 Kirk & Othmer *Encycl. Chem. Technol.* XIII. 551 Oxycellulose, when properly prepared, is a hemostatic material and is gradually absorbed by bodily fluids when it is used to pack wounds. 1963 [see *overbleached *ppl. a.*].

oxychlorocruorin (ǫ:ksiklōᵊrokrū·ǒrin). *Biochem.* [f. Oxy- 2 + *chlorocruorin* s.v. Chloro-¹.] The oxygenated form of chlorocruorin.

1870 *Jrnl. Anat. & Physiol.* IV. 129 (*caption*) Green blood of *Sabella ventilabrum*, shewing the two bands of Oxy-chlorocruorin. 1924 *Proc. Cambr. Philos. Soc.: Biol. Sci.* I. 217 The absorption bands of oxychlorocruorin and reduced chlorocruorin resemble those of oxy- and reduced haemoglobin shifted towards the red end of the spectrum. 1950 *Sci. News* XV. 89 Oxyhaemoglobin and oxychlorocruorin have each their characteristic absorption spectrum and the blood of *Serpula* shows both.

oxychromatin (ǫksikrōᵘ·mătin). *Biol.* [a. G. *oxychromatin* (M. Heidenhain 1894, in *Arch. f. mikrosk. Anat.* XLIII. 543), f. Gr. ὀξυ- sharp, acid: see *chromatin.] A supported component of chromatin characterized by a greater affinity for acid dyes and a smaller content of nucleic acid than chromosomal chromatin.

1895 *Jrnl. R. Microsc. Soc.* 159 'Oxychromatin' and 'cyanophilous granulation' are independent structural parts of the chromatin framework. 1924 E. G. Conklin in E. V. Cowdry *Gen. Cytol.* ix. 550 The oxychromatin which escapes into the cell body at mitoses is often more abundant than that which goes to form the chromosomes. 1948 W. Andrew tr. *E. D. P. de Robertis's Gen. Cytol.* vii. 140 With ultracentrifugation the nucleus is deformed and the nuclear structures are stratified in the following layers..: (1) nucleolus, (2) basichromatin, (3) oxychromatin, (4) karyolymph.

oxydase. Substitute for def.: obs. var. *oxidase. Add earlier and later examples.

1896 *Jrnl. Chem. Soc.* LXX. ii. 571 The author gives the generic term *oxydase* to laicase, tyrosinase, and other oxidising ferments of vegetable origin. 1929 R. P. Walton tr. *Waldschmidt-Leitz's Enzyme Actions* vii. 231 In these cases, special oxydases..appear to be present.

oxydoreductase, obs. var. *oxidoreductase.

oxygen. Add: **1.** Also *fig.*

1849 Lytton *Caxtons* I. ii. i. 45 Having thus exhausted all the oxygen of learning in that little receiver [*sc.* a preparatory school], my parents looked out for a wider range for my inspirations. 1932 *Sunday Times* 15 May 6 That cheerful noise which is the oxygen of 'society'.

b. An atom of oxygen.

1950 F. H. Hatch et al. *Petrol. Igneous Rocks* (ed. 10) i. ii. 68 The essential hydroxyl groups are included in the planes containing the 'free' oxygens in the tetrahedra. 1966 *Mineral. Mag.* XXXV. 1071 These compounds contain oxygens associated with three nearly equidistant protons forming H_3O^+ ions. 1974 *Nature* 4 Jan. 15/1 The main chain carbonyl oxygens were not resolved from the rest of the main chain, so that the orientation of the peptide bonds could not be determined directly.

3. b. *oxygen-carrier* (earlier and later examples), *lack, saturation, tension*; *oxygen-carrying* (examples), *-dependent, -free, -poor* adjs.; **oxygen bottle,** a cylinder of compressed or liquid oxygen; **oxygen debt** (see quot. 1923); **oxygen lance** (see *lance *sb.*¹ 6**); **oxygen mask,** a mask fitting over the nose and mouth through which oxygen or oxygen-enriched air may be supplied for breathing; **oxygen tent,** a tent-like enclosure for placing over a patient in order to provide him with an oxygen-enriched atmosphere.

1932 *Illustrierte Technische Wörterbücher* XVII. 234/1 *Sauerstoffbombe* (f.)—oxygen bottle—bombe (f) à oxygène—bombola (f) d'ossigeno. 1941 *Flight* 16 Jan. 48/1 The rigger changes the oxygen bottles and fits the starting motor to the aircraft. 1974 Hawkey & Bingham *Wild Card* xix. 156 The other [trolley], an anesthesia machine, carried three yoked oxygen bottles. 1888 *Jrnl. R. Microsc. Soc.* 596 Schunck..regards chlorophyll as a respiratory pigment, but probably a carbonic acid-carrier, not an oxygen-carrier. 1972 *Cytobiologie* V. 52 This was the first application of the perfusion medium with a fluorocarbon as oxygen carrier. 1916 A. P. Mathews *Physiol. Chem.* xi. 496 There may be in addition a union with the hemoglobin, which will retard its oxygen-carrying capacity. 1968 *Times* 13 Nov. 16/1 The beads may be minute clumps of haemoglobin, the oxygen-carrying protein. 1923 Hill & Lupton in *Q. Jrnl. Med.* XVI. 142 The 'oxygen debt' is defined as the total amount of oxygen used, after cessation of exercise, in recovery therefrom. 1947 T. K. Cureton et al. *Physical Fitness Appraisal* xiv. 437 The lactic acid [in the blood] increases very rapidly, with an estimated increment of 7 grams for each liter of oxygen debt. 1969 J. H. Green *Basic Clin. Physiol.* xi. 66/1 It is possible to run a short distance (100 yards) without breathing... After the exercise has been completed the subject breathes deeply and rapidly for the next few minutes in order to take in oxygen to 'repay' the oxygen debt. 1956 *Nature* 17 Mar. 531/1 Oxygen-dependent reactions. 1972 *Jrnl. Exper. Marine Biol. & Ecol.* IX. 217 The respiratory rate of the oxygen-dependent prosobranch, *Buccinum undatum* L., increases with decreasing salinity. 1933 *Mining & Metallurgy* XIV. 340/1 Oxygen-free high-conductivity copper..that is now being commercially offered for the first time represents a notable achievement in electro-metallurgy. 1972 *Radiation Res.* XLIX. 507 The oxygen-carrying capacity of *Busycon* and *Limulus* hemocyanins is eliminated following irradiation of the protein with cobalt-60 γ-rays in neutral, oxygen-free media. 1925 *Physiol. Rev.* V. 554 Carbon dioxide and oxygen lack produced marked increases in respiration with very little change in the reaction of the blood. 1963 R. P. Dales *Annelids* iv. 93 Among oligochaetes the abilities of *Tubifex* to withstand oxygen-lack are well known. 1920 *Abstr. Papers in Sci. Trans. & Periodicals* July 177 A description is given of the oxygen mask used by the French military aviators. 1930 E. Rice *Voy. to Purilia* i. 16 The air grew rarer... We were obliged to don the oxygen masks..so carefully and laboriously constructed for us. 1964 L. S. Brunner et al. *Text-bk. Medical-Surgical Nursing* xii. 189/1 Those individuals whose need for supplemental oxygen is greatest..are the very ones who are most prone to resist the application of an oxygen mask. 1975 *Times* 4 Sept. 1/8, I saw an air hostess run into the first-class compartment with an oxygen mask. 1951 M. Abercrombie et al. *Dict. Biol.* 128 *Lung*... Present in early fishes before origin of Amphibia, probably as an accessory breathing organ adapted to oxygen-poor fresh waters in which earliest vertebrates probably lived. 1969 *Listener* 6 Feb. 163/1 Mars has an atmosphere which is appreciable, even though it is too thin and too oxygen-poor to support any Earth creatures. 1942 *Electronic Engin.* XIV. 724 The ratio of their output currents will remain constant for any given degree of oxygen saturation. 1969 Crofton & Douglas *Respiratory Dis.* i. 33/1 The oxygen saturation is relatively uninfluenced until the partial pressure of oxygen in alveolar gas falls to relatively low levels. 1916 A. P. Mathews *Physiol. Chem.* xi. 481 The arterial blood had an oxygen tension varying in different experiments from 91·6–104·4 per cent of the tension in the alveolar air. 1953 J. Hunt *Ascent of Everest* 273 The respiratory centre in the brain..responds normally not to the oxygen tension of the blood..but to the direct effect of carbon dioxide tension of the arterial blood. 1965 B. E. Freeman tr. *Vandel's Biospeleol.* xviii. 318 The oxygen tension of subterranean waters is variable. [1921 *Jrnl. Physiol.* LV. p. xx (*heading*) A simple oxygen bed tent and its use to [*sic*] a case of œdema and chronic ulcer of the leg.] 1925 *Sci. Amer.* Sept. 181/2 (*caption*) A portable oxygen tent for pneumonia patients. 1974 C. Hill *Scorpion* 55 Michael was lying under an oxygen tent ..the top of his head covered in bandages.

oxygenase (ǫ·ksidʒĕnēiz, -s). *Biochem.* [a. G. *oxygenase* (Chodat & Bach 1903, in *Ber. d. Deut. Chem. Ges.* XXXVI. 607): see Oxygen and *-ase.] Any enzyme which catalyses the incorporation of molecular oxygen into a substrate; orig. used in the narrowest sense of *oxidase.

1903 *Jrnl. Chem. Soc.* LXXXIV. i. 378 Most oxydases contain principles of both types, and it is proposed to retain the term peroxydase for those substances..which are not themselves oxidisers, but impart activity to, and thus destroy, peroxides, whilst the new term, 'oxygenase', is proposed for those substances..which are capable of producing hydrogen peroxide, but leave it in an inactive condition. 1920 M. W. Onslow in *Biochem. Jrnl.* XIV. 536 The function of this additional enzyme is to catalyse the oxidation of the catechol substance with the formation of a peroxide... It is proposed to call this second enzyme an oxygenase, a term originally used by Chodat and Bach for the portion of an oxidase which can be replaced by hydrogen peroxide. 1964 [see *oxidase]. 1971 M. F. Mallette et al. *Introd. Biochem.* viii. 282 Both oxygenases and hydroxylases use O_2 to alter substrates... Both classes of enzymes reduce O_2 but do it by incorporating oxygen atoms into organic substrates. On the other hand, oxidases reduce O_2..and do not incorporate it into organic compounds.

oxygenator. Add: **c.** *Med.* An apparatus for oxygenating the blood.

1928 *Jrnl. Physiol.* LXVI. 443 Drinker, Drinker and Lund used a modification of Hooker's oxygenator in bone marrow perfusion experiments. 1961 [see *hole *sb.* 7 e]. 1968 *Sci. Jrnl.* Nov. 63/2 Attempts to replace the living heart and lungs by a mechanical pump and an artificial oxygenator were unsatisfactory.

oxygenless (ǫ·ksi͵dʒĕnles), *a.* [f. Oxygen + -less.] Not containing oxygen.

1935 E. R. Burroughs *Pirates of Venus* 46 Even though she [*sc.* the planet Venus] be oxygenless. 1963 I. Fleming *On H.M. Secret Service* ix. 98 James Bond followed her, holding his breath against the searing impact of the Arctic, oxygenless air. 1972 *Sci. Amer.* Apr. 58/2 We still have the 'fossils' of this life-style in the universal process of anaerobic (oxygenless) fermentation.

oxylith (ǫ·ksiliþ). Also **-lithe.** [ad. F. *oxylithe*, f. *oxy-* Oxy- 2 + *-lithe* -lith.] A commercial name for calcium peroxide, CaO_2, as used in breathing apparatus as a convenient source of oxygen (evolved by reaction with carbon dioxide).

1902 *Chem. News* 16 May 240/2 The recent invention of 'oxylith', due to M. Jaubert, will help to make the use of nascent oxygen still more wide in its applications. 1924 *Chambers's Jrnl.* Oct. 701/2 The helmet of this appliance..is supplied with a substance called 'oxylithe', which gives off pure oxygen when breathed upon. 1948 R. H. Davis *Breathing in Irrespirable Atmospheres* vi. 206 Where 'Oxylithe' was employed as the main source of oxygen in the earlier designs, it took a couple of minutes to evolve oxygen in sufficient quantity to allow work to begin.

oxyluciferin (ǫksilⁱusi·fĕrin). *Biochem.* [f. Oxy- 2 + *luciferin.] The oxidised form of (a) luciferin produced by the action of luciferase. (Cf. the note s.v. *LUCIFERIN.)

1919 E. N. HARVEY in *Jrnl. Gen. Physiol.* I. 135, I suggest also that luciferin when oxidized be designated oxyluciferin. **1953** J. RAMSBOTTOM *Mushrooms & Toadstools* xiv. 163 Luciferin is oxidised by luciferase in one part of a cell producing oxyluciferin which in another part is reduced again to luciferin. **1964** *Oceanogr. & Marine Biol.* II. 351 Chromatography yields three isolated substances, two of which are active in luminescence and have been designated oxyluciferin A and oxyluciferin B.

oxymoronic (ǫːksimōᵊrǫ·nik), *a.* [f. OXYMORON + -IC.] Suggestive of oxymoron; incongruous, self-contradictory. So **oxymoro·nically** *adv.*

1901 BEERBOHM *Around Theatres* (1924) I. 270 A little bore, whose oxymoronically belated-premature death we hail..as a merciful release. **1970** G. GREER *Female Eunuch* 164 It would be oxymoronic to claim to be gently, reliably or sensibly in love. **1972** P. GREEN *Shadow of Parthenon* 35 'Imperial democracy', that oxymoronic contradiction in terms. **1975** *Times Lit. Suppl.* 17 Oct. 1226/5 Professor Hardy's point..is signalled by the oxymoronic 'dubious consolations' of her title.

oxymyoglobin (ǫːksimə͡iˌǫglōᵘ·bin). *Biochem.* [f. OXY- 2 + *MYOGLOBIN.] The oxygenated form of myoglobin.

1935 *Physiol. Abstr.* XIX. 578 The dissociation curve of oxymyoglobin is a hyperbola. **1953** FRUTON & SIMMONDS *Gen. Biochem.* vi. 167 At a given oxygen pressure oxymyoglobin is less dissociated than oxyhemoglobin, i.e. myoglobin has a higher affinity for oxygen. **1974** M. D. RANKEN in Birch & Parker *Vitamin C* ix. 122 At the surface of fresh meat, in contact with oxygen, the colour is the bright red of oxymyoglobin.

ox yoke. [OX 5.] A yoke used for draught oxen. Also *transf.*

1573, 1688 [see OX 5]. **1785** G. WASHINGTON *Diary* 16 Nov. (1925) II. 441 A good Oxe Cart—2 Oxe yokes. **1809** *Austin Papers* (1924) I. 164 One Plough, one Harrow.. and two Ox yokes. **1847** in H. Howe *Hist. Coll. Ohio* 188 Journeys..of 20 or 50 miles, for the sole purpose of having the staple of an ox-yoke mended. **1879** B. F. TAYLOR *Summer-Savory* xvii. 138 Awkward H's like a pair of leaning bar-posts with one bar, and B's like ox-yokes. **1938** M. K. RAWLINGS *Yearling* iv. 41 Penny.. went to the sink-hole with a wooden ox-yoke supporting two wooden buckets over his thin shoulders.

oxyphil, *a.* Add: Also **-phile.** For 'acids' read 'acid dyes'. (Earlier and later examples.)

1893 *Brit. Med. Jrnl.* 25 Feb. 400/1 The complete histological differentiation of a leucocyte depends upon staining it in such a manner that all the oxyphile and basophile elements are brought out in relief. **1925** H. J. CONN et al. *Biol. Stains* vii. 79 Yellowish eosin..is used in various technics for staining the oxyphile granules of cells. **1970** *Jrnl. Path.* CII. 193 One of the adenomata in this series is composed of oxyphil cells and transitional oxyphil cells when viewed by light microscopy. **1976** *Clinical Endocrinol.* V. Suppl. 377 The one oxyphil adenoma tested by Schorr *et al.* (1972) showed no response.

oxyphilic (ǫksifi·lik), *a. Biol.* [f. prec. + -IC.] Readily stained by acid dyes; oxyphil.

1901 C. E. SIMON *Text-bk. Physiol. Chem.* xiii. 303 The granules which are found in certain forms of leucocytes are apparently of an albuminous nature. According to their affinity for acid, basic, or neutral dyes, they are termed oxyphilic, basophilic, and neutrophilic, respectively. **1973** *Cancer* XXXI. 253/1 The endoplasmic reticulum is poorly developed in oxyphilic cells, which means that protein-synthesis must be scanty.

oxyphilous (ǫksifiləs), *a. Biol.* [f. as prec. + -OUS.] = prec.

1893 *Brit. Med. Jrnl.* 25 Feb. 400/2 All the granules found in normal circulating leucocytes are oxyphilous. **1968** *Zeitschr. f. Mikrosk.-Anat. Forsch.* LXXIX. 551 Oxyphilous Welsh cells of the parathyroid glands have glandular functions.

oxyproline (ǫksiprōᵘ·līn). *Biochem.* [ad. G. *oxyprolin* (H. Leuchs 1905, in *Ber. d. Deut. Chem. Ges.* XXXVIII. 1937): see OXY- 2 and *PROLINE.] = *hydroxyproline* s.v. *HYDROXY-.

1928 *Physiol. Abstr.* XII. 599 Tetrasulphocyandiamminchromic acid..may be used to give crystalline precipitates with proline and oxyproline. **1931** *Chem. Rev.* IX. 264 Hammarsten..has synthesized γ-oxyproline. **1935** A. K. ANDERSON *Essent. Physiol. Chem.* xvi. 177 The pyrrol rings are present in the amino acids proline and oxyproline. **1972** *Biol. Abstr.* LIV. 4493/2 As silicosis progressed the quartz and oxyproline content in the lungs increased.

oxytetracycline (ǫːksitetrăsə͡i·klīn). *Pharm.* [f. OXY- 2 + *TETRACYCLINE.] The 5-hydroxy derivative, $C_{22}H_{24}N_2O_9$, of tetracycline (usu. administered in the form of its yellow hydrochloride), which is an antimicrobial substance produced by cultures of the bacterium *Streptomyces rimosus* and has actions and uses similar to those of other tetracyclines.

1953 *Jrnl. Amer. Med. Assoc.* 3 Jan. 46/1 Both compounds possess a common four-ringed skeleton, for which the generic term tetracycline has been proposed. They differ only in that aureomycin has a chlorine atom at ring one while terramycin has a hydroxyl group at ring three. The chemically descriptive generic names chlorotetracycline and oxytetracycline, respectively, have therefore been proposed for the two compounds. **1958** *Times* 29 Sept. 2/7 The promise of antibiotics as a means of controlling certain plant diseases has been brought a step nearer fulfilment by a recent Order which permits the use of streptomycin and oxytetracycline. **1966** *Economist* 9 Apr. 169/1 This February, Pfizer's patent monopoly on the drug, oxytetracycline, expired. **1969** CROFTON & DOUGLAS *Respiratory Dis.* xviii. 321/1 Sometimes oxytetracycline or chlortetracycline is better tolerated [than tetracycline]. **1974** R. M. KIRK et al. *Surgery* ii. 24 Oxytetracycline is given to prevent secondary infection.

oxytocin (ǫksitōᵘ·sin). *Med.* [f. OXYTOC(IC *a.* and *sb.* + -IN¹.] A hormone present in the neurohypophysis of mammals which stimulates uterine contractions and the ejection of milk from a lactating breast and is made synthetically for use in inducing labour and controlling bleeding after delivery.

1928 *Jrnl. Amer. Chem. Soc.* Feb. 575 α-Hypophamine is being supplied under the trade name of Oxytocin..and β-Hypophamine under the trade name Vasopressin... They were first supplied for clinical use in August, 1927. **1928** *Official Gaz.* (U.S. Patent Office) 11 Sept. 258/1 Parke, Davis & Company, Detroit, Mich... *Oxytocin* for preparation for stimulating contractions of uterine and other unstriped muscular fibers. Claims use since Sept. 15, 1927. **1930** *Druggists Circular* Oct. 60/2 In 1928 Oliver Kamm succeeded in separating the two principles of the posterior lobe of the pituitary body. One of them, which acts upon the uterus, Kamm named oxytocin. **1937** *Dispensatory U.S.A.* (ed. 22) 854/1 The oxytocic principle has been called pitocin, oxytocin, [etc.]. **1965** LEE & KNOWLES *Animal Hormones* ii. 29 The second hormone, oxytocin, appears to exert its action only in mammals, but it may play some part in oviposition in the other vertebrates. **1969** *Daily Tel.* 19 Dec. 11/8 Oxytocin is used regularly to start or speed up a labour that is lagging. **1974** *Nature* 20 Dec. 630/1 Neurones in the hypothalamus synthesise the hormones vasopressin and oxytocin. **1977** 'E. CRISPIN' *Glimpses of Moon* xii. 256 It read like an instruction from an obstetrician to a lady who..has been given oxytocin to hurry matters up.

Hence **oxyto·cinase** [*-ASE], an enzyme that inactivates oxytocin.

1949 *Chem. Abstr.* XLIII. 2330 (*heading*) Effect of cysteine and glutathione on the oxytocinase activity of blood plasma. **1974** PASSMORE & ROBSON *Compan. Med. Stud.* III. II. xl. 1/2 A serum oxytocinase which rapidly inactivates oxytocin appears in increasing amounts during pregnancy.

oxytonic (ǫksitǫ·nik), *a.* Also **oxyto·nical.** [f. OXYTONE *a.* and *sb.* + -IC.] Characterized by an oxytone; designating a language in which the majority of words are oxytones.

1890 *Century Dict.*, Oxytonical. **1954** PEI & GAYNOR *Dict. Linguistics* 156 *Oxytonic language*, a language in which the majority of the words bear the main accent on the last syllable. **1963** *Amer. Speech* XXXVIII. 217 Armenian, like French, is oxytonic; with rare exceptions, the stress in a word falls on the last syllable. **1972** HARTMANN & STORK *Dict. Lang. & Linguistics* 160/2 *Oxytonic language*, a language in which most words have fixed.. stress on the final syllable.

oy, oi (oi), *int.* [Yiddish.] An exclamation used by Yiddish-speakers to express dismay, grief, etc. Occas. in wider use. Also *oy vay, vey* [a. G. *Weh* woe] (see quot. 1968).

1892 I. ZANGWILL *Childr. Ghetto* I. xii. 270 The dispute thickened; the synagogue hummed with 'Ei's' and 'Oi's' not in concord. **1924** *Dialect Notes* V. 274 Exclamations in American English... Oy: —, — yoy. **1928** H. CRANE *Let.* 22 Feb. (1965) 317 Oy-oy-oy! I have just had my ninth snifter of Scotch. **1932** L. GOLDING *Magnolia Street* III. viii. 570 'And if you hadn't..oi! oi!' said Ada. 'It would have been awful!' **1934** WODEHOUSE *Right Ho, Jeeves* xi. 141 A story about a Scotchman, an Irishman, and a Jew... I said 'Hoots, mon,' 'Begorrah,' and 'Oy, oy.' **1939** MRS. P. CAMPBELL *Let.* 28 June in *B. Shaw & Mrs. Campbell* (1952) 332 A Jewish Mother... The Mothers dialogue consisting of: 'Oi; Oi; tch: tch.' **1959** B. KOPS *Hamlet of Stepney Green* I. 12 Children, oy vay, don't talk to me about children. **1963** V. NABOKOV *Gift* iii. 181 His trick of garbling Russian, in imitation of a farcical Jewish accent as when he said..'Oy, vat a mudnik!' **1968** L. ROSTEN *Joys of Yiddish* 14 Two *A*[lteren] *K*[ockern] had sat in silence on their favorite park bench for hours, lost in thought. Finally, one gave a long and languid '*Oy!*' The other replied, 'You're telling *me*?' *Ibid.* 273 *Oy* is often used as lead-off for '*oy vay!*' which means, literally, 'Oh, pain', but is used as an all-purpose ejaculation to express anything from trivial delight to abysmal woe. **1975** *New Yorker* 3 Mar. 34/3 The family gathered round for Passover. Oy, nephew! What's the world coming to. **1976** K. THACKERAY *Crownbird* v. 91 'Oy vey, but he's recovered well,' Stein thought.

‖**oyama** (ǫya·ma). [Jap.] = *ONNAGATA.

1963 *Guardian* 21 Jan. 9/3 The extraordinary verisimilitude achieved by the 'oyama' or actors playing female rôles. **1965** *This is Japan 1966* 51/2 He was considered to be the last of the great *oyama*, male performers of female roles on the Shimpa stage.

-oyl, ending of the names of acid radicals, formed on the names of the corresponding carboxylic acids ending in *-ic* or *-oic*; e.g. *FUMAROYL, *HEXANOYL.

1971 *Nomencl. Org. Chem.* (I.U.P.A.C.) (ed. 2) C. 185 The name of a univalent or bivalent acyl radical formed by removal of hydroxyl from all the carboxyl groups is derived from the name of the corresponding acid by changing the ending '-oic' to '-oyl'.

oyster. Add: **1. c.** *the world is my oyster*: the world offers opportunities for profit, etc.; also in extended uses.

1598 SHAKS. *Merry W.* II. ii. 2 Why then the world's mine Oyster, which I, with sword will open. **1930** J. A. WILLIAMSON *Short Hist. Brit. Expansion* (ed. 2) II. VI. ii. 183 *Laissez-faire*, with its cosmopolitan view of the world as the trader's oyster. *a* **1938** T. WOLFE *You can't go Home Again* (1940) III. xxix. 469 Drake was self-contained: the world his oyster, seas his pastures, mighty distances his wings. **1942** A. BRYANT *Yrs. of Endurance* xi. 230 He [*sc.* Napoleon] was not going to waste his incomparable genius to make the world—his oyster—safe for Barras and the plutocrats of the Luxembourg. **1949** A. MILLER *Death of Salesman* I. 39 The world is an oyster, but you don't crack it open on a mattress. **1975** *New Yorker* 26 May 66/3 A few weeks after the conference, he told American farmers that the world food market could 'be our oyster'. **1977** 'J. GASH' *Judas Pair* vi. 67 The world was my oyster. My uneasy mood had vanished.

d. A reserved or uncommunicative person.

1925 M. WILTSHIRE *Thursday's Child* xi. 221, I wouldn't mind betting Jane's worrying herself sick over it; and he —goodness knows what he's doing or feeling. I never saw such an oyster. **1930** J. B. PRIESTLEY *Angel Pavement* vi. 305, I never knew anybody so close, you old oyster you!

e. A type of unmoored submarine mine detonated magnetically or acoustically as a vessel passes over it. Also *attrib.*

1947 CROWTHER & WHIDDINGTON *Science at War* iv. 177 The mine mechanism [*i.e.* of German pressure mines] consisted of a rubber air bag with an aluminium diaphragm. With a change of pressure air escapes from the bag, the diaphragm is moved, and after a time closes an electrical detonating circuit. A change of about 1/1,000th in the total pressure, equivalent to that of about ½ inch of water, exerted for about six seconds, was needed to operate the mechanism. This device, called an 'oyster', is shown in Plate XLV. **1950** A. P. HERBERT *Independent Member* lii. 308 The enemy..had new terrors by then—the 'oyster' or pressure mine. **1955** J. F. TURNER *Service most Silent* xi. 155 For the first four years of the War both the Germans and ourselves were developing the top secret mine of the War—the oyster. *Ibid.*, The Luftwaffe produced 'acoustic oysters' and the Navy 'magnetic oysters'. **1965** K. LANGMAID *Approaches are Mined!* xiv. 240 The first 'Oyster' minefields were laid by German light craft on the night of the 6th/7th of June [1944].

4*. A greyish-white colour resembling that of an oyster. Cf. *5 c.

1922 *Daily Mail* 11 Dec. 14 (Advt.), Silk hose... In black, white,..peacock, flame, oyster. **1960** *Housewife* Apr. 97 Cotton sailcloth... In a choice of three good colours—oyster, light royal blue, or black. **1978** H. MACINNES *Prelude to Terror* ii. 18 A..study in greys, from silver carpeting to pale oyster walls.

4.** One of the cross-sections of wood in an oyster veneer.

1924 G. O. WHEELER *Old Eng. Furnit.* (ed. 3) iii. 22 These 'oysters' are often in kidney-shape and the welding of a mosaic was no easy task. **1974** *Country Life* 26 Sept. (Suppl.) 60 William III oyster olivewood chest. The top with concentric rings of oysters of decreasing size.

5. a. simple *attrib.*, as *oyster shoal*; connected with the taking, breeding, keeping, selling, or eating of oysters, as *oyster-bar* (examples), *-dish, house, -merchant, navy, pirate, saloon, season, -shop* (examples), *-smack* (examples), *-stall, stand, supper*; made of oysters, as *oyster cocktail, cracker, -patty* (examples), *-pie* (later examples), *-sauce* (earlier examples), *soup, stew, stuffing.*

1878 R. L. STEVENSON in *London* 8 June 441/1 They were driven by a sharp fall of sleet into an Oyster Bar. **1925** E. SITWELL *Troy Park* 74 That child is the small wicked ghost Of Metropoles and oyster bars. **1972** E. HARGREAVES *Fair Green Weed* i. 12 I've been eating something called escovitched fish in an oyster bar. **1895** *Funk's Stand. Dict.*, Oyster cocktail. **1905** *Granville Centennial Cook Bk.* 121 Oyster Cocktail. *c* **1938** [see *COCKTAIL 4]. **1957** M. McCARTHY *Memories Catholic Girlhood* viii. 203 Olympia oyster cocktail and devilled Dungeness crabs. **1975** M. ORR *Rich Girl, Poor Girl* (1977) xii. 147 The meal..began with an oyster cocktail and progressed to a cold Senegalese soup. **1873** *Kansas Mag.* III. 273/2 Our commissary department was poorly supplied.. four small oyster crackers. **1924** *Amer. Mercury* Apr. 430/1 The custom that some Baptist churches have fallen into of oyster crackers and cubes of bakers' bread in the Lord's supper is to my mind unscriptural. **1975** BYFIELD & TEDESCHI *Solemn High Murder* (1976) iii. 53 Baxter tore open a cellophane envelope of oyster crackers. **1865** GEO. ELIOT *Let.* 8 Jan. (1956) IV. 174, I am so much pleased with..the pretty oyster-dish. **1834** H. J. NOTT *Novellettes* I. 94 He can escape from the empty pageant to the substantial and homely comforts of a beefsteak or oyster house. **1949** *Fishing Gaz.* Oct. 96/2 Hampton oyster houses are George T. Elliott, M. F. Quinn, and J. S. Daly and Son. **1726** B. FRANKLIN *Jrnl. Voy. Philadelphia* in *Mem. Life & Writings* (1818) I. App. p. iii, The oyster-merchants fetch them..from other places. **1869** *Rep. Comm. Agric. 1868* (U.S. Dept. Agric.) 340 An oyster merchant of Rochelle, doing business with the growers of the adjacent islands of Oleron and Ré, will say £250,000 per annum. **1932** *Sun* (Baltimore) 19 Sept. 6/5 (*heading*) Sour note on a recent addition to the oyster navy. **1962** *Daily Progress* (Charlottesville, Va.) 21 Mar. 3 (*heading*) 'Oyster navy' gets radar. **1807** M. E. RUNDELL *New Syst. Dom. Cookery* 133 (*caption*) Oyster patties. **1843** *Ainsworth's Mag.* IV. 97 An eulogy of the excellence of Lord Marmiton's oyster patties. **1932** AUDEN in *Rev.*

Eng. Stud. (1978) Aug. 285 Over oyster patties, I'll explain it all. **1953** K. TENNANT *Joyful Condemned* vi. 51 Mrs. Mike was carrying a plate of oyster patties. **1851** A. O. HALL *Manhattaner* 59 Some of them [*sc.* mosquitoes] are dainty, and associate only with fat people whose nightmares are based upon turtle steaks and oyster pies. **1976** R. CONDON *Whisper of Axe* I. xxiii. 146 They ate oyster pie and crab cakes. **1903** J. LONDON *Let.* 9 Mar. (1966) 147 When the oyster pirates..arrived, they forced the two watchmen off into the water. **1930** J. DOS PASSOS *42nd Parallel* II. 133 Oyster pirates used to shanghai young fellers. **1833** *Knickerbocker* I. 117 To be seen about taverns and oyster saloons. **1905** J. C. LINCOLN *Partners of Tide* vi. 105 The pair entered a little battered restaurant with the sign 'Atwood's Oyster Saloon' over the door. **1727** 'E. DORRINGTON' *Hermit* I. 27 The boil'd Meat and Oyster-Sauce. **1798** JANE AUSTEN *Let.* 24 Oct. (1932) I. 9 We.. had some beef-steaks and a boiled fowl, but no oyster sauce. **1861** MRS. BEETON *Bk. Househ. Managem.* p. xxiv (Index), Oyster..season. **1866** 'F. KIRKLAND' *Pictorial Bk. Anecdotes* 181/2 [He] traded up and down the James and York rivers, especially during the oyster season. **1977** *Harpers & Queen* Nov. 276/3 When the British oyster season is over, the clam trade continues. **1827** J. L. WILLIAMS *View W. Florida* 16 The entrance to this bay is obstructed by sand bars and oyster shoals. **1823** in *Spirit of Public Jrnls.* (1825) 8 Charged with assaulting David Tullock, *Esq.* at an oyster-shop in Brydges-street. **1841** DICKENS *Old C. Shop* xxxix. 12 Kit, walking into an oyster-shop as bold as if he lived there. **1913** MRS. P. CAMPBELL *Let.* 25 Mar. in *B. Shaw & Mrs. Campbell* (1952) 102 Many a rendez-vous at Cheesmans oyster shop. **1802** E. WYNNE *Diary* 22 Oct. (1940) III. iv. 69 Several other sailors' bodies have been thrown on shore, it was an oyster smack that was lost. **1976** *Times* 27 Aug. 17/1 A string of oyster smacks..will be competing in the Thames Oyster Smack Race. **1741** E. SMITH *Compl. Housewife* (ed. 10) 62 (*heading*) Oyster soop. **1861** MRS. BEETON *Bk. Househ. Managem.* 103 Oyster soup. **1935** M. MORPHY *Recipes of all Nations* 599 *Oyster soup*.. is one of the favourite soups in America. **1836** DICKENS *Pickw.* (1837) xxii. 227 Here's a oyster-stall to every half-dozen houses. **1922** E. SITWELL *Façade* 15 Oyster-stall notes. **1830** *Boston Even. Transcript* 29 Sept. 2/4 The oyster stands in New Orleans have been leased for..the same price as last year. **1851** A. O. HALL *Manhattaner* 7 Oyster stands, where dirty mouths and flickering tallow candles grinned ghostly satisfaction. **1977** *Times* 14 May 13/4 For £4,000 to £6,000 each..you may be able to buy two Sèvres oyster-stands. **1846** D. CORCORAN *Pickings* 128 Mrs. Smith was never known to have an oyster stew of an evening that she did not divide it with Mrs. Jones. **1973** P. A. WHITNEY *Snowfire* xiii. 254 He..brought me back a bowl of hot oyster stew and crackers. **1935** M. MORPHY *Recipes of All Nations* 611 Oyster stuffings for poultry are frequently found in old English cookery books. **1971** M. G. EBERHART *Two Little Rich Girls* (1972) ix. 105 The dinner..with its oyster stuffing for the turkey and its huge mince pie. **1741** B. LYNDE *Diary* 17 Apr. (1880) 107 Oyster supper with all the Court. **1856** H. B. STOWE *Dred* II. 221 He drinks and frolics, and has his oyster-suppers. **1949** *Missouri Hist. Rev.* Apr. 215 He is uneasy at oyster-suppers at the 'Opera House'.

b. *oyster-eating* (examples), *-opener* (examples), *shucker*; also instrumental, as *oyster-covered* adj.

1882 W. D. HAY *Brighter Britain!* I. iii. 72 Oyster-covered rocks. **1905** *Westm. Gaz.* 10 Aug. 1/3 Oyster-covered iron beams and girders. **1933** *Sun* (Baltimore) 7 Aug. 14/2 An old-fashioned Southern Maryland 'oyster eatin''. **1977** *Times* 22 Jan. 12/3 The return to oyster-eating. **1827** W. CLARKE *Every Night Bk.* 62 If the visitor make an ally of the waiter or oyster-opener, he may often have people pointed out to him there, who are rather worth seeing. **1900** W. STEVENS *Let.* 21 Oct. (1967) 47 Fishmen, and grizzly oyster-openers. **1969** E. H. PINTO *Treen* 140 A simple but effective oyster opener, in Colchester Museum, is a wooden block, hollowed out to take a large oyster; [etc.]. **1898** GOULD *Pocket Med. Dict.* (ed. 2) 234 *Oyster-shuckers' keratitis*, a form due to corneal traumatism from pieces of embedded oyster-shell. **1969** L. HELLMAN *Unfinished Woman* vi. 61 The oyster shucker.. would open oysters for my father. **1973** *Daily Colonist* (Victoria, B.C.) 1 July 9/2 Rumor has it that the professional oyster shucker eventually becomes immune to the poison and simply counts his scars.

c. *oyster eye, kiss*; *oyster-coloured, -white* (examples) adjs.; also, further examples in the sense of oyster-coloured.

1901 *Sketch* 11 Sept. 303 Her wedding-dress of oyster-white satin. **1904** *Daily Chron.* 5 May 8/4 Women are wearing bronze shoes with their golden-brown costumes, ..oyster-coloured suede with a costume of that shade. **1920** S. LEWIS *Main St.* xi. 141 An oyster-coloured blouse. **1922** JOYCE *Ulysses* 114 Oyster eyes. **1931** J. CANNAN *High Table* xi. 168 The mother of the bride wore a handsome dress of oyster satin. **1938** S. BECKETT *Murphy* 117 Oyster kisses passed between them. **1951** [see *GIBSON[2]]. **1952** P. ATKEY *Juniper Rock* i. 5 A short, pink man in oyster silk pyjamas. **1958** L. DURRELL *Balthazar* i. 13 Pearl ground with shadowed oyster and violet reflections. **1960** *Harper's Bazaar* Apr. 84 A short narrow dress of de-lustred oyster satin. **1969** [see *Irish crochet* s.v. *IRISH *a.* 2 c]. **1974** N. MARSH *Black as he's Painted* i. 20 The glossy walls were an agreeable oyster-white. **1975** G. MOFFAT *Miss Pink* iii. 48 Bridget wearing oyster lace over silk. **1976** *Southern Even. Echo* (Southampton) 11 Nov. 9/1 The bride wore an oyster-coloured empire-line dress.

d. *oyster-boat* (later examples); hence *oyster-boatman*; *oyster-cellar* (earlier examples); *oyster-farm, -farming* (examples); hence *oyster farmer*; **oyster-crab** (later examples); **Oyster Feast,** a traditional feast held at Colchester to mark the beginning of the oyster-fishing season; **oyster-fish** (*b*) for '*Batrachus tau*' substitute '*Opsanus tau*'; (examples); (*c*) (examples); (*d*) (see quot. 1903); **oyster fitting** (see quot. 1940); **oyster-knife** (later examples); **oyster-like** *a.* (later examples); **oyster-man** (further examples); **oyster-piece**, a piece of oyster veneer; **oyster-plant,** (*a*) (later examples); (*b*) (examples); **oyster-scow** *U.S.*, a scow engaged in oyster-fishing; **oyster-tongs** (later examples); **oyster-veneer**, a whorled veneer obtained esp. from small boughs of trees; cf. *OYSTERING *vbl. sb.*; also *oyster-veneered* adj., *oyster-veneering*; **oyster walnut** (see quot. 1944); freq. *attrib.*

1813 J. K. PAULDING *Lay of Scottish Fiddle* i. 18 The sailors..urg'd in dreams the gallant chase Of oyster-boats far up the bay. **1891** *Scribner's Mag.* X. 472, I will try to describe how the deck of an oyster-boat must be trimmed for its work. **1859** G. A. SALA *Twice round Clock* 251 Listen to the slang of oyster-boatmen and bargees. **1830** J. F WATSON *Ann. Philadelphia* 220 Oyster Cellars..did not at first include gentlemen among their visiters. **1842** DICKENS *Amer. Notes* I. vi. 208 Lamps, marking the whereabouts of oyster-cellars. **1844** J. E. DEKAY *Zool. N.Y.* VI. 12 The *P[innotheres] depressum* of Say, is..the male, or we suppose the young, of the Common Oyster Crab. **1884** J. A. RYDER in G. B. Goode *Fisheries U.S.: Nat. Hist. Aquatic Animals* I. x. 744 Some Oysters were dredged up by the crew which contained some Oyster-crabs. **1902** H. L. WILSON *Spenders* 131 Now the oysters will be due—fine fat Buzzard's Bays—and oyster crabs. **1938** L. BEMELMANS *Life Class* I. iii. 49 All maîtres d'hôtel..are especially fond of little fried things.. whitebait, oyster crabs, fried scallops. **1960** C. M. YONGE *Oysters* vii. 118 An essentially parasitic crab which has been the cause of considerable damage.., especially in Delaware Bay, is the small Oyster Crab. **1940** *Sun* (Baltimore) 18 Oct. 3 Chesapeake oysters, which are now raised on 'oyster farms'. **1975** *Times* 24 Apr. 3/4 Their oyster farm is claimed to be the only one of its kind in Europe. **1946** *Nature* 26 Oct. 587/1 Many of the newly settled spat perish in the first weeks of sedentary life, and in spite of all the care of the oyster-farmers. **1953** *Sun* (Baltimore) 5 Feb. 19/5 If private leasing of such beds were allowed, they could produce enough seed to supply oyster 'farmers' their all-important seed oysters. **1977** *Harpers & Queen* Nov. 275/4 Fertilised eggs, which oyster farmers call..white, grey or black sick, depending on how ripe it is. **1943** *Sun* (Baltimore) 5 Feb. 10/1 A system of 'oyster farming' combining a free fishery with close State management. **1962** D. NICHOLS *Echinoderms* iii. 35 In the early days of oyster-farming the fishermen would drag a dredge across the beds to collect the starfish. **1974** *Country Life* 21 Nov. 1561/3 A high mercurial content in the water ..prevents oyster farming. **1888** E. L. CUTTS *Colchester* xviii. 171 The annual feast on the election of the mayor is called the Oyster Feast...people take it for granted that the feast derives its name from the bivalve for which the town is famous; but this origin of the name may be questioned. 'Oyster feasts' are common at the beginning of a new official reign in many places. **1924** F. MUIRHEAD *England* (ed. 2) 575 The opening of the oyster fishing is celebrated by an 'Oyster Feast' on Oct. 20th. **1934** A. E. HOUSMAN *Let.* 15 Sept. (1971) 360 The chief ambition of my life has long been to be invited to the Colchester Oyster Feast. **1972** R. COBB *Reactions to French Revolution* 4 He had once dressed up as a Roman Emperor for the carnival at the time of the Oyster Feast. **1855** S. F. BAIRD in *Rep. Bd. Regents Smithsonian Inst.* IX. 340 The toad-fish, or, as it is called at Beesley's point, the oyster-fish, on account of its frequenting the oyster beds, is one of the fisherman's pests. **1878** *Proc. U.S. Nat. Mus.* I. 374 *Tautoga omitis* [sic].—Oyster-fish. Rather common. **1884** G. B. GOODE *Nat. Hist. Aquatic Anim.* I. III. 251 The toad-fish, *Batrachus tau*, called also on the coast of New Jersey and in some parts of the Southern States 'Oyster-fish', is one of the most repulsive looking fishes upon our coast. **1903** T. H. BEAN *Fishes N.Y.* 598 This [*sc. Tautoga onitis*] is better known in New York as the blackfish; farther south it is styled..Moll, Will George and oyster fish. *Ibid.* 656 *Gobiosoma bosci*... Naked Goby; Mud Creeper; Oysterfish. **1940** *Sun* (Baltimore) 30 Apr. 6/3 The oyster fish, sometimes called 'devil fish' by local fishermen, has a big head and mouth with which it crushes oysters for food. **1962** K. F. LAGLER et al. *Ichthyology* xi. 361 In the oyster toadfish (*Opsanus tau*)..blood sugar levels are raised upon intramuscular injection of corticosteroid compounds. **1892** J. W. URQUHART *Electric Ship-Lighting* vii. 227 The oyster fitting, without the guard, is much used for cabins. **1940** *Chambers's Techn. Dict.* 606/2 *Oyster-fitting*, a bulkhead fitting designed to emit light on both sides of the bulkhead or other partition upon which it is mounted. **a 1841** W. P. HAWES *Sporting Scenes* (1842) II. 120 Oyster-knives and blood become well acquainted. **1907** *Yesterday's Shopping* (1969) 120/3 Place a stiff knife similar to an oyster knife between the rubber ring and flat metal top, and..it will easily come off. **1973** *Daily Colonist* (Victoria, B.C.) 1 July 9/1 An oyster knife..is obviously patterned on the rapier. **1937** *Daily Herald* 16 Feb. 19/6, I have never known Mr. Rinder so definitely oyster-like as when I tackled him yesterday on the line he proposed to take in the broadcast. **1975** *Country Life* 13 Sept. 1320/4 Its [*sc.* salsify's] stale fish flavour, described as oyster-like. *a* **1976** A. CHRISTIE *Autobiogr.* (1977) x. ii. 488 There was something oyster-like about Rosalind. **1753** in E. Singleton *Social N.Y. under Georges* (1902) 350, I am informed that an oysterman..may clear eight or ten shillings a day. **1853** O. S. FOWLER *Home for All* (rev. ed.) 23 Those persons who would economize, have only to order those very shells which the oyster-man has to pay to have carted from his cellar. **1955** *Times* 31 Aug. 5/1 But the oystermen of Cornwall eat the succulent grade four oyster with greater relish than its bigger brother. **1974** 'A. GARVE' *File on Lester* xxxix. 143, I talked first with some oystermen along the front here. **1925** Oyster piece [see *OYSTERING *vbl. sb.* b]. **1960** *Times* 9 Dec. 18/7 The beautiful 'oyster-piece' veneers and marquetry. **1973** *Daily Tel.* (Colour Suppl.) 16 Mar. 47/2 Laburnum wood which has a dark heart and a yellow sapring when cut across the grain produces highly decorative 'oyster pieces'. **1821** W. COBBETT *Amer. Gardener* iv. 257 Salsafy, called by some oyster plant, is good in soups, or to eat like the parsnip. **1841** *Cultivator* VIII. 114 Oyster Plant, or Salsify..after boiling soft, make gravy of flour, butter, etc. and add to them, and really they are rich substitutes for oysters. **1885** E. P. ROE *Nature's Serial Story* xxvi. 186 Will your nose become *retroussé* if I ask you to aid me in planting parsnips, oyster-plant, carrots and.. onions? **1938** R. GATHORNE-HARDY *Wild Flowers in Brit.* vi. 40 Another beautiful blue flower to be found on the coasts of Scotland and northern England is the uncommon Oyster Plant, *Mertensia maritima*,..which spreads its fat leaves and drooping blue flowers over the sea-shingle. **1960** *Oxf. Bk. Wild Flowers* 170/1 Sea Lungwort or Oyster Plant (*Mertensia maritima*)..is a rare plant of stony sea-shores in the north. **1972** Y. LOVELOCK *Vegetable Bk.* 201 The roots [of salsify] also are eaten..and are said to taste like asparagus; others suppose them to taste like oysters, from which belief it gains its name vegetable oyster and oyster plant. **1976** *Billings* (Montana) *Gaz.* 1 July 2-A/4 Ten percent vegetables and fruits: Beets, carrots, onion, oyster plant (salsify) rutabagas. **1824** *Nantucket Inquirer* 26 Jan. (Th.), He wore a hat of the new oyster-scow cut. **1856** *Dollar Times* (Cincinnati, Ohio) 11 Dec. 2/5 Our river boats are palaces of paint and gilding, but a leak from the bowsprit of an oyster-scow will sink one in fifteen minutes. **1835** J. J. AUDUBON *Ornith. Biogr.* III. 608 My host carried with him..a pair of oyster-tongs. **1949** R. J. SIM *Pages from Past Rural N.J.* 74 In oyster tongs the pin is thirty-two inches or more above the heads. **1909** G. O. WHEELER *Old English Furnit.* (ed. 2) iii. 115 Sections of small walnut branches were built in veneers,..resembling..oyster-shells, and.. this particular work has come to be classed as 'oyster veneer'. **1974** *Country Life* 30 May 1538/1 The use of walnut oyster-veneers in England is common. **1914** EBERLEIN & MCCLURE *Pract. Bk. Period Furnit.* 86 When the cabinets were 'oyster' veneered, inlaid with marqueterie or lacquered. **1976** *Country Life* 27 May (Suppl.) 48d/1 (Advt.), A rare 17th century oyster-veneered walnut side table. **1916** E. W. GREGORY *Furnit. Collector* vi. 91 The well-known 'oyster' veneering is also typical of the style. **1944** C. DREPPERD *Primer of Amer. Antiques* 241/2 *Oyster Walnut*, the burl in walnut having oyster shapes and forms in it and obvious when cut on the bias. A fine veneer pattern. **1972** *Country Life* 8 June (Suppl.) 51 A small William & Mary 'oyster walnut' chest of drawers.

oyster, *v.* Add: **b.** *trans.* To feed on oysters; with *up*.

1861 T. WINTHROP *Cecil Dreeme* 156 Boys, I've got a sick man to oyster up.

c. *intr.* To shut *up*; be silent. *slang.* Cf. *CLAM *v.*[4] 2.

1973 R. PARKES *Guardians* xii. 225 Once they got him down the station he oystered up proper. Not another word.

oystered (oi·stəɹd), *a.* [f. OYSTER *sb.* + -ED[2].] **1.** Of a veneer: bearing an oyster-shaped or whorled pattern.

1914 EBERLEIN & MCCLURE *Pract. Bk. Period Furnit.* ii. 57 The middle or end of the Carolean epoch when the whorled or 'oystered' veneer made from the transverse slices of small boughs came into vogue.

2. Eaten with oysters. *Nonce-use.*

1932 DYLAN THOMAS *Let.* (1966) 4 Oh, woe..unto Mumbles and the oystered beer.

oystering, *vbl. sb.* Add: **2.** Oyster veneer or work done with this.

1914 EBERLEIN & MCCLURE *Pract. Bk. Period Furnit.* iii. 90 Marqueterie, oystering and lacquer were freely used in their decorations. **1925** PENDEREL-BRODHURST & LAYTON *Gloss. Eng. Furnit.* 117 The slices are referred to as Oyster-pieces, and the arrangement as Oystering.

oyster-shell. Add: Also *fig.*

1876 TROLLOPE *Prime Minister* IV. vi. 87 When Aristides has been much too just the oyster-shells become numerous.

b. oyster-shell bark-louse *N. Amer.* = **oyster-shell scale* (*a*); **oyster-shell scale** *N. Amer.*, (*a*) a scale insect, *Lepidosaphes ulmi*, which attacks many trees and shrubs; (*b*) the disease produced by this insect, characterized by small curved scales on the plant's bark; **oyster-shell veneer, veneering** = *oyster veneer, veneering* s.v. *OYSTER 5d.

1868 *Rep. Comm. Agric. 1867* (U.S. Dept. Agric.) 73 The oyster shell bark louse or scale insect..is said to be exterminated by washing the tree with a mixture of two parts of soft soap, eight parts of water, and lime enough to give it the consistence of whitewash. **1877** *Rep. Vermont Board Agric.* IV. 150 Dr. Worcester has also shown me a branch covered with oyster shell bark-louse. *Ibid.*, The insect is shorter and stouter than that of the oyster shell scale. **1924** LAWRENCE & SKINNER *Boy in Bush* ii. 21 He was glad to reach the oyster-shell path running up Wellington Street. **1924** C. C. DEAM *Shrubs of Indiana* 233 Some individuals of several species are attacked and even killed both in cultivation and in the wild state by the oyster-shell scale. **1929** G. G. & F. GOULD *Period Furnit. Handbk.* xiv. 147 Veneer:..oyster-shell—in walnut, irregularly shaped oval pieces, cross sections cut from small boughs, the wood graining suggesting oyster-shells, popular in the late Charles II period. **1955** R. FASTNEDGE *Eng. Furnit. Styles* 286 This oystershell veneering, used for cabinet doors and drawer fronts, was introduced from Holland in the late seventeenth century. **1971** A. CHRISTIE *Nemesis* viii. 86 A William and Mary oyster-shell bureau. **1972** SWAN & PAPP *Common Insects N. Amer.* 163 Oystershell Scale: *lepidosaphes ulmi*... The armor is light to dark brown, shaped like a tiny oyster shell.

Ozalid (ōu·zălid). [Formed by reversing DIAZO- and inserting *l*.] A proprietary name used esp. in connection with a diazotype copying process in which the light-sensitive coating of the paper contains the coupling compound as well as the diazonium salt, so that the image may be made visible by exposure to gaseous ammonia. Hence, a photocopy produced by this process.

1924 *Trade Marks Jrnl.* 16 July 1608 Ozalid... Paper.., stationery, and bookbinding. Kalle & Co., Aktien Gesellschaft.., Biebrich-on-Rhine, Germany; manufacturers and merchants. **1928** *Official Gaz.* (U.S. Patent Office) 13 Nov. 292/2 Kalle & Co. Aktiengesellschaft, Wiesbaden-Biebrich, Germany. Filed Jan. 30, 1928. *Ozalid* for light-sensitive copying and photographic papers. Claims use since Mar. 19, 1923. **1929** *Encycl. Brit.* XVII. 803/1 G. Kögel has patented..the use of diazoanhydrides..for paper that may be used for the same purpose; this process is known as 'Ozalid'. **1939** *Thorpe's Dict. Appl. Chem.* (ed. 4) III. 589/2 Ozalide [*sic*] papers, which have largely displaced blueprint paper, are based on the principle that a light-sensitive diazoanhydride may be mixed with a phenol or aromatic amine without coupling until the mixture is rendered slightly alkaline. **1941** *Official Gaz.* (U.S. Patent Office) 23 Dec. 767/2 General Aniline & Film Corporation, New York, N.Y. Filed Oct. 22, 1941. *Ozalid.* For light-sensitive diazotype paper, cloths, films, etc., for machines for developing the photoprints thus produced and parts of such machines. Claims use for light-sensitive diazo type materials since Mar. 19, 1923; and for printing and developing machines since May 1, 1936. **1944** *Trade Marks Jrnl.* 12 Apr. 167/2 Ozalid... Photographic and photocopying apparatus, instruments, and utensils. Ozalid Company Limited,.. London,..manufacturers and merchants. **1967** V. STRAUSS *Printing Industry* v. 267/2 Diazo papers..are also known as Ozalids and whiteprints. **1970** E. A. D. HUTCHINGS *Survey of Printing Processes* vii. 114 Development of the intermediates is carried out in an Ozalid ammonia vapour dyeline machine. **1975** J. BUTCHER *Copy-editing* v. 61 The final proof is a photographic proof (usually an Ozalid).

Ozark (ōu·zāɹk). Also **Osark.** [ad. F. *aux Arcs* at the Quapaw, ult. ad. Illinois *akansea* Quapaw Indian.] The Quapaw, a North American Indian people, or perhaps a local group of this tribe.

1816 H. KER *Trav. Western Interior U.S.* 40 We were visited by a few of the Osark tribe of Indians, who came to us in canoes... They are called by the name of a river they inhabit, on the west side of the Mississippi. **1821** T. NUTTALL *Jrnl. Trav. Arkansa* vi. 81 The aborigines of this territory, now commonly called Arkansas or Quapaws and Osarks, do not..number more than about 200 warriors. **1910** F. W. HODGE *Handbk. Amer. Indians* II. 180/2 *Ozark*, a term at one time applied to a local band of Quapaw, from their residence in the Ozark mountain region of Missouri and Arkansas.

ozonation. (Further examples.)

1948 KIRK & OTHMER *Encycl. Chem. Technol.* II. 426 A triozonide is formed with difficulty by ozonation of benzene. **1972** *Adv. Chem.* CXII. 1 A competition exists during ozonation of olefins between ozonolysis and epoxide formation.

ozone. Add: **c. ozone-sonde,** a radiosonde for transmitting information on the ozone content of the atmosphere; also without hyphen as one word or two.

1960 *Monograph Internat. Geodetic & Geophysical Union* No. 3, 20 During the IGY many successful balloon soundings with the ozone-sonde were obtained. **1964** *Bull. Atomic Sci.* Jan. 29 In the past two years there has been an increased emphasis on several aspects of antarctic meteorology...albedo programs, meteorological studies aboard the Eltanin, and the inclusion of vertical coverage through..ozonesondes, and gammasondes. **1969** MCINTOSH & THOM *Essent. Meteorol.* vii. 111 One form of ozone sonde..is that devised by A. W. Brewer. Air is bubbled through a small electrolytic cell filled with neutral potassium iodide solution.

ozoner (ou·zōunəɹ). *U.S. slang.* [f. OZONE + -ER[1].] A drive-in cinema. Also *ozoner cinema.*

1948 *Time* 26 Apr. 96/2 This week, New York City will get its first 'ozoner': a 600-car..affair on Staten Island. **1949** *Sat. Rev. Lit.* (U.S.) 11 June 4/1 There are now between 1,000 and 2,000 drive-ins in the U.S...Hollywood calls them 'ozoners'. **1962** *Punch* 24 Jan. 167/1 Virtually every picture window of the motel rooms face[s] out on the ozoner cinema.

ozonide. Add: **2. a.** [ad. G. *ozonid* (C. Harries 1904, in *Ber. d. Deut. Chem. Ges.* XXXVII. 840).] Any of the compounds containing the ring C—O—O—C—O, which are formed by the addition of ozone to olefinic double bonds and are explosive oils or amorphous solids.

1904 *Jrnl. Chem. Soc.* LXXXVI. I. 361 The ozonides are mostly highly explosive. **1929** R. A. GORTNER *Outl. Biochem.* xxxi. 640 On treatment of the oleic acid ozonide with water, it decomposes into hydrogen peroxide, pelargonic acid, and azelaic acid semi-aldehyde. **1959** E. L. MASCALL *Pi in the High* 28 Though many facts that art. provides *Re* substances called Ozonides. **1968** R. O. C. NORMAN *Princ. Org. Synthesis* xviii. 505 Lithium aluminium hydride reduces ozonides to alcohols.

b. The ion O_3^-, or a salt of this ion.

1949 *Chem. Abstr.* XLIII. 4170 The compd. can be formulated K^+,O_3^-, and termed K ozonide. **1962** P. J. & B. DURRANT *Introd. Adv. Inorg. Chem.* xxi. 799 The ozonide ion, (O—O—O)⁻, is present in potassium ozonide, KO_3. **1966** *McGraw-Hill Encycl. Sci. & Technol.* XII. 409/2 Sodium also forms an ozonide, NaO_3, when ozone is passed into a solution of sodium in liquid ammonia.

ozonization. Add: **b.** Reaction with ozone, esp. in an ozonolysis process.

1906 *Jrnl. Chem. Soc.* XC. 227 The ozonisation of elaidic acid could only be carried out in chloroform solution. **1936** *Jrnl. Amer. Chem. Soc.* LVIII. 2272 The isolation of 1,2-diketones from the ozonization of disubstituted acetylenes. **1964** ROBERTS & CASERIO *Basic Princ. Org. Chem.* vii. 192 Ozonides..may explode violently and unpredictably. Ozonizations must therefore be carried out with due caution.

ozonize, *v.* Add: **2.** (Further examples.) Also, to cause to react with ozone.

1906 *Jrnl. Chem. Soc.* XC. 227 A solution of sodium oleate was ozonised and then evaporated under reduced pressure. **1930** *Jrnl. Amer. Chem. Soc.* LII. 2550 Methyl neopentyl ketone..and trimethylacetaldehyde were produced in the ratio of approximately 3·7 to 1 when di-isobutylene was ozonized and the ozonide hydrolyzed. **1968** *Adv. Chem. Ser.* LXXVII. lxii. 35 To determine what mechanistic pathways might be operating to account for the different cis-trans ratios, we have ozonized the olefin stereoisomers in the presence of the respective, necessary aldehydes. **1971** *Nature* 26 Nov. 213/1 The source [*sc.* mercury] was ozonized and mechanically spread on the Pt backing plate.

ozonolysis (ōuzǭnǫ·lĭsis). *Chem.* [f. OZON(E + -O + *-LYSIS.] The cleavage of double or triple carbon–carbon bonds by reaction with ozone.

1931 *Jrnl. Amer. Chem. Soc.* LIII. 358 In order to obtain the ketone indicated from hydrocarbon number 1 it is necessary to assume that the pinacolone rearrangement suggested by Butlerow has taken place during ozonolysis. **1936** *Jrnl. Org. Chem.* I. 145 The ozonolysis of triple bonds has been studied with..six acetylene representatives. **1951** I. L. FINAR *Org. Chem.* I. iv. 57 Ozonolysis..is probably the best method for determining the position of a double bond in any olefinic compound. **1971** I. G. GASS et al. *Understanding Earth* ix. 133 The ozonolysis products of the kerogens are aromatic in the Onverwacht.

Hence **ozonoly·tic** *a.*, involving ozonolysis.

1956 *Jrnl. Polymer Sci.* XXII. 213 A simple ozonolytic method has been developed which enables the natural rubber trunk chains of rubber-polymethyl methacrylate and rubber-polystyrene interpolymers to be degraded into low molecular weight fragments. **1972** *Angewandte Chemie* (Internat. Ed.) XI. 1089/2 (*heading*) Ozonolytic degradation of a catenane.

ozonosphere (ōuzōu·nosfiəɹ). *Meteorol.* [f. OZON(E + -O + SPHERE *sb.*] The region of the atmosphere where there is a significant concentration of ozone, at an altitude of 10 to 50 km. (6–30 miles); esp. the part between about 20 and 25 km (12–15 miles) where the concentration is greatest.

1933 *Jrnl. Inst. Electr. Engin.* LXXIII. 578/2 The upper part of the stratosphere is conveniently dealt with under a different name, even though there is no definite boundary between the stratosphere and the ozonosphere. **1951** *Jrnl. Brit. Interplanetary Soc.* X. 22 The composition up to the ozonosphere is then fairly well established. Above this both oxygen and nitrogen still form the major part of the atmosphere. **1963** *New Scientist* 1 Aug. 232/2 Apart from the effect that this might have in..giving us acute sunburn, there is another potentially important outcome of contaminating the ozonosphere. **1965** K. E. SPELLS in J. A. Gillies *Textbk. Aviation Physiol.* iii. 49 The region from about 12 to 22 miles altitude is sometimes called the ozonosphere.

P

P. Add: **I. 1.** *attrib.* Used *spec.* to designate one of the two main groups of languages which developed from Common Celtic, so called because its distinctive phonological features include the development of IE. **q^u* to *p*, as *P-Celtic*, *-division*, *-group*, etc.; *P-Celt*, a speaker of P-Celtic.

1891 J. RHYS in *Trans. Philol. Soc. 1891–4* 104 (*title*) The Celts and the other Aryans of the *P* and *Q* groups. *Ibid.* 111 We are entitled to conclude that the Q Celts arrived in the west before the P Celts, as they are found occupying the furthest parts of the Celtic area... The conclusion is scarcely to be avoided that the later comers, the P Celts, came as invaders and conquerors. **1892** [in Dict.]. **1913** J. M. JONES *Welsh Gram.* 1 Keltic: (*a*) the Q division, consisting of dialects in Gaul and Spain, and the Goidelic group, comprising Irish, Scotch Gaelic and Manx; (*b*) the P division, consisting of Gaulish, and the British group, comprising Welsh, Cornish and Breton. **1949** *Antiquity* XXIII. 23 By birth-place and blood, Kieran was closely associated with the P-Celtic tribe of Corcu-Loigde. *Ibid.* 27 The Ulaid (the Ulstermen of the Saga), were once P-Celts, in O'Rahilly's view. **1953** [see *BRITTONIC *a.* and *sb.*]. **1972** W. B. LOCKWOOD *Panorama Indo-Europ. Lang.* 74 The term Goidelic is chiefly used to denote Irish as distinct from British or, more technically speaking, to denote Q-Celtic as opposed to P-Celtic. **1977** *Word 1972* XXVIII. 133 One may wish to see Pictish interpreted as somewhat less different from Cumbric and the rest of insular p-Celtic than Jackson would argue.

4. *P.Z. exercise* (*R.N.*), an exercise at sea.

1905 *Trans. Inst. Naval Archit.* XLVII. II. 305 The P.Z. exercises have been so conducted as to be deceiving. **1916** 'TAFFRAIL' *Pincher Martin* viii. 140 Gunnery, gunnery, *toujours* gunnery—unless it was torpedo-running, steam tactics, or P.Z. Exercises—was carried on throughout the year. **1962** GRANVILLE *Dict. Sailors' Slang* 85/2 *PZ*, tactical exercise in the Fleet at sea in peacetime when the Code flags *PZ* were run up at the start of the exercise.

II. *p* = *piano* (examples); P., 'prompter side' in a theatre; cf. *P.S.* below; p, parental generation (see quot. 1902); p, p., pence, penny, in decimal currency (see *NEW *a.* 4); Pa, pascal; p. a., per annum (PER *prep.* I. 2); P.A., personal assistant; P.A. [see quot. 1972], a canvas climbing boot with a rubber sole strengthened with a steel plate; P.A., political agent, press agent, Press Association, programme assistant; P.A., PA, p.a., public address; P.A., power amplifier; PAL, phase alternation line (name of a colour television system); P. and O. (earlier example); PAR, precision approach radar; P.A.S., PAS, *para*-aminosalicylic acid; PAYE, P.A.Y.E., pay as you earn; PAYV, pay-as-you-view; P.B.I., Poor Bloody Infantry(man), so P.B. used with other sbs.; p.c., per cent; p.c., P.C., post-card; P.C. = Privy Councillor (examples); PC, propositional calculus (see *PROPOSITIONAL *a.* b); also *attrib.*; PCB, pcb, printed circuit board; (see also sense II. d below); PCM, pcm, pulse code modulation; PCP, phencyclidine; p.c.u., passenger car unit; P.D., p.d., potential difference; P.D., preventive detention (also, detainee); PDI, powered descent initiation (of a spacecraft); P.D.Q., p.d.q., pretty damn quick; P.E., physical education; P.E., p.e., plastic explosive; P.E.N., PEN, Poets, Playwrights, Editors, Essayists, and Novelists; PEP (*Radio*), peak envelope power; P.E.P., PEP, Political and Economic Planning; *p/e ratio*, price-earnings ratio; PERT (orig. *U.S.*), program(me) evaluation (and) review technique (orig., program(me) evaluation research task); (= **network analysis* b, esp. as used to deal with events of uncertain duration); P.E.S.C., Public Expenditure Survey Committee; p.f. (*Mus.*), pianoforte, [It. *piano forte*] soft then loud, [It. *più forte*] more loudly; p.f.a., P.F.A., pulverized fuel ash; PFC, p.f.c. (*U.S.*), Private 1st Class, poor foolish (forlorn, etc.) civilian; PG, parental guidance (*N. Amer.*, a cinema film classification); P.G., p.g., paying guest; hence p.g. *v. intr.*, to reside as a paying guest; PGR, P.G.R. [ad. G. *p.g.R.* (O. Veraguth 1907, in *Monatsschr. f. Psychiatrie und Neurol.* XXI. 387)], psychogalvanic reflex, response; Ph.D. [L. *Philosophiæ Doctor*], Doctor of Philosophy, Doctorate of Philosophy; P.I. (*U.S. slang*), pimp; PI, p.i., private investigator; PIB, Prices and Incomes Board; PIDE [Pg. *Polícia Internacional e de Defesa do Estado*], International Police for the Defence of the State; p-j, P.J., pyjama; PK., Pk., psychokinesis, psychokinetic (see quot. 1943); P.K.I. [Indonesian *Partai Komunis Indonésia*], Indonesian Communist Party; PKU (*Med.*), phenylketonuria; P.L.A., People's Liberation Army; P.L.A., Port of London Authority; P.L.M. [Fr. *Paris–Lyon–Méditerranée*], Paris–Lyons–Mediterranean (Railway); P.L.O., PLO, Palestine Liberation Organization; PL/1, PL/I (*Computers*), 'Programming Language One', a versatile and powerful high-level language designed to replace both Fortran and Cobol in their respective fields; PLP, P.L.P., Parliamentary Labour Party; PLSS, personal life support system; P.M., particular (*or* peculiar, *or* proper) metre; p.m. = afternoon (further examples); p.m., P.M., *post mortem*; P.M., Prime Minister; P.M.A. (*Dentistry*) (see quot. 1969); P.M.G., Postmaster General; P.M.S., pregnant mare's serum, or a gonadotrophic extract of it; PNdb, PNdB, perceived noise decibel(s) (see quot. 1959); P.N.E.U., Parents' National Educational Union; P.O., post office (examples); also, postal order; P.O.A., Probation of Offenders Act; P.O.D., pay on delivery; P.O.D. (*U.S.*), Post Office Department; P. of W., Prince of Wales; POL, petrol, oil, and lubricants; P.O.O., Post Office Order; POP, Post Office Preferred; P.O.P., POP, printing-out paper; POPOP [f. the repeated initials of PHENYL and *OXAZOLE, the molecule consisting of five such rings joined in this order], 1,4-di[2-(5-phenyloxazolyl)]benzene, a substance used in solution as a scintillator; POUM, P.O.U.M. [Sp. *Partido Obrero de Unificación Marxista*], Workers' Party of Marxist Unity; P.O.W., Prince of Wales; P.O.W., POW, prisoner of war; p.p., *per procurationem*, by proxy (examples); *pp* or *ppp* = *pianissimo* (examples); P-P, PP, pellagra-preventive or -preventing (formerly a designation of the vitamin now called niacin); ppb, p.p.b., parts per billion; P.P.C. (further examples); hence P.P.C. *v. intr.*; PPC, P.P.C., progressive patient care; P.P.D., PPD, purified protein derivative (of tuberculin); P.P.E., PPE, Politics, Philosophy, and Economics (a course of study at Oxford University); P.P.I., p.p.i., plan position indicator; PPK, *Polizei Pistole Kriminal* [G., police criminal pistol], a type of handgun; PPLO, pleuropneumonia-like organism(s); ppm, parts per million; P.P.S., Parliamentary Private Secretary; P.P.S., P.P.P.S., (*post*) *post post scriptum*; PPU, Peace Pledge Union; P.Q., PQ, parliamentary question; P.R., photographic reconnaissance; P.R., Pre-Raphaelite; P.R., prize ring; P.R., proportional representation; P.R., public relations; P.R., PR, Puerto Rico, Puerto Rican; P.R.A. (examples); P.R.B., Pre-Raphaelite Brother (-hood); P.R.O., Public Record Office; P.R.O., public relations officer; PROM, programmable read-only memory (cf. ROM s.v. *R II. 2 a); PROP, Preservation of the Rights of Prisoners; P.R.S., Performing Rights Society; P.S. = *post scriptum*, postscript (examples); P.S., 'prompter side' in a theatre; p.s.c., passed staff college; p.s.i.(a.), psi, pounds per square inch (absolute); P.S.V., p.s.v., public service vehicle; P.T., physical training; P.T., PT, purchase tax; P.T.A., Parent–Teacher Association; PT boat (*U.S.*), patrol torpedo boat; PTC, phenylthiocarbamide; P.T.I., physical training instructor; P.T.O. (examples); p.t.o., PTO, power take-off; Pty. (*Austral. commercial*), proprietary; P.U.O., pyrexia of unknown origin; P.U.S., PUS, Permanent Under-Secretary; pw, p.w., per week; P.W.D., Public Works Department; PWR, pressurized-water reactor; PX (*U.S. mil.*), Post Exchange. Also *PABA, *pH, *P-N-P, *P-TYPE.

1740 J. GRASSINEAU *Mus. Dict.* 173 *P*, in the Italian music, frequently signifies *piano*, which is what we called soft. **1888** KIPLING *Masque of Plenty* in *Departmental Ditties* (1890) 48 (*adagio dim.*) Fillèd with praise... (*p*) Ay, paint our swarthy billions The richest of vermilions. **1957** H. SHANET *Learn to read Music* IV. 123 Between *f* and *p*, there are *mezzo forte*.., and *mezzo piano* (medium soft). **1977** G. WARFIELD *How to write Music Manuscript* 133 Place a 'p' under the first note and a 'pp' under the last in these two examples. **1901** G. B. SHAW *Let.* 7 Nov. in *B. Shaw & Mrs. Campbell* (1952) 14 Titheradge's determination to die parrallel [*sic*] to the float with his heels O.P. and his head P..rather spoils the picture. **1933** P. GODFREY *Back-Stage* i. 18 The amber circuits in No. 1 batten, floats, and P. and O.P. perches. **1902** W. BATESON et al. *Rep. Evolution Comm. R. Soc.* I. 160 We suggest as a convenient designation for the parental generation the letter P. In crossing, the P generation are the pure forms. .. Starting from any subject-individual, P_2 is the grand-parental, P_3 the great-grandparental generation, and so on. **1918** BABCOCK & CLAUSEN *Genetics Rel. Agric.* x. 180 (*caption*) Re-appearance of parental values in the F_2 offspring. P_1 Leaf Factor. **1952** SRB & OWEN *General Genetics* ix. 164 Verify this by diagramming a sequence of crosses through F_2 where the P generation is the reciprocal of the one shown in the text. **1975** V. GRANT *Genetics of Flowering Plants* i. 9 The experimental results can be summarized as follows: P round yellow × wrinkled green. **1934** WEBSTER, *p.*,..penny. **1968** *Times* 17 Apr. 6/1 The 10p. and 5p. coins could appear in small change almost at once. **1973** *Guardian* 18 Dec. 13/3 We couldn't get away with a half p in tax evasion—but they do. **1976** 'W. TREVOR' *Children of Dynmouth* iv. 95 Yesterday had officially been the last day for entries, but he'd seen no reason to turn away the man's fifty p. **1964** H. S. HVISTENDAHL *Engin. Units* iii. 29 In the French decree of May 3rd, 1961, the name pascal (Pa), is adopted for the N/m^2. **1975** *Nature* 2 Oct. 371/2 The density of vitreous silica is affected irreversibly by the application of pressures of more than 2×10^9 Pa. *a* **1912** W. T. ROGERS *Dict. Abbrev.* (1913) 145/2 *p.a.*, *Per annum* (For the year). **1931** *Times* 16 Mar. 22/4 (Advt.), Present rental value £300–£350 p.a. **1955** *Times* 7 July 1/5 Salary, £1,200–£1,600 p.a., plus free furnished quarters, fuel, light, water. **1942** PARTRIDGE *Dict. Abbrev.* 73/1 *P.A.*... Personal Assistant. **1943** N. BALCHIN *Small Back Room* i. 14 D'you think Higgins goes in for women? We might hire him a suitable P.A. **1969** D. CLARK *Nobody's Perfect* ii. 61 Couldn't his P.A. have rung you when you got home? **1975** M. SINCLAIR *Long Time Sleeping* iii. 38 Gilbert Winter's office and the adjacent one of his long-suffering PA. **1963** [see *KLETTERSCHUH]. **1972** D. HASTON *In High Places* ii. 35 Neil and I [were] ahead leaving the other two arguing about who should wear the one pair of P.A.'s. (These are special boots for hard rock-climbing, with stiff, smooth rubber soles and canvas uppers. The initials are those of their inventor, Pierre Allain, a famous French climber before the Second World War.) **1913** E. M. FORSTER *Let.* 1 Jan. in *Hill of Devi* (1953) 25 The Political Agent from Neemuch..brought a party... The P.A...planted himself on the State for the night. **1937** F. STARK *Baghdad Sketches* 187 [They] send messages to the P.A. **1936** *Amer. Speech* XI. 220 In terms of the theater, the *P.A.* is the Press Agent. **1958** *Spectator* 11 July 53/2 The press box was empty except for PA and *The Times*. **1915** M. MACDONAGH *Diary* 6 Oct. in *London during Gt. War* (1935) II. iii. 80 My friend Howe, of the 'P.A.'. **1942** PARTRIDGE *Dict. Abbrev.* 73/1 *P.A.*... Publishers' Association. But also Press Association. **1972** D. MCLACHLAN *No Case for Crown* iii. 45 I'll deal with the P.A.; their news editor used to work under me. **1968** *Listener* 4 Apr. 442/3 Four of these programme assistants form the nucleus of Radio Sheffield's staff... My immediate task is to look at the material..left for me the previous night by one of the other PA's. **1936** *Amer. Speech* XI. 220 In radio, a *P.A.* system is a public address system. **1953** POHL & KORNBLUTH *Space Merchants* (1955) ii. 23 The PA system announced that my flight was ready. **1963** *Times Lit. Suppl.* 1 Mar. 156/1 Marlowe anticipated Whitman's barbaric yawp by setting up a national PA system of blank verse. **1964** S. BELLOW *Herzog* (1965) 35 Over the p.a. system the management begged the spectators not to throw pennies. **1940** *Chambers's Techn. Dict.* 608/1 *P.A.*, power amplifier. **1971** *Melody Maker* 4 Sept. 20 The giant PA's distort their guitars out of all recognition. **1963** J. R. DAVIES *Understanding Television* xiii. 485 Mention must be made of the recently introduced PAL system, developed by Telefunken... The PAL system has been investigated by the European Broadcasting Union... PAL is based on the N.T.S.C. system. **1968** *Listener* 21 Nov. 687/2 It's not quite true..that PAL and SECAM are 'irreconcilable' now that at least one inventor is trying to market a cheap conversion kit. **1975** *New Scientist* 31 July 274/1 Commercial TV resolution in the US is 525 lines, against Europe's PAL standard of 625 lines. **1863** DICKENS *Uncomm. Trav.* in *All Year Round* 6 June 350/2 The well-known regularity of the P. and O. Steamers. **1951** *Gloss. Aeronaut. Terms* (*B.S.I.*) III. 21 *Final controller*, a radar controller employed in the transmission of PAR talk-down instructions to the pilot of an aircraft on the final approach to the runway, and in passing monitoring information to the pilot when using a landing aid other than PAR. **1966** *McGraw-Hill Encycl. Sci. & Technol.* X. 578/2 In common practice, the ground PAR operators call instructions to the pilot. **1946** *Lancet* 5 Jan. 15/2 Treatment with *p*-aminosalicylic acid (P.A.S.) was given in three periods with concomitant falls in temperature. **1959** J. BRAINE *Vodi* vi. 85 They'd tried strep. and

P.A.S. **1971** *Brit. Jrnl. Dis. Chest* Jan. p. vi (Advt.), A choice of flavoured drinks... the acceptable way of taking PAS and Isoniazid. **1944** *Times* 4 Apr. 2/2 (*heading*) PAYE begins. **1956** 'C. Blackstock' *Dewey Death* iv. 89 Miss Holmes..[was] doggedly working out the P.A.Y.E. for the thirty members of I.L.D.A. staff. **1972** *Accountant* 21 Sept. 343/1 Scare stories..about the implications of the proposed letter suffixes to employees' PAYE code numbers, have been officially denounced. **1958** *Spectator* 27 June 829/2 The need is to make the idea of PAYV much more familiar than it is. There have been many references to it from time to time in the press in the last few years, but for some reason the idea has never caught on. **1916** *B.E.F. Times* 1 Dec. f. 4/1 So here's to the lads of the P.B.I. Who live in a ditch that never is dry. *a* **1918** J. T. B. McCudden *Five Yrs. in R. Flying Corps* (1919) 134 The famous Ypres salient..was by no means regarded with friendly feelings by the Infantry—or P.B.I. as they generally call themselves. **1946** *Jrnl. R. United Service Inst.* XCI. 52 He is the 'P.B.I.' of the service on whom the final success of the scheme depends. **1949** F. Swinnerton *Doctor's Wife comes to Stay* 149 He's only the P. B. Author. **1952** *Sunday Times* 14 Dec. 7/3 Procedural remedies are being sought, mostly by back-benchers—the 'P.B.I.' of Parliament. **1968** W. Winward *Conscripts* xii. 154 The p.b.i. gets the chopper, but never the officer. **1972** *Guardian* 1 Feb. 12/2 In the trenches the PBI.. await the order to go over the top. **1976** *Times Lit. Suppl.* 30 Jan. 106/1 The Crossman interpretation of the position of the MP whom he sees as the PBI of the mass party. **1874** 'Mark Twain' *Lett. to Publishers* (1967) 80 Bliss had contracted to pay me 10 p.c. on my next book... He paid 7½ p.c. on Roughing It and 5 p.c. on Innocents Abroad. **1931** *N. & Q.* 26 Dec. 465/2 A 10 p.c. solution of oxalic acid will be useful if ink-stains be present. **1889** E. C. Dowson *Let.* 21 Feb. (1967) 39, I enclose a P.C. wh. I had just written—it is no longer necessary—but you may as well post it. **1951** R. Macaulay *Lett. to Friend* (1961) 194, I had..a nice picture p.c. from Father Pedersen from Rome. **1881** E. W. Hamilton *Diary* 22 Nov. (1972) I. 185, I told Mr. G. he ought to make May a P.C. **1973** *Whitaker's Almanack 1974* 84 The Duke of Buccleuch and Queensberry, P.C., K.T., G.C.V.O., aged 78. **1960** P. H. Nidditch *Elem. Logic Sci. & Math.* 29 In a PC of the usual, axiomatic type the only definitions are those of connectives. **1965** Hughes & Londey *Elem. Formal Logic* xv. 101 In 1910, in the first volume of *Principia Mathematica*, Whitehead and Russell presented an axiomatization of PC. *Ibid.* xxix. 211 Their validity can be determined by PC methods alone. **1973** J. J. Zeman *Modal Logic* xi. 181 One might ask if there is a modal system bearing an analogous relationship to the classical PC. *Ibid.* xii. 191 The definition of complete modalization was extended to include certain PC theorems. **1977** *Engin. Materials & Design* Aug. 9/2 Thought to be the most powerful calculator/watch combination on the market, hybrid construction is used to mount the chips on a small pcb which also carries a miniature 5 by 4 matrix keyboard. **1977** *Gramophone* Nov. 960/3 It is not usual to mount heavy components on PCBs. **1947** *Bell Syst. Techn. Jrnl.* XXVI. 395 This paper describes an experiment in transmitting speech by PCM, or pulse code modulation. **1966** *Punch* 10 Aug. 224 PCM will enable each existing pair of telephone cables to carry twelve times as many conversations as before. **1972** [see *modulation 7]. **1977** *Broadcast* 7 Nov. 10/1 Sound radio signals..are distributed in pcm multiplex form along analogue television links. **1973** PCP [see *phencyclidine]. **1977** *Time* 18 July 35/3 Disturbing increases in the use of a dangerous new street drug called PCP. **1960** J. Drake in E. Davies *Roads* iv. 85 The term 'passenger car unit' or p.c.u. is used in capacity measurements to make allowance for mixed traffic—all motor vehicles count as one unit, except heavy goods vehicles, buses, and coaches which count three. On a road having moderately high volumes of heavy traffic it is found that the p.c.u. count is 50% more than that for motor vehicles. **1966** *New Scientist* 29 Sept. 711/3 The unit of traffic he used was the 'passenger-car unit' (pcu) which is employed by the Ministry of Transport. A bus is rated at 3 pcu, for example. **1887** W. E. Ayrton *Pract. Electr.* vii. 371 An influence machine can produce a P.D. between its terminals of some hundreds of thousands of volts. **1935** J. N. Friend *Text-bk. Physical Chem.* II. vii. 297 Experimental measurement of the P.D. between two liquids presents many difficulties. **1963** A. F. Abbott *Ordinary Level Physics* xxxvii. 487 The terminal p.d. is always less than the e.m.f., and the difference..represents the p.d. required to send the current through the internal resistance of the cell. **1956** 'C. Raven' *Underworld Nights* 30 The last I heard of him he was done for pinching a shaving brush from Woolworth's and sentenced to eight years P.D. under the new act. **1959** *New Statesman* 24 Jan. 102/2 My seven hosts were all preventive detainees (PDs) serving terms of five to 14 years imprisonment, and with three or more convictions. **1973** J. Wood *North Beat* vi. 81 The thought of preventive detention appalled him. There was no remission with P.D. **1969** *New Scientist* 17 July 115/1 The critical operation is then a 'three-phase powered descent initiation' or PDI, the braking manoeuvre which begins at this low point and reduces the vehicle's velocity to zero at a height of around 7000 feet. *c* **1875** B. Woolf *Mighty Dollar* in B. H. Clark *Favorite Amer. Plays 19th Cent.* (1943) 489 That's right, you'd better step P.D.Q., pretty damn quick. **1890** *Ladies' Home Jrnl.* July 12/4 The P. D. Q. Camera. **1891** Kipling *Life's Handicap* 189 He went as his instructions advised *p.d.q.*—which means 'with speed'. **1926** [see *make *v.*¹ 65 c]. **1961** B. E. Wallace *Death packs Suitcase* v. 55 I'd come back here P.D.Q., because here I'd know my way around. **1974** 'A. Haig' *Peruvian Printout* 33 Whoever is messing about with our computers, I want him found p.d.q. **1956** J. Edmundson *P.E. Teachers' Handbk.* vi. 30 Quite effective P.E. lessons can be taken in a classroom even with.. very limited space. **1973** J. Burrows *Like an Evening Gone* iii. 40 Sporting equipment of a modest kind,..a vaulting horse and a set of P.E. mats. **1976** 'W. Trevor' *Children of Dynmouth* v. 115 Stringer, the headmaster, was rubbish; the P.E. man went after the girls. **1949** F. S. Chapman *Jungle is Neutral* ii. 19 We piled the dicky high with Tommy-guns, cases of P.E. (plastic high explosive), grenades, and an assortment of demolition and incendiary devices. **1971** P. O'Donnell *Impossible Virgin* xiii. 261 He had some fuse and plastic explosive, but... using p.e. to set off a bullet would produce the wrong sort of noise. **1923** *Times* 2 May 11/3 Mr. John Galsworthy presided last night over a company of playwrights, poets, essayists, and novelists at an international dinner given by the P.E.N. Club. **1924** G. S. Gordon *Let.* 20 Sept. (1943) 176 A private dinner in the evening with the Stockholm Pen Club (P—poets; E—editors; N—novelists). **1931** T. E. Lawrence *Let.* 13 Apr. (1938) 718 The P.E.N. suggestion is rather astonishing. **1966** 'H. MacDiarmid' *Company I've Kept* xiii. 270 Saurat rendered great service to the International P.E.N., as one of its Vice-Presidents. **1969** L. Hellman *Unfinished Woman* xiii. 195 A reception for the president of PEN, an Englishman. **1956** *Proc. IRE* XLIV. 1710/1 For a 0·5 watt SSB signal (1w PEP) there is 0·095 watt in the AM component. **1971** *Gloss. Electrotechnical, Power Terms* (*B.S.I.*) III. vii. 23 *Peak envelope power; P.E.P.* of a radio transmitter. The power supplied to the aerial transmission line or specified artificial load by a transmitter during one radio frequency cycle at the highest crest of the modulation envelope, taken under conditions of normal operation. **1976** Perkowski & Stral *Joy of CB* vii. 70 As in AM transmissions, the peak envelope power (PEP) is still limited to 12 watts, but since the carrier is reduced or suppressed, additional power can be put into the sideband. **1933** *Planning* VI. 15 They began more than two years ago to study..the possibilities of renewing friction in..industry, agriculture, finance, the social services... The PEP budget..is raised entirely from among those interested in the work. **1941** J. S. Huxley *Uniqueness of Man* xi. 233 It [*sc.* group work] is far more necessary in social science, where various bodies, such as P.E.P., are studying how to perfect it as a research method. **1970** I. Sieff *Mem.* ix. 164, I would not want to try and write a history of PEP here if I could but I would like to say something about it. **1965** *Acronyms & Initialisms Dict.* (Gale Research Co.) 558 P/E, Price/Earnings Ratio (Relation between price of a company's stock and its annual net income). **1969** *Times* 30 Apr. 30/5 It leaves the historical p/e ratio on the ordinary shares..looking vulnerable for a newspaper company at 20.8. **1959** *Amer. Statistician* Apr. 10/1 This Program Evaluation and Review Technique (code-named PERT) is applied as a decision-making tool designed to save time in achieving end-objectives. **1960** *IRE Trans. Engin. Managem.* VII. 103/2 PERT (Program Evaluation and Review Technique) utilizes the network concept of R and D projects, and analyzes the 'time to completion' variable. **1962** [see *network analysis* s.v. *network 5]. **1964** A. Battersby *Network Analysis* ix. 134 Pollack has published a detailed description of how PERT was brought in to control the construction of the $47,000,000 Zero Gradient Synchrotron at the Argonne National Laboratory. **1969** J. Argenti *Managem. Techniques* 72 The technique known as PERT..is used when the duration of an activity is not accurately known. **1974** *Encycl. Brit. Macropædia* XIII. 600/1 Critical path method (CPM) is an optimizing procedure applicable only to certainty-type formulations of such problems. Project evaluation and review technique (PERT) is applicable to risk- as well as certainty-type formulations but does not always yield optimal solutions. *a* **1974** R. Crossman *Diaries* (1976) II. 126 Then we moved on to housing where we had a very strange situation because, after agreeing to the cuts PESC demanded, the Minister of Housing made an extraordinary Ministerial announcement virtually saying that the target of 500,000 houses a year had been abandoned. **1976** H. Wilson *Governance of Brit.* iii. 61 This meeting or 'PESC' was concerned not with detailed allocations of expenditure, as finally announced in February 1976, but with basic priorities. **1876** Stainer & Barrett *Dict. Mus. Terms* 348/2 *P.f.*, abb. of (1) Pianoforte. (2) *Piano, forte*, soft then loud. (3) *Più forte*, louder. **1938** *Oxf. Compan. Mus.* 712 *Pianoforte*,..often abbreviated pf. **1958** *Archit. Rev.* CXXIII. 326 The ground-floor walls are of cavity construction with an inner skin of insulating p.f.a. blocks and yellow bricks outside. **1970** *Sci. Jrnl.* Aug. 78/2 Marketing officers of the CEGB are today developing PFA sales for a wide range of civil engineering and building activities. **1941** *Amer. Speech* XVI. 167/2 PFC, Private 1st Class. **1947** *Ibid.* XXII. 112 References to rates and ranks are numerous. One variously caricatures *P.F.C.* ('private first class') as 'poor foolish civilian'... A *double P.F.C.*, however, is a corporal, since he has two chevrons on his sleeve. **1948** J. T. Appleby *Suffolk Summer* iii. 13 The third, an embittered P.F.C., did odd jobs of typing and message carrying. **1955** *Daily Progress* (Charlottesville, Va.) 24 Aug. 18/1 Pfc's with PhD's teach generals and others the fundamentals of atomic weapons. **1963** T. Pynchon *V.* i. 13, 'I would like to sing you a little song.' 'To celebrate your becoming a PFC' said Ploy... 'Pore Forlorn Civilian, We're goin to miss you so.' **1977** 'E. McBain' *Long Time no See* xii. 198 'A man named James Harris, served with the Army.'.. 'Rank?' 'Pfc.' **1972** *New Acronyms & Initialisms* (Gale Research Co.) 81/2 *PG*, parental guidance suggested (some material may not be suitable for pre-teenagers) (movie rating). **1974** *Daily Colonist* (Victoria, B.C.) 6 Oct. 27/5, 61 per cent rated the film PG (Parental Guidance) or G (General Audience). **1976** *New Yorker* 12 Jan. 70/2 Why would anybody want a PG-rated Peckinpah film? **1977** *Time* 11 Apr. 38/3 Modest, well crafted, less bloody and less bloody-minded than most TV shows, it is a PG film that any P ought to be happy to G the kids through. **1923** U. L. Silberrad *Lett. J. Armiter* ii. 49 They have made the suggestion that I should p.g. with them for the autumn and winter. **1925** F. Stark *Let.* 1 July (1974) I. 93, I am afraid I shall not be well enough to look after p.g.'s after all. **1933** M. Allingham *Sweet Danger* v. 62 We've got one P.G. already... She's been with us three years. **1959** D. Wallace *Richard & Lucy* v. 87 Terribly expensive rail fare, and they'd probably expect us to p.g. when we got there. **1972** *Times Lit. Suppl.* 28 Apr. 500/4 A decayed-gentlewoman's nice home for p gs. **1977** N. Slater *Crossfire* i. 22 I'm going to descend on you... I'd like to PG—handsome rental available. **1938** R. S. Woodworth *Exper. Psychol.* xiii. 277 The name 'psychogalvanic reflex' was introduced by Veraguth.., who made a comprehensive study of the Féré effect... In the present chapter we will call it PGR. **1949** *Brit. Jrnl. Psychol.* XL. 86 When the individuals' P.G.R. scores are obtained for a given attitude they must be expressed for each person relative to his own general P.G.R. reactivity. **1954** Woodworth & Schlosberg *Exper. Psychol.* (rev. ed.) vi. 137/2 The rapid changes in conductance have been studied extensively and suffer from too many names. The oldest is *psychogalvanic reflex* (PGR), but many dislike the implications that it is psychic or a reflex. **1962** *New Scientist* 22 Mar. 672 PGR (psychogalvanic response) records were taken for the same purpose. **1869** *Atlantic Monthly* Jan. 89/2 His cousin, the Ph.D. from Göttingen, cannot help despising a people who do not grow loud and red over Aryans and Turanians. **1903** W. James *Mem. & Stud.* (1911) 331 A Ph.D. in philosophy would prove little..as to one's ability to teach literature. *Ibid.*, He was of ultra Ph.D. quality. **1906** [see *D.Phil.* s.v. *D III. 3]. **1936** *Discovery* May 156 Julius Grant, Ph.D., M.Sc., F.I.C. **1966** J. Betjeman *High & Low* 40 Doubtless some pedant for his Ph.D. Has ascertained the facts. **1973** G. Mitchell *Murder of Busy Lizzie* xv. 174 Why should anybody want to strangle a harmless little Ph.D. like Mr Lovelaine? **1931** G. Irwin *Amer. Tramp & Underworld Slang* 144 *P.I.*, a pimp or pander, merely a euphemism by contraction. **1970** C. Major *Dict. Afro-Amer. Slang* 90 *P.I.*, pimp. **1960** *Acronyms Dict.* (Gale Research Co.) 165 PI..Private Investigator. **1970** G. F. Newman *Sir, You Bastard* vi. 170 The PI had his licence revoked. **1973** *Publishers Weekly* 13 Aug. 48/3 This is the third p.i. mystery featuring Shock and his partner. **1966** *Economist* 16 July 227/1 The Government should use the PIB only when it is ready to back the board's recommendations to the hilt. *a* **1974** R. Crossman *Diaries* (1975) I. 421 We can't afford to let the policy fail and yet quite soon we are going to face the 18-per-cent increase of army pay which the P.I.B. will almost certainly award. **1959** *Listener* 9 July 45/1 The widespread activities of the state security police, known as PIDE. **1970** *Ann. Reg. 1969* 276 On 19 November the [Portuguese] Government dissolved the PIDE and placed a similar organization under the direct control of the Ministry of the Interior. **1974** *Daily Tel.* 21 Aug. 4/7 The Portuguese Legion..was outlawed together with the PIDE/DGS. **1964** S. Bellow *Herzog* 257 Put on those p-j's now. **1967** R. De Sola *Abbrev. Dict.* (rev. ed.) 208/1 *Pj's*, peejays (pajamas). **1970** *New Yorker* 4 Oct. 122/3 (Advt.), Cotton sleep culotte rated perfect for P.J. parties. **1943** L. E. & J. B. Rhine in *Jrnl. Parapsychol.* VII. 20 This is the first of a long series of research reports describing experiments on what is called the 'psychokinetic' or 'PK' effect. The PK effect is colloquially called 'mind over matter', and means the direct influencing of a physical system by the action of a subject's effort, without any known intermediate energy or instrumentation. *Ibid.* 21 Up to the present, nothing has been published on the topic of the PK effect. **1949** *Mind* LVIII. 391 In PK the mind is supposed to cause changes in physical objects outside its own body, not by means of the nervous system and the muscular apparatus, but directly, by mere thought or 'will'. **1973** *Times* 4 Dec. 17/7 There is nothing new in PK (psychokinesis) and telepathy. **1976** *Times Lit. Suppl.* 13 Feb. 172/4 Demonstrating PK in chickens, and even in fertile eggs, which appear capable of influencing mentally an electronic randomizer controlling the switching mechanism of a lamp. **1939** J. S. Furnivall *Netherlands India* viii. 250 Semaoen, the leader of the revolutionary section, formed a Communist party (P.K.I.). **1944** B. H. M. Vlekke *Nusantara* xv. 341 On May 23, 1920, the Social Democrat Club of Semarang decided to take the name Communist Party of the Indies, in Malayan, *Perserikatan Kommunist di India* (P.K.I.). **1973** J. M. van der Kroef in R. F. Staar *Yearbk. Internat. Communist Affairs* 469 The oldest such party in Asia, the Communist Party of Indonesia (Partai Komunis Indonesia; PKI) formally came into existence on 23 May 1920 as an outgrowth of the 'Indies Social Democratic Association' founded six years previously by Dutch Marxists. **1964** *Observer* 19 July 8/6 The younger had been afflicted by the same dread disease—PKU (phenylketonuria)—which had produced retardation in her sister. **1976** *Lancet* 6 Nov. 1031/1 We have looked for differences in the mono-oxidation of phenylalanine between plasma (or serum) from normal persons and patients with P.K.U. Identification of different enzymatic activities within these two groups would be one of the first steps in the development of a test for diagnosing variants of P.K.U. **1962** E. Snow *Other Side of River* (1963) xxxix. 290 Chinese don't use the old word *ping*, or 'soldier', any more; the P.L.A. has only *chan-shih*, or 'fighters'. **1967** *Ann. Reg. 1966* 372 The Military Affairs Commission of the Central Committee appointed Mao's wife..'adviser on cultural work to the People's Liberation Army' (PLA). **1972** *Observer* 19 Nov. 8 The PLA is none the less a revolutionary army with traditions rooted in a guerrilla past. **1977** *Times* 12 Oct. (China Suppl.) p. iii/4 The People's Liberation Army, the PLA, is making little secret of its desire to modernize equipment under the leadership of Chairman Hua. **1925** *P.L.A. Monthly* Nov. 16/1 The warehouses of the P.L.A. become the Mecca of the woolbuyers of the world. *Ibid.* 22/1 Final tests preparatory to the opening of the P.L.A. automatic telephone system were carried out. **1936** *Discovery* Aug. 232/1 As for using it [*sc.* the Thames] for transport, that is left to P.L.A. tugs, brick-barges, and an occasional pleasure steamer. **1969** S. Hyland *Top Bloody Secret* i. 27 The PLA man in charge of the landing stage. **1898** W. J. Locke *Idols* xvi. 230 The great P.L.M. train carried Hugh swiftly northwards. **1919** R. Fry *Let.* 6 Oct. (1972) II. 458 The P.L.M. is really worse than the S.E.R... It's almost impossible to travel by it. **1948** W. Fortescue *Beauty for Ashes* xxxiii. 251 For the whole of my Paris visit..he was indefatigable in his attentions, finding a free Entr'aide car..to take me to my various destinations, and battling with the P.L.M. to get me a reserved seat and, if possible, a wagon-lit to take me to the South. **1972** R. Cobb *Reactions to French Revolution* iii. 87 The P.L.M... bypassed the river valley, to take in Montbard and Dijon. **1965** *Times* 23 Mar. 9/2 Ahmad Shukairy, leader of the Palestine Liberation Organization (P.L.O.) has extended his search for help to China. **1974** *Guardian* 23 Jan. 2/4 According to the official Egyptian news agency, Yasser Arafat, the PLO chairman, addressed a message disowning the PLO statement. **1974** *Jewish Chron.* 20 Dec. 11/1 The Palestinians, through the PLO, must show magnanimity and statesmanship. **1976** *Time* 27 Dec. 14/1 Although badly battered from its losing role in the Lebanese civil war, the P.L.O. remains an important force. **1965** *PL/I: Language Specifications* (IBM Form C28-6571-0) *title-page,* This manual is a description of the full facilities of PL/I to be implemented under Operating System/360. **1966** E. A. Weiss *PL/I Converter* p. iii, Many of the limitations..of FORTRAN have been eliminated in PL/I. **1970** A. Cameron et al. *Computers & Old Eng. Concordances* 27, I myself will be very surprised if the next generation of machines will not accept Fortran programming and probably Cobol, Algol, and PL I programming. **1972** *Computers & Humanities* VII. 12 Work in language computation is frequently done in PL/I. **1955** R. T. McKenzie *Brit. Pol. Parties* vii. 385 As a prelude to a discussion of the contemporary structure of the PLP it is necessary to recall that the party in Parliament from its earliest years was plagued by two problems. **1963** Butler & Freeman *Brit. Pol. Facts 1900–60* ii. 94 During the war-time coalition the P.L.P. elected an Administrative Committee of twelve, with Peers' representation, all of whom were non-ministers. **1974** *Times* 22 Mar. 1/8 (*heading*) Mr Mikardo elected PLP head. **1976** H. Wilson *Governance of Britain* viii. 160 A Labour prime minister has to operate in a number of intersecting party political circles. The first is PLP meetings. **1968** *McGraw-Hill Yearbk. Sci. & Technol.* 359/1 A portable life support system (PLSS) back pack will provide breathing oxygen, suit pressurization, carbon dioxide removal, liquid cooling and oxygen temperature control, biomedical monitoring package, suit pressure and high oxygen flow sensors, and communications. **1970** N. Armstrong et al. *First on Moon* iii. 63 Complete with the PLSS, the Armstrong and Aldrin suits weighed one hundred eighty-three pounds. **1764** A. Williams *Universal Psalmodist* (ed. 2) 87 Hallifax. Hymn 50th..P.M. *Ibid.* 91 Dalston. Psalm 122^d^ Dr W. P.M. **1798** [see Metre *sb.*¹ 1 b]. *a* **1912** W. T. Rogers *Dict. Abbrev.* (1913) 152/2 *P.M.* (mus.), peculiar metre (of hymns). *c* **1830** in M. Johnson *Amer. Advertising, 1800–1900* (1960), Worcester, Ms. and New York Mail Stage Line..leaves Worcester, Wednesday and Saturday mornings at 3, and arrives in Norwich at 4 same p.m. *Ibid.*, The Fanny..arrives in Norwich next morning; and in Worcester, by stage, in the p.m. **1845** *Punch* VIII. 54/2 The lights along the Hampstead Road still persist in turning day into night, and burning for several hours after P.M. **1965** *New Statesman* 23 Apr. 661/3 While I am abroad..entries must reach the office Monday p.m. **1974** F. Nolan *Oshawa Project* xx. 119 Staff meeting this pm at 1500 hours. **1911** Webster, *P.M.* or *p.m.*..post mortem, or post mortem examination. **1922** *Lancet* 12 Aug. 358/1 It seems possible that death resulted from a dislocation of the neck. Were the vertebræ examined p.m.? **1928** D. L. Sayers *Unpleasantness at Bellona Club* xvi. 187 The advisability of a P.M. in all cases of sudden death. **1938** S. Beckett *Murphy* xii. 259 They carried him into the p.m. room. **1973** R. Hill *Ruling Passion* I. ii. 15 We haven't had the PM yet, but the doctor was very certain it happened last evening. **1907** W. S. Churchill *Let.* 27 Mar. in R. S. Churchill *Winston Churchill* (1969) II. Compan. I. 653 Could not you or the PM send him a 'private & personal' urging him not to fail us. **1915** Lloyd George *Family Lett.* (1973) 178 It was found impossible ..for the P.M. to hold Exchequer during the time I am occupied in organising Munitions. **1972** M. Sinclair *Norslag* ii. 15 The P.M. wants you round at the Cabinet Office. **1948** Schour & Massler in *Jrnl. Dental Res.* XXVII. 733 A quantitative method of assessing the prevalence of gingivitis in large groups of persons is proposed. Each gingival unit consisting of a papillary portion (P), a marginal portion (M), and an attached portion (A) is examined and counted separately. This method is tentatively termed the P-M-A-Index (P-papillary gingivitis; M-marginal gingivitis; A-attached gingivitis). **1962** Blake & Trott *Periodontology* iii. 27 The difficulty of assessment of gingivitis has been partly overcome by the use of the P.M.A. index. **1969** *Gloss. Terms Dentistry (B.S.I.)* 67 *P.M.A. index* (papillary, marginal and attached index), an epidemiological index for scoring the extent of gingival inflammation. **1890** Webster, *P.M.G.*, Postmaster-general. **1908** G. B. Shaw *Coll. Lett.* (1972) II. 803 Your letter..did not overtake me until I arrived here (Bayreuth), too late for a rejoinder to the P.M.G. **1927** [see *Franking machine]. **1968** *Listener* 29 Aug. 285/2 Vague recent statements by the PMG, Mr Stonehouse. *a* **1974** R. Crossman *Diaries* (1976) II. 71 When Ted Short replaced Tony Benn as P.M.G. the Post Office was delighted. **1942** J. Hammond et al. in *Jrnl. Agric. Sci.* XXXII. 308 To avoid the constant use of cumbersome phrases, gonadotrophic extracts of the urine of pregnant women (chorionic gonadotrophin) are referred to throughout the text as 'U.P.', and extracts of the serum of pregnant mares as 'P.M.S.' **1957** *Times* 2 Dec. (Agric. Suppl.) p. vi/2 In experiments with Romney Marsh, Cheviot and Southdown sheep, P.M.S. injections have increased the number of lambs born of each ewe mated. **1970** W. H. Parker *Health & Dis. in Farm Animals* vii. 84 The method that appears most likely to succeed is a combination of progesterone and P.M.S. **1959** K. D. Kryter in *Jrnl. Acoustical Soc. Amer.* XXXI. 1425/1 The translation from perceived noisiness in noys to perceived noise level in PNdb is expressed by the equation PNdb = $(1.2T \log_{10} N)/0.03$, where N is the number of noys. By definition, the perceived noise level of sound 'X' (in PNdb) is the sound pressure level in db *re* 0·0002 μbar of the 910–1090 cps band of random noise that is judged by an average listener to be acceptable (or, inversely, as unacceptable) as sound 'X', under specified conditions of listening and testing. **1966** *Science* 18 Mar. 1346/3 As a practical matter, the loudness level, in phons, and the perceived noise level, in PNdb's, of a sound are usually calculated from acoustical measures of the sound rather than found by subjective judgement tests. **1971** *New Scientist* 18 Mar. 604/1 In calculating the NNI for any given point, a number of standard flight paths are assumed and the PNdB level for each type of aircraft moving along each possible flight path is then calculated, together with the number of aircraft movements. *a* **1912** W. T. Rogers *Dict. Abbrev.* (1913) 153/1 *P.N.E.U.*.., Parents' National Educational Union. **1931** *Times Educ. Suppl.* 14 Mar. 98/1 P.N.E.U. methods.. The paper on English Teaching..is of especial interest to the Parents' National Educational Union. **1972** R. Asher *Talking Sense* viii. 103, I was looking at the material my daughter of thirteen is studying at the P.N.E.U. school she attends. **1824** E. Weeton *Jrnl.* May (1969) II. 280, I wished to see the General Post Office.. I was close by the P.O., and could not tell which was it. **1861** Geo. Eliot *Let.* 17 May (1954) III. 415 You are at liberty to imagine a kiss from me, or else to accept a note for it payable at sight. They don't give *P.O.*'s for such payment here. **1891** A. Beardsley *Let.* 25 Dec. (1971) 31, I shall be glad of a few more copies of the November *Bee*, so enclosed PO for 1/-. **1973** *Guardian* 18 Apr. 12/3 Is not the ratio of inland to EEC-bound mail such that the PO (which is no longer G) would more than cover its costs. **1944** J. H. Bagot *Punitive Detention* i. 13 In the years 1936 to 1939 a marked tendency is disclosed for the proportions discharged P.O.A. and fined to decrease and for the proportion placed on probation to increase. **1945** *N. & Q.* 10 Mar. 106/1 'Dismissed P.O.A.' simply means that a case is dismissed under the Probation of Offenders Act, 1907.. Such dismissals are of such daily occurrence in the courts that P.O.A. are initials as commonly understood as are R.A.F. or Y.M.C.A. in their respective spheres. **1859** P.O.D. [see *C.O.D.]. **1890** Webster, *P.O.D.*, Post-Office Department; pay on delivery. **1870** A. J. Munby *Diary* 13 July in D. Hudson *Munby* (1972) 288 Today the Thames Embankment was opened, *not* by the Queen, but by the P. of W. and his sister Louise. **1974** *Listener* 3 Jan. 17/2 Lord Berners..invited a smart lady to luncheon to meet 'the P of W'. She arrived agog, expecting to meet the Prince of Wales and found it was the Provost of Worcester. **1944** *Times* 7 June 6/1 The operational planning for invasion had to be interpreted at an early stage in terms of P.O.L. requirements. **1955** *Bull. Atomic Sci.* Feb. 56/3 As it was, POL (gasoline and liquid fuels) *were* excluded from Pusan and unloaded by offshore floating lines. **1977** *R.A.F. News* 22 June–5 July 11/3 Training is centred on the ground attack role, with simulated attack profiles (SAPs) being flown against..POL objectives (Petrol, Oil, Lubricants). **1856** J. A. Symonds *Let.* 28 June (1967) I. 75 Thank Papa very much for the P.[ost] O.[ffice] O.[rder] which I got cashed without difficulty. **1886** W. S. Churchill *Let.* 13 July in R. S. Churchill *Winston Churchill* (1967) I. Compan. I. iv. 123, I received the P.O.O. which you sent me and am very thankful for it. **1966** Gurnett & Kyte *Cassell's Dict. Abbrev.* 169/2 *P.O.O.*, Post Office Order. **1968** *Which?* 11 Jan. 2/2 The Post Office have told us that they are introducing a new system of envelope sizing, called Post Office Preferred (POP). Packets which are not the size the Post Office prefers will not qualify for the cheapest postal rates. **1971** D. Potter *Brit. Eliz. Stamps* ix. 95 As part of the standardisation programme, the Post Office issued POP (Post Office Preferred) sizes during the course of 1968. **1895** W. K. Burton *Man. Photogr.* viii. 126 Paper for the [gelatino-chloride] process..is sold under various names... Examples are 'Solio-artistotype', 'Artisto-platino' and 'P.O.P.' **1925** P. R. Salmon *All about Photogr.* xx. 94 There is practically no difference between the cost of a finished print on P.O.P. and one on self-toning paper. **1972** A. Tyrrell *Basics of Reprogr.* vi. 105 POP should perhaps be remembered as more nearly a reprographic than a photographic process. **1955** *Science* 9 Dec. 1139/3 A solution of 0·4-percent PPO and 0·01-percent 1,4-di(5-phenyl-2-oxazolyl)benzene (POPOP) has been used, which gives..a pulse height of 121 percent. **1975** *McGraw-Hill Yearbk. Sci. & Technol.* 261/2 The scintillator dye POPOP, heated in an oven to a vapor pressure of about 10 torrs.., when pumped with 400 kW of ultraviolet light from a nitrogen laser, has produced 30 kW of tunable laser output. **1937** F. Borkenau *Spanish Cockpit* ii. 82 The depth of the antagonism between Esquerra and PSUC on the one hand and CNT and POUM on the other becomes intelligible. **1940** N. Mitford *Pigeon Pie* iii. 48 'It's Hitler and Stalin now, don't forget the wedding bells.' Mary had gone P.O.U.M., so she grudgingly conceded this point. **1916** F. M. Ford *Let.* 23 Aug. (1965) 69 The P.O.W.—who was quite unrecognizable, was perfectly businesslike. **1966** Gurnett & Kyte *Cassell's Dict. Abbrev.* 170/1 *P.O.W.*..Prince of Wales. **1919** W. H. Downing *Digger Dial.* 39 P.O.W., prisoner of war. **1941** *War Illustr.* 31 Jan. 101/1 P.O.W. camps in Germany and Poland are shown in this map. **1953** *News Chron.* 2 June 2/3 In Pusan..Pyun Yung Tai repeated his threat that foreign troops arriving to supervise P.o.W.s after a ceasefire would have to 'fight their way into Korea'. **1957** J. Braine *Room at Top* xiii. 128 What do you think a POW gets to eat? **1973** *Black Panther* 21 July 6/3 Former POW Sergeant Robert P. Chenoweth, 25, of Portland. **1882** R. Bithell *Counting-House Dict.* 235 *P.P. Endorsements.* Endorsements by procuration—that is, *per-procuration*... The following is the usual form of a per-pro endorsement. 'Pay to the Order of Blanc & Co. 'Per Pro Shipley & Sons. 'Thos. Brown.' **1882** [see Per *prep.* I. 7]. **1922** F. von Hügel *Let.* 29 Nov. (1927) 364 Yours very sincerely F. v. Hügel (pp. S.B.). **1967** E. Lemarchand *Death of Old Girl* i. 12 All the other letters can wait... Sign the ones we've done p.p. **1724** *Short Explic. Foreign Words in Mus. Bks.* 53 The letter P is often used as an Abbreviation of the Word *piano*: and PP as an Abbreviation of the Words *piu piano*: and PPP as an Abbreviation of the Word *pianissimo*. **1966** *Listener* 2 June 815/2 Helga Pilarczyk..often ignored the composer's repeated demands for *pp* or sometimes *ppp* singing. **1925** Goldberger & Tanner in *Public Health Rep.* (U.S. Public Health Service) XL. 77 It would seem as if the heretofore unrecognized pellagra-preventive factor, to which we shall hereafter refer as factor P-P, were capable of preventing the disease with little if any cooperation from the protein factor of the diet. **1926** —— in *Ibid.* XLI. 307 If the so-called growth-promoting water-soluble vitamin of the yeast is distinct from the antineuritic and from the P–P factor, then [etc.]. **1935** *Biochem. Jrnl.* XXIX. 2830 (*heading*) The vitamin B_2 complex. Differentiation of the antiblacktongue and the 'P.-P.' factors from lactoflavin and vitamin B_6. **1942** Bicknell & Prescott *Vitamins in Med.* v. 259 Nicotinic acid was at first hailed as the PP or pellagra preventing factor, but it is now known that pellagra is a multiple deficiency disease and that lack of nicotinic acid is only one of the factors in its causation. **1967** H. A. Guthrie *Introd. Nutrition* xii. 240/2 Niacin, another water-soluble vitamin identified with the B complex, has been known as nicotinic acid and as the pellagra preventative (P–P) factor. **1956** J. Cholak in P. L. Magill et al. *Air Pollution Handbk.* xi. 10 The normal fluoride content of the atmosphere is extremely low (2 to 8 ppb). **1970** *Nature* 25 July 403/1 Locally manufactured peanut butter was highly contaminated [with aflatoxin] in almost every case, with a mean approaching 500 p.p.b. **1975** *Ibid.* 23 Oct. 632/3 Figures in terms of p.p.b. (parts per 10^9) are as commonplace nowadays as p.p.m. once were and for some compounds analysts can measure as little as 1 part in 10^{12}. **1838** H. C. Robinson *Diary* 30 Oct. (1967) 190, I called with a p.p.c. card on Samuel Rogers. **1863** Mrs. Gaskell *Dark Night's Work* vii. 108, I don't see any reason he had to come calling and P.P.C.-ing. **1883** Kipling *Let.* 14 Aug. in C. E. Carrington *Rudyard Kipling* (1955) iv. 53, I distributed my P.P.C. cards. **1909** J. R. Ware *Passing Eng.* 191/1 *To P.P.C.* (*Soc.*, 1880 on), to quarrel and cut. **1966** Gurnett & Kyte *Cassell's Dict. Abbrev.* 170/1 *p.p.c.*, pour prendre congé, to take leave. **1960** *Brit. Med. Jrnl.* 10 Sept. 783/2 You cannot travel far in the United States hospital world nowadays before hearing the phrase 'progressive patient care' (P.P.C.)... P.P.C. is defined as 'the organization of facilities, services, and staff around the medical and nursing needs of the patient'. **1964** G. L. Cohen *What's Wrong with Hospitals?* vi. 128 The very consultants who attack P.P.C. for disrupting continuity of care champion the same idea in maternity units. **1934** *Amer. Rev. Tuberculosis* XXX. 766 Under current arrangements the Committee endorses the use of a special designation, namely 'Tuberculin, P.P.D. (Purified Protein Derivative)', by these two manufacturing houses. **1951** *Proc. R. Soc. Med.* XLIV. 1046 Even the best P.P.D. preparations on the market, of about 90% tuberculoprotein content, still contain appreciable quantities of polysaccharide and nucleic acid which are not known to be concerned in the intradermal tuberculin reaction at all. **1963** Lincoln & Sewell *Tuberculosis in Children* iii. 41 The Heaf test requires a special apparatus that makes 6 skin punctures 1 mm deep through a layer of concentrated PPD containing 100,000 TU per ml. **1955** *20th Cent.* June 584 Every university may have its department of economics or philosophy or sociology, but only Oxford —with or without sociology—has PPE. **1964** E. Waugh *Little Learning* viii. 173 A new, disreputable school named Modern Greats (now dubbed P.P.E.) was for 'publicists and politicians'. **1972** *Times Lit. Suppl.* 3 Nov. 1310/2 Edward Heath and Harold Wilson read PPE. **1945** *Electronic Engin.* XVII. 683/1 With the Battle of Britain by night must be associated..the use of G.C.I., or Ground Control Interception, which Dr. Denis Taylor developed, using the P.P.I. (Plan Position Indicator) for the first of its many applications. **1959** *New Scientist* 23 July 97/2 In the ppi system the position of the echoes with respect to the ship is built up in plan or map form on the face of a cathode ray tube. **1966** *McGraw-Hill Encycl. Sci. & Technol.* I. 163/2 PPI presentations also change with altitude and direction of approach, making identification more difficult. **1946** W. H. B. Smith *Walther Pistols* 26 The P.P.K. means *Polizeipistole Kriminal*, indicating that the arm is intended for detectives and other police not in uniform who need a smaller weapon which can be readily concealed about the person. **1948** —— *Small Arms of World* (ed. 4) 424 Characteristics of PPK Model: Length 5.8″. Barrel 3.25″. Weight 19 oz. Capacity 7. **1973** J. M. White *Garden Game* 173 The Jensen..had been thoroughly searched, but the PPK had been clipped back under the dash. **1975** J. McClure *Snake* iii. 36 Zondi..checked his PPK automatic. **1976** G. Seymour *Glory Boys* x. 121 For close protection work he favoured the PPK (Polizei Pistolen Kriminal) Walther... The PPK was a small weapon, manufactured..by..the Karl Walther factory at Ulm. **1947** *Proc. Soc. Exper. Biol. & Med.* LXIV. 165/2 The most reliable method for the identification of the P.P.L.O. is the use of stained agar preparations. *Ibid.*, The P.P.L.O. are resistant to sulfonamides and to penicillin. **1965** *Listener* 11 Mar. 372/1 Unlike viruses, PPLO can grow in the absence of living host cells. **1972** *Science* 5 May 504/1 The mycoplasmas (originally called pleuropneumonia-like organisms or PPLO) have been studied both by people who want to grow them for study because of their pathogenicity and small size and by people who want to get rid of them because they are common tissue culture contaminants. **1913** *Bull. Univ. Illinois: Water Survey Series* No. 10, 42 (*table*) Dissolved oxygen, p.p.m. **1948** *New Biol.* V. 64 At 1–5 ppm it can be used..as a means of inducing tomatoes to set without pollination. **1964** *Punch* 25 Nov. 806/2 A peregrine found dead on Lundy Island contained 78 ppm of total chlorinated hydrocarbon in its liver. **1936** H. Nicolson *Let.* 12 June (1966) 265 Then his P.P.S. took him by the arm and he left the House for ever. **1959** *Times* 23 Oct. 14/6 Mr. Barber had served as a whip before he became P.P.S. to the Prime Minister in February, 1958. **1973** O. Lancaster *Littlehampton Bequest* 94 At the last Government reshuffle he was appointed P.P.S. to the Minister of Exploitation. **1976** H. Wilson *Governance of Britain* ii. 30 Apart from this, my experience of consultation is that, in ninety per cent of the cases, the senior minister concerned recommended his own P.P.S. for promotion in his own or another department—advice I did not always follow. **1841** Dickens *Let.* 9 July (1969) II. 325 P.S. Half asleep... P.P.S. They speak Gaelic here. **1900** G. B. Shaw *Let.* 30 Dec. (1972) II. 216 PPS I have been reading 'Herod' (I never go to the theatre now). *c* **1921** E. E. Cummings *Sel. Lett.* (1969) 81 P.S. am waiting for you... P.P.S. Elaine writes your painting is awfully good... P.P.P.S. Enjoyed the Krazy [Kat] you sent B. **1967** *Listener* 21 Dec. 814/2 PS: There'll be a special Christmas edition of *Round the Horne*. PPS: The new series of *Round the Horne* starts in February. PPPS: No advertising. **1937** A. Huxley *Let.* 30 Mar. (1969) 416, I have talked to the secretary of the PPU and he agrees that it will be best to go ahead with the 6d. edition in paper. **1973** *Freedom* 1 Sept. 4/1 Convinced pacifists of the PPU type. **1948** *R.A.F. Rev.* Feb. 3 (*heading*) The path of the 'P.Q.'. **1962** *Observer* 6 May 21/5 The parliamentary question—the 'P.Q.' **1975** M. Sinclair *Long Time Sleeping* ix. 117 'Everything stops for a PQ,' he said... 'Is there a Parliamentary Question down?' Pringle asked. **1976** H. Wilson *Governance of Britain* vii. 132 Prime ministers approach the bi-weekly ordeal by questions in different frames of mind, but of two things I am sure: no prime minister looks forward to 'PQs' with anything but apprehension; every prime minister works long into the night on his answers. **1943** *Aeroplane Spotter* 3 Dec. 278 (*caption*) The De Havilland P.R. Mosquito. **1946** *R.A.F. Jrnl.* May 153 We are indebted for the photographs and specialized articles with which the P.R. people supplied us. **1958** *Times Lit. Suppl.* 24 Jan. 48/5 Another part of the secret was to have P.R. grouped together. **1851** *Art Jrnl.* July 186/2 A school..that..will continue to exist unless Mr. Ruskin and his friends the P.-R.s upset it. **1874** L. Troubridge *Life amongst Troubridges* (1966) ix. 75 Amy's present rage..is to make her room pre-Raphaelite, with a border of P.R. bulrushes all round it. **1829** P. Egan *Boxiana* 2nd Ser. II. 8 A boxer of considerable notoriety in the London P.R. **1863** 'Ouida' *Held in Bondage* I. iii. 64 Heroes of theTurf and the P.R. **1966** Gurnett & Kyte *Cassell's Dict. Abbrev.* 170/2 *P.R.*, Prize Ring. **1885** H. Sidgwick in A. & E. M. Sidgwick *Henry Sidgwick* (1906) 400 The application of the principle of P.R. to University Constituencies. **1909** (*heading*) P.R. Pamphlet No. 1 (Revised March 1909). **1924** [see *labour *sb.* 2 c]. **1935** H. Finer (*title*) The case against PR. **1974** *Times* 2 Mar. 14/4 If PR is to come in Britain the crucial issue is whether it is to be the single-member or multi-member kind. **1942** Partridge *Dict. Abbrev.* 77/1 *P.R.*.. Public Relations. (The publicity department of certain Services and Ministries.) **1944** A. Jacob *Traveller's War* 200 The remains of the P.R. unit set off down the desert road. **1963** H. Kubly *Whistling Zone* (1964) ii. xv. 177 Your students are giving you an excellent PR. **1977** *Time* 31 Jan. 48/3 The p.r. man behind this is the star. **1909** *Cent. Dict.* Suppl., *P.R.*, an abbreviation..(*b*) of *Porto Rico*. **1966** *Publ. Amer. Dial. Soc. 1964* xlii. 41 Terms used exclusively for Puerto Rican include..*P.R.* **1972** D. E. Westlake *Cops & Robbers* (1973) 9 There were no customers in there; just the Puerto Rican clerk... The PR was neutral as gray paint. **1895** G. B. Shaw *Our Theatres in Nineties* (1932) I. 32 If the friend of Sir Joshua Reynolds had been Sir David Garrick, and if every successive P.R.A. had had for his officially recognized peer the leading actor of his day. **1975** *Country Life* 18 Dec. 1736/2 Sir Gerald Kelly..the first of the televised art popularisers as PRA. **1849** D. G. Rossetti *Let.* 1 Oct. (1965) I. 73 Love to our family, the P.R.B., and all. **1850** W. M. Rossetti *P.R.B. Jrnl.* in *Preraphaelite Diaries & Lett.* (1900) 283 Collins has not established a claim to the P.R.B.-hood..the connexion would not be likely to promote the intimate friendly relations necessary between all P.R.B.'s. **1852** J. Brown *Let.* (1912) 128 The other morning I saw a scene which, were I a P.R.B. and a genius, I would make immortal. **1973** *Country Life* 8 Feb. 330/1 Rossetti is strangely well suited to one aspect of today's tastes... His aims went sensationally beyond those of his fellow members of the PRB. **1892** F. W. Maitland *Let.* 6 Sept. (1965) 105, I ought to be at P.R.O. next week. **1931** *N. & Q.* 5 Dec. 408/2, I cannot find the Returns of officers' services for these regiments at the P.R.O. **1958** *New Statesman* 6 Sept. 330/2 Farewell, adieu, BM and PRO, My time is up, reluctantly I go. **1941** H. Nicolson *Diary* 8 July (1967) 177, I drive down to White's Club with Duff [Cooper] and beg him to treat the P.R.O.s this afternoon with all gentleness. They are a touchy lot. **1966** 'H. MacDiarmid' *Company I've Kept* i. 22 Philip Jordan, Attlee's P.R.O., was with us. **1970** J. Tunstall *Westminster Lobby Correspondents* v. 56 The Prime Minister's scarcity value to the Lobby men allows him (a) to speak to the Lobby mainly through a P.R.O. and personally only on irregular occasions; (b) the P.R.O. still attracts a substantial daily attendance even when he says little. **1973** *Jrnl. Electrochem. Soc.* CXX. 1001 (*heading*) Reliability of NiCr 'fusible link' used in PROM's. **1977** *Sci. Amer.* Sept. 139/1 Information stored in ROM's and PROM's is nonvolatile. **1972** *Guardian* 1 Sept. 1/6 Prisoners were..vowing to stay up [on the roof] until the Home Office recognised the prisoners' union, PROP. *Ibid.* 1/8 PROP—'Preservation of the Rights of Prisoners'. **1973** D. Curtis *Dartmoor to Cambridge* xiii. 121 We decided to organise the British movement by forming a prisoners' union. That was the first step in the conception of PROP, the Preservation of the Rights of Prisoners, a movement that was destined to shake the British prison system to its core four years later. **1976** *Daily Mail* (Hull) 16 Dec. 11/4 PROP, the prisoners' rights organisation, is to hold its own public inquiry into the riot at Hull Jail. **1976** A. Miller *Inside Outside* xi. 176 Where PROP went wrong..was in inviting men to break the prison rules. **1927** *Melody Maker* Aug. 755/2, I am assuming..that the hall is not already licensed by the P.R.S. **1968** *Listener* 8 Aug. 177/3 A lot of the more superior publishers..weren't members of the PRS. **1616** T. Roe *Let.* 30 Nov. in *Embassy to Court of Gt. Mogul* (1899) II. 359 P.S.—I humbly desire your Honor to doe me the fauour to thanck Sir Thomas Smyth in my behalfe. **1757**, etc. P.S. [see main entry in Dict.]. **1771** J. Wedgwood *Let.* 11 May (1965) 108 PS The letter to which this is a ps I did not like to send by the post. **1842** Dickens *Let.* 1 May (1974) III. 228 Look over leaf for the PS. **1853** Mrs. Gaskell *Cranford* ix. 163 So she ended her letter; but in a P.S. she added, she thought she might as well tell me what was the peculiar attraction to Cranford just now. **1969** *Listener* 15 May 682/3 PS. These are only hints. Please do not repeat verbatim. **1790** P.S. [see O.P. s.v. *O 5 d]. **1838** R. B. Peake *Quarter to Nine* i, in B. Webster *Acting National Drama* II. 5 Apartment; Frolick's lodgings; closet door. Enter Mrs. Jervis, P.S. **1942** Partridge *Dict. Abbrev.* 78/2 *p.s.*, prompt side (of a theatre). Also *P.S.* **1896** *Oxfordshire Light Infantry Chron. 1895* 26 Lt.-Colonels... (1) Johnstone, J., *p.s.c.* 16 Mar. 92. **1920** *Punch* 24 Mar. 225/1 Upon my first arriving on his Staff he had said to me, 'Oh, by the way, P.S.C., of course?'.. 'You have Passed Staff College, of course?' he said a little less affably. **1972** *Times* 7 Sept. 16/2 Without the magic letters 'psc' (passed staff college) after their names their chances of being promoted above major are, at best, doubtful. **1944** E. W. F. Feller *Air Compressors* xiv. 438 Figure 410 shows the piping arrangement for the 250 psi method. **1959** *Motor* 2 Sept. 75/2 This is with 5·90–13 Goodyear tubed tyres, inflated to 26 p.s.i. back and front. **1968** M. Woodhouse *Rock Baby* xviii. 183 She fitted a little pressure gauge to the drill-guide... The needle on the gauge flicked across at once, to nine p.s.i. **1975** *Offshore Engineer* Sept. 44/1 Phillips has a contract with the British Gas Corporation (BGC) to meet the required amount per day at a specified pressure which is 1,000psi. **1951** psia [see *isentropically* adv. s.v. *iso-]. **1975** *Petroleum Rev.* XXIX. 91/1 The stabilised crude, with a vapour pressure of 5–7 psia, will be piped to the Greatham site. **1932** *Motor Transport* 28 Mar. 351/3 A bus driver who was refused a p.s.v. driving licence..has appealed with success to a bench of magistrates. **1944** L. D. Kitchin *Road Transport Law* 9/2 Every p.s.v., except those first registered on or before January 1, 1932, must be capable of turning in a circle not exceeding 60ft. **1972** *Police Rev.* 1 Dec. 1577/1 A licensed p.s.v. is not being used as a p.s.v. when it is not carrying passengers. **1922** T. E. Lawrence *Let.* 1 Sept. (1938) 364 If I can get able to sleep, and to eat the food, and to go through the P.T. I'll be all right. **1938** *Times* 14 Feb. 10/4 A Half-Day Course in P.T. **1965** W. Lamb *Posture & Gesture* viii. 107 If a woman she may be respected for her vigour but is too likely to be drained of feminine attractiveness—'P.T. hag' is the profession's own term. **1973** M. Amis *Rachel Papers* 137 The Darwin-born PT instructress, on the other hand, her glossy shoulder-muscles rippling in the ninety-degree heat, threw her bulk round the court in frank virility. **1958** *People* 4 May 2/1 (Advt.), Victor £498 plus £250 7s. PT. **1963** *Which?* Mar. 71/1 [Price] excluding 10 per cent P.T. **1966** *Punch* 27 July 132/2 The Government's determination not to flinch, if necessary, from a ten per cent PT increase on musical instruments? **1925** *Kansas City* (Missouri) *Star* 4 Feb. 11/1 (*heading*) P.-T.-A. plans celebration. **1962** L. Deighton *Ipcress File* xviii. 106 The old stuff about re-treads, P.T.A. meetings, and where to go for a good divorce. **1973** J. Burrows *Like an Evening Gone* iv. 47 We're doing a P.T.A. play at the school. **1976** *Publ. Amer. Dial. Soc. 1973* lx. 12 Mother of Informant 8. Active in church affairs and P.T.A. **1942** PT boat [see *expendable *a.*]. **1961** W. Vaughan-Thomas *Anzio* v. 67 On 28 January Clark himself, after being nearly killed on the deck of his PT boat, arrived at Anzio. **1974** *Lebende Sprachen* XIX. 38/1 US *PT boat*—BE/US *motor torpedo boat*, BEa. *E-boat*. Schnellboot. **1932** Blakeslee & Fox in *Jrnl. Heredity* XXIII. 97/1 The long name, phenyl-thio-carbamide, we are shortening to the nickname *P.T.C.*, an abbreviation which we shall use throughout this paper. *Ibid.* 98/1 To those who find P.T.C. strongly bitter, it seems incredible that any one could call it tasteless. **1965** *Punch* 10 Nov. 688/1 Tallness, or colour-blindness, or the ability to taste the substance known as PTC (phenylthiocarbamide) are inherited. **1976** PTC [see *phenylthiocarbamide* s.v. *phenyl 2 b]. **1909** *Army & Navy Gaz.* 1 May 430/3 Foil v. Foil (P.T.I's only). **1916** 'Taffrail' *Pincher Martin* iii. 45 The next turn was by the P.T.I. (Physical Training Instructor). **1964** J. Hale *Grudge Fight* vi. 92 Buck Jones the P.T.I. **1968** M. Woodhouse *Rock Baby* xxi. 202 He was wearing a sweatshirt and blue drill trousers, like a grossly overweight P.T.I. **1977** *R.A.F. News* 11–24 May 2/4 There will also be a trampoline display by PTIs of the RAF. **1859** Geo. Eliot *Let.* 24 Feb. (1954) III. 24 Yours ever truly George Eliot. P.T.O. I have reopened my letter to ask you [etc.]. **1902** H. G. Wells *Let.* 14 Feb. in *A. Bennett & H. G. Wells* (1960) 76 P.T.O. **1966** Gurnett & Kyte *Cassell's Dict. Abbrev.* 172/2 *P.T.O.*, Please Turn Over. **1951** A. B. Lees *Farming Machinery* xv. 144 If p.t.o.-driven trailers of compact design could be made available to hill farmers at an economic price they might well prove to be a major factor in increasing food production from marginal land. **1967** *Jane's Surface Skimmer Systems 1967–68* 64/2 Air can be supplied from a PTO-driven blower mounted on the tractor unit. **1973** *Country Life* 28 June 1904/2 The Bearcat combined roughage and grain grinder... Available as a pto driven static or trailed machine..[it] incorporates a pre-breaker with bevel edge. **1904** *Age* (Melbourne) 20 May 1 (Advt.), Ball and Welch Pty. Ltd. **1938** *Act* (Victoria) 3 *Geo. VI* no. 4602, sect. xxvi, § 5 The word 'proprietary' or the abbreviation thereof 'Pty.' shall form part of the name of a proprietary company. **1969** *Northern Territory News* (Darwin) 11 July 4/3 (Advt.), N.T. Real Estate Pty. Ltd. **1934** V. M. Yeates *Winged Victory* iii. ix. 365 'I wish you'd tell me what PUO means.' 'What do you want to know that for?' But the M.O. overcame his professional love of mystery, and added: 'It stands for Pyrexia of Unknown Origin.' **1964** M. Hynes *Med. Bacteriol.* (ed. 8) xii. 192 A clinical diagnosis of typhoid is rarely possible in the early stages, and the patient will be investigated as a case of 'P.U.O.' or pyrexia of unknown origin. **1976** *Proc. R. Soc. Med.* LXIX. 557/1, I..told him what a lot of interesting medical cases had come to the hospital under that useful army diagnosis of 'PUO'—pyrexia of unknown origin. **1933** C. Mackenzie *Water on Brain* viii. 112 'The P.U.S.?' 'The Permanent Under-Secretary,' Hunter-Hunt explained. **1974** P. Gore-Booth *With Great Truth & Respect* 324 What governed the whole of my life in this final period was the circumstance that, apart from the Secretary of State, the PUS was the only person in the Office whose obligation it was to have some knowledge of everything. **1939** *London Weekly Advertiser* 7 June 6/5, 35/- P.W. Incl. **1968** *Punch* 19 June 871/1 Let's be terribly sympathetic to the BOAC pilots, skilled, resourceful and too well-mannered actually to call their £30 pw pay rise offer 'insulting', the vogue word for this sort of thing. **1975** *Irish Times* 9 May 22/3 (Advt.), Rent inclusive of heating. £10 p.w. **1976** *Burnham-on-Sea Gaz.* 20 Apr. 7/7 (Advt.), I have sacked my advertising man. I have been paying him £1.15 pw and what do I get. **1909** *Cent. Dict.* Suppl., *P.W.D.*, an abbreviation of *Public Works Department*. **1922** G. Bell *Let.* 17 July (1927) II. xxii. 645 Mr. Cooke, Major Wilson and I accepted the invitation of Sabih Bey, Minister of P.W.D., to bathe from his house in Muadhdham. **1958** G. Durrell *Encounters with Animals* iv. 168 There was the little cockney P.W.D. man who..offered to drive me a hundred-odd miles, over atrocious African roads. **1971** *Illustr. Weekly India* 11 Apr. 45/3 Those of a structural nature which the P.W.D. were able and willing to solve. **1975** O. Sela *Bengali Inheritance* ix. 76 The flat was.. originally built for European PWD engineers. **1954** *Mech. Engin.* July 585/1 The Westinghouse Electric Corporation, as of July 1953, was assigned responsibility for the development and design of a pressurized light-water reactor (PWR). **1976** *New Scientist* 5 Aug. 290/2 PWRs are now better proven with a greater reliability than two years ago, and there are several large units now working in the US and West Germany. **1929** *Papers Mich. Acad. Sci., Arts & Lett.* X. 317/1 *PX*, post exchange. **1936** *Amer. Speech* XI. 62 The army took avidly to the name canteen—so avidly that after..the stores were officially re-named 'Post Exchanges', the name persisted... Even the modernistic abbreviation 'PX' does not seem to displace it. **1959** C. MacInnes *Absolute Beginners* 102 My ivy-league outfit a GI got for me last year from his PX. **1971** M. McCarthy *Birds of America* 184 If I give him a divorce, they'll take away my PX card and my QC privileges. **1975** *Publishers Weekly* 13 Jan. 59/1 Two American truck drivers get lost in Vietnam and take shelter in an abandoned supply depot that is still stocked with PX goodies like stereos, TVs and canned food.

b. *Teleph.* P = 'private' in PABX, private automatic branch exchange; PAX, private automatic exchange; PBX, private branch exchange; PMBX, private manual branch exchange.

1923 *P.O. Electr. Engineers' Jrnl.* XV. 309 On P.A.B.X.'s a jack is provided on the manual board for every line. **1976** *Computing Europe* 2 Sept. 5/2 Lines can be intercepted within buildings (particularly at PABXs or distribution boards) and even at Post Office telephone exchanges. **1923** *P.O. Electr. Engineers' Jrnl.* XV. 315 These plants are in some cases working as single P.A.X.'s. **1974** *Ibid.* Oct. *19* (Advt.), Pye Business Communications' capability in PAX and PABX telephone systems can improve the efficiency of your existing installation or provide you with a completely new system. **1976** *Eastern Even. News* (Norwich) 9 Dec. 16/2 (Advt.), Norwich Airport has a vacancy for a temporary Clerk/Telephonist (part-time) involving manual operation of a small PABX switchboard, some simple accounts and typing. **1917** G. D. Shepardson *Telephone Apparatus* xv. 253 The current through the talking subscriber's circuit experiences a considerable fall of potential due to the resistance in the trunk line between the control exchange battery and the P.B.X. board. **1940** R. Chandler *Farewell, my Lovely* xxxii. 240 A uniformed man dozed behind a pint-sized PBX set into the end of a scarred wooden counter. **1958** 'P. Bryant' *Two Hours to Doom* 19 He lifted the phone to the PBX. **1976** *National Observer* (U.S.) 10 Apr. 9/2 The FCC program, which takes effect Aug. 1 for the PBX, key, main, and coin telephones. **1932** Herbert & Procter *Telephony* (ed. 2) I. xiv. 614 Lines terminating on a P.M.B.X. are connected to consecutive jacks. *Ibid.* 619 The P.M.B.X. operator withdraws the plug from the exchange line jack. **1975** *Post Office Electr. Engineers' Jrnl.* LXVIII. 61/2 The PMBX No. 4 was originally designed to meet the requirements of single-position installations of up to 160 extensions.

c. p = *pico-, as in pF, picofarad(s).

1940 *Chambers's Techn. Dict.* 631/2 *pF.*, *pf.*, abbrev. for *pico-farad*. **1958** *Engineering* 21 Feb. 228/2 The sensitivity of the Tektor Major is better than 1·0 pF under all conditions.

d. P = 'poly-' in PCB, polychlorinated biphenyl; PTFE, polytetrafluoroethylene; PVA, (*a*) polyvinyl acetate; (*b*) polyvinyl alcohol; PVC, polyvinyl chloride; PVP, polyvinylpyrrolidone. (All these often occur with full stops, and some are occas. given in lower case letters.)

1966 *New Scientist* 15 Dec. 612/3 In Sweden, PCB is known to be used in electrical insulations, hydraulic oils, high-temperature and high-pressure lubricating oils, paints, lacquers and varnishes, and as pigments in various plastics. **1971** *Observer* 12 Dec. 4/3 Levels of PCBs..are roughly 10 to 100 times higher in plankton from the open ocean than from coastal waters. **1974** J. Burton *Pollution* v. 33 Thousands of seabirds died in the Irish Sea in 1969, and it is believed that PCB was responsible. **1977** *Jrnl. R. Soc. Arts* CXXV. 240/1 Our wildlife has..been affected by the accumulation of the persistent organochlorine pesticides and by PCBs. **1949** *Electronic Engin.* XXI. 220/1 Two new types of seals will shortly be available, one of which is made from an entirely new material, polytetrafluorethylene (P.T.F.E.). **1962** *Which?* Aug. 255/1 There are two kinds of non-stick frying pans—those with a silicone finish and those with a plastic called polytetrafluoroethylene, or PTFE. **1973** *Materials & Technol.* VI. viii. 545 Trade names of PTFE plastics include: Teflon (USA); Fluon (UK); and Hostaflon TF (Germany). **1943** Simonds & Ellis *Handbk. Plastics* viii. 393 (*table*) Polyvinyl alcohol 'PVA' Resin. *Ibid.* 1007 (*Gloss.*) Trade name/PVA Type/Polyvinyl alcohol Typical applications/Tubing, rubber substitute (see Resistoflex). **1960** *Farmer & Stockbreeder* 22 Mar. (Suppl.) 10/2 Again, modern materials come to the rescue, and this time it is the relatively new PVA (Polyvinyl acetate) emulsion. This is a synthetic resin which, when used in emulsion form and added to sand, cement, and certain aggregates, will give a jointless, waterproof floor. **1966** A. W. Lewis *Gloss. Woodworking Terms* 38 *Polyvinyl acetate* (*pva*), emulsion glue of a white creamy consistency. It is used cold and does not require a hardener. **1969** L. S. Mounts in W. R. R. Park *Plastics Film Technol.* v. 140 Three water soluble plastic films are currently produced from polyvinyl alcohol (PVA), methyl cellulose and polyethylene oxide. **1977** *36 Home Handyman Projects* (Austral. Home Jrnl.) 74/2 Cut thin strips of very thin felt and apply a PVA glue to one side of the felt. **1941** *Electronic Engin.* XIV. 541/2 Polyvinyl chloride and copolymers. Examples—Welvic, B.X.P.'s, 'P.V.C.', Chlorovene. **1957** *Economist* 12 Oct. 161/1 Similar plastic-coated steels, all using pvc, have been offered in the United States for some time. **1971** *New Scientist* 10 June 630 The PVC-coated fabrics that have previously been the main synthetic material used in women's footwear. **1972** *Country Life* 16 Mar. 612/1 Playing around with a few old bricks..and a cowl made of wire and pvc sacks. **1975** W. G. Roberts *Quest for Oil* (rev. ed.) vii. 77 Plastics, particular examples being Polythene, polystyrene, PVC and a number of synthetic resins. **1951** *Lancet* 19 May 1096/1 A Saline solution incorporating a p.v.p. compound was prepared and used in Germany with some success as a plasma substitute during the 1939–45 war. **1959** *Jrnl.*

Inst. Brewing LXV. 73/2 Beer can be chill-proofed, without risk of pasteurization haze, by adding PVP during storage in the cellar. **1966** J. A. BRYDSON *Plastics Materials* xiv. 286 In the field of cosmetics p.v.p. is used because of its unique property of forming loose addition compounds with skin and hair. Hair lacquers may be formulated based on 4–6% p.v.p. in ethyl alcohol. **1974** M. C. GERALD *Pharmacol.* ix 164 The plasma substitutes, dextran and polyvinylpyrrolidone, PVP.

III. 1. *P trap*, a trap consisting of a U bend the upper part of whose outlet arm is bent horizontal or nearly so.

1885 P. J. DAVIES *Stand. Pract. Plumbing* I. 103 Fig. 205 is the ordinary half ∽-trap, wrongly called ᴝ-trap. **1890** W. R. MAGUIRE *Domestic San. Drainage* vi. 206 No. 1 is the S-trap; No. 2, half S-trap; No. 3, P-trap. **1976** R. DAY *All about Plumbing* 64/1 In a ground floor w.c. it is usual to fit an S trap,..but in an upstairs floor w.c., a P trap is usually installed.

2. *p* or *P* (*Physics* and *Chem.*) = principal: orig. used to designate one of the four main series of lines in atomic spectra, but now more frequently applied to electronic orbitals, states, etc., possessing one unit of angular momentum.

1890 J. R. RYDBERG in *Phil. Mag.* XXIX. 335 A few examples will suffice to show the arrangement and the use of this system. K (D_1, 4) denotes the fourth line of the first diffuse series of the spectrum of potassium..Rb (P_{12}, 2) the second doublet of the principal group of Rb [etc.]. **1910** [see *F III. 1 j]. **1922, 1955** [see *D III. 3 b]. **1964** J. W. LINNETT *Electronic Struct. Molecules* ii. 29 In the oxygen atom two *2p* orbitals are half-filled..and so.. bonds can be formed to two hydrogen atoms.

3. [initial letter of *primary*.] Used, chiefly in *P wave*, to denote an earthquake wave of alternate compression and rarefaction (the faster of the two main kinds of wave transmitted through the earth).

1908 C. G. KNOTT *Physics Earthquake Phenomena* xi. 199 Although Rebeur Paschwitz had suggested the possibility, Oldham, of the Geological Survey of India, was the first clearly to establish the existence in the complete record of two distinct phases in the Preliminary Tremors. These will be distinguished as *P* and *S*. *Ibid.* xii. 225 (*heading*) Chordal and arcual speeds of P and S phases of preliminary tremors in earth-radius per minute. **1936** V. B. MACELWANE in Macelwane & Sohon *Introd. Theoret. Seismol.* I. ix. 248 When it became clear that the *P*-waves were of the condensation-rarefaction type and the *S*-waves of the shear type, and individual earthquakes had been observed at a sufficient number of stations, attempts were made to draw up time–distance curves for the arrival times and to correlate these with the time of occurrence of the earthquake. **1966** *McGraw-Hill Encycl. Sci. & Technol.* XII. 152/1 The seismic body waves (*P*, *S*, and composite types like *PS*) have predominant periods in the range 1–15 sec, with *P* and *S*, respectively, at the short-period and long-period end of this range. **1971** I. G. GASS et al. *Understanding Earth* iii. 54/1 The core-mantle boundary is marked by an abrupt reduction in the velocity of compressional or *P* earthquake waves.

4. On the analogy of *PH, used to denote the negative of the common logarithm of a concentration or activity expressed in moles per litre; similarly p*K*, the negative of the common logarithm of a dissociation constant; p*F* (see quot. 1971).

1924 N. H. FURMAN in H. S. Taylor *Treat. Physical Chem.* II. xiii. 828 By graphic interpolation, plotting —log *k* against pOH, we find pOH to be 5·1. **1929** H. T. S. BRITTON *Hydrogen Ions* iii. 43 The hydrogen-ion concentration has a *p*H value of $\frac{1}{2}pK_w$ at neutrality. **1935** R. K. SCHOFIELD in *Trans. 3rd Internat. Congr. Soil Sci.* II. 39 It has proved convenient to use a new scale, which I have called the pF scale, to express what has, in the previous pages, been called 'suction'... The symbol 'p' expresses its logarithmic character, while the symbol 'F' is intended to remind us that by defining pF as the logarithm of the height in centimetres of the water column needed to give the suction in question, we are really using the logarithm of a free energy difference measured on a gravity scale. **1946** LUTZ & CHANDLER *Forest Soils* ix. 292 Designation of the energy relations of soil water in terms of *pF* is analogous to specification of reaction in terms of *p*H. **1965** R. G. KAZMANN *Mod. Hydrol.* v. 141 The energy gradient of the soil (*pF*) works against the force of gravity. **1968** PASSMORE & ROBSON *Compan. Med. Stud.* I. vi. 5/2 In a solution containing a mixture of buffers the conjugate acid base ratio is determined at any pH by its p*K*. **1971** *Gloss. Soil Sci. Terms* (Soil Sci. Soc. Amer.) 12/2 *pF* (obsolete), the logarithm of the soil moisture tension expressed in centimeters height of a column of water. **1972** *Wastewater Engin.* (Metcalf & Eddy, Inc.) vii. 255 With pOH, which is defined as the negative logarithm of the hydroxyl-ion concentration, it can be seen..that, for water at 25°C, pH + pOH = 14. **1973** F. G. SHINSKEY *pH & pIon Control in Process & Waste Streams* i. 4 Increasing activity is indicated by a decreasing pIon.

5. *P-marker* (Linguistics) = *phrase-marker* (*PHRASE *sb.* 7).

1955 N. CHOMSKY *Logical Struct. Linguistic Theory* (microfilm, Mass. Inst. Technol.) x. 735 We define 'K is the P-marker of *Z*' as: K is the set of strings which appear as a line of one of the members of E, where E is an equivalence class of S_1-derivations of *Z*. **1963** CHOMSKY & MILLER in R. D. Luce et al. *Handbk. Math. Psychol.* II. 301 A grammatical transformation, then, is a mapping of *P*-markers into *P*-markers. **1964** E. BACH *Introd. Transformational Gram.* iii. 39 A representation of immediate constituent structure for a string, such as is given by a labeled bracketing or labeled tree, is called a *phrase marker* (P marker). **1967** D. G. HAYS *Introd. Computational Linguistics* xiii. 210 The parser would.. submit, to a higher level source-language processor or to a translator, base P-markers—constituency diagrams with all transformations undone. **1976** *Language* LII. 110 A successful asymmetrical derivation rule must operate on a P-marker and not on an individual lexical entry.

6. [repr. *proton*.] *p-process* (Astr.): a process believed to occur in stars by which heavy proton-rich nuclei are formed from other nuclei, esp. in circumstances of high proton flux such as may obtain in supernovae.

1956 F. HOYLE et al. in *Science* 5 Oct. 613/3 At such temperatures (*p*, γ) reactions occur in a time of the order of 10 seconds, even on the heaviest nuclei (*p*-process). **1957** *Rev. Mod. Physics* XXIX. 617/2 It is probable that the maximum number of protons which can be added to C^{12} through the duration of the *p* process is only two. **1977** J. NARLIKAR *Struct. Universe* ii. 50 Apart from these two processes there is a rarer process which produces proton-rich isotopes by exposing the r-process and s-process material to a fast flux of protons or of high-energy photons. This is known as the p-process.

paan (pān). [see PAN *sb.*[5]] = PAN *sb.*[5]; the leaf of the betel pepper, *Piper betle*, used to enclose slices of betel nut (*Areca catechu*) mixed with lime; also, the masticatory formed by this mixture. Also *attrib.*

1964 *New Statesman* 3 Apr. 517/3 Eating the green leaf called paan..and the nut of the betel palm..is common in India, in Malaya and in Ceylon... The best paan leaf comes from Banaras. **1967** SINGHA & MASSEY *Indian Dances* vi. 68 The betel or *paan* as it is called, is covered with silver leaf and sprinkled with rose water. **1971** *Illustr. Weekly India* 4 Apr. 48/1 Paan chewing is an ancient Indian habit. *Ibid.* 51/2 The Mughal rulers were great connoisseurs of paan. **1974** *Times* 7 Dec. 10/8 Paans, those leaf-wrapped chews.

‖ **pa'anga** (pā,ā·ŋgă). [Native.] The monetary unit of Tonga.

1966 *Times* 21 May 8 Tonga has decided against calling its new decimal currency unit the dollar because the native word, 'tola', also means a pig's snout, the soft end of a coconut, or, in vulgar language, a mouth. The new unit, to be introduced next year, will be called 'pa'anga', which has only two alternative meanings—a coin-shaped seed and, not surprisingly, money. **1973** *Whitaker's Almanac 1974* 986/2 Pa'anga (T$) of 100 *Seniti*.

paarlmoer, var. *PERLEMOEN.

PABA (pī:ē¡bī,ē¡·, pā·bā). *Pharm.* Also **Paba, paba.** [f. the initial letters of the formative elements of the chemical name.] = **para-aminobenzoic acid*.

1944 *Jrnl. Exper. Med.* LXXIX. 337 (*heading*) Comparison of PABA production by staphylococci (method of Lewis) with the concentration of sodium sulfathiazole required to inhibit *in vitro* growth of the cultures. **1945** *Proc. Soc. Exper. Biol. & Med.* LVIII. 262/1 In addition to its activity against typhus rickettsiae, preliminary experiments have shown that paba also inhibits growth of the rickettsiae of Rocky Mountain spotted fever. **1951** A. GROLLMAN *Pharmacol. & Therapeutics* xxvii. 606 The use of Paba has also been advocated in various 'collagen' diseases. **1963** *Times* 2 May 14/1 (Advt.), Para-amino-benzoic acid..has long been known simply as PABA which, even when pronounced 'pahbah' is clinically and aurally acceptable. **1966** *McGraw-Hill Encycl. Sci. & Technol.* XIII. 244/2 The mode of action of sulfonamides is considered to be an antimetabolite activity, dependent upon the inhibition of enzyme systems involving the essential PABA.

pablum (pæ·blŏm). Also **Pablum.** The proprietary name of a children's breakfast cereal. Also *fig.*

1932 *Official Gaz.* (U.S. Patent Office) 19 July 596/2 Mead Johnson & Company, Evansville, Indiana. Pablum. For specially prepared cereal food consisting of a mixture of wheat meal, to which have been added wheat embryo, dried yeast, powdered dehydrated alfalfa leaf and powdered beef bone prepared for human use. Claims use since June 4, 1932. **1941** *Trade Marks Jrnl.* 5 Feb. 47/2 Pablum... A food for infants and invalids. Mead Johnson & Company,..Evansville, State of Indiana, United States of America; manufacturers. **1953** POHL & KORNBLUTH *Space Merchants* i. 9 Over the breakfast juices and the children's pablum..they spoke persuasively to each other about how wise and brave they had been to apply for passage in the Venus rocket. **1956** P. FRANK *Forbidden Area* i. 40 He would want her to quit her job, and eventually..there would be children. She would find.. her research downgraded to equations involving boiled water, evaporated milk, Karo syrup, and pablum. **1964** A. TYLER *If Morning ever Comes* xi. 160 *Joanne* never picks up. I had to scrape pablum off the damn *toaster* this morning. **1970** *Listener* 22 Oct. 538 In one week Spiro Agnew ascribed moral decay to the universities, Dr Spock, and the Presidential Commission on Campus Unrest, which, he said, had produced a report which 'was sure to be taken as more pablum for the permissivists'. **1971** W. HILLEN *Blackwater River* ii. 9 After a start on pablum and eggs and milk..he developed into a strong dog. **1976** *Amer. N. & Q.* XIV. 147/2 Its [*sc.* Oscar Wilde's *The Happy Prince*] obvious allegory and its appeal to a patronizing benevolence are palatable as pablum, but hardly to be trusted to sustain Eliot's confused, but intellectual Fisher King.

Pabst (pabst). *U.S.* The name of a lager beer.

Registered in the U.S. as a proprietary name.

[**1906** *Official Gaz.* (U.S. Patent Office) 26 June 2969/2 Beer. Pabst Brewing Company, Milwaukee,..Used ten years..the name 'PABST' on the upper part of the band.] **1920** *Ibid.* 15 June 579/2 Pabst Brewing Company, Milwaukee..Pabst..Beer and Malt Extracts. *Claims use* since June, 1889. **1963** R. WELLEK in N. Frye *Romanticism Reconsidered* 112 'It is impossible to think seriously with words such as Classicism, Romanticism, Humanism, or Realism.'.. But of course these terms are not labels: they have a range of meaning very different from Pabst Blue Ribbon or Liebfrauenmilch. **1974** *Black World* Mar. 59/1 He opened the refrigerator. In its confines were two cans of Pabst. **1976** *Time* 27 Sept. 47/2 The room is a cacophony of the ping-pong-dingdingding of the pinball machine, the pop-fizz of another round of Pabst, [etc.]. **1977** *Time* 7 Feb. 60/1 Belting down tumblers of Jim Beam and Pabst, they compared horror stories.

pac (pæk). Also **pack.** *N. Amer.* [Of Lenape (Delaware) Indian origin.] **a.** (See quots. *a* 1877 and 1961; cf. *SHOEPACK.) **b.** With initial apostrophe, *ellipt.* for *SHOEPACK.

a **1877** KNIGHT *Dict. Mech.* II. 1590/1 *Pac; Pack*, a moccasin having a sole turned up and sewed to the upper. Though now made of leather of various kinds, the *pac*, as used by the Indians of the Six Nations, for instance, was made of hide boiled in tallow and wax; or of *tawed* hide subsequently stuffed with tallow or wax. **1922** *Outing* May 68/1 Footwear, pac boots 16 inches; rubber boots. **1931** 'GREY OWL' *Men of Last Frontier* 181 And here is where my hard-soled 'packs came in. **1944** *Sears, Roebuck Catal.* 345 Leather top work Pac... Not rationed... If you wear size 6½ or 7 shoe, order size 6 pac. **1961** WEBSTER 1616/1 *Pac* also *pack*,..2. a laced heelless sheepskin or felt shoe worn inside a boot or overshoe in cold weather. **1973** B. WRIGHT *Four Seasons North* 12 The trails are slippery in our rubber-soled pacs.

pace, *sb.*[1] Add: **III. 7. b.** *spec.*, in *Cricket*, the speed of a bowler's delivery; the velocity of a ball bowled. Also *ellipt.*, = pace-bowling.

1800 T. BOXALL *Rules & Instr. Cricket* 15, I think it very proper not to bowl always the same pace. *Ibid.* 34 The striker must judge for himself what pace the bowler is bowling. **1816** W. LAMBERT *Instr. & Rules Cricket* 18 Never bowl faster than you can do..well, varying your pace as you may judge proper. **1900** P. F. WARNER *Cricket in Many Climes* 90 In Cobb and Kelly the New York team had two capital bowlers. The former is right-hand, and varies his pace well. **1955** [see *back-lift* s.v. B*ACK- B]. **1976** *0–10 Cricket Scene* (Austral.) 7/1 Many [innings] have been an amazing barrage of brutal driving, hooking and cutting against both pace and spin.

c. *pace of the wicket, ground* (further examples).

1888 R. H. LYTTELTON in Steel & Lyttelton *Cricket* ii. 52 In back play, unless the ball is very short, the pace of the ground may beat a man. **1903** A. C. MACLAREN in H. G. Hutchinson *Cricket* ix. 252 Too much importance ought never to be attached to the opening game, owing to those who have not previously visited Australia being wholly unaccustomed..to the fast pace of the wicket. **1955** *Times* 9 May 15/1 He spun it, too, and one can imagine how dangerous he might be on wickets with any pace in them.

8. a. Later example with *hold*.

1893 *Nat. Observer* 30 Sept. 505/1 Watts would have made a better race with La Flèche if he had pushed to the front, since she can hold a hot pace.

b. *to go the pace* (further examples); *to set the pace* (examples).

1890 *Licensed Victuallers' Gaz.* 5 Dec. 363/1 Fresh from Oxford, Arthur had been going the pace. **1892** [see *BLIND *a.* (and *adv.*) 1 i]. **1905** A. BENNETT *Tales of Five Towns* I. 109 Well, you *have* been going the pace! We always knew you were a hot un, but really—. **1928** BARRIE *Peter Pan* I, in *Plays* 19 Nana must go about all her duties in a most ordinary manner..; naturalness must be her passion; indeed, it should be the aim of every one in the play, for which she is now setting the pace. **1928** E. WINGFIELD-STRATFORD *Hist. Brit. Civilization* II. iii. 1090 Britain was ceasing to set the pace to her neighbours; she was beginning to show signs of flagging in the race. **1958** *Engineering* 4 Apr. 424/2 Do things before anyone else not wait to see what someone else does—set the pace and keep them hopping.

IV. 14. pace-bowling (hence *pace bowler*), **pace-change, pace-man** (cf. senses 7 b, c above).

1951 *People* 3 June 8/6 Good news to-day about Alec Bedser and Trevor Bailey, the two pace bowlers likely to be chosen to open England's attack in the First Test. **1976** *Scotsman* 24 Dec. 15/7 But whatever flaws the Australian batting may suggest, their pace bowlers, Dennis Lillee and Jeff Thomson, seem the likeliest match-winners. **1958** *Listener* 16 Oct. 604/1 England had no powerful reserves of pace-bowling strength to call on. **1951** R. ROBINSON in A. Ross *Cricketer's Compan.* **1960** III. 396 Not satisfied with..a wide range of pace-changes, he rings in a leg-break or a round-armer now and again. **1974** *Times* 25 Nov. 10/2 Prasanna, coming in at No. 10, edged, slashed and drove the West Indies pacemen to distraction. **1976** *0–10 Cricket Scene* (Austral.) 11/1 The deadpan wickets in England were enough to cause a speedster to retire, but Lillee's speed genius and dedication earned him 21 wickets—more than any paceman on either side.

pace, *v.* Add: **2. a.** Also *fig.*

1921 W. DE LA MARE *Veil* 24 She paced in pride The uncharted paths men trace in ocean's foam. **1955** *Sci. News Let.* 26 Mar. 201/1 The red maple is one of the first trees to wear its now flower-patterned spring frock. Experts use it as a milestick for pacing spring weather northward because it is one of the few trees that grows from Florida to Quebec.

5. a. Also *transf.* and *fig.*

1961 A. BERKMAN *Singers' Gloss. Show Business* 65 *Pacing an act*, making a line-up plan of the songs used in an act, so that the interest and enthusiasm of the audience builds up to the end. **1962** *Listener* 31 May 947/1, I had been pacing him in meetings all over the country—that is, talking, to keep the crowd..until Cook should arrive. **1967** *Technology Week* 23 Jan. 64/1 The past history of the design and construction of the vehicles and their propulsion systems..has been paced by the major developments in the materials fields. **1968** *Globe & Mail* (Toronto) 15 Jan. 18/9 The Hawks outscored the Gens 4–1 in the third period to take the victory. Dennis Giannini paced the winners with two goals. **1968** P. OLIVER *Screening Blues* ii. 82 'Lining out' in which a lead singer paces a line and the congregation follows with the same line or a refrain response with a linear reply. **1969** *Times* 13 Dec. (Sat. Rev.) p. iv/4 He knows to a nicety just how to pace a book. **1973** *Internat. Herald Tribune* 15 June 15/4 In the American League, Jim Spencer drove in two runs, one with his third homer of the season, in the seventh, to pace Texas to a 4–2 triumph. **1977** *Sci. Amer.* June 138/3 It is the development of the remarkable military reconnaissance programs that has indirectly paced civilian technology in the postwar years.

b. *Med.* To make (the heart) beat at an appropriate rate by stimulating it with pulses of electricity.

1963 *Brit. Heart Jrnl.* XXV. 299 When the heart was paced by ventricular stimulation, mean left atrial pressure was higher..than when the atrium was paced at the same rate. **1973** SEGEL & SAMET in P. Samet *Cardiac Pacing* iv. 82 The coronary sinus provides another area from which the heart can be paced.

pace (pēi·si, pā·ke), *prep.* [L., abl. sing. of *pax* PEACE as used e.g. in phr. *pāce tuā* by your leave.] By the leave of (a person).

Used chiefly as a courteous or ironical apology for a contradiction or difference of opinion.

1863 *Fraser's Mag.* Nov. 662/1 Mendelssohn was an artist passionately devoted to his art, who (*pāce* Dr. Trench) regarded art as *virtù*. **1883** *Standard* 1 Sept. 2/2 *Pace* the late Sir George Cornewall Lewis, Mr. Scofield is right. **1911** *Chambers's Jrnl.* Nov. 720/1 The colour [of fruit]..is a tacit invitation (*pace* the gardener) to the feast. **1931** R. L. MÉGROZ *Joseph Conrad's Mind & Method* vii. 170 Stevenson..was regarded by the English critics who, (*pace* Mr. Olage) so dislike fine writing on fine subjects, as a master of prose in fiction. **1955** *Times* 7 July 9/6 Nor, *pace* Mr. Smith, was I for one moment defending immorality in the journalist. **1973** A. H. SOMMERSTEIN *Sound Pattern Anc. Greek* iv. 116 Indeed, pace Chomsky and Halle, we would probably want it to be impossible for mid glides to exist at all. **1974** 'M. UNDERWOOD' *Pinch of Snuff* iii. 23 It was something he greatly prized—*pace* Whitby-Stansford. **1976** *Conservation News* Nov./Dec. 4/2, I find (a) incredible (*pace* Herman Kahn).

b. In Latin phr. *pace tanti viri*: by the leave or favour of so great a man.

1771 SMOLLETT *Humph. Cl.* II. 101 Dr. Shaw..says, he has seen flakes of sulphur floating in the well.—*Pace tanti viri*; I, for my part, have never observed any thing like sulphur, either in or about the well. **1855** *Sat. Rev.* 8 Dec. 100/2 But who seeks for them in Harry Brougham's speeches, or even—*pace tanti viri* be it spoken—in Henry Lord Brougham's *Historical Sketches*? **1865** MILL *Exam. Hamilton's Philos.* xxvii. 544 Admiration, *pace tantorum virorum*, is a different thing from wonder.

paced, *a.* Add: **2.** Also *fig.*

1953 *Brit. Jrnl. Psychol.* Nov. 295 The task..was simply to touch the contact corresponding to the one lamp which was alight. In one condition (the 'paced' one) the lamp went out. *Ibid.* 296 Group II, which was paced, showed a fall-off. **1958** *Oxf. Univ. Gaz.* 27 Jan. 523/2 This year has seen the conclusion of a programme of work on 'Conditions influencing the rate of learning in paced and unpaced tasks'.

pace-maker. Add: **1. a.** Also, one of the leading runners in a race. Also *transf.*

1900 *Field* 4 Aug. 186/1 Up to this he had been one of the pacemakers, but even now he was not to be left behind. **1942** *Sun* (Baltimore) 29 Apr. 19/1 El Toreador scored by three parts of a length over Seaway, pacemaker for most of the mile and 70-yard route of the seventh event. **1951** R. & N. MCWHIRTER *Get to your Marks!* iii. 66 Latching on to an over-awed local pace-maker in a 3-man field, Whitfield swept through. **1957** J. PETERS et al. *Mod. Middle- & Long-Distance Running* xii. 55 He..missed a great opportunity of using Hansenne as a pacemaker. **1961** *Times* 11 Apr. 14/5 An athlete training with an automatic pacemaker. **1978** G. A. SHEEHAN *Running & Being* xii. 174 A pacemaker..had zeroed in on the perfect pace.

b. One who sets the rate of working for others or the standards to be achieved by others; a 'trend-setter'. Also *transf.*, of things.

1906 U. SINCLAIR *Jungle* xi. 130 They would get new pace-makers and pay them more. **1967** *Daily Tel.* 17 May 17/7 Public schools may well continue to act as pacemakers and trend-setters for this country's education as a whole. **1970** *Ibid.* 14 Feb. 9/8 Both Rameau and Gluck were pacemakers in their day, progressive composers who consciously set out to change the musical landscape of the society in which they lived. **1976** *Star* (Sheffield) 30 Nov. 14/4 Chris Guthrie's hopes of a return to face the Second Division's pacemakers Chelsea at Bramall Lane on Friday night soared today. **1977** *Times* 22 Dec. 12/5 Pacemakers to watch in 1978 are..good Victorian dining furniture, early Continental oak and walnut, and tallboys.

3. *Physiol.* **a.** That part of an animal's heart which determines the rate at which it contracts and where the contractions begin (in man and other mammals normally the sino-atrial node).

1910 *Heart* II. 39 The normal auricular complex is most closely simulated by beats excited from the neighbourhood of Keith and Flack's node. The pace-maker of the heart is therefore situated in the neighbourhood of the superior cavo-auricular junction. **1927** HALDANE & HUXLEY *Animal Biol.* vii. 146 In a mammal the beat starts at the entrance of the great veins to the right auricle in a special piece of tissue known as the 'pacemaker' which does not contract but stimulates the neighbouring muscle. **1951** *Ann. Surg.* CXXXIV. 8/2 Pratt..stated that the pacemaker is governed, at least in part, by the chemical content of venous blood returning to the right auricle. **1961** *Lancet* 9 Sept. 574/1 After a 550-volt shock complete auriculo-ventricular dissociation with a nodal or high bundle pacemaker at a rate of 30 per minute evolved spontaneously. **1968** PASSMORE & ROBSON *Compan. Med. Stud.* I. xxviii. 10/2 If the rate of discharge of the SA node is depressed, the portion of the heart with the next highest spontaneous discharge rate becomes the pacemaker, usually the AV [*sc.* atrioventricular] node.

b. A structure which controls the rate of rhythmic activity of an organ other than the heart.

1949 KOESTLER *Insight & Outlook* xx. 138 A certain region near the sinus end of the heart controls the rate of beat, and similar 'pacemakers' function in the stomach, the ureters, and so forth. **1963** R. P. DALES *Annelids* vi. 132 If there are two pacemakers maintaining two muscular activities it may well be asked if one can dominate the other. **1966** S. OCHS in E. E. Selkurt *Physiol.* (ed. 2) vi. 147 A pacemaker for rhythmicity of the EEG wave was located in the thalamus. **1974** MCLENNAN & SANDBERG *Synopsis Obstetr.* (ed. 9) x. 145 Any group of excited myometrial cells anywhere in the uterus may serve in the pacemaker role and initiate electrical propagation throughout the myometrium.

c. A man-made device which supplies electrical signals to the heart, stimulating it to beat at an appropriate rate.

1951 *Ann. Surg.* CXXXIV. 9/1 Our attention has been directed to the study of the problem of cardiac arrest to determine if the use of an electrical artificial pacemaker in resuscitation would be of value. **1963** *Daily Tel.* 16 Apr. 17/1 A transistorised pacemaker little bigger than a match box and weighing only a few ounces has been devised for implanting in the abdominal wall. **1967** *New Scientist* 9 Feb. 331/1 Battery-powered pacemakers normally need their batteries replacing after no more than 2–3 years, needing a surgical operation each time. **1974** *Times* 4 Mar. 6/6 He is to undergo an operation for the installation of a pacemaker to help him overcome a heart condition which has affected him on several recent occasions.

pa·ce-ma:king. [PACE *sb.*[1]] **1.** The act or practice of making or setting the pace for competitors in a race.

1896 ADE *Artie* xi. 94 Ain't I tellin' you that we done the pacemakin'? **1900** *Field* 8 Sept. 384/1 Pacemaking has long since exceeded the original function it was designed to fulfil as a preventive of waiting tactics in ordinary bicycle races. **1911** *Encycl. Brit.* XXIII. 854/1 An element unknown to sprinting enters into middle- and long-distance runs, namely that of pace-making. **1968** B. TULLOH *On Running* ix. 114 You can often help each other along by sharing the pacemaking.

2. *Med.* = *PACING *vbl. sb.* 3.

1963 *Amer. Jrnl. Cardiol.* XI. 594 (*heading*) Hemodynamic sequelae of idioventricular pacemaking in complete heart block. **1973** SCHERLAG & LAZZARA in P. Samet *Cardiac Pacing* xiii. 309 (*heading*) Pacemakers and pacemaking in the AV junction.

pa·ce-se:tter. [PACE *sb.*[1]] One who sets the pace, trend, or fashion. (Chiefly *fig.*)

1895 [see PACE *sb.*[1] 14]. **1946** *Sun* (Baltimore) 2 Aug. 14/1 Perlina, the early pacesetter, was second about two lengths in front of..White Ford. **1958** *Listener* 23 Oct. 653/3 The new middle-class society and the new pacesetters within it. **1961** *Times* 8 May 16/4 Music is limited to punctuation,..or the role of pace-setter for words and action. **1969** *Times* 22 Oct. (Ghana Suppl.) p. i/2 Ghana was the pacesetter for modern Africa when it became the first sub-Saharan black country to move from colonial status to independence. **1970** *Globe & Mail* (Toronto) 25 Sept. 31/7 Keith Alexander of Calgary continued to be the Canadian pacesetter, firing a 71 yesterday for a two-round total of 143. **1973** A. E. WILKERSON *Rights of Children* 307 The White House Conferences on Children have served since 1909 as pacesetters in child welfare. **1975** *N.Y. Times* 16 Oct. 43/7 'For all the city's problems, New York has been and will continue to be the pace-setter for a high quality of urban life in this country,' the developer said in an interview.

pa·ce-se:tting, *a.* [PACE *sb.*[1]] That sets the pace, trend, or fashion. (Chiefly *fig.*)

1965 *Economist* 13 Feb. 645/2 A moratorium on other settlements while a clearly 'pace-setting' wage claim for the year is under review. **1967** *Jane's Surface Skimmer Systems 1967–68* 1/1 If the pacesetting operations by British Rail and Hover-Lloyd alone cannot silence the sceptics, they can be invited to look to the Mediterranean. **1976** M. BIRMINGHAM *Heat of Sun* iii. 24 The educational initiative which the state had taken over in founding the pace-setting Achimota school.

pacey (pēi·si) *a.* Also **pacy.** [f. PACE *sb.*[1] + -Y[1].] Having pace or speed; fast. (*lit.* and *fig.*)

1906 J. J. MUNRO *Let. to F. J. Furnivall* (MS.) 25 Aug., In the practice of the day before yesterday, Cantab was perceptibly the pacier boat. **1927** *Observer* 29 May 28/4 These hitters, when once they get a real start, play havoc with pacey bowling. **1967** *Listener* 25 May 688/2 The production..is..pacey and vivid. **1968** *Daily Mirror* 27 Aug. 7/2 This is considered very pacey, which is the new word for trendy. Nobody, but nobody, says trendy any more. **1969** C. BOOKER *Neophiliacs* ii. 48 The whole world..had been reduced to the same grainy, pacy, ever more 'realistic' dream. **1969** *Pony* July 512/1 *Show Jumping Summer* is a 'pacey' book, in which events follow each other in quick succession. **1977** *Daily Tel.* 13 Jan. 17 (Advt.), The Celeste's low slung, pacey appearance isn't just for show. The 2 litre model has a top speed of 105 mph. **1977** *Times Lit. Suppl.* 11 Feb. 145/4 (Advt.), Pacy, turbulent story with an excellent and authentically researched diamond mining setting.

pachinko (pătʃi·ŋko). Also **pachinco.** [Jap. *pachin* onomatopœic word repr. the sound of something triggered off + *ko* dim. suffix.] A variety of pin-ball popular in Japan. Also *attrib.*

1953 *Encounter* Nov. 7/2 In Tokyo there are 5,000 registered *pachinko* halls. **1954** J. L. MORSE *Unicorn Bk. 1953* 262/1 An interesting development in Japan was the popular craze for *pachinko*, a kind of poor-man's pinball game. **1964** *Listener* 8 Oct. 540/2 Pachinko is played with handfuls of ball-bearings. You drop them, one by one, into the machine, flick them round, and if they land in a winning cup, the machine coughs back fifteen ball-bearings which are bought in the first place, twenty-five at a time, for fifty yen (one shilling). If you amass enough of them, they can be exchanged for prizes. **1971** *Guardian* 11 June 11/6 Pachinco machines, dozens of them side by side in rows..are all identical. A trigger shoots off a ball which may find its way into a slot and produce a jackpot of balls. **1973** A. BROINOWSKI *Take One Ambassador* v. 55 This [joint] next door's *pachinko*..reminds me of some of the leagues clubs at home. *Ibid.* 56 They'll [*sc.* the Japanese] ..spend their time in a useless game like this *pachinko*.

pachisi. Add: (Further examples.) Also played in other countries besides India. Also *attrib.*

The spellings *parcheesi* and *parchesi* are now usual.

1892–3 *T. Eaton & Co. Catal.* Fall & Winter 67/2 Games... Parcheesi, linen board, 50c. **1895** *Montgomery Ward Catal.* 235/3 Royal Game of Parchesi complete.. including..folding board,..8 dice,..and 16 counters. *a* **1910** 'O. HENRY' *Rolling Stones* (1916) 37 John Tom Little Bear, in full Indian chief's costume, drew crowds away from the parchesi sociables and government ownership conversaziones. **1948** C. MCCULLERS *Discovery of Christmas* in *Mademoiselle* Sept., Budge..was too little to count straight, to play Parcheesi, to wipe himself. **1950** O. NASH *Family Reunion* (1951) 15 They can't pass it in bridge or parchesi or backgammon. **1969** L. KENNEDY *Very Lovely People* i. 35 The first night we were there two girls came over with a parcheesi board, and for the next two months we played nothing but parcheesi. **1972** *Jrnl. Social Psychol.* LXXXVII. 108 This procedure was chosen over Vinacke's parchesi game and Gamson's simulated political convention to emphasize the relative importance of the subjects [*sic*] initial resources. **1972** *Listener* 13 July 51/3, I was playing a lot of board games at home. We had Pachisi, Monopoly..Chinese chequers and whatnot.

‖**pachuco** (pătʃu·ko). [a. Mexican Sp. *pachuco* flashily dressed, vulgar.] A juvenile delinquent of Mexican-American descent, esp. in the Los Angeles area; in extended use, a derogatory term for any Mexican-American. Also *attrib.*

1943 C. HIMES in *Crisis* July 200/1 *Pachuo* is a Mexican expression which originally meant 'bandit' but has degenerated by usage into a description of a juvenile delinquent... In Mexican districts in the county of Los Angeles, small bands of pachuos have organized into gangs to fight each other. **1944** *Time* 10 July 26/2 Pachuco... Mexican for zootsuiter. **1946** C. HIMES *Black on Black* (1973) 256 Some pachuco kids were ganged about the juke box, talking in Mex. **1947** *Common Ground* Summer 79/1 The Pachuco dialect is a mélange composed of *Caló*, Hispanicized English, Anglicized Spanish, and words of pure invention. **1950** G. C. BARKER (*title*) Pachuco: an American-Spanish argot and its social function in Tucson, Arizona. *Ibid.* (1958) 1. 13 In many cities of the American Southwest there are today Mexican-American boys who are known..as pachucos. These boys..may be distinguished by certain peculiar characteristics of dress, behavior, and language. **1954** J. STEINBECK *Sweet Thursday* 11 In Los Angeles..he led a gang of pachucos. **1966** T. PYNCHON *Crying of Lot 49* i. 11 Hostile Pachuco dialect, full of chingas and maricones. **1972** J. WAMBAUGH *Blue Knight* (1973) v. 70 *'Órale, panzón,'* he said, like a pachuco, which he put on for me. He spoke beautiful Spanish..but the barrios of El Paso Texas died hard. **1976** *Word 1971* XXVII. 294 Pachuco, also known as *tirili*, *tirilongo*, is used not only by felons, delinquents,..and others outside respectable society, but also by younger males throughout the Southwest as a street variety and for its slangy effect.

pachycaul (pæ·kikǭl), *sb.* (*a.*) *Bot.* [f. PACHY- + Gr. καυλ-ός stem, stalk.] A tree having a thick primary stem and few or no branches; also *attrib.* or as *adj.* Hence **pachycau·lous** *a.*; **pa·chycauly,** development of this type. Cf. *LEPTOCAUL *sb.* and *a.*

1949 E. J. H. CORNER in *Ann. Bot.* XIII. 392 The pachycaulous Cycad. *Ibid.* 393 The old clumsy pachycaul with massive and slow-growing branches. **1954** *Phytomorphology* IV. 264/1 In general, six effects accompany the transition from pachycauly to leptocauly. **1964** E. J. H. CORNER *Life of Plants* ix. 154 'Pachycaul' (with thick primary stem) denotes massive construction as of the rosette tree or cabbage tree. *Ibid.* 155 The pachycaul plants establish themselves by robust growth. **1967** E. A. MENNINGER *Fantastic Trees* 16 (*heading*) The pachycaulous trunks. *Ibid.*, One conspicuous example of this pachycaulous curiosity today in the forests of the Ivory

Coast and Nigeria is the aky tree, also called the forest papaw. Despite its enormous size..this tree's trunk is soft, porous, and spongelike, and it is generally unbranched. It is a living relic of an ancient age. **1973** A. J. Willis *Introd. Plant Ecol.* v. 55 A tendency to a pachycaul habit is seen in the ash, with its pinnate leaves and thick stubby twigs. **1974** *Kew Bull.* XXIX. 535 The pachycaul Giant Lobelias are some of the most spectacular plants of the tropical African highlands. *Ibid.* 549 In herbaceous species [of giant lobelia]..the development is similar to that of the forest pachycauls. **1974** *New Phytologist* LXXIII. 971, I propose a general hypothesis on the evolutionary trends involving pachycauly in *Senecio*. **1976** *Phil. Trans. R. Soc.* B. CCLXXIII. 359 The purpose of this account [of climbing species of *Ficus*] is to provide new evidence for the general theory of angiosperm evolution from pachycaul to leptocaul vegetation.

pachysandra (pæːkisæ·ndrǎ). [mod.L. (A. Michaux *Flora Boreali-Americana* (1803) II. 177), f. Gr. παχύς thick + ἀνήρ, ἀνδρό-ς male, in reference to the thick stamens of the male flowers.] A small evergreen subshrub of the genus so called, belonging to the family Buxaceæ, native to eastern North America or eastern Asia, and bearing white or pinkish-white flowers.

1813 W. T. Aiton *Hortus Kewensis* (ed. 2) V. 260 Trailing Pachysandra. Nat[ive] of North America. Intro[duced] 1800, by Messrs. Fraser. **1818** *Curtis's Bot. Mag.* XLV. 1964 Trailing Pachysandra... Pachysandra was first described in Michaux's Flora of North-America, and received its name from the remarkable thickness of its stamens. It has very little beauty to recommend it to the flower-garden; but the curious Botanist will regard it with some interest. **1914** W. J. Bean *Trees & Shrubs Hardy in Brit. Isles* II. 118 The Pachysandras thrive in any moist soil, and do not mind shade; they make neat tufts, but are of only moderate decorative value. **1941** R. S. Walker *Lookout* 52 Pachysandra, or mountain spurge, blooms in March and April in the rich soil in Lookout Mountain woods. **1961** *Amat. Gardening* 18 Nov. 1/1 The pachysandra is..one of those borderline plants that are half shrub half herbaceous perennial. **1975** *New Yorker* 23 June 38/3 Both laughing, he supervised John's spitting out the lettuce and paper and tobacco into the pachysandra.

pachytene (pæ·kitīn). *Cytology.* [ad. F. *pachytène* (H. von Winiwarter 1900, in *Arch. de Biol.* XVII. i. 63): see Pachy- and *-tene.] The third stage of the first meiotic prophase, following zygotene, during which the paired chromosomes shorten and thicken, the two chromatids of each separate, and exchange of segments between chromatids may occur.

[**1900** *Jrnl. R. Microsc. Soc.* 654 As the chromatic thread spreads itself again through the nuclear space, this duality disappears, and the thread is single, thick, and moniliform (pachytænic stage).] **1912** *Jrnl. Exper. Zool.* XIII. 378 All the threads still stain deeply and are very much thicker than in the leptotene-stage; hence these nuclei may be called the pachytene-nuclei. **1932** *Proc. 6th Internat. Congr. Genetics* I. 257 It is assumed that every chiasma represents a crossover which has occurred between two of the four chromatids at pachytene. **1965** Bell & Coombe tr. *Strasburger's Textbk. Bot.* 34 In pachytene the pairing of homologous chromosomes is completed. **1974** *Cytogenetics & Cell Genetics* XIII. 330 Breakdown of spermatogenesis at the pachytene stage of meiotic prophase was observed in most germ cells.

pacifarin (pǣsi·fǎrin). *Med.* [f. L. *pāci-f(ic)ār-e* to make peace + -in[1].] Any biologically produced substance which, when introduced into an organism, protects it from the harmful effects of an infection without killing the pathogen.

1963 H. A. Schneider in *Proc. Amer. Philos. Soc.* CVII. 445/2 As a new and third category of ecological ectocrines, which already embraces vitamins and antibiotics, we add as the first example of its class the substance I have described above, and name the class 'pacifarins' from the Latin verb 'pacificare', to make peace, to pacify. (I wish to thank my colleague, Dr. Ludwig Edelstein, for guiding me in this choice.) The particular pacifarin, the salmonellosis pacifarin, is, we believe, addressed only to the typhoid diseases, and for other diseases there are, we postulate, other pacifarins waiting to be identified. **1967** *Daily Tel.* 10 May 14/6 The basis of the discovery is that a microscopic amount of pacifarin extracted from wheat and dried egg-white will protect mice against infection by salmonella. **1975** *Infection & Immunity* XI. 69/2 Certain bacterial products other than enterobactin are also now known to possess pacifarin activity.

pacific, *a.* and *sb.* Add: **A.** *adj.* **2. b.** = *peaceful *a.* 4.

1906 *Chambers's Jrnl.* Jan. 61/2 It is by their mastery of the policy of 'pacific penetration' that the Chinese make themselves such formidable neighbours.

4. *pacific blockade* (see quots.).

1880 *Encycl. Brit.* XIII. 194/1 The right of 'pacific blockade', *i.e.*, the blockade of ports belonging to a nation with which we profess not to be at war, has been asserted in a few doubtful instances. **1889** A. C. Boyd *Wheaton's Elem. Internat. Law* (rev. ed.) iv. i. 404 The abovementioned proceedings against Greece and Brazil furnish instances of what is called 'pacific blockade'; the blockading power blockading the coast, or a certain portion of the coast, of the blockaded power, but declaring, at the same time, that a state of peace is maintained. **1895** T. A. Walker *Man. Public Internat. Law* ii. iv. 96 Pacific blockade consists in the cutting off by one state of communication with the ports or a particular portion of coast of another, otherwise than in the case of declared war, with the object of preventing commercial relations by sea. **1935** T. A. Taracouzio *Soviet Union & Internat. Law* x. 299 Another form of redress to which nations sometimes resort, and which is yet not considered war, is pacific blockade.

B. *sb.* **2. b.** *Pacific coast* (further examples), *coaster, Northwest, seaboard, state* (examples), *style*; **Pacific slope,** (*a*) (see quot. 1902); hence *Pacific sloper*; (*b*) an escape across the Pacific Ocean to avoid arrest (chiefly *Austral.* and *N.Z. slang*); **Pacific time,** time as reckoned on the 120th meridian west of Greenwich.

1872 R. G. McClellan *Golden State* xxxi. 523 The Pacific coast..contains an area equal to one-half of the whole territory of the Republic of America. **1948** *Denison* (Texas) *Herald* 2 July 12/2 The most valuable fish is the Pacific Coast salmon. **1970** J. H. Paterson *N. Amer.* (ed. 4) xix. 287/1 Like other Pacific coast cities, it has a small steel output, based on scrap. **1883** *Harper's Mag.* Nov. 943/1 [The completion of the Union Central route has not] given the 'boost' to California that the 'Pacific coasters' so fondly dreamed of. **1889** *Wealth & Resources of Oregon & Washington* (Union Pacific Railway Co.) 3 The resources and industries of the Pacific Northwest are so varied..as to not only suggest but enforce its consideration in sections. **1938** G. Cash *I like Brit. Columbia* 100 The Provincial Library at the Parliament Buildings is quite one of the most interesting in the Pacific Northwest. **1977** *Time* 12 Dec. 61/3 They take the armchair beachcomber on a scenic tour..past the cypresses of Monterey and the great coastal forests of the Pacific Northwest to the fog-shrouded Aleutians. **1838** *Knickerbocker* June 556 Where the prairie stretches away..shall sweep the long, hissing train of cars, crowded with passengers for the Pacific seaboard. **1845** J. C. Frémont *Rep. Exploring Expedition* 274 [We were] now about to turn the back upon the Pacific slope of our continent. **1855** [in Dict.]. **1901** Hall & Osborne *Sunshine & Surf* 38 There is such a thing known in Australia, America, and Canada as 'the Pacific slope', which, being interpreted, means a hurried departure, down to these regions [*sc.* Tahiti] of gentlemen who find these countries too hot to hold them. **1902** [in Dict.]. **1902** W. S. Walker *Zealandia's Guerdon* 292 Perhaps he [*sc.* the missing man] accomplished the 'Pacific Slope'. *Ibid.* 326 He [*sc.* the detective] has packed so many 'confidence men' off to penitentiary that the others have done the 'Pacific Slope' in various directions, chiefly towards Australia. **1915** H. B. Niver *Elem. Geogr.* 167/1 By means of irrigation, the Pacific Slope has become one of the greatest fruit-growing sections of the world. **1938** R. Gilkison *Early Days in Dunedin* xiii. 133 In the 'seventies and 'eighties many fraudulent debtors, embezzlers and rich thieves escaped from New Zealand before arrest, by doing what came to be known as the 'Pacific Slope'. **1945** Baker *Austral. Lang.* xiv. 243 *Eucalyptian, the Pacific slope,*..and *tiersman*, are not so important to our language that we could not do without them. Yet we would tend to class these as standard. **1954** E. Gunther in Freeman & Martin *Pacific Northwest* (ed. 2) 16 Salmon runs occur in all streams in the Pacific slope. **1876** *Benton Democrat* (Corvallis, Oregon) 18 Aug. 2/3 (*heading*) Pacific slopers. **1883** *Harper's Mag.* Mar. 648/1 'Well,' said the Pacific sloper, 'if it's a private funeral, what do they call it a reception for?' **1820** W. Tudor *Lett. on Eastern States* 57 When the future Pacific states come to be represented in congress. **1949** *Los Angeles Times* 6 Nov. 1/8 The overall increase for Pacific States is 5,251,000 or 53.9%. **1976** *National Observer* (U.S.) 2 Oct. 1/2, 16 South Atlantic and South Central states got back $11.5 billion more than they paid in taxes. Thirteen Pacific and Mountain states came out $10.6 billion ahead. **1959** *Wall St. Jrnl.* 13 July 1/4 Increasing numbers of home builders..are experimenting with the new style, often called..'Pacific style'. **1883** *N.Y. Herald* 18 Nov. 12/3 In the United States the standards will be known as the 'Eastern', 'Central', 'Mountain' and 'Pacific' times. **1958** 'Castle' & 'Hailey' *Flight into Danger* ii. 36 'How soon do you expect to land?' 'About five a.m., Pacific Time.' **1976** *National Observer* (U.S.) 7 Aug. 16/1 Broadcast times apply to Eastern and Pacific time zones.

c. Used to designate a type of steam locomotive with a 4-6-2 wheel arrangement designed to pull express passenger and freight trains; also *absol.*

1903 *Amer. Engineer & Railroad Jrnl.* Oct. 351 (*caption*) Pacific-4-6-2 Type Passenger Locomotive—Chicago, Rock Island and Pacific Railway. **1905** *Railroad Gaz.* 9 June 620/1 (*heading*) Pacific locomotive with superheater for the Erie Railroad. **1908** *Westm. Gaz.* 31 Dec. 3/1 The most interesting locomotive novelty of the year was the Great Western Company's 'Pacific' type of express engine. **1910** *Ibid.* 25 Jan. 2/1 French railways..built their first 'Pacific' not long before ours, and this season most of the 'Riviera' expresses will be horsed by these vast machines. **1938** L. M. Beebe *High Iron* iii. 97 The most important U.S.R.A. designs, for present purposes, fall into four wheel arrangements: the 4-6-2 or Pacific, the 4-8-2 or Mountain, the 2-8-2 or Mikado, and the 2-10-2 or Santa Fe types. **1972** B. C. Blanton *400,000 Miles by Rail* iii. 37/1 The last major rail trip I took with my parents was in November, 1910. Our route was over the Katy's rails to St. Louis. The *Katy Flyer* was now headed by a Pacific locomotive. *Ibid.*, The *Royal* Blue was advertised as a solid-vestibuled train... It was headed by a Pacific and carried a Pullman parlor-observation car with open platform. **1978** *Observer* 26 Mar. 2/5 'Swanage'..was built in 1950 and died in 1964. It is a 4-6-2 Pacific type.

pacification. Add: **a.** (Later examples.) spec. *U.S.*, a process or operation (usu. a military operation) designed to secure the peaceful cooperation of a population or an area where one's enemies are thought to be active.

1946 'G. Orwell' in *Horizon* XIII. 76 Defenceless villages are bombarded from the air, the inhabitants driven out into the countryside, the cattle machine-gunned, the huts set on fire with incendiary bullets: this is called *pacification*. **1966** *N.Y. Rev. Bks.* 3 Mar. 4/3 It would be wrong to predict a priori that President Johnson's new 'counter-insurgency' and 'pacification' programs, based on plans for economic and social development in the Southern villages, will fail as totally as did the quite similar plans sponsored by the French and later by the Diem regime. **1967** *New Yorker* 14 Oct. 55 For God's sake, Hinton! You mean all this time I've been talking about pacification you thought I meant *peace*? **1969** A. G. Frank *Latin Amer.* xxv. 401 The latest effort, for instance, is to have the Latin American military occupation forces improve their reputation in the countryside by undertaking Latin American versions of the imperialist 'pacification' program in Vietnam. **1969** *Listener* 12 June 814/2 US civilians are busy with pacification programmes to make the peasants more hostile to communism and more loyal to Saigon. **1974** *Black Panther* 16 Mar. 2/3 This prison we're in is a military camp and it has the most propagandist and pacification program in all the camps in America. **1974** *Encycl. Brit. Macropædia* XIII. 847/1 The formula that peace is the aim of war..has time and again been expressed in the paradoxical concept of pacification, which means exactly those violent actions through which an expanded area of peace shall be won and maintained.

pacificator. (Later examples.)

1907 G. B. Shaw *Let.* 10 June (1972) II. 692, I..have just created a scandal among the German pacificators by informing the leading Viennese newspaper that I consider disarmament..absurd. **1968** *Daily Tel.* (Colour Suppl.) 13 Dec. 43/4 Drink, in other words, is becoming the opium of the people: the great pacificator.

pacificism (pæsi·fisiz'm). [f. Pacific *a.* + -ism.] **a.** Rejection of war and violence as a matter of principle; = *pacifism. **b.** Advocacy of a peaceful policy; rejection of war in a particular instance.

As an ideological term *pacifism (influenced by Fr. *pacifisme*) is now the preferred form.

1910 W. James *Mem. & Stud.* (1911) xi. 283 Pacificism makes no converts from the military party. **1912** *Q. Rev.* July 203 With the old Pacificism, the Pacificism of the Quakers, of Tolstoi, and of all those who hold that war must not be tolerated..the world has long been familiar. **1916** G. G. Coulton (*title*) The main illusions of pacificism. **1920** *Q. Rev.* Oct. 396 The revolution [in Japan, 1868].. was a reaction against these centuries of pacificism. **1936** F. M. Ford *Let.* 20 Aug. (1965) 254, I am just on the verge of litigation with the Oxford University Press over modifications they have arbitrarily made in my pacificisms quasi-communism and other outrages that they have committed. **1957** A. J. P. Taylor *Trouble Makers* ii. 51 By 'pacificism' I mean the advocacy of a peaceful policy; by 'pacifism' (a word invented only in the twentieth century) the doctrine of non-resistance. **1978** J. Meyers *Katherine Mansfield* x. 131 Weekends [with Lady Ottoline Morrell] ..were characterized by high spirits and high-mindedness, pacificism, poetry and all that was ultra-modern in the arts.

pacificist (pæsi·fisist). [f. as prec. + -ist.] **a.** One who rejects war and violence as a matter of principle; = *pacifist *sb.* **b.** One who advocates a peaceful policy as the first and best resort (see prec., sense b). Also *attrib.* or as *adj.*

In sense a *pacifist (influenced by Fr. *pacifiste*) is now the preferred form.

1907 *Westm. Gaz.* 2 Apr. 2/2 We have..a picture of Germany going to war in order 'to demonstrate the futility of the dreams of the Pacificists'. **1908** *Ibid.* 4 June 5/1 It is not sufficient to simply call him 'Pacificist' to prevent him denouncing these follies anew. **1910** W. James *Mem. & Stud.* (1911) xi. 275 In my remarks, pacificist though I am, I will refuse to speak of the bestial side of the war-*régime*..and consider only the higher aspects of militaristic sentiment. **1910** [see *milk-blooded* s.v. *milk *sb.* 10]. **1912** *Q. Rev.* July 204 To make war impossible, the older Pacificists appealed to the heart and soul of man; the new Pacificists make their appeal to his pocket. *Ibid.* 217 In places he draws the usual Pacificist conclusion. **1919** J. Buchan *Mr. Standfast* i. 21 It was bad enough for anyone to have to pose as a pacificist, but for me, as strong as a bull and as sunburnt as a gipsy and not looking my forty years, it was a black disgrace. *Ibid.* 35 You were bidden..turn yourself from a successful general into a pacificist South African engineer. **1923** *Blackw. Mag.* June 822/2 These people are instinctive pacificists. **1923** R. Macaulay *Told by Idiot* iii. iv. 192 Stanley was in these days a stop-the-war, pacificist Little Englander, anti-militarist, anti-Chamberlain, anti-Concentration Camp. **1965** D. A. Martin *Pacifism* v. 73 The dissenting opposition to war discussed here is *pacificist* not pacifist. The dissenters did not hold that war was always wrong but that it should be avoided wherever humanly possible. **1966** *New Statesman* 3 June 815/2 We are all..'Pacificists' —that is, we believe that war should be avoided wherever humanly possible

pacifico (pasi·fiko). [Sp.] A person of pacific or peaceful character, *spec.* a native of Cuba or the Philippines who submitted without active opposition to Spanish occupation.

1897 R. H. Davis *Cuba in War Time* 41 His [*sc.* General Weyler's] object..was to prevent the pacificos from giving help to the insurgents. **1898** *Harper's Weekly* 19 Feb. 174/2 The pacificos who are in the fields supply the food for the army [*sc.* the insurgents in Cuba, February, 1898] and are under military supervision. **1905** A. G. Robinson *Cuba & Intervention* iii. 35 These became known as the *Pacificos*. **1916** G. B. Shaw in *To-day* 13 May 38/2 One who accidentally tackled Mr Ponsonby, and, miscalculating the mettle of the true British Pacifico, had his head heartily punched for his pains.

pacifier. Add: (Further examples.)
1956 H. GOLD *Man who was not with It* (1965) ii. 12 Telling *as if*, secure in morphine or other pacifiers,..we found in the show that forgotten moral thickness for which so many of us were sick. **1969** *Daily Tel.* 10 Nov. 2 By 1990 most of us..will be taking synthetic mood modifiers, pacifiers and general comforters.

2. A baby's dummy. *U.S.*
1904 F. CRISSEY *Tattlings Retired Politician* 367, I put away my teething ring and baby 'pacifier' several years ago. **1949** M. MEAD *Male & Female* xiii. 271 The very modern pediatrician may recommend a pacifier—the same old pacifier that still lingers on the back-street, in the little..drug stores. **1960** *Encounter* Mar. 19/2 Minnie Foote's baby got held up to see and dropped his pacifier in the box. **1963** M. MCCARTHY *Group* xiv. 321 Norine removed the pacifier from the baby's mouth. **1976** *Billings* (Montana) *Gaz.* 4 July 5-A/3 The government has closed the books on a case that started with the choking death of a five-month-old boy and ended with the recall of more than 100,000 baby pacifiers.

pacifism (pæ·sifiz'm). [ad. F. *pacifisme* (see quot. 1902): see -ISM, *PACIFICISM.] The policy or doctrine of rejecting war and every form of violent action as means of solving disputes, esp. in international affairs; the belief in and advocacy of peaceful methods as feasible and desirable alternatives to war.
1902 *Proc. 10th Universal Peace Congr.* 74 M. Emile Arnaud... Speaking at length, in French,..said:... The negative programme of Pacifism is anti-War-ism. **1906** *Times* 30 July 5/4 It can bring its naval policy into harmony with its foreign policy and give pledges to 'pacifism'. **1915** *National Rev.* Mar. 54 The greatest war in history is now being fought in the cause of Pacifism. **1917** *Atlantic Monthly* June 745/2 To such people pacifism is a religion, an interpretation of Christianity. **1919** G. B. SHAW *Heartbreak House* p. xviii, There was only one virtue, pugnacity: only one vice, pacifism. That is an essential condition of war. **1929** CHESTERTON *Thing* 111 Nothing that I say here has any connection with what is commonly called pacifism. I think that our friends and brethren fell ten years ago in a just war. **1935** *Fellowship* Mar. 3/1 Pacifism does not renounce the struggle, but carries it on with the more effective weapons of non-violence. **1936** A. HUXLEY in G. K. Hibbert *New Pacifism* ii. 39 Humanism was once a favourable environment for pacifism. It has now become wholly inimical. **1937** P. S. MUMFORD *Introd. Pacifism* i. 10 Pacifism is not simply a negative policy of refusing to fight. It is a constructive policy of showing that there are more powerful and better ways of opposing your enemies. **1941** A. HUXLEY *Let.* 17 Nov. (1969) 470 In war time, it would seem, psychological conditions are such that the application of pacifism to politics is for all practical purposes impossible. **1945** G. C. FIELD *Pacifism & Conscientious Objection* 4 Pacifism..is not one single, simple creed, but a number of creeds. **1955** *Bull. Atomic Sci.* Sept. 265 If armaments are not acceptable to the pacifist, does this mean that he will submit to the aggressor and meekly resign himself to what he considers evil? The answer is emphatically no. This is to confuse pacifism with appeasement. The pacifist is definitely not a passivist. **1957** A. J. P. TAYLOR *Trouble Makers* ii. 51 Even Bright, who was sometimes nearer to pacifism, did not plead 'that this country should remain without adequate and scientific means of defence'. **1964** GOULD & KOLB *Dict. Social Sci.* 481/2 Pacifism has never yet been adopted as official policy by any state. **1976** *Pacifist* Jan. 10/1 It is an integral part of pacifism not only to expect one's own freedom but also to allow everybody else *their* freedom. **1976** *Christian Cent.* 15 Sept. 753/2 Most American evangelicals have been less than enthusiastic about pacifism.

pacifist (pæ·sifist), *sb.* and *a.* [ad. F. *pacifiste*: see -IST, *PACIFICIST.] **A.** *sb.* A proponent or advocate of pacifism; one who believes in resort to peaceful alternatives to war as means of settling disputes. Also in Comb., as *pacifist-minded* adj.
1906 *Times* 30 July 5/4 The French 'Pacifists' will appeal to England's example in order to induce France also to cut down her naval programme. **1907** *Academy* 2 Mar. 204/2 In 1890 he [*sc.* Carducci] wrote on 'War' an ode that passionately condemned the Pacifists. **1917** *Atlantic Monthly* June 748/1 My friend is a pacifist because he dreads the tantalizing consequences upon himself of resisting aggression by violent physical methods. **1929** CHESTERTON *Thing* 133 One does not need to be a pacifist to think that gunpowder need hardly go on being useful on quite such a grand scale. **1930** W. S. CHURCHILL *My Early Life* xxvi. 346, I have always been against the Pacifists during the quarrel, and against the Jingoes at its close. **1930** *Sun* (Baltimore) 30 Dec. 7/3 Most people like to have their soldiers represented as brave... But not these German pacifists and defeatists. **1936** A. HUXLEY *Let.* 2 Mar. (1969) 401 What the pacifist suggests is the eminently reasonable course of using intelligent generosity to begin with—rather than waiting to use it till the evil act has been committed. **1937** P. S. MUMFORD *Introd. Pacifism* ii. 15 The Pacifist believes: 1. That war, *i.e.* mass murder, as a political policy is morally wrong, and consequently will never produce good results... 2. That security for nations, ideals or personal freedom can be obtained only by non-violent resistance, [etc.]. **1948** 'J. TEY' *Franchise Affair* xix. 225 The murderous rage that fills the pacifist-minded when their indignation is roused. **1961** E. S. TURNER *Phoney War* xiii. 179 There was an arrogance among certain militant pacifists which..prevented them from respecting the views of those who thought freedom worth fighting for. **1969** *Listener* 10 Apr. 505/3 Perhaps the oddest aspect of dispatches from Vietnam is that pacifist-minded conscripts are so readily made available to say they don't think words like honour and patriotism make any sense out there. **1970** R. SAMPSON *Anarchist Basis of Pacifism* 1 My usage of the term 'pacifist' includes only those who live by the principle that they will not intentionally take human life, cost what it may. **1974** A. PRICE *Other Paths to Glory* i. 18 'What did your father do in the last war?'.. 'He worked on a farm... He was a conscientious objector—a pacifist.'

B. *adj.* Of or pertaining to pacifism; characterized by rejection of war and belief in peaceful alternatives. Also **pacifi·stic** *a.*, suggestive of or inclined to pacifism; **pacifi·stically** *adv.*
1908 *Times Lit. Suppl.* 10 Dec. 453/3 He made a speech remarkable for its string of pacifist commonplaces. **1909** *Westm. Gaz.* 1 Sept. 9/1 Prussia was led to 1806–7 by pacifist and humanitarian ideas. **1918** A. HUXLEY *Let.* 3 Mar. (1969) 146 The one blow at the eleventh hour was the Vice Provost's refusal to allow De La Warr's article on Labour and the War to be printed, as being too revolutionary and pacifist. **1920** W. J. LOCKE *House of Baltazar* xxi. 256 It contained the names of representatives of all the disgruntled and pacifist factions in England. **1927** H. D. LASSWELL *Propaganda Technique in World War* iii. 62 H. G. Wells may be taken as an example of the pacifistically inclined Liberal..whose support of the War came at the cost of inner struggle. **1930** *Sun* (Baltimore) 31 Dec. 6/2 What Mr. Bouton characterizes as a peculiarly German Socialist, defeatist and pacifist attitude of 'a class apart' is far from that. **1936** A. HUXLEY *What are you going to do about It?* 4 It has seemed best to state the pacifist case in terms of a series of answers to common antipacifist objections. *Ibid.* 17 War..can only be prevented from breaking out if at least one government of an important sovereign state chooses to act pacifistically towards its neighbours. **1945** *Fellowship* Aug. 152/1 A fearful responsibility rests upon us who believe in the pacifist way. **1956** A. H. COMPTON *Atomic Quest* i. 37 The public attitude..had been strongly pacifistic. **1961** E. S. TURNER *Phoney War* xix. 278 Vendors of Fascist, Communist or pacifist literature were liable to be arrested. **1973** D. AARON *Unwritten War* III. viii. 108 Both [*sc.* William and Henry James] felt the need..to display a pacifistic heroism. **1976** *Pacifist* Jan. 5/2 It doesn't seem to me to be a pacifist way of overcoming things we dislike just to use our position of power (as parents or as government) to impose our will upon the people over whom we happen to have some influence.

pacing, *vbl. sb.* Add: **2.** *Cycle-Racing* and *Athletics.* The act of (tactical) pace-making, and hence of artificially increasing the speed of a competitor by allowing him to proceed in the slip-stream of a (usu. motorized) vehicle; also, the act of distributing effort carefully over a race to ensure optimum performance, esp. by utilizing the wind resistance offered by other competitors. Also *attrib.*
1895 G. L. HILLIER *Cycling* (ed. 5) 342 Appended are the Rules for 'Herne Hill Pacing', which, if strictly enforced, insure fair pacing all round... No pacer is to remain on the path, unless actually pacing. **1897** *Encycl. Sport* I. 62/1 (Athletics) *Pacing*, going in front so as to quicken the speed at which the race is being run, or at which some particular competitor is running. *Ibid.* 287/2 As a natural consequence the trade appeared upon the scene, the friendly character of the assemblies gradually disappeared, things became more business-like, pacing was supplied, tandems and often larger multicycles swooped down in shoals upon the highways. **1902** *Encycl. Brit.* XXVII. 327/2 The introduction of pacing by multicycles and motors next took from cycle racing what interest was left. **1935** *Encycl. Sports* 206/2 Surprising records have been created by pacing, since motorcycles and cars became available for this purpose, with wind-shields attached to the rear to protect the cyclist from wind resistance. These wind-shields also act as a sucker and help to draw him along. **1955** R. BANNISTER *First Four Minutes* x. 123 This was the first of many occasions when Chris Chataway helped me with the pacing in the early stages. **1974** *Encycl. Brit. Macropædia* XVIII. 544/2 Pacing styles have changed over the years, and this is particularly evident in mile running. The early style was to start fast, relax somewhat during the middle two laps, then finish as rapidly as possible. **1974** *Sunday Mirror* 21 July 38/1 Schaer..indulged in some unfair 'pacing', tucking himself in behind..Doyle and refusing official requests to move away.

3. *Med.* Artificial stimulation of the heart so as to make it beat at an appropriate rate. Cf. *PACE *v.* 5 b.
1962 *Lancet* 29 Dec. 1369/2 We report here our experience of artificial pacing in nineteen patients, with special emphasis on the management of Stokes-Adams attacks in hospital, and the emergency control of rhythm by the electrode catheter. **1969** J. P. P. STOCK *Diagnosis & Treatment of Cardiac Arrhythmias* x. 144 Paired pacing has been employed in severe heart failure to increase the force of contraction of the heart. **1975** J. FLEMING in F. J. Fawcett *Cardiol.* I. 24 Electrical pacing of the heart on a short or long term basis is now firmly established as a valuable measure.

pack, *sb.*[1] Add: **1. c.** (Later examples.)
1897 *Outing* XXX. 374/1 Men..shoulder their packs of general cussedness, and..hit the trail. **1962** J. BRAINE *Life at Top* vi. 101 Suddenly the pack was on my shoulders again; there was no quietness in the room.

d. *Photogr.* A set of two or three plates or films sensitive to different colours which are superimposed and exposed simultaneously. Cf. *BI-PACK, *TRI-PACK.
1907 *Brit. Jrnl. Photogr.* 19 July 547/2 By interspersing ..filters with films in sets for tri-chromatic negatives..the respective exposures can be made in rapid sequence without removing the pack from the camera. **1929** *Penrose Ann.* XXXI. 41 To assert that the colour analysis of the pack is equal to that of orthodox trichromatic work would be incorrect.

e. A knapsack, rucksack, usually with a wooden frame. Chiefly *Forces'* and *N.Z.*
1916 'BOYD CABLE' *Action Front* 49 The neutral ground ..was a sea of mud..littered with..packs which had been cut from or slipped from the shoulders of the wounded. **1925** FRASER & GIBBONS *Soldier & Sailor Words* 218 *Pack*, the infantry knapsack. **1958** *Tararua* XII. 27 Food and gear have to be carried. Everyone in New Zealand..puts it in a *pack*. **1968** *N.Z. Listener* 15 Mar. 6/1 You women can't go carrying all that stuff. Here, Joyce, give us your pack, Joyce! **1969** *Ibid.* 21 Feb. 4/1 Hobnail boots and canvas pack..just the gear for pushing through scrub and supplejack. **1971** *Ibid.* 22 Feb. 51/2 Pack carrying is still the same old personal battle between man and gravity. **1973** *Parade Sunday Bull.* (Philadelphia) 7 Oct. 31/2 Packs: Most versatile pack is a tubular metal pack frame, contoured to the body with a waist strap that transfers the weight to the legs and hip muscles.

f. A packet or package, esp. of cigarettes. More usual in the U.S. than in the U.K.
1924 *Saucy Stories* May 54/1 Miss de Rose..reached for a pack of Strikes. **1936** *Discovery* Nov. 345/2 Ten nuts are the equivalent of one pack of Golden Bat cigarettes. **1937** J. A. LEE *Civilian into Soldier* v. 219 He emptied his pack of issue cigarettes. **1951** *N.Y. Times* 14 June 22/6 It comes in a little pack. **1958** *Listener* 19 June 1015/1 Six packs of American cigarettes. **1959** *Housewife* June 80 The fine white Table Salt in the gaily coloured packs! **1959** N. MAILER *Advts. for Myself* (1961) 218 Stoned with lush, with pot,..Milltown, coffee, and two packs a day, I was working live, and overalert, and tiring into what felt like death. **1963** *B.S.I. News* Apr. 20/1 The 'shelf-appeal' pack designed to catch the eye of the ordinary shopper. **1974** 'J. LE CARRÉ' *Tinker, Tailor* xxiii. 201 Gerstmann was a chain-smoker: Camels. I sent out for several packs of them—*packs* is the American word?

g. The container into which a parachute is packed.
1926 *Sci. Amer.* Aug. 100/1 (*caption*) This photograph.. shows the pilot parachute just emerging from the pack. **1930** C. J. V. MURPHY *Parachute* 43 The jumper, with the pack strapped on his back, dived from the wing of a plane. **1940** *Aeroplane* 13 Sept. 298/2 A small pilot chute..pulls the main parachute out of its pack. **1969** D. DWIGGINS *Bailout* vi. 88, I would have to jump, but first squeeze from my turret and reach my parachute pack from its rack in the fuselage. **1976** A. WHITE *Long Silence* vii. 59 The snap when the fixed line broke open the pack, and the jerk when the pack pulled out the chute.

2. (Earlier and later examples as a measure of furs.)
1744 A. DOBBS *Acct. Countries adjoining Hudson's Bay* 39 He had four Packs of Beaver of 40 each. **1774** S. HEARNE *Jrnl.* 11 Oct. (1934) 122 By the Masters account ..65 or 70 Packs or Caggs, called by them Pieces, are put on board each canoe. *c* **1840** D. THOMPSON *Narr. Explorations W. Amer. 1784–1812* (1916) iv. 417, I traded three packs of Furrs (a pack is 90 lbs). **1961** PHILLIPS & SMURR *Fur Trade* II. 330 [He] fined him thirty packs of beaver, which was just the quantity he had.

3. c. *Rugby Football.* The forwards of a team, who form one half of the scrummage; also, the scrummage itself.
1887 M. SHEARMAN *Athletics & Football* II. iii. 305 The chief business of the half-back then became to snap up the ball..as soon as it came away from the pack. **1900** A. E. T. WATSON *Young Sportsman* 253 Form a compact scrummage with the heads down. Long and straggling packs are easily broken through. **1909** *Westm. Gaz.* 11 Dec. 20/2 Cambridge have an exceptionally fine pack, to whom they must look almost entirely for victory, their halves and three-quarters being but moderate. **1927** H. S. WALPOLE *Jeremy at Crale* xvi. 278 Mellon's probably the best three-quarter playing on any school side this season. But that needn't worry us. We've got a better pack than theirs. **1955** *Times* 1 Aug. 3/3 The British forwards.. were beaten time and again by the Rhodesian pack. **1960** E. S. & W. J. HIGHAM *High-Speed Rugby* III. xii. 147 Only those who have played in the pack know what will-power it sometimes requires to stand up from a scrum in the last ten minutes and force the weary legs to run. **1972** G. SLATTER *Football is Fifteen* i. 16 Tom Morrison, manager of the All Blacks, said only the forwards would know what the loss of Simpson meant to the pack. **1976** *Eastern Even. News* (Norwich) 29 Nov. 13/7 Pressure from Beccles led to a five-metre scrum where they pushed the Union pack back over the line to give Shannon a try.

d. The organizational unit of the Brownie and Wolf Cub movements.
1918 [see *BROWNIE[1] 2]. **1932** U. M. WILLIAMS *For Brownies* 111 Brown Owl is guarding the rest of the pack. **1945** 'GILCRAFT' *How to run a Pack* 5 The man or woman who in a weak moment has consented to run a Wolf Cub Pack. **1965** *Wolf Cub Jubilee Bk.* 31 Some Cub Packs in Canada have a real wolf's head on the top of their totem pole. **1973** *Guardian* 1 Apr. 11/3 Brown Owl said she'd understand if I wasn't quite happy in the pack.

e. In the war of 1939–45, a number of German submarines operating together.
1943 *Times* 13 Dec. 2/1 The story is told below of the defeat of a pack of U-boats in the North Atlantic. **1944** *Daily Tel.* 11 July 3 Captain Walker and his crew smashed U-boat packs lying across the Arctic and North Atlantic convoy routes. **1956** R. BRADDON *Nancy Wake* ix. 96 The Bay of Biscay was to be the main target area for U-Boat packs. **1961** S. E. ELLACOTT *Ships under Sea* x. 100 A common practice among U-boat packs was to lie in line at one- or two-mile intervals across a shipping lane. **1978** *Jrnl. R. Soc. Arts* CXXVI. 252/2 The German submarine packs..were threatening to starve us into submission.

11. b. *Surg.* A soft pad usu. composed of several layers of gauze sewn together, used esp. for wedging organs of the body during an operation.

1916 PARKER & BRECKINRIDGE *Surg. & Gynæcol. Nursing* xx. 263 At the Mayo clinic three sizes of packs are used, (1) 4 × 8 inches, (2) 5 inches by 3 yards, (3) 3 inches by 2 feet. The latter are used for packing about the gall-bladder. **1944** W. W. BABCOCK *Princ. & Pract. Surg.* xviii. 285 Salt packs consist of gauze soaked in 10 per cent hypertonic solution in which 5- or 10-grain tablets of sodium chloride are embedded. **1955** *Times* 15 July 11/4 The plaintiffs' cause of action was that during an operation on Mrs. Urry for the delivery of a child by lower Caesarian section, a swab or pack was left in her body. **1955** M. G. LYNCH in Ochsner & DeBakey *Christopher's Minor Surg.* (ed. 7) xxi. 500/1 Gelfoam packs will often control this bleeding. **1970** H. HAXTON *Surg. Techniques* vii. 45 Most bleeding can be controlled by the pressure of a pack or a finger on the right spot.

c. *Dentistry.* A substance applied in a plastic state to the gums around and between the teeth, subsequently hardening, to serve as a dressing after disease or surgery of periodontal tissue.

1923 A. W. WARD in *Jrnl. Amer. Dental Assoc.* X. 478/2 In order to avoid infection, pain, sensitiveness of the roots..I have devised a quick setting pack. This pack is mixed like cement and flowed between the teeth and all over the exposed surface. The tissues regenerate under the pack, which is allowed to remain four to six days after the operation. **1953** I. GLICKMAN *Clin. Periodontology* xliv. 743 The mixed pack is separated into small masses. *Ibid.* 746 If a portion of the pack fractures off within three days after it was placed, the entire pack should be replaced. **1974** D. L. ALLEN et al. *Periodontics for Dental Hygienist* (ed. 2) x. 206 The placement of a periodontal dressing or pack following surgery is extremely important.

d. = *face-pack* s.v. *FACE *sb.* 27.

1934 M. VERNI *Mod. Beauty Culture* I. v. 29/1 In many schools of beauty, the pupils are taught to sponge the face with hot water before applying the pack. **1944** R. G. HARRY *Mod. Cosmeticology* (ed. 2) v. 55 The tightening effect is produced by the drying of the pack, and is enhanced by the presence of albumin and/or certain gums. **1964** WELLS & LUBOWE *Cosmetics & Skin* II. vii. 202 The significant mechanism operative in the use of face packs is the drying of the pack on the skin surface. **1972** *Vogue* Jan. 15/2 To transform a dry skin..use this simple pack.

13. (Earlier example.)

1866 N. CHEVALIER *Reminisc. Journey across South Island* (typescript) 7 The pack [was] a strong heavy old chap, the third pretty good. The fourth a flea bitten Arab mare.

13*. Slang phr. *to send to the pack* (see quot. 1916); also *to go to the pack*, to lose a (high) position, to 'go to pieces', to deteriorate. Chiefly *Austral.* and *N.Z.*

1916 C. J. DENNIS *Songs Sentimental Bloke* 94 I've sent the leery bloke that bore me name Clean to the pack wivout one pearly tear. *Ibid.* 127 *To send to the pack*, to relegate to obscurity. **1919** W. H. DOWNING *Digger Dial.* 26 *Go to the pack*, deteriorate. **1934** T. WOOD *Cobbers* xvi. 200 The country was going to the pack. **1939** JOYCE *Finnegans Wake* 269 If she can't follow suit Renée goes to the pack. **1946** K. TENNANT *Lost Haven* (1947) xvi. 250 Everything'ull go to the pack unless they're let go home again. **1952** D. NILAND in *Coast to Coast 1951–52* 196, I can't let him go to the pack like that. **1958** G. CASEY *Snowball* 118 You wait till he gets a bit older. Them abos always go t' the pack. **1963** D. CRICK *Martin Place* 196 Things are goin' to the pack. If they get any shorter of work, they'll close down.

14. a. *pack-animal* (earlier example), *-dog*, *-mule* (earlier and later examples), *-pony* (examples). **c. pack-clouds** (*poet.*), densely massed clouds; **pack-drill,** also in phr. *no names, no pack-drill*: see *NAME *sb.* 1 h; **pack-frame,** a frame, usu. of metal, into which a knapsack or other pack is fitted for easier transport; **pack-ice** (earlier and later examples); **pack-leader,** the leader of a group of animals; **pack-peddler,** one who travels round from village to village with a pack of small items for sale; **pack-rat,** substitute for def.: the North American bushytailed woodrat, *Neotoma cinerea* (further examples); also *attrib.* and *fig.*; hence as *v. trans.*, to collect an assortment of objects, as a pack-rat does; **pack-sack,** the container into which goods comprising a pack are put, a rucksack; also *attrib.* in phr. *pack-sack citizen* (*Canad.*), a vagrant; **packshot,** in television advertising, a close-up picture of the advertised product in its wrappings; **pack-strap(s,** the strap or straps which secure a load round the forehead or shoulders of a person or to the back of a pack animal; **pack tactics,** the practice of German submarines of operating in groups; **pack-track, -trail,** a path or route suitable for a pack-train; **pack-train** (earlier and later examples).

1847 *Santa Fé* (New Mexico) *Republican* 16 Oct. 2/2 They left their wagons and took pack animals, and ten days' provisions. **1871** G. M. HOPKINS *Note-bks. & Papers* (1937) 141 If you look well at big pack-clouds. **1844** *New Orleans Picayune* 18 Mar. 38/1 The only assistant they took with them was an Indian-trained pack dog. **1913** I. COWIE *Company of Adventurers* 323 Pack-ponies were also used; also pack dogs, the latter bearing frequently burdens mountains high in comparison with their size. **1933** B. WILLOUGHBY *Alaskans All* 18 We four stood clinging to the collars of our pack dogs, wondering what marvels lay beyond. **1976** T. WALKER *Spatsizi* xii. 132 Travelling slowly with their pack dogs, they walked 150 miles through the mountains. **1955** E. HILLARY *High Adventure* vii. 118 Her [*sc.* the Sherpani's] method of carrying it [*sc.* her load] was with a headband, and as I had no pack frame with me I had to follow suit. **1963** *Guardian* 9 Aug. 7/4 To get to Dyrfjoll was a whole day's march from the nearest road and the pair used a sledge pack-frame on the way in. **1973** [see above sense 1 e]. **1976** G. MOFFAT *Over Sea to Death* x. 119 The paraphernalia of [mountain] rescue: rucksacks, pack frames, radio sets. **1850** R. A. GOODSIR *Arctic Voy. Baffin's Bay* 108 As long as there was a chance of procuring whales in Prince Regent's Inlet, he might have persevered..great as the risk would have been in pushing through the heavy pack-ice we had fallen in with. **1930** *Times Educ. Suppl.* 25 Jan. p. iv/1 From the air it was also observed that the great region of heavy pack-ice..gives place to waters comparatively little encumbered. **1965** *Kingston* (Ontario) *Whig-Standard* 3 Apr. 4/5 About 300,000 of these seals are killed on the pack ice every spring. **1975** *Nature* 18 Dec. 594/1 In the foraminifera-poor beds which we believe represent periods free, at least seasonally, of packice. **1902** J. H. M. ABBOTT *Tommy Cornstalk* 35 In work where there is a probability of being under fire..the pack-leader might be left behind. **1975** W. H. NESBITT in M. W. Fox *Wild Canids* xxvii. 394 The female pack leader [of a group of feral dogs] often 'scouted' ahead before moving the pack. **1835** A. UNDERWOOD in *Southwestern Hist. Q.* (1928–9) XXXII. 139 In company with Messrs. Money, Gay..and William Pruit attended by a Mexican with a pack mule we took our departure. **1839** Z. LEONARD *Adventures* (1904) 61 We now scattered over a considerable range of country for the purpose of hunting, leaving ten or twelve men only to bring on the pack-mules. **1909** W. R. Harris *Catholic Church in Utah* 128 We..entered a small mountain forest of pine trees in which we lost one of our pack mules. **1934** F. STARK *Valleys of Assassins* ii. 74, I..crouched with my back to the gale on the pack-mule. **1868** *Harper's Mag.* Aug. 348/2 Ten years ago a pack peddler went through the town. **1880** *Ibid.* Nov. 892/1 There was a pack peddler with smuggled shawls and laces at the door. **1944** G. WILSON *Passing Institutions* 70 We..married, and died in a small area, learning of the big outside world only through books and an occasional pack peddler or clock tinker who came in. **1870** DE B. R. KEIM *Sheridan's Troopers on Borders* 201 [Indians] drive the herds and pack-ponies, or else on foot lead them. **1923** J. H. COOK *50 Yrs. Old Frontier* 98 We used pack ponies on the return trip. **1936** D. MCCOWAN *Animals Canad. Rockies* xxii. 196 From the fact that it habitually transports sundry articles from one place to another the animal [*sc.* the wood rat], in the West, is commonly called Pack rat. **1955** PRIESTLEY & HAWKES *Journey down Rainbow* iii. 47 A mass of bat and pack-rat droppings. **1963** *Spectator* 21 June 803/2 Obsessed with some impulse, like a packrat fear of throwing anything away. **1966** H. MARRIOTT *Cariboo Cowboy* iii. 40, I had other visitors every so often in the shape of sharp-faced, long-tailed rats which were known as pack rats. **1970** R. LOWELL *Notebk.* 22 The horrifying mortmain of Ephemera: keys, drift, sea-urchin shells, Packratted off with joy. **1970** *Publishers' Weekly* 8 June 154 A pack rat is somebody who wants to have his own information material, his own personal library or files, even if this means indulging in a little petty thieving. **1973** *Ann. N.Y. Acad. Sci.* CCXI. 308 The sporadic pack-rat collecting we all do every day by habit amidst the print, graffiti, and speech that encompass our peculiar lives. **1973** 'D. SHANNON' *No Holiday for Crime* (1974) vi. 94 When I came to, they were busy as packrats carting stuff out. **1851** W. KELLY *Excursion to California* I. ix. 159 We, the packers, were now busily employed making pack-sacks of a uniform size. **1920** *Rod & Gun in Canada* Nov. 715/1 A good old-time packsack. **1966** *Globe & Mail* (Toronto) 18 Jan. B5/7 [He] was a pack-sack citizen and appeared on Skid Row streets..with..caulk boots which would be later hocked for the last bottle. **1970** 'E. LATHEN' *Pick up Sticks* (1971) viii. 70 The packsacks under Thatcher's chair contrasted strongly to the matched sets of luggage piled everywhere. **1960** O. SKILBECK *A B C of Film & TV* 94 *Pack Shot*, the egregious scene with which most T.V. 'Commercials' conclude: a C.U. of the Sponsor's wrapped product. **1966** G. N. LEECH *Eng. in Advertising* v. 42 In seven-second commercials there is little time to show anything except a title card or a 'pack shot' establishing a visual image of the product. **1969** *Focal Encycl. Film & Television Techniques* 128/1 Television advertising, for instance, makes much use of cinemacrography in the so-called 'pack shots' but these are normally filmed at a scale of less than 1:1. **1897** J. W. TYRRELL *Across Sub-Arctics of Canada* 12 Western half-breeds, trained in the use of the pack-straps as well as the paddle. *Ibid.* 70 We both took a turn at the pack-straps. **1902** S. E. WHITE *Blazed Trail* 113 The solitary man with the packstraps across his forehead and shoulders had never seen so many [wood creatures]. **1949** P. NEWTON *High Country Days* iv. 38 The swags..lashed together [on a pack-horse] with the long packstraps. **1956** M. DUGGAN *Immanuel's Land* 53 He walked along..with the packstraps cutting into his shoulders. **1956** H. S. M. KEMP *Northern Trader* 25 Our canoemen tied their packstraps around a hundred-pound piece, piled another hundred-pound piece atop it, squatted down cross-legged while they adjusted the headband, heaved themselves up and jogged off. **1960** B. CRUMP *Good Keen Man* 109 The only reason my pack-straps didn't go the same way was that I noticed Harry eyeing them. **1942** *Sun* (Baltimore) 21 Feb. 2/8 The Nazi in command of the U-boat fleet, had promised to use 'pack tactics' on the Eastern Atlantic and save the largest submarines and best crews for attacks off American shores, to cripple Allied tanker strength. **1944** *Hansard Commons* 7 Mar. 1897 It might have seemed as if perhaps after all, the U-boats with their pack tactics might defeat the convoy system. **1870** *App. Jrnls. House Reps. N.Z.* D. XL. 6 It will be desirable to connect them [*sc.* No Name diggings] by a metalled pack-track with Marsden to the Greenstone. **1930** L. G. D. ACLAND *Early Canterbury Runs* (ser. 1) ix. 219 It [*sc.* a hut] is miles by pack-track from the nearest neighbour. **1843** in *Utah Hist. Q.* (1929) II. 116 There is little grass in the mountains and the pack trail bad. **1911** *Daily Colonist* (Victoria, B.C.) 29 Apr. 17/6 The completion of a pack trail into the valley of the Naas. **1965** *Beaver* Autumn 54/1 Along the pack trail we met trappers coming out of the bush. **1849** K. WEBSTER *Diary* 19 June in *Gold Seekers of '49* (1917) iii. 50 It is said at Fort Kearney that the wagons passed here already this season, en route for California, number 5,400, and also three pack trains. **1862** R. C. MAYNE *Four Yrs. Brit. Columbia & Vancouver I.* 148 From thence pack-trains could make Alexandria.. in 14 or 15 days. **1922** *Beaver* Nov. 64/1 The daily progress of a pack train is a single drive of ten to fifteen miles. **1965** *Beautiful Brit. Columbia* Summer 9/1 He..operated a pack train for the Hudson's Bay Company.

pack, *v.*[1] Add: **I. 1. b.** (Later examples).

1831 *Reg. Deb. Congress U.S.* 8 Feb. 133 It is believed that, in Cincinnati alone, there were slaughtered and packed this year one hundred thousand hogs. **1852** *Trans. Mich. Agric. Soc.* III. 230 Mullet..are sometimes used as pan-fish, and are packed to a limited extent.

2. c. Now freq. without *up*. Also used in passive of a person: to have finished packing.

1906 'O. HENRY' in *N.Y. World Mag.* 1 July 8/1, I am packed and was to have left for the North Woods this morning. **1907** G. B. SHAW *John Bull's Other Island* I. 28 *Doyle*: Hodson. *Hodson*..: Did you call, sir? *Doyle*: Pack for me too. I'm going to Ireland with Mr. Broadbent. **1912** R. BROOKE *Old Vicarage Grantchester* (1916) 10 God! I will pack, and take a train, And get me to England once again! **1958** J. CANNAN *And be a Villain* iv. 83 I'm packed, but I must..tell them I'm leaving. **1962** J. BRAINE *Life at Top* xxii. 248, I turned away without speaking and went upstairs to pack. **1969** G. LYALL *Venus with Pistol* xxxv. 234 We're all packed up. I don't know if I've got all your things in the right bags. **1974** J. JOHNSTON *How Many Miles to Babylon?* 66, I have to catch the Dublin train. I..should go and pack.

d. *to pack up* (or *in*) (*intr.*), to stop working; to give up an enterprise; to surrender; to die; to cease to function; to collapse.

1925 FRASER & GIBBONS *Soldier & Sailor Words* 219 *Pack-up*.., *To*, to stop (as opposed to 'carry on'). To give up. To finish. To die. **1926** E. F. SPANNER *Naviators* i. 8 It was about five in the afternoon when Sir Joseph decided to pack up for the day. **1928** C. F. S. GAMBLE *Story N. Sea Air Station* xii. 201 To make matters worse another engine packed up, and this increased the stern list of the ship. **1940** 'GUN BUSTER' *Return via Dunkirk* II. xii. 174 The Belgians have packed up... They've laid down their arms. **1948** C. DAY LEWIS *Otterbury Incident* iv. 45 There seemed nothing to stop Toppy unless his voice packed up; so Ted and I left him. **1953** W. BURROUGHS *Junkie* (1972) vii. 70 He said, 'We've got to pack in. We can't last with this crowd.' **1956** 'J. WYNDHAM' *Seeds of Time* 87 The laterals aren't firing... I mean they *won't* fire. They've packed up. **1959** 'M. INNES' *Hare sitting Up* I. i. 17 The most surprising people will pack up under strain. **1962** *Economist* 3 Nov. 440/2 The Algerians seem to think that Mr Khemisti..broke off the talks as a gesture of solidarity with Cuba. But American reports suggest that it was the State Department itself that decided to pack in. **1967** J. L. ANDERSON *Vinland Voyage* 90 None of us had much confidence in it [*sc.* our ancient engine] and it packed up a few days later. **1973** A. BROINOWSKI *Take One Ambassador* i. 14 I'm Mrs Bert Norrice..Mr Norrice passed on last year..Bert's heart packed up. **1977** G. FISHER *Villain of Piece* iv. 40 Where is the nearest telephone?..It's packed in.

e. *to pack up* or *in* (*trans.*), to stop (doing something), to give up, finish with; freq. in phr. *to pack it up* (or *in*), to stop working, abandon an attempt, etc.; also as imp., be quiet, 'cut it out', behave yourself. *slang* and *colloq.*

1942 BERREY & VAN DEN BARK *Amer. Thes. Slang* § 205/4 *Stop talking*; '*shut up*',..pack it up. **1943** HUNT & PRINGLE *Service Slang* 50 *Pack it up* or *in*, stop talking or fooling; cut it out. **1945** J. B. PRIESTLEY *Three Men in New Suits* iv. 104 'Pack it up,' she warned him. **1949** 'G. ORWELL' *Nineteen Eighty-Four* I. viii. 86 'Oh, pack it in!' said the third man. **1951** A. BARON *Rosie Hogarth* 210 Pack it up, Joyce. I'm telling you. **1951** 'N. SHUTE' *Round Bend* 10 It looked as if the public were getting a bit tired of it. Sir Alan packed it up. **1953** W. BURROUGHS *Junkie* (1972) xii. 121 Every month or so she hires a new lover, gives him shirts and suits and wrist watches, and then packs him in when she has enough. **1959** 'O. MILLS' *Stairway to Murder* viii. 92, I packed up my job last week. .. I just told you... I packed in my job last week. **1963** N. HILLIARD *Piece of Land* 43 They saw nothing... About eight o'clock they decided to pack it in..headed back for town. **1971** B. W. ALDISS *Soldier Erect* 47 'Why don't you pack in ordering us about, Wally?' I asked. **1972** J. WILSON *Hide & Seek* viii. 137 Rob Millar didn't finish work until gone eleven, and then decided he'd have to pack it in. **1974** K. CLARK *Another Part of Wood* ii. 56 He had long ago 'packed it in', and spent his life sitting by the window dozing, with a volume of Pepys' Diary upside down on his knee. **1976** *News of World* 14 Mar. 11/2 He has been ordered to pack in his job and return for the final four weeks of term. **1977** *Daily Mirror* 18 Mar. 24 Hey! You! That's my missus—pack it in!

3. d. (Earlier example.)

1850 R. G. CUMMING *Five Yrs. Hunter's Life S. Afr.* II. 141 The ground all round was packed flat with their spoor.

f. *Theatr.* Phr. *to pack them in*: to attract a capacity audience. Also *transf.*

1943 *N.Y. Times* 9 May II. 5/4 Harry James and his band have been helping to pack them in at the Paramount. **1970** *Guardian* 31 July 9/3 Bolton's Octagon Theatre..is packing them in for Old Tyme Musical Hall. **1972** *Ibid.* 1 Dec. 11/1 She's still at it at 49; still packing 'em in, and getting the odd rave review. **1977** *New Statesman* 17 June 809/2 His rejigged Radio 4 *Today* programme is now packing the listeners in.

g. *Computers.* To compress (stored data) in a way that permits subsequent recovery; *spec.* to represent (two or more items of data) in a single word. Also *absol.*

1954 *Computers & Automation* Dec. 18/1 *Pack*, to combine several different brief fields of information into one machine word. **1959** M. H. Wrubel *Primer of Programming* viii. 189 If the data consist of only a few significant digits, two or more numbers can be 'packed' into a single 10-digit word. They will be transferred from the card to the machine as a 10-digit word, which must subsequently be 'unpacked' by an appropriate program. **1961** L. W. Hein *Introd. Electronic Data Processing* ix. 165 One of the bad situations is that of the 31-word record in a 60-word fixed record-length computer... A decision to pack means some rather complex programming. **1964** *IBM Systems Jrnl.* III. 125 Decimal digits, packed two to a byte, appear in fields of variable length (from 1 to 16 bytes). **1972** *Computer Jrnl.* XV. 199/1 A stream..might be formed by one stream function which unpacks words into bytes, followed by another one which packs them all up again. **1973** [see *packed *ppl. a.*[1] 1 c].

5. a. (Further examples.) Also of a group of runners in a long-distance race.

1844 in *Rep. U.S. Comm. Patents 1846* (1847) 34 It [*sc.* cotton] does not pack and becomes hard. **1887** A. W. Tourgée *Button's Inn* 200 It [*sc.* the storm] filled the road with a slippery mealy mass, which did not cling or pack. **1890–3** E. M. Taber *Stowe Notes, Lett. & Verses* (1913) 8 The snow packs so readily that I can walk without much difficulty. **1908** *Westm. Gaz.* 27 July 9/3 The failure of the British representatives..was undoubtedly due to their failure to 'pack' well.

b. (Later examples.)

1939–40 *Army & Navy Stores Catal.* 656/1 Foulard Silk [dressing gown]..of very light weight to pack small. **1946** *Mod. Lang. Notes* LXI. 444 This dress washes and irons and packs easily. **1974** *Janet Frazer Catal.* Spring & Summer 455/2 Pneumatic 'Igloo' tent... Packs away compactly.

c. Of the forwards in Rugby football: to form or take their places in the scrummage. Also const. *in* and *down*.

1874 *Rugby Union Football Ann. 1874–5* 15 A good forward will..pack in again at the back of the scrummage. **1887** M. Shearman *Athletics & Football* ii. iii. 313 There is many a good scrimmager who packs quickly. **1900** A. E. T Watson *Young Sportsman* 252 Be the first to form the scrummage and pack quickly. **1927** Wakefield & Marshall *Rugger* ii. iii. 162 If..his opponents have the right of putting the ball in, he ought to pack opposite their loose-head to be ready to check their scrum-half. **1949** *Rugby League Football* ('Know the Game' Series) 31 The front row forward who packs nearest to the referee has what is known as the 'loose head'. **1968** Hudson & Dyer *Your Bk. of Rugger* v. 49 'Number 8'..packs down in between the second row, with his back parallel to the ground and his feet spread evenly apart. **1970** G. Slatter *On the Ball* vi. 139 The scrum packs down on our 25-yard line and Haigh takes the ball.

6. c. *Surg.* To fill, wedge, or cover with a pack. Also *absol. to pack off*, to wedge (an internal organ) with packs so as to keep it away from a region of interest.

1889 Caird & Cathcart *Surg. Handbk.* vii. 53 The cavity of the nostril may be packed with a long strip of lint. **1897** Stimson & Rogers *Man. Operative Surg.* (ed. 3) i. 28 Much of the hemorrhage can be stopped..by packing with sponges or pads of gauze. **1906** H. M. Davies *Man. Minor Surgery & Bandaging* (ed. 13) ii. 36 Large pieces of gauze..are very convenient for packing off the intestines..from the rest of the abdomen. **1924** R. Howard *Surg. Emergencies* iv. 74 The site of the obstruction should be isolated..by..packing the surrounding intestine off with abdominal pads. **1940** R. Maingot *Abdominal Operations* I. i. ii. 46 The little sinus that remains may be lightly curetted out and packed with gauze which has been soaked in..penicillin. **1955** M. G. Lynch in Ochsner & DeBakey *Christopher's Minor Surg.* (ed. 7) xxi. 499/2 If the hemorrhage is severe..the nose should be packed. **1972** Nealon & Grossi in P. F. Nora *Operative Surg.* i. 7/2 The wound is packed open with gauze over a simple layer of nonadherent material.

7. (Further example.)

1910 C. E. Mulford *Hopalong Cassidy* xxxviii. 242 Hall carefully packed his pipe and puffed quickly.

b. Also const. *out*.

1932 C. C. Martindale *What are Saints?* 58, I had to go straight from Wesminster Cathedral..to a church in Chiswick,..packed out with people observing his [*sc.* St. Edward the Confessor's] feast-day. **1944** G. Texidor in D. M. Davin *N.Z. Short Stories* (1953) 301 The domain in front of the hotel was packed out with cars and lorries. **1973** *Times* 7 June 15/5 The Rolling Stones couldn't play the Ken Colyer Club one night and The Dimensions appeared instead... It was packed out. **1977** D. Clark *Gimmel Flask* vi. 101 This place is packed out for lunch.

c. *to pack them*, to hold back diarrhœa caused by nervousness; hence to be terrified. Also with explicit alternative objs. *Austral. slang.*

1951 E. Lambert *Twenty Thousand Thieves* 132 He's packing them badly. He's quite useless. **1952** T. A. G. Hungerford *Ridge & River* iii. 46, I suppose the poor cow *would* pack 'em a bit. He's on'y a kid, by the look of him. **1959** 'D. Forrest' *Last Blue Sea* 69 You know something, thought Ron Fisher, you're no good. You're packing them. **1961** R. Braddon *Naked Island* 44 'Who's panicking?' 'You are, son. Fair packing 'em, y'are.' **1971** D. Ireland *Unknown Industrial Prisoner* 132 They were packing the shits when he went off his head in the control room last time.

9. a. (Earlier examples.) Also, to carry in any manner; to wear habitually; to possess. Also *absol.*

1805 W. Clark *Jrnl.* 15 Dec. in Lewis & Clark *Orig. Jrnls. Lewis & Clark Expedition* (1905) III. xxi. 280 Proced up the 1st. right hand fork 4 miles & pack the meat from the woods to the canoes. **1816** U. Brown *Jrnl.* in *Maryland Hist. Mag.* (1916) XI. 360, I let him know that I..meant to hire a horse of him to pack our provisions. **1845** J. C. Frémont *Rep. Exploring Expedition* 73 It would have been a work of great time and labor to pack our baggage across the ridge. **1863** S. Butler *First Year in Canterbury Settlement* v. 61 The back country..is inaccessible by dray, so that all stores..have to be packed in and packed out on horseback. **1874** E. Eggleston *Circuit Rider* vii. 71 My shoes hurts my feet, an' I have to pack one of 'em in my hand most of the time. **1890** N. P. Langford *Vigilante Days* II. xviii. 282 No man that ever packed a star in this city can arrest me. **1902** A. H. Lewis *Wolfville Days* v. 61 He finds this person ain't packin' no gun. **1903** *Dialect Notes* II. 323, I never did pack a watch. **1913** [see *heft *v.*[1] 1]. **1927** *Amer. Speech* II. 361 He packed the child home. **1930** L. G. D. Acland *Early Canterbury Runs* (ser. 1) viii. 200 George Harper..used to pack the wool out on bullocks, three sacks on each. **1940** R. Chandler *Farewell, my Lovely* iii. 22 Don't you pack no rod? **1952** *Picture Post* 6 Dec. 37/2 A revival of flogging was in loud demand, and there was the barmaid who insisted she wouldn't feel safe until every policeman packed a gun. **1970** C. Wilson *Campbell of Yukon* ii. 9 Here the cargoes &c have to be 'packed' on the men's shoulders from water to water. **1973** *Washington Post* 5 Jan. B3/6 Actress Ali McGraw 'packs all the glamor of a worn-out sneaker'.

b. To travel with one's goods or merchandise in packs.

1842 M. Crawford *Jrnl.* (1897) 14 Some of the company preparing to pack from here. **1857** W. Chandless *Visit to Salt Lake* ii. vii. 264 Waggoning through the settlements..and thence 'packing' to California. **1903** S. E. White *Forest* ii. 15 Do not carry a coat..you will never wear it while packing. **1911** J. F. Wilson *Land Claimers* i. 1 It isn't much fun packing along that trail.

c. To be capable of delivering (a blow) with force; esp. in phr. *to pack a punch*; also *fig. colloq.*

1921 H. C. Witwer in *Collier's* 19 Feb. 22/3 He packed a wicked right and had stopped a lot of good men before Kid Roberts cut him short with a one-round knockout. **1922** E. O'Neill *Hairy Ape* (1923) i. 7 He packa da wallop, I tella you!..No fightin', maties. **1934** M. H. Weseen *Dict. Amer. Slang* 239 *Pack a terrific punch*, to hit hard, or to have the ability to do so. *a* **1938** T. Wolfe *Lett.* (1956) 45, I think my play 'The House' will 'pack a punch'. **1957** *Listener* 20 June 1008/1 An artist who packs such a violent literary punch might be expected to make use of a savage, expressionist line. **1958** Wodehouse *Cocktail Time* xvi. 137, I take it that she busted you one. .. These nannies pack a wicked punch. **1971** *Sunday Express* (Johannesburg) 28 Mar. 22/3 Like Kies, he packs a powerful punch, but he does not wade in like Jan. **1973** W. M. Duncan *Big Timer* xxi. 137 That Carver packed a wallop, didn't he? I should have plugged him sooner.

II. 10. b. Also *to go packing*.

1926 T. E. Lawrence *Seven Pillars* lxxxviii. 468 As both example and guilt were blatant, the others went packing into the far room while their chiefs forthwith executed sentence.

c. Const. *off*. Also, to die.

1766 Sewel & Buys *Compl. Dict. Eng. & Dutch* I. 549/3 To pack off, (to die) *Stërven*. **1914** W. Owen *Let.* 15 June (1967) 260 The alternative would be to come home immediately..and at once to pack off to some other part of the world. **1933** T. E. Lawrence *Let.* 10 Aug. (1938) 774, I would like myself and those I care for to pack off all together.

pack, *v.*[2] Restrict † *Obs.* to I and add: **II. 4.** (Later examples.) Also, to secure (a particular decision or result) by selecting or arranging the body of voters, etc.

1925 A. Toynbee *Survey Internat. Affairs 1920–23* 80 In order to prevent any possibility of 'packing' the vote, the date of residence was not fixed..as the day when the Treaty came into force, but as the day when it was signed. **1932** *Ann. Reg. 1931* ii. 275 China... Together with others from the Canton faction they issued a manifesto declaring that the elections to the Convention would be a fiasco, that the Convention would be 'packed' by Chiang, and that its whole purpose was to seat him more firmly in the dictatorship. **1955** *Times* 26 May 8/3 The Minister had tried to cloak the Bill with respectability but this had to be seen against his earlier statements about 'packing' the courts and the Senate. **1965** *Mod. Law Rev.* XXVIII. 517 He was not above packing the House in order to curb such activities. **1973** *Black Panther* 14 Apr. 12/2 The Supreme Court is being systematically packed despite the defeat of Carswell and Haynesworth. **1976** *Daily Tel.* 24 Apr. 2/6 Vauxhall Labour party is to meet..to investigate allegations that the general management committee is being improperly 'packed' with members to ensure the selection of a merchant banker to succeed the present MP.

5. (Further example.)

1927 *Amer. Speech* II. 352/2 They packed the deal on the other players.

packability (pækăbi·lĭti). [f. Packable *a.*: see *-bility.] The capacity to be packed; *spec.* of clothes and fabrics, the ability to be packed easily into, and to travel without damage in, a suitcase.

1958 *Vogue* May 108 A traveller's dream of packability, a pleated dress..that emerged uncreased after days in a suitcase. **1963** *New Yorker* 29 June 44/1 (Advt.), All the lightness, comfort, and packability that Arnel is famous for. **1967** *Daily Tel.* 24 Oct. 19 Dress and coat ensembles of great packability. **1977** *Shooting Times & Country Mag.* 13–19 Jan. 33/1 One of the main advantages of pistols—'packability'—is lost.

packable, *a.* Delete *rare* and add further examples. Also *ellipt.* as *sb.*

1932 *Times Lit. Suppl.* 21 Jan. 40/4 So easily packable, pocketable, readable a copy of the book. **1962** *Sunday Express* 30 Dec. 16/5 Opaque and eminently packable pyjamas. **1972** *New Yorker* 29 July 16/1 (*caption*) A packable that goes to town dressed up ndown! **1976** *Sci. Amer.* Feb. 123/3 In any Euclidean space an infinite set of boxes packable by a given brick has a finite subset of packable boxes that can be used for packing all the others.

package, *sb.* Add: **2. b.** *fig.* (See quots.) *slang.*

1933 *Sun* (Baltimore) 17 Aug. 8/6 The 'package', as the kidnapped victim is called, is rushed across the State line and delivered to the 'keepers'. **1935** A. J. Pollock *Underworld Speaks* 85/1 *Package*, the kidnaped victim. **1945** L. Shelly *Jive Talk Dict.* 15/2 *Package*, a girl. **1960** Wentworth & Flexner *Dict. Amer. Slang* 371/1 *Package*, an attractive, usu. small and neat, girl or young woman. **1963** *Listener* 4 Apr. 585/1 A 'package' was criminal jargon for a dead body with three or more bullets placed in a most efficient manner at the base of the skull.

3. b. *transf.* and *fig.* orig. *U.S.* A combination or collection of interdependent or related abstract entities. (Cf. Parcel *sb.* 7 b.) Hence *attrib.*, esp. (*a*) of negotiations, as *package deal*, a transaction or proposal agreed to as a whole, the less favourable items as well as the more favourable; so *package offer, proposal*, etc.; (*b*) of holidays, tours, etc., one in which all arrangements are the responsibility of agents; (*c*) of a series of acts in a vaudeville show, on television, etc. (For a considerable body of further evidence see *Amer. Speech* May 1958, 73 ff.)

Dict. Americanisms has an 1846 quot. for *package ticket* in the sense 'one entitling the holder to a specified number of journeys'.

1931 *Social Sci. Abstr.* 15838 Insurance in a 'package'... The exact size of the 'package' offered to any employee depends upon age, sex, and length of service. **1948** *Investor's Reader* 26 May 9 Often units of preferred and common shares are tied together in one big economy package which offers two for the price of one. **1951** W. F. Buckley *God & Man at Yale* 40 This report is primarily a highly controversial package of political and economic ideas. **1952** *N.Y. Herald Tribune* 9 Apr. 26/7 On this basis the [steel] industry is confronted not with a package [*sc.* the wage recommendations of the Wage Stabilization Board] costing 29.8 cents an hour, but one that will cost 59.6 cents. **1953** in *Amer. Speech* (1958) XXXIII. Suppl. 74 Eventually the agency offers a package—a violinist, a pianist, a singer, a quartet and perhaps a small string orchestra. **1958** *Economist* 8 Mar. 849/1 The [U.S.] Administration is thinking of proposing a simplified 'package' [for summit talks]. **1959** *Observer* 26 Apr. 6/2 The package would link the future of Berlin with a settlement of the German problem and European security. **1962** M. McLuhan *Gutenberg Galaxy* 128 (*heading*) The *camera obscura* anticipated Hollywood in turning the spectacle of the external world into a consumer commodity or package. **1965** *Melody Maker* 25 Sept. 20 Few fans will turn out every week for expensive concerts. Yet, in the past, some towns have had two or even three big packages in their area in one week. **1966** *Listener* 3 Mar. 300/2 It was the orthodox deflationary package that was to be expected in an off-year for the British balance of payments. **1967** M. McLuhan *Medium is Massage* 22 The mass audience..is..merely given packages of passive entertainment. **1968** *Globe & Mail* (Toronto) 3 Feb. B3/3 Although the Canadian union gained the greatest economic package in its 30-year history from the company the day before, hundreds of workers were reluctant to return to work. **1969** L. G. Arthur in A. E. Wilkerson *Rights of Children* (1973) 132 The great advancement of the juvenile courts is that they can be imaginative and flexible: that they can design a package of dispositions to fit the needs of a particular child. **1969** *Listener* 2 Jan. 31/2 You can arrange as part of your package to hire a car. **1970** *Daily Tel.* 3 Mar. 2/1 The Hillman Minx de Luxe model will also cease to be available, but a 'comfort' package of carpets and central console will be available for the Minx. **1972** *Guardian* 25 Mar. 1/1 Northern Ireland's Parliament at Stormont is to be prorogued for a year under the peace package of Ulster announced in the Commons yesterday. **1972** *Times* 16 Aug. 1/4 National bargaining on the unions' package claim... The whole package amounted to 40 per cent... Union officials at local level will now be able to pursue those parts of the package that have not been met. **1975** J. De Bres tr. *Mandel's Late Capitalism* xi. 358 The underdeveloped country sends its entire export package to the imperialist country. **1977** *Time* 17 Jan. 17/1 The Carter package offers something to just about everybody. **1977** 'A. Stuart' *Snap Judgement* 192 The tired tanned look of tourists at the end of a two-week package.

attrib. (*a*) **1951** *N.Y. Herald Tribune* 14 Dec., President Truman in effect wrapped up the whole subject of creeping corruption in his administration..into one package policy which he laid before the nation. **1952** *Ibid.* 4 Mar. 1/8 (*headline*) State to offer city 'Package' Aid Plan. *Ibid.*, The Dewey [State] administration was reported ready tonight to offer New York City a 'package' solution for the city budget crisis. **1952** *N.Y. Times* 9 Mar. 15/1 The plan for West German sovereignty was tied up in a 'package deal' with the plan for West Germany's military and financial contribution to Western defense. **1952** *N.Y. Herald Tribune* 19 May 14/3 The ensuing battle for diplomatic advantage..seemed pretty well played out by the end of April, when the United Nations Command made up its 'package' offer of settlement. **1955** *Times* 13 May 8/4

An attempt at some sort of 'package deal', whereby a disarmament settlement is made dependent on the solution of other world problems. **1963** *Ann. Reg. 1962* 247 The Chancellor..criticized the American suggestion for a 'package deal' with Moscow. **1964** M. McLuhan *Understanding Media* (1967) II. xxxi. 334 He tends instead to accept the full image as a package deal. **1967** *Listener* 20 July 74/2 In the peculiarly modern field of mass productive factory design, the so-called package-dealer holds sway, with his offer of a complete design-and-build service. **1972** *New Building* Oct. 11/3 Fully conscious of the wastefulness of normal tendering methods, Simonbuild consider their package deal system the only sensible and economic approach for the needs of today. **1972** Wodehouse *Pearls, Girls & Monty Bodkin* iii. 41 This step-daughter who had come to him as part of the package deal when he and Grayce were joined in holy wedlock. **1973** I. M. Sinclair *Vienna Convention on Law of Treaties* v. 141 But the 'package' proposal did not envisage any stage of compulsory arbitration or judicial settlement, except in relation to the *jus cogens* articles. **1976** *Economist* 16 Oct. 73/3 It now says that what Mr Smith accepted in his September 24th broadcast was not—as he says he was told it was—a package deal that had been firmly agreed upon with Mr Kissinger by Britain and the African presidents; it was merely a set of 'proposals'.

(*b*) **1952** *N.Y. Herald Tribune* 14 Apr. 6 (Advt.), Unique, new, all-expense fishing 'package' trips. **1952** *N.Y. World-Telegram & Sun* 29 Apr. 25/1 Eastern Air Lines has mapped out an ambitious schedule of package vacations. **1958** *New Statesman* 11 Oct. 502/2 The great increase in British visitors, however, has been in the less expensive areas, and this is reflected in the range of 'package' tours offered by the travel agencies. **1960** *News Chron.* 11 Apr. 9/4 Pony trekking..is probably the most popular of all the package-holidays. **1964** M. McLuhan *Understanding Media* (1967) II. xx. 212 They can have..Berlin or Venice in a package tour. **1967** *Spectator* 1 Dec. 699/3 Cut-price package trips [are] practically keeping the international airlines going during the slack season. **1971** *Daily Tel.* 9 Jan. 18/3 Moscow..is one place where the package tourist scores heavily over the independent tourist. **1973** J. Symons *Plot against Roger Rider* II. 45 Are they going to be stranded in a foreign city?.. Reassured, the package tourists sink into their seats. **1976** A. Grey *Bulgarian Exclusive* xiv. 99 A large Russian package tour group. **1976** *Field* 18 Nov. 980/2 We read of the pilgrimages to Eton..and the crowds who flocked there—'those package tourists of medieval times'. **1977** *Irish Times* 8 June 4/1 Mr. Adrian Hopkins, of Bray Travel, which organises package holidays in the Seychelles, said yesterday that they could have full refunds if they decided not to travel.

(*c*) **1946** *Sun* (Baltimore) 18 Feb. 11/5 The boys in blue finally have come up with touring package shows of their very own. **1952** *N.Y. Jrnl.-American* 23 May 13/1 Judy Garland and Sid Luft are investing close to $100,000 in producing their own package shows to tour the country. **1956** B. Holiday *Lady sings Blues* (1973) xx. 165 When theatre dates began to slack off, Mr. Levy decided to get together a whole package show, with me as the star and fronting the band. **1958** *Amer. Speech* XXXIII. (Suppl.) 73 A package show on radio or television may involve a number of varied performances given once a week throughout the year, with a core of main performers and with others who are brought on for one or more performances, but not for all. **1959** *Tatler* 1 Apr. 34/1 Stan Getz, star of last year's 'Jazz At The Philharmonic' package show in Britain.

c. Any related group of objects that is viewed or organized as a unit.

1947 Crowther & Whiddington *Science at War* Pl. ix (*caption*) A late model; it is a 'package', with magnetron and magnet complete with rectangular wave guide out of which power pours. **1952** *New Yorker* 12 Apr. 45 (Advt.), The big, beautiful, package that comprises the restaurants of Rockefeller Center. **1958** *Observer* 12 Oct. 1/3 The objectives of this lavish experiment were..to test the interaction of the three stages..and..to achieve a trajectory that could be controlled enough to put the final package within some 50,000 miles of the moon. **1962** F. I. Ordway et al. *Basic Astronautics* iv. 128 The cosmic ray package contains two proton monitors..and devices to detect electrons. **1962** S. Carpenter in *Into Orbit* 56 Another item which is thrown off, just before re-entry, is the package of three retro-rockets which ride strapped to the heatshield during most of the mission. **1965** *IEEE Trans. Reliability* XIV. 114 (*heading*) Impact testing of plug-in circuit packages for high reliability. **1968** *Times* 10 Dec. 6/7 The orbiting observatory carries two experimental packages, both intended to make observations in the ultraviolet region of the spectrum. **1970** *Sci. Amer.* Feb. 26/1 If..one wanted to design a central processor with 1,000 logic elements, one could begin by selecting 200 integrated-circuit packages, each containing an average of five gates of the kind desired. **1972** *Computers & Humanities* VII. 82 A collection of canned programs maintained as a unit is a library. If they are closely related in content, e.g., all statistical, then the library is a package. **1976** *Offshore Platforms & Pipelining* 23/2 The pump package of Noble's Rig 27 varies slightly from the specification guide. **1976** *Physics Bull.* May 202/3 A Japanese company has recently developed a multicolour three-dimensional image video package, using 35 mm film for the storage of the holograms, which is aimed at the advertising, educational, medical and recreational markets. **1977** *Modern Boating* (Austral.) Jan. 81/2 Every boat-trailer-motor package which goes out of their doors is fully equipped with the recommended number of fire extinguishers as well as all other recommended safety gear as part of the package.

d. Misc. *attrib.* uses of sense 3 a. (All *N. Amer.*)

1821 *Deb. Congress U.S.* (1855) 16th Congress 2 Sess. App. 1526 Package sales..by the assortments of merchandise they combine, excite most interest. **1888** M. Deland *John Ward* i. 2 They were at the mercy of Phibbs, the package man, who brought their wares on his slow, creaking cart..from Mercer. **1971** H. A. Smith *View from Chivo* xiii. 127 Jim Davey closed the package store two hours early and shut off all beer sales. **1976** *Amer. Speech 1974* XLIX. 115 *Package bar*, establishment that sells packaged goods (wine, beer, and hard liquor) as well as serves liquor by the drink.

package, *v.* [f. the sb.] *trans.* To wrap up, make into a package. Also *fig.* and *absol.*

1928 M. H. Weseen *Crowell's Dict. Eng. Gram.* 445 *Package*, commercial cant as a verb. **1947** M. McCarthy *On Contrary* (1961) 11 An image of happiness as packaged by the manufacturer. **1954** N. Tomalin in *Granta* 6 Nov. 21/1 Two licensed pigeon-feed sellers who..earn ten pounds a day, have factories in Ealing packaging the peas, and are worried acutely by their income tax. **1959** *Listener* 30 July 186/3 There is no lack of playwrights who carry on the old trade of packaging sentimental hokum into a tough shell. **1967** *Boston Sunday Herald* 26 Mar. VI. 7/6 Something for everybody is the way Air France describes its 1967 Jet Away Holidays tour program, recently packaged and distributed to travel agents. **1970** *Natural Hist.* Feb. 18/3 Philadelphia is now packaging its trash, putting it into empty coal cars and then shipping the material back to the strip mines as land fill. **1972** *New Yorker* 2 Dec. 162/2 The black films are packaged, financed, and sold by whites. **1976** N. Postman *Crazy Talk* 70 Billy Graham has packaged his 'message' in a way not unlike that in which Scope packages its 'message'. **1976** *NBR Marketplace* (Wellington) III. 5/1 It brings in its products from factories overseas (US, UK, Australia, and even Brazil) and packages here.

packageable (pæ·kėdʒăb'l), *a.* [f. *Package *v.* + -able.] Capable of being packaged, in the various senses of the verb.

1961 *Aeroplane* CI. 578/2 From the present generation of packageable propellents (e.g. nitric acid and a mixed amine fuel), a practical realizable specific impulse of about 245 sec. can be obtained. **1977** *Church Times* 6 May 7/1 Fundamentalism, like Maoist Marxism, is positive and highly packageable.

packaged (pæ·kėdʒd), *ppl. a.* [f. *Package *v.* + -ed[1].] Wrapped up, made into a package; pre-packed.

1933 R. Simmat *Princ. & Pract. Marketing* viii. 67 The various types of packaged product may be divided into two classifications—the liquid and the solid. **1934** S. B. Whipple *Noble Experiment* 173 The exorbitant prices for packaged spirits and wines. **1945** P. Cheyney *I'll say she Does!* ii. 41 This Confucius certainly knew his packaged goods. **1952** [see *knock-down *a.* 3]. **1958** *Times* 4 Aug. 9/2 The pile of débris that results from unpacking a pound of packaged biscuits has to be seen to be believed. **1964** M. McLuhan *Understanding Media* (1967) II. xx. 207 The age of the consumer of processed and packaged goods. **1969** *Jane's Freight Containers 1968–69* 184 Packaged Timber Berth.

b. *fig.*

1946 R. Blesh *Shining Trumpets* (1949) xiv. 325 The mediocre, but financially profitable slick packaged musical trash. **1947** *Richmond* (Virginia) *Times-Dispatch* 11 May 1-D/4 Scheduled for this Summer are some 14 weekly 'packaged' tours. **1951** *N.Y. Herald-Tribune* 24 Apr. 23/6 Fifteen 'packaged' lessons have been prepared. **1953** R. Chandler *Long Good-Bye* iv. 22 The goddam women will start..making up with the packaged charm. **1954** *Sun* (Baltimore) 16 Oct. 12/6 Many insurance companies offer homeowners a 'packaged' policy..at a saving over the cost of a multiplicity of policies each to cover a limited field. **1958** *Observer* 7 Dec. 15/6 Some of the units would be 'packaged' kitchens, bathrooms or bedrooms—that is to say, units with built-in furniture and fittings. **1959** *Economist* 7 Feb. 511/2 A packaged holiday, usually consisting of two weeks or ten days.. for an all-in charge that includes air ticket and hotel bill. **1959** *Listener* 23 Apr. 700/1 A foreign policy that is a packaged deal. **1961** L. MacNeice in *New Statesman* 30 June 1054/3 The weather is packaged and the spacemen In endless orbit. **1967** A. Cowan in Wills & Yearsley *Handbk. Managem. Technol.* 160 It is not possible to write a prescription which can be applied as a finite system to a business. This is a disappointment to those who hope that a neat, packaged solution can be found. **1970** *Daily Tel.* 10 Nov. 17/5 Even ghost-hunters have been offered a packaged tour of the haunted houses of England. **1975** *Times* 18 June 5/2 The packaged tourists pay homage and more solid currency to Anne Hathaway's cottage.

packager (pæ·kėdʒəɹ). [f. *Package *v.* + -er[1].] One who packages, in the various senses of the verb.

1959 *Wall St. Jrnl.* (Eastern ed.) 14 Jan. 1/1 They're rough-and-tough 'action-adventure' shows, and all have been produced by independent packagers—TV program producers who assemble the ingredients of story, director and cast, and then put them together to make a show. **1969** *Listener* 17 Apr. 538/1 'These two are the outstanding producers and packagers of guilt in our time,' whines Alexander Portnoy of his parents. **1976** *New Yorker* 19 Apr. 31/2 Morty Mann, the packager of 'Back-Chat', who claims to have lost 'a small fortune' in the enterprise, says that the program failed because the Prince just couldn't 'relate'. **1977** W. Marshall *Thin Air* ii. 22 We'll go and see your food packager.

packaging, *vbl. sb.* (in Dict. s.v. Package.) (Further examples.) Also *fig.*

1934 *Planning* II. xxxvi. 10 They must submit samples, manufacturing formula, chemical analysis.., description of process of manufacture and packaging. **1950** *Sunday Times* 7 May 8/4 It is apparent..that in the last 12 months packaging has improved considerably. **1954** *Economist* 20 Feb. 568/1 Some of the subsidiaries do 'quite a substantial amount of trade' in packaging materials. **1957** L. F. R. Williams *State of Israel* 96 Much attention is being paid to grading, packaging and marketing. **1962** *Rep. Comm. Broadcasting 1960* 34 in *Parl. Papers 1961–2* (Cmnd. 1753) IX. 259 A trivial presentation may consist ..in an excessive interest in smart 'packaging' at the expense of the contents of the package. **1962** M. McLuhan *Gutenberg Galaxy* 268 Language and the arts would..become mere packaging devices. **1976** R. Barnard *Little Local Murder* ix. 105 Slovenly shoppers who could be deceived by the most patently bogus special offer, the most obviously inflated packaging device. **1977** W. Marshall *Thin Air* ii. 24 I've seen the food packaging people... Apparently the packaging is done in the evenings.

packaway (pæ·kăwēi), *a.* [f. Pack *v.*[1] + Away *adv.*] Capable of being folded into a small space when not in use.

1957 *Archit. Rev.* CXXII. 355/3 Other garage doors will be shown... A new packaway door..which was exhibited in prototype at the last exhibition..has been modified and improved since. **1973** *Times* 4 May 15/1 Up in London's Seven Sisters Road, they are marketing the best value in child-to-adult, packaway bicycles I have seen. **1974** *Times* 5 Mar. 9/1 (*caption*) Those amorphous, ectoplasmic packaway jobs [*sc.* mackintoshes] the earnest tourists wear.

packed, *ppl. a.*[1] **1.** Add to def.: Of meals, packaged for transporting and eating on a picnic or in an informal manner.

1958 B. Pym *Glass of Blessings* xvi. 186 Sitting on mackintoshes, eating packed lunches..tramping home again through the rain—one can see how he would yearn after Portugal. **1959** 'M. Innes' *Hare sitting Up* III. i. 167 He'll be back in no time. With a nice packed lunch. **1965** E. Salter *Once upon a Tombstone* II. xvii. 152 How about a trip up the glacier? We could take a packed lunch and make a day of it. **1968** *Guardian* 30 Mar. 10/5 You can.. be met at Benbecula by a hired car with a packed meal in it. **1973** G. Mitchell *Murder of Busy Lizzie* iv. 49 We're going to explore the island. Do you think, Father, that we could ask for a packed lunch? **1976** *Times Lit. Suppl.* 5 Nov. 1398/4 What an outing that would have been; you would have needed a packed lunch.

b. *Med.* Applied to blood cells separated as much as possible from plasma (usu. by centrifugation); esp. in *packed-cell volume*, the proportion of a sample of blood, by volume, occupied by cells after they have been allowed to settle; cf. *hæmatocrit* s.v. *Hæmato-, hemato-.

1933 *Amer. Jrnl. Med. Sci.* CLXXXV. 59 Several students of the blood have again become interested in the determination of the volume of packed red cells by means of various types of hematocrit. **1943** *Lancet* 6 Nov. 576/2 The mean corpuscular hæmoglobin concentration, which is the ratio of the hæmoglobin content of the blood (grammes per 100 c.cm.) to the volume of the packed red cells (hæmatocrit). **1955** *Ibid.* 17 Dec. 1274/2 *Investigations.*—Blood-count: hæmoglobin 4·7 g. per 100 ml.; packed-cell volume 14%; mean corpuscular hæmoglobin concentration 33%; [etc.]. **1961** *Ibid.* 26 Aug. 490/1 A thirteen-year-old boy required a 250 ml. packed-cell transfusion every four to five weeks. **1967** S. Taylor et al. *Short Textbk. Surg.* i. 11 Packed-cell transfusions are viscid and slow to flow. **1974** *Jrnl. Appl. Physiol.* XXXVII. 976/1 These data were obtained under very carefully controlled conditions (e.g., careful measurement of packed cell volume and resistivity..). **1976** *Nature* 1–8 Jan. 47/2, 0.25 ml of packed cells were added to 2 ml of a medium.

c. *Computers.* Of, pertaining to, or being a decimal number stored with successive digits represented by successive half-bytes and the sign by the rightmost half-byte.

1964 *IBM Jrnl. Res. & Devel.* VIII. 95 (*in figure*) Packed decimal number. **1966** R. Silverstone in A. Opler *Programming the IBM System/360* xi. 126 All internal decimal arithmetic operation[s] must be performed in packed format. *Ibid.*, Since packed numbers require half as much space as zoned decimal numbers, they should be used in storing or writing intermediate files which are not to be directly printed. **1973** Murrill & Smith *Introd. Computer Sci.* vi. 219 To obtain the packed representation from the zoned (or unpacked) representation, we need only to (a) remove all zone fields and (b) transpose the sign and digit fields in the rightmost byte... Systems such as the IBM 360 have hardware instructions to 'pack' and 'unpack' decimal numbers.

packer[1]**.** Add: **3. a.** Also *Canad.* and *N.Z.* Also in extended use.

1859 *Brit. Colonist* (Victoria, B.C.) 6 June 2/3 The arrival of over one hundred pack mules from the Chilliwak country, where they have been wintering, and offers by the packers to take freight to Lytton City for eighteen cents, has failed to revive trade. **1874** A. Bathgate *Colonial Experiences* x. 135 The rear [of string of pack-horses was] brought up by the packer on horseback, his broad-brimmed wide-a-wake hat pulled well over his weather-beaten face. **1952** H. Innes *Campbell's Kingdom* 22, I was wakened with the news that the packer was in from Come Lucky and would be leaving after lunch. I was taken out and introduced to a great ox of a man who was loading groceries into an ex-army truck. **1958** G. Terry *Hist. & Legends of Chilcotin* 7 Tom Hutchinson was a packer and worked with a pack train of 300 mules between Yale and Barkerville. **1968** R. M. Patterson *Finlay's River* 101 When they travelled with horses they had, in him, a competent packer.

b. Also *Canad.* Also, a pack-dog.

1908 A. C. Laut *Conquest Gt. Northwest* II. 270 Getting two or three of the wise old bell-mares, that are in every string of packers, at the end of a long rope, the canoemen shot across the whirl of mid-stream and got footing on the opposite shore. **1944** J. Martin *Canad. Wilderness Trapping* 13 In spring and fall when it is impossible to haul your supplies, dogs come in handy as packers.

c. One who transports goods in a pack on

his back; also, in more recent use, one who carries a rucksack containing all the necessities of travelling. Chiefly *Canad.*

1873 G. M. Grant *Ocean to Ocean* 356 We could see that continuous labour for one or two years in solitary wilderness..as surveyor, transit-man..or even packer, is a totally different thing from taking a trip across the continent. **1892** E. S. Brookes *Frontier Life* xiii. 117, I have often watched the packers, who would carry a load of seventy-five pounds on their backs, through a rough survey line for six or seven weeks. **1921** A. Heming *Drama of Forests* 320 Upon the first his companion placed two more packs; then, stooping beneath the weight of 240 pounds, the packers at a jog-trot set off uphill and down, over rugged rocks and fallen timber. **1968** R. M. Patterson *Finlay's River* 29 He was a short, stocky man—the ideal build for a packer—and it was nothing for him to pack a two hundred-pound load over a long portage. **1974** *Weekend Mag.* (Montreal) 9 Mar. 20/3 It is something peculiar to the Spanish that they look on every packer as a hippie-freak—and they don't like hippie freaks.

4. (Further example.)

1902 *Census Bull.* (U.S.) No. 216. 28 June 61/1 Types succeed each other in the packer with 3-em space between the words, until a continuous line is formed.

5. (Examples.) For '*U.S.*' read 'orig. *U.S.*' and substitute for def.: A device inserted into an annular space in an oil well (such as that between the casing and the tubing) in order to block the flow of oil and gas.

1885 *Encycl. Brit.* XVIII. 718/1 An indiarubber packer is then attached in such a manner that within it the pipe that is above it slides in that which is below it, and the rubber is forced against the sides of the drill-hole. **1904** *Dialect Notes* II. 386 When a well has sufficient gas to flow its product through a two-inch pipe, but will not make its production through the casing, a packer is placed at or near the top of the sand to compel the gas or oil to relieve itself only through the tubing. **1922** D. T. Day *Handbk. Petroleum Industry* I. 291 The fundamental principle of all types of packers embodies the vertical compression and lateral expansion of a resilient substance ..between casing or tubing and the wall of the hole, between two strings of casing, or between tubing and casing. **1960** C. Gatlin *Petroleum Engin.* xiii. 256/1 The ratio of hole diameter to unexpanded packer diameter is kept as low as possible, and commonly ranges from 1·1 to 1·2. **1973** J. W. Jenner in Hobson & Pohl *Mod. Petroleum Technol.* (ed. 4) iv. 141 In some areas where the wells are not easily accessible..a packer is run on the tubing and set just above the pay zone. Completion fluid of high enough density to kill the well is contained in the annulus above the packer and production is via the tubing. **1977** *Sunday Times* 24 Apr. 17/4 The plug is called a packer, and it blocks off the bottom of the outer casing.

packer[2]. (Later example.)

1905 W. O'Brien *Recoll.* 295 Mr. Peter O'Brien.. afterwards earned the titles of Lord O'Brien of Kilfenora and..'Pether the Packer'.

packet, *sb.* Add: **1. f.** *slang* (chiefly *Mil.*). A bullet or other missile; hence, trouble, misfortune; *to stop* (or *cop*, etc.) *a packet*, to be killed or wounded; to get into trouble; to be reprimanded.

1917 P. MacGill *Brown Brethren* xx. 284 Wot's she doin' standin' out in the street like that?.. She'll stop a packet if she's not careful. **1925** Fraser & Gibbons *Soldier & Sailor Words* 219 *Packet*, a bullet wound, *e.g.* it would be said of a wounded man:—He 'stopped a packet' or 'bought a packet'—*i.e.*, got hit by a bullet. Also, any trouble or unexpected bad luck. **1933** D. L. Sayers *Murder must Advertise* vii. 120 I'm really fearfully sorry you copped that packet that was meant for me. **1946** J. Irving *Royal Navalese* 130 *Packet*, trouble, in some form or another. 'So-and-so caught his packet on the Russian convoys'... 'Smithie caught a packet from "The Bloke".' **1948** Partridge *Dict. Forces' Slang* 135 Blimey, old Bill didn't half cop a packet from the C.O. **1958** B. Hamilton *Too Much of Water* xi. 236, I was a bit vague as to when Swete got his packet. **1960** 'H. Carmichael' *Seeds of Hate* viii. 70 Frank Mitchell copped a packet on the river bank. **1978** A. Price *'44 Vintage* iii. 39 We've been disbanded... The same thing's happening to the 2nd Northants, they've caught a packet too.

g. A large sum of money. *slang.*

1922 M. Arlen *Piracy* III. viii. 214 Tarlyan and Cypress had both won a packet at *chemin de fer*. **1928** Wodehouse in *Strand Mag.* Aug. 114/1 'Get in on the short end,' said Aurelia earnestly, 'and you'll make a packet.' **1930** W. S. Maugham *Bread-Winner* II. 76 It cost me a packet. **1955** 'E. C. R. Lorac' *Ask Policeman* vii. 101 Lived in style for years and must have spent a packet. **1959** J. Fleming *Miss Bones* xv. 171 I've cleaned up a nice little packet..but Walpurgis still owes me quite a bit. **1966** J. Betjeman *High & Low* 74, I bet your racket brings you in a pretty packet. **1972** P. D. James *Unsuitable Job* iii. 80 That awful cross of roses... Poor old nanny, it must have cost her a packet.

h. *Physics.* A localized disturbance of a field or medium that retains its identity as it travels; usu. = *wave packet* (*wave *sb.* 10).

1928 *Proc. R. Soc.* A. CXVII. 278 We may imagine that by means of Heisenberg's γ-ray microscope we have detected an electron near a hydrogen nucleus in the form of a packet like (5·4) with x_0, etc., so adjusted that on the older quantum theory the particle would describe the nth circular quantum orbit. **1934** *Discovery* May 125/1 Photons (quanta or packets of electro-magnetic energy) are in general more efficient in bringing about atomic changes than particles of corresponding energy. **1956** A. A. Townsend *Struct. Turbulent Shear Flow* v. 102 If this is true, a packet of turbulent fluid that has been moved across the flow by large eddy motion will have a turbulent intensity determined by its rate of energy gain over a considerable part of its previous existence as turbulent fluid. **1970** *Nature* 29 Aug. 937/2 As long as the incoming packet is spatially sharp enough, the reflected packet will manifestly carry information about the scattering mass.

2. (Further examples.)

1852 J. R. Planché *Invisible Prince* ii. 14 Fierce whiskered gents,..Smoked bad cigars, on board the penny packets. *a* **1936** Kipling *Something of Myself* (1937) ii. 26 Turkey..turned up, usually a day or two late, by the Irish packet, aloof, inscrutable.

3. *packet-ship* (earlier examples), *-steamer*; *packet cigarettes, goods* (examples), *mix, soup, tea* (examples); **packet rat**, a derogatory name for a seaman, *spec.* one who specialized in the short voyage across the Atlantic.

1909 *Westm. Gaz.* 5 June 11/1 The demand for packet cigarettes..has given rise to the manufacture..of special brands. **1958** *Observer* 9 Feb. 5/3 Packet goods... Loose goods. **1977** 'J. Fraser' *Hearts Ease* ix. 103 Shelves of tinned and packet goods. **1968** D. E. Allen *Brit. Tastes* i. 35 Housewives in the South are fonder of all the speeded-up ways of cooking... Packet mixes are used with less compunction. **1894** Stevenson & Osbourne *Ebb-Tide* II. ix. 172, I fought my way, third mate, round the Cape Horn with a push of packet-rats that would have turned the devil out of hell and shut the door on him. **1906** *Daily Chron.* 11 Aug. 4/6 It is almost as far a cry from the days of the Liverpool 'packet rat' as it is from the craft of to-day to the 'coffin ships' of Plimsoll memory. **1920** *Punch* 7 Apr. 266/1 An' the blessed lights o' Liverpool a-winkin' through the rain To welcome us poor packet-rats come back to port again. **1935** J. Masefield *Victorious Troy* 68 'Who in hell said "Time, too?"' Cobb asked... 'Which of your damned packet-rats said "Time, too", then?' **1967** A. L. Lloyd *Folk Song in England* iv. 296 The packet-rats sailing under the house-flags of the Black Ball, Red Star, Dramatic and Swallowtail lines. **1782** R. Morris *Let.* 7 Oct. in J. Jay *Corr. & Public Papers* (1891) II. 349 Joshua Barney..[is] now commanding the Packet Ship *General Washington*. **1837** A. Langton *Jrnl.* in *Gentlewoman Upper Canada* (1950) 9, I should strongly recommend avoiding a crowded packet-ship..or perhaps a packet-ship at all. **1962** *Which?* Jan. 20/1 For convenience in shopping, the packet soups (the least heavy and bulky) are obviously better than the tinned soups. **1974** A. Ross *Bradford Business* 125 We stoked up hurriedly on packet soup and woody pork chops. **1865** T. P. Kettell *Hist. Great Rebellion* xx. 246 These two vessels had been packet-steamers, running to New York. **1883** E. Eggleston *Hoosier School-Boy* 115 The little packet-steamer was landing at the wharf. *c* **1870** in A. Davis *Package & Print* (1967) Pl. 192 (Advt.), Niblett's farm house bread stores... Agent for the celebrated packet tea. **1907** *Yesterday's Shopping* (1969) 1 Packet Teas packed on the estates in China and India. **1931** *N. & Q.* 14 Nov. 353/2 One of the earliest distributors of packet tea was the one-time old-fashioned firm of Horniman. **1976** *Times* 28 July 1/6 Packet tea and large, sliced loaves are among the eight foods for which manufacturers have voluntarily restricted prices.

packetarian (pækĕtēə·riăn). *U.S.* [f. Packet *sb.* 2 + *-arian.] One of the crew of a packet-boat.

1882 *Harper's Mag.* July 281/1 The typical 'Jack' of the pre-propeller age—the 'packetarian', and the able seaman of the clipper-ship fleet—has..utterly vanished. **1887** S. Samuels *From Forecastle to Cabin* 265 The 'packetarians' came last, and they invariably found themselves reduced to the same toggery in which they boarded the ship. **1930** R. Clements *Grey Seas* 110 No 'packetarians' these days, Mr. Findlay.

† packeteer (pækĕtīə·ɹ). *Obs.* except *Hist.* [f. Packet *sb.* + -eer.] **1.** *Canad.* A carrier (often an Indian) of letters and documents, esp. in the fur trade.

1784 J. Thomas in *Publ. Hudson's Bay Rec. Soc.* (1954) XVII. 27 Tradesmen at their separate employs, Hunters, Trappers, fishermen, and pacqueteers. **1943** *Beaver* Mar. 30/1 Mail packets were operated on a time-table, just as are mail flights by aeroplanes today. 'Packeteers' were never armed.

2. = *packetarian.

1922 *Short Stories* Feb. (early issue) 141/2 *Au revoir*, Joe Pichegru, you sun-smoked son of a packeteer!

packeter (pæ·kĕtəɹ). *Canad.* [f. Packet *sb.* + -er[1].] = *packeteer 1.

1893 J. Horden *Forty-Two Yrs. amongst Indians & Eskimo* xv. 147 The packeters returning from Abbitibbe with the letters..to Moose. *Ibid.* xvii. 169 The 'packeters' were espied crossing the river, in snow-shoes. **1961** J. W. Anderson *Fur Trader's Story* iii. 24 Others again would drive dog teams..while others would be 'packeters', hauling the mail..in winter.

pack-flat (equal stress), *a.* [f. Pack *v.*[1] + Flat *a., adv.*] Capable of being made into a flat package.

1951 *Good Housek. Home Encycl.* 107/2 Glass-top coffee table with pack-flat base. **1969** E. H. Pinto *Treen* 375 The 18th-century, 'pack-flat', mahogany wig stand..is exactly like modern travelling millinery stands. **1974** *Sunday Tel.* 6 Oct. 20/1 (Advt.), Sportsmans snug will keep you warm & dry in the worst weather! Full size 54″ × 30″ × 20″. Pack flat 30″ × 6″ × 2″.

packie (pæ·ki). *N.Z. colloq.* [f. Pack *sb.*[1] + -ie.] = *packman 2 b.

1945 J. D. Pascoe in *N.Z. Geographer* I. 20 Next on the list is the 'packie'—half-cook, half-handyman, always good with horses or mules—who takes blankets and provisions into 'camp'. **1947** P. Newton *Wayleggo* (1949) 14 The process is repeated, the 'packie' moving on again. **1963** *Weekly News* (Auckland) 8 May 39/1 The packie happened to come in that morning for more bread. **1972** P. Newton *Sheep Thief* iv. 31 An old packie by the name of Paddy Roper lost two of his team there.

packing, *vbl. sb.*[1] Add: **I. 1. c.** (Earlier example.)

1861 Geo. Eliot *Let.* 10 Dec. (1954) III. 472 As I hope the Florentine hydropathist may not be a quack as Dr. Gully at Malvern certainly is, I shall be disappointed if there is no good effect to be traced to judicious 'packing' and sitz baths.

d. The transporting of goods on pack animals.

1843 *Amer. Pioneer* II. 162 Merchandise..was principally carried on pack horses until after 1788. Packing continued to be an important business in Kentucky until 1795. *Ibid.* 215 The grain would not bear packing across the mountains; a horse could not carry more than four bushels of it. **1897** *Boston Daily Globe* (evening ed.) 4 Aug. 5/2 Prices for packing across the pass have risen. **1948** *Hungry Horse News* (Columbia Falls, Montana) 24 Sept. 8/1 Roy owns a valuable string of pack horses and does considerable packing for the forest service.

e. An extra charge added to the cost of delivered goods to cover the cost of packing them.

1901 *Pitman's Business Terms, Phr. & Abbrev.* 155 *Packing*... The *charge* made for packing. **1974** *Parker's Wholesale Catal.* (J. Parker Dutch Bulbs..Co.) Autumn 13/2 All our prices are inclusive of duty and packing.

f. The spatial arrangement of the constituent atoms of a crystalline structure relative to one another.

1917 [see *hexagonal *a.* 3]. **1945** C. W. Bunn *Chem. Crystallogr.* vii. 276 The mode of packing of atoms, ions, or molecules in crystals may be regarded as controlled by two principles—the principle of close packing.., and, where ions are concerned, the tendency for an electrically charged unit to surround itself with units of opposite charge. **1966** C. R. Tottle *Sci. Engin. Materials* iii. 54 The closeness of packing of atoms in a crystal lattice affects thermal and mechanical properties. **1973** H. D. Megaw *Crystal Struct.* ii. 54 Packing of ions as rigid spheres determines the coordination number (the number of anions surrounding a cation).

II. 2. b. *slang.* Food, particularly if of inferior quality.

1891 J. Bent *Criminal Life* 272 Packing,..food. **1925** Fraser & Gibbons *Soldier & Sailor Words* 219 *Packing*, rations. Food in general. **1973** 'P. Malloch' *Kickback* iv. 27 'When you've had the kind of packing I've had for three years, this is a treat.' He..began to eat.

III. 3. a. *packing-house* (examples), *-paper* (examples), *-plant, -room, -shed* (examples). **c. packing box** (earlier examples); also *attrib.* = **packing case*; **packing case**, also *attrib.* used disparagingly of a type of modern architecture alleged to resemble packing-cases in its regularity and monotony; **packing density** *Computers*, the density of stored information in terms of bits per unit of storage medium; **packing fraction** *Nuclear Physics*, 10,000 times $(M-A)/A$ (or $(M-A)/M$), where M is the atomic weight of a nucleus and A is its mass number; cf. *mass defect* s.v. *mass *sb.*[2] 10 d; **packing needle** (later examples); **packing station**, *spec.* an official depot where eggs are graded and packed; also (with hyphen) *attrib.*

1774 in *Mass. Hist. Soc. Coll.* (1914) LXXI. 214 To a packing Box £0. 9. 4. **1800** Jane Austen *Let.* 25 Oct. (1952) 77 The charge of 3*s* 6*d* for the Packing box. **1909** *Daily Chron.* 8 July 8/3 (*heading*) No 'packing box' houses. They are not turned out by the score or the hundred all to one pattern like packing cases. **1935** *Fortnightly* Apr. 410 So we are given the packing-case building—rectangular boxes with holes punched for doors and windows. **1961** *Times* 11 Apr. 4/2 Sir Jacob Epstein apparently intended a certain reproach to the 'packing-case' type of modern architecture in the bronze group, 'Pan'. **1958** *Wescon Convention Record of IRE* IV. 49/1 The first limitation in packing density is the number of pulses per inch that can be recorded on each track, which is limited by the basic resolution of the head and tape combination. **1967** McLachlan & Molsom *Data Processing* xi. 171 The speed of reading and writing..will depend upon the physical speed of the tape past the read/write head, and the packing density of the information written. **1927** F. W. Aston in *Proc. R. Soc.* A. CXV. 501 The mean gain or loss of mass per proton when the nuclear packing is changed from that of oxygen to that of the atom in question..will be called the 'packing fraction' of the atom and expressed in parts per 10,000. **1938** R. W. Lawson tr. *Hevesy & Paneth's Man. Radioactivity* (ed. 2) xix. 179 The idea of the 'packing fraction' has been introduced, by which we understand the difference between the mass of the atom and the integral part of its mass-number, divided by the mass-number. **1949** Friedlander & Kennedy *Introd. Radiochem.* ii. 38 The mass defect Δ is the difference between the atomic mass M and the mass number A: $\Delta = M - A$... The packing fraction f is the mass defect divided by the mass number: $f = \Delta/A$. (Sometimes f is defined as Δ/M; the difference is negligible.) **1955** A. E. S. Green *Nuclear Physics* ii. 55 Packing fractions are positive (0·6 to 0 mMU) for the stable nuclei from 1 to 20, negative (0 to −0·8 to 0 mMU for nuclei from 20 to 170, and positive again (0 to 0·6 mMU) for the very heavy nuclei. **1968** G. M. Mossop *Advanced Level Atomic Physics* ix. 150 The packing fraction is the mass defect per nucleon. **1834** C. F. Hoffman *Winter in West* (1835) II. xxxii. 136 One of the packing-houses, built of brick, and three stories high, is more than a hundred feet long, and proportionably wide. **1901** *Chambers's Jrnl.* Mar. 208/1 Two of the largest packing houses had in their cold-storage chambers no fewer than two hundred and sixteen million eggs. **1968** *Globe & Mail* (Toronto) 5 Feb. 5/4 He was leading the campaign to organize packinghouse workers. **1977** *Time* 22 Aug. 43/1 By 14 he had quit school and started work as a janitor and a packing-house laborer. **1880** L. Higgin *Handbk. Embroidery* iv. 34 It should now be braced with twine by means of a packing needle. **1937** A. M. Miall *Making Home Furnishings* x. 161 Thread your long curved packing needle with string, and with a few large stitches through the hessian secure the tops of the springs to it. **1861** D. G. Rossetti *Let.* Jan. (1965) II. 392, I shall have it printed on common brown packing-paper. **1939** *Army & Navy Stores Catal.* 305/2 Packing paper and cloth for export parcels. **1921** *Daily Colonist* (Victoria, B.C.) 17 Mar. 2/5 Representatives of ten national packing plant unions today pledged their support to the Amalgamated Order of Meat Cutters. *Ibid.* 9 Oct. 31/5 Fire, which apparently originated in a smokehouse last night, destroyed the packing plant of the H. F. Lewis Company. **1854** *Harper's Mag.* Mar. 456/1 The 'packing-room' is the loft of the gin-house. **1900** H. Lawson *On Track* 94 One day I went downstairs to the packing-room and saw a lot of phosphorus in jars of water. **1960** J. Betjeman *Summoned by Bells* ii. 12 Bang through the packing-room! **1901** *Chambers's Jrnl.* Feb. 99/1 An expert to accompany the fruit from the orchard, through the packing-shed, on to the port of shipment. **1946** K. Tennant *Lost Haven* (1947) vii. 100 Jack Starbrace had fallen over backwards into the packing shed. **1930** E. Brown *Brit. Poultry Husbandry* 347 Packing stations. **1938** L. Pearce-Gervis *Compl. Poultry Keeper & Farmer* v. 150 Each grade has its own particular colour..and contains the registered number of the packing station. **1960** *Farmer & Stockbreeder* 1 Mar. 55/3 Many of us..are not at all happy about current packing-station prices.

packing, *ppl. a.* Add: **2.** As the second element in adj. combs.: habitually carrying, esp. of a weapon, as *pistol-packing*, etc. (See *pack *v.*[1] 9 a.)

1936 E. Ambler *Dark Frontier* xi. 174 How do you suppose we're going to stop a mob of eight dagger-packing Greeks? **1943**, etc. [see *pistol-packing* ppl. adj. s.v. *pistol *sb.* 2]. **1959** *Times Lit. Suppl.* 13 Nov. 664/4 He is forced into carrying a Luger-packing German entomologist on a hunt for a rare and mysterious beetle.

packman. Add: **2. a.** *N. Amer.* One who transports goods by means of pack-animals or in a pack on his own back.

1828 in *Kansas Hist. Q.* (1936) Aug. 251, I & the two pack-men returned to the creek with six horses and all the baggage. **1847** *Ex. Doc. 31st U.S. Congress 1 Sess. House* (1849) No. 5. iii. 627 Two of Judge Burt's packmen arrived today for provisions to take to the parties south. **1908** W. R. Nursey *Story Isaac Brock* vi. 45 Brock would watch these packmen as, thus handicapped with a load weighing from two to five hundred pounds, they set out across the rough portage.

b. *N.Z.* A sheep-station handyman whose principal duties are conveying goods by pack-animal from camp to camp and cooking; hence also **packman-cook.**

1933 L. G. D. Acland in *Press* (Christchurch, N.Z.) 11 Nov. 15/7 *Packer, packman*, one who loads the packhorses and leads or drives them from camp to camp. He also cooks for the musterers. **1961** B. Crump *Hang on a Minute* 76 The packman-cook [on the sheep-station] was a muttering-to-himself old man called Joe. **1963** *Weekly News* (Auckland) 31 July 37/1 Packman-cook can be a tough job in some places. **1972** P. Newton *Sheep Thief* vii. 51 'Come and get it or I'll chuck it out.' The packman's rude yell rang through the hut and all hands stirred.

packsaddle, *v.* [f. the sb.] *trans.* To convey on a packsaddle.

1912 *Red Mag.* Mar. 508/1 They had a burro on another ledge of the estate, which packsaddled things in from where the stage dropped them.

pact, *v.* For *Obs.* read *rare* and add later example of sense b.

1940 *Economist* 6 Jan. 10/2 To-day Germany has pacted with Communism, Italy is neutral, the West fights Germany.

‖ **pacta sunt servanda** (pæ·kta sunt sɜːvæ·nda), *phr.* [L., lit. 'agreements must be kept': cf. Cicero *De Officiis* iii. xcii pacta et promissa semperne servanda sint; *Digesta Iustiniani* ii. xiv ideo servandum erit pactum conventum.] The principle, esp. in international law, that agreements are binding and inviolable.

1855 R. Phillimore *Commentaries upon Internat. Law* II. v. vi. 56 *Pacta sunt servanda* is the pervading maxim of International, as it was of Roman jurisprudence. **1925** E. Satow in *Cambr. Hist. Jrnl.* I. 295 (*heading*) *Pacta sunt servanda* or International Guarantee. **1939** E. H. Carr *Twenty Years' Crisis* xi. 232 War writers..have attempted to treat the rule *pacta sunt servanda* not merely as a fundamental rule of international law, but as the cornerstone of international society. **1945** J. L. Kunz in *Amer. Jrnl. Internat. Law* XXXIX. 197 *Pacta sunt servanda* means the institution, by general international law, of a special procedure—the treaty procedure—for the creation of international norms... Valid treaty norms must be kept, but they can, by appropriate procedures, be revised. *Pacta sunt servanda* means the inviolability, not the unchangeability, of treaties. **1958** *Reports of Judgments* (Internat. Court of Justice) 121 The maxim *pacta sunt servanda* is of special significance in considering this contention of the Government of Sweden. **1962** *Times* 27 June 8/6 The ordinary rule was that contracts were to be enforced—*pacta sunt servanda*. **1973** I. M. Sinclair *Vienna Convention on Law of Treaties* iii. 53 Article 26 of the Convention reproduces, in lapidary language, the basic principle *pacta sunt servanda*, designated by the Commission as 'the fundamental principle of the law of treaties'.

paction, *sb.* (Further examples.)

1856 Bouvier *Law Dict.* (ed. 6) II. 277 *Pactions*. International Law. When contracts between nations are to be performed by a single act, and their execution is at an end at once, they are not called treaties, but agreements, conventions or pactions. **1883** *Wharton's Law Lexicon* (ed. 7) 586/1 *Paction*, a bargain or covenant. **1964** *Mod. Law Rev.* XXVII. 314 In *Learmonth* v. *Sinclair's Trustees*..Moncrieff L.J.-C. said: ..Now custom, whether general or local, when it is effectual operates not by implied paction or contract but by law.

pacu. Also **paku.** Substitute for def.: A large, vegetarian, freshwater fish, *Colossoma nigripinnis*, belonging to the family Characidæ and native to the northern parts of South America. (Later examples.)

1938 A. H. Verrill *Strange Fish & their Stories* 218/1 Pacu. **1959** P. Capon *Amongst those Missing* 181 Not too bad, I guess. A paku, and two of those fish sort of like bream. **1962** D. W. Tucker tr. *Sterba's Freshwater Fishes of World* 112 (*caption*) The Pacu is a rarely-imported species from northern South America. **1974** H. MacInnes *Climb to Lost World* vi. 86 In the river there was plenty of Pakuweed, so called by the Indians because the Paku fish is supposed to feed on it. **1977** D. J. Coffey *Encycl. Aquarium Fish* 89/1 *Colossoma nigripinnis*. Pacu. 71 cm. (28 in.) This fish comes from the Amazon... Body colour is silver. The dorsal and anal fins are red in colour.

pacy, var. *pacey *a.*

pad, *sb.*[2] Add: **1. b.** *Austral. spec.* A track made by bullocks, cattle, camels, etc. Cf. *cattle-pad* s.v. *cattle 9.

1911 C. E. W. Bean *'Dreadnought' of Darling* xxiii. 207 The white track was the pad made by the feet of many camels. **1934** A. Russell *Tramp-Royal in Wild Australia* ii. 20 The pad was winding and rocky and scarcely discernible. One sometimes wondered if it really was a pad, so little did it look like one. **1941** I. L. Idriess *Great Boomerang* ix. 67 You'll see the pad leadin' back to the horse paddock. **1954** B. Miles *Stars my Blanket* xix. 138 In places we were able to follow a wandering bullock-pad. **1966** 'J. Hackston' *Father clears Out* 19 We almost wore a series of pads through the bush trailing it. **1968** K. Weatherly *Roo Shooter* 37 They strode down the cattle pad at a fast walk.

pad, *sb.*[3] Add: **I. 1. b.** A bed; hence, a lodging, a place to sleep; one's residence. Also, a room frequented by narcotic (esp. marijuana) users. *slang* (orig. *U.S.*).

1718 C. Hitching *Regulator* 19 The names of the Flash Words now in vogue amongst Thieves... The Padd, *alias* Bed [etc.]. **1846** *Swell's Night Guide* 67 The only question she asks is, 'vot pad do you vont?' **1914** Jackson & Hellyer *Vocab. Criminal Slang* 64 Pad.., a bed; a place to sleep. **1938** *New Yorker* 12 Mar. 36/3 Pads where semi-conscious smokers are robbed of their money are creeper joints. **1956** 'E. McBain' *Cop Hater* (1958) ix. 79 'If Ordiz is a junkie, what's he doing on Whore Street?' 'He's blind in some broad's pad.' **1959** [see *beatnik* s.v. *beat generation]. **1959** N. Mailer *Advts. for Myself* (1961) 346, I went with my wife and my friend..to a cold-water pad, south of the village. **1961** *Spectator* 25 Aug. 266 In this half world of cats, pads and hipsters there is a residual morality. **1965** 'Malcolm X' *Autobiogr.* 57 Cats' pads, where with the lights and the juke down mellow, everybody blew gage and juiced back and jumped. **1967** *Boston Sunday Herald* 26 Mar. iv. 1/3 'Four out of five times when we go into a pad where we have been told there is pot, we find it', says the detective. **1967** N. Lucas *C.I.D.* x. 134 A 'pad' is a bed—in a flat, a house, a bed-sitter or even in a shack. **1973** 'D. Shannon' *No Holiday for Crime* (1974) vi. 89 She's got a pad over on Nadeau Street. **1974** K. Millett *Flying* i. 26 The usual university ghetto pad, an old house gone hip. **1977** *Time* 17 Jan. 8/3 They later searched the apartments of several employees, as well as Starckmann's swank pad in Neuilly.

c. A padded cell: cf. Padded *ppl. a.*[2]

1938 S. Beckett *Murphy* 167 The padded cells, known to the wittier as the 'quiet rooms', 'rubber rooms' or, in a notable clip 'pads'. **1964** G. L. Cohen *What's Wrong with Hospitals?* vii. 147 The side-rooms are in fact 'pads' remaining from the pre-tranquillizer regime. **1965** *New Statesman* 23 July 119/2 Quondam padded cells, now pink and chintzy, are given to old reliables who could leave hospital if they had anywhere to go. 'Yes, we do keep two 'pads' for isolation purposes,' barked the burly N.C.O.

3. e. A strip of rubber (etc.) material fitted in the road which when depressed by traffic operates road signals. Cf. **detector-pad*.

1933 H. Watson *Street Traffic Flow* ix. 165 Electric contact pads or strips, called 'detectors' laid in the carriageway, and actuated by vehicles. **1935** *Times* 3 Dec. 11/4 The installation of pedestrian control signals, to be operated by traffic pads. *Ibid.*, The Hendon Council, however, did not consider that the provision of pad-operated pedestrian signals would serve the desired purpose on such a road. **1960** H. Manzoni in E. Davies *Roads* vii. 176 The signals are actuated by vehicles passing over a detector pad consisting of two hollow rubber treads.

f. = *launching pad* s.v. *launching *vbl. sb.* b.

1949 *Gloss. Guided Missile Terms* (GM 51/8) (Res. & Devel. Board, U.S. Dept. Defense) 75 *Pad*, a permanent or semipermanent base constructed to support a missile-launching device. **1953** *Air Univ. Q. Rev.* Fall 32 (*caption*) To withstand the pressures and intense heat of the exhaust blast during take-off, the 100-foot-square pad must be two-and-one-half feet thick. **1958** *Times* 1 Mar. 6/3 The missile had been on its pad for days before firing. **1964** Mrs. L. B. Johnson *White House Diary* 24 Mar. (1970) 101 Saturn I will be used to send an unmanned Apollo spacecraft into orbit—in fact, one is on the pad..now for launching later this spring. **1971** *Sci. Amer.* Sept. 229/3 In 1961..the Russians had just 14 big liquid-fuel SS-6's on open pads. **1973** *Times* 17 Oct. 1/4 Our Egyptian rockets ..are now on their pads ready to be launched by the single order to press a button.

g. A take-off or landing point for a helicopter.

1960 *Washington Post* 1 Dec. D13/1 The mushrooming uses to which the 100-by-100 foot concrete helicopter 'pad' at the Pentagon is being put today. **1972** L. Hancock *There's a Seal in my Sleeping Bag* ix. 238 We were walking along the boardwalk past the helicopter pad. **1974** *BP Shield Internat.* Oct. 18/2 With a slight bump and shudder, we landed on the helicopter pad. **1976** 'L. Black' *Healthy Way to Die* ii. 17 The circling helicopter was descending towards the pad. **1977** *Time* 31 Jan. 15/1 On the drive from a helicopter pad to his office, his swift-moving convoy was guarded by three select commando battalions.

h. = *cow-pad* (*cow *sb.*[1] 8).

1971 *New Scientist* 1 July 36/2 The dung is also the incubation medium of many helminth parasites of stock, the eggs of which are passed in the pads. **1973** *Nature* 30 Nov. 271/1 Such dung pads soon dry into a hard cake. **1974** *Sci. Amer.* Apr. 101/2 On the average 12 dung pads are dropped by a single adult bovine every day. **1976** *Australasian Express* 3 Sept. 2/1 Dung pads are being eaten at a rapid rate in the northern half of Australia.

III. 13*. A padding machine. Freq. *attrib.*

1935 *Textile World* LXXXV. 1860/2 Formation of the patches is a danger signal, however, and—as is true of all danger signals in the pad dyehouse—should be taken heed of at once if serious trouble is to be avoided. **1951** *Jrnl. Soc. Dyers & Colourists* LXVII. 508/1 In dyeing practice, the nearest approach to printing technique was the so-called pigment-padding process, where the vat dye was applied on the pad as a suspension of unreduced dye. **1955** *Ibid.* LXXI. 896/1 Difficulties may arise from this increase [in width], e.g. from wrinkles passing the pad nip. *Ibid.* 900/1 Does the preferential uptake of water by the dry cloth entering the pad box cause a slight change in the concentration of direct dye and give a length of cloth off shade at the beginning of a run? **1961** Cockett & Hilton *Dyeing of Cellulosic Fibres* xi. 358 The essential parts of a pad are a nip of two or more rollers, a trough, and means of applying pressure to the nip. **1966** *Encycl. Polymer Sci. & Technol.* V. 238 The machine consists of two or three squeeze rolls mounted over a shallow trough, or 'pad box', provided with guide rolls for the cloth.

13.** *Electr.* A resistance network inserted into a transmission line to attenuate all frequencies equally by a known amount.

1931 *Electronics* Feb. 508/1 The term 'pad' as commonly employed in connection with audio frequency circuits, refers to an attenuation device used to reduce the power at a point in a circuit by some desired value... Regarded as an electric circuit, a pad consists of a one-section artificial line whose elements are pure resistances. **1951** W. J. Creamer *Communication Networks & Lines* v. 46 Non-symmetrical pads may be employed for the purpose of matching impedances, but there will be a minimum loss below which it is not possible to go without getting into the difficulty of a negative resistance element. **1959** K. Henney *Radio Engin. Handbk.* (ed. 5) xxi. 22 The minimum attenuation setting of a ladder pad normally corresponds to its insertion loss, which amounts to approximately 2·5 db. **1967** D. H. Hamsher *Communication Syst. Engin. Handbk.* vi. 31 Two-wire trunk circuits may contain a switchable 2-db pad.

13*.** *U.S. slang.* (See quots.)

1970 *Daily Tel.* 27 Apr. 3 New York police have their own secret slang to deal with illegal business... A 'pad' is an establishment that provides police with regular payoffs. **1971** *N.Y. Times* 19 Oct. 47 The gamblers of the city paid off the policemen on a regular monthly basis after they had been placed on what is called 'the pad'. **1971** *Guardian* 28 Oct. 13/6 [He] was thrilled with becoming a plainclothesman because..'he was now on the pad'. The pad is the regular sum paid to officers for ignoring illegal activities. **1971** *Time* 1 Nov. 23 When a cop was transferred to a new post, the pad from his old station kept up for another two months. **1973** M. Truman *Harry S. Truman* iii. 72 In Kansas City there was a tradition of carrying one or two thousand city employees 'on the pad' without requiring them to show up for work.

IV. 14. *pad-foot* (examples), *-mark* (later examples); **pad eye** *Engin.* (see quot. 1909); **pad mangle**, a padding machine; **pad money** *U.S. slang* (see quots.); **pad-play** (examples); **pad room** *U.S.*, in a theatre, a waiting-room for performers; **pad-steam**, used *attrib.* and *absol.* to denote a process in which fabric is first padded and then steamed; **pad stitch** (see quot. 1968); also (with hyphen) as *vb.*; so **pad stitching; padstone** (see quots.).

1909 *Cent. Dict. Suppl.*, *Pad-eye*, in ship-building, a flat rectangular piece of metal with an eye or ring projecting edgewise from its surface, the whole forming one solid piece. It is attached to the surface on which it is placed by screws or rivets through the flat part. **1972** L. M. Harris *Introd. Deepwater Floating Drilling Operations* vi. 76 The principal use of buoys in floating-drilling operations is to mark anchors... The unit should have strong padeyes on top and bottom for attaching handling lines and pendants. **1976** *Offshore Platforms & Pipelining* 239/3 For added strength, cables are run from each corner of the frame to the existing pad eyes on the mass anchor. **1905** F. S. Robinson *Eng. Furnit.* xii. 181 The legs of these tables are somewhat too straight to be classed as cabriole, and have pad feet. **1955** R. Fastnedge *Eng. Furnit. Styles* 286 *Pad foot*, resembling the club foot but set on a disk. **1974** *Country Life* 7 Mar. (Suppl.) 40 A fine quality George II red walnut Armchair in original condition having cabriole legs and pad feet. **1955** *Jrnl. Soc. Dyers & Colourists* LXXI. 777/2 On leaving the pad-mangle, the goods should pass directly into a Mather & Platt ager. **1966** R. C. Cheetham *Dyeing Fibre Blends* i. 59 Piece-dyeing is usually carried out on a pad-mangle, with the least possible duration in the wet state. **1926** T. E. Lawrence *Seven Pillars* lxvi. 344 We..marched south..seeing tracks of gazelle..with, in one spot, stale padmarks of leopard. **1973** *Times* 14 Aug. 14/5 Only pad marks of mink were found. **1904** 'No. 1500' *Life in Sing Sing* 256/2 Pad money, money for lodgings. **1927** *Dial. Notes* V. 457 *Pad money*.., money for a night's lodging or for admission into an opium den. **1920** E. R. Wilson in P. F. Warner *Cricket* 94 [They] used to bowl round the wicket in order to get batsmen l.b.w. with their off break, which, if bowled over the wicket, permitted 'pad play'. **1956** N. Cardus *Close of Play* 15 Hobbs and Sutcliffe twice frustrated an Australian attack on 'sticky' pitches—on one of the most vicious of all, at Melbourne, largely by pad-play. **1960** J. Fingleton *Four Chukkas to Australia* 39 His reliance on so much pad-play had ruined his stroke-play. **1927** K. Nicholson *Barker* 149 *Pad room*, waiting room for performers. **1931** *Amer. Mercury* Nov. 353/2 *Pad room*, a dressing tent. **1945** *Textile World* Jan. 84 (*heading*) Pad-steam dyeing reaches volume production. **1961** Cockett & Hilton *Dyeing of Cellulosic Fibres* xi. 361 The several forms of pad-steam..give greater production because of their continuous character. **1966** *Encycl. Polymer Sci. & Technol.* V. 240 The Du Pont pad-steam process employs steam under controlled conditions to bring about dye fixation. **1924** W. D. F. Vincent et al. *Cutters' Pract. Guide Cutting & Making Body Coats* 30/3 Whether or not you pad-stitch the collar, or stitch together by machine, give it firmness as well as shape. **1964** *McCall's Sewing* ix. 126/2 *Pad stitch*, this stitch is very similar to diagonal basting stitch. **1968** J. Ironside *Fashion Alphabet* 84 *Pad-stitch*, 1. In Tailoring: A diagonal basting stitch used to hold interlining or canvas to fabric. 2. In Embroidery: Filling stitches over which fancy stitches are worked; used to give bulk. **1964** *McCall's Sewing* xiv. 254/1 End pad-stitching at seam line. **1963** *Gloss. Gen. Building Terms* (*B.S.I.*) 19 *Padstone*, a block of stone or concrete built into a wall to distribute the pressure from a concentrated load. **1964** J. S. Scott *Dict. Building* 222 *Padstone*, a stone or concrete pad in a wall.

pad, *v.*[1] Add: **1. c.** (Later examples.)

1904 [see *boot *sb.*[3] 1 c]. **1916** J. B. Cooper *Coo-oo-ee* x. 130 A dog with you breaks the lonesomeness of the bush, I know. We've padded the hoof together. **1966** 'J. Hackston' *Father clears Out* 108 When the people..missed the coach, and had to pad the hoof into the town.., they'd take the short cut. **1970** *N.Z. Listener* 21 Dec. 8/4 We pondered on the day years ago when we were padding the hoof ourselves.

2. b. Also of a person, and reduplicated *pad-pad*.

1899 C. J. C. Hyne *Further Adventures Capt. Kettle* v. 84 Naked feet pad-padded quickly up over the dust and grass. **1926** A. Bennett *Lord Raingo* i. ii. 7 A nice thing, that with five servants in the place, and him a millionaire, he should be reduced to padding about in his socks! **1966** 'J. Hackston' *Father clears Out* 84 Father was changing as we padded along. **1975** M. Bradbury *History Man* vii. 126 Felicity pads at Howard's side down the long bright passage.

pad, *v.*[2] Add: **2. b.** To extend or increase (an official list, expense account, claim for payment, etc.) with unauthorized or fraudulent items.

1913 *Maclean's Mag.* Mar. 104 (*heading*) Padding the expense account. *Ibid.* 105/2 To pad this account by magnifying the cost of hotel accommodation, meals and railway fare, was most distasteful to him. **1921** *Daily Colonist* (Victoria, B.C.) 23 Oct. 1/2 John W. Duncan, charged with padding a cheque.., was found not guilty. **1928** *Observer* 15 Apr. 12 They claim that the list of members..was heavily 'padded' by the inclusion of persons without their knowledge and consent. **1967** *Boston Sunday Herald* 26 Mar. iv. 3/1 Beating the system can be done by padding bills, adding a dollar here, two dollars there, for medical items, clothing and so forth. **1968** *Economist* 14 Dec. 27/2 A report by a Granada television team in Britain showed that the [voting] lists were padded. **1976** 'M. Albrand' *Taste of Terror* xi. 67 Forster never paid but preferred to be sent a bill in spite of the fact that he knew it was padded.

3. Substitute for def.: To impregnate *with* a liquid or paste by squeezing between rollers, the substance applied being either on one of the rollers or in a bath preceding them. (Further examples.)

1897 C. T. Davis *Manuf. Leather* (ed. 2) 324 They first pad the leather with a solution of alizarine rendered slightly alkaline with ammonia. **1927** C. E. Mullin *Acetate Silk* (1928) xxx. 375 In applying the developed colors on cotton, the fiber is usually first padded in the naphthol bath and then the color developed in a second bath. **1933** *Chem. Abstr.* XXVII. 2045 Fabrics having a cellulose acetate pile are printed or padded with a soln. of regenerated cellulose in caustic alkali to obtain a local or over-all deposition of cellulose. **1972** D. Hildebrand in K. Venkataraman *Chem. Synthetic Dyes* VI. iii. 431 The fabric which has been padded with dyestuff and anti-crease agent is stored in the presence of mineral acid as catalyst for 1–3 hours.

pada (pā·dă). Also **padam**. [Skr., = foot.] **a.** An Indian lyrical poem set to music. Also *attrib.*

1880 F. S. Growse *Mathurā* (ed. 2) 212 He is said to have written a Hindi poem called the Dasratna, together with a few short *Sākhis* and *Padas* in the same language. **1898** B. A. Pingle *Indian Mus.* (ed. 2) ii. 64 The Dhrupada is a later form of the original Padas or Bhajanas (prayer or praise). **1914** [see *bhajan]. **1957** O. Gosvami *Story Indian Mus.* xx. 212 The *Padam* is sung in the same way as the *Kriti*. **1967** Singha & Massey *Indian Dances* ii. 43 Padas are love lyrics which cover every conceivable aspect of love from the mystic and divine to the earthly and profane. **1968** *Jrnl. Mus. Acad. Madras* XXXIX. 102 Annamacharya says that the songs of one ignorant of the proper style and pattern of *pada*-composition..would be worthless. **1972** P. Holroyde *Indian Mus.* 275 Padams demand a very dramatized technique of mime gesture and facial expression. **1974** B. C. Deva *Indian Mus.* v. 76 The songs of Bhadrachala Ramadas..are referred to as pada-s.

b. A group of words forming a section of Sanskrit verse; a mode of reciting this.

1887 M. Monier-Williams *Brāhmanism & Hindūism* (ed. 3) xv. 409 These Vedic texts may be recited according to any one or more of the five different Pāthas, or modes of recitation, called Samhitā, Pada, Krama, Jaṭā, and Ghana. **1916** A. A. Macdonell *Vedic Gram. for Students* 449 A hemistich of two or more Pādas is treated as a unit. **1917** —— *Vedic Reader for Students* p. xiii, The earliest expedient of this kind was the formation of the Pada or 'word' text, in which all the words of the Saṃhitā text are separated and given in their original form as unaffected by the rules of Sandhi. **1965** *Language* XLI. 11 Three instances are accounted for by the pāda *devān devayaté yaja*. **1971** *Language* XLVII. 59 The first three pādas are hyposyllabic as transmitted.

padanda, var. *pedanda.

‖ **padang** (pa·daŋ). [Malay.] An open grassy space; a field, esp. a playing-field; also, scrub vegetation.

1915 *Blackw. Mag.* Dec. 793 Two others were caught near the Europe Hotel, sitting on the 'padang' by the sea. **1927** R. J. H. Sidney *In Brit. Malaya To-Day* 45 We are standing on my large verandah overlooking the school *padang*. **1933** L. Ainsworth *Confessions Planter in Malaya* 74 They had been given leave to gather on our Padang (a large field in the centre of all our coolie lines). *Ibid.* 182 The clubhouse is set in very pleasant surroundings, with a large padang, or playing-field, attached. **1952** P. W. Richards *Trop. Rain Forest* ix. 211 The vegetation was the so-called padang, a kind of heath-like scrub or poor forest. **1964** K. G. Tregonning *Hist. Mod. Malaya* x. 226 E. W. Birch..was one of those whose delight it was to see a *padang*, a shady playing field, laid out in every kampong of the State. **1972** *Malay Mail* (Kuala Lumpur) 25 May 4/5 The pasar malam..will be held at Dato Kramat padang from Wednesday. **1977** *Borneo Bull.* 7 May 4-A/2 Red Cross Day will be celebrated here tomorrow (Sunday) with a parade on the town padang followed by a ceremony in the Youth Centre.

padauk, var. Padouk (in Dict. and Suppl.).

padded, *ppl. a.*[2] For 'treated with a mordant in calico-printing' substitute: Impregnated throughout with a dye or the like by padding (see *pad *v.*[2] 3). (Further examples.) *padded cell* (examples); also *fig.* and *transf.*; also (with hyphen) *attrib.*; *padded room* (see quot. 1976); *padded shoulders*, the shoulders of a suit, etc., padded to give the appearance of breadth; also *fig.*; *padded soap*.

1891 S. P. Sadtler *Handbk. Industr. Org. Chem.* ii. 61 Soaps made in this way retain all the glycerine..and belong to the class known as 'filled' or 'padded' soaps. **1935** H. G. Wells *Things to Come* 14 The fact that in the future various light apparatus such as a portable radio, electric torch, notebook, will have to be carried on the person and that this will probably necessitate a widening of those broadly padded shoulders which are already necessary in the costume of contemporary men because of their wallets and fountain pens. *a* **1936** Kipling *Something of Myself* (1937) vii. 176 A 'comfortable nursery' proved to be a dark padded cell at the end of a discreet passage! **1959** N. N. Holland *First Mod. Comedies* 39 'Dapperwit' implies a comparison of clothes and wit, as though Dapperwit's pretensions to wit were a kind of padded shoulders to cover his actually feeble intelligence. **1961** Cockett & Hilton *Dyeing of Cellulosic Fibres* xi. 361 Where vat dyes are concerned, development of the padded goods with alkaline reducing agent may be carried out discontinuously on jigs. **1962** A. Nisbett *Technique Sound Studio* ii. 48 Of the various possible sound-deadening systems, it is best to try to avoid those which give a padded-cell effect. **1963** Wodehouse *Stiff Upper Lip, Jeeves* xxii. 167 Stiffy, who is pure padded cell from the foundations up, was planning to marry the Rev. H. P. Pinker. **1972** D. Hildebrand in K. Venkataraman *Chem. Synthetic Dyes* VI. iii. 424 If the substantivity of the dye is insufficient, the dye will migrate when the padded goods are dried under inhomogeneous drying conditions. **1973** *Jewish Chron.* 19 Jan. 14/5 To give readers some idea of what passes for dialogue in the padded cell of the drama department, here is the kind of exchange in which Mr Mackie specialises. **1976** *Amer. Speech* 1973 XLVIII. 207 An uncontrollable patient may be sent to the *quiet room* or *QR*, formerly called the *padded room*. **1977** *Time* 3 Jan. 56/3 You will recall that the last we saw of Inspector Clouseau he had succeeded in..driving his immediate superior, Chief Inspector Dreyfus, completely, totally, padded-cell mad.

padder, *sb.*[2] Add: **2.** A padding machine.

1927 C. E. Mullin *Acetate Silk* (1928) xxviii. 361 It is usually best to dye the acetate silk first and then cross-dye the cotton either in the padder or jig. **1955** *Jrnl. Soc. Dyers & Colourists* LXXI. 812/2 In order to get as good impregnation as possible before the fabric reaches the nip of the padder, this small volume is combined with a comparatively long path through the padder trough. **1971** E. I. Valko in H. Mark et al. *Chem. Aftertreatment of Textiles* iii. 105 Impregnation of fabric is frequently carried out by first immersing the fabric and then pulling it between the rolls of a padder.

3. *Electronics.* Also **padder capacitor, condenser.** A usu. adjustable capacitor connected in series in a tuned circuit in order to improve the tracking with another tuned circuit at low frequencies when the tuning of the two circuits is ganged (as in a superheterodyne). Cf. *trimmer.

1936 J. H. Reyner *Testing Radio Sets* (ed. 3) xiii. 190 (*in figure*) Padder. **1939** H. J. Hicks *Princ. & Pract. Radio Servicing* ii. 21 C10, C11, C12 and C13 are the trimmer and padder condensers employed in the oscillator circuit to make it track with the r.f. tuning condenser. **1950** A. Marcus *Radio Servicing* xi. 453 In addition to the series padder, a small trimmer capacitor is usually connected in parallel with the main tuning capacitor. **1971** A. Margolis *Mod. Radio Repair Techniques* vi. 82 To maintain the tracking difference, a smaller oscillator coil and padder capacitor is added to the circuit.

padding, *vbl. sb.*[2] Add: **1.** (Further examples, corresponding to *pad *v.*[2] 2 b and Pad *v.*[2] 3 in Dict. and Suppl.)

1954 *Jrnl. Soc. Dyers & Colourists* LXX. 383/2 The polymer emulsion..is then suitably diluted for application to the fabric, and applied by padding and drying. **1964** 'E. Lathen' *Accounting for Murder* (1965) x. 94 It would take more than a little juggling of expense accounts to explain the situation... Somebody must have gone into a panic about some minor padding. **1973** *Times* 31 July 1/8 Several delegations have submitted a variety of inflated expense statements ranging from high living to outright padding of the bills.

attrib. **1912** J. Hübner *Bleaching & Dyeing Veg. Fibrous Materials* xvi. 371 The padding machine may be used for..impregnating with the aniline solution in the dyeing of Aniline Black. **1935** *Chem. Abstr.* XXIX. 4179 Dyeing in concentrated dye bath... The mech. and operating details of padding mangles of various manuf. are described. **1963** A. J. Hall *Textile Sci.* iv. 193 The textile material..is impregnated evenly with the dye liquor with the aid of a so-called padding mangle. **1973** *Materials & Technol.* VI. vii. 461 The most popular type of padding machine has two or three rollers giving one or two immersions in the padding solution.

3. *Electronics.* The use of a padder; *padding capacitor* or *condenser* = *padder *sb.*[2] 3.

1935 A. T. Witts *Superheterodyne Receiver* iv. 37 Condenser C3, the padding condenser, has a capacity that is large in comparison with the tuning condenser C2, with the result that at the lower settings of the latter the padding condenser has very little effect. **1936** J. H. Reyner *Testing Radio Sets* (ed. 3) xiii. 190 The alternative method, that of padding and trimming, is usually adopted. *Ibid.* 191 We..have three variables, namely, the oscillator inductance, the parallel trimming condenser, and the series padding condenser, and three frequencies which are to be 'spot on'. **1946** C. A. Quarrington *Mod. Pract. Radio & Television* I. xviii. 140 The [condenser] vanes are shaped to give the necessary effect when working on the highest frequency band incorporated in the receiver, and the lower frequency band or bands are corrected by means of padding. *Ibid.* 141 The series condenser..is called the padding condenser and is usually..of the pre-set type..; the small parallel capacity..is called the trimming condenser, and is invariably of the pre-set type. **1962** J. H. & P. J. Reyner *Radio Communication* ix. 371 The padding and trimming capacitances must..be altered for each wave range and are usually..changed over by the switching which alters the coils.

4. padding stitch = **pad stitch*.

1913 M. E. Wilkinson *Embroidery Stitches* 123 *Padding stitch*, close Satin stitch worked over a raised or padded grounding. **1955** E. A. Mansfield *Clothing Construction* xv. 323/2 To shorten the fold-line so that the collar will lie close to the neck,..put in two rows of small padding stitches along the fold line.

paddle, *sb.*[1] Add: **III. 7. d.** In *Leather-making* (see quot.).

1885 C. T. Davis *Manuf. Leather* xviii. 356 The motion of the wheels causes the stock to move up in front, pass under the wheels, and down on the concave bottom to the back of the vat, and thus by means of the paddles, and the constant changing position of the stock a thorough and gentle agitation is maintained.

8. b. (Later examples.)

1970 *Wall St. Jrnl.* 16 June 1 The 'board of education', a paddle applied smartly to the backside, may be making a comeback in the classroom. **1977** *New Yorker* 30 May 27/1 One of the boys..was said to have been struck more than twenty times with a paddle.

c. A short-handled bat with a broad, flat blade, used in various ball games.

[**1925**: implied in **paddle tennis*]. **1935** Mason & Mitchell *Active Games & Contests* xxi. 388 Paddle Ball... This is an excellent game played with a paddle-tennis ball and paddle. **1949** P. B. Barringer *Natural Bent* xviii. 127 To play two-hole cat, four boys, two bases, a ball, and two bats were needed. These bats were sometimes called paddles. **1974** E. Tidyman *Dummy* vi. 80 He..accepted a challenge to play table tennis..offering the doctor instruction on the proper way to hold his paddle. **1975** *Oxf. Compan. Sports & Games* 745/1 Bigger and heavier paddles are used, and the ball may be played into court off the walls. **1976** *Webster's Sports Dict.* 299/2 The table tennis paddle is slightly smaller than the paddleball paddle.

9*. *Astronautics.* A paddle-shaped array of solar cells projecting from a spacecraft.

1959 *Listener* 13 Aug. 247/1 The four 'paddles' re-charge the satellite's batteries by converting sunlight into electricity. **1966** *Electronics* 17 Oct. 36 The two solar paddles each extend 19 feet from the Agena and together provide 15 kilowatts. **1972** *Nature* 17 Mar. 90/1 The solar paddles and antenna were also reported to be working satisfactorily.

IV. 10. *paddle-boat* (examples), *punt, steamer* (earlier example), *tug*; (sense 4) *paddle-foot*.

1874 J. W. LONG *Amer. Wild-Fowl Shooting* 79 Now the building of a paddle-boat is not so simple an under-taking as many of my readers may suppose. **1891** *Scribner's Mag.* X. 13 She was a paddle-boat, built of wood, and was 207 feet long. **1938** M. K. RAWLINGS *Yearling* xx. 261 The remaining bears were scrambling across the swamp like paddle boats, churning the water behind them. **1954** J. R. R. TOLKIEN *Fellowship of Ring* II. ix. 399 It wasn't a log, for it had paddle-feet. **1909** *Yachting Monthly* Dec. 93/2 The 'paddle punt' is about 14 ft. long, strongly built on the Deal model. **1918** N. DUNCAN *Battles Royal* IV. ii. 242 Old Elihu Maul, with a hook and line, had fished the Boiling Pot in civil weather from a paddle-punt. **1970** E. J. MARCH *Inshore Craft Gt. Brit.* II. ii. 82 The second class [*sc.* punts]..cost £12. Generally known as 'paddle punts', they were used for inshore fishing. **1886** *Outing* VIII. 26/1 The Ripple, [a] paddle steamer of the river steamer type. **1923** *Man. Seamanship* (Admiralty) II. viii. 152 For long tows at sea the screw tug is the most efficient, as owing to the propellers being totally submerged they are not affected by the sea to the same extent as paddle tugs. **1930** J. MASEFIELD *Wanderer of Liverpool* 15 The Paddle-tug Wrestler arrived at an hour ere flood. **1955** *Times* 6 June 6/6 Experience has shown that paddle tugs are more efficient than screw-driven tugs for work in confined basins because of their great manoeuvrability and power.

11. paddle ball, a game played with a light ball and wooden bat in a four-walled handball court; **paddle board,** (*b*) a wooden board for supporting a person in water, esp. when surfing; **paddle-box** (earlier and later examples); also *transf.*; **paddle foot** *U.S. slang,* (*a*) an infantryman; (*b*) a member of an airforce ground crew; (see also sense 10 above); † **paddle-plane** *Aeronaut.* = *cyclogiro, -gyro* s.v. *CYCLO-; **paddle tennis,** a type of tennis played in a small court with a sponge-rubber ball and wooden or plastic bat; **paddle-vat** = *paddle-tumbler*; **paddlewheeler,** a paddle steamer.

1935 Paddle ball [see sense 8 c above]. **1962** *Times* 14 Nov. 3/6 Games of..paddle-ball (Rugby fives with table tennis bats). **1973** *Daily Colonist* (Victoria, B.C.) 20 May 2/2 Our daughter..gets blisters on her soles after a hard game of tennis or paddle ball. **1975** *Listener* 9 Oct. 484/1 A *cinquantaine sportive* concern to keep fit through paddle ball at the Downtown Club. **1967** J. SEVERSON *Great Surfing* Gloss., *Paddleboard,* a square-sided, hollow surf-craft usually constructed of plywood. **1968** *Surfer Mag.* Jan. 56/1 He surfed a hollow paddle board that he made at home. **1974** 'R. B. DOMINIC' *Epitaph for Lobbyist* xvi. 139 He was going to find time for healthful exercise—paddle-board, or a few turns in the pool. **1833** *Chambers's Edin. Jrnl.* 1 June 140/2 The captain now takes his station on the paddle-box. **1908** G. B. SHAW *Let.* 31 Dec. (1972) II. 823 Charlotte wrecked it [*sc.* the car] the first day. The professional kept her in countenance by knocking off the paddle-box against the gate. *a* **1936** KIPLING *Something of Myself* (1937) iv. 102, I saw..a woman crouching on the paddle-box of a crowded boat. **1976** P. LOVESEY *Swing, swing Together* xxxvii. 175 A coat of white paint on the paddle-box, lifeboats and funnel. **1946** *Amer. Speech* XXI. 34/2 *Paddlefeet*.., Infantrymen. **1948** MENCKEN *Amer. Lang.* Suppl. II. 727 The airmen..use many derisory terms in speaking of themselves..*e.g.,*.. *paddlefoot*..for a member of the ground crew. **1950** *Life* 2 Jan. 98/2 Murray was a paddlefoot in Europe. **1957** *New Yorker* 23 Nov. 67/3 A paddlefoot mess officer in North Africa. **1960** WENTWORTH & FLEXNER *Dict. Amer. Slang* 372/1 *Paddlefoot*.., an infantry soldier. **1933** *Flight* 2 Feb. 107/2 Our Berlin correspondent indicates that the Rohrbach 'paddle plane' has the circumferential speed of the paddles approximately equal to the top speed. **1950** *Gloss. Aeronaut. Terms* (*B.S.I.*) I. 30 *Cyclogyro* (paddle-plane). **1925** *Playground* Mar. 710/1 He secured permission from Park Commissioner Francis B. Gallatin to mark several paddle tennis courts in Washington Square Park. **1944** F. G. MENKE *Encycl. Sports* (rev. ed.) 490 Frank P. Beal..originated Paddle Tennis in 1924 to provide children with a game that would teach them the rudiments of tennis. **1972** *N.Y. Times* 3 Nov. 22/4 (Advt.), A new recreational facility featuring tennis, paddletennis..and a barbeque and picnic area with charming pavilion has been completed. **1903** L. A. FLEMMING *Pract. Tanning* 23 Sheepskins are also very satisfactorily tanned with one-bath chrome liquors in paddle-vats. **1924** H. A. TRIPP *Shoalwater & Fairway* vii. 128 That Belle steamer was a mine-sweeper in the War, and jolly useful they found the old excursion paddle-wheelers. **1970** S. TRUEMAN *Intimate Hist. New Brunswick* vi. 83 He built the *Reindeer,* a paddlewheeler that easily outraced bigger and fancier river boats. **1976** *National Observer* (U.S.) 13 Mar. 8/1 (Advt.), Return to heartland America aboard the legendary paddlewheeler Delta Queen, or the luxurious new Mississippi Queen.

paddle, *sb.*³ Add: **2.** Usu. in form **paidle.** (Earlier example.) Also *attrib.*

1879 *Cases Court of Session, Scotl.* (ser. 4) VI. 1324 Nets ..often have also a barrel-shaped trap or paidle attached to them. **1882** *Ibid.* IX. 186 The respondents..earn part of their living by fishing on the shores of the Solway by means of small stake-nets, locally called 'paidle-nets'.

paddle, *sb.*⁴ Restrict †*rare* to sense in Dict. and add: **2.** (Also *Sc.* **paiddle, paidle.**) An act of paddling in mud or shallow water.

1866 W. GREGOR *Dial. Banffshire* 121 The twa bairns keepit a paidle..in the lint-colle, catchin' wattir-horse. **1880** LONGMUIR & DONALDSON *Jamieson's Etym. Dict. Scottish Lang.* (rev. ed.) III. 430/1 We..had a gran' paidle in the saut watter. **1896** A. M. BISSET *Poets Linlithgowshire* 188 But woe to the imp that..damm'd up the burn for a paiddle or wade. **1942** 'N. SHUTE' *Pied Piper* v. 106 Wouldn't you like to take your shoes off and have a paddle, then? **1976** *Morecambe Guardian* 7 Dec. 25/7 They decided to go for a swim and walked into the sea first for a paddle.

paddle, *sb.*⁵ Add: *Comb.* **paddle-over** [after WALK-OVER], an easy victory in a boat race.

1906 *Westm. Gaz.* 4 July 5/1 Little more than a paddle-over for the Cambridge men.

paddle, *v.*¹ Add: **II. 4.** (Later examples.)

1908 H. G. WELLS *War in Air* iii. 72 Then he got up, paddled about, rearranged the ballast bags on the floor,.. and turned over the maps on the locker. **1970** F. DURBRIDGE *P. Temple & Harkdale Robbery* v. 51 Tam Coley paddled cheerfully out [of the room] with a nod to Paul.

5. *Comb.* **paddle-pond,** a pond in which children may paddle.

1930 *Time & Tide* 14 Feb. 195/2 He saw that these spaces were..empty, and he resolved that some..of them should be filled; hence the goal-posts and paddle-ponds.

paddle, *v.*² Add: **2. b.** (Earlier and later examples.)

1828 J. HALL *Lett from West* 261 It seems that they were not so well skilled in navigation as the *Lady of the Lake,* who 'paddled her own canoe' very dexterously. **1834** W. G. SIMMS *Guy Rivers* II. 225 He guessed therefore, best haul off, and each..'must paddle his own canoe'. **1887** *Harper's Mag.* Mar. 547/1 They couldn't see how he was to paddle his canoe all alone by himself. **1924** [see *BUNCH *v.*² 1 c]. **1924** M. KENNEDY *Constant Nymph* xvii. 232 Why can't she leave the fellow to paddle his own canoe? **1949** *Time* 4 July 25/2 They seem more interested in paddling their own canoes than shaping a strong third force that would be the best weapon against the communism they all hate.

3. (Later examples.)

1919 L. F. CODY *Memories Buffalo Bill* 31, I had started from the porch to paddle every one of them [*sc.* the children]. **1976** 'D. HALLIDAY' *Dolly & Nanny Bird* iv. 48 The first thing a Maggie Bee nurse does in any British household is to ask the mother if she minds if the offspring get paddled from time to time.

4. To use a paddle, in various special senses of the sb.: (*a*) to stir or mix (molten ore) with a paddle; (*b*) to wash or dye (leather) by means of a paddle; (*c*) to stir (the lye in soap-making) with a paddle.

1873 E. SPON *Workshop Receipts* (ser. 1) 382/2 The paddling should be continued until a ring drawn with the spatula may be recognized. **1874** J. A. PHILLIPS *Elem. Metallurgy* 544 The pot-skimmings..are now thrown into the furnace and well paddled with the charge. **1909** H. G. BENNETT *Manuf. Leather* 171 When a quick and even colouring is desired..the goods may be paddled in the first liquors.

5. To use (something) like a paddle.

1929 W. DEEPING *Roper's Row* xxxii. 363 He spread his table napkin, and finding the soup too hot, paddled his spoon in it.

pa·ddle-fish. [f. PADDLE *sb.*¹ + FISH *sb.*¹] A large freshwater fish of the family Polyodontidæ, which includes the two genera *Polyodon* and *Psephurus,* characterized by a projection resembling a paddle attached to the upper part of its head.

[**1686** tr. *Relation Invasion Florida* xxiv. 121 We caught another sort of fish also, called *Pexe-palla,* the *Palat-fish*; the head of it is covered with a kind of an elbow-hood, the upper point whereof is shaped like a Palet or Lingel.] **1807, 1892** [in Dict. s.v. PADDLE *sb.*¹ 11]. **1908** *Century Mag.* July 457/1 In Louisiana it [*sc. Polyodon spatula*] is known as billfish, billdom, and paddlefish. **1948** *Sat. Rev. Lit.* (U.S.) 15 May 26/2 They were assailed by questions about the Paddlefish, the Brindled Stonecat, or the Tessellated Darter. **1962** K. F. LAGLER et al. *Ichthyol.* iv. 110 Examples of partly scaled fishes include the paddlefish (*Polyodon*)..that inhabits streams in Central North America and has also a near-relative, the fresh-water swordbill, *Psephurus,* in China. **1976** *Billings* (Montana) *Gaz.* 16 June 1-C/1 The paddlefish is a living fossil like the Coelacanth..and is found only in two places on earth, the Mississippi River and its tributaries and the Yangtze drainage in China.

2. = *oar-fish* (s.v. OAR *sb.* 6 in Dict. and Suppl.).

1953 *Sun* (Baltimore) 18 Sept. 11/5 One of the world's rarities, an oarfish, or paddle fish, believed to be the origin of sailors' tales of sea serpents, has been caught off Sydney Heads.

paddler¹. Add: **2.** *pl.* A child's waterproof knickers or overall.

1928 *Weekly Dispatch* 27 May 15/7 All-black bathing suits. Besides suits, there are the much needed rubber paddlers, caps, and shoes.

paddle-wheel. Add: **3.** A device shaped like the wheel of a paddle-boat, used in a game of chance.

1926 ADE *Let.* 26 Oct. (1973) 114 We had games as follows: one roulette, one hazard,..one wheel of fortune for cash, one paddle wheel for fancy baskets, dolls, boxes of candy etc. **1935** *Sun* (Baltimore) 22 July 7/4 Operation of paddle wheels, bingo devices and other alleged games of chance would no longer be tolerated. **1939** *Ibid.* 24 Apr. 18/1 Prince George's county..secured passage of a measure that would legalize not only pinball games, but bingo, paddle wheels and other similar devices. **1961** J. SCARNE *Compl. Guide Gambling* xix. 459 *Paddle wheel or raffle wheel,* a carnival wheel each of whose numbered sections contain one, two, or three numbers. Most such wheels have a counter laydown raffle chart on which bets are placed.

4. *attrib.* † **paddle-wheel aeroplane** or **aircraft** = *cyclogiro, -gyro* s.v. *CYCLO-.

1935 *Technical Rep. Aeronaut. Res. Committee 1933–34* I. 8 We have also considered a number of proposals for the construction of..paddlewheel aeroplanes. **1939** *Jrnl. R. Aeronaut. Soc.* XLIII. 756 Unusual aircraft such as flapping wing aircraft, paddle wheel aircraft, tail-first aeroplanes.

paddling *vbl. sb.*¹ (s.v. PADDLE *v.*¹ in Dict.) Add: *Comb.* **paddling pool.**

1932 T. SHARP *Town & Countryside* x. 204 These playgrounds should be equipped with swings,..and a sand-pit and perhaps a paddling pool. **1958** *Listener* 6 Nov. 727/1 Children's paddling pools. **1972** *Guardian* 1 Aug. 15/6 Emma went to the crèche-playgroup where there were swings, slides, books, a paddling-pool, a Wendy-house.

paddling, *vbl. sb.*² (s.v. PADDLE *v.*² in Dict.) (Further examples.)

1874 J. A. PHILLIPS *Elem. Metallurgy* 542 The alternate raking and paddling of the charge is continued at regular intervals. **1888** L. A. SMITH *Music of Waters* 325 The following is a specimen of the paddling-songs, which really form the principal water-music of the Tonga Islands. **1953** P. PROVENCHER *I live in Woods* i. 6 The crews commenced a lively paddling song on quitting the shore.

paddock, *sb.*² **1. c.** Substitute for def.: In Australia and New Zealand, any field or piece of land enclosed by fencing, irrespective of size or land use. (Further examples.)

1822 J. DIXON *Narr. Voy. New South Wales* 58, I saw a few paddocks of clover and English grasses, in as good condition as I have seen the same fields in England. **1847** A. HARRIS *Settlers & Convicts* xiv. 279 In ten months' time from their occupying the farm, there was one of the sides of a paddock fence put up. **1873** TROLLOPE *Austral. & N.Z.* II. xxiii. 368 Vast paddocks containing perhaps 20,000 acres each. **1911** C. E. W. BEAN *'Dreadnought' of Darling* i. 7 The Western Division is inhabited—indeed it is all fenced into paddocks. **1916** J. B. COOPER *Coo-oo-ee* ix. 115 Sandy was in his pumpkin paddock ('pumpkins were the things to feed pigs on'). **1924** H. T. GIBSON *That Gibbie Galoot* xv. 56 By the way, you Colonials call a field a paddock, or more often a paddeck. **1930** L. G. D. ACLAND *Early Canterbury Runs* (ser. 1) i. 7 In the early sixties..expense and the scarcity of water prevented much sub-division into paddocks on most of the plains stations. **1937** 'W. HATFIELD' *I find Australia* iv. 59 The 'horse-paddock' near the homestead was eight miles by eight, and that wasn't a big 'paddock'. **1957** *N.Z. Listener* 22 Nov. 4/3 'Creek' and 'paddock' are New Zealandisms, because they mean something quite different in the English of England. It is of some significance that Katherine Mansfield uses both words only in their New Zealand sense. **1962** J. FRAME *Edge of Alphabet* xv. 81 With the gate into the field (they call it paddock) shut. **1963** B. PEARSON *Coal Flat* xvii. 310 In the lush paddocks on the river flat, a few prosperous farmers ran sheep. **1968** K. WEATHERLY *Roo Shooter* 7 In the forty-five-thousand-acre paddock at the bottom of the rocky hill country the rains have scoured great washouts in the slopes. **1977** *National Times* (Austral.) 17 Jan. 16/4 (Advt.), Lot 7: Homestead Block: 166.05 ha (410 acres) Freehold, gently undulating country running down to river, subdivided into 9 paddocks.

3. (Further examples.)

1862 *Otago: Goldfields & Resources* 34 Sod walls..are largely used in making dams and 'paddocks'. **1874** A. BATHGATE *Colonial Experiences* viii. 93 This process is carried on for months, the tail-race being prolonged into the space from which the ground has been washed away, until a larger hole or 'paddock' is taken out, with precipitous sides, varying in height from a couple of feet to two hundred or more.

4. *paddock fence, gate* (later examples), *sheet*; **paddock-grazing,** in dairy farming, a method of pasture management developed by the French farmer, André Voisin, in which several fields are used in rotation; hence, as a back-formation, **paddock-graze** *v. trans.*

1864 R. HENNING *Let.* 4 Mar. (1966) 156 The 'Station Creek'..came down a roaring river..and swept down with it the whole of the paddock fence which crossed its bed, though it was built in that part of entire trunks of trees. **1908** E. J. BANFIELD *Confessions of Beachcomber* II. iii. 326 The tribe cut off the iron bracing from the paddock gates. **1911** C. E. W. BEAN *'Dreadnought' of Darling* i. 11 The coach had stopped at a paddock gate. **1969** 'J. ASHFORD' *Prisoner at Bar* v. 37 A herd of Frisians were paddock-grazing the nearest fields. **1960** *Farmer & Stockbreeder* 16 Feb. 77/3 It was no use introducing strip- or paddock-grazing unless this was accompanied by a marked increase in stocking. **1962** K. N. RUSSELL *Fishwick's Dairy Farming* (ed. 3) II. 228 This..is the gospel according to Voisin, whose system of rotational paddock grazing Mr. Pearson has recently adopted. **1970** C. S. BARNARD et al. *Milk Production* xv. 240 Paddock grazing is an alternative to strip grazing which obviates the daily task of moving electric fences. Semi-permanent fences are erected to create paddocks of a size and number that enable fresh grazing to be offered every 1–7 days. **1970** R. JEFFRIES *Dead Man's Bluff* ix. 85 The bloke who invented paddock grazing knew a thing or two. **1971** *Power Farming* Mar. 40/2 Paddock grazing is the modern way to really efficient grassland management. It enables grass to be accurately rationed ensuring that each cow has the correct intake of highly nutritious herbage, resulting in increased milk yield per acre and improved milk quality. **1975** *Country Life* 26 June 1702/3 Modern paddock-grazing owes much to the work of ICI..pioneers of the one-day, 21-paddock, two-sward system. **1963** E. H. EDWARDS *Saddlery* xxi. 160 The everyday exercise sheets..are the same shape as a paddock sheet, but usually a few inches larger. **1977** *Horse & Hound* 10 June 28/1 (Advt.), Coloured Rollers, For day rugs or paddock sheets.

paddock, *v.* Add: **1.** (Further examples.)

1873 TROLLOPE *Austral. & N.Z.* II. xii. 214 The sheep are all 'paddocked',—that is, kept in by fences,—so that shepherding is unnecessary. **1930** L. G. D. ACLAND *Early Canterbury Runs* (ser. 1) v. 111 He paddocked the sheep one night at the Rangitata Bridge. *Ibid.*, Meaning to have breakfast at the hotel where his sheep were paddocked. **1941** BAKER *N.Z. Slang* v. 40 *To paddock land*, to put up fences; *to paddock stock*, to put stock into a paddock.

2. Also, To excavate washdirt in shallow ground (see PADDOCK *sb.*[2] 3 a); occas. const. *out*.

1860 *National Mag.* VIII. 307/1 Those who have seen Chinamen at work 'paddocking' in the worn-out alluvial gold-diggings of Australia, can speak for their steady, untiring industry. **1863** V. PYKE in *App. Jrnls. House Reps. N.Z.* D. VI. 18 Many..who held river claims worked very successfully by wing dams, consisting of bags of sand laid into the stream, so as to cut off a portion of its bed, which, being drained by pumping, was paddocked out and passed through the cradle.

paddy, *sb.*[1] Add: **1.** Also, the rice plant. Now freq. written *padi*. (Further examples.)

1893 F. A. SWETTENHAM *About Perak* 41 The country for miles round Parit Buntar has been converted from jungle into fields of sugarcane and padi. **1894** [see *NASI]. **1900** C. O. BLAGDEN in W. W. Skeat *Malay Magic* iii. 58 In the inland villages it is regarded as a great crime to use the sickle (*sabit*) for cutting the *padi*. **1931** *Economist* 19 Dec. 1168/2 Thousands of acres of paddy are being planted in isolated plots that were merely abandoned swamps. **1943** *Sun* (Baltimore) 10 June 12/2 Unmilled or rough rice, growing or cut, is known as 'paddy'. **1966** S. M. SADEEK *Windswept & Other Stories* (1969) 2 The strong winds whistled their..tunes..through the whispering sugarcanes and the sheets and sheets of shimmering padi —green, or golden—under the tropic sun. **1969** J. M. GULLICK *Malaysia* ii. 47 'Padi' is the term for unhusked rice and is used to denote the rice plant. **1971** R. RUSSELL tr. *Ahmad's Shore & Wave* i. 9 All around is flat country.. and dotted about the plains are muddy bluish pools which from the air look like big pieces of blue glass set in the fields of green waving paddy. **1972** M. SHEPPARD *Taman Indera* 163 The grey water bottles are left to dry for two or three days and are then fired in a shallow trench, using coconut fibre, coconut shells and padi husks.

b. = *paddy-field*.

1948 *Amer. Speech* XXIII. 229/2 *Paddy*, a rice field. **1972** *Sci. Amer.* May 23/1 The entire immediate area had been a rice paddy, but during the years when no cultivation had occurred, the rice had been replaced by a very tall reed. **1974** *Encycl. Brit. Micropædia* VII. 668/3 *Paddy*, a wet field used for growing rice. **1974** *Indonesian Observer* 26 July 1/3 The President was informed that the irrigation project whose construction work was begun 1936 but stopped until 1971 will be capable of irrigating 50,330 hectares of paddies. **1974** *Nat. Geographic* Aug. 252 A tree-lined road cut through harvested grainfields and paddies resting under a crystal-blue sky.

3. *paddy-field* (further examples).

1937 *Discovery* Jan. 7/2 Spacious padi fields. **1971** *Illustr. Weekly India* 25 Apr. 42/1 The large tracts of golden paddy fields blended with the molten gold of Niger flowers. **1977** *Borneo Bull.* 7 May 1/5 Four people.. were electrocuted in a padi field at Kampong Keriam, near Tutong, last month when an overhead power cable collapsed on to the field.

Paddy, *sb.*[2] Add: **1.** Also used as a form of address, often felt to be derog., for an Irishman.

1907 G. B. SHAW *John Bull's Other Island* III. 75 *Hodson*... Dont you be taken in by my ole man, Paddy. *Matthew*... Paddy yourself! How dar you call me Paddy? **1916** 'TAFFRAIL' *Pincher Martin* ii. 29 'Stop yer bloomin' noise, Paddy!'.. And Pincher suffered no further inconvenience at the hands of Peter Flannagan.

c. The proprietary name of an Irish whiskey; a drink of this. Also (sometimes with lower-case initial) Irish whiskey generally.

1925 *Trade Marks Jrnl.* 23 Dec. 2827 Paddy... Whisky. Cork Distilleries Company, Limited,..Cork, Ireland; distillers. **1971** J. AIKEN *Nightly Deadshade* vii. 77 Milly is drinking port..and O'Grady, double Paddys. **1974** D. SEAMAN *Bomb that could Lip-Read* vii. 51 Will you gentlemen join me in a drink now?.. Three Paddies, then, is it? **1975** *New Yorker* 25 Aug. 40/3 Did she put Irish whiskey in your glass, that Paddy junk? We asked for Scotch. **1976** N. FREELING *Lake Isle* xx. 140 The drop of paddy's fearfully dear here. I've no opinion of the stuff the supermarket calls Scotch.

4. (Further examples.)

1929 J. OWEN *Shepherd & Child* i. 14 Tristina went—and that without pulling the door behind her 'in a paddy', as she would have done if the order had come from Miss Trellis. **1933** [see *IRISH *sb.* 5]. **1959** 'O. MILLS' *Stairway to Murder* v. 56 It was my awful temper. I used to get into the biggest paddies when I was a kiddie. **1959** I. & P. OPIE *Lore & Lang. Schoolch.* x. 178 They taunt the person:..'Don't get in a paddy.' **1975** J. COWLEY *Mandrake Root* (1976) xvi. 280 You're a pigheaded Stilwell... Got a real paddy when you let go.

7. In Black English, a white person; also *attrib.* or as *adj.*

1946 C. HIMES *Black on Black* (1973) 256 'Hey, don't spit in the sink where you wash the glasses,' some paddy down the bar said. **1962** [see *BOOT *sb.*[3] 1 e]. **1966** *Sat. Rev.* (U.S.) 15 Oct. 74/2 Man, how I hate Paddies (white people)! **1967** *Trans-Action* Apr. 6/1 This field worker.. had run with 'Paddy' (white), 'Chicano' (Mexican), and 'Blood' (Negro) sets since the age of twelve. **1970** R. D. ABRAHAMS *Positively Black* i. 8 The black became beautiful and the white became nothing but a honky and a paddy. **1972** J. WAMBAUGH *Blue Knight* (1973) xiv. 240, I spotted a paddy hustler taking a guy up the back stairs. *Ibid.* 241 Paddy hustling was always a Negro flimflam and that's where the name came from, but lately I've seen white hustlers using this scam on other paddies. **1973** D. BARNES *See the Woman* (1974) 68 'What are you?' Grear said to West. 'This paddy's interpreter?' *Ibid.* 70 Biggest paddy whore in Normandie Avenue. **1976** —— *Yesterday is Dead* (1977) II. 199 Hollister..found he was the only white face in the place... 'You know..I'm the only paddy in here.'

8. *Railway* and *Colliery slang.* (See quots.)

1965 H. SHEPPARD *Dict. Railway Slang* 8 *Paddy*, colliery train from mine to railhead. **1971** D. J. SMITH *Discovering Railwayana* x. 58 *Paddy*, train conveying coal from the pithead to distant sidings. **1977** *Guardian Weekly* 4 Dec. 19/4 Once out of the cage, there was a quarter of a mile to walk over pit railway sleepers, dodging heavy equipment, to the 'paddy' whose proper name is 'the endless rope haulage manrider'.

9. In *Combs.* of **Paddy** or **Paddy's**: **Paddy Doyle** *Services' slang*, confinement in the cells, esp. in phr. *to do*, or *doing*, *Paddy Doyle*; **Paddy's hurricane** *Naval slang*, a flat calm; **Paddy's lantern** *colloq.*, the moon; **Paddy('s) lucerne** *Austral.*, a local name for the tropical evergreen shrub, *Sida rhombifolia*, of the family Malvaceæ, a pest in parts of Australia, although cultivated elsewhere for the fibre it yields; **paddy mail** = sense 8 above; **paddy wagon** *slang* (orig. *U.S.*), a police van; occas., a police car; **Paddy Wester** *slang*, an inefficient or inexperienced seaman; (see also quots.).

1919 Paddy Doyle [see C.B. s.v. *C III. 3]. **1932** E. WEEKLEY *Words & Names* xii. 174 Doing '*Paddy Doyle*' as a euphemism for doing 'time' in the cells. **1948** PARTRIDGE *Dict. Forces' Slang* 136 *Paddy Doyle*, a lower-deck term for 'detention cell'—singular or collective. *a* **1865** SMYTH *Sailor's Word-bk.* (1867) 514 *Paddy's hurricane*, not wind enough to float the pennant. **1891** H. PATTERSON *Illustr. Naut. Dict.* 132 *Paddy's hurricane*, when there is little or no wind, so that the pennant hangs down alongside the mast. **1897** 'F. B. WILLIAMS' *On Many Seas* 43 We came on deck to find a 'Paddy's Hurricane'—a calm. **1903** A. SONNICHSEN *Deep Sea Vagabonds* vii. 114 The winds here never blew at all, or, after the manner of Paddy's hurricane, up and down. **1958** J. G. R. BISSET *Sail Ho!* v. 48 A dead calm was known as 'Paddy's hurricane'. **1933** P. A. EADDY *Hull Down* v. 104 Work round the deck and up aloft is a hundred times easier when 'Paddy's Lantern' is hung out. **1937** PARTRIDGE *Dict. Slang* 600/2 *Paddy's lantern*, the moon: nautical... Prob. after parish-lantern. **1898** MORRIS *Austral Eng.* 195/2 Hemp, Queensland,..name given to the common tropical weed *Sida rhombifolia*... Called also Paddy Lucerne. **1926** 'J. DOONE' *Timely Tips for New Australians* (Gloss.), Paddy's lucerne.—A prevalent type of weed. **1965** *Austral. Encycl.* VIII. 127/2 Paddy's lucerne is so tough and difficult to eradicate that it is reckoned one of the most formidable weed-pests in warmer parts of the Commonwealth. **1945** *Penguin New Writing* XXIII. 85 Colliers were drawn toward it from all the surrounding parts. His mate, Ron Loss, came in by the paddy-mail. **1976** *Star* (Sheffield) 29 Nov. 1/2 A man died today when ten miners were thrown from a paddy mail which crashed at a pit on the outskirts of Barnsley... The paddy mail—a train for carrying miners underground—struck a wooden roof support which had become dislodged, and was derailed. **1930** *Chicago Tribune* 26 Mar. 3/6 He was informed by the pink faced lockup keeper that all Chicago's 'paddy waggons' are motor driven. **1932** J. T. FARRELL *Young Lonigan* vi. 259 First thing you know they'll have you in a jam, and you'll be riding in the paddy wagon. **1946** C. HIMES *Black on Black* (1973) 260 The police..held all four of us there waiting for the ambulance and the paddy wagon. **1964** M. BANTON *Policeman in Community* iii. 51, 2 Patrolmen in a wagon ('Paddy-wagon' or 'Black Maria'). **1967** *N.Z. Listener* 20 Jan. 3/4 A policeman is my guide, and a paddy-wagon my carriage, for a late evening trip around the town's night-spots. **1972** H. C. RAE *Shooting Gallery* iv. 258 The Paddy-wagon, customarily on duty at the cul-de-sac beyond the junction. **1973** *Sunday Mail* (Brisbane) 18 Mar. 25/6 A Police paddy wagon..cruised by. **1974** *Times* 21 Sept. 14/2 Police, dogs, ambulances..a gigantic paddy-wagon. **1927** F. H. SHAW *Knocking Around* xiii. 125 He was not an actual Paddy-Wester, but he had sailed shipmates with many of them. **1929** F. C. BOWEN *Sea Slang* 100 *Paddy Wester*, a fake seaman with a dead man's discharge, after a notorious boarding-house keeper in Liverpool who shipped thousands of green men as A.B.'s for a consideration. **1937** PARTRIDGE *Dict. Slang* 600/1 *Paddy Wester*; occ. *paddywester*. A bogus seaman carrying a dead man's discharge-papers; a very incompetent or dissolute seaman. **1938** W. E. DEXTER *Rope-Yarns* 125 They had a pack of fake seamen sailing on dead men's discharges—a crew of 'Paddy Westers'.

paddy (pæ·di), *a.* [f. PAD *sb.*[3] + -Y[1].] Having pads; cushion-like; soft, mild; also, 'comfortable', placidly self-satisfied.

Not in common use. The contextual sense is not entirely clear in some of the examples.

1865 C. M. YONGE *Clever Woman* II. iii. 38 A pair of plump, paddy-looking old friends. **1873** —— *Pillars of House* II. xix. 156 The paddy good-natured face in bed. **1958** L. M. BOSTON *Chimneys of Green Knowe* 132 He was woken by Orlando's whiskery face poking him in the ear, and a paddy foot on his eyelid. **1962** N. MARSH *Hand in Glove* ii. 53 The impressive things about Sergeant Raikes were his size and his mildness... He said: 'Good afternoon, miss,' in a loud but paddy voice.

paddywhack, -wack. Add: **3.** Also in occas. use in *Austral.* and *N.Z.* (Examples.)

1898 B. KIRKBY *Lakeland Words* 111 Ah gev yon beggar paddy-whack fer his sauce, an' he'll nut fergit it in a hurry. **1923** G. WATSON *Roxburghshire Word-bk.* 227 *Paddy-whack*.., a stroke or blow; a whack or whacking. **1924** *Truth* (Sydney) 27 Apr. 6 *Paddywhack*, a beating. **1965** F. SARGESON *Mem. Peon* iv. 75 'Of course Michael is not going to be unsociable,' she announced. 'I'll have to give him a paddy-whack if he is.'

padenda, var. *PEDANDA.

padge (pædʒ). *dial.* Also **pudge.** [Cf. PUDGE[1].] The barn owl, *Tyto alba*, which has white plumage flecked with brown or grey. Also *attrib.*

1848 A. B. EVANS *Leicestershire Words* 65 Padge-owl, the common owl. **1881** *Ibid.* (new ed.) 208 Padge..the common barn-owl. **1885** C. SWAINSON *Provincial Names & Folklore Brit. Birds* 126 Familiar names [of the barn owl]... Padge, Pudge, or Pudge owl (Leicestershire). **1937** AUDEN in Auden & MacNeice *Lett. from Iceland* viii. 103, I'll never grant a more than passing beauty To pudge or pilewort, petty-chap or pooty.

padi, var. PADDY *sb.*[1] in Dict. and Suppl.

‖ **padkos** (pa·tkǫs). *S. Afr.* Also **padkost,** erron. **pat-koss.** [Afrikaans, f. *pad* road + *kos* (Du. *kost*) food.] Food for the journey; provisions.

1848 R. GRAY *Jrnl.* 16 Dec. (1849) 95 Having got careless as to our 'pat-cop' [*sic*] as we approached home, we fared but badly, and finished our meal by a draught of not the clearest water in the world. **1850** —— *Jrnl.* 6 Nov. (1851) 173, I was not allowed to depart without a good supply of pat-koss, and other comforts provided by the kindness of the parishioners. **1878** *Cape Monthly Mag.* Nov. 273 A dish of 'sesaties' and a couple of loaves..often formed part of the 'padkos'. **1895** in *Funk's Stand. Dict.*, Padkost. **1950** *Cape Times* 19 Sept. 14/1 With apples, biscuits and fish and chips as padkos, Mr. C. J. Kirstein..arrived..from Cape Town..in 12 hours, 45 minutes. **1957** —— 3 Apr. 9 (*heading*) 'Padkos' Passengers. *Ibid.*, One thing the South African Railways have always had to contend with is South Africa's habit of taking along 'padkos' on a journey. **1971** *Sunday Mail Mag.* (Brisbane) 24 Oct. 11/2 No Afrikaner ventures forth on a journey of more than a few miles without his padkos ('food for the road'), and our new friends were seemingly equipped for a fortnight's safari.

padouk. Also **padauk.** Substitute for def.: A large deciduous or evergreen tree of the genus *Pterocarpus*, belonging to the family Leguminosæ, esp. *P. soyauxii* of West Africa, *P. dalbergioides* of the Andaman Islands, and *P. macrocarpus* of Burma and Thailand; also, the reddish hardwood produced by these trees. Also *attrib.* (Earlier and later examples.)

1839 H. MALCOM *Trav. South-Eastern Asia* I. II. 189 The Pa-douk, or Mahogany.., is plenty in the upper provinces... It grows very large, and is mostly of the branched or knotty kind. **1858** C. T. WINTER *Six Months Brit. Burmah* xv. 115 The pa-douk..a highly ornamental evergreen tree with bright yellow papilionaceous flowers, which are very fragrant, exudes a gum. **1908** W. R. FISHER *Schlich's Man. Forestry* (ed. 2) V. 590 Many foreign woods are used for piano-cases—mahogany, American walnut and maple, padauk, satin wood, etc., ebony for keys, and Florida-cedar for the hammers. **1928** *Observer* 25 Mar. 13/2 Counter-tops at the Bank of England are made of Andaman padouk. **1930** *Times Lit. Suppl.* 5 June 483/3 He would be a tiro indeed who could mistake the fierce red and lively grain of padouk, or the dull heavy texture of sabicu for mahogany. **1956** *Handbk. Hardwoods* (Forest Prod. Res. Lab.) 182 Padouk wood is variable in texture. **1967** G. SIMS *Last Best Friend* vii. 61 The weight of the Padouk door might have been the first sign to the perceptive caller that this was a rather special house. **1973** *Times* 1 Feb. 19/3 In the furniture section padouk wood display cabinets..were selling in the £200–£500 range.

Padovan (pæ·dŏvăn), *sb.* and *a.* [f. It. *Padova* (see PADUAN *a.* and *sb.*) + -AN.] **A.** *sb.* = PADUAN *sb.* 1. **B.** *adj.* = PADUAN *a.*

1973 M. WEST *Salamander* i. 42 That girl in the Ferrari, she's a Venetian, a Veronese, a Padovan. **1978** *Sci. Amer.* June 26/1 Eighteen years a professor in Padua, he had published only two books, one an instruction manual.., the other a witty polemic against a Padovan student who had sought to rip off that very instruction book!

pædeia (paidai·ă). Also **paideia.** [a. Gr. παιδεία child-rearing, education.] In ancient Greek society: education or upbringing; more gen., a society's culture; the sum of physical and intellectual achievement to which the human body and mind can aspire. Also *transf.*

[**1875** F. HUEFFER tr. *Guhl & Koner's Life of Greeks & Romans* 196 The education proper of the boy (παιδεια) became a more public one, while the girl was brought up by the mother at home.] **1939** G. HIGHET tr. *Jaeger's*

Paideia I. II. iii. 283 The age of Sophocles saw the beginnings of an intellectual movement... This was the movement mentioned in our introductory chapter: it was *paideia*, education, or rather culture, in the narrower sense. The word paideia, which at its first appearance meant 'childrearing', and which in the fourth century, the Hellenistic, and the Imperial Roman ages constantly extended its connotation, was now for the first time connected with the highest aretê possible to man: it was used to denote the sum-total of all ideal perfections of mind and body. **1962** *Listener* 30 Aug. 323/2 The Lycurgan training for public service enriched Greek 'paedeia'. **1967** *Ibid.* 17 Aug. 201/3 Marx is..built into my intellectual experience, what the Greeks would have called my *paideia*. **1977** G. W. H. LAMPE *God as Spirit* ii. 49 Wisdom is a holy spirit of *paideia*, which, in opposition to materialistic (Epicurean) culture, is the disciplined observance of the Law.

pæderast. (Later examples.)

1925 R. FRY *Let.* 7 Sept. (1972) II. 581 We had a long talk on the tyranny of the Paederasts and Sapphists. **1935** E. E. CUMMINGS *Let.* 2 Jan. (1969) 131 Scientists are of course pederasts, as we neither know nor care; & unnaturally enough this natural history museum is a temple or cathedral of the scientific spirit. **1963** A. HERON *Towards Quaker View of Sex* 69 Socially the paederast is the most isolated of homosexuals. **1969** *Listener* 14 Aug. 205/3 A divorced woman on the throne of the House of Windsor would be a pretty big feather in the cap of that bunch of rootless intellectuals, alien Jews and international pederasts who call themselves the Labour Party. **1971** P. QUENNELL *Marcel Proust* 11 The sense of his own separateness, as a paederast who loved women,..and a sick man..intensified his gift of observation.

pædiatric (pīdi,æ·trik), *a. Med.* Also **pediatric.** [see PÆDO-, PEDO- and IATRIC *a.*] Of, pertaining to, or dealing with pædiatrics or the diseases of children.

1880 A. JACOBI in *Trans. Amer. Med. Assoc.* XXXI. 709 (*heading*) Address on the claims of paediatric medicine. **1894** [in Dict. s.v. PÆDO-, PEDO-]. **1927** W. P. LUCAS *Mod. Pract. Pediatrics* iii. 20 From the moment a child is conceived it is a pediatric problem. **1963** *Times* 16 May 13/3 For all these reasons it is not surprising that opinion among paediatricians and paediatric nurses is divided. **1965** *Math. in Biol. & Med.* (Med. Res. Council) v. 228 In a well known text book of paediatric surgery there is a photograph of nine children with tracheo-oesophageal fistula, successfully treated. **1973** D. MORLEY *Paediatric Priorities in Developing World* i. 1 Doctors with the relevant paediatric training can organize a service which will prevent more than one-half of the deaths in infancy and early childhood without awaiting any great change in environment.

Hence **pædia·trically** *adv.*

1949 M. MEAD *Male & Female* ix. 192 If her suckling of the child [is] replaced by a formula pediatrically prescribed—then also we may find very serious disturbances in maternal attitudes.

pædiatrician (pīdi,ătri·ʃăn). *Med.* Also **ped-.** [f. prec. + -ICIAN.] A specialist or expert in pædiatrics.

1903 *Med. Rec.* (N.Y.) LXIII. 513/2 Dr. L. Emmett Holt said he thought all pediatricians would agree that most of the cases which had given trouble in diagnosis were those in which there was a prolonged fever. **1932** *Lancet* 12 Nov. 1072/1 (*heading*) Congress of German pædiatricians in Vienna. **1959** *Times Lit. Suppl.* 13 Mar. 148/1 The authors, a pediatrician and a psychiatrist, show a broad understanding of the sociological scope of adolescents' difficulties. **1971** C. G. PARSONS in S. M. Bates *Pract. Paediatric Nursing* p. ix, Paediatricians have always depended on nurses to help children to settle into hospital..and to take the mother's place when she has to be separated from her baby. **1976** *Daily Tel.* 1 Mar. 2/1 Women who become pregnant despite being fitted with intra-uterine contraceptive devices..may risk giving birth to seriously malformed babies, a consultant paediatrician has warned.

pædiatrics (pīdi,æ·triks), *sb. pl.* (const. as *sing.*). *Med.* Also **ped-.** [f. as prec.: see -IC 2.] The branch of medical science dealing with the study of childhood and the diseases of children.

1884 (*periodical title*) Archives of pediatrics. **1924** *Glasgow Herald* 10 June 6 The new foundation is the Sampson-Gemmell Chair of Medical Pædiatrics at the Royal Hospital for Sick Children. **1946** *Nature* 24 Aug. 277/2 Geriatrics must also come to occupy a part not less important in medicine than pediatrics to-day. **1956** LD. AMULREE in A. Pryce-Jones *New Outl. Mod. Knowl.* 213 Infant and child welfare services are available in most civilized countries, and pediatrics and the care of children is becoming more and more a preventive service. **1975** *Physics Bull.* Oct. 458/1 (*caption*) In the field of paediatrics the x ray examination of infants and young children is a diagnostic procedure that is on the increase.

pædiatrist (pidəi·ătrist, pīdi,æ·trist). *Med.* Also **ped-.** [f. as prec. + -IST.] = *PÆDIATRICIAN. Also *attrib.* or as *adj.*

1897 [in Dict. s.v. PEDIATRIST]. **1928** O. WILKINSON *Strabismus* x. 143 The advice and insistent counsel of the family physician and the pediatrist. **1977** *Chicago Tribune* 2 Oct. XII. 12/2 (Advt.), 1 deluxe optometric or pediatrist suite.

pædogamy (pidǫ·gămi). *Biol.* Also (chiefly *U.S.*) **pedogamy.** [ad. G. *pädogamie*, *paedogamie* (M. Lühe 1902, in *Schriften d. Physikal.-ökonom. Gesellsch. Konigsberg, Sitzung biol. Sektion* XLIII. 5), f. PÆDO- + *-GAMY.] In certain protozoans, reproduction by the fusion of gametes derived from the same parent cell (see also quot. 1953).

1910 G. N. CALKINS *Protozool.* iv. 146 (*heading*) Fertilization by endogamy (pedogamy, Prowazek). **1953** R. P. HALL *Protozool.* ii. 80 Pedogamy appears to be an unusual type of syngamy in which the two gametes are not more than one or two cell-generations removed from a single gametocyte. **1965** POLJANSKIJ & CHEJSIN *Dogiel's Gen. Protozool.* (ed. 2) vii. 322 In certain cases sister individuals, originating from a single nucleus of one and the same mother cell, act as gametes. Phenomena of this type are known as paedogamy.

Hence **pædo·gamous** *a.*, of or pertaining to this type of reproduction.

1926 G. N. CALKINS *Biol. Protozoa* xi. 510 Fertilizations have been described as exogamous, endogamous, autogamous, or pædogamous. **1940** L. H. HYMAN *Invertebrates* I. iii. 161 The fertilization [of Myxosporidia] is seen to be a paedogamous autogamy.

pædogenesis (pīdodʒe·nĭsis). *Biol.* Also (chiefly *U.S.*) **pedo-.** [mod.L., coined in Ger. (K. von Baer 1866, in *Bull. Acad. Imp. Sci. St.-Pétersbourg* IX. 96), f. PÆDO- + GENESIS.] Reproduction by larval or immature forms of animals, esp. certain insects; cf. *NEOTENY b. Hence **pædogene·tic** *a.*, pertaining to or characterized by pædogenesis.

1871 W. S. DALLAS tr. O. von Grimm in *Ann. & Mag. Nat. Hist.* VIII. 32, I had before me an insect [*sc.* a species of *Chironomus*] which is subject to what Von Baer calls pædogenesis. *Ibid.* 36 Different animals may be subject to pædogenesis at different stages of development. **1888, 1889** [in Dict. s.v. PÆDO-, PEDO-]. **1891** F. V. THEOBALD *Acct. Brit. Flies* 42 The ovaries [of flies of the family Cecidomyidæ] become fully developed and bud off eggs; [*Note*] = Pædogenesis (i.e., the production of ova by the immature animal, and is in the insecta always parthenogenetic). **1895** D. SHARP in *Cambr. Nat. Hist.* V. iv. 142 A very rare kind of parthenogenesis, called paedogenesis, has been found to exist in two or three species of Diptera. **1920** H. REINHEIMER *Symbiosis* II. viii. 158 The 'wages' of a prolonged transgression against the law of Symbiosis is thus indeed death—in the shape of diathesis, dissolution, and of a kind of Paedogenesis—precocious sexuality. **1951** COLYER & HAMMOND *Flies Brit. Isles* iii. 71 Parthenogenetic reproduction by immature stages is known as paedogenesis. *Ibid.* iv. 83 Those [*Miastor* larvae] which are paedogenetic have no 'breast-bones', while those which will pupate and produce normal flies possess this organ. **1964** R. M. & J. W. FOX *Introd. Compar. Entomol.* vii. 243 Neoteny (pedogenesis) involves the precocious maturity of the ovary so that young are produced by a mother who has not reached the imaginal instar.

pædomorphic (pīdomǭ·ɹfik), *a.* Also **ped-.** [f. PÆDO- + MORPHIC *a.*] **1.** *Biol.* Exhibiting pædomorphism or pædomorphosis.

1891 *Proc. Acad. Nat. Sci. Philadelphia* 209 It might be expected that pedomorphic varieties closely resemble each other when the same disposition is exhibited in closely allied species. **1922** *Jrnl. Linn. Soc.* (*Zool.*) XXXV. 97 Crinoids are as 'pædomorphic' as any Perennibranchiate Amphibian. **1957** L. EISELEY *Immense Journey* 119 The pedomorphic features of man—his almost hairless body, his helpless childhood, his surprisingly developed brain. **1959** J. D. CLARK *Prehist. S. Afr.* iv. 90 The Boskop type exhibits a continuation of certain pedomorphic (infantile) characteristics into the adult state, as does the Bushman. **1965** B. E. FREEMAN tr. *Vandel's Biospeleol.* xi. 165 This feature may be considered in addition to that of small size, as a paedomorphic character. **1970** G. GREER *Female Eunuch* 31 This..is an observation which is frequently made about the whole female body, that it is infantilized or pedomorphic.

2. (After *anthropomorphic.*) Having (or attributing to other objects) the form or characteristics of a child.

1903 H. G. WELLS in *Fortn. Rev.* Jan. 184 He will look out on the world with anthropomorphic (or rather with pædomorphic) eyes. **1907** H. ELLIS in *19th Cent.* May 767 The Child..imagines a colossal magician, of anthropomorphic (if not paidomorphic) nature.

pædomorphism (pīdomǭ·ɹfiz'm). *Biol.* Also **ped-.** [f. PÆDO- + *-MORPHISM.] The retention of juvenile characteristics in certain adult mammals.

1891 *Proc. Acad. Nat. Sci. Philadelphia* 208 Dr. Harrison Allen spoke of the disposition occasionally exhibited in adult mammals, for the proportions of different parts of the body to remain as they were in the immature individuals... Dr. Allen proposed for this peculiarity the term pedomorphism. **1931** *Amer. Jrnl. Physical Anthropol.* XVI. 203 (*title*) Pedomorphism in the pre-Bushman skull. **1970** G. GREER *Female Eunuch* 333 The pedomorphism of women has always been remarked upon. **1973** B. J. WILLIAMS *Evolution & Human Origins* vii. 98/1 Paedomorphism is said to occur when certain developmental processes are retarded in such a way that important features of the larval or infantile form are maintained into sexual maturity.

pædomorphosis (pīdomǭ·ɹfŏsis, -mǭɹfōu·sis). *Biol.* [f. PÆDO- + MORPHOSIS.] Phylogenetic change indicated by the retention of juvenile characteristics in the adult form.

1922 W. GARSTANG in *Jrnl. Linnean Soc.* (*Zool.*) XXXV. 100 In other articles I propose to deal with the origin and significance of larval forms, and to draw attention to some further examples of the influence of larval characters upon adult organisation, to which I apply the term 'Pædomorphosis'. **1932** J. S. HUXLEY *Probl. Relative Growth* vii. 240 (*caption*) Diagram to illustrate positive and negative mutations in rate-factors, leading to recapitulation and paedomorphosis, respectively. **1965** B. E. FREEMAN tr. *Vandel's Biospeleol.* ix. 134 Partial neoteny, a phenomenon to which Garstang's term paedomorphosis may be more exactly applied. **1970** *Times Lit. Suppl.* 4 June 619/4 The most serious lacuna in the book is the absence of any mention of the part which the well-known principle of retardation of development, or paedomorphosis, has played in the evolution of man. **1971** [see *NEOTENY]. **1974** G. L. STEBBINS *Flowering Plants* xi. 249/2 The evolutionary mechanism by which this [*sc.* the evolution of herbs and subshrubs into shrubs or trees] could happen involves the principle of paedomorphosis.

pædophile (pī·dofəil), *sb.* and *a.* Also **pedo-.** [ad. Gr. παιδόφιλ-ος loving children (cf. -PHIL, -PHILE).] **A.** *sb.* A person with pædophilia. **B.** *adj.* = *PÆDOPHILIAC, -PHILIC *adjs.*

1951 *Group Psychotherapy* IV. 166 (*heading*) Psychodramatic treatment of a pedophile. **1954** *Jrnl. Projective Techniques* XVIII. 352/1 This sexualized view of a late middle-aged female, by a 26-year-old subject, reflects the strikingly immature confusion of sexual and maternal figures found in the pedophile group. **1975** *Sunday People* 1 June 2/6 Many paedophiles who read the article will have heard of P.A.L. for the first time and will be anxious that the organisation survives to continue this service. **1976** *Publishers Weekly* 23 Aug. 75/2 Hilary is nine... She's at the mercy of the old man she calls the Devil, actually a pathetic pedophile. **1977** *Sunday Times* 30 Jan. 41/2 The paedophile authors he discusses include the diarist Kilvert, Lewis Carroll..and J. M. Barrie.

pædophilia (pīdofi·liă). Also **pedo-,** † **paido-.** [f. PÆDO-, PEDO- + *-PHILIA, or f. as prec. + -IA[1].] An abnormal, esp. sexual, love of young children.

1906 H. ELLIS *Stud. Psychol. Sex* V. i. 11 Paidophilia or the love of children..may be included under this head [*sc.* abnormality]. **1926** *Med. Jrnl. & Rec.* CXXIV. 161/1 One must keep clearly in mind in dealing with pedophilia the distinction between that mediating homosexuality, and the much more pure perversion which is our subject. **1952** E. A. GUTHEIL tr. *Stekel's Patterns of Psychosexual Infantilism* i. 62 Some eager lady friends of the mistress of the house who expand their friendship to include the younger male generation, may be suspected of pedophilia. **1962** *Listener* 20 Sept. 438/1 The film certainly is not..a study in paedophilia, of a middle-aged professor's grotesque passion for a twelve-year-old girl. **1963** A. HERON *Towards Quaker View of Sex* 69 Paedophilia is not always homosexual. **1973** *Times Lit. Suppl.* 8 June 647/2 He was driven to a pedophilia in which he played the role of both parents to the children of his fancy.

Hence **pædophi·liac, -phi·lic** *adjs.*, pertaining to or characterized by pædophilia; also as *sb.*, a pædophilic person.

1927 *Psychoanal. Review* XIV. 191 It is only in rare cases that one encounters an individual who has pedophilic predilections and at the same time is suffering from venereal disease. *Ibid.*, Krafft-Ebing..in his attempt at psychological explanation falls back on 'a morbid disposition only' on the part of the pedophalic [*sic*] as the motivating factor. **1951** *Group Psychotherapy* IV. 170 He then insisted he had never had the slightest amount of pedophiliac desire, and that his crime was a total mystery to him. **1954** *Jrnl. Projective Techniques* XVIII. 348/1 The rapists probably do differ from the pedophiles, however, on the variable of aggression, the majority of the pedophilic acts having been of a passive and seductive nature. **1960** *Spectator* 8 July 69 The..survey..shows the paedophiliac to be a type altogether distinct from the adult-seeking homosexual. **1963** A. HERON *Towards Quaker View of Sex* 69 A variety of early experiences and inadequacies of upbringing..make the paedophilic especially sympathetic towards..the state of childhood and immaturity. **1974** J. BANCROFT *Deviant Sexual Behaviour* vi. 157 Paedophiliac offenders frequently have personalities in which self-deception and deception of others is marked. **1976** *Publishers Weekly* 26 Apr. 52/1 He contacted fellow pedophiliacs and through them was able to sample many kinds of young girls.

Paelignian (peli·gniăn, pəi-), *sb.* and *a.* Also **Pelignian.** [f. L. *P(a)eligni* + -AN.] **A.** *sb.* **a.** A member of an Oscan-Umbrian people centred on Corfinium in southern Italy. **b.** The language of this people. **B.** *adj.* Of or pertaining to this people or their language.

1600, etc. [see *MARRUCINIAN *sb.* and *a.*]. **1853** C. MERIVALE *Fall of Roman Republic* iii. 77 The Samnites and Pelignians reclaimed 4,000 of their own countrymen who had thus established themselves in the Latin town of Fregellæ. **1862** W. P. DICKSON tr. *Mommsen's Hist. Rome* II. xi. 332 When..the Samnites and Pælignians applied to the senate for a reduction of their contingents, their request was based on the ground that during recent years 4000 Samnite and Pælignian families had migrated to the Latin colony of Fregellæ. **1909** W. E. HEITLAND *Roman Republic* II. xliii. 434 For the revolted Allies some centre was necessary as the headquarters of the confederate government. This was found at Corfinium in the Paelignian country on the eastern side of the Apennine. **1933, 1939** [see *MARSIAN *sb.* and *a.*]. **1939** R. SYME *Roman Revolution* xiv. 193 The fierce Marsians and Paelignians had long and bitter memories. **1967** E. T. SALMON *Samnium & Samnites* iv. 177 Ovid..had his own Paelignian homeland in mind.

paella (pa,e·lă, pəi,e·lă). [Cat. *paella*, f. OFr. *paele* (mod. *poêle*), f. L. *patella* pan, dish.] A Spanish dish of rice with chicken, seafood, vegetables, etc., cooked and served in a large shallow pan. Also *fig.*

1892 *Encycl. Pract. Cookery* II. 84/2 *Paela*, a favourite Spanish dish containing the usual oil and garlic. **1926** B. REYNOLDS *Cocktail Continentale* 66 You lunch at Antiqua Casa Botin. Crab soup. Paella a la Valencian, a mixture of chicken, fish, meat, rice, vegetables, snails and clams. **1939** R. CAMPBELL *Flowering Rifle* II. 52 Dead Charlies climbing on each other's backs To make a huge paella of the plains. **1955** J. THOMAS *No Banners* viii. 69 An appetizing *paella* and a goblet of *vino tinto* for each man. **1960** 'W. HAGGARD' *Closed Circuit* x. 121 The food was excellent: he could give her the *paella* which he knew she loved, and now she was eating it with relish..her mouth still full of rice and chicken. **1965** *Punch* 24 Feb. 289/1 The locals mostly speak with a macaroni Italian accent, the Dons with some kind of *paella* Spanish. **1970** 'D. HALLIDAY' *Dolly & Cookie Bird* vii. 99 Paella with all the right things in it, squids and octopuses and chicken and lobster-tails and paprika and sherry and peas and onion and pimento and pork, all done with saffron rice. **1972** *Village Voice* (N.Y.) 1 June 24/3 The underworld provided the paella for the detective stories, including the celebrated 'Pinktoes'. **1976** *National Observer* (U.S.) 23 Oct. 19/3 The restaurant serves up an imaginative assortment of house specialities, many European inspired including..the Spanish Paella Valenciana.

‖ **paepae** (pai·pai). Also 9 **pi-pi**. Pl. **paepae**. [Native name.] **a.** An elevated stone platform on which Polynesian houses were often built. **b.** A paved area in front of some Polynesian buildings. **c.** A type of raft.

1846 H. MELVILLE *Typee* xxiv. 219 Like all the other edifices of any note, it was raised upon a small pi-pi of stones. **1919** *Century Mag.* Aug. 446/1, I sat..on the palm-shaded *paepae* of my cabin above the blue lagoon. **1923** R. LINTON *Material Culture of Marquesas Islands* 272 Many of the *paepae* on hill slopes were simple terraces with a trench at the rear to carry off water. *Ibid.* 273 The perfect *paepae* contains stones of three sorts. **1927** P. H. BUCK *Material Culture of Cook Islands* i. 39 In the well-preserved house site..the cobbled *paepae* terrace was a foot lower than the house terrace. **1930** —— *Samoan Material Culture* 56 When a high *paepae* platform was made, most of the posts did not reach the ground level. **1958** T. HEYERDAHL *Aku-Aku* x. 334, I was the man who had travelled to Raroia with my friends on a *pae-pae*. **1968** N. A. ROWE in T. Heyerdahl *Sea Routes to Polynesia* 205, I had wondered for many years what this could mean but I see now..that it was a reference to a raft or *pae-pae*. *Pae-pae* can also mean stone platform: hence the confusion. **1974** T. HEYERDAHL *Fatu-Hira* ii. 88 Here we stumbled upon human vestiges..mostly overgrown terrace walls and stone platforms, *pae-pae*, where native huts had once stood. *Ibid.* iv. 155 Some *paepae* had been declared *tabu* by ancient medicine men and often contained burials and old artifacts.

paff (pæf), *int.* Also **paf.** [Imit.] An expression of contempt. Also used to represent the sound of a blow.

1851 LONGFELLOW *Golden Legend* v. 242 These beggars ..Lamed and maimed, and fed upon chaff, Chaunting their wonderful piff and paff. **1897** *Pall Mall Gaz.* 28 Sept. 2/3 The combatants used their fists only... Paf! paf! one for you, and paf! paf! for your opponent. **1910** [see *CRASH *v.* 6a]. **1922** JOYCE *Ulysses* 40 What offence laid fire to their brains? Paff!

pagani·stic, *a.* [f. PAGAN *sb.* and *a.* + -ISTIC.] = PAGANISH *a.* 2.

1933 DYLAN THOMAS *Let.* (1966) 71 But the more paganistic..one becomes, the less one feels the desire to write. **1938** *Sun* (Baltimore) 14 Nov. 2/5 He will ignore the madman Hitler and his cripple-minded Goebbels with their paganistic philosophy. **1948** L. SPITZER *Linguistics & Lit. Hist.* v. 194 A comparison of Claudel's Christian ode with the paganistic ode of Ronsard.

page, *sb.*[1] Add: **I. 5. c.** (Examples in sense 'an attendant upon a legislative body'.)

1840 *Boston Even. Transcript* 18 Feb. 2/1 A page took them to the Clerk—the Clerk handed them to the Speaker. **1878** B. HARTE *Man on Beach* 104 Obtaining political influence through caucuses, I became at last page in the Senate. **1949** *Time* 27 June 61/1 The Capitol Page School ..is attended by the House's 49 page boys, the Senate's 21, the Supreme Court's four, and a few more Capitol-employed boys.

d. (Further examples.)

1955 *Times* 8 July 10/4 She was attended by two pages, James Mostyn and Viscount Quenington, two child bridesmaids, Harriet and Sarah Duckworth, and five older bridesmaids. **1973** 'M. YORKE' *Grave Matters* III. i. 54 Maybe he'll bring the girl to see us... Then you can start planning Andrew's page's outfit.

II. 9. *page-boy* (further examples); (*b*) used *attrib.* and *absol.* to designate a woman's hair-style in which the hair is worn in a long bob with the ends turned under and hanging on the shoulders; (*c*) = *PAGER *sb.*[3]

1874 A. J. MUNBY *Diary* 29 June in D. Hudson *Munby* (1972) 368 'Goodbye, William!' she said to the page boy who opened the hall door for us. **1939** R. CHANDLER *Big Sleep* i. 13 Her hair was a fine tawny wave cut much shorter than the current fashion of pageboy tresses curled in at the bottom. **1951** 'A. GARVE' *Murder in Moscow* i. 27 She still wore her fair hair in a fringe with a page-boy bob. **1961** L. P. HARTLEY *Two for River* 53 'Mr. Lenthall, please, Mr. Lenthall, please,' intoned a page-boy in a high-pitched nasal sing-song. **1971** *Guardian* 27 July 9/2 Hair is in long page-boy bobs with hair slides. **1973** *Times* 17 Jan. 4/5 The Post Office yesterday launched its radio 'pageboy', a tiny 'bleeper' which can be set off by a telephone call. **1975** H. MCCUTCHEON *Instrument of Vengeance* vi. 94 Her hair was..cut in pageboy style. **1976** G. MCDONALD *Confess, Fletch* (1977) xxvii. 125 Her hair was a perfect black, shining pageboy.

page, *sb.*[2] Add: **1.** Also, a complete leaf of a book, etc.

1728 SWIFT *Poetical Works* (1967) 346 Tim set the Volume on a Table, Read over here and there a Fable, And found, as he the pages twirl'd, The Monkey, who had seen the World. **1786** BURNS *Poems, chiefly in Scottish Dial.* 71 Now moths deform in shapeless tatters Their unknown pages. **1819** BYRON *Don Juan* I. xcv. 50 By the wind Even as the page is rustled while we look, So by the poesy of his own mind Over the mystic leaf his soul was shook. **1895** CONRAD *Almayer's Folly* 254 Books open with torn pages bestrewed the floor. **1919** G. B. SHAW *Great Catherine* 115 A play that will leave the reader as ignorant of Russian history as he may be now before he has turned the page. **1925** F. SCOTT FITZGERALD *Great Gatsby* iii. 55 Knew when to stop, too—didn't cut the pages. **1950** W. STEVENS *Auroras of Autumn* 99 On the pedestal, an ambitious page dog-eared. **1969** I. MURDOCH *Bruno's Dream* 27 He..folded the page into a paper dart. **1974** 'J. LE CARRÉ' *Tinker, Tailor* I. xiii. 113 The pages had been excised with a razor blade.

d. That which is (actually or notionally) written, printed, etc., on a page. Cf. sense 2 a.

1805 W. BLAKE *Let.* 19 Jan. (1966) 857 The first page of the Poem was beautifully executed. *c* **1862** E. DICKINSON *Poems* (1955) I. 376 Tell him the page I didn't write. **1903** G. B. SHAW *Revolutionist's Handbk.* viii, in *Man & Superman* 210 Whilst these pages are being written an English judge has sentenced a forger to twenty years penal servitude. **1951** L. HUGHES *Montage of Dream Deferred* 39 Up to my room, sit down, and write this page. **1966** *McGraw-Hill Encycl. Sci. & Technol.* V. 177/1 Railroads employ high-speed facsimile (several pages per minute) for the transmission of waybills. **1975** *Times* 24 Sept. 2/8 Using the Keypad, the user would call up the Viewdata service and select the 'pages' of information to be displayed on the television screen. **1978** *Broadcast* 6 Mar. 10/2 Viewdata's standard page of 24 lines of text requires 480 lines of actual picture information.

e. *Computers.* A division of the main store of a computer consisting of a certain number of 'words' (commonly a few thousand); also, a corresponding amount of data or part of a program.

1948 *Ann. Computation Lab. Harvard Univ.* XVI. 46 A 'page' number marks a section of 'blocks' in much the same fashion as the page of a book would contain several lines of data, while the block number identifies the line of data. **1962** *IRE Trans. Electronic Computers* XI. 226/2 The main core store is..partitioned into blocks..which for identification purposes are called pages. **1970** O. DOPPING *Computers & Data Processing* ix. 124 In systems with extensive core swapping it is advantageous to have the program subdivided into 'pages' of a prescribed size, e.g. 1,000 words, and consider primary storage to be subdivided into blocks, where each block has room for exactly one page.

3. *page-size*; *page-long* adj.; **page charge,** a fee of so much per page requested from an organization when a learned journal publishes a paper by one of its members; **page-galley,** (*a*) a galley containing enough type to print a page; (*b*) a galley proof on which the type has been divided into pages and numbered; **page printer,** a printer (sense 2) whose output is in the form of printed or typed pages; so **page-printing** *ppl. a.* and *vbl. sb.*; **page-proof** (examples); **page reference,** a reference to a specific page or group of pages in a book or periodical; **page-turner,** (*a*) a mechanical device for turning the pages of a book (so **page-turning** *ppl. a.*); (*b*) *fig.*, a very enjoyable or readable book; (*c*) one who turns the pages of a musician's score, usu. during a performance.

1966 *Jrnl. Amer. Chem. Soc.* 5 Feb. 8A/2 A page charge is assessed to cover in part the cost of publication. Payment is expected but is not a condition for publication. **1968** J. M. ZIMAN *Public Knowl.* vi. 117, I am informed that the decision of the referees on the paper is quite independent of whether this 'page charge' is honoured. **1969** *Physics Bull.* Jan. 23/1 Page charges were first introduced by the AIP in 1930 for *The Physical Review*..; for *The Physical Review*, for example, they currently amount to $60 a page. The charges, which are not mandatory, are paid by authors' institutions and are honoured by the majority of institutions... These are used to offset those items of expenditure classified as 'input' production costs; subscription prices are kept relatively low and are applied towards 'output' production costs. **1970** *Nature* 29 Aug. 892/1 The actual pressure behind page charges is the desire of each editor to keep the selling price of his journal within the means of the individual subscriber. **1927** R. B. MCKERROW *Introd. Bibliogr.* I. vi. 63 The page 'galley'... The compositors of the Elizabethan period normally finished a page of work at a time. **1964** F. BOWERS *Bibliogr. & Textual Crit.* III. i. 65 An example of the routine practice of the trade would be the transfer of lines of type from the stick directly into the Elizabethan page galley instead of the long or slip galley of later times. **1971** *Library* XXVI. 297 The earliest hint of a 'long' galley, as opposed to a 'square' or page galley, seems to appear in an 'oral testimony'..which claims that the news galley of 1770 contained at least 132 lines of matter in long primer between eighteen and twenty ems wide. This suggests a galley with dimensions of about 20 in. × 4 in. **1918** E. POUND *Let.* 4 June (1971) 136 You have got all the points I noted in the page-galleys, so I was right in not cabling about them. [**1975** J. BUTCHER *Copy-Editing* xii. 213 The printer may be asked to provide page-on-galley proofs. **1976** *Gloss. Documentation Terms* (*B.S.I.*) 46 *Page-on-galley proof*, a single-stage alternative to galley proof and page proof.] **1930** *Times Lit. Suppl.* 30 Oct. 886/2 The page-long questions and answers of the *cause célèbre*. **1961** *Times* 31 Aug. 11/1 These convoluted evocations, often in page-long parentheses. **1899** *Electrical Engineer* (N.Y.) 2 Mar. 249/2 There is..no simple page printer having such speed and such perfect control over page and line as is here secured. **1948** *Ann. Computation Lab. Harvard Univ.* XVI. 69 The output devices of the machine are page printers and tape punches. **1967** BURKHARD & CLARE in D. H. Hamsher *Communication Syst. Engin. Handbk.* ii. 30 Until recent years page printers were developed almost exclusively for teletype-writer use and were almost entirely mechanical. With a trend toward higher speeds and toward data applications many of the mechanisms are being replaced by electronic circuits. **1895** *Jrnl. U.S. Artillery* Oct. 593 (*heading*) Experimental use of the Essick page printing telegraph for transmitting information in sea-coast artillery firing 1895. **1959** J. W. FREEBODY *Telegr.* ii. 55/2 This machine, known as a teleprinter, printed the messages on a paper tape. In 1931, a page printing machine was introduced. **1881** W. WHITMAN 24 Aug. in *Daybooks & Notebooks* (1978) I. 256 The first batch of page-proofs of the new volume, to-day. **1901** T. L. DE VINNE *Pract. Typogr.: Correct Composition* xvi. 301 Page proofs seriously add to the expense of the work when the author makes much alteration. **1934, 1951** [see *GALLEY *sb.* 5b]. **1951** W. STEVENS *Let.* 30 July (1967) 724 On receipt of page proofs [I] will give them prompt attention. **1975** J. BUTCHER *Copy-Editing* v. 59 It is usually cheaper to proceed straight to page proof. **1925** *Manual of Style* (Univ. Chicago Press) (ed. 8) 195 Unfilled page references must be queried. **1953** R. L. COLLISON *Indexes & Indexing* I. 68 Page references should be carefully stated. **1971** *Nature* 30 Apr. 602/1 The index has suffered greatly from the speed of production, being incomplete both in subject matter and the page references given. **1975** J. BUTCHER *Copy-Editing* x. 184 Form of text reference. The author's name, date of publication and page reference (if one is needed) are given in parentheses. **1929** H. CRANE *Let.* 30 Aug. (1965) 344, I think we ought to change our plan regarding page size and use. **1946** *Nature* 24 Aug. 267/1 The members of the Institute hope that British periodicals which adopted reduced page-sizes as a war-time measure will as soon as possible revert to full size. **1969** *Daily Tel.* 11 Aug. 18/3 The page-turner, made of plywood, plastic toy gears and commonplace lamp batteries, operates with the user's suck or blow a miniature electrical device. **1974** *Publishers Weekly* 27 May 5/1 (Advt.), What happens next makes *Eagle in the Sky* a moving, exciting, and ultimately joyous page-turner. **1976** *Gramophone* Mar. 1482/1 As host of the first runthrough by the composer..of the *Elègie*, and page-turner at the English premieres of the two string sonatas, I may be forgiven for having a nostalgia for this music. **1976** *Washington Post* 19 Apr. C5/1 The last time I saw her she was up on that stage without an orchestra; just herself, the piano player, and the page turner. **1976** *Publishers Weekly* 19 Apr. 81/2 Like the other crime novels from the British author, this is a real page turner. **1969** *Daily Tel.* 11 Aug. 18/2 I've been using this page-turning gear without trouble for 18 months.

page, *v.*[1] Add: **c.** To send for, search for, or communicate with (a person) by means of a page; to have the name of (a person) called out by a page. Also in extended use (of various electrical or electronic devices). orig. *U.S.* So **pa·ging** *ppl. a.* and *vbl. sb.*[2]

1904 L. BELL *At Home with Jardines* 65 The name of Jardine was paged through the corridors and billiard-room and café. **1904** *Sun* (N.Y.) 21 Aug. 5 A bell boy is called. 'Here, page Mr. Smith, Room 186', the clerk will say. The process of 'paging' Mr. Smith consists of calling out his name in the dining and other public rooms of the hotel. **1916** H. L. WILSON *Somewhere in Red Gap* ix. 368 A.. mining promoter from Arizona..has himself paged by the boys about twenty times a day so folks will know how important he is. **1923** *Daily Mail* 31 July 6/5 The telephone operator..turned to me. 'Stay around awhile,' she instructed. 'I'll "page" you when I'm through.' **1936** H. F. OLSEN in *RCA Rev.* I. I. 58 (*heading*) General announce and paging systems. *Ibid.* 59 For certain types of general announce, paging, and sound distributing installations,..the intensity level required is relatively low. **1938** WODEHOUSE *Code of Woosters* xiii. 283 Jeeves, go and page Mr. Spode. Tell him I want him to come and put a bit of stuffing into my alibi. **1959** A. SEXTON in *Hudson Rev.* Spring 80 Out in the hall The intercom pages you. **1960** *IRE Trans. Vehicular Communications* Dec. 48 (*heading*) Personal radio paging in the VHF band. **1970** *Railway Mag.* Oct. 579/1 Post Office staff at Waterloo have been issued with two-way speech radio paging equipment supplied by Modern Telephones Limited to enable a central control point to speedily contact personnel handling letter bags on the platforms and concourse. **1971** *Daily Tel.* (Colour Suppl.) 22 Oct. 9/2 It works on the principle of the short-range radio paging systems used in factories and large-office complexes. **1973** *Times* 21 May (Telecommunications Suppl.) p. v/2 In connexion with pocket paging systems, dialling a code on the telephone will signal the appropriate paging receiver. The person paged will then dial a reply code on his nearest telephone. **1976** *New Yorker* 26 Jan. 54/2 We'd better have him paged. **1977** *Time* 2 May 49/1 A portable paging device about the size of a cigarette pack, the beeper is a mini-radio receiver that puts the person carrying it on instant call from office, home or anywhere else.

page, *v.*[2] Add: **3.** *intr.* To look *through* the pages of a book.

1943 *Amer. Speech* XVIII. 138 The following notes, taken as I paged through the book at random. **1966** E. PALMER *Plains of Camdeboo* xviii. 291 Paging through the books is an experience for every Palmer of every generation, for a single entry can recall a drama..forgotten for many years. **1970** *Physics Bull.* Sept. 401/1 The selection of a metal..for use in the body is not a simple matter which can be accomplished by paging through a handbook.

pageant, *sb.* Add: **2.** For *Obs.* read '*Obs.* exc. *Hist.*' and add later examples.

1825 T. SHARP *Diss. Pageants Coventry* 20 It is evident that the 'scaffolds' were placed upon wheels, and moved with the Pageant, to which it probably was attached. **1954** *Oxf. Jun. Encycl.* XII. 261/1 Each guild was usually responsible for one play, which was performed on a special two-decker waggon called a *Pageant.* **1960** Beckson & Ganz *Reader's Guide to Lit. Terms* (1961) 153 The pageant was built on wheels. **1974** S. J. Kahrl *Trad. Medieval Eng. Drama* ii. 36 What distinguishes the pageants referred to in this procession from the stages otherwise described is that the structures for the Jesse tree, for St John and St Edward, the four Cardinal Virtues, and the censing angels..are all built around permanent architectural features.

5. b. A spectacular representation (usually in the form of a procession) of scenes or events belonging to the past history of a place.

1883 D. Cook *On Stage* I. x. 219 In the pantomime season, or whenever any great pageant or spectacle is to be produced, these plots are of prodigious extent. **1905** *To-day* 7 June 180/2 The inhabitants are preparing a pageant. **1908** *Westm. Gaz.* 1 Oct. 2/3 On the sixth of these [days]..there will be presented a historical pageant. **1939** W. Ward *Theatre for Children* xiii. 248 Many playgrounds end their season with a festival or pageant in which every group has some part. **1970** Burton & Lane *New Directions* iii. 78 A great many pageants have been so gruesome—Merrie Englande with rain—the form has earned itself a bad reputation. **1977** K. O'Hara *Ghost of T. Penry* xvii. 173 It was that charity pageant the old mistress put on up Kelletts one year. She needed a robe for an archbishop..when they were acting a crowning.

6. b. *pageant cart, drama, -master* (later examples), *stage, vehicle, wagon; pageant-like* adj.

1974 S. J. Kahrl *Trad. Medieval Eng. Drama* ii. 39 Such structures occupy space, as they do in pictures of continental pageant carts. **1975** P. Happé *Eng. Mystery Plays* 27 The civic records of York and Chester show that the plays were performed on pageant carts. **1953** *Travel* Apr. 36/2 This spectacular pageant-drama is a civic non-profit enterprise of the twin cities of Hemet and San Jacinto in Riverside County, California. **1974** *Encycl. Brit. Macropædia* XIII. 862/1 The pageant dramas of the West have tended to be largely open-air performances given in front of mass audiences. **1933** R. Tuve *Seasons & Months* i. 41 A pageant-like processional march of familiar figures. **1973** M. Amis *Rachel Papers* 215 I've included a break-down of one of your more pageant-like essays. **1937** Auden *Spain* 11 Tomorrow the hour of the pageant-master and the musician. **1963** *Times* 17 Apr. 13/3 Miss Gwen Lally, O.B.E., pageant master, play producer, and lecturer, died on Sunday. **1977** *Daily Tel.* 23 June 18 Pageantmaster to Hammersmith & Fulham Silver Jubilee Committee. **1974** S. J. Kahrl *Trad. Medieval Eng. Drama* ii. 34 The most usual event which called for the erection of pageant stages in the street was a royal entry. **1825** T. Sharp *Diss. Pageants Coventry* 18 The different Companies Accounts..refer to the Pageant vehicles. **1932** T. W. Stevens *Theatre* vii. 61 The pageant wagon, interesting in itself, was a sterile device. **1958** A. C. Cawley *Wakefield Pageants* p. xxvi, A pageant-wagon with the superstructure of a ship, would have provided a strong scenic attraction for the *Processus Noe.* **1974** S. J. Kahrl *Trad. Medieval Eng. Drama* ii. 37 Nor, when we come to visualize the early pageant wagons as opposed to the fixed pageant stages, are we helped by the nature of the surviving evidence.

pageanteer. Delete †*Obs.* and add: **b.** One who takes part in a pageant (sense *5 b).

1910 *Daily Chron.* 11 Apr. 1/7 The pageanteers must be enjoying themselves all the time. **1927** *Daily Express* 15 July 2/4 The pageanteers—3,000 of them—assembled on the green and sang 'Land of Hope and Glory'.

pageantry. Add: **1.** (Later example.)

1908 *Daily Chron.* 21 July 4/6 The pageantry brings the classes together.

2. Also *fig.*

1909 E. Pound *Personae* 53 Slow-moving pageantry of hours.

paged, *a.* Add: **a.** (Further examples.)

1868 Geo. Eliot *Let.* 29 Apr. (1956) IV. 433 As I shall not see these paged sheets again, will you charitably assure me that the alterations are safely made? **1869** D. G. Rossetti *Let.* 21 Aug. (1965) II. 715 Replace it at the end of the first section of sonnets—not as paged. **1930** A. E. Housman *Let.* 29 June (1971) 297 In the paged proofs..I find that the printers have inserted..a comma.

c. *Computers.* Divided into pages (*page *sb.*[2] 1 e).

1966 *IEEE Trans. Electronic Computers* XV. 857/1 The relationship between hardware and software in a paged and segmented system environment greatly affects system performance. **1973** *Nature* 6 Apr. 361/2 Among the features that made it [*sc.* Atlas] one of the most advanced machines in the world at the time were a number of facilities that have since become standard such as its permanent master programme and paged store.

pager (pē·dʒəɹ), *sb.*[2] [f. Page *sb.*[2] + -er[1].] Following a numeral (usu. with hyphen): a book, newspaper or the like having the number of pages indicated by the numeral.

1966 'H. B. Taylor' *Triumvirate* i. 9 He'd gone all out on school supply ads..and turned out a thirty-two pager. **1973** *Times* 5 Sept. 18/7 The Fabian pamphlet, a 50-pager which should be out in a fortnight. **1977** *Times* 12 Sept. 12/6 Pamphlets on..how to get the most out of your phone service. This last is a 14-pager containing 59 pieces of information.

pager (pē·dʒəɹ), *sb.*[3] [f. Page *v.*[1] + -er[1].] A radio device that emits a sound when activated by a telephone call, used to contact a person carrying it.

1968 *Guardian* 10 Apr. 7/3 There are already..in this country devices called radio pagers. You carry in your pocket the pager, which is linked by radio connection to your telephone. When the telephone rings, the pager blips, and you can answer the call by speaking into the pager. As things stand the pager is illegal. **1973** *Sci. Amer.* Aug. 57 The receiving pager..has a range of 50 miles. It emits a tone when the person carrying it is wanted on the telephone. **1977** *Time* 2 May 49/1 Customers can either rent the pocket pagers..or buy them outright.

Paget (pæ·dʒėt). *Path.* The name of Sir James *Paget* (1814–99), English surgeon, used in the possessive to designate: **a.** A disease (also called *osteitis deformans*) that affects chiefly the elderly and is often symptomless, being characterized by the localized alteration of tissue in one or more bones (most often in the spine, skull, or pelvis), which become thickened and may undergo fracture or bending.

1877 *Guy's Hosp. Rep.* XXII. 337 (*heading*) Osteoporosis or Paget's osteitis deformans. **1889** *Index-Catal. Library Surg.-General's Office, U.S. Army* X. 353/2 (*heading*) Paget's disease of the bones. *See* osteitis deformans. **1939** *Times* 18 May 4/6 Dr. Alexander Wilson said that Mr. Desnos had Paget's disease—the bones of his skull were brittle and at least 50 per cent. softer than a normal skull. **1963** *Lancet* 5 Jan. 34/2 In Paget's disease stones are formed as a result of increased excretion of calcium due to increased turnover of bone. **1966** Wright & Symmers *Systemic Path.* II. 1390/2 Paget's disease is a precancerous condition. **1974** Passmore & Robson *Compan. Med. Stud.* III. xxvi. 17/2 Paget's disease is rarely a painful disorder in the absence of complications such as fracture, tumour or arthritis.

b. A reddish eczematous condition of the skin associated with cancer of the underlying tissue and usually occurring in the female nipple; freq. called *Paget's disease of the nipple*; so *Paget* († or *Paget's*) *cell*, a large cell with clear cytoplasm and hyperchromatic nuclei found in the epidermis of the affected area.

1880 *Brit. Med. Jrnl.* 24 Jan. 128/1 As attention was first called to it by Sir James Paget, he [*sc.* J. E. Erichsen] would suggest for it the name 'Paget's disease' of the nipple. **1910** *Jrnl. Cutaneous Dis.* XXVIII. 383 The epidermis..contained many of the large round, so-called Paget cells. **1917** *Lancet* 7 Apr. 519/2 The degenerate deeper layers of the epidermis..contain the large clear cells known as Paget's cells. **1923** *Brit. Jrnl. Surg.* XI. 317 Carcinoma in the breast, with which Paget's disease of the nipple is usually associated, is a primary carcinoma of the breast epithelium. **1954** *Jrnl. Obstetr. & Gynæcol.* LXI. 758 (*heading*) Histochemical characterization of the specific cells in Paget's disease of the vulva. **1966** Wright & Symmers *Systemic Path.* I. xxviii. 995/2 Paget's disease of the breast..accounts for between 2 and 3 per cent of all mammary carcinomas. *Ibid.* 996/2 Patients with Paget's disease are still very likely to be treated for supposed dermatitis of the nipple. **1974** Passmore & Robson *Compan. Med. Stud.* III. xxx. 9/2 Some believe that the Paget cells represent intra-epidermal spread of this [*sc.* cancer].

paging, *vbl. sb.*[1] Add: **2.** *Computers.* Division (of storage) into pages (*page *sb.*[2] 1 e); the transfer of pages between the central store and an auxiliary store.

1966 *IEEE Trans. Electronic Computers* XV. 855/1 The computer addressing techniques known as paging and segmentation will be familiar. **1970** O. Dopping *Computers & Data Processing* ix. 124 Paging systems and hardware relocation..are comparatively new inventions. **1972** *IEEE Trans. Computers* XXI. 1053/1 Under demand paging, a single program's execution and its resulting page swapping can be overlapped.

paging, *vbl. sb.*[2]: see *page *v.*[1] c.

pagoda. 5. pagoda sleeve (earlier and later examples).

1872 *Queen* 3 Feb. 71/2 Pagoda sleeves..embroidered all over. *Ibid.* 1 June 391/3 Pagoda sleeves with rich lace ruffles beneath. **1873** *Young Englishwoman* Apr. 183/1 The casaque..has a large pagoda sleeve. **1952** C. W. Cunnington *Eng. Women's Clothing* ii. 33 A 'pagoda sleeve' (long and narrow, opening some five or six inches above the wrist with small white undersleeves).

‖ **pagri** (pa·gri). Var. Puggree. Also *pagri-cloth.*

1901 [see Puggree 2]. **1930** *Aberdeen Press & Jrnl.* 22 Apr. 5/2 He has no British officers and no uniform except a distinguishing kind of pagri (head-dress). **1930** *Punch* 1 Oct. 392/2 Mr Thompson should not allow this bee to find a permanent home in his *pagri.* **1934** [see *drill *sb.*[5]]. **1974** 'B. Mather' *White Dacoit* 18 Sowars straightened tunics and pagris. **1978** 'M. M. Kaye' *Far Pavilions* vi. 98 She slept soundly..tied to him by a length of *pagri* (turban) cloth that prevented her from falling.

-pagus, *suffix*, f. Gr. πάγος that which is fixed (f. πηγνύναι to fasten), used to form the names of different kinds of Siamese twins according to their site of attachment; as *thoracopagus* s.v. Thoraco-.

pah, pa, *sb.* Add: (Further examples.)

The spelling *pa* is now the more usual.

1858 *App. Jrnls. House Reps. N.Z.* E. iv. 4 They seem ..at present inveterate in their adherence to their Native habits, and to their residence in Pas. **1863** T. Moser *Mahoe Leaves* 14 A pah is strictly a *fortified village*, but..a collection of huts forming a native settlement is generally called a pah now-a-days. **1880** J. C. Crawford *Recoll. Trav. N.Z. & Austral.* 28 A large pa (village) was visible at Pitone. **1900** H. Lawson *Over Sliprails* 82 Things, according to pa gossip, had gone wrong with her from the date of the tragedy. *Ibid.* 88 A poor pa outcast who had negro blood in her veins. **1905** J. M. Thomson *Bush Boys N.Z.* iii. 45 In every Maori 'pah' or village, there is one specially large 'whare', or house. **1911** W. H. Koebel *In Maoriland Bush* xii. 170 The old Maori did not appear to have lost caste among the brethren of his own race who still dwelt in their quaintly carved Pahs. **1920** *Outlook* (N.Z.) 29 Nov. 18/3 Her parish is roadless, deep ravines and steep hills separate pa from pa. **1938** R. Finlayson *Brown Man's Burden* 52 The old pa where many of the chieftain's ancestors and relatives were laid to rest on the topmost parapet. **1958** S. Ashton-Warner *Spinster* 72 When she got to the pa they cried in the Meeting House. **1959** G. Slatter *Gun in my Hand* 99 Unpainted whares at the pa with cardboard at the windows and new cars parked on the lawn. **1963** D. Adsett *Magpie Sings* 109 Perhaps they would go and live in the pa and get big and fat like lots of other Maori women.

‖ **paha** (pā·hă). Pl. **paha.** [Malay.] In Malaysia, a unit of weight used esp. for gold and equal to ¼ tahil, equivalent to ⅓ oz. (9·4 grammes-weight).

1839 T. J. Newbold *Pol. & Statistical Acct. Straits of Malacca* II. xiv. 236 A fine of ten tahils and one paha is to be exacted. **1947** R. O. Winstedt *Malays* 42 If the ordinary person pay five *paha* of gold in consideration of his low birth, then the marriage can take place.

Pahari (pahā·rī), *sb.* and *a.* Also **paharia, Pahaṛiya.** [Hind. *pahāṛī* (language) of the mountains, f. *pahāṛ* mountain.] **A.** *sb.* **a.** An Indo-Iranian language group to which belong the languages spoken in the lower ranges of the Himalayas from Nepal to Chamba. **b.** (Also **pahareen.**) A native or inhabitant of this region. **B.** *adj.* Of or pertaining to this region, its inhabitants, or the languages spoken by them.

The name was originally applied to one of the languages or dialects which formed the group (so quots. 1857, 1886).

1811, etc. [see *Maler *sb.* and *a.*]. **1857** *Jrnl. Asiatic Soc. Bengal* XXVI. 317 The languages included in..these two papers are..Dahi or Darhi..Dénwár..Pahi or Pahari, [etc.]. **1876** [see *Kashmir 1]. **1884** [see *Malto *sb.*]. **1886** Kipling *Plain Tales from Hills* (1888) 1 The Kotgarh Chaplain christened her Elizabeth, and 'Lispeth' is the Hill or *pahari* way of pronouncing it. **1887** R. N. Cust *Linguistic & Oriental Ess.* (ser. 2) iii. 73 It is..more convenient..to treat Hindi as the unit, and then allow full room to its magnificent dialects, such as..Bagri, Pahári, [etc.]. **1901** Kipling *Kim* iv. 93 'Huh! It is only a *pahari*' (a hillman), said Kim over his shoulder. 'Since when have the hill-asses owned all Hindustan?' *Ibid.* 107 A *pahareen*—a hillwoman of Dalhousie, my mother. **1905** *Daily Chron.* 9 Sept. 3/1 This particular district has been inhabited, since the British occupation, by two distinct races, the Santals and Paharias... The Paharias are a mountain race. **1908** T. G. Bailey *Lang. N. Himalayas* iii. p. i, Of these all, except Lāhulī, belong to what is at present called the Western Pahāṛī language of the Northern Group of the Sanskritic Aryan Family. **1916** G. A. Grierson *Linguistic Survey India* IX. iv. 1 The Pahāṛī languages fall into three main groups. *Ibid.* 2 The mass of the Aryan-speaking population of the Himalayan tract in which Pahāṛī is spoken belongs, in the West, to the Kanēt and, in the East, to the Khas caste. **1923** A. Turnbull *Nepali Gram. & Vocab.* (ed. 3) 1 They also frequently refer to the language as 'Pahāṛī', or 'Pahāṛiyā', though, strictly speaking, it is only one of the many forms of Pahāṛī. **1943** R. Godden *Rungli-Rungliot* 37 Monbad speaks Hindustani and Paharia. **1950** *Encycl. Brit.* XVIII. 773/2 The hill dialects, known as Pahari, are akin to the language spoken in Rajputana. **1971** *Hindustan Times* (New Delhi) 7 Apr. 7/3 Mr Khandalavala's books include Pahari Miniature Painting, an exhaustive survey of painting in the Punjab hills. **1974** *Encycl. Brit. Micropædia* VII. 676/3 *Pahari painting*, miniature painting and book illustration that developed in the independent states of the Himalayan foothills in India. **1974** *Listener* 31 Jan. 136/3 The shops are run by Sikhs: the Paharis, the hill people, are not really interested.

‖ **pahit** (pa·hit). [Malay, = bitter.] In full *gin pahit.* Gin and bitters.

1914 G. Frankau *Tid'apa* (1915) ii. 11 He had shouted for *pahit* and for *stinger* till the hot, strong bane of them swept In flame to each brain-cell's tinder. **1923** W. S. Maugham in *Nash's & Pall Mall Mag.* Apr. 32/1 The Irishman ordered a dry martini for her and a gin pahit for himself. **1932** —— *Book-Bag* 21 Shall you be ready for a gin pahit in ten minutes? **1961** Conyn & Marten *Bali Ballet Murder* iii. 41 *Gin pahit* as an aperitif. **1963** J. Kirkup *Tropic Temper* 213 Patrons are requested to reserve their tables for dinner before ordering their pahits. **1965** O. A. Mendelsohn *Dict. Drink* 251 *Pahit*, Malay Club term for long gin drink. **1968** *Punch* 12 June 852/2 There was the euphoria of foreseeing ourselves in Maugham fiction—white-tuxedoed dinner-parties, the fans turning on the ceiling, gin *pahits* on the veranda, humid adultery behind the jalousies.

Pahlavi, *a.* and *sb.* Add: (Earlier and later examples.) Also **Pehlavi, Pehlevee, Pehlevian.**

1773 W. Jones tr. *Astarabadi's Hist. Nader Shah* App. 159 Barzuien learned the Indian tongue, and, having..procured a copy of the book, translated it into the Pehlevian dialect: about an hundred and forty years after, his work was turned from Pehlevi into Arabick. **1777** J. RICHARDSON *Dict. Persian, Arabic, & Eng.* p. iv/2 The idiom of Farsistan (Persia Proper)..had an extensive range over the most civilized of the lower districts: whilst the Pehlavi prevailed chiefly around the Mazenderan or Caspian Sea. **1789** [see ZEND 1]. **1815** M. ELPHINSTONE *Acct. Kingdom of Caubul* II. iv. 191 Some of these Zend and Pehlevee words are, however, common to the Shanscrit. **1950** R. G. KENT *Old Persian* 6/2 Middle Iranian includes the Iranian dialects as they appear from about 300 B.C. to about 900 A.D. They are in general called Pahlavi. *Ibid.* 7/1 Arsacid Pahlavi was the official language of the Arsacid dynasty of Parthia, which ruled from 250 B.C. to 226 A.D... The Sasanian or Southwest Pahlavi was the official language of the Sasanian dynasty, which ruled from 226 A.D. until..652. **1968** K. JAHN *Rypka's Hist. Iranian Lit.* 34 There is a great wealth of Middle Persian book-literature, usually known as Pahlavi literature. The language is also called book-Pahlavi. **1972** W. B. LOCKWOOD *Panorama Indo-European Lang.* 235 Middle Persian or Pahlavi, as the language of this literature is also called.

‖ **pahoehoe** (pǎhō͞u·ihō͞uˌi). *Geol.* Also †**paho-ihoi.** [Hawaiian.] A form of solidified lava that is undulating or billowy in form and has a shiny appearance. Cf. *AA².

1859 [see *AA²]. **1864** R. ANDERSON *Hawaiian Islands* 142 The broken lava is piled ten or fifteen feet above the smooth, hard *pahoihoi.* **1869** *Q. Jrnl. Geol. Soc.* XXV. 434 From this a stream of the smooth satin-like lava called 'pahoehoe' in Hawaii flowed for a few hours. **1972** *Islander* (Victoria, B.C.) 24 Sept. 4/2 One is pahoehoe—a taffy-like lava that has hardened into folds and creases that give it a smooth, ropy look, like frosting that has spilled over the top of a cake. **1975** *Nature* 29 May 387/1 The eruptions of this period include two..which produced pahoehoe instead of the more normal aa flows of Etna.

paiche (pɑi·ʃe). [Amer. Sp.] = *ARAPAIMA, *PIRARUCÚ.

1961 E. S. HERALD *Living Fishes of World* 99/1 The largest species in the family [*sc.* Osteoglossidæ] is the fabulous *Arapaima gigas,* called paiche in Peru, pirarucú in Brazil, and arapaima in British Guiana. **1962** N. MAXWELL *Witch-Doctor's Apprentice* xx. 251 At each stop, the block of salt fish grew higher. It was all *paiche,* a giant fish often attaining a weight of more than two hundred pounds, which is found only in the Amazon River system. **1976** 'A. HALL' *Kobra Manifesto* xiii. 174 We were eating *paiche* with *farinha.*

paid, *ppl. a.* Add: **2.** (Further examples.)

1961 WEBSTER s.v., A good job and a paid vacation. **1967** *Listener* 30 Nov. 694/2 The shortening of hours of work, improvements in housing standards, paid holidays, the prohibition of child labour,..should all, on the face of it, have helped to intensify family cohesiveness. **1978** *Ibid.* 19 Jan. 78/3 After the Second World War, paid holidays became common.

4. a. *paid for,* esp., an instruction given to a dog that has 'earned' a reward; *paid-up* (earlier and further examples).

1848 MILL *Pol. Econ.* II. v. ix. 463 A known and large amount of paid-up capital. **1854** J. C. MAITLAND *Cat & Dog* 8 To please Lily, I learned to sit patiently watching the most tempting buttered crust on the ground under my nose, when she said 'Trust, Captain!' never dreaming of touching it till she gave the word of command, 'Now it is paid for;' when I ate it in a genteel and deliberate manner. **1874** 'MARK TWAIN' *Gilded Age* xlviii. 435 What the insurance companies call the 'endowment', or the 'paid-up' plan, by which a policy is secured after a certain time without further payment. **1913** [see *EXTENDED *ppl. a.* 2 c]. **1922** 'R. CROMPTON' *Just—William* xii. 238 They taught him to sit up and almost taught him 'Trust' and 'Paid For'. **1934** 'R. HULL' *Murder of my Aunt* ii. 107 It seemed eternity to me, and I suppose to So-so too, waiting for the glad sound of 'Paid for'. **1970** J. FLEMING *Young Man, I think you're Dying* ix. 127 The manner of dogs put on *Trust* for a biscuit, watching the biscuit until the words: *Paid for!*

b. In phr. *paid-up member,* a member of a club, society, etc., who has paid a subscription.

1959 H. HOBSON *Mission House Murder* xxvi. 176 A fully paid-up member of Medina, Soho's equivalent of the old Mafia. **1960** *News Chron.* 1 July 6/7 Prince Philip always..[visits] the club when he attends Cowes Week—he's a fully paid-up member. **1970** 'H. CARMICHAEL' *Remote Control* ii. 24 He was a paid-up member of the Kennel Club. **1976** *Conservation News* Nov./Dec. 12 That issue contained the application for non-voting tickets for paid-up members not attending as delegates.

paidle, var. PADDLE *sb.*³ in Dict. and Suppl.

paido-: see PÆDO-, PEDO-.

paigeite (pē̆i·dʒəit). *Min.* [f. the name of Sidney *Paige* (1880–1968), U.S. geologist + -ITE¹.] A borate of iron and magnesium, $(Fe^{II},Mg)_2Fe^{III}BO_5$ with more ferrous iron than magnesium, which is found as black orthorhombic crystals.

1908 KNOPF & SCHALLER in *Amer. Jrnl. Sci.* CLXXV. 324 The other mineral, for which we propose the name *paigeite,* in honor of Mr. Sidney Paige of the Geological Survey, was found at two localities, at Brooks Mountain [Alaska] in loose blocks, and at Ear Mountain, 40 miles to the northeast, *in situ.* **1954** [see *HULSITE]. **1961** *Doklady Earth Sci.* CXXXIV. 1004 (*heading*) On the discovery of warwickite and paigeite in Precambrian dolomitic marbles of North Korea.

‖ **pai-hua** (paiˌhwā). Also **bai hua, báihuà.** [Chinese *báihuà,* f. *bái* white, clear, plain + *huà* language, speech.] The standard written form of modern Chinese, based on the northern dialects, esp. that of Peking; the vernacular literary style (opp. *WENYEN). Also *attrib.* Cf. *PUTONGHUA.

1923 B. KARLGREN *Sound & Symbol in Chinese* iii. 37 Some modern newspapers have tried to introduce *pai hua* 'white language', i.e. vulgar style, colloquial, at least in one or two columns, but with no great success. **1932** O. M. GREEN in *Asiatic Rev.* XXVIII. 114 The Literary Revolution of 1917 to 1919..secured the adoption of the Pai Hua, the most widely spoken language in China, for all literary purposes. Not only newspapers and magazines but many standard works are now printed in the Pai Hua. **1936** N. WALES in E. Snow *Living China* 336 The healthy parvenu *pai-hua,* 'plain speech', literature of the people in the spoken language, ashamed of itself and despised and outcast by the *wen-yen literati.* **1937** E. SNOW *Red Star over China* i. 44 These Shensi hill people have a dialect of their own..but they understand *pai-hua,* or mandarin Chinese. **1950** J. DE FRANCIS *Nationalism & Lang. Reform in China* i. 7 The *paihua* or colloquial style was, roughly speaking, speech reduced to writing in the ideographic script. **1968** P. KRATOCHVÍL *Chinese Lang. Today* v. 163 Perhaps the most influential factor..was the outburst of writing in the new style which followed the rejection of *wényán.* This style called *the new báihuà,* or only *báihuà* (usually translated as 'vernacular'; the etymology of the Chinese term which means something like 'plain language' is not quite certain), grew partly out of the tradition of popular old *báihuà* writing mainly represented by the great medieval novels.

pai kau (pai kɑu). Also **pai kow, pie-gow.** [Cantonese, f. *p'ai* tablet + *kau* nine.] A Chinese gambling game played with dominoes.

1906 [see *CHUCK-A-LUCK]. **1969** R. C. BELL *Board & Table Games* II. vi. 102 Pai Kow is played with a full set of Chinese dominoes. **1972** *Guardian* 29 May 16/2 Mr Liu ..wants..to attract his countrymen away from Mah Jong and Pai Kau—a sort of dominoes played like poker. **1978** *Daily Tel.* 13 July 1/7 The legalising of exotic games such as fan tan and pai kau in casinos.

‖ **pailou** (pai:lō͞u·). [Chinese, f. *p'ai* tablet + *lou* tower.] An elaborate Chinese commemorative or ornamental gateway.

1836 J. F. DAVIS *Chinese* II. xviii. 321 The emperor occasionally orders a *pae-low* to be erected at the public expense. **1887** *Chinese Times* 1 Oct. 785/2 The homes of the dead, with their *p'ailou* and carved images of lions, sheep, &c. **1923** *Blackw. Mag.* Jan. 101/2 In front of one of them [*sc.* temples] stands a white stone *pailou,* which shines in the sunlight like a flamboyant Stonehenge trilith. **1947** *Archit. Rev.* CII. 13 The p'ailou is a commemorative gateway, set up either to mark a famous place or to serve as a monument to the dead and having three or five openings with double or triple lintels and tiled roofs. **1948** R. ALLEY *Gung Ho* 28 Under the great pailou framing the main street. **1958** W. WILLETTS *Chinese Art* II. viii. 736 This class of monumental stone arch or gateway... Commemorative or triumphal in function... *P'ai-lou* are almost always built of stone, in close imitation of a wooden prototype and with carpentry technique. They have one, three, or five openings. **1977** *N.Y. Rev. Bks.* 26 May 21/2 The destruction of Peking started in the 1950s, when all the pailous that spanned the main thoroughfares of the old city were eliminated.

pain, *sb.*¹ Add: **3. d.** *pain in the neck* (colloq.) (also simply *pain*), an annoying or tiresome person or thing; also, in same sense (but *vulg.*), *pain in the arse.* Also, *to give* (someone) *a pain* (*in the neck* or *arse*), to be annoying or tiresome (to someone).

1908 R. E. KNOWLES *Web of Time* xiv. 144 'There's naethin' like the guid auld oatmeal.' 'You Scotch folks give me a pain,' broke in David. **1912** *Maclean's Mag.* Nov. 68/1 Bill, you give me a pain. **1924** WODEHOUSE *Leave it to Psmith* ix. 188 He got there first, damn him! Wouldn't that give you a pain in the neck! **1933** E. B. WHITE *Let.* Mar. (1976) 112 All through the campaign I thought Mr. R. was something of a pain. **1934** [see *ASS]. **1937** [see *DINKUM *a.*]. **1941** W. A. PERCY *Lanterns on Levee* 77, I was a sickly youngster..a frail problem child, a pain in the neck. **1951** 'A. GARVE' *Murder in Moscow* x. 102 What do we really know of Mullett, except that he was a pain in the neck to everybody? **1958** *Spectator* 7 Feb. 175/3 The Liu was almost as big a pain in the neck as the previous night's Preziosilla. **1967** W. SOYINKA *Kongi's Harvest* 14 Your uncle is a pain in the neck. **1970** *Times* 7 Jan. 7/7 Anthony Quinn.. plays a wise, noble, feckless, life-loving Greek dispenser of advice, lay preacher and general pain in the neck. **1972** D. RAMSAY *Little Murder Music* 8 Hey, Jack, how does his royal pain in the ass intend to take the *Scherzo?* **1972** *Times* 13 Sept. 7/5 He represents about 1 per cent of the blokes... He is a pain. **1973** 'E. MCBAIN' *Hail to Chief* i. 6 Homicide cops..were pains in the ass to detectives actually..trying to solve murder cases. **1975** *New Yorker* 21 Apr. 103/3 She is a pain, and, unconsciously, the source of many of the troubles that follow. *Ibid.* 17 Nov. 125/1 Fiction, in whatever form, about real people is more often than not a pain, and sometimes downright pernicious. **1976** A. WHITE *Long Silence* xiv. 123 Lieutenant Otto Andersen..was a consistent pain in the arse to Colonel Birkenkamp, constantly reporting his men for slovenly dress. **1977** *Rolling Stone* 7 Apr. 12/2 It was an increasing pain in the ass to do the same material each night.

7. a. pain point *Physiol.* = **pain spot*; **pain spot** *Physiol.,* a small spot on the surface of the skin that is sensitive to pain; **pain-threshold,** the upper limit of tolerance to pain.

1897 tr. *T. Ribot's Psychol. of Emotions* 27 Goldscheider..admits pain-points (points sensible to pain), but not a specific organ for pain nor special nerves to transmit it. **1954** S. ROTHMAN *Physiol. & Biochem. Skin* v. 136/2 There is no doubt that itching is produced with great ease when the stimulus is weak and repetitive and when several pain points are stimulated simultaneously. **1888** W. STIRLING tr. *Landois's Text-bk. Human Physiol.* (ed. 3) xiv. 831 The pain-spots can be isolated by means of a needle, or electrically. **1927** HALDANE & HUXLEY *Animal Biol.* v. 126 Stimulation of a single pain-spot will only cause movement after a long time or never. **1973** C. P. SWANSON *Nat. Hist. Man* viii. 237/2 (*caption*) Pain spots on normal hands of two individuals. **1902** Pain-threshold [see *MISERY 8]. **1969** 'I. DRUMMOND' *Man with Tiny Head* xvi. 182 Sandro guessed that his pain-threshold would be high and that he would give nothing away.

b. *pain-shot* adj.

1911 BEERBOHM *Zuleika D.* iv. 44 He was gazing at the girl with pain-shot eyes.

c. *pain-giving, -killing, -relieving* adjs.

1889 'MARK TWAIN' *Connecticut Yankee* xviii. 215 The executioner..was a good, pains-taking and pain-giving official. **1890** W. JAMES *Princ. Psychol.* II. xxi. 306 Locke expressly makes the *pleasure-* or *pain-*giving quality to be the ultimate human criterion of anything's reality. **1934** R. BODLEY *Japanese Omelette* iv. 30 The geta..supposed to fit the sole of a Japanese foot..are, to my mind, the most paingiving form of footwear ever devised. **1964** J. J. WALSH *Understanding Paraplegia* iv. 24 In many cases, the so-called 'harmless' pain-killing drugs are not sufficiently strong to stop the pain. **1974** 'J. GRAHAM' *Bloody Passage* ix. 125 The pain-killing injection had helped. **1908** *Practitioner* Dec. 850 The experiment was absolute proof of the pain-relieving quality of congestion. **1935** *Discovery* Aug. 226/2 One very fortunate property which such a generator appears to possess is its pain-relieving virtue. **1966** *Lancet* 31 Dec. 1436/1 Digitalis, quinidine,.. and pain-relieving drugs were given when indicated to both groups.

d. pain-killer (earlier and later examples); **pain-proof** *a.,* having immunity from pain.

1853 *La Crosse* (Wisconsin) *Democrat* 7 June 2/4 Ayer's Cherry Pectoral, Perry Davis' Pain Killer. **1855** I. C. PRAY *Mem. J. G. Bennett* 200 The many pain-killers invented have diminished largely the amount of human suffering. **1863** W. B. CHEADLE *Jrnl. Trip across Canada* (1931) 102 Milton rubs his face with pain-killer. **1932** J. STEINBECK *Pastures of Heaven* x. 236 Pat could hear the sizzle of mentholatum and painkiller gushing from containers and boiling into the fire. **1959** [see *benzocaine* s.v. *BENZO-]. **1973** 'R. MACLEOD' *Burial in Portugal* iii. 68 Finding the painkiller tablets, he swallowed a couple. **1977** A. MORICE *Murder in Mimicry* I. iv. 33 In those days you had to get by with ordinary painkillers which were about as effective as a slug of brandy to a man having his leg amputated. **1903** 'MARK TWAIN' in *North Amer. Rev.* Jan. 3 No C[hristian] S[cience] family would consider itself..pain-proof without an Annex.

pain, *sb.*² **2.** *pain perdu* (later examples.)

1723 [see *CREAM *sb.*² 7 b]. **1941** W. A. PERCY *Lanterns on Levee* 11 Oh, the poor little boys who never put a lump of butter into steaming butter-bread (spoon-bread is the same thing) or lolled their tongues over pain-perdu. **1961** T. HENROT *Belgium* 189 *Pain-perdu*—rusk softened in warm, sweetened milk then browned in butter. **1972** *Guardian* 28 Jan. 9/5 Pain Perdu or Gilded Crusts..are very popular with children.

pain, *v.* **3.** (Later example.)

1885 W. PATER *Marius* II. 213 Christ, paining in him, set forth a copy to the rest.

painedly (pē̆i·ndli, pē̆i·nėdli), *adv.* [f. PAINED *ppl. a.* + -LY².] In a pained manner.

1921 D. H. LAWRENCE *England, my England* (1922) 270 Mr. Enderby looked up painedly. **1926** FOWLER *Mod. Eng. Usage* 418/2 *Painedly.* A bad form.

painfully, *adv.* Add: **4.** *fig.* Excessively, to an alarming degree.

1900 [see *EFFORTFUL *a.*]. **1909** A. LANCASTRE SALDANHA *Recoll.* xi. 151 Sir Robert Peel was painfully shy with strangers. **1941** N. COWARD *Australia Visited* i. 2 An R.A.F. plane which seemed to me almost painfully small. **1961** *Flying* (N.Y.) Feb. 33/1 At this point it should be painfully obvious that cities, being 'soft', and the people within them are ideally suited to destruction by nuclear weapons.

pa-in-law. *colloq.* = FATHER-IN-LAW.

1886 H. BAUMANN *Londinismen* 130/1 *Pa-in-law,*.. father-in-law. **1949** E. COXHEAD *Wind in West* xii. 289, I couldn't throw away the chance of poking my fingers into pa-in-law's pie. **1952** M. ALLINGHAM *Tiger in Smoke* xiv. 213 Are you worrying about..my future pa-in-law?

pai·nstakingness. [f. PAINSTAKING *a.* + -NESS.] The fact or habit of taking pains; assiduous effort.

1927 *Sunday Express* 19 June 19/3 The sportingness of owners, the painstakingness of trainers, and the brilliance of jockeys. **1936** *Times Lit. Suppl.* 2 May 366/3 His dicta are analysed by the author with the same painstakingness.

paint, *sb.* Add: **2. e.** Phr. *as smart* (*pretty,* etc.) *as paint*: superlatively smart, pretty, etc.

1850 F. E. SMEDLEY *Frank Fairleigh* xli. 340 Why, Oaklands, man, you are looking as fresh as paint; getting sound again, wind and limb, eh? **1883** R. L. STEVENSON *Treas. Isl.* viii. 65 You're a lad, you are, but you're as smart as paint. I see that when you first came in. **1905** *Tatler* 22 Feb. 306/3 Half the English [Rugby] side were played out twenty minutes before the end while the Irishmen were still as fresh as paint. **1918** A. QUILLER-COUCH *Foe-Farrell* 176 He stared..across at the grouped rustic buildings, all as pretty as paint. **1930** H. A. BRYDEN *Enchantments of Field* 187 After all, your hounds may be as handsome as paint, but if they fail you in nose, cry and hunting-power they are worse than useless. **1963** N. MARSH *Dead Water* (1964) iii. 58 Miss Emily arrived at noon on Monday. She had stayed overnight in Dorset and was fresh as paint. **1975** J. I. M. STEWART *Young Pattullo* ii. 40 Not always wholly agreeable, perhaps, but as clever as paint.

5*. *sb.* and *a.* = PINTO *a.* and *sb.* (Chiefly *U.S.*)

1848 BARTLETT *Dict. Amer.* 243 In some of the Southern States, a horse or other animal which is spotted, is called a *paint*. **1869** *Overland Monthly* III. 126 A black-and-white-paint horse, fifteen hands high. **1909** 'O. HENRY' *Roads of Destiny* vi. 96 Sam Kildrake's old paint hoss that killed hisself over-drinkin' on a hot day. **1948** *Sun* (Baltimore) 18 June 15/4 The Appaloosa somewhat resembles the paints, pintos and calicos, so popular with the plains Indians. **1955** W. FOSTER-HARRIS *Look of Old West* viii. 226 An animal violently splotched with different colors was called a paint. **1975** J. HANSEN *Trouble Maker* i. 2 She led out a little paint mare. *Ibid.* xii. 125 The sorrel followed the paint. **1976** *Billings* (Montana) *Gaz.* 2 July 11-C/6 (Advt.), 8 yr old paint gelding. Child broke. Possible show horse.

6. *paint-drum, -job, -oil* (earlier example), *-rag, -shop, -stoving, -work* (further examples); *paint-remover* (earlier and later examples), *-stripper, -thinner*; *paint-dappled, -daubed, -speckled* adjs.; **paint box** (earlier examples); **paint-brush** (*b*) = *Indian paint-brush* (*INDIAN A. 4 b); **paint card,** a card showing a graduated range of paint colours; also *fig.*; **paint frame** (examples); **paint-roller,** a roller covered in an absorbent material which holds paint to be applied to a surface; also *attrib.*; **paint spray,** a device for spraying paint on to a surface; hence *paint-spray* vb. trans., *paint-sprayed* ppl. adj.; **paint-stone,** a stone used as a source of paint.

1725 *New-England Courant* 8–15 Feb. 1/2, I would oblige every Sign-Painter to serve seven Years at College, before he presum'd to handle Pencil or Paint-Box. **1820** SHELLEY *Posthumous Poems* (1824) 62 Near that a dusty paint box, some old hooks. **1915** ARMSTRONG & THORNBER *Field Bk. Western Wild Flowers* 472 Paint Brush. *Castilleja miniata*. Red. Summer. Northwest. This is a very handsome kind, from one to four feet tall. **1968** MRS. L. B. JOHNSON *White House Diary* 9 Apr. (1970) 656 Great splashes of wildflowers began to appear along the road and in the pastures..pale pink buttercups, wild verbena, coral paint brush, Indian blanket. **1931** D. RUNYON *Guys & Dolls* (1932) xiii. 266 A nervous man ..with a blood pressure away up in the paint cards must live quietly. **1961** [see *grey scale* s.v. *GREY *a.* 8]. **1904** *Windsor Mag.* Jan. 234/1 He handed me a paint-dappled copper stencil-plate, two feet square. **1945** W. DE LA MARE *Burning-Glass* 54 A paint-daubed woman bound for lonely bed..Stood watching him. **1920** *Blackw. Mag.* Apr. 499 The paint-drums..had been jolted bodily from their lashings. **1901** C. MORRIS *Life on Stage* v. 31 Run upstairs to the paint-frame (three flights up) and ask the painter to put a little ad-libitum in this bottle for me. **1954** *Archit. Rev.* CXVI. 114 A similar movement may still be seen driving the paint-frame at the Leicester Theatre Royal. **1961** *New Statesman* 20 Jan. 81/1 Backstage, Mr Moro plans..a full-scale paint frame. **1970** *New Yorker* 14 Nov. 59/1 The danger is always that the result will be a paint job, very superficial. **1971** *New Scientist* 22 Apr. 224/3 An imaginative and informed paintjob can achieve things which no camera or CRT could ever do. **1978** G. VIDAL *Kalki* xi. 251 The White House (which needs a paint job). **1727** in *Maryland Hist. Mag.* (1923) XVIII. 227 Glass, Paint oile, Druggs and Stationary ware. **1938** N. MARSH *Artists in Crime* i. 4 The painter..found..a handkerchief that had been used as a paint-rag. **1975** N. FREELING *What are Bugles blowing For?* 73 The woman..was wiping dust off her hands with a paint-rag. **1885** *List of Subscribers, Classified* (United Telephone Co.) (ed. 6) 133 Manufacturers..Paint Remover. **1960** *Practical Wireless* XXXVI. 306/1 The enamel can then be softened..by immersing them in a paint remover for perhaps a quarter of an hour. **1962** L. DEIGHTON *Ipcress File* xx. 131 She offered me one of those menthol cigarettes that taste like paint remover. **1973** F. TAUBES *Painter's Dict.* 175 Paint remover is sold under various trade names, and each brand is of similar formulation. The fluid is used to remove old paint layers and oil-varnish films. **1951** N. & S. MAGER *Amer. Househ. Encycl.* 623 Paint rollers. **1954** *Good Housek. Home Encycl.* 208/1 *Paint Rollers*: Covered in lamb's wool on special felt,..these rollers are simple to use. **1958** *Times* 7 July 6/5 The latest paint roller improvement is a foolproof model which holds and automatically feeds the right amount of paint on to the surface. **1959** *Listener* 23 Apr. 739/1, I have been trying out the self-feeding paint rollers that have recently come on the market. **1971** *Handyman Which?* Nov. 25/2 There are lots of paint rollers and their prices vary..from 28p to about £2. **1866** *Oregon State Jrnl.* 23 June 3/4 Enquire of W. W. Winter, at paint shop under picture gallery. **1899** *Sat. Even. Post* 10 June 795 Eight hundred tons of white lead are ground in the paint shop every twelve months. **1949** J. H. OUSBEY *Cellulose Spraying* xv. 61 The bodies, on which the doors have already been hung, come to the paintshop by overhead conveyor and are in bare metal. **1973** *Times* 18 May 26/5 By eliminating the solvents and attendant fumes, Fiat said the danger to the lungs of paintshop employees is sharply reduced. **1922** JOYCE *Ulysses* 442 Their paint-speckled hats wag. **1962** *Punch* 11 July 57/1 Twenty thousand men downing paint-sprays at Dagenham. **1967** M. CHANDLER *Ceramics in Mod. World* iii. 99 Almost all products of this kind..are glazed by spraying, in much the same way as car bodies are paint-sprayed. **1971** *Money Which?* Mar. 69/1 Small tools, such as hand drills, paint sprays, and so on, are strictly speaking capital. **1973** *Scotsman* 13 Feb. 8/6 Dundee's modern shopping precinct has now been further decorated with paint-sprayed gang slogans. **1797** A. BARNARD *Let.* 29 Nov. in *S. Afr. a Century Ago* (1901) 121 The 'paint stone' is found in this neighbourhood [*sc.* Paarl] in quantities—namely, an impalpable powder which, mixed with oil, serves the country people with colour to paint their waggons, houses, etc. **1896** *13th Ann. Rep. U.S. Bureau Amer. Ethnol. 1891–92* 115 The articles known as paint-stones scarcely come under the head of implements... Most of them were used merely to furnish paint. **1951** *Engineering* 26 Jan. 100/2 An infra-red paint-stoving plant..is being used for stoving No. 20 gauge aluminium panels for omnibus bodies. **1962** W. D. HISLOP in H. W. Chatfield *Sci. Surface Coatings* xviii. 531 All paint stoving ovens can be a hazard as the solvent vapour/air mixture is a potential fire risk. **1971** *Morning Star* 13 Apr. 4/5 While this may only be washing-up liquid,..it could well be something far more dangerous, like bleach or paint-stripper. **1973** J. ROSSITER *Manipulators* iv. 37 Paint-stripper fluid poured lavishly over the enamel..had boiled large blisters. **1959** *Sears, Roebuck Catal.* Spring/Summer 1397/6 Paint Thinner. **1960** *Practical Wireless* XXXVI. 313/1 The following will be required:..paint, paint thinners and an artist's small brush. **1977** F. PARRISH *Fire in Barley* ix. 96 Two five-gallon drums... One was called paint-thinner, one creosote. **1933** L. A. G. STRONG *Sea Wall* i. 3 The mailboat..glided gracefully in, her white paintwork stained a rich orange. **1966** G. N. LEECH *Eng. in Advertising* v. 40 Handy Andy shifts grime from paintwork like this. **1973** *Handyman Which?* Aug. 104/1 Curtains..rubbing against a wall could, over a period of time, make marks on the paintwork.

paint, *v.*[1] Add: **9.** *to paint by number*(*s*: to paint in a picture supplied marked out into sections which are numbered according to the colour to be used; hence *paint-by-number*(*s*, *painting-by-number* attrib. phrs.

1970 *Women's Household* July 6/3, I..paint by number and plan to try painting soon. **1971** 'P. KAVANAGH' *Triumph of Evil* (1972) vi. 50 He even bought this terrible oil painting... It looked as though it had been painted by numbers. **1976** *Billings* (Montana) *Gaz.* 26 June 14-B/6 But paint-by-number artists have nothing on 11 men at Our Savior's Lutheran Church. Led by Merle Brunsvold, the men put together an electronic pipe organ kit. **1976** *Sunday Post* (Glasgow) 26 Dec. 9/2 Our other products, like playing cards, jigsaws, painting-by-number kits, &c. **1977** J. HODGINS *Invention of World* iii. 42 She..spent the afternoon doing a paint-by-numbers picture, in the living room.

11. paint out. d. *Naut.* = sense 3.

1902 B. LUBBOCK *Round the Horn* viii. 302 The great day for cleaning and painting out the half-deck has come... The steward also painted out his berth to-day. **1924** 'P. BLUNDELL' *Confessions of Seaman* ii. 28 When was it painted out last, I should like to know? **1963** S. HAYDEN *Wanderer* (1964) i. 8 You've painted her out—you've even changed her name?

12. a. *trans.* To cause to be displayed or represented on the screen of a cathode-ray tube.

1946 *Jrnl. Inst. Electr. Engin.* XCIII. IIIA. 147/2 When an echo or the background has been painted it rapidly fades away according to a law determined by the properties of the screen. **1949** *Jrnl. R. Aeronaut. Soc.* LIII. 436/1 It will be seen that the area of towering cumulo-nimbus clouds..are clearly painted on the PPI picture. **1960** J. D. HAIGH *Radiolocation Techniques* xii. 192 A photographic display of this kind has the advantage that the whole display is of uniform brightness as compared with a normal p.p.i. in which, at any one moment, only that portion of the picture actually being painted by the rotating time-base is at maximum brightness. **1960** *Proc. Inst. Electr. Engin.* CVII. B. Suppl. 19. 54/2 The display console has a double-deflection system consisting of the main deflection circuits..which position a spot on the tube face, and a second deflection coil..which paints a small raster about this position. **1977** *Sci. Amer.* Jan. 60/2 One kind of stimulus we find useful consists of a moving pattern of small, bright dots 'painted' on the screen of a cathode-ray tube with the aid of a computer.

b. *intr.* To show up on the screen of a cathode-ray tube. Also with *up*.

1946 *Jrnl. Inst. Electr. Engin.* XCIII. IIIA. 145/2 To obtain a satisfactory picture it is necessary to arrange that a fixed target 'paints' at approximately the same point on the screen for consecutive rotations of the aerial system. **1949** *Jrnl. R. Aeronaut. Soc.* LIII. 436/2 It was hoped to fly into some of the cloud forms, but the pilot decided that the risk of flying into any area which 'painted up' on the PPI tube was too great.

painted, *ppl. a.* Add: **4. painted beauty,** substitute for def.: a large North American butterfly, *Vanessa virginiana*, with black and white markings on its brownish-yellow wings; (examples); **painted lady,** (*d*) a name used in South Africa for several local species of gladiolus, distinguished by marks of a different colour on some of their petals; **painted terrapin, tortoise, turtle,** substitute for def.: a small American freshwater turtle of the genus *Chrysemys*, distinguished by red and yellow rings on its greenish-brown shell; (examples); **painted top-shell,** a littoral gastropod mollusc, *Calliostoma zizyphinum* (formerly *Trochus* or *Gibbula magus*), which has a vividly coloured conical shell.

1899 *Lippincott's Monthly Mag.* Oct. 631 The Painted Beauty and the Cosmopolitan resemble each other strongly. **1972** SWAN & PAPP *Common Insects N. Amer.* 237 Painted Beauty: *Vanessa virginiensis*... Also called American painted lady and Virginia lady. **1906** B. STONEMAN *Plants S. Afr.* xix. 198 Gladiolus... Painted Ladies and 'Kalkoentjes' belong here. Eighty-one species of this large genus are found in South Africa. **1927** [see *AANDBLOM]. **1972** *Stand. Encycl. S. Afr.* V. 201/2 The Cape species [of gladiolus] are known as pypies, afrikaners, painted ladies, bells. *Ibid.* 202/1 The painted ladies (e.g. *G. carneus*) have white or pink trumpet-shaped flowers with markings on the lower perianth lobes. **1839** STORER & PEABODY *Rep. Fishes, Reptiles & Birds Mass.* 208 *Chrysemys picta*... The painted Tortoise. **1842** J. E. DEKAY *Zool. N.Y.* III. 12 The Painted Tortoise..is unquestionably the handsomest of our fresh-water species. **1876** D. S. JORDAN *Man. Vertebrates Northern U.S.* 163 *C*[*hrysemys*] *picta* (Herm.) Ag. Painted Turtle. Mud Turtle... One of the most common turtles. **1904** W. T. HORNADAY *Amer. Nat. Hist.* xxxvii. 327/1 The Painted Terrapin, hitherto called at random the Painted 'Turtle' and Pond-'Tortoise', is perhaps the most widely distributed species..in the United States. **1949** *Life* 11 Apr. 81 A painted turtle cranes its neck in the spring sun. **1973** M. CROWELL *Greener Pastures* 200 We..pick up a painted turtle intent on crossing the road. **1865** J. G. WOOD *Common Shells of Sea-shore* xi. 100 The Painted Top-shell ..is rather boldly ridged. *Ibid.* 101 The name of Painted Top is given to it on account of the magnificent hues of the animal. **1901** E. STEP *Shell Life* xi. 205 The Painted Top-shell..is a very distinct species, the shape of the three largest of the 8 whorls giving the solid shell a decidedly turreted appearance. **1972** S. P. DANCE *Shells* 18 (*caption*) The Painted Top Shell is a gaily coloured species and has long tentacles.

painter[1]. Add: **4.** *painter-engraver, -etcher, -graver, -poet*; *painter-engraving, -etching*; **painter-like** *a.*, (*a*) resembling or characteristic of a painter; (*b*) picturesque, artistic; **painter's brush,** (*b*) = *Indian paint-brush* (*INDIAN A. 4 b); **painter's** (or **painters'**) **mussel,** the freshwater mussel, *Unio pictorum*.

1879 F. S. HADEN *About Etching* I. 18 We shall have to show that the adoption of the tool, (except in the case of the painter-engraver, who..was an original artist,) implies the practice of a secondary art. **1937** *Burlington Mag.* Feb. 77/1 Elevation to the level of painter-engravers such as Hausbuchmeister and Martin Schongauer. **1890** F. S. HADEN *Art of Painter-Etcher* 4 This great-master engraving, this original engraving, this painter-engraving. **1880** *Times* 23 Dec. 7/5 Society of Painter Etchers.— ..The society..has been formed to 'promote original etching and the interest of painters practising that branch of art'. **1920** E. H. HUBBARD *Etchings* 128 The work of 'painter-etchers' (men who execute original subjects direct on the plate). **1975** *Whitaker's Almanack 1976* 1104/2 Painter-Etchers and Engravers, Royal Society of.., 26 Conduit Street, W.1. **1890** F. S. HADEN *Art of Painter-Etcher* 5 The singular restriction of the Fine Arts to three—Oil painting, Sculpture, and Architecture, to the exclusion of Water Colour painting and Painter-Etching. **1879** —— *About Etching* II. 47 *Leyden, Lucas Van*.. A Flemish painter-graver of great reputation. **1738** J. F. FRITSCH tr. *De Lairesse's Art of Painting* I. VI. xv. 331 But since Beauty is attracting, and Deformity offensive, this certainly is true Painter-like, which supposes the best and most agreeable Objects. **1821** Painter-like [in Dict.]. **1845** R. FORD *Hand-bk. for Travellers Spain* II. 595/2 *Villafranca del Vierzo* is truly Swiss-like,.. with painter-like bridges. **1958** *Economist* 8 Nov. (Suppl.) 9/2 His painter-like method of composition 'over the whole surface at once'. **1909** *Daily Chron.* 17 Mar. 3/3 Mr. Graham is what may be termed a painter-poet. **1941** BLUNDEN *Thomas Hardy* 262 The painter-poet insists on being very much in the middle of things time and again in Hardy's verse. **1869** S. BOWLES *Our New West* v. 104 The painter's brush, as familiarly called here, is a new flower to me. **1899** S. HALE *Let.* 22 Apr. (1919) 345 Mariposa lilies, painter's-brush, poppies, and dozens of others. **1910** MRS. H. WARD *Canadian Born* x. 206 Anderson had brought her to a wild garden of incredible beauty... Painter's brush, harebell, speedwell, golden-brown gaillardias. [**1862** J. G. JEFFREYS *Brit. Conchol.* I. 34 *U*[*nio*] *pictorum*... Painters'. **1865** L. REEVE *Conchologia Iconica* XXV. s.v. Unio, species 123 The painters' Unio. Shell elongately oblong,..fulvous-olive.] **1896** L. E. ADAMS *Collector's Man. Brit. Land & Freshwater Shells* (ed. 2) 148 The 'Painters' Mussel' is found in similar localities to *U*[*nio*] *tumidus*. **1901** E. STEP *Shell Life* 111 The Painter's Mussel.., so called because the valves were formerly used to hold artists' colours. **1952** J. CLEGG *Freshwater Life* xvi. 268 The Painter's Mussel..has a long, thin shell, about two to three inches in length. **1974** M. SAUL *Shells* 87 The more solid valves of the Painter's Mussel..were used by artists throughout Europe to hold their colours.

painter[3]. (Earlier and further examples.)

1803 J. DAVIS *Trav. U.S.A.* 382 My master..said that I ought to live among *painters* and wolves, and sold me to a *Georgia* man for two hundred dollars. **1834** D. CROCKETT *Narr. Life* i. 5 This alarmed me, and I screamed out like a young painter. **1940** ARNOLD & HALE *Hot Irons* 9 You learn, accidentally, that a 'painter' is really a panther. **1972** *Amer. Speech 1968* XLIII. 218 Mountain cuisine consisted almost entirely of meat: rattlesnake,..*painter* (panther), and rabbit.

painterly, *a.* (*adv.*). Restrict *rare* to the advb. and add to def. of the adj.: *spec.* of a style of painting, characterized by qualities of colour, stroke, and texture rather than of contour or line. Also *transf.* (Further examples.)

1932 *Times Lit. Suppl.* 16 June 441/1 A linear style and a 'painterly' (a translation of the German word *malerisch*, which can also mean picturesque). **1942** *Burlington Mag.* Jan. 24/2 A technique which foreshadows the painterly methods of Watteau. **1950** *Eng. Stud.* XXXI. 166 One should not forget the exciting Kiplingesque rhythm..or the painterly qualities of the dramatic, colourful poem of Cummerbund, the monster of India. **1952** H. READ in P. & L. MURRAY tr. *H. Wölfflin's Classic Art* p. vi, One word, however, calls for comment—the word 'painterly', which has been invented to convey the meaning of the German word *malerisch*.. It stands for that depreciation and gradual obliteration of line (outline and tangible surface) and for the merging of these in a 'shifting semblance' of things—it is an attempt to represent the vague and impalpable essence of things. **1958** *Observer* 23 Mar. 16/5 Short lyrics of precision and beauty, painterly poems, touchingly infused with the poet's passion for what is beautiful. **1958** *Times* 24 July 5/2 His recent attempts to exchange a linear for a more painterly manner. **1962** *Punch* 1 Aug. 177/3 Alberta Wheeler, ex-night club dancer and painterly genius. **1963** *Guardian* 11 Mar. 7/2 He is becoming more painterly, his colour more subtle, and his surface dense with matter. **1969** H. E. BATES *Vanished World* xi. 147 It was not only the painterly quality of Crane's prose that attracted me. **1969** R. MAYER *Dict. Art Terms & Techniques* 276/1 *Painterly*, having the quality of expertly brushed workmanship... A term applied to the dominance of tonal masses over line as a means of defining form in painting, sculpture, and architecture. **1973** F. TAUBES *Painter's Dict.* 176 Botticelli is a linear painter, whilst Rembrandt's work would be considered painterly. **1973** *Times Lit. Suppl.* 3 Aug. 900/3 The painterly aspect of each drawing is never forgotten: apart from shading with chalk or wash, in order to enliven a line or contour, pastels are employed and often coloured paper used. **1974** A. DILLARD *Pilgrim at Tinker Creek* xv. 268 A photograph of earth from space, the planet so startlingly painterly and hung. **1978** P. PORTER *Cost of Seriousness* 2 Masts for Woodbridge Crowd three degrees of the horizon, edging A painterly Dutch sky.

Hence **pai·nterliness**, painterly quality.

1955 P. HERON *Changing Forms of Art* xiii. 202 Hilton's *conscious intention* has been to eliminate all charm, all painterliness, even that evidence of mastery of the material which is itself a seductive element in painting. **1958** S. SPENDER *Engaged in Writing* iii. 43 Marteau's very appearance transformed the atmosphere from the weighted inwardness of Bonvolio-directed programme music, to cracking outdoor painterliness. **1977** *Times Lit. Suppl.* 24 June 761/5 Manet's painterly procedures—as well as his acknowledged painterliness.

paint-in (pēⁱ·nt,in). [f. PAINT *v.*¹ + *-IN³.] A gathering for the purpose of painting; *spec.* an organized attempt to improve and draw attention to shabby or neglected buildings by cleaning and redecorating them.

1966 *Maclean's Mag.* 14 May 3 What is a Paint-In? Well, it's a protest, like a sit-in, except that people paint and other people gather round. **1969** *Time* 20 June 64 Jane Shay..organized a one-day paint-in by a group of Washington high school art students. **1969** *Parade* (N.Y.) 14 Dec. 12/2 A gigantic clean-up and paint-in began. **1974** *State* (Columbia, S. Carolina) 26 Apr. B-1/3 (*caption*) Gibson Hopper tries his hand at a paint-in during opening day of Fiesta '74.

painting, *vbl. sb.* Add: **6.** *painting-machine.*

1902 *Chambers's Jrnl.* Feb. 125/2 The spray painting-machine is brought into operation where large unbroken surfaces have to be covered. **1966** 'H. MACDIARMID' *Company I've Kept* ii. 59 A painting-machine like Jean Tinguely's to produce unexpected designs.

pair, *sb.*¹ Add: **I. 1. b.** *another* or *a different pair of shoes* (earlier and later examples).

1849 T. ARNOLD *Let.* 28 Aug. in *N.Z. Lett.* (1966) 135 Nothing is easier than to make a beautiful scheme of education on paper, but to make it work is 'quite another pair of shoes', as they say in New Zealand. **1931** G. B. SHAW *Widowers' Houses* III. 58 in *Works*, Dooty's another pair o' shoes. **1936** W. H. S. SMITH *Let.* 9 Aug. in *Young Man's Country* (1977) ii. 22 I've now had a good opportunity to get to know Hill... We haven't got many tastes in common, but I like him. Doha is a very different pair of shoes.

2. b. *Cricket.* = *a pair of spectacles* s.v. SPECTACLE *sb.*¹ 7c in Dict. and Suppl.

1862 *Bell's Life in London* 29 June 7/5 Obtained that unenviable score, 'a pair'. **1960** *Times* 22 June 5/3 Willett and Gibson each completed a perfunctory 'pair'. **1974** *Daily Tel.* 12 June 34/1 Engineer, looking to save his pair, would have been run out first ball if Amiss's throw ..had hit the stumps. **1977** *Sunday Times* 27 Feb. 29/7, I wouldn't swop that 'pair' for anything. It taught me much of life and cricket.

3. a. *happy pair*: see *HAPPY *a.* 3.

4. a. *to be a pair*: of persons, to be two of a kind, to be as bad as one another. *colloq.*

1840 THACKERAY in *Fraser's Mag.* Jan. 107/2 'I' faith, I believe you're a pair,' said Mr. Wood. 'Pray, sir, keep your tongue to yourself..' cried Mrs. Catherine, with proper spirit. **1914** G. B. SHAW *Fanny's First Play* I. 178 Dora: We both get a bit giddy when we're lighthearted. Him and me is a pair, I'm afraid. **1931** N. ALLINGHAM *Police at Funeral* v. 69 She was a damned bad-tempered old harpy! And so was Andrew—they were a pair. **1967** J. ROSENBERG *Double Darkness* I. i. 46 It's only her own respectability she thinks of. Like you. You're a pair. **1976** 'D. FLETCHER' *Don't whistle 'Macbeth'* 86 It's a creepy feeling... Aren't we a pair? Come on. Let's go back and cheer ourselves up.

c. Also, such an agreement between opposite sides. (Earlier and later examples.)

1819 C. ARBUTHNOT *Let.* 14 Mar (1941) 16 It is expected of them all to be there during the whole course of every evening, & that the coming down merely to get a pair will not do. **1965** *New Statesman* 19 Mar. 426/2 One minister.. was flatly refused a pair by his Tory opposite number. **1976** *Southern Even. Echo* (Southampton) 18 Nov. 3/4 Sir Harold had to cancel a flight to Geneva at the last minute because, he claimed, the Tories changed their minds about providing him with a pair in the Commons division.

f. *Mech.* Two mechanical elements that together constitute a kinematic pair (see *KINEMATIC *a.* b).

1876 A. B. W. KENNEDY tr. *Reuleaux's Kinematics of Machinery* i. 43 The kinematic elements of a machine are not employed singly, but always in pairs; or in other words,..the machine cannot so well be said to consist of elements as of pairs of elements. *Ibid.*, If a kinematic pair of elements be given, a definite motion can be obtained by means of them if one of the two be held fast or fixed in position. *Ibid.* xiii. 549 If we put a normal or normally crossed pair in place of one of the parallel pairs we obtain a chain which is constrained, and which contains five cylinder pairs. **1905** SMITH & MARX *Machine Design* i. 13 The helical surfaces by which a nut and screw engage with each other are called a twisting pair. **1969** G. D. REDFORD et al. *Mech. Technol.* ii. 24 Two links which interact directly with, and mutually constrain, each other form a kinematic pair. *Ibid.*, Shafts in plain bearings, pin-jointed links, slide bars and slide blocks, screw and nut assemblies are all forms of lower pairs. **1975** MABIE & OCVIRK *Mechanisms & Dynamics of Machinery* (ed. 3) i. 9 A pair that permits only relative rotation is a revolute or turning pair, and one that allows only sliding is a sliding pair.

g. In basket-making (see quots. 1910 and 1912).

1897 A. FIRTH *Cane Basket Work* vi. 42 Take No. 3 [spoke]..bringing it down beside No. 1 and behind No. 4.., making one 'pair' of ends turned down. The canes forming these 'pairs' must each in turn be kept side by side..and held perfectly flat under the thumb till the next 'pair' is down. **1904** O. T. MASON *Indian Basketry* I. iii. 94 *Two-rod foundation.*—One rod in this style lies on top of the other; the stitches pass over two rods in progress and under the upper one of the pair below, so that each stitch incloses three stems in a vertical series... The alternate rod, or the upper rod, in each pair will be inclosed in two series of stitches. **1910** *Encycl. Brit.* III. 482/2 The 'pair', two rods worked alternately one over the other, used for filling up bottoms and covers of round and oval baskets. **1912** T. OKEY *Introd. Basket-Making* 153 *Pair*, two rods of willow or cane worked alternately over and under each other—the reverse of a fitch. **1953** [see *FITCH *sb.*³].

h. Ellipt. for *a pair of breasts.*

1922 JOYCE *Ulysses* 231 Hell's delights! She has a fine pair. **1973** M. AMIS *Rachel Papers* 174 'Who was that tart you had round here before?' 'Gloria?' 'Yeah. Tell you what, she's got a right pair on her.'

II. 6. (Further examples of 'a pair of beads'.)

1880 J. H. SHORTHOUSE *John Inglesant* xx. 267 You remind me of some of the rich oratories I have seen..; where everything is beautiful and costly, but where a classic statue of Apollo stands by the side of a crucifix, a Venus with Our Lady, a Cupid near St. Michael, and a pair of beads hanging on Mercury's Caduceus. **1930** *Amer. Speech* V. 427 A necklace is sometimes called a *pair o' beads* in the Ozarks. **1962** A. JOBSON *Window in Suffolk* vi. 102 She would refer to a necklace as a pair of beads. **1976** *Publ. Amer. Dial. Soc.* 1973 LX. 16 One informant called it [*sc.* a string of beads] *a pair of beads.*

b. (Further examples.)

1836 DICKENS *Let. c* 24 Aug. (1965) I. 170 His notion of the Bedroom is rather more derived,..from his own fourth pair back. **1922** JOYCE *Ulysses* 316 And who was he, tell us? A nobody, two pair back and passages, at seven shillings a week.

7*. In roulette (with pronunc. pę̄r), an even number, or a number marked 'pair'.

1850, etc. [see *NOIR 2 a]. **1902** [see *IMPAIR *sb.*²]. **1953, 1969** [see *MANQUE]. **1973** [see *IMPAIR *sb.*²].

III. 8. pair-bond, the relationship formed during the courtship and mating of a pair of animals or two people; so **pair-bonding** *vbl. sb.*, the formation of such a relationship or the patterns of behaviour that help to establish it; **pair-feed** *v. trans.*, to feed two groups of (experimental animals) with a diet identical except for the item whose effects are being tested on one group; so **pair-fed** *ppl. a.*; **pair-formation,** the pairing of animals, esp. birds, in preparation for breeding; **pair-light,** a window of two lights (LIGHT *sb.* 10); **pair-mate** *v. trans.*, to test the sexual compatibility of (experimental animals) by allowing mating within and between each of two groups; also, to control the mating of (experimental animals) so that each male mates with only one female, or vice versa; so **pair-mating** *vbl. sb.*; **pair production** *Nuclear Physics*, the conversion of a gamma-ray photon into an electron and a positron.

[**1939** G. K. NOBLE in *Auk* LVI. 265 If pairs of birds or fishes are to form a bond between themselves they must develop behavior different from the feeding or locomotion of non-breeding members of the group.] **1940** D. LACK in *Condor* XLII. 282 In some species of birds, the sexes.. form a very temporary pair-bond. **1954** *Behaviour* VI. 279 The intruder male [*sc.* a zebra finch] succeeded in breaking the old pair-bond, won the female over, built her a new nest, and began a fresh cycle with her. **1963** *Listener* 31 Jan. 204/1 The two [*sc.* gannets] perform an elaborate mutual display which is concerned with strengthening the pair bond. *Ibid.* 204/2 The length and intensity of this display is greatest when the pair bond is weakest, that is, when the couple are newly mated. **1969** *Times* 11 Apr. 12/6 The..tree sparrow, a species in which the pair bond is usually strong. **1970** J. KEAR in J. H. Crook *Social Behaviour in Birds & Mammals* 358 The pair bond and its stability is obviously of great consequence to parental behaviour. **1974** *Country Life* 7 Mar. 491/1 In few mammals is the pair bond so strong;..a [beaver] couple may remain paired for up to 18 years. **1977** D. MORRIS *Manwatching* 88 A sign of old friendships or pair-bonds is that two people can sit together in a peaceful silence without feeling the need to keep up a stream of cheerful chatter. **1965** *New Scientist* 17 June 768/1 Pair-bonding..is the ornithologist's in-phrase for procreative conjunction between sexually ardent cocks and hens. **1967** D. MORRIS *Naked Ape* ii. 62 The pair-bonding mechanism in our species [*sc. Homo sapiens*], although very powerful, is far from perfect. **1978** *Listener* 12 Jan. 35/2 The interplanetary visitor..would quickly conceptualise pair-bonding in what we call marriage. **1972** *Science* 19 May 795/1 Rat litter-mates were pair-fed nutritionally adequate liquid diets. *Ibid.*, The animals fed alcohol had 72 percent more hydroxyproline in hepatic protein than did pair-fed controls. **1974** *Nature* 4 Jan. 48/2 Hamsters were made vitamin A deficient by maintenance on a vitamin A deficient diet starting at day 10–14 after birth; controls were pair-fed with the same diet supplemented with vitamin A... Tracheas were removed from the vitamin A deficient and pair-fed control hamsters. **1940** D. LACK in *Condor* XLII. 269 There is probably more ignorance concerning pair-formation than there is of any other aspect of bird behavior. **1950** *Brit. Birds* XLIII. 392 Pair-formation [of marsh-tits] takes place at all times of the year. **1967** A. MANNING *Introd. Animal Behaviour* v. 105 In some birds the female becomes dominant after pair formation. **1970** J. KEAR in J. H. Crook *Social Behaviour in Birds & Mammals* 358 Pair-formation itself is influenced by plumage changes, display and maturity. **1971** J. Z. YOUNG *Introd. Study Man* xxxiv. 484 Apparently in baboons and even chimpanzees and gorillas there is no long-lasting pair formation. **1868** G. M. HOPKINS *Jrnls. & Papers* (1959) 183 It [*sc.* a tower] is pierced with pair-lights first, higher with a triplet. **1944** *Genetics* XXIX. 526 One hundred and six Azusa wild males [*sc.* fruit-flies] were pair-mated to standard grade 20 Wooster bobbed females. *Ibid.* 529 Two genes were tested by each pair-mating. **1968** R. RIEGER et al. *Gloss. Genetics & Cytogenetics* 327 *Pair mating*, a procedure used to determine the degree of sexual isolation between two groups (A and B) of individuals. Separate tests of mating success are made for the four possible mating combinations. **1934** *Physical Rev.* XLV. 137/1 For energies above twenty million volts the predicted pair production is even greater than that computed by Oppenheimer and Plesset. **1958** W. K. MANSFIELD *Elem. Nucl. Physics* v. 43 The three methods of interaction of γ-rays with matter are Compton scattering, photo-electric absorption and pair production. **1973** L. J. TASSIE *Physics Elem. Particles* ii. 9 Electron–positron pair production has a threshold of 1·022 MeV. Pair production cannot occur in free space, because the conversion of a photon into a pair cannot conserve both total energy and momentum... Some other particle must be present.

pair, *v.*¹ Add: **3. b.** Also *absol.*

1841 E. C. GREY *Little Wife* II. vii. 61 If you go on pairing and matching in this manner..you will be the terror of the whole of the male species.

c. In the British Parliament and other legislative bodies: to bring (an opponent) into an agreement to abstain from voting on a given question or for a certain time.

1956 ABRAHAM & HAWTREY *Parl. Dict.* 127 If a member wishes to be absent from the House, he may arrange with a member of the opposite party, who also wishes to be absent, that neither shall attend the House, or at least vote in a division, for an agreed time. They are then said to be 'paired'. **1968** W. SAFIRE *New Lang. Politics* 315/2 When supporters of John F. Kennedy explained that their candidate was seriously ill at the time of the McCarthy censure, liberal Democrats refused to accept the excuse because, they argued, 'the Senator could have been paired against McCarthy'. **1973** *Courier & Advertiser* (Dundee) 21 Feb. 11/3 Mr Teddy Taylor (Cathcart), who did not vote, as he was 'paired' with Mr Ronald King Murray (Leith), said, 'It is a victory for the people.' **1974** *Times* 18 Mar. 2/8 The Conservatives have said that they will only pair sick MPs with sick MPs, and there are no invalids on the Tory side.

4. a. (Earlier and further Parliamentary examples.) Also of other legislative bodies.

1772 *Debates & Proc. Brit. House of Commons 1768–1770* 240 At dinner time many made no scruple, though the cause was not determined, of *pairing off*, as it is called; some pair'd off for every question in the election, others for a day, or a few hours only. **1811** T. CREEVEY *Let.* 21 Jan. in *Creevey Papers* (1963) iv. 76, I am not to vote to-night... Villiers won't release me from contract of pairing off. **1866** *Harper's Mag.* May 805/2 This vote was given under peculiar circumstances. Mr. Morrill, of Maine, had sometime previously 'paired off' with Mr. Wright of New Jersey, [etc].. **1964** MRS. L. B. JOHNSON *White House Diary* 8 Apr. (1970) 102 Those committed as being safe for the bill..those who were absent and might 'pair' if you got to them and could find them an opposite number. **1965** *New Statesman* 19 Mar. 426/2 It is further alleged that one Conservative, at least, saw fit to pair with two Labour members.

c. (Earlier example.)

1803 G. COLMAN *John Bull* I. 9 Come, Mrs. Brulgruddery, let you and I pair off, my lambkin.

d. In basket-making: to work two rods alternately one over the other.

1901 A. FIRTH *Cane Basket Work* (ser. 2) iv. 45 Pair round once to divide into twos, still keeping the central side spokes undivided. *Ibid.*, Now turn the basket upside down and pair round once, taking two lots of double spokes together each time, and keeping the row of pairing even with the edge of the weaving.

e. *to pair up*, to form couples, esp. (of birds) to form pairs in preparation for mating; also, to match.

1908 A. W. MYERS *Compl. Lawn Tennis Player* 134

The prevalent custom..is for the members to 'pair up' irrespective of style and temperament. **1920** E. O'NEILL *Beyond Horizon* II. 37 Don't you think them two'd pair up well? **1937** *Brit. Birds* XXX. 267 As soon as a couple of birds have paired up, they proceed to exclude other Grebes from a certain area. **1951** L. MACNEICE tr. *Goethe's Faust* 170 One's bosom finds this paper light to nurse, It pairs up snugly with a billet doux. **1965** D. LACK *Life of Robin* (ed. 4) v. 66 The blackbird apparently pairs up in late autumn.

paired, *ppl. a.* Add: **b.** Special collocations, as **paired associates,** stimulus material presented in pairs to test the strength of associations set up between them at a subsequent presentation of one of the pair; also (freq. in form *paired-associate*) *attrib.*; hence *paired association*; **paired comparison,** a method of testing the discriminations made between different examples of the same type of stimulus by presenting them for comparison in pairs; also *attrib.*

1937 *Jrnl. Exper. Psychol.* XX. 60 (*heading*) The influence of the relative order of presentation of original and interpolated paired associates. **1949** B. J. UNDERWOOD *Exper. Psychol.* ix. 287 The number of pairs in a paired-associate list has varied, but from 8 to 15 have commonly been employed. **1971** *Jrnl. Gen. Psychol.* LXXXV. 212 Some are variants of such tasks as those for memory span..and paired-associates learning. **1963** D. T. CAMPBELL in S. Koch *Psychol.* VI. 120 The preexperimental learning of the pro-Communists might be epitomized as a paired association of 'Communist—good'. **1901** E. B. TITCHENER *Exper. Psychol.* I. I. vii. 154 Smells have enough variety, but are extremely and insistently associative. However, it would be well worth while to apply the method of paired comparisons to them. **1937** G. W. ALLPORT *Personality* (1938) i. 5 The method of paired-comparison recommends itself as an objective and qualitative technique for studying judgments of the affective value of colors. **1951** S. S. STEVENS *Handbk. Exper. Psychol.* i. 28/1 Certain criteria of internal consistency, as in the method of paired comparisons. **1970** *Jrnl. Gen. Psychol.* LXXXII. 19 With the use of a paired-comparisons procedure, each group consisting of five animals was exposed to all three pairs.

pair-horse, *a.* Add: (Earlier and later examples.) Hence **pair-horsed** *a.*

1842 *Ainsworth's Mag.* II. 429 The 'Bath pair-horse Invalid' now drew up..for the elderly gentleman. **1902** [see *DIFFERENTIAL *a.* 4 b]. **1905** *Daily Chron.* 22 May 6/3 The costly motor-cars of the humble workmen and the pair-horsed carriages of the lordly labourers. **1910** A. BENNETT *Clayhanger* I. iii. 19 A couple of pair-horsed trams. **1914** CONRAD *Chance* I. vii. 193 Just then the racket was distracting, a pair-horse trolley lightly loaded with loose rods of iron passing slowly very near us.

pairing, *vbl. sb.*[1] Add: (Further examples.) (For quots. 1915, 1969 cf. *PAIR *sb.*[1] 4 f.) Also with *off* and *up.*

1792 J. PEARSON *Political Dict.* 40 Pairing-off. Two Sneaking Scoundrels, not worth a piece of dog's meat to either party. **1897** A. FIRTH *Cane Basket Work* ii. 18 To begin by pairing, place each weaver singly behind two consecutive spokes. *Ibid.* vii. 60 This last inch may be all 'pairing'..if preferred, but if woven in the ordinary way, a row or two of pairing must form the edge. **1901** M. WHITE *How to make Baskets* i. 6 Pairing may be used either with an odd or even number of spokes. **1908** *Westm. Gaz.* 19 Nov. 14/3 The question of pairing-up arose, and the other [tennis] players naturally awaited the Prince's choice. **1909** E. STRASBURGER in A. C. Seward *Darwin & Mod. Sci.* vi. 109 Attention was drawn to the fact that during the reducing division of nuclei which contain chromosomes of unequal size, gemini are constantly produced by the pairing of chromosomes of the same size. This led to the conclusion that the pairing chromosomes are homologous, and that one comes from the father, the other from the mother. **1915** R. F. MCKAY *Theory of Machines* viii. 89 Line contact is undesirable..in lower pairing. **1926** J. S. HUXLEY *Ess. Pop. Sci.* 175 In herons and egrets..it is not the male who seeks out territory long before pairing-up, but pairing-up occurs on the communal feeding-grounds. **1939** *Auk* LVI. 265 No bond in the strict sense of the word, that is a pairing off, is formed. **1953** N. TINBERGEN *Herring Gull's World* xii. 105 Settling upon a territory will not occur until after pairing-up. **1955** A. W. BOOTHER *Basketry for Beginners* 13 Reverse pairing, used in conjunction with pairing, makes an attractive decoration for a basket... Reverse pairing is also used on cane bottoms and lids of baskets. **1958** B. HAMILTON *Too Much of Water* ix. 204 It was, indeed, a day of pairings-off. Annie Maxwell and Fred Upcher seemed to have settled for one another's company. **1964** H. HODGES *Artifacts* x. 146 Pairing was done with two rods woven simultaneously so that they crossed between the stakes to produce an effect similar to twined weave. **1965** D. LACK *Life of Robin* (ed. 4) v. 65 Tradition assigns St. Valentine's Day for the pairing up of wild birds. **1969** G. D. REDFORD et al. *Mech. Technol.* ii. 24 In higher pairing, contact is usually along a line or at a point, and the motion is that of, or equivalent to, rolling. **1970** AMBROSE & EASTY *Cell Biol.* x. 326 The result of this process, which is known as synapsis or zygotene pairing, is that there is now a haploid number of chromosome pairs, which are called bivalents. **1971** *Sci. Amer.* Sept. 89/3 Light absorbed by a molecule kicks one of the electrons associated with the molecule into an excited energy state, thereby making the electron available for pairing with an electron from a neighbouring atom or molecule in an electron-pair bond.

b. pairing-call, a call used by birds during the mating season; **pairing-time** (earlier and later examples); also *transf.*

1911 J. A. THOMSON *Biol. Seasons* II. 149 The long-drawn-out, modulated pairing-call of many of the waders ..is on the border-line. **1742** W. ELLIS *Mod. Husbandman* July xvi. 85 Every Pheasant..that can be proved to be in the Mannor at Pairing-time. **1850** *Punch* 10 Aug. 62/2 Parliamentary Almanack.—Latter end of July, 'pairing' time begins. **1867** O. W. HOLMES in *Atlantic Almanac 1868* 2/2 On the 14th of February the windows fill with pictures for the most part odious, and meant for some nondescript class of males and females, their allusions having reference to Saint Valentine's day, the legendary pairing-time of the birds.

pair-oar. Add: Hence **pair-oared** *a.*

1901 *Chambers's Jrnl.* Feb. 129/2 It comes by way of the river, a rotten, old, pair-oared skiff. **1938** C. S. FORESTER *Ship of Line* i. 7 Hornblower took his seat in a pair oared wherry.

pair-royal. c. (Further example.)

1840 DE QUINCEY in *Blackw. Mag.* XLVIII. 516/2 The year 333 before Christ. Here we have another '*prial*', a prial of threes, for the *locus* of Alexander.

pairwise (pēᵊ·ɹwəiz), *adv.* and *a.* [f. PAIR *sb.*[1] + -WISE.] In or by pairs; with regard to pairing; forming a pair.

1831 [in Dict. s.v. PAIR *sb.*[1] 8]. **1876** [see *KINEMATIC *a.* b]. **1956** *Nature* 21 Jan. 127/2 In the tetramer, pairwise engagement of all the CONH groups is again geometrically possible. **1960** H. M. HOENIGSWALD *Language Change* xiii. 144 Pair-wise reconstructions from three related languages may probe the question of degrees of relationship within the language family. **1965** *Math. in Biol. & Med.* (Med. Res. Council) III. 126 An observer or observers willing to assign a ranking order to the pair-wise resemblances among the objects. **1969** *Word 1967* XXIII. 302 The characters can be anything at all as long as they are pairwise distinguishable. **1971** POWELL & HIGMAN *Finite Simple Groups* viii. 260 $K_1, \ldots, K_c$ are pairwise disjoint, non-empty subsets of *G*. **1972** *Computers & Humanities* VI. 184 Used in roll-call analysis to count pair-wise voting agreement on isolated roll-call votes. **1975** *Language* LI. 378 Even if we allow pairwise (non-linear) extrinsic ordering, the problem is not solved.

paisa (pai·sä). Pl. **paise, -a, paisas.** Now the usu. form of PICE. Now decimalized and equal in value to one-hundredth of a rupee in India (since 1957: see *NAYA PAISA), Pakistan (since 1966), and Nepal, and to one hundredth of a taka in Bangladesh.

1884 [see *DAM *sb.*[5]]. **1924** *Regions Beyond* XLV. 44 Flowers are scattered upon the waters, coins are dropped into the depths, perhaps only a paisa (farthing), but the giver is poor and needy. **1956**, etc. [see *NAYA PAISA.] **1959** [see *ANNA]. **1963** *Times* 8 May 21/4 Last year the Pakistan Government made a reduction of 40 per cent—from 25 paise to 15 paise per lb.—in export duty. **1969** *Sunday Tel.* 12 Jan. 7/3 Hashish candy..is available for 50 Nepalese paise. This is about 3d. **1969** *Enact* (Delhi) Dec. 7/3 Oh! You are a munim all over, always counting paisas. **1971** *Femina* (Bombay) 16 Apr. 55/1 Your family won't even know you've been counting every paise [*sic*]. **1975** *Bangladesh Observer* (Dacca) 26 July 2/4 (Advt.), Cement... Taka 7.50 (seven and paisa fifty) only per ton. **1978** L. HEREN *Growing up on The Times* v. 166 The more affluent Indians..gave beggars paise, or fractions of farthings.

paisano. Add: **2.** In Spanish-speaking areas: a fellow-countryman; a peasant. Also *attrib.*

1844 G. W. KENDALL *Narr. Santa Fé Expedition* II. 230 [He] invariably called me his paisano, or country man. **1890** C. F. LUMMIS *Land of Poco Tiempo* iv. 88 Every one was out, but they were no longer the friendly *paisanos* we had known. **1935** J. STEINBECK *Tortilla Flat* 11 What is a paisano?.. His ancestors have lived in California for a hundred or two years. **1940** E. FERGUSSON *Our Southwest* xiv. 247 The Spanish clustered in towns. They fought Indians only when they had to, to assure safety and security. Security was what the *paisano* wanted. **1969** A. MARIN *Rise with Wind* x. 118 Carrasco was one of the few *paisanos*..who wore civilian clothes. **1971** *Publishers' Weekly* 18 Oct. 25/2 There are many cookbooks exploring the gourmet or *paisano* delights of foreign countries and places. **1977** H. FAST *Immigrants* 6 No use, paisano. Come back next week, the week after.

Paisley (pēi·zli). The name of a town in Renfrewshire, Scotland, used *attrib.* or *absol.* to designate a garment or material made there or having the curvilinear design characteristic of cloth made there, or the pattern itself.

1834 Paisley shawl [see SHAWL *sb.* 2 a]. *c* **1860** [see *NORWICH]. **1866** R. S. CHARNOCK *Verba Nominalia* 215 *Paisley*, a shawl made at Paisley, co. Renfrew (Scotland); celebrated also for its manufactures of silk and other shawls, muslin, cotton thread, and ornamental fancy goods. **1898** *Daily News* 5 Mar. 6/4 If black stuffs were chosen, it was only that they might be trimmed with paisleys. **1900** *Ibid.* 28 Apr. 6/6 Paisley velvet is a favourite facing for collars and revers. **1911** *Daily Colonist* (Victoria, B.C.) 23 Apr. 7/1 (Advt.), Paisley silks. **1950** D. GASCOYNE *Vagrant* 15 Spread with a soft paisley-patterned cloth. **1951** E. PAUL *Springtime in Paris* vi. 125 One of the coffee-coloured men in a flashy paisley robe and wearing gold-bowed pince-nez. **1954** F. SARGESON in C. K. Stead *N.Z. Short Stories* (1966) 5 He hoped to better himself at the fine Paisley work. **1959** H. HOBSON *Mission House Murder* ii. 11 My Paisley silk bow-tie. **1964** *McCall's Sewing* iv. 58/2 *Paisley*, any cotton, wool, or rayon which is printed with the traditional scroll design which originated in Paisley, Scotland. **1966** R. THOMAS *Spy in Vodka* (1967) vii. 60 He wore a dark-blue flannel sports shirt, a blue and yellow Paisley ascot, a pair of grey flannels that must have cost sixty bucks, and black loafers. **1967** [see *NORWICH]. **1975** G. LYALL *Judas Country* xxii. 163 He had his old brownish Paisley-pattern silk scarf folded as a choker. **1976** *Evening Advertiser* (Swindon) 31 Dec. (Advt.), Fur coats, capes and foxes. Victorian nighties, petticoats and camisoles, silk and Paisley shawls, beaded and sequined garments... Buyer calling regularly in the area. **1977** J. FLEMING *Every Inch a Lady* xiii. 63 A Paisley-patterned scarf in blue and red silk. **1977** J. WAMBAUGH *Black Marble* (1978) viii. 105 The long-legged asthmatic..was trying to look dog show respectable in a three-button herringbone coat, gray woolen slacks and a paisley tie.

Paisleyite (pēi·zli,əit), *a.* and *sb.* [f. the name of Ian *Paisley* (b. 1926), Ulster Presbyterian minister and politician + -ITE[1].] **A.** *adj.* Of or pertaining to Ian Paisley or his followers. **B.** *sb.* A supporter of Ian Paisley and his advocacy of Protestant interests in Northern Ireland and the independence of Northern Ireland from the Republic of Ireland. So **Pai·sleyism,** the religious and political principles of Paisleyites.

1966 *Guardian* 18 July 4/5 Paisleyism might have been expected to cause alarm and fierce anger in the [Irish] Republic. *Ibid.* 25 July 1/2 A Government order restricting a Paisleyite march. **1966** *New Statesman* 30 Sept. 468/3 The Cormac Square riots, when the Paisleyites marched on the General Assembly of the Irish Presbyterian Church. **1968** *Listener* 19 Dec. 823/2 Through the day, groups of Paisleyites infiltrated into the cordoned-off city. **1969** *Daily Tel.* 26 Feb. 16 Mr. Roy Bradford.. increased his majority in his Belfast constituency.. despite the intervention of a Paisleyite candidate. **1970** *Guardian* 18 Apr. 11/5 The likelihood is that the Paisleyite opposition will increase its numbers in Stormont. **1976** J. CARROLL *Madonna Red* (1977) iii. 98 He knew the bitter energy that faith could release against Paisleyites and Jews. **1978** D. MURPHY *Place Apart* vii. 148 However people may disagree in their analyses of Paisley the man, everybody recognises the danger of Paisleyism the cult.

Paiute (pəi·ūt), *sb.* and *a.* Also 9 **Pah-Utah, Pah-Utche, Pah-Ute, Pa-Utah Pie-Utaw;** 9– **Piute.** [ad. Sp. *Payuta*, or ad. native name (perhaps *payiutsi* fish people), influenced by *Utah* and *Ute.*] **A.** *sb.* **a.** A Shoshonean Indian people inhabiting parts of Utah, northern Arizona, and southeastern Nevada (more fully *Southern Paiute*); also, a culturally similar Shoshonean people of western Nevada and adjacent parts of California, Oregon, and Idaho (*Northern Paiute*); a member of either of these peoples.

The Southern Paiute and Northern Paiute are not subdivisions of a single people; their languages are distinct, and their territories are not contiguous.

1827 D. T. POTTS in D. M. Frost *Notes on Gen. Ashley* (1960) 63 This river [*sc.* the Sevier] is inhabited by a numerous tribe of miserable Indians... They call themselves Pie-Utaws, and I suppose are derived from the same stock [as the Utaws]. **1827** J. SMITH in H. D. Carew *Hist. Pasadena* (1930) I. 136 Passing down this river some distance, I fell in with a nation of Indians who call themselves Pah Utches. **1860** MAYNE REID *Odd People* 329 In the western & southern division of the Great Basin, the Digger exists under the name of *Paiute*, or more properly, Pah-Utah—so-called from his supposed relationship with the tribe of the Utahs. **1881** *Encycl. Brit.* XII. 825/2 In California and the south-western States, occupied by the morally debased and physically degraded Pah-Utes. **1910** F. W. HODGE *Handbk. Amer. Indians* II. 186/2 Paiute... In common usage it has been applied at one time or another to most of the Shoshonean tribes of W. Utah, N. Arizona, S. Idaho, [etc.] **1937** R. H. LOWIE *Hist. Ethnol. Theory* vi. 55 Had he begun his studies among the Eskimo or Paiute, his general views might have been different. **1947** B. HAILE *Prayer Stick Cutting* 43 Neckbands..should be of otter or beaver skin obtained from the..Paiutes. **1952** J. R. SWANTON *Indian Tribes N. Amer.* 375 With the Bannock, the Northern Paiute constituted one dialectic group of the Shoshonean Branch of the Uto-Aztecan stock. *Ibid.* 381 The Southern Paiute belonged to the Ute-Chemehuevi group of the Shoshonean branch of the Uto-Aztecan stock. **1959** E. TUNIS *Indians* 107/2 The southern Paiute, the Bannock, and the Gosiute were typical 'tribes', though they were not actually organized as tribes. **1973** A. H. WHITEFORD *N. Amer. Indian Arts* 39 One-rod coiling was done by the Pomo and Paiute. **1974** A. MACLEAN *Breakheart Pass* i. 12 They say the Paiutes kill every white man on sight. **1977** H. LANDAR in T. A. Sebeok *Native Lang. Americas* II. III. 327 The term Snake, applied to the Northern Paiute of Oregon, is used of other Shoshonean groups as well.

b. Either of the languages of the Paiute, technically distinguished as *Southern Paiute* and *Northern Paiute.*

1915 *Everybody's Mag.* Oct. 461/2, I talked Piute to him all afternoon and he didn't understand a word of it. **1921** E. SAPIR *Language* 67 Paiute, for instance, may compound noun with noun. **1933** L. BLOOMFIELD *Language* iv. 72 The Shoshonean family (in southern California and eastward, including Ute, Paiute, Shoshone, Comanche, and Hopi). **1949** E. A. NIDA *Morphol.* (ed. 2) iv. 103 Alternating unvoicing and reduction as in Southern Paiute. **1975** *Language* LI. 124 Consider an alternating stress rule, such as that of Southern Paiute, which stresses every alternate vowel from left to right across a word. **1977** H. LANDAR in T. A. Sebeok *Native Lang. Americas* II. III. 327 Northern Paiute... 2,000 [speakers] in Nevada, California, Oregon and Idaho.

B. *adj.* Of or pertaining to the Paiute or their languages.

1845 J. C. FRÉMONT *Rep. Exploring Expedition* 260 They rarely carried home horses, on account of the difficulty..of guarding them..from the Pa-utah Indians. **1869** 'MARK TWAIN' *Innoc. Abr.* xx. 205 Tahoe means grasshoppers. It means grasshopper soup. It is Indian,.. They say it is Pi-ute—possibly it is Digger. **1938** W. DYK *Left Handed's Son of Old Man Hat* 11 A Paiute girl came to our place. **1949** *Natural Hist.* June 268/1 Major Powell..named it Tapeats Creek after a Paiute Indian in his employ. **1955** W. GADDIS *Recognitions* II. ii. 388 The Piute Indians followed the sun to that hole where it crawled in at the end of the earth. **1975** *Language* LI. 797 The Southern Paiute suffix -*ŋü* is restricted to true passives.

paiwari: see PIWARRIE in Dict. and Suppl.

pajala (pā·dʒălă). [Malay.] A type of boat used around the Macassar Strait (see quot. 1950).

1937 G. E. P. COLLINS *Makassar Sailing* 12 When the first stage is completed the ship is a pajala, a low undecked boat of island design. **1950** *Jrnl. Malayan Branch R. Asiatic Soc.* XXIII. 113 The Pajala is a beamy, undecked coasting boat which is normally fitted with a tripod mast setting a single, large rectangular sail. **1964** K. G. TREGONNING *Hist. Mod. Malaya* 59 There had been Bugis traders in Malayan waters for centuries. In the sixteenth century Malacca knew well their *pájalas*, their large prahus with a distinctive tripod mast and a deep oblong sail.

Pajarete, var. *PAXARETE.

Pajitanian, var. *PATJITANIAN *a.*

Pak (pæk), colloq. abbrev. of *Pakistan*, *PAKISTANI *sb.* and *a.*

[**1935** C. RAHMAT ALI (*title*) Pakistan, the fatherland of the Pak nation.] **1954** G. S. RAO *Indian Words in Eng.* 134/1 *Pak*, contraction of Pakistan. **1965** P. ROBINSON *Pakistani Agent* v. 74 It was obvious the Paks were up to some new game. **1967** *Guardian* 24 Aug. 6/6 The official Pakistan news service reported yesterday that 'indecent miscreants' are smuggling Pak grain into India. **1969** *Indian Express* (Bombay) 28 July 11/3 (*heading*) Pak separatist parties merge. **1971** M. KELLY *25th Hour* iii. 214, I don't see all this secrecy and drama. Smuggling us out like a load of Paks. **1971** *Sun* (Ceylon) 17 Sept. 6/4 (*heading*) Pak refugees hit by floods. **1974** *New Society* 13 June 627/3 The chauvinists' scenario runs on about filthy foreigners and Pak shopkeepers (they *do* stay open later). **1975** *Bangladesh Times* (Dacca) 27 July 6/1 (*heading*) Pak flood death toll rises to 49. **1977** *Private Eye* 13 May 7/3 The foreign mission which serves booze in limitless quantities is the Russian Embassy in Islamabad, 200 miles away and many alcoholics are now signing up to join the Pak-Soviet Friendship Societies.

pakapoo, pakapu (pæ·kăpū, pækăpū·). Also **pak-a-peu, puka pu,** etc. [Chinese]. A Chinese gambling game resembling lottery with sheets of paper so marked as to be indecipherable except to an initiate. Phr. *like a pakapoo ticket*, untidy, disordered (*Austral.*).

1911 L. STONE *Jonah* ix. 92 He had come down early to mark a pak-ah-pu ticket at the Chinaman's in Hay Street. **1913** *Chambers's Jrnl.* Feb. 155/1 All kinds of games of chance—'two up', 'pak-a-pu' (the latter a form of lottery imported by the Chinese). **1923** *Daily Mail* 12 Feb. 7 Five Chinese pleaded guilty at Liverpool Assizes to charges of running a gaming house... For the defence it was argued that Pak-a-Peu (or Puck-a-pu) was a game of skill. **1927** *Daily Express* 21 Sept. 7/2 A Japanese ship's captain..appealed against a conviction..for employing two other Japanese to sell chances in an unlawful lottery known as 'Puka pu'. 'It is a favourite game with the Japanese and Chinese and others living in Limehouse,' explained Mr. Horace Fenton. **1932** H. SIMPSON *Boomerang* x. 275 Brought in evidence two flimsy pieces of printed paper, one a pakapu bet, the other a five-pound-note. **1936** 'R. HYDE' *Passport to Hell* i. 10 Chinese grocery-shops, masonic clubs, and pakapoo saloons. **1951** E. LAMBERT *Twenty Thousand Thieves* (1952) ix. 89 Henry opened Dooley's pay-book, the pages of which showed liberal sprinklings of the red ink with which fines and convictions were entered. 'What a pay-book!' he sighed. Dooley grinned. 'Like a pak-a-poo ticket,' he agreed. **1959** BAKER *Drum* 133 *Marked like a pakapoo ticket*, confusedly or incomprehensibly marked. **1960** *N.Z. Listener* 22 July 9/2 Some of the last of the old Chinese dwellings of the opium-smoking and pakapoo-playing generation are being pulled down in Haining Street in Wellington. **1961** PARTRIDGE *Dict. Slang* Suppl. 1212/1 *Look like a pakapu ticket*, to be completely indecipherable: Australian (esp. Sydney) coll.: since ca. 1940. 'Pakapu is a Chinese gambling game, not unlike housie. A pakapu ticket, when filled, is covered with strange markings'. **1964** A. WYKES *Gambling* 330 The only illegal gambling games in New South Wales are *fan-tan*, another Chinese game called *pak-a-p*, and *two-up*.

pakaru, var. *PUCKEROO.

pak-choi (paktʃoi·). [Cantonese, lit. 'white vegetable'; cf. *PE-TSAI.] A Chinese species of cabbage, *Brassica chinensis*. Also *attrib.*

1847 R. FORTUNE *Three Years' Wanderings N. Provinces China* xvi. 306 The celebrated 'Pak-tsae', or white cabbage of Shastung and Peking, is a very different plant. **1894** *Bull. Cornell Univ. Agric. Exper. Station* LXVII. 183 The Pak-Choi, commonly called Chinese cabbage and frequently confounded with the Pe-Tsai..is a vegetable which never forms a head. **1900** L. H. BAILEY *Cycl. Amer. Hort.* I. 178/1 Pak-Choi Cabbage... This plant is grown by the American Chinese, and is occasionally seen in other gardens. **1931** H. C. THOMPSON *Vegetable Crops* (ed. 2) xix. 291 The Pak-choi varieties resemble swiss chard in habit of growth. The leaves are long, dark green and oblong or oval. This type does not form a solid head. **1969** *Oxf. Bk. Food Plants* 154/1 Pak-Choi (*Brassica chinensis*)..is more closely related to rape and swede than to the European cabbages... The plant does not form a heart and in appearance it resembles chard or spinach beet... Pak-choi does best when sown in July or August, to produce an autumn crop. **1972** Y. LOVELOCK *Vegetable Bk.* 72 The other [Chinese cabbage], Baak-choy (B[rassica] chinensis), is also called Chinese mustard, and is noted for its lack of smell when cooking.

pakeha. Delete || and add earlier and further examples.

1817 J. L. NICHOLAS *Narr. Voyage to N.Z.* I. v. 139 Many of them had never before..beheld an European, and to see *packaka kiki* (the white man eat,) was a novelty. **1838** J. S. POLACK *New Zealand* II. iii. 102 He [*sc.* the chief] said I was a pákeha maori or native white man. **1859** [see *beach-comber*]. **1933** *Bulletin* (Sydney) 13 Sept. 8/4 The first pakehas were not at all ethical—rough whalers and adventurers. **1938** [see *HALF-PIE *a.*]. **1938** R. FINLAYSON *Brown Man's Burden* 1 Rua came from Taupo to the coastal district to work on the farm of a Pakeha. **1959** G. SLATTER *Gun in my Hand* xxii. 224 The Maori must smile at the pakeha going all Maori when he's overseas. People on the ship to England wearing tikis and saying good kai this morning. **1960** *Guardian* 23 Sept. 13/1 Race relations in New Zealand..had been based on the absolute equality of Maori and Pakeha (European). **1963** *Evening Post* (Wellington, N.Z.) 25 July, Co-existence between Maoris and Pakehas had seriously affected Maori culture. **1978** *Islands* (N.Z.) Aug. 20 The pakehas' faces floated like white disks in a sea of brown.

pakhal (păkā·l). [Hind.: see PUCKAULY.] A vessel for carrying or keeping water, *spec.* a water-skin of leather.

1885 G. C. WHITWORTH *Anglo-Indian Dict.* s.v. *bhisti*, A double bag called a pakhāl, which is carried by a buffalo or bullock. **1892** W. WICKHAM *Milit. Transport India* xv. 147 The leather packháls or water bags should.. be dubbed before use. **1920** *Blackw. Mag.* Oct. 464/1 A couple of mules laden with metal pakhals of water. **1925** [see *CHAGAL].

||**pakhawaj** (pa·kawādʒ). [Hind.] A double-headed drum used in Indian music, esp. that of the northern part of the country.

1867 E. M. TAYLOR in *Proc. R. Irish Acad.* IX. 116 Perhaps the *pukhwaj* is employed more than the other [*sc.* the tabla] by Hindu professionals. **1921** H. A. POPLEY *Mus. India* vii. 121 The *Pakhawāj* is a drum slightly larger than the mṛidaiṅga but similar in shape, which is used in the north of India. **1957** *New Oxf. Hist. Mus.* I. iv. 222 Prominent in our days are the *pakhawaj* and the *tabla*. The former..has a clay body of irregular cylindrical shape, tapering slightly towards the left hand, with a large surface of parchment. **1969** R. SHANKAR *My Music, My Life* i. 41/1 The *pakhawaj*, a one-piece drum made of clay with two faces or heads, tuned to different pitches. **1977** B. C. DEVA *Mus. Instruments* 39 The *pakhavaj* is the king of drums in Hindustani music, though now it is more a constitutional monarch, respected from a distance.

Pakhto: see PUSHTOO *sb.* and *a.* in Dict. and Suppl.

Pakhtun (păktū·n), *sb.* and *a.* Also **Pakhtoon, Pakhtun,** etc., and in form **Pashtun, Pushtun.** [Pashto.] **A.** *sb.* A member of a Pashto-speaking tribal people, also called *PATHAN, inhabiting parts of south-east Afghanistan and north-west Pakistan; this people collectively. **B.** *adj.* Of or pertaining to this people.

1815 M. ELPHINSTONE *Acct. Kingdom of Caubul* II. i. 151 Their own name for their nation is Pooshtoon; in the plural, Pooshtauneh. The Berdooraunees pronounce this word Pookhtauneh. **1867** H. W. BELLEW *Dict. Pukkhto* p. vii, To have given place to all the words of those languages used in an unchanged form by Pukkhtūn authors, would have added unnecessarily to the bulk of the work. **1880** —— *Races of Afghanistan* vi. 56 The term Pathán is not a native word at all. It is the Hindustani form of the native word Pukhtána, which is the plural of Pukhtún, or Pakhtún..as it is pronounced by the Afrídí. And Pukhtún is the proper patronymic of the people inhabiting the country called Pukhtún-khwá, and speaking the language called Pukhtú or Pukhto. **1885** G. C. WHITWORTH *Anglo-Indian Dict.* 245/2 *Paṭhán* (Hindustáni, from the Pashṭo *pakhṭána*, the plural of *pakhtun*, the name of a people inhabiting the country called by Herodotus Pactiya.) **1906** A. HAMILTON *Afghanistan* x. 263 After the Afghans the dominant people are the Pukhtun or Pathans, represented by a variety of tribes. **1908** *Encycl. Relig. & Ethics* I. 158/2 The Afghans themselves prefer the designation Pushtūn or Pukhtūn, older form Pashtūn, Pakhtūn (whence their Indian name Pathān). **1940** P. SYKES *Hist. Afghanistan* I. i. 13 The Afghan nomads organized on a tribal system, whose true national name is Pashtun or Pakhtun, generally termed 'Pathan' by Europeans, belong to the Turko-Iranian type. **1955** *Times* 11 May 9/6 Even before 1947 the Pathans (or Pakhtoons, as they are called in their own tongue) had been claiming the right to independence. **1956** *Ann. Reg. 1955* 116 The Afghan Prime Minister..stated that the proposed merger of West Pakistan would never be accepted or recognized either by the 'Pakhtun nation' or by his Government. **1963** *Times* 13 May 9/5 One consequence expected from Sardar Muhammad Daud Khan's resignation was an improvement of relations between Afghanistan and its neighbour Pakistan... Afghanistan is so publicly committed to the cause of the Pakhtuns, however, that no sudden relinquishment can be expected. **1971** *Illustr. Weekly India* 18 Apr. 21/2 West Pakistan in order to consolidate the Baluchis and the Pakhtoons in its north-west, may be forced into a diversionary adventure in Kashmir. **1973** *Times* 27 July 16/5 An attempt was made to raise the Pakhtun flag on the banks of the Indus. **1974** *Encycl. Brit. Micropædia* VII. 783/1 The Pashtuns believe themselves to have originated in Afghanistan and to be descended from a common ancestor.

Paki (pæ·ki). *slang.* Also **Pakki, Pakky.** [Abbrev. of *PAKISTANI *sb.* and *a.*] A Pakistani, *spec.* an immigrant from Pakistan. Also *attrib.* and in *comb.*, as *Paki-bashing*, wanton physical assault on or other violence directed against Pakistani immigrants (hence *Paki-bash, Paki-basher*).

1964 *Guardian* 15 Apr. 8/4 Some big Paki over the water's got her set up for right trouble. **1969** B. KNOX *Tallyman* v. 94 Ali's a Paki—an' you know how it goes. Paki's pretty well look all the same to me. **1970** *Observer* 5 Apr. 3/2 The name of the game is Pakky Bashing... Any Asian careless enough to be walking the streets at night is a fool. **1970** *Daily Progress* (Charlottesville, Va.) 15 Apr. 7-c/2 They attack Asian immigrants, and term this 'paki-bashing'. **1972** J. BROWN *Chancer* iii. 47 Sergeant Burton and me, we broke in the Paki lodging house. **1973** C. MULLARD *Black Brit.* II. iv. 40 'Hunting the Barney'..a practice that has much in common with present-day 'Paki-bashing'. **1973** M. AMIS *Rachel Papers* 142 Joe, a young and ambitious cook, was fed up to the teeth with cooking steak and chips for the odd Pakki. **1975** J. SYMONS *Three Pipe Problem* v. 36 He wanted to send the nig nogs and the Pakis back where they belong, in the jungle. **1976** *Times* 20 Jan. 12/7 Argument over the precise number of Paki-bashers who can dance on the arms of a swastika. **1977** F. BRANSTON *Up & Coming Man* xii. 126 He let the half [of a house] he owned to a load of Pakis to use as a temple. **1977** *Daily Tel.* 17 Jan. 3/1 'Paki-busting' is suddenly a topical phrase in Canada. **1977** *Time* 12 Dec. 19/3 Bands of front backers, swinging fists and banner staves, have sallied into peaceful demonstrations by Indians and Pakistanis in what are cruelly called 'Paki bashes'.

pakihi (pā·kihī). Also **pakahi, paki.** [Maori.] An area of open, swampy, land, esp. characteristic of north-western parts of the South Island of New Zealand; also, the type of waterlogged soil associated with such land. Also *attrib.*

1861 J. VON HAAST *Rep. Topogr. & Geol. Explor. Nelson Province* iv. 131, I shall now enumerate the different pakis, or open tracts of land, and give a short description of them. **1871** C. L. MONEY *Knocking about in N.Z.* v. 63 We suddenly came out of the bush on to an open pakihi some miles in length. **1896** *N.Z. Alpine Jrnl.* II. 148 The only patch of rata bush on the flat, the rest being partly open 'pakihi' and partly covered with low scrub and timber. **1919** L. J. WILD *Soils & Manures in N.Z.* v. 53 Pakihi Soils of Westland..occur over considerable tracts of sour, swampy, but easily drained terrace lands. **1930** J. DEVANNY *Bushman Burke* 14 The supplies..had been packed by horse along a track cut out of the bush, and further, up towards the Ridge, the pakahi. **1947** P. NEWTON *Wayleggo* (1949) x. 110 Little pakihis ran up into the bush every here and there. **1959** A. MCLINTOCK *Descr. Atlas N.Z.* p. xiv, The soils in the scrub-covered terraces are gley podzols (pakihi). **1959** G. SLATTER *Gun in my Hand* 76 Green swamp-water, a tangle of blackberry or pakahi beside the twisting railway line. **1970** *N.Z. Listener* 7 Dec. 6/3 The 33 million acres of sour and barren 'pakihi' soil [on the West Coast of N.Z.]. *Ibid.* 6/5 So what about all that pakihi? It is red-brown, depressing land whose drainage is blocked by an impervious iron pan. **1972** P. NEWTON *Sheep Thief* ix. 72 He set off up the creek in search of the horses. He found them grazing in a little pakihi. **1973** *Massey Ferguson Rev.* (N.Z.) Mar.–Apr. 3/1 Two farmers a few miles away from Bald Hill have successfully transformed 170 acres of pakihi by using much the same over-sowing methods as the department.

Pakistani (pākistā·ni, pæk-), *sb.* and *a.* [f. the name *Pakistan* + *-I.] **A.** *sb.* A native or inhabitant of Pakistan, an independent state formed in 1947 as a homeland for the Muslims of India from parts of Punjab, Sind, Baluchistan and North-West Province (East Pakistan, formerly East Bengal, achieved independence as Bangladesh in 1971). **B.** *adj.* Of or pertaining to Pakistan, its natives, or its inhabitants.

1941 L. S. AMERY *Let.* 25 Jan. in J. Glendevon *Viceroy at Bay* (1971) xvi. 198 Jinnah and his Pakistanis. **1948** *Sunday Times* 2 May 4/5 No Pakistani I have met is yet ready to admit that the achievement was not worth the sacrifice. **1950** *Times* 6 Mar. 5/7 The Pakistani Government soon set about filling the gap, taking care to ensure that the tribal areas and their peoples benefit from the development of West Pakistan as a whole. **1951** W. I. JENNINGS *Commonwealth in Asia* viii. 117 No Indian—or for that matter Pakistani or Ceylonese—politician wishes to sit at the same table as a representative of the Union of South Africa. **1957** *Times* 19 Dec. 15/2 The agreement signed by the World Bank and Pakistani officials yesterday completes the initial financing of the newly formed Pakistan Industrial Credit and Investment Corporation. **1965** *New Statesman* 30 Apr. 670/1 In neighbouring Sparkbrook, where faded vermilion posters..stare down upon shabbily dressed Pakistanis. **1967** *Listener* 17 Aug. 211/3 Radio comics with their unending imitations of Pakistani bus conductors must find other targets. **1971** *Peace News* 28 Oct. 5/2 We understood that the Pakistani army was burning the villages in the area, in retaliation for the previous day's attack. **1973** M. AMIS *Rachel Papers* 186 When I surfaced, dragged along in a tide of fat-legged girls and torpid Pakistanis, . . there . . was Rachel. **1976** 'W. TREVOR' *Children of Dynmouth* iii. 77 He'd seen the Dynmouth Hards beating up the Pakistani from the steam laundry in a bus-shelter.

Pakki, Pakky, varr. *PAKI.

pakora (păkōə·ră). Also **pakhora.** [a. Hind. *pakoṛā* a dish of vegetables in grain-flour.] A savoury Indian dish consisting of diced or chopped vegetables coated in batter and deep fried.

1954 J. MASTERS *Bhowani Junction* xxiii. 192 Our guests will be here in half an hour, and I have forgotten to make pakhoras. **1962** R. P. JHABVALA *Get Ready for Battle* iii. 135 She took a bite from a cheese pakora. **1963** *Guardian* 1 May 6/5 She can make fresh pakoras . . dainty morsels of cauliflower, green pepper, onion, or slivers of potato, coated in highly seasoned batter and deep-fried in oil. **1971** *Femina* (Bombay) 30 Apr. 63/1 Even then they get only cold pakoras or oily potato chips. **1972** R. P. JHABVALA *New Dominion* II. 138 The tea . . was very nice. They had pakoras and samusas and all sorts of other things. **1978** *Times of India* 18 Mar. 13/6 Delicious smells from the neighbouring *halvai's* shop. He is frying *samosas, pakoras, jalebis* and other mouth-watering delicacies.

‖ **pak pai** (pak pai). [Cantonese, lit. 'white licence'.] In Hong Kong, a car used illegally as a taxi.

1972 *South China Morning Post* (Hong Kong) 4 Dec. 10/6 *Pak Pai*, a car which plies for hire, illegally. **1977** *Ibid.* 13 Apr. 11/7 Triad gangs are involved in the operation of extortion rackets with mini-buses, pak pais and goods vehicles illegally used for passengers in rural areas. **1977** 'J. LE CARRÉ' *Hon. Schoolboy* xix. 464 Collecting gambling debts from the *pak-pai* drivers.

paku, var. PACU (in Dict. and Suppl.).

pal, *sb.*[1] Add to definition: Now *colloq.* Also applied to a woman. (Further examples.)

1807 BYRON *Let.* 30 June in *Works* (1898) I. 130 'Better late than never, Pal,' is a saying . . applicable on the present occasion. **1841** S. BAMFORD *Passages in Life of Radical* (ed. 2) I. xxiv. 151 The thieves and their 'pals', as he termed the repulsive females. **1886** *Lantern* (New Orleans) 27 Oct. 2/3 Reynold Bowers and his pal, Jack Lacoste. **1890** KIPLING in *Pioneer Mail* 28 May 698/2, I was great pals with a man called Hicksey. **1924** F. M. FORD *Some do Not* I. ii. 50 Eunice Vanderdecken is a bitterly misjudged woman. She's a real good pal. **1936** M. DE LA ROCHE *Whiteoak Harvest* v. 79, I have talked to her . . as I couldn't to anyone else. . . Well, she's been a complete pal—if you know what I mean. **1963** *Listener* 14 Feb. 279/1 The local battalion, the Bradford Pals, was butchered at the Somme. **1972** J. PORTER *Meddler & her Murder* x. 128 Be a pal and shove the marge across.

pal, *v.* Add: Also, *to pal around with, up with.*

1915 R. LARDNER in *McClure's Mag.* Aug. 21/3, I and Lefty and Mike used to pal round together. **1926** G. HUNTING *Vicarion* vi. 103 And I shan't have time to compromise *you* when I can pal around with Charlemagne, or Valentino, or Rameses Second, or Kublai Khan! **1943** I. WOLFERT *Tucker's People* viii. 167 All those poor people . . were just like the people he palled around with. **1958** B. HAMILTON *Too Much of Water* xi. 249, I got tight one night with a chap I'd palled up with. **1975** *High Times* Dec. 24/1 Lenny picked up part of his *schtick* from the characters that he palled around with in New York. **1976** *New Society* 20 May 409/1 Y'know, who to pal up with. **1977** *Time* 28 Mar. 37/1 It has been reported that he occasionally palled around with gangsters on golf courses or in gambling casinos.

pala[1] (pā·lă). *Ent.* Pl. **palæ.** [a. L. *pāla* spade.] (See quot. 1906.) Hence **pa·lar** *a.*, of or pertaining to a pala.

1892 E. SAUNDERS *Hemiptera Heteroptera Brit. Islands* 336 *C[orixa] Fallenii*. . . The palæ of the male are truncate at the base. **1906** J. B. SMITH *Explanation Terms Entomol.* 95 Pala: the shovel-shaped tarsal joints in many aquatic *Heteroptera*. **1957** RICHARDS & DAVIES *Imms's Gen. Textbk. Entomol.* (ed. 9) III. 428 The pala is not a stridulatory organ, nor has it been shown conclusively that the peculiar strigil of these insects [*sc.* Corixidæ] is concerned with sound production. **1959** SOUTHWOOD & LESTON *Land & Water Bugs Brit. Isles* 387 Palar pegs numerous, extending in a row along most of the pala. *Ibid.* 388 Male palae more or less rounded on the top edge.

pala[2]: see PALLAH.

palace, *sb.*[1] Add: **1. e.** By metonymy, the monarch or monarchy.

1962 A. SAMPSON *Anat. Brit.* I. iii. 49 For much of this, it is unfair to blame the palace. Many of the pretensions spring from deeper causes than the monarchy. **1973** *Times* 14 Apr. (Nepal Suppl.) p. i/5 The primacy of the palace in the decision-making process was the principal feature of the constitution that King Mahendra introduced in 1962. **1974** *Listener* 14 Mar. 327/3, I thought the election was going to be a very close thing . . actually, the Conservatives have more votes than the Labour Party. But I think the choice made by the Palace was inevitable. **1974** *Times* 6 May 14/7 The Palace . . believed it did not *have* to accede to Mr Wilson's request.

4. (Later examples.) Also, *palace of varieties*, a variety theatre.

1899 BEERBOHM *More* 125 Oh, for the wasted glories of the old Oxford! Oh, for one hour in the Hoxton Palace of Varieties! **1902** O. WISTER *Virginian* xiii. 148, I came upon him one morning in Colonel Cyrus Jones's eating palace. **1933** P. GODFREY *Back-Stage* xiv. 179 Sir Oswald Stoll, by transforming the music-hall into the palace of varieties, achieved the same sort of result that Sir Joseph Lyons reached by converting tea-shops into Corner Houses. **1966** *Economist* 10 Dec. 1144/2 The plush restaurants . . have been supplanted by the palaces *à go-go*. **1973** A. MACVICAR *Painted Doll Affair* ii. 32 A toilet palace dominates the head of Inveraray pier. **1976** J. M. BROWNJOHN tr. *Kirst's Time for Payment* 28 There was a big medium-priced restaurant, a porn palace, a hair stylist.

6. b. *palace-bordered* adj.; **c. palace-car** (earlier and later U.S. examples); **palace coup** = **palace revolution*; **palace guard,** (*a*) one who guards a palace; (*b*) one who helps to protect a monarch, president, etc.; **palace-hotel** (earlier U.S. and later examples); **palace revolution** [cf. G. *palastrevolution*], the overthrowal of a sovereign, etc., without civil war, usu. by other members of the ruling group; also *fig.*; **palace style** *Archæol.*, a type of pottery associated with the Minoan palaces, or an imitation of this type.

1893 'MARK TWAIN' in *Century Mag.* Dec. 234/1 Along the palace-bordered canals of Venice. **1900** J. K. JEROME *Three Men on Bummel* viii. 174 Through Prague's dirty, palace-bordered alleys must have pressed often in hot haste blind Ziska and open-minded Wallenstein. **1868** *Dispatch & Vanguard* (San Francisco) 28 Mar. 1/1, I enjoyed the equivocal luxury of traveling in a 'palace' or 'sleeping car'. **1967** C. O. SKINNER *Madame Sarah* viii. 163 They travelled via . . three Pullmans . . and her own private car, known as a 'Palace Car'. **1970** *Guardian* 13 Jan. 1/2 Some kind of palace coup occurred in Biafra on Friday. . . The Biafran doves 'invited' their leader to step down. **1970** *Daily Tel.* 16 Feb. 16 This adds another possibility to those of a bid by Reed or a rival—a palace coup which would allow new management to be called in to put through an internal re-organisation. **1887** Palace-guard [in Dict.]. **1948** J. A. FARLEY *Jim Farley's Story* xxii. 232 Nathan Straus brought me word that the White House 'palace guard' realized the anti-Catholic campaign against me had failed. **1973** *Times* 11 May 1/1 This seemed his [*sc.* President Nixon's] most direct admission to date that he had allowed himself to be kept too isolated for too long by his departed 'palace guard'. **1870** J. D. SHERWOOD *Comic Hist. U.S.* 422 By the side of palace hotels, now gleaming along golden bays. **1884** *Century Mag.* Mar. 643/1 It [*sc.* Washington, D.C.] has no elevated railroads, no palace hotels, no mammoth elevators. **1934** G. B. SHAW *Too True to be Good* 11 Come to our palace hotels. **1969** *Sat. Rev.* (U.S.) 4 Jan. 64/2 Whether the world of the Superjet will allow the survival of the palace hotels is a question facing grand tours and grand tourists. **1904** Palace revolution [listed in Dict., sense 6 a]. **1907** J. LONDON *Iron Heel* xiv. 188 They will be like the guards of the palace in old Rome, and there will be palace revolutions whereby the labour castes will seize the reins of power. **1932** M. EASTMAN tr. *Trotsky's Hist. Russ. Revolution* I. 83 (*heading*) The Idea of a Palace Revolution. **1935** H. A. L. FISHER *Hist. Europe* I. xii. 143 The [Byzantine] state was shaken by palace revolutions and civil war. **1949** *Mind* LVIII. 500 The ensuing changes must be classed with the 'palace revolutions' of other histories, since they scarcely affected the structure of the state. **1958** *Times* 1 Mar. 7/6 The palace revolution in ski racing technique. **1972** H. KEMELMAN *Monday the Rabbi took Off* xix. 123 The Persian King feared a palace revolution by Haman and plotted with Esther to bring about his ruin. **1902** A. J. EVANS in *Ann. Brit. Sch. Athens 1900–1901* 51 (*heading*) Mycenaean painted pottery of the 'Palace Style'. *Ibid.*, The view that this in fact represents the indigenous 'Palace Style' of Knossos in its highest development is confirmed by the evident parallelism which its motives present to the decorative wall paintings of the building. **1913** R. A. S. MACALISTER *Philistines* i. 18 In Palestine and elsewhere occasional scraps of the 'palace' styles come to light. **1939** J. D. S. PENDLEBURY *Archæol. Crete* iv. 180 L.M. II, in fact, was, like M.M. II, a true Palace style, though even more restricted in being confined to Knossos alone. **1974** *Encycl. Brit. Macropædia* XIX. 275/2 Between 1450 and 1375 BC, Mycenaean taste reduced the spontaneity of the early Marine style to a rigid formality, thereby creating the monumental Palace style.

‖ **palacio** (păla·þyo, pălæ·sĭo). [Sp., palace.] A palace, or a country seat, or an official building (in Spain or the Spanish-speaking territories in the Americas); also, the name of a specific building, as the former residence of the Spanish and Mexican governors in Santa Fe, New Mexico, or the former hunting-lodge of the Spanish kings in the Coto Doñana, Sevilla.

1844 J. GREGG *Commerce Prairies* I. 203 These bricks are called *adobes*, and every edifice, from the church to the *palacio*, is constructed of the same stuff. **1885** *Weekly New Mexican Rev.* 18 June 4/1 There he erected a palacio. **1893** CHAPMAN & BUCK *Wild Spain* xxxii. 350 The head of our cavalcade sighted the welcome light displayed from the turrets of the ancient shooting lodge of Doñana. Though now in a state of partial ruin, the old Palacio still shows signs of former grandeur, and has been . . a favourite sporting retreat for more than one Spanish king. **1963** *Times* 27 Feb. 11/6 It was frequently visited for hunting parties by the Kings of Spain for whom was created the palacio or hunting-lodge which is still the only substantial habitation many miles from the nearest road. **1968** R. F. ADAMS *Western Words* (rev. ed.) 218/2 *Palacio*, what the early freighters called the Palace of Governors in Santa Fe. **1969** A. MARIN *Rise with Wind* xiv. 170 A four-story white-stucco *palacio*. **1975** N. LUARD *Robespierre Serial* xiii. 113 The *palacio* had been . . used by the Spanish Kings who'd come to the Coto to shoot. **1977** P. SOMERVILLE-LARGE *Eagles near Carcase* vii. 132, I worked at the *palacio* before I was married.

palæanthro·pic, *a.* Also **palæoanthropic** and with the prefix written **pale-.** [f. PALÆO-, PALEO- + ANTHROPIC *a.*] Of, pertaining to, or designating extinct prehistoric forms of man.

Quot. 1916 may represent an independent coinage.

1890 *Cent. Dict.* V, Paleo-anthropic. **1916** G. E. SMITH in *Amer. Museum Jrnl.* XVI. 325/2 If we refer to the epoch of the modern type of man as the Neoanthropic age, . . the Mousterian period and all of man's record that went before it can then be included in a Palæanthropic age. **1935** HUXLEY & HADDON *We Europeans* ii. 52 Modern types (Neanthropic) of man appear in Europe as the last ice-sheet began to retreat and the earlier types (Palæanthropic) seem to have disappeared. **1954** *Sci. Amer.* Sept. 52/3 Paleoanthropic man is clearly a tool user, a worker in stone and bone. **1962** C. S. COON *Origin of Races* viii. 334 How many grades . . shall we recognize in fossil and living men? . . A compromise nomenclature is Protoanthropic, Paleanthropic, and Neanthropic. **1973** B. J. WILLIAMS *Evolution & Human Origins* xi. 175/2 The paleanthropic line has included the finds of: Neandertal, Heidelberg, Peking, Java, Solo, Broken Hill (Rhodesia).

Palæarctic, *a.* Add: Also **Palearctic** and with lower-case initial. (Further examples.) Also *absol.*

The (incorrect) 1857 reference in Dict. is given below in corrected form as quot. 1858.

1858 P. L. SCLATER in *Jrnl. Linn. Soc.* (*Zool.*) II. 135, I think we may consider Africa, north of the Atlas, Europe and Northern Asia, to form one primary division of the earth's surface, for which the name Palæarctic or Northern Palæogean Region would be best applicable. **1951** *Antiquity* XXV. 69 If Odysseus began as a bear, as Rhys Carpenter asks us to believe, it is well to know how palæarctic that makes him. **1957** P. J. DARLINGTON *Zoogeogr.* vii. 438 The Palearctic is north-temperate with an arctic fringe. **1974** *Environmental Conservation* I. 7/2 Huge numbers of palaearctic birds overwinter in the savanna zones south of the Sahara.

Palæasiatic, var. *PALÆO-ASIATIC *sb.* and *a.*

palæencephalon (pæ:-, pī̆:liˌense·fălǫn). *Anat.* Also (chiefly *U.S.*) **paleencephalon.** [a. G. *palaeencephalon* (L. Edinger *Vorlesungen über den Bau der nervösen Zentralorgane des Menschen und der Tiere* (ed. 7, 1908) II. xvi. 241): see *PALÆO-, PALEO- b and ENCEPHALON.] The phylogenetically older portion of the brain, as contrasted with the neencephalon.

1917 *Jrnl. Compar. Neurol.* XXVIII. 216 It is becoming increasingly evident that the key to this difficult question is to be sought in the subcortical centers of the primitive types, that is, in the 'old brain' (palaeencephalon of Edinger, segmental apparatus of Adolf Meyer). **1972** [see *NEENCEPHALON].

palæo-, paleo-. Add: **palæoanthropic,** delete entry and see *PALÆANTHROPIC *a.*; **palæobathy·metry** *Geol.*, the bathymetric features of an area as they were at some period in the past; so **pa:læobathyme·tric** *a.*; **palæobio·logy,** the biology of fossil plants and animals; hence **pa:læobiolo·gic, -ical** *adjs.*, **palæobio·logist; palæoceanography,** etc., varr. *palæo-oceanography*, etc., below; **Palæocene,** delete entry and see *PALÆOCENE *a.*; **palæochem·istry,** (the study of) the chemical features of something as they were in the geological past; hence **palæoche·mical** *a.*; **pa·læo-current** *Geol.*, a current, usu. of water, which existed at some period in the past, as inferred from the features of sedimentary rocks; **pa:læoenvi·ronment,** an environment at a period in the past; hence **pa:læoenvironme·ntal** *a.*; **pa·læo-equator** *Geol.*, the equator as it was at some period in the past; hence **pa:læo-equato·rial** *a.*; **pa·læofield** *Geol.*, (the strength of) the earth's magnetic field at a period in the geological past; **palæogeo·graphy** *Geol.*, (the study of) geographical features at periods in the geological past; hence **palæogeo·grapher; pa:læogeogra·phic, -ical** *adjs.*; **pa:læogeogra·phically** *adv.*; **palæogeo·logy,** (the study or reconstruction of) the geological features of an area in past ages; hence **pa:læogeolo·gic, -ical** *adjs.*, **palæogeo·logist; pa:læogeomagne·tic** *a. Geol.*, of or pertaining to the magnetic field of the earth in the geological past; **pa:læogeophy·sics** *sb. pl.*, the study of the physical characteristics of the earth in past ages; hence **pa:læogeophy·sical** *a.*; **palæoge·otherm** *Geol.* [*geotherm* f. GEO- + *-therm*, after ISOTHERM, etc.], a pattern of temperature variation which existed in the earth's crust at some time in the past; so **pa:læogeothe·rmal** *a.*; **pa·læogra:vity** *Geol.*, the strength of the earth's gravity at some time in the past; **palæohydro·graphy** *Geol.*, (the study of) hydrographic features at periods in the geological past; **pa·læointe:nsity** *Geol.*, the intensity of a palæomagnetic field; **palæola·titude** *Geol.*, the latitude of a place at some period in the past; hence **pa:læolati-tu·dinal** *a.*; **palæolimno·logy,** (the study of) the conditions and processes occurring in lakes in the geological past; hence **pa:læolimnolo·gical** *a.*, **palæolimno·logist**; **pa:læolitholo·gic** *a. Geol.*, applied to a map showing the lithological features of an area at some period in the past; **palæolo·ngitude** *Geol.*, the longitude of a place at some period in the past; **palæo-meri·dian** *Geol.*, the meridian of a place at some period in the past; **pa:læometeoro·logy,** the study of atmospheric conditions at periods in the geological past; so **pa:læo-meteorolo·gical** *a.*, **-meteoro·logist**; **pa:læo-oceano·graphy** (also **palæoceanography**), (the study of) the conditions and processes occurring in oceans in the geological past; hence **pa:læ(o-)oceano·grapher**; **pa:læ(o-)oceano-gra·phic, -ical** *adjs.*; **palæopedo·logy** *Geol.*, (the study of) the features of soils in the geological past; hence **pa:læopedolo·gical** *a.*, **palæopedo·logist**; **pa:læophysio·graphy** *Geol.*, (the study of) the physical and topographical features of the earth's surface in the geological past; hence **pa:læophysiogra·phic, -gra·phical** *adjs.*; **pa:læophysio·grapher**; **pa·læoplain** *Geomorphol.*, a peneplain which existed at some period in the past and became overlain by other strata, being now buried or re-exposed; **pa·læopole** *Geol.*, a magnetic pole of the earth at a period in the past; **palæopsy·chic** *a. rare*, pertaining to the assumed (prehistoric) origins of behaviour patterns; so (also *rare*) **pa:læopsycho·logy, -ist**; **pa·læoradius** *Geol.*, the radius of the earth or another planet at some time in the past; **palæosali·nity** *Geol.*, the salinity of the environment in which a sedimentary deposit was laid down; **pa·læo-slope** *Geol.*, the former or original slope of a region, or its direction; **pa·læosol [*-SOL]**, a soil horizon which was formed as a soil in the geological past; hence **palæoso·lic** *a.*; **pa·læo-species** *Palæont.*, a species including a group of fossils from different geological formations that make up a chronological series; **pa·læo-structure** *Geol.*, the geological structure of an area at some period in the past; hence **palæo-stru·ctural** *a.*; **palæotechnic** *a.* (examples); *spec.* (see quot. 1960); **palæotecto·nic** *Geol.*, of or pertaining to tectonic features or events of previous stages in the earth's history; **pa·læotemperature,** the average climatic temperature at a particular place and time in the past; **palæothermo·metry,** the investigation of the temperature of climates and oceans in past ages; **palæotopo·graphy** *Geol.*, the topography of ancient landscapes, esp. as represented today by features that are buried or newly exhumed (cf. *PALÆOGEOMORPHOLOGY); hence **pa:læotopogra·phic, -gra·phical** *adjs.*, **pa:læotopogra·phically** *adv.*; **pa·læo-wind** *Geol.*, a prevailing wind that existed at some period in the past; freq. *attrib.*; **pa:læo-zo:ogeo·graphy,** the study of the distribution of fossil animal remains; hence **pa:læozo:o-geogra·phic** *a.*

1945 *Bull. Amer. Assoc. Petroleum Geologists* XXIX. 428 Maps of fossil distribution, with evaluation of the habitat of the organisms, add evidence. Thus from the lithology and fauna, it is possible to construct paleobathymetric maps. **1964** H. W. MENARD *Marine Geol. Pacific* vi. 138/1 Since most of the islands existed at about the same time.., a consistent paleobathymetric map can be drawn. **1959** *Jrnl. Paleont.* XXXIII. 944/2 Critical comparative study is also called for of the characteristics of sedimentary rocks in areas where there is possibility of reconstructing a reasonably objective paleobathymetry, as in the..Ventura Basin of California or other areas where the endemic fossils indicate a wide range of depth. **1971** *Nature* 2 Apr. 319/1 The magnitude of the cretaceous–Tertiary hiatus in the deep sea is therefore a function of palaeobathymetry with deeper water sections exhibiting a greater unconformity. **1948** *Bull. Geol. Soc. Amer.* LIX. 1337 (*heading*) Paleobiologic implications of the measurement of paleotemperatures. **1961** WEBSTER, Paleobiological. **1963** D. W. & E. E. HUMPHRIES tr. *Termier's Erosion & Sedimentation* ix. 192 Two palaeobiological aspects of this subject should be noted. **1974** *Nature* 15 Feb. 496/1 He [*sc.* D. M. S. Watson] joined Abel as one of the pioneers of palaeobiological thought. **1900** *Biol. Lect. Marine Biol. Lab. Woods Holl 1899* ix. 132 The method thus elaborated has been and is now in constant use by a number of paleobiologists. **1975** *Nature* 1 May 16/1 Because they have become excited by new biological concepts and wish to apply them to fossils, a number of young researchers would now prefer to call themselves palaeobiologists. **1893** S. S. BUCKMAN in *Q. Jrnl. Geol. Soc.* XLIX. 482 The term 'hemera' will therefore enable us to record our facts correctly; and its chief use will be in what I may call 'palæo-biology'. **1943** *Mind* LII. 127 One can hardly think of a scientific fact better and more impressively documented than the phylogenetic hierarchy, established as it is by the threefold evidence of embryology, comparative anatomy, and paleobiology. **1948** *Jrnl. Paleont.* XXII. 265/1 Paleobiology is..mainly biological in objectives, but many of its techniques are unknown to biology. **1973** P. TASCH (*title*) Paleobiology of the invertebrates: data retrieval from the fossil record. **1854** *Edin. New Philos. Jrnl.* LVI. 9 The palæophysics are hardly studied, and even less the palæochemistry. **1904** *Trans. Canad. Inst.* VII. 535 (*heading*) The palæochemistry of the ocean in relation to animal and vegetable protoplasm. **1926** *Physiol. Rev.* VI. 316 (*heading*) The paleochemistry of the body fluids and tissues. *Ibid.* 331 The high concentration of the salts, 2·852 per cent, in the serum of the lobster would appear to indicate that it is of neochemical rather than of paleochemical origin. **1942** *Proc. R. Irish Acad.* XLVIII. B. 119 An enquiry into oceanic palæochemistry and its bearing on the electrolytes of blood and cells. **1955** *Bull. Geol. Soc. Amer.* LXVI. 1606 (*heading*) Paleocurrents of Lake Superior Precambrian quartzites. **1971** *Nature* 28 May 245/2 A W.N.W. to N. palaeocurrent component predominates in the channel sandstones with pedogenic modification.. occurring on most proximal floodplain deposits. **1957** R. J. BRAIDWOOD in *Publ. National Research Council* (U.S.) No. 565. 16/2 This field or axis of interrelated disciplines (perhaps 'Pleistocene ecology' or 'paleo-environment' or 'Quaternary geography'—I shall not attempt to name it!) would definitely include Man as an element in, and a factor acting upon, the environmental scene. **1970** *Nature* 29 Aug. 944/2 The palaeoenvironment of the Neolithic occupation site. **1975** *Ibid.* 20 Mar. 187/2 Reconstructions of palaeoenvironments often rely heavily on fossils, and thus engender circular arguments about the habitats occupied by different elements in the fauna. **1961** *Micropaleontology* VII. 366/1 Preliminary results of analyses of these data, in terms of biotic diversity, show interesting parallels with independent evidence concerning paleoenvironmental changes and floral evolution. **1974** *Nature* 29 Mar. p. iv/3 (Advt.), An accompanying text describes each feature and discusses its..preservation and occurrence in sedimentary rocks, and significance for palaeoenvironmental reconstructions. **1976** *Ibid.* 20 May 223/1 These palaeoenvironmental similarities may be sufficient to explain the near identity of the two assemblages of microfossils. **1960** *Quaternary Res.* (Tokyo) May 212 (*heading*) The palaeoequator and its relation to the recent distributional area of *Coriaria*. **1962** *Nature* 3 Nov. 427/2 The estimates of palæolatitudes are generally low, ranging from 59° S.–44° N., with 76 per cent of the values lying within 20° of the palæoequator. **1973** *Sci. Amer.* Nov. 111/1 An eastward extrapolation of paleo-equator positions determined from deep-sea drilling, together with a westward extrapolation of crustal age.., enables us to estimate the location and age of a series of points where the East Pacific Ridge and earlier 'paleo-equators' once intersected. **1966** *Nature* 15 Oct. 247 (*heading*) Summary of estimates of palaeoequatorial [magnetic] intensity from igneous rocks in the temperature range 670° C to 500° C. **1968** *New Scientist* 4 Apr. 16/1 Since the newly acquired moment is proportional to the known field, and the natural moment of the virgin rock is proportional to the ancient field, a simple equation allows the 'palaeofield' to be calculated. **1975** *Nature* 27 Feb. 685/2 The obvious ways of obtaining a palaeofield from a rock containing thermoremanent magnetisation require that the rock be heated above its Curie point. **1911** *Bull. Geol. Soc. Amer.* XXII. 262 These results are of the greatest value to the paleogeographer. **1972** *Science* 12 May 665/2 A scholar who, as a paleogeographer, is not narrowly specialized in archeology or geology. **1906** *Bull. Geol. Soc. Amer.* XVII. 248 (*heading*) Paleogeographic charts. **1971** *Nature* 16 July 180/2 The evidence..was taken from two series of palaeogeographic maps showing the distribution of land and sea since the early Cambrian. **1882** E. HULL *Contrib. Physical Hist. Brit. Isles* I. iii. 19 In endeavouring to prepare a series of maps representing the palæo-geographical features of some region,..the requisite number of such maps and their proper order of succession..necessarily corresponds to those of the successive geological formations. *Ibid.* II. i. 55 (*heading*) Palæo-geographical and geological maps of the British Isles. **1956** L. J. WILLS *Concealed Coalfields* 6 The palaeogeographical treatment is capable of throwing new light on the problem of where the workable coals may originally have been deposited. **1965** B. E. FREEMAN tr. *Vandel's Biospeleol.* xvi. 274 A map of the distribution of the cavernicolous sphaeromids can easily be superimposed on the paleogeographical reconstruction of the Miocene epoch. **1934** *Bull. Amer. Assoc. Petroleum Geologists* XVIII. 784 (*heading*) Future research in paleogeographically favorable zones. **1969** BENNISON & WRIGHT *Geol. Hist. Brit. Isles* xi. 265 Permian outcrops in Ireland, though not extensive, are palaeogeographically important. **1881** R. ETHERIDGE in *Q. Jrnl. Geol. Soc.* XXXVII. 228 Could we strip off all the Secondary and Tertiary rocks, and reveal or expose the extension of the older or Palæozoic series towards Germany on the east, and France on the south, then the vexed question of the old physical geology and geography (palæogeography) of Britain and the relation and correlation of our area with that of Europe would be revealed. **1946** *Nature* 20 July 89/2 Grabau's widely ranging interests in stratigraphy, palæogeography, palæontology and sedimentation..were synthesized into a whole in his 'Principles of Stratigraphy' (1913). **1969** BENNISON & WRIGHT *Geol. Hist. Brit. Isles* i. 3 Changes in the distribution of land and sea, of the physiography of the land, and of climate have taken place and their study is called palaeogeography. **1971** I. G. GASS et al. *Understanding Earth* xx. 292/1 The direction of these currents can be established by studying the sedimentary structures the rocks contain; and this may assist in the determination of the palaeogeography of the times when sedimentation occurred. **1933** *Bull. Amer. Assoc. Petroleum Geologists* XVII. 1113 (*caption*) Paleogeologic map of United States at beginning of Lower Cretaceous or Comanche time, representing areal geology of surface upon which Cretaceous sediments were deposited. **1966** *McGraw-Hill Encycl. Sci. & Technol.* IX. 519/1 Paleogeologic maps, showing the pattern of rocks on the surface at a past time, aid in the interpretation of landforms. **1882** *Sci. Trans. R. Dublin Soc.* I. 257 (*heading*) Palæo-geological and geographical maps of the British Islands and the adjoining parts of the continent of Europe. **1940** *Geogr. Jrnl.* XCV. 208 The island re-emerged during the Tertiary from an ancient, drowned landmass named Palaeonotis, postulated by palaeogeologists..as having extended from Asia as far as New Caledonia. **1933** *Bull. Amer. Assoc. Petroleum Geologists* XVII. 1129 Northeastern Texas..is an excellent example of the application of paleogeology to the problem of the accumulation of oil and gas. **1959** P. C. BADGLEY *Struct. Methods Exploration Geologist* v. 128 Figure 138 indicates the paleogeology immediately below the pre-Cretaceous erosion surface. **1960** A. I. LEVORSEN *Paleogeologic Maps* i. 2 Paleogeology ignores all subsequent sedimentation, volcanism, and deformation, and requires that the geologist consider the geology as it was when it was being formed. **1962** *Jrnl. Geophysical Res.* LXVII. 3461/2 Since different parts of formations became magnetized at different times, secular variation of the paleogeomagnetic field must have produced a certain amount of scatter of the directions of magnetization. **1977** *Sci. Amer.* Dec. 42/1 The maps are computer-generated by rotation around the varying north paleogeomagnetic poles, the amount of rotation controlled by sea-floor magnetic measurements. **1965** *Phil. Trans. R. Soc.* A. CCLVIII. 1 Because no other palaeogeophysical record is comparable in scope, palaeomagnetic surveys in the different continents have led to important conclusions about the Earth's evolution. **1970** *Nature* 18 July 227/1 Palaeogeophysical studies to determine whether present day processes were equally valid in past geological time. **1959** *Geophysical Abstr.* No. 175. 374 'Paleogeophysics' includes all methods which can lead to an understanding of former physical conditions and processes in the earth during its evolution; it is a part of paleogeography. **1970** S. K. RUNCORN *Palaeogeophysics* iii. 17 The newest branch of palaeogeophysics is the record presumed to have been found in fossils of the biological rhythms of marine fauna. In the oceans it seems *a priori* reasonable to suppose that these biological clocks set themselves by the exactly periodic variations in their physical environment, which seem only to be the solar day, the synodical month and the tropical year. **1975** *Nature* 3 Apr. 406/2 The palaeogeotherms which existed in the upper mantle immediately before incorporation and transport of the xenoliths by kimberlite eruptions have been derived from data from large numbers of individual xenoliths. **1970** R. G. J. STRENS in S. K. Runcorn *Palaeogeophysics* xl. 383 Apart from their usefulness in studying palaeogravity and palaeogeothermal gradients, such geothermometers and geobarometers would be of inestimable value to petrologists. **1978** *Nature* 18 May 221/1 Much debate has centred upon whether some palaeogeothermal gradients are perturbed or not. **1970** R. G. J. STRENS in S. K. Runcorn *Palaeogeophysics* xl. 383 Prospects for measuring palaeogravity with an accuracy sufficient to detect major variations (> 10%) over the last 3000 m. yr appear good. **1978** *Nature* 12 Jan. 153/2 Hypotheses involving substantial changes in Earth radius over geological time can be tested by measuring palaeogravity at, or near, the Earth's surface. **1853** *Edin. New Philos. Jrnl.* LV. 298 (*heading*) On the palæohydrography and orography of the Earth's surface. **1933** W. J. ARKELL *Jurassic Syst. Gt. Brit.* xviii. 557 To do justice to the palæogeography of the Jurassic period..we should have to proceed systematically from the points of view of..palaeohydrography, palaeoceanography, palaeobiogeography, palaeoclimatology,..and many others. **1971** *Geol. Fŏrening. Stockholm Forhandl.* XCIII. 59 (*heading*) Foraminifera and the paleohydrography of the Arabian Sea. **1965** *Jrnl. Geomagnetism & Geoelectr.* XVII. 417 (*heading*) Preliminary results of investigations made to study the use of Indian pottery to determine the paleointensity of the geomagnetic field for United States 600–1400 A.D. **1974** *Nature* 17 May 227/2 If the Moon were uniformly magnetised, it would need to have had a dipole moment of about 10^{23} gauss cm^3 to give an ancient surface field of 2,000 gamma (γ) which is typical of several palaeointensity studies, although a much higher value has been reported. **1959** *Geophysical Jrnl.* II. 307 Thus the shape of the areas of confidence so calculated depends on the palaeolatitude. **1971** I. G. GASS et al. *Understanding Earth* xiii. 174/2 The study of wind systems associated with arid deposits of different ages gives evidence of palaeolatitudes and so has a bearing on continental drift. **1964** *Prof. Papers U.S. Geol. Survey* No. 501-C. 109/1 (*heading*) Paleolatitudinal distribution of ancient phosphorite. **1971** *Nature* 1 Jan. 17/1 The geometrical reconstruction presented here..was obtained using a palaeomagnetic computer program which plotted continental outlines in their palaeolatitudinal position relative to a pole determined palaeomagnetically. **1961** *Mem. Coll. Sci. Kyoto Univ.* B. XXVIII. 68 A paleolimnological study of deep core-samples will indicate not only the developmental history of Lake Biwa-ko but the whole Pleistocene climatic history of the East Asiatic continent. **1973** *Nature* 16 Mar. 184/1 This aspect of the palaeolimnological work is being pursued in greater detail by magnetic, chemical and botanical investigations of the most recent sediments in Lough Neagh. **1960** *Amer. Jrnl. Sci.* CCLVIII. A. 1 (*heading*) Wilmot Hyde Bradley. Geologist, geomorphologist, paleolimnologist, paleontologist, administrator. **1970** *Ann. Acad. Sci. Fennicae* A. 3. CV. 25 The two species *Bosmina coregoni* Baird and *B. longirostris* O. F. Müller..are of particular interest to limnologists and palaeolimnologists. **1942** *Amer. Jrnl. Sci.* CCXL. 237 One particularly significant contribution of paleolimnology to glacial geology may be the derivation of an absolute chronology on the basis of quantitative counts of microfossils. **1948** *Bull. Geol. Soc. Amer.* LIX. 641, I have selected three distinctive features of the Green River formation to interpret in terms of the paleolimnology of the Eocene Green River lakes. These are the carbonate sediments and carbonate minerals, the oil shales, and the varved sediments. **1973** *Jrnl. Phycol.* IX. 395/2 The algal senescence system may prove valuable in lacustrine paleolimnology as a simple but experimentally accessible analogy to the processes of chlorophyll degradation in the water column. **1945** *Bull. Amer. Assoc. Petroleum Geologists* XXIX. 427 Paleolithologic maps have lines, isoliths, connecting points of similar lithology and separating rocks of differing nature. **1966** *McGraw-Hill Encycl. Sci. & Technol.* IX. 519/1 Paleolithologic maps showing bottom sediment patterns suggest whether rocks were laid in depths of strong wave action or in quieter water of deeps or broad shoals. **1964** K. M. Creer in A. E. M. Nairn *Probl. Palaeoclimatol.* 274 Because of the assumed axial symmetry of the field, palaeomagnetic data cannot yield information about palaeolongitude. **1961** *Nature* 17 June 1097/2 Localities along the same palæo-meridian. **1965** *Phil. Trans. R. Soc.* A. CCLVIII. 27 A palaeomagnetic survey of a suite of rocks representing at least 10^4y thus provides information from which may be determined: (1) the palaeomagnetic latitude..of the sites, and (2) the palaeomeridian direction. **1901** *Q. Jrnl. Geol. Soc.* LVII. 405 (*heading*) A palaeometeorological explanation of some geological problems. **1962** Rex & Goldberg in M. N. Hill *Sea* I. v. 295 Deep-sea deposits provide excellent source areas for paleometeorological investigations provided eolian materials can be recognised. **1964** K. W. Butzer *Environment & Archeol.* xxii. 334 A great deal of more satisfactory paleoclimatic information must be available before this major barrier to paleometeorological study is removed. **1901** *Q. Jrnl. Geol. Soc.* LVII. 468 The palæometeorologist must work with the best material he can obtain, content with the enunciation of general principles, and with the solution of some of the more simple problems. **1854** *Edin. New Philos. Jrnl.* LVI. 9 We have got very few notions on palæometeorology and palæotemperature or thermics. **1901** *Q. Jrnl. Geol. Soc.* LVII. 469 Among the services which palæometeorology may hereafter render to the geologist..may be that of assisting him to determine the chronological relations of geological zones in different regions where no direct evidence..may be attainable. **1954** *Sci. News* XXXIII. 65 Paleoclimatology, the study of the climates of the past, is considerably more advanced than paleometeorology, the study of past weather. **1957** *Mem. Geol. Soc. Amer.* LXVII. II. xxiv. 684 The development of the method of paleotemperature research..using the $O^{16}:O^{18}$ ratio in carbonates and other solid salts of oxyacids has provided the most powerful single tool yet invented in the equipment of the paleo-oceanographer. **1945** Paleooceanographic [see *palæoclimatologic *a.*]. **1968** *Science* 29 Mar. 1461/1 The distribution of planktonic tests in fossil marine sediments are being used increasingly for paleo-oceanographic reconstructions. **1971** *Nature* 13 Aug. 469/1 Oxygen isotope and palaeontological determination of planktonic foraminifers allow us to make several generalizations on the palaeoceanographic history of the Arctic Ocean back to Mid Pliocene. **1971** *Ibid.* 30 Apr. 563/1 In the interesting palaeoceanographical model proposed by Bandy, a thermal maximum is indicated in marine conditions during the same 9–8 m.y. periods. **1933** Palæoceanography [see *palæohydrography* above]. **1957** *Mem. Geol. Soc. Amer.* LXVII. II. xxiv. 684 (*heading*) Future of the study of paleo-oceanography. **1972** *Nature* 17 Mar. 117/1 The gross geometric relationships of pelagic facies on a ridge system must be interpreted in the light of the spreading process itself before meaningful conclusions can be drawn about palaeoclimatology and palaeo-oceanography. **1927** B. B. Polynov *Contrib. Russ. Scientists to Paleopedology* 1 It is yet scarcely possible to speak of paleopedology, as of a scientific theory that has assumed a wholly definite shape. *Ibid.* 14 As one of the most interesting recent Ukrainian papers on pedology may be especially mentioned the paleopedological map of Ukraina, drawn by Makhov. **1943** *Amer. Jrnl. Sci.* CCXLI. 197 A great deal more must be learned about the soil formation before paleopedologists will understand the true significance of the soil bones. *Ibid.* 199 Because of the nature of the pedogenic fossils it cannot be expected that paleopedology ever will be able to deal with much more than the general types of the ancient soil formation and the changes in the geographical pattern of the zones and regions in which these types prevailed during the different geological periods. *Ibid.* 200 The true paleopedological formations are rather rare. **1971** G. Roeschmann in D. H. Yaalon *Paleopedology* 319 In future, paleopedologists and geologists will only obtain satisfactory results..if they work as a team. **1973** *N.Z. Jrnl. Geol. & Geophysics* XVI. 723 Such paleopedological evidence may be employed to confirm and extend the chronology of the later part of the New Zealand Quaternary. *Ibid.* 735 This identification of these ancient episodes of erosion depends on the identification of tephra formations and paleosols and is a logical application of paleopedology to environmental reconstruction. **1898** J. E. Marr *Princ. Stratigr. Geol.* x. 121 The palæo-physiographer..attempts to restore the physical conditions of greater thicknesses of deposit. **1950** *Bull. Illinois State Geol. Survey* No. 73. iii. 23 (*caption*) Paleophysiographic diagram of the bedrock topography of Illinois. **1954** W. D. Thornbury *Princ. Geomorphol.* ii. 31 (*caption*) A paleophysiographic diagram showing the major features of the preglacial topography of Illinois. **1898** J. E. Marr *Princ. Stratigr. Geol.* x. 122 The utmost that the maker of palæophysiographical maps can expect to indicate, when dealing with considerable thicknesses of strata, is an approximation to the mean position of the shore-lines of the period when these strata were deposited. **1882** E. Hull *Contrib. Physical Hist. Brit. Isles* p. v, I had intended giving the title of 'Palæo-Physiography of the British Islands' to this volume; but certain friends in whose judgment I have the most implicit confidence assured me that no one would have the slightest conception from such a title of the contents of my book. **1915** C. Schuchert *Text-bk. Geol.* II. xx. 450 There is..another record that has so far been almost refused recognition in our time-tables. This is the time evaluation of topographic form at any given stage of development (the physiography of the present, the paleophysiography of the past). **1900** R. T. Hill in *Topogr. Atlas U.S. Geol. Survey* Folio 3. 5/3 Destructional plains are sometimes evolved from constructional plains; the latter, after elevation in long erosion, are reduced in old age to the former. On the other hand, constructional plains are usually established upon areas which were once destructional plains. Ancient buried destructional plains thus veneered by constructional formations might be appropriately termed paleoplains. **1966** *Bull. Amer. Assoc. Petroleum Geologists* L. 2302/2 Farther west along the flank of the Canadian shield..a vast paleoplain..was covered by Lower Cretaceous (locally Upper Jurassic) sediments which include a high percentage of sandstone which could serve as reservoir. **1962** *Geofisica Pura e Appl.* LIII. 52 (*heading*) Rock magnetism and the earth's palaeopoles. **1971** I. G. Gass et al. *Understanding Earth* xv. 212 The evidence favouring drift including geomagnetic data (palaeopole investigations). **1904** G. S. Hall *Adolescence* II. xii. 194 The problem, whether there is any paleopsychic race element, is as inevitable as it is unanswerable. **1916** *N.Y. Med. Jrnl.* CIV. 1077/1 We wish to maintain the idea that there may be other types of fossils to be studied than those derived from plants and animals, namely thought fossils, and that to paleobotany and to paleozoology we may add a science of paleopsychology. The happiest ground of the paleopsychologist is ..in history, in literature, in..possibly diseases. **1960** *Geofisica Pura e Applicata* XLV. 116 The palaeo-radius corresponding to the time *t*. **1978** *Nature* 26 Jan. 316/1 Observations of the surface of Mercury and Mars by spacecraft enable constraints to be placed on the palaeo-radius of these extraterrestrial bodies. **1960** *Oil & Gas Jrnl.* 1 Feb. 154/1 A method for determining paleo-salinities..would also be of considerable practical value in the search for various types of mineral deposits and petroleum. **1972** *Marine Geol.* XII. 335 (*heading*) Pollen and paleosalinity analyses from a Holocene tidal marsh sequence. *Ibid.* 337 A method for determining paleosalinity was proposed by Nelson (1967) which utilized the relative proportions of iron and calcium phosphate in argillaceous sediments. **1957** *Bull. Geol. Soc. Amer.* LXVIII. 469/1 Mapping of cross-bedding and other primary current structures has proved useful in reconstruction of regional paleoslopes. **1965** *Bull. Amer. Assoc. Petroleum Geologists* XLIX. 341/1 Regional variation in stratigraphic position of the base of the landslide facies establishes the fact that the foot of the paleoslope migrated north-northwestwardly through time. **1975** Read & Watson *Introd. Geol.* II. I. iv. 82 Remarkably constant palaeocurrent directions determined from current-bedding throughout the Athabasca formation indicate a palaeoslope towards the west or north-west. **1950** Hunt & Sokoloff in *Prof. Papers U.S. Geol. Survey* No. 221. 109/1 An ancient soil, hereafter referred to as paleosol, has been dated..as pre-Wisconsin in the Lake Bonneville and Denver basins. **1954** W. D. Thornbury *Princ. Geomorphol.* iv. 82 Paleosols may be found on buried landscapes, on exhumed portions of ancient landscapes, or upon features of the present topography which are relicts of previous geomorphic cycles. **1968** R. W. Fairbridge *Encycl. Geomorphol.* 554/2 A lateritic crust is essentially a paleosol, and reflects a polycyclic regime, usually as a result of repeated alternation of hot, humid conditions developing laterite, with dry, evaporating conditions favoring crust development. **1975** *Nature* 20 Mar. 189/1 Palaeoenvironmental indicators in the sediments include polygonal desiccation cracks, calcretes and other palaeosols. **1956** *Soil Sci.* LXXXII. 441 Erosive stripping of the protective mantle of sediment in many places, however, resulted in the resurrection of the paleosolic profile *in toto*, so that now the paleosol occurs within the continuum of soils on the modern surface. **1965** R. V. Ruhe in Wright & Frey *Quaternary of U.S.* 759/2 These kinds of soil occur adjacent to each other and grade from one to another on the paleosolic surfaces of the older glacial tills. **1954** A. J. Cain *Animal Species* vii. 107 When good series are available, forms that seem to be good species at any one time may become indefinable since they are successive stages in a single evolutionary line... It is convenient to refer to such forms as palaeospecies. **1956** P. C. Sylvester-Bradley *Species Concept in Palaeont.* 2 A third concept is the result of projecting the biospecies into a third dimension, that of time. It is the concept..others have called the 'palaeospecies'. **1964** *Nature* 1 Aug. 451/1 A species in palæontology..is a fundamentally different kind of unit and has been called a chronospecies or palæospecies. **1974** *Ibid.* 1 Nov. 85/2 Physical anthropologists have expanded the concept of variability in palaeospecies making it possible to lump greater ranges of morphological variation within a single species. **1966** *Bull. Amer. Assoc. Petroleum Geologists* L. 2323/1 To demonstrate a logical method of paleostructural mapping by use of carefully selected isopachous intervals. **1972** *Internat. Geol. Rev.* XIV. 1320/1 In any platform region, paleostructural reconstructions should be preceded by a comprehensive study of the conditions of occurrence and distinctive lithologic features of the rocks. **1937** *Jrnl. Geol.* XLV. 51 A paleo-structure map of southeastern Missouri at the end of Lamotte time. **1970** *Israel Jrnl. Earth-Sci.* XIX. 141 Systematic study of the thickness of Senonian strata yields conflicting data regarding palaeostructure. **1904** P. Geddes *City Devel.* xxv. 175/1 Must we not, therefore, call this earlier and crude mechanical civilisation which still predominates among us the 'Palæotechnic' stage, and recognise that the formerly less prominent industrial peoples..are passing more quickly than we into the 'Neotechnic' stage? **1915** —— *Cities in Evolution* iv. 63 We may distinguish the earlier and ruder elements of the Industrial Age as Paleotechnic, the newer and still often incipient elements disengaging themselves from these as Neotechnic. **1934** Paleotechnic [see *eotechnic *a.*]. **1946** *Theology* XLIX. 94 The report..praises the past but its vision for the future is lighted less by a doctrine of the creation than by paleotechnic ideology. **1960** C. Winick *Dict. Anthropol.* 399/1 *Paleotechnic*, in the development of the techniques of western civilization, referring to the period in which mineral resources became prominent and coal power and iron were widely used. It flourished around 1750. The factory system, finance capital, and competition developed. **1973** *New Society* 7 June 543/2 Its automated ticket system..makes London's machines seem paleotechnic by comparison. **1947** *Jrnl. Geol.* LV. 311 (*caption*) Paleotectonic maps of the Cordilleran region in late Paleozoic time. Cross-ruled area is the volcanic archipelago and orogenic belt. Horizontally ruled areas were uplifted and eroded during the period designated. **1957** *Bull. Geol. Soc. Amer.* LXVIII. 151/2 These studies have revealed a paleotectonic framework composed of a geosynclinal basis in central Idaho and a relatively more stable cratonic shelf in southwestern Montana. **1975** *Nature* 10 July 117/1 The positions of Triassic seaways along the southern continental margin of the Tethys 'geosyncline' are defined by the effects of at least two main palaeotectonic events. **1854** Palæotemperature [see *palæometeorology* above]. **1948** *Science* 5 Nov. 492/1 This particular application of the chemical differences in the processes of isotopes occurred to me a year and a half ago, and since that time my colleagues and I have been trying to solve the several difficult problems encountered in making such measurements of paleotemperatures. **1969** *Nature* 4 Oct. 66/2 Recent palaeotemperature measurements obtained from Caribbean cores..suggest that the coldest part of the Weichselian was around 17000 years BP. **1957** *Chem. Abstr.* LI. 12773 (*heading*) Determination of climatic conditions of some regions of the U.S.S.R. in the Upper Cretaceous period by the method of isotopic paleothermometry. **1971** *Nature* 13 Aug. 466/2 Reconstruction of the climatic and hydrologic history of ocean basins has been based on either oxygen isotope palaeothermometry or studies of foraminiferal assemblages preserved in deep sea sediments. **1943** *Jrnl. Sedimentary Petrology* XIII. 111/1 Most paleotopographic maps pass under the name of structural maps but there is a distinct difference. **1960** M. S. Bishop *Subsurface Mapping* ix. 135 Oftentimes the gentle slopes of paleotopographic surfaces are indicative of much steeper dips on the underlying beds, especially if a major unconformity is being mapped. **1960** *Canad. Mining & Metallurg. Bull.* LIII. 535/2 The oil has accumulated beneath the unconformity and the accompanying 'caprock' wherever the subcrop trend of a reservoir bed crosses a paleotopographical ridge. **1966** *Bull. Amer. Assoc. Petroleum Geologists* L. 2296/1 These quantitative concepts are very useful in interpreting an area paleotopographically; *i.e.*, they keep the number of tributaries, lengths of streams, and channel slopes within specific limits according to geomorphological principles. **1943** *Jrnl. Sedimentary Petrology* XIII. 108 The search for new deposits of petroleum is aided by the use of special paleogeographic maps... Other types of maps that may be used show salinity, thickness of sands, paleogeology and paleotopography. **1970** *Jrnl. Geol. Soc. Australia* XVII. 39 The palaeotopography of an east–west valley on the eastern flank of the Great Divide is reconstructed from a consideration of early Tertiary and Palaeozoic rocks. **1957** *Bull. Geol. Soc. Amer.* LXVIII. 1870 (*heading*) Paleo-wind directions in late Paleozoic and early Mesozoic time on the Colorado Plateau as determined by cross-strata. **1964** *Sedimentology* III. 52 The directional features of the dunes suggest that the paleowind pattern was similar to the present-day pattern around Bermuda. **1975** *Nature* 3 Jan. 19/1 We recommend experimental and analytical study of these currents taking into account continental dispersion and palaeowinds. **1967** *Palaeogeogr., Palaeoclimatol., Palaeoecol.* III. 201 Palaeozoogeographic data are thought to be especially useful in establishing a timetable for continental drift. *Ibid.* 210 Many ammonite species were able to disperse widely. While this renders them excellent for purposes of correlation it reduces their importance for palaeozoogeography. **1972** *Nature* 7 Apr. 297/3 Succeeding chapters..examine..the palaeozoogeographic patterns in the fossil record. **1975** *Ibid.* 17 Apr. 556/3 Palaeozoogeography can only make sense as the evolution of organisms in space and time.

b. In anatomical terms designating parts of the brain which are considered to be of relatively ancient development phylogenetically, as *palæencephalon, *palæocerebellum, *palæocortex, *palæopallium, *palæostriatum, *palæothalamus. Cf. *neo- 1 e.

palæoanthropo·logy. Also (chiefly *U.S.*) **paleo-.** [ad. F. *paléoanthropologie* (P. Topinard *Élém. d'Anthrop. Gén.* (1885) vii. 177): see Anthropology.] The branch of anthropology concerned with the study of fossil hominids.

1916 *Bull. Amer. Mus. Nat. Hist.* XXXV. 347 Then follows..the conclusion to which all M. Boule's own researches in palænthropology [*sic*] and palæontology have evidently led him. **1935** *Times Lit. Suppl.* 14 Feb. 84/2 Dr. Leakey also..clearly sums up his results and shows their bearings on general palaeoanthropology and prehistory. **1957** *Antiquity* XXXI. 43 Rapid advances.. are being made in paleoanthropology at present. **1965** B. G. Campbell *Nomenclature of Hominidae* 3 New taxa are very rarely presented in palaeoanthropology according to the rules of the more recent zoological congresses. **1974** *Nature* 6 Sept. 10/2 Investigations of the development of locomotion within the hominid lineage provides one of the more active and fascinating areas of palaeoanthropology today. **1978** *Ibid.* 2 Mar. 10/3 Wherever physical anthropology is taught in British universities, palaeoanthropology is recognised as an important component of the courses.

Hence **pa:læoanthropolo·gical** *a.*; **pa:læoanthropo·logist,** an expert or specialist in palæoanthropology.

1934 Webster, Paleoanthropological,..paleoanthropologist. **1935** *Times Lit. Suppl.* 14 Feb. 84/3 The problem of the prehistorical, especially the palaeoanthropological, relations between East Africa and the rest of the continent. **1947** *Sci. News* V. 44 The palæanthropologists [*sic*] went on with their researches..in the hope of one day discovering the hypothetical 'Tertiary man'. **1969** *Times* 17 Jan. 13/6 Dr. Louis Leakey..has for the past 40 years been exploiting the rich palaeoanthropological deposits in the Olduvai Gorge. **1975** *Nature* 10 Apr. 478/3 Although the article admirably reflects recent work in East Africa, it does scant justice to the palaeoanthropological researches in the Transvaal over the past decade. **1978** *Ibid.* 22 June 589/3 In almost all circumstances it now seems important that palaeoanthropologists try to work with a set of alternative hypotheses rather than simply with one favourite interpretation.

Pa:læo-Asia·tic, *sb.* and *a.* Also **Palæoasiatic, Palæasiatic,** and with the prefix spelt **paleo-.** [f. PALÆO-, PALEO- + ASIATIC *a.* and *sb.*] = *PALÆO-SIBERIAN *sb.* and *a.*

1909 A. C. HADDON *Races of Man* 48 The..western, and northern Ural-Altaians form one division, which includes such peoples as the Ugrians (in part), Palæasiatics, some of the Tungus, and the true Mongols. **1925** L. H. D. BUXTON *Peoples of Asia* vii. 191 Some early type may, as one of the components of the highly complex physical form of the Koreans, include as a basis the aboriginal Palæasiatic type. **1929** —— *China* iii. 58 There is a clear division also between the Mongols and the Palaeasiatics, that is the old yellow-skinned tribes of north-eastern Asia, and other tribes on the north. **1932** [see *CHUKCHEE, CHUKCHI *sb.* and *a.*]. **1948** D. DIRINGER *Alphabet* I. ix. 157 The Chukcha..are a..Palæoasiatic, Mongoloid people. **1953** W. K. MATTHEWS *Struct. & Devel. Russian* I. iv. 76 A variety of languages (e.g. Caucasian, Uralian, and Palaeoasiatic). **1962** W. P. LEHMANN *Hist. Linguistics* ii. 44 Far to the east in Siberia the Palaeo-Asiatic or Hyberborean languages are spoken. **1976** *Language* LII. 482 The so-called Palaeo-Asiatic family..is..more a geographical convenience than a genetic grouping.

palæobathymetry, etc.: see *PALÆO-, PALEO-.

pa:læobioche·mistry. Also (chiefly *U.S.*) **paleo-.** [f. PALÆO-, PALEO- + *BIOCHEMISTRY.] The biochemistry of fossils and of organisms of the geological past, esp. as a means of investigating phylogeny; the investigation of the evolutionary development of biochemical processes.

1954 *Carnegie Inst. Yearbk. 1953–4* 97 (*heading*) Paleobiochemistry. **1966** *Science* 6 May 762/2 The Fig Tree organisms are comparable in size, shape, complexity of structure, and isolated habit to many modern bacillar bacteria. Although they may have had a nonphotosynthetic metabolism, there is insufficient information available about their paleobiochemistry to realistically evaluate such a suggestion. **1967** *Compar. Biochem. & Physiol.* XX. 553 (*heading*) Paleobiochemistry of molluscan shell proteins. **1969** *Collier's Encycl. Year Bk.* 406 In one of the first applications of paleobiochemistry it has been found that hydrocarbon compounds in rock 3 billion years old may be composed of fossilized chlorophyll. **1969** G. EGLINTON in Eglinton & Murphy *Org. Geochem.* ii. 21 Two main approaches can be taken to the biochemistry of organisms in past times. The first is to examine fossil specimens in the hope that some of the information is still there in the form of protein structure, secondary metabolites, etc... The second is to examine the biochemistry of present-day living organisms and make phylogenetic comparisons. From these one can attempt to infer evolutionary sequences in the development of biochemical processes..; this approach is known variously as paleobiochemistry, evolutionary biochemistry and chemical paleogenetics. **1969** M. FLORKIN in *Ibid.* xx. 498 Structurally preserved biopolymers kept *in situ* in their anatomical location in fossils..should constitute the most reliable material for studies in paleobiochemistry.

So **pa:læobioche·mical** *a.*

Quot. 1937 is an isolated example, unrelated to the later use of *palæobiochemistry*.

1937 *Bull. Amer. Assoc. Petroleum Geologists* XXI. 770 Theories which appear to be in part applicable to such an accumulation are (1) the existence of paleo-biochemical conditions associated with the shallow-water near-shore deposits which controlled the abundance of petroleum-forming organisms. [Etc.] **1972** *Science* 31 Mar. 1461 (*heading*) Amino acid composition of planktonic foraminifera: a paleobiochemical approach to evolution. **1973** *Nature* 20 July 182/2 The recognition that keratin can survive tens of millions of years..could lead to further discoveries, enabling more palaeobiochemical analyses to be undertaken.

pa:læobiogeo·graphy. Also (chiefly *U.S.*) **paleo-.** [f. PALÆO-, PALEO- + *BIOGEOGRAPHY.] The study of the distribution of fossil plants or animals.

1934 in WEBSTER. **1953** *Ecology* XXXIV. 811 (*heading*) A synthesis of paleobiogeography. **1961** P. E. CLOUD in M. Sears *Oceanogr.* II. 151 The patterns created in the struggle for perpetuity are the essence of descriptive biogeography and paleobiogeography. **1972** *Sci. Amer.* Mar. 12/2 He has written on such subjects as fossil carnivores, dating of early man,..evolutionary theory and paleobiogeography.

Hence **pa:læobiogeo·grapher,** an expert or specialist in palæobiogeography; **pa:læobi:-ogeogra·phic, -ical** *adjs.*

1953 *Ecology* XXXIV. 812/2 Then come the paleobiogeographic maps. **1958** *Bull. Geol. Soc. Amer.* LXIX. 107/1 The amount of detail that can be shown on a paleogeographic or paleobiogeographic map depends on the length of the time interval which it attempts to represent. **1961** P. E. CLOUD in M. Sears *Oceanogr.* II. 159 For the paleobiogeographer, it is essential not to confuse temperature subdivisions with geodetic terms. *Ibid.* 162 An important paleobiogeographical exception to the direction of size increase is provided in the case of the shelled invertebrates. **1970** *Spec. Papers Geol. Soc. Amer.* No. 124. 23 During the late Paleozoic, unequal distribution and dispersal of biotas created changing paleobiogeographic provinces. **1978** *Nature* 9 Mar. 159/1 Palaeobiogeographic evidence is thus compatible with seafloor spreading and palaeomagnetic data.

palæobiology, etc.: see *PALÆO-, PALEO-.

palæobotany, paleo-. Add: Hence also **pa:læobota·nically** *adv.*, in terms of or as regards palæobotany.

1934 *Bull. Amer. Assoc. Petroleum Geologists* XVIII. 1010 The Jackfork-Stanley is paleobotanically older than the Coal-bearing shale. **1968** R. W. FAIRBRIDGE *Encycl. Geomorphol.* 534/2 The last of the paleobotanically established Holocene stages is..also the historical period.

palæoceanography, etc.: see *palæo-oceanography* s.v. *PALÆO-, PALEO-.

Palæocene, delete entry in Dict. (s.v. PALÆO-, PALEO-) and substitute:

Palæocene (pæ·lĭˌo-, pēi·lĭˌosīn), *a. Geol.* Also (chiefly *U.S.*) **Paleocene.** [ad. F. *paléocène* (W. Ph. Schimper *Traité de Paléont. végétale* (1874) III. 680), f. *paléo-* PALÆO-, PALEO + Gr. *καινός* new, recent (cf. EOCENE, OLIGOCENE, etc.).] Of, pertaining to, or designating the lowest series of the Tertiary system, lying below the Eocene and comprising the Montian and perhaps the Danian stages; (formerly often not recognized as a distinct series but incorporated in the Eocene). Also *absol.*

1877 *Proc. Geol. Soc.* XXXIII. 83 An attempt has been made to establish a zone intermediate between the European Cretaceous and Eocene, under the title of Palæocene. **1877, 1899** [in Dict. s.v. PALÆO-, PALEO-]. **1921** A. W. GRABAU *Textbk. Geol.* II. xlv. 782 The Palæocene is not always recognized by American geologists, who class it as Lower or Basal Eocene. **1949** R. C. MOORE *Introd. Hist. Geol.* xvii. 399 In Europe and in North America, the Tertiary System is recognized as containing main divisions that in upward order are named Paleocene, Eocene, Oligocene, Miocene, and Pliocene. **1957** DUNBAR & RODGERS *Princ. Stratigr.* xvii. 298/1 The Paleocene is commonly not separated from the Eocene in Great Britain and France. **1965** KAY & COLBERT *Stratigr. & Life Hist.* xxiv. 617 There was an evolutionary explosion of mammals..with the advent of the Paleocene Epoch. **1969** [see *MONTIAN *a.*].

pa:læocerebe·llum. *Anat.* Also (chiefly *U.S.*) **paleo-.** [mod.L., f. *PALÆO-, PALEO- b + CEREBELLUM.] A phylogenetically older portion of the cerebellum, comprising mainly the anterior lobe, pyramid, and uvula.

1925, 1954 [see *NEOCEREBELLUM]. **1974** *Encycl. Brit. Macropædia* XII. 990/2 The anterior lobe of the cerebellum represents the paleocerebellum, an area that regulates equilibrium and muscle tone; it constitutes the main mass of the cerebellum in fish, reptiles, and birds.

So **pa:læocerebe·llar** *a.*, of or pertaining to the palæocerebellum.

1936 C. U. A. KAPPERS et al. *Compar. Anat. Nervous Syst. Vertebr.* I. vii. 777 The above mentioned group of authors has separated the cerebellum into a neocerebellar portion and a paleocerebellar portion. **1958** L. HAUSMAN *Clin. Neuroanat.* xxii. 203 (*heading*) Syndrome of paleocerebellar atrophy.

palæochemistry, etc.: see *PALÆO-, PALEO-.

pa·læoclimate. Also (chiefly *U.S.*) **paleo-.** [f. PALÆO, PALEO- + CLIMATE *sb.*] The climate at a period in the geological past.

1924 *Geol. Mag.* LXI. 512 Conclusions regarding palæoclimates. **1954** *Jrnl. Geol.* LXII. 229/1 The organism-induced differentiation in recording varying fractions of the environmental temperature ranges and the fact that these types of skeletal-temperature records are at present our sole sources of data for paleotemperature investigations introduce uncertainty in evaluation of amplitudes in paleoclimates. **1963** *Times* 7 Jan. 9/7 The geological evidence of palaeoclimates. **1974** *Encycl. Brit. Macropædia* XIII. 908/2 Many ingested seeds, hair, feathers, and small animal bones within the coprolites may provide a reliable estimate of the paleoclimate of the time.

So **pa:læoclima·tic** *a.*, of or pertaining to a palæoclimate.

1893 C. A. WHITE in *Rep. U.S. Nat. Museum 1892* 301 This subject relates to what may be designated as paleoclimatic conditions, that is, to formerly existing conditions, which in certain parts of the earth were more or less materially different from those which now exist in the same parts. **1946** F. E. ZEUNER *Dating Past* vi. 163 The number of Palaeolithic sites which can be dated on local palaeoclimatic evidence is as yet very small. **1977** A. HALLAM *Planet Earth* 171 The occurrence of ancient calcareous rocks can be used as a paleoclimatic indicator.

pa:læoclimato·logy. Also (chiefly *U.S.*) **paleo-.** [f. prec. + -OLOGY.] The study or investigation of palæoclimates.

1920 G. W. BERRY in *Ann. Rep. Board of Regents Smithsonian Inst. 1918* 298 In the interpretation of the far distant past paleobotany and..paleozoology contribute fundamental data to geology..; not only as comprising the subject matter of the biology of the past,..but in the elucidation of the climate and other physical conditions of past times, subjects which may be embraced under the terms of Paleoclimatology and Paleoecology. **1946** F. E. ZEUNER *Dating Past* v. 145 Combining the geological evidence with the astronomical time-scale by means of the radiation curves, an absolute chronology is obtained which can be regarded as sufficiently reliable for the purposes both of palaeoclimatology and prehistoric archeology. **1974** *Encycl. Brit. Micropædia* VII. 690/2 Most research in paleoclimatology centres on explaining (1) the warmth of the Northern Hemisphere land masses during at least 90 per cent of the last 570,000,000 years, (2) the semiperiodic occurrence of widespread glaciation.., and (3) the irregular advances and retreats of the ice sheets during the glacial periods.

Hence **pa:læoclimatolo·gic, -lo·gical** *adjs.*, **pa:læoclimatolo·gically** *adv.*; **pa:læoclimato·logist,** one who investigates palæoclimates.

1924 J. G. A. SKERL tr. *Wegener's Orig. Continents & Oceans* vi. 105 Information about deposits of rock-salt, which are so important for palæoclimatological purposes. **1927** *Geogr. Jrnl.* LXX. 167 For the palæoclimatologist.. Wegener's theory is a tempting haven of refuge from his perplexities. **1945** *Bull. Amer. Assoc. Petroleum Geologists* XXIX. 428 (*heading*) Paleoclimatologic and paleo-oceanographic maps. **1957** *Antiquity* XXXI. 78 The field research necessary for a meaningful paleoclimatological, paleobotanical, and paleozoological history of post-glacial south-western Asia is only beginning. **1963** *Amer. Jrnl. Sci.* CCLXI. 282 The hope that paleoclimatologic evidence may support or refute certain of the major rival hypotheses of global paleogeography. **1966** J. A. MABBUTT in G. H. Dury *Ess. Geomorphol.* 83 The zone offers a worthwhile challenge to the climatic geomorphologist,.. partly because of its situation in the palaeoclimatologically little-known Southern Hemisphere. **1968** *Economist* 3 Feb. 42/3 He..leaves one wondering once again whether the ups and downs of ancient history will ever be adequately understood until the palaeoclimatologists have done a proper job on the Mediterranean basin. **1972** *Nature* 17 Mar. 116/1 In either case, significant palaeoclimatological or palaeo-oceanographic variations might be detectable by analysis of the facies geometry.

palæoco·rtex. *Anat.* Also (chiefly *U.S.*) **paleo-.** [mod.L., f. *PALÆO-, PALEO- b + CORTEX.] A phylogenetically older portion of the cerebral cortex, which is coextensive with the palæopallium.

1909, 1947 [see *NEOCORTEX]. **1964** J. Z. YOUNG *Model of Brain* XIX. 306 In the vertebrate brain there are also such tiers of circuits provided, by the hypothalamus, thalamus, palaeocortex and neocortex.

Hence **palæoco·rtical** *a.*, of or pertaining to the palæocortex.

1909 *Arch. Neurol. & Psychiatry* IV. 162 The palæocortical arrangement..is not nearly as typical as in the ventral grey substance. **1964** J. Z. YOUNG *Model of Brain* vi. 110 The palaeocortical centres and basal parts of the forebrain are also concerned largely with 'motivation' as well as being involved in learning.

palæocurrent: see *PALÆO-, PALEO-.

pa:læoeco·logy. Also (chiefly *U.S.*) **paleo-.** [f. PALÆO-, PALEO- + *ECOLOGY.] The ecology of fossil plants and animals.

1898 C. MACMILLAN in *Minnesota Bot. Stud.* I. 950 Paleoecology might be defined as the science of adaptations of fossil organisms. **1916** F. E. CLEMENTS *Plant Succession* xii. 193 Paleo-ecology develops its most fascinating aspect when it reaches the Human period. **1942** *Bull. Amer. Assoc. Petroleum Geologists* XXVI. 1697 Paleoecology, both organic and sedimentary, is a fertile field for geologic research. **1969** *Beaver* Summer 36/2 Too little is known about too few of the insects in Canadian amber to draw conclusions about their palaeo-ecology. **1976** *Nature* 29 Jan. 350/3 Palaeoecology is primarily concerned with the reconstruction of past ecosystems from palaeontological and lithological evidence.

Hence **pa:læoecolo·gic, -ical** *adjs.*, **pa:læoecolo·gically** *adv.*; **palæoeco·logist,** an expert or specialist in palæoecology.

1934 WEBSTER, Paleoecologist. **1940** *Bull. Amer. Assoc. Petroleum Geologists* XXIV. 1196 (*heading*) Inferred and possible paleoecological effects of the water medium. **1940** *Jrnl. Paleont.* XIV. 320/2 In a problem of this kind the paleoecologist is greatly handicapped by the fact that every criterion available is susceptible of a variety of interpretations. **1954** *Jrnl. Geol.* LXII. 234/2 Paleoecological factors, such as wide fluctuations in salinity and insolation-induced temperatures, are insufficient for such mean growth temperatures. **1959** *Jrnl. Palæont.* XXXIII. 936/1 More in need of emphasis paleoecologically, the change from water to sediment or between sediment layers may be almost as profound as that from air to water. **1961** WEBSTER, Paleoecologic. **1963** POTTER & PETTIJOHN *Paleocurrents & Basin Anal.* i. 2 Knowledge of current direction is also useful in paleoecologic studies. **1975** *Nature* 6 Feb. 400/1 Palaeoecological studies suggest that the species [sc. *Armeria maritima*] was widespread in distribution during the cold and disturbed conditions at the close of the last glaciation. **1977** A. HALLAM *Planet Earth* 218 Because they are far more abundant, the invertebrate fossil faunas of the sea are of more importance to stratigraphers and paleoecologists than are the vertebrates.

palæoenvironment to **-geomagnetic:** see *PALÆO-, PALEO-.

pa:læogeomorphic (-dʒīˌomǭ·ɹfik), *a.* Chiefly *U.S.*, in the form **paleo-.** [f. PALÆO-, PALEO- + GEOMORPHIC *a.*] Of, pertaining to, or formed by buried relief features; palæogeomorphological.

1945 M. KAY in *Bull. Amer. Assoc. Petroleum Geologists* XXIX. 427 (*heading*) Paleogeomorphic maps. **1960** *Prof. Papers U.S. Geol. Survey* No. 400-B. 186/1 Because of the subtle nature of the topography of this disconformable surface a regional paleogeomorphic pattern has not been generally recognized or described. **1966** *Bull. Amer. Assoc. Petroleum Geologists* L. 2279/1 Kay (1945, p. 427), discussing 'paleogeomorphic maps', did not really do justice to Thornbury's later definition of paleogeomorphology, because he omitted all mention of the use of subsurface data in constructing such maps; his main concern was the separation of seas from lands. **1972** *Ibid.* LVI. 538/2 Paleogeomorphic traps are formed where ancient subaqueous or land surfaces and the relief features on them..are buried by younger strata of a different lithology.

pa:læogeomorpho·logy. Also (chiefly *U.S.*) **paleo-.** [f. PALÆO-, PALEO- + *GEOMORPHOLOGY.] The geomorphology of ancient landscapes, esp. as represented today by features that are buried or newly exhumed.

1954 W. D. THORNBURY *Princ. Geomorphol.* ii. 31 It might seem that the recognition of ancient erosion surfaces and the study of ancient topographies does not belong in the field of geomorphology, but the approach of the geomorphologist may be the most logical one. This aspect of geomorphology may well be called paleogeomorphology. **1966** R. MARTIN in *Bull. Amer. Assoc. Petroleum Geologists* L. 2278/1 Enlarging on Thornbury's concept, the writer groups under the term *paleogeomorphology* the study of all geomorphic phenomena which are recognizable in the subsurface and in outcrops of previously buried formations. **1968** R. W. FAIRBRIDGE *Encycl. Geomorphol.* 805/1 Paleogeomorphology is of practical importance insofar as many accumulations of oil, gas, certain ores and fresh water are related to buried relief features. **1972** *Geo Abstr.* A. 727 The palaeogeomorphology of the region is dominated by glacial features upon which karst features are now being superimposed.

Hence **pa:læogeomorpholo·gical, -lo·gic** *adjs.*; **pa:læogeomorpho·logist,** one who studies palæogeomorphology.

1960 *Canad. Mining & Metallurg. Bull.* LIII. 529/2 Buried relief features are of importance to the petroleum geologist whenever they lead to the trapping of hydrocarbons, either directly or indirectly. In areas where such features abound,..paleogeomorphological features rank in importance with sedimentation and structure as hydrocarbon trapping agents. **1963** *Oil & Gas Jrnl.* 21 Oct. 140/1 It is convenient for the paleogeomorphologist to know that water travelling at a certain speed can move particles of specific sizes and density. **1966** *Bull. Amer. Assoc. Petroleum Geologists* L. 2279/1 An important difference between stratigraphic and paleogeomorphologic traps is the pronounced three-dimensional aspect of the latter. *Ibid.* 2297/1 Although these [observations] have received practically no attention from 'modern' geomorphologists, they are of considerable importance to the paleogeomorphologist in the exploration for oil and gas. **1975** *Nature* 24 July 279/2 This work has resulted in the elucidation of the geographic extent, stratigraphic succession, facies change, palaeoenvironments and palaeogeomorphological setting of the basin.

palæogeophysical to **-hydrography:** see *PALÆO-, PALEO-.

Palæo-I·ndian, *sb.* and *a.* Also **PalæoIndian, Palæoindian, palæo-Indian,** and with prefix spelt **paleo-.** [f. PALÆO-, PALEO- + INDIAN *a.* and *sb.*] **A.** *sb.* **a.** The culture of the earliest Indian inhabitants of the Americas. **b.** One of these people. **B.** *adj.* Of or pertaining to Palæo-Indians or their culture.

1940 F. H. H. ROBERTS in *Smithsonian Misc. Coll.* C. 51 (*heading*) Developments in the problem of the North American Paleo-Indian. *Ibid.* 77 The morphological significance of the skeletons is considered..in conjunction with the other human remains attributed to the Paleo-Indian inhabitants. *Ibid.* 109 The work of recent years.. demonstrates that there actually was a Paleo-Indian. **1941** *Bull. Geol. Soc. Amer.* LII. 2001 Evidences of the Paleo-Indian of the late Pleistocene or Early Recent times are present in Alaska. **1943** *Acta Americana* I. II. 194 The causes of this rapid and widespread disappearance [of Pleistocene forms of animals] are not known. It has been suggested that the Paleo-Indians may have been a contributing factor. **1959** J. J. HONIGMANN *World of Man* xliii. 791 In Union County, New Mexico, a site containing remains of 32 bison, 19 projectile points, and other artifacts indicates a mass kill by Paleoindians. *Ibid.*, The Paleoindian period yields none of the elaborate portable and mural art characteristic of the Upper Paleolithic in Europe. **1968** R. W. FAIRBRIDGE *Encycl. Geomorphol.* 454/2 The lake [*sc.* Lake Agassiz] influenced the movements of early man (paleo-Indian cultures), and artifacts typical of the period 5000–9000 B.C. are found around its margins. **1972** *Science* 16 June 1211/2 Although the literature on North American PaleoIndians is quite extensive, most of this information has been derived from the analysis of kill sites, and only limited data on Paleo-Indian campsites have been available.

palæointensity to **-longitude:** see *PALÆO-, PALEO-.

palæoma·gnetism. *Geol.* Also (chiefly *U.S.*) **paleo-.** [f. PALÆO-, PALEO- + MAGNETISM.] (The study and interpretation of) the natural magnetism of rocks, which they are believed to have acquired at the time of their formation and is used as evidence for the past relationship of the rocks to each other and to the earth's magnetic field.

1854 *Edin. New Philos. Jrnl.* LVI. 9 The palæomagnetism..will also give rise to most interesting discoveries, and even to magnetical maps in the various geological periods. **1953** T. NAGATA *Rock-Magnetism* vi. 213 Other people might be concerned with rock-magnetism as the medium or the fossil of the geomagnetic field in the past geologic times, namely, as the tool for palaeomagnetism, since the knowledge of the secular variation of geomagnetic field throughout the whole life of the earth is one of the basic subjects in the modern geophysics. **1955** *Nature* 10 Sept. 505/1 (*heading*) Palæomagnetism of sediments from the Colorado Plateau. **1962** *Listener* 17 May 849/1 This new subject of palaeomagnetism enables us to track the movement of the magnetic poles relative to the continents. **1970** *Nature* 6 June 934/1 The motion of these plates with respect to the Earth's spin axis can be determined using the methods of palaeomagnetism. **1971** I. G. GASS et al. *Understanding Earth* xv. 222/2 One may use palaeomagnetism as a tool for verifying continental drift.

Hence **pa:læomagne·tic** *a.*, of or pertaining to palæomagnetism; **pa:læomagne·tically** *adv.*, by means of or as regards palæomagnetism; **palæoma·gnetist,** one who studies palæomagnetism.

1953 T. NAGATA *Rock-Magnetism* vi. 218 It seems that the Königsberger's [*sic*] conclusion quoted above is still substantially right at present and very useful as the criterion of available rock-magnetism for the palaeomagnetic purposes. **1957** *Adv. Physics* VI. 166 Drab deltaic sediments of a cool environment are palaeomagnetically unsuitable. **1960** *Bull. Geol. Soc. Amer.* LXXI. 763/2 The paleomagnetist would like to know if it is at all possible for a nonaxial dipole field to exist for a long period of time. **1969** BENNISON & WRIGHT *Geol. Hist. Brit. Isles* iii. 51 As well as the marked angular unconformity, there is a difference in the palaeomagnetic pole position of about 50° which may indicate that this part of the Lower Torridonian is much older than the upper groups. **1970** *New Scientist* 17 Dec. 491/1 A stern criticism which palaeomagnetists have always had to face..is over the long-term stability of the magnetic minerals within their rock samples. **1973** *Nature* 23 Feb. 497/2 It is not difficult to distinguish palaeomagnetically between polar wandering and continental drift if one or the other acts alone. **1977** A. HALLAM *Planet Earth* 143 Paleomagnetic studies have been vital in establishing the theory of plate tectonics.

palæomeridian to **-meteorology:** see *PALÆO-, PALEO-.

palæoniscoid, *sb.* and *a.* [f. mod.L. name of suborder Palæoniscoidei, f. generic name *Palæoniscus* (L. Agassiz *Recherches sur les Poissons fossiles* (1833) II. v. 41), f. PALÆO- + Gr. ὀνίσκος a sea-fish resembling cod + -OID.] **A.** *sb.* A fossil fish belonging to the suborder Palæoniscoidei, a group that includes elongate fishes with heterocercal tails and diamond-shaped scales. **B.** *adj.* Of or pertaining to a fish of this kind.

1895 B. DEAN *Fishes Living & Fossil* vii. 166 (*caption*) Palaeozoic Palaeoniscoid. **1928** *Palaeobiologica* I. 87 (*heading*) *Polypterus*, a palaeoniscoid? **1963** P. H. GREENWOOD *Norman's Hist. Fishes* (ed. 2) iv. 56 A modified palaeoniscoid scale occurs in the superorder Holostei, another group which is best known from extinct forms. **1968** A. S. ROMER *Procession of Life* viii. 161 A typical palaeoniscoid was a small, well-streamlined little fish, with thick shiny scales, long jaws with a powerful gape, and..a tail in which the fleshy, scale-covered tip of the body extends upward and backward to the tip of the fin. *Ibid.*, Today there survive only two small groups of palaeoniscoid descendants. **1974** D. & M. WEBSTER *Compar. Vertebr. Morphol.* viii. 162 True ganoid scales occurred in the palaeoniscoid fishes.

palæontography. Delete *rare*$^{-0}$ and add: (Examples.) So **palæonto·grapher,** a person engaged in the description of fossil animals and plants.

1924 P. GEDDES in P. Boardman *Worlds of Patrick Geddes* (1978) x. 357 The study of comparative religion too often readily gives an impression..[of] but the latest form of palaeontography and palaeography. **1973** *Nature* 1 June 308/2 The discussions liberally impinge on the cognate sciences of evolutionary palaeontography, biogeochemistry and statistics. *Ibid.* 308/3 It [*sc.* Schopf's *Models in Paleobiology*] should..infuse panic in the hearts of those palaeontographers who have got stuck in a rut.

palæo-oceanography, etc.: see *PALÆO-, PALEO-.

palæopa·llium. *Anat.* Also (chiefly *U.S.*) **paleo-,** and with hyphen. [mod.L., f. *PALÆO-, PALEO- b + *PALLIUM 3 d.] A phylogenetically older portion of the pallium of the brain, which comprises mainly the pyriform lobe (the hippocampal formation or archipallium is sometimes included).

1909 C. V. A. KAPPERS in *Arch. Neurol. & Psychiatry* IV. 161 This nervous substance, in order to distinguish it from the subventricular grey substance, should be called palæo-pallium. **1933** [see *ARCHIPALLIUM]. **1948** A. BRODAL *Neurol. Anat.* x. 324 (*caption*) In amphibians..a dorsal area is found between the hippocampal area (archipallium) and the piriform area (palæo-pallium). **1962** E. C. CROSBY et al. *Correl. Anat. Nerv. Syst.* vii. 411/1 'Paleopallium' is a term applied to the pyriform cortex; that is, to portions at least of the hippocampal gyrus. **1972** T. W. JENKINS *Functional Mammalian Neuroanat.* ii. 35/1 Based on the phylogenetic age, the olfactory cortex at the base of the brain, which is the older cortex is referred to as the archipallium (archicortex), or paleopallium (paleocortex).

Hence **palæopa·llial** *a.*, of or pertaining to the palæopallium.

1936 C. U. A. KAPPERS et al. *Compar. Anat. Nerv. Syst. Vertebr.* II. ix. 1482 In mammals the discharge paths between the archipallial, paleopallial, and archistriatal regions and the diencephalic centers are essentially those which have been described for lower forms. **1962** E. C. CROSBY et al. *Correl. Anat. Nerv. Syst.* vii. 411 The non-olfactory functions of paleopallial and archipallial areas may become dominant in higher mammals.

pa:læopatho·logy. Also (chiefly *U.S.*) **paleo-.** [f. PALÆO-, PALEO- + PATHOLOGY.] (The study of) the pathological conditions found in ancient human and animal remains.

1893 R. W. SHUFELDT in *Pop. Sci. Monthly* XLII. 679 Palæopathology..is a term here proposed under which may be described all diseased or pathological conditions found fossilized in the remains of extinct or fossil animals. **1923** R. L. MOODIE *Antiquity of Disease* iv. 66 Virchow, Mayer, Esper, Schmerling, and the other founders of paleopathology did their initial observations on the diseased bones of cave bears of Europe. **1952** *Bull. Hist. Med.* XXVI. 538 (*heading*) Evidence on the paleopathology of yaws. **1967** *Science* 11 Aug. 638/3 Since not only skeletal material but disease itself is the subject matter of paleopathology, many disciplines find a meeting ground in these studies. **1975** *Palestine Exploration Q.* CVII. 89 Excavated the cemeteries of four medieval leper hospitals in Denmark... Palaeopathology was, in this instance, able to contribute to clinical medicine.

Hence **pa:læopatholo·gic, -lo·gical** *adjs.*; **pa:læopatho·logist,** one who investigates or studies palæopathology.

1917 *Johns Hopkins Hosp. Bull.* XXVIII. 261/1 Another American investigator, Dr. Aleš Hrdlička, has developed intensively the palæopathological side in his numerous explorations and studies of the aborigines on this continent. *Ibid.*, A very remarkable exhibition of palæopathologic specimens in San Diego. **1939** *Brit. Jrnl. Tuberculosis* XXXIII. 148 Egypt has provided the anatomist and the anthropologist, no less than the archæologist and the palæopathologist, with unrivalled opportunities and an unprecedented wealth of material for the prosecution of their respective researches. **1966** O. TEMKIN in S. Jarcho *Human Palaeopath.* 34 Material from Ancient Egypt looms very large in the discussions of palaeopathologists. **1966** W. G. J. PUTSCHAR in *Ibid.* 60 In palaeopathological material we have only the mineralized portion of the affected bone available. **1967** *Amer. Jrnl. Roentgenology* XCIX. 712 The Mochica-Chinú civilizations developed in the coastal deserts of northern Perú and the dry desiccating sands of these areas have preserved large quantities of their skeletal remains in a remarkably good state for paleopathologic study. **1975** *Palestine Exploration Q.* CVII. 88 To rule out the possibility that they were the disease now known as leprosy..; an opinion supported by the palaeopathological evidence given below.

palæopedological to **-salinity:** see *PALÆO-, PALEO-.

Palæo-Sibe·rian, *sb.* and *a.* Also **palæo-Siberian, Palæosiberian,** and with the prefix spelt **paleo-.** [f. PALÆO-, PALEO- + SIBERIAN *a.* and *sb.*] **A.** *sb.* **a.** A member of any of several peoples of northern and eastern Siberia who are held to represent the earliest inhabitants of Siberia and whose languages do not belong to any of the major families. **b.** The Palæo-Siberian group of languages.

1914 M. A. CZAPLICKA *Aboriginal Siberia* ii. 15 If we are to provide a name for these unclassified tribes of the extreme north and east of Asia,..we would propose the name 'Palaeo-Siberians'... It implies a comparison and a contrast with the other tribes—Finnic, Mongolic, Turkic, Samoyedic, and Tungusic—who are comparatively recent comers to Siberia. **1965** *Language* XLI. 122 Soviet research in the rather exotic field of Paleosiberian. **1970** *Atlantic Monthly* Feb. 111 The Paleosiberians and a small Mongol enclave in Afghanistan..use these two methods of taking Soma. **1975** *Language* LI. 482 He suggests that the correspondence of certain Proto-Uralic items to those of other language families (e.g., Indo-European, Indo-Iranian, Turkic, Paleo-Siberian, and Eskimo) is due to an ancient areal affinity, not to linguistic relationship.

B. *adj.* Of, pertaining to, or designating Palæo-Siberians.

1923 R. B. DIXON *Racial Hist. Man* III. v. 334 The conclusion cannot be escaped that a relationship of some sort exists between these Palæo-Siberian peoples of Asia and the Indian tribes of the northwest coast of America. **1948** D. DIRINGER *Alphabet* 156 The aboriginal or Palaeo-Siberian group..are mainly nomad reindeer breeders and hunters. **1961** L. F. BROSNAHAN *Sounds of Language* viii. 177 The area of the simple stress accent is much larger: it extends..from the west and south of Europe and includes ..the..Mongolian, Tungus and Paleosiberian languages of eastern Asia. **1964** tr. *Levin & Potapov's Peoples of Siberia* 56 The characteristics..show an ancient paleo-Siberian race, features of which are observed in other Siberian tribes.

palæoslope to **-species:** see *PALÆO-, PALEO-.

pa:læostriatum (-strəi,ēi·tə̆m). *Anat.* Also (chiefly *U.S.*) **paleo-.** [mod.L (coined in Ger. by C. U. A. Kappers 1908, in *Anat. Anzeiger* XXXIII. 322), f. *PALÆO-, PALEO- b + *STRIATUM.] The phylogenetically older portion of the corpus striatum, consisting essentially of the globus pallidus. Hence **pa:læostria·tal** *a.*

1913 *Brain* XXXVI. 159 In analogy with the archistriatal commissure which connects the nuclei amygdalæ, and a possible commissure between the palæostriata in Meynert's commissure, such a connexion of the phylogenetically most recent parts of the striatum would not be improbable. **1921** TILNEY & RILEY *Form & Functions*

Cent. Nervous Syst. xliv. 805 In its process of evolution from the lower vertebrates to mammals, the primordial portion of the striate body corresponds to the globus pallidus. This structure may, therefore, be tentatively distinguished as the paleostriatum. *Ibid.* xlv. 819 This is known as the syndrome of the globus pallidus, juvenile paralysis agitans or the paleo-striatal syndrome of Ramsay Hunt. **1929** [see *NEOSTRIATUM]. **1936** C. U. A. KAPPERS et al. *Compar. Anat. Nervous Syst. Vertebr.* II. ix. 1369 The paleostriatal and neostriatal areas of birds and their reptilean equivalents are basal in origin. **1972** [see *NEOSTRIATUM].

palæostructural to **-temperature:** see *PALÆO-, PALEO-.

palæotha·lamus. *Anat.* Also (chiefly *U.S.*) paleo-. [mod.L., f. *PALÆO-, PALEO- b + THALAMUS.] The phylogenetically older portion of the thalamus, usu. taken to include its anterior and medial parts.

1920 S. W. RANSON *Anat. Nervous Syst.* 391/1 (Index), Palæothalamus. See *Thalamus, old.* **1921** TILNEY & RILEY *Form & Functions Cent. Nervous Syst.* xxxi. 560 The primitive pars thalamica is known as the paleothalamus. **1958** L. HAUSMAN *Clin. Neuroanat.* xxvii. 242 Phylogenetically, the hypothalamus, the epithalamus and part of the medial division of the dorsal thalamus constitute the old thalamus or paleothalamus. **1973** [see *NEOTHALAMUS].

palæothermometry to **-zoogeography:** see *PALÆO, PALEO-.

palæozoology. Add: (Further examples.)

1889 H. A. NICHOLSON in Nicholson & Lydekker *Man. Palæont.* (ed. 3) I. i. 3 Palæozoology and Palæobotany are inseparably connected with Neozoology and Neobotany. **1935** TWENHOFEL & SHROCK *Invertebr. Paleontol.* i. 1 Paleontology..may be divided into paleobotany, treating of fossil plants, and paleozoology, treating of fossil animals. **1953** E. S. BARGHOORN in H. Shapley *Climatic Change* xx. 238 Ecologic interpretation..will always require confirming evidence from the physical geology and paleozoölogy. **1978** D. BLOODWORTH *Crosstalk* iv. 38 A common interest in paleozoology.

palæozoological (earlier and later examples); hence also **pa:læozoo·logist**, a student of extinct or fossil animals.

1866 *Phil. Trans. R. Soc.* CLVI. 672 A complete Monograph of the structure and life-history of that organism [sc. *Pentacrinus*] would be one of the most valuable contributions which Palæo-zoological science could receive. **1909** WEBSTER, Paleozoölogist. **1947** *Jrnl. Paleontol.* XXI. 574/1 This seems to be the favored path of some paleontologists (or should I call them paleozoologists?). **1957** *Antiquity* XXXI. 78 The field research necessary for a meaningful paleoclimatological, paleobotanical, and paleozoological history of post-glacial south-western Asia is only beginning. **1972** D. BLOODWORTH *Any Number can Play* x. 81 Max..was a paleozoologist..doing some work on prehistoric monkeys.

Palaic (pălēⁱ·ik), *sb.* and *a.* [f. *Pala*, appar. a district of Asia Minor + -IC.] **A.** *sb.* The name of an Anatolian language, known from the Hittite archives. **B.** *adj.* Of or pertaining to this language.

1928 C. DAWSON *Age of Gods* xiii. 302 The Hittite archives also refer to three other tongues, Luvian, Palaic, and Harrian or Churrite. **1951** STURTEVANT & HAHN *Compar. Gram. Hittite Lang.* (ed. 2) I. i. 5 In the ritual of the deity Ziparwas certain passages are to be spoken *Pala-um-ni-li* 'in Palaic'. **1966** BIRNBAUM & PUHVEL *Anc. Indo-Europ. Dial.* 237 Watkins has..built a very ingenious hypothesis..on the brittle back of the Palaic hapax *malitanna. Ibid.* 243 Among verb stems, Luwian, Hieroglyphic, and Lycian *-s(s)-* contrasts with the Hittite and Palaic 'iterative' *-sk-*. **1972** W. B. LOCKWOOD *Panorama Indo-European Lang.* 263 Palaic was spoken in an area to the north of Hattusa, say in the province later known as Paphlagonia. It occurs solely in interpolations in the Hittite text in connection with the cult of the god Ziparwa. **1973** *Trans. Philol. Soc. 1971* 159 The Palaic particle, unlike the Lycian one, is connective and adversative. **1974** *Encycl. Brit. Macropædia* I. 834/1 An interrogative or relative pronoun *kui-* (compare Latin *quis*) is common to Hittite, Palaic, and Cuneiform Luwian.

palais de danse (pæle də daṅs). [Fr.] A public hall for dancing. Also *attrib.*, *fig.*, and *ellipt.* as **palais.**

1919 *Honey Pot* I. 14 The new Palais de Danse, which is to be opened on September 1st, is situated in Brook Green Road, two minutes walk from Hammersmith. **1926** *Punch* 13 Oct. 416/3 The young man you choose [as a dancing partner] out of a pen at sixpence a time at the Palais de Danse. **1928** *Melody Maker* Nov. 1193/3 Its rhythm had all the faults and few of the good points of the heavy 'Palais' style. **1940** HARRISSON & MADGE *War begins at Home* 225 The manager of a large suburban palais. **1946** J. AGATE *Contemporary Theatre 1944–5* 73 Yes, but have they [sc. Delibes, Offenbach, and Johann Strauss] the lush, treacly, palais-de-danse Orientalism dear to the British heart? **1958** *New Statesman* 25 Jan. 102/3 The good old-fashioned pit and palais muscians. **1964** W. G. RAFFÉ *Dict. Dance* 368/2 The Palais is an accepted town centre, replacing the mediaeval marriage-market, or the Victorian Assembly Rooms, as a place where eligible young people can meet matrimonial partners. **1966** *Listener* 19 May 711/2 A Tashkent spinning and weaving mill..had its own..palace of culture (depreciated term—shades of the Palais de Danse!) with singing, dancing, and dramatic activities. **1972** P. BLACK *Biggest Aspidistra* I. iii. 30 He [sc. Jack Payne] broke up his..group to take a job as pianist with a band at the Birmingham Palais (the huge public-hall fashion of dancing was spreading outward from London). **1975** R. BUTLER *Where all Girls are Sweeter* iv. 36 While others studied at night we headed for the nearest Palais de Danse. **1976** *Times* 7 Aug. 2/5 Mrs Stonehouse, who has been married for 27 years, met her husband at the Hammersmith Palais when he was in the RAF. **1978** *Radio Times* 28 Jan. 69/4 Britain is renowned for its dance-skaters and has the strongest tradition of *palais de danse* in the world.

‖ **Palais de Justice** (pale̜ də ʒüstis). [Fr., lit. 'palace of justice'.] In France (occas. elsewhere): a law court.

1792 T. BLAIKIE *Diary Scotch Gardener* (1931) 235, I told him..that I was here with a gang of theeves who had robbed my house..and the others and I [were] taken to the Palais de Justice. **1885** H. JAMES *Little Tour in France* xii. 92 His [sc. Jacques Cœur's] house..to-day is used as a Palais de Justice. **1962** N. FREELING *Love in Amsterdam* III. 133 At the Palais de Justice they made.. an impressive entrance. **1974** —— *Dressing of Diamond* 187 Like all public buildings in France, the Palais de Justice is ruled entirely by the concierge. **1978** W. GARNER *Möbius Trip* iii. 65 They drove back to the Palais de Justice, crossed the chill courtyard.

palais glide (pæ·le gləid). [f. *PALAIS (DE DANSE) + *GLIDE *sb.* 1 c.] A type of ballroom dance in which large groups dance together.

1938 A. MOORE *Ballroom Dancing* (ed. 2) VII. 251 The Palais Glide can hardly be termed a dance; it is reminiscent of the Gallop which has been a feature of Hunt Balls for many years... It can be danced to any Foxtrot tune.. and it is played at a tempo of about 30 bars a minute. **1939** *Britannica Bk. of Year* 196/2 Another instance of the desire to add more festiveness to British ballrooms has been the occasional introduction, at all kinds of dances, of the old 'Palais Glide'... This is even more of a romp than the 'Lambeth Walk'. **1969** *Listener* 8 May 640/1 The tune stayed alive in dance-halls where, during the 1930s, it could be used for the 'Palais Glide'. **1970** *Guardian* 24 Dec. 9/3 The girls..engaged in a perpetual Palais Glide, regardless of rhythm. **1974** R. INGHAM *Yoris* xvii. 54 Do you remember the Palais Glide?..Lovely dance.

‖ **Palais Royal** (pale̜ rwayal). The name of a Parisian theatre used *attrib.* to designate a type of indelicate farce said to be typical of this theatre.

1877 *Illustr. Sporting & Dramatic News* 21 Apr. 109/1 In my remarks about *Pink Dominos*..I alluded to the inevitable comparison that must be made between that piece and the other Palais Royal adaptations. *Ibid.* 20 Oct. 109/2, I consider the libretti of three-fourths of the French opéras-bouffes which have been translated..into English, practically and palpably cynical, and they are indecent withal. I may say the same of some Palais Royal pieces, mightily popular amongst us. **1951** N. MITFORD *Blessing* II. v. 195 What a curious thing—intrigues and misunderstandings, just like a Palais Royal farce. **1967** *Oxf. Compan. Theatre* (ed. 3) 715/1 In England the term 'Palais-Royal farce' was applied to the broad suggestiveness of such productions as *The Pink Dominos* (1877) and *The Girl from Maxim's* (1902).

palamino, var. *PALOMINO.

Palamite (pæ·lămait), *sb.* and *a.* *Eccl. Hist.* [f. the name of St. Gregory *Palamas*, an intellectual leader of the Hesychasts + -ITE¹.] **A.** *sb.* = HESYCHAST. **B.** *adj.* Of or pertaining to the Palamites or their doctrines; = HESYCHASTIC *a.* 2.

1859 *Encycl. Brit.* XVII. 177/1 At the councils which were severally held in 1341 and 1351 he [sc. Gregorius Palamas] pled the cause of his party, and so identified himself with the tenets he advocated that his fellow-sectarians were thenceforth called *Palamites.* **1877** MCCLINTOCK & STRONG *Cycl. Bibl. Lit.* VII. 547/2 The peculiar leading tenets of the Palamites were the existence of the mystical light discovered by the more eminent monks and recluses in their long exercises of abstract contemplation and prayer, and the uncreated nature of the light of Mount Tabor seen at the transfiguration of Christ. *Ibid.* 548/1 These alleged heresies were, however, mostly..the inferences deduced by Nicephorus Gregoras and other opponents from the Palamite dogma of uncreated light, and not the acknowledged tenets of the Palamite party. **1900** 'ODYSSEUS' *Turkey in Europe* vi. 252 The quarrel between the Palamites and Barlaamites, after distracting the Eastern Church, was at last settled by a Synod in a sense favourable to the former. **1949** E. L. MASCALL *Existence & Analogy* vi. 151 For the Thomist, supernatural grace means a communication of God himself to the creature... For the Palamite, it means a communication of the uncreated energy of God though not of his uncommunicable essence. **1957** *Oxf. Dict. Chr. Ch.* 633/2 In the second half of the 14th cent. Hesychasm was accepted throughout the Greek Church, its adherents being also generally known as 'Palamites'. **1961** *Times* 24 Nov. 14/4 Moghila did not admit the Palamite doctrine of energies. **1971** *Catholic Dict. Theol.* III. 15/1 This controversy, also known as the Palamite controversy.., was concerned not so much with the spiritual doctrine of the Hesychasts as with its ultimate theological and metaphysical justification.

‖ **palang** (pala·ŋ). *Borneo* and *Philippines.* [Native name.] (See quot. 1974.)

1959 T. HARRISSON *World Within* I. 59 The rapid spread of the *palang*, a cross-piece driven through the male penis, has shown that behind the easy acceptance of many upland women there is a readiness to react in a more elaborate and erotic manner. **1964** *Jrnl. Malaysian Branch R. Asiatic Soc.* XXXVII. 163, I have here chosen the term *palang* as the most widespread of the indigenous Bornean terms (cf. *utang*, etc.) and also the one known over parts of the outside world. *Ibid.* 164 It is safest to take the people nowadays called Kayans and some of the Kenyahs closely associated with them as the main west Borneo *palang* users in proto-historical times. **1974** S. E. MORISON *European Discovery of America: Southern Voyages* xvii. 422 The gentle Limasawans, says Pigafetta, went about nearly naked... Here, and at Cebu, he describes a sexual practice known as *palang*. 'The males, large and small, have their penis pierced from one side to the other near the head, with a gold or tin bolt as large as a goose quill. In each end of the bolt some have what resembles a star, with points; others are like the head of a cast nail... In the middle of the bolt is a hole, through which they urinate'. *Ibid.* 435 Although certain writers..have either omitted this story or called it one of Pigafetta's tall tales, *palang* did exist. It persists to this day in Borneo and parts of the Philippines.

† **palanthropic** (pælænþrǫ·pik), *a.* *Obs. rare.* [Irreg. f. PALÆO-, PALEO- + ANTHROPIC *a.*] = *PALÆANTHROPIC *a.*

1894 [see *NEANTHROPIC *a.*].

Palantype (pæ·lăntəip). [f. the name *Palan(que* (see quot. 1940) + TYPE *sb.*¹] The proprietary name of a machine for typing in shorthand; also, the system of shorthand used. Hence **pa·lantypist.**

1940 *Trade Marks Jrnl.* 14 Aug. 782/1 Palantype... Typewriters and parts thereof, typewriter inks, typewriter ribbons, typewriting paper, and stands for typewriters (not being furniture). Clementine Camille Marie Palanque, ..London,..manufacturer. **1959** *Times* 9 Apr. 3/1 Palantype operator..required by Uganda Government. **1959** *Economist* 23 May 745/2 The institute's courses range from the training of district officers to that of clerks, typists and palantypists. **1964** *Financial Times* 25 Feb. 6/7 The small nucleus of reporting palantypists, the ladies who translate scientific jargon into shorthand hieroglyphs on a small, silent, rubber keyboard—later to convert it back. **1970** *Nature* 12 Sept. 1090/2 Several major hurdles still have to be overcome to transpose the twenty-nine symbols of palantype, the British form of mechanical shorthand, into proper English.

‖ **palari** (pălā·ri). [Malay.] A type of boat (see quot. 1948).

1936 *Times Lit. Suppl.* 7 Nov. 899/3 He wanted a chance of seeing a *palari* working to windward in bad conditions. **1937** G. E. P. COLLINS *Makassar Sailing* 12 During the second stage, which turns a pajala into a palari, the sides are raised and a deck and high stern added. **1948** R. DE KERCHOVE *Internat. Maritime Dict.* 516/1 *Palari*, an East Indian trading boat from southern Celebes and eastern Madura... It is rigged with one or two masts. 2. In Macassar the term 'palari' refers to a fast-sailing pleasure craft with two masts and an elaborately carved stern. **1950** *Jrnl. Malayan Branch R. Asiatic Soc.* XXIII. 112 The Palari is now characterised by the possession of a double-ended hull with a heavy, tripartite bowsprit and a high, overhanging stern. **1964** K. G. TREGONNING *Hist. Mod. Malaya* 59 The Bugis copied their craft from the Portuguese, and the *pajala* was adapted into the famous *palari*, which..is..like a miniature seventeenth century fore and aft rigged galleon.

palarie (pălā·ri), *v.* *Tramps'* and *Circus slang.* Also **palari.** [ad. It. *parlare.*] *trans.* and *intr.* To talk, to speak. Cf. *PARLYAREE.

1846 *Swell's Night Guide* 77 The chanting cadger stalls the chummy's daughter off to a single padded lumber; ranks her of five bob and a bender;..palaries sweat patter, and nobbs on for more blunt. **1893** P. H. EMERSON *Signor Lippo* xx. 91 She looked for all the world like a gippo, and she knew all the cant, and used to palarie thick to the slaveys. **1933** E. SEAGO *Circus Company* iii. 29 A subject not meant for a 'gajo's' ears, to be checked immediately... 'Nante palari before the josher cul.'

palatal, *a.* and *sb.* Add: **A.** *adj.* **2.** (Earlier example.)

1728 CHAMBERS *Cycl.* s.v. T., The *T* is one of the five Consonants which the Abbot de Dangeau calls *Palatal.*

b. Of a sound change: occurring in the environment of a palatal consonant or vowel.

1888 H. SWEET *Hist. Eng. Sounds* 124 This *c*-smoothing is by the Germans called 'palatal-umlaut'. **1894** —— *Anglo-Saxon Reader* (ed. 7) p. xiv, Why then continue.. to call the change of *weorc* into *werc* 'palatal mutation', when the change is not a mutation, and is caused not by front, but invariably by back consonants? **1908** J. & E. M. WRIGHT *Old Eng. Gram.* iv. 28 Umlaut is of two kinds: Palatal and Guttural. Palatal umlaut, generally called *i*-umlaut, is the modification (palatalization) of an accented vowel through the influence of an *ĭ* or *j* which originally stood in the following syllable. **1914** H. C. WYLD *Short Hist. Eng.*, v. 75 'Palatal Mutation'. This term was suggested by Bülbring to denote primarily the loss in Anglian of the second element of the diphthong *ea* (which thus appears merely as *e*) before the consonant-groups *ht, hs, hþ*, when followed by a front vowel, or when final. **1939** *Trans. Philol. Soc.* 126 By the assumption that 'Breaking', 'Palatal Diphthongization', and 'Back-Mutation' were developments which can be dated within limits, a system of 'sound-changes' has been built up, which in some cases may be purely fictitious, in others only part of a long-drawn-out process. **1959** A. CAMPBELL *Old Eng. Gram.* v. 70 *Sċip* sheep, presumably from **sċēp* with palatal diphthongization of nW-S *sċēp.* **1975** LASS & ANDERSON *Old Eng. Phonol.* iv. 123 'Palatal diphthongization' of *ē̆*. As we show..there is no very good evidence for such a process in OE.

Hence **pa·latally** *adv.*, towards the palate; by means of the palate.

1934 *Dental Items of Interest* LVI. 206 Any extension of the preparation under the gingiva..palatally is to be avoided as being unnecessary. **1940** J. OSBORNE *Dental Mech.* xiv. 156 The use of black rubber palatally and lingually will give a better appearance to the finished denture. **1963** C. R. COWELL et al. *Inlays, Crowns, & Bridges* iv. 39 The withdrawal path must be inclined palatally. **1970** *Archivum Linguisticum* I. 7 When the following syllable contained an *i* the medial vowel could be palatally coloured.

palatalize, *v.* Add: Also *intr.*, to become palatal, to undergo palatalization.

1943 E. A. NIDA *Handbk. Descriptive Linguistics* II. v. 83 This may be the result of an original *e* which did palatalize but later this *e* changed to *a* and the palatalization remained. **1964** *Language* XL. 28 Cunter does not palatalize before unstressed /a/.., and..Trun does not palatalize before any allophone of /a/. **1973** J. M. ANDERSON *Struct. Aspects Lang. Change* 154 The frontal allophone of /g/ appears to have palatalized first.

palate, *v.* **2.** (Later example.)

1845 [see *BLANC 2].

Palatinate, *sb.* **1. c.** In small-type note, delete 'higher up the Rhine'.

palato-. Add: **palato-alveolar** *a.* (*Phonetics*) (see quots. 1932 and 1962); **palato-velar** (*Phonetics*) *a.*, articulated with the tongue in contact with the palate and velum simultaneously or successively; also either palatal or velar.

1932 D. JONES *Outl. Eng. Phonetics* (ed. 3) ix. 45 *Palato-alveolar*, articulated by the blade of the tongue against the teeth-ridge with raising of the main body of the tongue towards the palate. **1962** B. M. H. STRANG *Mod. Eng. Struct.* iii. 30 *Palato-alveolar* (tongue tip to palatal edge of alveolar ridge). **1964** R. H. ROBINS *Gen. Linguistics* iii. 101 Palato-alveolar fricatives. **1973** J. C. WELLS *Jamaican Pronunc. in London* i. 10 An unexpectedly large number of confusions between post-alveolar and palato-alveolar affricates turned up. **1895** P. GILES *Short Man. Compar. Philol.* II. viii. 113 Osthoff argues that there were originally three series of guttural consonants [in Indo-Germanic], making the velars which are not followed by *u̯* the third intermediate or 'palato-velar' series. **1902** E. W. SCRIPTURE *Elem. Exper. Phonetics* xxix. 443, 3d Series (middle and back of tongue).. k^2, g^2 palato-velar. **1935** W. F. TWADDELL *On defining Phoneme* v. 48 The 'p-phoneme' is therefore the sum of *all* those phonological differentiae which correspond to a bilabial articulation as opposed to alveolar or palato-velar, [etc.]. **1964** R. A. HALL *Introd. Linguistics* I. xvi. 96 In the case of French, we can, on the grounds of complementary distribution, bring bilabial and labio-dental together under 'labial' position; palatal and velar together under 'palato-velar'; and fricative and sibilant together under 'spirant' manner.

palatogram (pæ·lătogræm). *Phonetics.* [f. PALATO- + -GRAM.] A diagram produced by palatography.

1902 E. W. SCRIPTURE *Elem. Exper. Phonetics* xxi. 296 The diagram recording the contact of the tongue with the palate is called a 'palatogram'. *Ibid.* 298 The points at which the tongue touches the palate..in forming sounds can be registered by a mixture of meal and mucilage or by carmine water color or Chinese ink spread over the previously dried tongue. The sound is spoken naturally; the mouth is at once opened and the marks on the palate are observed... The results obtained are called 'palatograms'. **1917** *Nature* 4 Oct. 96/2 Palatograms will be found to corroborate observations of tongue-positions made by other methods. **1932** D. JONES *Outl. Eng. Phonetics* (ed. 3) xxi. 171 Fig. 97 is a palatogram of the sound *s*, as pronounced by me. **1948** J. R. FIRTH in *Bull. Sch. Orient. & Afr. Stud.* XII. IV. 859 Palatograms are not much use for any velar articulation, but throw light on many articulations forward of the soft palate. **1957** [see **linguistic analysis*].

palatography (pælătǫ·græfi). *Phonetics.* [f. PALATO- + -GRAPHY.] A technique of recording the position of the tongue during articulation from its contact with the hard palate. Hence **palatogra·phic** *a.*

1902 E. W. SCRIPTURE *Elem. Exper. Phonetics* xxi. 296 (*heading*) Tongue Contacts; Methods of Palatography; American, Irish and Hungarian Records. **1908** H. SWEET *Sounds of English* 108 There are other methods whose results are obtained only indirectly, such as the palatographic, by which 'palatograms' are made. **1917** *Nature* 4 Oct. 96/1 Palatography..consists in using a special kind of artificial palate, in order to find out what parts of the roof of the mouth are touched by the tongue in the production of different speech sounds. **1935** *Amer. Speech* X. 230/1 Extensive palatographic and kymographic study. **1940** *Ibid.* XV. 102/1 Palatography cannot be used extensively in the correction of foreign brogue and speech defects. **1948** J. R. FIRTH in *Bull. Sch. Orient. & Afr. Stud.* XII. IV. 863 The possibility of a large proportion of palatographic abstractions in any given language. **1957** D. ABERCROMBIE in *Zeitschr. für Phonetik* X. 21, I use the expression '*direct* palatography' to mean the investigation of articulatory movements by means of marks made directly on the roof of the mouth as distinct from the more usual technique which employs an artificial palate. **1960** P. STREVENS in *Lang. & Speech* III. 34 Palatographic studies..show that there are often large variations of the shape of the orifice.., within the speech of a single individual as well as between different speakers. **1970** *Times Lit. Suppl.* 23 July 817/1 The motion of the tongue in speech can be studied by 'dynamic palatography'. **1976** *Language* LII. 508 No mention is made of palatography as an observational technique.

‖**palatschinken** (pælătʃi·ŋkən), *pl.* [Austrian Ger. dial., f. Hungarian *palacsinta*, f. Rum. *plăcintă*, f. L. *placenta* a cake.] An Austrian dish of stuffed pancakes.

1929 K. BAEDEKER *Austria* p. xxvii, Farinaceous dishes. *Strudel*,..*Palatschinken*, pancakes [etc.]. **1941** 'R. WEST' *Black Lamb* (1942) I. 144 For the sweet course we were given two apiece of palatschinken, those pancakes stuffed with jam which one eats all over Central Europe. The Balkans inherited the recipe from the Byzantines, who ate them under the name of palacountas. **1952** I. RHODE *Viennese Cookery Bk.* v. 67 The pancakes in this chapter..are strictly Viennese—thin *Palatschinken* and the thick *Schmarren*... Although the name *Palatschinken* is a corruption of the Hungarian *Palacsinta*, these pancakes are more French in origin. **1963** R. CARRIER *Great Dishes of World* xv. 270 Just before serving, dust *palatschinken* with icing sugar. **1971** LYON & BENTON *Eggs, Milk & Cheese* 171 *Palatschinken with Chicken.* This is an Austrian form of pancake which can be used with different kinds of flavouring and stuffing.

Palaung (pălɑu·ŋ), *sb.* and *a.* Also 9 **Paloung, Poloung.** [Native name.] **A.** *sb.* **a.** A people of the Shan States of Burma; a member of any of the various tribes constituting this people. **b.** The Mon-Khmer language of this people. **B.** *adj.* Of or pertaining to this people or their language. Hence **Palau·ngic** *a.*

1860 F. MASON *Burmah* iii. 69 The Paloungs..are a Shan tribe found north and east of Bamoo. **1885** A. R. COLQUHOUN *Amongst Shans* v. 72 The Paloungs, or Poloungs, are darker and smaller than the Shans. *Ibid.* 75 The slopes of the hills to the west of Thai-nee are cultivated by the Paloungs. **1923** H. T. WHITE *Burma* xiii. 136 Palaungs, timid, peaceable folk, to the number of 144,000, are found principally in the Northern Shan States. *Ibid.* 140 The Austro-Asiatic family is represented by Môn-Hkmer [*sic*] languages, of which the most noticeable are Talaing..and Palaung. **1934** 'G. ORWELL' *Burmese Days* xi. 165 The Palaungs..admire long necks in women. **1942** J. L. CHRISTIAN *Mod. Burma* ii. 15 The Wa and Palaung tribal groups of the Shan hills belong to the Mon Khmer family. **1948** A. KROEBER *Anthropol.* (rev. ed.) x. 424 Asia is particularly rich in tribal societies with 'internally marginal' cultures. Examples are:.. Palaung, [etc.]. **1957** *Encycl. Brit.* XVII. 114/2 The Palaung is darker than the Shan in complexion. **1971** N. BIXLER *Burma* vi. 133 The Palaung, who live less than 3,000 feet above sea level and cannot grow opium, have within this century begun to specialize quite successfully in raising tea. **1974** *Encycl. Brit. Micropædia* VII. 688/2 *Palaungic languages*, branch of the Austroasiatic language family, including..Palaung, [etc.]. **1978** *Language* LIV. 206 The Mon-Khmer languages Palaung, Riang-Lang, and Praok.

palaver, *sb.* Add: Also † **palaber, palava.**

1. Also *fig.*

1951 DYLAN THOMAS in *World Rev.* Oct. 66 In his house on stilts high among beaks And palavers of birds.

2. b. (Earlier example.)

1744 A. HAMILTON *Itinerarium* (1948) 160 The pedlar.. sold some dear bargains to Mrs. Williams, and while he smoothed her up with palaber, the Bostoner amused her with religious cant.

† **c.** In West Africa: a dispute or contest. *Obs.*

c **1740** F. MOORE *Trav. Inland Afr.* (ed. 2) 221 They.. call a Dispute *a Palaver.* **1744** W. SMITH *New Voy. to Guinea* 32 The English..once had a Settlement upon Charles Island, but having a Pallaver with the Natives they..waded over from the Main; by which Surprize they got Possession, and beat the English off that Island. **1789** *Rep. Lords Comm. Council: Evidence* I. 5 in *Parl. Papers 1731–1800* (Brit. Libr.) LXXXIV, If any Dispute or *Palavers* arose between Two or more Persons, they called a Council of the head Men, where the Persons were tried.

d. Business, concern. *slang* and *African colloq.*

1899 C. J. C. HYNE *Further Adventures Capt. Kettle* 21 It's not your palaver..or mine. **1953** *Eng. Stud.* XXXIV. 286 [West Africa] That's your palaver.

e. Jargon. ?*U.S.* (*rare*).

1909 'MARK TWAIN' *Is Shakes. Dead?* vii. 74, I have been a quartz miner..and know all the palaver of that business.

f. In Africa: trouble.

1953 P. CHRISTOPHERSEN in *Eng. Stud.* XXXIV. 286 *Palaver*..is now part of Standard English in the sense of 'talk' or 'parley'. But in West Africa this meaning is obsolete. In Pidgin and very largely in Coast English the word has come to mean 'business' or 'trouble' (e.g... 'That has caused a lot of palaver' and 'He had some tummy palaver last week'). **1954** [see *D.O.* s.v. *D III. 3]. **1970** *Drum* (E. Afr. ed.) Feb. 39/2, I am a boy of 21 and I am still unemployed. I want a girl friend, someone to pet me. But I feel I should get a job before getting involved with woman palava.

palaver, *v.* Add: **3.** *intr.* const. *to*: to ask (someone) for something, to beg from. *slang.* ?*Obs.*

1858 A. MAYHEW *Paved with Gold* III. i. 255, I thought he was a 'queer gill' (suspicious) at first, and smoked us, from what he palavered to Phil when he gave him his 'deux-wins' (twopence). **1859** HOTTEN *Dict. Slang* 71 'Palaver to the nibs for a shant of bivvy,' ask the master for a quart of beer.

palazzo (păla·tso). [It.: see PALACE *sb.*¹] **1.** Pl. **palazzi.** A palatial mansion; a large and imposing building.

a **1666** EVELYN *Diary* an. 1644 (1955) II. 228 The Palazzo Barberini..I take to be as..princely an object, as any moderne building in Europ. **1758** M. W. MONTAGU *Let.* May (1967) III. 149 He brags..that you found the Palazzo very clean. **1892** W. JAMES *Let.* 28 Dec. (1920) I. 335 You seem to me something ideal, off there in your inaccessible Cambridge palazzo. **1924** M. ARLEN *Green Hat* v. 143 In drawing-rooms, up and down terraces of palazzos, in clubs and cabarets. **1930** E. POUND *XXX Cantos* xvii. 77 On past the palazzi. **1958** *Oxf. Mag.* 13 Mar. 357/2 What activities it [*sc.* the Institute of Statistics] wishes to pursue in the great *palazzo* which it now demands. **1962** A. SAMPSON *Anat. Brit.* v. 66 The taxis and government Humbers draw up outside the palazzi of Pall Mall, and bowlers and umbrellas disappear through the great stone doorways, acknowledged by reverent porters. **1968** 'E. LATHEN' *Stitch in Time* i. 1 The..Sloan Guaranty Trust, an opulent palazzo of glass, marble and brass that had replaced the stately and venerable edifice on Pearl Street. **1978** W. M. SPACKMAN *Armful of Warm Girl* 12 But now anyhow in her 73rd Street palazzo her phone rang.

2. Usu. as pl. **palazzos.** Loose, wide-legged trousers worn by women.

1972 *New Yorker* 9 Sept. 8/1 (Advt.), Our haltered palazzos come in champagne beige... The no-waistband, back-zip palazzos. **1973** *Harper's Bazaar* Apr. 5 (Advt.), Lollipops loll on a plunging palazzo... Shirring and sashing halt the halter above billowing pyjamas. **1973** *Telegraph* (Brisbane) 6 Sept. 18/2 Female employees..now are being permitted to wear the pants—in the form of trim pants suits, or, we guess, baggies—or palazzos, if they please.

3. *attrib.* and *Comb.*, as (sense 2) *palazzo outfit, pants, pyjamas, shape, suit, trouser*; **palazzo sleeve,** a wide, flowing sleeve.

1973 *Today's Health* Oct. 36/1 Linda stopped at the dry cleaners to pick up the flowered silk pallazzo [*sic*] outfit she planned to wear to the theater on Saturday. **1972** *New Yorker* 7 Oct. 18/1 (Advt.), Velvety fleece palazzo pants. **1973** *Woman's Day* Sept. 168/1 (Advt.), Choose from smashing palazzo pants and clothes with the bare look. **1966** *Listener* 3 Feb. 171/2 The mannequins start with a natural advantage over most other mortals. Who but they could wear palazzo pyjamas..made entirely of ostrich feathers. **1968** *N.Y. Times* 30 Apr. 52 All these varieties continued into the nineteen-sixties, when they were joined by such other forms as palazzo pajamas (wide enough to sweep around a palace in), culottes, pants dresses and pants suits. **1976** *Times* 1 Sept. (Fashion Suppl.) p. viii/5 Emilio Pucci..introduced..the famous palazzo pyjamas. **1973** *New Yorker* 17 Mar. 56 (Advt.), We like the palazzo shape as a slashback culotte. **1972** *Ibid.* 26 Aug. 55 (Advt.), Our fluid navy wool knit with permanent pleated polyester chiffon palazzo sleeves. **1974** *Country Life* 3–10 Jan. 55/1 Drip-dry dresses and palazzo suits. **1972** *N.Y. Times* 3 Nov. 11/4 (Advt.), The palazzo-trouser.

pale, *sb.*¹ Add: **4. e.** From 1791 to 1917, specified provinces and districts within which Russian Jews were required to reside.

The Russ. expression corresponding to 'pale of settlement' is *chertá osédlosti* (lit. 'boundary of settlement').

1890 A. READER *Russia & Jews* viii. 78 The Jews,..as soon as the contract was completed..had to return within the 'pale' of settlement. **1892** I. ZANGWILL *Children of Ghetto* III. 329 The whole history of her strange, unhappy race flashed through her mind... She was overwhelmed by the thought of its sons in every corner of the earth proclaiming to the sombre twilight sky the belief for which its generations had lived and died—the Jews of Russia sobbing it forth in their pale of enclosure. **1897** [see *GOLEM]. **1927** *New Statesman* 6 Nov. 104/1 Bolshevism, whilst destroying the livelihood of the Jewish masses in the so-called 'Pale'—small traders and artisans—has disorganised Russia's economic system. **1969** *Observer* 23 Feb. 23/2 With the Revolution in 1917, the Jews were released from the Pale and allowed to move in great numbers into Russia proper. **1976** *Times* 8 Apr. 11/3 Generally it has been held that Jews had arrived in what was known as the Pale of Settlement, between Russia and Poland, because they were driven there, under expulsion first from England and France, then from Germany. **1977** Y. MENUHIN *Unfinished Journey* i. 4 The Mnuchins..had settled in Gomel, a smallish city..at the very center of the Pale.

8. *pale-fence* (earlier examples), *-gate.*

1834 J. KEMPER in *Wisconsin State Hist. Soc. Coll* (1898) XIV. 423 In walking over the meadow..passed an indian burial place, 2 poles with white flags flying a pale fence partly surrounding the place. **1845** M. M. NOAH *Gleanings* 77 His house is..surrounded with a white pale fence. **1850** H. C. WATSON *Camp-Fires of Revolution* 28 Their ranks looked like a broken pale-fence. **1836** W. DUNLAP *Mem. Water Drinker* (1837) I. 12 It was..a ricketty wooden pale-gate drawn back by a chain and bullet.

pale, *sb.*² (Further example.)

1887 M. E. WILKINS *Humble Romance* 110 'It ain't so much the pale,' said Mrs. Potter, 'but thar's..a kind of a look around..the mouth that I've seen a good many times.'

pale, *a.* Add: **1. d.** *pale ale* (later examples); also *ellipt.*; *pale sherry*, a general term for light-coloured, dry sherries.

1833 C. REDDING *Hist. Mod. Wines* vi. 189 Pale sherry is made from the same grape as the brown, to the wine from which is added a couple of bottles of very pure brandy to each butt. **1846** R. FORD *Gatherings from Spain* xiv. 161 Pure genuine sherry..will stand the importer from 100 to 130 guineas in his cellar... The reader will now appreciate the bargains of those 'pale' and 'golden sherries' advertised in the English newspapers at 36*s.* the dozen, bottles included. **1849** Pale ale [see *brown sherry* s.v. *BROWN *a.* 7]. **1853** *Q. Jrnl. Chem. Soc.* V. 173 (*heading*) Alleged adulteration of pale ales by strychnine. **1891** in C. Ray *Compleat Imbiber* (1967) IX. 122 Pale Sherry..Per. Doz. 20/-. **1965** A. SICHEL *Penguin Bk. Wines* III. 231 Intermediate types of sherry are described as brown, light golden, pale, etc., and are for the most part excellent wines, blended to the taste and needs of importers. **1976** 'J. FRASER' *Who steals my Name?* ix. 104 Don't guzzle down that Clos de Vougoet as if it was Watney's Pale. That's worth six pounds a bottle. **1977** *Berry Bros. & Rudd Catal.* Apr. 6 South African Sherry...pale extra dry—per bottle £1·70.

e. Pale Brindled Beauty, a geometrid moth, *Apocheima pilosaria*, usually having light-coloured wings flecked with darker markings.

[**1803** A. H. HAWORTH *Lepidoptera Britannica* 274 (*heading*) The pale Brindle. **1824** G. SAMOUELLE *Entomologist's Useful Compendium* 363 The pale brindle. Trunks of trees.] **1860** H. N. HUMPHREYS *Genera Brit. Moths* 81 (*caption*) The Female of the Pale Brindled Beauty. **1908** R. SOUTH *Moths Brit. Isles* (ser. 2) 295 Pale Brindled Beauty... The fore wings of this species are greyish,.. sprinkled with darker grey or brownish. **1955** E. B. FORD *Moths* xiii. 191 A black form of the Pale Brindled Beauty has become well established in some of the industrial areas of the north and round London. **1964** *Sunday Times* (Colour Suppl.) 2 Feb. 33 (*caption*) The male Pale Brindled Beauty moth may have these typical markings, but others have black wings. **1966** *Punch* 30 Mar. 463/1 Some ancient apple trees,..generous hosts, in season, to the Capsid Bug and..the Pale Brindled Beauty.

4. *pale-blurred, -breasted, -lipped, -mouthed, -snowed, -starred; pale-gleaming, -glimmering* (example).

1918 D. H. LAWRENCE *New Poems* 32 Pale-blurred, with two round black drops..my own reflection! **1913** —— *Love Poems* 8 Pale-breasted throstles and a blackbird. **1921** W. DE LA MARE *Veil* 6 But with set, wild, unearthly eyes Pale-gleaming, fixed as if in fear, She couched in the water. **1954** J. R. R. TOLKIEN *Two Towers* III. iii. 52 Mist lay there, pale-glimmering in the last rays of the sickle moon. **1920** BLUNDEN *Waggoner* 33 But, alas, she falls in a swoon, Pale-lipped like a withering moon. **1820** KEATS *Ode to Psyche* in *Lamia & other Poems* 119 No shrine, no grove, no oracle, no heat Of pale-mouth'd prophet dreaming. *a* **1918** W. OWEN *Coll. Poems* (1963) 103 And when the land lay pale for them, pale-snowed. **1929** BLUNDEN *Near & Far* 46 While unamazed I view the siege of pale-starred horror raised By dawn.

b. Special Comb.: **pale crêpe** (or **crepe**) (**rubber**), crêpe rubber of a pale yellowish colour, made by treating the latex with a chemical such as sodium bisulphite to prevent its turning brown.

1913 *India-Rubber Jrnl.* XLVI. 222/1 The preparation of pale crepe..is confined to the plantation rubber industry. *Ibid.*, In the preparation of pale crepe rubber the latex is coagulated in volumes varying from a few gallons to 500 or 600 gallons. **1937** [see *CRÊPE 2]. **1938** C. F. FLINT *Chem. & Technol. Rubber Latex* iv. 126 Pale crêpe rubber may disappear from the market owing to the increasing use of latex for purposes for which pale crêpe was formerly used. **1970** *Encycl. Polymer Sci. & Technol.* XII. 187 Pale crepe is a long-established special rubber used for high-grade shoe soling and for applications needing a very light-colored, pure rubber.

pale, *v.*[2] Add: **1. b.** In phr. *to pale into insignificance*: to lose importance (freq. in comparison with a greater achievement).

1909 *Daily Graphic* 26 July 10/1 He..made a flight of twenty-five miles across country; but that, of course, pales into insignificance by the side of the Channel flight. **1966** *Listener* 27 Oct. 602/1 This..will..be a standard biography upon a scale which will make..the rest pale into insignificance.

Palearctic, var. PALÆARCTIC *a.* in Dict. and Suppl.

pale-face. Add: **2.** In American Negro use, a contemptuous term for a white man.

1945 MENCKEN *Amer. Lang.* Suppl. I. 637 The Negroes use various other sportive terms for whites, *e.g.*, *pale-face, chalk* and *milk.* **1964** *N.Y. Times Mag.* 23 Aug. 62/2 *Whitey*, the latest word of contempt for a white person, superseding *ofay* and..*paleface.* **1971** *Publ. Amer. Dial. Soc.* 1969 LI. 33 To Negroes, a white convict is a..*paddy, pale face.* **1971** E. E. LANDY *Underground Dict.* 145 *Pale face*, (B) white person.

Palekh (pā·lek). The name of a town in Ivanovo province in northwest U.S.S.R. used *attrib.* to designate the iconography for which the town was renowned in the 18th century, and also a type of miniature painting on such articles as boxes and trays which was developed there during the 19th century.

[**1916** R. NEWMARCH *Russian Arts* iii. 65 Palekh 'the heart-centre of Russian popular ikonography'.] **1960** *Guardian* 1 Dec. 10/6 A Russian and Bulgarian shop opens in London tomorrow... There should be a rush on.. examples of palekh iconography. **1963** M. CHAMOT *Russ. Painting & Sculpture* i. 7 The famous Palekh work, as it is called from the village where it is produced, is executed with incredible delicacy and carries on to this day something of the inventiveness and charm of early Russian Painting. **1964** *Punch* 16 Dec. p. xii, Gifts at the Russian Shop..include..Palekh painted boxes. **1976** *Times* 19 Mar. 16/6 A sale of Russian and Greek icons totalled £35,609... A private buyer paid £1,400 for an early nineteenth-century Palekh school calendar.

Palermitan (pălǝ·ɹmităn), *sb.* and *a.* [ad. It. *palermitano.*] **A.** *sb.* A native or inhabitant of the Sicilian town or province of Palermo. **B.** *adj.* Of, pertaining to, or characteristic of Palermo.

1673 J. RAY *Observations Journey Low-Countries* 279 There is a great emulation and enmity between the Palermitans and Messanese, which involves the whole Island. **1826** M. KELLY *Reminisc.* I. 80 The Palermitans are all fond of music. **1835** N. P. WILLIS *Pencillings by Way* I. xxi. 257 The oddity of the Palermitan style of building struck me forcibly. **1847** J. H. NEWMAN *Let.* 25 Aug. (1962) XII. 109 There was a Palermitan father at dinner. .. He has warmly invited us to Palermo. **1908** *Westm. Gaz.* 6 July 4/2 The editor..is a Palermitan, and his family is the Sicilian branch of the Roman Colonnas. **1936** G. F.-H. & J. BERKELEY *Italy in Making* II. xxii. 339 Even in Sicily, La Masa and his Palermitans would rise against Ferdinand with shouts of 'Viva Pio Nono!' **1961** *Times* 14 Jan. 9/2 Palermo's cathedral church..is in its own way more typically 'palermitan' than them all. **1968** D. M. SMITH *Medieval Sicily* x. 110 St. Cristina's fair during which Palermitans had had the valuable privilege of not paying customs or excise duty. **1978** *Harpers & Queen* Sept. 42/4 We had..spaghetti con sarda, a Palermitan dish, with sardines, fennel and raisins.

Palestine (pæ·lǝstəin). The name of a territory on the eastern shore of the Mediterranean (see next) used *attrib.* to designate a cream soup made from Jerusalem artichokes.

1834 J. ROMILLY *Diary* 13 Apr. (1967) 55 He told us that he had given Palestine Soup yesterday: he asked the B. of London the origin of the name..he told him it was because it was made of Jerusalem Artichokes. **1861** MRS. BEETON *Bk. Househ. Managem.* 912 (*heading*) Dinner for 6 persons... First course. Palestine soup. **1907** *Yesterday's Shopping* (1969) 41/1 Soups..Palestine—0/8½. **1929** A. E. HOUSMAN *Let.* 14 Sept. (1971) 284, I was however agreeably surprised by a Palestine soup which had not the faintest trace of artichoke. **1970** SIMON & HOWE *Dict. Gastron.* 287/1 *Palestine soup*, the term for a soup made of Jerusalem artichokes.

Palestinian (pæ:lĕsti·niăn), *a.* and *sb.* [f. *Palestine* (see below) + -IAN.]

The name *Palestine* is derived from Gr. Παλαιστίνη (used in early Christian writing), L. *Palaestina* (the name of the Roman province), and designates that territory on the eastern Mediterranean coast which in biblical times comprised the kingdoms of Israel and Judah. There have been many changes in the frontiers in the course of history. It was revived as an official political title for the land west of the Jordan mandated to Britain in 1920. Palestine ceased to exist as a political entity in 1948 when the state of Israel was established, but the name continues to be used to describe a geographical entity, particularly in the context of Arab aims for the resettlement of people who left the area when the state of Israel was established.

A. *adj.* Of, pertaining to, or connected with Palestine.

1875 *Encycl. Brit.* II. 181/1 The books bearing this name are not contained in the Jewish or Palestinian Canon. **1902** D. G. HOGARTH *Nearer East* 163 The Palestinian highlands. **1920** *Glasgow Herald* 13 July 6 Mr. Balfour said that for long he had been a convinced Zionist but..he never foresaw..that the great work of Palestinian reconstruction would happen so soon. **1934** [see *GÖTTERDÄMMERUNG]. **1936** A. W. CLAPHAM *Romanesque Archit.* v. 113 Certain churches in southern Italy..show evidence of being the product of the Palestinian school. **1936** *Discovery* Aug. 250/1 Palestinian objects of the Bronze Age. **1949** *Radio Times* 15 July 27/2 Musa Alami, a prominent Palestinian Arab. **1962** *New Jewish Encycl.* 476/1 The initial compilation of the Palestinian Talmud is ascribed to Rabbi Johanen ben Nappaha (third century). **1972** *Guardian* 4 Sept. 3/7 Black September operations do generate a local Palestinian activism. **1973** *Jewish Chron.* 2 Feb. 22/4 Eventually the teachings of the Palestinian Amoraim were gathered together to form the Palestinian Talmud. **1976** *Daily Tel.* 30 June 4/8 He accused the Syrians of collaborating with the Right-wing Christians to suppress the Palestinian commando movement. **1977** M. MAZZAWI in *Times* 13 June 14/1 This promise, coupled with 30 years' occupation of the country by Britain, and compounded by a decision of the United Nations in 1947, has resulted in the Palestinian people (who now number three million) being either in refugee camps, in exile, or under alien military rule.

B. *sb.* A native or inhabitant of Palestine in biblical or later times.

1905 *Daily Chron.* 31 July 5/3 Territorialists..flooded the hall with leaflets declaring that 200 Russian Palestinians were illegally present. **1909** *Ibid.* 9 Sept. 3/6 Those who are for a mass return to the country of their origin..are termed 'Palestinians'. **1920** *Glasgow Herald* 12 July 12 The higher ranks of the Civil Service..would consist mainly of British officials until an increasing number of Palestinians were fully qualified... Other ranks would be open to Palestinians, irrespective of creed. **1968** *Guardian* 12 May 9/3 The other card the Israelis reckon to play is the Palestinians' actual experience of Israeli occupation. **1973** *Ibid.* 21 Apr. 12/1 The Arabs..[must] put the rights of the Palestinians (to the exclusion of Israel) before anything else. **1974** *Times* 30 Oct. 15/3 King Husain ..is not himself a Palestinian and indeed has a vested interest in preventing the assertion of a distinct Palestinian identity. **1977** *Listener* 19 May 642/1, I do not necessarily equate the Palestinians with the PLO: can you rationally and logically expect me to go along with the covenant that says that the liberation of Palestine means to purge the Zionist presence from Palestine. **1977** M. MAZZAWI in *Times* 13 June 14/2 The Palestinians who left their homes were driven out by danger and threats. **1979** *Time* 13 Aug. 13/2 The Administration's first goal then, would be to bring Palestinians, perhaps even some P.L.O. officials, into the talks between the Israelis and the Egyptians on the future of the West Bank and Gaza.

Palestrinian (pælĕstri·niăn), *a.* [f. the name *Palestrin(a* (see below) + -IAN.] Of, pertaining to, or in the style of the Italian composer Giovanni Pierluigi da Palestrina (*c* 1525–94).

1954 *Grove's Dict. Mus.* (ed. 5) VI. 512/1 Equally important, in any examination of the Palestrinian style, is it to bear in mind the fact that the order of publication of such of his works as appeared in the composer's lifetime offers no reliable evidence as to date of composition. **1958** *Listener* 2 Oct. 540/1 There always was a Palestrinian tradition.

paletoted (pæ·lĕtōu:tėd), *a.* *nonce-wd.* [f. PALETOT + -ED[2].] Provided with, or wearing, a paletot.

1947 V. NABOKOV *Bend Sinister* 34 A mild bore who used to take out his two polite paletoted dachshunds at nightfall.

palette. Add: **1. c.** Of sounds (*spec.* in music): variety or range of tonal or instrumental colour (see COLOUR *sb.* 15).

1959 [see *DEBUSSYAN *a.* and *sb.*]. **1965** *Listener* 28 Oct. 680/2 If you want to be reminded of his mastery of the orchestra and the richness of his [*sc.* Ravel's] instrumental palette, listen again to *Daphnis et Chloé*, and the *Rapsodie espagnole.* **1975** *Broadcast* 3 Nov. 14/3 Relaxed circumambient dialogue... You may find Pinter's subdued palette somewhat baffling. **1977** *Listener* 7 Apr. 452/1 The shock of moving from one tonal palette to another.

3. (Further example.)

1887 D. MAGUIRE *Art of Massage* (ed. 4) 20 The palette, which is also called ferule, tapette, battoir,..is an instrument..ending at one extremity in a handle, and the other in a disc.

5*. In certain card games, a device used by the banker to facilitate the movement of cards and money.

1949 J. SCARNE *On Cards* (1955) xxi. 205 The croupier, squatting in the concavity of the kidney table, needs an ebony-finish palette to slide the cash and cards around. **1966** 'W. HAGGARD' *Power House* xi. 114 The croupier had one hand on the shoe, the other playing with the *palette.* **1968** D. TORR *Treason Line* 105 Vittoria's mother had invited him..for his dexterity in wielding the *palette.* As *chef de partie* in the high chair he could run a game of baccarat *banque* or chemin-de-fer as slickly as any professional.

palette-knife. a. Add to def.: Also used for spreading oil-paint on canvas. (Further examples.) Also *attrib.*

1785 J. REYNOLDS *Discourse to Students of R. Acad.* 28 Rembrandt, in order to take the advantage of accident, appears often to have used the palate-knife [*sic*] to lay his colours on the canvass. **1931** L. RICHMOND *Technique Oil Painting* xi. 86 With palette knife painting..the charm lies to a certain extent in accidental qualities. **1938** D. SHARP *Student's Bk. Oil Painting* vii. 45 A different style of work is palette-knife painting, and this method certainly gives a very fascinating texture to a picture. **1958** *Times* 11 Mar. 3/4 Aix-en-Provence has a 'Self-portrait' with heavy impasto ascribed to Rembrandt (which arrived there in 1863 a year or two before Cézanne painted his palette-knife studies of 'Uncle Dominique'). **1967** W. GAUNT *Compan. Painting* 93 Some equivalent of work with the spatula may be found in the practice of palette-knife painting. **1970** *Oxf. Compan. Art* 562/1 Some modern artists, working with palette knife or fingers or squeezing paint from the tube, have treated oil paint almost as if it were a substance for modelling.

b. A similar instrument used as a culinary tool.

1889 A. B. MARSHALL *Cookery Bk.* iii. 41 Royal Icing... Put on to the cake with a clean palette knife. **1906** MRS. BEETON *Bk. Househ. Managem.* xlvii. 1431 Scrape down the sides with a palette-knife, and with the point of the knife mix in all the material scraped down. **1951** E. DAVID *French Country Cooking* 20 A first-class pliable palette knife,..a selection of wooden spoons. **1975** *Habitat Catal.* 64 Kitchen equipment... Palette knife. Wood handle, steel blade.

Pali, *sb.* and *a.* Add: **3.** *Comb.*, as *Pali-Prakrit, -Pyu.*

1948 D. DIRINGER *Alphabet* vi. 388 Pali-Prakrit Sinhalese. This language..may be dated from the third century B.C. to about the fourth century A.D. *Ibid.* vii. 410 A mixed Pali-Pyu inscription.

paligorskite, obs. var. *PALYGORSKITE.

palilalia (pælilē̆i·liă). *Path.* [mod.L., ad. F. *palilalie* (A. Soques 1908, in *Rev. Neurol.* XVI. 340), f. Gr. πάλι-ν again + λαλιά talk, speech.] A speech disorder characterized by repetition of words, phrases, or sentences.

1908 *Index Medicus* VI. 157/1 (Index), Palilalia. **1927** *Jrnl. Neurol. & Psychopath.* VIII. 26 The palilalia (as with stammering) disappears during pre-formed speech automatisms, as for instance, when the patient reads aloud, sings or recites. **1934** *Jrnl. Amer. Med. Assoc.* 1 Dec. 1711/2 Those familiar with such symptoms as automatic writing, palilalia, perseveration and verbigeration are inclined to wonder whether or not the literary abnormalities in which she [*sc.* Gertrude Stein] indulges represent correlated distortions of the intellect. **1955** J. M. NIELSEN in A. B. Baker *Clin. Neurol.* I. iv. 376 Palilalia is a repetitive disturbance encountered in parkinsonism and in encephalitis (as representatives of organic causes), and in schizophrenia. **1961** W. R. BRAIN *Speech Disorders* vii. 107, I have once met with palilalia as a temporary phenomenon in a patient who suffered from compression of the medulla.

palimpsest, *sb.* and *a.* Add: **A.** *sb.* **2.** (Later *fig.* examples.)

1918 D. H. LAWRENCE *New Poems* 33 Darkness comes out of the earth..Wanes the old palimpsest. **1929** *Oxford Poetry* 17 The world is all a palimpsest That hails the spurious pugilist. **1949** 'G. ORWELL' *Nineteen Eighty-Four* I. iv. 42 All history was a palimpsest, scraped clean and re-inscribed exactly as often as was necessary. **1962** R. PAGE *Educ. Gardener* x. 294 In Italy every town and house..is a palimpsest of two or three thousand years of building and decay. **1977** *Times* 3 Sept. 9/1 Alan Watts will be principally remembered as the architect of that peculiar theological palimpsest which served as an ideology for the hippie generation: that odd blend of rural fundamentalism and eastern mysticism.

B. *adj.* **3.** *Petrogr.* Of a rock: partially preserving the texture it had prior to metamorphism. Also in *Geol.*, exhibiting features produced at two or more distinct periods.

1912 R. W. CLARK tr. *Weinschenk's Petrogr. Methods* x. 198 In the normal case the newly developed substance is confined strictly to the border of the original crystal, but the texture of the altered rock may be recognized excellently, palimsest [*sic*] structure. **1926** G. W. TYRRELL *Princ. Petrol.* xvi. 271 (*caption*) A palimpsest structure. Garnetiferous biotite-hornfels... Shows alternations of psammitic and pelitic sediments preserved, although the rock is thoroughly hornfelsed with the production of muscovite and biotite. **1951** TURNER & VERHOOGEN *Ign. & Metamorphic Petrol.* xx. 503 It frequently happens.. that fabric relicts (palimpsest structures), like mineral relicts, survive metamorphism and provide valuable indications of the parentage of the metamorphic rock. **1962** A. D. HOWARD in *Bull. Amer. Assoc. Petroleum Geologists* XLVI. 2255/1 A particularly interesting part of the anomaly is the drainage pattern, an unusual superposition of modern and ancient patterns that is convenient to refer to as palimpsest. In palimpsest drainage, the modern pattern is anomalous with respect to the older; it clearly indicates different topographic and possibly structural conditions at the time of development. **1972** D. J. P. SWIFT et al. *Shelf Sediment Transport* xxiii. 499 The floor of the central and southern Atlantic shelf is a palimpsest or multiple imprint surface.

palindrome, *sb.* and *a.* Add: **a.** *sb.* Also *transf.*: in *Mus.*, a piece of music of which the second half is the first half in retrograde motion; in *Biol.*, a palindromic sequence of nucleotides.

1947 E. BLOM *Everyman's Dict. Mus.* 430/1 *Palindrome*, a word or poem reading the same backwards as forwards. In m[usic] a piece constructed in the same way, more or less loosely, as e.g. the prelude and postlude in Hindemith's *Ludus tonalis*. **1961** *Listener* 21 Sept. 445/3 The palindrome is another symmetrical form that she has used several times, most notably and extendedly in the recent *Symphonies* where the strict symmetry of the reversed 'reprise' is relieved only by changes of scoring, [etc.]. **1963** *Ibid.* 28 Mar. 570/3 Huber..is obsessed with musical palindromes. **1974** WILSON & THOMAS in *Jrnl. Molecular Biol.* LXXXIV. 115 We call these regions in double-chain DNA palindromes, because, given the antiparallel arrangement of the polynucleotide chains, these sequences read the same both backwards and forwards. **1977** *Nature* 3 Nov. 10/2 If these inverted repeats are adjacent (forming a palindrome) renaturation produces a double-stranded hairpin. **1979** *Gramophone* Aug. 327/2 Hers is a gorgeous performance, and its orchestral match may be summarized by the moment when Berg moves into a palindrome.

palindromic, *a.* Add: More widely (esp. in *Math.* and *Mus.*), having a structure or composition that reads the same in both directions.

1957 W. J. REICHMANN *Fascination of Numbers* ix. 90 The most simple form of palindromic numbers is the one containing a number of identical digits. **1961** *Listener* 23 Nov. 889/1 Schönberg makes his ternary-form prelude in effect a prelude-and-fugue, the middle section being fugal, with a powerfully melodic subject of palindromic construction, and a counter-subject that is also palindromic. **1963** *Ibid.* 17 Jan. 140/3 This act is the only formal success, having clear-cut musical ideas worked out logically in a neat palindromic structure. **1964** A. H. BEILER *Recreations in Theory of Numbers* xx. 228 There are an infinite number of palindromic primes. Here are a few: 101, 131, 151, 181, 313. **1972** *Times* 1 Aug. 15/2 The sole point of this letter is the date [*sc.* 27.7.72] at its foot. Apart from the three rather less pleasing palindromes arising on the 27th of the 8th 9th and 11th months of this year, today's is the last palindromic date until 18.1.81. **1974** *Nature* 9 Aug. 467/2 The central assumption of my theory is that the nucleotide sequences at the ends of eukaryote linear DNA molecules are palindromic. **1975** W. SAFIRE *Before the Fall* 181 Prince Norodim Sihanouk, had been deposed by Lon Nol, his palindromic Prime Minister.

2. *Med.* Characterized by frequent, irregular recurrences of short-lived rheumatic attacks.

1941 HENCH & ROSENBERG in *Proc. Staff Meetings Mayo Clinic* XVI. 814 When an etiologic term cannot be applied, a distinctive descriptive term should be used. Such a designation we found in the term 'palindromic rheumatism', suggested to us by Profs. A. D. Fraser and A. L. Hench, respectively, of the departments of Ancient languages and of English literature of the University of Virginia. **1959** *Ann. Rheumatic Dis.* XVIII. 331/2 When the histories of patients with definite rheumatoid arthritis were reviewed, a palindromic or episodic type of onset was found in 10 to 15 per cent. *Ibid.*, Finger contractures had been a common feature during the palindromic phase. **1972** *Lancet* 5 Aug. 269/2 Palindromic rheumatism is a condition in which an acute arthritis develops over a few hours, lasts for a day or two, and disappears the way it came.

paling, *vbl. sb.*[1] **4.** *paling fence* (later U.S. examples).

1843 *Amer. Pioneer* II. 308 A strong body occupied the yard of Ebenezer Zane..using the paling fence as a cover. **1873** 'MARK TWAIN' & WARNER *Gilded Age* v. 60 Hawkins put up the first 'paling' fence that had ever adorned the village. **1901** MERWIN & WEBSTER *Calumet 'K'* v. 68 They were standing..near the paling fence which bounded the C. and S.C. right of way. **1925** W. J. BRYAN *Mem.* 17 Our yard was enclosed in the old-fashioned paling fence with a baseboard about a foot high.

palingenesis. Add: **3.** *Petrol.* [ad. Sw. *palingenes* (J. J. Sederholm 1907, in *Bull. Comm. Géol. Finlande* XXIII. 89).] The formation of a new magma by the remelting of existing rocks.

1907 J. J. SEDERHOLM in *Bull. Comm. Géol. Finlande* XXIII. 102 The granitic magma, once solidified and, in part, decomposed, undergoes again, when brought into the deeper parts of the earth, a resurrection, or, as the author expresses it, palingenesis. **1965** A. HOLMES *Princ. Physical Geol.* (ed. 2) xxx. 1131 The following list of the radiometric ages of some of the uplifted basement rocks shows how successfully they escaped the widespread palingenesis..that rejuvenated similar old rocks during the Nevadan orogenies farther west. **1974** L. N. KOGARKO in H. Sørensen *Alkaline Rocks* vi. 480/1 The significant reductions of the melting temperatures of rocks caused by the volatile components is probably of great importance for palingenesis.

palingenetic, *a.* (Examples corresponding to *PALINGENESIS 3.)

1942 M. P. BILLINGS *Structural Geol.* xv. 296 Palingenetic granites were actually molten and, in the simplest case, they have the same chemical composition as the rocks from which they were derived. **1974** BORODIN & PAVLENKO in H. Sørensen *Alkaline Rocks* vi. 523/1 In the Mongol–Tuva province palingenetic and metasomatic formations of alkaline rocks are widespread.

palinspastic (pælinspæ·stik), *a.* *Geol.* [f. Gr. πάλιν again + σπαστικ-ός drawing in (see SPASTIC *a.*).] Of a map or the like: representing layers of rock as returned to their supposed former positions. Hence **palinspa·stically** *adv.*, by means of such maps; **palinspa·stics** *sb. pl.*, the production of such maps.

1937 G. M. KAY in *Bull. Geol. Soc. Amer.* XLVIII. 291 The resulting map displays the several slices in their conceived relative positions... The name *palinspastic*..is proposed for base maps of this character. **1945** *Bull. Amer. Assoc. Petroleum Geologists* XXIX. 426 Palinspastics concern the placement of rocks in their relative original positions. *Ibid.* 435 Palinspastic maps..have been used to illustrate concepts of continental drift and of intracontinental movements in the development of mountain systems. **1969** J. F. DEWEY in M. Kay *N. Atlantic* xxiv. 331/2 No attempt was made in Figures 2 and 3 to reconstruct palinspastically the original shape of the paratectonic cover sequence, in terms of thickness or extent. **1971** *Nature* 2 Apr. 319/1 Fig. 2 is an upper Palaeocene palinspastic reconstruction of Fig. 1.

‖ **palio** (pæ·lio). Also 7, 8 pallio. [a. It. *palio*, ad. L. *pallium* a covering, cover.] A traditional horse-race held every July and August in the Italian city of Siena; a similar horse-race held in other Italian towns; the cloth or banner of velvet, silk, etc., given as the prize for this race.

1673 J. RAY *Observations Journey Low-Countries* 338 He entertains and diverts the Citizens of Florence..with sports and shows, especially races for prizes (Pallio's they call them). **1791** E. WYNNE *Diary* 4 Apr. (1935) I. iv. 60 The King of Naples arrived today [at Padua] and they prepare a Pallio for him. **1863** GEO. ELIOT *Romola* I. viii. 138 The Porta Santa Croce..where the richest of *Palii*, or velvet and brocade banners.., were..awaiting the winner or winner's owner. *Ibid.* xvi. 291 You are going towards the Piazza della Signoria...we shall perhaps see who has deserved the *palio* among these racers. **1873** S. & J. HORNER *Walks in Florence* I. xvii. 296 The Corso..was at one time celebrated for horse-races, in which the Florentine youth competed for a piece of cloth of gold, called the *Pallio*, and which gave its name to the diversion. **1881** K. BAEDEKER *Central Italy* (ed. 7) 21 On 2nd July and 15th August, horse-races, called *il Palio*, take place, presenting a very picturesque scene. **1902** E. G. GARDNER *Story of Siena* v. 131 The race is still called the Palio, from the rich stuff (now represented as a banner) given as prize. **1904** W. HEYWOOD *Palio & Ponte* I. i. 11 Besides the Palio of St John the Baptist, at Florence, another palio is referred to in the *Divina Commedia*. **1925** A. HUXLEY *Along Road* II. 100 The *Palio* itself—the painted banner which is given to the *contrada* whose horse wins the race. *Ibid.* 101 The Palio is probably the most dangerous flat-race in the world. **1930** E. POUND *XXX Cantos* xxiv. 109 Zohanne da Rimini Has won, the palio at Milan with our horse. **1970** C. FRY *Yard of Sun* I. 6 You know it is the first practice-run for the Palio—And you know this parish has got the best horse It has ever had. **1972** *Times* 18 Sept. 19/1 Over the weekend the historic Tuscan town was enlivened with.. the Palio horse race in Renaissance costumes. **1974** *Radio Times* 27 July–2 Aug. 33/2 Old traditions also continue [in Siena], like the famous annual horse-race, the *Palio*, held every summer on the city square.

‖ **paliotto** (pæliọ·to). [It.] The frontal painting on an altar-piece. Also *attrib.*

1937 *Burlington Mag.* July 18/1 The *St. Peter* paliotto of about 1280–85. **1958** *Times Lit. Suppl.* 27 June 356/3 'Judas receiving Payment', the 'Baptism of Christ' from the thirteenth-century St John *paliotto* in the Siena Gallery, the head of Pietro Lorenzetti's St Catherine of Alexandria, [etc.]. **1961** M. LEVY *Studio Dict. Art Terms* 82 Paliotto painting.

palisade, *sb.* Add: **3. d.** *Biol.* A region of parallel elongated cells, often at right angles to the surface of the structure of which they form part; *esp.* the palisade parenchyma of a leaf. Freq. *attrib.* (see sense 4).

1914 M. DRUMMOND tr. *Haberlandt's Physiol. Plant Anat.* vi. 263 A remarkable modification, and one which is of great importance for the understanding of the palisade form, is the so-called arm-palisade-cell; in this case the palisade, instead of consisting of entire cells, is made up of groups of cell-branches or -arms. **1956** R. W. EVANS *Histol. Appearances of Tumours* vi. 79 In one of Chase's tumours the cells tended to form palisades. **1965** BELL & COOMBE tr. *Strasburger's Textbk. Bot.* 349 The outer leaves on the southern sunny side of a tree commonly possess a deeper palisade..than the 'shade leaves' of the northern side. **1971** *Nature* 19 Feb. 561/1 Here the so-called palisades of Vogt are found: fine radial lines about 1 mm long and four per mm of the corneal circumference. **1972** *Arch. Dermatol.* CVI. 865/3 The schwann cells which are closely aggregated often appear to be arranged in palisades.

4. *palisade-trench.*

1935 *Proc. Prehistoric Soc.* I. 124 In this barrow the posts (set in a palisade-trench) were smaller. **1963** W. F. GRIMES in Foster & Alcock *Culture & Environment* v. 142 The entrance took the form of a passage between the ends of the bank which was defined by narrow trenches resembling palisade-trenches.

palisade, *v.* Add: **palisaded** *ppl. a.*, (*b*) *Med.*, consisting of, or arranged as in, a palisade (*PALISADE *sb.* 3 d); **palisading** *vbl. sb.*, (*b*) *Med.*, arrangement of cells in a palisade.

1951 M. S. MCKEEHAN in *Jrnl. Exper. Zool.* CXVII. 39 During the period of nuclear orientation, the lens ectoderm rapidly changes from a cuboidal to a high columnar epithelium. This phenomenon may be called 'palisading'. **1956** R. W. EVANS *Histol. Appearances of Tumours* xvi. 300 When palisading is present it is usually a conspicuous microscopical feature. *Ibid.* xix. 403 This palisaded columnar epithelium lies in contact with the adjacent fibrous tissue. **1966** WRIGHT & SYMMERS *Systemic Path.* II. xxxviii. 1435/1 The zones of necrosis..are surrounded by radially oriented ('palisaded') connective tissue cells. **1972** *Arch. Dermatol.* CVI. 865/1 The palisaded, encapsulated neuroma is a..benign cutaneous tumor. **1974** *Nature* 18 Jan. 145/1 This 'palisading' gives the lens anlage a regular appearance, but individual cells may deviate considerably from the columnar shape.

palisander (pælisæ·ndəɹ). Also **palissander.** [a. F. *palissandre, palisandre*, prob. of Amer. Ind. origin.] The hard, dark, black-streaked wood of the Brazilian tree, *Dalbergia nigra*, of the family Leguminosæ; also known as Brazilian rosewood. Cf. ROSEWOOD 1. Also *attrib.*

1843 C. HOLTZAPFFEL *Turning & Mech. Manipulation* I. 104 The furniture rose-wood..was afterwards imported as Jacaranda, Palisander, and Palaxander-wood, by which names it is still called on the Continent. **1902** G. S. BOULGER *Wood* II. 270 Palisander-wood... A valuable wood, chiefly used in pianofortes. **1930** *Heal & Son Catal.* 14 The timbers that invite the craftsman's hand.. Macassar Ebony, Amaranth and Palisander. **1936** *Burlington Mag.* Aug. 88/2 Furniture in mahogany, palissander, rose- or satinwood. **1941** *Archit. Rev.* LXXXIX. 16 (*caption*) The study, with palisander wood furniture. **1947** J. C. RICH *Materials & Methods Sculpture* x. 294 Brazilian rosewood, also known as Palisander and Jacaranda, is an extremely fine, rare, and expensive variety. **1957** *Times* 4 Nov. 13/1 There is plain Bangkok teak, and palisander wood from South America. **1966** *House & Garden* Dec. 57/1 The Clairtone [hi-fi]..is solid-state encased in rare Brazilian Palisander. **1971** *Country Life* 3 June 1361/1 The top is lined with gilt tooled leather in a surround of palisander wood. **1974** *Ibid.* 3 Oct. 939/1 (*caption*) An 18th-century secretaire bookcase in palissander wood attributed to William Vile. **1977** *Early Music* July 455 (Advt.), The Roessler 'Meister' range [of recorders] is available in rosewood, palisander, olivewood and boxwood.

palissy (pæ·lisi). The name of the French master potter Bernard *Palissy* (*c* 1510–*c* 1590), used *attrib.* to designate pottery made by him, his successors, or his imitators.

1858 TROLLOPE *Three Clerks* I. vii. 137 He..was inclined to ridicule the growing taste of the day for torsos, Palissy ware, and Assyrian monsters. **1867** G. M. HOPKINS *Jrnls. & Papers* (1959) 155 Dish of Palissy ware with a pike. **1900** F. LITCHFIELD *Pott. & Porc.* vii. 255 The manufacture of the Palissy ware was continued until the time of Henri IV. **1902** S. WEYMAN *In Kings' Byways* I. 68 The table gleamed with..Palissy ware and Cellini vases. **1969** S. SITWELL *Gothic Europe* xiv. 162 The rather horrible imitation Palissy pottery made in Portugal with fruit and vegetable and crustacean motifs.

pallasite. For *Min.* read *Geol.* and substitute for def.: Any of a class of stony-iron meteorites which consist largely of iron (usu. with a small proportion of nickel) and olivine. (Earlier and further examples.) Hence **pal-lasi·tic** *a.*

1868 *Geol. Mag.* V. 78 The arrangement of the meteorites in the museum of Berlin University, by M. G. Rose, is based on their mineral character, and forms two divisions —the metallic and the stony meteorites, the first containing meteoric iron and the Pallasite, the second the Chondrites, Howardites, [etc.]. **1920** *Mineral Mag.* XIX. 59 In most pallasites the iron is poor in nickel,.. and the olivine is correspondingly poor in ferrous oxide. **1956** *Nature* 28 Jan. 156/1 From 60 to 1,600 km. the material of the mantle is identified as dunite and from 1,600 to 3,000 km. it is taken as of the same composition as pallasitic meteorites. **1962** [see *MESOSIDERITE]. **1977** A. HALLAM *Planet Earth* 134/2 This led to the speculation that ancient peridots were extraterrestrial, extracted from the meteorites known as pallasites.

pallavi (pă·la·vi). Also **pallevi.** [Origin uncertain.] In the music of southern India, the first section of a song.

1891 C. R. DAY *Mus. & Mus. Instruments S. India* v. 60 Almost all [melodies] consist of a burden or refrain called Pallevi, a kind of answer to this refrain styled Anupallevi, and stanzas (called Charanam) of which there is usually an uneven number. These parts are in the several compositions arranged in different ways. **1914** A. H. F. STRANGWAYS *Mus. Hindostan* iii. 86 A *Pallavi* was then sung round. **1968** *Jrnl. Musical Acad. Madras* XXXIX. 26 A whole line of the Pallavi..had been absent from the piece as current. **1971** *Shankar's Weekly* (Delhi) 11 Apr. 23/1 The pallavi was set to Rupakam with a sub-initial take-off.

pallet, *sb.*[3] Add: **3. d.** A portable tray or platform used, esp. in conjunction with a fork-lift truck, for moving or stacking heavy loads in convenient units. Also *attrib.*

1921 R. V. WRIGHT et al. *Material Handling Cycl.* 97 *Pallet*, a flat platform..used to pile material on. **1948** *P.O. Telecomm. Jrnl.* I. IV. 119/2 A pallet is a double-faced wooden or metal platform with a space between the top and bottom faces significantly large to permit the entry of the forks of a forklift truck. **1958** [see *FORK *sb.* 16]. **1961** *Times* 10 June 11/6 Tomatoes..packed, 120 at a time, into 'pallets' or metal trays supplied by British Railways. **1963** *Times* 23 July 7/3 The soldiers will sit in what are called 'people pallets' which will be dropped from low-flying Lockheed C130 assault aircraft. The pallets, which hold 12, 24 or 48 men, will be carried on the open cargo ramp at the rear end of the aircraft. **1971** *Power Farming* Mar. 13/2 Five-ton high-lift pallet trailers were used to transport the carrots from the field to the packing station. **1974** *Guardian* 20 Mar. 5/4 Pack your goods onto a standard pallet up to 40″ × 48″... We lift the whole pallet and take it to any of..17 different European destinations. **1976** *Farnborough Internat. Exhib.* (Official Programme) 17 Hawker Siddeley Dynamics..has a £6m. contract to build experiment carrying pallets for Spacelab. **1978** S. BRILL *Teamsters* vii. 266 Pallets are the wooden trays under which any heavy cargo is loaded.

pallet (pæ·lėt), *v. rare.* [f. PALLET *sb.*[2]] *intr.* To lie *down* to sleep on or as on a pallet.

1921 G. C. SHEDD *Lady of Mystery House* xix. 263 He and I could pallet down on the porch.

palletization (pæ:lėtəizē[i]·ʃən). [f. *PALLETIZE *v.* + -ATION.] The action or process of palletizing or of becoming palletized. Also *attrib.*

1946 *Chem. Industries* Aug. 294 (*heading*) Palletization. **1957** *Economist* 19 Oct. 257 They will advise on palletisation, mechanical handling and other modern techniques. **1965** R. B. ORAM *Cargo Handling* v. 83 Whisky in cases and cartons, insulation material in bags and fire bricks; all this was cargo that lent itself to palletization. **1967** *Times Rev. Industry* Feb. 71/3 The introduction of more efficient cargo-handling techniques, i.e., palletisation, containerization, packaged timber, roll-on, roll-off, &c.

palletize (pæ·lėtəiz), *v.* [f. PALLET *sb.*[3] + -IZE.] *trans.* To place on a pallet; to transport on a pallet; to convert a loading system to the use of pallets. (See *PALLET *sb.*[3] 3 d.) So **pa·lletized** *ppl. a.*; **pa·lletizing** *vbl. sb.*

1954 in WEBSTER Add. **1959** *Times Rev. Industry* Apr. 77/2 Wagons specially designed for palletized loading. **1960** *Farmer & Stockbreeder* 1 Mar. 71/3 Palletizing, widely used in industry, and for fruit and potatoes, has not, it is believed, been used in this. **1964** *Economist* 3 Oct. 61/2 Goods being palletised in advance. **1967** *Jane's Surface Skimmer Systems 1967–68* 21/2 Palletised loads can be 'floated' in on hover-pallets supplied with air from the main compressor. **1970** *Financial Times* 13 Apr. 9/7 A feature of the building is that the structural steel frame is designed as a space frame to perform the function of storing palletised goods. **1977** *R.A.F. News* 22 June–5 July 3 (Advt.), Removals—Home and overseas Storage—Palletised containers.

pallial, *a.* Add: **b.** *Anat.* Of or pertaining to the pallium of the brain.

1901 [see *NEOPALLIUM]. **1933** *Proc. Nat. Acad. Sci.* XIX. 7 Below the reptiles the entire pallial field is dominated by the olfactory system. **1965** L. B. AREY *Developmental Anat.* (ed. 7) 495 [The commissures] cross partly in the lamina and partly in the fused adjacent portions of the median pallial walls.

pallite (pā·ləit). *Min.* [a. F. *pallite* (Capdecomme & Pulou 1954, in *Compt. Rend.* CCXXXIX. 288), f. *Pall-o*, the name of its locality in Senegal + -ITE[1].] A white or greyish ferrian variety of millisite.

1954 *Mineral. Abstr.* XII. 440 Two types of Ca-Al phosphates are distinguished: (1) Pallite..formed by the action of calcium phosphate on montmorillonite; (2) Crandallite..formed by the leaching of (1). **1960** *Amer. Mineralogist* XLV. 257 Uranium is present in amounts up to 140 ppm U in pallite.

pallium. Add: **3. d.** *Anat.* The wall of the cerebral hemispheres (including, in mod. use, the rhinencephalon). Cf. *ARCHI-, *NEO-, and *PALÆOPALLIUM.

1890 *Jrnl. Anat. & Physiol.* XXV. 106 When the surface of a cerebral hemisphere is carefully examined, it is seen to be capable of a natural division into two parts: a basal region, or Rhinencephalon, and a superior portion, or Pallium. **1901** *Ibid.* XXXV. 442 And His..freely admits that the rhinal fissure is the line of demarcation between the 'pallium' and the 'rhinencephalon'. **1934** L. B. AREY *Developmental Anat.* (ed. 3) xv. 414 The telencephalon consists of three regional parts. One is the corpus striatum... The second division is the rhinencephalon, or archipallium, while the remainder of the hemisphere makes up the neopallium. The last two portions comprise all of the externally visible hemispheres, and together may be called the pallium. **1948** A. BRODAL *Neurol. Anat.* 323 It is only in mammals that the dorsal cortex undergoes a marked development, and increases progressively in the phylogenetic ascent, to reach its peak of development in man, in whom it forms the bulk of the entire pallium. **1972** *Jrnl. Neurochem.* XIX. 2031 During the last third of the gestational period, the cerebral pallium of the rabbit develops from a primitive vesicle with a total weight of about 100 mg to a highly organised structure 10 times as large.

Pallottine (pæ·lŏtəin), *a.* and *sb.* [f. the name of Vincent *Pallotti* (1795–1850), an Italian priest who founded in 1835 the Society of the Catholic Apostolate, a society of R.C. priests, lay brothers, sisters, and associates, known formerly as the Pious Society of Missions, and known popularly as the Pallottine Fathers.] **A.** *adj.* Also **Pallottian, Pallotine.** Belonging or pertaining to the Society founded by Pallotti. **B.** *sb.* A member of the Society.

1890 *Tablet* 19 July 98/2 The English Pallotine Fathers (Society of Missions) have bought the Palazzo Caccia in Rome, and intend converting it into a seminary. **1894** M. E. HERBERT *Life Vincent Pallotti* xiv. 153 The Pallottine Sisters have also large schools adjoining the church. **1896** [see *CONSULTOR 1 b]. **1903** P. J. CHANDLERY *Pilgrim-Walks in Rome* xvi. 409 The church is served by the Pallotine Fathers. **1962** J. S. GAYNOR *Eng.-Speaking Pallottines* 5 They set about realising the Pallottian ideal in the world. **1962** *Times* 1 Sept. 8/3 Provincial of the Pallottine Fathers. **1971** *Shrewsbury Diocesan Year Bk.* 84 Pallottine Missionary Sisters, Pallotti Hall, Siddington, near Macclesfield. **1976** *Billings* (Montana) *Gaz.* 20 June 12-B/6 Church and state Saturday were ready to crack down on the Pallottine Fathers, an order of Roman Catholic priests dedicated to helping the poor abroad but accused of using millions in charitable funds for land ventures and loans to local politicians.

pally, *a.* See s.v. PAL *sb.*[1] in Dict. Add: (Later examples.) Also in the extended form **pally-wally.**

1915 H. L. WILSON *Ruggles of Red Gap* (1917) i. 9 The Honourable George..had..been almost quite too pally with him. **1922** J. CANNAN *Misty Valley* 282 If you cared for me it was not pally to let me go on doing things I didn't know were wrong. **1923** [see *hell-brew* s.v. *HELL *sb.* 11 a]. **1929** H. A. VACHELL *Virgin* i. 12 She had never been 'pally' with girls. **1936** W. R. TITTERTON *G. K. Chesterton* I. v. 60 [He] was on pally terms even with small shop-keepers, farmers and country squires. **1951** R. HOGGART *Auden* ii. 38 Auden often wobbles..from the pally to the patronising. **1954** F. BROWN in *Astounding Sci. Fiction* Sept. 16/2, I *like* quarrelling. If you're going to go namby-pamby and pally-wally on me, I'll go find someone else. **1974** S. GULLIVER *Vulcan Bulletins* 47 Why would Anscudden go along with stealing Javits' shipment? I thought they were supposed to be pally. **1976** *Scottish Rev.* Spring 9 She joined a Whist club and got very pally with another auld maid like herself.

pally (pæ·li). Colloq. abbrev. and spelling of *PALAIS DE DANCE.

1928 D. H. LAWRENCE *Lady Chatterley* xi. 189 The new girls in their silk stockings, the new collier lads lounging into the Pally or the Welfare. **1947** I. BROWN *Say Word* 72 Whether with hurdy-gurdy on the pavement or with boogie-woogie in the 'Pally', still they favour a word with rhyming syllables. **1948** *Amer. Speech* XXIII. 319/2 *Pally*, dance hall (in England abbreviation for Palais de Dance).

palm, *sb.*[1] Add: **7. a.** *palm-frond* (examples). **b.** *palm-flanked, -lined* adjs. **c. palm bottom,** a hollow or valley in which palms grow; **palm-branch** (later examples); **palm-cabbage** (later examples); **palm-heart** = *palm-cabbage* (cf. HEART *sb.* 18); **palm-hut,** a small cabin made from palm-trees; **palm-room,** a room, usu. in a hotel, adorned by potted palms; **palm-soap,** a soap made from palm-oil; **palm-squirrel,** a small, greyish-brown, tree squirrel with three white stripes along its back, belonging to the genus *Funambulus*, esp. *F. palmarum*, which is found in India; **palm-stand,** a stand for supporting a palm grown in a plant-pot; **palm-sugar** (later examples); **palm toddy** (later examples); **palm-wine** (further examples).

1902 D. G. HOGARTH *Nearer East* 141 Stony slopes.. only at very rare intervals relieved by palm bottoms. **1914** W. OWEN *Let.* 25 Feb. (1967) 235, I had huge success with my Costume: Nothing more elaborate than my Gown on my back a laurel wreath on my head, & a palm branch in the hand. **1928** D. H. LAWRENCE *Woman who rode Away* 16 Simply marvellous people! And the way they strewed palm-branches under her feet! **1977** H. KAPLAN *Damascus Cover* xii. 122 He was tied to the gate of the Al-Frange Synagogue... Then he was beaten with palm branches. **1966** E. J. H. CORNER *Nat. Hist. Palms* iv. 93 Not all palm-cabbages are edible. **1972** J. W. PURSEGLOVE *Tropical Crops: Monocotyledons* II. 443 The freshly cut terminal bud [of *Cocos nucifera*], known as palm cabbage, is considered a delicacy and may be eaten cooked or raw. **1928** H. CRANE *Let.* 31 Jan. (1965) 314 The great palm-flanked arena of Angelus Temple. **1938** M. K. RAWLINGS *Yearling* i. 5 The palm-frond mill-wheel must just brush the water's surface. **1972** 'M. RENAULT' *Persian Boy* xxvi. 349 He looked up at the waving palm-fronds, and played lazily with my hair. **1973** *Nat. Geographic* Feb. 211/1 On a plain before the fort of Rustaq, I sat on a palm-frond mat with a wiry old sheik. **1974** *Observer* (Colour Suppl.) 13 Oct. 20/3 (*caption*) Swinging from palm fronds like a teenage Tarzan, this Arab boy performs acrobatics for the benefit of admiring tourists at the oasis of Gafsa in Tunisia. [**1901** tr. C. G. O. Drude in L. H. Bailey *Cycl. Amer. Hort.* III. 1193/1 From many species are cut out the soft terminal bud (heart), which is eaten as Palm salad.] **1938** M. K. RAWLINGS *Yearling* xx. 250 He sliced the palm-hearts thinly. **1971** 'D. HALLIDAY' *Dolly & Doctor Bird* v. 67 We had palm hearts, a matter of flaccid white tubing, followed by prime rib steak. **1976** *Times* 1 June 6/3 We have found..tinned palm hearts and artichoke bottoms. **1930** R. MACAULAY *Staying with Relations* ii. 20 The forest would recede a little, and small clearings and plantations make themselves apparent.., with groups of palm huts dumped among them like beehives. **1936** *Discovery* Dec. 382/1 A riverside palm-hut. **1902** D. G. HOGARTH *Nearer East* 74 The abundant waters of its own palm-lined defiles. **1930** R. MACAULAY *Staying with Relations* xviii. 265 They rode into the bay, and saw before them the palm-lined harbour front of the Pacific's greatest pearl city. **1903** 'C. E. MERRIMAN' *Lett. from Son* 46, I met him in the palm room last night. **1930** E. POUND *XXX Cantos* xxix. 137 'No not in the palm-room.' The lady says it is Too cold in the palm-room. **1931** F. L. ALLEN *Only Yesterday* i. 11 In the more dimly lighted palm-room there may be a juvenile petting-party or two going on. **1846** *Jewish Manual, or Pract. Information Jewish & Mod. Cookery* Toilette iv. 212 Palm soap, Castille soap..should always be preferred. **1966** J. S. COX *Illustr. Dict. Hairdressing* 108/1 *Palm-soap*, a soda soap of palm oil. (*Piesse*). **1831** *Proc. Zool. Soc.* I. 103 The Palm Squirrel is very abundant in gardens in Dukhun. **1891** W. T. BLANFORD *Fauna Brit. India: Mammalia* II. 384 The cry of the palm-squirrel is a shrill chirp, resembling the note of a bird. **1908** *Westm. Gaz.* 15 June 5/3 The workers [*sc.* white ants] are preyed upon by true ants and many other insects;..by rats, mice, and palm-squirrels. **1955** I. T. SANDERSON *Living Mammals of World* 115/2 Palm-Squirrels... It is virtually impossible for the non-specialist to identify or even define this tribe. **1926** M. LEINSTER *Dew on Leaf* v. 55 A large writing-desk and shelf of books,..and a blackwood palm-stand, were some of the surrounding objects. **1937** M. COVARRUBIAS *Island of Bali* (1972) vi. 125 The child is weaned after three birthdays.., when the mother puts a mixture of lime and palm-sugar to her nipples. **1971** *Nat. Geographic* Mar. 344 (*caption*) Train of oxcarts, laden with baskets of palm sugar, rumbles toward a landing on the Irrawaddy River. **1950** 'D. DIVINE' *King of Fassarai* vii. 48 Fishing, canoe-building..and palm toddy. **1974** *Nat. Geographic* Dec. 754 A feast of marinated raw fish..was washed down with palm toddy. **1957** M. BANTON *W. Afr. City* iii. 52 Wartime prosperity multiplied the demand for palm-wine in Mende country. **1964** J. P. CLARK *Three Plays* 5 A big gourd of palm wine and three heads of kola-nut split before the dead of the land. **1969** J. M. GULLICK *Malaysia* i. 31 There may be a shop for the restricted sale of 'toddy' (palm wine). **1976** *Daily Times* (Lagos) 8 July 32/4 But Obadeya told the tribunal that he was in a palm-wine bar with Chidi that night.

palm, *sb.*[2] Add: **9.** *palm-reader*; **palm-ball** *U.S. Baseball*, a pitch of the ball gripped with the thumb and palm; **palm-print,** the impression left by the palm of the hand.

1948 *Richmond* (Virginia) *Times-Dispatch* 15 Mar. 17/4 The lanky Cincinnati Reds' sidewheeler has added a new pitch to his repertoire—a palm ball. **1950** *Sun* (Baltimore) 28 Aug. 16/2 He carries his own little notebook and can tell you many of the pitches he has made, when he threw the slider, the palm ball and even the gopher ball. **1973** *Times* 15 Aug. 7/3 There are numerous ways of hurling a ball legally to increase its effectiveness, such as the..screw-ball, the fork-ball and the palm-ball. **1976** *Webster's Sports Dict.* 300/2 *Palm ball*,..an off-speed pitch that is gripped between the thumb and the palm instead of with the ends of the fingers and that is thrown so that the fingers do not impart rotation to the ball. **1929** A. C. & C. EDINGTON *Studio Murder Myst.* xv. 202 In wearing gloves the criminal nearly always leaves a very legible palm print. **1946** *Nature* 12 Oct. 526/1 A drawing of a hand emphasizing the features of finger- and palm-print patterns is reproduced from this article. **1954** F. CHERRILL *Cherrill of Yard* vii. 69 'Are palm-prints as infallible as finger-prints?' he asked. **1955** *Times* 10 May 4/2 It had now been established that no two human beings had the same palm prints. **1967** N. LUCAS

C.I.D. v. 61 In 1930..for the first time, palm-print evidence was accepted in a criminal court. **1977** D. HARSENT *Dreams of Dead* 5 Her palm-print shrinks on the mirror as she turns away. **1920** R. MACAULAY *Potterism* III. ii. 131 She is the most wonderful palm reader and crystal gazer I have come across.

palm, *v.* Add: **1.** (Further examples.)

1974 *Guardian* 23 Sept. 24/8 Farmer palmed over a header from the impressive Thompson. **1976** *Wymondham & Attleborough Express* 3 Dec. 27/2 From the kick off the ball was put to Chambers on the wing and his hard shot was palmed into the path of Bartrum who put Pollastra 1-0 up in 45 seconds.

4. a. *spec.* in *U.S. Law* = *PASS *v.* 64 c.

1880 *Federal Reporter* (U.S.) I. 36 Nor is it necessary, in order to give a right to an injunction, that a specific trade-mark should be infringed, but it is sufficient that the court is satisfied that there was an intent on the part of the respondent to palm off his goods as the goods of the complainant. **1904** *Judicial & Statutory Definitions* VI. 5159/2 'To palm off' means to impose by fraud; to put off by inferior means. The language also imports that plaintiff must have been deceived and cheated by the representations, which he could not have been had he relied upon them. **1939** *Northeastern Reporter* XXI. 837/2 Defendants so conducted their business as to intentionally palm off on the public goods of the defendants as the goods of the plaintiff. **1956,** etc. [see *PALMING *vbl. sb.*[1] 2*]. **1973** *N.Y. Law Jrnl.* 17 Apr. 4/5 A claim that Borden attempted to 'palm off' its dried soup package as that of Lipton's.

b. Delete *rare* and add later examples.

1934 *Punch* 30 May 592/3, I lost seven holes running this morning absolutely and entirely because I had been palmed off with a little swine who sniffed whenever I was about to strike my ball. **1960** B. KOPS *Dream of Peter Mann* III. 66 We couldn't have our Superstore just yet and we were palmed off with promises.

Palmach (pa·lmaχ). Also ‖ **Palmakh.** [Heb. shortening of *p^{e}luggōṯ maḥaṣ* striking force.] A commando force of the Jewish *HAGANAH, active esp. during the war which preceded the formal establishment of the state of Israel in 1948, and incorporated in the Israeli national army in that year.

1945 *Times* 26 Sept. 5/7 The present strength of the *Haganah* itself is variously estimated at 50,000 to 75,000 men, with first-rate equipment,..and a motorized field force (*Palmakh*) capable of throwing in a task force of several thousand men at a few hours' notice at any threatened point of the country. **1949** KOESTLER *Promise & Fulfilment* III. i. 298 The military cadres of the extreme Left, *Palmach*, became the best and most ferocious shock troops. **1950** H. LEVIN *Jerusalem Embattled* 288 *Palmach* (Heb.), abbreviation for *Plugot Machatz*. Mobile detachment of the Jewish Defence Organization. **1955** S. D. GOITEIN *Jews & Arabs* viii. 224 The best boys of the *Palmach*, the 'Commandos' of the *Haganah*. **1960** H. AGAR *Saving Remnant* ix. 219 The Jews began the war with five thousand trained men: the *Palmach*, or shock companies of the Haganah. **1966** *New Statesman* 7 Oct. 506/2 He [*sc.* Ben Gurion] risked unpopularity in dissolving the Palmach, the crack commando troops who formed the potential core of a political and military elite. **1968** P. DURST *Badge of Infamy* iii. 27 There are a hundred of my old friends from the Palmach who would jump at the chance. **1971** *Guardian* 21 Oct. 7/5 The Palmach, the underground Jewish commando movement.

palmarosa (pæ:lmărōu·să). [It.]. **1.** *palmarosa oil,* an essential oil distilled from the grass *Cymbopogon martinii* var. *motia* and used in soaps, perfumes, and cosmetics.

1897 *Jrnl. Chem. Soc.* LXXII. I. 81 Palmarosa oil... This oil, formerly known as Turkish geranium oil, is prepared in the province of Bombay by distilling with water the leaves of a grass. **1902** C. SALTER tr. *Koller's Cosmetics* iv. 64 Palmarosa oil dissolves in 3 parts of 70 per cent. alcohol. **1923** W. A. POUCHER *Perfumes & Cosmetics* I. 105 Palmarosa oil is a useful adjunct in preparing almost any perfume of rose type. **1940** H. TROTTER *Man. Indian Forest Utilization* xiii. 243 Rosha grass oil..is also known as palmarosa or geranium oil. **1945** E. SAGARIN *Sci. & Art of Perfumery* iii. 33 Geraniol..is present in oil of citronella, gingergrass, palmarosa, attar of rose, and a host of others. **1950** E. GUENTHER *Essent. Oils* IV. 5 In India ..the bulk of commercial palmarosa oil originates. **1972** *Stand. Encycl. S. Afr.* V. 320/2 From others [*sc.* aromatic grasses]..essential oils like palmarosa oil and citronella oil are extracted.

2. In full, *palmarosa grass.* A tropical grass, *Cymbopogon martinii* var. *motia,* cultivated, esp. in India, for the sake of the essential oil it produces; also known as rosha grass.

1950 E. GUENTHER *Essent. Oils* IV. 9 Distillation of palmarosa grass in direct steam stills increased the yield of oil. *Ibid.* 13 All palmarosa plantings [in Java] were..in excellent condition. **1975** F. KENNETT *Hist. Perfume* ix. 183 Geraniol..can be obtained with greater facility and abundance from oils of citronella, geranium, or palmarossa [*sic*] grass.

Palm Beach. The name of a coastal resort in Florida, U.S.A., used to designate a kind of light-weight fabric used for clothing. Also *attrib.*, as *Palm Beach cloth, suit.*

Palm Beach is a proprietary name in the U.S. in this sense.

1915 *Policeman's Monthly* Sept. 21/2 A lady and a daughter thinking to give the husband a pleasant surprise, bought him a fine new silk 'Palm Beach' suit. **1915** *Official Gaz.* (U.S. Patent Office) 26 Oct. 1221/1 Palm Beach... Woolen piece goods, mohair piece goods, and piece goods of combinations of cotton, wool, mohair, alpaca, camel-hair, silk, and artificial silk. **1916** *Daily Colonist* (Victoria, B.C.) 2 July 6/1 (Advt.), Palm Beach Suits in an exceptionally fine quality of mercerized Palm Beach cloth. **1922** H. L. FOSTER *Adventures Trop. Tramp* i, I had just applied for a job as stoker, but a Palm Beach suit, a Panama hat, and a cane did not seem to be a convincing costume on the figure of an applicant for this position. **1928** —— *If you go to S. America* 17 In..tropical lands white linen or palm beach are desirable. **1928** *Daily Mail* 25 July 12/1 The ideal is a sports shirt with a low open neck, flannel trousers, and a jacket of the material used in Palm Beach suits. **1940** *Chambers's Techn. Dict.* 610/1 *Palm Beach,* a light fabric of plain weave made from cotton warp and lustre worsted weft, or entirely of cotton. **1959** J. THURBER *Years with Ross* vi. 99 Ingersoll had appeared..dressed in a Palm Beach suit. **1973** 'I. DRUMMOND' *Jaws of Watchdog* xi. 148 He was elegant in a white Palm Beach suit and a dark pink shirt.

palm court. Also with capital initials. [f. PALM *sb.*[1] + COURT *sb.*[1] I.] A large room or patio, esp. of a hotel, named from the palm-trees used as decoration. Now usu. in *attrib.* use, esp. **palm-court music,** the kind of light music associated with the palm court (also *ellipt.*); **palm-court orchestra,** a small band which plays such music.

These associations are now regarded as old-fashioned.

1908 *Westm. Gaz.* 12 Mar. 10/2 The lounge or palm-court of to-day was merely a revival of the Greek hall. **1910** *Bradshaw's Railway Guide* Apr. 1151 Plymouth, Royal Hotel..Magnificent Palm Court. Orchestra plays daily. **1930** E. WAUGH *Vile Bodies* x. 197 The manager of the 'Imperial'..upheld the integrity of British hotel-keeping. Tea, he explained, was served daily in the Palm Court, with orchestra on Thursdays and Sundays, between the hours of four and six. **1945** S. HUGHES in C. Madge *Pilot Papers* 89 The 'light' music public thinks of the music it wants in terms..of palm-court orchestras. **1955** *Radio Times* 22 Apr. 13/2 David Galliver sings with the Palm Court Orchestra in Grand Hotel at 9.0 tonight. **1959** *Observer* 21 June 18/4 The sugary tones of the Palm Court orchestra are never far away. **1962** *Ibid.* 28 Oct. 23/7 A retreat into daydream-fantasy that eventually either nauseates or numbs, as palm-court music does. **1966** M. BREWER *Man against Fear* xvi. 171, I recognised a popular Palm Court number from *Traviata.* **1969** *Times* 30 Apr. (Brighton Suppl.) p. i/3 The bingo hall with a palm court bar and lounge. **1970** E. LEE *Music of People* vii. 138 Music which would now be called 'Palm Court' was still widely popular. **1973** J. RYDER *Trevayne* (1974) vi. 50 Trevayne had gone to a corner pay phone to call his wife at the Plaza..but..he was told she wasn't in the Palm Court. **1977** J. WAINWRIGHT *Do Nothin'* viii. 124 He sometimes plays pure 'Palm Court'..without that extra lilt which can make a band swing.

palmer, *sb.*[1] **1.** Also *transf.*

1906 *Bungalow* Dec. 8/2 The exodus of these infatuated palmers is ever to the land of Shakespeare.

Palmerstonian (pāmǝɹstōu·niăn), *a.* [f. the name of Henry John Temple, Viscount *Palmerston,* English statesman (1784–1865) + -IAN.] Of, pertaining to, or characteristic of Lord Palmerston, or the forceful, assertive diplomacy associated with him. Also as *sb.*, a supporter of Lord Palmerston. So **Palmersto·nianism; Pa·lmerstonism.**

1854 *Punch* 17 June 246/2 We also wish he [*sc.* Lord Palmerston] would open a school in Downing Street wherein to furnish instruction in penmanship on the Palmerstonian system. **1858** *Illustr. News of World* 24 Apr. 187/1 Exposed to an attack from Palmerston and the Palmerstonians. *Ibid.* 5 June 283/2 Thunderbolts in the *Times* which made Mr. Disraeli, at Slough, virtuously protest against Palmerstonian corruption of the press. **1866** R. S. CHARNOCK *Verba Nominalia* 217 *Palmerstonism,* ..old-soldierism; soft-soap. **1898** *Westm. Gaz.* 14 Dec. 8/1 The revived Palmerstonianism of Lord Rosebery. **1900** [see *ELDONIAN *a.*]. **1927** *Observer* 20 Nov. 10/2 Because, in the hard old Palmerstonian phrase, we are not geese. **1928** *Ibid.* 11 Mar. 6/4 In private he was never chary of urging his chief to a more Palmerstonian line of policy. **1946** J. W. DAY *Harvest Adventure* xii. 195 One old man, with a Palmerstonian pippin face, in a full-skirted, snuff-coloured greatcoat with a velvet collar, talked of Culford as had done the beater half an hour before. **1954** A. J. P. TAYLOR *Struggle for Mastery in Europe 1848–1918* 414 Lansdowne did not need much encouragement to abandon the bankrupt Palmerstonian policy. **1966** *Economist* 12 Nov. 683/2 Palmerstonism was already hopelessly bankrupt. **1973** *Listener* 7 June 742/1 You will wonder why such a Palmerstonian view of television cuts any ice with the broadcasting authorities.

palmette. Add: **1.** (Later examples.) Also *transf.* and *attrib.*

1908 *Times Lit. Suppl.* 14 Aug. 260/2 From the tenth to the fourteenth century the palmette-motive disappears. **1931** A. ESDAILE *Student's Man. Bibliogr.* vi. 212 Two.. London binders..produced about 1815 some really beautiful bindings decorated with classical palmette borders. **1931** A. U. DILLEY *Oriental Rugs & Carpets* iii. 61 A fourth group of superior rugs, distinguished by pattern of palmette and now called Ispahan. **1975** *Ashmolean Mus. Rep. Visitors 1973–4* 17 A fragment of an Attic black-figure amphora decorated with a lotus and palmette pattern, languettes, and part of a battle scene.

palmetto. Add: **c.** *palmetto country, ground* (earlier example), *hat* (later examples), *juice, leaf* (further examples), *swamp, tree* (later example); *palmetto-thatched* adj.; also in sense 'thatched with palmetto leaves', as *palmetto cabin, house* (earlier example), *hut;* **palmetto brush,** a hard brush made from the roots of the palmetto; **palmetto bush,** a young or dwarfed plant of one of the species of palmetto; **palmetto cabbage** = *cabbage palmetto* (see sense b in Dict.); **palmetto flag** (examples); **Palmetto State** (examples).

1913 *Country Life* Nov. 94/3 For the making of palmetto brushes the problem is to remove the pith without destroying the fibres. **1784** T. HUTCHINS *Hist. Narr. Louisiana & W. Florida* 34 The whole is..covered with thick wood, Palmetto bushes, &c. **1812** *Niles' Reg.* III. 237/1 Many more must have been slain, but were hid from our view by the thick and high Palmetto bushes. **1901** *Scribner's Mag.* Apr. 433/1 Narrow grooves have been worn in the hillsides, divided one from the other by.. pyramids of earth and clay, crested with the stunted stems and roots of palmetto bushes. **1802** J. DRAYTON *View South-Carolina* 6 Their soil is of very sandy nature; producing..palmetto cabbage, palmetto royal, silk grass. **1870** *Amer. Naturalist* III. 458 With a palmetto cabin, plenty of oysters, game and fish, he lives a free and easy life. **1942** S. KENNEDY *Palmetto Country* 24 The Palmetto country rests upon what is geologically known as the Floridian plateau. **1860** in *South Carolina Hist. Mag.* (1964) LXIV. 156 This evening the Palmetto Flag was inaugurated. **1861** *Mitchell's Maritime Reg.* 403/2 The Peter Maxwell sailed off with the Palmetto flag flying at her main. **1744** F. MOORE *Voy. Georgia* 124 The Indians were prevailed upon to return to the Palmetto ground. **1877** E. S. WARD *Story of Avis* 410 She looked very young and girlish that day in her palmetto hat and white linen dress. **1889** G. W. CABLE in *Century Mag.* Feb. 516/2 Before the end of the month all the women in St. Martinville were wearing palmetto hats. **1974** 'B. MATHER' *White Dacoit* vi. 64 His hideous palmetto hat..flopped down over his face in a ragged veil. **1741** in *South Carolina Hist. Soc. Coll.* (1887) IV. 42 They came to some Palmetto Houses, where they halted about one hour. [**1731** M. CATESBY *Nat. Hist. Carolina* I. 69 A man..builds a hut with Palmetto-Leaves, for the shelter of himself and family while they stay.] **1739** W. STEPHENS *Jrnl.* 29 Dec. in *Colonial Rec. Georgia* (1906) IV. 480, I found them well covered from bad Weather, by a strong Palmeta Hut. **1741** in *South Carolina Hist. Soc. Coll.* (1887) IV. 33 The first Palmetto Hut on the sea beach.. where the Spaniards had once a lookout. **1845** T. J. GREEN *Jrnl. Texian Expedition* 152 Several were left on the road exhausted for the want of water and here they commenced unfortunately, the use of the palmetto juice as a substitute. **1731** Palmetto-leaf [see **palmetto hut*]. **1763** tr. Du Mont in *Le Page du Pratz' Hist. Louisiana* I. 351 Making thus the form of a house of an oblong square..and cover..with cypress-bark, or palmetto-leaves. **1880** G. W. CABLE *Grandissimes* xiv. 89 On it [*sc.* the floor] were here and there in places white mats woven of bleached palmetto leaf. **1891** *Harper's Mag.* Dec. 47/1 Perhaps the colonel would not wave the palmetto leaf too vigorously. **1976** C. LARSON *Muir's Blood* xxx. 159 Ferns as wide as palmetto leaves drooped and swayed. **1837** *Globe* (Washington) 14 Jan. 3/3 After exchanging all kinds of civilities..which induced them to believe that the Judge was certain of the Palmetto State. **1843** *Knickerbocker* XXI. 222 The merry days of good old Christmas are still observed in the Palmetto State. **1948** *Sat. Even. Post* 10 July 12/3 Although Palmetto State folks may have hesitated to brag the first year, they're safe now. **1974** *State* (Columbia, S. Carolina) 15 Feb. 1-A/3 Officials of the U.S. Justice Department firmly rejected a disputed reapportionment plan Thursday for the S.C. House of Representatives charging that it could deny equal voting rights to blacks in the Palmetto State. **1853** 'P. PAXTON' *Stray Yankee in Texas* 56 The '*marais*' or slough,..according to my friend Joe's account, changed into a 'branch'; then after running through a cypress brake or two, ultimately assumed the form of a palmetto swamp. **1888** G. W. CABLE *Bonaventure* 86 On a bank of this bayou..[stood] the palmetto-thatched fishing and hunting lodge. **1895** G. KING *New Orleans* 34 There is absolutely no seeing of Bienville's group of palmetto-thatched huts by the yellow currents of the Mississippi. **1908** *Daily Chron.* 1 Sept. 7/5 As they strolled together towards the palmetto-thatched, open-face camp fronting on Ruffle Lake. **1971** 'D. HALLIDAY' *Dolly & Doctor Bird* xiv. 202 Brady led me..up to the Begum's long palmetto-thatched bar. **1865** 'G. HAMILTON' *Skirmishes* xiii. 172 If he is concocting..rebellion, can he not go on just as blithely under the Stars and Stripes as under the Palmetto tree?

palmful, *sb.* (Later examples.)

a **1861** T. WINTHROP *John Brent* (1883) xxii. 194 They took their water by the throatful, not by the palmful. **1940** C. H. WARREN *Corn Country* 3 He pulled out a palmful of unprepared flour.

palmierite (pælmī·ěrǝit). *Min.* [ad. F. *palmiérite* (A. Lacroix 1907, in *Compt. Rend.* CXLIV. 1400), f. the name of Luigi *Palmier-i* (1807–1896), Italian meteorologist: see -ITE[1].] A sulphate of potassium, sodium, and lead, $(K,Na)_2Pb(SO_4)_2$, found as colourless hexagonal crystals.

1907 *Mineral. Mag.* XIV. 406 Palmierite..found enclosed in aphthitalite amongst the products of the Vesuvian eruption of April, 1906. **1954** *Mineral. Abstr.* XII. 332 Palmierite..was prepared as pearly scales by fusing a mixture of $PbSO_4$ and K_2SO_4.

palmiet (pa·lmit). [Afrikaans, a. Du., f. Sp. and Pg. *palmito,* dim. of *palma* palm.] A South African plant found in swamps and along river-banks, *Prionium serratum* (= *P.*

palmita), of the family Juncaceæ, which has a woody stem, topped with a cluster of long, narrow, serrated leaves two or three feet long, and small, greenish-gold flowers borne in a large panicle.

1785 G. FORSTER tr. *Sparrman's Voy. Cape Good Hope* I. iii. 42 A little river or stream covered with *palmites*, a kind of *acorus* with a thick stem and broad leaves, which grow out from the top, as they do in the palm-tree, a circumstance from which the plant takes its name. **1800** A. BARNARD *Let.* 14 May in *S. Afr. a Century Ago* (1901) xvii. 286, I am living out of town.., removed from all party work, except working parties in our fields, rooting up of palmite roots, and planting of fir trees and potatoes. **1822** W. J. BURCHELL *Trav. S. Afr.* I. iv. 89 The boors believe this brownness [of the water] to be caused by the great quantity of Palmite (Palmiet), which every where grows in these streams. *Ibid.* 91 Most of the rivers which we passed in this excursion, are choked up with the plant called *Palmiet* by the colonists, and from which this one [*sc.* river] derives its name. **1868** J. CHAPMAN *Trav. S. Afr.* I. ix. 193 The flower and root of the bulrush as well as the tsetla root or palmiet..forms the main article of the diet of the Makobas. **1871** H. H. DUGMORE *Reminisc. Albany Settler* I. 17 The beaver gave way to the home-made palmiet or coffee straw, and the tiger-skin cap. **1944** V. POHL *Adventures Boer Family* xvi. 106 The only hats they possessed were those made by my mother and Sophia from straw, *palmiet* (a water plant) or mealie leaves. **1952** *Cape Times* 20 Sept. 3/2 The boat..was steered to a clump of palmiet. **1973** *Stand. Encycl. S. Afr.* VIII. 439/2 Palmiet... This waterside plant..has a fairly stout, erect or decumbent, woody stem covered with old leaf-bases.

palming, *vbl. sb.*[1] Add: **2*.** *palming off* (U.S. Law) = *PASSING *vbl. sb.* 2 b. Also *attrib.*

1891 *Atlantic Reporter* XXI. 613/2 The language of the court imports an intentional deceit and palming off. **1925** *Federal Reporter* (1926) VII. 604/1 In the case at bar the means are as plainly unlawful as in the usual case of palming off. It is as unlawful to lie about the quality of one's wares as about their maker. **1942** *Ibid.* CXXIV. 706/1 Under Illinois law the 'palming off doctrine' is not treated as merely the designation of a typical class of cases of unfair competition, but as a rule of law itself. **1956** *Dior* v. *Milton* in *N.Y. Suppl.* 2nd Ser. CLV. 452 With the passage of those simple and halcyon days when the chief business malpractice was 'palming off', and with the development of more complex business relationships ..many courts..have extended the doctrine of unfair competition beyond the cases of 'palming off'. **1965** A. BOGSCH in *Ibid.* 329/2 The principle of 'passing off' or 'palming off'.

palm-leaf. Add: **c.** *palm-leaf book, fan, hat* (earlier example), *manuscript, roof*; **palm-leaf pattern,** a device resembling a palm-leaf used in the decoration of oriental carpets.

1937 M. COVARRUBIAS *Island of Bali* (1972) i. 7 The second half of the manuscript [of the Tjatur Yoga] is extremely obscure, full of errors, and appears incomplete, perhaps owing to careless copying of an older palm-leaf book. **1860** J. G. HOLLAND *Miss Gilbert's Career* viii. 132 Then Mrs. Ruggles helped herself to a palm-leaf fan. **1891** *Century Mag.* Mar. 734 Chad substituted a palm-leaf fan from the hall table. **1836** O. W. HOLMES *September Gale* 156 The wind whisked off my palm-leaf hat. **1948** D. DIRINGER *Alphabet* vi. 360 Many palm-leaf manuscripts.. are also written in this [Nagari] script. **1931** A. U. DILLEY *Oriental Rugs & Carpets* Pl. 28 (*caption*) Saraband Rug. Palm Leaf Pattern. **1930** R. MACAULAY *Staying with Relations* ix. 119 They..went to find her, but found nothing except wrecked posts and a smashed palm leaf roof sprawling on the shaken earth.

palm-tree. Add: **c.** Also *Comb.*, as **palm-tree justice,** justice summarily administered, usu. with little regard for legal principle or precedent (with reference to the Islamic cadi (see CADI) administering justice under a palm-tree: see also quot. 1634 for sense a in Dict.).

[**1916** A. UNDERHILL in *Shakespeare's England* I. xiii. 383 In Shakespeare's time the Court of Chancery was almost as unfettered by precedent as the typical Cadi under the Palm Tree.] **1959** *Sunday Times* 24 May 5/4 What are the origins and associations of the phrase..'palm-tree justice', which has recently been used several times by Her Majesty's Judges in legal contexts? **1963** *Times* 7 May 9/2 It would be perhaps rather hard luck for Simpson's now to have to part with their North Road site at prices which no longer represented modern prices. It would be no more than palm-tree justice. **1968** *Economist* 3 Feb. 42/3 In this period the [Roman] emperors themselves considered the letters that came up to them and dictated their answers personally: palm-tree justice was still obtainable.

palmy, *a.* Add: **2.** *palmy days* (earlier examples).

1837 DICKENS *Let.* 31 Jan. (1965) I. 232, I hope you will meet with every happiness that you picture to yourself in these palmy days. **1848** TROLLOPE *Kellys & O'Kellys* I. iv. 80 Mrs. Lynch had died before the commencement of Sim's palmy days. They had seen no company in her time.

Hence **pa·lmily** *adv.*; **pa·lminess.**

1886 G. B. SHAW *How to become Mus. Critic* (1960) 112 When old-fashioned people..regret the palmy days of the drama, superstitious ones are apt to take the desirability of palminess for granted... The young London play-goer can hardly judge; for he has no experience of palminess. *Ibid.*, A palmily stall-less pit.

Palmyrene (pæ·lmĭrīn, pælmaɪ·rīn), *sb.* and *a.* Also **Palmyre·nian.** [ad. L. *Palmyrēn-us*, f. Gr. *Παλμύρα*, L. *Palmyra* Palmyra.] **A.** *sb.* **a.** A native or inhabitant of the ancient city of Palmyra in Syria. **b.** The language and script in use at Palmyra. **B.** *adj.* Of or pertaining to Palmyra, its inhabitants, its language, or its script.

1609 HOLLAND tr. *Ammianus Marcellinus' Roman Hist.* 339 Praysing and extolling of her, as much as the Parthyans do Semiramis, Ægypt Cleopatra..or the Palmyrenes Zenobia. **1609** JONSON *Masque of Queenes* sig. E2[v] The ninth, in time, but equall in fame, and (the cause of it) vertue, was the chast Zenobia, Queene of the Palmyrenes. **1695** E. HALLEY in *Phil. Trans. R. Soc.* XIX. 161 But the Palmyrenes being informed of the Design [of M. Antonius to plunder Palmyra], took care to prevent them, and so escaped Plunder. *Ibid.* 172, I have taken care to have the Stone purposely viewed, as also to get from thence the exact Figure of the Syrian or Palmyrene Characters thereon... By the help of these, compared with two others.., I hope we may be able, one day, to make out the Palmyrene Alphabet. **1753** R. WOOD *Ruins of Palmyra* 6 Odenathus, a Palmyrene,..made so proper a use of this situation..as to get the balance of power into his hands. *Ibid.* 25 The ancient inscriptions we found at Palmyra were all Greek, or Palmyrene, except one in Latin. **1776** GIBBON *Decl. & F.* I. xi. 309 The emperor [Aurelian], by his salutory edicts, recalled the fugitives, and granted a general pardon to all who..had been engaged in the service of the Palmyrenian queen. *Ibid.* 310 They..engaged the Palmyrenians in a laborious pursuit. **1875** [see *NABATÆAN *sb.* and *a.*]. **1886** W. P. DICKSON tr. *Mommsen's Provinces Roman Empire* II. ix. 96 Even in votive inscriptions which Palmyrenes set up to their native gods in Rome, and in tombs of Palmyrene soldiers that died in Africa or Britain, the Palmyrene rendering is added. **1900** G. BELL *Let.* 20 May (1927) I. 108 As we drew near Palmyra, the hills were covered with the strangest buildings, great stone towers, four stories high, some more ruined and some less, standing together in groups or bordering the road. They are the famous Palmyrene tower tombs. **1932** D. & T. RICE tr. *Rostovtzeff's Caravan Cities* v. 149 The external aspect of Palmyrene culture strikes the eye with its complexity and peculiarity. **1948** D. DIRINGER *Alphabet* iv. 280 Cantineau considers the Syriac alphabet as related to the cursive Palmyrene, the former having been influenced by the latter thanks to the commercial activities of the Palmyrenians. **1957** *Encycl. Brit.* XVII. 162/2 The Palmyrene princes cherished the idea of an independent empire of their own. *Ibid.* 163/2 The technical terms of municipal government are mostly Greek, transliterated into Palmyrene. **1963** W. F. ALBRIGHT *Biblical Period from Abraham to Ezra* i. 9 Nearly all..parallels come from Nabataean or Palmyrene, as well as later Syrian inscriptions. **1972** P. M. FRASER *Ptolemaic Alexandria* I. i. 12 It was their destruction in the reign of Aurelian, at the time of the Palmyrene invasion, which led to the abandonment of Brucheion. **1978** *Times Lit. Suppl.* 3 Mar. 249/2 There is an interesting section discussing the scattered but far from negligible artistic traces left by Palmyrenes resident *in partibus*.

palo blanco (pa·lo bla·nko). *U.S.* [Amer. Sp., = 'white tree'.] A small tree or shrub of the genus *Celtis*, esp. *C. reticulata*, the western hackberry, belonging to the family Ulmaceæ, native to south-western North America and distinguished by its light-coloured bark, downy leaves, and red berries (see also quot. 1947).

1838 S. MAVERICK *Let.* 30 Dec. in 'R. M. Green' *Samuel Maverick* (1953) v. 83 Griffin & Granville can cut posts or pickets, and haul them to the (palo-blanco) hackberry tree. **1901** J. C. VAN DYKE *Desert* 147 All the common growths like the sage, the mesquite, the palo fierro, and the palo blanco, are blossom bearers. **1926** D. H. LAWRENCE *Plumed Serp.* xix. 326 The car went on, the great lights glaring upon the hedges of cactus and mesquite and palo blanco trees. **1927** —— *Mornings in Mexico* 33 A valley bed, where is..the *palo-blanco*..with big white flowers like pure white, crumpled cambric. **1938** L. N. GOODDING *Notes Native & Exotic Plants* (U.S. Dept. Agric. Soil Conservation Service) 52 Palo Blanco or White Bark Hackberry..furnishes shade along many of the dry washes. **1947** J. C. RICH *Materials & Methods Sculpture* x. 293 *Palo Blanco* means 'white wood' and the name is applied to many woods of different species. **1951** KEARNEY & PEEBLES *Arizona Flora* 220 *Celtis reticulata*... Netleaf hackberry, palo-blanco, sugar-berry. **1958** E. M. REISS *Garden of Chaparral* 140 Palo-blanco; Hackberry (*Celtis laevigata*). A thirty-foot tree with whitish bark which accounts for its local name. **1960** R. VINES *Trees, Shrubs & Woody Vines of Southwest* 203/2 A vernacular name [of *Celtis lindheimeri*] is Palo Blanco.

palo de hierro (pa·lo də hi,ē·ro). *U.S.* Also **palo fier(r)o.** [Amer. Sp., = 'iron tree'.] The Sonora or desert ironwood, *Olneya tesota*, of the family Leguminosæ, which bears racemes of white flowers; also used as a name for other trees producing particularly hard wood, or the wood itself.

1894 *Amer. Anthropologist* VII. 293 During the rest of the year the Indians devote themselves to..the gathering of the fruit of the cactus, mesquite beans, and the bean of the *palo fiero*. **1912** K. LUMHOLTZ *New Trails in Mexico* 224 All the mules, donkeys, and horses gathered at once around a lone but very large palo fiero tree to eat its dark green juicy leaves. **1931** W. A. DAYTON *Important Western Browse Plants* 86 Tesota (*Olneya tesota*) is variously known as arbol (or palo) de hierro, and desert (Mexican, or Sonora) ironwood. **1949** *Desert Mag.* June 22/2 The great washes along the highway were crowded with palo verde trees and ironwood, or palo fierro. **1951** KEARNEY & PEEBLES *Arizona Flora* 442 *Olneya Tesota*... Known commonly in Arizona as ironwood, or palo-de-hierro. **1963** W. J. SCHALDACH *Path to Enchantment* vi. 74 A tree unique in several ways is the ironwood, or *palo-fierro*. True to its name, the ironwood tree possesses wood so tough that it dulls an ax.

palomino (pælomī·no). orig. *U.S.* Also **palamino.** [Amer. Sp., a. Sp. *palomino* f. L. *palumbīnus* of or resembling a dove.] A light brown or cream-coloured horse with pale mane and tail, believed to have been developed from Arab stock. Also *attrib.*

1914 *Sunset* May 995/1 A Palomino stallion with arching neck and muscle-ridged barrel led the dozen brown and mottled mares of his seraglio up a silent hillside. **1932** H. W. BENTLEY *Dict. Spanish Terms in Eng.* 176 Palomino..A term commonly used in the Southwest and California to describe a horse of a silver yellow color. **1935** J. STEINBECK *Tortilla Flat* x. 180 You will ride a palomino horse. **1936** *New Yorker* 18 Apr. 12/3 He made a fine entrance on his palomino. **1949** *Esquire* Mar. 29/1 They'll reserve a golden palomino horse for you—all yours for the length of your stay. **1955** W. FOSTER-HARRIS *Look of Old West* viii. 239 Palominos are gold-colored horses, light tan or cream, with white manes—a color variant, not a breed. **1958** *Times* 18 Sept. 13/3 Her favourites are not only Arabs, but, also, Thoroughbreds, Percherons..with, as runners-up, Hackneys, Hunters, Palominos. **1959** *Sunday Express* 19 Apr. 5/6 Her Palamino pony-breeding business in Warwickshire. **1967** [see **circus-trick*]. **1973** *Country Life* 8 Mar. 654/3 (*heading*) British Palomino Society annual show. **1976** *Billings* (Montana) *Gaz.* 2 July 11-C/6 (Advt.), 4 year old Palamino mare. Good kid & ranch horse. $300.

2. A pale golden-brown colour.

1951 H. MACINNES *Neither Five nor Three* I. ii. 27 Her blonde palomino-rinsed head turned towards Mrs. Hershey. **1960** *Times* 31 Oct. 1/3 Mink Coat..and Palamino Stole. **1968** J. IRONSIDE *Fashion Alphabet* vii. 159 The mink breeders.., always searching for different colours...name each variety, the more generally known being:... Palomino..: Honey-gold.

palone (pălōu·n). *slang.* [Etym. uncertain; conceivably a phonet. var. of BLOWEN.] A derogatory term for a young woman; also, an effeminate man.

1934 P. ALLINGHAM *Cheapjack* xvi. 202 I'd rather 'andle a man any day than a lot of these silly palones. *Ibid.* 203 Charlie was not a lady's man, and by 'palones' he meant girls. **1947** *Penguin New Writing* XXIX. 99 The authentic flavour of life among the small-time spivs, of caffs and gaffs, grafter and palone. **1969** J. GARDNER *Complete State of Death* v. 66 There was another possibility. Hart could be a palone. Fanny Hart. No.

palooka (pălū·kă). *slang* (chiefly *U.S.*). Also **paluka, palooker.** [Orig. unknown.] An inferior or average prizefighter; any stupid or mediocre person; a lout. Also *attrib.*

1925 H. C. WITWER *Roughly Speaking* (1926) 287 Ben will make at palooka's pan over for you in any style you wish, Reverend Jephtha. **1927** D. HAMMETT in *Black Mask* Feb. 28/1 A paluka who leads with his right. **1932** WODEHOUSE *Hot Water* vi. 112 One of these palookas suddenly pulls out a young carving-knife and sticks me in the wish-bone with it. **1933** *Amer. Speech* Oct. 37/2 He still looks plenty good enough to take the English palooka. **1936** J. TULLEY *Bruiser* v. 48 Don't let these palookers around here laugh you outta seein' me go—all you'll ever get outta these stumble bums is the holes in the doughnuts. **1950** J. DEMPSEY *Championship Fighting* ii. 11 It was only natural that the tide of palooka experts should sweep into the amateur ranks. **1950** A. LOMAX *Mister Jelly Roll* (1952) 139 You won't kick me in the ass, because I can beat this palooka. **1977** *New Yorker* 8 Aug. 12/2 A romantic fable about a Philadelphia palooka who gains his manhood. **1978** *N.Y. Times* 27 Feb. c2/6 Leon Spinks..does not rate highly with at least one former heavyweight title holder. 'He is a palooka,' says Ingemar Johansson.

‖**palourde** (palu·ɹd). [Fr.] A marine bivalve mollusc belonging to the genus *Venerupis*; a Venus clam or carpet-shell. Cf. PULLET 2 in Dict. and Suppl.

[**1863** J. G. JEFFREYS *Brit. Conchology* II. 361 According to Collard de Cherres, the Breton designation is 'palourde'.] **1942** E. PAUL *Narrow St.* xxxiv. 303 Baby sea snails to be picked out with a pin; huge *palourdes* and giant snails; the tender coquilles St. Jacques. **1951** —— *Springtime in Paris* xi. 189 Sampling eagerly the oysters, clams, palourdes, cockles, mussels, snails, razor-fish or sea-urchins. **1960** E. DAVID *French Provincial Cooking* 141 We..cannot obtain the various kinds of exquisite little clams, the *praires*, the *palourdes* and the *clovisses* which one gets in France. **1976** *Times* 2 Oct. 10/2 Palourdes on a buttery spinach puree.

palo verde (pa·lo vē·ɹde). *U.S.* [Amer. Sp., = 'green tree'.] A name used for several small trees or shrubs belonging to the genera *Cercidium* or *Parkinsonia* of the family Leguminosæ, native to south-western North America and distinguished by green bark and racemes of yellow flowers. Also *attrib.*

1854 J. R. BARTLETT *Pers. Narr. Explor. Texas* II. 188 The vegetation consisted of mezquit and palo verde. **1860** *Proc. Calif. Acad. Sci.* II. 129 In the eastern part of the

Papagoria, the country is..covered with a low growth of *mesquite* and *palo verde* brush. **1881** *Amer. Naturalist* XV. 982 The 'Palo[v]erde' of the Mexicans...grows to be some fifteen or twenty feet high. **1891** [see *MESCAL 2]. **1913** *Rep. Brit. Assoc. Adv. Sci. 1912* 533 The valleys [in the Sonora Desert] contain in abundance trees—of which the most common are mesquito (*Prosopis velutina*) and paloverde (*Parkinsonia torreyana*)—shrubs and cacti. **1947** *Southern Sierran* May 4/2 The flaming red of the Ocotillo and the bright lemon yellow of the Palo Verde were outstanding. **1955** *Sci. Amer.* Apr. 72 (*caption*) Desert wash is traced by ironwood (*Olneya*) and paloverde (*Cercidium*) plants. **1969** T. H. EVERETT *Living Trees of World* 200/2 The Jerusalem thorn or palo verde..is not an Old World native but is indigenous from Texas to Argentina. **1972** Y. LOVELOCK *Vegetable Bk.* I. 177 Another close American relative [of the Judas tree] is the palo verde.., whose Spanish name refers to the distinctive green bark. **1974** P. A. MUNZ *Flora S. California* 437 *Cercidium* Tulasne. Palo Verde. Shrubs or small trees with green bark and ± spinose twigs. *Ibid.* 465 *Parkinsonia* L. Palo Verde. Low trees with green branches and twigs... *P. aculeata* L. Mexican Palo Verde.

palouser (pălū·zəɹ). *U.S. colloq.* [f. the *Palouse*, a region in the north-western U.S.] (See quots. 1918 and 1958.)

1903 *Outing* May 144/2 No, all were not British 're-mittance men', Arizona 'palousers', and bank clerks on the trail. **1918** *Dialect Notes* V. 27 *Palouser*, n. 1. A greenhorn; a country fellow. From the fact that the Palouse is a farming country. 2. A lantern made by attaching a bale, horizontally, to an empty can and by inserting a candle through a hole in the side. 3. A gorgeous sunset. From the circumstance that the sunsets in the Palouse are very magnificent. **1958** W. F. MCCULLOCH *Woods Words* 131 *Palouser*, a lantern made by sticking a candle through a hole in a tin can.

palp, *v.* Add: (Further example.)

1967 S. BECKETT *Stories & Texts for Nothing* III. 86 Palp your skull, seat of the understanding.

2. Short for PALPITATE *v.* 1.

1903 'MARJORIBANKS' *Fluff-Hunters* 30 Georgie panted and palped, and the old man gurgled and gasped. *Ibid.* 149 'I am Phyllis Tremayn!' exclaimed the excited bit of fat, palping all over.

palpable, *a.* **1. b.** (Further example.)

1974 *Nature* 22 Mar. 344/2 At 72 and 96 h the lesions were smaller but still palpable.

palpate, *v.* Add: Also *absol.* or *intr.*

1901 W. OSLER *Princ. & Pract. Med.* (ed. 4) 25 There may be early muscle rigidity and increased tension, and spasm on any attempt to palpate. **1963** D. G. W. CLYNE *Textbk. Gynaecol. & Obstetr.* xv. 374 The examiner..then gently palpates with the pulps of the fingers so as to distinguish between the soft, wedge-shaped breech and the hard, round ballottable head.

Hence **palpa·ting** *ppl. a.*

1901 G. R. BUTLER *Diagnostics Internal Med.* xxxiii. 431 The re-enforcement of the palpating hand by the other preserves the perceptive delicacy which the former would otherwise lose. **1974** PASSMORE & ROBSON *Compan. Med. Stud.* III. II. xxxix. 15/1 If the palpating fingers on the appropriate side can reach below the occipital prominence..the head is not engaged.

palping (pæ·lpiŋ), *ppl. a. rare.* [f. PALP *v.* + -ING².] That palps or feels.

1929 R. BRIDGES *Testament of Beauty* iv. 128 It thrusteth out its finely adapted tentacles in their first palping movements to the encounter of life.

palsa (pæ·lsă). *Geomorphol.* [ad. Sw. *palse*, *pals* (pl. *palsar*), introduced as a techn. term (*palse*) by Fries & Bergström 1910, in *Geol. Fören. i Stockholm Förhandl.* XXXII. 195, from Finnish and Lappish *palsa*. The pl. *palsen*, sometimes found in Eng., reflects Ger. usage.] A mound or ridge of peat covered with vegetation and containing a core of frozen peat or mineral soil in which are numerous ice lenses, occurring in subarctic regions (usu. in bogs).

1942 *Geogr. Rev.* XXXII. 420 Peat knobs in swamps and bogs and hillocks in tundra, commonly called *Palsen*, are described from northern Europe and Siberia in an extensive foreign literature. *Ibid.* 421 The solid cores of ice show that the mounds are not due solely to upward movement of fine material, as in the case of most *Palsen*. **1954** W. D. THORNBURY *Princ. Geomorphol.* iv. 89 On surfaces covered by a good growth of tundra vegetation low, rounded mounds composed of fine materials are often found. They are called earth hummocks or palsen. **1973** A. L. WASHBURN *Periglacial Processes* 152 The ice lenses generally distinguish palsas from pingos. **1973** *Nature* 9 Nov. 64/1 In Finland palsas are only found north of the coniferous forest limit.

palship. See s.v. PAL *sb.*¹ in Dict. Add: (Further examples.) Also *attrib.*

1916 [see *NEVER *adv.* 9]. **1936** P. M. CLARK *Autobiogr. Old Drifter* xiv. 200 The wonderful pal-ship of dogs is to me an everlasting delight. **1966** *Listener* 23 June 897/2 The whole feuding quartet had been invited..to join the presidential plane and put on a show of unanimity and palship. **1972** R. D. ABRAHAMS in T. Kochman *Rappin' & Stylin' Out* 236 The protected and licensed confines of palship groupings. **1974** *Publishers Weekly* 11 Feb. 56/2 His long, intimate palship with Marlon 'Bud' Brando.

palsy, *sb.* (*a.*) Add: **1. b. cerebral palsy**, any of various non-progressive forms of paralysis caused by damage to motor areas of the brain before or during birth, manifested in early childhood by weakness and imperfect control of the affected muscles; hence **cerebral-palsied** *a.*, affected with cerebral palsy; also *absol.*

[**1888** *Lancet* 14 Apr. 709/1 There are two classes of birth palsies, the 'peripheral' and the 'cerebral'.] **1889** W. OSLER *Cerebral Palsies of Children* i. 2 The cases are usually arranged under the generic terms cerebral palsies—the German *Cerebrale Kinderlähmung*—or spastic palsies, while the specific designation indicates the distribution of the paralysis, whether unilateral, bilateral, or paraplegic. **1940** *Jrnl. Amer. Med. Assoc.* 14 Dec. 2119/1 Treatment depends on..the particular kind of cerebral palsy: spastic, athetoid or ataxic. **1955** *Lancet* 15 Jan. 146/1 Cerebral palsies may occur in mentally normal and in mentally deficient subjects. **1961** *Ibid.* 19 Aug. 433/2 The Pædiatric Research Unit..is contributing to the study of..the special psychological problems of learning in cerebral-palsied children. **1973** *Times* 30 Oct. 2/7 Buildings and land housing St Margaret's School, Croydon, which provides specifically for the cerebral palsied, were leased rent-free to the school by two sisters. **1974** PASSMORE & ROBSON *Compan. Med. Stud.* III. II. xxxvi. 9/1 Many children with mild cerebral palsy require no medical treatment and, if they are of average intelligence, should be considered as normal children, though allowances may have to be made.

palsy (pæ·lzi), *sb.*² (*a.*²) *slang.* Also **palsie** and in extended forms **palsy-walsy, palsie-walsie, palsey-walsey.** [f. PAL *sb.*¹ + -SY.] **A.** *sb.* A friend, a 'pal'; a form of (ostensibly) friendly address.

1930 *Amer. Speech* Dec. 82 Call me Palsy. **1937** J. CURTIS *There ain't no Justice* xxvi. 287 What are you having, palsy-walsy? **1941** H. SMITH *Gang's All Here* 266 There was nothing to do but I must go along with them. I even went into SRO with them. Talk about palsy-walsies! **1945** P. CHEYNEY *I'll say she Does* i. 18 How come, palsie? **1945** E. WILSON *I am gazing into my 8-Ball* 118 Ratoff appealed to him. 'Look, palsy,' he said ,'whawt time I wawz in your house this morning?' **1962** *Coast to Coast 1961–62* 25 'Well, well, if it's not my old palsie-walsie Bert,' one of the detectives said. **1966** 'W. HAGGARD' *Power House* x. 111 There was nothing quite so expendable as dear old palsy-walsies who had by now outgrown their usefulness.

B. *adj.* Friendly, 'pally'. So **pa·lsy-wa:lsiness.**

1947 *Philadelphia Bull.* 17 Feb. 8/3 Army planes will drop on them pictures of General MacArthur and Hirohito in palsey-walsey attitudes, to convince them that hostilities have ceased. **1957** 'P. QUENTIN' *Suspicious Circ.* vii. 75 What if all that revolting *Daddy Long Legs* palsy-walsiness had been fake? **1959** 'J. R. MACDONALD' *Galton Case* (1960) xviii. 149 Him and Pete were palsy-walsy. **1962** BROWN & GILMAN in J. A. Fishman *Readings Sociol. of Lang.* (1968) 268 Very 'palsy' parents may invite their children to call them by first name. **1963** WODEHOUSE *Stiff Upper Lip, Jeeves* xiii. 101 What do you call it when a couple of nations start off by being all palsy walsy and then begin calling each other ticks and bounders? **1969** *Daily Tel.* (Colour Suppl.) 11 Apr. 41/4 The New York police and I are not too palsy right now. **1974** WODEHOUSE *Aunts aren't Gentlemen* vii. 56 Being a Communist, he was probably on palsy-walsy terms with half the big shots at the Kremlin. **1977** J. WAINWRIGHT *Pool of Tears* 218 He's one of those matey types... Very palsy-walsy.

palter, *v.* **1.** (Later example.)

1872 in C. Sumner *Wks.* VI. 34 Some weak-backed quietist, who, afraid to look this thing in the face, would palter weak commonplaces.

paludal, *a.* Add: Esp., of a plant, growing in marshy ground. Also, as *sb.*, a plant requiring a marshy habitat.

1847 H. C. WATSON *Cybele Britannica* I. 65 The proposed series of terms runs thus:—..Paludal. Plants of marshy ground, the roots of which are in water or wet ground most part of the year, or constantly. **1926** *Nat. Hist. Oxford District* 88 Many of these paludals..can grow equally well on either soil. **1932** G. C. DRUCE *Comital Flora Brit. Isles* p. xxv, The Hydrophytes or Water-loving plants..include first the Paludal or Marsh and Bog plants. **1974** *Kew Bull.* XXIX. 542 The paludal species [of giant lobelia]..have little secondary wood.

Paludrine (pæ·liudrīn). *Pharm.* Also **paludrine.** [f. L. *palūs, palūd-em* marsh + *-rine*, after *ATABRINE, *MEPACRINE.] A proprietary name for proguanil hydrochloride, used as an anti-malarial drug.

1944 *Trade Marks Jrnl.* 22 Mar. 127/2 Paludrine... Pharmaceutical substances for the treatment of malaria. Imperial Chemical (Pharmaceuticals) Limited,..Slough, Buckinghamshire; manufacturers and merchants. **1945** *Times* 6 Nov. 6/4 The new drug, which is to be distributed in a form known as Paludrine marks a revolutionary departure in anti-malarial research. **1951** 'N. SHUTE' *Round Bend* 288 Connie had taken Paludrine regularly.. and his malaria had not recurred. **1966** D. FORBES *Heart of Malaya* vi. 65, I..pour my tea and take a paludrine tablet with the first gulp. **1974** P. DICKINSON *Poison Oracle* iv. 111 The malaria season was not yet at its height, but he had been giving them both Paludrine. **1977** P. THEROUX *Consul's File* 45 They went off on one of their usual expeditions. No compass, no paludrine, no torch.

palus¹. Restrict *obs. rare* to sense in Dict. and add: **2.** With capital initial and pronunc. (palüs): a wine produced in the Palus region of Bordeaux in France. Also *attrib.*

1833 C. REDDING *Hist. Mod. Wines* v. 144 Bassens and Mondferrand grow the second class of Palus wines. **1861** MRS. BEETON *Bk. Househ. Managem.* 888 The genuine wines of Bordeaux are of great variety..and the principal vineyards are those of Medoc, Palus, Graves, and Blanche. **1953** E. HYAMS *Vineyards in England* 90 Such *palus* wines are good enough of their kind. **1968** *New Statesman* 29 Nov. 744/2 How many little Palus and/or Bourg wines reach the market as Médoc, or even as St Julien?

palygorskite (pæligǭ·ɹskəit). *Min.* Also † **paligorskite.** [ad. G. *paligorskit* (T. v. Ssaftschenkow 1862, in *Verh. d. k. Ges. für d. Ges. Mineral. zu St. Petersburg* 102), f. *Palȳgorsk*, name of a locality by the Popovka river in the Ukrainian S.S.R.: see -ITE¹.] A silicate of magnesium and aluminium that occurs as soft, light-coloured, fibrous layers and has a structure based on silica tetrahedra arranged in double chains.

1868 J. D. DANA *Syst. Min.* (ed. 5) 406 (*heading*) Paligorskite. **1916** *Chem. Abstr.* X. 581 (*heading*) Studies in the magnesian silicates. The group of zillerite, zermattite and palygorskite. **1921** *Mineral. Abstr.* I. 237 Paligorskite ('mountain-cork') from Billowitz near Brünn [Moravia]. **1968** I. KOSTOV *Mineral.* II. v. 352 Sepiolite can be dense or spongy..whereas palygorskite resembles leather or parchment... Both minerals are secondary products found in altered serpentinitic rocks in association with opal, dolomite, and other minerals. **1973** *Clay Minerals* X. 28 Under a binocular microscope, the palygorskite shows fine interwoven fibres similar to those of coarse-textured paper.

palynology (pæliṇǫ·lŏdʒi). [f. Gr. παλύνειν to sprinkle (cf. πάλη fine meal = L. *pollen*) + -OLOGY.] The study of the structure and dispersal of pollen grains and other spores, as indicators of plant geography, taxonomic characteristics of plants, fossils used in dating geological formations or archæological remains, or causative agents of allergic reactions. So **palynolo·gical** *a.*, of or pertaining to this study; **palynolo·gically** *adv.*; **palyno·logist**, a student of palynology.

1944 HYDE & WILLIAMS *Let.* 15 July in *Pollen Analysis Circular* 28 Oct. 6 We would therefore suggest palynology ..: the study of pollen and other spores and their dispersal, and applications thereof. We venture to hope that the sequence of consonants p-l-n, (suggesting pollen, but with a difference) and the general euphony of the new word may commend it to our fellow workers in this field. **1944** H. A. HYDE in *Museums Jrnl.* XLIV. 146/1 In view of the admitted inadequacy of the expression pollen analysis it has recently been proposed to substitute for it the new word palynology (Gk. παλύνω (paluno), I scatter; πάλη (pale), meal): the study of pollens and other plant spores and their dispersal, and applications thereof. **1946** *Svensk Bot. Tidskr.* XL. 303 (*title*) Palynological aspects of the pioneer phase in the immigration of the Swedish flora. **1953** *Proc. 7th Pacific Sci. Congr.* V. 172 It is a matter of no small concern to palynologists and plant geographers that our [*sc.* New Zealand's] peat deposits are being greatly modified by draining and burning. **1956** H. GODWIN *Hist. Brit. Flora* iii. 48/1 They [*sc.* pollen-grains] confer much increased sensitiveness and power upon the palynological technique. **1958** *Antiquity* XXXII. 54 Palynology, or the science of pollen analysis, has developed during the past three decades into a major source of knowledge of the past. **1959** *Micropaleont.* V. 27/2 Several samples were investigated palynologically in order to confirm, if possible, the supposed Pleistocene age. **1962** *Courier-Mail* (Brisbane) 10 Sept. 15/9 (Advt.), A major oil company..is setting up a regional stratigraphic laboratory in Perth, Western Australia. A palynologist is required to organise and run the palynological section of this laboratory. **1963** G. ERDTMAN in A. & D. Löve *N. Atlantic Biota* 367 (*title*) Palynology and Pleistocene ecology. **1972** *Courier-Mail* (Brisbane) 15 Apr. 9/7 (Advt.), B.O.C. of Australia Limited..requires a Senior Palynology Technician to supervise its laboratory staff. **1973** *Microscopy* XXXII. 319 This same resistance to attack permits the palynologist to employ selective oxidation techniques to concentrate microfossils from peats and coals. **1973** *Nature* 16 Mar. 187/1 These [*sc.* Pleistocene sediments] were analysed palynologically, and indicated four or five alterations of pluvial and interpluvial conditions. *Ibid.* 8 June 342/1 The date of the appearance of marine grasses is not traceable by palynology because they produce pollen without exine, and so are not fossilized. **1975** *Times* 27 May 14/6 The lake beds [of Hoxne] contain fossil pollen and constitute the palynological type site of the Hoxnian Interglacial.

pamaquin (pæ·măkwin). *Pharm.* Also **-ine.** [f. P(ENTYL + *A(MINO- + *M(ETHOXY- + *-a-* + QUIN(OLINE.] An orange-yellow crystalline salt, $C_{19}H_{29}N_3O.C_{23}H_{16}O_6$, which is a toxic compound formerly used in the treatment of malaria. Cf. *PLASMOCHIN, *PLASMOQUINE.

1941 *Brit. Pharmacopœia 1932* Add. IV. 24 Pamaquin is the 6-methoxy-8-[ω-diethylamino-α-methylbutyl]-amino-quinoline salt of 2:2′-dihydroxy-1:1′-dinaphthylmethane-3:3′-dicarboxylic acid. **1951** A. GROLLMAN *Pharmacol. & Therapeutics* xxxiii. 483 Because of its toxicity and the availability of safer and better drugs, pamaquine is no longer of therapeutic importance. **1961** *New Scientist* 4 May 261/1 The anti-malarial drugs pamaquin and primaquine produce anaemia in certain susceptible persons. **1974** B. G. Maegraith in A. W. Woodruff *Med. in Tropics* ii. 65/1 The 8-aminoquinoline most widely given [for vivax malaria] is primaquine; pamaquine or quinocide are alternatives.

pa·mby, shortening of Namby-pamby *a.*

1823 Byron *Let.* 25 Jan. in *Wks.* (1901) VI. 164, I will bet you a flask of Falernum that the most stilted parts of the political *Age of Bronze*, and the most pamby portions of the Toobonai Islands, will be the most agreeable to the enlightened public. **1947** I. Brown *Say Word* 89 Defeating the accusation that..Ambrose [Philips] composed nothing but 'pamby' stuff.

pampa. 2. pampas deer, substitute *'Blastoceros bezoarticus'* for Latin name in def.; (earlier and later examples); **pampas flicker,** a black, white, and yellow woodpecker, *Colaptes campestris,* found in the eastern part of South America; **pampas fox,** one of several small mammals resembling a fox or a dog, esp. *Dusicyon gymnocercus,* or Azara's fox, found in eastern and southern parts of South America; **pampas woodpecker** = *pampas flicker* above.

1860 Mayne Reid *Odd People* 446 A man on foot can approach much nearer to any game, than if he were mounted upon a horse. This is true..also of the large pampas deer. **1972** G. K. Whitehead *Deer of World* iv. 63 The Pampas deer is the most elegant of all the South American deer. **1912** Brabourne & Chubb *Birds S. Amer.* I. 168 *Colaptes... campestris...* Pampas Flicker. Carpentero. **1926** *Bull. U.S. Nat. Mus.* No. 133. 223 In habit and general appearance the pampas flicker differs little from the familiar *Colaptes aureus* of the eastern United States. **1957** M. H. Mitchell *Obs. Birds S.E. Brazil* 120 Pampas Flickers, on first sight or hearing, immediately recall to the northerner *Colaptes aureus.* **1923** *Proc. Biol. Soc. Washington* XXXVI. 55 Specimens from the high savanna of Bogotá..indicate that the pampa fox of this area is a depauperate pallid race of the lowland *Cerdocyon thous.* **1956** G. Durrell *Drunken Forest* v. 105 He was a small, delicately made, grey pampas fox, with slender legs and enormous brush and eager brown eyes. **1972** *Vogue* Jan. 12/2 South American fur rugs..viscacha, guanaco, grey and pampas foxes. **1975** H. J. Stains in M. W. Fox *Wild Canids* i. 13 The pampas fox is found in Paraguay and southeastern Brazil south through the pampas region of Argentina. **1870** *Proc. Zool. Soc.* 705 (*title*) Notes on the habits of the pampas woodpecker.

pampano, var. Pompano (in Dict. and Suppl.).

1931 [see *carangid *a.* and *sb.*]. **1971** P. Crampton tr. *Heyerdahl's Ra Expeditions* ix. 198 A fat little pampano fish..waggled its tail. *Ibid.* xi. 297 We had pampano among the pilot fish underneath us.

pampas-grass. Add: The Latin name of the plant is now *Cortaderia selloana.* (Further examples.)

1851 Lindley & Paxton *Paxton's Flower Garden* I. 175 This noble plant, now called the Pampas Grass, in consequence of its inhabiting the vast plains of S. America so named, has been introduced within a few years through Mr. Moore, of the Glasnevin Botanic Garden. **1900** L. H. Bailey *Cycl. Amer. Hort.* II. 703/1 The popular name 'Pampas Grass' is now unchangeable, but the plant does not grow on the pampas or vast grassy plains of South America, but in the mountains. **1934** C. Lambert *Music Ho!* ii. 76 A Picasso reproduction is not considered 'amusing' unless flanked by pampas grass. **1950** G. Brenan *Face of Spain* iii. 56 Red branched tamarisks and tufts of pampas grass. **1973** F. A. Boddy *Foliage Plants* vii. 126 The pampas grass..makes such a splendid specimen plant in a lawn, with or without its great feathery plumes in the autumn.

pamphleteer, *v.* Add: **a.** (Earlier and later examples.) Also, to engage in propaganda involving the issue or distribution of pamphlets. Also *fig.*

1698 E. Ward *Trip to Jamaica* 3 The condition of an author is much like that of a strumpet... If the reason be requir'd Why we betake our selves to so scandalous a profession as whoring or pamphleteering, the same excusive answer will serve us both. **1897** *Granta* 24 Apr. 264/2 The result..will be a compromise, which will permanently injure that future of women's education, which has been endangered enough already by the impatient folly of those who try to do a century's work in a week of garrulity and pamphleteering. **1930** T. S. Eliot tr. *St.-J. Perse's Anabasis* 39 Let me go alone with the airs of the night, among the pamphleteering Princes. **1938** E. Wilson *Triple Thinkers* 284 Long-range literature attempts to sum up wide areas and long periods of human experience... Short-range literature preaches and pamphleteers with the view to an immediate affect. **1943** *Sun* (Baltimore) 22 June 1/4 OWI officials acknowledged that they have 'pamphleteered' several times in the past. **1976** *Time* 27 Dec. 5/1 Since when is pamphleteering per se bad manners or bad art in theatre or film, with such historic examples as Ibsen, Shaw, Eisenstein and Odets?

b. *trans.* To influence or persuade by means of pamphlets. *rare.*

1944 G. B. Shaw *Everybody's Pol. What's What?* iii. 29 The peasants and peasant soldiers, neither of them Communists, but all more or less talked and pamphleteered and journalized into believing that the Bolsheviks were the boys to give them land and peace.

pampsychism (and derivs.): see *panpsychism.

pan, *sb.*[1] Add: **1. c.** (Further and *fig.* examples of a lavatory.)

1919 R. Fry *Let.* May (1972) II. 451 A real Victorian W.C. with a pull up plug... But..there's no sham Chinese landscape in the pan. **1961** Partridge *Dict. Slang.* Suppl. 1212/2 *Down the pan...* A Cockney equivalent of *down the drain*, ruined with no chances left. **1972** J. Wainwright *Requiem for Loser* iv. 75 A race from one shithouse to the next. A lifetime of sitting on the pan. **1974** *Listener* 14 Mar. 347/3 'It's just money down the pan,' said one pensioner.

e. *on the pan* (U.S.), under reprimand or adverse criticism (said of a person).

1923 H. C. Witwer *Fighting Blood* v. 140 Even when the newspapers puts him on the pan..the safe-playing, money-grabbing middleweight king just laughs at us. **1937** C. Boothe *Women* i. i. 9 *Edith.* I'll bet you had me on the pan. *Sylvia.* I never say behind my friends' backs what I won't say to their faces. I said you ought to diet. **1939** A. Aylesworth in *Better English* May 13/1 Five college professors sitting around a table... A sixth professor who wasn't there because he had snagged a job at a better institution, was on the pan. MacSnuft leaned across at the rest of us and contributed: 'He's an ignoramus!' **1941** J. Smiley *Hash House Lingo* 41 *On the pan,* being reprimanded.

f. A metal drum in a West Indian steel band. Also, steel-band music and the way of life associated with it.

1955 *New Commonwealth* 28 Nov. (Suppl.) p. xix/1 To make a 'pan' the end of a metal oil drum is cut off and the bottom of the circular pan so formed is shaped into sections by beating and chiselling. **1958** J. P. Hickerton *Caribbean Kallaloo* i. 15 The steel bands have reached a high pitch of virtuosity... 'Beating the pan' is a West Indian passion, and we once discovered an old man sitting outside our back gate beating out a rhythm on our upturned rubbish bin. **1960** *Times* 17 Sept. 7/7 In Trinidad a steelband is known as a 'pan-side' and the word 'pan' has two connotations. The first refers to the instrument, the second to a way of musical life. Pan, the instrument, is..a tuned gong, made from the top of a 44-gallon steel barrel. *Ibid.*, The intermarriage of musical cultures—the offspring of which is pan. Pan is the core of national culture and the first expression of a truly West-Indian art-form. **1973** *Trinidad Guardian* 1 Feb. 8/5 The question of having tuners specialise in particular pans.

5. c. = **skid-pan.*

1966 T. Wisdom *High-Performance Driving* ii. 30 The first skid pan was introduced at Chiswick [in 1922]. On this 'pan' solid-tyred K and D buses were put through their paces. *Ibid.* 31 'Pans'—circular areas covered with a mixture of grease or oil and water—were by now out of date.

6. c. A face. (Perh. influenced by *to shut one's pan* s.v. sense 4 b. Cf. also *dead-pan *a., sb., adv.,* and *v.*) *slang* (orig. *U.S.*).

1923 [see *heebie-jeebie(s)]. **1931** E. Linklater *Juan in Amer.* iii. viii. 262, I never want to see that pan of yours again! **1943** Hunt & Pringle *Service Slang* 50 *Pan,* slang for face. **1944** E. B. White *Let.* 8 Oct. (1976) 260 He starts toward her bearing a bouquet of American Beauty roses, and falls on his pan before he gets there. **1972** *Jazz & Blues* Nov. 11/4 This must have been funny enough when it happened; relayed through the medium of Rich's sourly contemptuous pickled-walnut pan. **1977** *Rolling Stone* 13 Jan. 41/2 As Belushi filled out the registration card, the manager remarked with a deadly pan: 'Write down the name of the person you're staying with.'

10*. Severe or dismissive criticism. orig. *U.S. colloq.*

1936 *Esquire* Sept. 160/3 A pan on a show is a damp blanket. **1958** *Spectator* 24 Oct. 543/1 'Is it a pan?' asked the reporter from *Time* hopefully... 'No, bigod, it's a smashin' crit.' **1960** P. Tompkins *To a Young Actress* 60 The notice in *Punch* appeared next to a long pan of *Back to Methuselah.* **1972** *N.Y. Times* 3 Nov. 24/5 This Hunanese restaurant... Appraisals..included the whole possible spectrum of opinion from rave to pan. **1977** *Zigzag* Apr. 34/1 Afterwards they wrote a pan and then had a huge article criticising the pan.

11. a. *pan-load;* (sense *1 f) *pan music.*

1939 J. Steinbeck *Grapes of Wrath* xxii. 414 Ma had taken up a panload of brown pone. **1963** *Which?* 6 Feb. 48/2 Each [dish-washing machine] had to deal..with three separate assortments of dishes, which we call *standard, capacity* and *pan* loads respectively. **1960** *Times* 17 Sept. 7/7 Pan music casts a spell of enchantment on the Trinidadian... The essential feature of pan music is that the melody is carried by one instrument at a time while the others play more or less 'free' variations on the theme. **1977** *Times* 14 May 12/4 'Pan' music, as the drums are called, originated in Trinidad.

b. pan-broiling *vbl. sb.* (hence, as a back-formation, *pan-broil* vb.) (see quot. 1970); **pan-man** (earlier example); (*b*) one who plays the pan (sense *1 f) in a steelband; **pan-scourer, -scrubber,** a scourer, often in the form of a wire pad, for cleaning pans; **pan-side** *West Indian* (see quot.).

1950 L. H. Gross *Meats, Poultry & Game* 14 Rib steaks —Broil, or pan-broil. **1970** Simon & Howe *Dict. Gastron.* 287/2 *Pan-broil.* An American cooking term meaning to cook meat in a hot pan with almost no fat, pouring off fat as it accumulates. **1896** F. M. Farmer *Boston Cooking-School Cook Bk.* ii. 22 When coal is not used, or a fire is not in condition for broiling, a plan for *pan broiling* has been adopted. This is done by placing food to be cooked in a hissing hot frying-pan, turning often as in broiling. **1832** A. Davis in P. D. Curtin *Two Jamaicas* (1955) 234 One stocker-man, one pan-man, three boiler-men... These were all slaves. **1959** W. A. Simmonds *'Pan'—Story of Steelband* 15 In order to understand fully the story of the Pan, one must understand the Panmen, who drew their music from every source that is Trinidadian. **1960** *Times* 17 Sept. 7/7 Some people say that the 'pan-men' take themselves too seriously. **1974** *Trinidad Guardian* 2 Nov. 9/2 Pan men would be trained to become teaching assistants. **1959** 'A. Gilbert' *Death takes Wife* ix. 112 'Packet of pan-scourers,' she said. **1960** *Guardian* 19 Sept. 6/4 The very first electric pan scourer. **1971** C. Bonington *Annapurna South Face* App. B. 252 Pan-scourers..24. **1926–7** *Army & Navy Stores Catal.* 118/3 *Pan scrubber.* A Metal Sponge for cleaning pots, pans, etc. **1960** *John o' London's* 14 Apr. 440/2 The sound of a wire pan-scrubber chasing grease round a frying pan. **1960** Pan-side [see sense 1 f above].

pan, pán, *sb.*[5] Add: **2.** *attrib.* and *Comb.*, as *pan-box, -chewing, -garden, -juice;* **panwala, -wallah** [see Wallah], a person who sells pans.

1922 E. M. Forster *Abinger Harvest* (1936) 314 Bidar.. has produced beautiful pan-boxes of a lead alloy inlaid with silver. **1939** R. Godden *Black Narcissus* v. 53 A peon..who carried the General's pan-box. **1892** *Chambers's Jrnl.* 14 May 320 After a long course of pawn-chewing, the utterance becomes thick and indistinct, and the teeth black. **1923** *Blackw. Mag.* Dec. 769/1 In one of these pan-gardens, as they are called, a boar had taken up his quarters. **1901** Kipling *Kim* ii. 47 He spat red *pan*-juice on the floor. **1955** R. P. Jhabvala *To whom she Will* xxvi. 186 He stopped at a pānwala's and..asked for a pān with cardamons and aniseed. *Ibid.* 294 The stalls of pānwalas are found everywhere, and they sell not only pāns but also cigarettes, matches, mineral drinks, biscuits, hard-boiled eggs and anything else suitable for a quick cheap snack. **1969** *Hindusthan Stand.* (Calcutta) 5 Aug. 2/4 As one waits..for the panwallah to stuff a betel leaf with hot or sweet masallah..and roll it into a shapely pan. **1975** O. Sela *Bengali Inheritance* xix. 166 That bloody pan-wallah..lied to you.

‖ **pan** (ban), *sb.*[6] [Chinese *bǎn* slab.] A Chinese percussion instrument (see quots.).

1872 *Catal. Special Exhib. Anc. Mus. Instr. S. Kensington Museum* viii. 39 Pan. A piece of wood, with a groove cut nearly through its substance, and bamboo sticks for percussion. Used principally by Chinese beggars. **1954** *Grove's Dict. Mus.* (ed. 5) II. 234/1 *P'ai-pan* (or *pan*), percussion clapper. A popular instrument consisting of two slabs of the red wood *huai*, attached by a silk cord, on which a third slab is struck to beat time. **1975** C. P. Mackerras *Chinese Theatre in Mod. Times* viii. 131 (*caption*) The *pan* (clapper) consists of three pieces of wood, two of them fastened together (patterned surface visible), the other behind.

pan, *sb.*[7] *Cinemat.* [Abbrev. Panorama or Panoramic *a.*] **1.** The action of panning a camera (see *pan *v.*[3]); a panoramic sequence.

1922 *Opportunities Motion Pict. Industry* 111 *Pan..,* moving the camera up and down or from side to side to follow the action from one place to another. **1931** J. H. Reyner *Cine-Photogr. for Amateurs* viii. 92 *Rapid pan.* An exception to this slow movement is the case of the rapid panoram which is sometimes necessary in order to keep a moving object within the field of vision. **1937** H. B. Abbott *Compl. 9·5-mm. Cinematographer* vi. 88 A satisfactory 'pan' can sometimes be effected by slowly turning the camera on its tripod screw. **1942** *Amer. Cinematographer* May 235/2 The layout-man..figures out all of the camera moves such as..pans (following a character along). **1960** C. Morris *Unloved* in D. Wilson *Television Playwright* 447 Camera panning, moves round a stone seat... As the car circles, the pan reveals a boy on the stone seat apparently sketching the front façade. **1962** *Listener* 5 Apr. 596/2 The opening shot of *Exodus* is a huge 200-degree pan across the landscape and coastline of Cyprus. **1970** *Daily Tel.* (Colour Suppl.) 3 July 23 A tripod's a bit of a bind to lug around but it does give a rock steadiness and a touch of professionalism, especially on pans and telephoto shots. **1977** *Spare Rib* June 42/2 A story unfolded in a series of 360° camera pans.

2. *attrib.* and *Comb.*, as *pan shot, -tilt;* **pan-and-tilt** *a.*, used with reference to a tripod or other unit that allows the camera to move in both horizontal and vertical planes; **pan head** (see quot.).

[**1937** H. B. Abbott *Compl. 9·5-mm. Cinematographer* v. 69 The metal top has both pan and tilt movements with locking device for each.] **1938** G. H. Sewell *Amateur Film-Making* iii. 34 The ideal tripod..should also incorporate a 'pan-and-tilt' head. **1962** M. Bardwell *Amateur Cinematogr.* ii. 32 A tripod must not only give firm support—it must also allow controlled horizontal and vertical movement. This is achieved by means of a 'pan-and-tilt' head, which also enables you to lock the camera in position at almost any angle. **1977** *Offshore Engineer* May 97/2 It occupies only a fraction of the space normally dedicated to a camera mounted on a pan and tilt unit. **1940** *Amer. Speech* XV. 359/2 *Pan head,* the mechanism at the top of a tripod which permits the camera to be moved in both horizontal and vertical planes. **1941** Steinbeck & Ricketts *Sea of Cortez* xxiii. 223 We made jerky little pan shots back and forth. **1956** L. Mallory *Ciné Camera Secrets* 20 Pan shots must be slow and even. **1975** *New Yorker* 26 May 113/3 An 'atmospheric' tape background such as accompanies pan shots over bleak, windswept headlands. **1970** *Ibid.* 3 Oct. 108/3 Two.. spots..could be directed by means of pan-tilt.

‖ **p'an** (pan), *sb. Archæol.* [Chinese *pán.*] A vessel or wash basin.

1958 W. Willetts *Chinese Art* I. iii. 154 It is not altogether certain that *p'an* date back as far as Shang-Yin times. **1973** *Genius of China* 57/2 Dish on a high foot *p'an*, of burnished black pottery. 1977 Kwang-chih Chang *Archaeol. Anc. China* (ed. 3) vii. 368 Water utensils: p'an, i, chien, yii, p'en, cheng, chu, wan.

pan, *v.*[1] Add: **1. a.** (Earlier example.)
1839 *Amer. Railroad Jrnl.* VIII. 99 Old machines are invariably burnt up, and the ashes 'panned out' for the fine gold that has lodged in the joints of the wood.

b. (Earlier example.)
1850 N. Kingsley *Diary* 27 May (1914) 123 About 200 Indians & squaws came down and began to pan all around us.

4. a. (Earlier examples.)
1849 J. D. Dana *Mineral.* (ed. 2) 317 Gravel or soil..is said to *pan well* or *pan poorly* according to the result. 1866 'Mark Twain' *Lett. from Hawaii* (1967) 85 In the mining camps of California..it is etiquette to say, 'Here's hoping your dirt'll pan out gay.'

b. (Earlier and later examples.) Also, to work out, to have a result (not necessarily something favourable).
1868 F. Whymper *Trav. Alaska* 282 'It panned out well' means that 'it gave good returns'. 1870 'Mark Twain' *Lett. to Publishers* (1967) 31 January and November didn't pan out as well as December. 1884 *Brandon* (Manitoba) *Blade* 24 Jan. 4/3 If the domineering Attorney-General 'pans out' well during the coming session he will probably be the man. 1923 Wodehouse *Adv. Sally* xiv. 177 He was hoping all along that this fight would pan out big and that he'd be able to pay you back what you had loaned him. 1925 A. Huxley *Let.* 16 Sept. (1969) 253 However, I shall see how things pan out when I get there. 1947 'N. Shute' *Chequer Board* vii. 191, I think it may pan out all right. 1956 S. Bellow *Seize Day* (1957) i. 23 If I don't pan out as an actor I can still go back to school. 1967 *Electronics* 6 Mar. 316/2 Machines that automatically feed and place flatpacks on printed circuit boards haven't panned out, largely because girls with tweezers excel at gently handling the fragile IC packages. 1972 *Daily Tel.* 14 Dec. 5 But Dr Brett cautioned that what sounds exciting from the Moon does not always pan out in the laboratory. 1977 P. Dickinson *Walking Dead* i. v. 69 They decided to give it a year and see how it all panned out.

c. To speak freely or at length; to expatiate.
1871 [see sense 4 b in Dict.]. 1915 W. J. Locke *Jaffery* xxi. 291 I'm panning out about this, because it seems so deuced interesting. 1917 —— *Red Planet* xv. 182, I had.. made up my mind to pan out to you like this. 1928 *Observer* 18 Mar. 9/3 Mr. Lewis..resists even the temptation to 'pan out' about that obviously born temptress.

7. *trans.* To criticize severely; to judge (a performance) to be unsuccessful or inadequate. orig. *U.S. colloq.*
1911 G. Ade in *Chicago Daily News* 16 Dec. 28/2 They would open up on Rufus and Pan him to a Whisper. 1914 *Sat. Even. Post* 7 Mar. 7/3 Kelly got nasty and begun to pan me for quitting and for the way I played. 1926 S. Lewis *Mantrap* xii. 150 I've never done one single thing to give her any excuse for panning me. 1927 *Vanity Fair* XXIX. 134/3 Will Shakespeare..was panned by the critics because he delved into the argot of his day to put it over. 1935 *Hot News* Apr. 14/3 Don't mistake me. I am not panning 'Hawk' as a player. 1938 G. Heyer *Blunt Instrument* iii. 52 'I have no dealings with actresses.' 'Well, then, stop panning them.' 1939 'N. Blake' *Smiler with Knife* v. 78 The lurid headline, 'Famous Woman Explorer Pans Domesticity.' 1947 R. Chandler *Let.* 8 Mar. in *R. Chandler Speaking* (1966) 137 MacCarthy panned me, said the toughness was largely bluff. 1960 *Daily Mail* 27 Apr. 8/8 The idea that critics like panning shows is a myth. 1971 *Sunday Times* (Johannesburg) *News Mag.* 28 Mar. 6/1 Dirk de Villiers' latest South African film drama..is being panned by the critics. 1974 *Times* 2 Oct. 14/5 The play was roundly panned by many of our correspondents. 1977 *Time* 26 Dec. 36/2 Colleagues are quick to pan Simon in return: 'The Count Dracula of critics!'

pan (pæn), *v.*[3] *Cinemat.* [Abbrev. Panorama or Panoramic *a.*] **1.** *trans.* **a.** To follow or pass along (a person or object) with a camera.
1913 *Sat. Even. Post* 1 Nov. 64/3 We'll 'pan' you right down the middle of the picture to the raft. 1960 N. Kneale *Mrs. Wickens in Fall* in D. Wilson *Television Playwright* 167 The Camera pans him away. He calls to the two Englishwomen.

b. To turn (a cine or television camera) in a horizontal plane, esp. in order to keep a moving object in view.
1930 *Electronics* Nov. 373/2 With the advent of sound, the operation of 'panning' the camera to afford a changing point of view became a more complicated process. 1956 *Railway Mag.* Nov. 779/1 Taking up a stance broadside to his target, he 'panned' his camera—that is, swung the camera round with the train—so that the engine remained in the same portion of the viewfinder throughout. 1973 P. L. Cave *Speed Freaks* v. 43 Gerry panned the camera slowly over the remnants of the once-beautiful TR6. 1977 *Film & Television Technician* Feb. 4/2 The camera is supported by a counterweighted arm, and the arm is attached to a harness worn by the operator. The camera floats in space and the operator can pan, tilt, or crane it with one hand.

2. *intr.* Of a camera: to swing from one scene to another, or along objects or a place; to give a panoramic view in closing up to an object or a place.
1931 R. Dykes *Amateur Cinematographer's Handbk.* iii. 31 The tilting handle..is used to panoram down into valleys... It is also used to 'pan' up cathedral spires. 1932 A. Buchanan *Films* vi. 174 The camera 'pans' around the room, bringing to view the shabby furniture. 1936 *Words* Oct. 6/1 One of those inserts in which the camera seems to swing, or 'pan' dizzily from action going on in one place to what is going on in another. 1960 N. Kneale *Quatermass & Pit* i. 11 The camera pans, to take in all that remains of a little working-class street. 1963 *Listener* 14 Feb. 300/3 The camera pans over photographs of tribesmen. 1971 *Daily Tel.* 21 Aug. 7/2 A camera panned dramatically in on a manorial notice. 1975 *New Yorker* 19 May 81/1 Then the camera moves to a worker with a cart, and pans with him to the end of the assembly line.

pan (pæn), *a.* Abbrev. of *panchromatic *a.* Also *ellipt.* for *panchromatic film.*
1940 *Amer. Speech* XV. 357 'Going to use pan or N.C.?' 'Neither. Ortho.' 1940 'C. I. Jacobson' *Developing* 106 On no account must the dark green safelight provided for pan materials be used. 1954 C. Wallace *Enjoy your Photogr.* iv. 44 Pan films photograph reds well. 1969 J. Elliot *Duel* i. iv. 82, I brought ten thousand feet of pan but only three of high speed for interiors.

pan-. Add: **1. pan-Celtic** *a.* (earlier and later examples); hence (as a back-formation) **pan-Celt**, one who believes in the unity of all the Celtic peoples; **pan-Orthodoxy** (earlier example); **pan-Tura·nian** *a.*, embracing all the speakers of Ural-Altaic languages; hence **pan-Tura·nianism, -Tura·nism**, the principle of a union of all speakers of these languages.
1904 *Westm. Gaz.* 3 Sept. 3/2 The Pan-Celts also considered..the question of clothes, and it appears that Ireland is in need of a satisfactory and distinctive national costume. 1955 R. Graves *Crowning Privilege* 155, I was introduced to Welsh poetry nearly fifty years ago, when my father became an enthusiastic pan-Celt; and, this noun being new to Merioneth where we lived, he had a famous argument with Mr Postoffice-Griffiths as to whether it would count as one word in a telegram. 1891 Yeats *Let.* Nov. (1954) 181 He [*sc.* Ernest Rhys] has a kind of Pan-Celtic enthusiasm. 1973 *Stornoway Gaz.* 24 Feb. 9/2 (*caption*) Discussing the programme for the Pan-Celtic Week, to be held in Killarney, Ireland, during May 12–20. 1900 'Odysseus' *Turkey in Europe* vi. 286 But Panorthodoxy, if I may use the word, tends to regard Russia as the head, not only of the Slav races, but of all orthodox nations. 1926 *Glasgow Herald* 3 Apr. 5/1 The Pan-Turanian movement..began not more than 40 years ago. 1950 E. H. Carr *Bolshevik Rev.* I. xi. 338 The pan-Turanian aspirations of the 'young Bokhara' movement. 1926 *Glasgow Herald* 3 Apr. 5/1 The alphabet of the West will..give a new aspect to Pan-Turanianism. 1932 *Times Lit. Suppl.* 21 July 525/2 A policy which..has been based in turn upon Panislamism, Ottomanism, Panturanianism. 1974 *Encycl. Brit. Macropædia* XIII. 789/2 Pan-Turanianism developed from a now much-disputed 19th-century theory of the common origin of Turkish, Mongol, Tungus, Finnish, Hungarian, and other languages; in certain very limited circles it looked forward to a great political federation of speakers of these languages. 1977 *Guardian Weekly* 25 Dec. 8/1 Panturanism (the dream of uniting the Turks in Asia with those of Turkey).

2. pananthropism (further examples); **pa:n-cytope·nia** (also *erron.* **-pœnia**) *Path.* [*-penia], a condition in which the blood shows a relative deficiency of all three cellular components (erythrocytes, leucocytes, and platelets); **pan-diato·nicism** (see quot. 1937); hence **pan-diato·nic** *a.*; **pa:nencephali·tis** *Path.* [prob. coined in Ger.: cf. G. *panenzephalitisch* adj., *panenzephalomyelitis* (H. Pette 1938, in *Münch. med. Wochenschr.* 29 July 1138/2), *panencephalitis* (Pette & Döring 1939, in *Deutsch. Zeitschr. f. Nervenheilkunde* CXLIX. 32)], a rare form of encephalitis in which both the grey matter and the white matter are affected and there is a gradual but progressive loss of mental and motor functions; **panen-theism** (further examples); hence **pane·ntheist** *a.* and *sb.*, **panenthei·stic** *a.*; **panhy:popitu·itar-ism** *Path.* (see quot. 1941); **pano·ral** *a. Dentistry*, of or pertaining to radiography of the whole mouth in one exposure; **panspo·roblast** *Zool.*, a structure formed by protozoans of the subclass Neosporidia, comprising several sporoblasts and two other cells; **pansysto·lic** *a. Med.*, (of a heart murmur) continuing throughout a systole; **panthelism** (earlier and later examples); **pantropic** (-trōᵘ·pic, -trǫ·pic) *a. Med.* [*-tropic], attacking or affecting many kinds of tissue indiscriminately; **pan-tropical** *a.*, of plants or animals, found in all regions of the tropics; also, including all tropical areas.
1879 J. J. G. Wilkinson *Let.* 20 May in R. B. Perry *Tht. & Char. W. James* (1935) I. 27 Nothing is left to my apprehension but pananthropism, a composite form of pantheism. 1936 *Theology* XXXIII. 265 The poem is an impassioned plea for the truth not of Pantheism but of Pananthropism. 1944 W. Dameshek *Leukopenia & Agranulocytosis* ii. 44 The designation of pancytopenia may be applied to conditions in the blood in which there is a well-defined reduction in red cells, white cells and platelets. 1956 M. W. Wintrobe *Clin. Hematol.* (ed. 4) xi. 560 Pancytopenia is not a disease entity but rather a triad which is found under a number of different circumstances. 1974 *Nature* 17 May 263 Three patients, two males and a female, were studied: two suffered from aplastic anaemia and one from a pre-leukaemic state with pancytopoenia. 1937 N. Slonimsky *Mus. since 1900* (1938) p. xxii, Pan-diatonicism sanctions the simultaneous use of any or all seven tones of the diatonic scale, with the bass determining the harmony. *Ibid.*, Gebrauchsmusik, proletarian music, and most forms of absolute music make use of pan-diatonic technique. 1963 *Times* 13 May 8/2 The immense profusion of counterpoint was under complete control, and the pandiatonic climaxes were shattering. 1970 *Composer & Conductor* Aug. 6/1, I myself [*sc.* N. Slonimsky] ventured into musical neologism with Pandiatonicism to describe a 20th-century technique in which all seven tones of the diatonic scale are used freely in dissonant combinations. 1950 *Brain* LXXIII. 150 Perhaps the term 'Pan-encephalitis' already adopted by Pette (1942) for forms which attack both grey and white matter could be usefully employed here, i.e. 'Sub-acute sclerosing pan-encephalitis'. 1974 *Sci. Amer.* Feb. 35/1 In 1969..measles virus was isolated from brain cells of patients suffering from the brain inflammation called subacute sclerosing panencephalitis (SSPE). 1940 *Theology* XL. 270 He [*sc.* Eckehart] oscillates between non-duality and modified duality, between pantheism and panentheism. 1959 I. Epstein *Judaism* 244 Cordovero.. safeguards the theistic position by defining his attitude in the formula: 'God is all reality, but not all reality *is* God'—an attitude which came to be known in modern philosophy as 'panentheism'. 1970 P. Bertocci *Person God Is* xi. 207, I shall..argue that a temporalistic form of personalistic theism (not pantheism, not panentheism) can reasonably illuminate what we actually do find in human experience and the world. 1959 W. N. Pittenger *Word Incarnate* vii. 155 They [*sc.* 'Hartshorne and the other theistic 'process' philosophers'] ..offer us a *pan-en-theist* view of the world which presents God and his creation, supremely God and man, in continued and intimate relationship. 1974 *Church Times* 22 Nov. 15/1 We regret that, in Canon David Edwards's review of Martin Thornton's *My God*, Fr. Thornton was described as a 'pantheist'. This was a misprint for 'panentheist'. 1918 M. D. Petre *Modernism* viii. 177, I..began slowly to form an optimistic and panentheistic belief. 1959 W. N. Pittenger *Word Incarnate* vii. 200 A panentheistic conception, in which God is seen as above and beyond the world yet ceaselessly active in it and intimately related to it. 1970 P. Bertocci *Person God Is* xi. 221 But persons have too much autonomy, and God has too much autonomy, in 'essence' and 'content', to fit into a part–whole model, either in the 'organic' sense or the panentheistic. 1941 F. Albright et al. in *Trans. Assoc. Amer. Physicians* LVI. 48 By 'panhypopituitarism' is meant a condition in which the anterior pituitary gland as a whole has impaired function. 1954 K. E. Paschkis et al. *Clin. Endocrinol.* xiii. 293 Tendency to hypoglycemia..is regularly present in panhypopituitarism. 1972 *Obstetrics & Gynecol.* XXXIX. 397/1 In a woman hypophysectomized at the time a craniopharyngioma was performed and who showed full panhypopituitarism, several regimens of human menopausal gonadotropin..failed to induce ovulation. 1977 *Lancet* 9 Apr. 779/2 The underlying pituitary tumour was not diagnosed until she presented with panhypopituitarism at the age of 76 (serum-prolactin 950 μg/l). 1959 *Dental Practitioner* X. 270 (*heading*) Pan-oral radiology. The most recent advance in dental radiography. 1967 L. M. Ennis et al. *Dental Roentgenol.* (ed. 6) x. 287 (*caption*) Exposure mechanism and shieldings used ..for the panoral technic. 1893 R. R. Gurley in *Bull. U.S. Fish Comm. 1891* 408 *Pansporoblast*, the transparent plasma-sphere formed by the condensation of a portion of the plasma around one of the numerous nuclei of the endoplasm of the myxosporidium; in distinction from the sporoblasts which result from the segmentation of the pansporoblast. 1932 Borradaile & Potts *Invertebrata* ii. 93 In the syncytium,..there arise..bodies known as pansporoblasts, each composed of a couple of envelope cells with one or more cells known as sporoblasts. 1973 K. G. Grell *Protozool.* 464 In most species [of *Myxosporidia*] the sporoblast forms several spores. It is then referred to as a pansporoblast. 1954 *Brit. Heart Jrnl.* XVI. 257 A pan-systolic apical murmur was always associated with some degree of regurgitation at operation. 1966 *Lancet* 24 Dec. 1389/2 There was a harsh pansystolic murmur..radiating into the axilla. 1896 W. Caldwell *Schopenhauer's Syst.* i. 37 Though Schopenhauer's system has a strong materialistic colouring it is not materialism. It is rather animism or panpsychism (panthelism, in point of fact). 1917 *Encycl. Relig. & Ethics* IX. 612/1 The affirmation that the real is irrational (a blind will, panthelism [πᾶν + ἐθέλω]) in Schopenhauer's pessimism. 1937 *Jrnl. Path. & Bacteriol.* XLIV. 410 The neurotropic virus protects to a certain extent against the pantropic strain. 1967 *Res. Vet. Sci.* VIII. 414 Antibodies will persist..for many years in the sera of cattle and sheep infected with pantropic virus. 1937 *Discovery* Sept. 263/1 Its [*sc.* the fern, *Ceratopteris thalictroides*'] distribution is pan-tropical. 1946 *Nature* 20 July 86/1 The once-popular 'tiger nut' (swellings on the rhizomes of a pan-tropical water sedge). 1953 *New Biol.* XV. 35 The Scale Insect *Aspidotus destructor* is a pan-tropical species which is found wherever the coconut palm grows. 1967 *Palaeogeogr., Palaeoclimatol., Palaeoecol.* III. 203 There are no pan-tropical mammals, as there are pan-tropical plants. 1976 *Nature* 19 Feb. 528/2 A demonstrably Australian flora with many common pan-tropical plants missing.

panache. Add: **2.** *fig.* Display, swagger, verve.
1898 Thomas & Guillemard tr. *Rostand's Cyrano de Bergerac* v. vi. 294 *Cyrano*... One thing is left, that, void of stain or smutch, I bear away despite you... *Roxane*... 'Tis?... *Cyrano*... My *panache*. 1900 J. T. Grein *Dramatic Crit.* (1902) III. 65 No one displayed that 'panache' which is the paramount demand of romantic comedy. 1903 G. B. Shaw *Man & Superman* p. xxxi, Shakespear..never conceived how any man who was not a fool could, like Bunyan's hero..with the panache of a millionaire, bequeath 'my sword to him that shall succeed me in my pilgrimage, and my courage and skill to him that can get it'. 1932 R. Fry *Characteristics French Art* iii. 53 In real life the fun of soldiering, its bustle, its swagger, its panache, sometimes leads to being mutilated. 1949 F. Maclean *Eastern Approaches* iii. vi. 370 His must have been, I think, an engaging character, a mixture of

southern *panache*, rustic guile, and a childlike desire to please. **1960** D. WALKER *Where High Winds Blow* II. viii. 117 Mac wore his flying clothes, the half-laced boots and the old suède jacket; but with his clean blue shirt and a silk handkerchief knotted at his neck, he had a workaday panache. **1972** D. FRANCIS *Smokescreen* v. 58 A certain *panache* about him, but also some of the ruthless cynicism of experienced journalists. **1976** *New Yorker* 22 Mar. 128/3 When he did join the Maquis, late in March, 1944, Malraux exhibited his customary panache. **1978** *Listener* 12 Jan. 49/1 He plays the piano with panache, but cannot read music.

Panadol (pæ·nădǫl). *Pharm.* Also **panadol.** A proprietary name for paracetamol.

1955 *Trade Marks Jrnl.* 14 Dec. 1231/2 Panadol... All goods included in class 5 [*sc.* pharmaceutical, veterinary, and sanitary substances, etc.] for sale in the United Kingdom. Bayer Products Limited,..Kingston-on-Thames, Surrey; merchants and manufacturers. **1959** WILSON & SCHILD *Appl. Pharmacol.* (ed. 9) xvi. 326 The analgesic activity of N-acetyl p-aminophenol (paracetamol, panadol)..has been shown to be about as great as that of the parent compounds. **1967** M. CULPAN *In Deadly Vein* viii. 176 A low table—with..a couple of novels, and a bottle of Panadol tablets. **1971** D. LAMBERT in C. Bonington *Annapurna South Face* 293 The majority who attended had to be given some form of placebo, and panadol or aspirin were found best for this purpose. **1975** *Sunday Times* 16 Nov. 44/3, I was going crazy trying to find things: the Panadol for my husband's head.

Pan-African, *a.* Add: (Later examples.) Also, of, pertaining to, or comprising all the peoples of Africa generally.

1944 *Ann. Reg. 1943* 132 Sir Godfrey Huggins, Prime Minister of Southern Rhodesia,..foreshadowed a possible Pan-African Council to coordinate problems common to African countries. **1955** [see next]. **1960** *Times* 29 Sept. (Nigeria Suppl.) p. xii/2 Dr. Nkrumah's pan-African way of thinking. **1962** *Listener* 25 Jan. 157/1 The Ghana Government has also tried to promote pan-African schemes of unity. **1967** *Freedomways* VII. 174 It is only by planning along Pan-African lines ourselves can Africa hope to free herself. **1973** *Caribbean Contact* Feb. 16/2 Garvey's views in the 1920's already foreshadow the later Pan African movement. **1975** C. E. GRIFFITH *Afr. Dream* viii. 105 The pan-African advocate was disturbed by contemporary works which assigned Africans last place among the three major races of the world.

Pan-Africanism (pæn,æ·frikăniz'm). [f. PAN-AFRICAN *a.* + -ISM.] A movement which advocates the political union of all the indigenous inhabitants of Africa; the ideals of this movement. Hence **Pan-A·fricanist** *sb.*, an advocate or supporter of Pan-Africanism, also as *adj.*, of or pertaining to Pan-Africanism.

1955 B. TIMOTHY *Kwame Nkrumah* iii. 38 In October, 1945, the fifth International Conference of the Pan-African Congress was held in Manchester... The proceedings of the Conference were conducted under the joint chairmanship of..Dr. P. Milliard, and Dr. W. E. B. Du Bois, who gave birth to Pan-Africanism. **1959** *Cape Times* 7 Apr. 1/7 African leaders from all parts of the Union decided to establish the Pan Africanist Congress. **1960** *Times* 22 Mar. 12/1 The Pan-Africanists' campaign against the pass laws exploded today on the banks of the Vaal river. **1963** *Listener* 17 Jan. 110/1 The fourth political ideal, Pan-Africanism, or continental federation. **1973** S. HENDERSON *Understanding New Black Poetry* 17 The changing world in which Black Americans of the post-World War II generation found themselves, a world in which articulate men and women rediscovered Africa and Pan-Africanism. **1973** *Black World* Mar. 53/2 An indiscriminate listing of pan-Africanist and Africanist resources. **1975** *Times Lit. Suppl.* 17 Oct. 1238/5 Like many pan-Africanists from the New World, there was often an element of utopianism in Delany's vision of Africa. **1976** *Survey* Summer–Autumn 289 Among black people outside there was often a strong link between Marxism and pan-Africanism. *Ibid.*, Black Americans and West Indians who were pan-Africanists were disproportionately left of centre in their political ideologies.

Panag(h)ia (pænaiyī·ă), now the usual spelling of PANHAGIA. Also, an image or representation of the Virgin Mary.

1910 *New Schaff-Herzog Encycl. Relig. Knowl.* VIII. 327/1 Panagia ('All Holy'), the usual (though not official) title of the virgin in the Greek Church. **1911** [see *HODEGETRIA]. **1931** *Times Lit. Suppl.* 19 Mar. 231/2 Devotees who implore the Panagia of Kykko for rain or the Panagia of Tenos for health. **1958** L. DURRELL *Balthazar* vi. 135 'I ask you to sleep with him as I would ask the Panaghia to come down and bless him while he sleeps—like in the old ikons.' How..Greek! **1961** D. ATTWATER *Christian Churches of East* I. 223 *Panagia*.., 'all-holy', used for the Mother of God as we say 'our Lady'. Also another name for the *enkolpion*.

panagraphic, etc., varr. *PANOGRAPHIC, etc.

Panama. Add: *Panama disease*, a vascular wilt disease of banana trees, caused by the soil-borne fungus *Fusarium oxysporum* f. sp. *cubense*, and characterized by the yellowing and wilting of the leaves, first described from infected trees in Central America in 1910; *Panama fever* (earlier and later examples); *Panama hat* (further examples); **Panama** *sb.* (earlier and later examples); *Panama hat palm, plant*, the screw-pine, *Carludovica palmata*, which produces leaves used in the manufacture of Panama hats; = *JIPIJAPA a; *Panama red*, a local variety of marijuana grown in Panama.

1910 E. ESSED in *Ann. Bot.* XXIV. 488 The Panama Disease.—Preliminary Notice.—This fungoid disease on the *Musa sapientum* var. *Gros Michel* was, it seems, first detected in Central America. **1913** W. FAWCETT *Banana* xiii. 87 The true Panama disease also exists in Trinidad. **1934** A. HUXLEY *Beyond Mexique Bay* 16 That insidious Panama Disease..has ruined so many [banana] plantations throughout the Caribbean. **1949** *Caribbean Q.* I. III. 43 Bananas resistant to Panama disease..are being grown commercially. **1956** H. G. DE LISSER *Cup & Lip* x. 119, I instructed him to go to Napleton to see Sampson about the treatment of Panama Disease. **1969** *New Scientist* 16 Jan. 142/2 Panama disease of bananas is not controlled by eliminating the pathogen but by selecting resistant strains of banana. **1972** J. W. PURSEGLOVE *Tropical Crops: Monocotyledons* II. 368 Panama disease, also known as banana wilt and vascular wilt,..is one of the world's most catastrophic plant diseases. **1850** J. L. TYSON *Diary of Physician in Calif.* 29 The so-called *Panama fever* rarely occurs, unless previous disease has wasted the powers. **1868** *Overland Monthly* Dec. 561/1 After hearing all about how she felt, his diagnosis was a mild case of fever—Panama fever. **1940** F. RIESENBERG *Golden Gate* 109 Complaints charged that the frequent burials at sea resulted from improper care of those who had contracted 'Panama fever' or 'yellow fever'. **1856** C. M. YONGE *Daisy Chain* II. xi. 455 Dr. Spencer was in the hall, with his bamboo, his great Panama hat, and grey loose coat. **1916** 'TAFFRAIL' *Pincher Martin* iii. 34 Vernon Hatherley, the lieutenant-commander (T.), clad in an ancient Panamá hat and a suit of indescribable overalls. **1974** *Country Life* 4 Apr. 816/1 Simple panama hat with gros-grain ribbon. **1931** P. C. STANDLEY in *Publ. Field Mus. Nat. Hist. Bot. Ser.* X. 117 *Carludovica palmata*... Panama hat palm... Common in wet forest; ranging to Guatemala and southward to Peru. **1941** T. H. GOODSPEED *Plant Hunters in Andes* v. 146 Along such forest margins small species of bamboo, 'Panama hat' palms, tree ferns, the ginger, and other attractive plants disported themselves. **1954** R. W. SCHERY *Plants for Man* vii. 176/1 The Panama hat palm..grows wild in most of the American tropics. **1972** J. W. PURSEGLOVE *Tropical Crops: Monocotyledons* I. 94 Panama Hat Plant. ..occurs wild in the humid forests of Central America. **1967** *Boston Sunday Herald* 26 Mar. IV. 1/1 Traffic in marijuana—Acapulco Gold and the better quality Panama Red and Yakatanga Purple—out of Mexico has steadily increased in the last three years. **1972** *Last Whole Earth Catalog* (Portola Inst.) 62/3 Acapulco Gold, Panama Red and other strains of grass are reputed to be particularly potent.

1848 *Colburn's United Service Mag.* III. 67 One veteran in a panama and rosette deputed by the body, addressed me in Spanish. **1873** J. MILLER *Life amongst Modocs* 44 He could not push his panama any further back. **1975** G. AVERY *Childhood's Pattern* ix. 216 School uniform was no badge of servitude... Nobody sat viciously on their Panamas.

Panaman (pæ·nămăn), *sb.* and *a.* [f. PANAMA + -AN.] = *PANAMANIAN *a.* and *sb.* Also **Pana·mic** *a.*

1901 W. H. DALL in *Proc. U.S. Nat. Museum* XXIII. 285 The northern limit of the Panamic fauna is Point Conception, California. **1904** *Sun* (N.Y.) 25 Feb. 2/6 The constitution settled the question of what the people of that republic are to be called by specifying that they are 'Panamans'. **1906** W. F. JOHNSON *Four Centuries of Panama Canal* (1907) xx. 360 The Panaman sense of justice is as highly cultivated, and the Panaman sensitiveness to and resentment of injustice are as keen as our own. **1913** E. PEIXOTTO *Pacific Shores from Panama* 26 Verandas..overhang all the thoroughfares, and the indolent Panamans spend much of their time upon them or lounging about the..cafés and hostelries. **1937** *Times Lit. Suppl.* 22 May 397/3 The friction between Yanqui indifference to diplomatic etiquette and Panaman pride are all candidly described here.

Panamanian (pænămēi·niăn), *a.* and *sb.* Also † **Panamenian.** [Irreg., f. PANAMA + *-n-* + -IAN.] **A.** *adj.* Of or pertaining to Panama. **B.** *sb.* A native or inhabitant of Panama.

The form with medial *-e-* (quots. 1869, 1892) is an adaptation of the Spanish term *Panameño*.

1855 R. TOMES *Panama in 1855* vii. 216, I had no means of judging of the intimate character of the Panamanian dames. **1869** PIM & SEEMANN *Dottings in Panama* xi. 184 The Panamenians displayed great heroism, but.. the buccaneers could not be repulsed. **1889** W. NELSON *Five Yrs. Panama* 50 The native Panamanians being great stay-at-homes. **1892** J. BORNN in G. S. Minot *Hist. Panama* xv. 74 The Buccaneer..desired..precious metals and stones... But their search for these disclosed to them the fact that the Panamenian had provided against this emergency by placing these aboard a ship, with orders to sail away if the city should fall. **1906** M. A. CHATFIELD *Let.* 21 Jan. in *Light on Dark Places at Panama* (1908) 45 The best [hotel], the Central, charged $4.00 gold per day, $8.00 Panamanian. **1913** *Chambers's Jrnl.* July 503/2 Travelling without any Spanish and without binoculars puts one wholly at the mercy of the secretive Panamánian or the wily Indian. **1934** [see *HONDURAN, HONDUREAN *a.* and *sb.*]. **1959** *Listener* 23 Apr. 718/1 A former Panamanian ambassador in London. **1964** *Daily Tel.* 11 Jan. 16/6 Panamanian claims to sovereignty over the Canal Zone. **1976** *Times* 5 Feb. 20/4 The Lloyd's report shows that 14 of last year's casualties were registered under the Panamanian flag. **1976** *Sci. Amer.* Sept. 140/2 Nicolás Ardito Barletti, a Panamanian, attempted to place a value on the social benefit from research.

Pan-American, *a.* (Further examples.)

1927 *New Republic* 21 Sept. 110/1 The existence of the Pan-American Union, and the calling of an occasional Pan-American Congress, should not deceive anyone as to the predominant position of the United States in this hemisphere. **1934** A. HUXLEY *Beyond Mexique Bay* 200 Pan-American Airways..are responsible for the long-distance international services. **1966** *Times* 28 Feb. (Canada Suppl.) p. xiv/5 Canada's 1967 Pan-American Games.

Pan-Americanism. Add: (Further examples.) Also, a movement towards better commercial and cultural relations among American nations.

1915 W. WILSON *Public Papers* (1926) III. 409 This is Pan-Americanism. It has none of the spirit of empire in it. **1954** H. C. ALLEN *Gt. Brit. & United States* xiv. 526 His Pan-Americanism, which aimed at the economic and political consolidation of the Western hemisphere,..led him to leap into action on the Isthmian issue. **1966** *Oxf. Compan. Amer. Hist.* 611/2 Pan-Americanism, a new contribution to U.S. policy during the 1880's,..was formulated by Secretary of State Blaine.

Pan-Arabism (pæn,æ·răbiz'm). [f. PAN- + ARAB *sb.* and *a.* + -ISM.] The ideal of political union of all the Arab states; a movement advocating such a union. Hence **Pan-A·rab** *a.* and *sb.*, **Pan-A·rabic** *a.*, **Pan-A·rabist.**

1930 *Encycl. Social Sci.* III. 148/2 Pan-Arabism is scarcely more possible when Moslems speaking the Arabic language are ruled in such diverse ways as in French North Africa, Egypt, Syria, Iraq and the divisions of Arabia. **1939** *Asia* Aug. 450 (*heading*) Pan-Arab nationalism. **1958** *Spectator* 7 Feb. 159/1 In a sense pan-Arabism proved Farouk's downfall. *Ibid.* 1 Aug. 155/3 By joining the UAS the ruler [of Kuwait] would preserve his sheikdom and his subjects would have their pan-Arabic aspirations satisfied. **1959** *Times* 10 Mar. 11/2 This uncertainty at the top is bound to encourage others, who know more clearly what they want, to take over, whether they are pan-Arabists or Communists, idealists or self-seekers. **1962** *Listener* 1 Mar. 365/1 To young Arab Nationalists—to young Pan-Arabists everywhere—Egypt under President Nasser seemed destined to unite the Arab world. *Ibid.* 5 Apr. 597/1 The Ba'ath leaders are doctrinaire pan-Arabs of the frontier-smashing variety. **1963** M. KHADDURI *Mod. Libya* xi. 330 At the outset, those who advocated Pan-Arabism were limited to the articulate intelligentsia who had received their education in neighboring Arab countries. **1968** *Listener* 15 Aug. 195/2 The commandos themselves are pan-Arab in a new sense... The fedayin have no state. **1974** *Florida FL Reporter* XIII. 52/1 They admitted that each had also learnt (besides Classical Arabic) a pan-Arabic Standard dialect. **1975** N. LUARD *Robespierre Serial* iv. 16 Twice Saudi-Arabian delegate to Pan-Arab conferences. **1978** *Times* 10 Aug. 12/7 Messianic Pan-Arabism was rapidly declining, while the Arab national state triumphed.

panarchy. (Later example.)

1948 L. MACNEICE *Holes in Sky* 49 He is separate too, who had but now ascended Into the panarchy of created things Wearing his halo cocked.

panary, *a.* (Further examples.)

1875 *Encycl. Brit.* III. 254 The so-called panary fermentation in bread-making is a true alcoholic fermention [*sic*]. **1942** *Proc. Food Group* V. 70/1 During the latter half of the last century the microbiological aspect of panary fermentation attracted considerable attention. **1971** A. R. DANIEL *Bakers' Dict.* (ed. 2) 139/2 *Panary fermentation*, the fermentation of bread dough.

panatela (pænăte·lă). Also **panatella, panetela.** [Amer. Sp., a long, thin biscuit, etc.] **a.** A long, slender cigar tapering at the sealed end. Also *attrib.* **b.** A cigarette made of Central or South American marijuana.

1901 'H. MCHUGH' *Down Line* 32 A young chap..who had been out in the smoking room working faithfully on one of those pajama panatella cigars. **1904** W. STEVENS *Let.* May (1967) 74 My idea of life is a fine evening..+ a soft, full Panatela. **1906** L. J. VANCE *Terence O'Rourke* II. i. 190 Gravely he inspected the end of the commendable panetela, which he was enjoying by the grace of Chambret; and he puffed upon it furiously, twinkling upon his friend through a pillar of smoke. **1912** G. FRANKAU *One of Us* v. 41 Apart, unmoved, behind his Panatela, Old Hiram stood, of journalists surrounded. **1928** ADE *Let.* 27 May (1973) 130 For many years after I took up the writing game I smoked whatever was readily obtainable, with a preference for a mild Havana Cigar of the Panatella shape. **1943** R. CHANDLER *Lady in Lake* (1944) ii. 9 He reached himself a panatela..and lit it. **1946** MEZZROW & WOLFE *Really Blues* xii. 229 Some Spanish guys..rolled it [*sc.* marijuana] in a different sized paper, about half an inch longer than mine and much thinner, and they called their product a 'panatella'. **1956** B. HOLIDAY *Lady sings Blues* (1973) iv. 43 'Girl,' he said, 'come *here*. Jimmy's got the best panatella you ever smoked in your life.' **1969** R. R. LINGEMAN *Drugs from A to Z* 194 *Panatella*.., bigger, fatter, more potent marijuana cigarette made of Central or South American marijuana. **1970** E. MCGIRR *Death pays Wages* vii. 156 The Sergeant produced a small box of midget panatellas and a box of matches.

Panatrope (pæ·nătrōup). Also **panotrope** and with small initial. [f. *pana-*, *pano-*, of unknown origin + Gr. τροπή turn, turning.] The proprietary name of a form of (electric) record-player capable of relatively loud reproduction.

1926 *Glasgow Herald* 5 Oct. 5 There was no graduation of musical vibrations that the 'Panatrope' could not reproduce. **1928** E. WAUGH *Decline & Fall* II. iii. 168 In a minute the panatrope was playing, David and Martin were dancing, and Peter was making cocktails. **1933** *Punch* 16 Aug. 181/1 Whatever you may lack in the way of plush seats and panotropes you wouldn't see that at an ordinary cinema. *c* **1940** DYLAN THOMAS & DAVENPORT *Death of King's Canary* (1976) vii. 125 A panatrope sounded over the crack of rifles, the smashing of crockery, the complaining of beasts. **1954** *Trade Marks Jrnl.* 15 Sept. 921/1 Panatrope... Gramophones, radio gramophones, apparatus and instruments for recording and reproducing sound, parts and fittings..for all the aforesaid goods; and gramophone needles and gramophone records. The Decca Record Company Limited,..London,..manufacturers. **1961** *Times* 28 Mar. 12/7 They must now man the ticket office, sell programmes, start the recalcitrant generator, warm up the panotrope. **1968** D. BRAITHWAITE *Fairground Archit.* 165 *Panatrope*, successor to the mechanical organ—gramophone turntables, amplifier and loudspeakers relaying noisy pop records. **1978** C. HUMPHREYS *Both Sides Circle* x. 114, I had a fight with the representative of the firm who had hired us the panatrope, or long-playing record machine.

Panavision (pæ·nǎvizən). [f. PAN(ORAMA + *a* + VISION *sb.*] A proprietary name for a type of anamorphic lens; *loosely*, wide-screen cinematography. Also *fig.*

1955 *Jrnl. Soc. Motion Pict. & Television Engin.* LXIV. 233/1 Anamorphic printer lenses used..are the Tushinsky and Panavision. **1963** *Punch* 3 July 30/1 Panavision and colour make the whole thing incongruously cheerful to look at. **1967** *Trade Marks Jrnl.* 24 May 669/2 Panavision... Cinematographic and photographic apparatus..; anamorphic lenses... Panavision Incorporated.., City of Los Angeles. **1973** W. DANCY in S. Henderson *Understanding New Black Poetry* 300 Frail we cringe before Dante's Italic vision Its cineramic focus and panavision scale Swells brain-mind.

pancake, *sb.* Add **1.** Further examples of phr. *as flat as a pancake* (and varr.). Also used with reference to the *fig.* senses of FLAT *a.*

1761 STERNE *Tr. Shandy* III. xxvii. 138 He has crush'd his nose..as flat as a pancake to his face. **1830** MARRYAT *King's Own* I. xvii. 261 Under which it had lain, jammed as flat as a pancake. **1909** *Dialect Notes* III. 411 *Flatter than a pancake*, very flat, of persons and things. **1921** GALSWORTHY *To Let* I. ix. 79 Fleur was not yet home... Here were her aunt, and her cousins the Cardigans, and this fellow Profond, and everything flat as a pancake for the want of her. **1922** JOYCE *Ulysses* 735 The last [stout] they sent from O Rourkes was as flat as a pancake. **1936** 'G. ORWELL' *Keep Aspidistra Flying* i. 15 He was nearly thirty and had accomplished nothing; only his miserable book of poems that had fallen flatter than any pancake. **1959** *Daily Tel.* 14 Mar. 6 His statement to the House of Commons yesterday fell as flat as a pancake.

2. f. A type of flat hat. *U.S.*

1875 E. S. NADAL *Impressions London Social Life* 143 The cap was peculiar, though about the year '56 we had something like it called the 'Pancake'. **1945** *Amer. Speech* XX. 233/1 She had on her duty dress and a French pancake. *Ibid.* 234/1 *French pancake*, flat hat. **1957** M. B. PICKEN *Fashion Dict.* 241/2 *Pancake beret*, broad flat beret. **1975** G. HOWELL *In Vogue* 188 (*caption*) Pancake and huge gloves in looped emerald green crochet. **1976** M. & G. GORDON *Ordeal* (1977) xiii. 92 She wore..a pancake Stetson that she could tilt over her face.

g. A vertical descent made by an aircraft in a level position (see quot. 1918[1]); the landing of an aircraft in an emergency with the undercarriage retracted (see **pancake landing*).

1912 *Aero* Mar. 66/1 Pride cometh before a pancake. **1913** C. MELLOR *Airman* 25 Landings must be 'normal'—not of the 'pancake' order. **1914** HAMEL & TURNER *Flying* 66 He must be able to learn how to make a fairly safe 'pancake'. **1918** H. BARBER *Aeroplane Speaks* (ed. 6) 14 *Pancakes*, pilot's slang for stalling an aeroplane and dropping like a pancake. **1918** COWLEY & LEVY *Aeronautics* x. 225 Dangerous consequences due to a landing of a pancake type are usually guarded against by a strong under-carriage and by the insertion of shock absorbers. **1974** P. WRIGHT *Lang. Brit. Industry* 5 In the R.A.F. during the last war crash landings were *pancakes*.

h. An opaque facial treatment used as a base for make-up. *Freq. attrib.*, as *pancake make-up*. orig. *U.S.*

1937 *Official Gaz.* (U.S. Patent Office) 13 July 251/1 Max Factor & Co., Los Angeles, Calif... Pan-cake. The word 'cake' is disclaimed apart from the mark. For cosmetic in the nature of a solidified cream used for a make-up base. **1940** *Sears Catal.* Spring/Summer 99 (*caption*) Pan-Cake Makeup. **1946** *Trade Marks Jrnl.* 15 May 244/2 Pancake... Cosmetic preparations for toilet use and for use in theatrical, motion picture, television, and photographic make-up. Max Factor & Co..., Hollywood, United States of America; manufacturers. **1951** H. MACINNES *Neither Five nor Three* I. v. 66 Miss Guttman's face flushed with pleasure even under the pan-cake make-up. **1953** *New Yorker* 13 June 61/1 Like his Cabinet members, he used pancake makeup. **1955** W. GADDIS *Recognitions* III. ii. 737 It's too bad they didn't get some pancake on him before he went up. **1960** L. COOPER *Accomplices* II. ii. 84 A private life that you can put on over your real one..like your pancake make-up. **1962** E. O'BRIEN *Lonely Girl* ii. 22, I put pancake on Baba's back to hide her spots. **1970** *Sunday Times* 3 May 28/6 Women take hours getting themselves done up to attract men, slapping on pancake, painting their eyes. **1975** J. CROSBY *Affair of Strangers* iii. 25 Chantal wore only light pancake, dimming but not obliterating the brown skin. **1975** *Daily Colonist* (Victoria, B.C.) 20 June 4/6 The candidate had ugly mannish hands and, under the heavy pancake make-up, the suspicion of beard stubble. **1978** *Chicago* June 14/3, I didn't used to wear pancake at all—it was a macho thing with me. But now I do.

3. pancake batter, the mixture from which pancakes are made; **pancake coil** *Electr.*, any flat or very short inductance coil (see quots.); **pancake descent, landing** [cf. *PANCAKE *v.* b], the landing of an aircraft in an emergency with the undercarriage retracted; **pancake race,** a race held on Shrove Tuesday, in which the participants are required to toss pancakes as they run; **pancake roll** (see quot. 1967).

1739 E. SMITH *Compl. Housewife* (ed. 9) 114 Mix all well together a little thicker than pancake batter. **1747** H. GLASSE *Art of Cookery* vii. 69 Make it up into a thick Batter with Flour, like a Pancake Batter. **1965** A. CHRISTIE *At Bertram's Hotel* xi. 103 She made herself three pancakes with the pancake batter. **1910** H. M. HOBART *Dict. Electr. Engin.* I. 108 *Pancake coil*, a flat former-wound coil used in the construction of the early smooth-core rotating armatures of alternators. The term is also sometimes applied to the flat separately insulated unit coil used in modern high-pressure transformers. **1921** *Physical Rev.* XVIII. 138 Coursey's curves do not cover the case of coils whose radial dimension exceeds the axial (pancake coils). **1940** *Chambers's Techn. Dict.* 611/1 *Pancake coil*, an inductance coil in which the windings are arranged spirally, in the form of a flat disc. **1960** COOKE & MARKUS *Electronics & Nucleonics Dict.* 322/2 *Pancake coil*, a coil having a diameter appreciably greater than its length. **1961** *Guardian* 18 Jan. 1/1 The transformer..will be made up of a series of 'pancake' coils of primary and secondary windings. **1914** W. J. CLAXTON *Mastery of Air* xlviii. 249 It is considered faulty piloting to make a pancake descent where there is ample landing space. **1928** Pancake landing [see *LEVEL *v.*[1] 5*]. **1938** *Encycl. Brit. Bk. of Year* 57/2 Nothing better could be expected than a 'pancake' landing which would destroy the under-carriage without seriously injuring the crew. **1960** WENTWORTH & FLEXNER *Dict. Amer. Slang* 374/1 *Pancake landing*, Specif., in aviation, the act or instance of landing an airplane on its fusilage rather than on its wheels, done when the landing gear is damaged. **1951** *Sun* (Baltimore) 17 Jan. 3/2 (*caption*) Mrs. Virginia Leete ..takes a spill in the snow during a practice run..in preparation for the annual pancake race scheduled for Shrove Tuesday. **1955** *Ibid.* 23 Feb. 2/3 Pancake races have featured Shrove Tuesday observances in Olney for some 510 years. **1967** D. BRICE *Folk-Carol of England* iii. 86 The well-known 'pancake race' that takes place in the Buckinghamshire village [of Olney] every Shrove Tuesday. **1972** *Guardian* 15 Jan. 14/5 Shrovetide brings pancake races like that at Olney in Buckinghamshire, with housewives tossing pancakes as they belt along. **1976** *Times* 3 Mar. 14/6 The annual women's pancake races in Lincoln's Inn Fields. **1967** *Observer* (Colour Suppl.) 30 Apr. 38/4 *Pancake roll*, a pancake with savoury meat and vegetable fillings, deep fried. **1968** R. V. BESTE *Repeat Instructions* xi. 121 They had a more adventurous meal than the..vegetable chop suey and pancake rolls he usually ordered. **1969** O. BLAKESTON *For crying out Shroud* vii. 59 Jim orders fried oysters and crispy pancake rolls. **1976** M. BUTTERWORTH *Remains to be Seen* iv. 68 The diligent Chinese..laboured over their crab foo yung and their crispy pancake rolls.

pancake, *v.* **a.** (In Dict. s.v. PANCAKE *sb.*) Delete *nonce-wd.* and add later examples (chiefly as ppl. adj.). Also *fig.* and in sense *2 h of the sb.

1941 *Time* 6 Oct. 17/1 A..near-hurricane..that killed three people, leveled grain fields, pancaked buildings, blocked highways. *Ibid.* 20 Oct. 2/1 Starting the bill in the House, with a steam roller set to pancake all opposition. **1942** *Capital* (Topeka, Kansas) 15 Mar. (*caption*) Sure! He's pancaked 17 guys in a row! Hits like a train at a grade crossing. **1948** L. MACNEICE *Holes in Sky* 13 They tell me report at the first police station. But the station is pancaked—so what can I do? **1953** DYLAN THOMAS *Let.* 22 June (1966) 409 Sober, airsick, pancaked flat, I saw these intelligent old friends as a warren full of blockish stinkers. **1973** R. L. SIMON *Big Fix* vii. 50 His face was pancaked in layers, his hair lacquered. **1974** *Listener* 23 May 678/2 Rows of pancaked Cadillacs and burnt-out Rolls-Royces. **1977** *S. Wales Echo* 18 Jan. 1/4 Police reported 21 confirmed deaths but said it was likely 60 to 70 more bodies remained in a pancaked carriage crushed to a quarter of its bulk by a giant slab of concrete weighing hundreds of tons.

b. *Aeronaut. intr.* Of an aircraft: to descend rapidly in a level position in stalled flight, *spec.* to land in this manner in an emergency with the undercarriage retracted (cf. **pancake landing*). Of the pilot: to cause an aircraft to pancake. Also *transf.* and *fig.* Hence **pa·ncaking** *vbl. sb.*

1911 *Aero* Aug. 136/2 In the meanwhile Conway Jenkins had..'pancaked' badly, and smashed it pretty conclusively. **1912** *Ibid.* Mar. 66/1 He..then shut off his engine, calmly waiting for the machine to return to the ground, which it did with a resultant bump, commonly known to the aviation world as pancaking (falling flatly). **1914** *Aeronaut. Jrnl.* Oct. 316 *Pancake, to*, to descend steeply, with the wings at a very large angle of incidence, like a parachute. **1914** H. M. BUIST *Aircraft in German War* 35 The craft pancaking, diving and banking are monoplanes. **1916** C. WINCHESTER *Flying Men* 68 So ..the 'pancaking' of aircraft is not an advisable method of landing. **1920** *19th Cent.* Mar. 570 This pancaking device by which the National Socialists tried at the last moment to save the crash. **1928** C. F. S. GAMBLE *Story N. Sea Air Station* xv. 263, I took my chance and about 10 feet up 'pancaked'—a horrid crash. **1929** E. W. SPRINGS *Above Bright Blue Sky* 73, I came out of the spin at five hundred feet and pancaked in the reserve lines. **1936** F. CLUNE *Roaming round Darling* xxv. 271 All at once she [*sc.* a lorry] slithered like hell, and, knifing a corner, pancaked on to a mulga-tree. **1938** *Daily Progress* (Charlottesville, Va.) 30 July 1/8 He suggested the planes might be ordered to comb isolated mountain forests on the Pacific side of Luzon Island on the possibility the 'Clipper' pancaked into the trees. **1943** P. BRENNAN et al. *Spitfires over Malta* 91, I told my boys to pancake as soon as they had finished engaging. **1950** *Gloss. Aeronaut. Terms* (*B.S.I.*) I. 12 *Pancaking*, the alighting of an aircraft at an abnormally high rate of descent or low forward speed. **1952** M. TRIPP *Faith is Windsock* vi. 97 'Beany Able funnels; we are on three engines and must land.' 'Pancake, Able.' 'Able pancaking.' **1962** R. W. CLARK *Rise of Boffins* ii. 53 Another great time-saver was the use of a code for passing instructions to the fighters, and such R.A.F. terms as.. 'pancake' (for land), were invented during these experiments. **1977** *Listener* 28 Apr. 559/2 His plane..pancaked into it. The Germans..came out..to take him and the plane.

panchama (pa·ntʃāmă). *India.* [Skr., = fifth.] A member of the fifth division of early Indian society, outside the four main divisions of Brahmin, Kshatrya, Vasiya and Sudra; a pariah, an outcaste. This caste was also called *Pancham Bandam.*

1800 F. BUCHANAN *Jrnl.* 30 Apr. in *Journey from Madras* (1807) I. i. 19 Their farms they chiefly cultivate by slaves of the inferiour casts, called Súdra, and Panchum Bundum. The Panchum Bundum are by far the most hardy and laborious people of the country. **1874** *Madras Census Rep. 1871* I. xi. 168 We now come to that great division of the people, spoken of by themselves as the 'fifth caste', and described by Buchanan and other writers as the *Pancham Bandam.* **1909** E. THURSTON *Castes & Tribes of S. India* VI. 44 The Government ruled that there is no objection to the proposal that Paraiyas and kindred classes should be designated Panchama Bandham or Panchama in future, but it would be simpler to style them the fifth class. *Ibid.*, Panchama students under training as teachers get stipends at rates nearly double of those for ordinary Hindus. **1917** *Rangoon Gaz.* 10 Oct. 12/1 A mass meeting of Panchamas (depressed classes) was held in Madras. **1932** G. S. GHURYE *Caste & Race in India* i. 10 In the Tamil and Malayalam regions..sometimes the village is divided into three parts: that occupied by the dominant caste in the village or by the Brahmins, that allotted to the Sūdras, and the one reserved for the Panchamas or untouchables. **1968** N. W. ROSS *Hinduism, Buddhism, Zen* 29 Outside the four main caste divisions,..there has also existed from the earliest times a group familiarly known as the Untouchables. They were called Panchamas, literally 'the fifths'.

panchayat. (Now the normal spelling.) Add: (Later examples.) Also *attrib.* Hence **panchayat samiti** [f. Hindi *samiti* committee].

1881 E. B. EASTWICK *Murray's Handbk. Bombay Presidency* (ed. 2) II. 141/1 In order to see the Towers of Silence, permission must be obtained from the Secretary to the Pârsî Panchâyat. **1893** KIPLING *Many Inventions* 84 Create, further, councils other than the panchayats of headmen, village by village and district by district. **1945** 'P. WOODRUFF' *Call Next Witness* 14 He was chairman of the village panchayat, the court which could try the smallest local offences. **1955** *Times* 29 Aug. 9/6 Mansingh tried to negotiate peace at a special meeting of the Panchayats, or village councils. **1963** *Times* 11 Mar. 11/7 The emphasis was corrected and laid on agricultural production—but no sooner than the establishment of *panchayat raj* had led villagers to express their needs more outspokenly, and their satisfaction had become the business of the village politicians. **1963** *Economist* 23 Nov. 752/1 His [the King of Nepal's] system of 'panchayat democracy', an elaborate four-tier edifice of indirect elections. **1965** E. LINTON *World in Grain of Sand* vi. 73 Were all members of the Panchayat present? No. Then send for them! Panchayats, literally meaning 'councils of five', have existed in villages since ancient times... Numbers need not necessarily be confined to five. **1969** *Listener* 2 Jan. 5/1 The panchayat system is little more popular than Pakistan's basic democracy. **1969** *National Herald* (New Delhi) 29 July 7/4 Mr. Thana Ram, pradhan of panchayat samiti, has criticised the demotion of education extension officers who have completed five years of service. **1971** *Hindustan Times Weekly* (New Delhi) 4 Apr. 8/2 The Agriculture Refinance Corporation will provide Rs 25 lakhs for disbursement as loans among the orange-growers of Halrapatan panchayat samiti in Halawar district. **1971** *Nat. Geographic* Nov. 662/1 Panchayat means 'five elders', a traditional informal council that runs the affairs of Nepalese villages. **1973** *Times* 14 Apr. (Nepal Suppl.) p. i/5 Limited popular representation is permitted through a pyramidal structure of partly elected and partly nominated *panchayats*, or councils, beginning at the village level. **1976** D. HIRO *Inside India Today* 50 What then emerged was a three-tiered system whereby the old district boards..were replaced by zilla parishads (i.e. district councils) with responsibility for co-ordinating development plans to be channelled through panchayat samitis (i.e. council committees) consisting of a number of popularly elected panchayats encompassing one or more villages—all interlinked through indirect elections. This system, popularly known as the panchayat raj, was first introduced in..1959.

panchen pan,tʃěn). *Tibet.* Also **Banchen, Pantchan,** etc. [Tibetan, abbrev. of *paṇḍita-chen-po* great learned one (cf. PUNDIT).] A Tibetan Buddhist title of respect, applied *esp.* to the lama of Tashi Lhunpo, who is held to be the reincarnation of Buddha Amitbha and is next in importance to the Dalai Lama, being styled the *Panchen Lama* or *Panchen Rinpoche* (rinpoche = precious, jewel). Cf. *RINPOCHE.

1763 J. BELL *Trav. from St. Petersburg* I. 284 The Kontaysha is of the same profession with the Delay-Lama... I am informed there is a third Lama, called Bogdu-Pantzin, of still greater authority... He lives.. near the frontiers of the Great Mogul. **1784** S. TURNER *Let.* 2 Mar. in *Acct. Embassy to Court of Teshoo Lama in Tibet* (1800) III. 373, I was..strongly dissuaded by the Regent Punjun Irtinnee. **1794** A. DALRYMPLE *Oriental Repertory* II. 273 This Pantchan-lama is the Second Person of Tibeth and of all the Lama-Hierarchy. *Ibid.* 274 The Pan-tchan..asked permission of his Majesty to proceed to the Capital of the Empire. **1800** S. TURNER *Acct. Embassy to Court of Teshoo Lama in Tibet* II. viii. 325 *Punjin Rimbochay*, Great Apostolic Master; the mitred professors of religion. **1834** C. GÜTZLAFF *Sk. Chinese Hist.* II. xvii. 64 One of the chiefs of Tibet, on hearing of the death of Banchen Lama at Peking, had gone to Nepaul with an immense treasure. **1851** H. T. PRINSEP *Tibet, Tartary & Mongolia* 108 The highest of existing regenerate Boodhs are the Delai Lama of Lassa; the Bandshan Remboochi, of Teeshoo Loomboo, the same who was visited by Captain Turner, in the time of Warren Hastings. **1876** C. R. MARKHAM *Narr. Bogle & Manning* p. cxi, The Pundit went..to Teshu Lumbo, to do homage to the Teshu Lama or Panchen Rimboché, a boy eleven years old. **1895** L. A. WADDELL *Buddhism of Tibet* x. 235 The Sa-kya Grand Lāmas had been called 'Pan-ch'en', or the 'Great doctor' from the twelfth century. **1925** *Glasgow Herald* 13 Apr. 9 The Panchan Lama is one of the two lama popes, the other being the Dalai Lama, or Ocean Priest, who resides at Lhassa. **1931** C. BELL *Relig. of Tibet* xii. 155 During the reign of the eighth Dalai Lama it is the Panchen Rim-po-che who looms largest in Tibetan history. **1935** *Discovery* Aug. 239/2 On the high altar itself the central position was occupied by an excellent photograph of the Panchen Lama. **1956** K. W. MORGAN *Path of Buddha* vi. 256 The present Panchen Lama is the ninth in succession and was selected jointly by the former National Government of China and the followers of the exiled Panchen Lama. **1962** *Listener* 12 July 71/1 People interested in Tibetan institutions will also pay attention to the few pages devoted to the Panchen Lama. **1964** J. P. MITTER *Betrayal of Tibet* 98 The Chinese Amban violated the Trade Regulations of 1908 by forbidding the Pan-chen Lama and his officials to communicate with the British Trade Agent at Gyantse. **1978** *Guardian* 25 Feb. 6/8 The Panchen Lama..remained behind in Tibet when the Dalai Lama and other religious leaders fled to India in 1959.

panchromatic (pænˌkrŏmæ·tik), *a.* [f. PAN- + CHROMATIC *a.*] **1.** *Photogr.* Sensitive (though not equally so) to light of all colours in the visible range. Also *ellipt.*, a panchromatic emulsion or plate.

1903, etc. [see *ORTHOCHROMATIC *a.* 1]. **1906** *Chambers's Jrnl.* May 416/2 This layer..is re-covered with yet another layer of panchromatic, and sensitised. **1921** *Glasgow Herald* 6 Apr. 7 My dark-room lamp has three interchangeable safe-lights,..one a dark green for panchromatics. **1952** *Proc. R. Soc. Edin.* A. LXIII. 206 The usual type of orthochromatic emulsion is a little slow to this radiation, but a panchromatic emulsion might record some red. **1978** *SLR Camera* Aug. 82/1 Panchromatic film—the type almost exclusively used these days for normal photography—..is very much more sensitive to blue and blue-green, than the eye, but less sensitive to green, yellow and orange.

2. = POLYCHROMATIC *a.*

1971 J. MCCLURE *Steam Pig* iii. 39 The poser of the panchromatic panties. **1975** M. KENYON *Mr Big* xix. 180 Two boisterous black girls in patched panchromatic trousers.

Hence **panchro·matize** *v. trans.*, to render panchromatic; **panchro·matizing** *vbl. sb.*

1922 E. J. WALL *Pract. Color Photogr.* ii. 15 Many dyes have been suggested for panchromatizing. **1925** —— *Hist. Three-Color Photogr.* vii. 246 A. Miethe recommended the following mixture for panchromatizing plates. **1960** K. M. HORNSBY tr. *P. Glafkidès' Photogr. Chem.* II. xxxv. 729 To make them [*sc.* photographic emulsions] sensitive to the other colours, green, yellow, red and infra red—or to ortho- or panchromatize as we say—it is necessary to incorporate certain special dyes.

panchronic (pænˌkrǫ·nik), *a.* *Linguistics.* [tr. F. *panchronique* (F. de Saussure *a* 1913, in *Cours de Linguistique générale* (1916) I. iii. 138), f. PAN- 2 + CHRONIC *a.*] Pertaining to or designating linguistic study applied to all languages at all stages of their development. Also **panchroni·stic** *a.* Hence **panchro·nically** *adv.*; **pa·nchrony.**

1931 *Amer. Jrnl. Philol.* LII. 79 Scientific grammar must be based on a combination of ideo(syn)chrony and panchrony. **1939** L. H. GRAY *Foundations of Lang.* 24 The components of such a panchronic grammar, which may technically be termed *general grammar*, will be few in number. **1949** *Archivum Linguisticum* I. II. 127 On the *panchronistic* plane, there is the usual argument of the complete diversity of words for the same idea in different languages. **1951** S. ULLMANN *Princ. Semantics* v. 261 He [*sc.* de Saussure] did admit the possibility of 'panchronistic laws' resembling the universal regularities of natural science, e.g. the ubiquitousness of sound-change. **1952** *Times Lit. Suppl.* 10 Oct. 659/3 A final chapter, devoted to panchronistic or general semantics, is merely a programmatic sketch. **1957** *Archivum Linguisticum* IX. II. 81 Finally, hyper- and hypocharacterization may be used panchronically. **1964** *Ibid.* XVI. I. 23 Clusters so shaped may panchronically tend to undergo just this development. **1966** M. PEI *Gloss. Ling. Terminol.* 192 *Panchronic grammar*, applicable to all languages and at all historical stages of their development. **1969** *Eng. Stud.* L. 417 General phonetics is by definition synchronic, or rather panchronic. *Ibid.* 422 Comparatism was supposed ..to lead to diachrony, not to the establishment of common, general features of language, to panchrony. **1974** R. A. HALL *External Hist. Romance Lang.* 4 The panchronic approach treats those aspects of language for which the passage of time is not relevant. **1978** *Language* LIV. 238/2 In Chapter V, he treats 'Lingua, stile, dialetti'.. from a primarily panchronic point of view.

‖**panchshila** (pɑnʃī·la). Also **panchsheel, panchsila,** and as two words. [Hindi and Skr., f. *panch* five, *shila* foundation.] The five principles of peaceful relations formulated between India and China (and, by extension, other communist countries).

The five principles, stated in the preamble of a treaty signed by India and China in April 1954, are: 1. Mutual respect for each other's territorial integrity and sovereignty. 2. Non-aggression. 3. Non-interference in each other's internal affairs. 4. Equality and mutual benefit. 5. Peaceful co-existence.

1955 *Times* 18 July 7/5 After analysing the popular enthusiasm in Russia over the Nehru visit, the newspaper [sc. *Times of India*] says, 'It would be foolish, even dangerous, to work oneself up into a frenzy of apocalyptic fervour and hail those who hailed our Prime Minister as comrades good and true demonstrating in their mammoth enthusiasm the resolve to march in step to the golden melody of Panchshila.' **1958** *Times* 4 July 9/3 India tried to act upon the principles of *panchsila*, and did not wish to interfere in other people's affairs. **1959** *Manch. Guardian* 15 Aug. 5/4 China has slapped India's face, and the Panchshilas (the 'five principles of co-existence') have popped. **1961** *Economist* 2 Dec. 939/2 India was drawing up the *Panch Shila*—the five principles of peaceful co-existence—with the Chinese. **1965** J. NEHRU in A. Appadorai *Documents Political Thought* (1976) II. 739 Panchsheel has begun to acquire a specific meaning and significance in world affairs. **1967** L. J. KAVIC *India's Quest for Security* iii. 59 On 1 August 1955, a joint communiqué issued in Kathmandu by representatives of the Nepalese and Chinese governments declared that an agreement had been reached which affirmed panch sheel as the basis of Sino-Nepalese relations. **1978** L. HEREN *Growing up on The Times* v. 178 Despite the Indian name, the *panchsila* were of Chinese origin, and were written into the preamble of the Sino-Indian Tibetan Treaty on the instance of Peking.

pancreatectomy (pæ:ŋkrīˌăte·ktŏmi). *Surg.* [f. Gr. stem παγκρεατ- (PANCREAS) + *-ECTOMY.] Excision of the pancreas.

1900 in DORLAND *Med. Dict.* **1903** W. S. BICKHAM *Text-bk. Operative Surg.* v. 834 Anatomically, complete pancreatectomy is very difficult. **1968** *New Scientist* 27 June 701/2 Pancreas transplantation..might also be useful..where pancreatectomy is needed because of malignancy. **1974** R. M. KIRK et al. *Surgery* vi. 112 Occasionally distal pancreatectomy, the removal of ductal stones, and drainage of the cut end of the pancreas into the jejunum, improves the patient. **1977** *Proc. R. Soc. Med.* LXX. 160/1 One man of 44 died of massive haemorrhage the day after a complicated procedure to relieve intestinal and biliary obstruction, following a pancreatectomy less than three weeks previously.

Hence **pa:ncreate·ctomize** *v. trans.*, to excise the pancreas of; **pa:ncreate·ctomized** *ppl. a.*

1912 *Amer. Jrnl. Physiol.* XXX. 341 The glycolytic action of muscle extracts of both normal and pancreatectomized animals has been tested. **1960** *Recent Progress Hormone Res.* XVI. 503 Rats were fasted and underfed for 8–10 days and then pancreatectomized. **1965** LEE & KNOWLES *Animal Hormones* vii. 111 If a dog is pancreatectomized and the circulation connected to one, two or three pancreases from normal dogs, the blood glucose is normal in the pancreatectomized animal, irrespective of the number of the pancreases utilized.

pancreatico-. Add: **pancrea:ticoduoden-e·ctomy** = **pancreatoduodenectomy*.

1941 *Ann. Surg.* CXIV. 612 Until 1935, pancreaticoduodenectomy for cancer involving the pancreas was not attempted. **1973** V. L. STEVENSON *Biliary Tract Surg. & Cholangiogr.* xii. 124 Those undergoing pancreaticoduodenectomy generally afforded a longer survival than those undergoing palliation.

pancreato-, comb. form (= PANCREATICO-), as in **pancrea:toduodene·ctomy** (see quot. 1928); **pa:ncreato·graphy**, radiological examination of the pancreas.

1928 R. J. E. SCOTT *Gould's Med. Dict.* (ed. 2) 1044/2 *Pancreatoduodenectomy*, excision of the head of the pancreas with the surrounding loop of duodenum. **1937** *Surg., Gynecol. & Obstetr.* LXV. 681 (*heading*) Resection of head of pancreas and duodenum for carcinoma—pancreatoduodenectomy. **1977** *Proc. R. Soc. Med.* LXX. 153/1 Unfortunately, Whipple's operation or pancreatoduodenectomy for carcinoma of the head of the pancreas was seldom possible. **1971** RAINS & CAPPER *Bailey & Love's Short Pract. Surg.* (ed. 15) xlii. 877 (*heading*) Pancreatography. **1977** *Lancet* 9 July 68/1 A screening test which makes possible the detection of pancreatic disease at an early stage and gives an indication for invasive procedures such as endoscopic pancreatography and selective arteriography is urgently needed.

pancreozymin (pæŋkrīˌozəi·min). *Biochem.* [f. PANCRE(AS + -O + ZYMIN.] A hormone which stimulates the production of enzymes by the pancreas.

1943 HARPER & RAPER in *Jrnl. Physiol.* CII. 116 We have obtained preparations which increase the output of enzymes from the cat's pancreas without having any secretin activity... For the active substance producing this effect we suggest the name 'Pancreozymin'. **1956** *Nature* 7 Jan. 22/2 Cholinergic drugs and pancreozymin in the pancreas, and acetylcholine and adrenalin in the salivary glands, all stimulate the secretion of protein. **1965** LEE & KNOWLES *Animal Hormones* viii. 120 It may be that under normal conditions both secretin and pancreozymin are released together. **1974** R. M. KIRK et al. *Surgery* vi. 110 Pancreozymin..is liberated in response to the presence of protein and fat in the duodenum.

pancuronium (pænkiŭrōu·niŏm). *Pharm.* [f. *pan-*, of uncertain etym. + CUR(ARE + *-ONIUM.] A steroid whose bromide is used as a neuromuscular blocking agent.

1967 *Brit. Jrnl. Anæsthesia* XXXIX. 775/1 Pancuronium bromide (NA97), was first synthesized in 1964 by Hewett and Savage (1966, personal communication). **1976** *Billings* (Montana) *Gaz.* 17 June 1-D/6 Many of the breathing failures at the hospital were caused when unknown assailants injected patients with a potentially lethal muscle-paralyzing drug, pancuronium bromide. **1976** *Lancet* 18 Dec. 1334/1 One group of eight patients received general anæsthesia with thiopenthone, suxamethonium chloride, pancuronium bromide or gallamine, and enflurane ('Ethrane') with nitrous oxide plus oxygen.

panda. Add: **2.** A large, black and white, bear-like mammal, *Ailuropoda melanoleuca*, native to limited, mountainous areas of forest in China, where the first scientific description of it was made by the French missionary, Armand David (1826–1900), in 1869; formerly known as the parti-coloured bear, until its zoological relationship to the red panda was established in 1901.

1901 E. R. LANKESTER in *Trans. Linn. Soc.* (*Zool.*) VIII. 165 *Æluropus* must be removed from association with the Bears..and is no longer to be spoken of as 'the Parti-coloured Bear', but as 'the Great Panda'. **1928** *Proc. Zool. Soc.* 975 The systematic position of the Giant Panda..is a question about which there has been much disagreement amongst zoologists. **1933** *Discovery* Mar. 91/1 In outward appearance there is considerable difference between these two animals, the giant panda.. being very bear-like, while the little panda is about the size and somewhat the shape of a cat. **1939** *Daily Mail* 12 Apr. 8/4 This sickly sentimental panda plague has infected far more people than can ever hope to eye it in the flesh... Would-be fashionable young women are carrying panda mascots. **1940** N. MITFORD *Pigeon Pie* ix. 140 Ming, the panda, would soon eat no food until one of them was played to her. **1943** *Jrnl. Mammalogy* XXIV. 267 The New York Zoological Society has recently acquired a pair of giant pandas... The principal natural diet of the panda is bamboo. **1966** R. & D. MORRIS *Men & Pandas* vi. 105 There were panda postcards.., panda toys (almost obliterating the teddy bear for a brief period), panda novelties, panda strip-cartoons, panda brooches, and pandá hats. **1973** *Times* 2 May 9/8 Children [in Peking] played a multitude of games including 'feed the panda', a variation on 'pin the tail on the donkey'. **1976** *Times Lit. Suppl.* 27 Feb. 231/5 It is rumoured that China has sited her nuclear testing grounds not far away from Panda country.

b. Used *attrib.* to designate a type of pedestrian crossing (see quot. 1962[1]). Also *absol.*

1962 *Daily Tel.* 7 Mar. 15/7 'Panda' pedestrian crossings are to be introduced..to supplement zebra crossings. Their warning lights will be operated by push-buttons and they will be given a 12-month trial. *Ibid.*, Differences in appearance between the 'Pandas' and the zebras are that the black-and-white carriageway markings at the 'Pandas' will be altered in shape from rectangles to blunted chevrons. **1962** *Times* 3 Apr. 12/6 Panda crossings, introduced yesterday, held up Croydon's evening traffic. **1963** *Times* 24 May 17/4 The amber lights system used on panda crossings was so complex and ambiguous that the ordinary driver could not understand it. **1965** A. CHRISTIE *At Bertram's Hotel* xi. 106 On the whole, the Canon was not what we would call accident prone... Whilst taking no care or thought, they could still survive even a Panda crossing.

c. A police patrol car, so named from the resemblance of a broad white stripe on the car to the markings of the giant panda. Also *attrib. colloq.*

1966 *Guardian* 13 Sept. 8/4 Special one-man patrol cars—painted blue with a broad white stripe and known as 'Pandas'. **1969** J. WAINWRIGHT *Take-Over Men* i. 13 What about your Panda Patrols? Your closed-circuit television? **1970** *Times* 17 Mar. 2 Five children, who.. helped catch two thieves, are to be given a ride in a police panda car. **1971** *Daily Tel.* 10 May 2/2 It was felt that panda drivers should be warned that the vehicles were not meant to be pursuit cars. **1974** 'A. GILBERT' *Nice Little Killing* vi. 82 He got out his old second-hand car—the village bobby didn't rate a panda.

pandaite (pæ·ndăˌəit). *Min.* Also **pandaïte.** [f. *Panda*, the name of the hill in Mbeya, Tanzania, where it was first found + -ITE[1].] A hydrated oxide of barium, strontium, niobium, and titanium, $(Ba,Sr)(Nb,Ti)_2$-$(O,H_2O)_7$, belonging to the pyrochlore group and found as yellow or white octahedral crystals.

1959 E. JÄGER et al. in *Mineral. Mag.* XXXII. 24 Some authors prefer to include under pyrochlore all the members of the group. Others give distinct names to the various members of this group. We prefer the latter and therefore propose to give the mineral described above the name of *pandaite* (after Panda Hill). This name shall be used for those minerals of the pyrochlore group in which Ba predominates over other elements in the *A* positions. **1971** *Mineralium Deposita* VI. 154/2 This pandaite shows large deficiencies in A ions and only 20–25% of the A positions are occupied. *Ibid.* 155/1 The mineral from Bingo [in the Congo] is a hydrated rare-earth variety of pandaïte. **1977** *Amer. Mineralogist* LXII. 407 *Pandaite*.. is a synonym for *bariopyrochlore*. The name should be dropped.

pandal. Add: Now usu. with pronunc. (pændā·l). (Further examples.)

1929 F. T. Jesse *Lacquer Lady* I. xii. 86 Her mother, the Kalawoon's wife, was running the pandal or festival pavilion for Thibaw. **1956** *Times* 13 Jan. 3/3 All the music is amplified, since the temporary *pandal*, which is the equivalent of an Eisteddfod 'tent', seats nearly 1,500 people. **1962** *Housewife* (Ceylon) Feb. 19 It was decided to hold the reception at the 39th lane sports club, where there was ample room for two large pandals to be erected. **1963** *Guardian* 11 Apr. 11/3 The Hindu wedding, celebrated under the flowered palm leaf pandal. **1971** *Weekend* (Ceylon) 8 Aug. 3/3 Permanent pandals will be built to decorate the entrances to sacred cities. **1977** *Oxford Mission Q. Paper* Jan.–Mar. 10 An enormous *pandal* had been erected which covered the whole area on the south side of the church, and the altar was placed on a mound in the middle of it.

pandan[2] (pæ·ndăn). Also **pandang.** [Malay.] = *Pandanus.

1777 [see Pandanus]. **1783** W. Marsden *Hist. Sumatra* 87 Of the *pandan*, which is a shrub with very long prickly leaves, like those of the pine apple or aloe, there are many varieties. **1935** I. H. Burkill *Dict. Econ. Products Malay Peninsula* II. 1646 The compound pine-apple-like fruit of a *Pandan* is composed of the fused fruits of the individual flowers. **1954** R. E. Holttum *Plant Life Malaya* ii. 23 Pandans have much in common with palms. **1959** 'M. Derby' *Tigress* iii. 125 A clump of *pandan*..edged the near end of the pool. **1972** M. Sheppard *Taman Indera* 158 Pandan leaves are used to make mats of finer quality, for sitting, praying or sleeping on.

pandanus. Substitute for etym. and def.: [mod. L. (G. E. Rumphius *Herbarium Amboinense* (1743) IV. 139/1), f. Malay *pandan*.] A tree or shrub of the genus so called, belonging to the family Pandanaceæ, native to Malaysia, tropical Africa, or Australia, and distinguished by forked trunks with thick aerial roots, long, narrow, prickly leaves arranged in spiral tufts, and large, sometimes edible fruits resembling a pineapple. Also *attrib.* (Add earlier and later examples.)

1830 J. Lindley *Introd. Nat. Syst. Bot.* 285 The seeds of Pandanus are eatable. **1908** E. J. Banfield *Confessions of Beachcomber* I. i. 15 Groups of pandanus palms bearing massive orange-coloured fruits. **1915** *Chambers's Jrnl.* Nov. 698/1 A net..is woven from a strong fibre found in a species of pandanus-tree. **1936** I. L. Idriess *Cattle King* xxxvi. 314 Plenty of water there, rock-bound rivers, pandanus-palm creeks, grass, trees, lily-covered lagoons. **1946** —— *In Crocodile Land* i. 5 They chopped pandanus nuts for breakfast. **1964** R. Perry *World of Tiger* xv. 231 The palms and pandanus wilderness in southern parts of the Island [*sc.* Java]. **1971** *World Archaeol.* III. 140 Unworked river pebbles, used for such purposes as breaking bones and crushing pigments or pandanus nuts. **1977** *Bulletin* (Sydney) 22 Jan. 65/1 The spindly eucalypts and pandanus palms in the Alligator River district were filled with the rasping shriek of millions of cicadas and crickets.

2. The fibre produced from pandanus leaves or the material woven from it. Also *attrib.*

1894 [in Dict.]. **1930** M. Mead *Growing up in New Guinea* ix. 156 A pandanus rain mat is a clumsy thing to carry about. **1963** *House & Garden* Feb. 61/2 Storage unit..teak, with pandanus grasscloth doors. **1971** *Daily Tel.* 23 Dec. 3/7 The children [of Pitcairn Island] will have found their presents in pandanus-leaf baskets suspended by the front porch or above their beds. **1972** M. Sheppard *Taman Indera* 141 The floor is hard and smooth and there is usually a low platform at one end on which spectators can sit, cross-legged, on pandanus mats. **1974** *Nat. Geographic* Dec. 778/1 The scene was one from yesterday—the pandanus-thatched houses under the palms, the circle of grinning, tattooed men.

pandect. Add: **2. b.** A manuscript volume containing all the books of the bible.

1887 F. J. A. Hort in *Academy* 26 Feb. 148/2 There cannot now be a shadow of doubt that the Codex Amiatinus is the 'Pandect' which Ceolfrid sent as a present to Gregory II. **1893** E. G. Browne *Lessons Early Eng. Church Hist.* 68 A pandect means a copy of the whole Bible. **1912** D. S. Boutflower *Life of Ceolfrid* 69 He [*sc.* Ceolfrid] caused three Pandects to be transcribed. **1969** *Jrnl. Brit. Archaeol. Assoc.* XXXII. 1 One of the three pandects, as they were then called (complete bibles in one volume) has survived miraculously intact. This is the Codex Amiatinus.

pandemoniac, *a.* Add: **c.** as *sb.* A pandemoniac person; a denizen of Pandemonium. *rare.*

1923 Galsworthy *Captures* 81 Success, power, wealth —those aims of profiteers and premiers, pedagogues and pandemoniacs.

pandiagonal (pæ:nˌdəiˌæ·gŏnăl), *a. Math.* [f. Pan- + Diagonal *a.*] Used to describe a magic square with the property that, if any number of columns be removed from one side of the diagram and added *en bloc* to the other, another magic square results.

1897 *Amer. Jrnl. Math.* XIX. 99 The square A is magic because each row, column, and diagonal has the same sum, 175; it is pandiagonal because not only the two main diagonals, but also the twelve broken diagonals..have each the same sum. **1919** *Monist* XXIX. 308 Magic squares of order ≡ 2 (mod. 4) made with consecutive numbers cannot be pandiagonal. **1939** H. S. M. Coxeter *Ball's Math. Recreations & Ess.* (ed. 11) vii. 203 A magic pandiagonal square of the fourth order..was inscribed at Khojuraho, India, as long ago as the eleventh or twelfth century. **1976** *Sci. Amer.* Jan. 120/1 And it is pandiagonal (sometimes called Nasik or diabolic), which means that its broken diagonals add up to 65, the constant.

Hence **pa:ndia·gonally** *adv.*

1911 W. W. R. Ball *Math. Recreations & Ess.* (ed. 5) vii. 157 If a pandiagonal square be cut into two pieces along a line between any two rows or any two columns, and the two pieces be interchanged, the new square so formed will be also pandiagonally magic.

pan-drop. *Sc.* [f. Pan *sb.*[1] + Drop *sb.* 10 e.] A hard, peppermint-flavoured sweet, shaped like a flattened sphere.

1877 *Encycl. Brit.* VI. 257/1 A core or centre of some kind is required, and this may consist either of a seed or fruit..; or it may be a small lozenge, as in the case of pan drops. **1904** 'H. Foulis' *Erchie* v. 29, I thoucht it was pan-drops ye cam' oot for, or conversation-losengers. **1927** *Glasgow Herald* 7 Sept. 12/7 An' there's nae mae tears since ye've got him wi' the poke o' pan-draps in his han'. **1956** C. M. Costie *Benjie's Bodle* 106 Wir haean a duff, an' treacle..an twa pan drops. **1964** *Scotsman* 14 Oct. 5 What was described in court as 'a classical line of traditional Scottish sweet—pan drops'. **1966** W. Merrilees *Short Arm of Law* 184 These..were not chocolates at all but hard peppermint sweets..pan-drops as we called them in Scotland.

pandurina (pæ:ndiūrī·nă). [It., f. *pandura* (see Pandora[2], pandore) + dim. suffix *-ina*.] A small musical instrument of the mandoline type.

1893 J. S. Shedlock tr. *Riemann's Dict. Mus.* 53/1 *Bandola.* (Span.), Bandolon, Bandora, Bandura, an instrument of the lute family, with a smaller or larger number of steel or catgut strings, which were plucked with the finger like the Pandora, Pandura, Pandurina, [etc.]. **1910** F. W. Galpin *Old Eng. Instruments of Mus.* iii. 40 At this period [*sc.* the sixteenth century] there was another small instrument called by Prætorius *Mandürichen* or *Pandurina*, which could be conveniently carried under the cloak. **1938** *Oxf. Compan. Mus.* 683/1 *Pandurina*, a very small instrument of the lute type, strung with wire—probably the ancestor of the mandoline. **1954** *Grove's Dict. Mus.* (ed. 5) V. 549/1 The pandurina returned to popularity, particularly about 1760–80, under the name Milanese mandoline. **1976** D. Munrow *Instruments Middle Ages & Renaissance* 79/3 Praetorius..also mentions a smaller size [of mandora], the *pandurina*, with four strings tuned to g, d′, g′, d″.

pandy, *sb.*[1] Add: **b.** *attrib.* and *Comb.*, as *pandybat.*

1916 Joyce *Portrait of Artist* (1969) i. 49 Fleming held out his hand. The pandybat came down on it with a loud smacking sound. **1922** —— *Ulysses* 547 Twice loudly a pandybat cracks.

Pandy (pæ·ndi). *Med.* The name of Kalman *Pandy* (b. 1868), Hungarian neurologist, used *attrib.* or in the possessive to denote a reaction or test he devised for globulins in the spinal fluid, in which a sample is treated with a dilute aqueous solution of phenol.

1916 L. F. Barker *Monographic Med.* II. 83 Pandy's test has not received the attention it deserves. **1933** W. R. Brain *Dis. Nervous Syst.* 113 Pandy's reaction is the most sensitive, and may yield a weakly positive result with normal fluids. **1963** *Lancet* 12 Jan. 108/1 Lumbar puncture on the ninth day of the illness yielded clear fluid..; the Pandy test was negative.

pane, *sb.*[1] **II. 4.** Delete † *Obs.* and add later example.

1912 T. D. Atkinson *Eng. & Welsh Cathedrals* 268 The north pane of the cloisters with its sunny aspect.

10. A sheet or page of stamps.

1912 *Chambers's Jrnl.* Nov. 749/1 The print would have represented a 'pane' of one hundred and twenty stamps. **1916** F. J. Melville *Postage Stamps in Making* I. xvi. 173 Where the sheet is in panes, only the pane containing the defective print is discarded. **1971** D. Potter *Brit. Eliz. Stamps* viii. 83 From September 1967 until May 1968 only 6s booklets contained Machin Head stamps, with three panes of 4ds. *Ibid.* xv. 174 In those days British stamps were printed by typography, and the printers' rule placed round the edge of the panes relieved the edges of the plates from the pressure which always falls more heavily on those parts. Marginal arrows..indicate the points of division into counter book panes, less unwieldy than complete sheets.

panel, *sb.*[1] Add: **II. 5. b.** Also, *spec.* a list or group of people called upon to advise, judge, take part in a discussion or contest, etc. (Further examples.)

1934 G. B. Shaw *Too True to be Good* 24 The formation of panels of tested persons eligible for the different grades in the governmental hierarchy. **1947** *Ann. Reg. 1946* 53 The method of forming panels for juvenile courts. **1952** W. J. H. Sprott *Social Psychol.* vi. 103 Another device for assessing the attitudes of special groups of people is to use panels of respondents who are prepared to give their views on expert or general questions. **1958** *New Statesman* 1 Feb. 127/2 Perhaps..he believes the Brainstrusters really are equipped to pronounce themselves upon, virtually, anything... Radio and television have given a great impetus here. 'Do the panel think that there is an after life?' **1958** *Listener* 4 Dec. 916/1 A small panel of experts who were also good broadcasters. **1959** *Times* 28 Feb. 7/4 If one of those contests which require the competitor to list a number of items in order of popularity were to turn its attention to the months of the year, the panel of judges (each one an expert) would surely find February at the bottom of the poll. **1961** *Which?* Sept. 231/2 The assessments were made by a panel of people experienced in listening to tape recorders. **1962** *Listen* 1 Feb. 211/2 It was a panel of architects of many nationalities who sketched out the main design. **1966** *Ibid.* 4 Aug. 168/1, I thought the panel skirted the subject. Why the BBC did not have a child psychologist on it I cannot guess. **1967** C. L. Wrenn *Word & Symbol* 11 The committee of scholars who translated the *New English Bible* New Testament..sought..to weld the whole into agreeable and dignified English with the aid of a 'literary panel'. **1973** *N.Y. Law Jrnl.* 31 Aug. 1/6 In reversing and remanding the case to the Southern District, the Second Circuit panel assigned it to Judge Constance Baker Motley. **1975** *Irish Times* 10 May 3/4 They named a panel of players from which the Ballybofey line-out will be chosen tomorrow. **1976** *Horse & Hound* 3 Dec. 54/3 He introduced a panel of experts for an open forum and considerable discussion ensued. **1977** *Sunday Express* 30 Jan. 31/5 It is customary for the touring side to see the full panel of Test umpires in action in the games outside the Tests.

c. The official list of doctors in a district who accepted patients under the National Health Insurance Act of 1913 (since superseded by the National Health Service Act of 1946). *On the panel,* (*a*) of doctors, registered as accepting patients thus; (*b*) of patients, under the care of a 'panel doctor'; also in extended use.

1913 *Punch* 30 July 101/1 The proposed Laureate was a medical man and not on a panel. **1914** *Times* 12 Feb. 6/5 Of these [doctors] 1500 are already on the panel for the county. **1914** T. Smith *Everybody's Guide Insurance Acts* (ed. 3) 124 Which practitioners are collectively to be known as 'the panel'. **1957** R. Hoggart *Uses of Literacy* i. 21 Almost every worker has been on the 'panel' at the local doctor's. **1964** G. L. Cohen *What's Wrong with Hospitals?* i. 22 Working people still talk about 'going on the Panel' when they're off sick, and don't see why they should use another term. **1974** *Daily Tel.* (Colour Suppl.) 29 Mar. 19/2 The average GP has 2,460 people on his panel. **1975** P. G. Winslow *Death of Angel* v. 117 It's the National Health... If only the government had left things alone, like they always was, with the Panel. **1976** 'J. Bell' *Trouble in Hunter Ward* i. 6 There were thousands of Health Service patients who put themselves upon their doctor's panel because they could no longer, after the war, afford to be private patients.

III. 9. f. A section of a tapestry or other ornamental work, usu. one surrounded by a decorative border. Also, a tapestry regarded as a whole.

1856 O. Jones *Gram. Ornament* xvi, The painter began to usurp the office of the scribe... We have the first stage ..where a geometrical arrangement is obtained with conventional ornament enclosing gold panels, on which are painted groups of flowers. **1911** *Encycl. Brit.* XXVI. 405/1 Other tapestries..are fantastic with schemes of abstract ornament into which are introduced as subsidiary details figure subjects set in panels and medallions. **1918** G. L. Hunter *Decorative Textiles* xii. 243 Tapestry screen panels woven in New York. **1923** F. de Zulueta *Embroideries M. Stuart & E. Talbot* 10 This again is a green velvet curtain, measuring 7½ × 6 feet and mounting twenty-four needle-work panels. *Ibid.* 15 If the centrepiece is not enough, there is the octagonal panel immediately above it. **1946** H. Léjard *French Tapestry* 24 The tapestry panels intended for the decoration of the same room soon came to be composed on related themes. **1953** E. Fisher *Swedish Embroidery* 38 The stimulating colours of this unique hanging panel can be seen in the colour reproductions. **1964** D. DuBon *Tapestries S. H. Kress Coll. at Philad. Mus. of Art: Hist. Constantine* 20 The sarcophagus is framed by an oval wreath of ribbon within an oval panel, bound laurel leaves with a shell form at the top and bottom. *Ibid.* 21 The ornament surrounding the central panels on all of the over-doors is similar. **1965** P. Hentgès tr. *Biryukova's Hermitage, Leningrad: Gothic & Renaiss. Tapestries* Pl. 33 The left-hand panel shows the betrothal of Mary and Joseph. **1974** *Encycl. Brit. Macropædia* XVII. 1055/1 A tapestry set is a group of individual panels related by subject, style, and workmanship and intended to be hung together.

g. One of the shaped sections of a parachute.

1930 O. H. Kneen *Everyman's Bk. Flying* xii. 223 Two men straighten out the twelve 'panels' of silk. **1938** *Flight* 25 Aug. 168c/1 The canopy, which is 24ft. in diameter, is made up of 24 triangular gores cut from high-quality silk. Each gore is composed of four panels, the stitching of which forms a zig-zag pattern round the complete canopy. **1974** *Encycl. Brit. Micropædia* VII. 740/2 The canopy is given extraordinary strength by fabrication from up to 28 separate panels, or gores, each made up of smaller sections.

10. b. Also *transf.*

1898 C. H. Turner in J. Hastings *Dict. Bible* I. 421/1 This picture is cut up, as it were, into six panels, each labelled with a general summary of progress. **1927** A. H.

McNeile *Introd. New Testament* 79 He [*sc.* St. Luke] cuts the history into 'panels'.

IV. 14. a. (Later example in sense of an oil painting on a wooden board.)

1956 Hedström & Taylor tr. *Bergström's Dutch Still-Life Painting* 58 We may now compare Bosschaert's panel with two early works by other artists... The farther edge of the table is considerably more than half way up the panel.

c. A leaf or section of a folding screen or triptych, etc. Also *fig.*

1880 E. Glaister *Needlework* vi. 62 Panel screens..are excellent subjects for fine embroidery. **1896** F. Simmonds tr. *Ricci's Correggio* vii. 122 On the high altar of the oratory..there was once a triptych, the central panel of which represented Christ. **1936** E. G. Troche *Painting in Netherlands* 26/2 Possibly half of a diptych, of which the panel with Our Lady is now lost. **1959** P. & L. Murray *Dict. Art & Artists* 324 Usually the central panel [of a triptych] is twice the width of the wings, so that they can be folded over it to protect it. **1967** N. Amphoux tr. *Troyat's Tolstoy* (1970) II. viii. 223 In painting the third panel of his triptych he had, as in *Boyhood*, combined the story of his friends, the Islenyevs, with his own. **1970** *Oxf. Compan. Art* 494/1 Panel painting was not developed fully until altars were furnished with painted retables.

15*. A control panel or instrument panel.

1897 E. Wilson *Electr. Traction* x. 219 The panel system of switchboards, whereby the various switches, complete for a given purpose, can be mounted on a panel of slate or marble and placed in line with those already installed. **1923**, etc. [see *control panel* s.v. *control *sb.* 5]. **1926** *Wireless World* 8 Dec. 760/3 A neat method of mounting a flash lamp bulb so that it may..illuminate the panel and tuning dials at night. **1929** V. W. Pagé *Ford Model 'A' Car* ix. 314 Remove the four screws which hold the instrument panel in place and pull panel back. **1933**, etc. [see *instrument panel* s.v. *instrument *sb.* 6]. **1940** *Railway Signalling & Communications* xix. 353 Points within 350 yds. of the signal box are mechanically operated by levers and the signals by switches on the panel. **1941** G. E. Irvin *Aircraft Instruments* xvii. 438 Large transport planes carrying two pilots require a dual set of instruments. This necessitates a large panel. **1964** M. Allward *Inside Jet Airliner* v. 39 The main panels contain the indicators and controls for the hydraulic and electrical systems, engine and fuel functioning, anti-icing and air-conditioning. **1969** T. C. Millington *Hillman Imps* x. 117 It is just possible to contrive a panel to mount two 2 in. gauges immediately above the speedometer. **1977** D. Beaty *Excellency* i. 8 He..clambered gingerly inside the fuselage..ran his fingers round the dusty panel.

VI. 20. (sense *5 b) *panel discussion, member*; (sense *5 c) *panel system*; (sense 14 a) *panel painter*; **panel analysis** *Sociol.*, analysis of attitude changes using the panel technique (see below); **panel-back** *a.*, applied to chairs with panelled backs (see quot. 1925); also *absol.* as *sb.*; **panel-beater,** one whose occupation is beating out the metal panels of motor vehicles; hence *panel beating*; **panel board** (see quot. 1954); **panel doctor,** formerly, a doctor registered as accepting patients under the National Insurance Act of 1913; **panel fence** *U.S.*, a fence constructed in panels or sections (see Panel *sb.*^{1} 8); **panel fire** = **panel heater*; **panel-game** (examples); (*b*) a 'quiz' or similar game played before an audience by a small group of people; hence *panel gamester*; **panel gauge** (see quot. 1966); **panel heater,** an electrically-heated panel mounted on a wall; hence *panel-heated* adj., *panel heating*; **panel-house** (earlier and later examples); **panel patient,** one who received medical treatment from a doctor under the Insurance Act of 1913; **panel pin,** a kind of thin nail, usu. having a tapered head, for securing panels; **panel practitioner** = **panel doctor*; **panel-robbery,** the business of a panel-thief; **panel saw,** a fine-toothed saw used for cutting out panels; **panel show** = **panel-game* (b); **panel stamp,** a stamp for decorating the panels in the cover of a book; hence *panel-stamped* adj.; **panel study** *Sociol.*, an investigation of attitude changes using a constant set of people and comparing each individual's opinions at different points in time; **panel technique** *Sociol.*, the technique used in panel studies; **panel-thief** (earlier and later examples); **panel truck** *U.S.*, a small lorry or van with a closed body; **panel van** *Austral.* = **panel truck*; **panel wall,** (*a*) a division between two panels in a coal mine; (*b*) a wall in a building that does not bear any structural weight; hence *panel-walled* adj.; **panel warming,** warming by means of panel heaters.

1968 *Internat. Encycl. Social Sci.* XI. 371/1 Panel analysis gives rise to the study of an aspect of social change that tends to be neglected in studies of aggregate trends. **1969** J. J. Linz in Dogan & Rokkan *Quantitative Ecol. Anal. Social Sci.* v. 102 The possibility of using ecological units for a kind of panel analysis of aggregate data to explore problems of change over time. **1904** P. Macquoid *Hist. Eng. Furnit.* ix. 223 The late panel-back chair..dated 1691. **1925** Penderel-Brodhurst & Layton *Gloss. Eng. Furnit.* 119 *Panel-back or wainscot chair*, a cumbrous high-seated oak chair with heavy legs, stretchers, and high wainscotted back, in use in Tudor and Jacobean times. **1975** *Oxf. Compan. Decorative Arts* 360/2 The panel-back chair (which was also panelled beneath the arms and seat) was to establish for two centuries the standard pattern of the chair with back of square or rectangular shape. *Ibid.* 361/1 Richly upholstered chairs..were found with more refined types of panel-backs. **1908** *Daily Chron.* 21 Feb. 10/7 (Advt.), Panel beaters, used to hammering landaulette..panels in steel and aluminium. **1973** J. Wainwright *Devil you Don't* 14 The mechanics and panel-beaters working Sunday, double-time. **1978** *Cornish Guardian* 27 Apr. 6/1 (Advt.), Qualified mechanic and/or Panel Beater Sprayer required. **1968** *Gloss. Terms Mechanized & Hand Sheet Metal Work* (*B.S.I.*) 15 *Panel beating*, a method of roughly forming a hollow body, usually by hammer blows. **1972** K. Bonfiglioli *Don't point that Thing at Me* iii. 21 Moishe Spinoza Barzilai is, as a matter of fact, Basil Wayne & Co., the great coach-builders of whom even you, ignorant readers, must have heard, although not point one per cent of you will ever afford his lovely panel-beating, still less his princely upholstery. **1932** Panel-board [see *corner-block* s.v. *corner *sb.*^{1} 16]. **1954** *Paper Terminol.* (Spalding & Hodge) 43 *Panel boards*, thick, tough, rigid boards made in various ways... Used in the manufacture of cars and in the building trade. **1972** *Gloss. Terms Timber* (*B.S.I.*) 27 *Panel-board*, fibre building board generally made from wood fibres. **1936** Panel discussion [see *creative *a.* 1 d]. **1956** W. H. Whyte *Organization Man* (1957) 55 It had started conventionally enough with a panel discussion in which I and two other men spoke. **1971** *Archivum Linguisticum* II. 20 A recent investigation of recorded panel discussions has shown that the average length of a unit of intonation used by the ten Present-English speakers involved was 5·3 (institutional) words. **1913** *Punch* 12 Feb. 127/2 To ask the Secretary of the Treasury if he could state the total population of the island of Canna, and who is the panel doctor. **1932** Kipling *Limits & Renewals* 300 A private party of thirty-two gentlemen and ladies,..all near enough neighbours in Shoreditch to use the same panel-doctor, poured into that man's consulting-room. **1957** R. Hoggart *Uses of Literacy* iii. 63 Working-class people have had years of experience of waiting at labour-exchanges, at the panel doctor's and at hospitals. **1800** W. Tatham *Hist. & Pract. Ess. Tobacco* 10 The *worm* or *pannel* fence,..consists of malled rails. **1858** J. A. Warder *Hedges & Evergreens* 113 A half-acre lot, with a seven foot panel-fence on one side and a hedge on the other. **1949** W. Faulkner *Knight's Gambit* 154 They would ride past mile after mile of white-painted panel fence. **1951** *Southern Folklore Q.* June 130 'Farm Fences' ..pictures a panel fence adapted to rocky fields. **1934** *Archit. Rev.* LXXV. 110/1 Panel fires are less than five years old. **1844** G. Wilkes *Mysteries of Tombs* 54/1, I forgot to mention..that Malinda Hoag was convicted..in robbing a countryman of $54 by the panel game. **1857** *Porter's Spirit of Times* 5 Dec. 213/3 Females are employed as decoy-ducks to induce the yokels from the rural districts into places of unquestionable character, where they are sure to be plundered of their money by the panel-game. **1928** Panel game [see *creep *sb.* 1 e]. **1953** *Evening News* 2 Jan. 5/3 The first edition of the new TV panel game 'Down You Go' was not an unqualified success. **1957** P. Wildeblood *Main Chance* 55 A singularly witless panel-game in which the contestants, in turn, thought of somebody whom they would like to be and their fellow-panellists had to guess the name. **1971** *Morning Star* 25 June 3/6 The new [radio] shows vary from current affairs, comedy, court dramas, Radio 4's answer to 'World in Action', and panel games. **1976** *Dumfries & Galloway Standard* 25 Dec. 9/3 The weather has continued to play havoc with the football programme and to reduce the 'Pools' to something of a 'panel game'. **1969** *Listener* 6 Sept. 308 Gilbert Harding..brought a compelling viewability to everything he did, whether as panel-gamester.. or television cook and general pundit. **1909** *Cent. Dict. Suppl.*, Panel-gage. **1966** A. W. Lewis *Gloss. Woodworking Terms* 34 *Panel gauge*, marking gauge with a long stem and extra-wide stock for gauging the widths of wide boards. **1936** *Archit. Rev.* LXXIX. 109/2 The library is panel-heated, the criss-cross net-work of heating tubes being woven round the slots of the skylights. **1951** *Good Housek. Home Encycl.* 11/1 An electric fire..in the form of a panel heater mounted on the wall. **1928** *Domestic Engin.* XLVIII. 101 (*heading*) The physical and physiological effects of panel heating. **1848** 'N. Buntline' *Mysteries & Miseries N.Y.* III. 44 This is a panel-house and I have led a bad, bad life for many a year. **1948** [see *lush *sb.*^{2} 2]. **1967** *Parade* (Austral.) Oct. 61/3 After that Katie Marks and her gang decided to branch out into the panel-house racket—a brothel equipped with sliding panels which allowed thieves to rifle clients' clothing. **1938** *Public Opinion Q.* Oct. 602 A small magazine.. which is published expressly for panel members. **1952** *Radio Times* 15 Aug. 37/2 What makes *What's My Line?* so popular? The personalities of the panel members, certainly. **1975** *Listener* 2 Jan. 21/3 What was spent on running the Arts Council? How many artists sat on your panels: who were they: who were the other panel-members? **1911** *Encycl. Brit.* XXVI. 405/2 The earlier painters whether illuminators of MSS. or wall and panel painters. **1937** *Burlington Mag.* Feb. 77/2 The group of Upper Rhenish panel-painters. **1954** M. Rickert *Painting in Brit.: Middle Ages* v. 120 The ability of Matthew Paris as a panel painter. **1913** *Outlook* 23 Aug. 247/1 Green tickets such as are used by ordinary panel patients when temporarily from home. **1924** J. Buchan *Three Hostages* i. 12 He would pay three visits a day to a panel patient, which shows the kind of fellow he was. **1950** T. H. Marshall *Citizenship & Social Class* 57 The early health service added 'panel patient' to our vocabulary of social class. **1964** A. Briggs in S. Nowell-Smith *Edwardian England* ii. 91 Other persons earning less than £160 a year could insure themselves voluntarily and become 'panel patients'. **1977** *Lancet* 8 Oct. 776/1 He took on no panel patients. **1951** *Good Housek. Home Encycl.* 320/1 Secure the glass..with a small sprig or panel pin. **1957** *Practical Wireless* XXXIII. 542/1 Fix the panel to the base with panel pins or small screws. **1960** *Farmer & Stockbreeder* 8 Mar. (Suppl.) 5/2 Take piece P and pin it to the frame with deep-drive panel pins, making sure hole S lines up with the drawer space. **1914** *Aberdeen Univ. Rev.* Nov. 50 The Panel practitioner being obliged to provide only what is termed ordinary medical treatment. **1922** *Encycl. Brit.* XXXI. 384/2 Medical men who act as panel practitioners continued to recommend their panel patients to the hospitals in increasing numbers. **1882** *Harper's Mag.* Feb. 400/1 Stories designed to teach our girls that theft, and arson, and panel-robbery..are the noblest exploits in which they can engage. **1754** *South Carolina Gaz.* 1 Jan. 2/2 Thomas Evance Has just imported..tenent, pannel and compass Saws. **1964** W. L. Goodman *Hist. Woodworking Tools* 151 The Hand, Panel, and Ripping Saws, ranging from 10 in. to 30 in. **1954** G. Marx *Let.* 16 Aug. (1967) 93 The gibbering idiots on panel shows, quiz shows, and other half hours of tripe. **1958** M. Dickens *Man Overboard* vii. 99 That long-lipped ass from the panel show. **1893** *Portfolio* XXIV. 55 John Reynes..often used a large panel stamp, representing the instruments of the Passion treated as a coat-of-arms. **1961** T. Landau *Encycl. Librarianship* (ed. 2) 52/2 Many elaborate panel stamps and roll stamps appear in the 14th and 15th centuries. **1952** J. Carter *ABC for Bk.-Collectors* 130 *Panel-stamped*, a term used by writers on book-binding to describe leather bindings of the 15th and 16th centuries decorated in blind with engraved blocks. **1958** M. Argyle *Relig. Behaviour* iii. 22 Panel studies in which the same subjects are repeatedly studied while their attitudes are changing. **1963** T. & P. Morris *Pentonville* vii. 182 Panel studies by Fiedler and Bass..indicate that inmate attitudes undergo a kind of cyclical change. **1964** M. Argyle *Psychol. & Social Probl.* xiii. 165 Panel studies during election campaigns have shown that there are some individuals who are more likely to change their voting intention than others. **1913** *Act* 3 & 4 *Geo. V* c. 37 § 11 Medical treatment under the panel system. **1926** *Encycl. Brit.* II. 861 At the time of its initiation the panel system met with great opposition from the medical profession. **1938** *Public Opinion Q.* Oct. 596 Instead of taking a new sample for each poll, repeated interviews with the same group of people have been tried. The experiences met with and the problems involved in such a panel technique will be discussed here. **1949** R. K. Merton *Social Theory* I. iii. 107 We may anticipate that the recent introduction of the panel technique—the repeated interviewing of the same group of informants—will in due course more sharply focus the attention of social psychologists upon the theory of attitude formation. **1844** G. Wilkes *Mysteries of Tombs* 48/1 Oh, he's a panel thief. **1947** *True* Nov. 69/1 The two lawyers had in addition the business of every free-lance safecracker, forger,..and panel thief whose business was worth having. **1937** Panel truck [see *bookmobile* s.v. *book *sb.* 18]. **1966** H. Kemelman *Saturday Rabbi went Hungry* v. 31 A light panel truck bearing the sign Jackson's Liquor Mart drove up. **1973** *Black World* Jan. 58/1 The panel truck followed. **1976** *CB Mag.* June 40/1 The Army Reserve Sergeant and afternoon soap opera buff suddenly switched on his headlights and churned onto the roadway in pursuit of a panel truck. **1969** *Age* (Melbourne) 24 May 60/11 (Advt.), Falcon panel van, 1962 mod[el]. **1977** *Western Morning News* 1 Sept. 6/2 (Advt.), Volkswagen LT 31 Panel Van, white, petrol. **1839** Ure *Dict. Arts* 976 Through the panel walls roads and air-courses are driven. **1962** *Listener* 11 Jan. 64/1 They have shown how sensitively the new and economical materials like concrete frames and panel walls can be handled. **1957** J. Kerouac *On Road* (1958) I. xi. 64 We had our headquarters in the main building, just a wooden contraption with panel-walled offices. **1934** *Times* 19 Feb. 20/5 They have got the latest ideas in panel warming, and the heat required in the type foundry is also supplied by gas.

panel, *v.* Add: **7.** Also *absol.*

1908 *Westm. Gaz.* 14 Mar. 13/2 All the gauzy fabrics will panel well.

panellist (pæ·nĕlist). Also (chiefly *U.S.*) **panelist.** [f. Panel *sb.*^{1} 5 b + -ist.] **a.** A panel doctor. **b.** A member of a discussion panel, committee, group of judges, etc., esp. one taking part in a radio or television programme.

1937 G. Frankau *More of Us* 14 Alas! Came dawn when local panelist Pronounced Jack's Ladye Alice a cadaver. **1952** *N.Y. Times* 14 June 13 Bennett Cerf.. television panelist and anthologist, has compiled another book of humor. **1955** *Picture Post* 14 May 10/3 This programme concludes with a gay, exciting parlour variation on musical chairs, in which the panellists exchange faces. **1958** K. Amis *I like it Here* iii. 36 Bowen..had something of the air of a television panellist. **1958** *New Statesman* 19 Apr. 501/1 A member of the audience has a go first; the panellists comment on what he has said; and he has a final brief right of reply. **1959** *Encounter* Dec. 52/1 The panelists at the Socialist meeting. **1971** C. Fick *Danziger Transcript* (1973) 131, I picked up a few bucks being a panelist on one of those Sunday political shows on TV. **1974** H. L. Foster *Ribbin'* vii. 316 Panel presentations were followed by ten small group meetings with panelists, former addicts and parents of addicts leading discussions. **1976** *Nature* 15 Apr. 633/2 Indeed the effect at the lower concentration of bitterness investigated was so marked that four out of the five panellists could detect no bitterness at all after presaturation of their tongues with sucrose.

‖**panem et circenses** (pæ·nem et sɜːke·nzīz). [L.] = *bread and circuses* (*bread *sb.* 2 g).

1787 P. H. Maty tr. *Riesbeck's Trav. Germany* I. xxvi. 303 Every thing here cries out *panem et circenses*, and the multitude seem to have no other wishes than to have their paunches well filled, and a theatrical entertainment by way of dessert. **1864** C. M. Yonge *Bk. Golden Deeds* 100 Their [*sc.* the Romans'] cry was that they wanted *panem ac Circenses.* **1903** G. B. Shaw *Man & Superman* p. xxiv, At this moment the Roman decadent phase of *panem et circenses* is being inaugurated under our eyes. **1928** D. H.

LAWRENCE *Lady Chatterley* xiii. 219 The masses are unalterable... Panem et circenses! **1961** D. L. MUNBY *God & Rich Society* iii. 61 Leaders who..win votes by offering *panem et circenses* to those they despise. **1966** *Listener* 29 Sept. 458/2 Sir Joseph Hutchinson is concerned with the provision of *panem*, but what of *circenses* for a *populus* with vast leisure time created by cybernation?

panetela, var. *PANATELA.

Paneth (pæ·neþ). *Histology.* The name of Joseph *Paneth* (1857–90), Austrian physiologist, used *attrib.*, in the possessive, and with *of* to designate a secretory cell present at the base of the crypts of Lieberkühn in the small intestine, and also the eosinophilic granules characteristic of their cytoplasm.

1899 *Veterinarian* LXXII. 555 These granular cells of Paneth showed the same reaction, and I was forced to conclude that they were mucus-forming. *Ibid.* 560 The cytoplasm in some instances has been observed to contain granules—Paneth's granules. **1938** *Gray's Anat.* (ed. 27) 1329 The deeper cells, especially in the duodenal glands, contain granules which stain characteristically with phosphotungstic haematoxylin and are termed granules of Paneth. **1968** PASSMORE & ROBSON *Compan. Med. Stud.* I. xxx. 21/1 There are only about a dozen Paneth cells in each crypt, but because of the enormous number of crypts the total mass of Paneth cells is large. **1976** *Cell & Tissue Kinetics* IX. 72 The number and localization of Paneth cells was not affected by changes in crypt cell kinetics during recovery after irradiation.

‖ **panettone** (panětō·ne). Also **panetone.** Pl. **panetto·ni.** [It.] A rich Italian bread made with eggs, fruit, and butter.

1922 D. H. LAWRENCE *Aaron's Rod* xvii. 251 He shoved a lump of cake—or rather panetone, good currant loaf—through the window, with a knife to cut it. **1938** JOYCE *Let.* 20 Apr. (1966) III. 420, I spent all Easter Day with Lucia,..eating *panettoni di Milano* and fooling generally. **1967** *Economist* 28 Oct. 450/3 Motta's success is inevitably connected to 'panettone', a traditional Milanese Christmas cake. Owing to Motta's successful marketing of this one hand-made product, 'panettone' is now all over Italy, the recognised symbol of Christmas, perhaps even more so than the Christmas tree and the crib. **1969** R. & D. DE SOLA *Dict. Cooking* 167/1 *Panettone*: (Italian—a kind of cake bread) Often orange flavoured and raisin filled. **1972** L. O'DONNELL *Phone Calls* iv. 48 She..pushed forward a plate on which there was a high glossy cake with only one slice cut out of it. 'Please, have some *panetone.* Is very good—.' **1978** *Nieman-Marcus Christmas Bk.* 91 From Italy, the traditional semi-sweet panettone..bread studded with candied fruits and nuts.

Pan-Europe·an, *a.* [f. PAN- + EUROPEAN *a.*] Pertaining to, affecting, or extending over the whole of Europe. Hence **Pan-Europe·anism.**

1901 CONRAD & HUEFFER *Inheritors* viii. 117 There was an 'All Round the World Cable Company'.., and a 'Pan-European Railway, Exploration, and Civilization Company' that let in light in dark places. **1931** *Ann. Reg. 1930* 172 This same trend in Italian policy was also manifested in Italy's reply to M. Briand's 'Pan-European' proposal in the course of which the Fascist Government declared its disagreement with any scheme of this kind which excluded Turkey and Russia. **1942** L. B. NAMIER *Conflicts* 2 The two great nations of Central Europe..burdened with Pan-European past..remained in a condition of political disunion and dynastic subdivision. **1961** *Guardian* 9 June 8/6 The later Pan-Europeanism of this loneliest of poets [*sc.* Rilke]. **1966** *New Statesman* 14 Oct. 540/2 This journal repeatedly emphasised that the famous breeze of European competition, or the large accumulations of capital open to pan-European industries, were no substitute for a successful socialist economy. **1979** *Daily Tel.* 20 Jan. 16/6 The new flowers..have been put through their paces under the Fleuroselect scheme which is run by a pan-European organisation for testing them.., with a secretariat in The Hague.

panfan (pæ·nfæn). *Geomorphol.* [f. PAN- + FAN *sb.*[1]] = *PEDIPLAIN.

1915 A. C. LAWSON in *Univ. California Publ. Geol.* IX. III. 33 The surface thus evolved is, in its ideal completion, wholly one of aggradation, a vast alluvial fan surface to which for convenience in discussion I propose to give the name *panfan.* **1931** *Jrnl. Geol.* XXXIX. 138 Pediments are essentially compound graded flood plains excavated by ephemeral streams. As their growth corrodes the mountain mass they eventually coalesce to form smooth graded domes to which Lawson applied the term 'panfan' ..—a name that is etymologically unfortunate because these features are not concerned with alluvial fans at all. **1933** *Geol. Mag.* LXX. 345 The rock-floors of the desert, known as pediments and panfans. **1954** W. D. THORNBURY *Princ. Geomorphol.* xi. 291 Lawson (1915) proposed the term *panfan* to designate 'an end stage in the process of geomorphic development in an arid region in the same sense that the peneplain is an end stage of the general process of degradation in a humid climate'. He also recognized that both peneplains and panfans represent penultimate rather than ultimate stages of degradation. **1974** [see *PEDIPLAIN].

panfish. 1. (Earlier and later examples.)

1833 J. F. WATSON *Hist. Tales Philad.* 49 Before the house flows a small but deep creek, abounding in pan-fish. **1838** J. F. COOPER *Home as Found* II. v. 71 The Egyptians use them as a pan-fish. **1852** *Trans. Mich. Agric. Soc.* III. 226 These little fish are sometimes used as pan-fish. **1888** G. B. GOODE *Amer. Fishes* 36 In season the White Perch is *the* pan-fish, excelled by none. **1969** R. & D. DE SOLA *Dict. Cooking* 167/1 *Panfish*, any fish suitable for frying, usually hand-caught fish like sunfish or catfish. **1970** *Globe & Mail* (Toronto) 26 Sept. 40/5 In addition to the ancestral stock of Atlantic salmon, Lavalee Lake holds bass, pan fish.

panfry (pæ·nfrai), *v.* Chiefly *N. Amer.* [f. PAN *sb.*[1] + FRY *v.*[1]] *trans.* and *intr.* To fry in a pan with shallow fat. Also *transf.* So **pa·n-fried** *ppl. a.*

1942 M. K. RAWLINGS *Cross Creek Cookery* Pan-Fried Young Quail or Dove. **1957** J. KEROUAC *On Road* (1958) x. 174 That pan-fried chow mein flavored air. **1973** *Sat. Rev. World* (U.S.) 18 Dec. 48/3 It [*sc.* the Kahala's Maile Room] imports filets of trevally from New Zealand..and panfries them with tomatoes. **1974** *Globe & Mail* (Toronto) 20 Mar. 35/1 Ling or freshwater cod can be cooked in a variety of ways—the simplest being to panfry. **1976** *Woman's Day* (N.Y.) Nov. 104 Panfried liver and onions. **1977** *N.Z. Jrnl. Agric.* Jan. 63/1 Grill or pan-fry the bacon.

pang (pæŋ), *sb.*[2] [Echoic.] Vocal imitation of a short, resonant sound, such as that produced by a drum, a horse's hoof, etc.; a sound of this character.

1925 E. SITWELL *Troy Park* 65 As the hoofèd sound of a drum marched on With a pang like darkness. **1955** E. POUND *Classic Anthol.* III. 188 Every man eager to pace the stallions, 'Pang, pang' and Rein bells chink. **1958** L. DURRELL *Mountolive* vii. 144 There were two excellent hard courts which rang all day to the pang of racquets. **1958** —— *Balthazar* vii. 155 The tattling flutes and the pang of drums.

panga[1] (pā·ŋgă). Also **ponga, pongo.** [a. Amer. Sp. *panga* a boat.] A flat-bottomed boat with rising stem and stern.

1927 G. BRADFORD *Gloss. Sea Terms* 124/2 *Panga*, a flat-bottomed rowboat of Central America. **1948** R. DE KERCHOVE *Internat. Maritime Dict.* 517/1 *Panga*, a dug-out canoe from Panama, double-ended with rising stem and stern. These craft are about 18 ft. long by 4 ft. 6 in. wide and are cut out of one cedar log. **1970** *National Fisherman* Jan. 18B/4 The chaser-skiffs, also called speed-boats or pongos, are lowered overboard. **1971** *Islander* (Victoria, B.C.) 4 July 15/3 The reds and greens and yellows of the double-ended pongas which the lobster and bonito fishermen took far out to sea. **1978** *Daily Colonist* (Victoria, B.C.) 7 May 17/2 We haul anchor as soon as the ship-to-shore shuttle, called a panga, brings aboard the last of our cruise-mates.

panga[2] (pæ·ŋgă). [Swahili.] A large knife used in Africa either as an implement or as a weapon. Also *attrib.*

1935 E. HEMINGWAY *Green Hills Afr.* (1936) IV. i. 216 Chopping our way through with the long brush knives that are called pangas. **1952** *Time* 3 Nov. 36 Once pooh-poohed as mere 'press exaggeration', the Mau Mau have already mutilated scores of whites and 'loyal' blacks, with their favorite weapon, the *panga*—a long, machete-like knife. *Ibid.* 10 Nov. 38/3 On the front of the governor's car waved his official flag: two crossed *pangas* (broad-bladed African knives used to chop bananas). The *pangas* seemed symbolic last week, for Kenya Colony, the brightest jewel in Britain's East African Empire, is bleeding badly in a *panga* war. **1953** *Ibid.* 12 Jan. 26/1 There was a noise at the door, a shout, and a gang of Mau Mau thugs, led by the ranch's male cook, burst into the living room, brandishing *panga* knives. **1953** *Newsweek* 6 Apr. 38/3 As the villagers ran from their blazing homes, waiting Mau Maus struck them down with *pangas* (long knives) and hatchets. **1954** D. H. RAWCLIFFE *Struggle for Kenya* ix. 86 The isolated loyalist groups in the reserves.. were still armed with little more than *pangas* and spears. **1955** O. MEEKER *Report on Afr.* xii. 199 But until I reached Kenya no-one said a word about the Mau Mau terrorists, secret society oaths, the long knives called *pangas*, or the other Kikuyu specialities. **1964** C. WILLOCK *Enormous Zoo* viii. 138 African butchers sharpened their pangas on stone. **1969** *Daily Tel.* 28 Oct. 16 An African Presbyterian Minister was killed by a panga gang for refusing to take Kikuyu tribal oaths. **1972** J. MCCLURE *Caterpillar Cop* iii. 34 'I hear the murder was sometime around six.'.. 'Usual bit of passion and panga.' **1976** *Maclean's Mag.* 6 Sept. 51/2 Zulu mobs rampaged through Soweto armed with pangas (cane cutters), axes, spears, and knives. **1976** *Survey* Summer-Autumn 303 Forest fighters had..often only the ordinary rural blade of East Africa, the *panga.* **1977** D. BEATY *Excellency* xii. 139 The soldiers had taken out panga knives and were cutting down thorn bush and scrub.

Pangæa (pændʒī·ă). *Geol.* [f. PAN- + Gr. γαῖα land, earth.

The name is freq. stated to have been coined by A. Wegener 1914, in *Die Entstehung der Kontinente und Ozeane*, but it has not been found in the 1st ed. of that book (actually published in 1915); *Pangäa* does occur in ed. 2 (1920), p. 120, but with no indication that Wegener is coining it.]

A vast continental area or supercontinent comprising all the continental crust of the earth which is postulated to have existed in late Palæozoic or Mesozoic times before breaking up into Gondwanaland and Laurasia.

1924 J. G. A. SKERL tr. *Wegener's Orig. Continents & Oceans* xiii. 192 Thus the Pangæa of the Carboniferous era had already an anterior margin (America), which became folded (Precordilleras)..; and a posterior margin (Asia), from which littoral ranges and fragments became detached, and remained fast in the sima of the Pacific as groups of islands. **1928** C. SCHUCHERT in *Theory Continental Drift* (Amer. Assoc. Petroleum Geol.) 106 The rifting of Pangaea and the floating away of Australasia, Antarctica, and the Americas are said to have begun east of Africa in Jurassic time and west of Euro-Africa in early Cretaceous time. **1958** *Continental Drift* (Tasmania Univ. Geol. Dept.) 177 Apart from the dissociation of Pangaea into independent Laurasia and Gondwana, the fundamental picture is much as Wegener saw it. **1971** I. G. GASS et al. *Understanding Earth* xv. 230/2 Before the Pangaea of Permo-Triassic time was formed, one must envisage a different mosaic of continental fragments reassembled in a different way. **1974** *Sci. Amer.* Apr. 81/1 Ancient ocean currents in the vicinity of Pangaea, the single 'supercontinent' that is believed to have existed near the beginning of the Triassic period some 225 million years ago, are indicated here. **1977** *Ibid.* Mar. 92/3 About 600 million or perhaps one billion years ago the ancestors of all the present continents were evidently combined into one immense supercontinent, named Pangaea, which may have come into existence as much as 2.7 billion years ago.

Pangan (pæ·ŋgăn). [Malay, = 'forest country'.] = NEGRITO.

1839 T. J. NEWBOLD *Pol. & Statistical Acct. Straits of Malacca* II. v. 60 In the interior of Pakaa, an aboriginal race is said to exist, termed Pangan. **1929** A. CHAMBERS tr. *Schebesta's Among Forest Dwarfs Malaya* v. 162 From the Malays in Tadoh I first heard the word *Pangan.* This was the name they gave to the Orang-Utan tribes. **1947** R. O. WINSTEDT *Malays* 8 The oldest of Malaya's existing races anthropologically is the Negrito, termed Semang in Perak and Pangan in Kelantan. **1965** R. MCKIE *Company of Animals* i. 35 Pangans had been digging with fire-hardened sticks for tubers, and later we found one of the small camps of these jungle aborigines.

Pangasinan (pāngāsī·nā·n). Pl. **Pangasinans, Pangasinanes.** [Native name.] **a.** (A member of) a people inhabiting the central area of the Luzon district of the Republic of the Philippines. **b.** The Austronesian language of this people.

1840 [see *ILOCANO]. **1885** [see *IBANAG *sb.* and *a.*]. **1948** D. DIRINGER *Alphabet* vii. 432 The other important vernaculars spoken by the Filipinos are: (1) Pangasinan, [etc.]. **1954** PEI & GAYNOR *Dict. Linguistics* 158 *Pangasinan*, a language spoken in the Philippine Islands by almost 400,000 persons; a member of the Indonesian sub-family of the Malayo-Polynesian family of languages. **1964** E. BACH *Introd. Transformational Gram.* v. 89 Some languages that have been worked on from this point of view..are English,..Pangasinan. **1974** *Encycl. Brit. Micropædia* VII. 717/a *Pangasinan*, eighth largest cultural-linguistic group in the Republic of the Philippines. They occupy the central area of the province of Pangasinan in Luzon.

pangeran (pæŋgěræ·n). Also **pangarang.** [Malay.] A Malay prince or noble.

1817 T. S. RAFFLES *Hist. Java* I. ii. 79 His [*sc.* the sovereign's] family are called *Pang'érans.* **1821** J. LEYDEN tr. *Malay Annals* viii. 272 The pangeran of Surabaya.. came to Malaca. **1831** *Canton Miscellany* II. 79 The Princes or Pangarangs who were seated on chairs walked with us. **1900** CONRAD *Ld. Jim* xx. 219 He came into the Council-hall where all the rajahs, pangerans, and head-men were assembled, with the queen,..reclining on a high couch under a canopy.

Pan-Ge·rmanist. [f. PAN-GERMAN *a.* and *sb.* + -IST.] A supporter of Pan-Germanism. Also *attrib.*

1909 *Daily Chron.* 25 June 4/6 A racing yacht devised, built, and..manned in Germany—an object of idolatry ..to the Pan-Germanists. **1914** *Atlantic Monthly* Oct. 448/2 The schemes of the Pan-Germanists indeed reach to the creation of a vast confederation of states. **1939** *Tablet* 3 June 706/1 He defends himself as best he can against the Pan-Germanist propaganda of the turbulent German minority. **1957** ELLIOTT & SUMMERSKILL *Dict. Politics* 251 Pan-Germanists have advocated particularly the absorption into Germany of the German-speaking provinces of Austria. **1974** *Encycl. Brit. Micropædia* VII. 717/b Pan-Germanists continued to press for expansion; the most articulate and active force toward that end was Hitler and the Nazi Party.

Hence **Pan-Germani·stic** *a.*, of, pertaining to, or supporting Pan-Germanism.

1915 *World's Work* (N.Y.) Aug. 456/1 To block the Pan-Germanistic plan.

panghulu, var. *PENGHULU.

panglima (pănglī·mă). Also **penglima.** [Malay *pĕnglima.*] A Malay leader of secondary rank; a Malay chief.

1839 T. J. NEWBOLD *Pol. & Statistical Acct. Straits of Malacca* I. v. 237 For further security, two panglimas sat on each side. **1900** W. W. SKEAT *Malay Magic* 169 Two swords were produced and placed crosswise, and a couple of Panglimas selected for the dance. **1939** A. KEITH *Land below Wind* xv. 264 The Penglima, or native chief..met our *perahus* with much ceremony.

Pangloss (pæ·nglǫs). Name of the philosopher and tutor in Voltaire's *Candide* (1759) who believes that 'all is for the best in the best of all possible worlds', used allusively for one who is optimistic regardless of the circumstances. Also *attrib.* Hence **Pa·nglossism,** an unrealistically optimistic attitude or saying; **Panglo·ssic** *a.*, characteristic of Pangloss.

1844 DISRAELI *Coningsby* I. II. i. 153 The political Panglosses who..were continually proving that this was the best of all possible governments. **1926** J. S. Huxley *Ess. Pop. Sci.* xii. 147 This conclusion, from its inception with some of the Stoics to its Panglossic latter end in certain evolutionists, he dismisses. **1928** A. Huxley in *Life & Letters* 1 Oct. 345 We are to interpret them, Pangloss fashion, in terms of preconceived philosophy. **1931** *Times Lit. Suppl.* 10 Dec. 994/4 We can best envisage him..still the sworn disciple of Pangloss the optimist. **1959** *Encounter* Nov. 66/2 He includes..some of his pet Panglossisms, such as that learning is happiness. **1964** *Economist* 11 July 128/2 This is cheerfulness raised to the level of Panglossism. **1973** *Listener* 5 Apr. 438/1 The [Egyptian] regime's official Dr. Pangloss, Culture Minister Dr Abdel Khader Hatem.

Panglo·ssian, *a.* and *sb.* [f. prec. + -ian.] **A.** *adj.* Of, pertaining to, or characteristic of the philosophy of Pangloss. **B.** *sb.* One who shares this philosophy.

1831 Disraeli *Young Duke* I. i. iii. 23 He was quite disembarrassed of that Panglossian philosophy, which had hitherto induced him to believe, that the Earl of Fitz-pompey was the best of all possible uncles. **1922** Hardy *Late Lyrics* Apol. p. xi, Hence should anything of this sort in the following adumbrations seem 'queer'—should any of them seem to good Panglossians to embody strange and disrespectful conceptions of this best of all possible worlds, I apologize; but cannot help it. **1936** G. B. Shaw *Simpleton* Pref. 3 If author and journalist are both placid Panglossians, convinced that their civilization is the best of all possible civilizations..there is no trouble. **1937** A. Huxley *Ends & Means* vii. 68 In those who make the identification it induces a kind of busy, Panglossian fatalism. **1957** M. McCarthy *Memories Catholic Girlhood* p. xxiv, Some of my relations philosophize to this effect, in a somewhat Panglossian style. **1967** *Guardian* 17 May 1/3 This somewhat Panglossian interpretation of the significance of General de Gaulle's press conference. **1976** *Nature* 18 Mar. 196/2 The first, and most widely appreciated, is the old Panglossian fallacy that natural selection favours adaptations that are good for the species as a whole, rather than acting at the level of the individual.

Pangola, var. *Pongola.

pangram (pæ·ngræm). [f. Pan- + -gram.] A sentence containing all the letters of the alphabet (see also quot. 1953). So **pangramma·tic** *a.*

1933 M. E. Ohaver *Cryptogram Solving* 31 Pangrammatic, containing all the letters of the alphabet. **1953** W. R. Trask tr. *Curtius's European Lit.* xv. 283 The 'pangrammatic' affection, which consists in having as many successive words as possible begin with the same letters. **1963** *Medium Ævum* XXXII. 149 'Pangrammatic' verses are far older than the thirteenth century. **1964** *Sci. Amer.* Sept. 222 The pangram, an ancient form of word play, is an attempt to get the maximum number of different letters into a sentence of minimum length. **1965** *Time* 17 Sept. 72 Also represented: Sotadic [palindromic] verses, pangrammatic rubaiyat and problems in alphametics (alphabet arithmetic).

panhandle, *sb.* Add: Also applied to territories outside the U.S.A. (Earlier and later examples.)

1856 *Porter's Spirit of Times* 8 Nov. 159/1 He was from old Virginny—from what, he said, they called the *Pan-handle.* **1861** *Vanity Fair* (N.Y.) 25 May 246/2 We will wrap the flag of our fathers around the 'Pan Handle' of Virginia, and upset the entire dish of Old Dominion Secession. **1877** E. E. Hale *G.T.T.* 30 So they..whirled relentlessly across the Pan Handle by which domestic name that funny strip of West Virginia is known which shoots up like an inverted icicle between Pennsylvania and Ohio. **1932** *Atlantic Monthly* Mar. 295/1 Your atlas will show that Idaho has a panhandle jutting up to the Canadian border. **1952** B. Ulanov *Hist. Jazz in Amer.* (1958) iv. 33 Jack Teagarden, a big burly Texan with an infectious Panhandle accent in his singing, has always been associated with the blues. **1960** *20th Cent.* Mar. 248 The 'panhandle' of North Wiltshire near Lechlade. **1967** *Economist* 14 Oct. 141/2 These targets are usually in the 'panhandle', as Americans call the thin southern part of North Vietnam. **1974** *Union* (S. Carolina) *Daily Times* 22 Apr. 1/3 Mt. Hermon straddles the Lebanese-Syrian border and is just north of the Israeli panhandle. **1977** *Time* 7 Mar. 52/1 In a grimy arc, from Nebraska through the plains of Kansas and Colorado, on into the panhandles of Oklahoma and Texas, scenes right out of *The Grapes of Wrath* suddenly materialized in the swirl of dust billowing up to 12,000 feet.

2. The act of begging (cf. next).

1849 J. J. Hooper in *Spirit of Times* 14 Apr. 87/3 The elephant was the great point of attraction. 'I want his hide and frame for a corn crib,' said a fellow from the Pan-Handle Beat. **1894** *Harper's Weekly* 5 May 429/2 'Workin' the pan-handle.' 'Eh?' 'I mean, are you beggin'?' **1900** Ade *More Fables* 142 He usually found some one waiting on the Door-Step to give him the Sign of Distress and work the fraternal Pan-Handle on him. **1942** Berrey & Van den Bark *Amer. Thes. Slang* § 486/2 *A solicitation,*.. panhandle.

Hence (sense 1) **pa·nhandled** *a.*

1976 T. Stoppard *Dirty Linen* 65 Enormous women in taffeta dresses stir the air with panhandled fans.

panhandle (pæ·nhænd'l), *v. slang.* (orig. and chiefly *U.S.*). [Back-formation from next.] *trans.* and *intr.* To beg (from); to steal or purloin. Hence **pa·nhandling** *vbl. sb.* and *ppl. a.*

1903 *N.Y. Even. Post* 9 Dec. 1 The prisoners were members of a 'panhandling' corporation which operated extensively throughout the financial district. **1904** G. H. Lorimer *Old Gorgon Graham* 53 A lot of men..who wouldn't think of asking for money, will panhandle both sides of a street for favors. **1907** 'O. Henry' *Strictly Business* (1910) xix. 242 He felt his sleeve grasped and held. Suspecting that he was about to be panhandled, he turned a cold and unprofitable face, and saw that his captor was—Dawe. **1931** 'D. Stiff' *Milk & Honey Route* viii. 84 Domestic panhandling, or hitting back doors,.. seems to be on the decline. **1932** L. C. Douglas *Forgive us our Trespasses* (1937) xiv. 276 It's never been in a suppliant attitude, panhandling the brethren and sisters for sixpences to pay the parson's coal-bill. **1951** E. Paul *Springtime in Paris* xi. 198 The street music..was strictly for panhandling—stray accordion players, atrocious old fiddlers, and half-crazed women with cracked voices and maudlin lyrics. **1959** *Times Lit. Suppl.* 6 Nov. p. xxxv/5 A poor art scholar..has his precious manuscript on Giotto destroyed by the panhandling Jewish refugee from Israel. **1973** 'A. Blaisdell' *Crime by Chance* (1974) ix. 173, I ain't had a bite to eat since yesterday. I was in that bar panhandlin'. **1976** *Yellowstone Explorer* July 1/3 The absence of bears along the park's roads is a major concern of visitors, especially those who were here just a few years ago and saw literally dozens of bears panhandling picnic items passing cars. **1977** *It* June 5/2 They tackled the dilemma facing anyone who has been pan-handled—'Why don't I take this poor bastard home with me,'—and they did it on a massive scale.

panhandler (pæ·nˌhæ:ndləɹ). [f. Panhandle *sb.* in Dict. and Suppl. or *panhandle *v.* + -er¹.] **1.** A beggar. *slang* (orig. *U.S.*).

1897 F. Moss *Amer. Metropolis* II. vii. 393 A party of petty thieves and 'pan-handlers' (able-bodied street beggars), went into the 'Morgue'. **1899** Ade *Doc. Horne* xxiii. 255 The freckled boy then announced that he had 'sized' the hustler for a 'panhandler' from the start. **1909** [see *lone *a.* 3 c]. **1929** *Daily Tel.* 8 Jan. 11/6 Large profits from begging in the rich Fifth Avenue business districts have produced a 'king of the pan-handlers'. **1954** *Manch. Guardian Weekly* 30 Dec. 14/3 The delicatessen stores alone in this city [*sc.* New York] would make the Phoenicians feel like pan-handlers and the merchant princes of Venice like fugitives from a soup kitchen. **1962** H. Hood in R. Weaver *Canad. Short Stories* (1968) 2nd Ser. 202 In a minute they would speak to him. They always did, drunks and panhandlers. **1966** F. Shaw et al. *Lern Yerself Scouse A pan'andler,* a scrounger of food. **1973** 'E. McBain' *Hail to Chief* vi. 113 Don't..start screaming if a panhandler taps you on the shoulder. He may only want a quarter for a drink. **1975** *Globe & Mail* (Toronto) 5 July 2/1 Panhandlers..urinate in doorways, sleep in the streets. **1978** G. Vidal *Kalki* vi. 136 First they would approach a well-dressed person of the sort who would normally run a mile to avoid a panhandler for god, any god.

2. (With capital initial.) A native or inhabitant of a Panhandle.

1936 *Sun* (Baltimore) 12 May 12/5 If the gentleman from Texas wants us to revise our lingo so that it meets the approval of the Panhandlers, the least he could do is offer a substitute for the word he wishes eliminated. **1940** E. Fergusson *Our Southwest* xviii. 335, I talked all this over with a native-born Panhandler. **1949** *10 Story Western* May 28/2 He remembered how it was down there in the Panhandle—how the Panhandlers hated these Rio Valley floaters as no Idaho man could.

Panhonlib (pænhǫnli·b). [f. *Pan*ama, *Hon*duras, *Lib*eria.] Designating a merchant ship of Panama, Honduras, and Liberia flying a 'flag of convenience'. Cf. *flag *sb.*⁴ 1 f, *Panlibhonco.

1958 *Times* 1 Apr. 11/5 There has recently been an intensification of the campaign against registration of ships, particularly tankers, under what have come to be known as 'PanHonLib' flags. **1958** [see *Panlibhonco]. **1962** S. G. Sturmey *Brit. Shipping & World Competition* 228 Few British owners have sought Panholib registration.

panic, *sb.*¹ **b. panic-grass** (earlier and later examples).

1597 Gerard *Herball* i. 7 Pannicke grasse is garnished with chaffe and downie tufts. **1870** W. Robinson *Wild Garden* ii. 121 Twiggy Panic Grass..is an elegant plant. **1901** C. T. Mohr *Plant Life Alabama* 355 Wiry Panic-Grass... Exposed places in light soil. **1929** Weaver & Clements *Plant Ecol.* vii. 134 (*caption*) Competition between tall panic grass and evening primrose. **1963** Gleason & Cronquist *Man. Vascular Plants North-eastern U.S.* 101 Panic grass. Spikelets lanceolate or hisiform to ovate.

panic, *a.* and *sb.*² Add: **B.** *sb.*² **2. c.** *fig.* A noteworthy or amusing person, thing, or situation.

1936 R. Ackland *After October* i. 47 Oh, my dear, aren't you *swell*! All grown up and sophisticated. Doesn't she look a panic, Timmy? *Ibid.* 49 My dear, it was a panic! **1946** T. Williams *27 Wagons Cotton* iii. 27 *Flora*: Says—(She goes off into another spasm of laughter.) *Jake*: What ever he said must've been a panic!

3. a. (Earlier U.S. examples.)

1842 *Southern Q. Rev.* I. 88 The sudden and violent contraction of 1833..produced the scenes of what is usually termed the 'panic session'. **1854** T. H. Benton *30 Years' View* I. 369/2 On the second day of December, 1833, commenced the first session of the Twenty-third Congress, commonly called the Panic Session.

3. b. panic bolt, a special bolt for a door designed to unfasten readily in emergencies; **panic button,** a switch or button for operating various devices in emergencies (see quots.); also *fig.* in phr. *hit, press, the panic button,* to become over-excited, take emergency measures (the origin of the expression is discussed in *Amer. Speech* XXXI (1956) no. 3, 240); **panic buying,** the buying in large quantities of goods of which a shortage is threatened or suspected; hence (as a back-formation) **panic-buy** *v.*; **panic party** (see quots. 1929, 1943); **panic stations,** a state of emergency (freq. *fig.*); **panic-stricken** *a.* (earlier and later examples); **panic-striking,** causing, or likely to cause, a panic; **panic-struck** *a.* (earlier examples).

1930 *Aberdeen Press & Jrnl.* 1 May 7/3 When he took the cinema in July, 1928, he put panic bolts on the wooden door..where there were ordinary slip bolts before. **1940** *Chambers's Techn. Dict.* 611/2 *Panic bolt,* a special form of door-bolt which is released by pressure at the middle of the door; commonly used on exit-doors in public buildings. **1964** J. S. Scott *Dict. Building* 223 *Panic bolt,* a door bolt often used at the double exit doors of theatres. It is opened by pressure from inside on to a horizontal bar within the door at waist height. **1972** *Times* 28 Dec. 1/8 London fire brigade checked the new arrangements last night and said that 'panic bolts' on the inside complied with regulations. **1955** *Amer. Speech* XXX. 117 *Hit the panic button,* panic, get excited. **1956** *Ibid.* XXXI. 240 Discussion with several pilots..reveals at least four buttons or switches, each one of which may be referred to as the 'panic button'. **1958** *Ibid.* XXXIII. 183 *Panic button,* the release button on the one-point release harness worn by the smokejumper. When a jumper is hung up in a tree,..he twists a metal knob (the 'panic button') on his harness fifteen degrees to the left and hits it. This releases the webbing straps of the harness, and the entire parachute and harness fall off. 'I hit the panic button and let down about sixty feet.' **1959** *Times* 9 Mar. 13/4 *Hit the panic button,* get over-excited. **1962** *Review & Herald* 25 Oct. 24/3 Dr. Franklin Clark Fry, president of the Lutheran Church in America, warned here that the time is coming for world Christian missions 'to press the panic button', because Christianity is dying out. **1970** *Washington Post* 30 Sept. D4/5, I haven't thrown the panic button yet and I'm not going to. **1970** D. Francis *Rat Race* iv. 45 Someone in the control tower had pressed the panic button. Fire engines screamed up. **1970** *Motoring Which?* July 113/1 As a last resort, pressing the 'panic-button' would 'dump' the craft, but could cause damage on a hard surface. **1972** T. Ardies *This Suitcase* viii. 71 The President reacted reasonably enough. He didn't push the panic button... He..ordered a stand-by alert. **1973** *Listener* 15 Feb. 200/3 The panic-button was pressed: foreign-exchange markets slammed their doors. **1974** *Scottish Daily Express* 14 Oct. 1/6 But one grocery chain manager stressed last night there was no immediate need for customers to panic buy as stocks were high and many stores' supplies were still unaffected by the strike. **1974** *Times* 15 Nov. 18/3, I had already panic-bought five gallons of petrol..saving 42p on next week's prices. **1942** *Washington Post* 23 Nov. 11/6 An anti-hoarding regulation for householders..to curb panic-buying of foods. **1949** *Sun* (Baltimore) 2 Dec. 4/5 There is no question but that panic buying has contributed to the current price rise. **1972** *Guardian* 18 Aug. 13 Concern over the number of mortgages available in the future and fears that selling [houses] could become more difficult have created a flood of panic-selling (which makes a change from panic-buying). **1973** *Times* 7 Dec. 18/8 Panic buying of spirits in the High Street, caused largely by forecasts of the shortage. **1974** *Guardian* 19 Jan. 20/2 Panic-buying would in itself lead to 'artificial shortages'. **1919** *Boy's Own Paper* XLI. ix. 456/2 The 'Farnborough'..disembarked a 'panic party'..to pretend that the officers and crew were abandoning their ship. **1929** *Papers Mich. Acad. Sci., Arts, & Lett.* X. 313 *Panic party,* a feigned demonstration of alarm or panic on board a decoy (mystery) ship in order to lure the commander of a submarine alongside. When a mystery ship was torpedoed, the panic party took to the boats, apparently abandoning the vessel, but always leaving on board another crew to man the guns and finish the submarine if it came near enough. **1929** F. C. Bowen *Sea Slang* 100 *Panic Party,* the men whose job it was to leave a Decoy Ship (Q-boat) in disorder when a German submarine opened fire. **1932** 'N. Shute' *Lonely Road* vii. 144 They shelled the panic party in the boats. **1943** Baker *Dict. Austral. Slang* (ed. 3) 57 *Panic party,* any rush move (Digger slang). **1961** in Partridge *Dict. Slang* Suppl. 1213/1 *Panic stations, be at,* to be prepared for the worst. **1963** 'J. Prescot' *Case for Hearing* iii. 53 Someone has been into Greenwood's again ..and got away with another three hundred... The police seem to be at panic stations about it. **1972** A. Draper *Death Penalty* xviii. 113 Let's face it, Caleb, you'll be the first to run to panic stations. **1804** M. Hays *Harry Clinton* xxxii. 199 A ladder was..speedily brought, the panic-stricken family assisted to descend, and charitably conducted to a neighbouring inn. **1904** [see *Dixie² 1 b]. **1977** M. T. Bloom *13th Man* iii. 39 They both turned their faces to me and the car and they looked panic-stricken, stuck in place. **1851** H. Melville *Moby Dick* III. vii. 56 Pip loved life, and all life's peaceable securities; so that the panic-striking business in which he had somehow unaccountably become entrapped, had most sadly blurred his brightness. **1934** R. Campbell *Broken Record* ii. 46 A senseless, dutiful exposure of panic-striking and depressing facts is worse than any amount of mischievous lying. **1776** J. Thacher *Mil. Jrnl.* (1823) 70 [Washington] made every effort to rally them, but without success; they were so panic struck that even the shadow of an enemy seemed to increase their precipitate flight. **1835** J. E. Alexander *Sk. Portugal* vi. 139 The Miguelites at last became panic-struck.

panic, *v.* Delete (*nonce-wd.*) and add later examples.

1917 'Contact' *Airman's Outings* 184 Nothing seems to panic the Boche more than a sudden swoop by a low-flying aeroplane. **1919** H. L. Wilson *Ma Pettengill* iv. 127 He was sure going to annoy Ben from time to time, even if he didn't panic him much. **1932** Kipling *Limits & Renewals* 169 Then I'd come round the corner and hailed him, and that panicked him. **1932** *New Yorker* 4 June 46/1 Gough..had a violence and fervor on the platform which packed them and panicked them everywhere. **1957** *Economist* 30 Nov. 795/1 The markets are healthy and not likely to be panicked into headlong fall. **1966** A. Sachs *Jail Diary* xxi. 189 That will panic the Whites in South Africa even further. **1971** *Daily Tel.* 2 Nov. 2/5 A radio dramatisation of H. G. Wells's 'War of the Worlds'.. panicked thousands throughout America in 1938. **1974** 'M. Innes' *Appleby's Other Story* xi. 93 At least it panicked her. She came..to tell me a pack of lies. **1975** *Daily Tel.* 1 May 13/6 When I received a tax demand asking for £600 by Tuesday it panics me completely. **1977** *Time* 23 May 24/3 The Defense Secretary is by no means panicked.

2. *intr.* To get into a panic, to lose one's head.

1910 Kipling *Divers. Creatures* (1917) 310 Jules was, so to speak, panicking in a water-tight flat through his unfortunate lack of language. **1921** 'Sapper' *Man in Ratcatcher* 30 For a few agonizing seconds..she panicked; then..she pulled herself together and tried to stop him. **1924** M. Newman *Consummation* v. xxii. 240 They panicked one night, started rapid fire and killed two of their own men. **1930** J. Cannan *No Walls of Jasper* 196 Martin helped Phyl to unpack. All at once she panicked, rummaging wildly among the paper in the tea-basket and saying, 'Good heavens, Martin! there's no sugar for his tea!' **1946** M. Peake *Titus Groan* 371 Swelter,..thinking the thin man to have panicked, pursued him. **1958** N. Marsh *Singing in Shrouds* (1959) xi. 235 I'd had one or two drinks over the eight and I suppose that's why I panicked. **1971** *Radio Times* 4 Nov. 72/4 Their headmaster..rather panicked at the word 'drug'. **1975** P. Somerville-Large *Couch of Earth* iii. 48, I thought you might have panicked and hared off.

Hence **pa·nicked** *ppl. a.*, stricken with panic; also *fig.*

1916 G. Frankau *Guns* 15 His panicked watchers spy us, a droning threat in the void. **1920** E. Sitwell *Wooden Pegasus* 107 The light falls like a rain of panick'd leaves Through the gold heart of eves. **1978** R. Lewis *Uncertain Sound* iii. 80 With a sense of panicked claustrophobia I felt I had to get out of the office.

panicky, *a.* Add: **b.** quasi-*sb.* That which is panicky.

1924 Galsworthy *White Monkey* i. xii. 96 'That appears to savour of the panicky,' he said.

panicum (pæ·nikə̆m). [L. name of a type of millet, adopted by Linnæus (*Species Plantarum* (1753) I. 55) and earlier botanists as the name of a genus.] A grass belonging to the large genus so called, including the European millet, *Panicum miliaceum*, and several other important cereals or fodder grasses; = Panic *sb.*[1]

1844 J. D. Hooker *Let.* 10 Feb. in L. Huxley *Life J. D. Hooker* (1918) I. viii. 169 Fancy two new Panicums; I cannot make them agree with any others. **1870** W. Robinson *Wild Garden* ii. 121 Elegant Panicum... America. Annual... Banks, slopes, fringes of shrubberies. **1932** *Discovery* Jan. 24/2 A shade plant grows rankly and below is a mat of *Panicum* to the exclusion of everything else. **1966** C. A. W. Guggisberg *S. O. S. Rhino* iv. 92 *Panicum*, which grows to a fair height, is eaten more especially when short, and the rhino have a tendency to keep it down. **1968** F. W. Gould *Grass Systematics* 214 Bulb Panicum is an important forage grass of the southwestern mountain ranges.

‖ **panier de crabes** (pa·nye də krab). [Fr., lit. basket of crabs.] An internal struggle, a 'rat race'.

1963 *Economist* 30 Mar. 1218/2 The visitor is..not able to move around in this communist *panier de crabes*. **1979** *Dædalus* Summer 137 In what the French would term the *panier de crabes* of sixteenth century Toledan society.

Paninean (pæni·niăn), *a.* Also **Paninian.** [f. Skr. *Pāṇiniyā* in the same sense (also used), f. the name *Pāṇini*: see below.] Of or pertaining to the Sanskrit grammar of Pāṇini (6th or 5th c. b.c.); adhering to the rules formulated by Pāṇini.

1801 H. T. Colebrooke in *Asiatic Researches* VII. 204 A performance, such as the Pániníya grammar, must inevitably contain many errors... The studied brevity of the Pániníya Sútras renders them in the highest degree obscure. **1807** W. Jones *Wks.* IV. 107 Asked what he thought of the Pániníya, he answered very expressively, that 'it was a forest'. **1879** W. D. Whitney *Skr. Gram.* ii. 9 The Paninean scheme..classes *a* as guttural. **1900** A. A. Macdonell *Hist. Skr. Lit.* ix. 268 But the most important information we have of pre-Pāninean grammar is that found in Yāska's work. **1915** S. K. Belvalkar *Acct. Syst. Skr. Gram.* 43 For most of those writers who followed Kaiyyata there was very little original work in the Pāṇinīya school that was left to be done. **1929** L. Bloomfield in *Language* V. 273 A brief survey of both the Pāṇinean and the later systems is given by Belvalkar. **1967** S. M. Katre *Pāṇinian Stud.* I. p. viii, With the resurgent interest in linguistic studies..it is appropriate that Pāṇinian studies should form part of the Building Centenary and Silver Jubilee Series. **1977** *Language* LIII. 222 Given the above, it is not impossible that Kātyāyana and Patañjali might have suggested additions or modifications to Pāṇinian rules.

pani-wallah. *India.* [f. Hindi *pānī* water + Wallah.] A water-carrier (see also quot. 1957).

1934 'G. Orwell' *Burmese Days* xxv. 368 Ba Pe is pani-wallah in the same house at sixteen rupees a month. **1936** W. H. S. Smith *Let.* 2 Aug. in *Young Man's Country* (1977) ii. 20 My nice young pani-wallah has had to return to Rajshahi. **1957** D. G. O. Baillie *Sea Affair* 244 *Pani-wallahs*..are not really watermen at all, but oilmen, or greasers. **1960** *Times* 16 Mar. (Canberra Suppl.) p. xiv/6 Greasers are called panniwallahs, where 'panni' means water (once a more popular lubricant than grease). **1971** *Blitz* (Bombay) 6 Mar. 9/2 Householders are cursing him loudly, calling him 'paniwala maharaj'.

Panjabi: see *Punjabi *sb.* and *a.*

panji(e, varr. *punji.

panjrapol, var. *pinjrapol.

Panlibhonco (pænlibhǫ·nkǫ). [f. *Pan*ama, *Lib*eria, *Hon*duras, *Co*sta Rica.] Designating or pertaining to a merchant ship of Panama, Liberia, Honduras, and Costa Rica flying a 'flag of convenience'. Cf. *Flag *sb.*[4] 1 f, *Panhonlib.

1958 *Hansard Lords* 20 Mar. 369 We have to be very careful lest any action taken by Her Majesty's Government may harm British shipping more than 'Panlibhonco' owners. **1958** *Times* 14 Nov. 13/3 This great and growing block of virtually stateless tonnage—the tonnage of what is commonly known as 'PanHonLib' or 'Panlibhonco'. *Ibid.* 15 Nov. 8/2 Many of the big Panlibhonco fleets pay rates well above the average. **1959** P. Padfield *Sea is Magic Carpet* vi. 97 We sunbathed and watched the tankers sweep by on either side—many of them magnificent, streamlined beasts of the PanLibHonCo variety.

pan-loaf. (In Dict. s.v. Pan *sb.*[1] 11 b.) Add: Chiefly *Sc.* (later examples). Also used *fig.* of an affected or cultured accent, or of someone whose behaviour is regarded as pretentious, this usage originating in the fact that a pan loaf, being more expensive, was a sign of affluence. Hence **pan-loafy** *a.*

1906 'H. Foulis' *Vital Spark* i. 5 Four men and a derrick, and a water-butt and a pan loaf in the fo'c'sle. **1907** J. Kirkland *Mod. Baker* I. 112 Tin or Pan Loaves... Scotch pan loaves..are generally baked four in a pan, and to ensure that they separate with a smooth face each loaf is greased on the ends before being placed in the tin. **1922** Joyce *Ulysses* 143 They buy..four slices of panloaf at the north city dining rooms in Marlborough street. **1946** 'D. Twitter' *Tales o' the Toonie* 48, I warned Sarah Amelia no' tae start speakin' pan-loafy fin I wiz wi' her. She thrapit doon my thrapple that if I spak braid Farfar fowk wud tak me for a Turk. **1947** H. W. Pryde *First Bk. McFlannels* vi. 61 An' yer pan-loaf talk! 'Good-marning, Mrs. McTweed,' says you, 'fehn weather we've heving for this tehm of the year!' **1957** *Bulletin* (Glasgow) 25 Feb. 11/2 Pan loaves are coming back into favour again. **1959** M. Pugh *Chancer* 61 'The little kids used to shout, "Grey breeks, grey breeks, let's hear you speaking pan-loafy,"' she said... An all girls' school where they paid fees and wore grey uniforms and didn't talk in the local accent was splendidly ridiculous. **1964** *Weekly Scotsman* 16 June 8 Ah dinna like her, she's oafy pan loaf. **1973** Boyd & Parkes *Dark Number* v. 58 Him and his fancy clothes and his pan-loaf accent and his money! Why couldn't he stay on his own side of the tracks? **1974** *New Society* 28 Feb. 500/3 It was the authentic voice of the people of Glasgow.., and not the 'pan-loaf' (falsely polished) accents of the Scottish BBC. **1976** *Scotsman* 24 Dec. (Weekend Suppl.) 1/7 His pan-loaf accent would make you die. He's gettin' ready, y'see, to be a great sports commentator on the telly after he's made his mark in athletics.

panmixia. Also **panmixis, panmixy.** Add to def.: Now used to mean random mating within a breeding population. Also *transf.* (Further examples.)

1889 [see *Galton]. **1890** W. James *Princ. Psychol.* II. xxviii. 687 The obsolescence of disused organs he [*sc.* Weismann] explains very satisfactorily..by his theory of panmixy. **1896** A. Tille in T. Common tr. *Nietzsche's Case of Wagner* p. x, In a tribe the members of which.. assist each other in every kind of danger natural selection must soon come to an end, a kind of panmixy must arise and lead to a rapid decline. **1909** W. M. Urban *Valuation* xi. 341 Social pan-mixia, the breaking down of class barriers, makes impossible that fixity and contrast of ideals. **1943** *Genetics* XXVIII. 114 Mass selection..is all that can occur under panmixia. **1949** Darlington & Mather *Elem. Genetics* 408 Panmixis, unrestricted Random Mating. Properly excluded by any restriction, but sometimes used where random mating is assumed within the operation of a restriction, especially with dioecy in animals. **1955** *New Biol.* XVIII. 35 Panmixia or random mating..does not mean promiscuity. **1968** J. W. Purseglove *Tropical Crops: Dicotyledons* II. 360 Panmixia: by growing a number of c[ulti]v[ar]s together and hand-pollinating between them a highly variable population can be synthesized. **1971** L. N. Morris *Human Populations* (1972) ii. 34 Panmixis does not take place within the total [human] species.

2. In form **panmixis.** A population within which random mating takes place.

1968 J. W. Purseglove *Tropical Crops: Dicotyledons* II. 360 In Uganda a panmixis of 19 [*Gossypium*] *latifolium* c[ulti]v[ar]s from a number of countries was chosen.

Hence **panmi·ctic** *a.*, characterized by panmixia.

1943 *Genetics* XXVIII. 117 The term random breeding or panmictic unit will be used for any local population of the same effective size as the parental group. **1971** *Nature* 12 Feb. 468/1 It is possible that in animal species.. well able to migrate, no local population is sufficiently isolated to prevent the entire species or subspecies forming effectively one panmictic population. **1975** S. K. Jain in Frankel & Hawkes *Crop Genetic Resources* ii. 18 All individuals within a colony might be one panmictic group.

panne. Delete ‖ and add earlier and later examples.

1794 A. Young *Trav. France* (ed. 2) I. ii. xix. 550 St. Omers. There is a manufacture of..a kind of stuff called *pannes*. **1919** [see *Bud *sb.*[1] 3d]. **1923** [see *marocain]. **1940** *Chambers's Techn. Dict.* 611/2 *Panne velvet*, a warp pile fabric with silk pile; used for dresses and furnishings. **1972** *New Yorker* 7 Oct. 24/1 (Advt.), Pants are perfect for evening when they're lush panne velvet. **1977** *Vogue* Dec. 124/3 *Big sister*..in chocolate brown panne velvet.

pannier, *sb.*[1] Add: **6. pannier bag,** a bag or similar container (usu. one of a pair) placed above or to the side of the rear wheel of a bicycle or motor cycle; also *ellipt.*; **pannier pocket,** a large pocket attached to the side of a skirt or dress; **pannier tank,** a type of small steam locomotive which has a water tank on each side of the boiler.

1939–40 *Army & Navy Stores Catal.* 783/3 Cycle accessories..pannier bags and carriers. **1959** I. Jefferies *Thirteen Days* (1961) i. 9, I was forced to pull off the road... I had a bottle of cold beer..in the pannier. *Ibid.* xi. 170, I was taking the letters out of the pannier bag when the phone rang. **1975** J. Wood *North Kill* x. 139 The speaker kicked his bike into life... The others were storing their cleaning materials into side pannier bags. **1976** *Times* 27 Aug. 12/8 The world's most expensive bicycle... For nearly £600 you get neither mudguards nor pannier bags, and not even a rear reflector. **1922** Joyce *Ulysses* 501 Those pannier pockets of the skirt.. are devised to suggest bunchiness of the hip. **1973** *Times* 11 Dec. 13/3 Bill's new skirt with its slung pannier pockets is pretty. **1949** C. J. Allen *Locomotive Pract. & Performance 20th Cent.* vi. 65 Shunting on all railways is entrusted in large measure to small 0-6-0 tanks (pannier tanks on the Western Region). **1950** H. C. Webster *Railways for All* ix. 83 Frequently such locomotives carry the water in tanks fitted on top of the boiler and are therefore termed 'saddle tanks'. Others carry the water in two tanks secured high up along the boiler sides, and these are known as 'pannier tanks'. **1957** *Railway Mag.* Nov. 751/2 Today 0-6-0 pannier-tanks usually deal with the traffic. **1970** *Ibid.* Oct. 549 (*caption*) Wellington to Much Wenlock afternoon passenger train..headed by 0-6-0 pannier-tank No. 7754. **1973** *Country Life* 8 Mar. 593 A type peculiar to the GWR—the pannier tank..these modest 0-6-0 engines, which carried their water in 'panniers' at either side of the boiler.

panniform, *a. Bot.* [f. L. *pannus* cloth + -form.] = Pannose *a.*

1894 J. M. Crombie *Monogr. Lichens Brit.* I. 238 The thalline reactions, in conjunction with the general aspect of the plant, show that it belongs to *P[armelia] revoluta*, produced no doubt by a panniform condition of this species. **1921** A. L. Smith *Handbk. Brit. Lichens* 141 *Panniform, Pannose*, felted. **1957** Snell & Dick *Gloss. Mycol.* 110/1 Panniform. Having a felted or matted appearance.

pannikin. Add: **a.** (Further examples.)

1908 E. J. Banfield *Confessions of Beachcomber* ii. i. 280 One day a bucket of milk was brought to the camp at dinner-time and served out with pannikins. **1911** C. E. W. Bean *'Dreadnought' of Darling* xxxii. 282 There was a case of pannikins that had come up as freight. **1924** *Truth* (Sydney) 27 Apr. 6 *Pannikin*, small drinking vessel, made out of tin, carried by the sundowner, and tied to his billy. **1936** I. L. Idriess *Cattle King* ii. 14 The boy stared, then snatching his pannikin pushed the reluctant foal away and commenced milking the mare. **1945** Baker *Austral. Lang.* 169 *A friendly pannikin*, a drink with a companion.

b. The head; in slang phr. *off one's pannikin*, off one's head.

1895 C. Crowe *Austral. Slang Dict.* 56 *Off his pannikin*, silly. **1899** 'S. Rudd' in Murdoch & Drake-Brockman *Austral. Short Stories* (1951) 110, I seen 'im just now up in your paddick, an' he's clean off he's pannikin. **1916** C. J. Dennis *Moods of Ginger Mick* 126 Per'aps I'm orf me pannikin wiv' sittin' in the sun. **1934** B. Penton *Landtakers* (1935) iv. vii. 360 He's gone raving off his pannikin in Sydney.

c. = *pannikin-boss.*

c **1926** 'Mixer' *Transport Workers' Song Bk.* 7 My power is such to make or break—I'm a pannikin, get me?

Comb. **pannikin-boss** (later examples).

1930 L. G. D. Acland *Early Canterbury Runs* (ser. 1) v. 105 At 'smoke-oh' he used to take a standing jump over a bale of wool and then Brucksaw, the 'pannikin boss' (head general hand), used to carry it out of the shed singlehanded. **1936** A. Russell *Gone Nomad* ix. 70 There in the Silver City a telegram awaited me. It contained the offer of a job, that of 'pannikin-boss' and book-keeper on a sheep run east of Broken Hill, on the Milparinka Track. **1959** D. Hewett *Bobbin Up* viii. 97 All this unshakable distrust of the pannikin boss, the boss's man..the lowest of the low in a world where dog ate dog. **1966** G. W. Turner *Eng. Lang. Austral. & N.Z.* vii. 146 The manager of a sheepstation was called a *pannikin boss*, a term I have heard used..for a foreman on building jobs in New Zealand. **1969** D. Niland *Dead Men Running* iv. 98 Father Vaughan seemed to project himself as no more than the mouthpiece of a pannikin boss of a God who sounded like a brutal and violent pirate.

panning, *vbl. sb.* Add: **1.** Also with *out.*
1839 *Amer. Railroad Jrnl.* VIII. 99 This operation is continued until all the sand is removed, and nothing but the gold left. It is called 'panning out'. **1872** 'MARK TWAIN' *Roughing It* lxi. 443 'Panning out' refers to the washing process by which the grains of gold are separated from the dirt.

c. The action of denouncing or criticizing severely. (Cf. *PAN *v.*[1] 7.)
1914 *Sat. Even. Post* 15 Aug. 9/1 Speed sure got a pannin' in the clubhouse... Everybody..roasted him, but it didn't do no good. **1946** *Jazz Writings* 21/2 All this sounds like a merciless panning, I'm afraid, and yet it is kindly meant. **1958** *Spectator* 16 May 624/2 The Council of Industrial Design's exhibition..has had a panning from the design critics. Speaking..as a consumer, I agree with the criticism. **1960** *News Chron.* 27 Feb. 4/8 It was about the only thing in the show which did not get a panning from the critics.

e. *attrib.*, as *panning test, trough.*
1850 N. KINGSLEY *Diary* 17 May (1914) 122 Stoped down to day and made a panning trough to pour quicksilver from the riffler into and fix the pump. **1951** *Oxf. Jun. Encycl.* VII. 21/1 One of the oldest methods of assay ..is the miner's concentration or 'panning' test.

2. *Agric.* The action of PAN *v.*[1] 6: the hardening of a layer of soil.
1939 *Geogr. Jrnl.* XCIV. 468 A heavy black clay of undetermined depth without any evidence of panning, no iron concentrations and no characteristics of laterite. **1960** *Farmer & Stockbreeder* 26 Jan. 78/3, I am completely convinced that a panning effect is negligible compared with that of a plough. **1971** *Power Farming* Mar. 50/2 (Advt.), Even in sticky conditions the Soilmaster acts efficiently without 'bulldozing'—Positively no panning. Before buying a new cultivator get the facts on the Soilmaster range.

pa·nning, *vbl. sb.*[2] [f. *PAN *v.*[3] + -ING[1].] The action of *PAN *v.*[3] Also *attrib.*, esp. in *panning shot.*
1917 C. N. BENNETT *Guide to Kinematogr.* ii. 22 Sweeping round the camera from side to side is called panoraming or 'panning'. **1939** G. GREENE *Lawless Roads* vi. 147 If I had moved a camera all round..the little plaza in a panning shot. **1946** *Electronic Engin.* XVIII. 207 The trick of camera panning from one speaker to another. **1953** K. REISZ *Technique Film Editing* ii. 42 A scene.. shot from a large number of set-ups, some of them with a panning or tracking camera. **1967** *Spectator* 6 Oct. 392/2 The producer..was not helped by his camera crews, who, if their panning shots were tremulous, zoomed in on things like homing missiles. **1969** *Amat. Photographer* 23 Apr. 51/4 When you are forced to work more or less broadside-on,..swing the camera as you expose in the same direction as the movement. This technique, known as 'panning', is much used by press photographers. **1977** *Radio Times* 28 May 17/1 A long panning shot across some velvet cushions.

Pannonian, *a.* (Earlier and later examples.)
1605 BACON *Adv. Learning* II. f. 70[v] We see a notable example in Tacitus of two Stage-plaiers, Percennius and Vibulenus, who by their facultie of playing, put the Pannonian armies into an extreame tumulte and combustion. **1912** *Q. Rev.* Oct. 335 His happiest days were certainly spent away from Rome in German and Pannonian wars. **1975** R. BROWNING *Emperor Julian* i. 13 Decius, a Pannonian senator who found himself proclaimed emperor against his will in 249. **1976** *Classical Q.* XXVI. 302 It was established in Dalmatia in or soon after A.D. 9, in the wake of the Pannonian uprising.

pannus. Add: **2.** *Path.* A layer of granulation tissue that forms by a thickening of the synovial membrane and tends to spread over and absorb adjacent cartilage in a joint affected by rheumatoid arthritis.
1904 *Boston Med. & Surg. Jrnl.* 17 Nov. With the swelling which results the membrane at times extends in or over the cartilage, forming a pannus, and wherever this persists for any length of time.., the cartilage under the pannus is more or less absorbed. **1929** R. PEMBERTON *Arthritis & Rheumatoid Conditions* iii. 53 The proliferation of the synovial membrane causes a layer of granulation tissue to extend in the form of a thin pannus more or less completely over the joint cartilage. **1973** *Nature* 14 Dec. 419/1 The pannus of the rheumatoid joint has the ability to produce an active collagenase and invade and degrade cartilage *in vitro.*

panoche (panǫ·tʃi). *U.S.* Also **panocha, penoche, penuche.** [Amer. Sp., 'brown sugar'.]
1. A type of coarse brown sugar.
1847 *Californian* 10 Apr. 3/2 The cargo consists of 180 bales..of Mexican Sugar; 30 Packages Panoche and one Bale of Zarapies. **1856** L. J. F. JAEGER *Jrnl.* 17 Aug. in *S. Calif. Hist. Soc. Publ.* (1928) XIV. 124 Had to leave 3 cargoes of flour and one fanega of beans & ½ cargo of panocha. **1881** H. T. WILLIAMS *Pacific Tourist* 300/2 The ordinary brown sugar (panoche) of the Mexicans is also obtained from this plant. **1887** *Outing* Apr. 10/2 It is ordinarily made of corn, roasted and crushed and slightly sweetened, the most common sweetening being *panoche*, a crude sugar. **1936** J. A. MCKENNA *Black Range Tales* 52 With ten pounds of jerky, a cone of *penoche* or pressed brown sugar, and a serape, or gray blanket, a Mexican is fitted for a trip of several hundred miles through the mountains.

2. A kind of sweet resembling fudge, made with brown sugar, butter, milk or cream, and nuts. Also *fig.*
1872 *Rep. Indian Affairs 1871* (U.S.) 359, I doubt the good policy of issuing bread, and at times candy (panoche), to the pupils. **1921** M. L. MATTHEWS *Foods & Cookery* 274 Panocha... Mix sugar, milk, and salt. Boil until it reaches the 'soft-ball' stage. **1930** *Sunset* Dec. 30/2 At lower left are seen fondant-dipped and penoche-dipped figs and prunes. **1949** *Arizona Q.* Autumn 255 He made the most luscious panocha and rich syrups, which he sold to the public. **1949** *Chicago Tribune* 28 Sept. II. 2/2 Our recipe for Butterscotch Cake, and Penoche Icing, is printed on the recipe folder. **1952** J. STEINBECK *East of Eden* xix. 226 Faye twisted around in her chair to reach a piece of brown panocha studded with walnuts. When she spoke it was around a mouth full of candy. **1966** *Cookies & Candies* (Better Homes & Gardens) 79/2 Penuche. Rich and creamy brown-sugar fudge. A favorite of grandmothers (granddads, too!) **1968** *Cook's & Diner's Dict.* (Funk & Wagnalls) 167/2 Pe-nu-che..A candy made with brown sugar..Also called panocha. **1971** *Islander* (Victoria, B.C.) 7 Feb. 14/1 There are recipes for all the classic home candies like fudge, butterscotch, penuche, etc. **1976** *Publishers Weekly* 29 Mar. 59/3 With its story of aggressive hatred.., murder attempts.., a later revealed illegitimate birth, and a love interest as well, it's a well-iced piece of penuche.

panographic (pænogræ·fik), *a. Dentistry.* Also **panagraphic.** [f. PANO(RAMIC *a.* + RADIO)GRAPHIC *a.*] Of, pertaining to, or designating radiography of several teeth and the adjacent bones in a single exposure by means of a small X-ray source placed inside the mouth and a film outside it.
1952 *Jrnl. Dental Res.* XXXI. 165 In the evaluation of the panographic technique it is well to remember that it must be judged as an adjunct to conventional radiography and not as a substitute for it. **1963** *Dental Radiogr. & Photogr.* XXXVI. 81/2 (*caption*) Panagraphic equipment and technic for the maxilla and the mandible. **1967** *Amer. Jrnl. Roentgenology* CI. 989/2 (*caption*) Panographic study reveals a large expansile cystic lesion in the right mandible, proven to be a dental cyst.

Hence **pa·nograph,** (*a*) a panographic radiograph; (*b*) an X-ray machine for use in panography; **pano·graphy,** panographic radiography.
1961 *Oral Surg., Oral Med., Oral Path.* XIV. 1178 (*heading*) Panagraphy. *Ibid.* 1179 The x-ray tube used in the Panagraph is the Swiss Panoramix tube. **1963** BLACKMAN & POYTON *Man. Dental & Oral Radiogr.* xvi. 160 (*caption*) Panagraph of lower jaw showing unerupted and supernumerary teeth. **1967** *Amer. Jrnl. Roentgenology* CI. 988/1 Panography is a radiographic technique recently described by Blackman for use predominantly in dentistry. **1969** WUEHRMANN & MANSON-HING *Dental Radiol.* (ed. 2) viii. 161 Panagraphy suggests a technic to study structures in a panoramic fashion. The Panagraph or Panoramix is an x-ray machine utilizing an intraoral source of radiation to expose film placed extraorally. *Ibid.* 163 The main advantages of the Panagraph appear to be that it is relatively portable, is easy to operate, and may be used effectively for mass dental radiography.

panoply, *v.* **b.** (Earlier and later examples.)
1873 'MARK TWAIN' *Gilded Age* xxxii. 290 It would be.. judicious to send her forth well panoplied for her work. —So he had added new and still richer costumes to her wardrobe, and assisted their attractions with costly jewelry. **1880** —— *Tramp Abroad* xxviii. 284, I and my agent panoplied ourselves in walking costume. **1940** 'GUN BUSTER' *Return via Dunkirk* I. i. 11, I was panoplied for War.

panopticon. 1. b. (Earlier example.)
1850 *Deed of Settlement of Royal Panopticon of Science & Art* 1 Royal Panopticon of Science and Art. An institution for Scientific exhibitions and for promoting discoveries in arts manufactures.

panora·m, *v.* [A shortening of PANORAMIC *a.*] *intr.* = *PAN *v.*[3] Hence **panora·ming** *vbl. sb.*
1915 *Wells Fargo Messenger* Oct. 18/3 We are before the Erie cut, and as the camera 'panorams' around, we get a glimpse of our splendid Eleventh Avenue Stable in Jersey City. **1938** G. H. SEWELL *Amateur Film-Making* ix. 80 The revolution of a camera on its vertical axis, so that it covers the features of a landscape, is known as 'panoraming' or 'panning'. *Ibid.* 81 To panoram with a hand-held camera, set your feet firmly on the ground,.. brace yourself up and turn from the hips.

panorama. Add: **1. b.** (Earlier examples.)
1813 M. EDGEWORTH *Let.* 16 May (1971) 56 Pray do not think because I name these fine people..that my poor little head is turned... Be assured that the whole panorama passes before me as a panorama. **1818** 'T. BROWN' *Brighton* I. p. xi, A novel should be a panorama of life; and we trust that our *views* will be found correct in the present one.

2. (Earlier example.)
1805 M. WILMOT *Russ. Jrnls.* (1934) 151 Up at Cock Crow to drive to Sparrow Mount from which spot Moscow is seen as a Panorama, & a most exquisite view it is indeed.

pan-pie. *U.S.* [f. PAN *sb.*[1] + PIE *sb.*[2]] = PANDOWDY.
1723 J. NOTT *Cook's & Confectioner's Dict.* sig. Y8[v] This Paste is proper for Pan pies that are set on the Table without a Desert or Banquet of sweet Meats. **1862** 'G. HAMILTON' *Country Living* 70 No pan-pie with hot brown bread on Sunday morning. **1883** *Rep. Maine Board Agric. 1882* 403 You have all heard of the pan-dowdy, or pan-pie, the pride of our grandmothers.

panplain (pæ·nplē͡ⁱn). *Physical Geogr.* Also **-plane.** [f. PAN- + PLAIN *sb.*[1]] A plain formed by the coalescence of previously separate flood-plains.
1933 C. H. CRICKMAY in *Geol. Mag.* LXX. 345 We would expect the growing floodplains to become confluent, making one broad universal plain shared by all the streams of the region. The surface will be flat, and will have a general slope like that which now characterizes the lower floodplains of great rivers. The only relief will be remnants of some of the interfluves which may persist as low monadnocks. This plain, formed of floodplains joined by their own growth, may be called a panplain. **1942** O. D. VON ENGELN *Geomorphol.* vi. 97 Eventually the level surfaces of adjacent stream floors, concurrently developed by such planation, become confluent and a panplane, a very level plain with a general downward inclination, is produced. **1960** B. W. SPARKS *Geomorphol.* xv. 340 There seems little doubt that river planation is an important agency of erosion,..but whether these can extend indefinitely to form a panplain seems more doubtful. **1967** J. HAYS in Jennings & Mabbutt *Landform Stud. Austral. & New Guinea* ix. 200 Near Darwin, the panplains of north-flowing and west-flowing streams have coalesced.

panplanation (pæ:nplǣnē͡ⁱ·ʃən). *Physical Geogr.* [f. PAN- + *PLANATION, after *PANPLAIN.] The formation of a panplain.
1933 C. H. CRICKMAY in *Geol. Mag.* LXX. 345 The essential difference between panplanation and peneplanation is that the former starts from the lower floodplains of rivers and grows laterally in all landward directions, whereas the latter is of universal occurrence. **1942** O. D. VON ENGELN *Geomorphol.* xvi. 356 It is now considered improbable that flood-plain accumulation and panplanation (Crickmay, C. H., 1933) combined..could completely dispose of all relief in a peneplaned region. **1970** R. J. SMALL *Study of Landforms* v. 168 Many authorities have regarded lateral plantation by running water as a major factor in the formation of desert surfaces.., and a process akin to panplanation has been assumed by some to account for savanna plains.

panpot (pæ·npǫt), *sb.* [f. *pan(oramic) pot(entiometer).*] A kind of potentiometer used to vary the apparent position of a sound source by varying the strengths of the signals to individual speakers without changing the total signal strength.
1941 *Jrnl. Soc. Motion Pict. Engin.* XXXVII. 130 A special 3-circuit differential junction network, nicknamed 'The Panpot', is used to dub one original track onto one, any two ,or all three of our Fantasound program tracks. **1964** H. B. HADDEN *Pract. Stereophony* iii. 39 To present a monophonic signal, as a point source at a given position.., a control known as a 'panoramic potentiometer' is employed... This control, known as a 'panpot' for short, is a two-gang fader with the two halves arranged back to back, so that as the gain of one half of the particular channel is increased, the other half is decreased. **1975** *Gramophone* Dec. 1122/1 The deck was plugged into a large discothèque type console with a quadrophonic panpot in the middle.

Hence **pa·npot** *v. trans.*, to process by means of a panpot; **pa·npotted** *ppl. a.*, **pa·npotting** *vbl. sb.*
1973 *Jrnl. Audio Engin. Soc.* XXI. 3/2 The recording may..be made by 'pan-potting' sounds into the channels to stimulate [*read* simulate] pickup by directional microphones. **1976** *Gramophone* Jan. 1269/1 This 'panpotting' method also enabled the balance to be adjusted after the recording session. *Ibid.* 1269/2 The medium is largely confined to pan-potted multi-track material.

panpsychism (pænsəi·kiz'm). *Philos.* Also **pampsychism.** [PAN-.] (See quot. 1901.) Hence **panpsy·chic** *a.*, pertaining to or based on panpsychism; **panpsy·chist,** one who believes in panpsychism; also *attrib.* or as *adj.*; **panpsychi·stic** *a.*, connected with or characterized by panpsychism; **panpsychi·stically** *adv.*
1879 G. H. LEWES *Mind as Function of Organism* ii. 34 We must therefore pronounce against the hypothesis of Panpsychism. **1881** W. JAMES in *Unitarian Rev.* Nov. 415 All modern thought converges toward idealistic or, as I should rather call them, pan-psychic, conclusions. **1901** Panpsychism [in Dict. s.v. PAN- 2]. **1903** C. A. STRONG *Why Mind has Body* p. vi, Hence I think panpsychists are justified in maintaining that with their principles they are able to explain the connection of mind and body. *Ibid.*, I have chosen my title with the object of putting this panpsychist pretension distinctly on record. **1904** J. MCCABE tr. *Haeckel's Wonders of Life* xv. 354 His [*sc.* Fechner's] system is..panpsychistic and at the same time pantheistic. **1911** J. WARD *Realm of Ends* i. 20 To this principle pampsychism appeals. *Ibid.* 21 On this, the pampsychist view, Nature..resolves into a plurality of conative individuals. *Ibid.* iii. 62 The pampsychist.. maintains..that at all events there are no things wholly inert. **1924** B. EDGELL *Theories of Memory* 133 The present writer has failed to find any link between M. Bergson's pampsychism and his individualism. **1935** R. B. PERRY *Tht. & Char. W. James* II. 443 Whether this 'beyond', this thing-in-itself, shall be interpreted panpsychistically, is questioned and again left unsettled. **1937** A. H. MURRAY *Philos. of James Ward* v. 98 The pampsychistic solution, at which he arrives, dates back to Leibniz and earlier. **1940** *Mind* XLIX. 43 Berkeley probably saw that pampsychism, for him, spelled pantheism. *Ibid.* 45 With this new background the Berkeleian immaterialism took on a new aspect; it is no longer pampsychist. **1955** H. J. KOREN *Introd. Philos. Animate Nature* I. i. 35 The ancient hylozoists..and modern panpsychists..imply or state that all things are alive. **1959** *Chambers's Encycl.* XII. 718/2 Should pampsychism replace the older hylozoism, the truth being that the inner side of everything is its

soul, the outer aspect observable by an outsider being its body? **1968** F. COPLESTON *Hist. Philos.* VIII. v. xvii. 393 Neither Strong nor Drake meant to imply that stones, for instance, are conscious. Their panpsychism was linked with the idea of emergent evolution. **1973** *Nature* 20 July 183/1 At one time he expressed panpsychic ideas, thinking there could be some consciousness even in a mug, but later was prepared to restrict it to animals with a nervous system. **1975** C. BURT *ESP & Psychol.* vi. 99 Theists and panpsychists..have no qualms about ascribing minds to human beings.

panpygoptosis (pæːnpəigoptōᵘ·sis). *nonce-wd.* [A fanciful formation combining the elements PAN-, PYGO-, OPTO-, -OSIS.] = *duck's disease* s.v. *DUCK *sb.*[1] 12. Hence **panpy:g-opto·tic** *a.*

1938 S. BECKETT *Murphy* v. 97 Duck's disease is a distressing pathological condition in which the thighs are suppressed and the buttocks spring directly from behind the knees, aptly described in Steiss's nosonomy as Panpygoptosis. *Ibid.* 104 Miss Dew's control, a panpygoptotic Manichee of the fourth century,..had not..been raised so wholly a spiritual body as yet to sit down with much more comfort than she had in the natural.

Pan-Roman, Panroman (pæːn,rōᵘ·măn). [PAN- + ROMAN *sb.*[1] 3.] An artificial language invented for universal use by H. Molenaar; also known as *UNIVERSAL.

1907 W. J. CLARK *Internat. Lang.* II. vi. 103 The last few years have produced quite a crop of artificial languages..Idiom Neutral; Pan-Roman or Universal, by Dr. Molenaar; Latino sine flexione [etc.]. *Ibid.* 105 The victorious Esperantists..poke fun at these new-fangled schemes. A parody in Esperanto verse..narrates the fickleness of Pan-Roman and how it changed into Universal. **1922** *Nature* CIX. 494/1 A language of the Neo-Latin type, somewhat similar to Neutral Idiom, is the 'Panroman' (or 'Universal') of the German positivist and pacifist, Dr. H. Molenaar. **1927** E. S. PANKHURST *Delphos* vi. 81 Universal (1903), later called Panroman (1906), by Dr. H. Molenaar, is another neo-Latin language.

‖ **pansala** (pɒ·nsālă). [Sinhala, f. *pan* leaf + *sala* dwelling, f. Skr. *parnaśālā*, Pali *pannasālā*.] A Buddhist temple or monastery; orig., a forest hut constructed from leaves.

1850 R. S. HARDY *Eastern Monachism* xiii. 129 The dwelling of the priest is called a pansala, from pan, leaves, and sala, a dwelling, or a place to which any one is accustomed to resort, from a root which signifies to go. **1913** L. WOOLF *Village in Jungle* i. 12 He had fallen ill.. and had stayed for a month or two in the priest's pansala. **1927** *Missionary Herald* Sept. 219/2 Mr. Weeratua went to see him at his pansala and talked to him about Christ. **1956** R. PIERIS *Sinhalese Social Organization* II. ix. 73 There was, in almost every village, temple land, the property of which was vested in..a local *vihāra* or *pansala*.

pan-se·xual, *a.* [f. PAN- 2 + SEXUAL *a.*] Of or pertaining to pan-sexualism; that is not limited in sexual choice; **pan-se·xualism,** the view that the sex instinct plays a part in all human thought and activity and is the chief or only source of energy. Hence **pan-se·xualist** *a.*, pertaining to the theory of pansexualism; **pan-sexu·ality.**

1917 C. R. PAYNE tr. *Pfister's Psycho-anal. Method* 60 Which..has brought the reproach of 'pansexualism' against psychoanalysis. **1922** J. STRACHEY tr. *Freud's Group Psychol.* iv. 39 Psycho-analysis, then gives these love instincts the name of sexual instincts... The majority of 'educated' people have regarded this nomenclature as an insult, and have taken their revenge by retorting upon psycho-analysis with the reproach of 'pan-sexualism'. **1926** W. MCDOUGALL *Outl. Abnormal Psychol.* i. 20 It has led Freud.., as Janet has said, to construct 'an enormous system of medical philosophy', the theory of Pansexuality. *Ibid.* vi. 131 Freud, in accordance with his pansexualist tendency, expressed the opinion [etc.]. *Ibid.* xviii. 314 The dogma that the Œdipus complex is present in all men is the principal instrument of the pansexual theory. **1972** *Jrnl. Social Psychol.* LXXXVII. 51 In the beginning the human organism has the potential of pansexuality. **1974** *Observer* 7 Apr. 36/6 Eventually, no doubt, some biographer will tell us how far he [*sc.* H. de Montherlant] was homosexual, heterosexual or—as seems to be suggested by some discreet passages about bestiality and incest—pansexual. **1977** *Guardian Weekly* 7 Aug. 18/2 An exquisitely Victorian taste for extravagant, pansexual erotic fantasy.

pansified (pæ·nzifəid), *ppl. a.* [f. PANSY + -FY + -ED[1].] Excessively stylized or adorned; affected, effeminate.

1941 C. KING *Diary* 17 July in *With Malice toward None* (1970) 135 These birds from Portland Place...think anything said with feeling is rather vulgar, so usually give out a very pansified BBC message. **1944** 'G. ORWELL' *Crit. Ess.* (1951) 145 The rather pansified drawings of youths. **1959** W. D. PEREIRA *North Flight* iv. 56 You don't know this place. Like a pansified rabbit warren. Architect designed. **1973** *Listener* 20 Dec. 860/3 Hervey's relationship with..the pansified international Algarotti. **1976** *Ibid.* 27 May 679/1 Being not only a Londoner, but a central Londoner,..I can breakfast and dine in my pansified quarters in the heart of the soft South, having spent most of the intervening time in the gritty, bracing, humorous, individualistic North.

panspermy. Add: (The usual form is now **panspermia.**) In recent use applied to the idea that micro-organisms or chemical precursors of life are present in space and able to initiate life on reaching a suitable planet. (Further examples.)

1908 H. BORNS tr. *Arrhenius' Worlds in Making* viii. 217 The so-called theory of panspermia really shows a way. According to this theory life-giving seeds are drifting about in space. They encounter the planets, and fill their surfaces with life as soon as the necessary conditions for the existence of organic beings are established. **1938** S. MORGULIS tr. *Oparin's Origin of Life* ii. 39 At the beginning of the twentieth century the idea of the transfer of genus from one celestial body to another was again revived in the form of the so-called theory of panspermia, originated by the great Swedish physical chemist S. Arrhenius. **1970** *Daily Tel.* 9 Jan. 19 The theory of 'panspermia', the idea that the seeds of life drift through the Galaxy until they find a planet on which to settle, was eagerly discussed on the..final day of the moon-rock conference in Houston. **1971** I. G. GASS et al. *Understanding Earth* ix. 140/2 The hypothesis of 'panspermia'..is an old one which has never found much favour. **1975** *Times Lit. Suppl.* 25 July 846/3 The possibility of panspermia—the idea, recently revived by Leslie Orgel and Nobel laureate Francis Crick, that life did not originate on earth at all, but arrived here from elsewhere in the universe.

panstick (pæ·nstik). Also **Pan-Stik** (proprietary name). [f. *PAN(CAKE *sb.* 2 h + STICK *sb.*[1]] A kind of matt cosmetic in the form of a stick.

1949 *Trade Marks Jrnl.* 10 Aug. 705/2 Pan-Stik... Non-medicated toilet preparations, cosmetic preparations and perfumes. Max Factor & Company.., Los Angeles, State of California, United States of America; manufacturers. **1962** *New Statesman* 18 May 708/2 We were crushed in the toilets. All round girls smeared on pan-stick. 'I can't go with him, he's too short.' 'All the grey glitter I put on me hair come off on his cheek and I hadn't the heart to tell him.' **1967** *Guardian* 1 Feb. 6/6 The kids I meet..just don't wash enough. And they plaster their faces..with layers of cover creams, and thick tinted foundations and then probably panstick make-up as well. **1973** J. BURROWS *Like an Evening Gone* i. 13 Talk..as superficial as panstick.

pansy, *sb.* Add: **1. c.** *pansy-coloured* (further example), *-dark, -purple* (further example).

1909 *Daily Chron.* 18 Mar. 10/3 Lady Kenmare in black and Georgiana Lady Dudley, tall and beautiful in pansy-coloured cloth, were Lady Mayo's assistants. **1862** G. M. HOPKINS *Vision of Mermaids* (1929), Their pansy-dark or bronzen locks were strung With coral shells. **1940** C. DAY LEWIS tr. *Virgil's Georgics* IV. 89 Eridanus, than which through fertile lands no river Rushes with more momentum to the pansy-purple sea.

2. The colour of a pansy; *spec.* a shade of blue or purple.

1914 JOYCE *Dubliners* 227 A red-faced young woman, dressed in pansy. **1926** *Eaton's News Weekly* 26 June 13/1 Bathing suit...in blue, cardinal, pansy, black. **1935** *Amer. Speech* X. 193/2 The following terms are applied to blue..: *slate, aster, indigo, pansy,* [etc.].

3. An effeminate man; a male homosexual.

1929 M. LIEF *Hangover* 210 'Say, what do you know about this?' he said. 'One of those pansies was trying to date me up!' **1937** M. ALLINGHAM *Dancers in Mourning* xiv. 192 You don't want to feel that every other user of the road privately feels that your club is nothing but a pack of pansies on bicycles. **1947** A. P. GASKELL in D. M. Davin *N.Z. Short Stories* (1953) 276 He struck a chesty attitude standing naked on the seat. 'Do I look like a pansy?' 'Not with that thing.' **1956** [see *CAMP *a.* (and *sb.*[5])]. **1957** [see *boy friend, boy-friend* s.v. *BOY *sb.*[1] 7]. **1960** J. BETJEMAN *Summoned by Bells* ix. 98 There Bignose plays the organ And the pansies all sing flat. **1967** G. JACKSON *Let.* 16 May in *Soledad Brother* (1971) 115 They make emotional pansies of the boys with that sanctimonious dogma. **1971** F. FORSYTH *Day of Jackal* xx. 335, I don't like you in that stuff. It makes you look like all those nasty pansies back in there. **1975** *Amer. N. & Q.* XIII. 146/2 Evidence that Sir Thopas is a 'pansy' or a 'queer', who would be ridiculed as a homosexual. **1976** BOTHAM & DONNELLY *Valentino* vii. 52 A group of degenerate art students, most of whom he considered pansies.

b. *Comb.*, as *pansy-ass, -boy.*

1934 *New Statesman* 15 Sept. 318/2 Reminiscences of the fate of Heines and Röhm were reflected in shouts about 'pansy-boys'. **1976** N. THORNBURG *Cutter & Bone* viii. 192 He learned all about the ingratitude and stupidity of the man's..pansy-ass sons.

pa·nsy, *a.* [f. *PANSY *sb.* 3.] Effeminate; homosexual; affected. So **pa·nsyish** *a.*

1929 J. DEVANNY *Riven* xvii. 112 'Thanks. Don't bother.' The voice was warm... A rich telephone voice. To an artist a pansy voice; a purple pansy. **1934** M. HODGE *Wind & Rain* III. 83 She'll forget all about it, in the arms of Roger Cole! I think he's pansy, anyhow. **1942** E. PAUL *Narrow St.* xxxvi. 323 Pierre..started sending affectionate notes to certain homosexual French officers who were rabidly anti-Left... One by one, these pansy reactionaries began to disappear from their units. **1951** 'E. CRISPIN' *Long Divorce* viii. 84 I'd want her to be walking out with a decent lad, not a pansy little foreign gramophone-record. **1953** E. TAYLOR *Sleeping Beauty* ii. 27 Laurence leant awkwardly against the chimney-piece in a rather pansyish pose. **1971** *Daily Tel.* 21 Aug. 3/4 'Most of these new designs are too pansy, too effeminate,' said Leading Seaman Robert Nelson.

pa·nsy, *v.* [f. *PANSY *sb.* 3] **a.** *trans.* To dress or adorn in an affected or effeminate manner. Freq. *refl.* and const. *up.* **b.** *intr.* To act or walk in an effeminate manner.

1946 'BRAHMS' & 'SIMON' *Trottie True* 154 Luke Lovelock had pansied himself into a feature of every fashionable production. Luke had such perfect taste. **1951** N. MARSH *Opening Night* i. 27 The theatre was shut dahn for a long while until they 'ad it all altered and pansied up. **1966** J. WAINWRIGHT *Crystallised Carbon Pig* xxxix. 172 Originally, his hair had been mousy brown. He'd tried to pansy himself up—and failed. **1972** M. KENYON *Shooting of Dan McGrew* i. 10 It's over a month old..and the last word from McGrew before he went pansying off.

pant (pænt), *sb.*[3] [sing. back-formation f. PANTS *sb. pl.*] **1.** = PANTS *sb. pl. U.S.*

1893 H. A. SHANDS *Some Peculiarities of Speech in Mississippi* 49 *Pant*.., an abbreviation of *pantaloons,* used by clerks in dry-goods stores. They say: 'I have a pant that I can sell you,' etc. Of course, *pants* is a well-known abbreviation, but I think *pant* is rather a new word. **1936** A. L. HENCH (*MS. note dated Feb.*), For six or seven years now, I have been hearing clothes dealers speak of a pair of pants as 'a fine pant'. The reasoning seems to be that if a pile of pairs of pants is *pants*, then one pair is a *pant*. **1962** *L. L. Bean Catal.* Spring 10 A practical and well made pant for general sportswear. **1976** *Billings* (Montana) *Gaz.* 16 June 3-A/4 (Advt.), You just can't beat the value of this 3-piece jacket/dress/pant ensemble at our irresistible price... The pull-on pant makes a good thing better.

2. *attrib.* and *Comb.*, as *pant-leg, look*; **pant-coat,** a women's coat designed for wearing with trousers; **pantdress,** a dress with a divided skirt; **pantskirt,** a divided skirt; **pant suit, pantsuit** = *trouser suit.*

1970 *N.Y. Post* 16 Dec. 6 Pantcoat, on duty for wintry weather and for city traffic. **1974** *New Yorker* 25 Feb. 62/1 (Advt.), A great pantcoat: this Weatherbee, with its easy swing and snappy fit. **1964** *Women's Wear Daily* 30 Nov. 44 Julie Isles..likes the pantdress that stops just above the knee. **1967** *Maclean's Mag.* Dec. 35 At far left a Persian pantdress in pure wool (with a matching mini-nightie, about $60). **1968** Pantdress [see *pantskirt* below]. **1956** H. GOLD *Man who was not with It* (1965) ix. 73 The pantleg was sticky where it was bruised. **1974** D. RICHARDS *Coming of Winter* i. 6 He moved uphill very quickly, his boots and pantlegs soaking from the water. **1976** *New Yorker* 5 Jan. 22/3 We glanced down the row and saw..the next straightening the pant leg over his right calf in a single motion, and so on. **1970** *Women's Wear Daily* 23 Nov. 31/2, I think another pant look will take over. **1964** *Times* 3 Aug. 11 The pants and pantskirt as shown by Marc Bohan at Dior are for the country and around the house. **1968** *N.Y. Times* 15 July 43 This time, it is a more coordinated trend—pant-skirts, pant-dresses, pant-suits, tops and pants and so on. **1977** *Evening Post* (Nottingham) 27 Jan. 9/5 Stride ahead in this all-season look of a classic shirt paired with a trim pant-skirt. **1966** *Sun* 15 June 3/1 'At least they didn't come in trouser suits.' Two girls did. One wore a pant suit in pink and green linen. **1968** *Telegraph* (Brisbane) 24 Oct. 31/6 Model Kelly shows off the latest pantsuit in white stretch towelling. **1970** *Harrods Christmas Catal.* 14/1 Pant suit hangers. **1975** *N.Y. Times* 8 Sept. 33/4 Another woman.. sits by herself looking aloof, brushing hairs off her well-pressed rust pantsuit.

pant-. Add: **Panta·rchic** *a.*, of or pertaining to a pantarchy.

1883 L. F. WARD *Dynamic Sociol.* I. 466 The cosmopolitan, or pantarchic stage.

pantaleon. (Earlier example.)

1757 A. LINDE tr. *Keysler's Trav. Germany* IV. lxxxvi. 125 M. Panthaleon Hebenstreit, never refuses to gratify strangers with a sight of the Panthaleon, a musical instrument called by his own name, who was the inventor of it.

pantalettes, *sb. pl.* Add: Also (in *sing.*) **pantelette.** (Earlier and later examples.)

1834 *Knickerbocker* IV. 117 In the first place, in their blushing girlhood, they assume the pantalettes, or little pantaloons. **1838** *Southern Lit. Messenger* IV. 28/1 Two pretty sisters, in pantalettes, waited on table. **1922** JOYCE *Ulysses* 528 The scanty, daringly short skirt, riding up at the knee to show a peep of white pantelette, is a potent weapon. **1975** R. PLAYER *Let's talk of Graves* iii. 78 Little girls in pantalettes bowled their hoops.

pantee, see *PANTIES *sb. pl.*

Panthalassa (pænþælæ·sā). *Geol.* Also **panthalassa.** [f. PAN- + Gr. θάλασσα sea.] A universal sea or single ocean, such as would have surrounded *PANGÆA.

1893 E. SUESS in *Natural Sci.* II. 186 We might.. rather be induced to infer that in Prepalæozoic times there may have existed a universal hydrosphere or panthalassa covering the whole of the planet. **1924** J. G. A. SKERL tr. *Wegener's Orig. Continents & Oceans* x. 149 It is ..not improbable that in the most ancient 'pre-geological times' the film of sial..could then have been..only about 30 km. thick, and have been covered with a 'Panthalassa' ..which probably left exposed only small proportions, or none at all, of the earth's surface. **1937** A. L. DU TOIT *Our Wandering Continents* x. 210 The Drift Hypothesis.. has to view the great geosynclinal seaways of earlier geological history as branches, albeit important ones, of a universal ocean or 'Panthalassa', which was transformed into the present oceans through the horizontal drifting of the crustal blocks. **1970** R. S. DIETZ in Johnson & Smith *Megatectonics Continents & Oceans* iii. 36 (*caption*) Accretionary development of two supercontinents (Laurasia and Gondwana)..producing two supercontinents of equal area, surrounded by the equatorial universal ocean of Panthalassa. *Ibid.* iii. 43 The Pacific Ocean may be regarded as the remnant of Panthalassa, with the Atlantic, Arctic, and Indian Oceans being mostly rift oceans.

pantheize (pæ·nþi,əiz), *v. rare.* [f. PANTHE(IST + -IZE I.] To imbue with the characteristics and ideas of pantheism; to make compatible with pantheism.

1909 W. JAMES *Pluralistic Universe* iii. 118 Theologians have felt its irrationality acutely, and the 'fall', the predestination, and the election which the situation involves have given them more trouble than anything else in their attempt to pantheize Christianity.

panther. Add: **3. b.** *ellipt.* f. *Black Panther* s.v. *BLACK *a.* 19; also used *attrib.* or as *adj.*

1968 *Guardian* 28 June 20/7 The Panthers wear a uniform consisting of Black Leather jacket and beret. **1968** *Listener* 5 Sept. 290/2 The hotel cops, baited in the beginning not only by rocks and bottles but by language of insane obscenity, and having waded into the advance guard of panthers, militants white and black, perambulating trouble-makers, then went berserk. **1970** G. JACKSON *Let.* 4 Apr. in *Soledad Brother* (1971) 220 The young Panther party member, our vanguard, must be embraced, protected, allowed to develop. **1972** J. MILLS *Report to Commissioner* 120 The Panthers are worse than the Shylocks. They won't let you alone. **1973** E. BULLINS *Theme is Blackness* 141 A Black Panther selling Panther newspapers. *Ibid.*, Say, brother..you Panthers sell papers just like the Muslims..don't cha? **1973** *Black Panther* 3 Mar. 8/1 Yet there are some people who say..that Panther rhetoric invites repression and destruction.

5. panther juice, panther('s) piss, panther sweat, strong liquor, usu. spirits, esp. of local or home manufacture; *ellipt.* **panther,** gin.

1942 BERREY & VAN DEN BARK *Amer. Thes. Slang* § 100/9 *Gin*,..panther. **1960** WENTWORTH & FLEXNER *Dict. Amer. Slang* 374/2 *Panther*,..inferior liquor, esp. gin. From 'panther sweat'. **1960** J. PHILIPS *Whisper Town* (1961) I. i. 4 Here's your panther juice, Judge. **1941** BAKER *Dict. Austral. Slang* 52 *Panther's p—s*, liquor, esp. spirits. **1946** T. HEGGEN *Mister Roberts* 134 'That whiskey they make,' said Dowdy, 'is really panther-piss.' **1955** W. GADDIS *Recognitions* II. i. 308 Yeah? Well did you ever drink panther piss? the liquid fuel out of torpedoes? **1973** 'B. MATHER' *Snowline* v. 57 Locally distilled stuff of the genus known as panther piss. **1929** *Amer. Speech* IV. 386 Whiskey is sometimes called *donk* or *mule* because of its..'kick'... *Panther-sweat*..and *rat-track whiskey* are less easily classified.

panti-, see next.

panties (pæ·ntiz), *sb. pl.* Also occas. **pantees.** [dim. of PANTS *sb. pl.*] **1. a.** Men's trousers or shorts. Usu. in derog. contexts.

1845 *Knickerbocker* XXVI. 433 If your panties weren't sheeted home at the bottom, you'd out-jump a monkey. **1848** W. E. BURTON *Waggeries* 19, I hadn't on nothin'..only a blue cotting shirt and sail-cloth pantys. *Ibid.* 95 I've a Colt's revolver in each pantey's pocket. **1910** KIPLING *Divers. Creatures* (1917) 310 The umpires, all in short panties, conferred. **1928** *Weekly Dispatch* 27 May 15/7 Panties for boys and skirts for girls..are being made *very* short. **1930** E. POUND *XXX Cantos* xviii. 82 And he was my gawd scared out of his panties.

b. Short-legged or legless knickers worn by women and girls.

1908 M. MORGAN *How to dress Doll* vi. 59 The undergarment is..easily made, for the little waist and panties are cut in one piece. **1932** *New Yorker* 11 June 40/1 There is a lace brassière top on a circular satin slip, and panties..are built in underneath. **1958** *Times* 25 Apr. 13/3 Brand new ex-Wren officers' silk/wool panties. **1969** M. PEI *Words in Sheep's Clothing* (1970) v. 34 'Panties'..short, abbreviated pants worn by women and children (men, as everyone knows, wear shorts, not panties). **1972** F. WARNER *Maquettes* 39 Bra and panties. **1976** J. CROSBY *Snake* (1977) xxxv. 216 She..picked up her panties, and slipped them on. After that the sweater, the skirt, stockings, and shoes.

c. Also *transf.* and *fig.*

1909 *Sat. Even. Post* 24 Apr. 15/3 New York..would be inhabited by cow-persons in décolleté leather panties. **1936** L. C. DOUGLAS *White Banners* ii. 42 There won't be any French chops with pink panties and a little bite of meat about the size of a peppermint lozenge. **1949** *Sat. Even. Post* 26 Mar. 35/2 Large bottles in woven straw panties stood on the checked table top.

2. *sing.*, as **pantie, panty.** = sense 1 b above. Also *attrib.* orig. *U.S.*

1932 *New Yorker* 11 June 28 (Advt.), If ever a garment could outwit that old ogre depression, it's the pantie in this picture... It is made of celanese. **1939** *Reader's Digest* May 107/2 There is nothing so mournful as a pantie manufacturer who cannot get space in the pantie section [of the garment-making area of New York City]. **1951** C. W. & P. CUNNINGTON *Hist. Underclothes* 246 For sports, pantie trunks and pantie briefs. **1960** *Harper's Bazaar* Apr. 56/1 Striped pantie; boned perforated foam bra. **1961** *New Yorker* 2 Dec. 48 Rogers places you there in the briefest baby doll and matching panty. **1970** *Focus* June 11/3 No apparent dye loss when washed, but pantie part shrank an inch all round.

3. *Comb.* of **pantee, panti, pantie, panty. a.** In names of women's undergarments combining the function of panties with that of some other undergarment, as *panty-belt, -blouse, -brassière, -girdle, -hose, -stockings, -tights.*

1957 A. ADBURGHAM in *Punch* 27 Mar. 419/1 How pert the little pantie-belt, blue-spotted, with its blue-spotted suspenders to match. **1961** S. PRICE *Just for Record* iii. 26 The sort of birds I lie me down with..shimmy out of their pantie-belts. **1971** *Guardian* 24 Aug. 9/1 Pantie-blouses are..the newest thing in all-in-one garments. **1925** *Ladies' Home Jrnl.* May 87/3 Panty-brassiere, $12. **1941** HERMER & MAY *Havana Mañana* 43 We recommend panty-girdles of mesh elastic and net or lace bras. **1946** [see *LASTEX]. **1961** *She* Feb. 42 Au Fait's panty girdle..evenly supports tummy, behind, hips and thighs. **1961** *Housewife* Apr. 103/1 Wear a strong pantie-girdle—not a roll-on. **1968** J. IRONSIDE *Fashion Alphabet* 71 *Panti-girdle*, lightly elasticated briefs, exercising some control over bulges. **1972** E. T. RENBOURN *Materials & Clothing in Health & Dis.* xix. 387 The pantie-girdle syndrome has crept into the recent literature. Here, marked constriction of the circulation of the upper thigh..leads to aching legs and..swelling ankles. **1972** J. WAMBAUGH *Blue Knight* (1973) vii. 98 A micro-mini that showed her red-flowered panty girdle when she sat down. **1963** *N.Y. Times* 22 Dec. 19 Our exclusive panti-hose... She'll enjoy the comfort and freedom of..panty tops and micromesh stockings, all in one. No garters, no seams. **1967** *Vogue* 15 Oct. 16 (Advt.), For 12/11 you can treat yourself to Panti-hose seam tights. **1970** *Focus* June 9/2 Invented ten years ago, tights (or pantie-hose) gained ground with the advent of the mini-skirt in 1968. **1970** *Toronto Daily Star* 24 Sept. 38/8 (Advt.), The first quality panty hose at a sensible price. **1972** G. V. HIGGINS *Friends E. Coyle* xviii. 108 She don't own no pants... Wears them panty hose. **1975** *Publishers Weekly* 1 Dec. 67/2 The type of wan, lightweight heroine who can't support her own pantyhose let alone a mystery novel. **1976** M. SPARK *Takeover* iv. 41 She pulled, through her dress, at the top of her panty-hose, setting herself to rights like a schoolgirl. **1966** P. O'DONNELL *Sabre-Tooth* vii. 104 The combined pantie-stockings she always wore. **1968** S. E. ELLACOTT *Everyday Things in Eng. 1914–1968* iv. 69 For some years previously [to 1966], during cold weather, women had worn 'tights' (pantee stockings), and these were now developed in sheer nylon for everyday wear with mini-skirts. **1968** *Vogue* 15 Apr. 92 Pantie-stockings,..3 gns. **1971** *Sunday Nation* (Nairobi) 11 Apr. 37/1 (Advt.), Stockings, Panty-stockings..Tights. **1971** *Guardian* 24 Aug. 9/1 Stocking tights and pantie stockings. **1970** *Guardian Weekly* 11 Apr. 14 'Sorry,' the man in overalls said. 'We're right out of them. What about a pair of panti-tights?' **1970** G. F. NEWMAN *Sir, You Bastard* viii. 207 Her lunch-break dash to Selfridges for pantie-tights, or whatever.

b. *spec.* **panty leg,** the leg part of a pair of panties; (with hyphen) *attrib.*, having such legs; **panty raid** *U.S.*, a prank involving the raiding of women's rooms for trophies of underwear; also *transf.* or *fig.*; **panty-waist** *U.S.*, (*a*) a sissy, a coward; used *attrib.*, effeminate, weak; (*b*) (*rare*) a garment, usu. for children, consisting of panties attached to a bodice.

1908 M. MORGAN *How to dress Doll* vi. 61 Face the armholes, neck and panty legs with a narrow facing. **1963** *New Yorker* 8 June 62 Favorite panty-leg bathing suit. **1966** *Time* 2 Dec. 53 Gold and silver pantyleg stockings..are selling so fast stores can't keep them in stock. **1952** *Stars & Stripes* (Pacific ed.) 21 May 2/3 A wild wave of panty raids swept a dozen college campuses Monday night... The [Univ. of] Colorado raid was staged by 1500 male students intent on seizing intimate trophies of lingerie. *Ibid.* 2/5 More than 1000 Northwestern university male students Monday went on a gleeful 'panty raid', stealing 'all the underwear in sight' and carrying a bewildered police sergeant on their shoulders. **1953** *Newsweek* 11 May 94/1 Traditionally, American undergraduates seem to regard the coming of spring as the rightful time to raise various kinds of hell. Be it goldfish eating, panty raids, or general disturbance of the town peace, boys will be boys, and, more recently, girls will be girls. **1957** TURNER & KILLIAN *Collective Behavior* 208 The fad may also exist as a *permission* to act contrary to the folkways and mores, as in the example of college 'panty raids'. **1968** *Listener* 3 Oct. 428/2 'I think we should organise a political panty raid.' There is little organised opposition to the radicals from other students, although one group did deplore 'holding members of the administration captive and burning irreplaceable files of professors who are unsympathetic.' **1936** *Amer. Speech* XI. 280/1 *Panty-waist*, a sissy. **1937** *Sun* (Baltimore) 28 Apr. 6 (Advt.), Now Mike don't be calling *me* a panty waist. **1939** C. MORLEY *Kitty Foyle* 15 Some of my pantywaists and nightgowns. **1942** *Short Guide Gt. Brit.* (U.S. War Dept.) 5 The English language didn't spread across the oceans and over the mountains and jungles and swamps of the world because these people were panty-waists. **1951** M. McLUHAN *Mech. Bride* (1967) 125/1 No panty-waist humanitarianism here. **1952** N. SPAIN in C. Asquith *Second Ghost Bk.* 33, I should have said that I was pretty tough... I didn't do too badly in the War. I was in the Marines and they don't encourage panty waists in the Marines. **1971** 'A. BURGESS' *MF* x. 116 Some goddam British poet with one of these pantiwaist names, like Vere de Vere. **1971** H. A. SMITH *View from Chivo* i. 7 He is a pantywaist kind of fellow, very *dainty* about things. **1975** *Daily Colonist* (Victoria, B.C.) 30 July 5/3 When they [*sc.* the police] do lay hands on the culprits and get them to the courtroom they are let down by our pantywaist judges.

pantile. 1. c. Delete † *Obs.* and add later examples.

1831 M. EDGEWORTH *Let.* 16 Apr. (1971) 525 Yesterday I went to Tunbridge Wells.., saw the Pantiles... The pantiles looked to me wondrous small and narrow and the roof over the row too low. **1907** *Daily Chron.* 29 Jan. 8/5 It is at the east end of the Pantiles that the original spring,..comes to the surface. **1936** *N. & Q.* 26 Dec. 461/2 The old Chapel of Ease..at entrance to the Pantiles, Tunbridge Wells..was built in 1684. *Ibid.*, When I was at school at Tunbridge Wells..I used to be taken to a church, close to the Pantiles. **1974** *Encycl. Brit. Micropædia* X. 179/1 The Pantiles Parade, with the original chalybeate spring..is preserved.

pantiled *a.* (later examples.)

1951 [see *mansarded* adj. s.v. *MANSARD]. **1963** *Guardian* 5 Mar. 7/2 A precipitous assembly of orange pantiled houses. **1978** M. BUTTERWORTH *X marks Spot* III. i. 121 They passed over a red pantiled roof of a farmhouse.

panting, *vbl. sb.* Add: **b.** *spec.* In Shipbuilding: the movement of the plates of the ship's hull under stress, esp. occurring at the fore and aft ends of the ship. Also *attrib.*, often in names of structures designed to prevent such movement.

1885 H. PAASCH *From Keel to Truck* 24/1 *Panting* (of a ship). **1899** E. L. ATTWOOD *Text-bk. Theoret. Naval Archit.* 212 Panting beams and stringers to be fitted at the after end. **1904** A. C. HOLMS *Pract. Shipbuilding* I. ix. 105 At the stern, panting stresses are usually unimportant. **1922** C. M. SWAINSTON *Reed's Seamanship* (ed. 23) I. 187 The principal methods to resist panting are:—Closer spacing of frames, double frames, an extra tier of beams called *panting beams*, broadening of the stringers called *panting stringers*, [etc.]. **1927** G. BRADFORD *Gloss. Sea Terms* 124 *Panting strains*, those produced by..the pressing in and out of a ship's plates due to the pressure of the waves. *Ibid.* 125 The *panting stringers* reinforce the plates against these stresses, along the sides, and *panting beams* and *frames* at the bow. **1961** F. H. BURGESS *Dict. Sailing* 156 *Panting*, the vibrations of the forward plates caused by the variable resistance of the water. *Ibid.*, *Panting beam*, a strengthened beam fitted forward to decrease vibration.

pantless (pæ·ntlės), *a.* [f. *PANT *sb.*[3] + -LESS.] Wearing no pants.

1880 S. LAKEMAN *What I saw in Kaffir-Land* xi. 136 They [*sc.* Cape baboons] shot from branch to branch,..like flying fish, or as pantless Zazel shoots from the cannon's mouth to her swinging rope. **1948** D. BALLANTYNE *Cunninghams* 260 Three pantless Maori kids met him. **1969** N. BEHN *Shadowboxer* (1970) ix. 79 He stared directly up the plump pantless female thighs. **1971** W. HANLEY *Blue Dreams* xxi. 331 Then, bra-ed but pantless, she moved toward Walter.

panto (pæ·nto). [Abbrev. PANTOMIME *sb.* (*a.*).] = PANTOMIME *sb.* (*a.*) 3 in Dict. and Suppl.; also *attrib.*

1852 E. L. BLANCHARD *Jrnl.* 15 Sept. in Scott & Howard *Life E. L. Blanchard* (1891) I. 98 At home till 5 p.m. fixing on titles for pantos... Arrange for panto with Smith for Drury. **1914** C. MACKENZIE *Sinister St.* II. IV. ii. 865 'You're on the stage, aren't you?' 'I usually get into panto,' she admitted. **1922** JOYCE *Ulysses* 533 Immoral panto boys in flesh tights. **1929** J. B. PRIESTLEY *Good Companions* II. i. 251 That's right. A lot of experience. C.P. work, halls, panto, low comedy in legit., know it all. **1937** G. FRANKAU *More of Us* xi. 121 Eke tho' of words bard still commands a brainful Which she can still make dance like panto elves. **1962** *Oxford Times* 1 June 23/4 Orsino and Viola..the latter part, although difficult in its mixture of boyishness and charm, should not really be played as a principal boy in panto. **1968** *Listener* 26 Dec. 871/3 Nor has the standard of the witless, panto-type sketches been raised. **1969** *Ibid.* 28 May 663/1, I was glad that Hazel Hughes should play her..like Kenneth Williams as painless panto dame. **1976** *Sunday Post* (Glasgow) 26 Dec. 3/3 She was transporting it from Calderpark Zoo to the Pavilion panto, where it was due to appear in the cartoon spot featuring TV personality Glen Michael. **1977** *R.A.F. News* 11–24 May 3/5 The organizers ran an 'ad lib' version of the panto 'Cinderella'.

pantocain (pæ·ntokēin). *Pharm.* Also **-caine.** [a. G. *pantocain*, f. Gr. παντο- PANTO- + *-cain*, after G. *cocain* COCAINE.] The hydrochloride salt, $C_{15}H_{24}N_2O_2{\cdot}HCl$, of a diamino-ester which is used as a local anæsthetic; also called *amethocaine* or *tetracaine hydrochloride*.

1931 *Manuf. Chem.* II. 105/1 The new local anæsthetic of the I.G. Farbenindustrie, Pantocain,..has been systematically evolved from the novocaine series and is the hydrochloride of *p*-butylaminobenzyldimethylamino-ethanol. **1937** *Brit. Med. Jrnl.* 20 Nov. 1036/2 Local infiltration with 0·5 per cent. pantocaine caused excessive oedema of the lids and face..and intense itching. **1942** PARSONS & STALLARD *Dis. Eye* (ed. 10) xxi. 431 Particles of lime must be perseveringly picked out with forceps, after previous application of pantocain. **1970** *Brain Res.* XIX. 102 The neck afferents were eliminated by..the blockage of afferent fibers by Pantocain injection into the intervertebral foramen.

Pantocrator (pæntǫ·krătəɹ). Also **Pantokrator.** [ad. Gr. παντοκράτωρ almighty.] With reference to God or Christ: the Almighty, all-ruler; hence, an artistic representation of the figure of Christ, esp. as a characteristic form in Byzantine art.

1871 RUSKIN *Fors Clavigera Letter 12* 11 In the Apocalypse it is 'Lord, All governing'—Pantocrator—which we weakly translate 'Almighty'. **1911** O. M. DALTON *Byzantine Art & Archaeol.* xii. 672 In the Last Judgement, and as the Pantokrator, Christ is bearded, because in his function as Judge he is regarded as merely continuing his earthly mission. **1931** *Antiquity* V. 508 With the exception of the Pantocrator in the dome..the Daphni mosaics belong to the pictorial, representational, Hellenic tradition. **1947** C. STEWART *Byzantine Legacy* v. 111 The condition of the Church of Christ Pantocrator is typical of many. **1950** A. HUXLEY *Themes & Variations* 174 Young Domenikos received a sound Greek education and studied painting... That indecently human personage—was that supposed to be the Pantocrator? **1962** *New Statesman* 25 May 768/3 It [*sc.* a cathedral tapestry] fails to achieve the commanding presence of a Byzantine pantocrator. **1963** D. T. RICE *Art of Byzantine Era* 88 In Basil's church the bust of Christ Pantocrator dominated the building from the dome. **1970** *Oxf. Compan. Art* 182/1

The Iconoclastic crisis..culminated in the formation of a new religious iconography... It was then that the decorative scheme of the Byzantine church was fixed..: in the dome the Pantocrator (Christ the Ruler) surrounded by archangels. **1974** D. YARWOOD *Archit. Europe* iii. 110/2 The mosaics and frescoes..of the dome..illustrate the Christ Pantocrator in all His Glory.

Hence **pantocr·atic** *a. rare.*

1949 AUDEN *Under Sirius* in *Horizon* Oct. 210 And out of the open sky The pantocratic riddle breaks;—'Who are you and why?'

pantograph, *sb.* Add: **c.** A jointed, self-adjusting framework on the top of an electric locomotive for conveying the current from overhead wires.

1907 F. H. DAVIES *Elect. Power & Traction* xxiii. 269 The..collecting gear is that known as the pantograph, and the object..is to permit of high speed running and reversal of direction without any corresponding adjustment of the gear. **1920** *Glasgow Herald* 23 Sept. 7 Electric locomotives can..be fitted..with pantograph collectors. **1930** *Engineering* 20 June 793/3 Only one pantograph was used at all speeds, so long as the current did not exceed 1800 amps. **1957** *Railway Mag.* Mar. 159/2 The pantograph is raised by pressing the push-button in the driving trailer. **1970** *Daily Mail* 8 Jan. 1/4 The pantograph..appears to have jumped on top of the wire instead of running beneath it. **1977** *Modern Railways* Dec. 492/1 The primary reason for the central position was power collection problems at high speed in a two-power-car formation if each power car had its own pantograph.

d. Used of other mechanisms in the form of a movable diamond-shaped trellis or lazy tongs.

1942 *Archit. Rev.* XCII. 46 (*caption*) The early tube carriages of 1906, *seqq.*, had pantograph doors at both ends. **1975** *Observer* 9 Mar. 33/5 The driver's screen-wiper is a pantograph type and sweeps a commendably large area but the passenger's section of the screen has a big unswept corner.

pantograph (pæ·ntŏgrɑf), *v.* [f. the sb.] *trans.* To enlarge by means of a pantograph. Cf. PANTOGRAPHING *vbl. sb.* in Dict.

1934 in WEBSTER. **1936** J. AGATE in *Sunday Times* 12 Apr. 5/1 Can a drop-earring be pantographed to chandelier-size without loss of exquisiteness?

pantographically, *adv.* (Examples.)

1911 E. C. WORDEN *Nitrocellulose Industry* II. xiv. 697 These enamels may be closely imitated..by taking a given pattern, enlarging it pantographically or otherwise, [etc.]. **1945** F. J. CAMM et al. *Newnes Plastics Manual* xii. 135 This machine [*sc.* the 'Keller' die-sinking machine] will produce all kinds of dies and jigs by a process of copying from a pattern pantographically.

pantoic (pæntōᵘ·ik), *a. Chem.* [f. as *PANTOYL + -IC.] *pantoic acid*, the unstable parent carboxylic acid $C_6H_{12}O_4$, of the pantoyl radicle.

1945 *Jrnl. Biol. Chem.* CLXI. 513 In connection with studies on the antagonistic action of pantoyltaurine on salicylate inhibition of *Escherichia coli* we have observed that pantoic acid, or, more properly, the pantoate ion, is more active than pantolactone. **1966** *McGraw-Hill Encycl. Sci. & Technol.* XIV. 259/2 α-Ketoisovaleric acid ..is also a precursor of leucine and of the pantoic acid moiety of pantothenic acid.

Hence **pa·ntoate**, the anion, or a salt or ester, of pantoic acid.

1945 [see above]. **1968** *Compar. Biochem. & Physiol.* XXVII. 647 Pantothenate and pantoate inhibit the growth of *Trypanosoma lewisi in vitro.*

pantomime, *sb.* (*a*). **3.** Add to def.: By the 20th century, the traditional form changed, with the loss of the pantaloon and harlequin features. The entertainment, primarily for children, is now based on the dramatization of a fairy tale or nursery story, and includes songs and topical jokes, buffoonery and slapstick, and standard characters such as a pantomime 'dame', played by a man, a leading boy, played by a woman, and a pantomime animal, e.g. horse, cat, goose, played by actors dressed in a comic costume, with some regional variations. (Further examples.)

1896 *Pall Mall Mag.* Oct. 302/1 She was still playing principal boy in the pantomime—a gay, gallant Prince, in plumed cap and tights. **1901** R. J. BROADBENT *Hist. Pantomime* xxi. 225 Present-day Pantomime, with the immense sums spent annually on its gorgeous spectacular display and costly dresses..is a subject that is well known to us all... The best parts are, as a general rule, allotted to music-hall 'stars' whose names will draw the most money. **1911** *Times* 7 Nov. 9/4 Some of us would have passed through a childhood of tasteless pantomimes, lacking the most exciting of their three annual thrills, which were always the clown, the 'principal boy', and 'Jimmie' Glover. **1950** *Oxf. Jun. Encycl.* IX. 273/2 Pantomimes of to-day are on a splendidly lavish scale, with hundreds of performers. They all have their stock characters... They provide many of the catch phrases and popular songs of the season during their long runs.., often from Christmas till Lent. **1965** D. ARUNDELL *Story of Sadler's Wells* xii. 149 Phelps began his 1847–8 season on 23rd August..with of course a grand pantomime at Christmas (pantomime now meaning the extravaganza fairy-tale as we understand it today). **1978** *Times Lit. Suppl.* 24 Feb. 247/2 The town is agog over the annual pantomime which opens on Boxing Day.

b. *transf.* and *fig.*

1781 G. SELWYN *Let.* 27 Feb. in *15th Rep. R. Comm. Hist. Manuscripts* App. VI. 464 in *Parl. Papers 1897* (C. 8551) LI. 1, I believe there is no actor upon the stage of either theatre who, repeating what the author has wrote, does not, at the same time, recite his own private sentiments oftener, than our pantomimes in Parliament. **1837** DICKENS *Let.* 13 Feb. (1965) I. 236 Oliver and the Pantomime of Life are both finished, and with the Printer. **1941** *Penguin New Writing* III. 109 It's a proper pantomime. The old Tabbies'll have to mind their dignities if they steps out to-day. **1972** *Times* 7 Aug. (Jamaica Suppl.) p. v/4 The uniquely Jamaican 'pantomime'..has evolved into the musical comedy formula incorporating topical allusions..along with folklore characters.

5. Further *attrib.* and *Comb.* examples.

1765 H. TIMBERLAKE *Mem.* 80 [The Cherokees] are.. very dexterous at pantomime dances; several of which I have seen performed that were very diverting. **1883** D. COOK *On Stage* I. x. 219 In the pantomime season, or whenever any great pageant or spectacle is to be produced, these plots are of prodigious extent. **1901** R. J. BROADBENT *Hist. Pantomime* xix. 196 This clashing.. cannot but..adversely affect the box-office receipts, unless, of course the Pantomime-goer makes a point of 'doing the round'. **1908** G. B. SHAW *Pen Portraits* (1932) 74 A pantomime animal with two men in it is a mistake when the two are not very carefully paired. **1919** —— *Great Catherine* 114 They..produced scene after scene of.. tragic relief in the torture chamber with the monarch as pantomime demon committing real atrocities. **1922** JOYCE *Ulysses* 431 In pantomime dame's stringed mobcap, crinoline and bustle, widow Twankey's blouse..and cameo brooch. **1935** T. S. ELIOT *Murder in Cath.* i. 41 All things are unreal, Unreal or disappointing: The Catherine wheel, the pantomime cat, The prizes given at the children's party. **1939** —— *Old Possum's Pract. Cats* 37 In the Pantomime season I never fell flat. **1946** M. DICKENS *Happy Prisoner* ix. 189 He had been afraid they were going to guy her up like a pantomime dame. **1967** *Listener* 19 Oct. 513/2 Everyone will want to see Alec Guinness do his pantomime-dame act in *Wise Child.* **1973** 'A. HALL' *Tango Briefing* viii. 99 Whether you die like a man or the back end of a pantomime horse you're going to stop breathing. **1976** M. GILBERT *Night of Twelfth* xvii. 156 Think of old Dip in a wig and falsies. He'd look like a pantomime dame.

pantomime, *v.* Add: **1.** Also, to behave as though in a pantomime.

1958 *Spectator* 8 Aug. 187/2 The vanity of a Lloyd George or a Ramsay MacDonald, who preferred pantomiming round the world in a continual circus to staying put where they belonged.

Hence **pa·ntomimed** *ppl. a.*

1950 A. RONELL in Manvell & Huntley *Technique Film Music* (1957) iii. 137 His pantomimed thoughts find voice through the inflection of instruments whose colours express Harpo's spirited style.

pa·ntomimish, *a.* [PANTOMIME *sb.* (*a.*) + -ISH[1].] = PANTOMIMIC *a.* 2.

1923 *Glasgow Herald* 3 Feb. 6/6 A few veterans may recall how pantomimish Mr. Gladstone looked when..he borrowed the hat of a colleague.

pantomography (pæntŏmǫ·grăfi). *Med.* [f. PAN(ORAMIC *a.* + *TOMOGRAPHY.] A form of tomography for obtaining radiographs of curved layers of an object, *spec.* the teeth and jaws, by rotation of the body and film during exposure; a further modification of the technique is *ORTHOPANTOMOGRAPHY.

1952 Y. V. PAATERO in *Suomen Hammaslääkäriseuran Toimituksia* XLVIII. 7 Pantomography—a tomographic method for roentgenographing curved surfaces. **1954** —— in *Acta Radiologica* XLI. 321 A new method of tomographic roentgenography (which I subsequently named pantomography.) *Ibid.* 326 Since the roentgen beam in pantomography is relatively narrow, it is obvious that secondary radiation emanates from only a narrow portion of the object. **1956** K. C. CLARK *Positioning in Radiog.* (ed. 7) xxviii. 536/2 Pantomography..By this method of simultaneous movement of head and film in front of the slit diaphragm of the tube, a progressive panoramic view of the whole jaw is produced. **1969** G. J. VAN DER PLAATS *Med. X-Ray Technique* (ed. 3) iv. 104 Pantomography is mainly applied in dental radiography.

Hence **panto·mogram**, a radiograph obtained by pantomography; **panto·mograph** (see quot. 1954[1]); **pa:ntomogra·phic, -gra·phical** *adjs.*

1952 Y. V. PAATERO in *Suomen Hammaslääkäriseuran Toimituksia* XLVIII. 7 Divergence of rays in pantomographical roentgenography. *Ibid.*, Taking of lateral roentgenograms of jaw with the pantomographic method. **1954** —— in *Acta Radiologica* XLI. 321 *Pantomograph*, a device used with a normal roentgen apparatus, which produces pantomographic roentgenograms = pantomograms. *Ibid.*, Thus, pantomographic roentgenography must be distinguished from all previous tomographic methods which produce roentgenographic representations of level surfaces. *Ibid.* 326 The pantomograph used rotates around its axis once every 20 seconds.

pantonal (pænˌtōᵘ·nəl), *a.* [PAN- + TONAL *a.*] Used as a synonym for 'atonal', in twelve-tone music; including all tonalities; hence **panto·nalism, pantona·lity.**

1958 R. R. RETI *Tonality, Atonality, Pantonality* III. iii. 70 The question of how in the realm of pantonality the problem of consonance and dissonance is treated. *Ibid.*, 73 The first example tending towards the pantonal, the second towards the atonal concept. **1961** *Times* 6 Dec. 17/6 It is true enough that a crowd of Muscovites do not sing pantonal fugues. **1963** *Listener* 31 Jan. 220/3 In some sections I have expanded this pantonality into harmonic structures which vertically include up to twenty-three notes. **1966** *Ibid.* 19 May 736/1 Schoenberg disliked the word 'atonal', and preferred the expression 'pantonal', inclusive of all tonalities. **1970** W. APEL *Harvard Dict. Mus.* (ed. 2) 640/1 *Pantonality, pantonal,* the inclusion of all tonalities. The terms are sometimes used instead of atonality and atonal.

Pantopon (pæ·ntopǫn). *Pharm.* Also **pantopon.** [f. PANT- + OP(IUM *sb.* + *-on.*] A proprietary name in the U.S. for a mixture of the hydrochlorides of the opium alkaloids. Cf. *OMNOPON.

1909 *Chem. Abstr.* III. 944 Pantopon..contains according to Sahli..all the opium alkaloids. 1g. = 5g. opium. **1910** *Official Gaz.* (U.S. Patent Office) 1 Feb. 183/1 F. Hoffmann-La Roche & Co., Basel, Switzerland. Filed Sept. 8, 1909. *Pantopon...* A pharmaceutical preparation containing all the alkaloids of opium in an easily-soluble state and in a form suitable for subcutaneous injections. **1940** H. A. MCGUIGAN *Appl. Pharmacol.* 524 It is claimed that pantopon causes less depression of the respiration, less nausea, and has a slower and more prolonged action [than morphine]. **1953** W. BURROUGHS *Junkie* (1972) xii. 121 Lupita sells her stuff in papers. It is supposed to be heroin. Actually, it is pantopon cut with milk sugar and some other crap. **1972** *Biol. Abstr.* LIV. 1738/2 The changes in histamine may have been affected by the narcotics—amobarbital and Pantopon.

pantothenic (pæntoþe·nik), *a. Biochem.* [f. Gr. πάντοθεν from every side (f. παντο- PANTO-) + -IC.] *pantothenic acid*: an oily, optically active carboxylic acid, $HOCH_2C(CH_3)_2$-$CHOH{\cdot}CO{\cdot}NH(CH_2)_2COOH$, which is widely distributed in plant and animal tissues (mainly in combined form as coenzyme A), is essential for the growth of yeast and certain bacteria, and is a member of the vitamin B complex.

1933 R. J. WILLIAMS et al. in *Jrnl. Amer. Chem. Soc.* LV. 2925 We can safely regard the activity [in stimulating the growth of yeast] as due to a single acid. Since this acid appears to be of very widespread occurrence..we have tentatively called it 'pantothenic' acid. **1953** J. RAMSBOTTOM *Mushrooms & Toadstools* viii. 82 Some strains of *Saccharomyces cerevisiae* require inositol, biotin, aneurin, pantothenic acid and other factors. **1960** *Times* 2 July 2/6 Certain..vitamins [in royal jelly]..are almost entirely members of the B-complex, and include an unusually high proportion of pantothenic acid. **1974** PASSMORE & ROBSON *Compan. Med. Stud.* III. I. xxiv. 30/1 Pantothenic acid deficiency has been considered, on the basis of therapeutic trials, to be the cause of the burning feet syndrome.

Hence **pantothe·nate**, the anion, or an ester or salt, of pantothenic acid.

1941 *Chem. Abstr.* XXXV. 3606 $[\alpha]^{24}_D$ for the pantothenate ion is calcd. to be −26·8°. **1955** *Sci. News Let.* 1 Oct. 211/1 The cancer cells, Dr. Eagle finds, need these seven vitamins: choline, folic acid, nicotinamide, pantothenate, pyridoxal, riboflavin and thiamine. **1974** R. W. DOSKOTCH in W. O. Foye *Princ. Med. Chem.* xxv. 613/2 The commercial synthesis of calcium pantothenate starts with isobutyraldehyde and formaldehyde.

pantothermal (pæntoþɜ̄·ɹmăl), *a.* [f. PANTO- + THERMAL *a.*] Able to stand a wide range of temperature.

1906 *Athenæum* 10 Feb. 175/1 A revision of all captures ..appeared to show one species..as cosmopolitan and pantothermal.

pantoyl (pæ·ntoil, pæ·ntoˌəil). *Biochem.* [f. *PANTO(THENIC *a.* + -YL.] The optically active radical $HOCH_2C(CH_3)_2CH(OH)CO$—, present in pantothenic acid.

1942 BARNETT & ROBINSON in *Biochem. Jrnl.* XXXVI. 357 Dr. McIlwain..suggested a simplified nomenclature, following which we have adopted a system based on the name 'pantoyl' for the α:γ-dihydroxy-β:β-dimethyl-γ-butyryl radicle. **1971** *Analytical Biochem.* XLII. 8 Pantoyl lactone, the other product of hydrolysis of pantothenates, can be easily and directly evaluated by gas chromatography, providing a simpler method for the quantitation of Vitamin B_5.

Hence **pantoyltau·rine,** a sulphonic acid, $C_8H_{17}O_6NS$, which inhibits the action of pantothenic acid in microorganisms.

1942 *Biochem. Jrnl.* XXXVI. 366 The degree of inhibition by pantoyltaurine depends on the amount of pantothenic acid present in the medium. **1954** E. E. SNELL in Sebrell & Harris *Vitamins* II. ix. 680 Addition of pantoyltaurine increased the lag phase and decreased the rate of growth during the first half of the logarithmic phase of *Streptococcus hemolyticus.* **1968** *Compar. Biochem. & Physiol.* XXVII. 649 When pantoyltaurine, an analogue of pantothenic acid, was incorporated into the culture media, inhibition of growth [of *Trypanosoma lewisi*] was observed.

pantry, *sb.* Add: **1. b.** Used in the names of tea rooms and cafés.

1948 J. BETJEMAN *Sel. Poems* 79 The shops..on the Esplanade—The Circulating Library, the Stores, Jill's Pantry. **1958** J. CANNAN *And be a Villain* i. 16 Pam's Pantry started to serve tea at three-thirty. **1967** M. KENYON *Whole Hog* xvii. 169 They agreed on the Pancake Pantry..Liz said the pancakes were good. **1971** S. PHILLIPS *Death in Sheep's Clothing* iv. 36 A teashop known as *Pam's Pantry*..with fresh chintz curtains, flowers on each tiny oak table, and a lot of unidentifiable brass objects hanging from the beams.

2. *pantry work*; **pantry-maid**, a maidservant who has duties in the pantry.

1921 *Dict. Occup. Terms* (1927) § 900 *Pantry maid*.. washes china and glass and cleans up in pantry. **1928** *Daily Tel.* 5 June 4/7 He had paid her 22s a week as a pantrymaid. **1973** *Courier & Advertiser* (Dundee) 12 Jan. 1/3 (Advt.), Part-Time woman required for general cleaning and pantry work in hotel.

pants, *sb. pl.* Add: **1. a.** No longer 'chiefly U.S.'. Now used for trousers, worn by either men or women, and no longer considered vulgar. **b.** Now used for underpants, panties, or shorts worn as an outer garment: cf. *hot pants* (*HOT *a.* 12 c). (Earlier and later examples.)

1840 E. A. Poe *Peter Pendulum* in *Burton's Gentleman's Mag.* Feb. 88 Standing on one leg three hours, to show off new-touch strapped pants. **1928** R. Campbell *Wayzgoose* ii. 58 Through pants and vest the God explored. **1930** H. G. Wells *Autocracy of Mr. Parham* II. i. 95 He grows more and more independent of the idea that his pants are him. **1940** O. Nash *Face is Familiar* 91 Sure, deck your lower limbs in pants. **1951** T. Sterling *House without Door* xiii. 152 She chose her blue underwear... She laid the pants and brassière on her bed. **1956** H. Gold *Man who was not with It* (1965) i. 5 Grack.. plucked a tricksie in shorts as she wiggled by. He took the thin pants between his horny fingers. **1964, 1968** [see *pantskirt* s.v. *PANT *sb.*[3] 2]. **1971** *New Yorker* 11 Sept. 12/1 (Advt.), The back-zippered tunic is a great topper for skirts and pants. **1973** N. Moss *What's the Difference?* p. ix, I heard an American student at Cambridge University telling some English friends how he climbed over a locked gate to get into his college and tore his pants, and one of them asked in confusion, 'But how could you tear your pants without tearing your trousers?' **1976** *National Observer* (U.S.) 20 Nov. 13/2 The men in flannel shirts and work pants stood in the driveway outside the hillside house and talked about Vivien Kellems.

c. Slang phr. *to be caught with one's pants down*: in a state of embarrassing unpreparedness. orig. *U.S.*

1932 *Amer. Speech* VII. 330 To be caught with one's pants down, to be caught off guard. **1943** N. Balchin *Small Back Room* xiv. 164 We just let him carry on alone. Now, we're caught with our pants down, with nobody knowing anything about the damned thing. **1959** *Times Lit. Suppl.* 10 July 407/2 Here were the 'better elements' caught with their pants down, as Americans coarsely put it. **1963** P. McCutchan *Man from Moscow* iii. 36 There was..four days to go before the arrival of the Foreign Ministers but the West was not going to be caught with its pants down. **1974** 'M. Innes' *Appleby's Other Story* xvi. 133 He overheard Maurice Tytherton, in a great fury, say something to his nephew about having caught him with his pants down. **1976** N. Thornburg *Cutter & Bone* v. 129 His record..did not amount to much more than indiscretion, an embarrassing talent for getting caught with his pants down.

d. Slang phr. *to bore* (or *scare, talk*, etc.) *the pants off* (someone): to bring about (the action of the verb) to a state of extremity.

1933 E. O'Neill *Ah, Wilderness!* I. 38, I tell you you scared the pants off him. **1934** E. Waugh *Handful of Dust* iii. 133 She bores my pants off, but she's a good trier. **1937** N. Coward *Present Indicative* IV. 164 Even if I had known then how much time and ink he [*sc.* a critic] was going to waste in the future roasting the pants off me, I [etc.]. **1939** E. B. White *Quo Vadimus?* II. 65 And if I *did* have a butler named Fish, wouldn't I kid the pants off him? **1940** O. Nash *Face is Familiar* 74 And that Mrs Comfitmonger while pounding her beat has dealt with personalities who would scare the pants off Lombroso. **1953** H. Clevely *Public Enemy* i. 2 'Did you win?' 'We took the pants right off them.' **1956** B. Holiday *Lady sings Blues* (1973) i. 6 Once a girl hit me on the nose and it just about finished me. I took my gloves off and beat the pants off her. **1966** R. Ellison in A. Chapman *New Black Voices* (1972) 402 Where does that idea come from?.. One place (which almost frightened the pants off me) was in *Commentary*. **1968** M. Woodhouse *Rock Baby* vi. 51 He..told me there was an international athletics meeting at White City..and that Denmark would undoubtedly thrash the pants off us. **1972** G. Bromley *In Absence of Body* ix. 119 Usually they take the pants off us, which is not surprising—they play regularly and it's our only game. **1975** 'W. Haggard' *Scorpion's Tale* ii. 23 There's some stupid story the island is haunted... there's something which scares the pants off the local peasantry.

e. In other phrases: *to wear the pants*: to be the dominant member of a household; *to keep one's pants on*: to keep calm, not to panic or get angry; (*by*) *the seat of one's pants*: in the handling of an aeroplane, car, etc.: (by) human instinct or experience, as opposed to technical aid or scientific knowledge. Also in extended uses and with hyphens (*seat-of-the-pants*) as adj. phr.

1931 *Amer. Mercury* Nov. 331/1 He claimed that Peggy was bossy, that she wore the pants and gave orders to Pal. **1936** J. Steinbeck *In Dubious Battle* vi. 83 'I wish it would start,' Jim said... 'Keep your pants on,' said Mac. **1942** *Harper's Mag.* May 626/2 When you check your instruments you find it is doing a correct job of flying and that the seat of your pants and your eyes would have tricked you had you been allowed to do the 'co-ordinating'. **1947** *Richmond* (Virginia) *Times-Dispatch* 26 Dec. 2/3 Even expert flyers can't tell by the feeling in 'the seat of their pants' when an airplane is about to stall. **1957** L. P. Hartley *Hireling* x. 77 She's older than he is and she wears the pants. **1958** *Listener* 20 Nov. 835/3 That's no help to the man who's driving by the seat of his pants, as we used to say in the R.A.F. police. **1965** R. Sheckley *Game of X* (1966) xxi. 146 Flying *was* in fact extremely difficult, but..I was just one of those seat-of-the-pants naturals who instinctively do everything right. **1971** *Sunday Nation* (Nairobi) 11 Apr. 29/1 The type of car which I have just put through one of my seat-of-the-pants road tests—the Alfa-Romeo 1300 GT Junior. **1972** *Times* 18 Sept. 20/4 There was a feeling among the workforce that the firm was being run 'by the seat of the pants'. **1973** E. Bullins *Theme is Blackness* 68 [Mother] Now, put it some place where they'll be safe..understand? Safe! [Daddy] Okay..okay..Matilda..just keep your pants on, will ya? **1977** M. Walker *National Front* i. 17 Mussolini had governed by the seat of his pants, guided in part by his early Socialism, in part by his..bombastic nationalism and above all..by his flair for presentation and publicity. **1978** R. Jansson *News Caper* viii. 85 Thackray was not looking at the instruments... Perhaps that was what they meant by flying by the seat of the pants.

3. *attrib.* and *Comb.*, as *pants pocket*; **pants dress**, a dress with a divided skirt; **pants rabbit** *U.S. slang* (chiefly *Mil.*), a body louse; **pants skirt** = *pantskirt* s.v. *PANT *sb.*[3] 2; **pants suit** = **pant suit*, **trouser suit*.

1964 *Women's Wear Daily* 30 Nov. 4 Catherine Deneuve ordered at Heim a pantsdress in multicolored striped chiffon. **1969** *Sears Catal.* Spring/Summer 32 Floral print especially smart in this pants dress because it's done in navy and white. **1931** E. O'Neill *The Hunted* IV, in *Mourning becomes Electra* (1932) 170 He fumbles in his pants pocket. **1951** T. Sterling *House without Door* vi. 78 He walked down the stairs, struggling for change in his pants pocket. **1974** R. B. Parker *Godwulf Manuscript* xii. 99, I took a jackknife out of my pants pocket. **1918** *Nat. Geogr. Mag.* June 499 They call the things 'pants rabbits' and 'seam squirrels'. **1928** W. H. Upson *Me & Henry & Artillery* 11 Some of the wise crackers in the battery used to call them pants-rabbits, which is not real scientific, as they usually roam around your back and shoulders and seldom hit below the belt. **1937** J. Steinbeck *Of Mice & Men* ii. 36 What the hell kind of bed you giving us, anyways? We don't want no pants rabbits. **1964** *Glamour* July 77 A blouse that looks like challis edged in wool lace, with a wine-dark leather pants-skirt. **1969** *Sears Catal.* Spring/Summer 34 Plaid pants skirt. Twill. Front panel hides plaid culotte. **1964** *Glamour* Dec. 112, 1 and 2 [*sc.* jacket and pants] make a pants-suit that's very current and handsome. **1968** Mrs. L. B. Johnson *White House Diary* 26 June (1970) 691, I changed into a beige pants suit. **1975** *New Yorker* 5 May 81/3 Elizabeth Franz..looked fine in a becoming pants suit.

pantun. Add: (Earlier and later examples.) Also *attrib.*

1783 W. Marsden *Hist. Sumatra* 162 The essentials in the composition of the *pantoon*..are the rythmus and the figure, particularly the latter, which they consider as the life and spirit of the poetry. **1821** J. Leyden tr. *Malay Annals* 83 They sing of it in Pantuns. *Ibid.* 259 There came a Pantun poet, who was famous for his skill in horsemanship. **1964** M. Taib bin Osman in Wang Gung-Wu *Malaysia* III. xv. 211 The *pantun* can be considered as folk-ditty; it is used on almost all occasions in Malay life. **1970** *New Yorker* 14 Nov. 58/1 She drafted three poems—another rondeau, a pantoum, and a cynghanedd. **1975** 'G. Black' *Big Wind* x. 183 She was singing a Malay *pantun*, a verse form tending to the obscene.

panty, see *PANTIES *sb. pl.*

|| **panung** (pā·nuŋ). [Thai.] A Siamese garment, worn by men and women, consisting of a long piece of cloth draped round the lower part of the body.

1857 J. Bowring *Kingdom & People of Siam* I. 132 Of the garments worn by the Siamese, the *panung*..is worn round the waist and thighs. **1886** *Pall Mall Gaz.* 3 Aug. 4/1 Two men dressed in their ordinary garb—only a dark blue 'panung' about their loins (all Siamese wear the panung). **1928** *Daily Express* 13 Mar. 12/2 The Eton crop in Bangkok is as old as the 'panung'—that peculiar garment worn by men and women alike, which resembles a cross between a 'sarong' and a baby's napkin. **1958** *Listener* 18 Dec. 1039/3 Siamese girls..wear their traditional *panung*, or slim skirt folded in front adapted from their own *pasin*.

panzer (pæ·nzəɪ, || pa·ntsər). [G., 'mail, coat of mail'.] Used *attrib.*, of or pertaining to a German armoured unit; also in G. form *Panzerdivision*. As *sb.*, a panzer unit or a member of such a unit. Also *transf.* and *fig.*

1940 *Economist* 20 Apr. 729/1 It is more than silly..to calculate the speed at which Germany's *panzerdivisionen* could traverse the Hungarian plain. **1940** *Topeka* (Kansas) *Daily Capital* 24 June 1 b Delegations deploying to stop Willkie's 'panzer' wire attacks. **1941** *Hutchinson's Pict. Hist. War* 19 Mar.–13 May 189 An Imperial division concentrated round Bengazi was left in the air when the German Panzer inrush swept aside the British armoured brigade. **1942** *R.A.F. Jrnl.* 3 Oct. 5 You were in danger of breaking your leg by falling over a complete panzer division of dachshunds moving from bar to shove ha'penny table on a broad front. **1943** E. J. Pratt *Coll. Poems* (1958) I. 82 And what specific can unmesh The tangle of civilian flesh From the traction of the panzers? **1945** Koestler *Yogi & Commissar* III. iv. 250 Geniuses are panzer-spearheads. **1949** —— *Promise & Fulfilment* II. iii. 234 Just after Glubb's panzers had begun the shelling of the Jewish quarter. **1962** *Listener* 28 June 1117/1 German Panzer troops arriving in Wales last week. *a* **1963** S. Plath *Ariel* (1965) 55, I have always been scared of *you*, with your Luftwaffe..your Aryan eye, bright blue Panzer-man, panzer-man, O You. **1965** *New Statesman* 14 May 759/1 They tried to defend the Book of Genesis against Darwin's *panzers*. **1969** G. Macbeth *War Quartet* 74 Each panzer was a coiled spring, oiled For instant action. **1973** R. Lewis *Blood Money* iii. 30 He served in North Africa during the Second World War in the Panzer Corps. **1975** *Times* 24 June 4/7 Three new brigades have been added to the West German army... The number of tanks in a Panzer battalion is being reduced. **1976** A. White *Long Silence* ix. 83 A lean panzer major walked fro m the other half track.

|| **pao-chia** (bɑuˌdʒyā). Also **pao chia, paochia.** [Chinese *bǎojia.*] In China, a system by which households were organized for the purposes of administration. Also *attrib.*

1937 E. Snow *Red Star over China* II. i. 50 The *pao-chia* system, an ancient method of controlling the peasantry.. is now being widely imposed..by the Kuomintang in China and the Japanese in Manchukuo. *Pao-chia* literally means 'guaranteed armour'. **1959** C. K. Yang *Chinese Village in Early Communist Transition* vii. 103 To increase the effectiveness of governing such a large population.. there had developed the system of collective responsibility, or *pao chia*, rooted far back in Chinese history, especially in the 'new policy' of the Sung prime minister Wang An-shih. **1965** J. Ch'ên *Mao & Chinese Revolution* (1967) I. xi. 246 In the 'orderly' areas, they used the age-old system of collective responsibility known as the *pao-chia*—every 100 families were organized into a *chia* and every 1,000 families into a *pao* in which all members were made responsible for each other's actions. **1973** T. R. Tregear *Chinese* iii. 68 Law and order are maintained very largely through a modification of the old *pao chia* system by which every group of ten households was held responsible for the behaviour of its own members.

|| **pao-tzu** (bɑuˌdzə̄). Also **bao zi.** [Chinese *bāozi.*] A steamed roll with savoury or sweet fillings.

1956 B. Y. Chao *How to cook & eat in Chinese* II. xx. 228 When *man-t'ou*, or Steamed Bread, is filled with stuffing, then it is *pao-tzŭ*. **1972** K. Lo *Chinese Food* I. 61 The miniature *pao-tzu* (steamed buns with various fillings) are sometimes steamed first and finally fried until they are crisp, and served as crispy savouries. *Ibid.* III. 233 *Pao-tzu* are meant to be eaten on their own, like hot sandwiches. **1973** T. R. Tregear *Chinese* iv. 93 The staple diet is boiled millet or kaoliang, *pao tzu* (steamed bread), *tu fu* (bean curd) and vegetables. **1978** *Nagel's Encycl.-Guide: China* 376 The same variety of preparation is to be found in the different sorts of *bao zi*, or rolls stuffed with vegetables and meat (*cai rou bao zi*), or meat alone (*tian jin bao zi*).

pap, *sb.*[2] Add: **1.** *fig.* (Further examples.) Also, *spec.* in *U.S.*, a political appointment or grant; patronage, 'graft'.

1825 *Delaware* (Ohio) *Patron* 10 Feb. 3/2 An irresistible desire..to serve the state, and to taste a little of the 'Treasury Pap', impelled us towards the capital. **1841** *Congress. Globe* 26th Congress 2 Sess. App. 300/2 The very new States are nursed from their chrysalis territorial condition into existence upon Federal pap from the Executive spoon. **1862** in J. B. Ranck *Albert Gallatin Brown* (1937) 217 Young, strong men..were feeding on government pap whilst wounded soldiers..were in a state of positive want. **1894** *Voice* (N.Y.) 6 Sept. 1/6 The Prohibition Party is the only party that is not controlled by public pap-seeking politicians. **1965** *Chicago Schools Jrnl.* Feb. 197/2 Most of the new clientele will have little taste for or interest in traditional literary values. This does not mean that we should give them over to pap. **1976** *Sounds* 11 Dec. 34/2 To describe this record as 'maudlin pap' must be extremely hurtful to Bernie Taupin. His lyrics are the result of his own poignant experience of a broken marriage. **1977** *Lebende Sprachen* XXII. 10/2 The spoils of office, the rewards for political activities..are called sweets, fat, spices, pap (baby food), plum, pie, persimmon, melon, pork, grease, and gravy. **1977** *Rolling Stone* 21 Apr. 84/3 Spector retreated into an increasingly contrived world of sound, lavishing his skill and money on cutting..such soft-core pap as the Righteous Brothers 'Unchained Melody'.

3. *pap-food*; **pap-warmer**, formerly, a contrivance for keeping food or drink warm, usu. incorporating a night-lamp.

1905 *Daily Chron.* 13 May 4/5 Too prolonged use of artificially digested and 'pap-foods' must be avoided. **1920** W. J. Pountney *Old Bristol Potteries* x. 141 Another most interesting piece..is a caudle cup or pap warmer. **1961** L. G. G. Ramsey *Connoisseur New Guide Antique Eng. Pott., Porc. & Glass* 66 Food warmers, catalogued as pap-warmers, performed the duties of night-light shelter as well as keeping liquids warm enough to drink during the night. **1969** E. H. Pinto *Treen* 122 The majority of wooden night-light holders are combined with pap warmers.

pap (pæp), *sb.*[3] Abbreviation of Papa[1]. Also applied to an older man. Chiefly *U.S.*

1844 *Knickerbocker* XXIII. 15 They said, pap wasn't at home. **1854** M. J. Holmes *Tempest & Sunshine* v. 69 Come here, and shake your old pap's paw. **1886** C. M. Yonge *Chantry House* I. xxi. 207 She never took liberties with him, nor called him Pap or any other ridiculous name. **1899** A. Nicholas *Idyl of Wabash* 53 His pap left him right smart of a lump. **1924** W. M. Raine *Troubled Waters* ii. 24 There can't any of you..run me out the way you did Pap Thomson. **1955** D. W. Maurer in *Publ. Amer. Dial. Soc.* XXIV. 105 A *pappy* (or *pap*) is an elderly man.

Pap (pæp), *sb.*[4] Also **pap.** Abbrev. of *Papanicolaou (used only *attrib.*).

1963 Greisheimer & Troyer *Physiol. & Anat.* (ed. 8) xx. 789 The so-called 'Pap' test is so named after Papanicolaou, who with Stockard called attention to the importance of the changes in the vaginal epithelium first in lower animals in connection with estrous cycles. **1969** *Awake!* 8 Nov. 15/1 A study conducted at the University of Chicago 'reportedly shows a sixfold increase in positive Pap smears..among women who have taken oral contraceptives'. **1973** *Sci. Amer.* July 22/3 Of the estimated 2·6 million women served last year by organized family-planning programs,..eight in 10 had annual breast examinations and Pap tests. **1973** *Nation* (Barbados) 16 Dec. 10/4 I'd like to see all of the women who should be having pap smears coaxed into their doctor's offices. **1977** *Spare Rib* May 20/4 Pap smear and breast cancer tests could have been lost.

pap, *v.*[1] Add: **3.** To make into pap.
1927 *Observer* 6 Feb. 14/4 This does not mean papping food for babes; it means speaking intelligibly to grown-ups.

papa[1]. Add: **2.** *transf.* **a.** A woman's lover or husband. *U.S. slang.*
1904 'No. 1500' *Life in Sing Sing* 261, I blew out and rung in with a couple of penny-weighters. A Tommy and his papa... I left them and went with two expert thieves who make it a practice to rob jewelers, a woman and her lover. **1926** L. Hughes in *New Republic* 14 Apr. 223/2, I met a yellow papa, He took my last thin dime... I give it to him cause I loved him But I'll have more sense next time. **1942** —— *Shakespeare in Harlem* 107 That's one time, pretty papa, You'll sure stay in your place. You was a mighty lover and you Ruled me many years. **1960** Wentworth & Flexner *Dict. Amer. Slang* 375 *Papa*, a male lover.
b. Phr. *tell papa*, confide in the speaker.
1929 E. Wallace *Red Aces* v. 48 'Tell papa,' he said. **1961** A. Christie *Pale Horse* xvi. 166 'Come now, tell Papa', said the odious Bradley.
3. *attrib.* or as *adj.*, paternal.
1900 'S. Grand' *Babs* (1901) lxxv. 350 So long as he does not assume papa airs with me, I don't mind.

papa[3] (pā·pā). [Maori.] A soft bluish clay or mudstone found in the North Island of New Zealand.
1873 J. H. H. St. John *Pakeha Rambles through Maori Lands* xi. 183 We descended a steep slide into..a river with a bed of papa rock. **1892** E. S. Brookes *Frontier Life* xvii. 150 The country [Taranaki]..is principally composed of papa rock. **1905** J. M. Thomson *Bush Boys N.Z.* ix. 62 That Papa Rock is beastly stuff to slip... The Papa Rock, of which many of the cliffs in the bush country in New Zealand are formed, is really a very hard blue clay. **1909** G. H. Scholefield *N.Z. in Evolution* i. 12 *Papa* country produces the readiest crops of grass. **1911** W. H. Koebel *In Maoriland Bush* xxiii. 239 The track.. has dented a passage upon the soft pa-pa rock. **1921** H. Guthrie-Smith *Tutira* ii. 9 The materials of which the station is formed are marl or 'papa', sandstone, sandy marl, limestone, and conglomerate. **1949** F. Sargeson *I saw in my Dream* ii. xiii. 128 Nearly all the soil had slipped away and left only great faces of papa. **1969** —— *Joy of Worm* iii. 105 The river had been willing..to slide in casual ripples over slabs of papa, as though to look more closely at a tiny curve of beach.

‖**papabile** (papā·bile), *a.* [It.; cf. Papable *a.*] Of a prelate: worthy of becoming Pope; having good prospects of being elected Pope. Also in pl. form *papabili* and in L. form *papabilis*. Also as *sb.*, a prelate regarded as a possible Pope (during a conclave).
1934 G. Seldes *Vatican* v. 94 Certain cardinals always are *papabili*, or in line for the papacy. **1935** V. Pirie *Triple Crown* 9 Not too many virtues were necessary for a candidate to be considered 'papabile', that is, acceptable to a reasonable amount of voters. **1938** *Times Lit. Suppl.* 1 Jan. 6/2 At the next Conclave he was *papabilis*. **1939** *Daily Tel.* 11 Feb. 12 Cardinal Hlond..and Cardinal Copello..are both considered papabile. **1958** *Times* 29 Oct. 11/3 A number of the younger Cardinals..will still be *papabili* at the next election. **1958** *New Statesman* 1 Nov. 583/3 This week, there were scarcely half-a-dozen *papabili* and the only suitable 'neutral', Roncalli, was 76. **1963** *Times* 4 June 10/1 Cardinals Montini of Milan, Lecaro of Bologna, and Siri of Genoa remain, however, among the *papabile*. **1963** *Economist* 29 June 1342/1 He, alone among the *papabile* cardinals, made a point of nailing his ..colours to the mast. **1973** A. Mann *Tiara* viii. 71 His own integrity, combined with his consummate administrative ability, led many observers to consider him the most *papabile* of the European Cardinals. **1976** *Church Times* 9 July 14/3 The other Italian '*papabile*' figures are numerous. **1978** *Guardian Weekly* 10 Sept. 11/1 The cardinals, who had a wide range of ten papabili to choose from.

papacy. Add: ¶ **2. b.** = Papism.
1914 *Trans. Shropshire Archæol. & Nat. Hist. Soc.* IV. 45 Mr. Jermor seems to have been himself suspected of a leaning towards papacy.

papadam, papadum, varr. Popadam.

Papago (pæ·păgo, pā·păgo), *sb.* and *a.* [Sp., ad. native name.] **A.** *sb.* **a.** An Indian people of the south-western U.S. and northern Mexico; a member of this people. **b.** The Uto-Aztecan language of this people and (in some uses) of the closely related Pima Indians; also called Pima. **B.** *adj.* Of or pertaining to the Papago or their language.
1839 A. Forbes *California* 162 On the River Gila.. Papaga, 4000. **1864** *Harper's Mag.* Dec. 25/1 The Papago Indians also do good service by..killing the hostile savages. **1875** *Encycl. Brit.* II. 538/2 The inhabitants of Arizona are mostly Indians... 4000 Papagoes, a wandering tribe in the south-eastern part of the territory, have no grounds allotted them. **1878** R. J. Hinton *Hand-bk. Arizona* 227 South and west of these lie the old Papago villages and wells. **1911** H. B. Wright *Winning of Barbara Worth* 101 She pointed to a smoky, copper-colored Papago in a green headcloth and decorated shirt. **1912** K. Lumholtz *New Trails in Mexico* 185 Hydrophobia is called in Papago *nótakik*. **1936** *Univ. Arizona Gen. Bull.* iii. 118 These caterpillars feed on a spreading four-o'clock or on the Papago spinach on the desert. **1946** E. E. Cummings *Let.* 31 Jan. (1969) 170, I sat opposite a Papago Indian. **1964** E. A. Nida *Toward Sci. Transl.* viii. 162 Certain problems of translating magic incantations of the Papago Indians of Southern Arizona. **1968** P. M. Postal *Aspects Phonol. Theory* i. 10 The situation described here is based to a certain limited extent on that existing in Papago, a Uto-Aztecan language of the American Southwest. **1973** A. H. Whiteford *N. Amer. Indian Arts* 13 Modeling and paddling is a techniques..till used by the Papago and Yuma of Arizona. **1977** *Language* LIII. 459 L now recognizes..that Papago *hi̵ji̵l* and *PaPay* ..probably do not belong in this cognate set.

papagoite (păpă·gōu,əit). *Min.* [f. prec. + -ite[1].] A basic silicate of calcium, copper, and aluminium, approximately $CaCuAlSi_2O_6(OH)_3$, which is found as blue monoclinic crystals.
1960 Hutton & Vlisidis in *Amer. Mineralogist* XLV. 600 The mineral described herein has been named papagoite after the Indian tribe that inhabited the area in which the active mining center of Ajo is situated. **1965** *Mineral. Abstr.* XVII. 359/2 Papagoite from the type deposit at the Ajo Mine, Arizona.., is monoclinic, with *a* 12·94, *b* 11·52, *c* 4·68Å, *β* 100°30′; space group *C* 2/*m*.

papaia, var. *papaya*: see Papaw.
1914 R. Brooke *Let.* Feb. in E. Marsh *Rupert Brooke* (1918) 108 Great squelchy tropical fruits, custard-apples, papaia, pomegranate,..and the rest. **1932** W. S. Maugham *Narrow Corner* xix. 143 Breakfast in the little hotels in the Dutch East Indies is served at a very early hour. It never varies. Papaia, *œufs sur le plat*, cold meat, and Edam cheese.

papain. Add to def.: which is used to assist the digestion of patients suffering from chronic dyspepsia and gastritis, as a meat tenderizer, and in clarifying beverages. **b.** The pure crystalline protease extracted from papaya latex. (Further examples.)
1937 *Science* 22 Oct. 379/1 (*heading*) Crystalline papain. **1943** Sumner & Somers *Chem. & Methods of Enzymes* 158 The impure papain of commerce is a mixture of two distinct enzymes. **1963** *Daily Tel.* 14 June 17/6 British meat traders are concerned about the use of papain, an enzyme preparation, injected into animals before they are slaughtered, to produce artificially tenderised meat. **1969** T. C. Thorstensen *Pract. Leather Technol.* vi. 100 The enzyme papain introduced into this system exhibited very strong unhairing action. **1972** *Materials & Technol.* V. xix. 700 Papain is a relatively small enzyme, with a molecular weight of 21 000 and an isoelectric point of 8·75.

papalist. Add: Also *attrib.*
1903 *Eng. Hist. Rev.* XVIII. 482 What little significance lies in the expression depends on Llywelyn's clerk's serving up to the papalist primate the conventional phraseology of Roman documents. **1964** P. F. Anson *Bishops at Large* ix. 325 The year 1920 saw the first of several Anglo-Catholic Congresses, and with them a rapid increase of baroque and rococo furnishings in Anglican Papalist churches.

Papality. (Later example in pl.)
1826 W. S. Landor *Imag. Conv.* (ed. 2) I. viii. 163 He resisted the authority of the pope, and refuted the doctrine of transubstantiation, with several other papalities.

papaloi (pa·pa,lwa). [ad. Haitian Creole *papalwa*, f. *papa* father + *lwa* *loa[2].] A voodoo priest. Cf. *mamaloi.
1884 S. St. John *Hayti* v. 184 He again consulted the Papaloi or priest. *Ibid.* v. 194 The Haytians have corrupted the compounds Papa Roi and Maman Roi into Papaloi and Mamanloi. **1935** [see *mamaloi]. **1965** J. von Sternberg *Fun in Chinese Laundry* i. 16 My mind seems full of stealth, it has no goal, no conclusions, and no ambitions, as if a Haitian 'papa loi' had made me into a zombie. **1976** *Billings* (Montana) *Gaz.* 11 July 2-F/5 So he consulted the voodoo 'papaloi', who diagnosed the ailment as a minor spell which had been laid on him by an enemy.

Papanicolaou (pæ:pănikŏlā·ū, pæpăni·kŏlau). *Med.* The name of George Nicholas *Papanicolaou* (1883–1962), Greek-born U.S. anatomist, used *attrib.* and in the possessive with reference to a technique he devised for examining exfoliated or secreted cells, used chiefly as a means of detecting cancer, esp. of the vagina, cervix, and uterus.
1947 *Surg., Gynecol. & Obstetr.* LXXXV. 275 (*heading*) Modifications of the Papanicolaou technique. *Ibid.* 276/2 A number of flakes..were prepared with Papanicolaou's stain. **1956** *Nature* 18 Feb. 330/1 The cells were smeared on microscopical slides coated with egg-albumin or human serum and fixed in Papanicolaou's fixative. **1958** E. Day in R. W. Raven *Cancer* III. xxii. 450 In taking cervical smears by the Papanicolaou method a cotton-tipped applicator is used. **1966** W. H. Cole in R. W. Cumley et al. *Recent Adv. Diagnosis of Cancer* 183 The Papanicolaou stain (1942) represents one of the greatest advances in diagnosis and treatment of cancer during the past several decades. **1972** Graham & Urbach in J. H. Graham et al. *Dermal Path.* xxx. 675/1 During the past three decades the Papanicolaou technique, or various modifications of this method, has been applied to most organ tissues where secretions, exudates, or exfoliated cells can be obtained.

‖ **paparazzo** (paparā·tso). Pl. **paparazzi.** [It.] A free-lance photographer who pursues celebrities to take their pictures. Also *attrib.*
1968 *Daily Tel.* (Colour Suppl.) 29 Nov. 66/4 The anticipated horde of detested *paparazzi*—those scavenging Italian street photographers whose sole purpose appears to be to make every film celebrity's life a misery. **1972** W. Garner *Ditto, Brother Rat!* xxii. 163 Pik..hoisted his camera and began zip-click-zipping at the delegation like a *paparazzo* who's suddenly found nothing between him and royalty in the nude. **1972** *N.Y. Times* 6 July 1 United States District Court Judge Irving Ben Cooper ruled yesterday that the activities of Ronald E. Galella, the self-styled 'paparazzo' photographer, had 'relentlessly invaded' the right to privacy of Mrs. Aristotle Onassis. **1974** V. Gielgud *In Such a Night* vii. 64 The Roman *paparazzi*..are so frequently the terror of film-actors with thin skins. **1974** *Times Lit. Suppl.* 20 Dec. 1439/4 The London Clinic which she had entered a week before with the defiant exclamation to the vulturine *paparazzi* at the entrance, 'Don't think I'm coming here to die, I'm not.' **1977** *Maclean's Mag.* 21 Mar. 64/1 If Margaret was troubled by the publicity or the paparazzi that followed her during her New York stay, she certainly didn't show it.

papaumu (papa,u·mu). *N.Z.* Also **papauma.** [Maori.] A small evergreen tree or shrub, *Griselinia littoralis*, belonging to the family Cornaceæ, native to New Zealand, and distinguished by thick, ovate leaves with shiny upper surfaces; = *broad-leaf* s.v. *broad *a.* D. 2.
1882 W. D. Hay *Brighter Britain!* II. vi. 199 The Karamu or Papaumu.., a family of pretty flowering shrubs. **1928** Cockayne & Turner *Trees N.Z.* 57 Papaumu, Broadleaf. A small tree, 30–50 ft. high, or a shrub, with short irregular trunk. **1956** [see *broad-leaf]. **1966** *Encycl. N.Z.* I. 252/1 Broadleaf, papauma (*Griselinia littoralis*)..is a common hardwood tree throughout the mixed and beech forests.

papaw. The spelling **pawpaw** is now more frequent; cf. *papaya.
1. a. (Later examples.)
1902 *Westm. Gaz.* 24 Dec. 1/3 The little mustard and cress seeds out of the paw-paws. **1908** E. J. Banfield *Confessions of Beachcomber* i. i. 43 Until we grew fruit, the papaw, the quickest and amongst the best, vegetables were more necessary. **1918** *Chambers's Jrnl.* Oct. 669/2 The great golden paw-paw..brought in showers to the earth by a shake of the tree. **1936** *Geogr. Jrnl.* LXXXVIII. 330 Such sub-tropical fruits as bananas, pineapples, pawpaws. **1953** G. Durrell *Overloaded Ark* vi. 106 The cook.. overbalanced into a basket containing eggs and some very ripe and soft pawpaw. **1972** Y. Lovelock *Veg. Bk.* i. 109 The melon tree.., of Central American origin, bears fruit known as pawpaw or papaya.
b. For 'N.O. *Papayaceæ*' substitute 'family Caricaceæ'. (Later examples.)
1920 *Nature* 2 Sept. 36/1 A fungus..causes powdery mildew on the leaves of the pawpaw plant. **1948** *Archit. Rev.* CIV. 94 In a forest of bamboo, palm, bread-fruit and paw-paw trees the white temples rear their phenomenal towers. **1958** J. Carew *Black Midas* iv. 64 We walked past banana, paw-paw, and cocoa trees. **1964** D. Varaday *Gara-Yaka* xi. 96, I intended placing thorn fences around the paw-paw trees. **1966** B. Kimenye *Kalasanda Revisited* 23 Anna remained as alien to Kalasanda as an orange in a papaw tree.
2. (Later examples.)
1882 *Cornhill Mag.* May 580 Often we pass by groves of young paw-paws. **1925** C. E. Mulford *Cottonwood Gulch* xi. 148 You let me catch you foolin' 'round this ranch an' I'll turn you into pulp as soft as a paw-paws! **1969** *Northwest* (*Sunday Oregonian Mag.*) 14 Dec. 19/1 The fragrant aroma and rich flavor of the Pawpaw is reminiscent of many tropical favorites. **1970** B. Miles *Bluebells & Bittersweet* iv. 47/3 *Asimina triloba* (pawpaw)... Large drooping leaves give this a tropical look, and solitary dark-purple, bell-shaped flowers about 2 inches across in May are followed by strange cylindrical fruits 3 to 7 inches long... Pawpaws are difficult to move.
3*. (Usu. with initial capital.) In Jamaica, a slave brought from the region of West Africa so called, in Dahomey, near the town of Ouidah. *Obs.* exc. *Hist.*
1707 H. Sloane *Voy. Jamaica* I. p. liv, The Negros called Papas have most of these scarifications. **1725** *Ibid.* II. 376 Its [*sc.* belly-ach-weed's] use was first made known in Jamaica, by Papau-Negros, and thence call'd Papau-weed. **1740** C. Leslie *New Hist. Jamaica* xi. 307 They generally believe there are Two Gods..; the first they call Naskew in the Papaw language. **1774** E. Long *Hist. Jamaica* II. iii. iii. 425 In 1769, several new masks appeared; the Ebos, the Papaws, &c. having their respective Connús, male and female, who were dressed in a very laughable style. **1793** B. Edwards *Hist. Brit. Colonies W. Indies* II. iii. 73, I now proceed to the people of Whidah, or Fida. The Negroes of this country are called generally in the West Indies Papaws. **1949** *Caribbean Q.* I. i. 11, 33 were Nagoes and 24 Pawpaws from the Slave Coast.

papaya, now freq. used as an alternative to Papaw 1. (Examples.)
1769 [see Papaw 1]. **1832** W. C. Bryant *Poems* (N.Y.) 82 For thee the wild grape glistens, On sunny knoll and

tree, And stoops the slim papaya With yellow fruit for thee. **1874** E. Lear *Indian Jrnl.* (1953) 57 Bits of palmyra-palm, papaya, and dark clumps of oak-like trees around. **1920** W. Popenoe *Man. Tropical & Subtropical Fruits* vii. 229 The fruit of the papaya, as well as all other parts of the plant, contains a milky juice. **1933** H. Allen *Anthony Adverse* VI. xxxix. 571 The papayas were already prodigious and there were shiploads of bananas. **1937** M. Covarrubias *Island of Bali* (1972) iii. 39 Dark green island of tall palms, breadfruit, mango, papaya, and banana trees. **1962** A. Huxley *Island* xi. 177 Gardens shaded by palms and papayas and bread-fruit trees. **1965** *Austral. Women's Weekly* 20 Jan. 25/1 This same cook.. concocted mango and papaya soufflés of a texture I'd never before encountered. **1966** D. Forbes *Heart of Malaya* i. 16 There were..groves of papaya and clumps of coco-nut palms beside them. **1969** *Oxf. Bk. Food Plants* 114/1 Papaya (*Carica papaya*) is also commonly known as 'pawpaw' (sometimes spelt papaw). A native of tropical America, it is now widely planted all over the tropics. **1972** *Kent Life* July 82/2 Fresh juicy pineapple or papayas put out the fires in your mouth. **1974** T. Heyerdahl *Fatu-Hiva* ix. 318 The papaya was another strictly tropical American plant, and two varieties grew in the Marquesas. **1977** *New Yorker* 25 July 20/3 He bought papaya and melon for dinner every day.

Pape (pēɪp). *Sc.* and *Ulster*. Also **pape.** [f. Pope *sb.*[1] or as shortening of Papist.] An opprobrious term for a Roman Catholic.

1935 L. Kerr *Woman of Glenshiels* iv. 56 Mary... wouldn't click with a 'pape' or a boy who whistled after them. **1939** Joyce *Finnegans Wake* iii. 440 Skim over *Through Hell with the Papes* (mostly boys) by the divine comic Denti Alligator. **1957** *Bulletin* (Glasgow) 11 Oct. 15/3 Lucas had been drinking. When charged he said, 'I set the house on fire to burn these Papes and Niggers.' **1968** J. Braine *Crying Game* v. 118 Adam's a good Catholic... It's smart to be a Pape now. *Ibid.* xii. 217 When I marry..it must be a Catholic... I mean, who else would I marry but a Pape? **1970** G. M. Fraser *General danced at Dawn* 48 Years later, when he led a famous league side out to play Celtic, this same corporal, having said his Hail-Mary and fingered his crucifix, instructed his team, 'Awright, fellas, let's get stuck intae these Papes.' **1972** *Listener* 7 Sept. 304/3 Gerry Fitt has been bawling about the number of Roman Catholics..who have been found shot dead... Gerry deduces that the dead papes have been killed by Protestant guns. **1974** *Socialist Worker* 2 Nov. 11/1 During my childhood it was constantly hammered home to me that I should be a good boy at school, that I shouldn't question what my elders told me, and that I should join the Orange Lodge because the 'Papes' are bastards.

† **papelito** (papĕlī·to). *Obs.* [a. Sp. *papelito* slip of paper, bit of paper (cf. *papelillo* cigarette).] A cigarette.

1845 R. Ford *Hand-bk. for Travellers Spain* II. 784 So they jogged on, smoking their *papelitos*, to the Escorial. **1861** L. Wraxall tr. *Aimard's Freebooters* xvi. 211 He rolled a husk cigarette..lit his papelito, and was soon surrounded by a dense cloud of bluish and fragrant smoke. **1867** 'Ouida' *Under Two Flags* I. i. 15 Something to drink and something to smoke, were it only a glass of brown sherry and a little papelito.

paper, *sb.* Add: **1. d.** (Further examples of *on paper*.) *paper-and-pencil* (*attrib.*): executed in writing, carried out with paper and pencil.

1788 *Amer. Museum* III. 336/2 The form of their constitution, as it is on paper, admits not of coercion. But necessity introduced it in practice. **1948** [see *conniption]. **1965** N. Chomsky *Aspects of Theory of Syntax* i. 10 Let us use the term 'acceptable' to refer to utterances that are..comprehensible without paper-and-pencil analysis. **1971** *Jrnl. Gen. Psychol.* Oct. 308 The five measures described here—three paper-and-pencil inventories and two visual tasks—all appear to be concerned with a central phenomenon, that of the individual's need to maintain an optimal level of stimulus input or variability. **1972** *Jrnl. Social Psychol.* LXXXVII. 156 Test anxiety scales are typically self-report, paper-and-pencil measures. **1973** *Jrnl. Genetic Psychol.* Sept. 35 The measure of approach was a paper and pencil measure. **1973** D. Westheimer *Going Public* i. 19 For every point it goes up you've made yourselves a hundred twenty seven thou five hundred dollars. On paper. I must warn you that paper profits are often illusory. **1976** *Verbatim* Sept. 5/2 Six nifty paper-and-pencil games. **1977** *World of Cricket Monthly* June 82/3 On paper, Hampshire looked a short-odds bet for any of the one-day competitions.

2. Delete †*Obs.* and add later examples.

1966 *Rep. Comm. Inquiry Univ. Oxf.* I. 241 Upon this depends the ability of the Vice-Chancellor to make himself felt, his capacity to think ahead and to give a lead without having continually to submerge himself in paper. *Ibid.* 253 Only thus can it [*sc.* the General Board] see over the top of the piles of paper and look at those general topics..which ought to be its principal concern. **1977** D. Aitkin *Second Chair* ii. 19 Watch out that you don't get smothered in paper. That foxy little friend of ours wants you to do all his hackwork while he..thinks great thoughts.

3. (Further examples.)

c **1722** Ld. Mar *Legacy to Scotl.* (1896) 201 The paper could not exceed more than a certain quantity..in proportion to the specie in the nation. **1850** Thackeray *Pendennis* II. xxvi. 259 It was whispered among the tradesmen, bill-discounters, and others..that the Captain's 'paper' was henceforth of no value. **1906** *Westm. Gaz.* 20 Oct. 12/2 Without..feeling—as he puts it—that he is 'a pawn with a breech-loader on an open-air chessboard, to be moved at the bidding of a despotic keeper who only takes paper'. **1925** [see *hot *a.* 7 e]. **1930** *Liberty* 5 July 23/2 Next day the news cracks about a twenty-grand payroll robbery at the factory in Sheffield. Bob comes in at night loaded with paper and gives me five hundred bucks of it. **1937** E. Snow *Red Star over China* vi. iv. 234 Only Soviet paper was in use, except in the border counties, where White paper was also accepted. **1949** J. Cary *Fearful Joy* 255 Now they've got some loose paper they're going to make it float. **1969** *Times* 26 Mar. 28/8 A 'proper' level for three-month paper is thought to be about $8\frac{3}{8}$ per cent compared with a frequently quoted level of between $9\frac{3}{16}$ and $8\frac{7}{8}$ per cent. **1977** *Law Rep.* 5 July 620 The bank..also bought them, in the recognised international market in what was called 'medium-term paper'.

4. a. (Earlier and later examples.)

1785 *Apol. Life G. A. Bellamy* (ed. 2) II. xliii. 114 The piece [*sc. Romeo and Juliet* at Drury Lane and Covent Garden] was performed so many nights, that the public as well as the performers were tired and disgusted with it. We, [at Drury Lane] however, got the advantage of some nights. But this was not done without a great deal of paper, which was bestowed upon the occasion. **1820** C. Mathews *Let.* in A. Mathews *Mem. Charles Mathews* (1839) III. 165 He had spoken to the cash-taker of the rooms, who said, this is *all* the money (not much), and there's plenty of paper. **1825** P. Egan *Life of Actor* iv. 144 '*Theatrical paper*' has been frequently known to *silence* many a harsh tongue; and also to change the looks of an angry creditor. **1927** *Vanity Fair* XXIX. 132/3 'Paper' is a pass. **1951** 'J. Tey' *Daughter of Time* ii. 21 Johnny Garson can tell you how much paper there is in the house what time he is sobbing his heart out.

b. (Later examples.)

1929 M. A. Gill *Underworld Slang* 9/2 *Paper*, marked playing cards. **1938** H. Asbury *Sucker's Progress* 37 In the early days of Poker the marked cards used by sharpers were prepared beforehand by the gamblers themselves, and were known as 'paper'; or were marked during the process of the game with the finger nail or a needle point embedded in a ring.

c. *U.S.* A forged cheque or document.

1850 [see *kite-flying *vbl. sb.* 2]. **1925** *Flynn's* 7 Mar. 191/2 *Paper*,..forged notes or checks. **1930** *Liberty* 19 July 27/1, I turn out bills of sale by the dozen. I don't like to do it as it is not playing square with my dealers. They don't know they're getting worthless papers.

d. *U.S.* Posters or similar publicity material. Also individual singular: a poster or placard.

1878 *Harper's Mag.* Mar. 599/2 Struggling families who have 'one room to let', or..a modest paper in a window 'Boarders wanted'. **1896** *N.Y. Dramatic News* 18 July 12/1 Car No. 6..was here July 7–8, posting very attractive paper, which reads 'coming soon'. **1903** W. C. Thompson *On Road with Circus* i. 23 The posters and lithographs sent out in advance are 'paper'. **1942** Berrey & Van den Bark *Amer. Thes. Slang* § 571/6 *Paper*, posters.

6. c. (Earlier examples.)

a **1746** M. Leapor *Poems* (1748) I. 5 Let Isabel unload her aking Head Of twisted Papers, and of binding Lead. **1772** J. Woodforde *Diary* 21 Apr. (1924) I. 114 We.. caught my Sister Jane at table with her hair up in papers. **1819** Keats *Let.* 16 Apr. (1958) II. 92 Do you put your hair in papers of a night? **1838** Dickens *Nickleby* (1839) vii. 60 The lady..was dressed in a dimity night jacket with her hair in papers.

d. *U.S.* A playing card. (Cf. sense 4 b in Dict. and Suppl.).

1842 *Southern Lit. Messenger* VIII. 412/1, I found myself..around a table in a corner, and the 'papers' in motion. **1862** O. W. Norton *Army Lett.* (1903) 41 Those whose taste inclines them that way are playing with the 'spotted papers'. **1935** A. J. Pollock *Underworld Speaks* 86/1 *Papers*, playing cards.

7. d. (Later examples.)

1914 E. A. Powell *Fighting in Flanders* ii. 45 One never stirred out of doors in Antwerp without one's papers, which had to be shown before one could gain admission to the post office..or any other public buildings. **1960** O. Manning *Great Fortune* ii. 142 Recalled to his regiment. His papers came yesterday and off he had to go. **1960** *Victorian Studies* June 326 Those, like Captain Gadsby..in the end sent in their papers for the sake of their wife and family. **1963** R. D. Symons *Many Trails* xi. 110 The great steam-engine..was attended by a proper steam engineer, with 'papers'. **1966** *Listener* 24 Feb. 267/2 The Moscovite lives by the rules. 'Without "papers" a man is nothing,' my exasperated interpreter once asserted. **1970** *Globe & Mail* (Toronto) 28 Sept. 29/2 (Advt.), Applicant must possess thorough knowledge of hot water heating systems and preferably possess engineers papers. **1977** H. Kaplan *Damascus Cover* xiv. 140 Some [Nazis]..proceeded to Rome and Geneva where clandestine processing stations..supplied them with the papers necessary for travel to the Middle East.

8. b. = Wall-paper.

1764 in E. Singleton *Social N.Y. under Georges* (1902) 43 The Dining-Room is 14 × 19, hung with genteel Paper; the Entry or Passage from the Door, is hung with the same. **1830** M. Edgeworth *Let.* 17 Nov. (1971) 430 When I went down to the library..I was charmed even with the fuschia-trellis looking paper. **1873** C. M. Yonge *Pillars of House* II. xiv. 53 What our paper may have been in its earlier stages of existence I am not prepared to say; but since I can remember..the wall presented every *nuance* of purplish salmon. **1945** *Catal. Exhib. Eng. & Hist. Wallpapers* (Central Inst. Art & Design) 6 The most beautiful of all..are the hand-painted Chinese papers. **1967** Wodehouse *Company for Henry* iv. 57 His spiritual home would have been some such establishment as Edgar Allen Poe's House of Usher, into which he would have fitted like the paper on the wall. **1975** 'A. Hall' *Mandarin Cypher* vii. 104 We had all the paper off the wall at the Hong Kong Cathay [Hotel].

c. *pl.* The publicity afforded by the newspapers; esp. in phr. *to make the papers*: to gain publicity.

1963 'A. Gilbert' *Ring for Noose* viii. 97 At all events he hadn't made the morning papers. **1967** Wodehouse *Company for Henry* iii. 47 One of these days that woman is going to get herself Into The Papers. **1972** *Village Voice* (N.Y.) 1 June 16/2 Through many lonely months McGovern had trouble making the papers.

10. a. (Further examples.)

1594 T. Nash *Unfortunate Traveller* sig. H 4[v] As if it had beene a candle in a paper lanterne. **1723** J. Nott *Cook's & Confectioner's Dict.* sig. Cc 2[v] (*heading*) To dry Plums..when they are dry put them into Paper Bags full of small Holes, and hang them up. **1723** *Amer. Weekly Mercury* 7 Nov. 2/2 The natural Situation of these Counties and the Practice of our Neighbours, has laid us [of Penna.] under the necessity of coming into a Paper Currency. *a* **1790** B. Franklin *Autobiogr.* in *Writings* (1905) I. 306 The wealthy inhabitants..being against all paper currency. *Ibid.*, I wrote and printed an anonymous pamphlet.. entitled 'The Nature and Necessity of a Paper Currency'. **1796** Jane Austen *Let.* 9 Jan. (1952) 3 We have trimmed up and given away all the old paper hats of Mamma's manufacture. **1808** *Ibid.* 24 Oct. 225 We do not want amusement: bilbocatch,..spillikins, paper ships, riddles, conundrums, and cards..keep us well employed. **1864** *Harper's Mag.* Dec. 58/2 With an umbrella and a shawl, inclosing a box of paper collars. **1867** J. Laing *Theory of Business* vi. 77 With Austria, Russia, America, and other countries using paper currencies..the par is exceedingly uncertain. **1870** J. K. Medbery *Men & Mysteries Wall St.* 23 A broker cannot..innocently fling a 'paper dart' at a neighbour without being amerced ten dollars. **1899** 'Mark Twain' in *Forum* (N.Y.) Mar. 31 A billionaire in a paper-collar, a king in a breech-clout. **1905** *Daily Chron.* 15 May 8/5 There is a craze just now for 'paper hats'. It sounds crude, but the smartest and prettiest tricornes, mushrooms, and shady river hats are daintily woven from a soft paper. **1907** *Yesterday's Shopping* (1969) 352 c/1 *Paper d'oyleys.* Star pattern. **1913** C. Mackenzie *Sinister St.* I. ii. iv. 190 They threw paper darts and paper pellets with unerring aim. **1922** Joyce *Ulysses* 423 A bandy child..with a papershuttlecock. **1934** A. Huxley *Beyond Mexique Bay* 6 He..decreed.. that we should be given paper hats, balloons, and cardboard trumpets. **1935** H. Edib *Clown & his Daughter* xlii. 233 Women distributing sweets in coloured paper bags passed in and out of the audience. **1951** 'J. Tey' *Daughter of Time* i. 17 She was carrying various paper bags and a small tight bunch of anemones. **1951** R. W. Jones *Thomson's Dict. Banking* (ed. 10) 452/1 *Paper currency*, the paper instruments such as bank notes, cheques, bills, and other forms which take the place of money and act as a currency or circulating medium. **1955** A. Marshall *I can jump Puddles* (1956) xix. 136 'Skeeter couldn't fight his way out of a paper bag,' Joe asserted. **1958** Paper doily [see *doily *sb.* or *a.*]. **1969** 'H. Pentecost' *Girl Watcher's Funeral* (1970) ii. i. 94 That first punch..smashed through my guard like a paper doyley. **1972** M. Woodhouse *Mama Doll* xi. 145 Andy Dylan made paper darts. **1973** M. Amis *Rachel Papers* 153 Not, for her, the wet Brillo-pad, nor the paper-bagful of kedgeree. **1973** J. Leasor *Mandarin Gold* ii. 18 Paper lanterns were glittering above shop fronts and over stalls. **1974** *Sunday Times* (Colour Suppl.) 17 Feb. 55/3 Strange how people assume at once the personalities of their paper hats. That man, for instance, in a boiled shirt and three exiguous Red Indian feathers. **1974** M. G. Eberhart *Danger Money* xiii. 134 Shoes, stockings and paper tissues littered the room. **1975** *New Yorker* 3 Mar. 38/3 She never got over her spending a hundred and twenty-five dollars on paper lanterns for the engagement party. **1977** R. Barnard *Death on High C's* ix. 87 She went through men like other women go through paper tissues.

b. (Earlier example of *paper ship* in *fig.* use.)

1854 *2nd Rep. Select Comm. Emigrant Ships* 61 in *Parl. Papers* XIII. 267 These advertisers...have a kind of arrangement with the owners of vessels; they are like recruiters, they collect emigrants; their ships are known in the trade by the name of 'paper' ships.

c. (Further examples.)

1809 'D. Knickerbocker' *Hist. N.Y.* I. iv. iv. 231 This all potent word, which served as his touchstone in politics, at once explains the whole system of proclamations, protests, empty threats, windmills, trumpeters, and paper war. **1826** M. Kelly *Reminisc.* II. 119 Most of the popular songs which he sang in Sacchini's operas were composed by himself, although the credit of them was given to Sacchini; but upon a severe quarrel between them, Rauzzini, in a paper war, actually avowed himself the author of them, and accused Sacchini of the greatest ingratitude. **1963** D. Ogilvy *Confessions Advertising Man* (1964) i. 15, I abhor people who wage paper-warfare. **1970** *Times* 13 Feb. 10/5 In the much larger Arab world, it is a paper war for many people.

d. (Further examples.)

1803 *Deb. Congress U.S.* 23 Feb. (1851) 129 Paper blockades were substituted for actual ones, and the staple commodities of our country lay perishing in our storehouses. **1812** *Boston Gaz.* 20 July 1/5 The paper-blockades, which have justly occasioned so much irritation, are now abandoned. **1932** *Sun* (Baltimore) 15 Aug. 7/5 It was granted there might be a half-dozen 'paper' agreements at least..from the conference. **1941** J. S. Huxley *Uniqueness of Man* xiii. 270 Hedonism, like utilitarianism, is another of those paper schemes, beautifully logical, that just are not true. **1960** *Washington Post* 27 Nov. E 3 At least 70 anti Castro groups have been formed in Miami, but many of them are paper organizations. **1965** A. Nicol *Truly Married Woman* 43 One more week towards the time when Olu Jones and his brethren would take over. He was not worried, however, Perhaps ..because I have paper qualifications. **1970** *New York* 16 Nov. 54/3 Abbie is a simple bourgeois basket case, a paper Yippie, and over 30 anyway. **1973** *Time* 25 June 66/2 Lloyd also has a number of paper companies set up in Liechtenstein. **1977** E. Ambler *Send No More Roses* xi. 266 A chain of twenty different corporations..all making paper profits. **1978** *Jrnl. R. Soc. Arts* CXXVI. 607/2 These targets are real, and not just paper objectives.

11. a. *paper-clip* (further examples); so *paper-clip* vb.

1904 Chesterton *Nap. Notting Hill* iii. ii. 151 One of those queer little shops..which must be called toy-shops only because toys..predominate; for the remainder of goods seem to consist of almost everything else in the world—tobacco, exercise-books,..halfpenny paper clips. **1921** V. Sackville-West *Orchard & Vineyard* 97, I watched..And thought how London clerks with paper-clips Had filed the bills of lading of those ships. **1962** A. Nisbett *Technique Sound Studio* ii. 40 Thin paper..individually paper-clipped to thick paper or card. **1963** A. Ross *Australia 63* ii. 49 The two banks of the city paper-clipped together by harp-like steel bridges. **1969** P. Highsmith *Tremor of Forgery* xi. 101 Ingham paper-clipped his notes and put them on a corner of his desk. **1973** *Time* 25 June 44/2 With roads, the North Vietnamese can bring in the stuff of life—the paper clips for a bureaucracy, the beginning of a postal system, school supplies, the works. **1974** H. L. Foster *Ribbin'* vi. 284 He entered, took a tray of paper clips from her desk and sat down on a chair directly in front of her. **1976** *New Yorker* 1 Mar. 64/2 The note was paper-clipped to a collection of President Nixon's Vietnamization speeches. **1978** N. Freeling *Night Lords* xv. 64 A thin pile of letter paper, neatly squared off and paper-clipped by her fair hand.

b. *paper-keeper.*

1927 *Daily Tel.* 3 May 3 In the opinion of the Postmaster-General the paperkeepers were amply remunerated at the present rates. **1970** *Ibid.* 12 Jan. 1/6 There would be a series of strikes by 10,000 messengers and paper-keepers in Whitehall. *Ibid.*, One effect of the strike..will be that documents will not be circulated to departments by the paper-keepers.

c. *paper-bound* (examples) (see also sense 12 below), *-collared* (example), *-covered* (further examples), *-insulated*, *-soled*, *-wrapped* adjs.

1882 W. Whitman *Daybks. & Notebks.* (1978) II. 287 Paper-bound L of G with revisions prop. **1901** *Sketch* 24 July 26/2 The unsold paper-bound books in Germany are returned to the publisher, who re-binds them. **1928** A. Huxley *Let.* 12 Dec. (1969) 304 He'd be able to get rid of the paper bound copies at the same time. **1942** E. Waugh *Put out More Flags* i. 32 The Vichy water and the paper bound-volume of Balzac on the table before her..spoke of what..she would have called her 'personality'. **1976** *National Observer* (U.S.) 2 Oct. 14/4, I disappeared into the bathroom..with a jar of bath salts and a paper-bound novel. **1874** A. Bathgate *Colonial Experiences* viii. 86 A section of the community known as the 'paper-collared swells', who are the government officials, medical men, bank employees *et hoc genus omne.* **1867** Geo. Eliot *Let.* 21 Mar. (1956) IV. 354 People write..to tell me of one paper-covered American copy of Felix Holt being brought to Europe. **1923** J. M. Murry *Pencillings* 18 The paper-covered book, in fact, a rough and ready test of literary curiosity. **1952** *Amer. Speech* XXVII. 149 The paper-covered book in the United States is earning a place for itself much above that of the 'paper-back' and 'dime novel'. **1978** *Jrnl. R. Soc. Arts* CXXVI. 702/1 To have a catalogue of all the Institute's *dix-huitième* drawings in the small compass of a paper-covered 8vo volume including a coloured illustration of every one of them, is most valuable. **1900** *Jrnl. Inst. Electr. Engin.* Dec. (Advt., verso rear cover), Diatrine paper-insulated..cables. **1967** *IEEE Trans. Power Apparatus & Systems* LXXXVI. 34 (*heading*) Drying and impregnation of paper-insulated power cables. **1902** Conrad *Typhoon* ii. 19 A mournful,..Chinaman, walking behind in paper-soled silk shoes, and who also carried an umbrella. **1973** M. Amis *Rachel Papers* 32 An old woman passed by surreptitiously dropping paper-wrapped sugar-lumps on to the chair opposite.

d. *paper-hearted*, *-thin* (freq. *fig.*), *-white* (later examples).

1939 Dylan Thomas *Let.* Mar. (1966) 226 The English poets now are such a..paperhearted crowd you could blow them down with one bellow out of a done lung. **1929** E. Bowen *Last September* vii. 85 The door went paper-thin as they raised their voices. **1939** 'N. Blake' *Smiler with Knife* 99 His old, paper-thin voice. **1971** *Guardian* 17 Sept. 4/6, I do want to dedicate what is left of my life..to..this paper-thin thing of law and order. **1977** *Guardian Weekly* 28 Aug. 3/1 Even a paper thin majority in favour of the rule at Congress would ensure TGWU support. **1978** B. Norman *To nick Good Body* vii. 57 There was this thumping in their bedroom. Paper-thin the walls are in those houses. **1976** *Liverpool Echo* 24 Nov. 5/4 The Government's paper-thin majority. **1806** *Curtis's Bot. Mag.* XXIV. 947 (*heading*) Italian or paper-white Narcissus. **1938** [see *grandiflora *a.*]. **1957** L. Durrell *Justine* 66 They [*sc.* Egyptian women] have become tuns of pleasure, rolling on paper-white blue-veined legs. **1973** J. Burrows *Like an Evening Gone* xi. 128 [He] had turned paper-white when given the news. **1977** P. Moyes *To kill Coconut* v. 66 Paper-white legs proclaimed him a new arrival.

12. paper-board; delete †*obs.* and add later examples; (*b*) *pl.* boards with a paper cover, used in book-binding; **paper boat,** (*a*) a model boat made from folded paper; (*b*) a lightly made vessel; **paperbound** *sb.* (see sense 11 c above) (chiefly *U.S.*) = *paperback; **paper box,** (*a*) a box made of paper; (*b*) a box in which to keep papers; **paper cable,** an electric cable insulated with paper; **paper cap,** (*a*) a cap made of usu. coloured paper and worn at festivals, parties, etc.; (*b*) a cap made of paper worn by carpenters and other workmen; **paper chain,** a chain made of usu. coloured paper as a decoration, esp. at Christmas; **paper-chase,** also *transf.* and *fig.*; **paper-chewing** *slang* (*rare*), official correspondence; **paper chromatogram** *Chem.*, a chromatogram made on a paper support; **paper chromatography** *Chem.*, the separation of substances by chromatography on a paper support; hence *paper chromatographic* adj., *paper-chromatographically* adv.; **paper cover,** (*a*) see quot. 1960; (*b*) = *paperback; **paper cup,** a drinking cup made of thin cardboard; **paper-cutter** (earlier and later examples); **paper doll,** (*a*) a doll-shaped figure cut or folded from a sheet of paper; (*b*) *U.S. slang*: (see quots. 1968–70, 1970); **paper dress,** an inexpensive disposable dress made of paper; **paper dust** *Printing* (see quot. 1964); **paper-feed,** a device for inserting sheets of paper into a typewriter, printing machine, or the like; **paper flower,** (*a*) an imitation flower made from paper; (*b*) *U.S.*, a name used for several plants with flowers of a papery texture, esp. *Psilostrophe cooperi*, a small shrub of the family Compositæ, native to south-western desert areas of the United States and bearing panicles of yellow flowers; **paper-folding,** the making of objects by folding paper, origami; **paper game,** a game played using pencil and paper; **paper gold** = *special drawing rights* (*special *a.* 3 d); **paper guide,** an adjustable device on a typewriter for ensuring that the left edge of each sheet of paper is inserted at the same place; **paper handkerchief,** a disposable handkerchief made from soft tissue paper; **paper hankie, hanky** *colloq.*, = **paper handkerchief*; **paper kiosk,** a kiosk at which newspapers are sold; **paper-making wasp** = *paper-wasp*; **paper man,** a musician, esp. a drummer, who plays from written music; **paper-match** = *book match* (*book *sb.* 18); **paper napkin,** a disposable table-napkin made of paper; **paper nylon,** a stiff paper-like form of nylon; **paper pattern,** a pattern cut out of paper; *spec.* a dressmaking pattern printed on paper, now usu. on tissue paper with printed instructions; **paper plate,** (*a*) a disposable plate made of paper or cardboard; (*b*) a specially treated paper used as an offset printing plate in certain office duplicating machines; **paper ribbon,** (*a*) = *paper tape* below; (*b*) = *paper streamer* below; **paper-round,** the job of regularly delivering newspapers; the particular route covered; **paper route** *U.S.*, = *paper-round* above; **paper run** *N.Z.*, = *paper-round* above; **paper sack,** (*a*) *U.S.* a paper bag; (*b*) a large sack-like container made of strong paper; **paper sculpture,** the making of three-dimensional structures from one or more pieces of paper by folding, cutting, etc.; **paper shale** *Geol.*, shale which readily splits into very thin paper-like laminæ; **paper-shell** (earlier and later examples); so **paper-shelled** *a.*, having a very thin shell; **paper shredder,** a machine that tears up esp. secret documents into small unreadable fragments; so *paper-shredding* adj.; **paper streamer,** a long narrow strip of coloured paper used as a decoration, etc.; **paper-taffeta,** a lightweight taffeta with a crisp papery finish; **paper tape,** tape made of paper; *esp.* such on which data is represented by means of holes punched in it; freq. *attrib.*; cf. Tape *sb.*[1] 2 b, *perforated tape* (*perforated *ppl. a.* 1), *punched tape* (*punched *ppl. a.* 2); **paper tiger** [tr. a Chinese expression first used by Chairman Mao], a person, country, etc., that appears outwardly powerful or important but is actually weak or ineffective; **paper towel,** a small disposable towel made of absorbent paper; **paper tower,** the part of a Monotype machine (*monotype *sb.* 3) in which the perforated paper tape is held; **paper town** *N. Amer.*, (*a*) a town that is projected or promoted but not always actually founded; (*b*) a town or city supported by the paper-making industry; **paper ware,** (articles made of) papier-mâché; **paper-work,** (*c*) (earlier example); (*d*) work done on paper, the filling-in of esp. official forms, the keeping of administrative records.

1888 C. T. Jacobi *Printers' Vocab.* 95 *Paper boards*, a term applied to cheap bindings in boards, but with paper instead of cloth sides. **1929** A. J. Vaughan *Mod. Bookbinding* iv. 216 *Paper or Cloth Boards*, a binding consisting of a case made from a paper or cloth cover. **1944** *Sun* (Baltimore) 9 Jan. 3/5 The Robert Gair Company plant, manufacturing paperboard for containers and boxes for war purposes, was shut down today because of a lack of wastepaper. **1959** R. Hostettler et al. *Technical Terms Printing Industry* (ed. 3) 103/1 (Bound) in paper boards. **1959** A. McLintock *Descr. Atlas N.Z.* 59 The value of production of pulp, paper, and paperboard for 1956–7 was £12·4 million. **1961** J. Carter *ABC for Bk.-Collectors* (ed. 3) 143 Notwithstanding that 'original boards'..are in fact covered with paper, the term *paper boards*, if used of any but quite modern books..suggests boards..covered with paper of a plain colour, usually not the original binding. **1965** B. J. Kirkpatrick *Bibliogr. E. M. Forster* 47 Pale green paper boards; printed in black on upper cover. **1971** *New Scientist* 27 Apr. 259/2 Scrap paper..is used to make some forms of paperboard for packaging. ? **1846** Mrs. Gaskell *Let.* (1966) 48 All the children were very kind to Florence, and made her paper boxes, and boats. **1863** Dickens in *All Year Round* 26 Sept. 108/1 My voyages (in paper boats) among savages often yield me matter for reflection at home. **1929** F. C. Bowen *Sea Slang* 101 *Paper boat*, a lightly-built vessel of any sort, but particularly applied to paddle excursion steamers. **1931** R. Campbell *Georgiad* III. 61 The anecdotes Of Alfred's cakes and Shelley's paper boats. **1961** F. H. Burgess *Dict. Sailing* 156 *Paper boat*, any boat with very thin planking. **1964** M. Clive *Day of Reckoning* viii. 73 Parlour tricks, such as making cocked hats out of newspaper or paper boats from half-sheets of writing paper. **1978** *Listener* 12 Jan. 57/2 A parting gift from his cell-mate..a little paper boat..not more than two or three millimetres long. **1961** *Spectator* 26 May 765 (Advt.), Yale Paperbounds. Yale University Press. **1970** *Scholarly Publishing* I. 419 Yale Fastbacks will be made available as paperbounds, at low cost, and they will often reflect the newest techniques of rapid book production. **1973** *Publishers Weekly* 7 May 10 (Advt.), Now *The Divine Vision* is a Quest paperbound. **1754** *Connoisseur* I. 189 The man of taste takes his Strasburgh veritable tabac from a right Paris paper-box, and the pretty fellow uses a box of polished metal, that by often opening it he may have the opportunity of stealing a glance at his own sweet person reflected in the lid of it. **1757** in S. M. Hamilton *Lett. to Washington* (1899) II. 80 Paper Box of Tarsils..1. **1776** J. Wedgwood *Let.* 14 July (1965) 195 They have not much expectation in those articles (unless in very cheap paper Boxes) from any market where they have the French for their Rivals. **1861** D. G. Rossetti *Let.* 19 Jan. (1965) II. 389 Will you tell her we are very thankful for her paper-box, which is very useful? **1869** *Boyd's Business Directory N.Y. State* 460 H. Lettington, Manufacturer of Paper Boxes. **1913** J. London *Valley of Moon* I. xi. 96 As if I didn't know..how long you worked in..the paper-box factory. **1926–7** *Army & Navy Stores Catal.* 383/2 Paper boxes, japanned tin. **1893** W. J. Hopkins *Telephone Lines* xiv. 209 In the paper cables made by John A. Roebling & Sons Company, two paper strips are laid on lengthwise, as loosely as possible, being held in place by thread wound about them. **1936** *Economist* 22 Feb. 437/1 The board intended to extend the business of the company into new lines, the main business being the manufacture of paper cables. **1973** R. W. Sillars *Electr. Insulating Materials* v. 88 Drying of high voltage oil-filled paper cables..is more critical than transformer drying, for the stress at working voltage is considerably higher and therefore discharge is more difficult to avoid. **1809** 'D. Knickerbocker' *Hist. N.Y.* II. vi. viii. 162 Little urchins..followed in droves after the drums, with paper caps on their heads. **1835** Dickens *Sk. Boz.* (1836) 1st Ser. II. 149 An unshaven, dirty, sottish-looking fellow, whose tarnished paper-cap..communicates an additionally repulsive expression to his very uninviting countenance. **1887** Kipling *Plain Tales from Hills* (1888) 231 A big blue paper cap from a cracker. **1967** C. V. Bark *See Living Crocodiles* iii. 44 The guests wore paper caps and pulled crackers. **1974** L. Lamb *Man in Mist* vi. 37, I can well remember when carpenters and masons wore paper caps, as they still do in Italy and in Tenniel's *Alice.* **1943** N. Balchin *Small Back Room* iii. 31 It's a damned shame we haven't got a few paper chains and a bit of misletoe for the old boy. **1971** M. McCarthy *Birds of America* 31 He..preferred the [Christmas] tree..with..the paper chains he cut and pasted. **1973** E. Jong *Half-Lives* 82, I tie you to the bed with paper chains. **1914** Paperchase [see **cyclecar*]. **1932** *Times Lit. Suppl.* 9 June 425/4 This is not the usual paper-chase of clues from crime to detection. **1977** *Arab Times* 14 Nov. 2/1 Now, in what local journalists call the great paper chase, three newspapers for blacks are competing at the newsstands. **1934** 'G. Orwell' *Burmese Days* ii. 30, I can't stick my bloody office..signing one chit after another. Paper-chewing. *Ibid.* 38 All this paper-chewing and chit-passing. **1944** *Biochem. Jrnl.* XXXVIII. 231/2 The paper chromatograms are by no means united to the separation of aminoacids. **1972** K. Narita in M. Funatsu et al. *Proteins* II. 246 Radioactivity of acetylglycylserine was almost the same as that found in the material which stayed at the origin on the paper chromatogram. **1956** *Nature* 7 Jan. 22/1 He described preliminary studies on the successful paper-chromatographic separation of intact tissue phospholipids. **1971** *Jrnl. Chromatogr.* LX. 381 Almost the entire present knowledge on the composition of human urinary sugar content in health and disease can be ascribed to paper chromatographic studies. **1966** *Bot. Mag.* (Tokyo) LXXIX. 507 Three amino acids are formed that can be identified paper-chromatographically. **1948** *Science* 7 May 483/2 It appears that..paper chromatography will be found to be an increasingly important research tool in analyzing for amino acids. **1971** C. T. Kenner *Analyt. Separations & Determinations* xv. 282 Two-dimensional paper chromatography is used to separate complex mixtures of amino acids produced by hydrolysis of protein. **1856** Geo. Eliot *Let.* 24 Dec. (1954) II. 282 George definitely votes for..boards. He thinks a paper cover for a philosophical book a bad augury. **1903** [in Dict., 10 a]. **1913** T. E. Lawrence *Let.* 5 Apr. (1938) 152 If you have any cheap paper covered copy..(paper-covers are customs free)..I would be exceedingly grateful. **1952** *Amer. Speech* XXVII. 149 It is not clear whether the *Matrix*..uses *limp-cover* in contradistinction to *hard-cover* or *paper-cover*. **1960** G. A. Glaister *Gloss. Bk.* 295/1 *Paper covers*, a style of binding much used for cheap reprints, and, especially on the Continent, for original works in which no boards are used, and the stiff paper cover which encloses the book is adhered to the back. **1907** *Yesterday's Shopping* (1969) 352E/2 Paper drinking cups, complete with holders. **1939** G. Greene *Lawless Roads* xi. 272 The odious child takes all the paper cups from the water-tap by the lavatory. **1971** J. Henderson *Copperhead* (1972) xv. 191 A girl appeared with..the usual paper cups. **1978** R. Hill *Pinch of Snuff* xxiv. 239 She..poured tea from the flask into the paper cups. *a* **1828** D. Wordsworth *Jrnl.* (1941) II. 128, I purchased a ladle and a paper-cutter..made by the peasants of these mountains. **1969** *New Yorker* 14 June 46/3 His overhead is hit with his whole arm—no mere flick of the wrist. The arm comes down like the moving part of a paper cutter. **1849** G. S. Appleton *Mother Goose in Hieroglyphicks* (1963) (Advt., recto rear cover), Chandler's paper dolls of the latest Paris fashions. No. 1—Carrie, with her Dresses and Bonnets. **1903** H. Keller *Story my Life* I. ii. 12 Two little children..were busy cutting out paper dolls. **1968–70** *Current Slang* (Univ. S. Dakota) III–IV. 81 *Make like a paper doll, and cut out*,..to leave. **1970** C. Major *Dict. Afro-Amer. Slang* 89 *Paper doll*,..to play hookey from school; to leave. **1972** T. I. Elliott in *Kawai's Origami* (ed. 4) p. iv, Playing with paper dolls is for girls, and the closest a guy approaches a paper doll is in the famous song where he buys 'a paper doll that other fellows will not steal'. **1976** *New Yorker* 15 Nov. 50/2 Maria undresses her paper doll and deliberately rips a feather off its hat. **1966** *Listener* 15 Dec. 893/1 This ..is the year of the paper dress that can be worn and then tossed in the waste basket. *Ibid.* 893/2 Paper-dress fabrics take colour well, and can be shortened with scissors. **1967** *Observer* 21 May 28/6 The best use so far of so-called 'paper' dresses—as instant summer bargains to be chucked away with no regrets. **1970** *New Society* 5 Mar. 385/2 It's a market that started developing in the fifties, boomed briefly in the mid-sixties with gimmicks like paper dresses, reassessed itself and looks set for a genuine boom in the mid-seventies. **1906** E. Dyson *Fact'ry 'Ands* iii. 27 Over these [*sc.* side-whiskers] the feathery paper-dust collected till they looked like the wings of an adolescent gosling. **1964** *Gloss. Letterpress Rotary Printing Terms* (*B.S.I.*) 5 *Paper dust or fluff*, fibre (fluff) or loading (dust) which leaves the web as it passes through the printing press or slitters. **1971** *Engineering* Apr. 79 (Advt.), Clean air in every facet of industry... Paper dust. **1920** H. Etheridge *Dict. Typewriting* 177 The paper feed of a typewriter consists of a paper roller (or platen) and two or more small feed rollers, which latter are kept in contact with the platen by means of springs, to allow of different thicknesses of paper being inserted. **1960** *Times* 24 Feb. 9/2 New fast paper-feed with integrated controls to reduce hand-movement. **1961** T. Landau *Encycl. Librarianship* (ed. 2) 120/2 The modern electric duplicator with its automatic paper-feed, counting mechanism and automatic stopping device, is a highly efficient and economical machine. **1967** Karch & Buber *Offset Processes* ix. 369 The delivery paper-feed control..controls the feed of paper from the delivery end. **1854** *Rep. Trans. Pennsylvania State Agric. Soc.* 176 The first premium on paper flowers, is awarded to No. 177. **1892** *Jrnl. Amer. Folk-Lore* V. 99 *Xeranthemum, Helichrysum*, paper-flowers. **1915** Armstrong & Thornber *Field Bk. Western Wild Flowers* 542 Paper Flowers. *Psilostrophe Cooperi*. Yellow. Spring. Southwest. **1935** R. Macaulay *Personal Pleasures* 256 Like those Japanese paper flowers which gently unfold and bloom in bowls of water..the mind puts out boughs and sprigs of blossom and ripe fruits, inebriating and enticing the charmed soul. **1972** *Islander* (Victoria, B.C.) 2 Apr. 2/3 Paper-flower and sundrop raced up the hills. **1974** C. Fremlin *By Horror Haunted* 94 Just look at all these mats, and doilies, and paper flowers! **1893** T. S. Row (*title*) Geometric exercises in paper folding. **1905** *Westm. Gaz.* 30 Sept. 13/2 Paper folding has long been a favourite amusement in our Kindergartens. **1908** W. F. White *Scrap-bk. Elem. Math.* 144 (*heading*) Symmetry Illustrated by Paper Folding. **1968** [see *origami]. **1972** T. I. Elliott tr. *Kawai's Origami* (ed. 4) p. i, Origami, paper-folding, can be enjoyed by children and adults alike. **1879** C. M. Yonge *Magnum Bonum* III. xxxv. 759 To listen to an exposition of the microphone, to share in a Shakespeare reading, or worse still, in a paper game, was..such a bore. **1934** E. Waugh *Handful of Dust* i. 21 'No paper games?' 'Oh, no, nothing like that. A certain amount of bridge and backgammon and low poker.' **1961** A. Wilson *Old Men at Zoo* iii. 125, I felt..that it would not be long before we were involved in paper games or even a sing-song round the piano. **1975** R. Player *Let's talk of Graves* iv. 108 We played games—paper games and Ludo. **1966** *Wall St. Jrnl.* 1 Dec. 5/2 World monetary reform negotiators removed some of the major stumbling blocks in their path to creating 'paper gold', although many more still remain. **1971** *Daily Tel.* 10 May 14 'Paper gold'..is a credit, listed in a computer in Washington, for each country which is a member of the International Monetary Fund. The members agree to use it to pay debts among themselves under certain rules, the only one of which need bother us is that no one except governments ever owns 'paper gold'. **1973** *Times* 15 Nov. 25/6 The nations of the world should start doing something to find a more catchy name for the Special Drawing Right, whose popular (well, fairly popular) nickname of 'paper gold' has recently been coming under attack in Britain. **1978** *Guardian Weekly* 19 Nov. 5/1 An agreement..to begin to phase out the world role of the United States dollar and its progressive replacement with so called 'paper gold', the basket of international currencies known as the IMF Special Drawing Rights. **1952** Leslie & Pepe *Methods of Teaching Typing Simplified* i. 9 Paper guide should be set and paper inserted by the teacher. **1962** *Which?* Dec. 354 Only four of the machines..had a paper guide for helping to get the left edge of the paper at the same place each time. **1970** L. Gartside *Teaching Business Subjects* viii. 173 Adjustment of margin stops with special reference to the paper-guide. **1907** *Yesterday's Shopping* (1969) 510/1 Handkerchiefs, Paper (Medicated)—These soft, silky papers are specially prepared for invalids, and are invaluable to sufferers from bronchial affections, catarrh, &c. **1939** R. Stout *Red Threads* (1941) viii. 109 A luxury brand of paper handkerchief, used for wiping creams from the skin. **1954** I. Murdoch *Under Net* iv. 62, I was choking and sneezing and using up a sackful of paper handkerchiefs. **1976** P. Ferris *Detective* i. 2 Rubbing the sweat off his bald head with a paper handkerchief. **1969** *Woman* 19 July 9/2 What man will pick up a dropped paper hanky? **1970** A. Ross *Manchester Thing* 66 Purse, loose change, paper hankies, comb—that kind of stuff. **1974** N. Freeling *Dressing of Diamond* 171 Vera..gave him a paper hanky. Bernard..mopped at his face. **1935** E. Bowen *House in Paris* i. 11 A paper kiosk opened to take its stock in. **1867** *Amer. Naturalist* I. 140 The odor that arises from the Tarantula killer when she uses her sting..resembles the odor of the paper-making wasp (Vespa), only much stronger. **1936** *Metronome* Feb. 21/4 *Paper man*, drummer who plays only what's written. **1936** *Delineator* CXXIX. 10/3 We have heard that no music is used... No, indeed! *Papermen* are not welcome in this esoteric milieu. **1970** C. Major *Dict. Afro-Amer. Slang* 89 *Paper man*, musician..who plays according to written music. **1832** F. Trollope *Dom. Manners Amer.* II. xxvi. 74 Four inkwipers, three paper-matches, and a paste-board watch-case. **1844** Dickens *Mart. Chuz.* xlv. 519 Little Ruth.. had a particular interest in some delicate paper-matches on the chimney-piece: wondering who could have made them. **1895** *Montgomery Ward Catal.* 109/1 Paper Napkins ..for tourists, travelers, lawn parties, lunches, picnics. **1945** G. Brooks in S. Henderson *Understanding New Black Poetry* (1973) 175 Some paper napkins in a water glass. **1972** L. Lamb *Picture Frame* xiv. 122 He put in his order, saw it..served in paper napkins on plates. **1959** J. T. Story *Mix me a Person* iv. 42 The fossilised remains of juke boxes and female frolic skeletons in paper-nylon slips. **1960** C. MacInnes *Mr. Love & Justice* 82 The man in Italian drape.., the woman with..paper nylon petticoat and white stilettos. **1702** Pepys *Let.* 13 Sept. (1926) II. 272 A strict measure cutt in paper of the originall writeing..and..a strict copy taken of the sayd writeing.. one copy thereof and of the paper-patterne, attested by the Doctor, to bee delivered to him. **1833** in A. Adburgham *Shops & Shopping* (1964) iv. 40 A great variety of Morning, Dinner, Evening, Ball & Opera Dresses,..which are made in models and full-size Paper Patterns. **1909** G. Stratton-Porter *Girl of Limberlost* iv. 54 Margaret Sinton was busy with the gingham and the intricate paper pattern. **1969** *Times* 30 Sept. 15/2 Sales of paper patterns —an invention claimed by an American, Mrs. Butterick more than 100 years ago but almost certainly extant in London earlier—are quoted at more than 22 million per year. **1974** M. Cecil *Heroines in Love* iv. 84 Paper patterns for home dressmaking. **1723** J. Nott *Cook's & Confectioner's Dict.* sig. B2^v Almond Bisket..bake them on Paper-Plates in a moderate Oven. **1948** R. R. Karch *Graphic Arts Procedures* viii. 242 Three kinds of plates are used on the Multilith Duplicators. On the paper plate provided for one-run jobs, you can type, write, letter, draw, paint, rule, or trace the image desired in special inks. The plate is then placed on the press without further preparation. **1966** 'D. Shannon' *With a Vengeance* (1968) iii. 48 [He] confiscated one of the hot cookies she'd just transferred to the paper plate. **1971** R. K. Smith *Ransom* (1972) iv. 167 Greer took the paper plate of hamburgers in one hand..and walked to the standup counter. **1975** *New Yorker* 16 June 25/2 Some girls went to wash their hands, and others..killed time by wearing paper plates on their heads. **1976** *Times* 1 Apr. 32/9 (Advt.), Multilith paper plates, large surplus stock, variety of sizes. **1876** Paper ribbon [see Perforator 1]. **1888** *Encycl. Brit.* XXIII. 120/2 The paper ribbon R is moved forward by its centre row of holes. **1903** [see *paper tape* below]. **1922** [see *paper tower* below]. **1935** G. Greene *Basement Room* 102 He hadn't blown whistles or thrown paper ribbons. **1965** Paper ribbon [see *monotype *sb.* 3]. **1948** C. Day Lewis *Otterbury Incident* iv. 47, I asked if he'd let me take on part of his paper-round that evening. **1960** C. Dale *Spring of Love* i. 22 If I'm ever hard up for a job I'll come to you for a paper round... So if you ever need a paper boy, remember yours truly. **1971** C. Storr *Thursday* i. 15 The paper-round money had to provide Thursday with the things other children got without having to work. **1868** *Figaro* (San Francisco) 23 July 2/1 A Paper Route—One of the best on the most substantial city daily. **1929** T. Wolfe *Look Homeward, Angel* (1930) xxvi. 349 He found a substitute for his paper route. **1973** *Publishers Weekly* 19 Nov. 60/3 Isabelle gets to use some of that energy taking over her brother's paper route. **1975** *New Yorker* 28 July 28 (*caption*) Thank goodness, Winant has got himself a paper route, so we have a little something coming in. **1948** D. Ballantyne *Cunninghams* I. viii. 48 Gilbert wanted..a bike for Christmas so's he could have a paper run. **1904** *Dialect Notes* II. 420 Put the apples in a paper *sack*. **1940** W. Faulkner *Hamlet* III. ii. 207 The note was in pencil, on a scrap torn from a paper sack, unsigned. *Ibid.* IV. i. 279 Eck had gone on into the store and emerged with a paper sack, from which he took a segment of cheese. **1944** *Chicago Daily News* 14 July 9/2 She carried a thermos jug of coffee and a couple of sandwiches in a paper sack to eat on the bus. **1955** *Times* 5 July (Reed Suppl.) p. iii/5 In little more than twenty-five years the development of the multi-wall paper sack, in which Medway Paper Sacks Limited has been largely instrumental, has established new standards of efficiency, convenience and cleanliness in the packaging of powdered and granular products. **1971** 'R. Macdonald' *Underground Man* xi. 74, I..had a double hamburger with a paper sack of French fried potatoes. **1974** S. Marcus *Minding Store* (1975) ix. 185 A little old lady in shabby clothes, carrying a paper sack instead of a handbag. **1946** A. Sadler *Paper Sculpture* 17 Paper Sculpture ..is composed of sheets of finished paper, so rolled, bent, scored, cut and folded, that it makes a desired form. **1957** B. Angrave *Sculpture in Paper* 24 A legend has already grown up that modern paper sculpture was born in Poland, and is a development of the folk-art paper-cut tradition in that country. **1973** 'D. Halliday' *Dolly & Starry Bird* viii. 111 A fantasia of pure abstract design; a garden of convoluted plastic as fine as paper sculpture. **1978** *Cornish Guardian* 27 Apr. 33/5 Mrs. Phillips, president, welcomed Mrs. Spargo who gave a talk and demonstration of her paper sculpture. **1877** Paper shale [in Dict., sense 10 b]. **1931** *Prof. Papers U.S. Geol. Survey* No. 168, 7/2 'Paper shale' is the term applied to finely laminated claystones, siltstones, mudstones, and marlstones that show a pronounced tendency to part along the closely spaced bedding planes. **1969** Bennison & Wright *Geol. Hist. Brit. Isles* xiii. 292 An abundant fauna of ammonites and lamellibranchs is present, except in thin paper-shales. **1884** G. B. Goode *Fisheries U.S.: Nat. Hist. Aquatic Animals* 776 The terms 'Soft Crab', 'Paper-shell', and 'Buckler' denote the different stages of consistency of the shell. **1912** *Outing* Oct. 377/1 The only difference between the so-called 'paper-shell' pecan and the fruit from wild trees is that the former has been grown on a budded or grafted tree. **1945** *New England Homestead* 27 Oct. 20/2 Paper-shell pecan in Shell 50¢ per pound. **1948** F. N. Howes *Nuts* 110 Among the many varieties [of almond] cultivated in France are those that range from the thinnest of shells or 'paper shells' to thick hard-shelled forms. **1969** R. & D. De Sola *Dict. Cooking* 167/2 Papershell: Soft-shell pecan. **1974** *Anderson* (S. Carolina) *Independent* 22 Apr. 5A/3 Georgia is the leader in the production of papershell pecans in this country. **1911** Webster, Paper-shelled, *a.* Having a very thin shell, as a paper-shelled almond, or a crab whose shell is beginning to harden. **1946** *Nat. Geogr. Mag.* Apr. 526/2 Immediately after molting the animal [*sc.* a lobster] is soft-shelled. In a few days it is paper-shelled. **1948** F. N. Howes *Nuts* 110 It is usual to classify almonds according to the thickness of the shell—thin- or paper-shelled, soft-shelled and thick- or hard-shelled. **1962** L. Deighton *Ipcress File* xxx. 195 A small machine like a typewriter carriage. It was a paper shredder. Jay fed the sheet in and pressed a button. It disappeared. **1973** 'D. Jordan' *Nile Green* xiii. 54 The House has an obsession with security so it provides paper shredders on every floor. **1958** S. Hyland *Who goes Hang?* xxxii. 137 John Wintour's bankruptcy..was now officially expunged..by..the paper-shredding machines. **1968** A. Diment *Bang Bang Birds* i. ii. 14, I fed the telex strip into my paper-shredding device. **1930** A. P. Herbert *Water Gipsies* xxv. 373 It was a Gala Night; and the waiters were distributing paper streamers, balloons, dolls, squeakers and fans. **1935** C. Isherwood *Mr. Norris changes Trains* iii. 41 The ruffled plumes of a paper streamer..stirring like seaweed in the draught from an electric fan. **1941** M. Treadgold *We couldn't leave Dinah* xvii. 266 A box of crackers and paper streamers left over from the famous Carnival. **1969** N. Freeling *Tsing-Boum* xvi. 117 Broken paper streamers knee deep. **1957** M. B. Picken *Fashion Dict.* 344/1 *Paper taffeta*, crisp lightweight taffeta with a somewhat papery feel. **1963** *Times* 27 Feb. 12/2 The bride, who was given away by her father, wore a gown of white paper taffeta, the bodice and trained-skirt trimmed with knife-pleated frilling. **1972** *Vogue* 15 Mar. 3/2 Plaid paper taffeta dress. **1890** *Electrician* 4 July 233/2 Each of these styles can be pressed against the paper tape by the armature of a corresponding electromagnet. **1903** C. H. Sewall *Wireless Telegr.* III. 133 There is a telegraphic apparatus known as the 'Wheatstone', in which a paper ribbon is first perforated and then sent through a machine, recording at the distant end with ink marks upon paper tape. **1924** P. J. Risdon *Wireless* xvi. 135 When the operator depresses the keys,.. instead of typing letters and figures, it perforates the paper tape with holes corresponding to the dots and dashes of the Morse code. **1943** *Rep. Progress Appl. Chem.* XXVIII. 131 In the standard test for the adhesive power of gummed paper tape the sample is moistened under standard conditions. **1961** *Times* 3 Oct. (Computer Suppl.) p. vi/4 Each day the paper-tape readers feed into the computer more than nine million characters relating to long-distance calls. **1971** *Ann. Rep. Curators Bodl. Libr. 1969–70* 45 The correction of records..suffered from rapid changes of the staff operating the paper-tape typewriters. **1975** J. B. Harley *O.S. Maps* i. 14 The names are then typed on a 'Monotype' keyboard which reproduces them on punched paper tape to operate the filmsetter. **1952** 'Han Suyin' *Many-Splendoured Thing* v. 313 America is only a paper tiger... That's what the Peking government says. **1958** *Peking Rev.* 11 Nov. 7 In August 1946 Comrade Mao Tse Tung gave an interview to the American journalist Anna Louise Strong and expressed his famous view point that all reactionaries are paper tigers. **1963** *Economist* 12 Jan. 98/1 In the Chinese view, the 'rotten, decadent, paper-tiger nature' of imperialism cannot change. **1973** *Black Panther* 10 Nov. 14/3 Our minority may be powerful now, but in the end even that power will prove to be a paper tiger once the people unite. **1976** J. Snow *Cricket Rebel* 25 We [*sc.* Sussex] were something of paper tigers when it came to the championship games. **1943** D. Baker *Trio* I. 55 She jerked a paper towel off the roller and did a careful job of drying. **1953** *Times* 31 Oct. 1/11 Many paper manufactures, including..paper towels and handkerchiefs. **1972** *Guardian* 17 May 9/5 Plain coloured paper towels cost 17p for a two-roll pack. **1975** *New Yorker* 8 Dec. 41/2 The stenographers and typists had to make do with paper towels that scratched when new and dissolved when damp. **1916** *Monotype System* (Lanston Monotype Machine Co.) Gloss. p. lxvi, Paper Tower... The mechanism of both the Keyboard and Casting Machine..that carries the paper ribbon and advances it one marginal perforation for each character, or space, struck at the Keyboard or cast at the Casting Machine. *Ibid.* xi. 35 The operator has only to turn the small Valve Handle.. at the left side of the bottom of the Paper Tower. **1922** *Casting Machine Adjustments* (Lanston Monotype Machine Co.) 17 The Paper Tower is the controlling mechanism of the Casting Machine. In it is placed the paper ribbon prepared at the Keyboard by the compositor, and the ribbon compels the Casting Machine to produce the characters required. *Ibid.*, The Paper Tower mechanism provides that the advance of the paper will be absolute. **1951** S. Jennett *Making of Bks.* iv. 68 Above the keybank [of the Monotype] is the paper-tower, in which is a roll of paper perforated along the edges like cine-film. **1819** E. Evans *Pedestrious Tour* 228 On this river too is General Simcoe's paper town called London. **1943** T. Pratt *Barefoot Mailman* xi. 90 How do we know you are not a paper-town shark yourself? How do we know you have not come here to boom our city to false values? **1948** E. N. Dick *Dixie Frontier* 151 Many towns..never got beyond the stage of 'paper towns'. **1957** B. Hutchison *Canada: Tomorrow's Giant* 307 Logging camps, mills, paper towns, the new aluminium town of Kitimat..pour their products into Vancouver. **1959** *Tararua* XIII. 49 *Paper road* and *paper town*..describe those roads and towns which have been surveyed but whose actual existence has got no further than the maps. **1969** H. Horwood *Newfoundland* i. 4 Driving back through the star-studded night towards the paper town of Grand Falls. **1925** G. Dickinson *Eng. Papier-Mâché* i. 3 In 1772 Henry Clay, japanner, of Birmingham, invented a material which had certain heat-resisting properties, that made it suitable for japanning or lacquering processes. The body of the material was made by pasting sheets of paper together, and the articles made from it were called 'paper ware'. **1969** *Canad. Antiques Collector* Jan. 8/1 The craze for making 'Paper-ware' spread from the 17th to the 19th century, when recipes for making and decorating bowls, vases and plates, were printed in such papers as the '*Gentleman's Magazine*'. **1889** W. FRASER *Words on Wellington* 136, I have heard it said that a vivâ voce examination is not fair upon a young man; and that, what at Oxford we call 'paper work' should be used for military examinations. **1917** R. KIPLING *Let.* in C. E. Carrington *Rudyard Kipling* (1955) xvii. 445 Both sides groan together over the enormous amount of unnecessary paper-work. **1958** I. MURDOCH *Bell* viii. 120 Time was badly needed to catch up on the paper work of the previous week. **1961** [see *feed-house* s.v. *FEED *sb.* 6]. **1969** J. ARGENTI *Managem. Techniques* v. 24 Too much paperwork. Symptoms: masses of complicated forms. **1971** S. HILL *Strange Meeting* ii. 123 They sat in their dug-out in the evening, reading or doing paperwork, listening to the gramophone. **1973** C. BONINGTON *Next Horizon* xxi. 290 Back to Base Camp, to start wading through the mass of paper-work which the end of the expedition.. entailed. **1977** *New Yorker* 8 Aug. 68/3 (Advt.), We do the paperwork, you do the legwork.

paper, *v.* Add: **3. e.** Fig. phr. *to paper over*: temporarily to conceal; esp. in phr. *to paper over the cracks* (see *CRACK *sb.* 7 f).

1955 *Times* 16 Nov. 10/5 This document was treated by the western Ministers as no more than an attempt to paper over the complete divergence in policy. **1957** *Economist* 28 Dec. 1114/2 The party's usual split has been papered over. **1966** J. DEAKIN *Lobbyists* 79 Not even the impressive legislative accomplishments under Lyndon Johnson can paper over Congress's serious..frailties. **1969** *Sunday Sun* (Baltimore) 16 Mar. K 1/3 The two sides were still able to paper over their differences and agree to a compromise program. **1974** *Times* 6 Apr. 1/2 Mrs Meir has persuaded the party previously to paper over such differences.

4. b. (Earlier and later examples.)

1859 E. FITZBALL 35 *Yrs. Dram. Author's Life* II. 113 The second night comes, the unfailing 'Lady of Lyons'... House well papered, but badly *gilt*—calls similar. **1959** *Times* 3 Nov. 15/3 'Papering a house' is all very well when a company is playing to empty stalls, but is hardly a good idea when the house is full. **1973** *Courier-Mail* (Brisbane) 26 July 9/5 Surely the theatre could..at least have 'papered' the house with complementary guests for the opening if the box office was looking so poorly. **1978** A. MORICE *Murder by Proxy* xx. 155 We should be playing to an audience of approximately thirty-five, about two thirds of it papered.

6. *intr.* and *trans.* To pass forged cheques; to defraud by issuing forged cheques. Also in extended use. *U.S. slang.*

1925 *Flynn's* 7 Mar. 191/2 *Paper*,..to pass worthless or forged checks. **1941** *Amer. Speech* XVI. 248/2 *To paper the burg*, to pass a quantity of forged checks. **1958** *Daily News* (N.Y.) 16 Apr. 60 Helped by phony..credentials and a blonde, a former stable boy..papered Queens and Long Island with $10,000 to $15,000 worth of bum checks. **1976** SCOTT & KOSKI *Walk-In* xi. 63, I want to know that this *is* Li we're dealing with and not some ringer they've papered on us.

7. *trans.* To preserve (insects) by storing them in triangular packets made of folded paper.

[**1894** W. F. KIRBY *Hand-bk. Lepidoptera* I. p. lii, Collectors abroad generally put their captures into papers folded to resemble a triangular envelope. *Ibid.* p. lv, The cheapest way of buying Butterflies is to buy miscellaneous lots at an auction, especially lots in papers.] **1955** WAGSTAFFE & FIDLER *Preservation Nat. Hist. Specimens* I. 186 Specimens may often have to be stored for considerable periods before they can be set to form part of the permanent collection. The usual method of storing such specimens is to 'paper' them.

‖ **paperasserie** (papərasəri). [Fr.] An accumulation of paper-work; administrative red tape.

1928 *Observer* 22 July 12 The Frenchman loves to make fun of 'paperasserie', the elaborate and meticulous bureaucracy, whose spirit he really admires in his heart. **1955** D. BARTON *Glorious Life* 123 Even though I make a great parade of enthusiasm and am far too conscientious about my work.., all this *paperasserie* is not my element. **1965** *New Statesman* 21 May 809/1 The complaints universally made against Indian administrators today—delay and file-passing—seem to be just the complaints that Curzon made against the British administrators of his time. His first battle was against paperasserie.

paperback (pē̆i·pəɹbæk). Also **paper-back.** [f. PAPER *sb.* + BACK *sb.*[1]] A book with a paper back or cover. Also *attrib.*, and as *v. trans.*, to publish in a paperback edition.

1899 [in Dict. s.v. PAPER *sb.* 12]. **1954** etc. [see *HARDBACK 2]. **1957** *Times Lit. Suppl.* 12 July i/2 The revolution wrought in the world of books by the emergence of the paperback can best be measured by comparing a classical private library with a contemporary collection of books. *Ibid.* ii/3 In one way or another most English publishers have accepted, and come to terms with, the paperback revolution. **1960** *N.Y. Times Mag.* 5 June 2 Has Emily Post been paper-backed? **1962** A. HUXLEY *Let.* 11 Feb. (1969) 929 In this context see the list of 112 exercises in awareness..printed at the end of *Zen Flesh, Zen Bones* (now in paperback). **1963** *Sunday Times* (Colour Suppl.) 24 Nov. 23/2 They paperback their *World of Art* series at 18s. **1964** M. MCLUHAN *Understanding Media* (1967) II. xxxi. 347 The paperback, especially in its highbrow form, was tried in America in the 1920s and thirties and forties. It was not, however, until 1953 that it suddenly became acceptable. **1968** *Guardian* 27 Apr. 7/1 The worse the rubbish the wider the market: trash is paperbacked in many languages. **1971** *Country Life* 18 Feb. 381/2 His *Highland Year*..which is already in three editions and about to make paperback, is followed by *Highland Deer Forest*. **1971** *New Scientist* 19 Aug. 433/1 It looks as if most people are going to have to wait for the paperback. **1973** 'M. INNES' *Appleby's Answer* xvii. 149 The paperback rights..would pay for far more than Miss Pringle's customary inexpensive holiday. **1974** *Times* 28 Feb. 15/8 Paperback rights bring £27,000 bid... Hardback rights in Britain are held by Alison Press. **1975** *Bookseller* 11 Oct. 2038/2 The book was called *Harris in Wonderland*, and Cape published it. It was adapted for radio, and paperbacked in Hungary, of all places. **1976** H. M. HARRISON in Aldiss & Harrison *Decade the 1950s* 12 With the coming of the paperback revolution..SF found new places to go.

So **pa·per-backed** *a.* or *ppl. a.*, having a paper back, published in paper-back form; also (*fig.*), lacking in strength, feeble.

1888 KIPLING *Soldiers Three* (1889) 52 'Push, men!' sez Crook; 'Push ye paper-backed beggars!' he sez. **1903** *Work* 14 Mar. 89/3 (*heading*) Handy method of binding paper-backed books. **1909** *Chambers's Jrnl.* Sept. 610/2 The man then buys a paper-backed novel for fourpence-halfpenny. **1932** D. L. SAYERS *Have his Carcase* x. 116 One or two paper-backed books. **1957** *Times Lit. Suppl.* 12 July p. ii/3 American bookstalls and bookshops are nowadays crowded with solid, well made, often highbrow but still paperbacked volumes. **1968** *Guardian* 29 July 20/8 Paperbacked D. H. Lawrence floods the bookshops. **1974** C. FREMLIN *By Horror Haunted* 58 Years of..reading of lurid paper-backed stories under the desks at school had not provided him with this sort of solid..information.

pa·per-bark. [f. PAPER *sb.* + BARK *sb.*[1]] **1.** A name used for several Australian trees distinguished by flaky layers of pale bark, esp. *Melaleuca leucadendron*, the cajeput, and other members of the genus *Melaleuca*, belonging to the family Myrtaceæ. Also *attrib.*

1842 *Western Australia* 81 It [*sc.* the Melaleuca, or tea-tree] is sometimes known by the name of the paper-bark tree, from the multitudinous layers (some hundreds) of which the bark is composed. These layers are very thin, and are loosely attached to each other, peeling off like the bark of the English birch. **1846, 1866** [see PAPER *sb.* 12]. **1908** E. J. BANFIELD *Confessions of Beachcomber* I. vi. 216 Few of the forest trees are more picturesque than the paper-bark or tea-tree..of free and stately growth, the bark white. **1920** B. CRONIN *Timber Wolves* 88 From the paper-bark swamps came the reverberating boom of frogs. **1924** LAWRENCE & SKINNER *Boy in Bush* 100 It was salty paper-bark country. **1946** K. TENNANT *Lost Haven* (1947) 2 Wide, soggy moors..from which the great, white paper-barks tower. **1957** P. WHITE *Voss* 59 She walked in the garden, amongst the camellia bushes..and the scurfy native paperbarks. **1961** A. UPFIELD *Bony & White Savage* ix. 78 A ring of paperbark trees, all grey-white of trunk and branch... He was able to tear off a strip, to find it composed of layer above layer of paper-thin wafers... Under the outer one the wafers were flesh-coloured. **1969** *Northern Territory News* (Darwin) *Focus '69* 85/1, I took up my most pleasant sentry duties amongst the paperbark trees.

2. The durable bark of *Melaleuca leucadendron.*

1857 J. ASKEW *Voy. Austral. & N.Z.* 433 The dead bodies are burnt or buried, though some in North Australia place the corpse in the paper bark of the tea-tree, and deposit it in a hollow tree. **1908** E. J. BANFIELD *Confessions of Beachcomber* I. ii. 82 It became necessary..to keep the ridge covering of paper-bark in position. **1941** I. L. IDRIESS *Great Boomerang* iv. 28 It was she who found him paperbark and fashioned his first sandals.

3. paper-bark maple, *Acer griseum*, a maple native to central China, introduced into Europe in 1901, and characterized by flaky, light brown bark; **paper-bark tea-tree, ti-tree** = sense 1 above.

1927 A. REHDER *Man. Cultivated Trees N. Amer.* 577 Paperbark M[aple]. Tree to 8 m., with cinnamon-brown bark separating in thin papery flakes. **1938** *Amer. Nurseryman* 15 Oct. 3/3 The leaves of the paperbark maple..are finely and thickly hairy underneath. **1969** T. H. EVERETT *Living Trees of World* 223/1 The paper-bark maple (*A[cer] griseum* of western China is remarkable for its beautiful rich cinnamon brown bark which peels in broad paper-thin strips. **1974** A. MITCHELL *Field Guide Trees Britain* 349 Paper-bark Maple... Now much planted in gardens. **1967** A. RULE *Forests Austral.* xiv. 154 An enterprising firm manufactures cork from the bark of the paperbark tea tree. **1944** *Living off Land* vii. 137 Open-grained Timbers... Paper-bark Ti-tree [etc.].

papered, *ppl. a.* Add: **a.** (Further examples.)

a **1828** D. WORDSWORTH *Jrnl.* (1941) II. 335 The little room so snug—the carpets—the papered walls. **1846** *Jewish Manual, or Pract. Information Jewish & Mod. Cookery* vi. 158 Bake in a papered tin. **1860** F. NIGHTINGALE *Notes on Nursing* ii. 16 Old papered walls of years' standing..are..ready sources of impurity to the air. **1977** M. T. BLOOM *13th Man* ii. 13 The papered corridors had the palpable feel of transitoriness, of waiting to be called—up or out.

b. *slang.* Of a theatre, etc.: filled by means of free passes.

1936 *Amer. Speech* XI. 221 The house will be *papered*, which means that free passes to the show will be given away. **1959** *Oxf. Mag.* 12 Feb. 244/1 Last week the B.B.C. was able to fill the Festival Hall decently full (even allowing for 'papered' seats). **1974** *Plain Dealer* (Cleveland, Ohio) 27 Oct. 2-C/3 If there is a large crowd at ringside the suspicion will be a papered house, for the government doesn't want the world to see an empty stadium.

2. Of insects in a collection, stored in triangular packets made of folded paper.

1937 C. LONGFIELD *Dragonflies Brit. Isles* 27 Preserving the brilliant colours after death is extraordinarily difficult, and for that reason a 'pinned' or 'papered' collection of dragonflies is often very disappointing. **1955** WAGSTAFFE & FIDLER *Preservation Nat. Hist. Specimens* I. 187 (*caption*) Box for storing papered insects.

paperer. Add: (Further examples of sense 'a paper-hanger'.)

1837 J. ROMILLY *Diary* 25 May (1967) 119 Set the Painters & Paperers to work in the new house. **1928** A. HUXLEY *Let.* 8 Oct. (1969) 302 The house is in a state of chaos—painters and paperers still at work, furniture huddled here and there.

b. *slang.* One who issues or receives free passes to a theatre, etc.

1885 *Referee* 14 June 3/3 Results showed that the 'paperer' understood his business. **1895** *Punch* May 230/1, I took Lil, Dannel's youngest, larst week to the play with some tickets I'd got. Well paperers mustn't be choosers.

paper-hanger. Add: **1.** (Earlier and later examples.)

1796 M. EDGWORTH *Parent's Assistant* (ed. 2) 164 A new carpenter and paper-hanger..were appointed. **1969** *New Yorker* 12 Apr. 80/2 'We'll be as busy as one-armed paperhangers,' says Lind. **1975** *Ibid.* 21 Apr. 95/1 According to some twenty separate lists that were obtained from underwriters' manuals..occupations that various insurance companies consider to be grounds for rejection of applications for auto insurance, or acceptance only after careful study or on a restricted basis, included those of.. paperhangers,..sports coaches and assistants, travelling salesmen,..and doctors.

2. *slang.* (orig. *U.S.*). One who passes forged or fraudulent cheques; a forger.

1914 JACKSON & HELLYER *Vocab. Criminal Slang* 101 Whoever thoughtlessly leaves his check book in accessible places incurs the jeopardy of..personal loss, seeing that 'paper hangers' are vigilant in the search for these. **1938** *Detective Fiction Weekly* 23 Apr. 73/1 Next to the con man is the 'paperhanger' or a 'writer of sad, short stories', these terms referring to a forger. **1941** J. G. BRANDON *Death in Quarry* xiii. 126 'Paper-hanger,' McCarthy echoed. 'That's a new one on me, William.' 'Passin' the snide, sir,' Withers informed him. 'Passing flash paper. Bank of Elegance stuff.' **1945** L. SHELLY *Jive Talk Dict.* 31 *Paper hanger*, one who deals in counterfeit money. **1976** *Times Lit. Suppl.* 16 Apr. 457/4 A legendary confidence man and 'paperhanger' (described as 'a criminal who specialises in hanging, or passing on stolen or counterfeit securities on brokerage houses, insurance companies, and individuals').

paper-hanging. Add: **2. b.** The affixing of bills, advertisements, etc., on a bill-board or hoarding.

1851 DICKENS in *Househ. Words* 22 Mar. 604/2 [I] Hired a large one [*sc.* hoarding]..let out places on it, and called it 'The External Paper-Hanging Station'. **1961** *Times* 21 June 13/6 A hundred years ago 'paper hanging' (a term for bill-posting inherited from the eighteenth century) was an irresponsible and pirate trade.

3. *slang.* (orig. *U.S.*). The passing of forged cheques; forging.

1927 *Dialect Notes* V. 458 *Paper hanging*,..passing forged cheques. **1930** *Detective Fiction Weekly* 30 Aug. 697/2 'Paperhanging', or passing fictitious checks..is not always a mere matter of offering a check to a merchant and trusting to luck that he will cash it. Many tradesmen make it a rule never to cash a check for a stranger, unless it be a pay check or a certified check; but a clever paper-hanger can get around this easily enough. **1932** *Evening Sun* (Baltimore) 9 Dec. 31/5 *Paper hanging*, forging. **1975** C. WESTON *Susannah Screaming* (1976) viii. 42 From paperhanging to murder—that's a pretty big jump. **1976** A. SCHROEDER *Shaking it Rough* 95 It all involved paper-hanging—fake credit cards, rubber checks, [etc.].

papering, *vbl. sb.* Add: **1.** (Further examples.)

1841 THACKERAY *Gt. Hoggarty Diamond* (1849) x. 130 The painting, papering, and carpeting of my house. **1855** MRS. GASKELL *North & South* I. viii. 97 It needed the pretty light papering of the rooms to reconcile them to Milton. **1928** A. HUXLEY *Let.* 25 Oct. (1969) 302 The main work is done..all painting and papering. **1975** P. DICKINSON *Lively Dead* xxi. 125, I do want to get the papering done before my son comes back. He's an absolute devil with glue.

2. (See quot. 1966.)

1798 JANE AUSTEN *Let.* 1 Dec. (1952) 35 My long hair is always plaited up out of sight, and my short hair curls well enough to want no papering. **1815** R. FENTON *Mem. Old Wig* 9 Having undergone the varied ordeal of papering, pinching, crimping, baking, and torture a thousand ways, I was promoted to thatch the cranium of the notorious judge Jefferies. **1966** J. S. COX *Illustr. Dict. Hairdressing* 108/1 *Papering*, 18th cent. term for placing the paper papillotes around the wound hair preparatory to pinching it with hot pinching irons.

papery, *a.* Add: Also *fig.*

1924 R. FRY *Let.* 27 June (1972) II. 554 Ingres's *Stratonice* is a shock..it's so thin and papery. **1937** D. CANFIELD *Fables for Parents* (1938) 55 It was..more apparent that it was a papery idea out of a book.

Paphlagonian (pæflăgōu·niăn), *a.* and *sb.* [f. Gr. Παφλαγωνία, L. *Paphlagonia*, an ancient region in northern Asia Minor + -AN.] **A.** *adj.* Of or pertaining to Paphlagonia or its inhabitants. **B.** *sb.* A native or inhabitant of Paphlagonia.

Also (spelt *Paflagonian*) with reference to the fictional people in Thackeray's *The Rose and the Ring.*

1596 T. NASHE *Have with you to Saffron-Walden* sig. O2ᵛ, Procris and Cephalus, and a number of Pamphlagonian things more, that it would rust & yron spot paper, to have but one sillable of their names breathed over it. **1607** TOPSELL *Foure-f. Beasts* 291 Touching the Paphlagonians about the education of their horsses see more among the Venetians. *Ibid.* 562 The Paphlagonians, which before the Troyan warre were called *Eneti*, and afterwards *Veneti*. **1748** HUME *Philos. Ess. conc. Human Understanding* x. 189 The Impostor..was enabled to proceed, from his ignorant Paphlagonians, to the inlisting of Votaries, even among the Grecian Philosophers. **1855** THACKERAY *Rose & Ring* i. 4 Two nations which had been engaged in bloody and expensive wars, as the Paflagonians and the Crimeans had been. *Ibid.* ii. 5 The Paflagonian nobility did not care who was king. **1954** T. GUNN *Fighting Terms* 32 Here in a cave the Paphlagonian King Crouched. **1974** *Encycl. Brit. Micropædia* VII. 734/1 The Paphlagonians were one of the most ancient peoples of Anatolia.

papia, var. *PAPAYA.

1921 *Outward Bound* Feb. 69/1 The natives..kept bringing fresh fruit to our view—mangoes and custard apples and papia.

‖ **Papiamento** (pæpyäme·nto). Also **Papiamentu.** [Sp.] A Spanish-based creole language of Curaçao, Aruba, and Bonaire, in the Caribbean Sea.

1949 *Caribbean Q.* I. III. 36 The remnants of the African culture, are fast disappearing... There are no signs, however, that their language, the papiamento, which is still in use everywhere, will disappear. **1953** *Ibid.* III. I. 27 Dialects such as Papiamento..were unworthy of the grammarians' labour. **1956** *Publ. Amer. Dial. Soc.* XXVI. 11 The derivative of Spanish spoken in Curaçao (called Papiamentu or Papiamento), of French in Haïti (Creole), of English in Guiana (Ningro-Tongo), in the West Indies, and in South Carolina (Gullah) are some examples of languages which can either be regarded as dialects of the colonial languages or as new languages of their own. **1967** *Language* XLIII. 818 Papiamentu 'may well represent a fusion of two earlier pidgins or creoles'. **1972** J. L. DILLARD *Black English* i. 24 Some of them [*sc.* pidgin and creole languages] are vehicles of education and literature, like Papiamento, whose speakers have profited from an enlightened Dutch attitude toward languages. **1974** R. A. HALL *External Hist. Romance Lang.* vii. 157 In other languages, however, such as Papiamentu, the dominant lexical influence in later centuries has come from a non-Romance language, in this case Dutch. **1976** *San Francisco Examiner & Chron.* 13 June (Travel Suppl.) 8/3 Although Papiamento is spoken on radio and TV, and newspapers and books are printed in it, the official language on the island [*sc.* Aruba] is Dutch.

‖ **papier** (papye). The French word for 'paper' used in various phrases, as **papier collé** (kǫle) ['gummed paper'], a collage made from paper; also *attrib.*; **papier déchiré** (deʃire), paper torn haphazardly for making collages; a collage made of such paper; **papier poudré** (pūdre), a paper impregnated with face-powder. See also PAPIER MÂCHÉ in Dict. and Suppl.

1907 *Yesterday's Shopping* (1969) 539/1 Papier Poudre. In 3 shades, white, rose and rachel... These exquisitely perfumed leaves are designed to supersede the use of 'puff and powder box'. **1919** R. FIRBANK *Valmouth* xi. 189 'A book is anathema to her.' 'Even a *papier poudré* one; for, when I gave her my little precious volume of *blanc de perle* in order to rub her nose, she started grating her teeth at me.' **1935** D. GASCOYNE *Short Survey Surrealism* v. 107 The *papiers collés* of Picasso and Braque (newspaper, wallpaper, cigarette packets). **1959** *Listener* 30 Apr. 766/3 It is a picture as utterly *original* as the first *papiers collés*. *Ibid.* 19 Nov. 868/1 Arp even welcomed the ravages wrought by time on his own works, and started to help nature along by doing the destruction for her, making *collages* of *papiers déchirés*, roughly and haphazardly torn. **1960** E. H. GOMBRICH *Art & Illusion* x. 356 His [*sc.* Picasso's] more playful creations, such as his *papiers déchirés*. **1960** D. HOLMAN-HUNT *My Grandmothers & I* iv. 121 Grandmother was scrubbing her nose with a sheet of Papier Poudre. **1962** *Listener* 15 Feb. 305/1 In using the technique of *papier collé* they were substituting fragments of reality itself for the earlier fragmented images of reality. *Ibid.*, Their *papier collé* pictures. **1963** *Times* 8 Feb. 14/3 The reliefs..and the sculpture..are built up of plywood layers treated in the manner of a *papier dechiré* collage. **1965** *New Statesman* 12 Nov. 758/2 The introduction of *trompe-l'œil* and *papier-collé*. **1973** *Country Life* 1 Mar. 556/3 Tiny booklets..containing *papier poudre*, for 12p..very popular years ago for taking the shine off noses. It works.

‖ **papier mâché.** Add: Also *fig.*

1818 'T. BROWN' *Brighton* I. i. 13 He has a clay-cold heart, and a mere papier maché mind. **1920** F. M. FORD *Let.* 24 July (1965) 115 The plaster Pillars of the State and the papier maché hearts of men. **1977** *Broadcast* 7 Feb. 7/2 It's unlikely that he would want to be party to a papier maché exercise.

papilio (păpi·lio). [a. L. *pāpilio* butterfly, adopted as a generic name by Linnæus in *Systema Naturæ* (ed. 10, 1758) I. 458.] A swallow-tail butterfly belonging to the large genus so called, frequently distinguished by tail-like projections on the hind pair of wings; formerly, any butterfly.

1789 *Loiterer* 26 Sept. 9 The Wings of Moths, and Papilios. **1835** J. DUNCAN *Brit. Butterflies* 92 The word *Papilio* was used by Linnaeus in the comprehensive sense which he was accustomed to attach to such terms, to designate generically all the diurnal lepidoptera. **1932** J. S. HUXLEY *Probl. Relative Growth* ii. 55 Many of these [*sc.* holometabolous insects] possess organs which increase in relative size with increase of absolute size of body..[like] the 'tail' on the hind wing of Papilios. **1936** *Discovery* July 213/2 Many large Papilios were flying about. **1965** R. MCKIE *Company of Animals* xiii. 178 Papilios and pierids and danaids, the Browns, the Blues, the Skippers, and many many more. **1972** L. E. CHADWICK tr. *Linsenmaier's Insects of World* 41/1 The males [of *Papilio dardanus*] occur throughout the range in the normal, long-tailed costume of the papilios.

papillœdema (pæpilidī·mă). *Ophthalm.* Also (chiefly *U.S.*) **papilledema.** [f. PAPILL(A + ŒDEMA, as repr. G. *papillenödem* (A. Eloching 1895, in *A. von Græfe's Arch. für Opthhalm.* XLI. II. 276).] Non-inflammatory swelling of the optic disc due to increased intracranial pressure on the optic nerve, usu. as a result of a tumour or abscess of the brain.

1908 J. H. PARSONS *Path. of Eye* IV. xxvii. 1349, I suggest the use of the term 'papillœdema' to replace 'choked disc' (Stauungspapille). **1922** R. F. MOORE *Med. Ophthalm.* i. 23 In a few cases papillœdema runs its course to complete subsidence in one eye, the other remaining normal throughout. **1950** BERENS & SIEGEL *Encycl. of Eye* 34 Papilledema is a common finding in increased pressure, although it is by no means an early sign. **1961** *Times* 11 May 9/1 The pathogenesis of papilloedema. **1972** *Pediatrics* XLIX. 248/1 Papilledema in a patient with cyanotic congenital heart disease is not necessarily a sign of brain abscess. **1977** *Proc. R. Soc. Med.* LXX. 235/2 Acute blockage of the shunt is usually obvious because of the clinical signs, the most valuable being bradycardia. Papillœdema is not to be relied upon.

papillon (pa·piyoṅ). [a. F. *papillon* butterfly.] A breed of toy dog related to the spaniel, having a white coat with a few darker patches, esp. on the head, and erect ears resembling the shape of a butterfly's wings. Also *attrib.*

1907 R. LEIGHTON *New Bk. Dog* XVII. lxi. 536/1 A very engaging little dog is the Papillon, or Squirrel Spaniel. *Ibid.* 536/2 The name Papillon is obviously given to the dog in reference to its ears, which stand out large and erect like the wings of a butterfly, heavily feathered. **1910** *Encycl. Brit.* VIII. 376/1 At the annual show of the Kennel Club in the autumn of 1905..additional breeds..[were] Chesapeake Bay dogs, Chihuahuas, Papillons and Roseneath terriers. **1924** *Glasgow Herald* 4 Apr. 8 A new toy dog has been brought from Belgium, the Papillon. It is very small, weighing when full grown 3 to 5 lb. **1927** M. B. COOPER in C. C. Sanderson *Pedigree Dogs* 341 The Papillon or Butterfly dog was first introduced into England in any number in 1923. **1929** R. GRAVES *Poems* 25 Those pugs and papillons and in-betweens. **1960** *Times* 11 Mar. 1/7 (Advt.), Adorable Papillon Puppies. **1971** F. HAMILTON *World Encycl. Dogs* 541 The Papillon has bred true to type for some 700 years or more, as can be verified in the art galleries and museums of the world. **1972** *N.Y. Times* 4 June 6/2 Deja..has been best Papillon 125 of the 135 times he has been shown.

papillote. Add: **1.** (Further examples.) Also *fig.*

1848 THACKERAY *Van. Fair* xliii. 392 Glorvina, trembling with all the papillotes. **1860** QUEEN VICTORIA *Let.* 3 Nov. in R. Fulford *Dearest Child* (1964) 278 We drove over..to Clifden which unfortunately was en papillotte. **1959** S. G. FLITMAN *Craft of Ladies' Hairdressing* viii. 74 For years the posticheur had used papilottes (small triangles of paper) to hold damp flat curls until they were dried.

attrib. **1960** CUNNINGTON & BEARD *Dict. Eng. Costume* 156/1 *Papillotte comb*.., a decorative comb of tortoiseshell. **1966** J. S. COX *Illustr. Dict. Hairdressing* 108/2 *Papilotte tongs*, pinching irons.

2. A paper wrapper, usu. greased, in which certain types of meat and fish are cooked or served.

1818 T. MOORE *Fudge Fam. Paris* v. 38 One's hair and one's cutlets both *en papilotte*. **1868** M. JEWRY *Warne's Model Cookery* 296/2 Wrap them [*sc.* mutton cutlets] in buttered papers... The fat of the dressed meat is absorbed in the papillotes. **1959** R. POSTGATE *Good Food Guide 1959–1960* 109 Tamar salmon en papillotte, ham soufflé, or chicken à la crème, may appear on the menu. **1961** *Guardian* 10 Mar. 10/6 Trout can..be grilled..in paper-bags (*papillotes*)...first spread the inside of the *papillote* generously with maître d'hôtel batter.

Papist. Add: **3.** An imitator or follower of the poet, Alexander Pope. Also *attrib.*

a **1849** H. COLERIDGE *Ess. & Marginalia* (1851) II. 118 Nor would so many really monotonous jinglers have passed for correct, orthodox Papists. **1902** F. HARRISON *John Ruskin* ii. 22 Many a prize poem has had worse couplets in the Papist vein than these on Etna.

papodam, -dum, varr. POPADAM (in Dict. and Suppl.).

papolater (pēⁱpǫ·lătəɹ). [f. L. *pāpa* pope + *-later* (see -LATRY).] One who practises papolatry.

1913 A. FORTESCUE *Lesser Eastern Churches* i. 4 We are Creed-tamperers, Papolaters, gross disturbers of the peace by our shameless way of sending missionaries.

papoose. Add: **b. papoose-root,** a perennial plant, *Caulophyllum thalictrioides*, of the family Berberidaceæ, native to eastern North America, and bearing panicles of small yellowish flowers and blue berries; the thick, twisted root was formerly used medicinally. (Earlier and later examples.)

1815 D. DRAKE *Nat. View Cincinnati* ii. 85 Poppoos root. **1843** J. TORREY *Flora N.Y.* I. 33 Blue Cohosh. Pappoose-root... The root of this plant is in some repute as a diuretic and bitter. **1943** R. PEATTIE *Great Smokies* 190 The old wives of the mountains today are not averse to..giving their teething children a little papooseroot.

papovavirus (păpōᵘ·văvəⁱᵊrɒs). *Microbiol.* Also **papova virus.** [See quot. 1962.] Any of a group of small animal viruses which includes those causing polyoma, papilloma, sarcoma, and warts, the members of which consist of double-stranded DNA in an icosahedral capsid with no envelope.

1962 J. L. MELNICK in *Science* 30 Mar. 1128 In the course of work in this laboratory with papilloma (wart) virus of man, polyoma virus of mice, and vacuolating virus of monkeys, I have been made conscious of the similarities in properties between each of them and papilloma virus of rabbits. This has led me to group these viruses together in the pa'po'va virus group, the name being derived from the first two letters of each virus name: *pa*pilloma, *po*lyoma, *va*cuolating, in the order in which the viruses became known. *Ibid.* 1129 The papova viruses contain DNA. **1969** S. T. LYLES *Biol. Microorganisms* xxvi. 536 Papovaviruses characteristically produce warts in human infections; the most common type is the *verruca vulgaris*, called the common wart. **1973** R. G. KRUEGER et al. *Introd. Microbiol.* xxi. 562/1 Members of the papovavirus group can produce tumours readily when injected into tissues of immunologically undeveloped neonatal animals and with difficulty when injected into older animals. **1977** *Proc. R. Soc. Med.* LXX. 393/2 Dulbecco (1976) has recently considered evidence suggesting that cellular mutations may be needed for the full expression of cell transformation by papova viruses.

Pappenheimer (pæ·pĕnhəi·məɹ). *Med.* [The name of Alwin M. *Pappenheimer* (b. 1908), U.S. biochemist, who described such bodies in 1945 (*Q. Jrnl. Med.* XXXVIII. 75).] *Pappenheimer('s) body*: a siderosome that stains with Romanowsky's or Wright's stain.

1947 MCFADZEAN & DAVIS in *Glasgow Med. Jrnl.* XXVIII. 238 Preparations of the peripheral blood of this case were sent to Dr. Pappenheimer, who..confirmed their apparent identity with those studied by him... We shall in this paper refer to these inclusion bodies as Pappenheimer's bodies. *Ibid.* 255 It would appear that the siderotic granules described by Grüneberg..and by Doniach *et al.*..are probably similar to the Pappenheimer bodies. **1966** J. W. LINMAN *Princ. Hematol.* iii. 63 Siderocytes are red cells that contain one or more hemosiderin granules; these inclusion bodies..are usually demonstrable only with special stains, such as Prussian blue. Occasionally they are associated with sufficient basophilic material to be evident with Romanowsky stains and are then referred to as Pappenheimer bodies. **1972** W. J. WILLIAMS et al. *Hematol.* viii. 80/2 Siderosomes staining with Wright's stain have been called Pappenheimer bodies.

pappy, *sb.*¹ Add: Also **pappie.** Delete 'Now *rare*' and add further examples.

1909 JOYCE *Let.* 29 July (1966) II. 230 All are delighted with Georgie, specially Pappie. **1918** —— *Exiles* 20 Do you want to speak to my pappie? **1929** W. FAULKNER *Sartoris* III. iv. 206 Whut you hear, pappy? **1962** L. DEIGHTON *Ipcress File* xx. 130 My pappy used to say, 'Drink Scotch by itself, with rye mix a little water.' **1963** M. DUGGAN in C. K. Stead *N.Z. Short Stories* (1966) 109 Fanny never chattered much and less than ever in the presence of her pappy. **1978** D. BAGLEY *Flyaway* xxix. 280 He wanted to find his Pappy's airplane.

paprika (pæ·prikă, pa·prikă, păprī·kă). [Hungarian, f. Serbo-Croat *pàpar* pepper (see H. H. Bielfeldt 1965, in *Sitzungsber. d. deutsch. Akad. d. Wissensch. zu Berlin: Klasse für Sprachen, Literatur u. Kunst* I. 20).] **1.** A condiment made from the dried, ground fruits of certain varieties of the sweet pepper, *Capsicum annuum*. Also *attrib.* and *fig.*

1896 J. T. LAW *Grocer's Manual* 521/1 Paprika, or Hungarian Red Pepper. **1897** *Sears, Roebuck Catal.* 9/3 Pure Ground Spices..Paprika—Hungarian (¼lb boxes), sweet pepper. **1898** C. H. SENN *Culinary Encycl.* 70 *Paprika*, Hungarian red pepper. A kind of sweet capsicum of a brilliant scarlet colour. **1908** *Daily Chron.* 29 Apr. 9/6 Beat together, adding oil every two minutes; paprika to taste. **1918** A. QUILLER-COUCH *Foe-Farrell* 91 You rubbed a soupsong of garlic into them with three drops of paprika. **1930** *Time & Tide* 14 Feb. 206/2 The Master of the pig-stick had a face and a temper as scarlet as paprika. **1962** H. T. MOORE *Coll. Lett. D. H. Lawrence* I. p. x, He [*sc.* Lawrence] often sprinkled in the paprika of gossip. **1974** *Times* 14 Mar. 11/5 Prawn cocktail... Garnish with a sprinkling of paprika pepper. **1976** *Times* 3 Mar. 13/6 A touch of paprika in the finale was not allowed to lessen appreciation of contrapuntal cunning.

2. One of several European varieties of the sweet pepper, *Capsicum annuum*, bearing mildly flavoured fruits.

1925 J. A. HAMMERTON *Countries of World* V. 3586/1 Onions, garlic, paprika (Turkish pepper), beans and cabbage are common [in Serbia]. **1941** 'R. WEST' *Black*

Lamb II. 55 Tomatoes and paprikas glowed their different reds. **1960** E. DAVID *French Provincial Cooking* 96 Red or green sweet peppers, also called capsicums. The pimientos of Spain, paprika peppers of Hungary and peperoni of Italy. **1969** *Oxf. Bk. Food Plants* 128/1 In general, the term 'paprika' is applied to European types [of sweet pepper] with large mild fruits; Spanish paprikas are called pimiento. **1978** *Times* 16 Mar. 25/4 The paprikas grow freely [under glass] as though Holland were a tropical country.

3. The orange-red colour of paprika. Also *attrib.*

1934 in WEBSTER. **1938** L. BEMELMANS *Life Class* II. vii. 191 The little rough-haired dachshund, almost paprika red. **1972** *Guardian* 11 Aug. 9/6 The colour combinations are..lemon with navy/lemon plaid, and paprika with wine/yellow plaid. **1976** *National Observer* (U.S.) 22 May 19/3 (Advt.), Any body looks better in our ribknit turtleneck... One size fits all men. Colors: Natural, Yellow, Paprika, Forest Green, Light Blue, Navy.

4. Used *attrib.* to designate various dishes flavoured with either the condiment or the vegetable.

1935 M. MORPHY *Recipes of All Nations* 337 Among the most famous of all Hungarian dishes are..their paprikas ..being divided into pörkölt, the paprika dish without sour cream, and the other being paprika dishes containing sour cream. *Ibid.* 345 Pork chops with paprika sauce. *c* **1938** *Fortnum & Mason Price List* 26/2 Paprika Chicken—per tin 2/6. **1963** *Guardian* 25 Jan. 10/6 An excellent Viennese meal which included paprika chicken (strictly speaking a dish of Hungarian antecedents). **1966** *Harrods Food News* Sept. 2/1 Paprika Goulash—2 [Portions] 11/6. **1968** R. V. BESTE *Repeat Instructions* xiv. 145 He ordered Bulgarian salata, paprika chicken and a bottle of Riesling. **1969** R. & D. DE SOLA *Dict. Cooking* 168/1 *Paprika butter*, butter sauce colored and flavored with paprika. **1977** K. BENTON *Red Hen Conspiracy* ix. 53 The table was set with dishes..ranging from the delicate flesh tones of Parma ham, the rusty scarlet of paprika sausage, [etc.].

paprikahuhn (păpri:kăhū·n). Also (pl.) **-hühner.** [G., = paprika chicken.] An Austrian dish, perhaps of Hungarian origin, consisting of poached chicken in a rich cream sauce flavoured with paprika.

1905 K. BAEDEKER *Austria-Hungary* p. xvii, Some of the Austrian dishes have curious names;..'Gulyás', Hungarian baked meat, peppered; 'Paprikahuhn', fowl prepared in a similar way. **1906** [see *GOULASH 1]. **1957** S. STRONG *Good Food from Vienna* 112 Chicken Paprika (Paprika Hühner)... This is a typical Viennese dish deriving from Hungary and should on no account be missed. **1965** R. PHILPOT *Viennese Cookery* 95 Paprikahuhn... Get a good spring chicken..two ounces of butter, a medium-sized onion,..very mild paprika,..tomatoes,..chicken stock, double cream. **1969** B. SIAS *Chicken Cookbook* 426 Paprika Huhn—Paprika Chicken—Austria's most famous chicken dish, even though Hungary has a claim on it. **1975** *Times* 9 Aug. 8/5 The *Paprikahuhn* proved as bland as baby food.

† **Papua** (pæ·pŭă, -iŭă). Also **Papoo, Papu.** *Obs.* [ad. Malay *papuah, pĕpuah* frizzled.] = *PAPUAN *sb.* 1.

1619 W. PHILLIP tr. *Schouten's Relation of Voiage from Straights of Magelan* 62 Wee thought those people to be Papoos, for all their haire was short, and they eate Betell and Chalke mingled with it. *Ibid.* 66 A kind of ill favoured people, all Papoos, their haire short, and curled, having rings in their noses and eares, and..hogs teeth hanging about their neckes. **1684** LOCKE *Jrnl.* 20 Apr. in K. Dewhurst *John Locke* (1963) 242 Amongst the draughts he had of severall Esterne people in their natural colours and habits were the Kakerlacks and Papu's. *Ibid.*, The Papua was an olive coloured man with a taile. **1840** *Penny Cycl.* XVII. 219/2 Along the coast of the western half of the island are the Papuas, who have received that name from the Malays, in which language the word signifies 'frizzled hair'. **1845** *Encycl. Metrop.* XXV. 239/1 The Papúas of New Guinea..seem to approach more nearly to the make and strength of the African. **1885** *Encycl. Brit.* XVIII. 231/1 New Guinea..and other islands peopled by Papuas.

Papuan (pæ·piŭăn), *sb.* and *a.* [f. *Papua* (see prec.), formerly a name for the island of New Guinea and later for a territory consisting of its south-eastern part (now incorporated in the state of Papua New Guinea, independent since 1975): see -AN.] **A.** *sb.* **1.** A native or inhabitant of Papua (or Papua New Guinea); also, a member of the racial type found there.

1814 J. MAVER tr. *J. Martinez De Zúniga's Hist. View Philippine Islands* I. p. xii, It is generally allowed that the language spoken by the Papuans, Samangs, and Negritos of the Philippines, and adjacent islands, is totally different from the Malayan. **1869** A. R. WALLACE *Malay Archipelago* II. xl. 445 In stature the Papuan decidedly surpasses the Malay. **1876** *Encycl. Brit.* V. 790/2 The rite of circumcision..is still kept up..among the Papuans. **1902** *Chambers's Jrnl.* May 287/2 [With] the Negro..he throws in the Papuans and Malays, who have black or olive skins. **1913** J. G. FRAZER *Belief in Immortality* I. ix. 190 The Papuans, a tall, dark-skinned, frizzly-haired race, inhabit apparently the greater part of New Guinea, including the whole of the western and central portions of the island. **1954** M. K. WILSON tr. *Lorenz's Man meets Dog* p. ix, Even highly civilized peoples..were accustomed to treat their prisoners no better than domestic animals... The Papuans eat them even to-day with excellent appetite. **1975** J. VAN DE WETERING *Outsider in Amsterdam* (1976) i. 12 Suddenly de Gier knew what this man had to be. Not a Negro but a Papuan.

2. The Papuan group of languages.

1925 H. MURRAY *Papua of Today* ii. 33 The Territory shows even a greater variety of languages. These languages are classified as Papuan and Melanesian. **1939** L. H. GRAY *Foundations of Lang.* 388 The Dravidian family seems to be isolated within India, all attempts to connect it either with Uralic, Altaic, Elamite, Subaraean, Burushaskī, Andamanese, Australian, or Papuan having proved unsuccessful. **1949** M. MEAD *Male & Female* 416 The Arapesh are a Papuan-speaking people. **1960** C. WINICK *Dict. Anthropol.* 401/1 *Papuan*, a New Guinea linguistic stock, non-Melanesian or non-Austronesian. **1978** *Language* LIV. 467 This vast area contains two well-established language families (Austronesian and Australian), as well as a bewildering congeries of seemingly diverse speech communities centering in New Guinea which until recent years were known only under the negative collective label 'Papuan' (= non-Austronesian, non-Australian).

B. *adj.* **1.** Of, pertaining to, or characteristic of Papua (or Papua New Guinea) or its inhabitants.

1869 A. R. WALLACE *Malay Archipelago* II. xl. 449 These people..are tall and well-made, with Papuan features, and curly hair. **1875** *Encycl. Brit.* III. 739/1 The Papuan Subregion..comprises, besides the large and imperfectly-known island whence its name is derived, three other provinces, which may be named the Timorese, the Celebesian, and the Moluccan. **1930** A. HUXLEY *Let.* 7 Jan. (1969) 326 The way every trace of beauty, originality, charm, nobility, existing in the various indigenous arts and crafts—from Papuan and Melanesian to Chinese and Indian—had been utterly stamped out. **1957** P. WORSLEY *Trumpet shall Sound* v. 98 Its leader..declared that he was charged by God to convert his Papuan fellows. **1973** A. BEHREND *Samarai Affair* xii. 124 A small roundish lump now shrunken and indeterminate but once the head of a Papuan tribesman.

2. *spec.* Of or pertaining to a group of non-Austronesian languages spoken in Papua (or Papua New Guinea).

1885 *Encycl. Brit.* XVIII. 780/1 Still less known are the Papuan or Negrito languages, belonging to the black race with frizzled hair inhabiting most of New Guinea, and found also in the interior of some of the other islands having been driven from the coasts by superior intruders of the Malay race. **1908** T. G. TUCKER *Introd. Nat. Hist. Language* 145 The Papuan languages, in New Guinea and some smaller islands, breaking the geographical continuity of the Malayo-Polynesian family. **1912** J. H. P. MURRAY *Papua* v. 135 The languages of the islands at the east end of Papua are all classed as Melanesian, with the exception of Rossel Island, the language of which is considered to be Papuan. *Ibid.* v. 137 The language is..unmusical in sound... It seems to be a Papuan language. **1925** —— *Papua of To-Day* ii. 33 The Papuan and Australian languages meet,..in Torres Straits. **1933** L. BLOOMFIELD *Language* iv. 71 The other families of this part of the earth have been little studied; the Papuan family, on New Guinea and adjacent islands, and the Australian language. **1943** *Official Handbk. New Guinea* v. 343 The Papuan languages..are said to differ as much among themselves as do the languages of the Indo-European group. **1957** *Oceania* XXVIII. 159 There is a distant genetic relationship between a group of Papuan (non-Austronesian) languages in the Vogelkop peninsula of Netherlands New Guinea and the equally non-Austronesian languages of North Halmahera. **1971** LAYCOCK & VOORHOEVE in *Current Trends in Linguistics* VIII. 509 It is rare for speakers of Papuan languages to have a name for themselves. **1975** *Encycl. Papua & New Guinea* II. 610/2 The Papuan languages are not a single family.

papulate (pæ·piulĕt), *a.* [f. PAPULA + -ATE[2] 2.] = PAPULATED *a.*

1876 J. S. BRISTOWE *Treat. Theory & Pract. Med.* II. ii. 318 Not unfrequently these patches are papulate,.. gyrate, or marginate.

papyro-. Add: **papyro·grapher**, a writer on papyrus; **papyrolo·gical** *a.*, pertaining to or dealing with papyrology; **papyro·logist**, a student of papyrology.

c **1904** *Encycl. Dict.* Suppl., Papyrological. **1906** J. H. MOULTON *Gram. N.T. Greek* I. 159 In the less educated papyrographers we find blunders of this kind. **1922** *Glasgow Herald* 14 Apr. 5/2 A most helpful Guide prepared..by the well-known papyrologist Mr. H. I. Bell. **1925** H. S. JONES in *Liddell & Scott's Greek-Eng. Lexicon* (1940) I. Pref. p. viii, Mr. H. Idris Bell..has supplied valuable notes on recent papyrological publications. **1939** A. TOYNBEE *Study of Hist.* VI. 74 The benefit of half a century of papyrological enterprise and ingenuity. **1968** *Sunday Times* 25 Aug. 3/5 He spent his winters as a young papyrologist excavating the rubbish-mounds of Græco-Roman cities in Egypt for the significant 'waste-paper' of a forgotten civilization. **1977** *Times* 28 Oct. 14/3 A famous lost play of antiquity has been discovered ..among the Oxyrhyncus papyri,..by Professor Eric Turner, the great papyrologist.

par, *sb.*[1] Add: **2. b. mint par**: see *MINT *sb.*[1] 6. **c.** (Earlier and later examples.) Also **no par**, having no face value.

1848 W. ARMSTRONG *Stocks* 5 The par value of any stock is that proportion of the capital stock which it represents [etc.]. **1952** *Economist* 27 Dec. 904 No par value shares were not endorsed by the Cohen Committee when it studied the company law nearly ten years ago, and Sir John Barlow's private Bill, which sought to make no par value shares permissible, went virtually unsupported by the City and by the Government. *Ibid.*, The n.p.v. share is distrusted on the Left,..simply because it tells the truth about an equity share in a way that the share with a nominal or unrealistic par value never could. **1960** NANASSY & SELDEN *Business Dict.* 142 *No par value*, refers to stock issued with no par value printed on the face. Each share represents a fractional part of the total value of the business. **1964** *Financial Times* 25 Feb. 5/2 The shares will have a par value of Kr. 100 each. **1973** D. WESTHEIMER *Going Public* i. 18 There's not a high degree of relationship between par value and what a share of stock will bring on the market.

3. b. (Further examples.)

1776 H. NEWDIGATE *Let.* in A. E. Newdigate-Newdegate *Cheverels* (1898) i. 11 As to my Spirits they are rather above than below par. *c* **1793–4** JANE AUSTEN *Lady Susan* (1925) 111 Sir James is certainly under par. **1880** GEO. ELIOT *Let.* 1 Aug. (1956) VII. 308 These conditions found him a little below par from long protracted anxiety and excitement... But..he has been getting strong again. **1934** G. B. SHAW *Too True to be Good* I. 31 There is nothing constitutionally wrong. A little below par: that is all. **1940** WODEHOUSE *Quick Service* x. 104 Mrs. Chavender's Pekinese..had woken up that morning a little below par, and Sally was driving her and it to the veterinary surgeon in Lewes. **1958** A. HUXLEY *Brave New World Revisited* (1959) viii. 99 Whenever anyone felt depressed or below par, he would swallow a tablet or two of a chemical compound called Soma.

4. Substitute for def.: The number of strokes which a first-class player should normally require for a hole or course, calculated from the length of the holes with two putts for each green, and in some cases taking account of difficulties and obstacles in the course. Add further examples. Also *fig.*, **par for the course** (see quot. 1961[1]).

1924 J. BRAID *Golf Guide* 164 *Par Play*, perfect golf without flukes. Thus, if a green can be reached in two strokes, the hole is a Par four; two putts being allowed on each green. **1947** *Partisan Rev.* XIV. 363 Nancy had married and moved to San Francisco and had had three children immediately. 'Par for the course,' said Seymour to Jasper. **1957** *Encycl. Brit.* X. 507/1 Distance is the chief factor in determining the par for a hole. Following are the divisions: all distances up to 250 yd., par 3; 251 to 445, par 4; 446 to 600, par 5; more than 600, par 6. **1961** PARTRIDGE *Dict. Slang* Suppl. 1213/2 *Par for the course, that's* (*just*) *about*, that's pretty normal; that's what, after all, you can expect. Canadian c.p.: since ca. 1946. Ex golf. **1961** M. BEADLE *These Ruins are Inhabited* (1963) x. 137 While waiting..I caught a fragment of another subscriber's telephone conversation. This is also par for the course in making an Oxford phone call. **1973** A. MACVICAR *Painted Doll Affair* viii. 96 Let's see if you can still keep shooting all these pars and birdies. **1974** *Encycl. Brit. Macropædia* VIII. 250/2 Par is essentially a U.S. term that came into use in the early 1900s as a base for computing handicaps under the system devised by L. Calkins of Plainfield, New Jersey. **1975** A. BERGMAN *Hollywood & Le Vine* (1976) ix. 129 I'm not sure about his sex life... But that's par for the course out here, you don't even give it a second thought. **1976** *Scotsman* 15 Dec. 19/8 A perfect approach gave him another birdie at the thirteenth and with pars at the other inward holes he set a target which was not successfully challenged all day. **1977** *Times* 23 Mar. 16/8 *Mail* readers ..will, it is true, be getting their news a day later than you who take *The Times*, but that is about par for the course.

par, *sb.*[4] (Earlier and later examples.)

1844 E. L. BLANCHARD *Diary* 27 Sept. in Scott & Howard *Life E. L. Blanchard* (1891) I. 36 Wrote some little pars for Alderton about 'screw Penholder'. **1854** GEO. ELIOT *Let.* 17 May (1954) II. 155, I intend to have the first sentence or par[agraph] in every § of the appendix in italics. **1928** D. L. SAYERS *Unpleasantness at Bellona Club* i. 9, I am ready to sacrifice my nearest and dearest in order to curry favour with the police and get a par. in the papers. **1969** *Daily Tel.* (Colour Suppl.) 31 Oct. 21/2 A story that the *Daily News* would splash might make only a couple of pars well back in the [*New York*] *Times.* **1973** K. GILES *File on Death* v. 119 There was a par. in the evening papers. **1976** *Listener* 2 Dec. 712/3 My business [as television reviewer] is not to bore the readers, to get 'em in the first par and bounce 'em with a last par they'll remember.

par, *v.*[2] Restrict *rare* to sense in Dict. and add: **2.** *Golf.* To complete (a hole or a course) with a score equal to par.

1961 WEBSTER s.v., [3]*Par*.., to make a golf score on (a hole) equal to par. **1974** *Spartanburg* (S. Carolina) *Herald* 19 Apr. B5/1 Heard, who parred the course Wednesday, said he was driving badly 'but I chipped and putted very well.' **1976** *Scotsman* 24 Dec. (Weekend Suppl.), We won every par five we parred. **1977** *Evening Post* (Nottingham) 24 Jan. 16/6 He parred the next nine holes before his second bogey of the day at the 18th.

par, *prep.* Add: **2.** *par exemple* (examples); *par parenthèse* (earlier examples).

1791 A. S. DAMER *Let.* 18 Aug. in 'L. Melville' *Berry Papers* (1914) 63 They have seen her, and..admire her talents, and, *par parenthèse*, I do really believe that he means to marry her. **1847** in F. A. Kemble *Rec. Later Life* (1882) III. 264 There are a few expressions I should like to have stricken out of it, *par exemple*, I hate the word *stink.* **1847** C. BRONTË *Jane Eyre* I. xii. 204 This, *par parenthèse*, will be thought cool language. **1853** THACKERAY *Let.* in H. Ritchie *Lett. A. T. Ritchie* (1924) iv. 49 (This is par parenthèse). **1857** C. KINGSLEY *Two Yrs. Ago* I. p. ix, 'You shall see enough to-day..*Par exemple*—' And Claude pointed to the clean large fields. **1863** GEO. ELIOT *Let.* 4 Dec. (1956) IV. 118 Miss Hennell is staying there and writes me word that Miss Remond is a fellow guest lecturing (par parenthèse) on Slavery. **1867** H. JAMES *Let.* 22 Nov. in R. B. Perry *Tht. & Char. W. James* (1935) I. 251 Tonight, *par exemple*, I am going into town to see the French actors. **1878** —— *Europeans* I. iii. 111

'Ah, par exemple!' cried the young man. 'You deserve that I should never leave you.' **1889** E. DOWSON *Let.* 30 Jan. (1967) 30 Is he *the* Coquelin, par exemple or is he another? **1916** E. POUND in *Lett. J. Joyce* (1966) II. 375 And par exemple, the 'practical' Pinker was able to do less than I was.

para[1]. (Further examples.)

1907 [see *DINAR b]. **1935** H. EDIB *Clown & his Daughter* xvii. 90 'Rabia Abla, ten paras' worth of chewing-gum!' shouted a shrill voice from the street. **1960** O. MANNING *Great Fortune* I. 12 He took the coins from his pocket... They comprised a few *lire, filler* and *para*. **1971** *Daily Tel.* 18 Sept. 7/7 The first stamps issued in 1941 took the form of the Yugoslavian issues overprinted 'NEZAVISNA DRZAVA HRVATSKA' (Independent State, Croatia). Denominations ranged from 50 paras to 5·50 dinars. **1971** *Whitaker's Almanack 1972* 988 Dinar of 100 Old Dinars or 100 Paras.

Pará[2]. Add: Also **Para** and in some collocations **para**. The seaport is now usu. known as Belém, *Pará* being the name of the state in which it is situated.

Pará grass, (*b*) substitute for def.: a forage grass, *Panicum purpurascens*, native to Brazil but widely cultivated in tropical or sub-tropical regions; (later examples); **Pará-nut** (later examples); **Pará rubber** (earlier and later examples).

1916 L. H. BAILEY *Stand. Cycl. Hort.* V. 2453/1 Pará-Grass... Intro[duced] from Brazil. *P[anicum] numidianum*, Lam., is a closely related species of the E. Indies, sometimes confused with the true para-grass. **1929** J. W. BEWS *World's Grasses* vi. 230 'Para grass' (a perennial, with stout stolons, as much as 15 feet long..)..is cultivated for forage. **1958** J. CAREW *Black Midas* iv. 65 Here and there amidst lotus lilies, reeds or paragrass were alligator's eyes. **1968** E. LOVELACE *Schoolmaster* xiv. 221 Silence, and the many fingers of para grass at the roadside ..gesturing skyward. **1973** TOTHILL & HACKER *Grasses S.E. Queensland* I. 17 Para grass..is an introduced pasture grass which is planted in wet places. **1884** *Encycl. Brit.* XVII. 761/1 Para-nut or Brazil-nut oil, yielded by the kernels of *Bertholletia excelsa*, is employed in South America as a food-oil and for soap-making. **1931** B. MIALL tr. *Guenther's Naturalist in Brazil* iv. 77 It [*sc.* the sapucaja] yields..edible fruits..whose nuts, known to the trade as Pará-nuts, appear on our Christmas dinner-tables as Brazil-nuts. **1857** T. HANCOCK *Personal Narr. Caoutchouc* 281 (Index), Para rubber. **1860** *Chem. News* 25 Aug. 125/1 The Para rubber, which is of a superior quality, is generally sent in the shape termed bottle rubber. **1947** J. C. RICH *Materials & Methods of Sculpture* v. 98 Clarke states that the rubber cement can be made by dissolving ½ ounce of caoutchouc (para rubber) in 25 ounces of benzene. **1968** A. S. CRAIG *Dict. Rubber Technol.* (1969) 112 Para rubber was the best variety of all wild rubber but the advent of plantation rubber steadily reduced its importance until it is now of little significance in world rubber production.

b. Used *absol.* for *Pará rubber*.

1897 [in Dict.]. **1922** [see *OVERVULCANIZE *v.*]. **1954** H. J. STERN *Rubber* i. 17 Apart from some domestic consumption the wild rubber of South America is now of small commercial importance, although the so-called 'fine hard Para' is still favoured in some quarters. **1963** A. S. CRAIG *Rubber Technol.* iii. 18 As late as 1920, the best quality of Para (pa-rá) rubber (known as 'Fine Hard Para') was the standard by which the newer plantation rubbers were judged.

para[3] (pā·ră). [Maori.] A New Zealand name for the large, evergreen fern, *Marattia salicina*, or its swollen rhizome, formerly used as food.

1855 J. D. HOOKER *Bot. Antarctic Voy.: Flora Novæ-Zelandiæ* II. 49 *Marattia salicina*... Northern and eastern parts of the Northern Island... Nat[ive] name, 'Para',.. (Cultivated at Kew.). **1890** H. C. FIELD *Ferns of N.Z.* 153 *Marattia fraxinea*..'Para', 'Para reka', or 'Para tawhiti' of the Maoris. 'Horse-shoe fern' of Europeans. **1906** T. F. CHEESEMAN *Man. N.Z. Flora* 1026 Para; Parareka... The large starchy rhizome was formerly eaten by the Maoris, and hence the plant was occasionally cultivated near their villages. It is now fast becoming rare. **1921** [see *king fern* s.v. *KING *sb.* 13 c]. **1946** *Jrnl. Polynesian Soc.* LV. 149 If there is no distinguishing suffix para is understood to mean the fern-tuber [of *Marattia fraxinea*].

para[4] (pæ·ră). Abbrev. of PARAGRAPH *sb.*

1859 J. BLACKWOOD *Let.* 18 Apr. in *Geo. Eliot Lett.* (1954) III. 52 We had better set a paragraph afloat... If you send a para(graph) to me here I will set it afloat among the Edinr. papers. **1885** R. KIPLING *Let.* 26 Sept. in C. E. Carrington *Rudyard Kipling* (1955) iv. 70 How am I to tackle your letter... Para. two from the butt end asks me if I know *The City of Dreadful Night*. **1938** 'G. ORWELL' in *New English Weekly* 9 June 169/1 Casual half-inch paras in every issue of the newspapers. **1951** WODEHOUSE *Old Reliable* x. 123 There is a morality clause in my contract..Para Six. **1972** 'G. BLACK' *Bitter Tea* (1973) viii. 124 After this 'Dealer' para the news of your sunk ship could push them to a decision.

para[5] (pæ·ră), *a.* (*adv.*) [f. PARA-[1].] **1.** *Chem.* (Now usu. italicized.) Characterized by or relating to (substitution at) two opposite carbon atoms in a benzene ring; at a position opposite *to* some (specified) substituent in a benzene ring. Also as *adv.*

1876, etc. [see *ORTHO *a.* (*adv.*) 1]. **1903** A. J. WALKER tr. *Holleman's Text-bk. Org. Chem.* II. 446 There remains no possibility, except the *para*-structure, for the third hydroxybenzoïc acid melting at 210°. **1938** L. F. FIESER in H. Gilman *Org. Chem.* I. ii. 132 The para coupling of a free phenol is regarded as a 1,4-addition to the conjugated system of the nucleus, followed by loss of water. **1949** [see *ORIENT *v.* 4 a]. **1968** R. O. C. NORMAN *Princ. Org. Synthesis* xii. 402 The inductive effect is relayed through one more carbon atom than is the case for *ortho* or *para* substitution. **1972** R. A. JACKSON *Mechanism* ii. 12 Explanations based on the resonance effects of the methyl group do not..explain the more pronounced effect of *meta* compared with *para* substitution.

2. *para* (or *Para*) *red*, any of various dyes that consist chiefly of the coupling product of diazotized paranitraniline and β-naphthol and are used in printing inks and paints.

1907 *Jrnl. Soc. Dyers & Colourists* XXIII. 20/2 Para red discharges on indigo have been produced for the last ten years. **1930** A. W. C. HARRISON *Manuf. Lakes & Precipitated Pigments* xii. 163 When Para red is present in old water paint on a wall surface, it is again best to remove the old material. **1967** [see *FIRE-RED *sb.*].

3. See *PARA-[1] 3.

para[6] (pæ·ră). *Obstetr.* [the ending of *nullipara, primipara, multipara.*] A woman who has had a specified number of confinements, as indicated by a preceding or following numeral.

1881 *Trans. Edin. Obstetr. Soc.* VI. 70 Of the 48 cases, 26 were primiparæ and 22 multiparæ, as follows: ii. paræ, 11; iii. paræ, 4; [etc.]. **1908** *Practitioner* Aug. 312 Fromme records the case of a vi-para, aged 34, who developed pyæmia after an abortion. **1923** *Jrnl. Obstetr. & Gynæcol.* XXX. 568 In one patient, a iii-para,..the second stage of labour occupied 1½ hours. **1950** *Amer. Jrnl. Obstetr. & Gynecol.* LIX. 737 The second maternal death occurred in a 40-year-old, para ii, gravida iv, whose diabetes was of two years' standing. **1966** *Fertility & Sterility* XVII. 336 A 24-year-old para 2 who had menstrual irregularity prior to insertion of the spiral. **1967** [see *MULTIPARA]. **1977** *Lancet* 23 Apr. 910/1 A 36-week gestation 2·2 kg Black male infant was born to a 36-year-old gravida 7, para 5 mother by vaginal delivery.

para[7] (pæ·ră). Abbrev. of *PARATROOPER.

In early quots. a. Fr. *para*, abbrev. *parachutiste*.

1958 *Spectator* 20 June 807/2 This has not greatly endeared him to the 'paras'. **1962** A. BUCHWALD *How Much is that in Dollars?* 15 My son assured me paras could never land in the Parc Monceau. **1966** M. CATTO *Bird on Wing* ii. 24 Louis..had been a captain in the *paras*. He had learned certain things in Algeria. **1967** L. FORRESTER *Girl called Fathom* xii. 148 Commandant Daniel Jules Delavigne, late of the Paras—Indo-China, Algeria. **1972** *Listener* 9 Nov. 625 The First Battalion of the Parachute Regiment pulls out of Northern Ireland at the end of the month... Incidents like Bloody Sunday..have earned the Paras a reputation for toughness. **1973** *Ibid.* 26 Apr. 534/1 A gun battle between the Paras and the Provos. **1977** J. CARTWRIGHT *Fighting Men* vii. 95 Right, paras get ready to jump.

para[8] (pæ·ră). Slang abbrev. of PARAPLEGIC *a.*

1961 PARTRIDGE *Dict. Slang* Suppl. 1213/2 *Para.* 2. A *para*plegic (a spinal-cord paralytic): Canadian doctors' and nurses': since ca. 1946. **1969** *Sun* (Melbourne) 18 Apr. 7/3 I'd like to say it's a disgrace that quadras (quadraplegics) and paras (paraplegics) have to wait so long before courts get around to clearing up the mess.

para-[1]. Add: **1.** (The less important terms beginning with this prefix, other than those in *Chem.*, are placed below; the description under this sense in Dict. is not applicable to all of them.) **parabro·nchus** *Zool.*, any of the minutest ramifications of the bronchi in the lung of a bird; **parace·llular** *a.*, passing or situated alongside and between cells; **parace·rvical** *a.*, pertaining to or designating the region surrounding the cervix; hence **parace·rvically** *adv.*; **para-church** (see quot. 1970); **paraconfo·rmity** *Geol.* = *NON-SEQUENCE; **parafi·scal** *a.*, ancillary to or containing elements not usually regarded as fiscal; **pa:rageosy·ncline** *Geol.*, (*a*) a geosyncline situated at the edge of a continental kratogen (craton) (? *obs.*); (*b*) a geosyncline situated within an older kratogen (craton); [in sense (*b*) ad. G. *parageosynklinale* (H. Stille 1935, in *Sitzungsber. d. preuss. Akad. d. Wissensch.* (*Phys.-mat. Kl.*) 182)]; hence **pa:rageosyncli·nal** *a.*; **paragnath** (pæ·răgnæþ), **paragnathus** (pără·-gnăþǝs) *Zool.* (usu. in pl. **-gnaths,- gnatha**) [Gr. γνάθ-ος jaw], (*a*) one of the pair of lobes forming the lower lip in most Crustacea; (*b*) one of the pair of lobes forming the hypopharynx in certain insects; (*c*) one of several paired, tooth-like scales found inside the mouth of certain annelid worms; **pa·ragneiss** *Petrogr.* [a. G. *paragneiss* (H. Rosenbusch *Elem. d. Gesteinlehre* (1898) 467)], gneiss derived from sedimentary rocks; **paragno·sis** [GNOSIS], knowledge which is beyond that which can be accounted for by known methods; so **pa·ragnost**, a person possessing or allegedly possessing powers of clairvoyance or foreknowledge; **paragno·stic** *a.*; **paragra·mmatism,** the confused or incomplete use of grammatical structures found in certain forms of speech disturbance; so **paragramma·tic, -gramma·tical** *adjs.*; **parahippoca·mpal** *Anat.* [HIPPOCAMPUS], a gyrus on the inferior surface of each cerebral hemisphere that posteriorly is continuous via the isthmus with the cingulate gyrus and anteriorly ends in the uncus; **parakerato·tic** *a. Path.*, affected by or symptomatic of parakeratosis; **paralexia** (further example); **paralitu·rgical** *a.*, parallel or ancillary to the liturgy; **parame·nstruum** [MENSTRUUM], the period of eight days consisting of the first four days of each menstruation and the preceding four days; hence **parame·nstrual** *a.*; **parame·trial** *a.*, of or pertaining to the parametrium; **parametritis,** add: [coined in Ger. by R. Virchow 1862, in *Arch. f. path. Anat. u. Physiol.* XXIII. 416: see quot. 1869] (earlier example); **parametrium,** add: [back-formation from prec.] (examples); **paramnesia,** add: [ad. F. *paramnesie* (Lordat *Analyse de la Parole* (1843) 31]; now usu. = *DÉJÀ VU a; (examples); hence **paramne·sic** *a.*; **parana·sal** *a. Anat.*, situated beside the nose: the epithet of certain sinuses; **parano·tum** *Ent.* (pl. **-nota)** [NOTUM], in certain insects, a lateral expansion of the dorsal part of a thoracic segment; so **parano·tal** *a.*; **paraphasia** (further examples; see also quot. 1972); **paraphysical** *a.*, add: of or pertaining to physical phenomena for which no adequate scientific explanation exists; **parapoli·tical** *a.* (see quot. 1965); **parapsy·chic** *a.*, of or pertaining to mental phenomena etc., for which no adequate scientific explanation exists; also **parapsy·chical** *a.*; **parareli·gious** *a.*, parallel to, or outside, the sphere of orthodox religion; **parasagi·ttal** *a. Anat.*, situated adjacent or parallel to the sagittal plane; †**parasyna·psis** *Cytology*, the side-by-side pairing of chromosomes at meiosis; hence **parasyna·ptic** *a.*, **-syna·ptically** *adv.*; †**parasynde·sis** *Cytology* [ad. G. *parasyndese* (V. Häcker 1907, in *Ergebnisse und Fortschritte der Zool.* I. 74), f. Gr. σύνδεσις binding together] = *parasynapsis* above; hence **parasynde·tically** *adv.*; **paratecto·nic** *a. Geol.*, (*a*) accompanying deformation (? *obs.*); (*b*) [ad. G. *paratektonik* sb. (H. Stille *Einführing in den Bau Amerikas* (1940) i. 9)], formed by, or of the nature of, a deformation which is chiefly epeirogenic and produces relatively simple, broad folds such as those in Germany north of the Alps (believed to be characteristic of parageosynclines); cf. *orthotectonic* adj. s.v. *ORTHO- 1; **parate·rminal** *a. Anat.*, epithet of a strip of cortex in the rhinencephalon that lies immediately in front of the lamina terminalis at the anterior end of the third ventricle and superiorly is continuous with the indusium griseum; chiefly in *paraterminal gyrus* (or † *body*); **parathe·cium** *Bot.* [THECIUM], in cup fungi and lichens, the outer, dark-coloured layer of an apothecium; so **parathe·cial** *a.*; **parathyroid,** add: [ad. mod.L. (*glandula*) *parathyreoidea* (coined in Sw. by I. Sandström 1880, in *Upsala Läkareförenings Förhandl.* XV. 466)]; freq. *attrib.* or as *adj.*, esp. in *parathyroid gland, hormone* (= *PARATHORMONE); (earlier and later examples); **para·tomous** *a.*, (*a*) (in Dict. as main entry); (*b*) *Zool.*, of or pertaining to paratomy; **para·tomy** *Zool.* [ad. G. *paratomie* (F. von Wagner 1890, in *Zool. Jahrbücher. Abth. für Anat.* IV. 393): see -TOMY], in certain annelid worms, asexual reproduction in which new organs are developed before the division of the animal into two or more parts; **paratra·cheal** *a. Bot.*, describing the structure of wood in which the position of the parenchyma depends on that of the vessels; **paraventri·cular** *a. Anat.*, situated next to a ventricle: epithet of (*a*) a nucleus in the hypothalamus situated above the supra-optic nucleus, and (*b*) one of the mid-line nuclei of each thalamus.

1893 A. NEWTON *Dict. Birds* II. 522 Secondary Bronchi.., besides opening into Air-sacs, send off a number of radially-arranged parabronchia [*sic*], all of which extend to and end blindly near the surface of the Lungs. **1971** *Sci. Amer.* Dec. 75/1 The bird lung is perforated by the finest branches of the bronchial system, which are called parabronchi. **1900** G. EISEN in *Jrnl. Morphol.* XVII. 16,

I designate as paracellular bodies numerous non-cellular bodies situated between the regular cells of the testes. **1977** *Lancet* 15 Jan. 139/2 During intestinal secretion considerable ion movement occurs by a paracellular route via lateral intercellular spaces and the so-called tight junctions rather than through the cells. **1922** R. T. Frank *Gynecol. & Obstetr. Path.* xii. 439 Three zones [of pelvic connective tissue spaces] are readily demonstrable —a para-vesical, para-cervical and para-rectal one. **1945** *Amer. Jrnl. Obstetr. & Gynecol.* L. 527 (*heading*) Paracervical anesthesia for the relief of labor pains. *Ibid.* 532 The injection of anesthetic solutions paracervically produces prompt relief from the pain caused by uterine contractions. **1977** *Lancet* 29 Jan. 260/1, I learnt my lesson whilst demonstrating to a colleague how simple is a termination of pregnancy using paracervical block as a local anæsthetic. **1970** *Guardian Weekly* 12 Dec. 14 Groups that don't attract or seek publicity, that meet in upper rooms... This is sometimes called the para-church, the church of the future which is beginning to take shape. **1976** *Church Times* 17 Dec. 6/3 The author shows that the 'underground' churches that sprang up in the late 1960s have rightly given place to a new form—namely the 'para-church', or alternative church—which exists alongside the institutional churches. **1957** Dunbar & Rodgers *Princ. Stratigr.* vi. 119/2 We propose to restrict the term *disconformity* to the third type, in which two units of stratified rocks are parallel but the surface of unconformity is an old erosion surface of appreciable relief, and to introduce a new term *paraconformity* for the fourth type, in which the beds are parallel and the contact is a simple bedding plane. **1975** *Nature* 3 Jan. 15/1 Here we use the term unconformity to refer to a significant gap (demonstrated or inferred) in the stratigraphic record (disconformity or paraconformity). **1968** *Economist* 30 Nov. 66/3 Either it would mean higher prices for French farmers..or else some parafiscal expedient to prevent this which would be a breach in the whole common price principle. **1974** B. Pearce tr. *Amin's Accumulation on World Scale* I. ii. 257 It is not practicable to take a share of their profits away from these enterprises by fiscal or parafiscal measures. **1978** *Guardian Weekly* 26 Mar. 12/1 Sums collected as parafiscal levies..by employer associations. **1956** L. V. de Sitter *Struct. Geol.* xxiv. 346 The blocks or nuclei sometimes became partly nuclear (parageosynclinal) basins, and partly remained continuously above sea level. **1961** *Jrnl. Geol.* LXIX. 650/2 Northern Sakhalin..was characterized during the Tertiary by parageosynclinal conditions. **1923** C. Schuchert in *Bull. Geol. Soc. Amer.* XXXIV. 199 These recording basins can not be grouped into any of the mentioned types of geosynclines, since some of them have oceanic depths, but all are actually a part of the Asiatic continent. They are marginal geosynclines or parageosynclines (geosynclines beside a continent). **1936** tr. H. Stille in *Bull. Amer. Assoc. Petroleum Geologists* XX. 853 Less intense orogenies..may take place in areas prepared by having been 'special basins' (parageosynclines) in regions that had become consolidated earlier. **1941** *Ibid.* XXV. 1403 The influx of orthogeosynclinal clastics into the Artinskian parageosyncline (in the sense of Stille) is comparable with the invasion of Ouachita-derived geosynclinal sediments into the base of the Strawn in the Oklahoman geosyncline. **1968** R. W. Fairbridge *Encycl. Geomorphol.* 446/2 A ring of Paleozoic basins ('parageosynclines') surrounds both the Canadian and the Scandinavian shields. **1888** Rolleston & Jackson *Forms Animal Life* (ed. 2) 170 The sides of the mouth [of the common crayfish] are overhung by the bases of the mandibles, and behind the latter are two small soft lobes united by the posterior margin of the mouth. These lobes are the paragnatha, metastoma, or lower lip. **1921** *Psyche* XXVIII. 86, I would claim that the so-called 'superlinguæ' of insects most emphatically do represent the paragnaths of Crustacea. **1952** R. C. Moore et al. *Invertebr. Fossils* xi. 454/2 (*caption*) Morphologic features of worms... Paragnaths. One or more pairs of minute denticulate distal plates. **1963** R. P. Dales *Annelids* ii. 43 Between this muscular part or 'pharynx' and the mouth [of nereids] is a membraneous buccal tube bearing small immovable teeth or paragnaths. **1902** A. Harker *Petrol.* (ed. 3) xxii. 331 All these have the chemical composition of sedimentary rocks; Rosenbusch styles them 'parageneisses', in contra-distinction to 'orthogneisses', which have the composition of, and are believed to represent, igneous rocks. **1932** Paragneiss [see *orthogneiss* s.v. *ortho- 1]. **1965** *Mem. Geol. Survey Dept. Malawi* No. 3 vii. 102 The dominant paragneisses in the hilly area around the Chaumbwi vent are quartzo-feldspathic granulites which occur as belts up to 1,100 yards wide. **1933** 'W. Carington' *Death of Materialism* viii. 193, I shall..use the words 'paragnosis', 'paragnostic' and the like; the point being that all the phenomena I have in mind..show signs of the possession or acquisition of knowledge (gnosis) which is, *prima facie*, beyond (para) what can be ascribed to the operation of classical law. **1946** G. N. M. Tyrrell *Personality of Man* v. 53 *Paragnosis*, awareness of additional to normal knowledge. **1964** J. H. Pollack *Croiset* (1965) i. 14 His mentor, Professor W. H. C. Tenhaeff, calls him a 'paragnost', a word which he coined in 1932. **1973** *Radio Times* 1 Nov. 67/4 More Things in Heaven and Earth... Gerard Croiset paragnost and healer. **1958** Goodglass & Hunt in Saporta & Bastian *Psycholinguistics* (1961) 449/1 Most authorities have distinguished between an 'agrammatic' form [of aphasia], marked by simplification and loss of grammatical detail, and a 'paragrammatic' form, marked by confused and incomplete, but not necessarily simplified constructions. **1962** Fish & Stanton tr. *Kleist's Sensory Aphasia* v. 71 'Then it is left had'..is paragrammatical. **1924** A. A. Brill tr. *Bleuler's Textbk. Psychiatry* xiii. 397 At times grammar fails them [*sc.* schizophrenics] (paragrammatism). Many words are used incorrectly. **1946** *Brit. Jrnl. Psychol.* XXXVII. 11 Paraphasia and paragrammatism are generally associated with the receptive ('temporal') syndromes. **1961** W. R. Brain *Speech Disorders* iv. 43 Sentence-deafness is characterized by a difficulty in understanding sentences and by 'paragrammatism' in expression, a term intended by Kleist to describe confusion in the use and order of words and grammatical forms. **1962** Fish & Stanton tr. *Kleist's Sensory Aphasia* v. 67 (*heading*) Sentence deafness and its abortive form with paragrammatism. **1958** *Gray's Anat.* (ed. 32) 1031 The parahippocampal gyrus..commences at the isthmus, where it is directly continuous with the gyrus cinguli, and passes forwards bounded on its lateral side by the collateral and rhinal Sulci. **1969** Truex & Carpenter *Human Neuroanat.* (ed. 6) xxi. 522/2 The lateral olfactory stria, the uncus, and the anterior part of the parahippocampal gyrus constitute the..pyriform lobe. **1972** M. L. Barr *Human Nervous Syst.* xiii. 213/1 The parahippocampal gyrus..hooks sharply backward as the uncus. **1943** *Arch. Dermatol. & Syphilol.* XLVII. 9 In an area above a large focal infiltration of the cutis the epidermis was thin and covered by a condensed parakeratotic horny layer. **1973** *Internat. Jrnl. Dermatol.* XII. 153/1 This histologic picture consists of a parakeratotic column that stains lighter than the adjacent stratum corneum on hematoxylin and eosin stains. **1950** *Jrnl. Speech & Hearing Disorders* XV. 291/1 Paralexia is defined as the substitution of any other word or words for the given symbol in reading. **1977** *Times Lit. Suppl.* 25 Feb. 225/1 Much hagiographical material was transmitted through the liturgy. Eventually, miracle plays based on saints' lives made their appearance as a paraliturgical halfway-house between ritual and drama. **1978** G. Wainwright in C. Jones et al. *Study of Liturgy* II. I. i. 38 Paraliturgical activities flourished: the Stations of the Cross, the rosary, the cult of the Sacred Heart. **1968** *Sunday Times* 29 Dec. 3 The para-menstrual failure rate in 'O' level candidates was 17 per cent. for girls whose menstrual loss lasted up to four days. **1966** K. Dalton in *Proc. R. Soc. Med.* LIX. 1015/2 *Paramenstruum* is used in this study for the four days immediately before menstruation and the first four days of menstruation. **1970** *Times* 30 Sept. 14 Recent studies have shown that in women half of all medical and surgical admissions to hospital occur during the paramenstruum. **1976** *Drive* Sept.–Oct. 31/2 The paramenstruum (the four days before menstruation and the first four days of blood-loss). **1903** *St. Louis Med. Rev.* XLVII. 449/2, I advised that the patient submit to examination under anesthesia, when the obstructing mass could be cleared away and the extent of the parametrial involvement approximately determined. **1962** J. W. Huffman *Gynecol. & Obstetr.* vi. 140/2 Cervical tears at labor may extend upward into the..parametrial tissues. **1869** J. M. Duncan *Pract. Treat. Perimetritis & Parametritis* 4 It is..to Virchow that I am indebted for the suggestion of the chief terms I propose to use habitually. Taking example from the heart and other organs, he proposes to use *peri* to imply inflammation of serous membrane, and he uses *para* to imply inflammation of [adjacent] cellular or connective tissue... *Perimetritis*, then, will strictly imply inflammation of the uterine peritoneum. *Parametritis* will imply inflammation of the cellular tissue in connection with the uterus. **1878** tr. *H. von Ziemssen's Cycl. Pract. Med.* VIII. 281 These abnormal conditions in the parametrium are described by various authors under different names..: for example, phlegmon of the pelvis (Erichsen), parametritis phlegmonosa (Virchow), and purulent oedema (Pirogoff). **1908** *Practitioner* Aug. 312 Nine days later rigors commenced, and in the right parametrium there was a diffuse infiltration, though thrombosed veins were not palpable. **1967** G. M. Wyburn et al. *Conc. Anat.* i. 43 The general condensation of tissue around the base of the broad ligament and lower end of the cervix of the uterus is known as 'parametrium'. **1888** *Amer. Jrnl. Psychol.* I. 735 Several philosophers..have noticed that illusions of memory occur in dreams; and, judging from the writer's own experience, such phenomena are not uncommon. Several dreams illustrative of paramnesia have come to my notice. **1941** *Mind* L. 323 However strong the feeling that this has all happened before, it may turn out that one is not remembering, but suffering from paramnesia, a feeling of *déjà vu*. **1961** J. Heller *Catch-22* (1962) xx. 202 The subtle, recurring confusion between illusion and reality that was characteristic of paramnesia fascinated the chaplain. **1897** *Mind* VI. 285, I frequently read a new poem with a vague sense of familiarity, but such an experience never puts on a really paramnesic character, as I quickly realise that it is explainable by the fact that the writer of the poem has fallen under the influence of Heine, or Tennyson, or Rosetti, as the case may be. **1963** *Lancet* 19 Jan. 164/2, I emerged from my paramnesic reverie to see the two attendants pursuing me across the hall. **1909** J. P. Schaeffer in *Univ. Pennsylvania Med. Bull.* XXII. 235/1 While making a study of the sinus maxillaris..my attention was called to some anatomical conditions which to my mind are of great importance in arriving at the etiology, diagnosis, and proper treatment of some affections of this paranasal chamber. **1954** L. B. Arey *Developmental Anat.* (ed. 6) xxvi. 528 Lodged within the adjoining bones, and in communication with the nasal cavity, are several irregular chambers known collectively as the paranasal sinuses. **1973** J. Davies in Paparella & Shumrick *Otolaryngology* I. iii. 166/2 The paranasal air sinuses comprise the maxillary, the ethmoidal, the frontal, and the sphenoidal sinuses. **1916** G. C. Crampton in *Jrnl. N.Y. Entomol. Soc.* XXIV. 8, I would refer to these lateral folds as the 'paranota', regardless of whether they are entirely tergal in origin, or entirely pleural, or a combination of both. The theories dealing with this origin of the wings may therefore be referred to as the paranotal theories. **1935** R. E. Snodgrass *Princ. Insect Morphol.* viii. 158 A third stage was inaugurated with the transformation of the paranotal lobes of the mesothorax and the metathorax into movable organs of true flight. **1964** R. M. & J. W. Fox *Introd. Compar. Entomol.* iv. 112 Although no insect, living or fossil, is known to have paranota that can be clearly interpreted as precursory to wings, paranota are present in certain living insects. **1973** *Nature* 16 Nov. 127/1 He [*sc.* G. C. Crampton] pronounced judgment unequivocally in favour of the paranotal theory. **1946** Paraphasia [see *paragrammatism* above]. **1959** Schuell & Jenkins in H. Schuell *Aphasia* (1974) xi. 212 Jargon and paraphasia were present. **1972** *Sci. Amer.* Apr. 78/2 Verbal paraphasia is the substitution of one word or phrase for another... Literal or phonemic paraphasia is the substitution of incorrect sounds in otherwise correct words. **1933** O. Lodge in T. Besterman tr. *Driesch's Psychical Res.* p. ix, For the experimental establishment of reality the paraphysical stand first, although they are admittedly on a lower plane and have less important consequences than the psychical variety. **1934** *Mind* XLIII. 255 The 'theories' of psychical research in their application to 'paraphysical' and 'parapsychical' phenomena. **1961** *Ann. Reg. 1960* 420 A lady had bought an instrument which was claimed by its maker to be capable of diagnosis and treatment on a para-physical plane. **1965** D. Easton *Framework Polit. Anal.* iv. 52, I shall refer to the internal political groups and organizations as *parapolitical systems* and retain the concept 'political system' for political life in the most inclusive unit being analyzed, namely, in a society. **1968** F. G. Bailey in M. J. Swartz *Local-Level Politics* (1969) xiii. 281 My hope..is a model for all kinds of politics in village India, and beyond that for politics in all parapolitical situations. **1971** P. A. Allum *Politics & Society Post-War Naples* (1973) vi. 166 Party and para-political organisation membership is a *sine qua non* of a successful candidature. **1911** H. Carrington in *Flournoy's Spiritism & Psychol.* i. 39 The most striking case of this character which I have encountered is that of Mme. Guelt, in which parapsychic gifts and tendencies were manifested in four generations of her family. **1930** D. Ibberson tr. *Oesterreich's Possession* II. vii. 267 Accounts of the parapsychic performances of the mediums are not susceptible of subsequent proof. **1918** D. Wright in *Boirac's Psychic Sci.* p. v, Unless we choose to coin a special word for the purpose, such as 'parapsychical', as suggested by Dr. Boirac. **1957** Rhine & Pratt *Parapsychol.* i. 5 The observations and events dealt with in parapsychology—parapsychical phenomena—are associated in some central way with *living* organisms. **1966** *New Statesman* 18 Feb. 229/2 These uncommitted people were unable to take up new religions, but they could adopt a set of parareligious dogma if it was called scientific. **1974** *Daily Colonist* (Victoria, B.C.) 31 May 7/6 What is usually involved in 'black magic' here is not really necromancy or witchcraft, but rather 'anteria', a parareligious form of African origin and related to Macumba in Brazil and voodoo in Haiti. **1909** *Cent. Dict.* Suppl., Parasagittal. **1925** *Jrnl. Compar. Neurol.* XXXIX. 200 (*caption*) Parasagittal section near the median line, showing the tractus olfacto-tuberalis and its connections. **1929** Brain & Strauss *Recent Adv. Neurol.* iv. 57 Parasagittal meningiomas..arise from the wall of the superior longitudinal sinus. **1969** D. Sutton *Textbk. Radiol.* lix. 1051/2 Parasagittal tumours being in the midline, and often bilateral, are better shown by encephalography than angiography. **1975** *Nature* 6 Mar. 48/2 Parasagittal crests relatively far apart and meeting posteriorly almost at posterior border of frontoparietal. **1909** E. B. Wilson in *Jrnl. Exper. Zool.* VI. 84 Pyrrochoris shows a close similarity to Tomopteris... This comparison has convinced me that synapsis occurs at the same period in both—whether by parasynapsis (side to side union) or telosynapsis (end to end union). [*Note*] I have for some years made use of these terms in my lectures on cytology. **1912, 1925** [see *parasyndesis* below]. **1932** *Proc. 6th Internat. Congr. Genetics* II. 319 Parasynapsis may be demonstrated..by observation of actual side-by-side association of homologous chromosomes or chromosome-segments at zygotene. **1956** *Biol. Abstr.* XXX. II. (Index), Parasynapsis. (*See* Chromosomes; Meiosis.) **1910** *Ann. Bot.* XXIV. 727 Grégoire.., while agreeing with the parasynaptic chromosome formation, put a different interpretation on to the 'gamosomes' and 'zygosomes' of Strasburger and Miyake. **1912** *Jrnl. Exper. Zool.* XIII. 394 Bivalent segments, each consisting of two chromosomes in parasynaptic union. **1921** *Ann. Bot.* XXXV. 386 Both the telosynaptic and the parasynaptic methods of synapsis may occur, the latter perhaps more largely in forms with long thready chromosomes and the former with short and stout chromosomes. **1929** *Jrnl. Genetics* XXI. 46 In *Prunus cerasus*..the method of pairing is parasynaptic, judging from the occurrence of diplotene chiasmata and their occasional persistence to metaphase as interstitial exchanges. **1910** *Ann. Bot.* XXIV. 752 Whether these univalent strands join with their homologous pairs telosynaptically or parasynaptically, or by any other intermediate method between these two extremes, resolves itself merely into a question of non-essential detail. **1926** *Genetics* XI. 274 It was thought that one could differentiate in a triploid between splitting and parasynaptic union of chromosome threads, because it seemed possible that the three threads might all unite parasynaptically. **1911** *Jrnl. Morphol.* XXII. 754 The main difference between the views of parasyndesis and metasyndesis lies in the interpretation of the longitudinal cleft of the gemini. **1912** *Jrnl. Exper. Zool.* XIII. 392 Do they [*sc.* the chromatin-elements] conjugate side by side (parasynapsis, parasyndesis), end to end (telosynapsis, metasyndesis) or in both ways? **1925** E. B. Wilson *Cell* (ed. 3) vi. 509 Evidence has steadily accumulated to show that in a large class of cases synapsis involves a side-by-side union of the synaptic mates (parasynapsis or parasyndesis) instead of an end-to-end union ..as was formerly supposed. **1911** *Jrnl. Morphol.* XXII. 750 The chromosomes conjugate parasyndetically. **1929** *Jrnl. Genetics* XIX. 171 She found a continuous spireme composed of parasyndetically paired threads alternating with single ones. **1938** Knopf & Ingerson *Struct. Petrology* viii. 110 Such a structure is a typical paratectonic crystallization under conditions of differential displacement. **1956** L. V. de Sitter *Struct. Geol.* i. 15 Paratectonic Regions contain curved folds, predominantly of concentric type without thickening of the strata in the hinges, accompanied by faulting which is secondary to the folding. **1969** *Mem. Amer. Assoc. Petroleum Geologists* XII. xxiv. 309/1 South of the fundamental Highland Boundary fault zone, inliers of the paratectonic Caledonides consist of Cambrian through Lower Devonian strata typified by simpler upright fold styles and a low degree of metamorphism. **1973** *Nature* 5 Oct. 244/2 Thickening of crust in paratectonic orogeny when two continental plates collide. **1901** G. E. Smith in *Jrnl. Anat. & Physiol.* XXXV. 434 The..'paraterminal body' is a structure of great morphological interest and importance, the essential unity of which has not hitherto been recognised. **1935** *Gray's Anat.* (ed. 26) 964 Immediately in front of the lamina terminalis and almost co-extensive with it, there is a narrow, triangular field of grey matter, which is termed the paraterminal gyrus (paraterminal body). **1951** O. Larsell *Anat. Nervous Syst.* (ed. 2) xvii.

428 The septal or paraterminal area...includes the gray substance of the basal portion of the cerebral hemisphere extending from the region of the anterior commissure to the caudal end of the anterior olfactory nucleus. **1921** A. L. Smith *Handbk. Brit. Lichens* 141/1 Parathecium, layer surrounding the thecium (hymenium). **1973** M. A. Letrouit-Galinou in Ahmadjian & Hale *Lichens* ii. 76 The parathecial apparatus..comprises (1) a parathecium, often cup-shaped, flaring, and composed of filaments which..are elongated and branched [etc.]. **1895** *Jrnl. Physiol.* XVIII. p. xxx, The tissue of the parathyroid gland does not at all resemble that of the thyroid in its adult form. **1925** *Jrnl. Biol. Chem.* LXIII. 395 (*heading*) The extraction of a parathyroid hormone which will prevent or control parathyroid tetany and which regulates the level of blood calcium. **1948** Martin & Hynes *Clin. Endocrinol.* v. 101 Four parathyroid glands are normally situated at the posterior extremities of the lateral lobes of the thyroid. **1960** *Farmer & Stockbreeder* 1 Mar. 136/1 There are two parathyroids in the bird. **1968** *Times* 10 Feb. 5/2 Parathyroid hormone is produced by the parathyroid glands, situated in the neck. **1930** J. Stephenson *Oligochaeta* xiii. 522 It would seem that regeneration after separation is the more primitive form; regeneration before separation a more recent development; the first is called..architomy, the second paratomy. **1963** R. P. Dales *Annelids* viii. 161 The fragmentation of an individual into two or more parts may be referred to as 'scissiparity', either before ('architomy') or after ('paratomy') formation of heads on the parts which break away. *Ibid.* 162 In this genus [sc. *Trypanosyllis*] a series may be traced from *T. coeliaca*, in which simple paratomous stolonization occurs. **1908** Paratracheal [see *metatracheal* s.v. *META- 4]. **1933** *Tropical Woods* XXXVI. 9 *Paratracheal Parenchyma*, aggregated wood parenchyma in association with the vessels or vascular tracheids. **1965** K. Esau *Plant Anat.* (ed. 2) xi. 258 The phylogenetic sequence among the distributional types of wood parenchyma is from the diffuse arrangement to the other apotracheal and the paratracheal types. **1935** J. C. White *Autonomic Nervous Syst.* iii. 19 There is a good deal of evidence that the paraventricular nuclei [*sic*] preside over the sympathetic system. **1942** F. A. Mettler *Neuroanat.* xiv. 321 More diffuse cells scattered about in the ventricular wall are collectively called the paraventricular nuclei.. and represent what is left of a system which, in lower forms, interrelates the two thalami. **1945** *Jrnl. Compar. Neurol.* LXXXIII. 11 Here [*sc.* laterally] the anterior paraventricular nucleus becomes a thin, vertical strip of cells. *Ibid.*, Ventrally and dorsally the posterior paraventricular nucleus fades into the surrounding periventricular gray. **1972** M. L. Barr *Human Nervous Syst.* xi. 190/2 The precursors of vasopressin and oxytocin appear in the cytoplasm of cells of the supraoptic and paraventricular nuclei as neurosecretory droplets or granules.

2. a. paraca·sein, a phosphoprotein produced as a calcium compound in the form of a curd by the action of rennet on milk; hence **paraca·seinate,** a compound of paracasein with a metal; **paraformaldehyde** (examples); also called **pa·raform; paramy·osin,** a protein which forms the thick filaments of the contractile units of molluscan muscle; **parapro·tein** [a. G. *paraprotein* (K. Apitz 1940, in *Virchows Arch.* CCCVI. 685)], any of various proteins found in the blood only in certain diseases (as myelomatosis); hence **pa:raproteinæ·mia** [ad. G. *paraproteinämie* (K. Apitz, loc. cit.), f. Gr. *αἷμα* blood], the presence of paraproteins in the blood; **pa:rarosa·niline** [ad. G. *pararosanilin* (E. & O. Fischer 1878, in *Ann. der Chem.* CXCIV. 266)], a colourless, crystalline alcohol $(H_2NC_6H_4)_3COH$, which is used in making triphenylmethane dyes and whose red hydrochloride is used as a biological stain.

1906 Paracasein [see *CASEINOGEN]. **1937** A. L. & K. G. B. Winton *Struct. Foods* III. 184 Paracasein at 5° and 23°C. has 1·5 times as much base-combining power as casein. **1959** Jenness & Patton *Princ. Dairy Chem.* x. 314 In view of the close similarity between the casein and paracasein, it is not surprising that the mechanism of the primary action of rennin has long remained obscure. **1961** Paracasein [see *CASEINOGEN]. **1907** *Chem. Abstr.* I. 1740 Pure neutral sodium caseinate and sodium paracaseinate solutions..are not precipitated by saturation with pure sodium chloride. **1937** A. L. & K. G. B. Winton *Struct. Foods* III. 185 Rennet-casein..consists of calcium paracaseinate, formed from the calcium caseinate associated with dicalcium phosphate carried down mechanically. **1913** *Jrnl. Industr. & Engin. Chem.* June 508/1 We have succeeded..in producing a fusible phenol resin by heating ..paradioxydiphenylmethan with 10 grams of paraform. **1932** I. D. Garard *Introd. Org. Chem.* vi. 79 Paraformaldehyde is made into candles and sold for fumigating purposes under the name of *paraform*. The heat of the burning candle converts the paraform into formaldehyde. **1966** *McGraw-Hill Encycl. Sci. & Technol.* V. 472/1 It [*sc.* formaldehyde] is also sold as the solid hydrated polymer known as paraformaldehyde or paraform. **1894** *Jrnl. Chem. Soc.* LXVI. I. 487 Methylal is readily obtained by this method from paraformaldehyde and methylic alcohol. **1913** J. Walker *Org. Chem. for Students of Med.* 40 Paraformaldehyde is largely used as a source of formaldehyde for the purpose of disinfecting rooms, clothing, etc. **1951** Kirk & Othmer *Encycl. Chem. Technol.* VI. 861 On heating, paraformaldehyde depolymerizes to yield a mixture of monomeric formaldehyde gas and water vapor. **1946** C. E. Hall et al. in *Biol. Bull.* XC. 44 Since this protein can be identified by electron microscope observation and x-ray diffraction it merits a distinguishing name and is therefore designated as *paramyosin*. **1963** *Jrnl. Molecular Biol.* VII. 234 Light scattering, viscosity and sedimentation experiments on solutions of *Venus mercenaria* paramyosin show that the paramyosin molecule is a rod, 1330 Å long and 20 Å in diameter, and has a mass of 220,000 atomic mass units. **1972** *Biochemistry* (Easton, Pa.) XI. 4532/1 The paramyosin molecules align to form a bipolar core of the thick filament which is covered by a surface layer of myosin. **1949** *Chem. Abstr.* XLIII. 9097 The paraproteins have a different structural analysis than plasma protein. **1961** *Lancet* 9 Sept. 603/2 Large errors may arise if the urinary protein consists of a paraprotein, such as Bence Jones'. **1972** *Jrnl. Immunol.* CIX. 511/2 No feline paraproteins have been characterized physically or chemically. **1958** *Arch. Internal Med.* CII. 618/1 This method to this day has been used clinically as a method of evaluating dysproteinemias and paraproteinemias in disease states. **1972** *Clin. & Exper. Immunol.* XI. 488 There were six patients whose disease was associated with an IgM paraproteinaemia..and another six without a paraproteinaemia. **1879** *Jrnl. Chem. Soc.* XXXVI. 385 Pararosaniline is the name applied by the authors to the colouring matter derived from paratoluidine. **1926** J. Read *Text-bk. Org. Chem.* xi. 203 By replacing six hydrogen atoms in the molecule of the magenta dye, pararosaniline, with six methyl groups, a deep violet dye, known as 'crystal violet' is produced. **1971** E. Gurr *Synthetic Dyes* 81 Fuschin basic..is, in fact a hybrid mixture of the chlorides of pararosaniline, rosaniline and new magenta.

b. para-aminosalicy·lic acid, a colourless crystalline compound, $HOOC·C_6H_3(OH)(NH_2)$, which is used (usually with isoniazid) in treating tuberculosis; **pa:ra-dichlor(o)be·nzene,** a colourless crystalline compound, $C_6H_4Cl_2$, that has a low melting point and is used as a moth-proofing agent; **paranitra·niline,** a pale yellow crystalline compound, $H_2NC_6H_4NO_2$, used in making azo dyes; **para-phe:nylenedi·amine,** a colourless, crystalline compound, $C_6H_4(NH_2)_2$, used as a photographic developer, for dyeing hair and fur, and for making safranine and sulphur dyes; **paraxy·lene,** an isomer of xylene that melts to a colourless liquid at room temperature and is now obtained from petroleum naphtha for use esp. as a source of terephthalic acid.

1946 *Lancet* 5 Jan. 15/1 (*heading*) *Para*-aminosalicylic acid in the treatment of tuberculosis. **1954** S. Duke-Elder *Parsons' Dis. Eye* (ed. 12) x. 120 For the common ophthalmological infections, however, the most important compounds are the sulphonamides, the sulphones and para-amino-salicylic acid. **1966** *McGraw-Hill Encycl. Sci. & Technol.* I. 320/1 *para*-Aminosalicylic acid (PAS) was synthesized in 1901. **1876** *Jrnl. Chem. Soc.* XXIX. 81 By heating equal molecules of chlorobenzenesulphonic chloride and phosphorus pentachloride to 200°–220°, paradichlorobenzene, melting at 53°, and boiling at 172°–174°, is formed. **1938** *Forum & Century* (N.Y.) Feb. 96/2 There is probably no better moth protection than paradichlorbenzene crystals. **1965** Zigrosser & Gaehde *Guide to Collecting Orig. Prints* vii. 113 Preventative measures [against microbiological infection of prints], however, can be taken by placing open containers of paradichlorobenzene crystals upon the storage shelves. **1872** Para-nitraniline [in Dict.]. **1918** C. M. Whittaker *Applic. Coal Tar Dyestuffs* vi. 87 The first stable form of diazotized paranitraniline manufactured commercially was nitrosamine red. **1963** A. J. Hall *Textile Sci.* iv. 181 A deep bright red shade developed in the fabric as the result of formation within the fibres of an insoluble pigment by coupling of the beta-naphthol with the diazotised paranitraniline. **1873** *Jrnl. Chem. Soc.* XXVI. 167 Dinitrobenzene was reduced by means of tin and hydrochloric acid; the bromine was eliminated by the nascent hydrogen and paraphenylenediamine was formed. **1906** *Jrnl. Soc. Dyers & Colourists* XXII. 77/1 Paraphenylenediamine is employed by furriers for dyeing pelts, and it has been used also as a hair dye. **1966** L. F. A. Mason *Photogr. Processing Chem.* i. 25 Although these paraphenylenediamine derivatives are stable in acid solution or as salts in the solid state, the free bases..readily oxidise and are not very soluble. **1873** *Jrnl. Chem. Soc.* XXVI. 272 The author, by acting upon isoxylene and paraxylene with benzyl chloride, in presence of zinc, has obtained benzylisoxylene and benzylparaxylene. **1954** R. W. Moncrieff *Artificial Fibres* (ed. 2) xxi. 265 Development of a method for making large quantities of *para*-xylene proved to be difficult and delayed the manufacture of Terylene in the United Kingdom, but in America the Standard Oil Co. have developed a method of making it from petroleum. **1969** Para-xylene [see *feedstock* s.v. *FEED *sb.* 7]. **1975** W. G. Roberts *Quest for Oil* (rev. ed.) ix. 95 Very pure aromatic compounds such as paraxylene, which is used in synthetic fibre manufacture.

c. Names of minerals having a chemical composition the same as or similar to those to the names of which *para-* is prefixed, but a different crystal structure: **parabu·tlerite** [f. *butlerite* (f. the name of Gordon *Butler* (1881–1961), U.S. geologist)], a basic hydrated sulphate of ferric iron, $FeSO_4(OH)·2H_2O$, found as orange orthorhombic crystals; **parahopeite** (-hōu·pəit), a hydrated zinc phosphate, $Zn_3(PO_4)_2·4H_2O$, found as colourless, transparent, triclinic crystals; **paralau·rionite,** a hydroxide and chloride of lead, Pb(OH)Cl, found as colourless, transparent, monoclinic crystals; **paramela·conite,** an oxide of copper, CuO, in which some of the bivalent copper (typically about a quarter) is replaced by monovalent copper and which is found as black tetragonal crystals; **parara·mmelsbergite,** an arsenide of nickel, $NiAs_2$, that occurs as white, opaque, tabular crystals that alter to erythrite when exposed; **paratacamite** (pæ̆:ræ̆tăkā·məit), a secondary mineral that is a basic chloride of copper, $Cu_2(OH)_3Cl$, and is found as green to greenish black hexagonal crystals; **parate·llurite,** an oxide of tellurium, TeO_2, found as soft, white or yellow tetragonal crystals with a waxy lustre; **paravau·xite,** a secondary mineral that is a hydrated basic phosphate of ferrous iron and aluminium, $FeAl_2(PO_4)_2(OH)_2.8H_2O$, and occurs as brittle, whitish or colourless, triclinic crystals, usu. in association with vauxite and wavellite; **parawo·llastonite,** the monoclinic form of the calcium silicate, $CaSiO_3$, of which wollastonite is the commoner triclinic form, both occurring as intergrowths with one another.

1938 M. C. Bandy in *Amer. Mineralogist* XXIII. 742 Parabutlerite $Fe(SO_4)(OH).2H_2O$. A basic hydrate of iron of this same composition has already been described as the mineral butlerite and as an artificial compound in the system $Fe_2O_3–SO_3–H_2–H_2O$. **1968** I. Kostov *Mineral.* 499 Metahohmannite, parabutlerite, and fibroferrite..occur as yellow crusts or reniform aggregates with fibrous texture, products of weathering of pyritic deposits. **1907** *Nature* 12 Dec. 143/1 Another new species, named parahopeite, has the same chemical composition as hopeite, $Zn_3P_2O_8.4H_2O$, but is anorthic. **1908** L. J. Spencer in *Mineral. Mag.* XV. 18 Parahopeite. This name I propose to give to a new species of hydrous zinc phosphate, identical with hopeite in chemical composition, but differing from both α-hopeite and β-hopeite in physical and crystallographic characters. **1955** *Mineral. Abstr.* XII. 479 Preliminary note on the occurrence of parahopeite and tarbuttite..in the Kef Semmah mine [in Algeria]. **1974** *Mineral. Mag.* XXXIX. 684 Several uncommon phosphate minerals including tarbuttite, parahopeite, scholzite, and collinsite occur in near-surface gossans in the Reaphook Hill zinc prospect [in South Australia]. **1899** G. F. H. Smith in *Mineral. Mag.* XII. 102 On some of the specimens [of lead slags from Laurium] a new mineral, paralaurionite, was found, which possesses the same chemical composition as laurionite. **1950** *Mineral. Mag.* XXIX. 341 About 1942 paralaurionite was identified in a suite of minerals from the Mammoth mine, Tiger, Arizona. **1891** G. A. Koenig in *Proc. Acad. Nat. Sci. Philadelphia* 289 The tetragonal crystals are so unique in their appearance, that they should be accorded the rank of a very distinct species, and the name *Paramelaconite* is proposed for them. **1941** *Amer. Mineralogist* XXVI. 659 The paramelaconite occurs as stout prismatic crystals up to 3 cm. in length. **1962** *Ibid.* XLVII. 779 On a recent collecting trip to the Algomah mine [in Michigan] a few massive pieces of paramelaconite were found. **1939** M. A. Peacock in *Ibid.* Dec. II. 11 Recently described materials provisionally named rammelsbergite.., from Cobalt, Ontario, and Elk Lake, Ontario, give identical *x*-ray powder photographs unlike those of from Schneeberg and Eisleben... The Canadian mineral is thus a distinct species for which the name *pararammelsbergite* is proposed. **1967** *Canad. Mineralogist* IX. 129 Pararammelsbergite has vacant arsenic lattice positions which are occupied in part by excess metal atoms. **1972** *Amer. Mineralogist* LVII. 1 Pararammelsbergite ($NiAs_2$) is orthorhombic.., space group *Pbca*, $Z = 8$. **1905** *Nature* 13 Apr. 574/2 This new mineral, to which the name paratacamite was given [by Prior and Smith], has the same chemical composition as atacamite. **1950** *Mineral. Mag.* XXIX. 280 It is paratacamite, not atacamite that occurs at the famous Cornish locality, Botallack mine, St. Just. **1960** Switzer & Swanson in *Amer. Mineralogist* XLV. 1272 Orthorhombic TeO_2 is found in nature as tellurite. The tetragonal form, well known as a chemical compound, has been found associated with tellurite and native tellurium at Cananea, Sonora, Mexico. The name paratellurite is proposed for the new mineral. **1973** *Chem. Abstr.* 8 Oct. 489/2 In an acoustooptic light deflector, frequency modulated acoustic shear waves propagate in the [110] direction in paratellurite (TeO_2). **1922** S. G. Gordon in *Science* 14 July 50/1 Preliminary notes on vauxite and paravauxite. Among the mineral specimens collected on the Vaux-Academy Andean expedition of 1921 are two that have proved to be new. **1944** *Proc. Acad. Nat. Sci. Philadelphia* XCVI. 339 Vauxite, paravauxite, metavauxite, and childrenite are secondary phosphates, derived from solution of apatite by supergene waters, and deposited usually upon wavellite. **1968** I. Kostov *Mineral.* 452 Paravauxite and gordonite have perfect {010} cleavage. **1935** M. A. Peacock in *Amer. Jrnl. Sci.* XXX. 525 It thus seems necessary to regard the triclinic modification as the normal one properly entitled to the name wollastonite; the name parawollastonite is, therefore, proposed for the rarer monoclinic modification. **1963** W. A. Deer et al. *Rock-forming Min.* II. 172 The distinction between wollastonite and parawollastonite is based on the extinction angle $\beta:y$, which is 3°–5° in wollastonite and 0° in monoclinic parawollastonite. *Ibid.* 173 Parawollastonite, identified by single-crystal X-ray photographs, has been recorded from Monte Somma, Vesuvius, ..from Crestmore, California.., and from Csiklova, Roumania.

3. *Physics* and *Chem.* Of, pertaining to, or designating the form of some homonuclear diatomic molecules in which (as in parahydrogen) the two nuclei have antiparallel spins (see also quot. 1940[2] s.v. *ORTHO- 3); also used similarly with reference to the electronic spins of helium. Also as an independent word.

1927, etc. [see *ORTHO- 3].

para-³, comb. form of PARACHUTE *sb.* **a.** With sbs., denoting 'dropped by parachute', 'trained or equipped for descending by parachute', as *para-bomb, -cargo, -commando, -girl, -marine, -mine, -nurse, -pa(c)k* (hence *-packed* adj.), *-pooch, -spy*. Also *PARADOCTOR, *PARADROP *sb.* and *v.*, *PARAFOIL, *PARAGLIDER, PARAKITE (in Dict. and Suppl.), *PARAMEDIC¹, *PARA-RESCUE, *PARASCENDING *vbl. sb.*, *PARATROOPS *sb. pl.*, *PARAWING. **b. parabrake,** a parachute which opens behind an aircraft and acts as a brake; **parafrag bomb,** a bomb dropped by parachute which bursts into fragments on hitting its target; **parajump** = *JUMP *sb.*¹ 1 c; so **parajumping** *vbl. sb.*; **parajute,** a parachute made of jute; **parapants,** women's knickers made from parachute silk; **paraplane,** (see quot. 1942); **parasheet,** (see quot. 1951); **paraski** *attrib.*, (*a*) designating a parachute trooper trained to ski from the point where he lands; (*b*) designating a sport in which skiers ski from a place to which they have dropped by parachute; **paraskier,** a paraski trooper; **paraspotter,** a person who watches for enemy parachute landings.

1943 *Time* 18 Oct. 36/2 Parabombs burst above the ground, spray their fragments with telling effect. **1951** Parabrake [see *DROGUE 3]. **1954** *Britannica Bk. of Year* 638/1 The verbal shorthand habitual to members of the armed forces produced such contractions as *parabrake*, a parachute used to slow down an aeroplane on landing. **1967** N. E. BORDEN *Jet-Engine Fund.* 97 Military fighters release a parachute, called a parabrake, from their tail as soon as their wheels contact the runway. **1951** R. MALKIN *Boxcars in Sky* 172 As for military paracargo, however, the picture is entirely different. **1965** *Britannica Bk. of Year* (U.S.) 869/2 *Para commando, n.*, a parachute commando, as in the Congolese army. **1967** *Economist* 30 Sept. 1180/1 The Israelis train Mr Mobutu's crack corps, the para-commandos. **1978** *Guardian Weekly* 18 June 16/3 The bigger white community in Likasi..has told the Belgian Government it would leave en masse if the paracommandos go. **1944** *Tuscaloosa* (Alabama) *News* 5 Oct. 1 This..Jap Sally plane went up in smoke a few seconds after this picture was taken—destroyed by parafrag bombs. **1972** *Courier-Mail* (Brisbane) 16 May 1/7 Lucky paragirl Jackie Smith fell from 2400 ft. into the sea when her parachute failed to open during a week-end skydiving show—and lived. **1973** *Jewish Chron.* 9 Feb. 15/2 The nearest your reporter came to hearing fighting words from Israel's paragirls. **1971** *Islander* (Victoria, B.C.) 20 June 3/4 Most parajump clubs in Canada are affiliated with the Canada Sport Parachute Association. **1977** *R.A.F. News* 30 Mar.–12 Apr. 3/3 The £16 fee (lower than that charged by similar, civilian para-jump clubs) covers the cost of membership. *Ibid.* 3/4 A halt had been called to any para-jumping that week-end. **1956** W. SLIM *Defeat into Victory* 225 In a month we had a parajute that was eighty-five per cent as efficient and reliable as the most elaborate parachute. It was made entirely of jute. **1973** J. LUCAS *Big Umbrella* x. 108 The parajutes were not intended for man-carrying, but about 100,000 of them were used for supply-dropping in the Burma campaign. *Ibid.* 107 The 'parajute'..had no large vent in the apex, but several smaller ones all over, and it was only about one-seventh less efficient than the standard silk parachute. **1944** *Veterans' Weekly* (Lincoln, Nebraska) 15 Dec. 2 Oliver N. Magee, paramarine, son of War Dad and Mrs..Magee [etc.]. **1969** *TV Times* (Austral.) 22 Jan. 27 He is aided by the tough leader of a group of paramarines. **1944** in *Amer. Speech* (1945) XX. 221 Nazi para-mines nearly blocked supply lines. **1942** A. M. LOW *Parachutes* p. x, A paranurse is..a nurse dropped by parachute. **1946** *B.B.C. War Report* 234 Suddenly the pilot called our attention to the parapacks coming out from the aircraft in front of us. *Ibid.*, There go the parapacks from the formation ahead of us—yellow, brown, red, drifting down gently, dropping their containers. **1950** in *Amer. Speech* (1956) XXXI. 62 A resupply mission was flown in the afternoon—with a drop of parapaks and other supplies simulated. **1954** *N.Y. Times Mag.* 6 June 79/2 Captain Schweiter slapped the switch controlling the parapacks (belly bundles), bellowed: 'Follow me,' and jumped. **1945** *Birmingham* (Alabama) *News* 27 Mar. 1/5 Allied Airborne troops and parapacked supplies are shown as they plummeted down five miles beyond the Rhine. **1944** *Time* 10 Apr. 12/3 Parapants. In Manhattan, Mrs. Virginia Bell Jack received from her Thunderbolt-pilot husband in England a pair of real silk (German parachute) panties. **1942** A. M. LOW *Parachutes* 111 In Russia, some years ago, a young engineer, B. Pavlov, invented what he called a 'paraplane' which consisted essentially of two wings made of heavy linen stretched over a duralumin framework. These were strapped to the back of the parachutist and enabled him to glide before opening his parachute. **1974** *Sport Parachutist* June 18/1 Ten paraplane jumpers who are all..experienced paraplane flyers. **1944** *N.Y. Times* 26 Apr. 5/6 St. Bernard Qualifies as 'Parapooch' for Army. Major [*sc.* a St. Bernard dog] has made seven high altitude jumps with a regular size parachute. **1951** W. D. BROWN *Parachutes* 315 *Parasheet*, a parachute constructed from one piece of fabric (or from several pieces with their warps parallel) in the form of a regular polygon, with the rigging lines attached to the apexes of the polygon. **1973** J. LUCAS *Big Umbrella* x. 110 Para-*sheets*, which acted like parachutes but were formed of strips of fabric rather than gores, were used for these [*sc.* slow-falling parachute flares]. *Ibid.*, A pair of para-sheets were used for each flare to increase stability. **1942** *Christian Science Monitor* 26 Mar. 3 Para-ski troopers of the 503rd Parachute Battalion. **1974** *Sport Parachutist* June 26 (*heading*) German Para-Ski Championships. **1942** *Christian Science Monitor* 26 Mar. 3 'Let 'Er Buck' Is War Cry of Para-Skiers. **1976** *National Observer* (U.S.) 13 Mar. 6/3 Para-skiers make 3,000-foot parachute jumps from a hovering helicopter and attempt to land precisely on a four-inch disk, then they race against the clock down a giant slalom course. **1940** in *Amer. Speech* (1944) XIX. 12/2, Britain has 400,000 paraspotters ready to fight parachutists. **1943** *Daily Express* 10 Sept. 1/5 (*headline*) Para-spies dropped in Germany.

para-aminobenzoic (pæ:ră,ămīnobenzōᵘ·ik), *a.* [f. PARA-¹ 2 b + *aminobenzoic* s.v. *AMINO-.] *para-aminobenzoic acid*: the *para*-isomer of aminobenzoic acid, which is sometimes considered a member of the vitamin-B group, is widely distributed in plant and animal tissue, has the ability to neutralize the bacteriostatic effects of the sulphonamides, and has been used in the treatment of rickettsial infections, esp. typhus and Rocky Mountain spotted fever. Abbrev. *PABA.

1906 *Proc. R. Soc.* A. LXXVIII. 82 (*heading*) Methyl derivatives of para-aminobenzoic acid. **1940** *Nature* 28 Dec. 838/2 (*heading*) Para-amino benzoic acid as a bacterial growth factor. **1963** [see *PABA].

para-aminosalicylic acid: see *PARA-¹ 2 b.

para-aortic (pæ:ră,e,ǭ·ɹtik), *a.* *Anat.* [f. PARA-¹ + AORTIC *a.*] Situated beside the aorta; used chiefly (in *para-aortic body*) as an epithet of certain paraganglia.

1927 *Jrnl. Anat.* LXI. 317 The pre- and para-aortic tissue of a 16-week embryo from the region of the suprarenal glands is seen on section to contain the semilunar ganglia, collections of haemo-lymphoid tissue, and other encapsuled masses (the Zuckerkandl anlage). **1952** *Ibid.* LXXXVI. 357 Wrete (1927) observed the continuity of the chromaffin bodies of the para-aortic region with the chromaffin tissue of the adrenal glands. *Ibid.* 358 Because of the lack of uniformity in the interpretation of the 'paraganglia', it has been replaced in the present investigation by the topographical term 'para-aortic bodies'. A para-aortic body is defined as an encapsulated collection of chromaffin cells lying in intimate contact with the sympathetic nervous system and yielding a pressor substance after extraction. **1959** R. D. LOCKHART et al. *Anat. Human Body* 488/2 The paraganglia, small brownish masses,..are similar to the suprarenal medulla... The largest masses, the para-aortic bodies, a third of an inch long at birth, lie on each side of the inferior mesenteric artery. **1965** [see *PARAGANGLION]. **1973** *Gray's Anat.* (ed. 35) 144/1 Chromaffin organs are found in connection with certain..of the secondary plexuses of the sympathetic system; the largest members of this series are the para-aortic bodies,..commonly termed paraganglia. *Ibid.* 1381/2 The para-aortic bodies..attain their maximum size in the first three years of post-natal life, when the largest takes the form of two elongated brownish bodies..which lie on each side of the inferior mesenteric artery. *Ibid.*, The chromaffin cells of the paraganglia and para-aortic bodies.

parabasal, *a.* (*sb.*) Add: **2.** *Zool.* [in this sense a. G. *parabasal* (C. Janicki 1911, in *Biol. Centralbl.* XXXI. 321).] Applied to the kinetoplast (sense *a) of protozoa; chiefly in *parabasal body*. Also *ellipt.*

1912 E. A. MINCHIN *Introd. Study Protozoa* vi. 89 The ring of blepharoplasts in *Lophomonas* is supported on the edge of a membranous structure,..which in its turn is surrounded by a peculiar striated body, the 'collar' of Grassi, or 'parabasal apparatus' of Janicki. **1924** HEGNER & TALIAFERRO *Human Protozool.* v. 127 Most of the members of the genus [*Trypanosoma*] are characterized by the possession of a more or less spindle-shaped body, a central nucleus, and a spherical or rod-shaped parabasal body, with which is closely associated a small blepharoplast and a flagellum. **1925**, etc. [see *KINETOPLAST]. **1973** K. G. GRELL *Protozool.* 17 Trichomonads have only a single, though occasionally branched, parabasal body which is anchored at the base of the flagella and can either wind about an axostyle or follow a straight course to the posterior end.

3. *Med.* Applied to cells from the layers of stratified epithelium just above the deepest (basal) layer of cells.

1948 G. N. PAPANICOLAOU et al. *Epithelia of Woman's Reproductive Organs* ix. 38 The parabasal postpartum cells..show a greater variety in size and form, somewhat larger nuclei, extensive vacuolization, and a tendency to congregate into larger groups. **1960** *Obstetr. & Gynecol.* XVI. 407/2 Deep in the layers of the epithelia are the parabasal cells, which cover the basal germinal layer of cells and are characterized by dense, thick cytoplasm with vesicular nuclei. **1972** *Acta Cytologica* XVI. 382/2 The presence [in amniotic fluid] of parabasal cells in excess of 70 per cent suggests a fetal weight of less than 500 gms.

parabasis. Add: (Further examples.) Also *transf.*, any digression in which the author addresses the audience on personal or topical matters.

1949 *Oxf. Classical Dict.* 216/2 *Parabasis* (addresses to audience separated by brief chants). **1952** F. H. DUDDEN *Henry Fielding* I. p. v, In the frequent parabases intercalated in his novels..[Fielding] has laid open his innermost self. **1965** *New Statesman* 30 Apr. 694/2 This is Coward's exercise in parabasis form: a lightly fictionalised justification of his way of theatre, acting and life. **1974** *Encycl. Brit. Micropædia* VII. 511/1 The *parabasis*, in which the chorus addresses the audience on the topics of the day and hurls scurrilous criticism at prominent citizens.

Parabellum (pærăbe·lŏm). Also **parabellum.** [f. L. *parā* imp. of *parāre* to prepare + *bellum* war (see quot. 1970).] The proprietary name of a make of automatic pistol or machine-gun. Also *attrib.*

1904 [see *LUGER]. **1918** E. S. FARROW *Dict. Mil. Terms* 432 *Parabellum Gun*, a German aëroplane gun of small caliber. It has a belt of cartridges which contains not less than a thousand projectiles. **1924** *Blackw. Mag.* Feb. 157/1 The vessel..carried two old-pattern Maxims and a German Parabellum, mounted for anti-aircraft fire. **1962** E. AMBLER *Light of Day* ii. 46 Six Parabellum pistols. **1970** R. A. STEINDLER *Firearms Dict.* 165 Based on the Latin 'Si vis pacem, para bellum' ('If you want peace, prepare for war.'),..the word Parabellum is the protected tradename of Mauser & D.W.M. **1973** J. WAINWRIGHT *Pride of Pigs* 127 A German gun..Official title—the German parabellum P'08, military automatic pistol... the Luger. **1974** S. GULLIVER *Vulcan Bulletins* 18 The 9mm jacketed Parabellum rounds used in..Stens and Sterlings.

parabiont (pærăbəi·ǫnt). *Biol.* [f. PARA-¹ + Gr. βιουντ-, pr. pple. stem of βιοῦν to live, f. βίος life.] An animal subjected to a parabiotic union.

1935 *Proc. Soc. Exper. Biol. & Med.* XXXIII. 568 Since the serum from each parabiont agglutinated the cells of both Pearlneck and Ring dove, it would seem that cellular differences were present other than those peculiar to each of the 2 species. **1955** *Anatomical Rec.* CXII. 225 The lateral one-third of the adjacent kidneys in each parabiont was excised. **1970** *Nature* 19 Dec. 1186/2 The abdominal cavities of the parabionts were connected by a common free canal.

parabiosis (pærăbəi,ōᵘ·sis). *Biol.* [mod.L., ad. F. *parabiose* (A. Forel 1898, in *Bull. de la Société Vaudoise des Sciences Naturelles* XXXIV. 380), f. PARA-¹ + Gr. βίωσις way of life (f. βίος life).] The anatomical union of a pair of organisms either natural or produced by surgery; the state of being so joined.

1908 *N.Y. Med. Jrnl.* LXXXVII. 374/1 Sauerbruch and Heyde give the name parabiosis to the new condition produced in animals which are experimented upon when they are organically connected together in an artificial manner. **1930** *Physiol. Rev.* X. 589 Parabiosis is a skin flap union, (to which is usually added peritoneal union), in which two whole organisms, instead of parts of organisms, are joined to each other. **1952** *New Biol.* XII. 46 Referring to the vascular anastomosis normally occurring between dizygotic bovine twins as 'nature's experiment in parabiosis'. **1955** *Anatomical Rec.* CXXII. 226 From parabiotic pairs formed between rats approximately 21 days of age, 12 pairs in successful parabiosis were chosen. **1962** D. J. B. ASHLEY *Human Intersex* iv. 58 Natural embryonic parabiosis has been observed in three instances in man. **1965** LEE & KNOWLES *Animal Hormones* iii. 64 If a male and a female salamander are joined by parabiosis (this allows the blood of the two animals to mix), a blood-borne substance from the male will lead to complete involution of the ovaries.

parabiotic (pærăbəi,ǫ·tik), *a.* *Biol.* [f. PARA-¹ + BIOTIC *a.*] Of, pertaining to, or existing in parabiosis.

1911 *Arch. Internal Med.* VII. 396 The reaction appeared very clearly after a parabiotic union of a tuberculous and healthy guinea-pig. **1930** *Physiol. Rev.* X. 591 Each of the parabiotic individuals continues, therefore, to a certain extent, to live its own life. **1935** *Proc. Soc. Exper. Biol. & Med.* XXXIII. 568 Each member of a pair of parabiotic twins developed antibodies against the red cells of the other. **1955** [see prec.]. **1970** *Nature* 19 Dec. 1186/2 Two months later when the animals became accustomed to the parabiotic condition, they were again anaesthetized with ether and the abdominal cavities opened.

Hence **parabio·tically** *adv.*, so as to produce parabiosis.

1915 *Arch. Internal Med.* XV. 45 Forschbach united dogs parabiotically, bringing peritoneal cavities and homologous layers of the parietes into continuity. **1961** *Lancet* 23 Sept. 707/1 If a cockroach thus rendered 'arhythmic' is joined parabiotically to a normal cockroach, its activity is restored.

parable, *sb.* Add: **e.** *parable-art, -opera, -play.*

1935 AUDEN in G. Grigson *Arts To-Day* 20 There must always be two kinds of art, escape-art..and parable-art, that art which shall teach man to unlearn hatred and learn love. **1976** *Listener* 8 July 27/1 Auden both devised and named the literary genre—'parable-art'—that the decade [of the 1930s] demanded. **1976** *National Observer* (U.S.) 18 Dec. 18/1 Britten composed in almost all the musical forms available to him—and even invented one, the parable opera, such as *Curlew River* and *The Prodigal Son*, in which a moral lesson was set forth in direct and easily assimilable musical terms. **1941** L. MACNEICE *Poetry of Yeats* 187 Thirdly, there are those plays which are near to fable or which might be called parable-plays —*The King's Threshold* (1904).

parablepsia, var. PARABLEPSIS. **parablepsy** (further example).

1913 F. W. HALL *Compan. Classical Texts* 154 Lipography (parablepsia), or simple omission of any kind.

1934 L. F. POWELL in G. B. Hill *Boswell's Life of Johnson* II. 370 Power..government (*by parablepsy*).

parabolic, *a.* and *sb.* **A.** *adj.* **2.** (Further examples.)

1955 *Sci. Amer.* Mar. 38/1 A parabolic 'dish', either solid or made of a wire screen, reflects incoming radio waves to a focal point, where a small dipole or rod picks up the energy. **1960** *Practical Wireless* XXXVI. 391/1 The radio telescope, a parabolic mirror of 83ft diameter.. scans the sky. **1962** A. NISBETT *Technique Sound Studio* i. 23 An assembly consisting of a cardioid or omnidirectional microphone fitted at the focus of a parabolic reflector is also strongly directional. **1965** P. WAYRE *Wind in Reeds* vi. 74 Separate E.M.I. recording equipment, including..a microphone which could be used in conjunction with a parabolic reflector. **1969** *Times* 4 Feb. 13/3 He seems to have recorded pulses of energy by means of a large array of parabolic mirrors. **1977** P. HILL *Fanatics* 38 Could we have a parabolic microphone in the control flat?

parabolicalism (pærăbǫ·likăliz'm). *rare.* [-ISM.] Parabolical character; matter which is parabolical.

1854 C. WALTON *Notes Biogr. W. Law* 238 The deeply experienced spiritual man..will be much disappointed.. at finding so much deep experience buried in such a huge mass of parabolicalism and idiocratic deformity.

parabolize, *v.* Add: Hence **para:boliza·tion,** the process of making parabolic or paraboloidal.

1903 *Sci. Amer. Suppl.* 17 Oct. 23232/3 Draper's method of 'parabolization by measure'.

parabutlerite, -casein(ate): see *PARA-[1] 2 c, 2 a.

paracentric (pærăse·ntrik), *a.*[2] *Cytology.* [f. PARA-[1]: cf. *-CENTRIC 2.] Involving only the part of a chromosome at one side of the centromere. Opp. *PERICENTRIC *a.* 2.

1938 H. J. MULLER in *Collecting Net* XIII. 187/2 If the breaks were to one side of the centromere, the inversion may be termed 'paracentric', and it will be noted that the proportions of the two arms, and hence the general shape of the chromosome as seen at mitosis, is not changed. But if the breaks included the centromere between them, being 'pericentric', the mitotic chromosome will have the relative sizes of its two arms altered, except in the special case in which the two distal sections are sensibly equal in size. **1957** C. P. SWANSON *Cytol. & Cytogenetics* xv. 485 Paracentric inversions are by far the most common type of aberration found in natural populations. **1975** *Nature* 3 July 40/1 Heterozygosity for a paracentric inversion, that is, a structural rearrangement in which a chromosome segment that does not include the centromere is rotated through 180°, results in suppression of recombination in the inversion region.

paracetamol (pærăsī·tămǫl). *Pharm.* [f. *para-acetyl*amino*phenol*, its chemical name.] A white crystalline compound, $C_8H_9NO_2$, with mild analgesic and antipyretic properties; a tablet of this.

1957 *Approved Names* (Brit. Pharmacopœia Comm.), Paracetamol. **1963** *Brit. Pharmaceutical Codex* 564 Paracetamol..is a suitable alternative for patients sensitive to aspirin. **1971** *Daily Tel.* 18 June 13/4 The active ingredients of pain-killing drugs that can be bought at the chemist are only two, namely paracetamol and aspirin. **1972** J. GILL *Tenant* III. ii. 92 Denis still had his headache when he woke and he went into the bathroom and took Paracetamol. **1976** *Liverpool Echo* 23 Nov. 1/8 Open verdict recorded by Merseyside Coroner at inquest into death of A— C— (32),..who died..of paracetamol poisoning. **1977** *Listener* 28 Apr. 563/3 An obligatory late-night snack for all production staff of toasted cheese and paracetamols..and who knows what new programmes would result.

parachor (pæ·răkǫɪ). *Chem.* [f. PARA-[1] + Gr. χορός (= dance, but taken by the coiner, in mistake for χώρα, as = space).] A numerical quantity (found empirically to be constant over a wide range of temperature) equal to the molecular weight of a liquid multiplied by the fourth root of its surface tension and divided by the difference between its density and that of its vapour.

1924 S. SUGDEN in *Jrnl. Chem. Soc.* CXXV. I. 1178 The quantity *P* can be regarded as function of chemical composition. For saturated substances, *P* is an additive function... It is proposed to name this quantity the parachor ..to signify comparative volume. **1940** GLASSTONE *Text-bk. Physical Chem.* viii. 517 The mean parachor equivalent of the —NC group, in a number of alkyl and aryl isocyanides, is 66; this corresponds closely to that required for the structure $—N^+ \equiv C^-$, thus N(12·5), C(4·8), triple bond (46·6), making a total of 63·9. The alternative structure —N=C would have a parachor equivalent of only 40·6. **1956** I. L. FINAR *Org. Chem.* II. i. 9 A comparison of parachors of different liquids gives a comparison of molecular volumes at temperatures at which liquids have the same surface tension. **1974** *Nature* 22 Nov. 296/2 For a given salt, k_s was proportional to the characteristic volume of the non-electrolyte which in $m^3\ mol^{-1}$ equals the parachor (calculated in the usual way in c.g.s. units) × 10^{-6}.

para-church: see *PARA-[1] 1.

parachute, *sb.* Add: **1.** Now more commonly used for descent from an aircraft. (Further examples.)

1938 *Britannica Bk. of Year* 79/1 Parachuting..seems to be considered as a kind of popular amusement for everybody in Russia and France if performed with stiff parachutes on ropes from special jumping towers. **1940** *Chambers's Techn. Dict.* 613/1 *Free parachute*, a parachute to be released or opened by the falling person. **1974** *Encycl. Brit. Micropædia* VII. 740/3 Sport parachutes have large holes that permit the air to escape and drive the parachute in the direction opposite the hole, much like a low-power jet engine.

2. (Further examples.)

1930 R. CAMPBELL *Adamastor* 50 The proud White gannet in his parachute of snow. **1947** AUDEN *Age of Anxiety* v. 112 In pelagic meadows The plankton open their parachutes.

5. Dropped by or attached to a parachute, as *parachute bomb, flare, light, mine, pack, rocket, signal*; designating part of a parachute, as *parachute cord, harness, ring*; using a parachute, as *parachute drop, jump* (so *jumper, jumping* vbl. sb.), *skiing* vbl. sb., *system, troops*; for, involving or consisting of parachute troops, as *parachute aircraft, attack, battalion, brigade, landing, regiment, wing*; resembling or acting as a parachute, as *parachute garment, spinnaker*; used for making parachutes, as *parachute nylon, silk*; **parachute assembly** (see quot. 1951); **parachute course,** a course of instruction in parachuting; **parachute tower,** a tower from which one may make a parachute jump.

1962 G. CHATTERTON *Wings of Pegasus* 32 There was a very limited number of tug aircraft and parachute aircraft. **1951** *Gloss. Aeronaut. Terms* (*B.S.I.*) III. 14 *Parachute assembly*, a parachute complete with all equipment for deployment and for harnessing a load. **1978** T. ALLBEURY *Lantern Network* iv. 36 They clambered into the thick parachute assemblies. **1941** *Hutchinson's Pict. Hist. War* 22 Jan.–18 Mar. 74 We must all be prepared to meet gas attacks, parachute attacks, with constancy, forethought and practised skill. **1942** Parachute battalion [see **para-ski* s.v. *PARA-[3]]. **1912** *Sci. Amer.* 16 Nov. 422/1 A Parachute bomb for Aeronautic Use... The bomb is provided with a small parachute which quickly destroys the horizontal velocity communicated by the airship. **1943** *Hutchinson's Pict. Hist. War* 25 Nov. 1942–16 Feb. 1943 148 Groundstaff of the R.A.F. loading parachute bombs into Hampden aircraft. **1974** *Times* 19 Apr. 15/4 The 1st Parachute Brigade fighting in North Africa. **1941** 'R. CROMPTON' *William does his Bit* viii. 193 Robert's got a bit of German parachute cord. **1976** A. WHITE *Long Silence* xi. 101 We checked ourselves for climbing. It was very similar to checking ourselves for a parachute jump... I had taken a loop of nylon parachute cord with me. **1946** R. CAPELL *Simiomata* I. 13 Tzigantis, having got round rules excluding men of his age, obtained the privilege of a parachute course. **1977** D. SEAMAN *Committee* 151 Like every one else in the Department, Walters had done his parachute course. **1928** *Even. News* 5 May 5/3 There will be wing walking and a parachute drop by Miss June. **1974** 'H. CARMICHAEL' *Motive* iii. 31 A sky-diver in a delayed parachute drop. **1918** *War Illustr.* 13 July 372/2 We saw flashes far to the south—shrapnel, star-shells, and parachute flares. **1941** A. O. POLLARD *Bombers over Reich* 46 So we dropped another parachute flare, which.. showed wreckage lying all over the place. **1974** S. GULLIVER *Vulcan Bulletins* 130 Wire-guided missiles, small aerial incendiaries, parachute flares. **1912** C. B. HAYWARD *Pract. Aeronaut.* 690 (*heading*) Parachute garment as a safeguard. *Ibid.*, A parachute garment has been devised to ease the shock of the fall. **1929** F. P. GIBBONS *Red Napoleon* 231, I made a last inspection of my parachute harness. **1958** G. DUTTON in B. James *Austral. Short Stories* (1963) 292 His shirt clung..to.. the parachute harness. **1978** T. ALLBEURY *Lantern Network* iv. 36 He..checked all the straps on her parachute harness. **1970** Parachute jump [see *JUMP *sb.*[1] 1 c]. **1977** *Listener* 28 July 104/3, I had hoped to be making my first parachute jump..that Saturday. **1912** C. B. HAYWARD *Pract. Aeronaut.* 161 The parachute jumper insisted on going up at least a thousand feet for the first trial. **1932** AUDEN *Orators* II. 71 The Mimosa's affair with the parachute jumper. **1952** *Chambers's Jrnl.* May 261/1 Parachute-jumping is the field of aviation in which the monopoly belongs to the Soviet Union. **1969** *Listener* 20 Feb. 255/1, I won the Northern Junior Sky-Diving Championship, but have given up parachute-jumping at least for the time being. **1974** *Encycl. Brit. Micropædia* VII. 741/1 The sport of parachute jumping is usually governed by the parachute branch of the national aeronautic club. **1976** A. WHITE *Long Silence* i. 14 Can he climb?.. Parachute jumping? **1940** W. S. CHURCHILL *Into Battle* (1941) 222 If parachute landings were attempted..these unfortunate people would be far better out of the way. **1942** E. WAUGH *Put out More Flags* 247 Parachute landings were looked for hourly. **1876** VOYLE & STEVENSON *Mil. Dict.* (ed. 3) 285/2 *Parachute light*, a suspended light, invented by Colonel (now General) Boxer R.A., and which is used for the same purpose as *ground light* balls..viz. to light up the enemy's works and working parties. **1918** E. S. FARROW *Dict. Mil. Terms* 432 *Parachute Lights*, rockets or flares fired electrically from the pilot's seat, through a tube. **1940** *Hutchinson's Pict. Hist. War* 20 Dec. 1939–13 Feb. 1940 2 When the 'parachute' and magnetic mines were first used in the war, many people assumed that the Allies were taken by surprise. **1961** B. FERGUSSON *Watery Maze* i. 44 The Germans dropped some parachute mines into the harbour. **1974** N. FREELING *Dressing of Diamond* 90 It was indeed difficult to see what a human agency could do, short of a few parachute mines. **1972** J. POYER *Chinese Agenda* (1973) v. 42 Mountain tents of very light-weight, close-woven parachute nylon. **1977** *New Yorker* 12 Sept. 101 Two parachute nylon traveling bags. **1975** T. ALLBEURY *Special Collection* iv. 20 There was ample room for..the parachute pack. **1977** P. WAY *Super-Celeste* II. 57 Bosco.. pulled the green apple on the oxygen cylinder attached to his parachute pack. **1972** Parachute regiment [see *PARA[7]]. **1973** *New Statesman* 28 Sept. 410/3 Reaction against the cloistered Hampstead life drove him into the Parachute Regiment. **1977** *R.A.F. News* 11–24 May 20/6 The Dakota..stands outside the Parachute Regiment's museum at Aldershot. **1930** C. DIXON *Parachuting* 53 He will then pull out the parachute ring in the front of his harness which will open the pack to let the parachute fly out. **1935** *Discovery* Feb. 43/2 The multi-tube parachute rocket used for the Harz Mountain experiments. **1976** *Star-Phoenix* (Saskatoon) 23 June 52/4 Since many rescues have to be performed at night or in darkened, stormy conditions, he suggested police and other officials involved in rescues carry illuminating parachute rockets. **1937** *Discovery* June 187/2 The manufacture of marine signals,..parachute signals,..railway flares. **1962** M. DUFFY *That's how it Was* xvi. 131 She was juggling with some pieces of parachute silk she had been given, trying to shape them to a pair of cami-knickers. **1977** J. CLEARY *High Road to China* i. 28 A length of old parachute silk was a curtain that hid..our skimpy wardrobe. **1971** *Bahamanian Rev.* Nov. 15/2 For those who like to be on the water as well as in it, water skiing is available at the larger hotel beaches. The more daring may wish to sample parachute skiing. In this unique sport, the skiers use the wind and motion of the boat to climb on the lift of a parachute and soar perhaps a hundred feet in the air for a thrilling ride. **1932** *Yachting* Oct. 68/1 That the 'parachute' spinnaker—or 'double' spinnaker, if you prefer—has come to stay is pretty evident to those who have given it any kind of a fair trial. **1964** M. WEEKS *Compl. Boating Encycl.* 398/1 *Parachute spinnaker*, a large, wide spinnaker introduced in 1927 by the Swedish yachtsman Sven Salén. **1971** *Daily Tel.* 1 July 30/6 After aerodynamically braking in the atmosphere the parachute system was put into action and before landing the soft-landing engines were fired. **1946** A. LEE *German Air Force* 37 This stage [in training, etc.] recalls the parachute tower in the Park of Rest and Culture at Moscow. **1938** *Jrnl. R. Aeronaut. Soc.* XLII. 840 It appears that the landing of parachute troops will require special sighting devices. **1942** *R.A.F. Jrnl.* 18 Apr. 29, 700 parachute troops were landed. **1978** *Listener* 9 Mar. 307/1 Malthausen..held whole armies of capable men and women who hoped that Allied parachute troops.. would drop on, or near enough to, the camps. **1958** P. KEMP *No Colours or Crest* xii. 264 As a further precaution we had to remove our badges of rank and parachute wings. **1973** *Times* 18 Oct. 18 General Amin..arrived in Amman earlier this week wearing Israeli parachute wings.

Hence **pa·rachutage,** a drop of supplies, etc. by parachute; **pa·rachuter,** a parachutist; **pa·rachutal** *a.*; **pa·rachutic** *a.* (sense 2). (See also next.)

1905 *Spectator* 14 Jan. 47/1 A parachutic arboreal serpent is not an impossible animal. **1930** *Flight* 21 Feb. 240/1 The last part of the lecture was devoted mainly to a discussion of vertical descent and to the parachutal efficiency of the autogiro. **1940** Parachuter [see *CHUTIST, 'CHUTIST]. **1941** R. GREENWOOD *Mr. Bunting at War* xvi. 221, I learnt it in case I meet any parachuters. **1945** G. MILLAR *Maquis* iii. 38, I told myself it was risky to sleep in bed so near the parachutage. **1956** R. BRADDON *Nancy Wake* xiii. 141 Whenever a parachutage was due, the B.B.C. would issue the special code phrase.

parachute, *v.* (In Dict. s.v. PARACHUTE *sb.*) Add: **a.** *trans.* (Further examples.) (Also **parachuted** *ppl. a.* **b.** *intr.* (Earlier and later examples.) Also, to use a parachute. **parachuting** *vbl. sb.* (further examples).

1860 W. H. RUSSELL *My Diary in India* II. ix. 174 And thus, with an able-bodied aborigen holding on by my tunic-tails behind,..I parachuted down. **1914** G. B. SHAW *Misalliance* 46 *Tarleton*... Been up much? *Lina.* Not in an aeroplane. Ive parachuted; but thats child's play. **1930** E. W. HENDY *Wild Exmoor* 245 Meadow-pipits parachuted down to the brink. **1938** Parachuting [see *PARACHUTE *sb.* 1]. **1945** G. MILLAR *Maquis* xv. 316 One pair of the high brown American parachuting-boots. **1946** *News Chron.* 2 Mar. 3 Brig. Nicholls was parachuted into Albania in October, 1943. **1956** 'C. BLACKSTOCK' *Dewey Death* ii. 27 He was with the Resistance... They parachuted him down into France. **1969** N. FREELING *Tsing Boum* xvii. 130 They came out at night to steal parachuted supplies. **1971** *Sci. Amer.* Sept. 230/1 It parachuted down over the open Pacific. **1974** *Times* 19 Apr. 15/4 Corporal Jackie Smith, the only girl Red Devil.. [has] considerable parachuting talent... You can 'buy' the weather by paying to travel wherever it's suitable for parachuting. **1977** *R.A.F. News* 11–24 May 3/6 An instructor in high-altitude parachuting at Abingdon. **1977** *New Yorker* 20 June 90/3 The connecting roads between tanks and parachuted troops are single lanes.

c. *fig.* Const. *in* or *into*. *trans.* To appoint or elect an outsider in such a way as to disregard the existing hierarchy; *intr.* to obtain a position in such a way. Also **parachuting (in)** *vbl. sb.*

1954 B. & R. NORTH tr. *Duverger's Pol. Parties* II. iii. 357 The 'parachuting' of candidates, so developed in the first proportional elections when some deputies had never set foot in their constituency before being elected, was radically impossible in the arrondissement system. **1968** *Listener* 13 June 759/3 Too many of the existing hierarchy are civil servants 'parachuted' in from outside. **1968** D. STUEBING *Trudeau: Man for Tomorrow* v. 39 Trudeau was accused of parachuting into Mount Royal, the term in this sense implying that the candidate was dropped into the riding under party sponsorship and over the objections of the riding association. **1971** P. A. ALLUM *Politics & Society Post-War Naples* (1973) vi. 180 A controversial example of the 'parachuting' of a candidate into the constituency was the transfer and inclusion in the list in 1968 of the Parisian correspondent of *L'Unità*, Maria-Antonietta Macciocchi. **1973** *Globe & Mail* (Toronto) 9 June 6/2 Mr. Roberts prudently concluded that local Liberals would resist if an officer from the Prime Minister's office parachuted into the riding to push aside a respectable candidate, and a woman at that. **1973** *Times* 13 July 5/1 The 'parachuting in' of two young men at a relatively senior level caused some bitter feelings among existing Commission staff, who saw their promotion prospects threatened. **1975** *Globe & Mail* (Toronto) 4 Mar. 6/2 Competent French-Canadians develop a sense of frustration and inferiority. They move more slowly and in smaller numbers up through the middle ranks. To redress the balance, the Government has to parachute French-Canadians from outside the civil service into senior positions. This parachuting produces complaints from English Canada about 'The French' taking over the Government.

parachutist. Add to def.: Now more commonly one who makes a parachute descent from an aircraft, esp. a soldier dropped by parachute. (Further examples.)

1888 *Sci. Amer.* 13 Oct. 231/1 An American Parachutist in England. **1927** *Illustr. London News* 10 Sept. 406 (*caption*) The perilous work of the parachutist. **1936** [see **ankle-boot*]. **1940** *Hutchinson's Pict. Hist. War* 10 Apr.–11 May 114 Another photograph showing large numbers of Red Army parachutists falling from troop-carrying aircraft during Soviet Army manoeuvres. **1946** *B.B.C. War Report* 78 Parachutists were to do the job, but in the darkness and bad weather the paratroops were widely scattered and only 150 men reached the rendezvous for the attack. **1972** *Daily Tel.* (Colour Suppl.) 7 Jan. 11/4 Parachutists compete in individual aerial acrobatics or accuracy work. **1974** *Times* 19 Apr. 15/5 A sports parachutist just starting out could expect to spend £500 on his kit. **1976** A. WHITE *Long Silence* i. 14 He'll also need to be a parachutist and rock-climber.

paraclinical (pærăkli·nikăl), *a. Med.* [f. PARA-[1] + CLINICAL *a.*] Of or pertaining to the branches of medicine, esp. the laboratory sciences, that provide a service for patients without direct involvement in their care.

1961 *Lancet* 29 July 255/2 In each case paraclinical laboratories have been included in the main complex of buildings. **1968** *Rep. R. Comm. Med. Educ. 1965–8* 85 in *Parl. Papers 1967–8* (Cmnd. 3569) XXV. 569 A course of clinical instruction which includes..such paraclinical subjects as pathology and microbiology. **1971** *Inside Kenya Today* Mar. 15/2 The A.I.D. regional programme has given assistance to the Veterinary Faculty..including commodities necessary for the construction and equipping of a paraclinical building.

paracone (pæ·răkōun). [f. PARA-[1] + CONE *sb.*[1]] An external cusp on the front, outer corner of a mammalian upper molar tooth.

1888 H. F. OSBORN in *Amer. Naturalist* XXII. 1072 (*table*) Proposed terms... Paracone. **1896** *Proc. Zool. Soc.* 563 The first two upper molars [of the hedgehog] are.. provided with two well-developed external cones, the paracone and metacone. **1922** W. K. GREGORY *Origin & Evolution Human Dentition* I. 74 It seems very likely that the high apex of the upper-molar crowns [in the marsupial mole] is really the paracone. **1934** W. E. LE GROS CLARK *Early Forerunners of Man* iv. 71 The premolars of a generalized mammal would be of simple form with a single pointed cusp which in the upper teeth is called the paracone and in the lower the protoconid. **1971** W. A. CLEMENS in A. A. Dahlberg *Dental Morphol. & Evolution* x. 187 The paracone and metacone of Cretaceous marsupials were maintained at approximately equal height.

paraconformity: see *PARA-[1] 1.

paraconid (pærăkōu·nid). [f. *PARACON(E + *-ID[5].] A cusp on a mammalian lower molar tooth corresponding to the paracone on an upper molar.

1888 H. F. OSBORN in *Amer. Naturalist* XXII. 1072 (*table*) Proposed terms... Paraconid. *Ibid.* 1076 As the hypocone develops, the paraconid recedes. **1896** *Proc. Zool. Soc.* 564 The ordinal position of the paraconid in the ontogeny may seem rather strange. **1904**, etc. [see *METACONID]. **1922** W. K. GREGORY *Origin & Evolution Human Dentition* I. 84 It seems probable that the paraconid, metaconid, and entoconid, arose *in situ* on the slopes of the protoconid. **1970** *Nature* 25 July 356/1 The presence of a paraconid in such a position is more characteristic of fossil lemuroids and omomyoids. **1975** [see *METACONID].

paracrine (pæ·răkrīn), *a. Physiol.* [ad. G. *parakrin*, f. Gr. παρα- PARA-[1] + κρίν-ειν to separate (cf. *ENDOCRINE *a.* and *sb.*).] Used of the action of a hormone whose effects are only local, and of the tissues which release and respond to such a hormone.

1972 F. FEYRTER in *Endocrinol. 1971* 137 The hypothesis of the peripheral entodermal endocrine (paracrine) glands was confirmed (1) by the evidence of a pressor agent in the enteral carcinoid.., (2) by the discovery of the islet cells of the pancreatic duct with A and B cells, their endocrine function having already been established. **1976** *Nature* 8 July 92/3 The actions of this hormone are paracrine, directed that is to neighbouring cells and tissue, rather than truly endocrine. **1978** *Ibid.* 20 Apr. 730/2 Further investigations related to the possible release of other endogenous substances or peptides, such as vasopressin or those of the paracrine system of the gut, where enkephalin immunoreactivity has been demonstrated, are needed.

paracrystal (pæ·răkristăl). [f. PARA-[1] + CRYSTAL *sb.* and *a.*] An assemblage of particles that has some degree of order but is not a true crystal.

1933 *Trans. Faraday Soc.* XXIX. 1019 On addition of acetone to a cold saturated solution in acetic ester of phytosterin valerate the latter..separates out as a paracrystal. **1953** S. E. LURIA *Gen. Virol.* v. 94 In the needles, which should more correctly be called 'paracrystals', the individual rods are oriented sidewise with great regularity. **1956** *Nature* 10 Mar. 473/1 The great regularity of plant viruses is shown even more strikingly by their ability to form crystals (or paracrystals) which give good X-ray photographs. **1970** *Jrnl. Biochem.* (Tokyo) LXVIII. 885/1 Paracrystals are formed by side-by-side association of F-actin particles in the presence of an excess amount of $MgCl_2$.

Hence **paracry·stalline** *a.*, of the nature of a paracrystal; **pa:racrystalli·nity.**

1933 *Trans. Faraday Soc.* XXIX. 1027 An especially strong paracrystallinity is to be ascribed to the paracrystalline sperm heads of Sepia officinalis. **1950** W. J. MOORE *Physical Chem.* xiv. 408 The compound ethylanisol-paraäminocinnamate passes through three distinct paracrystalline phases between 83° and 139°. **1964** G. H. HAGGIS et al. *Introd. Molecular Biol.* xi. 283 The haemoglobin in cells which had taken up the sickle shape was in para-crystalline, or tactoid form. **1974** *Amer. Jrnl. Anat.* CXXXIX. 135 Paracrystalline aggregates of microtubules were observed by electron microscopy in some cells of the anterior pituitary glands from ten untreated chinchillas.

parade, *sb.* Add: **I. 2. b.** (Later example.)

1930 E. RAYMOND *Jesting Army* I. iii. 45 A medical officer..and the whole of his Sick Parade ran.

3. c. Easter Parade, a crowd of promenaders in new clothes at Eastertime; a parade or pageant held at Eastertime. Hence **Easter-Parading** *vbl. sb.*

1904 'O. HENRY' in *N.Y. World Mag.* 27 Mar. 10/4 Will it tire you to be told again that Aileen was beautiful? Had she..joined the Easter parade,..you would have hastened to say so yourself. **1933** I. BERLIN *Easter Parade* (song), In your Easter bonnet..you'll be the grandest lady In that Easter Parade. **1942** O. NASH *Good Intentions* 5 Life is an Easter Parade. **1968** *New Statesman* 26 Apr. 544/3 In a sense, I suppose, this informal Easter Parading..is a middle-class demo. **1973** *Times* 24 Apr. 12/7 Several thousand people turned up at Battersea Park for the Easter Parade.

d. *transf. spec.* of broadcasting, a sequence or recital of forthcoming programmes, events, etc.

1947 *Radio Times* (Scottish ed.) 2 May 8/1 Scottish Programme Parade. **1948** *Broadcasting in West* (B.B.C.), Listen to your regional Programme Parade at 8.10 a.m. daily. **1962** *Rep. Comm. Broadcasting 1960* 255 in *Parl. Papers 1961–2* (Cmnd. 1753) IX. 259 Broadcast of a half-hour 'parade' of new advertisements.

5. (Further examples.) Now freq. used of a row of shops in a town, and of the street in which they are situated.

1766 C. ANSTEY *New Bath Guide* ix. 57 Whether thou art wont to rove By Parade, or Orange Grove,..In the Circus or the Square. **1791** F. BURNEY *Jrnl.* 20 Aug. (1972) I. 35 O how I have thought..of my poor Mrs. Thrale!—I went to look..at the House on the North Parade where we dwelt. **1885** *List of Subscribers, Brighton* (South of Eng. Telephone Co.) 5 Vizer E.B...154, Marine-parade. **1968** R. K. COX *Retail Site Assessment* ii. 15 Most new shopping centres..have broken away from the old strip parades which usually face each other across heavy inter-town traffic. **1970** *Times* 9 Mar. 15/2 It is convenient for the local shopper to have a compact shopping area..to provide in modern terms the facilities offered by the small local 'parades' of the 1930s. **1976** *Derbyshire Times* (Peak ed.) 3 Sept. 18/6 (Advt.), A vacant shop having a total area of 710 sq. feet, situated in a parade of shops and in a busy location. **1976** P. HILL *Hunters* viii. 95 The small parade of shops near the village hall.

7. *parade horse*; **parade drum,** a large drum played at a parade.

1963 M. LAURENCE in R. Weaver *Canad. Short Stories* (1968) 2nd Ser. 115 From Captain Fossey..the boy learned how to play the parade drum. **1967** W. SOYINKA *Kongi's Harvest* 64 The Big parade drum is heard. **1894** *Rep. Vermont Board Agric.* XIV. 123 The descendants of Woodbury Morgan..possess that peculiar qualification necessary for the parade horse. **1968** 'J. LE CARRÉ' *Small Town in Germany* ii. 21 Lieff, an empty-headed parade horse from Protocol Department, sat on his left. **1974** —— *Tinker, Tailor* xvi. 132, I refuse to bequeath my life's work to a parade horse.

parade, *v.* Add: **1. b.** *intr. Mil.* Of troops, to assemble for parade. Also *transf.*

1802 C. JAMES *New Mil. Dict.*, *To parade*, to assemble in a prescribed regular manner, for the purpose of being inspected, exercised, or mustered. **1811** *Gen. Regulations* (Army) 102 All Guards are to parade with shouldered Arms. **1914** T. A. BAGGS *Back from Front* xxiv. 122 We paraded for marching at 9 a.m., and set off with two manacled prisoners..before us. **1916** W. OWEN *Let.* 1 Feb. (1967) 377 Of course I 'paraded sick', but having no rash, I just have to crouch in my Hut. **1930** E. RAYMOND *Jesting Army* III. ii. 292 The working parties parade under the trees at nine o'clock. **1964** M. BANTON *Policeman in Community* ii. 15 He 'parades' at the beat box where he meets the constable coming off duty.

parade-ground. orig. *U.S.* [PARADE *sb.*] A place where troops parade; now the more usual term than PARADE *sb.* 4.

1724 [see PARADE *sb.* 7]. **1843** N. BOONE *Jrnl.* 31 July in L. Pelzer *Marches of Dragoons* (1917) 237 By one o'clock our command was formed on the parade ground of Fort Gibson. **1846** T. L. MCKENNEY *Mem.* I. v. 103 The level of the ground, and its freedom from undergrowth, were such as to give it the appearance of a parade ground. **1891** *Century Mag.* Mar. 715 The rats were so numerous that they were common sights on the parade-ground. **1933** H. H. SYMONDS *Walking in Lake District* ii. 44 Before reaching the camp you pass..the 'parade ground', a large square of cleared ground. **1975** J. CLEARY *Safe House* i. 18 Camp 93...long huts, a parade ground with a pock-marked surface. **1977** D. BEATY *Excellency* xx. 221 The Major led the way outside... The parade ground..was floodlit.

b. *transf.* and *attrib.*, esp. in phr. *parade-ground bearing, manner, voice*, etc.

1863 'G. HAMILTON' *Gala-Days* 174 Besides abundance of food and parade ground, these happy fowls have a very agreeable prospect. **1867** A. D. WHITNEY *Summer in L. Goldthwaite's Life* vi. 129 Clothes-lines like a parade-ground of telegraphs. **1892** *Harper's Mag.* Dec. 137 Both dismounted at the parade-ground gate. **1932** *Times Lit. Suppl.* 29 Sept. 693/4 The preposterous chief constable is of no use at all, and his parade-ground manners make a suitable contrast to Colonel Gethryn's cool and gentlemanly efficiency. **1937** 'M. INNES' *Hamlet, Revenge!* I. iv. 74 The precocious bass, favoured on public-school parade-grounds. **1937** J. R. FIRTH *Tongues of Men* 41 There is a well-known Prussian parade-ground type of voice. **1944** J. D. CARR *Till Death do us Part* i. 8 Major Horace Price..had made a trumpet of his hands and was addressing them in a parade-ground voice. **1961** M. BEADLE *These Ruins are Inhabited* (1963) ii. 28 He expected the boys to have a parade-ground bearing. *a* **1963** S. PLATH *Crossing Water* (1971) 23 Pawing like paradeground horses. **1964** L. DEIGHTON *Funeral in Berlin* iv. 25 The parade ground of Europe has always been that vast area.. that stretches eastward from the Elbe. **1965** *New Statesman* 9 Apr. 558/3 In a peremptory parade-ground voice Lord Balniel repeatedly bellowed the name of the current occupant of the chair ('Sir Herbert!' 'Sir Samuel!') in an effort to raise points of order. **1973** 'M. INNES' *Appleby's Answer* xvi. 138 He had a..parade-ground manner. **1976** R. CONDON *Whisper of Axe* I. xxi. 130 A spit-and-polish, parade-ground major. **1978** R. LEWIS *Uncertain Sound* vi. 189 He was all tension..no longer the stiff, military, parade ground bearing.

paradichlorobenzene: see *PARA-[1] 2 b.

paradiddle (pæ·rădid'l). *Mus.* [Echoic.] A basic drum roll, produced by alternate beating with the left-hand and right-hand drumsticks.

1927 *Melody Maker* Aug. 804/3 The ordinary paradiddle is greatly to be recommended. This is a wonderful exercise for getting out of 'one-hand' playing, and there are some variations of this beat which are invaluable to the dance drummer. **1934** *Metronome* Feb. 47 Either the single paradiddle or the flam paradiddle may be used during a marching step. **1941** *Amer. Speech* XVI. 229/2 The ramatacue and the paradiddle are advanced rhythmic drum movements, the words possibly being onomatopoeic. **1956** L. MCINTOSH *Oxford Folly* 153 Fiona thought hard for a moment of a negro Staff-Sergeant in the American Air Force whom she had once seen throwing the whole of the University Jazz Club into a prolonged ecstasy with an erotic and protracted paradiddle... But the drumsticks in her inexpert hands refused to make a smooth roll. **1960** K. AMIS *Take Girl like You* xvii. 210 A great saccharine growl came from the organ and a slow-motion paradiddle from the drums. **1961** A. BAINES *Mus. Instruments* 337 At a steady march tempo, with eight strokes on the drum in each bar, the sound of the paradiddle is fascinating. **1976** D. MUNROW *Instruments Middle Ages & Renaissance* 33/4 The specialized techniques of the side drum, such as the roll, flam, drag, and paradiddle developed in the first instance to fulfil a practical object: to encourage friend and frighten the foe.

paradigm. Add: **1. b.** *attrib.*, as **paradigm case,** a case or instance to be regarded as representative or typical.

1955 J. L. AUSTIN *How to do Things with Words* (1962) xi. 132 We were content to refer to 'statements' as the typical or paradigm case. **1962** *Listener* 4 Oct. 516/1 Plato's morality is supported and underlined by his theory of Forms, according to which mathematics is the paradigm case of knowledge. **1965** *Mod. Law Rev.* XXVIII. 509 The paradigm case at first instance—the core situation—appears to absorb so much attention that little concern is expended on the appeal process. **1974** *Jrnl. Philos.* LXXI. 337 Nagel employs a fairly standard 'paradigm case argument' in his analysis. **1977** *Canad. Jrnl. Linguistics* XXII. I. 13 A paradigm case is Anderson's description of Breton vowel lowering.

3. b. *transf.* and *fig.*

1929 C. DAY LEWIS *Transitional Poem* II. 25, I would be pædagogue—hear poplar, lime And oak recite the seasons' paradigm. **1964** *Listener* 6 Aug. 200/2 If one uses the word 'paradigm' as Wittgenstein himself used it, to denote a logical or conceptual structure serving us as a form of thought within a given area of experience. **1966** A. F. PARKER-RHODES in *Automatic Transl. of Lang.* (NATO Summer School, Venice, 1962) 173 The concept of paradigm thus enables us to approach the problem of mathematizing the process of syntactic description with greatly enhanced resources. **1970** *Eng. Stud.* LI. 18 Although Ohmann determines objective criteria to state the similarity (and at the same time the dissimilarity), there still remains a whole paradigm of related structures out of which the author has to choose the particular alternative(s) to match the marked term with. *Ibid.* 46 But, of course, for her Edwardian family life is a convenient paradigm of civilisation as a whole. **1973** C. Sagan *Cosmic Connection* (1974) xxiii. 155 There is a generation of men and women for whom..the Moon was the paradigm of the unattainable. **1973** *Times Lit. Suppl.* 2 Mar. 238/4 The unfolding of terror and duplicity which follows is easily seen as a paradigm of the suppression of Dubček's liberalizing administration. **1973** *Nature* 6 July 59/3 The use of induced epilepsy as an 'interfering technique' in the study of learning and memory paradigms. **1975** *Language* LI. 1009 The publication of Chomsky's *Syntactic structures* provided a new paradigm for linguistics. **1976** T. Eagleton *Crit. & Ideology* i. 19 In the drive for order, proportion and propriety, the demand for socially cohesive categories of Nature and Reason,..history once again selects criticism as both paradigm and instrument of such a project. **1976** *Language* LII. 286 As for the periods in between the quantum leaps, Kuhn contends that each period of normal science in the development of a scientific discipline corresponds to one and only one methodological framework or *paradigm*. In a nutshell, paradigms are 'universally recognized scientific achievements that for a time provide model problems and solutions to a community of practitioners'. **1976** F. Zweig *New Acquisitive Society* ii. x. 132 The television set ..is the paradigm of consumer culture, with its disarming passivity prone to desires divorced from action.

paradigmatic, *a.* Add: (Further examples.) **b.** *Linguistics.* Belonging to a set of linguistically associated forms. Cf. Paradigm 3.

1662 [see *agogic *a.* 1]. **1948** J. R. Firth in E. P. Hamp et al. *Readings in Linguistics II* (1966) 175 Most phoneticians..have continued to elaborate the analysis of words... Such studies I should describe as paradigmatic and monosystemic in principle. **1953** C. E. Bazell *Linguistic Form* 43 A special instance of paradigmatic indiscreteness of phonic character is afforded by English æ. **1964** *Eng. Stud.* XLV. 388 The concept of an active selective function of what has been called a paradigmatic frame does not serve teleological explanation of linguistic history. **1964** R. H. Robins *Gen. Linguistics* 49 Paradigmatic relations are those holding between comparable elements at particular places in structures. **1965** M. I. Finley in *New Statesman* 11 June 926/1 The authors do not distinguish between history as a systematic discipline and Aristotle's or Machiavelli's use of the past as a quarry for data for his social and political theories ('paradigmatic history', that has been called). **1972** W. Labov *Language in Inner City* v. 215 Larry is a paradigmatic speaker of black English vernacular as opposed to standard English. **1973** J. M. Anderson *Struct. Aspects Lang. Change* 124 In some cases syntagmatic influence may be the dominant force..; at other periods and under different conditions, paradigmatic forces may be stronger. **1973** *Black World* Sept. 51 A violence that becomes, in Wright's vision, paradigmatic of the entire spectrum of violence Blacks experience in this country. **1974** *Nature* 16 Aug. 609/1 Most of the philosophers of science..take the Comtean view, of physics as the paradigmatic science. **1975** *Language* LI. 665 Halle 1973 argues that paradigmatic information should be represented in the dictionary. **1976** *Times Lit. Suppl.* 23 Jan. 88/3 To his contemporaries Defoe was insignificant except as the paradigmatic Grub Street hack. **1977** *Church Times* 18 Feb. 6/3 Even if the (New Testament) accounts have been stylised, they have nonetheless a paradigmatic trustworthiness, an incontestable inner truth.

paradigmatically, *adv.* (Further examples.)

1953 C. E. Bazell *Linguistic Form* 7 An allomorph is paradigmatically relevant. **1960** C. Geertz in J. A. Fishman *Readings Sociol. of Lang.* (1968) 283, I offer the accompanying three charts depicting paradigmatically how a single sentence alters within each of the [Javanese] dialects and among them. **1964** R. H. Robins *Gen. Linguistics* 49 The status of a particular case as a grammatical category applicable to certain word endings in a language like Latin is stated..paradigmatically in terms of the number of different cases formally marked in the language. **1967** D. Cooper *Psychiatry & Anti-Psychiatry* p. xii, The third chapter seeks paradigmatically to make intelligible the patient-career of one young diagnosed schizophrenic in terms of the nature of his family world and the key events that have happened in it. **1971** T. F. Mitchell in *Archivum Linguisticum* II. 49 Within such a selection of phrases, *working* is definable as adjectival on the basis of the relationships it accretes paradigmatically.. and syntagmatically. **1976** *Amer. Speech 1974* XLIX. 79 These relationships are seen..as constituting the basis for lexical sets paradigmatically.

paradise, *sb.* Add: **1. c.** *ellipt.* The plumage of a bird of paradise (cf. Bird *sb.* 7).

1905 E. Wharton *House of Mirth* ii. x. 446 Mrs. Trenor's hat? The one with the green Paradise? **1928** *Daily Express* 24 May 5/3 The same firm was responsible for wonderful curls of shaded paradise,..toning from dark to palest beige tones.

3. c. *Assoc. Football.* (With capital initial.) A name given to Celtic Park, Glasgow, the home ground of the Celtic Football Club.

1946 C. A. Oakley *Second City* iii. 168 Celtic Park.. seemed so palatial, in odd comparison with an adjacent graveyard, that it was described as the 'Paradise'. **1958** C. Tully *Passed to You* xxii. 92 One of the best things about being at Paradise is that you're pretty certain to move in good company... You'll go a long way before you meet a better bunch than the Tims of Parkhead.

8. *paradise garden*; **paradise crane,** the blue or Stanley crane, *Anthropoides paradisea*, found in South Africa and distinguished by a cluster of very long, black tail feathers.

1906 *Daily Chron.* 8 May 7/4 His consignment..included..three paradise cranes, five wolves and seven baboons. **1958** E. T. Gilliard *Living Birds of World* 146/1 Other species [of crane] are named for their ornamental plumage, coloration, wattles or geographical ranges—as, for example..the Paradise or Stanley Crane.. of southern Africa; and the Crowned Crane. **1910** O. Lindemann tr. *Delius's Village Romeo & Juliet* 178, I know another place not very far from here where we'll be quite unknown. 'Tis the Paradise Garden. *Ibid.* 192 Der Paradiesgarten... The Paradisegarden. **1972** *Country Life* 23 Mar. 682/3 It has been suggested that such places as this, in which an attempt is made to bring together plants from all parts of the world, should be known as paradise gardens. **1977** A. Wilson *Strange Ride R. Kipling* iv. 221 The Woolsack [*sc.* their South African house] was a delight to the whole Kipling family. .. For the children..it was clearly a Paradise garden.

paradoctor (pæ·rădǫ:ktəɹ). Chiefly *U.S.* [f. *para-³ + Doctor *sb.* 6.] A doctor who is parachuted to patients in remote areas.

1944 *Time* 10 July 92/3 He is one of six paradoctors attached to the Search and Rescue Station of the Second Air Force. **1947** *Birmingham* (Alabama) *News* 30 May 1/7 A paradoctor from Athens..parachuted into the jungle. **1949** *Ibid.* 7 Aug. 1/7 Dr...Little,..former Army paradoctor, gave first aid to the injured.

parador (pæ·rădōᵊɹ). Pl. **paradores.** [Sp. *parador* inn, hostel.] Formerly an inn or hotel in Spain, now used as the name of a chain of hotels owned and administered by the Spanish government. Also *attrib.*

1845 R. Ford *Hand-bk. for Travellers Spain* II. 569/1 *La de Navarra*, near the Pla. Mayor, is but a mere *parador.* **1927** C. Connolly *Let.* 13 Feb. in *Romantic Friendship* (1975) 257 Roach I feel was..at home in the straw strewn venta or the noisy parador. **1960** *News Chron.* 10 Mar. 8/6 Castles in Spain have become paradores, Government run hotels. **1966** *Vogue* Nov. 182/3 Gran Canaria..here the broad terrace of a government parador looks out across a contorted volcanic landscape. **1973** *Country Life* 22 Nov. 1688/1 The needs of tourists can provide new functions..for historic buildings. Examples are the parador hotels in Spain.

parados. Add: **b.** The rear wall of a trench. Also *fig.*

1917 A. G. Empey *Over Top* 303 *Parados*, the rear wall of a trench which the Germans continually fill with bits of shell and rifle bullets. Tommy doesn't mind how many they put in the parados. **1938** H. G. Wells *Apropos of Dolores* iv. 139 Much of this discourse flowed over me. I did my best to keep my head down beneath the level of parapet and parados. **1957** P. Kemp *Mine were of Trouble* iv. 79, I saw Frejo and Santo Domingo on top of the parados.

paradosis (păræ·dŏsis). *Theol.* [Gr. παράδοσις, a handing down, a tradition.] A historical tradition, *spec.* relating to the teachings of Christ and of his disciples; teaching based on this tradition.

1950 L. S. Thornton *Revelation & Mod. World* ix. 285 The apostolic *paradosis* was embodied, not only in the apostolic writings, but also in the accredited teachers of the Catholic Church who could show their 'didactic successions' from the apostles. **1953** *Scottish Jrnl. Theol.* VI. 117 This is a tradition, a *paradosis* which does not fall under the condemnation which Jesus pronounces with regard to the *paradosis* in general. **1956** *Ibid.* IX. 434 Cullmann's thesis is that Paul was able to accord a higher place to the *paradosis* he had received, despite the fact that Jesus had denounced the high place accorded to *paradosis* in Judaism. **1958** A. Richardson *Introd. Theol. N.T.* xvi. 365 We must not make the mistake of the older NT critics who thought that what was to be interpreted was a number of ancient documents, which could be more objectively judged if they were isolated from the paradosis of the Church. **1973** *Amer. Jrnl. Philol.* XCIV. 320 Modern editors treat χειᾷ as a reasoned Triclinian conjecture. But χειᾷ proves almost certainly to be nothing but a further perversion of an already corrupt paradosis.

paradox, *sb.* (*a.*) Add: **2. a.** *spec.* in *Literary Criticism.*

1939 Brooks & Warren *Understanding Poetry* vi. 637 *Paradox*, a statement which seems on the surface contradictory, but which involves an element of truth. Because of the element of contrast between the form of the statement and its true implications, paradox is closely related to irony. **1942** C. Brooks in A. Tate *Language of Poetry* 37 Few of us are prepared to accept the statement that the language of poetry is the language of paradox... Yet there is a sense in which paradox is the language appropriate and inevitable to poetry. **1947** —— *Well-Wrought Urn* 230 Paradox, as a device for contrasting the conventional views of a situation, or the limited and special view of it such as those taken in practical and scientific discourse, with a more inclusive view. **1960** *Commentary* Nov. 369 He had been instructed in *paradox, tension*, and *ambiguity* in a course called 'Introduction to Literature'.

c. *Logic.* A statement or proposition which, from an acceptable premise and despite sound reasoning, leads to a conclusion that is against sense, logically unacceptable, or self-contradictory; freq. distinguished by name, esp. of its propounder or of the type of problem it raises. Cf. *liar 1 d, *Russell's paradox* s.v. *Russell.

1903 B. Russell *Princ. Math.* xliii. 358 This paradox, which, as I shall show, is strictly correlative to the Achilles, may be called for convenience the Tristram Shandy. **1921** W. E. Johnson *Logic* I. iii. 45 The paradox of implication assumes many forms, some of which are not easily recognised as involving mere varieties of the same fundamental principle. **1948** H. C. Brodie in Brodie & Coleman *Chwistek's Limits of Sci.* p. xxxiii, Typical of such paradoxes is the contradiction of Burali-Forti. **1950** R. Carnap *Logical Found. Probability* vii. 469 This is an instance of what Hempel calls the paradox of confirmation. **1955** A. N. Prior *Formal Logic* iii. i. 224 As with Lewis's paradoxes, these appear less startling when the definitions of the terms used are considered. **1966** W. V. Quine *Ways of Paradox* i. 7 The paradoxes in this class are called antinomies, and it is they that bring on the crises in thought. An antinomy produces a self contradiction by accepted ways of reasoning. **1971** *Brit. Jrnl. Philos. Sci.* XXII. 337 The Nelson-Grelling paradox requires separate notice, because it can be presented with an explicit distinction between predicative phrases and what they are supposed to express. **1972** T. Stoppard *Jumpers* i. 29 Zeno overlooked the fallacy which is exemplified at its most picturesque in his famous paradoxes, which showed in every way but experience that an arrow could never reach its target. **1973** J. L. Mackie *Truth, Probability & Paradox* vi. 237 There is a group of paradoxes..which includes the Epimenides and other forms of the liar, heterologicality, Russell's class paradox..and so on.

paradoxical, *a.* Add: **3. b.** Applied to sleep that is characterized by increased physiological and mental activity (e.g. rapid eye-movements and dreaming in man) and normally alternates with longer periods of orthodox sleep.

[**1959** Jouvet & Michel in *Compt. Rend. Soc. de Biol.* CLIII. 422 Cette phase est suivie d'une 'phase paradoxale' dont l'activité est extrêmement caractéristique.] **1962** I. Oswald *Sleeping & Waking* i. 16 (*heading*) 'Paradoxical phase' of sleep in the cat. **1969** *Sci. Jrnl.* Dec. 78/3 The brainwaves of paradoxical sleep are more like those during normal wakefulness. **1970** *New Scientist* 23 Apr. 170/2 After about an hour of this orthodox sleep phase..paradoxical sleep begins and lasts about 10 minutes before orthodox sleep is resumed. The electrical brain waves and many other bodily functions during paradoxical sleep are different—..most muscles become quite flaccid and their reflexes are lost; the penis is erect; the heart, breathing and blood pressure are irregular; [etc.]. **1974** *Times* 4 Sept. 6/7 There was increasing evidence of a 90-minute rhythm in both sleep and waking activity. Paradoxical sleep (when dreaming) occurred every 90 minutes. **1977** D. Morris *Manwatching* 315 So it is safe to assume that the total of 1½ hours of Paradoxical Sleep we have each night really does represent 1½ hours of actual dreaming.

paradoxician (pæ:rădǫksi·ʃăn). *rare.* [f. Paradox *sb.* + -ician.] One who deals in paradoxes; a paradoxer.

1909 W. J. Locke *Septimus* xvi. 186 Sypher was not convinced by the airy paradoxician.

paradoxling (pæ·rădǫ:ksliŋ). *nonce-wd.* [f. Paradox *sb.* + -ling¹ 2.] A statement or tenet that is slightly paradoxical.

1863 G. M. Hopkins *Let.* 10 July (1956) 199 Yes. You are a Fool. I can shew it syllogistically, by an Epimedicu-lum or paradoxling.

paradoxographical, *a.* Delete *nonce-wd.* and add later example.

1904 W. H. Stevenson in *Eng. Hist. Rev.* Jan. 139 He assigns the younger periplus to the Alexandrian or post-Alexandrian times on account of its paradoxographical character.

paradrop (pæ·rădrǫp), *sb.* and *v.* [f. *para-³ + *drop *sb.* 12 g or Drop *v.*] **A.** *sb.* The dropping from aircraft of men or supplies by parachute. **B.** *v. trans.* To drop (men or supplies) in this way. Hence **paradro·pping** *vbl. sb.*

1948 *Shell Aviation News* No. 118. 9/1 Back at the main supply base of Shell-Mera a radio message is received from this headquarters for a paradrop and feverish activity ensues. **1950** *Birmingham* (Alabama) *News* 27 Nov. 28/3 An Iuka man was one of the pilots who para-dropped more than 4,000 men of the 11th Airborne on an arc between the North Korean cities of Sukcon and Sunchow. **1952** *Time* 31 Mar. 71/2 (Advt.), Here, it paradrops vital supplies 'up front'. **1961** *Flight* LXXX. 371/2 The rear ramp allows paradropping. **1971** *Morning Star* 26 June 1 Liberation troops inspecting a U.S. ammunition paradrop captured in the far north of South Vietnam.

parafango (pæ:răfa·ŋgo). [f. Para(ffin *sb.* + *fango.] A mixture of mud and paraffin wax used for medicinal purposes (see quots.).

1969 *Daily Tel.* 25 June 15/6 Other new treatments recently introduced at Henlow include..the parafango, a mixture of mud and paraffin wax for spot reducing, arthritis and rheumatism. **1970** *Guardian* 4 Apr. 11/7 Parafango is the technical term for warm wax or mud baths.

parafe, *v.* App. var. of Paraph *v.* 2.

1922 Joyce *Ulysses* 212 Farrell parafes his polysyllables.

paraffin, *sb.* Add: **4.** *paraffin heater, stove, tin*; **paraffin oil** (later examples); **paraffin test** (see quots.).

1939–40 *Army & Navy Stores Catal.* 191/3 Coleman Paraffin Heater..Burns ordinary paraffin oil. **1975**

J. McClure *Snake* iv. 59 She had dumped..that very serviceable old paraffin heater, that was only a little rusty, on her new rubbish tip. **1976** *Sunday Mail* (Glasgow) 21 Nov., It is a disgrace that people who have worked hard all their days should be forced to use paraffin heaters because they cannot afford their electricity bills. **1949** Paraffin oil [see *kerosene]. **1950** *Sci. News* XV. 99 Serum from the umbilical cord can be guaranteed to increase haemoglobin production in rats only if collected under paraffin oil, that is, when protected from the oxygen of the air. **1966** M. Woodhouse *Tree Frog* xvi. 123 There was a pressure cooker and two large paraffin stoves. **1978** 'L. Black' *Foursome* ii. 18 The fug of the small wooden shed heated by a paraffin stove. **1950** *Ellery Queen's Mystery Mag.* Oct. 101/1 'What's a paraffin test?' asked Nicky... 'Every gun..has a certain amount of backfire. Some of the gunpowder flashes back and is embedded in the hand of the man that fires. They coat his hand with hot paraffin and then draw it off like a glove. They then test it for gunpowder..and if it's positive, it means that the man fired the gun.' **1974** R. B. Parker *Godwulf Manuscript* iii. 23 A paraffin test. When you fire a handgun cordite particles impregnate your skin. A lab man puts paraffin over it, lets it dry, peels it off, and tests it. The particles show up in the wax. **1935** H. Edib *Clown & his Daughter* lv. 342 Some of them brought empty paraffin-tins. **1937** K. Blixen *Out of Afr.* i. 12 The Swahili town..was built mostly out of old paraffin tins hammered flat.

paraffiny (pæ·răfini), *a.* [f. Paraffin *sb.* + -y[1].] Of, belonging to, or suggestive of paraffin; covered or smeared with paraffin; smelling of paraffin.

1902 Conrad *Youth* 21 The ascending air was hot, and had a heavy, sooty, paraffiny smell. **1925** B. Beetham in E. F. Norton *Fight for Everest, 1924* iii. vi. 368 Paraffiny fingers will taint the whole canteen. **1952** 'J. Tey' *Singing Sands* vi. 93 A large wooden tray of tuppenny buns... They were crummy and depressed-looking,..and they smelled very faintly of paraffin...the paraffiny buns and the margarine.

Parafilm (pæ·răfilm). Also **parafilm.** A proprietary name for certain thermoplastic materials (see quots. 1952, 1956).

1934 *Official Gaz.* (U.S. Patent Office) 18 Sept. 520/2 Marathon Paper Mills Co., Rothschild, Wis. Filed July 23, 1934, *Parafilm*. For moistureproof, self-sealing flat wrapper, claims use July 11, 1934. **1952** *Trade Marks Jrnl.* 21 May 472/1 Parafilm... Backing cloth, being piece goods..consisting of textile material coated with a thermoplastic substance containing rubber, the textile material predominating, for use in the manufacture of boots and shoes. Lindsay & Williams Limited,..Manchester..; manufacturers. **1956** *Ibid.* 8 Feb. 131/2 Parafilm... Electrical insulation identification tape. Lindsay & Williams Limited,..Manchester..; manufacturers. *Ibid.* 26 Sept. 947/2 Parafilm... Thermoplastic materials in the form of sheets, ribbons and tapes, none being textiles... Lindsay & Williams Limited,..Manchester..; manufacturers. **1967** K. M. Smith *Insect Virology* xi. 214 Recently..the animal membrane has been replaced by stretched Parafilm. **1974** *Nature* 3 May 85/1 The mouthparts of a dehydrated tick were inserted through a wax-coated parafilm membrane up to the base of the palps.

parafiscal, *a.*: see *para-[1] 1.

parafoil (pæ·răfoil). Also **para-foil.** [f. *para-[3] + *aero)foil.] A structure of fabric designed to function as both a parachute and an aerofoil, providing lift that enables the wearer to glide.

1967 *N.Y. Times* 13 Aug. 15 A revolutionary parachute invention..known as the para-foil, would enable pilots bailing out over enemy territory to glide like birds until they reached safety. **1968** *Sunday Times* 28 Sept. 5/1 Air fills the cells of his parafoil and flows over the upper surface, creating 'lift', as with an aeroplane. **1975** *Sci. Amer.* Mar. 122/3 A major breakthrough was the invention of an inflatable multicell airfoil of fabric by D. C. Jalbert of Boca Raton, Fla... It is called the Para-Foil... Its shape in the form of a rigid, low-speed wing, is maintained entirely by air that enters openings at the leading edge to build up internal pressure. On landing the Para-Foil..can be collapsed into a manageable bundle of lines and cloth. One can also jump with it from an aeroplane. **1976** *Listener* 8 July 30/3 We sent up a parafoil instead, an amazing American invention without any rigid structure, a mixture of balloon, parachute, aerofoil and kite, which instantly climbs to the permitted height of 200 feet.

parafolli·cular, *a.* *Anat.* [f. Para-[1] + Follicular *a.*] Situated near to, or around, a follicle: applied to cells found between the follicles of the mammalian thyroid gland, which secrete the hormone thyrocalcitonin.

1932 J. F. Nonidez in *Amer. Jrnl. Anat.* XLIX. 479 In the following pages the large epithelial cells with argyrophile granules will be termed 'parafollicular' cells, since they lie in the interstitial spaces in close proximity to the follicles from the epithelium of which they arose. **1968** H. Rasmussen in R. H. Williams *Textbk. Endocrinol.* (ed. 4) xi. 877/2 Between the follicles [of the thyroid gland] are groups of epithelial cells variously described as interstitial cells, mitochondrial-rich, or parafollicular cells. **1975** Francis & Martin *Introd. Human Anat.* (ed. 7) viii. 267 The ultimo-branchial body, an integral part of the thyroid, in man is represented by the parafollicular or C cells.

paraform(aldehyde: see *para-[1] 2 a.

parafovea (pærăfōu·viă). *Anat.* Also with hyphen. [f. Para-[1] + Fovea, or as back-formation from next.] An annular area of the retina immediately surrounding the fovea centralis. Cf. *perifovea.

1941 S. L. Polyak *Retina* xvi. 211 The parafoveal region or parafovea is the intermediate belt of the central area [of the retina]. **1944** *Jrnl. Optical Soc. Amer.* XXXIV. 713/1 Rods, though absent from the fovea, appear in the parafovea and increase to a maximum density within the area of the retina to which the bright field image is projected. **1960** R. A. Weale *Eye & its Function* v. 65 The corneo-lenticular system cannot form a sharp and undistorted image outside an area called the para-fovea. This surrounds the macula and would be covered by the image of a circular disc subtending at the eye an angular diameter of some 20°. **1970** J. A. Howard *Aerial Photo-Ecol.* xiii. 141 The fovea is most sensitive to green light at 0·555μ whilst in subdued light the para-fovea responds most to light at 0·515μ.

parafoveal (pærăfōu·viăl), *a.* *Anat.* [f. Para-[1] + Fovea + -al.] Of or pertaining to the parafovea; adjacent to the fovea.

1925 *Brit. Jrnl. Ophthalm.* IX. 53 Frequently [in macular disease] the paracentral or parafoveal elements are mainly involved. **1941** [see prec.]. **1959** S. Duke-Elder *Parsons' Dis. Eye* (ed. 13) xxii. 321 Central serous retinopathy..is presumably caused by exudation from the parafoveal capillaries, probably of toxic or allergic origin. **1971** *Jrnl. Gen. Psychol.* LXXXIV. 48 The considerable amount of stray light..stimulates parafoveal rods.

Hence **parafo·veally** *adv.*, in a parafoveal manner; by means of the parafovea.

1960 *New Scientist* 10 Nov. 1267/2 When an object is seen parafoveally or peripherally, detail is not perceived; the object is seen as a comparatively vague shape, and the eye in these regions is sensitive mainly to motion. **1963** *Jrnl. Psychol.* LV. 394 Brightness enhancement was measurably present for part-spectrum impingements presented parafoveally under the proper conditions of intermittency.

paraganglioma (pærăgæŋgliōu·mă). *Path.* Pl. **-omas, -omata.** [ad. F. *paragangliome* (Alezais & Peyron 1908, in *Compt. Rend. des Séances de la Soc. de Biol.* LXV. 746): see next and *-oma.] A tumour thought to arise from a paraganglion (in its wider sense) or the adrenal medulla; *esp.* one of non-chromaffin tissue. Cf. *phæochromocytoma.

1914 *Surg., Gynecol. & Obstetr.* XVIII. 209/1 Whenever a tumor of a paraganglion—a paraganglioma—is suspected, it should be fixed in a solution containing chromic acid or its salts. **1925** *Amer. Jrnl. Anat.* XXXIV. 89 By far the greater number of pathologists believe in a vascular origin for the growths of the carotid body... Some later workers would call these tumors 'paragangliomas'. **1948** Martin & Hynes *Clin. Endocrinol.* vii. 144 Chromaffin tumours. These uncommon tumours include the phæochromocytomata which arise from chromophile cells of the adrenal medulla, and the paragangliomata which originate from chromaffin tissue in the intrathoracic cervical chain, the carotid bodies, or the organs of Zuckerkandl. **1956** H. M. Zimmerman et al. *Atlas Tumors Nervous Syst.* 177/1 The chromaffin tumors are found most commonly in the adrenal medulla... They are called pheochromocytomas (chromaffin tumor, functionally active paraganglioma)... The term 'paraganglioma' is best used for the non-secretory and hence non-chromaffin tumors of the paraganglionic tissues. **1974** Passmore & Robson *Compan. Med. Stud.* III. i. xvii. 37/1 Glomus jugulare tumours. These are another example of non-chromaffin paragangliomata; they..grow in the connective tissue that lies between the bulb of the internal jugular vein and the floor of the middle ear.

Hence **pa:raganglio·matous** *a.*

1965 *Jrnl. Clin. Path.* XVIII. 291/2 Medullary carcinoma may resemble various neural or paragangliomatous tumours.

paraganglion (pærăgæ·ŋgliən). *Anat.* Pl. **-ia.** [a. G. *paraganglion* (A. Kohn 1900, in *Arch. f. mikrosk. Anat.* LVI. 130): see Para-[1] and Ganglion.] Any of several highly vascular groups of chromaffin cells that are similar to those of the adrenal medulla and in position and development are closely associated with the sympathetic nerve trunks; also applied to some structures now recognized as non-chromaffin (see quots. 1940, 1962).

1907 *Med. Rec.* (N.Y.) 3 Aug. 188/2 These occur in the medullary substance of the adrenal bodies, in the so-called paraganglia of the same organs. **1930** Maksimov & Bloom *Textbk. Histol.* xxxiv. 709 These paraganglia include the carotid gland and widespread, rather small accumulations of cells in the retroperitoneum which are often spoken of as the organs of Zuckerkandl. **1937** *Contrib. Embryol.* XXVI. 17 A study of the development of the carotid body..has left me unconvinced that it can be regarded as a paraganglion in the strict sense of the term. *A priori*..the term paraganglion means a structure of which the essential cells are derived in their entirety from the nervous system. **1940** *Q. Rev. Biol.* XV. 167/2 Recently..a distinction has been made between chromaffin and non-chromaffin paraganglia. **1962** E. C. Crosby et al. *Correl. Anat. Nerv. Syst.* viii. 545/1 Small collections of cells found in relation with certain blood vessels constitute the carotid body, the aortic bodies, the jugular body..and the coccygeal body. .. Although sometimes referred to as paraganglia, as the term is used in its wider sense, these cell masses usually contain no chromaffin cells and are unlike the chromaffin bodies in other ways as well. **1965** Lee & Knowles *Animal Hormones* iv. 85 In mammals additional chromaffin tissue may be found in the lower part of the abdominal aorta (para-aortic glands), or in contact with sympathetic ganglia (paraganglia).

Hence **pa:raganglio·nic** *a.*

1937 *Contrib. Embryol.* XXVI. 27 (*caption*) Reconstruction of the branchial-arch arteries in a 26-mm. human embryo to show positions in which 'paraganglionic' tissue can be found. **1959** W. Andrew *Textbk. Compar. Histol.* xiii. 530 No true carotid body is present in fishes, amphibians, and reptiles. It is only in birds and mammals that the paraganglionic cells in this region form an organ.

paragenesis. Add: Pl. **-geneses** (-dʒe·nèsīz). **2.** Substitute for def.: The occurrence together of different minerals, esp. as reflecting the conditions of their formation; a set of minerals occurring together or with a given mineral; also, the sequence and periods of formation of the constituent minerals. (Earlier and later examples.)

1853 *Edin. New Philos. Jrnl.* LIV. 324 By the paragenesis of minerals he [*sc.* Breithaupt] understands the more or less definite mode of association, by means of which he endeavours to determine their relative age. **1871** J. H. Collins *Handbk. Mineral. Cornwall & Devon* 71 A more strict paragenesis would deal with those groups of minerals which are immediately associated with each other. **1934** *Q. Jrnl. Geol. Soc.* XC. 338 Sillimanite has been abundantly developed alongside some quartz veins... This paragenesis forms a selvedge between quartz veins and the biotite-muscovite-schist. **1951** *Mineral. Mag.* XXIX. 677 The paragenesis sylvine-halite - magnesite - quartz - anhydrite - (carnallite).. first makes its appearance in the halite zone. **1954** R. L. Parker tr. *Niggli's Rocks & Mineral Deposits* iv. 128 Another method..consists in constructing theoretical (so-called normative) mineral associations..to constitute idealized parageneses under certain physical-chemical conditions. **1966** E. W. Heinrich *Geol. of Carbonatites* vii. 233 (*caption*) Paragenesis (from oldest to youngest): (1) some cerite.., (2a) bastnäsite.., (2b) monazite, (3) parisite, (3b) sahamalite. **1974** *Nature* 22 Nov. 336/1 The mineral parageneses of alkali pegmatites are not considered in detail.

paragenetic, *a.* Add: **c.** *Min.* Involving or pertaining to paragenesis (sense *2). Hence **paragene·tically** *adv.*

1853 *Edin. New Philos. Jrnl.* LIV. 325 The paragenetic phenomena met with in druses..indicates that the deposition of some more recent minerals has taken place more readily upon certain of the pre-existing minerals than upon others. **1963** *Mineral. Abstr.* XVI. 166/1 Paragenetically, pitchblende is associated with calcite, quartz, [etc.]. **1966** E. W. Heinrich *Geol. of Carbonatites* vii. 182 All the other sulfides..are not only uncommon to very rare but, unlike most of the pyrite, are usually paragenetically late. **1974** *Nature* 15 Mar. 261/2 Miyashiro distinguishes, somewhat anomalously, some subfacies on the basis of facies series, even though paragenetic criteria may not be available.

parageosyncline, -al: see *para-[1] 1.

paraglider (pæ·răgləidəɹ). [f. *para-[3] + Glider.] A large kite-like structure composed of two flexible triangular sections joined side by side, and designed to glide with a passive load or with a pilot to control its flight.

Whether this is the sense in quot. 1942 is uncertain.

1942 A. M. Low *Parachutes* 223 There have been occasions when Russian pilots with their machines damaged have dived them straight on to their targets. No real importance attaches to these 'human bombs'... Paragliders released from aircraft may prove quite another story. **1960** F. M. Rogallo et al. *Prelim. Investigation of Paraglider* (NASA TN D-443) 4 In evaluating the paraglider concept in a practical application as a reentry vehicle, calculations were made by using equations of motion involving two degrees of freedom. *Ibid.* 8 The results of this study indicate that this flexible-lifting-surface concept may provide a lightweight controllable paraglider for manned space vehicles. **1961** *Flight* LXXX. 651/2 There are two recovery systems that are now being seriously considered for application to the Saturn system —the Rogallo or paraglider wing, and the parachute recovery. **1966** [see *low-altitude* s.v. *low *a.* 20]. **1973** *Daily Colonist* (Victoria, B.C.) 3 May 1/7 A 27-year-old father of three was killed Wednesday when his lightweight para-glider plunged 200 feet to the ground.

paragnath(us to **-gnostic:** see *para-[1] 1.

paragogic, *a.* (Further examples.)

1827 [see *asyllabic *a.*]. **1968** W. S. Allen *Vox Graeca* iv. 95 Adding the so-called ν ἐφελκυστικόν (alias 'paragogic ν'). **1972** *Language* XLVIII. 35 The development of such 'paragogic' vowels is known also from Ukrainian and Czech dialects. **1975** *Canad. Jrnl. Linguistics* XX. 61 Portuguese phonotactics generally does not tolerate word-final stops; thus, borrowed words ending in a stop receive a paragogic final *e*: *time* 'team', *clube* 'club', etc.

paragon, *sb.* (*a.*) **6.** Delete † *Obs.* and add later examples. Usu. written **paragone.**

1848 J. D. Dana *Man. Mineral.* vii. 349 The *Nero-antico* marble of the Italians is an ancient deep black marble; the *paragone* is a modern one, of a fine black color, from Bergamo. **1888** G. H. Blagrove *Marble Decoration* 68 In Italy a black marble, sometimes called Paragone, is found mixed with marble of inferior quality at Castle Nuovo, in Piedmont [etc.]. **1894** H. W. Pullen *Handbk. Anc. Roman Marbles* II. 140 The term Paragone has..been loosely applied to several very black columns, such as those at a Tomb in the Winter Choir of St. John Lateran. **1955** M. H. Grant *Marbles & Granites of World* 71 Paragone. [Locality.] Bergamo, Italy. [Characteristics.] A pure, fine black.

paragonimiasis (pæ:răgonimǝi·ăsis). *Med.* [f. mod.L. *Paragonim-us*, generic name (f. Para-[1] + Gr. γόνιμος productive, fertile, f. root γεν-, γον- to produce) + *-iasis.] Infestation with worms of the genus *Paragonimus*, esp. the lung fluke, which results from eating infected crustacea and is marked at first by abdominal pains and later by a persistent cough and expectoration of blood.

1907 *Allbutt's Syst. Med.* (ed. 2) II. II. 861 The symptoms of paragonimiasis, or endemic hæmoptysis as it is sometimes designated, are a chronic cough—usually worst in the morning, a persistent pneumonic-like sputum in which ova abound, and recurring attacks of more or less profuse hæmoptysis. **1935** *Nature* 26 Oct. 674/1 There is fortunately no reason for anticipating that the crab will introduce into Europe the lung disease, paragonimiasis, of which it is one of the vectors in the Far East. **1961** L. E. Bollo *Introd. Med. & Med. Terminol.* xiv. 167 Paragonimiasis (caused by the lung fluke *Paragonimus westermani*) is common in Korea, Japan, the Philippine Islands, and parts of China. **1973** Kun-Yen Huang in J. R. Quinn *Med. & Public Health China* 258 Although careful roentgenological examinations..may differentiate paragonimiasis from tuberculosis, the diagnosis of paragonimiasis relies primarily on the demonstration of parasite ova in the sputum or an intradermal or CF test with antigen prepared from adult worms.

paragrammatism, etc.: see *para-[1] 1.

paragraph, *sb.* Add: **2. c.** *transf.* A distinct passage or section in a musical composition.

1959 *Listener* 16 July 114/2 The opening paragraph of the Fifth Symphony..takes the old-type dirge..as its model. **1975** *Gramophone* Sept. 466/3 In the slow movements and the cadenzas he shows himself to be capable of shaping long paragraphs with real discrimination. **1977** *Listener* 12 May 628/3 The opening..is one of the most difficult in the symphonic repertory..creating a tension from which the big first paragraph must be felt to spring.

3*. In Ice-skating, used *attrib.* and *absol.* with reference to the manner in which various figures are performed in competitions.

1930 T. D. Richardson *Mod. Figure Skating* xx. 184 Let me give a few suggestions of figures requiring the utmost technique; rockers and counters in eight form; three rocker three, and three counter three in paragraph form, i.e. making an eight formed figure. **1948** —— *Compl. Figure Skater* ix. 79 (*caption*) The first of the 'paragraph' figures—one foot eight forward. **1952** E. Jones *Elements Figure Skating* (ed. 2) vi. 127 The complete paragraph consists in order of a half-circle on the right outside edge, a full circle on the right inside edge, then a take-off on to the left foot, a half-circle on the left inside edge and finally a full circle on the left outside edge..this means describing three circles,..all in exact line with one another, all of equal size and symmetrically constructed. **1959** T. D. Richardson *Girls' Bk. Skating* iv. 57 All you have to do..is to apply your knowledge of the components when putting figures into paragraph form. **1967** *Daily Tel.* 1 Mar. 12/6 The powerful East German later narrowed the gap with her more consistent second tracing, the backward paragraph three. **1973** *Times* 7 Feb. 15/8 On the second figure, the paragraph-loop, he was beaten.

4. paragraph mark = Paragraph *sb.* 1.

1855 *N. & Q.* 29 Dec. 521/2 The old paragraph mark, ¶, he [*sc.* Bilderdijk] considers to be the Roman P. **1956** H. Williamson *Methods Bk. Design* ix. 119 If indention is not used, the typographer will have to find some other means of indicating the start of a new paragraph, such as a drop initial or a paragraph mark—¶.

paragraph, *v.* Add: **3.** Also *fig.* Cf. Punctuate *v.* 3 b.

1909 H. G. Wells *Ann Veronica* ix. 168 Ramage looked at her, and then fell into deep reflection as the waiter came to paragraph their talk again. **1959** *Vogue* Dec. 91 A soft dress in pure silk is scoop-necked and paragraphed with a lightly tying belt.

pa·ragraphed, *ppl. a.* [f. Paragraph *v.* + -ed[1].] Mentioned or written about in a newspaper paragraph.

1898 G. B. Shaw *Plays Pleasant* Pref. p. ix, The much paragraphed 'brilliancy' of *Arms and the Man.* **1928** *Manch. Guardian Weekly* 17 Aug. 135/2 A new comedy and the first visit to Manchester of a much-paragraphed young actress brought a large and eager audience to the Palace. **1930** *London Mercury* Feb. 319 He realised..that if he ever linked his future with a member of the opposite sex, it would not be with any such perfect and paragraphed ecstasy as Dandylion or Clytemnestra.

paragraphist. Add: (Earlier U.S. examples.)

1790 *Gazette of U.S.* 27 Nov. 655/1 A paragraphist in the General Advertiser of Thursday last. **1792** T. Jefferson *Writings* (1854) III. 467 One of its principal ministers enlists himself as an anonymous writer or paragraphist.

Paraguay. Add: Also with pronunc. (-gwǝi). **1.** (Earlier and later examples of *Paraguay tea.*)

1793 B. Edwards *Hist. Brit. Colonies W. Indies* I. 476 Ilex Cassine. Paraguay Tea. **1825** J. C. Loudon *Encycl. Agric.* I. 200 Paraguay tea..is used [in Brazil] as a substitute for that of China. **1839** W. Parish *Buenos Ayres* xv. 347 Even the yerba-maté, or Paraguay tea..is now introduced from the southern provinces of Brazil. **1856** *Househ. Words* 3 May 377/2 An eligible draught presents itself in the shape of Yerva de Paraguay, or Paraguay tea. **1924** Record & Mell *Timbers Trop. Amer.* II. 92 Holly bushes, the source of the famous Brazilian or Paraguay tea or 'herva mate'. **1937** A. F. Hill *Econ. Bot.* xxi. 510 Paraguay tea..is next to coffee, tea, and cocoa in importance.

Paraguayan (pærăgwē̆l·ăn, -gwǝi·ăn), *a.* and *sb.* Also 7 **Paragueyan,** 9 **Paraguarian.** [f. Paraguay + -an.] **A.** *adj.* Of or belonging to Paraguay or its inhabitants; produced in or characteristic of Paraguay. **B.** *sb.* A native or inhabitant of Paraguay.

1693 P. Gordon *Geogr. Anatomized* II. iv. 192 The Paraguayans are reported to be a people of very tall and big bodies, yet extraordinarily nimble and much given to running. **1699** *Ibid.* (ed. 2) II. ii. 283 The opposite Place of the Globe to Japan, is that part of the Paragueyan Ocean, lying between 340 and 350 Degrees of Longitude, with 30 and 40 Degrees of Southern Latitude. **1832** J. Bell *Syst. Geogr.* VI. I. 238 The Paraguarians collected an army of 6,000 men. **1856** C. Kingsley *Misc.* (1859) II. 18 Very interesting also..are..scattered hints as to the qualities of the Paraguayans themselves. **1884** R. G. Watson *Spanish & Portuguese S. Amer. Colonial Period* I. xvi. 273 Two Fathers, accompanied by thirty Paraguayan disciples, set out. **1901** *Chambers's Jrnl.* Sept. 623/2 The Paraguayans are ominously polite. **1935** P. de Ronde *Paraguay* iii. 43 From the unions between the Spanish and the natives there evolved in course of time the present Paraguayan race. **1956** G. Durrell *Drunken Forest* iii. 62 Our housekeeper, a dark-skinned, dark-eyed Paraguayan woman. **1957** P. Kemp *Mine were of Trouble* vi. 114 He had smuggled arms to one or other of the belligerents in the Gran Chaco war—I think to the Paraguayans. **1973** G. Greene *Honorary Consul* v. ii. 264 He does not think in terms of Paraguayans, Peruvians, Bolivians, Argentinians. **1977** *Gramophone* Dec. 1106/1 Agustin Barrios, the Paraguayan guitarist and composer.

paragutta (pærăgɒ·tă). [f. Para-[1] + Gutta[2].] A material derived from rubber and gutta percha used for insulating telephone cables.

1931 A. R. Kemp in *Jrnl. Franklin Inst.* CCXI. 37 An insulation called paragutta has been developed which as the name suggests is derived essentially from rubber and gutta percha. **1959** J. W. Freebody *Telegr.* xvii. 671/2 Paragutta, which has a specific capacitance of 2·6, eventually replaced gutta percha for the insulation of more modern cables.

parahelium (stress variable). Also **par-helium.** [f. *para-[1] 3 + Helium.] The form of helium whose spectrum does not exhibit the fine structure of orthohelium, owing to the spins of the two orbital electrons being antiparallel.

1896 Runge & Paschen in *Astrophysical Jrnl.* III. 18 We come to the conclusion that clèveite gas consists of two elements, one corresponding to the second and third series (single lines), and the other corresponding to the fifth and sixth series (double lines..). If this is true, the name *Helium* should be given only to the second element... The first element Professor Stoney has proposed to call *Parhelium.* **1903** A. M. Clerke *Probl. Astrophysics* v. 58 'Parhelium' may then safely be treated as fictitious. **1922, 1961** [see *orthohelium]. **1974** G. Reece tr. *Hund's Hist. Quantum Theory* iv. 60 Runge and Paschen were able to add series for O, S, Se and He in 1895–7. They discovered the two spectral systems of orthohelium and parahelium in the process.

parahippocampal, -hopeite: see *para-[1] 1, 2 c.

parahormone (pærăhǫ·ɹmōun). *Physiol.* Also † **parhormone.** [a. F. *parhormone* (E. Gley 1911, in *Rev. Scientifique* 11 Mar. 262): see Para-[1] and *hormone.] A product of metabolism which has a secondary hormonal role.

1918 M. Fishberg tr. *E. Gley's Internal Secretions* 154 At most we might apply the term *parhormones* to the excretory products which play only an accessory rôle as excitants, reserving the name of hormones for the specific glandular products. **1922** R. G. Hoskins in L. F. Barker et al. *Endocrinol. & Metabolism* I. I. 8 For nonspecific regulatory substances such as carbon dioxid, Gley has proposed the designation 'parhormones'. **1935** *Biol. Rev.* X. 440 Water..could presumably be classified as a parahormone for renal function. **1948** C. D. Turner *Gen. Endocrinol.* ii. 65 The synthesis, storage and release of sugar by the liver is not a true endocrine activity, since glucose is not a specific product of this organ. Sugar and such materials are important metabolites and may be designated as parahormones.

parahydrogen (stress variable). Also **para hydrogen** and with hyphen. [f. *para-[1] 3 + Hydrogen, as tr. G. *parawasserstoff* (Bonhoeffer & Harteck 1929, in *Naturwissenschaften* XVII. 182/1), coined on the analogy of *par(a)helium* (see quot. 1935 s.v. *orthohydrogen).] The form of molecular hydrogen in which the two nuclei in the molecule have antiparallel spins, so that the spectrum exhibits no hyperfine structure. Cf. *orthohydrogen.

1929 *Industr. & Engin. Chem.* 10 July 6/1 At room temperatures and atmospheric pressure in glass vessels para-hydrogen is a stable gas. **1935**, etc. [see *orthohydrogen]. **1969** H. T. Evans tr. *G. Hägg's Gen. & Inorg. Chem.* xviii. 452 The melting and boiling points of parahydrogen are approximately 0·1° lower than for ordinary hydrogen.

para-influenza (pæ:ră,influ,e·nză). *Biol.* Also **parainfluenza.** [f. Para-[1] + Influenza.] Any of a group of paramyxoviruses which resemble the influenza viruses and include the one causing croup; (orig. classed as myxoviruses before paramyxoviruses were recognized as a separate group). Usu. *attrib.*, esp. in *para-influenza virus.*

1959 C. H. Andrewes et al. in *Virology* VIII. 129 (*heading*) Para-influenza viruses 1, 2, and 3: suggested names for recently described myxoviruses. *Ibid.* 130 The following names are accordingly proposed: Sendai (including HA2). *Myxovirus para-influenzae 1* (Para-influenza 1). CA virus: *Myxovirus para-influenzae 2* (Para-influenza 2). HA1: *Myxovirus para-influenzae 3* (Para-influenza 3). **1959** *Brit. Med. Bull.* XV. 221/2 It seems..that the Far Eastern strain of para-influenza 1 virus (Sendai) is endemic in laboratory mice and very probably pathogenic for pigs and man also. *Ibid.* 222/1 Para-influenza 2. This virus was called CA (croup-associated) by Chanock (1956). It was independently described by Beale and his colleagues as the virus of acute laryngotracheobronchitis of children. **1965** C. Andrewes *Common Cold* xi. 98 Para-influenza infections are mainly seen in children in whom they cause respiratory infections of all degrees of severity up to fatal pneumonia. **1974** *Nature* 23 Aug. 650/2 As *in vivo* hybridisation seems to have permitted a human tumour to become..unusually lethal in the hamster,..similar mechanisms may be implicated in human cancer, particularly when such fusing agents as parainfluenza viruses are prevalent in man.

parajou·rnalism. orig. *U.S.* [f. Para-[1] past, beyond, contrary to + Journalism.] A type of unconventional journalism not primarily concerned with the reporting of facts. So **parajou·rnalist, parajournali·stic** *a.*

1965 D. Macdonald in *N.Y. Rev. Bks.* 26 Aug. 3/1 A new kind of journalism is being born, or spawned. It might be called 'parajournalism', from the Greek *para*, 'beside' or 'against': something similar in form but different in function. **1966** *New Statesman* 4 Mar. 300/1 The second achievement is 'parajournalism'—Dwight Macdonald's word. **1966** *Atlantic Monthly* June 89 MacDonald..castigates a Wolfe review of Mailer's latest novel and berates the reviewer as again playing parajournalist because his technique was 'to jeer at the author's private life and personality—or rather his *persona*.' **1970** *Americana Ann.* 503/1 A wave of parajournalistic publications, the so-called underground press, was mounting a serious challenge to established dailies. **1972** *Times Lit. Suppl.* 21 Apr. 444/1 (Advt.), 'What is now called parajournalism—writing it the way it happened' (Daily Mirror). **1978** *New York* 3 Apr. 81/2 Charlie, the megalomaniacal parajournalist.

parakeelya (pærăkī·lyă). *Austral.* Also **parake(e)lia, parakilja, parakylia.** [Aboriginal name.] An annual or perennial herb belonging to the genus *Calandrinia*, of the family Portulacaceæ, native to Australia and America and bearing succulent leaves and clusters of reddish flowers. Also *attrib.*

1898 D. W. Carnegie *Spinifex & Sand* vii. 216 Given 'parakeelia' every second night or so a camel would never want to drink at all. **1921** *Trans. R. Soc. S. Austral.* XLV. 11 The common parakeelya at Tarcoola..appears to be this species [sc. *Calandrinia polyandra*]. **1931** I. L. Idriess *Lasseter's Last Ride* xii. 99 The secret was in the Parakelia grass. In appearance something like ice-plant, its thick leaves were stored with water. **1934** [see *claytonia]. **1935** H. H. Finlayson *Red Centre* iii. 33 One can only refer to the sprightly purple and yellow flowered succulents, the parakeelia and munyeroo. **1944** F. Clune *Red Heart* 36 Crushed parakelia weed, broken mulga bough..—it was by signs such as these that the trackers deduced the course of the wayfarer. **1959** *Listener* 7 May 785/1 It [*sc.* the landscape] is ablaze with the scarlet of Sturt's desert pea, with cerise-coloured parakelia. **1965** *Austral. Encycl.* VI. 480/1 Parakeelya (Parakilja), the aboriginal name for several species of fleshy herbs in the genus *Calandrinia* (family Portulacaceae) which can thrive in the most arid parts of inland Australia. **1967** O. Ruhen in *Coast to Coast 1965–66* 189 A few parakeelya leaves can evoke the blessed relief of flowing saliva. **1972** Y. Lovelock *Vegetable Bk.* I. 193 The aborigines bake the succulent leaves of the parakilja..with bark as a food; the plant was once eaten by the early settlers.

parakite. Add: **2.** In modern use applied to a parachute kite which is towed along against the wind by a motorboat, car, or other fast vehicle. So **pa·rakiting,** the sport of soaring when harnessed to a parakite.

1962 *Aeroplane* CII. 233/2 Para kite.—First trials of the Lemoigne parachute kite have taken place in England... Mr. Walter Neumark remained at about 150 ft. for over 5 minutes while moored to the towing car. **1964** T. W. Willans *Parachuting & Skydiving* v. 50 The Lemoigne parakite of the 1960s—a sort of ascending parachute, a few of which had found their way from France into England. **1970** *Time* 30 Mar. 42/1 In parakiting, the water skier becomes airborne when the trailing parachute pops open. **1978** *Lancashire Life* Apr. 50 (*caption*) Instead of hang gliding's crunch-down, parakiting's finale is a splash-down: on this occasion, in an icy sea. *Ibid.*, Stan Lyons was the guinea-pig—the man setting out to make Morecambe's first parakite flight between the Stone Jetty and West End Pier.

paralanguage (pæ:rǎlæ·ŋgwėdʒ). *Linguistics.* [f. PARA-[1] alongside + LANGUAGE *sb.*[1]] The system of non-phonemic but vocal factors in speech, such as tone of voice, tempo of speech, and sighing, by which communication is assisted. Cf. *KINESICS.

Some authorities also include in paralanguage such adjuncts of speech as gesture and facial expression.

1958 G. L. TRAGER in *Studies in Linguistics* XIII. 4 The vocalizations and voice qualities together are being called *paralanguage* (a term suggested by A. A. Hill). **1959** H. L. SMITH in *College English* XX. 172/2 Speech does not take place in a vacuum but is surrounded, as it were, by patterned bodily motions—the *kinesic* system—and by systematically analyzable vocalizations, or *paralanguage.* **1964** *Language* XL. 202 Trager's 1958 paper outlined a taxonomic system for the analysis of the phenomena of paralanguage. **1965** [see *morpheme-like* s.v. *MORPHEME c]. **1967** *Jrnl. Eng. Linguistics* I. 28 *Paralanguage*, the non-linguistic but communicatively significant orchestration of the stream of speech, involving such phenomena as abnormally high or low pitch, abnormally fast or slow tempo, abnormal loudness or softness, drawl, clipping, rasp, openness, and the like. **1972** W. M. AUSTIN in A. L. Davis *Culture, Class, & Lang. Variety* viii. 159 We judge the dynamic and effective speaker by his use of kinesics and paralanguage as well as language. **1978** *Verbatim* May 15/2 That particular methodology called generative-transformational did not include paralanguage, kinesics, or cultural influences.

paralaurionite, -lexia: see *PARA-[1] 2 c, 1.

paralegal (pæ:rǎlī·gǎl), *a.* and *sb.* Chiefly *N. Amer.* [f. PARA-[1] + LEGAL *a.*] **A.** *adj.* Of or pertaining to auxiliary aspects of the law. **B.** *sb.* One trained in subsidiary legal matters, though not fully qualified as a lawyer, etc.; a legal aide.

1972 *N.Y. Law Jrnl.* 22 Aug. 2/7 (Advt.), Para-legals (that is, legal assistants or paraprofessionals) are used by an ever-increasing number of prominent attorneys to reduce their unwanted load of paralegal matters and free up their time to render legal advice more efficiently. **1975** *Daily Colonist* (Victoria, B.C.) 23 Aug. 1/1 Miss Lissell intends to take a two-year para-legal course at one of the Vancouver colleges. **1977** *Times* 12 July 4/6 If legal aid was not available, the staff of the first-tier agency, who would have some paralegal training, would try to help. **1977** *N.Y. Rev. Bks.* 15 Sept. 55/2 (Advt.), Smith College graduate. Economics major. Financial, law and management background. Light skills. Seeks position as paralegal, office manager, social secretary, coordinator, etc.

paralic (pǎræ·lik), *a. Geol.* [ad. G. *paralisch* (C. F. Naumann *Lehrb. d. Geognosie* (1852) II. II. vii. 452), f. Gr. παράλ-ιος by the sea (see PARALIAN): see -IC.] Formed or having occurred in shallow water near the sea.

[**1911**: see *LIMNIC *a.*] **1914** H. RIES *Econ. Geol.* (ed. 4) i. 13 A distinction is, however, sometimes made between (1) limnetic coals..; and (2) paralic coals, or those derived from plant remains which collected in marshes near the sea border. **1940**, etc. [see *LIMNIC *a.*]. **1963** D. W. & E. E. HUMPHRIES tr. *Termier's Erosion & Sedimentation* i. 30 There was an extension of warm marine faunas, a large distribution of paralic flora and the development of lateritic soils. **1966** *McGraw-Hill Encycl. Sci. & Technol.* XII. 142/2 The molasse is a product of paralic sedimentation. **1977** A. HALLAM *Planet Earth* 154 The seams formed from peats in coastal-swamp environments (paralic coals) are characteristically relatively thin after compaction.

paralinguistic (pæ:rǎliŋgwi·stik), *a.* and *sb. Linguistics.* [f. PARA-[1] alongside + LINGUISTIC *a.* and *sb.*; cf. *PARALANGUAGE.] **A.** *adj.* Of or pertaining to paralanguage; of or pertaining to vocal communication effected non-phonemically by tone of voice, tempo of speech, etc. So **pa:ralingui·stically** *adv.* Cf. *KINESIC *a.*

1958 A. A. HILL *Introd. Ling. Struct.* xxi. 409 The paralinguistic area investigated by Birdwhistell has been called by him kinesics. **1959** [see *KINESIC *a.*]. **1964** G. L. TRAGER in D. Abercrombie et al. *Daniel Jones* 267 It has become possible to separate out paralinguistic pitch phenomena from those of language proper. **1964** CRYSTAL & QUIRK (*title*) Systems of prosodic and paralinguistic features in English. **1965** *Canad. Jrnl. Linguistics* XI. 36 This is linguistically and paralinguistically irrelevant. **1967** M. ARGYLE *Psychol. Interpersonal Behaviour* v. 89 People are often quite unaware of the emotive, paralinguistic aspects of their speech—they do not realize how cross they sound, for instance. **1971** M. L. SAMUELS in A. J. Aitken et al. *Edin. Stud. Eng. & Scots* 5 A paralinguistic feature like an unusual voice-quality is found to accompany an unusual phonetic system. **1976** *Amer. Speech 1974* XLIX. 286 Nonverbal, paralinguistic features related to male/female language involve voice pitch, body language and facial expression, and the place of silence in sex-role communication.

B. *sb.* (in form a *pl.*) [-ICS.] The study of paralanguage; non-phonemic factors of vocal communication. Cf. *KINESICS.

1958 A. A. HILL *Introd. Ling. Struct.* xxi. 408 A part of communication activity which is outside the area of microlinguistics..is what can be called paralinguistics. **1958** G. L. TRAGER in *Studies in Linguistics* XIII. 4 The words *paralinguistic* and *paralinguistics* are self-explanatory. **1962** D. H. HYMES in J. A. Fishman *Readings Sociol. of Lang.* (1968) 106 Features of speech, such as tone of voice and hesitation pauses,..phenomena which have recently been systematized in a preliminary way under the heading of 'paralinguistics'. **1972** *Sci. Amer.* Sept. 60/1 The most probable links to investigate exist within human paralinguistics: the extensive array of facial expressions, body postures, hand signals and vocal tones and emphases that we use to supplement verbal speech. **1973** *Archivum Linguisticum* IV. 53 *Linguistic levels*..Grammar, lexis, phonology, semantics, graphology, phonetics, paralinguistics.

parallax. Add: **3.** Special comb.: **parallax error**, error in reading an instrument caused by parallax when the scale and the indicator are not precisely coincident.

1901 C. J. LEAPER *Graduated Exercises Elem. Pract. Physics* p. iii/1 (Index), Parallax error. **1906** BOWER & SATTERLY *Pract. Physics* v. 83 The reading, especially of the burette, is very liable to parallax error. **1967** *Electronics* 6 Mar. 117/2 With analog instruments..operator and parallax errors, meter movement wear and aging often reduce their nominal accuracies.

parallel, *a.* and *sb.* Add: **A.** *adj.* **1.** *parallel bars* (earlier and later examples); also *fig.*

1868 TROLLOPE *He knew he was Right* (1869) I. iii. 17 Certain poles and sticks and parallel bars with which feats of activity might be practised. **1878** [see *HORIZONTAL *a.* (*sb.*) 2 b]. **1962** H. C. WESTON *Sight, Light & Work* (ed. 2) viii. 225 Various objects have been suggested and used, such as the 'parallel-bar' test-object of Luckiesh. **1964** G. C. KUNZLE *Parallel Bars* 19 The parallel bars are the most interesting and varied of all the pieces of apparatus. **1973** J. FLEMING *You won't let me Finish* vii. 52 He was in the small gym giving exhibitions of walking along the parallel bars on his hands.

b. *parallel text*, one of two or more versions of a literary work, etc., printed in a format which allows direct textual comparison, freq. on facing or consecutive pages of the same volume; a text of different versions of a work set out in such a way; also (with hyphen) *attrib.*; *parallel tracking*, tracking in which the pick-up is kept tangential to the record groove by a rectilinear motion of the arm; freq. *attrib.*; *parallel turn*, a swing in skiing, with the skis kept parallel to each other.

Delete *parallel circuit* and see instead sense A. 1 d below.

1870 F. J. FURNIVALL *Chaucer Soc. Six-Text Print of Chaucer's Canterbury Tales in Parallel Columns* (verso rear cover of first section), The issue for 1870 is, in the First Series, XIV. The Miller's, Reeve's, and Cook's Tales, with an Appendix of the Spurious Tale of Gamelyn, in 6 parallel Texts. **1871** —— (*title*) Chaucer Society one-text print of Chaucer's minor poems, being the best text of each poem in the parallel-text edition. **1877** *Trans. Philol. Soc. 1875–76* 10 The two best features of our editing are minute accuracy and fullness of material. Hence our parallel-text editions. **1889** C. PLUMMER *Two Saxon Chrons. Parallel* p. viii, This, the first of our two parallel texts, is commonly known as the Parker MS. **1941** *B.B.C. Gloss. Broadcasting Terms* 22 Parallel tracking unit. **1954** BRODERMAN & MCPARTLIN *Ski-ing for Beginners* ix. 77 The Parallel Turn is a speed turn. **1962** A. NISBETT *Technique Sound Studio* viii. 145 Where parallel tracking arms are used, calibration above the track is a fairly simple matter. (But parallel tracking..has not proved itself in practice.) **1963** *Amer. Speech* XXXVIII. 206 An especially fast kind of short parallel turn. **1971** (*title*) William Wordsworth: The Prelude: A parallel text. **1978** *N. & Q.* Feb. 75/2 Mrs. Bawcutt's own admirable parallel-text edition..will doubtless remain standard.

d. *Electr.* Involving connection in parallel (cf. sense B. 6 in Dict. and Suppl.).

[**1884** *Jrnl. Soc. Telegr. Engin.* XIII. 497 These two machines..may be connected in one of two ways: they may be in parallel circuit with regard to the external conductor..; or they may be coupled in series.] **1886** *Electrician* 19 Feb. 296/2 The three direct systems are the parallel, series, and parallel-series methods of attaching lamps to the main conductors. **1891** J. W. URQUHART *Dynamo Construction* xvi. 232 For many years this difficulty stood in the way of parallel working with dynamo machines. **1940** *Chambers's Techn. Dict.* 614/2 *Parallel feed*, a method of connecting the anode of a thermionic valve to the high-tension supply through a high resistance or inductance, whilst the a.c. circuits are connected through a condenser. The d.c. and a.c. components of the anode current are thereby separated. **1962** [see sense *B. 6].

2. c. (Further examples.)

1953 K. REISZ *Technique Film Editing* i. 20 Porter himself developed this kind of parallel action editing further in his subsequent films. *Ibid.* 281 *Parallel action*, device of narrative construction in which the development of two pieces of action is represented simultaneously by showing first a fragment of one, then a fragment of the other, and so on alternately.

d. *Computers.* Involving the concurrent or simultaneous performance of certain operations; functioning in this way.

1948 *Math. Tables & Other Aids to Computation* III. 149 The use of plugboard facilities and punched cards permits parallel operation (as distinguished from sequence operation), with further gain in efficiency. **1963** W. H. WARE *Digital Computer Technol. & Design* II. xi. 3 Parallel arithmetic tends to be faster than serial arithmetic because it performs operations in all columns at once, rather than in one column at a time. **1974** P. H. ENSLOW *Multiprocessors & Parallel Processing* i. 1 This book focuses on ..the integration of multiple functional units into a multiprocessing or parallel processing system.

e. S. Afr. *parallel development* = **separate development.*

1950 *Ann. Reg. 1949* 140 The conflict between the Southern Rhodesian policy of 'parallel development' with its emphasis on permanent European control, and the United Kingdom policy of partnership leading to self-government. **1971** *Weekend World* (Johannesburg) 9 May 3/4 Chief George agreed with an Opposition claim that parallel development in the Republic meant that the Europeans were in the sky and Africans were in the mud.

f. S. Afr. *parallel-medium*, used *attrib.* to designate schooling or a school in which instruction is given through the medium of more than one language.

1958 *Cape Argus* 10 Dec. 20/5 The classroom instruction given in Afrikaans-medium classes in a parallel-medium school would be as Afrikaans as instruction given in the classes of an exclusively single-medium Afrikaans school. **1971** *Sunday Times* (Johannesburg) (Business Section) 28 Mar. 4/2 (Advt.), Separate English and Afrikaans medium primary schooling, and parallel-medium schooling to matriculation standard is available.

g. Biol. *parallel evolution* = *PARALLELISM 7.

1963 E. MAYR *Animal Species & Evolution* xix. 609 There are numerous cases of..parallel evolution in the animal and plant kingdoms. **1972** *Canad. Jrnl. Earth Sci.* IX. 1032/1 The shell shape of *C[olus] brevis* closely resembles that of *A[tractodon] stonei* and provides a striking example of parallel evolution in response to parallel selective pressures.

3*. *parallel cousin* = *ortho-cousin* (*ORTHO- 1).

1936 R. FIRTH *We, the Tikopia* vi. 221 The differentiation between cross-cousin and parallel cousin is certainly not one of the outstanding features of the Tikopia kinship system. **1949** F. EGGAN in M. Fortes *Social Struct.* 124 Parallel cousins are treated as siblings, whereas cross-cousins are differentiated. **1970** E. LEACH *Lévi-Strauss* 121 A parallel cousin..is a cousin of the type 'mother's sister's child' or 'father's brother's child'. **1972** [see *ortho-cousin* s.v. *ORTHO- 1].

b. Forming adjectival phrases with sbs., as *parallel-jaw(s)*, *-plate.*

1951 *Good Housek. Home Encycl.* 325/2 The bench.. having..a parallel-jaw vice at the other end. **1962** L. S. SASIENI *Princ. & Pract. Optical Dispensing* ix. 214 Parallel jaw pliers. **1971** B. SCHARF *Engin. & its Lang.* viii. 60 (*caption*) Parallel jaw vice. **1926** *Encycl. Brit.* II. 331/2 The parallel plate method..for measuring the *absolute* conductivity of air. **1962** CORSON & LORRAIN *Introd. Electromagn. Fields* ii. 37 If one plate of a parallel-plate capacitor is charged on one face, an equal and opposite charge must exist on the opposite plate of the capacitor.

B. *sb.* **I. 1.** (Further example.)

1972 *Sci. Amer.* Dec. 102/1 Circles of varying radii that go around the hole or center of the torus on parallel planes are called parallels.

II. 6. *in parallel* (earlier and later examples): in *Electr.* also said of individual circuit components connected by such wires, so that a current is divided between them; also *transf.*

Delete the cross-reference to sense A. 1 b and see instead sense A. 1 d above.

1884 *Jrnl. Soc. Telegr. Engin.* XIII. 529 The two alternate-current generators cannot work in series;..they can work in parallel. **1943** C. L. BOLTZ *Basic Radio* i. 21 A voltmeter is always connected in parallel with whatever part of a circuit across which we wish to measure the electrical pressure. **1949** E. P. ABRAHAM et al. in H. W. Florey et al. *Antibiotics* II. xv. 644 The basic unit.., of which there were six working in parallel, was a glass tube containing amyl acetate. **1962** D. F. SHAW *Introd. Electronics* iii. 51 The capacitance *C* is connected in parallel with the combination *L* and *R*. **1962** *Newnes Conc. Encycl. Electr. Engin.* 569/2 *Parallel operation.* The operation of generators or transformers in parallel implies equality of terminal voltage. **1971** *Sci. Amer.* June 31/3 This could be accomplished by using a flow rate of 2,300 gallons per minute with two pumps operating in parallel.

7. b. (Further examples.) Also *in parallel* (without *with*), concurrently, simultaneously.

1938 *New Statesman* 7 May 796/2 Nor..does it seem right to attribute to 'the scholastic tradition of the universities' of the time, the failure of social studies to grow.. in parallel with the natural sciences. **195/** R. K. RICHARDS *Digital Computer Components* viii. 365 By transmitting all bits of a word to and from storage simultaneously or 'in parallel' a great increase in the speed of operation can be obtained in comparison with the transmission of one bit at a time. **1969** P. B. JORDAIN *Condensed Computer Encycl.* 373 By searching all (or very many cells) in parallel, the time of the operation is greatly reduced. **1971** *Sci. Amer.* Sept. 45/1 In parallel with the increase in carbon dioxide in the atmosphere there has also been a rise in suspended particulate contamination. **1977** *New Scientist* 21 Apr. 140/1 ILLIAC IV is actually a group of 64 individual computers working in parallel and linked to a one billion bit binary memory.

parallel, *v.* **6.** Delete ? *Obs.* and add later examples.

1907 *Smart Set* Mar. 52/2 He..recognizes the truth that so easily their paths might have paralleled if events had only favored. **1977** *Zigzag* Mar. 21/1 Then it parallels to R&B in quite a few ways.

9. *trans.* To connect (electrical apparatus) in parallel. Const. *with.*

1902 *Electr. Rev.* 27 June 1056/2 (*heading*) Apparatus for paralleling alternators. **1903** T. SEWELL *Elem. Electr. Engin.* (ed. 2) xviii. 379 There is not so much danger in paralleling machines which have iron cored armatures, for their self-induction prevents a dangerous current from flowing. **1921** [see *PHASE *v.* 5 a]. **1952** G. V. MUELLER *Alternating-Current Machines* ix. 339 When a shunt generator is to be paralleled with an operating d-c system, it is driven at its rated speed by a prime mover. **1965** *Wireless World* Sept. 431/1 They [*sc.* thyristors] may be used singly to give a 2A d.c. output or they may be paralleled to give any desired output provided that suitable arrangements are made for simultaneous firing.

parallelepipedal, *a.* (s.v. PARALLELEPIPED). (Earlier and later examples.)

1754 *New & Compl. Dict. Arts & Sci.* II. 1394/1 The capacities of all sorts of vessels.., as cubical, parallelopipedal, cylindrical,..&c. are computed. **1950** L. R. UNDERWOOD *Rolling of Metals* I. iv. 83 If a rectangular network of lines on the bar before rolling is still rectangular after rolling, then the total deformation may be regarded as parallelopipedal. **1974** *Chem. Physics* VI. 2/2 The term 'unit cell' will be retained here..to mean the parallelepipedal cell (whether primitive or multiple) used by crystallographers.

parallelism. Add: **2.** (Further examples.)

1962 *Listener* 5 Apr. 606/2 The success of *apartheid* or parallelism or separate development—call it what you will—is dependent on educating the Bantu to take over all their responsibilities themselves. **1968** *Economist* 4 May 18/2 'Parallelism' in the activities of party and state can be eliminated quite simply by emphasising that the party is the boss and the government merely its executive servant [in Romania]. **1972** *Nature* 8 Dec. 339/2 A rough parallelism between the histories of the Iceland and Hawaii plumes is noteworthy.

b. (Further example.)

1955 P. W. STALLMAR in *College English* XVII. 25/1 For relationships between works that are not necessarily borrowings of the one from the other, I would use the general label 'parallelism'. The differentia of the parallelism is, I suggest, that a parallelism is not necessarily a conscious borrowing.

3. Also in Anglo-Saxon poetry.

1813 J. J. CONYBEARE in *Archaeologia* XVII. 269 The parallelism (if I may be so allowed to term it) of the Anglo-Saxon writers... The poems attributed to Cædmon afford innumerable instances of the same figure. **1876** H. SWEET *Anglo-Saxon Reader* p. xcix, There is also a tendency to parallelism, or repetition of the same idea in different words. The last half of one line is often connected with the first half of the next in this way. **1935** A. C. BARTLETT *Larger Rhet. Patterns Anglo-Saxon Poetry* iii. 30 Every literary model impelled the Anglo-Saxon toward structural parallelism in pairs. **1938** A. CAMPBELL *Battle of Brunanburh* 38 The sentence structure is essentially that of the older verse, with its free use of parallelism both of expressions and sentences. **1977** J. A. CUDDON *Dict. Lit. Terms* 471 Parallelism is common in poetry of the oral tradition—for instance, in *Beowulf.*

6. *Psychol.* The theory that mental (psychic) and physical processes are concomitant and that any change in the one will be correspondingly reflected in the other.

1860 J. D. MORELL tr. *Fichte's Contrib. Mental Philos.* iii. 41 How far into details this parallelism between the mind and the world reaches, it is the province of psychology to show. **1877** *Illustr. London News* 5 May 427/1 As to the relation of mind to matter, he held that there is an exact parallelism of mental and material events..as two aspects of the same thing. **1891** M. E. LOWNDES tr. *Höffding's Outl. Psychol.* ii. 64 Both the *parallelism* and the *proportionality* between the activity of consciousness and cerebral activity point to an *identity* at bottom. **1902** *Encycl. Brit.* XXXII. 66/2 The last of these [*sc.* the Monism of Spinoza, which reduced matter and mind to parallel attributes of the One Substance]—severed, however, from Spinoza's metaphysics—is now the prevailing theory, and to it the term *Psychophysical Parallelism* most properly applies. **1925** C. D. BROAD *Mind & its Place* iii. 121 Psycho-neural Parallelism has also a positive side. **1956** [see *INTERACTIONISM]. **1976** *Progress in Sci. Culture* (E. Majorana Centre) Spring 11 If we are to avoid falling into parallelism with its self-stultifying philosophy of determinism, we have to develop a dualist-interactionist philosophy according to which the self-conscious mind has an identity and activity that are not entirely dependent on brain events.

7. *Biol.* The development of similar characteristics by two related groups of animals or plants, in response to similar environmental pressures.

1887 E. D. COPE *Origin of Fittest* ii. 98 Among the higher groups [of Lacertilia Leptoglossa] the parallelisms lie in the arrangement..of the head shields. **1898** A. S. WOODWARD *Outl. Vertebr. Palæont.* p. xxiii, The case of the horses is often cited as suggesting that such a parallelism in evolution may have occurred. **1907** V. L. KELLOGG *Darwinism To-Day* viii. 279 (*heading*) Parallelisms in variation. **1934** W. E. LE GROS CLARK *Early Forerunners of Man* i. 6 If this thesis is carried to a logical conclusion, it will necessarily demand a much greater scope for the phenomenon of parallelism or convergence in evolution. **1961** G. G. SIMPSON *Princ. Animal Taxon.* iii. 78 Parallelism is the development of similar characters separately in two or more lineages of common ancestry and on the basis of, or channeled by, characteristics of that ancestry. *Ibid.* 103 Parallelism may be difficult or practically impossible to distinguish from homology on one hand and convergence on the other. **1967** R. E. BLACKWELDER *Taxon.* iv. 139 Parallelism..differs from convergence in that the development of the similar features is the result of and is channelled by a common ancestry.

b. *Anthrop.* A similarity between the evolution and achievements of different cultures.

1937 R. H. LOWIE *Hist. Ethnol. Theory* xi. 190 Schmidt differs from Morgan mainly in denying universal parallelism, *unilinear* evolution. **1949** G. P. MURDOCK *Social Struct.* vii. 116 The extraordinary extent of parallelism, both in kinship terminology and in types of kin and local groups. **1958** E. A. HOEBEL *Man in Primitive World* (ed. 2) xxxiv. 607 Very little attention has been given to parallelism, or independent invention, in this discussion for the reason that relatively few of the total mass of cultural traits possessed and shared by the peoples of the world have been invented more than once. **1958** F. M. KEESING *Cultural Anthropol.* vi. 148 Anthropologists.. have therefore been critical of attempts to read historical connections into what they regard as an instance of parallelism between Old and New World cultural elements.

parallelist. 2. Delete *nonce-use* and add further examples (cf. *PARALLELISM 6, 7). Also *attrib.* or as *adj.*

1903 C. A. STRONG *Why Mind has Body* I. i. 23 The parallelist hypothesis. *Ibid.* vii. 126 The two arguments most commonly appealed to by parallelists. **1925** C. D. BROAD *Mind & its Place* iii. 124 The orthodox Parallelist ..goes much further. **1937** R. H. LOWIE *Hist. Ethnol. Theory* v. 44 McLennan was essentially a parallelist. 'All the races of men have had..a development from savagery of the same general character.' *Ibid.* 48 Apart from the parallelist faith in universal stages, we note the erroneous idea that totemism generally implies worship. **1950** R. PIDDINGTON *Introd. Social Anthropol.* I. i. 27 Obviously, claimed the parallelists, there had been no contact between these peoples, and the similarity in custom must be explained by the operation of similar psychological processes in the two widely separated areas. **1976** *Progress in Sci. Culture* (E. Majorana Centre) Spring 11 It is not in question that the happenings in the cerebral cortex are *necessary* for the experience of consciousness... However, it must not be naively assumed that these brain events are *sufficient* for the conscious experiences... This in fact is the parallelist position.

parallelistic *a.* (further examples).

1904 G. S. FULLERTON *Syst. Metaphysics* xxi. 341 He quite wrecks his parallelistic formula. **1934** [see *INTERACTIONISM]. **1946** *Brit. Jrnl. Psychol.* Jan. 52 It was precisely because in the *Manual* Stout endeavoured to exclude philosophical discussion that his parallelistic conclusion remained, as *mere* parallelism must..remain, an exasperating mystery.

parallelity (pærăle·lĭti). [f. PARALLEL *a.* and *sb.* + -ITY.] The state or condition of being parallel (*lit.* and *fig.*); parallelism.

1953 *Cases Court of Session, Scotl.* 290 There is no parallelity or necessary mutual dependence between the two inquiries. **1970** *Physics Bull.* Feb. 71/1 In the spaghetti, adjacent lengths tend to lie somewhere near to parallelity without achieving exact alignment.

parallelization (s.v. PARALLELIZE *v.*). (Further examples.)

1892 J. NASMITH *Students' Cotton Spinning* v. 150 Its result is to effect a much greater parallelisation of the fibres in the carded sliver. **1922** *Bull. Geol. Soc. Amer.* XXXIII. 443 From the meteorological standpoint such a far-reaching parallelization of the fluctuations of the weather from one year to the other, in Sweden and North America, is surprising. **1933** *Trans. Faraday Soc.* XXIX. 211 The process of parallelisation of long thin bodies.

paralog (pæ·rălǫg). [f. PARA-[1] + Gr. λόγ-ος word.] (See quot. 1968.)

1951 TRAGER & SMITH *Outl. Eng. Struct.* 85 The instances just cited are examples of the use of different *paralogs*, a paralog being one of the forms constituting an inflectional paradigm. **1968** J. JUNG *Verbal Learning* iii. 30 Nonsense syllables and other laboratory learning materials, such as trigrams and paralogs. Trigrams are nonsense syllables, that is, a trigram is any three-letter combination which does not form a word. Paralogs or dissyllables are verbal units containing two syllables and range from meaningless units to actual words. **1970** *Jrnl. Gen. Psychol.* LXXXIII. 55 The nonsense words..were five paralogs with approximately equal, low levels of association value.

paralogia (pærălōu·dʒiă). *Med.* [f. PARA-[1] + *-logia* (see -LOGY and -IA[1]).] (See quots.)

1811 R. HOOPER *Lexicon Medicum* 596/1 *Paralogia*, a delirium in which the patient talks wildly. **1857** R. G. MAYNE *Expos. Lex. Med. Sci.* (1860) 877/1 *Paralogia*,.. term for a slight degree of madness or of delirium. **1900** GOULD *Dict. Med.* (ed. 5) 973/1 *Paralogia*, difficulty in thinking logically. **1905** S. PATON *Psychiatry* xiv. 383 Another important symptom [of dementia præcox]..is the grotesque irrelevancy exhibited in replying to questions (Paralogia). **1919** R. M. BARCLAY tr. *Kraepelin's Dementia Praecox & Paraphrenia* ii. 21 Evasion or paralogia consists in this, that the idea which is next in the chain of thought is suppressed and replaced by another which is related to it. **1923** STEDMAN *Med. Dict.* (ed. 7) 737/1 *Paralogia*, false reasoning, involving self-deception. **1965** *New Scientist* 25 Nov. 605/1 The disorders of generalization are..subdivided into lowering of the level of generalization and distortion of generalization. The..latter seems to be the same as Kleist's 'paralogia' and Cameron's 'overinclusion'.

paralyse, *v.* Add: **2.** (Later examples.) Also with constr.

1871 L. W. M. LOCKHART *Fair to See* II. xxv. 280 He saw all this, quite paralysed out of the power of surprise or wrath. **1890** *Congress. Rec.* 19 May 4933/1 You boast about what you have done for the American farmer... What audacity! It paralyzes me. **1900** *Dialect Notes* II. 47 *Paralyze*... In phrase 'to *paralyze* the professor'; to make a perfect recitation.

paralysedly (pæ·răləizdli), *adv.* [f. PARALYSED *ppl. a.* + -LY[2].] In a paralysed manner.

1876 R. BROUGHTON *Joan* III. I. xxxiii. 48 As she so paralysedly sits the door opens softly.

pa·ralysingly, *adv.* [f. PARALYSING *ppl. adj.* + -LY[2].] In a paralysing manner.

In quot. used hyperbolically.

1926 *Socialist Rev.* Dec. 21 The paralysingly stupid 70/- a week shipping or insurance clerk.

paralysis. Add: **1. b.** *general paralysis* (earlier and later examples); also called *general paralysis of the insane* [tr. F. *paralysie générale des aliénés* (L. F. Calmeil *De la Paralysie considérée chez les Aliénés* (1826) 9], and now recognized as a form of neurosyphilis. So *general paralytic*, an individual with general paralysis.

1820 *Edin. Med. & Surg. Jrnl.* XVI. 373 Dissection of a case of general paralysis... The disease of the brain seemed to have originated in indolence and chagrin from the sudden loss of fortune. **1847** *Further Rep. Commissioners in Lunacy* 46 in *Parl. Papers* (Brit. Libr.) XLIX. 291 The forms of insanity, which are occasioned by extreme indigence and privation,..are of the worst kind, and..many of them have invariably a fatal termination. [*Note*] This is particularly observable in the very frequent form of paralysis, termed the general paralysis of the insane. **1856** *Jrnl. Mental Sci.* III. 170 General paralytics are not malignant, and although sometimes furious, their passion is gusty and transient. *Ibid.* 172 In general paralysis, the pathological conditions of which involve the whole nervous system, the excito motory sensibility is almost abolished. **1925** *Amer. Speech* I. 24/2 The disease 'general paralysis', also known as paresis, usually is spoken of as softening of the brain. **1930** *Daily Express* 8 Sept. 1/1 Formerly every person developing general paralysis of the insane died after a period of distressing symptoms and agony. **1941** T. WARWICK *Handbk. Venereal Dis.* v. 53 The great majority of general paralytics are men. **1964** KING & NICOL *Venereal Dis.* v. 62 In all cases of general paralysis, tests of the mental status should be carried out. **1970** W. J. BROWN et al. *Syphilis & Other Venereal Dis.* vii. 125 The common types of neurosyphilis are tabes dorsalis, general paralysis of the insane, and meningovascular neurosyphilis.

c. *paralysis agitans* [L. *agitans* shaking], Parkinson's disease, shaking palsy.

1817 J. PARKINSON *Ess. Shaking Palsy* in M. Critchley *James Parkinson* (1955) 153 (*heading*) Shaking palsy. (*Paralysis Agitans.*) **1845** *Encycl. Metrop.* VII. 548/2 Paralysis Agitans..consists of a feeble trembling action of the muscles, not amounting to palsy. **1888** W. R. GOWERS *Man. Dis. Nervous Syst.* II. 594 The great characteristic of the tremor of paralysis agitans is, as Parkinson pointed out, that it continues during rest. **1909** [see *PARKINSON[1]]. **1941** *Brit. Jrnl. Psychol.* XXXII. 5 Only a few years after the conclusion of the peace he fell a tragic victim to that incurably fatal disease of the central nervous system, paralysis agitans. **1973** *Neurology* XXIII. 215 (*heading*) Prevalence of neoplasms and causes of death in paralysis agitans.

paralytic, *a.* and *sb.* Add: **A.** *adj.* **1. b.** Of a (form of) disease: characterized by paralysis.

1890 F. TAYLOR *Man. Pract. Med.* 279 (*heading*) General paralysis of the insane (paralytic dementia). **1948** O. BRELAND *Animal Facts & Fallacies* i. 45 The bats also transmit diseases... One of the worst is the frequently fatal paralytic rabies which has occasionally been transmitted to human beings. **1951** WHITBY & HYNES *Med. Bacteriol.* (ed. 5) xxiv. 408 This preparalytic stage may progress no further... On the other hand paralysis or encephalitic symptoms may appear after a few hours (paralytic poliomyelitis). **1974** H. MACINNES *Climb to Lost World* ii. 33 My first reaction was to telephone our local doctor: 'Dr. Mackenzie, have you any idea where I can get a vaccine for Paralytic Rabies?' **1976** *Yorkshire Even. Press* 9 Dec. 1/5 A seven-month-old baby from Kippax, near Leeds, is in hospital with paralytic polio according to health authorities.

3. d. Intoxicated; incapably drunk. *slang.*

a **1921** E. W. HORNUNG in *Penguin Bk. Austral. Ballads* (1964) 103 The shanty-keeper *he* was just as steady as a rock, And me as paralytic as a fool. **1927** *Daily Express* 23 Nov. 7 Woman at the Thames Court: I was not drunk. I was suffering from paralysis. Mr. Cairns: I have heard being drunk called being paralytic. **1958** [see *HONKERS *a.*]. **1966** F. SHAW et al. *Lern Yerself Scouse* 76 Half-dreaming, half-par'latic on me back.

paralytically, *adv.* Add: Also *fig.* (see prec.)

1969 *Sunday Times* (Colour Suppl.) 16 Feb. 38/2, I was paralytically drunk.

paramagnet (pærămæ·gnėt). [Back-formation from next, after *magnet* and *magnetic*.] A paramagnetic body or substance.

1909 in *Cent. Dict.* Suppl. **1973** *Nature* 21/28 Dec. 445/1 Only above 100 K does the material become a self-respecting paramagnet, with thermally randomised spins.

paramagnetic, *a.* Add: **1.** (Earlier and additional examples.) This sense is now *Obs.*, having been superseded by the next.

1850 W. WHEWELL *Let.* (1876) II. 364 [*To Faraday.*] Hence it would appear, that the two classes of magnetic bodies are those which place their length *parallel* or *according* to the terrestrial magnetic lines, and those which place their length *transverse* to such lines. Keeping the preposition *dia* for the latter, the preposition *para* or *ana* might be used for the former; perhaps *para* would be best as the word *parallel*..would be a technical memory for it. Thus we should have this distribution—Paramagnetic: Iron, Nickel, Cobalt, &c. Diamagnetic: Bismuth, Phosphor, &c. If you like *anamagnetic* better than *paramagnetic*, as meaning magnetic *according to* our standard, terrestrial magnetism, I see no objection. **1880** [see *FERROMAGNETIC *a.* 1].

2. a. Of a body or substance: very weakly attracted by the poles of a magnet but not retaining any permanent magnetism; having a susceptibility that is positive but small, so that the relative permeability is only slightly greater than one and hysteresis does not occur. **b.** Characteristic of or pertaining to paramagnetism. Cf. *FERROMAGNETIC *a.* 2 and the note there.

1896, etc. [see *FERROMAGNETIC *a.* 2]. **1902** *Encycl. Brit.* XXX. 430/2 The magnetic susceptibility of a vacuum..is 0, that of a diamagnetic substance..has a negative value, while the susceptibility of paramagnetic and ferromagnetic substances..is positive. **1903** *Proc. R. Soc.* LXXI. 239 The law of Curie, that the susceptibility of weak paramagnetic substances is inversely proportional to the absolute temperature. **1931** S. R. WILLIAMS *Mag. Phenomena* v. 159 Oxygen, palladium, air, glass, porcelain, and $FeSO_4$ were some of the paramagnetic bodies studied by Curie. **1958** N. CUSACK *Electr. & Magn. Prop. Solids* xii. 269 At a critical temperature, called the Curie point.., ferromagnetic matter undergoes a phase transition and becomes paramagnetic. **1966** C. R. TOTTLE *Sci. Engin. Materials* vi. 133 Curie..deduced the law for paramagnetic susceptibility.

B. *sb.* A paramagnetic body or substance.

1855 *Phil. Mag.* IX. 293 The assertions I have made regarding mutual influence..are confirmed amply by experiment for paramagnetics. **1911** *Encycl. Brit.* XVII. 324/1 Between the ferromagnetics and the paramagnetics there is an enormous gap. **1914, 1962** [see *FERROMAGNETIC *sb.*]. **1966** C. R. TOTTLE *Sci. Engin. Materials* vi. 134 The group of elements iron, cobalt, nickel demonstrates this. Below a certain critical temperature these elements remain permanently magnetized after removal of the external field... Above it, the materials behave as normal paramagnetics.

paramagnetically, *adv.* (Examples.)

1883 *Encycl. Brit.* XV. 248/2 By virtue of differential action, a body may behave paramagnetically or diamagnetically according as it is placed in a less or in a more permeable medium than itself. **1974** *Nature* 31 May 426/1 The reduction at 25° C of the cytochrome c_3 from *Desulfovibrio vulgaris*..has been studied by following the paramagnetically shifted NMR resonances which lie to very low field.

paramagnetism. Add: (Earlier and later examples.) Now distinguished from *FERROMAGNETISM, but formerly synonymous with it.

1850 W. WHEWELL *Let.* (1876) II. 365 [*To Faraday.*] Will it not do to talk of iron, nickel, &c., as *paramagnetic*, and glass, phosphorus, &c., as *diamagnetic*? Then this new branch of science, for so, of course, it will soon become, will be *Paramagnetism*. **1930** [see *FERROMAGNETISM]. **1958** N. CUSACK *Electr. & Magn. Prop. Solids* xiii. 291 All matter possesses a basic diamagnetism but where there are carriers, e.g. free electrons in metals,..the orientation of the carriers in the field direction gives a paramagnetism which usually masks the diamagnetism. **1964** J. W. LINNETT *Electronic Struct. Molecules* iii. 53 The paramagnetism of the ground state of O_2.

paramedian, *a.* (Examples.)

1890 BILLINGS *Med. Dict.* II. 289/1 Paramedian sulcus. **1928** [see *INDUCTION 9 b]. **1962** *Lancet* 19 May 1049/2 The abdomen was opened through a long left paramedian incision. **1977** *Ibid.* 28 May 1128/1 Patients in whom a midline or paramedian incision was made were not included.

paramedic[1] (pærămeˑdik). orig. *U.S.* Also para-medic. [f. *PARA-[3] + MEDIC *a.* and *sb.*] A person trained to be dropped by parachute to give medical aid.

1951 *Sunday Mirror* (N.Y.) 8 Apr. 3 Para-medics from air-sea rescue squadrons..were in the search planes. **1957** *Time* 2 Sept. 35/2 A C-47 with a paramedic aboard started to track his flight. **1961** *Daily Tel.* 27 Feb. 18/2 The group's nucleus consists of six 'paramedics'. These are practised parachutists with a medical background. **1964** J. MASTERS *Trial at Monomoy* vii. 225 Why didn't they send a plane down with skis, paramedics, radios, food? **1974** *Spartanburg* (S. Carolina) *Herald* 25 Apr. A2/5 He hopes the state pilot, advanced course for paramedics will be available to local EMS technicians by August or September. **1974** *Courier-Mail* (Brisbane) 17 Sept. 11/4 (*caption*) Dummy United States Air Force para-medic, dressed in full gear, at the jump position of a door of a U.S.A.F. Hercules rescue aircraft.

paramedic[2] (pærămeˑdik). [f. *PARAMEDIC(AL *a.*[1] and *sb.* (cf. MEDIC *a.* and *sb.*).] A paramedical worker; = *PARAMEDICAL *sb.* Also *attrib.* or as *adj.*

1970 *Time* 9 Nov. 38 More than 40 training programs for doctors assistants are under way across the country. The graduates..are tagged with clumsy names—paramedic, clinical associate, health practitioner. *Ibid.*, Paramedic studies are wide-ranging—from community health to bacteriology and psychosomatic medicine, plus techniques such as regulating intravenous infusions and operating respirators. **1974** *Telegraph* (Brisbane) 27 Feb. 32/2 Paramedics tried artificial respiration, but to no avail. **1974** *Aiken* (S. Carolina) *Standard* 22 Apr. 4-A/1 Paramedic Services and the city police will provide first aid and protection during the walk. **1975** *Daily Tel.* 29 Sept. 3/1 The *Lancet* report gives details of 600 such operations, 366 performed by medical auxiliaries or 'paramedics' as they are described. The rest were carried out by qualified doctors. **1976** *Amer. Speech 1973* XLVIII. 195 Also of invaluable help to the nurse are the *paramedic personnel*, frequently shortened to *paramedics*. In their ranks we find those employees trained to read slides in the laboratory or to assist the doctor and nurse with other medical tasks. **1976** *Sci. Amer.* Sept. 72/3 (Advt.), Heart pacemakers, paramedic telecare units and ultrasonic cardioscopes—all are outgrowths of space technology. **1977** *It* May 21/2 They also have a fully-equipped ambulance, manned by State-certified paramedics and emergency medical technicians.

paramedical (pærămeˑdikăl), *a.*[1] and *sb.* [f. PARA-[1] + MEDICAL *a.* and *sb.*] **A.** *adj.* Supplementary to or supporting the work of medically qualified personnel.

1921 *Lancet* 15 Oct. 814/1 Para medical research. The report for 1920–21 of the Committee of the Privy Council for Scientific and Industrial Research touches the fringe of several medical problems and describes work linked at several points with that being undertaken under the auspices of the Medical Research Council. **1952** C. P. BLACKER *Eugenics* 303 Marriage guidance, premarital examinations, eugenic prognosis, birth control, and treatment of infecundity have recently been described as 'para-medical services'. **1962** *Times* 2 Mar. 5/7 Nurses and other paramedical personnel. **1969** *Nature* 15 Feb. 604/1 If a student failed to complete the medical course, he would at least have a qualification that would enable him to take up a career in some non-medical or paramedical field. **1972** *Sci. Amer.* Feb. 117/1 Intended largely for paramedical students, nurses and technicians, it presents..a review of the general structure of the body. **1977** *Private Eye* 1 Apr. 7/3 New ventures in the paramedical field include Polyglot Schools (UK) limited.. who canvass doctors in the Harley Street area with their scheme, 'Arabic for the Medical Professions'.

B. *sb.* A paramedical worker.

1972 *Guardian* 23 Oct. 11/1 It was suggested that abortion be delegated to paramedicals. **1974** *Financial Times* 5 July 1/8 It was announced on Wednesday that the committee, which is looking at nurses' and midwives' salaries, will also make recommendations for the 'paramedicals'. **1975** *Nature* 21 Aug. 610/3 [In China] barefoot doctors..are called 'doctors', not paramedicals or auxiliaries. **1976** *Times Lit. Suppl.* 16 July 872/5 The enlistment of para-medicals to perform the tasks of health care.

paramedical (pærămeˑdikăl), *a.*[2] [f. *PARA-[3] + MEDICAL *a.* and *sb.*] Trained in parachuting and competent to give medical aid.

1962 *Flight Internat.* LXXXI. 227/1 The Near East Air Force 'para-medical' team in Cyprus. **1974** *Telegraph* (Brisbane) 17 Sept. 34/1 An American paramedical airman will parachute into the water off Redland Bay..as part of a simulated search and rescue operation.

paramelaconite: see *PARA-[1] 2 c.

paramenstruum: see *PARA-[1] 1.

parameter. Add: **2.** (Examples in *Computing.*)

1954 *Computers & Automation* Dec. 18/1 *Parameter*, in a subroutine, a quantity which may be given different values when the subroutine is used in different parts of one main routine, but which usually remains unchanged throughout any one such use. **1958** *Communications* (Assoc. Computing Machinery) Dec. 16 A procedure..is a closed and self-contained process with a fixed ordered set of input and output parameters. **1965** [see *keyboarded* ppl. adj. s.v. *KEYBOARD *v.*]. **1969** *Computers & Humanities* III. 278 Thus input parameters were included to specify page width and length, and the dictionary was photo-offset. **1973** C. W. GEAR *Introd. Computer Sci.* v. 201 A and B are input parameters, so they can be given values by any expression when the subroutine is called. **1973** MURRILL & SMITH *Introd. Computer Sci.* 585 Through the use of arguments and parameters, subroutines and functions can be used throughout a program to perform identical operations upon many different data items.

b. Delete †*Obs.* (Later examples.)

1963 R. H. MERSON in M. Roy *Dynamics of Satellites* 83 The values of the six basic elements at a given time..are determined from a set of observations by a differential correction technique... In addition to the estimates of the orbital parameters, estimates of their variances and covariances are also determined. **1967** *Technology Week* 20 Feb. 13 Orbital parameters were apogee—817·2 mi.; perigee—128 mi.; inclination—48·4 degrees, and period 100·3 minutes. **1975** *Nature* 18 Sept. 184/2 Even though a few comets with hyperbolic orbits have been seen, Whipple's calculations show that for four candidates—the only ones..with well determined parameters—the chance of any one having arrived on such an orbit from interstellar space is less than 1 in 10^4.

d. *Math.* An independent variable in terms of which each co-ordinate of a point is expressed, independently of the other co-ordinates.

1873 G. SALMON *Treat. Higher Plane Curves* (ed. 2) viii. 317 The coordinates x', y', z' are..expressible as quadric functions of a parameter θ. **1907** GRACE & ROSENBERG *Coordinate Geom.* xvi. 220 If we can find simple expressions for the coordinates of points on a conic in terms of. one variable quantity, a point on the curve may be looked on as determined by a definite value of the variable, the variable being usually called the parameter. **1937** MICHELL & BELZ *Elem. Math. Analysis* I. vii. 401 Taking $x^2/a^2 - y^2/b^2 = 1$, (a, b positive), as the equation of the hyperbola, we can evidently write $x = \pm a \cosh \phi$, $y = b \sinh \phi$, introducing ϕ as parameter. **1969** J. J. STOKER *Differential Geom.* iv. 75 As with curves, the surface parameters are to a considerable degree arbitrary; in fact, parameters u, v can be replaced by new parameters through the equations $\bar{u} = \phi_1(u, v)$, $\bar{v} = \phi_2(u, v)$, provided that the Jacobian $\partial(\bar{u}, \bar{v})/(u, v)$ is different from zero.

e. *Electr.* Any of several numerical quantities that can be used jointly to characterize a network.

1911 *Trans. Amer. Inst. Electr. Engin.* XXX. 885 The impedances required to make a normal type of network of the requisite number of parameters equivalent to the given network under specified conditions of operation. **1930** T. E. SHEA *Transmission Networks & Wave Filters* iii. 71 Any network having one pair of input and one pair of output terminals may be completely represented..by a T network (or network having any form providing at least three independent parameters) as far as external current and voltage conditions are concerned. **1962** SIMPSON & RICHARDS *Physical Princ. Junction Transistors* v. 82 The *h*'s define the following circuit parameters: $h_{11} = h_i$ = input impedance with output short-circuited.., $h_{12} = h_r$ = reverse voltage ratio with input open-circuited. **1966** R. H. MATTSON *Electronics* ix. 381 The *y* parameters are used when discussing feedback amplifiers and pentode amplifiers. The *h* parameters are used when discussing transistor circuits.

f. *Statistics.* A numerical characteristic of a population (as distinguished from a 'statistic', which relates to a sample).

1922 R. A. FISHER in *Phil. Trans. R. Soc.* A. CCXXII. 311 The law of distribution of this hypothetical population is specified by relatively few parameters. *Ibid.* 313 These involve the choice of methods of calculating from a sample statistical derivates, or as we shall call them statistics, which are designed to estimate the values of the parameters of the hypothetical population. **1939** A. E. TRELOAR *Elem. Statistical Reasoning* x. 130 The true sampling error of each sample mean and standard deviation, so far as those statistics form estimates of the corresponding parameters, may be expressed as [etc.]. **1962** E. S. KEEPING *Introd. Statistical Inference* v. 95 If.. the population is assumed to be normal, as far as a particular variate is concerned, the density function for this variate will contain two parameters, μ and σ, which are the population mean and standard deviation respectively. **1975** HARNETT & MURPHY *Introd. Statistical Anal.* i. 5 The numerical characteristics of a sample are used to estimate the parameters of the parent population from which this sample was drawn. A numerical characteristic used for this purpose is referred to as a sample statistic, or usually just a statistic.

3. In extended use: any distinguishing or defining characteristic or feature, esp. one that may be measured or quantified; an element or aspect *of* anything; *loosely*, a boundary or limit.

1927 *Proc. R. Soc.* A. CXIII. 642 In the case of phenacite, the symmetry of the structure imposes no limitations on the position of the seven atoms in the molecule, so that twenty-one parameters are required to define the structure. **1934** *Ibid.* CXLVI. 570 Few of the structures of hydrated salts have as yet been found. This may be due to the large numbers of parameters usually involved, which, in the absence of any general laws concerning water of crystallization, makes the analysis very difficult. **1939** BREVOORT & JOYNER *Cooling on Front of Air-Cooled Engine Cylinder* (NACA Techn. Rep. No. 674) 1/1 These results are introductory to the study of front cooling and show the general effect of the several test parameters. **1950** J. C. SLATER *Microwave Electronics* x. 230 The quantity, *x*..occurs frequently in klystron theory and is called the bunching parameter. **1957** *Times* 11 Sept. 6/2 The principle that it was possible to specify the sounds of speech in terms of six parameters or factors, which might be considered as functions of time. **1961** *Jrnl. Speech & Hearing Res.* IV. 10/1 There is some evidence..that parameters other than the formant frequencies may influence human judgement of vowel qualities. **1962** *Rep. Comm. Broadcasting 1960* 335 in *Parl. Papers 1961–2* (Cmnd. 1753) IX. 259 Many Western European countries..are considering whether there would be advantage in using..the technical parameters they already use for 625-line standards in the 7 Mc/s channels of Bands I and III. **1964** A. EDEL in I. L. Horowitz *New Sociol.* xiv. 220 A theory of human society is seen to involve a specific picture of the nature of man. We would then say that a social theory has a human-nature parameter. **1965** *Listener* 9 Dec. 943/2 There remains the bulk of those for whom politics is a parameter of life rather like the weather. **1967** *Economist* 16 Dec. 1157/1 A second, even bigger generator of 1,300 MW was also contracted for... With these orders, practically every existing parameter of power generating practice has been exceeded. **1970** *Time* 3 Aug. 9 The fact that Nixon was willing to make his chastisement public suggests..that the President at least understands 'the parameters of the problem'. **1971** *Jrnl. Gen. Psychol.* LXXXIV. 18 Three phenomena corresponding to the three major parameters of color—brightness, hue, and saturation. **1972** *Nature* 18 Feb. 373/2 In Fig. 2 ozone and radon concentrations together with various meteorological parameters are shown for two consecutive Saturdays. **1973** *N.Y. Times Mag.* 25 Feb. 71/4 It carries, to begin with, the liberal presumption that the mind of man can in fact comprehend the major parameters of the world we inhabit. **1975** D. M. DAVIN *Closing Times* p. xviii, There are parameters to these recollections which may not be immediately apparent: the world of learning..and the war... My chief parameter, however, is that of art. **1975** *Times* 14 Oct. 15/4 The considerable element of indeterminacy which exists within the parameters of the parole system. **1975** *Publishers Weekly* 27 Oct. 20/1 One disappointment for the publishers is that it [*sc.* the High Court decision] fails to provide any clear guidelines on the larger issue of the parameters of Government secrecy. **1976** *Listener* 30 Sept. 419/3 Carter, who has made the running so far by raising the debate beyond the orthodox economic and financial political parameters. **1976** H. Young *Crossman Affair* i. 19 At this meeting a word was first spoken and a concept first articulated which later came to dominate the Crossman Diaries case. The word was 'parameters'... Sir John Hunt, in giving guidance on the limits within which an edited version of Crossman would have to be prepared, now formalized into a set of rules his interpretation of past practice... These parameters, or limits, excluded four particular areas from detailed report or discussion.

para:meteriza·tion. Also para:metriza·tion. [f. as next + -ation.] The action of parameterizing; a parametric representation.

1939 H. Weyl *Classical Groups* ii. 56 (*heading*) Cayley's rational parametrization of the orthogonal group. **1964** L. Wilets *Theories Nuclear Fission* ii. 14 (*heading*) Parameterization of the nuclear surface. **1970** I. E. McCarthy *Nuclear Reactions* I. iii. 69 To facilitate numerical calculations the following parametrization is used. **1972** A. W. F. Edwards *Likelihood* vi. 127 In view of the relatively high conformation of $\hat{x}$ and $\hat{y}$ the former parametrization in p and r is more suitable. **1975** *Physics Bull.* July 323/3 The required degree of accuracy is established at the beginning by a theoretical study using the virial coefficients of the post Newtonian parameterization expansion for the viable gravitation theories. **1976** *European Econ. Rev.* VIII. 287 The TF form, a finite parametrization of the well-known final form, is appropriate for control and forecasting.

parameterize (pǎræ·mɪ̆tərəiz), *v.* Also **parametrize.** [f. Parameter + -ize.] *trans.* To describe or represent in terms of a parameter.

1940 E. T. Bell *Devel. Math.* xv. 322 The wave surface in optics, parametrized by elliptic functions. **1949** [see *interval *sb.* 6* b]. **1964** *Ann. Rev. Automatic Programming* IV. 125 A translation algorithm is presented, capable of being conveniently parameterized for various source language-target language pairs. **1970** *New Scientist* 9 Apr. 76/2 The nuclear charge distribution..can be parametrized directly using a suitable mathematical form which does not necessarily have fundamental significance. **1973** *Nature* 14 Sept. 61/1 Cigarette smoking is parametrized by the number smoked daily both before pregnancy and after the fourth month. **1974** *Ibid.* 20/27 Dec. 673/1 The zonal velocity (parameterised by Λ) leads to a secular change in i as the value of ω of the satellite orbit changes.

Hence **para·meterized** *ppl. a.*, **para·meterizing** *vbl. sb.*

1962 [see *magnetosonic* adj. s.v. *magneto-]. **1964** *Ann. Rev. Automatic Programming* IV. 125 (*heading*) A parameterized compiler based on mechanical linguistics. **1971** *Physics Bull.* Jan. 24/2 Only the large scale physics of the atmosphere is well represented in our models and the subgrid scale physics..can only be included in some parametrized form.

parametral, *a.* (Further example.)

Except in *Cryst.*, *parametric* is the usual adj.

1973 H. D. Megaw *Crystal Struct.* v. 103 The plane used to define the axial ratios *a*:*b*:*c*, the parametral plane, is (111).

parametrial: see *para-[1] 1.

parametric, *a.*[1] Add: (Further examples.) *parametric curve*, a curve obtained by keeping constant one of the parameters in the parametric equations of a surface; *parametric equation*, one of a set of equations each of which expresses one of the co-ordinates of a curve or surface as a function of one or more parameters (*parameter 2 d).

This, rather than *parametral* or *parametrical*, is the usual adj. (except in *Cryst.*: cf. *parametral *a.*).

1900 *Trans. Amer. Math. Soc.* I. 461 (*heading*) Parametric representation of the fundamental quadric. **1909** L. P. Eisenhart *Treat. Differential Geom. Curves & Surfaces* i. 1 (*heading*) Parametric equations of a curve. *Ibid.* ii. 55 Upon a surface (2) there lie an infinity of curves whose equations are given by equations (2), when u is constant, each constant value of v determining a curve... In a similar way, there is an infinite family of curves v = *const.* The curves of these two families are called the parametric curves for the given equations of the surface. **1942** C. H. Lehmann *Analytic Geom.* xi. 229 The parametric equations of a specific locus are not unique. *Ibid.* 230 Find the rectangular equation of the curve whose parametric equations are $x = 2 + 3 \tan \theta$, $y = 1 + 4 \sec \theta$. **1969** J. J. Stoker *Differential Geom.* ii. 14 Many important results in differential geometry can often be made direct and easy to achieve once a special parametric representation has been tactfully chosen.

b. *Electronics.* Applied to devices and processes in which amplification or frequency conversion is obtained by applying a signal to a non-linear device that is modulated by a pumping frequency, so that there is a transfer of power from the latter to the output, which in general can include the sum and difference frequencies.

So called because the action of the pumping frequency is to modulate the parameters of the non-linear device.

1957 *RCA Rev.* XVIII. 578 (*heading*) Theory of parametric amplification using nonlinear reactances. *Ibid.* 579 In this paper the parametric amplifier is analyzed in terms of an equivalent circuit using a nonlinear inductance. **1961** *Guardian* 14 Feb. 24/1 The so-called 'parametric amplifiers'..can increase the sensitivity of radio reception over great distances. **1968** Angelakos & Everhart *Microwave Communications* iv. 82 A parametric amplifier converts power at one frequency (from a source generally called the pump) into power at another frequency, the signal frequency... The pump voltage is mixed with the signal voltage by a nonlinear reactance, which in microwave systems is generally a varactor diode. **1971** *Physics Bull.* Aug. 464/3 Parametric conversions of waves to other frequencies are familiar in the field of nonlinear optics. **1972** *Sci. Amer.* Sept. 136/3 In present-day satellite-communication terminals the maser amplifier has given way to the cooled parametric amplifier, which combines low-noise performance with an even wider bandwidth. **1972** Zernike & Midwinter *Appl. Nonlinear Optics* (1973) vii. 153 The parametric up-converter is a special case of sum-frequency generation. Similarly, the parametric amplifier and the parametric oscillator are special cases of difference-frequency generation.

parametrically (pærǎme·trikǎli), *adv.* [f. Parametric *a.*[1]: see -ly[2].] In terms of a parameter or parameters.

1894 C. A. Scott *Introd. Acct. Plane Analyt. Geom.* v. 89 The possibility of expressing the coordinates of a point on a curve parametrically. **1940** E. T. Bell *Devel. Math.* xv. 322 Kummer's (1864) quartic surface..is the so-called singular surface of the quadratic line complex, and ..is represented parametrically. **1962** W. B. Thompson *Introd. Plasma Physics* v. 86 The coordinates (X, Y) can be given parametrically in terms of the phase velocity $v(\theta)$ and the angle between the wave vector and the magnetic field. **1968** C. G. Kuper *Introd. Theory Superconductivity* xii. 202 The probability of occupation of a given single-particle state will depend parametrically on the *whole* distribution of quasiparticles, but not on the detailed question of whether some other particular state is occupied.

parametritius, -metrium: see *para-[1] 1.

parametrize, -metrization: varr. *parameterize *v.*, -meterization.

parametron (pǎræ·mɪ̆trǫn). *Electronics.* [f. Parametr(ic *a.*[1] + *-on*; coined in Jap. by E. Goto 1955, in *Denki Tsūshin Gakkai Zasshi* XXX. 770.] A digital storage element consisting of a parametric oscillator in which the digit is represented by the phase (0° or 180°, corresponding to 1 or 0) of the output signal relative to that of an applied reference signal of the same frequency.

1956 *ETJ of Japan* June 64 A new type of electronic computer component called the 'parametron' was invented by Ei-ichi Goto of the Faculty of Science, University of Tokyo, in spring of 1954. **1957** *Jrnl. Sci. Res. Inst.* (Tokyo) LI. 59 (*caption*) A parametron unit; an exciting current is supplied from 1, causing an oscillation in the L-L′-C circuit. Input and output lines are 2 and 3 respectively. **1960** T. E. Ivall *Electronic Computers* (ed. 2) xiii. 234 The parametron requires no valves or transistors, only passive reactive elements, and being therefore extremely stable, reliable and long-lived, is ideally suited for use in digital computers. The main limitation is that because several cycles of oscillation are required to establish a binary digit,..the digit rate is necessarily low. **1967** R. K. Richards *Electronic Digital Components & Circuits* vi. 337 Parametrons quickly became very popular with Japanese computer manufacturers... However, not one computer employing parametrons is known to have been built or designed in the United States.

paramilitary (pærǎmi·litǎri), *a.* [f. Para-[1] + Military *a.*] Of or pertaining to an organization, unit, force, etc., whose function or status is ancillary or analogous to that of military forces, but which is not a professional military force. Also as *sb.* Hence **parami·litarism.**

1935 *Ann. Reg. 1934* 96 A difficult problem has been raised in regard to the so-called 'para-military training', *i.e.*, the military training outside the Army of men of military age. **1936** *Punch* 1 Apr. 376/1 Let us at once impale the new and unnecessary mongrel 'paramilitary'—'paramilitary forces (S.A., S.S., Labour Corps and other organisations)'... Why not 'semi-military', 'quasi-military', or even 'sub-military'? **1949** F. Maclean *Eastern Approaches* III. xvii. 516 The military and paramilitary forces which they [*sc.* the quisling administrations] had raised had either surrendered or else were withdrawing northwards. **1958** *Listener* 14 Aug. 238/2 The Nazi storm-trooper is preceded by a hardly less 'heroic' communist in his paramilitary uniform. **1962** *Times Lit. Suppl.* 16 Feb. 102/1 Lawrence of Arabia was almost a paramilitary symbol as long ago as 1917. **1969** *New Statesman* 11 Apr. 499/2 The Israelis were to receive unofficial guarantees that a UN presence, or paramilitary force as it was termed, would be stationed on the Israeli-Egyptian border. **1970** *New Yorker* 14 Feb. 33 An editorial in the Times..talked about the Panthers' 'Mao-Marxist ideology and Fascist paramilitarism'. **1972** J. McClure *Caterpillar Cop* xii. 199 I'd forgotten you chappies were really a para-military outfit. **1974** J. White tr. *Poulantzas's Fascism & Dictatorship* III. ii. 102 Party representation was short-circuited by the formation of para-military organizations. **1976** *Times* 9 Mar. 16/8 The para-militaries are no longer prepared to be used..unless they have a say in the running of the country [*sc.* Ulster]. **1976** *Listener* 16 Sept. 325/3 To change the climate within which the paramilitaries operate. **1977** M. Walker *National Front* i. 18 Although Mussolini had specifically warned him against building a para-military force in Britain, Mosley was convinced..that he needed a corps of tough stewards to guarantee order at his meetings.

paramnesia, -ic: see *para-[1] 1.

paramount, *a.* Add: **1. c.** *paramount chief*, esp. in African countries, a tribal chief of the highest order, whose authority extends over an entire district.

1844 in F. Brownlee *Transkeian Native Territories: Hist. Rec.* (1923) 92 Treaty of Amity entered into..on behalf of Her Britannic Majesty, of the one part, and Faku, Paramount Chief of the Amapondo Nation. *a* **1882** G. W. Stow *Native Races S. Afr.* (1905) x. 183 They acknowledged a Bushman captain..as their great chief, who..was succeeded by 'Khiba, or 'Kheba, who was the paramount chief over the men of the caves. **1885** in F. Brownlee *Transkeian Native Territories: Hist. Rec.* (1923) 20 Some of these clans..depended directly upon the paramount chief, others were grouped under a sub-chief. **1919** G. M. Theal *Ethnogr. & Condit. S. Afr. before 1505* (ed. 2) x. 212 Sometimes the heads of the clans were members of the family of the paramount chief. **1928** G. P. Lestrade in A. M. Duggan-Cronin *Bantu Tribes S. Afr.* I. I. 18 The petty chiefs, each of whom is responsible to the paramount chief for the maintenance of good order in his section of the tribe, share in..privileges at the chief's pleasure. **1948** B. G. M. Sundkler *Bantu Prophets S. Afr.* ii. 38 As the Queen of England was the head of the English Church, so the Paramount Chief of the Tembu should be the *summus episcopus* of the new religious organization. **1954** E. A. Hoebel *Law of Primitive Man* viii. 193 Every village, which belongs to a subclan, has its headman... If an ordinary headman, a lesser chief..his powers extend only to the boundaries of his own village. If he is a full chief..his influence will spread over several villages and their subchiefs. If he is a paramount chief among the full chiefs, it will extend over an entire district. **1957** P. Worsley *Trumpet shall Sound* vi. 119 Three of the Paramount Chiefs failed to report the movement to Government. **1965** A. Nicol *Truly Married Woman* 87 His main preoccupation was to find ways of slighting the neighbouring and more powerful provincial Paramount Chief. **1971** *Rand Daily Mail* 4 Dec. 3/4 No member of your Government should consider his position to be more important and exalted than that of the Paramount Chief. **1974** *Afr. Encycl.* 505/1 The policy of 'separate development'..which led to the establishment of the Transkei has been opposed by the leader of the 'True' Thembu, Paramount Chief Saberta Dalinyebo. **1976** *Times* 26 Oct. 8/4 Dr. Nicolaas Diederichs, the President of South Africa, handed over a copy of the Transkei Act to the country's first Prime Minister, Paramount Chief Kaiser Matanzima.

paramountly, *adv.* (Later examples.)

1962 S. E. Finer *Man on Horseback* v. 65 The so-called 'Free Officers'..regrouped and decided to overthrow the régime, and paramountly the king who headed it. **1971** *Country Life* 19 Aug. 464/1 The tragedy is that man..still constitutes..the paramountly weak link.

paramyosin: see *para-[1] 2 a.

paramyxovirus (pærǎmi·ksovəiᵊrɒ̆s). *Biol.* [f. Para-[1] + *myxovirus.] Any of a group of related viruses which includes the para-influenza viruses and those causing mumps, measles, distemper, and rinderpest, and which differ from the myxoviruses in their larger and more variable size and in being hæmolytic.

1962 [see *myxovirus]. **1968** *Times* 27 Nov. 9/3 Mumps, a disease which is caused by one of the paramyxoviruses. **1969** A. Cohen *Textbk. Med. Virol.* vi. 71 Myxoviruses are characterized by particles whose size varies from 800 to 1100 Å in diameter, and whose helical internal component is 90 Å wide and lightly packed inside the envelope. Paramyxoviruses..are characterized by larger sized particles, 1000–5000 Å in diameter, whose internal component is 180 Å wide and more loosely packed within the virus envelope. Morphological differences between myxoviruses and paramyxoviruses are associated with some differences of biological activity. **1974** [see *myxovirus].

Parana (parǎ·nǎ). Also **Paraná.** The name of a river and a province in Brazil, used *attrib.*, usu. in **Parana pine,** to designate a large evergreen tree, *Araucaria angustifolia*, of the family Pinaceæ, found in the high plateau region of south-western Brazil, Paraguay, and northern Argentina; also, the light-coloured, softwood timber obtained from this tree.

1923 Dallimore & Jackson *Handbk. Coniferæ* 153 Araucaria brasiliensis, Loudon. Parana Pine; Parana Wood. **1924** Record & Mell *Timbers Trop. Amer.* II. 92 The Paraná pine is the most extensively exploited timber in South America. **1959** *Archit. Rev.* CXXV. 333/2 Natural wood, parana pine, oak and western red cedar. **1964** *Listener* 17 Sept. 428/3 Paraná pine..—highly polished—forms the glistening verandah floor. **1971** N. E. Hickin *Wood Preservation* 15 *Araucaria angustifolia* from Argentina and South Brazil is Parana Pine. **1977** *Irish Press* 29 Sept. 16/1 (Advt.), Unique solid Parana Pine bunk beds, £59.

paranasal: see *para-[1] 1.

paranatal (pærǎnēⁱ·tǎl), *a.* *Med.* [f. Para-[1] + Natal *a.*[1] and *sb.*] Of or pertaining to the time shortly before and after birth.

Orig. given a broader meaning (quot. 1940).

1940 F. Schreiber in *Jrnl. Pediatrics* XVI. 297 (*heading*) Neurologic sequelae of paranatal asphyxia. [*Note*] The term *paranatal* has been coined to designate the entire period of fetal life, the period of birth, and the neonatal period within which the results of occurrences during the first two periods may become manifest. **1954** *Jrnl. Amer. Med. Assoc.* 19 June 719/1 Proponents of the brain injury hypothesis state that in most cases anoxia during the prenatal and paranatal periods has resulted in brain damage. **1964** *Jrnl. Nerv. & Mental Dis.* CXXXIX. 357 (*heading*) Pre- and paranatal factors in mental disorders of children. **1971** C. B. COURVILLE *Birth & Brain Damage* xi. 197 (*caption*) Gliosis, the most significant tissue reaction in paranatal anoxia. **1976** *Word 1971* XXVII. 62 The developing human foetus..is 'practicing', in amniotic fluid, those neuromuscular gestures which will lead, in air, to paranatal cry and neonatal cry specifically.

paranemic (pærănī·mik), *a.* [f. PARA-¹ + Gr. νῆμα thread + -IC.] Of, pertaining to, or designating two or more like helices coiled together side by side in such a way that they may be fully separated without being unwound. Opp. *PLECTONEMIC *a.*

1941 [see *PLECTONEMIC *a.*]. **1950** *Biol. Rev.* XXV. 500 Until quite recently almost all observers were agreed that the plectonemic spiral was characteristic of mitosis and the paranemic of meiosis (meaning the first meiotic division). **1953** WATSON & CRICK in *Cold Spring Harbor Symp. Quant. Biol.* XVIII. 129/2 With paranemic coiling, the specific pairing of bases [in DNA] would not allow the successive residues of each helix to be in equivalent orientation with regard to the helical axis. **1974** F. CRICK in *Nature* 26 Apr. 767/2 Looking back, I think we deserve some credit..for our forthright stand against paranemic (as opposed to plectonemic) coiling.

parang. (Earlier and later examples.)

1839 [see *KLEYWANG]. **1966** D. FORBES *Heart of Malaya* v. 60 A full-blooded *amok*, slaughtering every man, woman and child in reach with the snaky kris or the curved parang. **1967** J. CLEARY *Long Pursuit* iii. 81 They cut branches from the mangroves with a parang they had found in the boat. **1972** [see *JACK *sb.*⁴ b]. **1976** 'G. BLACK' *Moon for Killers* ix. 109 The rent in the cloudbank ..its edges as rough as a wound made with a *parang*.

parangi (păræ·ŋgi). Also 9 **parangy.** [Sinhalese *parangi (lede)*, lit. '(disease of) foreigners', i.e. the Portuguese (= Skr. *phiraṅga* 'Frankish', European), f. Pg. *Frangue*, name given by the Moors to Frenchmen, Spaniards, and European Christians generally (cf. FERINGHEE).] The name given in Sri Lanka to a disease now known to be identical with yaws.

1821 H. MARSHALL *Notes Med. Topogr. Interior Ceylon* iii. 43 There is a complaint mentioned in the Kandyan medical works, called *parangy lede* (Parangy disease). *Ibid.*, *Parangy lede* seems to have been originally intended to denominate a new disease;..it may perhaps be inferred that the term meant Portuguese disease. There is, however, no tradition among the Kandyans respecting the importation of a disease. *Ibid.* 44 Many of the cutaneous affections which they denominate *parangy*, are evidently herpetic, and cannot be referred to a syphilitic origin. **1882** *Med. Times & Gaz.* 14 Jan. 30/1 The diseases which parangi resembles are syphilis and its various manifestations, lupus leprosy, and frambœsia. **1913** L. WOOLF *Village in Jungle* i. 11 There were few in the village without the filthy sores of parangi, their legs eaten out to the bone with the yellow, sweating ulcers.

paranitraniline: see *PARA-¹ 2 b.

‖ **paranjah** (parandʒā·). [a. Russ. *parandzhá*, ult. f. Arabic.] A long wide robe with a (horse-)hair veil worn by Muslim women.

1928 *Daily Express* 7 Dec. 9 The women, completely covered from head to foot by the hideous 'paranjas' (veils), watch the proceedings from the far off roof-tops. **1947** *New Times* 20 June 24/2 In the streets of Sarajevo you may meet Moslem women wearing the paranja. But you needn't be surprised if the muffled figure under the black horsehair veil turns out to be a local women's leader. **1954** KOESTLER *Invis. Writing* II. xii. 141 The doors of the harems were thrown wide open; the sack-like *paranjahs* and black veils fell.

paranoia, paranœa. Add: The form **paranœa** is now *obs.* The various forms of the disorder are now usu. considered as belonging to the schizophrenic group of mental illness. Also in trivial use. (Earlier and later examples.)

1811 R. HOOPER *Lexicon Medicum* 596/2 *Paranœa*, alienation of the mind; defect of judgment. **1848** DUNGLISON *Dict. Med. Sci.* (ed. 7) 625/2 *Paranœa*, delirium, dementia. **1918** [see *neuropsychosis* s.v. *NEURO-]. **1940** HINSIE & SHATZKY *Psychiatric Dict.* 395/2 Perhaps no term in psychiatry has undergone wider variations of meaning than the term paranoia. **1954** W. MAYER-GROSS et al. *Clin. Psychiatry* iv. 158 Much of the age-old controversy on 'paranoia' has arisen from the difficulty of distinguishing between paranoid reactions and paranoid schizophrenia. *Ibid.* vi. 256 The effort to maintain paranoia as a distinct condition has also failed. **1957** V. NABOKOV *Pnin* iv. 96 There is nothing more banal and more bourgeois than paranoia. **1970** HINSIE & CAMPBELL *Psychiatric Dict.* (ed. 4) 540/2 Several types of paranoia have been described on the basis of the type of delusion that predominates: litigious, depressed, persecutory, grandiose, erotic.., and infidelity. *Ibid.* 541/2 The patient with amorous paranoia develops delusions of marital infidelity in relation to his spouse. **1972** *Encycl. Psychol.* II. 366/1 Paranoia...was thought to be distinct from the group of schizophrenias because it did not lead to deterioration. This is not now thought to be the case. **1977** *Time* 16 May 56/3 They constitute what has become a standard trip down paranoia lane.

paranoiac, *a.* and *sb.* Add: (Later examples.)

1902 [see *ASSOCIATION 9]. **1914** A. A. BRILL tr. *Freud's Psychopathol. Everyday Life* xii. 309 The gap between the paranoiac's displacement and that of superstition is narrower than appears at first sight. **1935** D. GASCOYNE *Short Survey Surrealism* v. 102 Dali claims that it is the paranoiac faculty that enables him to discover a head where there was, until he looked at it, only an African village. **1937** *Brit. Jrnl. Psychol.* XXVII. 245 It has frequently been suggested that those who come much in contact with paranoiacs tend themselves in time to exhibit paranoid symptoms. **1952** A. HUXLEY *Let.* 20 May (1969) 645 Boastful in an altogether childish way, mildly paranoiac, but well-meaning. **1977** A. SHERIDAN tr. *Lacan's Écrits* i. 3 The social dialectic that structures human knowledge as paranoiac. **1978** J. BLACKBURN *Dead Man's Handle* i. 20 Paranoiacs and schizophrenics like George Heath and Neville Haigh, and the Boston Strangler.

Hence **paranoi·acally** *adv.*, in a paranoiac manner.

1964 P. F. ANSON *Bishops at Large* vi. 213 He continued to build castles in the air,..paranoiacally refusing to face up to reality. **1976** *Listener* 22 Apr. 505/1 The girl next door is already out there, doing her yoga and singing paranoiacally.

paranoic, *a.* Add: (Further examples.)

1952 W. J. H. SPROTT *Social Psychol.* 244 The Haida Chief whose relative has died suspects supernatural persecution; with us he would be labelled 'paranoic' and sent for 'treatment'. **1977** *Times Lit. Suppl.* 15 Apr. 462/2 His paranoic dislike not only of Robert Ferguson. *Ibid.* 1 July 799/3 The paranoic fantasies to which Bely was prey in 1916, when he believed that he was a 'human bomb', under surveillance from 'a dark-skinned man in a bowler hat'.

Hence **parano·ically** *adv.*

1976 *Times Lit. Suppl.* 28 May 648/1 The outline of a paranoically hostile Soviet Union.

paranoid (pæ·rănoid), *a.* and *sb.* [Irreg. f. PARANOIA + -OID.] **A.** *adj.* Resembling or characterized by paranoia; also used *colloq.*, *transf.*, and *fig.* So **paranoi·dal** *a.*

1904 *Brit. Med. Jrnl.* 15 Oct. 972 The collective grouping of hebephrenia, katanoia, and the paranoid forms makes so vast a congeries that it is impossible to perceive any connecting link between the items of the mass. **1904** tr. *Kraepelin's Lect. Clin. Psychiatry* 151 Paranoidal forms of Dementia Præcox. **1919** R. M. BARCLAY tr. *Kraepelin's Dementia Praecox & Paraphrenia* 195 Paranoid Weak-mindedness. *Ibid.* 252 Paranoid Forms. *Ibid.* 253 Delusions and hallucinations of quite the same kind, as we see them in paranoid cases, occur also in most of the remaining forms of dementia præcox. **1954** KOESTLER *Invis. Writing* xxv. 270 The paranoid tendencies inherent in the movement. **1961** L. MUMFORD *City in Hist.* ii. 39 A paranoid psychal structure was preserved and transmitted by the walled city. **1967** M. ARGYLE *Psychol. Interpersonal Behaviour* viii. 135 *Paranoid reactions* are closely related to schizophrenia. Where there is personality disintegration but with rather more systematic delusions this is called paranoid schizophrenia. **1970** *Guardian Weekly* 28 Feb. 19/1 The sort of international news letters run by paranoid ex-generals. **1974** *Guardian* 13 June 10/3 Those paranoid placards with their Red Rats and Hot Seats for Traitors and Fry 'em.

B. *sb.* A person afflicted with, or showing symptoms of, paranoia.

1922 *Brit. Jrnl. Psychol.* Oct. 113 In discussing the case of paranoids, Neisser writes, 'the patient is progressively less able to exert an independent control over the course of his presentations'. **1938** S. BECKETT *Murphy* ix. 167 Paranoids, feverishly covering sheets of paper with complaints against their treatment. **1950** T. SUGRUE in M. Hay *Foot of Pride* p. xix, The rabble-rousing race bigots who peddle hate and fear to simpletons and paranoids. **1958** *Times Lit. Suppl.* 5 Sept. 495/4 The racy blend of anecdote and psychological jargon produce..a basic Hindu paranoid with suppressed homosexual tendencies, who is never precisely related to particular Hindus. **1967** *Listener* 9 Feb. 186/2 Naive Russian advisers might even believe that only the paranoid would see a Russian defence system as threatening the United States. **1967** M. ARGYLE *Psychol. Interpersonal Behaviour* viii. 136 Paranoids feel that they are being plotted against, spied upon, or otherwise victimized, and that this is the explanation of their failures. **1976** G. MCDONALD *Confess, Fletch* (1977) xiii. 55 Even paranoids have enemies.

parano·rmal, *a.* [PARA-¹.] Applied to observed phenomena or powers which are presumed to operate according to natural laws beyond or outside those considered normal or known; also *absol.* Hence **paranorma·lity,** the state or character of being paranormal; **parano·rmally** *adv.* Cf. SUPERNORMAL *a.*

1920 WEBSTER Add., Paranormal. **1935** *Discovery* May 138 (*caption*) The paranormal displacement of a handkerchief actuated electrically the flashlight by which this photograph was taken. **1950** A. HUXLEY *Themes & Variations* 133 The general tendency of ideas to embody themselves at any price and by fair means or foul, normally or paranormally. **1955** —— *Let.* 30 June (1969) 749 Two 'sensitives', one who specializes in paranormal diagnosis, the other a 'healer'. **1958** J. BLISH *Case of Conscience* (1959) i. 82 He has no belief in the supernatural—or, as we're calling it in our barbarous jargon these days, the 'paranormal'. **1959** *Listener* 11 June 1032/3 Her judgments will be equally remote from dogmatic incredulity and uncritical acceptance of claims to paranormality. **1961** W. H. SALTER *Zoar* ii. 15 'Paranormal' has now in general use taken the place of 'supernormal'. *Ibid.* vi. 69 They were convinced that the moulds were produced paranormally by 'Ideoplasmy'. **1968** *New Scientist* 24 Oct. 209/2 The out-of-the-body or 'ecsomatic' experience has long been familiar to students of the paranormal. **1973** *Daily Colonist* (Victoria, B.C.) 19 Apr. 5/2 Critics who dislike the seemingly paranormal condemn the claims with a vehemence beyond objective scientific candor. **1973** *Daily Tel.* (Colour Suppl.) 30 Nov. 26/1 The individuals who have been at the receiving end of the paranormally-transmitted information. *Ibid.* 31/3 Jung was to claim that if he had his life over again, it would have been devoted to the study of the paranormal. **1975** *Nature* 10 Apr. 470/2 Among the claims made are that plasticity of metal was paranormally produced. **1976** 'J. ROSS' *I know what it's like to Die* xxv. 157 Rogers' belief..in the paranormality of Pybus's experiment with the two dead bodies. **1977** *N.Y. Rev. Bks.* 13 Oct. 45/2 The enormous qualitative difference between testing psychics for paranormal powers, and experimentation in *all other* branches of science.

paranotal, -notum: see *PARA-¹ 1.

Paranthropus (pæræ·nþrǫpǒs, pærænþrōᵘ·pǒs). [mod.L. (R. Broom 1938, in *Nature* 27 Aug. 379/1), f. PARA-¹ + Gr. ἄνθρωπος man.] A fossil hominid first described from remains found at Kromdraai and other sites in southern Africa, formerly included in the genus so called, and now usually included in the species *Australopithecus robustus*.

1941 R. BROOM in *Nature* 5 July 13/1 We have a good lower jaw of Paranthropus. Its teeth are almost typically human. **1946** *Transvaal Mus. Mem.* II. iii. 85 In the male Plesianthropus the anterior surface of the maxilla is essentially similar to that in the female, and thus unlike that in the presumably male Paranthropus. *Ibid.* 92 The Paranthropus skull resembles the living anthropoids much more than it does man. **1953** [see *AUSTRALOPITHECUS]. **1959** J. D. CLARK *Prehist. S. Afr.* iii. 62 Now, however, anatomists are agreed that only one generic form is represented in the Man-ape remains but that two specific forms exist—*Australopithecus* and a later, more specialized form, *Paranthropus*. **1961** *Lancet* 30 Sept. 768/1 The existence of a *Paranthropus*-like form at Olduvai and later at Swartkrans and Kromdraai..seems to suggest that this genus..was moving out peripherally from a central African habitat. **1971** S. A. BARNETT *Human Species* (ed. 5) iv. 100 There are..some more recently discovered forms ('Paranthropus') which were probably above the average height of modern man.

paranym (pæ·rănim). [f. PARA-¹ + *-nym* in ANTONYM, PARONYM, SYNONYM *sb.*, etc.] **a.** A near synonym. *rare.* **b.** (See quot. 1976.)

1963 L. HOGBEN *Essential World Eng.* 11 The L.E.S.U. [*sc.* List of Essential Semantic Units] cites non-essential paranyms for new terms even if definable by reference to terms which appear earlier in the list. **1976** *Listener* 17 June 773/3 A newspaper columnist has recently been collecting what he calls 'paranyms'—words whose meaning is generally the opposite of that intended by the speaker, such as 'provisional' or 'liberation' or 'rationalise'. The writer Brian Aldiss thereupon contributed an example he had found in the New Testament: ' "everlasting life"; in other words "death" '. **1977** *Sunday Times* 2 Jan. 32/4 What a year for paranyms. Never before can so many decent, explicit words have utterly altered their meaning to conceal an evasion or untruth.

parapet. Add: **1.** *spec.* a bank of earth in front of a military trench. Also *fig.*

1916 J. BUCHAN *Greenmantle* xx. 266 A crump took the parapet of the trench. **1918** 'R. WEST' *Return of Soldier* i. 6 On the war-films I have seen men slip down..from the trench parapet. **1928** BLUNDEN *Undertones of War* 317 It seems, as now I wake and brood, And know my hour's decrepitude, That on some dewy parapet The centuries' spirit gazes yet. **1929** 'C. EDMONDS' *Subaltern's War* i. 25 A head and shoulders, seen from the sniper's loophole, leaping past a gap in the enemy's parapet. **1954** W. FAULKNER *Fable* 25 He saw only a few figures crouching along his own parapet. **1975** *Times* 14 July 13/1 The Leader of the House, to whom the Prime Minister..will yield the honour of going over the parapet first. **1975** *Listener* 14 Aug. 207/1 Some TV performers..have been howitzered into the mud... A few have had the sense to learn..to keep their heads behind the parapet. **1977** H. FAST *Immigrants* III. 171 The men were leaning high on the parapet, staring out over the ruptured, wire-strewn earth that separated them from the enemy.

4. *parapet mounting.*

1914 *Illustr. London News* 29 Aug. 332/2 A Hotchkiss machine-gun on a parapet mounting.

paraphasia: see *PARA-¹ 1; **paraphenylenediamine:** see *PARA-¹ 2 b.

paraphilia (pærăfi·liă). [f. PARA-¹ + Gr. φιλία affection.] Perverted sexual desires. Hence **paraphi·liac, paraphi·lic** *adjs.* and *sbs.*

1925 J. S. VAN TESLAAR tr. *Stekel's Peculiarities of Behav.* II. 341 *Paraphilia*, interest in perversions. **1935** L. BRINK tr. *Stekel's Sadism & Masochism* I. iv. 100 If the patient can be brought to normal sexual relations, the paraphiliac impulses recede into the background. **1958** *Times Lit. Suppl.* 31 Oct. 619/2 Stekel..says that pluralistic orgies are tribal in derivation, and that frequently the paraphiliac who engages in them seeks a family combination. **1960** *Arch. Gen. Psychiatry* III. 442/1 He was allegedly heterosexually quite adequate (by using different paraphilic fantasies during coitus). **1962** C. ALLEN *Textbk. Psychosexual Disorders* I. v. 73 We regard the paraphylics [*sic*] divisible into three degrees. **1971** *Nature* 16 Apr. 433/2 Contact with urine plays little part in human relations, though it may be emphasized in paraphilias. **1977** *Proc. R. Soc. Med.* LXX. 792/2 Some patients have fantasies which involve masochistic or other paraphilic activity. **1977** E. J. TRIMMER et al. *Visual Dict. Sex* (1978) i. 12 The common paraphilias that we choose to call sexual perversions today, were defined by the Greeks as being parallel to love.

paraphony, anglicized form of PARAPHONIA.

1919 H. J. WATT *Found. Music* 157 The term paraphony was used by several later writers, Thrasyllus, Bacchius and Gaudentius. **1924** T. H. Y. TROTTER *Music & Mind* 154 The words 'symphony', 'paraphony', and 'diaphony' are used to express more or less complete unity and dissonance.

Hence **paraphonic** *a.* (later example); **parapho·nically** *adv.*

1919 H. J. WATT *Found. Music* 156 For the proper flow of simultaneous melodies intervals must either be themselves actually paraphonic or they must be used paraphonically.

pa:raphrasabi·lity. [f. PARAPHRASABLE *a.* + -ITY.] The capacity of being paraphrasable.

1965 *Amer. Philos. Q.* II. 185/2 Paraphrasability is generally regarded as the central issue. **1965** *Times Lit. Suppl.* 25 Nov. 1082/4 He brings the [Wittgensteinian] technique to bear on two aesthetic problems: the paraphrasability of poems and the tonality of atonal music. **1977** *Amer. Speech 1975* L. 82 Constructions in which the modifier is the author of the headword, such as *Zunser's hymn*, also vary in their paraphrasability with *have*.

paraphrasable, *a.* (Later examples.)

1936 F. R. LEAVIS *Revaluation* v. 155 It is difficult not to believe, after reading, say, Book II of *The Prelude*, that one has been reading a paraphrasable argument. **1952** *Essays in Crit.* II. 106 If it is self-sufficient (that is, if it yields a paraphrasable meaning answering the normal demands of logic and syntax). **1966** *Listener* 25 Aug. 282/1 Mr Lodge carefully demolishes the view that the novel is reducible to its paraphrasable and translatable content. **1970** *Language* XLVI. 831 The adjectives shown..are normally considered stative..and they are indeed paraphrasable with active verbs.

paraphrase, *sb.* Add: **1.** (Examples of a musical passage.)

1880 GROVE *Dict. Mus.* II. 741/2 His [*sc.* Liszt's] transcriptions, paraphrases, and arrangements, comprise not only vocal and orchestral works of German, French, Italian, and Russian composers, but also the national melodies of Europe, Asia, etc. **1900** L. GODOWSKY *Let.* 24 Dec. in H. C. Schonberg *Great Pianists* (1964) xxiv. 320, I came out to play my seven Chopin paraphrases and Weber's 'Invitation'. **1944** W. APEL *Harvard Dict. Mus.* 554/1 Liszt's paraphrases on Wagnerian operas. **1963** H. C. SCHONBERG *Great Pianists* (1964) xxiv. 322 Big technicians will occasionally attempt his paraphrase on *Fledermaus*. **1976** *Gramophone* Apr. 1598/2 Liszt's *Eugene Onegin* paraphrase is not one of his most elaborate, nor his finest, but it has the authentic glitter, and a most enjoyable flair.

e. *transf.* In art, the representation of a subject in a realistic or other manner so as to convey its essential qualities.

1951 G. SUTHERLAND in *Listener* 6 Sept. 378/1, I feel that now we can perhaps enlarge the field of painting by setting our emotional paraphrases of reality—they themselves have been conceived more optically—within the ambience of optical reality. **1962** R. G. HAGGAR *Dict. Art Terms* 246/2 *Paraphrase.* The term is used by Graham Sutherland to explain the nature of his realist art, implying that he seeks to express the character and mood of the landscape or object which inspires him by other and general forms which do not constitute 'views'. **1962** *Listener* 26 July 134/1, I believe that in the case of a portrait, there are two ways of doing it. One..is the real paraphrase such as Picasso does. **1965** *New Statesman* 14 May 775/1 His line overstates and under-praises, as in the paraphrase of a Cranach nude.

paraphrase, *v.* Add: **1.** (Later examples of *fig.* use, *spec.* in art.) Cf. prec.

1961 D. COOPER *Work of Graham Sutherland* II. 14 He [*sc.* Sutherland] found that when he paraphrased what he saw he had captured more of 'the essence or the *gesture* of reality.' **1962** *Listener* 26 July 134/1, I might have wanted to paraphrase a landscape.

paraphrastical, *a.* Delete 'Now *rare* or *Obs.*' and add later examples.

1960 *Spectator* 30 Sept. 497 No don with simple-minded paraphrastical or reductive tastes [etc.]. **1977** *Archivum Linguisticum* VIII. 10 This paraphrastical relation..does not characterize the respective sentences of [examples] (67)–(72).

paraphrenia (pærăfrī·niă). [ad. F. *paraphrénie* f. PARA-[1] + Gr. φρήν mind + -IA[1].] A form of mental disorder; a term sometimes used to refer to mental disorders of the paranoid and schizophrenic varieties. Hence **paraphre·nic** *a.*

[**1846** DUNGLISON *Dict. Med. Sci.* (ed. 6) 552/1 *Paraphrénie*, insanity.] **1890** in BILLINGS *Med. Dict.* II. 290. **1917** C. R. PAYNE tr. *Pfister's Psychoanal. Method* 522 Dementia praecox (schizophrenia according to Bleuler, paraphrenia according to Freud). **1919** R. M. BARCLAY tr. *Kraepelin's Dementia Praecox & Paraphrenia* 2 It seems to me that the term 'paraphrenia', which is now no longer in common use, is in the meantime suitable as the name of the morbid forms thus delimited. **1934** WEBSTER, Paraphrenic. **1952** PURVES-STEWART & WORSTER-DROUGHT *Diagnosis of Nervous Dis.* (ed. 10) xxii. 737 The term paraphrenia is applied to those cases of paranoidal schizophrenia who retain their personality... Paraphrenic symptoms usually develop later in life than those of the ordinary paranoidal type, often as late as the menopause. **1958** *Daily Tel.* 30 June 10/4 The effect was found to be beneficial even with some of the seriously disturbed paraphrenic patients. **1962** HENDERSON & GILLESPIE *Text-bk. Psychiatry* (ed. 9) xii. 291 We would..suggest that the term paraphrenia should be discarded, as it does not serve any useful purpose. **1973** T. & R. MILLON *Abnormal Behav.* (1974) xvii. 381 The closest approximation to what we have termed paraphrenia may be found in the DSM-II descriptive text of 'schizophrenia, paranoid type'.

paraphysical: see *PARA-[1] I.

paraplegic, *a.* Add: **B.** *sb.* A person with paraplegia.

1890 W. JAMES *Princ. Psychol.* I. ii. 16 Paraplegics draw up their legs when tickled. **1950** *Time* 31 July 39/1 The story of war-wounded paraplegics makes a powerful and moving salute to the human spirit. **1970** C. HAMPTON *Philanthropist* iii. 26 Like realizing that Socialism is about as much use to this country as—a pogo-stick to a paraplegic. **1975** *Oxford Times* 12 Dec. 4/4 Her son had been a paraplegic since he injured his spine in a fall four years ago.

||**parapluie** (pæräplüi). [Fr.] An umbrella.

The word had wide literary currency in the 19th c.

1781 H. NEWDIGATE *Let.* 30 Sept. in A. E. Newdigate-Newdegate *Cheverels* (1898) iii. 35 It has poured all this Day..but with ye help of Pattins & Parapluies we got to ye Well. **1790** E. HELME tr. *Le Vaillant's Trav. Afr.* I. ii. 32 He that takes the East side of the mountain should carry his *paraplue* [sic], while he that takes the West would have occasion for his *parasol*. **1813** M. EDGEWORTH *Let.* 31 May (1971) 69 A shower came on and all the dressed groups were forced to take shelter under trees and parapluies. **1827** M. WILMOT *Jrnl.* 21 Aug. in *More Lett.* (1935) 291 Both wet, but not very bad as they had parapluis [*sic*]. **1847** *Punch* 6 Feb. 62/2 Our umbrellas..bear no announcement of some new pill... The *parapluie* is destined to become a tremendous vehicle for information. **1970** T. S. CRAWFORD *Hist. Umbrella* viii. 158 In the 1880s, the French author, Uzanne, was implying that certain French 'gentlemen' armed with *parapluies* were in the habit of preying on girls..on rainy evenings.

parapolitical: see *PARA-[1] I.

parapraxia (pærăpræ·ksiă). Also **parapra·xis**, *pl.* **-es.** [f. PARA-[1] + *-PRAXIA.] The faulty performance of an intended act; in psycho-analysis, a minor error said to reveal a subconscious motive.

1912 STEDMAN *Med. Dict.* (ed. 2) 657/2 *Parapraxia*, a condition..in which there is a defective performance of certain purposive acts. **1937** tr. *Freud's Gen. Sel. Wks.* i. 25 That group of everyday mental phenomena whose study has become a technical help for psycho-analysis. These are the bungling of acts (parapraxes) among normal men as well as among neurotics. **1953** M. CRITCHLEY *Parietal Lobes* v. 160 The patient, requested to make a particular movement, may do something quite different (parapraxia or parakinesis). **1959** *Observer* 1 Feb. 19/4 Such forces in scientists may produce quite unpredictable parapraxes in their experimental work. **1969** P. ANDERSON in Cockburn & Blackburn *Student Power* 261 No appeal to the conventions of drawing-room conversation can controvert the parapraxes of the couch. **1975** *Times Lit. Suppl.* 4 July 713/1 Have we recognized a bit of the Latin Mass?.. An astronomical reference? A Freudian parapraxis? **1975** *New Society* 11 Sept. 600/3 All too many malapropisms and misprints (or are they parapraxes? We get, for instance, 'He apostasises', followed by a quotation from Mill, for 'He apostrophises'.).

paraprofessional (pæ:răprofe·ʃənăl). [f. PARA-[1] + PROFESSIONAL *a.* (*sb.*).] A person without professional training to whom a particular aspect of a professional task is delegated. Also as *adj.*, of or pertaining to such a person.

1967 *Maclean's Mag.* May 64 There is some talk now of using para-professional help, trained on the job like internes. In some schools, mothers already are supervising lunch hours and study periods. **1968** *Bull. Council for Basic Educ.* (U.S.) June 2 The future student..would discover other quaint educational terms which are currently fashionable... 'Paraprofessional' is one, meaning a mother who helps the kindergarten teacher in putting on children's overshoes. **1971** *Harvard Business Rec.* Nov.–Dec. 39/2 The understandable reluctance of the physician to delegate tasks to paraprofessionals. **1972** *N.Y. Law Jrnl.* 22 Aug. 3/5 Another paraprofessional in our office is a retired police officer, presently responsible for..important trial preparation functions. **1974** *Yale Law Jrnl.* LXXXIII. 806 In many professions greater use of paraprofessional employees could help to solve problems in the delivery of professional services. **1975** *Publishers Weekly* 22 Sept. 89/1 A paraprofessional's view of how to survive breast cancer. **1976** *Maclean's Mag.* 17 May 26/1 Basford also stressed the need for developing native lawyers and para-professional court workers for small settlements. **1976** *Times Lit. Suppl.* 16 July 872/4 The personal service ideologies of medical professionals, paraprofessionals, indigenous non-professionals.

paraprotein(æmia: see *PARA-[1] 2 a.

parapsoriasis (pæ:răsorəi·ăsis). *Med.* [mod.L. (coined in Fr. by L. Brocq 1902, in *Ann. de Dermatol. et de Syphiligr.* III. 446), f. PARA-[1] + PSORIASIS.] Any of various rare chronic diseases of the skin which resemble psoriasis and are characterized by red scaly patches, resistance to treatment, and lack of subjective symptoms.

1906 DORLAND *Med. Dict.* (ed. 4) 526/1 *Parapsoriasis*, a chronic skin-disease resembling psoriasis and lichen. **1920** J. M. H. MACLEOD *Dis. of Skin* xxvii. 844 Brocq has divided the parapsoriasis group into three varieties namely: Parapsoriasis en gouttes, P. lichénoïde, P. en plaques. **1936** *Practitioners Libr. Med. & Surg.* X. vi. 617 Much of the confusion that has been occasioned by parapsoriasis is attributable to its widely differing clinical types and its multitudinous nomenclature. **1956** D. M. PILLSBURY et al. *Dermatol.* xxxii. 744 The original definition of parapsoriasis was a chronic eruption resembling psoriasis and having no acute manifestations. *Ibid.*, Lichenoid parapsoriasis is the parapsoriasis analogue of lichen planus. **1961** R. D. BAKER *Essent. Path.* xx. 540 There are other histologically identifiable noninfectious dermatoses in addition to psoriasis and pityriasis rosea. These include parapsoriasis, lichen planus and several other rare conditions. **1968** A. J. ROOK et al. *Textbk. Dermatol.* I. 804/2 The terms guttate parapsoriasis and varicelliform parapsoriasis are still frequently used as synonyms for pityriasis lichenoides chronica and pityriasis lichenoides acuta, respectively.

parapsychic(al: see *PARA-[1] I.

parapsycho·logy. [PARA-[1].] The science or study of phenomena which lie outside the sphere of orthodox psychology. Cf. *METAPSYCHICS *sb. pl.* Hence **parapsycholo·gical** *a.*, **parapsycholo·gically** *adv.*; **parapsycho·logist.**

1924 *Times Lit. Suppl.* 10 Jan. 27/2 Its inherent merit..renders the publication a noteworthy and welcome contribution to parapsychological literature. **1927** H. DRIESCH in C. Murchison *Case Psychical Belief* 164 The philosophic importance of Parapsychology. **1936** *Discovery* Dec. 396/1 The book [sc. *The Modern Dowser*]..should be useful to the would-be dowser and of interest to the parapsychologist. **1954** M. LOWRY *Let.* 10 May (1967) 369 You were so sporting as to write us parapsychologically suspecting some Lowry misery-grisery. **1957** RHINE & PRATT *Parapsychol.* i. 12 The term parapsychology was adapted from the German word *Parapsychologie*... It means the same as the older English expression, *psychical research*, and the French, *métapsychique*. **1967** A. WILSON *No Laughing Matter* I. 12 Alas for the limits of our parapsychological knowledge. **1973** *Daily Tel.* (Colour Suppl.) 30 Nov. 33/1 The Russians, who had previously persecuted parapsychologists as bourgeois deviationists, began to encourage research, doubtless with their space communications system in mind. **1975** *Sci. Amer.* Oct. 117/3 Whenever a major experiment, such as the SRI test of Targ's ESP machine, is a conspicuous failure, parapsychologists themselves become strongly motivated to give reasons for the failure. **1976** *Listener* 3 June 698/3 Once you postulate psychic communication..you are really committed to a whole new dimension... You can't sell parapsychology by the yard. **1977** *Church Times* 7 Apr. 6/1 They accept the reality of the 'Easter experience' understood psychologically, perhaps parapsychologically.

paraquat (pæ·răkwǫt, -kwæt). [f. PARA-[1] 2 b + QUAT(ERNARY *a.* and *sb.*

So called from the fact that the bond between the two pyridyl groups is in the *para* position with respect to their quaternary nitrogen atoms.]

Any salt, esp. the dichloride or dimethylsulphate (both crystalline and water-soluble), of the 1,1′-dimethyl-4,4′-bipyridylium ion, $(\text{—}C_5H_4\overset{+}{N}\cdot CH_3)_2$, a quick-acting contact herbicide that is rendered inactive by the soil.

1961 *Weed Abstr.* X. 572 *Paraquat di(methyl sulphate), previously PP.910, a new herbicide.* Publ. Plant Protection Ltd., 1961, pp. 6. Paraquat (1,1′-dimethyl-4,4′-bipyridylium) is the name given to the free radicle. Two salts are currently under test, the di(methyl sulphate) (PP.910) and the dichloride (PP.148)... Paraquat salts are very rapidly absorbed into the aerial parts of plants. **1962** *New Scientist* 6 Sept. 490/1 The active ingredient—paraquat—is a member of a family of herbicidal chemicals (quaternary salts of bipyridyls). **1962** *Listener* 15 Nov. 836/1 A new family of weed-killing substances based on 'paraquat' may herald a new agricultural revolution. Paraquat is almost a total weed-killer but is especially useful in killing grasses. **1965** *Economist* 5 June 1193/2 The 'Paraquat' herbicides, used in ploughless cultivation. **1968** *Times* 17 Dec. 10/5 The weedkiller paraquat..is highly poisonous but is swiftly broken down to harmless components by bacteria in the soil. **1972** *Country Life* 20 Jan. 169 The advent of paraquat was one of the most important developments in British farming in the 1960's. **1974** *Daily Tel.* 2 Feb. 1/1 The weedkiller paraquat has been officially declared a poison... Only registered pharmacists or firms will be able to sell paraquat, and only people engaged in agriculture or horticulture will be able to buy it. **1974** *Times* 2 Feb. 4/2 At least twenty deaths in Britain in the past 10 years are known to have been caused by paraquat. In almost all cases death followed the decanting of agricultural paraquat solutions into soft drink bottles. Granular preparations containing less than 5 per cent of paraquat salts are not affected by the new controls. **1977** *Jrnl. R. Soc. Arts* CXXV. 567/2 Paraquat acts..by killing the green top growth of all plants and is inactivated by soil.

pararammelsbergite, -religious: see *PARA-[1] 2 c, I.

para-rescue (pæ·răre:skiu). [f. *PARA-[3] + RESCUE *sb.*] A rescue carried out by a parachutist or parachutists. Chiefly *attrib.* and *Comb.*

1950 *N.Y. Times* 30 Jan. 20/2 A para-rescue crew is being held in readiness here and will be sent out at once if the ground party finds any trace of the missing transport. **1961** *Aeroplane* C. 458/1 A ground search party and 12 trained pararescue men are included. **1968** *Washington Post* 4 July A 11/6, I realized there was a guy in green bending over me... He was the chopper's para-rescueman. **1973** *Maclean's Mag.* July 58/3 Gathercole..told Mooddy to direct..a helicopter and a Hercules with a pararescue team, piloted by Captain Neil Toby.

para-rhyme, pararhyme (pæ·rărəim). [f. PARA-[1] + RHYME *sb.*] A half-rhyme, with the same consonant pattern but vowel variation.

In English poetry particularly associated with Wilfred Owen (1893–1918).

1931 E. BLUNDEN in W. Owen *Poems* 28 Having discovered and practised this para-rhyme, Owen became aware that it would serve him infinitely in the voicing of emotion and imagination... By means of it he creates remoteness, darkness, emptiness, shock, echo, the last word. **1939** *Eng. Stud.* XXI. 99 He [*sc.* Wilfred Owen] had invented what has been called pararhymes. Choosing words built upon the same framework of consonants but different vowels, he played with this blend of similarity and dissimilarity..placating the ear while disturbing it. **1951** [see *DISSONANTAL *a.*]. **1961** *Listener* 23 Nov. 863/1 Owen muted the rhythms of the romantics by the use of pararhyme. **1975** *Ibid.* 9 Jan. 69/1 [Wilfred] Owen had taught him pararhyme, but [Keith] Douglas uses both pararhyme and assonance.

pararosaniline, -sagittal: see *PARA-[1] 2 a, I.

parascending (pæ·răsendiŋ), *vbl. sb.* [f. *PARA-[3] + ASCENDING *vbl. sb.*] A sport in which participants, wearing open parachutes, are towed behind a vehicle to gain height before release for a conventional parachute descent, usu. towards a predetermined target area. Hence **pa·rascender,** one who takes part in this sport.

1970 *Policy, Organisation & Rules of Scout Assoc.* III. 169 In order to ensure the safe control of the sport of Parascending within the Scout Movement the following safety regulations must be applied. **1973** J. LUCAS *Big Umbrella* xiii. 137 The advent of multiple aerofoil parachutes has led to a challenging new kind of fun-jumping—parascending, which is enjoying increasing popularity among children as well as adults. Parascending is practised at sea as well as on land. One girl, towed by a motor boat, travelled more than half-way across the English Channel by parachute. On land, the parachutist takes off with the aid of a towing vehicle, such as a Land-Rover. *Ibid.*, Parascending made its first appearance in Britain in 1962, and has gained a firm foothold in the sporting world. **1973** *Daily Tel.* 28 Feb. 16/4 (*heading*) Parascenders split from parent group. *Ibid.*, Parascending..has become independent of the British Parachute Association. *Ibid.* 16 July 12/4 The parascender..chooses the point of release and tries to hit the centre of the target, five and a half inches across. **1975** *Valiant* 30 Aug. 1 Parascending is a new all-action sport. **1978** *Observer* (Colour Suppl.) 9 Apr. 43/4 Two helpers hold the parachute open, the Land-Rover moves forward and the parascender soars into the air.

parascience (pæ·răsəiˌĕns). [f. PARA-[1] + SCIENCE.] The study of phenomena assumed to be beyond the scope of scientific inquiry or for which no scientific explanation exists. So **pa:rascienti·fic** *a.*, **-sci·entist.**

1953 *Mind* LXII. 360 [The fallacy] that I know about thinking by 'observing' myself thinking, whereby thought is transformed into a paraphysical object studied by a parascience of introspection. **1961** *Times Lit. Suppl.* 1 Sept. 577/3 Time Travel, like hyperspace, is one of the classical Science-Fiction presumptions which, though abstruse mathematical discussion may give it para-scientific justification, is essentially a basis for fantasy. **1974** *Nature* 8 Nov. 129/1 So much of the interpreting, let alone the theorising, of parascientists and parathinkers is based on seemingly natural occurrences which either cannot be fully corroborated according to the rules of evidence, or cannot be properly repeated according to the rules of experiment. **1975** *Ibid.* 6 Nov. 22/1, I lumped them all [*sc.* telepathy, telekinesis, parapsychology, etc.] under the title 'parascience'. **1976** *Word 1971* XXVII. 77 As we know very little about human language (a fact..little known to most parascientists..), any approach toward its analysis may contribute something to our understanding of the subject.

parasexual (pærăse·ksiuăl), *a. Genetics.* [f. PARA-[1] + SEXUAL *a.*] Involving, exhibiting, or being a process by which recombination of genes from different individuals occurs without meiosis.

1954 G. PONTECORVO in *Proc. 9th Internat. Congr. Genetics* 192 In the last ten years, processes other than standard sexual reproduction, and yet resulting in recombination of hereditary properties, have come to light in microorganisms of widely different groups... The purpose of the present paper is to give a summary of the work which has led, in our Laboratory, to the discovery in the filamentous fungi of another of these mechanisms, which could be called 'para-sexual'. This mechanism, based on *mitotic* segregation and recombination, occurs side by side with a standard sexual cycle in one of the three species investigated. **1962** *Ann. Rev. Microbiol.* XVI. 39 Using parasexual processes, 40 markers have been assigned to eight linkage groups in *A[spergillus] nidulans.* **1962** G. DALLDORF *Fungi & Fungous Dis.* x. 135 Even in asexual fungi, recombinant types may arise through a parasexual process. **1970** J. WEBSTER *Introd. Fungi* 161 The occurrence of parasexual recombination explains how variation can occur in Fungi Imperfecti. **1974** *Nature* 27 Sept. 321/2 Genetic analysis of their development [*sc.* that of cellular slime moulds] has been hampered by the apparent absence of a true sexual cycle, although progress has been made in parasexual genetic analysis. **1977** P. B. & J. S. MEDAWAR *Life Sci.* iii. 39 In some bacteria..the sexual process is restricted to something that amounts to hardly more than the infection of one bacterium by nucleic acid from another—the 'parasexual' process that lies at the root of the enormously important phenomenon of bacterial transformation.

Hence **pa:rasexua·lity,** the parasexual process.

1959 *Mycologia* LI. 109 Somatic recombination or parasexuality..reassorts genetic characters of heterokaryotic components in a vegetative system to yield products that are comparable to the meiotic products of the sexual process. **1974** *Nature* 18 Jan. 142/1 Using an improved version of the methods employing parasexuality.., we have selected axenic resegregants carrying various markers from non-axenic strains.

parashoot (pæ·răʃūt), *sb. rare.* [Alteration of PARACHUTE *sb.* after SHOOT *sb.*[1], SHOOT *v.*] (See quot.)

1940 [see *CHUTIST, 'CHUTIST].

parashot (pæ·răʃǫt). [f. *PARA-[3] + SHOT *sb.*[1]] In the war of 1939–45, a member of the British Home Guard whose task was to shoot down enemy parachutists. Also *attrib.* So **pa·ra-shoot** *v. trans.*; **pa·rashooter.**

1940 *Star* 14 May 8/5 (*caption*) 'What are you doing with that gun?' 'I'm practising-to-parashoot Germans!' **1940** *Daily Mirror* 17 May 5/2 Over a quarter of a million had applied to join Britain's parashooters by midnight on Wednesday, the War Office stated last night. **1940** Parashot [see *PARATROOPS *sb. pl.*]. **1940** *Star* 22 May 8/2 Clubs' part in fight against parachute troops... The appeal for parashooters has brought rifle shooting into the news. Clubs are offering free instruction to applicants. **1940** *Economist* 8 June 1005/2 Air-raids will precede invasion; and the transfer of wardens and other civil defence workers to become Ironsides and parashooters..should be stopped immediately. **1940** *New Yorker* 29 June 46/3 A movement to provide parashots with hand grenades. **1941** A. CHRISTIE *N or M?* vi. 85 I've got to go to a meeting about this Parashot business, raising a corps of local volunteers. **1942** A. M. LOW *Parachutes* p. x, Parashot, the word coined by the newspapers in the summer of 1940 to describe gentlemen with shotguns seeking enemy parachutists. **1944** *Ourselves in Wartime* 129 The village men lined up..to join the local Defence Volunteers. The 'Parashooters' they called themselves in those days, when everyone thought the enemy might drop on us from the sky just in the same way as he had done over the Low Countries.

parasitæmia (pæ:răsəitī·miă). *Path.* Also (chiefly *U.S.*) **-emia.** [f. PARASIT(E *sb.* + Gr. αἷμα blood: see -IA[1].] The presence of demonstrable parasites in the circulation.

1947 DORLAND & MILLER *Med. Dict.* (ed. 21) 1066/2 *Parasitemia*, the presence of parasites (especially malarial parasites) in the blood. **1956** *Nature* 21 Jan. 133/1 In December 1952, N'Dama 151 was challenged with a strain of *T[rypanosoma] vivax*..; a low-grade intermittent parasitæmia persisted until August 1953, after which time no parasites were detected in the blood. **1972** *Ann. Trop. Med. & Parasitol.* LXVII. 390 A direct counting technique for estimating high parasitaemias of *Babesia argentina* is described. **1973** B. J. WILLIAMS *Evolution & Human Origins* v. 80/2 He confirmed Beet's observation that the incidence of parasitemia was less in *AS* individuals than it was in *AA* individuals.

parasite, *sb.* Add: **4. parasite drag** *Aeronaut.*, the drag of all parts of an aircraft other than that induced by the lift or due to the lifting surface (quot. 1927 represents a broader use); **parasite (jet) fighter** *Aeronaut.*, an aircraft carried by and operating from another aircraft; **parasite resistance** *Aeronaut.* = **parasite drag.*

1927 V. W. PAGE *Mod. Aircraft* (1928) iv. 134 The parasite drag results from friction of the air on the parts of the airplane, including the wings, tail, fuselage, landing gear, etc., and from the eddies set up by these parts when in motion. **1934** *Jrnl. R. Aeronaut. Soc.* XXXXIII. 459 For aeroplanes of normal design, the ratio of induced drag to parasite drag was very low at high speeds. **1958** *Guided Missiles* (U.S. Dept. Air Force) ii. 24/2 Both parasite and induced drag vary as the square of the velocity. **1965** C. N. VAN DEVENTER *Introd. Gen. Aeronaut.* iv. 59/1 The resistance of parts that do not contribute to lift is called parasite drag. **1948** *Daily Progress* (Charlottesville, Va.) 2 Jan. 10/1 A new jet fighter plane is expected soon to start and end a flight high in the sky for the first time in history. This is the McDonnell XP-85, known as a 'parasite' fighter because it is based on a larger craft. **1948** *Shell Aviation News* No. 121. 6/3 The Air Force has announced the building by McDonnell of a parasite jet fighter..designed to be carried in the front bomb-bay of Consolidated's B-36. It has no landing gear and is launched and picked-up by means of a retractable hook which engages in an eye on the mother plane. **1977** *New Scientist* 25 Aug. 489/4 In the immediate post-war years the US Army Air Force test launched the diminutive McDonnell XF-85 Goblin parasite fighter from the bomb bay of a Boeing B-29 bomber. **1918** WEBSTER Add., Parasite resistance. **1921** *Flight* XIII. 509/2 Great reduction in parasite resistance..is brought about by the cantilever construction. **1929** *Aircraft Engineering* Mar. 10 Giant seaplanes are another story... Aerodynamically they are disappointingly full of parasite resistance.

parasite, *v.* Add: **1.** (Later example.)

1932 [see *GAZOOMPH *v.*].

2. (Later examples.) Also *fig.*

1882 *Amer. Naturalist* XVI. 150, I had the opportunity of examining a larva..parasited by an allied species. **1963** *Guardian* 14 June 10/2 The cuckoo bees Psithyrus..parasite the Bombex. **1968** *Daily Tel.* (Colour Suppl.) 8 Nov. 12/3 Viruses are incomplete cells. They exist by parasiting 'proper' cells, and getting into them. **1969** K. GILES *Death cracks Bottle* vii. 83 The only worry I had was that he might be parasiting the business stone dry. **1976** *Eastern Daily Press* (Norwich) 19 Nov. 12/2 Beds of pelargoniums ..heavily parasited by this rust.

parasitic, *a.* Add: **3. c.** Applied to trades: † (*a*) see quot. 1909; (*b*) non-productive.

1909 *Q. Rev.* Jan. 83 The so-called parasitic trades—that is, trades in which it is alleged that workers who have incomes or maintenances derived from sources other than their wages underbid those who live entirely on their wages. **1926** *Spectator* 19 June 1032/1 Far too much still goes in what we may call parasitic middlemen's profits.

4. Applied to unwanted subsidiary phenomena and effects in physical apparatus, esp. in electronic devices and electrical machinery.

1889 *Telegraphic Jrnl.* 1 Nov. 497/1 If..the iron core were solid, the E.M.Fs. induced in it would..cause enormous currents to flow... They are currents which could not be utilised... By suitably dividing the iron core..these so-called parasitic currents may be rendered almost negligible. **1921** *Wireless World* 15 Oct. 437/1 The..parasitic noise which abounds in amplifiers wired on the usual principle. **1927** V. W. PAGÉ *Mod. Aircraft* (1928) vi. 206 (*heading*) Reduction of parasitic resistance. **1943** F. E. TERMAN *Radio Engineers' Handbk.* VI. 498 Parasitic oscillations..are very likely to occur when large tubes are employed because of the long leads, large interelectrode capacities, and relatively high values of transconductance involved. **1958** NAYLER & SAUNDERS *Handbk. Aircraft Industry* viii. 125 In modern aircraft the 'parasitic' drag due to extraneous items..has been largely eliminated. **1959** *Listener* 25 June 1109/1 They are electric insulators and therefore do not carry parasitic electric currents (so-called eddy currents) when their magnetization changes rapidly. **1967** *Electronics* 6 Mar. 251/1 With discrete components, parasitic capacitance from the diodes' packages increased the over-all capacitance. **1972** *Sci. Amer.* Aug. 19/2 The Wankel operates with less friction than a conventional engine... The lower friction alone means decreased parasitic losses and can be translated directly into an increase in fuel economy.

5. *parasitic bronchitis* = *HOOSE; *parasitic gastritis, gastro-enteritis,* in cattle, horses, or other domesticated animals, a gastric inflammation caused by parasitic nematode worms.

1925 *Vet. Rec.* 19 Dec. 1137/1 Parasitic bronchitis is also known as husk, hoose, verminous bronchitis, or paper skin. It is a bronchial irritation, arising from the presence in the air passages of nematode parasites. **1942** *Skandinavisk Veterinär-Tidskrift* XXXII. 488 (*title*) On parasitic gastritis in the horse. **1947** *New Biol.* III. 49 The inflammation of the alimentary tract of sheep (and of that of other farm animals also) which is caused by parasitic roundworms is called by the veterinarian parasitic gastro-enteritis. **1951** *Vet. Rec.* 22 Dec. 864/2 The literature presents certain references to the occurrence of parasitic bronchitis in adult cattle. **1965** *Ibid.* 9 Oct. 1196/1 Field investigations into parasitic gastro-enteritis in the west of Scotland showed that *Ostertagia ostertagi* was the predominant parasite. *Ibid.*, In Great Britain, outbreaks of bovine parasitic gastritis have been reported for many years. **1967** W. R. KELLY *Vet. Clin. Diagnosis* vi. 27/2 (*caption*) Moderate degree of dyspnoea in a yearling heifer suffering from parasitic bronchitis.

6. Applied to an aerial that is not electrically connected to a transmitter or receiver.

1936 L. S. PALMER *Wireless Engin.* xii. 469 Antenna B is not directly energised from the power source, but receives its current through the induction and radiation field of the directly energised antenna A. Antenna B..is sometimes called a parasitic antenna. **1947** C. E. TIBBS *Frequency Modulation Engin.* vi. 114 When the parasitic aerial is at resonance.., and the separation between it and the energised aerial is held at 0·1λ, maximum radiation is in the direction of the parasitic aerial, which is then called a 'director'. **1970** J. EARL *Tuners & Amplifiers* v. 113 When a reflector and directors (called parasitic elements because they are not electrically connected to the dipole) are added to the system the centre impedance of the dipole falls well below 75Ω.

B. *sb. pl. Electronics.* Parasitic oscillations.

1943 F. E. TERMAN *Radio Engineers' Handbk.* VI. 498 Parasitics cause reduction in the power at the desired mode of operation, introduce spurious frequencies, give rise to distortion in linear amplifiers and modulators,..etc. **1967** *Electronics* 6 Mar. 177/2 (Advt.), 'Strays', 'streaks', 'parasitics'..you may forget them all.

parasitism. 1. (Further examples.)

1974 *Times* 19 June 16/5 One of them [*sc.* Russian Jews], Vitali Rubin, was..told that he had 15 days to get a job, otherwise he would be tried for parasitism, a charge entailing a heavy prison sentence. **1975** *Nature*

17 Apr. 554/3 Methods mentioned include the issue of call-up papers for retraining in the Soviet Army.., prosecution for 'parasitism' (being without employment, although the scientists concerned have been deprived of their jobs as a result of applications for exit visas), [etc.]. **1976** *Ibid.* 3 June 363/1 Some 20 scientists called in to regional police headquarters in Moscow were told that if they did not commence working within two weeks they would be charged under the 'parasitism' law, which covers such offences as prostitution, drug addiction, and alcoholism.

parasitization (pærăsitəizēⁱ·ʃən, pærăsəit-əizēⁱ·ʃən). [f. PARASITIZ(E *v.* + -ATION.] The infestation of a plant or animal by a parasite.

1932 J. S. HUXLEY *Probl. Relative Growth* i. 38 Parasitization of Inachus with Sacculina..actually increases the growth-ratio of the female abdomen. **1946** *Nature* 3 Aug. 174/1 A team of workers is co-operating on different aspects of the work, namely, rate of growth, parasitization-rates and mortality. **1950** *Hilgardia* XIX. 422 There was a slight drop in the population (probably due to *Apanteles* parasitization). **1953** *New Biol.* XIV. 100 Parasitization of the larvae [of wheat blossom midges] does not prevent them from feeding. **1962** GORDON & LAVOIPIERRE *Entomol. for Students of Med.* xxxii. 201 A few days after parasitisation has occurred the site occupied in the skin by the larva assumes the appearance of a boil-like swelling. **1975** *Nature* 29 May 403/1, I examined the effects of parasitisation on tumorigenesis by parasitising *vg tu*²⁸ larvae.

parasitize, *v.* Add: Now usu. with pronunc. (pæ·răsitəiz). Also *intr.* Also *fig.* (Later examples.)

1915 W. B. HERMS *Med. & Vet. Entomol.* ii. 7 That an animal is parasitized does not necessarily involve it in death. **1922** W. M. WHEELER *Social Life Insects* v. 197 Our bodies, our domestic animals and food plants, dwellings, stored foods, clothing and refuse support such numbers of greedy organisms, and we parasitize on one another to such an extent that the biologist marvels how the race can survive. *Ibid.* 198 The thoroughly parasitized host must abandon all hope of being an end in itself. **1934** J. S. HUXLEY *Sci. Res. & Social Needs* vii. 111 New suburbs, almost all in ribbon development, have been allowed to parasitize the road. **1955** *Sci. Amer.* Apr. 98/3 Viruses.. used to be thought of solely as foreign intruders—strangers to the cells they invade and parasitize. **1956** T. W. M. CAMERON *Parasites* 235 In some cases (*Leishmania*) the phagocytic cells themselves are parasitized. **1970** *Nature* 25 July 382/1 Mice were infected with..erythrocytes parasitized with the NK 65 strain of *Plasmodium berghei.* **1974** *Sci. Amer.* Oct. 98/3 The estrildid finches parasitized by these two related widow-bird species are also two species of the same genus, *Uraeginthus.* **1977** *N.Z. Jrnl. Agric.* Jan. 21/3, 90 per cent of the caterpillars were parasitised.

parasitoid (pæ·răsitoid), *sb.* and *a.* [a. mod. L. *Parasitoïdea* (O. M. Reuter *Lebensgewohnheiten und Instinkte der Insekten* (1913) v. 53), f. PARASIT(E *sb.* + -OID.] An insect, esp. one belonging to the orders Hymenoptera or Diptera, whose larva lives as an internal parasite which eventually kills its host. Also as *adj.*, of or pertaining to an insect of this kind.

1922 W. M. WHEELER *Social Life Insects* ii. 46 Recent studies of the parasitic, or as I prefer to call them with O. M. Reuter, the 'parasitoid' Hymenoptera. *Ibid.*, The parasitoids exhibit another peculiarity. **1941** J. S. HUXLEY *Uniqueness of Man* v. 135 There exist fully formed adult insects—a beetle or two, and several parasitoid wasplike creatures—of smaller bulk than the human ovum. **1971** *Nature* 12 Feb. 508/1 Many viruses, bacteria, fungi and insect parasitoids can attack insects. **1972** L. E. CHADWICK tr. *Linsenmaier's Insects of World* 300/1 Since most 'parasites' of the Hymenoptera destroy the host, they are not true parasites. Instead they are more accurately called parasitic predators or parasitoids. *Ibid.*, Although it is important to know the distinction between parasites and parasitoids, in actual practice even entomologists tend to use the word parasite for both. **1974** *Nature* 22 Feb. 572/1 A parasitoid fly was suspected as the cause of death.

parasitological, *a.* Add: (Later examples.)

1921 H. G. PONTING *Gt. White South* 115 On the south side..was Dr. Atkinson's parasitological laboratory. **1962** J. D. SMYTH *Introd. Animal Parasitol.* ii. 8 The question of the part played by environmental conditions in controlling the development of the parasite is..one scarcely touched on by modern parasitological research. **1971** *Nature* 16 July 209/2 Both these organisms have been widely used in parasitological research.

Hence **parasitolo·gically** *adv.*

1976 *Nature* 15 Apr. 608/2 Our experimental group consisted of 100 male and female white laboratory mice, strain ICR, from 3 weeks to 3 months old, which had been standardised both microbiologically and parasitologically (specific pathogen-free). **1977** *Lancet* 21 May 1095/1 Stool samples can be negative for *Giardia lamblia* even in parasitologically confirmed cases of giardiasis.

parasitopolis (pæ:răsəitǫ·pǒlis). [f. Gr. παράσιτο-ς PARASITE *sb.* + πόλις city; see -POLIS.] A parasite city; a city that is over-developed and economically non-productive.

1927 P. GEDDES in A. Defries *Interpreter* viii. 199 In all the great cities..you have in progress the history of Rome in its decline and fall. Beginning as Polis—the city, it developed into Metro-polis—the capital; but this into Megalo-polis—or city overgrown... Next, with its ample supply of 'bread and shows' (nowadays called 'budget') it was Parasito-polis, with degeneration accordingly. Thus, all manner of diseases, bodily, mental, moral: hence Patholo-polis, and finally,..Necro-polis—city of the dead. **1945** L. MUMFORD in *Archit. Rev.* XCVII. 7/1 But one outstanding fact must first be frankly acknowledged: the Parasitopolis of the late nineteenth century has already become the spectral Necropolis of the mid-twentieth century. **1961** —— *City in Hist.* viii. 234 Parasitopolis had become Pathopolis; and even further, Pathopolis had turned into Psycho-pathopolis, with a Nero or a Caligula as absolute ruler.

parasol, *sb.* Add: **2. b.** An aircraft having wings raised above the fuselage. Also *attrib.* and *Comb.*

1914 *Aeroplane* 29 Jan. 110/1 M. Gilbert has been flying another 'parasol', 60-h.p. *Ibid.*, The 'parasol' monoplane ..has been fitted with a new..Gnome [engine]. **1930** *Flight* 8 Aug. 896/1 The machine used by Lombardi was a Fiat 'A.S.1' parasol monoplane. **1940** *Jrnl. R. Aeronaut. Soc.* XLIV. 661 Outboard tanks were employed with the Junkers J.21/22 parasol fighters. **1952** A. Y. BRAMBLE *Air-Plane Flight* xi. 161 The high-wing type was sometimes known as the 'parasol' type, especially when the wing was carried on struts rising above the main structure of the fuselage. **1969** K. MUNSON *Pioneer Aircraft 1903–14* 131/1 A few R.E.P. parasol-winged monoplanes were in French and R.N.A.S. service during the early part of the war.

para-state (pæ·răstēⁱt). [f. PARA-¹ + STATE *sb.* IV.] An institution or body which takes on some of the roles of civil government or political authority; an agency through which the state works indirectly. Also *attrib.* Hence **parasta·tal** *a.* and *sb.*

1959 *Listener* 5 Feb. 245/2 He [*sc.* Lenin] described the proletarian dictatorship as a sort of a para-state.., a state progressively dissolving in society and working towards its own extinction. **1966** *Economist* 24 Sept. 1233/3 Since the [Tunisian] government is only too keen to load off its shares.., there is developing a group of what are called para-state industries, with both government and private capital. **1969** *Nationalist* (Dar es Salaam) 25 Jan. 1/4 The Vice-President told the workers that the aim of opening TANU branches in industries and parastatal organisations was to strengthen the political role of the Party. **1969** *Reporter* (Nairobi) 13 June 20/3, 65 per cent of parastatal investment would also come from within the country. **1971** *Guardian Weekly* 23 Oct. 6 The parastatals were still almost wholly outside central control. **1971** P. A. ALLUM *Politics & Society Post-War Naples* (1973) i. 38 The public administration groups a plethora of institutions and para-state agencies...prefecture, field offices of ministries, municipalities, state banks (Bank of Naples) ISVEIMER, IRI, ENI, etc. **1974** J. WHITE tr. *Poulantzas's Fascism & Dictatorship* III. i. 74 A whole series of hidden parallel networks, operating as the channels of real communication of real power and decisions, varying from the emergence of pressure groups and private militia..to the setting up of virtual para-state networks. **1974** *Daily News* (Tanzania) 13 Sept. 5/6 Employees of hotels, bars and parastatal organisations in Shinyanga Region who fail to enrol in adult education courses by the end of this month will be sacked. **1976** *Nigerian Herald* 20 July 5/1 In terms of depth of investigation and the sheer volume of assignment, the Odje Commission of Inquiry, which probed parastatals in the Bendel State, is remarkably unprecedented.

parasymbiosis (pæ:răsimbəiōᵘ·sis, -biōᵘ·sis). *Biol.* [a. G. *parasymbiose* (W. Zopf 1897, in *Ber. Deutsch. Bot. Ges.* XV. 90), f. PARA-¹ + SYMBIOSIS.] The relationship between a free-living lichen and an organism (either a fungus or another lichen) which infests it and establishes a symbiotic relationship with the algæ of the lichen. So **pa:rasymbio·tic** *a.*, of or pertaining to such an association; **para-sy·mbiont**, an organism involved in an association of this kind.

1897 *Jrnl. R. Microsc. Soc.* 228 Prof. W. Zopf finds fresh confirmation of his theory that many of the fungi which grow on lichens are not true parasites, but have a kind of symbiotic relationship to the host, which he terms parasymbiosis, the hyphæ of the 'parasite' enveloping the algal constituent of the lichen, without inflicting any injury upon it. **1921** A. L. SMITH *Lichens* vi. 264 Zopf found several instances of such parasymbiosis in his study of fungal parasites. *Ibid.*, There occur in lichens, certain parasites classed as fungi which at an early stage are more or less parasymbionts of the host. *Ibid.* 265 Tobler has added two more of these parasymbiotic species on the border line between lichens and fungi. **1952** Parasymbiont [see *LICHENIZED *ppl. a.* b]. **1967** M. E. HALE *Biol. Lichens* x. 155 This [*sc.* the order Lecanorales] includes..the parasymbiotic lichen fungi. *Ibid.*, Other parasymbionts are classified under appropriate fungal families.

pa:rasympathe·tic, *a. Anat.* [PARA-¹.] Of, pertaining to, or designating one of the major divisions of the autonomic nervous system, distinguished from the sympathetic system by its place of origin, its use of acetylcholine as a transmitter, and its general association with rest and recuperation rather than alertness. Also *absol.*, the parasympathetic system.

1905 J. N. LANGLEY in *Jrnl. Physiol.* XXXIII. 403, I use the word para-sympathetic for the cranial and sacral autonomic systems. **1920** *Gray's Anat.* (ed. 21) 768 The peripheral part [of the autonomic system] is..arranged in two subsidiary systems—the parasympathetic system and the sympathetic system. **1925** *Jrnl. Physiol.* LX. p. ix, The absence of effect of pilocarpine and atropine on muscle tonus indicates that the parasympathetics do not control the tonus of voluntary muscle. **1940** [see *MUSCARINE]. **1946** *Nature* 10 Aug. 207/1 Most internal organs have a double nerve supply of which one is excitatory (sympathetic) and the other inhibitory (parasympathetic), that is, they work against each other. **1948** A. BRODAL *Neurol. Anat.* xi. 340 From the anatomical arrangement of the sympathetic and parasympathetic it is also to be inferred that the former must be involved predominantly as a whole in diffuse reactions, affecting the entire organism, whereas in the latter, the structural organization permits more restricted, localized effects. **1954** S. DUKE-ELDER *Parsons' Dis. Eye* (ed. 12) v. 68 A second type of drug acts as a parasympathetic stimulant. **1967** G. M. WYBURN et al. *Conc. Anat.* iii. 92/1 Branches from the sympathetic and the vagus (the parasympathetic) form plexuses in relation to the arch of the aorta and the bifurcation of the trachea. **1968** PASSMORE & ROBSON *Compan. Med. Stud.* I. xxiv. 90/2 Overall parasympathetic activity corresponds roughly to the picture of an old man asleep after dinner, i.e. slow heart, small pupils, constricted bronchioles and noisy breathing, salivary secretion, vigorous peristalsis. **1972** J. A. WILSON *Princ. Animal Physiol.* xi. 416/2 That part of the autonomic nervous system originating in the thorocolumbar portion of the spinal cord is the sympathetic division; that part originating in the other three segments of the central nervous system is the parasympathetic system. **1977** D. MORRIS *Manwatching* 166 Whenever we are called upon to perform some intense, violent activity, the sympathetic system takes over and pours adrenalin into the blood, temporarily dominating the keep-calm parasympathetic system.

Hence **pa:rasympathe·tically** *adv.*

1957 *Jrnl. Nerv. & Mental Dis.* CXXV. 463/1 For the most part a situation in which the sympathetic nervous activity is high inhibits parasympathetically innervated consummatory reactions. **1978** A. WINGATE in M. U. Barnard et al. *Human Sexuality for Health Professionals* iii. 18 The first phase [of the male sexual response]..is parasympathetically mediated.

pa:rasympatholy·tic, *a.* (*sb.*) *Pharm.* [f. prec. + -O + *-LYTIC.] Annulling or opposing the physiological action of the parasympathetic nervous system. Also as *sb.*, a substance which does this.

1949 *Jrnl. Pharmacol. & Exper. Therap.* XCV. 53 There is need for a simple *in vivo* assay for the study of parasympatholytic agents. **1960** A. BURGER *Medicinal Chem.* (ed. 2) liii. 1147/2 Diphemanil methylsulfate is a parasympatholytic agent which blocks the cholinergic impulse to the eccrine sweat glands. **1969** *Scand. Jrnl. Gastroenterol.* IV. 641/1 The following parasympatholytics were applied: atropine, Isopropamide.., and Gastrixone. **1973** *Jrnl. Pharmacol. & Exper. Therap.* CLXXXVII. 293/2 The mechanism for this parasympatholytic augmentation of dopamine's pressor and inotropic actions is not clear and may involve an interaction between dopamine and acetylcholine within the central nervous system.

parasy:mpathomime·tic, *a.* (*sb.*) *Pharm.* [f. as prec. + -O + MIMETIC *a.* (and *sb.*).] Producing physiological effects characteristic of the action of the parasympathetic nervous system by promoting stimulation of parasympathetic nerves. Also as *sb.*, a substance which does this, either by mimicking the action of acetylcholine or by interfering with that of cholinesterase.

[**1940** *Q. Jrnl. Med.* IX. 239 Observations on the effect of parasympathetic-mimetic drugs have been made.] **1946** *Jrnl. Pharmacol. & Exper. Therap.* LXXXVII. 31 A range of doses of eleven parasympathomimetic drugs (acetylcholine, mecholyl, [etc.]..) was administered subcutaneously. **1968** W. C. BOWMAN et al. *Textbk. Pharmacol.* xxviii. 702 In addition to their important muscarinic actions, many parasympathomimetic drugs exert other actions at different sites. For example, acetylcholine itself..stimulates ganglion cells and striated muscle. **1972** *Exper. Neurol.* XXXIV. 355 (*heading*) The central activity of parasympathomimetics on gastric secretory function. **1974** *Ann. Internal Med.* LXXXI. 49/1 All parasympathomimetic maneuvers and drugs affect arrhythmias by causing local release of acetylcholine in cardiac tissues. **1974** M. C. GERALD *Pharmacol.* v. 103 Analogous terms are used for drugs modifying cholinergic activity, that is, cholinergic or parasympathomimetic agents and cholinergic blocking agents.

parasynapsis to **-tacamite:** see *PARA-¹.

parataxic (pærătæ·ksik), *a. Psychol.* [f. PARA- I + TAX(IS 6 + -IC.] A term used mainly by H. S. Sullivan to describe the mode in which subconscious attitudes or emotions affect overt interpersonal relationships. See also *PROTOTAXIC *a.*, *SYNTAXIC *a.*

1938 H. S. SULLIVAN in *Psychiatry* I. 125/2 A *parataxic* situation, a much more complicated entity in that two of the *four* or more persons now concerned, while illusory, are real antagonists to any collaboration of A and Mrs. A. Our Mr. A has become multiplex. **1945** P. MULLAHY in *Ibid.* VIII. 184/1 With the development of the parataxic mode of symbol activity, the original undifferentiated wholeness, oneness, of experience is broken. **1961** J. A. C. BROWN *Freud & Post-Freudians* ix. 168 By a process of what Sullivan describes as 'parataxic distortion' one may attribute to others traits taken from significant people in one's past. **1970** HINSIE & CAMPBELL *Psychiatric Dict.*

(ed. 4) 222/2 One way to learn what is true and what is parataxic in thinking or feelings about another is to compare one's evaluations with those of others. **1973** *Jrnl. Genetic Psychol.* CXXIII. 338 The extent to which a person distorts his perception of the norm for self-acceptance by attributing his own high or low acceptance of self to the average person is termed 'parataxic distortion'.

paratectonic to **-terminal:** see *PARA-[1].

paratha (parāthā·). [Hindi *parāṭhā*.] In India and among Indian communities outside India: a variety of unleavened bread fried in butter, ghee, etc., on a griddle.

1935 M. MORPHY *Recipes of All Nations* 691 *Paratha* (Indian bread)..as Chapati, but the dough..is..fried in butter on the griddle. **1960** R. P. JHABVALA *Householder* i. 46 Her eyes were modestly lowered and she appeared intent on preparing dough for parathas. **1964** S. M. SADEEK *Windswept & Other Stories* (1969) 13 The wife and two daughters of the East Indian headman were busy with the cooking of the curry-mutton..the rice and paratha rotie. **1971** *Hindustan Times Weekly Rev.* (New Delhi) 4 Apr. p. iv/5 Have you ever tried mashing up left-over *gobhi, aloo,* or *matar bhujia* and using it as a filling for stuffed *parathas*? **1977** *New Society* 3 Feb. 242/1 While others were still wondering whether chapatis were folded or flat, I was boldly ordering poppadoms and parathas.

parathecial, -ium: see *PARA-[1] I.

parathion (pærăþəi·ǫn). [f. the elements PARA-[1] 2 b and THIO- in its chemical names + *-n.*] An organophosphorus insecticide which is also highly toxic to mammals and is available in commercial preparations similar to those of malathion; diethyl-*p*-nitrophenylthiophosphate, $(C_2H_5O)_2 \cdot PS \cdot O \cdot C_6H_4NO_2$.

1947 *Jrnl. Econ. Entomol.* XL. 915/2 (*heading*) Parathion for control of green peach aphid. *Ibid.*, Parathion may be formulated into emulsions, dusts and wettable powders. **1953** *Sci. Amer.* July 62/2 A slow-acting insecticide—e.g., parathion—may have a devastating effect on a bee colony. **1958** E. HYAMS *Taking it Easy* II. 198, I noticed Red Spider mite on some newly-budded peach trees... I went to my small store of parathion. **1960** *Jrnl. R. Hort. Soc.* LXXXV. III. 127 A parathion smoke was used and..200 dead beetles were collected from the floor and staging. **1970** *Daily Tel.* 22 Aug. 3/1 On the fruit and vegetable farms of California..it is not uncommon for workers coming in contact with parathion to faint, become nauseated, or go into convulsions. **1977** *Jrnl. R. Soc. Arts* CXXV. 566/2 In 1950 parathion, the first of many powerful organic phosphorus materials, gave positive control of Red Spider Mites.

parathormone (pærăþǭ·ɹmōᵘn). *Physiol.* [Blend of *parath(yroid* (s.v. PARA-[1] I) and *HORMONE.] A polypeptide hormone secreted by the parathyroid glands of higher vertebrates, which increases the amount of calcium in the blood by its action on bones, kidneys, and gut.

Registered in the U.S.A. as a proprietary name, although its protection lapsed in 1966.

1925 *Official Gaz.* (U.S. Patent Office) 17 Nov. 591/1 Eli Lilly & Company, Indianapolis, Ind. Filed Oct. 1, 1925. *Para-thor-mone*... Medicine or Pharmaceutical Preparation. Claims use since Sept. 1, 1925. **1926** *Encycl. Brit.* III. 147/2 Collip prepared from the [parathyroid] glands an extract, parathormone, which is capable, when injected subcutaneously into parathyroidectomised dogs, of promptly removing the symptoms of tetany. **1948** MARTIN & HYNES *Clinical Endocrinol.* v. 101 Parathormone is a protein substance obtainable in solid, but not crystalline, form by acid extraction of fresh parathyroid tissue. **1965** LEE & KNOWLES *Animal Hormones* vi. 104 It would appear that the rate of secretion of parathormone is controlled by the level of the blood calcium.

pa:rathyroide·ctomy. [f. *parathyroid* s.v. PARA-[1] I in Dict. and Suppl. + *-ECTOMY.] Excision of the parathyroids, or a portion of them.

1903 *Med. News* (Philadelphia) 31 Oct. 823/2 Various detailed studies of the results of complete and partial parathyroidectomy have..been made. **1921** *Times Lit. Suppl.* 12 Nov. 898/2 The primary effect in both parathyroidectomy and guanidine poisoning is an abnormal breakdown of tissue proteins. **1971** *New Scientist* 19 Aug. 437/3, I recently had a parathyroidectomy, which was followed, 48 hours later, by acute hypocalcaemia. The effects of this were according to the text book—tingling limbs and fuzzy-headedness. **1974** F. ELLIS in R. M. Kirk et al. *Surgery* viii. 171 Correction of calcium metabolism defects by the use of vitamin D for rickets and osteomalacia, and by parathyroidectomy for hyperparathyroidism.

Hence **pa:rathyroide·ctomize** *v. trans.*, to deprive of the parathyroids; **pa:rathyroide·ctomized** *ppl. a.*

1903 *Med. News* (Philadelphia) 31 Oct. 823/2 The condition into which these parathyroidectomized animals fall after a few days is..as follows. **1922** *Endocrinology* VI. 222 When a litter of eight pure black rats 75 days old..was parathyroidectomized all but two survived the 48 hour period. **1965** LEE & KNOWLES *Animal Hormones* vi. 107 In the female duck oestrogen administration leads to an elevation of the blood calcium, but it is without effect in the parathyroidectomized animal. **1972** *Jrnl. Endocrinol.* LIV. 107 Bone loss did not occur in parathyroidectomized dogs.

paratomous, *a.* Add: **2.** (See s.v. *PARA-[1] I.)

paratomy: see *PARA-[1] I.

paratonal (pærătōᵘ·năl), *a. Linguistics.* [f. PARA-[1] + TONAL *a.*] Ancillary to tone; *spec.* of or pertaining to a range of features, excluding pitch, associated with a particular tone.

1966 H. L. SHORTO in C. E. Bazell *In Memory of J. R. Firth* 399 The paratonal register distinction is broadly similar to that described for Cambodian by Henderson. Its exponents are distributed throughout the articulatory complex but exclude pitch features.

paratone (pæ·rătōᵘn). *Linguistics.* [f. PARA-[1] + TONE *sb.* I.] A postulated tonal unit of a sequence of simple tone-groups, in which information concerning sentence-type, the speaker's attitude, etc. is conveyed. Also *attrib.* Hence **paratona·lity; paratoni·city.**

1973 A. FOX in *Archivum Linguisticum* IV. 21 As far as the paratone-group is concerned, we may identify three kinds of choice which parallel exactly those applicable to the tone-group. By the side of tonality we may have 'paratonality', which is concerned with the number of paratone-groups in the utterance. Since the position of the major tone-group within the paratone-group is variable, we must also have a 'paratonicity' system to locate it..; and parallel to the choice of tone we may have a choice of 'paratone', that is, of the specific tone-sequence to be used.

paratonic, *a.* **2.** Add: In general, applied to plant movements caused by external stimuli (e.g. tropisms and kineses). [First formed in this sense as G. *paratonisch* (J. Sachs *Lehrb. der Bot.* (1868) III. i. 517).]

1910 J. M. COULTER et al. *Textbk. Bot.* I. II. 454 The terminal leaflet of *Desmodium gyrans*, like leaves of other members of the bean family, exhibits paratonic movements (i.e. those due to special stimuli, not tonic; opposed to autonomic). **1973** A. CRONQUIST *Basic Bot.* xxvi. 412/2 Some growth movements are self-controlled (autonomic); others are induced by external stimuli (paratonic)... Paratonic movements are further classified as tropisms and nasties.

paratracheal: see *PARA-[1] I.

para-transit (pæ·rătræ:nzit). Also as one word. [f. PARA-[1] + TRANSIT *sb.*] Public transport of a flexible, informal kind (see quots.). Also *attrib.*

1973 *Technology Rev.* July-Aug. 46/2 Modes such as taxis, jitneys, dial-a-ride, car pools, subscription buses, and minicars, the modes we collectively call 'para-transit'. **1974** R. KIRBY et al. (*title*) Para-transit: neglected options for urban mobility. **1977** *Chicago Tribune* 2 Oct. XII. 37/7 (Advt.), Transit manager to implement and supervise innovated public paratransit system in growth suburb NW of Chicago. System will consist of subscription mini-bus and dial-a-ride van service. **1978** *Paratransit: Rep. 40th Round Table Transport Econ.* (Europ. Conf. Ministers of Transport) i. 9 'Paratransit'..embraces a series of transport modes, organisational procedures and services falling broadly *midway* between two pre-eminent types of conventional transport, i.e. private cars and public transport services.

paratroops (pæ·rătrūps), *sb. pl.* [f. *PARA-[3] + TROOP *sb.* 2.] A body of soldiers dropped by parachute from aircraft flying over enemy territory. Also, in the singular, = *PARATROOPER below. Also *attrib.* and *fig.*

1940 *Daily Express* 16 May 3/1 Parashots—the new Local Defence Volunteers now being enrolled to deal with paratroops dropped from planes—will have uniforms of overall material. **1940** *N. & Q.* 29 June 459/1 Parachutists dropped as troops, or to establish themselves in the enemy's country..have now been shortened to 'paratroops'. **1940** *English Digest* Sept. 43 Copford, East Anglia, has a nasty lesson in store for any paratroops who may land there. **1941** *Aeronautics* Apr. 41/1 Paratroops. Better late than never! Parachute troops, originally developed by the Russians..were used by the British early in February. **1941** *Time* 14 July 19/2 Boys and girls..were organized as paratroop detectors. **1942** in *Amer. Speech* (1943) XVIII. 64/2 George Hopkins had made 2,300 parachute jumps..before enlisting as a paratroop. **1942** *Time* 17 Aug. 38 He was transferred to paratroop service. **1943** *Illustr. London News* 17 July 71 (*caption*), A paratroop about to land, with feet together and knees bent ready to take the shock. **1944** *Times* 18 Mar. 4/7 A big-scale exercise with paratroops..was in progress at one point. **1946** A. R. D. FAIRBURN in Chapman & Bennett *Anthol. N.Z. Verse* (1956) 106 Love's paratroops have hit the ground. **1956** *Nature* 4 Feb. 218/1 During the Second World War he [*sc.* Dr. P. B. Walker] was responsible at the Ministry of Aircraft Production for the supervision of the design of gliders and paratroop aircraft. **1958** *Spectator* 20 June 807/2 The attitude of many French paratroop officers towards General Raoul Salan. **1966** *New Scientist* 22 Sept. 659/3 Emotional sweating..has been reported in paratroops before jumping. **1973** 'R. MACLEOD' *Burial in Portugal* i. 18 She'd been young, she'd married a pair of paratroop wings. **1977** *R.A.F. News* 27 Apr.–10 May 13/1 To give them a detailed refresher course on formation flying and paratroop dropping, the film company enlisted the help of the RAF.

Hence **pa·ratroo:per,** a soldier of this kind; also, an aeroplane transporting paratroops.

1941 *Time* 4 Aug. 20/1 The paratroopers..had never been in an airplane when it was landed. **1943** J. STEINBECK *Once there was a War* (1959) 228 The lieutenant wanted to look back to see whether any of the paratroopers were in sight. **1945** *Times* 12 Jan. 8/3 The trial of..an American paratrooper..has been fixed for Tuesday next. **1946** *R.A.F. Jrnl.* May 180 There were..three distinct types of *Halifax* Glider Tugs and Paratroopers. **1956** *Flight* 8 June 748/2 As a paratrooper the Beverley carries 70 soldiers. **1957** *Economist* 5 Oct. 39/1 The dispatch of paratroopers to Little Rock was a painful blow to Americans. **1962** *Times* 29 Mar. 15/5 For the paratroopers the sheer luck of their landing place meant..the difference between a swift regrouping or death in the air.

paratrophic (pærătrōᵘ·fik), *a. Biol.* [ad. G. *paratroph* (A. Fischer *Vorlesungen über Bakterien* (1897) v. 47), f. PARA-[1]: see TROPHIC *a.* (*sb.*).] Needing live organic matter for nutrition.

1900 A. C. JONES tr. *Fischer's Struct. & Functions Bacteria* v. 49 The paratrophic group includes all those bacteria that can exist only within the living tissues of other organisms. **1902** [see *METATROPHIC *a.*]. **1919** F. O. BOWER *Bot. Living Plant* XXX. 460 On the basis of nutrition Bacteria have been classified into three groups:.. (iii) Paratrophic, those which develop normally only within the living tissues of other organisms, and are true, and obligatory parasites, such as the germs of Tubercle or Diphtheria. **1930** S. THOMAS *Bacteriol.* (ed. 2) xiv. 228 The paratrophic organisms..must have living organic matter from which to get all or part of their food requirements.

paratype (pæ·rătəip). *Taxonomy.* [f. PARA-[1] + TYPE *sb.*[1]] A specimen from a group that includes the one designated as the nomenclatural type of a species in its first description, but not the type itself.

1893 O. THOMAS in *Proc. Zool. Soc.* 242 Since the other specimens mentioned or enumerated..in the original description are of unquestionably great value in a typical sense, they ought also to have a name and might be called 'para-types' (or side-types). *Ibid.*, A Para-type is a specimen belonging to the original series but not the type, in cases where the author has himself selected a type. It should, however, be one of the specimens mentioned or enumerated in the original description. **1914** *Brit. Mus. Return* 171 in *Parl. Papers* LXXI. 193 Two paratypes of a new species of River-crab from Cochin. **1933** *Jrnl. R. Soc. W. Austral.* XIX. 15 The type specimen is being presented to the Western Australian Museum and a paratype to the British Museum. **1943** [see *ISOTYPE 3]. **1951** G. H. M. LAWRENCE *Taxon. Vascular Plants* ix. 204 A paratype is a specimen cited with the original description, other than the holotype. **1956** *Internat. Code Bot. Nomencl.* ii. 15 A paratype is a specimen cited with the original description other than the holotype or isotype(s). **1962** GORDON & LAVOIPIERRE *Entomol. for Students of Med.* liii. 325 Specimens other than the holotype which the author used when describing the species are known as the 'paratypes'. **1964** *Internat. Code Zool. Nomencl.* xvi. 79 After the holotype has been labelled, each remaining specimen (if any) of the type-series should be conspicuously labelled 'paratype', in order clearly to identify the components of the original type-series. **1971** *Nature* 30 July 311/2 It [*sc.* the skull of a fossil hominid] resembles the paratype from Bed II (Olduvai H. 13) in both cranial and dental characters.

paratyphoid (pærătəi·foid), *sb.* (*a.*) *Path.* [f. PARA-[1] + TYPHOID *a.* (*sb.*).] A fever similar in symptoms to, but generally milder than, typhoid fever, from which it can be distinguished bacteriologically. Freq. *attrib.* or as *adj.*, esp. in *paratyphoid fever.*

1902 *Amer. Jrnl. Med. Sci.* CXXIII. 977 Paratyphoid fever closely resembles typhoid in its course, temperature curve, and abdominal symptoms. **1904** *Jrnl. R. Microsc. Soc.* June 369 If there is suspicion of para-typhoid (or dysentery) the agglutination of the colonies in question must be investigated with the specific serum of this disease. **1948** MORGAN & CHEEVER in R. J. Dubos *Bacterial & Mycotic Infections of Man* xvii. 384/2 *Salmonella paratyphi* is found only in man where it has been described as one cause of paratyphoid fever. **1965** HARGREAVES & MORRISON *Pract. Trop. Med.* ii. 91 Paratyphoid infections are caused by *S[almonella] paratyphosus A., S. paratyphosus B* and *S. paratyphosus C.* In general paratyphoid A occurs in the tropics whilst B infections are met with more frequently in temperate zones. Paratyphoid C occurs in the Indian subcontinent, the Middle East and the Balkans. **1972** HOOK & JOHNSON in P. D. Hoeprich *Infectious Dis.* lv. 588/2 Members of the genus *Salmonella* other than *S. typhi* can produce an illness with all the clinical characteristics of typhoid fever—paratyphoid fever.

parautochthonous (pærǭtǫ·kþŏnəs), *a. Geol.* [f. PARA-[1] + AUTOCHTHONOUS *a.*; prob. orig. formed in Ger.] Intermediate in character between autochthonous and allochthonous.

1927 L. W. COLLET *Struct. Alps* I. vi. 20 The Morcles Nappe and similar parautochthonous folds. **1935** E. B. BAILEY *Tectonic Ess.* iii. 34 In parautochthonous folds and thrust-masses (Arnold Heim) the travel of the rock has been considerable or great, according to ordinary standards, but small in the Alpine scale of magnitudes. **1962** READ & WATSON *Introd. Geol.* I. x. 580 Parautochthonous granites have travelled only a short distance from their place of origin. **1963** J. G. RAMSAY in Johnson & Stewart *Brit. Caledonides* vii. 166 It is not certain where these pieces have their roots. They might be parautochthonous folds, but some evidence seems to indicate that a few might represent the noses of nappes.

paravane (pæ·răvēⁱn). [f. PARA-[2] + VANE.] An apparatus, fitted with vanes to keep it at a constant depth, designed to be towed at the bows of a vessel in order to clear its path from mines, cut the moorings of submerged mines, or destroy hostile submarines. Also *attrib.* Also *Aeronaut.*, a towing device (see quot. 1959).

1919 *Daily Mail* 6 Jan. 6/2 Like many other great conceptions, the paravane seems a quite simple thing. *Ibid.*, On one occasion last year a flotilla of light cruisers found themselves in a minefield, and by using the paravane they were able to cut their way safely through it. *Ibid.*, The paravane was invented by Lieut. Dennis Burney, R.N. **1920** *Rep. Brit. Assoc. Adv. Sci. 1919* 273 The Paravane has been developed as a weapon to fulfill two purposes:—(1) To attack a submarine. (2) To protect vessels from moored mines. **1920** [see *OTTER *sb.* 4 c]. **1920** *Glasgow Herald* 8 Oct. 10 Nor was part of the manufacturing profits in respect of paravane systems supplied to the Navy paid by the Government. *Ibid.* 5 Nov. 11 The 'paravane' is a name invented in or about 1916 to denote a particular kind or type of water kite of special shape and material and with special appliances. It was evolved and developed and in 1916 was adopted by the naval authorities as standard. **1922** *Encycl. Brit.* XXXII. 33/1 Paravane, a naval device used in the World War first for attacking submerged submarines and subsequently for protecting vessels against mines and for cutting up hostile minefields. The name of Acting-Comm. C. D. Burney is especially associated with its design and development. **1948** R. DE KERCHOVE *Internat. Maritime Dict.* 519/2 Two paravanes are towed, one on each side of the ship, by means of specially constructed wire towropes. **1959** J. L. NAYLER *Dict. Aeronaut. Engin.* 186 *Paravane*, a kite-shaped device by means of which a wire is kept at an angle from a towing vehicle. This device is used at Woomera, towed behind an aircraft, in snatch recovery methods for intercepting guided missiles towards the end of their flights.

paraventricular: see *PARA-¹ 1.

paravertebral (pærăvɜ̄·ɹtĭbrăl), *a. Med.* [f. PARA-¹ + VERTEBRAL *a.*] Situated or occurring beside the vertebral column or a vertebra.

1893 DUNGLISON *Dict. Med. Sci.* (ed. 21) 822/1 *Paravertebral*, situate beside or in the vicinity of the vertebral column. **1923** R. E. FARR tr. H. Braun in *Pract. Local Anesthesia* v. 123 Paravertebral anesthesia had been employed quite extensively in abdominal surgery. **1934** *Practitioners Libr. Med. & Surg.* V. xiii. 854 The sympathetic nerves pass from the higher centers in the midbrain down the spinal cord and then out into the paravertebral sympathetic chain. **1963** *Lancet* 12 Jan. 85/2 The patient was given..paravertebral block with 1% procaine. **1967** J. J. BONICA *Princ. & Pract. Obstetr. Analgesia & Anesthesia* I. xxxvii. 643/2 Each thoracic paravertebral space contains loose areolar and fatty tissue.

paravisual (pærăvi·ʒiuăl, -vi·ziuăl), *a.* [f. PARA-¹ + VISUAL *a.*] Conveying information visually but not requiring a person's direct gaze.

1960 *Aeroplane* XCVIII. 764/1 Airborne experience with the Smiths Para-Visual Director system will leave the newcomer with a strong conviction that this new flight-director/instrument-flying concept must inevitably alter present ideas about weather minima and automatic-landing prospects. **1964** M. ALLWARD *Inside Jet Airliner* vii. 53 Three little instruments called Para-Visual Directors mounted in line along the top of the instrument panels in front of each pilot. **1968** G. D. P. WORTHINGTON *Airline Instrument Flying* xvi. 256 The Para-visual Director is designed to apply command information in regard to pitch and bank through a rotating 'barber's pole' display which is so located that it is within the pilot's general field of vision but outside the limits of his direct field of vision. The direction of rotation of the pole applies a signal in the pilot's peripheral field of vision which demands fly up or fly down in the case of the pitch bars, or fly left or fly right in the case of the bank presentation.

parawing (pæ·răwiŋ). *Aeronaut.* Also **para wing.** [f. *PARA-³ + WING *sb.*] A parachute device having a flat inflatable wing in place of the more usual umbrella, allowing greater manœuvrability.

1960 R. L. NAESETH *Exploratory Study of Parawing as High-Lift Device for Aircraft* (NASA TN D-629) 1 A wind-tunnel investigation was made of the high-lift capabilities of two supersonic airplane configurations equipped with auxiliary parawings which are lightweight, stowable, fabric wings of parachute-like construction that may be used for take-off and landing. **1964** *Engineering* 7 Feb. 237/1 All of these gliders make use of the fact that the parawing is simple and cheap enough to be expendable. **1966** *Guardian* 12 May 14/5 Inflated triangular 'parawings' are being tested by the US army for possible use in place of parachutes. The parawing, which can be folded, packed and released like a parachute, inflates on opening into a flattened triangular dirigible that glides and maneuvres through the air. **1973** D. POYNTER *Hang Gliding* ii. 54 The idea of a limp para wing was presented to NASA as a reentry vehicle and millions of dollars were spent in research and tests... Stiffened Para Wings have performed much better than the limp models.

parawollastonite: see *PARA-¹ 2 c.

paraxial, *a.* Add: **b.** *Optics.* Situated close to the axis of an optical system, and (if linear) virtually parallel to it; of or pertaining to such a region.

1906 H. D. TAYLOR *Syst. Appl. Optics* iv. 55 The ultimate or paraxial rays. **1930** L. C. MARTIN *Introd. Appl. Optics* I. i. 17 Imagine..that the point P is brought so close to the axis that the inclination of the ray to the axis becomes very small; these conditions are characteristic of a 'paraxial' ray. **1934** W. H. A. FINCHAM *Optics* v. 83 For light in the paraxial region the angles of incidence and refraction will be very small, and may be considered as proportional to their sines in applying the law of refraction. **1974** W. T. WELFORD *Aberrations Symmetr. Optical Systems* iii. 17 We..define the domain of paraxial or Gaussian optics to be close enough to the axis to ensure that all terms of higher order of magnitude than quadratic in *x* and *y* are to be neglected.

Hence **para·xially** *adv.*, adjacent to or virtually parallel to an axis.

The 1905 reference given in quot. 1909 is incorrect and has not been traced.

1909 *Cent. Dict.* Suppl., *Paraxially*, in *zoöl.*, in such a way as to lie on each side of the long axis (of the body). *Proc. Roy. Soc.* (London), Feb., 1905, p. 318. **1927** V. T. SAUNDERS *Light* iii. 38 If a single ray is incident on the mirror through the principal focus it is seen to be reflected paraxially. **1950** H. H. HOPKINS *Wave Theory of Aberrations* 162 The paraxial equations..refer to rays which are limitingly close to the axis. Since, however, the equations are linear in the angles *u*, *α*, *i* rays at finite apertures may be traced paraxially.

paraxylene: see *PARA-¹ 2 b.

parca, var. *PARKA.

parcel, *sb.* **4. b.** Delete *local* and add further examples.

1887 R. HUNT *Brit. Mining* (ed. 2) 911/2 A parcel of ore is a pile or heap of copper or lead ore dressed for sale. **1898** *Barrier Weekly Post* 29 Oct. 13 [They] received satisfactory prices for their parcels. **1958** M. D. BERRINGTON *Stones of Fire* 20 They gradually collected a 'parcel' of choice stones. **1965** G. T. WILLIAMS *Econ. Geol. N.Z.* viii. 119/1 Increase in the price of gold resulted in renewed activity in 1935 and a certain amount of prospecting and development ensued for over a decade, though apparently only one parcel of 400 tons was treated.

7. d. A large amount of money gained or lost. *slang.*

1903 A. M. BINSTEAD *Pitcher in Paradise* vii. 172 'Aye, it's a pinch for t'pair of 'em, y'r Graace', roared Old Jack, with much warmth; 'an' what's moo-re, if y'r Graace doesn't *pack oop a reglar parcel* over 'em, why—why, A'al *never* speak to y'r Graace on a racecourse agin!' **1922** E. WALLACE *Flying Fifty-Five* x. 56 In the argot of his kind he had 'packed up a parcel' over the disqualification of Fifty-Five. **1923** WODEHOUSE *Inimitable Jeeves* xii. 131 'But if you haven't dropped a parcel over the race,' I said, 'why are you looking so rattled?' *Ibid.* xiv. 162, I think I can put you in the way of winning a parcel on the Mothers' Sack Race.

10. parcel bomb, a bomb wrapped up so as to resemble a parcel; **parcel(s) shelf, tray**, a shelf or tray upon which parcels may be placed, esp. in a motor vehicle; **parcel tanker**, a vessel designed to carry various liquids with separate piping and tanks.

1950 *Times* 22 Aug. 3/1 Injured by parcel bomb. A small parcel addressed to Mr. Thomas Rose..blew up when he opened it on Sunday night. **1966** 'A. HALL' *9th Directive* iv. 44 There's a dozen ways—prussic acid..the parcel bomb. **1974** *Guardian* 25 Jan. 24/5 Police scientific experts are examining the remains of a parcel bomb which exploded in an Israeli bank in the City of London yesterday. **1977** *New Society* 27 Jan. 163/3 The weekend parcel-bomb murder of Jason Moyo. **1951** *Motor* 2 May 386/3 There are two useful parcel shelves unobtrusively located beneath the front seat cushions. **1953** *Motor* 9 Dec. 728/3 Large cases..have to be lifted over a somewhat high rear bulkhead, and then slid forward into place below the rear parcels shelf. **1973** *Country Life* 31 May 1547/2 Stowage capacity is also good for a large car... There is..a useful parcel shelf. **1974** 'J. Ross' *Burning of Billy Toober* i. 9 He placed the pipe in the parcels shelf. **1976** *Chrysler World of Motoring* '77 15/4 With the parcel shelf folded away, and the rear seat folded flat, you've suddenly got 49 cu. ft. **1973** *Sea Breezes* May 297/1 The typical modern purpose-built parcel tanker is a complex and expensive investment. **1974** *Times* 31 May (Poseidonia Suppl.) p. iii/4 Parcel tankers have been developed which have the ability to carry incompatible chemicals in separate tanks. **1950** *Motor* 19 Apr. 372/3 There is a parcel tray of generous size below the instrument panel. **1956** *Motor* 24 Oct. 525 (*caption*) Air for de-misting this window is blown through the slots seen here on the parcel tray.

B. *adv.* or quasi-*adv.* or *adj.* **1. c.** Also with vbl. sbs.

1867 [see PARCEL-GILDING]. **1902** A. H. HIORNS *Metal-Colouring & Bronzing* (ed. 2) III. 243 (*heading*) Parcel coppering or bronzing as applied to fine zinc castings. **1907** *Handbk. Electro-Plating* (W. Canning & Co.) (ed. 3) 64 (*heading*) Parcel-plating. Plating articles in two or three colours. **1911** S. FIELD *Princ. Electro-Deposition* xii. 175 Partial deposition..is, in the case of copper, called parcel coppering. **1925** FIELD & BONNEY *Chem. Coloring of Metals* xiii. 166 'Parcel plating'..is applicable to all deposited metals. **1971** T. C. COLLOCOTT *Dict. Sci. & Technol.* 855/2 *Parcel plating*, the electrodeposition of a metal over a selected area of an article, the remainder being covered with a nonconductor in order to prevent deposition.

parcelization (pāːɹsĕləizēi·ʃən). Also **parcellization.** [f. PARCEL *sb.* + -IZATION.] = PARCELLATION.

1960 E. R. GOODMAN in J. A. Fishman *Readings Sociol. of Lang.* (1968) 725 The treatment of the Moslem peoples of the Soviet Union provides the clearest illustration of this policy of parcelization. In an effort to avoid the creation of a large Moslem state in the Volga-Urals area, the Soviet regime created separate Bashkir and Tartar ASSRs. **1963** *Listener* 21 Feb. 322/1 Parcelization gets worse and worse. *Ibid.* 322/2 Even such an obvious reform as a change in the law which permits parcelization seemed to be viewed with suspicion. **1975** DJURFELDT & LINDBERG *Behind Poverty* 124 The parcellization of land among many small owners.

pa·rcellate, *v. rare.* [f. PARCEL *v.* + -ATE³ or as back-formation from next.] *trans.* To divide into separate parcels or portions. So **pa·rcellated** *ppl. a.*

1934 WEBSTER, Parcellate. **1971** *Country Life* 3 June 1374/1 About 50 [vine] growers among the 1,700 whose heavily parcellated strips dominate the district. **1978** *Ibid.* 7 Sept. 642/1 The 100 growers concerned..now have an average of 800 square metres of consolidated vineyard in place of the 200 square metres of parcellated terraces they formerly had to work.

parcellation. (Later example.)

1965 K. H. CONNELL in Glass & Eversley *Population in Hist.* xvii. 429 Connaught..was..the province where parcellation of the land was most acute.

parcel post. (Earlier examples.)

1837 *9th Rep. Comm. Managem. Post-Office* 28 in *Parl. Papers* XXXIV. 431 Would it not occasion great delay if you made a parcel-post of it to that extent? **1843** *Rep. Sel. Comm. Postage* 41 in *Parl. Papers* VIII. 1 The Banghy post of the East Indies is a parcel post; the maximum of weight appears to be about 15 lb.

parch, *sb.*¹ Restrict *rare* to sense in Dict. and add: **2.** *attrib.*, as **parch mark** *Archæol.*, a localized discoloration of the ground in dry weather over buried remains.

1947 *Antiquity* XXI. 82 The crop's growth had not improved matters, and curiously enough there did not seem to be any 'parch-marks'. **1977** *Times* 19 Sept. 3/2 The latest discovery emerged partly through last summer's drought. Parch marks on the ground disclosed regular lines of Roman trench work.

‖**parch** (pāɹχ), *sb.*² *rare.* [W. *parch* reverence, *parchedig* reverend.] In Wales: a clergyman.

1944 DYLAN THOMAS *Let.* 21 Sept. (1966) 267 Hearing rise slimy from the Welsh lechered Caves the cries of parchs and their flocks. **1953** —— *Under Milk Wood* (1954) 20 A beer-tent black with parchs.

parcheesi: see *PACHISI.

parchment, *sb.* Add: **2. b.** A certificate; *spec.* (see quot. 1962).

1888 C. M. YONGE *Our New Mistress* ii. 14 She had been two years from her training college, and had an excellent parchment and report from the place she had left. **1914** 'BARTIMEUS' *Naval Occasions* xxii. 206 The sailor himself..describes his Certificate as his 'Discharge'. In Accountant circles in which the thing circulates it is known as a 'Parchment'. A Service Certificate..is a double sheet of parchment with printed headings, foolscap size. **1962** GRANVILLE *Dict. Sailors' Slang* 86/1 *Parchment*, naval rating's service certificate on which his character and abilities are assessed by the commanding officer of each ship in which he has served.

3*. A colour resembling that of parchment.

1934 BRIT. COLOUR COUNCIL *Dict. Colour Standards* 58 Parchment. B.C.C. 165. General representation of samples submitted by Textile and other Colour Using Industries. **1947** J. H. BUSTANOBY *Princ. Color & Color Mixing* IV. 68 Parchment. A pale tint of brown, resembling the prepared and polished skin of sheep, goats, lambs, young calves, and other animals, used for writing, painting, engraving, etc. **1970** P. WEST *Words for Deaf Daughter* vi. 117 Old golds, and parchments (the tone, not the stuff). **1974** *Simpson (Piccadilly) Catal.* Christmas 15 Cable cardigan... Parchment, vicuna colour or light green.

4. a. Also, parchment-coloured.

1939–40 *Army & Navy Stores Catal.* 637/2 Satin, marocain, etc...in Oyster, Pearl and Parchment shades. **1959** *Sears, Roebuck Catal.* Spring/Summer 1224/1 Vitreous china Bathroom Fixtures..Frosty pink, Parchment beige, Sage green. *Ibid.* 618/3 Rayon Fortisan [curtains] ..Frosty pink, Parchment ivory. **1977** *Times* 29 Dec. 17/7 (Advt.), Mercedes-Benz..Magnetic blue/parchment velour.

b. *parchment-coloured* adj.; **parchment window** *Obs. Canad.*, a window-pane made of parchment.

1932 W. FAULKNER *Light in August* vi. 115 Always against her eyelids was that..parchmentcolored face watching her. **1936** —— *Absalom, Absalom!* viii. 335 The slight dowdy woman..with parchment-colored skin. **1979** *Country Life* 9 Aug. 431/3, I have included photographs.. of two intarsia sweaters... I particularly like the parchment-coloured one. **1775** HEARNE & TURNOR *Jrnls.* (1934) 182 The Carpenter Employed nailing on a set of new Parchment windows. **1882** *Royal Readers* (Canada) v. 435 He [*sc.* Robert Campbell] and his companions were forced to use for food the parchment windows of their hut.

parchment-lace. For †*Obs.* read '*Obs.* exc. *Hist.*' and add further examples.

1905 N. H. MOORE *Lace Bk.* II. 62 The English term for this old Guipure was 'Parchment Lace'. **1930** P. G. TRENDELL *Guide to Collection of Lace* (Victoria & Albert

Mus.) 6 In England there was frequent mention of 'parchment lace' in Queen Mary's reign. **1960** C. W. Cunnington et al. *Dict. Eng. Costume* 268/1 *Parchment lace.* 16th and 17th c's. A lace usually of gold or silver but occasionally of coloured silks.

par-cook (pā·ɹkuk), *v. rare.* [After Parboil *v.* 2.] *trans.* To cook partially.

1927 *Daily Express* 17 Nov. 5/2 The chicken was par-cooked and cooled, the stock being set aside for next day.

pardalote. Add to etym. after '*Pardalotus*' (L. J. P. Vieillot *Analyse d'une nouvelle Ornithologie* (1816) 31). (Earlier and later examples); = *diamond-bird* s.v. Diamond *sb.* 12.

[**1826** J. F. Stephens in G. Shaw *Gen. Zool.* XIII. II. 252 Olive-green Pardalotus, with the back spotted with fulvous.] **1894** A. Newton *Dict. Birds* III. 684 *Pardalote*, see *Diamond-bird.* **1901** A. J. Campbell *Nests & Eggs Austral. Birds* I. 441 The Red-tipped Pardalote occasionally breeds underground. **1961** *Coast to Coast 1959–60* 63 He pointed to where some pardalotes and sitellas were fluttering about the drooping branch of pepper-tree. **1965** *Austral. Encycl.* VI. 481/1 Pardalotes, a group of very small, insectivorous, tree-haunting birds (genus *Pardalotus*)... Most are brightly coloured and liberally spotted, hence the term 'pardalote' and the alternative name 'diamond-bird'. **1975** I. Rowley *Bird Life* iii. 40 Pardalotes and shrike-tits may turn to bark searching.

pardessus. Restrict *Obs.* to sense in Dict. and add: **1.** (Earlier example.)

1843 *Godey's Lady's Bk.* Nov. 240 *Pardessus.*—At the present moment this most useful appendage to a lady's out-door costume, is more than ever in request.

2. Mus. *pardessus de viole* (də viǫl) [F. *par-dessus* adv.], a small treble viol, played esp. in France during the eighteenth century; also *ellipt.* as *pardessus.*

1889 Grove *Dict. Mus.* IV. 277/2 The five-stringed Treble Viol survived longest in France where it was called 'Quinton' or 'Pardessus de Viole'. **1893** J. S. Shedlock tr. *Riemann's Dict. Mus.* 832/2 The violin quietly took the place of the 'Pardessus de viole' in the band of viols, for the highest part. **1941** N. Bessarabov *Anc. Europ. Mus. Instruments* IV. 303 The *quinton* is very often confused with the *pardessus de viole*, which also has five strings. These instruments belong to different families: the *quinton* is a true violin, and the *pardessus de viole* (the high treble) is a viol. **1954** *Grove's Dict. Mus.* (ed. 5) VIII. 804/2 A small sopranino viol was evolved, called a *pardessus de viole*, which was in all respects a true viol, but suited to a tuning a fourth above the treble. *Ibid.*, All sizes of viols, even the smallest *pardessus*.., must be held downward resting on or between the knees. **1961** T. Dart in A. Baines *Mus. Instruments* vii. 189 A tiny viol—the *pardessus de viole*—found an admirer or two among the court ladies of France. **1974** *Early Music* Jan. 75/3 Several pardessus de viole, the smallest of the viols, cultivated by court ladies of the time. **1976** *Ibid.* July 361/1 The pardessus is built like a small treble viol, with deep ribs, flat back and frets.

pardner (pā·ɹdnəɹ). *colloq.* (orig. *U.S.*). Also †**pardener.** Var. Partner *sb.* Cf. Pard[2].

1795 B. Dearborn *Columbian Gram.* 137 Improprieties, commonly called Vulgarisms... Pardener for Partner. **1837** A. Sherwood *Gazetteer Georgia* (ed. 3) 71 *Pardner*, for partner. **1847** F. A. Buck *Let.* 23 Feb. in *Yankee Trader in Gold Rush* (1930) 4 Mr. Johnson has taken a pardner, a Mr. Hollister, who appears to be a very smart man. *Ibid.* 5 The young lady who was my pardner gave me a private lesson beforehand so that I walked through it pretty well. **1857** *Observer* 12 Apr. 2/4 The Punch and Judy man..cleared from £2 to £3 a week, he and his 'pardner'. *a* **1861** T. Winthrop *John Brent* (1862) vii. 71, I don't mean sech. I mean jolly dogs, like me and my pardener. *Ibid.* xiii. 140 'Pardners for a kerdrille!' cried Jake. **1864** Dickens *Mut. Fr.* (1865) I. I. i. 4 'Arn't been eating nothing as has disagreed with you, have you, pardner?' 'Why, yes, I have,' said Gaffer. 'I have been swallowing too much of that word, Pardner. I am no pardner of yours.' **1875** J. Miller *First Fam'lies Sierras* (1876) v. 55 That evening Limber Tim..told..what a hero his 'pardner' had become. **1882** D. Pidgeon *Engineer's Holiday* I. xvii. 200 The mine is worked by two 'pardners' who dig and wash by turns. **1907** S. E. White *Arizona Nights* I. xi. 178 It's money I haven't got, and can't get unless I let somebody in as pardner. **1926** *Ladies' Home Jrnl.* Nov. 24 'There', she added as she crouched once more beside her pardner. **1952** M. Allingham *Tiger in Smoke* xiii. 196 'Now, pardner,' he said. They were both great readers of Westerns. **1973** R. Perry *Nowhere Man* iv. 59 'Well, pardner,' he said.. overdoing both the western accent and the sarcasm, 'it seems I'm stuck with you.'

pardon, *sb.*[1] Add: **6. d.** Ellipt. for *I beg your pardon* (see sense 6 in Dict.). *colloq.*

1898 G. B. Shaw *Man of Destiny* 161 *Giuseppe* (coming to the foot of the couch) Pardon. Your excellency is so unlike other great men. **1914** —— *Fanny's First Play* III. 221 *Knox*... You sit there after carrying on with my daughter, and tell me coolly youre married... *Duvallet.* Pardon. Carrying on? What does that mean? **1930** J. Cannan *No Walls of Jasper* xv. 277 Julian said, 'That's all nonsense. You're drunk.'.. 'Pardon?' said Eric. **1930** A. P. Herbert *Water Gipsies* xiii. 178 To gain time she said 'Pardon?' and Mr. Baxter had to repeat his question. **1951** [see *Grant *v.* 4 e]. **1954** A. S. C. Ross in *Neuphilol. Mitt.* LV. 45 *Pardon!* is used by the non-U in three main ways:—1) if the hearer does not hear the speaker properly; 2) as an apology (e.g. on brushing by someone in a passage; 3) after hiccupping or belching. **1978** I. Murdoch *Sea* 211 'Did you destroy the letter?' 'Pardon?' 'Did you destroy the letter?' 'Yes.'

‖ **pare** (pā·re), *sb.*[2] *N.Z.* [Maori.] A lintel in a Maori building.

1897 A. Hamilton *Maori Art* (1901) II. 156 The small doorway has the usual *pare* or *korupe* over it with a single figure in the centre, and the bird-headed monsters at the ends. **1911** *Dominion Museum Bull.* (N.Z.) No. 3. 106 From the Salem Museum comes also the photograph of a *pare* or door-lintel... This *pare* can be definitely located, from the style of carving, as having been made in the Bay of Plenty District. **1927, 1949** [see *Korupe]. **1950** *N.Z. Jrnl. Agric.* May 501 The dark-brown pare or korupe framing the window..is a modern totara carving. **1962** N. Davis in Davis & Wrenn *Eng. & Medieval Stud.* 324 The central group on a lintel (*pare*) from Porangahau, Hawke's Bay.

pared, *ppl. a.* (In Dict. s.v. Pare *v.*[1]) Add: Also with *down.*

1974 *Country Life* 21 Feb. 398/2 The pared-down practicality of mini skirts and boots. **1977** *Rolling Stone* 30 June 98/2 The arrangements are just pared-down versions of the originals.

Paree (pærī·). *colloq.* [Repr. the Fr. pronunc. of *Paris.*] Paris; esp. in phr. *gay Paree.*

1848 F. A. Durivage *Stray Subjects* 116 Walk in, gentlemen, and see the collection.., which beats the Zoological Gardens all holler, and can't be come over by the Gardens des Plantys in Par-*ee!* **1903** Mrs. G. de H. Vaizey *Pixie O'Shaughnessy* xvi. 171 The Major..revived recollections of an old visit to 'Paree'. **1930** E. Waugh *Labels* 21 There are good young men saving up their money for a beano in 'Gay Paree'. **1964** 'P. Loraine' *Day of Arrow* i. 12 The porter, putting on a weary archness reserved for British and American visitors to *Paree.* **1974** *Times* 9 Feb. 10/5 The prize: a second honeymoon in—guess where? You've got it—Gay Paree.

pareiasaur (pǎrəi·ăsǭɹ). Also (erron.) **pariasaur.** [f. mod.L. name of suborder *Pareiasauria*, f. generic name *Pareiasaurus*: see following entry.] A herbivorous fossil reptile of the group once included in the suborder Pareiasauria, known from Permian remains found in southern and eastern Africa, eastern Europe, and Russia, now classified as the superfamily Pareiasauroidea of the suborder Procolophonia. So **pareiasau·rian** *sb.* Also as *adj.*, of or pertaining to an animal of this type.

1905 E. R. Lankester *Extinct Animals* v. 220 These Pariasaurs were about as big as well grown cattle, but not so high on the legs. **1927** Haldane & Huxley *Animal Biol.* xi. 242 (*caption*) Primitive type [of reptile] (Pareiosaurian [*sic*]). **1933** A. S. Romer *Vertebr. Paleont.* vi. 129 A more advanced type..is that of the pareiasaurs of the Middle and Upper Permian of Europe and Africa. **1966** E. Palmer *Plains of Camdeboo* vi. 105 The great 'Cheek-Lizards', the Pareiasaurs,..were found..in the lowest and oldest zone of the Beaufort series. **1971** E. C. Olson *Vertebr. Paleozool.* viii. 315 The main link between procolophons and pareiasaurs is provided by *Rhipaeosaurus. Ibid.*, *Rhipaeosaurus* has a dentition that appears somewhat like that to be expected in an ancestral pareiasaurian. *Ibid.*, The skull..has a somewhat pareiasaurian and somewhat procolophonian look. **1975** *Nature* 3 Apr. 415/1 The first..is an exposure of the Madumabisa Mudstones yielding abundant therapsid and some pareiasaur remains. **1977** A. Hallam *Planet Earth* 270 The second group were the pareiasaurs, which were up to 3m..long.

pareiasaurus (pǎrəi:ăsǭ·rǒs). Also (erron.) **pariasaurus.** [mod.L. (R. Owen *Descr. & Illustr. Catal. Fossil Reptilia S. Afr.* (1876) 7), f. Gr. παρειά cheek + σαῦρος lizard.] = prec.

1876 R. Owen *Descr. & Illustr. Catal. Fossil Reptilia S. Afr.* 10 (*caption*) A vertebra from the hinder part of the dorsal, or from the lumbar, region of a *Pareiasaurus.* **1905** E. R. Lankester *Extinct Animals* v. 218 (*caption*) Photograph of a skeleton of Pariasaurus. **1959** *Times* 19 June 7/5 Those [animals] like the pareiasaurus..have gradually become extinct.

‖**parens patriæ** (pæ:renz pæ·tri,i). *Law.* [mod.L., lit. 'parent of the country'.] The sovereign, or some other authority, regarded as the guardian or protector of citizens who are unable to protect themselves.

1764 T. Cunningham *New & Compl. Law-Dict.* II. s.v. Ideots and Lunaticks § 2, It seems to be agreed at this day, that the King as *parens patriæ* hath the protection of all his subjects, and that in a more particular manner he is to take care of all those who, by reason of their imbecillity and want of understanding, are incapable of taking care of themselves. **1883** *Wharton's Law Lexicon* (ed. 7) 593/2 *Parens patriæ*, the sovereign, as *parens patriæ*, has a kind of guardianship over various classes of persons, who, from their legal disability, stand in need of protection, such as infants, idiots, and lunatics. **1955** *Times* 25 May 15/2 Was it prepared, as regarded a subject of her Majesty and having regard to the jurisdiction which they exercised on her Majesty's behalf as *parens patriae*, to send the child away to become a citizen of another country? **1973** *N.Y. Law Jrnl.* 20 July 1/1 A Court of Appeals has upheld the right of a state to sue to enjoin antitrust violations as parens patriae for its citizens. **1976** *Howard Jrnl.* XV. I. 51 A legal rational was discovered in the ancient doctrine of parens patriae. **1976** *Washington Post* 19 Apr. A22/4 These bills contain a so-called *parens patriae* provision permitting state attorneys general—directly or by hiring outside attorneys—to bring a class action for alleged anti-trust infractions.

parent, *sb.* Add: **1.** *parent-in-law* (further examples).

1932 E. E. Evans-Pritchard in *Sociologus* VIII. 411 There may be difficulty later with his parents-in-law because he has taken no steps to protect their daughter from the perils of child-birth. **1937** R. H. Lowie *Hist. Ethnol. Theory* vii. 78 This typical parallelist cites many instances of African, American, Australian, and Asiatic parent-in-law avoidance. **1972** D. Bloodworth *Any Number can Play* ix. 71 An agent..with parents-in-law in Peking was obviously open to pressure. **1976** *Southern Even. Echo* (Southampton) 10 Nov. 24/7 His wife Josephine and five-year-old son Simon, were at Heathrow Airport yesterday, together with his parents-in-law.

4. b. *Nuclear Sci.* A nuclide that becomes transformed into another nuclide (the 'daughter') by nuclear disintegration.

1905 E. Rutherford in *Phil. Mag.* X. 294 The experiment..was also utilized to prove that radium E was the parent of the α ray product radium F. **1950** [see *Daughter 6 d]. **1961** G. R. Choppin *Exper. Nucl. Chem.* vi. 82 If the parent is shorter lived than the daughter, the daughter activity will grow to some maximum value, then decay with its own characteristic half life. **1972** Smith & Stokes *Princ. Atomic & Nucl. Physics* xii. 364 The number of atoms of the daughter nuclide decays with either the daughter's or the parent's half-life, whichever is the larger.

5. a. (Further examples.)

1896 [see *Division 1 f]. **1905** E. Rutherford in *Phil. Mag.* X. 295 The activity of the successive product, when in equilibrium with the parent substance, can be utilized to determine the period of a substance which itself does not emit rays. **1909** J. Joly *Radioactivity & Geol.* iii. 57 Detrital sediments are 67 per cent. of the total parent igneous rocks. **1914** *Phil. Mag.* XXVIII. 837 It is possible from the disintegration equations of uranium and thorium, and the atomic weights of the parent elements, to calculate the atomic weights of the end products. **1934** M. Bodkin *Archetypal Patterns in Poetry* 329 In the psychological study of poetry it seems to me to have value, partly because it helps us to relate to the facts of poetic experience, those facts which Freud has formulated under the hypothesis of the parent-imago, or super-ego. **1955** [see *daughter atom* s.v. *Daughter 7 c]. **1956** *Nature* 11 Feb. 248/1 The fact that the chief expressive movements are the same throughout the world he regards as affording an argument that we are descended from a single parent-stock. **1957** G. E. Hutchinson *Treat. Limnol.* I. xv. 829 One of these isotopes, mesothorium 1, has a half life..long enough for it to undergo some geochemical migration with radium, independently of the parent element thorium. **1967** H. Hellman *Controlled Guidance Syst.* vi. 158 The 'parent' aircraft can carry a larger transmitter and transmitting antenna than the missile can. **1971** I. G. Gass et al. *Understanding Earth* viii. 121/1 The abundance of the common chondrites indicates that most of the parent bodies must have had similar compositions. **1978** *Jrnl. R. Soc. Arts* CXXVI. 686/1 In many cases the mechanical properties of EB welds remain unchanged from those of the parent metal

c. parent–child, used *attrib.* of or pertaining to both a parent and a child, esp. in phr. *parent-child relationship*; **parent company,** a company of which other companies are subsidiaries; **parent figure,** one who is regarded as having some of the characteristics of a parent; **parent language,** a language from which certain other languages are derived; **parents' day,** a day on which parents visit their children's school; **parent ship,** a ship which protects smaller vessels or which acts as a base for ships or aircraft; **parents' meeting,** a meeting of parents with their children's teachers at a school; **parent–teacher,** used *attrib.* of or pertaining to parents and the teachers of their children, chiefly in phr. **parent–teacher association,** a local organization of parents and teachers established to promote closer relations and improve educational facilities; *abbrev.* P.T.A. s.v. *P II.

1928 in *Smith Coll. Stud. Social Work* (1931) I. 411 (*title*) A study of parent-child dependency. **1939** Auden in *I Believe* (1940) 26 The family is based on inequality, the parent-child relationship. **1942** H. Nicolson *Diary* 28 Aug. (1967) 239 Will that child not come to..lose that atmosphere of sacrifice-gratitude which is the best parent-child relationship? **1965** M. Morse *Unattached* i. 70 Strained parent-child relationships were characteristic of the unattached in all areas. **1972** *Guardian* 11 Aug. 9/6 The idea is..for parent-child involvement in getting the maximum from the material. **1869** *Bradshaw's Railway Manual* XXI. 5 They would soon be enabled to declare a dividend equal to that of the parent company. **1943** J. D. Dawson *Tunisian Battle* i. 21 Six Simcas, small cars similar to Fiats but manufactured in France for the parent Italian company. **1970** T. Lupton *Managem. & Social Sci.* (ed. 2) ii. 47 The American parent company..had taken steps to reduce labour costs. **1976** *Times* 1 Mar. 12/4 The British Government did not bind the American parent company [of Chrysler] to continue its operations in Britain for any specific period. **1960** I. Bennett *Delinquent & Neurotic Children* i. 11 The same process that occurs in the rearing of every child, i.e. that of identifying with the parent-figure and incorporating his ideals. **1976** S. Hynes *Auden Generation* ii. 51 In the war, young men ..were faced with a real challenge which was yet like a school game: highly competitive..and earning..the approval of parent-figures. **1905** O. Jespersen *Growth & Struct. Eng. Lang.* ii. 19 The Arian language..was in course of time differentiated into all these languages, or as the same fact is generally expressed in a metaphor of dubious value, was the parent-language from which all these languages have descended. **1933** L. BLOOMFIELD *Language* xviii. 298 In the case of the Romance languages, we have written records of this parent language, namely, Latin. **1965** H. A. GLEASON *Linguistics & Eng. Gram.* 33 This reconstructed parent language is now generally called Proto-Indo-European,..abbreviated PIE. **1971** D. CRYSTAL *Linguistics* 154 This parent language (*Ursprache*) was probably more inflected than any of the attested languages. **1973** *Times* 31 Oct. 10/4 This was certainly parents' day with a difference. Small groups were escorted round the buildings and shown classrooms stacked with books on Marxism, on Russian geography and on Cuba. **1973** *Listener* 15 Nov. 675/3 Parents' Day at their son's prep school. **1976** C. STORR *Unnatural Fathers* v. 60 She and Martin..always appeared together at the parents' days at their children's schools. **1933** *Jane's Fighting Ships* 148/3 Beskytteren... Cruising speed is 9 kts... Serves as parent ship for aircraft. **1961** F. H. BURGESS *Dict. Sailing* 157 *Parent ship*, a mother ship to several smaller ones. **1972** *Guardian* 17 Oct. 19/8 The parents who never come to a parents' meeting or try ..to help or influence their children's school. **1973** 'J. PATRICK' *Glasgow Gang Observed* viii. 79 He simulated the voice of a form teacher at a parents' meeting. **1915** (*title*) Parent-teacher associations in the rural and village schools of Oregon. **1916** *Ann. Amer. Acad. Pol. & Social Sci.* LXVII. 139 The Congress [of Mothers and Parent-Teacher Associations] assumed the task of organizing Parent-Teacher Associations in every school. **1951** M. MCLUHAN *Mech. Bride* (1967) 126/2 There is in the parent-teacher relationship a basic violation of the idea of equality. **1957** *Times* 16 Sept. 11/5 The National Federation of Parent-Teacher Associations, formed last year, seeks to promote closer relations between parents and teachers mainly by practical means. **1968** *Daily Tel.* 12 Nov. 21 (*heading*) Parent-teacher link guide for schools. **1973** *Times* 10 Apr. 3/2 In an ideal world all schools would have parent-teacher associations.

parent, *v. trans.* Delete *rare* and add later examples. Hence **pa·rented** *ppl. a.* (cf. PARENTED *a.* in Dict. and Suppl.).

1904 BELLOC *Avril* I. 4 Literary..epochs..are.. definitely parented. We know their special stuff and harmony. We can show..the parts meeting and blending. **1954** E. H. W. MEYERSTEIN *Verse Lett. to Five Friends* 2 One so quick, so parented, as you Needed but *time*, to feed her fancies new. **1957** *Times* 7 May 6/5 It is almost heaven-sent that the Suez Canal Company, with its position and its money, should be wanting to parent the idea [of a Channel tunnel]. **1975** *Listener* 13 Mar. 340/3 Over 75 couples..have already been approved as adoptive or foster-parents... Many..are most suitable candidates to parent the child in question.

2. *intr.* To be a parent. Hence **pa·renting** *vbl. sb.*; also *attrib.*

1959 *Britannica Bk. of Year* 547/1 *Parenting*, the supervision by parents of their children. **1970** F. DODSON (*title*) How to parent. **1970** L. B. AMES in *Ibid.* p. xi, New parents have a great deal to learn from those already experienced in what Dr. Fitzhugh Dodson calls the art of parenting. **1972** *Times* 30 Oct. 8/3 The single-minded, unconditional desire..to provide a loving, caring home, which is the hallmark of good parenting. **1973** A. E. WILKERSON *Rights of Children* 305 While making available to parents the range of resources necessary for effective parenting, we need to be more explicit about the social expectations of parents. *Ibid.* 308 The price of waiting indeterminably for parents who cannot or will not develop acceptable parenting requirements is paid by the child. **1975** *N.Y. Times* 16 Sept. 84 Because of all the changes in American society, we are losing our intuitive ability to parent. **1976** *Guardian* 16 Aug. 9/3 Energy gone, parenting is handed over to the parent-substitute, the teak box in the corner.

parentalism (păre·ntăliz'm). [f. PARENTAL *a.* + -ISM.] The character or quality of a parent.

1878 W. L. BLACKLEY in *19th Cent.* Nov. 838 What some folk sneer at under the name of 'parentalism'. **1923** *Daily Mail* 4 Oct. 7/2 The parentalism of our laws, with their mixture of foolish prohibitions and foolish laxities.

parentcraft (pēə·rĕntkrɑft). Also with hyphen. [f. PARENT *sb.* + CRAFT *sb.*] The 'craft' or business of a parent; knowledge of, and skill in, the rearing of children.

1930 *Lancet* 22 Mar. 672/1 (*heading*) The teaching of parentcraft. **1945** *Times* 10 Mar. 8/2 The Ministry were discussing various schemes regarding children under two, and they had lately set up a committee to go into the question of parentcraft. **1958** *Times* 7 July (National Health Service Suppl.) p. xii/1 It [*sc.* maternity care] should also include guidance in parent-craft and in problems associated with infertility and family planning. **1973** *Guardian* 3 Apr. 18/2 A school can teach good parentcraft, both explicitly and implicitly. **1976** *Oxford Times* 10 Dec. 17/1 This state of affairs has certainly been fostered by the voluntary parentcraft classes organised by doctors, midwives and health visitors.

parented, *a.* Add: Also not in comb.: having parents.

1974 *Times Lit. Suppl.* 11 Oct. 1109/1 The orphan.. tearfully watching his parented friends go off to camp.

parentela (pærĕntī·la). *Biol.* [a. L. *parentēla* relationship, f. *parent-*, stem of *parens* parent.] The set of all descendants of a particular pair of individuals.

1927 J. F. VAN BEMMELEN in *Proc. Sect. Sci. Kon. Akad. Wetensch. Amsterdam* XXX. 772 The pedigree itself forms a so-called Parentela, which means a survey of all the descendants of a certain pair. **1932** *Proc. 6th Internat. Congr. Genetics* II. 7 The Table of Descendants is better called the parentela. There are two kinds: the definite or closed parentela and the indefinite or open parentela. Only the latter is important for research in heredity. **1946** R. R. GATES *Human Genetics* II. xxix. 1320 The members of this parentela were also small as children.

parentelic (pærĕnte·lik), *a.* [f. as prec. + -IC.] Of or pertaining to relationship based on common ancestry.

1895 POLLOCK & MAITLAND *Hist. Eng. Law* II. 294 In a parentelic scheme my great-nephew, since he springs from my father, is nearer to me than my first cousin. **1957** *Jrnl. R. Anthrop. Inst.* Jan. 40 The other entrenched law, åsetasrett, shows the same emphasis but it operates in close conjunction with the law of inheritance which is based on quite different principles, namely the equality of spouses, bilateral affiliation, and equality of siblings. A full discussion of this law and of the parentelic system that it employs is out of place here.

parenteral (păre·ntərăl), *a. Med.* [f. PARA-[1] + Gr. ἔντερ-ον intestine + -AL.] Involving the introduction of a substance into the body other than by the alimentary tract. Also as *sb.*, a preparation for parenteral administration. Hence **pare·nterally** *adv.*

1910 *Lippincott's New Med. Dict.* 692/1 *Parenteral, -ly*, not by way of the digestive tract. **1912** A. E. TAYLOR *Digestion & Metabolism* viii. 467 The secretions of the intestine and of the pancreas are toxic on parenteral introduction. **1916** A. J. SMITH tr. *O. von Fürth's Probl. Physiol. & Path. Chem. of Metabolism* ii. 48 The toxic effect of the parenterally introduced trypsin. **1949** E. P. ABRAHAM et al. in H. W. Florey et al. *Antibiotics* II. xv. 639 Such a test could scarcely be expected to give an accurate forecast of the effect of a drug administered by mouth or parenterally for the treatment of a generalized infection. **1957** *Obstetr. & Gynecol.* X. 261/2 Esterification of the different steroid preparations resulted in longer-acting, oil-soluble, nonirritating parenterals being made available for clinical use. **1971** *Nature* 12 Nov. 101/2 Excitatory effects of amphetamine administered parenterally in other regions of the brain. **1974** R. M. KIRK et al. *Surgery* iii. 38 When it cannot be given into the gut, it must be administered parenterally. **1974** PASSMORE & ROBSON *Compan. Med. Stud.* III. II. l. 11/1 In experienced hands, complete parenteral nutrition is a safe if time-consuming form of therapy.

parenthesis. Add: **3. c.** *Logic.* Such curved lines (brackets) or other symbols used in the notation of formal logic to punctuate a proposition or to indicate that the expression they contain forms a unit within the whole proposition; also *attrib.* and *comb.* as **parenthesis-free** *a.*, a term referring to notation, esp. that of Łukasiewicz, which eliminates the need for such symbols.

1918 C. I. LEWIS *Survey Symbolic Logic* iv. 233 For any function of one variable we here omit any parenthesis around the variable. **1940** W. V. QUINE *Math. Logic* i. 40 The parenthesis notation formulated at the beginning of the section is retained. **1954** I. M. COPI *Symbolic Logic* viii. 253 (*heading*) A parenthesis-free notation. **1959** O. BIRD tr. *Bocheński's Precis of Math. Logic* v. 82 In this it is better to use the Peano–Russell notation with parentheses, since its similarities to algebra facilitate the 'multiplication'. **1963** O. WOJTASIEWICZ tr. *Łukasiewicz's Elem. Math. Logic* p. ix, I enumerate here the more important new results whose authorship, I think, I may ascribe to myself. They are as follows: 1. The parenthesis-free notation of expressions in the sentential calculus and in Aristotle's syllogistic. **1965** DICKOFF & JAMES *Symbolic Logic* Pref., The parenthesis-free Lukasiewicz notation was especially convenient. **1976** H. LEBLANC *Truth-Value Semantics* i. 11 When no ambiguity threatens, we shall omit the outer parentheses of conditionals, conjunctives..and biconditionals.

parenthesize, *v.* Add: **1. a.** So **parenthesized** *ppl. a.*

1940 W. V. QUINE *Math. Logic* i. 39 It may be bounded at its other end by the limit of that parenthesized expression. **1971** *Amer. Jrnl. Physics* XXXIX. 501/1 The first parenthesized term in the final member of [equation] (29). **1973** A. H. SOMMERSTEIN *Sound Pattern Anc. Greek* i. 6 A schema with parentheses abbreviates a sequence of rules with and without the parenthesized elements, the longest first.

parenthetical, *a.* Add: **B.** as *sb.*

1957 *Publ. Amer. Dial. Soc.* XXVIII. 73 We may divide the segmental tentations according to position into three groups: initials, parentheticals, and finals. **1977** *Canad. Jrnl. Linguistics* 1976 XXI. II. 166 Parentheticals containing 'do'.

parent-in-law: see PARENT *sb.* 1 in Dict. and Suppl.

pareo, var. *PAREU.

pareœan (pærē·ăn), *a.* and *sb. Anthrop.* [f. PARA-[1] + Gr. ἑῷ-ος dawn, eastern + -AN.] **A.** *adj.* Designating a Southern Mongol people, esp. those found in and near China, perhaps to distinguish them from the older Chinese stock whose myths spoke of themselves as the people of the dawn. **B.** *sb.* A member of this people.

1904 T. W. KINGSMILL in *Jrnl. R. Asiatic Soc.* (North China Branch) XXXV. 95 In the Mantses, and in a less degree in..the Lolos, the yellow pigment, characteristic of the Pareæan [*sic*] races, is either altogether absent or at most slightly developed. **1909** A. C. HADDON *Races of Man* 18 (*heading*) Indo-Chinese, Pareœans or Southern Mongols. **1929** L. H. D. BUXTON *China* iii. 44 The Chinese belong to the southern or 'Pareoean' branch of that great group of humanity which is usually called 'Yellow Man' or 'Mongolian'. *Ibid.* 45 Pareoean (παρῃοῖος), 'from beside the east', is a term originally proposed by T. W. Kingsmill and now definitely adopted by Haddon for the group frequently known as 'southern Mongols'. **1931** C. G. SELIGMAN in W. Rose *Outl. Mod. Knowl.* 443 The Southern Mongols, who in recent literature are tending more and more to be called Pareoean. **1957** *Encycl. Brit.* XVIII. 866/2 In Korea there is a narrow belt which forms a connecting link between the northern and the Pareoean peoples. The latter differ most strikingly from their northern neighbours in having less prominent cheek-bones and a broadish nose.

parera (pa·rerā). [Maori.] A New Zealand name for the grey duck, *Anas superciliosa*, found in many islands of the South Pacific region.

1835 W. YATE *Acct. N.Z.* (ed. 2) ii. 57 *Parera*, or Wild Duck—These birds exactly resemble the common English wild-duck. They are of a fine flavour. **1855** R. TAYLOR *Te Ika a Maui* xxv. 407 Parera, turuki..the duck; very similar to the wild duck of England. **1894** C. W. RICHMOND *Let.* 22 Mar. in *Richmond–Atkinson Papers* (1960) II. x. 597 Your Uncle James got a pot-shot at a lot of parera (grey duck) and knocked over *seven*. **1930** W. R. B. OLIVER *N.Z. Birds* 215 Grey Duck. Parera. **1966** R. A. FALLA et al. *Field Guide to Birds N.Z.* 90 Grey Duck *Anas superciliosa*... Maori name: Parera.

parergon. Add: **2.** (Further examples.) Also a work, composition, etc., that is secondary to or a derivative of a larger or greater work; an opusculum.

1928 W. M. WHEELER *Foibles of Insects & Men* p. vii, For some time friends have been urging me to republish in book form some of my papers which have appeared in various scientific journals. The continued demand for these parerga..suggests that they may, perhaps, be of interest to readers who do not habitually consult scientific journals. **1957** H. NICOLSON *Let.* 2 Oct. (1968) 339, I don't think that you [*sc.* Vita Sackville-West] will really go down to posterity as a writer of gardening articles. You will be remembered as a poet... So your gardening things will be regarded as a mere *parergon* ('a bye-work'), like the flute-playing of Frederick the Great. **1963** *Times* 15 Feb. 6/6 At the end of the programme he and his orchestra played the suite of Symphonic Dances from *West Side Story*, a parergon of the musical show, and a very distinguished one. **1975** A. MIMS tr. N. Kazantzakis *Let.* in *Nikos Kazantzakis* IV. 526, I think that my whole soul..is crystallized in the *Odyssey*. All the other works are parergons. **1975** *Times Lit. Suppl.* 16 May 531/2 Henry Bradley's *The Making of English*..is what it is only because it arose as an inspired parergon to its author's main work as co-editor of the great Oxford Dictionary.

pareschatology (pæ:reskătǫ·lŏdʒi). *Theol.* [f. Gr. παρέσχατο-ς penultimate + -LOGY.] A term introduced for theories about human life after physical death and before the final resolution.

1976 J. HICK *Death & Eternal Life* i. 22 Whereas eschatology is the doctrine of the *eschata* or last things, and thus of the ultimate state of man, pareschatology is, by analogy, the doctrine of the *para-eschata*, or next-to-last things, and thus of the human future between the present life and man's ultimate state. *Ibid.* iv. 34 The rather rare Greek word *pareschatos* means 'penultimate' or 'next-to-last', and enables us to coin 'pareschatology' as the study of the next-to-last things, on analogy with 'eschatology', the study of the last things. I am grateful to my colleague Michael Goulder for this useful word. **1977** *Theol. Today* XXXIV. 182 His own constructive proposal for a 'pareschatology' is a form of the doctrine of resurrection expanded to include what he calls 'vertical' as opposed to 'horizontal' reincarnation. **1977** *Times Lit. Suppl.* 1 Apr. 390/4 He examines in detail Western and Eastern pareschatologies (ie, pictures of what happens between death and an ultimate state).

Paretan (parē·tən, -ī·tən), *a.* and *sb.* Also **Paretian** (-ʃən). [f. *PARET(O + -AN, -IAN.] **A.** *adj.* Of or pertaining to Pareto or his economic or sociological theories or methods. **B.** *sb.* A follower of Pareto or someone who adheres to his theories or methods. Hence **Pare·tanism.**

1936 WIRTH & SHILS tr. *Mannheim's Ideology & Utopia* v. 279 From Nietzsche the lines of development lead to the Freudian and Paretian theories of original impulses. **1949** R. K. MERTON *Social Theory* viii. 219 Not only ideological analysis..but also..Marxism, semanticism, propaganda analysis, Paretanism and..functional analysis have..a similar outlook on the role of ideas. **1965** *McGraw-Hill Dict. Mod. Econ.* 369 A situation is not a Paretian or social optimum if it is possible..to make one person better off without making another person (or persons) worse off. **1969** D. MACRAE in Ionescu & Gellner *Populism* 153 For over a century ideologies have been regarded as epiphenomena by sociologists and political scientists. As such Marxists have 'unmasked' them, Paretans treated them as the verbal derivations of non-logical sentiments,..Freudians psycho-analysed them, and so on. **1969** R. WOLLHEIM *Family Romance* 170 A pupil asked me a question about Paretan *optima*.

paretic, *a.* Add: **B.** *sb.* A person affected with paresis.

1881 *Brit. Med. Jrnl.* 12 Mar. 394/1 Local anæsthesia seems..the rule with paretics. **1924** [see *CONFABULATE *v.* 2]. **1957** J. KEROUAC *On Road* (1958) II. vi. 142 An old college schoolmate whose father, a mad paretic, had died and left a fortune. **1972** *Brit. Jrnl. Psychiatry* CXXI. 146/1 Quite a few paretics can be rehabilitated following a complete treatment.

Pareto (parē·to, -ī·to). The name of the Italian economist and sociologist, Vilfredo *Pareto* (1848–1923), used *attrib.* and in the possessive to indicate his theories or methods and esp. the law, or mathematical formula, in which he claimed that the distribution of income for any society could be expressed.

1920 A. C. PIGOU *Econ. of Welfare* v. ii. 699 When these points are conceded, the general defence of 'Pareto's law' as a law of even limited necessity rapidly crumbles. **1930** E. R. A. SELIGMAN in *Political Sci. Q.* XLV. 341. His *Cours d'économie politique*..contained among other notable contributions the first formulation of the principle which subsequently became known as Pareto's law. This was a generalization which attempted to express the relation between the amount of income and the number of its recipients. **1937** YULE & KENDALL *Introd. Theory Statistics* (ed. 11) vi. 100 In economic statistics this form of distribution [*sc.* the extremely asymmetrical] is particularly characteristic of the distribution of wealth in the population at large.., and the curve to which it gives rise has been called the 'Pareto line', after Vilfredo Pareto. **1949** [see *ERGODICITY]. **1962** *Times Lit. Suppl.* 24 Aug. 634/1 The Pareto coefficients measuring such interspatial and intertemporal differentials of remuneration show 'a very considerable consistency'. **1967** [see *IMPOSSIBILITY 4]. **1968** *Internat. Encycl. Social Sci.* XI. 406/1 Thus, Pareto's law is nothing else than the ordinary negative exponential distribution, truncated at the left to log *h.* **1971** I. J. GOOD in *Public Choice* X. 99 The definition of a Pareto-optimal set is a set such that every point outside it is dominated by at least one point inside it, whereas no point inside it is dominated by any other point in it. **1974** *Encycl. Brit. Macropædia* XIX. 680/1 The right-hand tail of the Pareto curve for *disposable* income distribution is curved downward considerably by taxation. **1974** *Times* 25 Mar. 17/8 We were warned of the dangers of Pareto's law—to spend 80 per cent of the time on 20 per cent of the people.

pareu (pā·re,u). Also **pariu, pareo.** [Native Polynesian name.] A skirt worn by men and women in Polynesia, made of a single straight piece of cloth, usu. of printed cotton. So **pareu cloth,** the cloth of which this and other Polynesian garments are made.

1860 MAYNE REID *Odd People* 211 There is but one 'garment' to be described, and that is the 'pareu', which will be better understood, perhaps, by calling it a 'petticoat'. **1894** STEVENSON & OSBOURNE *Ebb-Tide* I. i. 13, I saw a man in a *pariu*, and with a mat under his arm, come along the beach from the town. **1914** R. BROOKE *Let.* 5 Apr. (1968) 574 I'll wind my parea [*sic*] tighter round my middle & go & pull out the canoes & we'll all jump in. **1914** —— *Let.* 24 May (1968) 588 Raymond Buildings must be littered with dropped smocks. May I add a well-worn *paréo* to the heap on Friday week—a day or two after you get this? **1919** *Century Mag.* Aug. 452/2 The light fell upon..the men,..catching ruddy gleams from red *pareus*. **1919** W. S. MAUGHAM *Moon & Sixpence* liii. 230 The *pareo* is a long strip of trade cotton... It is worn round the waist and hangs to the knees. **1932** —— *Narrow Corner* ix. 46 In a little while a blackfellow, wearing nothing but a pareo, came along. **1949** P. H. BUCK *Coming of Maori* (1950) II. v. 158 The women's skirt, termed *pareu* in the Cook and Society Islands, was a wider piece of material wound around the waist and descending to above the knees for single girls and below the knees for married women. **1961** *Sunday Express* 26 Nov. 21/1 A gorgeous young Polynesian girl..was wearing a native *pareu*,—a sort of wrap-around costume of flowered cloth. **1969** R. T. WILCOX *Dict. Costume* (1970) 259/2 *Pareu, pareo*, a Polynesian skirt or loincloth of standard size and colors, a rectangle printed with conventional flower designs. **1972** *Islander* (Victoria, B.C.) 16 Apr. 2/1 The children also discovered..pareu cloth at 89c a yard. This brightly colored, boldly designed cloth is used all over the Pacific for virtually all clothing, as well as for bed-covers, drapes, room dividers and tablecloths. **1974** T. HEYERDAHL *Fatu-Hiva* i. 41 To walk in the woods and hills of Papenoo was sheer pleasure, for there we wore only an airy *pareu*, and the temperature felt like a pleasant dream.

parfait (pā·ɹfē¹). [a. F. *parfait* sb., absolute use of *parfait* PERFECT *a.*] A rich iced pudding of whipped cream, eggs, etc.; also, ice cream, fruit, syrup, whipped cream, etc., arranged in layers and served in a tall glass. Also *attrib.*

1894 C. RANHOFER *Epicurean* 994 Parfait with Nougat and with Almonds. **1906** [see *MOUSSE]. **1932** 'N. SHUTE' *Lonely Road* iv. 67 The parfaits came, and proved to be a tinned peach and ice mixed up together in a cup. **1936** G. GREENE *Gun for Sale* i. 11 He stared with distaste at the long list of sweet iced drinks, of *parfaits* and sundaes and *coupes* and splits. **1948** *Good Housek. Cookery Bk.* II. 490 A Parfait..is usually understood to be a rather rich form of Mousse, light for the reason that it contains whipped whites of eggs. **1953** E. TAYLOR *Sleeping Beauty* ix. 161 Sundaes, shakes, parfaits, whips, melbas. **1969** R. & D. DE SOLA *Dict. Cooking* 168/2 *Parfait*, dessert made of alternate layers of ice cream, fruit, syrup, and whipped cream. *Ibid., Parfait glass*, tall narrow glass used for serving parfaits. **1978** *Monitor* (McAllen, Texas) 25 June 1E Mayan Parfait is a smooth, rich mix of vanilla ice cream layered between a banana-nut frozen confection. *Ibid.*, Parfait glasses are perfect for showing off this pretty dessert.

‖ **Parfait Amour** (pā:ɹfē¹t amū³·ɹ). [Fr., lit. 'perfect love'.] A sweet, spiced liqueur.

1818 T. MOORE *Fudge Fam. Paris* 25 A neat glass of *parfait-amour* which one sips Just as if bottled velvet tipp'd over one's lips! **1862** C. SCHULTZ *Manual for Manuf. Cordials &c.* 183 *Parfait Amour*... 8 ounces of cedrat rinds. 4 do. lemon peels. ½ do. cloves. Ground; macerate for 24 hours with 3 gallons of alcohol, 95 per cent, and 3½ gallons of water..distil from off the water 3 gallons of flavored alcohol; add 30 lbs. of sugar dissolved in 5⅛ gallons of water; color deep red, and filter. **1877** [see *orange bitters* s.v. *ORANGE *sb.*¹ 7 a]. **1950** O. A. MENDELSOHN *Earnest Drinker* xvii. 130 The bright purplish tint of such a liqueur as *Parfait Amour* is..as artificial an effect as possible. **1965** *House & Garden* Dec. 90/3 *Parfait Amour.* Sweet and heavy taste and colouring. **1972** N. FREELING *Long Silence* II. 156 She..was being given a choice between crème de cacao, crème de banane and a mauve concoction known to Holland as Parfait Amour.

parfleche. Add: Also **-flash.** (Earlier and later examples.) Occas. *fig.* Hence **parfle·ched** *a.*, made or covered with parfleche.

1827 E. ERMATINGER in *Trans. R. Soc. Canada 1912* (1913) VI. II. 110 We embarked with crews and cargoes as follows: viz..1 pack Parfleches. **1845** J. C. FRÉMONT *Rep. Exploring Expedition* 237 Some of us had the misfortune to wear moccasins with parflêche soles, so slippery that we could not keep our feet. **1850** L. H. GARRARD *Wah-to-Yah* vii. 106 With a sole of *par-fleche*, lapping over on top of the foot. **1867** *Harper's Mag.* Oct. 584/2 The *teet-sock* or *parfleche* is generally made of a dried buffalo hide, the hair of which has been beaten off with a stone..; it is then cut in the shape of an envelope. *a* **1918** G. STUART *40 Yrs. on Frontier* (1925) II. 40 [The medicine man] usually had a highly ornamental parflash, in which he kept one or more fetishes. **1938** P. H. GODSELL *Red Hunters of Snows* 33 Here braves..stored..commodities in painted parfleche bags for the forthcoming journey to York Factory. **1940** F. NIVEN *Mine Inheritance* 61, I saw her bending over another parflèched box in front of the tent and taking out two long, gleaming knives. **1952** *Beaver* June 6/1 The hides were manufactured into robes or were divested of their hair and made into tepee covers, clothing, moccasins, *parfléche* trunks and shields. **1956** V. FISHER *Pemmican* 199 The old man's face was a parfleche of seams. **1972** D. KENNEDY *Recoll. Assiniboine Chief* 92 These parfleches were made from flint hides with the hair scraped off. They were decorated with colours in geometric designs. **1973** A. H. WHITEFORD *N. Amer. Indian Arts* 78 Parfleches are large envelopes of rawhide used in the Plains to pack dried food and other things. **1974** *Sci. Amer.* Jan. 129/1 These modern ingenuities do not overshadow the photographs within: a parfleche, a yurt or an old folding feather-bed-in-a-chest.

parfocal (pāɹfōu·kăl), *a.* [f. PAR *sb.*¹ + FOCAL *a.*] Having or pertaining to the property that corresponding focal points of different lenses lie in the same plane, so that they may be interchanged without the need to adjust the focus. Const. *with.*

1886 *Microsc. Bull. & Sci. News* Aug. 31/1 Referring to the article in the April issue..on 'changing eye-pieces without altering focus, etc.', we announce that we are prepared to furnish eye-pieces, as there described... We have named these eye-pieces *parfocal*, meaning 'of equal focus'. **1944** C. P. SHILLABER *Photomicrography* iii. 234 The objectives are said to be parfocal with each other when one setting of the microscope will serve to focus all four objectives. **1955** *Sci. Amer.* Feb. 122/2 This is called 'parfocal' mounting, and it saves a lot of time when, for example, you are searching your collection for a specific type of crystal, surface texture or color to match an unknown mineral. **1965** J. R. BENFORD in R. Kingslake *Appl. Optics & Optical Engin.* III. iv. 167 The 3·5× objective is a comparatively recent 'telephoto' construction, designed to be parfocal with the high-power objectives. **1970** R. P. LOVELAND *Photomicrography* I. iii. 114 The rotating objective holder is the most convenient in use when the objectives are parfocal. **1976** *Physics Bull.* Nov. 511/1 To meet the recently increased demand for low magnification objectives, a parfocal distance of 45 mm has been employed. **1979** *Nature* 1 Mar. p. xxiii, All optical components are parfocal and permanently centred.

Hence **parfoca·lity,** the property of being parfocal; **parfo·cally** *adv.*

1965 J. R. BENFORD in R. Kingslake *Appl. Optics & Optical Engin.* III. iv. 165 Tightening one of these and loosening the other provide a precise means of moving the objective lens up and down to bring about the desired parfocality setting, so that objectives on a multiple nosepiece can be interchanged without losing focus. **1971** J. H. RICHARDSON *Optical Microscopy for Materials Sci.* i. 41 Parfocality is not an inherent property of an objective, but is rather a convenience often provided on the more modern microscopes. **1974** *Physics Bull.* May 197/2 For optical measurements the instrument has a high pressure xenon arc lamp and six pairs of matched condenser and objective lenses mounted parfocally in turrets.

parfocalize (pāɹfōu·kăləiz), *v.* [f. prec. + -IZE.] *trans.* To make parfocal. So **parfo:calization,** the action or result of parfocalization.

1944 C. P. SHILLABER *Photomicrography* iii. 234 As a rule parfocalization can be attained for all microscope objectives except those of great focal length. **1958** G. H. NEEDHAM *Pract. Use Microscope* xv. 234/2 On the modern, routine stands these three or four objectives are parfocalized on the revolving nosepiece so that after focusing with the low dry, the high dry may be swung into position without racking the body tube up. **1965** J. R. BENFORD in R. Kingslake *Appl. Optics & Optical Engin.* III. iv. 165 The second adjustment is to parfocalize the objective.

‖ **parfumerie** (parfümərī). [Fr.] A factory which produces, or a (department of a) shop which sells, perfume.

1842 POE *Mystery of Marie Rogêt* in *Ladies' Compan.* (N.Y.) Dec. 97/2 The disappearance of..Marie Rogêt from the *parfumerie* of Monsieur Le Blanc. **1855** S. WHITING *Heliondé* iii. 125 The department of parfumerie would have used up a whole continent of 'sweet gul',..steppes of lavender, [etc.]. **1951** W. SANSOM *Face of Innocence* 138 In Eve's parfumerie shadowy with scent and cool with pale attendants. **1970** 'S. TROY' *Blind Man's Garden* vi. 63 They were sitting in André's office at the *parfumerie.* **1977** *Time* 11 Apr. 29/3 They are fellow clerks in the same Budapest *parfumerie.*

parge, *v.* Delete ? *Obs.* and add later example.

1908 G. P. BANKART *Art of Plasterer* vi. 77 'Lambert's Farm', in the parish of Great Tey, Essex, has a parged front.

pargeter. Delete † *Obs.*, remove restriction of *pargetter* to 6–9, and add later examples.

1936 S. R. JONES *Eng. Village Homes* vi. 96 Men who dabbed on the clay were 'daubers', and those responsible for working the plaster were 'playsterers' or 'pargetters'. **1951** LAMBERT & MARX *Eng. Popular Art* iii. 48 In the nineteenth century the pargeter sometimes turned his hand to making plaques for inn signs. **1968** J. ARNOLD *Shell Bk. Country Crafts* iii. 55 This includes millwrights, masons, thatchers, sawyers, drystone-wallers and pargetters.

pa·rgetry. [f. PARGET *sb.* + -RY]. = PARGET *sb.* 2.

1908 G. P. BANKART *Art of Plasterer* vi. 64 (*caption*) Pargetry on House in High Street, Maidstone, now pulled down. **1936** S. R. JONES *Eng. Village Homes* vi. 97 Thought in design, and capacity to invent suitable tools for working, brought a good deal of variety to pargetry, as may be seen in roughcast and those numerous pricked, combed and scratched arrangements once known as arrowheads, tortoise-shell, zig-zag, herring-bone, basket-work, scallops, interlacing squares and wavy lines.

parge-work (in Dict. s.v. PARGE *v.*). Delete † and add later examples. Hence **pa·rge-worker.** Also *parge decoration*, etc.

1906 *Essex Rev.* XV. 162 The unique designs in parge-work on its front. **1908** G. P. BANKART *Art of Plasterer* vi. 58 One form of parge decoration consisted of a simple type of incising, or cutting patterns through the top layer of plaster down to the coating underneath. *Ibid.* 79 The favourite spots of the parge-worker were over-mantels, gable ends, and lunettes, [etc]. **1940** *Chambers's Techn. Dict.* 617/1 *Parge-work* (*Build.*), an ancient form of external plastering with a mixture similar to that used in *pargetting*..chimneys. **1951** LAMBERT & MARX *Eng. Popular Art* iii. 48 This 'parge work' ornament was very popular in the sixteenth, seventeenth and eighteenth centuries. At Ipswich there are numerous examples of external parge decorations from about 1557.

parging (pā·ɹdʒiŋ), *vbl. sb.* [f. PARGE *v.* + -ING¹.] = PARGETING *vbl. sb.*

1897 F. C. MOORE *How to build Home* iii. 34 The parging or plastering of the inside of the flue is permitted. **1903** *Eng. Dial. Dict.* IV. 423/2 *Parging*..(1) the lining of a chimney..(2) a ceiling. **1940** *Chambers's Techn. Dict.* 617/1 *Parge-work*... Also called *parging.* **1964** J. S. SCOTT *Dict. Building* 224 Pargeting or parging or pargeting.

pargyline (pā·ɹgilīn). *Pharm.* [Etym. unkn.] A monoamine oxidase inhibitor used in the treatment of benign hypertension, usu. in the form of the hydrochloride, a white crystalline powder; *N*-methyl-*N*-prop-2-ynylbenzyl-amine, $C_6H_5CH_2N(CH_3)CH_2C{:}CH$.

1961 *Current Therapeutic Res.* III. 381 Pargyline hydrochloride appears to be a potent antihypertensive agent, the maximal effect of which is manifested slowly. **1963** *Yearbk. Drug Therapy* 85 (*heading*) Antihypertensive properties of pargyline hydrochloride (Eutonyl): new nonhydrazine monoamine oxidase inhibitor. **1970** PASSMORE & ROBSON *Compan. Med. Stud.* II. viii. 10/2 Pargyline, a nonhydrazine compound, possesses modest anti-hypertensive potency and its effect begins several days after the drug is given and continues for 2–3 weeks after treatment is stopped. **1972** [see *methyldopa* s.v. *METHYL c]. **1977** *Lancet* 6 Aug. 275/1 Plasma-prolactin levels doubled in depressive patients treated with the monoamine-oxidase inhibitors, clorgyline and pargyline.

parhelium, obs. var. PARHELION, var. *PARAHELIUM.

parhormone, obs. var. *PARAHORMONE.

pariah. Add: Also freq. with pronunc. (părəi·ă). **4. b. pariah brig,** a sea-vessel built in India.

1929 F. C. BOWEN *Sea Slang* 101 *Pariah brigs*, deep-sea native vessels in India. **1935** M. H. BEATTIE *On Hooghly* 116 She was what was termed a pariah brig, or native craft, which would find her way to Kedgeree and there pick up a native pilot. **1946** 'SHALIMAR' *Ships & Men* 122 Indian pariah brigs were taken up to replace coasting steamers.

pariahdom (further examples); also **pa·riah-hood, pa·riahism, pa·riahship.**
1887 *Globe* 22 Oct. 1/4 It is astonishing that any person ..should regard the national uniform as a badge of pariah-ism. **1894** *Work & Workers* June 258/2 Ostracism from the class carries with it..hopeless, entire pariahdom. **1897** W. J. LOCKE *Derelicts* xx. 256 Forgetful of the gaol and his pariahdom. **1906** —— *Beloved Vagabond* (1908) vi. 68 They walked on together, and I dropped behind, suddenly realising my pariahdom. **1920** *Edin. Rev.* Jan. 18 The possibility of intermarriage is the crucial test of equality of consideration; its absence sets a stamp of servility and pariahship on the proscribed caste. **1936** W. FAULKNER *Absalom, Absalom!* 334 Rode the two horses through that night..in something very like pariah-hood. **1945** R. HARGREAVES *Enemy at Gate* 19 This choice aggregation of desperadoes and 'poor masterless men', welded into that solidarity of pariahdom which is the outlaws' primary source of strength. **1967** H. ARENDT *Orig. Totalitarianism* (new ed.) iii. 68 Disraeli ..discovered the secret of how to preserve luck, that natural miracle of pariahdom. **1977** *New Yorker* 15 Aug. 70/2 Moynihan is the strongest force in the attempt to shift New York out of the congressional pariahdom to which it has long been consigned.

Parian, *a.* (*sb.*) Add: **A.** *adj.* **1.** *Parian Chronicle,* add: a further fragment was found in 1897 and is kept on Paros.

3. *Parian cement,* a plaster similar to Keene's cement but prepared with borax in place of alum.

1858 P. L. SIMMONDS *Dict. Trade Products* 276/1 *Parian-cement,* a fine or coarse cement, according to the purpose for which it is to be used. **1880** *Encycl. Brit.* XI. 351/2 Parian cement is plaster hardened with water containing 10 per cent. of borax. **1949** KIRK & OTHMER *Encycl. Chem. Technol.* III. 443 Keene's cement is the best known of the hard-plaster group, others, differing only slightly, being Parian cement and Martin's cement.

B. *sb.* **1.** A native or inhabitant of Paros.

1550 T. NICOLLS tr. *Thucydides' Hystory* [*Peloponnesian War*] IV. xiii. sig. u6 Being nyghe the towne of Thase, whyche was a colonie of the Paryans, distante frome Amphipolis aboute one journey by sea. **1629** HOBBES tr. *Thucydides' Hist. Peloponnesian Warre* IV. 270 Thasus (which is an island, and a colonie of the Parians, distant from Amphipolus, about halfe a dayes sayle). **1753** W. SMITH tr. *Thucydides' Hist. Peloponnesian War* II. IV. 85 Thasus is an island, a colony of the Parians, and distant about half a day's sail from Amphipolis. **1845** *Encycl. Metrop.* XVII. 487/2 Themistocles made the Parians pay severely for their perfidy to Aristides. **1911** *Encycl. Brit.* XX. 861/1 So high was the reputation of the Parians that they were chosen by the people of Miletus to arbitrate in a party dispute. **1960** R. CARPENTER *Greek Sculpture* i. 14 The Parians..had acquired the craft in Egypt. **1978** CARSON & CLARK *Paros* (rev. ed.) 5 Campers have established a good reputation among Parians.

2. (See sense 2 in Dict.)

3. = **Parian cement.*

1886 H. C. SEDDON *Builder's Work* vi. 238 Parian is a white cement. **1967** A. G. GEESON *Building Sci. Materials* (ed. 2) II. i. 56 Adhesion on Keene's or Parian is notoriously poor.

paribuntal (pæri̇̆bʌ·ntăl). [f. *Par*acale, *Para*ñaque, *Par*ang or *Par*asan, places in the Philippines + *BUNTAL.] A fine straw.

1926 *Vogue* May 105 An attractive summer model is carried out in paribuntal, a new fine straw. **1935** *Times* 17 June 11/3 For a tall girl there is a charming wide brimmed hat in brown paribuntal. **1963** *Harper's Bazaar* May 47 The hat..in cream paribuntal. *Ibid.* 49 The hat..in white paribuntal overlaid with toast paillasson straw.

parichnos (pari·knǫs). [a. F. *parichnos* (C. E. Bertrand 1891, in *Trav. & Mém. Facultés de Lille* II. VI. 84), f. PARA-[1] + Gk. ἴχνος track, trace.] A strand of tissue found beside the leaf traces in fossil plants of the family Lepidodendraceæ. Also *attrib.*

1893 W. C. WILLIAMSON in *Phil. Trans. R. Soc.* B. CLXXXIV. 10 Since I agree with M. Bertrand on this point, I shall accept and employ his name of parichnos. **1906** *Ann. Bot.* XX. 269 (*title*) On the presence of a parichnos in recent plants. *Ibid.*, The term Parichnos was used by Bertrand to designate the thin-walled parenchymatous strand of tissue, occurring in *Lepidodendron Harcourtii,* which accompanies the leaf-trace on the posterior side during its outward journey. **1935** F. O. BOWER *Primitive Land Plants.* xii. 234 These lateral pits are connected internally with the parichnos. **1969** F. E. ROUND *Introd. Lower Plants* xi. 135 Two structures entirely unknown in modern lycopods occur on either side of the leaf trace—these are the parichnos scars. *Ibid.*, There may be two other scars beneath the leaf scar which are also parichnos strands branching off those entering the leaf.

parietal, *a.* (*sb.*) Add: **1. a.** *parietal eye,* in the tuatara and many lizards, a structure of unknown function, resembling an eye and situated in the upper part of the skull beneath an opening in the parietal bone.

1886 W. B. SPENCER in *Nature* 13 May 35/1 In formation of the paired eyes [of *Hatteria punctata*] invagination to form an optic cup takes place, whilst apparently it does not do so in the case of what may be called the parietal eye. **1911** *Phil. Trans. R. Soc.* B. CCI. 264 The pineal or parietal eye in Sphenodon is..the left-hand member of the original pair of pineal outgrowths. **1937** *Discovery* May 135/1 The so-called third eye of the tuatara..is sometimes known as the parietal or pineal eye. **1969** A. BELLAIRS *Life of Reptiles* I. vi. 232 In many lizards the parietal eye seems to play some part in regulating the amount of time spent basking.

2. (Later examples.)

1968 'E. LATHEN' *Come to Dust* (1969) xiv. 140 Two young women had been discovered at a time and in circumstances all too clearly proscribed by the parietal rules and Brunswick's honor system. **1972** A. ULAM *Fall of Amer. Univ.* iii. 106 In any case in most schools, certainly at Harvard, the formerly idiotically strict parietal rules had been eroded by the sixties to sensibly hypocritical proportions. **1973** E. TAYLOR *Serpent under It* (1974) xxi. 177 The kinds of things that stir them [*sc.* students] up these days are parietal hours and open admissions and black studies. **1977** *National Observer* (U.S.) 1 Jan. 10/4 Parietal rules were ignored and, later, abandoned.

3. (Further example.)

1916 [see *MURAL *a.*[1] 2].

B. *sb.* **2.** *pl.* (see quot.) *U.S. slang.*

1967 *N.Y. Times* 17 Dec. IV. 9 Yale students..have rejoined the nationwide battle for liberalized 'parietals'—campus term for women's visiting hours in male dormitories, or vice-versa.

parietin (părəi·ėtin). *Chem.* and *Bot.* [f. L. *parietinus* of or belonging to walls (f. *pariēs, pariet-* wall), in the fem. a specific epithet of the lichen *Xanthoria parietina* from which the compound was obtained: see -IN[1].] An anthraquinone derivative present as an orange-yellow pigment in some lichens; 1:8-dihydroxy-3-methoxy-6-methylanthraquinone, $C_{16}H_{12}O_5$.

1844 R. D. THOMSON in *Proc. Philos. Soc. Glasgow* I. IX. 187, I have succeeded in obtaining the colouring matter, or *Parietin,* as I propose to term it, in the form of needles. **1894** *Jrnl. Chem. Soc.* LXVI. I. 541 The colouring matter.. may be extracted by means of benzene without destroying the lichen. It crystallises in small, golden-yellow needles which are soluble in alkalis with blood-red coloration... The authors consider this colouring matter to be a dihydroxyanthraquinone, and propose for it the name *chrysophyscin*... The colouring matter was termed parietin by Thomsen [*sic*]. **1921** A. L. SMITH *Handbk. Brit. Lichens* 44 The species [of *Xanthoria*] grow most freely in maritime districts, and are bright-yellow in the open where the acid substance parietin..is freely formed. *Ibid.*, Parietin is produced in more or less abundance in the thallus of most species [of *Placodium*], and in the apothecia of all except *Pl. repellens* which is probably an impoverished form. **1966** *New Phytologist* LXV. 211 Unlike the species of *Peltigera,* those of *Xanthoria* are relatively rich in 'lichen acids' such as parietin and atranorin. **1967** M. E. HALE *Biol. Lichens* viii. 105 The following four pigments are also common to non-lichenized fungi: endocrocin and parietin, both anthraquinones, and polyporic and thelephoric acids, both terphenylquinones.

‖ **parigot** (parigo), *a. colloq.* [Fr.] Of an accent, etc.: Parisian. Also as *sb.*, Parisian French.

1974 N. FREELING *Dressing of Diamond* 175 'What sort of accent would you call that, Johnny?' 'Overlaid,' said the technician stolidly. 'Predominance parigot.' 'Parigot hell, that's peasant... Peasant who went up to Ivry and acquired the rhythms.' *Ibid.* 202 A young or youngish woman who speaks with something of a parigot accent. **1977** *Times Lit. Suppl.* 6 May 546/5 French, in this case the most idiomatic 1977 Parigot French.

pari mutuel. Add: Now usu. **pari-mutuel** and sing. (Further examples.) **b.** The booth at which such bets are placed, or the machine which issues tickets recording such bets.

1888 [see *FAR-EASTERN *a.*]. **1891** *Harper's Mag.* Mar. 511/1 For this rough horde of human beings the only interest that the races offered was the betting..by means of the mutual pool or *pari mutuel* system. **1913** 'F. SUMMERVILLE' *Spirit of Paris* v. 38 But there is a great keenness on the animals too, and men and women bet at the *pari-mutuel* with much earnestness. **1923** E. HEMINGWAY *Three Stories & Ten Poems* 43 The gong going for dear life and the pari mutuel wickets rattling down. **1931** E. WAUGH *Remote People* 12 There had been a horse-race ..with a pari-mutuel. **1934** 'A. BRIDGE' *Ginger Griffin* xvi. 200 They strolled towards the *pari-mutuel* windows, which extended in a long row between the paddock and the grand-stand. **1955** 'S. RANSOME' *Deadly Bedfellows* xiii. 123 The legislature..will choose to legalise *pari-mutuel* horse-racing. **1964** A. WYKES *Gambling* viii. 191 The pari-mutuel system (which was devised in 1872 by a French chemist named Pierre Oller). **1969** C. DRUMMOND *Odds on Death* ii. 43 The big market is not the parimutuel —totaliser, call it what you will—but book-making, legal and illegal. **1971** L. KOPPETT *N.Y. Times Guide Spectator Sports* x. 172 Pari-mutuel betting refers to a system in which all the participating bettors are betting against each other. **1973** D. FRANCIS in *Winter's Crimes 5* 115 It meant hanging around the pari-mutuel with your eyes open. **1976** *Maclean's Mag.* 12 Jan. 34/1 The state bicentennial commission raised $845,000 from the taxes on one extra day of betting at pari-mutuel outlets.

paring, *vbl. sb.* Add: **4.** *paring bee*: for U.S. read N. Amer. and add earlier and later examples; *paring-chisel* (later examples), *frolic, gouge, -knife* (later examples).

1830 J. PICKERING *Emigration* 72 A paring 'bee', or 'be', [is] an assemblage of neighbours invited to one house, to prepare apples for drying. **1845** *Lowell* (Mass.) *Offering* V. 269 When we were about to have a paring bee we sent our invitations a day or two previous. **1850** *Knickerbocker* XXXV. 24 Give me the real paring-bee reels and jigs before all your waltzes and Spanish dances. **1857** *Quinland* I. 191 Went this evening..with the young people to a paring-bee at Squire Carter's. **1933** E. C. GUILLET *Early Life Upper Canada* 195 A paring bee produced large numbers of strings of dried apples, and these were suspended from the ceiling of kitchen or attic. **1895** *Montgomery Ward Catal.* Spring & Summer 365/2 Barton's paring chisels. **1940** *Chambers's Techn. Dict.* 617/1 *Paring chisel* (*Carp., Join.*), a long chisel with a thinner blade than a firmer tool, used for finishing off work by hand. **1964** W. L. GOODMAN *Hist. Woodworking Tools* 33 Plate 1 of the 'Charpente' article shows a workman using the paring-chisel end of this tool. **1968** J. ARNOLD *Shell Bk. Country Crafts* 287 Each blade produced may be compared very roughly to a carpenter's paring-chisel in having a bevel along its two sides. **1974** P. W. BLANDFORD *Country Craft Tools* v. 76 A longer and thinner chisel for hand pressure only was called a 'paring' or 'heading' chisel. **1931** V. P. SEARY *Romance Marit. Provinces* 177 Another sort of frolic was the 'paring frolic', when young men and girls gathered to pare and slice apples, that they might be dried out and kept throughout the winter. **1909** WEBSTER, Paring gouge. **1940** *Chambers's Techn. Dict.* 617/2 *Paring gouge* (*Carp. etc.*), a gouge having the bevel ground upon the inside or concave face of the cutting edge. **1966** A. W. LEWIS *Gloss. Woodworking Terms* 39 A paring gouge is a long thin scribing gouge. **1908** *Sears, Roebuck Catal.* 768/1 Kitchen or paring knives... Length of blade, 3 inches. **1925** *Scribner's Mag.* Oct. 430/1 She was rubbing the paring-knife across her fingers to free them from dirt and water. **1968** J. ARNOLD *Shell Bk. Country Crafts* 139 The box contains hammer, pritchel, buffer, paring-knife, pincers and, of course, a supply of nails.

Paris. Add: Also, in names of articles associated with or designed in Paris, esp. with an implication of being fashionable, exclusive, or expensive, as *Paris cloth, cut, dress, felt, gown, hat, net, shirt*; **Paris binding** (see quot. 1964); **Paris cap** (see quot.); **Paris embroidery** (see quots.); **Paris green** (earlier and later examples); also used as an insecticide.

1918 E. & M. WALLBANK *Dress Cutting & Making* x. 65 For binding skirt seams, use ½″ lute or Paris binding with one edge folded over rather less than half the width. **1964** C. PENTON *ABC of Sewing* 64/1 *Paris binding,* a braid ½″ wide used for covering raw edges cut on the straight, and slip-stitched to the fabric beneath. **1966** J. S. COX *Illustr. Dict. Hairdressing* 109/1 *Paris cap,* a woman's head-dress of the mid-sixteenth century. It fitted the head closely with a jewelled band running over the top of the head and ending in a point on the cheeks. **1960** C. W. CUNNINGTON et al. *Dict. Eng. Costume* 268/1 *Paris Cloth, Toile de Paris.* Med. and 17th c. Originally a fine white linen; later a woollen cloth. **1748** SMOLLETT *R. Random* II. xlv. 80 In the evening, [I] dressed myself in a plain suit of the true Paris cut. **1959** J. BRAINE *Vodi* xiv. 195 The rather cold-eyed girl with the Paris dress and the real pearls. **1973** H. MCCLOY *Change of Heart* ii. 17 The black dress was Paris and so at least four years old... Yet old as it was that Paris dress made every other dress in the room look shapeless. **1882** CAULFEILD & SAWARD *Dict. Needlework* 378/1 *Paris Embroidery.*—This is a simple variety of Satin Stitch worked upon Piqué with fine white cord for washing articles, and upon coloured rep silk, or fine cloth with filoselles for other materials. **1957** M. B. PICKEN *Fashion Dict.* 243/2 *Paris embroidery,* white cord embroidery on piqué. **1969** R. T. WILCOX *Dict. Costume* (1970) 259/2 *Paris embroidery,* a fine white cord embroidery appliquéd in satin stitch on piqué. Used in washable linens and garment accessories. **1853** J. B. FELT *Customs New Eng.* 119 They were at first called *sombreros,..slouches,* and *California hats,..*but latterly, by some, *Paris felts.* **1839** F. A. KEMBLE *Jrnl. Residence Georgian Plantation* (1863) 346 A Paris gown and bonnet might have been in equal danger of shocking his prejudices. **1896** E. TURNER *Little Larrikin* xiii. 141 The commanding presence in the Paris gown. **1913** A. BENNETT *Regent* II. viii. 219 Elegant women wearing Paris or almost-Paris gowns. **1965** ROACH & EICHER *Dress, Adornment, & Social Order* 396 Writer sees Hollywood fashions beginning to take some of the prestige away from Paris gowns in the 1930's. **1868** *Amer. Agriculturist* XXVII. 321 The following is going the rounds of the press 'Sure death to Potato Bugs: Take 1 lb. Paris green, 2 lbs. pulverized lime. Mix together, and sprinkle the vines.' We consider this unsafe, as..Paris green is a compound of arsenic and copper, and a deadly poison. **1902** *Encycl. Brit.* XXVIII. 530/2 The best fruit farmers spray fruit trees regularly in the early spring..with quassia and soft soap and paraffin emulsions, and a very few with Paris green only. **1966** LOCKHART & WISEMAN *Introd. Crop Husbandry* vii. 231 Baits such as Paris green. **1845** G. DODD *Brit. Manuf.* 5th Ser. 172 The plush for the larger number of silk hats is woven in Lancashire; but for 'Paris hats', as they are called, it is woven in France. **1906** E. DYSON *Fact'ry 'Ands* vii. 87 A man in a long frock coat, a high, glittering, Paris hat. **1951** C. PORTER *Kiss me Kate* 108 Mr. Harris, plutocrat, Wants to give my cheek a pat, If the Harris pat Means a Paris hat—Bé-bé. **1957** M. B. PICKEN *Fashion Dict.* 165/2 *Paris hat,* high silk hat worn by men. **1759** *Newport* (Rhode Island) *Mercury* 26 June 4/3 To be sold by Jacob Richardson,..plain Gauze, Parisnets, gimp and floss Garland. **1766** C. ANSTEY *New Bath Guide* iii. 23 Stomachers and Parisnets. **1882** CAULFEILD & SAWARD *Dict. Needlework* 378/1 *Paris net,* a description of Net employed in Millinery. **1937** N. COWARD *Present Indicative* I. 28, I can smell the eau-de-Cologne, see..the stripes on his Paris shirt.

parish, *sb.* Add: **2. e.** *transf.* and *fig.* (also influenced by sense 1).

1940 AUDEN *Another Time* 52 The ape Is really at home in the parish Of grimacing and licking. **1941** —— *New Year Let.* I. 25 However miserable may be Our parish of immediacy. **1951** *Times* 1 Jan. 7/6 Covering the whole of the F.E.A.F. [*sc.* Far East Air Force] area,.. two impressions stand out..the vastness of its 'parish' and of its commitments..and the slenderness of the aircraft resources at its disposal. **1958** P. KEMP *No Colours or Crest* viii. 153 My parish includes not only the old frontiers of Albania, but the new regions incorporated into the country by the Axis. **1976** *Shooting Times & Country Mag.* 16–22 Dec. 13/2 Others—in the north—consider they are too far south, while in the south some consider they are too far north! In fact, WAGBI is based almost equally between their interests, bordered by the 'parish' of Northern Ireland; the North of Scotland; Cornwall and Kent. **1977** D. BEATY *Excellency* ii. 25 From British Embassies and High Commissions all over the world came messages reporting reactions of their parishes to the recent events.

7. a. *parish doctor* (examples), *mag, magazine* (examples); *parish relief* (further examples). **b. parish communion, Eucharist,** a communion service held as the principal service of the day (usu. Sunday), and at which most of the congregation communicate; **parish mass,** a mass celebrated in a parish church, *spec.* = **parish communion* (quot. 1763 is a fortuitous collocation); **parish pump,** used allusively (often *attrib.* or as *adj.*) to denote political speakers and their speeches, and other matters, that are limited in scope, outlook, or knowledge, or of local importance only; hence **parish pumper,** one who is concerned with parish-pump politics; **parish pumpery,** concern with local matters only, parochialism; **parish-pumpish** *a.*, limited in outlook and interests, parochial; **parish rig** (see quots.); **parish-rigged** *a.* (later examples); **parish school** *Sc.* and *N. Amer.*, = *parochial school* (*PAROCHIAL *a.* (*sb.*) 1a); so *parish schoolmaster* (the collocation in quot. 1788 may be fortuitous); **parish work,** the work or duty of attending to the poor and sick of a parish; pastoral work in a parish.

1936 *Church Q. Rev.* Oct.–Dec. 103 There will naturally be no later Solemn Eucharist, and only provision earlier for those who cannot possibly attend the Parish Communion. **1937** A. G. HEBERT *Parish Communion* i. 3 By 'the Parish Communion' is meant the celebration of the Holy Eucharist, with the communion of the people, in a parish church, as the chief service of the day, or, better, as the assembly of the Christian community for the worship of God. **1953** [see *MORCELLATED *ppl. a.*]. **1968** L. DEWAR *Outl. Anglican Moral Theol.* vii. 171 The rise of the 'Parish Communion' in the last thirty or forty years..is one of the most remarkable phenomena in the history of the Church of England. **1972** C. STEPHENSON *Merrily on High* ii. 36 It was his custom to go to Holy Communion on the first Sunday in the month, but when a new vicar started a parish communion..my father felt it his duty to back him up and became a weekly communicant. **1975** *Church Times* 8 Aug. 6/5 The Sunday Parish Communion at 9.15 a.m. had been pioneered, though not originated, by St. John's Newcastle, in 1927. **1848** *Punch* 12 Feb. 59 (*caption*) Well, young man. So you wish to be engaged as Parish Doctor? *c* **1875** 'BRENDA' *Froggy's Little Brother* new ed.) ix. 115 It turned out to be only the parish doctor come to see little Deb Blunt. **1977** R. L. WOLFF *Gains & Losses* viii. 425 The parish doctor is a rich man, a scientist. **1936** E. UNDERHILL *Worship* v. 94 The choral Parish Eucharist, the Roman Catholic rite of Benediction,..or any other truly congregational service where the general movement is understood, and hymns, chants, and actions are familiar to all. **1965** C. E. POCKNEE *Parson's Handbk.* (ed. 13) p. xii, The whole trend of Sunday morning worship as manifested today in the Parish Eucharist had been foreshadowed by John Wordsworth in *The Ministry of Grace* (1901). *a* **1966** M. ALLINGHAM *Cargo of Eagles* (1968) xii. 140 The vicar called to leave 'is compliments and a parish mag. **1888** C. M. YONGE *Our New Mistress* ii. 14 As had been put into the 'Parish Magazine', she had been two years from her training college. **1926** S. T. WARNER *Lolly Willowes* I. 67 The parish magazine said: 'The vicar had scarcely left East Bingham when war was declared.' **1955** M. ALLINGHAM *Beckoning Lady* ii. 19 He'd ploughed down there through the snow to take her the parish magazine. **1974** *Times* 8 Mar. 16/8 The editor of *The Shoreham Gazette*, a parish magazine, boasts that he is the first to get into print with a prayer for the new government. **1976** *Deeside Advertiser* 9 Dec., In his parish magazine the Vicar of Shotton has warned parishioners to be prepared for disturbances during Midnight Mass on Christmas Eve. **1763** C. CORDELL *Divine Office for Use of Laity* I. p. vi, the prayers, publications, and familiar instructions used at the Parish-Mass, on Sundays. **1929** S. LESLIE *Anglo-Catholic* xx. 275 The following morning Jasper did not return from saying the Parish Mass in time for his early breakfast. **1958** S. NEILL *Anglicanism* xiv. 403 In many parishes the 'Parish Mass' is followed by a parish breakfast. **1965** C. E. POCKNEE *Parson's Handbk.* (ed. 13) ii. 22 The parson must think out whether he intends to develop the Parish Mass with a choir as his chief act of Sunday morning worship. **1970** H. BRAUN *Parish Churches* xvii. 206 While the sermon has always played a part in the parish Mass, no architectural provision for its delivery appears to have been made until late in the Middle Ages. **1915** *Truth* 21 Apr. 620/1 They are the last word in parochialism; but the table is their parish pump and the croupier is the beadle. **1923** *Daily Mail* 12 Mar. 5 Parish pump politicians distort every word they [*sc.* statesmen] utter. **1923** U. L. SILBERRAD *Lett. J. Armiter* x. 211 The to-dos we make over our own parish pump matters. **1961** A. WILSON *Old Men at Zoo* i. 11 The Treasury job..had called for a good measure of toughness; after it, Regent's Park affairs smelt a little of the parish pump. **1962** *Punch* 14 Feb. 285/1 Parish Pump radio, when it comes, may be the biggest draw yet. **1962** *Radio Times* 22 Nov. 40/2 In 'Talking Point' we introduce a bit of controversy to avoid being too parish-pump. **1963** *Times* 27 Feb. 8/6 Resistance from parish-pump politics is clearly being encountered; hostility to fresh ideas seems inevitable in a country that has some 38,000 communes containing fewer than 500 people. **1973** *Times* 6 June 18/2 Graham Tope, a Liberal, swept to victory..on a platform of community politics, or the politics of the parish pump. **1977** *N.Y. Rev. Bks.* 9 June 32/4 The news they brought did nothing to still those local manifestations around the parish pumps which had been the very essence of the Old Republic in its Golden Age. **1978** G. GREENE *Human Factor* I. i. 14, I don't think I've voted since the war. The issues nowadays so often seem—well, a bit parish pump. **1963** *Economist* 29 June 1387 Worthy parish-pumpers would do well on the enclave councils. **1979** G. POTTINGER *Secretaries of State for Scotland 1926–76* xv. 163 To combat apathy at local elections it was hoped that the top tier would offer an avenue to aspiring politicians, while parish-pumpery would find their satisfaction in the second one. **1962** *Economist* 5 May 425/1 The rest of the country may simply shrug its shoulders at London's enduring parish-pumpery. **1968** *Listener* 29 Feb. 283/2 It all sounds incredibly parish pumpish, but..the parish pump is extremely important when you live next door to it. **1864** R. A. ARNOLD *Hist. Cotton Famine* vi. 179 One or two members of the Manchester Committee..evidently considered that all subscriptions should be applied to supplement parish relief. **1949** N. MITFORD *Love in Cold Climate* xiii. 134 Uncle Matthew..was quite certain in his own mind that he would end up on parish relief. **1937** PARTRIDGE *Dict. Slang* 606/1 *Parish-rig*, a poorly found ship or an ill-clothed man. **1958** J. BISSET *Sail Ho!* 36 These men [*sc.* pierhead jumpers] usually had nothing except the clothes they stood up in—known as a 'parish rig'. **1933** P. A. EADDY *Hull Down* 135 A couple of the new hands who had been shipped just before we left Portland had come aboard pretty well 'parish rigged', to use an old sailor term for a man going to sea short of clothes. **1962** A. G. COURSE *Dict. Naut. Terms* 145 When a seaman joins a ship with few clothes and little working gear he is said to be 'parish rigged'... The term came to be used afterwards with reference to the ships themselves, so that if they had a minimum of sails, spares and gear to start a voyage they were said to be 'parish rigged'. **1968** L. MORTON *Long Wake* i. 15, I joined *Beeswing* in what in those days was called 'Parish rigged' [*sic*], in other words with little or no kit. **1794** J. MUIRHEAD in J. Sinclair *Statist. Acct. Scotl.* XI. 81 A parish school is now a momentary, or at least a temporary employment, for some necessitous person of ability. **1812** Parish school [in Dict.]. **1875** G. MACDONALD *Malcolm* I. vii. 67 A cottage rather larger than the rest, which stood close by the churchyard gate. It was the parish school. **1910** J. KERR *Scottish Educ.* 196 The name, parish schools, conveys no definite idea of the very varied character of the work done in them. **1964** *Winnipeg Tribune* 27 Feb. 1/5 Parish schools deserve a measure of public support, in keeping always with the overall resources of the community and without detriment to the public school system. **1788** P. M. FRENEAU *Misc. Wks.* 371 She would have killed the parish schoolmaster with the cluva-stick. **1929** J. B. PHILIP *Weelum* 11 More than a hundred years ago, the Parish Schoolmaster, who was also a poet, often wandered here. **1873** MRS. H. WOOD in *Argosy* XVI. 133 Parish work is not to everyone's taste. **1885** C. M. YONGE *Nuttie's Father* I. xiv. 163 She had a practical soul for parish work, and could appreciate..the exertions made for people of the classes she had always supposed too bad or else too well off to come under clerical supervision. **1911** W. OWEN *Let.* 18 June (1967) 75 To become the 'assistant' of some hard-worked or studiously inclined parson, helping in parish work, correspondence etc.

parish, *v.* Add: **b.** Of a clergyman: to do parish work. *rare.*

1880 J. GOTT *Lett.* (1918) 132 The growth and gymnastics of the mind, the mind with which one prays and parishes.

‖ **parishad** (pāriʃa·d). [Bengali and Hindi, f. Skr. *parishad* an assembly, council, f. *pári* around, about + *sad, sídati* to sit down.] In India and Bangladesh: an assembly, group, or council; also *attrib.* Also *zil(l)a parishad,* a district council.

1919 R. MOOKERJI *Local Govt. Anc. India* i. 29 The communal life of ancient India..sought to express itself through a variety of institutions, civic and municipal, industrial and commercial, political and religious... The following, for example, are the terms we generally come across in our literature, viz. *kula,..pariṣat, charana.* **1932** V. R. R. DIKSHITAR *Mauryan Polity* iii. 97 This passage only corroborates our view that the *pariṣad* (Council) exercised real executive powers. **1959** R. S. SHARMA *Aspects Polit. Ideas & Inst. Anc. India* xiii. 191 The influence of caste is to be also seen in some of the collective institutions such as the *pariṣad.* **1963** B. A. SALETORE *Anc. Indian Polit. Thought & Inst.* v. v. 417 The term *pariṣad*, which was confined originally in the Vedic days only to a congregation or assembly of learned men, seems to have been used in a wider sense of a council or assembly of ministers by the time of Pāṇini. **1971** *National Herald* (Lucknow) 1 Apr. 3/6 The commission will also go into the wage structure of employees of local bodies, zila parishads, town areas, notified areas, municipalties, [etc.]. **1975** *Bangladesh Times* 23 July 2/3 One Nagoruddin Mondal, member Bilasbari union parishad under Badalgaehi Police station has been suspended for selling relief goods in black market and the misuse of test relief fund. **1976** *CRC Jrnl.* July 5/3 There was a very wide representation, from Trade Unions..Vishwa and Parishad groups. **1976** D. HIRO *Inside India Today* 50 What then emerged was a three-tiered system whereby the old district boards.. were replaced by zilla parishads (i.e. district councils) with responsibility for co-ordinating development plans to be channelled through panchayat samitis (i.e. council committees). **1977** *Bangladesh Times* 20 Jan. 1 The district-wise break-ups of the Union Parishads where polls took place on Wednesday are Dacca and Sylhet 18 each.

parishionate (pări·ʃənĕit). [f. PARISHION(ER + -ATE[1].] Body of parishioners.

1910 *Tablet* 3 Sept. 363 The archiepiscopal diocese with its parishionate of nearly four million souls.

Parisian, *sb.* and *a.* Add: **A.** *sb.* **b.** The French spoken in or associated with Paris.

1841 M. EDGEWORTH *Let.* 23 Mar. (1971) 587 Educated at Paris and all proper—'hors les p-s and b-s and c-s' which could not pass surely..for true Parisian. **1846** R. FORD *Gatherings from Spain* xi. 119 Their silly grandees murder the glorious Castilian tongue, by substituting what they fancy is pure Parisian. **1909** W. J. LOCKE *Septimus* xii. 177 Peculiar vocables which she had learnt at school, and which Hégisippe declared to be the purest Parisian he had ever heard an Englishwoman use. **1932** KIPLING *Limits & Renewals* 322 His speech—to suit his hearers—ran From pure Parisian to gross peasant. **1969** [see *GRENADIAN *a.* and *sb.*]. **1976** 'TREVANIAN' *Main* (1977) iii. 59 Guttmann speaks up in his precise European French, the kind Canadians call 'Parisian', but which is really modelled on the French of Tours.

B. *adj.* Special Combs.: **Parisian cloth** (see quot.); **Parisian French** = *sb.* b. above; **Parisian ivory,** an early type of celluloid; **Parisian matins** (later example); **Parisian pattern** (see quot.); **Parisian stitch** (see quot.).

1960 C. W. CUNNINGTON et al. *Dict. Eng. Costume* 268/1 *Parisian Cloth*, 19th c., an English textile of cotton warp and worsted weft. **1974** E. AMBLER *Dr. Frigo* I. 20 He speaks Parisian French. **1976** E. BERCKMAN *Be All & End All* v. 59 Cecil spoke Parisian French and he himself hated the English. **1921** *Daily Colonist* (Victoria, B.C.) 26 Oct. 9/1 (Advt.), A new display of Parisian ivory. **1962** P. O'BRIAN tr. *Erlanger's St. Bartholomew's Night* iv. 162 At four o'clock in the morning the tocsin in Saint-Germain l'Auxerrois had begun ringing for what history was to call the Parisian matins. **1964** W. L. GOODMAN *Hist. Woodworking Tools* 34 This tool [*sc.* twybill] is 2ft. 6in. long, has no handle, and is described as the 'Parisian pattern'. **1934** M. THOMAS *Dict. Embroidery Stitches* 157 *Parisian stitch*.., a Canvas Stitch, consisting of upright stitches worked alternately over one and three horizontal threads of the canvas.

Parisianize, *v.* Add: Also *refl.* Hence also **Pari·sianized** *ppl. a.*

1897 [see *BOULEVARDED *a.*]. **1913** E. WHARTON *Custom of Country* xii. 156 Mrs. Harvey Shallum, a showy Parisianized figure. **1916** W. J. LOCKE *Wonderful Year* xv. 220 The last thing a solid and virtuous citizen of Central France desires to do in Paris is to Parisianize himself. **1962** *Punch* 28 Nov. 783/1 This fashion should not be a Parisianised version from Bond Street.

parity[1]. Add: **1. b.** A state in which two countries potentially hostile to one another have equal strategic resources, used *spec.* of the capacities in nuclear weapons of the U.S. and the U.S.S.R.

1955 *Bull. Atomic Sci.* Mar. 100/2 To try to achieve parity in conventional weapons would mean such a regimentation of our industry and manpower that we would lose the freedom we seek to preserve. **1965** H. KAHN *On Escalation* 295 The term 'parity' is shorthand for 'nuclear parity' or 'strategic parity'. Parity exists when neither side obtains any important strategic technical advantages ..from its central war forces. **1971** *Human World* Nov. 20 In the last five or six years the Russians have achieved nuclear-missile parity with the United States.

c. In phr. *parity of esteem*, the state or condition of being regarded as equal, used *spec.* of the status of administratively comparable educational institutions.

1961 D. JENKINS *Equality & Excellence* vi. 112 The authors of the 1944 [Education] Act..enunciated their principle..that there should be 'parity of esteem' for all forms of secondary education. **1961** *Guardian* 3 Apr. 3/2 The training colleges must aim high... Parity of esteem with the universities must be earned. **1966** D. JENKINS *Educated Society* ii. 63 There has to be 'parity of esteem' as between the various sections of the community. **1966** *Rep. Comm. Inquiry Univ. Oxf.* I. 117 We are convinced that undergraduate and postgraduate education should enjoy parity of esteem. **1974** *Listener* 23 May 661/3 If they [*sc.* polytechnics] could accept the challenge that they can offer a different kind of degree from well-established universities, they might get something like parity of esteem.

4. b. The oddness or evenness of a number, or of the number characteristic of something.

1915 P. A. MACMAHON *Combinatory Analysis* I. III. vi. 139 (*heading*) The parity of the greater index. **1949** G. & R. C. JAMES *Math. Dict.* 258/1 If two integers are both odd or both even they are said to have the same parity; if one is odd and the other even they are said to have different parity. **1960** G. N. LANCE *Numerical Methods for High Speed Computers* i. 10 The extended word should always have odd parity unless binary digits have been lost or gained during the transfer of the word from one part of the machine to another. **1966** R. R. ARNOLD et al. *Introd. Data Processing* xiv. 268/2 Codes that use an odd number of bits are said to have an odd parity. Codes that use an even number of bits are said to have an even parity. **1971** HUNTER & MONK *Algebra & Number Syst.* ii. 28 Let us.. say that *b* is related to *a*, when the positive integer *b* has the same parity as the positive integer *a*, that is when *a* and *b* are either both odd or both even. **1975** J. FINKEL *Computer-Aided Experimentation* xvii. 374 Parity is computed by adding the total number of 'ones' in a word. If the total is an even number and even parity is desired, the parity bit is stored as a 'zero'.

c. *Physics.* The property of having or being a spatial wave function that remains the same (has even parity) or changes sign (has odd parity) when a change of sign is applied to the co-ordinates; also (*charge parity, G-parity*), the same property with respect to certain other symmetry operations (see quots. 1964, 1970); the value of the quantum number (eigen-value) representing such a property (+1 for even parity, −1 for odd parity).

1939 *Physical Rev.* LVI. 526/2 Only the selection rules for *J* and parity would remain valid ($\Delta J = \pm 1$ or 0, no change in parity allowed). **1953** *Ann. Rev. Nuclear Sci.* II. 240 Means are available..for determining the angular momentum and parity change carried off by the emitted radiation. **1955** R. D. EVANS *Atomic Nucleus* iv. 174 The parity of an isolated system is a constant of its motion and cannot be changed by any internal processes. Only if radiation or a particle enters or leaves the system..can the parity change. **1956** *Canad. Jrnl. Physics* XXXIV. 1110 There is..evidence for spin and parity assignment of $\frac{1}{2}(+)$ for the C^{15} ground state. **1957** *Times* 11 Nov. 11/5 The launching of an Earth satellite is of less fundamental importance than..the failure of the law of parity conservation. **1964** G. KÄLLÉN *Elem. Particle Physics* xii. 316 We can describe the *G*-operation as a charge conjugation followed by a rotation [in isospin space] through the angle π around the 1-axis. The eigenvalue of this operator is usually referred to as 'G-parity'. *Ibid.* 317 *G*-parity is a conserved quantum number in all reactions involving strong interactions. **1968** M. S. LIVINGSTON *Particle Physics* vii. 134 The parity of a wave function representing a system of particles includes the intrinsic parities of each of the individual particles and also depends on the relative angular momentum of the several particles. **1969** *Observer* 13 Apr. 2/6 Certain particles do not obey..the parity (or P) principle. This P principle says, in effect, that nature does not 'know' the difference between left and right. **1970** MARTIN & SPEARMAN *Elem. Particle Theory* v. 237 We define an operation *C* as the mapping of a physical system into another physical system in which each particle has been replaced by one with the opposite value of charge, baryon number, (lepton number) and strangeness... The eigenstates of *C* have eigenvalue either +1 or −1, that is they have either even or odd charge parity. **1973** L. J. TASSIE *Physics Elem. Particles* iii. 32 When discussing the parity of the π^-, we assumed that the proton and the neutron have the same intrinsic parity. If we assume that the proton and the neutron have opposite intrinsic parities, then we find that the π^- and the π^0 have opposite intrinsic parities... We choose the parities for different charge states to give the simplest scheme.

5. c. An agreed price for agricultural produce, relative to other commodities.

1941 *Time* 2 June (Air Exp. Ed.) 2/3 'Parity' is a political concept which holds that the farmer should receive prices for his products which will give him a purchasing power (in terms of other commodities) equal to that which he had in the period 1909–14. **1977** *Askov* (Minnesota) *American* 31 Mar. 1/2 The milk price support increase to 83 percent of parity will have a positive impact on Minnesota dairy farmers.

d. The value of one currency in terms of another or others, as agreed by the procedures of the International Monetary Fund, which became effective on 1 March 1947.

1945 *Ann. Reg. 1944* I. ii. 41 All transactions between the Fund and members were to be at par, and all transactions in member currencies at rates within an agreed percentage of parity. **1949** *Britannica Bk. of Year* 254/2 Mexico temporarily suspended exchange transactions by the Central bank on July 22, 1948, pending the establishment of a new parity. Although the new parity had not been announced, the Bank of Mexico was authorized to engage in free market transactions. **1971** *Daily Tel.* 10 May 14 The major countries agree..that if..the price of their own currency in relation to any other foreign exchange moves to more than 1 p.c. away from the fixed price (called parity), they will intervene. **1971** *Ibid.* 11 May 1/3 The Swiss franc closed below its new parity of 4·08 to the dollar. **1976** *Shooting Times & Country Mag.* 18–24 Nov. 28/2 Doubtless the parity of the pound sterling against other currencies is leaning..in favour of the visitor.

7. *parity level, price*; **parity bit** *Computers*, a bit that is automatically made 1 or 0 so as to make the parity of the word or set containing it either odd or even, as previously determined; **parity check** *Computers*, a check on the correctness of a set of binary digits that involves ascertaining the parity of a number derived from the set in a predetermined way; so **parity checking** *vbl. sb.*; **parity digit** *Computers* = *parity bit* above.

1957 D. D. MCCRACKEN *Digital Computer Programming* xii. 151 A common system is to assign six bits to each character... The six bits and the parity bit are then recorded in a row, which requires a seven-channel tape. **1975** J. FINKEL *Computer-Aided Experimentation* xvii. 373 The parity bit is computed by the memory write hardware before storing a word. When a word is fetched from storage the parity bit is recomputed, and if it does not agree with the parity bit appended to the word an interrupt is issued. **1950** R. W. HAMMING in *Bell Syst. Techn. Jrnl.* XXIX. 150 The type of check used..will be called a parity check. The above was an even parity check; had we used an odd number of 1's to determine the setting of the check position it would have been an odd parity check. **1958** *IRE Trans. Electronic Computers* VII. 207/1 If the specified number of ONE digits is even the parity check digit is a zero. If the number of ONE digits is odd the parity check digit is a one. **1970** N. R. SCOTT *Electronic Computer Technol.* v. 220 'Digital' parity checks..depend upon the digits of the number and not upon the significance attached to the digits by virtue of their position... The numerical parity check..is a function of the number represented by the digits but not a function of the digits themselves. **1972** *Computers & Humanities* VI. 149 One channel is reserved for the internal control, the parity check. **1958** *IRE Trans. Electronic Computers* VII. 207/1 Parity checking usually is defined for the binary system in terms of the odd or evenness of the number of ONE digits in a specified block of binary digits. **1966** R. R. ARNOLD et al. *Introd. Data Processing* xiv. 268/1 Parity checking is a built-in self-checking feature utilized in most magnetic tape as well as paper tape coding methods. **1954** *Computers & Automation* Dec. 18/1 *Parity check*, use of a digit (called the 'parity digit') carried along as a check. **1959** S. H. HOLLINGDALE *High Speed Computing* ii. 27 Some computers are designed to deal with numbers which contain an extra digit, known as the parity digit. **1970** N. R. SCOTT *Electronic Computer Technol.* v. 217 The correct parity digit is attached to the digit group at the source, and then the augmented group is tested upon reception to determine whether the parity digit and the message digits are still in agreement. **1907** *Daily Chron.* 3 Oct. 2/1 Opening under the parity level prices continued to lose ground every hour up to the close. **1909** *Westm. Gaz.* 20 May 12/4 The parity price of Amalgamated was 85 3–16. **1937** MCINTOSH & ORR *Pract. Agric. for High Schools* 15 Show the actual and parity prices of the major farm products. **1955** *Times* 24 Aug. 7/2 American farm prices are kept relatively high and often above world prices by the arrangements whereby the Government must buy certain produce for stock when its price falls to certain specified percentages of so-called 'parity prices'.

pariu, var. *PAREU.

park, *sb.* Add: **2. a.** Also, an enclosed piece of ground, of considerable extent, where animals are exhibited to the public (either as the primary function of that 'park' or as a secondary attraction). See also **safari park*, **zoological park*.

1909 ELLIOT & THACKER tr. *Hagenbeck's Beasts & Men* ii. 40, I wished my new park to be a great and enduring example of the benefits that can be wrought by giving the animals as much freedom and placing them in as natural an environment as possible. **1914** E. VELVIN *From Jungle to Zoo* xxiii. 336 There are 139 employees engaged in taking care of the ground and collections of this Park [*sc.* the New York Zoological Park]. **1976** W. BLUNT *Ark in Park* i. 15 William the Conqueror established or perhaps took over an already existing animal park at Woodstock, near Oxford. **1977** *Belfast Tel.* 22 Feb., The initiation of compulsory safety programmes at wild life parks and circuses.

b. Add to def.: or for the preservation of wild life. (Further examples.)

1895 ROOSEVELT & GRINNELL *Hunting in Many Lands* 400 The preservation of elk, deer, antelope and the carnivora is assured... Their wide distribution within the Park,..added to the danger attendant on killing them within the Park, is a sufficient protection. **1922** *Baedeker's Dominion of Canada* (ed. 4) vii. 309 About 3M. to the S. of Lamont lies the pretty Elk Island Park.., one of the Canadian National Parks.., 16 sq. M. in area and including elk, deer, moose, and buffalo. **1926** *Encycl. Brit.* II. 1020/1 In Canada since 1910 the following national game preserves, bearing the name of parks, have been established... Nemiskam National Park.., an antelope preserve in southeastern Alberta [etc]. **1957** *Ibid.* XXIII. 603/1 The Serengeti National park.. preserves the finest remaining assembly of the plains game of Africa. **1959** *Chambers's Encycl.* IX. 705/1 In African parks the emphasis is on wild life conservation and public access is strictly controlled. **1974** *Afr. Encycl.* 362/1 *National parks* are areas of land where large numbers of wild animals live in natural surroundings. **1975** *Islander* (Victoria, B.C.) 31 Aug. 4/1, I got to see the first of the wild animals for which Africa is famous. This was in the Game Park at Lake Nakuru. **1978** K. TURNER *Serengeti Home* i. 1 This was my first visit to the Serengeti, a vast wildlife park in Tanganyika, now Tanzania.

c. A sports ground or stadium; *spec.* (*a*) in the U.S., a baseball field (cf. *ball park* s.v. *BALL *sb.*[1] 21); (*b*) a football field or stadium; also in the names of football teams.

1867 *Chicago Times* 25 July 5/2 These cars connect with the stock-yards dummy, which runs to within a short distance of the park. **1880** *Times* 8 Nov. 11/3 Notts v. Glasgow Queen's-Park. This match was played at Nottingham on Saturday, and ended in favour of Queen's-park by four goals to three. **1892** J. HIGSON *Hist. Salford Football Club* 18 Our first ground was the Peel Park cricket ground. *Ibid.* 96 The first game they played with us was against Birkenhead Park. **1902** *'Golden Penny' Football Album 1901–2* 32/3 The record gate at an International match is £4,387 9s. 6d. for Scotland v. England, at Celtic Park, Glasgow, in 1900. **1917** C. MATHEWSON *Second Base Sloan* 217 Which way is the park from here, please? **1948** S. MATTHEWS *Feet First* xii. 66 The first thought that flashed through my anxious mind was Hampden Park. Would this injury keep me out of the England team to play Scotland? **1974** *Linlithgowshire Jrnl. & Gaz.* 16 Aug. 12/5 Old favourite Paddy Buckley led the Bo'ness team on to the park on Saturday. **1974** *Sunday Tel.* 8 Sept. 33/6 Middlesbrough began as if they were going to sweep Chelsea off the park. **1976** E. DUNPHY *Only a Game?* i. 31 He'd been troubled by knee injuries ever since Palace kicked us off the park the year they got promotion. **1976** *Scotsman* 27 Dec. 10/5 The sad sight of fighting on the terracing and terrified youngsters spilling on to the park.

d. *industrial park*: see *INDUSTRIAL *a.* e.

3. c. *U.S.* An enclosure into which animals are driven for slaughter; a corral. *Obs.*

c **1797** in L. F. R. Masson *Les Bourgeois de la Compagnie du Nord-Ouest* (1889) I. 280 The chief of the park thinks that if he were to eat any of this meat thus killed, it would be out of his power to make buffaloes enter his park ever after; so he must have meat killed in the open field for his own use. **1805** M. LEWIS in Lewis & Clark *Orig. Jrnls. Lewis & Clark Expedition* (1904) I. 313 There was a park which they had formed of timber and brush, for the purpose of taking the cabrie or antelope. **1820** D. W. HARMON *Jrnl. Voy. & Trav. Interior N. Amer.* 99 The Natives..killed upwards of eighty [buffalo] by driving them into a park, made for that purpose. **1839** Z. LEONARD *Adventures* (1904) 224 After travelling a short distance we arrived at a large pen, enclosing about three-fourths of an acre, which they call a park or correll.

4. b. (See quots.)

1950 *Amer. Speech* XXV. 163 The meaning of *park* as 'any grassy piece of level land enclosed by trees, hills, or mountains' has become, or at least is fast becoming, the central meaning of the word [in Colorado]. **1961** *Ibid.* XXXVI. 269 *Park* means either 'mountain meadow' or 'clearing', from the foothills communities westward; especially in the northwest it is likely to mean both.

5. b. An open space, a building, or underground accommodation, in or near a city or town, where cars and other vehicles can be left; = *car-park* (*CAR *sb.*[1] 6). Also *transf.* See also **caravan park*.

1916 A. BENNETT *Lion's Share* xxiii. 162 Audrey's motor-car..was waiting in the automobile park outside the principal gates. **1925** *Times* 14 Apr. 8/5 The Automobile Association..has put forward a scheme for the construction of motor parks below ground. **1929, 1944** [see *air park* s.v. *AIR *sb.*[1] III. 7]. **1970** *Times* 9 Feb. 13/4 Underground there will be a park for up to 2,200 cars. **1972** R. HILL *Fairly Dangerous Thing* I. i. 11 The park was quite full and he would probably never have noticed the two-tone Consul if it hadn't begun to move.

c. In a motor vehicle with automatic transmission: the position of the selector lever in which the gears are locked, preventing the vehicle from moving.

1963 *Which? Car Suppl.* Oct. 116/1 P meant *Park*. This position could only be engaged with the car at rest and it served as a transmission brake which would hold the car on a hill. *Ibid.* 116/2 If the engine was started with the lever at *Park* and it was running quickly, the car would tend to jerk backwards as the lever was passed through *Reverse* on its way to *Drive*. **1965** PRIESTLEY & WISDOM *Good Driving* v. 40 In *Park* the gearbox is locked and thus the car is completely immobilized. **1967** *Times* 31 Mar. 3/7 It is obvious that in using a car with automatic transmission it is of the utmost importance that drivers should ensure that the lever is in the 'park' position, while they use the handle. **1972** D. E. WESTLAKE *Cops & Robbers* (1973) i. 15 He shifted into drive, caught up, and shifted back into park. **1977** J. CLEARY *Vortex* viii. 208 Stenhouse moved the gear-lever from *Park* to *Drive* and the car started to move forward.

7. park bench, a bench in a park provided for the public; also *attrib.*; **park-ranger, -warden,** an official responsible for the patrolling and maintenance of a national park; **park-way,** add: freq. **parkway** (as one word); (*a*) for *U.S.* read orig. *U.S.*, and add earlier and later examples; (*b*) a name given to a railway station with extensive parking facilities, situated on the outskirts of a city for the use of travellers into the city centre; also *attrib.*

1906 *Daily Chron.* 6 Sept. 3/2 When a Park-bench orator has shouted at you for a quarter of an hour, you cease to be able to attend. **1908** *Busy Man's Mag.* Mar. 63/2 So amiably and with gusto he economized, sleeping in the moonlight upon a park bench and following the marvels of the water front by day. **1946** A. CLARKE *Second Kiss* 14 That park bench in the rain, the dredge of leaves, I sat there wrapped in miserable sleeves. **1965** *Listener* 11 Nov. 763/1 Those tendencies of sloth and indolence which..have marked me out as a friend of park-bench philosophers. **1976** 'O. BLEECK' *No Questions Asked* xii. 137 If I weren't here, you could find a priest or a psychiatrist or just somebody on a park bench. **1912** J. B. BICKERSTETH *Let.* 20 June in *Land of Open Doors* (1914) 150 Next day, after seeing the park ranger about the burial place, the doctor and I went down..to a place where there is a flat stretch of land. **1940** E. FERGUSSON *Our Southwest* 144 Park rangers now assiduously police almost two million acres of land. **1963** *Weekly News* (Auckland) 15 May 30/2 The maintenance of bush tracks and huts is almost a full-time occupation for the park rangers [at the Fiordland National Park]. **1972** G. DURRELL *Catch me a Colobus* ix. 192, I felt that, if we talked to the park rangers, they would be sure to give us information about the whereabouts of the Teporingoes. **1977** *Borneo Bull.* 7 May 4-A/1 Park rangers, who have continued to look for him, found some traces. **1936** D. MCCOWAN *Animals Canad. Rockies* vii. 62 Bill Hartley.. is Park Warden at Glacier in British Columbia. **1964** C. WILLOCK *Enormous Zoo* ix. 159 The park warden is more than an impresario. **1973** *Times* 9 Feb. 9/1 In the party will be..an Ethiopian Government minister, and national park wardens. **1887** *Visit to States* (ser. 1) xxix. 378 This broad parkway has a magnificent drive on either side of a central walk for pedestrians. **1929** *Times* 23 Jan. 20 Parkway system near New York City. **1937** *Times* 13 Apr. (Suppl.) p. x/2 The plan may provide for orbital and radial roads, parkways, viaducts and tunnels, communications to aerodromes, railway stations, and docks. **1938** *Archit. Rev.* LXXXIV. 238/3 The city of Stockholm, which has had the foresight to buy up large tracts of land in its neighbourhood, has been able to plan a system of 'Parkways'. Initially an American development the 'Parkway' represents a form of planning which might with advantage be extensively used in the English countryside. **1939,** etc. Parkway [see *clover-leaf* s.v. *CLOVER *sb.* 4]. **1944** *Ann. Reg. 1943* 58 An easy flow of open space from.. parkway to green wedge, and from green wedge to Green Belt. **1958** *Listener* 23 Oct. 642/1 The development of the

Wythenshawe estate by the City of Manchester..with its beautifully landscaped parkway—the first, I think, in this country. **1972** *Modern Railways* July 271 The Western Region recently commissioned two new stations, one completely new at Bristol Parkway. **1973** *Bulletin* (Sydney) 25 Aug. 11 Canberra's major new freeway-type road which is the subject of a major 'environmental impact investigation' is now styled the Molonglo Parkway. **1976** P. R. WHITE *Planning for Public Transport* viii. 155 The 'parkway' stations opened by British Rail in recent years, notably that at Bristol, offer undoubted evidence of cars being abandoned by their users in favour of a rail journey. **1977** *Evening Gaz.* (Middlesbrough) 11 Jan. 1/4 The route of their return to the Royal Yacht will be made by the Mandale Interchange and the new Parkway.

park, *v.* Add: **2. b.** To place or leave (a vehicle or the like), usu. temporarily, in a park (sense *5 b), at the side of the road, or elsewhere. orig. *U.S.*

1864 J. S. BILLINGS in F. H. Garrison *John Shaw Billings* (1915) 95 The trains are parked along the edge of the river. **1867** A. D. RICHARDSON *Beyond Mississippi* 79 At night the wagons are parked in a circle. **1900** *Congress. Rec* 2 Feb. 1445/1 No part of said street..shall be used for depot purposes, or railroad yard, or for the purpose of switching, shifting, or parking cars. **1911** *N.Y. Even. Post* 29 Nov. 16 The train was parked near the Union Station and was visited by hundreds of townsfolk and countrymen. **1921** *Daily Colonist* (Victoria, B.C.) 13 Mar. 6/2, I am now in the position of fearing to leave my car anywhere at all in the central part of the city lest I should be parking it where it should not be. **1925** WODEHOUSE *Carry on, Jeeves!* vi. 156 It was about an hour later that I shoved my way out to where I had parked the car. **1929** J. B. PRIESTLEY *Good Companions* I. iv. 139 They were not able to keep the van with them, but had to..park it up a side-street in a line of other cars and carts and caravans. **1938** *Times* 25 Feb. 15/2 The Chinese..state that over 40 Japanese aeroplanes were observed parked on the airfield. **1969** *Highway Code* 22 Make sure you always park your vehicle safely. **1974** *Nature* 15 Nov. 185/3 Down by the river, in the specially built loop for parking punts, the economic crisis seemed a thousand light years away.

c. *transf.* To place or leave (a person or thing) in a suitable or convenient place until required; to put aside for a while. Also *refl.*

1908 *St. George's Rev.* July 282 The children being parked' in their own schoolyards. **1922** *Atlantic Monthly* June 773 High-school girls..'park' their corsets when they go to dances. **1923** WODEHOUSE *Inimitable Jeeves* iv. 40 At this point the brother, who after shedding a floppy overcoat and parking his hat on a chair had been standing by..gave a little cough. *Ibid.* ix. 94 The policeman, having retrieved a piece of chewing-gum from the underside of a chair, where he had parked it against a rainy day, went off into a corner. **1927** *Evening Standard* 7 Dec. 19/1 Then I suppose I park myself here. **1938** E. WAUGH *Scoop* I. v. 81 A voice said in English, 'Anyone mind if I park myself here?' and a stranger stood at the table. **1949** R. HARVEY *Curtain Time* 66 So for Hattie the Grand Opera House, Daly's Theatre, Wallack's, Booth's, Tony Pastor's Variety Theatre and Niblo's Garden became familiar enchanted night nurseries where her father would park her, safe and amused, until his meeting was over. **1960** E. W. HILDICK *Jim Starling & Colonel* xv. 137 Come on, dad! Park yerself! **1968** [see *BOOSTER 2 c]. **1971** 'A. BURGESS' *MF* xiv. 158 His companion had parked his black lenses on his brow. **1972** J. PHILIPS *Vanishing Senator* (1973) III. iii. 139 Peter crawled round to the other side of the bed where his aluminium leg was parked. **1978** G. GREENE *Human Factor* III. ii. 117 The girl was parking her gum on the back of the telephone directory while she got down to a long satisfactory conversation.

d. *intr.* To take up a position in or as in a park; to place a vehicle in a park or elsewhere; to occupy a suitable or stationary position; to stay where one is.

1865 O. W. NORTON *Army Lett.* (1903) 255 The wagons parked behind the stables to wait orders. **1926** G. FRANKAU *My Unsentimental Journey* xi. 149 There, Stidger put on his brakes, 'parked', took out the inevitable keys to lock his gear-lever and ignition-switch. **1929** *Strand Mag.* Feb. 183 'I want them' persisted the other and I guess I'm parking right here until I do get 'em'. **1948** *Democrat* 1 Jan. 4/2 Drivers now can park or back into alleys or up to loading platforms with much greater ease. **1959** *Daily Tel.* 24 Mar. 9/3 Besides asking motorists not to park on main roads, he urged them to use alternative routes. **1966** P. MOLONEY *Plea for Mersey* 51 Not hardened junkies, when deprived of dope, Ere felt such anger..As Scouseville driver seeking space to park.

parka (pā·ɹkă). Also **parkha**; (all †) **parca, parkee, parki.** Pl. **parkas** (northern Canada **parki**). [Aleutian, from Russ. *párka* skin jacket.] An outer garment or long jacket with a hood attached, made of skins and worn by Eskimos; a similar garment, usu. of windproof fabric, worn by mountaineers, skiers, etc. Also *attrib.*

1780 W. COXE *Acct. Russ. Discoveries* 256 The inhabitants of Alaxa, Umnak, Unalaksha..wear coats (parki) made of bird skins. **1813** G. H. VON LANGSDORFF *Voy. & Trav.* II. ii. 37 They are called *parka*, and are worn sometimes with one side outwards sometimes with the other. **1818** V. M. GOLOVNIN *Narr. Captivity in Japan* I. i. 32 The women wore parkis made of the skin of birds with the feathers outward. **1851** J. RICHARDSON *Arctic Searching Exped.* II. 379 (*heading*) Eskimo vocabulary. English... *Parka*... Kuskutchewak... atkuk. **1907** R. W. SERVICE *Songs of Sourdough* 56 Talk of your cold! through the parka's fold it stabbed like a driven nail. **1910** —— *Ballads of Cheechako* 25 My eyes were seared, yet thralled I peered through the parka hood nigh blind. **1922** *Chambers's Jrnl.* Feb. 137/1 He had no snowshoes, no parki, and he did not see the dense black blizzard sweeping up from the north-west. **1922** *19th Cent.* Feb. 269 They changed their drill parkees for coats of caribou fur. **1926** *Spectator* 18 Sept. 408/2 The woodsman of the north..wears no fur, unless it be a little trimming round the neck of the 'parca'. **1934** *Sun* (Baltimore) 31 Jan. 3/3 Stocky Indians and Eskimos, fur-trimmed parkas and mukluks, miners with violent red and green plaid shirts,..—these characterized the simpler functions at crossroad taverns. **1948** *Manch. Guardian Weekly* 1 Jan. 9 Your correspondent will now buckle on his parka, latch his skis, and take off. **1955** E. HILLARY *High Adventure* 37 We took possession of our own equipment—..double-layered windproof parkas. **1958** *Tararua* XII. 31 *Parka.* This name is the only one used in New Zealand for the hooded garment based on that of the Eskimos. *Anorak* seems to be common in England. **1958** L. WHISHAW *As far as You'll take Me* vii. 94, I spent a wonderful couple of hours trying on fabulous parkas (pronounced parkees in the North). **1963** *Times* 25 Feb. (Canada Suppl.) p. xv/1 Eskimo children..Huddled inside their sealskin *parkhas* and warmed by the low flame of a blubber lantern,..may listen spellbound to stories of the powers of Talluliyuk the seal-goddess. **1968** *Globe & Mail* (Toronto) 17 Feb. 1/7 Busloads of parka-clad workers..arrived almost hourly yesterday at Elliot Lake's two hotels. **1973** *Guardian* 10 Apr. 13/2 Fox-trimmed parka with shirred waist. **1973** A. H. WHITEFORD *N. Amer. Indian Arts* 86 The Kutchin made fine tailored skin skirts, parkas, and one-piece leggings and moccasins. **1976** *Evening Post* (Nottingham) 14 Dec. 1/6 A boy's parka coat worth £4·50 was stolen from the cloakroom of the Chaucer Junior School, Ilkeston. **1978** *Times* 23 Feb. 13/6, I wore a silk Chinese padded jacket under my parkha.

park-and-ride (pā:ɹkˌănd,rəi·d), *a.* [f. PARK *v.* + AND *conj.* + RIDE *v.*] Designating or pertaining to a system whereby commuters and other visitors travel by private car to car-parks situated on the outskirts of a city, and continue their journey to the centre of the city by means of public transport. Also as *sb.*

1966 *Leicester Mercury* 30 Dec. 24/3 Park 'n' Ride was the success of the year. **1968** *Economist* 20 Apr. 48 Public transport to those facilities, largely by rail (incorporating park-and-ride stations), must be built up. **1971** *Sunday Times* (Johannesburg) (Business Section) 28 Mar. 7/4 He wants to attract shoppers to the city centre by way of off-street parking and establish 'park-and-ride' schemes outside the city with a speedy bus service to the downtown area. **1973** *Times* 28 Feb. (Victoria Centre, Nottingham Suppl.) p. iii/3 (*heading*) 'Park-and-ride' can beat the traffic problem. **1974** *Drive* Autumn 110/1 Public transport improvements now in operation include a park-and-ride service, catering for the parking of 250 cars..and distribution of the occupants from a site $1\frac{1}{2}$ miles south of the city centre. **1977** *Modern Railways* Dec. 461/3 Perhaps we can hope for improved road/rail interchange or even park-and-ride facilities to woo potential rail commuters.

Park Avenue. Name of a street in New York City, U.S.A., used *attrib.* and as *adj.* to designate the fashionable and luxurious style of life for which it is noted.

1956 R. MACAULAY *Towers of Trebizond* vi. 59 Mrs. Van Damm looked very handsome and bland, with blue hair and eyes and Park Avenue clothes. **1971** M. BABSON *Cover-up Story* vi. 67 Lou-Ann isn't Park Avenue Hillbilly material... Hillbilly, yes. Park Avenue, no. **1975** J. HONE *Sixth Directorate* iv. 149 She had all the rare finesse of a Park Avenue debutante. **1976** *National Observer* (U.S.) 13 Mar. 7/1 They know we run a Park Avenue operation at Marquette, that we SRO the joint. The kids realize that by playing at Marquette they'll be constantly in the limelight and get good pro contracts.

parked, *ppl. a.* (Further examples.)

1919 C. P. THOMPSON *Cocktails* 176 The old farm where the V.A.D. drivers were cleaning their parked ambulances. **1932** *Daily Tel.* 23 May 8/6 In view of..the parked cars using the park, it was felt that it was an injustice that the horse-rider should be solely blamed for damage to the turf. **1962** [see *DOUBLE-PARK *v.*]. **1973** *Daily Tel.* 19 June 3/1 A visitor to Gatwick Airport complained yesterday that he had been able to walk unchallenged up to a parked airliner. **1976** C. BERMANT *Coming Home* II. i. 113 One can hardly move for tourists and traffic and parked cars.

parker[2] (pā·ɹkəɹ). [f. PARK *v.* + -ER[1].] **1.** One who parks a vehicle.

1930 M. McCLINTOCK *Rep. Parking & Garage Probl. Washington* 78 (*caption*) Street obstruction by a desperate parker. **1959** *Encounter* Aug. 32/2 He's used to pinching parkers on the broad highway. **1959** *Times* 8 Dec. 5/6 Mr. Marples gave an example of the immunity these all-day parkers have enjoyed. **1974** W. GARNER *Big enough Wreath* xi. 151 Smith had the luck to find a car leaving the meter. He reversed fast..cutting out another would-be parker.

2. *Austral. colloq.* = **parking light.* Usu. *pl.*

1967 S. H. COURTIER *Murder's Burning* xiii. 187 Mr. Proctor switched on his tail lights and parkers. **1971** R. DENTRY *Encounter at Kharmel* x. 179 Keep out of the way as soon as you see me switch the parkers on. **1971** *Southerly* XXXI. 71 A prowl car told us to switch our parkers on.

Pa·rker[3]. [Name of the manufacturing company.] The proprietary name of a pen made by the Parker Pen Company.

1906 *Official Gaz.* (U.S. Patent Office) 2 Oct. 1507/2 Parker Pen Company, Janesville, Wis... Used ten years Parker..for Fountain-pens. **1914** *Trade Marks Jrnl.* 5 Aug. 1229 'Parker' Fountain Pens, not of Precious Metal or imitation thereof. The Parker Pen Company..Wisconsin, United States of America. **1923** *Official Gaz.* (U.S. Patent Office) 2 Jan. 18/1 The Parker Pen Co., Janesville, Wis... Parker..Fountain Pens and Mechanical Pencils. Claims use since 1891 on fountain pens; since 1921 on mechanical pencils. **1935** *Trade Marks Jrnl.* 5 June 718/1 Parker... Fountain pens and propelling pencils (none being of precious metal or of imitation precious metal) and desk stands (not of precious metal or imitation precious metal) for pens. The Parker Pen Company..Wisconsin, United States of America. **1959** I. JEFFERIES *Thirteen Days* (1961) x. 143, I reckon I'll get a Parker 51, a gold one. **1974** 'E. ANTHONY' *Malaspiga Exit* ii. 44 An assortment of pens from ball-point to gold-nibbed Parkers. **1976** 'Z. STONE' *Modigliani Scandal* I. iv. 38 He filled up the form with the gold Parker in his pocket.

parkerite (pā·ɹkərəit). *Min.* [f. the name of R. L. *Parker* (b. 1893) of Zurich + -ITE[1].] A sulphide of nickel, bismuth, and lead, $Ni_3(Bi,Pb)_2S_2$, occurring as orthorhombic crystals with a metallic lustre.

1936 D. L. SCHOLTZ in *Publ. Univ. Pretoria* 2nd Ser. I. 186 The new minerals F and G were first recognised towards the end of the year 1932..when the writer benefited greatly by the valued advice and criticism of Professors P. Niggli and R. Parker. The author, therefore, proposes the name 'Niggliite' for the former (F), and 'Parkerite' for the latter (G). **1943** *Amer. Mineralogist* XXVIII. 345 Single grains of parkerite..are bright bronze coloured with brilliant metallic lustre on fresh fractures, becoming darker and dull on tarnished surfaces. **1969** *Canad. Mineralogist* IX. 610 The parkerite in the Great Slave Lake area occurs as small inclusions in niccolite and is associated with native bismuth.

Parkerizing (pā·ɹkərəiziŋ), *vbl. sb.* [f. the name of the *Parker* Rust-Proof Co. of America (incorporated 1915), which introduced the process.] A rust-proofing process in which iron or steel is given a protective coating of phosphate by immersing it for a short time in a hot acidic solution of a metal phosphate (usu. manganese dihydrogen phosphate).

A proprietary name in the U.S.A.

1919 *Chem. & Metall. Engin.* 31 Dec. 787/2 Messrs. Allen and Richards were mainly responsible for changes in the Coslett process, which made its present modification one of the most simple methods of rust prevention. Their patented modification in use today is known as 'Parkerizing'. **1932** *Metal Industry* XL. 369/2 The basis of the Parkerizing process is a solution of a prepared powder, which consists essentially of manganese dihydrogen phosphate. **1949** *Official Gaz.* (U.S. Patent Office) 24 May 984/1 Parker Rust Proof Company, Detroit, Mich... Certification mark. 'Protected by Parkerizing for rust resistance.'.. Claims use since Mar. 15, 1936. **1954** E. MOLLOY *Electro-Plating & Corrosion Prevention* xiii. 213 'Parkerising' is applied to cameras and instruments, rifles, typewriters, chains, bolts, nuts, tacks, and so on. **1976** J. A. VON FRAUNHOFER *Basic Metal Finishing* xiii. 147 The original Coslett process, based on phosphoric acid containing zinc phosphate, has been superseded by the accelerated Parkerising, Bonderising and similar processes.

So **Pa·rkerize** *v. trans.*, to treat in this way; **Pa·rkerized** *ppl. a.*, a proprietary name applied to articles so treated.

1922 *Raw Material* V. 438/2 Heavy castings of intricate shape, containing irregular cavities, can be completely Parkerized. *Ibid.* 439/1 On structural iron work, heavy Parkerized coatings can be produced. **1932** *Metal Industry* XL. 369/2 The Parkerized surface is..excellent for absorbing and retaining paint, lacquer or enamel. **1939** BURNS & SCHUH *Protective Coatings for Metals* xvi. 375 It is possible to Parkerize zinc coatings. **1942** *Trade Marks Jrnl.* 20 May 205/2 Parkerized... Hand tools and side arms. The Pyrene Company Limited,..Brentford, Middlesex; manufacturers. *Ibid.* 2 Dec. 505/2 Parkerized... Small domestic utensils and containers, non-electric instruments for cleaning purposes..all being goods of common metal; steel wool. The Pyrene Company Limited,..Brentford, Middlesex; manufacturers and merchants. **1961** *Chem. Abstr.* LV. 8883 (*heading*) The resistance of parkerised iron in polar marine climatic conditions.

† **Pa:rker's ceme·nt.** *Obs.* except *Hist.* [Named after James *Parker*, who patented it in England in 1796.] = *Roman cement* s.v. ROMAN *a.*[1] 16 c.

1814 *Trans. Geol. Soc.* II. 193 This place is particularly known on account of its furnishing abundance of the septaria, from which that excellent material for building under water and for stucco is made, known by the name of Parker's cement. **1839** *Penny Cycl.* XV. 420/1 The mortars made with them are called hydraulic mortars. Of these, Parker's cement is a well known kind. **1889** W. A. TILDEN *Watts' Man. Chem.* I. 337 Parker's or Roman cement is made in this manner from the nodular masses of calcareo-argillaceous ironstone found in the London clay. **1917** E. A. DANCASTER in G. Martin *Industr. & Manuf. Chem.: Inorg.* II. 85 The first of the natural cements was prepared by James Parker towards the end of the eighteenth century. It was known at first as Parker's cement, but was afterwards called Roman cement, by which name it is still known.

Parkes (pāɹks). *Metallurgy.* [Name of Alexander *Parkes* (1813–90), English chemist and inventor, who first patented the process in 1850 (*Brit. Pat. 13,118*).] *Parkes* (or † *Parkes'*, ¶ *Parke's*) *process*: a process for removing silver and gold from lead by adding zinc to the molten lead, so that the precious metals form an alloy with the zinc and collect on the surface.

1857 PHILLIPS & DARLINGTON *Rec. Mining & Metallurgy* 180 (*heading*) Parkes' process for desilverizing lead. **1892** W. CROOKES tr. *R. von Wagner's Man. Chem. Technol.* II. 180 A further advantage of the Parkes process is that a minimum proportion of gold, present in the work-lead, can be first extracted by a small addition of zinc..whilst the subsequent main quantity of silver extracted..is free from gold. **1912** J. W. MELLOR *Mod. Inorg. Chem.* xxi. 382 Lead can be desilverized by means of Pattinson's or Parkes' process. **1923** U. R. EVANS *Metals & Metallic Compounds* IV. 268 Parke's process.. only serves to remove silver and gold, and would leave the objectionable impurities in the lead. **1940** *Chambers's Techn. Dict.* 617/2 Parke's process. **1969** R. F. LANG tr. *Henglein's Chem. Technol.* 531 The refining of crude lead takes place in two steps: 1. refining proper... 2. desilvering by the aid of Zn (Parkes process).

Parkesine (pā·ɹksīn). Now *Hist.* [f. prec. + -INE^5.] A substance more or less identical with celluloid, based on pyroxylin and castor oil or camphor.

1862 *Chem. News* 9 Aug. 75/2 Parkesine.—A number of pretty and useful articles, formed of a material which the inventor, Mr. Parkes, has named after himself, are exhibited in Case 1112, Class IV. The basis of this material is the mixture of collodion and castor oil. **1868** *Chambers's Encycl.* X. 679/1 Parkesine was first shewn in quantity at the International Exhibition of 1862. **1911** E. C. WORDEN *Nitrocellulose Industry* I. xi. 364 Lewthwaite utilized the patented product of A. Parkes (called Parkesine) by ornamenting, embossing, and printing, and treated it in a manner similar to real leather. **1958** *Times* 25 Mar. (Careers in Industry Suppl.) p. xii/3 'Parkesine' was the forerunner of 'xylonite' and is identical with 'celluloid', the American article which in the 1870's was the first commercially satisfactory plastics product. **1964** V. E. YARSLEY et al. *Cellulosic Plastics* xv. 181 The celluloid of the Parkesine process was produced by squeezing out the dough between rolls and subsequently removing the residual volatile solvent.

parkie, parky (pā·ɹki). *colloq.* (chiefly *Sc.* and *north.*). [f. PARK *sb.* 2 + -Y^6, -IE.] A park-keeper.

[**1939** JOYCE *Finnegans Wake* 587 Touching our Phoenix Rangers' nuisance at the meeting of the waitresses,.. and those pest of parkies, twitch, thistle and charlock.] **1953** *Scottish Jrnl. Theol.* VI. 424 [Schopenhauer] one day sat hunched up on a seat in the Tiergarten, sunk in profound reflection. A *Parkaufseher*, or as we should say 'parky', saw him and not unnaturally put him down as at least a suspicious character. **1957** J. KIRKUP *Only Child* 124 We lived in mortal terror of being caught by the parky. **1965** *Listener* 4 Nov. 720/1 The Parkie's usually an auld man and he cannie climb the poles. **1971** *Sunday Times* 9 May 34 It's just coats on the ground and the parkies chase us at least once a month for doing something wrong. **1975** *Scottish Field* Apr. 4/3 You had to be on the lookout for the Parky if, as was likely, you had nipped on to the Alexandra Park golf course] without paying.

parkin. (Earlier and later examples.)

1800 D. WORDSWORTH *Jrnl.* 6 Nov. (1941) I. 71, I was baking bread, dinner, and parkins. **1968** E. R. BUCKLER *Ox Bells & Fireflies* xix. 268 Two women had brought oatmeal parkins on cake plates that were exactly alike. **1973** *New Society* 20 Dec. 709/3 The re-birth of interest in regional specialities like parkin (a rich, dark gingerbread, eaten with cheese).

parking, *vbl. sb.* **2.** Add to def.: Also, in some regions of the U.S., a strip of grass between the footpath and the curb. Also **parking strip.**

1945 *Amer. Speech* XX. 154/1 *Parking*, the grassed area between curbing and sidewalk. The term is used by some Minnesotans instead of *Boulevard*, by others as an alternate. **1963** R. I. McDAVID *Mencken's Amer. Lang.* 667 In the Minneapolis area it [sc. *boulevard*] designates the grass strip between the sidewalk and the curb, elsewhere called a *tree lawn* or a *parking strip*. **1964** *Amer. Speech* XXXIX. 293 That strip of grass and weeds between the sidewalk and the curb..seems to be most commonly called *tree lawn* or *parking strip*... I use the colorless *parking* from the language of relatives in Iowa. **1966** *Inland* (Inland Steel Co., Chicago) Autumn 16/2 For the grass strip between sidewalk and street there is a bewildering array of local terms:..*parking* in Illinois. **1969** *Better Homes & Gardens* (U.S.) Apr. 85 They look best when used in a formal manner, such as in pairs on front parkings or equally spaced along property lines.

3. The placing or leaving of a vehicle or vehicles in a park (*PARK *sb.* 5b), at the side of the road, or elsewhere. Also *transf.*

1926 *Rep. Commissioner Police Metropolis 1925* 17 in *Parl. Papers* (Cmd. 2660) XV. 239 Parking of Cars.—The arrangements tentatively made by Police for parking cars on certain highways have been given statutory effect. **1929** *Minnesota Alumni Weekly* June 619 The new space along with a lot now used for parking will be seeded. **1931** *Times Lit. Suppl.* 15 Oct. 789/2 Let off with a caution at Marlborough-street for improper parking of his car. **1959** *Daily Tel.* 24 Mar. 9/2 A possible ban on parking on main roads was hinted at yesterday. **1961** *Product Engineering* 14 Aug. 34/1 Additional symbols of status are granted, such as reserved parking, distinctive badge passes.., and a difference in the treatment of financial progress through merit. **1970** *R.A.C. Guide & Handbk. 1970–71* 63/2 Where unexpired time is shown on the meter at the time of parking this period may be used without payment. **1977** 'M. UNDERWOOD' *Fatal Trip* i. 7 A re-arrangement of her domestic routine including the parking of Simon on a good-natured neighbour.

b. *attrib.* and *Comb.*, as *parking apron, area, attendant, fee, fine, garage, offence, place, space*; **parking bay**, a recess at the side of a road or other space allocated for parking a vehicle; **parking brake**, a brake provided on a motor vehicle or trailer for holding it at rest; **parking deck** [*DECK *sb.*^{1} 3 b], a floor of a building used as a parking place for vehicles; also, a multi-storey car park; **parking disc**: see *DISC *sb.* 2f; **parking lamp, light**, a small (often detachable) light on a motor vehicle for indicating its position when parked at night; = *SIDE-LIGHT; **parking lot** orig. *U.S.*, a plot of ground used for the parking of vehicles; **parking meter** orig. *U.S.*, a coin-operated meter which registers the time a vehicle has been parked; **parking orbit**, an orbit around the earth or some other planet from which a space vehicle can be launched farther into space; **parking strip** (see quots.); **parking tag, ticket** orig. *U.S.*, a ticket attached by an official to a vehicle which has violated parking regulations; **parking warden** = **traffic warden*.

1974 HAWKEY & BINGHAM *Wild Card* i. 20 The mile-long journey to the parking apron. **1961** R. A. FUTTERMAN *Future of our Cities* iii. 62 Less ambitious freeway plans may be more successful—especially when the roadways and interchanges are raised, allowing for cross access at many points and providing parking areas below the ramp. **1966** 'A. HALL' *9th Directive* vii. 63 A car had come into the parking area. **1977** E. LEONARD *Unknown Man No. 89* xxi. 212 He..crossed the parking area to the front entrance. **1941** B. SCHULBERG *What makes Sammy Run?* iii. 48 He was on speaking terms with everybody, the parking attendant, the hat-check girl. **1962** J. BRIERLEY *Parking of Motor Vehicles* 298 *Parking attendant*, a person authorized by or on behalf of a council or parking authority to supervise a parking place. **1973** A. MANN *Tiara* ix. 87 He handed the Maserati over to a parking attendant of the Automobile Club. **1962** J. BRIERLEY *Parking of Motor Vehicles* v. 49 A parking bay 18 feet long will be long enough for the majority of modern cars. **1972** *Times* 26 Jan. 6/1 The notice was given to comply with the provisions for rent revision contained in an underlease for a flat on the seventh and eighth floors of Ambassador House and a parking bay. **1976** T. HEALD *Let Sleeping Dogs Die* viii. 167 The van ahead berthed in a parking bay. **1944** L. D. KITCHIN *Road Transport Law* 41/4 It is an offence to leave a vehicle without stopping the engine..and applying the parking brake. **1959** E. K. WENLOCK *Kitchin's Road Transport Law* (ed. 12) 20/1 On all trailers exceeding 2 cwt unladen the braking system must also be capable of acting as a parking brake to prevent at least two wheels from revolving. **1967** *Gloss. Caravan Terms (B.S.I.)* 2 *Parking brakes*, brakes for holding the caravan when at rest, usually the overrun brakes or power brakes provided with additional means of manual application. **1974** *New Yorker* 25 Feb. 44/3 He went into a double-parking maneuver that culminated as, with a flourish, he pulled at the parking-brake handle. **1970** Parking deck [see *DECK *sb.*^{1} 3b]. **1972** *Graphic* (Tuscaloosa, Alabama) 30 Nov. 12/3 The County Commission Tuesday formally adopted a multi-level parking deck to be constructed adjacent to the County Jail. **1972** *Birmingham* (Alabama) *News* 17 Dec. 4A/1 With two parking deck sites assured..the property surrounding the station could be purchased and the proposed seven-story structure built in an L-shape. **1974** *Tuscaloosa* (Alabama) *News* 17 Feb. 3D/2 The authority was to build a parking deck for the downtown area. **1932** *Autocar* 9 Sept. 469, I have only once, in two years, been asked to pay a parking fee. **1963** P. HALL *London 2000* v. 111 One exception, which parking fees do not meet, is the extra congestion in the very short morning and evening rush periods. **1971** 'S. SMITH' *Grave Affair* ix. 134 Horsham Police were surprised to receive payment of the £2 parking fine on the Cortina... It came in a plain manilla envelope,..and inside were two pound notes and the parking ticket. **1972** P. D. JAMES *Unsuitable Job* iv. 117 She daren't risk a parking fine nor the impounding of the car. **1977** D. WILLIAMS *Treasure by Degrees* xviii. 166 Miss Stopps was not the type of citizen who would ignore a parking fine demand. **1948** *Sun* (Baltimore) 18 Feb. 10/2 There will undoubtedly be debates as to whether the commission should build and operate parking garages as public enterprises. **1974** M. G. EBERHART *Danger Money* (1975) xi. 118 Greg drove..to a parking garage where he left the car and hailed a taxi. **1976** *Billings* (Montana) *Gaz.* 1 July 3-B/2 Bids to construct Billings first municipally owned parking garage have all been rejected as being at least $300,000 too high. **1926–7** *Army & Navy Stores Catal.* 1134/1 Motor lamps..parking lamp... Burns very small amount of current. **1957** E. K. WENLOCK *Kitchin's Road Transport Law* (ed. 11) 60/1 Parking lamps which can be used only on certain vehicles..must show a 1in diameter white light to the front and a 1in diameter red light to the rear. **1972** *Daily Tel.* 27 Apr. 19/6 Motorists will be able to discard their clip-on auxiliary parking lamps after Sunday next, when standardised regulations for parking without lights come into effect throughout the country. **1938** H. A. TRIPP *Road Traffic & its Control* III. ix. 160 'Parking lights' of extremely low power (in order to economise current) are fitted to some cars. **1943** R. CHANDLER *Lady in Lake* (1944) xxiv. 136 A motor purled gently in the car with the parking lights on it. **1973** 'B. MATHER' *Snowline* xiv. 171 It was a car running on its parking lights. **1924** H. CROY *R.F.D. No. 3* 172 Some of the people still lingered under the arc light, with its summer collection of bugs still in it, waiting for the two to come from the parking lot. **1930** M. McCLINTOCK *Rep. Parking & Garage Probl. Washington* 19 Parking lot rates average substantially lower than those for garages. **1958** *New Statesman* 1 Nov. 590/3 Partial overbuilding of these parking lots would do little to disguise the inherent visual bleakness of conception. **1972** *Times* 18 Mar. 8/7 People who in Leeds, for instance, will have stepped across the parking lot from rehearsals in the Playhouse to others in the studio. **1976** H. NIELSEN *Brink of Murder* ix. 81 Simon found the restaurant..and drove into the parking lot. [**1935** *Pop. Sci. Monthly* Aug. 33/3 (*heading*) Curb-parking meter times autoist's stay.] **1936** *Amer. City* Jan. 95/3 In July..there came to the attention of the officials in Dallas a device known as the parking meter. **1938** *Encycl. Brit. Bk. of Year* 649/2 Many cities have installed parking meters, usually requiring the deposit of five cents per hour for permission to park at the kerb. **1949** *Chicago Daily News* 11 Aug. 3/4 A runaway horse and wagon collided with a parking meter. **1956** *Planning* XXII. 210 There has been much discussion of the merits of coin-in-slot parking meters as a means of enforcing time limits. **1958** *Observer* 13 July 7/8 Six hundred parking meters, the first in Britain, came into operation in Mayfair on Thursday morning. **1966** *New Scientist* 24 Nov. 447/1 The psychological effect of the parking meter is always diluted by the element of gambling involved. **1974** *Guardian* 24 Jan. 28/4 Increases in parking meter charges. **1959** M. SUMMERTON *Small Wilderness* i. 21 Once..he'd let me off a parking offence. **1960** G. MIKES *How to be Inimitable* 60 The most heinous offence known to the Police is officially called 'obstructing the Queen's Highway'. The Queen is brought into it to underline the close connection between a parking offence and high treason. **1960** *Aeroplane* XCIX. 496/1 Such a satellite could be launched for immediate interception, or placed in a 'parking' orbit, always ready to intercept, interrogate or inspect in detail another object orbiting in space. **1961** *Flight* LXXIX. 426/1 Injection into 'parking orbit', which places the vehicle at the proper location in space for departure into the desired lunar trajectory. **1970** *New Scientist* 2 July 21 The spacecraft goes on into a parking orbit and the two boosters coast down to land. **1925** *Act* 15 & 16 *Geo. V* c. 71 §68 (9) In this section the expression 'parking place' means a place where vehicles, or vehicles of any particular class or description, may wait. **1941** Parking-place [see *BINDI-EYE]. **1975** N. LUARD *Robespierre Serial* ii. 6 It's the residents coming back from work; they've got permits for the parking-places. **1924** *Collier's* 5 Jan. 17/2 Secretary Mellon has asked permission to move the Washington Monument so as to get more parking space. **1926** Parking space [see *car-park* s.v. *CAR *sb.*^{1} 6]. **1941** G. MARX *Let.* 25 July (1967) 29 Parking space is at a premium around this ramshackle building. **1971** A. PRICE *Alamut Ambush* iii. 35 His mind on a parking space thirty yards ahead. **1961** *New Left Rev.* July–Aug. 57/2 In front of the garages and kitchens are cobbled parking strips which absorb oil stains and from which moving traffic is kept by low bollards. **1966** *Inland* (Inland Steel Co., Chicago) Autumn 16/2 For the grass strip between sidewalk and street there is a bewildering array of local terms:..*parking strip*..in Illinois. **1956** 'E. McBAIN' *Cop Hater* (1958) iii. 28 Anybody who ever got a parking tag is automatically a cop hater. **1968** *Globe & Mail* (Toronto) 17 Feb. 5/8 More than $6-million of this amount came from the magistrates' courts. About $1,850,000 came from parking tags. **1977** *Time* 22 Aug. 34 (*caption*) The telltale parking tag and Deputy Craig Glassman with hate letters from his neighbor. **1947** *Denver Post* 2 Mar. A1/2 Parking tickets no longer could be fixed. **1951** T. STERLING *House without Door* vii. 80 These old bastards haven't even read a parking ticket for the last twenty years. **1959** W. R. BIRD *These are Maritimes* x. 300 He took an old parking ticket out of his pocket. **1971** [see *parking fine* above]. **1973** H. GILBERT *Hotels with Empty Rooms* xvi. 137 The car stood where they had left it. A parking ticket had been inserted under the right-hand windscreen-wiper. **1966** P. MOLONEY *Plea for Mersey* 51 This sentinel your chariot will keep Till Parking Wardens, roused up from their sleep, Espy the yellow in the monster's face, And mark the car, with symbol of disgrace. **1974** L. DEIGHTON *Spy Story* xiii. 130, I watched two parking wardens clobber a delivery van.

Parkinson^1 (pā·ɹkinsǝn). The name of James *Parkinson* (1755–1824), English surgeon and palæontologist, used in **Parkinson's disease** [tr. F. *maladie de Parkinson* (J. M. Charcot 1876, in *Progrès médical* 2 Dec. 838/2)], a chronic, slowly progressive disorder of the central nervous system that occurs chiefly in later life as a result of degenerative changes in the brain and produces tremor, rigidity of the limbs, and slowness and imprecision of movement (described by Parkinson, under the names *shaking palsy* and *paralysis agitans*, in *An Essay on the Shaking Palsy* (1817)); **Parkinson syndrome** = *PARKINSONISM.

1877 G. SIGERSON tr. D.-M. Bourneville in *Charcot's Lect. Dis. Nervous Syst.* (ser. 1) v. 144 This man, aged 50 years, was attacked by 'Parkinson's disease' in consequence of a strong emotion occasioned by the attempts of the Federalists, during the time of the Commune, to incorporate him in their battalions. **1888** W. R. GOWERS *Man. Dis. Nervous Syst.* II. 589 From the fact that it was first fully described by Parkinson in 1817, it has been called 'Parkinson's disease', but the name which he gave to it of 'shaking palsy' is both apt and adequate. **1909** *Practitioner* Feb. 290 In Parkinson's disease (paralysis agitans), the drug produced considerable decrease in all the cases. **1933** [see *HOFFMANN 3]. **1950** A. HUXLEY *Let.* 19 July (1969) 627 Poor Osbert [Sitwell] has got Parkinson's disease and has started to tremble. **1955** *Sci. News Let.* 20 Aug. 120/2 A drug of the antihistamine class has helped almost half of a group of patients suffering with the Parkinson syndrome, best known to the layman as shaking palsy. **1970** [see *DOPA]. **1973** *Sci. Amer.* July 98/3 Symptoms of Parkinson's disease..include active features such as tremor and muscular rigidity and negative features such as slowness in the initiation of movement and loss of the usual facial expression of emotions.

Parkinson^2 (pā·ɹkinsǝn). The name of Cyril Northcote *Parkinson* (b. 1909), historian and journalist, used in the possessive to denote the 'law' propounded by him, that work expands to fill the time available for its completion. Also *transf.*

1955 *Economist* 19 Nov. 635/1 Before the discovery of a new scientific law—herewith presented to the public for the first time, and to be called Parkinson's Law—there has.. been insufficient recognition of the implications of this fact in the field of public administration. **1957** C. N. PARKINSON (*title*) Parkinson's law. **1957** *N.Y. Times* 5 May III. 1/7 Parkinson's Law is that British Government employes multiply by about 5 per cent a year even though their total work output does not increase in proportion. **1958** C. N. PARKINSON *Parkinson's Law* (U.K. ed.) 4 Parkinson's Law or the Rising Pyramid. Work expands so as to fill the time available for its completion. **1958** N. MACKENZIE *Conviction* 15 Our civil servants are bureaucratic slaves to Parkinson's Law. **1958** *Times* 3 July 11/6 An extension of Parkinson's Law to the parliamentary system establishes that the British instinct 'is to form two opposing teams, with referee and linesmen, and let them debate until they exhaust themselves'. **1960** *Guardian* 22 July 10/4 There is some 'Parkinson's law' that cars increase in numbers to fill..any space made available. **1962** *Lancet* 28 Apr. 898/2 The transportation of anything to high camps is subject to Parkinson's law: the greater the weight, the greater the number of porters; the greater the number of porters, the greater the weight of supplies; the greater the weight of supplies, the greater the number of porters. **1964** M. ARGYLE *Psychol. & Social Probl.* xiv. 172 Studies of factories, hospitals and school districts of different sizes show that larger ones have if anything a lower proportion of administrators, so that Parkinson's law is by no means generally true. **1966** R. H. ROBINS *Gen. Linguistics within Liberal Educ.* 15 A sort of Parkinson's Law applies in vocabulary: the meaning range of a word expands to fill the available space. **1972** *Daily Tel.* 3 Feb. 14 The engineers will tell you that, once it is built, the traffic will be there; and this, alas, is true, for Parkinson's Law ensures that traffic expands to fill the space available. **1974** L. DEIGHTON *Spy Story* xiii. 127 Before we had the security cards, there had been no delays. I was a victim of some Parkinson's law of proliferating security. **1978** *Cornish Guardian* 27 Apr. 3/1 Having spent the money, they then see the need to take on scores of new planners and technical officers. It was Parkinson's Law gone mad.

Hence **Parkinso·nian** *a.*[2], of or pertaining to Parkinson or his law; also as *sb.*[2], a believer in this law; **Pa·rkinsonism**[2], the principle or doctrine reflected in Parkinson's law; an instance of this.

1957 *Life* 15 Apr. 57/1 Maybe where the squeeze ought to be applied hardest is on 'Parkinsonism', that trend for every bureau to proliferate. **1959** *Times* 3 Mar. 3/7 A port scene by Seurat, compounded of a thousand 'pointillist' dots must seem to Parkinsonians like a troupe of typists at £12 a week and 10 clerks at £20 and a dozen 'high executives' at £5,000 a year all busily employed in the composition and dispatch of a 'Yours of the 9th to hand'. *Ibid.* 5 May 11/5 They seem, perhaps, to be in some danger of falling into the (Parkinsonian?) trap of treating theoretical maxima as practical minima. **1960** *N.Y. Times* 31 Jan. 56/3 Professor Parkinson's book, 'Parkinson's Law', expounding this and other Parkinsonisms, was published in 1957. **1962** *Daily Tel.* 14 Mar. 12/2 The LCC has built up some efficient teams, with high status and pay at the top, for supervising its many services. Though some of these may smack of Parkinsonian internal empire building, many are good. **1964** R. BRADDON *Year Angry Rabbit* iv. 33 Committees of otherwise useless Civil Servants (whose numbers had swollen to quite terrifying and parkinsonian proportions since World War II). **1964** *New Society* 29 Oct. 6/2 In spite of the charges of Parkinsonism, Mr. Wilson's administration is fairly orthodox in its size and structure. **1968** A. DIMENT *Bang Bang Birds* ii. 15 At the outset it was just a little sub-department but by inevitable Parkinsonian growth it had assumed an identity of its own. **1971** C. RUSSELL *Crisis of Parliaments* III. i. 110 The Parkinsonian process by which people administering particular subjects under the Chamber acquired subordinates and a formal organization was accelerated by the increase in government business. **1975** M. SINCLAIR *Long Time Sleeping* xiv. 166 The best of all Parkinsonian models—when he had little to do he did nothing; when overstretched he always managed to fit extra into the day.

Parkinsonian (pāɹkinsōᵘ·niăn), *sb.*[1] and *a.*[1] *Med.* Also **parkinsonian.** [f. *PARKINSON[1] + -IAN.] **A.** *sb.* A person affected with Parkinsonism.

1899 CHURCH & PETERSON *Nervous & Mental Dis.* VII. iii. 516 The gait of Parkinsonians is strikingly peculiar. **1949** *Lancet* 26 Feb. 364/2 The parkinsonian has difficulty in starting to walk, and in stopping when once started. **1973** M. RIKLAN *L-Dopa & Parkinsonism* iii. 185 In the usual therapeutic dosages, L-Dopa has a wide variety of behavioral effects, both positive and negative, on the behavior of the parkinsonian.

B. *adj.* Characteristic of or affected with Parkinsonism.

1906 P. STEWART *Diagnosis Nervous Dis.* xvii. 243 The posture and gait of *paralysis agitans* are diagnostic... In a well-marked case the patient stands with the trunk stooping forwards, the face appearing 'starched' and expressionless—the so-called 'Parkinsonian mask', in which there is little or no emotional play of features. **1930** *Arch. Ophthalm.* IV. 364 Neurologic examination revealed a characteristic postencephalitic parkinsonian facies, gait and attitude. **1933** W. R. BRAIN *Dis. Nervous Syst.* viii. 447 The Parkinsonian gait..is usually slow, shuffling, and composed of small steps. **1970** *Nature* 4 Apr. 23/2 It is likely..that at least 50 per cent of the total Parkinsonian population may obtain benefit from L-dopa.

Parkinsonism (pā·ɹkinsǫniz'm). *Med.* Also **parkinsonism.** [f. *PARKINSON[1] + -ISM.] **a.** The group of symptoms seen esp. in Parkinson's disease, but occurring also in other cerebral disorders. **b.** = **Parkinson's disease.*

1923 *Brain* XLVI. 268 Post-encephalitic Parkinsonism is usually due to degeneration of the substantia nigra. **1949** *Lancet* 12 Feb. 258/1 A patient with advanced parkinsonism..was bedridden owing to extreme rigidity. **1954** H. H. MORRITT in L. J. Doshay *Parkinsonism & its Treatment* i. 3 Two striking characteristics of the symptoms of parkinsonism are their relationship to emotional tension and their disappearance in sleep. **1966** WRIGHT & SYMMERS *Systemic Path.* II. xxxiv. 1292/2 Tremor and rigidity may develop in other diseases, and it is usual to refer to this syndrome as Parkinsonism. Postencephalitic Parkinsonism..is the most familiar example of this disability; it also occurs in chronic manganese poisoning and in patients who have survived severe carbon monoxide or nitrous oxide intoxication. **1970** *Times* 29 Apr. 2/3 There are about 60,000 sufferers from Parkinsonism in England and Wales. **1974** E. AMBLER *Dr. Frigo* II. 110 If you can catch Parkinsonism in the early stages treatment nowadays can do a lot to help the patient.

parkland (pā·ɹklænd). [PARK *sb.* 7.] **1.** An area of grassland scattered with occasional clumps of trees. Also *attrib.*

1907 H. A. KENNEDY *New Canada* 182 Very soon the parklands of the north were all behind us. **1909** E. WARMING *Oecol. Plants* lxxxix. 325 We may cite the 'park-lands' of eastern Asia, where grassland has become occupied by trees and shrubs. **1920** H. G. WELLS *Outl. Hist.* 84/2 They were forest and parkland peoples without horses. *Ibid.* 267/2 A slow change in climate..was replacing the swamps and forests and parklands of South Russia ..by steppes. **1926** TANSLEY & CHIPP *Study of Vegetation* x. 209 Parkland..aptly describes the great stretches of country which in Africa almost completely surround the Closed Forest... The characteristic feature of the Parkland is grass, interspersed with trees. **1948** A. L. RAND *Mammals E. Rockies* 110 The parklands of central Alberta. **1953** *Canad. Geogr. Jrnl.* XLVI. 240/1 This fact would seem to urge caution in the extension of irrigation northward into the parkland belt. **1960** N. POLUNIN *Introd. Plant Geogr.* xiv. 441 Savanna-woodlands or 'parklands' are often found where the rainless period is more prolonged and the annual rainfall less heavy than in true closed forest. **1968** R. M. PATTERSON *Finlay's River* 3 It [*sc.* a relief map] has been carefully painted with the varying greens and yellows that indicate the different kinds of forest, parkland and tundra.

2. Land given over to the cultivation of a park or parks (PARK *sb.* 1 b).

1937 *Proc. Prehist. Soc.* III. 73 The edges of the barrow are turfed and merge into undisturbed parkland. **1952** *Antiquity* XXVI. 161 The houses of Stowe or Wimpole or Castle Howard were being absorbed into their parklands. **1954** M. BERESFORD *Lost Villages* i. 28 The parkland.. was both attractive to the eye and useful to the pocket. **1959** *Geogr. Rev.* XLIX. 28 A thousand acres of parkland was deliberately left unaltered. **1977** *Times* 26 Nov. 28/5 (Advt.), Enjoy a weekend in the country at a beautiful Georgian Rectory in 26 acres of parkland.

3. *Canad.* **a.** A parcel of land required by law to be set aside for public recreation and wildlife conservation.

1957 *Financial Post* (Toronto) 29 June 23/3 Every major Canadian city knows it should be providing 10 acres of parkland for every 1,000 people. **1977** *Little Cataraqui Environment Assoc. Newsletter* Nov. 1 The [conservation] authority will maintain this land as a natural parkland, paying both taxes to the city and maintenance costs.

b. A national or provincial park.

1958 *Maclean's Mag.* 10 May 8/1 We do, of course, sometimes set aside tracts of country for recreation and so forth—and we say these are in perpetuity; but this phrase only seems to mean until the parkland is needed for logging, or mining. **1971** *Weekend Mag.* (Montreal) 21 Aug. 9/2 Quebec..now has an accelerated program attending to some 25,000 square miles of developed and partially developed parkland.

Park Lane (pāɹk lēⁱn). The name of a fashionable London street used as a symbol of wealth and breeding and the social attitudes they imply. Hence **Park Lane-ite.**

1880 TROLLOPE *Duke's Children* II. vii. 78 Park Lane was sweeter than the Fifth Avenue. Lord Silverbridge was nicer than the bank clerk. **1906** *Westm. Gaz.* 27 Apr. 1/3 The attitude of this lady of the ballad is a common one among the Park-lanes of every land. **1936** 'J. TEY' *Shilling for Candles* vii. 73 What I'd like to know is if that method goes in Pimlico or if you keep it for Park Lane. **1944** M. LASKI *Love on Supertax* ii. 27 Would you yourself be quite happy to see your children playing with scrubbed little brats from Park Lane? **1961** A. SMITH *East-Enders* ii. 29 If they want to live like Park Lane-ites they should live in Park Lane.

parklet (pā·ɹklėt). [dim. of PARK *sb.*] A small park in an urban area.

1966 *Listener* 27 Jan. 135/1 The charming little 'parklets' ..have real herbaceous borders. **1968** MRS. L. B. JOHNSON *White House Diary* 2 Oct. (1970) 715 These two small parklets on Hobart Street in a low-income area were a gift to the city by David Lloyd Kreeger.

parky, *a.*[1] Delete *rare,* and add earlier and later examples.

1831 M. EDGEWORTH *Let.* 11 Apr. (1971) 517 We came to a beautiful parky place where Dr. Fitton flourishes for the summer. **1955** R. P. HOBSON *Nothing too Good for Cowboy* v. 43 Cow tracks fanned out through the parky poplar country leaving a messy swath many yards wide. **1973** R. D. SYMONS *Where Wagon Led* III. x. 181 The country around Turtleford was parky, with aspen bluffs and just the odd spruce.

parky, *a.*[2] (Earlier and later examples.)

1895 *Sporting Times* 9 Feb. 1/4 A toff came and ordered a pint of hot, As he said that the weather was parkey. **1916** 'TAFFRAIL' *Pincher Martin* xi. 191 'Strewth!..it's a bit parky, ain't it? **1969** J. CLARKE *Foxon's Hole* xxv. 153 Gawaine ventured to say that it was a fine day... 'Ah. Parky, though. Shouldn't wunner if we 'ad a bit o' snow.' **1970** *Kenya Farmer* Feb. 36/3 All our visitors seem to labour under the delusion that it should be warm and sunny all twenty four hours... They are utterly demoralised by our parky nights on the farm. **1975** T. HEALD *Deadline* v. 99 'Cold isn't it?' 'Pretty parky.'

parky: see *PARKIE.

‖ **parlando** (pāɹlæ·ndo), *a.*, *adv.*, and *sb. Mus.* [It.] A direction that a passage is to be played or sung 'as if speaking', in an expressive or declamatory manner.

1876 STAINER & BARRETT *Dict. Mus. Terms* 342/2 *Parlando, Parlante (It.)*, in a declamatory manner, as if speaking. **1880** GROVE *Dict. Mus.* II. 650/2 *Parlando, Parlante*, 'speaking'. A direction allowing greater freedom in rendering than *cantando* or *cantabile*, and yet referring to the same kind of expression. **1930** *Time & Tide* 7 June 745/1 Against a dissonant pianoforte accompaniment, the voice disclaims monotonously in the 'parlando' style. **1944** W. APEL *Harvard Dict. Mus.* 554/1 Parlando occurs particularly in rapid tempo when the syllables of the text change with every note... In connection with instrumental music, parlando (*parlante*) calls for an expressive declamation, suggestive of speech or song. **1955** *Times* 27 May 13/4 Miss Nancy Evans sang 'The Water Mill' too slowly and with too much tone—this is a *parlando* song. **1960** *Times* 23 May 16/7 A..lyrical setting of the Bible story, involving..choral parlando. **1970** *Daily Tel.* 28 Sept. 11/3 Where he perhaps carried relaxation a shade too far ..was in a habit, during less important recitative-like passages, of lapsing occasionally into a toneless parlando of too vaguely defined pitch. **1977** *Gramophone* Dec. 1098/3 Brahms to them is a romantic to the hilt, and they go out of their way to extract the maximum *parlando*-type expression from every phrase.

parlary, var. *PARLYAREE.

parlay (pā·ɹlēⁱ), *sb. U.S.* [Now the more usual form of PARLEY *sb.*[4]] A cumulative series of bets in which winnings accruing from one transaction are transferred to the next. Also *attrib.* See also PARLEY *sb.*[4]

1927 *National Turf Digest* (U.S.) Jan. 19/1 From the standpoint of the bookmaker..no money coming from a winning horse can be 'iffed' to a parlay on that same horse and another. **1928** *Ibid.* Feb. 91/1 A parlay player cannot protect himself against a changed track condition, a change of jockeys, or added starters. **1932** D. RUNYON in *Collier's* 26 Mar. 40/2 He has a dispute with Sorrowful about a parlay on the races the day before. **1946** *Sun* (Baltimore) 2 Apr. 26/4 A $2 parlay would have paid $10,906.70. **1957** *New Yorker* 2 Nov. 105/1 Colonel Martingale..has figured out that a parlay on the same horses would have paid $4,045.58. **1963** T. PYNCHON *V.* vii. 158 Both, together, were like a parlay of horses, capable of a whole arrived at by some operation more alien than simple addition of parts. **1976** *New Yorker* 23 Feb. 85/2 Well, all the players who made parlays on the Proud horses—Birdie and Delta—clicked.

parlay (pā·ɹlēⁱ), *v.* [Now the more usual form of PARLEY *v.*[2]] **1.** See PARLEY *v.*[2]

2. *trans.* To increase (capital) by means of gambling; more generally, to exploit (a circumstance) for gain, to transform (an asset, advantage, etc.) *into* something considerably greater or more valuable. Also *absol. U.S. colloq.*

1942 *San Francisco Examiner* 5 May 18/5 As far as the girl who was kicked off the '36 Olympic team and parlayed it into a million dollars or so, is concerned, water these days is strictly for drinking and bathing. **1947** *Life* 20 Jan. 89/2 Only 25 years ago trucking firms consisted of a few men with strong backs and iron nerves who parlayed their savings into creaky trucks and did their bookkeeping on backs of envelopes. **1949** *Sat. Even. Post.* 25 June 32 H. J. Heinz..parlayed a pickle into one of the most valuable family heirlooms in America. **1952** *Sun* (Baltimore) 8 Oct. 11/2 She would like to parlay an original 'People's Union' fund of $100 into lots more and start in motion her mailing plan for errant politicians. **1956** B. HOLIDAY *Lady sings Blues* (1973) vi. 57, I hoped he could shoot enough dice to parlay it into a bill big enough I didn't have to feel ashamed to send home. **1964** 'E. MCBAIN' *Axe* v. 78 Cards... Dice. Anything where he can parlay a small stake into some quick cash. **1972** *Publishers' Weekly* 17 Jan. 56/3 His family had parlayed the sum awarded him by the court into millions. **1973** *Times Lit. Suppl.* 28 Sept. 1131/3 Parlaying his genuine physical tragedy, by unspoken comparison, into a certificate of literary genius. **1975** *High Times* Dec. 106/2 (Advt.), I have parlayed $146 into $90,000. **1976** *Wood Sci.* VIII. 180 These findings may be parlayed into savings in sample size in future experiments on the strength of lumber. **1977** *New Society* 5 May 236/3 Former pupils who had parlayed a third-class degree into £7,000 a year and ten minutes' teaching a week. **1977** *Time* 27 June 15/1 Rainer Werner Fassbinder, 31, the *Wunderkind* of low-budget West German cinema,..is about to parlay his critical acclaim into box office success as an international director.

‖ **parlementaire** (pārlĕmantę̄r'). [Fr., f. *parlementer* to discuss terms, to parley.] = PARLIAMENTARY *sb.* 3.

1918 E. S. FARROW *Dict. Mil. Terms* 434 *Parlementaire,* in the French services the term meaning a bearer of a flag of truce. **1931** *Economist* 14 Nov. 892/2 The Japanese expeditionary force..began by sending parlementaires to the local Chinese military commander..who agreed to withdraw his troops ten kilometres. **1945** R. Hargreaves *Enemy at Gate* 230 Terms having been refused his *parlementaires*, Osman was left with no option but to submit in unconditional surrender. **1945** C. S. Forester *Commodore* xxii. 253 'French or Russian, sir,' said the parlementaire 'they will die unless they receive speedy aid.' **1950** W. S. Churchill *Second World War* (1951) IV. ii. xxiv. 376 At dawn on the 21st General Klopper sent out a parlementaire with an offer to capitulate, and at 7.45 a.m. German officers came to his headquarters and accepted his surrender.

parley, *v.*[2] Add: (Earlier and later examples in form *parlee.*)

The usual spelling is now *parlay.

1890 J. P. Quinn *Fools of Fortune* ii. ii. 194 Almost all [faro] bankers will allow a player to 'parlee' as the percentage is largely in favor of the bank. **1903** Ade *People you Know* 110 He wanted to parlee a $2 Silver Certificate and bring home enough to pay the National Debt.

parliament, *sb.*[1] Add: **3. e.** *Act of Parliament clock*, a type of wall clock produced in the 18th century for use in inns and taverns and characterized by a black or green dial with gold numerals over which there was no glass. The name arose from the popular belief that such clocks were acquired by innkeepers in order to attract custom after Parliament imposed a tax on clocks and watches in 1797.

1899 F. J. Britten *Old Clocks & Watches* 337 In country inns and other places Act of Parliament clocks may still occasionally be seen. **1917** A. Hayden *Chats on Old Clocks* iv. 124 It is supposed that these clocks suddenly came into being when private clocks were taxed. Owing to such a deep-seated belief they are always known throughout the country as 'Act of Parliament' clocks. But they were used earlier than the Act of 1797, and were probably ordinary inn clocks in common use about that time. **1952** J. Gloag *Short Dict. Furnit.* 191 *Coaching Inn Clock*..Such clocks have been misnamed Parliament or Act of Parliament clocks, on the assumption that they were introduced and used extensively by innkeepers after Pitt's Act of 1797 (under which clocks and watches were taxed) presumably to save customers..buying a watch or clock and then paying tax on it—not a plausible theory. **1960** *House & Garden* Apr. 100/1 The round-faced Act of Parliament clock..is two feet across. **1962** *Kent & Sussex Courier* 19 Oct. 6/6 The Rose and Crown Hotel boasts the town's oldest public clock. A fine example of an Act of Parliament clock, it was made in 1797 and now stands in the entrance hall.

5. c. (Further examples.)

1905 R. B. Smith *Bird Life* x. 386 Two such 'Parliaments of rooks' I have had the opportunity of watching, from early times. **1939** C. E. Hare *Lang. Field Sports* xxiii. 192 The modern accepted rook term is believed to be *parliament*, but no authority for this can be traced. **1968** J. Lipton *Exaltation of Larks* 57 (*caption*) A parliament of owls.

9. parliament-gingerbread (example); **parliament hinge** (example).

1861 C. M. Yonge *Stokesley Secret* iii. 39 A stall full of parliament gingerbread. **1841** C. Cist *Cincinnati in 1841* 247 The lighter castings kept in hardware stores—butt and parliament hinges, for example—will be made here.

pa:rliamentariza·tion. [f. Parliamentary *a.* + -ization.] The act or process of becoming parliamentary in character or in means of government.

1924 *Contemp. Rev.* Aug. 256 The book deals..with the progress of the ideas of Parliamentarisation and racial self-determination under the stress of war. **1974** J. White tr. *Poulantzas's Fascism & Dictatorship* iii. iii. 132 The peace pact and the parliamentarization of the fascist movement were resented. **1975** *Times Lit. Suppl.* 12 Sept. 1028/2 *Gesellschaft, Parlament und Regierung* is concerned with the painful evolution of German parliamentarism and its weaknesses both before and after the First World War. More specifically, Dr Ritter's own introduction asks why those forces that might, on the strength of their economic resources, have pressed for parliamentarization..failed to mount an effective challenge to the traditional elites.

parliamentary, *a.* Add: **1.** (Further examples.)

Parliamentary Commissioner (*for Administration*) = *Ombudsman; *Parliamentary Counsel*, barristers employed as established civil servants to draft government bills and amendments; *Parliamentary Private Secretary*, a member of Parliament who acts as assistant to a government minister; the post has no official status and is unpaid.

1833 *Rep. Select Comm. Establ. House of Commons* 163 in *Parl. Papers* XII. 341 You are Parliamentary Counsel to the Treasury?—I am. **1850** *Rep. Sel. Comm. Official Salaries* 8 in *Parl. Papers* XV. 179 Both the Secretaries to the Treasury..are most responsible officers. With regard to the Parliamentary secretaryship, which I once held myself, I do not know so difficult or so disagreeable office in the Government. **1858** H. G. G. Grey *Parliamentary Govt.* vi. 90 Our whole system of Parliamentary Government rests..upon the Ministers of the Crown possessing such authority in Parliament as to enable them generally to direct its proceedings. **1872** Disraeli in *Times* 4 Apr. 5/2, I believe that, without party, Parliamentary government is impossible. **1886** *Whitaker's Almanack 1887* 156/1 Office of Parliamentary Counsel,—Spring Gardens. *Parliamentary Counsel*, Hen. Jenkyns, C.B. **1917** *H.M. Ministers & Heads of Public Departments* (Stationery Office) 1 Parliamentary Private Secretary... Capt. Hon. W. Ormsby-Gore, M.P. **1918** *Act* 8 *Geo. V* c. 3 § 1 (1) A Secretary who shall discharge the functions both of a parliamentary secretary to the Board and a parliamentary under-secretary to the Secretary of State. **1930** W. K. Hancock *Australia* x. 210 The practice of the Australian Labour party makes England's classic philosophy of parliamentary government appear strangely artless and out of date. **1930** A. J. Balfour *Chapters of Autobiogr.* viii. 103 On taking his new post, he [*sc.* Salisbury in 1878 when he became Foreign Secretary] asked me to become his Parliamentary Private Secretary. **1939** W. I. Jennings *Parliament* vii. 229 A department official and the draftsman are seated in the 'box' and communications pass through his parliamentary private secretary or 'fetch-and-carry' man. **1954** H. Morrison *Govt. & Parliament* iv. 66 The life of the Parliamentary Secretary can be interesting and fairly full, or, on the other hand, uninteresting and rather empty. **1966** *Listener* 11 Aug. 194/2 Sir Edmund Compton, Comptroller and Auditor-General, is to be Britain's first Parliamentary Commissioner, or Ombudsman. **1968** T. Stoppard *Real Inspector Hound* 11 I dream of champions chopped down by rabbit-punching sparring partners while eternal bridesmaids turn and rape the bridegrooms over the sausage rolls and parliamentary private secretaries plant bombs in the Minister's Humber. **1969** *Times* 2 May 22/1 The work of the Parliamentary Counsel is not widely known. They draft the Government's Parliamentary Bills. *a* **1974** R. Crossman *Diaries* (1975) I. 42 What was a bit crazy was to put Charles Snow in as his Parliamentary Secretary. *Ibid.* 239 Whereas the parliamentary draftsman who has worked on my Bill is superb, in the Ministry I feel we could have got a far stronger team together if we hadn't relied so entirely on the administrative class. **1976** *Daily Tel.* 20 July 1/2 An issue which has split both Ministers and the different wings of the Parliamentary Labour party. **1976** B. Kemp *Sir Robert Walpole* iv. 79 Walpole and the other ministers cannot be called the 'executive'... Their relation to parliament cannot be called 'parliamentary government', if by this is meant a state of affairs where the 'executive power and the power of legislation are virtually united in the same hands'. **1976** H. Wilson *Governance of Britain* ii. 32 When choosing ministers of state and parliamentary under-secretaries, the prime minister would naturally consult—or at least inform—the Cabinet minister concerned.

2. c. (See quot.)

1886 J. Barrowman *Gloss. Scotch Mining Terms* 49 *Parliamentary pit*, an outlet pit required by statute.

‖ **parloir** (pārlwār). [Fr.: see Parlour.] A room in a monastery or convent used for conversation with people from outside, or among the inmates; = Parlour B. 1. Also, a similar room in a prison.

1728 Chambers *Cycl.* II. 354/2 *Parloir, Parlour*, in Nunneries, a little Room, or Closet, where People talk to the Nuns, thro' a kind of grated Window... Antiently, there were also Parlours in the Convents of Monks, where the Novices used to converse together at the Hours of Recreation. **1924** A. D. Sedgwick *Little French Girl* iii. vi. 276 She might have sat, in her early convent days, giving an account of herself in the *parloir*..to the relative who had come to pay her a weekly visit. **1927** J. Rhys *Left Bank* 43 The old man and the little boy were the last of the queue of people waiting..to be admitted to the *parloir*—a row of little boxes where on certain days prisoners may speak to their friends through a grating. **1955** J. Thomas *No Banners* xxv. 248 His camp bed had been installed in the narrow, steel-barred passage dividing the two sections of the *parloir* or visiting cell.

parlour. Add: **2. e.** In *attrib.* use with the names of outdoor games which have been adapted to a smaller scale for use indoors.

1872 A. Elliot *Within Doors* 45 Numerous Parlour Games have recently been introduced... Such are Parlour Croquet,..Parlour Billiards, [etc.]. **1881** *Cassell's Bk. In-Door Amusem.* 74 The game described in this book as German Balls is sometimes also known as Parlour Bowls. **1887** E. Custer *Tenting on Plains* xv. 501 A game of parlor croquet was proposed. **1895** *Montgomery Ward Catal.* 235/3 Parlor Tennis. This new and fascinating game is arranged for parlor or lawn use and is played with 12 light rubber balls... Parlor Quoits..consists of two turned posts..and four quoits five inches in diameter. **1899** Beerbohm *More* 140 Playing parlour-golf with his only child. **1901** Parlour cricket [see *dart *sb.* 1 d]. **1926–7** *Army & Navy Stores Catal.* 854/3 The parlour golf hole... For practising 'putting' indoors.

f. In *attrib.* use applied to persons of comfortable or prosperous circumstances who profess support, usu. of a non-participatory nature, for radical, extreme, or revolutionary political movements, as *parlour Bolshevik, communist, socialist*, etc. Hence *parlour Bolshevism, socialism.*

1910 *Ann. Library Index 1909* 273 (*title*) Parlour socialists. **1915** T. Dreiser *Let.* 26 Apr. in *Lett. H. L. Mencken* (1961) 68, I hold no brief for the parlor radical. **1918** [see *Bolshevism]. **1922** R. Nevill *Yesterday & Today* i. 14 What may be called 'Society Socialism' is an entirely modern development, pretty well limited to England and America where the 'Parlour Socialist' has become recognized as a regular type. **1926** G. Frankau *My Unsentimental Journey* iv. 56 The audience..were only 'parlour Bolsheviks'. **1929** F. P. Gibbons *Red Napoleon* 67 Margot was more than a parlour pink; she was an ardent internationalist. **1930** H. G. Wells *Autocracy of Mr. Parham* ii. i. 86 Don't imagine we are that mysterious unseen power, the Money Power, your parlour Bolsheviks talk about. **1938** G. T. Garratt *Shadow of Swastika* 201 Mr. Neville Chamberlain remained..invincible because of his backing amongst the very wealthy and influential parlour fascists outside. **1939** C. Isherwood *Goodbye to Berlin* 105 Wasn't I a bit of a sham..with my arty talk..and my newly-acquired parlour-socialism? **1954** Koestler *Invis. Writing* iii. 40 The most fashionable poet among the snobs and parlour-Communists of the period was Bertold Brecht. **1960** *News Chron.* 22 June 6/5 A wonderfully reactionary view of country life. It makes John Buchan look a 'parlour pink'. **1969** *Times* 24 Mar. 7/7 Cripps..had just come into notoriety before the war as a 'parlour Bolshevist' of a high intellectual order. **1973** K. Giles *File on Death* vi. 156 A parlour pink! Did he have anything to contribute? **1976** S. Hynes *Auden Generation* x. 367 The stock notion of the 'thirties writer as a *New Country* parlour-communist.

4. For *U.S.* read orig. *U.S.* (Examples.)

1884 Ice cream parlor [see *ice-cream *attrib.*]. **1908**, etc. Beauty parlour [see **beauty parlour* s.v. *beauty *sb.* III]. **1912** Manicure parlor [see *manicure *sb.* 2]. **1913**, etc. Massage parlour [see *massage *sb.* b]. **1927** E. Glyn *'It'* xiii. 122 'The Oak Parlour', a new little restaurant. **1928** *Daily Express* 22 Oct. 1/3 The bodies of the boys will be kept in sealed caskets in an 'undertaking parlour' until the mother is well enough to attend the funeral. **1942** H. C. Bailey *Dead Man's Shoes* xxvi. 100 Pat's Parlour, a tea shop for holiday visitors. **1952** S. Selvon *Brighter Sun* iv. 63 He was listless and dull, and attracted very little business, though his was the only well-stocked parlour in that part of Barataria. **1963** H. Garner in R. Weaver *Canad. Short Stories* (1968) 2nd Ser. 41, I tried a couple of beer parlours, but couldn't stand the noise and laughter. **1973** W. McCarthy *Detail* ii. 115 Stuart..went to the adjoining pizza parlour. **1974** *Listener* 8 Aug. 168/3 Model industrial communities, with sun-lamp parlours.

b. *ellipt.* form of *milking-parlour* s.v. *milking *vbl. sb.* 4.

1950 *N.Z. Jrnl. Agric.* June 541/1 Near Davis [California] I visited some dairies using the 'parlour' system of milking. **1973** *Country Life* 28 June 1904/1 Development work on milking machinery..directed at speeding the movement of cows through the parlour.

6. *parlour game* (earlier and later examples), *pastime, politics*; **parlour-boarder** (earlier examples); **parlour-girl** *U.S.*, = Parlour-maid; **parlour-house**, (*a*) a house having a parlour; (*b*) *U.S. slang*, an expensive type of brothel; **parlour-jumper** *slang*, one who robs rooms (see quot. 1938); **parlour man**, a male domestic servant; = *house-parlourman* s.v. *house *sb.*[1] 23; (the sense in quot. 1851 is uncertain); **parlour melodeon** *U.S.*, a kind of parlour organ; **parlour-organ** (examples); **parlour-palm**, the aspidistra; **parlour-piece**, a slight entertainment suitable for performance in a parlour; **parlour social** *U.S.*, = *house-rent party* s.v. *house *sb.*[1] 23; **parlour trick**, (*b*) an amusing 'turn' or trick performed, often by an animal, as entertainment.

1777 P. Thicknesse *Year's Journey* I. ii. 12 The Prieure of this convent..had received, as parlour boarders, some English ladies of very suspicious characters. **1812** *Theatrical Inquisitor* I. 211, I am a parlour boarder at Mrs. Twizzle's school. **1872** Parlour game [see sense 2 e above]. **1923** W. de la Mare *Riddle* 127 She *talks* to you; but it's all make-believe. It's all a 'parlour game'. **1958** Wodehouse *Cocktail Time* xviii. 157 The television set..was now deep in one of those parlour games designed for the feeble-minded trade. **1975** *Listener* 28 Aug. 279/1 At this season of the year, the listener to Radio 4 cannot expect much more than..parlour games. **1863** A. D. Whitney *Faith Gartney's Girlhood* iii. 9 The parlor-girl made her appearance with her mop and tub. **1875** Mrs. Stowe *We & Neighbors* xxxiv. 323 Maggie was parlor-girl and waitress, and a good one too. **1872** E. Crapsey *Nether Side N.Y.* 142 A most deplorable change..greatly decreasing the number of parlor houses, while houses of assignation have multiplied. **1924** in Henderson & Maddock *Housing Acts* (1930) 431 Appropriate normal rents may be fixed for different classes of houses, *e.g.* parlour and non-parlour. **1926** J. Black *You can't Win* iv. 28 Women who kept 'parlor houses' in the Tenderloin district. **1927** St. John Ervine *Wayward Man* i. i. 3 Three shops, four parlour-houses... The front of his house looked like that of any other parlour-house, but if a passer-by had peeped through the window he would have seen, not, as he might have expected, a small d'oyley-covered table, bearing a pot of geraniums or [etc.]. **1927** F. E. Fremantle *Housing of Nation* 40 At Roehampton the cost of a parlour house rose to £1,750. **1975** J. Gores *Hammett* (1976) v. 38 The parlor houses, cribs, brothels and bagnios had disappeared..and a thousand prostitutes had been thrown out of work. **1977** *Belfast Tel.* 19 Jan. 25/3 (Advt.), Parlour house, off Newtonards Rd., good condition. **1898** *Daily Tel.* 4 Aug. 3/2 A constable explained that the prisoner..was known as a 'parlour-jumper'... He went in for robbing rooms. **1938** F. D. Sharpe *Sharpe of Flying Squad* xv. 170 'Parlour Jumpers'..went round knocking on doors until they found a temporarily unoccupied house or flat, when they would force a way in and collect everything of value.., put it in the table cloth ..and walk out. **1851** H. Melville *Moby Dick* II. xiv. 121 Beale's..frontispiece, boats attacking Sperm whales, though no doubt calculated to excite the civil scepticism of some parlour men, is admirably correct..in its general effect. **1922** *Glasgow Herald* 31 Oct. 7/1 The men who have disappointed as 'housemen' and 'parlourmen' are for the most part ex-Service men..prepared to do anything to get a job. **1960** *Times* 5 Jan. 3/3 (Advt.), Cook and Butler/House Parlourman required for Surrey;..excellent kitchen; own redecorated flat. **1909** 'O. Henry' *Roads of Destiny* vii. 107 The natives were panning out enough from the beach sands to buy all the rum, red calico, and parlour melodeons in the world. **1845** in C. Cist *Cincinnati Misc.* I. 179/1 'I was on a visit to Vermont, a few weeks since,' said he, 'and intended to buy a parlor Organ.' **1943** A. G. Powell *I can go Home Again* 96 There was an ordinary parlor organ, but on the days in which Old Lady McCan..attended services the organ in the Baptist

Church could not be used. **1904** *Amateur Gardener's Diary* 145 *Aspidistra* (Parlour Palm), one of the hardiest of in-door plants, as it will survive dust and even the fumes of gas. **1876** G. M. HOPKINS *Poems* (1967) 65 And ever, if bound here hardest home, You've parlour-pastime left. **1938** *Amer. Speech* XIII. 255 Most of the music..played on these many pianos was..'light classical', and in anthologies the terms 'salon music' and 'parlor pieces' were used. **1957** T. HUGHES *Hawk in Rain* 20 (*title*) Parlour-piece. **1940** H. G. WELLS *New World Order* § 1. 18 This is no small affair of parlour politics we have to consider. **1956** Parlour social [see *house-party* s.v. *HOUSE *sb.*[1] 23]. **1966** W. T. E. KIRKEBY *Ain't Misbehavin'* iv. 39 Another and popular way to meet expenses was the parlour social or, as it later became familiarly known, the 'rent-party'. **1922** R. LEIGHTON *Compl. Bk. Dog* vii. 99 He [*sc.* the Chow Chow]..often has a clever gift for parlour tricks. **1961** *Times* 7 Jan. 7/7 The art of skiing is..gradually suffering conversion into a gigantic outdoor parlour trick.

parlyaree (pāliā·rī). Also **parlary.** [f. It. *parlare* to speak, talk.] A form of slang used by actors and showmen, particularly in the 18th and 19th centuries, and characterized by Italianate vocabulary. Cf. *PALARIE *v.*

The word appears to be related to *nanty parnarly* recorded in Barrère & Leland *Dict. Slang* (1890) II. 81/2.

1933 PARTRIDGE *Slang To-day & Yesterday* iii. 223 Until about the end of the eighteenth century, actors were so despised that, in self-protection, they had certain words that, properly, should be described as cant and were actually known as Parlyaree. **1933** *Times Lit. Suppl.* 15 June 412/3 Circus slang is a nineteenth-century offshoot from the Parlyaree of the seventeenth and eighteenth centuries. **1950** PARTRIDGE *Here, There & Everywhere* 117 It was among showmen and strolling players that parlyaree originated. *Ibid.* 122 Most parlyaree-speakers prefer a *carser* or *carsey*, ie. a house, when they can get it. *Ibid.* 125 Parlyaree..is a glossary, a vocabulary, not a complete language. **1952** GRANVILLE *Dict. Theatr. Terms* 132 *Parlyaree* (occasionally *parlary*). Little is known about this language which has neither accidence nor syntax of its own but is built on a base of Italian words and phrases, whereon cant terms and illiteracies are piled. **1960** J. FRANKLYN *Dict. Rhyming Slang* 106/1 The term [*sc.* parlamaree] is obviously a mispronunciation of Parlyaree, the language of the Circus. **1960** *Spectator* 11 Mar. 355 The canting jargon of the Victorian fairgrounds known as 'parlyaree'.

parm (pāɹm). Colloq. contraction of *pardon (me)*.

1945 A. KOBER *Parm Me* 180 Parm me fa conterdicting. **1957** J. BLISH *Fallen Star* vii. 101, I was hun'ry. Parm me. **1967** C. DRUMMOND *Death at Furlong Post* xiv. 171 'Piss off,' said Hart. 'Parm?' **1973** K. GILES *File on Death* v. 144 Parm me, sir, but I've got me good name to consider.

Parma[1] (pā·ɹmă). The name of a city in northern Italy, used *attrib.* or *absol.* to designate products associated with the region, as **Parma ham,** a local type of ham which is eaten uncooked; **Parma violet,** (*a*) a cultivated violet with double, scented flowers, usually light or deep purple, belonging to a group of cultivars of *Viola alba*; a crystallized flower of this kind; (*b*) a perfume manufactured from a flower of this type or imitating its scent; (*c*) a deep or medium shade of purple.

[**1960** E. DAVID *French Provincial Cooking* 134 It is a common misconception that all hams eaten raw, including that of Parma, are smoked.] **1964** A. LAUNAY *Caviare & After* vii. 54 The Bayonne and Parma hams are served raw. **1966** 'J. MELVILLE' *Nell Alone* i. 21 She's doing a lot of eating..Parma ham, tinned stuff, the best coffee. **1971** *Sunday Times* (Colour Suppl.) 27 June 50/3 Parma ham..and Westphalian smoked ham, all eaten raw, have always been popular with gourmets. **1976** E. WARD *Hanged Man* xx. 118 Eggs and Parma ham and oven-hot bread and coffee. **1856, 1880** Parma violet [see VIOLET *sb.*[1] 2 a]. **1907** *Yesterday's Shopping* (1969) 521/1 Perfumes... Opoponax. Parma Violet. Peau d'Espagne. **1919** K. MANSFIELD in *Art & Lett.* II. 155 A stout lady in blue serge, with a bunch of artificial 'parmas' at her bosom. **1922** *Weekly Dispatch* 10 Dec. 15 A leather set in the new shade of violet. Something between purple and parma, this hue will soon be the rage. **1923** *Daily Mail* 7 Feb. 1 (Advt.), Black, Navy,..Parma. *Ibid.* 12 Feb. 1 (Advt.), Shades: Fawn, Grey, Lovat, Parma, Browns. **1932** *New Flora & Silva* IV. 190 The origin of the Parma Violet has never been satisfactorily elucidated... There are many violets growing round Naples, but none..which I have seen suggest themselves as parents of the Parma. **1938** G. L. ZAMBRA *Violets* vii. 62 The family of Parma violets gives the sweetest perfume, the longest flowering season, and the handsomest foliage of all the double violets. **1954** 'M. COST' *Invitation from Minerva* 96 A frock..parma-violet in colour. **1956** *Punch* 23 May 626/1 If the modest violet is employed it must be..a shameless bunch of Parmas. **1963** R. D. MEIKLE *Garden Flowers* 105 The delicious Parma Violet, with smaller, rather glossy leaves, and slender-stalked flowers, is probably a form of *Viola alba* Bess., found wild (with innumerable variations) over most of the Mediterranean area and Asia Minor. **1970** *Observer* 1 Feb. 32/7 Dior: Parma violet coat. **1970** I. ORIGO *Images & Shadows* ii. 60 The ladies in summer gowns..leaving behind them a faint aroma of lavender and Parma violet. **1974** *Country Life* 25 Apr. 1025/2 Using parma violet or electric blue, she sprinkles these vibrating colours through the wardrobe. **1977** *Times* 14 June 18/6 Women in the chocolate factory..place walnuts and Parma violets on to the store's handmade confectionery.

parma[2] (pā·ɹmă). *Geol.* (See quots.)

1888 *Encycl. Brit.* XXIV. 4/1 The section [of the Urals] between the 64th and 61st parallels has..a wholly distinct character... From the broad plateaus, or *parmas*, which stretch towards the north-west, it might be conjectured..that the structure is more complicated. **1904** *Amer. Jrnl. Sci.* CLXVIII. 469 This may mean that no true axis or 'parma' was in existence during Richmond time, but it does seem to show that the Wabash parma at least indicates the strike for the then highest land. **1904** tr. *Suess' Face of Earth* I. II. xii. 601 We see great folded chains merge with gradually flattening undulations into the similar foreland, where they form secondary folds, or 'parmas'—this is the case in the Urals and the Appalachians. **1913** A. W. GRABAU *Princ. Stratigr.* xx. 808 Many of the low-dipping domes are perceptible as such only by the erosion which has removed their central portion, often leaving a topographic depression. Such low domes have also been called parmas. **1957** *Gloss. Geol.* (Amer. Geol. Inst.) 212/2 *Parma*, a low dome or quaquaversal.

Parmentier (pāɹma·ṅti͵e), *a.* [f. the name of Antoine A. *Parmentier* (1737–1813), French agriculturalist, who popularized potatoes in France.] In cookery, made with or accompanied by potatoes.

1906 *Mrs. Beeton's Bk. Househ. Managem.* 1314 *Parmentier eggs*... Poach the eggs in salted water flavoured with lemon-juice, and place them carefully in the halved potatoes. **1929** A. E. HOUSMAN *Let.* 14 Sept. (1971) 284 Food not varied or inventive, especially soup: I do not mind Santé twice in ten days, but Parmentier I do. **1951** *Good Housek. Home Encycl.* 580/2 *Parmentier*, the name of the man who introduced the potato into France... The term is now applied to a number of potato dishes... Parmentier soup. **1963** A. L. SIMON *Guide Good Food & Wines* 38/1 In culinary parlance *Parmentier* always means potatoes; it is the homage of French cooks to Parmentier, who introduced potatoes in France. **1965** *House & Garden* Dec. 84/2 *Parmentier*. Named after the man who did so much to improve the cultivation of potatoes in France..and so, naturally, means potatoes.

Parmesan, *a.* and *sb.* Add: **A.** *adj.* (Later examples.)

1885 [see *EDAM]. **1946** G. MILLAR *Horned Pigeon* iii. 47 Denis Patchett..stole a large lump of Parmesan cheese from one of our guards.

B. *sb.* (Later examples.)

1876 [see *BRIE]. **1960** [see *CANNELLONI *sb. pl.*]. **1971** *Sunday Times* (Colour Suppl.) 28 Mar. 39/2 Parmesan is a cheese with remarkable keeping qualities.

parnas(s (pāɹnā·s). Pl. **parnassim** (pāɹnasī·m). [Heb.] The lay head of a Jewish synagogue congregation.

1831 [see *MAHAMAD]. **1892** I. ZANGWILL *Childr. Ghetto* I. 97 Michael Birnbaum was a great man in the little local synagogue... He had been successively *Gabbai* and *Parnass*, or treasurer and president. **1907** —— *Ghetto Comedies* 76 The Great Synagogue..struck a note of modern English gaiety,..looking towards the box of the *Parnass* and *Gabbai*, she saw it was occupied by officers with gold sashes. *Ibid.* 122 The *Parnass* proffered his presidential hand in pious congratulation. **1932** C. ROTH *Hist. Marranos* 247 The community boasted a model organisation. The power of the *Parnasim*, the elected Wardens, was autocratic, as offenders like Benedict Spinoza or Uriel Acosta learned to their cost. **1949** *Spectator* 4 Nov. 595/2 The *Parnas Presidente*, the President of the Wardens of the Synagogue. **1962** B. ABRAHAMS tr. *Life Glückel of Hameln* ii. 18 My father has been *parnass* for many years. [*Note*] In Glückel's time the office of *parnass* (president or warden [of the synagogue]) was a monthly one. **1967** D. T. KAUFFMAN *Dict. Relig. Terms* 346/1 *Parnas steward*, lay president of a synagogue congregation.

parnassia (pāɹnæ·siă). [mod.L. (Linnæus *Hortus Cliffortianus* (1737) 113), f. PARNASS(US + IA[1].] A small perennial herb of the genus so called, belonging to the family Saxifragaceæ, native to temperate or cold regions of the northern hemisphere, and bearing radical ovate or cordate leaves and white or pale yellow flowers; = *grass of Parnassus* s.v. PARNASSUS c.

1772 R. WESTON *Universal Botanist* II. 546 Parnassia, Grass of Parnassus. **1793** J. E. SMITH *Eng. Bot.* II. 82 The Parnassia agrees with Saxifraga in the wonderful œconomy of its impregnation. **1883** W. ROBINSON *Eng. Flower Garden* 207/2 In many of our moist heaths and bogs the Marsh Parnassia..is not unfrequently met with. **1941** W. A. PERCY *Lanterns on Levee* ix. 97 In the streams where the iris forgathered there are parnassia, the snowdrop's only kin. **1951** *Dict. Gardening* (R. Hort. Soc.) III. 1485/1 The Parnassias are hardy, and succeed in moist, peat soils.

Parnassian, *a.* and *sb.* Add: **A.** *adj.* **1. c.** Of or pertaining to sense *B. 1 c. **B.** *sb.* **1. c.** *spec.* In the writings of G. M. Hopkins, a second kind of poetry, which can only be written by poets but which is not the language of inspiration.

1864 G. M. HOPKINS *Let.* 10 Sept. (1956) 216 *Parnassian* then is that language which genius speaks as fitted to its exaltation, and place among other genius, but does not sing..in its flights. Great men, poets I mean, have each their own dialect as it were of Parnassian, formed generally as they go on writing, and at last,—this is the point to be marked,—they can see things in this Parnassian way and describe them in this Parnassian tongue, without further effort of inspiration. *Ibid.* 217 In Parnassian pieces you feel that if you were the poet you could have gone on as he has done, you see yourself doing it, only with the difference that if you actually try to find you cannot write his Parnassian. *Ibid.* 218, I believe that when a poet palls on us it is because of his Parnassian.

Parnassianism (pāɹnæ·siăniz'm). [f. PARNASSIAN *a.* 1 b + -ISM.] The Parnassian style in poetry.

1905 *Times* 4 Oct. 6/2 He began to write the sonnets which attracted the attention of the most expert connoisseurs in Parnassianism. **1922** *Freeman* (N.Y.) 26 Apr. 105 Parnassianism means objectivity, impassivity, attention to line and image rather than to colour and music and vague suggestiveness. **1927** *Observer* 11 Sept. 7/3 Parnassianism, Symbolism, and the Ecole Roman have all had their day. **1967** *Guardian* 19 May 7/2 Some of the poems are too deliberate, Parnassian... And very splendid, too, parnassianism at that level.

Parnate (pā·ɹnēit). *Pharm.* A proprietary name for the drug tranylcypromine.

1960 *Official Gaz.* (U.S. Patent Office) 17 May TM112/2 Smith Kline & French Laboratories, Philadelphia, Pa. Filed Oct. 19, 1959. *Parnate* for anti-depressant. First use Oct. 6, 1959. **1960** *Trade Marks Jrnl.* 29 Dec. 1681/1 Parnate... Preparations and substances in capsule or tablet form for use in medicine and pharmacy. Smith Kline & French Laboratories Limited,..Welwyn Garden City, Hertfordshire; manufacturing chemists. **1964** *New Statesman* 6 Mar. 354/1 An American anti-depressant drug—Parnate or tranylcypromine—has been declared unsafe by the US Food and Drug Administration. **1965** J. POLLITT *Depression & its Treatment* iv. 56 The monoamine oxidase inhibitors include several members, among them phenelzine (Nardil), iproniazid (Marsilid),..and tranylcypromine (Parnate). **1970** *Daily Tel.* 7 July 3/3 The result of eating cheese with the drug Parnate was to trigger off fatal side-effects. **1976** *Ibid.* 11 Mar. 19/4 She was taking Parnate, which is a very strong drug. If mixed with alcohol it could have a most terrible effect.

Parnellite. (Earlier and later examples.)

1881 E. W. HAMILTON *Diary* 26 Jan. (1972) I. 102 This nettled the Parnellites, and they intimated they would fight to the death. **1882** *Ibid.* 30 Apr. 259 Wednesday was quite an important day, as it was taken up by the discussion of the bill brought in by the Parnellite party, with the name of Parnell himself on the bill. **1892** W. B. YEATS *Lett.* (1954) 222 Parnellite Dublin and the Parnellite young men in the country parts. **1931** *Times Lit. Suppl.* 17 Sept. 708/1 His anecdote of the Parnellite in an Irish theatre. **1936** W. B. YEATS *Poems* (1957) 586 Come gather round me, Parnellites, And praise our chosen man. **1939** JOYCE *Finnegans Wake* 307 Are Parnellites Just towards Henry Tudor?

parochial, *a.* (*sb.*) Add: **1. a.** *parochial school* (*Sc.* and *N. Amer.*): a school established and maintained by a religious body. Hence *parochial schoolmaster*. (See also *parish school* s.v. *PARISH *sb.* 7 b.)

1755 in *Sc. Nat. Dict.* (1968) VII. 37/2 How great importance it would be both to the College and the Parish to have a Parochial School. **1791** A. MURRAY in J. Sinclair *Statist. Acct. Scotl.* I. 457 The parochial schools are by no means supplied with such enlightened teachers as those that were formerly instrumental in diffusing this knowledge. **1792** D. MCDOUGAL in *Ibid.* III. 188 The parochial schoolmaster teaches Latin, English, Gaelic, [etc.]. *a* **1817** [in Dict.]. **1832** *Chambers's Edin. Jrnl.* I. 226/2 Acts of Parliament..have considerably enlarged the salaries of the parochial schoolmasters. **1851** C. CIST *Sk. Cincinnati in 1851* 58 Parochial Schools. The Catholic schools are the only ones which are strictly parochial. **1860** *Nor' Wester* (Red River Settlement) 14 Feb. 2/1 The Parochial Schools of our Protestant population speak for themselves, and I am sorry that they should have found disparagement at the hands of your correspondent. **1876** J. GRANT *Hist. Burgh & Parish Schools Scotl.* 100 The teacher of the burgh and parochial school was invariably session clerk and precentor. **1904** F. CRISSEY *Tattlings Retired Politician* 263 When he [*sc.* the Governor] was renominated the parochial school teachers camped on his trail and made it some hot for him. **1926** J. B. RITCHIE *Forres* 74 It was held that the Grammar School of Forres had never been a parochial school. **1955** *Western Star* (Corner Brook, Newfoundland) 10 Mar. 2/3 An amendment to the Municipal Act..would allow municipalities to exempt parochial schools from taxation. **1964** *Calgary Herald* 11 Feb. 15 Premier Roblin Monday proposed a partial solution to the dilemma of Manitoba's parochial schools. **1972** *Lebende Sprachen* XVIII. 35/2 US *parochial school*—BE/US *denominational school*. **1976** *Globe & Mail* (Toronto) 16 Jan. 29/8, I attended parochial school in Winnipeg. That meant I was Roman Catholic, that I ate fishcakes on Friday and smelled of candle wax and incense. **1978** *Times* 30 Jan. 12/5 As soon as you get more than half black in a school then the whites..put their youngsters in to private and parochial schools.

parochially, *adv.* (Later examples.)

1929 S. LESLIE *Anglo-Catholic* xiii. 182 He could never tell the truth to his father, since the Canon had parochially decreed that his cryptic daughter-in-law was no fit person to live in the parish. **1971** *Daily Tel.* 19 June 15/1 This [tax] relief has been very limited in its scope and I doubt whether its passing will be more than parochially mourned. **1977** *Ibid.* 19 Apr. 12 For a flower festival to open its golden jubilee celebrations at Addington Palace, Croydon, next month the Royal School of Church Music plans to have desert flowers from Southern California, orchids from Singapore and proteas from South Africa to demonstrate its ecumenism. More parochially, though, displays from this country will be the responsibility of the Surrey Flower Arrangers' Association.

parodic, *a.*[2] Delete *rare* and add later examples.

1962 D. LESSING *Golden Notebk.* IV. 529 The word *correct* had an echoing parodic twang. **1974** C. A. PATRIDES *Eng. Poems George Herbert* 9 Herbert looked beyond the Bible for parodic purposes. **1976** *Archivum Linguisticum* VII. 27 H. B. Richardson..follows Meyer-Lübke in suggesting *escuerzo* < *scorteum*, 'made of leather', meaning in 1544c 'toad'; this is possible, given the parodic context (the mock planctus for Urraca).

parodistic, *a.* (Later examples.)

1937 *Scrutiny* VI. 298 His [*sc.* Lord Berners']..measure is by no means summed up in his satirical and parodistic pieces. **1949** KOESTLER *Insight & Outlook* 427 Freud distinguished between the comic effects of imitation as such, and the parodistic attitude which usually accompanies it. **1975** *Times Lit. Suppl.* 21 Oct. 1305/1, I must record my partial disappointment, both at the parodistic and the confessional level. **1977** *Gramophone* June 106/3 The parodistic 'Danzon' is also, I think, the most entertaining of the three dances from Bernstein's ballet *Fancy Free.*

parœcious, *a.* (Earlier and later examples.)

1882 *Encycl. Brit.* XIV. 718/2 They [*sc.* the antheridia] are usually seated in the axils of modified leaves (perigonial), sometimes appearing..on special branches of the same plant (parœcious). **1912** S. M. MACVICAR *Student's Handbk. Brit. Hepatics* p. xix, In some cases they [*sc.* the antheridia] occur below the female inflorescence,..usually making this 'paroicous' [*sic*] form of inflorescence easy to recognize. **1968** E. V. WATSON *Brit. Mosses & Liverworts* (ed. 2) 34 Paroecious, bearing antheridia and archegonia close together, but not mixed, the antheridia being in the axils of bracts below those that surround the archegonia.

parole, *sb.* Add: **1. a.** Now generally used for a system of conditional release of selected prisoners before they have completed their sentences. (Further examples.) **b.** (Further example.)

1908 J. M. SULLIVAN *Criminal Slang* 18 *Parole,* released from prison, not a pardon. **1939** JOYCE *Finnegans Wake* 246 So they must have their final since he's on parole. **1966** *Listener* 3 Mar. 301/2 Parole was introduced in the United States—at the Elmira Reformatory in New York—in 1876; today some form of parole is in use in all the fifty States, as well as in the separate Federal prison system. **1972** J. GORES *Dead Skip* (1973) xvi. 116 We go see his parole officer. If he was sent up two years ago and is out now, he's on parole. **1974** *Times* 17 Apr. 14/1 Only a minority of the prisoners are getting a parole. *Ibid.* 14/2 Since the parole system began on April 1, 1968, about 14,000 prisoners have been paroled and about 1,550 are on parole at any one time.

2*. *Linguistics.* With pronunc. (parǫl). [f. *parole* in sense '(spoken) word, utterance'.] The actual linguistic behaviour of individuals, in contrast to the linguistic system (opp. *LANGUE 3).

1935 W. F. TWADDELL in *Lang. Monogr.* XVI. 40 The utterance occurs, it is speech, 'parole'; the form exists, so to say, it is a part of the language, 'langue'. **1939** L. H. GRAY *Foundations of Lang.* ii. 18 The third part of our definition of language..is obviously concerned almost exclusively with *langage* rather than with *langue* or *parole.* **1953,** etc. [see *LANGUE 3]. **1959** W. BASKIN tr. *F. de Saussure's Course in Gen. Linguistics* (1960) 13 Execution is always individual, and the individual is always its master: I shall call the executive side *speaking* (*parole*). **1968** J. LYONS *Introd. Theoret. Linguistics* i. 51 Let us follow de Saussure, and say that all those who 'speak English' (or are 'speakers of English') share a particular *langue* and that the set of utterances which they produce when they are 'speaking English' constitute instances of *parole.* **1971** D. CRYSTAL *Linguistics* 162 This leads to the correlative Saussurean concept of *parole,* the actual, concrete act of speaking. **1974** R. QUIRK *Linguist & Eng. Lang.* iii. 47 Every individual has a unique *parole,* a unique realization of what is possible in the language of his time and place. But at the same time this is not to deny that the *parole* of some individuals is more interesting than that of others. **1976** *Language* LII. 93 The particular contextual variant of the adjective may vary for each parole application.

3. *parole board, clinic, matron, officer, scheme, sponsor, system.*

[**1908** *Charities & Commons* 26 Sept. 730/2 Clearly the Board of Parole is acting adversely to its own rule.] **1916** *N.Y. Times* 9 Jan. IV. 19/4 There will be weekly meetings ..of the Parole Board. **1938** C. HIMES *Black on Black* (1973) 163 He beseeched God to bless the warder and the deputy warder and the chaplain and the guards and the parole board and the outside judges and the governor and the sovereign state itself. **1956** B. HOLIDAY *Lady sings Blues* (1973) xix. 158 If I had been a booster or a petty thief I'd have the parole board helping me to get a job. **1972** 'W. HAGGARD' *Protectors* v. 63 Jack would be out in around five years, even less if the Parole Board were helpful. **1974** *Times* 17 Apr. 14 Prisoner's cases are considered by the local review committee..and are then referred..to the Parole Board for England and Wales. **1939** *Sun* (Baltimore) 22 Nov. 9/2 The State hospital system will institute an extensive program of parole clinics within the next few weeks to provide a follow-up service for furloughed and discharged patients which authorities believe may tend to curtail readmissions. **1907** *Charities & Commons* 24 Aug. 609/2 Three parole officers and one parole matron have been added to the police department. **1949** *Times-Picayune* (New Orleans) *Mag.* 13 Nov. 23/3 He became chief probation and parole officer for the federal court. **1970** G. JACKSON *Let.* Apr. in *Soledad Brother* (1971) 51 Parole officers have sent brothers back to the joint for selling newspapers. **1974** *Guidelines to Volunteer Services* (N.Y. State, Dept. Correctional Services) 36 *Parole officer,* title. A law enforcement officer, peace officer specifically charged with the supervision, and other related duties, of inmates who are released from correctional facilities via parole or some other form of conditional release. They are professional caseworkers in a law enforcement setting. **1973** *Daily Tel.* 20 June 8/6 During the five years of the parole scheme, only 36 of the 11,055 paroled from sentences for crimes of sex or violence had been further convicted of similar offences. **1973** *Philadelphia Inquirer* (Today Suppl.) 7 Oct. 14/3 The Rev. Anthony Velasquez, his parole sponsor, insists that 'Tony has never had a fair trial.' **1900** *Congress. Rec.* 24 Jan. 1130/2 We have in that State what is known as the parole system. Prisoners are put out on their good behavior. **1952** *Manch. Guardian Weekly* 8 May 4 The parole system should be reformed and speeded up. **1973** *Guardian* 31 Jan. 6/1 Lord Hunt..said the parole system had been operating for five years and had shown a low failure rate in terms of recalling of prisoners.

parole, *v.* **2.** (Earlier and later examples.)

1790 D. FANNING *Narrative* (1861) 33, I then parolled the prisoners, except 30, which I sent to Wilmington. **1948** *Chicago Daily News* 27 Feb. 1/6 Another of those parolled..put up $5,000 as a fee. **1973** *Publishers' Weekly* 2 Apr. 61/2 The murders took place in 1934. Mrs. Judd was parolled in 1971. **1974** [see *PAROLE *sb.* 1]. **1975** *Daily Tel.* 3 Apr. 3/4 The two Great Train robbers paroled from jail yesterday had each served more than their legal minimum sentences.

paroled, *ppl. a.* (Earlier and later examples.)

1865 L. N. BOUDRYE *Hist. Rec. Fifth N.Y. Cavalry* 196 It is remarkable how readily paroled Rebel soldiers affiliate with us. **1908** *Independent* (N.Y.) 16 Jan. 146/2 Of his one thousand and seven or eight paroled men, up to this evening, seventy-seven have fallen. **1925** *Scribner's Mag.* Oct. 410/1 A large proportion of paroled prisoners have been reclaimed from their evil ways by this judicious system. **1966** *Listener* 4 Aug. 155/1 There may be one or more conditions attached to it, and failure to observe them may cause the paroled prisoner to be returned to prison to finish his sentence. **1972** J. GORES *Dead Skip* (1973) xviii. 131 I'm looking for a paroled con named Howard Odum.

parolee (pǎrōu·lī·). [f. PAROLE *sb.* or *v.* + -EE[1].] One who is released on parole.

1916 *Dialect Notes* IV. 327 *Parolee*.., one to whom parole is granted, esp. one sentenced to jail or reformatory or penitentiary who is released 'on parole'. **1934** *Sun* (Baltimore) 3 Dec. 8/3 One of the defects in the system in Baltimore is obvious—lack of supervision of parolees because of inadequate funds. **1937** *Ibid.* 9 Feb. 15/7 (*headline*) Parolee held in murder. **1938** *Yale Rev.* XXVIII. 157 The large majority of parolees are out to-day under such conditions as those which have just been described. **1957** V. NABOKOV *Pnin* 46 The Nansen Passport (a kind of parolee's card issued to Russian émigrés). **1964** M. ARGYLE *Psychol. & Social Probl.* v. 72 Shaw also organized a good deal of local support and sympathy for parolees and ex-convicts. **1973** *Publishers Weekly* 3 Dec. 40/1 In 1971, Long Island University opened its doors to young parolees. The ex-prisoners lived with the other students.. except that they were closely supervised by their parole officer. **1975** *Times Lit. Suppl.* 26 Sept. 1100/2 The process of making parole decisions, and the subsequent supervision of parolees, must be looked at from the viewpoint of all the various participants—prisoners, prison staff, paroling authority and parole supervisors.

parolein (pæ·rǒlīn). *Pharm.* Also **-oleine.** [f. PAR(AFFIN *sb.* + L. *ole-um* oil + -IN[1], -INE[5].] = *liquid paraffin* s.v. *LIQUID *a.* 7.

Formerly a proprietary name in the U.K.

1892 MARTINDALE *Extra Pharmacopœia* (ed. 7) 311 Paroleine, a still more fluid odourless petroleum, or Adepsine Oil..are used..more especially as bases for Laryngeal and Nasal Spray Solutions or Pigments. **1908** *Practitioner* Apr. 441 A parolein spray containing a little oil of eucalyptus. **1964** S. DUKE-ELDER *Parsons' Dis. Eye* (ed. 14) xv. 184 Local treatment consists in relieving the dryness with methylcellulose, parolein or weak alkaline solutions.

paromomycin (pæ:romomǝi·sin). *Pharm.* [f. Gr. παρόμοιος closely resembling (f. παρ- (see PARA-[1]) + ὅμοιος resembling): see *-MYCIN.] A broad-spectrum antibiotic that is a mixture of the sulphates of certain substances (chemically related to neomycin) produced by some strains of the bacterium *Streptomyces rimosus,* and is given orally in the treatment of intestinal infections. Also called *paromomycin sulphate.*

1956 *Brit. Pat.* 797,568 Paromomycin is a stable amorphous white substance which is very soluble in water, moderately soluble in methanol and sparingly soluble in absolute ethanol. **1964** M. HYNES *Med. Bacteriol.* (ed. 8) x. 138 Kanamycin..and paromomycin..are chemically similar to neomycin (and streptomycin) and have much the same properties. **1969** J. H. THOMPSON in J. A. Bevan *Essent. Pharmacol.* li. 545 Paromomycin sulphate (Humatin) is usually prescribed as 10 to 25 mg per kilogram per day. *Ibid.,* Paromomycin has been used in the treatment of intestinal amebiasis, trichomoniasis, some types of bacterial dysentery, preoperatively to suppress the colonic flora, and in hepatic coma and precoma. **1974** *Indian Jrnl. Med. Res.* LXII. 495 Streptomycin and paromomycin were selected for treatment of cholera carriers at Hongkong.

parotidectomy (pǎrǫ:tide·ktǒmi). *Surg.* [f. PAROTID *sb.* + *-ECTOMY.] Excision of the parotid gland.

1893 DUNGLISON *Dict. Med. Sci.* (ed. 21) 825/1 *Parotidectomy,* operation for excision of the parotid gland. **1951** MARSHALL & MILES in *Surg. Pract. Lahey Clinic* 122 The operation may be altered to extensive subtotal parotidectomy. **1974** *Lancet* 7 Dec. 1353/2 The patient's left parotid gland was explored, found to contain a mixed tumour in the deep lobe and a total parotidectomy was performed. **1974** J. D. MAYNARD in R. M. Kirk et al. *Surgery* ix. 201 Intraoral duct ligation may lead to parotid atrophy and cessation of symptoms in some cases, otherwise conservative parotidectomy must be considered.

Parousia (pǎrū·ziǎ). *Theol.* Also **parousia.** [ad. Gr. παρουσία presence, in N.T. (Matth. xxiv. 27, etc.) used as below.] The Second Coming or Advent of Christ. Also *transf.*

1875 *Expositor* May 385 The feverish expectation of a visible *parousia* was requiring modification. **1895** *Dublin Rev.* Apr. 334 The date of Our Lord's second coming, the Parousia. **1910** W. MONTGOMERY tr. *Schweitzer's Quest Historical Jesus* xix. 360 The Parousia of the Son of Man is to be preceded according to the Messianic dogma by a time of strife and confusion. **1918** J. H. LECKIE *World to Come* ii. 66 The Church has held its belief in the Parousia in varying forms throughout the ages. **1927** A. H. MCNEILE *Introd. New Testament* 112 At the end of his [*sc.* St. Paul's] life, the thought of the Parousia..had practically faded from his mind. **1936** A. M. RAMSEY *Gospel & Catholic Ch.* iii. 42 Christ is in us—yet the Parousia is in the future. **1941** AUDEN *New Year Let.* 39 Thus *Wordsworth*.. Saw in the fall of the Bastille The Parousia of liberty. **1964** *Listener* 27 Feb. 352/1 Your personal Parousia, the Biggest Show on Earth! **1969** A. T. HANSON in A. Richardson *Dict. Christian Theol.* 113/2 The complaint that the *parousia* (coming) had not arrived as expected. **1977** *Illustr. London News* Nov. 50/4 A pale yellow cross is just visible against a background of deeper yellow... Austin Winkley [the architect] calls it a Parousia cross, significant of the mysterious end of a mysterious journey. **1977** G. W. H. LAMPE *God as Spirit* iii. 65 The presence of the Spirit is..a substitute for the early *parousia* that had at first been expected.

Hence **Parou:siama·nia,** excitement or frenzy aroused by the thought of the Parousia.

1904 *Amer. Jrnl. Relig. Psychol. & Educ.* May 40 Men chanted, raved, spoke in unknown tongues, prophesied, gazed up into heaven all day, longed for vision, with a real parusiamania.

Parowax (pæ·rowæks). Also **parowax.** [f. *paro-* (f. PARA(FFIN *sb.*) + WAX *sb.*[1]] A proprietary name in the U.S. for paraffin wax.

1909 *Official Gaz.* (U.S. Patent Office) 7 Dec. 301/2 Standard Oil Company... *Parowax.* Particular description of goods.—Paraffin. **1926** *Daily Colonist* (Victoria, B.C.) 4 July 2/1 (Advt.), Parowax, for sealing, lb. 15c. **1945** *Industr. & Engin. Chem.* June 518/2 To extend the series of *n*-paraffins into the range of higher paraffins, Parowax was used. Fractional crystallization..showed the composition to be substantially normal paraffins... The paraffins ranged from C_{20} to C_{28}, with an average number of 23·8 carbon atoms. **1974** J. E. UNDERHILL *Wild Berries Pacific Northwest* 23 Cook until thick, then pour into hot sterilized jars, and seal promptly, with parowax or tight lids.

paroxytonization (parǫ:ksitǒnǝizēi·ʃǝn). [f. PAROXYTONIZE *v.* + -ATION.] The rule which places stress on the penultimate syllable.

1973 A. H. SOMMERSTEIN *Sound Pattern Anc. Greek* v. 177 This rule..changes all properispomenon words ending in *-ks* to paroxytones: (221) Paroxytonization. [+sharp] →[-falling]/—C_0Vks[+WB.].

parp (pāɹp), *sb.* [Echoic.] A honking noise, *spec.* that of a car horn. Hence as *v. intr.,* to make such a noise; also *trans.*

1951 E. BLYTON *Big Noddy Bk.* 51 Noddy had a good little hooter on his car. When he pressed it it said 'Pip-Pip', and sometimes 'Poop-Poop', and sometimes 'Parp-Parp'. **1953** —— *Noddy at Seaside* 14 'Parp-parp-parp!' Yes, that was Noddy's little car, longing to be taken out into the sunshine for a drive. *Ibid.* 16 'Parp-parp!' said the little car excitedly. **1958** [see *BLEEP *sb.*]. **1968** S. CHALLIS *Death on Quiet Beach* v. 69 Outside his hotel, a horn suddenly parped. **1973** M. AMIS *Rachel Papers* 124 To break her reverie I parped the horn.

parquet. Add: (Now usu. with pronunc. pā·ɹkēi.) **4.** *parquet floor* (earlier examples); **parquet carpet,** a patterned square of carpet.

1902 Parquet carpet [see *art square* s.v. *ART *sb.* V]. **1819** M. WILMOT *More Lett.* (1935) 20 Fruit and flowers dirt cheap—parqué flours—*Carpits* if you chuse to give a daughters dowery for them. **1833** PRINCESS ELIZABETH *Let.* 28 Dec. (1898) 213 And the doctor said with those shoes she might now walk about the parquet floors. **1865** M. EYRE *Lady's Walks S. of France* xxxi. 330 The *parquet* floors are undusted, unwaxed, and unswept.

parrot, *sb.* Add: **4.** *parrot-cry* (earlier and later examples), *-learning, -phrase* (examples), *-pie, -shooting, -voice; parrot-bright, -plumed, -sharp* adjs.; *parrot-fashion* adj. and adv.; **parrot-bill,** (*c*) applied *attrib.* and *absol.* to a type of cutting-tool the blades of which resemble a beak; **parrot disease, fever** = PSITTACOSIS in Dict. and Suppl.; **parrot snake** (see quot. 1931); **parrot tulip,** substitute for def.: a variety of tulip with fringed and ruffled petals, often of variegated colours; (earlier and later examples).

1971 *Power Farming* Mar. 46/4 Stem cutting...parrot bill shears may be used. **1972** *Country Life* 23 Mar. 690/3

After this major excitement a willow lapses into humdrummery and can be lopped with the parrot-bill. **1920** E. SITWELL *Wooden Pegasus* 24 From her fan, sliding slow, Parrot-bright fire's feathers. **1937** —— *I live under Black Sun* 89 Giving a little girl a forbidden parrot-bright apple. **1837** J. S. MILL in *Westm. Rev.* XXVIII. 3 There would be an end to the parrot cry of 'Do not endanger the Ministry'. **1956** [see *EYEBROW 1 c]. **1963** *Times* 20 Feb. 4/7 Such attacks are only worth noticing because they have tended to become a parrot cry. **1977** *Socialist Press* 2 Mar. 7/5 'If you have a case, why don't you go to an industrial tribunal', has become the favourite parrot cry of every barrack room lawyer crossing the picket line. **1908** *Spratt's Parrot Culture* 29 Should a room have become infected with the parrot disease..it will be needful to have it fumigated with sulphur. **1930** *Daily Express* 6 Feb. 11/5 They [*sc.* alarming facts] concerned that dread illness, psittacosis, or parrot disease, of which a number of cases have occurred lately in London and Birmingham. **1955** *Times* 8 June 6/4 A case of psittacosis (parrot disease) has occurred in the aircraft-carrier Centaur, which berthed here to-day on her return from the Mediterranean. **1951** *Mind* LX. 346 People just know it by heart and recite it parrot-fashion. **1956** D. ABERCROMBIE *Probl. & Princ.* 25 Parrot-fashion teaching is apt to result from regarding reasoned explanation as 'unnatural'. **1977** 'F. CLIFFORD' *Ten Minutes on June Morning* 111 Reassurances..were passed on, parrot-fashion, without knowledge or understanding. **1955** *Sci. News Let.* 3 Sept. 148/2 Viral hepatitis, better known to the layman as jaundice; psittacosis or parrot fever; rabies; smallpox; yellow fever; the common cold,..are other of the virus diseases. **1957** O. BRELAND *Animal Friends & Foes* ii. 63 This malady has also been called parrot fever, because the first known human cases were traced to sick parrots. **1973** 'D. SHANNON' *No Holiday for Crime* (1974) i. 9 The stolen goods had been..tropical parrots, and..one of the San Diego detectives had subsequently succumbed to parrot fever. **1901** G. G. COULTON *Public Schools & Public Needs* 312 We cannot prevent..mere parrot-learning, from counting somewhat..against real culture. **1977** *Observer* 20 Mar. 13/3 There seem to be two potent reasons why memorising (or 'parrot-learning', as people ignorant of the mental capacities of parrots sometimes call it) should once more become a staple component of curricula. **1891** O. WILDE *Pict. Dorian Gray* v. 89 'Foolish child! foolish child!' was the parrot-phrase flung in answer. **1958** *People* 4 May 4/2, I can get no comment except the parrot-phrase: 'The Home Secretary is still considering this case.' **1907** P. FOUNTAIN *Rambles Austral. Naturalist* ii. 8 Parrot-shooting is a favourite sport in Australia. *Ibid.*, Parrot-pie is as much esteemed in Australia as rook-pie in England. **1923** E. SITWELL *Bucolic Comedies* 25 Who came from the parrot-plumed sea. **1936** —— *Victoria of Eng.* ii. 33 Her dark parrot-sharp face. **1931** R. L. DITMARS *Snakes of World* Pl. 19 (*caption*) Green Tree Snake; Chocoya or Parrot Snake, *Leptophis occidentalis*. Found from Guatemala to northern South America. Uniform leaf-green with two hair-like strips on the back. **1958** J. CAREW *Wild Coast* ii. 28 A green parrot-snake slithered down a coconut tree. [**1829** J. C. LOUDON *Encycl. Plants* 266 One of the latest London catalogues (Mason's) enumerates six sorts of early blowing tulips; four perroquets or middle blowers; twenty-two double sorts.] **1856** C. M. YONGE *Daisy Chain* II. xxi. 586 She was nothing better than a parrot-tulip, stuck up in a parterre. **1890** O. WILDE *Pict. Dorian Gray* iii, in *Lippincott's Monthly Mag.* July 22 Some large blue china jars, filled with parrot-tulips, were ranged on the mantel-shelf. **1911** J. WEATHERS *Bulb Bk.* 441/2 Parrot or Dragon Tulips. These curious-looking and remarkable Tulips are believed to be derived from *T[ulipa] viridiflora*. **1932** A. J. MACSELF *Bulbs* v. 58 The Cottage, Darwin, and Parrot tulips..require similar general treatment. **1971** R. GENDERS *Collecting Antique Plants* viii. 191 Early Parrot tulips are depicted in a water colour drawing about 1700... The artist is Herman Henstenburg. **1925** R. FRY *Let.* 1 May (1972) II. 568 A lady with a parrot voice screaming that she wanted a Picasso of the blue period. **1975** C. FREMLIN *Long Shadow* v. 37 'Very well, thank you,' she heard her parrot voice saying..to the two or three people who rang up.

parrot, *v.* Add: **1.** (Later example.)

1970 C. HAMPTON *Philanthropist* iv. 49 Will you please stop parroting on about breakfast?

2. (Later examples.)

1965 *Austral. Women's Weekly* 20 Jan. 48/1 'I'll wait,' he said. 'He'll wait,' she parroted. **1968** *Language* XLIV. 204 School textbooks..had simply parroted a series of rules. **1971** *Nature* 13 Aug. 456/2 Thus a child who produces the correct response when asked the AC question may do so by parroting a verbal label picked up during the initial comparisons. **1976** *Amer. Speech 1973* XLVIII. 259 She quickly muddies the water when she parrots the creed that all languages and dialects are equally fit to express 'concepts such as time or relativity'. **1977** *Spare Rib* Jan. 11/1 The catechism, which we had to be able to parrot, went into the different sorts of sins at great length.

parroting *vbl. sb.* (later examples.)

1934 E. POUND *Let.* 30 Dec. (1971) 263 Mr. Croft seems to me an idiot... His kind of parroting seems to me exactly what does keep people from studying the classics. **1951** G. HUMPHREY *Thinking* iii. 223 Much 'parroting' is not entirely meaningless. **1971** *Daily Tel.* 1 Nov. 5/7 Rote learning—learning something by constant repetition or 'parroting'—free recall and other memory tests were included.

pa·rroted, *ppl. a.* [f. PARROT *v.* + -ED[1].] That is repeated mechanically in the manner of a parrot.

1927 M. SADLEIR *Trollope: a Comm.* 295 Wherever he appears as..waverer from their parrotted idealisms, Sir Thomas Underwood is Trollope himself. **1966** *Listener* 30 June 949/1 This romanticism is probably a reaction from thousands of inane, parroted essays. **1969** *Daily Tel.* 5 Sept. 17 Underpaid teachers whose mission it was to hammer into my brain..the parroted conjugations of Latin verbs.

parrot-house. A building in a zoological garden in which parrots are kept; freq. in *transf.* or *fig.* use *esp.* with reference to loud or raucous noise.

1872 GEO. ELIOT *Middlem.* I. II. xv. 251 Our chat would be thin and eager, as if delivered from a camp-stool in a parrot-house. **1923** H. C. BAILEY *Mr Fortune's Practice* vii. 186 It is an old-fashioned orphanage..as noisy as the parrot house. **1929** J. BUCHAN *Courts of Morning* I. 35 Yanqui youth..is chronically alcoholic and amorous, and its manners are a brilliant copy of the parrot-house. **1945** E. WAUGH *Brideshead Revisited* II. i. 216 The parrot-house fever of my wife's party. **1959** *Times* 2 Mar. 3/3 Without Mias to coordinate them, there was the tell-tale, parrothouse chatter of half a dozen leaders. **1967** 'S. WOODS' *And shame Devil* 126 A clamour in many ways reminiscent of the Parrot House at the Zoo. **1977** 'M. UNDERWOOD' *Murder with Malice* xxiii. 209 The courtroom became a parrot-house of chatter as people pushed towards the exits.

parse, *v.* Add: **a.** In extended use in computational linguistics, to analyse (a string) into syntactic components to test its conformability to a given grammar.

1962 J. J. ROBINSON *Prelim. Codes & Rules Automatic Parsing of English* (Rand Corp. Memo. RM-339-PR) p. v, This Memorandum presents a set of grammar codes and rules for analyzing, or 'parsing', English sentences automatically on a digital computer. *Ibid.* iii. 34 All the words in the string being parsed have been accounted for. **1963** *Communications Assoc. Computing Machinery* VI. 669/1 It will parse strings describable in essentially Backus Normal Form. **1967** D. G. HAYS *Introd. Computational Linguistics* viii. 148 First, we transcribe the grammar, omitting all context restrictions. Obviously, the new grammar parses every string acceptable to the old one and if the restrictions are not vacuous it either assigns extra structures to some acceptable strings or accepts some additional strings, and may do both. **1975** J. S. ROHL *Introd. Compiler Writing* xiii. 226 For syntax analysis it is convenient to have the definitions in an analytic form, so that we can analyse or parse a string of characters to see whether they conform to the grammar.

b. *fig.* (Later example.)

1965 P. KAEL *I lost it at Movies* 9 A movie had to tell some kind of story that held together: a plot had to parse.

c. *transf.* To examine or analyse minutely.

1788 F. GROSE *Rules for drawing Caricaturas* 14 When a caricaturist wishes to delineate any face..he may commit it to his memory, by parsing it in his mind (as the school-boys term it). **1860** *Leisure Hour* 9 Aug. 507/2 Let him soak and remove the leather covering, parsing his way, as it were, by minute examination. **1931** *Times Lit. Suppl.* 7 May 353/3 Reade's biographer is confronted with the necessity of, as it were, 'parsing' a character which..does not make sense. **1962** P. TOMPKINS *Spy in Rome* xxxi. 307 Franco spoke Italian with a slightly foreign (or aristocratic) accent—depending on which way the listener chose to parse it.

Hence **parsed** *ppl. a.*; **parsing** *vbl. sb.* (further examples); also *attrib.* or as *ppl. a.*

1962 J. J. ROBINSON *Prelim. Codes & Rules Automatic Parsing of English* (Rand Corp. Memo. RM-339-PR) i. 2 The English codes and parsing rules being developed at RAND are essentially a machine grammar. **1963** *Communications Assoc. Computing Machinery* VI. 669/1 The automatic parsing algorithms..simplify compiler construction but contribute little to the production of 'optimized' machine code, for example. **1964** *Ibid.* VII. 131/2 The right side of the algorithm..in effect runs the input string backwards..until the tentatively parsed word is reached. *Ibid.*, An example of a syntactically ambiguous phrase is 'medical schools and hospitals of Boston' which actually has five possible parsings: ((MS)AH)OB; (MS)A(HOB); (M(SAH))OB; M((SAH)OB); M(SA(HOB)). **1967** D. G. HAYS *Introd. Computational Linguistics* vi. 107 A systematic answer to questions like this, determining the exact sequence in which reductions will be made to any particular string, is the basis for a parsing strategy. *Ibid.* 114 Only complete parsing of a string reveals that any part of a tentative parsing is correct. **1971** E. WILSON in R. A. Wisbey *Computer in Lit. & Ling. Res.* v. 210 This definition it attempts to transform into an equivalent definition which can be parsed by a one-track algorithm. If it succeeds, SID can be made to generate this parsing algorithm. **1972** J. A. N. LEE *Computer Semantics* v. 273 The form of text which is generated by the analyzer, we shall name the parsed text, which may take the form of a syntactic tree or a phrase marked string.

parse (pāɹz, -s), *sb.* [f. the vb.] The action or result of parsing.

1963 *Communications Assoc. Computing Machinery* VI. 670/1 In the algorithm presented here, all possible parses are carried along as shown below in the progressing parse of *abce* according to the syntax of the earlier example. When the symbol *e* is encountered, Parse 1 cannot be continued and is dropped, leaving Parse 2 as the correct one. **1973** W. M. WAITE *Implementing Software for Non-Numeric Appl.* viii. 292 Both pattern-directed and string-directed scans have been used for parsing algorithms. If a pattern-directed scan is used, the procedure is known as a 'top-to-bottom' or 'top-down' parse; a string-directed scan yields a 'bottom-to-top' or 'bottom-up' parse.

parsec (pā·ɹsek). *Astr.* [f. PAR(ALLAX + SEC(OND *sb.*[1]] A unit of length equal to the distance at which a star would have a heliocentric parallax of one second of arc, viz. 3·09 × 10^{16} metres (19·2 × 10^{12} miles, 3·26 light-years), approximately.

1913 F. W. DYSON in *Monthly Notices R. Astron. Soc.* LXXIII. 342 There is need for a name for this unit of distance... Professor Turner suggests *Parsec*, which may be taken as an abbreviated form of 'a distance corresponding to a parallax of one second'. **1921** *Glasgow Herald* 11 July 4 He estimates the distance of the object as 140 parsecs or four times the distance of the Hyades cluster. **1955** *Sci. News Let.* 29 Jan. 71/2 These hydrogen clouds have diameters of several parsecs, one parsec being the distance light travels in 3·26 years. **1962** F. I. ORDWAY et al. *Basic Astronautics* vi. 290 Within 5 parsecs (16·5 light years) of the Sun, 53 individual stars have been counted, the nearest of which is Proxima Centauri, 25 trillion miles away. **1974** S. V. M. CLUBE in R. H. Stoy *Everyman's Astron.* viii. 309 The nearest star clusters are the Pleiades and Hyades which are at distances of 130 and 40 parsecs respectively and therefore beyond the reach of trigonometric parallax determinations. **1977** *Time* 30 May 42/2 The four of them are even now setting out to deliver the secret plans to rebel headquarters, light-years and parsecs away.

‖ **parsemé** (pārsĕme), *a.* [Fr., pa. pple. of *parsemer* to sprinkle, strew f. L. *per-* through + *sēmināre* to sow.] Sprinkled or strewn (with); used *esp.* in embroidery with reference to the decoration of fabrics and costumes.

1814 M. BIRKBECK *Notes Journey through France* App. 14 The numerous longitudinal ridges..with which this charming country is, 'parsemé', appear to be the venerable remains of the ancient surface. **1832** F. TROLLOPE *Dom. Manners Amer.* I. vi. 74 She was preparing to set to work in a yellow dress parsemé with red roses... I thought it was a pity to spoil so fine a gown. **1883** H. C. DENT *Jrnl.* 9 June in *Year in Brazil* (1886) i. 4 The country on the north bank has a low coastline, *parsemé* with red-roofed white houses. **1890** O. WILDE *Pict. Dorian Gray* ix, in *Lippincott's Monthly Mag.* July 71 A skull-cap *parsemé* with pearls. **1905** *Athenæum* 17 June 760 The rise of a new conception of design, with figures and ornaments parsemé on a velvet ground,..in the fifteenth century.

parser. Add: Also, a computer program for parsing.

1965 *Communications Assoc. Computing Machinery* VIII. 688/1 In testing the program on 300 basic English sentences Knowlton's parser produced 137 correct parsings and 44 incorrect ones. **1967** D. G. HAYS *Introd. Computational Linguistics* vi. 116 Whereas the other parsers considered..have generally operated more or less from left to right on the string, or from right to left, this one operates by choosing..the top of the dependency structure, and working downward. **1970** *Computers & Humanities* V. 25 More computational parsers are being written following the generative-transformational model than any other. **1977** E. VON GLASERSFELD in D. M. Rumbaugh *Lang. Learning by Chimpanzee* v. 121 The parser, however, can handle a lexicon of 250 items.

parsettensite (pāɹse·tĕnzəit). *Min.* [ad. G. *parsettensit* (J. Jakob 1923, in *Schweiz. min. und petrogr. Mitt.* III. 227), f. Alp *Parsettens*, name of the locality in Val d'Err, Graubünden, E. Switzerland where it was first found: see -ITE[1] 2 b.] A basic silicate of manganese that often contains appreciable potassium and occurs as copper-red masses.

1924 *Mineral. Abstr.* II. 251 Parsettensite..occurs as a filling in rather thick veins. **1962** W. A. DEER et al. *Rock-forming Min.* III. 103 Parsettensite..was shown by Fankuchen..to be a manganese stilpnomelane, and it is proposed to retain this name to describe varieties rich in manganese. **1968** I. KOSTOV *Mineral.* 362 Transitional towards the vermiculite group are stilpnomelane, ekmanite, and parsettensite, with formulas similar to those of the illites but as a rule without aluminium in tetrahedral coordination.

Parseval (pā·ɹsĕvăl). Also **Parsefal.** [The name of the inventor, the German engineer August von *Parseval* (1861–1942).] A type of non-rigid dirigible airship formerly in use in Germany.

[**1908** W. H. STORY tr. *Hildebrandt's Airships* viii. 85 (*caption*) Major Parseval's dirigible balloon.] **1909** *Chambers's Jrnl.* Oct. 660/2 At present the airship fleet consists of three Zeppelins, three Parsefals, and two Gross dirigibles. *Ibid.*, It is of the Parsefal type. **1910** C. C. TURNER *Aerial Navig. To-day* xxiv. 295 The 'Parseval' is a non-rigid balloon with a cubic capacity of 190,000 cubic feet... It is rounded at the front and pointed at the rear. **1931** C. ST. J. SPRIGG *Airship* viii. 106 In its final form the Parseval was not much smaller than the early Zeppelins, and was of a good streamline shape. *Ibid.* 110 Two of the Parseval type were built by Messrs. Vickers under licence. **1957** *Encycl. Brit.* I. 465/1 Maj. August von Parseval in 1906 constructed for the German army the first in a series of some 28 Parseval pressure type airships which were built from that date until 1929. **1959** J. A. SINCLAIR *Famous Airships of World* iii. 30 In Germany, Major von Parseval..in 1911 constructed the *Parseval No. 3*... The steel tube car carried 12 passengers. **1971** R. JACKSON *Airships* v. 112 On the outbreak of war, the Astra-Torres and the Parseval were immediately allocated to coastal patrol duties.

parsimony. Add: **c.** Also, the principle that organisms tend towards economy of action in learning or in fulfilling their needs.

1931 D. K. ADAMS in *Brit. Jrnl. Psychol.* XXII. 153 This economy upon repetition or, better, the property (we shall call it parsimony) of which it is simply one manifestation, is a fundamental property of a certain class of bodies. *Ibid.*, I think that parsimony is a property of all organisms. **1948** E. R. HILGARD *Theories of Learning* xi. 295 The process of need satiation is regulated by a principle called 'parsimony'. That is a preference for short-cuts, described by others as the principle of least action. **1955** *Sci. Amer.* June 68/1 This is the grand overriding law of the parsimony of nature: every action within a system is executed with the least possible expenditure of energy.

d. (Further examples.) Also *parsimony, principle of parsimony*.

1933 J. C. FLÜGEL *Hundred Years Psychol.* ii. 124 The 'law of parsimony', according to which we must always explain animal behaviour in terms of the simplest mental processes that will account for the facts. **1957** R. K. MERTON *Social Theory* (rev. ed.) viii. 259 The theoretical objective of *parsimony*, found whenever several empirical generalizations are derived from a more general formulation. **1970** M. H. MARX *Learning: Theories* I. i. 16/2 The principle of parsimony, often called William of Occam's razor or Lloyd Morgan's canon,..is a rough guideline to the acceptability of hypotheses and principles. *Ibid.* 17/1 The failure to accept the principle of parsimony results in the overloading of relatively untested..ideas. **1972** *Encycl. Psychol.* I. 202/2 The essential similarity between classical and operant conditioning has led students to pose questions about the parsimony or necessity of more than one principle to account for this type of learning.

pars intermedia (pāɹz intəɹmī·diă). *Anat.* [mod.L., = 'middle part'.] A layer of tissue in the hypophysis between the anterior and posterior lobes (sometimes regarded as a part of the anterior lobe).

1908 P. T. HERRING in *Q. Jrnl. Exper. Physiol.* I. 132 It is convenient to consider as the anterior lobe only that portion of it which has already been distinguished from the 'pars intermedia'. **1912** H. CUSHING *Pituitary Body & its Disorders* I. 4 The posterior lobe comprises the pars nervosa..and its epithelial investment (pars intermedia of Herring). **1926**, etc. [see *neuro-intermediate* adj. s.v. *NEURO-]. **1932** [see *INTERMEDIN]. **1962** E. C. CROSBY et al. *Correl. Anat. Nerv. Syst.* vi. 323/2 From Rathke's pouch, an embryonic diverticulum from the roof of the stomadeum, are derived the pars distalis, pars intermedia, and pars tuberalis. **1968** W. C. BOWMAN et al. *Textbk. Pharmacol.* xiv. 365 The hormone of the pars intermedia (the melanocyte stimulating hormone, MSH) stimulates dispersion of the melanin granules in melanocytes of the skin of fish, amphibia and reptiles, with a resulting darkening of the skin.

parsley. Add: **3.** *parsley-dark* adj.; **parsley butterfly** *U.S.*, the black swallowtail butterfly, *Papilio polyxenes asterius*; **parsley caterpillar** *U.S.*, the larva of the anise swallowtail butterfly, *Papilio zelicaon*, which is a pest of umbelliferous plants in western North America; **parsley frog**, a spadefoot toad, *Pelodytes punctatus*, found in western Europe; **parsley green**, a colouring additive used in cookery; **parsley-leaved elder**, a cultivated variety of the elder, *Sambucus nigra* var. *laciniata*, distinguished by its cut leaves; **parsley sauce**, a white sauce flavoured with parsley; **parsley-worm** *U.S.*, the larva of the parsley butterfly, which is a pest of umbelliferous plants.

1889 S. H. SCUDDER *Butterflies Eastern U.S.* II. 1353 Papilio Polyxenes.—The black swallow-tail... Parsley butterfly (Emmons). **1926** E. O. ESSIG *Insects Western N. Amer.* xxvii. 634 The western parsley caterpillar, *Papilio zelicaon*,..is yellow or orange and black. **1962** METCALF & FLINT *Destructive & Useful Insects* (ed. 4) xiv. 598 In the West it [*sc.* the parsleyworm] is replaced by the western parsley caterpillar. **1920** E. SITWELL *Wooden Pegasus* 31 Face as white as any clock's Cased in parsley-dark curled locks. **1897** *Proc. Zool. Soc.* 577 (*title*) On the structure and development of the hypobranchial skeleton of the Parsley-Frog. **1934** J. FLETCHER tr. *Rostand's Toads* vii. 72 In a pond near Paris..the larvae of the Common Frog were in the North and West;..those of the Parsley Frog, the South-east. **1960** R. MERTENS *World of Amphibians & Reptiles* ii. 34 The parsley frog (*Pelodytes*).. occurs only in south-western Europe and the Caucasus. **1845** E. ACTON *Mod. Cookery* iv. 151 (*heading*) Parsley green, for colouring sauces. Gather a quantity of young parsley,..pound it in a mortar,..set it into a pan of boiling water. **1731** P. MILLER *Gardeners Dict.* s.v. Sambucus. The Cut or Parsley-leav'd Elder. **1838** J. C. LOUDON *Aboretum* II. 1028 The Parsley-leaved Elder; has the leaflets cut into fine segments. **1904** E. STEP *Wayside & Woodland Trees* 125 An Elder with its leaflets deeply cut into very slender lobes...is an escape from cultivation—a garden variety (*laciniata*) known as the Cut-leaved or Parsley-leaved Elder. **1836** E. COPLEY *Cook's Compl. Guide* II. v. 359 *Parsley Sauce.* Boil a bunch of green parsley in salt and water for five minutes; when done, chop it fine, put in half a pint of bechamel sauce, or good melted butter. **1877** E. S. DALLAS *Kettner's Bk. of Table* 329 *Parsley Sauce.*..is generally in England given to what in the French kitchen is known as maître d'hôtel sauce. **1965** R. CARRIER *Cookbk.* ii. 90 (*heading*) English parsley sauce. **1978** *Listener* 23 Mar. 366/1, I've just dialled for the weather... There was a slight crossed line. The outlook is warm with parsley sauce, Regulo 7. **1842** T. W. HARRIS *Insects Injurious to Vegetation* 211 In the month of June, there may be found, on the leaves of the parsley and carrot, certain caterpillars, more commonly called parsley-worms. **1972** SWAN & PAPP *Common Insects N. Amer.* 204 Black Swallowtail (Parsleyworm). *Papilio polyxenes asterius.*

parsnip. Add: **1. c.** In various colloq. or slang expressions: *before you can say parsnips*, very rapidly, 'in the twinkling of an eye'; *to look parsnips*, to look sour or displeased; *I beg your parsnips*, joc. alteration of 'I beg your pardon'.

1803 G. COLMAN *John Bull* II. ii. 18 'You'll come back again,' says she—'That's what I will, before you can say, parsnips, my darling,' says he. **1837** J. HOOK *Jack Brag* II. iv. 167 'I'm delighted,' said Jack, looking parsnips. **1886** H. BAUMANN *Londinismen* 131/2 *Parsnip*,..I beg ~s (statt pardon) bitt' um Entschuldigung. **1922** JOYCE *Ulysses* 297 Who said Christ is good?—I beg your parsnips, says Alf.—Is that a good Christ, says Bob Doran, to take away poor little Willy Dignam?

3. *parsnip soup*; **parsnip butterfly, swallow-tail** = *parsley butterfly* s.v. *PARSLEY 3; **parsnip web-worm** *N. Amer.*, the larva of a moth, *Depressaria pastinacella*, a pest of parsnips and related plants.

1867 *Amer. Naturalist* I. 220 The Parsnip butterfly (*Papilio Asterias*) may be seen flying over the beds of parsnips. **1845** E. ACTON *Mod. Cookery* i. 25 (*heading*) Parsnip soup. Dissolve,..four ounces and a half of good butter,..and slice in directly two pounds of sweet tender parsnips. **1942** E. O. ESSIG *College Entomol.* xxxi. 503 *Papilio ajax* Linn. Parsnip swallowtail. **1888** *Insect Life* I. 94 The Parsnip Web-worm... We found this insect extremely common in the stems of Wild Parsnips. **1928** METCALF & FLINT *Destructive & Useful Insects* xvi. 509 Parsnip Webworm... The flower heads of parsnip and celery are webbed together with silk and devoured by small yellow, greenish or grayish caterpillars covered with small black spots. **1954** BORROR & DELONG *Introd. Study Insects* xxvi. 536 The parsnip webworm..attacks parsnips, celery, and related plants.

parson. Add: **6. d. parson's table** *U.S.*, a small, simple, wooden table with a square top supported at each corner by straight legs.

1969 *Sears Catal.* Spring/Summer 1385/1 Parson's Tables. Avocado green. **1973** R. HAYES *Hungarian Game* xlvi. 271 Except for a matched set of Sheraton chairs, a salon mirror and a parson's table, the landing was empty. **1976** *Billings* (Montana) *Gaz.* 24 June 7-F/6 (Advt.), 16 × 16" parsons tables.

Parsonian (pāɹsōᵘ·niăn), *a.* *Sociol.* [f. the name of Talcott *Parsons* (1902–), Amer. sociologist + -IAN.] Of or relating to the theories of action and change within a society or culture put forward by Parsons, or to his structural-functional method of analysing a social system. Hence **Parso·nianism**, the views or theories of Parsons.

1961 A. HACKER in M. Black *Social Theories of Talcott Parsons* 298 One obstacle to a Parsonian theory of class and power may not be easy to overcome. **1970** TOURAINE & PÉCAUT in I. L. Horowitz *Masses in Lat. Amer.* iii. 68 If the Parsonian categories are to be directly applied, it should be possible to define a system of values. **1973** J. REX *Discovering Sociol.* ix. 117 As Parsonianism developed, and as the attack upon it and its ideological offspring rumbled on. **1974** R. JESSOP *Traditionalism, Conservatism & Brit. Polit. Culture* i. 23 In addition to the well-known Parsonian pattern-variables, there are others developed specifically for political analysis and relevant to the problems in hand. **1977** *Times Lit. Suppl.* 25 Feb. 198/3 The family thus functioned, in the best Parsonian fashion, as the principal agent of 'socialization'. *Ibid.*, Mr. Gutman never does tell us what he means by 'socialization', and his implicit Parsonianism hardly does justice to Talcott Parsons.

parsonical, *a.* (Later examples.)

1902 *Irish Rosary* VI. 77/2 His (*sc.* Herrick's) verse..is on the whole more poetical than *parsonical*. **1972** *Times* 13 Oct. 3/6, I never wear a parsonical collar unless someone asks me to. **1976** *Church Times* 20 Aug. 7/3 The advent of the tape-recorder has, one hopes, eradicated the worst aberrations of the parsonical voice.

parsonify, *v.* (In Dict. s.v. PARSON). Add: (Further examples.) Also, to make into a parson.

1737 J. THOMSON *Let.* 12 Jan. in W. Goodhugh *Eng. Gentl. Libr. Man.* (1827) 262, I have not yet seen the round man of God to be. He is to be parsonifyed a few days hence. **1926** tr. *William II's Early Life* iii. 19 He.. left all dogmas and creeds severely alone. They were, in his view,..apt to 'parsonify' the grand and simple outline of the Christian Faith.

parsonsite (pā·ɹsənzəit). *Min.* [a. F. *parsonsite* (A. Schoep 1923, in *Compt. Rend.* CLXXVI. 173), f. the name of Arthur L. *Parsons* (b. 1873), Canadian mineralogist: see -ITE[1] 2 b.] A hydrated phosphate of lead and uranium, $Pb_2(UO_2)(PO_4)_2.2H_2O$, found as crusts and powdery aggregates of transparent or translucent, minute, lath-like crystals.

1923 *Chem. Abstr.* XVII. 1776 (*heading*) Parsonsite, a new radioactive mineral. **1950** *Amer. Mineralogist* XXXV. 247 Parsonsite occurs at the Ruggles pegmatite near Grafton Center, Grafton County, New Hampshire, as crusts of microscopic spicular or lath-like crystals... The parsonsite is associated with autunite and phosphuranylite and all of these have ultimately been derived from the alteration of the primary uraninite. **1964** *Bull. U.S. Geol. Survey* No. 1064. 233 Parsonsite probably is monoclinic, but the possibility of triclinic symmetry cannot be ruled out.

‖ **pars pro toto** (pāɹz prōᵘ tōᵘ·to). [L., = 'a part for the whole'.] A part considered as representative of the whole. Also *attrib.*

1702 [see SYNECDOCHICAL *a.*]. **1958** W. STARK *Sociol. of Knowl.* 156 The fallacy of *pars pro toto*—taking the part for the whole. **1965** *Eng. Stud.* XLVI. 55 It is a *pars pro toto* figure, just as *rand* is used to refer not only to the metal border or ring round the wooden board but also to the shield as such. **1970** *Jrnl. Gen. Psychol.* LXXXIII. 66 The tendency to combine areas of questionable form into strange or absurd entities or the *pars pro toto* effect.

part, *sb.* (*adv.*) Add: **I. 2. d.** Each of the separate or separable pieces that go to make up a machine or the like. Also *attrib.* in *pl.*

1886 D. CLERK *Gas Engine* 5 Fig. 3 is a sectional elevation of the first engine, showing the principal working parts. *Ibid.* 8 Barnett's second engine..is double-acting, and therefore requires a greater number of parts. **1890** W. ROBINSON *Gas & Petroleum Engines* ii. 11 The wearing parts can be easily taken out and, when worn, replaced by duplicates. **1897** *Trans. Inst. Naval Archit.* XXXVIII. 217 Set of accessories, spare parts, and securing gear. **1923** *Radio Times* 28 Sept. 6 (Advt.), The user of the 'Gecophone'..may desire to purchase in his own locality spares and replacement parts. **1939** G. W. STUBBINGS *Diseases Electr. Machinery* iii. 60 A.C. transformers..are entirely static and have no moving parts. **1939** H. R. SIMONDS *Industr. Plastics* (1940) ix. 244 The average household refrigerator has more than 20 important plastics parts. **1947** W. W. MCCULLOUGH *Electr. Motor Maintenance* ii. 13 Worn parts should be replaced promptly. **1968** *Amer. Speech* 1967 XLII. 40 Owner's manuals, parts catalogues, motoring publications from abroad. **1971** *Good Motoring* Sept. 4/1 It was driven by Billy Mackay, a VW Motor parts manager in Scotland. **1974** *Daily Tel.* 4 Dec. 12/3 On average, parts for a Renault 12TL are 77 per cent. more expensive than for the Austin Allegro 1300. **1975** *Sci. Amer.* Feb. 25/2 Industry mass-produces parts in great variety and number. **1976** *Nature* 1 Apr. 391/3 Two fibres, called Kevlar and Kevlar 49 by Dupont,..look likely to be used in tyre belting and in composites for body armour and aircraft parts.

3. (Later *absol.* (*euphem.*) examples.)

1942 BERREY & VAN DEN BARK *Amer. Thes. Slang* §121/37 *Genitals*,..parts. **1958** S. A. GRAU *Hard Blue Sky* 152 The young girls giggled and felt a hot touch in their parts. **1968** J. UPDIKE *Couples* ii. 141 'Oh you have big—' 'Parts?' **1977** 'J. LE CARRÉ' *Hon. Schoolboy* ii. 41 The devil's red-hot wind would burn his parts to a frazzle.

IV. 17. (Earlier and later examples.)

1871 'MARK TWAIN' in *Galaxy* Aug. 284/1 He..brushed his hair with elaborate care,..accomplishing an accurate 'part' behind. **1933** J. STEINBECK *To God Unknown* (1935) viii. 61 He raked a nervous hand through his hair and destroyed the careful part. **1970** *Globe Mag.* (Toronto) 26 Sept. 19/2 (Advt.), Balding! So you moved your part down over your ear. **1972** D. RAMSAY *Little Murder Music* 123 A shoulder-length fall of blue-black hair divided by a snow-white part in centre. **1976** 'R. MACDONALD' *Blue Hammer* xxiv. 126 The part in her hair was white and straight.

V. 19. a. part of speech: also (with hyphens) *attrib.*

1933 L. BLOOMFIELD *Language* i. 17 Even the fundamental features of Indo-European grammar, such as, especially, the part-of-speech system, are by no means universal in human speech. **1964** *Language* XL. 167 One-syllable words, graphemically defined, have the same part-of-speech assignments when checked against standard dictionaries.

VI. 29. part-playing, playing in parts (sense 10 in Dict.); **part-score** *Bridge* (see quot. 1936); **part–whole** *a.*, of or pertaining to the relationship of a part or parts to a whole; **part-work**, (*a*) used *attrib.* to designate a system of part-time work; (*b*) a book or the like published in parts; also *attrib.*

1946 R. BLESH *Shining Trumpets* (1949) i. 18 *Tempo*: I. Strict tempo or controlled acceleration. II. Moderate, never too fast. Relaxed, and with room for improvised part-playing. **1960** *Times* 29 Feb. 15/1 Balanced part-playing and clear harmonic progression appeared to dominate his intentions to the detriment of artistic communication. **1932** *Official Syst. Contract Bridge* 187 (*heading*) Bidding against a side which has a part score. **1936** E. CULBERTSON *Contract Bridge Complete* 17 *Part-score*, (1) A contract of less than game; (2) the points earned for the making of such a contract. **1973** *Times* 20 Oct. 11/3 You then run the risk of missing a game unless you have a part-score. **1949** M. MEAD *Male & Female* iii. 73 The Balinese child..develops a part–whole relationship to the world, in which each part of his body is a whole, and yet each is part of the whole. **1953** C. E. BAZELL *Linguistic Form* 107 It is likely that, as soon as the part–whole rather than the member–class terminology is used, the ostensible criteria for phonemic analysis should be transferred to the analysis of phonemic parts. **1972** *Language* XLVIII. 452 Semantic analysis based on a strict part–whole conception of meaning. **1966** *Economist* 26 Mar. 1231/1 One of the aims of the part-work system is to increase the sum of technically trained people in the rural areas. **1969** *Times* 13 Mar. 20/7 (Advt.), Part work publishing. *Ibid.*, Part-works now account for more than 10 per cent of all money spent on periodicals. **1971** *Guardian* 22 Oct. 9/2 'World of Wildlife' is the latest in a string of partwork publications... Partworks began in the mid-eighteenth century when the 'Encyclopaedia Britannica' found itself unable to raise sufficient funds to publish all the volumes in one go. **1975** *Nature* 24 Jan. 227/2 Dr Magnus Pyke..currently to be seen on British television, advertising the appearance of a new partwork about science.

B. c. *part-cause* (later examples); **part-exchange**, a transaction in which the owner of an article exchanges it for another (usu. new) article and pays a sum of money to cover the difference between the value of the two articles; hence as *v. trans.*, to exchange (something) in this way; also *fig.*; **part-load** (see quot.

1971); **part-pay**, a part of one's pay; *spec.* that part paid to whalemen before the start of a voyage.

1878 C. Read *On Theory of Logic* 130 It is certain that C is a Cause or Part-Cause of E. **1901** H. H. Joachim *Study Ethics of Spinoza* 169 In our ignorance we attribute these qualities of sensation directly to the external bodies, which are at most their part-causes. **1932** H. H. Price *Perception* viii. 270 One needs..to know that any material thing is a part-cause of the sense-data belonging to it. **1964** M. Argyle *Psychol. & Social Probl.* v. 61 Different part-causes combine together, so that if one is very strong, or if several of them add together, the result is a delinquent. Each part-cause has a known statistical weight over a large sample, so that it is possible to estimate the chances that a given person will be a delinquent. **1926** *Punch* 10 Nov. 505/3 A correspondent writes to know if, when the new wave-lengths come into force, the old ones will be accepted in part-exchange. **1929** *Melody Maker* Jan. 18 (Advt.), Your present instrument in part exchange. **1931** D. L. Sayers *Five Red Herrings* xx. 218 He had something to do with the second-hand motor trade and was taking the bike in part-exchange for something. **1961** *Guardian* 12 June 2/3 The urge to part-exchange my car comes upon me. **1968** *Listener* 30 May 711/1 One way is to resolve to *part-exchange* an idea long before it has been driven down to the rims. **1972** *Daily Tel.* 10 Oct. 3/3 He part-exchanged his old power-boat for the Carnation in 1970. **1973** *Times* 25 Oct. 38/7 (Advt.), Steinway and Sons..are prepared to purchase or take part exchange pianos of their own or other makes. **1976** *Leicester Trader* 24 Nov. 21/2 They do part-exchanges, offer an excellent after-sales service and an insurance repair service. **1969** *Jane's Freight Containers 1968–69* 315/1, 20% will go to wagon-load and 80% to LCL, or part-load. **1971** M. Tak *Truck Talk* 115 *Part load*, a consignment to a destination that is less than a complete trailer load. **1850** H. Melville *White Jacket* II. xxxvii. 234 There were instances of men in the Neversink receiving money in part pay for work done for private individuals. **1851** —— *Moby Dick* III. xlix. 309, I hope my poor mother's drawn my part-pay ere this.

part, *v.* Add: **3.** Also *to part brass-rags*: see *brass *sb.* 7.

4. c. (*d*) Usu. *to part off.* (Examples.)

1923 C. M. Linley *Lathe Users' Handbk.* vii. 118 In bar work, as each piece is finished, it is parted off. **1945** W. C. Durney *Capstan & Turret Lathes* iii. 78 Mount a parting off tool in one of the remaining stations of the rear square turret and locate a longitudinal stop to part off the bar ¼ in. from the collet face. **1948** L. H. Sparey *Amateur's Lathe* x. 126/1 When work of large diameter must be parted-off, it is not advisable to make the part in one cut. **1958** C. T. Bower *Aids to Workshop Pract.* viii. 94 The parting-off tool shown..has been designed for use on a 3½-in. centre lathe to enable work gripped in the chuck to be parted off without jamming.

6. d. (Earlier and later examples.) Also const. *up* (*Austral.* and *N.Z. colloq.*).

1864 Hotten *Slang Dict.* 196 *Part*, to pay, restore, give up; 'he's a right un, he is; I know he'd part.'.. The term is in general use in *Sporting* circles. **1889** *Bulletin* (Sydney) 21 Sept. 20/1 An' then they reckoned I'd been usin' 'em [*sc.* double-headed pennies in a game of two-up] all the time, and they made me part up. **1913** E. Wharton *Custom of Country* II. xiv. 202 People said of him that he 'didn't care to part'. **1933** A. G. Macdonell *England, their England* xv. 267 Might squeeze another hundred [pounds]... Not more. He doesn't part easily. **1943** *Amer. Speech* XVIII. 92 Words and phrases..which deserve to be recorded in any attempt to convey something of the flavour of the colloquial speech of the country [*sc.* New Zealand]...*to part up*, to pay up. **1946** F. Sargeson *That Summer* 152 Ted got more but of course there was his wife, and he had to part up. **1952** Wodehouse *Barmy in Wonderland* viii. 81 Fanny won't part. She's so tight she could carry an armful of eels up two flights of stairs and not drop one. **1953** K. Tennant *Joyful Condemned* iv. 39, I guess Rene might part up to know who her mum was. **1966** Wodehouse *Plum Pie* i. 17 Uncle Tom..had to foot the bills. He has the stuff in sackfuls, but he hates to part. **1970** J. Aiken *Embroidered Sunset* x. 209 'So where are all the old girl's pictures?' 'Scattered all over the village. Nobody will part; they are thought to be lucky.'

Partaga (pāɹtā·gă). The proprietary name of a brand of Havana cigar.

1862 *Illustr. Catal. Internat. Exhib., Industr. Dept., Brit. Div.* I. No. 869 The exhibitors are manufacturers of the following Cigars:—..Cubas. Partagas. Salvadoras. **1865** *Dublin Univ. Mag.* Apr. 378/1 By-and-by, after smoking two or three Partagas, I may recollect some lunatic who would do such an absurd thing. **1871** M. Legrand *Cambridge Freshman* 145 The O'Higgins was accommodated with a prime Partaga. **1878** *Trade Marks Jrnl.* 17 Apr. 264/1 Design patent. Partagas... Juan Antonio Bances, of and on behalf of the firm of Bances and Co.,..Havana, Cuba; manufacturers of cigars, cigarettes, and picadura. **1908** *Ibid.* 3 June 921 Partagas... Cigars. Cifuentes, Fernandez y Ca.,..Havana, Cuba; cigar manufacturers. **1930** A. Bennett *Imperial Palace* xvi. 100 Evelyn took a cigar out of a box of Partagas. *Ibid.* xxiii. 145 Oldham handed Partaga cigars, and, the table having been cleared of all but finger-bowls, ash-trays and cigars,..disappeared. **1973** J. M. White *Garden Game* 115 Our cigars..were Partagas, and merited careful attention.

partake, *v.* Add: **1. b.** Also *absol.*

1844 D. B. Reid *Illustr. Theory & Pract. Ventilation* 181 Nor was any of the members aware..that they had partaken more heartily than usual. **1870** J. P. Smith *Widow Goldsmith's Daughter* ix. 144 Chris could not touch anything, but the widow partook with the particular relish which a well-spent morning gave her. **1974** J. McClure *Gooseberry Fool* v. 80 He hardly ever drank... He didn't often partake, but then it was also bloody hot.

parthenocarpy (pā·ɹpĕnokāɹpi). *Bot.* [a. G. *parthenocarpie* (F. Noll 1902, in *Sitzungsber. d. Niederrheinischen Ges. für Natur- und Heilkunde* 160), f. Gr. παρθένο-ς virgin + καρπός fruit + -y[3].] The development of a fruit without fertilization having taken place in the plant producing it. Hence **pa:rthenoca·rpic** *a.*, of a fruit, produced without prior fertilization; **pa:rthenoca·rpically** *adv.*

1911 J. M. Coulter et al. *Textbk. Bot.* II. 917 In striking contrast to ordinary fruit production is parthenocarpy, or the development of fruit without the fusion of gametes. *Ibid.*, Plants with parthenocarpic fruits are.. propagated vegetatively. **1924** M. Skene *Biol. Flowering Plants* v. 406 An embryo may develop without fertilisation having occurred. Corresponding to this parthenogenesis we have parthenocarpy, where a fruit is produced without any seeds. **1929** *Nature* 13 July 63/2 Triploids occur..with partial parthenocarpy in the cultivated apples. **1949** *Endeavour* VIII. 191/1 Even in plants which normally produce seeded fruits, parthenocarpy may occur spasmodically. *Ibid.* 191/2 Parthenocarpic fruits often differ from seeded fruits of the same variety, not only in size and shape but in chemical composition. **1951** *New Biol.* XI. 72 There is virtually no fertilization in the seedless edible varieties [of banana], the fruits being formed parthenocarpically. **1960** *New Scientist* 11 Feb. 322/3 Such parthenocarpic fruits contain no viable seed. **1965** K. Esau *Plant Anat.* (ed. 2) xix. 586 Formation of a fruit may also occur without seed development and without fertilization, a phenomenon known as parthenocarpy.

parthenogenesis. (Further examples.)

1902 D. H. Campbell *Univ. Text-bk. Bot.* v. 122 In one species of Chara, *C. crinita*, the oöspores are developed without fertilization—one of the few well-authenticated cases of parthenogenesis. **1936** [see *eutelegenesis]. **1950** *Adv. Genetics* III. 195 In vertebrata normal parthenogenesis is unknown (with the possible exception of certain fish hybrids). **1965** Bell & Coombe tr. *Strasburger's Textbk. Bot.* 203 There are exceptions in which a sexual cell will germinate and undergo development without fertilization. This phenomenon is referred to as parthenogenesis. Habitual parthenogenesis is that occurring when egg cells germinate regularly without fertilization.

parthenogenetic, *a.* **1.** (Further examples.)

1884 *Q. Jrnl. Microsc. Sci.* XXIV. 266 In certain cases, the oospores become normally developed and capable of germination without any male organs being formed at all... Pringsheim himself termed these oospores parthenogenetic. **1936** [see *amphidiploid *a.* and *sb.*]. **1950** *Adv. Genetics* III. 195 Some big animal groups are wholly (or almost wholly) characterized by parthenogenetic reproduction. **1965** B. E. Freeman tr. *Vandel's Biospeleol.* ix. 110 *E*[*laphoidella*] *bidens*, a species with parthenogenetic reproduction, is cosmopolitan.

parthenogenetically, *adv.* (Further examples.)

1884 *Q. Jrnl. Microsc. Sci.* XXIV. 281 *Ascobolus furfuraceus* probably produces its fructification parthenogenetically. **1895** *Ann. Bot.* IX. 638 In *S*[*aprolegnia*] *mixta*..we conclude that fertilization frequently takes place, but in default of its occurrence the oosphere may develop parthenogenetically. **1924** *Jrnl. Agric. Res.* XXVII. 513 The stem-mother is always wingless and gives birth to living young parthenogenetically. **1938** [see *apomict]. **1950** *Adv. Genetics* III. 195 Some vertebrata have been artificially induced to reproduce parthenogenetically. **1972** *Nature* 28 Jan. 196/1 Microtubule proteins are still synthesized in parthenogenetically activated, nucleated half-eggs.

parthenogenone (pā:ɹpĕno,dʒe·nōun). *Zool.* [f. Parthenogen(esis + *-one*.] An organism of parthenogenetic origin, having only one parent.

1957 R. A. Beatty *Parthenogenesis & Polyploidy in Mammalian Devel.* i. 4 Parthenogenesis will be considered here as a term applicable not only to born young but also to embryos and foetuses, the parthenogenetic organism being called a parthenogenone. **1970** *Sci. Jrnl.* June 42/3 The human population, by virtue of its enormous size, could indeed contain a few parthenogenones. **1973** *Nature* 13 Apr. 475/2 [Mouse] eggs were examined under the × 50 magnification of a Wild dissecting microscope to determine the overall frequency and types of parthenogenones induced. **1977** *Ibid.* 6 Jan. 53/2 Diploid and haploid parthenogenones evidently possess the capacity to form teratomas and give rise to differentiated tissues.

Parthenopean (pā:ɹpĕnŏpī·ăn), *a.* [ad. It. *Partenopea*, f. L. *Parthenopēi-us* belonging to Naples (f. *Parthenopē* Naples) + -an.] Of or belonging to Naples; applied *esp.* to the short-lived republic established in Naples by French revolutionary forces in 1799.

1799 Nelson *Let.* 19 Jan. (1845) III. 236 The Parthenopien Republic is forming. **1858** S. Horner tr. *Colletta's Hist. Kingdom of Naples* I. iv. ii. 341 The day had arrived when the Parthenopean Republic was to be abandoned to her own resources. **1879** *Encycl. Brit.* IX. 79/1 The French, entering the city after a furious but undisciplined resistance by the lazzaroni, established with the aid of the citizens and nobles the 'Parthenopean Republic'. **1894** C. E. Clement *Naples* vi. 156 Vesuvius..sent forth a brilliant flame, which the Neapolitans regarded as an omen of future prosperity. Thus was the Parthenopean Republic established. **1900** P. Orsi *Mod. Italy* ii. 45 It was then that the Parthenopæan Republic—so-called from the ancient name of the city—was proclaimed at Naples. **1903** C. Giglioli (*title*) Naples in 1799: an account of the revolution of 1799 and of the rise and fall of the Parthenopean Republic. **1915** C. Mackenzie *Guy & Pauline* 284 They would travel farther south and perhaps come to that Parthenopean shore calling to him still now from the few days he had spent upon its silver heights and beside its azure waters. **1921** *Q. Rev.* Apr. 365 The relationship of the Parthenopean Republic to the Mother-Republic of France, could not be safely dealt with in a public print. **1925** L. V. Bertarelli *S. Italy* 262 Burdensome taxation ..aroused the Neapolitans to insurrection under Masaniello in 1647, but his 'Parthenopean Republic' endured only a few months... In 1799..Gen. Championnet, at the head of a Napoleonic army, founded the second Parthenopean Republic. **1956** H. Acton *Bourbons of Naples* xvii. 333 The Parthenopean Republic was installed by conquest, and the French army of occupation was its only solid prop. **1974** *Encycl. Brit. Macropædia* IX. 1156/1 Thus was born the Parthenopean Republic, which..was the most democratic of the Italian states set up between 1796 and 1799.

Parthian, *a.* and *sb.* Add: **B.** *sb.* **2.** The Iranian language of the Parthians; = Pahlavi *a.* and *sb.* Also as *adj.*

1932 W. L. Graff *Lang.* x. 373 For a time Armenian was deemed to be an Iranian dialect on account of the large number of Parthian (Persian) words in its vocabulary. **1933** L. Bloomfield *Language* iv. 63 Discoveries of manuscript fragments in Chinese Turkestan gave us knowledge of other medieval Iranian languages, which have been identified as Parthian, Sogdian, and Sakian. **1939** L. H. Gray *Foundations of Lang.* 320 We have a fair amount of material in some other Middle Iranian dialects, notably *Middle Parthian* north of Persia. **1944** *Trans. Philol. Soc. 1942* 44 Scripts used in Iran in ancient times.. derive from the Aramaic script of twenty-two letters (not counting..Chinese for Middle Persian and Parthian). **1954** M. Boyce *Manichaean Hymn-Cycles in Parthian* 1 There are in Parthian three long texts which are divided into sections known as *handāms* or 'limbs'. **1972** W. B. Lockwood *Panorama Indo-European Lang.* 236 The Manicheans borrowed the Estrangelo Syriac script and used it to write other Middle Iranian languages as well, i.e. Parthian and Sogdian.

parti. Add: **2.** *parti pris* (further examples). Also *attrib.* and as *pred. adj.*

1885 [see *faute de mieux]. **1905** R. Broughton *Waif's Progress* xxiv. 268 It can be no *parti pris* that has dwindled her to half her size. **1923** H. Crane *Let.* 18 Feb. (1965) 125 In his letter his partis pris emotionalism was too evident to convince his readers properly. **1958** L. Durrell *Mountolive* v. 103 Personally I think we both have made a mess of it, and I have no *parti-pris* in the matter. **1959** *Times* 31 Dec. 11/3 Professor Brinton is not *parti pris* as Lecky and Westermarck were. **1973** *Times Lit. Suppl.* 15 June 660/5 With none of the characters in Lawrence's life is he *parti-pris*. **1974** *Broadcast* 9 Dec. 17/2 Most discussion about advertising is conducted on a basis of *parti pris*. **1977** *N.Y. Rev. Bks.* 9 June 21/2 The ideological *parti-pris* of these last two sources does not invalidate their generally rigorous and sound historical documentation.

partial, *a.* (*sb.*) Add: **3. b.** (*a*) (Further examples.) (*c*) *partial fractions*: the simpler fractions as the sum of which a compound fraction can be expressed; (*d*) *partial product*: (i) the product of one term of a multiplicand and one term of its multiplier; (ii) the product of the first *n* terms of a series, where *n* is a finite integer (including 1); (*e*) *partial sum*: (see quot. 1973); (*f*) *partial ordering* or *order*: a transitive antisymmetrical relation among the elements of a set, which is not necessarily informative about each pair of elements; (*g*) *partial pivoting*: see *pivoting *vbl. sb.* 2.

1889 W. W. Johnson *Treat. Ordinary & Partial Differential Equations* xi. 288 An equation..giving the value of a single partial derivative, or more generally an equation giving a relation between the several partial derivatives of a function of two or more independent variables, is called a partial differential equation. **1975** F. G. Hagin *First Course Differential Equations* i. 32 Another important concept is the partial derivative... Recall that this can be computed simply by treating y as a constant and differentiating F as a function of x.

1816 Peacock & Herschel tr. *Lacroix's Elem. Treat. Differential & Integral Calculus* II. 186 The general method of integrating differentials of the above form, consists in decomposing them into others, whose denominators are more simple, which we designate by the name of partial fractions. **1908** G. H. Hardy *Course Pure Math.* vi. 198 It is very often convenient, in differentiating a rational function, to employ the method of partial fractions. **1975** Flanders & Price *Algebra* vi. 207 In general, $\frac{ax+b}{(x-r)(x-s)} = \frac{A}{x-r} + \frac{B}{x-s}$ for suitable constants A and B. This expression is called the partial fraction decomposition of the given rational function.

c **1823** *New Pract. Builder* 554 The sum of all the partial products will be the answer. **1959** G. & R. C. James *Math. Dict.* 285/1 *Partial product*, the product of the multiplicand and one digit of the multiplier, when the latter contains more than one digit. **1977** *Sci. Amer.* Sept. 82/2 Since each digit of the multiplier must be either a 0 or a 1, each partial product formed must be equal either to zero or to the multiplicand.

1966 W. Rudin *Real & Complex Analysis* xv. 290 The p_n are the partial products of the infinite product. **1972** A. G. Howson *Handbk. Terms Algebra & Anal.* xxviii. 145 Given a sequence (a_n) of non-zero real or complex numbers we form a second sequence (P_n) whose terms are the partial products $P_n = \prod_{k=0}^{n} a_k = a_0 a_1 \ldots a_n$.

1926 BROMWICH & MACROBERT *Introd. Theory Infinite Series* (ed. 2) 540 (Index), Partial Sum of Fourier Series. **1928** R. C. YOUNG tr. *Knopp's Theory & Appl. Infinite Series* ii. 99 An infinite series is a new symbol for a definite sequence of numbers deducible from it, namely the sequence of its partial sums. **1973** D. BALL *Introd. Real Anal.* iv. 71 The sum of the first n terms of a series $a_1 + a_2 + a_3 + a_4 + a_5 + \ldots$ is called the nth partial sum. **1941** BIRKHOFF & MACLANE *Survey Mod. Algebra* xi. 326 (*heading*) Partial orderings. **1964** T. O. MOORE *Elem. Gen. Topology* vii. 126 Many writers require that a partial ordering be reflexive; some do not. We choose not to do so in this book. **1972** A. G. HOWSON *Handbk. Terms Algebra & Anal.* iii. 18 A binary relation on a set X which is reflexive, transitive and antisymmetric is called a partial order of X. A set with a partial order is known as a poset.

f. *partial pressure*: the pressure that would be exerted by a gas in a given mixture if it alone occupied the space.

1857 H. E. ROSCOE tr. *Bunsen's Gasometry* 131 The quantity of each constituent gas absorbed, is proportional to the pressure on that constituent part..; and these pressures may be distinguished as 'partial pressures', in contradistinction to the 'total pressures' of the whole mixture. **1899** J. WALKER *Introd. Physical Chem.* vii. 55 When a mixture of gases dissolves in a liquid, each component dissolves according to its own partial pressure. **1968** *Brit. Med. Bull.* XXIV. 249/2 The changes in composition of the body when the CO_2 partial pressure..is raised or lowered. **1971** *Physics Bull.* Feb. 83/3 The UKAEA's pulsed electrolytic hygrometer..can measure water in a gas down to a partial pressure of 10^{-7} atm.

g. Dentistry. *partial denture*: a denture that replaces one or more, but not all, of the natural teeth of one set.

1860 J. RICHARDSON *Pract. Treat. Mech. Dentistry* xv. 374 (*heading*) Partial dentures constructed in a base of vulcanizable gums. **1921** D. GABELL *Prosthetic Dentistry* ix. 206 Partial dentures should slide smoothly and tightly into place and rest evenly on their supports. **1975** H. THOMSON *Occlusion* xi. 215 With the exception of the canine an abutment tooth for a partial denture should have two roots.

h. Chem. *partial valency* [tr. G. *partialvalenz* (J. Thiele 1899, in *Ann. d. Chem.* CCCVI. 89)]: a partially unsatisfied valency formerly attributed to some atoms in unsaturated compounds to account for the addition reactions of olefins and the stability of the benzene ring.

1899 *Jrnl. Chem. Soc.* LXXVI. I. 554 The author holds the view that, in unsaturated compounds, whilst two affinities of every atom which participates in the double linking are occupied with those of the contiguous atom, the combining energy is not completely absorbed, so that the atoms in question still possess valency (*Partialvalenz*), and it is in this partial valency that the source of additive capacity is to be found. **1937** H. B. WATSON *Mod. Theories Org. Chem.* viii. 105 The reactivity of the olefinic linkage was attributed to the incomplete saturation of the affinities of the doubly bound carbon atoms, which were thus regarded as possessing free 'partial valencies'. **1964** N. G. CLARK *Mod. Org. Chem.* xix. 394 When applied to a conjugated system, such as occurs in buta-1,3-diene, Thiele postulated the union of the centre pair of partial valencies, thus creating a relatively inert type of double bond between C_2 and C_3, and leaving reactive partial valencies only at C_1 and C_4.

i. Dentistry. *partial veneer*: used *attrib.* to designate a crown consisting of a covering of three or more, but not all, of the surfaces of a tooth (the labial or buccal enamel being left exposed).

1928 *Jrnl. Amer. Dental Assoc.* Oct. 1919/2 The cast restoration is indicated in most other locations where esthetics will permit its use... One of the greatest fields of usefulness is in the construction of abutment pieces of the inlay, partial and full veneer types. **1940** S. D. TYLMAN *Theory & Pract. Crown & Bridge Prosthesis* xxvii. 332 (*heading*) The preparation of anterior teeth for partial veneer crowns. *Ibid.*, The partial veneer retainer is indicated primarily in bridge prosthesis when two or more missing teeth are restored. **1963** C. R. COWELL et al. *Inlays, Crowns, & Bridges* ix. 98 Although a well-constructed partial veneer crown shows little gold, an alternative preparation should be undertaken if a patient is anxious to avoid showing any gold.

j. *partial title* (see quots.).

1938 L. M. HARROD *Librarians' Gloss.* 113 *Partial title*, one which consists of only a part of the title as given on the title-page. **1967** *Anglo-Amer. Catal. Rules: Brit. Text* 267 *Partial title entry*, an added entry made under a secondary part of the title as given on the title page, e.g. a catchword title, subtitle, or alternative title.

k. *Cryst.* Of a dislocation: such that the displacement involved, as represented by the Burgers vector, is not an integral multiple of the lattice spacing.

1951 F. C. FRANK in *Phil. Mag.* XLII. 816 Unlike an ordinary twin-boundary, a translation-twin-boundary need not go right through the crystal. When it does not, its edge in the interior of the crystal is a dislocation. It will be called an imperfect dislocation (alternatively, a partial dislocation) in contrast with perfect dislocations which are surrounded entirely by good crystal. **1960** [see *GLIDE *sb.* 4*]. **1966** C. R. TOTTLE *Sci. Engin. Materials* iv. 101 Metals such as copper, silver, and gold have low values of this stacking-fault energy, and so readily form partial dislocations. **1976** M. T. SPRACKLING *Plastic Deformation Simple Ionic Crystals* iv. 51 A strip of stacking fault extending through a crystal has two opposite sides terminated by partial dislocations.

l. Physics. *partial wave* (see quot. 1971).

1953 R. G. SACHS *Nuclear Theory* iv. 65 The straightforward analysis of a scattering problem involving a short-range potential makes use of the method of partial waves. **1970** I. E. MCCARTHY *Nuclear Reactions* I. i. 13 Large values of l correspond to trajectories which miss the nucleus. Therefore the effect of the nuclear forces is noticeable only in the first few partial waves. **1971** *Physics Bull.* Sept. 516/2 Any wavefunction describing a quantum mechanical system can be expanded in terms of eigenfunctions of angular momentum ('partial waves') characterized by an integer l ranging from zero to infinity; usually only a finite number of partial waves is required to specify the system.

m. *partial drought*: see *DROUGHT 2.

B. *sb.* **2.** *Cryst.* A partial dislocation (see sense 3 k above).

1952 READ & SHOCKLEY in W. Shockley et al. *Imperfections in nearly Perfect Crystals* ii. 85 It was first pointed out by Heidenreich and Shockley that a dislocation having a ½ [110] slip vector (taking the lattice constant as unit length) in a face-centered cubic crystal could lower its energy by dissociating into two partials (Shockley partials) having slip vectors ⅙ [211] and ⅙ [121], respectively, and connected by a stacking fault. **1967** A. H. COTTRELL *Introd. Metall.* xvii. 280 The more widely the partials are separated initially, the more the energy required to bring them together to form the constriction and the more rare is the cross-slip. **1969** tr. *Kubo & Nagamiya's Solid State Physics* v. iii. 752 The characteristic of Shockley partials is that they together with their stacking faults can move and slip freely inside the slip planes.

partial (pā·ɪʃăl), *v. Statistics.* [f. PARTIAL *a.* (*sb.*)] *partial out* (trans.): to eliminate (a factor or variable) during analysis so as to remove its influence when considering the relationship between other variables.

1932 *Brit. Jrnl. Psychol.* XXIII. 184 This figure [for mean concrete imagery] is reduced..when the influence of visual verbal imagery is 'partialled out'. **1940** G. H. THOMSON *Anal. Performance Test Scores* ii. 9 The form of distribution of age is not very important since age was partialled out. **1949** BRUNER & POSTMAN in J. S. Bruner *Beyond Information Given* (1974) iv. 73 We cannot partial out the differential effect of serial position of a card, whether first or third or fifth in the series, independently of the kinds of experience the subject had before being presented any given card. **1972** *Visible Language* Winter 57 For eighth graders there is no relation between linear spatial ability and either word or nonsense anagram performance when decentration is partialled out. **1976** *Nature* 24 June 689/1 When the effect of air temperature was partialled out..a rise in adjusted oral temperature was found in the 6 d following.

partially, *adv.* Add: **II. 2. b.** (Further examples.) *partially ordered* (Math.), having a partial ordering (see *PARTIAL *a.* (*sb.*) 3 b (*f*)).

1941 BIRKHOFF & MACLANE *Survey Mod. Algebra* xi. 326 Partially ordered systems with a finite number of elements can be conveniently represented by diagrams. **1949** Partially-sighted [see *dark-ground* s.v. *DARK *a.* 13c]. **1971** *Optometry Today* (Amer. Optometric Assoc.) 15 Partially-sighted and legally-blind persons must first be located. **1974** HILTON & WU *Course in Mod. Algebra* 2 *Zorn's lemma.* Every inductive partially ordered set has a maximal element.

participant, *a.* and *sb.* Add: **B.** *sb.* **1.** Also *attrib.* and *Comb.* **participant democracy** = **participatory democracy*; **participant observer,** a research worker (esp. in the social sciences) who, while apparently belonging to the group under observation, is gathering information about it for the study team; hence **participant observation, observing,** this method of research.

1924 E. C. LINDEMAN *Social Discovery* II. viii. 191 For experimental purposes the coöperating observers have been called '*participant observers*'. The term implies, not that the observers are participating in the study but that they are participating in the activities of the group being observed. **1933** HADER & LINDEMAN *Dynamic Social Res.* x. 147 (*heading*) Participant observing as a technique for psycho-social research. *Ibid.* 148 *Participant Observation* is based on the theory that an interpretation of an event can only be approximately correct when it is a composite of two points of view, the *outside* and the *inside*. **1948** *Mind* LVII. 510 Anthropologists, psychologists and administrators will all offer their contributions, making use of social surveys, opinion polls, official statistics, time-budgets, interviews of various types, 'participant-observers', and new techniques of self-observation. **1971** G. K. ROBERTS *Dict. Polit. Analysis* 144 Ethical and practical problems are raised connected with the concealed 'dual role' of the participant observer. *Ibid.*, Several advantages are served by participant observation rather than external observation or interview techniques. **1971** *Sci. Amer.* Mar. 72 These 'alternative institutions' frequently emphasize values similar to those of a therapeutic community: group cohesion and commitment;..and 'participant democracy', meaning involvement of the entire group in decision-making. **1976** *Word 1971* XXVII. 421 Classical anthropological techniques were used in our research: participant observation, interviews, sociological data surveys, questionnaires, and so on. **1977** *Jrnl. R. Soc. Arts* CXXV. 198/1 Some concern is also paid to academic ethics; and research involving, for example, joining a political or aberrant social group so that one can be a participant observer—the new academic name for *snoop*—or the manipulation of people as subjects for research purposes, may not get very far.

participating, *ppl. a.* (Further examples of the sense 'profit-sharing'.)

1930 *Daily Express* 6 Nov. 14/3 The dividend on the Participating Preferred Ordinary shares is again made up to the maximum of 9 per cent. by the recommendation of a final dividend of 5¼ per cent. **1952** *Prentice-Hall Encycl. Dict. Business* 458/1 Participating insurance is a plan of insurance under which the policyholder receives dividends from his insurance company. *Ibid.* 626/1 *Participating* preferred stock gives the stockholder the right to receive dividends beyond the fixed rate. *Ibid.* 626/2 A company with two kinds of preferred stock might have one class participating, and the other non-participating. **1957** CLARK & GOTTFRIED *Dict. Business & Finance* 268/2 Practically all mutual insurance company policies, and some stock insurance company policies, are participating policies. *Ibid.* 337/1 Typically the participating stock receives dividends at a fixed rate, after which the common stock receives the excess up to a given amount. **1959** L. E. DAVIDS *Dict. Insurance* 158 *Participating insurance*, insurance on which the policyholder is entitled to share in the surplus earnings of the company through dividends which reflect the difference between the premium charged and actual experience. **1964** *Lebende Sprachen* IX. 100/2 Participating bonds share in the profits of the insuring company in addition to receiving a fixed rate of interest. **1974** *Terminol. Managem. & Financial Accountancy* (Inst. Cost and Managem. Accountants) 61 *Participating preference shares*, shares which usually entitle the holder to a fixed dividend, and to participate in any surplus profits after payment of dividends at a specified rate on the ordinary share.

participation. Add: **2. b.** *spec.* the active involvement of members of a community or organization in decisions which affect their lives and work. Cf. *audience participation* s.v. *AUDIENCE 7 d.

1939 *Amer. Speech* XIV. 254 *Teacher placement,..pupil participation,..language usage* are a few typical examples of the monstrosities I refer to. **1944** H. P. FAIRCHILD *Dict. Sociol.* 213/2 *Participation*, entry into, identification with, as through communication or common activity, some defined social situation. **1948** A. L. KROEBER *Anthropol.* (rev. ed.) ix. 347 The second mechanism making for participation of the young in their culture, and their putting into society, is education. **1964** M. ARGYLE *Psychol. & Social Probl.* viii. 113 One way of allowing greater participation is through the use of democratic techniques of supervision. **1968** *Guardian* 13 July 9/2 General de Gaulle's social reform programme, summed up by the slogan 'Participation'. *Ibid.* 10 Sept. 8/5 Participation begins when employees at all levels feel that their own supervisors enlist their help to get what has to be done at their own level performed expeditiously. **1970** *Ibid.* 5 May 13/2 Students have shown no more enthusiasm for 'participation' than did French workers when General de Gaulle proposed it to them. **1974** *Listener* 28 Feb. 276/3 Publicity for proposals is easy, but..effective participation is much more difficult..there is a need to involve all sectors of the community in any debate on proposals. **1976** *Which?* May 110/3 So it's important to make sure that the major issues that you think affect your area do get discussed, and one of the purposes of the public participation legislation is that the public should be involved at the formative stage. **1977** *Times* 25 Feb. 1/7 The unions had an essential role in any system for developing participation.

c. A participating bond or share.

1931 *Economist* 5 Dec. 1057/1 In Germany, foreign exchange (by which is meant foreign notes, claims, bills of exchange, cheques and gold in any form, but not foreign bonds or shares or other industrial participations, except bonds acquired after July 12th) must, within three days after acquisition, be sold to the Reichsbank. **1968** *Globe & Mail* (Toronto) 13 Feb. B2/4 In addition to long-term bonds with call provisions, the new mortgage bank would sell participation certificates on the mortgage holdings in its secondary market operations portfolio.

d. participation mystique, imaginative identification with people and objects outside oneself, regarded as an attribute of primitive peoples by the French anthropologist Lucien Lévy-Bruhl (1857–1939); merging of the individual consciousness with that of a group or with the external world.

Discussed by Lévy-Bruhl in *Les fonctions mentales dans les sociétés inférieures* (1910) I. ii. 78, etc.

1927 A. HUXLEY *Proper Stud.* 77 A subjectivized world, with which the observer lives in a state of what Lévy-Bruhl calls '*participation mystique*', is unamenable to scientific treatment. **1933** DELL & BAYNES tr. *Jung's Mod. Man in Search of Soul* viii. 198 The secret of artistic creation and of the effectiveness of art is to be found in a return to the state of *participation mystique*—to that level of experience at which it is man who lives, and not the individual, and at which the weal or woe of the single human being does not count, but only human existence. **1949** D. MACARDLE *Children of Europe* I. i. 20 Powerful, also, is a deeper source of unrest—a *participation mystique*—the craving, much stronger in some races than in others, which makes individuals long to merge in the herd. **1956** F. HERBERT *Dragon in Sea* (1960) 36 *Religious services*, thought Ramsey... *Participation Mystique!* **1957** N. FRYE *Anat. Crit.* 295 College yells, sing-songs, and similar forms of *participation mystique*. **1966** J. B. PRIESTLEY *Moments* 228 In our early childhood..we exist in a state that a French anthropologist has called *participation mystique*. **1974** *Times* 23 May 10/5 As one who has never visited the Indian sub-continent, nothing I have read has..given me so much the sense of *participation mystique* in a civilisation..the antithesis of our own.

participational (pāɹtisipēɪ·ʃənəl), *a.* [f. PARTICIPATION + -AL.] Involving or requiring participation.

1959 *Times* 18 June (Queen in Canada Suppl.) p. xv/4 Recreational pursuits turn to swimming, fishing and 'participational' outdoor life. **1964** M. McLuhan *Understanding Media* ix. 82 Electric technology seems to favor the inclusive and participational spoken word over the specialist written word. *Ibid.* xvii. 168 This participational and do-it-yourself aspect of the electric technology. **1970** *Americana Ann.* 687 The $30 million Ontario Science Center opened in September in Toronto. The Center features hundreds of 'participational' exhibits that are operated by push buttons. **1971** *Guardian Weekly* 19 June 12 In spite of its premature closing, the participational section of the Morris exhibition was valuable because of the discussion and thought it provoked among artists and public alike.

participative, *a.* Add: (Later examples.)

1975 *Church Times* 22 Aug. 13/4 (Advt.), Many Clergy have benefited from our open consultations on running the local church... Ecumenical and participative methods of learning. *Ibid.* 3 Oct. 6/3 Those who are not so high-minded..might be dedicated to sabotage a new system as it staggered forward to achieve a new, different and participative venture.

b. In business administration: pertaining to or characterized by the sharing of the decision-making process with either (*a*) the lower grades of management, or (*b*) the workers.

1961 B. von H. Gilmer *Industrial Psychol.* v. xiv. 303 Gradually industrial organizations moved towards *participative management*, still leaving the worker in the position of having someone else plan for him... Participative management aimed higher, giving increased status to the people in middle management. **1965** R. C. Sampson *Managing the Managers* xii. 193 In participative coaching, a manager works with the executive, both in problem-solving and learning situations, in such a way that the subordinate retains the decision-making function and learns as the result of the experience. **1966** *New Statesman* 19 Aug. 255/3 There is growing interest in 'participative' and even democratic styles of management. **1972** *Jrnl. Social Psychol.* LXXXVII. 100 They [*sc.* Blake and Mouton] indicate that..participative leadership..can create conditions where work group standards are high. **1973** *Nature* 6 Apr. 381/1 The view that a boss-and-minion society can be replaced by something more cooperative and participative. **1976** *Birmingham Post* 16 Dec. 6/6 Another important feature of such improvements programmes is participative training to change attitudes, open minds and spread awareness and knowledge of control and improvement techniques. **1977** *Jrnl. R. Soc. Arts* CXXV. 671/2, I think we have now moved out of the participative area, in terms of management; I think Bullock is maybe ten years out of date.

participatory, *a.* Add to def.: *spec.* in government, etc., involving members of the community in decisions; allowing members of the general public to take part, as *participatory art, broadcasting, democracy, radio, television, theatre.*

1968 *N.Y. Times* 6 May 46 Both the Negroes and the antiwar groups have made use of the politics of marches, sit-ins and mass demonstrations. But those who practice this 'participatory democracy' can ultimately achieve their objectives only if they work through electoral processes and win control of Congress and the Presidency. **1968** *N.Y. Rev. Bks.* 11 July 31/2 Those who really are committed to 'participatory democracy' and hence insist on participating directly and fully in all forms of social life that can rightly command their allegiance, are separated by an ideological abyss from those traditional representatives of 'representative democracy'. **1968** *Guardian* 10 Oct. 2/5 The prevailing catechism..requires all 'dialogue' to be 'meaningful' and democracy itself to be 'participatory'. **1970** *Time* 23 Feb. 68 These ventures in dramatic exploration are also intimately related to an attempt to bridge the we–they gap in the actor–audience relationship—what is popularly called 'participatory' theater. **1970** *Sat. Rev.* (U.S.) 30 May 9/2 The most dramatic action of the early New Left was the journey hundreds of young people took in the summer of 1963 to live and work in Mississippi, helping Negroes organize themselves... The main slogan of that movement..was 'participatory democracy'. **1972** *Listener* 17 Aug. 197/3 Participatory broadcasting could be seen as a threat to the impartial provision of facts on the air. **1972** *Guardian* 2 Sept. 10/3 The best of BBC participatory local radio. *Ibid.* 6 Nov. 10/6 The BBC is to start 'participatory' television... A trial run of 50 weekly programmes, each devised by community or pressure groups on their own terms. **1977** *Times* 10 Aug. 14/7 That most trendy of activities, participatory art.

† **participled** (pā·ɹtisip'ld), *a. Obs.* [f. Participle *sb.* 2 + -ed².] Euphemism for 'damned' or 'confounded'.

1887 *Sat. Rev.* 17 Dec. 815 Thucydides.., by the way, was a participled Tory, like Clarendon, Gibbon, Tacitus, and all the greatest historians.

parti·ckler, *sb.* and *a.* (*adv.*) Also **partiklar, partic'lar.** ¶ With distortion of spelling to indicate an uneducated pronunciation of Particular *a.* and *sb.* (*adv.*)

1833 Dickens *Let.* ? Jan. (1965) I. 14, I am so anxious to hear the *particklers.* **1837** —— *Pickw.* xv. 147 He wants you partickler; and no one else'll do. *Ibid.* xliv. 482 Vich is your partickler wanity? **1871** *Harper's Mag.* Oct. 690 Ef Pat Role, or any other consarned Irishman, kicks up a muss 'bout these yer diggins, he'll kotch *partic'lar* lightnin'. *c* **1875** 'Brenda' *Froggy's Little Brother* (new ed.) ii. 22, I feels quite well, sir..and I wants to go home partiklar. **1901** M. Franklin *My Brilliant Career* xvii. 150 The boss is so dashed partickler too.

particle, *sb.* Add: **1.** (Later example.)

1881 'Mark Twain' *Prince & Pauper* xxxi. 374 Now began a movement of the gorgeous particles of that official group.

2. (Further examples.) In *Physics* now applied esp. to the constituents of atoms and to other sub-atomic entities (some of which are now regarded as likely to be composite in nature). Cf. *alpha particle* s.v. *Alpha 3 e, *elementary particle* s.v. *Elementary *a.* 6.

1898 J. J. Thomson *Discharge Electr. through Gases* 189 The other theory..regards the cathode rays as marking the course of a stream of negatively electrified particles. **1942** H. Dingle *Sub-Atomic Physics* i. 12 We next assume that the atoms of all bodies are constructed from three kinds of particles—one positively electrified (the proton), one negatively electrified (the electron), and one unelectrified (the neutron). **1968** M. S. Livingston *Particle Physics* iv. 77 By this time [*sc.* 1947] the definition of elementary particles had expanded to include more than the components of atoms. It now included particles created in nuclear decay processes, such as pions and muons..; it also included antiparticles, although the positron was the only example which had been observed... The list of elementary particles jumped to over 30 within the next 8 years. **1969** *Times* 8 Jan. 12/2 This star.. would consist entirely of the nuclear particles called neutrons. **1970** P. H. A. Sneath *Planets & Life* i. 24 Modern physics has demonstrated the existence of a large number of 'smaller' subatomic particles, some of them very short-lived, and it has recently been suggested that they are all composed of yet 'smaller' particles, called quarks.

3. (Further examples.)

1924 O. Jespersen *Philos. Gram.* 87, I therefore propose to revert to the old terminology by which these four classes [*sc.* adverbs, prepositions, conjunctions, and interjections] are treated as one called 'particles'. **1933** O. Jespersen *Essent. Eng. Gram.* vii. 69 Some particles can be used in one capacity only, others may be used now as adverbs, now as prepositions, and now as conjunctions, others again in two of these capacities. **1935** H. Straumann *Newspaper Headlines* 56 Particles, then, are all those words which cannot be looked upon as nominals, verbals, and neutrals. **1964** A. S. C. Ross *Essent. Eng. Gram.* 18 English consists of *words* and *particles.* The main difference between these two things is that the class of words is very numerous and can be added to at will, whereas the class of particles is rather small and cannot be added to at will. **1965** *Eng. Stud.* XLVI. 439 By 'particles' he [*sc.* A. S. C. Ross] means, not only prepositions, articles, indefinite pronouns, etc., but also prefixes, suffixes and inflectional endings. **1977** M. Cohen *Sensible Words* i. 40 Particles..are the grammatical functions that serve what Arnaud called the reasoning and ordering operations of the mind.

b. The preposition-like word which forms part of a complex (phrasal) verb and which can be optionally separated from the verb in certain constructions. Also *attrib.*

1925 Grattan & Gurrey *Our Living Lang.* xii. 80 When, therefore, such words [as in He has run *up* a bill] differ clearly from the ordinary adverb, it is advisable to give them a more precise label: Verbal Particles. **1957** N. Chomsky *Syntactic Struct.* vii. 76 Further investigation of the verb phrase shows that there is a general verb + complement..construction that behaves very much like the verb + particle construction. **1964** Katz & Postal *Integr. Theory Ling. Descr.* (1965) iii. 41 The particle inversion transformation..inverts the particle of a certain set of complex verbs with their Noun Phrase objects. **1968** Jacobs & Rosenbaum *Eng. Transformational Gram.* xiii. 102 Some sentences contain words known as *verb particles* in their verb phrases. *Ibid.* 103 When question sentences containing verb particles are generated, the particle *must* remain in its original position. *Ibid.* 104 The transformation responsible for introducing a particle segment into the structure is called the *particle segment transformation*, or more simply, the particle transformation. *Ibid.* 106 The particle movement transformation is normally optional. **1968** R. W. Langacker *Lang. & its Struct.* 118 The Particle Shift rule.. separates a verb and a particle by placing the particle after the following direct object noun phrase. **1974** McArthur & Atkins *Dict. Eng. Phrasal Verbs* 5 Phrasal verbs..are, usually, combinations of simple, monosyllabic verbs (put, take, get etc.) and members of a set of particles (on, up, out etc.).

4. *attrib.* and *Comb.*, as *particle-size; particle-accelerating, -like* adjs.; **particle accelerator** = *Accelerator e; **particle physics,** the branch of physics concerned with the properties, relationships, and interactions of sub-atomic particles; so **particle physicist.** See also sense 3 b above.

1947 *Electronics* Dec. 82/1 An electrostatic particle-accelerating machine called a Van de Graaf generator. **1959** *Sunday Times* 5 Apr. 8/6 The particle-accelerating machines of the nuclear physicist. **1975** *Nature* 2 Oct. 360/2 Work has thrived on the use of pulsed sources, including particle-accelerating machines, for neutron diffraction experiments. **1946** *Physical Rev.* LXX. 91/1 (*heading*) Particle accelerators as mass analyzers. **1968** *Times* 21 Dec. 13/7 Bubble chambers..are used in conjunction with powerful particle accelerators—machines that produce beams of high energy particles—to study how subatomic particles interact. **1977** D. Bagley *Enemy* xvii. 145 Microbiology isn't like atomics; you don't need a particle accelerator costing a hundred million. **1959** G. Troup *Masers* ii. 14 The 'wave-like' aspects of radiation have been stressed rather more than the 'particle-like' aspects. **1973** *Sci. Amer.* Oct. 104/2 Dirac called his hypothetical particlelike holes positrons. **1977** *Ibid.* Apr. 116/1 Allowance must be made for wavelike properties, such as interference, diffraction and polarization, and for particlelike properties, such as the momentum carried by a beam of light. **1969** *New Scientist* 24 Apr. 171/1 What the high-energy particle physicists are witnessing..is evidently a yet further spectrum of some kind. **1971** *Ibid.* 5 Aug. 334 Even particle physicists and molecular biologists would be hard put to point to new discoveries, insights and ideas rivalling those in the field of astronomy..since 1961. **1946** *Proc. Amer. Philos. Soc.* XC. 44/2 Some of the outstanding experimental problems in elementary particle physics—problems concerned with electrons and positrons, nuclear explosions, neutrino physics, and most of all with the meson. *Ibid.* 47/1 Elementary particle physics..will get sources of energetic particles and use these sources to study the transformations of the elementary particles. **1962** Livingston & Blewett *Particle Accelerators* p. v, Phenomena in nuclear physics and high-energy particle physics. **1969** *New Scientist* 24 Apr. 171/1 In 20th century particle physics there has been a continuous progression from the world of the atom,..through the MeV world of nuclear physics..to the present perplexing phenomena of the GeV world created by the big particle accelerators. **1946** *Nature* 21 Dec. 908/2 Particle-size in silts and sands. **1966** D. G. Brandon *Mod. Techniques Metallogr.* v. 249 There is very little to be said about the quantitative analysis of particle-size or grain-size distributions.

particle board. [f. Particle *sb.* 2 + Board *sb.* 1.] (See quot. 1957.)

1957 *Brit. Commonwealth Forest Terminol.* II. 29 *Board, particle*, a board (sheet) constituted from fragments of wood (chips, shavings, sawdust, etc.) and/or other vegetable materials that have been partly or wholly comminuted and then consolidated by pressure, heat, etc., with or without binders and supplementary material. **1959** *Times Rev. Industry* Apr. 91/3 Particle board is a building board made by bonding woodflakes or shavings under heat and pressure with the aid of a resin adhesive. **1966** A. W. Lewis *Gloss. Woodworking Terms* 55 Manufactured boards..include hardboard, chipboard or particle board, plywood, and laminboard. **1973** *Time* 25 June 29/1 (Advt.), We manufacture and distribute building materials, including plywood, particleboard, sidings, prefinished paneling, and adhesives. **1973** *Globe & Mail* (Toronto) 4 Aug. 8/4 In 1970 a lumber company owned by New Brunswick industrialist K. C. Irving obtained cutting rights in the area and was expected to put up a particle-board plant. **1977** *36 Home Handyman Projects* (Austral. Home Jrnl.) 6/1 Here we show how to make some great seating from particle board—it's simple to make, can look elegant or casual and..it's so comfortable.

parti-colour, *a.* (*sb.*) Delete *Obs.* and add: esp. in reference to a dog's coat, marked in patches of two distinct colours. As *sb.*, a dog whose coat is coloured in this way.

1945 C. L. B. Hubbard *Observer's Bk. Dogs* 113 Pekingese... Colour red, tricolour, parti-colour. **1961** C. H. D. Todd *Popular Whippet* vi. 90 Like most judges.. I dislike a 'butterfly nose', but it is permissible in a parti-colour. **1971** F. Hamilton *World Encycl. Dogs* 200 Colors [of Tibetan terriers] are white, golden, cream, gray or smoke, black particolor and tricolor. *Ibid.* 262 In particolors [*sc.* cocker spaniels], the contrasting color must be ten per cent or more.

parti-colour, *v.* Delete † *Obs.* and add later example.

1971 F. Meynell *My Lives* xi. 168 A man..can paint.. or decorate a room or parti-colour a motor-car.

parti-coloured, *a.* Add: esp., in reference to dogs, having a coat marked with two or more colours in distinct patches.

1879–81 V. Shaw *Illustr. Bk. Dog* xxvi. 185 Parti-coloured dogs [*sc.* Pomeranians] are much objected to. **1922** R. Leighton *Compl. Bk. Dog* 285 All colours [of Pekingese] allowable, red, fawn, black, black and tan, sable, brindle, white and parti-coloured.

particular, *a.* and *sb.* Add: **I. 2.** *particular average* (examples).

1773 *Encycl. Brit.* I. 506/1 The simple or particular average..consists in the extraordinary expences incurred for the ship alone, or for the merchandizes alone. **1895** W. Gow *Marine Insurance* xii. 208 The repairs of damage of the nature of particular average are confined to what will put the vessel in the same state of efficiency as she was in before the accident which rendered these repairs necessary. **1960** Dover & Calver *Banker's Guide Marine Insurance of Goods* 287 If incurred as a consequence of a peril insured against, particular average is made good by underwriters subject to the conditions of the policy. **1974** L. E. Davids *Dict. Insurance* (ed. 4) 203 *Particular average*, loss borne by one of a number of carriers in marine insurance, such as partial loss of cargo, hull, or freight, falling entirely on the interest concerned.

7. e. *in a particular condition*, pregnant. (Cf. *Interesting *ppl. a.* 3.)

1922 Joyce *Ulysses* 411 All these little attentions would enable ladies who were in a particular condition to pass the intervening months in a most enjoyable manner.

8. a. (Further example.)

1813 Jane Austen *Let.* 26 Oct. (1952) 359 Your Saturday's Letter..was quite as long & as particular as I could expect.

10. (Later examples.)

1932 *Punch* 2 Nov. 488/1 He was rather particular what he ate and drank. **1933** D. C. Peel *Life's Enchanted Cup* xiv. 176 Mothers who were 'particular' used to see to it that their girls went to dances with other girls well known to them.

10*. *particular integral* (Math.): **a.** A solution of a differential equation obtained by assigning values to the arbitrary constants of the complete primitive of the equation. Also called *particular solution.*

1814 P. BARLOW *New Math. & Philos. Dict., Particular Integral*, in the Integral Calculus, is that which arises in the integration of any differential equation, by giving a particular value to the arbitrary quantity or quantities that enter into the general integral. **1885** A. R. FORSYTH *Treat. Differential Equations* iii. 49 The primitive then consists of two parts: First, the quantity η, which is called the Particular Integral and is any solution whatever (the simpler the better) of the original equation; Second, the quantity Y, which is called the Complementary Function. **1897** D. A. MURRAY *Introd. Course Differential Equations* i. 6 The solution which contains a number of arbitrary constants equal to the order of the equation, is called the general solution or the complete integral. Solutions obtained therefrom, by giving particular values to the constants, are called particular solutions. **1958** G. E. H. REUTER *Elem. Differential Equations & Operators* i. 5 General solution = particular solution plus complementary function. **1966** S. ROSS *Introd. Ordinary Differential Equations* iv. 95 Consider the differential equation $\frac{d^2y}{dx^2}+y=x$... A particular integral is given by $y_P=x$.

† **b.** A solution of a differential equation which cannot be obtained by assigning values to any or all of the arbitrary constants of the complete primitive; now called *singular solution*. *Obs.*

1820 G. PEACOCK *Coll. Examples Appl. Differential & Integral Calculus* II. xi. 477 A particular integral of the original equation, involving only one arbitrary function. **1845** *Encycl. Metrop.* II. 23 This value of *y* satisfies the proposed equation; but as it cannot be derived from the complete integral we have obtained above by assuming a particular value for one of the arbitrary constants, it ought to be considered as a particular integral.

particularism. 1. (Later example.)

1969 J. E. DITTES in Lindzey & Aronson *Handbk. Social Psychol.* (ed. 2) V. 633 Religious ideology tends to promote a concept of social exclusiveness or 'particularism'..especially with notions of..special election as a member of a divinely chosen group.

2. (Further examples.)

1955 *Bull. Atomic Sci.* Apr. 142/2 The humanitarian theme of the two preceding centuries certainly persisted, but universalism yielded step by step to national particularism which was in many respects naïve but which became increasingly noticeable among European scientists and scholars. **1964** *Welsh Hist. Rev.* II. 147 The breakdown of local particularisms in general elections..was resented in some quarters. **1973** *Daily Tel.* 4 May 18 He attacks the concept of youth particularism, stating that as a group youth has few common interests or problems. **1975** *New Left Rev.* Nov.–Dec. 1 The intrinsically uneven and combined development of capitalism and imperialism were bound to intensify..national particularism and antagonism.

3. (Further and *transf.* examples.)

1912 *Q. Rev.* Jan. 212 A recognition of Albanian particularism would create a precedent of which all other nationalities would take advantage. **1965** *Mod. Law Rev.* XXVIII. v. 616 He may well be right in affirming that regional particularism..call[s] for a redrawing along provincial lines. **1976** M. A. JONES *Old World Ties Amer. Ethnic Groups* 13 Particularism..had for centuries kept the German states apart.

4. (Later example.)

1936 *Nature* 25 Apr. 681/1 The advance of science is along two roads: the first is in the direction of greater intensity, particularism and of empiricism, and the second, from intensity, particularism and empiricism, towards extensity, generalisation and synthesis.

5. *Philos.* The fact or quality of being concerned with elements that have a particular (as opposed to universal) application, or to which no general standard is applicable.

1939 J. DEWEY in P. A. Schilpp *Philos. J. Dewey* 544 In philosophy there is also the need to find an alternative for that combination of atomistic particularism with respect to empirical material and Platonic *a priori* realism with respect to universals. **1943** *Mind* LII. 140 Almost every philosophical term which connotes a tendency to particularism may be predicated of the Berkeley of this early period. **1963** R. M. HARE *Freedom & Reason* ii. 19 Such a philosopher could indeed embrace..the extremest form of particularism.

b. *Sociol.* and *Econ.* In some analyses of social and economic organization, a name that characterizes the particular or fixed nature of a role or element, as contrasted with the universal, general, or mobile nature of other elements or roles.

1949 T. PARSONS *Ess. Sociol. Theory* viii. 197 In all these cases though in different ways and degrees, particularism tends to replace universalism. **1951** PARSONS & SHILS *Toward Gen. Theory of Action* II. i. 98 The pattern variables most relevant to the description of the normative patterns governing roles..are achievement–ascription and universalism–particularism. **1959** B. F. HOSELITZ *Sociol. Aspects Econ. Growth* (1960) ii. 32 We must not expect the principle of particularism in assigning economic roles to appear in complete purity in all societies on a low level of economic advancement. **1964** T. PARSONS *Ess. Sociol. Theory* (rev. ed.) 16 On the level of the research techniques he [*sc.* Weber] used, the broad contrasts, e.g. as between Chinese traditionalistic particularism and Western universalistic 'rationalism', were unmistakable. **1969** I. DEUTSCHER *Marxism in our Time* (1971) 190 The growth of bureaucracy was further stimulated by the breaking down of feudal particularism and the formation of a market on a national scale.

particularist, *sb.* (*a.*) (Further examples.)

1935 *Jrnl. Gen. Psychol.* XII. 55 For the same reason we cannot accept the definition proposed by the extreme particularist. **1939** E. MUIR *Present Age* 160 But he remained an inveterate particularist; his philosophy is not an organic whole, but is made up of a number of peculiar ideas. **1963** R. M. HARE *Freedom & Reason* ii. 18 A particularist (if I may use that name for the opposite of a universalist). *Ibid.* 20 It is quite impossible for a naturalist to be, consistently, any sort of particularist. **1968** D. M. MURPHY tr. *Gelin's Concept of Man in Bible* iv. 63 In the Bible there is a universalist outlook and a particularist outlook.

particularistic, *a.* (Further examples.)

1937 T. PARSONS *Struct. Soc. Action* III. xv. 551 The whole Chinese social structure accepted and sanctioned by the Confucian ethics was a predominantly 'particularistic' structure of relationships. **1955** M. GLUCKMAN *Custom & Conflict in Afr.* v. 123 She also brings out the particularistic nature of their answer to the problem, what is man? **1956** *Jrnl. Theol. Stud.* VII. 99 Both the universalistic and the particularistic strands in their teaching. **1964** GOULD & KOLB *Dict. Social Sci.* 489/1 He may decide to be particularistic, treating them 'in accordance with their standing in some particular relationship to him or his collectivity, independently of the objects' subsumibility under a general norm'. **1970** J. COTLER in I. L. Horowitz *Masses in Lat. Amer.* xii. 426 Through the ..particularistic pattern in which juridical and political authorities are designated, the Pisac mestizos become political figures. **1972** *Science* 9 June 1094/3 The differentiation of scholarship within a field into a variety of highly particularistic specialties reduces the potential for the type of behavior associated with intellectuality. **1974** tr. *Wertheim's Evolution & Revolution* i. 51 Popular emancipation movements do not stress an abstract universalism as their main ideology, but rather strike a note of particularistic loyalties.

So **particulari·stically** *adv.*

1951 PARSONS & SHILS *Toward Gen. Theory Action* 260 A specific situation vis-à-vis particularistically designated persons. **1963** R. M. HARE *Freedom & Reason* ii. 20 The particularistically inclined non-naturalist.

particularity. Add: **1.** (Further examples.) *spec.* in *Theology*, with ref. to Christ as the incarnation of God as a particular human being at a particular time and place.

1930 E. HOSKYNS in Bell & Deissmann *Mysterium Christi* 89 The philosopher should..make sense of it [*sc.* revelation] by some other means than by obscuring the particularity of the Old Testament and by refusing to recognize that in the end the particularity of the Old Testament is only intelligible in the light of its narrowed fulfilment in Jesus, the Messiah, and of its expanded fulfilment in the Church. **1966** G. W. H. LAMPE in Lampe & Mackinnon *Resurrection* vii. 92 The Incarnation necessarily involves particularity. If the Word was truly made flesh then he had to be incarnate as a certain individual man in a particular time and place. **1969** T. F. TORRANCE *Theol. Sci.* iii. 140 God reveals Himself in the contingent particularity and sheer singularity of Jesus Christ. **1975** *Listener* 17 July 92/2 She seems to lack awareness of individuals in the particularity of each. **1979** B. HEBBLETHWAITE in M. Goulder *Incarnation & Myth* iv. 93 The inevitable limitations of that particularity are overcome ..by his spiritual and sacramental presence and activity, by means of which God's personal self-revelation in Jesus is universalized.

5. Delete † *Obs.* and add later examples.

1961 W. HERBERG in *Webster* s.v., Fixing exclusively on the particularities of the current situation. **1977** *Times Lit. Suppl.* 11 Feb. 148/3 Sociologists are notorious for their use of generalizing terms that ride roughshod over the particularities of history.

particulate, *a.* Add: (Earlier and later examples.)

1871 *Q. Jrnl. Microsc. Sci.* XI. 325 It may be supposed either that the germinal substance is universally and equally distributed, *i.e.* dissolved in such liquids, or that it is unequally distributed or particulate. **1962** F. I. ORDWAY et al. *Basic Astronautics* iv. 120 Interstellar and interplanetary particulate matter. **1966** *McGraw-Hill Encycl. Sci. & Technol.* IX. 197/2 Beta rays are particulate radiation consisting of electrons or positrons emitted from a nucleus during β-decay. **1974** *Environmental Conservation* I. 16 The addition of carbon dioxide and particulate matter to the atmosphere by mankind.

b. (Further examples.) *particulate inheritance*, the manifestation in offspring of discrete characters each inherited from one or other of the parents.

1886 F. GALTON in *Rep. Brit. Assoc. Adv. Sci. 1885* 1213 To express this aspect of inheritance, where particle proceeds from particle, we may conveniently describe it as 'particulate'. **1889** —— *Nat. Inheritance* ii. 8 The exact meaning of Particulate Inheritance, namely, that each piece of the new structure is derived from a corresponding piece of some older one. **1930** R. A. FISHER *Genetical Theory Nat. Selection* i. 1 The need for an alternative to blending inheritance was certainly felt by Darwin, though probably he never worked out a distinct idea of a particulate theory. *Ibid.* 8 Apart from dominance and linkage, ..all the main characteristics of the Mendelian system flow from assumptions of particulate inheritance of the simplest character, and could have been deduced *a priori*. **1971** J. Z. YOUNG *Introd. Study Man* xxviii. 392 (*heading*) Genes and their mutations. Particulate inheritance.

B. *sb.* A particulate substance; particulate material. Also *attrib.*

1960 *New Scientist* 13 Oct. 1001/3 The future will see the ultra-centrifuge used more and more as a tool to determine the physical structure of specific parts of such macromolecules as the nucleoproteins, coenzymes and cell particulates. **1971** *Nature* 20 Aug. 553/2 Airborne particulate was collected on 0·45 μm 'Millipore' membrane filters. **1973** *Physics Bull.* May 314/3 Methods for the elemental analysis of air particulates. **1974** *Post-Herald* (Birmingham, Alabama) 29 June A7/3 The Jefferson County particulate count has exceeded the 260 level 82 times during the past year. **1976** *Sci. Amer.* July 77 The emission of particulates is reduced by the liberal use of filters.

partier (pā·ɹtiəɹ). *colloq.* [f. PARTY *sb.* 9 + -ER[1].] One who likes to give or attend parties.

1965 J. HART *File for Death* xii. 94 Jinsie most certainly did not care for the 'partiers'. **1973** *Daily Colonist* (Victoria, B.C.) 16 Sept. 13/3 Thor said he understood the hesitancy of many landlords to rent to male rather than female students. Women are generally neater than men, he concedes, and are not partiers.

pa·rtified, *ppl. a. colloq.* [f. PARTY *sb.* 9 + -FY + -ED[1].] Dressed up for a party.

1928 *Sunday Express* 13 May 16/4 He couldn't quite get over the queerness of seeing Bobs with feathers on her head and white gloves up to her shoulders—and that strip of train on the ground..the thought of a word used by his childhood's nurse to denote a certain standard of sartorial tribute to 'occasions'. 'You look so frightfully "partified",' he added. **1969** A. CHRISTIE *Hallowe'en Party* i. 9 They look good and partified.

parti-generic (pā·ɹti͵dʒene·rik), *a. Linguistics.* [f. PARTI-[2] + GENERIC *a.* (*sb.*)] Referring to an indefinite amount or sub-set of a whole.

1939 P. CHRISTOPHERSEN *Articles* ii. 33 Continuate-words have only zero-form and *the*-form. The former is used when the thing meant is viewed as unlimited or having indefinite limits. We can distinguish three different significations of the zero-form: (1) The whole genus everywhere and at all times (*toto-generic sense*)... (2) An indefinite amount of the genus (*parti-generic sense*). *Ibid.* 34 (3) (In negative phrases) nothing of the genus (*nulli-generic sense*). **1962** J. SÖDERLIND in F. Behre *Contrib. Eng. Syntax* 103 They [*sc.* 'uncountables and plural countables' in zero-form] then refer either to the whole genus of their content (toto-generic sense) or to some indefinite amount or number of it (parti-generic sense).

parting, *vbl. sb.* Add: **2. a.** (*b*) *parting off*: the separation of a piece from a longer length (cf. *PART *v.* 4 c (*d*)). Freq. *attrib.*

1905 J. HORNER *Tools for Engineers & Woodworkers* v. 60 Tools for parting off..have clearance both behind and below. Being generally very thin at the cutting end, this is commonly reduced from a bar of greater width, in order to afford sufficient width and rigidity for clamping in the tool-holder. **1923** C. M. LINLEY *Lathe Users' Handbk.* v. 88 In capstan work where parting-off tools are in continual use..I have used milling cutters or slitting saws as tools with great success. **1950** C. T. BOWER in A. W. Judge *Machine Tools & Operations* II. viii. 186 The parting-off saw shown..has been evolved for cutting off non-ferrous extrusions or bars up to 4 in. by 2½ in. deep. **1977** C. R. SHOTBOLT *Technician Workshop Processes & Materials* I. vii. 84/1 The draw tube and the back end of the collet are hollow to permit bars to be fed through the spindle for repetition turning and parting-off of workpieces.

7. a. (Further examples of *parting shot*.) Cf. *Parthian shot* s.v. PARTHIAN *a.*

1906 GALSWORTHY *Man of Property* III. ix. 372 He could not resist a parting shot. 'H'mm! All flourishing at home? Any little Soameses yet?' **1957** P. WORSLEY *Trumpet shall Sound* iii. 67 Dasiga..finally left with a parting-shot of 'unintelligible gibberish'. **1962** P. VAN GREENAWAY *Crucified City* xiii. 136 Still Creston permitted himself a parting shot. 'I suppose we're going through the whole farce again?' **1963** *Daily Tel.* 19 Aug. 8/6 It was also something of a parting shot, following a 100 yards victory in 9·9 sec. **1967** T. STOPPARD *Rosencrantz & Guildenstern* II. 57 He smiles briefly at them without mirth, and starts to back out, his parting shot rising again.

parti pris: see PARTI 2 in Dict. and Suppl.

‖ **Parti Québecois** (parti kebękwa). *Canad.* [Fr., f. PARTI + *QUÉBECOIS *a.*] A French-Canadian political party which advocates greater autonomy for Quebec. Also *attrib.*

1968 *Times* 30 Oct. 4/7 After many years as the first official champions of the separatist cause in Quebec, Le Rassemblement pour l'Indépendence Nationale (R.I.N.) has decided to join forces with Mr. Rene Levesque's new Parti Québecois which until recently was Le Mouvement Souveraineté-Association (M.S.A.). **1970** *Globe & Mail* (Toronto) 27 Apr. 4 Rene Levesque, the Parti Quebecois leader. **1972** *Maclean's Mag.* Mar. 8/2 It is interesting to note that the Parti Québécois..has managed to affect the terrorist movement. **1976** *Southern Even. Echo* (Southampton) 16 Nov. 1/2 Parti Quebecois won a clear majority of seats in the Quebec National Assembly. **1978** *Times* 20 Mar. 5/6 On the Parti Québecois social policies, Mr Lévesque said that it was a left-of-centre party.

partisan, *sb.*[1] Add: **2. c.** In the war of 1939–45, a guerrilla, esp. one working in enemy-occupied territory in Eastern Europe and the Balkans, *spec.* in Yugoslavia. Also *attrib.*

1939 C. GUBBINS (*title*) Partisan leader's handbook. **1942** *Daily Tel.* 22 May 1/3 Behind the fighting front the Russian 'partisan front' in the German rear forms a skeleton army. **1944** *Hutchinson's Pict. Hist. War* 27 Oct. 1943–11 Apr. 1944 414 In the autumn of 1941 Marshal Tito's partisans began a wild and furious war for existence against the Germans... The partisan movement soon outstripped in numbers the forces of General Mikhailovitch. **1958** P. KEMP *No Colours or Crest* vi. 100 He arrived with thirty Partisans, saying he intended to lay an ambush in exactly the same place as ours. **1965** B. SWEET-ESCOTT *Baker St. Irreg.* vii. 191 Maclean and Velebit were mainly concerned to obtain British training for a Yugoslav tank regiment and a fighter squadron, and to get a fleet of light craft for a partisan navy. *Ibid.* 193 His assignment had been to make contact with the Bulgarian partisans. **1968** *New Left Rev.* Jan.–Feb. 67 During the Second World War I had no doubts about which side I was on in the struggle, let us say, between the Yugoslav Partisans and the Nazi occupation forces. **1974** tr. *Sniečkus's Soviet Lithuania* 47 The Lithuanian people gave every possible aid to the partisans, whom they regarded as true patriots. **1978** A. PRICE *'44 Vintage* xix. 220 He got back in..in 1939... France in '40, then the Middle East... And finally Yugoslavia as a weapons adviser to a big Partisan outfit.

partisanery (pāɹtizæ·nəri). *rare.* [f. PARTISAN, PARTIZAN *sb.*[1] *(a.)* + -ERY.] A partisan feeling or act.

1911 G. B. SHAW *Getting Married* Pref. 119 Such paltry follies and sentimentalities, snobberies and partisaneries, as ignorance can understand and irresponsibility relish.

partisanly, *adv.* (Earlier and later examples.)

1866 H. SIDGWICK *Let.* 7 Nov. in A. & E. M. Sidgwick *Henry Sidgwick* (1906) 153 To ensure no..votes be lost, partisanly speaking. **1976** *Church Times* 9 July 12/4, I wish I could understand why so many Christians feel so strongly—or so partisanly—about events in South Africa. **1977** *Times Lit. Suppl.* 27 May 644/3, I may be partisanly over-optimistic about the ability of the Sussex Constabulary to stand up to Mother Ancilla.

partita (pāɹtī·tă). *Mus.* [It.] An air with variations; a suite.

1880 GROVE *Dict. Mus.* II. 656/1 He [*sc.* Bach] also wrote three Partitas (in the Suite-form) for the lute. The name has very seldom been used since Bach... But in the modern rage for revivals it may possibly reappear. **1925** *Chambers's Jrnl.* 31 Oct. 755/1 In such a week Mr Samuel has played sixteen preludes and fugues, ten French suites, partitas and English suites. **1948** *Times* 30 July 7/3 Mr. Vaughan Williams's most recent work, a Partita for strings, was given its first concert performance at the Albert Hall last evening. **1967** I. SPINK *Hist. Approach Mus. Form* iii. 67 Bach clearly distinguishes the forms in his six sonatas for violin alone by calling those in church style 'sonatas' and those in chamber style 'partitas'.

partition, *sb.* Add: **1. a.** esp. the division of a country into two or more nations; *spec.* *(a)* the division of Ireland into Northern Ireland and the Irish Republic; *(b)* the division of the Indian sub-continent into India and Pakistan in 1947. Hence **parti·tionist,** one who advocates partition; also as *adj.*

1919 *Times* 25 Jan. 9/5 (*headline*) Irish Unionist breach. New League against Partition. *Ibid.* 27 Jan. 9/4 The principles of the [Anti-Partition] League were defined as follows:—To maintain the legislative union of Great Britain and Ireland, to secure Ireland against partition, and to safeguard the liberties and interests of Irish Unionists. **1919** P. S. O'HEGARTY *Ulster* 1 In North Down the Independent vote was counted as Partitionist. **1921** *Spectator* 4 June 713/2 Partition has come to be reckoned the unforgivable sin by the Sinn Feiners. The worst thing a man can be called is a partitionist. **1938** *Ann. Reg. 1937* 256 The World Zionist Executive, sitting in Jerusalem, formally resolved that the Zionist Organization would resist any attempt to curtail the rights of the Jews as defined in the Mandate, either by Partition or any other measure. **1941** K. CHANDRA *Tragedy of Jinnah* xv. 220 Many schemes of partition of India on communal basis [*sic*] were put forward by a few fanatics, off and on. **1945** *Ann. Reg. 1944* 164 This weakening of Mr. Gandhi's hitherto uncompromising opposition to partition was denounced by the Hindu Mahasabha and the Sikhs and caused much misgiving in Congress circles. **1948** *Ann. Reg. 1947* 153 The Muslims having voted for partition of India, the Hindus and Sikhs then voted for the partition of two Provinces, and the frontiers of Pakistan were thus drawn in the midst of the Punjab and Bengal. **1955** R. P. JHABVALA *To whom she Will* vi. 43 Hari Sahni's family.. were Punjabi Indians who in 1947, at the time of Partition, had had to leave their native Lahore. **1959** P. COLUM *Arthur Griffith* II. iv. 121 The Irish people were now shown that this claim would be countered by a move for Partition. **1967** P. M. HUBBARD *Custom of Country* (1969) vii. 81, I agreed I was English, and he said, 'Ah, then you will have been a government servant out here before Partition.' **1971** R. DENTRY *Encounter at Kharmel* iii. 58 There hasn't been a tribal rising..since the Partition troubles died down. **1972** A. BOYD *Brian Faulkner* i. 12 the issue, as in all previous elections, was partition. **1973** *Archivum Linguisticum* IV. 42 In the Indo-Pakistan subcontinent before partition..Delhi and Lucknow were recognized as the places where 'they spoke the best Urdu'. **1975** *Guardian* 24 Feb. 9/6 Just as in every other country that has fallen for the silly expedient of Partition—Ireland, Korea, Vietnam—nobody profits but the politicians.

d. *Physical Chem.* The distribution of a solute between two immiscible or slightly miscible solvents in contact with one another, in accordance with its differing solubility in each. Cf. *partition coefficient* (sense *10).

1861 *Nat. Philos. for Use of Schools: Chem. & Chemical Analysis* ii. 44 Partition of Elements.—Affinities are sometimes modified by circumstances which might not be supposed likely to produce any effect: thus, the more difficult solubility of one of the compounds present in a solution. **1898** C. L. SPEYERS *Text-bk. Physical Chem.* v. 119 (*heading*) Partition of substance between two solvents. **1950** F. HAUROWITZ *Chem. & Biol. Proteins* iii. 21 Synge..has made use of the partition of amino acids between water and..organic solvents which are immiscible with but partly soluble in water. **1970** SHERMA & ZWEIG in G. Zweig et al. *Paper Chromatogr. & Electrophoresis* (1971) II. ii. 11 The paper..acts by a combination of partition, adsorption, and ion exchange.

6. b. *Math.* A collection of non-empty subsets of a given set such that each element of the latter is a member of exactly one of the subsets; a way of dividing a set thus.

1905 J. PIERPONT *Lect. Theory Functions Real Variables* I. ii. 82 Let α be any number of $\Re$; we can use it to throw all numbers of $\Re$ into two classes A, B. In A we put all numbers $<\alpha$; in B all numbers $>\alpha$. The number α we may put in A or B. This division of the numbers of $\Re$ into two classes we call a partition. **1937** MICHELL & BELZ *Elem. Math. Analysis* II. xxi. 1051 The notion of partitions of the rationals forms the basis of Dedekind's treatment of real numbers. **1968** E. T. COPSON *Metric Spaces* i. 12 If $\sim$ is an equivalence relation on a set E, two equivalence classes are either identical or have no common member; the collection of all equivalence classes is a partition of E. **1972** A. G. HOWSON *Handbk. Terms Algebra & Anal.* xxiv. 118 A finite set of points $P=\{a_0,\ldots, a_n\}$ satisfying the above requirements, i.e. $a=a_0<a_1<a_2<\ldots<a_n=b$, is known as a partition of the interval $\leqslant a, b\geqslant$.

10. *partition fence*; **partition chromatography,** chromatography which utilizes the differing solubilities of the components of a mixture in a liquid sorbent (chosen to be immiscible with the carrier if this is a liquid); *spec.* that in which the sorbent is a polar liquid and the carrier a less polar liquid; hence **partition-chromatogram, -chromatographic** *a.*; **partition coefficient** *Physical Chem.* [tr. F. *coefficient de partage* (Berthelot & Jungfleisch 1872, in *Ann. de Chim. et de Physique* XXVI. 398)], the ratio of the concentrations of a solute in each of two immiscible or slightly miscible liquids, or two solids, when it is in equilibrium across the interface between them; **partition function** *Physics,* a sum of the form $\sum_i \Omega_i \exp(-E_i/kT)$ (where Ω_i is the degeneracy of the state with energy E_i, k is Boltzmann's constant, and T the absolute temperature), or an analogous integral, which enters into the expression for the distribution of the particles of a system among different energy states and other thermodynamic quantities; symbol Z; **partition treaty** (earlier example).

1944 *Biochem. Jrnl.* XXXVIII. 286/2 On paper strip partition chromatograms..a number of free peptides travel as reasonably narrow bands whose presence can be revealed by treatment with ninhydrin. *Ibid.* 65/1 We record here some technical aspects of the experience which we have gained in the use of our partition chromatographic method..for the quantitative analysis of amino-acid mixtures. **1968** *Jrnl. Chromatogr.* XXXVII. 97 Partition systems..are much less likely to hinder complete recovery of unchanged, separated components. Hence there is an interest in developing practically useful liquid partition chromatographic systems. **1943** A. H. GORDON et al. in *Biochem. Jrnl.* XXXVII. 79/1 In the present paper we report new applications and developments of partition chromatography* (Martin & Synge, 1941*b*) in the study of amino-acids and peptides. [*Note*]* We employ the term 'partition chromatography' at the suggestion of Dr. E. Lester Smith, to distinguish it from the classical adsorption chromatography. Our earlier term 'liquid-liquid chromatography' was liable to confusion with the fractional elution procedure sometimes called 'liquid chromatography'. **1966** *McGraw-Hill Encycl. Sci. & Technol.* III. 94/2 Volatile, nonpolar substances such as hydrocarbons may be examined by gas adsorption or gas partition chromatography... Weakly polar substances such as alcohols..are examined by adsorption or partition chromatography. *Ibid.* 95/2 With the phases reversed, that is with the polar phase as the wash liquid and the less polar phase fixed in the support, the method is known as reversed phase partition chromatography. It provides a chromatographic sequence the inverse of that produced by partition chromatography. **1967** M. E. HALE *Biol. Lichens* viii. 130 It is only in the past 15 years that the development of partition chromatography has brought a rapid and sure means of identifying plant products within the reach of taxonomists and physiologists. **1891** *Jrnl. Chem. Soc.* LX. II. 1148 (*heading*) Relation between affinity and partition coefficients in immiscible solvents. **1925** *Jrnl. Iron & Steel Inst.* CXII. 492 Variations in the concentration of cementite can be studied by means of the position of the Curie point, which allows of ascertaining variations in the partition coefficient of manganese between the carbide and the ferrite according to the annealing temperature. **1964** G. I. BROWN *Introd. Physical Chem.* xxi. 235 Suppose that 100 cc. of benzene is available for extracting a solute, X, dissolved in 100 cc. of water, and that the partition coefficient of X between benzene and water is 5. **1639** *Early Rec. Dedham, Mass.* (1892) III. 51 A ptićon [*sc.* partition] fence in the same. **1748** *New Hampsh. Probate Rec.* (1916) III. 608 [This land is] to be possess'd and enjoy'd by them..as ye partition fence between them now stands. **1870** *Rep. Comm. Agric. 1869* (U.S. Dept. Agric.) 395 Partition fences must be proof against sheep. **1927** FISHER & HARTREE tr. *Born's Mech. Atom* 3 The so-called partition function (Zustandsintegral). **1970** P. W. ATKINS *Molecular Quantum Mech.* x. 392 The proportion of molecules in the rotational state J is given by $Z^{-1}(2J+1)\times\exp\{-E(J)/kT\}$, where Z is the rotational partition function. **1711** SWIFT *Conduct of Allies* 15 The Violation of the Partition-Treaty, by the French.

partition, *v.* Add: **1. c.** *Math.* To subdivide by means of a partition (sense *6b).

1943 K. MATHER *Statist. Anal. Biol.* xi. 180 A compound χ^2 can be partitioned into simple components each dependent on a single comparison and each taking 1 degree of freedom. **1959** PERFECT & PETERSEN tr. *Alexandroff's Introd. Theory of Groups* vi. 67 Every group may be partitioned into classes of mutually conjugate elements. **1966** S. BEER *Decision & Control* vi. 106 The set of commercial responsibilities is partitioned, for example, into home sales (heavy), home sales (light) and export sales. **1968** E. T. COPSON *Metric Spaces* v. 68 We can partition this set into two separated sets.

partless, *a.* **3.** (Later examples.)

a **1868** G. M. HOPKINS *Poems* (1967) 36 Your parley was not done and there! You went into the partless air. **1904** G. S. FULLERTON *Syst. Metaphysics* xxv. 410 An unanalyzable and part-less thing like the percept. **1972** *Sci. Amer.* Aug. 8/2 Democritus..desired that his atoms be partless, a property they were to have in common with geometrical points.

partner, *sb.* Add: **3. e.** *Biol.* Each of a pair or group of symbiotically associated organisms.

1924 J. A. THOMSON *Sci. Old & New* xxvii. 147 The fungus partners, which supply the water and salts, sometimes get the upper hand and absorb their partner algae, without which, however, they cannot continue to live. **1925** R. S. LULL *Ways of Life* ii. 39 Both partners [of a lichen] combine, when they come to the formation of sexual reproductive bodies. **1970** *Canad. Jrnl. Zool.* XLVIII. 371 (*heading*) The association of *Calliactis tricolor* with its pagurid, calappid, and majid partners in the Caribbean.

f. partners' (also **partner's, partners**) **(pedestal) desk** (see quot. 1952).

1946 *Connoisseur* Dec. p. i (Advt.), Mahogany Partners' Pedestal Desk in style of William Kent. *Circa* 1745. **1950** *Apollo Misc.* p. ix (*caption*) A fine mahogany pedestal partners' desk. **1952** J. GLOAG *Short Dict. Furnit.* 351 *Partners' desk,* a large flat-topped kneehole desk, at which two people may sit, facing each other. The term is probably of 19th century origin. **1971** J. LEASOR *Love-All* iii. 36 His eighteenth-century partner's desk was covered with polished leather. **1974** *Country Life* 11 Apr. (Suppl.) 70 Handsome Partners Desk... The Desk is fitted with five drawers each side.

partner, *v.* Add: **3.** *intr.* (cf. next). **a.** To associate or work as partners. **b.** To associate or join *with* as a partner.

1961 A. B. MAYSE in *Webster* s.v., Him and me, we partnered once. **1961** R. O. BOWEN in *Ibid.*, He still partnered with Tom on the piers. **1968** *Globe & Mail* (Toronto) (Mag.) 17 Feb. 9/2 In 1929 he partnered with a U.S. businessman, Ben Raeburn, to publish a series of 'forbidden' sex books. **1977** *Bangladesh Times* 19 Jan. 5/1 Partnering with Habib against Tipu and Haroon, the foursome played perhaps the most evenly contested matches in Bangladesh tennis to date.

partnering (pā·ɹtnəriŋ), *vbl. sb.* [f. PARTNER *v.* + -ING[1].] Association as partners; the action or work of a partner.

1897 S. & B. WEBB *Industr. Democr.* II. 475 Occasionally the employer has tried to have only one boy-piecer to two spinners. This system, called 'joining' or 'partnering', is always resisted by the union. **1963** *Times* 8 Jan. 4/1 His partnering proved adequate and his dancing showed vitality and breadth. **1975** 'M. FONTEYN' *Autobiogr.* I. iv. 41 This impromptu lesson stood me in good stead after I joined the ballet and sometimes danced with boys as new to partnering as I was. **1976** U. HOLDEN *String Horses* vii. 80 Wait until you try my partnering. I'll take a turn with you both.

partnership. Add: **1.** (Further examples.) Now esp. of relationships in industry and politics.

1933 *Planning* 25 Apr. 2 It aims at giving labour effective partnership in industry and at creating a new attitude of mind to replace sterile hostilities. **1941** *Ann. Reg. 1940* 140 The attainment by India of free and equal partnership in the British Commonwealth. **1959** *Times Lit. Suppl.* 31 July 449/2 It has been a cardinal principle in Rhodesia that the way should be open not for *apartheid* but for partnership, and that the new State will avoid the racial impasse of the Union. **1976** *Star* (Sheffield) 30 Nov. 14/7 Dennis Amiss and Brearley, the opening partnership which England hope will serve them throughout the forthcoming Test series with India, made a quiet start to their alliance when they launched the innings. **1977** *World of Cricket Monthly* June 31/2 He and Kallicharran set about repairing the damage with a fourth-wicket partnership of 90 in 85 minutes and 20 overs.

partness (pā·ɹtnės). Also **part-ness.** [f. PART *sb.* + -NESS.] The fact or quality of being partial or incomplete.

1925 D. H. LAWRENCE *Let.* ? 26 Jan. (1962) II. 828 Any relation based on the one half—say the delicate spiritual half alone—inevitably brings revulsion and betrayal. It is halfness, or partness, which causes Judas. **1945** KOESTLER *Yogi & Commissar* 240 Isolation destroys their very character of 'part-ness'. *Ibid.* 253 A 'vertical' approach which brings to the dry concepts of part-ness, love and all-oneness the igniting spark of experienced reality.

parton (pā·ɹtǫn). *Nuclear Physics.* [f. PART(ICLE *sb.* + *-ON[1].] Each of the hypothetical point-like constituents of the nucleon that were invoked by R. P. Feynman to explain the way the nucleon inelastically scatters electrons of very high energy.

The printed coinage was published after the term had been given currency by Feynman in discussions.

1969 *New Scientist* 26 June 679/2 A similar 'current bun' concept of the proton is implied by the so-called 'parton' theory of Feynmann [*sic*]. **1969** R. P. FEYNMAN in C. N.

Yang et al. *High Energy Collisions* 241, I call the fundamental bare particles of my underlying field theory 'partons'. **1973** *Sci. Amer.* Aug. 34/3 There is some evidence that partons and quarks are the same, although they have been postulated in different ways. **1974** M. L. PERL *High Energy Hadron Physics* xx. 482 We take the partons to be point particles with fixed mass and fixed internal quantum numbers... The quark model discussed in Ch. 14 is a particular form of the parton model in which the partons have been assigned a particular set of internal quantum numbers.

part-owner. Add: Also stressed **pa:rt-ow·ner.** Hence (stress variable) **part-own** *v. trans.*; **part-ownership.**

1890 *Act* 53 & 54 *Vict.* c. 39 §2 Joint tenancy, tenancy in common, joint property, common property, or part ownership does not of itself create a partnership as to anything so held or owned. **1969** R. ESSER *Hot Potato* 42 He..part-owned a night club. **1974** *Listener* 10 Oct. 460/3 A mainly middle-class constituency was told of his part-ownership of a factory. **1975** D. BLOODWORTH *Clients of Omega* iv. 31 This mighty organization..covers two thousand factories, banks and businesses... It part-owns a high percentage of them. **1977** M. T. BLOOM *Thirteenth Man* (1978) ii. 26 Now he was wealthy enough to have..part-ownership of a private bank.

partridge. Add: **5.** *partridge pie*; **partridge bush** = PARTRIDGE-BERRY b; **partridge plum,** the fruit of the partridge-berry; **partridge (berry) vine** (examples).

1843 *Amer. Pioneer* II. 125 The vivid green leaves and bright scarlet berries of the 'partridge bush', or 'Checkerberry'. **1723** J. NOTT *Cook's & Confectioner's Dict.* sig. y7 (*heading*) To make a Partridge Pye. **1757** EARL OF BUCKINGHAM *Let.* Sept. in *Lett. to & from Henrietta, Countess of Suffolk* (1824) II. 239 If the partridge-pie gives you as much pleasure as your letter did to me. **1963** A. L. SIMON *Guide Good Food & Wines* 579/2 Partridge pie. **1872** MRS. STOWE in *Christian Union* 3 Jan. 32/3 Little Love gathered stores of bright checker berries and partridge plums. **1868** H. W. BEECHER *Norwood* 91 Here the little queen took on airs, and sent her Ethiop..[for] some partridge-berry vines from the edge of the wood. **1880** *Harper's Mag.* Nov. 864/1 Here are soft beds of rich green moss studded with scarlet berries of wintergreen and partridge vine. **1913** W. P. EATON *Barn Doors & Byways* 245 We have come upon ferns still flaunting through the snow and partridge berry vines; scratched up into sight by some hungry bird. **1940** *Sun* (Baltimore) 9 Dec. 8/4 In Christmas seasons when holly berries are comparatively scarce, the berries of the smoke bush come as a substitute, and often of the dogwood and of the partridge vines in the woodlands.

part-time (pā:ɹt,təi·m), *a.* [PART *sb.* (*adv.*) B. c.] Employed, occurring, lasting, etc., for part of the time or for less than the customary time. Also as *adv.* Cf. *FULL TIME.

1891, 1896 [see PART *sb.* (*adv.*) B. c]. **1931** *Times Lit. Suppl.* 14 May 380/3 The legislation of 1919..has put some 10,000 small farmers and 20,000 men upon part-time and spare-time holdings. **1955** *Times* 1 July 10/7 The chairman need devote only part of his time to the board. Most of the members should be part-time. **1959** *New Statesman* 23 May 710/2 Are married women who worked part-time for years after the war, but are now being squeezed out, to be compensated? **1965** M. MORSE *Unattached* i. 33 She began studying part-time for G.C.E. 'O' levels. **1973** *Fisheries Fact Sheet* (Environment Canada Fisheries & Marine Service) No. 1. 4/3 Winter fishing..is carried on by teams of men, many of whom are only part-time fishermen.

Hence **part-ti·mer,** a part-time worker, student, or the like.

1927 *Daily Tel.* 3 May 3 (*heading*) Part-timers employed. **1936** A. G. STREET *Gentleman of Party* vii. 134 The dairyman's eldest son, George, went to work as a part-timer at ten years of age. **1939** *Rostrum* (N.Z.) 7 Some grove of Academe where part-timers will have no place. **1952** G. WILSON *Julien Ware* 19 The part-timers were a handful of men engaged by John Cecil for a couple of months at the peak of each year. **1972** *Daily Tel.* 25 Apr. 7/2 Places for at least one million full-time students in 1980 would be planned, with a comparable provision for part-timers. **1976** *Listener* 2 Dec. 712/2 What is often seen as a part-time job is further split among several part-timers: the *Times* has four people who review [TV] programmes.

parturiate, *v.* **a.** (Later example.)

1922 JOYCE *Ulysses* 206, I am big with child... Let me parturiate!

parturient, *a.* Add: **B.** *sb.* A parturient woman.

1956 *Amer. Jrnl. Obstetr. & Gynecol.* LXXI. 1251 A clinical program was set up to evaluate the effects of chlorpromazine on the parturient during the first and second stages of labor. **1958** R. LIDDELL *Morea* II. viii. 192 No birth or death might take place in the sacred enclosure, and the dying or parturient had to be carried hastily on to the hills. **1974** R. WINSTON tr. *Wunderlich's Secret of Crete* xxv. 334 Many highborn young ladies brought children into the world in this way; the infants were ascribed to the god in whose sanctuary these women had been temple servants or whose medical men had taken care of the parturient.

part-way (pā:ɹtwē^i^), *adv.* Also **part way, partway.** [PART *sb.* (*adv.*) B. c.] Part of the way; a certain distance along the way; to some extent; partly.

1859 MRS. GASKELL *Lett.* (1966) 530 Flossy is gone to school..at Knutsford. I took her part way on Tuesday last. **1875** [see PART *sb.* (*adv.*) B. c]. **1930** BLUNDEN *De Bello Germanico* 15 Half-ruined houses, with sacks stretched partway over some windows. **1954** *Essays in Crit.* July 320 It is unbearable for a man or woman to be faced with anything less than a person—and thus, tragically, even part-way unbearable to be faced only with other human persons, where the personal relationship is inevitably enmeshed in material situations. **1968** C. HELMERICKS *Down Wild River North* I. ii. 22 Starting off toward Billings, we learned partway there that the road was blocked. **1976** I. LEVIN *Boys from Brazil* i. 34 He stopped and rewound part-way and replayed a few bits. **1978** *Sci. Amer.* Feb. 68/1 When a peg is partway into a hole, it can wobble back and forth a good deal farther than the clearance itself.

party, *sb.* Add: **II. 6. c.** *spec.* (freq. with capital initial) *the party*: the Communist Party.

1920 *Times* 5 Oct. 14/3 (*heading*) Realities of Russia. Iron Rule of 'The Party'. **1922** E. P. OPPENHEIM *Great Prince Shan* iv. 38 'Her father at present represents the shipping interests of Russia and England. He is one of the authorised consuls.' 'Is he of the party?' **1928** E. & C. PAUL tr. *Stalin's Leninism* I. 168 The central unit of organisation is the Party. **1936** A. HUXLEY *Eyeless in Gaza* xxii. 316 One joined the Party, one distributed literature. **1943** KOESTLER *Arrival & Departure* I. 18 He had courage, but he could not adapt himself to changes in the tactics of the movement. That's why he had to leave the Party. **1959** *Times Lit. Suppl.* 11 Sept. 575/4 The recent dramatic dismissal of the Kerala Government by the President of India..is certain to influence the attitude of the Party towards legally constituted authority. **1975** *New Left Rev.* Nov.–Dec. 65 A whole series of import-export co-operatives..pay a tithe of their profits to the party.

9. b. Phrases: *the party is over*: enjoyment must stop; the happy or easy times are at an end; *to keep the party clean*: to act responsibly; to conform to accepted patterns of behaviour.

1937 M. ALLINGHAM *Dancers in Mourning* xxvii. 328 'You've made up yer mind to go to-day? It's a lovely day.' His wistfulness was pathetic, and Campion felt sudden sympathy for him. 'I'm afraid so,' he murmured. 'The party's over. Sorry.' **1938** E. WAUGH *Scoop* III. 210 'The party's over,' said Bannister... 'From tomorrow onward, I shall get a daily pile of bumf from the Ministry.' **1959** *Times* 7 Nov. 7/4 Then they [*sc.* young people] should be invited to cooperate in keeping the party clean and so ensuring that the letting off of fireworks is kept within bounds. **1965** D. FRANCIS *For Kicks* vi. 91 'Do your dress up,' I said. 'Why? Are you impotent after all, Danny boy?' 'Do your dress up,' I repeated. 'The party's over.' **1975** *Times* 10 May 1/1 Local government.. is coming to realize that, for the time being, the party is over. **1977** *Time* 22 Aug. 5/1 Now in the '70s, the party is over. **1977** PARTRIDGE *Dict. Catch Phrases* 131/1 *Keep the party clean!*.. Don't talk smut or tell dirty stories; don't act loosely or indelicately. A correspondent..commented thus: 'But the speaker often does not quite mean it. "Give me my hat and knickers," she said. "I thought you were going to keep the party clean."' **1978** D. MURPHY *Place Apart* xi. 243 To them [*sc.* Provos] their campaign is..a conventional war, and they want to keep the party clean.

c. An attack, a combat, or fight; an operation, or a unit engaged in an operation. *Armed services' slang.*

1942 'B. J. ELLAN' *Spitfire!* v. 23, I just fired when something came into my sights and then turned like hell as something fired at me! What a party! **1942** *R.A.F. Jrnl.* 27 June 7 Confirmation came through that the big party was on. And that the target was Cologne. **1943** P. BRENNAN et al. *Spitfires over Malta* 18 This party is about 40 miles North, coming South. **1946** J. IRVING *Royal Navalese* 131 A good example of naval understatement for, in one sense, a 'party' can mean quite a tough fight while it lasts. **1959** *Times Lit. Suppl.* 7 Aug. p. iii/3 Classic understating metaphors like 'having a party'.. had their value in time of war when men had to accept as steadfastly and as mildly as they could the possibility of their own violent and horrible deaths.

III. 14. c. A telephone subscriber; a person using a telephone.

At first used only with reference to party lines (*PARTY LINE 2), *subscriber* being the usual term.

1912 J. POOLE *Pract. Telephone Handbk.* (ed. 5) xxxii. 531 Party lines up to 4 stations on a line can be worked on the automatic by giving each of the parties on the line a separate number and multipleing the lines on four sets of connectors. **1938** C. W. WILMAN *Automatic Telephony* (ed. 2) xix. 185 All incoming calls are received at one of the ordinary telephones, from which they can be transferred to the wanted party. **1955** W. GADDIS *Recognitions* II. v. 508, I think we got a crossed wire, would the other parties mind hanging up. **1973** *Times* 23 May 8/7, I heard him say: 'I am receiving a report on that right now' to the party on the other end.

V. 19. (sense 6 or *6 c) *party boss, card, caucus, cell, conference, congress, convention, discipline, government* (earlier example), *hack, image, label, leader* (later examples), *list* (later example), *loyalty, machine, manager, meeting, member, membership, -mindedness, passion, platform, point, -political* adj. (examples; also ellipt., a party-political broadcast), *politician, politics* (later example), *press, question, rally, secret, -state, system, worker*; *party-bound* adj.; (sense 8) *party-boat* (N. Amer.) (hence as *v. intr.*); (sense 9) *party call, dress, game, girl, -giving* (earlier and later examples), *-going, mood, piece, record, thrower, trick*; *party-frocked, -like* adjs.; **party manners,** good manners, best behaviour; **party piano,** a boogie-woogie or barrel-house style of piano-playing; **party plan,** a sales strategy by which goods are displayed or demonstrated at a party in a private house; also *attrib.*; **party poop, pooper** *U.S. slang*, one who throws a gloom over social enjoyment; **party spirit,** (*a*) feeling of solidarity with and support for one's political party (in Dict.); (*b*) feeling or atmosphere of festivity.

1937 E. HEMINGWAY *To have & have Not* I. i. 14 You party-boat captains. *Ibid.* 28, I..went party-boating and broke out this sword-fishing in Cuba. **1963** J. T. ROWLAND *North to Adventure* i. 27 She [*sc.* a sloop] had a long, open cockpit and a small cuddy, since it was his intention to rent her as a party boat. **1909** *Times* 27 Apr. 4/5 There would thus be a good chance of undermining the 'party boss'. **1938** *Ann. Reg. 1937* 320 The men and the movement, the party and the party bosses, the national aims of the Third Reich. **1977** J. CLEARY *Vortex* ii. 32 He had never been able to make his mark with any of the state's party bosses. **1908** *Westm. Gaz.* 30 Dec. 4/3 The one honest solution which is constantly shirked by those who are either party-bound or who..hope for a secular solution. **1936** WIRTH & SHILS tr. *Mannheim's Ideology & Utopia* iii. 136 Those whose standpoints are party-bound are finding it necessary to have a broader perspective. **1910** J. W. TOMPKINS *Mothers & Fathers* 144 They only came twice, and those were party calls. **1935** N. MITCHISON *We have been Warned* II. 209 He had very few papers..his trade union card, and his Party card. **1970** *Guardian* 10 Mar. 13/1 Union leaders must talk to Ministers, whatever the shade of their party cards. **1977** P. JOHNSON *Enemies of Society* xiv. 185 Such a brutal division can only be maintained by laws of status and privilege—a nobility by birth, or by party card. **1882** W. M. THAYER *From Log Cabin to White House* 300 Garfield..was nominated by acclamation at the party caucus, and unanimously elected. **1977** *N.Z. Herald* 5 Jan. 1–6/3 The party caucus has long functioned as part and parcel of New Zealand politics. **1949** *Ann. Reg. 1948* 285 There were 25,635 party cells in all sections of the country's structure and economy. **1978** F. MACLEAN *Take Nine Spies* iv. 132 The Party..[was] using him to organize Party cells and cadres and study-groups. **1935** N. MITCHISON *We have been Warned* IV. 381 It was the best Party Conference he'd been at. **1969** *Listener* 12 June 827/1 The Party Conference defeated Gaitskell..on the question of nuclear weapons. **1954** B. & R. NORTH tr. *Duverger's Pol. Parties* II. i. 273 After 1935 the army played a part of first-rate importance in the party Congresses at Nuremberg. **1977** W. WEAVER tr. *Morante's Hist.* (1978) 341 The Party Congress had been held in Rome. **1881** *Nation* (N.Y.) XXXIII. 4 The slipshod method in which the Vice-President is commonly chosen by party conventions. **1976** *National Observer* (U.S.) 1 May 4/5 The rural followers of William Jennings Bryan fought Al Smith's city legions at the party convention in New York City. **1830** *Deb. Congress U.S.* 9 Feb. 149/2 The provisional power of removal from office by a President..[should not] be exercised..in the corrupting spirit of 'party discipline'. **1909** H. ZIMMERN tr. *Nietzsche's Human, All-too-human* I. 181 The old obsequiousness.. still survives in party-feeling and party-discipline. **1933** *Discovery* Feb. 64/1 The English party system has many advantages, but it also has the disadvantage that party-discipline and party-loyalty do sometimes exercise a prejudicial, cramping or numbing effect on the mind and actions of individual members of the House of Commons. **1961** W. A. SWANBERG *Citizen Hearst* IV. iii. 213 He.. came to be regarded..as a professional radical leading a small pack of obedient terriers whose constant snapping was demoralizing to party discipline. **1873** 'S. COOLIDGE' *What Katy did at School* (1874) x. 175 Elsie is much excited over the party dresses which Mrs. Hall is having made for her. **1960** [see *COVER-UP *attrib.* or quasi-*adj.*]. **1973** G. GREENE *Honorary Consul* IV. ii. 195 A pale-faced child of three..dressed in a blue party dress. **1960** *Times* 3 Aug. 5/2 A juvenile delinquent cousin who appears.. party-frocked in the second [act]. **1929** G. MITCHELL *Mystery of Butcher's Shop* xvii. 192 Idiotic invitations to play silly party games with pencils and paper. **1972** *Guardian* 14 Mar. 14/6 Party game time. What do the following have in common? **1936** *Sun* (Baltimore) 20 Apr. 3/1 A 'party girl's' flat was hunted by police today as the probable scene of the slaying of Arthur P. Hewitt, rich retired contractor. **1960** A. WEST *Trend is Up* vii. 298 He had never thought of asking himself what she was, inside of the hard shell of her disguise as the party girl who would go the limit for fun. **1968** *Globe & Mail* (Toronto) 11 July 5/2 The prostitutes and partygirls who hang around the beer parlors are having poor pickings, police say. **1977** *Time* 26 Dec. 36/1 He characterized Sylvia Miles as a 'party girl and gate crasher'. **1864** TROLLOPE *Small House at Allington* II. xxiii. 242 Nor had they any ground on which to stand, except the party-giving ground. **1963** *Times Lit. Suppl.* 10 May 345/2 A sensible guide to party-giving of every sort. **1864** TROLLOPE *Small House at Allington* II. xxvi. 274, I knew it wasn't to be all party-going and that sort of thing. **1973** *Listener* 14 June 805/2, I am probably..cloistered..when it comes to party-going, but I do hear a lot of talk and gossip. **1977** M. HINXMAN *One-Way Cemetery* xvi. 119 She didn't feel up to party-going and I sympathized. **1869** R. F. D. PALGRAVE *House of Commons* 22 This system is called party government. **1899** BEERBOHM *More* 89, I should be glad to see..his office held by an artist, not by a party-hack. **1974** E. AMBLER *Dr. Frigo* II. 73 Your father's party needed a Cavour... All they had were party hacks. [**1908** G. WALLAS *Human Nature in Politics* iii. 84 A party..is primarily a name, which, like other names, calls up when it is heard or seen an 'image' that shades imperceptibly into the voluntary realisation of its meaning.] **1960** BUTLER & ROSE *Brit. Gen. Election 1959* iii. 17 In the two years before the 1959 election the Conservative party engaged in a public relations campaign...the term 'party image' was continually invoked. **1962** *Listener* 19 Apr. 702/2 In the discussion of the Party Image in the same programme, the Liberals appeared to me to come out best. **1931** G. B. SHAW *Fabian Ess. Socialism* Pref. p. xiv, Candidates with a party label, pledged to vote for their party right or wrong.

1882 A. Bain *John Stuart Mill* ii. 60 That his father would have made an able minister or party-leader, we must cheerfully allow. 1974 E. Ambler *Dr. Frigo* I. 56 The loss of our Party leader..was a demoralizing blow. 1976 *Encounter* June 78/2 The party leader believes in himself, and his supporters believe in him because he is *their* leader. 1832 Dickens *Let.* 30 July (1965) I. 7, I give you this early notice not because there is anything formal or party like in the arrangements. 1968 *Listener* 20 June 806/2 Freedom and participation in one's place of work are to replace constituency or 'party list' democratic choice. 1882 A. Bain *John Stuart Mill* iv. 125 He set a good example of perfect party loyalty, combined with the assertion of difference of opinion on particular questions. 1968 W. Safire *New Lang. Politics* 321/1 'Sometimes party loyalty asks too much,' said John F. Kennedy to a Democratic friend, excusing him for supporting Republican Leverett Saltonstall for Senator of Massachusetts. 1891 'O. Thanet' *Otto the Knight* 266 He can't be trusted to run the office as a party machine, and Milton Bedford can! 1918 *Observer* 29 Sept. 6/2 No serious citizen..can doubt..what is imperatively demanded by the interests of the nation, no matter what may be the interests of some caucuses and party-machines. 1939 *War Illustr.* 2 Dec. 375/3 Even in Germany itself there are millions who stand aloof from the seething mass of criminality and corruption constituted by the Nazi party machine. 1972 *Guardian* 8 June 12/2 The wholehearted support of the party machine rather than just a resigned tokenism. 1977 *Cleethorpes News* 6 May 7/4 It is a moot point whether they do much good because, like other party machines, the Conservative local unit functions day-in and day-out pretty successfully. 1881 *Bradstreet's* IV. 305 The voters of Kings county have usually been relied upon by party managers. 1885 W. Harris *Hist. Radical Party* ii. 19 That great body of the people who were too frequently regarded by placemen and party managers as machines to be used and property to be disposed of. 1930 A. Harris tr. *P. Cohen-Portheim's England, the Unknown Isle* iv. 45 When we get into our party clothes we put on our party manners and party conversation with them. 1931 R. R. Marett in W. Rose *Outl. Mod. Knowledge* 422 After much steam has been blown off, all cheerfully assume their party-manners. 1969 'J. Morris' *Fever Grass* ii. 22 A child suddenly remembering its party manners. 1974 G. Jenkins *Bridge of Magpies* xii. 178 Judging from what I've seen of their party manners, it won't be a pretty operation. 1931 H. Nicolson *Diary* 22 Sept. (1966) 91 Party-meeting at 11.30. 1976 S. Hynes *Auden Generation* v. 138 *It's a Battlefield*..is full of Communists, and a long scene is devoted to a Party meeting. 1920 S. Lewis *Main St.* x. 116 He's a socialist..a regular old-line party-member. 1942 [see *fellow-traveller 2]. 1974 'J. Le Carré' *Tinker, Tailor* xvii. 147 His father was a docker..and a Party member. 1972 *Listener* 20 July 69/2 According to the proposed Democratic Party charter, there would be a national dues-paying party membership. 1976 S. Hynes *Auden Generation* ix. 317 For Upward, Party membership seems to have been a mode of salvation in a desperate time. 1957 R. N. C. Hunt *Guide to Communist Jargon* xxxii. 110 *Party-mindedness* ('Partiinost') was given its classical formulation by Lenin in his polemic with Peter Struve of the middle 'nineties, when he laid down that 'Materialism involves party-mindedness, since it compels us in evaluating anything which takes place openly and directly to adopt the standpoint of a specific social group'. 1958 *Ann. Reg. 1957* 209 Leading writers.. were reminded that negative features of Soviet life could be criticized only from the standpoint of 'Party-mindedness' (*partiynost*) i.e. recognition that all defects were being successfully overcome by the Party. 1973 H. McCloy *Change of Heart* ix. 104 I'm hardly in a party mood. My father is still unconscious. 1976 G. Sims *End of Web* xvii. 116 Being quite sober and not in a party mood they shared a feeling of detachment. 1838 J. S. Mill in *Westm. Rev.* XXXII. 246 The 'Standard'..on this occasion has merged the party passions..in the sympathy of talent for talent. 1945 W. S. Churchill *Victory* (1946) 193 If party passions, doctrines, and ambitions were to dominate our life for any lengthy period, [etc.]. 1942 C. E. Smith *Jazz Record Bk.* 81 The 'party piano' style, a growth that owes more to oldtime blues playing than to any other one source, was already a flourishing development in the 1930's. 1946 R. Blesh *Shining Trumpets* xiv. 337 A number of gifted Harlem pianists in the 'party-piano' tradition. 1962 *Listener* 6 Sept. 367/1 A late-night series of party pieces. 1967 'P. Loraine' *W.I.L. One to Curtis* i. 20 It's been my party piece for over a year now: not *family* parties, I hasten to add. 1969 E. H. Pinto *Treen* 86 Although all these spoons could be used,..one feels that they were very much 'party pieces'. 1973 *Times* 25 Apr. 10/1 (Advt.), Scott James of Westminster distribute a superb range of family clothing direct to the consumer, through party plan and catalogue selling techniques. 1976 *Billings* (Montana) *Gaz.* 30 June 5-D/3 (Advt.), Montana owned firm looking for party plan representatives in Billings area. Work your own hours for good commission. 1977 *Evening Gaz.* (Middlesbrough) 11 Jan. 10/2 (Advt.), Party Plan demonstrators, car available for ambitious applicant. 1848 J. R. Lowell *Biglow Papers* 1st Ser. 111 It gives a Party Platform, tu, jest level with the mind Of..honest folks thet mean to go it blind. 1964 Gould & Kolb *Dict. Social Sci.* 484/1 A *party platform* is a general statement of principles, policies, and issues, and a programme of promises which the party pledges to enact into legislation. 1972 *Jrnl. Social Psychol.* LXXXVII. 46 Public opinion should not be a major concern of political leaders in writing party platforms. 1957 *Times* 14 May 11/2 There was an admirable absence of rancour or effort to make party points when the decision to afford British ships the facilities for using the Suez Canal again was announced in the House of Commons yesterday. 1886 G. Whetenall *Echetlus* i. 60 Let us consider shortly some of these results, the common phenomena of our party-political life. 1910 Party-political [see *cartoon *sb.* 2]. 1947 *Radio Times* 14 Mar. 1/1 Party political broadcasts of a controversial character are to be resumed. 1966 *New Statesman* 4 Mar. 289/1, I am.. unable to watch party-politicals at all. 1974 *Guardian* 23 Jan. 1/1 A plan to shorten 'News at Ten' to make way for a party political broadcast. 1977 *Jrnl. R. Soc. Arts* CXXV. 467/1 Such questions are..essentially political, though not necessarily party-political. 1831 J. S. Mill in *Examiner* 9 Jan. 20/2 They who prefer the ravings of a party politician to the musings of a recluse, may consult a late article in Blackwood's Magazine. 1922 *Brit. Jrnl. Psychol.* Oct. 116 The 'party politics complex' in the mind of the party politician. 1942 L. B. Namier *Conflicts* 200 It is of paramount importance that the extent to which our present constitutional system is bound up with party organisations and party politics should be fully understood. 1961 *Middle East Jrnl.* XV. 6 The bulk of the preparation had..proceeded under the supervision of the Ministry of the Interior, whose officials are barred from party activity and probably generally disinterested in party politics. 1969 *New Yorker* 11 Oct. 53/1 They pecked the hostess farewell, apologized in unison for being party poops. 1954 *Amer. Speech* XXIX. 293 Such comic masterpieces as *lounge lizard* and *party pooper* are of American origin. 1956 in Wentworth & Flexner *Dict. Amer. Slang* (1960) 377/1 No one can call Mr. Bulganin and Mr. Khrushchev party poopers... The Russian leaders demonstrated their suavity and cleverness at the party. 1842 Dickens *Let.* 1 Apr. (1974) III. 176 The silly, drivelling, slanderous, wicked, monstrous Party Press. 1950 *Middle East Jrnl.* Apr. 168 With one full-fledged *journal d'information*..a party press..Egyptian journalism can look to an interesting future. 1803 *Deb. Congress U.S.* 6 Jan. (1851) 337 This ought not to be made a party question. 1885 A. Crump *Formation Polit. Opinion* 152 The position was now far too grave to be treated as a party question. 1941 'G. Orwell' *Lion & Unicorn* i. 16 No party rallies, no Youth Movements. 1959 I. Jefferies *Thirteen Days* vi. 75 A single truck stuck out like a top hat at a Party rally. 1964 *Amer. Folk Music Occasional* i. 10 Under-the-Counter 'party' records provide a traditional version of *The Eddystone Light*. 1968 P. Oliver *Screening Blues* vi. 175 The cheapened styles of the party records which have a large illicit sale in the white society. 1855 Tennyson *Maud* xxv. 91 And another, a statesman there, betraying His party-secret, fool, to the press. 1711, 1882 Party-spirit [in Dict.]. 1941 N. Marsh *Death & Dancing Footman* (1942) viii. 151 He's gone into a huddle over the fire and does *not* exactly manifest the party spirit. 1971 S. Jepson *Let. to Dead Girl* xix. 218 I'm not ungregarious but I'm quite incapable of the party spirit in a roomful of people busy smoking themselves into lung cancer. 1974 J. White tr. *Poulantzas's Fascism & Dictatorship* iii. ii. 113 It is unnecessary to go into details of the continuous contradictions between big capital and the Nazi party-state. 1977 P. Johnson *Enemies of Society* vi. 78 Nazi Germany was equally frank in imposing control of labour and eliminating all foci of political and economic power other than the party-state. 1824 J. S. Mill in *Westm. Rev.* I. 530 Here..the evils of the party system are most clearly shown. 1959 B. & R. North tr. *Duverger's Pol. Parties* (ed. 2) ii. 203 With the exception of the single-party states, several parties coexist in each country: the forms and modes of their coexistence define the 'party system' of the particular country being considered. 1961 *How-to-do-it-Encycl.* (Mechanix Illustr.) I. 12 If you are a party thrower, you may need added capacity. 1962 *Listener* 22 Feb. 347/3 One friend of mine, a compulsive party thrower, had four flats in five months. 1929 *Radio Times* 8 Nov. 390/1 Tony Monke..has been persuaded to execute his best party trick of standing on his head. 1892 *Courier-Jrnl.* (Louisville, Kentucky) 2 Oct. 1/7 The 'party workers'..were well represented. 1935 N. Mitchison *We have been Warned* i. 51 The thick sense of urgency and seriousness which was beginning to show among the Party workers. 1974 *Listener* 14 Mar. 330/2 On election day, my wife and I..did the traditional tour..to thank and encourage the party workers.

party, *v.* Restrict †*Obs. rare* to senses in Dict. and add: **3.** *N. Amer.* **a.** *intr.* To give a party; to attend a party; to have a good time. **b.** *trans.* To entertain (someone) at a party; to accompany to a party. Hence **pa·rtying** *vbl. sb.* and *ppl. a.*

1922 E. E. Cummings *Let.* 5 Dec. (1969) 91 Haven't seen Vanity All Is Fair in? but have extensively partyed with Er former Heditor. 1948 *Penguin New Writing* XXXV. 106 Between times, when they were not drinking at the cafés, partying, writing, or making love, they talked a lot and did a certain amount of thinking. 1953 *N.Y. Times Bk. Rev.* 12 July 8/1 The delegates and guests..were partied to a crisp. 1953 W. P. McGivern *Big Heat* iv. 54 A woman..waiting up for a partying teenage daughter. 1957 M. Millar *Soft Talkers* 97 All those times when I was so ill I could scarcely move and he went off partying. 1963 D. B. Hughes *Expendable Man* (1964) ii. 30 You can't imagine the entertainment she's had.. every club on the campus has partied her. 1967 [see *joiner *sb.* 1 b]. 1970 N. Armstrong et al. *First on Moon* ii. 42 There was so much partying that not a few people wondered about the size of the national hangover. 1971 J. Philips *Escape a Killer* (1972) i. iii. 34 You're to drive into New York..stay there a few days... Peter will party you around. 1973 *Islander* (Victoria, B.C.) 25 Feb. 6/3 Everybody crowded in, the home brew arrived and we partied until 4 in the morning. 1976 H. Nielsen *Brink of Murder* xx. 177 A small crowd..who had been partying on another boat. 1977 *Time* 31 Jan. 31/1 Outgoing Democratic National Committee Chairman Robert Strauss partied along with singer Helen Reddy and actor Alan Alda. *Ibid.* 25 Apr. 48/3 Los Angeles rockers do not lack for private places in which to party. 1977 *Daily Tel.* 9 Apr. 15/6 Mrs Trudeau returned to Ottawa after a week-end of partying in Toronto with the Rolling Stones.

partyism. (In Dict. s.v. Party *sb.*) (Earlier example.)

1842 *Amer. Pioneer* I. 278 Partyism or love of party is the vibratory motion.

partyless (pā·ɹtilės), *a.* [f. Party *sb.* + -less.] Not having or not belonging to a political party.

1896 *N.Y. Voice* 9 July 2/4 This means..a reign of straight-out, inexorable, sectless, seminaryless, partyless righteousness in citizenship. 1909 *Westm. Gaz.* 15 Mar. 2/1 In 1901 Francis Ferdinand was practically alone, partyless. 1963 *Times* 2 Feb. 9/2 Mr. Nkomo, the partyless but undoubted African Nationalist leader. 1966 N. Nicolson in H. Nicolson *Diaries & Lett.* 66 Harold Nicolson, being partyless, was one of the first to join him. 1977 *Times* 15 Nov. 15/2 Nepal will stick to its 'partyless panchayat' rather than risk..one man one vote.

party line. [f. Party *sb.* + Line *sb.*[2]] **1.** A policy adopted by a political party; an area of policy or 'line' separating the policy of one political party from that of another. Also *transf.* and (with hyphen) *attrib.*

1834 T. H. Benton *30 Years' View* (1854) I. 431/2 Look at the vote in the Senate upon the adoption of the resolution, also as clearly defined by a party line as any party question can ever be expected to be. 1904 G. B. Shaw *Common Sense of Municipal Trading* xi. 105 A councillor selected on strict party lines. 1915 Mrs. H. Ward *Eltham Ho.* xiv. 268 The dogged adherence to the traditional party lines and shibboleths on the part of the average British voter. 1937 C. Connolly in L. Russell *Press Gang!* 95 The kind of bullets they keep for reviewers who step across the party line. 1942 Z. N. Hurston in A. Dundes *Mother Wit* (1973) 32/2, I am a mixed-blood,.. but I differ from the party line in that I neither consider it an honor nor a shame. 1948 *Daily Ardmoreite* (Ardmore, Okla.) 2 May 5/4 On party-line votes, this will give the democrats guarantee of a two-thirds majority. 1957 *Times Lit. Suppl.* 27 Dec. 782/3 Mr Dawson's party-line pronouncements on such subjects as contraception or the mediative role of the Church. 1966 *Listener* 10 Mar. 357/2 When any of his whig friends deviated from the party-line, the old pedant laid into them. 1975 J. P. Morgan *House of Lords & Labour Govt.* iv. 134 It can be safely concluded that, for whatever reason, there is such a phenomenon as party-line voting in the Lords. 1976 S. Hynes *Auden Generation* vi. 171 This party-line definition of proletarian art. 1977 A. Ecclestone *Staircase for Silence* v. 88 He was well aware of the faith-destroying outcome of the dogmatism of the party-line, whether in Church or State.

2. [*Party *sb.* 14 c.] A telephone line shared by two or more subscribers. Also *transf.* and (with hyphen) *attrib.*

1893 W. J. Hopkins *Telephone Lines* i. 4 When 'party lines', so called, are used, they should be connected according to the 'bridging-bell' method. 1901 *Ann. Rep. Amer. Telephone & Telegr. Co. 1900* The general adoption of..party lines..has attracted many thousands of subscribers. 1930 *Telegraph & Telephone Jrnl.* XVI. 115/2 The 'party line' is not so rife in this country as in America. *Ibid.* 119/2 The number of rural party lines at Dec. 31, 1929 was 10,322. 1933 *Punch* 10 May 508/1 If you take a real personal interest in your fellow-beings as I do, I should advise all those living in the country to have a party-line. 1959 *Ibid.* 19 Aug. 30/3 The new 'party-line' electronic stethoscope..allows up to four doctors to listen to a patient's heart simultaneously. 1973 M. Russell *Double Hit* vi. 44 He overheard things on our party line.

Hence **pa:rty-li·ner,** one who follows the line adopted by a political party. Also *transf.* So **pa:rty-li·ning** *vbl. sb.*

1940 *Common Sense* (N.Y.) Feb. 21/2 Right now a Communist Party-liner does not have a ghost of a chance in the A.F. of T. 1943 *Sun* (Baltimore) 28 Sept. 12/2 The speech he [*sc.* Earl Browder] has just made at Chicago is fully as brash as anything he said before Marshal Stalin disowned him and other party-liners outside of Russia by liquidating the Communist Internationale in May of this year. 1948 *Daily Mail* 7 Feb. 2/6 When the party-liner squawks an indignant protest he is at once knocked off his perch. 1949 *Virginia Q. Rev.* Winter 44 For the past eleven years he has allied himself with, and never broken on any significant issue from, the 'party-liners'. 1958 *Spectator* 27 June 846/3 Large immigrant colonies of Poles, Lithuanians and others who were not easily taken in by Soviet party-lining. 1966 *Economist* 1 Oct. 39/3 The Chinese here—Nationalists and party-liners alike..are clearly confused. 1969 *Guardian* 31 July 5/3 The..gulf.. between..party-liners and deviationists. 1973 C. Mullard *Black Brit.* ix. 106 Good councillors who find themselves in disagreement with their party's views on race can be removed and replaced with party-liners.

party-man. Add: **2.** (Further examples.)

1933 *Discovery* Feb. 64/1 M. Briand, not at all a 'party' or 'group' man in his later career, also had his own personal following of deputies. 1938 W. S. Churchill *Into Battle* (1941) 15 The Fascists of Italy, the Party-men, are asking themselves whether all this is to the permanent safety..of their native land. 1946 'G. Orwell' *Crit. Ess.* 136 The young G.P.U. man..is the typical 'good party man'.

3. One who frequently attends or gives parties.

1936 *Mademoiselle* Apr. 20/1 The true Party Man possesses a *je ne sais quoi* which lends a rich grace to the most distinguished party. 1963 *Times* 14 Jan. 9/4 The non-party man (speaking in the social rather than the political sense) is saddened by the occasional receipt of invitations... How does one become a successful party man?

partyness (pā·ɹtinės). Also **party-ness.** [f. Party *sb.* + -ness.] **a.** Party-mindedness (see quot. 1976). **b.** The state or condition of being a political party.

1952 *Mind* LXI. 120 It is, of course, a principle of Marxism-Leninism that philosophy should be written in a 'party spirit', with 'partyness'. This principle..originated with Lenin. 1969 P. Worsley in Ionescu & Gellner *Populism* 228 Professor Brough Macpherson has described ..the United Farmers of Alberta,..and its successor, Social Credit... Macpherson..labels this a 'quasi-party' system: not 'non-party', because institutionalized opposition and other..manifestations of 'party-ness' still persisted. **1976** *Russ. Rev.* (N.Y.) XXXV. 69 Lenin advocated the principle of *partiinost*, a concept roughly translatable as 'partyness', the constant referral to party policy as the inspiration and guide to action.

parvenu, *sb.* and *a.* Add: **A.** *sb.* (Further examples.)

1944 PARTRIDGE *Here, There & Everywhere* (1950) 54 A word begins its career as a *parvenu*. **1955** *Times* 20 Aug. 7/7 To such a man the Jews are not only aggressors and common thieves but parvenus too. **1978** P. VAN GREENAWAY *Man called Scavener* vii. 95 Genealogy..attracts a growing body of parvenus.

B. *adj.* (Earlier and later examples.)

1828 J. S. MILL in *Westm. Rev.* IX. 290 No one licked the dust before the *parvenu* emperor with greater *gusto* than the abbé Maury. **1958** *Times* 12 Nov. 3/5 She sounds a *parvenu* proletarian, if such a fancy be comprehended. **1978** *Amer. N. & Q.* XVII. 31/2 Some of the parvenu universities are rapidly approaching maturity.

parvenuess (pāɹvěniu͵e·s). *rare.* [-ESS[1].] A female parvenu.

1903 'O. HENRY' in *Everybody's Mag.* July 59/2 As proud and satisfied as a prince that's abjured a two-hundred-dollar crown for a million-dollar parvenuess.

parvovirus (pā·ɹvovəiə·rǒs). *Microbiol.* [f. L. *parv-us* small + -O[1] + VIRUS.] Any of a group of very small animal viruses consisting of single-stranded DNA in an icosahedral capsid without an envelope and occurring in a wide variety of vertebrates.

1965 *Proposals & Recomm. Provisional Committee Nomencl. Viruses* in *Ann. de l'Inst. Pasteur* CIX. 629 (*table*) Parvovirus. **1968** RHODES & VAN ROOYEN *Textbk. Virol.* (ed. 5) III. 352/2 Johnson..has isolated and identified the virus of feline panleukopenia (or feline enteritis) as a parvovirus. **1974** J. A. ROSE in Fraenkel-Conrat & Wagner *Comprehensive Virol.* III. i. 50 The biological significance of most of the parvoviruses is still obscure. Only the feline and related viruses are known to cause disease naturally, but the pathogenicity of rodent viruses under experimental conditions indicates that other disease potentials may exist... Because of their latency and hardiness, parvoviruses must always be considered as potential contaminants of cells, other virus stocks, and certain vaccines. **1976** FENNER & WHITE *Med. Virol.* (ed. 2) xxii. 424 There is current controversy about whether two important human pathogens, hepatitis A virus and the Norwalk agent of gastroenteritis, are parvoviruses or picornaviruses, but the former seems more likely.

parylene (pæ·rilīn). Also **Parylene.** [f. *par(ax)ylene* s.v. PARA-[1] 2 b.] Any of several transparent thermoplastic polymers of para-xylene or its substituted derivatives that are obtained as thin films or particles by condensation of the vapour of the monomer.

1965 *N.Y. Times* 18 Feb. 43 The product, named parylene, has been successfully used as a dielectric..on capacitors. **1965** *Mod. Plastics* Mar. 113/2 The simplest member of the family is parylene N. A chlorinated member, designated parylene C, is also available. **1969** C. A. HARPER *Handbk. Electronic Packaging* vii. 43 The basic member of the series, called Parylene N, is poly-para-xylylene, a completely linear, highly crystalline material. *Ibid.*, The parylenes are produced by vapor-phase deposition in a variety of forms. **1975** J. A. BRYDSON *Plastics Materials* (ed. 3) xxi. 470 With both Parylene materials the polymers have molecular weights of the order of 500,000.

‖**pas.** Add: **2.** *pas d'action*, a thematic dance or mime; *pas de basque*, a dance step derived from Basque national dances; *pas de bourrée*: see *BOURRÉE 2; *pas de chat* (see quot. 1957); *pas de cheval* (see quots.); *pas de deux* (earlier and later examples; also *transf.* and *fig.*); *pas de quatre*, a dance or figure for four persons; *pas de trois*, a dance or figure for three persons; also *transf.* and *fig.*; *pas seul* (examples).

1951 *Ballet Ann.* V. 25 He has a superb plastic imagination which he showed even in that wickedly conceived *pas d'action* to the music of Tristan. **1957** G. B. L. WILSON *Dict. Ballet* 206 *Pas d'action*, lit. action dance. A dance expressive of a theme or telling a story, in opposition to absolute dance—e.g. the Rose Adagio in *Sleeping Beauty*. **1818** T. WILSON *Quadrille & Cotillion Panorama* 100 *Pas de basque*, a Step used in Quadrille Dancing. **1865** MRS. GASKELL *Lett.* (1966) 748 The neat maid servant had performed a sort of 'pas-de-basque', hopping & sliding with more grace than security to the dishes she held. **1892** E. SCOTT *Dancing* ix. 119 Remember, in performing a *gavotte*, that the French *pas de basque* is employed, in which the first two movements are made to one count of the music. **1948** *Ballet Ann.* II. 144 To see a Basque dancer perform the *pas de basque* is to realise the true nature of that step. The soft, cat-like landing gives an impression of immense strength and of power in reserve. **1964** J. F. & T. M. FLETT *Trad. Dancing in Scotl.* viii. 190 In reel tempo the commonest setting step was the pas de Basque. **1968** J. WINEARLS *Mod. Dance* (ed. 2) iii. 88 The pas de basque lends itself to many rhythmic and expressive variations. **1914** T. & M. W. KINNEY *Dance* iv. 90 In this group might appropriately be included *pas de bourrée dessus-dessous* (i.e., in front and behind); *glissades*; *petits battements*; and the devilish-looking little *pas-de-chat*. **1916** *Dancing Times* Sept. 327 [Espinosa's] 'Syllabus of Dancing.'.. Steps.—..pas de basque, pas de chat, pas de cheval. **1922** BEAUMONT & IDZIKOWSKI *Man. Classical Theatr. Dancing* II. v. 197 *Pas de chat.* This *pas* is composed of *three* movements, generally executed *en diagonale.* **1953** E. TAYLOR *Sleeping Beauty* vi. 114 The staggered thumps of children practising a *pas de chat.* *Ibid.* 116 She was still humming the *pas de chat* tune. **1957** G. B. L. WILSON *Dict. Ballet* 207 *Pas de chat*, lit. a cat's step. A springing movement in which one foot jumps over the other, executed on the diagonal. A jumping step in which the feet are one after the other drawn up to the knee of the opposite leg... Also called pas de papillon. **1976** *New Yorker* 15 Nov. 111/1 The pas-de-chat/pirouette ending of the second variation, nowadays done at the New York City Ballet as a line of brisés, gave her no difficulty. **1916** Pas de cheval [see *pas de chat* above]. **1930** CRASKE & BEAUMONT *Theory & Pract. Allegro in Classical Ballet* 41 Pas de cheval. Stand erect in the centre of the room and face 2, with the head upright [etc.]. **1957** G. B. L. WILSON *Dict. Ballet* 207 *Pas de cheval*, a pawing movement of one foot while the dancer hops on the other. **1762** G.-A. GALLINI *Treat. Art Dancing* 282 Venus and Adonis form a *pas-de-deux*, or duet-dance. **1775** H. WALPOLE *Let.* 23 Aug. in *Corr.* (1965) XXXII. 255, I was not so struck with the dancing as I expected, except with a *pas de deux* by the Marquis de Noailles and Madame Nolstein. **1802** [see *ENSEMBLE *sb.* 1]. **1806** E. FREMANTLE in *Wynne Diaries* (1940) III. 265 The grand Ballet..has fine effect... Des Hayes pas de deux with his wife quite beautiful. **1808** T. ASHE *Trav. Amer.* III. xxxv. 118 The Waltz had most votaries; the *Pas de deux* next. **1955** *Times* 5 July 14/1 The choreography is designedly adventurous,..particularly in the long central section which is set as a *pas de deux.* **1960** [see *pas de trois* below]. **1962** *Listener* 13 Sept. 380/2 Dr Adenauer would have to go faster and further in the *pas de deux* to convince himself and his people that 'the Franco-German alliance is what counts'. **1973** *Times Lit. Suppl.* 26 Oct. 1324/1 Between them they perform a ritual examination of conscience, a *pas de deux* in which they are painfully at cross-purposes. **1978** *Times* 27 May 14/7 This was no ordinary *debut* performance in the *corps de ballet*, but was a solo performance in a *pas de deux* specially introduced for her. **1978** *Country Life* 27 July 220/2 She..rode side-saddle in the pas-de-deux dressage with David Hunt. **1882** *Standard* 26 Dec. 5 The famous *pas de quatre* which had the effect of killing the Ballet in England. **1890** [see *GAIETY 4]. **1897** G. BELL *Let.* 28 Jan. (1927) I. iii. 42 There is a rather nice sort of variant of the 'pas de quatre' which they call the 'pas de patineur' which I quickly learnt. **1902** CHESTERTON *Twelve Types* 43 His metre is a bounding 'pas de quatre'. **1978** *Times* 9 Mar. 13/6 Ashton's *pas de quatre* and Neapolitan dance. **1762** G.-A. GALLINI *Treat. Art Dancing* 280 A *pas-de-trois* or trio-dance follows. **1773** H. WALPOLE *Let.* 3 Apr. in *Corr.* (1965) XXXII. 116 Lord Delawar's two eldest daughters and the Ancaster infanta performed a *pas de trois* as well as Mlle Heinel. **1794** [see DIVERTISSEMENT 2]. **1823** T. CREEVEY *Let.* 14 Feb. in *Creevey Papers* (1963) xi. 190 We went to our *own* playhouse, where we saw 1st a *pas de trois* between Wilson, Hobhouse and Canning, and then a *pas de deux* between Broughman and Canning. **1957** G. B. L. WILSON *Dict. Ballet* 208 *Pas de trois* (de quatre, de cinq, de six, etc.), a dance for three (four, five, six, etc.) persons. **1960** A. PODHAJSKY *Spanish Riding School Vienna* 40 The 'Pas de Deux' or 'Pas de Trois' demands perfectly trained horses which allow themselves to be led by the rider both as regards keeping time and performing the steps with great precision. **1976** *New Yorker* 9 Feb. 95/1 There is a gracious and supple, long-limbed pas de trois..in which the boy holds an invisible lute or mandolin. **1977** D. WILLIAMS *Treasure by Degrees* vi. 55 The Dean's violent about-turn led him straight into the arms of Amelia Hatch... She, in turn, recoiled on to Witaker so that all three had momentarily become engaged in a curious *pas de trois* for ill-matched performers. **1813** BYRON *Waltz* 14 Not decent David, when, before the ark, His grand pas-seul excited some remark. **1830** R. BARTON tr. *Blasis's Code of Terpsichore* v. 354 From time to time these bacchanalia are interrupted by *pas seuls* and *pas de deux.* **1832** F. TROLLOPE *Dom. Manners Amer.* I. xiii. 188 Had Mercury stepped down, and danced a *pas seul* upon earth, his godship could not have produced a more violent sensation. **1839** DICKENS *Nickleby* xlviii. 473 A castanet pas seul by the Infant Phenomenon. **1849** THACKERAY *Pendennis* I. xxvii. 260 Now the young ladies went over to Pen's side, and Cornet Perch performed a *pas seul* in his turn. **1863** MRS. GASKELL *Sylvia's Lovers* I. xiii. 291 Philip hardly knew what he said in reply, the mention of that *pas-seul* lifted such a weight off his heart. **1939** JOYCE *Let.* 28 Jan. (1966) III. 436, I am afraid the traditional *pas seul* with high kicking effects..will be beyond my powers this year of grace. **1955** *Times* 29 Aug. 10/5 If Mr. Ashton has not succeeded in making the love-duet the climax of his work he has almost compensated for it in Juliet's pas seul after the marriage in Friar Laurence's cell. **1978** S. ROSENFELD *Temples of Thespis* iv. 71 Little Chatterley, as the black slave, was admired for his *pas seul.*

pasa doble: see *PASO DOBLE.

‖**pasar** (pæ·sāɹ). [Indonesian *pasar*, perh. f. Pers. *bāzār* market.] A market in Indonesia and Malaysia. So **pasar gelap** [Indonesian *gelap* dark], black market; **pasar malam** [Indonesian *malam* night], a fair.

1958 H. FORSTER *Flowering Lotus* ii. 26 The women ..walked miles from their villages..to the big *pasar*, the covered market. **1959** 'M. DERBY' *Tigress* iv. 154 The *pasar gelap* or black market trade with Sumatra was risky but profitable. **1961** CONYN & MARTEN *Bali Ballet Murder* xvi. 175, I shall ask the cook to go to the *pasar.* **1972** *Malay Mail* (Kuala Lumpur) 25 May 4/5 The pasar malam in Gurney Drive will end on Tuesday.

Pascal (pæska·l). [The name of Blaise *Pascal* (1623–62), French scholar and scientist.] **1.** Math. *Pascal's triangle*: a triangular array of numbers in which those at the ends of the rows are 1 and each of the others is the sum of the nearest two numbers in the row above, the apex, 1, being at the top. [Described in Pascal's *Traité du Triangle Arithmetique* (1665).]

1886 G. CHRYSTAL *Algebra* I. iv. 65 (*heading*) Pascal's triangle generalised. **1977** R. E. MEGILL *Introd. Risk Analysis* vii. 67 You can construct a triangle, called Pascal's triangle, from the binomial expansions just reviewed.

2. Written **pascal** (pæ·skăl). The unit of pressure in the M.K.S. system (now incorporated into the International System of Units), equal to one newton per square metre (approximately 0·000,145 p.s.i., $9{\cdot}9 \times 10^{-6}$ atmosphere, or 0·102 kilogramme-force per sq. cm.). Abbrev. Pa.

1956 KAYE & LABY *Tables Physical & Chem. Constants* (ed. 11) 7 (*table*) Pascal. **1964** H. S. HVISTENDAHL *Engin. Units* iii. 29 In the French decree of May 3rd, 1961, the name pascal (Pa), is adopted for the N/m^2,..although that name has not yet received international recognition. **1972** *Physics Bull.* Jan. 40/1 The 14th General conference of Weights and Measures (CGPM) met in Paris on 4–7 October 1971... Amongst the main decisions taken by the conference were the final adoption..of the 'pascal' (Pa) as the SI unit of pressure ($N\,m^{-2}$) and the 'siemens' (S) as the SI unit of conductance (Ω^{-1}). **1974** *B.S.I. News* Sept. 12/2 The pascal is advised by the aircraft industry..as the best unit to use in their fields. **1975** *Sci. Amer.* Feb. 110/2 The manual uses the MKS pressure unit, the pascal, almost throughout. **1976** *Nature* 29 Apr. 745/3 A Pascal of pressure on top of your head Is the same push that butter exerts on sliced bread.

Pascalian (pæskā·liăn), *sb.* and *a.* [f. prec. + -IAN.] **A.** *sb.* An admirer or adherent of Pascal (see prec. (etym.)); an interpreter of his works. **B.** *adj.* Of or pertaining to Pascal or to his ideas and philosophy.

1929 A. HUXLEY *Do What you Will* 235, I now propose to write of Pascal. As a positivist first of all... More sympathetically next, in the guise of a Pascalian. **1930** tr. *Chevalier's Pascal* i. 26 Charron's work contained, as it were, the germ of Pascalian apologetics; at any rate we find in it a great deal of material that Pascal was to utilize after changing its order. **1937** A. HUXLEY *Ends & Means* xv. 304 There is, however, an element of truth in the Pascalian doctrine. **1937** *Sunday Times* 25 Apr. 8/3 The truth is Pascalian Christianity is only fit for heroes and saints; it is not a possible life for ordinary men. **1948** *Scottish Jrnl. Theol.* I. 98 A full length study of Pascal by an established Pascalian scholar. **1971** G. STEINER *In Bluebeard's Castle* iii. 64 We are forced now to return to an earlier, Pascalian pessimism, to a model of history whose logic derives from a postulate of original sin. **1973** *Listener* 6 Sept. 298/1 The man who finds himself suddenly independent in this way will then fall prey to Pascalian despair, existential anguish, dereliction. **1977** *N.Y. Rev. Bks.* 14 Apr. 26/4 Sennett is thus an atheist about social science, but a Pascalian about society.

Pascarete, var. *PAXARETE.

Pa·schaltide. [f. PASCHAL *a.* + TIDE *sb.*] The period following Easter Sunday, esp. Easter Week.

1894 G. F. X. GRIFFITH tr. *Fouard's St. Paul* xv. 349 The octave of Paschal-tide, a rite of Jewish origin. **1974** *Oxf. Dict. Chr. Ch.* (ed. 2) 1038/1 *Paschaltide*, the period in the ecclesiastical year immediately after Easter.

Paschen[1] (pæ·ʃən). *Physics.* The name of L. C. H. Friedrich *Paschen* (1865–1947), German physicist, used *attrib.* and in the possessive to designate certain phenomena he discovered, as **Paschen('s) curve,** a graph of the breakdown voltage in a gas against the product of pressure and interelectrode distance; **Paschen's law,** the law that at a constant temperature the breakdown voltage in any given gas depends only on the product of the pressure and the interelectrode distance (formulated by Paschen in *Ann. d. Physik und Chem.* (1889) XXXVII. 90); **Paschen series,** a series of lines in the infra-red part of the spectrum of atomic hydrogen, with wave numbers represented by $R(1/3^2 - 1/m^2)$ (where R is the Rydberg constant and $m = 4, 5, \ldots$), of which the first line has a wavelength of 1857 nanometres and the series limit is at 821 nanometres.

1903 *Proc. R. Soc.* LXXI. 375 A general application of Paschen's law demands that the minimum spark potential must be a physical constant for each gas. **1922** Paschen series [see *LYMAN]. **1957** A. F. MONYPENNY tr. *Penning's Electr. Discharges in Gases* vi. 32 (*caption*) Paschen curves for breakdown between flat iron plates in various gases and gas mixtures. **1967** *IEEE Trans. Electr. Insulation* II. 82/1 In accordance with Paschen's curve, equally large discharge voltages could also result for very small voids. **1967** Paschen series [see *LYMAN]. **1968** G. F. WESTON *Cold Cathode Glow Discharge Tubes* ii. 59 For the case of a non-uniform field Paschen's law relating breakdown to gap width and pressure no longer holds.

Paschen[2] (pæ·ʃən). *Med.* The name of Enrique *Paschen* (1860–1936), Mexican-born bacteriologist, used *attrib.* in **Paschen body,** each of the particles making up one of the cytoplasmic inclusions found in epithelial

cells in cases of smallpox (described by Paschen in *Münch. med. Wochenschr.* (1906) 4 Dec. 2391).
1931 *Jrnl. Path. & Bacteriol.* XXXIV. 122 A preparation is shown which demonstrates the presence of elementary bodies precisely similar to the Paschen and Borrel bodies. **1974** J. D. ACTON et al. *Fund. Med. Virol.* xi. 167 Although the poxviruses are DNA viruses, they replicate in the cytoplasm and produce characteristic cytoplasmic inclusions called Guarnieri bodies; the inclusions are composed of a dense aggregation of many virus particles. Virus particles are also referred to as 'elementary bodies' or Paschen bodies.

Paschen–Back effect (pæ:ʃən bæ·k). *Physics.* [f. *PASCHEN[1] + the name of Ernst E. A. *Back* (1881–1959), German physicist, who jointly published a description of the effect in 1913 (*Ann. der Physik* XXXIX. 897).] An effect observed when a source of spectral lines is in a magnetic field so strong that the resultant splitting of each line is comparable in magnitude to the separation of the lines in a multiplet, the spacing of the lines corresponding to the normal Zeeman effect rather than the anomalous Zeeman effect generally observed at lower field strengths.
1923 H. L. BROSE tr. *Sommerfeld's Atomic Struct. & Spectral Lines* vi. 389 The Paschen–Back effect links together only such lines as belong together in a series as multiplicities. **1964** G. W. KING *Spectrosc. & Molecular Struct.* iii. 109 A magnetic field that would be strong enough to produce a resolvable splitting of nuclear Zeeman lines is usually more than sufficient to uncouple **I*** from **J*** and cause them to precess independently around the *z* axis, giving a nuclear Paschen–Back effect instead. **1970** G. K. WOODGATE *Elem. Atomic Struct.* viii. 150 This strong-field limit of the Zeeman effect is called the Paschen–Back effect.

pascual, *a.* Add: esp. describing plants growing in pasture or grassland. Also as *sb.*, a pascual plant.
1847 H. C. WATSON *Cybele Britannica* I. 65 The proposed series of terms runs thus:—1. Pratal... 2. Pascual. —Plants of pastures and grassy commons, where the herbage is usually less luxuriant than in the meadowlands, [etc.]. *Ibid.* 67 The pratal plants are occasionally pascual plants, as Phleum pratense; the pascuals are in turn ericetals, as Prunella vulgaris. **1926** G. C. DRUCE in J. J. Walker *Nat. Hist. Oxf. Distr.* 96 *Carex tomentosa* L., usually classed as a paludal, is a pascual in its only known Oxford locality near Burford.

Pascuan (pæ·skiuăn), *a.* and *sb.* [a. F. *Pascuan* (H. Lavachery 1935).] **A.** *adj.* Of or pertaining to Easter Island in the South Pacific, its inhabitants, or its script. **B.** *sb.* **a.** A native or inhabitant of Easter Island. **b.** The script used by the inhabitants of Easter Island. So **pascuense** *a.* and *sb.*
[**1935** H. LAVACHERY *Ile de Pâques* i. 16 Ici la naiveté des Espagnols apparaît non moins admirable que l'ingéniosité des Pascuans.] **1940** B. BONNERJEA in *N. & Q.* 17 Feb. 110/2, I have used the term 'Pascuans'—following Lavachery—in place of the more cumbersome English expression 'Easter Islanders'. *Ibid.* 111/1 It is an undeniable fact that the Pascuans are Polynesians. *Ibid.*, Since the..discovery of the Pascuan script, numerous articles have been written on the subject. **1948** D. DIRINGER *Alphabet* 137 According to local traditions, Hotumatua, an ancestor of the Pascuans..came to the island.. and brought with him 67 inscribed wooden tablets. **1960** J. FUENTES *Dict. & Gram. Easter Island Lang.* 591 The spoken language keeps some of the old Pascuense characteristics, that is to say, the Pascuense before assimilating modern foreign expressions.

‖**pas devant les enfants** (pā dəvaṅ lezaṅfaṅ). [F.] Not in front of the children, used of an expression or action that requires discretion. Also *transf.* and *ellipt.*, *pas devant*, and as *adj.*
1951 N. MITFORD *Blessing* I. xv. 153 'Adultery is for when you're older, darling.' 'Oh I see. A sort of pas devant thing?' **1953** D. PARRY *Going Up—Going Down* i. 21 Mrs. Tyndale was holding forth in that extraordinary *pas-devant* French which the upper-class English used to speak so confidently. **1955** L. P. HARTLEY *Perfect Woman* vii. 65 'There's something I want to say to you. *Mais pas devant les enfants,*' he went on heavily. **1958** M. SPARK *Robinson* v. 51 'Pas devant,' said Tom Wells, casting his eyes towards the child. **1962** *Listener* 7 June 975/2 There is a sickening folklore of *pas devant*—'not in front of the children'—which excludes children from some of the very conversations that would show their parents as people with strong interests. **1962** *Times* 6 Aug. 9/3 It will be a mistake for the War Office to adopt a *pas devant les enfants* attitude. **1968** J. FLEMING *Kill or Cure* vii. 87 *Pas devant les enfants*; such bad form having rows before one's—friends. **1971** O. NORTON *Corpse-Bird Cries* v. 85 '*Pas devant les opérateurs*,' I said. I knew what manual [telephone] exchanges can be. **1974** J. JOHNSTON *How Many Miles to Babylon?* 7 'Dr. Desmond is an ass.' 'Frederick, pas devant —.' **1978** D. BLOODWORTH *Crosstalk* xxxix. 311 You mean *pas devant les enfants terribles*.. Not in front of the CIA?

pasear (paseā·r), *v.* and *sb.* *slang* and *U.S. dial.* [See *PASEO.] **A.** *vb. intr.* To take a paseo or walk. **B.** *sb.* = *PASEO. Also *attrib.*
1840 R. H. DANA *Two Yrs. before Mast* xxviii. 313 He was going to paseár with our captain a little. **1847** *Calif. Star* (San Francisco) 24 July 2/3, I am told this *pasear* over the mountains, will cost the Commodore [Stockton] five thousand dollars. **1878** B. HARTE *Man on Beach* 112, I was reck'nin' on taking a little *pasear* with you. **1892** STEVENSON & OSBOURNE *Wrecker* xii. 192, I tell you, Mr. Dodd, it was a queer thing to see me and the old lady taking a *pasear* in the garden, and the old man scowling at us over the pickets. **1903** CONRAD & HUEFFER *Romance* III. iii. 141, I just come from taking a pasear that way. **1914** *Sunset* July 64/1 It was the pasear madness that made despairing feet give way to auto tires—it is the undiminishing nature of pasear joys that is stretching the eighteen-million-dollar highway through the state. **1948** *Popular Western* June 16/2 Yuh're takin' a little *pasear* to the penitentiary in Walla Walla.

pasel, var. *PASSEL.

‖**paseo** (pāse·o). [Sp. *paseo* walk, *pasear* to walk.] In Spain and southwestern parts of the United States, a walk taken at a leisurely pace for exercise, amusement, or the like; any trip or outing of a similar nature; (concretely) a street or promenade; a parade, a procession, *spec.* at a bull-fight.
1832 W. IRVING *Leg. Alhambra* 111 An alameda, or public walk..not so fashionable as the more modern and splendid paseo of the Xenil. **1840** R. H. DANA *Two Yrs. before Mast* xxii. 219 The theme of..conversation..in our afternoon's *paséo* upon the beach, was the ship. **1897** 'H. S. MERRIMAN' *In Kedar's Tents* xviii. 205 He..proposed to Julia that they should take a 'paseo' in the garden. **1902** *Out West* Dec. 683 Such bosoming of motherly hills, knee-deep with winter wild flowers, as you may have unrolled to you in an afternoon's *paseo* from the metropolis. **1920** *Glasgow Herald* 22 Sept. 8/5 The greater companies..have built model towns, intersected with finely laid-out paseos and plazas, for their employees. **1927** E. HEMINGWAY *Men without Women* (1928) 29 They formed up for the paseo as soon as the bull had gone through. **1950** G. BRENAN *Face of Spain* ix. 187 It was the hour of the evening *paseo*: the girls were in their best frocks; the young men had oiled and smoothed their hair. **1967** MCCORMICK & MASCAREÑAS *Compl. Aficionado* iii. 72 You will now show me how to walk in the *paseo*. **1974** *Times* 2 May 17/2 Less than a decade ago, the *paseos* and boulevards were crowded on sunny days with strollers... Madrid has sacrificed these shady strolling places. **1976** E. P. BENSON *Bulls of Ronda* iv. 25 The stewards..led the *paseo*; the matadors were next, followed by the *bandilleros*... The bull..came charging into the arena. **1977** P. SOMERVILLE-LARGE *Eagles near Carcase* v. 91 Evening was being heralded..by the emergence of the *paseo*, if the three youths..and the four fat girls in black could be so described.

pash (pæʃ), *sb.* and *a.* *colloq.* **A.** *sb.* Abbreviation of PASSION; esp. in phr. *to have a pash for*, to be infatuated with, to have a 'crush' on; *transf.* a person who is the object of an infatuation. **B.** *adj.* Abbreviation of PASSIONATE *a.*
1914 *N.Y. World Mag.* 1 Nov. 5/6 There wasn't much 'pash' about it. **1920** F. SCOTT FITZGERALD *This Side of Paradise* (1921) 52 That isn't as pash as some of them. **1922** C. E. M. JOAD *Highbrows* iii. 102, I have met such a duck of a man. You'll never believe! I've quite a pash for him. **1924** P. MARKS *Plastic Age* 24 Let's go the movies.. Gloria Nielsen is there and she's a pash baby. **1930** A. HUXLEY *Brief Candles* 217 Miss Figgis, the classical mistress, had been her pash for more than a year. **1930** WODEHOUSE *Very Good, Jeeves!* x. 257 The last bloke in the world..who you would think would ever fall a victim to the divine pash. **1934** G. GREENE *It's a Battlefield* 168 When you've got a pash for someone like I have, anybody's better than nothing. **1937** AUDEN & MACNEICE *Lett. from Iceland* 17 Sometimes containing frank demands for cash, Sometimes sly hints at a platonic pash. **1952** [see *CRUSH *sb.* 2 d]. **1955** AUDEN *Shield of Achilles* i. 30 As when past Iseult's tower you floated The willow pash-notes of wanted Tristram. **1972** J. MCCLURE *Caterpillar Cop* xiii. 209 'You know her then?' 'Oh sure. Had a pash for her big sister once.' **1975** J. HITCHMAN *Such a Strange Lady* iii. 36 In her efforts to get over her 'pash' on Dr. Allen she became extremely bossy.

Pashto. Now the usual spelling of PUSHTOO, -TU *sb.* and *a.* in Dict. and Suppl.

Pashtun, var. *PAKHTUN.

pasmo (pæ·zmo). [Amer. Sp., f. Sp. *pasmo* spasm.] A disease of flax, first reported from the Argentine in 1911, caused by the fungus *Mycosphaerella linorum*, and distinguished by circular brown or yellowish lesions on the leaves and stems of the plants affected. Also *attrib.*
1926 W. E. BRENTZEL in *Jrnl. Agric. Res.* XXXII. 25 (*title*) The pasmo disease of flax. *Ibid.*, The disease of flax called 'pasmo' in South America..caused great injury to flax in Argentina. **1942** *N.Z. Jrnl. Sci. & Technol.* A. XXIV. 102 Pasmo disease of flax is of almost world-wide occurrence. **1946** *Nature* 16 Nov. 723/1 The dreaded Pasmo disease was first described from the Argentine in 1911, reached Europe in 1936, and spread to five countries by 1942. **1958** *New Biol.* XXVII. 21 A number of fungi responsible for causing diseases of flax are seed-borne. The principal parasites in this group and the diseases they cause are..*Botrytis cinerea* Fr. (grey mould),..and *Sphaerella linorum* Wollenw. (pasmo). **1974** E. C. STACEY *Peace Country Heritage* ii. 121 They [*sc.* flax varieties] had been bred for resistance to pasmo and other diseases.

paso (pa·so). [Sp.] An image, or group of images, representing Passion scenes, carried in procession as part of Holy Week observances in Spain.
1923 *Chambers's Jrnl.* Apr. 213/1 Away goes the paso across the square. **1939** SPENDER & GILI tr. *Lorca's Poems* 19 (*title*) Paso. *Ibid.* 141 [Note] *Paso*, image, or group of images, representing a scene from the Passion of Christ, carried in procession during Holy Week, particularly in Andalusia. **1950** G. BRENAN *Face of Spain* viii. 178 Making our way into another church, we found the *pasos*, or floats holding images, pulled out into the nave in preparation for the Easter processions. *Ibid.*, One particularly large *paso*, supported on cart wheels, showed the scene of Christ being whipped by Roman soldiers. **1970** 'D. HALLIDAY' *Dolly & Cookie Bird* x. 155 The procession..got moving again...the paso of the poor hunting bishop [*sc.* St. Hubert] came rollicking past.

paso doble (pa:so do·ble). Also (erron.) **pasa doble,** and as one word. [f. Sp. *paso* step + *doble* double.] A quick Spanish dance-step; the music for such a dance.
1927 V. SILVESTER *Mod. Ballroom Dancing* 121 The *Paso Doble* is danced very little in this country, but it is popular in certain parts of the Continent. It is often referred to as the Spanish one-step. The walk is short and springy, not unlike a very modified Quickstep. **1934** C. LAMBERT *Music Ho!* II. 94 The Russian folk dance gives way to the pasodoblé of the street band. **1939** E. AMBLER *Mask of Dimitrios* vi. 101 An accordion band was playing a *paso-doble*. **1948** F. BORROWS *Theory & Technique Lat.-Amer. Dancing* iv. 156 Paso Doble music is in march time. **1955** W. GADDIS *Recognitions* III. iii. 771 An old man with a battered guitar..had two tunes, one a vaguely recognizable pasa doble. **1959** *Listener* 18 June 1059/2 The band plays a tinny *paso doble.* **1971** *New Scientist* 22 Apr. 219/1 The only sensuality indulged.. would be a quick routine or two from the pas a doble [*sic*] or the slow foxtrot. **1973** *Times* 23 Apr. 6/2 The baby-faced couples who dance the samba..and Pasodoble..are sometimes a bit short of Latin-American fire. **1974** *Times* 7 Jan. 5/8 There is Italian smooch-song and Spanish light music, pasadoble and tango. **1975** 'M. FONTEYN' *Autobiogr.* I. iii. 35 At every tea-dance in the..Hotel we waltzed and fox-trotted and danced the *paso-doble*, he so tall and me a little shrimp of eleven years.

paspalum (pæ·spălə̆m). [mod.L. (Linnæus *Systema Naturæ* (ed. 10, 1759) II. 855), f. Gk. πάσπαλος a kind of millet.] An annual or perennial grass of the genus so called, native to warm regions, especially South America, and cultivated elsewhere for fodder. Also *attrib.*
1772 R. WESTON *Universal Botanist* III. 547 Round-flowered American Paspalum. **1857** *Ann. Rep. Mass. Board Agric.* IV. 84 Hairy Slender Paspalum..has an erect or decumbent, slender culm, from one to two feet high. **1884** G. VASEY *Agric. Grasses U.S.* 31 *Paspalum laeve.* (Smooth paspalum.) This species grows from 2 to 4 feet high. ..*Paspalum dilitatum.* (Hairy-flowered paspalum.) **1906** *Chambers's Jrnl.* 24 Feb. 207/2 Paspalum Grass..has been known in the United States since 1880, where it is called hairy and flowered paspalum. **1926** *Brit. Weekly* 12 Aug. 392/3 There's a corner of paspalum down there on the creek that would do your two eyes good to see. **1929** *Contrib. U.S. Nat. Herbarium* XXVIII. I. 4 Paspalum-grass..was introduced into the southern United States from Uruguay or Argentina about the middle of the last century. *Ibid.* 5 The seeds of paspalum are eaten by a large number of birds. **1940** A. UPFIELD *Bushranger of Skies* x. 111 Bony stepped off the veranda.. and..trod the yielding paspalum grass lawn to arrive at the bottom fence. **1962** *Coast to Coast 1961–62* 94 In no time weeds and paspalum had hidden the grave. **1970** A. T. SEMPLE *Grassland Improvement* 381/2 Brownseed paspalum. **1977** *N.Z. Jrnl. Agric.* Jan. 52/3 Rhizomatous grasses—such as paspalum..—are not controlled with paraquat.

pasquinade, *sb.* (Later examples.)
1934 W. GERHARDI *Resurrection* xv. 43 A man famous for his evil tongue came up and..delivered himself of a long pasquinade at the expense of my friend. **1946** W. S. MAUGHAM *Then & Now* xxxv. 204 A cold shiver ran down his spine at the thought of the pasquinades, the epigrams that his misadventure would suggest. **1977** *Times Lit. Suppl.* 6 May 572/1 The famous pasquinade: 'quod non fecerunt barbari fecerunt Barberini'.

pass, *sb.*[1] Add: **3. b.** *to sell the pass*: see SELL *v.* 7 g.

pass, *sb.*[2] Add: **I. 1. a.** (Further examples.)
1966 *B.B.C. Handbk.* 53 Previously we had to snatch in a hit or miss fashion at 'passes' as *Telstar* or one of its cousins streaked from horizon to horizon. **1967** *Technology Week* 23 Jan. 28/2 Primary function of the subsystem is to correct the flight trajectory to assure a close pass by Mars. **1968** M. WOODHOUSE *Rock Baby* xvi. 153, I don't say it was impossible to spot, but.., short of an overhead pass by a very low-flying helicopter, I thought it would pass muster. **1974** *Nature* 4 Jan. 24/1 The orbit is near-polar with the north-going passes on the nightside at about 2230 LT, and the south-going passes on the dayside at about 1030 LT. **1977** *Offshore Engineer* Apr. 28/1 It is followed up by an external welder or 'bug', which completes a 3 mm weld thickness in one pass over wall thicknesses above 9·6 mm.
c. *Bridge.* The act of declining to make a bid.
1923 M. C. WORK *Auction Bridge of 1924* 497 Business Pass, a pass which indicates to the partner, who has made an Information Double, that the existing declaration will be remunerative. **1927** [see *AUCTION *sb.* 2 c]. **1958** *Listener* 25 Dec. 1094/3, I agree with West's opening pass and with his next bid of Two No Trumps. **1959** *Ibid.* 15 Jan. 146/1 After two passes, South opened Three Spades.

1959 Reese & Dormer *Bridge Player's Dict.* 165 West's double is for a take-out and East's pass is a penalty pass. **1977** *Times* 14 May 12/7 Hands which were so freakish that an unorthodox pass was the only road to safety.

d. *Computers.* A passage of data through a computer for processing; a single cycle of reading, processing, and writing; the performance of a particular kind of operation on each in turn of a set of data.

1954 *Jrnl. Assoc. Computing Machinery* I. 151/1 A single pass of the data through the 702 may be enough to carry out..a statistical analysis. **1961** *Ibid.* VIII. 46 Passes are continued until no item is exchanged during a given pass... This signals that all items have been sorted. **1968** *Amer. Documentation* Jan. 78/1 During one pass all elements which have already been classed in a particular category are retrieved. A second retrieval pass is then made to retrieve all remaining elements which have headwords or definitions which match those of items retrieved on the first pass. **1968** G. Emery *Electronic Data Processing* ii. 10 Figure 1.5 shows a single job, made up of three separate runs... Runs are sometimes subdivided further into separate passes—sorting runs are an example. **1975** H. Lorin *Sorting* i. 6 A pass of Linear Selection involves selecting the element with the lowest key on the list to be sorted and placing it on a growing output list. Additional passes are made until the output list is complete.

II. 7. a. Also phr. (*to come to*) *a pretty pass*, (to reach) a regrettable state of affairs.

1842 [see Pretty *a.* 3 c]. **1843** Dickens *Mart. Chuz.* (1844) xiv. 178, I need be departing, with all speed, for another country; for I have come to a pretty pass in this! **1876** H. Melville *Clarel* II. iv. xvi. 501 'Was ever Saracen so bold!' 'Well, things have come to pretty pass—The mysteries slobbered by an ass!' **1909** *Dialect Notes* III. 359 *Pretty pass*,..a peculiar or astounding situation, an abnormal condition: used in derogatory sense. **1955** *Times* 5 Aug. 10/4 Things, one felt, must have reached a pretty pass if the big banks, or any one of the big banks, had run into the same squalid staffing problems as the National Coal Board or the chain groceries. **1970** *Brewer's Dict. Phr. & Fable* (rev. ed.) 808/1 *A pretty pass*, a difficult or deplorable state of affairs.

III. 8. b. (Further examples.)

1919 [see *leaf *sb.*[2]]. **1939** Joyce *Finnegans Wake* iii. 507 Such my billet. Buy a barrack pass. **1955** 'N. Shute' *Requiem for Wren* iii. 67 Before she had been a year at Ford Janet came to look forward to her next pass with something close to apprehension. **1955** [see *bind *v.* 23].

e. (Examples.)

1838 *Actors by Daylight* I. 141 Give the Mounseer a pass to the pit. **1944** J. W. Krutch *Samuel Johnson* (1945) viii. 210 Johnson..complained that Garrick had just refused him a pass to the theater for Miss Williams because..he saw no reason why he should give away a ticket to what he knew was going to be a full house. **1961** Bowman & Ball *Theatre Lang.* 250 *Pass*, a permit to admit a person into a theatre without a ticket. British: *complimentary ticket.* **1977** *Times* 22 Apr. 11/1 Forging free passes to movie theatres.

f. In South Africa and (formerly in) Rhodesia, a document issued to non-white residents (now usu. one which it is obligatory for them to carry), authorizing and regulating their movement and residence in particular areas.

1828 J. Philip *Res. S. Afr.* I. 167 Among the many hardships to which the Hottentot is subject by this proclamation, one must advert to the Law of Passes, contained in the 16th article. **1899** W. J. K. Little *Sk. & Stud. S. Afr.* ii. i. 127 It was required that he [*sc.* a Hottentot] should have..a 'pass' or certificate when moving from place to place, and should be fined or punished as a vagrant if unable, when required, to produce this pass. **1901** *Natives S. Afr.* x. 165 Every native on entering a district, being in possession of the pass required by the existing Pass Law, was directed to repair to the district office and get a pass and badge. **1902** in *Statute Law of Transvaal* (1910) II. 871 Any native found in any street public place or thoroughfare..between the hours of nine pm. and four am. without a written pass or certificate.. shall be liable to a fine. **1914** in *Statute Law of S. Rhodesia* (1923) II. 273 Every native shall be bound, on demand made by any Pass Officer, to state all the particulars required to be entered upon his pass or certificate. **1914** in *Ibid.* (1939) II. 286 To amend and consolidate the law relating to native's passes. *Ibid.*, 287 Every male native within the Colony over the apparent age of fourteen years shall register himself at the proper pass office. **1928** R. R. R. Dhlomo *Afr. Tragedy* 21 There was no necessity for him to go to the Pass Office and spend half a day there waiting for his pass to be endorsed. **1941** C. W. de Kiewiet *Hist. S. Afr.* 45 They were naturally inclined to arrest the Hottentot as a vagabond and compel him to take service or achieve the same result by refusing him the pass or certificate without which he could not move from one district to another. **1948** *Rep. Native Laws Comm. 1946–48* (Dept. Native Affairs, S. Afr.) 26/1 It is not always clear whether a particular document can rightly be described as a pass or not. Neither from European nor from Native witnesses did we receive a satisfactory definition, but we think it would be correct to say that in the mind of the Natives a document is a pass, to which they object, if it is a document—(*a*) which is not carried by all races, but only by people of a particular race; and which either (*b*) is connected with restriction of the freedom of movement of the person concerned; or (*c*) must at all times be carried by the person concerned on his body, since the law lays the obligation on him of producing it on demand to the police and certain other officials and the mere failure to produce it is by itself a punishable offence. **1949** *Handbk. Race Relations S. Afr.* 275 The tendency was to equate a pass with a document controlling movement. Clearly however, the pass has acquired a wider connotation to-day. **1952** *Statutes Union S. Afr.* 1013 To repeal the laws relating to the carrying of passes by natives; to provide for the issue of reference books to natives. **1956** D. Jacobson *Dance in Sun* 51 I've been to the police and told them to chase him away, but they looked at his passes and said his passes were in order. **1964** *Ann. Reg. 1963* 327 All adults were entitled to vote, provided that they had registered and that this fact had been recorded on their identity cards or 'passes'. **1968** R. Griffiths *Man of River* 137 But they must! At all times they must carry their passes! **1971** T. Sharpe *Riotous Assembly* ii. 10 Verkramp confessed himself satisfied with the experiment and the milk delivery boy was charged with being out without a Pass. **1972** P. Driscoll *Wilby Conspiracy* (1973) iii. 40 The black man shuffled forward, reaching automatically for his pass, and the constable paged through the green booklet. **1977** *Times* 5 Nov. 15/1 The tribal homelands are henceforth to issue travel documents to their nationals, a more dignified card of identity. But these, even if upgraded to passport status upon independence, will serve the police and the Ministry of Bantu Affairs as well as the passes. Possession of one will be needed to apply for a job in white South Africa.

IV. 11. b. An amorous advance, esp. in phr. *to make a pass at* (someone). *colloq.*

1928 J. P. McEvoy *Show Girl* 27 Almost all parties look alike at the takeoff—a few high balls, a few dunces, and the boys getting merry and making preliminary passes. **1936** D. Parker *Not so Deep as a Well* 70 Men seldom make passes At girls who wear glasses. **1938** G. Greene *Brighton Rock* i. i. 21 He made no immediate pass at Ida in the taxi. **1939** C. R. Cooper *Designs in Scarlet* ii. 14 The girl sipped idly at her drink, swallowing with it her disgust that she should be forced to stick with a deado when she might be making a pass at a 'gentleman'. **1942** E. Waugh *Put out More Flags* 173 What are you doing now besides making passes at Susie? **1944** Auden *For Time Being* ii. 31 His progress from outrage to outrage would not relent before the gross climax of His making, horror unspeakable, a pass at her virgin self. **1945** J. Steinbeck *Cannery Row* xxix. 190, I been over there. He never made a pass at me. **1952** W. Plomer *Museum Pieces* ix. 68 Since my visit to the painting room he had almost completely hidden from me the feelings which seemed to have driven him to make a pass at me. **1957** J. Braine *Room at Top* vii. 70 A little gentle flirtation, even a discreet sort of pass, would have changed her attitude entirely. **1959** 'D. Buckingham' *Wind Tunnel* xv. 127 Male passes were nothing new to Janet. **1972** J. Gores *Dead Skip* (1973) xiii. 89 As for making a pass at her, he'd as soon have made one at his five-year-old daughter. Sex was for home. **1973** 'D. Shannon' *No Holiday for Crime* (1974) iv. 58 If he started to get fresh, threw a pass, she could just walk off. **1978** D. Devine *Sunk without Trace* ii. 23 He cast round for ulterior motives. Was she perhaps making a pass at him?

12. a. (U.S. examples.)

1944 N. Mailer *Calculus at Heaven* in E. Seaver *Cross-Section* 345 Sergeant! Did I ever tellya how I got to throw a pass in the Red Bank game one year? **1961** J. S. Salak *Dict. Amer. Sports* 319 *Pass* (baseball, softball), base on balls. **1970** *Washington Post* 30 Sept. D4/3 Shugars..has been very accurate this year, completing 37 of 78 passes for 376 yards and a 47 per cent average. **1972** *N.Y. Times* 4 June 5/2 He has been throwing passes in casual workouts.

b. In real tennis, a service which drops in the pass-court; in lawn tennis, a shot which succeeds in passing the racket of an opponent.

1888 *Encycl. Brit.* XXIII. 179/2 A pass counts for nothing but annuls a previous fault. **1900** in A. E. T. Watson *Young Sportsman* 614 A 'pass' shall not neutralise a previous fault. **1911** *Encycl. Brit.* XXVI. 627/2 'Pass': a service in which the ball drops beyond the pass-line; the service in this case does not count, but a 'pass' does not annul a previous fault, as was once the case. **1961** F. C. Avis *Sportsman's Gloss.* 259/2 *Pass*..Passing shot. **1962** *Times* 27 Apr. 4/1 A mixture of lobs and angled passes. **1975** *Oxf. Compan. Sports & Games* 825/1 The remainder of the winning area is the 'pass court' and, if the ball falls there, 'pass' is called and a let played. **1978** *Times* 4 July 19/4 Newcombe actually reached set point with a glorious backhand cross-court pass off second service.

13. (Further examples.)

1939 [see *lap *sb.*[3] 2 e]. **1967** A. H. Cottrell *Introd. Metall.* xxii. 439 For the first few passes the draught (i.e. reduction of cross-section) is light... Reductions of 10–50 per cent per pass are then used.

13*. In full, *food-pass*. Among certain birds of prey, the habit of passing food from one bird to another while in flight.

1931 D. Nethersole-Thompson in *Brit. Birds* XXV. 147 During the early stages of incubation the food 'pass' of the Hobbies may be occasionally witnessed. **1940** H. F. Witherby et al. *Handbk. Brit. Birds* III. 19 During this period [of incubation] male feeds hen both by food pass and by calling hen off to adjoining perch. **1948** B. H. Ryves *Bird Life in Cornwall* vi. 93 The aerial 'pass' of a kill is spectacular. **1956** D. A. Bannerman *Birds Brit. Isles* V. 182 Excellent views of the food-pass of the cock to the hen [marsh harrier] were also witnessed. *Ibid.* 195 Some account of the serious business of the 'pass' will be given. **1970** E. Hosking *Eye for Bird* xi. 157 They [*sc.* a pair of hobbies] rolled over, swung up their feet and passed food from one to the other. It is the speed and precise flight control which makes the hobby's food-pass so exhilarating to watch.

V. 15. (Further examples.)

1930 *Engineering* 12 Dec. 759/2 The drawing of the strip through the pass of the rolls. **1939** [see *lap *sb.*[3] 2 e]. **1960** D. J. O. Brandt *Manuf. Iron & Steel* (ed. 2) xxxiii. 249 The most commonly used passes in bar and rod rolling are the diamond, the diagonal, the oval, and to finish with, the round.

VI. 17. a. (*a*) (sense 4) *pass class, coach, degree* (further examples), *examination* (earlier example), *mark, moderations* (colloq. *mods*), *rate*; (*b*) (sense *8 f) *pass-bearing* adj.; *pass office, regulation, system.*

1943 E. H. Brookes *Bantu in S. Afr. Life* v. 11 The provisions of the Act under which Industrial Councils are formed do not apply to 'pass-bearing Natives'. **1953** K. Amis *Lucky Jim* viii. 82 Of course, their problems down there are very different... The Pass classes in particular. **1908** E. M. Sneyd-Kynnersley *H.M.I.* xi. 110 He had taken refuge in a Hall. There he exhausted the pass-coaches of Oxford. **1915** W. S. Maugham *Of Human Bondage* xxvi. 109 When he only got a pass degree his friends were astonished. **1919** Mencken *Amer. Lang.* 105 His [*sc.* an English university man's] daily speech is full of terms unintelligible to an American student, for example, *wrangler, tripos, head, pass-degree* and *don.* **1948** M. Laski *Tory Heaven* i. 5 After reading for a Pass Degree at Oxford, James had..been sent to..an uncle's rubber-plantation in Malaya. **1861** Mill *Repr. Govt.* xiv. 259 A mere pass examination never, in the long run, does more than exclude absolute dunces. **1911** W. Owen *Let.* Sept. (1967) 79 Have I passed? I do think so! even in Arith. & Geometry. At least I have done enough right to score pass marks. **1957** *Economist* 12 Oct. 104/1 It is often assumed that there is a common pass mark for the whole of each county, but there can hardly be that until the school bus is replaced by each child's own jet propelled transport. **1977** P. Strevens *New Orientations Teaching Eng.* ii. 34 In many countries..the effective criterion for success in an English-language course has been to achieve the pass mark in an examination set and marked in Britain. **1969** G. Smith in *Lett. Aldous Huxley* 11, 1913... October: H. enters Balliol and prepares for Pass Moderations. **1912** *Rep. Brit. Assoc. Adv. Sci. 1911* 219 The opinion has been expressed that Pass Mods. is not a bad thing. **1928** Pass office [see sense 8 f above]. **1948** *Rep. Native Laws Comm. 1946–48* (Dept. Native Affairs, S. Afr.) 66/2 Any Native *entering* the Province must proceed to the nearest Pass Office (or to the nearest Pass Office to his destination if entering by rail) and take out an *Inward Pass.* **1953** P. Abrahams *Return to Goli* iv. ii. 129 He was soon picked up outside the Pass Office by one of the touts or 'runners' who look out for unemployed Africans. **1973** *Morning Star* 18 May 4/2 In the schools in the countryside the average pass rate was more than 95 per cent. **1976** *Daily Mail* (Hull) 16 Dec., Their pass rate of 79 per cent from 77 entries was better than most he had seen. **1948** *Rep. Native Laws Comm. 1946–48* (Dept. Native Affairs, S. Afr.) 33/1 If in course of time, as matters develop, the pass regulations fall into entire disuse, the laws authorising their application may well disappear from the statute book. **1859** *Queenstown Free Press* 2 Mar. (Pettman), Upon more occasions than one I have endeavoured to bring to the notice of the public the evils of the Pass system. **1936** *New Statesman* 11 July 46/1, I badly wanted to know whether God approved of the colour bar and the Pass system for natives. **1939** J. S. Marais *Cape Coloured People* p. viii, The pass system as applied to the Coloured north of the Orange, was abolished by the Natives (Urban Areas) Act of 1923. **1972** P. Driscoll *Wilby Conspiracy* (1973) vi. 74 A national campaign among Africans against the pass system.

b. passband, a frequency band within which signals are transmitted by a filter without attenuation; **pass-burner** *Southern Africa*, an African who burns his pass in protest against the pass laws; hence **pass-burning** *vbl. sb.*; **pass check** (examples); **pass court** *Real Tennis* (see quots.); **pass door** (further examples); **pass duty**, a duty levied on goods entering a territory; **pass lamp**, a lamp on a motor vehicle for use in fog; **pass law** *Southern Africa*, a law regulating the carrying of passes (see sense 8 f above); **pass light** = **pass lamp*; so **pass-lighting**; **pass line** *Real Tennis*, the line between the pass-court and the service court; **pass pawn**, a passed pawn; **pass play** *Amer. Football*, a sequence of passes between members of the same team; **pass raid**, in South Africa, a raid on African premises by the white authorities to check that passes are in order.

1922 G. A. Campbell in *Bell Syst. Techn. Jrnl.* Nov. 15 The pass band and stop band characteristics of wave-filters are concretely illustrated..by the curves of Figs. 8–13. *Ibid.* 26 Each state holds for one or more continuous bands of frequencies; these bands have been distinguished as stop bands and pass bands. **1965** *Wireless World* Sept. 459/1 The low-frequency passband of the filter. **1970** J. Earl *Tuners & Amplifiers* v. 102 A BBC station at ±75kHz deviation with a modulation frequency of 15kHz..would call for a passband of about 180kHz for the best results. **1970** *Nature* 12 Dec. 1069/2 A 30 Å passband Faby–Perot type filter was used to isolate the line. **1953** P. Abrahams *Return to Goli* vi. i. 190 Strikers and pass-burners were jailed and shot down in large numbers. **1961** *Economist* 4 Nov. 415/1, 2,072 [Northern Rhodesians] were convicted on charges of stoning, pass-burning, arson, road-blocking, and the like. **1844** J. Cowell *30 Yrs. among Players* i. xi. 27 We agreed to pay the extra three and sixpence and go into the boxes; but as to obtaining a pass check, it was impossible. **1858** G. A. Sala *Twice round Clock* in *Welcome Guest* 22 May 60/1 There is a theatrical pass-check, and the thumb of a white kid glove, very dirty, lying..at the back [of the hansom]. **1961** Bowman & Ball *Theatre Lang.* 250 *Pass check*, a re-admission pass for a spectator who leaves the theatre temporarily. British: *pass-out check.* **1900** G. E. A. Ross in A. E. T. Watson *Young Sportsman* 608 The pass-court is the area enclosed by the pass-line, the service-line, the end-wall and the main-wall. **1961** J. S. Salak *Dict. Amer. Sports* 320 *Pass court* (court tennis)—the part of the floor on the hazard side that lies between the main wall, the grille wall, the pass line (but not including the pass line), and the service line (including the service line). **1975** Pass court [see sense 12 b above]. **1937** N. Coward *Present Indicative* viii. 313 At the final curtain there was booing... I dashed through the pass door and on to the stage as quickly as I could. **1939** JOYCE *Finnegans Wake* I. 146 The little passdoor, I go you before, so, and you're at my apron stage. **1950** 'J. TEY' *To love & be Wise* xviii. 233 Marta..came down to the edge of the stage... 'Come through the pass door, will you?' **1970** A. MORICE *Death in Grand Manor* x. 103 Be an angel, Annie, and show Miss Crichton to the pass door. **1909** *Daily Chron.* 20 Feb. 4/4 Opium..is grown in the Native States, the Government levying a heavy pass duty on its entrance to British territory. **1948** *Times* 14 Jan. 2/5 It has been found that the low-mounted passlamp is especially liable to cause dazzle. **1897** A. MILNER *Let.* 12 Aug. in C. Headlam *Milner Papers* (1931) I. vi. 194 If they do exempt Cape Boys from the degrading provisions of the Pass Law. **1901** Pass law [see sense 8 f above]. **1921** *Outward Bound* May 46/2 Soon after that, all my own boys cleared one night... I would not report them, that was not my way, let the pass-law say what it pleased. I don't hold with pass-law slavery. **1948** *Rep. Native Laws Comm. 1946–48* (Dept. Native Affairs, S. Afr.) 26/1 They regard even the certificates of exemption, which are issued to them as evidence of exemption from the pass laws, as passes; for only Natives require them, and they must be produced at any time on demand by an authorised official. **1956** T. HUDDLESTON *Naught for your Comfort* ii. 30 Another consequence of the pass laws—a consequence known to every intelligent South African at all interested in penal reform—is that it leads to an absolute contempt for the law. **1960** *Observer* 27 Mar. 16/4 Throughout South Africa's history, the pass laws have caused more bitter resentment than any other grievance. **1971** *Rand Daily Mail* 4 Dec. 1/1 It is where family life—the very basis of stability in traditional African societies—is being devastated by the pass laws and other apartheid regulations. **1974** A. WILLIAMS *Gentleman Traitor* xiii. 213 Two African youths had been arrested for breaking the Pass Laws. **1977** *Times* 16 Feb. 8/3 Legislation tabled in Parliament [in South Africa] today proposes the doubling of fines for violations of the country's pass laws. **1977** *Time* 2 May 22/3 The 'pass laws'—which control the movement of blacks into white areas—cost South Africa no less than $130 million a year to administer. **1938** *Times* 20 July 12/5 A rubber footrest for the clutch foot in which is the switch to cut out the head-lamps and put on a pass-light. **1948** *Times* 14 Jan. 2/5 Three-quarters of the cases of dazzle are caused by dipped headlights and pass lights. **1959** *Motor Manual* (ed. 36) vi. 181 The so-called spotlight ..provides a concentrated beam, but of more general use is the pass-light or fog-lamp, which is designed to throw a broad, flat beam with a fairly sharply defined top edge. **1965** PRIESTLEY & WISDOM *Good Driving* ii. 21 Many cars are fitted with 'fog' or 'pass' lights. **1938** *Times* 14 Oct. 11/1 Radio sets, permanent jacking systems, and an arrangement of pass-lighting which conduces to safety are outstanding features in standardization this year. **1888** *Encycl. Brit.* XXIII. 179/2 A 'pass' [is called] if the ball has gone beyond the pass line. **1911** *Ibid.* XXVI. 627/1 The pass-line is drawn 7 ft. 8 in. from the main wall. **1935** *Encycl. Sports* 619/2 On the 'hazard side' of the court..is traced the 'service line'..and at right angles to this again is the 'pass line'. **1961** J. S. SALAK *Dict. Amer. Sports* 321 *Pass line* (court tennis)—the line on the floor nearest the grille and extending from the service line to the grille wall. **1908** *Daily Chron.* 29 Sept. 1/6 Lasker has a pass pawn, but..a draw appears probable. **1968** *Globe & Mail* (Toronto) 11 July 32/5 Turek scored on a 71-yard pass play with Joe Zuger. **1969** *Official Playing Rules Canad. Football* 29 For interference on a forward pass play see Rule 6, Section 4. **1970** *Toronto Daily Star* 24 Sept. 17/7 Eckman added Ticats' clinching touchdown a few minutes later when he shook off a blitzing B.C. lineman and ran seven yards on a broken pass play. **1958** *New Statesman* 8 Nov. 619/3 'Pass raids' are so commonplace in Johannesburg that even few liberal whites experience any real shock when they see a group of 10 or 20 Africans under police guard on a street corner, waiting to become part of the more than a thousand of their kind who, every day of the year, spend at least a day in custody because their papers are not in order. **1971** *Rand Daily Mail* 27 Mar. 1/1 To this is added perpetual insecurity, the harassment of pass raids and the miseries of life below the poverty datum line.

pass, *v.* Add: **A.** *intr.* **II. 5. a.** (Later examples.)

1933 M. GRANT *Conquest of Continent* 269 This enables some of these light Negroes to 'pass' as Whites. **1948** *Time* 16 Feb. 25/1 Possibly as many as 5,000,000 people with 'a determinable part' of Negro blood are now 'passing' as whites.

c. (Later example.)

1895 *Century Mag.* Sept. 676/2 It was a poor thing for the Bruce boys to do, to try to pass upon him like this.

d. To be held or accepted as a member of a religious or ethnic group other than one's own. Used esp. of a person of Negro ancestry who is held to be or regards himself as a white person.

1935 H. W. HORWILL *Dict. Mod. Amer. Usage* 224/2 In Am. there are many persons with a strain of Negro blood in whom this heritage of colour is so inconspicuous that they might easily be supposed to be of pure white lineage. If such persons leave their Negro associations and succeed in becoming accepted as Whites, they are said to *pass.* **1938** I. GOLDBERG *Wonder of Words* vi. 118 There are other Jews who resembling, psychologically, the troubled Negro—try to 'pass', which is the Negro term for being taken as a White. **1952** M. STEEN *Phoenix Rising* vii. 170 Coloured people who hide their origin and live as whites are said to 'pass'. **1953** E. H. BROOKES *S. Afr. in Changing World* vii. 147 Because of the permutations of nature, a coloured man white enough to 'pass' can have children or grandchildren who look 'Coloured'. **1955** D. VIKLUND tr. *Tingsten's Probl. S. Afr.* xiii. 148 There are two coloured brothers. One of them manages to 'pass' and becomes a barrister, a respectable member of white Cape society. **1960** D. JACOBSON *Evidence of Love* 92 He could 'pass' in the Transvaal, very easily, she thought. **1963** M. McCARTHY *Group* xiv. 319 'Freddy's parents were trying to pass,' she went on sombrely. 'Like so many rich German Jews.' **1966** K. L. MORGAN in A. Dundes *Mother Wit* (1973) 606/2 The children used to love to come to Philadelphia with Caddy because there they could pass and have fun. **1971** *Encycl. Judaica* X. 60 At the height of 19th-century liberalism in Europe and America, it was possible for some Jews to 'pass' without doing anything more than simply ceasing to function in any Jewish association. **1976** *Wilson Q.* Autumn 87 Acceptable pigmentation plus wealth and influence were necessary for persons who hoped to obtain the *limpeza-de-sangue* document. But how dark one could be and still 'pass' varied from region to region.

VI. 15. (Further examples.)

1907 G. B. SHAW *Major Barbara* II. 222 Youd pass still. Why didnt you dye your hair. **1962** J. BRAINE *Life at Top* xv. 191 She said: 'He's a lovely little boy.' 'He'll pass,' I said absently.

IX. 21. c. (Later *transf.* example.)

1917 ADE *Let.* 29 July (1973) 68 If you want me to pass upon the sub-titles, I shall be glad to do so and if I change them it will be to make them more compact and not more intricate.

XI. 26. b. (Further examples.) Also, in Bridge and other card games, to decline to make a bid. Also *fig.*

1869 'MARK TWAIN' *Innoc. Abr.* xxxiv. 375 Jack said, 'I pass'—he plays euchre sometimes—and we all passed in turn. **1908** R. F. FOSTER *Auction Bridge* 29 The player on his left must either pass, or make a better declaration, or 'double'. **1918** [see *GO *v.* 78 k]. **1929** M. C. WORK *Compl. Contract Bridge* 42 South..bids one No Trump: North..passes. **1959** REESE & DORMER *Bridge Player's Dict.* 163 North, not being obliged to keep the bidding open, might pass. **1964** *Official Encycl. Bridge* 414/2 *Pass*, a call by which a player indicates that, at that turn, he does not choose to contract for a number of odd tricks at any denomination, nor does he choose, at that turn, to double a contract of the opponents or redouble a contract by his side that opponents have already doubled. **1976** L. SANDERS *Hamlet Warning* (1977) xxv. 216 'If you want to run up and take a look..' 'I'll pass. If you've seen one cannonball, you've seen them all.' **1976** *Washington Post* 15 Oct. A 23/3 The Washington Post passed. It made no mention whatsoever of what the committee had to say about the news media.

d. In dominoes, to miss a turn when one does not have a suitable number.

1960 R. C. BELL *Board & Table Games* I. 169 When one player has drawn all but the last two dominoes from the pool, and can neither make a ten, nor play a matador, he says, 'pass'. *Ibid.* 170 When a player is unable to make a match he calls 'pass', and the next player tries.

B. *trans.* **I. 29. c.** (Earlier and later examples.)

1870 J. K. MEDBERY *Men & Mysteries Wall St.* 137 To 'pass' a dividend... A dividend is said to be passed when the directors vote against declaring it. **1903** *Forum* (N.Y.) Oct. 209 Concerns which not only passed dividends..but went bankrupt. **1965** PERRY & RYDER *Thomson's Dict. Banking* (ed. 11) 422/2 *Passing a dividend*, a term used when a company decides not to pay a dividend.

see *BUCK *sb.*[9]; *to pass the word* (colloq., orig.

C. Causative uses. **III. 46. a.** *to pass the buck*: *Naut.*), to convey information orally; to issue an oral order or instruction.

1843 S. LEECH *30 Yrs. from Home* ix. 186 Her officer.. so exasperated our captain that he passed the word to fire into her. *Ibid.* x. 218, I heard the order from an officer, of 'Pass the word for the boy Leech'. **1884** *Naval Encycl.* 636/2 *To pass the word* for a man is to summon him by name, the cry being repeated by the boatswain's mates on all decks. **1901** G. B. SHAW *Caesar & Cleopatra* II. 133 Pass the word to the guard; and fetch my armor. **1910** H. Y. MOFFAT *From Ship's-Boy to Skipper* iii. 39 He called to the sentry: 'Pass the word for the boy Moffat.' **1924** J. BUCHAN *Three Hostages* vi. 96, I will visit it as a man..to see about the meter... Macgillivray will pass the word for me. **1946** E. O'NEILL *Iceman Cometh* III. 184 They know I was framed. And once they've passed the word, it's as good as done, law or no law. **1961** *Sat. Even. Post* 3 June 60/2 Hundreds of men are required to pass the word to the button pushers and to push the buttons.

IV. 52. a. *to pass a* (or *the*) *remark*: to make an observation or comment, esp. one that is gratuitously sarcastic or depreciatory; freq. *pl. colloq.*

1899 R. WHITEING *No. 5 John St.* xxi. 218, I didn't sye I 'ad nothin' to sye to 'im. I only passed the remark. **1924** KIPLING *Debits & Credits* (1926) 157 ''E *could* pass remarks, too!' Humberstall recited..a fragment..ending with, 'You lazy-minded, lousy-headed, long-trousered, perfumed perookier.' *Ibid.*, Macklin had a wonderful way o' passing remarks on a man's civil life; an' he put it about that our B.S.M. had run a dope an' dolly-shop with a Chinese woman. **1929** J. B. PRIESTLEY *Good Companions* II. v. 370 'Dewn't you be so personal', said Mr. Jerningham... 'You're always passing remawks.' **1933** C. MACKENZIE *Water on Brain* x. 142, I only passed the remark to Mr Wigmore yesterday, 'Mr Wigmore,' I said, 'people are getting pre-war again.' **1934** R. FERGUSON *Celebrated Sequels* 134 Were they or were they not laughing and passing remarks? **1939** JOYCE *Finnegans Wake* 463 He is looking aged with his pebbled eyes, and johnnythin too, from livicking onpidgins' ifs with puffins' ands, he's been slanderising himself, but I pass no remark. **1941** E. BOWEN *Look at Roses* 103, I merely passed the remark. There's no harm in my passing a remark occasionally. **1958** J. CANNAN *And be a Villain* iii. 70 I'll tell him you've broken off your engagement and not to pass any remarks. **1962** —— *All is Discovered* ii. 43, I passed a remark about her being indoors. I don't like her. **1975** C. STORR *Chinese Egg* xxvi. 168 He called her Fatty..and passed remarks about her figure.

c. *to pass the time of day* (further examples).

1851 [see TIME *sb.* 28 b]. **1936** 'F. GERALD' *Millionaire in Memories* xii. 316, I was riding home after doing some work on my racecourse and I pulled up at Swanson's swagger camp to pass the time of day. **1960** G. DURRELL *Zoo in Luggage* viii. 192, I was passing the time of day with the garage man. **1965** N. GULBENKIAN *Pantaraxia* xi. 230 Joe Boyle, one of the directors of the Royal Dutch Shell..went to see my father, as though merely to pass the time of day. **1965** *Listener* 23 Sept. 453/2 The English chaps would pretend..to be very friendly and jovial and pass the time of day and that sort of thing. **1978** M. GIROUARD *Life in Eng. Country House* v. 147 The King.. was then conveyed to the prince's bedchamber, where *he* passed the time of day for a few minutes.

V. 54. (Earlier example.)

1859 L. WRAXALL tr. *Mem. J. E. Robert-Houdin* I. viii. 157 He also said, in allusion to the ace of hearts, which he had 'passed' on one of the most beautiful women in the room: 'Will you be kind enough, madam, to lay your hand on your heart?'

D. With prepositions and adverbs.

I. With prepositions. **57. pass over—. a.** (Further examples.)

1749 *Apol. Life B.-M. Carew* 125 Passing over this Ferry they came into Rhode Island. **1874** J. W. DRAPER *Hist. Conflict Relig. & Sci.* vi. 161 The distance passed over in a voyage from Italy to the Gulf of Guinea.

58. pass through—. e. To follow a ritual of going through a narrow opening in a natural object such as a cleft tree or rock, etc., in the belief that the object will prove a barrier to evil or will absorb illness. Also *trans.*, in causal senses. Hence **passing-through** *sb.*

1804 *Gentl. Mag.* Oct. 909/1 Rowe's son was passed through the present tree in 1792, at the age of one or two. **1846** *Athenæum* 5 Sept. 909/1 A second point arises upon the 'passing through'... The passing through a cleft or aperture in a rock is a medical superstition..found in many countries. **1900** C. HOSE in *Geogr. Jrnl.* XVI. 45 The funeral procession climbed the mound on which the ceremony was situated, passing through the V of the cleft stick in single file. **1913** J. G. FRAZER *Golden Bough: Balder the Beautiful* (ed. 3) II. xi. 176 The words uttered by the mourners in passing through the cloven stick shew clearly that they believe the stick to act as a barrier or fence, on the further side of which they leave behind the ghost. *Ibid.* 184 In Scotland children who suffered from hectic fever and consumptive patients used to be healed by passing thrice through a circular wreath of woodbine. **1961** C. HOLE *Encycl. Superstitions* 21 A young ash-sapling was split, and the child was passed through it, three or nine times. **1968** *Proc. Amer. Philos. Soc.* CXII. 388/1 Passing-through rituals in the earth usually involved grassy terrain, where sod could be cut, piled, and arched to make a passageway. *Ibid.* 391/1 Prevention of disease by passing through seems more pronounced in passing through stones than in other kinds of rituals involving passing through.

II. With adverbs. **63. pass in.** *to pass in one's cheques*: see also *CHECK *sb.*[1] 15; *to pass in one's chips*: see *CHIP *sb.*[1] 2 e; also *absol.*; *to pass in one's marble*: see *MARBLE *sb.* 4 b.

1904 *N.Y. Even. Jrnl.* 3 May 2 'I may die' he told friends, 'and I want to breathe American air again before I pass in.'

b. *trans.* To withdraw from an auction sale because of failure to reach the reserve price. *Austral.* and *N.Z.*

1973 *Sun-Herald* (Sydney) 26 Aug. 23/2 The house was passed in at $37,000—the reserve was $42,000. **1977** *N.Z. Herald* 5 Jan. 1-11/10 What seemed to be unrealistic prices asked for by vendors in general resulted in 60 of the 99 lots on offer at a thoroughbred sale at Alexandra Park yesterday being passed in.

64. pass off. b. (Earlier examples.)

1787 J. WOODFORDE *Diary* 4 Dec. (1926) II. 356 Everything passed of [*sic*] as agreeable as one might expect from such a Meeting. **1788** E. SHERIDAN *Jrnl.* (1960) 107 All pass'd off very well—My Father a little stately at first but soon thoroughly cordial with his Son. *Ibid.* 141 Our day pass'd off very well—no awkwardness or unpleasantness of any kind.

c. *spec.* in *Law*, to represent (goods, etc.) as those of another.

1884 [in Dict.]. **1900**, etc. [see *PASSING *vbl. sb.* 2 b]. **1902** *Encycl. Brit.* XXXIII. 388/1 No trader is entitled to 'pass-off' his goods as those of another... Even if the 'passing-off' is done innocently it will be restrained. **1972** WHITE & JACOB *Kerly's Law of Trade Marks* (ed. 10) xvi. 362 The question whether the use of particular words or badges is calculated to pass off the defendant's goods as those of the plaintiff is often one of difficulty.

65. pass on. c. *intr.* To proceed from one existence or activity to another; *spec.* to die.

1804–1820 W. BLAKE *Jerusalem* III, in *Compl. Writings* (1972) 714 So Men pass on: but States remain permanent for ever. **1884** *150th Anniv. Settlement of Boscawen & Webster, New Hampsh.* 44 They have all passed on to become soldiers of the unseen army. **1920** R. MACAULAY *Potterism* III. ii. 131 If I have to pass on before Percy, he will be left bereaved indeed. **1923** *Amer. Mag.* June 15/1 The murderer took poison and so the two passed on. **1925** *Nat. Geogr. Mag.* XLVII. 489/2 His mother now dwells in comfort..while his father has passed on. **1928** L. NORTH *Parasites* 77 When my dad passed on there was just enough insurance to have let me finish up. **1930** 'E. QUEEN' *French Powder Myst.* xxxv. 274 Bernice [should] come in for a good share of Cyrus's estate when Cyrus should pass on. **1945** A. HUXLEY *Time must have Stop* vi. 66 'They don't die,' said Mrs. Gamble. 'They pass on.' **1946** E. O'NEILL *Iceman Cometh* I. 89 Too late! The old Doc has passed on to his Maker. **1960** S. KAUFFMAN *If it be Love* i. 12 'Margaret passed on.' William winced.. when someone used a euphemism for 'died'. **1973** A. BROINOWSKI *Take One Ambassador* i. 14 I'm Mrs Bert Norrice, well, Mrs Fern Norrice these days, since Mr

Norrice passed on last year. **1977** B. PYM *Quartet in Autumn* i. 10 Old Snowy had long since died, 'passed on' or 'been taken', however one liked to put it.

66. pass out. c. *intr.* (*a*) to die; (*b*) to faint, become unconscious; also, *to pass out cold*. *colloq.*

1899 *Westm. Gaz.* 6 Mar. 2/1 Another [spirit] who passed out' with consumption is heard coughing. **1924** P. MARKS *Plastic Age* i. 12 He left us a whole lot of jack when he passed out. **1927** *Hutchinson's Myst. Story Mag.* Feb. 80 First, the name of the dead relative or friend, then when they passed out. **1939** JOYCE *Finnegans Wake* 627, I am passing out. O bitter ending! **1968** *Publ. Amer. Dial. Soc.* 1966 XLVI. 28 *Pass out*, die—'When he passed out, he was buried with his dogs.'

1915 C. MATHEWSON *Catcher Craig* i. 9 They sure do work you hard over there. I worked in the stock-room one summer and nearly passed out! **1918** J. M. GRIDER *War Birds* (1927) 97 We..carried him home after he passed out. **1924** P. MARKS *Plastic Age* xxii. 254 A man 'passed out cold' and had to be carried from the gymnasium. **1935** J. T. FARRELL *Guillotine Party* 191 Young Johnny Herbert had gotten drunk for the first time in his life and he'd passed out like a light. **1936** WODEHOUSE *Laughing Gas* ii. 26, I broke off here, because she had fainted... She slid sideways along the seat and quietly passed out. **1939** J. B. PRIESTLEY *Let People Sing* vii. 167 He's a big success in the cocktail bar... Does a few little tricks now and then, an' they nearly pass out. **1942** D. POWELL *Time to be Born* (1943) x. 245 'What'll we do if he passes out in your place?' Corinne asked. 'I'll look after him,' said Vicky. **1947** 'N. SHUTE' *Chequer Board* i. 3, I suddenly passed out cold... I passed out cold and fell down..on the floor. *a* **1953** E. O'NEILL *Hughie* (1962) 22, I got scared he'd pass out with excitement. **1974** D. GRAY *Dead Give Away* ix. 95 'How has she taken it?' 'Badly... She passed out when I told her.'

d. *trans.* To knock unconscious. *Austral. slang.*

1906 E. DYSON *Fact'ry 'Ands* xii. 151 He promised to show Feathers a 'boshter knack for passing out gazobs'.

e. *intr.* To complete a course of instruction, etc., successfully; to graduate. Also *trans.*, to undergo (a course of instruction); to allow or enable (someone) to pass out.

1916 *Daily Colonist* (Victoria, B.C.) 28 July 4/7 Midshipman Robert W. Wood..passed out first in 1914 both in the college and in ships. **1920** *Discovery* Mar. 77/2 Airship pilots..are required to pass-out a course in free ballooning, which includes a night flight and a solo flight. *a* **1968** S. FAESSLER in R. Weaver *Canad. Short Stories* (1968) 2nd Ser. 335 My plan, after being passed out of Grade VIII, was to go..to Harbord Collegiate. **1968** J. SANGSTER *Touchfeather* ii. 8, I romped through the training, passing out with the highest marks anyone could remember.

f. To hand out or distribute.

1926 *Publishers' Weekly* 10 July 116 Librarians..are eager and willing to pass out catalogs that have won their confidence. **1927** *Ibid.* 12 Feb. 599 On that day she had passed out 130 books. **1964** MRS. L. B. JOHNSON *White House Diary* 5 June (1970) 154, I was impressed that Charlotte Ford said, 'I'll do anything you want me to do. Type, pass out cards, anything.' **1973** R. HILL *Ruling Passion* III. iii. 179 He passed out some photostatted sheets. **1978** *Detroit Free Press* 2 Apr. 8E/1 Allow the ATF to lift licenses from dealers at any time in the future for the most minor of errors in complicated bookkeeping procedures, as well as pass out $10,000 fines.

g. *Bridge.* Of the players: to make three consecutive passes following (a bid), the auction thus ending and this bid becoming the contract; to make no positive bid at all in (a hand). Usu. in *passive.*

1959 *Listener* 19 Mar. 530/3 The fourth hand bid Three Spades which was passed out. **1960** T. REESE *Play Bridge with Reese* 91 Partner now surprises me by going five hearts. That is passed out. **1969** A. TRUSCOTT *Gt. Bridge Scandal* 307 A two notrump opening bid that has been passed out.

67. pass over. b. (Later examples.)

1794 W. BLAKE *Urizen* IV, in *Compl. Writings* (1972) 228 And a second Age passed over, And a state of dismal woe. **1795–1804** —— *Vala* V, in *Compl. Writings* (1972) 307 Till many a morn & many a night pass'd over in dire woe. **1840** R. H. DANA *Two Yrs. before Mast* xxiv. 250 The night passed over without any trouble. **1878** R. L. STEVENSON in *London* 6 July 10/1 The journey passed over without much incident.

h. To convey across; to transport.

1832 N. WYETH *Jrnl.* 18 June in *Corr. & Jrnls.* (1899) 157 Reached the place for fording the platte. 19th, Passed over my goods during a severe wind without accident.

i. To die.

Associated esp. with spiritualism.

1909 *Review of Reviews* Feb. 123/2 His automatic writing..came..through the same friend through whom he has constantly communicated ever since he passed over. **1928** *Daily Mail* 7 Aug. 16/5 This doctor was now with my mother, who had recently passed over. **1930** D. L. SAYERS *Strong Poison* xvi. 209, I have had the most marvellous talks with the dear ones who have passed over. **1938** AUDEN & ISHERWOOD *On Frontier* III. i. 89 Those who have passed over are all very happy. He said the Other Side was difficult to describe. **1958** C. WATSON *Coffin scarcely Used* ii. 18 If the living's good and bad mixed, then those who've passed over are two sorts as well. **1974** J. STUBBS *Painted Face* vii. 108, I wonder if her poor husband ever read those diaries, after she passed over?

69. pass up. To give up or abandon (a course of action, etc.); to decline or refuse to have (further) dealings with (someone or something); to reject (something) on the terms offered; to renounce or forgo (an opportunity, prospect, etc.). orig. *U.S.*

1896 ADE *Artie* i. 5 If he gets on a street-car where I am, I get off and walk. That ain't no lie. I pass him up. *Ibid.* xii. 112 Well, I guess I'll pass up the whole thing. **1906** H. D. PITTMAN *Belle of Bluegrass Country* vii. 108 'I know,' he continued, 'when I've got enough. I pass this little town up.' **1923** R. D. PAINE *Comrades of Rolling Ocean* ii. 33 My duty is to stand by the family... That is why I passed up college. **1926** *N.Y. Times Mag.* 13 Aug. 1 He was sent to the U.S. Senate, but on his own terms, having previously passed up the Senatorship rather than take it on the terms of others. **1931** W. G. MCADOO *Crowded Yrs.* xxxii. 503 This would have been congenial work..but I had to pass it up. **1932** WODEHOUSE *Hot Water* xi. 188 And those jewels? You're really going to pass them up? **1939** —— *Uncle Fred in Springtime* i. 19 Your name..will be mud if you pass up an excellent bet like old Horace Davenport. **1943** R. FROST *Let.* Feb. (1972) 241, I am lucky to be getting lectures still at here and there a college and feel I mustn't pass any of them up. **1948** L. A. G. STRONG *Trevannion* v. 98, I don't like to see a good man waste himself. Pass up his opportunities. **1951** E. PAUL *Springtime in Paris* xvi. 310 'You mean that miserable bookworm turned her down, when she offered herself? He's a cad.' 'Don't say that... He didn't pass her up.' **1956** 'A. GILBERT' *And Death came Too* xiv. 146 Eventually he agreed to take the case (his heel of Achilles being an inability to pass up a chance of wiping the official eye). **1962** *Listener* 26 Apr. 722/2 They passed up opportunities of wealth and property. **1964** MRS. L. B. JOHNSON *White House Diary* 6 July (1970) 175 When Lyndon insisted that I go over to the Scharnhorst Ranch with him, it was one last chance that I couldn't pass up. **1969** AUDEN *City without Walls* 48 If you pass up a dame, you've yourself to blame, For shame is neurotic, so snatch! **1972** J. POTTS *Trouble-Maker* (1973) x. 72 All false leads so far, but they can't afford to pass any of them up. **1975** *Times Lit. Suppl.* 11 Apr. 401/1 When the book does put reproductions of two states of the same etching side by side..Mr Passeron passes up the opportunity to discuss the meaning of the changes made. **1976** *Daily Tel.* 26 Oct. 17/1 He had passed up a job offer with a large accounting firm to cruise the South Seas.

passable, *a.* Add: **8.** as *sb.* A person or thing that is passable.

1908 *Westm. Gaz.* 26 June 2/1 Among such offspring there would be a small class of 'desirables', a large class of 'passables', and a small class of 'undesirables'.

passade. Add: **4.** (With pronunc. ‖ pasād.) A transitory love affair; a passing romance.

1931 *Times Lit. Suppl.* 19 Feb. 134/2 His [*sc.* Mérimée's] singular *passade* with George Sand. **1934** H. G. WELLS *Exper. Autobiogr.* II. vii. 465 The French..distinguish between the *passade*, a stroke of mutual attraction that may happen to any couple, and a real love affair. In theory, I was now to have *passades*. *Ibid.* 466 For women even more than for men, the frequent *passade* seems unattractive. **1937** —— *Brynhild* ix. 176 This lady had experienced two *grand passions* and a vast number of minor *passades*... The term *passade* was new to Brynhild. She tried to imagine the technique of a *passade*. **1938** —— *Apropos of Dolores* iv. 158 She has a wonderful French word 'passades'. She may have *passades*. Possibly with rather scared youngish men. **1973** WODEHOUSE *Bachelors Anonymous* viii. 88 'Sure I did, the first moment I got here,' said Mr Llewellyn, feeling it unnecessary to complicate things by mentioning his *passade* with Miss Vera Dalrymple.

passage, *sb.* Add: **I. 1. e.** (*b*) *bird of passage* (further examples); esp. = *passage-migrant* (sense 16 b below); *fig.* (earlier and later examples). Also (*slang*), a tramp.

1728 CHAMBERS *Cycl.* II. 758/2 Birds of Passage, are such as only come at certain Seasons, and then disappear again. **1763** J. BELL *Trav. from St. Petersburg* I. 188 As for water-fowl..they are also birds of passage. **1771** SMOLLETT *Humph. Cl.* I. 150 The..entertainments of Bath are over for this season; and all our gay birds of passage have taken their flight to Bristol-well, Tunbridge..*&c.* **1785** E. SHERIDAN *Jrnl.* (1960) 52 Our young Man is I find only a Bird of passage so the lady will be our only dinner companion. **1789** G. WHITE *Selborne* I. x. 29 Mr. Stillingfleet makes a question whether the blackcap (*motacilla atricapilla*) be a bird of passage or not. **1853** DICKENS *Bleak Ho.* xl. 398 My Lady has been but poorly..when she was here as a bird of passage—like. **1879** MRS. C. COOK *Comic Hist. N.S.W.* 49 It was a speculation by a bird of passage, one (poor little) Sparrow. **1893** A. NEWTON *Dict. Birds* II. 550/1 Others again—and these are strictly speaking the 'Birds of Passage'—which shew themselves but twice a year, passing through the country without staying long in it. **1896** E. DOWSON *Let.* c 4 June (1967) 366 People arrive daily; most of them, however, birds of passage. **1945** BAKER *Austral. Lang.* 103 *Traveller* and *commercial traveller*, together with *food inspector*, *bird of passage*, *wallaby tracker*, *tourist*, *footman* and *professional pedestrian*, are often applied to itinerants. **1960** *Guardian* 13 Oct. 12/3 As a 'bird of passage' the graduate tended to be supernumerary in the various departments. **1963** *Times* 20 Apr. 5/4 There is a need to differentiate between the birds of passage and those who give a lifetime to the profession.

2. c. *rites of passage*: see *RITE 1 d.

4. b. *to work one's passage*: see WORK *v.* 12 h in Dict. and Suppl.

7. (Further examples.)

1931 J. T. ADAMS *Epic of Amer.* ix. 240 The passage of a more stringent fugitive-slave law. **1968** *Globe & Mail* (Toronto) 3 Feb. 3/5 She rejected a request from Edward Schreyer (NDP, Springfield) that passage of the clause be postponed until members had had a chance to think about it. **1974** *Encycl. Brit. Macropædia* VII. 875/2 He could not prevent the passage of the bill.

10. b. *Med.* and *Biol.* A stage in the maintenance of a strain of micro-organisms or cells, from inoculation into a host organism or culture medium, through a period of multiplication, to extraction; the process of passing micro-organisms or cells through a series of hosts or cultures in this way, so as to maintain them or modify their virulence. Freq. with pronunc. (pæsā·ʒ).

1896 [in Dict., sense 10]. **1926** G. H. SMITH tr. *F. d'Herelle's Bacteriophage* iv. 160 The virulence of a bacteriophage may be exalted by successive passages in suspensions of a susceptible bacterium. **1945** *Jrnl. Immunol.* LI. 390 A chorio-allantoic suspension of the 259th chick embryo passage. **1947** *Jrnl. Exper. Med.* LXXXV. 24 The virus was maintained by occasional lung passage in albino Swiss mice. **1973** *Nature* 18 May 163/1 These tumours are transplantable and have been transplanted for up to six consecutive passages.

III. 13. b. (Further example.)

1920 *Brit. Mus. Return* 115 in *Parl. Papers* XXXVI. 673 The threatened extermination of the Elephants in the Addo Bush..has led to the passage of a number of letters between the Museum and various writers.

14. e. Add to def.: *spec.*, an area of a picture where one tone merges into another; the technique of achieving this effect.

1961 M. LEVY *Studio Dict. Art Terms* 84 *Passage*... Also used to describe the transition from one tone to another, by means of a half-tone. **1962** *Listener* 15 Feb. 304/1 They [*sc.* the Cubists] exaggerated his [*sc.* Cézanne's] use of his device known as *passage* by which the near end of a plane is clearly defined while the far end dissolves into space. **1962** R. G. HAGGAR *Dict. Art Terms* 247/2 *Passage*, a term used to describe a certain area of paint on a picture where one color or tone merges into another, where some special technique has been used, or where there may be over-painting by another hand. **1967** J. N. BARRON *Lang. of Painting* 143 These passages are used to relate volumes or three-dimensional forms to the two-dimensional picture frame.

V. 16. b. passage-free *adv.*, free of charge for passage or conveyance; **passage grave** *Archæol.*, an underground burial chamber connected with the surface by a passage; also *attrib.*; **passage-migrant**, a bird that stays for a short time in an area on the route of its migration to summer or winter quarters; also *fig.*; **passage-work** *Mus.*, a passage of a composition which calls for virtuosic display; the execution of such a passage.

1928 *Daily Express* 28 Aug. 3/7 She..brings to Canada almost passage-free any man of good health and physique who is an experienced agriculturist. **1888** F. H. WOODS tr. *Montelius's Civilisation of Sweden* i. 30 The graves of this period are commonly described as 'dolmens' (*stendösar*), 'passage-graves' (*gånggrifter*), and 'stone cists' (*hällkistor*). **1919** [see *boat-axe* s.v. *BOAT *sb.* 3]. **1934** *Discovery* Mar. 66/2 Soon after 4,000 B.C. began the neolithic civilization marked by great stone tombs, first dolmens then passage-graves, and lastly long stone cists. **1943** J. & C. HAWKES *Prehist. Brit.* ii. 45 The men who introduced passage-grave architecture and art seem to have reached Ireland from Portugal and south-west Spain. **1958** F. E. ZEUNER *Dating Past* (ed. 4) 81 This leaves only something like 200 years for that part of the Neolithic in Denmark which is clearly anterior to the arrival of the Bronze Age Beaker folk in Britain, namely all that preceding the middle of the Passage Grave period. **1963** E. S. WOOD *Collins Field Guide Archaeol.* I. iv. 57 Passage Graves have a chamber, round, square or with side chambers, connected by a narrow passage to the outside of the usually round mound or cairn which covers it. **1970** *Canad. Antiques Collector* Nov. 19/1 The shape of Knowth differs from other known passage graves in Ireland. **1934** INGRAM & SALMON *Birds in Brit. To-day* xiii. 115 Records of small parties [of Scandinavian lesser black-backed gulls].. occurring as passage-migrants, especially in spring, should be considered extremely doubtful. **1940** H. F. WITHERBY et al. *Handbk. Brit. Birds* III. 12 Distribution [of peregrine falcon].—British Isles.—Resident and passage-migrant. **1964** *Oxf. Bk. Birds* 74/1 Ruffs and reeves used to breed in Britain, but now they are mainly passage migrants..; a few spend the winter and summer. **1976** N. ROBERTS *Face of France* iv. 47 In the past they [*sc.* the French] did indeed accept Black immigrants, and particularly passage migrants, happily enough. **1977** *Times* 18 Aug. 14/6 Formby Point is a haunt of passage-migrants. **1920** *Musical Times* LXI. 159 The Fantasia is mere passage-work of the most desolating description. **1931** G. JACOB *Orchestral Technique* iii. 25 Of course arpeggios and passage-work generally can freely *pass through* this part of the compass. **1959** *Times* 13 Nov. 15/4 Some of his faster passage-work (notably in Beethoven's semi-quavers) tended to sound scratchy. **1966** *Listener* 10 Feb. 219/1 The passage work sounded anything but assured and intonation was distinctly impure. **1972** *Daily Tel.* 11 Jan. 9/4 The choral singing..was sonorously centred and admirably articulated in quickfire passage-work. **1977** *Gramophone* Sept. 423/1 All three of these concertos are well constructed and melodious, sometimes with brilliant passage-work for the soloist.

passage, *v.*[2] Add: **3.** *Med.* and *Biol.* To subject a strain of (micro-organisms or cells) to a passage (sense *10 b). In *Med.* usu. with pronunc. (pæsā·ʒ).

1927 *Brit. Jrnl. Dermatol.* XXXIX. 7 Although the herpetic strain has been submitted to intracerebral passages for 4 years, it is still far from being as virulent or 'neurotropic' as the lethargica strain which has been passaged for 18 months only. **1952** *Jrnl. Exper. Med.* XCV. 260 All [influenza strains] were prepared from allantoic fluid passaged in 10 to 11 day old embryos. **1973** R. G. KRUEGER et al. *Introd. Microbiol.* xix. 514/1 The higher the donor species lies on the evolutionary scale, the more times one can passage that species' tissue *in vitro*. **1973** *Nature* 18 May 163/2 Non-infected, non-transformed hamster cells passaged *in vitro* fifteen times failed to develop tumours in 1-day-old hamsters.

passage-money. (Further examples.)
1833 *Chambers's Edin. Jrnl.* 25 May 140/3 Hereabout the captain collects the passage-money. **1889** F. D. Lugard *Diary* 31 Dec. (1959) I. i. 60 Rs. 300 is I think very moderate. He asks no passage money &c. and speaks the language. **1966** *Times* (Australia Suppl.) 28 Mar. p. xv/1, I am not talking about cultural encouragement, only passage money.

passage-way. (Earlier N. Amer. examples.)
1649 *Rec. Early Hist. Boston* (1877) II. 98 Wm. Franklin is fined 20s. for disablinge the passage way. **1715** in *Cambridge* (Mass.) *Reg. Bk.* (1896) 276 It is Neither Needfull nor convenient for to have a passage Way thro' Said Dickson's lot. **1846** T. L. McKenney *Mem.* I. ix. 191 On reaching the War Department I was met in the passage-way by the Hon. James Barbour.

passalid (pæ·sălid), *a.* (*sb.*) *Ent.* [f. mod.L. family name *Passalidæ*, f. the generic name *Passalus* (J. C. Fabricius *Entomologia Systematica* (1792) I. II. 240), f. Gr. πάσσαλος peg, in allusion to the shape of the insect: see -id[3].] Belonging to the family Passalidæ, which includes black or dark brown beetles with slightly flattened bodies, found in decaying wood in warm forest regions. Also as *sb.*, a beetle belonging to this family.
1904 G. J. Arrow in *Trans. Entomol. Soc. London* 748 The Passalid beetle stridulates by the opposition of certain stout spines upon the wings to other spines..upon the antepenultimate dorsal segment. **1916** *Records Indian Museum* XII. 138 Madame Merian's larva can no longer be regarded as a Passalid. **1927** *Chambers's Jrnl.* 20 Aug. 601/1 The whole Passalid family lives in rotten tree-stumps. **1959** E. F. Linssen *Beetles Brit. Isles* I. 44 The Passalid beetles are so interesting and of such exceeding importance to the comparative study of the social behaviour of insects that the reader may wish to know more about them. **1972** L. E. Chadwick tr. *Linsenmaier's Insects of World* 155/2 Famous for their family life are the passalid beetles.

Passamaquoddy (pæ:sămăkwǫ·di). Also 8 **Passamaquoda, Pesmaquady.** [Micmac, = 'place where pollack are plentiful', with reference to Passamaquoddy Bay.] (A member of) a tribe of North American Indians nearly identical in language and culture to the Maliseet and inhabiting parts of south-east Maine and (formerly) south-west New Brunswick; the Algonquian language of this tribe. Also *attrib.* or as *adj.*
1726 J. Gyles in *Maine Hist. Soc. Coll.* (1853) III. 357 Memorandom of ye No of Indians in each tribe from 16 years of age... Pesmaquady Indians 30. **1759** T. Pownall in *Ibid.* (1857) V. 371 Zacharie was asked what Tribe he was of, ansd Passamaquoda. **1842** *Wasp* (Nauvoo, Illinois) 3 Sept. 3/1 Our Passamaquoddy Indians are divided into two political parties, between which a good deal of acrimonious feeling exists. **1857** *Porter's Spirit of Times* 11 July 292/2 Much interest was felt in the birch canoe race, between some Indians of the Passamaquoddy, Penobscot and Micmac tribes. **1910** F. W. Hodge *Handbk. Amer. Indians* II. 207/2 Passamaquoddy... A small tribe belonging to the Abnaki confederacy... They formerly occupied all the region about Passamaquoddy bay and on St Croix r and Schoodic lake, on the boundary between Maine and New Brunswick. **1912** *28th Ann. Rep. U.S. Bureau Amer. Ethnol. 1906–7* 259 The consonantic clusters of Passamaquoddy. *Ibid.* 285 The Passamaquoddy independent mode. **1917** *Internat. Jrnl. Amer. Linguistics* I. 58/1 The Passamaquoddies live about four hundred strong at Pleasant Point... It is safe to estimate that about a thousand persons still speak Passamaquoddy. *Ibid.* 58/2, I intend to publish shortly a complete chrestomathy of Passamaquoddy tales. **1935** *Explorations & Field Work Smithsonian Inst. 1934* 85 Probably all the Passamaquoddy have white blood in varying degrees. *Ibid.* 88 Passamaquoddy (as is the case with other Eastern Algonquian languages) has deviated from the normal type. *Ibid.* (*caption*) Alexander Spain, a Passamaquoddy. **1957** *Encycl. Brit.* I. 49/2 They [*sc.* the Abnaki] included the.. Passamaquoddy. **1974** *Encycl. Brit. Micropædia* VII. 786/1 In 1969 there were two Passamaquoddy reservations in Maine. **1977** C. F. & F. M. Voegelin *Classification & Index World's Lang.* 17 Passamaquoddy... D[ialect] also Malecite... 9,000–10,000 [speakers]. New Brunswick, Maine, and adjacent Quebec. **1978** *Times* 11 Jan. 7/3 In Maine, the Passamaquoddy and Penobscot Indians are claiming..nearly two thirds of the entire state.

passback (pɑ·sbæk). [f. Pass *v.* + Back *adv.*] **a.** *Amer. Football.* = *snap-back. **b.** *Association Football*, etc. A defensive pass directed backwards to a team-mate, usu. the goalkeeper.
1934 in Webster. **1947** *Richmond* (Virginia) *Times-Dispatch* 16 Nov. 8B/7 For the first time in the game Filer called play No. 43. The passback came directly to the big fullback. **1976** *Scottish Daily Express* 23 Dec. 12/5 Goalkeeper Ted McPheat dropped a passback at the feet of Mike Lafnach. **1976** *Sunday Post* (Glasgow) 26 Dec. 35/3 If there's a better fetch-and-carry midfield man in the country than Lex Richardson (as long as he doesn't attempt passbacks) I'd like to see him.

pass-book. Add: **1.** (Further examples.)
1902 G. Meredith *Let.* ? 20 Apr. (1970) III. 1441, I do not see in my pass-book the Swedish £15. **1916** *Banking Publicity* Oct. 1/1 It is not more necessary for the banker to advertise who would have men and women leave their money with nothing more than a passbook to carry home in place of it? **1922** Joyce *Ulysses* 707 A bank passbook issued by the Ulster Bank, College Green branch showing statement of a/c for halfyear ending 31 December 1903. *Ibid.* 710 The endowment policy, the bank passbook, the certificate of the possession of scrip. **1949** G. B. Shaw *Buoyant Billions* III. 30 What money I need appears to my credit in my bank passbook as cash or dividends on the few investments my stockbroker has advised. **1954** R. Gittings *John Keats: Living Year* v. 49 A small red leather wallet with a tuck-in flap, rather like a bank passbook. **1977** *Time* 28 Feb. 38/1 If the salesman had $2,000 or more in a savings account, he could borrow on his passbook and pay 1% more in interest on his loan than he received in interest on his savings.
2. (Earlier and later examples.)
1833 *Chambers's Edin. Jrnl.* II. 321/1 [Are there] no unheard-of overcharges in those pass-books I see flying about like evil spirits? **1861** Mrs. Beeton *Bk. Househ. Managem.* 1108 The 'pass-books' employed backwards and forwards between bakers, butchers, and the like domestic traders, and their customers. **1972** *Lebende Sprachen* XVII. 34/1 US passbook—BE credit sales book, roundsman's book.
3. *S. Afr.* = *pass *sb.*[2] 8 f.
Usu. written as two words without hyphen.
1961 T. Matshikiza *Chocolates for my Wife* 88 The sergeant..thumbed querulously through each ninety-six paged pass book. **1963** K. Mackenzie *Dragon to Kill* xvi. 181 The police came to know about the evidence he could give in this case when they arrested him again, on a charge involving forged pass books. **1971** *Post* (Golden City, S. Afr.) 21 Mar. 7 Bishop Alpheus Zulu, who was arrested a week ago for not carrying his pass book. **1972** P. Driscoll *Wilby Conspiracy* (1973) vi. 74 People were advised..to destroy the pass books which the law required them to carry. **1973** *Times* 21 Sept. 15/5 Sizwe appropriates the dead man's name and pass book.

pass-by. Add: **3. a.** (Further examples.)
1911 *Act* 1 & 2 *Geo. V* c. 50 § 43(3) Where, in the case of any mine, sets or trains of tubs are coupled or uncoupled at the face, or at the pass-bye next the face. **1967** *Gloss. Mining Terms* (*B.S.I.*) x. 11 *Pass-by*, 1. A siding in an underground haulage track having a turnout at both ends to the main line... 2. A loop of track around the shift at the pit bottom.
b. A place on a plate-rail (Plate *sb.* 8) where vehicles can pass. Also *attrib.*
1797 J. Curr *Pract. Coal Viewer* 26 Pass bye plates. Useful for 2 horses going contrary ways and passing each other with a draught of corves. *Ibid.* 27 Supposing a branch of road is required to be made to a new pit, one end of the above described pass bye..will accommodate such purpose.

passé, *a.* Add: **B.** as *sb.* In Ballet (see quot. 1948). Also *attrib.*
1948 A. Chujoy tr. *Vaganova's Basic Princ. Classical Ballet* vi. 65 Passé corresponds to its French meaning (passed). It is an auxiliary movement which transfers (passes) the leg from one position into another. If you are standing in développé effacé forward and you wish to bring the leg back into arabesque without doing a grand rond de jambe, you bend the leg at the knee, leaving it at a height of 90°, brush the toe of that foot past the standing leg and bring it out into arabesque. The passing the leg through this path is called passé. **1957** T. Mara *Second Steps in Ballet* 41 *Passé*... This means to pass the foot to a position at the knee in preparation for opening it in the *développé*. The right foot is strongly pointed at the little hollow of the supporting knee. **1959** B. & P. Fletcher *How to improve your Ballet Dancing* ix. 100 Relevé to passé position on left toe with right toe touching inside supporting knee. **1967** G. Grant *Tech. Man. & Dict. Classical Ballet* (ed. 2) 75 *Passé*,..is an auxiliary movement in which the foot of the working leg passes the knee of the supporting leg from one position to another (as, for example, in développé passé en avant) or one leg passes the other in the air (as in jeté passé en avant) or one foot is picked up and passes in back or in front of the supporting leg (as in chassé passé).

‖ **passe** (pas). [Fr., f. *passer* to pass: see quot. 1903.] In roulette, the section of the cloth covering the numbers 19 to 36; a bet placed on this section.
1850, etc. [see *noir 2 a]. **1902** *Encycl. Brit.* XXXII. 304/1 *Pair* indicates even numbers, *impair* odd numbers; *manque* includes the numbers from 1 to 18; *passe*, from 19 to 36. **1903** 'L. Hoffmann' *Card & Table Games* (ed. 3) 649 So called because in this event the ball 'fails' (Fr. *manque*) to fall into a higher number than 18. *Passe* is so called because the ball 'passes' that number. **1923**, etc. [see *manque]. **1937** G. Frankau *More of Us* vii. 76 By plying rake on impair, manque, passe, parity, or any number you might put your fish on. **1971** P. O'Neil-Dunne *Roulette for Millions* iv. 38 The roulette table is divided into six areas which, starting from the top nearest the wheel, are labelled: *manque* for low; *passe* for high; *impair* for odds; *pair* for evens.

passe-. Add: passe colmar (earlier and later examples); usu. with capital initials.
1837 *Amer. Q. Rev.* XXI. 377 We could speak of others just coming into notice, such as the passe colmar. **1860** R. Hogg *Fruit Manual* 204 Passe Colmar... An excellent pear. Ripe during November and December. **1928** H. B. Tukey *Pear* x. 108 Passe Colmar..and other winter sorts sometimes shrivel and rot before reaching an edible condition.

passed, *ppl. a.* Add: **3.** *passed-out*: unconscious, *spec.* through alcoholic drink. *colloq.*
1927 *Amer. Speech* II. 277 *Passed out*, intoxicated. **1939** G. Greene *Lawless Roads* iii. 95 The blue soda-water bottles and the passed-out Mexican.

‖**passeggiata** (pasėdʒiā·tă). [It., = walk, promenade.] A leisurely walk; a regular stroll.
1967 *Listener* 30 Mar. 434/2 They step out together like a mother and children on a walk, or an Italian family making a *passeggiata*. **1969** Hurd & Osmond *Smile on Face of Tiger* v. 141 In the canyons of the Chinese town the deafening *passegiata* [*sic*] of the poor, dressed in their holiday best. **1971** N. Fisher *Rise at Dawn* viii. 137 We drove into Viareggio one evening. It was the hour of the *passeggiata*... The pavements thronged with strolling families. **1973** *Sat. Rev. Society* (U.S.) Feb. 19/3 The *passeggiata* after working hours of citizens along the Via dei Caizaiuoli. **1978** 'A. Stuart' *Vicious Circles* 4, I found myself peacefully watching the flow of people.. taking their passegiata, or shopping.

‖**passéisme** (paseiz'm). [Fr.] Adherence to and regard for the traditions and values of the past, esp. in the arts. So **passéist(e)**, a traditionalist, one who is backward-looking (also *attrib.* or as *adj.*).
1914 Wyndham Lewis *Let.* 14 June (1963) 62 There are certain artists in England who do not belong to the Royal Academy nor to any of the passéist groups, and who do not on that account agree with the futurism of Sig. Marinetti. **1927** R. Fry *Let.* 4 Aug. (1972) II. 603 I've never been a Passéist—I was a Futurist but I have gradually trained myself to be a Presentist. **1943** Wyndham Lewis *Let.* 15 Oct. (1963) 368, I remember that clown Marinetti (the 'father of fascism') and his bellowings about 'passéisme' and his proposal to destroy all the pictures and buildings reminding people of the Past in Italy. **1953** —— *Let.* 23 Nov. (1963) 552 In editing *Blast* I regarded the contributions of Ezra as compromisingly passéiste. **1962** *Times* 12 Apr. 18/5 Delacroix was far more of a *passéiste* than the author suggests. **1968** *Listener* 29 Feb. 259/1 The old conflict between *passéiste* faculty and *antipasséiste* students is over.

passel (pæ·səl). Also **pasel, passle, pazil.** *dial.* and *U.S. colloq.* var. Parcel *sb.* 6.
1835 A. B. Longstreet *Georgia Scenes* 195 'How did you come on raisin' chickens this year, Mis' Shad?' 'La Messy, honey! I have had mighty bad luck. I had the prettiest pasel you most ever seed till the varment took to killin 'em.' **1865** W. B. Forfar *Kynance Cove* vii. 43 She ax'd about 'n a fine passle more than she wud ef he'd been a stranger. **1871** E. Eggleston *Hoosier Schoolmaster* 169 A passel of thieves. **1881** *Atlantic Monthly* June 740/1 A passel o' folks. **1889** T. E. Brown *Manx Witch* 16 She knocked two dishes And a pazil of plates there off the dresser. **1890** S. S. Buckman *John Darke's Sojourn in Cotteswolds* ii. 6 Lor, thur wur quite a passel o' volk altogither. **1893** H. A. Shands *Some Peculiarities of Speech in Mississippi* 49 *Passle* (pæsel). Used to some extent by all classes, but principally by the uneducated, to mean a *parcel*, not in the sense of a small bundle or a small quantity, but in that of a considerable number; as, 'There was a whole *passle* of hogs in the yard'; i.e. there were a good many. The word has, perhaps, a somewhat larger meaning than *a good many*, but denotes less than a multitude. This word is used in Kentucky, but is becoming rare there. **1903** K. D. Wiggin *Rebecca* xix. 202 Then you can explain, if you can, who gave you any authority to invite a passel of strangers to stay here overnight. **1906** Kipling *Puck of Pook's Hill* 264 'Twas a passel o' nosense talk. **1935** Z. N. Hurston *Mules & Men* I. vii. 151 A man had a wife and a whole passle of young 'uns. **1936** [see *no-'count *a.*]. **1948** *Sun* (Baltimore) 3 Dec. 14/2 Who wants to gamble that a passel of bureaucrats in a planned economy could have shown similar bounce in the face of adversity? **1957** W. C. Handy *Father of Blues* vi. 80 We had to absorb a 'passel' of oratory of the brand served by some Southern politicians just this side of the turn of the century. **1972** M. J. Bosse *Incident at Naha* iii. 134 'He'll forget,' I declared, thinking of the wives and the passel of kids. **1973** *Science* 12 Jan. 162/1 But the AAAS did succeed in having a passel of young activists evicted from the meeting's main registration area. **1973** D. Westheimer *Going Public* iv. 54 How'd you like to make yourself a passel of money without hardly havin' to do any work? **1977** *Time* 20 June 47/2 She plays a small rancher who pools her resources with neighboring Landowner James Caan to fight off greedy Cattle Baron Jason Robards and a passel of oil companies lusting after their range land.

passementerie. Add: Also **pasmentier.** (Earlier and later examples.)
1794 A. Young *Trav. France* (ed. 2) I. xix. 550 They assert their *pasmentiers* of silk and cotton mixed, to be cheaper than any similar fabric in England. **1903** [see *dangly *a.*]. **1933** M. de la Roche *Master of Jalna* viii. 100 'Put a frill on it,' he suggested. 'A frill! A frill of what?' 'Would *passementerie* do?' he asked. **1936** M. Mitchell *Gone with Wind* xii. 232 Her stout bosom heaved violently beneath its glittering passementerie trimmings.

passenger. Add: **3. b.** Ellipt. for *passenger train. colloq.*

1886 H. Baumann *Londinismen* 132/1 *Passenger*,.. passenger-train. **1920** 'O. Douglas' *Penny Plain* xxiii. 259 He could spend ecstatic days watching every 'passenger' and every 'goods' that rushed..along the permanent way. **1962** 'D. Shannon' *Extra Kill* ix. 145 I'd just taken a couple to the Union Station, I guess to make the Owl for San Francisco—only passenger I know of leaving about then.

6. For *slang* read *colloq.* and add to def.: Also, in extended uses, one who takes a passive role in a group activity, enterprise, etc., making no personal contribution and requiring the continuous support of the rest. (Earlier and later examples.)

1852 J. F. Bateman *Aquatic Notes* iii. 23 Some University scratch Four-oared Races were rowed... Here would be seen three good oars endeavouring to row along a passenger', of some eleven stone weight. **1908** *Animal Managem.* 297 A sick or lame ox should be removed from the span at once, as he..is in fact 'a passenger', and has to be dragged along by the others. **1914** *Daily Mail* 6 Apr. 9/4 There was not a passenger in any division of the winning team. **1932** Auden *Orators* I. 19 We simply can't afford any passengers or skrimshankers. **1932** *Times Educ. Suppl.* 6 Aug. 301/2 It is a lucky school that has no passenger on its staff. **1946** D. Hamson *We fell among Greeks* iv. 47 We nearly had to shoot both of them later on at different times, because they were lazy and untrustworthy and we had no room for 'passengers'. **1948** 'N. Shute' *No Highway* xi. 288 As a scientist from Farnborough I was expected to be a passenger, useless in the woods. **1949** 'J. Tey' *Brat Farrar* xx. 185 You cannot expect to carry two adults as passengers in the estate... They are both capable of earning their own living. **1951** J. B. Priestley *Festival at Farbridge* II. ii. 319 Theodore plodded on, like a man walking on a hot afternoon to some place he hated. 'I'm beginning to feel I'm almost a passenger.' **1957** *Listener* 28 Nov. 882/2 More women have had to learn to become self-reliant in the mountains, or at least not to be mere passengers. **1961** A. Wilson *Old Men at Zoo* ii. 79 If you haven't any appreciation at all for serious research work, then the sooner you get out..the better. We're carrying enough passengers already. **1964** J. Masters *Trial at Monomoy* vii. 219 I'd want to do my share of work. I don't want to be a passenger. **1971** L. P. Davies *Shadow Before* v. 49 The scheme was really yours in the first place. Jack Latham wasn't much more than a passenger. **1971** R. J. White *Second-Hand Tomb* vii. 72 It was..an affection born of patronage. Pamela was so obviously a passenger.

7. a. *passenger cabin, car* (earlier and later examples), *carriage* (examples), *depot* (examples), *door, elevator, lift, line, list, lounge* (spec. in an airport), *manifest, plane, seat, side, terminal, trade* (examples), *traffic* (earlier and later examples), *train* (earlier and later examples), *way, window*; *passenger-carrying* adj.; *passengerless* adj. and adv.

1946 R. A. McFarland *Human Factors Air Transport Design* xi. 492 The general arrangement of the passenger cabin will naturally vary with the type of service for which the plane will be used. **1952** *Shell Aviation News* No. 166. 24 (*caption*) Cutaway drawing showing interior arrangement of the 44-passenger Convair-Liner 340. Forward of the passenger cabin is a large compartment for baggage and cargo. **1832** *Amer. Railroad Jrnl.* I. 305/3 Arrived, 9 passenger cars with 71 passengers. **1847** *Hunt's Merchants' Mag.* XVI. 211 Attached to this station, are also..two wood and water stations..a brass foundry, passenger car house, passenger rooms, offices &c. **1968** *Globe & Mail* (Toronto) 3 Feb. B 3/3 Extensive absenteeism by members of local 444 of the United Auto Workers forced a shutdown of the passenger car lines yesterday at the Windsor plant of Chrysler Canada Ltd. **1975** A. Bergman *Hollywood & LeVine* xiv. 211 Some Indian children waved at the train. They..stopped to stare at the silver blur of passenger cars. **1977** *Reinforced Plastics* XXI. 22/3 Engineering plastics materials have been used for many years for the production of cooling fans for passenger car engines. **1838** *Mechanics' Mag.* 13 Oct. 32/1 The *passenger carriages* of the American railways are extremely large and commodious. They are seated for 60 passengers, and are made so high in the roof, that the tallest person may stand upright in them without inconvenience. **1879** *Harper's Mag.* July 165 A bustling little locomotive with one passenger-carriage comes whistling down the valley. **1978** N. Marsh *Grave Mistake* vii. 210 A slow train with a passenger carriage. **1909** *Daily Chron.* 8 Sept. 1/6 He was placed third in the speed contest, fourth in the Gordon-Bennett Cup contest, and second in the passenger-carrying competition. **1928** *Manch. Guardian Weekly* 21 Sept. 224/4 It is with this passenger-carrying airship that the Germans hope to fly across the Atlantic. **1937** *Discovery* Sept. 270/2 The ultimate aim of all such experiments is the production of a passenger-carrying rocket plane. **1967** *Jane's Surface Skimmer Systems 1967–68* 87/2 The PT 20, a 27-ton boat for 75 passengers, is considered by Supramar to be the smallest size hydrofoil suitable for passenger-carrying coastal services. **1849** *Hunt's Merchants' Mag.* XX. 342 A spacious freight and passenger depot..has been completed in the lower part of Detroit. **1958** *Amer. Speech* XXXIII. 145 Though both units are likely to be in the same building, separate reference is sometimes made to the *freight depot* and the *passenger depot.* **1952** *Shell Aviation News* No. 165. 24 It is authorized that 87 occupants may be carried in aircraft with six exits, and one passenger door in the passenger area. **1968** K. Bird *Smash Glass Image* xii. 149 The dark-green Seat swung into the kerb... The passenger door opened. **1974** 'J. Le Carré' *Tinker, Tailor* xxxv. 311 In one of these blaring side-streets..Ricki Tarr would unlock the passenger door and hold him up at gun-point. **1886** J. A. Porter *New Stand. Guide Washington* 205 The building..is furnished with passenger-elevator, steam-heating, deposit-vaults, speaking tubes. **1919** C. Morley *Haunted Bookshop* iv. 87 Maybe he had no right to be riding in the passenger elevator. **1926** *Scribner's Mag.* Aug. 196/1 We ain't no trunks. Take us up in a passenger-elevator. **1906** *Westm. Gaz.* 11 Dec. 6/3 One would almost imagine that the running of a passengerless train from station to station,..would 'grow' on the conductors. **1952** R. Finlayson *Schooner came to Atia* 110 He was soon back, passengerless. **1907** *Shipping World* 16 Jan. 111 (Advt.), S.S. 'Lusitania' is being fitted with Passenger Lifts. **1931** *Times* 16 Mar. 21/7 An unique and beautifully-fitted flat, ideally situated and equipped with constant hot water, central heating, passenger and service lifts. **1938** M. Allingham *Fashion in Shrouds* xv. 248 They came up in a small handworked passenger lift to a front door. **1975** D. Bloodworth *Clients of Omega* xxii. 207 Dr. Moondance..will take the fast number one passenger lift to the fiftieth floor. **1851** *Min. Proc. Inst. Civil Engin.* X. 255 Owing to the different value now put upon the resistances to railway trains at high velocities,..good gradients had become relatively of less importance on passenger lines. **1843** Dickens *Mart. Chuz.* (1844) xvi. 196 I've just now sent a boy up to your office with the passenger-list. **1869** 'Mark Twain' *Innoc. Abr.* xx. 199 We had the whole passenger list for company. **1928** Kipling *Bk. of Words* 268 H.M.S. Great Britain carries a passenger list..of forty-five millions. **1931** —— *Limits & Renewals* (1932) 189 It's on the back of the passenger-list. **1958** B. Hamilton *Too Much of Water* ii. 23 A copy of the Passenger List which he had found in his cabin. **1973** A. Price *October Men* ii. 31 He was on the passenger list... It was an ordinary scheduled flight. **1969** D. Barron *Man who was There* i. 14, I..was considering looking for Gregory beyond the confines of the passenger lounge when they began to broadcast the announcement of our impending departure. **1970** M. Pereira *Pigeon's Blood* viii. 95 The Hall..for obvious reasons, was the only way of leaving the Passenger Lounge. **1971** Passenger manifest [see *manifest *sb.* 3]. **1976** B. Jackson *Flameout* (1977) ix. 149 I've..got the list of cargo... And the passenger manifest. **1931** W. L. Smith *Air Transport Operation* i. 5 The cost per passenger mile is about 7 cents for the largest passenger planes. *Ibid.* 4 In about the same period [12 yrs.], the capacity of passenger planes has increased from 2 to 30 passengers. **1937** *Discovery* May 164/1 The Pan-American Grace Company converted one of its passenger planes into a cargo plane. **1970** 'D. Holliday' *Dolly & Cookie Bird* viii. 124 Every now and then a big passenger plane would come droning in. **1975** S. Johnson *Urbane Guerilla* III. 114 The US..has banned shipment of nuclear material by passenger plane. **1937** M. Allingham *Dancers in Mourning* xxiv. 299 The body lay doubled up on the floor with..its head jammed against the front of the passenger seat. **1962** D. Francis *Dead Cert* xvii. 187 Pete himself poked his big bald head out of the passenger seat and called to me. **1972** *Guardian* 5 Dec. 7/2 Travel organisers..[must] keep within the terms and conditions of their licences... The licence will cost £250 a year plus 2p for each one-way passenger seat authorized by it. **1977** B. Pym *Quartet in Autumn* x. 91 Ken stuck in the passenger seat of a car on test. **1969** J. Gardner *Compl. State of Death* x. 216 He removed the bar, gently placed it on the passenger-side floor. **1972** *Country Life* 15 June 1577/2 A large glove box on the passenger side and a smaller one for the driver. **1976** *New Yorker* 16 Feb. 76/2 More personnel are needed at passenger terminals than at freight terminals relative to the value of their respective services. **1780** A. Young *Tour in Ireland* II. vi. 30 At the ports of Belfast, Derry, &c. the *passenger trade* as they called it, had long been a regular branch of commerce, which employed several ships, and consisted in carrying people to America. **1866** 'Mark Twain' *Lett. from Hawaii* (1967) 21 The sailing vessels..[are] too slow and uncertain to build up the passenger trade. **1972** 'G. Black' *Bitter Tea* (1973) vii. 110 The public is held back by a long counter..only we don't have much public really, not being in the passenger trade. **1836** *Mechanics' Mag.* 15 Oct. 30/1 No credit whatever was taken in the Eastern Counties Railway estimates for any of the passenger-traffic from *transmarine* sources, as that traffic was, at best, of a contingent character. **1883** W. H. Maw *Recent Pract. Marine Engin.* I. 117/2 In the case of a larger launch 40 ft. long fitted with engines of twenty indicated horse-power, and employed for passenger traffic on the River Dart, the average [fuel] consumption per week is but 10 cwt. **1933** S. L. Miller *Inland Transportation* xxi. 361 Efforts to increase the volume of railway passenger traffic have been in the past decade increasingly active. **1963** N. Wymer *Behind Scenes at London Airport* i. 17 The 'Short-haul' Building, opened in 1955, is for passenger traffic to and from Europe. **1976** Passenger traffic [see *private motoring* s.v. *private *a.* (*sb.*) 4c]. **1836** *Mechanics' Mag.* 5 Nov. 83/1 What is the usual weight you carry in one of your trains; your passenger train?—Forty or fifty tons; no, not more than thirty to forty tons, carriages and passengers together. **1937** *Discovery* Mar. 88/2 Each [van]..is vacuum fitted and fully equipped for working on fast passenger trains. **1976** *Daily Tel.* 20 July 4/1 Last Thursday he left Nairobi in a passenger train for Kampala. **1908** *Westm. Gaz.* 14 Mar. 2/1 Using the parallel of the street..he claimed that the river should be regarded as a passenger way. **1971** R. Petrie *Thorne in Flesh* xiv. 175 There was a large, dark saloon parked at the kerb... The nearside passenger window slid down and Tina called to him. **1977** P. Hill *Fanatics* 145 Dice..wound down the passenger window.

b. Special Comb., as **passenger-mile**, a unit of measurement representing one passenger travelling a distance of one mile; hence *passenger-mileage*; also *passenger-kilometre* (abbrev. *km.*).

1900 *Geogr. Jrnl.* XVI. 221 The number of passengers carried in 1898 was 126 millions, the number of passenger-kilometres amounting to 4439 millions. **1903** E. Johnson *Amer. Railway Transportation* x. 140 An equal mileage of road accommodates a much greater traffic in Europe than in the United States. This is shown by dividing the total number of miles traveled by all passengers (the 'passenger miles') by the miles of railroad. **1930** *Flight* 28 Nov. 1381/2 Taking paying passengers only, the figure becomes 41 passenger-miles. **1936** *Jrnl. R. Aeronaut. Soc.* XL. 850 The criterion then being the number of passenger miles flown per period. **1943** *Ibid.* XLVII. 249 An expectation that the accident rate can..be reduced to a long-term average of no more than 1·0 fatality per 100,000,000 passenger-miles. **1962** R. B. Fuller *Epic Poem on Industrialization* 219 Passenger miles per capita per annum By all modes of transport Represents a smoothly ascending Curve. **1971** *Guardian* 13 July 2/2 TWA on its own rates as the world's second largest airline—in terms of passenger-miles—behind United, the American domestic operator. **1974** *State* (Columbia, S. Carolina) 1 Apr. 2-A/2 (Advt.), If your carpool cars average, say, 13 miles to the gallon and you share costs with three others, you are paying for only one gallon in four, and you're getting 52 passenger miles-per-gallon. **1976** P. R. White *Planning for Public Transport* viii. 175 Of the 29000 million or more passenger-km generated on the BR system each year about 45 per cent are classified as intercity. **1978** *Jrnl. R. Soc. Arts* CXXVI. 427/1 In London Transport, we have adopted as our corporate aim the maximization of passenger-mileage within the financial resources available to us from fares and grants.

pa·ssengered, *a. rare.* [f. Passenger + -ed[2].] Of a vehicle, ship, etc.: carrying or occupied by passengers.

1929 R. Graves *Poems* 27 That was the hospital-boat of twelve years back, Passengered as before with doubt and dying. **1955** W. Gaddis *Recognitions* III. i. 723 Traffic often consists only in the gay orange garbage carts, passengered by black vultures.

passenger-pigeon. Add to def.: The bird became extinct in 1914. (Later examples.)

1907 W. B. Mershon *Passenger Pigeon* p. ix, As recently as 1880 the Passenger Pigeon was thronging in countless millions through large areas of the Middle West. **1955** A. W. Schorger *Passenger Pigeon* ix. 229 The passenger pigeon became extinct through such constant persecution that it was unable to raise sufficient young to perpetuate the race. **1967** D. Goodwin *Pigeons & Doves of World* 203 The Passenger Pigeon shares with the Dodo the doubtful fame of being one of the two best known species that have been exterminated by man. **1972** G. Durrell *Catch me a Colobus* x. 213 It was impossible, everyone thought, that the Passenger pigeon (so delicious to eat and so plentiful) could ever be exterminated... The last Passenger pigeon in the world died in the Cincinnati zoo in 1914. **1975** *New Yorker* 7 Apr. 45/1, I saw the last passenger-pigeon flocks in Iowa.

passe-partout, *sb.* Add: **2. c.** A kind of adhesive tape or paper used for framing photographs and for other purposes. Also *attrib.* and as *vb. trans.*

1909 *Cent. Dict.* Suppl. 952/1 *Passepartout*,..to place in a passe-partout frame. **1910** V. Tree *Let.* 13 Nov. in *Castles in Air* (1926) 54, I have found a manufacturer of *passe-partouts* for my flower and French costume prints. **1910–11** *T. Eaton & Co. Catal.* Fall & Winter 144/1 Passepartout binding, black, green, brown, grey, red and white. **1928** *Daily Express* 17 May 9/4 A favourite occupation is evidently to 'passe-partout' their pictures. **1954** *Paper Terminol.* (Spalding & Hodge) 44 *Passe-partout*, a strong embossed paper, gummed on one side and sold in coils about 1 in. wide. It is made in many colours and is used for picture mounting and the binding of lantern slides. **1969** R. Blythe *Akenfield* viii. 136 Passe-partouted photographs of their sons and daughters..hang on long strings from the picture rail. **1978** J. Goodman *Last Sentence* iii. 112 Haphazardly hung photographs, all framed amateurishly with passe-partout.

passer. Add: **3. b.** In ball games, a player who passes the ball to another player (cf. Pass *v.* 46 b).

1905 *Westm. Gaz.* 12 Dec. 9/2 From a clever pass—the 'passer' could not be distinguished in the fog—Parker feinted and swerved cleverly, scored behind the posts, and an easy goal resulted from Nesbitt's kick. **1970** *Washington Post* 30 Sept. D 4/3 If he played the whole season, he would rank among the top passers in the country. **1972** J. Mosedale *Football* ii. 18 Clark was his team's leading passer. **1973** *Times* 25 Jan. 12/8 Ian's a much better passer of the ball on the ground.

c. In various trades, a person who examines materials or manufactures to ensure that they are of the required quality, workmanship, etc. (see Pass *v.* 45 b).

1921 *Glasgow Herald* 21 June 9/7 The proposed reduction is 3d. per hour in respect of measure cutters,..fitters-up, tailors' pressers, machinists, passers, etc.

d. One who receives and passes on counterfeit money. *slang.* (Cf. Pass *v.* 46 c.)

1929 *Detective Fiction Weekly* 25 May 683/1 The dealer calls the carrier..they meet..and..a few bills are handed out as a sample. The carrier calls the 'shovers', sometimes known as 'passers' or 'pushers' who begin to operate. To this class belong the men who actually place the bogus money in circulation. **1955** W. Gaddis *Recognitions* II. v. 490 I'm going out to meet a passer, to hand this stuff over to him. It's all arranged and paid for. *Ibid.*, It's always trouble with the middleman and the passers that get you pulled in.

4. One who 'passes' as a member of an ethnic group other than his own. (Cf. *pass *v.* 5 d.)

1953 P. Abrahams *Return to Goli* II. iv. 64 If the passing is successful even the parents of the passer cease to know him or her. **1956** L. Kuper *Passive Resistance in S. Afr.* I. ii. 66 The psychology implicit in apartheid legislation is the psychology of the coloured man who has successfully 'passed' into the white group. Over the generations, there would have been inculcated into the successful 'passer' the dominant value that 'whiteness is all'.

5. One who sells drugs illicitly.

1955 [see *meet *sb.* 1 b]. **1956** *Sun* (Baltimore) 26 July

14/1 This is an Act of the utmost severity, even providing the death penalty for 'passers' under certain circumstances.

passe-temps. ? Delete †*Obs.* and add later examples.

1840 GEO. ELIOT *Let.* 20 July (1954) I. 60 It [sc. *Don Quixote*] is a charming passe-temps (a word by the bye that I ought to have outlawed long ago). **1848** T. ARNOLD *N.Z. Lett.* (1966) 27 One cannot be always reading and this sail-making forms a very agreeable passe-temps. **1891** W. FRASER *Disraeli & his Day* 344 After many dreary weeks of solitude at the 'Three Cups' hotel, the only *passe-temps* being to watch the corpses, removed from the sunk-fort, of soldiers who died daily of small-pox, the Election took place.

pass–fail (equal stress), *a.* [f. PASS *v.* 17 + FAIL *v.* 14.] Of or pertaining to passing and failing (in an examination or the like); applied *spec.* to methods of assessing examination performance in terms simply of success or failure, without further reference to the individual standards attained.

1959 *Psychol. Rev.* LXVI. 62/2 Using pass-fail scoring on all eighteen tests, the test-subject matrix was 91.8 per cent reproducible. **1963** *Times* 2 Dec. 11/7, I would like to suggest a Use of English paper on a five-point scale with no pass-fail line drawn. **1966** *Crimson-White* (Univ. of Alabama) 1 Dec. 4/3 On the last SRI poll, students were asked to give their opinion on a system known as 'pass-fail electives'. Under this system a student could take 2 or 3 electives while he was here at the University and not have to worry about his grade. **1970** *Times* 20 Apr. 2, I believe we have gained a great deal in suggesting grading instead of somewhat more rigid pass-fail standards. **1972** *Sat. Rev.* (U.S.) 4 Mar. 49/2 All courses are given on a pass/fail basis. **1973** *Harvard Law School Bull.* Apr. 18/2 A strictly pass-fail grading system.

‖**passglas** (pa·sglas). Also **pass glas**, and in anglicized form **pass glass** (pɑs glɑs). Pl. ‖**passgläser, pass glasses.** [Ger.] A tall, cylindrical drinking glass decorated with parallel rings or a spiral down its length.

1897 A. HARTSHORNE *Old Eng. Glasses* 68 Touching the Passglas, its usual type was a tall cylindrical vessel.. spaced, by fine wheeled stringings, into divisions for measuring and controlling the drinking. *Ibid.*, Rembrandt,..in his portrait by himself at Dresden, holds up exactly such a Rhine-land Passglas. *Ibid.* 81 Certain rare Pass glasses are ornamented with figures of knaves from playing cards, painted in enamel on white grounds. **1907** E. DILLON *Glass* xvi. 273 The tall *pass*-glass..is dated 1662. **1926** W. BUCKLEY *European Glass* 54 The Pass-glas is a typical German form which was made chiefly during the 17th century. It is always cylindrical, and is decorated by a stringing which sometimes encircles the glass spirally and at other times forms a number of rings more or less equidistant from one another. **1942** *Burlington Mag.* Dec. 299/1 The vessels depicted in Dutch still-life paintings are in fact as often of German as of Italian form—the *Roemer*, the *Passglas*,..are as commonly seen as the Italianate 'winged' goblets. **1960** H. HAYWARD *Antique Coll.* 211/1 *Passglas*,..a German glass beaker encircled by a notched spiral thread dividing it into equal parts so that the glass could be passed from guest to guest allowing each his allotted share. **1965** A. VON SALDERN *German Enameled Glass* 145 Cylindrical Stangen with horizontal rings in multicolored enamel—so-called Pass glasses..are derived from similar glasses with applied rigaree bands or spirals; each horizontal ring is called a Pass... In drinking, the trick was to bring the wine or beer down exactly to the level of one of the rings.

‖**pas si bête** (pɑ̄ *si* bɛ̄t). [Fr.] Not so foolish; 'not that stupid' (said of the speaker or of someone other than the speaker). Also (in quot. 1924), not so bad.

1840 THACKERAY in *Fraser's Mag.* June 727/2, I am not holding up the whole affair as a masterpiece—*pas si bête*. **1849** —— *Pendennis* I. xxix. 283 'Emily was always as stupid as an owl,' said Miss Blenkinsop. 'Eh! pas si bête,' the old Peer said. **1862** W. COLLINS *No Name* II. 82, I am not fool enough to open it. *Pas si bête*, as we used to say in the English circle at Zurich... *Pas si bête!* **1923** GALSWORTHY *Captures* 247 Why suppose one's family superior to other people's? *Pas si bête!* **1924** J. BUCHAN *Three Hostages* xii. 179 'What about the weather?' I asked anxiously. '*Pas si bête*,' he said, sniffing. 'The wind is pretty sure to go down.' **1939** N. MARSH *Overture to Death* xvi. 183 'Try us,' suggested the young man. 'Pas si bête,' said Alleyn, 'I want my lunch.' **1965** N. FREELING *Criminal Conversation* II. i. 102 You see how the parallel fails?.. *Pas si bête*.

passimeter (pӑsi·mɪ̆təɹ). Also (erron.) **passimetre.** [f. PASS *v.* or PASS(ENGER + -METER.] An automatic machine for supplying public transport passengers with tickets and recording the number of people who pass through.

1921 *Railway Gaz.* 2 Dec. 860/2 There are three separate registering cyclometers... The first registers the dating and cancellation of each ticket, setting the passenger free to proceed through the 'passimeter', whereby another cyclometer automatically records his passage. **1923** *Westm. Gaz.* 11 Aug. 6/4 Fifteen passimeters will be installed, and..it is hoped..to eliminate booking queues. **1927** *Observer* 16 Jan. 18/2 The work of substituting passimeters for the booking offices is now in progress. **1928** *Daily Express* 10 May 9 What a contrast with the modern **'passimetre'**, the glitter of green and white tile, the silent motion of escalators! **1928** J. P. THOMAS *Handling London's Undergr. Traffic* xii. 156 The first passimeter booking-office was introduced at Kilburn Park in 1921. **1964** *Guardian* 26 June 5/2 Central London is to have six experimental 'standee' buses, on which a single coin fare will be placed in a 'passimeter'. *Ibid.* 1 Dec. 4/2 On the six fast 'standee' buses which London Transport hopes to introduce next year..the fare..will be placed in a 'passimeter'.

passing, *vbl. sb.* Add: **1. a.** (Examples in sense *5d of the vb.)

1926 C. VAN VECHTEN *Nigger Heaven* 286 *Passing*, passing for white. **1952** L. MARQUARD *Peoples & Policies S. Afr.* iii. 77 Though..it is impossible to say how many coloured have succeeded in 'passing'—that is, in being fully accepted as European—'passing' has certainly occurred. **1952** M. STEEN *Phoenix Rising* vii. 176 Those who succeed in 'passing' live their lives in mortal terror of being found out. **1953** [see *PASSER 4]. **1958** S. E. HYMAN in A. Dundes *Mother Wit* (1973) 46/2 The account of lynching, passing, discrimination, or varieties of resistance. **1961** *Guardian* 4 May 10/4 'Passing', the word used to describe Negroes merging indistinguishably into a white community in America. **1973** G. D. BERREMAN *Caste in Mod. World* 10/2 The response of *Burakumin* to their birth-ascribed status is that common to all low castes: accommodation on the most part, and occasional 'passing'... As in all societies passing is difficult and stressful, for the fear of discovery and the necessary loss or attenuation of family contacts are traumatic.

b. *spec.* in ball games, the action of transferring (the ball) to another player (see sense 46b of the vb.). Also *absol.*

1882 *Blackburn Times* 1 Apr. 6/3 While the Rovers worked their way towards their opponents' goal by passing, the Etonians did so by rushes. **1889, 1892** [in Dict.]. **1906** GALLAHER & STEAD *Compl. Rugby Footballer* 85 A player's object in passing the ball is to give possession of it to a colleague who is in a better position for making further headway with it than he is himself. **1952** J. B. PICK *Phoenix Dict. Games* 1. 63 This..ensures that the passing will be precise. **1960** E. S. & W. J. HIGHAM *High Speed Rugby* 5 A method of passing the ball in which the outside elbow is bent upwards.

2. b. With *off*: see sense 64c of the vb. in Dict. and Suppl.

1900 *Rep. Patent Cases* (Patent Office) 15 Aug. 482 In the *Yorkshire Relish* case the inference was drawn that the mere use of a name implied passing off. **1902** [see *PASS v. 64c]. **1908** *Westm. Gaz.* 30 Apr. 9/2 Damages were claimed by the plaintiff for alleged libel, and the passing off of a story written by her in 1895 and 1896. Defendants denied that there was any libel or passing off. **1959** *Times* 6 Feb. 17/1 His action against them for alleged libel and passing off. **1960** *Times* 20 Sept. (Pure Food Suppl.) p. i/5 There still remains..the possibility of verbal passing-off at the time of sale. **1962** *Listener* 15 Mar. 457/1 We might ..be called upon to change our law in respect of 'passing-off'. Broadly speaking, this is selling one's own goods or services in a way which deceives the public into thinking that they are those of some other trader. **1970** WHITE & JACOB *Patents* III. viii. 65 In an action for passing-off the plaintiff must in practice prove that he has extensive enough goodwill for his goods to be recognised by members of the public.

3. (Earlier and later examples.)

1848 E. C. P. in C. H. Hartshorne *Eng. Medieval Embroidery* 113 A rich gold thread, called passing, or tambour. **1880** L. HIGGIN *Handbk. Embroidery* i. 8 *Gold and silver passing*, a very fine kind of thread. **1957** M. B. PICKEN *Fashion Dict.* 349/2 *Passing*, smooth, flattened thread made by twisting strands of gold or silver around a strand of silk. **1960** B. SNOOK *Eng. Hist. Embroidery* 48 A very fine flexible metal thread called 'passing' was known to the Elizabethans.

4. a. passing door *Mining*, an arrangement of doors in a gallery that enables people to pass through while preventing the free passage of air currents; **passing novel** (see quot.); **passing place** (*c*) on a narrow or single track road.

1839 URE *Dict. Arts* 989 Passing doors..may be substituted in any place for a passage where there is a stopping. **1964** J. H. CLARKE *Harlem* 345 James Weldon Johnson..wrote 'passing' novels, i.e. novels about Negroes who were able to pass as whites. **1951** N. M. GUNN *Well at World's End* xxiv. 210 The lorry swung into a 'passing place' with squealing brakes. **1963** P. MACTYRE *Fish on Hook* v. 73 He pulled ponderously into the next passing-place, to allow the vehicle behind to overtake. **1972** *Times* 16 Oct. 13/6 It's a single track road, with passing places not very close together—and of course heavy lorries can't back. **1973** G. MOFFAT *Lady with Cool Eye* vii. 74 A narrow tarred track..only wide enough for one vehicle. At intervals there were passing-places.

b. With advbs., as *passing-off action*; *passing-out examination, inspection, parade*; *passing-through ritual*.

1925 F. I. SCHECHTER *Hist. Found. Law Trade-Marks* i. 10 Lord Chancellor Halsbury, in analyzing the plaintiff's pleadings in a 'passing-off' action, stated that such an action 'has been a well recognized cause of action, certainly for the last two hundred and fifty years'. **1946** *Nature* 2 Nov. 604/1 Traders were obliged to rely on cumbersome and expensive passing-off actions to protect their name and goods. **1970** WHITE & JACOB *Patents* III. viii. 66 Many businesses do not keep their trade marks fully and validly registered, so that resort to a passing-off action may always be necessary to cover flaws in the trade-mark position. **1976** *Century of Trade Marks* (Patent Office) i. 2/2 In France ..there is at least one recorded instance in the 16th Century of what would be called today a passing-off action, in which the defendant was subjected to a perpetual injunction and made to pay heavy costs. **1916** *Daily Colonist* (Victoria, B.C.) 28 July 4/7 He came out first in the recent passing-out examinations. **1973** *Soviet Weekly* 5 May 2/3 Moscow School of Choreography..has begun its passing-out examinations. **1930** *Times Educ. Suppl.* 2 Aug. 340/3 The passing-out inspection of aircraft apprentices..was held on Tuesday. **1955** *Times* 11 Aug. 6/5 The Sudan defence force to-day held the first passing-out parade of officer cadets since the Sudanization of the force. **1971** B. W. ALDISS *Soldier Erect* 156 The C.O. of Kanchapur spoke to us on passing-out parade. **1973** 'S. HARVESTER' *Corner of Playground* I. v. 38 Officer cadets due to receive their commissions at the passing-out parade. **1969** *Times* 19 Mar. 4/4 The wedding ring and the custom of the groom carrying his bride over the threshold may be relics of the 'passing through' rituals.

passing, *ppl. a.* Add: **2. c.** *passing show*, the spectacle of contemporary life; an entertainment using as material current events and interests, a revue.

1908 *Sears, Roebuck Catal.* 1047/3 A whole passing show... Your friends grotesquely photographed... By getting a focus on passing pedestrians, horses, cars, etc., the most ludicrous pictures are witnessed. **1915** (*title of journal*) The passing show. **1915** A. WIMPERIS (*title of revue*) Passing show. **1956** *B.B.C. Handbk. 1957* 31 To keep the listener fully in touch with the 'passing show' of contemporary life. **1968** *N.Y. City* (Michelin Tire Corp.) 81 In 1864, Tony Pastor's Opera House made vaudeville fashionable...the 'revue' or 'passing show' caught on in the 90's. **1976** *Scottish Rev.* Summer 9 Reason tends to be hostile to the passing show, tends to view reality as an eternity of fixed types amenable to the eye of reason.

passing-by. Restrict †*Obs.* to sense in Dict. and add: **b.** The action of ignoring or neglecting.

1909 *Westm. Gaz.* 6 May 8/3 The ousting of home-bred meat, and the passing-by of the market by the great importers.

passing-note. (Earlier example.)

1730 *Short Treat. Harmony* v. 28 We make use of the Second, the Seventh, and of the Fourth as Discords or Passing Notes.

passion, *sb.* Add: **1. c.** Also, a dramatic setting of the Passion of Christ; = *passion-play*.

1823 W. HONE *Anc. Mysteries Described* 169 In 1298, the passion was played at Friuli. **1903** E. K. CHAMBERS *Mediæval Stage* II. xxii. 129 There were performances of Passions in Reading in 1508, in Dublin in 1528, [etc.]. **1962** R. SOUTHERN *Seven Ages of Theatre* 107 The *Passion* of Mons may well have run to ninety-eight separate representations of 'scenes'.

2. b. A narrative account of the passion of a martyr.

1904 T. SHEARMAN *Veneration of S. Agnes* 90 Helen of Rossow, or Roswitha, a Benedictine nun of the Convent of Gandersheim, Saxony, wrote poems in the 10th century, 'to replace,' as she says in her preface, 'the pagan passions which dishonour the profane drama, by the triumphs of the Christian heroines, the chaste spouses who are admitted to the Nuptials of the Lamb.' **1913** E. R. BARKER *Rome of Pilgrims* xiii. 183 In an eighth-century manuscript there is a note that Passions are to be read at Office in the Church of S. Peter. *Ibid.* xiv. 192 It is always the conventional version of a Passion which is reproduced in numerous manuscripts. *Ibid.* 195 For this saint ..there exists not only the contemporary Passion, but also a series of records. **1927** F. J. E. RABY *Hist. Christian-Latin Poetry* ii. 56 His poem was used as a basis for later prose passions of Cassian.

11. a. *passion-clouded, -dimmed, -frantic, -pale, -pastured, -plunged, -wearied* adjs.

1925 W. B. YEATS *Vision* III. 183 Aristophanes' passion-clouded eye. **1899** —— *Wind among Reeds* 26 Because your crying brings to my mind Passion-dimmed eyes and long heavy hair. **1916** A. HUXLEY *Burning Wheel* 29 So, troubled, passion-frantic, The poet's mind boils gold and amethyst. **1889** O. WILDE in *19th Cent.* Jan. 47 The passion-pale face of Andromeda. *c* **1865** G. M. HOPKINS *Voice from World* in *Poems* (1967) 125 How turn my passion-pastured thought To gentle manna and simple bread? **1876** —— *Wreck of Deutschland* xxxiii, in *Poems* (1967) 62 Our passion-plungèd giant risen, The Christ of the Father compassionate, fetched in the storm of his strides. **1881** O. WILDE *Poems* 4 With passion-wearied face.

b. passion-fruit, add to def.: esp. *Passiflora edulis*, the granadilla, which produces egg-shaped fruit with reddish-purple, slightly wrinkled skin and sweet yellow pulp surrounding small black seeds; (further examples); **passion killers** *slang* (see quots.); **passion play** (earlier and later examples); also *transf.*; **passion vine** (earlier and later examples); **passion wagon** *slang* (see quot. 1948).

1867 R. HENNING *Let.* 18 Feb. (1966) 234, I have also been making some passionfruit jelly. **1908** E. J. BANFIELD *Confessions of Beachcomber* I. vi. 192 There may be some who do not know that the humble papaw..belongs to the passion-fruit family. **1934** T. WOOD *Cobbers* xvii. 217 Passion fruit, squeezed into a wineglass, mixed with cream and sugar and a spoonful of sherry, has a rich smoothness. **1961** L. VAN DER POST *Heart of Hunter* I. ii. 27 His old lady, dark and wrinkled with age like a passion fruit about to fall. **1969** *Oxf. Bk. Food Plants* 98/1 Passion Fruit or Purple Granadilla (*Passiflora edulis*). A perennial climbing plant, originally native to Brazil but now widely planted in the tropics, it is also sufficiently hardy to be grown in some Mediterranean countries. **1974** *Herald* (Melbourne) 5 Apr. 23/1 Pavlova,..a crusty meringue-like sweet-cake made from egg whites and sugar and topped with whipped cream and, usually, passionfruit. **1976** *Observer* 17 Oct. 36/3 (Advt.), Easy to grow delicious passion fruits. Our own specially cultivated pot-grown species of Granadilla for fruiting in Britain. **1977** 'E. CRISPIN' *Glimpses of Moon* xii. 235 The infant Grand Duchess..lisps a request for a glass of..passion-fruit juice. **1943** C. H. WARD-JACKSON *Piece of Cake* 47 *Passion killers*, service knickers issued to air-women. **1946** J. IRVING *Royal Navalese* 136 An elastic-bound bifurcated undergarment said to be worn in the women's Services and known..as 'passion-killers'. **1974** *Times* 17 Dec. 12/5 Stout fleecy lined drawers..which would have been called by this generation 'passion-killers'. **1870** in J. Brown *Lett.* (1912) 378 I was very much touched by the Passion-play, and wrote some very bad verses at Ammergau. **1965** B. SWEET-ESCOTT *Baker St. Irreg.* iii. 90 It turned out to be..the ritual passion play on the 10th of the month of Muharram which commemorates the death of Hassan. **1975** *Listener* 10 Apr. 472/3 Going to Oberammergau to the Passion Play. **1853** 'P. PAXTON' *Stray Yankee in Texas* 57 The 'passion vine' with its singular flower and luscious fruit. **1862** R. HENNING *Let.* 23 Sept. (1966) 100 A veranda covered with passion-vine and a garden full of petunias in most brilliant flower. **1946** *Coast to Coast 1945* 64 Let his girls dig in the orchard or chip around the passion-vines. **1957** M. WEST *Kundu* ii. 19 A passion vine trailing over a bamboo summer-house. **1969** *West Australians* 5 July 41/7 (Advt.), Nellie Kelly the amazing grafted passion vine. **1948** PARTRIDGE *Dict. Forces' Slang* 137 *Passion waggon*, truck taking men for a day's, or part of a day's, leave, into a town or place of entertainment. **1961** *New Left Rev.* Jan.–Feb. 24/2 He knows every girl who comes out the base on Saturday on the passion-wagon.

passionful, *a.* Add: **2. b.** Subject to or susceptible to passion.

1902 *Amer. Anthropologist* Jan.–Mar. 33 The savage man conceived the diverse bodies collectively constituting his environment..to be living, thinking, willing, passionful beings.

Hence **pa·ssionfulness,** the state or quality of being passionful.

1922 *Glasgow Herald* 16 Dec. 10/6 Several members..by their passionfullness of heart and uncontrollable spirit had..broken the order and decorum of the House of Commons.

Passionist, *sb.* (*a.*) Add: **1. a.** (Earlier and later examples.)

1832 G. SPENCER *Let.* 7 June in C. R. Leetham *Luigi Gentili* (1965) iii. 40 The General of the Passionists. **1839** LD. SHREWSBURY *Let.* 16 Apr. in E. S. Purcell *Life & Lett. A. P. de Lisle* (1900) I. vi. 105, I have seen Lord Clifford, Father Glover and the Passionists. **1957** *Oxf. Dict. Chr. Ch.* 1022/2 In 1841 the Passionists came to England, where they were the first religious after the Reformation to lead a strict community life and wear their habit in public. **1967** D. T. KAUFFMAN *Dict. Relig. Terms* 347/1 Passionists wear black garments and heart-shaped badges symbolizing the Passion. **1975** R. PLAYER *Let's talk of Graves* iii. 89 Father Dominic the Passionist who received our dear Newman into Christ's Church.

b. (Earlier and later examples.)

1844 A. P. DE LISLE *Jrnl.* 8 July in E. S. Purcell *Life & Lett. A. P. de Lisle* (1900) I. vii. 118 The Superior of the Passionist Monks called upon us. **1911** *Encycl. Brit.* XX. 887/1 The order of Passionist Fathers,..was founded by St Paul of the Cross..in 1720. **1975** *Irish Times* 30 May 16/1 The fact that in Ireland strong religious piety co-exists with fierce sectarian hatreds is lamentable and points to a need for a questioning of the reality of religious beliefs, President O Dalaigh states in an interview in the current issue of the Passionist magazine, the Cross.

Passion Sunday. Add: (In the R.C. Ch. suppressed as a separate observance in 1969.)

passion-tide. (Earlier examples.)

1847 *Dublin Rev.* Mar. 25 The physical cause of our Lord's death is a subject..adapted to the season of Lent and Passion-tide. **1849** J. H. NEWMAN *Discourses to Mixed Congreg.* xv. 323 Though at this season [*Note* Passion-tide] many words would be out of place.

passival, *a.* Restrict *rare* to sense in Dict. and add: **b.** Semantically passive, *spec. passival verb*, an intransitive verb with a quasi-passive meaning.

1892 H. SWEET *New Eng. Gram.* I. 90 *The book sells well, meat will not keep in hot weather*... We call *sells* and *keep* in such constructions passival verbs. **1926** H. POUTSMA *Gram. Late Mod. Eng.* II. II. xlvi. 64 Sweet..calls the verbs thus used passival verbs. **1950** *Eng. Stud.* XXXI. 156 It is generally said that in a sentence like *His books don't sell* the verb is active in form, but passive in meaning, what is 'really' meant being *His books are not sold*. In accordance with this theory verbs used in this way are sometimes called active-passive or passival. **1961** Y. OLSSON *On Syntax Eng. Verb* vii. 180 That article, which..rightly rejects the analysis of such collocations as 'active-passive or passival'. **1963** F. T. VISSER *Hist. Syntax Eng. Lang.* I. ii. 152 (*heading*) Intransitive verbs used to represent the action as quasi-automatic, or self-originated. (Sweet's 'passival verbs'; Jespersen's 'activo-passive' use.)

passivate (pæ·sivēⁱt), *v.* [f. PASSIV(E *a.* and *sb.* + -ATE³.] **a.** *trans.* To render (metal) passive (PASSIVE *a.* 7 b in Dict. and Suppl.), e.g. to prevent corrosion.

1913 *Chem. News* 28 Nov. 259/1 We assume the passive state of metals (which can be passivated) to be the normal state. **1916** *Jrnl. Chem. Soc.* CIX. 1365 Hittorf has passivated chromium by anodic treatment in hydriodic acid. **1961** *Flight* LXXIX. 747/1 All surfaces that are to be in contact with HTP [*sc.* High Test Peroxide] must be 'passivated' to prevent surface decomposition. **1967** *Times Rev. Industry* Apr. 80/1 Unpainted non-stainless steel parts are cadmium plated and passivated for use at temperatures below 200 degrees centigrade. **1973** *Sci. Amer.* June 119/2 The brass or iron piping and fittings you use must be degreased, nitrogen-purged and passivated in a dilute stream of the fluorine, allowed to enter slowly enough to form a metal-fluoride film on the surface.

b. *trans.* To give (semiconducting material) a protective coating of some relatively inert material in order to protect it from contamination.

1964 *IBM Jrnl. Res. & Devel.* VIII. 368 (*heading*) Space-charge model for surface potential shifts in silicon passivated with thin insulating layers. **1969** GRAY & SEARLE *Electronic Princ.* v. 176 The oxide layer is said to passivate the semiconductor surface. **1972** PLANER & PHILLIPS *Thick Film Circuits* xi. 123 Active devices..are passivated with a layer of glass or silicon monoxide.

Hence **pa·ssivated** *ppl. a.*, **pa·ssivating** *vbl. sb.* and *ppl. a.*

1914 *Trans. Faraday Soc.* IX. 261 The amount of hydrogen..is too small to counteract the passivating action of the potassium hydroxide. **1919** H. P. TIEMANN *Iron & Steel* (ed. 2) 364 Iron in this condition has been termed passive, passivated, passivified, inactive, altered, or prepared. **1941** *Nature* 28 June 803/1 An electro-formed nickel-surfaced mould is..made and a coat of nickel..applied to the outer passivated nickel face. **1959** C. F. CORFE in *Control in Electroplating* iii. 57 (*heading*) Passivating dips. **1963** *Engineering* 27 Dec. 814/1 Passivated and hardened stainless steel is used for the housings. **1967** *Electronics* 6 Mar. 281/2 The silicon planar passivated construction employed provides long-term parameter stability. **1974** J. A. VON FRAUNHOFER *Concise Corrosion Sci.* viii. 79 Nitrates are poor passivating agents since they..are only sluggishly reduced. **1978** *Gramophone* Jan. 1334/3 The main chassis is constructed from passivated steel.

passivation (pæsivēⁱ·ʃən). [f. as prec. + -ATION.] The process of passivating.

1912 *Trans. Faraday Soc.* VIII. 234 (*heading*) Direct experiments on the passivation of metals. **1925** *Jrnl. Iron & Steel Inst.* CXI. 601 The anodic passivation of iron in sodium sulphate solution is demonstrated experimentally. **1956** *Nature* 17 Mar. 508/1 The mechanism of metallic corrosion, oxidation and passivation processes. **1964** *IBM Jrnl. Res. & Devel.* VIII. 385/1 Films..used for surface passivation of semiconductor devices. **1969** *Jane's Freight Containers 1968–69* 484/1 Approximate cost £1,450, depending on optional customer requirements for:—separate compartments,..passivation, fork-lift pockets, etc. **1972** PLANER & PHILLIPS *Thick Film Circuits* xi. 123 Passivation with silicon nitride yields a considerably increased protection against ionic contamination.

passivator (pæ·sivēⁱtəɹ). [f. as prec. + -OR.] A passivating agent.

1935 F. N. SPELLER *Corrosion* (ed. 2) ix. 378 Passivators may be used effectively to retard corrosion in refrigerating systems or anti-freezing mixtures. **1951** *Engineering* 28 Dec. 819/3 The oxidation, which causes sludging and the formation of acids, may be prevented by using an inhibited oil. The substances employed for this purpose include catalyst passivators and de-activators. **1974** J. A. VON FRAUNHOFER *Concise Corrosion Sci.* viii. 79 Passivators or Type IIIA inhibitors... Generally these substances are oxidising agents with redox potentials that are more noble than that of the metal and they are readily reduced.

passive, *a.* and *sb.* Add: **A.** *adj.* **7. b.** Also, applied to substances that are normally reactive. (Earlier and later examples.)

1836 *Phil. Mag.* IX. 54 The third wire can make indifferent or passive a fourth one, and so on. *Ibid.*, Direct contact between the two wires..is not an indispensably necessary condition for communicating chemical activity from the active wire to the passive one; for any metal..renders the same service. **1940** *Nature* 19 Oct. 506/1 The addition of a sufficient amount of chromium to iron confers upon the iron the property of producing spontaneously upon its surface a passive and resistant film as a result of contact with the atmosphere or with certain aqueous environments. Such passive films, if mechanically damaged, are self-repairing. **1965** D. ABBOTT *Inorg. Chem.* x. 447 Nitric acid renders some metals completely passive, e.g. iron and nickel are rendered passive by the concentrated acid.

c. Of a trade balance: unfavourable; with debits greater than credits; *passive rate* (see quot. 1972).

1930 *Economist* 15 Mar. 587/2 The passive balance of Kr. 25 million was quite normal for the time of the year, as there is always an excess of imports during the winter months. **1936** K. A. H. EGERTON *Bower's Dict. Econ. Terms* (ed. 10) 119 *Passive trade balance*, a balance of imports in excess of exports—another term for 'unfavourable trade balance'. **1940** G. CROWTHER *Outl. Money* viii. 298 Following the usual terminology we can say that the balance of trade between the two countries was unfavourable (or 'passive') to Switzerland. **1972** *Times* 29 Dec. 15/1 It has also been accepted that the annual rate of monetary growth should be curbed gradually rather than suddenly until it reaches a 'passive' rate—the planned rate of economic growth plus the going rate of inflationary expectations.

d. *Immunol.* [tr. G. *passiv* (given this sense by P. Ehrlich 1892, in *Zeitschr. f. Hygiene und Infectionskrankheiten* XII. 189).] Produced by or involving the introduction into the body of antibodies of external origin.

1895 *Science Progress* III. 204 'Passive immunity', a term first employed by Ehrlich. **1898** R. T. HEWLETT *Man. Bacteriol.* v. 123 'Passive immunity' is soon lost, but..is transmitted to the fœtus. **1935** F. P. GAY et al. *Agents of Dis.* xxii. 450 Passive transfer occurs naturally from immune mothers to their offspring. **1970** W. H. PARKER *Health & Dis. in Farm Animals* ix. 114 Natural passive immunity is acquired from the first meals of colostrum. **1974** R. M. KIRK et al. *Surgery* ii. 33 Passive immunity is often transmitted to humans by using the serum from a highly immunised horse.

e. *Chess.* Designating a sacrifice (*a*) in which a piece or pawn attacked by an opponent's move is left to be captured; (*b*) that an opponent need not accept.

1907 S. S. BLACKBURNE *Terms & Themes Chess Probl.* 87 *Sacrificing*, offering a White man to be captured. If a man or men already *en prise* be left so, this may be called a 'passive sacrifice'. **1924** A. EMERY *Chess Sacrifices & Traps* II. 40 In general, 'passive' sacrifices like that in No. 1—where, the Queen being attacked, Alekhine calmly allows it to be taken—are more pleasing than the 'active' variety. **1935** J. DU MONT tr. *Spielmann's Art of Sacrifice in Chess* I. 2 Under the heading 'form', there are two types, namely active and passive. In making a distinction between these two types, the deciding factor, from a scientific point of view, would be whether the sacrifice arises from a move made for the purpose, or from a raid by the enemy... For reasons of practicability, however, it has seemed to me better to make the distinction a different one, namely, whether acceptance of the proffered sacrifice is compulsory or not. Those which must be accepted I call active, the others passive. **1968** P. H. CLARKE tr. *Vuković's Chess Sacrifice* i. 12 Passive sacrifices have the drawback that they can be declined; they can, as it were, be ignored.

f. *Psychol.* Of, relating to or characteristic of the female or the inactive role in a sexual relationship, freq. associated with masochism in psychoanalytic theory; that fails or refuses to respond with, or shows an abnormal lack of, activity.

1916 A. A. BRILL tr. *Freud's Leonardo da Vinci* ii. 39 Strangely enough this phantasy is altogether of a passive character; it resembles certain dreams and phantasies of women and of passive homosexuals who play the feminine part in sexual relations. **1921** *Internat. Jrnl. Psycho-Anal.* II. 439 The author comes to the conclusion that masochism has to be considered as the result and expression of the primacy of passive partial impulses. **1935** *Ibid.* XVI. 337 The sexual aims of the little boy's incestuous wishes are clearly passive. **1940** HENDERSON & GILLESPIE *Text-bk. Psychiatry* (ed. 5) 312 Predominantly inadequate or passive, this again is an important and numerous group. **1969** R. L. KELLEY in Solomon & Patch *Handbk. Psychiatry* xlii. 521 Severe characterologic problems such as sexual perversion, alcoholism..and passive dependent personality. **1973** L. C. KOLB *Mod. Clin. Psychiatry* (ed. 8) vi. 93/1 In this type the personality contains a considerable element of aggression..expressed by passive measures, such as sullenness, stubbornness, procrastination [etc.].

g. *Electronics.* Containing no source of e.m.f.

1924 K. S. JOHNSON *Transmission Circuits Teleph. Communication* xi. 121 The transmission properties of passive networks may often be best determined by considering them as equivalent to lines having smoothly distributed constants. **1930** T. E. SHEA *Transmission Networks & Wave Filters* ii. 43 A network composed only of inductances, capacitances, and resistances is a passive network. **1965** *Wireless World* July 332/1 In the so-called hybrid circuit,..the active elements..are formed in the silicon slice by the normal planar process, but..the passive elements (resistors, capacitors and conductors) are deposited as thin films on to the thermally grown silicon dioxide protective coating. **1970** J. EARL *Tuners & Amplifiers* ii. 29 A junction diode is equivalent to the thermionic valve diode, a transistor to a thermionic valve and an IC to a multiplicity of active and passive devices and components.

h. *Linguistics.* Of vocabulary, etc.: that is recognized and understood but through inability, lack of assurance, or for some other reason, is not used by the auditor or reader himself.

1935 G. K. ZIPF *Psycho-Biol. of Lang.* (1936) v. 220 The auditor's passive vocabulary (i.e. the words which the auditor can understand). **1966** J. DERRICK *Teaching Eng. to Immigrants* ii. 99 Most stories will contain far more material than the pupils are expected to reproduce themselves (i.e. relying on and helping to build up their 'passive' or recognition vocabulary). **1976** *Word 1971* XXVII. 85 Grammont reported and demonstrated that 'passive language' precedes 'active language'.

i. Of radar, homing systems, etc.: relying on radiation generated by the target. Of a satellite, space relay station, etc.: not generating any signal.

1954 K. W. GATLAND *Devel. Guided Missile* (ed. 2) iii. 67 A missile can be homed on to its target..by..'passive' homing (whereby the missile homes on to a source of energy radiated by the target). **1960** *N.Y. Times* 9 Oct. E 9/6 Echo, a 'passive' satellite, reflects or bounces radio signals sent from one station back to another point on the earth. **1962** J. CLEMOW *Missile Guidance* ii. 45 It is possible to have a passive radar system where a receiver carried in the missile detects the direction of the source of radar signals from the target. **1966** *McGraw-Hill Encycl. Sci. & Technol.* XII. 504/2 Modern submarines carry passive sonar apparatus which is believed to be capable of detecting ships as far away as 100 miles. **1967** H. HELLMAN *Controlled Guidance Syst.* vi. 161 Additional advantages of passive systems are that they emit no telltale signals to aid the enemy, and the guidance equipment is kept to a bare minimum. **1969** *Proc. IEEE* LVII. 427/1 Passive remote sensing at microwave frequencies has applications which range from meteorology to oceanography and geology.

B. *sb.* **1. b.** *pl.* In pillow-lace making, the bobbins holding the threads which correspond to the warp threads in weaving.

1907 MINCOFF & MARRIAGE *Pillow Lace* vii. 89 The other pairs which these [*sc.* the wefts] must cross are called the 'passives'. **1953** M. POWYS *Lace & Lace-Making* iv. 20 This makes the connection and the worker bobbins pass back again across the passives. *Ibid.* xi. 186 The bobbins hanging straight down are called the 'passives'.

passive resistance. (In Dict. s.v. RESISTANCE 1 b.) Add: (Further examples.) Now mostly used of refusal to comply with demands or legal requirements imposed by a government or other authority.

1883 *Encycl. Brit.* XX. 147/2 The student of English constitutional history will observe the success with which they [*sc.* the Quakers] have, by the mere force of passive resistance, obtained from the legislature and courts indulgence for all their scruples and a recognition of the legal validity of their customs. **1909** J. J. DOKE *Indian Patriot in S. Afr.* ii. 5 The Passive Resistance movement had come into prominence [in 1907]. **1927** C. BERGMANN *Hist. Reparations* xxiii. 173 (*heading*) Force and passive resistance. *Ibid.* 180 The military invasion of the Ruhr District was met by the German people and the German Government with an attitude which has become generally known as passive resistance. **1928** V. G. DESAI tr. *Gandhi's Satyagraha in S. Afr.* xii. 172 None of us knew what name to give to our movement. I then [*sc.* in 1906] used the term 'passive resistance' in describing it. **1930** *Economist* 22 Mar. 631/1 The Education Bill, which was the cause of the bitter religious controversy that gave rise to the passive resistance movement. **1936** [see *CONSCIENTIOUS *a.* 2]. **1942** E. PAUL *Narrow St.* vi. 46 Unable to collect reparations, on account of German poverty and 'passive resistance' which became spasmodically impassive, Poincaré declared an embargo on iron and steel into Germany. **1950** G. BRENAN *Face of Spain* vii. 167 The land is difficult to legislate for, and those who own it are past masters in passive resistance. **1974** J. WHITE tr. *Poulantzas's Fascism & Dictatorship* IV. ii. 170 In July 1923, with..the failure of passive resistance in the Ruhr, ..there was a situation of open crisis.

Hence **passive-resi·stant, -resi·ster,** one who practises passive resistance; **passive-resi·stful** *a.*, expressive of passive resistance. Also **passive-resist** *v. intr.* (*rare*), to practise passive resistance.

1904 G. B. SHAW in *Daily Mail* 27 Feb. 4/4 They look at me with volumes of reproach in their earnest, passive-resistful eyes. **1906** Passive resister [see *LIPPY *a.* 2]. **1907** G. B. SHAW *John Bull's Other Island* Pref. p. xxx, The warcry of the Passive Resisters is Voltaire's warcry, 'Écrasez l'infâme'. **1936** M. PLOWMAN *Faith called Pacifism* 86 It was as a passive resister that the greatest revolutionary in the world became the greatest social force in the world. **1949** KOESTLER *Promise & Fulfilment* I. xii. 131 The soldiers were confronted with the grotesque task of dragging the passive resistants..into barbed-wire cages for interrogation. **1952** B. WOLFE *Limbo* (1953) xvii. 255 Couldn't you just lie down and passive-resist? **1968** *Punch* 2 Oct. 474/1 He incurred much unpopularity as a Passive Resister, which is what people called those who refused to pay their rates towards the upkeep of Church Schools.

† **passivication** (pæ̆sivikēⁱ·ʃən). *Obs.* [Irreg. f. PASSIVE *a.* and *sb.* + *-ication*, after nouns of action like *application, publication*.] = *PASSIVATION.

1922 *Trans. Faraday Soc.* XVIII. 4 (*heading*) Anodic passivication. **1942** R. T. ROLFE *Steels for User* (ed. 2) x. 300 Owing to passivication of the surface by nitriding, no corrosion was found to occur.

† **passivification** (pæ̆si:vifikēⁱ·ʃən). *Obs.* [f. as prec.: see -FICATION.] = *PASSIVATION.

1907 *Jrnl. Soc. Chem. Industry* 31 Aug. 900/2 Retardation of passivification is brought about..by making the liquid in question less oxidizing. **1937** *Jrnl. Iron & Steel Inst.* CXXXV. 301A (*heading*) Passivification and activation of chromium-iron alloys.

† **passivifier** (pæ̆si·vifəiəɹ). *Obs.* [f. next + -ER¹.] = *PASSIVATOR.

1911 J. N. FRIEND *Corrosion of Iron & Steel* 298 Passivifiers are oxidizers. **1921** *Jrnl. Chem. Soc.* CXIX. 946 All passivifiers are not oxidisers, hydronitric acid being a case in point.

† **passivify** (pæ̆si·vifəi), *v. Obs.* [f. PASSIV(E *a.* and *sb.* + -IFY.] *trans.* = *PASSIVATE *v.* a.

1907 *Jrnl. Soc. Chem. Industry* 31 Aug. 902/1 All the solutions enumerated above that passivify iron contain an oxy-anion. **1934** *Jrnl. Iron & Steel Inst.* CXXIX. 619 The addition of easily passivified metals, such as chromium and nickel, to iron yields alloys which are more easily passivified than iron itself.

Hence **passi·vified** *ppl. a.*, **passi·vifying** *vbl. sb.* and *ppl. a.*

1907 *Jrnl. Soc. Chem. Industry* 31 Aug. 903/2 The passivifying of an iron anode. **1911** J. N. FRIEND *Corrosion of Iron & Steel* xii. 189 (*heading*) The characteristic properties of passivified iron. **1915** *Jrnl. Physical Chem.* XIX. 644 It is..possible that both nitrous acid and nitrogen peroxide may be passivifying agents. **1919** [see *PASSIVATED *ppl. a.*]. **1934** [see above]. **1934** *Jrnl. R. Aeronaut. Soc.* XXXVIII. 425 An alkaline pigment, such as zinc oxide or a passivifying pigment, like zinc chromate. **1938** *Jrnl. Iron & Steel Inst.* CXXXVIII. 404A, Strong nitric acid acted primarily as a cleaner, but had some value as a passivifying agent.

passivism (pæ·siviz'm). [f. PASSIV(E *a.* and *sb.* + -ISM.] An abnormal state of passivity, esp. that of a male who accepts or desires the passive role in a sexual relationship.

1903 H. ELLIS *Stud. Psychol. Sex* III. 93 Stefanowsky, who also discussed this condition [*sc.* masochism]..termed it passivism. **1940** HINSIE & SHATZKY *Psychiatric Dict.* 403/2 *Passivism*, a form of sexual perversion in which the subject, usually male, is submissive to the will of the partner in the unnatural sexual practices. **1961** *Brit. Med. Dict.* 1060/1 *Passivism*, a type of sexual perversion characterized by submission of one partner (usually the male) to unnatural sexual practices desired by the other partner, who may be of either sex.

passivist (pæ·sivist). [f. PASSIV(E *a.* and *sb.* + -IST.] One who or that which is characterized by passivity, *spec.* (*a*) a (male) person who abnormally accepts or desires a passive sexual role (see *PASSIVISM); (*b*) an opponent of active participation in war. Also *attrib.* or as *adj.*

1895 [see *MASOCHIST]. **1942** PARTRIDGE *Usage & Abusage* (1947) 222/2 There is, in cultured usage, a tendency to make *pacifist* an active, *passivist* an inactive, indeed a negatively passive, opponent of war. **1945** K. R. POPPER *Open Society* II. xxiii. 201 It continues on the lines of Kant's criticism of what we may term the 'passivist' theory of knowledge. **1955** *Bull. Atomic Sci.* Sept. 265/3 But if armaments are not acceptable to the pacifist, does this mean that he will submit to the aggressor and meekly resign himself to what he considers evil? The answer is emphatically no. This is to confuse pacifism with appeasement. The pacifist is definitely not a passivist. **1957** P. WORSLEY *Trumpet shall Sound* 236 The basic division,..is not between millenarian and non-millenarian movements but between activist and passivist movements. **1961** *Brit. Med. Dict.* 1060/1 *Passivist*, anyone who is the subject of passivism.

passivity. Add: **2. a.** (Later examples.)

1958 T. D. WELDON *Kant's Critique of Pure Reason* (ed. 2) iv. 132 Thus there really is a marked distinction between the activity of the understanding and the passivity of sensibility. **1967** G. H. VON WRIGHT in N. Rescher *Logic of Decision* 130 He [*sc.* the agent] can do nothing to produce a change..or to prevent a change which independently of him happens. We may call this case [of impotence] (forced) passivity.

4. b. Substitute for def.: The state of chemical inactivity that is produced in some normally reactive metals following a slight initial attack. (Further examples.)

1881 *Jrnl. Chem. Soc.* XL. 344 Passivity may be induced in a rod of iron by the immersion of a part only in concentrated nitric acid. **1940** GLASSTONE *Text-bk. Physical Chem.* xii. 1010 The resemblances between a metal rendered passive by chemical and electrochemical methods is very marked, and there is little doubt that the fundamental cause of passivity is the same in each case. *Ibid.* 1011 In certain cases the dissolution of an anode is prevented by a visible film, e.g., lead dioxide on a lead anode in dilute sulfuric acid: this effect has been called 'mechanical passivity', but it is probably not fundamentally different from electrochemical passivity. **1966** *McGraw-Hill Encycl. Sci. & Technol.* III. 488/1 Passivity is usually due to surface films which act as barriers between the metal and its environment... Aluminum is a reactive metal, but it is widely used for corrosion applications because of protection by a stable aluminum oxide film.

5. *Psychol.* The state or condition of being abnormally inactive or lacking in normal responsiveness (see *PASSIVE *a.* 7 f); also *attrib.*

1927 HENDERSON & GILLESPIE *Text-bk. Psychiatry* 88 In other cases the patient believes that someone reads his thoughts... These later conditions are examples of 'passivity'. **1952** W. WOLFF *Threshold of Abnormal* xviii. 436 Passivity may appear as apathy, as anxiety, as helplessness. **1955** *Psychiatric Q.* XXIX. 604 Nowhere is it more difficult to decide whether passivity is an ego defense mechanism or an instinctual gratification than in the study of masochism. **1958** M. E. SPIRO *Children of Kibbutz* IV. vii. 146 Play among the two younger groups is marked by an aimlessness and passivity that are two of its most characteristic features. **1968** W. WEISS in Lindzey & Aronson *Handbk. Social Psychol.* (ed. 2) V. 113 Television may reinforce withdrawal and passivity when these preexisted or are latent, but does not create them. **1969** W. MAYER-GROSS et al. *Clin. Psychiatry* (ed. 3) v. 270 The passivity phenomena in which this loss of [self] is best seen are indeed very characteristic of schizophrenia.

passivizable (pæsivəi·zăb'l), *a. Gram.* [f. as next + -ABLE.] Able to undergo passivization; meeting the structural analysis for the passive transformation. So **pa:ssivizabi·lity.**

1970 N. CHOMSKY in Jacobs & Rosenbaum *Readings Eng. Transformational Gram.* 203 Passivizability is a property of verbs. **1972** A. MAKKAI *Idiom Struct. Eng.* 152 The tournure *kick the bucket*, per se, is not passivizable. **1978** *Language* LIV. 172 Phrases are apt to be passivizable if 'they perform the same function as single verbs'.

passivization (pæ:sivəizēⁱ·ʃən). *Gram.* [f. next + -ATION.] Conversion into the passive form.

1965 N. CHOMSKY *Aspects of Theory of Syntax* ii. 104 It accounts automatically for the restriction of passivization to Verbs that take Manner Adverbials freely. *Ibid.* 229 The sentences 'I regard John as pompous', 'it struck me blind',..are freely subject to passivization. **1968** *Language* XLIV. 230 The syntactic motivation for this treatment comes from the fact that the verbs that can undergo passivization are restricted to those that take manner adverbials freely. **1970** *Ibid.* XLVI. 466 Whatever the machinery may be to handle these cases, it can clearly also handle constraints on the passivization of verbs like *condescend*. **1971** J. M. ANDERSON *Gram. of Case* ix. 132 Both 'primary' and 'secondary' passivization.., as well as the two kinds of object ('direct' and 'indirect') are allowed for in this way. **1976** J. S. GRUBER *Lexical Struct. Syntax & Semantics* I. iv. 98 The deletion of *for* in certain complement constructions apparently applies after passivization.

passivize (pæ·sivəiz), *v.* [f. PASSIV(E *a.* and *sb.* + -IZE.] † **1.** = *PASSIVATE *v.* a. *Obs.*

1910 *Jrnl. Physical Chem.* XIV. 731 When the current is interrupted after the anode has been passivized, the potential of the anode rises slowly. **1912** *Trans. Faraday Soc.* VIII. 279 One of the slabs was 'passivized' and then allowed to regain its normal state.

2. *Gram.* **a.** *trans.* To convert into the passive form. **b.** *intr.* To be subject to conversion into the passive.

1965 N. CHOMSKY *Aspects of Theory of Syntax* 229 Such sentences as 'John strikes me as pompous', 'his remarks impress me as unintelligible' do not passivize. **1972** R. A. PALMATIER *Gloss. Eng. Transformational Gram.* 120 The application of the passive transformation, by which the sentence is said to have been passivized. **1973** *Amer. Speech 1969* XLIV. 212 There are certain transitive combinations which are phrasal verbs although they do not passivize. **1977** *Verbatim* Feb. 10/1 Thus, transitive verbs in idiomatic expressions frequently will not passivize (*the cowboy kicked the bucket*, but not *the bucket was kicked by the cowboy*). **1978** *Language* LIV. 93 Causation is a transitive process which can be passivized.

Hence **pa·ssivized** *ppl. a.*, **pa·ssivizing** *vbl. sb.*

1975 *Language* LI. 792 Under Hasegawa's analysis, the passivized clause originates as an object complement. **1977** *Trans. Philol. Soc. 1975* 219 It is clear that the passivized/intransitivized sense continued for some. *Ibid.* Assuming that both reflexive and passivizing/intransitivizing functions passed into the Suffix verbs..we have a source for the four functional types having middle-voice forms which are found in Lowland Eastern Cushitic now. **1978** *Amer. Speech* LIII. 25 Between the passivized versions of the following sentence, only the one in which the deep-structure subject has been deleted can be interpreted impersonally.

passle, var. *PASSEL.

passman. Add: **b.** [see PASS *sb.*² 8.] A prisoner who is allowed to leave his cell. *slang.*

1965 B. KNOX *Taste of Proof* iii. 49 The passmen, the privileged, trusted prisoners. **1973** J. PATRICK *Glasgow Gang Observed* ix. 82 He had envied the 'passmen', boys who in the afternoon were permitted to leave their cells to scrub floors and polish shoes.

pass-out (pɑ·s,ɑut). [PASS-.] **a.** (A document giving) permission to leave and re-enter a theatre, etc.; also *attrib.* in *pass-out check, ticket.*

1894, 1896 [in Dict. s.v. PASS-]. **1907** *Daily Chron.* 29 Aug. 5/6 He begged for a pass-out ticket to see how his old friends were doing down below. **1922** JOYCE *Ulysses* 106 No fear of anyone getting out, no passout checks. **1952** GRANVILLE *Dict. Theatr. Terms* 133 *Pass-out checks*, a ticket given by the usher to permit a patron to re-enter the theatre if he, or she, leaves during the interval. **1959** K. WATERHOUSE *Billy Liar* xii. 159 The Roxy was unguarded. They dodged in, giggling... 'Where's yer pass-outs, you two?' yelled Stamp. 'Hey, mister, they're getting in for nix!' **1962** J. WAIN *Strike Father Dead* 60, I stuck to Lucille till the dance ended. At one point she suggested that we should get pass-outs and go out for a drink. **1968** C. DRUMMOND *Death & Leaping Ladies* iii. 61 No need for pass-outs... I'm the Manager. The pub's okay.

b. A fit of unconsciousness. Also, one who has become unconscious (cf. *PASS *v.* 66 c).

1946 E. O'NEILL *Iceman Cometh* II. 115 He puts his head back on his arms and closes his eyes, but this time his habitual pass-out has a quality of hiding. **1949** *Esquire's Handbk. for Hosts* 272 There is small pleasure to be derived from finding yourself with an eighteen-year-old passout on your hands. **1967** E. FENWICK *Passenger* iv. 31 She slept like a pass-out, a total, never making a sign of any kind of consciousness.

passover. Add: **4. b.** A path or pass over hills.

1839 Z. LEONARD *Adventures* (1904) 230 We..continued all day without any interruption, and in the evening encamped at the foot of the passover.

passo·verish, *a.* [f. PASSOVER + -ISH¹.] Suggestive of the passover.

1921 A. HUXLEY *Crome Yellow* xxviii. 299 The disorganized, passoverish meal that took the place of dinner on this festal day. **1930** H. G. WELLS *Autocracy of Mr. Parham* II. iii. 106 After an exceptionally passoverish dinner at Marmion House.

passport, *sb.*¹ Add: **6.** *passport holder, number, office, officer, official*; **passport control,** (*a*) regulation of the issuing and inspecting of passports; (*b*) the department or office at a port, airport, etc., which checks passports; **passport photo(graph),** (*a*) the identification photograph in a passport; (*b*) a photograph of the size required for passports.

1947 AUDEN *Age of Anxiety* I. 17 An ordered world Of planned pleasures and passport-control. **1948** M. LASKI *Tory Heaven* i. 6 A lifetime of devoted service in Passport Control. **1960** 'R. EAST' *Kingston Black* vi. 60 Passport control would report when she left the country and returned. **1966** C. MACKENZIE *My Life & Times* V. 43 We were lucky to have a Minister like Sir Francis Elliot..; he agreed to this experiment in passport control. **1973** W. MCCARTHY *Detail* iii. 150 He walked across the airport towards passport control. **1976** *CRC Jrnl.* July 3/2 The UK passport holders from East Africa have a right to settle in Britain. **1971** M. KELLY *25th Hour* i. 15 He opened the other page..closed the passport and held it out... He took a pen..and wrote something down. I said, 'What's that?' 'Your passport number.' **1976** 'M. BARAK' *Secret List H. Roehm* xiv. 139 He checked names, addresses, and passport numbers. **1849** I. SPENCER *Let.* 14 Aug. in U. Young *Life Fr. Ignatius Spencer* (1933) III. ii. 165, I write from the Belgian passport office. **1975** *Times* 14 June 6/3 Long queues form at passport offices [in Angola] and 40,000 passports are already on order from Lisbon. **1950** P. BOTTOME *Under Skin* i. 16 The passport officers are in the dining saloon. **1958** L. VAN DER POST *Lost World of Kalahari* viii. 193 There was a group of vigilant painted animals assembled on a ledge rather like passport officers at a frontier. **1975** D. BLOODWORTH *Clients of Omega* xxiv. 235 The Passport Officer said..'May I see your passport, please?' **1922** M. ARLEN *Piracy* III. vi. 89 The passport officials at the ports. **1961** J. BARLOW *Term of Trial* I. vi. 127, I got my passport photo to show you. **1975** 'A. HALL' *Mandarin Cypher* x. 150 Passport photos are only ever good for a giggle. **1935** J. BUCHAN *House of Four Winds* iii. 84 The passport photograph isn't unlike him. **1939** G. GREENE *Confid. Agent* I. ii. 50 Life seemed determined to make him look less and less like his passport photograph. **1965** G. LYALL *Midnight plus One* ii. 17 There is one passport photograph only. **1966** N. FREELING *King of Rainy Country* 85 Switzerland confirmed that nobody would bother checking such well known passport photographs.

passportless, *a.* (Further examples.)

1919 J. BUCHAN *Mr. Standfast* v. 96 It seemed to me that, in spite of being passportless, I might be able somehow to make my way. **1968** *Punch* 16 Oct. 525/2 The Common Market..envisages a common nationality and a passportless society for most of Western Europe. **1970** *Guardian* 24 Mar. 11/3 Europe's airport lounges are still littered with passportless Kenyan Asians. **1973** *Daily Tel.* 5 Apr. 8/3 Passportless, on the run, he escapes into the Connecticut woods.

pass-through (pɑ·sþrū), *a.* and *sb.* [f. vbl. phr. *to pass through*: s.v. PASS *v.* 58.] **A.** *adj.* **1.** Through which something may be passed.

1955 *Sun* (Baltimore) 24 Aug. 12/4 An arm length's [*sic*] away via the 'pass-through' window is the kitchen range. **1976** C. LARSON *Muir's Blood* (1978) xxix. 153 The phone rang..while Blixen was lifting it from his crowded breakfast table to the pass-through bar.

2. Of costs, etc.: that are passed on to the buyer; that are chargeable to the customer.

1972 *Time* 17 Apr. 44/1 The commission may order an end to 'pass-through' profits. At present, businessmen are allowed to pass along to customers not only their increases in costs, but also to tack on their standard profit margins. **1976** *National Observer* (U.S.) 14 Feb. 17/3 'Political' ads are also excluded from pass-through expenses in most states, such as those that promote offshore oil and gas drilling.

B. *sb.* **1.** A passage; a means of passing through; *spec.* a hatch through which food, etc., is passed.

1958 *Washington Post* 16 Aug. B3/2 (Advt.), Over-size dining-family room served by louvered pass-through from kitchen. **1959** 'S. RANSOME' *I'll die for You* iii. 37 Anne..began piling the breakfast dishes in the pass-through to the kitchen. **1971** *Daily Colonist* (Victoria, B.C.) 21 Oct. 15/1 Como sawed through two vertical bars in his cell into the passageway, and then 'enlarged a food pass-through' to get into an outside corridor. **1976** C. WESTON *Rouse Demon* (1977) xx. 94 Through the bar-type pass-through into the kitchen they could see a rusty stove. **1977** *Austral. House & Garden* Jan. 58/1 Above the stove the pass-through overlooks the informal dining room.

b. *fig.* A route for money, profits, or investments. *N. Amer.*

1968 *Economist* 18 May 77/2 Last March Ottawa promised to make sure that its banks and other financial intermediaries here would not permit American investors to use Canada as a pass-through for funds destined for the Euro-dollar market.

2. An act of passing through or passing on.

1975 *Sci. Amer.* June 55/1 The beams collide at two regions on the perimeter of the ring... The probability of even a single e^-e^+ annihilation in any one pass-through of the bunches is quite low. **1976** *Billings* (Montana) *Gaz.* 16 June 5-A/3 O'Leary took the position that a Supreme Court decision of last Dec. 30, which permitted a temporary pass-through of Montana Power's higher Canadian-gas costs, has the effect of also authorizing reduced rates on an interim basis.

passway (pɑ·swēɪ). [PASS *sb.*[1]] **a.** A means of passing; a passage or gangway. **b.** = PASS *sb.*[1] 3.

1825 *Mechanics' Mag.* IV. 203/1, I hope we shall have a better passway than the present, otherwise we shall have the bridge down again. **1835** A. B. LONGSTREET *Georgia Scenes* 99 These were the only passways to the interior. **1874** J. W. LONG *Amer. Wild-Fowl Shooting* 161 There is a good passway for flight shooting. *Ibid.* 245 Good sport may then be had on the passways. **1889** 'C. E. CRADDOCK' *Despot of Broomsedge Cove* xiv. 267 Through the broad passways he could see the white frost gleam responsive upon the expanse of the fields. **1889** *Harper's Mag.* Aug. 390/2 Our family carriage..is left out in the streets along with many others to block up the passway. **1920** *Blackw. Mag.* June 817/1 There is only one pass-way through the wild hills at the back..—a narrow defile.

past, *ppl. a.* and *sb.* Add: **A.** *ppl. a.* **4.** *past tense*: also *attrib.* and in extended uses; *past participle* (examples); *past-participial* adj.

1798 J. H. TOOKE *Diversions of Purley* (ed. 2) I. viii. 263 The adjective *Less* and the comparative *Less* are the imperative..; and the superlative *Least* is the past participle. **1892** W. W. SKEAT *Primer Eng. Etym.* ix. 104 The suffix so common in Lat. past participles, as in *amā-tus*.., loved. The corresponding past participial suffix in E. is *-d*, as in *dea-d*.., orig. a past participle. **1937** *Jrnl. Eng. & Gmc. Philol.* XXXVI. 474 The strong vowel is divided into classes..according to the vowel of the past and ignoring the past participle vowel. **1961** R. B. LONG *Sentence & its Parts* vii. 167 Where main predicators are past-tense forms, common-mode predicators in subordinate clauses..are likely to be past-tense too if a choice between past forms and presents is possible. *Ibid.* xviii. 406 Latin past-participial stems are commonly marked..by the use of either the letter *t* or the letter *s*. **1961** B. MALAMUD *New Life* (1962) 290, I did—ah—see one but that's all past tense. **1976** H. MACINNES *Agent in Place* xxviii. 286 No need to think anything. It's all past tense now. **1976** *National Observer* (U.S.) 27 Mar. 19/3 Vidal's spicy past-tense peep show adds seasoning to this year's version. **1976** G. L. BROOK *Lang. Shakespeare* iii. 110 The present participle is normally active and the past participle is normally passive. **1977** *Word* 1972 XXVIII. 98, 89·5 percent of all past-tense environments preserve lenition.

B. *sb.* **1.** Phr. *a thing of the past.*

1863 *Athenæum* 15 Aug. 200/3 Even in America the woman-doctor is an eccentricity, and most probably will in a few years be a thing of the past. **1903** G. B. SHAW *Man & Superman* III. 92 Do not ask me how old I was—as if I were a thing of the past. I am 77. **1952** E. O'NEILL *Moon for Misbegotten* I. 43 Who told you I fall for the dainty dolls? That's all a thing of the past. **1961** NEW ENG. BIBLE *Luke* xvi. 9 When money is a thing of the past. **1977** C. ALLEN *Raj* i. 21/2 By the 1880s the discomfort of travelling by *palkee* (palanquin)..was already becoming a thing of the past.

C. Also from B, as *past-coloured, -dissecting, -done* adjs.; **past-future** *a.* (Gram.), of a tense: expressing an action or a state viewed as future in relation to a given past time; **past-president**, one who has been a president.

1939 S. SPENDER *Still Centre* 24 In the past-coloured pigment of the mind's eye They feed and fly and dwell. **1939** L. MACNEICE *Autumn Jrnl.* 18 The final cure is not in his past-dissecting fingers. **1762** STERNE *Tr. Shandy* VI. xxi. 89 Chatting..upon past-done deeds. **1925** GRATTAN & GURREY *Our living Lang.* 230 The Past-Future Tense (a)..(a) He said he should (would) write, etc. *Ibid.*, The Past-Future-Continuous Tense (b)..(b) He said he should (would) be writing, etc. *Ibid.*, The Past-Future-Perfect Tense (c)..(c) He said he should (would) have written, etc. *Ibid.*, The Past-Future-Perfect-Continuous Tense (d)..(d) He said he should (would) have been writing, etc. **1961** R. B. LONG *Sentence & its Parts* v. 127 Progressive-aspect forms..sometimes emphasize..in past-perfect and past-future tenses closeness to a past time that is central in the attention at the moment. **1903** *Nature* 12 Feb. 348/2 James Glaisher..was also a past-president of the Royal Meteorological Society. **1961** *Newark* (New Jersey) *Even. News* 22 Mar. 25 He regretted Hughes had made a personal attack on a past president.

past, *prep.* and *adv.* Add: **A.** *prep.* **1. c.** (later example.)

1967 M. FORSTER *Trav. Maudie Tipstaff* I. v. 98 In Maudie's opinion, no woman could get past forty and still have those needs.

2. b. (Further examples.) spec. *to get past*, to pass, to overtake.

1857 T. HUGHES *Tom Brown's School Days* I. v. 109 They're the bounds. As soon as the ball gets past them, it's in touch, and out of play. **1906** GALLAHER & STEAD *Compl. Rugby Footballer* xix. 262 We don't think Scoular was to blame for allowing Smith to get past him and score. **1971** *Croquet Gaz.* July 14/2 The..Singles..were won by Lady Ursula Abbey who just got past Mrs. Temple in a close and protracted final. **1977** *Daily Express* 29 Mar. 32/4 England put nine goals past Luxemburg 16 years ago in the away leg of a World Cup qualifier.

3. a. *past praying for* (later examples); also loosely, beyond hope (of cure, recovery, etc.).

1881 G. M. HOPKINS *Lett. to R. Bridges* (1955) 126, I have become very musical of late... I could make great progress—not in execution: that is past praying for—but in composition and understanding. **1897** *Cornh. Mag.* June 830 The man who can deliberately set aside his own personal knowledge and the gift of reason and common-sense with which God has endowed him,..is indeed 'past praying for'. **1902** H. JAMES *Wings of Dove* I. i. 5 The precious name..in spite of the harm her wretched father had done it..was not yet past praying for. **1909** KIPLING *Rewards & Fairies* (1910) 46 I've seen her walk to her own mirror by bye-ends, and the woman that cannot walk straight *there* is past praying for. **1939** C. DAY LEWIS *Child of Misfortune* III. i. 264 Everything's past praying for. **1962** J. LUDWIG in R. Weaver *Canad. Short Stories* (1968) 2nd Ser. 255 Sidney was past praying for, she herself couldn't have kids.

b. Esp. in phr. *not to put it* (or *anything*) *past* (*someone*), to think (a person) quite capable of performing a specific action, or behaving in a specified way.

1870 G. M. HOPKINS *Jrnls. & Papers* (1959) 198 Br. Yates gave me the following Irish expressions—*I wouldn't put it past you* or *I wouldn't doubt you* = It is just what I should expect of you. **1894** SOMERVILLE & 'ROSS' *Real Charlotte* I. v. 63, I wouldn't put it past Charlotte to be trying to ketch Mr. Dysart. **1912** J. N. MCILWRAITH *Diana of Quebec* xvii. 259, I did not put it past her to have a desire to meet the scoundrel once more, since I had assured her he was really a Green Mountain Boy. **1916** H. L. WILSON *Somewhere in Red Gap* vi. 272, I wouldn't put it past him that he had old Jerry kicked on purpose to-day! **1922** JOYCE *Ulysses* 733, I wouldn't put it past him. **1929** W. FAULKNER *Sound & Fury* 251 I'm not surprised though... I wouldn't put anything past you. **1930** J. B. PRIESTLEY *Angel Pavement* v. 214, I believe he waits until he has the tickets, then rings you up that morning and makes it up... I wouldn't put it past him. **1946** K. TENNANT *Lost Haven* (1947) xv. 240 'Bracewell is a boy any mother could trust.' 'Don't you be too sure.. I wouldn't put anything past that little devil.' **1953** S. BECKETT *Watt* 16 Poor woman, God forgive her, said Telty. Faith I wouldn't put it past him, said Mr Hackett. **1961** 'E. LATHEN' *Banking on Death* (1962) i. 5, I wouldn't put it past him to do this deliberately. **1976** M. BIRMINGHAM *Heat of Sun* ix. 159 'Do you think she could possibly consider killing justified for the sake of her deprived flock?' 'I wouldn't put it past her'.

2. *past it* (slang), incompetent through senility, etc., no longer competent, ineffective after long use; (quot. 1864) dead. Also (with hyphen) *attrib.*

1864 C. M. YONGE *Trial* II. xi. 197 'He is almost past it,' said Tom, 'but..he may be roused by my voice.' **1928** E. WALLACE *Flying Squad* xv. 130 He was a handy old chap—but he was getting rather past it. **1950** 'J. GUTHRIE' *Is this what I Wanted?* ii. 37 One never dreamed of going to them for advice. The fact was they were past it; they had lived their lives. **1959** *Listener* 22 Jan. 154/1 They never knew much about it anyway... Ramsay was past it then. **1972** K. BONFIGLIOLI *Don't point that Thing at Me* xiv. 118 The faded allure of portly, past-it Mortdecai. **1974** M. BABSON *Stalking Lamb* xix. 138 'You're getting past it, Ma.' Aaron seemed obscurely satisfied by her display of weakness. **1978** *Times Lit. Suppl.* 1 Dec. 1388/2 Not for him the slumped envy of the past-it fantasizer.

C. a. *past-prayer*; **past-pointing** *Med.* [tr. G. *vorbeizeigen* (R. Bárány 1910, in *Wien. med. Wochenschr.* LX. 2036)], pointing to one side of an object that a person intends to point at, e.g. after being spun round, as a diagnostic test.

1916 *N.Y. Med. Jrnl.* 15 July 100/2 Movement of the endolymph in the semicircular canals in a given direction, stimulates the sensitive hair cells in these canals, and produces definite phenomena. These phenomena are: 1, A twitching of the eyes or nystagmus of a certain type; 2, vertigo; 3, so-called 'past pointing'; 4, falling reactions. **1934** R. R. GRINKER *Neurology* xiii. 372 In cerebellar disturbances if a past pointing does occur it is outward, no matter where the lesion. **1977** J. MACLEOD *Davidson's Princ. & Pract. Med.* (ed. 12) xiv. 662 If a movement is attempted with the eyes closed the finger overshoots towards the side of the cerebellar lesion ('past-pointing'). **1876** G. M. HOPKINS *Wreck of Deutschland* xxxiii, in *Poems* (1967) 62 A vein for the visiting of the past-prayer, pent in prison, The-last-breath penitent spirits.

pasta (pæ·stă). [It., = PASTE *sb.*] A generic name for various forms of Italian dough mixtures or 'pastes', as macaroni, spaghetti, vermicelli, etc. Also *attrib.* and *Comb.*

[**1673** J. RAY *Observations Journey Low-Countries* 405 *Paste* made into strings like pack-thread or thongs of whitleather (which if greater they call *Macaroni*, if lesser *Vermicelli*) they cut in pieces and put in their pots as we do oat-meal to make their *menestra* or broth of.] **1874** R. H. BUSK *Folk-Lore of Rome* 118 There was a dish of 'pasta' heaped up like a mountain. **1927** F. STARK *Lett. from Syria* (1942) i. 13 They were preparing us a gigantic *pasta asciutta*. **1934** *Discovery* Aug. 215/1 What these country folk do not know about the preparation of *pasta* in its various forms of macaroni, spaghetti, tagliatelli and so on,..is not worth knowing. **1946** C. P. STEWART *Her Husband's House* xx. 134 She slapped a sheet of pasta down upon the..table. **1958** *Woman* 8 Feb. 23/1 British manufacturers are now successfully making pasta products. **1959** *Sunday Times* 22 Mar. 5/4 Pasta-loving Italian girls carry too much weight around the hips. **1973** *Times* 1 Dec. 6/5 The pasta-makers have stopped delivering spaghetti and other products to the shops. **1974** *Guardian* 31 Jan. 12/4 Trials have been made here to grow the durum or 'pasta' wheat, from which macaroni is made. **1976** *New Yorker* 15 Nov. 51/3 'George would be pleased to hear that,' Lenore says, lifting a small piece of pasta to her lips.

pastance. (Later *arch.* example.)

1906 *Outlook* 7 Apr. 471/2 During the dog-days..the grouse, the pheasant, and the fox are..withdrawn by the needs of Nature from their altruistic task of providing pastance for the gentlemen of England.

paste, *sb.* Add: **8.** *paste-brush* (also in sense 1); *paste-pot* (earlier examples); **paste-bodied** *a.*, of porcelain (see quots.); **paste-cutter** (earlier example); **paste grain,** also, occas. used of morocco; (further examples); **paste-wash** *sb.* (examples); hence **paste-wash** *v.*, to apply a mixture of paste and water to leather bindings, in order to improve the surface before lettering or decoration is applied; hence *paste-washing* vbl. sb.; **paste-water** (further examples).

1915 R. L. Hobson *Chinese Pott. & Porc.* II. ix. 141 Steatitic porcelain,..with the body..composed of *hua shih*..is light to handle, and opaque; and the body has a dry, earthy appearance, though it is of fine grain and unctuous to touch. It is variously named by the Chinese *sha-t'ai* (sand bodied) and *chiang-t'ai* (paste bodied). **1936** *Burlington Mag.* Jan. 10/1 Many fine specimens of a 'soft paste' white porcelain (paste-bodied the Chinese call it). **1964** M. Medley *Handbk. Chinese Art* 63/1 *Chiang-t'ai*, 'paste bodied' wares made from a fine-grained white firing clay, often miscalled 'soft paste'. These wares occur mainly from the 18th century onward. **1846** *Jewish Manual, or Pract. Information Jewish & Mod. Cookery* vi. 106 Beat the yolk of an egg, dip a paste-brush into it, and lay it on the crust before baking. **1845** E. Acton *Mod. Cookery* i. 5 Divide the bread into dice, or cut it with a deep paste-cutter into any other form. **1923** H. A. Maddox *Dict. Stationery* 59 Pastegrain.—Also abbreviated to P.G., but more correctly specified as pastegrain roan. Comprises the thin grain side of a split sheepskin, mechanically grained with a cracked or fissured pattern and stiffened slightly by pasting on the back... In the fancy trade P.G. roan is elaborately but erroneously described as French morocco. **1963** B. C. Middleton *Hist. Eng. Craft Bookbinding Technique* xi. 122 In the 30s and 40s of the nineteenth century hard- and paste-grain morocco replaced straight-grain morocco and russia for use on fine bindings. **1845** *Ainsworth's Mag.* VII. 27 Elliston now demanded the paste-pot. **1857** N. W. T. Root *School Amusements* 207 A large scrap-book is prepared, a committee of selection is chosen, a paste-pot made ready, and contributions are invited. **1880** J. W. Zaehnsdorf *Art of Bookbinding* 116 The porous varieties [of leather] must be paste-washed carefully. *Ibid.* 174 Paste-wash.—Paste diluted with water. **1946** E. Diehl *Bookbinding* II. xxii. 327 When leathers such as calf, sheep, or russia are used, they should be paste-washed before tooling, in order to fill up the many fine pores. *Ibid.*, Calf and other very porous leathers require a heavier paste wash than morocco or levant. **1963** B. C. Middleton *Hist. Eng. Craft Bookbinding Technique* xiv. 211 Paste-wash, glaire, glue-size, yolk of egg and boot and furniture polishes have been used on leather, but mainly to improve the surface. **1921** *Librarian* Nov. 74 Pastewashing and varnishing tends to crack and destroy the leather, and does not soften or preserve it in the slightest degree. **1946** E. Diehl *Bookbinding* II. xxii. 327, I do not approve of paste-washing or sizing leather if it can be avoided. **1880** J. W. Zaehnsdorf *Art of Bookbinding* 116 The non-porous leathers need only be washed with thin paste water or vinegar. **1901** D. Cockerell *Bookbinding* xiv. 198 Paste-water is paste and water well beaten up to form a milky liquid.

paste, *v.* Add: **1.** *to paste down*, to line the cover of a book by attaching half the end-paper to it.

1835 'J. A. Arnett' *Bibliopegia* I. 67 When dry, the end papers are pasted down, and the work finished. **1880** J. W. Zaehnsdorf *Art of Bookbinding* viii. 35 When the book is to be pasted down, the ends [*sc.* end-papers] are lifted from the book. **1901** D. Cockerell *Bookbinding* xvii. 254 To paste down end papers, the book is placed on the block with the board open. **1963** B. C. Middleton *Hist. Eng. Craft Bookbinding Technique* xiii. 203 Until, roughly, the end of the first quarter of the nineteenth century the endpapers of all grades of bindings were pasted down without being trimmed.

4. (Earlier and later examples.) Also, to inflict heavy damage on by bombing or shelling; in *Cricket*, to hit (a ball, the bowling) hard.

1846 *Swell's Night Guide* 58 They pasted his nibs, and scarpered rumbo. **1911** *Daily Colonist* (Victoria, B.C.) 30 Apr. (Mag.) 10/1 As the ducks kept coming round the point the shooters in the canoes had a great opportunity of pasting them. **1924** A. C. Maclaren *Cricket Old & New* xiii. 128 Many and many a short ball bowled by Gregory in the Test Matches of 1921, would have been pasted to the square leg boundary in the days 'when Plancus was consul'. **1930** *Strand Mag.* May 348/1 The Major was gazing at Trout's forehead, where the stick had pasted him. **1934** D. L. Sayers *Nine Tailors* III. 275 Deacon..pastes the fellow one. **1942** *Hutchinson's Pict. Hist. War* 18 Mar.–9 June 23 (*caption*) The nose of a Westland Whirlwind single-seater fighter... The Whirlwind has been used with much success for 'pasting' enemy aerodromes. **1955** M. Allingham *Beckoning Lady* ix. 127 He came to this part of the country in 1942 when London was being pasted. **1973** A. Mann *Tiara* ii. 17 [He] used to play for Yorkshire. Let's go down and watch him paste the bowling. **1977** *New Yorker* 25 July 70/3 She guessed correctly each time just where Mrs. King, in charge of the forecourt, would be pasting her volley.

pasteboard, *sb.* (*a.*). **3. c.** (Earlier examples.)

1856 'Ockside' & 'Doesticks' *Hist. & Rec. Elephant Club* 29 Putting his physiognomy before the seven by nine aperture through which the money goes in and the pasteboard comes out. **1873** J. H. Beadle *Undevel. West* xxxvi. 771 The call of 'Tickets, gents', showed one man without the pasteboard.

paste-down (pē̆ⁱ·stˌdaun). [f. Paste *v.* 5 + Down *adv.* 1.] In modern bindings, that part of the end-paper which is pasted to the inside of the cover of a book; in earlier bindings, a piece of paper or parchment used as a lining inside a cover.

Replaces def. s.v. Paste *v.* 5 in Dict.

1888 C. T. Jacobi *Printers' Vocab.* 97 *Paste-downs*, the blank flyleaves, sometimes coloured, at either end of a book which are pasted down on the covers. **1901** D. Cockerell *Bookbinding* xvii. 254 One of the paste-down papers is then stretched over the board. *Ibid.* 256 All rubbing down must be done through paper, or the 'paste-down' will be soiled. **1934** *Yorkshire Archæol. Jrnl.* XXXI. 338 The paste-down and recto of the fly-leaf are blank. **1954** N. R. Ker (*title*) Fragments of medieval manuscripts used as pastedowns in Oxford bindings. **1963** *Times* 11 June 5/7 A collection of leaves and fragments from manuscripts..which had been used as pastedowns in later bindings went to Quaritch. **1972** P. Gaskell *New Introd. Bibliogr.* 148 Then the endpapers were sewn on... Their purpose was, as paste-downs, to reinforce the joints of the covers.

paste-in (pē̆ⁱ·stˌin), *a.* and *sb.* [f. Paste *v.* 5 + In *adv.* 1.] **A.** *adj.* Pasted in, inserted by pasting. Also, of a scrapbook, etc., containing blank paper on which cuttings or pictures may be pasted. **B.** *sb.* A correction or illustration printed separately from the main text of a book, and attached to the relevant page by its inner edge being pasted to the margin.

1902 [see Paste *v.* 5]. **1907** *Yesterday's Shopping* (1969) 436A (*heading*) Paste-in Albums for Photographs, &c. **1939** *Library* XIX. 486 When, more than a month after the publication of the *Lyrical Ballads*, 1800, Wordsworth received copies of Volume II, he was greatly irritated to find that the lower half of page 210..was blank... There exist at least two specimens of a paste-in supplying the fifteen missing lines... Each of the two specimens is pasted to the inner margin of page 211 to open out onto the blank on page 210. **1960** *Times* 13 Oct. 15/7 Where paste-ins have become puckered, wavy lines must be expected. **1971** L. M. Harrod *Librarians' Gloss.* (ed. 3) 488 Paste-in. 1. A correction or addition to the text supplied after the sheets have been printed, and tipped into the book opposite the place to which it refers... 2. A separately printed illustration or map, cut to the size of the book, and the inner edge pasted into the text before gathering.

pastel². Add: **3.** Also applied to soft or subdued shades used generally in textiles, interior decoration, etc.

1926–7 *Army & Navy Stores Catal.* 678/1 Gloves.. washable suède, light grey, pastelle, or white. **1934** *Archit. Rev.* LXXV. 14/2 There is, for instance, a stone known as Quartzite, which..when worked to a rough surface provides an everlasting wall lining in a variety of cool pastel shades. **1951** *Good Housek. Home Encycl.* 19/1 Upholstered fibre furniture..is available in various pastel shades. **1970** H. Ratcliffe *Home Decorating* xiii. 84/2 White plus a colour is a tint, white plus colour plus grey or black is a pastel shade. **1974** N. Freeling *Dressing of Diamond* 96 A glimpse of pastel green tiles. **1976** *Star* (Sheffield) 26 Nov. 24 (Advt.), 1976 (P) Cavalier 1600 L 4-door. In pastel beige. Fitted radio.

4. *pastel-coloured*, *-tinted* adjs.

1932 *Daily Tel.* 25 Apr. 4/4 Pearls on Pastel Gowns. Pearls are to be worn even more than usual this season. The reason is the vogue for pastel coloured gowns. **1978** B. Freemantle *Clap Hands* iv. 26 A fine-featured.. man who affected pastel coloured shirts with matching socks. **1922** H. Crane *Let.* 2 Mar. (1965) 80 Delicate pastel tinted flowers. **1952** *Granta* 29 Nov. 8/1 We find it agreeable to place a Victorian chair or print among the blond woods and foam rubber, or to hang pastel-tinted antlers on the wall near a mobile.

paster. Add: **2.** For *U.S.* read 'orig. *U.S.*' (Earlier example.) Also, a piece of adhesive paper used for various other purposes.

1870 *Congress. Globe* 13 Apr. 2659/3 There were ten tickets..which were scratched and had pasters with the name of Caleb N. Taylor. **1882** *Nation* (N.Y.) 6 July 7/2 The Erie and Central Railroads have made the attempt to rid themselves of all liabilities..by putting a 'paster' on their bills of lading. **1906** *World's Work* (N.Y.) May 7511/1 You may read upon its label that it has been 'U.S. Government Inspected'. The paster on the box from which it came assures us again of that fact.

paste-up (pē̆ⁱ·stˌʌp). [f. Paste *v.* 5 + Up *adv.*¹ 21.] **1.** A plan of a page or group of pages, with the position of text, illustrations, etc., indicated. Also *attrib.*

1930 Freshwater & Bastien *Pitman's Dict. Advertising & Printing* i. 186/2 A proof with blocks, blue prints, or odd pieces of type matter pasted up in position is termed a paste-up. **1948** H. Missingham *Student's Guide Commercial Art* II. 76 Paste-up. The various components of the complete layout pasted together on a card to form the complete advertisement. **1949** Melcher & Larrick *Printing & Promotion Handbk.* 202/1 Extreme neatness is not necessary on a paste-up dummy. *Ibid.*, There are many tricks to paste-up technique. **1967** E. Chambers *Photolitho-Offset* iii. 35 This key drawing or paste-up, as it is often called, should at least include all type pulls. **1975** J. Butcher *Copy-Editing* v. 61 In the paste-up the illustrations are represented by photocopies, rough sketches or just empty rectangles. **1977** *Sci. Amer.* Sept. 95/3 (Advt.), In May, 1977 we announced KODAK MX-929 Resist, for use in an arrangement for translating a paste-up of a newspaper page to metal by scanning with a He-Ne laser and modulating an argon ion laser to expose the resist.

2. A piece of paper or cardboard with a newspaper or book clipping, etc., pasted to it. Also *transf.*

1944 *Daily Progress* (Charlottesville, Va.) 11 Mar. 8/6 Simple paper paste-ups a child could do. **1953** *Amer. Speech* XXVIII. 81 The D[*ictionary of*] A[*mericanisms*].. had the benefit of but a mere 300,000 quotation slips... Nor did this number represent fresh materials only, for it included thousands of paste-ups from its predecessors. **1972** D. H. Laurence *Coll. Letters G. B. Shaw* II. p. xviii, Making paste-ups of previously published correspondence. *a* **1974** R. Crossman *Diaries* (1975) I. 401 The following weekend my red box contained the paste-up of all the extracts and they included one or two absolutely unequivocal statements. **1977** *Times Lit. Suppl.* 3 June 682/1 His novel is a carefully constructed, defiantly random paste-up of *faits divers*.

Pasteur (pastö·r). The name of *Pasteur* (see Pasteur *v.*) used *attrib.* and † in the possessive to designate apparatus he devised and effects he discovered, as **Pasteur effect,** the effect of oxygen of inhibiting fermentation in favour of respiration in certain organisms and tissues; formerly called the **Pasteur reaction*; **Pasteur('s) flask,** a glass flask with an elongated neck bent downwards so that micro-organisms in the air cannot contaminate its contents; **Pasteur('s) pipette,** a sterile pipette which at one end has a plug of cotton-wool or the like and a rubber bulb and at the other terminates as a capillary tube whose end is sealed at the time of drawing and not broken until the pipette is to be used; also, in mod. use, a pipette bought for similar purposes but not sterilized, plugged, or sealed; **Pasteur reaction** [after G. *Pasteursche reaktion* (O. Warburg 1926, in *Biochem. Zeitschr.* CLXXII. 435)] = **Pasteur effect*.

1935 *Nature* 15 June 995/2 (*heading*) Mechanism of the Pasteur effect. **1942** O. Meyerhof et al. *Symposium Respiratory Enzymes* 48 Most doubly equipped organisms possess in the Pasteur effect a regulatory device that enables them to use, as occasion demands, either their aerobic or their anaerobic systems. **1953** Fruton & Simmonds *Gen. Biochem.* xx. 483 Under anaerobic conditions the rate of consumption of carbohydrate by muscle tissue is approximately six to eight times that observed under aerobic conditions... This inhibition, by oxygen, of the rate of carbohydrate breakdown is frequently termed the Pasteur effect. **1971** I. G. Gass et al. *Understanding Earth* x. 146/2 In many primitive organisms, the change-over from fermentation to respiration occurs when oxygen reaches about 1 per cent of its present concentration in the atmosphere. Pasteur pointed out this effect..during his study of the spoilage of wines, so it is known as the 'Pasteur effect'. [**1876** tr. *Schützenberger's On Fermentation* II. iii. 327 (*heading*) M. Pasteur's flask to deprive the air of its germs.] **1882** W. W. Cheyne *Antiseptic Surg.* i. 17 Mr. Lister has found that in Pasteur's flasks with the long open necks, no floating dust is present after what was originally there has settled. **1913** G. Martin *Industr. & Manuf. Chem.: Organic* v. i. 231 A pure culture in sterilised wort is obtained by inoculating from each separate colony nutrient sterilised wort contained in a Pasteur's flask. *Ibid.*, A small amount of pure yeast culture from a Pasteur flask. **1969** R. K. Das *Industr. Chem.* II. xvi. 221 The sterile wort is inoculated with pure culture (from the Pasteur flask). **1902** J. W. H. Eyre *Elem. Bacteriol. Technique* i. 21 (*heading*) Capillary pipettes or Pasteur's pipettes. **1903** Swithinbank & Newman *Bacteriol. of Milk* 547 (*heading*) Method of making a Pasteur pipette. **1972** *Jrnl. Endocrinol.* LIV. 108 Fluid from control and test dishes was removed with a sterile Pasteur pipette. **1930** *Biochem. Jrnl.* XXIV. 1302 Ethyl *iso*cyanide is therefore said to be a specific inhibitor of the Pasteur reaction, *i.e.* of the reaction between respiration and fermentation, using the latter term to include glycolysis. **1966** Irvine & James tr. *Lundegårdh's Plant Physiol.* iv. 193 The exact position of the Pasteur reaction in the glycolysis chain..cannot be very easily determined.

pasteurella (pastöre·lă). Pl. **-ellæ, -ellas.** [mod.L. (V. Trevisan 1887, in *Rendiconti Reale Istituto Lombardo di Scienze e Lettere* XX. 94), f. prec. + *-ella*, diminutive ending.] A bacterium of the genus so called, which includes those causing plague and other acute infectious diseases in man, other mammals, and birds.

1913 H. J. Hutchens tr. *Besson's Pract. Bacteriol.* xxviii. 446 Lignières..came to the conclusion that varieties of the Pasteurella could be distinguished by means of their pathogenic properties. *Ibid.* 447 Organisms of the pasteurella group are..v ry pleomorphic. **1929** G. F. Petrie in *Syst. Bacteriol.* (Med. Res. Council) III. 139 The plague bacillus..is generally considered to be a member of the Pasteurella group. **1929** H. Schütze in *Ibid.* IV. 447 (*heading*) Pasteurellas in man. **1949** *Vet. Rec.* 5 Feb. 64/1 (*title*) Pneumonia in sheep associated with infection by a pasteurella-like organism. **1961** *Lancet* 7 Oct. 812/2 Organisms of the pasteurella group are non-motile aerobic gram-negative rods. **1963** Jubb & Kennedy *Path. Domestic Animals* I. iii. 172/1 A complete separation of the different strains of the pathogenic pasteurellae has still to be determined. **1974** Q. N. Myrvik et al. *Fund. Med. Bacteriol. & Mycol.* xxiv. 309 The pasteurellae..are parasites and pathogens for an unusually wide range of animal species.

pasteurellosis (pa:störelōᵘ·sis). *Med.* and *Vet. Sci.* Pl. **-oses.** [ad. F. *pasteurellose* (J. Lignières 1901, in *Ann. Inst. Pasteur* XV. 734), f. prec. + -osis.] An infection produced by a bacterium of the genus *Pasteurella*.

1902 *Nature* 29 May 120/1 The name pasteurelloses is applied to a group of diseases of the same type, including typhoid fever and pneumonia of the horse, chicken cholera and hæmorrhagic septicæmia of the sheep, ox, and pig. **1913** H. J. Hutchens tr. *Besson's Pract. Bacteriol.* xxviii. 447 (*heading*) The pasteurelloses and plague in animals. **1925** *Jrnl. Hygiene* XXIV. 66 Deaths due to Pasteurella and deaths in which no evidence of pasteurellosis was found..were grouped together. **1929** [see *barbone]. **1963** Jubb & Kennedy *Path. Domestic Animals* I. iii.

172/1 In the various hosts, pasteurellosis may take a variety of forms. **1966** *Daily Tel.* 4 Nov. 13/4 He has pasteurellosis too, or 'pseudo-tuberculosis', also found in voles, sparrows, magpies, wrens, swallows, and, especially wood pigeons. More important, children can be affected—it causes a swelling of the glands that may be mistaken for appendicitis.

pasteurize, *v.* **1.** Delete the first clause of def. and add: To kill most but not all of the micro-organisms present in (food) so as to render its consumption safe and to improve its keeping quality (as by heat treatment or irradiation). (Add further examples.)

Distinguished from *sterilize*, which implies the killing of all the micro-organisms.

1945 *ABC of Cookery* (Ministry of Food) vi. 19 Unless milk has come from a herd of tuberculin tested cows or has been pasteurized it should be scalded or boiled before drinking. **1959** *Internat. Jrnl. Appl. Radiation & Isotopes* VI. 205/2 Packaging does not present a problem for foods 'pasteurized' by radiation. **1966** *Proc. Internat. Symp. Food Irradiation* (Internat. Atomic Energy Agency) 842 The cost of pasteurizing food (300 000 to 500 000 rads) should be less than one-tenth the cost of radio-sterilization. **1970** *Preservation of Fish by Irradiation* (United Nations F.A.O.) 3 A test was..developed for evaluating whether or not there exists a botulinum Type E hazard in fish fillets pasteurized with gamma radiation.

pasteurization (further examples); **pasteurized** *ppl. a.*, also *fig.*; also **pa·steurizing** *ppl. a.*

1957 *Jrnl. Appl. Bacteriol.* XX. 286 For meat processing, two different types of treatment have been envisaged. One is complete sterilization... The other process, which is becoming known as 'pasteurization', consists in decreasing the bacterial numbers sufficiently to give a substantial increase in storage life, usually under refrigeration. Doses from 5×10^4 to 5×10^5 rads have been suggested as giving useful results. **1959** *Internat. Jrnl. Appl. Radiation & Isotopes* VI. 143/1 Some species of fish stand up better to irradiation than others and..these when subjected to only pasteurizing levels suffer none of the undesirable changes produced by sterilization. **1962** *Listener* 13 Sept. 406/2 After Mr Kokoschka's verve and spontaneity our average spoken word sounds pasteurized and insipid both in substance and expression. **1966** *Proc. Internat. Symp. Food Irradiation* (Internat. Atomic Energy Agency) 527 With the exception of thiamine, no significant changes occurred in the water-soluble vitamins of haddock fillets and clam meats subjected to pasteurizing doses of radiation. *Ibid.* 549 (*heading*) Investigations on pasteurization of cold marinades by ^{60}Co gamma rays. **1973** STEWART & AMERINE *Introd. Food Sci.* v. 203 Radiation dosages for pasteurization are only about a tenth of that [*sic*] required for sterilization. **1976** *National Observer* (U.S.) 19 June 20/5 The pasteurised, homogenised, tanned, toothy, breasty, false-lashed, make-up-larded, honey cascade-haired beings thrust upon us as representatives of young womanhood. **1976** N. FREELING *Lake Isle* vi. 38 Castang, though a youngish cop with a university degree, didn't think much of his more pasteurized colleagues.

pasticcio. Add: Also in the orig. It. sense, a pie containing numerous ingredients, of which macaroni and some form of meat are the chief constituents. (Further examples of senses in Dict.)

1907 JOYCE *Let.* 18 Feb. (1966) II. 216, I have made a lovely pasticcio, it seems. **1923** *Mrs. Beeton's Bk. Househ. Managem.* 1326 *Pasticcio Maccharóni.* (*Macaroni Pie*). *Ingredients.*—½ of a lb. of cold beef or mutton, ½ an onion, 3 or 4 tomatoes, ¼ of a lb. of macaroni, breadcrumbs, grated cheese, stock, salt, pepper, nutmeg. **1937** M. MORPHY *Good Food from Italy* 63 Pasticcio di maccheroni (Ferrara). **1967** *Listener* 19 Jan. 107/1 The *pasticcio*, the medley of movements contributed by different composers. **1973** *Guardian* 14 Apr. 5/4 Anyone at sea among unfamiliar Italian dishes would be well rewarded by going straight for such specialities as Pasticcio. **1973** J. WAINWRIGHT *Touch of Malice* 63 Fernlea Autumn Fair..had ended up as a crummy, screaming pasticcio of brash lights and belching noise. **1974** *Listener* 28 Feb. 282/3 Next year Handel supplied..*Deborah*, largely a *pasticcio* over which he took little trouble. **1976** *Survey* Summer–Autumn 322 The contents turn out to be a pasticcio of themes rather tenuously connected.

pastiche, *sb.* Add: Now in more general use than *pasticcio*. (Further and *attrib.* examples.)

1934 C. LAMBERT *Music Ho!* I. 20 The illogicality of some of the present-day pastiches may give you 'a rare turn'. **1955** *Times* 11 May 7/5 At the Players' we are still basking in the glory of having started *The Boy Friend* on its historic career, and to attempt *pastiche* again would have been an affront to the theatrical gods. **1961** *Listener* 7 Sept. 335/1 The subject that lies at the back of popular writing on contemporary themes is sociology: it is the Americans who have sold best—Whyte, Riesman, Galbraith, the pastiche merchants Wright Mills and Vance Packard. *Ibid.* 5 Oct. 508/1 The new examination is *not* conceived as a pastiche of the G.C.E. **1964** *Ibid.* 16 Apr. 649/1 Henze is sometimes called an eclectic composer.. an inference that he is the worse for being a pasticheur... Henze's interest in pastiche has long since died a natural death. **1978** *Listener* 2 Feb. 158/2 Such genre pastiches as the recent film, *Chinatown*.

pasti·che, *v.* [f. the sb.] **a.** *intr.* To create pastiches. Also const. *about*. **b.** *trans.* To copy or imitate the style of. Hence **pasti·ching** *vbl. sb.*

1957 *Listener* 26 Dec. 1082/2, I pastiche of course and exaggerate, but that is the kind of thing. **1962** D. LESSING *Golden Noteb.* III. 375 Well, Anna, and how do you describe all this pastiching about? **1965** R. G. COHN *Toward Poems of Mallarmé* 6 Rimbaud..'pastiched' Mallarmé's *Les Fleurs*. **1970** *Times* 17 Oct. 20 The unfortunate Victorian habit of 'reviving', that is, pastiching, the Renaissance, the Baroque and just about every other style of the past. **1973** *Nature* 11 May 49/2 A device for selecting as university students only those who have already demonstrated that they can survive a university course as pastiched at school.

‖ **pasticheur** (pastiʃör). [Fr., f. PASTICHE.] An artist who imitates the style of another artist.

1912 R. FRY *Let.* 3 Feb. (1972) I. 353 One doesn't like to be called a *pasticheur*... I've always been searching for a style to express my *petite sensation* in. **1913** *Nation* 2 Aug. 676 A skill which might lead him [*sc.* C. Brancuzi], in default of any overpowering imaginative purpose, to become a brilliant *pasticheur*. **1934** C. LAMBERT *Music Ho!* v. 329 The dog-Latin classicism of the post-war pasticheurs. **1944** *Burlington Mag.* Mar. 71/2 Steer, on the other hand, was a *pasticheur* and to say of him that he 'was beyond doubt the greatest of our landscape painters since Turner and Constable'..is as meaningless as it is ridiculous. **1958** *Observer* 7 Dec. 16/4 The obvious accusation against Betjeman is that he is a pasticheur—and it is certainly true that he has scarcely ever written a poem which was not, quite consciously, in the manner of someone else. **1964** [see *PASTICHE *sb.*]. **1973** *Daily Tel.* 9 Apr. 5 For many he [*sc.* Picasso] was one of the great creators of his age. To others he was at best an accomplished pasticheur and at worst a mountebank. **1976** *Gramophone* Apr. 1643/3 Karg-Elert (1877–1933) was a pasticheur, too, and even a consciously humorous parodist in some of his miniatures.

pastie (pēⁱ·sti). [f. PASTE *v.* + -Y^6, -IE.] (Chiefly *pl.*) A covering for the nipple of a woman's breast.

1961 *Washington Post* 17 May A3/6 Miss Mason was lying on the floor with nothing on except the scantiest of brassieres, known in the trade as 'pasties'. **1964** *Punch* 29 July 164/3 The young ladies [of the *Folies Bergère*] have been bidden [in New York]..to wear, in the cause of innocence, two 'pasties'. **1969** *Sunday Truth* (Brisbane) 23 Nov. 10/4 Stripper Sharon was promoting a Valley nightclub, wearing nothing on top but a couple of pasties to keep her modest. **1973** 'E. MCBAIN' *Let's hear It* viii. 123 Topless dancing, in this city, was something more than topless—the something more being pasties or filmy brassieres. **1975** *New Society* 23 Oct. 198/3 Go-go dancers in New York are not allowed to dance completely nude; they wear G-strings and mini bras or nipple-covering 'pasties'... For the dancers to get a tip, the 'pasties' usually have to come off.

‖ **pastiglia** (pastī·lyă). *Art.* Also **pastiglio.** [It., = paste.] A kind of stucco (see quots.). Also *attrib.*

1927 EBERLEIN & RAMSDELL *Pract. Bk. Ital., Span., & Portuguese Furnit.* 36 The process of *pastiglia* decoration ..consisted in covering the *cassone*, cabinet, or whatever the piece of furniture might be with coarse linen or fine canvas, strained or glued over both the moulded and flat surfaces. Over this were painted successive coats of *pastiglia*, a thick creamy mixture of *gesso*, which dried and hardened rapidly. **1938** L. E. COTCHETT *Evol. Furnit.* ii. 21 Canvas was..painted with several coats of *pastiglia* or gesso. **1959** L. A. BOGER *Compl. Guide Furnit. Styles* iii. 27/2 Pastiglia work as a form of decoration is chiefly identified with the 15th century. **1969** R. MAYER *Dict. Art Terms & Techniques* 284/2 (*caption*) Italian casetta (casket) of the latter half of the 15th century, ornamented in pastiglia relief. **1977** *Technical Bull.* (National Gallery) Sept. 3/2 The top corners of the eight panels..were decorated in pastiglio.

pastil, pastille, *sb.* Add: **2. b.** *Med.* A small disc of barium platinocyanide whose gradual change of colour when exposed to X-rays was formerly used as an indication of the dose delivered.

1906 *Sci. Abstr.* A. IX. 49 (*heading*) Use of platinocyanide pastilles in radiotherapy. **1922** G. W. C. KAYE *Pract. Appl. X-Rays* iv. 71 Of all the various intensity measurers, the pastille finds the most favour with medical men in this country. *Ibid.*, The pastille is placed at a specified distance from the anticathode of the bulb, and the colour is matched against one of a number of standard tints. **1956** C. W. WILSON *Radium Therapy* (ed. 2) iv. 74 Sabouraud.. made use of the fact that a pastille of barium platinocyanide turns from apple green to reddish brown when irradiated by X-rays.

5. pastille-burner = CASSOLETTE 2; **pastille dose** *Med.*, an obsolete unit of radiation dose corresponding to a change from one standard colour to another of a pastille (sense *2 b).

1904 A. HAYDEN *Chats on Eng. China* i. 11 Crown Derby Pastille-Burner. **1957** MANKOWITZ & HAGGAR *Conc. Encycl. Eng. Pott. & Porc.* 32/2 There is..a red script mark 'P. Bradley 1828' on a pastille burner probably of Coalport manufacture in the National Museum of Wales. **1971** *Country Life* 7 Oct. 922/2 The larger sizes [of pottery model houses] have a hole in their back, being intended for use as nightlights or pastille burners. **1909** *Lancet* 15 May 1380/1 A Sabouraud pastille dose with the anticathode at 6½ inches from the nearest point of the scalp is given to the vertex, occiput, lower occiput, right side and left side in succession. **1935** *Nature* 14 Dec. 960/2 The ionisation unit of X-ray quantity, the röntgen, has practically replaced the older arbitrary standards such as the pastille dose. **1950** WALTER & MILLER *Short Textbk. Radiotherapy* x. 243 The 'pastille dose'..has now been completely superseded and there is no justification for its continued use.

pastillage (pæ·stilėdʒ, ‖ pastiyāʒ). [Fr., lit. compression of paste into blocks.] **1.** *Pottery.* (See quot. 1940.)

1901 W. P. RIX tr. *Bourry's Treat. Ceramic Industries* II. ix. 427 This method of decoration is known as 'pastillage'. **1940** *Chambers's Techn. Dict.* 619/2 *Pastillage*, dot and dribble designs made with coloured slip, which is dribbled from a container with a flexible base and a spout. **1947** *Horizon* June 369 There must be hundreds of years difference between the coarse idols obtained by a process of *pastillage* and the delicately coloured and modelled figures of the kind reproduced here. **1962** G. KINNELL tr. *Lehmann's Pre-Columbian Ceramics* I. ii. 19 The *pastillage* technique used in the decoration. *Ibid.* II. i. 40 The eyes, almost always slanted, are indicated by incisions or *pastillage*. **1974** SAVAGE & NEWMAN *Illustr. Dict. Ceramics* 214 *Pastillage..*, slip applied by trailing through a quill.

2. A type of icing.

[**1951** *Good Housek. Home Encycl.* 499/1 The special stiff royal icing..(called pastillage in French).] **1963** *Times* 20 Apr. 10/3 The cake is decorated with 46 lb. of marzipan and 25 lb. of royal icing and pastillage.

pastilled (pæ·stild), *a. rare.* [f. PASTIL, PASTILLE *sb.* + -ED^2.] Subjected to the effect of a medicated pastille.

1935 E. M. FORSTER *Abinger Harvest* (1936) 101 The clearing of pastilled throats.

pasting, *vbl. sb.* Add: **1.** (Earlier example of *pasting-lace*.)

1846 G. DODD *Brit. Manuf.* 6th Ser. v. 132 Coach-trimmings... 'Pasting-lace', about half an inch broad..is employed to cover and hide rows of tacks.

3. (Further examples.) Also *fig.*

1922 G. B. SHAW *Let.* in *To a Young Actress* (1960) 24 There is nothing for your soul in Shakespear..but there is plenty of pasting for your ear; and you need an exquisite ear for tragedy. **1930** *Collier's* 1 Feb. 44/2 Instead of being mad at Lillian and giving her a pasting for such goings on, Wilbur is somewhat pleased. **1942** *R.A.F. Jrnl.* 3 Oct. 33 We were getting a pasting. Everything going up in smoke and everything coming down with a bang. **1950** J. D. MACDONALD *Brass Cupcake* (1955) x. 105 Fictional heroes..can bounce back from a pasting that should have put them in hospital beds. **1953** in Wentworth & Flexner *Dict. Amer. Slang* (1960) 377/2 [The] Philadelphia A's took a 13–10 pasting from the Washington Senators. **1974** *Times* 14 Jan. 3/7 Some managers have taken a real pasting when things have gone wrong. **1976** *Listener* 1 Apr. 409/2 'More embarrassing interviews..and more feeble comedy sketches.'.. Was it fair to give a show such a pasting in advance?

pastis (pæ·stis). [Fr.] An aperitif made from aniseed.

1926 'C. BARRY' *Detective's Holiday* vi. 51 'Have your tea if you like, but I will drink a "*pastis*".' 'A matter of taste, *mon ami*,' Gilmartin replied. 'To me your terrible aniseed smells like a pharmacy.' **1942** W. SANSOM in *Penguin New Writing* XIV. 72 Jean was saying, 'Damn that waiter! Why must he bring me quinquina instead of pastis?' **1955** *Times* 8 Aug. 8/7 No longer the friendly gossip at the pump, no longer the fraternal glass of pastis on the terrace of the Auberge de la Pageole. **1958** X. FIELDING *Corsair Country* viii. 165 Even obvious Europeans like the pastis-drinkers in the bar. **1959** *Encounter* Oct. 53/1 Spain for the bull-fights, Provence for the *pastis*. **1967** A. LICHINE *Encycl. Wines* 396/2 *Pastis*, the aperitif of Marseilles. Pastis is made on an alcohol base with herb flavourings, notably liquorice. **1973** P. O'DONNELL *Silver Mistress* ii. 24 He had called at the auberge to drink a pastis.

pastism (pɑ·stiz'm). [f. PAST *sb.* + -ISM.] Memory of, nostalgia for, the past.

1921 W. DE MORGAN *Old Man's Youth* xxvii. 258 The late fifties were still under the spell of Pastism. **1962** *Listener* 30 Aug. 326/3 The *Jugendbewegung* was sterile 'past-ism' by contrast with contemporary futurism.

pastless (pɑ·stlės), *a.* [f. PAST *sb.* + -LESS.] Without a past; having no history.

1954 W. FAULKNER *Fable* 21 The perfect soldier: pastless, unhampered, and complete. **1965** P. ROGERS in *Granta* Summer 12/1 It's all very well being pastless in a moment of existential dilemma. **1971** S. CAVEL *World Viewed* 97 His people are without fantasy (hence pastless and futureless, hence presentless).

past-mistress. Add: (Later examples.) Also written without hyphen.

1915 [see *COCK-AND-BULL 3]. **1939** A. THIRKELL *Before Lunch* iii. 56 Mrs. Middleton was a past mistress in the art of keeping a staff. **1974** G. BUTLER *Coffin for Canary* vi. 72, I would meet reproachful gazes from Sarah. She was a past mistress in the art of giving me such a look.

pastness. Delete *rare* and add later examples.

1890 W. JAMES *Princ. Psychol.* I. xv. 605 They are associated with other things which for us signify pastness. But how do these things get *their* pastness? What is the *original* of our experience of pastness, from whence we get the meaning of the term? **1919** T. S. ELIOT *Sel. Essays* (1951) 14 The historical sense involves a perception, not only of the pastness of the past, but of its presence. **1925** C. D. BROAD *Mind & its Place* v. 262 The very same characteristic..we took to be 'pastness' in other situations. **1941** F. MATTHIESSEN *Amer. Renaissance* XIV. iv. 654 He did not so often think of the presentness of the past as of the pastness of the present, of its illimitable shadowy extensions backward to the roots of history. **1954** K. TILLOTSON *Novels of Eighteen-Forties* I. 111 The Brontës..turn from the present, emphasizing their choice by a specified..'pastness'. **1973** A. H. SOMMERSTEIN

Sound Pattern Anc. Greek ii. 63 The verb whose pastness brings the rule into operation may be in the infinitive or participial form. **1977** *Theology* LXXX. 201 The faith of the communion of saints..confers on the death of Jesus at least one kind of capacity to survive 'pastness' and to become in a valid sense objectively present for us.

pastoral. Add: **A.** *adj.* **2. b.** *pastoral lease*, in Australia and New Zealand, a lease of land for sheep or cattle farming.

1850 *Papers Rel. Crown Lands in Austral. Colonies* 95 in *Parl. Papers* XXXVII. 287 You are empowered to grant pastoral leases for eight years... No leases.. whether pastoral or tillage leases, are to convey a perpetual right of renewal. **1894** W. Epps *Land Syst. Australasia* 154 In the event of a renewal of any pastoral lease being determined upon, it must be offered at auction 12 months before the expiry of the term. **1924** S. H. Roberts *Hist. Austral. Land Settlement* 293 Thus, after ten years of waste, the resumed areas of 1884, both in the centre and the west, were again placed under pastoral lease. **1948** V. Palmer *Golconda* iii. 18 Nominally the country around was held on pastoral lease by an old cattleman named Gourlay. **1950** *N.Z. Jrnl. Agric.* Nov. 413/2 At this period of Canterbury's development it would not have been possible for many of the so-called squatters to make a profit out of grazing sheep if they had been required to freehold the land. Though the pastoral lease was a partial answer, it did not give any security of tenure. **1953** A. Upfield *Murder must Wait* xix. 169 Prospecting pastoral leases in the far north of South Australia. **1959** A. McLintock *Descr. Atlas N.Z.* 38 With the growth in sheep numbers, regulations covering the granting of pastoral leases were laid down.

4. *pastoral letter* = Pastoral *sb.* 5 b.

1885 *Encycl. Brit.* XVIII. 351/2 *Pastoral letter*, a letter addressed, in his pastoral capacity, by a bishop to his clergy, or the laity of his diocese, or both. **1957** *Oxf. Dict. Chr. Ch.* 1023/2 *Pastoral letters*,..official letters addressed by a bishop to all members of his diocese.

B. *sb.* **3. a.** (Later examples.)

1949 *Poetry* (Chicago) LXXXIII 245 Pastoral. In Empson, a frequent literary device 'of putting the complex into the simple' by a process of inversion; e.g., the last shall be first, a little child shall lead them, etc. 'The essential trick of the old pastoral, which was felt to imply a beautiful relation between rich and poor, was to make simple people express strong feelings (felt as the most universal subject, something fundamentally true about everybody) in learned and fashionable language (so that you wrote about the best subject in the best way).' **1957** N. Frye *Anat. Crit.* 43 The pastoral of popular modern literature is the Western Story.

pastoralia (pɑstōrā·liă). [L., neut. pl. of *pastōrālis*, Pastoral *a.*] Things having relation to spiritual care or guidance; the duties of a pastor.

1959 *Listener* 26 Feb. 379/3 Mr. McCulloch seems,..to be reaching towards not a blank rejection but..towards an existential theology and pastoralia. **1962** G. Lawton *John Wesley's English* 261 It is..a little classic of pastoralia. **1973** *Church Times* 20 July 2/2 The Rev. John Elford..specialises in ethics, philosophy and pastoralia. **1975** M. Sullivan *Watch how you Go* iii. 57 The new Warden lectured in Church History and Doctrine and gave us a full course in Pastoralia. **1977** *Church Times* 7 Apr. 11/5 Pastoralia was the soft edge of the traditional three-year course [for ordinands].

pastoralism. (Further examples.)

1959 *Economist* 7 Feb. 489/2 The economy of West Germany today is something very different from the 'pastoralism' of the Morgenthau Plan. **1973** *Nature* 28 Sept. 194/2 The human response to the low and highly variable rainfall..is nomadic pastoralism, which is a very functionally adapted form of life. **1974** F. Emery *Oxfordshire Landscape* i. 36 Neolithic settlers..liked to graze their cattle, pigs and sheep in the woods and clearings; together with this strong pastoralism they retained a high degree of skill in hunting and snaring wild animals. **1976** *Sci. Amer.* Sept. 170/2 In traditional agriculture and pastoralism ruminants also represent a means of storing and transporting food supplies.

pastoralist. 2. (Further examples.)

1911 J. Collier *Pastoral Age in Australasia* iii. 16 The pastoralist, however, needs something more than level and spacious lands; he needs water and grass. **1926** *Daily Colonist* (Victoria, B.C.) 10 Jan. 1/5 A sheep calendar is to be issued, illustrating the various acts to be engaged in by the pastoralist in care of his flock. **1941** I. L. Idriess *Great Boomerang* v. 35 Coastal pastoralists [in Australia] generally speak of a beast or beasts to the acre. **1973** *Sci. Amer.* July 74/3, I obtained more responses from the herders of Kapsirika than from the farmers of Sasur. This was partly because polygamous marriages are twice as common among the pastoralists. **1975** *Nature* 15 May 180/2 A highland ridge, supporting an agricultural population of some 2.2 million, cuts into a semi-desert lowland ('Issa and Ogaden) which is seven times greater in area, with a population in normal times of up to 0.5 million pastoralists. **1977** *Caravan World* (Austral.) Jan. 107/1 The road..proved a lifeline to the pastoralists of the west.

pastoraliza·tion. [f. Pastoralize *v.* + -ation.] The fact or process of pastoralizing land, *spec.* the restoration of an industrial area to agriculture.

1949 I. Deutscher *Stalin* 501 Even as late as September 1944 both Roosevelt and Churchill were still to favour plans for the 'pastoralization' of Germany which were to deprive Germany of her heavy industry. **1964** F. Crouzet in *Jrnl. Econ. Hist.* Dec. 573 Because of the permanent injury inflicted on many Continental industries by interruption of overseas trade, the war brought about a lasting de-industrialization or pastoralization of large areas. **1975** T. Balogh in *Times Lit. Suppl.* 10 Oct. 1212/2 Reparations based on dismantling factories—pastoralization—a policy on which the Russians and Americans at first agreed, could of course not really be pursued.

‖ **pastorela, -ella** (pastŏre·lă). [Prov., Pg.: see Pastorel, Pastourelle.] = *pastourelle b.

1878 F. Hueffer *Troubadours* i. viii. 77 Guiraut Riquier is the Provençal representative of the 'Pastorela', or 'Pastoreta', the shepherd's song. **1885** *Encycl. Brit.* XIX. 555/2 The effects of Diniz's influence pervade the whole of Portuguese poetry, for not only was he in his pastorellas the forerunner of the great pastoral school, but..he..perpetuated..lyric forms of great beauty. **1899** J. H. Smith *Troubadours at Home* II. 451 The *pastorela*, *alba*, and *balada* were popular forms, and for that reason pretty much ignored by the troubadours. **1910** E. Pound *Spirit of Romance* iii. 58 The Pastorella has a peculiar interest in so far as it is one of the roots of modern drama. **1925** A. F. G. Bell *Portuguese Lit.* ii.53 Airas Nunez.. wrote a *pastorela* in the manner of the trouvères. **1931** [see next]. **1960** Beckson & Ganz *Reader's Guide to Lit. Terms* (1961) 159 *Pastourelle* (*Pastorella*), a type of medieval lyric in dialogue form in which a knight or a man of equivalent social rank attempts to court a shepherdess. **1976** M. Bogin *Women Troubadours* 40 The refrain.., common in some of the more popular song forms such as..the *pastorela*.

‖ **pastoreta** (pastŏre·tă). [Prov.] = prec.

1867 *Chambers's Encycl.* IX. 560/2 They [*sc.* the troubadours] even descended to depict the life of the peasantry, and sang their adventures with shepherdesses, &c. in *pastoretas* and *vaqueyras*. **1878** [see prec.]. **1931** W. P. Jones *Pastourelle* i. 6 The pastourelle takes its name.. from its principal actor, the shepherdess herself... The name was perhaps applied first to the Provençal specimens, the *pastorela* or *pas[t]oreta*.

‖ **pastorie** (pastori·). *S. Afr.* [Afrikaans, = Du. *pastorie*, ad. med.L. *pastoria*.] The dwelling of a pastor of the Dutch Reformed Church or one of its sister churches: a parsonage.

[**1856** E. M. Murray *Let.* 20 Sept. in J. Murray *Young Mrs. Murray* (1954) 11 Bloemfontein Parsonage (or Pastorie as the Dutch call it).] **1934** E. A. Walker *Gt. Trek* vii. 217 A house was provided for public worship at the capital, and granted an erf for the metropolitan church and another alongside it for the *pastorie*. **1944** L. Smit *Sudden South-Easter* 8 He had received a telephone call asking him to supper at the Pastorie. **1946** *Cape Times* 26 Jan. 11/7 Smoke was..seen coming from the thatched roof of the Dutch Reformed Pastorie. **1958** *Ibid.* 19 Nov. 5/6 On the site..a second pastorie will be built.

pastourelle. Add: **b.** A medieval lyric whose theme is love for a shepherdess. Also *attrib.*

1882 A. B. Grosart *Spenser's Compl. Wks.* III. p. li, Equally vital to an adequate apprehension and comprehension of Spenser as a pastoral poet, is a like vision and grasp of the mediæval *pastourelle*, or courting of a shepherdess by a man of rank. **1908** *Mod. Philol.* VI. 33 A *pastourelle* is a simple poem set in a rustic scene, graceful and trifling in tone, describing the meeting of a man of culture and an *ingenue*, generally a shepherdess. **1929** C. R. Baskervill *Elizabethan Jig* i. i. 26 The dominance of the pastourelle figure Marian in the Robin Hood cycle would argue for song drama. *Ibid.* i. viii. 253 The rôle of the Gentleman, recalling that of the gentleman or knight of the pastourelles who pursues the sweetheart of the shepherd or clown. **1933** R. Tuve *Seasons & Months* iv. 97 The lady is the one figure in the spring landscape that we may come to expect..in *aube*, *pastourelle* or *chanson de danse*. **1965** P. Dronke *Med. Latin & Rise Europ. Love-Lyric* I. iv. 214 The motif of the young girl scolded or beaten by her parents..on account of her lover is most frequent in the *pastourelle*.

pastrami (pæstrā·mi). [Yiddish, f. Rum. *pastramă*, f. *păstra* to preserve.] A smoked beef, usu. prepared from a shoulder cut, highly seasoned and eaten hot or cold. Also *attrib.*

1940 G. Marx *Groucho Lett.* (1967) 45 The catering was delegated to Levitoff, the demon pastrami prince. **1941** L. G. Blochman *See you at Morgue* (1946) xxiv. 164 The hot pastrami sandwich on rye. **1945** A. Kober *Parm Me* 110 Mr. Freidkin was..eating a plate of pastrami and eggs. **1953** W. P. McGivern *Big Heat* ix. 111 He liked Jewish food..sour red cabbage, pastrami, cheese cake. **1961** E. Hunter *Mothers & Daughters* ii. 160 She..unwrapped the pastrami sandwich. **1962** J. Ludwig in R. Weaver *Canad. Short Stories* (1968) 2nd Ser. 239 The air inside was like a home-made mist—garlic pickles, pastrami, salami. **1967** M. Waldo *Internat. Encycl. Cooking* II. 477/2 *Pastrami* (Jewish), a cut of beef, usually the shoulder, highly seasoned (especially with garlic) and smoked. Cut into thin slices, it is served either hot or cold. **1973** *New Yorker* 24 Feb. 114/2 The sandwich makers at the counter always maintain rigid queue discipline while hand-slicing a high-quality pastrami on rye. **1976** *Time* 27 Dec. 31/1 One child conquered her stage fright by downing a quick pizza and a hot pastrami.

pastry. Add: **1. b.** = Paste *sb.* i.

1845 E. Acton *Mod. Cookery* xvi. 402 This glazing answers also very well,..if used before the pastry is baked. **1892** A. B. Marshall *Larger Cookery Bk.* xiv. 528 Prepare a pastry fleur case with paste as below and cook it as for Fleur of Apples. **1906** *Mrs. Beeton's Bk. Househ. Managem.* xxxi. 883 The pastry may be used at once, but it will be lighter if allowed to stand for 1 hour in a cool place before being used. **1948** *Good Housek. Cookery Bk.* ii. 408 Fold the pastry in three, folding the first lap away from you and the second one towards you. *Ibid.* 409 Roll the pastry about ¼ inch thick. **1952** F. Dale *Ambitious Cook* 51 Roll out the pastry thinly into a strip 4 in. wide. **1970** Simon & Howe *Dict. Gastron.* 290/1 *Pastry*, a paste, usually a fat-and-flour mixture with water or other liquid added to make a dough for shaping and baking. Also the product of the baking.

c. A small confection made wholly or partly of pastry.

1906 *Mrs. Beeton's Bk. Househ. Managem.* xxxi. 879 Since the dinner *à la Russe* banished almost everything of an edible nature from the table, any talent in this direction has been chiefly expended on small pastries. **1929** E. J. Kollist *French Pastry* ii. 15 This cream is used for various pastries (Tartelettes), gâteaux, petits-fours, etc. **1935** D. L. Sayers *Gaudy Night* xix. 395 A plateful of synthetic pastries in Ye Olde Worlde Tudor Tea-Shoppe. **1938** H. Robertson *Cassell's New Cookery Bk.* 420 Pastries are baked in a hot oven. **1957** S. Strong *Good Food from Vienna* 181 (*heading*) How to enter earthly heaven by way of Viennese pastries, cakes, bakery and torten. **1960** E. David *French Provincial Cooking* 435 The ingredients of good pastries..are very expensive. **1972** 'M. Yorke' *Silent Witness* vi. 125 They carried a box of cream pastries..and said they had come to tea. **1973** 'J. Ashford' *Double Run* viii. 60 In a café..he ate a stale pastry and half drank a cup of very peculiar-tasting coffee.

4. *pastry-brush*, *chef*, *-scraper*, *shop* (later examples).

[**1907** *Yesterday's Shopping* (1969) 115/1 Brushes, &c., Pastry, tin bound or boxwood.] **1948** P. Harben *Way to Cook* (rev. ed.) x. 203 Moisten right round the edge of your sheet of paste (a pastry brush is the best tool for this job). **1976** M. Patten *Barbecue* 25/2 Glaze (brush) with beaten egg; use a pastry brush for this. **1961** *N.Y. Times* 3 July 13/5 A dedication to decoration worthy of a pastry chef creating a wedding cake for [etc.]. **1971** R. Thomas *Backup Men* ix. 82 Check out the new pastry chef. **1974** *John O'Groat Jrnl.* (Wick) 6 Sept. 8/1 *Pastry chef*, Post House Hotel, Aviemore, requires a Pastry Chef. **1962** *Listener* 22 Nov. 887/1 Pastry scraper, mixing spoon, and pastry brush. **1782** J. Woodforde *Diary* 25 May (1926) II. 26, I dined at a pastry shop on 3 Cheese Cakes. **1977** 'S. Leys' *Chinese Shadows* (1978) ii. 68 The local pastry shop..sells..strudels and little pink marzipan pigs.

pasture, *sb.* Add: **4. b.** Also phr. *pastures new.*

[**1638** Milton *Lycidas* in *Iusta Eduardo King* ii. 25 To morrow to fresh woods and pastures new.] **1906** G. Ade (*title*) In pastures new. **1922** Joyce *Ulysses* 645 Wrapped in the arms of Murphy, as the adage has it, dreaming of fresh fields and pastures new. **1975** L. Gillen *Return to Deepwater* i. 6 He had always resolutely refused to leave his native heath..and..had never felt the need to seek pastures new. **1977** *It* June 5/2 Some of this third group came to London to lead the winos and the rejects out to pastures new and they used 66 as a clearing house.

6. *pasture-field* (later examples), *ground* (U.S. examples).

1874 G. M. Hopkins *Jrnls. & Papers* (1959) 251, I sat down in the lap or fold of a steep slanting pasturefield. **1922** Joyce *Ulysses* 407 A region where grey twilight ever descends, never falls on wide sage-green pasturefields. **1949** K. M. Wells *Owl Pen Reader* (1969) ii. 196 Even the mill-pond is vanished. The old pond bottom is now part of a tree-spangled pasture field. **1668** in *Connecticut Hist. Soc. Coll.* (1912) XIV. 21 All that percell of pasture Ground lyeing on the east Side. **1775** J. Nourse in *Jrnl. Amer. Hist.* (1925) XIX. 351 Water enough for Cattle may be kept all the year here for pasture grounds. **1789** J. Morse *Amer. Geogr.* 381 On the north end it subsides gradually into extensive pasture-grounds. **1841** H. S. Foote *Texas & Texans* I. 14 The tide of indiscriminate havoc..[marked] its dreadful course with..the spoliation of her fair plantations and pasture-grounds.

pasture, *v.* Add: **3.** Also, to use (land) as pasture; to feed cattle on (land).

1901 J. Muir *Our National Parks* 5 The great Central Valley of California..is ploughed and pastured out of existence, gone forever. **1976** L. Sanders *Hamlet Warning* (1977) iv. 39 The ranch seems in good shape. He pastures about four hundred head of cattle on it.

pasture land. Also **pasture-land, pastureland.** Grass land used or suitable for the grazing of cattle or sheep; pasturage. Also *fig.*

1591 [in Dict. s.v. Pasture *sb.* 6]. **1669** J. Worlidge *Systema Agriculturae* 15 Meadow and Pasture Lands are of..considerable use and advantage to the Husband-man. **1718** *New Hampsh. Probate Rec.* (1914) II. 4, I give and bequeath unto my son..two thirds of my pasture lands. **1786** G. Washington *Diaries* (1925) III. 108, I..directed the best plowman at it to break up about 10 Acres of Pasture land. **1867** 'T. Lackland' *Homespun* i. 65, I believe in my heart that this same huckleberry field..is a real pasture-land for the spirit of the boy. **1885** *Outing* VII. 58/1 Fortunately I live within a mile of real pasture-land and forest. **1920** W. D. Howells *Vacation of Kelwyns* 146 They all struck through the woods into a piece of pasture-land beyond. **1922** Joyce *Ulysses* 124 Of bosky grove and undulating plain and luscious pastureland of vernal green. *Ibid.* 290 Sheep and pigs and heavyhooved kine from pasturelands of Lush and Rush and Carrickmines. **1966** *New Statesman* 23 Dec. 928/2 The pasturelands of higher output and industrial efficiency and competiveness.

pasty, *sb.* Add: (Further examples.) Now usu. a small pastry turnover containing meat and vegetables (see **Cornish pasty*), or fruit. Also *transf.*

1877 *N. & Q.* 14 Apr. 297 *The Divisions of an Orange...* The word 'pasty' is used in Cornwall, from the likeness to the shape of the Cornish pasty baked without a dish. **1880** M. A. COURTNEY in Courtney & Couch *Gloss. Words Cornwall* 41/2 *Pasty*, a meat and potatoe or fruit turnover. **1906** J. H. HARRIS *Cornish Saints & Sinners* (ed. 2) xx. 194 When small, a pasty is a snack; when large, it's a meal... The home of the pasty is Cornwall. **1966** *Times* 28 Dec. 9/7 Cornwall is as protective about its pasties as Devon is about its cream. **1972** K. STEWART '*Times' Cookery Bk.* xvi. 213 (*heading*) Chicken liver and bacon pasties. **1978** R. BUSBY *Garvey's Code* x. 119 Cooper collected a couple of pasties in a paper bag.

pasty, *a.* Add *fig.* examples.
1909 *Westm. Gaz.* 28 Jan. 4/1 The pasty feeling of exhaustion usually experienced at the end of a long [railway] journey. **1926** E. O'NEILL *Great God Brown* 100 A little dab of pasty resignation here and there—and even broken hearts may be repaired to do yeoman service!

pat, *sb.*[1] Add: **I. 2. b.** (Further fig. examples.)
1933 E. O'NEILL *Ah, Wilderness!* (1934) I. 41 He gives him an approving pat on the back. **1952** M. ALLINGHAM *Tiger in Smoke* iv. 81 He had liked the boy... The present assignment had been in the nature of a personal pat on the head for him. **1969** *Listener* 15 May 698/2 A pat on the back for the regional bulletin *South-East*, which gave Eastbourne's maligned medical officer a chance to explain ..what he really meant about the artificial prolongation of life into living death. **1973** L. MEYNELL *Thirteen Trumpeters* vi. 100 If I could dive like that—well, I'd give myself a big pat on the back.

II. 3. c. = **cow-pad, -pat.* Also of other animals.
1940 F. SARGESON *Man & Wife* (1944) 22 On cold mornings we'd watch out, and whenever a cow dropped a nice big pat we'd race for it, and the one who got there first wouldn't let the others put their feet in. **1957** V. NABOKOV *Pnin* iii. 63 The bright pat of dog dirt somebody had already slipped upon. **1959** C. T. M. HERRIOT tr. *Voisin's Grass Productivity* II. 115 The scattering of dung pats over the whole area of a pasture could make the cattle anything but willing to graze. **1966** 'J. HACKSTON' *Father clears Out* 181 A cow,..will,..in a most flagrant manner, deposit a pat fair bang in the bail. **1973** G. MITCHELL *Murder of Busy Lizzie* iv. 51 The rough road.. was muddy with the tramplings of cattle and plentifully endowed with large pats of cow-dung.

Pat, *sb.*[2] (Earlier example.)
1806 *Port Folio* (Philad.) 11 Oct. 221/2 A company of honest Pats in the purlieus of St. Giles's.

pat, on one's: see *PAT MALONE.

pat, *v.*[1] Add: **5.** *to pat on the back* (earlier and later examples).
1821 M. EDGEWORTH *Let.* 18 Nov. (1971) 270 Sydney Smith who wrote the review..first patted his friend Holford on the back and then cut him up. **1866** *Galaxy* I. 750 It seems as if John Bull would never have done patting us on the back for our performance of a very plain and simple duty. **1946** E. O'NEILL *Iceman Cometh* (1947) III. 148 Dey all pat me on de back and say, 'Joe, you sure is white.' **1973** *Washington Post* 13 Jan. B 8/6 'We broke our arm, trying to pat ourselves on the back,' is the way Wood now describes the ad.

pat, *adv.* and *a.* **3. b.** (Earlier example.)
c **1868** *How Gamblers Win* 51 When quick work is to be made with a victim, 'pat hands', in other words, hands which fall complete,..are given out.

pata (pa·tă). *Indian Art.* [Skr. *pata.*] Cloth, canvas; a picture painted on a scroll of canvas.
1948 T. BHATTACHARYYA *Study on Vāstuvidyā* 261 A mere representation of a temple, building, idol and the like, either in sculpture..or a painting on paṭa. **1963** —— *Canons of Indian Art* xxx. 373 The Kātyāyana Saṃhitā prescribes worship of image (Pratimā) or drawings on Pata (paint on canvas). *Ibid.* 382 Paintings on canvas having the form of a scroll were known as paṭas. *Ibid.* 383 Such paṭas were commonly shown along with explanatory songs in East Bengal fairs. **1970** *Centennial Acquisitions Mus. Fine Arts, Boston* 43 (*caption*) Mandala of Eight Bodhisattvas..probably the earliest known example of Nepali painting of the type known as pata. **1974** *Times* 30 Apr. 18/6 The top price was paid for..a Nepalese pata depicting the mandala of a Tantric deity. **1976** *Sunday Standard* (Bombay) 5 Sept. 9/7 The patas, or painted scrolls, are specimens of folk-art in Bengal.

pataca (pătā·kă). [Sp. and Pg.] **1.** = PATACOON. *Obs.* except *Hist.*
1875 C. SCHREIBER *Jrnl.* (1911) I. 415 We found him to be a stupid old man,..selling bars of iron to people who paid him in heavy patacas. **1948** C. R. BOXER *Fidalgos in Far East 1550–1770* vi. 102 The 1625 Voyage..netted Dom Francisco Mascarenhas a personal profit of 26,000 *patacas* (silver dollars).

2. The monetary unit of Macao, and, formerly, of Timor; also, a coin of this value; also *attrib.*
1928 *Whitaker's Almanack 1929* 804/2 *Macao*, in China, on the Canton River..total trade 1926–27, *Patacas* 25,057,898. *Portuguese Timor*..(the budget includes a loan to be realized of *Patacas* 1,120,074); total trade 1926–27, *Patacas* 3,178,439. **1967** 'A. CORDELL' *Bright Cantonese* x. 109 One..came over..with his girl..a pataca woman... For her the big black Mozambiques would pay about two or three patacas a night. **1968** *Economist* 16 Nov. 39/2 In exchange for the grant of.. franchises to import gold, the government now charges the syndicate a tax of 7.60 patacas an ounce. **1977** *Times* 16 Apr. 11/3 The Macanese *pataca* is at par with the Hongkong dollar... But get rid of any *patacas* before returning to Hongkong, where they are not generally accepted.

Patagonian, *a.* and *sb.* Add: **A.** *adj.* **2.** *Patagonian cavy, hare*, a large rodent, *Dolichotis patagona*, belonging to the cavy family and found in southern parts of South America; = MARA[1].
1833 [see MARA]. **1910** *Encycl. Brit.* V. 586/2 A very different animal is the Patagonian cavy, or mara.., the typical representative of a genus characterized by long limbs, comparatively large ears, and a short tail. **1961** G. DURRELL *Whispering Land* i. 43 Small, desert-like areas seemed to be favoured by that curious animal, the Patagonian hare... They had blunt, rather hare-like faces, small, neat, rabbit-shaped ears, neat forequarters with slender forelegs. But the hindquarters were large and muscular in comparison, with powerful hind-legs. **1965** D. MORRIS *Mammals* 226 The Mara, or Patagonian Cavy, is the most hare-like of all the rodents. **1971** L. H. MATTHEWS *Life of Mammals* II. vii. 205 When they run.. they hop with a gait much resembling that of a rabbit—this gait, and the long ears and legs, have earned them the misnomer of Patagonian hare.

pataka (pā·tākā). [Maori.] In New Zealand, a Maori storehouse for food, raised off the ground on poles.
1842 W. R. WADE *Journey N. Island N.Z.* vi. 151 In the pa, a large elaborately carved pataka, or kumara store, supported on four strong wooden pillars, attracted my attention. **1843** E. DIEFFENBACH *Trav. N.Z.* II. v. 70 A third sort of structure are the provision-houses (pataka), which are built on poles to prevent rats from entering them. **1949** P. H. BUCK *Coming of Maori* (1950) II. i. 106 In order to store the preserved food, special storehouses (*pataka*) had to be built. *Ibid.* ii. 132 The best *pataka* were much more extensively carved than the meeting houses, to outward appearance. **1950** *N.Z. Jrnl. Agric.* May 502/3 The carved pile of a pataka, a storehouse, [is a] choice example of age-old Native arts. **1967** A. & D. REID *Paddle Wheels on Wanganui* 33 A few other scattered cottages, whares, and patakas belonging to the Maori residents and a few odd ancillary sheds and outbuildings completed the layout.

pataphysics (pætăfi·ziks), *sb. pl.* (const. as sing.) Also **'pataphysics.** [ad. Gr. τὰ ἐπὶ τὰ μεταφυσικά 'the (works) imposed on the Metaphysics' (see METAPHYSICS *sb. pl.*).] The study of a realm additional to metaphysics, a concept introduced by Alfred Jarry (1873–1907), French writer and dramatist of the absurd. Hence **pataphy·sical** *a.*, **pataphysi·cian.**
[**1911** A. JARRY (*title*) Gestes et opinions du docteur Faustroll, pataphysicien.] **1945** C. CONNOLLY tr. *Jarry's Ubu Cocu* in *Horizon* Dec. 375 What's all this? Monsieur Ubu, sometime King of Poland and Aragon, Professor of Pataphysics? That makes no sense at all. *Ibid.* 376 Remember that you are conversing with a famous pataphysician... Pataphysics is a branch of science which we have invented and for which a crying need is generally experienced. **1960** *Evergreen Rev.* May–June 131 'Pataphysics..is the science of that which is superinduced upon metaphysics... 'Pataphysics is the science of imaginary solutions. **1971** LENNON & MCCARTNEY in A. Aldridge *Beatles' Illustr. Lyrics* II. 106 Joan was quizzical studied pataphysical Science in the home Late night all alone with a test-tube. **1973** *Times Lit. Suppl.* 13 Apr. 415/4 That dogged pedantry which is perversely common among 'pataphysicians like himself. **1975** *Physics Bull.* Feb. 61/1 Perhaps it should also be mentioned here the existence of another 'physics'—'pataphysics', an invention of Alfred Jarry, probably the father of the Dada movement.

Patarin, -ene, *a.* (Examples.)
1926 A. L. MAYCOCK *Inquisition* iv. 89 In February 1231 a number of Patarin heretics were arrested in Rome. **1934** R. MACAULAY *Going Abroad* ii. 33 It was odd how those dear people inclined to the Patarine heresy. **1968** *Trans. R. Hist. Soc.* XVIII. 25 After 1056, its [*sc.* Milan's] order and independence were rudely challenged when the Patarene movement gave rise to nineteen years of civil strife.

Patau (pæ·tau). *Path.* [Name of K. *Patau* of Germany, who with others described the condition in 1960 (*Lancet* 9 Apr. 790).] *Patau('s) syndrome*: a syndrome due to trisomy and marked by mental retardation, seizures, cleft lip and palate, and other congenital anomalies, and usu. resulting in death soon after birth.
1964 GORLIN & PINDBORG *Syndromes of Head & Neck* xvii. 80 (*heading*) Trisomy 13–15 syndrome (Patau's syndrome, trisomy D_1). **1971** LEVITAN & MONTAGU *Textbk. Human Genetics* iii. 76 (*caption*) The shortness of the neck and low-set malformed ears are also found frequently in the Patau (D_1) syndrome. **1976** W. L. L. REES *Short Textbk. Psychiatry* (ed. 2) xxviii. 255 Patau's syndrome is due to an extra chromosome of the D group. **1978** D. A. P. EVANS in R. B. Scott *Price's Textbk. Pract. Med.* (ed. 12) IV. 354/2 Mongolism (Down's syndrome) is caused by trisomy 21 and the much rarer Edwards and Patau syndromes..by trisomy 18 and 13 respectively.

Patavinian (pætăvi·niăn). [f. L. *Patavīn-us* (see PATAVINITY) + -IAN.] A native or inhabitant of Padua (formerly Patavinium); *spec.* Livy. Also †**Pa·tavin(e** *obs.*
1611 CORYAT *Crudities* 129 The Romanes..priviledged them..that the Pataulnes should give their suffrages in the election of the Romane Magistrates. *Ibid.* 131 Three [statues] are of that famous Historian Titus Livius, who was borne and brought vp in Padua: the other three of other worthy Patauins. **1771** C. BURNEY *Present State of Mus. France & Italy* 124 He died universally regretted by the Patavinians. **1924** *Glasgow Herald* 6 Sept. 4/2 Livy.. does not make the actual route clear, for among the Patavinians excellent geographical accuracy is not included. **1932** E. WEEKLEY *Words & Names* 149 Virgil the Mantuan, Livy the Patavinian.

pat-ball. Substitute for def.: A game in which a ball is hit back and forth between two players. Also used as a contemptuous name for lawn tennis, especially when not played vigorously; also, tactical slow and gentle play in lawn tennis. (Further examples.) Also *fig.*
1890 S. W. GORE in *Tennis, Lawn Tennis, Rackets, Fives* (Badminton Libr.) 282 This derisive name of 'patball' was applied to lawn tennis by tennis and racket players, who maintained that, from the absence of backor side-walls, it was impossible to hit hard without sending the ball out of court. *Ibid.* 285 The final blow to the 'pat-ball' game was given by the brothers Renshaw when they discovered that they could stand back at the serviceline, and..volley. **1900** *Captain* IV. 26/1 In the summer, a great form of 'eccer' is 'patters', a corruption of 'patball', *i.e.* tennis. **1904** J. P. PARET *Lawn Tennis* ii. 13 The next three years have been aptly described by an English historian as 'the era of pat-ball'. **1923** *Daily Mail* 28 Apr. 11 At this stage Mishu played 'pat ball'..and Norton wisely did likewise, for in slowing the pace he affected Mishu's game. **1927** *Daily Tel.* 21 June 12/3 No one would have guessed..that the mild game derisively nicknamed 'patball'..would develop so rapidly into this highly exacting and arduous exercise. **1944** C. DILKE in *Wine & Food* No. 41. 16 He might have been back at the Eureka tennis club..watching the nymphs who played patball on summer evenings. **1955** *Times* 20 June 9/4 Lawn tennis was still known as pat-ball when I was an undergraduate. **1959** *Economist* 18 July 150/3 An astonishing amount of rather owlish erudition and a no less astonishingly patball standard of controversy. **1963** *Times* 23 Apr. 13/4 No contestant..at Wimbledon would care to have his sport spoken of as pat-ball. **1973** P. GEDDES *Ottawa Allegation* xii. 160 When they spoke during the journey, it was like pat-ball. **1977** J. WAINWRIGHT *Do Nothin'* vi. 102 A kiosk means a telephone call. Where to go next. Maybe another kiosk, for another call. A crazy, pat-ball game that could stretch forever.

patch, *sb.*[1] Add: **1. d.** (Further examples.)
1912 'AURORA' *Jock Scott* i. 4 He passed out of the *Britannia* a midshipman and was wearing his patches the day he left... Naval cadets wear a little bit of white twist on their coat collars, while a full-blown midshipman has a patch of white cloth about two inches square instead. **1970** N. ARMSTRONG et al. *First on Moon* v. 107 John Young's wife..designed a handsome red Roman numeral X for the patch he and Mike Collins wore on Gemini 10. **1974** R. B. PARKER *Godwulf Manuscript* i. 8 A fatigue jacket with a staff sergeant's stripes, a Seventh Division patch.

3. e. The area which is assigned to a policeman as his responsibility; a policeman's 'beat'. Also *transf.*
1963 *T.V. Times* (Austral.) 18 Apr. 10/2 *Patch*, a police area: as in 'It's on my patch'. **1965** 'W. HAGGARD' *Hard Sell* xii. 126 I'm a foreign official on another man's patch. I'm quite without standing. **1965** J. WAINWRIGHT *Death in Sleeping City* II. 123 My patch in the city. I'm not like you—a county officer. **1969** D. DEVINE *Death is my Bridegroom* xi. 113 Smith was from the south and had never before turned up in Christie's patch. **1975** J. SYMONS *Three Pipe Problem* xvi. 157 Either he gets off your patch or he finds his reputation as an art dealer ruined.

5. b. *transf.* With qualifying adj.: a period of time with a particular characteristic.
1926 WODEHOUSE *Heart of Goof* i. 32 How like life it all was!.. We strike a good patch and are beginning to think pretty well of ourselves, and along comes a George Parsloe. **1928** *Daily Express* 6 July 9/3 He dreaded to think what would happen to Kent if those players had a month's bad patch. **1958** *Daily Sketch* 2 June 12/4 A friend helps you over a sticky patch in the afternoon. **1974** I. MURDOCH *Sacred & Profane Love Machine* 213 If there were bad patches I've simply forgotten them. **1976** J. M. BROWNJOHN tr. *Kirst's Time for Payment* v. 114 All new businesses go through a sticky patch, but it's only temporary.

6. f. A temporary electrical connection. Usu. *attrib.* (see *patch bay*, etc., in sense *8).
1923 *Bell Syst. Techn. Jrnl.* II. 123 A temporary [telephone] connection made in this manner..is called a 'patch'. **1937** *Printers' Ink Monthly* May 40/1 *Patch*, a temporary and removable connection on studio equipment. **1977** R. L. DUNCAN *Temple Dogs* (1978) II. 259 He just called computer, requested a patch on the Metro interface. He wants to know what the Tokyo police have picked up.

7. patch-up. Also as *adj.*
1904 *Westm. Gaz.* 30 Sept. 2/1 The kind of patch-up policy which he would accept for the next election. **1971** 'H. CALVIN' *Poison Chasers* v. 74 There may be some value in a patch-up operation. **1974** P. FLOWER *Odd Job* ii. 16 His patch-up jobs on furniture.

8. patch bay, an area in an analogue computer that receives one or more removable patchboards; **patch-board,** a plug-board, esp. one in an analogue computer or similar device; **patch cord,** an insulated lead with a plug at each end, used for making connections between the sockets of a patch-board or different pieces of electronic apparatus; **patch fox,** a North American red fox, *Vulpes Fulva*, in its yellowish colour phase, or the skin of such an animal;

= CROSS-FOX; **patch lead** = *patch cord* above; **patch panel** *sb.*[2] = *patch-board* above; (cf. PATCH-PANEL *sb.* and *a.* in Dict.); **patch-plug** = *patch cord* above; **patch pocket,** a pocket consisting of a piece of cloth sewn on like a patch.

1948 Patch bay [see *patch cord* below]. **1962** HUSKEY & KORN *Computer Handbk.* iv. 26 Most multipurpose electronic analog computers are programmed by means of a patchboard system which comprises (1) a patchbay with spring-contact terminations for the computing elements and (2) interchangeable removable problem boards which carry the actual interconnecting patchcords. **1949** *Math. Tables & Other Aids to Computation* III. 512 Receptacle patch-board for 500 element connections and 25 main busses. **1961** G. MILLERSON *Technique Television Production* i. 17 Tape recorders, racks of audio amplifiers, patchboards and an electronic reverberation unit, complete the general set-up. **1971** J. H. SMITH *Digital Logic* ii. 28 The inputs and outputs of the logic elements, and the connections to the switched inputs, external terminals and indicator lamps are brought out to a programming device consisting of a patchboard and detachable panel. **1938** G. E. STERLING *Radio Manual* (ed. 3) vii. 442 The input may be connected to a terminal board in rear or to normal-through standard double patch-cord jacks at front of panel. **1948** *Electronics* July 119/3 To set up the computer the elements are connected..by means of patch cords joining the proper inputs and outputs through the patch bay. **1967** [see *patch panel* below]. **1971** J. H. SMITH *Digital Logic* ii. 28 Switching problems are set up by using patch cords on the front panel. **1835** Patch fox [see *LORD *sb.* 16]. **1930** *Economist* 4 Jan. 10/2 The highest priced fur in 1927–8 was silver fox..; cross or patch fox was second. **1942** M. BOSANQUET *Saddlebags for Suitcases* 48 The most common of these [variations] is the 'cross' or 'patch' fox, which is yellow with a dark cross or patch across the shoulders. **1964** C. P. GILBERT *Design & Use Electronic Analogue Computers* vi. 364 The dotted line in Fig. 6.7(*d*) encloses all the sockets within reach of amplifier 3 using short patch leads. **1971** J. H. SMITH *Digital Logic* ii. 18 The reader is advised to have at least 50 patch leads to connect the circuits together. **1952** G. A. & T. M. KORN *Electronic Analog Computers* viii. 339 It should..be possible to provide so-called removable patch panels of the type used in the IBM punched-card machines. **1967** *N.Y. Times* 9 Jan. 140 Basically, an analog computer consists of an assembly of individual electronic computing elements that can be interconnected by means of a 'patch panel' outside the machine. This panel is a terminal board with holes, each hole facing an internal contact. The computer operator uses 'patch cords' (wire connectors) to interconnect specific holes for the kind of operation he wants the machine to perform. **1973** *Physics Bull.* Aug. 500/2 The new system, PB100, is a large, sophisticated unit..for rapidly simulating complex digital, analogue or hybrid systems. It features removable patch panels each of which will accommodate up to 44 dual-in-line integrated circuits. **1962** *Gloss. Terms Automatic Data Processing* (*B.S.I.*) 82 *Patchcord*, [deprecated synonym] *patchplug*, in a.d.p. a connector used to interconnect the sockets of a plugboard. **1964** G. A. & T. M. KORN *Electronic Analog & Hybrid Computers* xi. 443 With a separate copper-bar signal ground behind the patchbay.., we can use the patchbay shielding as a relay ground and return each relay-coil connection through a single patchplug grounded to its shield. **1895** *Montgomery Ward Catal.* 556/1 Coat, three-button sack, four patch pockets. **1908** *Times* (Weekly ed.) 14 Aug. p. iii/3 There are two deep patch pockets..for carrying fly-book and sandwich-case. **1928** *Daily Express* 22 May 5/2 A plain, collarless coat.. with two large patch pockets. **1973** 'D. RUTHERFORD' *Kick Start* iv. 86 He wore an expensive tropical suit with patch pockets and a waist belt. **1976** *Horse & Hound* 3 Dec. 24/1 (Advt.), Two large patch pockets,..and adjustable rear belt make this a smart comfortable coat.

patch, *v.* Add: **1.** Also *absol.*

1870 J. P. SMITH *Widow Goldsmith's Daughter* xviii. 287, I could patch and darn for you.

8. *Electronics.* **a.** *trans.* To connect temporarily; also with *in, into*; similarly to *patch out* (see quot. 1940[2]). **b.** *intr.* To be temporarily connected. **c.** *trans.* To represent or simulate by means of temporary connections.

[**1923**: implied in *PATCHING *vbl. sb.*[1] 1.] **1937** *Printers' Ink Monthly* May 40/1 *Patch it in*, to tie together various pieces of apparatus to form a circuit. **1940** *Chambers's Techn. Dict.* 619/2 *Patch*, to join together units of apparatus..by flexible cords terminated on plugs, which are inserted into break-jacks bridged across the terminations of each unit. *Ibid.*, *Patch in* and *patch out*, the temporary connexion (*patching in*) of spare apparatus in a circuit with patch cords, defective apparatus being thereby *patched out.* **1948** *Electronics* July 120/2 Two inverting or summing amplifiers in the computer unit..are patched to the servo as illustrated. **1962** HUSKEY & KORN *Computer Handbk.* iv. 36 The small extra cost of duplicate resistors for a few plug-in patchboards is negligible compared with the almost incredible nuisance of patching, say, a summing integrator with patchcord connections alone. **1964** C. P. GILBERT *Design & Use Electronic Analogue Computers* vi. 363 In Fig. 6.7(*d*) unit 2 can patch directly into units 1 and 3, unit 3 can patch directly into units 2 and 4, and so on. **1966** *Times* 21 Sept. (Ascension Island Suppl.) p. iv/3, I recently picked up this telephone and asked the communications centre..to patch me in on the network. **1971** J. H. SMITH *Digital Logic* v. 79 Electronic control systems can be quickly developed by patching the required design on a simulator. **1975** J. GRADY *Shadow of Condor* (1976) xii. 190 Kevin used the powerful radio in his car to call CIA headquarters in Langley, Virginia. The technicians there patched his radio call into the old man's office phone.

patched, *ppl. a.* Add: *patched-up* (later examples). So *patched-together.*

1905 *Daily Chron.* 13 Feb. 5/1 Japan will tolerate no patched-up peace. **1916** H. G. WELLS *Mr. Britling* III. i. 385 It was the queer halting telling of a patched-together tale. **1935** T. S. ELIOT *Murder in Cath.* i. 16 Peace, but not the kiss of peace. A patched up affair, if you ask my opinion. **1954** KOESTLER *Invis. Writing* xxii. 249 To emerge in the end with a more or less successfully patched-up personality. **1972** *Listener* 21 Dec. 872/1 A young man who deals in patched-up cars.

patchily, *adv.* (In Dict. s.v. PATCHY *a.*) (Further examples.)

1972 *Daily Tel.* 24 Apr. 14/8 Anyone who bites or licks her lips to concentrate will soon look patchily fungoid rather than trendy. **1974** I. MURDOCH *Sacred & Profane Love Machine* 144 His face patchily pink. **1975** G. LYALL *Judas Country* xxx. 220 I stepped cautiously out into the patchily-lit alley.

patchiness. (Earlier example.)

a **1828** D. WORDSWORTH *Jrnl.* (1941) II. 93 The character of the Lake..is of free cheerfulness...it is not *disturbed* by buildings. *I* complained not of *patchiness* or *spottiness.*

patching, *vbl. sb.*[1] **1.** (Further examples: cf. *PATCH *v.* 8.)

1923 *Bell Syst. Techn. Jrnl.* II. 123 In open-wire installations it has been the practice to equip each line circuit.. with a full complement of jacks suited to provide the maximum degree of flexibility in 'patching'. *Ibid.* 132 With this arrangement of apparatus, any 'ringer'..may be connected temporarily to the system by means of 'patching' cords. **1948** J. ATKINSON *Herbert & Proctor's Telephony* (new ed.) I. xvii. 346 (*caption*) Patching jack at incoming end of order wire. *Ibid.* xxi. 473 The junctions are routed through break jacks on the test jack frame and a small cord shelf accommodates a number of patching-out cords to facilitate temporary changes. **1964** C. P. GILBERT *Design & Use Electronic Analogue Computers* vi. 361 To interconnect the amplifiers, leads with a plug at each end would be inserted into the appropriate sockets giving what is known as simple direct 'patching'. *Ibid.*, The patching is carried out on the plug board before it is inserted into the 'patch' panel. **1964** G. A. & T. M. KORN *Electronic Analog & Hybrid Computers* xi. 443 Iterative differential analyzers..require frequent patching of integrator and memory control circuits.

3. (Earlier example.)

1835 A. B. LONGSTREET *Georgia Scenes* 286 He..drew out his patching, found the most even part of it, [etc.].

patchless (pæ·tʃlès), *a.* [f. PATCH *sb.*[1] + -LESS.] Not having or exhibiting patches. (In quot. fig.)

1927 *Observer* 1 May 6 Hundreds of different..things are mentioned; but the mentionings are all woven into a seamless, patchless, and nowhere ragged history of the subject.

patchouli'd (pătʃū·lid), *a. poet.* Also **patchoulied.** [f. PATCHOULI + -ED[2].] Perfumed with patchouli.

1925 H. ACTON in *Oxf. Poetry* 7 The pulsing cafés and patchouli'd vamps. **1929** W. DE LA MARE in H. Granville-Barker *Eighteen-Seventies* iii. 51 The patchoulied nosegay of artifice. **1943** D. GASCOYNE *Poems 1937–42* 42 Tenebrous lanes Down which at times patchouli'd ghosts flit by.

patch panel[2]: see s.v. *PATCH *sb.*[1] 6.

pa·tch test. *Med.* [f. PATCH *sb.*[1] + TEST *sb.*[1]] A test for determining a patient's sensitivity to a substance, by applying to his skin a patch made of or containing it, and noting whether erythema is produced. Hence (with hyphen) as *vb. trans.*, to subject to such a test; also **pa·tch-testing** *vbl. sb.*

1933 R. W. & R. M. B. MACKENNA *Dis. Skin* (ed. 3) xv. 320 Recently the 'patch' or 'contact eczema' test has been much used to determine whether or not a patient is susceptible to an external irritant. **1956** *Brit. Med. Jrnl.* 21 Jan. 148/1 She was patch-tested to nylon stockings of three shades and gave positive reactions to all of them. **1963** *Lancet* 5 Jan. 61/2 The patient was patch-tested with the sample that he had provided, and whereas the control patch remained unaffected, the test patch became reddened in three days, and redder and scaly in a week. **1963** V. J. FONTANA in F. Speer *Allergic Child* xv. 223 Patch testing is a helpful procedure in eliciting the specific cause in many types of contact dermatitis. **1967** *Oceanogr. & Marine Biol.* V. 366 Patch testing with pieces of the polyzoon..have confirmed that the *Alcyonidium* is the causative agent. **1968** A. ROOK et al. *Textbk. Dermatol.* I. xiv. 301/1 The patch-test was first devised by Jadassolm 1896 and later brought into general use by Bloch. *Ibid.* 310/1 Any patch-test involves a risk of sensitization.

patchwork. Add: **4. a.** and **b.** Also *fig.*

1905 *Daily Chron.* 30 Aug. 5/6 A rupture is preferable to a patch-work peace. **1933** CHESTERTON *All I Survey* ix. 45, I am afraid of the Patchwork Peril, which is all colours and none. **1951** M. MCLUHAN *Mech. Bride* (1967) 144/2 Everyone is intellectually and emotionally a patchwork quilt of occupied and unoccupied territory. **1956** H. J. PATON in H. D. Lewis *Contemp. Brit. Philos.* (ser. 3) 348, I never had any use for the patchwork theory popular at that time, which supposed his [*sc.* Kant's] work to be a mass of contradictions. **1977** P. SCUPHAM *Hinterland* 3 Now, the celebrated Ride stiffly through a patchwork multitude.

Hence **pa·tchworker,** a maker of patchwork; also *fig.*; **pa·tchworky** *a.* [-Y[1]], resembling or suggestive of patchwork.

1844 *Ainsworth's Mag.* VI. 112 A patchworker of the piquant anecdotes of the newest French memoirs. **1884** E. W. HAMILTON *Diary* 29 Mar. (1972) II. 585 The exterior [of the house, Coombe Warren] is picturesque, but almost *too* unsymmetrical and 'patch-work-y'. **1888** *Advance* (Chicago) 3 May 275/1 It would quicken the zeal of the little patchworkers also, if they could see how pretty their gay quilts look upon the beds. **1906** *Speaker* 20 Oct. 71/2 To a foreign student London presents..a patchworky spectacle. **1972** *New Yorker* 26 Aug. 50/1 (*caption*) Tie on this patchworky, wrap-around skirt. **1977** R. RICHARDSON *Discovering Patchwork* (rear cover), This book..should..have much to offer the experienced patch-worker.

patchy, *a.*[1] Add: (Further examples.) Also, occurring only in patches, or at separate points; irregular, spasmodic.

1905 *Sat. Westm. Gaz.* 16 Dec. 15/1 That evening I noticed a peculiarity in the pit's applause. It was 'patchy'. **1921** *Ampleforth Jrnl.* Jan. 139 Scent was patchy and a good deal of lifting was necessary to maintain the line. **1957** [see *CONTAGIOUS *a.* 8]. **1967** W. CARR *Daily Tel. Beauty Bk.* 23 Those who freckle have only groups of pigment-producing cells, providing patchy, inefficient protection. **1971** *Nature* 30 July 352/2 The survey is patchy and by no means as up to date as one expects. **1976** *Shooting Times & Country Mag.* 16–22 Dec. 38/1 Many countries report varied and patchy scent.

pâté. Add: **1.** *pâté de foie gras*, now used chiefly of the goose-liver filling only: cf. next (further examples).

1863 G. MEREDITH *Let.* 19 July (1970) I. 217 Did you have salmon at Strasbourg—and pâté de foie gras—it's not a good place for the latter. **1876** GEO. ELIOT *Dan. Der.* III. VI. xlviii. 343, I can't eat *pâté de foie gras.* **1892** A. B. MARSHALL *Larger Cookery Bk.* vi. 253 Cut up the contents of a small tin of *pâté de foie gras.* **1960** E. DAVID *French Provincial Cooking* 35 His *pâté de foie gras* and *mousse de foies de volaille*, smooth, pink, and marbled with green pistachio nuts and black truffles,..were as good and delicate as they looked.

b. A paste made from liver or other meats. So *pâté de campagne*, a coarse pork and liver pâté; *pâté en croûte*, a pâté baked in a pastry surround; *pâté maison*, a pâté cooked according to the recipe of a particular restaurant.

1901 C. H. SENN *New Cent. Cookery Bk.* xxii. 399 Fleurettes de Foie Gras (Foie Gras with Mayonnaise).—1 medium-sized tin or terrine of foie gras pâté, 1 truffle [etc.]. **1931** X. M. BOULESTIN *What shall we have To-day?* 84 Let the *pâté* get cold in the larder with a weight over it. Serve in the *terrine* in which it has cooked. **1948** *Good Housek. Cookery Bk.* II. 74 Liver and other savoury pâtés ..may be served as an hors d'oeuvre. **1931** J. BERJANE *French Dishes for Eng. Tables* x. 152 Pâté de Campagne (*foie de porc*) Gascon... Chop up the liver and the fat [etc.]. **1966** P. V. PRICE *France: Food & Wine Guide* 101 A *pâté de campagne* will be a rather rough-cut *pâté.* **1967** V. CANNING *Python Project* ii. 31 He was not English. The French accent was as thick and meaty as *pâté de campagne.* c **1938** *Fortnum & Mason Price List* 29/2 Pâté en croutes (October to March). **1961** S. BECK et al. *Mastering Art of French Cooking* ix. 569 The recipe we have chosen to illustrate *pâté en croûte* is boned duck stuffed, reformed, surrounded with decorated pastry, and baked. **1967** A. CHRISTIE *Endless Night* xiii. 113 We had brought *pâté en croûte* with us and French bread. **1947** M. MCCARTHY *On Contrary* (1962) 6 *Open City*,..Oscar Wilde, a reprint of Henry James were *paté de maison* to this lady who wanted the definitive flapjack. **1956** M. LASKI in *Observer* 14 Oct. 17/4 It is..misleading to say that..*pâté de foie gras* is known under the names *pâté de foie, pâté de campagne, pâté maison.* **1963** R. CARRIER *Great Dishes of World* 40 Every French restaurant boasts its *pâté maison.* **1967** *Listener* 20 Apr. 533/3 The standardization and mass-production of food extends beyond the same tinned '*pâté maison*'..wherever one goes.

‖ **pâte** (pāt). [Fr., = PASTE *sb.*] **a. pâte** (erron. **pâté**) **brisée** (pāt brīze), short pastry.

1845 E. ACTON *Mod. Cookery* xvi. 405 Pate brisee, or French crust for hot or cold meat-pies. **1960** E. DAVID *French Provincial Cooking* 205 This is one version of the *pâte brisée*..used for most open tarts in French cookery. **1978** *N.Y. Times* 29 Mar. c. 6/6 A pâté brisée is one of the best sweet pastry doughs.

b. The clay from which porcelain is made. So **pâte dure** (pāt diūəɪ), hard clay; **pâte-sur-pâte** (pāt siūər pāt), clay applied in layers to form relief decoration; **pâte tendre** (pāt taṅdr), soft clay.

1863 W. CHAFFERS *Marks Pott. & Porc.* 163 Porcelain of the *pâte tendre* has the appearance of an unctuous white enamel, like cream;..the *pâte tendre* is also soft in another sense, being unable to bear so great a degree of furnace heat as the hard porcelain. *Ibid.*, The *pâte dure*, or true porcelain, is of the whiteness of milk, and feels to the touch of a hard and cold nature. **1870** C. SCHREIBER *Jrnl.* (1911) I. 71 We found an exquisite pâte tendre St. Cloud group. **1881** C. C. HARRISON *Woman's Handiwork* II. 104 To Minton's unmatched artist, Solon, the world is indebted for an exquisite style of ceramic ornamentation, low relief carving in clay, known as pâte-sur-pâte. **1890** [see *KUTANI]. **1899** R. GLAZIER *Man. Hist. Ornament* 83 Porcelain is technically known under the terms 'hard paste' ('pâte dure') and 'soft' ('pâte tendre'). **1904** H. JAMES *Golden Bowl* I. viii. 149 He had handled nothing so precious as the Principino..whom he could manipulate.. as he couldn't a correspondingly rare morsel of an earlier *pâte tendre.* **1932** R. FRY *Characteristics of French Art* III. 66 He loved to feel the *pâte tendre* of a piece of fine pottery. **1947** J. C. RICH *Materials & Methods of Sculpture* ii. 44 *Pâte sur pâte* is the phrase applied to a method of modeling very low reliefs with slip. **1959** *Times* 3 Oct. 9/5 Her sister Florence, who specialized in birds..and also painted in *pâte sur pâte.* **1964** H. HODGES *Artifacts* i. 33 In a process known as pâte-sur-pâte, clay made to the consistency of a thin paste may be painted on, layer by layer, to produce low relief modelling. **1972** *Country Life* 20 Jan. 152/2 They are early Minton pâte-sur-pâte, their maker the technically gifted Marc Louis Solon. **1974** SAVAGE & NEWMAN *Illustr. Dict. Ceramics* 215 *Pâte dure*, the French term for hard-paste porcelain. **1976** *Times Lit. Suppl.* 3 Sept. 1074/4 A display of Minton *pâte-sur-pâte* wares.

c. pâte de verre (pāt də vɛr), powdered glass that has been refired.

1907 E. DILLON *Glass* xxii. 359 Of quite another nature is the *pâte de verre*, a substance somewhat of the nature of a glass frit, which has been made use of by the French sculptor, M. Henri Cros, in the modelling of polychrome reliefs and friezes. **1961** E. M. ELVILLE *Collector's Dict. Glass* 178/2 [James] Tassie's medium was a finely powdered potash-lead glass, or pâte-de-verre. **1978** *Guardian Weekly* 9 Apr. 14/4 Sofas are covered in bright prints, lamps are pink or blue *pate de verre*.

patellectomy (pætĕle·ktŏmi). *Surg.* [f. PATELL(A + *-ECTOMY.] Surgical removal of the patella.

1940 *Q. Cumulative Index Medicus* XXVIII. 706/1 Patellectomy in therapy of recidivating dislocations. **1944** *Surg., Gynecol., & Obstetr.* LXXIX. 536/1 These observations..suggest that routine total patellectomy for fracture of the patella in the human may be folly. **1977** *Proc. R. Soc. Med.* LXX. 258/2 All had been considered for surgical treatment, including patellectomy.

patellofemoral (păte:lofe·mŏrăl), *a. Anat.* [f. PATELL(A + -O + FEMORAL *a.* and *sb.*] Of or pertaining to the patella and the femur.

1934 in WEBSTER. **1964** J. McM. MENNELL *Joint Pain* xii. 126 (*heading*) The patellofemoral joint. **1978** *Sci. Amer.* Jan. 44/3 The [knee] joint includes two articulations, or movable parts, that transmit force and relative motion. One is the patellofemoral bearing surface between the patella (the kneecap) and the femur (the thighbone).

patent, *a.* Add: **2.** (Further examples.) *patent house, theatre*, a theatre established by Royal Patent; *spec.* in London, the theatres of Covent Garden and Drury Lane, whose Patents were granted by Charles II in 1662.

1835 DICKENS *Sk. Boz* (1837) 2nd Ser. 166 Why were they not engaged at one of the patent theatres? *c* **1844** C. GORE in M. R. Booth *Eng. Plays of 19th Cent.* (1973) III. 16 The disproportion and caricature *established into the custom of the stage* by the exigencies of our colossal patent theatres. **1891** [in Dict.]. **1932** *Times Lit. Suppl.* 24 Nov. 888/3 In 1832, however, the fashion [of stalls] spread at last to the patent houses. **1973** M. R. BOOTH *Eng. Plays of 19th Cent.* III. 1 Social and political change, the enlarging of the patent theatres, the broadening and inevitable coarsening of audience tastes—all this brought with it a demand for a new kind of comedy. **1973** *Times Lit. Suppl.* 19 Oct. 1272/2 During the period 1740–80 there were only two patent theatres in London: Drury Lane and Covent Garden. Unlicensed theatres were confined to musical performances, and dubiously legal public 'rehearsals' of plays.

3. *patent food*, a proprietary food preparation; *patent insides, outsides* (see quot. 1970); *patent leather* (see LEATHER *sb.* 1); also *ellipt.*, a patent leather boot or shoe; also *fig.*; *patent log*, a mechanical device for measuring the speed of a ship; *patent medicine*, a proprietary medicine manufactured under patent; *patent sail*, an automatically controlled windmill sail (see quots.); *patent still* [patented by Aeneas Coffey in 1830], a type of still for the continuous production of alcohol of greater strength and purity than is obtainable in a pot still, steam being used to heat the wash directly and carry off the alcoholic vapour; freq. *attrib.*

1871 *London Jrnl.* Apr. (Advt.), Dr. Ridge's patent food. **1903** 'A. MCNEILL' *Egregious English* 56 Mammas.. who suckle their children out of patent-food tins. **1925** *Scribner's Mag.* Sept. 274/2 Even the 'quick lunch' takes time, so a widely advertised patent food is put up in tablet form, to be eaten at the business desk itself. **1929** GALSWORTHY *Exiled* II. 66, I have recently had to make a series of pictures for a patent food called Vital. **1964** M. LASKI in S. Nowell-Smith *Edwardian England* iv. 205 The richer parents..were more likely to feed the infant on one of the many patent foods. **1882** I. M. RITTENHOUSE *Jrnl.* 8 June in *Maud* (1939) 103 The funny places in all the old patent-insides of newspapers talk about the sweet girl graduate. **1931** *Sat. Even. Post* 28 Feb. 129/2 Some publishers bought patent insides, which were the interior pages of the newspaper ready printed for use. **1968** E. RUSSENHOLT *Heart of Continent* IV. xiii. 243 The 'St. James Leader'..is an 8-page weekly (including 'patent insides'). **1970** R. K. KENT *Lang. Journalism* 98 *Patent insides* (or *outsides*), features or other syndicated material that come to a newspaper already printed on inside (or first and last) pages; readyprint pages. **1829** *Poulson's Amer. Daily Advertiser* (Philad.) 25 Apr. 3/5 Just received, an extensive assortment of Japanned Patent Leather, of superior quality. **1846** A. J. H. DUGANNE *Daguerreotype Miniature* 7 A pair of patent-leather boots and a Polka hat were the extremes of his apparel. **1849** G. G. FOSTER *New York in Slices* 64 Our young gentlemen..thus preserve their patent-leathers. **1882** *Encycl. Brit.* XIV. 387/2 *Patent or Enamelled Leather.*—Leather finished with a brilliant, smooth, and glossy surface, used for dress boots and shoes,..is known under a variety of names, as lacquered, varnished, japanned, and enamelled leather, &c. **1890** O. WILDE *Pict. Dorian Gray* i, in *Lippincott's Monthly Mag.* July 8 Lord Henry..tapped the toe of his patent-leather boot. **1905** H. A. VACHELL *Hill* ii. 29 He had to varnish Grieve's patent-leathers for Sunday. **1910** J. W. TOMPKINS *Mothers & Fathers* 356 [He was] humbly removing the overshoes that covered Mr. Hammond's patent leathers. **1955** [see *LAIR *sb.*[4]]. **1976** BOTHAM & DONNELLY *Valentino* iv. 35 Rodolpho reached up a hand to pat his patent leather hair into place. **1876** Patent log [see LOG *sb.*[1] 5]. **1940** *Chambers's Techn. Dict.* 509/1 The modern *patent* (or *taffrail*) *log* mechanically indicates the rate of travel by means of a submerged fly or rotator, whose revolutions are conveyed to a register on the rail of the vessel by a braided hemp line secured to the rotator. **1961** F. H. BURGESS *Dict. Sailing* 157 *Patent log*, a mechanical device with which a rotator is used, to work a dial indicating the distance run through the water. **1770** *Essex Gaz.* (Salem, Mass.) 17 Apr. 4/4 To be sold by Benjamin Eaton..in Marblehead..a collection of genuine patent medicines. **1799** [in Dict.]. **1830** SCOTT *Lett. Demonology* v. 144 The proprietor of a patent medicine, who should in those days have attested his having wrought such miracles as we see sometimes advertised. **1866** 'MARK TWAIN' *Speeches* (1923) 7 It is said by some..that Kanakas won't lie, but I know they *will* lie..lie like patent-medicine advertisements. **1887** [in Dict.]. **1888** G. B. SHAW *Let.* 20 Sept. (1965) I. 198 Nearly all the citizens..buy immense quantities of charms called patent medicines. **1901** *Chambers's Jrnl.* Jan. 63/1 Soaps, patent medicines, chocolates..are the things most advertised. **1914** *Rep. Sel. Comm. Patent Medicines* p. xii, in *Parl. Papers* IX, Patent and proprietary medicines differ very widely in character. At one end of the scale is the valuable scientific preparation; at the other end is the mere vulgar swindle. **1961** *Today's Health* Feb. 30/2 The medical device pirate of today, of course, is a far more sophisticated operator than his predecessor of yesteryear—the gallus-snapping hawker of snake oil and other patent medicines. **1978** P. BAILEY *Leisure & Class in Victorian Eng.* i. 15 Street preachers, stump orators and patent medicine salesmen. **1871** *Lancaster Intelligencer* 3 Apr., The editor who surrenders control of one-half of his paper to some manufacturer of patent-outsides, may make a slight reduction in his current expenses, but in the end he will lose both money and influence. **1890** *Boston Jrnl.* 7 Mar. 4/5 He was running his patent outsides for country newspapers. **1945** *Archit. Rev.* XCVIII. 72/2 In 1807 Sir William Cubitt invented what has even since been called 'patent sail'. **1968** J. ARNOLD *Shell Bk. Country Crafts* 170 This was the patent sail and enabled adjustment to the wind to be made without interrupting the milling. **1973** J. VINCE *Discovering Windmills* (ed. 3) 21 The most significant improvement in sail design came about in 1807 when William Cubbitt [*sic*] invented his patent sail. This retained Meikle's shutters, but they were controlled automatically by a weight suspended outside the mill. **1887** A. BARNARD *Whisky Distilleries of U.K.* 12 Blenders without number can be found who will strenuously affirm that to give the public a moderate priced article with sufficient age, there is no way but to use good old Patent Still Grain Spirit as a basis. *Ibid.* (Advt.), Flemming, Bennet & McLaren... Makers of Fire Stills, Steam Stills, Coffey's Patent Stills,..&c. **1906** *Daily Chron.* 27 Feb. 1/7 The North London magistrate held that patent-still spirit was not whisky. **1934** J. I. DAVIS *Beginner's Guide Wines & Spirits* viii. 85 Irish Whisky is always 'pot-stilled'... Some Scotch Whisky is so made, but most of it is manufactured in a patent still, which completes the distillation in one operation. **1937** *Thorpe's Dict. Appl. Chem.* (ed. 4) I. 178/1 The spirit produced in these 'patent stills'..has been used only to a limited extent for the production of spirit for whisky blending... The great bulk goes into industry for use as a raw material or as a technical solvent. **1968** I. C. TAYLOR *Highland Whisky* (An Comunn Gaidhealach) 3 The practice of blending pot-still and patent-still whiskies began about 1860.

patent, *sb.* Add: **6.** *patent agent.*

1860 BARTLETT *Dict. Amer.* (ed. 3) 310 *Patent Agent*, one who procures patents for inventors. **1884** *List of Subscribers* (London & Globe Telephone Co.), Haseltine, Lake & Co...Patent Agents. **1957** *Encycl. Brit.* XVII. 371/1 Patents are usually, although not necessarily, obtained through the intervention of 'patent agents'. **1959** *Digest of Patent & Other Cases* (Patent Office) II. 778 A person who lodges and signs a complete specification as Agent for Applicant does not thereby describe himself as a Patent Agent.

patent, *v.* Add: **1.** (Earlier examples.)

1789 J. MORSE *Amer. Geogr.* 261 They..patented away to their particular favorites, a very great proportion of the whole province. **1831** J. M. PECK *Guide for Emigrants* III. 319 The Military Bounty Tract..was set apart by Congress and patented for soldiers who served in the last war.

3. (Earlier examples.)

1675 *Calendar Virginia State Papers* (1875) I. 8 Major Lawrence Smith..did patent foure thousand six hundred acres of land. **1815** D. DRAKE *Nat. View Cincinnati* i. 51 The following is the course pursued in locating and patenting these lands.

5. *Metallurgy.* To subject to the process of 'patenting' (see *PATENTING *vbl. sb.* b).

1922 J. W. URQUHART *Steel Thermal Treatment* xi. 271 The process known as 'patenting' wire is of recent origin. **1932** BARR & HONEYMAN *Steel* xix. 102 The rods require to be patented once only.

patented *ppl. a.* (examples in sense *5 of the vb.).

1891 J. B. SMITH *Wire* i. 60 'Patented or improved steel wire' implies that which has been treated by a patented or special 'improving process' of annealing, hardening, and tempering. **1916** D. K. BULLENS *Steel & its Heat Treatment* xvi. 402 The high strength and toughness of patented wire are due to its carbon condition and its peculiar structure. **1956** A. K. OSBORNE *Encycl. Iron & Steel Industry* 307/2 Best patented steel wire is wire intended for the production of steel cables which has been drawn to a maximum stress of between 80 to 90 tons per sq. in.

patentability. (In Dict. s.v. PATENTABLE *a.*) Further examples.

1946 *Nature* 23 Nov. 726/1 In these circumstances the requirements for patentability as a selection from the general disclosure or claim are discovery of a previously unrecognized advantage.., and limitation to a manufacture based on that discovery. **1972** *N.Y. Law Jrnl.* 10 Oct. 5/2 The general level of innovation necessary to sustain patentability remains the same. **1972** *Sci. Amer.* Oct. 45/3 Novelty, though essential for patentability, does not guarantee utility. **1978** *Nature* 22 June 584/1 Patent law has not yet got to grips with the problem of genetically-engineered bacteria, both in terms of their patentability and of the particular difficulties there might be in storing bacteria whose claim to originality lies in the properties possessed by a plasmid.

patentable, *a.* (Earlier and later examples.)

1817 *Niles' Reg.* XII. 283/2 The improvement relied on by Witness was not useful, and consequently not a patentable improvement under the patent law. **1977** *New Scientist* 7 Apr. 24/2 Although computer programs are not as such patentable, computer hardware can be protected.

patentably (pēi·tĕntăbli), *adv.* [f. PATENTABLE *a.* + -LY[2].] In a way that satisfies the conditions for patenting anything.

1903 *Sci. Amer.* 28 Feb. 159/1 Patents have been granted in Great Britain..without any enquiry to learn whether the inventions were patentably new.

patenter. For *Obs. rare*$^{-1}$ read *rare* and add further example.

1883 E. W. HAMILTON *Diary* 25 Mar. (1972) II. 413 The only other person at dinner was Lane Fox, the inventor and patenter of an electric lighting system.

patenting, *vbl. sb.* Add: **b.** *Metallurgy.* In the manufacture of wire, a process for improving ductility similar to normalizing, but involving cooling in either air or molten lead or salt.

The subject of *Brit. Patent 1104* (granted to J. Horsfall in 1854).

1891 J. B. SMITH *Wire* i. 60 'The patenting or improving' of steel wire is..an occult process..for each manufacturer has his own..special methods. **1916** D. K. BULLENS *Steel & its Heat Treatment* xvii. 405 The structure obtained by patenting permits much further cold drawing than does the structure obtained by annealing. **1921** L. AITCHISON *Engin. Steels* viii. 275 The patenting furnace is a long, open-ended chamber. **1945** *Engineers' Digest* VI. 169 (*heading*) Direct resistance heating of salt baths for the patenting of steel wire. **1961** *Engineering* 14 Apr. 516/2 A batch of 24 wires is fed through the 60 ft patenting furnace at a time, being heated to 950°C.

pater. Add: **3. b.** spec. *Anthropol.* The legal father.

1949, etc. [see *GENITOR[2] b]. **1951** E. E. EVANS-PRITCHARD *Kinship & Marriage among Nuer* 113 The children clearly regard themselves as members of a legal family to which the brother of their pater does not belong, although he is their foster-father, and may also be their genitor. **1955** M. GLUCKMAN *Custom & Conflict in Afr.* iii. 71 In these institutions physiological paternity is distinguished from social fatherhood—as anthropologists put it, the *pater* need not be the *genitor*.

pateras, var. *PATTRESS.

Pateresque (pēi:təre·sk), *a.* [f. the name of Walter Horatio *Pater* (1839–94), English writer and critic.] Resembling the style of Pater's writing or his method of criticism. So **Paterian** (pēitīə·riăn), *a.*

1903 BEERBOHM *Around Theatres* (1953) 274 One reason why this book is so fresh and welcome is that we see for the first time the Pateresque manner and method of criticism applied to current dramatic art. 'Pateresque' is no slight. **1905** *Westm. Gaz.* 24 July 14/1 The definition of the priest's 'triumph' as that of 'achieving as much faith as possible in an age of negation' recalls a passage from Bishop Blougram, but is truly Pateresque in its expression. **1938** L. P. SMITH *Unforgotten Years* viii. 207 The record of an attempt to see things elegantly and nobly in the Paterian spirit. **1939** *Scrutiny* VII. IV. 442 For years he cultivated a Paterian manner in his own writing. **1944** W. STEVENS *Let.* 27 Mar. (1967) 463 He considers my poems to be expressions of Paterian hedonism. **1965** K. GRAHAM *Eng. Crit. of Novel* iii. 93 An interesting Pateresque attempt to explain the flaws..in terms of form alone. **1977** R. L. WOLFF *Gains & Losses* ii. 188 This Paterian Christianity is astonishingly like Paterian paganism.

paternal, *a.* Add: **1. b. paternal roof,** the home of one's father.

1828 CARLYLE in *Edin. Rev.* Dec. 293 But now, at this early age, he quits the paternal roof. **1845** J. PORTER *Thaddeus of Warsaw* (new ed.) xliii. 475 Longing earnestly for a temporary sanctuary under his friend's paternal roof. **1861** J. W. CARLYLE *Let.* 22 Sept. (1883) III. 91 If you are returned to 'the paternal roof', no need almost of this letter.

paternalist (pătə̄·ɹnălist), *a.* [see -IST.] = PATERNALISTIC *a.*

1928 *Britain's Industr. Future* (Liberal Industr. Inquiry) III. xviii. 237 'Welfare work' has an unpleasant paternalist and patronising sound.

paternalistic, *a.* Add: (Later examples.) Hence **paternali·stically** *adv.*

1918 *Nation* (N.Y.) 7 Feb. p. xii/2 It is perhaps as well that a paternalistic Government, with unlimited power of taxation to make good the deficit, is behind it. **1918** E. H. Griggs *Soul of Democracy* xviii. 125 The breakdown of paternalistically achieved efficiency has been evident in Germany's utter failure to understand, [etc.]. **1961** *Daily Tel.* 24 Apr. 12 They are humble people, Europeans, half-castes and Africans, whose only crime is to have pursued their livelihoods unprotestingly under a paternalistic Government which is now challenged by the spread of black nationalism. **1966** *Listener* 16 June 889/1 I felt the face of Britain was reasonably presented in this paternalistic atmosphere. **1976** *Daily Mirror* 16 July 5/7 That puts him on the side of the Labour unions, who are uneasy about Carter, a paternalistic employer.

paternalized (pătɜ̄·ɹnăləiz'd), *ppl. a.* [f. as Paternalism + -ize + -ed[1].] Characterized by or subjected to paternalism.

1903 *Electr. World & Engin.* 11 Apr. 597 The socialistic spirit..that would have every man on the pay roll of the State or the municipality in a vast series of paternalised institutions.

paternity. Add: **5.** *attrib.* and *Comb.*, as *paternity case, leave, suit*; **paternity test**, a blood test used to assess or discount the likelihood of paternity in a particular case; hence **paternity-testing** *vbl. sb.*

1940 D. MacCarthy *Drama* 104 In the opening scene we have seen him confronted, as a soldier in authority, with a paternity case he cannot solve. **1973** *Guardian* 4 June 9/1 Imagine the day when firms allow their male employees paternity leave to be with their wives during the last part of their pregnancies and the first days in the life of their children. **1975** *Times* 12 Mar. 3/1 The Greater London Council..agreed tonight that fathers on their staff should normally be allowed up to five days paternity leave. **1977** *Spare Rib* June 18/3 We're also now pressing for paternity leave, realising it's a joint thing. **1975** J. McClure *Snake* viii. 108 See a doctor, get some pills... Paternity suits I don't contest, madam. **1977** D. Anthony *Stud Game* iii. 21, I can imagine the damage a paternity suit would do. But I'm broke, and the baby's due in less than five months. **1926** R. J. E. Scott *Gould's Med. Dict.* 773/2 Mayoral and Jiminez paternity test. **1943** D. Harley *Medico-Legal Blood Group Determination* vi. 44 (*heading*) Paternity tests. **1960** I. A. Stanton *Dict. for Med. Secretaries* 113/1 *Paternity test*, blood comparison tests to rule out the possibility of paternity. **1968** F. E. Camps *Gradwohl's Legal Med.* (ed. 2) xiii. 171/1 Anti-S [antibody] has been found sufficiently often for it to be used economically for paternity testing. **1972** B. Knight *Legal Aspects Med. Practice* xxiii. 196 Certain haemoglobin-binding proteins in human serum, called haptoglobins, can be detected by electrophoresis... Their inheritance is..determined on fixed genetic principles, thus making them of use in paternity testing.

paternoster, *sb.* Add: **4. c.** A lift consisting of a succession of doorless compartments on an endless chain in continuous slow motion that allows entry at any time. Also *paternoster lift.*

1912 *Engineering Index* XXXI. 72/2 The 'Paternoster' continuous elevator (Ascensori a movimento continuo, o ascensori 'Paternoster'). U. Quintavalle. An endless chain elevator with several compartments... *L'Industria*—Mar. 10 1912. **1937** *Discovery* Dec. 388/2 Lifts and conveyors of the 'Paternoster' type have been installed. **1971** R. Lewis *Error of Judgment* vi. 205 He and the victim of his attack were on a small square landing at the end of the corridor and directly in front of the paternosters. **1973** *Times* 24 Dec. 4/3 Instead of orthodox lifts, the architects..use 'paternosters', continually moving, doorless two-person lifts which reduce waiting. **1977** *Times* 19 Feb. 2/3 Passenger-carrying 'paternoster' lifts consisting of continuous chains of small cars.

6. paternoster lake *Physical Geogr.*, each of a line of lakes in a glaciated valley.

1942 C. A. Cotton *Climatic Accidents in Landscape-Making* xix. 256 If the step-tread basins are occupied by lakes..these may follow one another like beads upon a string—'paternoster lakes'. **1968** R. W. Fairbridge *Encycl. Geomorphol.* 468/2 Since the floor of a glaciated valley is often undulating..or with a step-like rock floor.., it is sometimes marked by a succession of lakes.. rather fancifully named paternoster lakes.

Paterson (pæ·təɹsən). *Austral.* The surname of an Australian family, used in *Paterson's curse*, a blue-flowered weed, *Echium plantagineum*, of the family Boraginaceæ which is said to have spread from their garden near Albury, New South Wales, in the 1890s.

1905 *Agric. Gaz. New South Wales* XVI. 268 That 'Paterson's Curse' produces some feed is undoubted, but it is a smothering, rough, coarse plant, whose room is far better than its company. **1922** G. M. Thomson *Naturalisation of Animals & Plants in N.Z.* iii. 445 It [sc. *Echium plantagineum*] is a serious pest in some parts of Australia, where it is known as 'Paterson's Curse'. **1926** F. W. Hilgendorf *Weeds N.Z.* vi. 144 Paterson's Curse..is the local name of this weed where it is commonest in New Zealand, viz. in the Thames and neighbouring districts. **1930** A. J. Ewart *Flora of Victoria* 971 Paterson's Curse... A weed proclaimed for the whole state. **1970** R. M. Moore *Austral. Grasslands* xii. 189/2 Paterson's curse..has a wide distribution in South Australia, Victoria, and southern New South Wales.

patesi (pătē·si). [erron. transliteration of Sumerian *ensi.*] The ruler of a Sumerian city-state; a petty sovereign or priest-king. Hence **pate·siship**, the office or position of a patesi.

1894 A. H. Sayce *Primer of Assyriol.* iii. 45 At a later date Tello lost its independence, and its rulers became merely patesis or high-priests. **1910** L. W. King *Hist. Sumer & Akkad* iv. 101 The human kings and patesis were nothing more than ministers, or agents, appointed to carry out their will. **1927** Peake & Fleure *Priests & Kings* 178 The Sumerian patesi was a magistrate who performed sacred or priestly functions. **1928** C. L. Woolley *Sumerians* v. 138 Only in Nippur did the patesiship continue to descend from father to son.

path, *sb.* Add: **1. d.** *Physiol.* = *pathway 2 a.

1881 A. L. Ranney *Appl. Anat. Nervous Syst.* iii. 299 It is as certainly proved that the motor impulses travel along the anterior half of the spinal cord, while the path of sensory impressions is intimately associated with the posterior half. **1902** H. E. Santee *Anat. Brain & Spinal Cord* (ed. 2) x. 190 The sensory paths conduct two varieties of impulse. *Ibid.* 195 There are two auditory paths, the Cochlear and the Vestibular. **1942** F. A. Mettler *Neuroanat.* x. 201 There are thus two paths for delicate tactile sensations: a long, crossed path and an uncrossed one. **1950** *Physiol. Rev.* XXX. 461 An extrapyramidal path..appears to diverge from the cortico-spinal tract in the pons.

e. *Biochem.* A metabolic pathway (*pathway 2 b).

1909 A. E. Garrod *Inborn Errors Metabolism* i. 7 This conception of the permanency of the metabolic paths is no new one. **1927** M. Bodansky *Introd. Physiol. Chem.* xi. 270 The possible paths of metabolism of this amino acid are the following. **1935** C. F. & G. T. Cori in Harrow & Sherwin *Textbk. Biochem.* xx. 553 With the enzyme systems existing in muscle it seems more probable..that cleavage products of glycogen are led into the lactic acid path.

f. A schedule which is allotted to or is available to an individual train over a given route.

1961 *Guardian* 28 Apr. 30/4 The code..will indicate the class of train..and the number of its 'path' on operational timing. **1971** D. J. Smith *Discovering Railwayana* x. 60 *Train path*, vacant line in the timetable which may be used by an extra train. **1977** *Modern Railways* Dec. 463/3 Through freight traffic can be a problem too, some of these trains have paths at the busiest times.

3. b. *Math.* A continuous mapping of a real interval into a space.

1939 M. H. A. Newman *Elem. Topology of Plane Sets of Points* vi. 143 Paths and loops are not merely sets of points. **1956** E. M. Patterson *Topology* iv. 76 A path in a topological space T is a continuous mapping $\alpha : C \to T$ of the space C, that is the set of real numbers u satisfying $0 \leqslant u \leqslant 1$ with the usual topology, into T. **1974** L. Loomis *Calculus* xi. 437 A parametric representation of a curve is often called a path. Sometimes we call the curve itself a path.

5. path-breaker [tr. G. *bahnbrecher*], one who or something which breaks open a path; a pioneer; so *path-breaking* adj. [G. *bahnbrechend*]; **path difference** *Physics*, difference in path length; **path-finder**, (*a*) (further examples); also *fig.*; (*b*) an aircraft or its pilot sent ahead of bombing aircraft to locate and mark out the target for attack; **path-finding**, the state of being a path-finder; also *attrib.*; **path length** *Physics*, the length of the path followed by a light ray, sound wave, or the like (in the case of light usu. after allowing for the retarding effect of the medium: cf. *optical path* s.v. *optical *a.* 6); **path-master** *N. Amer.* (see quot. 1869).

1905 *Daily Chron.* 15 Nov. 4/3 A gentle path-breaker in her chosen..field of the delineation of child life and child millinery. **1913** *Q. Rev.* Oct. 407 The late Frederic Seebohm's 'English Village Community' was literally a path-breaker. **1914** R. M. Jones *Spiritual Reformers 16th & 17th Cent.* iv. 46 A man of heroic spirit and a path-breaking genius. **1973** *Times Lit. Suppl.* 27 Apr. 466/3 Not an epoch-making or path-breaking book. **1978** *Sci. Amer.* Feb. 131/3 His words apply equally well to other path-breaking discoveries in physics. **1929** J. K. Robertson *Introd. Physical Optics* ix. 186 If the thickness of the film gradually increases, the path difference between..pairs of interfering rays will do so also and consequently the face of the film will be alternately light and dark. **1962** A. Nisbett *Technique Sound Studio* i. 28 (*caption*) The effective path difference (i.e. the extra distance travelled by the [sound] wave to reach the back of the ribbon 1) is equivalent to the distance D round the magnet pole-piece 2. **1866** *Harper's Mag.* June 28/1 The great Path-finder, unfortunately for himself, took the wrong path. **1898** W. James *Coll. Ess. & Rev.* (1920) 408 Philosophers are after all like poets. They are path-finders. **1932** C. Fuller *Louis Trigardt's Trek* 18 These were the 'path-finders' of the greater movement that followed in their wake. **1943** *Times* 25 Nov. 4/4 Red tracer bullets were continually fired from the ground at the pathfinders' flares. **1944** [see *marker 3 c]. **1946** *R.A.F. Jrnl.* May 168 For the crews of Bomber Command's Pathfinder Force it was all a question of time. **1959** R. Collier *City that wouldn't Die* i. 22 As pathfinders their function was to spotlight the target..with thousands of chandelier flares and incendiary bombs. **1973** *Nature* 2 Mar. 67/1 He was an inventor and an innovator, a path-finder and prognosticator. **1977** 10 June 16/3 A former wartime Path-finder with DFC and Bar. **1888** Path-finding [in Dict.]. **1943** *Jane's All World's Aircraft 1942* p. iv/2 The success.. was contributed to by the introduction of the system of path-finding. **1944** *Living off Land* iv. 85 Accurate path-finding in the bush..tests your common sense. **1948** H. Brighouse in J. Marriott *Best One-Act Plays 1946–47* 145 Well, pathfinding for Bomber Command..so a bit of marine navigation wasn't beyond me. **1961** *Listener* 30 Nov. 908/1 The development of radio aids and path-finding techniques was proceeding. **1978** R. V. Jones *Most Secret War* xviii. 148 KGr 100's pathfinding role. **1949** S. Silver *Microwave Antenna* iv. 123 Fermat's principle: The optical ray or rays from a source at a point P_1 to a point of observation P_2 is the curve along which the optical path length is stationary with respect to infinitesimal variations of path. **1956** *Nature* 10 Mar. 469/1 The summary of section A contains a useful review ..of resonance and pulse velocity tests... An important omission..is mention of the practical difficulty of measuring path-lengths sufficiently accurately in testing in-situ concrete structures by the pulse velocity method. **1971** *New Scientist* 3 June 566/1 Long path-length spectroscopy is made plausible by the combination of high intensity and directionality. **1799** *Upper Canada Gaz.* (York, Ontario) 29 June 3/2 The public are much indebted to Mr. John McDougal, who was appointed one of the path-masters at the last town meeting, for his great assiduity and care in getting the streets cleared of the many and dangerous (especially at night) constructions therein. **1869** *Rep. Comm. Agric. 1868* (U.S. Dept. Agric.) 348 The immediate supervision of construction and repairs is generally under the direction of local 'road supervisors', or 'path masters', as they are termed in some districts. **1959** *Maclean's Mag.* 20 June 83/2 The name was changed about 40 years ago because Gottlieb Watts, town path-master, could not spell it. **1968** E. S. Russenholt *Heart of Continent* iv. xi. 206 The Department of Agriculture orders that pathmasters cut weedy grain, and have the work charged to landowners.

path. (pæþ). Also written without full stop. Abbrev. of Pathology. Freq. *attrib.*

1937 'J. Bell' *Murder in Hospital* xii. 233 He does not appear to have had any path. tests done. **1944** H. Ashton *Yeoman's Hospital* xi. 239, I always hoped he'd land that job he wanted..in the Path. Lab. there. **1965** K. Giles *Some Beasts no More* v. 137 Sir Shelly diagnosed leukemia and it was confirmed by path. Prognosis was twelve months. **1968** C. Watson *Charity ends at Home* vii. 90 He's like a kid in the bath when he gets into that path lab. **1972** *Guardian* 20 June 16/4 People rather miss out on their psychi, because it happens to coincide with path finals. **1978** N. Freeling *Night Lords* xiv. 61 You find a suicide which..is a phony. We wait for the path. report.

Pathan (pătā·n). Also 7 **Pattan, Puttan,** 8 **Patan,** 9 **Puthan.** [Hind., f. Pashto *Pakhtun.*] The name of a Pashto-speaking people inhabiting parts of south-east Afghanistan and north-west Pakistan, also called *Pakhtun. Also *attrib.* or as *adj.*

1638 T. Herbert *Trav.* (ed. 2) 64 Most of her Pattans were slaine. **1787** C. Hamilton *Hist. Relation Rohilla Afgans N. Provinces Hindostan* 53 The tribe of Afgans denominated Rohees, or Rohillas, (so termed from Roh, which in the Pâtan dialect signifies a mountainous country.) **1792** *Asiatick Researches* III. 6 The principal inhabitants of the mountains, called Pársici,..seem to have been destroyed or expelled by the numerous tribes of Afgháns or Patans. **1851** H. B. Edwardes *Year on Punjab Frontier* I. 78, The people whom we geographically call Afghans, style themselves nationally Puthâns. **1864** *Athenæum* 5 Nov. 598/3 Pathans and Sikhs inspired them with feelings very little removed from panic. **1901** Kipling *Kim* vii. 173 Except for Mahbub Ali, and he is a Pathan, I have no friend save thee, Holy One. **1903** *Strand Mag.* May 530/1 A swarthy Pathan face grinned wickedly over a rubble heap. *Ibid.* 530/2 To compete with the..Pathan in his own hills. **1915** R. W. Campbell *Private Spud Tamson* iii. 23 Once on the Frontier of India he had slaughtered ten bloodthirsty Pathans in the space of an hour. **1930** *N.Y. Times* 6 Feb. 22/6 His [*sc.* Kipling's] commissioners, syces, Pathans, and budmashes continue to be as well known as the fascinating denizens of the animal kingdom celebrated in 'The Jungle Books'. **1958** A. Toynbee *East to West* 128 That British century had already brought the modern world to the threshold of the Pathan highlander's hovel. **1968** *Economist* 16 Nov. 31/1 Extremists..argue that the Pathans, like the Nagas, were never part of pre-partition India and should therefore be allowed to determine their own future. **1971** R. Dentry *Encounter at Kharmel* iii. 58 Your Pathan tribesman is a realist. He enjoys cutting throats. **1973** *Times* 27 July 16/3 The Pathans are estimated to account for half the present population of Afghanistan. **1976** *Spare Rib* Nov. 12/1 It was the case of a Pathan family. The Pathans are often very orthodox Muslims—sometimes religious fanatics.

pathetic, *a.* (*sb.*) Add: **A. 4.** So in phr. *pathetic fallacy*, first used by John Ruskin (see quot. 1856 in Dict.) to describe the attribution of human response or emotion to inanimate nature.

1856 [in Dict.]. **1856** Geo. Eliot in *Westm. Rev.* Apr. 631 Mr. Ruskin..enters on his special subject, namely, landscape painting. With that intense interest in landscape which is a peculiar characteristic of modern times, is associated the 'Pathetic Fallacy'—the transference to external objects of the spectator's own emotions. **1895** C. H. Herford *Spenser's Shepheards Calender* p. xlviii, Pastoral nature is founded upon the 'pathetic fallacy'. **1906** W. W. Greg *Pastoral Poetry & Pastoral Drama* 93 We have here a specific inversion of the 'pathetic fallacy'. **1930** H. S. V. Jones *Spenser Handbk.* iii. 64 Each elegy opens with an apostrophe to the poet's verse, and each illustrates what Ruskin called the 'pathetic fallacy'. **1930** L. Powys (*title*) The pathetic fallacy: a study of Christianity. **1959** *Listener* 6 Aug. 223/2 Many awaited death.. while the pathetic fallacy laboured away with ill winds and rain. **1968** *Ibid.* 18 Jan. 68/3 To believe that a television station should be part of its audience could seem like the Pathetic Fallacy (Communications Division), a piece of electronic anthropomorphism. **1975** M. C. Davis *Near Woods* v. 83 The next morning I fell under the spell of literature's pathetic fallacy at nearly every step. **1977** D WATKIN *Morality & Archit.* II. ii. 38 Le Corbusier's argument..combines succinctly the pathetic fallacies we are investigating: that particular types of architectural form are morally regenerative and physically health-giving.

6. Miserably inadequate; so poor as to be ridiculous. *colloq.*

1937 PARTRIDGE *Dict. Slang* 609/2 *Pathetic*, ludicrous. **1969** *Listener* 10 July 41/1 The military government clearly thinks it is established for good. The alleged plots against it are either mythical or, when genuine, pathetic. **1974** *Liverpool Echo* (Football ed.) 26 Oct. 3/2 The standard of refereeing in English soccer is pathetic. There is no consistency.

Pathet Lao (pǎte·t lɑu). [Laotian Thai, lit. 'land of the Lao'.] A communist guerrilla movement and political party (after December 1975 the ruling party) in Laos. Also *attrib.*

1954 *Times* 10 May 6/3 Earlier in the day statements by the two leaders—Mr. Son Ngoc Minh for the Khmer and Mr. Souvannouvong for the Pathet Lao—had been distributed to the Press... The Pathet Lao claim was to control half the territory. **1966** 'A. HALL' *9th Directive* xxvi. 236 The territory..is in the hands of the Pathet Lao, which takes orders from Peking. **1968** H. TOYE *Laos* v. 136 It was not long before they reached an area where the local Pathet Lao organization could protect them. **1970** LANGER & ZASLOFF *N. Vietnam & Pathet Lao* vi. 100 Prior to the Geneva Conference of 1962, the Soviet advisory role to the Pathet Lao had been very brief. **1970** *Peace News* 8 May 3/2 A Cambodian Communist Party has existed since the end of the second world war, when it fought shoulder-to-shoulder with the Pathet Lao, and the Vietminh. **1977** *Bangladesh Times* 20 Jan. 7/4 The Laotian authorities have set up a committee to censor every thing written, sung, recited or danced, the Pathet Lao news agency Khao San reported today.

pathic, *sb.* and *a.* Add: **A.** *sb.* **1.** (Later example.)

1972 STEDMAN *Med. Dict.* (ed. 22) 930/1 *Pathic*, a person who assumes the passive role in any abnormal sexual act.

B. *adj.* **1.** (Later example.)

1959 *N. & Q.* Dec. 435/2 The Pardoner's pathic role in the perverted relationship thus suggested is clearly indicated in A 691.

2. Delete *rare*⁻⁰ and add later examples. Also, that suffers from disease or disorder.

1902 W. A. HAMMOND *Aristotle's Psychol.* p. lxviii, Desire, as Aristotle employs it, is not a purely pathic or affective element. **1940** HINSIE & SHATZKY *Psychiatric Dict.* 404/1 *Pathic*,..pertaining to or affected by disease or disorder. **1951** S. F. NADEL *Found. Social Anthropol.* xi. 291 Vague states of feeling ('pathic states', as they have been called). **1973** M. AMIS *Rachel Papers* 148 Rachel received this idiot outpouring with a pathic nod.

Hence **pa·thically** *adv.*, in a passive manner.

1934 *Mind* XLIII. 300 The root notion..seems to be that the given must be passively, or (should I say?) pathically received.

patho-. Add: **pathobio·logy,** the study of the biological processes associated with diseased or injured tissue.

1971 LAVIA & HILL *Princ. Pathobiol.* i. 4 This is the subject of pathobiology—the alterations in normal biological mechanisms that occur in response to injury. **1972** *Lancet* 20 May 1104/1 Pathobiology (a trendy name for general pathology) seems to be a fashionable subject in the United States. **1975** *Amer. Jrnl. Path.* LXXIX. 183 Pathobiology of an endocrine disease.

pathogen. Substitute for def.: Any agent that causes disease, esp. a micro-organism. Add further examples.

1942 E. C. STAKMAN in *Aerobiology* (Amer. Assoc. Adv. Sci. Publ. No. 17) 2/1 The possible aerial dissemination of pathogens of domestic animals by air currents is a relatively unexplored field. **1970** M. TRESHOW *Environment & Plant Response* ii. 17 Contrary to common belief, a pathogen technically does not have to be an organism or virus. A pathogen can be any component of the physical environment, including adverse climate, soil, or air relations. **1972** *Daily Colonist* (Victoria, B.C.) 8 Feb. 6/2 Diener said the new agent, which he described as a 'novel type of pathogen' or disease-causing agent, is about 80 times smaller than the smallest known virus.

pathogenesis. Add: Hence **pathogene·tically, pathoge·nically** *advs.*, as regards pathogenesis.

1904 *Brit. Med. Jrnl.* 10 Sept. 559 The cells pathogenically affected by a toxin may not be the cells of origin of antitoxin. **1928** *Amer. Jrnl. Path.* IV. 632 Primary and secondary contracted kidneys in this respect are pathogenetically identical. **1972** ARONSON & ELLIOTT *Ocular Inflammation* xi. 258/2 Pathogenetically, the diffuse fundus lesion presents as a disseminated metastatic choroiditis,..relatively early in life.

pathography. (In Dict. s.v. PATHO-.) Add: **b.** The, or a, study of the life and character of an individual or community as influenced by a disease.

1917 C. R. PAYNE tr. *Pfister's Psychoanal. Method* xxvii. 573 The history of the Catholic sainthood affords the analytic pathography an inexhaustible material. **1959** *New Statesman* 28 Nov. 760/2 The founder of Protestantism with his fits of melancholia, his anxiety attacks, night sweats, and anguish about concupiscence, is an obvious subject for historical pathography. **1972** Q. BELL *Virginia Woolf* II. i. 20 The Japanese psychiatrist Mme Miyeko Kamiya is, I believe, preparing a pathography of Virginia Woolf.

Hence **patho·grapher,** one who writes a pathography.

1974 *Times Lit. Suppl.* 15 Mar. 256/4 The pathographer must allow for the language and limitations of the theory.

pathological, *a.* Add: **1. b.** (Later examples.) Also in more general use.

1921 R. S. WOODWORTH *Psychol.* (1922) i. 16 The pathological method..traces the decay or demoralization of mental life instead of its growth. **1933** E. GLOVER in S. Lorand *Psycho-Anal. Today* 192 (*title*) Pathological character formation. **1949** *Sat. Rev. Lit.* (U.S.) 25 June 11/1 For Ford, you see, was what those who were not charmed by him insisted upon describing as a pathological liar. **1951** V. NABOKOV *Speak, Memory* ii. 32 Age had developed in her a pathological stinginess. **1951** M. LOWRY *Let.* 25 Aug. (1967) 256 A himself is an almost pathological liar. **1971** *Jrnl. Gen. Psychol.* LXXXV. 64 In fact.. pathological anxiety might..represent a heightened susceptibility to over-arousal.

2. (Earlier examples.)

1796 F. A. NITSCH *Gen. View Kant's Princ. concerning Man* 195 The pathological interest aims at the agreeable and pleasing consequences of an action. **1798** A. F. M. WILLICH *Elem. Critical Philos.* 101 A rational observance of pathological laws.

3. *Math.* Grossly abnormal in properties or behaviour, as compared with the well-behaved functions normally encountered in classical applications (see quots. 1946, 1960).

1939 I. S. SOKOLNIKOFF *Advanced Calculus* iv. 105 Such pathological behavior of continuous functions led to a careful inquiry into the meaning of such geometrical concepts as the area under a curve. **1946** H. & B. S. JEFFREYS *Methods Math. Physics* i. 17 We can speak of a function of *x* that is equal to 1 if *x* is rational but to 0 if *x* is irrational. Such a function would be fairly regarded by a physicist as pathological, and he is interested in a much narrower class of functions, roughly speaking such as can be represented by graphs. **1960** *New Scientist* 25 Aug. 537/2 The term 'pathological functions' does not name any specific functions... It is applied rather informally to functions whose behaviour appears delinquent to those who expect mathematical functions to correspond only with physical events or, conversely, to possess only properties that can be represented by a graph or in a computer. Often the 'pathological' features concern continuity and smoothness. **1968** FOX & MAYERS *Computing Methods for Scientists & Engineers* ix. 179 Examples could be constructed of pathological repeated inaccurate consistency. **1971** D. W. SCIAMA *Mod. Cosmol.* viii. 113 In this case the geometry of space is said to be hyperbolic... The volume of the space is infinite except in pathological cases that need not concern us.

pathologically, *adv.* Add: **1. b.** Corresponding to sense *1 b of the adj.: morbidly; abnormally.

1933 *Mind* XLII. 138 In the expression of his feelings and appreciations he was almost pathologically reticent. **1978** P. G. WINSLOW *Coppergold* 75 She was pathologically jealous.

pathologist. Add: (See quots.)

1971 *Lancet* 29 May 1124/1 A pathologist (O.E.D., probably about 1905) is 'One versed in pathology: a student of or writer upon diseases' and pathology 'treats of the causes and nature of diseases'. Even at that time, when departments of pathology were beginning to be usual in medical schools and several specialised journals included the word in their titles, that was a little out of date... The word was already used chiefly for practitioners of laboratory medicine. By the thirties it had differentiated further: non-specialised laboratory doctors called themselves 'clinical pathologists', but used alone the word was increasingly limited to practitioners of the oldest branch of the trade, morbid-anatomy-histopathology. The N.H.S. has partly reversed this trend, advertising posts, for instance, as 'pathologist with a special interest in bacteriology'. The Royal College of Pathologists goes even further, being anxious to include the non-medical biochemists, though there is..a backwoods faction which challenges the propriety of calling anyone non-medical a pathologist. **1977** *Role & Membership of College* (R. College of Pathologists) 5 The pathologist can be defined as a medical (or dental) graduate who has ultimate responsibility for the diagnostic tests performed in the pathology laboratory and for the advice given to clinicians on the selection and interpretation of tests.

pathology. 1. c. (Examples in further extended senses.)

1972 W. LABOV *Language in Inner City* iv. 134 There is evidence from linguistic pathology that a deep-seated knowledge of this fact may be present in native speakers. **1972** T. KOCHMAN *Rappin' & Stylin' Out* p. xi, This book is an attempt to get beyond what Albert Murray has called the 'fakelore of black pathology' and its corollary, the 'folklore of white supremacy'. **1977** D. M. SMITH *Human Geogr.* x. 278 The major metropolitan states with their high general *average* affluence levels clearly experience high levels of social pathology.

patholopolis (pæþǒlǫ·pǒlis). [f. Gr. παθολογικός, f. πάθος suffering, disease + πόλις city; see PATHOLOGIC *a.*, -POLIS.] A diseased or morally degenerate city.

1927, 1961 [see *PARASITOPOLIS].

pathophysiology (pæ:þofiziǫ·lǒdʒi). *Med.* [f. PATHO- + PHYSIOLOGY.] The physiological processes associated with disease or injury; the study of such processes.

1952 *Adv. Internal Med.* V. 428 Abnormalities in protein metabolism form the central problem in the pathophysiology of multiple myeloma. **1962** *Lancet* 2 June 1172/2 An analysis of the pathophysiology of these disturbances may further our understanding of cerebral function. **1972** *Ibid.* 20 May 1104/1 It is impossible to keep up with all trends in pathophysiology. **1974** M. C. GERALD *Pharmacol.* xvi. 296 We may anticipate that the etiology of these disorders will be better understood with future advances in the pathophysiology and biochemistry of mental disease. **1975** *Nature* 3 Jan. 77/2 A symposium on the pathophysiology and clinical aspects of pain.

Hence **pa:thophysiolo·gic, -physiolo·gical** *adjs.*, of or involving abnormal physiological processes; pertaining to pathophysiology, **pa:thophysiolo·gically** *adv.*, as regards pathophysiology.

1952 *Adv. Internal Med.* V. 398 From the pathophysiologic point of view, the most interesting part of the myeloma problem is the disturbance of protein metabolism. **1960** (*title*) Works of the Institute of Higher Nervous Activity. Pathophysiological series. (Academy of Sciences of the U.S.S.R.) **1962** H. G. KEITEL *Pathophysiol. & Treatment of Body Fluid Disturbances* i. 12 In many illnesses the anatomical, biochemical, and pathophysiological characteristics of the associated fluid derangement and their successful treatment have been fairly clearly defined. **1973** WASSERMAN & BROWN in Holland & Frei *Cancer Med.* xix. 1367/1 The pathophysiologic mechanisms responsible for these symptoms. **1973** *Sci. Amer.* Sept. 121/3 Selective errors in the metabolism of the monamines in specific areas of the brain may be the pathophysiological basis for psychotic disorders. **1976** *Nature* 29 July 397/2 This..results in a chronic murine hepatosplenic disease which closely resembles, pathophysiologically, human chronic schistosomiasis.

pathosticate (pǎþǫ·stikēᵢt), *v. nonce-wd.* [joc. f. PATHOS + PATHE)TICATE *v.*] *intr.* To induce pathos by melodramatic writing.

1901 G. B. SHAW *Cashel Byron's Profession* (rev. ed.) Pref. p. xii, In novel-writing there are two trustworthy dodges for capturing the public. One is to slaughter a child and pathosticate over its deathbed for a whole chapter.

pathway. Add: **2. a.** *Physiol.* A chain of nerve cells forming a continuous route along which impulses of a particular kind habitually travel.

1924 R. M. OGDEN tr. *Koffka's Growth of Mind* iv. 235 Von Kries pointed out that the arousal of associations can not be explained on the basis of a mere 'pathway'-hypothesis which assumes that nervous excitations travel along fixed paths. **1934** J. H. GLOBUS *Neuroanat.* (ed. 6) 63 There will now be no difficulty in linking up the chain of nuclei and tracts, which form the optic pathways. **1952** W. F. T. TATLOW et al. *Synopsis Neurol.* ix. 162 Hyperalgesia.—Occurs when visceral and somatic (deep or superficial) afferents share pain pathway, so that on simultaneous stimulation, summation of subliminal stimuli can occur. **1971** *Sci. Amer.* July 48/2 The pathways extending from the brain to the lower spinal cord are some two feet long. **1972** *Science* 5 May 536/2 The descending cortical and brainstem pathways to the spinal cord represent the main instrument by which the brain controls movements.

b. The sequence of reactions undergone by a compound or class of compounds in a natural environment, esp. a living organism.

1927 M. BODANSKY *Introd. Physiol. Chem.* xi. 271 Another pathway of metabolism has been suggested, namely one involving the conversion of arginine into guanidinebutyric acid,..which by β-oxidation would yield guanidine acetic acid. **1947** *Growth* XI. 232 The pathway of galactose fermentation [in yeast]. **1961** *Proc. Nat. Acad. Sci.* XLVII. 378 (*heading*) Transformation studies on the linkage of markers in the tryptophen pathway in *Bacillus subtilis.* **1967** M. E. HALE *Biol. Lichens* viii. 106 The biosynthetic pathways by which they appear to be synthesized. **1971** *Sci. Amer.* Sept. 45/2 The carbon dioxide pathways in our biosphere. **1971** *Nature* 17 Sept. 163/2 His latest experiments are an attempt to identify the pathway of incorporation of ^{3}H-thymine into DNA. **1973** *Ibid.* 13 Apr. 453/1 This information will be required..to elucidate the pathways and interactions of mercury in the estuarine and marine environment.

-pathy. Add: **2.** Forming the names of bodily disorders of a specified part (as MYOPATHY) or kind (IDIOPATHY).

patience, *sb.* Add: **6.** *patience board, card* (further examples).

1907 *Yesterday's Shopping* (1969) 379/2 Patience and 'Pigmy' Cards. Rounded corners, printed backs, two packs in a box. *Ibid.* 380/1 Patience Board With Cards. **1916** J. BUCHAN *Greenmantle* ii. 24 From his pocket he had taken a pack of Patience cards and had begun to play the game called the Double Napoleon. **1926–7** *Army & Navy Stores Catal.* 392 Patience Board. For playing the game of Patience off the table.

patience-dock. 1. (Earlier and later examples.)

[**1640** J. PARKINSON *Theatrum Botanicum* II. iii. 154 Garden Patience is a Docke bearing the name of Rhubarbe, for some small purging quality therein.] **1820** T. GREEN *Universal Herbal* II. 498 *Rumex Patientia*; Patience Dock, or Rhubarb. **1822** J. C. LOUDON *Encycl. Gardening* 715 Herb Patience, or Patience Dock..is a hardy perennial plant, a native of Italy, introduced in

1573. **1859** *Trans. Illinois Agric. Soc.* III. 513 Patience dock comes early, and makes good greens. **1972** Y. LOVELOCK *Vegetable Bk.* I. 218 The spinach dock..is used in the early spring..and goes by such names as patience and patient dock. **1973** C. A. WILSON *Food & Drink in Britain* vi. 204 Many other large-leaved green plants were employed in this pottage, including orache, clary, mallows, patience dock, borage and bugloss.

patient, *a.* and *sb.* Add: **A. 4.** *spec.* in *Grammar* (see quot.).

1939 L. H. GRAY *Foundations of Lang.* xii. 374 A distinction is drawn between the ergative case as the logical subject of a transitive verb and the patient case as the subject of an intransitive verb.

5. patient Lucy orig. *U.S.*, = *busy Lizzie* s.v. *BUSY *a.* 11.

1946 M. FREE *All about House Plants* xvii. 161 The names Patience Plant and Patient Lucy are interesting examples of how the original meaning of a plant name can be reversed. The vernacular names are derived from the botanical name *Impatiens*,..referring to the sudden bursting of the seed pods. **1956** [see *BUSY *a.* 11]. **1977** K. & G. BECKETT *Illustr. Encycl. Indoor Plants* 110/2 Busy Lizzie; Patient Lucy; Sultana. A familiar house plant, native to tropical Africa.

B. *sb.* **4.** *spec.* in *Grammar*.

1968 J. LYONS *Introd. Theoret. Linguistics* viii. 342 But this conflicts with the notion of the subject as the 'actor', rather than the 'goal' (or 'patient'). **1971** J. ANDERSON *Grammar of Case* ix. 140 Accounts of transitivity conducted in terms of 'actor-action-patient'. [*Ibid.* iv. 52 The labels 'ergative' and 'nominative' are usually used with respect to..an inflectional..system; alternative terms are 'actif'/'nominatif' (Lafitte, 1962) 'agens'/'patiens' (Troubetzkoy, 1929).] **1975** *Language* LI. 806 It is significant that the suffix has come to designate the agent or instrument of the verbal activity in certain daughters—but not the patient, product, or location of the verbal activity.

pa·tienthood. [f. PATIENT *sb.* 2 + -HOOD.] The state or condition of being a patient.

1970 *New Yorker* 14 Nov. 108 Millions of boys..live, as Captain Ahab says, with half of their heart and with only one of their lungs, and the world is the worse for it. Now and again, however, an individual is called upon..to lift his individual patienthood to the level of a universal one and to try to solve for all what he could not solve for himself alone. **1971** *Harper's Mag.* May 111/2 Hers [*sc.* R. Mackenzie's] is the best account of the psychology of patienthood in a modern hospital I've ever read.

‖**patiki** (pā·tiki). *N.Z.* [Maori.] A local name for a flat-fish belonging to one of several species of *Rhombosolea* found in New Zealand waters; cf. FLOUNDER *sb.*[1] 1.

[**1820** *Gram. & Vocab. Lang. N.Z.* (Church Missionary Soc.) 190 Patiki, *s.* a fish so called.] **1838** J. S. POLACK *New Zealand* I. ix. 322 The *pâtiki*, between the large flounder and the sole, is equally excellent with the European fish. **1843** *N.Z. Jrnl.* No. 92 177/2 The natives.. brought in an abundant supply of fine fish; mullet,.. patiki, (the flounder of Europe) and other delicious species. **1855** R. TAYLOR *Te Ika a Maui* xxv. 412 *Patiki*, common name for the sole and flat-fish. **1879** *Trans. N.Z. Inst.* XII. 316 Large *Patiki*, flat fish, are occasionally speared up the river. **1949** P. H. BUCK *Coming of Maori* (1950) II. xiii. 321 One [rafter-painting] design, in which the field was roughly divided into lozenge-shaped areas, was named *patiki* (flounder) from its outline.

patina. Add: **2.** Also *fig.*

1933 H. NICOLSON *Diary* 24 Feb. (1966) 140 He says what the Americans lack is *patina*. **1955** KOESTLER *Trail of Dinosaur* 79 This tendency prompts people to have their wall-brackets and picture-frames artificially dirtied to lend them the patina of age; so let us call it the 'patina-snobbery'. **1957** R. HOGGART *Uses of Literacy* ix. 227 He develops a strong patina of resistance, a thick and solid skin for not taking notice. **1967** N. MAILER *Cannibals & Christians* I. 13 It gives them all a high instant patina, their skin responding to the call of the wild. **1977** *Time* 18 July 28/2 Defending the rights of homosexuals.., she mingled with and took on some of the patina of the loony left. **1978** J. THOMSON *Question of Identity* x. 97 The disorder was not a mere evening's untidiness. It had taken time to build up that rich patina of squalor.

Hence **pa·tinaed** *a.*, covered with a patina, patinated; also *fig.*

1948 W. FAULKNER *Intruder in Dust* (1949) xi. 244 Took from the inside coat pocket a leather snap-purse patina-ed like old silver and almost as big as Miss Habersham's handbag. **1968** D. MURPHY tr. *Gelin's Concept of Man in Bible* vii. 117 This is what I call a 'patinaed' reading.

patinate (pæ·tinēit), *v.* [f. PATINA 2 + -ATE[3].] *trans.* To cause to develop a patina; to cover with a patina. Also *fig.* So **pa·tinated** *ppl. a.*, **pa·tinating** *vbl. sb.*

1880 Patinated [in Dict. s.v. PATINA]. **1920** WEBSTER, Patinate. **1934** J. & C. GORDON *Portuguese Somersault* x. 237 Roofs of rich red-tile, patinated with lichens of varied tints. **1957** *Encycl. Brit.* IX. 382/2 When patinated flint occurs in gravels containing iron salts a yellow staining, producing the well-known ochreous patina, results. *Ibid.* XX. 231/2 The slower the patinating the more artistic the results is a good general rule to follow. **1957** *New Yorker* 6 Apr. 31 The riches Ian had inherited were so blindingly brand-new that it had taken time and pains to patinate them with good manners and good taste. **1969** L. R. ROGERS *Sculpture* vi. 210 Most sculptors today prefer a patina to a clean bronze surface and use acids..to patinate their work. **1970** G. SAVAGE *Dict. Antiques* 312/2 Handsomely patinated bronzes are much sought. **1974** K. CLARK *Another Part of Wood* iii. 103, I learnt a great deal from some lectures on the fascinating subject of Aristotle's *Poetics* by a richly patinated character named Farquharson.

patination. (Further examples.)

1936 *Bull. Raffles Museum, Singapore* Ser. B. No. 1. 53 The neolithic implements of Puming and Pajitan..have practically no patination at all. **1947** J. C. RICH *Materials & Methods Sculpture* vii. 199 The patination of metals is a highly specialized art. **1960** H. HAYWARD *Antique Coll.* 212/2 Patination and colour pose problems to a faker. **1970** *Cabinet Maker & Retail Furnisher* 30 Oct. 301/2 The optional antique patination is hand-dyed. **1973** *Country Life* 27 Sept. (Suppl.) 91 Jacobean oak court cupboard of excellent colour and patination. **1975** *Nature* 7 Aug. 469/1 The bifaces from that site do not, on the whole, have a dark-brown polish but have a grey to white, calcareous patination or no patination at all.

patine. (Further examples.)

1910 G. B. SHAW *Let* 18 Sept. (1972) II. 942 Back in the dark [in a rowing-boat], without compass,..49 strokes to the minute striking patines of white fire from the Atlantic. **1940** *Harper's Mag.* Nov. 566 Her [*sc.* a pilgrim hawk's] back was an indefinable hue of iron; only a slight patine of the ruddiness of youth still shone on it. **1966** M. M. PEGLER *Dict. Interior Design* (1967) 326 *Patina or Patine*, a greenish coating on the surface of old bronze.

patine (pæ̆tī·n), *v.* [f. PATINA.] *trans.* To coat or cover with a patina (sense 2). Also *fig.* Hence **pati·ning** *vbl. sb.*

1896 A. H. KEANE *Ethnol.* v. 84 Many [flints] have been deeply patined and rusted sometimes even right through. **1936** L. P. SMITH *Reperusals & Re-Collections* i. 2 Time and history adds to their significance; it patines and mellows them. **1947** J. C. RICH *Materials & Methods Sculpture* vii. 200 Brass can be patined in several colors. *Ibid.* 209 Iron and steel can be patined a blue-black by the application of a hot solution composed of 10 grains of sodium thiosulphate to each ounce of water. *Ibid.* 403/2 (Index) Chemical methods of patining bronze.

patinize (pæ·tĭnəiz), *v.* [f. as prec. + -IZE.] *trans.* To coat with or as with a patina. Hence **pa·tinizing** *vbl. sb.*

1904 *Sci. Amer. Suppl.* 27 Feb. 23548/1 The patinizing of zinc articles has become a very important question in the art industry.

patio. Add: **1.** Also in extended uses not in Spanish or Spanish-American contexts, a courtyard or enclosure; a paved area belonging to a house and usu. adjoining it. (Further examples.)

1891 KIPLING *City of Dreadful Night* vi. 36 The central square, the *patio* or whatever it must be called, reeks. **1941** B. SCHULBERG *What makes Sammy Run?* xi. 271 He was..dancing with her out on the patio to the rhumba orchestra. **1947** *Chicago Maroon* 25 July 2/1 Tables will be set up in the patio with free cokes, and a faculty member or new student from each state will be on hand to welcome new students. **1949** *Here & Now* (N.Z.) Oct. 22/2 The patio is really an extra room without a roof. It is protected on three sides by the house itself and on the north by the bank. **1955** J. CANNAN *Long Shadows* i. 16 The addition of two bathrooms built over a sun-room, which reduced the sooty little triangular garden to a size convenient to the construction of a *patio*. **1957** C. BROOKE-ROSE *Languages of Love* 23 Bernard sat now in an imitation *patio* under an imitation palm-tree. **1959** *Observer* 22 Mar. 1/1 But behind is a small golf course and a patio where a naval commander could be seen arranging the cushions. Filipino mess boys have polished up the interior. **1959** N. MAILER *Advts. for Myself* (1961) 378 Eitel is smoking a cigarette on the patio. **1968** *Globe & Mail* (Toronto) 17 Feb. 45 (Advt.), Detached 4-bedroom home on large fenced lot, beautiful patio. **1969** *Daily Tel.* 11 Nov. 17 Shops, dotted about among tree-strewn patios, fountains and open-air cafés [in Paris]. **1972** [see *LIMBO[3]]. **1973** *Irish Times* 2 Mar. 22/8 (Advt.), Bungalow: Dundrum—Scandinavian style, central heating, living room.. looking onto secluded patio. **1976** E. SCARROW *N.Z. Vegetable Gardening Guide* 5 A number of vegetables can be grown..in tubs or pots on a patio. **1977** *Austral. House & Garden* Jan. 39/2 This sunny family room has one wall of glass looking out to the plant-hung pergola and patio and the lush small garden.

2. (Earlier and later examples.) So *patio process*.

1845 *Chem. Gaz.* 1 Sept. 373 The preparation of magistral, an indispensable agent in the amalgamation by *patio*. **1856** *Hutching's Mag.* Sept. 104/1 The ore deposited on the *patio*, another set of laborers engage in separating the large lumps and reducing them to the size of common paving stones. **1863** *Proc. Calif. Acad. Nat. Sci.* II. 133 No experiments have been made in working this ore by the *patio* or Spanish-American amalgamation process. **1867** J. A. PHILIPS *Mining & Metall. Gold & Silver* xvi. 334 At the hacienda of Regla..the patio, comprising an area an acre and a half in extent, is carefully covered with a wooden floor. **1896** C. H. SHINN *Story of Mine* 82 He treated them [*sc.* silver sulphurets] with the chemicals of the *patio* process. **1913** *Trans. Inst. Mining & Metallurgy* XXII. 661 The ore is received in the 'patio' or yard adjoining the mill, where it is weighed. **1974** *Encycl. Brit. Micropædia* VII. 664/1 The patio, or Mexican, process of separating silver from the ore by amalgamation with quicksilver was perfected in Pachuca by Bartolomé de Medina in the 16th century.

3. *attrib.* and *Comb.*, as *patio block, furniture, garden, model, stand*; **patio door**, a large, glass, sliding door leading to a garden or balcony.

1973 *Houston* (Texas) *Chron. Mag. People, Places, Pleasures* 14 Oct. 3 (Advt.), 7½″×16″ concrete patio blocks. **1979** *Sci. Amer.* Apr. 110/2 The concrete slabs were 'patio blocks' that weigh 6·5 kilograms and were 40 centimeters long, 19 centimeters wide and four centimeters thick. **1973** *Daily Tel.* 10 July 15/1 Usually the patio door is a replacement for the rather clumsy French doors which were put in by the thousand between the wars... The new sliding patio doors are vastly superior. A complete wall of glass, they can be five feet wide or even extend, with several panels, up to 24ft wide. Usually they are around 7ft high. *Ibid.* 21 July 3 (Advt.), We are Patio Door specialists. **1975** *Oxford Jrnl.* 31 Jan. 9 (Advt.), Add a new dimension to your living. With patio doors that slide open at a touch on warm summer days and close snugly to seal out the rain and draughts of winter. Their slim aluminium frames won't warp or need painting. **1976** *Homes & Gardens* July 116/2 Although patio doors are becoming an increasingly popular feature in houses, as yet there is no safety legislation governing their manufacture. **1969** *Sears Catal.* Spring/Summer 9 Moderately priced all-wood patio furniture. **1973** C. WILLIAMS *Man on Leash* (1974) i. 5 The standard small swimming pool and sundeck with patio furniture and umbrellas. **1912** J. LONDON *Let.* 18 Jan. (1966) 360, I should like to see a novel of mine come out from the presses back of the patio garden. **1976** *Outdoor Living* (N.Z.) I. II. 44 For the patio garden in the ideal location on the sunny side of the house the list of plants is unending. **1969** *Sears Catal.* Spring/Summer 13 Patio model [gas-fired grill] with its own 18-inch diameter mounting base. *Ibid.* Barbecue on patio stand.

patisserie. Add: Also **pâtisserie.** (Further examples.)

1802 [see *CONFITURE]. **1912** R. K. WOOD *Tourist's Russia* ii. 34 All the larger cities have good patisserie shops where afternoon tea is served à la Russe. **1960** E. DAVID *French Provincial Cooking* 434 Elaborate *pâtisserie* and confectionery require practical experience and knowledge of an art quite distinct from that of normal household cookery. **1974** *Times* 25 Feb. 8/7 She gives a Viennese tea concert, at which the audience..claps with fingers sticky from the patisserie. **1976** *Times* 1 June 6/2 For patisseries we can recommend Toutaubeurre.

b. A shop which sells *pâtisserie*; a pastry-cook's.

[**1884** F. E. A. GASC *Dict. French & Eng. Lang.* (ed. 3) 410/2 *Pâtisserie*,..pastry; pastry-work *or* making *or* business; biscuit-baking *or* bakery.] **1903** F. B. SMITH *How Paris amuses Itself* ii. 48 One of the most doleful sights I have seen in Paris was a sad-looking gentleman in black sitting at a cold marble-topped table of an expensive *patisserie* lunching on a weak cup of tea and a plate of cream-puffs. **1927** E. BOWEN *Hotel* xv. 181 Will you come to tea with me and Victor at the Pâtisserie? **1930** *Chambers's Jrnl.* 15 Nov. 800/1 'Let's go and get tea at a café.' The idea found instant acceptance; three or four hundred yards from the hotel we found a good *pâtisserie* and we were soon..drinking excellent tea. **1949** A. WILSON *Wrong Set* 161 It was so cool inside the patisserie that Jeremy would gladly have stayed on there for ever. **1966** A. CHRISTIE *Third Girl* i. 5 A brioche..from the fourth shop he had tried. It was a Danish *patisserie* but infinitely superior to the so-called French one near by. **1975** N. LUARD *Robespierre Serial* ii. 6 The patisserie at the corner of the Rue Vaumar.

‖ **pâtissier, patissier** (pati·sie). [Fr.] One who makes *pâtisserie*; a pastry-cook.

1924 A. D. SEDGWICK *Little French Girl* IV. vi. 346 She had to buy a *baba-au-rhum*..and asked André to drive them across to the *pâtissier's*. **1960** E. DAVID *French Provincial Cooking* 434 A French housewife..is able to order what she requires..from that local *pâtissier* whom she knows to be most skilful and to use only the finest ingredients. **1961** A. WESKER *Kitchen* 59 *Paul.* But then I think: I should stop making pastries?... *Kevin.* Hush pâtissier! Hush! **1972** *Times* 29 July 9/3 Try the specialities of Catalan pâtissiers. **1975** *Sat. Rev.* (U.S.) 15 Nov. 50/1 Michel, the *chef de cuisine*, and André, the *pâtissier*.

Patjitanian (pædʒitā·niăn), *a. Archæol.* Also **Pajitanian.** [f. *Pajitan*, a town on the south coast of central Java + -IAN.] Of or pertaining to Pajitan or the Early Palaeolithic chopper culture discovered near there in 1935. Also *absol.*, the Patjitanian chopper industry.

[**1936** G. H. R. VON KOENIGSWALD in *Bull. Raffles Museum, Singapore* Ser. B No. 1. 52 In October, 1935, the author was travelling with Mr. M. W. F. Tweedie, Curator of the Raffles Museum, in Central Java. During this trip we discovered on the 4th of October, a new site with big stone implements of various types, including, for the first time in Java, hand-axes... The site is near Pajitan, a town on the south coast of Central Java.] **1943** H. DE TERRA in *Trans. Amer. Philos. Soc.* XXXII. 458/2 It was from the basal stratum of the 10-m. terrace that we extracted a few rolled implements of 'Patjitanian' type. *Ibid.* 459/1 My impression is that the question of the absolute age of the Patjitanian industry can be determined only when the terrace geology of the region is known. **1944** H. L. MOVIUS *Early Man & Pleistocene Stratigr. S. & E. Asia* 90/2 The Patjitanian should be placed probably in the second half of the Second Interglacial. *Ibid.* 91/1 The Patjitanian implements include many large, massive forms which have been crudely worked. **1949** K. P. OAKLEY *Man the Tool-Maker* viii. 70 No implements were found with the remains of the Java Man, *Pithecanthropus erectus*, but beds of slightly later age in Java have yielded the Patjitanian industry.., which recalls some of the artifacts of the related Pekin Man. **1964** M. W. THOMPSON tr. *Semenov's Prehist. Technol.* II. ii. 36/2 The rough hand-axes of Java (Pajitanian)..are very inexpressive stone objects. **1969** COLES & HIGGS *Archaeol. Early Man* xx. 390 A small number of Patjitanian artefacts might well be described as handaxes in African contexts. *Ibid.* 391 The stratigraphical position of the Patjitanian is not well-established, because much of this material is in a derived state in recent gravels of the

Basoka River. **1974** *Encycl. Brit. Micropædia* II. 887/1 These traditions [of stone tools] include..the Patjitanian industry, Java (associated with Java man at Sangiran and Trinil).

Pat Malone (pæt mălōᵘ·n). *Rhyming slang* (orig. and chiefly *Austral.*). = Own *a.* 3. Also *ellipt.* **pat.**

1908 Mrs. A. Gunn *We of Never-Never* xii. 146 He travels day after day and month after month, practically alone—'on me Pat Malone', he calls it. **1908** *Austral. Mag.* 1 Nov. 1251 'On my own' (by myself) became 'on my Pat Malone' and subsequently 'on my Pat' a very general expression nowadays. **1916** C. J. Dennis *Moods of Ginger Mick* 110 But, torkin' straight, the Janes 'as done their bit. I'd like to 'ug the lot, orl on me pat! **1930** *Bulletin* (Sydney) 12 Mar. 47/1 On your pat now, aren't you? When did the old man go away? **1937** E. Hill *Great Austral. Loneliness* i. 22 If I was out there on me Pat Malone for too long—. **1943** N. Marsh *Colour Scheme* ix. 156 We're dopey if we let that bloke go off on his pat. **1948** V. Palmer *Golconda* xv. 120 Perhaps if I start off [singing this duet] on my pat there's some of you will take pity and not see me left. **1952** J. Cleary *Sundowners* 276 First the missus died, then a coupla months later he went, and I was left on me pat malone. **1959** C. MacInnes *Absolute Beginners* 58 Standing there all on his Pat Malone. **1966** 'L. Lane' *ABZ of Scouse* 110 *On me tod*, by myself. An alternative phrase is *on me pat.* **1966** G. W. Turner *Eng. Lang. Austral. & N.Z.* vi. 119 *On one's pat* 'alone'.. has reached New Zealand. **1971** *Private Eye* 2 July 16 Pat malone again! Cripes I am cheesed.

Patna (pæ·tnă). The name of a district in north central Bihar, India, used *attrib.* in **Patna rice,** a small-grained rice, used principally in curries and other savoury dishes. Also *ellipt.*

1845 [see *Carolina]. **1861** Mrs. Beeton *Bk. Househ. Managem.* 473 Well wash 1 lb. of the best Patna rice. **1868** *M. Jewry Warne's Model Cookery* 75/2 One and a half pound of whole Carolina or Patna rice. **1888** Kipling *Story of Gadsbys* 48 A spattering gale of Best Patna... Throws half-a-pound of rice at G. **1902** 'Ketab' *Indian Dishes for Eng. Tables* 3 Patna rice is the best for boiling and should increase in boiling to about three times its bulk when raw. Good Patna rice has fine, rather long grains, and should be of a pale straw colour when rubbed to remove the dust. **1948** *Good Housek. Cookery Bk.* 400 For plain boiled rice, curries, risotto, and such dishes, in which the aim is to keep the grains separate, the Indian varieties of rice, such as Patna and Burma, are best. **1952** F. White *Good Eng. Food* II. vi. 145 Wash ½ lb. of Patna rice. **1960** E. David *French Provincial Cooking* 97 The long-grained rice which we call Patna is usually known in France as *riz caroline.* **1965** *Guardian* 6 Aug. 6/1 Long thin Patna for its dry separate grains to accompany curries. **1970** Simon & Howe *Dict. Gastron.* 327/1 What we call Patna rice is Patna seed type. Very little of so-called Patna rice comes from Bihar, but the name is reserved for good quality long grain rice.

patois. Add: **b*.** The folk or Creole speech of the English-speaking Caribbean (esp. Jamaica).

1934 J. Rhys *Voy. in Dark* I. vi. 83 She said something in patois and went on washing up. **1953** *Caribbean Q.* III. I. 24 The hybrid dialects of French origin which in philology come under the heading *Creole.* In Trinidad the word used to denote these dialects is *Patois.* **1970** *Caribbean Stud.* July 108 *Patois*, used by many Jamaicans in reference to Jamaican Creole. **1971** *Caribbean Q.* XVII. II. 13 Same name, different referent..patois.

patootie (pătū·ti). *U.S. slang.* [Perh. a corruption of *potato* (see quot. 1921).] A sweetheart, girl-friend; a pretty girl.

1921 *Dialect Notes* V. 110 *Patootie*,..Sweetheart. Reported from four different localities [in California]. Etymology unknown. Suggested, by sweetheart and sweet potato. **1923** G. McKnight *Eng. Words* iv. 61 In the vocabulary of modern youth, chivalry is dead... A girl.. if she is popular..is a *darb*, a *peach*,..a *sweet patootie.* **1935** *Nation* (N.Y.) 15 May 562/2 He calls the object of his affection a 'hot patootie'. **1948** Lait & Mortimer *New York: Confidential!* I. vi. 61 New Yorkers..tell their patooties how pretty they are. **1950** *Times-Herald* (Washington) 27 Jan. I. 14/3 A batch of pretty-panned patooties. **1958** P. De Vries *Mackerel Plaza* 149 You like to shake a leg with a hot patootie now and then, do you? **1977** *New Yorker* 26 Sept. 32/1 She was, successively,..the wife and/or sweet patootie of the quartet.

patrass, var. *pattress.

patri- (pæ·tri, pēⁱ·tri), used as the combining form of L. *pater* (*patr-is*) father, in words used in connection with the prominence of males and the importance of relationship on the male side in social organization. Some examples are given below as main words. Cf. also Patriarch *sb.*, Patriarchal *a.*, etc., in Dict.

‖ **patria** (pæ·triă, pēⁱ·triă). [ad. L. *patria*, fatherland.] Native country; homeland; also, heaven, as the region from which the soul is exiled while on earth and to which it longs to return.

a **1914** Joyce *Stephen Hero* (1944) xix. 64 He refused therefore to set out for any task if he had first to prejudice his success by oaths to his patria. **1919** G. B. Shaw *What I really wrote about War* (1931) 352 As all the delegations have a different patria, and every patria has moral pretensions intolerable to and incompatible with the moral pretensions of all the other patrias, patriotism has to be dropped before any discussion is possible. **1936** H. G. Wells *Anat. Frustration* iv. 46 The causes and devotions, the churches and organizations, the patrias and gangs, the family honour and the caste duty, to which the imagination of man..has clung. **1957** G. V. Smithers in *Medium Ævum* XXVI. 151 The use elsewhere of *ælþeodig(-nes)* to render *peregrinus, peregrinatio*..shows that *elþeodigra eard* here means the heavenly home (*patria*) of good Christians (*peregrini*). **1959** C. S. Lewis *Let.* 5 Nov. (1966) 289 It is just when there seems to be most of Heaven already here that I come nearest to longing for a *patria.* **1965** J. C. Pope in *Franciplegius* 182 The word *elþeodig* here is used with reference to the idea that good Christians are exiles and aliens on earth, destined to travel as *peregrini* toward their *patria* in heaven. **1977** *N.Y. Rev. Bks.* 26 May 30/3 The attachment of the creoles to what they had come to regard as their *patria*—a land of eternal spring as eulogized by local poets in baroque extravaganzas—required spiritual patrons which they could genuinely call their own.

patrial, *a.* (*sb.*) Restrict *rare* to senses in Dict. and add: **3.** *spec.* Having the right of abode in the U.K. Also as *sb.*, one who has this right.

1971 *Sunday Times* 24 Jan. 11/1 The draft Bill..lays down that a patrial basically is: 1. A person born in the UK or one of whose parents or grandparents were; 2. A naturalised citizen; 3. A former citizen of the Commonwealth already resident in Britain. **1971** *Times* 25 Feb. 4/4 Anyone who is patrial will be exempt from deportation. *Ibid.* 15/1 A new distinction is being drawn between patrials, who will be free of immigration control, and non-patrials who will require work permits. **1971** *Sunday Times* 28 Feb. 12/1 Conferring full patrial status on grandchildren of people born here has some strange implications. **1973** C. Mullard *Black Brit.* v. 62 [The 1971 Immigration Bill] created a new 'right of abode' for a certain category of Commonwealth immigrant, 'patrials'. **1973** Ld. Boyle in N. Fisher *Iain Macleod* 20 Secondly, Macleod's compassion, and his strongly felt concern for the fair treatment of individuals, extended beyond those fellow-citizens who have come to be defined as 'patrials'. **1976** *Equals* Dec. 7/5 Foreign nations and people from the old Commonwealth (excluding 'patrials' and those on working holidays) made up the remainder.

So **pa·trialism, pa·trialization.**

1971 *Sunday Times* 24 Jan. 11/2 At the end of the probationary period, the work permit holder will be able to apply for 'patrialisation'. *Ibid.*, 'Patrialism' is intended to clear it all up once and for all. **1971** *Times* 25 Feb. 4/4 Patrialism is a thin disguise for whites, albeit from the Commonwealth.

patriality (pēⁱtriæ·lĭti). [f. prec. + -ity.] Eligibility for or right to patrial status (*patrial *a.* (*sb.*) 3).

1971 *Guardian Weekly* 6 Mar. 8 In some cases, where patriality depends on ancestral connection, a certificate issued through the British High Commissioner will be needed as proof of that right. **1971** *Guardian* 9 Mar. 12/4 Mr Maudling denied that the 'patriality' concept was racialist. **1971** *Times* 19 Mar. 3 The jurists were also concerned that people arriving without work permits or certificates of patriality would be sent back to their countries of origin. **1973** *Daily Tel.* 22 Sept. 18 A woman cannot transmit United Kingdom citizenship or patriality to a man by marriage. **1974** *Ibid.* 31 Oct. 7/3 Although a passport was not essential legally to leave or re-enter the country, it had strong evidentiary value of 'patriality'. **1978** R. Maudling *Mem.* xi. 159 The solution we found was the introduction of the new concept of patriality.

patria·rchalist. [f. Patriarchal *a.* + -ist.] One who advocates or approves of a patriarchal system of society or government.

1923 *Contemp. Rev.* Oct. 450 The mutual contempt of the patriarchalist and the feminist is identical in its sources..with the mutual contempt of the 'tough' and the 'tender' races.

Patriarchist (pēⁱ·triāɹkist). [f. Patriarch *sb.* + -ist.] A supporter of the Patriarch of Constantinople against the Exarch of Bulgaria during the schism of 1872–1945. Also *attrib.*

1903, etc. [see *Exarchist]. **1903** *Daily Chron.* 23 Sept. 3/5 They [*sc.* the Vlachs] are attached to the Greek or Patriarchist party. **1907** A. Fortescue *Orthod. Eastern Ch.* IV. x. 320 The Patriarchists..stand by the Patriarch of Constantinople. **1921** *Contemp. Rev.* May 587 Bulgarian Patriarchists—*i.e.* Bulgarians who affect the Greek religion..are numbered with the Greek inhabitants. **1972** D. Dakin *Unification of Greece* ix. 129 Vatikiotis.. reported that Greek intervention would be welcomed by the Slav-speaking patriarchists. *Ibid.* xii. 160 It was precisely in those regions where the exarchist and patriarchist school populations were evenly matched that the struggle between the two Churches was fiercest.

patriate (pēⁱ·triēⁱt), *v. Canad.* [f. Re)patriate *v.*] *trans.* To bring (legislation) under the constitutional authority of an autonomous country, used with reference to laws passed on behalf of that country by its former mother-country.

1966 *Deb. Commons Canada* 28 Jan. 373/2 *Mr. T. C. Douglas* (*Burnaby-Coquitlam*):..would the Prime Minister care to indicate to the house what action the government now proposes to take with a view to having a constitution in Canada amendable by Canadians? *Right Hon. L. B. Pearson* (*Prime Minister*):..we intend to do everything we can to have the constitution of Canada repatriated, or patriated. **1976** *Daily Gleaner* (Fredericton, New Brunswick) 12 Apr. 3 (*heading*) Trudeau wants serious bid to patriate constitution. *Ibid.*, He set out three possible ways of patriating the constitution, the British North America Act. **1978** *Globe & Mail* (Toronto) 2 Jan. 10/3 These things 10 years ago were..almost academic exercises and when Victoria failed nobody saw it as a.. tragedy—so Trudeau didn't succeed in patriating the constitution.

Hence **patria·tion,** the act or process of patriating; also *attrib.*

1976 *Globe & Mail* (Toronto) 20 Apr. 6/2 Haven't there been hundreds of spontaneous demonstrations across the country in support of unilateral patriation of the constitution? *Ibid.* 16 Aug. 5/6 The talks will be the most extensive on patriation of the BNA Act since the inconclusive Victoria conference in 1971. **1976** *Daily Colonist* (Victoria, B.C.) 3 Oct. 1/7 (*heading*) Patriation formula. **1978** *Globe & Mail* (Toronto) 13 Feb. 7/5 Mr. Ryan urged Premier Robert Bourassa to take a firm stand, and to refuse any patriation of Canada's constitution.

Patrician, *a.*[2] Delete *rare* and add earlier and later examples.

1872 A. T. de Vere *Legends St. Patrick* p. x, In the legends of the Patrician Cycle the chief-loving old Bard is ever mournful. **1932** *Universe* 26 Feb. 3/2 The Patrician sites in Co. Down. **1933** *Clergy Rev.* May 382 A normal development of the Patrician system of organization. **1950** *Month* May 379 Five chapters..with an introduction on Patrician scholarship past and present. **1963** *Times Lit. Suppl.* 19 Apr. 264/2 The Patrician controversy.

patricentric (pætrise·ntrik), *a.* [f. *patri- + Centric *a.*] Emphasizing, organized around, or dominated by the father or male line.

1949 R. K. Merton *Social Theory* viii. 244 Freud himself was in his patricentric character, a typical representative of a society which demands obedience. **1957** V. W. Turner *Schism & Continuity in Afr. Society* vii. 222 The patricentric family..is attached to a locality.

patri-clan (pæ·triklæn). [f. *patri- + Clan *sb.*] A patrilineal kin group or clan; also, *occas.*, the clan of the father.

1937 W. E. Lawrence in G. P. Murdock *Stud. Sci. of Society* 319 'Patri-clan' and 'matri-clan', denoting small exogamous kin-groups with patrilineal and matrilineal descent respectively, are suggested to eliminate monotonous repetition of adjectives. **1957** *Contrib. Indian Sociol.* I. 52 Incidentally, 'patri-clan' is not taken here in the sense of 'patrilineal clan', but of the father's clan. **1959** G. D. Mitchell *Sociol.* iv. 69 The Tallensi seem to make a distinction between offences committed by a man with a member of the same patri-clan, such as with a paternal aunt, daughter, or sister,..and offences committed by a man with the wife of a member of the same patri-clan, such as the wife of a father, brother, or son. **1975** G. A. Collier *Fields in Tzotzil* iii. 61 The second, not so widely accepted by scholars, is that Mayah social structure was and is characterized by patrilocal extended families, patrilineages, and, in some cases, fully developed patriclans. **1978** *Language* LIV. 214 It seems likely that vocabulary replacement and differentiation relate to the development of the lexical encoding or indexing of other sociolinguistic variables, e.g. patri-clan affiliation.

patrilateral (pætrilæ·tĕrăl), *a.* [f. *patri- + Lateral *a.*] (See quot. 1964.)

1949 N. Fortes *Social Struct.* 70 Ashanti say..that a person can claim house-room in the house of a patrilateral kinsman. **1957** V. W. Turner *Schism & Continuity in Afr. Society* vii. 222 Kafumbu's..followers were a group of uterine siblings and their children, related to him by ties of marriage and patrilateral cross-cousinship. **1964** Gould & Kolb *Dict. Social Sci.* 486/2 *Patrilateral* is sometimes used as a synonym for *patrilineal*... It is more usual nowadays to use the term for relationships traced through the father in a matrilineal system..or for relatives on the father's side in a non-unilineal kinship system. **1969** M. Fortes *Kinship & Social Order* (1970) II. xi. 201 Patrilateral connections are, as a rule, recognized among the offspring of men whose own fathers were the sons of one man, that is, among the children of parallel cousins, but rarely beyond that stage. **1973** *Times Lit. Suppl.* 6 July 787/2 That ideal marriage partner, the father's brother's daughter... It looks well, in Kabyl society, for a man to marry his patrilateral parallel cousin.

patriline (pæ·trilәin). [f. *patri- + Line *sb.*[2] 24.] A patrilineal line of descent.

1957, etc. [see *matriline]. **1972** P. Laslett *Household & Family in Past Time* i. 18 A patriline, that is a succession of male heads of household directly descended from each other.

patrilineage (pætrili·nĭĕdʒ). [f. *patri- + *lineage 2 c.] Patrilineal lineage.

1949 J. F. Holleman *Pattern of Hera Kinship* i. 1 The relationships and their respective terminology have to be seen in the framework of patrilineages. **1955** [see *linearity]. **1957** V. W. Turner *Schism & Continuity in Afr. Society* vii. 222 A system of patrilineages..requires virilocal marriage. **1969** *Tanzania Notes & Rec.* July 10 All minor local government posts, with the exception of the necessarily localised village headmen, had been consistently awarded not only to men resident in the chief's settlement, but also only to men from his own immediate patrilineage.

patrilineal (pætrili·nĭăl), *a.* [f. *patri- + Lineal *a.*] Of, pertaining to, or recognizing kinship with and descent through the father or the male line.

1904, 1906 [see *matrilineal *a.*]. **1923** A. L. Kroeber *Anthropol.* xiii. 356 Within each area or type of culture the matrilineal tribes manifest superiority over the patrilineal tribes in a preponderance of cultural aspects. **1936** R. FIRTH *We, the Tikopia* vi. 226 In this, such aggregations differ from the ordinary *paito*..which are patrilineal kinship groups of exclusive membership. **1951** [see *MATRILINEAL *a.*]. **1957** V. W. TURNER *Schism & Continuity in Afr. Society* viii. 236 This virtual equality between family and lineage as principles of local organization is at least partially responsible for the merging of patrilineal and matrilineal kin as joint members of a single genealogical generation. **1966** *Punch* 17 Aug. 262/2 There is much good sense in a matrilineal society. One suddenly finds oneself asking if it isn't perhaps the patrilineal one which is out of date? **1974** *Encycl. Brit. Micropædia* III. 484/3 Patrilineal (or agnatic) systems, in which the relationships through the father are emphasized.

Hence **patrili·neally** *adv.*

1934 in WEBSTER. **1954** J. LAYARD in E. E. Evans-Pritchard et al. *Inst. Primitive Society* v. 55 Even in England, which is predominantly patrilineal, we now have a Queen, and though she succeeds to the throne patrilineally, her son will succeed matrilineally, through her. **1955** HOMANS & SCHNEIDER *Marriage, Authority & Final Causes* 13 The only difference is that the men of B lineage, defined either patrilineally or matrilineally [etc.].

patrilinear (pætrili·niǎɹ). [f. *PATRI- + LINEAR *a.*] = *PATRILINEAL *a.*

1913 [see *MATRILINEAR *a.*]. **1926** *Contemp. Rev.* Apr. 528 Among the Bakitara, a patrilinear people, Canon Roscoe shows that on a man's death the sister of the heir entered [etc.]. **1939** JOYCE *Finnegans Wake* 279 Pot price pon patrilinear plop. **1943** *Nature* 18 Sept. 317/2 The historic change from matrilinear to patrilinear inheritance has also led to important conflicts. **1950** [see *MATRILINEAR *a.*].

patriliny (pæ·trilini). [f. *PATRI- + LIN(E *sb.*[2] + -Y[3].] The observance of patrilineal descent and kinship.

1906 N. W. THOMAS *Kinship Organisations & Group Marriage Austral.* ii. 21 It is unnecessary to go into the complicated question of the relation of brother-inheritance to matriliny and patriliny. **1949** M. FORTES *Social Struct.* 76 Patriliny is not legally recognized. **1957** *Jrnl. R. Anthrop. Inst.* Jan. 40 If it were the only rule determining the rights of descendants we should be inclined to describe Norwegian kinship as based strongly on patriliny and primogeniture. **1965** [see *MATRILINY]. **1974** *Encycl. Brit. Micropædia* III. 484/3 Under a patriliny, a man (or woman) is linked to his (or her) sons and daughters, his sons' children, his sons' sons' children, and so on.

patrilocal (pætrilō̆u·kăl). [f. *PATRI- + LOCAL *a.*] Applied to the custom in certain social groups for a married couple to settle in the husband's home or community.

1906 N. W. THOMAS *Kinship Organisations & Group Marriage Austral.* iii. 30 When the husband removes and lives in his wife's group the marriage is *matrilocal*; if the wife removes it is *patrilocal*. **1920** *Q. Rev.* July 168 How could it be otherwise wherever..patrilocal marriage occurs in conjunction with matrilineal descent? **1949** M. FORTES *Social Struct.* 70 Households with male heads can be..'patrilocal', that is, made up of a man and his dependants by marriage and paternity. **1965** L. STONE *Crisis of Aristocracy* XI. iii. 634 To use the terminology of the sociologists, temporary patrilocal residence was the norm. **1971** *Sci. Amer.* Dec. 93/3 Marriage is patrilocal among the peoples of the Upper Congo.

Hence **patriloca·lity**, the custom of patrilocal residence; **patrilo·cally** *adv.*, in a patrilocal manner.

1949 M. GLUCKMAN in M. Fortes *Social Struct.* 146 Members of these tribes, who..usually marry patrilocally, have been migrating into central Barotseland. **1951** E. E. EVANS-PRITCHARD *Social Anthropol.* ii. 34 He [*sc.* MCLENNAN] suggested how patriliny might have developed out of matriliny through a combination of the customs of polyandry and patrilocality. **1952** M. N. SRINIVAS *Relig. & Society among Coorgs of S. India* v. 125 Men, thanks to patrilocality, are assured of continuous residence. **1969** *Language* XLV. 468 In this large household, inheritance by males followed their right to reside patrilocally.

patrimonial, *a.* Add: **1. b.** *patrimonial seas, waters*, etc., an area extending beyond territorial waters, the natural resources of which are the property of the coastal nation though ships and aircraft of other countries have freedom of passage through it.

1973 *Caribbean Contact* Jan. 12/3 One such [new] concept is that of 'patrimonial' waters which Foreign Minister Calvani [of Venezuela] defined thus: 'A coastal nation exercises rights of sovereignty over its natural resources, both renewable and non-renewable, that are found in the waters, the ocean floor and the subfloor of a zone adjacent to territorial waters'. **1973** *Nature* 14 Sept. 63/1 In essence next year's conference is intended to sort out the whole of the law of the sea, a brief that not only includes fishing and mineral and hydrocarbon rights in territorial waters, the so-called patrimonial waters, on the high seas and on the deep ocean floor, but also [etc.]. *Ibid.* 63/2 A number of developing nations took the stance..that patrimonial seas should be established that extend for 200 miles or to the outer edge of the continental shelf, whichever is the greater. **1973** *Internat. & Compar. Law Q.* XXII. IV. 668 The patrimonial sea can be briefly defined as an economic zone not more than 200 miles in breadth from the base line of the territorial sea (the limit of which shall not exceed 12 miles), where there will be freedom of navigation and overflight for the ships and aircraft of all nations, but in that zone the coastal state will have an exclusive right to all resources.

2. *Sociol.* A term used by Max Weber to designate a traditional type of social structure in which the chief or ruler maintains authority through his officials, army, etc., who are retained by him and whose loyalty is to him personally. Hence **patrimo·nialism,** a system of patrimonial authority.

1946 GERTH & MILLS tr. M. Weber in *From Max Weber* (1947) xi. 297 As a rule, this meant that princely prerogatives became *patrimonial* in nature. Patrimonialism can also develop from pure patriarchism through the disintegration of the patriarchical master's strict authority. **1947** HENDERSON & PARSONS tr. *Weber's Theory Social & Econ. Organization* iii. 318 The primary external support of patrimonial authority is a staff of slaves, coloni, or conscripted subjects, or, in order to enlist its members' self-interest.., of mercenary bodyguards and armies. **1968** E. FISCHOFF et al. tr. *Weber's Econ. & Society* I. iii. 232 Where domination is primarily traditional, even though it is exercised by virtue of the ruler's personal autonomy, it will be called *patrimonial authority*. *Ibid.*, Patrimonial authority under which the administrative staff appropriates particular powers and the corresponding economic assets. *Ibid.* III. xvi. 1366 The patrimonial structure of the Roman ruling stratum. **1968** M. ILFORD tr. *Freund's Sociol. of Max Weber* iv. 236 The old bureaucracies were essentially patrimonial in character. **1968** *World Politics* XX. 195 Patrimonial rulers..endeavour to maximize their personal control. *Ibid.*, Lately, some attempts, primarily in the field of African studies, have been made to remember the meaning of patrimonialism. **1970** H. BIENEN in Huntington & Moore *Authoritarian Politics in Mod. Society* 119 His [*sc.* Zolberg's] party-state emerges as a system where bureaucratic and patrimonial features coexist. **1974** tr. *Wertheim's Evolution & Revolution* i. 27 Weber's 'patrimonial bureaucracy', as a sub-type of a feudal political structure, comes much nearer to historical reality.

patriot, *sb.* Add: **2. d.** In the war of 1939–45, *spec.* a loyal inhabitant of a country overrun by the enemy, esp. a member of a resistance movement. Also *attrib.*

1945 *News Chron.* 7 May 1/5 The formal liberation of Denmark had begun. Actually the patriots had started it much earlier... When we landed the Danish patriots.. had the situation under complete control. In patriot cars,..we drove down streets lined with cheering Danes. **1959** *Listener* 23 Apr. 727/2 Wingate's leadership of the ill-found 'Patriot' forces [in Ethiopia] was audacious.

3. *U.S.* **Patriots' Day,** anniversary of the Battle of Lexington and Concord in the American Revolution, 19 April 1775, observed since 1894 as a legal holiday in Maine and Massachusetts.

1897 *Boston Even. Transcript* 18 Apr. 8/4 Lowell mill agents, having heard the indignant protest against the running of machinery in the mills Patriots' Day, have decided to reconsider their action. **1909** *Springfield* (Mass.) *Weekly Republ.* 22 Apr. 11 The celebration of Patriots' day, the 134th anniversary of the battles at Lexington and Concord. The day is a legal holiday in Massachusetts and Maine. **1925** *Boston Even. Transcript* 21 Apr. 10/1 Sesquicentennial of Patriots' Day passes into history. **1948** *Daily Ardmoreite* (Ardmore, Okla.) 18 Apr. 14/7 They are down to play a second game in the afternoon, since it's Patriot's day in Boston.

patrioteer (pē̆itriǒtīə·ɹ). [f. PATRIOT *sb.* + -EER.] One who makes a public display of patriotism; one whose patriotism is spurious and insincere. Also *attrib.*

1928 *Amer. Speech* III. 262 The second camp is made up of nationalists, or, if you will, of patrioteers. **1935** *Evening Sun* (Baltimore) 11 Apr. 27/2 Some British patrioteer has grown terribly excited over the possibility that Soviet arguments broadcast from Moscow may be so strong.. as to sweep the masses of Englishmen from their political moorings. **1939** *Time* 27 Feb. 9/1 By patrioteer *Time* means to describe the professional patriot, the kind of refuge-seeking scoundrel who waves a red-white-&-blue handkerchief when he should be wiping his own nose. **1941** 'FANFARLO' in *Penguin New Writing* X. 112 A patrioteer is very simply a man who will cut his country's throat to an old tune. **1954** *Manch. Guardian Weekly* 18 Feb. 9 Talking in 'patrioteer' terms. **1954** *Birmingham* (Alabama) *News* 14 Apr. 10 They are quick to detect the phony and they can distinguish a patriot from a patrioteer. **1954** D. RIESMAN *Individualism Reconsidered* III. vii. 137 Mr. MacLeish has suffered greatly from patrioteers. **1956** C. W. MILLS *Power Elite* xii. 271 The American elite have not remained as patrioteer essayists have described them to us.

patripotestal (pætripǒte·stăl), *a.* [f. *PATRI- + POTESTAL *a.*] Characterized by the exercise of authority by the father or his relatives in a family or household.

1906 N. W. THOMAS *Kinship Organisations & Group Marriage Austral.* i. 8 Three main types of family may be distinguished: (1) patripotestal, (2) matripotestal, (*a*) direct, and (*b*) indirect, in which the authority is wielded by the father, mother, and mother's relatives, in particular her brothers, respectively. **1944** H. P. FAIRCHILD *Dict. Sociol.* 215/2 *Patripotestal*, characterized by the exercise of authority, especially in the family or household, by the father or paternal grandfather. **1952** A. R. RADCLIFFE-BROWN *Struct. & Function Primitive Society* i. 22 A society may be called patriarchal when descent is patrilineal.., marriage is patrilocal.., and the family is patripotestal (i.e. the authority is in the hands of the father or his relatives). **1964** GOULD & KOLB *Dict. Social Sci.* 486/2 *Patripotestal* modes of social organization. **1972** D. DAVIES *Dict. Anthropol.* 144/1 *Patripotestal*, the holding of authority over a family by the father or his relative

patrist (pæ·trist). *Psychol.* [f. *PATR(I- + -IST.] A term applied to someone whose behaviour or attitude is influenced or dominated by the father. Also *attrib.*

1953 G. R. TAYLOR *Sex in Hist.* iv. 77 Though I am no great lover of jargon, it would be tedious to refer continually to persons who have modelled themselves on their fathers. I shall therefore speak of them as patrists. **1958** —— *Angel-Makers* xiii. 272 The patrist accepts learning in the sense of mere erudition..but deeply distrusts all original inquiry. **1958** *Sunday Times* 27 Apr. 6/3 The 'Patrists', in the shape of the commercial middle class. **1977** E. J. TRIMMER et al. *Visual Dict. Sex* (1978) xxii. 248 Male-dominated or patrist societies.. tend to a certain stern prudishness.

patroclinous (pætroklai·nəs), *a.* *Biol.* [f. Gr. πατήρ, πατρ- father + κλίν-ειν to lean + -OUS.] Resembling the male rather than the female parent in inherited characters; involving or possessing a tendency to inherit a character or characters from the male parent only. So **pa·trocliny,** patroclinous inheritance.

1913 *Jrnl. Exper. Zool.* XV. 590 For comparison I give the F_2 from normal males by sisters such as those to which I mated the patroclinous males. **1917** *Genetics* II. 247 The hybrids in these reciprocal crosses resemble the pollen parent strongly, i.e., they are strongly patroclinous. *Ibid.*, So far as the vegetative characters are concerned patrocliny can not be ascribed to either of the hybrids. **1936** *Ibid.* XXI. 592 It has also been shown that X chromosome inversion heterozygotes give rise to patroclinous males among their progeny. **1973** *Nature* 26 Oct. 439/2 Stimulated by Richard Goldschmidt's erroneous explanation of patroclinous inheritance in *Oenothera*.

patrol, *sb.* Add: **1. c.** A reconnaissance flight by military aircraft.

1917 *Flying* 19 Dec. 347/3 A low patrol over the Fleet was carried out by three Flight-Lieutenants in Sopwith machines, during which they encountered and attacked a number of hostile craft. **1957** *Economist* 7 Dec. 836/2 To guard against surprise attack, bombers flying on patrol from Britain carry hydrogen bombs.

3. b. A unit of scouts or guides consisting of from six to eight members.

1908 R. S. S. BADEN-POWELL *Scouting for Boys* 22 A troop consists of not less than three patrols... A patrol consists of six scouts. **1908** *Scout* 18 Apr. 20/2 Several patrols together can form a 'Troop' under an officer called a Scout-master. **1917** R. E. PHILIPPS *Patrol System* ii. 13 Here is the Patrol, consisting of six, seven, or eight boys. **1946** C. CHRISTIAN *Seventh Magpie* xix. 216 Her bulging haversack bumping against her, to the extreme peril of the patrol milk supply she was carrying. **1974** *Policy, Organisation & Rules of Scout Assoc.* (ed. 3) 124 The Troop is composed of Patrols, each consisting of six to eight Scouts, including the Patrol Leader and Assistant Patrol Leader. **1977** *Guider* July 315/2 Estimated publication date is 1st September 1977, so you need to tell your Patrols about it *now* and encourage them to have a money-raising effort during the school holidays.

4. *patrol-craft, system, watch*; **patrol car,** a motor car employed by the police on patrol; **patrol leader,** (*a*) the boy scout in charge of a patrol (sense *3 b); (*b*) the leader of a military patrol; **patrol officer,** a representative of the Australian government in Papua New Guinea; **patrol-wagon:** for *U.S.* read *N. Amer.*; (*a*) (earlier and later examples).

1931 *Chicago Police Problems* v. 88 Each district normally has two small patrol cars. **1951** A. MARTIENSSEN *Crime & Police* iv. 49 In the Aberdeen system, the patrol cars and the beat constables have been formed into teams. **1967** N. LUCAS *C.I.D.* vi. 70 The Information Room put out an all car call for any disengaged patrols to join in the pursuit of the stolen Rover. Five patrol cars responded to the call. **1977** 'E. MCBAIN' *Long Time no See* i. 9 A radio motor patrol car was angle-parked into the curb. **1930** *Times Lit. Suppl.* 9 May 379/2 Officers who served in the French mine-sweepers and patrol-craft during the War. **1908** *Scout* 18 Apr. 20/2 One boy is then chosen as Patrol Leader to command the patrol. **1918** E. S. FARROW *Dict. Mil. Terms* 438 Patrol leaders. **1929** E. K. WADE *Twenty-One Years of Scouting* vi. 193 Patrol leaders have taken closer command of their Patrols. **1973** *Guardian* 11 Apr. 11/4 One of my best friends used to be a patrol leader. **1977** M. JANCATH *Seatag* II. i. 63 He rifled through the files... 'Dishonourable discharge..Patrol leader Aden.' **1924** 'R. DALY' *Outpost* i. 11 'In my district,' put in Jessel amiably, 'there's a regulation that no patrol-officer shall be a married man.' **1935** *Discovery* Nov. 346/1 Local conditions fully justify the title of knights errant to the patrol officers and other members of the administration of Papua. **1964** *Mod. Encycl. Austral. & N.Z.* 790/1 Districts are divided into sub-districts in charge of an Assistant District Officer (A.D.O.), who has assistance from Patrol Officers (P.O.). **1880** A. W. TOURGÉE *Fool's Errand* II. xii. 507 The old 'patrol' system of the antebellum days..was also one of the active causes of the rapid spread of the Klan. **1966** *Listener* 20 Oct. 571/1 Baden-Powell..dreamed up the patrol system: autonomous groups of boys, whose leaders plan the troop programme together with the scoutmaster. **1887** *Courier-Jrnl.* (Louisville, Kentucky) 22 Jan. 3/5 The patrol wagon, filled with officers, was driven to the place at a breakneck speed. **1921** *Daily Colonist* (Victoria, B.C.) 5 Apr. 7/1 Dr. Tomalin was called and attended to the unfortunate man and Sergeant Blackstock and Constable Walton attended with the patrol wagon and removed him to the Jubilee Hospital. **1974** *Amer. Speech 1971* XLVI. 78 Large police van: paddy wagon, van, Black Maria, patrol wagon, patrol. **1810** *Boston* (Registry Dept.) *Records* (1904) 33rd Rep. 426 Return of the patrole watch read. **1821** *Ibid.* (1909) 39th Rep. 227 Granting permission for private patrole watches.

patrol, *v.* Add: **1.** Also, to act as patrol in an aircraft.

1940 [see *dive-bomb* vb. s.v. *DIVE *v.*].

patrolette (pătrōu·le·t). [f. PATROL(MAN + -ETTE.] A woman or girl on patrolling duty.

1960 *Oxford Times* 1 Jan. 1/7 The Oxford office of the Royal Automobile Club invites applications from Young Ladies for the duties of patrolette. **1973** *Daily Tel.* 3 Jan. 10/3 Patrolettes and radio rescue mechanics also have new gear.

patroller. Delete *rare* and add earlier and later examples.

1744 *Bristol* (Va.) *Vestry Bk.* (1898) 118 To Burwell Green for his Levy, Being a patroler, 50. **1901** B. T. WASHINGTON *Up from Slavery* 77 The 'patrollers' were bands of white men..organized largely for the purposes of regulating the conduct of the slaves at night. **1938** W. FAULKNER *Unvanquished* 18 Into this room they would be fetched to face the Patroller. **1968** [see *KETCH *v.*[2]]. **1972** R. ADAMS *Watership Down* xlix. 401 Without Campion, probably not one rabbit would have got back to Efrafa. As it was, all his skill as a patroller could not bring home half of those who had come to Watership.

patrolman. For 'Chiefly *U.S.*' read 'orig. *U.S.*' and add: **a.** (Further examples.)

1902 *Chambers's Jrnl.* Oct. 673/2 Nor is this all. He is well off, even if he never rises beyond the grade of patrolman. **1955** W. GADDIS *Recognitions* II. vii. 644 The patrolman turned his attention to his charge. **1970** P. LAURIE *Scotland Yard* iii. 70 Very occasionally a patrolman meets crime in progress. **1974** *Anderson* (S. Carolina) *Independent* 20 Apr. 1B/4 Participating in the investigation and arrests were..Patrolmen Jerry Gambrell and Jimmy McKinney of the Anderson police. **1977** 'J. FRASER' *Hearts Ease* ii. 12 The two police patrolmen were..directing traffic.

c. In general senses.

1867 J. M. CRAWFORD *Mosby* 330 [They] captured five patrolmen, from whom..they succeeded in obtaining the countersign. **1878** *Harper's Mag.* Feb. 331/2 Each patrolman will carry a beach lantern. **1900** J. LONDON *Let.* 31 Jan. (1966) 86, I was..a fish patrolman, a longshoreman, and a general sort of bay-faring adventurer. **1945** *Seafarers' Log* 22 June 6/1 The SS Prospector of the Alcoa SS Company, paid off here in an Army Base, and two Patrolmen managed to get aboard her. **1959** *Times* 14 Aug. 15/2 A beach patrolman said, [etc.]. **1965** M. SPARK *Mandelbaum Gate* iii. 69 The hill road to the Potter's Field bordered on disputed territory, and wanderers in the area were likely to be shot at by the patrolmen of either country. **1966** R. & D. MORRIS *Men & Pandas* v. 90 An exhausted zoo patrolman. **1974** *Country Life* 5 Dec. 1772/3 All AA patrolmen carry a copy.

patron, *sb.* Add: **III. 6.** (Further examples.) Also, a similar person in N. American waters.

1777 P. THICKNESSE *Year's Journey* I. viii. 59 The *Patron* of the barge..affected to shew how much skill was necessary to guide it through the main arch. **1817** J. BRADBURY *Trav. Interior Amer.* 192 Her crew consisted of five French Creoles, four of whom were oarsmen, and the fifth steered the boat, he is called the *patron.* **1849** T. T. JOHNSON *Sights in Gold Region* 12 The Creoles..were generally the patrones or captains, and the owners of the boats. **1906** [see *BOSMAN]. **1968** R. F. ADAMS *Western Words* (rev. ed.) 222/1 *Patron*, a trader's name for the head of a barge engaged in the Missouri River fur trade. In river boating, a rudder man on a mackinaw.

8. (Later examples.) Also with reference to countries other than Spain.

1973 *Times* 25 Aug. 12/4 To them a good restaurant without the patron's presence is a paradox. **1978** T. ALLBEURY *Lantern Network* iii. 46 They..sat..in the warmth of a small restaurant... The *patron* moved among his customers.

8*. *U.S.* and *Canad.* (with capital initial). A member of a political association, in full *Patrons of Husbandry* (or *Industry*), founded in the U.S.A. in 1867, or of a similar association founded in Canada in 1891, for the promotion of farming interests. Now chiefly *Hist.*

1873 *N.Y. Times* 3 July 1/2 The organization known as the Patrons of Husbandry originated in Washington in 1867, and the National Grange was organized in December of that year in this city. **1880** [see GRANGE *sb.* 5]. **1894** *Weekly Globe* (Toronto) 23 May 1 Mr John A. Leitch, the Conservative candidate for West Middlesex.. said:—'The Patron Order was originated in the Western States, and was imported into Canada by dissatisfied politicians.' **1903** J. S. WILLISON *Sir Wilfrid Laurier & Liberal Party* II. xxvi. 281 The position of the Liberals was also measurably affected by their practical alliance for the campaign of 1896 with Mr. D'Alton McCarthy and the Patrons of Industry... The Patrons were an off-shoot from the farmers' organizations of the United States, and their demands embraced simplification of the laws and machinery of government, limitation of public subsidies, protection against industrial combinations, and a tariff for revenue. **1914** W. S. WALLACE in Shortt & Doughty *Canada & its Provinces* XVII. 173 Patrons, as they were called *tout court*, were representatives of the farming class. **1932** A. BRADY *Canada* iii. 104 The new organization, known as the Patrons of Industry, succeeded in 1894 in electing sixteen of its nominees to the legislature of Ontario. **1962** *New Democrat* Oct. 3/2 In 1894 the Patrons of Industry elected 14 members to the Ontario legislature. **1963** A. S. MORTON *Kingdom of Canada* 382 The Patrons did everything the Grangers did, but they added a special emphasis on co-operation. **1977** *Canad. Hist. Rev.* LVIII. 401 McCarthy gravitated further from the Conservatives, emerging as an Independent in 1893 and an ally in all but name of the Liberals and Patrons in 1896.

patronage, *sb.* Add: **3. f.** *Rom. Antiq.* The rights and duties or position of a patron (sense 2 b).

1697 [see CLIENTSHIP]. **1885** *Encycl. Brit.* XVIII. 413/1 The patronage and the clientage were alike hereditary.

6. (sense 4) *patronage curse, -monger, polity, system*; **Patronage Secretary** (earlier examples); so *Patronage Secretaryship.*

1907 *Daily Chron.* 18 July 3/6 The patronage curse.. has received the benediction of a Liberal Government. **1968** *Economist* 28 Dec. 21/2 It seemed unquestionably right to establish the teaching profession as a separate civil service beyond the reach of politicians and patronage-mongers. **1971** P. A. ALLUM *Politics & Society Post-War Naples* (1973) iv. 98 The patronage polity has been absorbed within the parliamentary system despite the contradictions between them. **1852** DISRAELI *Lord George Bentinck* xvii. 314 Sir Robert appointed the man of the world financial secretary of the treasury..and entrusted to the student, under the usual title of patronage secretary of the treasury, the management of the house of commons. **1873** TROLLOPE *Phineas Redux* (1874) I. xvi. 127 Roby.. was at this moment Mr. Daubeny's head whip and patronage secretary. **1909** *Westm. Gaz.* 16 Sept. 9/2 When he laid down the Patronage Secretaryship he assumed the offices of Lord Privy Seal and Chancellor of the Duchy of Lancaster. **1802** *Deb. Congress U.S.* 18 Feb. (1851) 580 A variety of circumstances..gave the patronage system the preponderancy, during the first three Presidential terms of election. **1976** *National Observer* (U.S.) 24 Apr. 16/4 The patronage system in the nation's fourth-largest city remains intact, and it is expected that the power it wields will be utilized with considerable impact.

‖ **patronat** (patronā). [Fr.] An organization of industrial employers in France; French employers collectively.

1958 *Economist* 15 Nov. 616/1 There are certainly two distinct attitudes in France. One group, which includes the *patronat* or employers' federation, seems opposed to any sort of free trade area on terms possible for Britain. **1963** *Times* 13 Feb. 9/1 Against this it is argued that in 1958 the Common Market seemed to the French *patronat* a dangerous experiment, whereas now it is an established international entity. **1971** *Guardian* 15 July 16/4 We still have to decide whether the enlarged EEC will..take the place of the UK in EFTA..or whether it will insist on rules leading to tighter harmonisation... The Patronat has declared itself firmly in favour of the second solution. **1972** LD. GLADWYN *Mem.* xvii. 306, I dwelt at length on the very considerable opposition in France to the entry of the UK into the Common Market... For their part, the Patronat, having accepted the Common Market, still maintained an uncompromising opposition..to any reduction of the Common External Tariff.

patronite (pæ̆trōu·nəit). *Min.* [f. the name *Patron* (see quot. 1906) + -ITE[1].] A black, lustrous, fine-grained mixture of vanadium sulphides that occurs in Peru and is exploited as a source of vanadium.

1906 F. HEWETT in *Engin. & Mining Jrnl.* LXXXII. 385 There was discovered, on Nov. 20, 1905, in the neighborhood of Cerro de Pasco, Peru, a new material containing vanadium... The material..was taken to Señor Antenor Riza Patron, metallurgist of the Huaracucar smelter, nine miles from Cerro de Pasco... It is suggested, in appreciation of the work of the discoverer of the material, Señor Antenor Riza Patron, that it be given the name 'patronite'. **1922** *Amer. Jrnl. Sci.* CCIII. 200 The real patronite is a black mineral of fine grain and metallic luster. In polished section it is shown to consist of a very fine-grained mixture of three minerals. **1946** J. R. PARTINGTON *Gen. & Inorg. Chem.* xxi. 644 Vanadium is widely distributed, the principal ores being carnotite.., vanadinite.., and especially the impure sulphide patronite found at 17,000 ft. in the Peruvian Andes and in North Rhodesia. **1968** I. KOSTOV *Mineral.* 146 Patronite is found as graphite-like masses associated with bravoite, native sulphur, bituminous substances, quartz and other minerals in Minas Ragra in Peru.

‖ **patronne** (patrǫn). [Fr.] A woman who is the owner or the wife of the owner of a business, esp. a café, hotel, or restaurant (in quot. 1777, a barge).

1777 P. THICKNESSE *Year's Journey* I. vii. 51 Your female *Patronne*..for they are all conducted by females. **1898** W. J. LOCKE *Idols* xxiii. 324 The little inn came in sight... The buxom *patronne*..was grinding coffee. **1921** *Spectator* 9 Apr. 465/1 The *patronne* came in, and gave me a liqueur glass of rum. **1942** E. PAUL *Narrow St.* v. 40 He had found that Madame Sara, as he called his *patronne*, was one of the gentlest and most patient women alive. **1955** *Times* 8 Aug. 8/7 Madame Ribard, the patronne, had surpassed herself; an omelette aux champignons that melted in the mouth, [etc.]. **1973** P. O'DONNELL *Silver Mistress* i. 15 'What about your reputation with the patron?' 'Patronne. What will really shock Mme. Martine is giving us separate rooms.'

patronomate (pætrǫ·nǒmēit). [f. Gr. πατρονόμ(ος (f. πατήρ father + νέμειν to rule), the title of certain magistrates at Sparta + -ATE[1].] The office of a *patronomos* in Hellenistic Sparta.

1910 *Year's Work Class. Stud.* 68 The election of 'Divine Lycurgus' to the eponymous patronomate at Sparta for a series of years.

patsy (pæ·tsi), *sb. slang* (orig. *U.S.*). [Origin unknown.] A person who is ridiculed, deceived, blamed, or victimized.

1903 'H. MCHUGH' *Back to Woods* 68 I'm the Patsy, oh, maybe! **1920** ADE *Hand-Made Fables* 76 Sometimes they ask him to come back and be the Village Patsy once more. **1927** [see *BUILD-UP a]. **1953** WODEHOUSE *Performing Flea* 205 That gentle pity which the kind-hearted always feel when they regard the fellow whom Fate has called upon to be the Patsy, the Squidge or, putting it another way, the man who has been left holding the baby. **1954** J. STEINBECK *Sweet Thursday* vii. 45 She's making a patsy of you. **1960** *Analog Science Fact/Fiction* Oct. 151/1 We had to have a patsy—some one to put the blame on. **1967** *Punch* 8 Feb. 211/3 Blamey blunders about, the perfect patsy, while we watch the real sex-maniac at work. **1970** J. H. GRAY *Boy from Winnipeg* 57, I had grown somewhat more able to take care of myself and hence had ceased to be the school patsy. **1971** *Times Lit. Suppl.* 26 Nov. 1467/3 The police are what they would call 'the patsies', the focus for popular discontent. **1974** *Daily Tel.* 17 Apr. 1/8 [He] said yesterday he was not going to be turned into a scapegoat. 'Whatever happens I am not going to be the patsy in this business.' **1977** *Rolling Stone* 13 Jan. 32/2 He felt Silkwood had possibly been a pawn or a patsy. **1977** *Time* 9 May 24/1 Or would the politically inexperienced Frost prove a patsy and let Nixon filibuster with those same skillful diversions that always seemed to be the answers but never were?

patsy (pæ·tsi), *a.* *U.S. slang.* [Origin unknown.] Satisfactory, all right.

1930 *Amer. Mercury* Dec. 457/1 *Patsy*, all right. 'The mutt offices patsy and we walk into a collar.' **1935** A. J. POLLOCK *Underworld Speaks* 86/1 *Patsy*, satisfactory; O.K.; when high pressure salesmen guarantee stock purchaser not to lose and get back money invested with profit in (90) days. **1941** J. SMILEY *Hash House Lingo* 42 *Patsy*, all right. **1950** H. E. GOLDIN *Dict. Amer. Underworld Lingo* 153/1 *Patsy*, a. (Rare) All right; okay; trustworthy.

pattawalla (pa·tăwǫlă). Also **pattawala, puttiwala,** etc. [ad. Hind. *patta-wālā* one wearing a belt: see PUTTEE, WALLAH.] In India, a messenger or servant.

1878 MONIER WILLIAMS *Mod. India* 34 Here and there a belted Government servant (called a Patti-wālā, or Patta-wālā, because distinguished by a belt)—all within call—all ready to answer..to the Sahib's summons, and eager to execute his behests. **1881** E. M. GUTHRIE *Life in Western India* I. vi. 12 Behind M— stood the tall and handsome Jew, G—'s writer, and the putthawaller, with his badge of office. **1949** R. LAWRENCE *Indian Embers* 23 Pattawallas in stiff white, with scarlet belts and turbans, were salaaming deeply. **1971** A. D. GORWALA *Queen of Beauty* 79 Give me a cup of coffee too and tell your pattawalla not to come in and not to let anyone else in.

patte. Add: **3.** *patte de velours* (də vəlūr), the velvet paw (of a cat; i.e. a paw with the claws held in): used *fig.* indicative of resolution or inflexibility combined with apparent softness or gentleness. Cf. *IRON *a.* 3 c.

1853 C. BRONTË *Villette* III. xxxiii. 84 She played before me the amiable; offered me patte de velours; caressed, flattered, fawned on me. **a 1855** —— *Professor* (1857) I. xi. 185 The soft touch of a patte de velours. **1859** LYTTON *What will he do with It?* III. VII. xviii. 150, I always felt that she had the claws of a tigress under her *patte de velours*! **1881** *Atlantic Monthly* Jan. 137/2 An innocent-looking creature, with feline manners, *pattes de velours*, and such claws! **1904** P. PENNINGTON *Diary* 1 Jan. in *Woman Rice Planter* (1913) ii. 59 One is so apt to forget that the 'patte de velours' which every one uses in polite society is even more of a help in dealing with the most ignorant.

patten, *sb.* **6. patten-shoe**: delete † and add later examples.

1957 R. LISTER *Decorative Wrought Ironwork* 231 *Patten shoe*, in farriery, a shoe used for a hip-shot horse. Its underside is forged into a hollow hemisphere. **1963** *Times* 25 Feb. 1/7 Sometimes it was necessary to rest a leg that was strained, so a Patten shoe was obtained which had a raised heel to relax the back tendon of the leg while the horse was resting after muscular injury.

patter, *sb.*[1] Add: **2.** Now *spec.*, the speech of a comedian or a stage magician.

1949 *Amer. Speech* XXIV. 40 Anything he says while performing is *patter*, and he almost never says silk handkerchief, but simply calls it a *silk*. **1952** GRANVILLE *Dict. Theatr. Terms* 134 *Patter*, quick speeches uttered between their songs by music-hall comedians. **1965** G. MELLY *Owning-Up* vi. 59, I can still remember some of the abysmal patter which he delivered. **1976** *Liverpool Echo* 6 Dec. 10/5 Songs and patter formed the mainstay of his senior citizens' act which has already won awards and will doubtless claim more.

3. *patter-act*; **patter-song** (earlier and later examples).

1972 *Times* 24 June 11/3 A patter act is usually written so that the lines sometimes don't finish. **1823** C. MATHEWS *Let.* 23 Feb. in A. Mathews *Mem. Charles Mathews* (1839) III. xvii. 385 The only striking subject for a patter-song is the inordinate love of title. **1839** J. ADOLPHUS *Mem. John Bannister* I. xii. 234 It formed the precedent for what are now, in the technical slang, called 'patter songs'. **1965** *Listener* 23 Dec. 1050/2 The Barber himself a buffo bass,.. has a famous Gilbertian patter song, with compound rhyming. **1975** *Ibid.* 13 Mar. 328/3 His characters, his funny voices, his patter song.

patter, *sb.*[2] Add: freq. in phr. *the patter of little* (or *tiny*) *feet*: used to suggest the presence of young children or the expectation of the birth of a child. See PATTERING *vbl. sb.*[2] and *ppl. a.*[2] in Dict. and Suppl.

1863 LONGFELLOW *Tales of Wayside Inn* 209, I hear in the chamber above me The patter of little feet, The sound of a door that is opened, And voices soft and sweet. **1883** [in Dict.]. **1924** N. Coward *Rat Trap* III. 68 And we're to expect little clinging fingers and the patter of tiny feet. **1945** E. Bowen *Demon Lover* 66 They knew there was going to be the patter of little feet. I wasn't actually *born*..till 1918. **1966** *Guardian* 29 Dec. 14/1 At any time now, the patter of little feet is expected to indicate that Helga's dream has at last come true... Helga is a polar bear. **1972** *Daily Tel.* 8 May 12 Amen Court.. resounds with the patter of tiny feet... The Rev. Patrick Tuft, the Succentor, has become the father of triplet boys. **1977** *Times* 29 Oct. 20/1 Expectant motherhood these days is marked less by the patter of tiny feet than the tinkling of cash registers.

patter, *v.*[1] Add: **4.** Also *transf.*

1905 B. Tarkington *In Arena* 259 Between the acts the orchestra pattered ragtime and inanities from the new comic operas.

pattering, *vbl. sb.*[2] and *ppl. a.*[2] Add: Freq. with allusion to *patter *sb.*[2]

1849 Longfellow *Kavanagh* xi. 40 With these day-dreams mingled confusedly the pattering of little feet. **1884** [in Dict.]. **1903** Beerbohm *Around Theatres* (1953) 257 Napoleon may..drill a squad of small children. But ..his motive..was not a delight in pattering feet and chubby cheeks. **1955** M. Ewer *No Abiding Place* vii. 112 No pattering feet on the way? **1962** A. Lejeune *Duel in Shadows* vi. 81 All was sweetness and light,..and the pattering of tiny feet round the Christmas tree.

pattern, *sb.* Add: **2. b.** A model or design in dressmaking, *spec.* a paper pattern from which material for a garment can be cut out and sewn together.

1792 Jane Austen *Catharine* in *Wks.* (1954) VI. 207, I expect a new Cap from Town... Every Body will be longing for the pattern. **1811** —— *Sense & Sens.* I. xxi. 281 Taking patterns of some elegant new dress. **1890–1** *T. Eaton & Co. Catal.* Fall & Winter 52/1 Ours is the only store in Toronto where you can get Butterick's dress patterns. *Ibid.* 52/2 By means of a system invented..by the Buttericks, each pattern is graded to suit every size in which it is furnished. **1911** O. Onions *Widdershins* 183 A mass of tissue-paper patterns and buckram linings. **1964** *McCall's Sewing* ii. 15 Without patterns, home-sewing would probably be a lost art... Not every pattern style will look equally well on everyone. **1974** D. Kyle *Raft of Swords* vi. 60 The women sew mini-dresses from McCall patterns.

8. c. *fig.* An arrangement or order of things or activity in abstract senses; order or form discernible in things, actions, ideas, situations, etc. Freq. with *of*, as *pattern of behaviour* = *behaviour pattern* (see *behaviour 6), and as second element with defining word.

1901 G. B. Shaw *Admirable Bashville* II. i. 309 Fates That weave my thread of life in ruder patterns Than these. **1906** C. S. Sherrington *Integrative Action Nervous Syst.* v. 176 (*caption*) The cutaneous fields of the 'scratch-reflex', the 'flexion-reflex', the 'extensor-thrust', are areas which in nowise fit in with the pattern of the cutaneous fields of the afferent spinal roots. **1915** V. Woolf *Voyage Out* xxii. 366 According to him, too, there was an order, a pattern which made life reasonable, or, if that word was foolish, made it of deep interest anyhow, for sometimes it seemed possible to understand why things happened as they did. *Ibid.* xxiv. 385 Perhaps, then, everyone really knew as she knew now where they were going; and things formed themselves into a pattern not only for her, but for them, and in that pattern lay satisfaction and meaning. **1922** Joyce *Ulysses* 562 Arabesquing wearily, they weave a pattern on the floor. **1927** E. O'Neill *Marco Millions* III. 152 The young boys and girls take up their censers and dance their pattern out backward, preceded by the musicians. **1933** H. G. Wells *Shape of Things to Come* III. §6. 301 Old habits of thought, old values, old patterns of conduct. **1933** T. S. Eliot *Use of Poetry* 88 There is something integral about such greatness, and something significant in his place in the pattern of history. **1936** *Nature* 18 Jan. 87/2 In these sections..there are interesting analyses..of the technological and economic patterns observable in material culture. **1936** A. Huxley *Olive Tree* 290 Our habits are not those of the Romans, Greeks and Hebrews... Patterns of behaviour change. **1937** —— *Ends & Means* iii. 22 Every culture is full of arbitrary and fortuitous associations of behaviour-patterns, thought-patterns, feeling-patterns. *Ibid.* 23 Thought-patterns, feeling-patterns and action-patterns..have seemed in their time inevitable and natural. **1945** T. S. Eliot *What is a Classic?* 32 Each literature has its greatness, not in isolation, but because of its place in a larger pattern, a pattern set in Rome. **1951** J. M. Fraser *Psychol.* III. xx. 236 Different patterns of relationships will develop according to what kind of task the group happens to be engaged in. **1956** A. C. Guyton *Textbk. Med. Physiol.* xlvii. 591 Sensory impulses from the eyes, the ears, the proprioceptors, etc.,..assess whether or not the nail is being hammered and, if not, change the pattern of movement so that it will be hammered. **1956** *B.B.C. Handbk. 1957* 115 Reference has already been made..to the pattern of viewing by those having sets equipped for both BBC and ITA programmes. **1958** *Spectator* 30 May 692/1 A study..of the patterns of marriage. **1958** *Listener* 12 June 964/1 How the railways ought to behave in fixing the pattern of their charges. **1958** *Spectator* 8 Aug. 204/1 The pattern of supply is constantly changing. **1959** H. Gardner *Business of Crit.* II. iii. 148 Both a study of the patterns of images, and their part in the structure of a poem, and the knowledge of ideas, theories, and beliefs current in a period are of great value as tools in an interpreter's hands. **1968** P. B. Weiz *Elem. Zool.* viii. 123/2 A given external stimulus usually leads to the completion of several or many simultaneous reflex responses, all occurring as a single, integrated pattern of activity. **1976** *Sci. Amer.* Jan. 96/2 The limited evidence on other mammals suggests a different pattern of evolution.

d. *Linguistics.* A discernible order or arrangement in some branch of language, esp. in phonology.

1921 E. Sapir *Language* iii. 56 Every language, then, is characterized as much by its ideal system of sounds and by the underlying phonetic pattern (system, one might term it, of symbolic atoms) as by a definite grammatical structure. **1926** *Germanic Rev.* I. I. 49 The Indo-European consonant pattern differed radically from that of Sanskrit. **1933** L. Bloomfield *Language* 136 The structural pattern leads us to recognize also compound phonemes. **1935** G. K. Zipf *Psycho-Biol. of Lang.* v. 195 The only difference between a *pattern* and a *configuration* is that the former is the more generic and collective term. One infers the nature of speech-patterns from the exemplifications of the patterns, i.e. the configurations of speech-elements. **1951** *Language* XXVII. 295 This explicit talk about the fact of patterning makes possible the distinction between the grammar (specific pattern) and grammaticalness (degree of patterning) of language. **1960** *Language Learning* X. I. 59 No two languages have the same set of patterns of pronunciation, words, and syntax. **1963** C. Fries *Linguistics & Reading* ii. 67 The habits of pronunciation that the child develops in learning his native language are not habits of producing and hearing the separate sounds as isolatable items in individual words but rather habits of patterns of functioning contrasts in the unique structured system of a particular language. **1968** Chomsky & Halle (*title*) The sound pattern of English. **1972** M. L. Samuels *Linguistic Evol.* xiii. 160 Noticeable in the Middle and Early Modern periods is the start of a new pattern of quantitative gradation in the verb.

e. *Physiol.* A particular sequence or arrangement of nerve impulses, in time and space, that is correlated with a particular sensation.

1947 W. E. Le Gros Clark *Anat. Pattern* 7 The multiple nerve fibres approach the spot from different directions through the cutaneous nerve plexus, so that stimulation of a sensory spot gives rise to nerve impulses which reach the central nervous system by different routes, and thus lead to some specific pattern of excitation there. **1955** *Brain* LXXVIII. 586 There has been a revulsion from the ..idea of the nervous system as a telephone exchange, and this has found one expression in the suggestion that a specific cutaneous sensation results when the brain receives from the skin impulses which make up a characteristic pattern. **1961** T. L. Peele *Neuroanat. Basis Clin. Neurol.* (ed. 2) xix. 448 A 'touch' pattern requires more large fibers than a 'pain' pattern. **1969** Melzack & Wall in K. H. Pribram *Brain & Behav.* II. 145 The pattern theory proposed by Weddell and Sinclair, then, fails as a satisfactory theory of pain. **1975** —— in M. Weisenberg *Pain* i. 12/1 There can no longer be any doubt that temporal and spatial patterns of nerve impulses provide the basis of our sensory perceptions.

11. (Earlier and later examples.)

1859 'Stonehenge' *Shot-Gun and Sporting-Rifle* I. ii. 14 So much depends on the pattern made at thirty and forty yards by the gun intended to be used. *Ibid.* III. i. 175 A gun can only be made to combine a certain amount of strength with regularity of pattern. *Ibid.* 176 They shall give such a pattern on the target as will prevent the escape of a partridge or grouse. **1961** C. Willock *Death in Covert* ii. 34 Pattern..is the spread of the shot. **1972** *Shooting Times & Country Mag.* 1 July 14/2 The more the manufacture of shotgun ammunition is influenced by the needs of competitive clay pigeon shooting, the more it will repay game and pigeon shooters to check that they are not getting unduly close patterns. **1976** *Shooting Mag.* Dec. 52/2 A new game cartridge,..features the exclusive Monowad, claimed by the manufacturers to deliver up to 10 per cent more pellets inside the pattern.

13. b. *pattern discrimination, -quality, recognition*; **pattern baldness,** baldness in which there is a gradual loss of hair in accordance with a characteristic pattern, as in the receding hair-line that commonly occurs in men as they grow older; **pattern body** *rare*, a dress pattern taken from an existing dress; **pattern-bomb** *v.*, to bomb a target from aircraft according to a prescribed pattern in order to obtain maximum effect; so **pattern-bombing** *vbl. sb.*; **pattern book** (*a*) (earlier and later examples); also *transf.* and *fig.*; **pattern card** (earlier and later examples); also *fig.*; **pattern congruity** *Linguistics*, conformity to the structure of a language, esp. the phonological structure; **pattern darning,** a type of embroidery in which darning stitches are used to form a design, freq. as a geometric background; also *pattern darn*; **pattern-maker,** (*b*) (earlier example); **pattern-making** (further examples); **pattern-paper,** the paper from which a pattern (sense *2 b) is made; **pattern practice,** in learning a foreign language, intensive repetition of its distinctive constructions and patterns; **pattern setter** (*b*), anyone or anything that establishes a pattern or precedent; so *pattern-setting* adj.; **pattern shop** (examples); **pattern variable** *Sociol.*, a term used by Talcott Parsons in his attempt to define social action as the choice between five main dichotomous patterns of behaviour; also *attrib.*; **pattern-welding,** a technique used by the Anglo-Saxons for forging sword blades; also, a piece of pattern-welded metal; so **pattern-welded** *a.*

1916 *Jrnl. Heredity* VII. 349/2 Congenital baldness must not be confused with pattern baldness. **1956** C. Auerbach *Genetics in Atomic Age* 16 The so-called pattern-baldness of men is due to a mutated gene which acts most effectively on the background of a male constitution. **1974** *Jrnl. Clin. Endocrinol. & Metabolism* XXXIX. 1012/1 Androgens may paradoxically cause male pattern baldness in individuals with a genetic predisposition. **1819** M. Edgeworth *Let.* 28 Jan. (1971) 165 The gown..is made by the very best dressmaker in Paris by a pattern body which I got my dear Fan to take from a gown of yours. **1943** *Jane's All World's Aircraft* 23a/1 The air targets could be pattern-bombed so that a bomb fell in every area of 50 square yards. **1944** *Britannica Bk. of Year* 770/1 *Pattern-bomb*,..to bomb, from a number of aircraft, in such a way that the relative position of the craft determines the 'pattern' of the bombs when they strike, so as to cover the target in a desired manner. **1947** *Sun* (Baltimore) 29 Mar. 2/2 Sending a fleet of jetpropelled planes from the Kurile islands (north of Japan) to pattern-bomb all of America. **1940** *War Illustr.* 5 Jan. 555 (*caption*) Wellingtons preparing for 'pattern bombing'. **1941** E. C. Shepherd *Mil. Aeroplane* 4 Anti-aircraft fire can..break up the formations so that mass bombing or pattern bombing becomes impossible. **1948** E. Waugh *Loved One* 78 You couldn't really get away from the war even there. The ladies didn't seem to have a mind for anything higher than pattern-bombing. **1973** *Times* 6 June 19/5 It was subjected to air bombardment..by a process of deliberate and sustained 'pattern bombing' which wiped out the little town. **1774** N. Cresswell *Jrnl.* 7 Apr. (1925) 9 Spent the evening with Mr. Longsdon, who gave me a pattern Book and desires me to do some business for him. **1821** P. Egan *Real Life in London* I. vi. 91 And was followed by a servant with pattern-books, the other apparatus of his trade. **1846** [see *East-end]. **1950** E. H. Gombrich *Story of Art* x. 141 It was in the thirteenth century that artists did occasionally abandon their pattern book altogether. **1959** *Times* 5 Nov. 15/2 Mr. Busch knows his job..but his people are pattern-book and never suprise. **1978** Cadogan & Craig *Women & Children First* viii. 165 Lorna moves in a world of Women's Institute whist-drives..and Weldon's pattern books. **1773** J. Wedgwood *Let.* 21 Nov. (1965) 155 Voyer's Seals are sad trash, but Boden & Smiths were mounting half a Groce of them..to be sent..as Pattern Cards. **1821** P. Egan *Life in London* II. i. 136 Mr. Primefit, of Regent-street, was..ordered to attend upon Mr. Hawthorn, with his pattern-card, to take orders. **1881** [see *beveller]. **1970** G. Heyer *Charity Girl* i. 17, I shall attend Hetta's wedding... I daresay Hetta will be better off with her pattern-card. **1934** *Language* X. 124 The criterion of pattern congruity. Particular formulations must be congruous with the general phonemic pattern of the given language. **1941** *Ibid.* XVII. 229 That /č, ǰ, š, ž/ are unit phonemes appears partly from their distribution.., partly from their behavior in clusters... There may be some dialects in which they can be analyzed as /tj, dj, sj, zj/ respectively, but considerations of pattern congruity make this unlikely. **1964** E. Bach *Introd. Transformational Gram.* viii. 178 It seems natural to identify simplicity with the number of symbol tokens.. in the grammar. We would exclude from our count symbols of metatheory..and count as single symbols..the primes of the various parts of the grammar. This consideration seems to underlie many statements about 'pattern congruity' and the like. **1906** Mrs. A. H. Christie *Embroidery & Tapestry Weaving* ix. 197 The second kind is called pattern darning; in it the stitches are picked up in some regular order, so that they form various geometrical patterns over the surface. *Ibid.* 199 Samplers ..may be seen entirely filled with these pattern darns. **1915** M. Symonds *Elem. Embroidery* xii. 138 Pattern darning is also used for backgrounds, in which cases the linen..should be strong but not woven too closely. **1932** D. C. Minter *Mod. Needlecraft* 14/1 Pattern darning.. consists of the regular picking up of threads in such a way as to cover a background of a design with a pattern. **1967** E. Short *Embroidery & Fabric Collage* i. 34 Bead embroidery must give a raised texture, shadow work or pattern darning a relatively smooth surface. **1951** S. S. Stevens *Handbk. Exper. Psychol.* xx. 764/2 So far we have dealt only with pattern discriminations: the capacity to tell the difference between a triangle and a circle or between an upright triangle and an inverted triangle, and so on. **1851** C. Cist *Sk. Cincinnati in 1851* xv. 297 He engaged in the foundry..as pattern-maker. **1934** C. Lambert *Music Ho!* III. 143 We must not think, however, that the modified internationalism of the eighteenth century is any more a permanent and integral part of musical tradition than the objective pattern-making of the period. **1937** H. Read *Art & Society* i. 23 But from the normal point of view we have to explain..the almost complete atrophy of the artistic impulse in man—at least the disappearance of the individual work of art in an undifferentiated mass of pattern-making as monotonous as the standardized products of our own machine age. **1926** J. Masefield *Odtaa* iii. 59 She picked up some pattern-paper..snipped it with scissors..and then shook it out as a sort of cape or shawl of lace. **1944** C. Fries *Intensive Course in Eng. for Latin-Amer. Students* VI. 1 A..class hour is given to the 'pattern practice' and drill. *Ibid.* 2 (*heading*) Pattern practice in conversation. **1948** *Language Learning* I. I. 27 This type of completely oral pattern practice approximates the language activity involved in free conversation while..it provides the concentrated practice of simple imitation. **1960** N. Brooks *Language & Lang. Learning* iv. 49 Pattern practice, which opens the door to analogy, may be called the antithesis of paraphrasing. **1932** H. H. Price *Perception* viii. 243 AB.. is a *sensible* complex... It means also that the complex AB has a certain characteristic which we may call *sensible pattern-quality*. **1938** R. G. Collingwood *Princ. Art* x. 233 A new pattern-quality emerging from a particular way of combining psychical experiences. **1976** *Shooting Times & Country Mag.* 16–22 Dec. 14/2 It is not a high-velocity cartridge: a type which, in certain guns, so often gives hostages to fortune in the shape of pattern quality, so vital for satisfactory full-range work. **1959** *Proc. Eastern Joint Computer Conf.* 225/1 These approaches prove..to center upon analysis of the specific characteristics of patterns into parts, followed by a synthesis of the whole from the parts. In these studies, pattern recognition of the whole, that is, Gestalt recognition, was chosen as a more fruitful avenue of approach. **1964** J. Z. Young *Model of Brain* xix. 312 There is every reason to think that similar arrangements are an essential part of the pattern-recognition systems of the brain. **1970** O. Dopping *Computers & Data Processing* xi. 173 Automatic recognition of characters is a special case of a more general problem, called pattern recognition. **1974** W. R. Adey et al. *Brain Mechanisms & Control of Behav.* xi. 474 There has been a very earnest search for computer methods of pattern recognition. **1976** *Gloss. Documentation Terms* (*B.S.I.*) 47 *Pattern recognition*, machine-sensing or identification of visible patterns. **1899** W. James *Talks to Teachers* 213 We, here in America, through following a succession of pattern-setters whom it is now impossible to trace,..have at last settled down collectively into what, for better or worse, is our own characteristic national type. **1902** —— *Var. Relig. Exper.* i. 6 It would profit us little to study this second-hand religious life. We must make search rather for the original experiences which were the pattern-setters to all this mass of suggested feeling and imitated conduct. **1973** *Tucson* (Arizona) *Daily Citizen* 22 Aug. 2 The UAW has made good use of the 'strike target' strategy it dreamed up in 1955 to put added pressure on one auto company to agree to a pattern-setting contract. **1878** *Harper's Mag.* Apr. 648/1 Here is the great hall of the pattern shop fragrant with new wood. **1916** 'Taffrail' *Pincher Martin* xiv. 256 Before joining the destroyer he had been at the College at Dartmouth, teaching the naval cadets their business in the pattern-shop. **1964** S. Crawford *Basic Engin. Processes* (1969) x. 234 A finished component drawing is sent to the pattern shop providing all essential information. **1951** Parsons & Shils *Toward Gen. Theory Action* ii. 48 The pattern-variable scheme defines a set of five dichotomies. Any course by any actor involves (according to theory) a pattern of choices with respect to these five sets of alternatives. **1959** D. Martindale in L. Gross *Symposium Sociol. Theory* ii. ii. 76 In explaining this surprise, Parsons is led to assign importance to all sorts of factors not even mentioned in his set of pattern variables. **1964** I. L. Horowitz *New Sociol.* 15 The long trek from an action context to a paradigm for describing all types of action in a four-part pattern variable is no better..than Hegel..ending with..the perfect equation of Reason equating itself. **1948** H. Maryon in *Proc. Cambr. Antiquarian Soc.* XLI. 76 The welding of these swords represents an excessively difficult operation. I do not know of finer smith's work... I have named the technique 'pattern welding'... Examples of pattern-welding range in date from the third century to the Viking Age. **1956** *Nature* 29 Dec. 1432/2 (*caption*) Modern pattern-welded sword: experiment No. 7. *Ibid.*, Welding also came to be used successfully..in delicate work, involving the 'piling' of many sheets into a composite laminate, and developing into pattern-welding. *Ibid.* 1433/1 Most pattern-welded swords are so corroded that..[metallographic study] is not possible. **1962** H. R. E. Davidson *Sword in Anglo-Saxon England* i. 25 The ninth-century sword from the Palace of Westminster..had a pattern-welded blade. *Ibid.* 29 A means of re-using old strips of pattern-welding from worn swords to make a new blade. *Ibid.* 30 Short swords made by the pattern-welded technique. *Ibid.* 32 By the ninth century the art of pattern-welding was on the decline. **1964** H. Hodges *Artifacts* v. 88 In this process, known as pattern welding, case-hardened bars of iron were piled or faggotted white hot and forged. **1975** *Anglo-Saxon England* IV. 179 The technique of pattern-welding died out during the tenth and eleventh centuries.

pattern, *v.* Add: **6.** Also const. *after*, to take (someone or something) as a model or example (*absol.* use of sense 2), *U.S.* Now *rare.*

1878 J. H. Beadle *Western Wilds* xxii. 356 That was a nice family for us Americans to pattern after, wasn't it? **1884** 'C. E. Craddock' *In Tennessee Mts.* i. 4 They dunno what he patterned arter.

7. b. To order or arrange (a number of things) into a pattern; to design or organize (something) for a specific purpose. Also *intr.*, to form or cast a pattern (*rare*).

1931 W. Stevens *Harmonium* 133 A pale silver patterned on the deck And made one think of porcelain chocolate And pied umbrellas. **1967** *Boston Sunday Herald* 14 May ii. 13/2 (Advt.), The s.s. Rotterdam.. patterned for epicures,..art connoisseurs, and other bon vivants. **1967** *Times Rev. Industry* July 89/1 Organisations tend to be patterned for a variety of reasons. **1971** J. Z. Young *Introd. Study Man* iii. 47 The essence of the operation that we call coding is that events patterned in one medium are made to correspond to events patterned in another. **1972** *Where* Feb. 40/1 The borders of the new jigsaw are becoming clear, even if we haven't found and patterned all the pieces yet. **1977** *Sci. Amer.* Sept. 124/3 The uppermost layers of integrated circuits are formed by depositing and patterning thin films.

c. *intr. Linguistics.* To make, fall into, or form part of a pattern (*pattern *sb.* 8 d).

1942 *Amer. Speech* XVII. 147 They pattern congruently with the similarly distributed varieties of /p/ and /k/. **1951** Trager & Smith *Outl. Eng. Struct.* ii. 53 The distributional gaps are often found to pattern as if they were themselves partials with phonemic content. **1963** *Amer. Speech* XXXVIII. 53 Most natural languages, including English, do not pattern on the finite-state model, which cannot handle certain regular processes of sentence formation. **1965** *Word Study* Feb. 7/2 We should distinguish between prepositions (which always have an object, occasionally elliptical) and verbal particles (which pattern with transitive and intransitive verbs alike). **1971** D. Crystal *Linguistics* 89 The way words pattern in sequences to form sentences.

patternation (pætəɹnēⁱ·ʃən). [f. Pattern *sb.* + -ation.] The fact or action of forming, or conforming to, a pattern; *spec.* non-uniformity in the distribution of spray from a jet.

1946 M. Peake *Titus Groan* 399 Her hips..swayed when she talked.., they did all but chime as her sharp, unpleasant voice..dictated their figure-of-eight (bird's-eye view, cross-section) patternations. **1947** *Shell Aviation News* No. 110 21/3 Atomizers may, in some cases, be subjected to radical distribution tests, a specialized species of patternation with the main object of measuring the variation of spray density at different radial distances from the spray axis. **1949** *Jrnl. R. Aeronaut. Soc.* LIII. 161/1 The use of specialised atomising jets with their accompanying troubles of penetration and patternation is avoided. **1955** *Jrnl. Brit. Interplanetary Soc.* XIV. 218 By this time patternation tests were carried out [on a combustion chamber injector] as well as calibrations.

patterned, *ppl. a.* Add: **a.** (Further examples.) Also, conforming with, or forming, an arrangement or pattern.

1930 E. Pound *XXX Cantos* v. 19 Ecbatan, City of patterned streets. **1961** *Lancet* 29 July 259/2 The release from patterned behaviour forced the choice between good and evil. **1964** Gould & Kolb *Dict. Social Sci.* 480/2 These..represent potentialities for the most varied outcomes, yet outcomes extremely patterned culturally. **1967** E. Short *Embroidery & Fabric Collage* iii. 64 When wall papers, patterned fabrics and carpets are used any embroidery must be more carefully considered to avoid a 'messy' effect. **1970** G. A. & A. G. Theodorson *Mod. Dict. Sociol.* 293 *Patterned evasion*, a regularised way of deviating from an established social norm. **1973** *Technical Translation Bull.* XIX. 103 *Patterned glass* is the name used where the patterns are distinctive and fancy, e.g. Arctic, Hammered, Moroccan (traditional patterns still going strong) or modern types such as 'Mersey' or 'Manhattan'. **1973** J. M. White *Garden Game* 64 A bright flower-patterned cretonne. **1977** *Jersey Even. Post* 26 July 10/1 Her bridesmaid..wore a long, tiered empire-line voile dress, made of a yellow and red floral patterned material.

b. *patterned ground* (Physical Geogr.): ground showing a definite pattern of stones, fissures, vegetation, etc. (commonly polygons, rings, or stripes), such as is typical of periglacial regions.

1950 A. L. Washburn in *Revue Canad. de Géogr.* IV. 8 The terms *Rutmark, Strukturboden..stone polygons, mud circles, soil circles, mud polygons, soil polygons, fissure polygons, tundra polygons, stone stripes, soil stripes, solifluction stripes* and others have all been used to describe features here collectively named *patterned ground* for want of a satisfactory collective term in English... The writer would restrict the use of *patterned ground* to more or less symmetrical features. **1956** *Bull. Geol. Soc. Amer.* LXVII. 846/1 Frost wedging in bedrock is capable of developing several varieties of patterned ground, all intimately associated with bedrock structure. **1973** *Nature Physical Sci.* 4 June 85/2 This mechanism creates the *gilgai* of clay-rich and commonly alluvial soils in many hot sub-humid to semi-arid regions of the world. These structures are forms of patterned ground, having a surface expression as roughly polygonal to rectilinear-parallel systems of low ridges between hollows.

patterning, *vbl. sb.* Add: Also, the fact or process of forming (part of) an abstract pattern, as of behaviour, speech, etc. (Further examples.)

1921 E. Sapir *Language* iv. 61 It also has a definite feeling for patterning on the level of grammatical formation. **1937** B. L. Whorf in *Language* (1945) XXI. 1 This view loses sight of various word-classes that are marked not by morphemic tags but by types of patterning. **1939** J. Dollard et al. *Frustration & Aggression* vii. 152 Traditional patterning identifies another group of circumstances in which the aggression may be expressed. **1952** *Internat. Jrnl. Psycho-Anal.* XXXIII. 411/2 Certain fundamental relationships, resulting in characteristic pregenital patterning..are offered here. **1961** R. B. Long *Sentence & its Parts* i. 22 In *he's sort of nice* the relationship is similarly upside down: *he's rather nice* shows the syntactically more ordinary patterning. **1963** *Lancet* 12 Jan. 67/1 The inseparability of genetic and environmental influences should not deter us from the study of isolated aspects of growth and patterning. **1964** *Amer. Speech* XXXIX. 140 Nineteenth- and twentieth-century works that discover and elucidate structural patterning in one or more languages. *Ibid.*, It is..in the gradually developed concept of patterning that the structural teachings of our own day are rooted. **1964** M. Critchley *Developmental Dyslexia* xiii. 79 The evolution of behaviour can be 'conceptualised' as the process of development of intersensory patterning. **1973** *Word 1970* XXVI. 122 A deep sense of the presence of patterning in the phenomena of man. *Ibid.*, To extend the scope of linguistic inquiry.. to include..verbal art, cultural symbolism and patterning, and so on.

patternism (pæ·tǝɹniz'm). [f. Pattern *sb.* + -ism.] A name given (chiefly by its critics) to a way of describing religions (esp. those of the ancient Near East) not on the basis of historical development but on the basis of common and recurrent patterns; also, a mode of literary appreciation based on recurrent patterns. Hence **pa·tternist**, a proponent of this theory (also *attrib.* or as *adj.*).

1951 H. Frankfort *Problem of Similarity in Anc. Near Eastern Religions* 10 One may admit the close relationship between the myths and rites of a religion..without falling into the error of those 'functionalist' and 'patternist' authors who declare that a myth is merely the spoken accompaniment of ritual. **1956** *Jrnl. Theol. Stud.* VII. 276 The absurdity of labelling scholars holding such divergent views on the subject of 'patternism'..as the 'Scandinavian' school of patternists. *Ibid.* 277 It must be admitted that some of the Scandinavian patternists have carried their interpretation of the Old Testament to lengths which invite criticism. **1957** *Scottish Jrnl. Theol.* X. 95 This volume is all the more welcome because since Professor Hooke edited *Myth and Ritual*, he has often been unjustly held responsible for all the vagaries of the wildest of the patternists. *Ibid.*, Not all will agree with Dr Hooke's patternist explanation of Elijah on Carmel and away to Horeb. **1961** *Times Lit. Suppl.* 17 Feb. p. xiii/3 Another interesting feature of Dr. Carrington's 'patternism' is his suggestion that Mark has divided his narrative into five divisions.

patternization (pæ:təɹnəizēⁱ·ʃən). [f. Patternize *v.* + -ation.] Arrangement in a pattern. Cf. *patternation.

1938 *Mind* XLVII. 379 When he discusses the patternisation of a square of dots he makes a series of remarks which are so significant that we must quote them at length. **1960** R. Carpenter *Greek Sculpture* viii. 217 the patternization of the..underlying muscular structure.

patternless, *a.* Add: **c.** Formless; conforming to, or possessing, no discernible arrangement or pattern.

1960 R. Carpenter *Greek Sculpture* ix. 243 The patternless tangle of shadow in hair and beard. **1963** *Times* 20 May 4/7 Tambling was the man for the quick break and almost stole two more goals near the end to make nonsense of all Sunderland's patternless hammering. **1975** *Sci. Amer.* May 47/2 Clearly a more sensible definition of randomness is required, one that does not contradict the intuitive concept of a 'patternless' number.

patteroller (pæ·tərōᵘləɹ). Also **pateroller, patter(-)roller.** Southern U.S. varr. Patroller; *spec.* a person who watched and restricted the movements of Blacks by night. *Obs.* except *hist.*

c **1862** J. C. Harris *Uncle Remus & Friends* (1892) 196 He sing en he play—oh, gals, go 'way! Whar de patter-roller never kin see. **1893** *Nation* (N.Y.) 7 Sept. 173/1 Ability to write meant ability to counterfeit passes which would outwit the ignorant midnight 'patterrollers'. **1899** B. W. Green *Word-bk. Virginia Folk-speech* 268 *Patteroller*, a patroller. **1917** *Dialect Notes* IV. 385 *Pateroller.* Night-guard over negro slaves on an ante-bellum plantation. Ky. **1928** S. V. Benét *John Brown's Body* 40 He's friends with de ha'nts and steel won't touch him But the paterollers is sure to cotch him. **1936** M. Mitchell *Gone with Wind* xvii. 307 What are you boys doing so far from Tara? You've run away, I'll be bound. Don't you know the patterollers will get you sure? **1964** R. Hayden in *Negro Digest* June 47 Moon so bright and no place to hide, The cry up and the patterollers riding.

patters (pæ·təɹz). *University slang.* [f. first syllable of Pat-ball (in Dict. and Suppl.) + *-er[6].] A university students' name for tennis.

1900 *Captain* IV. 26/1 In the Summer, a great form of 'eccer' is 'patters', a corruption of 'patball', *i.e.* tennis. **1912** A. F. Wilding *On Court & Off* v. 103 A tremendous amount of 'patters', as tennis is popularly called, is played at the University.

Pattinson (pæ·tinsən). *Metallurgy.* [Name of Hugh Lee *Pattinson* (1796–1858), English metallurgical chemist, who patented the process in 1833 (*Brit. Pat. 6497*).] *Pattinson('s) process*: a process formerly used for desilverizing and purifying lead (see quot. 1881).

1856 W. A. Miller *Elem. Chem.* II. xvi. 994 (*heading*) Concentration of silver in lead by Pattinson's process. **1881** [see Pattinsonize *v.*]. **1912** [see *Parkes]. **1946** *Thorpe's Dict. Appl. Chem.* (ed. 4) VII. 224/1 The value of the Pattinson process as a means of purifying lead is shown by the fact that lead to be used for white-lead making was frequently Pattinsonized, although the amount of silver present was too small to repay the cost of its recovery. **1964** H. Hodges *Artifacts* vi. 93 This method of enriching a lead alloy is now known as Pattinson's process.

pattoon, obs. var. Patten *sb.*

1715 *Boston News-Let.* 17 Oct. 2/2 All Persons may have Boots, Shoes, Pattoons, or anything belonging to that Trade mended. **1743** *Ibid.* 3 Feb., To be Sold.. Women's & Children's Shoes & Pattoons.

pattress (pæ·trės). Also **pat(t)rass, pateras.** [(Corruption of) *pateras*, pl. of Patera.] A wooden or plastic block attached to a surface to carry a gas bracket, electric light switch, ceiling rose, or the like; the base of a wall socket. Also *pattress block, box.*

1886 J. Black *Gas Fitting* v. 35 Screw on the pattress blocks, pendants and brackets. **1900** P. N. Hasluck *Pract. Gas-Fitting* iv. 80 The wooden block or pattress is now placed over the tube-bit, the screwed end being passed through the hole in the centre. **1905** C. C. Metcalfe *Prac. Electr. Wiring* ii. 33 Casing brought from skirting board to pateras..will hardly be noticeable. **1928** Maycock & Kemp *Electr. Wiring* (ed. 6) iii. 292 Single- and two-circuit fixture blocks,..are virtually ceiling-rose blocks embedded in hard-wood pattrasses, and without covers. **1934** *Pract. Electr. Engineer* II. 310/2 The pattrasses are marked off and drilled, for the fixing and cable holes on their faces, and the conduit entry holes at their sides. **1969** A. J. Coker *Electr. Wiring* (ed. 7) v. 81 Pattress boxes are also available to convert flush-type to surface mounting. *Ibid.* 83 For fixing and wiring a surface socket-outlet, the circuit cables are first passed through a suitable knockout in the pattress block. **1973** G. A. T. BURDETT *Householder's Electr. Guide* xi. 85 These switches are mounted on moulded plastic surface pattress boxes or metal boxes which are sunk into the wall flush with the plaster. **1976** *Pract. Householder* Nov. 66/3 The ceiling roses will, or should be, mounted on pattress blocks but there is unlikely to be an earth.

patty-cake. **2.** Delete '¶ Error for PAT-A-CAKE' and substitute 'U.S. var. PAT-A-CAKE'. (Later examples.) Also *fig.*

1950 O. NASH *Family Reunion* (1951) 11 All of Granny's muscles ache From half an hour of patty-cake. **1972** *Bankers' Mag.* (Boston, Mass.) Winter 93/2 The crushing price increases that are putting the older fixed incomers on welfare don't emanate from the big firms that are assumed to be playing patty cake with the unions. **1976** *Word 1971* XXVII. 34 Laura loves to play patty-cake. She laughs and flaps her hands together. She will respond to the words alone, but she does not respond to the motions alone. **1976** M. MACHLIN *Pipeline* xxxviii. 412 Ever since we started this damn pipeline, Golconda has been playing patty-cake with Friends of the Earth and all the rest.

‖**patu** (pā·tu). *N.Z.* Also 8–9 **pat(t)oo.** Also in redupl. form. [Maori.] A short club-like weapon with sharpened edges made of stone, whalebone, or nephrite, used for striking rather than thrusting.

1769 J. COOK *Jrnl.* 12 Nov. (1955) I. 200 They have short Truncheons about a foot long, which they call Pattoo Pattoos, some made of wood some of bone and others of stone. **1770** J. BANKS *Endeavour Jrnl.* (1962) II. 26 *Patoo patoos* as they calld them, a kind of small hand bludgeon of stone, bone or hard wood most admirably calculated for the cracking of skulls. **1817** J. L. NICHOLAS *Narr. Voyage to N.Z.* I. iii. 89 The men in the canoe.. exhibited..mats, spears, hooks, fishing-lines, thread, *pattoo pattoos* (war implements). **1882** T. H. POTTS *Out in Open* 82 It [*sc.* fern-root] was soaked, roasted, and repeatedly beaten with a small club (patu) on a large smooth stone, till it was supple. **1921** H. GUTHRIE-SMITH *Tutira* x. 77 Tua Kiaki pulled out a *patu* concealed beneath his mat, and with it there and then slew Te Mautaranui. **1949** P. H. BUCK *Coming of Maori* (1950) II. xi. 277 The short clubs (*patu poto*)..are made in three types: the *mere*, *kotiate*, and *wahaika*..the whalebone clubs carrying the descriptive name of *patu paraoa* (*patu*, club; *paraoa* whalebone). **1974** *Nat. Geographic* Dec. 760 (*caption*) This Tahitian war club is older than the similar patu of the New Zealand Maori.

patulin (pæ·tiŭlin). *Biochem.* [f. L. *patul-um*, specific epithet of the mould, neut. of *patulus* (see PATULOUS *a.*): see -IN[1].] A colourless crystalline antibiotic compound, C_7H_6O, that was obtained from the mould *Penicillium patulum* and afterwards found to be identical with *CLAVACIN and *CLAVIFORMIN.

1943 H. RAISTRICK in *Lancet* 20 Nov. 625/1 Some time ago a metabolic product of *Penicillium patulum* Bainier which had not been previously encountered here was isolated and shown to have antibacterial properties; it has now been identified as anhydro-3-hydroxymethylene-tetrahydro-γ-pyrone-2-carboxylic acid, and has been given the shorter name of 'patulin'. **1947** *Sci. News* V. 98 In 1943 there was a report that a substance..called patulin had proved powerful in treating colds. Further tests on more people showed no significant improvement, however. **1953** [see *CLAVATIN]. **1965** *New Scientist* 28 Oct. 253/2 He also worked out the structure of the remarkable mould product patulin, which, because of its unusual properties, was at that period a substance of considerable interest.

Patum Peperium (pā·tŏm pepīə·riŏm). [Invented name based loosely on L. *piper* pepper: *patum* is fanciful.] A commercial name for a savoury paste; = *Gentleman's Relish* s.v. *GENTLEMAN 7 c.

1884 M. L. ALLEN *Breakfast Dishes* 82 That made by C. Osborne of London, 'Patum Piperium, or Anchovy Paste,' recommended by author as the very best made. **1907** [see **Gentleman's Relish*]. **1935** *Discovery* Dec. 364/1 There used to be in Victorian times—perhaps it still exists—a breakfast compound known as 'Patum Peperium, the Gentleman's Relish'—salted anchovy with a dash of pepper. **1976** *Times* 26 Mar. 14/4 Patum Peperium, the anchovy paste known as gentleman's relish.

paturon (pæ·tiurǫn). [a. Fr. (P. Lyonet *Recherches sur l'anatomie et les métamorphoses de différentes espèces d'Insectes* (a 1789, published 1832) 76, f. Gk. πατ-εῖν to tread + οὐρ-ά tail + *-on*.] = *FALX.

1926 T. H. SAVORY *Brit. Spiders* v. 44 The poison fangs or chelicerae..are two-jointed and unchelate. Various names have been given to these joints; we prefer Lyonnet's terms, unguis and paturon. **1951** LOCKET & MILLIDGE *Brit. Spiders* I. iii. 25 The chelicerae consist of two segments, the basal, called the paturon, and an apical one called the fang. **1970** K. R. SNOW *Arachnids* iv. 38 The appendages of the first segment, the chelicerae, are composed of two podomeres: a basal podomere or paturon and a distal unguis or fang.

patwari (pætwā·ri), var. PUTWARY.

1819 F. HAMILTON *Acct. Kingdom Nepal* II. i. 155 A Patwari or clerk..has one-half ana on the rupee of rent. **1873** E. BALFOUR *Cycl. India* (ed. 2) IV. 457/2 *Patwari*.., a village accountant, responsible for keeping the accounts of the village, noticing changes in the list of proprietors, [etc.]. **1913** J. H. MORRISON *On Trail of Pioneers* xiii. 60 The headman of the village is the patél, and, assisting him, is the patwari or village clerk, usually a Brahmin, who keeps a record of the village lands. **1931** E. A. H. BLUNT *Caste System N. India* xi. 222 The numerous class of *patwaris* (keepers of the village revenue records) consists almost entirely of Kayasthas: and as the *patwari* has a bad name for chicanery, the better class Kayasthas affect to despise this occupation. **1948** 'P. WOODRUFF' *Whatever Dies* 180 The patwari, who is the local representative of the government and looks after some sixty or eighty villages. **1958** O. LEWIS *Village Life N. India* iii. 95 The plots were never..officially registered, because the *patvari* [sic] wanted 30 rupees for the registration, which the villagers refused to pay.

patzer (pæ·tsəɹ). *slang.* [Origin uncertain: cf. G. *patzen* to bungle.] In chess: a poor player, a 'rabbit'.

1959 *S. Afr. Chess-Player* VII. 11 That patzer Grivainis got Evans with an opening trap, but now the difference in strength begins to show. **1960** WENTWORTH & FLEXNER *Dict. Amer. Slang* 378/1 *Patzer*, an inferior chess player. Although said to be from the Yiddish, there is no Yiddish, German, or Hebrew word or word combination to suggest it. Prob. from 'patsy' with the familiar '-er' ending added. **1965** tr. *A. D. de Groot's Thought & Choice in Chess* p. v, Why do masters find the good moves that patzers overlook? **1972** *Daily Tel.* 28 July 15/4 So Fischer after beating off a ferocious attack..'played like a patzer', said one American Grandmaster, 'went to sleep on the job', said another. **1978** *New Statesman* 27 Oct. 556/2 He appears (or perhaps pretends) to be as tempted as the average patzer, by any old poisoned pawn, and has to have his folly explained to him.

paua (pā·wă). *N.Z.* Also **pawa.** [Maori.] A large gastropod mollusc of the genus *Haliotis*, esp. *H. iris*, which attaches itself to rocks by suction and is sometimes collected and used for food. Also *attrib.* Cf. *ABALONE, ORMER.

[**1820** *Gram. & Vocab. Lang. N.Z.* (Church Missionary Soc.) 191 Paua, *s.* a shell-fish so called.] **1846** C. HEAPHY *Jrnl.* 6 Apr. in N. M. Taylor *Early Travellers N.Z.* (1959) 211 The mutton fish, or *pawa*, although resembling india rubber in toughness and colour, is very excellent and substantial food for explorers. *Ibid.* July 244 At Tunupoho we obtained twenty *paua* or 'mutton fish'. **1949** P. H. BUCK *Coming of Maori* (1950) I. ii. 13 The shores [of the Chatham Islands] yielded quantities of shell fish which included the *paua*. **1959** M. SHADBOLT *New Zealanders* 120 He would feel underwater, knife in hand, for the pauas. *Ibid.* 125 He heard them talking quietly in the kitchen as they prepared the meal, hammering soft the paua-steaks. **1963** *Times* 12 Jan. 1/5 This exotic New Zealand delicacy prepared from Paua (Par-War) Clams delicately flavoured with Asparagus is now obtainable from leading delicatessen and high-class food stores throughout the United Kingdom. **1966** J. K. BAXTER *Pig Island Lett.* 13 A corrugated shack With fried pauas in the pan.

2. In full, *paua shell*. The oval shell of this mollusc, which may be as much as six inches long and two deep, distinguished by the row of holes along the back and the blue, green, and pink nacreous lining, which is used to make jewellery or other ornaments.

1873 J. H. H. ST. JOHN *Pakeha Rambles through Maori Lands* vii. 131 The eyes [of a carving] are formed of the inner coating of the 'pawa' shell, a kind of blueish mother of pearl. **1882** T. H. POTTS *Out in Open* 162 Immense heaps of paua shells..show how largely these substantial mollusks were consumed. **1920** 'K. MANSFIELD' *Bliss* 43 Chocolate custard which she had decided to serve in the pawa shell. **1931** *Times Educ. Suppl.* 11 July p. ii, (*caption*) Elaborate carving on a gateway of a Maori village... The white spots are pieces of pawa shell let into the wood. **1936** 'R. HYDE' *Check to your King* xvii. 203 The women cut their flesh with thin paua shell. **1936** N. MARSH *Death in Ecstasy* ii. 22 A figure carved in wood with protruding tongue and eyes made of pawa shell. **1949** E. DE MAUNY *Huntsman in Career* ii. 104 On top of the bookcase were pawa shell ashtrays. **1958** S. ASHTON-WARNER *Spinster* 162 The released mind revolves, flashing different colours like a paua. **1959** M. SHADBOLT *New Zealanders* 157 The large clean paua-shell ashtray gleaming copper and purple colours.

paucal (pǭ·kăl), *a.* *Gram.* [f. L. *paucus* few: see -AL.] Applied to a 'number' or inflected form denoting more than two but fewer than the number denoted by the plural. Hence **pauca·lity.**

1964 R. H. ROBINS *Gen. Linguistics* vi. 247 A few [languages] have four [numbers], singular, dual, trial or 'paucal'..and plural. **1966** J. E. BUSE in C. E. Bazell *In Memory of J. R. Firth* 52 These systems relate ultimately ..to the activity of counting and the resultant concepts of singularity, duality, plurality, paucality and multiplicity. *Ibid.* 58 Filling Place 1 in the structure is a commutation of *t-* and absence, the latter marking the possessed as paucal. **1973** *Archivum Linguisticum* IV. 39 The..'little plural' or 'paucal' form xoxaat 'a few peaches'. **1977** *Canad. Jrnl. Linguistics 1976* XXI. II. 217 Faced with a system like than of Fijian, where there is a further distinction between trial (or paucal) and multiple within plural (Milner 1956), the reapplication of non-minimal membership would have to operate within two branches of the resulting tree diagram.

pauci-. Add: Also in *Min.*, as **paucili·thionite** [LITHIONITE], a hypothetical end-member of the lepidolite system (see quot. 1942).

1942 A. N. WINCHELL in *Amer. Mineralogist* XXVII. 117 The second end-member [of the lepidolite system] ($K_2Li_3Al_5Si_6O_{20}F_4$) has no name and no varietal name in the literature seems to be appropriate. In these circumstances the writer would suggest that it be called paucilithionite. **1963** *Mineral. Abstr.* XVI. 189/2, 142 Chemical analyses of lithium micas from the literature have been transformed to the molecules polylithionite, paucilithionite, muscovite, and siderophyllite.

Pauillac (po͵i·yak). [Fr., f. the name of a commune in the department of Gironde, France.] Claret produced in Pauillac. Also *attrib.* passing into *adj.*

1858 [see MARGAUX]. **1897** A. BEARDSLEY *Let.* c 27 Apr. (1971) 310 The Pauillac at Lapérouse is *excellent*! only 2 fr. a bottle. **1920** G. SAINTSBURY *Notes Cellar-Bk.* iv. 66 Margaux..and Pauillac..have very much fewer tricks played on them. **1966** H. YOXALL *Fashion of Life* xxv. 246, I..could separate, among the Médocs, the red Graves, Pauillacs, Margaux, St Juliens and St Estèphes. **1968** *Guardian* 29 Mar. 9/4 Ch. Ponter Canet, the best so far, with a fine Pauillac bouquet and taste. **1977** B. ROUECHÉ *Fago* I. ii. 19, I slipped the wine out of its paper bag. It was a good Bordeaux, a Pauillac of the Haute-Médoc.

Paul. Add: **3. Paul Pry:** substitute for def.: name of a very inquisitive character in a U.S. song of 1820; often used allusively (also *attrib.*). (Later examples.)

1928 E. WALLACE *Double* xiii. 208 There are lots of quiet little nooks and places where a fellow can sit without a lot of Paul Prys seeing him. **1934** *Sun* (Baltimore) 27 Apr. 12/2 The Senate's theory that the way to enforce the tax laws is to give the Paul Prys of every community access to the private details of every man's gross and net income. **1956** H. G. DE LISSER *Cup & Lip* ix. 109 It would be ruinous to a doctor to be known as a paul pry. **1978** H. C. RAE *Sullivan* I. ii. 24 Twenty-five thousand dollars?..It's the going rate for a quiet investigation, a straight Paul Pry?

b. Hence **Paul-Prying** *vbl. sb.*; **Paul Pryism,** the conduct of a Paul Pry.

1927 *Daily Express* 6 Oct. 8/2 These restrictions were imposed during the war... Their maintenance to-day is simply part of that fussy Paul Pryism which covers the State with ridicule. **1960** *Times* 4 Mar. 13/7 The straitest champion of marital fidelity would, surely, not defend such monstrous Paul Prying.

4*. Paul Jones [the name of John *Paul Jones* (1747–92), Scottish-born naval officer noted for his victories for the Americans during the War of Independence]: a ballroom dance during which the dancers change partners after circling in concentric rings of men and women. Also *attrib.* and *fig.*

1920 *Atlantic Monthly* July 89/1 The whole sprightly, smiling, hand-clapping population seems engaged in one vast 'Paul Jones'..with no one..refusing to join the dance. **1934** *Punch* 14 Feb. 174/1 There was nothing doing in the matter of Paul Joneses, from which even the most emphatic protestations could not give us release. **1938** *Times* 10 Jan. 10/4 The 'party' began with 'I've been to Harlem', a change-partner dance of the 'Paul Jones' type sung to the pure English harvest-home tune, 'I've been to France and I've been to Dover'. **1942** M. DICKENS *One Pair of Feet* vii. 147 A blond A.C.2 whom I had picked up in the Paul Jones. **1958** L. DURRELL *Balthazar* xiii. 233 But now the band had begun to play a Paul Jones (perhaps the very dance in which Arnauti first met Justine?). **1967** *Times Rev. Industry* May 58/3 Driving a private car is often a death-defying Paul Jones with an endless succession of lorries. **1972** V. CANNING *Rainbird Pattern* iv. 66 Harriet..was seduced in the back of the officer's car while Grace was dancing a Paul Jones.

Paul–Bunnell (pǭl bɒne·l). *Path.* The names of J. R. *Paul* (1893–1936) and W. W. *Bunnell* (1902–1965), U.S. physicians, used *attrib.* and *absol.* with reference to a test first described by them in 1932, in which the presence of an antibody reaction to the red blood cells of sheep confirms a diagnosis of infectious mononucleosis (glandular fever).

1938 *Amer. Jrnl. Med. Sci.* CXCVI. 79 The diagnosis was established by the clinical course, confirmed by a characteristic blood smear and a positive Paul–Bunnell test. **1952** *Brit. Med. Jrnl.* 22 Mar. 637/1 The Paul-Bunnell reaction was positive in a dilution of 1 in 28. **1958** *Woman* 27 Sept. 70/3 A special blood test, a Paul–Bunnell test, proved that it could only be gladular fever. **1970** PASSMORE & ROBSON *Compan. Med. Stud.* II. xviii. 116/2 In some cases [of glandular fever], a heterophile antibody capable of agglutinating sheep erythrocytes appears (Paul–Bunnell antibody). **1976** *Lancet* 11 Dec. 1297/1 Paul Bunnell, blood cultures, electrocardiogram, and chest X-ray were all normal.

Pauli (pau·li). *Physics.* The name of Wolfgang *Pauli* (1900–58), Austrian-born physicist, used *attrib.* and in the possessive to designate the **exclusion principle*, which he enunciated in 1925 (*Zeitschr. f. Physik* XXXI. 765–83).

1926 *Jrnl. Optical Soc. Amer.* XIII. 10 By means of schemes (7) and (8) we easily can write down the $\overline{m}_r$ and $\overline{m}_k$ values observing Pauli's principle. *Ibid.*, the period is closed with the *N*th electron where the Pauli principle gives only a $^1S_0$ term. **1926** *Physical Rev.* XXVIII. 339 Whether the impossibility of obtaining coordination for equivalent electrons is directly connected with Pauli's exclusion principle is difficult to say. **1928, 1930** [see **exclusion principle*]. **1946** J. R. PARTINGTON *Gen. & Inorg. Chem.* x. 257 For an atom containing more than one electron, the maximum number of electrons in each shell is fixed by Pauli's exclusion principle. **1968** C. G. KUPER *Introd. Theory Superconductivity* ix. 157 The wave function (9.51) is antisymmetric against interchange of particles, and therefore automatically satisfies the Pauli exclusion principle. **1974** G. REECE tr. *Hund's Hist. Quantum Theory* xiii. 181 The spin of the electron had hitherto been taken into account only in so far as it had no consequence beyond the Pauli principle.

Paulicianism. (In Dict. s.v. PAULICIAN *sb.* and *a.*) (Examples.)

1839 *Penny Cycl.* XIV. 385/1 The Manichæan doctrines..continued to have supporters, under their new name of Paulicianism, till a very late period. **1874** J. H. BLUNT *Dict. Sects* 414/2 From the close of the eleventh century Paulicianism as such ceases to be significant. **1941** [see *BOGOMIL, -MILE]. **1967** N. G. GARSOIAN (*title*) The Paulician heresy. A study of the origin and development of Paulicianism in Armenia and the eastern provinces of the Byzantine empire.

Paulinism. (In Dict. s.v. PAULINE *a.* and *sb.*) Add: (Later examples.)

1910 J. MOFFATT *Paul & Paulinism* II. 33 Paulinism.. was the outcome of the apostle's attempt to hunt out for himself the relations of the Lord Jesus Christ to God, the Law, the universe, and the church. **1916** G. B SHAW *Androcles & Lion* Pref. p. xci, The Christianity of Jesus failed completely to establish itself politically and socially, ..whilst Paulinism overran the whole western civilized world.

b. An expression or feature characteristic of St. Paul.

1927 A. H. MCNEILE *Introd. New Testament* iv. 65 The presence in *Mark* of 'Paulinisms' or other features thought to be secondary on subjective grounds.

Paulist (pau·list), anglicized f. *PAULISTA. Hence **Pauli·stic** *a.*

1900 Paulist [see MAMELUCO]. **1942** A. ST. JAMES tr. *Zweig's Brazil* 214 Anyone still desirous of seeing something of the Paulistic type of the nineteenth century habitation had better hurry.

Paulista (pauli·stă). Also with lower-case initial. [Pg., f. *São Paulo* (see below) + *-ista* -IST.] **a.** A person of mixed Portuguese and Brazilian Indian descent; *spec.* one of the explorers and settlers of the hinterlands of southern Brazil. (*Obs.* exc. *hist.*). **b.** A native or inhabitant of the city of São Paulo in southern Brazil.

1817 SOUTHEY *Hist. Brazil* II. xxiii. 300 The Paulistas have acted so memorable a part in Brazil and Paraguay that it becomes of importance to trace their history distinctly, and clear it from fables and misrepresentations. **1884** R. G. WATSON *Span. & Portug. S. Amer.* II. xi. 169 The search for the precious metals had long shared with slave-hunting the efforts of the *Paulistas* and others. *Ibid.* 174 *Minas Geraes* soon acquired the unenviable notoriety..of being the most turbulent settlement in *Brazil*. Its people were divided into two classes, called.. *Paulistas* and *Florasteiros* or strangers. **1896** A. H. KEANE *Ethnol.* vii. 152 In Brazil the famous '*Paulistas*' (so called from the province of São Paulo), a cross between the first Portuguese immigrants and the aborigines, have always been the most vigorous and enterprising section of the community. **1910** *Encycl. Brit.* VII. 677/2 Cuyabá was founded in 1719 by Paulista gold hunters. **1932** W. S. ROBERTSON *Hist. Lat.-Amer. Nations* (ed. 2) vi. 123 'Paulistas', as the half-breed adventurers from São Paulo were called, gradually penetrated farther and farther into the interior. **1942** A. ST. JAMES tr. *Zweig's Brazil* 211 During the seventeenth and eighteenth centuries on the banks of the little river Tieté there lies a small unimportant town, more headquarters and camp than a permanent settlement of those roaming gangs, the Paulistas, who roved through the whole country..in search of loot. *Ibid.* 218 The Paulistas have a most competitive attitude toward Rio de Janeiro, and the desire not to appear inferior or less artistic. **1944** S. PUTNAM tr. *E. de Cunha's Rebellion in Backlands* ii. 63 The Paulista—and this name, in its historic signification, takes in the sons of Rio de Janeiro, Minas, São Paulo, and regions south—now arose as an autonomous type, adventurous, rebellious, freedom-loving. **1966** *Economist* 3 Sept. 902 Pleasure-loving *cariocas* (those who live in Rio), economically eager *paulistas* (those who live in São Paulo). **1976** R. PERRY *One Good Death* v. 75 The daily nightmare that many Paulistas called travelling home from work.

paulownia. Also (erron.) **pawlonia.** Substitute for etym. and def.: [mod.L. (P. F. von Siebold & J. G. Zuccarini *Flora Japonica* (1835) I. 25), f. the patronymic of Anna *Paulowna* (1795–1865), daughter of Tsar Paul I and wife of William II of the Netherlands.] A deciduous tree of the genus so called, esp. *P. tomentosa*, belonging to the family Scrophulariaceæ, native to China or Japan, and bearing panicles of bell-shaped blue or lilac flowers. Also *attrib.* (Earlier and later examples.)

1843 *Paxton's Mag. Bot.* X. 7 *Paulownia imperialis* (Imperial Paulownia).. A considerable quantity of this noble tree has lately been introduced to Britain. **1901** L. H. BAILEY *Cycl. Amer. Hort.* III. 1224/1 The Paulownia is one of the most conspicuous flowering trees in spring. **1971** *Country Life* 1 Apr. 741/1 A potentially large shrub or tree,..like the..tree of heaven (*Ailanthus*) or pawlonia. **1973** C. LLOYD *Foliage Plants* x. 189 A group of paulownia seedlings, grown and pruned for their enormous, furry, heart-shaped leaves. **1976** P. QUENNELL *Marble Foot* v. 182 The local carpenter made me a large knee-desk of silvery pawlonia wood.

paunch, *v.*[1] Restrict 'Now *rare* or *dial.*' to senses 1, 3 and 4 and add: **2.** (Further examples.)

1906 *Chambers's Jrnl.* Sept. 681/2 The animals [*sc.* rabbits] have to be killed, bled, and paunched. **1952** F. WHITE *Good Eng. Food* II. 111 One of the things I had to do before I was twenty was to paunch and skin a hare.

pauperization. (Earlier and later examples.)

1838 W. HOWITT *Rural Life Eng.* II. III. ii. 149 The working classes..what distress, what pauperization.. they have gone through. **1955** *Times* 6 July 10/3 The recent C.G.T. congress..insisted that revolutionary action was the only remedy to the 'progressive pauperization' of the working class under capitalism. **1971** J. J. SHAPIRO tr. *Habermas's Toward Rational Society* vi. 110 Underprivileged groups are not social classes... Their *disfranchisement* and pauperization no longer coincide with *exploitation*. **1974** J. WHITE tr. *Poulantzas's Fascism & Dictatorship* v. iii. 259 In this process of pauperization, artisans and traders lost almost half their income.

‖ **paupiettes** (popiet), *sb. pl.* Also in *sing.* [Fr.] The current form of POUPIETS. (See quots.)

1889 A. FILIPPINI *Table* 241 Panpiette [*sic*] of Veal à la Faubonne. **1892** A. B. MARSHALL *Larger Cookery Bk.* iv. 86 Eel paupiettes à la Française. **1906** *Mrs. Beeton's Bk. Househ. Managem.* lxii. 1666 *Paupiettes* (Fr.), slices of meat or fish rolled with forcemeat. **1936** LUCAS & HUME *Au Petit Cordon Bleu* 174 *Paupiette*, a thin slice of meat or..fish, sometimes spread with a farce, then rolled up and tied with white cotton. **1948** *Good Housek. Cookery Bk.* II. 141 Glazed paupiettes of sole. **1970** SIMON & HOWE *Dict. Gastron.* 291/2 *Paupiettes*, thinly sliced pieces of meat used as wrappers for various meat or forcemeat fillings. Also, in Escoffier's usage, fillets of sole and cabbage leaves used in the same way. The meat slices are spread with a well-spiced forcemeat and rolled up. Wrapped up in thin slices of fat bacon, they are tied up with cotton thread to be braised, baked or casseroled. Bacon and thread are removed before serving. **1975** J. SYMONS *Three Pipe Problem* xvi. 159 The soup was followed by what Sue called paupiettes de porc, pancakes with some sort of minced pork filling. **1976** *Evening Advertiser* (Swindon) 31 Dec. 13/1 (Advt.), Scottish restaurant menu at £7.00 inclusive with..Paupiette of Plaice 'Auchenshuggle'.

pause, *sb.* Add: **1. d.** (See quot. 1966.) Also *fig.*

1962 *Listener* 29 Mar. 549/2 The point is clearly made by General Norstad, who says..that what he needs in order to impose what he calls the pause, in order to identify a threat, in order to relieve himself of the intolerable choice between retreating and using nuclear weapons, is thirty divisions. *Ibid.* 19 Apr. 674/1 The time has come to declare a 'pause' on the culture-front. **1966** SCHWARZ & HADIK *Strategic Terminol.* 85 *Pause*, in the defense of Western Europe, a moment of reflection imposed on any aggressor before the defense resorts to nuclear weapons.

2. (Later examples.) In *Linguistics*, spec. the break marking juncture, sometimes regarded as having phonemic status.

1933 L. BLOOMFIELD *Language* xii. 185 Since the constituents of phrases are free forms, the speaker may separate them by means of *pauses*. Pauses are mostly non-distinctive; they occur chiefly when the constituents are long phrases; in English they are usually preceded by a pause-pitch. **1948** *Language* XXIV. 19 Some utterances contain a perceptible time-interval during which none of the vocal organs perceptibly articulates... Such a time-interval is an *internal pause*... The absence of speech before or after an utterance is an *external pause*. **1950** *Ibid.* XXVI. 97 Pause may be regarded as a kind of zero phone, characterized by a complete lack of qualities. **1951** *Ibid.* XXVII. 520 An interrupted sequence is considered to include the phoneme of *pause*. **1952** W. P. LEHMANN *Proto-Indo-European Phonol.* ii. 10 Choice of positional variant in PIE was determined by preceding and following phoneme, group of phonemes, or pause. **1957** B. DEUTSCH *Poetry Handbk.* (1958) 35 The pause in the last foot of the second line is made more emphatic because the words conclude the line and the poem as well. **1968** J. LYONS *Introd. Theoret. Linguistics* v. 200 The native speaker is able to actualize the 'potential pauses' in his utterances when he wishes to, even though he does not do this normally. **1972** M. L. SAMUELS *Linguistic Evol.* ii. 13 Unvoicing of final consonants (i.e. voicing is not maintained till the end of the word, especially before a pause).

5. *pause-filler, -linking, -marker, -pattern, rhythm, -substitute*; *pause-giving* ppl. adj.; **pause-pitch,** the pitch pattern which characteristically precedes a pause in utterance.

1967 A. LASKI *Seven Other Years* i. 13 It sounded like the kind of remark which is made as a pause-filler. **1887** A. SETH *Hegelianism* ii. 74 [T. H.] Green..constantly assumes a stream of sensations as the material upon which the pause-giving and rationally constitutive activity of thought is exercised. **1963** *Economist* 9 Nov. 577/1 Papers with..pause-giving titles. **1970** *Canad. Jrnl. Linguistics* XV. 112 Thus, if the pause-linking rule was solely phonological we would have no way of determining whether or not it applies to these phrases. **1956** *Kenyon Rev.* XVIII. 433 The lesser pause-markers: comma, colon and semi-colon. **1965** *Times Lit. Suppl.* 25 Nov. 1070/3 New sentence-shapes, new pause-patterns. **1933** L. BLOOMFIELD *Language* vii. 115 We must recognize *pause-pitch* or *suspension-pitch* [,], which consists of a rise of pitch before a pause within a sentence. It is used.. to show that the sentence is not ending at a point where otherwise the phrasal form would make the end of a sentence possible: *I was waiting there* [,] *when in came the man.* **1902** E. W. SCRIPTURE *Elem. Exper. Phonetics* xxxvi. 517 A tone may be sounded for a definite time at definite intervals. The result is a 'rhythm of sound and pause,' or..a 'pause rhythm'. **1964** J. L. M. TRIM in D. Abercrombie et al. *Daniel Jones* 375 Major tone-groups.. are followed by a pause, or pause-substitute.

pause, *v.*[1] Add: **3.** *trans.* To cause to stop temporarily.

a **1542** WYATT *Coll. Poems* (1969) 104 Sorowfull david.. yt..pausid his plaint and layd adown his harp. **1908** A. S. M. HUTCHINSON *Once aboard Lugger* II. ii. 101 The strain on his invention paused him.

pauseful, *a.* Add: **b.** That causes a pause. (Cf. PAUSEFULLY *adv.*)

1958 *Times* 5 May 12/5 A pauseful finger was being laid upon his life.

pauw (pāu, ‖pōu), var. PAAUW. Cf. *POUW.

1800 G. YONGE in G. M. Theal *Rec. Cape Colony* (1898) III. 197 Pauws or Wild Peacocks are become extremely scarce. **1838** [see *GOMPAAUW, GOMPAUW]. **1886** G. A. FARINI *Through Kalahari Desert* v. 62, I saw a large *pauw* out in the open. **1939** S. CLOETE *Watch for Dawn* iii. 39 To make this feast there had been a great killing: of oxen,..of wildfowl, guineas, pauws, and pheasants.

pav[1]**.** (pæv). Abbreviation of PAVILION *sb.* (sense 6): *spec.* (*a*) the London Pavilion (a music-hall and theatre, later a cinema); (*b*) a cricket pavilion.

1864 HOTTEN *Slang Dict.* 197 *Pav.*, the Pavilion Theatre,—sometimes called the P.V., *i.e.*, pe-ve. **1892** *Idler* Mar. 127 One Saturday night, I wended my way to the 'Pav.'. **1901** *To-Day* 26 Sept. 266/1 The retiring victim [*sc.* a stumped batsman] came back to the Pav. **1903** [see *CART *v.* 1 d]. **1934** *Observer* 1 Apr. 18/1 That long-established landmark, the London Pavilion (better known to its habitues as 'the Pav.') is following the example already set it by the Empire and the Alhambra and 'going over to the pictures'. **1978** *Guardian* 20 Mar. 9/1 St. B's always had them, especially behind the cricket pavs. **1978** L. MEYNELL *Papersnake* i. 10, I had gone over to the sports pavilion, 'the Pav'..to make sure the gear was all right for the match.

pav[2]**.** Abbreviation of *PAVLOVA. *Austral.* and *N.Z.*

1966 G. W. TURNER *Eng. Lang. Austral. & N.Z.* viii. 173 *Pavlova cake*, a meringue sweet, sometimes shortened to *pav.* **1974** *Herald* (Melbourne) 5 Apr. 23/1 The pavlova (now fondly abbreviated to the 'pav').

pave, *v.* Add: **1. c.** To form a pavement for; to be a pavement under.

1821 SHELLEY *Epipsych.* 15 The air-like waves Of wonder-level dream, whose tremulous floor Paved her light steps.

2. c. To write interlinear or marginal translations in (a Latin or Greek text-book). *School slang.*

1888 [implied in *PAVING *vbl. sb.*]. **1897** A. SIDGWICK in P. A. Barnett *Teaching & Organisation* 308 Cases of dishonesty are pretty certain to turn up..to 'pave' the text, *i.e.* write the English down at the side. **1940** M. MARPLES *Public School Slang* 52 A common word of special meaning is pave, which denotes the practice of writing the English meaning above words in a Greek or Latin text.

pave, *sb.* (Earlier examples.)

1835 *Southern Lit. Messenger* I. 357, I met a friend on the *pave* last week. **1859** [see NYMPH 2 b]. **1880** J. BOWICK *Montrose Characters* 138 Gaun pauchlin' alang the pave.

pavement, *sb.* Add: **1.** (Further examples.) Also (without *a*), paving.

a **1817** [see *KNOWING *ppl. a.* 3]. **1843** A. B. BLACKIE *Wood Pavement* 13 The efficient labour of a horse on Wooden Pavement, compared with that of the same horse on a perfectly consolidated Macadamized road, being as 42 to 17. **1900** T. AITKEN *Road Making* ix. 300 Streets of many English towns are still paved with cobbles, but these are being gradually replaced by better descriptions of pavement. **1947** *Engineering News-Record* 16 Oct. 534/3 The surface of the runways, which it is hoped will be adequate for the pavement base, will be finally solidified by a 'super-compactor' unit. **1952** *Jrnl. R. Aeronaut. Soc.* LVI. 879/1 The pavement must be capable of carrying with safety the heaviest aircraft. **1977** *Bitumen* (Shell Internat. Petroleum Co.) 7 Shell companies' main interest in bitumen technology has been the engineering properties of bitumen and the structural design of roads and airfield pavements.

b. For '*obs.*' read '*obs.* exc. *techn.* and *U.S.*' Hence (*techn.* and *U.S.*), the roadway as distinct from the adjacent footway. (Further examples.)

1877 D. K. CLARK in Law & Clark *Construction of Roads* 12 The surface of the pavement soon became very uneven, and not unfrequently sunk so much as to form hollows, which rendered it..dangerous to horses and carriages. **1918** E. POOLE *Dark People* i. 5 You could see the sidewalks on either hand, but the dark wooden pavement of the street was almost lost in shadows. **1935** H. W. HORWILL *Dict. Mod. Amer. Usage* 226/1 When preparations were being made in Washington for a procession.., the newspapers of the city complained that in Pennsylvania Avenue the grandstands filled the sidewalk and compelled pedestrians to walk on the pavement. **1939**

Liverpool Daily Post 9 Nov. 3/2 When any road works are about to be undertaken, a notice headed 'Reconstruction of Pavement' is exhibited near the scene of operations, stating that the 'pavement of this thoroughfare' is shortly to be reconstructed. It is invariably the roadway, and not the sidewalk, which in these cases receives attention. **1958** *Engineering* 4 Apr. 441/3 It will also be a double carriageway,..comprising 7 in of granular fill on which will be laid 11 in of reinforced concrete, placed in a single pass for the full 24 ft width of each pavement. **1966** R. ASHWORTH *Highway Engin.* x. 171 The modern road pavement is usually composed of several layers of material of differing quality; the strongest material being placed uppermost and forming the actual running surface. **1971** D. HAMILTON *Poisoners* x. 78 She was barreling out on.. the road that'll take you clear down Baja California to La Paz, if you and your vehicle are tough enough to make it... The pavement ends about ninety miles south of Ensenada at present. After that, things get pretty rough. **1976** *Billings* (Montana) *Gaz.* 17 June 1-A/4 A southern Indiana woman died when her car skidded out of control on wet pavement.

f. (See quot. 1965.)

1899 P. DEARMER *Parson's Handbk.* v. 128 The thurifer and boat-bearer..go to the right of the priest, as he stands on the pavement. **1908** *Ritual Notes* (ed. 5) II. 59/3 When the Deacon descends to the pavement, the Thurifer will stand at his right. **1922** C. MACKENZIE *Altar Steps* xix. 212 The baldacchino was given by one rich old lady, the pavement of the church by another. **1936** *Server's Manual* 6 Go and stand in some convenient place on the 'pavement' of the sanctuary. **1965** C. E. POCKNEE *Parson's Handbk.* (ed. 13) ii. 23 The pavement, i.e. the level of the sanctuary between the lowest step before the altar and the communicants' rail, should extend to six feet at the very least. *Ibid.* ix. 98 He remains standing on the pavement swinging the censer until the hymn or psalm is finished. **1978** *Church Times* 20 Jan. 3/4 An application was made for a faculty to remove the sanctuary pavement and transfer from a columbarium underneath 177 caskets containing..cremated remains.

2. (Further examples.)

1931 J. R. NORMAN *Hist. Fishes* vii. 126 They [*sc.* the teeth of Nurse Sharks and Hounds] are arranged in pavement fashion, and all or most of the rows are in use at the same time. **1971** P. J. P. WHITEHEAD tr. *Budker's Life of Sharks* iii. 41 The only sharks having teeth in a 'pavement' are those belonging to the genera *Mustelus, Hexanchus* and *Heterodontus.*

b. *Geol.* A horizontal or gently sloping expanse of bare rock.

1827 G. P. SCROPE *Mem. Geol. Central France* vii. 154 The lower portion of this bed is very beautifully columnar, the upper obscurely so; this latter has been in parts destroyed, and a pavement or causeway left, formed by an assemblage of upright and almost geometrically regular columns fitted together with the utmost symmetry. **1932** C. R. LONGWELL et al. *Physical Geol.* vii. 157 Many gentle slopes above the levels of the playas are floored with 'desert pavements' consisting of pebbles fitted so closely together and with their top surfaces so even that the general effect suggests a mosaic. **1937** WOOLDRIDGE & MORGAN *Physical Basis Geogr.* xix. 288 Bare limestone surfaces commonly show a widening of joints by solution, or in extreme cases, a complex fretting or fluting of the surface... Limestone pavements tending to this type are called 'clints' or 'grykes' in the North of England. **1954** J. F. KIRKALDY *Gen. Princ. Geol.* vi. 69 The direction of ice movement can also be proved if glaciated pavements can be found. These are surfaces of rock, hard enough to be smoothed and polished by the ice and showing striations caused by the harder rocks dragged across them by the ice. **1965** *Proc. Geologists' Assoc.* LXXVI. 421 Carboniferous limestone in Great Britain and Ireland is frequently exposed in broad, curiously sculptured plateaux termed pavements. **1977** *Oxf. Diocesan Mag.* Nov. 10/1 We have botanized over a limestone 'pavement' in Westmoreland, several bogs in Scotland, [etc.].

4. *pavement café*; **pavement-pounder** *slang*, a policeman; **pavement princess** *Citizens Band Radio slang* (see quots.); **pavement-toothed** *a.*, having teeth arranged in a pavement (see sense 2).

1953 *Observer* 10 May 5/4 It isn't worth..doing much about pavement cafés or open-air dancing. **1972** J. AITKEN *Butterfly Picnic* i. 12 Several pavement cafés were thronged with elderly men. **1942** BERREY & VAN DEN BARK *Amer. Thes. Slang* § 460/17 *Policeman*..ossifer, pavement pounder, P.D. **1947** K. JAEDIKER *Tall, Dark & Dead* vii. 102 Neal had put out a teletype for my car, and some Brooklyn pavement-pounder had spotted it. **1959** I. & P. OPIE *Lore & Lang. Schoolch.* xvii. 369 There are, in the London area, at least thirty nicknames... Nobby, Pavement Pounder, Peeler, Robert, [etc.]. **1976** L. DILLS *CB Slanguage Dict.* (rev. ed.) 53 *Pavement princess*, roadside or truckstop prostitute. **1976** *Time* 10 May 79/2 Prostitutes ('pavement princesses') who plug their charms on CB have become so common that there is even a song about them. **1976** *Daily Tel.* (Colour Suppl.) 16 July 10/2 Car-borne prostitutes..describe themselves as 'a dream for sale' in the West..a 'pavement princess' and a 'snuff-dipper' in the East. **1904** *Nature* 5 May 13/1 He discusses the affinities of the pavement-toothed genus Endothiodon.

pavement, *v.* Add: (Later example.) Also *transf.* Hence **pa·vementing** *vbl. sb.*

1930 R. CLEMENTS *Grey Seas* 126 The blown, empty sky, pavemented by the tossing sea. **1977** *Lancet* 20 Aug. 402/2 At 30 and 60 min, these showed an inflammatory reaction to both solutions with pavementing of polymorphs and a perivascular infiltrate.

paver. Add: **1. b.** A machine for depositing and spreading material for a road, etc., as it travels.

1947 *Engineering News-Record* 16 Oct. 535/3 A paver was used to mix the soil-cement and to deposit it along the pipe line as required. **1955** *Concrete Roads* (Road Research Lab.) xv. 279 For large works, pavers which consist of a non-tilting mixer mounted on crawler tracks are sometimes convenient. **1972** *Travelling* Autumn 33/2 The concrete slab will be laid with a very high accuracy using a purpose built slip form paver. **1977** *Bitumen* (Shell Internat. Petroleum Co.) 5 The mixes are laid by various types of mechanical paver.

Pavian (pā·viăn), *sb.* and *a.* [f. *Pavia* name of a city of northern Italy (L. *Ticinum*) + -AN.] **A.** *adj.* Of, pertaining to, or characteristic of Pavia or its people. **B.** *sb.* A native or inhabitant of Pavia.

1856 O. JONES *Gram. Ornament* xvii. 5 Our woodcuts, selected from the Piscina of the High Altar, furnish some idea of the general style of the Pavian arabesques. **1888** W. BENHAM tr. *Platina's Lives of Popes* I. 260 John the Fourteenth, a Roman, or, as some will have it, a Pavian. **1936** A. W. CLAPHAM *Romanesque Archit.* iii. 62 In some of the Pavian churches an acanthus decoration is to be met with, consisting of a regular diaper or brocade pattern of palmette leaves. **1940** G. F.-H. & J. BERKELEY *Italy in Making* III. viii. 202 The Pavian student volunteers had occupied Colà.

pavilion, *sb.* Add: **6.** (Earlier examples of use in *Cricket.*)

1799 *Times* 1 June 3/4 The colours..were presented.. to the corps in Lord's cricket ground... After the military ceremony was over, the Earl and Countess..partook of a cold collation provided for them in the pavillion. **1853** F. GALE *Public School Matches* 10 All of a sudden the bell from the Pavilion strikes up, and the ground is gradually cleared.

7. b. (Later examples.)

1938 *Amer. Speech* XIII. 228/1 A *ward* is a unit or division in the hospital, often called a *floor, pavilion*, or by the number or letter under which it is listed. **1973** *Lancet* 7 July 33/1 Princess Alexandra Eye Pavilion, Royal Infirmary of Edinburgh.

pavillon. Add: **2.** *pavillon chinois* (ʃīnwa) = *Chinese pavilion*, **jingling Johnny* (*a*).

1876 STAINER & BARRETT *Dict. Mus. Terms* 347/1 *Pavillon chinois*, an instrument consisting of little bells attached to a staff. **1920, 1970** [see *JINGLING *ppl. a.*].

paving, *vbl. sb.* Add: **a.** (Examples in sense *2 c of the vb.)

1888 H. LOGEMAN *Rule of S. Benet* p. xxxvi, Dr. Thompson..said that the Rugby boys' slang term for this process was *paving*—paving smooth (I suppose) the rough road of learning Latin. **1914** 'I. HAY' *Lighter Side School Life* v. 138 He is greatly addicted to a more venial crime known as 'paving'. The paver prepares his translation in the orthodox manner, but whenever he has occasion to look up a word in a lexicon he scribbles its meaning in the margin of the text, or, more frequently, just over the word itself, to guard against loss of memory on the morrow. **1958** L. FOSTER in *Aspects of Translation* 10 The 'paving' of books by schoolboys and the old-fashioned classical 'literal crib' are rather different cases of translations intended to facilitate comprehension of the original text, not to supplant it.

b. *paving-block, -sand* (later example).

1911 *Daily Colonist* (Victoria, B.C.) 1 Apr. 7/3 The city will purchase from the Michigan Puget Sound Lumber Company a quantity of wood paving blocks sufficient to complete the pavement on View Street. **1968** J. ARNOLD *Shell Bk. Country Crafts* xxxi. 332 The Scots pine is planted cultivated and felled..for the primary purpose of providing pit-props and telephone poles, railway sleepers and at one time for paving-blocks. **1934** *Ledger-Dispatch* (Norfolk, Va.) 11 June 7/8 There is glass sand, moulding sand, building, paving, grinding and polishing sand.

pavisand (pæ·visænd), *v.* [f. PAVISADE.] *intr.* To display a formidable array of clothing and ornament; to flaunt one's appearance. Hence **pa·visander.**

1910 KIPLING *Rewards & Fairies* 297 Forth she come pavisanding like a peacock—stuff, ruff, stomacher and all. **1950** I. BROWN *Having Last Word* 90, I can picture Queen Elizabeth pavisanding at times. *Ibid.*, Among great pavisanders also was Milton's Delilah.

Pavlov (pa·vlǫf, pæ·vlǫv). Also **Pavloff,** etc. The name of the Russian physiologist Ivan Petrovich *Pavlov* (1849–1936), used *attrib.* or in the possessive to designate aspects of his work, esp. those connected with conditioning the salivary reflexes of a dog to the mental stimulus of the sound of a bell.

1911 STEDMAN *Med. Dict.* 644/2 *Pavloff method*,..a quantitative study of the modifications of the salivary reflexes caused by psychic reactions. **1922** K. DUNLAP *Elements Sci. Psychol.* xiv. 303 The development of the auditory-salivary reaction in Pavloff's dog. **1933** J. C. FLÜGEL *Hundred Years Psychol.* xi. 208 He became much concerned with Pavlov's conditioned reflex and the psychology of food. **1949** KOESTLER *Insight & Outlook* xxviii. 379 The Pavlov-trained dog, when faced with an ambiguous stimulus,..becomes deranged in all his reflexes. **1967** *Listener* 3 Aug. 138/2, I had a kind of Pavlov-dog reaction, shaking with nerves, because I'd been very nervous when I'd done that first film nine years before. **1974** *Sunday Times* (Colour Suppl.) 27 Oct. 30/4 Such de- or re-conditioning is quick, cheap, and, like Pavlov's bells, it gets results. **1976** A. WHITE *Long Silence* ii. 19 You're not a Pavlov dog, trained to bark when I ring a bell. You have a mind of your own.

pavlova (pævlōu·vă). *Austral.* and *N.Z.* [f. the name of Anna *Pavlova* (1885–1931), Russian ballerina.] A dessert or cake, now usually one made with meringue, whipped cream, and fruit. Also *attrib.*

1927 *Davis Dainty Dishes* (ed. 6) (Davis Gelatine, N.Z., Ltd.) 11 Pavlova... Dissolve all but a teaspoonful of Gelatine in the hot water, and all the sugar except a dessertspoonful [etc.]. **1929** K. MCKAY *Pract. Home Cookery* 155/1 *Pavlova cakes*... Cook like meringues... They are delightful and simple to make besides being a novelty. **1952** *Weekly News* (Auckland) 30 July 14/4 (*heading*) Soft-centred Pavlova Cake. *Ibid.*, R.J.S. (Nelson) writes:—Could you give me a recipe for making a pavlova with a soft centre? *Ibid.*, Most good pavlova recipes are soft inside. **1952** B. NILSON *Penguin Cookery Bk.* xviii. 396 Pavlova Cake (to use as a cake or cold sweet). **1957** *Daily Mail* 7 Oct. 11/4 Pavlova. *Ingredients*: 3 egg whites 6 oz. castor sugar 1 teaspoonful vanilla 1 teaspoonful vinegar 1 teaspoonful cornflour ½ pint double cream (whipped and flavoured) 16 oz can Australian pineapple or apricots cherries angelica. **1958** *N.Z. News* 2 Dec. 10/2 Supper included some renowned New Zealand dishes such as pavlova, whitebait, and oysters. **1960** I. CROSS *Backward Sex* 85 I'll give you some of Mum's pavlova cake for supper. **1964** *Guardian* 18 Apr. 5/4 A Pavlova..is a meringue basket so called because it spreads out like the skirts of a ballerina. **1968** *N.Z. News* 11 Dec. 11/5 Pavlova cake—the New Zealand and Australian sweet—is believed to have been created as a compliment to the famous dancer when she visited those countries. **1972** V. C. CLINTON-BADDELEY *To study Long Silence* v. 191 A *Pavlova*—a New Zealand speciality of choice fresh fruit and whipped cream wrapped in meringue-like base. **1975** *Times* 16 Dec. 12/4 A Pavlova, an Australian dessert..a meringue with cream, passion fruit, ice cream and strawberries.

Pavlovian (pævlōu·viăn), *a.* [f. *PAVLOV + -IAN.] Of, pertaining to, or connected with Pavlov, his theories, experiments, or methods. Also in extended and weakened senses.

1931 A. HUXLEY *Let.* 24 Aug. (1969) 351 The effects of such sociological reforms as Pavlovian conditioning of all children. **1951** H. HUMPHREY *Thinking* 6 In the Pavlovian system,..we have an attempt to account objectively for all psychological facts in terms of the primary interaction of organism and environment. **1952** V. NABOKOV *Nabokov's Dozen* (1959) 206 A mad Pavlovian world where..variations in simple visual values influence and gradually replace flavour. **1963** A. HERON *Towards Quaker View of Sex* 67 Some recoveries with 'deconditioning' treatment along Pavlovian lines. **1974** *Daily Tel.* 8 Feb. 8/2 The report does not hesitate to name names, a procedure that will inevitably touch off a Pavlovian response from Leftist circles to deride it as a 'Reds under the Beds' scare. **1976** *Survey* Winter 24 The Soviet Union.. managed to exploit the South African issue in order to create the well-known Pavlovian reflex all through Black Africa. **1977** *Meanjin* XXXVI. 1. 108 The adroit orchestration of comedy..that is, the patrons were not treated as a collection of complete Pavlovian half-wits.

‖ **pavor.** Restrict *Obs. rare*—⁰ to sense in Dict. and add: **b. pavor nocturnus** [L. *nocturnus* nocturnal], a sudden and inexplicable terror which may afflict a sleeping person, esp. a child, in the night; = *night-terror* s.v. NIGHT *sb.* 14; similarly **pavor diurnus** [L. *diurnus* belonging to the day] (see quot. 1940).

[**1848** DUNGLISON *Dict. Med. Sci.* (ed. 7) 634/1 *Pavores nocturni seu dormientium*, fear during sleep.] **1889** *Albany Med. Ann.* June 200 The victim of night terrors, or *pavor nocturnus*, experiences an awful, unpleasant, terror stricken disturbance of the mind. **1889** J. THOMSON tr. *Henoch's Lect. Children's Dis.* I. 241 One of the rare cases of pavor diurnus which I have seen affected the son of an actor (7 years old), a nervous, anaemic, delicate child. **1900** *Lancet* 3 Feb. 292/1 Two cases of pavor diurnus..have recently been under my care. **1915** J. N. HALL *Borderline Dis.* I. iii. 96 Nightmare in adults and pavor nocturnus in young children are vivid dreams with sensations of oppression in the chest, of horror, and inability to escape some impending catastrophe. **1927** W. P. LUCAS *Mod. Pract. Pediatr.* II. xii. 698 Pavor diurnus is more rarely seen than night terrors but is more significant of a disorder of the nervous system. **1940** HINSIE & SHATZKY *Psychiatric Dict.* 406/1 *Pavor diurnus*, fear reactions which occur in the young child during the afternoon nap, similar to night terrors but not so frequently taking place as the latter. **1950** J. STRACHEY tr. *Freud's Totem & Taboo* iv. 128 Phobias of this type..are, in my opinion, at least as common in childhood as *pavor nocturnus*. **1966** *Sci. & Psychoanal.* IX. 176 The purposiveness of the rumination is seen in the fact that..the event does ultimately become commonplace... The suggestion is strong that the *pavor nocturnus* of the child may have a similar accustomizing function.

pavvy (pæ·vi). Also **pavy.** Abbreviation of PAVILION *sb.* Cf. *PAV¹.

1899 KIPLING *Stalky & Co.* 159 Forty shillin's or a month for hackin' the chucker-out of the Pavvy on the shins. **1900** FARMER *Public School Word-Bk.* 146 *Pavvy, The* (Harrow).—The pavilion on the cricket-ground. **1905** H. A. VACHELL *Hill* v. 117, I say, there's going to be a ruction in front of the Pavvy. Come on! **1961** PARTRIDGE *Dict. Slang* Suppl. 1215/1 *Pavy, the*,..The pavilion: Harrovian:..Hence, at certain other Public Schools': c. 20.

paw, *sb.*¹ Add: **4.** *paw-mark, print* (also *fig.*); also *pawful.*

1925 F. M. FORD *No More Parades* ii. 73 She resembled a white Persian cat luxuriating, sticking out a tentative pawful of expanding claws. **1964** D. VARADAY *Gara-Yaka*

xix. 173 The invaders replied very effectively to the warnings, and the Prodigal and his family [of lions] had a pawful of trouble. **1894** 'MARK TWAIN' in *Century Mag.* June 234/2 Are you going to ornament the royal palaces with nigger paw-marks? **1929** D. H. LAWRENCE *Lett.* (1932) 833 Such dark paw-marks of the wind on the sea! **1975** *Sunday Times* 16 Nov. 44/4 Every pawmark shows up on those virgin white surfaces. **1925** *Scribner's Mag.* July 33/1, I saw..the curious paw print of a porcupine, with its little pebbled markings. **1938** M. K. RAWLINGS *Yearling* iv. 35 All about were the paw-prints of the small things. **1963** *Times* 25 Jan. 12/7 The badger, whose paw-prints are square-fronted and easily recognizable, is better off. **1968** C. NICOLE *Self Lovers* vii. 88 The whole thing has his pawprints all over it. His speciality is taking his victims swimming at dawn. **1977** D. HARSENT *Dreams of Dead* 55 Dark ooze by the apple tree stippled with massive paw-prints.

paw (pǭ), *sb.*⁴ *U.S.* = PA.

1903 *Dialect Notes* II. 324 *Paw, maw,* nouns. Father; mother. (In the North *pa; ma.*) **1919** E. O'NEILL *Rope* in *Moon of Caribees* 183 Come on back to the house, Paw. It's gittin' near supper time. **1929** W. FAULKNER *Sound & Fury* 46 Your paw told you to stay out that tree. **1933** J. V. ALLEN *Cowboy Lore* IV. 67 He said he had to leave his home, his paw had married twice. **1935** Z. N. HURSTON *Mules & Men* I. vii. 163 His paw said, 'Son, Ah don't see how you gointer do dat.' **1939** in *Jrnl. Amer. Folklore* LII. 108 I am Peetie Wheet Straw, the devil's son-in-law, The woman I married, old Satan was her paw. **1942** ADE *Let.* 1 Feb. (1973) 228 The little red school-house is a thing of the past but don't forget that it turned out some of our best people, including possibly your paw and maw and, certainly, your grandparents. **1968** E. J. GAINES *Bloodline* 247 He follow his mom and paw out the house **1975** J. GORES *Hammett* (1976) xiv. 102 'What's the brother's name?' 'Don't rightly know. May be my paw—.'

paw, *v.* **3. a.** Now esp. to fondle (usu. a woman) lasciviously. Also const. *about, over.*

1902 ADE *Girl Proposition* 58 He told himself that he was a Chump for continuing to worship one who could be pawed over and man-handled by anything that wore a Derby Hat. **1918** H. G. WELLS *Joan & Peter* xi. 387 A fellow had to..watch..Joan being ordered about and..*pawed* about. **1928** A. HUXLEY *Point Counter Point* xi. 176 Other men were liable to pounce on you and try to paw you about and kiss you. **1934** E. O'NEILL *Days without End* II. 70 Walter was drunk, pawing over his latest female. **1942** A. CHRISTIE *Body in Library* ii. 24, I hate to see a girl..who..lets a disgusting Central European paw her about. **1955** G. FREEMAN *Liberty Man* I. iii. 51 Maureen had been mad for him to go on pawing her for hours last night. **1959** 'C. CARNAC' *Death of Lady Killer* xii. 136 A real dirty tyke he was, always trying to paw any woman within reach. **1975** J. I. M. STEWART *Young Pattullo* vii. 153 Fish, who had decent feelings, would have preferred to be pawed in privacy. **1978** D. BLOODWORTH *Crosstalk* xxxi. 240 The outraged shopper said..that when he saw her looking at him he had winked and pawed her.

pawa, var. *PAUA.

‖ **pawang** (pā·waŋ). Also (*rare*) **puwang.** [Malay.] A Malay sorcerer or medicine-man; a wizard or witch; a wise man, expert.

1821 J. LEYDEN tr. *Malay Annals* 51 He immediately ordered an artificer to be sent for, named Pawang Bentan. **1839** T. J. NEWBOLD *Pol. & Statistical Acct. Straits of Malacca* II. viii. 98 They have 'wise men', or Puwangs, who pretend to be able to ascertain the most favourable spots for sinking a mine. **1893** F. A. SWETTENHAM *About Perak* 33 A Malay Páwang (medicine-man) has the same sort of nose for tin that a truffle dog has for truffles. **1906** *Macm. Mag.* Aug. 778 An old *pawang*, or sorcerer, stepped forward with a bunch of twigs of a tree for which a tiger is thought to have a peculiar dread. **1907** F. A. SWETTENHAM *Brit. Malaya* vii. 156 When a patient becomes dangerously ill..it is common..to call in a *pâwang*, a kind of wizard or witch, who tries by incantations and other forms of the black art to lure the evil spirit from his prey. **1933** L. AINSWORTH *Confessions Planter in Malaya* 128 A 'Pawang' or witch doctor was called, and for the sum of twenty dollars he agreed to perform the complete ceremony. **1965** C. SHUTTLEWORTH *Malayan Safari* ii. 34 Contact with the spirit world is only made through the medium of the tribal *pawangs* or medicine-men. **1972** M. SHEPPARD *Taman Indera* 94 *Pawang*, an expert in any art believed to involve the use of magic.

pawing, *vbl. sb.* and *ppl. a.* (Further examples, esp. of sense *3 a).

1749 J. CLELAND *Mem. Woman Pleasure* II. 134 The tiresome pawing and toying. **1906** E. NESBIT *Railway Children* xii. 256 Like most boys..[he] hated..kissing and holding of hands. He called all such things 'pawing'. **1931** W. FAULKNER *Sanctuary* xix. 205 Impassable, swinging hands with their escorts, objects of casual and puppyish pawings, they dawdled up the hill toward the college. **1935** *Scrutiny* IV. 128 Revolutionary feeling is for her bound up with an incessant kissing and pawing between and among the sexes. **1951** J. C. FENNESSY *Sonnet in Bottle* III. v. 82 Their pawing hands stretched out..to feel and finger their prisoners. **1977** H. OSBORNE *White Poppy* xxix. 194 A certain amount of kissing and pawing, but absolutely no more. **1978** *Times* 7 Sept. 13/3 Ladies never touch their gentlemen in public... Pawing and clinging, with its nasty carnal implications, is reserved for..foreign adventuresses.

pawkily, *adv.* Add later non-dial. examples.

1963 *Times* 21 May 4/5 The Essex batsmen, only partially inhibited by the cold, pushed the score pawkily along, sending up the 50 in just over the hour. **1971** *Guardian* 8 Sept. 8/3 His pawkily British sense of humour.

pawky, *a.* Add later non-dial. examples.

1935 K. A. PORTER *Flowering Judas* 112 He went on in his pawky way trying to make clear to her his mystical faith in these men who went ragged and hungry. **1966** *Listener* 3 Feb. 171/2 With these advantages, and his convivial, pawky wit, which was enjoyed as much over the port wine as it was over tea in the withdrawing room, Radcliffe's progress was remarkable. **1970** *Daily Tel.* 10 Nov. 12/3 Beethoven's Trio in B flat, Opus 11, on the other hand, was given a rather pawky performance, and the first movement, especially, was robbed of weight by the over detached articulation. **1973** *Daily Record* (Glasgow) 6 Aug. 6/3 Her other pawky comments include: T is for *Training*: This is entered into with particular vigour by the Reserve Team, so that they may escape relegation to the First Eleven. **1976** W. GÉRIN *E. Gaskell* xiv. 146 Mr. Brontë could..be witty and pawky as his later letters to Mrs. Gaskell show.

pawl, *v.* Add: Also **pall. 2. a.** Also, to detect.

1859 HOTTEN *Dict. Slang* 71 *Pall* to detect. **1975** H. R. F. KEATING *Remarkable Case* viii. 92 She's been palled once..a-trying ter get a look at that door.

pawlonia, var. *PAULOWNIA.

pawn, *sb.*¹ Add: **c.** *pawn end-game*; **pawn chain,** an unbroken diagonal line of pawns extending across several adjacent files; **pawn skeleton,** the structure of the pawns at the end of a chess opening; **pawn storm,** an attacking advance of pawns against a castled king.

[**1818** W. S. KENNY *Pract. Chess Exercises* 45 This is better than breaking his chain of pawns.] **1937** M. EUWE *Strategy & Tactics in Chess* iii. 50 An immobile sequence of Pawns is called a pawn-chain. **1957** L. BARDEN *Guide to Chess Openings* v. 105/2 White is hoping to safeguard the base of his pawn-chain. **1973** *Sci. Amer.* June 104/2 The program now is sophisticated enough to execute very simple positional ideas such as creating pawn chains, striving for control of the center and so forth. **1939** A. ALEKHINE *My Best Games of Chess* 86/2 K-K4, P-QKt4!.. with a won Pawn end-game. **1914** J. DU MONT tr. *Lasker's Chess Strategy* (1915) iv. 26 Each opening is characterised by a well-defined pawn formation... Naturally the formation of a pawn skeleton is not an independent factor. **1927** *Brit. Chess Mag.* XLVII. 170 First you must learn the normal Pawn skeleton of the opening very thoroughly. **1950** R. N. COLES *Chess-Player's Week-End Bk.* 11 If the pawn skeleton remained sound, the game could be continued from one phase to another. **1926** *Brit. Chess Mag.* XLVI. 134 Herr Bachmann makes it plain that such 'modern' tactics as..the Pawn-storm against the opponent's Castled position..are not 'modern' at all. **1957** L. BARDEN *Guide to Chess Openings* iv. 69/2 If White can carry through a pawn storm and advance his KBP to KB6 then Black will be completely throttled.

pawn, *sb.*² **4.** Add: †**pawn party,** app. a game resembling blindman's buff. *Obs.*

1831 H. SMITH *Festivals Games, & Amusem.* (N.Y.) 330 The village and country lasses enjoy their *spinning* and *quilting* bevies, singing-schools, and *pawn* parties, with at least an equal zest. **1952** *Amer. Speech* XXVII. 47 A pawn party must have been something like blindman's buff.

pawn, *v.* Add: **d.** *Stock Exchange.* To deposit (stock) with a bank as security.

1902 *Encycl. Brit.* XXXII. 866/1 So much stock is 'pawned' with banks that the conclusions arrived at by the jobbers from examining only what they are carrying over themselves are liable to be falsified.

Pawnee (pǭnī·), *sb.*² Also 8–9 **Pane.** [ad. Canad. F. *Pani*, f. Ioway-Oto *panyi*.] † **a.** The Wichita Indians, *spec.* the Wichita and Tawehash bands of the Red River of Oklahoma and Texas. *Obs.*

1770 P. PITTMAN *Present State Europ. Settlem. on Mississippi* 40 The Arcansas or Quapas Indians..bring in very frequently young prisoners and horses from the Cadodaquias, Paneise, Podoquias, &c. of which they dispose to the best advantage. **1803** in C. E. Carter *Territorial Papers U.S.* (1940) IX. 74 The length of Red River is not known, it is Six or seven hundred Miles to the Pawnie or Towiash Indians. **1830** in *Ibid.* (1954) XXI. 215 The settlers are in continual alarm from the Pawnee Indians.

b. A confederacy of Caddoan Indians, formerly inhabiting the Loup, Platte, and Republican River valleys in Nebraska; a member of this group of tribes. Also *attrib.* or as *adj.*

1778 J. CARVER *Trav. N.-Amer.* 118 This is the road they [*sc.* Indians] take when their war parties make their excursions upon the Pawnees. **1794** [see *MANDAN *a.* and *sb.*]. **1806** Z. M. PIKE *Jrnl.* 22 Sept. in *Acct. Expeditions Sources Mississippi* (1810) II. 140 [I] met a Pawnee hunter. **1810** [see *KIOWA *sb.*]. **1827** J. F. COOPER *Prairie* II. xi. 177 He will never see a Pawnee become a Sioux. **1841** J. WILLIAMS *Narr. Tour Indiana to Oregon* (1921) 31 The Caws..told me that the Pawnees were a bad nation, and that they had a battle with them. **1868** *N.Y. Herald* 31 July 5/3 A large band of the Sioux and Cheyennes had attacked a small party of the Pawnee scouts. **1890** J. G. FRAZER *Golden Bough* I. iii. 381 The Pawnees annually sacrificed a human victim in spring when they sowed their fields. **1901** 'MARK TWAIN' in *N. Amer. Rev.* Feb. 163 The oldest Americans are the Pawnees. **1925** Z. A. TILGHMAN *Dugout* 13 The Pawnees were late going south that year. **1946** G. FOREMAN *Last Trek of Indians* 242 The Sioux made two more raids, killing a Pawnee each time. **1959** E. TUNIS *Indians* 84/1 Many tribes had broken off from them in that time and some had moved northward up the river valleys—the Pawnee to Nebraska, the Arikara to North Dakota, for instance. **1969** *Observer* (Colour Suppl.) 18 May 32/2 Mrs Hines was brought up in a Pawnee Indian school where bull-hide boots were compulsory. **1972** *N.Y. Times* 3 Nov. 78/4 Earlier, Mrs. Martha Gras, a 71-year-old Pawnee Indian, appeared to sum up the sentiment of the Indian gathering.

c. The Caddoan language of these people.

1806 Z. M. PIKE *Let.* 2 Oct. in *Acct. Expeditions Sources Mississippi* (1810) App. II. 48, I asked..[for] a Tetau prisoner who spoke Pawnee, to serve as an interpreter. **1821** J. FOWLER *Jrnl.* (1898) 55 Mr. Roy—He Spoke Some Pane and (in) that language our Councils Ware Held. **1877** L. H. MORGAN *Anc. Society* III. iii. 440 In Mandan my brother's wife is my wife, and in Pawnee.. the same. **1965** *Canad. Jrnl. Linguistics* X. 105 The structure of Pawnee as compared with Oneida. **1968** R. W. LANGACKER *Language & its Struct.* viii. 231 Other families found in this area [*sc.* the Great Plains] are Caddoan (Wichita, Caddo, Arikara, Pawnee), [etc.].

d. Special combs.: (in sense a) **Pawnee pic, pique** (see also quot. 1916); (in sense b) **Pawnee lands,** reservations of Pawnee Indians; **Pawnee Loups, Mohas, Republics, Republicans,** sub-tribes of the larger Pawnee confederacy.

1931 *Amer. Speech* VII. 4 The 'Indian reserves' were frequently referred to as the 'Pawnee lands', 'Otoe Lands', or 'Indian territory'. **1806** in *Deb. Congress U.S.* (1852) 9th Congress 2 Sess., App. 1046 Pānias Loups (or Wolves)... These are also a branch of the Panias proper. **1823** E. JAMES *Acct. Expedition Rocky Mts.* II. 165 The camp had been occupied by a war party of Skeeree or Pawnee Loup Indians. **1847** D. COYNER *Lost Trappers* (1859) 62 As Doranto proved to be a son of a grand chief of the Pawnee Loups, he was greatly prized as a captive. **1843** N. BOONE *Let.* 11 Aug. in L. Pelzer *Marches of Dragoons in Mississippi Valley* (1917) 187 Whether this was caused by a fear that we'd frighten off the buffalo, or not, they kept up a continual alarm of Pawnee Mohas. **1806** in *Deb. Congress U.S.* (1852) 9th Congress 2 Sess., App. 1075 Pania Piqûe... [Also called] Paunee Piqûe. **1856** J. P. BECKWOURTH *Life* ii. 26 The Pawnee Pics or Tattoed Pawnees. **1916** THOBURN *Hist. Oklahoma* I. 124 The confusion of the two tribes was doubtless due to the French traders and trappers, who called the Wichitas 'Pawnee Piques', i.e. 'Tattooed Pawnees', hence the corrupted American term, Pawnee Pict. **1836** L. FORD in *Army & Navy Chron.* 19 May 312/1 The Pawnee Loups, Pawnee Republics, [etc.].. lie upon the Loup fork of the Platte, twenty or thirty miles distant from the Grand Pawnee village. **1917** WILL & HYDE *Corn among Indians of Upper Missouri* 145 The Pawnee Republics had only enough corn to thicken their soup. **1806** in *Deb. Congress U.S.* (1852) 9th Congress 2 Sess., App. 1045 Pānias proper and Pānias Republican live in the same village. **1810** Z. M. PIKE *Acct. Expeditions Sources Mississippi* App. II. 14 On the La Platte, reside the grand Pawnee village, and the Pawnee loups on one of its branches, with whom the Pawnee Republicans are at war. **1823** E. JAMES *Acct. Expedition Rocky Mts.* I. 159 They arrived about noon, seventy in number, consisting of individuals of each of the three tribes called *Grand Pawnees, Pawnee Republicans,* and *Pawnee Loups.*

pawn-haus, var. *PONHAUS.

pax¹**.** Add: **1. a.** (Examples of *pax Romana.*)

Cf. Pliny, *Nat. Hist.* XXVII. 3 immensa Romanae pacis maiestate.

1884 W. J. CLARKE tr. *Duruy & Mahaffy's Hist. Rome* II. I. xxxiv. 201 Later, another form expressed the advantage, which was the compensation for this imperious sway, *pax romana*, that 'Roman peace' destined to draw the nations together and blend all languages,.. whose boundless majesty, *immensa romanæ pacis majestas*, the nations will honour with sincere homage. **1888** *Encycl. Brit.* XXIII. 591/1 The *pax Romana* died with the empire. **1934** G. B. SHAW *On Rocks* Pref. 183 We Romans have purchased the *pax Romana* with our blood. **1956** A. TOYNBEE *Historian's Approach to Relig.* II. xvi. 212 The final collapse of the *Pax Romana* in the third century. **1974** *Encycl. Brit. Macropædia* II. 371/2 This Pax Romana..ensured the survival and eventual transmission of the classical heritage.

a*. Also combined freely with Latinized adjs. to form phrases on the model of *pax Romana,* as *pax aeronautica, Americana, atomica, Britannica, Communistica, Egyptiana, hispanica, Sovietica.*

1933 M. ARLEN *Man's Mortality* ix. 180 These privately-owned stations..were of immense service to inter-communication throughout the world... They were the visible symbols of the pax aeronautica. **1967** 'R. RAINE' *Wreath for Amer.* xxv. 182 The whole Western world..is living under..a Pax Americana, just as the world once lived in peace under a Pax Britannica. **1971** *Newsweek* 18 Oct. 17 In the opinion of many European experts, the Kremlin has a more ambitious objective: to alter the staus quo by exchanging the *Pax Americana* for a *Pax Sovietica.* **1976** *Times Lit. Suppl.* 26 Nov. 1488/5 The 'Pax Americana', a phrase which several contributors toss about carelessly, is and was a myth, if meant to take in the world as a whole. There has not been so much peace since the Second World War for the right term to be either Pax or Americana. **1966** R. ARDREY *Territorial Imperative* (1967) viii. 283 Pessimism, under the rule of a *Pax Britannica*, was a dirty little luxury which any could afford; under a *pax atomica* it carries small selective value. **1969** W. GARNER *Us or Them War* xxv. 203 I'll give you a toast, girl. The *pax atomica*! Long may it last! **1886** *Jrnl. R. United Service Inst.* May 865 We should see Pax Britannica far transcend what Pliny called the 'immensa Romanæ Pacis Majestas'. **1899** [in Dict.] **1939** E. H. CARR *Twenty Years' Crisis* v. 104 In the past, Roman and British imperialism were commended to the world in the guise of the *pax Romana* and the *pax Britannica*. **1960** *Times* 29 Sept. (Nigeria Suppl.) p. x/3 As a result of the *Pax Britannica*..the population has increased steadily. **1967** J. CLEARY *Long Pursuit* v. 113 We brought peace to this part of the world, Pax Britannica is more than just a phrase. **1969** J. MANDER *Static Society* ii. 83 It brought greater stability..than did the *pax britannica*. **1973** *Listener* 1 Feb. 146/2 In the 19th century, the British Navy dictated the Pax Britannica and more or less guaranteed a century of peace. **1946** H. NICOLSON *Diary* 22 Aug. (1968) 75 They [*sc.* the Russians] believe that.. people will say in the end, 'Anything for peace', and will accept the Pax Scythica or Communistica. **1961** L. MUMFORD *City in Hist.* iii. 88 There may well have been [in ancient Egypt] a long period, a Pax Egyptiana, that relaxed both the internal tensions and the need for external protection. **1969** J. MANDER *Static Society* ii. 83 The centuries of peace under the *pax hispanica* that shielded Latin Americans. **1945** A. HUXLEY *Let.* 7 May (1969) 522 One can only hope that the Pax Sovietica may last as long as the Pax Romana. **1969** *Sunday Times* 19 Oct. 49 There won't be a Pax Sovietica or anything like it, because the world is too big to be governed by anybody. **1977** *Time* 29 Aug. 19/3 Bell-bottom denims, miniskirts and platform shoes have turned Ulan Bator's girls into the prettiest within the Pax Sovietica.

d. *Pax Romana*, also the name of an international organization of Roman Catholic students.

1957 M. P. FOGARTY *Christian Democracy in W. Europe* xvii. 263 Catholic graduates of all faculties are linked up through *Pax Romana* which also includes students. **1967** D. T. KAUFFMAN *Dict. Relig. Terms* 349/1 *Pax Romana*, world organization of Catholic students. In Europe it is called the International Movement of Catholic Students.

Paxarete (paχăre·tə). Also **Pajarete, Pascarete, Paxarette.** [f. *Paxarete*, a small town in the Jerez district of Spain.] A mixture of fortified wine and boiled-down grape juice, formerly drunk as a sherry, now used primarily for colouring or sweetening sherry or whisky.

1827 SCOTT *Chron. Canongate* 1st Ser. II. vi. 151 When they were comfortably seated over a bottle of Paxarete. **1846** R. FORD *Gatherings from Spain* xiv. 152 It is of this grape that the rich and luscious sweet wine called *Pajarete* is made. **1891** in C. Ray *Compleat Imbiber* (1967) IX. 122 Sherry... Paxerette. **1920** G. SAINTSBURY *Notes on Cellar-Bk.* ii. 18 Light Spanish wines..for instance, the lighter Paxarettes..which most literary people to-day associate only with Sir Telegraph in 'Melincourt'. **1958** A. L. SIMON *Dict. Wines* 122/1 The *Pajarete* or *Paxarete* liqueur wine..is mostly used for sweetening high-class sweet sherries. **1965** O. A. MENDELSOHN *Dict. Drink* 254 *Paxarete*, Spanish compound wine, also known as Pedro Ximénèz, made by fortifying *arrope* (concentrated grape juice)... Also known as *pascarete* and *pajarete*.

paxillar, *a.* (Example.)

1900 *Proc. Zool. Soc.* 292 Paxillar crowns are very large and oval.

paxillose, *a.* Add: **c.** Provided with paxillæ; paxillate.

1900 *Proc. Zool. Soc.* 290 The abactinal surface is paxillose, each paxillus having a circular crown of about eight papillæ, the centre being usually smooth.

Paxolin (pæ·ksŏlin). Also **paxolin.** A proprietary name for a type of laminated plastic widely used as an electrical insulating material.

1918 *Trade Marks Jrnl.* 23 Jan. 86 Paxolin... Electrical insulating preparations... The Micanite & Insulators Company, Limited,..London,..manufacturers. **1924** *Harmsworth's Wireless Encycl.* III. 1529/1 Paxolin is an insulating material made of paper impregnated with a varnish consisting of phenol and formaldehyde. **1944** *Electronic Engin.* XVI. 385/3 The objective lens was mounted inside a piece of paxolin tubing. **1958** *Official Gaz.* (U.S. Patent Office) 28 Oct. TM 135/2 The Micanite & Insulators Company Limited, London, England, Filed Feb. 14, 1958. Paxolin... For electrical insulating materials. **1960** *Practical Wireless* XXXVI. 413/1 To make such a screen, a piece of thin insulating material such as paxolin is wound with 26 s.w.g. wire. **1962** N. H. CODLING in G. A. T. Burdett *Automatic Control Handbk.* viii. 16 Characteristics of grade S5 silicone glass Paxolin are given in Table 9. **1965** *Wireless World* Aug. 377/1 Each unit has been assembled on a paxolin board using connecting pins.

pay, *sb.* Add: **4.** †**b.** In early N. Amer. colonial use, any article used as a medium of payment. *Obs.*

1663 *Early Rec. Portsmouth, Rhode Island* (1901) 118 To sell the tounes cow..for wompom or other pay. **1681** *Town Rec. Topsfield, Mass.* (1917) I. 34/2 Twente pownd of it in siluer forti five pownd in other pay as namli in Corne porke and beefe. **1794** S. KNIGHT *Jrnl.* (1825) 42 Pay is Grain, Pork, Beef, &c. at the prices sett by the General Court that year. **1767** in *Essex Inst. Hist. Coll.* (1912) XLVIII. 75 And if you should purchase light pay, then proceed for Turks island.

5. (Later examples.)

1873 *Trans. Illinois Dept. Agric.* X. 249 Many farmers were very slow pay. **1926** J. BLACK *You can't Win* iv. 28 They were good pay, but he could not get away from his work at the right hour to find them. **1973** R. THOMAS *If you can't be Good* (1974) xii. 103 Everybody in town is falling over each other to give him credit—even though he's a slow pay.

6. (Earlier and later examples.) Also, one of oil or natural gas. Also *concr.*, the bed itself.

1857 J. D. BORTHWICK *Three Yrs. in Calif.* vii. 140 After prospecting a little, we soon found a spot on the bank of the stream which we judged would yield us pretty fair pay for our labor. **1868** *Rep. J. Ross Browne Mineral Resources West of Rocky Mts.* (U.S. Treasury Dept.) 101 In 1866 they struck into pay and erected a 10-stamp mill, which is driven by a hurdy-gurdy wheel. **1933** E. CALDWELL *God's Little Acre* i. 2 I've been digging in this land close on fifteen years now, and..I figure we're going to strike pay pretty soon. **1975** [see *pay zone* s.v. *PAY- 2]. **1977** R. E. MEGILL *Introd. Risk Analysis* ix. 107 Every oil or gas field has a certain areal size, a thickness of the producing formation and a recovery per foot of pay.

7. Short for PAYMASTER. *slang.*

1878 F. DAVENPORT *On Man-of-War* 114 While the boy went forward after the steward, Pay regarded the omelet gloomily. **1914** 'BARTIMEUS' *Naval Occasions* xxiii. 216 Give it a shake, Pay, and put it on like a man! **1916** 'TAFFRAIL' *Pincher Martin* x. 173 Cashley, the fleet paymaster, was vainly endeavouring to get up a four at auction bridge... 'Going to take a hand?'..'Bridge,..not to-night, Pay; thanks, all the same.' **1942** [see *BOFFIN 1]. **1944** K. D. MCCRACKEN *Baby Flat-Top* 57 The Head of the Supply Department is known universally as 'Pay'.

pay, *v.*[1] Add: **2. d.** *not if you paid me, him,* etc.: under no circumstances; not at all.

1896 KIPLING *Seven Seas* 153 He couldn't lie if you paid him, and he'd starve before he stole! **1910** E. M. FORSTER *Howards End* xxiv. 201, I couldn't live near her if you paid me. **1952** M. ALLINGHAM *Tiger in Smoke* iv. 67, I shan't sleep, you know, I couldn't if you paid me. **1959** M. SUMMERTON *Small Wilderness* i. 8 Six months ago I was all set to read law, now I wouldn't go back to swotting if you paid me. **1979** R. JEFFRIES *Murder begets Murder* iii. 19, I wouldn't stay on here if you paid me to. The moment I've sorted everything out I'm off.

3. b. *pay out* (later examples).

1914 D. H. LAWRENCE *Widowing of Mrs. Holroyd* III. 66 He'd say to himself he'd pay me out. That's what he always does say, 'I'll pay thee out for that bit—I'll ma'e thee regret it.' **1940** G. D. H. & M. COLE *Counterpoint Murder* v. 51 He told Best to do it just in order to annoy him, to pay him out. **1951** M. KENNEDY *Lucy Carmichael* I. v. 36 I'm paid out for saying I wouldn't have a wreath. I thought a sort of vague cloud round my head would look nice. **1978** J. THOMSON *Question of Identity* xiii. 140 It was his way of paying out Maguire for giving him the push.

5. b. *to pay in* (later examples.)

1951 R. W. JONES *Thomson's Dict. Banking* (ed. 10) 468/2 Paying-in slips may also contain a notice requesting customers to cross all cheques before paying them in. **1961** NEW ENG. BIBLE *Matt.* xvii. 27 Take the first fish that comes to the hook, open its mouth, and you will find a silver coin; take that and pay it in; it will meet the tax for us both. **1978** N. J. CRISP *London Deal* v. 93, I didn't pay that money in, and no one else paid it in..and handed me the slip.

c. *to pay with the fore-topsail*: to leave port without paying one's debts or creditors. *Naut. slang.*

1843 J. F. COOPER *Ned Myers* 149 We sailed next morning, and I paid for the poor 'nigger' with the foretopsail. **1850** H. MELVILLE *White Jacket* I. ii. 5 The *middies* were busy raising loans to liquidate the demands of their laundress, or else—in the navy phrase—preparing to pay their creditors *with a flying fore-topsail*. **1910** D. W. BONE *Brassbounder* 262 Paid 'ee wi' tawps'l sheets, didn't 'e? **1929** F. C. BOWEN *Sea Slang* 101 *Pay debts with the fore topsail*, to slip away to sea in debt.

6. c. *pay up* (examples in *absol.* use).

1941 J. D. CARR *Case of Constant Suicides* xiv. 190 The insurance companies would have been compelled to pay up. **1972** *Daily Tel.* 13 Jan. 13/3 More than 100,000 TV licence bilkers have paid up since an anti-evasion campaign was launched last October. **1978** N. MARSH *Grave Mistake* ii. 43 I'm always having to yank him out of trouble... I'll go on paying up, I suppose.

9. b. *pay in*: to make (regular) contributions *to* a fund.

1911 *Rep. Labour & Social Conditions in Germany* (Tariff Reform League) III. 71 Men must pay in to the trade society to which they transfer their labour. *Ibid.* 82 Employees..commence to pay into State fund when 16 years old.

10. Also *to pay out.*

1909 'O. HENRY' *Roads of Destiny* xii. 193 Nobody in the bank knows those notes as I do. Some of 'em are a little wobbly on their legs, and some are mavericks without extra many brands on their backs, but they'll most all pay out at the round-up.

c. *pay off*: to succeed; to be profitable or advantageous; to show results.

1951 R. MALKIN *Boxcars in Sky* 118 It was the Big Briefing which, eventually, would pay off in plenty of free space outside the advertising columns. **1953** J. WAIN *Hurry on Down* iv. 73 Like a good many insane actions, it paid off. **1957** *Listener* 7 Nov. 757/1 Still, the cool piece of blackmail and bluff paid off. **1959** *Ibid.* 4 June 969/2 There are signs, already, that this policy of patience is paying off. **1962** A. SHEPARD in *Into Orbit* 104, I could feel that all the training we had gone through with the blockhouse crew and booster crew was really paying off down there. **1967** *Technology Week* 23 Jan. 61/1 (Advt.), Our aim is to make current space hardware and experience pay off for the national space program. **1971** R. DENTRY *Encounter at Kharmel* ix. 150 Your hunch had better pay off. The Tal's the last possibility. **1978** T. ALLBEURY *Lantern Network* viii. 93 By mid-May the training had begun to pay off.

13. Also *transf.*

1962 H. HOOD in R. Weaver *Canad. Short Stories* (1968) 2nd Ser. 211 He paid out a little string and began to run across the parking lot towards the main building. **1976** D. CLARK *Dread & Water* ii. 52 'Roped together?' 'Just like the book says... He went first and I payed out... I hadn't enough hands to cling tightly and pay out the rope'.

pay-. Add: **1. b.** *pay-check, -cheque, code, -envelope* (examples), *packet, -scale.* **c.** *pay-box* (esp. = *BOX OFFICE 1), *-desk, -night* (earlier and later examples), *-table* (later examples), *-window.* **d.** *pay-bed, -school, -toilet, ward.*

1895 *Brit. Med. Jrnl.* 2 Mar. 501/2 In opening..certain pay beds the Committee of Management had simply felt that they were carrying out what they were bound to do under the constitution of the hospital. **1928** *Daily Express* 19 July 9/4 The special committee appointed..to consider the needs of the professional and middle classes recommend that additional 'pay-beds' should be provided for them by the hospitals. **1934** *Lancet* 23 June 1371/2 To establish pay-beds for patients of moderate means. **1969** 'W. HAGGARD' *Doubtful Disciple* v. 52 In his pay-bed in the hospital Jacky D was depressed. **1974** *Times* 6 Nov. 2/8 The Owen working party..is discussing the new consultant contract and the pay-bed issue. **1976** H. WILSON *Governance of Britain* iv. 86 Fresh concern arose about government legislation and action in connection with pay-beds and private practice, in October and December 1975. **1851** DICKENS in *Househ. Words* 30 Aug. 531/2 He darts upon my luggage..pays certain francs for it, to a certain functionary behind a Pigeon Hole, like a pay-box at a Theatre. **1889** J. K. JEROME *Three Men in Boat* xix. 313 We attracted a good deal of attention at the Alhambra. On our presenting ourselves at the pay-box we..were informed that we were half-an-hour behind our time. **1952** V. GOLLANCZ *My Dear Timothy* 20 The practice was to open this door, and let people up the long staircase to a point a little short of the pay-box. **1975** N. LUARD *Travelling Horseman* iii. 71 The butler who'd..contact[ed] them from a street pay-box. **1904** 'O. HENRY' in *Everybody's Mag.* Aug. 240/1 Joe Wheeler signs the voucher for his pay-check. **1964** MRS. L. B. JOHNSON *White House Diary* 24 Apr. (1970) 122 How sensible these girls are to be starting on a skill that they can exchange for a paycheck almost anywhere. **1977** *Time* 10 Oct. 56/2 Chicagoans tell of a local executive who has supposedly never spent a paycheck in 30 years but lives entirely off the expense account. **1930** J. COLLIER *His Monkey Wife* xvii. 243 You take your pay cheque at the end of the week without making a lot of fuss about the size of it. **1973** J. WAINWRIGHT *Touch of Malice* 71 The inconvenience went with the rank and the pay-cheque. **1976** *Sunday Mail* (Glasgow) 21 Nov., And that wouldn't come into line with the Government's pay code which..limited everyone to £6 a week. **1898** A. BENNETT *Man from North* vii. 50 Jenkins eagerly drew Richard's attention to the girl at the pay-desk. **1919** W. DEEPING *Second Youth* vii. 64 Nearly always she sat at the same table near the pay-desk. **1932** D. L. SAYERS *Have his Carcase* xxx. 395 Bunter was four behind him in the queue at the pay-desk. **1909** *Sat. Even. Post* 5 June 17/1 (*heading*), The pay envelopes of the stars. **1911** E. FERBER *Dawn O'Hara* iv. 46 My bank account has always been an all too small pay envelope at the end of each week. **1973** E. TAYLOR *Serpent under It* (1974) xi. 172 Mr. Ramsay finally rrremembered that the rrrest of us like to eat, and left the pay envelopes. **1820** C. MATHEWS *Let.* 25 July in A. Mathews *Mem. Charles Mathews* (1839) III. vii. 148 The common outcry was against Saturday for a second performance, as it is pay-night, and the worst night in the week. **1970** G. GREER *Female Eunuch* 288 They have taken the pay packet out of the old man's pocket when he has finally arrived home on pay-night. **1941** 'N. BLAKE' *Case of Abominable Snowman* ix. 101 A stoppage of work and less money in the pay-packet on Fridays. **1973** *Times* 1 Jan. 3/2 Miners' institute libraries..were financed by pennies from miners' pay packets. **1976** *Norwich Mercury* 19 Nov. 1/4 Many firms find that a hamper is much appreciated by the workforce rather than '£10 in the pay packet', particularly as payment is subject to tax but a hamper is not. **1961** *Lancet* 9 Sept. 595/1 Our results make it possible to establish a pay-scale, based on production. **1976** F. MUIR *Frank Muir Bk.* 95 Teaching..became a respectable profession..with its own union to keep an eye on pay scales. **1856** X. D. MACLEOD *Biogr. F. Wood* 191 The cost to us in taxation is not one fifth the usual expense for an ordinary pay-school education. **1936** M. MITCHELL *Gone with Wind* v. lii. 905 There were no free schools. Few had money to send their children to pay schools. **1915** KIPLING *New Army* 29 The men..saluted emphatically at the pay-table, and fell back with their emoluments. **1965** 'LAUCHMONEN' *Old Thom's Harvest* xvi. 181 Every Saturday..the men were at the paytable in the ball-field. **1977** *Times Lit. Suppl.* 25 Mar. 334/5 His now receptive mind drifts back into the past where he is, once again, leader and paymaster of a racially mixed crew... The ghosts of the men again come forward to the paytable. **1946** E. HODGINS *Mr. Blandings builds his Dream House* ix. 132, I wouldn't come back here if you had a pay toilet. **1947** AUDEN *Age of Anxiety* (1948) iii. 72 The scene has all the signs of a facetious culture, Publishing houses, pawnshops, and pay-toilets. **1968** *Listener* 7 Nov. 610/1 There's a song about not having a dime for a pay toilet, and another one about the sexual relevance of Kleenex. **1976** *New Yorker* 15 Nov. 66/2 There was a character named Exotica A La Carte, who lived on the proceeds of a string of pay toilets. **1895** *Brit. Med. Jrnl.* 2 Mar. 502/1 It is desirable that the system of pay wards now in operation be so modified that the patients in those wards may..be attended in the hospital by outside practitioners of their own selection. **1934** *Archit. Rev.* LXXV. 92/1 The first doorway has a glass window which serves as a pay-window. **1977** A. C. H. SMITH *Jericho Gun* i. 16 It's a winning ticket... If you present it at the Tote pay window, even you might get some money back.

2. *pay-dirt* (further examples); also *fig.*; *-ground, -rock* (examples), *-streak* (examples), *zone* (later examples).

1866 *Dublin Rev.* Jan. 10 Even officers of men-of-war were seized by the gold mania, and 'ran' to soil their white hands in the precious 'pay-dirt'. **1930** E. RICE *Voy. to*

Purilia xvii. 249 As one elderly prospector expressed it: 'Thar's pay dirt in them thar hills.' **1935** *Motion Picture* Nov. 46/2 Frances Langford, the cutie whose 'pay dirt' reaches $1,000 per week. **1948** A. Huxley *Ape & Essence* (1949) 132 We see Loola standing in a three-foot hole wearily digging... 'When you hit the pay dirt..come and report to us.' **1953** *Economist* 24 Oct. 248 Senator McCarthy may have struck pay-dirt at last. **1967** *Ibid.* 26 Aug. 721/3 Senator Dirksen..applauds the President for permitting the bombers to attack targets within ten miles of the Chinese frontier: 'We seem to be getting close to paydirt.' **1972** *Lebende Sprachen* XVII. 34/1 US pay dirt—BE/US workable ore-bearing soil. **1973** C. Callow *Power from Sea* ii. 60 The thickness of the 'pay dirt'—that is the width of the sand in which the gas was contained. **1977** *Rolling Stone* 21 Apr. 88/3 Bowie hits celestial pay dirt on one of the pieces. **1927** *Daily Tel.* 25 Oct. 2/7 The results, taken in conjunction with the pay ground passed through the haulage, gives promise of..an important shoot. **1862** 'Mark Twain' *Let.* 8 Feb. (1920) 51 We'll have a mill-site, water power, and pay-rock, all handy. **1947** W. A. Chalfant *Gold, Guns, & Ghost Towns* 141 Thompson and Ramsay prospected over the same ground ..and struck some pay rock that was almost the pure stuff. **1856** *Daily Even. Bulletin* (San Francisco) 11 Oct. 1/1 These lucky miners worked one, two, and even three years, to reach the pay streak. **1910** R. W. Service *Ballads of Cheechako* 68 Late in the year he struck it rich, the real pay-streak at last. **1965** G. J. Williams *Econ. Geol. N.Z.* vii. 80/1 The gold is distributed over the schist bottom in more or less orientated paystreaks trending north-westerly. **1977** *New Yorker* 20 June 85/1 A pay streak appeared to be there, and what was needed now was a means of moving gravel in a major way. **1973** C. Callow *Power from Sea* ii. 61 The yield was 3.6 million cubic feet a day and the 'pay zone' was 64 feet thick. **1975** *Offshore* Sept. 75/2 It encountered three pay zones between 8,468 ft and 9,595 ft, with about 130 ft of net oil pay and a smaller zone of about eight ft of gas pay.

3. pay-back, the fact or action of paying back; reward or return, *spec.* the net return in profits from an investment project equal to the initial capital outlay; also *attrib.*; also as *adj.*, retaliatory.

1959 *Wall St. Jrnl.* (Eastern ed.) 31 Mar. 13/1 The pay-back order affects only the Star-Bulletin and not the union. **1965** H. I. Ansoff *Corporate Strategy* ii. 14 Three common methods for evaluation are the payback period, the internal rate of discount, and the net present worth. **1970** M. Kelly *Spinifex* iii. 63 'I can remember him taking part in a big pay-back raid a few years later.' 'Pay-back?' 'Pidgen for vendetta——.' **1971** C. R. W. Wysock Wright in B. de Ferranti *Living with Computer* iii. 22 This necessary investment in good education is essential although the payback may only be in the long term. **1972** *Accountant* 28 Sept. 391/2 You simply cannot say that.. discounted cash flow is superior to payback. **1973** *Sunday Times* (Colour Suppl.) 10 June 46/2 Such 'payback', or revenge killings, are common in the Highlands. **1977** *Irish Times* 8 June 10/7 It would, he said, depress cash flow and would lengthen the payback period for the mine's capital cost.

b. pay-as-you-earn, applied to a system of collecting income tax where the tax payable is deducted by employers from current earnings; **pay-as-you-enter,** applied to a system of collecting fares in public transport where passengers pay the driver on entering the vehicle; **pay-as-you-go,** applied to a system of paying or discharging obligations as they are incurred; **pay-as-you-see,** applied to a system of supplying an extra television channel to viewers paying either by subscription or by inserting coins into a box attached to the television receiver; **pay-as-you-use,** applied to a system of paying for an article while it is being used; **pay-as-you-view** = **pay-as-you-see*.

1943 *Daily Tel.* 22 Apr. 3 As to deduction of income-tax from wages he warned the House of the experiences of other countries which had attempted the 'pay-as-you-earn' idea. **1972** *Accountant* 6 Apr. 445/2 Pay-as-you-earn rates for 1972 are so much higher than last year that they could raise the tax take by the equivalent of some £1,500 million. **1908** *Sci. Amer.* 1 Feb. 76/2 (*heading*) A new type of fare register to be used on the New York pay-as-you-enter cars. *Ibid.*, The pay-as-you-enter cars which it is proposed to install on the New York city lines will be equipped with a device for collecting and automatically registering fares. **1913** *Chambers's Jrnl.* Aug. 623/1 This [system of tram-car operation] is the 'pay as you enter', or as it is termed briefly the 'paye' system. **1966** *Daily Tel.* 12 Sept. 20/3 A bus driver in Brighton collecting a fare from a passenger yesterday when the country's first pay-as-you-enter, one-man operated double deck bus service began for a experimental period. **1840** *Farmers' Cabinet* 15 May 319/1 Pay as you go..is the truest economy. **1888** J. Bryce *Amer. Commonwealth* II. lxvi. 507 'Pay as You Go' Convention! **1936** M. W. Childs *Sweden* xii. 214 The central government has consistently followed a pay-as-you-go tax policy. **1969** *Times* 30 Apr. 26/2 The rate of contribution needed from employees and employers jointly to finance the proposed State pensions on a 'pay-as-you-go' basis would increase from 7.7 per cent of earnings in 1972–73 to 11.4 per cent in 2002–03. *a* **1974** R. Crossman *Diaries* (1977) III. 176 We must therefore really accept pay-as-you-go. **1978** *Dumfries & Galloway Standard* 21 Oct. 5/7 (Advt.), It's pay-as-you-go; no big quarterly shocks. **1955** *Times* 6 Apr. 6/6 Sir Alexander Korda intends to seek permission of the United Kingdom authorities to operate 'pay as you see' television. **1962** *Variety* 22 Aug. 3 It's perhaps significant that all, or just about all, film distributors are leasing pictures to the Paramount-owned International Telemeter pay-as-you-see video in Etobicoke, Toronto suburb. **1929** *Radio Times* 8 Nov. 453/1 Place your order.. immediately, 'Pay as you use' terms can be arranged. **1961** *Engineering* 1 Sept. 257/1 Pay-as-you-use techniques covering the leasing of vehicles, machinery and equipment of all kinds are to be introduced into Britain. **1958** *Spectator* 11 July 61/3 The vital issue of whether a Pay-As-You-View television service is allowed to operate in this country. **1963** *Ann. Reg. 1962* 443 Other recommendations of the [Pilkington] Committee were that pay-as-you-view television..should be rejected.

c. *pay-on-* —: denoting a system of paying for a service when the action expressed has been performed or fulfilled.

1899 J. London *Let.* 29 July (1966) 46 And with these pay-on-acceptance fellows, did you ever get your check at the same time you were notified of acceptance? **1960** *Guardian* 11 Apr. 8/3 London's new..bus which..has the pay-on-entry system. **1961** *Daily Tel.* 23 May 17/6 (*heading*) 'Pay-on-reply' telephoning. *Ibid.*, Post Office engineers yesterday demonstrated the new 'pay-on-answer' coin boxes in seven telephone kiosks in the centre of Dartford, Kent.

4. Special combs. of Pay *sb.*, as **paybob** *slang*, = Paymaster; **pay freeze** = **pay pause*; **pay pause,** a period during which no wage or salary increases should occur, esp. as proposed in 1961 in the U.K.; **pay phone** orig. *U.S.*, a telephone that operates or connects the caller when coins are inserted; **pay-rise,** a wage or salary increase; **pay station** *U.S.*, (*a*) a public call-office; (*b*) a public telephone-booth; **pay-telephone** = **pay phone*; **pay television** = **pay-TV*; **pay-tone** (see quot. 1962); **pay-train** (see quot. 1969); **pay-TV,** a system of television based on the pay-as-you-see principle (see sense *3 b).

1916 'Taffrail' *Pincher Martin* viii. 125 Carn't yer get a hadvance o' money from th' paybob? **1962** Granville *Dict. Sailors' Slang* 87/1 *Paybob*, senior accountant officer. **1978** *Navy News* Dec. 6/1 The paybob and his chum never batted an eyelid as I signed my chit and I often wonder if they paid the difference. **1961** *New Scientist* 7 Sept. 568 The Chancellor of the Exchequer's pay-freeze. **1972** *Listener* 23 Nov. 690/3 The pay and wage freeze is a shoddy compilation. Over two million workers demanding pay rises are trapped in the freeze. **1975** *Guardian* 21 Jan. 26/3 The Chancellor..said there was no question of a pay freeze in the foreseeable future. **1961** *Daily Tel.* 19 Sept. 1/8 The increases for primary and secondary schools will cost £42 million a year, £5½ million less than the Burnham recommendation rejected by the Government on account of the 'pay pause'. **1969** C. Booker *Neophiliacs* vi. 158 On 25 July [1961], the Government mustered all the paraphernalia to meet a major crisis, from a 7 per cent Bank Rate to Selwyn Lloyd's celebrated 'Pay Pause', the first recent peacetime attempt by a Government to impose an overall regulation of wage increases. **1977** *Evening Post* (Nottingham) 27 Jan. 5/1 When the pay pause was relaxed for doctors earning over £8,000, it was decided not to pay the increment for another year. **1936** L. Duncan *Over Wall* ii. 31 He would then go to one of the pay phones. **1952** W. R. Burnett *Vanity Row* (1953) xiii. 90 'Where you calling from?' 'A pay-phone.' **1973** W. McCarthy *Detail* iii. 215 He gave the agent the number of a pay-phone in Burbank. **1975** *New Yorker* 27 Oct. 32/1 There are six pay phones downstairs and only five of them work. **1976** *Daily Express* 1 July 14/2 In April 1976 I asked the Post Office to change my business phone to a pay phone. **1936** J. Steinbeck *In Dubious Battle* iii. 26 Hell, we don't want only temporary pay-rises. **1957** P. Worsley *Trumpet shall Sound* x. 197 The soldiers of the Pacific Islands Regiment had achieved pay-rises. **1923** M. Watts *L. Nichols* 209 [He] rushed off to the nearest telephone pay station to call up the Grace house. **1948** *Time* 21 June 2 When you drop a nickel in a pay station and dial a call..as many as 1000 telephone relays go into action. **1973** W. McCarthy *Detail* iii. 215 He would like you to call this number...it is a pay station. **1974** *Spartanburg* (S. Carolina) *Herald* 24 Apr. A3/4 Police said Norton had answered a call from two men using a pay station, asking that a cab pick them up at a motel. **1963** A. Orlov *Handbk. Intelligence* xiii. 153 The agent avails himself of the forthcoming 'pay telephone' conversation with his superior. **1964** *Punch* 13 May 702/2 A man known to have installed a pay-telephone. **1971** A. Hunter *Gently at Gallop* viii. 89 There was a pay-telephone for customers. He fed in a coin and dialled the police-station. **1976** *Billings* (Montana) *Gaz.* 28 June 6-A/3 The chairman of the American Telephone and Telegraph Co. said Sunday a pay telephone call probably will cost a quarter in most places. **1957** *Economist* 28 Sept. 1028/2 The Federal Communications Commission has tentatively opened the airwaves to 'pay television'. **1962** *Rep. Comm. Broadcasting 1960* 262 in *Parl. Papers 1961–2* (Cmnd. 1753) IX. 259 'Subscription television' (or 'toll' or 'pay' television, as it is variously called) involves a third method of paying. **1973** *Listener* 31 May 706/1 'The big news in cable now is Pay.' He meant pay television. **1962** *Sunday Express* 4 Feb. 12 The pips are the pay-tone signal, which tells the caller that you have picked up the receiver and it is time for him to put in the coins. **1972** J. Wainwright *Night is Time to Die* (1974) 167 On S.T.D., a call-box is a dead give-away by the pay tone! **1968** D. I. Gordon in *Regional Hist. Railway Gt. Brit.* V. xii. 232 The Eastern Region is making a gallant fight. Conductor guards and the whole concept of the 'basic' railway with its Pay Trains, fast and well-integrated services, [etc.]..are all features of the current scene. **1969** *Railway Mag.* CXV. 169/2 Conductor/Guard workings ('pay trains') began on January 19 between Newcastle and Carlisle. *Ibid.* 473/2 From June 15, 'paytrains'—on which tickets are issued by the guard—were introduced by the Eastern Region. **1972** *Times* 15 June 3/1 Public transport, even in an age of one-man buses, 'pay-trains', and automatic fare collection, is much more labour intensive than other industries. **1976** P. R. White *Planning for Public Transport* ii. 53 Little detail is recorded of trip patterns on 'paytrain' services. **1956** *Britannica Bk. of Year* 492/2 Also introduced from the United States—though not yet fully accepted into British English—were such expressions as Pay TV, [etc.]. **1960** *News Chron.* 29 June 4/6 'Pay-TV', a system whereby you put some coins in a slot at the top of the set and are rewarded by several hours uninterrupted viewing. **1972** *Listener* 8 June 773/2 Pay-TV was expensive and offered very little that was new. **1976** J. Lund *Ultimate* vi. 57 He looked at the pay TV programme—'Jaws' showing on odd days it said.

payability. Delete *rare* and add later examples.

1933 *Flight* 30 Mar. 296/1 We have on occasion discussed with Mr. C. C. Walker the subject of 'payability' of aircraft. **1955** *Times* 3 May 17/5 The 170 feet sampled assayed 182.32 dwts. over 5.12 inches or 933 inch-dwts. at a payability of 100 per cent. **1971** *Daily Tel.* 11 Oct. 17 The payability is low as advance development is now confined largely to the flanks of the mine where values are inclined to be more scattered.

payables (pēi·ăb'lz), *sb. pl. Comm.* [f. the adj.] Debts that one owes; liabilities. Cf. *Receivable *sb.* 3.

1972 *Accountant* 12 Oct. 445/2 Money and receivables and payables. **1977** *Sci. Amer.* Apr. 95/1 (Advt.), You also get a complete package of programs for general ledger, payables, receivables, payroll, and inventory. **1977** *Detroit Free Press* 11 Dec. 18-D/7 (Advt.), Bookkeeper part-time. Full charge, receivable, payables, invoicing, and payroll.

pay-day. Add: (Further examples.)

1897 [see **account day*]. **1895** [see *Name-day 3]. **1916** 'Taffrail' *Pincher Martin* viii. 147 'Our ship's company made a bit of a pay-day over it.' 'Pay-day!' 'Ow d' yer mean?'.. 'Bettin'!' **1930** R. Campbell *Adamastor* 33 We attend the Great Inspection, The Roll-call of the Resurrection, The pay-day of Eternity. **1944** Dylan Thomas *Lett.* (1966) 262 I'll be up in London..always on payday Fridays. **1972** *Daily Tel.* 4 July 32/6 She laughed and replied 'They will have to do. It's the only pair I've got till pay day.'

b. Wages; the amount paid to a person on pay-day. *Naut.*

1915 D. W. Bone *Broken Stowage* 239 We had fondly hoped to be strutting on Liverpool streets with our women folk, a twelve-months' 'pay day' in our pockets. **1922** E. O'Neill *Anna Christie* (1923) ii. 60 'Tis no more drinking and roving about I'd be doing then, but giving my pay-day into her hand and staying at home with her as meek as a lamb. **1932** J. W. Harris *Days of Endeavour* 20 The Bos'n, his fat pay-day having dwindled away..had sailed.

paying, *vbl. sb.*[1] Add: **2. b.** *paying-in slip*: in *Banking*, a form listing cash, cheques, etc. which are paid in to the credit of an account; *paying-off pennant* (or *pendant*): a pennant flown by a homeward-bound naval ship or by a merchant vessel that will shortly discharge all hands.

1898 H. T. Easton *Work of Bank* iv. 26 The 'paying-in' slip can be utilised for pasting in the cash-book and ledger. **1968** 'C. Aird' *Henrietta Who?* x. 91 According to the paying-in slips, she always handed it over herself. **1974** 'S. Woods' *Done to Death* 50 When she makes up her paying-in slip for the Bank whatever cash there is has been taken over the counter. **1977** *Grimsby Even. Tel.* 14 May 5/8 Mrs. —— said she had signed other names 'on bank paying-in slips and things like that'. **1914** 'Bartimeus' *Naval Occasions* xxiii. 212 The paying-off pendant looks as if it were impatient. **1927** B. M. Chambers *Salt Junk* 50 At last the great day came: the hoisting of the paying-off pendant, a yard for every day of the commission. It was so long that the gilded bladder on the end fouled the houses which bordered the creek. **1954** Bradford & Quill *Gloss. Sea Terms* 142/2 *Paying-off pennant*, flown by a naval vessel when homeward bound from a foreign station. **1961** F. H. Burgess *Dict. Sailing* 158 *Paying off pennant*, an extremely long pennant hoisted as a sign that a ship is shortly 'paying off'. **1977** *Navy News* Aug. 40 H.M.S. Matapan enters Portsmouth Harbour for the last time, paying off pennant suspended from a large balloon.

paying, *ppl. a.* Add: (Earlier and later examples.) *paying guest*: a lodger.

1853 E. Clacy *Lady's Visit Gold Diggings Austral.* 111 The two holes were 'bottomed' before noon with no paying result. **1871** *Trans. Illinois Agric. Soc.* VIII. 238 We need not expect to get a paying crop from stiff clays. **1872** Geo. Eliot *Middlem.* IV. viii. 363 His skill was relied on by many paying patients. **1879** Trollope *John Caldigate* I. x. 135 'It's a paying concern, I suppose,' said Caldigate. 'It has paid;.. Whether it's played out or not, I'm not so sure...' **1895** G. Gissing *Paying Guest* i. 7 It's a very common arrangement nowadays, you know; they are called 'paying guests'. **1900** Paying guest [in Dict.]. **1929** E. F. Benson *Paying Guests* i. 9 Never had Wentworth and Balmoral and..Belvoir entertained so continuous a complement of paying guests. **1957** J. Braine *Room at Top* i. 16 Her voice paused perceptibly at the word *lodger* as if considering..the euphemisms—paying guest..and so on. **1958** J. Cannan *And be a Villain* vii. 148 Next pew—paying patients..then the doctors, the colleagues 'showing up'.

pay-load (pēi·lōud). [f. Pay- + Load *sb.*] **a.** The part of an aircraft's load from which revenue is derived; the passengers, mail, or cargo carried by an aircraft.

1930 *Times* 12 Nov. 11/4 Her [*sc.* a flying-boat's] range is determined by the amount of 'pay' load she has to carry. **1933** *Discovery* Dec. 367/2 There is no reason why the pay load should not be decreased to give an increased range but it could not carry a paying load for 2,000 miles. **1936** *Economist* 25 Apr. 190/1 From the operational aspect, the key factor of seasonal pay-loads is still present, and this must necessarily limit the prospects of large profits. **1946** R. A. McFarland *Human Factors Air Transport Design* x. 406 It is often contended that extra crew members replace passengers and payload. **1951** 'N. Shute' *Round Bend* 145 They pulled out a revised crew accommodation ..and added a hundred and ten pounds to the payload. **1955** *Sci. Amer.* Jan. 38/2 Helicopter designers are now busily engaged in harnessing jet engines to helicopters to raise their speed, range and payload. **1970** H. A. Taylor *Airspeed Aircraft since 1931* 170 It is practicable to use short, lightweight loading ramps which can be carried in the aircraft with a minimum loss of space and payload. **1978** *Jrnl. R. Soc. Arts* CXXVI. 685/1 The benefits of such scaling will be greatest on aircraft having the lowest percentages by weight of payload.

b. The bombs, warhead, etc., carried by an aircraft or rocket; the instruments, equipment, manned capsule, etc., carried by a rocket.

1936 *Sky* Nov. 7/3 Let the littlest and middlesize rocket serve as the 'pay load' of the biggest rocket. **1941** D. Garnet *War in Air* ii. 12 The British Bomber..could carry less petrol and more bombs, that is to say a higher 'pay-load' of bombs than the German Bomber. **1946** J. P. Baxter *Scientists Against Time* ii. 35 Allied scientists and intelligence officers racked their brains to determine what would be the pay load in these long-range missiles. **1955** *Times* 6 Aug. 6/1 The payload would be instruments capable of recording conditions outside the atmosphere and a telemetering apparatus to transmit findings to base. **1962** F. I. Ordway et al. *Basic Astronautics* iv. 121 Sounding rockets..with 50-lb payloads designed to analyze the results of these atomic explosions. **1970** *New Scientist* 8 Oct. 77/3 The proposed payload of the US space shuttle has come down some 50 per cent in the last three months. **1974** *Globe & Mail* (Toronto) 22 Oct. 7/1 In 1972, former President Richard Nixon.. promised that NASA would launch all foreign payloads intended for peaceful purposes under basically the same conditions that apply in the United States.

c. Goods, etc., carried on a road vehicle. Also *transf.* and *fig.*

1938 *Nation* (N.Y.) 13 Aug. 144/1 The trucks have to carry all their own gas, oil, and water..which does not leave much room for pay load. **1960** E. L. Cornwell *Commercial Road Vehicles* ix. 250 The articulated vehicle, weight for weight, generally has a rather lower payload capacity than a rigid vehicle. **1967** G. F. Fiennes *I tried to run a Railway* vii. 84 We have the pay load of some 500 tons transferred between road and rail by some six men. **1968** D. Braithwaite *Fairground Archit.* 88 But the electric 'Scenic'..constituted the heaviest pay load ever and often required the attendance of two traction engines. **1971** M. Tak *Truck Talk* 115 *Pay load*, the cargo or freight that a trucker hauls. **1971** C. Bonington *Annapurna South Face* vii. 85 Another factor one had to reckon with was that people moving back up the mountain, as opposed to ferrying, could carry only a very limited payload of supplies, if any, since they would be carrying their own personal equipment. **1976** P. R. White *Planning for Public Transport* x. 215 Although offering similar weight: payload characteristics as does an internal combustion engine and its fuel tank, such a 'fuel' would require large amounts of energy for its creation. **1978** J. B. Hilton *Some run Crooked* xiii. 132 Once the watertable overflows, there are gullies adding their pay-load from both sides.

So **Payloader, pay-**, the proprietary name of a type of heavy mobile machine used for lifting and loading.

1953 *Sun* (Baltimore) 12 Oct. 14/5 The Coast Guard informed Rukert Terminals Corporation that pay loaders could not be used in the bottom of the holds to remove the fertilizer because of possible fire hazard. The loaders are scoops operated by gasoline. **1957** *Muck Shifter* June 340/1 (*heading*) 'Four-in-one' attachment. The entire line of four-wheel-drive Hough 'Payloader' tractor-shovels will now offer Drott '4-in-1' buckets as optional equipment. **1959** *Trade Marks Jrnl.* 27 May 548/1 Payloader... Lifting, loading and mechanical handling machines and mechanisms and parts of all these goods.. The Frank G. Hough Co. Libertyville, State of Illinois, United States of America; manufacturers. **1963** T. Pynchon *V.* xii. 347 Someday there would be cranes, dump trucks, payloaders, bulldozers to come and level the neighbourhood. **1965** *Courier-Mail* (Brisbane) 10 Nov. 1/6 A man was killed at Mica Creek power station yesterday when a payloader he was driving overturned. **1969** *Jane's Freight Containers 1968–69* 267/1 The ancillary equipment is composed of..two 1.8 cu m payloaders, one 25 ton side-loader and several heavy-duty fork-lifts. **1977** G. A. Browne *Slide* xxii. 180 A heavy-duty ditch digger..called a payloader because of its combination digging-conveying system.

Payne's grey (pēinz grēi). [f. the name of William *Payne* (fl. 1800), English artist, + Grey *sb.*] A composite pigment composed of blue, red, black, and white permanent pigments, used esp. for watercolours.

1835 [see *neutral *a.* 3 c]. **1886** H. C. Standage *Artists' Man. Pigments* vi. 68 Payne's grey resembles neutral tint in being a compound colour. **1888** [see Grey *sb.* 4 e]. **1924** [see *neutral *a.* 3 c]. **1934** H. Hiler *Notes Technique Painting* ii. 133 As to the prepared greys,.. Payne's Grey, etc., they are usually mixed by the manufacturers. **1959** *Listener* 13 Aug. 254/3 The embellishment of the same green, sometimes with a touch of Payne's grey, fields. **1979** *Dryad Crafts* 49/4 Oil Colours... Payne's Grey.

pay-off. Also **payoff.** [f. vbl. phr. *to pay off* (in various senses): see Pay *v.*[1]] **1. a.** Winnings from gambling or the paying of these. Also *attrib.*

1905 F. Hutchison *Johnnie the Gent* 63 An' then there's the know-it-all-bloke that has just beat a couple of races, wit' about an ounce each way or maybe a deuce to peek. Oh, he's the wisest guy that ever give the pay-off gazebo the lofty leer when he reached for his dough. **1938** G. Greene *Brighton Rock* iv. i. 149 'I've won, Pinkie. A tenner.'.. A young man with oiled hair stood on a wooden step paying out money... Spicer called out to him..: 'Well, Sammy, now the pay-off.' **1943** *Sun* (Baltimore) 22 Apr. 18/1 This crowd backed New Moon confidently, the final payoff being $3.90 for $2. **1964** A. Wykes *Gambling* vi. 142 If he throws a natural or crap,.. the payoff odds will be considerably smaller. **1967** *Listener* 10 Aug. 168/2 A zero-sum game is one in which the pay-offs cancel out to zero—I've won sixpence, you're sixpence down. **1970** *Globe & Mail* (Toronto) 28 Sept. 20/2 How about the $800 daily double payoff the track made one day on a bet that never was made. Is that not bookmaking?

b. *Criminals' slang.* A confidence trick in which the victim is encouraged to venture a large sum of money by the success of a bet, investment, etc., involving a small sum or one furnished by the confidence tricksters. Also, one who employs this confidence trick (= *pay-off man* (*a*) (sense 5 below)).

1915 G. Bronson-Howard *God's Man* iii. iii. 197 Specialists in check-raising, wireless wire-tapping, 'the match', 'the pay-off', and cards. **1928** [see *creep *sb.* 1 d]. **1935** *Evening News* 29 June 3/2 The sucker is induced to put a small sum into one venture. His winnings are promptly paid and he has visions. This is the '*pay-off*'. **1938** P. J. Smith *Con Man* ix. 192 It is to his genius that the successful swindle known as the 'Pay Off' was attributed. **1943** *Police Jrnl.* Mar. 69 *Pay off*, a confidence trick—Stock Exchange fraud.

c. The return on an investment; profit. Also, the point at which an investment begins to yield profit.

1955 *Times* 5 Aug. 9/7 Countries which entered on the first stage would be relying on the second stage for their 'pay off'. **1969** *Daily Tel.* 11 Mar. 6/1 Profits in the past two years have been held back by the Woolco development and the pay-off here still could be a long way away. **1974** *Nature* 1 Feb. 248/1 The spending proposals entail vast concentration of resources in areas which are likely to have a quick payoff. **1974** *Information Handbk. 1974–5* (Shell Internat. Petroleum Co.) 64 A major oilfield can represent an investment as high as £400 million and it may take several years to reach pay-off. **1977** *Jrnl. R. Soc. Arts* CXXV. 58/2 The second problem..was to ensure that a fairly early pay off was secured from the new investment—and this in an industry where long lead times seemed inevitable. **1978** *N.Y. Times* 30 Mar. d. 5/3 The payoff in high-technology fields is extraordinarily great.

2. The payment of bribes; graft. Also, a sum of money given as a bribe. Also *attrib.*

1930 (*film title*) The Big Payoff. **1935** D. Lamson *We who are about to Die* xi. 193 Witnesses, juries, pay-off, fixin's—don't matter what it is... There ain't nothin' he won't do, long as you got the potatoes. **1938** R. Chandler in *Dime Detective Mag.* Jan. 62/1 He took my gun and his payoff money. **1950** *Sat. Even. Post* 27 May 20/1, I saw that in the Navy there's a lot of pay-off [graft]. **1958** S. Ellin *Eighth Circle* (1959) ii. iii. 44, I never took a penny of pay-off money since I got into the Department. **1971** R. Dentry *Encounter at Kharmel* xii. 219 *Money* for everything you've been through—a piddling wee payoff to close our mouths? **1976** *National Observer* (U.S.) 4 Dec. 2/2 Tanaka is one of several Japanese officials accused of receiving $12 million in pay-offs from Lockheed for promotion of the company's sales in Japan. **1977** *New Yorker* 22 Aug. 70/1 The scandal involving alleged political payoffs by agents of the South Korean government..first broke last year.

3. *Criminals' slang.* The division of the proceeds after a robbery.

1931 G. Irwin *Amer. Tramp & Underworld Slang* 141 *Pay off*, the division of spoils after a robbery. **1935** N. Ersine *Underworld & Prison Slang* 56 *Payoff*,..the end of a job and the splitting of the loot. **1935** A. J. Pollock *Underworld Speaks* 86/2 *Pay off joint*, place where the plunder (loot) is divided.

4. *transf.* and *fig.* Result, outcome, conclusion; return, recompense; punishment; the settling of accounts (in criminal contexts, esp. by murder). Also, a decisive or crucial factor; 'the ultimate'; 'the limit'. Also *attrib.*

It proved unrealistic to attempt to separate the examples that follow into clearly distinct sections. Many of them stand contextually at the border of at least two senses or embrace more than one sense.

1927 *Vanity Fair* Nov. 67/2 Conway's 'That's the pay off!' is swiftly making the rounds. It is employed when one enthusiastically describes anything that is first-rate: the acme, the last word! **1928** J. P. McEvoy *Show Girl* xiii. 195, I thought show business was all laughter and applause... It's a headache. It's a pain anywhere you sit. And then imagine falling in love on top of it. That's the pay-off. **1930** P. Annixter in *Flynn's* 11 Oct. 690 (*title*) The pay-off. **1932** *News* (San Francisco) 6 Aug. 12/3, I wanted to take one of those pictures which show how the greatest pitchers of the game hold their pay-off deliveries. **1937** N. Coward *Present Indicative* vii. 295, I had..lived far too strenuously. This [*sc.* a nervous breakdown] was the pay-off. **1937** *Sun* (Baltimore) 4 Aug. 14/1 The white-hulled defender isn't as impressive out of the water as the polished blue challenger but that isn't the payoff in this million-dollar sport. **1940** J. G. Brandon *Gang War!* ix. 93 It's a gang 'knock-off', or 'pay-off', whichever you like. **1944** *Sun* (Baltimore) 1 Nov. 1/5 The payoff is that there is no such thing as an effective Japanese fleet today. **1952** C. Day Lewis tr. *Virgil's Aeneid* ix. 189 The Fates and Venus have had their pay-off, in that the Trojans Have reached our fertile land of Ausonia. **1953** R. Lehmann *Echoing Grove* 42 The final pay-off, the practical one that always has to be gone through when there has been a death. **1957** *Times* 1 Oct. 11 It may be true, as Mr. Wilson said, that this economic crisis is 'the pay-off for the Government's policy on the past six years'. **1958** K. Amis *I like it Here* 200 He'd carried on in the same sort of way before, explaining he was part of the history of the English novel and all the rest of it, but this was really the pay-off. **1958** *Times* 8 May 11/6 To these crews, their terrible bomb loads are the devastating pay-off element of a daring formula: at war—to prevent war. **1970** G. Greer *Female Eunuch* 156 All that they have offered in the name of generosity and altruism has been part of an assumed transaction, in which they were entitled to a certain payoff. **1970** G. F. Newman *Sir, You Bastard* v. 149 All the inconvenience and suffering, and this was the payoff. **1971** R. Dentry *Encounter at Kharmel* xii. 199 There was nothing to be gained from beating the hell out of this foul-mouthed creep... The pay off could wait. **1976** *Survey* Summer-Autumn 45 Among the less apparent payoffs, one might well ponder the changes in regard to superficially non-political facets of Soviet life. **1977** *Time* 28 Feb. 8/2 Danish Premier Anker Jørgensen wagered his political future in January and last week collected the payoff.

b. The climax or dénouement of a story, play, etc.; the point or crux of a story, etc. Cf. *pay-off line* (sense 5 below).

1947 Wodehouse *Full Moon* vii. 141 A raconteur of established reputation expects something better than silence when he comes to the pay-off of one of his best stories. **1962** W. Nowottny *Lang. Poets Use* iv. 96 Marvell's poem has its 'pay-off' in the ambiguity of the *da capo* with which the poem comes to a conclusion. **1969** *Listener* 15 May 698/1 Some failed even to detect the snook being cocked at them in Mary's climactic confession that she'd 'always worry about Jim'—a pay-off one could take nostalgically or ironically.

5. Special combs.: **pay-off line**, the point of a story; the 'punch-line' of a story, limerick, etc.; **pay-off man** *Criminals' slang*, (*a*) a confidence trickster; (*b*) the cashier of a gang of criminals; **pay-off matrix, table** *Game Theory*, an array specifying the utilities to the players of all the possible outcomes of a game.

1934 J. O'Hara *Appointment in Samarra* (1935) i. 16 And they always knew when to laugh, even when it was a Catholic joke, because Reilly signalled the pay-off line by slapping his leg just before it was delivered. **1944** [see *bar-fly* s.v. *bar *sb.*[1] 30]. **1965** N. Coghill in J. Gibb *Light on C. S. Lewis* 61 We all laughed at this pay-off line. **1927** *Fresno* (Calif.) *Bee* 9 June 1/3 The complaint asserts that Justice of the Peace Murphy was introduced to Frank E. Howell, former deputy sheriff, who was alleged to have been the 'pay-off' man of the contractors. **1928** M. C. Sharpe *Chicago May* 286 *Pay-off men*,..confidence men (or women). **1932** *Sun* (Baltimore) 27 Apr. 15/7 There were frequent references to checks made payable by Plummer to an unidentified 'pay-off' man. **1934** [see *number *sb.* 3 e]. **1935** A. Squire *Sing Sing Doctor* v. 59 They surrounded themselves with bodyguards, flunkies, killers, fixers, pay-off men. **1938** D. Castle *Do Your Own Time* 287 *Pay-off man*, cashier of a mob. **1952** J. C. C. McKinsey *Introd. Theory of Games* i. 7 We shall henceforth describe such a game as this by giving merely the payoff matrix. **1971** D. C. Hague *Managerial Econ.* vii. 138 The columns show the result of each act... The rows show the events leading to these possible results. Table 11 is therefore known as a payoff matrix (or table). **1974** Anton & Kolman *Appl. Finite Math.* viii. 361 Games of the type described in this example are called matrix games and the matrix is called the payoff matrix. **1976** *Nature* 8 Apr. 481/1 He..assigned payoffs for winning, losing, getting injured in an escalated fight and so on, and used these values to construct a payoff matrix for each strategy against all others.

payola (pēi͵ōu·lă). *colloq.* (orig. *U.S.*). [f. Pay *sb.* or *v.*[1] + *-ola.] A secret or indirect payment or bribe to a person to use his position, influence, etc., to promote a commercial product, service, etc.; *spec.* such a payment to a disc-jockey for 'plugging' a record or song.

1938 *Variety* 19 Oct. 41 (*heading*) Plug payolas perplexed. *Ibid.*, The payola element had made their deals with bandleaders on the expectation that they continue to get 19c, thereby making it profitable to do business with the plug at a rate of around 10c a point. **1953** *Time* 23 Feb. 56/3 A world where *cut-ins* (giving a performer a share of a song's profits), *hot stoves* (open bribes) and other forms of *payola* were standing operating procedure. **1958** S. Ellin *Eighth Circle* (1959) ii. vii. 84 The unerring way he gravitated toward the graft, the payola, the swindle. **1966** T. Pynchon *Crying of Lot 49* iii. 61 They got the contracts. All drawn up in most kosher fashion, Manfred. If there was payola in there, I doubt it got written down. **1969** N. Cohn *A WopBopaLooBop* (1970) v. 51 There was a huge scandal about in 1959, the payola fuss, and a lot of people came crashing down. **1969** [see *dropsy *sb.* 4]. **1972** P. Black *Biggest Aspidistra* i. iii. 30 Gramophone records began to take over from sheet music and presented fresh temptations... Plugging re-emerged under the name of payola. **1974** *Guardian* 5 Nov. 7/2 Miss Squires and Mr Dabbs appeared in the dock together accused of 'payola' corruption. **1974** *Daily Tel.* 18 Nov. 6/1 There is growing talk of abuse of power by leading figures within the country's political establishment..at the expense of both Western businessmen and of the Kenyan people, involving payola for 'services rendered'. **1976** *Observer* 7 Nov. 1/6 (*heading*) Lockheed payola. A Spanish air force general and a colonel secretly managed the Lockheed Aircraft Corporation's sales in Spain and earned commissions worth £170,000 each. **1977** *Time* 31 Jan. 13/1 In the process of popularizing their products, the competing firms created a payola monster. They began slipping money as well as footwear to the stars of their choice.

pay-out. [f. vbl. phr. *to pay out* (see PAY *v.*[1] 5 b, 13).] The fact or action of paying out; the amount paid out (see also quot. 1904). Also, a place (in a shop, etc.) where payment is made.

1904 *Dialect Notes* II. 386 *Pay out*, n. Said of a well which more than returns the expense of drilling and pumping, or the capital invested in it. **1959** W. S. EVANS *Petroleum in E. Hemisphere* 19 As a result of the relatively low 'going' price for crude, his payout may be considerably longer than will be satisfactory, particularly if the price weakens further. **1960** *Guardian* 18 Dec. 5/1 The payout of stage artists by manufacturers for an advertising plug slipped into the artist's act. **1968** *Nature* 23 Nov. 752/1 Ross identified the bottom by a decrease in the rate of pay out of line from the free-spooling reel... An abrupt decrease in the rate of pay-out was indicative of bottom contact. **1970** *Globe & Mail* (Toronto) 25 Sept. B10/6 Profit..will not increase above last year's $1.05 a share because of payouts on long-range marketing programs. **1977** J. WAINWRIGHT *Day of Peppercorn Kill* 70 At the payout, she wrote a cheque. **1977** A. MORICE *Scared to Death* iv. 25 She had set off towards the pay-out windows to collect her winnings.

pay-roll, payroll. [PAY- 1.] The total amount to be paid to employees in a specified period; also, (a list of) employees receiving regular pay. Freq. in phr. *on the payroll*: employed by a particular company or person. Also *fig.*

1740 C. CIBBER *Apol. for Life* xiii. 257 The Rate of their respective Salaries were only enter'd in our daily Pay-Roll. **1775** *Rec. New Hampsh. Comm. Safety* in *New Hampsh. Hist. Soc. Coll.* (1863) VII. 26 Examined and allowed Capt. Crafford's pay Roll of his men engaged for fourteen days. **1780** *Calendar Virginia State Papers* (1875) I. 387 Enclose pay roll & account for purchase of kettles and dutch-ovens. **1840, 1898** [in Dict. s.v. PAY- 1 b]. **1921** C. E. MULFORD *Bar-20 Three* viii. 96 Looks like some Greaser had a grudge agin' him—somebody he's mebby fired off his payroll, or suspected of cattle-liftin'. *Ibid.* ix. 113, I ain't on Kane's payroll—yet. **1958** *Punch* 23 July 98/1 Skilled British agents are showing cause why they should be retained on the pay-roll. **1964** MRS. L. B. JOHNSON *White House Diary* 11 Jan. (1970) 39 On to Goldsmith Mill where a payroll of about a hundred had been saved by the joint work of the Community and the ARA. **1968** *Time* 17 May 66 Despite all the fuss at Columbia over IDA, none of its professors are actually on the IDA payroll. **1973** 'H. HOWARD' *Highway to Murder* viii. 98 Nobody on my payroll had anything to do with Vince Portelli's killing. **1977** *New Yorker* 29 Aug. 87/1 The Italian anarchists who were convicted of murdering two men while stealing a payroll in South Braintree, Massachusetts, in 1920 were executed on August 23, 1927.

2. *attrib.*, as *pay-roll index*; **pay-roll tax**, a tax levied on businesses according to the number of persons employed or on the wages-bill of the business.

1934 *Planning* II. xxxi. 7 The United Kingdom possesses nothing comparable to the payroll index, which is one of the major instruments of economic measurement in the United States. **1935** *N.Y. Times* 16 Jan. 2/6 The plans sent to the President by his Cabinet Committee included: unemployment insurance, financed, in part, at least by a payroll tax. **1937** M. NEWCOMER in *Stud. in Current Tax Probl.* 39 The new payroll taxes for unemployment insurance and old-age benefits will eventually become an important factor in the tax burden. **1971** *Sunday Australian* 8 Aug. 5/4 Australia's State schools paid about $15 million in payroll tax in the last financial year. **1976** in R. Crossman *Diaries* II. 58 Selective Employment Tax. A payroll tax paid by employers with some rebate for industrial enterprises.

‖ **Pays du Tendre** (pei dü tãndr'). Also with lower-case initials. [ad. Fr. *pays de Tendre*, with ref. to *Tendre*, an imaginary country whose topography symbolized aspects of love, devised by Madeleine de Scudéry (1607–1701) in her novel *Clélie* (1654–60).] Matters concerning love; the 'region' of the affections.

1910 W. J. LOCKE *Simon* viii. 113 A crock..with one foot in the grave has no business to put the other into the *Pays du Tendre*. **1913** —— *Stella Maris* xv. 200 Herold.. adventured with her into the Land of Tenderness—the *Pays du Tendre* of the old French romanticists. **1938** *Times Lit. Suppl.* 15 Jan. 43/3 The heroine's first excursion into the *pays du tendre* ends abruptly with the young man's betrothal to another girl. **1939** *Ibid.* 1 July 387/2 Mastery of this familiar type in the *pays du tendre*.. is a handsome equipment for story-telling. *a* **1976** A. CHRISTIE *Autobiogr.* (1977) IV. i. 168 The art of flirtation.. was an approximation, I think, to what the old troubadours called '*le pays du tendre*'.

Pazand (pā·zænd). Also **Pazend.** [f. Pers. *pā-zand* interpretation of the Zend: see ZEND-AVESTA.] A transcription of, or the method of transcribing Persian sacred texts from Pahlavi (see PAHLAVI *a.* and *sb.* in Dict. and Suppl.) into the script of the Avesta. Freq. *attrib.*, designating this mode of transcription.

[**1700** T. HYDE *Hist. Relig. Vet. Pers.* xxvi. 338 Literæ.. quæ..apud incolas vulgò audiunt..Character Zundicus, vel si Anglicè loquimur, the Zund Character; à quo aliquantulum differt Character Pazendicus.] **1772** J. SWINTON in *Phil. Trans. R. Soc.* LXI. 354 It not a little resembles that endued with the power of the short A, deduced from the Zend and Pazend, by Dr. Hyde. **1871** E. W. WEST (*title*) The book of the Mainyo-i-Khard. The Pazand and Sanskrit text... With an English translation, a glossary of the Pazand text.., a sketch of Pazand grammar, and an introduction. **1928** E. G. BROWNE *Lit. Hist. Persia* I. ii. 77 Hence the so-called Pázend and Pársí books, which are merely transciptions of Pahlawí books into the unambiguous Avestic and Arabic characters respectively, all the Huzvárish, or Aramaic, words being replaced by their Persian equivalents, or supposed equivalents. *Ibid.* 81 Just as *Zend* is the 'explanation' of an Avestic text in Pahlawí, so is *Pázend* (= *paiti-zainti*) a re-explanation' of a Pahlawí text by transcribing it into a character less ambiguous than the Pahlawí script, and substituting the proper Persian words for their respective Huzvárish equivalents. When the Avesta character is used for this transcription, the result is called 'Pázend'; when the Persian (*i.e.*, the Arabic) character is adopted, the term 'Pársí' is often substituted. In either case the product is simply an archaic or archaistic...form of 'modern' (*i.e.* post-Muhammadan) Persian, from which the whole Aramaic element has disappeared. **1934** *Trans. Philol. Soc. 1933* 56 There are reasons for believing that these Pāzand writers were active in the Central region from Kāšān to Yazd and Kirmān. **1939** L. H. GRAY *Foundations of Lang.* 319 This 'Book-Pāhlavī'..falls into two types: *Huzvarišn*, in which Semitic (Syriac) words are written, but with Iranian inflexions..; and *Pāzand*, which uses only Iranian. **1948** D. DIRINGER *Alphabet* 308 The most famous of the Persian indigenous scripts is the Pazand or Avesta alphabet, the script of the sacred Persian literature. **1968** M. BOYCE in *Handbuch der Orientalistik* IV. i. 47 It survives only in a mediaeval Sanskrit version, and in Pazand i.e. Middle Persian transcribed in mediaeval times out of Pahlavi into Avestan script. **1968** P. VAN POPTA-HOPE tr. *Rypka's Hist. Iranian Lit.* 34 In the Arab period Iranian Zoroastrian writers turned to new alphabets and attempted to use them for writing down Middle Persian texts phonetically. The writings in the Avestan alphabet are called *Pāzand*, those in the Arabic consonantal writing are called Pārsī. **1972** W. B. LOCKWOOD *Panorama Indo-European Lang.* xii. 235 Sometimes Pahlavi texts are found transcribed into vocalised Avestan script.., such texts being called Pazend.

pazazz, pazzazz. varr. *PIZZAZZ.

pazil, var. *PASSEL.

pea[1]. Add: **I. 1. d.** In the West Indies and southern U.S.A., a name for the seeds of various other legumes, including the red pea, *Vigna unguiculata*, and the Gungo pea, *Cajanus cajan*; esp. in phrase *pea(s) and rice*, the name of a local dish.

1928 FREEMAN & WILLIAMS *Useful & Ornamental Plants Trinidad & Tobago* (ed. 2) 166 Vigna sesquipedalis... Yard Bean. Bodi... The young pods are edible as French beans and also the ripe dry beans. V[igna] sinensis. Cow Pea. Black Eye Pea. **1930** B. S. RHETT *200 Yrs. Charleston Cooking* 59 (*heading*) Peas and rice pilau. **1969** *Daily Tel.* 11 Jan. 14/1 [In Jamaica] 'peas' are not peas at all but kidney beans. **1970** M. SLATER *Caribbean Cooking* 32 'Peas and Rice'..is cooked on every island. **1971** *Bahamas* XXIII. iii. 33/1 Being a true native son [of the Bahamas], Sidney Poitier sometimes has irresistible urges to devour such disastrous delicacies as pea 'n' rice or pea soup. **1972** C. D. ADAMS *Flowering Plants of Jamaica* 364 Vigna..cultivated in many varieties; native of tropical Asia; Black Eye Pea, Cow Pea, etc. **1973** *Advocate-News* (Barbados) 22 Jan. 13/3 (Advt.), Today's menu: Fried and boiled chicken,..dry peas or split peas and rice.

e. [In allusion to the pea used by a thimble-rigger.] A favourite; a horse likely to win. *Sporting slang* (*obs.* exc. *Austral.*). Also *transf.* someone in a favoured or favourable position, a person with authority (*Austral. colloq.*).

1888 *Sporting Life* 11 Dec. 4/4 Sweeny..forced the fighting, and was still the pea when 'Time!' was called. **1891** *Licensed Victuallers' Gaz.* 20 Mar. 187/3 Well, Albert, now what is the pea? we asked, hurrying towards the paddock. **1900** E. WELLS *Chestnuts* xxiii. 227 Informed me that the right pea for the race was 'L'Abbesse de Jouarre'. **1911** E. DYSON *Benno* xvi. 206 Mr. Dickson ..ran his eye down the card and chanced it. 'Dandy's the P,' he said. 'Put yer whole week's wash on Dandy, 'n hold me responsible if the goods ain't delivered.' **1953** BAKER *Australia Speaks* v. 118 Other expressions used by racing fans include: *pea*, a horse that is being ridden to win, especially when there is a doubt about the genuineness of other runners. **1958** F. HARDY *Four-Legged Lottery* xxv. 190 I've got the tip about it. Old Dapper Dan earwigged at the track. Swordsman is the pea. **1969** M. CALTHORPE *Defectors* iii. 17 'For the time being, I'm satisfied.' 'You're the pea,' Mick said. **1973** A. BUZO *Rooted* III. iii. 92 He's had his eye on her for some time, you know, but I'm the pea, she said. **1974** *Sun-Herald* (Sydney) 1 Sept. 15 The usual assumption has been that the Social Security Minister, Mr Hayden, 41, would move into the Treasury... Recent events have cast some doubts on that. The Deputy Prime Minister and Overseas Trade Minister, Dr Cairns, now seems the 'pea' for any change at the Treasury.

II. 5. b. = *pea-coal* (see sense 7 in Dict.); *pl.*, coals of a very small size.

1880 [see *EGG *sb.* 3 b]. **1886** J. BARROWMAN *Gloss. Scotch Mining Terms* 50 *Peas*, coal a grade smaller than nuts. **1905** A. S. CUNNINGHAM *Rambles in Scoonie & Wemyss* 260 Most of the trebles, nuts, beans and peas produced at Wemyss colliery are treated by the washer. **1930** *Engineering* 5 Dec. 708/1 The employment of anthracite duffs in place of washed grains and peas. **1949** *Black Diamond* 26 Feb. 54/3 Prices range as follows:..nut and pea, $3.50–$4.50.

III. 7. *pea-crop* (earlier example), *-field*, *patch*, *-seed*; **pea coffee** *U.S. obs.*, a beverage made by boiling roasted peas; **pea-combed** *a.*, of poultry, having a pea-comb; **pea-crab** (later examples); **pea-dodger** *Austral.* = BOWLER[3]; **pea-flour** (later examples); **pea gravel**, gravel consisting of particles similar in size to peas; **pea-lamp**, a very small, round electric lamp such as is often used as an indicator light; **pea-moth**, substitute for def.: the larva of the moth *Cydia nigricana*, which feeds on peas; (examples); **pea-shooter** (*a*) (earlier examples); **pea-stick** (earlier and later examples); **pea-viner**, a machine for picking, washing, and grading peas.

1805 T. E. WHITE *Jrnl.* 14 July (1904) 24, I drank three or four cups of pea coffee and then went to bed. **1818** 'A. BURTON' *Adventures J. Newcome* II. 112 Pea-coffee, Hurry-hush, and Chowder. **1851** H. MELVILLE *Moby Dick* I. ii. 14 The very spot for cheap lodgings, and the best of pea coffee. **1868** DARWIN *Variation of Animals & Plants under Domestication* I. vii. 254 In some breeds the comb is double..; it is triple in the pea-combed Brahmas. **1922** R. C. PUNNETT *Mendelism* (ed. 6) 32 The pea-combed bird contains the factor for pea but not that for rose. **1901** M. NEWBIGIN *Life by Seashore* x. 202 The tribe Catometopa..includes the curious pea-crab, *Pinnotheres pisum*, found inside the bivalves. **1960** C. M. YONGE *Oysters* vii. 118 The hundred or so species of Pea Crabs, most of which inhabit the mantle-cavity of various species of bivalves. **1978** G. DURRELL *Garden of Gods* iv. 88 It was he..who had got me the biggest clam shell in my collection and, moreover, with the two tiny parasitic pea-crabs still inside. **1732** W. ELLIS *Pract. Farmer* 39 This [weed] I cannot say will utterly destroy the Pea-Crop, but will so cripple it, as not to be a quarter Value. **1933** *Bulletin* (Sydney) 5 Apr. 12/3 'Elizabeth Owen':.. the different terms applied to 'bowler' hats—I have also heard them called 'egg-boiler' and 'pea-dodgers'. **1959** BAKER *Drum* (1960) II. 133 *Peadodger*, a bowler hat. [**1677** W. HUBBARD *Narr. Troubles with Indians in New-England* I. 24 If there were Indians in the Neck they should send them about a Peas-field not far off.] **1972** D. HASTON *In High Places* iii. 44 The trip was planned in the pubs of the pea-fields of Kent, where we had been supplementing our meagre incomes. **1881** Pea-flour [see *FLADBROD, -BRÖD]. **1915** D. H. LAWRENCE *Rainbow* ii. 46 The vicar put pea-flower [*sic*] into the crocuses, for his bees to roll in. **1928** E. E. BAUER *Highway Materials* xii. 122 After the bituminous material has been applied, the entire surface must be covered with an application of pea gravel. **1962** R. PAGE *Educ. Gardener* x. 277, I devised a very simple arrangement of areas of fine pea gravel and panels of grass. **1963** *Times* 16 Feb. 11/3 A bed of well weathered clinker ash, or small well washed pea gravel say 8 in. deep is placed on the floor of the greenhouse. **1973** C. WILLIAMS *Man on Leash* (1974) ix. 140 Bare planks..and then another two steps down onto the grating crunch of pea gravel. **1938** G. H. SEWELL *Amateur Film-Making* ii. 20 The glowing filament of a pea lamp. **1950** *Electronic Engin.* XXII. 413/1 The output of this amplifier was used to light a pea-lamp mounted alongside the microphone. [**1859** S. J. WILKINSON *Brit. Tortrices* 230 The larva [of *Endopisa nigricana*] feeds on the growing and unripe seeds of the Pea.] **1881** E. A. ORMEROD *Man. Injurious Insects* 131 Pea Moth... The caterpillars of this Moth cause the 'worm-eaten' or 'maggoty' Peas often found in old pods. **1931** G. S. CHAPPELL *Gardener's Friend* 153 The lupines..have inherited from their lowly ancestry an appeal to..wire-worms and pea moths. **1964** F. G. W. & M. G. JONES *Pests of Field Crops* v. 93 The pea moth has become increasingly important with the intensive cultivation of peas in certain areas of Britain. **1972** *Arable Farmer* Feb. 55/2 Folithion (insecticide for pea moth control from Bayer Agrochem). **1834** *Knickerbocker* III. 35 Didn't I turn that pied heifer of yourn into my pea patch. **1863** 'G. HAMILTON' *Gala-Days* 34 No premonition floated over from that adjoining pea-patch. **1941** J. STUART *Men of Mountains* 120 Tear off the damn Dingus silk shirts..for to make skeery-cows out'n for the pea patch! **1744** W. ELLIS *Mod. Husbandman* Feb. v. 29 When Horse-bean and Pea-seed are to be sown together.. the stated Allowance..is..two-third Parts Beans, and one-third Part Pease. **1946** *Nature* 31 Aug. 293/1 The fungus was grown in various modifications of Czapek-Dox medium with addition of manganese sulphate, in some cases with pea-seed extract. **1960** *Farmer & Stock-breeder* 16 Feb. 97/1 It is in practice difficult to get the fertilizer below the peas without forcing the pea-seed coulters into a too-shallow position. **1803** J. RUSSELL *Jrnl.* 23 Sept. in S. Walpole *Life Ld. John Russell* (1889) I. i. 6 The boys play at hoops, peg-tops, and pea-shooters. **1833** *Boy's Week-Day Bk.* 210 When you shoot a pea through your pea-shooter, it is quite as well to know that the natives of Macoushie shoot arrows in the same manner. **1745** J. MACSPARRAN *Letter Bk.* (1899) 27 Harry is come home..& has bro't home Pea Sticks. **1971** *Country Life* 2 Sept. 580/2 Most of the cut wood has its uses with the seasonal demand for pea sticks and bean poles. **1973** *Daily Tel.* 7 July 7/8 What can we stake our herbaceous plants with..now that you can no longer get pea sticks? **1943** C. CROW *Great Amer. Customer* 179 The pea viner is perhaps the most marvelous of them all. Vines fresh from the field are fed into the robot which hulls the peas, grades them as to size, and sends them on their way to the cooker. **1952** J. W. DAY *New Yeomen of Eng.* ii. 32 This giant pea-viner..deals with a ton of peas an hour. It picks them from the vines, washes, and grades them.

Peabody (pī·bǫdi). *U.S.* The name Peabody used *absol.* or *attrib.* in **Peabody bird** to designate the white-throated sparrow, *Zonotrichia* *albicollis*, whose call is said to resemble 'Sam Peabody, Peabody, Peabody'.

1865 E. A. SAMUELS in *Rep. Comm. Agric. 1864* (U.S. Dept. Agric.) 422 White-throated Sparrow—Peabody Bird—Wheat Bird... This beautiful sparrow arrives in Massachusetts by the first week in April. **1903** *N.Y. Even. Post* (Sat. Suppl.) 24 Oct. 1/1 That lovely bird, the white-throated sparrow, which under the name of 'Peabody bird' is well known in the North. **1917** W. P. EATON *Green Trails* 16 All day long in this pasture the Peabodies, or White-throated sparrows, sing their flutelike call. **1939** R. T. PETERSON *Field Guide Birds East of Rockies* 159 Song, several clear, pensive whistled notes, easily imitated. The White-throat is often called the 'Peabody bird' by New Englanders who fancy these whistled notes sound like Old Sam Peabody, Peabody, Peabody. **1940** E. T. SETON *Trail of Artist-Naturalist* 224 The night singer of the Assiniboine, was neither more nor less than the white-throated sparrow, the Peabody bird of New England, the nightingale of the farther north. **1964** A. WETMORE et al. *Song & Garden Birds N. Amer.* 369/2 The Peabody bird is in best voice in his summer home.

peace, *sb.* Add: **I. 4. c.** (Later examples.) Also, an action symbolizing the kiss of peace. Now usu. a light embrace, a hand-shake, or a bow.

1935 D. H. HISLOP *Our Heritage in Public Worship* xi. 243 Here, either before or after the Peace, in many rites is placed the Creed. **1957** *Oxf. Dict. Chr. Ch.* 771/1 Originally an actual kiss, the form of the Peace has been modified in all rites. **1974** R. J. HALLIBURTON in R. C. D. Jasper *Eucharist Today* vii. 90 The rubric in Series 3 gives no directions as to how the Peace is to be given. **1975** C. F. BAZLEY in C. O. Buchanan *Further Anglican Liturgies* x. 183 The Peace (in Chile called the Holy Kiss or the Love Embrace) is not included as a formal part of the service itself. **1976** *Church Times* 9 July 13/1 In recent years we have been bombarded with all kinds of fanciful and eccentric changes in the liturgy, of which 'the peace', in all its constantly changing forms, is surely the most ludicrous. *Ibid.* 8 Oct. 9/2 Staid churchwardens embraced others in the congregation during the giving of the Peace with a warmth and friendliness that they would have found difficult to express in a parish church. **1977** *Theology* LXXX. 175 The representation of 'the giving of the peace' by, rather oddly, shaking hands with one's neighbour.

7. b. In alliterative association with *plenty*.

1393, etc. [see PLENTY *sb.* 3]. **1596** SPENSER *Prothalamion* vi, Let endlesse Peace your steadfast hearts accord, And blessed Plentie wait vpon you[r] bord. **1703** *New Hist. Trojan Wars* III. 17 Now the Wars are done, and Peace and Plenty are pouring in upon us. **1713** POPE *Windsor-Forest* 2 And Peace and Plenty tell, a Stuart reigns. **1823** BYRON *Age of Bronze* xv. 32 How rich is Britain! not indeed in mines, Or peace, or plenty, corn or oil, or wines. **1949** W. S. MAUGHAM *Writer's Notebk.* 306 The world has always been a place of turmoil. There have been short periods of peace and plenty, but they are exceptional.

7*. With initial capital. A vigorous hybrid tea rose bearing large yellow flowers shaded with pink, belonging to a variety developed by Francis Meilland, French nurseryman, in 1939, and introduced into cultivation in 1942. Also *attrib.*

1944 R. PYLE *Let.* in A. Ridge *For Love of Rose* (1965) xii. 210 We are persuaded that this greatest new rose of our time should be named for the world's greatest desire: Peace. **1945** *Los Angeles Times* 30 Apr. I. 11/1 Today's main event [at the Pacific Rose Society show] was the official christening of the newly developed Peace rose. **1945** *Horticulture* 15 Sept. 409/2 The new rose Peace, which seems to be causing a furore, is another of many good roses coming to us from France. **1950** A. S. THOMAS *Better Roses* ix. 93 Mme A. Meilland was listed and sold in France in 1942 under this, its original and therefore correct name, but in Germany it has always been called Gloria Dei, and in Italy Gioia, while it was introduced into America in 1945 and sold under the title of Peace, its fourth name. **1963** W. BLUNT *Of Flowers & Village* 89 *R[osa] Andersonii.* Like a phlox-pink wild rose. Peace. For Mrs. Benham, who has promised to plant it where it can't be seen from the house. **1965** L. MEYNELL *Double Fault* II. v. 174 A heaped profusion of Peace roses looked superb in a large silver bowl. **1976** E. B. LE GRICE *Rose Growing Compl.* (ed. 2) xii. 192 Abroad this [*sc.* 1946] was the year of 'Peace' (Meilland) which was to have a profound effect on all rose breeding everywhere, giving a new standard in growth, health and size of bush and flower. **1978** M. DUFFY *Housespy* i. 9 The dusk was still full of the scent of Peace roses.

II. 8. a. (Earlier and later examples of attrib. use.)

1882 E. W. HAMILTON *Diary* 3 Sept. (1972) I. 332 Mr. G. wrote the other day a capital letter to Mr. Richard putting the war in Egypt in a light which would be likely to convince the strongest 'peace-at-any-price' person. **1910** BEERBOHM *Around Theatres* (1953) 579, I myself am not such a peace-at-any-price man as to be frightened away.

b. (Later example.)

1973 *Washington Post* 13 Jan. A23/3 President Nixon stated in Kentucky that we now had in our grasp a peace with honor instead of a peace with surrender.

14*. *no peace for the wicked* [Isaiah xlviii. 22, lvii. 21]: no rest or tranquillity for (the speaker); incessant anxiety, responsibility, or work.

1944 A. THIRKELL *Headmistress* iv. 86 'It's for Dr. Perry..' 'No peace for the wicked,' said Dr. Perry. **1953** D. PARRY *Going up—Going Down* iv. 128 'No peace for the wicked,' she said. 'But I expect it will be quiet from now on.' **1967** 'F. CLIFFORD' *All Men are Lonely Now* I. v. 89 The painters are descending on us tomorrow... Couldn't happen at a worse time, but there's no peace for the wicked is there?

III. 15. a. Freq. in senses: founded, held, organized, propounded, etc., to promote peace or end a specified war; advocated by pacifists; as *peace activist, advocate, aim, area, bloc, campaigner, conference, convention, crank, demonstration, -feeler, -fighter, formula, -front, march, marcher, -mediator, meeting, -mentality, mission, move, movement, negotiation, offensive, offer, petition, plan, propaganda, rally, society, symbol, terms, walk.* **b.** *peace-commanding, -conferring, -inspiring* (earlier example), *-loving* (later examples), *-promoting* adjs. **c.** *peace-calm, -complacent, -inspired, -minded* adjs. **d. Peace Corps,** orig. *U.S.* (see quot. 1962); **peace economy,** an economy, characteristic of peace-time, in which a large part of the labour force produces goods for export (as opposed to being engaged in arms production, etc.); **peace establishment** (earlier example); **peace-game** [after *war-game* s.v. WAR *sb.*[1] 11 in Dict. and Suppl.], an exercise in the maintenance of international peace; hence **peace-gaming** *vbl. sb.*; **peace-guild** (example); **peace line,** a line of demarcation drawn to avert conflict; **Peace People** (see quots.); **peace pledge,** (*b*) an undertaking to abstain from fighting, or to seek peace (in industrial relations); **peace prize,** an award (as a **Nobel prize*) presented for a contribution to the prevention of war; **peace sign,** a sign of peace made by holding up the hand with palm out-turned and the first two fingers in a V-shape; **peace talk,** conversation or discussion about peace or the ending of hostilities; *spec.* in *pl.*, a conference or series of discussions aimed at achieving peace in particular circumstances; hence **peace-talker, peace-talking** *vbl. sb.*

1968 *Listener* 31 Oct. 566/1 Those peace activists who at last year's Pentagon demonstration announced that they were going to make the Defence Department levitate 300 feet in the air. **1906** *Westm. Gaz.* 24 Mar. 6/3 Master of counsel sage and fluent pen, Peace-advocate, averse from warlike act. **1910** W. JAMES *Mem. & Stud.* (1911) xi. 284 Our socialistic peace-advocates all believe absolutely in this world's values. **1940** *Economist* 6 Jan. 9/2 The French have not fed much fuel to the idealist fire which has raged in this country over the discussion of peace aims. **1957** *Ibid.* 28 Sept. 1000/1 Replace alliances by security pacts—create 'peace areas' (ranging from southern Asia to the Baltic). **1939** W. S. CHURCHILL *Into Battle* (1941) 94 The first [step]..is the full inclusion of Soviet Russia in our defensive peace bloc. **1939** R. CAMPBELL *Flowering Rifle* I. 15 And loosing these in turn to drink and graze The peace-calm waters and the flowery ways. **1954** B. & R. NORTH tr. *Duverger's Pol. Parties* I. ii. 109 A large number of Europeans, very far removed from Communism, are..vulnerable to the attacks of the Peace Campaigners. **1807** J. BARLOW *Columbiad* x. 359 Enlighten'd interest, moral sense at length Combine their aids to elevate her strength, Lead o'er the world her peace-commanding sway. **1928** S. SASSOON *Heart's Journey* 31 Paid, with a pile of peace-complacent stone. **1889** *Cent. Dict. Peace convention* or *conference*, same as *Peace congress.* **1899** *Hazell's Ann. 1900* 462/1 A Peace Conference was held at the Hague in May, June, and July '99. **1919** G. B. SHAW *Peace Conference Hints* i. 7 Before the Peace Conference can be discussed with any profit, it must be approached in the light of the facts. **1933** *Radio Times* 14 Apr. 75/1 The war was newly over... There was a tremendous fuss of coming and going across the Channel..politicians..busy with the Peace Conference. **1978** *Times* 26 July 13/3 A strong performance of *The Green Table*..Kurt Jooss's allegory of the sometimes fatal effects of peace conferences. **1909** W. JAMES *Pluralistic Universe* iii. 128 It [*sc.* the absolute] might, with all its defects, be, on account of its peace-conferring power and its formal grandeur, more rational than anything else in the field. **1885** W. P. & F. J. GARRISON *Life W. L. Garrison* II. 230 The Peace Convention held in Boston, September.., 1838. **1960** H. HUMPHREY in *Congress. Rec.* 15 June 12634/3 Mr. President, I introduce..a bill to establish a Peace Corps of American young men to assist the peoples of the underdeveloped areas of the world to learn the basic skills necessary to combat poverty, disease, illiteracy and hunger. **1962** *Ann. Reg. 1961* 175 The Peace Corps was officially set up on 1 March as an organization to train and send American volunteers for service in foreign countries to help meet the need for skilled manpower. **1967** *Economist* 2 Sept. 785/2 Japan's version of the peace corps is getting into its stride. **1970** *Times* 19 Mar. (Liberia Suppl.) p. i/4 Sturdy American girls in Bermuda shorts earnestly go about the business of the Peace Corps. **1974** 'G. BLACK' *Golden Cockatrice* iii. 48 The Peace Corps phase in Manila..followed by free-lancing in refugee camps outside Kowloon. **1916** D. H. LAWRENCE *Let.* 11 Dec. (1962) I. 491 Fusty, fuzzy peace-cranks and lovers of humanity are the devil. **1935** A. HUXLEY *Let.* 5 June (1969) 395 His hobby is congresses and he has already organized one peace demonstration—at Amsterdam in 32, I think. **1910** W. JAMES *Mem. & Stud.* (1911) xi. 283 The military party..says..that mankind cannot *afford* to adopt a peace-economy. **1948** G. CROWTHER *Outl. Money* (rev. ed.) viii. 267 A peace economy..is chiefly interested in selling to foreign countries, a war economy in buying from them. **1766** in *Rep. on MSS. Mrs. Stopford-Sackville* III in *Parl. Papers 1904* (Cd. 1892) XLVII. I, I see no end of the load imposed upon us, as our peace establishment is so far beyond the ordinary supplies. **1942** H. NICOLSON *Diaries & Lett.* (1967) 225 There are all sorts of rumours... Germany is putting out peace-feelers. **1972** J. WILLIAMS *Home Fronts* v. 94 The Allies' curt rejection of peace feelers put out by the Chancellor. **1958** *New Statesman* 23 Aug. 230/1 Until last year Paul Robeson and Howard Fast ranked with the Dean of Canterbury as the foremost 'peace-fighters' of the English-speaking world. **1974** *Times* 16 Feb. 1/4 The chances of a peace formula emerging from the Pay Board's enquiry into the relative position of miners' pay. **1977** *Times* 17 Aug. 2/7 Postal workers..agreed on a peace formula after a five-day dispute. **1939** H. NICOLSON *Diary* 22 Aug. (1966) 411 This smashes our peace-front. **1968** *Guardian* 2 Dec. 9/8, I.. believe..that..practical pacifism [is] a reasonable goal. I am currently engaged in talking to computers about this in an elaborate peace game. **1968** *Economist* 23 Nov. 72/2 More attention should be paid to using these techniques for what he calls 'peace gaming'. **1913** *Encycl. Relig. & Ethics* VI. 215/1 The *frith gild*, or *peace gild*, so called, refers to an occasional feature of town life in Northern Europe from the 6th century. **1909** *Westm. Gaz.* 1 Sept. 9/1 The reactionary Holy Alliance was also a peace-inspired measure. **1828** DISRAELI *Voy. Capt. Popanilla* x. 119 The calm and peace-inspiring crosier. **1957** *Economist* 19 Oct. 209/2 When Japanese fishermen are apprehended in Peace Line violations, they are brought to Korea and given fair and open trials. **1969** *Times* 10 Sept. 1/1 (*heading*) Army 'peace line' to replace barricades across Belfast. *Ibid.* 1/2 General Sir Ian Freeland..said that troops would start building 'peace-line' barricades today. **1972** *Belfast Tel.* 12 Oct. 6/6 No doubt when the other volumes make the shops, Ulster will get its dishonourable mentions—no-go area, provo, peaceline. **1930** R. A. KNOX *Caliban in Grub St.* xiii. 212 Telling us to be honest and sincere and peace-loving. **1944** *Ann. Reg. 1943* 83 A general international organisation, based on the principle of the sovereign equality of all peace-loving States. **1955** *Ann. Reg. 1954* 191 Broadcasts to foreign audiences continued to extol the full religious freedom allegedly existing in the U.S.S.R., and to court the 'peace-loving' Catholics. **1970** V. CANNING *Great Affair* xii. 207 Basically I am a simple, peace-loving, even a dull person. **1977** T. ALLBEURY *Man with President's Mind* xiii. 131 The peace-loving American people. **1977** *Ann. Reg. 1976* 485 There are still certain forces who are bent on a return to cold war politics, which led to the division of the continent into opposing blocs. Communist Parties and other democratic and peace-loving forces have fought against and continue to fight against these policies. **1961** A. WESKER *Kitchen* 58 Did you go on that peace march yesterday? **1975** P. HARCOURT *Fair Exchange* 46, I proposed to wait until the Peace March had gone by. **1961** *Listener* 12 Oct. 548/2 The Western peace marchers approaching Moscow. **1972** J. WAMBAUGH *Blue Knight* (1973) vi. 77 Lieutenant Hilliard..was a cool old head and wouldn't get into a flap over fifteen peace marchers. **1884** Peace-mediator [see *HONEST *a.* 3e]. **1939** C. DAY LEWIS *Child of Misfortune* III. i. 260 Sitting on the platform at peace meetings. **1935** A. P. HERBERT *What a Word!* 243 Get your angles straight on air-mindedness, class-consciousness, peace-mentality, stomach-awareness. **1939** *War Illustr.* 14 Oct. p. ii/3 To-day an inoffensive peace-minded majority of the German people are being unwillingly dragged by a bloody-minded minority of their race along the road of doom. **1967** *Freedomways* VII. 118 Miss Barbara Deming..has been very active in the Peace Movement (she has taken part in a 'peace walk'..and a peace mission to Saigon in order to protest the war). **1976** R. MOORE *Dubai* i. 10 We [Americans] have a peace mission actively working to avoid war in the Middle East. **1940** H. NICOLSON *Diary* 16 July (1967) 102 We may be faced at any moment by a German peace move, and..a purely negative attitude is not sufficient. **1977** *Listener* 18 Aug. 195/1 If..the peace moves collapse..what will happen to the insecure régimes in Egypt and Syria? **1953** M. MCCARTHY in *Reporter* (N.Y.) 22 Dec. 33/3 My fiancé.. had known the organizer for years, perhaps from the peace movement. **1975** *Guardian* 2 Dec. 6/6 Defence Counsel..accused the prosecution of conducting a smear campaign against the British peace movement. **1912** Peace negotiation [see WILL *v.*[1] 46]. **1918**, etc. Peace offensive [see *OFFENSIVE *sb.* 2]. **1977** *Time* 3 Jan. 46/1 While Assad and Sadat have captured world headlines with talk of a peace offensive, Rabin has been attacked at home for being timid and indecisive. **1918** C. P. SCOTT in D. Ayerst *Guardian* (1971) xxvii. 410 The peace offers of the Emperor Karl, so insultingly and stupidly turned down by Clemenceau. **1966** N. NICOLSON in H. Nicolson *Diaries & Lett. 1930–39* 412 Hitler opened his attack on Poland as planned, claiming that the Poles had rejected his peace-offer. **1976** *Times* 19 Oct. 12/1 The Peace People, this misleadingly trendy title now adopted by the [Ulster] women's peace movement. **1977** *Time* 22 Aug. 6/2 A year ago last week, Catholics Betty Williams and Mairead Corrigan founded the so-called Peace People's Movement, which has attracted mass support from both Catholics and Protestants. **1977** *Arab Times* 14 Dec. 2/6 Mrs. Williams added: 'I am angry, the Peace People are angry that war at home dribbles on, and around the world we see the same stupidity gathering momentum for far worse wars than the little one which the little population of Northern Ireland has had to endure.' **1940** H. NICOLSON *Diary* 19 Sept. (1967) 116 Already the Communists are getting people in the shelters to sign a peace-petition to Churchill. **1955** *Treatm. Brit. P.O.W.'s in Korea* (H.M.S.O.) 11 From lectures on 'peace'..it was but a short step..to the production of 'peace' propaganda and 'peace' petitions by prisoners. **1968** *Listener* 3 Oct. 429/1 The process has apparently forced the Israelis to clarify their position with a 'peace plan'. **1977** A. WILSON *Strange Ride R. Kipling* vii. 306 The Pope put forward his peace plan in 1917. **1935** H. R. L. SHEPPARD *We say No* p. x, To give Pacifist opinion a chance to crystallize, I launched my Peace Pledge. **1956** A. H. COMPTON *Atomic Quest* 296 The 'Stockholm Peace Pledge.' In this 'peace pledge' a prime point was again made of outlawing atomic weapons. **1974** W. FOLEY *Child in Forest* II. 247 This group of young left-wing idealists..belonged..to the Peace Pledge Union. **1976** *Daily Mirror* 12 Nov. 2 Jack Jones yesterday declared: 'There will be *no* dock strike.' The Transport Union leader's peace pledge came amid dockland fury at the crippling of the Dock Work Regulation Bill in the Commons. **1902** *Idler* Nov. 244/2 The commission appointed to decide the peace prize. **1974** *Encycl. Brit. Micropædia* IV. 875/2 [Dag Hammarskjöld] was posthumously awarded the Nobel Peace Prize for 1961. **1906** *Westm. Gaz.* 12 Mar. 2/2 We certainly hope and believe that the Government will act in a peace-promoting spirit. **1929** D. H. LAWRENCE *Pansies* 85 Loud peace propaganda makes war seem imminent. **1955** Peace propaganda [see **peace petition*]. **1951** 'A. GARVE' *Murder in Moscow* iii. 43, I attended a great 'peace' rally at the Bolshoi Theatre. **1975** P. HARCOURT *Fair Exchange* 41 It's not a political rally. It's a peace rally. **1969** *New Yorker* 30 Aug. 21/2 Just as it finished, an Army helicopter flew over. The whole crowd..looked up and waved their forefingers in the peace sign. **1973** D. WESTHEIMER *Going Public* iv. 67 She raised her hand in a peace sign... He realized it was not the peace sign at all. To those of the old woman's generation it was V for Victory. **1976** *Scotsman* 20 Nov., (*caption*) Brian Robertson (right) gives the 'peace sign' as he leaves the High Court handcuffed to Jeremy Salmon. **1816** N. WORCESTER *Friend of Peace* I. vii. 30 (*heading*) First annual Report of the Massachusetts Peace Society. **1970** *Time* 2 Nov. 6 *American Opinion*..compared the familiar peace symbol to an anti-Christian 'broken cross'. .. The peace design was devised in Britain for the first Ban-the-Bomb Aldermaston march in 1958. **1972** *Times* 4 Aug. 1/2 He..is..said to have cut the peace symbol (the nuclear disarmament insignia) into the ice with his skates. **1789** J. STEELE *Papers* (1924) I. 51, I only mean to hold a peace talk. **1800** B. HAWKINS in *Georgia Hist. Soc. Coll.* (1848) III. i. 72 Peace talks are always addressed to the cabin of the Mic-co. **1852** J. REYNOLDS *Pioneer Hist. Illinois* 165 All the 'peace talks' ever presented to the red men, could not have kept them in peace, under these circumstances. **1918** W. OWEN *Let.* 10 Oct. (1967) 583 Tonight I must stand before them [*sc.* my company] & promulgate this General Order: 'Peace talk in any form is to cease in Fourth Army. All ranks are warned against the disturbing influence of dangerous peace talk.' **1930** J. CANNAN *No Walls of Jasper* 63 Look at the newspapers! Nothing but peace talk. **1958** *Times Lit. Suppl.* 10 Jan. 21/4 The campaign ended, un-Napoleonically, in the feeble peace-talks of Villafranca. **1973** *Times* 9 Nov. 1/1 Israel and Egypt have accepted a ceasefire agreement that could lead to Middle East peace talks by the end of the year. **1968** *Punch* 15 May 693/1 This is no surprise to the Korean peace talkers. **1917** D. H. LAWRENCE *Look! We have come Through!* 126 Everything was tainted with myself..nations, armies, war, peace-talking. **1935** MRS. BELLOC LOWNDES *Diary* 19 Dec.(1971) 136 Wickham Steed..talked with great excitement of what has happened over the offer of peace terms to Italy and Abyssinia. **1976** *Classical Q.* XXVI. 272 Andocides does not deal explicitly with the question of the status of the Greeks of Asia in the proposed peace-terms. **1967** Peace walk [see **peace mission*].

peaceful, *a.* Add: **4. a.** Not violating or infringing peace; used esp. of methods for effecting purposes for which force, violence, or war, is an alternative or more obvious means.

1876 G. HOWELL *Handy-Bk. of Labour Laws* (ed. 2) ii. 29 Peaceful picketing is no longer prohibited, for, although the Government refused..to legalise 'peaceful persuasion', yet it was distinctly declared that it was legal under the Act. **1902** *Engineering* 28 Mar. 413/3 The methods of trade unions run within the line of the law, with the single exception of the form of intimidation known as 'peaceful picketing'. **1903** E. GREY in *Hansard Commons* 18 Feb. 245 Russia seems undoubtedly..to be carrying on a process of absorption in Persia, and it is being done by what, I think, a French writer has called peaceful penetration. **1906** *Act* 6 *Edw. VII* c. 47 § 2 *marg.*, Peaceful picketing. **1909** *Westm. Gaz.* 7 Aug. 7/2 English proposals for the peaceful penetration of China from Burma have varied considerably since 1831. **1916** *Q. Rev.* Apr. 571 A regular system of 'peaceful picketing' was set up; and wounded heroes in mufti found white feathers thrust upon them by well-meaning females. **1930** *Economist* 18 Jan. 122/2 If Canada has been subjected to peaceful penetration by the economic forces of the United States it is because [etc.]. **1935** *Discovery* Nov. 320/1 It [*sc.* the spread of grasshoppers from Angará] is rather a matter of 'peaceful penetration', of infiltration, proceeding slowly and imperceptibly through the ages. **1950** *Chambers's Encycl.* XIII. 726/1 The Conspiracy and Protection of Property Act..in effect conceded the right to strike and reinstated peaceful picketing in a modified form. **1961** *U.S. Peace Corps Fact Bk.* 22 If it is decided to make a small shift which may be required from military aid or special assistance funds, in order to carry out the purposes of the Mutual Security Act through this new peaceful program, this will be a hopeful sign to the world. **1962** N. S. FALCONE *Labor Law* xi. 343 Peaceful picketing conducted at the premises of neutral employers was for the purpose of informing the public of a primary dispute and was not intended to bring about any work stoppage among the neutral employees.

b. *peaceful coexistence*: in the foreign policy of Soviet Russia, a concept of varying emphasis referring to relations with the capitalist West. Also *transf.* and *fig.*

In recent years *peaceful coexistence* has implied avoidance of nuclear confrontation. (Quot. 1920, cited from Carew Hunt *A Guide to Communist Jargon* (1957) 27, could not be verified as no copy of the newspaper appears to have survived.)

1920 *N.Y. Even. Jrnl.* 18 Feb., [Interview with Lenin] Our plans in Asia? The same as in Europe: peaceful coexistence with the peoples, with the workers and peasants of all nations. **1952** *Times* 2 Apr. 3/3 (*heading*) The invitations are..careful to emphasize the peaceful coexistence theme... The conference is based on the assumption..that mutually advantageous economic cooperation between Socialist and capitalist countries is quite possible. **1954** *Time* 4 Oct. 32/1 Attlee's men replied with one of those ingenious compromises that make peaceful coexistence possible between the two wings of the Labor Party: a policy favoring arms and sovereignty for the Germans but also offering to 'consider' some more Big Three talks with the Russians. **1956** R. MACAULAY *Towers of Trebizond* vi. 62 Turks do not believe in peaceful co-existence with Russia, they never have, and Father Chantry-Pigg agrees with them. **1959** *Listener* 26 Mar. 539/2 Both the Communist Party and the Church [in Poland] benefit immensely from the unprecedented type of peaceful coexistence they have worked out together. **1961** *Times* 2 Jan. 8/3 Mr. Khrushchev,..at a New Year banquet..in the Kremlin,..raised his glass and bade the whole company drink to peaceful coexistence. **1973** *Time* 25 June 31/3 Articles have appeared..applauding Brezhnev's peaceful-coexistence policy. **1977** *Lancet* 29 Oct. 903/2 Many microorganisms have been accused; so far, none have fulfilled Koch's postulates and some are known to live in peaceful coexistence with the healthy gut.

peacefully, *adv.* (Examples in sense *4 a of PEACEFUL *a.*)

1904 *Minutes of Evid. R. Comm. Trade Disputes* 262/1 in *Parl. Papers 1906* (Cd. 2826) LVI. 137, I have never seen picketing conducted peacefully yet. **1920** *Act* 10 & 11 *Geo. V* c. 55 § 2 (1) No such regulation shall make it an offence for any person or persons..peacefully to persuade any other person or persons to take part in a strike. **1935** E. WEEKLEY *Something about Words* i. 25 Unfortunately, 'refined' American is also penetrating peacefully, and I confidently expect that the English undertaker will soon describe himself as a *mortician*. **1961** *Nation* (N.Y.) 11 Nov. 371/3 Khrushchev..would like, above all, the Berlin and German problems to be settled peacefully.

peace-keeper. Add: Also, an organization that keeps or maintains the peace; one regularly employed in the maintenance of peace between nations or communities; a soldier in a force so employed. So **pea·ce-keeping** *vbl. sb.* (freq. *attrib.*).

1961 *Times* 2 Oct. 13/3 Budgetary procedures..including the cost of peace-keeping operations. **1961** *Guardian* 24 Oct. 8/3 The problems of a disarmed world, peace-keeping machinery, etc. **1963** *Times* 22 Apr. 11/3 The development of the United Nations as a peacekeeping organization will be seriously hampered before the summer is out if its present financial difficulties are not solved. **1964** *Daily Tel.* 17 Jan. 12/2 The sending of some international peacekeeping force has become a matter of extreme urgency. **1964** *Manch. Guardian Weekly* 5 Mar. 1 If an international truce force went to the island [*sc.* Cyprus], Turkey would forgo its right to intervene for three months... This is..a rare declaration of faith in the United Nations as a peace-keeper. **1965** *Spectator* 15 Jan. 76/2 Peace-keeping is the basic function of the United Nations. **1965** *Maclean's Mag.* 1 Dec. 16 Lieutenant-General Burns..was the first of a new breed of international trouble-shooters who now try to halt the escalators of war by policing cease-fires—the Canadian peacekeepers. **1973** *Times* 17 Sept. 16/8 Peacekeeping is..a purely temporary role; a permanently-active peacekeeper must in the end become an irritant. **1977** R. HOLLAND *Self & Social Context* ix. 274 The forces of capital and labour face each other unmediated by the normal peace-keeping functions of police intermediaries. **1978** *Globe & Mail* (Toronto) 20 Oct. 10/6 Although Mr. Jamieson refused to commit Canadian forces to a peacekeeping force in the territory, he indicated he was moving in that direction.

peacemonger. Add: (Further examples.) So **pea·cemongering** *vbl. sb.*

1928 *Funk's Stand. Dict.* II. 1815/2 Peacemongering, *n.* **1949** *N.Y. Times* 26 June IV. 1/2 Peacemongers, apparently in the hope that East-West tension would be lessened and the West's position softened. **1967** *Economist* 1 Apr. 26/3 He need not seek the political kudos that holders of other offices may hope to gain by public peacemongering. **1969** *Guardian* 18 Sept. 3/1 Peace-mongers who prolong the Vietnam war.

peacenik (pī·snik). [f. PEACE *sb.* + *-NIK.] A member of a pacifist movement, esp. when regarded as a 'hippy'; freq. *spec.* an opponent of the military intervention of the United States in Vietnam. Also *attrib.*

1965 *Time* 23 Apr. 13/2 (*heading*) War & Peaceniks. **1965** *San Francisco Examiner* 6 Sept. 14/2 Dean Plapowski..described himself as a 'peacenik'. This, he explained, 'is probably a beatnik who's got himself hung up in pacifist and non-violent activity'. **1966** *Guardian* 17 Aug. 9/2 The 60-year-old Judge is not suspected of 'peacenik' sympathies. **1971** *Ibid.* 14 July 11/5 The air base appears to treat its peaceniks with an easy tolerance. **1974** K. MILLETT *Flying* (1975) I. 117 A tenement crammed with peaceniks who have painted the word *love* across their brickfront. **1975** P. HARCOURT *Fair Exchange* I. 56 Who is this peacenik anyway?

peace-officer. (Later examples.)

1959 JOWITT *Dict. Eng. Law* II. 1320/1 *Peace officer*, a constable, coroner, justice or sheriff. **1965** *Economist* 7 Aug. p. xi/3 The officers in charge of these [S. African local labour] bureaus are now being designated 'peace officers', and have powers of arrest and search of houses. **1973** *Black Panther* 16 June 12/3 The scores of uniformed 'peace officers'. **1976** *Columbus* (Montana) *News* 10 June 1/3 They had hoped more residents would attend to express their wishes about having a full-time peace officer.

peace-time, peacetime. Also **peace time.** [PEACE *sb.* 15.] The time when a country is not at war. Also *U.S.* (with pl.), a period during which no declaration of war is in force. Also *attrib.*

1551 R. ROBINSON tr. *More's Utopia* I. sig. C v recto, The hole realme is fylled and besieged wyth hierede soldiours in peace tyme, yf that be peace. **1917** A. G. EMPEY *Over Top* 311 *Territorial*, a peace-time soldier with the same status as the American militiaman. **1923** *Man. Seamanship* (Admiralty) II. 5 In peace time at sea. **1938** *Sun* (Baltimore) 16 Apr. 8/3 His [*sc.* Roosevelt's] savage attacks in 1932 upon Mr. Hoover's Administration as the greatest spender of all peacetimes. **1940** *Economist* 5 Oct. 426/2 Already its price is more than four times the peacetime level. **1942** *Short Guide Gt. Brit.* (U.S. War Dept.) 23 Most British food is imported even in peacetimes. **1952** R. KNOX *Hidden Stream* xii. 106 I should want to take a good look round, as we did in the days of old-fashioned, peace-time shopping. **1955** *Times* 5 July 10/1 After transfer the Royal Navy will continue to enjoy the facilities of the Simonstown base in peace-time. **1968** S. HYNES *Edwardian Turn of Mind* viii. 273 That curious last-minute plunge toward the twentieth century that marked so strikingly that last peace-time summer. **1971** S. HILL *Strange Meeting* iii. 188, I hope all the rest will not be spoilt for leave, or peace-time. **1971** W. H. MCNEILL in A. Bullock *20th Cent.* 47/1 War-born techniques of administrative mobilization were carried over into peacetime.

peach, *sb.*[1] Add: **1. b.** *slang.* Someone or something of exceptional worth or quality; someone or something particularly suitable or desirable, esp. an attractive young woman.

1754 E. TURNER *Let.* 16 Aug. in Dickins & Stanton *18th-Cent. Corresp.* (1910) 238, I had almost forgot that orange Peach, your Niece. **1863** B. HARTE in *Daily Even. Bull.* (San Francisco) 9 Dec. 5/3 Phrases such as camps may teach,..Such as 'Bully!' 'Them's the Peach!' **1888** *Puck* (U.S.) XXII. 415/2 An' two young darters—one eighteen. A reg'ler peach. **1904** W. H. SMITH *Promoters* vii. 134 You're a brick! You're a peach! **1907** *Punch* 2 Jan. 13/2 Prof. Br—ce: H'm! Nice pleasant expression! One who was not a purist in language might almost describe him as a '*peach*'. **1917** WODEHOUSE *Man with Two Left Feet* 62 Opinions differ about girls. One man's peach..is another man's poison. **1919** H. L. WILSON *Ma Pettengill* iv. 111, I..landed a hard right on the side of his jaw and dropped him just like that. It was one peach I handed him and he slumped down like a sack of mush. **1924** 'J. SUTHERLAND' *Circle of Stars* xii. 126 It's a peach of a storm, and it's getting worse every moment. **1925** F. SCOTT FITZGERALD *Let.* June (1964) 484 He's a peach of a fellow and absolutely first-rate. **1930** 'R. CROMPTON' *William—the Bad* i. 19 Now would you think that a peach like her would fall for a fat-headed chump like that? **1943** E. B. WHITE *Let.* 1 Jan. (1976) 236 You were a peach to give me such a good present. **1949** *Sunday World-Herald Mag.* (Omaha, Nebraska) 1 May 2/1 The new recipe for making a peach cordial: Buy her a drink. **1974** *Times* 1 Apr. 12/4 She had, of course, a peach of a subject. **1976** *Derbyshire Times* (Peak ed.) 3 Sept. 22/6 (Advt.), 1972 Peugeot 504, white, 34,000, a real peach, £1,395. **1976** P. DICKINSON *King & Joker* iv. 46 Louise had a history essay, a real peach for which she'd only needed to look up a few dates. **1977** D. FRANCIS *Risk* xiv. 179 Dad's brought the detestable Lida... Actually I would have liked it..if he'd fallen for a peach.

c. *peaches and cream*: used *attrib.* and *absol.* to designate a fair complexion characterized by creamy skin and pink cheeks.

1901 ADE *Forty Mod. Fables* 188 Give me some perfumed Dope that will restore a Peaches and Cream Complexion. **1967** 'D. SHANNON' *Rain with Violence* (1969) i. 10 Carole had very blonde hair..and a peaches-and-cream skin. **1969** 'J. ASHFORD' *Prisoner at Bar* vii. 62 She had the perfect peaches-and-cream beauty that was often called classical English. **1975** *New Yorker* 9 June 46/3 She had a real peaches-and-cream complexion and a trim figure. **1978** J. W. WAINWRIGHT *Jury People* lxii. 211 His complexion..was pure 'peaches and cream'.

4. (Earlier examples.)

1809 M. L. WEEMS *Life Gen. F. Marion* viii. 74 Suppose you take a glass of Peach. **1845** J. J. HOOPER *Some Adventures Simon Suggs* v. 53 Thar's koniac, and old peach, and rectified.

6. *peach-orchard* (examples); also with names of colours; designating that shade of the colour which is shown by the peach, as *peach-beige, -green, -pink, -red*; **peach aphid, aphis,** one of several aphides infesting peach trees, esp. the peach-potato aphis, *Myzus persicae*; **peach-black** (examples); **peach-brandy** (earlier and later examples); **peach cobbler** *U.S.*, a cobbler (sense 4) made with peaches; **peach fly** = **peach aphid*; **peach leaf-curl** = *leaf-curl* (*b*) s.v. *LEAF *sb.*[1] 17; **peach Melba**: see *MELBA; **peach oak** (examples); **peach-potato aphid, aphis,** an aphis, *Myzus persicæ*, which causes leaf-curl in peach trees and other plants, and also transmits many plant virus diseases; **Peach State,** a sobriquet of the State of Georgia in the U.S.; **peach-worm** (examples); **peach yellows,** substitute for first part of def.: a virus disease affecting cultivated peach-trees, esp. in the United States; (examples).

1909 F. V. THEOBALD *Insect & Other Allied Pests* 324 Peach Aphides... At least four species of aphis attack the peach in this country. **1937** A. M. MASSEE *Pests of Fruit & Hops* vii. 163 The Peach Aphis has been recorded on a very large number of host plants, including fruit trees. **1942** *Phytopathology* XXXII. 93 (*title*) A virosis-like injury of snapdragons caused by feeding of peach aphid. **1963** *Jrnl. Insect Physiol.* IX. 875 (*title*) Some amino acid requirements of the green peach aphid, *Myzus persicae*. **1927** Peach-beige [see *GRÈGE *a.* and *sb.*]. [**1835** G. FIELD *Chromatogr.* 265 (Index), Black..Peach-stone 180. *Ibid.* xxi. 180 Similar blacks are prepared of vine twigs and tendrils,..also from peach-stones, &c. whence Almond black.] **1869** T. W. SALTER *Field's Chromatogr.* (new ed.) xxi. 407 *Peach Black*, or Almond Black, made by burning the stones of fruits, the shell of the cocoa-nut, &c., is a violet-black, once much used by Parisian artists. **1948** F. A. STAPLES *Watercolour Painting* (1951) i. 3 You will want to add the following to the palette: Raw Sienna,.. New Blue and Peach Black. **1963** *Times* 6 May 16/3 Many students will remember how much 'Corfi' enjoyed laying a wash of thickly sedimented peach black and raw sienna on a drawing that had taken weeks to prepare. **1711** W. Byrd *Secret Diary* 9 Sept. (1941) 403 After drinking two drams of peach brandy we returned to Mrs. Randolph's. *c* **1780** [see **apple-brandy*]. **1965** Amerine & Singleton *Wine* xvii. 268 Wines were made also from peaches and distilled into peach brandy. **1976** J. McClure *Rogue Eagle* vii. 129 As peach brandy goes, this is among the best *sluks* I've ever tasted. **1859** Bartlett *Dict. Amer.* (ed. 2) 90 *Cobbler*... According to the fruit, it is an apple or a peach cobbler. **1880** [see *cobbler 4]. **1947** *Reader's Digest* Apr. 130/2 You could smell a peach cobbler all through dinner. **1976** *National Observer* (U.S.) 28 Aug. 14/3 Peach cobbler (*recipe follows*). **1865** *Our Young Folks* I. 715 The peach-fly was thus kept from laying its eggs in the soft bark at the surface of the ground. **1905** *Chambers's Jrnl.* May 368/1 The peach..is not now obtainable, through the inroads of the peach-fly. **1971** J. Drummond *Farewell Party* 8 A great sunset...a wash of peach-green that ran across the sky. [**1887** *Bot. Gaz.* XII. 216 (*title*) The 'Curl' of Peach Leaves. *Ibid.* Pl. xiii. (*caption*) Knowles on Peach Curl. **1888** *Amer. Naturalist* XXII. 738 *T*[*aphrina*] *deformans* Tul., causing the 'peach curl' of the leaves of the peach tree.] **1899** *Bull. Cornell Univ. Agric. Exper. Station* CLXIV. 371 Peach leaf-curl is a disease which has long been known to the orchardist as well as to the botanist; and since the seasons of 1897 and 1898 there are probably very few peach growers..who are unfamiliar with the disease. **1904** *Westm. Gaz.* 6 Oct. 10/2 A fungus disease called peach leaf-curl..does injury to the extent of £600,000 annually in the United States. **1920** P. J. Fryer *Insect Pests & Fungus Dis.* xxxv. 557 Peach Leaf Curl... Plants Attacked. Peaches, nectarines and almonds. **1955** H. Wormald *Dis. Fruit & Hops* (ed. 3) vii. 172 Peach Leaf Curl..is found not only on peaches but also on nectarines and almonds. **1976** *Country Life* 18 Mar. 685/3 Garlic is said to protect peaches from peach-leaf curl. **1835** J. Martin *New Gazetteer Virginia* 209 Peach oak (so called from the resemblance of its leaves to that of the peach tree). **1897** G. B. Sudworth *Nomencl. Arborescent Flora U.S.* 177 *Quercus phellos* Linn. Willow Oak... Common Names... Peach Oak (N.J., Del., Ohio). **1676** T. Glover in *Phil. Trans. R. Soc.* XI. 628 Here are likewise great Peach-Orchards, which bear..an infinite quantity of Peaches. **1758** *Calendar Virginia State Papers* (1875) I. 257 We..overtook them at a peach orchard. *c* **1805** D. McClure *Diary* (1899) 68 Between the house & the bank of the River was a..peach orchard. *a* **1936** Kipling *Something of Myself* (1937) vi. 170 A bull-kudu.. would jump the seven-foot fence round our little peach orchard. **1955** W. Moore *Bring Jubilee* xix. 185, I made my way towards a farm on which there was a wheat-field and a peach orchard. **1974** *Sat. Rev. World* (U.S.) 2 Nov. 32/3 A long valley, green and golden with peach orchards —Canada's peach heartland. **1926** M. Leinster *Dew on Leaf* i. vii. 97 Ah Dai fingered and thumbed a fragment of the peach-pink silk he had unfurled for her inspection. **1934** A. Huxley *Beyond Mexique Bay* 2 The last word in cocktail bars and peach-pink sanitary fittings. **1956** R. Macaulay *Towers of Trebizond* xiv. 171 Through the windows I saw the circle of the Circassian mountains, indigo and brown and peach-pink in the sunset. [**1931** K. M. Smith *Textbk. Agric. Entomol.* vi. 50 (*heading*) Potato and Peach Aphis.] **1951** *New Biol.* XI. 51 The peach-potato aphid..is the main carrier of the known plant virus diseases throughout the world. **1959** *Times* 27 July 9/5 The aphids responsible for spreading the viruses—mainly the peach-potato aphid *Myzus persicae* —are able to multiply on the [potato] crop during the summer. **1975** D. S. Hill *Agric. Insect Pests of Tropics* v. 163/1 Peach-Potato Aphid... Peach (primary host)... Potato (secondary host), and polyphagous on many other crop plants and weeds. **1926** M. Leinster *Dew on Leaf* 114 My unborn son waits to clutch my heart-strings with peach-red fingers, with the call of flesh to flesh. **1935** W. de la Mare *Poems, 1919–1934* 377 Peach-red carnelian, apple-green chrysoprase, Amber and coral and orient pearl! **1941** G. E. Shankle *State Names* (rev. ed.) ii. 110 Georgia was nicknamed *The Peach State* in 1939 because 'peaches have been an important product of Georgia since the middle of the sixteenth century'. **1954** *Nat. Geogr. Mag.* Mar. 318/1 Georgia's automobile license plates carry the legend, 'Peach State'. **1970** G. Payton *Webster's Dict. Proper Names* 515/1 *Peach State*, a nickname for Georgia, where peaches are now a valuable crop in the center and south. **1976** *S. Wales Echo* 26 Nov. 2/5 With out-of-state tourists flocking to Jimmy Carter's home town in Plains, Georgia, officials are looking for ways to lure the visitors to the peach state's other attractions. **1814** *Cramer's Pittsburgh Mag. Almanac 1815* 55 (*heading*) Remedy for the Peach Worm. *a* **1817** T. Dwight *Trav. New-Eng.* (1821) I. 76 The Peach Worm has been known here for about fifty years; and is now become very common. **1856** *Rep. Comm. Patents: Agric. 1855* (U.S. Dept. Agric.) 299 The ravages of the peach-worm have proved more extensive than usual. [**1808** R. Peters in *Mem. Philad. Soc. for Promoting Agric.* I. 23 Mr. H. begins to suffer by the disease, I call the 'yellows'. *Ibid.* 24 The 'yellows' are seen making destructive ravages in Mr. Heston's peach plantation.] **1888** *Bull. U.S. Dept. Agric. Bot. Div.* IX. 9 Peach yellows appears to be confined exclusively to the Eastern United States. **1928** F. T. Brooks *Plant Dis.* iii. 23 The only means of checking the spread of Peach Yellows is to destroy affected trees as soon as seen. **1956** H. W. Anderson *Dis. Fruit Crops* vii. 265 Peach yellows is undoubtedly of American origin. **1974** K. M. Smith *Plant Viruses* (ed. 5) i. 2 Two years later [*sc.* 1888], Erwin F. Smith proved that the disease known as 'peach yellows' was also communicable and could be transmitted by budding.

peach, *v.* Add: **2.** Also const. *on.*

1881 *Punch* 26 Nov. 241/2 Eve flirted with Jerrem; Adam, enraged, 'peached' on Jerrem. **1927** Kipling *Limits & Renewals* (1932) 170 Will and I wouldn't have peached on him. **1966** *New Statesman* 1 July 9/2 The other members of the gang..would not hesitate to peach on him if it would serve their purpose. **1976** *National Observer* (U.S.) 17 July 17/3 Middle-level bureaucrats cravenly peach on their bosses everytime one of them does something the tiniest bit illegal, like violate the Constitution. **1978** P. Lovesey *Waxwork* 123, I shan't ask you to peach on one of your neighbours... What I want from you is the name and address of the supplier.

peach-bloom. Add: **b.** (Example.)

1923 D. H. Lawrence *Birds, Beasts & Flowers* 13 Why, from silvery peach-bloom—..This rolling, dropping, heavy globule?

c. A pink colour characteristic of the monochrome glazes on some Chinese porcelain; the glaze itself; = Peach-blow a, b. Also *attrib.*

1886 [see Peach-blow]. **1898** W. G. Gulland *Chinese Porc.* I. 139 The following are the names by which some of the colours met with are generally indicated:—..Lavender Clair de lune Peach bloom [etc.]. **1900** F. Litchfield *Pott. & Porc.* vii. 109 Some charming results were obtained in many of those beautiful self colours that collectors delight in; amongst others,..coral, lilac, peach bloom, crushed strawberry [etc.]. **1902** W. G. Gulland *Chinese Porc.* II. 360 Here we have..peach bloom employed along with other coloured glazes in the decoration of white porcelain. **1906** [see *crushed *ppl. a.* 3]. **1937** *Burlington Mag.* Oct. 195/1 Thus, such apparent mysteries as double crackle,..the achievement of peach bloom, the splashes in Chün glazes..are all comfortably disposed of. **1970** *Oxf. Compan. Art* 235/2 Many people consider the most admirable wares of the K'ang Hsi period to be those with monochrome glazes... The brilliant red *sang-de-bœuf* and soft pink 'peachbloom' celadon.

peach-blow. Add: **a.** (Earlier and later examples.)

1829 T. Flint *George Mason* 32 The Red Bud in a thousand places was one compact tuft of peach-blow flowers. **1837** J. L. Williams *Terr. Florida* 75 This bird is of a peach-blow colour. **1922** H. Shoemaker *Allegheny Episodes* xxv. 344 Her skin was transparently white, and the delicate peach-blow color in her cheeks was too hectic to betoken good health.

d. A type of glass of a similar colour.

[**1886** *Official Gaz.* (U.S. Patent Office) 20 July 236/2 13,523 Glass Table-Ware and Fancy Glass Articles.. Frederick S. Shirley, New Bedford, Mass... Used since July 1, 1885 'The word "peach".'] **1886** *Pottery & Glassware Reporter* 4 Nov. 21/2 In recent years four novelties have been brought out by the New England Glass Works, under Mr. Libbey's administration. We refer to the Amberina, Pomona, Peachblow, and Agata grades of goods. **1930** L. W. Watkins *Cambridge Glass 1818–1888* 156 The peach blow glass took its name from the Chinese peach blow porcelain... The New England [Glass Co.] peach blow is one of the loveliest and most unusual things in American glass. In color it shades by imperceptible degrees from white to a deep rose. **1933** *Antiques* (U.S.) Aug. 48 (*heading*) Peachblow Glass. *Ibid.*, Among those glass collectors who are more susceptible to color than to antiquity, 'peachblow items' are highly valued. **1944** R. W. Lee *Victorian Glass* xxii. 561 None of the glass factories at which Peachblow was produced adhered either to the shapes or to the purposes of the Peachblow porcelains. **1972** K. M. Wilson *New England Glass* vii. 352 Both the Mount Washington Peachblow and the New England Wild Rose are to be found in their natural state and also with a 'plush', or satin finish. **1975** *Daily Colonist* (Victoria, B.C.) 26 Oct. 30/6 Peachblow originated with Hobbs Brockunier around 1883. It is lined with white and shades from yellow to peach.

peacherino (pītʃərī·no). *slang* (chiefly *U.S.*). [Fanciful f. *Peach *sb.*[1] 1 b.] = *Peach *sb.*[1] 1 b. Also **peacheri·ne, peacheroo·.**

1900 *Dialect Notes* II. 48 *Peacherine*,..synonym for peach. [**1900** *Polk's Kansas State Gazetteer* IX. 695 (Advt.), As a hero you'll forever Take the 'peacherino' yam.] **1905** A. M. Binstead *Mop Fair* iii. 47 Archie, who had undertaken not only to give the Dragoon a merry evening, but to ring in miracles on him in the peacherino line,..repented the loss of all his addresses. **1908** G. H. Lorimer *Jack Spurlock* iv. 71, I went up in the air like an old wife happening by the office and discovering her husband dictating to a new blonde peacherino instead of old reliable. **1910** S. E. White *Rules of Game* iii. xv. 273 Plant has a drag with Chairman Gay; don't know what it is, but it's a good one, a peacherino. **1928** *Chambers's Jrnl.* Feb. 98/2 Though Captain Reginald saw little of her except at meals, he realised that here indeed was a 'peacherino'. **1966** M. Woodhouse *Tree Frog* xxiii. 171 'She [*sc.* an aeroplane] 's a peach,' he said. 'A real peacheroo.' **1967** C. Rougvie *When Johnny Died* iv. 88 When I was his age, they were hauling them out from under me... And all young peacherinos, too. **1970** R. Goldman *Sob Story* in *This Side of Parodies* (*National Lampoon*, U.S.) (1974) 78 'What do you think?' I asked. 'Isn't she a peacheroo?'

peachy, *a.* Add: (Later examples not referring to the complexion.)

1973 *Country Life* 15 Feb. 425/2 Their frosted bronzed peachy-pink lipstick. **1976** *Vogue* 15 Mar. 19/1 (Advt.), One (Barley Sugar) is a peachy sort of shade.

2. *slang.* Attractive, outstanding, marvellous, etc.

1926 E. Glyn *Love's Blindness* ii. 25 He..whispered to the man behind him——'Peachy bit in the eighth row—— Look at the pearls.' **1929** S. Anderson in *Mercury Story Bk.* 228 It was a peachy time for me. **1932** J. T. Farrell *Young Lonigan* iv. 193 He told himself that Airedales were peachy dogs, they were fighters, they could swim and liked the water, and they were smart. **1942** O. Nash *Good Intentions* 27 Do you know a picture program that Mr Oglethrip would find simply peachy? **1973** D. Westheimer *Going Public* xi. 166 How about it, fellows?.. Isn't it a peachy idea? **1976** 'W. Trevor' *Children of Dynmouth* v. 115 Your mum has a touch of style, Kate. I heard that remarked in a vegetable shop. I'd call her an eyeful, Kate. Peachy. **1977** *Time* 10 Jan. 28/3 Carter vowed that his Administration would not let New York City go into bankruptcy... Asked for a reaction to the meeting, Carey beamed; 'Peachy'.

b. *peachy-keen* adj. *U.S. slang* (see quot. 1960).

1960 Wentworth & Flexner *Dict. Amer. Slang* 379/2 *Peachy-keen adj.* 1 Excellent; fine... 2 All right; fair; not good enough to warrant enthusiasm but adequate. **1969** N. Cohn *A WopBopaLooBop* (1970) v. 50 We dig America. We think it's really peachy-keen. **1975** J. Grady *Shadow of Condor* (1976) iii. 52 Everything in Montana is peachy keen.

peacify (pī·sifəi), *v. rare.* [f. Peace *sb.* + -ify, influenced by Pacify *v.*] To make calm, to pacify.

1845 [see *nursery language* s.v. *nursery 8 a]. **1922** Joyce *Ulysses* 335 Joe and little Alf round him..trying to peacify him. **1942** Berrey & Van den Bark *Amer. Thes. Slang* § 269/1 *Peacify*, to pacify.

pea-coat. (Earlier and later examples.)

1790 *Pennsylvania Packet* 4 Jan. 2/2 There are now lodged in the said Office..1 pea coat;..1 coatee [etc.]. **1842** Dickens *Amer. Notes* II. viii. 244 The hoarse pilot, wrapped and muffled in pea-coats and shawls. **1974** *New Yorker* 25 Feb. 80/2 Neatly dressed in a sort of modified peacoat of generally Edwardian cut. **1976** *National Observer* (U.S.) 17 July 16/6 His youth was not exactly the Andy Hardy story. He got into trouble with teen-age drinking. At one point, he lived in a car; at another he fenced hot peacoats.

peacock, *sb.* Add: **4*.** Short for *peacock-blue.* Also *attrib.* or as *adj.*

1873 L. Troubridge *Life amongst Troubridges* (1966) viii. 60 A peacock grosgrain and white lace bonnet. **1881** C. C. Harrison *Woman's Handiwork* iii. 165 Peacock, turquoise, celestine, drake's neck, Damascus blue and robin's-egg blue. **1897** W. B. Yeats *Tables of Law & Adoration of Magi* 35 When the peacock curtains had closed behind us. **1922** *Daily Mail* 11 Dec. 14 (Advt.), Frock... In Brown, Lemon, Peacock, Rose, Mauve. **1924** C. Mackenzie *Heavenly Ladder* i. 11 He..sat for awhile on the sweet short grass of Pendhu cliffs, contemplating the peacock sea below. **1963** *New Yorker* 29 June 44 Sizes 8–18. Cranberry, peacock, olive. **1971** 'D. Halliday' *Dolly & Doctor Bird* xii. 166 The sea lay clear as shellac underneath us, jade and turquoise, cerulean and peacock.

5. a. *peacock colour* (earlier example), *-grey.*

1598 R. Haydocke tr. *Lomazzo's Tracte containing Artes of Curious Paintinge, Caruinge, Buildinge* iii. x. 110 The shaddowes of the simple and immixt colours of the thirde degree, suppose the aggate colour, are burnt oker, darke blew, peacocke colour [etc.]. **1935** Dylan Thomas *Sel. Lett.* (1966) 153 You write better when you've got someone..sneering when you go purple & using a cruel pencil over your choicest peacock-greys.

b. Peacock Alley *U.S.*, the name given to the main corridor of the original Waldorf-Astoria Hotel in New York, where fashionable people promenaded; hence the main corridor of other hotels; also *attrib.*; **peacock-blue** (earlier and later examples); **peacock butterfly,** for '*Vanessa Io*' substitute '*Inachis io*'; (earlier and later examples); **peacock copper,** substitute for def.: iridescent copper ore ('peacock ore'), esp. chalcopyrite or bornite; (examples); **peacock mottle** (see quots.); **peacock ore,** add: = *peacock copper* (in Dict. and Suppl.); (further examples); **peacock pheasant,** a small, south-east Asian pheasant belonging to the genus *Polyplectron*, whose markings resemble those of a peacock.

1906 *N.Y. Times* 2 Dec. iii. 7/2 The Waldorf-Astoria is the New York headquarters of Kalamazoo, Michigan, and Brassband, Wisconsin. Its main corridor is known as Peacock Alley. To sit there five minutes makes a man a representative American. **1925** E. Hungerford *Story of Waldorf-Astoria* vii. 139 The outstanding feature of this ground floor was a huge corridor—in after years to be known, somewhat irreverently, as 'Peacock Alley'— which was to run practically the entire length of the building, parallel to Thirty-fourth Street. **1930** J. Dos Passos *42nd Parallel* ii. 156 Seedy-respectable or Peacock Alley clothes. **1932** L. C. Douglas *Forgive us our Trespasses* (1937) x. 212 The peacock-alley of the hotel, stuffily scented, was daily, gravely, tallied off for Joan. **1974** *Washington Post* 20 Dec. d8/5 The Carr project included: Total restoration of the Willard's..public rooms and the famous Peacock Alley. **1881** C. C. Harrison *Woman's Handiwork* i. 65 The curtains made of peacock blue, are bordered with..bands of turquoise blue serge. **1882** H. P. Grattan in *Theatre* June 348 Fashion..was carried to the verge of caricature. Crimson and peacock blue stocks, three layers of different coloured underwaistcoats, [etc.]. **1968** R. H. R. Smithies *Shoplifter* (1969) vii. 151 An improbable peacock blue evening jacket. *c* **1760** B. Wilkes *Eng. Moths & Butterflies* iii. i. 55 The peacock-butterfly. You must look for the Caterpillar that produces this Fly in the great Stinging-Nettle. **1906** R. South *Butterflies Brit. Isles* 73 Usually the Peacock butterfly assumes the perfect state but once in the year. **1965** P. Wayre *Wind in Reeds* ix. 114 Tortoiseshell and peacock butterflies feed on the nectar. **1976** *Cumberland News* 3 Dec. 8/7 Mr Jack Thirlwell showed his prize winning films on the life style of the swallow tail and peacock butterflies. **1858** Greg & Lettsom *Man. Mineral. Gt. Brit. & Ireland* 340 At Great Crinnis, St. Austell, in the neighbourhood of which town the mines produce the finest iridescent massive variety [of chalcopyrite], known as peacock copper. **1897** *Slocan* (Brit. Columbia) *Pioneer*

4 Sept. 1/6 The Michigan claim on Toad mountain is showing up well, some very fine grey copper and peacock copper having been encountered. **1937** A. F. ROGERS *Introd. Study Minerals* (ed. 3) 300 Chalcopyrite... Color brass yellow, often with an iridescent tarnish, hence the name 'peacock copper'. **1924** G. O. WHEELER *Old English Furnit.* (ed. 3) xii. 278 Another variety [of mottle in mahogany] was once termed peacock mottle from its supposed resemblance to the tail of that bird. **1968** *Canad. Antiques Collector* Aug. 24/2 *Honeycomb or peacock mottle.* This is a variety of figure remarkable for its fine appearance; it is associated almost entirely with the mahoganies. **1911** *State* (Cape Town) Nov. 487 The ore is principally bornite—peacock-ore as it is often called on account of its beautiful iridescent colouring. **1964** H. HODGES *Artifacts* iv. 65 This group includes..the iron sulphide minerals chalcopyrites (copper pyrites, $Cu_2Fe_2S_4$) and bornite (peacock ore, Cu_5FeS_4). **1977** A. HALLAM *Planet Earth* 124 (*caption*) Bornite, an important ore of copper, is often called 'peacock ore' for its iridescent tarnish. **1864** *Proc. Zool. Soc.* 373 From Calcutta... 1 Peacock Pheasant. **1906** *Macm. Mag.* Aug. 779 A peacock-pheasant..ceased its clamour. **1922** C. W. BEEBE *Monogr. Pheasants* IV. 55 Peacock pheasants..are birds of the lowland forests. **1964** A. L. THOMSON *New Dict. Birds* 627/2 The peacock pheasants *Polyplectron* spp. form a very distinct genus of small pheasants with long tails and a grey or brown plumage marked with metallic green and purple ocellae on the mantle, wings, and tail.

peacock, *v.* Add: **3.** *Austral.* (See quot. 1898.) *Obs.* exc. *hist.*

1898 MORRIS *Austral. Eng.* 344/2 To *peacock* a piece of country means to pick out the *eyes* of the land by selecting or buying up the choice pieces and water-frontages, so that the adjoining territory is practically useless to any one else. **1928** 'BRENT OF BIN BIN' *Up Country* xxi. 347 They had been able to 'peacock' their runs and safeguard their holdings. **1959** BAKER *Drum* (1960) i. 14 Droughts and the activities of small selectors who 'peacocked' or 'picked the eyes out of' the country..capped the pioneers' woes.

Peacockian (pīkǫ·kiăn), *a.* and *sb.* [f. the name of Thomas Love *Peacock* (1785–1866), English novelist and poet + -IAN.] **A.** *adj.* Pertaining to or characteristic of Thomas Love Peacock or his works.

1886 *Macm. Mag.* Apr. 424/2 It is not necessary..to be a believer in education, or in telegraphs, or in majorities, in order to feel the repulsion which some people evidently feel for the Peacockian treatment. **1904** A. B. YOUNG *Life & Novels T. L. Peacock* 31 The squire's chief interest in the novel..seems to be mainly 'pushing' the bottle round, while that of Dr. Gaster, the first of many clergymen who figure in the Peacockian novels, is that of emptying it. **1927** J. B. PRIESTLEY *T. L. Peacock* vi. 160 His manner and talk are all his own and have the Peacockian sparkle and salty tang. **1930** *Times Lit. Suppl.* 13 Mar. 210/2 The Peacockian Mr. Dottery easily wins our affections. **1954** R. MACAULAY *Last Lett. to Friend* (1962) 145 It is a kind of Peacockian set of imaginary discussions between a group of people. **1963** *Listener* 21 Mar. 531/1 The visitors are all rather Peacockian. **1972** *Guardian* 20 Jan. 11/4 The Open House by Michael Innes... Sir John Appleby..intrudes on Peacockian mansion, and, overnight, identifies killer and unravels inheritance tangle. **1978** P. VAN GREENAWAY *Man called Scavener* iii. 34 A Peacockian world where conversation grows more polished than the superb sideboard.

B. *sb.* An admirer or devotee of Peacock and his writings.

1886 *Macm. Mag.* Apr. 420/2 One piece of verse..the 'War-song of Dinas Vawr'..has had some vogue, but the rest is only known to Peacockians. **1911** C. VAN DOREN *Life T. L. Peacock* xi. 277 Peacockians are wont to plume themselves upon a taste denied to the vulgar. **1973** *Times* 22 Mar. 12/3 An actor and Peacockian of some wit and taste.

peacocking, *vbl. sb.* Add: **b.** *Austral.* (See quots.) *Obs.* exc. *hist.*

1894 W. EPPS *Land Syst. Australasia* iii. 28 When the immediate advent of selectors to a run became probable, the lessees endeavoured to circumvent them by dummying all the positions which offered the best means of blocking the selectors from getting to water. This system, commonly known as 'peacocking', was assisted by the use of Volunteer Land Orders. **1965** *Austral. Encycl.* V. 234/1 Many of the counter-tactics employed by pastoralists were equally indefensible, notably the purchase of sites to prevent selectors from getting to water ('peacocking').

peacockly, *a.* and *adv.* For *Obs.* read '*Obs.* exc. *arch.*' and add: **b.** (Later example.)

1941 E. R. EDDISON *Fish Dinner* (1968) viii. 132 His coming hither but yesterday, most peacockly strained to the height of your philosophy and at an undue hour of eleven o'clock in the night.., was with purpose.

peacockry. [f. PEACOCK *sb.* + -RY.] = PEACOCKERY.

1909 *Daily Chron.* 14 Aug. 2/3 At Siena you leave Pinturicchio's 'peacockry' in the Cathedral library only to meet a bevy of youths with striped legs, tight doublets, and feathered caps tossing banners down the street of St. Catherine. **1932** *Times Educ. Suppl.* 6 Aug. 305/4 A fault among boys was what was called 'peacockry', when their vanity caused them to pinch anything to adorn their person. **1967** D. BEYFUS in L. Deighton *London Dossier* 229 Traditional British lairs of masculine peacockry.

pea-flower. **a.** (Later examples.)

1946 D. C. PEATTIE *Road of Naturalist* i. 20 In the innocent phase of spring there had bloomed an astragalus, very like a lupine, but straggling, crazy, clouded, its pea flowers sickly pink. **1977** M. ALLAN *Darwin & his Flowers* iv. 78 He found six adesmias-shrubs with pea-flowers.

pea-jacket. (Earlier and later examples.)

1721 *Amer. Weekly Mercury* 23 Mar. 2/2 Clothed with a double-breasted Pee-Jacket. **1848** A. BRONTË *Tenant of Wildfell Hall* III. xv. 301 A dubious, sidelong glance at my splashed, grey trousers and rough P jacket. **1898** F. H. SMITH *C. West* iii. 36 He had left his pea-jacket in the cabin. **1922** W. S. MAUGHAM *On Chinese Screen* xlvii. 186 A pea-jacket such as you see in Leech's pictures of the sea-faring man. **1968** *Wall St. Jrnl.* 19 Feb. 1/1 A long-haired Berkeley student wearing a *Kill for Peace* button in the lapel of his black pea jacket. **1976** *Time* 20 Dec. 17/1 In his Navy pea jacket and worn brown boots,.. Jordan loped down the Senate halls, looking like the country boy he tries hard to remain.

Peak, *sb.*[1] **3.** (Later examples applied to millstones.)

1933 *Times Lit. Suppl.* 14 Dec. 891/1 We are given..a notice of the mill's character..down to the quality of millstones—Peak or French burr. **1936** *Ibid.* 16 May 416/4 A very individual vocabulary whose words, such as..peak or French burr-stones..will soon be a dead if not a forgotten language.

peak, *sb.*[2] Add: **I. 1. f.** Delete *Obs.* and add later examples.

1938 A. MORRIS *Step-by-Step Method Water Waving* 39 (*caption*) Hair line showing peak and receding part over eyes. **1951** A. SETON *Foxfire* ii. 42 She had soft hair.., and it curled all around her heart-shaped face. Really heart-shaped, because a widow's peak cleft the white forehead. **1971** W. COOPER *Hair* vii. 206 In English folklore, if a woman's hair grows to a point low on the brow, it is said to indicate that she will live to be a widow, and so it is often called a 'widow's peak'. **1978** 'M. M. KAYE' *Far Pavilions* xxiii. 339 A small muslin turban..covered her hair and showed only the deep widow's peak in the angle where its folds crossed.

II. 5. c. *spec.* one on a graph. Cf. sense *5 e.

1922 *Encycl. Brit.* XXXII. 1024/1 The potential difference of the arc electrodes is an irregular curve with sharp peaks. **1926** W. R. INGE *Lay Thoughts* II. i. 89 If we look at a chart of the births and deaths in Germany for the two generations before the Great War we shall see that each war is marked by a peak in the line showing the death rate and a ravine in the line showing the birth rate. **1968** *Brit. Med. Bull.* XXIV. 212/1 The corresponding histogram of conjugated bilirubin is markedly bimodal, and also shows an artificial peak at 0·5 mg. (100 ml.).

e. A highest point in a period of any varying quantity, as electric power, traffic flow, prices, etc.; the time when this occurs; a culminating point or climax. Cf. sense *5 c.

1902 *Encycl. Brit.* XXV. 35/1 Accumulators will take the peaks of the load, relieving the machinery from sudden jerks. **1923** *Daily Mail* 28 May 4 We have long since passed the peak in this unpleasant business. **1923** *Westm. Gaz.* 11 Aug. 6/4 During the morning, evening and theatre peaks, two escalators in each group can be run in either an upward or downward direction. **1943** *Sun* (Baltimore) 2 July 17/1 Steels enjoyed a last minute upswing and assorted favorites emerged..a number at three year peaks. **1962** A. NISBETT *Technique Sound Studio* iii. 63 The closer one gets to an open piano, the more the transients associated with the strike tone will be apparent; at their strongest..they may be difficult to control without ..risking momentary distortion on the peaks. **1967** *Listener* 23 Mar. 386/2 The nuclear disarmament campaign was already past its peak. **1968** *Brit. Med. Bull.* XXIV. 219/2 This is a continuous-flow analyser with its output arranged so that individual results are produced as voltage peaks following one another at intervals. **1971** *Hi-Fi Sound* Feb. 68/2 It is a basic hi-fi requirement that peaks should be accommodated without serious distortion. **1976** *Daily Tel.* 20 July 1/5 At the peak of the wages rush last year, the annual rate of increase of earnings reached 30 per cent.

f. *Phonetics.* The most prominent sound in a syllable with regard to sonority.

1935 J. S. KENYON *Amer. Pronunc.* (ed. 6) 69 The phonetic center, or 'peak' of a syllable is its point of greatest sonority. **1942** BLOCH & TRAGER *Outl. Linguistic Analysis* 22 The sounds which constitute the peaks of sonority are called syllabic. **1960** E. SIVERTSEN *Cockney Phonol.* ii. 23 Stressed simple syllable peaks do not occur before juncture, and there are other limitations in the distribution of unstressed peaks in this position. **1964** E. PALMER tr. *Martinet's Elem. Gen. Linguistics* ii. 52 A consonant like [l] when placed between consonants of lesser perceptibility or audibility such as [p] and [k], may function as syllable peaks. **1965** W. S. ALLEN *Vox Latina* 2 Sounds which may function either as peaks or as valleys of prominence, whilst classified as vowels in their peak (or 'nuclear') function, are generally termed semivowels..in their valley (or 'marginal') function.

g. *Surfing.* The highest point of a wave.

1963 *Surfing Yearbk.* 42/2 *Peak*, the highest point of the wave. **1965** FARRELLY & MCGREGOR *This Surfing Life* iv. 44/2 On most occasions in this sort of surf you take off straight down the peak. **1965** J. M. KELLY *Surf & Sea* ii. 26 The wind blows gently into the faces of the white-crested waves. It holds up their peaks giving you time to speed away on the clear green slopes before they break. **1968** *Surfer Mag.* Jan. 48/1 The way the peak was breaking didn't offer many rights.

III. 6. (sense *5 e) *peak-clipping, -limiting*; (sense *5 f) *peak nucleus, satellite*; *peak-bearded, -capped* (examples), *-crested* adjs.; **peak experience,** the momentary awareness of joy or fulfilment akin to ecstasy, of a higher and different quality from ordinary life, experienced by some people; **peak factor** *Electr.*, the ratio of the maximum value (or the difference between the maximum and minimum values) of a wave to the r.m.s. value; **peak listening** (see sense *7 a); **peak programme meter** (see quot. 1941); **peak shaving,** storage of part of the gas produced when demand is low so that it can be used to increase the supply at times of peak demand; **peak-to-peak** *a.* and *adv.*, (measured or expressed as the difference) between extreme values of a periodically varying quantity; also called **peak-to-valley** (*rare*); similarly **peak-to-mean** *a.*; **peak viewing** (see sense *7 a); **peak voltmeter** *Electr.*, a voltmeter that measures the peak value of an alternating voltage.

1905 *Daily Chron.* 12 Aug. 5/2 At one carriage a little baby-girl was held up by its mother to kiss farewell to a peak-bearded gloire bluejacket. **1972** *Drive* Spring 147/1 A peak-capped driver at the helm of a Rolls-Royce Corniche. **1976** *Field* 30 Dec. 1275/3 A peak-capped figure on one knee beside a folded stretcher. **1961** *Which?* July 156/1 There are two accepted methods for achieving loudness compression. One is called A.V.C. and the other peak clipping. **1975** G. J. KING *Audio Handbk.* iii. 60 For example, if the 1 kHz input sensitivity is 2 mV and peak clipping..occurs at 20 mV, the overload margin is said to be 10:1 or 20 dB. **1879, 1881** Peak crested [see *BLONDINETTE]. **1962** A. H. MASLOW *Toward Psychol. of Being* III. vi. 69 An attempt to generalize in a single description some of these basic cognitive happenings... These and other moments of highest happiness and fulfilment I shall call the peak-experiences. **1969** H. GEIGER in Sutich & Vich *Readings Humanistic Psychol.* xvii. 307 If..there should come a kind of 'social' peak experience..a new rhythm of humane historical relationships could be established in the world. **1975** *Sat. Rev.* (U.S.) 22 Feb. 20/2, I underwent a religious-like peak experience in which the presence of divinity became almost palpable. **1976** N. POSTMAN *Crazy Talk* 85 Bombing the Vietnamese back to the Stone Age was quite possibly a 'peak experience' for millions of Americans. **1914** Peak factor [see *CREST *sb.*[1] 7 e]. **1963** WILLIAMS & PRIGMORE *Electr. Engin.* vii. 185 When deciding whether a particular voltage can be safely applied to an insulator, the r.m.s. value must be multiplied by the peak factor. **1970** *IEEE Trans. Information Theory* XVI. 86/1 The perceptual quality of synthetic speech signals depends to some extent on the 'peak-factor' (defined here as the difference between the maximum and minimum amplitudes of a signal divided by its root-mean-square value). *Ibid.*, FM signals have low peak factors. **1959** *B.S.I. News* Dec. 14 Recommendations regarding automatic gain control or peak limiting have also been excluded. **1960** E. SIVERTSEN *Cockney Phonol.* ii. 13 A simple peak consists of one of the six vowels. A complex peak consists of one of the six vowels as peak nucleus plus one of the peak satellites [h j w]. **1941** *B.B.C. Gloss. Broadcasting Terms* 23 *Peak programme meter*, instrument used (especially for the purpose of facilitating control) to measure the volume of programme peaks, averaged over a period of less than one-hundredth of a second. **1962** A. NISBETT *Technique Sound Studio* v. 94 There are several types of meter that can be used to line up equipment or check for overmodulation; but a 'peak programme meter' (PPM) seems to be the most satisfactory instrument. **1960** Peak satellite [see *peak nucleus* above]. **1960** *Wall St. Jrnl.* 5 Oct. 10/2 Pilot plants were being planned in this country a quarter century ago..looking for economic means of 'peak showing.' This is the practice in which standby sources of supply are used to meet demand at peak periods. **1973** *Times* 30 July 11/3 Both are designed to absorbe the stresses imposed on tüe gas supply system by a very cold day throughout the country in the depth of winter. The remedy is termed peak shaving. **1965** *Wireless World* July 329/1 A recording level indicator should essentially be a peak registering type because music has a large peak-to-mean ratio. **1962** SIMPSON & RICHARDS *Physical Princ. Junction Transistors* ix. 219 The shift due to the rise in ambient temperature is thus relatively small and can be tolerated for peak-to-peak output-current swings of about 7 mA. **1967** *Electronics* 6 Mar. 80/2 (Advt.), Model 900 Nanovolt Galvanometer. Noise: Less than 2 nV or (2 pA) peak-to-peak for all source resistances. **1973** *Nature* 9 Nov. 72/2 During the eclipse itself the stability of the aircraft was excellent: pitch $\lesssim 0{\cdot}1°$, roll $\lesssim 0{\cdot}5°$ (peak-to-peak values). **1974** HARVEY & BOHLMAN *Stereo F.M. Radio Handbk.* ii. 21 The peak-to-peak amplitude of the second harmonic between the collector and the tap on the coil is limited to approximately twice the line supply voltage. **1957** *Physical Rev.* CV. 1416/2 Nuclear emulsion as a target was found to have a significantly weaker asymmetry (peak-to-valley ratio of $1{\cdot}40 \pm 0{\cdot}07$). **1924** *Jrnl. Sci. Instrum.* I. 281 A compact peak voltmeter, using a thermionic rectifier for measuring positive and negative peak voltages up to 600 volts, is described. **1967** *IEEE Trans. Electr. Insulation* II. 80/2 The peak voltmeter may find wide application in corona routine measurements.

7. Passing into *adj.* **a.** Characterized by or pertaining to a greatest value or largest number; *peak-listening, -viewing*, listening to the radio, or viewing of television, by the largest audience of the day; freq. *attrib.* (from a false analysis of phrases like *peak listening-period* as *peak-listening period*).

1903 *Electr. World & Engin.* 9 May 789/1 The direct-current ends of these rotary converters are often worked in multiple with an old generating station..during the peak-hours. **1924** *Westm. Gaz.* 8 Aug. 3/4 A drop of nearly £40,000,000 in pensions expenditure since the 'peak' year of 1920–21 is mentioned. **1937** *Archit. Rev.* LXXXII. (Suppl.) 1 Traffic congestion at the 'peak hours' is deplorable. **1946** *Vogue* June 2/2 The Sunday evening peak-listening series, 'The Challenge of our Time'. **1948** E. WAUGH *Loved One* 57 It was as though..his speech came from some distant and august studio; everything he said might have been for a peak-hour listening period. 1949 *Radio Times* 15 July 31/2 Leonard Hooper, a..dining-car attendant, tells you something about his work..especially during the holiday peak periods. 1960 M. O'Conor et al. *Children & Television Programmes* iii. 8 Pressures of different kinds and degrees exist to compel the television organizations to seek very large audiences for at least some of the programmes placed within the peak viewing period. 1962 L. Deighton *Ipcress File* xxv. 158 One long fluorescent day punctuated by interrogations like TV commercials in a peak hour play. 1966 *B.B.C. Handbk.* 14 A serious endeavour to improve the range of peak-time programmes. 1966 *Listener* 5 May 643/2 The peak age [for juvenile crime] is during the last year at school. 1969 G. Rees *St Michael* xv. 184 It was not until 1948 that the figures of turnover exceeded those of the previous peak year of 1941. 1974 *Times* 19 Dec. 2/7 The fare rises..will not arrest traffic growth. Peak services to holiday areas..are being increased. 1976 *Jrnl. R. Soc. Arts* June 360/2 It would have been stupid and arrogant to think that 'Nobody will want all that news at the peak hour' or 'They ought to have half an hour's news, it is good for them.' 1977 *Herald* (Melbourne) 18 Jan. 1/1 A packed peak-hour express train tore down an overhead bridge.

b. Greatest; that is a maximum.

1903 [see *LOAD *sb.* 3 f]. 1930 *Daily Express* 6 Sept. 10/1 Ordinary shares..reached a peak price of 26s. 10½d. during the 'boom'. 1946 *R.A.F. Jrnl.* May 180 At peak production, the Halifax group turned out one complete aircraft every working hour. 1949 R.-M. S. Heffner *Gen. Phonetics* II. v. 79 Two resonators with peak resonances below 1,200 cycles per second. 1950 *Engineering* 10 Feb. 168/2 Each cylinder of a multi-cylinder engine may be fitted with one of these gauges, and the peak pressures attained..are then read at a glance. 1958 *Times Rev. Industry* May 24/3 Important for the overall economy of gas supply are the processes used to produce for peak loads. 1959 *Ann. Reg. 1958* 431 Mr. John Davis..anticipated attendance at the cinemas would have dropped during 1958 to..just over half the peak audiences achieved in the years immediately after the war. 1973 S. Fisher *Female Orgasm* vii. 202 Ideation and fantasy do not..play a large or consistent role during the peak arousal phase.

peak, *v.*[2] Add: **1.** Also const. *up*. (Further examples.)

1929 R. Bridges *Testament of Beauty* i. 23 Untill the pyramid in geometrical enormity peak'd true. 1962 T. Masters *Surfing made Easy* 65 *Peak up*, when a swell begins to break. 1965 J. M. Kelly *Surf & Sea* iii. 39 This is where the wave peaks up and first starts breaking. 1968 W. Warwick *Surfriding in N.Z.* 10/3 If you find the wave you have caught is peaking up further along the beach from you, paddle towards the peak. 1976 *Woman's Day* (N.Y.) Nov. 100/2 Don't overpluck, overpencil or change the place where your brows peak.

b. *fig.* To reach the highest point; to attain maximum intensity, activity, etc.

1958 *Bird Migration* I. I. 2 Common and Black-headed Gulls were usually present, the former peaking at 32 on 14th, the latter at 27 on 30th. 1961 T. H. White *Making of President 1960* xii. 299 There were now eighteen days left to the campaign, and Mr. Nixon was free to take the gloves off and 'peak' in his own manner. 1966 *Punch* 24 Aug. 283/1 Athletes are an awkward squad... Why does a young man fail to reach his potential on the day?.. His anxiety level is so high that he peaks too early. 1968 *Guardian* 21 Sept. 1/1 My campaign, according to the polls and surveys, has not peaked too soon. 1971 *Nature* 29 Jan. 304/2 Instead, the spectrum peaks around 4 keV and falls rapidly to both higher and lower photon energies. 1973 *Times Lit. Suppl.* 6 Apr. 366/5 That wild, speculative spirit peaked in 1929. 1974 *Sci. Amer.* Sept. 143/2 Only at relatively high occupational levels do the average earnings of men peak at the same time that the needs of their families are also peaking, that is, when the children are adolescent and of college age. 1975 *Listener* 8 May 615/1 Like so many of his ink, Man Ray peaked early, and turned dilettante. 1976 *Publishers Weekly* 26 Apr. 52/3 Growth, the very life-blood of corporate capitalism, has peaked in our time and now begun a decline towards what Jones calls 'a permanent recession'. 1977 *Horse & Hound* 25 Mar. 55/1 The eight [riders] named have been asked to programme their potential horses to 'peak' at this time but without too many competitions in advance.

c. To level *out* after reaching a peak.

1958 *Washington Post* 2 June A12/5 The Commissioner of the Bureau of Labor Statistics says the cost of living index is 'peaking out'. He follows this with the even more remarkable statement that the index may creep up further this summer after peaking out now. 1967 *Technology Week* 23 Jan. 55/3 When we learn just a trifle more about the hormonal control of brain development, these phenomena will peak out in human interest. 1971 *Daily Tel.* 2 Mar. 18/6 Since margins peaked out in the latter half of 1969 returns have not been so impressive and the rate of profit growth between the two halves has slackened from 7 p.c. to 5 p.c. 1977 *Time* 29 Aug. 46/3 General Motors shares peaked out at almost 114 in 1965 and are now down to around 65.

d. To have a peak experience (see *PEAK *sb.*[2] 6).

1970 J. Howard *Please Touch* 20 People who 'peak' can transcend the mundane and feel ecstatically fulfilled. 1972 *Village Voice* (N.Y.) 1 June 78/4 The hill with the tall fir cross, only 30 yards from where Michael and Ellen and I had peaked on the acid.

2. Add to first part of def.: to bring to a peak or maximum. Also const. *up*. (Examples.)

1957 *Practical Wireless* XXXIII. 718/2 When a station is found, the trimmers of range 5 are adjusted to peak it up. 1960 *Ibid.* XXXVI. 375/2 Trimmers can be peaked for minimum meter reading. 1961 T. H. White *Making of President 1960* xii. 296 He might move his campaign into its third, or final phase, 'peaking' it for impact on the week end before election. 1962 A. Nisbett *Technique Sound Studio* ix. 158 As the scene comes to a close the speech is faded down and the effects are lifted to swamp the line. Then after the effects have been peaked for a few seconds they too can be slowly faded out. *Ibid.* 263 *Peak up*, lift the volume either of an individual component of a mix, or of the entire programme.

peak, *v.*[3] **b.** (Earlier examples.)

1836 N. Isaacs *Trav. E. Afr.* II. 347 They immediately hauled down their sail, peaked their oars. 1849 J. F. Cooper *Sea Lions* I. xi. 156 The men now 'peaked' their oars, as it is termed; or they placed the handles in cleets made to receive them, leaving the blades elevated in the air, so as to be quite clear of the water. 1851 H. Melville *Moby Dick* II. vi. 42 The boat's five oars were seen simultaneously peaked.

peaked, *a.* **1.** (Further examples.) Cf. *PEAK *sb.*[2] 5 e.

1952 [see *KURTOSIS]. 1965 *Wireless World* July 329/1 The frequency of the peaked response is accordingly altered by switching each arm capacitance of the parallel-T network. 1968 A. J. Merrett *Executive Remuneration in U.K.* p. xiii, The indivisible nature of many executive roles..necessitates great personal involvement,..and the strain of an erratic and highly peaked work load.

3. *peaked-faced, -looking* adjs.

1891 'L. Malet' *Wages of Sin* I. I. iii. 56 It 'ud aggravate a saint, that it would, to hear you so taken up with a little peaked-faced bit of a maid. 1889 C. King *Queen of Bedlam* xiv. 188 Randall M'Lean, very white and 'peaked' looking, was sitting propped up in bed.

pea·kiness. [f. Peaky *a.*[1] + -ness.] Peaked or pointed character.

1921 L. B. Turner *Wireless Telegr.* iii. 22 The 'peakiness' of this curve measures the 'sharpness of tuning'. 1924 W. Deeping *Three Rooms* ii. 12 That slight peakiness about the chin, the ugly lines in the throat.

Peakland (pī·klænd). [See Peak *sb.*[1]] The Peak District of Derbyshire; = Peak *sb.*[1]

924, 1610 [see Peak *sb.*[1] 1]. 1891 J. Leyland *Peak of Derbyshire* I. 1 The 'Peak of Derbyshire' is a term which, to many, does not carry with it a very definite signification, for although most of the favourite resorts of tourists are known to lie within Peakland, few have inquired as to the boundaries of that district. 1909 *Westm. Gaz.* 5 Apr. 8/1 The death occurred..on Sunday night of..one of the best known figures among Peakland agriculturalists. *a* 1917 R. M. Gilchrist *Peakland Faggot* (1926) 97 The moon..foresaw a tragi-comedy in Peakland. 1926 E. Phillpotts in *Ibid.* p. viii, His [*sc.* Gilchrist's] incomparable pictures of Peakland were only won from long and self-denying service..in the courts and sanctities of the place and people. 1931 H. Walker (*title*) Peakland poems. 1974 *Country Life* 12 Dec. 1867/1 The strange disappearance of a Peakland river.

peaky, *a.*[1] Add: **3.** Special collocations, as **peaky blinder**, formerly, a hooligan active in the Birmingham area and distinguished by his hat, worn pulled into a peak over the eyes.

1896 *Birmingham Daily Argus* 17 Nov. 2/3 Is there..any Volunteer officer who will come down and captain a company of budding 'peaky blinders'? 1898 *Daily News* 22 Oct. 2/5 The woman..saw the two 'peaky blinders' leaving on Thursday morning. 1901 *N. & Q.* Feb. 94/2 *Peakyblinder*.., the 'larrikins', 'ruffiers', or 'hoodlums' of the Midlands are thus known from a custom they adopted of wearing the peak of their cap drawn down over their eyes when at their nefarious practices. 1971 B. Sleigh *Smell of Privet* x. 82 A mission in..Birmingham which took in some of the notorious Peaky Blinders.

peaky, peeky, *a.*[2] Add: (Earlier example.)

1821 M. Edgeworth *Let.* 23 Oct. (1971) 240 Poor young Worthington himself is rather peeky-weakee. He has a sore throat.

b. *Comb.*, as *peaky-faced* adj.

1906 *Westm. Gaz.* 12 May 11/2 A peaky-faced boy of about nine. 1910 *Chambers's Jrnl.* Jan. 53/1 He looked at the peaky-faced boy with the scared black eyes.

pealer[2] (pī·ləɪ). *U.S.* [var. *PEELER[1] 3.] A person who displays exceptional aptitude or enthusiasm *for* an activity.

1834 S. Smith *Sel. Lett. J. Downing* 142 Pennsylvany chaps are real pealers for electing folks when they take hold. 1869 [see Staver *sb.*[2]].

peanut. For 'a native of the West Indies and West Africa' substitute 'native to South America'; = Ground-nut 2. Add earlier and later examples.

1807 *Salmagundi* 27 June 240 Young seniors go down to the flag-staff to buy peanuts, and beer. 1937 A. F. Hill *Econ. Bot.* xvi. 358 The peanut is a native of Brazil but was early carried to the Old World tropics by the Portuguese explorers. It was brought to Virginia from Africa by the slaves and is now one of the most important crops of the south. 1967 N. Freeling *Strike Out* 96 His wife was..reading Proust and eating peanuts. 1968 J. W. Purseglove *Tropical Crops: Dicotyledons* I. 225 More than half the edible peanut stocks of the United States are used for peanut butter.

b. *peanut farmer* (so *-farming*), *oil, -seller, -shell, vendor; peanut-brained* adj.; **peanut boy** *U.S.*, a boy who sells peanuts and other wares; **peanut brittle**, a brittle toffee with roasted peanuts in it; **peanut butter**, a paste made with ground roasted peanuts; also *attrib.*; **peanut candy** *U.S.*, candy with roasted peanuts in it; **peanut gallery** *U.S. slang*, the top gallery in a theatre; **peanut-parcher** *U.S.*, = **peanut-roaster* (*b*), also *attrib.*; **peanut politician** *U.S.*, one who deals in peanut politics; **peanut roaster** *U.S.*, (*a*) a machine in which peanuts are roasted; (*b*) *fig.* a piece of machinery that puffs or hisses; **peanut stand** *U.S.*, a booth, stall, or stand where peanuts, etc., are sold; **peanut valve** *Electronics*, a type of small thermionic valve (see quots.); also *ellipt.*

1857 *Porter's Spirit of Times* 5 Sept. 12/1 At length the mare reached the quarter pole, where a little pea-nut boy had stationed himself. 1873 'Mark Twain' *Gilded Age* xxxvi. 333 In the cars,..the peanut-boy..always hands you out a book of murders if you are fond of theology. 1922 Joyce *Ulysses* 421 Come on, you doggone, bullnecked, beetlebrowed, hogjowled, peanutbrained, weaseleyed fourflushers, false alarms and excess baggage! 1903 *N.Y. Even. Post* 2 Oct. 7 To prescribe that all records [of great eating] henceforth shall be measured in peanut brittle. 1947 J. Bertram *Shadow of War* 336 The same jasmine tea, the same peanut brittle. 1965 Mrs. L. B. Johnson *White House Diary* 14 Feb. (1970) 244 Luci came bounding in this morning, to give her daddy a box of peanut brittle for his Valentine. 1976 *Monitor* (McAllen, Texas) 30 Sept. 8C/7 Crunchy peanut brittle, chock-full of tasty, nutritious peanuts, isn't difficult to make if you remember to spread the candy thinly on the cookie sheet. 1903 *Harper's Mag.* Oct. 981 Four sandwiches... Two of wholewheat bread with peanut butter. 1926–7 *Army & Navy Stores Catal.* 2/2 Peanut Butter jars—each 1/-. 1974 'R. B. Dominic' *Epitaph for Lobbyist* xiii. 113 A carnival with peanut butter fudge made by the Soroptimists. 1977 *Time* 14 Mar. 42/2, I grew up on peanut butter sandwiches. 1856 Mrs. Stowe *Dred* I. iv. 51 Dancing, flirting, writing love-letters, and all other enormities down to eating pea-nut candy. 1901 B. Matthews *Notes on Speech-Making* 53 Some postprandial addresses..resemble the peanut candy where you cannot see the candy for the peanuts. 1976 *Time* 27 Dec. 23/3 He met Carter at a commission conference in 1973 and was one of the few who early took the peanut farmer's presidential aspirations seriously. 1977 *Time* 3 Jan. 13/2 As President Harry Truman was saved from haberdashing by failure, Jimmy Carter was saved from peanut farming by success. 1888 *Lippincott's Monthly Mag.* XLII. 734 Go to the lowest theatre in any of our large cities, or..mark what is called the 'Family Circle' by theatre proprietors and to the general world is more felicitously known as the 'Peanut Gallery'. 1945 *New Yorker* 5 May 15/1 We were sitting in the peanut gallery of the Opera House. 1975 *Audubon* Nov. 26/3, I can hear the laughter down in the pit and up in the peanut gallery. 1976 *National Observer* (U.S.) 21 Aug. 12/1 Sitting in the peanut gallery with her two young daughters, she admitted: 'I wouldn't miss it for the world. I grew up watching it.' 1882 H. H. Kane *Opium-Smoking* 35 A small glass lamp with a glass cover, perforated just above the flame, and in which sweet or peanut oil is burned. 1912 A. H. Lewis *Apaches N.Y.* 132 He trimmed the peanut-oil lamp. 1973 R. Thomas *If you can't be Good* (1974) ii. 13 The reports of mine that did surface were major scandals... The Peanut Oil King Affair comes to mind. 1929 W. Faulkner *Sartoris* (1932) III. 261 'Narcissa'll take you..in her car.'.. 'In that little peanut-parcher?' 1942 —— *Go down, Moses* 228 The diminutive locomotive and its shrill peanut-parcher whistle. 1954 —— *Fable* 393 The shrill peanut-parcher whistle which did not presage the lurch [of the train]. 1931 W. G. McAdoo *Crowded Yrs.* xii. 191 Any Democratic Cabinet, if not actually deficient mentally, consists of adolescents and small peanut politicians. 1977 *Lebende Sprachen* XXII. 10/2 A politician who is merely interested in small advantages is a *peanut politician*. 1902 *Sears, Roebuck Catal.* 589/3 The Boss Peanut and Coffee Roaster is the only successful roaster on the market. 1904 'O. Henry' in *N.Y. World Mag.* 22 May 4/2 The whistle of a peanut-roaster puffed a hot scream into his ear. 1939 *These are our Lives* (Federal Writers' Project, U.S.) 283 [He] drew out a gallon at a time as needed for his peanut roaster. 1942 Berrey & Van den Bark *Amer. Thes. Slang* § 769/2 *Peanut roaster*, an intake manifold with a leak. 1960 Wentworth & Flexner *Dict. Amer. Slang* 379/2 *Peanut-roaster*,..a small locomotive..an old or ramshackle automobile. 1971 M. Tak *Truck Talk* 116 *Peanut roaster*, an intake manifold with a leak. 1971 'D. Halliday' *Dolly & Doctor Bird* iii. 33 Peanut-sellers and newsvendors have free access to the front door. 1856 Mrs. Stowe *Dred* I. i. 9 'There isn't one of the train that I would give *that* for!', said she, flirting a shower of peanut-shells into the air. 1862 'Mark Twain' *Let.* 8 Feb. (1917) I. iii. 67 He hasn't business talent enough to carry on a peanut stand. 1864 T. Pastor *'444' Combination Songster* 66 A blackguard by the name of McCarty..was book-keeper to a peanut-stand, And sold apples by the dozen. 1919 [see *FRANKFURTER]. 1947 *Time* 27 Jan. 58/2 He was always dabbling shrewdly in dry cleaning stores and peanut stands. 1923 G. Parr *Princ. & Pract. Wireless Transmission* viii. 119 A valve which has proved very popular in America both on account of its size and low current consumption is that known as the Polar 'Pea-nut' valve. The bulb is tubular, its dimensions being 2 in. long by ½ in. diameter, and is fitted with a bayonet cap similar to the ordinary incandescent bulb. The valve requires only ·25 ampere at ·08 to 1 volt, and has a life double that of the ordinary tungsten valve. 1924 [see *DETECTOR 3]. 1930 *B.B.C. Year-bk. 1931* 448/2 *Peanut Valve*, a type of three-electrode receiving valve requiring low filament current and anode voltage. The dimensions of the valve are very small and it is therefore of use where space and small battery consumption are a consideration. 1910 G. B. McCutcheon *Rose in Ring* 56 The lowliest peanut-vender was laughing in his sleeve at the sleuth. 1978 S. Naipaul *North of South* II. v. 209 The peanut vendor was guilty of waging capitalist war against socialist society.

2. a. *pl.* Something small, trivial, or unimportant; *spec.* a small sum of money, esp. when regarded as inadequate payment. orig. *U.S. slang*.

1934 H. N. Rose *Thesaurus of Slang* iii. 35/2 *Small robbery*,..peanuts; ex: The job was peanuts. **1936** *Metronome* Feb. 21/4 *Peanuts*, any pay from a nickel a night and down. **1941** B. Schulberg *What makes Sammy Run?* viii. 176 They got you working for peanuts. **1946** J. B. Priestley *Bright Day* x. 285 'How was the poker game?' 'Peanuts. All I got was about twenty-five dollars and a headache.' **1959** J. Osborne *World of Paul Slickey* II. x. 87 There's a thousand pounds a week from record sales..it ain't peanuts. **1968** *Globe & Mail* (Toronto) 13 Jan. 29/2 All this is peanuts compared to the steady core of 3,600 ministers who make up the United Church clergy. **1973** *Scotsman* 13 Feb. 8/5 A salary of £3000 a year is peanuts for a man at the top of his profession. **1975** *New Yorker* 26 May 23 (Advt.), Being in a region may be your only chance to sample the local delicacies. And the cost? Peanuts. **1977** *Time Out* 17 June 15/1 The *New Review*'s share of the budget is a much criticised 10% of the total, yet it's peanuts.

b. A small or unimportant person. Also in more specialized contexts (see quots.).

1942 Berrey & Van den Bark *Amer. Thes. Slang* § 389/1 *Insignificant or petty person*,..palooka, peanut, person of straw, picayune, [etc.]. *Ibid.*, Peanuts, rubbish, small fry, small potatoes *or* punkins, trash, truck, *persons of no consequence*. *Ibid.* § 429/4 *Small person*,..peanut, peewee, picayune. **1945** Baker *Austral. Lang.* viii. 157 *Peanut*, a simple-minded soldier. **1963** *Australasian Post* 14 Mar. 51/1 'And what,' I asked cheerfully, 'was this peanut's particular whinge?' **1968** *Daily Mail* 16 Mar. 6/4 Mods are the traditional enemies of Rockers, but there were no Mods that night... 'They're scared of us... We call them peanuts.' **1969** *Daily Mirror* 3 Sept. 12/4 The youths were peanuts, or skin-heads. **1970** *Observer* (Colour Suppl.) 12 Apr. 46/3 Once me and my mates used to go around robbing peanuts—mod girls.

3. *attrib.* passing into *adj.* Trivial, worthless.

1836 W. Dunlap *Thirty Years Ago* II. iii. 25 They were your pea-nut fellows, I suppose. **1854** *Congress. Globe* 19 May 1230/3, I know them—a set of peanut agitators and Peter Funk philanthropists. **1892** *Congress. Rec.* 18 June 5394/2 This country is not a peanut institution; it is a great country. **1910** G. B. McCutcheon *Rose in Ring* 203, I suppose that peanut aristocrat friend of yours has told you it ain't swell or proper to wear tights.

pear, *sb.* Add: **5. pear-apple,** (*b*) the fruit of a prickly pear, a cactus belonging to the genus *Opuntia*; **pear-blight** (*a*), add: = *fire-blight* s.v. *Fire *sb.* B. 5 (earlier and later examples); **pear-drop,** (*c*) used *attrib.* of parts of furniture, etc., shaped like pears; **pear midge,** a small gall midge, *Contarinia pyrivora*, whose larvae damage the fruit of pear trees; **pear-wood,** (*b*) the wood of one of several West African trees, esp. *Guarea cedrata*.

1898 H. S. Canfield *Maid of Frontier* 205 He knew.. which of the 'pear apples' were good to eat. **1854** E. Emmons *Agric. N.Y.* V. 165 Atmospheric Blight..proves itself to be independent of the cause that sometimes produces the pear blight. **1924** *Phytopathology* XIV. 478 (*title*) Experiments in the control of cankers of pear blight. **1961** A. Schoenfeld tr. *Stapp's Bacterial Plant Pathogens* II. 134 This disease, variously called 'fire blight', 'blossom blight', 'fruit blight', 'twig blight', 'apple blight', or 'pear blight', according to the place affected, is one of the most dangerous and dreaded tree diseases of North America. **1978** A. Huxley *Illustr. Hist. Gardening* v. 176 Pear blight was specifically described as 'a vegetable apoplexy'. **1914** Eberlein & McClure *Pract. Bk. Period Furnit.* i. 27 It is necessary for us to know whether a chest or cupboard ought to have knobs, pear drop or bail handles. **1925** Penderel-Brodhurst & Layton *Gloss. Eng. Furnit.* 121 *Pear-drop-handle*, a small pendent brass handle in pear-shape form, which came into use in England in the Restoration period. *Ibid.* 122 *Pear-drop ornament*, an ornament usually decorating the upper portion of a plain frieze,..consisting of a series of Gothic arches in relief with drops at the lower points suggesting capitals. **1960** H. Hayward *Antique Coll.* 213/1 *Pear-drop moulding*, a moulding, found below a plain cornice on late 18th cent. bookcases, carved in a repetitive design of inverted pear-shaped forms. **1884** E. A. Ormerod *Rep. Observations Injurious Insects 1883* 53 The Pear Midge is a very small two-winged gnat fly. **1920** P. J. Fryer *Insect Pests & Fungus Dis.* xvi. 234 The pear midge..is a destructive pest on fruit. **1956** Peairs & Davidson *Insect Pests* (ed. 5) xvii. 442 The pear midge is an introduced insect, present in the northeastern states for over 50 years. **1973** H. Martin *Sci. Princ. Crop Protection* (ed. 6) xv. 358 He [*sc.* F. V. Theobald] observed the extermination of the pear midge..by fowls penned under the attacked trees. **1915** J. H. Holland *Useful Plants Nigeria* III. 419 One of the finest timber trees in W. Africa [is *Mimusops Djave*], sold in Europe as 'African Pear Wood'. **1922** W. Schlich *Man. Forestry* (ed. 4) I. II. 320 The most prominent species [in Sierra Leone] are given as:—..red ironwood, very common. A species of Mimusops known as pearwood [etc.]. **1937** J. M. Dalziel *Useful Plants W. Trop. Afr.* 357 M[*anilkara*] *lacera*...African pearwood. *Ibid.*, M[*imusops*] *djave*... African pearwood. **1950** C. W. Bond *Colonial Timbers* 77 Guarea (Nigerian pearwood). **1961** F. R. Irvine *Woody Plants of Ghana* 519 *Guarea cedrata*... The names 'Nigerian Pearwood', 'Nigerian Cedar', and 'Cedar Mahogany', formerly given for this tree, are dropped as likely to cause confusion. **1971** F. H. Titmuss *Commerc. Timbers of World* (ed. 4) 134 Two species of *Guarea*..may be included in consignments of this timber, which has occasionally been sold as Nigerian Pearwood.

pearceite (pīə·ɹsəit). *Min.* [f. the name of Richard *Pearce* (1837–1927), British-born metallurgist and chemist + -ite[1].] A black, lustrous, brittle sulphide of silver and arsenic, $Ag_{16}As_8S_{11}$, that occurs as tabular crystals and usu. contains copper in place of some of the silver.

1896 S. L. Penfield in *Amer. Jrnl. Sci.* CLII. 18 The author proposes that hereafter the name polybasite shall be restricted to the antimony compound..and to make of the corresponding arsenic compound..a distinct species. For the arsenical mineral he takes pleasure in proposing the name *pearceite* as a compliment to his friend, Dr. Richard Pearce, of Denver. **1942** *Econ. Geol.* XXXVII. 491 Pearceite, recognizable only in polished section, is almost invariably associated with pyrargyrite. **1963** *Amer. Mineralogist* XLVIII. 567 The traditional polybasite and pearceite actually are members of two separate solid solution series in which Sb and As substitute mutually. **1968** I. Kostov *Mineral.* 173 The crystals of pearceite, polybasite, and xanthoconite are pseudohexagonal platy {001}.

pearl, *sb.*[1] Add: **I. 1. d.** (Earlier example of *Roman pearl*.) *essence of pearl*: now usu. called *pearl essence* (see sense *18); also prepared from the scales of other fish (as the herring).

1805 C. Wilmot *Let.* 26 Aug. in *Russ. Jrnls.* (1934) I. 170 A dress of white crape & roman pearls & white cameo ornaments.

II. 12. (Earlier example.)

1872 *Young Englishwoman* Oct. 543/1 *Ether pearls*, small round capsules about the size of a pea, are of marvellous efficacy in instantly calming attacks of Asthma.

16. b. Applied to an electric light bulb that is frosted on the inside so as to diffuse the light.

1930 *Engineering* 21 Mar. 393/1 The panels are illuminated from behind by a standard 40-watt 'pearl' lamp backed by aluminium reflectors. **1938** *Times* 3 Feb. 17/1 The conclusion reached is that lamps of the pearl type give a 7½ per cent better light than the opal type at present in use. **1972** 'R. Crawford' *Whip Hand* I. iii. 12 A single pearl bulb lit the store.

III. 17. a. *pearl necklace, -rope, string, stud.* **b.** *pearl-making, -sliding* adjs. **c.** *pearl-enamelled, -flushed, -hung, -paved* adjs. **d.** *pearl-tinted* adj. **e.** *pearl-bright, -grey* (later examples); also as sb., *-pale* adjs.

1914 G. Frankau *Tid'apa* (1915) v. 29 Pearl-bright under purple eyelids the unshed dew of a tear. **1943** D. Gascoyne *Poems 1937–42* 60 Like Some priceless pearl-enamelled toy. **1952** R. Campbell tr. *Baudelaire's Poems* 193 While Phoebe sheers Through pearl-flushed hours, To rain down tears In glittering showers. **1875** J. Blackwood *Let.* 30 Nov. in *Geo. Eliot Lett.* (1956) VI. 195, I rather lean to the pearl grey which he has told me is the name of the colour. **1931** V. Woolf *Waves* 110 Among the lustrous green, pink, pearl-grey women stand upright the bodies of men. **1969** in Halpert & Story *Christmas Mumming in Newfoundland* 182 Costumes used for disguise are listed:..fancy vests, beaver hats, pearl-gray spats. **1976** *Eastern Even. News* (Norwich) 9 Dec. 18/2 (Advt.), 1973 Capri 1600XL, pearl grey, 44,934, £1280. **1965** F. Sargeson *Mem. Peon* vi. 181 A short distance from my Leonora's pearl-hung ear. **1924** J. A. Thomson *Science Old & New* xx. 110 It seems highly probable that the walls of the pearl-making sac are in a state of inflammation. **1708** J. Lovett *Let.* 1 May in M. M. Verney *Verney Lett.* (1930) I. xii. 202 Tell Deare Bess her Pearle Necklas is come. **1819** M. Wilmot *Let.* 8 Dec. (1935) 33, I can wear my pearl necklace clasped with the amathyst behind. **1972** J. Wilson *Hide & Seek* ii. 35 He reached for her imitation pearl necklace. **1895** W. B. Yeats *Poems* 6 A pearl-pale, high-born lady. **1908** *Westm. Gaz.* 30 Dec. 2/3 There, in 'the Garden' roofed with glass, He flutes on the pearl-paved ridge of dawn. **1925** E. Sitwell *Troy Park* 75 And there the pearlropes fall like shawls. **1948** C. Day Lewis *Poems 1943–47* 15 What unseen clue Threads my pearl-sliding hours. **1939** L. M. Montgomery *Anne of Ingleside* xxi. 142 'Aren't those pearl strings pretty?'..'You'd almost think they were real.' **1927** E. Glyn *'It'* xix. 172 His shirt with its incomparable two pearl studs. **1975** S. Lauder *Killing Time on Corvo* i. 8 Her plain grey suit and hat, pearl studs, gloves. **1908** *Daily Chron.* 29 Sept. 7/5 He..entered the deserted garden where pearl-tinted spikes of iris perfumed the air.

18. pearl-berry, also *fig.*; **pearl essence, pearlessence,** essence of pearl (see Pearl *sb.*[1] 1 d in Dict. and Suppl.), or a synthetic imitation of this; **pearl-fish,** (*c*) = *fierasfer; **pearl-white** *a.*, add to def.: orig. used of *pearlware; also *ellipt.* as *sb.* = *pearlware (earlier and later examples).

1924 E. Sitwell *Sleeping Beauty* xvii. 67 And the pearl-berries of the snow upon dark bushes freeze. **1921** *Sci. Amer.* 12 Mar. 213/3 'Essence d'Orient' was easily manufactured, which was readily given the name of 'pearl essence' by the Bureau of Fisheries. **1946** Simonds & Bregman *Finishing Metal Products* (ed. 2) xxviii. 279 Pearl essence is used to substitute for metal powder finishes on everything from women's compacts and cosmetic containers to heavy industrial equipment and machinery. **1961** *Soap, Perfumery & Cosmetics* XXXIV. 60/3 By crushing or pulverising, natural and synthetic pearl essences lose part of their brilliance and become dull or greyish. **1972** P. G. I. Lauffer in Balsam & Sagarin *Cosmetics* (ed. 2) I. xii. 370 Natural pearlessence, consisting of a castor oil suspension of guanine crystals prepared from fish scales, produces a beautiful pearly luster when added to lipsticks. **1905** D. S. Jordan *Guide to Study of Fishes* II. xxix. 522 In the little group of pearl-fishes, called Fierasferidæ or Carapidæ, the body is eel-shaped with a rather large head. **1972** J. Binyon *Physiol. of Echinoderms* vi. 72 The famous pearl fish *Carapus* (= *Fierasfer*) *bermudiensis*..seems to live indefinitely in the cloaca and respiratory trees of this holothurian without ill-effect. **1779** J. Wedgwood *Let.* 19 June (1965) 236, I thank her majesty for the honor she has done to the *Pearl White*, and hope it will have due influence upon all her loyal subjects. **1866** E. Meteyard *Life J. Wedgwood* II. x. 482 An Italian order furnishes the accompanying tureen and plate in pearl-white ware. **1884** [see *creation 5c]. **1914** G. Frankau *Tid'apa* (1915) vi. 34 Pearl-white 'gainst the darkling lustre at the black-pearl plinth of the capes. **1937** V. Woolf *Years* 295 The road stretched pearl-white in front of them. **1956** G. Durrell *My Family* xvi. 218 The curve of pearl-white sand was backed by the great lily-covered dune behind.

pearl, *v.*[1] Add: **5. b.** To refine (potassium carbonate) in the preparation of pearl-ash.

1850 *Rep. Comm. Patents 1849* (U.S.) I. 176 The process of first roasting or heating the ashes..and then pearling in the pearling oven.

8. b. *Surfing.* (See quots.)

1962 [see *pearling *vbl. sb.* 4]. **1967** J. Severson *Great Surfing* Gloss., *Pearl* or *pearling*, while riding, the nose of the surfboard goes beneath the surface and continues downward, usually throwing the rider off (originally taken from pearl diving). **1970** *Studies in English* (Univ. Cape Town) I. 31 A milder form of wipe-out occurs when the surfboard *pearls*, in other words, the nose of the surfboard knifes under the water surface, usually throwing the surfer off. Variations on this expression include to *pearl-dive*, to *nose*, and to *plough*. **1971** *Ibid.* II. 27 If he is too far forward on the board the nose may dig in and the board *pearl* (shortened form of *pearl-dive*).

pearl-diver. Add: **b.** A person who washes crockery in a café or restaurant. So **pearl-diving** *vbl. sb.* (in this sense). *slang* (orig *U.S.*).

1913 E. A. Brown *Broke* iii. 29, I am in line for a pearl-diver's (dishwasher's) job tomorrow. **1930** J. Dos Passos *42nd Parallel* v. 402 He got a job pearldiving in a lunch-room. **1956** *Amer. Speech* XXXI. 151 *Pearl diver*, a dishwasher in a logging cookhouse. **1970** *Daily Progress* (Charlottesville, Va.) 15 Jan. 3B/5 Euphemism has upgraded other jobs. In parts of the country, dishwashers have been called utensil maintenance men, though back at the sink they still may be 'pearl divers'. **1970** C. Kersh *Aggravations M. Ashe* viii. 100 In the catering pearl diving is slang for dish washing.

pearler (pɜ̄·ɹləɹ), *sb.*[2] *N.Z.* and *Austral. slang.* [Var. Purler.] Something excellent or outstanding; a 'beauty'.

1941 Baker *N.Z. Slang* vi. 51 Expressions..in constant use by our youngsters..swinjer pearler stunner snorter. **1965** *Telegraph* (Brisbane) 5 July 8 *Ripsnorter* (or pearler, bosker, boshter). **1980** *Weekend Australian* 16 Aug. 13 Flo's 35-minute speech was a pearler.

pearlescent (pɜ̄ɹle·sĕnt), *a.* and *sb.* [f. Pearl *sb.*[1] + -escent.] **A.** *adj.* Having or producing an appearance of mother-of-pearl.

1949 *Industr. Finishing* (Indianapolis) Oct. 115 (Advt.), Chem-Scale pearlescent finishes are very effective for artificial pearls, costume jewelry,..etc. **1966** *Vogue* Dec. 84/3 New pearlescent lipsticks. **1972** A. Maruszewski in Balsam & Sagarin *Cosmetics* (ed. 2) I. xi. 357 The pearl material is not to be roller milled or colloid milled, since this tends to destroy the pearlescent property of the material.

B. *sb.* A pearlescent material or finish.

1960 *Times* 6 Jan. 15/4 The Carinex range includes basic polymers... A wide range of colours..include such special effects as pearlescents, tinsels and fluorescents. **1972** A. Maruszewski in Balsam & Sagarin *Cosmetics* (ed. 2) I. xi. 357 There is another pearlescent available under the tradename of Bilite. Chemically it is bismuth oxychloride deposited epitaxially on thin platelets of white mica. **1975** P. Browne *Bodywork Maintenance* ix. 102/1 Acrylics loaded with pearlescents also give an iridescent effect.

So **pearle·scence,** a pearlescent effect or material.

1953 *Organic Finishing* July 12/1 There is now more attention being directed to the production of 'Pearlescence' than to the duplication of the natural product known..as Pearl Essence. We may tentatively define Pearlescence as that action on light which results in a pearly lustrous appearance. **1969** *New Scientist* 2 Oct. 26/2 One of M. Pariat's most appealing products is known as 'pearlescence'. Essentially it consists of including crystals of polycarbonate of bismuth or lead during the final calendering stage of cardboard production. **1973** J. B. Wilkinson et al. *Harry's Cosmeticology* xvi. 205 Attempts to counteract this tendency..tend to decrease the pearlescence of the enamels.

Pearl Harbour. [The name (*Pearl Harbor*) of a U.S. naval base on Oahu, one of the Hawaiian Islands: tr. Hawaiian *Wai Momi*, lit. 'pearl waters'.] Used with direct allusion to the military attack by Japanese aircraft on Pearl Harbour on 7 December 1941, which, delivered without a declaration of war, severely damaged the surprised U.S. Pacific fleet and began the Pacific phase of the war of 1939–45. Also *transf.* and *fig.* Hence as *v. trans.*, to attack suddenly and effectively.

1942 *Progressive* 31 Jan. 272/2 Compare these recently abandoned myths in Britain with the pre-Pearl Harbor folklore about the Japanese which prevailed in the United States. **1942** *Capital* (Topeka, Kansas) 20 Mar. 15/3 Delay along this line is the delay that spells Pearl Harbor to the vital industrial nerve centers of our economy. **1945** Koestler *Twilight Bar* II. 44 Maybe they are doing a Pearl Harbour on us. **1955** *Times* 22 Aug. 7/2 This dangerous local situation could be the result of military aggression or of political subversion. In fact, the real danger is not now so much of an 'atomic Pearl Harbour' as of a new Sarajevo murder, building up into a major atomic war. **1959** *Economist* 10 Jan. 99/2 It will put a premium on

'Pearl Harbour' tactics to knock out opposing missiles before they leave the ground. **1963** *Guardian* 8 Jan. 8/4 No aggressor would dare to Pearl-Harbour any member nation of this club. **1974** *Ibid.* 25 Mar. 15/4 Hornby was working for the Japanese Ministry of Education when Pearl Harbour came. **1975** *Listener* 14 Aug. 211/1 In 1970, Aston Villa were relegated to the third division. Eric Woodward, the commercial manager, describes that as 'our Pearl Harbour'. **1978** *Times* 20 May 14/2 Mrs Thatcher was caught with the Sunday morning Pearl Harbour attack by Mr Peregrine Worsthorne..in last week's *Sunday Telegraph*.

pearling, *vbl. sb.* Add: **1. b.** *pearling lugger* (see quot. 1948).

1924 G. H. P. MUHLHAUSER *Cruise of Amaryllis* v. 233 A fair number of Australian 'black fellows' are to be found among the crews of the pearling 'luggers', as they are called, though really ketches. **1930** *Mariner's Mirror* XVI. 192 The pearling 'luggers' of the Torres Straits are usually ketch-rigged. **1948** R. DE KERCHOVE *Internat. Maritime Dict.* 525/1 *Pearl lugger, pearling lugger,* a local name given in northwest Australia to small ketch-rigged boats employed in pearl fisheries. **1978** O. WHITE *Silent Reach* vi. 71 It takes a different kind of knowhow to cut oyster rafts adrift or..sink pearling luggers..from the knowhow needed to dynamite windmills.

2. c. Decoration of furniture or architecture with pearl-shaped carving.

1899 R. GLAZIER *Man. Hist. Ornament* 43 Later Norman work is very rich,..the lozenge and the beading or pearling. **1914** EBERLEIN & MCCLURE *Pract. Bk. Period Furnit.* 222 Besides these we find reeding, fluting, beading, pearling, spandrel fans, rosettes, and ribbons. **1925** PENDEREL-BRODHURST & LAYTON *Gloss. Eng. Furnit.* 122 *Pearling,* a series of rounded forms of the same size or graded, in more or less relief, used as a decoration on furniture. **1966** M. M. PEGLER *Dict. Interior Design* (1967) 328 *Pearling,* a series of rounded forms of the same size, or graduated like a string of beads. The pearling was used as a furniture embellishment, either in straight lines, arced, or swagged.

4. *Surfing.* (See *PEARL *v.*[1] 8 b.)

1962 T. MASTERS *Surfing made Easy* 65 Pearling, when the nose of the surfboard goes under the water during a ride. **1965** J. POLLARD *Surfrider* ii. 18 The tendency of the nose of the board to dip into the water is 'pearling'. **1968** *Surfer Mag.* Jan. 56/1 The nose was curved to avoid pearling.

pearlite. Add: **2.** (Earlier and later examples.)

1888 H. M. HOWE in *Engin. & Mining Jrnl.* 18 Aug. 132 Minerals which compose iron. Name suggested here... Pearlyte. A mixture of about ⅔ ferrite and ⅓ cementite. **1966** C. R. TOTTLE *Sci. Engin. Materials* x. 228 A two-phase alloy will tend to corrode more readily because an electrochemical cell will be set up between the different areas. Mild steel, containing ferrite (pure iron) and pearlite (a eutectoid, itself two-phase), shows this. **1977** *Sci. Amer.* Oct. 127/1 The presence of pearlite in an iron artifact is a clear indication that the artifact has been carburized.

Hence **pearli·tic** *a.*

1904 *Proc. Inst. Mech. Engin.* Nov. 1149 'Sorbitic' steels..are produced by a much more rapid cooling than is necessary to produce the 'pearlitic' steels. **1947** *Nature* 11 Jan. 50/1 Ordinary cast iron has a mixed ferritic–pearlitic matrix, and the engineering irons are usually fully pearlitic. **1962** *B.S.I. News* June 12/2 Draft proposals considered by the committee related to chemical composition, mechanical properties and methods of test for blackheart, whiteheart and pearlitic malleable iron.

pearlized (pɜ̄·ɹlaizd), *ppl. a.* [f. PEARL *sb.*[1] + -IZE + -ED[1].] Treated so as to resemble mother-of-pearl or to convey a suggestion of mother-of-pearl.

1955 *Britannica Bk. of Year* (U.S.) 681/2 Pearlized and luster leathers were extremely important in women's shoes and colours ranged all the way from pastels to black. **1955** *Wall St. Jrnl.* 21 Nov. 5/2 Retailers note that round, perforated pearlized beads are taxable, and oval ones aren't. **1957** *New Yorker* 1 June 70/1 For town as well as the seashore, there are hats the size of beach umbrellas—sailors of white pearlized straw with straight brims, and sailors of white starched straw curled up at the edges. **1958** *Observer* 17 Aug. 7/4 A coat of pearlised suede lined in cotton. **1969** *Guardian* 12 Aug. 7/2 Transparent make-up..available in three pearlised tan shades. **1972** 'J. MELVILLE' *Ironwood* vi. 89 The names slid easily between her pearlised lips. **1976** *Morecambe Guardian* 7 Dec. 5/1 For a children's party, she made a table arrangement using a soft toy toad, on an oasis shaped like a toadstool, decorated with apples, seed pods and pearlised foliage.

pea·rlware. Also **pearl ware.** White-coloured pottery ware, orig. manufactured by Josiah Wedgwood.

1922 W. BURTON *J. Wedgwood & his Pottery* iv. 37 This 'pearl' ware, as Wedgwood made it, differed somewhat in composition from his cream ware, for it contained a larger proportion of ground flint and china-stone. **1948** W. B. HONEY *Wedgwood Ware* ii. 10 The 'pearl-ware' was chiefly used for tea-services made in rivalry with porcelain. **1953** W. MANKOWITZ *Wedgwood* ii. 44 The peak production period for pearlware is the first quarter of the nineteenth century. **1961** *Times* 8 Apr. 11/6 Cream-coloured earthenware and the harder, whiter pearlware. **1969** *Canad. Antiques Collector* Feb. 14/2 Round about the year 1800 this model must have been turned out by the dozen, sometimes, as in this instance, in pearlware, [etc.]. **1975** *Daily Tel.* 5 Feb. 12/5 A Leeds pearlware figure of a horse, 17 ins high, was bought anonymously for £1,350 at Sotheby's yesterday.

pearly, *a.* (*adv. sb.*) Add: **3. b.** *pearly gates*: the gates of heaven as described in Rev. xxi. 21, used allusively.

1853 [in Dict.]. **1927** H. CRANE *Let.* 29 May (1965) 300 If I can avoid the pearly gates long enough I may do better. **1953** [see *DODGER *a.*]. **1969** J. WAINWRIGHT *Big Tickle* 72 Dago said: 'A shiv kick—and pearly gates.' **1973** J. PORTER *It's Murder with Dover* xvi. 162, I heard somebody'd pushed that Marsh cat through dem pearly gates. **1977** *Gay News* 24 Mar. 21/4 Perfection's death to me, the pearly gates, and I do think pearl's awfully vulgar for gates.

c. *Pearly King* (or *Queen*): a leading London costermonger, dressed in festive costume covered with pearl-buttons.

1933 *Times* 26 Aug. 9/5, I wrote..to 'Snowy Tabram, Pearly King, Islington,' asking him when and where the annual meeting of the Pearlies would take place. **1934** *Times* 1 June 13/3 The Rev. A. D. Belden..unveiled yesterday..a statue of Henry Croft, the 'pearly king', who died four years ago. The statue represents Mr. Croft in his 'pearly king' clothes with top hat. **1935** F. W. TICKNER *London through Ages* xiv. 286 (*caption*) 'Pearly King and Queen' of the Costermongers. **1942** WYNDHAM LEWIS *Let.* 27 Jan. (1963) 315 They go about talking to themselves—in the purest idiom of the Pearly King. **1963** *Times* 16 May 15/5 Reminding me of one of the 'Pearly Kings' or button-covered costermongers that I had seen in London when I was a boy. **1967** E. SHORT *Embroidery & Fabric Collage* ii. 41 Most pearly kings and queens design and make their own costumes, the decoration being made up entirely of pearl buttons sewn on the fabric of the suit or dress. **1975** *Evening News* 26 Apr. 4/1 Pearly King Bill Davison raised thousands of pounds for charity. **1977** *Times* 28 Jan. 16/6 The silver-painted London double decker, decorated with Cockney slogans, pictures of buskers and an advertisement for an insurance company, is the contribution of the Pearly kings and queens of London to the Queen's silver jubilee, and will be used to raise money for a recently-formed Pearlies' charity appeal.

4. (Earlier and later examples of *pearly grey.*)

1845 *Punch* VIII. 247 The following terms..may be used pretty much at random: 'Chiaroscuro', 'texture', 'pearly greys', 'foxy browns'. **1978** I. MURDOCH *Sea* 437 A thick clammy pearly-grey mist surrounded the house.

B. as *adv.* (Further examples.)

1891 KIPLING *Light that Failed* xiii. 249 Maisie lifted up her face, and it was pearly white. 'No! No! Not blind! I won't have him blind!' **1952** A. G. L. HELLYER *Sanders' Encycl. Gardening* (ed. 22) 241 *H[ymenanthera] crassifolia,* yellow, pansy-like flowers, succeeded by pearly-white berries in autumn.

C. *sb.* Add to def.: Also, the pearl-buttons themselves. (Further examples.)

1898 J. D. BRAYSHAW *Slum Silhouettes* 142 He'd..a blue coat and weskit with the artfullest little pearlies you ever see. **1914** 'BARTIMEUS' *Naval Occasions* xviii. 156 What time the citizen ashore donned 'pearlies' or broadcloth and shut up shop. **1935** P. COHEN-PORTHEIM *Spirit of London* viii. 99 There are still costermongers in their 'pearlies' (one of the prettiest dresses to be found anywhere). **1949** R. GRAVES *Seven Days in New Crete* 123 'But you should see my gala suit! It is in rain-grey linen, covered with little pearl-buttons.'.. He went off to buy his pearlies. **1957** *Encycl. Brit.* VI. 511/1 (*caption*) London costermonger family of the Victorian age. These costumes, with their rich embroidery of pearl buttons or 'pearlies', are now used rarely, and only on festive occasions.

b. A costermonger or a pearly king (or queen).

1928 *Daily Express* 27 June 13/3 It is given to few men to be popular alike with princes and 'pearlies'. **1959** *Manch. Guardian* 4 Aug. 4/7 Hampstead Bank Holidays.. felt the loss of..the beery men, the pearlies, and the 'Stout Parties'. **1974** *Times* 20 Aug. 12/2 There will be 'three Pearlies including the Pearly King of London'. **1977** [see sense 3 c above].

Pearson (pīə·ɹsən). *Statistics.* The name of Karl *Pearson* (1857–1936), English mathematician, used *attrib.* and in the possessive to designate: **a.** The members of a family of curves described by him in 1895, which include many probability distribution functions.

1908 *Biometrika* VI. 4 Consequently a curve of Prof. Pearson's Type III may be expected to fit the distribution of s^2. **1927** H. L. RIETZ *Math. Statistics* iii. 58 The method of moments plays an essential rôle in the Pearson system of frequency curves. **1936** *Statistical Res. Mem.* I. 41 A better approximation to $p(L_1')$ might be obtained if a Pearson Type I curve were fitted with the correct first four moment coefficients. **1974** P. LUMB in I. K. Lee *Soil Mech.* iii. 51 Some of the most useful standard forms are members of the Pearson family of distributions defined by

$$\frac{\mathrm{d}}{\mathrm{d}x}\{\log g(x)\} = \frac{x-c_0}{c_1+c_2x+c_3x^2}.$$

b. A measure of the skewness of statistical distributions, proposed by him in 1895.

1911 G. U. YULE *Introd. Theory Statistics* viii. 150 There is, however, only one generally recognised measure of skewness, and that is Pearson's measure..—

$$\text{skewness} = \frac{\text{mean} - \text{mode}}{\text{standard deviation}}\ldots$$

The numerator of the above fraction may..be replaced approximately by 3 (mean − median). **1925** F. C. MILLS *Statistical Methods* v. 168 Pearson's formula for measuring skewness. **1962** *Lebende Sprachen* VII. 114/1 Pearson measure of skewness.

c. The product–moment correlation coefficient (see *PRODUCT *sb.*[1] 6).

1912 *Jrnl. R. Statistical Soc.* LXXV. 609 Professor Pearson's coefficient..was described and its use illustrated in two memoirs published in 1900. **1957** KENDALL & BUCKLAND *Dict. Statistical Terms* 215 The product-moment coefficient of correlation is sometimes referred to as the Pearson coefficient of correlation because of K. Pearson's part in introducing it into general use. **1973** L. D. PHILLIPS *Bayesian Statistics* x. 207 The correlation coefficient (or Pearson product-moment correlation coefficient, as it is sometimes called) is usually designated by r and is defined as $r = \dfrac{\Sigma Z_x Z_y}{N-1}$. *Ibid.* xii. 294 Transform the ranks into normal scores, compute the Pearson-r between the pairs of scores and use the inference method just discussed.

d. The chi-square test.

1912 *Jrnl. Exper. Zool.* XIII. 203 Pearson's test depends upon a variable χ_2[*sic*]$=S\{(m_r - m_r')^2/m_r\}$ where m_r is the theoretical frequency and m_r' the observed. **1969** H. O. LANCASTER *Chi-Squared Distribution* ix. 175 With several degrees of freedom, for class frequencies of 5 or more, the distributions of the Pearson χ^2 approximate satisfactorily to the asymptotic or theoretical χ^2 distributions.

e. A set of formulæ described by him in 1899, used for estimating human stature from the length of limb bones.

1925 S. SMITH *Forensic Med.* v. 53 (*heading*) Pearson's formulæ. **1947** *Sci. News* IV. 40 Pearson..compiled tables relating the length of certain of the arm and leg bones to the total height of the body. These Pearson formulas are quite remarkable in their accuracy. **1966** R. JACKSON *Crime Doctors* 25 Simpson measured the only intact bone he had—the upper part of the left arm—and, using Pearson's formula, concluded that the bones were those of a woman who had been slightly over five feet tall.

Pearsonian (pīəɹsǭu·niăn), *a. Statistics.* [f. prec. + -IAN.] Of or originated by Karl Pearson (see prec.); used esp. with ref. to senses a and b s.v. *PEARSON.

1907 F. B. WYATT in W. P. Elderton *Frequency-Curves* p. v, In January, 1903, Mr. W. Palin Elderton read before the Institute of Actuaries an interesting paper dealing with the application of the Pearsonian frequency-curves to the graduation of a mortality experience. **1927** H. L. RIETZ *Math. Statistics* iv. 82 The degree of correlation is often measured by the Pearsonian coefficient of correlation represented by the letter r. **1969** *Computers & Humanities* III. 145 The correlation coefficient used here is the Pearsonian product-moment correlation. **1972** R. B. CAIN *Elem. Statistical Concepts* xix. 163 The Pearsonian coefficient of skewness brings out the relation between the mean and the median in a skewed distribution which has exactly one mode.

pearten (pīə·ɹtən), *v. dial.* [f. PEART *a.* + -EN[5].] *trans.* and *intr.* To cheer up; to become more lively or sprightly; to hasten. Freq. const. *up*.

1879–81 G. F. JACKSON *Shropshire Word-bk.* 317 *Peärten, peärtle,*..to revive; to enliven; to cheer. (1) 'Oh! yo'n soon *pearten* up, yo' beginnen to look better a' ready'. (2) ''Er quite *pyurtled* 'im ŏop w'en 'er come wŏam'. **1895** [see *DRUTHER]. **1896** G. F. NORTHALL *Warwickshire Word-bk.* 169. **1909** *Dialect Notes* III. 356 *Pearten, v.i.* and *tr.* To hasten, go faster: often with *up*. 'We will have to *pearten up* if we expect to get there on time.' **1949** H. HORNSBY *Lonesome Valley* v. 70 Crit seemed to pearten up at that. **1951** H. GILES *Harbin's Ridge* xvi. 139 But when he peartened up, we all took fresh heart.

peasant, *sb.* Add: **1.** Substitute for def.: One who lives in the country and works on land which he has the right to use, relying for his subsistence mainly on the produce of his own labour and that of his household, and forming part of a larger culture and society in which he is subject to the political control of outside groups; also, loosely, a rural labourer. (Further examples.)

Circumstances have changed considerably since the publication of the Dictionary and although modern sociologists agree that a 'peasant' works the land, the more wealthy peasants may also be land-owners, rentiers, hirers of labour, etc., and in these capacities share interests with completely different social groups. Hence in the analysis of many rural societies divisions within the class frequently have to be made.

1850 H. MACFARLANE tr. *Marx & Engels's Manifesto of German Communist Party* in *Red Republican* 16 Nov. 171/2 The small manufacturers, shopkeepers, proprietors, peasants, &c., all fight against the Bourgeoisie, in order to defend their position as small Capitalists. They are, therefore, not revolutionary but conservative. **1926** E. & C. PAUL tr. *Marx's Eighteenth Brumaire of L. Bonaparte* vii. 137 The interests of the peasants no longer coincide, as during the reign of the first Napoleon, with the interests of the bourgeoisie, with the interests of capital. There is now a conflict of interests. The peasants, therefore, find their natural allies and leaders in the urban proletariat, whose mission it is to subvert the bourgeois order of society. **1927** M. J. OLGIN tr. *Engels's Peasant War in Germany* 18 The small peasants (bigger peasants belong to the bourgeoisie) are not homogeneous. They are either in serfdom bound to their lords and masters,..or they are tenants, whose situation is almost equal to that of the Irish. **1933** E. & C. PAUL tr. *Stalin's Leninism* II. 205 In the conditions prevailing in our country, the peasantry consists of various social groups,..the poor peasants, the middle peasants, and the kulaks. It is obvious that our attitude to these various groups cannot be identical. The poor peasant is the *support* of the working class, the middle peasant is the *ally*, the kulak is the *class enemy*—such is our attitude to these respective social groups. **1934** *Encycl. Social Sci.* XII. 48/2 The term peasantry has undergone many changes in meaning in the past and is still subject to various interpretations. Common to all the shifting meanings, however, is a view of the peasant as a tiller of the soil to whom the land which he and his family work offers both a home and a living. **1938** tr. *Lenin's Sel. Wks.* X. 223 The big peasants (*Grossbauern*) are the capitalist *entrepreneurs* in agriculture who..employ several wage workers and are connected with the 'peasantry' only by their low cultural level, habits of life and the manual labour they themselves perform on their farms. These constitute the largest of the bourgeois strata, and they are the..enemies of the revolutionary proletariat. **1948** A. L. Kroeber *Anthropol.* (rev. ed.) vii. 284 Peasants are definitely rural—yet live in relation to market towns; they form a class segment of a larger population which usually contains also urban centers, sometimes metropolitan capitals. **1951** Bonner & Burns tr. *Marx's Theories of Surplus Value* B. v. 192 In the capitalist mode of production the independent peasant or handicraftsman is sundered into two persons. As owner of the means of production he is capitalist, as worker he is his own wage worker. **1954** tr. *Mao Tse-tung's Sel. Wks.* I. 139 The rich peasant as a rule possesses land... The exploitation the rich peasant practises is chiefly that of hired labour. *Ibid.*, In many cases the middle peasant possesses land. The middle peasant relies wholly or mainly on his own labour as the source of his income. *Ibid.* 140 As a rule the poor peasant has to rent land for cultivation and, exploited by others, has to pay land rent and interest on loans and hire out a small part of his labour. **1956** R. Redfield *Peasant Society & Culture* i. 27 Those peoples are to be included in the cluster I shall call peasants who have..this in common: their agriculture is a livelihood and a way of life, not a business for profit. **1966** E. Wolf *Peasants* 3 Peasants..are rural cultivators whose surpluses are transferred to a dominant group of rulers that uses the surpluses both to underwrite its own standard of living and to distribute the remainder to groups in society that do not farm but must be fed for their specific goods and services in turn. **1969** *Internat. Social Sci. Jrnl.* XXI. 286 A peasant may be at one and the same time owner, renter, share-cropper, labourer for his neighbours and seasonal hand on a near-by plantation. Each different involvement aligns him differently with his fellows and with the outside world. **1971** tr. E. Feder in T. Shanin *Peasants & Peasant Societies* vii. 90 But while the landed elite [in Latin America] has no interest in the peasants' aspirations and keeps aloof from their world, it is still keenly aware of its obligations to keep the peasants in check and subservient. **1975** J. A. Hellman tr. *Stavenhagen's Social Classes in Agrarian Societies* v. 65 A useful distinction is sometimes made between tribal peoples, peasants, and modern farmers... In contrast to tribal or primitive peoples, peasant societies do form part of wider economic, social, and political units.

β. Later examples of *paysan* (now a gallicism). Also *attrib.* or as *adj.*

1801 C. Wilmot *Let.* 5 Dec. in *Irish Peer* (1920) 9 We met a young Paysan Savant. **1872** *Young Englishwoman* Oct. 542/1 The *paysan* blouse, so much in fashion now, has brought into favour the plain broad stitched hem. **1891** E. Dowson *Let.* 1 July (1967) 206 This is the queerest little auberge imaginable, quite *paysan*, but full of excellent folk. **1949** W. Stevens *Let.* 13 Oct. (1967) 650, I shall feel sorry about paysans and tepid by the time this reaches you.

c. Delete †*Obs.* and add later examples. Now *slang*, usu. implying ignorance, stupidity, or boorishness. Cf. *Farmer² 7 c.

1943 Baker *Dict. Austral. Slang* (ed. 3) 58 *Peasant*, an ordinary rank. (R.A.A.F. slang.) **1947** S. Bellow *Victim* i. 10 She showed such a dread of hospitals that at last he exclaimed, 'Don't be such a peasant, Elena!' **1957** *Sunday Mail* (Glasgow) 10 Feb. 11 *Peasant*—an older person who does not..understand the goings-on of teenagers. **1958** *Listener* 14 Aug. 247/3 People who dress conventionally are called [by teddy-boys] 'peasants'. **1961** G. Smith *Business of Loving* v. 161 Laura took me out riding... I'm a complete peasant in this, but she's an expert. **1964** G. Lyall *Most Dangerous Game* xix. 146 Alone? Of course I'm not alone, you—you peasant. D' you think I drive myself? **1966** H. Kemelman *Saturday the Rabbi went Hungry* (1967) iii. 27 Well, let the big boys worry, I'm just one of the peasants.

2. a. *peasant-boy* (earlier example), *-farmer* (earlier and later examples), *girl*, *-novelist*, *owner*, *-poet*, *-proprietor* (examples), *-soldier*, *tenant*, *woman*, *-worker*; *peasant farming*; *peasant proprietorship* (further examples).

1852 Dickens *Bleak Ho.* xxxi. 307 Mr. Skimpole..sang one [*sc.* a ballad] about a Peasant boy. **1848** Mill *Pol. Econ.* I. I. iv. 72 When a peasant farmer or proprietor lives on the produce of his land. **1906** *Daily Chron.* 21 Mar. 6/6 Of peasant-farmer stock, the elder Bunsen..became tutor in an English family. **1978** R. Mitchison *Life in Scotland* iii. 47 If a man had failed as a peasant farmer there might well be no work for him as a farm labourer. **1936** tr. *Lenin's Sel. Wks.* III. 183 Landlord farming evolves in a capitalist way... Peasant farming also evolves in a capitalist way and gives rise to a rural bourgeoisie and a rural proletariat. **1952** *Oxf. Jun. Encycl.* VI. 135/2 Peasant farming is the general rule in France, Germany, the countries of northern Europe, and all through central Europe, as well as in the greater part of Asia. **1883** C. M. Yonge *Stray Pearls* I. ix. 99 She kept the cows and knitted like a peasant girl. **1915** D. H. Lawrence *Rainbow* x. 250 Peasant-girls with wreaths of blue flowers in their hair. **1976** Scott & Koski *Walk-In* (1977) xix. 124 The second [woman] giggled like some empty-headed peasant girl. **1907** *Westm. Gaz.* 21 Nov. 12/2 A new book by Peter Rosegger, the Styrian peasant-novelist,..will be published on November 25. **1951** D. Mitrany *Marx against Peasant* xii. 201 In both countries [*sc.* France and Italy] the Communists have made great efforts to win influence in the countryside, especially among landless labourers and peasant tenants, who themselves hope to become peasant owners. **1974** J. White tr. *Poulantzas's Fascism & Dictatorship* vi. i. 275 The small peasant owners are the 'rural petty bourgeoisie' *par excellence.* **1857** Bagehot *Coll. Wks.* (1965) II. 24 The eager peasant-poet was at fault in the..refinements of the..drawing-room. **1794** A. Young *Trav. France* (ed. 2) I. xix. 542 *Caussade.*—This country is full of peasant proprietors of land. **1899** G. B. Shaw *Let.* c 23–24 Dec. (1972) II. 121 You have to deal with a war [*sc.* the Boer war] declared by a peasant-proprietor State. **1974** *Encycl. Brit. Macropædia* VI. 1064/2 Indispensable though his [*sc.* the local craftsman's] services may be, they do not give him equality with his peasant-proprietor neighbours. **1960** R. K. Webb *Harriet Martineau* xi. 338 The abuses of peasant proprietorship in France. **1974** *Encycl. Brit. Macropædia* VI. 256/1 In agriculture, peasant proprietorship or large private estates—particularly for export products—remained the general rule [in developing non-Communist countries]. **1966** *Sociol. Rev.* XIV. 21 By cultural intercourse and intermixture, if not by indoctrination, the peasant-soldier is taught to think in wide national, and not village-limited terms. **1978** D. Bloodworth *Crosstalk* xvi. 130 Wang, a peasant soldier..cunning in detail..but devoid of broad perception. **1951** Peasant tenant [see *peasant owner* above]. **1856** Dickens *Dorrit* (1857) ii. i. 323 The child carried in a sling by the laden peasant woman..was quieted with picked-up grapes. **1891** Hardy *Tess* II. v. xxv. 209 You are an unapprehending peasant woman. **1977** G. Butler *Brides of Friedberg* vi. 155 In the woods..a group of peasant women were gathering wood. **1962** E. Snow *Other Side of River: Red China Today* (1963) xviii. 134 Another peasant-worker dictatorship was proclaimed as a local soviet on November 18 in an area far removed from Tsalin. **1972** H. C. Stevens tr. *Galeski's Basic Concepts Rural Sociol.* vii. 174 The most numerous social categories in the Polish village today are (1) peasant owners of family farms, and (2) the highly diversified category of 'peasant-workers', i.e. families living in the village and..combining work on a farm with regular employment outside the village.

b. *peasant art*, *class*, *community*, *family*, *group*, *league*, *mind*, *revolution*, *society*, *style*; **peasant economy**, an economy in which the family is the basic unit of production.

1934 A. Huxley *Beyond Mexique Bay* 197 It is a typical semi-sophisticated peasant art. **1961** L. G. G. Ramsey *Connoisseur New Guide Antique Eng. Pott., Porc. & Glass* 72 The simple vigour and ingenuousness of a 'peasant' art. **1866** *Chambers's Encycl.* VIII. 379/1 Communal government is the fundamental principle of all the rights of the peasant class. **1954** B. & R. North tr. *Duverger's Pol. Parties* ii. i. 265 It [*sc.* the Communist party in the Soviet Union] liquidated the 'Kulaks' and the land-owning middle class, and for a long time it gave the working class of the towns preponderance over a peasant class that was actually more numerous. **1974** *Encycl. Brit. Macropædia* VIII. 1164/2 The [European feudal] aristocrats considered both their own and the peasant class to be permanent, God-given arrangements of hereditary status. **1951** R. Firth *Elem. Social Organiz.* v. 166 In various peasant communities in parts of Africa..new art sanctions have been provided in modern workshops. **1974** *Encycl. Brit. Macropædia* VIII. 1164/1 In Africa, scattered peasant communities occur in the upland areas of the Mediterranean shore. **1951** R. Firth *Elem. Social Organiz.* iii. 87 The term peasant has primarily an economic referent. By a peasant economy one means a system of small-scale producers, with a simple technology and equipment, often relying primarily for their subsistence on what they themselves produce. **1966** D. Thorner et al. *A. V. Chayanov on Theory of Peasant Econ.* p. v, The most sophisticated and best documented studies of the theory and problems of peasant economy in the half-century from 1880 to 1930 were written by Russians. **1975** J. A. Hellman tr. *Stavenhagen's Social Classes in Agrarian Societies* v. 65 Peasant economy tends towards self-sufficiency and the household is the main unit for production and consumption, based on the intensive use of family labor. **1926** E. & C. Paul tr. *Marx's Eighteenth Brumaire of L. Bonaparte* vii. 133 In so far as millions of families live in economic circumstances which distinguish their mode of life, their interests, and their culture, from those of other classes, and make them hostile to other classes, these peasant families form a class. But in so far as the tie between the peasants is merely one of propinquity, and..the identity of their interests has failed to find expression in a community..or in a political organization, these peasant families do not form a class. **1974** tr. *Sniečkus's Soviet Lithuania* 75 Inefficient, semi-natural farms, unbearable tax burdens, and constant anxiety over the future—such was the lot of many, many peasant families. **1934** *Encycl. Social Sci.* XII. 52/2 Even within a single country such as Germany local differences—physiographic, economic, historical—make for a very considerable variation among peasant groups. **1974** *Encycl. Brit. Macropædia* III. 151/1 Through illegal peasant leagues, founded in the late 1950s, and legitimate rural unions, which were authorized in 1962, many [Brazilian] peasants were able for the first time to make their needs known to the political leaders. **1975** *New Left Rev.* Nov.–Dec. 65 Their peasant leagues performed well in the clerical dominated countryside. **1911** J. London *Let.* 8 Jan. (1966) 330 Charmian has no peasant-mind. **1941** Wyndham Lewis *Let.* 22 Nov. (1963) 310 The stuffy conservatism of the land-locked peasant-mind. **1974** M. B. Brown *Econ. of Imperialism* xiii. 327 We could still see bourgeois and peasant revolutions which fall far short of socialism. **1949** E. Coxhead *Wind in West* vii. 176 Hermia..would frequently deplore the Fascist trend latent in peasant societies. **1964** Gould & Kolb *Dict. Social Sci.* 490/2 The term *peasant society* has long referred to Europe, changing in meaning as the industrial revolution has brought about changes in European life. Usage of the term..has recently been extended to native populations of much of the world, especially as former primitive societies have come to resemble the old European peasantry. **1974** *Encycl. Brit. Micropædia* VII. 823/3 In peasant society ultimate control of the means of production is usually not in the hands of the primary producers. **1952** G. Bemrose *19th Cent. Eng. Pott. & Porc.* vi. 31 A good deal of our unlettered art, especially the so-called peasant style, appears to lie dormant in our racial consciousness. **1973** *Times* 24 Aug. 2/2 She was wearing a cream-coloured peasant-style blouse with blue smocking at the neck and cuffs.

c. In crafts, fashion, etc.: in the style of articles produced by peasants or of clothes worn by them, as *peasant blouse*, *dress*, *skirt*, *sleeve*, *tapestry*, *weave*.

1953 'T. Sturgeon' *More than Human* iii. 167 Janie in a peasant blouse, with a straight spear of morning sunlight bent and moulded to her bare shoulder. **1963** 'E. McBain' *Ten plus One* (1964) xii. 137 She wore one of these very low-cut peasant blouses. **1970** *New Yorker* 15 Sept. 1 (Advt.), The cultivated peasant dress is news. **1960** C. W. Cunnington et al. *Dict. Eng. Costume* 158/1 *Peasant skirt*, 1885. A full round tennis skirt made with 2 or 3 wide tucks and a fall of lace. **1965** 'M. Neville' *Ladies in Dark* viii. 74 She was wearing a peasant skirt and blouse. **1911** *Daily Colonist* (Victoria, B.C.) 8 Apr. 20/2 (Advt.), The new peasant sleeves are featured in the waist part of these garments. **1900** *Archit. Rev.* June p. xxii/2 A twin bedstead..is covered with peasant tapestry designed by Mr. Godfrey Blunt. **1962** L. Deighton *Ipcress File* vii. 45 The rugs..of simple dark-toned peasant weaves. **1975** I. S. Black *Man on Bridge* v. 66 A peasant-weave curtain covered the window.

3. *peasant-minded* adj.

1961 J. Barlow *Term of Trial* i. iii. 53 The louts are essentially peasant-minded about sex.

peasantism (pe·zăntiz'm). [f. Peasant *sb.* + -ism.] **a.** The doctrine that political power should be in the hands of the peasants; also = *Narodnikism. Hence **pea·santist** *sb.* and *a.*

1894 P. Milyoukov in *Athenæum* 7 July 23/3 'Peasantism' [in Russia] puts its faith exclusively in the character and 'spirit' of the people. *Ibid.*, The programme of the 'peasantists' (*Narodnuichestvo*)..was subjected to analysis and discussion. *Ibid.*, Another section of our Radical party..contributed much to the criticism of the 'peasantist' programme. **1963** *Times* 3 May 12/6 Colonel Turkesh listed nine principles which..constituted the doctrine of his group. Many of these appeared to be vague abstractions, including such curiosities as 'peasantism', 'freedomism', and 'developmentism'. **1969** G. Ionescu in Ionescu & Gellner *Populism* 99 Peasantism, born in Eastern Europe in the twentieth century,..takes the individual peasant explicitly as its social prototype..blends its social-economic doctrines with a strong nationalistic concern..and it claims that the peasantry is entitled as a class to the leadership of the political society. **1969** A. Walicki in *Ibid.* 104 Denmark was and remained the model..for most East European peasantists. *Ibid.* 106 A dictatorial peasantry-class of some of the peasantist régimes in power after the First World War (and especially that of Stambolisky in Bulgaria).

b. = Peasanthood.

1901 M. Franklin *My Brilliant Career* v. 25 My parents..had dropped from swelldom to peasantism.

c. A proposal or movement for the diffusion of art among the peasants.

1903 L. F. Ward *Pure Sociol.* 454 There is probably something in the doctrine of 'peasantism', which seeks to rescue art from the exclusive control of the leisure class.

peasantize (pe·zăntəiz), *v. rare.* [-ize.] *refl.* To make (oneself) into a peasant.

1904 G. S. Hall *Adolescence* II. 513 They go West, to the colonies, the slums; devise new enterprises, sometimes almost want to peasantize themselves and fall in love with wheel-grease and the smell of the barnyard.

peasantry. Add: **1.** (Further examples.)

See *peasant *sb.* 1 and note there.

1933 E. & C. Paul tr. *Stalin's Leninism* II. 206 Why is the peasantry described [by Lenin] as the last capitalist class? Because of the two main classes of which our society is composed, the peasantry is a class whose economy is based on private property and small commodity production. Because the peasantry, as long as it remains a peasantry, living by small commodity production, will throw up capitalists from its ranks. **1934** *Encycl. Social Sci.* XII. 51/2 In the strongholds of European peasantry—the states formed in the western provinces of the former Russian Empire, the Danube basin and the Balkans—the peasants won a leading position after the World War when the great landed proprietors were compelled to surrender both their land and their dominant political status. **1936** tr. *Lenin's Sel. Wks.* III. 183 The better the condition of the 'commune', the greater the prosperity of the peasantry in general, the more rapid is the process of differentiation among the peasantry into antagonistic classes of capitalist agriculture. **1951** R. Firth *Elem. Social Organiz.* iii. 87 It is this close economic and social..attachment to the soil that is historically one of the main distinguishing features of a European peasantry. **1964** A. R. Holmberg in H. F. Dobyns et al. *Peasants, Power, & Appl. Social Change* (1971) ii. 33 More than 50 percent of the world's population is peasantry, the large majority of which lives in the so-called underdeveloped countries or newly emerging nations, under natural conditions and social structures that have denied peasants effective participation in the modernization process. **1966** *Sociol. Rev.* XIV. 6 The peasantry consist of small producers on land who, with the help of simple equipment and the labour of their families, produce mainly for their own consumption, and for the fulfilment of their duties to the holders of political and economic power. **1966** E. Wolf *Peasants* 11 It is only when a cultivator is integrated into a new society with a state—that is, when the cultivator becomes subject to the demands and sanctions of power-holders outside his social stratum—that we can appropriately speak of peasantry. **1971** I. Deutscher *Marxism in our Time* i. 28 We see all over the West the disappearance of those middle classes that were supposed to constitute the conservative foundation of capitalism; of the small-owning, small-holding peasantry. **1975** J. A. HELLMAN tr. *Stavenhagen's Social Classes in Agrarian Societies* v. 66 For some students, peasantries are merely holdovers from pre-capitalist times, which tend to disappear as capitalism develops. While this may be the case in Western Europe, the situation in the underdeveloped countries is quite different. Here we still have hundreds of millions of peasants ..who are well integrated into the colonial or underdeveloped capitalist system and who, if present trends continue, will maintain peasant characteristics for many generations.

2. (Later examples.)

1937 *Observer* 17 Oct. 19/2, I find it hard to believe that anybody, having read or seen 'The Power of Darkness', would not instantly swear..to remove from himself any traces of peasantry that he might possess.

pea·santy, *a.* [-Y^1.] = PEASANTLY *a.*

1933 *Times Lit. Suppl.* 8 June 400/2 Dark peasanty men. **1970** *Daily Tel.* 4 May 13 The peasanty voile top we've photographed over calico trousers is in fact sold as a mini dress.

pease, *sb.* Add: **5. pease-brose:** see BROSE b.

1811 W. AITON *Gen. View Agric. Ayr* 271 A few [late peas] are thrown in among the beans when sown broadcast. They are..made into meal for a species of pottage called 'pease-brose'. **1861** R. LEIGHTON *Rhymes & Poems* (ed. 2) 12 'Pease Brose to dinner! brose alone! With neither boil nor stew! But say, what did you breakfast on?' They answer '*Pease Brose too.*' **1922** R. THOMAS *Sandie McWhustler's Waddin'* v. 52 He was sittin' in his sark sleeves an' suppin' his pease-brose. *c* **1965** *Rebels Ceilidh Song Bk.* No. 2. 15 It'll be pease brose again.

pea-soup. Add: **a.** *pea-soup fog* (earlier and later examples); also *absol.*

1849 H. MELVILLE *Jrnl. Visit to London & Continent* (1948) 45 Upon sallying out this morning encountered the oldfashioned pea soup London fog. **1887** *S. Austral. Advertiser* 8 Jan. 4/7 A month or two ago London experienced a succession of 'pea-soup fog' days. **1965** MRS. L. B. JOHNSON *White House Diary* 7 Apr. (1970) 256 We flew in pea soup and uncertainty. **1976** J. LEE *Ninth Man* 10 He couldn't see more than fifteen or twenty feet through this pea soup. **1978** 'M. M. KAYE' *Far Pavilions* xix. 283 Londoners groping through a pea-soup fog.

b. A French Canadian; the French spoken in Canada. *N. Amer. slang.*

1896 G. PARKER *Pomp of Lavilettes* 60 Yes, an' dey call us Johnny Pea-soups. **1912** B. HEENEY *Pickanock* 22 Pea-soup! I never drink with the likes of you, Pauquett! **1931** 'D. STIFF' *Milk & Honey Route* iii. 38 A Canadian Frenchman is a 'Canuck' or sometimes a 'pea soup'. **1937** PARTRIDGE *Dict. Slang* 612/1 *Talk pea-soup*, to talk French-Canadian. **1945** H. MACLENNAN *Two Solitudes* 49 Listen, you goddam peasoup, you too fast with your mouth. **1959** J. W. GODSELL *I was no Lady* x. 170 I'm going to the Halfway right now to fix that damned Pea-soup. **1965** *Globe & Mail* (Toronto) 13 Oct. 6/3 Our childhood forays in Ottawa between pea-soup and English-speaking gangs.

pea-sou·per. *colloq.* [f. PEA-SOUP + -ER^1.] **1.** A pea-soupy or thick yellow fog. Also *pea-souper fog.*

1890 J. PAYN *Notes from 'News'* 8 The fogs we have had this year have been made too much of... You could see something in them if you looked long enough, which is not the case of a genuine Peasouper. **1907** *Daily Chron.* 30 Nov. 4/4 A country cousin who wishes to see and breathe and mingle in a metropolitan pea-souper. **1926** *Chambers's Jrnl.* Mar. 192/1 The fog..became dense—a real pea-souper. **1954** M. SHARP *Gipsy in Parlour* v. 62 The coal-burning London of my childhood was undoubtedly foggier than the London of to-day: the legend of the pea-souper, like all legends, has its roots in fact. **1973** H. CARVIC *Miss Seeton Sings* (1974) 196 Fog had clamped down on Paris... The scene reminded Miss Seeton of the London pea-soupers of her childhood. **1975** G. HOWELL *In Vogue* 4/2 There were high prices and strikes, peasouper fogs, and precious little coal. **1978** *Jrnl. R. Soc. Arts* CXXVI. 490/2 Pea-souper fogs are no longer experienced in London or in other cities.

2. = *PEA-SOUP b.

1942 BERREY & VAN DEN BARK *Amer. Thes. Slang* §385/5 Pea-souper, *a French-Canadian.* **1962** *Maclean's Mag.* 2 June 51/2 And *then* we can highstick those pea-soupers. **1966** [see *JOE *sb.*^{2} 7]. **1968** P. C. NEWMAN *Distemper of our Times* xix. 257 You're selling Canada to the pea-soupers!

peat^1. Add: **2*.** A dark brown resembling the colour of peat.

1971 *Homes & Gardens* Sept. 84 Quite a lot of dark browns (anything from donkey to peat.) **1975** *Times* 7 Oct. 11/4 Long-sleeve sweater..in colours loganberry, peat, brown, and mid-blue. **1978** *Country Life* 16 Nov. 1685/1 There is nothing brash about Biba colours. Moss, peat, [etc.].

3. a. *peat-ditch, -land, -pulp, -smoke* (later examples). **b.** *peat-cutter* (later examples), *-digger* (examples). **c.** *peat-stained* adj. Also similative, as *peat-black, -brown* adjs. and sbs.

1961 R. S. THOMAS *Tares* 35 Nerves strengthened with tea, Peat-black. **1898** B. KIRKBY *Lakeland Words* 160 *Peat-broon*, t' colour of a dried peat, er bit of undyed woo'. **1906** *Westm. Gaz.* 9 Aug. 10/1 A rush-grown pool of peat-brown water. **1962** D. FRANCIS *Dead Cert* xv. 173 My suit was a filthy peat-brown. **1963** *Times* 10 June 14/6, I followed a track that was once used by peat cutters. **1969** E. H. PINTO *Treen* 94/2 A peat cutter is a square-ended spade of normal length, with a right-angled, forward projecting blade at one side, like the breast plough. **1774** T. PENNANT *Tour in Scotl. & Voy. Hebrides 1772* I. 66 By the imprudence of the peat-diggers, who were continually working on that side [of the moss]. **1894** A. GORDON *Northward Ho!* 202 The peat-digger was the most notorious carouser in Carglen. **1978** *Maledicta* II. 167 *Peat-digger*, any rural Irish person. **1903** G. W. HARTLEY *Wild Sport* i. 11 Jumping in and out of crumbling peat-ditches. **1907** *Daily Chron.* 1 Oct. 8/1 They wandered hand in hand across the peatland and the marshes. **1973** MOORE & BELLAMY (*title*) Peatlands. **1977** *Undercurrents* June–July 40 They are tackling the problems of what to do with bull calves, a large acreage of peatland and the need to produce extremely high quality winter fodder in a high rainfall area. **1908** *Chambers's Jrnl.* Jan. 122/2 The latest development in the production of peat-pulp is being made in Sweden. **1922** JOYCE *Ulysses* 184 The peatsmoke is going to his head. **1971** *Country Life* 4 Nov. 1226/1, I may be prompted by something to recall the scent of peat-smoke. **1903** G. W. HARTLEY *Wild Sports* ix. 193 Its contents were for the thick-set, peat-stained beast standing a little to the right.

d. peat-bog, also *attrib.*

1965 G. M. BROWN in *New Statesman* 9 July 52/2 Being under age And wringing peatbog whisky from a clout Into a secret kettle.

pea-time. *U.S. colloq.* [f. PEA^1 7.] The season in which peas ripen. So *fig.* in phr. *the last of pea-time*: the last stage of anything, the end of one's life; *pea-time is past*: a thing is finished.

1834 [see *LAST *a.* 1 d.]. **1850** 'M. TENSAS' *Odd Leaves Life Louisiana Swamp Doctor* 174 It war the last of pea-time with me, sure, if I didn't rise 'fore bar did. **1862** J. R. LOWELL in *Atlantic Monthly* Jan. 128 Ther' 's ollers chaps a-hangin' roun thet can't see pea-time's past. **1867** —— *Biglow Papers* 2nd Ser. I. p. lviii, *Last of pea-time*, to be hard up. **1889** 'C. E. CRADDOCK' *Despot of Broomsedge Cove* x. 174 Ye oughter git some air an' light, Marcelly; ye look like the las' o' pea-time. **1893** M. A. OWEN *Voodoo Tales* 199 'Deed my gyarden am a-lookin' mighty bad. Hit look mo' lak de las' o' pea-time den de fust o' truck-time. **1904** [see *LAST *a.* 1 d]. **1911** R. D. SAUNDERS *Col. Todhunter* 108 'What on earth's the matter, Bill?' he asked. 'You look like the last of pea-times.' **1923** *Dialect Notes* V. 238 Utterly worn out. 'He looks like the *last o' pea-time.*'

‖**peau de chagrin** (pō: də ʃagræ·ṅ). [Fr., lit. 'skin of grained leather'.] The title of a novel by Balzac (1831), in which a piece of shagreen diminishes in size as wishes are granted through its magic power, used *fig.* or allusively to indicate the progressive diminution of the human life-span.

1861 GEO. ELIOT *Let.* 31 Dec. (1954) III. 475 The years of retrieval keep shrinking—the terrible *peau de chagrin* whose outline narrows..with our ebbing life. **1910** W. J. LOCKE *Simon* v. 56, I see my little allotted span of life shrinking visibly, like the *peau de chagrin.* **1946** L. P. HARTLEY *Sixth Heaven* v. 111 Money..[is] really like the Peau de Chagrin, and dwindles with every wish.

peau-de-soie. (Further examples.)

1912 C. MACKENZIE *Carnival* iv. 38 But when his grand-daughter,..all chiffon and ostrich plumes, took her upon a *peau de soie* lap..Jenny thought she had never experienced any sensation half so delicious. **1930** R. CUTHILL tr. *Schober's Silk* iv. 272 *Peau de Soie.*—A close, firm silk fabric. Weave: eight- or ten-shaft twill. **1958** *Times* 16 Oct. 14/3 The bride..wore a gown of pearl coloured peau-de-soie with a train. **1974** *Times-Picayune* (New Orleans) 15 Aug. v. 6 The bride..wore a peau de soie gown.

‖ **Peau d'Espagne** (pō:dèspa·ny). Also with lower-case initials. [Fr., lit. 'skin of Spain'.] **a.** A perfumed leather. Cf. *Spanish leather* s.v. SPANISH *a.* 2 b. **b.** A scent supposedly suggestive of the aroma of this leather.

1855 G. W. S. PIESSE *Art of Perfumery* vii. 143 Peau d'Espagne, or Spanish skin, is nothing more than highly perfumed leather. *Ibid.*, Finally, each double skin, now called peau d'Espagne, is to be enveloped in some pretty silk or satin, and finished off to the taste of the vender. **1898** *Junior Army & Navy Stores Catal.* 190/1 Atkinson's Perfumes..Peau d'Espagne, in Fancy Ribbon Sachets.. each 1/6. **1906** 'O. HENRY' *Four Million* (1916) 112 A 200-pound woman breathing a flavour of Camembert cheese and Peau d'Espagne. **1907** *Yesterday's Shopping* (1969) 37/2 *Soaps*..Peau d'Espagne—box of 3 tablets 4/9. **1912** *Maclean's Mag.* Jan. 262/2 When his mother swept into the dining-room at meal-times, her hair faultlessly arranged, and wafting *peau d'Espagne* as she moved, Eugene followed in her wake like a small dog. **1919** [see *OTTO^1]. **1922** JOYCE *Ulysses* 747 That cheap peau despagne that faded and left a stink on you. **1942** E. BOWEN *Seven Winters* 31 She used *Peau d'Espagne* scent. **1972** T. MCLAUGHLIN *Gilded Lily* vi. 70 The combination of perfume and leather could be obtained also in the form of *peau d'Espagne*, small perfumed pieces of leather that were used like lavender sachets or pot-pourri bags to hang in cupboards or tuck into pockets of clothes.

‖**peau d'orange** (pō dorā·ṅʒ). *Med.* [Fr., = 'orange-peel'.] A characteristic pitted appearance of the skin of the breast in some cases of breast cancer.

[**1875** *Nouveau Dict. de Méd. et de Chirurgie Pratiques* XXI. 569 La peau, au lieu d'être d'un blanc rosé, est.. comparable, comme l'a si bien fait remarquer Nélaton, á la peau d'orange. **1882** A. NÉLATON *Élements de Path. Chirurg.* (ed. 2) V. xxi. 148 Quelquefois la peau de la mamelle, suivant la comparaison du Dr Mauduyt, ressemble à une peau d'orange.] **1898** A. M. SHEILD *Clin. Treat. Dis. Breast* ix. 346 The skin..has that coarse pitted aspect to which the terms 'peau d'orange' and 'pigskin saddle' appearance have been well applied. **1948** C. ENGLISH *Dis. Breast* xi. 75 In the early stages the growth is entirely unattached to the overlying skin, but later dimpling of the skin occurs, and a condition known as 'peau d'orange' follows. **1974** R. M. KIRK et al. *Surgery* iv. 62 Invaded lymphatics are blocked causing overlying lymphoedema of the skin known as peau d'orange.

pea-vine. For 'Pea Vine of California' substitute 'a valuable fodder plant'. (Earlier and later examples.)

1675 J. FENWICK in *Pennsylvania Mag. Hist. & Biogr.* (1882) VI. 89 You have Grass as high as a Man's Knees.. interlac'd with Pea-Vines, and other Weeds that Cattel much delight in. **1880** *Harper's Mag.* June 23/1 A search was instituted—under the bed, in the bed,..behind the wood-pile and in the pea-vines. **1910** *Chambers's Jrnl.* June 364/1 A little beetle has climbed up the pea-vine and laid its eggs in the pod. **1973** R. D. SYMONS *Where Wagon Led* VI. xvii. 271 Both horses and cattle thrived on the good grass and plentiful pea vine.

2. pea-vine hay, the dried stalks and foliage of a pea-vine.

1846 V. AIMÉ *Plantation Diary* (1878) 111 Peavine hay is excellent this year, the vine being still green and juicy. **1860** *Southern Cultivator* XVIII. 211 A little corn with Pea Vine Hay will keep them fat. **1932** W. KELLEY *Inchin' Along* 55 Everybody knows there is nothing a mule likes better than pea-vine hay with the peas left on.

peb (peb), abbrev. *PEBBLE *sb.* 1 c. *Austral. slang.*

1903 R. BEDFORD *True Eyes* 129 The session broke up—pebs and donahs wandered off in couples. **1916** C. J. DENNIS *Moods of Ginger Mick* 114 They wus pebs, they wus norks, they wus reel naughty boys. **1916** —— *Songs Sentimental Bloke* 127 *Peb*, a flash fellow, a 'larrikin'. *a* **1943** L. ESSON in *Penguin Bk. Austral. Ballads* (1964) 233 'E's the bloke to fite, 'E's the peb, gorblime. **1959** BAKER *Drum* (1960) 133 *Peb*, a larrikin.

pebble, *sb.* **1. c.** For (*Australian slang*) read *slang* (chiefly *Austral.*) and add earlier and later examples. Also, a term of affection (applied to a person or animal). Phr. (*as*) *game as a pebble* (see quot. 1959) (*obs.*).

1829 P. EGAN *Boxiana* 2nd Ser. II. 20 Hudson, as *game* as a pebble, stuck to his man like glue. **1851** 'W. T. MONCRIEFF' *Scamps of London* III. i. 56, in *Sel. Dram. Wks.* I, Now, my pebbles, I'll give you a toast. *c* **1863** T. TAYLOR *Ticket-of-Leave Man* I. 11 Doctor? Nay; I'm as game as a pebble and as stell as a tree! **1874** M. CLARKE *His Natural Life* IV. vii. 415 'You're not such a pebble as folks seem to think,' grinned Frere. **1888** 'R. BOLDREWOOD' *Robbery under Arms* III. ix. 123 Then the Turon favourite—a real game pebble of a little horse—began to show up. **1893** K. MACKAY *Out Back* 188 Cabbage Tree Ned is as game as a pebble, and may try to dash through in spite of us. **1901** E. DYSON in *Bulletin Story Bk* 134 The Imp.., game as a pebble, despite his age and infirmities. **1918** C. FEATHERSTONHAUGH *After Many Days* 227 Traveller was game as a pebble, and he just passed Quadrant on the post and no more. **1945** BAKER *Austral. Lang.* iv. 88 *Game as a pebble*... (a *pebble* is a person, especially a larrikin, or an animal hard to control.). **1959** —— *Drum* (1960) 133 *Pebble*, a person (occasionally a horse) hard to control. Whence, *game as a pebble*, extremely courageous. **1974** D. STUART *Prince of My Country* 166 He was as hard as nails and as game as a pebble.

d. Colloq. phr. *the only pebble on the beach* and varr., the only person or thing to be considered in a particular situation; used *spec.* (usu. in negative contexts) with reference to an eligible man or woman.

1896 H. BRAISTED (*song-title*) You're not the only pebble on the beach. *Ibid.*, If you want to win her hand, Let the maiden understand That she's not the only pebble on the beach! **1906** E. DYSON *Fact'ry 'Ands* x. 128 S' elp me shicker, Twenty, you was the on'y pebble. **1924** H. DE SÉLINCOURT *Cricket Match* v. 156 There were other pebbles on the beach beside him. **1927** S. SPAETH *Weep some more, my Lady* x. 259 Another phrase that became a recognized part of the English language was 'You're not the only pebble on the beach', made into a song by Harry Braisted and Stanley Carter. **1930** M. KENNEDY *Fool of Family* vii. 66, I won't look at your damned things... You think you're the only pebble on the beach. **1933** E. O'NEILL *Ah, Wilderness!* I. 19 What do I care for him? He's not the only pebble on the beach. **1933** D. L. SAYERS *Hangman's Holiday* 193 The Birmingham–London express reached Rugby at 10.24, departing again at 10.28. But, swift and impressive as it was, it was not the only, or the most important, pebble on the station beach, for over against it upon the down line was the Irish Mail. **1936** G. B. SHAW *Simpleton* II. 73 The British Empire was not the only pebble on the beach. **1945** 'P. WENTWORTH' *Clock strikes Twelve* ii. 15 A heart-to-heart talk with someone who makes me feel I'm the only pebble on the beach. **1977** *World of Cricket Monthly* June 87/1 He was not the only pebble on the Middlesbrough beach.

5. a. *pebble brooch* (earlier example); *pebble (eye)glasses, lens, spectacles.*

1818 M. EDGEWORTH *Let.* 21 Dec. (1971) 150 This little pebble brooch will reach you I hope just in time for you to give it..to Harriette for a Christmas box. **1933** C. ST. J. SPRIGG *Fatality in Fleet Street* i. 14 His beady eyes regarded the Chief coldly behind his pebble eye-glasses. **1938** E. AMBLER *Cause for Alarm* xvi. 206 The pair of thick pebble glasses..rendered me practically blind. **1958** P. MORTIMER *Daddy's gone a-Hunting* ii. 11 A stern little girl in thick pebble glasses. **1972** M. WOODHOUSE *Mama Doll* ii. 4 A short fat man with mad bushy hair and pebble glasses. **1977** J. AIKEN *Last Movement*

i. 14 His eyes myopic behind thick pebble glasses. **1955** H. SPRING *These Lovers fled Away* 437 The spectacles now had pebble lenses. **1958** *Spectator* 30 May 687/3 The sadistic young slug of a lodger with dirty finger-nails and pebble-lens spectacles. **1964** R. CHURCH *Voyage Home* viii. 166 Thick, pebble lenses, flashed at me like headlamps. **1955** H. SPRING *These Lovers fled Away* 142 He was a dark, robust-looking youth, with flaring nostrils and pebble spectacles. **1976** 'W. TREVOR' *Children of Dynmouth* v. 115 He wore thick pebble spectacles, behind which his eyes were unnaturally magnified.

b. *pebble-lensed, -like* adjs.; **pebble-beached** *a. slang,* (*a*) penniless, destitute; (*b*) dazed, absent-minded; **pebble-bed,** (*a*) *Geol.*, a conglomerate that contains pebbles, esp. one from which they readily work loose with weathering; (*b*) *Nuclear Sci.*, used *attrib.* to designate a nuclear reactor in which the fuel elements are in the form of pellets having an outer layer of moderator; **pebble chopper** *Archæol.*, a primitive chopping tool made from a pebble (see *pebble tool* below); **pebble culture,** name given to a culture which uses pebbles as materials for tools, identified orig. in Africa but now known to have existed also in America, Asia, and Europe; **pebble dash** (examples); **pebble dashing** (examples); **pebble grain,** a patterned grain produced by pebbling (see PEBBLE *v.* 3); **pebble-grained** *adj.*, (*a*) having a pattern produced by pebbling; (*b*) of lenses etc., having the appearance of pebble (see sense 2 b in Dict.); **pebble tool** *Archæol.*, a primitive tool made by chipping and shaping pebbles, thought to be the earliest use of stone tools by man; **pebble weave,** a weave producing a rough surface.

1890 in Barrère & Leland *Dict. Slang* II. 120/2 He had arrived at a crisis of impecuniosity compared to which the small circumstance of being pebble-beached and stony-broke might be described as comparative affluence. **1897** *Sporting Times* 3 July 1/4 She was absolutely stony, pebble-beached to all the world. **1934** WODEHOUSE *Right Ho, Jeeves* xvii. 216 Gussie..switched on that pebble-beached smile again and tacked down to the edge of the platform. **1851** *Q. Jrnl. Geol. Soc.* VII. 77 The valley is.. so encumbered with detritus of the overlying and reaggregated pebble beds, that except at the town of Vichy it is almost impossible to make good observations. **1914** J. PARK *Text-bk. Geol.* xxviii. 377 The three main divisions of the Trias recognised in the British Isles are:—3. Rhætic... 2. Keuper... 1. Bunter... The Bunter consists of red and variously hued sandstones and conglomerates or pebble beds of fluviatile or fluvio-lacustrine origin. **1961** *New Scientist* 16 Mar. 695/1 W. Germany is to have what is probably the first operational 'pebble-bed' reactor... The fuel elements are balls of graphite with centres of uranium carbide. **1969** *Financial Times* 9 Jan. 7/6 The experimental 'pebble bed' reactor at Juelich more closely approaches the idea of a nuclear system into which fuel is simply shovelled. **1969** BENNISON & WRIGHT *Geol. Hist. Brit. Isles* xii. 274 The Bunter Pebble Beds characteristically occur in the Midlands... The name Pebble Beds is a descriptive term and the formation comprises sandstone with pebbles. **1959** J. D. CLARK *Prehist. S. Afr.* v. 115 Some of these flakes were struck from cores and were not simply the waste flakes removed in preparing the pebble-chopper. **1964** JENNINGS & NORBECK *Prehist. Man in New World* 164 At the basal level Butler places the Congdon I complex—peripherally flaked pebble choppers. **1974** *Encycl. Brit. Micropædia* VII. 825/3 *Pebble chopper,* or pebble tool, primordial cutting tool, examples of which have been dated at over 2,500 years BC. **1931** J. D. SOLOMON in L. S. B. Leakey *Stone Age Cultures Kenya Colony* 264 Mr. C. van Riet Lowe..has studied the terraces of the Vaal River, and finds... (i) High terrace, with coarse gravel containing what may be a pebble-culture. **1955** *Sci. Amer.* Aug. 50/2 He has found two teeth of the man-ape in a deposit together with crudely chipped stone tools of the 'pebble culture'. **1970** J. D. CLARK *Prehist. Afr.* ii. 68 It is a common misconception that the Oldowan tools were made from pebbles and the term 'Pebble Culture' has been used as synonymous with Oldowan. **1902** *Ann. Rep. Board of Regents Smithsonian Inst. 1901* 106 A cheap frame construction was used, the sides of which were treated with pebble-dash and the roof made of asphalted felt covered with crushed slag. **1911** *Encycl. Brit.* XXI. 785/1 *Rough-cast* or *Pebble-dash* plastering is a rough form of external plastering in much use for country houses. **1960** [see *GOD-WOTTERY]. **1973** G. MOFFAT *Deviant Death* iv. 54 A dull collection of pebble dash houses and wood trim in cardinal colours. **1940** *Chambers's Techn. Dict.* 621/1 *Pebble-dashing* (*Plast.*), a rough finish given to a wall by coating it with plaster, on to which, while it is still soft, small stones and liquid lime are thrown. **1978** *Lancashire Life* Sept. 3/2 (Advt.), A detached house.., built approximately 1938 of brick with pebbledashing to most elevations. **1897** *Sears, Roebuck Catal.* 194/3 Child's pebble grain school shoe. **1931** W. FAULKNER *Sanctuary* xv. 133 Disembodied voices blaring from imitation wood cabinets or pebble-grain horn-mouths above the rapt faces. **1969** R. T. WILCOX *Dict. Costume* (1970) 263/2 *Pebble grain,*..a leather, imitation leather or fabric given a grained surface by running it between rollers under pressure. **1971** 'O. BLEECK' *Thief who painted Sunlight* (1972) xiv. 123 His black, pebble-grained loafers were burnished and gleaming. **1973** W. M. DUNCAN *Big Timer* i. 10 Pale blue eyes which stared myopically from behind thick pebble-grained glasses. **1968** F. MULLALLY *Munich Involvement* iii. 21 The woman..hesitated, blinking at Sullivan through pebble-lensed glasses. **1975** D. PITTS *This City is Ours* xix. 65 [He] peered..through heavy, pebble-lensed glasses. **1977** 'E. CRISPIN' *Glimpses of Moon* xiii. 284 Long-haired, pebble-lensed cissies in white coats. **1924** W. DE LA MARE *Ding Dong Bell* 56 The pebble-like tattling of a robin. **1960** C. DAY LEWIS *Buried Day* 220 His stony eyes behind pebble-like glasses. **1931** J. D. SOLOMON in L. S. B. Leakey *Stone Age Cultures Kenya Colony* 263 We thus seem to have the following succession of events in East Africa during the Pleistocene: (i) Wet period..which coincided with the epoch of the man who made pebble-tools (Kafuan). **1959** J. D. CLARK *Prehist. S. Afr.* iv. 74 It is an open question whether *Australopithecus* could have made pebble-tools, the earliest examples of intentionally made implements known. **1961** *Times* 5 Sept. 13/5 In fact..*Australopithecinae* had been found at four or five sites in association with pebble-tools. **1973** B. J. WILLIAMS *Evolution & Human Origins* ix. 148/2 These are often referred to as 'pebble-tools', as they usually represent river pebbles that have been fractured in such a way that a cutting edge is produced. **1941** *Archit. Rev.* LXXXIX. 40 The floor is close-carpeted with a grey 'pebble-weave' material. **1958** *Woman's Jrnl.* Mar. 3 (Advt.), Classic casual in pebbleweave. **1969** R. T. WILCOX *Dict. Costume* (1970) 263/2 *Pebble weave,* a rough-surfaced fabric produced by weaving together shrunken, twisted yarns.

pebbled, *a.* Add: **1. b.** Of spectacles, etc.: made with or having the appearance of pebble lenses. Also *fig.*

1939 JOYCE *Finnegans Wake* 463 He is looking aged with his pebbled eyes. **1959** *Listener* 5 Mar. 406/2 Eccentric bookworms with pebbled glasses and bulging foreheads. **1969** R. PETRIE *Despatch of Dove* i. 10 He watched minutely from behind thick-pebbled lenses. **1978** M. BUTTERWORTH *X marks Spot* 18 Shrewd eyes glittered behind pebbled lenses.

pebbly, *a.* Add: **2.** *fig.* Resembling pebbles; uneven; *esp.* of textiles: having a rough surface.

1793 H. FUSELI in *Analytical Rev.* Jan. 2 The hoarseness of Northern language bound in pebbly monosyllables. **1923** [see *ARMURE]. **1936** CHESTERTON *Autobiogr.* 148 They had shiny pebbly eyes. **1955** *New Yorker* 19 Mar. 100 Done in pebbly navy wool, with deep raglan sleeves. **1964** *McCall's Sewing* i. 8/1 A pebbly crêpe will not noticeably add pounds, but a very rough, nubbly wool tweed may have a decided effect.

Pebidian (pĕbi·diăn), *a. Geol.* [See quot. 1877 and -AN.] Epithet of a thick sequence of volcanic rocks of Pre-Cambrian age exposed in Preseli, SW Wales. Also *absol.*

1877 H. HICKS in *Q. Jrnl. Geol. Soc.* XXIII. 230, I propose now to divide the Pre-Cambrian rocks [in the vicinity of St. David's] into two distinct series under the local names of Dimetian..for the lower, and Pebidian (*Pebidiauc* being the name of the division or hundred in which the rocks are chiefly exposed) for the upper series. **1880** *Ibid.* XXXVI. 538, I have long been disposed to consider the felspathic series in Shropshire, or at least the Lilleshall group, as representing the Pebidian. **1937** PRINGLE & GEORGE *S. Wales* ii. 15 In the neighbourhood of St. David's, the Pebidian tuffs occupy a broad anticlinal area which extends inland for several miles in an east-north-east direction. **1969** BENNISON & WRIGHT *Geol. Hist. Brit. Isles* iv. 80 The Caerfai Series commences with a reddish basal conglomerate, some of the pebbles being derived from the adjacent Precambrian volcanics, the Pebidian.

pébrine. Add to etymology: (A. de Quatrefages 1858, in *Comptes Rendus* XLVII. 530). Substitute for def.: A disease of silkworms, caused by the microsporidian parasite *Nosema bombycis* (cf. *NOSEMA), and characterized by the appearance of dark spots on the insect, whose growth is stunted. (Further examples.)

1873 A. S. PACKARD *Our Common Insects* iii. 47 The still more formidable disease called pebrine is thought to be of vegetable origin. **1911** *Proc. Zool. Soc.* 625 The parasite *Nosema apis* was closely allied to that of pébrine, the silkworm disease due to *Nosema bombycis.* **1912** E. A. MINCHIN *Introd. Study Protozoa* xvi. 412 The Microsporidia first attained an unenviable notoriety through the ravages caused by *Nosema bombycis*, the cause of 'pébrine' or silkworm-disease. **1964** T. C. CHENG *Biol. Animal Parasites* v. 141/2 *Nosema bombycis* is parasitic in silkworms and causes the fatal pébrine disease. **1972** SWAN & PAPP *Common Insects N. Amer.* 291 The microsporidian disease is called *pebrine* in France for the telltale spots on the infected silkworm. **1973** M. A. SLEIGH *Biol. Protozoa* x. 245 *Nosema bombycis*, is responsible for the pebrine disease of silkworms, in which tissue cells of any type may be infected at any stage of growth.

pec (pek). *N. Amer. slang.* Also **peck.** [abbrev. PECTORAL *sb.* and *a.*] = PECTORAL *sb.* 3. Usu. *pl.*

1966 L. COHEN *Beautiful Losers* (1970) ii. 159, I saw you with massive lower pecs and horseshoe triceps, with bulk and definition simultaneously. **1972** B. RODGERS *Queens' Vernacular* 147 *Pecks,* pectoral muscles. **1977** *Gay News* 24 Mar. 23/1 He sought only the most virile men—the brutes with watermelon-sized pecs and pea-sized heads.

pecan. Add: Also **pecon.** For '*Carya olivæformis*' substitute '*Carya illinoensis*'. (Further examples.)

1797 A. ELLICOTT *Let.* 1 Apr. in C. V. Mathews *Andrew Ellicott* (1908) 152, I have a large Keg of Pecon Nuts put up for you. **1818** G. FLAGG *Let.* 12 Sept. in *Trans. Illinois State Hist. Soc. 1910* (1912) 158, I have seen some [hogs] as fat upon Hickorynuts, Acorns, Pecons & Walnuts as ever I did those that were fatted upon Corn. **1969** *Oxf. Bk. Food Plants* 28/2 Nowadays, pecans can be bought in many British shops. *Ibid.*, The Pecan is a large tree up to 170 feet high, with grey, furrowed bark. **1975** *New Yorker* 3 Feb. 25/2 The cake..was made of thin layers of yellow sponge cake and filled with a whipped cream laced with brandy, pecans, and a special coffee extract.

c. *pecan pie.*

1936 F. M. FARMER *Boston Cooking-School Cook Bk.* (new ed.) 633 Pecan Pie... 3 eggs... 1 cup light corn syrup... 1 cup finely chopped pecans. **1976** *Express-News* (San Antonio, Texas) 2 Oct. 3-E/4 The specialty-of-the-house dessert—which is made every day—is pecan pie. **1976** *Listener* 22 July 86/1 Ordinary Southern food..fried chicken and pecan pie.

peccaminous, *a.* Delete †*Obs.* and add later examples.

Still *rare* It is the kind of word that Joyce may have picked up from the *O.E.D.*

1922 JOYCE *Ulysses* 720 A volume of peccaminous pornographical tendency entitled *Sweets of Sin.* **1939** —— *Finnegans Wake* 288 To put off the barcelonas from their peccaminous corpulums.

pêche à la Melba, pêche Melba: see *MELBA.

pecia (pī·siă). Pl. **peciæ, pecie, pecias.** [a. med.L. *pecia* PIECE *sb.*] A gathering of a manuscript, usu. a gathering of four leaves. **pecia system,** a system of copying pecia by pecia.

1908 H. HALL *Stud. in Eng. Official Hist. Documents* III. 380 A rarer term [in Palæography] occurs in the use of *peciae* to denote the component parts of a file of loose documents. **1912** E. M. THOMPSON *Introd. Gr. & Lat. Palaeogr.* 68 A survival of the ancient method of calculating [*sc.* the remuneration of scribes] has been found in the practice..in the middle ages, of paying by the *pecia* of sixteen columns, each of sixty-two lines with thirty-two letters to the line. **1930** R. STEELE in *Library* XI. 230 The pecia is a unit, devised mainly for estimating the rate of payment to the copyist, which seems to have arisen in the University of Bologna early in the thirteenth century. **1934** LITTLE & PELSTER *Oxford Theol. 1282–1302* I. v. 56 (*heading*) The pecia and some characteristics of Oxford scholastic manuscripts. *Ibid.* 57 The *pecia* is originally, according to the researches of Savigny and Destrez, a piece of parchment which when folded contains two sheets, i.e. 4 leaves on 8 pages. As copyists were frequently paid according to the number of *pecie* which they had written, the beginning of a new *pecia* in the original examples was not infrequently marked in the copies by a *p* or *pe*[a] with the corresponding numeral. **1935** *Times Lit. Suppl.* 14 Dec. 858/3 The *pecia* was the loose quire, generally of four folios or eight pages, lent out by an approved 'stationer' to be copied. **1958** C. H. TALBOT in Wormald & Wright *Eng. Library before 1700* iv. 67 The unit of their [*sc.* the university scribes'] work was the *pecia*, a technical term (borrowed no doubt from the tanners and parchment makers) designating a sheep-skin which could be treated for writing on. *Ibid.* 68 The size of the *pecia* appears to have differed somewhat in the manuscripts we know, but the general conclusion seems to be that it was a sextern. **1963** R. A. B. MYNORS *Catal. MSS. Balliol Coll.* 43 The care with which it is written and its *peciae* are marked might suggest that it was intended to be kept..as a standard copy. **1964** G. POLLARD in *Beiträge zum Berufsbeurussstein des Mittelalterlichen Menschen* (Miscellanea Mediaevalia III) 338 (*heading*) The pecia system. **1972** E. J. DOBSON *Eng. Text of Ancrene Riwle* p. x, It must have been one of two copies made simultaneously from a single exemplar by a form of the pecia system. **1976** A. G. JUDY *Kilwardby's De Ortu Scientiarum* p. xxi, There would have been exactly eighteen pecias in this copy.

peck, *sb.*[3] Add: **4. peck-right,** in a group of birds, the way in which those of higher rank are able to attack those lower in the hierarchy, without provoking an attack in return; cf. *PECK-ORDER, *PECKING-ORDER.

1931 W. C. ALLEE *Animal Aggregations* xix. 344 Hens with this power [of pecking inferiors] are said to have the 'peck-right' over those submitting to the pecking. **1954** FISHER & LOCKLEY *Sea-Birds* vii. 170 There is [among gulls], as in domestic hens, a definite order of precedence, or peck-right. **1962** J. C. WELTY *Life of Birds* x. 184/2 The dominant bird is said to possess a peck right over the subordinate bird.

peck (pek), abbrev. *PECKERWOOD b. *U.S. Black slang.*

1932 *Evening Sun* (Baltimore) 9 Dec. 31/5 *Peck,* a white person. **1964** O. HARRINGTON in J. H. Clarke *Harlem* 96 Every member loved Old Snakes and every school-child knew that he'd once been caught in a Texas mob which was joyously barbecuing another Negro. And when old Snakes began laughing the pecks stared in amazement and let him walk right through. **1969** C. BROWN in A. Chapman *New Black Voices* (1972) 183 A poor white peck will cuss. A poor white peck will cuss worse'n a nigger. I am talking about white men who ain't poor like them pecks. **1970** C. MAJOR *Dict. Afro-Amer. Slang* 90 *Peck,* white person.

peck, *v.* Add: **1. c.** To kiss perfunctorily; to give a peck (PECK *sb.*[3] 1) to.

1969 *New Yorker* 11 Oct. 53/1 They pecked the hostess farewell. **1977** C. MCCULLOUGH *Thorn Birds* xv. 343 Meggie leaned over to peck her brothers on their cheeks self-consciously.

peckawood: see *PECKERWOOD b.

pecked, *ppl. a.* Add: *spec.* in *Archæol.*: consisting of or characterized by pecked strokes or marks (see PECK *v.*[1] 5); *pecked curve, line* (further examples).

1959 J. D. CLARK *Prehist. S. Afr.* Pl. 12 (*caption*) Fine example of an eland in a pecked engraving style, Transvaal. **1963** *Field Archaeol.* (Ordnance Survey) (ed. 4) 43 The earth-fast boulder decorated with pecked marks and designs of uncertain age and significance is a common feature in many parts of Britain north of the Trent. *Ibid.*, Other pecked figures of axes are known elsewhere. **1971** *Nature* 21 May 160/1 This ungual must be rotated through an angle of 180° around its longitudinal axis (pecked line in Fig. 2*F*). **1975** J. B. HARLEY *O.S. Maps* iii. 33 Overhead features, distinguished by pecked lines, are shown when they are of a size and character to be useful features. **1976** *Nature* 29 Apr. 772/1 In Fig. 2 the pecked curve represents the 3-block running mean of February maximum temperatures for six stations surrounding the tree location.

pecker. Add: **1. c.** Abbrev. of *PECKERWOOD b. *slang.*

1966 R. G. TOEPFER *Witness* xvi. 127 Not a chance. These peckers know that as well as me.

3. a. (Further examples.)

In view of sense *3 b a use commonly avoided by British travellers in the U.S.

1901 R. C. LEHMANN *Anni Fugaces* 56 Weighed down by debt they yet keep up their pecker. **1918** GALSWORTHY *Five Tales* iv. 162 Keep your pecker up, and get off abroad. **1922** JOYCE *Ulysses* 320 Keep your pecker up, says Joe. She'd have won the money only for the other dog. **1928** A. MERRITT *Seven Footprints to Satan* xiii. 180, I was talkin' loud to keep my pecker up. **1934** F. W. CROFTS *12.30 from Croydon* xix. 263 Charles could not eat, in spite of the rough kindness of one of the warders, who adjured him to keep his pecker up. **1973** N. MOSS *What's the Difference?* 44/1 The Englishman in North America should beware of using the phrase 'keep your pecker up'.

b. The penis. *slang* (chiefly *U.S.*).

1902 FARMER & HENLEY *Slang* V. 289/2 The *penis*.. pecker. **1936** H. MILLER *Black Spring* 142 Ought to stand on Times Square with my pecker in my hand and piss in the gutter. **1949** —— *Sexus* I. iii. 114 Walking towards the house I open my fly and let my pecker out. **1958** N. LEVINE *Canada made Me* ii. 57 Ground sunflower seeds... This will make your pecker stand up to no end of punishment. **1960** E. L. WALLANT *Human Season* ix. 97 You know how it is when the ol' pecker ain't what it used to be, hah, hah! **1964** *Amer. Folk Music Occasional* I. 12 There is a house down in New Orleans, They call it The Rising Sun, When you want to get your pecker spoilt, That's where you get it done. **1967** I. A. BARAKA in W. King *Black Short Story Anthol.* (1972) 125 Oh, Lucasta, find me here on the bed, with hard pecker and dirty feet. **1969** K. VONNEGUT *Slaughterhouse-Five* v. 107 Billy took his pecker out, there in the prison night, and peed and peed on the ground. **1971** F. NORMAN *Dodgem-Greaser* iii. 45, I unzipped my fly and exposed my pecker to the night air with one deft flick of my finger. **1975** R. H. RIMMER *Premar Experiments* (1976) i. 27 Tony's pecker would no sooner get inside me than he'd pop off.

4. pecker-head *U.S. slang*, an aggressive objectionable person.

1955 *Time* 14 Nov. 116/2 When the girl's husband.., a got-rich peckerhead, finds out about that hotel visit, he ravishes his wife, just to even the score. **1977** E. LEONARD *Unknown Man No. 89* xxiii. 239 Them peckerheads'd never make it.

peckerwood (pe·kəɹwud). *U.S.* [f. WOODPECKER with reversal of the two elements.] **a.** A woodpecker. *dial.*

1859 BARTLETT *Dict. Amer.* (ed. 2) 314 *Peckerwood*, Western for Woodpecker. **1893** H. A. SHANDS *Some Peculiarities of Speech in Mississippi* 49 *Peckerwood*, woodpecker. Bartlett says that this word is Western. It is also heard very frequently in Mississippi, as in Tennessee. **1909** F. B. CALHOUN *Miss Minerva* 140 A big, red-headed peckerwood. **1926** E. M. ROBERTS *Time of Man* 153 Not had the sense of a pecker-wood. **1935** Z. N. HURSTON *Mules & Men* I. vi. 137 Ah wasn't gointer kill no ole tough peckerwood for you to eat, baby. **1940** R. WOOD *Amer. Mother Goose* 55 Peckerwood a-settin' on a swingin' limb, Blue-bird a-buildin' in the garden. **1947** J. H. BROWN *Outdoors Unlimited* 76 Sitting there watching the jays and peckerwoods and listening to the distant shrillings of a hawk, I thought Lucius looked tougher than a pine-knot. **1968** *Harper's Mag.* Sept. 61/1, I even liked what the kids at Tuskegee Institute called 'those crazy li'l ol' peckerwoods'.

b. *slang.* Also *peckawood.* A white person, esp. a poor one. Also *transf.*

1929 T. GORDON *Born to Be* 236 *Peckerwood*, a poor white man. **1929** C. MCKAY *Banjo* 217 For example, we have words like ofay..peckawood..and so on. **1941** W. C. HANDY *Father of Blues* vi. 86 Mound Bayou had no such words addressed to 'peckerwoods' or 'rednecks'. **1942** W. FAULKNER *Go Down, Moses* 255 Even a Delta peckerwood would look after even a draggle-tail better than that. **1947** *Sat. Rev. Lit.* (U.S.) 29 Mar. 13/2 There is a difference between white plantation people and the white 'peckerwoods' of the hills. **1966** R. G. TOEPFER *Witness* ii. 11 They was three peckerwoods had the boy. **1967** C. MAJOR in A. Chapman *New Black Voices* (1972) 299 How come so many Of us niggers Are dying over there In that white Man's war They say more of us Are dying Than them peckerwoods & it just Don't make sense. **1967** *Trans-Action* Apr. 27/2 There is a social distinction here between the white elite and the 'redneck' or 'peckerwood' families. **1967** *N.Y. Times* 7 Sept. 42/4 When I tried to get into the black caucus, they said, 'No peckerwoods allowed in here, Sonny.' **1974** *New Yorker* 29 Apr. 94/2 A horse can be well one day and a sick peckerwood the next. **1974** E. BRAWLEY *Rap* (1975) II. xxiv. 374 And we done, peckerwood, we finished.

Peckham (pe·kăm). [Name of a suburb of London.] **a.** Used in various joc. phrases, esp. with play on peck = food, to eat (PECK *sb.*[3] 3, PECK *v.*[1] 4). (See quots.)

Neither this sense nor the next seems to have much currency outside dicts.

1788 GROSE *Dict. Vulgar T.* (ed. 2) s.v. *All Holiday.* It is all holiday at Peckham, or it is all holiday with him; a saying signifying that it is all over with the business or person spoken of or alluded to. **1823** 'J. BEE' *Slang* 134 *Peckham* (going to), dinner. 'All holiday at Peckham'—no appetite. 'No Peckham for Ben, he's been to Clapham,' i.e. is indisposed, in a certain way. Peckish—hungry. **1864** HOTTEN *Slang Dict.* 198 *Peckham*, a facetious meaning of the name of this district, implying a dinner; 'all holiday at Peckham', *i.e. nothing to eat.* **1902** FARMER & HENLEY *Slang* V. 157/1 *Peckham.* To have (or spend) a holiday at Peckham, *verb phr.* (old)—To have nothing to eat. Going to Peckham = going to dinner. **1922** A. M. HYAMSON *Dict. Eng. Phr.* 267/2 *Peckham, To go to*, to go to dinner. **1970** *Brewer's Dict. Phr. & Fable* (rev. ed.) 814/2 *All holiday at Peckham*,..no appetite, not peckish.

b. *Peckham rye*, tie. *Rhyming slang.*

1925 FRASER & GIBBONS *Soldier & Sailor Words* 221 *Peckham rye*, tie. (Rhyming slang). **1960** J. FRANKLYN *Dict. Rhyming Slang* 106/2 *Peckham Rye*, tie (necktie). 19 C., and by far the most usual term. **1973** B. AYLWIN *Load of Cockney Cobblers* 84 Tie. Peckham Rye.

peck horn (pe·k hǭɹn). *Jazz slang.* Also with hyphen and as one word. [Origin uncertain.] A mellophone, saxophone, or similar instrument.

1936 *Amer. Mercury* May p. x/2 *Peck horn*, mellophone. **1942** BERREY & VAN DEN BARK *Amer. Thes. Slang* § 377/8 (*Alto*) *peck horn*, an alto horn or mellophone. **1948** MENCKEN *Amer. Lang.* Suppl. II. 705 It [*sc.* jive] arose in the honky-tonks and tingle-tangles of the pre-jazz era, and many of its current names for musical instruments go back to that era or even beyond, *e.g.*,..*pretzel* or *peckhorn* for a French horn. **1961** *Down Beat* 13 Apr. 37 This set contains a good sampling of his abilities on trumpet, alto, baritone, and the oddball peckhorn. **1966** *New Yorker* 25 June 44/2 The band generally had two trombones, three trumpets, a bass horn and a baritone horn, a peck horn, a clarinet. *Ibid.* 46/3 From the age of eight I played the upright alto—the peck horn—in my father's band. **1970** C. MAJOR *Dict. Afro-Amer. Slang* 90 *Peck horn*,..mellophone or saxophone. **1975** *Sunday Times* (Colour Suppl.) 12 July 47/1 Straight band singers were unknown in the Twenties—everyone, even Bing Crosby, had an instrument to hold. 'I had a peckhorn, like a flugelhorn.'

pecking order (pe·kiŋ ǭːɹdəɹ). [f. PECKING *vbl. sb.*[1] + ORDER *sb.*, tr. G. *hackliste* (T. J. Schjelderup-Ebbe 1922, in *Zeitschr. für Psychologie* LXXXVIII. 227).] **1.** A pattern of behaviour first observed in hens and later recognized in other groups of social animals, in which those of high rank within the group are able to attack those of lower rank without provoking an attack in return.

1928 A. HUXLEY *Point Counter Point* xxvi. 438 Observing the habitual and almost sacred 'pecking order' which prevails among the hens in his poultry yard..the politician will meditate on the Catholic hierarchy and Fascism. **1939** *Auk* LVI. 263 A position in the pecking order is not..always determined at the first meeting. **1952** M. K. WILSON tr. *Lorenz's King Solomon's Ring* xi. 147 This can be convincingly demonstrated by the existence of an order of rank, known to animal psychologists as the 'pecking order'. **1965** *Listener* 10 June 861/1 Normal monkeys, like many other kinds of animals, form a sort of pecking order. **1972** *Country Life* 9 Mar. 541/1 The fat little bantam hen, who proved first in the pecking order..quickly asserted herself. **1974** *Times Lit. Suppl.* 4 Oct. 1088/4 The term 'pecking order' has become part of common parlance... After a brief trial of strength, every animal in the flock or the herd learns to know its place.

2. *transf.* A hierarchy based on rank or status.

1955 H. NICOLSON *Good Behaviour* i. 7 In a perfect classless society..similar pecking orders must exist. **1957** L. DURRELL *Justine* I. 64 There is a Pecking Order among diplomats as there is among poultry. **1959** G. ENDORE *Detour through Devon* 11 The pecking order obtains among cars on the road as well as among chickens in the barnyard. **1959** T. H. WHITE *Godstone & Blackymor* 172 The ghosts..may have taken precedence in a kind of pecking-order, by virtue of the number of pipes which they could claim. **1961** *Times Lit. Suppl.* 29 Dec. 925/2 Man has animal instincts, instincts for desiring and holding territory and property, for creating a pecking order of dominance and hence status. **1962** *Observer* 25 Nov. 3/2 One of the most disastrous weaknesses of our whole educational system is its insistence on preserving formal hierarchies, a sort of academic pecking order. **1967** J. POTTER *Foul Play* xvi. 184 The inspector had a pretty low rating in the CID's pecking order... His office overlooked an unbroken expanse of sooty wall. **1967** M. ARGYLE *Psychol. Interpersonal Behaviour* iv. 70 Groups develop definite 'pecking orders' in terms of amount of speech and influence permitted. **1973** *Nature* 30 Nov. 318/1 One of the interpenetrating pecking orders that bedevil life in universities is the hard science/soft science hierarchy. **1976** H. WILSON *Governance of Britain* ii. 23 My own procedure was to rely on the order of precedence within the Cabinet, the so-called 'pecking-order', making clear that the second in the list chairs Cabinet.

peck-order (pe·kˌǭɹdəɹ). [f. PECK *sb.*[3] + ORDER *sb.*, tr. G. *hackliste* (T. J. Schjelderup-Ebbe 1922, in *Zeitschr. für Psychologie* LXXXVIII. 227).] = prec., sense 1.

1931 W. C. ALLEE *Animal Aggregations* xix. 344 The 'peck-order' decides which birds may peck others without being pecked in return. **1939** G. K. NOBLE in *Auk* LVI. 264 A peck order..does not appear unless the birds [*sc.* night herons] are crowded together in a strange area. **1955** *Brit. Jrnl. Animal Behaviour* III. 94/2 It is now recognized that the peck-order forms the basis of all group behaviour in adult chickens. **1966** *New Scientist* 26 May 536/1 Wolves live in groups, in which certain individuals are dominant: that is, they have prior access to food, females and other amenities. This sort of arrangement may be called a peck order.

2. *transf.* = prec., sense 2.

1953 A. UPFIELD *Murder must Wait* xvi. 138 Amid the lower Australian peck order..wines are imbibed from the bottle. **1962** A. SAMPSON *Anat. Brit.* I. x. 150 The Inns [of Court] have their own elaborate snobberies and peck-order. **1965** *Punch* 17 Mar. 389/1 Dons have always had an instinctive feeling for prestige, not to say 'peck-order'. **1971** W. J. BURLEY *Guilt Edged* ix. 149 The human peck-order is far more subtle than that of the hen-house.

Peck's bad boy, *phr. U.S. slang.* The name of a fictional character created by George Wilbur Peck (1840–1916) used allusively of an unruly or mischievous child. Also *attrib.* or as *adj.*

1883 *Peck's Sun* 14 July 1/6 The [cuff] buttons are.. gold..and on the back they are engraved 'Geo. W. Peck, Milwaukee, from his newsboy friends of Chicago', and on top of the Russia leather case are the words, 'From Peck's Bad Boys'. **1933** E. O'NEILL *Ah, Wilderness!* I. 19 Sid Davis, his brother-in-law, is forty-five, short and fat, bald-headed, with the Puckish face of a Peck's Bad Boy who has never grown up. **1946** *True* Apr. 34/1 Insulting the advertisers has become Big Business with the Peck's Bad Boy of Radio. **1967** *Atlantic Monthly* Feb. 4 [Governor George] Wallace's motives—ego, a Peck's-bad-boy desire to make trouble, a yen to see just what would happen if a presidential election were thrown into the House of Representatives, or a combination of all these—do not actually matter. **1970** *Time* 22 June 78/2 The book is an earnest effort by Della Femina to buttress his reputation as the Peck's Bad Boy of Advertising. **1977** *Redbook* Mar. 226/3 'I'm going to be forty years old.' He laughs with disbelief. 'It blows my mind.' Yet he sounds curiously unchanged, still the exuberant Peck's Bad Boy of whatever revolution comes to hand, still taunting the establishment. **1977** *Time* 19 Sept. 56/1 Now, in an attempt to break the longest winning streak in modern sports history, a new challenger from Down Under named *Australia* is squaring off with the 1974 U.S. defender, *Courageous*, skippered by Turner—the Peck's Bad Boy of yachting—in the waters off Newport, R.I.

Pecksniff. Add: Also as *v. intr.* Hence **Pecksniffery** (later example); **Pecksniffian** *a.* (earlier and further examples); **Pecksni·ffianly, Pecksni·ffingly** *advbs.*, in a manner resembling Pecksniff. Also *Comb.*, as *pecksniff-shark* (nonce use).

1851 J. CHAPMAN *Diary* 1 July in G. S. Haight *Geo. Eliot & J. Chapman* (1940) 188 Mr B. put on such an exquisitely saintlike Pecksniffian aspect as to seem nearly in heaven. **1894** LLOYD GEORGE *Family Lett.* (1973) 73 That pecksniffian young gent will have to climb down a peg or two. **1903** G. B. SHAW *Let.* 26 Dec. (1972) II. 386 And that you are to come Pecksniffing at me in this fashion. **1913** WYNDHAM LEWIS *Lett.* (1963) 50 A new form of fish in the troubled waters of Art..the Pecksniff-shark, a timid but voracious journalistic monster. **1914** KIPLING *Lett. of Travel* (1920) 232 A government which is not a government but the disconnected satrapy of a half-dead empire, controlled pecksniffingly by a Power which is not a Power but an Agency. **1915** G. B. SHAW *Pen Portraits* (1931) 116 To lie—lie impudently, snobbishly, spitefully, Pecksniffianly, Tartuffily. **1926** A. HUXLEY *Let.* 25 Dec. (1969) 278, I would have made him survive into the Pecksniffian epoch. **1945** R. HARGREAVES *Enemy at Gate* 212 The Tsar himself, temporarily assuming the mantle of Mr. Gladstone's best Pecksniffian manner, continued to give whining expression to pious hopes for some sort of accommodation. **1947** K. S. SORABJI *Mi contra Fa* x. 87 He is apparently unaware..that he is..submitting himself to the judgment of his own upper classes... This is surely nonconformist Pecksniffery gone mad. **1959** J. BRAINE *Vodi* ix. 131 At least it was recognisably the work of a human being, even if he were a greedy Pecksniffian old get who used to sneak around the factory in carpet slippers. **1963** *Times* 22 Apr. 11/1 Disgust at the Pecksniffian pose that the ruling party has shown in denying the blatantly obvious. **1971** M. S. HOWARD *Jonathan Cape* vii. 111 Edward Garnett poured scorn on the Pecksniffery of these British officials.

Peclet (pe·kle). Also **Péclet.** [Name of J. C. E. *Peclet* (1793–1857), French physicist; adopted in this context by H. Gröber *Die Grundgesetze der Wärmeleitung und des Wärmeüberganges* (1921) ii. 168.] *Peclet number*: a dimensionless parameter used in calculations of heat transfer between a moving fluid and a solid body, equivalent to the product of the Reynolds number and the Prandtl number, viz. Dvc_p/k, where D is a characteristic length of the body, v is the speed of the fluid past it, c_p is the heat capacity of unit volume of the fluid at constant pressure, and k is its thermal conductivity.

1933 W. H. MCADAMS *Heat Transmission* vii. 173 Equations of this form, expressing hD/k in terms of the

Peclet number DGc_p/k are used by many German writers such as Nusselt and Grober. **1956** GLASSTONE *Princ. Nucl. Reactor Engin.* xi. 679 For the correlation of heat-transfer data it is now appropriate to use another dimensionless modulus, namely, the Peclet number, Pe. **1958** [see *NUSSELT]. **1974** F. M. WHITE *Viscous Fluid Flow* ii. 89 In low-speed flows (V_0 less than 30 percent of the speed of sound), we can usually neglect both the pressure term and the dissipation term, leaving only the Peclet number (*RePr*) as the single important parameter.

pecon: see *PECAN.

pecoraite (pĭkǭ·rǎ,əit). *Min.* [f. the name of William T. *Pecora* (b. 1913), U.S. geologist + -ITE¹.] A nickel silicate, $Ni_3Si_2O_5(OH)_4$, found as green monoclinic crystals in the Wolf Creek meteorite in Australia.

1969 G. T. FAUST et al. in *Science* 4 July 59/3 A green mineral of the serpentine group, rich in nickel, was described..from the Wolf Creek meteorite in the desert of Western Australia. This mineral is the nickel analog of the well-known magnesium silicate, clinochrysotile. The new mineral is named pecoraite after Dr. William T. Pecora, Director of the U.S. Geological Survey, in recognition of his contributions..to the mineralogy and geology of nickel silicate deposits in North America and South America. **1973** *Mineral. Mag.* XXXIX. 113 Pecoraite.. was found as fracture fillings in the Wolf Creek meteorite of Western Australia.

‖**pecorino** (pekŏrī·no). [It., f. *pecora* sheep.] An Italian cheese made from ewes' milk.

1931 C. L. T. BEECHING *Law's Grocer's Man.* (ed. 3) 242/1 '*Pecorino Romano' type, 'Moliterno' type...* They must be kept in a dry and fresh room, turned every week and oiled with linseed oil when they begin to get mouldy. **1954** E. DAVID *Italian Food* 301, I always buy *pecorino* when I see it in London, for its taste evokes memories of good country food..and coarse red wine. **1958** J. LODWICK *Bid Soldiers Shoot* vi. 166, I was given a slice of.. Italian *pecorino* cheese, some maps, and five gold sovereigns, two of them Victorias. **1967** T. A. LAYTON *Wine & Food Soc. Guide Cheese & Cheese Cookery* 84 When cured for only 5–8 months Pecorino is eaten as a table cheese. **1970** I. ORIGO *Images & Shadows* ix. 205 The delicious sheep's-milk cheese, *pecorino*, which is a speciality of this region. **1973** *Country Life* 8 Mar. 570/3 Women used to come..to milk the ewes, and to make..the Roquefort..or the *pecorino*.

pectase. Add: (Further examples.) Now usu. called *PECTINESTERASE.

1945 [see *PECTINESTERASE]. **1972** [see *PECTINASE].

pectic, *a.* Add: Also, of or pertaining to pectin. (Further examples.)

1930 [see *GALACTURONIC *a.*]. **1964** D. D. DAVIES et al. *Plant Biochem.* iii. 147 Pectic acid is the simplest pectic substance and is the basis of the others. Pure pectic acid appears to be an unbranched chain of α-1,4 linked D-galacturonic acid units which are present in the C-1 chair form..of the pyranose ring. Any compound of this structure which is large enough to possess colloidal properties is classed as a pectic acid. Most pectic acids appear to contain about 100 units with a minimum of approximately 5 units. **1972** [see *PECTINASE].

b. Applied to a class of substances that includes the pectins and other colloidal polymers of galacturonic acid.

1889 *Chem. News* 1 Nov. 221/2 The author [*sc.* L. Mangin] shows the presence of pectic compounds in vegetable membranes. **1913** HAAS & HILL *Introd. Chem. Plant Products* II. 126 Comparatively little is known about the chemistry of pectin or the pectic bodies, as there appear to be several of these substances. **1957** E. V. MILLER *Chem. Plants* i. 14 Pectin is perhaps the pectic compound with which the layman is most familiar. **1966** R. M. DEVLIN *Plant Physiol.* vii. 137 During the ripening of the fruit, protopectin is converted into the more soluble pectic substances—pectin and pectic acid. **1973** J. A. GOSS *Physiol. Plants* xvi. 344 In contrast to the other pectic substances, pectin is water-soluble, and is located in the protoplasm of the cell.

pectin. Add: Now recognized as having a variable composition but being principally a high-molecular-weight polymer of partially methylated galacturonic acid in which galactose and arabinose residues are also present. (Further examples.)

1913, etc. [see *PECTIC *a.* b]. **1917, 1930** [see *GALACTURONIC *a.*] **1964** B. NILSON *Pears Family Cookbk.* 223/2 Over-ripe fruit will not set so well because it will contain less pectin. **1972** *Materials & Technol.* V. xix. 703 Pectins, which occur only in certain plant tissues, are polymers of galacturonic acid linked by α-1,4-glycosidic units, with about two thirds of the carboxylic acid groups esterified with methanol. **1975** D. GREEN *Food & Drink from your Garden* I. vii. 65 Flowers yield very little sugar, but their musts will release no pectins (the glue-like substances holding plant tissues together) and so will clear easily.

b. Any of the pectic substances.

1896 *Jrnl. Chem. Soc.* LXX. I. 7 Pectin Substances... Many attempts have been made to establish a relationship between pectins and vegetable gums (carbohydrates). **1929** R. A. GORTNER *Outl. Biochem.* xxvii. 584 The pectin producing these jellies is the only water-soluble member of a group of related compounds known as the 'pectic substances', or sometimes called the 'pectins'. **1931** E. C. MILLER *Plant Physiol.* i. 12 It is now fairly well established that these substances are not chemically combined with cellulose, although they are closely associated with it, so that they are classified under the general name of the 'pectic compounds' or 'pectins'. **1966** NOWAKOWSKI & CLARKE tr. *Kretovich's Princ. Plant Biochem.* ii. 86 The ripening of fruits is characterized by the conversion of insoluble into soluble pectin.

† **2.** *attrib.* in the sense of *PECTIC *a.* b. *Obs.*

1877 *Jrnl. Chem. Soc.* XXXII. 502 The formula of the group of pectin bodies. **1895** F. E. WEISS tr. *Sorauer's Pop. Treat. Physiol. Plants* vi. 123 Together with gums and acids we often find substances consisting also of carbon, hydrogen, and oxygen, which form gelatinous masses on boiling, and are termed pectin substances. **1900** A. J. EWART tr. *Pfeffer's Physiol. Plants* I. viii. 477 Many gums..seem to be in part allied to pectin substances.

pectinase (pe·ktinēiz, -s). *Biochem.* [a. F. *pectinase* (E. Bourquelot 1899, in *Jrnl. de Pharm. et de Chimie* IX. 567): see PECTIN and *-ASE.] An enzyme found in plants and in certain bacteria and fungi which hydrolyses pectin to its constituent monosaccharides.

1899 *Jrnl. Chem. Soc.* LXXVI. I. 652 In all probability it is a new ferment and the name pectinase is suggested for it. **1929** R. A. GORTNER *Outl. Biochem.* xxvii. 593 Pectinase hydrolyzes pectin (and possibly pectic acid) to its simple components, sugars and galacturonic acid. **1953** F. T. BROOKS *Plant Dis.* (ed. 2) x. 156 Brown..has indicated that the enzyme (pectinase) or enzyme complex of *B. cinerea* which softens the cell walls probably also kills the host protoplasm. **1972** *Materials & Technol.* V. 703 They [*sc.* the pectic enzymes] can be broadly classified,.. into two sub-groups. These are the polygalacturonases, which cleave glycosidic linkages between adjoining galacturonic acid units, and the pectic methyl esterases... The two groups were formerly known, respectively, as pectinases and pectases.

pectinesterase (pektine·stərēiz, -s). *Biochem.* Also **pectin esterase.** [f. PECTIN + *ESTERASE.] An enzyme found in plants and in certain bacteria and fungi, which hydrolyses pectin to pectic acid and methanol; = PECTASE, *PECTINMETHYLESTERASE.

1945 LINEWEAVER & BALLOU in *Arch. Biochem.* VI. 373 The enzyme that acts on pectin and causes gelation in the presence of calcium has been known as pectase... Since the enzyme hydrolyzes the ester bonds in pectin we propose the name pectinesterase, which indicates the esterase character of the enzyme. **1956** *New Biol.* XX. 96 It was concluded that the enzyme pectinesterase was responsible, at least in part, for the development of disease symptoms [in the tomato shoots]. **1966** *McGraw-Hill Encycl. Sci. & Technol.* IX. 609/1 With the enzyme, pectin esterase, obtained from such sources as roots, leaves, and fruits of all higher plants and also from a number of microorganisms, the ester groups are quickly removed. **1975** *Biochim. & Biophys. Acta* CCCLXXVII. 408 The ability of *B. cinerea* polygalacturonase to degrade pectin N.F. was connected with the presence of pectinesterase in the preparation.

pe:ctinme:thyle·sterase. *Biochem.* Also **pectin methylesterase,** and with hyphen. [f. PECTIN + METHYL + *ESTERASE.] = *PECTINESTERASE.

1945 MCCOLLOCH & KERTESZ in *Jrnl. Biol. Chem.* CLX. 149 Two enzymes which act on soluble pectic substances are recognized at the present time; namely, pectin-polygalacturonase (PG),..and pectin-methylesterase (PM), which catalyses the hydrolysis of the methyl ester groups. **1954** *Biol. Abstr.* XXVIII. 27349 The purpose of the study was to determine the extent to which several plant pathogens produced pectinmethylesterase..and polygalacturonase. **1966** [see *PECTINESTERASE]. **1975** *Phytochemistry* XIV. 109/2 No attempt was made to determine if pectin was being degraded..by the two step reaction catalyzed by pectinmethylesterase and endo-polygalacturonase.

pectoral, *sb.* **1. c.** For †*Obs.* read '*Obs.* exc. *Hist.*' and add: also, a piece of armour to protect the breast of a horse: cf. sense 1 b.

1656 [see PEITREL, PEYTREL, PETREL *sb.*]. **1786** F. GROSE *Treat. Anc. Armour & Weapons* 30 The Poitrinal, Pectoral, or Breast Plate was formed of plates of metal rivetted together. **1821** in G. F. Laking *Catal. European Armour & Arms in Wallace Collection* (1900) 315 Armour of the Elector Joseph of Bavaria on horseback. This superb suit of black and gold, with the pectoral, chanfron, and other trappings for the horse, of the finest workmanship of the time of Henry VIII. **1824** S. R. MEYRICK *Crit. Inquiry Antient Armour* III. Gloss. s.v. Pectorale, Sometimes the ends of the pectoral were raised so high as to protect the abdomen of the knight.

peculant (pe·kiŭlănt), *a. rare.* [ad. L. *pecūlant-em*, pres. pple. of *pecūlārī* to embezzle.] = next.

1920 *Glasgow Herald* 16 Aug. 8/3 Conveying large sums of money into their own pockets without having to resort to the clumsy methods practised by peculant contractors ..in the Napoleonic wars.

peculative (pe·kiŭlătiv), *a.* [f. PECULATE *v.* + -IVE.] That practises embezzlement or peculation.

1909 GALSWORTHY *Fraternity* xii. 102 Unlike other clubs, it..had special arrangements for the safety of umbrellas and such books as had not yet vanished from the library; not, of course, owing to any peculative tendency among its members, but because, after interchanging their ideas, those members would depart,..each grasping some material object in his hand. **1921** *Times Lit. Suppl.* 10 Feb. 84/3 The taxes so rapaciously collected by a host of peculative Turkish officials.

peculiar, *a.* and *sb.* Add: **A.** *adj.* **1. c.** *Astr.* Applied to the motion or velocity of a celestial object relative to a group of objects of the same kind; *spec.* that of a star in the frame of reference in which the average velocity of the stars in the neighbourhood of the sun is zero.

[**1890** A. M. CLERKE *Syst. Stars* xxii. 340 The motus peculiaris itself is only a projection upon the sphere of a line of travel which may make any angle with the line of sight.] **1927** H. N. RUSSELL et al. *Astron.* II. xix. 668 The peculair motions of the fainter stars are more rapid than those of the brighter. **1936** E. HUBBLE *Realm of Nebulæ* v. 106 It was expected that, when the solar motion was removed, the residual, peculiar motions of the nebulæ would be much smaller than the observed velocities and.. that they would be distributed at random. **1967** R. KURTH *Introd. Stellar Statistics* ii. 14 The parallactic and peculiar motions of the stars close to the Sun..can be estimated if the hypothesis..is adopted that the average of the peculiar motions vanishes. **1975** G. O. ABELL *Exploration of Universe* (ed. 3) xx. 396/1 The space velocity of a star, its motion with respect to the sun, is made up of both the star's peculiar velocity and a component due to solar motion. **1978** PASACHOFF & KUTNER *University Astron.* iii. 62 Most peculiar velocities are a few tens of km/sec; very few are above 100 km/sec. *Ibid.* 64 If we observe a large number of stars, their peculiar motions, since they are random, will average to about zero.

4. b. *Astr.* Of a galaxy: not belonging to any of the types, elliptical, spiral, and irregular, which include almost all galaxies.

1936 E. HUBBLE *Realm of Nebulæ* ii. 47 The remaining irregulars might be arbitrarily placed in the regular sequence as highly peculiar objects. **1959** *Listener* 31 Dec. 1152/1 There are a few galaxies that do not fit conveniently into this classification of spirals, ellipticals, and irregulars. These are the 'peculiar' galaxies. **1972** JASTROW & THOMPSON *Astron.* 213 In all the cases that have been examined thus far, the unusual event that altered the appearance of the peculiar galaxy seems to have been either a *collision* with another galaxy, or a gigantic *explosion* within the galaxy. **1973** *Sci. Amer.* Dec. 39/1 One or 2 percent, however, do not conform. Because of their bizarre appearance or unusual spectra they are known to astronomers as 'peculiar' galaxies.

ped². Add: (Further examples.) Now chiefly *U.S.*

1897 *National Police Gaz.* (U.S.) 26 May 10/4 The consensus of opinion is that the Irish-Scots ped. came to the mark in the pink of condition. **1962** *N.Y. Times* 26 Jan. 1/3 'Peds' is short for pedestrians in traffic engineers' jargon. **1973** D. BARNES *See the Woman* I. 134 A ped about three-quarters of a block away.

ped³ (ped). *Soil Science.* [f. Gr. πέδ-ον ground, earth.] (See quot. 1958.)

1951 *Soil Survey Manual* (U.S. Dept. Agric. Handbk. No. 18) 225 An individual natural soil aggregate is called a ped, in contrast to (1) a clod, caused by disturbance.., (2) a fragment caused by rupture.., or (3) a concretion caused by local concentrations of compounds that irreversibly cement the soil grains together. **1958** *U.S. Dept. Agric. Yearbk.* 1957 764/1 *Ped*, an individual natural soil aggregate such as a crumb, prism, or block, in contrast to a clod, which is a mass of soil brought about by digging or other disturbance. **1971** R. L. DONAHUE et al. *Soils* (ed. 3) ii. 41 There are four principal types of soil structure: 1. Platy. Peds exhibit a matted, flattened, or compressed appearance... 4. Spheroidal. Peds are imperfect spheres like marbles, but are usually smaller. **1972** J. G. CRUICKSHANK *Soil Geogr.* iii. 79 Clayey soils also tend to develop large columnar peds which on shrinking produce non-capillary pores.

ped-, form of *PEDO- used before a vowel (as in *PEDALFER).

pedagoguery, (*b*). (Earlier example.)

1872 F. HALL *Recent Exempl. False Philol.* 31 It is not because of any poverty of matter for remark in the head-long sciolism of the one and in the piddling pedagoguery of the other.

pedagoguette (pedăgǫge·t). *nonce-wd.* [f. PEDAGOGUE + -ETTE.] A school-mistress.

1960 V. NABOKOV *Invitation to Beheading* viii. 87 The strident commands of the red-haired 'pedagoguette'.

pedal, *sb.* Add: **1. b.** *soft pedal*: see also as main entry in Suppl.

2. b. *spec.* Such a lever forming one of the controls in a motor vehicle; often *attrib.*

1902 W. W. BEAUMONT in A. C. Harmsworth et al. *Motors* x. 219 The friction of the band on the drum..pulls on the band in the same direction as the pedal. *Ibid.* 220 A good form of brake is that..in which the pull on the rod F from pedal E pulls the arm D. **1909** *Westm. Gaz.* 4 Feb. 4/2 It seems to me that to dismantle the universal joint and pedal-gear means taking them out. **1926** *Scribner's Mag.* Aug. 153/1 The girl was satiated with speed. She relaxed the pressure of her foot on the pedal, and leaned back in her seat. 'Some car!' she said. **1929** *Times* 5 Nov. 7/5 The clutch pedal-shaft bearings have grease valves. **1962** *Which? Car Suppl.* Oct. 128/2 Most drivers liked the pedal controls in the VW 1500. *Ibid.* 129/1 The pedal control layouts..were generally liked. **1974** *Country Life* 21 Mar. 659/2 Pedals are nicely positioned for heel and toe driving. **1976** 'E. MCBAIN' *Guns* (1977) vi. 139 Great day for a robbery... Your driver hit the gas pedal and off you went.

4. Also *transf.*

1892 G. B. SHAW *Let.* 21 Apr. (1965) I. 337 Her voice has become much more powerful—quite Hyde Parkian in its pedal notes. 1905 *Daily Chron.* 25 Sept. 6/4 He did all that the pedal-notes of his magnificent voice could do toward realising..a character not wholly suited to his temperament.

b. On some brass and wind instruments, = FUNDAMENTAL *sb.* 2; usu. *attrib.*, as *pedal note, tone*.

1856 M. C. CLARKE tr. *Berlioz's Treat. Mod. Instrumentation* 153/2 All trombones..possess..three notes; which are..called pedals... Supposing that the bass trombone possesses the first only of these pedal notes..it would still be of great value for certain effects. *Ibid.* 154/1 The vibrations of the pedal notes are slow, and require much wind. 1938 *Oxf. Compan. Mus.* 953/2 The actual fundamental notes are not so easy to produce [on a trombone] as the harmonics above them; they are spoken of as *Pedal Notes*—possibly because they are considered to be useful for the holding of a 'pedal', in the sense in which the word is used in the terminology of harmony.., or else, as Berlioz suggests, from their resemblance to the low pedal notes of an organ. 1944 W. APEL *Harvard Dict. Mus.* 340/1 Owing to the narrow bore..the lowest tone of this series (pedal tone) is practically unobtainable. *Ibid.* 817/1 Another term for the fundamental tone is pedal tone... A distinction is made between whole-tube instruments.. producing the pedal tone, and half-tube instruments. 1954 *Grove's Dict. Mus.* (ed. 5) VI. 608/1 These prime notes, the lowest proper tones of the instrument,..are known as pedal notes... A pedal note always stands for the first note or No. 1 in the harmonic series. On trumpets and some other instruments the pedal notes are practically impossible. 1959 *Collins Mus. Encycl.* 491/2 *Pedal*,..the fundamental (or first note of the harmonic series) on a brass instrument. A few of these notes can be produced with a slack lip on the trombone, the tuba and the B♭ section of the double horn. 1961 C. W. MONK in A. Baines *Mus. Instruments* xi. 283 This gives *E* as the bottom note of the trombone's continuous scale, leaving a gap down to the less-used fundamental or 'pedal' notes from the first-position *B'*♭ downwards.

6. (Earlier example.)

1849 H. MELVILLE *Mardi* II. xliv. 204 To cool his heated pedals, he established..stopping-places.

7. *pedal-bike, cycle, cyclist, work*; *pedal-operated* adj.; **pedal bin**, a rubbish bin with a lid which is opened by means of a pedal; **pedal boat**, a boat, usu. a pleasure boat, propelled by means of pedals; also **pedal-driven boat; pedal car**, a car, usu. a child's toy, propelled by means of pedals; **pedal clarinet** (or **clarionet**), a clarinet sounding an octave below the bass clarinet; **pedal-craft**, pedal boats; **pedal entry**, in organ music, a point where a theme or figure is introduced on the pedal stops; also *transf.* and *fig.*; **pedal point** (earlier and later examples); also fig.; **pedal pusher**, a cyclist; hence in *pl.* (orig. *U.S.*), a type of girls' or women's trousers, reaching only just below the knee, suitable for wearing when cycling; also (with hyphen) *attrib.*; **pedal steel guitar**, an electric guitar fixed on a stand and connected to pedals by which the tension of the strings can be altered to produce glissando effects; also **pedal guitar, pedal steel; pedal wireless**, a small radio transceiver, with a generator powered by a foot-pedal, providing a means of communication in the Australian out-back; also **pedal radio, pedal set.**

1974 'A. GILBERT' *Nice Little Killing* vi. 83 I've been travelling around on a pedal-bike. 1951 *Catal. of Exhibits, South Bank Exhib., Festival of Britain* 52/1 'Binette' pedal bin. *Ibid.* 124/1 Pedal bin for soiled napkins. 1958 *Engineering* 7 Mar. 320/2 Polythene is used widely: for pedal bins, trug baskets,..and watering cans. 1966 N. FREELING *Dresden Green* I. 14 He..picked up his pedal bin (emptied that and every morning into one of the big dustbins). 1977 J. HEALD *Just Desserts* i. 14 An empty magnum of Château Waitrose by the pedal bin in the kitchen. 1951 *Go* Apr.–May There are little safe pedal-boats for venturing on to the lake. 1958 *New Yorker* 13 Sept. 130/3 (Advt.), The Yacht club with pedal boats, water skiing, skin diving. 1959 *Encounter* Oct. 17/2 The animated statue who looks after the pedal-boats. 1951 *Catal. of Exhibits, South Bank Exhib., Festival of Britain* 126/2 Pedalcar, 'Austin 40'. 1968 *Radio Times* 28 Nov. 6 A pedal car, a doll's pram, a trike or a bike. 1973 *Guardian* 11 June 6 The event for Formula One pedal cars was part of the RAC L-Driver of the Year finals. 1892 *Orchestral Times* Jan. 6/2 Messrs. F. Besson & Co.'s inventive faculty seems inexhaustible... That eminent firm has recently given us..the 'Pedal' Clarionet (contra-bass clarionet). *Ibid.* 7/2 The 'Pedal' Clarionet is the deepest-voiced instrument ever constructed for orchestral use... The fingering of the pedal clarionet is similar to the ordinary clarionet. 1911 *Encycl. Brit.* XXI. 36/2 *Pedal clarinet*, a contrabass instrument invented in 1891 by M. F. Besson to complete the quartet of clarinets..; it is constructed on practically the same principles as the clarinet, and consists of a tube 10 ft. long..doubled up twice upon itself. 1959 *Collins Mus. Encycl.* 491/2 *Pedal Clarinet*, another name for the Contrabass Clarinet. 1961 J. A. MACGILLIVRAY in A. Baines *Mus. Instruments* x. 260 Of those [*sc.* contrabass clarinets] in B♭, an octave below the bass clarinet, Fontaine-Besson's 'Pedal clarinet' was the first to arouse much interest. 1966 *Listener* 27 Oct. 632/2 He includes such rare instruments as..pedal-clarinet. 1957 G. BELLAIRS *Death in High Provence* ix. 105 Families.. sporting on the beaches, little pedal-craft skimming across the water. 1937 R. F. BROAD *Motor Driving made Easy* (ed. 6) vii. 94 A moment ago we used the word 'cyclist'. By this term is generally understood the pedal-cycle user. 1963 *Times* 5 Mar. 6/3 Motor cycle casualties fell by 7,632..and pedal-cycle casualties by 3,974. 1973 J. WAINWRIGHT *Pride of Pigs* 69 Sykes arrived in a Cortina. The postman arrived *with* a pedal cycle—pushing it. 1974 *Times* 8 Feb. 15 The local authority provides a pedal cycle speedway track. 1931 *Highway Code* 12 Certain of the rules for drivers of motor vehicles..also apply ..to pedal cyclists. 1974 L. LAMB *Man in Mist* vii. 43 The early evening shoal of pedal cyclists. 1927 *Sunday Express* 14 Aug. 1 Mr. E. P. Tierney..collapsed yesterday when attempting to carry out a test in his 12-foot pedal-driven boat Carrie, with which he had planned to cross the Atlantic. 1928 AUDEN in *Oxf. Poetry* 2 We sang Our descant until love one day, That pedal-entry in the fugue Roared in, swept soul and knees away. 1932 —— *Orators* I. 30 The bowel tremors at the pedal-entry. 1970 A. BELLOW *Illustr. Hist. Guitar* vii. 154 An even more unusual guitar, known as a 'pedal guitar', was constructed by Eduard Bayer. 1908 *Westm. Gaz.* 20 Oct. 4/3 A similar powered car..with patent pedal-operated plate clutch. *Ibid.* 10 Dec. 4/2 (*heading*) Pedal-operated car. 1936 *Discovery* July 224/2 A pedal-operated volume-control [on an electronic piano]. 1960 *Farmer & Stockbreeder* 5 Jan. 95/2 This pedal-operated device counteracts wheel-spin. 1964 W. L. GOODMAN *Hist. Woodworking Tools* 153 Holding his work in a vertical, pedal-operated vice or 'horse'. 1852 J. HULLAH *Gram. Musical Harmony* xxvii. 71 From a very obvious and effective mode of using these (foot) keys has arisen the term *pedal point*, by which is understood a note maintained during several successive changes of chords, or passages of melody. 1974 *Publishers Weekly* 16 Dec. 49/1 These tales are generally of high standard... But the insistent pedal point theme, the overwhelming atmosphere of misery.., makes this one to be taken in small doses. 1977 *New Yorker* 16 May 139/1 Hindemith's Requiem opens with a slow instrumental prelude, a four-note tolling ostinato over a pedal point. 1934 M. H. WESEEN *Dict. Amer. Slang* xvii. 262 *Pedal pusher*,—a bicycle rider, especially in a race. 1942 [see *PEDALLER]. 1944 *Life* 28 Aug. 65/2 When college girls took to riding bicycles in slacks, they first rolled up one trouser leg, then rolled up both. This..has now produced a trim variety of long shorts, called 'pedal pushers'. 1945 *Liberty* 1 Sept. 68 Miss McCardell..borrowed little-boy pants for 'pedal-pushers', the knee length shorts. 1957 H. ROOSENBURG *Walls came tumbling Down* vii. 189 His trousers had shrunk to the size of pedal-pushers. 1959 M. STEEN *Tower* I. vii. 92 A girl in..blue pedal-pusher jeans. 1960 S. PLEYDELL *Festival for Gilbert* i. 10 Black pedal-pusher trousers. 1971 Pedal-pusher [see *HAPPI-COAT]. 1959 *Manch. Guardian* 5 Aug. 5/4 All the aeroplane, the pedal-radio..and, latterly, the road-train have done to break down the isolation of life in inland central Australia. 1944 *Living off Land* iv. 77 Cars, trucks, aircraft, and radio pedal-sets, have put an end to the old era of isolation. 1949 H. M. MADELEY *Australia* xxxiv. 138 These pedal sets are in mining camps, in lonely houses, in police stations, in nursing homes. 1976 *Gramophone* Aug. 351/3 Paul Cotton..and Rusty Young (pedal steel, dobro, mandolin etc.) excel instrumentally. 1977 *Zigzag* Mar. 30/1 This coupled with Mike Utley's delicate piano and Al Perkins' unobtrusive pedal steel makes the track one of the standout cuts on the first side. 1969 *Listener* 20 Mar. 398/3 It features another splendid electronic invention, the pedal steel guitar which..specialises in vertiginous slides and swoops. 1969 *Rolling Stone* 28 June 17/1 Today's added use of drums, pedal steel guitar,..even harpsichord have [*sic*] made some arrangements far more complete. 1940 BAYNE & LAZARUS *Austral. Community* II. 76 Messages are sent out and received by means of the pedal wireless or transceiver (invented by the Australian Inland Mission and now much improved). 1944 F. CLUNE *Red Heart* 7 The combination of pedal-wireless sets, to call the doctor, and of aeroplanes, to bring him to the patient, is a triumph of modern times. 1963 A. LUBBOCK *Austral. Roundabout* 25 The hundreds of transceiver or pedal-wireless sets. 1944 R. LEHMANN *Ballad & Source* 96, I was already practising my technique for Bicyclists' Dashing Hill—a piece of frantic momentum-gathering pedal work.

pedal, *a.* Add: **1. b.** *pedal bone*, the lowest phalangeal bone in a horse's foot; = *coffin-bone* (COFFIN *sb.* 13).

1881 *Encycl. Brit.* XII. 178/1 A powerful tendon..passes down over the..phalanges, to be inserted mainly into the upper edge of the anterior surface of the last phalanx or pedal bone. 1920 F. T. BARTON *Horse* xiii. 107 Two tendons pass down the back of the foot,..the former being attached to the lower surface of the pedal-bone. 1973 EDWARDS & GEDDES *Compl. Bk. Horse* III. iii. 113/1 The end bone of the leg is the pedal bone..which corresponds to the last bone in the second finger of man. *Ibid.*, The pedal bone is roughly the shape of the foot and is of pumice-like consistency.

pedal (pe·dăl), *a.*[2] [ad. It. *pedale*: see PEDAL *sb.*] Applied to the lower and thicker part of a kind of straw grown in Italy for plaiting; *ellipt.*, a special plait made from this straw, usually having five or seven strands. (Hence *five-* or *seven-ends pedal*.)

1887 *Encycl. Brit.* XXII. 593/2 The straw of Tuscany, specially grown for plaiting, is distinguished into three qualities,—..from the third quality, *Santa Fioro*, only 'Tuscan pedals' and braids are plaited. 1907 *Yesterday's Shopping* (1969) 894 Fine pedal 'Homburg'... Fine pedal straw. 1923 *Daily Mail* 7 Feb. 1 (Advt.), Italian pedal straw hats... These hats are very soft and pliable, made of seven ends pedal. 1930 *Times* 13 Mar. 11/6 Fine pedal straw has returned, and is seen in a brimmed hat.., with the new sweeping line. 1962 A. SOUTHERN *Millinery* ii. 30 The fancy band straws and pedal come into this [*sc.* real Italian straws] group, the latter being dyed into fashion shades.

pedal, *v.* Add: **a.** Also of a pianoforte or similar instrument. Also *trans.*, to use the pedals in playing (a passage of music, etc.); also, to use the pedals of.

1889 *Cent. Dict.* s.v., *Pedal*..*v.i.*,..to work a pedal; use the pedals, as of a piano, organ, bicycle, etc. 1909, etc. [see *PEDALLING *vbl. sb.*]. 1922 S. GREW *Art of Player-Piano* iv. 23 We correct the first condition..by ceasing to pedal for a moment or two. *Ibid.* xviii. 112 An attempt..to 'pedal' the piece in the way it is 'fingered' for the pianist. 1922 JOYCE *Ulysses* 259 Upholding the lid he..gazed..at the oblique triple (piano!) wires. He pressed.., soft pedalling a triple of keys. 1938 F. C. RAUSER tr. *Leimer & Gieseking's Rhythmics* vii. 48 All of Beethoven's Sonatas can be properly pedalled by means of the time-tread. 1954 T. A. JOHNSON *Princ. Pianoforte Pedalling* 10 It is sometimes permissible to pedal certain staccato passages. 1961 C. CLUTTON in A. Baines *Mus. Instruments* v. 93 John Field..was the first person to develop the use of the sustaining pedal as part of his technique, and, like Chopin, he pedalled after the note. 1975 H. FERGUSON *Keyboard Interpretation* ix. 66 The passage must be pedaled thus. 1978 *Gramophone* July 231/1 The ending of 'Ende vom Lied'..is deeply impressive—I only wish he had not pedalled.

b. Also in *refl.*, *pass.*, and *fig.* uses.

1896 *Queen* 25 Jan. 169/2 If young ladies are to be allowed to pedal themselves about in..London, then it will certainly be necessary to provide..some proper escort. 1924 GALSWORTHY *White Monkey* II. xi. 208 'Well,' said Michael, '*I* think we shall pedal through yet.' 1955 G. GREENE *Quiet American* IV. ii. 243, I found a trishaw and was pedalled home. 1973 D. MAY *Laughter in Djakarta* viii. 132 A betjak came along the street, pedalled by a very young smooth-faced boy. 1977 *Daily Express* 29 Jan. 35/2 Derek Underwood pedalling slowly backwards before clutching it in his hands to send Gavaskar miserably away to an accompaniment of boos and jeers from the 40,000 crowd.

pedalfer (pědæ·lfəɹ). *Soil Sci.* [f. *PED- + AL(UMINIUM + L. *fer-rum* iron.] A soil in which there is no layer of accumulated calcium carbonate but in which oxides of iron and aluminium have tended to accumulate (generally acidic and characteristic of humid climates). Cf. *PEDOCAL.

1928 [see *PEDOCAL]. 1930 L. A. WOLFANGER *Major Soil Divisions of U.S.* iv. 100 The agriculture of the pedalfers is characterized by its wealth in crop variety and its extended development of crop centers. 1965 B. T. BUNTING *Geogr. Soil* viii. 95 Accumulation of Fe and Al oxides at depth is characteristic..of pedalfers, especially of podzols. 1972 C. B. HUNT *Geol. Soils* viii. 167 The significant feature of pedalfers is that moisture is sufficient to wet the soil to its capacity..and to allow excess water to.. remove the soluble constituents. 1977 A. HALLAM *Planet Earth* 179 These ideas were accepted in the USA, and the concepts of pedalfers and pedocals added: pedalfers are leached soils in humid areas where aluminium and iron accumulate in the B horizon.

Hence **pedalfe·ric** *a.*

1928 [see *PEDOCALIC *a.*]. 1930 L. A. WOLFANGER *Major Soil Divisions of U.S.* iv. 101 Although several of these crops are also grown in noteworthy quantity in the pedalferic zone, the chief production areas..are included within the pedocalic division.

Pedaline (pe·dăləin, -īn). Also with lower-case initial. [f. *PEDAL *a.*[2] + -INE[4].] A synthetic straw (see quot. 1957). Also *Pedaline straw*.

1927 *Daily Express* 16 Feb. 4/2 (Advt.), Women's becoming hats of Pedaline Straw, trimmed and bound with Ribbon Velvet. *Ibid.* 14 Mar. 5/3 (*heading*) Fashion's new vocabulary... The following are a few additions made to her vocabulary this spring by Dame Fashion:—..*pedaline*, a new type of plait for millinery, having a polished effect. 1942 J. G. DONY *Hist. Straw Hat Industry* v. 96 (*caption*) Pedaline, a Japanese imitation of a Swiss braid... Coburg pedaline, a Japanese braid. 1957 M. B. PICKEN *Fashion Dict.* 337 *Pedaline*,..synthetic straw made of hemp fiber covered with Cellophane and woven between cotton threads. Made chiefly in Japan.

pedaller, pedaler. Add: (Further examples in var. senses.) Also in *pl.*, a name for *pedal pushers* s.v. *PEDAL *sb.* 7.

The spelling *pedaler* is predominantly *N. Amer.*

1922 S. GREW *Art of Player-Piano* 17 Effects in the music which you cannot hope to create until you are an experienced pedaller. 1942 BERREY & VAN DEN BARK *Amer. Thes. Slang* § 426/10 *Bicyclist*,..pedaler, pedal pusher. 1945 *Consumers' Guide* (U.S.) July 6 Another part of the Clothes Magic show illustrated what had been done in a 'make over and make do' program... Pedalers (bicycle shorts) from G.I. pants, and a stunning beach ensemble..from a discarded evening dress were a few of the other things shown. 1953 BERREY & VAN DEN BARK *Amer. Thes. Slang* (1954) (ed. 2) § 87/15 *Pedalers, pedal pushers*, bicycle shorts that end just below the knee. 1972 *Village Voice* (N.Y.) 1 June 26/2 In an era of precious pedalers, back to nature sentimentalists, and ecology moralizers, Jack La Lanne is an honest, straightforward salesman. 1974 *Times* 12 Nov. 14/7 It seems against the interests of the environment to chase away harmless pedallers with a polluting petrol-engined monster. 1976 A. HILL *Summer's End* ii. 25 I'd got a pedaller that would run alright. No brakes, no mudguards. But I could pedal it. 1977 *Times* 14 June 16/7 Readers..keep complaining about the 'tedious' routine of having to apply to the Cyclists Touring Club for tickets to take their bicycles free on trains. More than 10,000 pedallers have done it without making a fuss.

pedalling, *vbl. sb.* Add: (Further examples.) Also *fig.* Also with reference to propelling a sled. Also as *ppl. a.*

1909 J. HOFMANN *Piano Playing* 42 Harmonic clarity in pedalling is the basis, but it is only the basis; it is not all that constitutes an artistic treatment of the pedal. 1911 H. BROWER *Art of Pianist* xiv. 170 Imagine what a performance of the compositions of Chopin or Liszt would sound like, deprived of proper pedaling. 1916 JOYCE *Portrait of Artist* (1969) v. 190 'It may be uphill pedalling at first. Take Mr. Moonan. He was a long time before he got to the top.'.. 'I may not have his talent.' 1925 E. H. YOUNG *William* iv. 38 A ringing of bicycle bells was heard, and then two pedalling figures.. appeared. 1936 Y. BOWEN (*title*) Pedalling the modern pianoforte. 1938 F. C. RAUSER tr. *Leimer & Gieseking's Rhythmics* vii. 57 It is possible to play a *glissando* with uninterrupted pedalling. 1948 A. FOLDES *Keys to Keyboard* (1950) viii. 50 Pedalling is one of the most complicated processes in piano playing. 1954 T. A. JOHNSON *Princ. Pianoforte Pedalling* 9 (*heading*), Pedalling of Arpeggios. 1954 *Grove's Dict. Mus.* (ed. 5) VI. 345/2 We must now consider the subject of pedalling... To look at the pedal-board is often impossible and rarely helpful. 1972 *Evening Telegram* (St. John's, Newfoundland) 24 June 14/3 Pedalling is an art and must be done smoothly, in order not to jerk the sled. 1973 *Guardian* 17 Feb. 15/2 In Britain..pedalling for pleasure is undergoing a sort of mini-renaissance. 1973 K. A. LEIBOVITCH tr. *Neuhaus's Art of Piano Playing* 165 How sad that such a great pianist as Schnabel..showed his lack of understanding in his inappropriate pedalling.

pedalo (pe·dălo). [f. PEDAL *sb.* + *-o^{2}.] A small pedal-operated pleasure boat used on lakes and at the sea-side.

The spelling in quot. 1962 is unusual.

1959 *News Chron.* 4 Dec. 3/7 One rescue team..manned a four-seat 'Pedalo' found on an untouched part of the beach. 1962 'O. MILLS' *Headlines make Murder* xviii. 199 A shilling-an-hour pedallo. 1969 *Daily Tel.* 21 Apr. 11/5 So many beaches today are crowded with water-skiers, canoeists, *pedaloes* and sailing boats that accidents are on the increase. 1973 W. FAIRCHILD *Swiss Arrangement* v. 61 The water was glass calm and children in pedalos glided in all directions. 1976 *Daily Tel.* 20 July 15/5 A man armed with a bottle defied an RAF helicopter and two lifeboats which tried to rescue him from a drifting pedalo four miles off Margate last night. 1977 *Navy News* Feb. 18/1 Glancing through a scuttle after reading the papers lately, a member of the Andrew might have expected to see a pedalo forging ahead of his fuel-saving warship.

‖**pedanda** (pedæ·ndă). Also **padanda, padenda,** and with capital initial. [Balinese, = 'bearer of the staff'.] In Bali, a Brahman priest. Also *attrib.*

1817 T. S. RAFFLES *Hist. Java* II. p. ccxxxix, The duties and ceremonies of religion, the conducting of which is in the hands of..learned Brahmins called *Padénda.* 1877 *Jrnl. R. Asiatic Soc.* IX. 113 The *Padandas* are Brahmans who have received a complete education from another *Padanda* (their *Guru*). They must be thoroughly acquainted with religion and with literature. In order to become a Padanda, they undergo all kinds of tests... The mark of the dignity is a staff, *danda,* which they receive from the Guru... After this staff they are called *Padanda,* that is, 'bearing a staff.' 1924 T. DE KLEEN *Mudrās* 23 Although the Balinese in general are a polite and hospitable people, the *Pedandas* showed themselves very reserved, sometimes obviously hostile. *Ibid.* 27 My *Pedanda* friends in Sidemen. 1936 R. GORIS in *Netherlands Indies* 16 Feb. 71/1 There are in Bali both Padandas 'Shiva' and Padandas 'Buda'. *Ibid.* 77/1 Every bench of magistrates in Bali must have at least one Padanda sitting on it as a judge. 1937 M. COVARRUBIAS *Island of Bali* (1972) ix. 293 The *pedandas* still exert a powerful influence on Balinese life despite the fact that their relations with the people were never intimate; they represent the law, and the judges of the high native courts..are still *pedandas* in the majority. 1953 J. BELO *Bali: Temple Festival* 4 The temple priests who are the guardians of these temples have not studied as have the Brahmana high priests, the *pedanda,* who are often scholars and learned men. 1961 P. KEMP *Alms for Oblivion* vii. 116 Priests wear white, and a high priest or *pedanda* goes bareheaded and carries a staff surmounted by a crystal ball.

‖**pedang** (pĕdæ·ŋ). [Malay.] A type of sword (see quots.).

1817 T. S. RAFFLES *Hist. Java* vi. 296 The *pedáng, bandól,* [etc.]..are varieties of sword. 1911 *Encycl. Brit.* XVII. 477/1 The Malays use..long swords of ordinary pattern called *pedang.* 1936 G. B. GARDNER *Keris & Other Malay Weapons* iii. 69 Theoretically this is any type of sword of foreign origin... The *pĕdang* may be straight or curved.

peddler (pe·dləɹ). [var. PEDLAR *sb.*] In this spelling, used to denote anyone who peddles goods in some way illicitly, as stolen goods, forged notes, illegal drugs, etc.

The spelling was mainly confined to the U.S. until the 1960s, and the word is still commonly written as *pedlar* in the U.K. even in the sense defined above.

1872 G. P. BURNHAM *Mem. U.S. Secret Service* p. vii, *Peddler,* an itinerant counterfeit money-seller. 1929 M. A. GILL *Underworld Slang, Peddlers,* drug bootleggers. 1930 [see *drug-peddler* s.v. *DRUG *sb.*^{1} 1 b]. 1935 *Jrnl. Abnormal Psychol.* XXX. 363 *Peddler,* an inmate who steals and sells state property. 1935 N. ERSINE *Underworld & Prison Slang* 57 *Pint peddler,* a petty bootlegger who carries a number of pints of liquor about his person. He usually hangs around poolrooms. *a* 1953 E. O'NEILL *Hughie* (1959) 27 Take my tip, pal, and don't never try to buy from a dope peddler. 1953 W. BURROUGHS *Junkie* (1972) ii. 29 In fact, a peddler should not come right out and say he is a peddler... Everyone knows that he himself is the connection, but it is bad form to say so. *Ibid.* iv. 41 A peddler..was pushing Mexican H on 103rd and Broadway. 1978 T. WILLIAMSON *Technicians of Death* vi. 44 They're ready to deal in junk [*sc.* drugs]... Fringe groups..will start feeding the peddlers. 1978 *Guardian* 25 Aug. 11/6 The officials even wanted me to identify the street peddler from whom I bought a copy of the English book.

pedestal, *sb.* Add: **1. b.** Used *fig.* in phr. *to put* (or *place,* etc.) *on a pedestal,* to regard as highly admirable or important; to accord an important place to; to exalt or magnify.

1859 [see SEAT *v.* 1 a *fig.*]. 1882 R. L. STEVENSON *Familiar Stud. Men & Bks.* 158 This is to put friendship on a pedestal indeed. 1916 G. B. SHAW *Pygmalion* 205 She wishes she could get him alone..and just drag him off his pedestal and see him making love like any common man. 1922 JOYCE *Ulysses* 638 They discovered..that their idol had feet of clay, after placing him upon a pedestal. 1930 A. ROOSEVELT in H. Powell *Last Paradise* p. xiii, In the United States we are so used to work that we can't conceive of life without it. We have placed work on a pedestal. It is our God. 1957 D. ROBINS *Noble One* xvi. 152 He had unconsciously put her on a pedestal. 1968 *Listener* 3 Oct. 440/3 When somebody becomes prime minister they're immediately put on a pedestal... Well, Ramsay fell off his pedestal. 1975 *Ibid.* 18 Dec. 815/1 The doctor is on a pedestal? Yes, unapproachable, because his expertise sets him apart.

3. c. (Later examples.)

1896 *Heal & Son Catal.: Bedsteads, etc.* 170 Washstand.., Chamber Pedestal, Towel Horse. 1959 W. S. SHARPS *Dict. Cinematogr.* 116 *Pedestal,* a simple vertical support for a film projector. 1960 O. SKILBECK *ABC of Film & TV* 95 *Pedestal,* a simple, high Dolly, used in T.V. 1961 G. MILLERSON *Technique Television Production* iii. 23 A one-man camera mounting, the pedestal has high manoeuvrability. *Ibid.* 24 The pedestal column is telescopic. 1971 *Nature* 9 July 98/1 The fines were mounted on the electron microscope pedestal with a drop of absolute methanol. 1975 J. RATHBONE *Kill Cure* I. iv. 22 The cracked W.C. pedestal did not bear looking into.

d. *Television.* The level of the video signal voltage during line blanking; also, this part of the signal.

1937 *Electronics* June 15/2 From the shading panel the signal goes to a control amplifier where the pedestal level is set. This pedestal is a voltage level corresponding to black, or slightly 'blacker than black', on which the synchronizing impulses are placed and which exists throughout the return trace of the cathode beam. 1951 R. B. DOME *Television Princ.* ix. 214 The width of the horizontal synchronizing pulse is approximately half the width of its pedestal. 1956 M. SLURZBERG et al. *Essent. Television* ii. 24 The blanking signal is often referred to as a pedestal on which the synchronizing pulses are mounted. 1972 F. H. BELT *How to interpret T.V. Waveforms* 101 Video looks okay at first glance, although actually it's compressed a bit at the black end (up near where the sync pedestals should be). Also, blanking (the sync pedestal) appears widened.

4. *pedestal base, cupboard, dancing, desk*; **pedestal (wash) basin,** a wash basin with a single columnar support; **pedestal mat,** a mat which fits around the base of a lavatory pedestal; **pedestal table** (examples); also used of other types of table; also *pedestal writing table*; **pedestal vase,** a vase with a pedestal base.

1948 A. LANE *Greek Pott.* ii. 9 Wide and shallow with pedestal bases. 1978 *N.Y. Times* 30 Mar. B21/9 (Advt.), Pedestal base dining tables. 1967 J. MORRISON in *Coast to Coast 1965–66* 140 There was no pedestal basin and no tap. 1896 *Heal & Son Catal.: Bedsteads, etc.* 194 Pedestal Cupboard. 1959 G. SAVAGE *Antique Collector's Handbk.* 122 Pedestal cupboards, surmounted by urns, appear quite frequently. 1906 *Daily Chron.* 12 Mar. 7/1 Mrs. Lannon said pedestal dancing was not a speciality, but they had introduced it. 1952 J. GLOAG *Short Dict. Furnit.* 353 Small pedestal desks were introduced early in the 18th century. 1957 V. NABOKOV *Pnin* iii. 69 It [*sc.* a room] had come with two ignoble chairs..and a humble pedestal desk of indeterminable wood. 1970 *Country Life* 1 Oct. (Suppl.) 48B/1 A very fine quality Hepplewhite mahogany Pedestal Desk with bow front and dummy drawers. 1962 *Guardian* 5 Dec. 6/3 Matching bathroom sets..bath mat, pedestal mat, lavatory seat cover. 1972 *Ibid.* 23 Feb. 18/5 Matching bathmats..pedestal mats, and loo seat covers. 1939 *Army & Navy Stores Catal.* 1032 Bedside pedestal table..With half door..or full door. *Ibid.,* Kidney Shape Pedestal Table, fitted with six drawers. 1952 J. GLOAG *Short Dict. Furnit.* 355 *Pedestal table,* a term sometimes used for round, oval, square, or rectangular tables that are supported by a single pillar or column which rests upon a stabilising base. 1966 M. M. PEGLER *Dict. Interior Design* (1967) 329 The pedestal table is also a popular modern design with the table surface resting on a thin support which flares outward as it reaches the floor. 1975 *Habitat Catal.* 35 Pedestal table. Spun aluminium base..melamine laminate top. 1960 K. M. KENYON *Archaeol. in Holy Land* vii. 171 Neither pedestal vases..nor flaring carinated bowls..are found. 1967 *Gloss. Sanitation Terms* (*B.S.I.*) 62 *Pedestal wash basin,* a wash basin supported from the floor by a column-shaped base. 1883 *Heal & Son Catal.: Bedsteads, etc.* 193 Pedestal Writing Table,..Leather Top.

pedestrian, *a.* and *sb.* Add: **B.** *sb.* **b.** *rare.* One who is dull, prosaic, or uninspired.

1969 D. F. HORROBIN *Sci. is God* iii. 24 These..purveyors of ideas..irritate intensely those pedestrian men who feel that they never have enough information for the proposal of a hypothesis. Unfortunately, for the pedestrians, it is the dreamers who tend to steal most of the scientific glory.

c. *attrib.* and *Comb. pedestrian-operated* adj.; **pedestrian crossing,** a marked section of the roadway where pedestrians crossing the road are given precedence over vehicular traffic; **pedestrian deck,** a series of pavements or walk-ways, usu. built above ground level and often roofed, reserved for pedestrians; **pedestrian precinct,** an area reserved for pedestrians only, usu. in a town centre or shopping centre.

1935 *Punch* 3 Apr. 374 (*caption*) Sorry, old man, but my wife has just signalled that she has thought of a name for our new dog, and I'm dashing along to the next pedestrian crossing so that I can go over and hear it. 1936 [see *BELISHA BEACON]. 1950 *Ann. Reg. 1949* 473 The plaintiff..was crossing a street..by means of a controlled pedestrian crossing. 1973 D. MILLER *Chinese Jade Affair* xvii. 164 The light at the intersection caught us..and my glamorous chauffeur brought the little Fiat to a halt just a yard or so the wrong side of the pedestrian crossing. 1976 *Evening Post* (Nottingham) 15 Dec. 2/5 We have suggested to the City Planners that a pedestrian crossing.. would be desirable on safety grounds. 1962 *Listener* 24 May 903/2 The pedestrian deck planned for the now abandoned project for a new town in Hook, Hampshire. 1963 *House & Garden* Mar. 35/2 Andover will also have its pedestrian deck, 15 feet above a ground level complex of footways and underpasses. 1937 *Daily Herald* 21 Jan. 3/7 No pedestrian operated signals for crossing places. 1938 H. A. TRIPP *Road Traffic* xii. 269 (*heading*) Pedestrian-operated signals. Signals fitted with buttons to be pressed by pedestrians desiring to cross the road are employed. 1953 F. GIBBERD *Town Design* v. 121 A system of pedestrian precincts as short cuts between shopping streets can be developed in a large centre. 1960 *New Left Rev.* July–Aug. 23/1 He proposed to ring the centre with an elaborate motor road, and to turn the entire central area..into a pedestrian precinct. 1971 P. GRESSWELL *Environment* 183 Pedestrian precincts include roads and other areas closed to traffic. 1977 *Belfast Tel.* 24 Jan. 5/1 The police officers chased the gunmen through a pedestrian precinct into Water Street.

pedestrianize, *v.* Add: **b.** *intr.* To produce something commonplace or unremarkable; *trans.* to make (something) commonplace or prosaic.

1838 W. HOWITT *Rural Life Eng.* II. I. iii. 57 We want a designer for wood-cuts..who would pedestrianize in simple style. 1945 W. DE LA MARE in *Trans. R. Soc. Lit.* XXII. 99 Genius originates what talent pedestrianizes.

c. To make accessible only to pedestrians; to make into a pedestrian precinct.

1963 *Observer* 15 Dec. 6/6 He [*sc.* Prof. Buchanan] even suggested that some of these central streets..should be closed to traffic and, in the jargon, pedestrianised. 1969 *Daily Tel.* 15 Nov. 7 (*caption*) Chancellors Way..which will become pedestrianised when the new building..is completed. 1971 *Hansard Lords: Official Rep. Comm. Highways Bill, 1st Sitting 28 Apr.* 11/1 The need for this provision is particularly clear where the street pattern in historic towns is being redesigned, and where it is designed to 'pedestrianise' a street and to construct a new road to give access to shop premises. 1973 *Guardian* 12 Oct. 15/2 The great effort to pedestrianise Carnaby Street. 1977 *Listener* 17 Feb. 207/3 All the streets around here—for the first time in Paris—have been pedestrianized.

Hence **pede·strianized** *ppl. a.*; **pedes:trianiza·tion.**

1964 *Listener* 3 Sept. 341/1 We have a maze of medieval alleys..—ideal for pedestrianization. 1966 *Economist* 2 Apr. p. xv/1 After a look at what is for sale in those urbanely pedestrianised shops, one is tempted to scream it. 1967 *Times Rev. Industry* Oct. 52/3 The medieval road pattern in the city centre..is 'natural for pedestrians' and he has an experimental scheme for pedestrianization of the upper High Street. 1971 P. GRESSWELL *Environment* 182 Pedestrianisation is a clumsy word to describe a simple process: closing shopping streets to traffic. 1972 *Times* 30 Dec. 16/4 The £45,000 scheme will provide 370 yards of 'pedestrianized' roadway. 1973 *Country Life* 15 Nov. 1575/2 It is to be hoped that extensive pedestrianisation and a one-way baffle system may be considered. 1974 *Oxford Times* 18 Oct. 4 Members agreed to stick to their policy of banning all but emergency ambulances from pedestrianised streets and bus lanes. 1977 *Lancashire Life* Aug. 34/1 The proof of Blackburn's pedestrianisation is in its perambulation.

pedgill (pe·dʒ'l), *v. dial.* [Cf. PEGGLE *v.*]. To work hard and painstakingly *at*; to plod or persevere.

1913 D. H. LAWRENCE *Let.* 12 Jan. (1962) I. 175 The thought of you pedgilling away at the novel frets me. 1915 —— *Rainbow* i. 8 But at drawing, his hand swung naturally in big, bold lines, rather lax, so that it was cruel for him to pedgill away at the lace designing, working from the tiny squares of his paper, counting and plotting and niggling.

pediatric, etc.: see *PÆDIATRIC *a.*, etc.

pedicab (pe·dikæb). Also **peddicab.** [f. PEDI- + CAB *sb.*^{3}] A small pedal-operated vehicle, usu. a tricycle, serving as a taxi in countries of the Far East. Also *attrib.*

1948 *Time* 22 Nov. 15/2 The usual crush of pedicabs surged down the street. 1951 *N.Y. Herald-Tribune* 26 Mar. 1/7 The rickishaw and peddicab boys. 1953 *Here & Now* (N.Z.) July 17/1 Trishaw, or pedicab: 'a tricycle affair for one or two passengers, pedalled by a driver. In the larger cities [in China], the trishaw has almost completely replaced the rickshaw.' 1966 D. FORBES *Heart of Malaya* x. 119 He hired his pedicab for one dollar a day. 1971 *Nat. Geographic* Jan. 21 Java's tricycle taxis—rear-driven pedicabs called *betjaks*—also haul freight through city streets. 1974 *Times* 30 Apr. 8/3 In Saigon a pedicab driver set fire to himself outside the President's palace. 1977 *Time* 14 Feb. 41/3 A pedicab parked in the lobby.

pedicure, *sb.* Add: **1.** Also *fig.*
1918 A. QUILLER-COUCH *Stud. in Lit.* 1st Ser. 271 Against this positive deed of friendship and thirty years of devotion little is set by sneering at Watts as 'a pedicure of the Muses'.

2. (Further examples.)
1900 [see *face-massage* s.v. *FACE *sb.* 26]. **1907** *Yesterday's Shopping* (1969) 538/2 Pedicure Scissors—2/6. Pedicure Cases—each 7/6. **1953** J. GORDON *Beauty Bk.* xvi. 167 The instruments you use for a pedicure should not be used for a manicure. *Ibid.*, *Pedicure routine*.. Remove all varnish with a pad of cotton-wool. **1974** *Times* 27 Aug. 9/2 Services..include waxing, manicure, pedicure.

pedigree, *sb.* Add: **2. d.** *colloq.* The 'life history' of a person or thing. Also, a person's criminal record. **pedigree-man** (see quot. 1923).
1903 *Dialect Notes* II. 324 *Pedigree*,..history. 'If he doesn't go straight I'll tell his pedigree.' Not applying to family descent, but to personal history. *a* **1911** D. G. PHILLIPS *Susan Lenox* (1917) II. xvii. 397 'I run her in myself.' 'Oh, she's got a record... Why the hell didn't you say so?' 'I thought you remembered. You took her pedigree.' **1923** J. MANCHON *Le Slang* 220 *Pedigree-man*,..un récidiviste, un cheval de retour. **1942** BERREY & VAN DEN BARK *Amer. Thes. Slang* §477/5 *Pedigree*, a prisoner's police record. **1964** 'D. SHANNON' *Root of All Evil* (1966) ix. 123 Dorothy had a little pedigree for shoplifting. **1969** C. IRVING *Fake!* (1970) xii. 147 Another element in the 'pedigree' of the painting was a certificate from a prior owner, usually one of several well-known collectors. **1975** *Times* 22 Aug. 3/3 It has been decided to establish a national register to check the pedigrees of vehicles, particularly their milages.

5. pedigree-stick, a stick carved to record the genealogy or history of a tribe.
1893 *Jrnl. Anthrop. Inst.* XXII. 319 Had the Polynesians any means of recording degrees of descent?.. *Aufau fetii* is 'the genealogy of a family', and must have been a staff bound in some especial manner to serve the purpose of a pedigree-stick. *Ibid.* 320 An undoubted pedigree-stick..is figured..in Roth's translation of Crozet's 'Voyage to Tasmania', where it is described as 'a staff recording the history of the Ngati-Rangi Tribe' of New Zealand. **1895** A. C. HADDON *Evol. Art* II. iv. 273 These carved shafts of sacred paddles and adzes were pedigree-sticks. **1908** *Encycl. Relig. & Ethics* I. 826/2 Colley March first suggested that the carved shafts of the sacred paddles and adzes were pedigree-sticks, the patterns being 'the multitudinous human links between the divine ancestor and the chief of the living tribe'.

pedigreed, *a.* Add: (Later examples.)
1916 *Mem. N.Y. Bot. Garden* VI. 353 The possibility of cross-sterility between sister plants of a seed progeny was proven and the interrelations of sterility studied in a pedigreed seed progeny. **1971** *Farmer & Stockbreeder* 23 Feb. 53/3 (Advt.), Ayr Bull Sale..Pedigreed, Milk Recorded and Brucellosis Accredited Ayrshire Bull Stirks. **1976** J. VAN DE WETERING *Tumbleweed* vii. 65 He is a pedigreed cat. **1977** *New Yorker* 11 July 70/1, I saw a sled being pulled by an Irish setter, another by a mongrel collie, a third by a pedigreed scottie.

b. Having a criminal record. Cf. *PEDIGREE *sb.* 2 d.
1935 *Amer. Speech* X. 13/1 To have one's record in the possession of the police;..*pedigreed.* **1942** BERREY & VAN DEN BARK *Amer. Thes. Slang* § 461/3 *Pedigreed crook*, one with a police record. **1971** 'A. BLAISDELL' *Practice to Deceive* viii. 112 Rodriguez and D'Arcy were out again hunting the pedigreed sex fiends.

pediment[1]. Add: **1. b.** *Geomorphol.* A broad, gently sloping, eroded rock surface that extends outwards from the abrupt foot of a mountain in arid and semi-arid regions and is usu. slightly concave and partly or wholly covered with a thin layer of alluvium.
This is not the sense in quots. 1882, where the word denotes steep rock slopes roughly triangular in shape, more like architectural pediments.
[**1882** C. E. DUTTON *Tertiary Hist. Grand Cañon District* v. 85 Just opposite to us the pediments seem half buried, or rather half risen out of the valley alluvium. *Ibid.*, Between the alcoves the projecting pediments present gable-ends towards the valley-plain.] **1897** W. J. MCGEE in *Bull. Geol. Soc. Amer.* VIII. 92 The tide-carved coast cuts a typical granitic butte..rising sharply from the inclined foot-slope of Sierra Seri, yet the rugged-faced knob is seen to surmount a granite pediment nearly half a mile across in the line of section. **1922** *Bull. U.S. Geol. Survey* No. 730. 52 The mountains of the Papago country rise from plains which are similar in form to the alluvial plains that commonly front mountains of an arid region, but large parts of the plains are without alluvial cover and are composed of solid rock. These plains are called 'mountain pediments', a term suggested by McGee's usage. *Ibid.* 58 A mountain pediment buried in alluvium may be called a concealed pediment. **1933** [see *PANFAN]. **1935** [see *PEDIPLAIN]. **1960** B. W. SPARKS *Geomorphol.* xi. 257 The sharp break of slope between the pediment and the mountain front seems to point to a change of operative process, but there is no agreement as to the nature of the processes involved. **1974** [see *PEDIPLAIN]. **1977** A. HALLAM *Planet Earth* 85 The low-angle (generally less than about 8°) concave surfaces which coalesce to form the pediplains are called pediments. *Ibid.*, More recently it has been argued that pediments develop through surface and subsurface weathering.

3. pediment pass *Geomorphol.* (see quot. 1930).
1930 C. SAUER in *Univ. Calif. Publ. Geogr.* III. 370 Under less advanced conditions of pediment development we find narrow, flat, rock-floored tongues extending back from the general pediment, but still penetrating along the mountain sufficiently to meet another pediment slope extending into the mountain front from the other side... To distinguish this less advanced feature from the broad saddle plains..we may call it a pediment pass. **1974** C. H. CRICKMAY *Work of River* viii. 206 In a few places, the upper end of the pediment is the smoothly rounded summit of a pediment pass, or rock floored gap through a low mountain ridge.

pedimentation (pedimentēi·ʃən). *Geomorphol.* [f. PEDIMENT[1] + -ATION.] The formation of a pediment.
1948 *Bull. Geol. Soc. Amer.* LIX. 372 Down the slope from the knickpoint pedimentation rapidly reaches stability. **1962** L. C. KING *Morphol. Earth* v. 146 Together, scarp retreat (by gully-head erosion and mass slipping of material) and pedimentation (by bedrock levelling and sheet-waste removal) are the most potent agents modifying epigene landscapes. **1973** *Nature* 9 Nov. 75/2 Recession of valley nickpoints inland from the coastal margin was followed by valley widening, scarp retreat and pedimentation, leading ultimately to the formation of gently undulating pediplains or erosion surfaces.

pedimented, *a.* Add: **2.** *Geomorphol.* Characterized by the presence of pediments (*PEDIMENT[1] 1 b).
1949 *Geol. Mag.* LXXXVI. 249 Pedimented landscapes consist essentially of hillslopes and of pediments. **1960** B. W. SPARKS *Geomorphol.* xi. 258 Landscapes resembling the pedimented areas of the arid south-western parts of the United States are found on an altogether larger scale in Africa.

pediocratic (pediǫkræ·tik), *a.* *Geol.* [f. Gr. πεδίον a plain + κράτ-ος strength + -IC.] Characterized by an overall lessening of relief as a result of erosion predominating over crustal upheaval.
1924 W. RAMSAY in *Geol. Mag.* LXI. 155 During anorogenic periods, again, the continents become more or less peneplained. I call such a condition pediocratic. **1929** L. J. WILLS *Physiogr. Evol. Britain* ii. 7 Even in the pediocratic periods, the non-spectacular phenomena of erosion and deposition, and the ordered changes in the life of the world, given the requisite length of time, produce equally profound modifications in its physiography. **1961** [see *OROCRATIC *a.*].

pediplain (pe·diplēin). *Geomorphol.* [f. PEDI(MENT[1] + PLAIN *sb.*[1]] An extensive plain formed in a desert by the coalescence of neighbouring pediments (believed to represent a late stage in the cycle of erosion in arid and semi-arid climates). Cf. *PEDIPLANE.
1935 MAXSON & ANDERSON in *Jrnl. Geol.* XLIII. 94 Widely extending rock-cut and alluviated surfaces of this type formed by the coalescence of a number of pediments and occasional desert domes may be called 'pediplains'. **1968** C. R. TWIDALE *Geomorphol.* xi. 308 Pediplains,.. like peneplains, are surfaces of low relief, but generally differ from the latter in a number of respects. They are smoother, and less dissected.., they are mostly dominated by concave profiles, and meet the adjacent uplands in a piedmont angle. **1973** [see *PEDIMENTATION]. **1974** C. H. CRICKMAY *Work of River* viii. 211 Where pediments are sufficiently extensive to be conjoint and broadly continuous, the whole is termed a pediplain or a panfan. **1977** A. HALLAM *Planet Earth* 190 The continents as a whole were, however, almost completely worn down to pediplains.

Hence **pe·diplained** *a.*
1970 R. J. SMALL *Study of Landforms* ii. 28 This is one of the explanations of the development, on the pediplained surfaces of South America, Africa and Australia, of very hard weathering crusts.

pediplanation (pediplănēi·ʃən). *Geomorphol.* [f. *PEDI(PLANE, *PEDI(PLAIN + *PLANATION.] Erosion to, or the formation of, a pediplain (or pediplane).
1942 A. D. HOWARD in *Jrnl. Geomorphol.* V. 11 *Pediplanation* may be applied as a general term to the process of formation of pediplanes. **1948** *Proc. Geol. Soc. S. Afr.* L. p. xxvii, Every one of these features is ubiquitous on the terrains of Southern and Central Africa, clear proof that the landscape of those regions has evolved through pediplanation. **1963** D. W. & E. E. HUMPHRIES tr. *Termier's Erosion & Sedimentation* ii. 40 It is on plateaus, sometimes uplifted and peneplained (often those which have undergone initial pediplanation) that desert dunes (Sahara) and ice caps (Scandinavia) have developed. **1975** *Nature* 31 July 442/1 Part 2 discusses the character and development of the tropical terrain and includes chapters ..on pediments and pediplanation.

pediplane (pe·diplēin). *Geomorphol.* [f. PEDI(MENT[1] + PLANE *sb.*[3]] A piedmont slope in arid and semi-arid regions comprising a pediment and a peripediment (or just one of these, if the other is not present). Cf. *PEDIPLAIN.
1942 A. D. HOWARD in *Jrnl. Geomorphol.* V. 11 The writer proposes the term *pediplane* as a general term for all degradational piedmont surfaces produced in arid climates which are either exposed or covered by a veneer of contemporary alluvium no thicker than that which can be moved during floods. *Ibid.* 13 In some localities the upland rocks may be extremely resistant or the basin rocks may be extremely weak... In such regions the pediplane will truncate basin sediments almost exclusively and will consist largely of peripediment. **1948** *Bull. Geol. Soc. Amer.* LIX. 370 In regions of rising base level the pediplane will be made up for the most part of a peripediment, and the pediment as a near-mountain zone cut on solid rock is sometimes overlooked. **1955** *Proc. Geologists' Assoc.* LXVI. 173 The combined pediment and peripediment may then be described as a pediplane (Howard, 1942).

pediscope, var. *PEDOSCOPE.

pediunker (pedĭˌɒ·ŋkəɪ). [Etym. unknown]. A name for the grey petrel, *Procellaria cinerea*, originally used in the island of Tristan da Cunha, where this bird is common.
1910 K. M. BARROW *Three Yrs. in Tristan da Cunha* 275 The 'Pediunker' lays in May and June; it is like a petrel. **1923** A. H. MACKLIN in F. Wild *Shackleton's Last Voy.* xii. 253 Gordon Glass had with him his dog, which occasionally discovered a 'pediunker', a species of seabird which frequents the island [*sc.* Tristan da Cunha]. **1952** J. FISHER *Fulmar* xvi. 381 Barnacles on birds are rare, though they have been found in the tail-feathers of the sub-antarctic *Adamastor cinereus*, the pediunker or grey petrel. **1967** B. ROBERTS *Wilson's Birds of Antarctic* 139/2 Grey Petrel or Pediunker, *Procellaria cinerea.* Drawings of a recently killed adult ♂.

pedo- (pe·do, pedǫ·, pĭdǫ·), or before a vowel **ped-**, repr. Gr. πέδον ground, earth, is used in the sense 'soil' in *PEDOLOGY and other technical terms.

pedocal (pe·dokæl). *Soil Sci.* [f. *PEDO- + CAL(CIUM.] A soil that contains a layer of accumulated calcium carbonate (generally characteristic of dry climates). Cf. *PEDALFER.
1928 C. F. MARBUT in *Proc. & Papers 1st Internat. Congr. Soil Sci.* IV. 20 A formal definition of the two groups is as follows: I. Includes all soils in whose maturely developed profiles no higher percentage of lime carbonate is found than in the parent material beneath them and in which either a shifting or an accumulation of sesquioxide and in many cases both, has taken place. II. Includes all soils with fully developed profiles in which lime carbonate is found on some horizon in the solum in higher percentage than in the parent geological formation beneath... The name *Pedalfers* is suggested as a designation for the soils of group I, and *Pedocals* for those of group II. **1938** *Nature* 21 May 925/2 It has been generally accepted that the climate of Great Britain is too wet for pedocals to develop. **1949** F. J. PETTIJOHN *Sedimentary Rocks* xii. 384 The pedalfers and pedocals are subdivided into many soil types. **1968** [see *halomorphic* adj. s.v. *HALO-]. **1972** J. G. CRUICKSHANK *Soil Geogr.* v. 158 Marbut..established a classification that became the most widely known of the schemes based on soil genesis, in which he made the two-fold primary sub-division between the leached soils (pedalfers) and the non-leached (pedocals) freely drained soils. **1977** A. HALLAM *Planet Earth* 179 These ideas were accepted in the USA, and the concepts of pedalfers and pedocals added: pedalfers are leached soils in humid areas where aluminium and iron accumulate in the B horizon, and pedocals occur in more arid regions.

Hence **pedoca·lic** *a.*
1928 *Proc. & Papers 1st Internat. Congr. Soil Sci.* IV. 23 Most of the groups of Pedalferic soils in category V were defined by Russian pedologists, but they made no attempt to differentiate the Pedocalic soils on the same basis since the Eurasian conditions do not present an opportunity for doing it. **1938** *Nature* 21 May 925/1 (*heading*) Pedocalic tendencies in soils of southern England. **1941** H. JENNY *Factors Soil Formation* vi. 191 Not all soils that are embraced by the area labeled as pedocals contain lime horizons. Only those soils which have the required normal topography and which have attained sufficient maturity deserve the attribute pedocalic.

pedogenesis (pedodʒe·nėsis). [f. *PEDO- + -GENESIS.] Soil formation.
1936 J. S. JOFFE *Pedology* vi. 134 From the point of view of pedogenesis, the classification of the soil-forming processes, in their broad aspects, should hinge on the elements of climate. **1943** *Proc. Soil Sci. Soc. Amer.* VII. 187/1 Most investigations on mechanical separates of the soil have dealt with the physical aspects of the subject, with no relation to pedogenesis and agropedologic implications. **1963** D. W. & E. E. HUMPHRIES tr. *Termier's Erosion & Sedimentation* vi. 135 During pedogenesis (soil formation), the nature of the alteration of the titanium minerals depends more upon chemical diagenetic environmental conditions than on the nature of the parent rock. **1972** J. G. CRUICKSHANK *Soil Geogr.* ii. 42 As part of the role of climate in pedogenesis, its moisture and temperature components also affect the rate of decay and incorporation into the soil of surface organic litter.

Hence **pedogene·tic, -gene·tical** *adjs.* = *PEDOGENIC *a.*; **pedogene·tically** *adv.*
1946 *Soil Sci.* LXI. 389 Each soil series..is thus pedogenetically connected with ten other series. **1950** *Ann. Assoc. Amer. Geographers* XL. 218 Within these pedogenetic regions no one of the weathering processes occurs exclusively. **1963** D. W. & E. E. HUMPHRIES tr. *Termier's Erosion & Sedimentation* vi. 153 Butterlin (1958) believes that these soils are formed by the pedogenetic alteration of the limestones. **1978** *Nature* 30 Mar. 477/3 Work on pedogenetical formations and Quaternary deposits in central and northern Dobrudja. *Ibid.* 28 Sept. 285/2 Deeper, pedogenetically differentiated profiles in relict areas immune from rapid denudation.

pedogenic (pedodʒe·nik), *a.* [f. *PEDO- + *-GENIC.] Soil-forming.
1924 *Geol. Mag.* LXI. 448 (*heading*) The pedogenic processes. [*Note*] I am indebted to my friend Dr. Edward Greenly, F.G.S., for this convenient term, which aptly describes the processes of soil formation and metamorphism. **1936** *Nature* 24 Oct. 729/2 The effect of human interference as a pedogenic factor was raised in the discussion. **1943** [see *palæopedology* s.v. *PALÆO-, PALEO-]. **1975**

Nature 20 Feb. 617/2 The carbonate nodules which occur in the Pleistocene but not in the Holocene portions of the core are regarded as pedogenic and as symptomatic of a soil climate drier than the present one.

Hence **pedoge·nically** *adv.*

1972 J. G. CRUICKSHANK *Soil Geogr.* iii. 74 The upper boundary is obvious, but the lower one may be either the maximum plant rooting depth or the base of the pedogenically altered material.

pedology (pe-, pĭdǫ·lŏdʒi). [f. *PEDO- + -OLOGY. Cf. G. *pedologie* (e.g. F. A. Fallou *Pedologie* (1862) I. 9), Russ. *pedológiya* (e.g. *Entsikl. Slovar'* (1898) XXIVA s.v. *pochvovedenie*; *Pochvovedenie* (1900) II. 140, (1902) IV. 1; the Fr. title of this periodical was *La Pédologie* from its inception in 1899).

The usual Russ. word for the subject has always been *pochvovédenie*, lit. 'soil science' (cf. G. *bodenkunde*, given by Fallou as a synonym of *pedologie*). The Eng. word *pedology* occurs in the galley proofs of an unpublished dict. of *c* 1900–10, according to L. D. Stamp *Gloss. Geogr. Terms* (1961) 358, but prob. only in reference to foreign equivalents.]

The scientific study of soil, esp. its formation, nature, and classification; soil science.

[**1923** M. M. McCOOL et al. in *Soil Sci.* XVI. 106 It places soil study on a natural basis and in fact lays the foundation of a new science which we might name, podology.] **1924** G. W. ROBINSON in *Geol. Mag.* LXI. 444 (*heading*) Pedology as a branch of geology. [*Note*] The writer ventures to hope that this convenient term (Gr. πέδον = soil or earth) will be more generally used to describe the scientific study of soils. **1926** TANSLEY & CHIPP *Study of Vegetation* vii. 114 The science of the soil (sometimes called pedology) has made very great strides within the past quarter of a century. **1938** A. B. YOLLAND tr. *A. A. J. de Sigmond's Princ. Soil Sci.* 1 The first to try to liberate soil science from this position was the German geologist Frederick Augustus Fallon, who, however, by basing his soil classification upon geological-petrographic principles unconsciously subordinated pedology to geology. **1958** I. W. CORNWALL *Soils for Archaeologist* 13 For information about the earth the archaeologist turns first to the sciences of geology, geography and pedology (soil-science). **1973** *Nature* 27 July p. ii/1 (Advt.), Scientists interested in sediments and in allied fields such as pedology, geomorphology, soils engineering and cement technology will find in this book a valuable research tool.

Hence **pedolo·gic, -lo·gical** *adjs.*, of or pertaining to pedology or soil; **pedolo·gically** *adv.*, in pedological terms; as regards pedology; **pedo·logist,** one who studies pedology.

1924 *Geol. Mag.* LXI. 450 Among mature soils, i.e. among soils which have reached a state of pedological equilibrium. *Ibid.* 454 The remaining class in Glinka's scheme is only of limited interest for western European pedologists. **1927** C. F. MARBUT tr. *Glinka's Great Soil Groups* 5 The distribution of such soil units also would be the same as that of the rocks from which derived and would be petrographic rather than pedologic. **1932** *Proc. & Papers 2nd Internat. Congr. Soil Sci.* V. 1 If it be pedologically justifiable to grant the type status to podzols. **1945** *Antiquity* XIX. 172 The pedological characters of Anglesey by which vegetation would be affected and to a large extent controlled. **1963** D. W. & E. E. HUMPHRIES tr. *Termier's Erosion & Sedimentation* ix. 192 Sedimentation in these basins..depends to a large extent on the pedologic evolution of the continents. **1964** R. FEYS in A. E. M. Nairn *Probl. Palaeoclimatol.* iii. 68 The sandstone is derived from sand which has been pedologically altered and mechanically sorted. **1972** J. G. CRUICKSHANK *Soil Geogr.* v. 159 The Marbut classification also influenced pedologists on an international level because it was discussed at international soil congresses in 1927, 1932, and 1935. **1974** *Nature* 4 Jan. 74/1 There was no known method by which termites or pedological processes could bring about the observed accumulation of calcium carbonate in termite mounds.

pedon (pe·dǫn). *Soil Sci.* [a. Gr. πέδον ground, earth.] A notional column of soil that extends vertically from the surface to the parent material and is of sufficient area (usu. at least a square metre) to be representative of the surrounding soil and its horizons.

1960 SIMONSON & GARDINER in *Trans. 7th Internat. Congr. Soil Sci.* IV. 128 Nature of the Pedon. It has recently been proposed that the term, pedon.., be used as a generic term for small basic soil entities. [*Note*] The term was proposed by Guy D. Smith. *Ibid.* 129 A pedon consists of a small volume of soil which includes the full solum and the upper part of the unconsolidated parent material.., is usually less than 2 meters in depth, and has a lateral cross section that is roughly circular or hexagonal in shape and between 1 and 10 square meters in size. **1972** J. G. CRUICKSHANK *Soil Geogr.* iii. 76 Pedons have such minimal horizontal area that often they fail to reflect important features of the larger soil body. **1973** THOMPSON & TROEH *Soils & Soil Fertility* (ed. 3) xvi. 369 Soils with large variations in their properties within short horizontal distances are allowed to have pedons as large as 10 sq m.. so that their properties may be fully represented.

pedophilia, etc., varr. *PÆDOPHILIA, etc.

pedoscope (pe·dŏskōup). Also **pediscope.** [f. PEDI- (erron. *pedo-*) + -SCOPE.] An X-ray machine for showing the fitting and movement of the feet inside shoes (formerly common in shoe shops).

1923 *Chambers's Jrnl.* Aug. 560/1 The machine used is called the pedoscope. **1959** *Times* 30 Apr. 6/5 The use of pedoscopes, although frowned on by the Medical Research Council, was not diminishing. **1967** *Punch* 22 Nov. 792/3 In one of the earliest scenes Harry, given a vacuum flask to smuggle to Helsinki, finds out what is inside by putting it under the X-ray of a shoe-shop's pediscope.

pedosphere (pe·dosfīəɹ). *Geol.* [f. *PEDO- + SPHERE *sb.*] The earth's soil layer.

1938 S. MATTSON in *Lantbrukshögskolans Ann.* V. 261 Soils might be said to represent the sum of the mechanical and the products of the chemical interaction of the four spheres: the lithosphere, the hydrosphere, the atmosphere and the biosphere. They constitute a dispersed system in which the material from these four spheres alternate as dispersed phase and dispersion medium. To this sphere of spheres the name of pedosphere has been given. **1946** *Nature* 6 July 31/1 G. A. Maximovich..has calculated the average porosities of different types of rocks and has also calculated the average porosities of the geospheres. These, in percentages, are as follows: pedosphere (soils), 55; [etc.]. **1968** R. W. FAIRBRIDGE *Encycl. Geomorphol.* 416/1 On top of this [*sc.* the lithosphere] the continents have an additional soil layer or pedosphere with a depth generally of only 1–2 meters.

Pedrail (pe·drēil). *Obs.* exc. *Hist.* [f. PED(I- + RAIL *sb.*[2]] A type of traction engine, patented in 1899 and 1902 by B. J. Diplock; it moves forward by means of articulated feet, instead of wheels, which support rollers upon which run rails fixed to the vehicle itself.

1902 *Daily Chron.* 29 Dec. 6/6 A recent invention of Mr. Diplock—the 'Pedrail'—was exhibited. **1903** *Ibid.* 23 Nov. 6/4 The Pedrail was primarily designed as a traction engine for the transport of heavy goods on common roads. **1908** *Chambers's Jrnl.* Mar. 270/1 The ped-rail traction-engine—an engine equipped with a number of feet placed around the periphery of its driving-wheels, thereby imparting a walking action. **1916** *Ibid.* Feb. 83/1 This device is called the pedrail, and consists of a flat chain round the wheels.., the chain being armed with discs offering a flat surface to the ground. **1959** W. J. HUGHES *Cent. of Traction Engines* xvi. 212 At the beginning of 1902 some interesting experiments were being carried out with Diplock's 'Pedrail' engine... The particular engine under notice..besides having the Pedrail wheels,..had four-wheel drive. **1960** R. H. CLARK *Devel. Engl. Traction Engine* xiv. 291 In Diplock's Pedrail the rail (the bottom concave run) runs over the feet by virtue of the rollers interposed between them.

pedro (pe·dro). Also with capital initial. [f. Sancho *Pedro*, the name of a U.S. card game.] **a.** A variant of the card game Sancho Pedro in which the sancho, or nine of trumps, does not count. **b.** The name for the five of trumps in such games. Cf. *CINCH *sb.* 3, *SANCHO[2].

1874 *Reno* (Nevada) *Crescent* 8 May 2/3 The five of trumps is 'pedro'. **1876** *Avalanche* (Silver City, Idaho) 15 Mar. 2/3 Whist, pedro, pool.., etc., seem to be flourishing pastimes. **1880** W. B. DICK *Amer. Hoyle* (ed. 13) 210 Pedro may be taken with any trump higher than the Five. **1929** R. S. & H. M. LYND *Middletown* 281 The growing rigidity of the social system today is centering parties more and more upon cards, pedro among the workers and bridge among the others. **1944** A. H. MOREHEAD *Pocket Bk. Games* 199 Auction Pitch has many variants. Most of them—Pedro, Pedro Sancho, Dom Pedro, Snoozer—have been swallowed up by their own ultimate creation, Cinch. **1947** *Sat. Even. Post* 17 May 102/3 He operates a pedro game.

pee (pī), *v.*[2] *colloq.* [f. initial letter of PISS *v.*] **1.** *intr.* To urinate. Hence **pee·ing** *vbl. sb.*

1879–80 *Pearl* (1970) 216 Your private parts, or cunny, Should not be let for money, They're only meant to pee with. **1886** in F. T. ELWORTHY *West Somerset Word-Bk.* **1929** C. CONNOLLY *Let.* Nov. in *Romantic Friendship* (1975) 329 It [*sc.* a kinkajou] seemed just a machine for shitting and peeing. **1932** AUDEN *Orators* II. 78 The boys, out of control, imbibe Vimto through india-rubber tubing, openly pee into the ink-pots. **1948** M. MCCARTHY in *Partisan Rev.* Mar. 227 'My God', you yell..'can't a man pee in his own house?' **1960** C. DAY LEWIS *Buried Day* 74 How to leave the room during lessons—I solved..by peeing in my trousers. **1963** M. MCCARTHY *Group* iii. 56 Anybody..who wandered in to pee during a cocktail party. **1965** J. R. HETHERINGTON *Selina's Aunt* 50, I could laugh till I peed. **1966** A. LA BERN *Goodbye Piccadilly* xi. 109, I kept wanting to pee every few minutes. **1969** P. ROTH *Portnoy's Complaint* 132 Here is how I learnt to pee into the bowl like a big man. **1971** N. SAUNDERS *Alternative London* (ed. 2) 236 As above for ladies, not so easily cured though peeing just after sex is meant to help. **1973** M. AMIS *Rachel Papers* 74 She looked fretful, importunate, almost bouncing up and down, like a little girl wanting to pee. **1975** *Sunday Times* (Colour Suppl.) 23 Feb. 26/2 The guys were forever peeing over the side so there was piss everywhere.

2. a. *trans.* To wet by urinating.

1788 E. PICKEN *Epitaph Favourite Cat* in *Poems & Epistles* 47 He never stealt, though he was poor, Nor ever pee'd his master's floor. **1948** D. BALLANTYNE *Cunninghams* 219 She nearly pees her pants every time he kids to her.

b. *refl.* To urinate into one's clothes; esp. (hyperbolically) in phr. *to pee oneself laughing.*

1946 G. KERSH *Clean, Bright & Slightly Oiled* i. 4 Even the Sarn-Major peed 'imself laughing. **1962** K. ORVIS *Damned & Destroyed* xv. 104 You did wrong to hit..so much... I peed myself. **1978** R. BUSBY *Garvey's Code* xii. 168 He must've realized what was going to happen.. because he peed himself right there.

pee (pī), *sb.*[5] [f. prec.] **1.** An act of urination.

1902 R. MACLAGAN *Evil Eye* 51 The milk has gone along with the pee. **1946** G. MILLAR *Horned Pigeon* xii. 156 The urinals alone would have a monument the size of London's Cenotaph... When they opened the sewer trap in the monumental pee-house great clouds of mosquitoes..rose from the opening. **1951** S. SPENDER *World within World* 273 In Russia it's so cold that when you do a pee, you can break it off in sticks. **1958** L. DURRELL *Mountolive* xiii. 244, I must just do a pee. **1966** J. CHAMIER *Cannonball* xiii. 119 Best go and have a pee, lad. **1973** *Daily Tel.* (Colour Suppl.) 23 Feb. 54/1 If people came in just to use the lavatory, he would ask them for their address 'in case I need a pee when I'm passing your house'.

2. Urine.

1961 H. RUDD *Shores of Schizophrenia* in *My Escape from CIA* (1966) 10 That gloomy, hideous building, with its smell of cedar sawdust and stale, infantile pee. **1968** R. P. WARREN *Incarnations* 43 Jesus, Wouldn't just *being* be enough without Having to have the pee..knocked out of You by a 1957 yellow Cadillac. **1971** J. OSBORNE *West of Suez* I. 42 Do you know what the cure for chilblains was then? Soaking your feet and hands in your own pee. **1976** P. CAVE *High Flying Birds* ii. 16 Sarcasm runs off on them like pee on a plastic bedsheet.

pee (pī), *sb.*[6] *colloq.* [f. initial letter of PENNY.] Representing the pronunciation of the initial letter of 'penny', i.e. a new penny, a unit of decimal currency introduced in Britain on 15 Feb. 1971. See also *p* s.v. *P II, *PENNY I. 1.

The pronunciation of *p.* as (pī) is common in everyday speech but is avoided by many people, who prefer (pe·ni) (as singular) and (pens) (as pl.).

1971 *Observer* 14 Feb. 9/5 Everyone at the Decimal Currency Board has taken to calling new pence 'pee'. **1972** *Daily Tel.* 9 Aug. 16 If Mr Broca had contacted us we would have sold him one not for 'seventy-eight pees', but for 69p. **1974** *Punch* 6 Mar. 362/2 The Scandinavian revenue men..intimating that it's either an immediate fifty pee in the £ or chuck the belongings back into the red-spotted hankie and ring up a mini cab. **1974** R. RENDELL *Face of Trespass* ii. 23 May I trouble you for forty-two pee? **1974** *Observer* (Colour Suppl.) 15 Dec. 13/4 Few could be bothered to say 'new pence' for the decimal stuff, so we used 'pee', and that is what we are lumbered with today. **1976** *Times Lit. Suppl.* 2 Apr. 388/1 A small boy on the loose in London with a million pound picture in a laundry bag and 'two pee' in his pocket. **1977** *Transatlantic Rev.* LX. 187 He was accosted by a group of rotting cider bums: 'Mister..we just need ten pee to get ourselves another bottle.'

peek, *sb.*[1] (Earlier and later examples.)

1844 'J. SLICK' *High Life N.Y.* II. 41, I jest give a peak in for a minit, and streaked it upstairs. **1869** L. M. ALCOTT *Little Women* II. xx. 300 'Ain't it a sight to see her settin' there,'..muttered old Hannah, who could not resist frequent 'peeks' through the slide. **1938** E. AMBLER *Cause for Alarm* vii. 116 Supposing you take an occasional peek at these other guys' hands, tell me what you see. **1969** *Daily Mail* 16 Jan. 5/1 After insertion into Earth orbit I had a lot of tests to perform on the spacecraft systems but, like all the rookies before me, I must confess to a sneak peek out of the window. **1973** P. EVANS *Bodyguard Man* 10, I poked my head out and took a peek. **1974** *Black World* Sept. 40 When you get inside cock your eyes ace-deuce and snatch a peek around. **1976** *National Observer* (U.S.) 24 Jan. 19/2 He was to proceed to Cairo, take a peek at Mecca, and head west across the bulge of Africa until he either sighted the Niger or fell into it.

b. *Comb.*, as *peek-hole*, a peep-hole.

1910 'MARK TWAIN' *Speeches* 222, I peeked through the little peek-holes they have in theatre curtains. **1927** G. ADE et al. *Let.* 4 Mar. (1973) 117 Gibraltar..is honeycombed with tunnels, which the visitor is not permitted to see, and from those tunnels there are peek-holes out of which guns can be pointed in any direction. **1927** *Sat. Even. Post* 24 Dec. 12/2 That's Fred's peek hole, where he sees out of. **1930** E. POUND *XXX Cantos* xvii. 79 One eye for the sea, for that peek-hole.

peek, *v.*[1] Add: (Further examples.) Also, to glance *at*. Hence **pee·king** *vbl. sb.*

1928 *Publishers' Weekly* 22 Sept. 1120/1 One cannot escape the temptation to peek at prices however and I found one marked six shillings and took it. **1947** AUDEN *Age of Anxiety* (1948) ii. 38 Pushing through brambles, I peeked out at Her fascination. **1953** *Manch. Guardian Weekly* 29 Jan. 4 A coloured butler peeked out of a cream-coloured door. **1962** K. ORVIS *Damned & Destroyed* vii. 49 When I went in [to jail] they didn't even ask for peekings. **1968** *Globe & Mail* (Toronto) 15 Jan. 21/7 Jerry Tighe, of Whitworth College in Spokane, came close to a fall in the men's two miles when he peeked over his shoulder to check the field. **1973** 'S. HARVESTER' *Corner of Playground* III. i. 165 Are you so bored with me you must peek at other men? **1973** *Black World* June 10/2 The vain Southern belle who undresses in front of the stable boy and then tells her 'Daddy' that he peeked. **1973** *Radio Times* 20 Dec. 100/4 What's he getting for Christmas?.. 'Absolutely no peeking before Christmas morning.' **1976** D. HEFFRON *Crusty Crossed* ix. 71 'It's time you learned the difference,' she called out after me, 'between high-class spying and low-down peeking.'

peek-bo, peek-a-boo. Delete 'now chiefly *U.S.*' and add further examples. Also *attrib.* and as *vb.*

The spelling *peek-a-boo* is now usual.

1903 [see *high sign* s.v. *HIGH *a.* 21]. **1922** JOYCE *Ulysses* 46 Peekaboo. I see you. **1940** S. O'CASEY *Let.* 19 May (1975) I. 862 I'm..kicking football with Niall; & peek a boo with Shivaun. **1950** G. BARKER *True Confession* ii. 10 But Memory flirts with seven veils Peekabooing the accidental. **1960** *Times* 22 June 5/5 Covering up behind his high 'peek-a-boo' guard, he [*sc.* Floyd Patterson] rode out the brief crisis. **1967** S. BECKETT *Stories & Texts for Nothing* 124 But peekaboo here I come again, just when most needed.

b. Used *attrib.* and *absol.* of various garments decorated with holes (see quots.).

1895 *Montgomery Ward Catal.* 306/3 Child's Sun Bonnet, made of printed lawn, peek-a-boo front. **1906** *Daily Chron.* 16 Aug. 8/1 The dreamer is embowered in soft cushions, and being punted by a River Girl, in a peek-a-boo blouse—all grace and lissomness and tan and bare arms. **1906** *Springfield* (Mass.) *Weekly Republ.* 10 May 13 In San Francisco there is no winter suit and summer suit. The same medium-weight garment is worn the year round and the peek-a-boo waist is unknown. **1907** *Westm. Gaz.* 21 Sept. 3/2 'The Peek-a-boo blouse'..is as popular here as in America. **1910** 'Mark Twain' *Speeches* 87 Why not adopt some of the women's styles?.. Take the peek-a-boo waist, for instance. **1913** *Maclean's Mag.* Aug. 103/1 The wars upon cigarettes, bridge whist and peekaboo waists are passing madnesses. **1930** M. Sullivan *Our Times* III. 499 A shirt-waist, supposed to be an extreme of daring, in which embroidered perforations permitted sight of female epidermis upon the arms and as much as two inches below the nape of the neck, was called the 'peek-a-boo'. **1957** M. B. Picken *Fashion Dict.* 246/2 *Peek-a-boo waist*, shirt-waist of eyelet or sheer fabric. **1959** J. Braine *Vodi* xiv. 195 The peekaboo blouse..now seemed vulgar, a barmaid's uniform. *Ibid.* 196 A naughty little girl who wore peekaboo blouses. **1969** R. T. Wilcox *Dict. Costume* (1970) 263/2 *Peek-a-boo blouse*, a shirtwaist of sheer lawn, voile or eyelet embroidery, a popular fashion of the 1890's and the first decade of the twentieth century. It was worn over a lacy, frilled corset cover. **1972** 'E. McBain' *Sadie when she Died* x. 107 Carella..wondered if he should tell Teddy about the brunette in the peekaboo blouse.

c. Used *attrib.* and *absol.* of a woman's hairstyle (see quots.).

1948 M. M. Miller *Winchester's Screen Encycl.* 117/2 Her 'peek-a-boo' style secured major part for her, under new name Veronica Lake. **1966** J. S. Cox *Illustr. Dict. Hairdressing* 109/2 *Peekaboo locks*, hanging hair that partly conceals the face and eyes. **1968** J. Ironside *Fashion Alphabet* 195 *Peek-a-boo*, hair style that originated..in 1941. The hair was cut so that it hung about 8 inches below the shoulders; in front it covered one eye and was softly waved to the end. **1973** *Daily Tel.* 9 July 17/3 Veronica Lake, the filmstar who was famous in the 1940s for her 'peek-a-boo' hairstyle, died in Vermont, America, on Saturday of acute hepatitis. *Ibid.*, The peek-a-boo hairstyle—long blonde tresses hanging over her right eye—disappeared in 1943 after the United States Government made an official request to Paramount to cut her hair.

peel, *sb.*[1] Add: **4.** (Further examples in spelling *pele.*)

1888 W. W. Tomlinson *Comprehensive Guide Northumberland* 156 Jutting crags..and lofty precipices, constitute the natural defences of the pele on three sides. **1921** P. S. Allen *Let.* 21 Sept. (1939) 180 It is built out of the Prior's Lodgings, and includes a regular 'pele tower' such as line the Border: low towers with immensely thick walls—this one 7 ft. thick at the bottom, but with mural chambers and staircases. **1964** *Dumfries & Galloway Standard* 8 July 7, The lost Dalswinton, Conggleton and Wigtown, the pele at Lochmaben are a story in themselves. **1973** Fedden & Joekes *National Trust Guide* 656 *Pele, pele tower*, a small or moderate-sized tower or keep which is easily defended. Peculiar to houses or castles on both sides of the Scottish border. Generally built between the 13th and 15th centuries.

6. peel-tower (further examples of spelling *pele-tower*).

1935 *Hist. Northumberland* XIV. 79 This [*sc.* Henry VIII to Charles I] forms a continuously evolving period, at first characterised by the erection of pele towers and bastle houses. **1965** N. Ridley *Portrait of Northumberland* 21 Scattered over wide areas of Northumberland are the Pele towers... These Pele towers were fortified dwellings, where the cattle could be driven into the ground floor rooms, to protect them from the Reivers and Moss Troopers. **1973** Fedden & Joekes *National Trust Guide* 325 Consequently a wide area is studded with massive pele towers, commonly with a vaulted chamber on the ground floor into which cattle might be driven at the first warning of raiders, and upper storeys arranged for human occupation. **1980** *Historic Houses, Castles & Gardens* 48/3 Hutton-in-the-Forest..14th cent. Pele Tower with later additions.

peel, *sb.*[3] Add: **2.** *Rugby Football.* The action of peeling from a set formation (see *peel *v.*[1] 5 g).

1973 *Scotsman* 21 Feb. 18/6 Thus, when it comes to deflecting the ball for a peel, Strachan prefers to operate from No. 8 where there is a little more scope for manoeuvre. **1978** *Sunday Express* 19 Mar. 31/4 From yet another winning line-out by Martin, Graham Price slipped him a pass on the peel and Edwards lofted over a towering drop goal.

peel, *sb.*[4] (Later examples.)

1890 J. Kerr *Hist. Curling* 240 He absolutely refused to play his stone on one occasion when the game stood peels. **1918** *Kelso Chron.* 4 Oct. 3 The players were 'peels' at 12. **1956** in *Sc. Nat. Dict.* (1968) VII. 70/2 The sides finished peels.

peel (pīl), *sb.*[6] [see *peel *v.*[3]] In Croquet, the action of peeling.

1907 C. D. Locock *Mod. Croquet Tactics* xi. 145 The croquet term 'Peel' is derived from the eminent player of that name. *Ibid.* 146 This peeling generally..takes place in the course of a single break; but sometimes, and especially in Doubles, it is worth while to go for a peel on the captain of the other side. **1914** Ld. Tollemache *Croquet* xviii. 111 In Handicap games it is frequently impossible to win without a Peel of some sort. **1932** *Times Lit. Suppl.* 18 Aug. 580/2 Like golfers its [*sc.* croquet's] devotees discuss it in mystical terms of 'tices', 'peels' and 'three-ball breaks'. **1953** *Times* 17 Feb. 3/7 Cotter used the turn to its fullest advantage and finished the match with a triple peel. **1974** *Observer* 23 June 40/3 Triple peels (three in a row) were commonplace at Cheltenham.

peel, *v.*[1] Add: **3. b.** (Further examples.) Also, to remove or separate (a label, bank-note, etc.) by peeling. Also *fig.*

1868 Browning *Ring & Bk.* I. 17 Also he peeled off that last scandal-rag Of Nepotism. **1896** 'Mark Twain' in *Harper's Mag.* Aug. 358/1 He peeled off one of his bulliest old-time blessings, with as many layers to it as an onion. **1946** E. O'Neill *Iceman Cometh* (1947) i. 75 He pulls a big roll from his pocket and peels off a ten-dollar bill. **1971** M. McCarthy *Birds of America* 181 With his thumbnail, unobtrusively, he peeled off the price-tag. **1977** *Monitor* (McAllen, Texas) 31 May 1B/1 She got out of the car and peeled off her gloves. **1977** H. Fast *Immigrants* I. 35 He..took out a wad of bills, peeling off two fives and two singles. **1978** D. Murphy *Place Apart* xii. 259 We *must* peel off the terrorist labels and look at the individuals underneath.

e. *to peel one's eyes*: to keep one's eyes peeled. See Peeled 4 b in Dict. and Suppl.

1875 J. G. Holland *Sevenoaks* xii. 161 An' peel yer eyes, Mike, for I'm goin' to show ye some thin' that'll s'prise ye. **1947** A. Miller *All my Sons* I. 12 Now go out, and keep both eyes peeled... A policeman don't ask questions. Now peel them eyes! **1976** T. Heald *Let Sleeping Dogs Die* v. 99 I've been peeling my eyes... There are some funny goings-on going on.

5. a. (Further examples.) Also const. *off.*

1879 *Boy's Own Paper* 18 Jan. 2/1 'Look sharp and peel!' cried our captain. So we hurried to the tent and promptly divested ourselves of our outer garments. **1922** [see *dishybilly]. **1922** Joyce *Ulysses* 490 Come and I'll peel off. **1950** *Variety* 13 Dec. 1/5 The gals are peelin' in 23 clubs through Los Angeles County.

e. *to peel off, away* (Aeronaut.): to veer from a straight course, esp. one alongside another aircraft; to break away from an airborne formation. (Said of the aircraft or of the pilot.) Also *transf.*

1941 *Christian Science Monitor* 6 Mar. 4/8 Other fanciful R.A.F. Terms include..'peeling off', for veering away from another aircraft. **1941** *N.Y. Times* 27 July 21/2 To 'peel off' is to curve away from another aircraft—the movement as one machine comes up close to another and then slants away is supposed to resemble the act of peeling off the skin of a banana. **1941** *Reader's Digest* Dec. 59/2 Our fighters seemed to be doing a good job on the Huns because only one peeled off to attack us. **1943** Hunt & Pringle *Service Slang* 51 *Peel off*,..to break away from a formation in order to meet an attack, or to leave a squadron to initiate an attack. **1945** *News Chron.* 7 June 3/1 The Spitfire came out of the clouds high above us, peeled off in our direction, circled around for a bit and then, apparently satisfied, made off. **1953** 'N. Shute' *In Wet* vii. 212 He dismissed the escort [of fighter aircraft].., and they peeled away up into the clear blue sky. **1976** A. White *Long Silence* vii. 53 We had picked up our fighter escort... Every so often, one of them would peel off and sweep an observation circuit. **1976** *Shooting Times & Country Mag.* 16–22 Dec. 29/2, I shot at another goose which peeled off, flew fluttering for a hundred yards, and then windmilled down stone dead. **1977** M. Babson *Lord Mayor of Death* xviii. 191 The police car..peeled away from the procession and sped for open ground.

f. To leave, depart; to move *off* in another direction. Also *transf.* and *fig.*

1952 S. Selvon *Brighter Sun* iii. 52 'Well, one for de road, Ah peeling off now,' and after the drink he waved his hand and departed. **1958** *Times Lit. Suppl.* 31 Oct. 621/3 The drug-peddling charlatan artist peels off with the German homosexual who has more money than he knows what to do with. **1960** *Tamarack Rev.* xiv. 25 The way he have it figure out, if he stay in the work he have now, he going to be able to peel off and spend the summer on the Continent. **1968** *Surfer Mag.* Jan. 47/3 Ten-foot waves that peel off in good right and left slides. **1968** W. Warwick *Surfriding in N.Z.* 21/2 When waves break over a sandbar they tend to either dump or peel off along the beach depending on the level of the tide. **1970** N. Armstrong et al. *First on Moon* ii. 38 Just short of the point where a main highway peels off westward.., motels and cocktail lounges..nest alongside gleaming new buildings. **1974** D. Gray *Dead Give Away* v. 54 'What do we do between tea and dinner?' asked Tony. 'I peel off to my room and read,' said Bob. **1976** *Sounds* 11 Dec. 29/4 The rhythm picks up and Ponty and Stuermer run up and down a soaring, emotive riff together before peeling off to indulge in their own fantasies in turn.

g. *spec.* In Rugby football, to move *off* in various directions from a set formation. Also const. without *off.*

1960 *Times* 24 Oct. 14/1 It was a joy to watch the smooth way in which they peeled off from a tight scrummage. **1960** *Rugby World* Nov. 6/2 From the line-out.. they aim to burst through frontally, either by the now familiar 'peeling off' method introduced by their late captain, Lucien Mias, or by extending the line and creating gaps through which a break can be made. **1963** *Times* 28 Jan. 4/6 Abetted by little Lacroix at their heels, they peeled off in all directions in concerted changes of the focal point of attack. **1970** *Times* 13 Apr. 6 Wiltshire peeled from the lineout for a try after five minutes of incessant pressure. **1977** *Western Mail* (Cardiff) 5 Mar. 18/1 They were trailing only 6-7 at the interval after No. 8 Roger Lane had peeled from a close range scrum to put Adrian Jones diving at full stretch for a try.

peel, *v.*[2] Add: Also in wider use in *Curling.* (Later examples.)

1921 *Glasgow Herald* 25 Aug. 4/7 The Scottish Tourists ..played a two-rink game [of bowls] at Balham yesterday, 'peeling' at 19 on one and losing the other by 12. **1950** *Scotsman* 9 Aug. 7/3 The players peeled at several stages in the game and were 17–17 at the seventeenth end. **1962** *Even. Dispatch* (Edinburgh) 29 Jan. 7 The last named fought back in the closing stages to peel the game [*sc.* curling] at 11 at the 13th. **1969** R. Welsh *Beginner's Guide Curling* iv. 33 *Peels*, to be equal in shots. **1971** *Rand Daily Mail* 27 Mar. 23/3 Thomson..came back into the game and peeled 15–15 on the 20th end.

peel (pīl), *v.*[3] [f. the name of Walter H. *Peel*, founder of the All England Croquet Assoc. and a leading exponent of the practice.] In Croquet, to send a ball other than one's own through a hoop. So **pee·ling** *vbl. sb.*[2], **peeled** *ppl. a.*[2]

1899 L. B. Williams *Croquet* iv. 123 Closely allied to this idea that the partners must be kept together at all hazards and, in a measure, dependent upon it, is the notion that it is a player's duty to put his partner through a hoop when the balls are both for the same point. This manœuvre is occasionally necessary, especially at the last hoop. It is called 'peeling', after its greatest exponent, the late Mr. Walter Peel... Mr. Peel practised it with great accuracy and success. **1914** Ld. Tollemache *Croquet* xviii. 110 The attempt is sometimes made in the second break to 'Peel' your first ball through its remaining Hoops during the course of your second break. **1960** E. P. C. Cotter *Tackle Croquet this Way* 77 To peel is to cause a ball other than the striker's ball to run its hoop in order. *Ibid.* 78 You can peel firmly and confidently, and there is less chance of Black sticking in the hoop. **1961** *Croquet* ('Know the Game' Series) 36/1 *Peel*, to send a ball other than your own through its own hoop. **1966** Miller & Thorp *Croquet* ix. 86 The better players are capable of peeling a ball through two or three hoops during a break... A ball peeled through its hoop in order scores that hoop. **1976** *Denbighshire Free Press* 8 Dec. 12/5 (Advt.), Do you find Croquet, the Croquet of Breaks and Bisques, baffling? Or do you Peel with consummate ease?

peelable (pī·lăb'l), *a.* [f. Peel *v.*[1] + -able.] Suitable for peeling, capable of being peeled. Hence **peelabi·lity.**

1958 [see *cellulose *sb.* c]. **1966** G. N. Leech *Eng. in Advertising* xx. 178 *Peelability*..is not the sort of quality one would normally have occasion to mention, in talking about oranges or anything else. **1971** D. Potter *Brit. Eliz. Stamps* xv. 163 A good-quality hinge is almost completely peelable. **1976** *Wireless World* Nov. 11 The reverse side..is covered by a peelable, tough vinyl insulation.

peeled, *ppl. a.*[1] Add: **4. b.** Now also *U.K.* (Further examples.)

1853 *Daily Morning Herald* (St. Louis, Missouri) 6 Jan. 2/1 Young man! Keep your eye peeled when you are after the women. **1872** E. Eggleston *End of World* xxvii. 186 [It would] teach the fellow to let monte alone, and keep his eyes peeled when he traveled. **1886** H. Stevens *Recoll. J. Lenox* 45 In reading catalogues and reports from all parts of the world, one eye at least was always kept peeled for his desiderata. **1906** *Springfield* (Mass.) *Weekly Republ.* 20 Sept. 16 The carpenters..are keeping their 'eyes peeled' for the many coins which have..slid between the planks. **1918** E. O'Neill in *Smart Set* June 96 We'll have to keep an eye peeled from now on. I know 'em. **1923** L. J. Vance *Baroque* xvi. 95 He sent a request to the door-porter to keep an eye peeled and let him know if the cab.. seemed disposed to tarry in the offing. **1945** E. Newhouse in *55 Short Stories from New Yorker* (1949) 238 Keep your eyes peeled and let me know if you come across Aladdin's lamp. **1956** B. Holiday *Lady sings Blues* (1973) xxi. 167 If you're doing something wrong, you *know* it and you've got at least one eye peeled looking for trouble. **1974** 'R. Tate' *Birds of Bloodied Feather* viii. 163 Keep your eyes peeled for a break in the mist.

peeler[1]. **2. b.** Delete '*Sc.* and *north. Irel.*' and add: Also *attrib.* (Later examples.)

1911 C. O. Minchin *Sea-Fishing* xvii. 245 When the cold outer shell has cracked and is ready to fall, and the new soft shell beneath is growing to replace it, the crab is called a 'peeler', and is then in the best condition for bait. **1934** *Sun* (Baltimore) 27 July 9/8 Hook-and-line fishermen can scarcely buy the popular peeler crab bait for fishing. **1956** M. Kennedy *Salt-Water Angling* x. 321 The crab is perhaps most useful as a bait shortly before it moults—when it has developed the new shell beneath the old one,..the angler anticipating nature by stripping the old shell off it. In this stage it is known variously as a peeler, peel, pill or shedder crab. **1971** *Angling Times* 10 June 3 Van driver Colin drifted his peeler crab bait around the rocks on float tackle. **1976** *Scottish Daily Express* 24 Dec. 12/6 For the smaller fish, rag and lugworm, soft peeler crab and strips of herring or mackerel are usually acceptable.

3. *U.S.* An exceptional or noteworthy example of anything; *spec.* a violent storm.

1823 J. F. Cooper *Pioneers* I. xv. 212 It's a peeler without, I can tell you, good woman. **1834** C. A. Davis *Lett. J. Downing* 331 The Captain was all the while boastin of [his boat] the 'Two Pollies'; and well he might, for she was a peeler. **1861** *Entertaining Things* I. 197 The gale..was a steady hard blow, what sailors call a peeler.

b. A person of exceptional or unusual qualities; a lively or energetic person.

1833 S. Smith *Life & Writings J. Downing* 218 Them are Pennsylvany chaps are real peelers for electing folks when they take hold. **1834** C. A. Davis *Lett. J. Downing* 88 If he does turn broker, you'll hear more on him; for he's a peeler I tell you. **1844** 'J. Slick' *High Life N.Y.* I. 82, I was talking with a rare peeler of a gal. **1869** Mrs. Stowe *Oldtown Folks* 117 She was spoken of with applause under such titles as 'a staver', 'a peeler', 'a roarer to work'. **1881** W. M. Thayer *From Log Cabin to White House* xiii. 207 He's a peeler for work, too; ain't afraid to dirty hisself.

4. One who removes his clothing: *spec.* a pugilist ready to strip for a fight.

1852 *As Good as Comedy* iv. 56 'I know you hain't got the teeth to raise the skin of that varmint.' 'Hain't I, then? Just you try it, then,..and see if I ain't a peeler.' 'Will you peel?' 'Won't I, then?' 'Jake, my boy, I've come here to-day to strip the skin off you altogether.'

b. A strip-tease artist; a stripper.

1951 *Variety* 20 June 53/2 (*heading*) Old Peelers Fade Away in St. Louis Crackdown. *Ibid.*, A steady exodus from the city of strippers in..St. Louis has been reported... It results from the crackdown of the law, with the peelers being replaced by jugglers, singers and hula dancers. **1951** Green & Laurie *Show Biz* 570/2 *Peeler*, stripteaser. **1955** *Variety* 9 Mar. 62/4 Chicago, for years a stripper's haven, is now seriously beset by a dearth of peelers. **1961** A. Berkman *Singers' Gloss. Show Business* 66 *Peeler*,..strip-teaser.

5. *U.S.* A cowboy.

1894 O. Wister *Out West: Jrnls. & Lett.* (1958) 198 *Peeler*, cowpuncher. **1902** *Out West* June 623 The 7 TX peelers is all in on this play,..and the 10 EC outfit will want a hand too. **1903** [see *ACT *v.* 9 f]. **1914** B. M. Bower *Flying U Ranch* 7 This is Mr. Mig-u-ell Rapponi, boys—a peeler straight from the Golden Gate. **1937** *Dialect Notes* VI. 618 Used in its strictest sense, the *peeler* refers to the cowpuncher who rides into the herd and 'cuts' out the horse desired. **1943** L. V. Hamner *Short Grass* 163 The driver, or 'peeler', rode the wheel horse and guides the whole team with one line.

6. In full, *peeler log*. The trunk of a tree, esp. a softwood one, suitable for the manufacture of veneer by the use of a rotary lathe, which peels thin sheets of wood from the log.

1935 *Timberman* Dec. 3/2 Some studies should be undertaken at once to determine the economic limits of the Douglas fir peelers... The log scarcity has brought forth the Veneer specialist, who makes a business of producing and preparing peeler logs for the plywood trade. **1942** Wood & Linn *Plywoods* vi. 179 From the [North American Pacific Coast] forests the 'peeler' logs, in lengths up to 40 feet, are conveyed by water, rail or road to the plywood mills. **1948** *Q. Jrnl. Forestry* XLII. 33 Poplar plywood could be manufactured if more peeler logs were grown. **1958** W. F. McCulloch *Woods Words* 133 Peeler... A log suitable for plywood. **1966** A. W. Lewis *Gloss. Woodworking Terms* 65 *Peeler log*, log from which veneer is cut by the rotary process of peeling. **1973** *Nature West Coast* 62 Wood [of grand fir] is used for pulp, lumber and peelers (core stock for plywood).

peeling, *vbl. sb.* Add: **1. d.** (Further example.)

1938 [see *OUTSTRIP *v.*[2]].

peel-off (pī·lǫf), *sb.* and *a.* [f. phr. *to peel off*: see Peel *v.*[1] 3, 5 in Dict. and Suppl.] **A.** *sb.* The action of peeling off. **B.** *adj.* Designating or pertaining to this action. Also *fig.*

1939 *Flight* 18 May 504a (*caption*) The peel-off. Westland Lysander monoplanes..start a mock dive-bombing attack. **1962** D. Warner *Death of Bogey* iv. vi. 168 The Lanes did the peel-off. Ran it by lorry. **1972** D. E. Westlake *Cops & Robbers* (1973) xi. 149 They'd busily switched the license plates on the squad car and put the new peel-off numbers on its sides.

peely-wally (pī·liwǫli), *a. Sc.* Also **peelie-wallie** and as one word. ['Orig. prob. imit. of a whining, feeble sound' (*Sc. Nat. Dict.*). Cf. Eng. dial. *pee-wee* whining, small (E.D.D.), and Wallydrag.] Pale, feeble, sickly, ill-looking.

1832 A. Henderson *Proverbs* 208 *Peelie*, thin; meagre. —*Peelie-wallie*, thin; sickly. **1833** J. Kennedy *Geordie Chalmers* 81 But may I ride on the win' wi' auld Nanee Logan, the witch o' Glenteerie, when I gang to siccan a peely-wally concern again! **1895** W. Stewart *Lilts* 104 The sun sen's forth its flickerin' rays, Fu' peely-wally wan. **1904** 'H. Foulis' *Erchie* xii. 73, I was a kind o' eccentric peely-wally soul, because I sometimes dried the dishes. **1932** 'L. G. Gibbon' *Sunset Song* 278 And damn it, if before a twelvemonth was up she didn't have a bairn, a peely-wally girl. **1945** B. Fergusson *Lowland Soldier* 25 Ye'd say he was thin, Peelywally, bow-leggit and shilpit. **1962** A. MacLeod *Eighth Seal* vi. 71 The wee Englishman is too peelywally to start any scrapping. **1966** K. White *Lett. from Gourgounel* 96 A snail..her long peelie-wallie neck with two horns slowly prodding the air.

peen, *sb.* Add: Now usu. written **pein** (pīn, pēⁱn). Add to def.: Hence, the other end of a hammer-head from the face, whether sharp-edged or rounded. (Further examples.)

1885 *Spons' Mechanics' Own Bk.* 84 This process is termed 'paning' or 'pening', from the pane or pene of the hammer being generally used to perform it. **1904** W. H. Van Dervoort *Mod. Machine Shop Tools* (ed. 4) i. 17 The machinist hammer..is made of high-grade steel, carefully tempered on head and pene. **1939** *Specification for Hand Hammers* (*B.S.I.*) 7 On completion, the forgings shall be hardened on the striking faces and peins only. *Ibid.* 12 (*caption*) Engineer's ball pein hammer. **1943** D. J. Swartz et al. *Fund. Shopwork* (1945) i. 27 The peen hammer is widely used. The head is so shaped that one end, called the peen, can be used to produce dents or depressions or to set up tension in metal. **1947** J. C. Rich *Materials & Methods Sculpture* vi. 182 In working the heavier thicknesses of $\frac{5}{8}$ inch and the $\frac{3}{8}$ inch, larger ball pein hammers are required. **1961** *B.S.I. News* Oct. 24/1 Most of the trouble was due to..heads too hard on either the striking face or the pein. **1964** S. Crawford *Basic Engin. Processes* i. 16 The three types of hammer most generally used by the fitter are (a) Ball Pein, (b) Cross Pein, and (c) Straight Pein... All three are of a standard shape at the striking face end but can be readily identified by the shape of the opposite end known as the pein. **1971** B. Scharf *Engin. & its Lang.* ix. 63 Ball-pein hammers have one ball-shaped end (pein, peen) for hand-riveting or burring over.

peen, pene, *v.* Delete '*Obs.* exc. *dial.*' and add examples of the sense: To strike with the pein of a hammer. (Usu. written **peen.**)

1888 J. Rose *Mod. Machine-Shop Pract.* II. xxv. 162/2 The side faces of the arms would require to be pened. **1902** *Internat. Libr. Technol.* IV. § 44.22 Iron may be stretched by peening it; that is, by striking it with the peen of a hammer. This method is often used to loosen a collar or a nut. **1941** A. C. Davies *Sci. & Pract. of Welding* ii. 118 In the arc welding of cast iron the risk of fracture is definitely reduced if the short beads of weld metal are lightly peened immediately after they have been laid. **1950** *Engineering* 31 Mar. 345/3 Each run of weld is peened before the next run is applied. **1964** S. Crawford *Basic Engin. Processes* i. 16 The bench fitter frequently uses different types of hand hammers for fitting operations requiring force, e.g...peening over the end of rivets. **1977** *Good Motoring* Mar. 32/2 A leak between two cylinders caused through a plug in the underside of the head which had been 'very poorly peened in place'.

Hence **pee·ning** *vbl. sb.* (see also *shot peening* s.v. *SHOT *sb.*[1] 30).

1885 [see *PEEN *sb.*]. **1905** W. S. Leonard *Machine-Shop Tools & Methods* (ed. 3) ii. 33 The peening affects only the outer surface of the shaft, and the turning removes this outer surface, thereby partially neutralizing the effect of the peening. **1907** *English Mechanic* 23 Aug. 49/1 After the bottom is slipped on the paning down can be done with a paning hammer.., or..with a sheet-metal worker's common hammer. **1960** *Times Rev. Industry* Jan. 36/2 The peening of springs for increasing the fatigue life, particularly for the motor industry, can be done in air operated plant as well as the airless type. **1964** J. G. Tweeddale *Mech. Properties of Metals* vii. 125 Residual stresses may be induced in several ways, such as surface rolling and peening. Peening can take the form of hammer peening or shot peening.

peent (pīnt), *sb. N. Amer.* Also **peeent.** [Echoic.] A representation of the high whistling sound emitted by a woodcock. Also *attrib.*

1895 F. M. Chapman *Handbk. Birds of Eastern N. Amer.* 153 [The Woodcock] begins on the ground with a formal, periodic *peent, peent*, an incongrous preparation for the wild flight that follows. **1925** E. H. Forbush *Birds Massachusetts* I. 386 Voice [of woodcock].—A nasal 'peent' something like common note of Nighthawk. **1931** *Sun* (Baltimore) 11 Apr. 4/7, I heard a woodcock, 'peent' sing, And I saw a hum-bird rise. **1944** L. A. Hausman *Illustr. Encycl. Amer. Birds* 438/2 This song [of the woodcock] is introduced, and concluded, by a series of nasal peeent notes, much like the flying calls of the Nighthawk. **1953** Murphy & Amadon *Land Birds Amer.* iii. 83/1 Both before and after these flights, they [*sc.* Woodcocks] utter a nasal call, usually written as peent. **1965** A. Wetmore et al. *Water, Prey, & Game Birds N. Amer.* 330/1 The woodcock zigzags rapidly down to earth with chirping notes. He struts across a patch of open ground, sounds his peent notes again, then soars to repeat the aerial act.

peent (pīnt), *v. N. Amer.* [f. the sb.] **a.** *intr.* To emit a high whistling sound characteristic of a woodcock. **b.** *trans.* To utter by making such a sound. So **pee·nting** *vbl. sb.*

1897 F. M. Chapman *Bird-Life* vii. 103 Unless disturbed, he [*sc.* the woodcock] will probably return to near the spot from which he started and at once resume his *peenting*. **1956** Peterson & Fisher *Wild Amer.* v. 56 Over downtown roof-gardens the 'peenting' of cruising nighthawks can often be heard. **1973** M. Crowell *Greener Pastures* 197, I hear a woodcock 'peenting' over on apple tree hill. **1976** *Kingston* (Ontario) *Whig-Standard* 22 Oct. 14/1 Often, shortly after sunset, the male [woodcock] peents a nasal sound. *Ibid.*, Once landed, the peenting resumes.

peeny-wally (pī·niwǭli). Also **peeni(e)wally, peeny(-wauly).** [Etym. uncertain; perh. *PEELY-WALLY infl. by Jamaican dial. *peeny* small (see also E.D.D.).] A Jamaican name for a firefly, esp. the largest of those found on the island, *Pyrophorus plagiophthalmus.*

1907 W. Jekyll *Jamaican Song & Story* ii. 184 'Peeny' is the Candlefly, which shines like my donkey's coat. **1961** F. G. Cassidy *Jamaica Talk* xiii. 292 The big one [*sc.* firefly] is also *peeny* or *peeny-wauly*, an unexplained word, though *wauly* may refer to its shining 'eyes'. **1962** S. Wynter *Hills of Hebron* i. 23 When the rains stopped, the 'peeniwallies', hundreds of them, fluttered transparent wings against the lamp. **1971** *Islander* (Victoria, B.C.) 17 Jan. 2/3 These fireflies are affectionately called 'peeniewallies' by the islanders [*sc.* Jamaicans].

peep, *sb.*[1] Add: **2. b.** A slight sound or utterance; a single item or piece of information, chiefly in neg. contexts. Cf. Pip *sb.*[2] 1 b.

1903 in *Eng. Dial. Dict.* **1908** R. W. Chambers *Firing Line* xxiv. 411 Nobody's heard a peep from you. What on earth do you mean by this? **1928** S. Lewis *Man who knew Coolidge* I. 13 I'd never made a peep about how maybe it'd be a good stunt for him to go out and maybe earn a little money on the side. **1954** *Picture Post* 2 Jan. 34/3 'One more peep out of you, Mister, and I'll get the boys to push you and your b— stall in the oggin', which was a nearby canal. *a* **1974** R. Crossman *Diaries* (1975) I. 275 Not a peep came out of any of them. **1974** T. P. Whitney tr. *Solzhenitsyn's Gulag Archipel.* I. i. 10 They take you from a military hospital with a temperature of 102, as they did with Ans Bernshtein, and the doctor will not raise a peep about your arrest. **1977** P. Cosgrave *Cheyney's Law* v. 47, I know coppers... They're not supposed to be able to take it... But there's not been a peep out of him... Maybe..he's tougher than you are.

4. a. Delete *Obs.* and substitute for def.: A young chicken. (Later *U.S.* examples.) Cf. *PEE-PEE[1].

1931 *Amer. Speech* VII. 20 Peeps. Little chickens. **1935** *Ibid.* X. 171/1 Peep. A chick just hatched, or a small chicken. **1943** *Sun* (Baltimore) 10 Aug. 10/3 The Boonsboro *Times* reports the birth there of a 'peep' with no eyes and no sign of an eye.

peep, *sb.*[2] Add: **1. d.** *dial.* and *U.S.* After a negative, a short interval (of sleep), a wink.

1905 R. Beach *Pardners* (1912) ii. 49 Most people called him crazy, 'cause he had fits of goin' for days without a peep.

4. peep-joint, a place where striptease is performed; **peep-machine,** a machine through which a peep-show is seen; **peep-toe** *attrib.*, designating a kind of shoe whose tip is cut away allowing the toes to be seen; also *absol.*; also **peep-toed** *a.*

1960 *News Chron.* 23 Sept. 10/1 Jayne is..head stripper in the Pink Flamingo, a gilded peep-joint. **1938** G. Greene *Brighton Rock* iii. ii. 117 The motor-track, the shooting booths and peep machines. *Ibid.* iii. iii. 130 Framed snapshots of King Edward VII (Prince of Wales) in a yachting cap and a background of peep machines. **1939** *Vogue* 3 May 5 (Advt.), Blue calf thonging and heel sets off this peep-toe sandal in blue calf, 45/9. **1940** *Ibid.* June 14 (Advt.), Only Joyce..would think of using duckskin and calf in this peep-toe creation for your every leisure hour. **1957** *Observer* 25 Aug. 11/7 A young French lady named Tracy, in peeptoe shoes and ice-blue, skintight gown with a good deal of cleavage. **1960** *News Chron.* 6 June 5/2 A blade in a tweed coat and peep-toe sandals. **1968** J. Ironside *Fashion Alphabet* 133 *Peeptoe*, a rather coy name for any shoe, usually court or slingback, from which the toe-cap is cut away to expose part of the toes. **1969** E. Wilson *Hist. Shoe Fashions* xx. 247 The war years of 1939–45 saw..a heavy restriction in shoe-making materials... Peep-toes and big chunky trimmings decorated the very popular court shoe. **1976** *Vogue* 15 Mar. 77 Pale blue and navy peep-toe sandals. **1953** K. Tennant *Joyful Condemned* xix. 173 A really pretty pair of peep-toed, high-heeled sandals.

peep (pīp), *sb.*[4] *U.S.* [see quot. 1943.] = *JEEP *sb.*

Sources are divided as to whether peep should designate a vehicle larger or smaller than a jeep, but are agreed in referring both terms to the same type of vehicle.

1941 *N.Y. Herald Tribune* 28 June 14/3 Peep (son of a jeep) means a bantam car. **1941** *N.Y. Times* 26 Oct. xx. 3/2 The one-half ton 'jeep' command reconnaissance car, its name taken from the model designation 'G.P.', and one-quarter ton 'peep' reconnaissance cars are combat vehicles. **1943** *Amer. N. & Q.* III. 137/1, I laid down an editorial ukase that the $\frac{1}{4}$-ton truck was thereafter to be the 'jeep' and the $\frac{1}{2}$-ton the 'peep'. **1946** *Amer. Speech* XXI. 245 In the Armored Force..the $\frac{1}{4}$-ton 4 by 4 is always a *peep*, the term 'jeep' being applied to the command and reconnaissance car. **1953** M. Bury *Rolling Wheels* 242 G.I.'s called a command car a *jeep*, called what you call a jeep, a *peep*—and bicycles were called *creeps!* **1962** *Amer. Speech* XXXVII. 78 The peep proved as versatile as the jeep, and had the advantages of a lower silhouette, less gasoline consumption, cheaper production, and the occupation of less cargo space when shipped.

peep, *v.*[1] Add: **2. b.** To betray a confidence; to inform. Also *trans.*

1911 J. London *Let.* 6 Mar. (1966) 340 The convicts are few and far between who come out and dare to peep a word of what they know. *Ibid.* I have known ex-cons who became dead for peeping. **1950** H. E. Goldin *Dict. Amer. Underworld Lingo* 154/2 *Peep*, to betray associates; to give information to the police.

peep-bo. Add: (Further examples.) Hence **pee·p-boing** *vbl. sb.*

1818 'A. Burton' *Adventures J. Newcome* ii. 114 His Toes played peep-boh through his Shoes. **1828** A. Royall *Black Bk.* II. 137, I was not disposed to play at peep-bo with him. **1853** Mrs. Gaskell *Ruth* I. vi. 145 After some 'peep-boing', she was about to snatch a kiss, when Harry ..hit Ruth a great blow on the face. **1974** P. Dickinson *Poison Oracle* vi. 153 Dorah and Peggy were playing peep-bo round a hut.

pee-pee[1] (pī·pī). *U.S.* [Perh. onomatopœic, f. the sound made by the birds.] A young chicken, or, esp. in Jamaica, a young turkey.

1890 *Dialect Notes* I. 74 Pee-pee..a very small chicken. Eastern Pennsylvania. **1927** Anderson & Cundall *Jamaica Negro Proverbs & Sayings* 73 Cuss John Crow 'peel-head', turkey pee-pee bex [i.e. little turkey angry]. **1950** *Publ. Amer. Dial. Soc.* xiv. 51 Pee-pee: *excl.* A call to turkeys. Imitative of the cry of the poults. **1953** *Amer. Speech* XXVIII. 252 Pee-pee... A newborn or very young chick. **1961** F. G. Cassidy *Jamaica Talk* v. 104 Young fowl, usually turkeys, are called pee-pees.

pee-pee[2] (pī·pī). [redupl. *PEE *sb.*[5]] = *PEE *sb.*[5]

1923 J. Manchon *Le Slang* 220 To do peepee. **1941** E. P. O'Donnell *Great Big Doorstep* x. 143 Commado said, 'When them twins get in the show like lass time, one's gotta make pee-pee, the udda one gotta climb on the seat [etc.].' **1962** B. J. Friedman *Stern* i. 58 Do you still make peepee in your pants? **1972** H. C. Rae *Shooting Gallery* iv. 263 Time stopped. The pee-pee was cold and swollen in her tummy.

peeper[1]. **2. b.** Substitute for def.: A small tree-frog of the genus *Hyla*, esp. *H. crucifer*, found in eastern North America. (Earlier and later examples.)

1857 S. H. Hammond *Wild Northern Scenes* 30 All is still now, save the piping notes of the little peeper along the shore. **1906** M. C. Dickerson *Frog Bk.* 139 There are few people in the eastern United States who do not know the voices of the Spring Peepers... The Peepers have spring in their hearts. **1938** J. W. Lippincott *Animal Neighbours* (1940) xx. 192 The ridiculously small spring frog or peeper, an inch and a quarter long, comes first, sometime in March. **1961** D. M. Cochran *Living Amphibians of World* 113/1 The spring peeper, *Hyla crucifer*, is one of the earliest of the frogs to appear in spring. **1976** *Yankee* Apr. 78/2 Nearly every Easterner..has heard the spring peeper's song.

peeper[2]. Add: **1. b.** A private detective or investigator; occas., a policeman.

1940 R. Chandler *Farewell, my Lovely* xxiii. 177 Peeper, huh, pally? From the big bad burg, huh? **1943** —— *Lady in Lake* (1944) xxxv. 185 Don't bother to call your house-peeper... I'm allergic to house-peepers. **1968** R. Clapperton *No News on Monday* iii. 25 Police protection for a peeper. What kind of advertisement is that? **1968** E. McGirr *Lead-Lined Coffin* ii. 64 He..flipped the wallet open. 'A peeper,' he said. **1970** G. F. Newman *Sir, You Bastard* ii. 54 'I have an arrangement with the peeper across the road. He's had a lean time lately.' His voice was level. Moving towards him, Angie said: 'Policemen are different.' **1975** R. L. Simon *Wild Turkey* xxii. 160 What kind of bullshit are you throwing around, peeper? You want me to slap you in the can?

2. (Further examples.)

1858 A. Mayhew *Paved with Gold* ii. xii. 191 They went to work slogging, Jack delivering a 'head-acher'.. and Ned one not to be worked at on the 'peepers'. **1901** 'H. McHugh' *John Henry* 93, I hate to have a girl plant her pleading peepers on me. **1908** A. N. Lyons *Arthur's* i. ii. 10, I jerked me peeper round, an' there was a girl squattin' on a tar barrel. **1928** E. Wallace *Double* xiii. 204 Unless your poor old peepers are going wrong you would have seen them. **1937** G. Frankau *More of Us* iv. 42 She winked one peeper; But Innocent's eyes, downcast, still withheld her man Glances he craved. **1968** A. Diment *Bang Bang Birds* vii. 108 There was a leer in his rheumy peepers as he gave Marianne a mental strip. **1978** J. Symons *Blackheath Poisonings* iii. 153 He had lost an eye long ago in the Ashanti campaign... 'I'm lucky to be alive, but I lost one of my peepers.'

peep-hole. Add: (Further examples.) Also *transf.* and *attrib.*

1952 E. F. Davies *Illyrian Venture* xi. 209 Every sentry looked in frequently through the peep-hole in the door. **1962** *Gloss. Terms Glass Industry (B.S.I.)* 17 *Peephole*, a small opening in a furnace wall through which observations are made. **1963** *New Yorker* 15 June 98/3 (Advt.), These fully washable shorties..sport dainty floral sprays of peephole petals. **1978** W. H. Jobson *To die a Little* ix. 148 Every now and again someone lifted the flap of the round peephole in the [cell] door.

peepie-creepie (pī·pikrī·pi). [f. Peep *v.*[2] + -ie and Creep *v.* + ie.] A portable television camera used for close shots on location.

1952 *Time* 14 July 22/3 Most startling TV innovation was a portable camera known as the walkie-lookie, or peepie-creepie, with which the enterprising TV reporter could sneak up to Mr. Delegate and catch him yelling his head off or scratching his nose. **1952** *Newsweek* 21 July 53 NBC's walkie-lookie, or 'peepie-creepie', was not a singular success in its debut. **1953** A. K. C. Ottaway *Educ. & Society* 82 Here it was that the 'peepie-creepie' also called the 'walkie-lookie' began to achieve prominence. **1954** F. G. Cassidy *Robertson's Devel. Mod. Eng.* (ed. 2) viii. 188 *Walky-talky* (a portable radio..), and its recent offspring *peepie-creepie* (a portable television camera).

peeping, *ppl. a.*[2] Add: (Later allusive examples of *Peeping Tom.*) Now freq. written *peeping Tom* and usu. applied to a prying person, esp. with connotations of prurience; one who obtains gratification from furtively observing women not fully clothed or the sexual activity of others, = *voyeur. Also *transf.*, *fig.*, and *attrib.* Hence *peeping Tommery*, the activity of a peeping Tom; also *peeping Tom-ism.*

1915 R. Frost *Let.* 11 Nov. (1964) 17 She executes a frightfulness. Somewhere else she brings in the Peeping-Tom idea. **1926** G. Hunting *Vicarion* ii. 38 What sort was a man who did not instinctively respect the privacy of others?—not mere physical privacy, on which any Peeping Tom might intrude, but the infinitely more intimate thing, to spy upon which was violation. **1933** *Week-End Rev.* 8 July 34/2, I can assure you that neither reporters nor sub-editors find satisfaction in playing the rôle of Paul Pry or Nosey Parker or Peeping Tom. **1955** *Sun* (Baltimore) 7 Nov. 30/7 The House Judiciary Committee is sending its general counsel here from Washington today to attend the City Council hearing on a bill to outlaw electronic 'peeping toms'. **1958** *Times* 12 Nov. 3/4 The curiously prosaic *bizarreries* of Magritte, and the peeping-Tom eroticism of such basically crude pictures as those of Labisse and Delvaux, are of the 'photographic' kind. **1960** *Spectator* 21 Oct. 602/3 Those semi-nude gambols [in a cinema film]..break any feeling of reality second by second by giving one a sense of peeping-tommery. **1963** A. Heron *Towards Quaker View of Sex* 67 Exhibitionism and the associated disorder Voyeurism (peeping-tom) involve sexual pleasure obtained respectively from displaying the naked body..or from observing the sexual acts or organs of other people. **1966** Auden *About House* 42 Peeping Toms Are never praised, like novelists or bird watchers, For their keenness of observation. **1966** *Guardian* 26 Mar. 1/6 They've had Peeping Tom cameras and now they've got eavesdropping microphones. **1972** W. P. McGivern *Caprifoil* i. 9 Surveillance was a constantly expanding and proliferating industry... He did have a professional view of this constantly expanding peeping Tom-ism, and it was a sour one. **1974** M. Kelly *That Girl in Alley* vii. 120 To avoid bringing myself into suspicion of peeping-tommery I moved a few steps down the yard, out of sight of the drilling class. **1977** *Transatlantic Rev.* lx. 38 At various times during the preceding year, there had been complaints of Peeping Toms.

peep of day. Add: **2.** *peep-of-day boys* (earlier and later examples). Also *transf.*

1780 A. Young *Tour in Ireland* ii. vi. 30 In England we have heard much of whiteboys, steelboys, oakboys, peep-of-day-boys, &c... All but the whiteboys were among the manufacturing protestants in the north. **1922** Joyce *Ulysses* 44 Raw facebones under his peep of day boy's hat.

peep-show. Add: (Earlier and later examples.) Also *attrib.*

1851 *Househ. Words* II. 290/1 There were tambourines, books, work-boxes..peep-show boxes, all kinds of boxes. **1894** [see *donkey-ride* s.v. *donkey 3 a]. **1914** G. B. Shaw *Misalliance* 67, I did a cheap trip to Folkestone. I spent sevenpence on dropping pennies into silly automatic machines and peepshows of rowdy girls having a jolly time. **1937** L. MacNeice *Poems* 110 It's no go the merry-goround, it's no go the rickshaw, All we want is a limousine and a ticket for the peepshow. **1941** J. Masefield *In Mill* 110, I had seen him box in one of the little primitive peep-show cinemas. **1951** M. McLuhan *Mech. Bride* (1967) 48/1 *Sexual Behavior in the Human Male* is a penny arcade peep show given the chrome treatment of scientific charts and figures. **1973** *Times* 22 Mar. 8/7 The bookshops, the peep shows, the pornographic cinemas..are all nasty. **1976** *National Observer* (U.S.) 18 Dec. 1/3 It sits in leased quarters on the eighth floor of a commercial building in a neighborhood of numerous adult book-stores and peep-show parlors on 9th street in Washington.

peepy, *a.* (Earlier and later examples.)

1833 *Chambers's Edin. Jrnl.* 5 Jan. 385/1 He is then a poor, peepy wretch, with blear eyes. *Ibid.* 27 Apr. 97/3 The contrast..between the meaning of the words, and the poor, peepy..voice in which they are given. **1939** N. Marsh *Overture to Death* xii. 117 It was the pot-boy, very tousled and peepy, and accompanied by a gust of stale beer. Alleyn thought that he looked like all pot-boys at dawn throughout time and space.

peer, *sb.* Add: **2. b.** *Anthropol.* and *Sociol.* An equal; a contemporary; a member of the same age-group or social set. Also *attrib.* (see also sense 6 a below).

1944 C. M. Tryon in *Nat. Soc. Study Educ. Yearbk.* (U.S.) i. xii. 233 Although in meeting some adult standards girls must undergo less change than boys, in their relation to their own peer culture they must often be more adaptive in relation to changing requirements. **1953** A. K. C. Ottaway *Educ. & Society* 109 What is called 'peer culture', in other words the community of the same age, has a very great influence on the individual. **1958** W. J. H. Sprott *Human Groups* 71 Wherever there is an adolescent 'peer-culture' it will have an influence which competes with that of the home. **1964** Minturn & Lambert *Mothers of Six Cultures* 288 Nuclear family cultures are least punitive of peer-to-peer aggression. **1966** Bereiter & Engelmann *Teaching Disadvantaged Children* i. 18 In reading down the list of contrasts between the home and the nursery school environment, one finds..the same contrast could be drawn between the upper-middle-class and the lower-class child's environment: adult versus peer contacts, [etc.]. **1966** *Listener* 14 Apr. 535/2 With their peers—that is, people of the same age, sex, and status—adolescents really experience for the first time relationships embodying equality and democracy. **1971** *New Society* 18 Nov. 975/2, I have discovered that wild-born monkeys spend more time watching a live peer, than themselves, in mirrors. **1972** *Where* Mar. 95/3 You need to consider the quality of the relationship which exists between your son and the teachers, your son and his peers, and between you and the teachers. **1972** *Jrnl. Social Psychol.* LXXXVI. 111 A subject receiving positive evaluations from a group of his peers was more active in the group. **1973** *Jrnl. Genetic Psychol.* CXXII. 263 Studies of human peer-social behavior in the preschool period. *Ibid.* 275 Retrospection and Peer-Perception scores did not differ from each other. *Ibid.* CXXIII. 124 Firstborn children have greater verbal facility, and there is evidence that they have more successful relationships with their teachers than do the later born although later born are more often successful in their peer relationships. **1975** *Nature* 4 Dec. 382/1 At the heart of the inquiry is the so-called peer-review system, which is used in some shape or form by virtually every government agency which supports academic research. **1977** *Listener* 7 Apr. 427/3 In the relatively public competition between rival research groups seeking financial support, there is no practical alternative to 'peer review' by committees of experts in the relevant fields. **1977** *Sci. Amer.* Sept. 177/3 Alternatively a distributed-processing system can be organized into a peer structure. All the computers..can communicate with one another on an equal footing.

4. Now also a man elevated to the peerage on a non-hereditary basis; = *life peer* s.v. Life *sb.* 17 in Dict. and Suppl. Also = *Peeress in her own right.*

1869 [see *life-peer* s.v. Life *sb.* 17]. **1958** *Oxford Mail* 21 July 1/7 The announcement will enable the lifepeers to take their seats in the Lords in time for the opening of the next session of Parliament in November. It will be the first time women peers have been allowed to sit in the Lords. **1958** *Times* 24 July 8/7 The main point of this interim constitutional reform [*sc.* introduction of life peerages] was to enlarge Labour representation in the Upper House with working peers. **1974** *Observer* (Colour Suppl.) 24 Mar. 30/1 'We are very passionate that we are not peeresses; peeresses are the wives of peers...' Now lavatories are discreetly marked 'Peers' and 'Women Peers'.

6. a. (sense *2 b) **peer group,** a group of people, freq. a group of adolescents, of the same age or social status.

1943 Breckenridge & Vincent *Child Devel.* xiii. 463 Although the adolescent declares his independence of adult standards and controls, he is actually very dependent upon conformity with his peer group. **1948** J. H. S. Bossard *Sociol. of Child Devel.* vi. xxi. 494 This element of antagonism between peer groups and adults has been fostered through the years in a great many ways. **1957** P. Lafitte *Person in Psychol.* viii. 104 Their standing in their peer group at school. **1959** *Listener* 19 Feb. 324/2 Each man's situation is slightly different from those of his peer-group. **1961** [see *inner *a.* (*sb.*[2]) 1 n]. **1964** Gould & Kolb *Dict. Social Sci.* 297/1 One of these concepts is that of *peer group* which commonly refers to a group of homogeneous age composition. There is no reason, however, why this term cannot be applied to a group whose members are equal in some respect other than age. **1964** M. Argyle *Psychol. & Social Probl.* xv. 187 Young people between puberty and marriage are consciously aware of belonging to this peer-group, wear distinctive clothes, meet in groups at coffee-bars, [etc.]. **1966** *Listener* 14 Apr. 535/2 The gang is a relatively authoritarian form of peer group. **1972** J. L. Dillard *Black English* i. 34 In the ghetto culture, peer group relations govern the social activity, including language, of the child to a degree far beyond its importance among middle-class whites. **1976** *Broadcast* 29 Mar. 19/1 A desire..to be seen to be involved with peer-group heroes.

peerie (pīə·ri), *a.* (*sb.*) *Sc.* (now only *Orkney* and *Shetland*). [Etym. uncertain: see S.N.D.] **A.** *adj.* Small, diminutive. Also in special collocations (see quots. and S.N.D.).

1808 Jamieson, *Peerie, adj.*, little, small. *A peerie foal*, a small bannock or cake, Orkn. Shetl. **1868** D. Gorrie *Summers & Winters in Orkneys* 12 An Oyce or inlet, locally termed the 'Peerie Sea'. **1871** R. Cowie *Shetland* ii. iv. 149 The *peerie* steamer—as the natives call her, in contradistinction to the larger one trading to the south. **1884** *Rep. H.M. Comm. Inquiry Crofters Highlands Scotl.* 1404 in *Parl. Papers* (C. 3980) XXXIV, The possession of even four ures of land constitutes the proprietor a small, or, in the vernacular, 'peerie' laird. **1891** J. J. H. Burgess *Rasmie's Büddie* 80 An sün her peerie winkie haands O' cockaloories bricht wis fu. **1916** G. W. Hoggan in B. Thynne *Shetland Sheep-Dog* 14 The 'peerie' Shetland Collie... These 'peerie things' are seldom seen outside—probably for fear of being tramped on. **1921** *Glasgow Herald* 1 Jan. 6/7 The mill stood..right on top of the sluice through which the waters of the bay rushed into the 'Peerie (little) Sea'. **1922** J. Firth *Reminisc. Orkney Parish* (ed. 2) 75 Sometimes as many as half-a-dozen women were called to the house..to keep away the 'peerie-folk'—those unearthly visitants who were particularly busy when a new arrival came. **1929** E. Linklater *White-Maa's Saga* 72 The world's nae comin' to an end for a peerie while yet. **1948** C. L. B. Hubbard *Dogs in Brit.* xviii. 205 In its home islands it [*sc.* the Shetland sheepdog] is known as the Tounie Dog or Peerie Dog. **1956** C. M. Costie *Benjie's Bodle* 58 Afore he kent whar he was the Peerie Laird wad be pitten tae the horn. **1959** I. & P. Opie *Lore & Lang. Schoolch.* x. 182 There she goes, there she goes, Peerie heels and pointed toes. **1978** *New Shetlander* Summer 22/2 Whaur is du gaun, du peerie boy, Wi dee face laek a smoored fire? *Ibid.* 28/2 Da Maister sat in a peerie hoose Wi Jordan's water rinnin near.

B. as *sb.* A Shetland sheep-dog.

1949 K. M. Wells *Owl Pen Reader* (1969) ii. 211 Shetland Sheep Dogs do possess the seeing eye,.. Shetland Sheep Dogs were once called 'Peeries' or 'Fairy Dogs'. **1971** F. Hamilton *World Encycl. Dogs* 96 Shetland Sheepdog, Shetland Collie, Miniature Collie, Shetland, Sheltie, Toonie or Peerie—at some time or other the Sheltie has answered to all these names.

peeta, var. *pita[2].

peeve (pīv), *v.* orig. *U.S.* [Back-formation f. Peevish *a.*] *trans.* and *intr.* To irritate, exasperate; to grumble, complain petulantly. So **peeved** (pīvd) *ppl. a.*, irritated, annoyed.

1908 G. V. Hobart *Go to It* 31 It may be interesting to some people, but it gets me peeved. **1912** Ade *Knocking Neighbors* 10 The Waiter peeved at being slipped a paltry $1.60. **1919** Wodehouse *Damsel in Distress* xxi. 242 About a million other people who'll be most frightfully peeved at my doing the Wedding Glide without consulting them. **1923** H. G. Wells *Men like Gods* i. i. 5 Liberalism would never do anything more for ever than sit.. grumbling and peeving. **1926** *Bulletin* (Glasgow) 17 June 5, I have a letter to-day from a peeved smoker..on the huge profits disclosed by the big tobacco combines. **1934** R. Macaulay *Going Abroad* xvii. 139, I suppose he'd peeved me in some way. **1937** G. Frankau *More of Us* v. 62 'Just look at that,' peeved she, one slim hand plucking High from her ankles' grace, the limbs' frail sheath. **1945** *Sun* (Baltimore) 7 Dec. 8/1 Mighty peeved at that, Lorena outs with a derringer and marches the bachelor to the nearest J.P. **1966** I. Jefferies *House-Surgeon* v. 101 'They were peeved, like little school-kids.'.. 'Who peeved them, Harry?' **1975** *Daily Mail* 13 June 7/4 The agency won't talk about the work; its executives are rather peeved that the news has got out.

peeve (pīv), *sb.* orig. *U.S.* [f. the vb.] A grumble, a (cause of) complaint or irritation; a peevish humour; *pet peeve*, a special or recurring source of irritation.

It is not certain that the sb. is intended in quot. 1911.

1911 *Dialect Notes* III. 549 Some common cases of 'back-formations', or 'back-shortenings', are..*peeve*. **1919** C. H. DARLING *Jargon Bk.* 25 *Pet peeve*, the thing that provokes you the most. **1920** S. LEWIS *Main St.* 293 You're simply hot and tired, and trying to work off your peeve on me. **1936** R. E. SHERWOOD *Idiot's Delight* III. 141 Every time yon get yourself into a peeve, you take it out on us. **1945** *Southwest Rev.* Summer 330/2 Such misrepresentation of this lovable American character is my pet peeve. **1963** B. S. JOHNSON *Travelling People* i. 21 Henry thought he could afford to indulge in a Peeve... This was very quickly achieved by concentrating his mind on as many of the disasters of his past as were conveniently on short call from his memory. **1973** 'TREVANIAN' *Loo Sanction* 12 His peeve lasted only a second. **1975** *Bibliognost* Aug. 27 My pet peeve? Scouts and dealers who don't identify themselves and expect you to pull out the best books in the store. **1976** *National Observer* (U.S.) 7 Feb. 8/4 Poorly designed parking garages have riled me for a long time, but they've become a full-fledged pet peeve in recent years.

peever (pī·vəɹ). *Sc.* Also **peaver, peevor, peiver.** [Origin unknown.] The stone, piece of pottery, or the like, used in hopscotch. Also (freq. pl.) the game itself.

a **1850** in *Sc. Nat. Dict.* (1968) VII. 78/1 s.v. peever. **1856** J. STRANG *Glasgow & its Clubs* 218 The young misses indulged in scoring the flagstones with their peevers, for the purpose of playing at pal-lall. **1887** D. DONALDSON Jamieson, Suppl., Add. 314/2 *Peever*, the pitcher or flat stone with which the children's game of *beds* or *pallall* is played; the game is therefore sometimes called '*peever*' or '*the peever*'. West of S. **1901** R. C. MACLAGAN *Games Argyleshire* 134 Pieces of broken pottery are by Lowlanders called *Lalies*, and the broken bottom of a bowl, a *laly*, is also called a peaver. **1921** *Edinburgh Even. News* 13 June 4 Chalking and disfiguring the street playing 'peevers'. **1931** A. J. CRONIN *Hatter's Castle* III. ix. 616 We'll be lookin' on at a game o' peever next if we're not careful, like a band o' silly lassies. **1962** *3rd Stat. Acct. Scotl.* XII. xii. 147 Peevors is still played on traditional stances. **1966** *Daily Tel.* 5 Nov. 13/8 Mr. Alex Lynch says that in Scotland hopscotch is known as 'peevers'.

pee-wee. Add: **2.** For '*Grallina picata*' substitute '*Grallina cyanoleuca*'. (Examples.)

1898 [see *MUDLARK *sb.* 3 c]. **1911** LUCAS & LE SOUËF *Birds Austral.* 340 The familiar shrill and rather whistling cry gives it [*sc.* the magpie lark] the common name of the Pee-wee or Pee-wit. **1947** *Coast to Coast 1946* 27 He can see a black-and-white bird, a pee-wee, that runs along the path between the rushes. **1956** A. BELL *Some Common Austral. Birds* 96 The Pee-wee is vigorous and unusually widespread. **1968** K. WEATHERLY *Roo Shooter* 119 There was a peewee that visited him often through the day.

3. (Further examples.) Also, usu. *attrib.* or as *adj.*, small, tiny, composed of children, and *transf.* of animals or things, and *fig.* (*attrib.*). *N. Amer.* and *dial.*

1877 F. ROSS et al. *Gloss. Words Holderness* 106/1 *Peewee*, adj. small; diminutive. **1930** *Amer. Speech* VI. 133 *Peewee soft song man*, petty confidence worker. **1935** *Ibid.* X. 271/2 *Peewees*, small, stunted pigs or lambs. **1936** *Time* 6 Apr. 45/1 Merciless, ignorant, lecherous, full of peewee patriotics, he wages senseless war against the Hill People. **1946** MEZZROW & WOLFE *Really Blues* (1957) vi. 69 A peewee jockey whose onliest riding crop was a stick of marihuana. **1952** *Daily News* (N.Y.) 13 Aug. C 16/3 The Bantams, an organization of men who are what they themselves call 'peewees and proud of it' with 5 [foot] 4 [inch]..Lenny Herman as spokesman. **1958** *Cut Knife* (Saskatchewan) *Grinder* 6 Feb. 1/5 The Cut Knife PeeWees were hosts to the Unity team and defeated them. **1965** *Western Wonderland* (Seattle) Apr. 22/1 The nine sorting categories [of logs]..are: hemlock; sawlogs..peewees.. and lastly, boomsticks. **1968** *Globe & Mail* (Toronto) 17 Feb. 44 Suburban Duberger defeated nearby Vanier 4-2.. in the ninth annual international pee-wee hockey tournament. **1970** C. MAJOR *Dict. Afro-Amer. Slang* 90 *Pee wee*, small; a very narrowly rolled marijuana cigarette. **1973** *New York* 26 Mar. 52/2 Why should the Rangers concern themselves with Cub Scouts and peewee players. *Ibid.* 54/3 With the sportswriters giving better notices to the peewees. **1975** *New Yorker* 12 May 113/1 All he comes up with is a cosmetic trick—a peewee Watergate analogy—by using the blunder as evidence that the producer whom Tod works for is corrupt.

b. *spec.* A small marble.

1848 BARTLETT *Dict. Amer.* 246 *Pee-wee*, the name given by boys to a little marble. **1862** C. C. ROBINSON *Dial. Leeds* 383 *Pey-wey*, a very small marble. **1902** FARMER & HENLEY *Slang* V. 160/2 *Pee-wee*... 3. (school).—A small marble. **1941** BAKER *Dict. Austral. Slang* 53 *Peewee*, a small yellow marble. **1951** J. FRAME *Lagoon* 122, I had pee-wees and bully taws and changers that weren't made of glass.

peeweep, peweep, piewipe. Add: **b.** *transf.* (See quot. 1966.) *rare.*

a **1902** S. BUTLER *Way of all Flesh* (1903) xl. 179 Looking for a watch and purse on Battersby piewipes was very like looking for a needle in a bundle of hay. **1966** S. H. BURTON in *Ibid.* (new ed.) 391 'Piewipes' is a dialect word for lapwings—birds that are noted for building nests so well camouflaged that they are very difficult to see. The sense seems to be that the Battersby 'piewipes' are moorlands; barren featureless land affording natural camouflage.

peg, *sb.*[1] Add: **1. e.** *off the peg* adv. phr. and (with hyphens) adj. phr.: said of (the purchase of) ready-made clothes from the peg on which they hang in a shop; available for immediate purchase or use. Also *transf.* and *fig.*

[**1879–81** G. F. JACKSON *Shropshire Word-bk.* 44 *Bought off the pegs*, said contemptuously of second-hand or 'slopmade' clothing.] *a* **1916** R. ASQUITH in Spender & Asquith *Life H. H. Asquith* (1932) II. xlviii. 234 Love ready-made or glamour off the peg. **1922** *19th Cent.* June 1026 Before the war the average undergraduate was..garbed in a 'sports' coat obviously 'off the peg'. **1926** M. A. VON ARNIM *Introd. to Sally* vi. 74 The poor Pinners would have to buy clothes off the peg. **1954** J. BETJEMAN *Few Late Chrysanthemums* 84 An officer's lady—and more so Than those who buy off the peg. **1957** *Economist* 28 Dec. 1120/2 There simply is no such thing as suitable spectacles 'off the peg'. **1959** [see *bar-tacking* s.v. *BAR *sb.*[1] 30]. **1959** *Daily Tel.* 4 May 13 (*heading*) Off-the-Peg thrills of the Law. **1963** *Times* 19 Feb. 18/2 Shipowners may before long buy vessels 'off the peg' instead of each vessel's being an individual tailor-made job. **1971** *Daily Tel.* 8 Nov. 12/3 Her clothes are mostly bought 'off the peg' in Zurich boutiques. **1974** *Country Life* 28 Mar. 732/1 Georgian sash windows.. have been replaced by off-the-peg glass rectangles. **1975** *Times* 11 Mar. (Italian Industry Suppl.) p. vii/4 It was the equivalent of the passage from bespoke to off-the-peg tailoring. **1977** *Navy News* June 22 (Advt.), Every Officer and Rating may be fitted immediately 'off the peg'.

f. *West Indies.* A segment of a citrus fruit. (Perh. a different word: cf. PIG *sb.*[1] 8 c.)

1909 *Cent. Dict.* Suppl. 960/2 *Peg*... One of the cells or natural divisions into which an orange may be separated after removing the skin. [West Indies.] **1956** J. HEARNE *Stranger at Gate* i. 9 He moved his hand and closed it on.. the..tangerine..stripping the soft skin from the fruit and cramming the pegs into his mouth. **1971** *Caribbean Q.* XVII. II. 14 Different name, same referent..feg/fig/peg/plug/sprig (of orange). **1973** *N.Y. Times* 3 June L 19/1 A section of an orange..is..called..'peg'.

g. *Railways.* A semaphore signal.

1911 C. E. W. BEAN '*Dreadnought' of Darling* xxxiii. 288 Recollec' that cove with a red beard we come on camped by the railway peg near Nine Mile Tank..? **1971** D. J. SMITH *Discovering Railwayana* x. 58 *Peg*, signal.

2. f. *Cricket.* A stump.

1865 *Bell's Life in London* 1 July 9/2 Griffith then bowling Davis's centre peg. **1901** H. BLEACKLEY *Tales of Stumps* i. 31 Little Tommy tossed a slow long-hop on the leg peg,..and Nat managed to fumble it away for two. **1909** *Westm. Gaz.* 15 July 12/1 He was beaten by another fine ball from Smith, which, after pitching well outside the off peg, broke across the wicket and hit the top of the leg stump. **1972** R. ROBINSON *Wildest Tests* xi. 120 Cunis swung one so late and so far that it hit Gandotra's leg peg.

g. *Mountaineering.* = *PITON 2. Also in *Comb.*

1920 G. W. YOUNG *Mountain Craft* iv. 201 My party has taken pegs three times in all, as a precaution, and used one once (on a new descent). **1946** J. E. Q. BARFORD *Climbing in Brit.* ii. 25 Pegs or large nails with rings in one end, which are driven into rocks to provide an anchor where no natural one exists. **1957** *Times Lit. Suppl.* 1 Nov. 655/2 The 'peg-bashers' have concentrated their main attention on short ferocious overhangs. **1971** [see *IRONMONGERY 1 d]. **1973** C. BONINGTON *Next Horizon* viii. 120 We fully expected our route to be high-standard peg-climbing the whole way.

3. b. *Mil. slang.* A charge. Usu. in phr. *on the peg*, on a charge, under arrest.

1890 BARRÈRE & LELAND *Dict. Slang* II. 122/2 *On the peg* (military), to be under arrest... The expression is also used when a soldier is put under stoppages. **1919** [see *FOR *prep.* 13 e]. **1923** J. MANCHON *Le Slang* 220 *To whip..on the peg*, mettre..aux arrêts. **1941** *Amer. Speech* XVI. 186/2 *On the peg*, under charge for misdemeanor.

5. (Further examples.) Also *absol.* and const. *for.*

1852 GEO. ELIOT *Let.* 24–25 July (1954) II. 50 The publishing world seems utterly stagnant—nothing coming out which would do as a peg for an article. **1909** J. R. WARE *Passing Eng.* 194/1 *Peg* (*Theatrical*, 1884). Sensation point or effect of a piece. Something upon which the actors ..can build up a scene. **1929** D. H. LAWRENCE *Phoenix II* (1968) 590 And as for his relation to his women..they are pegs to hang clothes on, and there's an end of them. **1930** E. POUND *XXX Cantos* vii. 26 The Elysée carries a name on And the bus behind me gives me a date for peg. **1953** A. HUXLEY *Let.* 19 July (1969) 678, I have been asked..to do an article on recent developments in parapsychology, using your forthcoming book as the peg on which to hang my remarks. **1966** *Listener* 10 Feb. 221/2 The event itself seemed too slight a peg on which to hang a sixty-minute programme. **1972** *Guardian* 11 Sept. 8/6 Newspapermen..with their contempt for yesterday's story, their embarrassment when confronted with masterpieces lacking any evident 'peg'. **1976** *Times Lit. Suppl.* 13 Feb. 174/3 Dr Hacking uses this theme as a series of pegs on which to hang his discussions of particular authors' philosophies of language.

11. peg-bag, a bag used as a container for clothes-pegs; **peg-basket,** a repository for clothes-pegs; **peg-board,** (*a*) (further examples); (*b*) a board having regularly spaced holes for holding hooks on which objects can be hung; hence **peg-boarding; peg-box, pegbox,** a structure at the head of instruments of the lute or violin type, where the strings are attached to the tuning-pegs; **peg doll,** a doll made from a clothes peg or similar piece of wood; **peg-house** *slang*, (*a*) a public-house (see sense 6 in Dict.); (*b*) a brothel or meeting-place for male homosexuals (U.S.); **peg leg** (earlier and later examples); also *transf.* and as *v. intr.*, to move with a limp or a stiff gait (see also quot. 1932); **peg-legged** *a.*, having a peg leg (also *transf.*); **peg-legger,** one having a peg leg; *slang*, a beggar; **peg-man** (*b*), a workman who lasts pegged boots or shoes; **peg-pot** = *peg-tankard*; **peg-rent,** cloak-room charges; **peg rhizoid,** in certain liverworts of the order Marchantiales, a rhizoid distinguished by peg-like processes on the inner surface; **peg-tankard** (later example).

1951 J. FLEMING *Man who looked Back* xl. 145 She gathered up her arty peg-bag. **1972** P. FLOWER *Cobweb* III. 92 Already a faithful clientele. What d'you think about tea cosies and table-mats, peg bags, teapot stands and so on? **1914** D. H. LAWRENCE *Widowing of Mrs. Holroyd* I. i. 12 Jack, can you go and take the stockings in for me?..Minnie, you take the peg-basket. **1951** *Catal. of Exhibits, South Bank Exhib., Festival of Britain* 152/1 Pegboard; Educational Supply Association Ltd. **1960** *Guardian* 24 Feb. 13/5 A peg board lining to the door..for extensive hanging purposes. **1962** E. GODFREY *Retail Selling & Organization* ii. 19 It [*sc.* the counter] will be replaced by shelving, pegboard or tiered stands. **1967** R. WHITEHEAD in Wills & Yearsley *Handbk. Managem. Technol.* 69 Those wonderful pegboard systems and elaborate charts designed along foolproof lines to check the flow of work are notorious for the way they fail to work. **1971** *Femina* (Bombay) 30 Apr. 27/3 Picture puzzles, pegboard, block building..sharpen motor skills. **1975** P. G. WINSLOW *Death of Angel* iv. 96 The shed was deep... Piles of what looked like sheets of metal lay along one side. Tools hung from a pegboard in the back. **1960** *Woman's Realm* 2 Apr. 10/3 Sheets of pegboarding..make a..useful space for hanging utensils. **1962** *Friend* 3 Aug. 946/2 The most expensive item was peg-boarding for the ceiling. **1883** GROVE *Dict. Mus.* III. 81/2 It [*sc.* the rebec] was shaped like the half of a pear, and was everywhere solid except at the two extremities, the upper of which was formed into a peg-box identical with that still in use, and surmounted by a carved human head. **1938** *Oxf. Compan. Mus.* 524/1 The head [of the lute], containing the peg-box, is generally bent back at an angle from the neck. **1961** M. W. PRYNNE in A. Baines *Mus. Instruments* vii. 158 For balance, the bent-back pegbox has to be as light as possible with very slender pegs or 'lute-pins'. **1976** D. MUNROW *Instruments Middle Ages & Renaissance* 25/4 From the twelfth to the fourteenth century, the instrument is regularly referred to in French literature as *mandoire* or sometimes *mandola* and illustrations often reveal the instrument's most recognizable feature; its sickle-shaped pegbox. **1950** *Dryad Catal.* 96 Peg doll. Height 11"—Each 4/6. **1951** *Notes Coll. Dolls & Figurines* (Wenham, Mass., Hist. Assoc.) 50 The popular wooden play doll commonly called 'Peg-doll', 'Penny-wood', was born in the Thuringian forest. **1969** [see **Flanders baby*]. **1972** *Times* 30 June 18/2 Nanny..is one of a series of pretty peg dolls all dressed in the fashions of 1870 servants... They are..made from genuine dolly pegs, hand painted and dressed by Somerset craftsmen. **1922** C. AIKEN *Jig of Forslin* 40 And once I murdered, by the waterfront: A drunken sailor, in a peg-house brawl. **1931** 'D. STIFF' *Milk & Honey Route* 211 Peg house, a place where, if the hobo wishes, he may meet *Angelina*. **1942** BERREY & VAN DEN BARK *Amer. Thes. Slang* § 507/4 *Peg house*, a male homosexual brothel or gathering place. **1972** R. A. WILSON *Playboy's Bk. Forbidden Words* 222 A 'peg-boy' is a young male who prostitutes himself to homosexuals; 'peg-house', a homosexual brothel. There is an unsubstantiated story that boys in East Indian peg-houses were required to sit on pegs between customers, giving them permanently dilated anuses. **1769** J. WEDGWOOD *Let.* 6 Dec. (1965) 88 The peg leg is much wanted. **1932** *Amer. Speech* VII. 269 When cable-tools alternately strike bottom and miss in drilling, they are said to *peg-leg*. **1969** D. FRANCIS *Enquiry* xiv. 190, I peg-legged up the back drive. **1971** M. TAK *Truck Talk* 116 *Peg leg*, (1) the first rear axle of a tandem-axle tractor when it has only single tires... (2) a three-legged trailer... (3) a trailer with one broken dolly. **1974** *Daily Tel.* 3 Sept. 14/6 During the 1914–18 war more than 20,000 men with legs amputated were fitted with clumsy wooden 'peg-legs'. **1967** B. PATTEN *Little Johnny's Confession* 18 It should scatter woodworm into the bedrooms of all peglegged men. **1974** H. L. FOSTER *Ribbin'* vi. 245 The current trend is..ankle-length, peg-legged jeans and platform shoes in the city. **1937** PARTRIDGE *Dict. Slang* 615/2 *Peg-legger*, a beggar... Either rhyming s[lang] or ex the preceding [*sc.* peg-leg]. **1943** *Bournemouth Daily Echo* 28 Oct. 2/3 Another 'peg-legger'—as the one-legged men call themselves—was Marine Edgar Saunders. **1897** S. & B. WEBB *Industr. Democracy* I. 418 'Lasters'..(in hand-sewn work these are known as 'makers', in 'pegged work'..they are called 'pegmen' or 'rivetters'). **1903** *Athenæum* 24 Jan. 122/1 In 1873 a peg-pot similarly engraved..was offered to the city, but declined. **1911** *Chambers's Jrnl.* Feb. 115/1 The man who likes to eat a meal without worry lest somebody should exchange hats with him..must pay peg-rent. **1911** J. M. COULTER et al. *Textbk. Bot.* II. i. 516 In the Marchantiaceae, rhizoids are of two kinds, plane rhizoids.. and peg rhizoids, in which the cell wall grows out internally into peg-like or antler-like projections. **1958** *New Biol.* XXVII. 90 One of the peculiarities of *Marchantia* is that these rhizoids are of two kinds, smooth rhizoids ..and 'peg rhizoids' which have numerous peg-like thickenings on the inner surface of the wall jutting into the cell cavity. **1969** F. E. ROUND *Introd. Lower Plants* viii. 102 (*caption*) Section through a pore region of *Conocephalum*, note photosynthetic filaments, peg and smooth rhizoids and amphigastrium. **1967** *Times* 7 Mar. 21/6 (Advt.), A York peg tankard, by John Plummer, circa 1695.

peg, *v.* Add: **1. c.** Also, in extended uses, to fix (a price, wage, etc.) at a certain level; to set a value on (a currency) in relation to gold or another currency; to set a numerical or quantitative limit on (something). (Further examples.)

1933 *Ann. Reg. 1932* 26 Shortly afterwards the Bank rate was considerably reduced, and sterling was effectively 'pegged' at a gold value of about 15*s.* **1933** *Sun* (Baltimore) 13 July 10/2 The British went off gold after a strenuous effort to maintain gold parity in 1931 and it can hardly be proved that England's trade balance has improved sufficiently to permit pegging the pound at any such figure. *Ibid.* 21 July 2/4 The market was 'pegged' once before this year... The fluctuations in wheat at that time were limited to 5 cents a bushel. **1940** *New Statesman* 13 Apr. 485 The dual system..of rationing by amount and of pegging prices is anomalous. **1944** AUDEN *Sea & Mirror* in *For Time Being* i. 5 When he learns the price is pegged to his valuation. **1949** KOESTLER *Promise & Fulfilment* 292 It is a kind of aseptic social operation, and as wages are pegged to the cost-of-living index, there is no occasion even for local strikes. **1954** *Birmingham* (Alabama) *News* 17 Feb. 1/6 The old method pegged unemployment at 2,259,000 the first week in January. **1959** *Punch* 19 Aug. 30/1 Inflation can be licked by other means, by pegging wages and profits, increasing productivity and output,.. and so on. *Ibid.* 30/2, I have already encouraged my teenagers to peg their consumption of sweets, soft drinks, records, cosmetics and cycle accessories in the hope of bringing manufacturers to heel. **1965** *Listener* 20 May 728/1 There is room for scepticism about the machinery which is supposed to peg these rents at a 'fair' level. **1970** *Times* 18 Dec. 2/5 The orchestras have had their grants pegged for three years and are in a serious position. **1971** *Morning Star* 10 May 1/5 The mark will be allowed to float, meaning its parity will no longer be pegged against the dollar. **1977** *Evening Post* (Nottingham) 27 Jan. 5/4 Planners hope to peg the cost of the tour at £60 or less per tourist.

d. *fig.* To categorize; to form an opinion of (someone, occas. something). Freq. in phr. *to have* (someone or something) *pegged*: to have a fixed opinion of (that person or thing). *N. Amer. colloq.*

1920 *Collier's* 31 July 29/2, I had him pegged from the go in for what he *is*—one of them tea-room boys which will stop at nothin' but work! **1926** J. BLACK *You can't Win* xxi. 320 The expression, 'I have him pegged', which has crept into common usage, is thieves' slang..and has nothing to do with the game of cribbage. **1940** J. O'HARA *Pal Joey* 175, I tho't I could peg a joint like that from 2 mi. away. **1949** *New Yorker* 12 Nov. 28/3 An elderly lady..who pegged him looked back, and then winked. **1959** J. LUDWIG in R. Weaver *Canad. Short Stories* (1968) 2nd. Ser. 232 Naturally Mitchell has her pegged: doesn't he know this shopping trip is a fake? **1967** M. REYNOLDS *After Some Tomorrow* 12, I peg him as a holier than thou cloddy. **1968** H. WAUGH *Con Game* ix. 91, I always knew she was a slut. An ignorant, stupid child. I pegged her from the start. **1972** D. LEES *Zodiac* 40, I had her pegged as a bit of a nut. **1976** *Publishers Weekly* 18 Oct. 52/1 Combine the pace of a Disney film with the reassurance of characters clearly good or evil and you will quickly peg what Nicolaysen's chase adventure has going for it.

2. d. To fasten the soles on to (boots or shoes) with wooden pegs.

1850 *Rep. Comm. Patents 1849* (U.S.) 295 Improvement in Machines for Pegging Boots and Shoes. **1858** [see PEGGED *ppl. a.*]. **1895** *Montgomery Ward Catal.* 511/1 Ladies' Heavy Pegged Shoes. **1940** *Chambers's Techn. Dict.* 622/2 *Pegged-sole shoes*, a type of footwear in which the outer sole is attached to the inner sole and the upper by two or more rows of pegs; used for sea boots.

e. To insert small wooden pegs into the stalks of (tobacco).

1850 *Rep. Comm. Patents: Agric. 1849* (U.S. Dept. Agric.) 321 'Pegging' tobacco..is done by driving little pegs, about six inches long and half an inch or less square, into the stalk about four inches from the big end of the stalk. **1968** *Publ. Amer. Dial. Soc. 1966* XLV. 19 It's hard work to peg tobacco.

f. *Cricket.* To drive pegs into (the face of a bat) (see quot. 1934).

1853 F. GALE *Public School Matches* 17 The captain is going in. An old bat, well pegged but very clean, looks like business. **1906** A. E. KNIGHT *Compl. Cricketer* ii. 48 Pegging down the bat is simple, but destructive and ineffective. **1934** W. J. LEWIS *Lang. Cricket* 186 *To peg a bat*, to drive a few small pegs into the face of a bat as a remedial measure when the grain of the wood has risen with use.

4. b. *peg back*, (*a*) (Racing): of a horse, to pull past, overtake (another horse); also, to gain on another horse by (a specified distance); (*b*) in a game: to pick up (a point or advantage) or to change (the score) so as to reduce or eliminate an opponent's lead.

1928 *Sunday Express* 24 June 22/3 He came..in the last furlong to peg back the flying French colt. **1932** *New Yorker* 14 May 52/2 Burgoo King pegged him back three furlongs from home. **1971** *Sunday Nation* (Nairobi) 11 Apr. 44/4 Owen de Souza pegged one back for Blues in the dying minutes when he converted a penalty-push. **1977** D. FRANCIS *Risk* ii. 18 Open ditch next; Tapestry met it just right and we pegged back a length in mid-air. **1978** *Rugby World* Apr. 4/1 The Irish side had given all Wales a fright by pegging the score back to 13–13 after the visitors had gone 13–3 in front.

10. *peg along* (further U.S. example); *peg away* (earlier and later examples).

1818 KEATS *Let.* 24 Jan. (1958) I. 216 The musicians began pegging & fagging away at an overture. **1882** 'MARK TWAIN' *Lett. to Publishers* (1967) 158, I still lack about 30,000 words... I shall peg along, day by day. **1956** *People* 13 May 1/6, I have just kept pegging away year after year. **1978** L. DEIGHTON *SS-GB* xiv. 115 How I envied you doing Greats, while I pegged away at my Civil Law.

13. g. To hang (washing) with pegs from a clothes-line.

1922 D. H. LAWRENCE *England, my England* 102 Helped his wife to peg out the washing on the clothes line in the meadow. **1974** *Country Life* 21 Mar. 633/1 The foreground girls selfconsciously pegging out the washing. **1978** J. THOMSON *Question of Identity* xii. 115 Betty Lovell was pegging out sheets on a washing-line.

Pegamoid (pe·gămoid). Also **pegamoid.** A trade name for a kind of waterproof cloth or imitation leather used in upholstery, bookbinding, etc. Also *attrib.* and *fig.*

1895 *Current Hist.* V. 731 It is claimed for 'pegamoid', a product recently placed on the markets of Europe, that it will render materials of any kind absolutely impervious to water. **1896** *Westm. Gaz.* 10 June 5/2 By imposing it on cotton cloth or impregnating it 'Pegamoid' can be turned to many and varied purposes. **1909** *Pract. Upholstery* 12 Pegamoid Cloth. This is one of the better class imitation leathers, and is obtainable in a large variety of 'grains', colours, and qualities. **1922** *Daily Mail* 10 Nov. 15 (Advt.), Seats in red, brown, green or blue rexine, pegamoid or velvet. **1957** L. DURRELL *Justine* I. 21 He is a pegamoid sloth of a man, a vast slow fellow. **1959** B. RUCK *Romantic Afterthought* xxxiv. 180 The pegamoid-covered chair.

Pegasean, *a.* (Later example.)

1923 'R. CROMPTON' *William Again* iv. 59 'I feel'—his Pegascan imagination soared aloft on daring wings—'I feel 's if I might *die* if I went to church this mornin' feelin' 's ill as I do now.'

pegasse (pĕgæ·s). Also **pegass.** [Etym. unknown.] A kind of peaty soil found in the Caribbean and northern S. America.

1924 *Chambers's Jrnl.* July 475/1 Suckers should be planted..15 feet apart on pegass or peat soil. **1949** *Caribbean Q.* I. III. 42 Experiments in Surinam seem to show that the pegasse lands..can be used to grow bananas. **1959** *Listener* 17 Sept. 435/1 The north-west of Guiana is a place of countless ridges of hills islanded in a sea of pegasse swamp. **1974** *Encycl. Brit. Macropædia* VIII. 507/1 *Pegasse* soil, a type of tropical peat, occurs behind the coastal clays and along the river estuaries.

pegged, *ppl. a.* (Later examples.)

1960 H. HAYWARD *Antique Coll.* 214/1 *Pegged construction*, furniture made by joiners constructed with mortice and tenon joints, the tenon being held in the mortice by a square peg, riven or split from green wood. **1966** A. W. LEWIS *Gloss. Woodworking Terms* 100 *Pegged or pinned tenon*, tenoned joint which is fixed by having a hole drilled through it near the shoulder and a wood pin inserted. **1967** *Wall St. Jrnl.* 9 Feb. 1/4 Mr. Glick..wears pegged pants, boots and an Army jacket. **1968** *Globe & Mail* (Toronto) 17 Feb. 46 (Advt.), Recreation room with bar and pegged floor. **1973** *N.Y. Law Jrnl.* 19 July 16/8 (Advt.), Parquet and pegged oak floors. **1974** *Times* 7 Mar. 2/6 Growers in Holland and Germany received government help through pegged oil prices.

pegging, *vbl. sb.* Add: **1. a.** (Later examples.)

1926 T. E. LAWRENCE *Seven Pillars* lxvii. 352 They told me something of Davenport's work: of his continual pegging away in Abdulla's sector. **1931** *Observer* 11 Jan. 19/1 Mr. Scultin's views about the pegging of wages are unknown. **1948** G. CROWTHER *Outl. Money* (rev. ed.) viii. 248 'Pegging' has usually meant 'pegging up', but we can invent the term 'pegging down' for the practice that grew up among some governments in the nineteen-thirties of maintaining their currencies at a fixed undervaluation. **1977** *Times* 24 Dec. 9/3 Continental motoring will be given added impetus..by the pegging of most cross-Channel ferry prices.

b. *level-pegging*: see as main entry in Suppl.

peggotty (pe·gǒti). Also **peggitty, peggoty, pegity,** and with capital initial. [Fanciful extension of PEG *sb.*[1]] A children's board game in which four players in turn place pegs in holes, the object being to complete a row of five pegs.

Pegity is registered in the U.S. as a proprietary name.

1925 *Official Gaz.* (U.S. Patent Office) 31 Mar. 996/2 Parker Bros... *Pegity.* Game of the Type of 'Go-Bang'. Played with Pegs, for Adults and Children. **1929** *Games & Toys* July 66/1 Pegity..is one of the most interesting board games ever devised. **1950** *Oxf. Jun. Encycl.* IX. 73/1 Peggotty, a very simple modern game on the Noughts and Crosses principle, is played by four players who take it in turn to stick coloured wooden pegs into holes in the board, the winner being the first to get five pegs in a row. **1958** M. STEWART *Nine Coaches Waiting* iv. 45, I brought you a game..called Peggitty. **1974** P. DICKINSON *Poison Oracle* ii. 60 Tribesmen..played their stone-age version of peggoty in noisy groups.

peggy, *sb.* Add: **5.** *Naut. slang.* A ship's mess-steward or menial.

1902 A. B. LUBBOCK *Round the Horn* iii. 105 An institution on board a sailing-ship is 'peggy'. Each of us take it in turn, and peggy has to fetch the grub from the galley. **1929** F. C. BOWEN *Sea Slang* 102 *Peggy*, the man who looks after the seamen's and the firemen's messes in a modern liner. In the old sailing days it was applied to the ship's boy or to a hand who was called upon to do all the odd jobs in a watch. **1930** 'GREENHORN' *Tinker, Tailor* viii. 191 The sailors' Peggy is a kind of fo'c'sle steward, and.. he has to wash up the pots and pans in the forrard galley, clean out the fo'c'sle, make the bunks, and generally keep the sailors' quarters swept and garnished. **1946** J. IRVING *Royal Navalese* 133 *Peggy*, an Ordinary Seaman detailed to act as Petty Officers' mess-man. **1967** S. WATERS *Indentures Indorsed* i. 11, I was initiated into the mysteries of acting as 'Peggy'. As the name implies this menial does all the domestic chores. **1972** *Courier-Mail* (Brisbane) 19 July 24/3 Some waterfront employers think Peggy should do other work..between tea breaks and lunch.

6. (See quots.) [Perh. a different word.]

1940 *Chambers's Techn. Dict.* 622/2 *Peggies*, slates 10–14 in. long. **1959** *Archit. Rev.* CXXV. 292 *Peggies*, small sizes of slates of random sizes which are sold by weight.

7. peggy bag, a style of women's hand-bag orig. having side handles and outside pockets; **peggy-work** *Naut. slang*, the work of a peggy (sense *5).

1920 *Scot at Hame an' Abroad* 1 July 5/3 Mirren had a wheen peppermints in her peggy bag. **1922** *Daily Mail* 11 Dec. 13 (Advt.), Peggy bags with side handle and two outside pockets. **1939–40** *Army & Navy Stores Catal.* 874/4 Peggy Bag, in plain Calf..with divided inner compartment and mirror. **1974** *Trafford Catal.* Spring–Summer 182/2 Classic 'peggy' bag with twin easy-to-get-at compartments..twin handle length straps. **1959** SCOTT-SHAWE & WYKES *Mariner's Tale* I. iii. 29, I was escaping my peggy-work in the *Ashmore*'s galley.

pego (pī·go). *slang.* [Origin unknown.] The penis.

1680 in Rochester *Poems* 36 As oft as Finger, Dildoe, Pego, Rape, The Virgin Hymen, she repaires the Gap. **1691** E. WARD *Poet's Ramble* 10 *Pego*, like an upstart Hector,..Would fain have Rul'd as Lord Protector: In-flam'd by one so like a Goddess, I scarce could keep him in my Codpiece. *c* **1763** J. WILKES *Ess. on Woman* 19 Then shall man's pride and pego comprehend His actions and erections, use and end. **1788** GROSE *Dict. Vulgar T.* (ed. 2), *Pego*, the penis of man or beast. **1879–80** *Pearl* (1970) 250 This made Neddy's Pego, accustomed to sprout, Shrink into his belly, and turn up his snout. **1974** H. R. F. KEATING *Underside* ix. 90 There's some as likes..her dirty old fingers round their pego.

peg-top, pegtop. Add: **1. a.** (Earlier U.S. and later examples.)

1788 *Massachusetts Spy* 3 Apr. 4/3 Children's Books... Memoirs of a Pegtop. By the Author of, The Adventures of a Pincushion. **1923** D. H. LAWRENCE *Birds, Beasts & Flowers* 171 Chieftains, three of them abreast, on foot Strut like peg-tops. **1978** *Country Life* 14 Dec. 2103/2 Tops: humming tops, peg tops, optical tops, gyroscopes.

b. (Earlier and later examples.)

1803 [see *pea-shooter* s.v. *PEA[1] 7]. **1931** P. GUEDALLA *Duke* I. iv. 22 Nor do the martial virtues thrive upon a simple diet of peg-top and battledore.

2. (Earlier example.)

1858 *Punch* 15 May 202/2 The fashion of trowsers improves, if anything, in ridicule. Henceforth pegtops are split.

3. peg-top pants, = *peg-top trousers*; **peg-top skirt,** a skirt that is wide at the top and narrow at the bottom.

1917 *Times* 24 Jan. 9/5, I noticed yesterday in the leading papers the leading *couturiers* announced the 'new peg-top skirt, cut on most becoming lines'. **1923** E. B. WHITE *Let.* Feb. (1976) 63 A stunning suit—real western cut with peg top pants and everything. **1956** *Punch* 15 Aug. 190/3 This Autumn Collection..emphasizing a belted natural waist-line, short peg-top skirts, and a wrapped-up look. **1970** *Daily Tel.* 23 July 15 Pegtop pants were Patou's big contribution to yesterday's fashion scene. **1972** J. MINIFIE *Homesteader* xvii. 146 The baggy end of a drummer's blue peg-top pants. **1975** G. HOWELL *In Vogue* 222 Schiaparelli's slim silhouette with..peg-top skirt.

pegtopped, *ppl.a.* Add: **pegtopped skirt** = **peg-top skirt.*

1959 *News Chron.* 22 July 3/3 Gently fitted jackets over stiffened pegtopped skirts. **1973** *Country Life* 8 Mar. 632/3 If this peg-topped, tapered, pencil skirt does catch on there will be resounding cheers from the girdle manufacturers.

Peguan (pe·giuăn), *sb.* and *a.* Also **Pegue, Peguer.** [f. the place-name *Pegu* (see below) + -AN.] **A.** *sb.* **a.** A native or inhabitant of the city or district of Pegu in southern Burma, the ancient capital of the Mon (*MON *sb.*[2] and *a.*) people. **b.** The language of the people of Pegu. **B.** *adj.* (Also **Pegu,** the place-name used *attrib.*) Of or pertaining to these people.

c **1591** R. FITCH in Hakluyt *Princ. Navigations* (1599) II. I. 262 The Pegues if they have a sute in the law which is so doubtfull that they cannot well determine it, put two long canes into the water..and there sit men to iudge, and they both do diue vnder the water. **1727** A. HAMILTON *New Acct. E. Indies* II. xxxvi. 36 The *Peguer* finding that he could not recover his Lands without foreign Aid and Assistance, invited the Portuguese. *Ibid.* 37 Neither the Siamers not the Peguers..understood the use of Fire Arms. *c* **1759** [see *KAREN *sb.* 1]. **1800** M. SYMES *Acct. Embassy to Ava* 12 The power of the Peguers now seemed hastening to its wane. **1828** [see *MON *sb.*[2] and *a.*]. **1834** *Chinese Repository* II. 504 The most important is the *Peguan.* **1851** *Ibid.* XX. 345 Frequent wars with the northern Siamese and the Peguans, or *Mons.* **1858** C. T. WINTER *Six Months Brit. Burmah* ii. 15 The inhabitants consist principally of Burmans and Peguans. **1874** J. M. HASWELL *Gram. Notes & Vocab. Peguan Lang.* p. vi, I sent a list of over sixty Peguan words to missionaries among the Kohls. **1910** L. MILNE *Shans at Home* i. 26 A vassal of the Pegu King. *Ibid.* 27 The conquering army of the Pegu king. **1920** G. A. GRIERSON *Linguistic Survey India: Index of Lang.-Names* 164 Peguan..According to the Burma Linguistic Survey, a form of Mōn (3) spoken in Amherst District. **1932** J. G. SCOTT *Burma & Beyond* i. 16 The Khmêr went, or were pushed, farther east,..but the Mōn remained behind, and came to be known to the early merchant adventurers as Peguans. **1942** J. L. CHRISTIAN *Mod. Burma* ii. 12 The Mons, known also as Talaings or Peguans, are an ancient race. **1955** E. MANNIN *Land of Crested Lion* xv. 190 The gift of a wealthy Pegu donor. **1956** *Introducing Burma* 38 The Mon Khmer Branch consists of the Mon Group comprising—Talaing (Mon, Peguan, Martabanèse) which are spoken in the Pegu and Tenasserim Divisions. **1973** J. M. & E. G. MARING *Hist. & Cultural Dict. Burma* 147 *Mon*, A lowland Mon-Khmer ethnolinguistic group of Mongoloid racial stock... Synonyms: *Mon̄*, *Mun*, *Peguan*, *Talaing*.

peh, var. *P'O.

Peierls (pəi·ərlz). *Physics.* The name of Sir Rudolf *Peierls* (b. 1907), German-born physicist, used *attrib.* with reference to a spatially periodic distortion of a linear chain of atoms or molecules in certain solids, adduced to explain an observed change from a conducting to a semiconducting or insulating state at low temperatures.

Described by Peierls in *Quantum Theory of Solids* (1955) 108.

1973 *Solid State Communications* XII. 1130/2 The important question is whether or not one can stabilize such a system just above the Peierls transition.., so that on lowering the temperature the superconducting state becomes truly stable. **1973** *Physical Rev.* VIII. B. 574/2 The experimental superperiod of 8 × 2·88 Å due to the platinum atoms is..in exact agreement with the expected superperiod as due to a 'Peierls distortion'. **1979** *Sci. Amer.* Oct. 54/3 The Peierls transition..comes about through a periodic distortion of the lattice.

pein, var. PEEN *sb.* (in Dict. and Suppl.).

‖ **peineta** (pĕine·tă). [Sp.] An ornamental comb worn by Spanish women with a mantilla.

1935 *Discovery* Oct. 307/2 The *peineta*, or ornamental high shell-comb which together with the *mantilla* constitutes the national head-dress of Spanish women. **1939** SPENDER & GILI tr. *Lorca's Poems* 23 *Calañés* and tall *peinetas*.

Peirce (pɒ̄ɪs). The name of the American philosopher and logician Charles Sanders *Peirce* (1839–1914) used in the possessive to indicate his theories or methods, esp. as **Peirce's Law**, a logical formula relating to implication (see quot. 1967).

1918 C. I. LEWIS *Survey Symbolic Logic* i. 100 By a further important modification of Peirce's method, a theoretically adequate logic of mathematics may be obtained. **1934** W. V. QUINE *Syst. Logistic* vii. 64 p ⊃ q. ⊃ p: ⊃ p This is Peirce's law... The theorem has been so named by Łukasiewicz. **1949** *Jrnl. Philos.* XLVI. 513 This paper assumes Peirce's semiotic as the basis for a discussion..of the logical paradoxes. **1954** I. M. COPI *Symbolic Logic* iii. 64 Assuming Peirce's Law false leads to a contradiction. **1955** A. N. PRIOR *Formal Logic* I. iii. 50 And so *p* is true (by 'Peirce's law'). **1967** S. C. KLEENE *Math. Logic* § 3. 13 ((P ⊃ Q) ⊃ P) ⊃ P. (Peirce's law, 1885). **1972** LAMBERT & VAN FRAASSEN *Derivation* 49 The following principle is known as Peirce's Law.

Peircian (pɒ̄·ɪsiăn), *a.* [f. prec. + -IAN.] Of or relating to the American philosopher, Charles Sanders Peirce, his theories or methods.

1905 *Mind* XIV. 237 The Peircian pragmatist. **1949** *Mind* LVIII. 130 Mr. Feibleman is a well-known Peircian scholar. **1952** *Mind* LXI. 205 This surely manifests a thoroughly Peircean attitude. **1965** *Amer. Philos. Q.* II. 115/2 We mobilize the Peircean idea of an inductive community. **1978** N. JARDINE in Hookway & Pettit *Action & Interpretation* 123 Such a picture of scientific progress may encourage, though it does not entail, a Peircean vision of an ultimate science, an omega of human knowledge in which the essences of all things are revealed.

Peisistratid, var. *PISISTRATID *sb.* and *a.*

peitrel, *sb.* For †*Obs.* read '†*Obs.* except *Hist.*' and add: The spelling **peytral** is now preferred by the best authorities. (Later examples.)

1894 H. A. L. DILLON in W. J. Loftie *Authorised Guide to Tower of London* (ed. 2) 147 Note also the horse armour consisting of the chanfrein for the head, the crinet for the neck, and the bard protecting the body, that is, the peytral on the chest, the flanches on the sides, and the crupper covering the hinder portion of the horse. **1926** *Fine Armour* (Christie's Sale Catal. 29 June) 4 A Peytrel for the Horse, of three plates of plain bright steel. *Ibid.* 15 A Horse Chanfron and Peytrel Plates. **1929** *Archaeologia* LXXIX. 242 The two sales of the armoury of Prince Radziwill..included no less than 22 chanfrons and 15 peytrals of Maximilian date. **1953** *Proc. Prehistoric Soc.* XIX. 175 The object was claimed to be a 'peytrel' or chest ornament for a small horse. **1962** J. MANN *Wallace Coll. Catal.: European Arms & Armour* I. 12 *Peytral* of five large plates. **1967** *Punch* 29 Nov. 809/3 If some hulking great brute..were to straddle an already overburdened war-horse, the whole caboodle would collapse in a sorry ruin of pauldron and salade, breastplate and roundel, cantle, crupper, greave, flanchard, peytral, chanfron and crinet.

pejoration. Add: **b.** *Linguistics.* The development of a less favourable meaning or of unpleasant connotations of a word.

1889 in *Cent. Dict.* **1939** L. H. GRAY *Foundations of Lang.* ix. 259 Their [*sc.* words'] degeneration (technically termed *pejoration*;..) is often due to a selection and specialisation of some ethically lower connotation which may be implied in them. **1956** *Archivum Linguisticum* VIII. 74 And is not pejoration a general feature of semantic development? **1966** *Word Study* Dec. 7/1 Perhaps Walt Disney would be interested in the pejoration and 'spread' of the name for his major cartoon character to a word now so loosely defined that it might some day take three dictionary columns to list. **1975** *Amer. Speech 1972* XLVII. 295 In the case of two English words, borrowing [in German] has resulted in pejoration.

pejorism. Delete *nonce-wd.* and add later example.

1910 R. BROOKE *Let.* 7 Nov. (1968) 261 Pejorism is the Art of thinking things Worse than they Are in order that you may thereby be the more powerfully impelled to Better them.

pejorist (pī·dʒŏrist, pe·dʒŏrist). [f. as PEJORISM + -IST, after *pessimist.*] One who believes that the world is becoming worse.

1919 W. DE MORGAN *Old Madhouse* i. 3 Are we the better or the worse off by the change? The Optimist says better, the Pessimist says worse. I think the present writer must be sitting on a fence—a pejorist, suppose we say, since jargon is in vogue nowadays. **1932** *Times Lit. Suppl.* 14 July 508/4 Between optimists and pessimists there are those who style themselves..bonists, malists and pejorists. **1933** A. E. HOUSMAN *Let.* 5 Feb. (1971) 329, I am not a pessimist but a pejorist (as George Eliot said she was not an optimist but a meliorist). **1958** *Listener* 31 July 171/3 Why he [*sc.* A. E. Housman] was impelled to rape the major pejorists of five literatures for phrase and form to enable him to make poetry of his own predicament.

pekan. For '*Mustela pennanti*' substitute '*Martes pennanti*'. (Earlier and later examples.)

1760 T. JEFFERYS *Nat. & Civil Hist. French Dominions* I. 37 The fur of this animal [*sc.* a kind of pole-cat], as also that of the Pekan, another creature of the wild-cat kind,.. are what is called the *Menuë Peleterie*, or lesser furs. **1771** T. PENNANT *Synopsis Quadrupeds* 224 The *Pekan* and *Vison* of M. de Buffon resemble each other so nearly, that I do not separate them. **1870** J. YEATS *Nat. Hist. Commerce* II. 270 The pekan inhabits North America, and is also called Hudson's Bay Sable. **1910** E. T. SETON *Life-Hist. Northern Animals* II. 926 The name 'Pekan', first recorded by Charlevoix (1744) and popularized by Buffon 1765, is the Abenaki name, adopted without change. **1963** R. D. SYMONS *Many Trails* xvii. 177 It was one of the loveliest and rarest of fur-bearers—a pekan or fisher. **1973** R. FIENNES *Headless Valley* v. 93 Pekans are better known as Fishers which is strange since they never fish.

Peke (pīk). Also **Pek, Pekie.** Abbreviation of *PEKIN(G)ESE *sb.* c.

1915 *Vanity Fair* (N.Y.) Jan. 52/1 England has known the Peke for some time. **1920** *Chambers's Jrnl.* 21 Feb. 177/2 Adjoining were the kennels where the Pekies live. **1922** W. J. LOCKE *Tale of Triona* ix. 105 Instead of pulling your weight you think it's your right to sit on a cushion, a passenger—or a Pekie dog—and let other people pull you. **1924** GALSWORTHY *White Monkey* II. iv. 157 I'll see what I can do, if you'll lend me your Peke for an hour or so. **1926** *Spectator* 22 May 859/2 A young lady of fashion happens to be travelling to-day..with a couple of wardrobe trunks and a fortune in sables, satchels, vanity cases, also a 'Pek'. **1936** [see *ICKLE *a.*]. **1956** E. BERCKMAN *Beckoning Dream* xiii. 95 The vacant eyes, round like a Peke's. **1973** *Listener* 9 Aug. 181/3 He gave me my first dog..a tiny Pekinese puppy... He came and broke the news to me about the death of that particular peke.

Pekin. Add: Also (now more usually) **Peking.**

The distribution of the spellings *Peking* and *Pekin* is uneven: for convenience, in sense 3 below, the spelling *Peking* is given but in some of the *attrib.* and *Comb.* uses *Pekin* occurs with equal or greater frequency.

1. a. (Further example.)

1954 'M. COST' *Invitation from Minerva* 105 The mahogany bed was draped with Pekin.

b. A type of Chinese rug or carpet.

1904 M. B. LANGTON *How to know Oriental Rugs* viii. 223 The Peking, Tientsin, and Samarkand are the only varieties known in this country. **1913** G. G. LEWIS *Pract. Bk. Oriental Rugs* (rev. ed.) 303 Those [rugs] which reach our own shores are generally divided into three classes according to the districts from which they came, namely, Pekin, Tientsin and Thibet. **1962** C. W. JACOBSEN *Oriental Rugs* 270 The Peking is a medium priced rug, costing much less than the Sarouk and half that of a good Kirman.

c. = **Peking duck* (a).

1885 *Encycl. Brit.* XIX. 647/1 The Pekin, a white breed with pale yellowish tint in the plumage, and a very bright orange bill. **1902** *Ibid.* XXXI. 882/2 Some duck-farmers in England have..also adopted the Peking. **1972** *Guardian* 24 May 9/1 You've got your Peking, your Aylesbury, your Muscovy.

3. *attrib.* & *Comb.*, as *Peking carpet, crepe, rug*; **Peking duck,** (*a*) a large white duck with yellow bill and legs, belonging to a breed imported from China to Britain and the U.S.A. in 1873; (*b*) a speciality of Chinese cuisine; **Peking Labrador** (see quot.); **Peking man**, a fossil hominid, *Homo erectus pekinensis*, first described in 1926 from remains found in caves near the village of Choukoutien; **Peking opera**, a stylized form of opera which evolved in China during the nineteenth century; *Peking point* (see quot.); **Peking spaniel** = *PEKIN(G)ESE *sb.* c; **Peking stripe** (see quots.).

1969 G. SIMS *Sand Dollar* i. 14 He slumped down further in the chair, letting his feet sink deep into the Pekin washed-silk carpet. **1971** *Nat. Geographic* Oct. 548/2 The Westerner who makes his way past the propaganda finds Shantung silk, Swatow lace, Peking carpets. **1972** P. L. PHILLIPS tr. *Formenton's Oriental Rugs & Carpets* 237 (*caption*) Typical Pekin carpet woven in the second half of the nineteenth century. **1895** *Montgomery Ward Catal.* 7/2 Pekin Crepe or Momie Cloth, 29 inches wide, used for fancy party dresses, draperies, etc. **1880** L. WRIGHT *Illustr. Bk. Poultry* (rev. ed.) xxxv. 541 The Pekin Duck is one of the most valuable of recent introductions... The Pekin Duck differs from all others in the shape and carriage of its body, which is a peculiar boat or barge shape. **1902** *Encycl. Brit.* XXXI. 882/2 In America the Peking duck is universally used, and has been made by selection both larger and a better layer. **1955** F. OLIVER *Chinese Cooking* ii. 53 Peking Duck..is one of the great Chinese dishes and was always on the banquet menu in Peking. **1973** L. HELLMAN *Pentimento* (1974) 185, I was driving back to the farm trying not to listen to the noise that came from two crates of Pekin ducks. **1964** LEE SU JAN *Fine Art of Chinese Cooking* xii. 94 The recipe for the authentic Peking Duck appears in this chapter. The incomparable flavour of the duck is a result of the vapours of the wine, soy sauce, and other condiments penetrating the meat. **1973** *Country Life* 15 Mar. 699/1 The infinite variety of Chinese food, with classic dishes such as Peking duck and shark's fin soup. **1974** *Encycl. Brit. Macropædia* VII. 943/2 The greatest of all delicacies of this region is of course the Peking duck. This elaborate, world-renowned dish requires lengthy preparation and is served in three separate courses. **1975** *Nature* 6 Mar. 12/3 The Peking duck originated in China and was first noted in the U.S.A. around 1870. **1960** C. W. CUNNINGTON et al. *Dict. Eng. Costume* 268/2 *Pekin Labrador*,..a Pekin silk flowered in wreaths. **1926** *Peking Leader* 24 Oct. in *Bull. Peking Soc. Nat. Hist.* (1928) II. IV. p. xvii (*heading*) Notable archaeologists deliver addresses at 'Peking Man' meeting. *Ibid.* p. xix, His [*sc.* J. G. Andersson's] work..culminated in the discovery of the two teeth of the 'Peking Man' (Dr. Andersson did not call the ancient inhabitant by that title, but probably this will be his popular designation). **1929** *Times* 30 Dec. 9/4 The Peking man is considered to antedate Neanderthal man, and is held to be nearer the genus *Homo* than the Piltdown and Java types. **1937** *Discovery* Jan. 27/1 'Peking Man' Skulls. A fifth skull, which may prove to be the most important of all, has been found at Choukoutien. **1946** J. S. HUXLEY *Unesco* i. 10 They [*sc.* man's innate mental powers] certainly were improved..in the earliest stages of his career, from Pekin man through the Neanderthalers to our own species. **1955** *Proc. Prehist. Soc.* XXI. 39 The oldest undoubted hearths are those recorded in the Choukoutien caves, occupied by Peking Man at the beginning of the second interglacial period. **1973** *Listener* 10 May 605/2 The classical find of *Homo erectus* was..made in China. He is Peking man, about four hundred thousand years old. **1976** *Times Lit. Suppl.* 7 May 544/5 There is an interesting, if speculative, account of the nature, habits and affinities of Peking Man. **1954** *Folk Arts of New China* 41 Peking Opera is traditionally played by men even to the female characters. Peking Opera has no sets or scenery. **1965** S. KNIGHT *Let.* 1 Oct. in *Window on Shanghai* (1967) xv. 65 Extracts from Peking opera—three modern and one ancient, the story of how the Monkey King ate the peaches of Immortality. **1968** *Guardian* 4 Nov. 7/5 Peking opera.. is extremely formal, a mixture of song, dance, music, and acting. Each movement and gesture and every word sung or recited is synchronised with the music. **1970** W. APEL *Harvard Dict. Music* (ed. 2) 153/1 The Peking opera has a short history (*c.* 100 years). Although the highly stylized singing and acting demands a cultivated taste, the Peking opera remains the most popular musical art form. **1971** *Guardian* 28 Dec. 12/3 The essence..is communicated to the children through slides, films..revolutionary Peking opera, books, posters. **1973** *Listener* 19 July 84/3 After 1949, a great attempt was made to play down what had become the Court opera—Peking opera—and to encourage the local traditions. **1974** *Encycl. Brit. Macropædia* XII. 675/2 Credit for the beginning of Peking opera is given to actors from Anhwei appearing in Peking in the 1790s. But Peking opera really combines elements from many different earlier forms and, like Western grand opera, can be considered to be a 19th-century product. **1960** C. W. CUNNINGTON et al. *Dict. Eng. Costume* 268/2 *Pekin point*,..a very rich white silk painted with flowers or bouquets with foliage, with a light mixture of gold in the pattern. **1962** C. W. JACOBSEN *Oriental Rugs* 270 A Peking rug is a Chinese design rug, hand woven in Japan. **1913** A. CONAN DOYLE *Poison Belt* (ed. 2) v. 163 There were three gaily dressed women, all young and beautiful, one of them with a Peking spaniel upon her lap. **1908** *Dry Goods Economist* 13 June 81/3 Pékiné, or pekin stripes.—A design in stripes of alternating colors, the stripes usually being of equal widths. **1960** C. W. CUNNINGTON et al. *Dict. Eng. Costume* 268/2 *Pekin*,..a silk textile of the nature of taffeta, having fine stripes running through it; hence 'Pekin stripes'.

Pekin(g)ese (pīkinī·z, pīkiŋī·z), *sb.* and *a.* [f. *Pekin(g)* (see PEKIN) + -ESE.] **A.** *sb.* **a.** A native or inhabitant of Peking. **b.** The form of Chinese used in Peking. **c.** A Pekingese dog. **B.** *adj.* Of or pertaining to Peking; applied esp. to a breed of dwarf pug-dogs with long, silky hair, obtained originally from the Imperial Palace at Peking; *Pekinese stitch*, a stitch in embroidery.

1849 *Ann. Propag. Faith* Mar. 94, I have been informed that you speak..Pekinese. **1866** *Leisure Hour* XV. 45/2 (*heading*) Peking and the Pekingese. **1879** *Good Words* 745/1 It is old and stiff like Pekingese Buddhism. **1888**

Peel City Guardian 14 Apr. 281/5 A singular Pekingese New Year custom is mentioned in the Shen Pao. **1898** *Kennel Gaz.* June 266/2 Foreign Dogs..Pekin Primula.. (Pekinese Spaniel). *Ibid.* July 299/3 Foreign Dogs. Jock (Pekinese Pug). **1902** *Ibid.* Jan. 19/1 In the hurried departure of the Court from Pekin during the late war.. not a single Pekinese Spaniel was left to..be annexed as loot. *Ibid.* Apr. 127/3 In future the breeds will be known as 'Japanese' and 'Pekinese' only, and neither the term spaniel nor pug added. A separate Classification on the Register of Breeds has also been given to 'Pekinese'. **1904** H. COMPTON *20th Cent. Dog* I. 261 It is now more than forty years since the first specimens of the Pekinese dog, or lion-dog of China, were imported into England. *Ibid.* 262 Thirty years had to elapse before the Pekinese dog became—I cannot call it popularised..but rather say, in evidence. **1906** *Field* 20 Oct. 663/2 Pekingese were forward in strong numbers, the best dog weighing [etc.]. **1910** *Encycl. Brit.* VI. 216/2 Cantonese is supposed to approximate most nearly to the primitive language of antiquity, whereas Pekingese perhaps has receded farthest from it. **1914** R. B. LEE *Hist. & Descr. Mod. Dogs Gt. Brit. & Ireland (Non-Sporting Division)* (ed. 3) Add. p. i, Many additions to the classification..have been made... The most remarkable instance..is that of the Pekingese. *Ibid.* p. v, An ideal Pekingese must have a long coat with a thick undercoat, straight and soft, neither curled nor wavy, the feather on thighs and legs long and profuse. The tail should be carried high on the loins in a loose curl. **1919** G. B. SHAW *Heartbreak House* II. 81 She has the Ancient Mariner on a string like a Pekinese dog. **1920** *19th Cent.* Sept. 384 The Grand Duchess Tatiana carried in her arms her little Pekingese dog. **1931** A. C. DIXEY *Lion Dog of Peking* III. i. 150 The Pekingese is above all fearless and sporting. **1932** D. C. MINTER *Mod. Needlecraft* 46/1 Pekinese stitch..is..most effective... A study of Chinese work will show this stitch worked..in fine silks to give beautiful graded effects. **1934** M. THOMAS *Dict. Embroidery Stitches* 159 Pekinese Stitch may be used as a line stitch or as a solid filling where shading is necessary, and is very pretty and braid-like in effect. **1935** [see *CRISP *sb.* 7]. **1950** D. JONES *Phoneme* vi. 17 In Pekingese, too, we find that the difference between the first (high-level) and third (low-rising) tones is accompanied by a difference of vowel quality and of length. **1958** *Proc. 8th Internat. Congr. Linguists* 764 Language reform in China covers the reform of the Chinese script and the standardization of Pekingese as the national language. **1960** B. SNOOK *Eng. Hist. Embroidery* 50 The stitches used [*sc.* in Black work] include chain, back, sword, Pekinese,..and speckling. **1969** *Queen* 17–30 Sept. 14/2 The hot sour soup ..and Peking duck are authentic examples of the subtle art of Pekingese cuisine. **1970** *Language* XLVI. 675 Even though Pekingese is hardly a rugged testing-ground for methods of describing phonotactic distributions..it might offer a very real test for certain kinds of prosodic analysis. **1976** A. POWELL *Infants of Spring* iii. 51 A conspicuous member of the household was Pekoe, my mother's pekinese, so huge in size that he was once mistaken for a St Bernard puppy.

Pekin(g)ology (pīkiŋǫ·lŏdʒi, pīkiŋ-). [f. *Pekin(g)* (see PEKIN) + -OLOGY.] The study of Chinese politics and current affairs.

1962 *Economist* 21 Apr. 228/1 Pekinology is the murkiest of arts, and it takes something like extra-sensory perception to glean much about Chinese policy from the session. **1966** *N.Y. Times* 3 Apr. IV. 6 Practitioners of the recondite art of Pekinology say that if Chairman Mao died tomorrow the party leadership probably would fall. **1976** *Pacific Affairs* XLIX. 126 Inevitably, a study of China's past zone of expansion leads geographically up to and into the zone of Russia's more recent expansion, and here power-politics, geo-politics, Kremlinology and Pekinology raise their hydra heads.

So **Pekin(g)o·logist**, an expert on or student of Chinese politics and current affairs.

1962 *Economist* 21 Apr. 228/2 He [*sc.* Chou En-Lai] mentioned light and heavy industry in that order (which is the kind of clue that Pekinologists have to fall back on). **1966** *Guardian* 27 July 8/6 If Mao wasn't actually ailing through all these months of secluded speculation, what was he doing? Our tame Pekinologist suggests: training for his epic swim. **1968** W. SAFIRE *New Lang. Politics* 76/1 A new synonym for China watcher is 'Pekingologist', coined on the analogy of Kremlinologist. **1969** *Punch* 2 Apr. 478 Fleet Street is said to be desperate for reliable Pekinologists who can churn out a thousand weekly words on the Chinese enigma. **1972** D. BLOODWORTH *Any Number can Play* xvi. 150 They've had the pekinologists declaring Mao dead, blind, gaga.

peko, var. *PIKAU *sb.*

pelagic, *a.* Add: Also applied *spec.* to the environment in any part of the sea away from the littoral and benthic regions and to marine life at any depth that is independent of these regions. (Further examples.)

1882 *Nature* 5 Oct. 559/1, I have spoken of pelagic life as belonging to the surface waters of the ocean..; but,.. it is impossible as yet to limit definitely the range of pelagic forms in depth, and we shall even have to refer to some connections of the fauna of the deep ocean bottom with that of the surface. Pelagic life then includes the inhabitants of the whole ocean waters, excluding those belonging to the bottom and shores. **1891** MURRAY & RENARD in *Rep. Sci. Results Voy. H.M.S. Challenger: Deep-Sea Deposits* iv. 251 We would suggest that the term oceanic Plankton be subdivided into pelagic Plankton for the animals living in the waters from the surface to 100 fathoms, zonary Plankton for those living in the intermediate zones between 100 fathoms from the surface and 100 fathoms from the bottom,..and abyssal Plankton for those living within 100 fathoms from the bottom over pelagic deposits. **1912** MURRAY & HJORT *Depths of Ocean* ix. 562 The conception of a 'pelagic' mode of life, originally associated with the animal-life of the ocean-surface, thus gradually proved to hold true for life in mid-water also... The main characteristic of pelagic life is its independence of the bottom. **1954** N. B. MARSHALL *Aspects Deep Sea Biol.* v. 89 Swimming and floating between the surface and the deep-sea floor are the pelagic animals. **1957** *Mem. Geol. Soc. Amer.* No. 67. I. xxii. 643 The distinction between pelagic and benthic species in these depths is difficult in many cases and depends on how far from the bottom a species must live in order to be considered pelagic. *Ibid.* 645 As yet nothing is known about pelagic animals from depths greater than 6000 meters—*i.e.*, from the trenches. *Ibid.* II. vi. 97 The subdivision of the water above the bottom, the great pelagic region, is more satisfactorily established. **1962** K. F. LAGLER et al. *Ichthyol.* xiv. 468 Marine fishes may be classed into three main categories: (*a*) the shore or shelf fauna..; (*b*) the pelagic or open sea fishes, generally living near the surface of tropical and warm-temperature seas..; (*c*) deepsea or abyssal forms, inhabiting depths greater than 100 fathoms. **1969** [see *NEKTON]. **1970** D. A. ROSS *Introd. Oceanogr.* vi. 140 The pelagic realm can be subdivided into the neritic environment (the water that overlies the continental shelf) and the oceanic environment (the water of the deep sea). **1974** [see *NERITIC *a.*].

b. Similarly applied to whaling and whalers.

1941 J. S. HUXLEY *Uniqueness of Man* viii. 184 With the advent of pelagic whaling it seemed certain that, unless international regulation of the industry were achieved, whales would certainly become exceedingly scarce, and some species might be wiped out. **1958** *Times* 12 Nov. 11/6 The total number of whales caught last year by pelagic or factory ship expeditions in the Antarctic in 69 catching days was 35,977. **1974** *Nature* 4 Oct. 367/2 If the 1974–75 quotas for pelagic whaling in the Southern hemisphere are reached..the catch of all species next season may reach 380 thousand tons.

c. Of sea-bed material: formed within the sea itself, rather than transported from the land.

1884 MURRAY & RENARD in *Proc. R. Soc. Edin.* XII. 515 The following table shows the nomenclature we have adopted:—Terrigenous deposits... Pelagic deposits. **1891** —— *Rep. Deep-Sea Deposits* iii. 185 From the point of view of their composition, as well as of their geographical and bathymetrical position, Marine Deposits may be separated into two great divisions, viz. (I.) Pelagic Deposits—those formed towards the centres of the great oceans, and made up chiefly of the remains of pelagic organisms along with the ultimate products arising from the decomposition of rocks and minerals; and (II.) Terrigenous Deposits. **1959** A. HARDY *Fish & Fisheries* v. 103 Pelagic deposits..cover the floor of the great oceans in the depths beyond the edge of the shelf. **1970** D. A. ROSS *Introd. Oceanogr.* viii. 297 Deep-sea sediments can be divided into two major groups: pelagic sediments and terrigenous sediments.

d. = *LIMNETIC *a.*

1899 G. C. WHIPPLE *Microsc. Drinking-Water* viii. 105 The plants and animals that inhabit lakes and ponds may be classified according to their habitat... The limnetic or pelagic organisms are those that make their home in the open water. **1955** C. C. DAVIS *Marine & Fresh-Water Plankton* i. 11 Lakes may be subdivided into horizontal and vertical portions. Horizontally, the relatively shallow area close to shore..is called the littoral region, while the region of open water is known as the limnetic (or pelagic) region. **1975** G. A. COLE *Textbk. Limnol.* ii. 9/1 Beyond the pond weeds..is the open water. This is the limnetic or pelagic zone, a region in the lake where shore and bottom have lessened influence.

e. Of birds: inhabiting regions of open sea beyond the edges of a continental shelf, feeding on plankton and other marine organisms, and returning to shore only in the breeding season.

1935 V. C. WYNNE-EDWARDS in *Proc. Boston Soc. Nat. Hist.* XL. 240 The typical species of these three communities [of birds] in the temperate North Atlantic might be separated as follows: 1. Inshore... 2. Offshore... 3. Pelagic. *Ibid.* 241 Pelagic birds..feed chiefly on plankton. **1936** R. C. MURPHY *Oceanic Birds S. Amer.* I. II. 323 South America..is the longest mass of land lying in the relatively open oceans of the southern hemisphere... It is natural..that nearly all the genera, and a large proportion of the species of southern-hemisphere pelagic birds should occur within the limits of the field. **1954** FISHER & LOCKLEY *Sea-Birds* vii. 170 Little is known of the construction of pelagic flocks. **1974** A. DILLARD *Pilgrim at Tinker Creek* x. 165 The oceanic breeding grounds of pelagic birds are as teeming and cluttered as any human Calcutta.

pelagically (pĭlæ·dʒikăli), *adv.* [f. prec.: see -LY[2].] In pelagic regions.

1966 R. M. LOCKLEY *Grey Seal, Common Seal* x. 129 Seals which breed pelagically on floating icefields are threatened by fishers who hunt them today by boat, helicopter and light aircraft. **1975** *Nature* 8 May 100/3 Introductions, the American smelt and the alewife, dominated the main trench and were also common pelagically.

pelandok (pəlændǫ·k). Also **plandok.** [Malay.] The lesser mouse-deer, *Tragulus javanicus*, native to parts of south-east Asia.

1821 J. LEYDEN tr. *Malay Annals* 89 One of his dogs roused a white pelandok. **1836** J. Low *Diss. Soil & Agric. Penang* iii. 188 The *plandok*, or cheurotin [*sic*] of Buffon, or hornless deer, about the size of a hare, is plentiful. **1839** T. J. NEWBOLD *Pol. & Statistical Acct. Straits of Malacca* I. vii. 436 The Plandok is a favourite animal among the Malays, and frequently alluded to both in their prose compositions and poems. **1900** W. MAXWELL in W. W. Skeat *Malay Magic* v. 113 There lived a man whose wife.. was seized with a violent longing for the meat of the *pelandok* (mouse-deer). **1905** *Outing* Jan. 469/2 It may be anything from a *plandok* (mouse deer) to a tiger. **1958** [see *KIDANG]. **1962** *Listener* 22 Nov. 878/2 The spider being here [*sc.* in Africa] what the *plandok* is in Malaya, a jungle Till Eulenspiegel. **1965** C. SHUTTLEWORTH *Malayan Safari* ii. 26 The flesh of the pelandok is extremely edible, and he is hunted constantly. **1969** LD. MEDWAY *Wild Mammals Malaya* 106/1 Lesser Mouse-deer. Pelandok, Kanchil... Largely nocturnal; generally solitary.

pelargonidin (pelāɪgōᵘ·nĭdin). *Chem.* [a. G. *pelargonidin* (R. Willstätter 1914, in *Sitzungsber. d. k. preuss. Akad. d. Wissensch.* 405), f. as next: see *-IDIN.] An anthocyanidin (usu. isolated as the chloride, $C_{15}H_{11}O_5Cl$) that is the aglycone of pelargonin and many other red plant pigments.

1914 *Chem. Abstr.* VIII. 3421 The pelargonin of the scarlet pelargona flower on hydrolysis gave 2 mols. dextrose and 1 mol. of pelargonidin, $C_{15}H_{11}O_6Cl$ [*sic*]. **1934** *Jrnl. Chem. Soc.* 1612 The orange-scarlet nasturtium contains a pelargonidin 3-bioside, the red *gloxinia* flowers are coloured by a pelargonidin rhamnoglycoside, and pelargonidin 3-glycosides occur in scarlet carnations, strawberries,..and in other flowers. **1937** [see *DELPHINIDIN]. **1965** [see *PEONIDIN]. **1966** [see *CYANIDIN]. **1974** *Phytochemistry* XIII. 2002 The major anthocyanins were dentified as the 3-glucoside, 3-galactoside, 3-rutinoside and 3-robinobioside of pelargonidin.

pelargonin (pelāɪgōᵘ·nin). *Chem.* [a. G. *pelargonin* (R. Willstätter 1914, in *Sitzungsber. d. k. preuss. Akad. d. Wissensch.* 405), f. G. *pelargonie* or mod.L. PELARGONIUM: see -IN[1].] An anthocyanin (usu. isolated as the red chloride, $C_{27}H_{31}O_{15}Cl$) that is the colouring matter of zonal pelargoniums and on hydrolysis gives pelargonidin and glucose.

1914 [see *PELARGONIDIN]. **1934** C. C. STEELE *Introd. Plant Biochem.* xix. 221 The different species of *Primula* contain different delphinidin derivatives, while cyanin and pelargonin predominate in different coloured varieties of *Pelargonium zonale.* **1956** I. L. FINAR *Org. Chem.* II. xv. 585 Pelargonidin chloride, $C_{15}H_{11}O_5Cl$. This is formed, together with two molecules of glucose, when pelargonin chloride is hydrolysed with hydrochloric acid.

Pelasgian, *a.* and *sb.* Add: **b.** (Earlier and later examples.) Also, the Indo-European language attributed to the pre-Hellenic population of Greece and the Aegean. Also *attrib.*

a **1490** J. SKELTON tr. *Diodorus Siculus' Bibliotheca Historica* (1956) I. IV. 321 Summe call theym Pelasgians by encheson that they first proceded from theym of Pelasgye which colaterallyth vnto the Grecians. **1875** *Calcutta Rev.* LXI. 4 The Celts..were followed by the so-called Pelasgians, who then separated into Greeks and Latins. **1939** L. H. GRAY *Foundations of Lang.* 376 N. Marr..held that Caucasian was..cognate with Basque, Etruscan, Pelasgian, and other 'Mediterranean' tongues. **1954** PEI & GAYNOR *Dict. Linguistics* 163 *Pelasgian*, an extinct language of southern Europe, variously described as Mediterranean or Japhetic, and said to have been linked with Caucasian, Basque and Etruscan. **1966** *Lingua* XVI. 277 The discussion of Pelasgian phonology offers nothing new. **1972** W. B. LOCKWOOD *Panorama Indo-European Lang.* 12 Pelasgian was apparently a living language locally in the Aegean until the fifth century B.C.

Hence **Pela·sgianist**, a student of the Pelasgian language.

1965 *Lingua* XIII. 349, I propose to examine..in section E those 'Pelasgian' etymologies which have been agreed by three or more Pelasgianists with no dissentient. **1967** *Ibid.* XVIII. 148 Errors made with 'Pelasgian' are characterized by the effort *to cling to the customary conceptions*..both on the side of the adversaries of 'Pelasgian' and on the side of the 'Pelasgianists' themselves. **1970** *Trans. Philol. Soc.* 1969 84 This [*sc.* reconstruction of a language from its loan-words in another language] is the desperate hazard attempted by the school of 'Pelasgianists'.

Pelasgic, *a.* Add: **b.** *sb.* = *PELASGIAN b above.

1966 E. P. HAMP in Birnbaum & Puhvel *Anc. Indo-European Dial.* 114 It is convenient here to reproduce Georgiev's subgrouping of Indo-European..: Central: Greek, Daco-Mysian.., Indo-Iranian, Phrygian-Armenian, Thracian, Pelasgic.

pele, var. *PEEL *sb.*[1] 4.

Peléan (pėlī·ăn), *a.* *Geol.* Also **Peléean, Pelean,** and with small initial letter. [f. the name of Mount *Pelée*, a volcano on the island of Martinique, W. Indies, which erupted in this way in 1902: see -AN.] Of, pertaining to, or designating a type of volcanic eruption characterized by the lateral emission of *nuées ardentes* from a point of weakness in the flank and the vertical extrusion of very viscous lava in the centre which tends to become consolidated as a solid plug.

1903 ANDERSON & FLETT in *Phil. Trans. R. Soc.* A. CC. 499 We propose to adopt the term 'A Peléan Eruption' to designate this group of phenomena. **1934** C. R. LONGWELL et al. *Outl. Physical Geol.* x. 189 The Peléean phase is the most violently explosive of all. *Ibid.* 191 The extraordinary features of a Peléean cloud are that it is emitted as a horizontal blast from beneath the lava plug in the summit of the volcano; that it carries with it an enormous amount of rock fragments, [etc.]. **1935** *Publ. Carnegie Inst. Washington* No. 458. 97 The general morphological features of the Peléan summit are those of an ancient crater wall, remaining in place on all sides but one. **1938** [see *bread-crust bomb* s.v. *BREAD *sb.* 10]. **1944** C. A. COTTON *Volcanoes* xii. 183 The chief product of both Vulcanian and Pelean eruptions is ash. **1965** A. HOLMES *Princ. Physical Geol.* (ed. 2) xii. 310 There are *nuée ardente* eruptions that differ in certain fundamental ways from those described as Peléan. **1972** G. A. MACDONALD *Volcanoes* x. 226 Two of the greatest Peléean eruptions of recent years are those of Bezymianny, Kamchatka, in 1956, and Mt. Lamington, New Guinea, in 1951. **1976** P. FRANCIS *Volcanoes* iii. 116 The presence of such a dome is sometimes considered to be a characteristic feature of Peléean eruptions.

pelerine. Add: **b. pelerine stitch** (see quots.).
1926 J. CHAMBERLAIN *Hosiery, Yarns & Fabrics* vi. 128 The Pelerine Stitch has a limited application as a shawl stitch, but modern variations of it are used for producing (1) cellular fabric; (2) in-turned welt... This stitch or combination of stitches is based on the transferring of a formed sinker loop to one or two needles. **1950** '*Mercury*' *Dict. Textile Terms* 392/1 *Pelerine stitches*, these stitches are produced by meshing the upper and lower components of a single loop together at the next course. Modifications of these stitches produce raised designs and places and eyelet holes. By meshing the lower components of the first row of loops to a subsequent row a hem or welt is produced on a plain fabric.

pelican. Add: **5.*** With capital initial: the proprietary name of a series of non-fiction books published by Penguin Books; a book in this series.
1937 *Bookseller* 3 Feb. 147 (Advt.), A glance at the magnificent first list below will reveal the general nature of *Pelican Books*, a new series of popular books on science, astronomy, archæology, politics, economics, history, etc. **1942** *Scrutiny* X. IV. 385 Enough passages like the above could be found..to yield Professor Stebbing cannon-fodder for at least a chapter, if not for a whole Pelican. **1948** G. V. GALWEY *Lift & Drop* vi. 158 He.. began to study the book-shelves... There was..a fair showing of Pelicans. **1953** E. SIMON *Past Masters* I. i. 15 He published a Pelican on his work under Chrichton in the Islands, which I thought you might have seen. **1957** R. HOGGART *Uses of Literacy* viii. 210 There are the dailies and weeklies,..the Penguins and the Pelicans. *Ibid.* xi. 261 They are in the habit today of buying copies of Pelicans. **1957** *Trade Marks Jrnl.* 22 May 532/1 Pelican... Printed books, being literary, dramatic, musical or artistic works, but not including books relating to pelicans. Penguin Books Limited,..Harmondsworth, County of Middlesex; manufacturers and publishers. **1966** 'L. BLACK' *Bait* viii. 128 He was reading a paper-back... It appeared to be a Pelican. **1968** *Guardian* 26 Sept. 11/1 By the time of the first Pelicans Penguins (the mother birds) were, of course, well established... Pelicans were born in 1937, the inheritors of a half century and more of self-education.

5.** In full *pelican crossing*: a pedestrian-crossing controlled by push-buttons (see quot. 1966).
1966 *Evening Standard* 26 May 11/6 We hope the Ministry will install 'pelicans'..in the town. Pelicans would be safer than zebras and easily understood by the public—the pedestrian just pushes a button which operates red, amber and green lights telling motorists when to stop. **1969** *Daily Tel.* 9 July 17/7 Another type of push-button pedestrian-controlled crossings—to be known as Pelicans—will come into operation on Monday. *Ibid.*, Instead of the white 'X', the Pelican (*pe*destrian *li*ght *con*trolled) crossing will show a green signal to a driver until a pedestrian presses the button to start the signal sequence. **1974** *Country Life* 30 May 1332/2 A Minister stating that 'pelicans will be interchangeable with zebras' ..was referring to the replacement of the sturdy and familiar orange beacons at the kerbside by the flashing lights and little coloured men... A circular from the DoE elucidates some of the mysteries of the pelican crossing. **1975** *Times* 22 Sept. 12/5 Question time at council meetings is peppered with inquiries and entreaties about zebra and pelican crossings and such like. **1976** *New Scientist* 24 June 702/1 The GLC survey..studied 40 pelicans which had been converted from zebras. **1976** *Flintshire Leader* 10 Dec. 1 Residents of Oakenholt are ready to block the main road through the village in their campaign for a pelican crossing.

6. Pelican flag *U.S.*, the flag of the State of Louisiana; **Pelican State** *U.S.*, a sobriquet of the State of Louisiana.
1860 *Charleston* (S. Carolina) *Mercury* 25 Dec. 4/5 The Pelican flag of Louisiana was unfurled in the streets, amid tremendous cheering... The Pelican flag consists of a red star upon a white field, with the ancient Louisiana emblem of a Pelican feeding her young. **1865** A. D. RICHARDSON *Secret Service* 40 There were Pelican flags, and Lone Star flags, and devices, unlike anything in the heavens above. **1859** *Harper's Mag.* May 853/2 A well-known writer in the Pelican State writes us a good thing from one of his little folks. **1934** G. E. SHANKLE *State Names* 119 The name, the *Pelican State* was given to Louisiana from the fact that this bird is so frequently seen along the streams..which fact caused it to be chosen as the emblem in the state coat of arms. **1949** *Times-Picayune* (New Orleans) *Mag.* 27 Nov. 53/2 Now Mississippi has nosed out the Pelican State. **1959** E. A. DAVIS (*title*) Louisiana: the Pelican State. **1974** *Encycl. Brit. Micropædia* X. 272 (*table*) State nickname(s) or slogan... Louisiana..Pelican state.

pe·lican, *v. rare*—¹. [f. the sb.] *trans.* To swallow or eat like a pelican.
1953 DYLAN THOMAS *Under Milk Wood* (1954) 65 And she bursts into tears, and, in the middle of her salty howling, nimbly spears a small flatfish and pelicans it whole.

pelike (pe·līki, pelī·ki). *Gr. Antiq.* Also **pelice, pellice.** Pl. **pelikai.** [ad. Gr. πελίκα a wooden bowl, pitcher.] A type of amphora with an ovoid body, wide mouth, and broad base used for holding wine or water.
1873 S. & J. HORNER *Walks in Florence* II. 435 On a Pellice, a vase rarely found in Etruria, and belonging to the most perfect style of art.., is the figure of a man binding up the arm of a youth. **1891** NETTLESHIP & SANDYS *Seyffert's Dict. Classical Antiquities* 685 (*caption*) Various shapes of Greek vases...*pĕlĭkē*. **1902** J. H. HUDDILSTON *Lessons from Greek Pott.* I. 75 The largest group is found on the Louvre pelike, where, although there are no persons, in addition to those named by Homer,..are two women, introduced..to remind us of Briseis. **1928** J. D. BEAZLEY *Greek Vases in Poland* iii. 64 His pictures, which are chiefly on small hydriai, small pelikai, and marriage-vases, are usually taken from the life of woman. **1936** *Burlington Mag.* May 253/1 A *pelice* with snarling lion and lioness. **1967** R. S. FOLSOM *Handbk. Greek Pottery* 159 The name pelike was applied by early archaeologists to the one-piece amphora with a sagging belly and broad neck. In fact the name appears to have no justification, but is retained for convenience. The form first appeared about 520 B.C. and lasted until the 4th century B.C. **1971** *Ashmolean Mus. Rep. Visitors 1970* 9 A notable addition to the collection of Athenian red-figure vases is a pelike, of the 4th century B.C.

Pelion (pī·li,ǫn). The name of a mountain in Thessaly, used in phr. *to pile* (or *heap*) *Pelion upon Ossa* (or *Ossa upon Pelion*) [tr. Virgil *Georgics* I. 281 *imponere Pelio Ossam*]: to add to what is already great; to add difficulty to difficulty. Also in similar phrases.
1589 A. FLEMING tr. *Virgil's Georgiks* I. 10 Thrise did they trie and giue assay vpon mount Pelius, To lay the mountaine Ossa. **1594** NASHE *Unfortunate Traveller* sig. C4ᵛ Whosoeuer seekes by headlong meanes to enter into Heauen..shall with the Gyaunts..be ouer-whelmed with Mount Ossa and Peleon. **1609** DEKKER *Guls Horne-Booke* 30 By talking and laughing..you heape Pelion vpon Ossa, glory vpon glory. **1628** T. MAY tr. *Virgil's Georgicks* I. 14 Thrice they indeavour'd with strong hand to place the mountain Ossa on high Pelion. *a* **1734** R. NORTH *Examen* (1740) II. v. 336 It is a Pelion upon Ossa to set Power over Power. **1919** G. B. SHAW in *Shaw on Shakespeare* (1962) 257, I might pile Pelion on Ossa with illustrations of the passages that might very well be cut out of Shakespear's plays. **1927** C. A. & M. R. BEARD *Rise Amer. Civilization* I. xii. 565 In piling Ossa on Pelion, Webster did not overlook mundane considerations—the economic and political substance of the pending issue, the sale of those annoying western lands. **1957** PARTRIDGE *English gone Wrong* i. 12 'To *categorize*' and *categorization*, and those Pelion-upon-Ossa horrifics, *recategorize* and *recategorization*. **1967** *Word Study* Mar. 3/1 We discover Mount Pelion piled on Ossa, however, when we note that our teachers are even more conservative than their conservative textbooks. **1976** *Times* 28 Apr. 14/8 Piling Pelion upon Ossa (a nasty habit that foreigners are much given to) they..calculate the rate of inflation in Britain.

peliosis (peliōᵘ·sis). *Path.* [mod.L. (F. Swediaur *Novum Nosologiæ Methodicæ Systema* (1812) I. p. xxiii, II. 173), f. Gr. πελίωσις extravasation of blood, f. πελιός livid.] = PURPURA 1; *peliosis rheumatica* [Gr. ῥευματικός subject to a discharge], an uncommon disease characterized by localized eruptions of the skin and mucous membranes, and associated with arthritis; (now usu. regarded as the same as *Henoch–Schönlein purpura* s.v. *HENOCH).
1839 DUNGLISON *Dict. Med. Sci.* (ed. 2) 772/1 *Peliosis*, purpura hæmorrhagica. **1850** A. T. THOMSON *Pract. Treat. Dis. affecting Skin* v. 338 Under the term Peliosis, or Purpura rheumatica, Schönlein describes a disease which has been termed by others Roseola rheumatica. In this disease local extravasations occur in the skin, and erythematous patches about the joints, which are swollen and painful. **1861** *New Sydenham Soc. Yr.-bk. 1860* 403 (*heading*) On 'peliosis rheumatica' of children. **1868** C. H. FAGGE et al. tr. *Hebra's Dis. of Skin* II. xxviii. 422 Alibert ..makes unnecessary distinctions between peliosis (purpura) and petechiæ. **1911** *Brit. Med. Jrnl.* 11 Feb. 331/2 That peliosis rheumatica is never of rheumatic origin is hardly capable of proof. **1968** CHAMPION & WILKINSON in A. J. Rook et al. *Textbk. Dermatol.* I. xvii. 428/1 The separation of Schönlein's 'peliosis rheumatica' [from the Henoch-Schönlein syndrome] is no longer justified.

pelisse. 2. b. (Earlier and later examples.)
1805 T. FREMANTLE in *Wynne Diaries* (1940) III. 234 Mistress Tittler with a black Velour pelisse, tell her I desire she will not spoil it until I come home. **1807** JANE AUSTEN *Let.* 7 Jan. (1952) 173 Caroline's new pelisse depended upon her mother's being able or not to come so far in the chair. **1828** M. O'BRIEN *Jrnl.* 20 Oct. (1968) I. 19 Mary set to work on a pelisse for the baby. **1922** JOYCE *Ulysses* 490 In babylinen and pelisse, bigheaded, with a caul of dark hair.

Pell (pel). *Math.* [See PELLIAN *a.*] *Pell('s) equation*: any Diophantine equation of the form $ax^2 - y^2 = 1$ (a, x, and y being integers). Also *absol.*
1910 *Encycl. Brit.* I. 617/2 Although Pell had nothing to do with the solution, posterity has termed the equation Pell's Equation. **1912** E. E. WHITFORD (*thesis title*) The Pell equation. **1966** OGILVY & ANDERSON *Excursions in Number Theory* x. 129 It turns out that the equation $y^2 - Nx^2 = 1$ known as Pell's equation, has solutions in integers whenever N is not a perfect square. **1974** *Sci. Amer.* July 116/3 Whenever the coefficient is not a square the Pell has an infinity of solutions. *Ibid.* 120/2 The general Pell equation, a key to so much of this kind of number analysis.

Pellegrini–Stieda (pe:legrīni,ʃtī·dă). *Med.* The names of Augusto *Pellegrini* (*c* 1880–*c* 1940), Italian physician, and Alfred *Stieda* (1869–1945), German physician, used *attrib.* and in the possessive to designate a condition described by them in 1905 and 1908 respectively, in which ossification of the tibial collateral ligament of the knee occurs as a result of injury. [Named by R. Petrignani 1930, in *Contributions à l'Étude de la Maladie de Pellegrini-Stieda* (Thèse, Paris) 14.]
1932 *Amer. Jrnl. Roentgenology* XXVIII. 97/2 Pellegrini-Stieda's disease is of importance from its medicolegal aspect. **1945** *Surg., Gynecol. & Obstetr.* LXXXI. 212/1 The imposing name of 'Pellegrini-Stieda disease' is misleading. It implies that the one finding of the calcification over the adductor tubercle is a disease complex. **1971** A. A. MICHELE *You don't have to Ache* v. 128 A fairly common condition in men between the ages of 24 and 40 years, is hardening and calcification of the ligament at the inner side of the knee joint (Pelligrini Steida [*sic*] disorder).

pellet, *sb.*¹ Add: **2. c.** = CAST *sb.* 19.
1802 G. MONTAGU *Ornith. Dict.* I. s.v. *Owl*, White. Their food is chiefly mice, which they swallow whole, and.. eject the bones and fur in large pellets, which are termed castings. **1834** R. MUDIE *Feathered Tribes Brit. Islands* I. 141 Mice are preferred to birds, the feathers being more untractable than the fur, both in swallowing, and in casting pellets or quids. **1895** *U.S. Dept. Agric. Yearbk. 1894* 217 These masses, known as 'pellets' are regurgitated before fresh food is taken. **1905** *Daily News* 5 Jan. 4/3 The brown owl's pellet very rarely contains the remains of shrews. **1948** *Brit. Birds* XLI. 290, I found a secluded coomb..which, judging by the quantity of droppings and pellets below the ledges, had been used as a roosting place by a number of Ravens. **1964** A. L. THOMSON *New Dict. Birds* 608/2 Pellets are best known in respect of birds-of-prey, but..birds of very widely differing species regularly eject pellets. **1971** S. HILL *Strange Meeting* i. 31 The small, bleached bones from the owls' pellets.

d. The droppings of various small animals, esp. the rabbit, which reingests some of them.
1919 'W. N. P. BARBELLION' *Diary* 14 Apr. (1920) 129 Those sand dunes! Their characteristic feature was rabbits' skulls..and the little round dry pellets of rabbits, more numberless than the snail shells. **1939** *Nature* 10 June 982/2 Numerous coccidial oocysts were also found in the stomach pellets of the control rabbit..which appeared to prove the fæcal origin of the pellets. **1956** THOMPSON & WORDEN *Rabbit* iii. 27 A blinded rabbit took pellets direct from its anus. **1964** R. M. LOCKLEY *Private Life Rabbit* ii. 32 At night their pellets were dropped along the boundary fence. **1972** R. ADAMS *Watership Down* l. 405 Under snow they [*sc.* rabbits] may stay underground for days at a time, feeding only by chewing pellets.

3. (Later example.)
1971 *Country Life* 27 May 1303/2 A purely secular goblet..its date 1664, its so-far unidentified maker's mark 'P.D.' with three pellets above, a cinquefoil below.

5. pellet bomb, a type of anti-personnel bomb; **pellet mill,** an apparatus for pelleting powders.
1970 *Guardian* 10 Mar. 12 Anti-personnel bombs..the same pellet bombs which figured so prominently in North Vietnamese protests. They are dropped in canisters..the bomblets, each a bit bigger than a man's fist, might go on exploding for two days. **1970** *Peace News* 3 Apr. 5/3 An unexploded pellet bomb she had touched while digging in the fields. **1950** J. H. PERRY *Chem. Engineers' Handbk.* (ed. 3) 1189/1 Pellet mills are designed to agglomerate permeable free-flowing materials into pellet form. **1971** *Power Farming* Mar. 22/1 Demand for cubed and pelleted feed has led to the development of the Cubamix single unit mobile feed plant... The equipment comprises the grinding and mixing section as already used on the company's Grindamix model and a separately driven Simon Barron pellet mill.

pellet, *v.* Add: Pples. **pelleted, -eting** (occas. incorrectly -etting). **a.** Restrict † (*obs.*) to the second def. and add later examples of the sense: to form or shape into pellets; *esp.* to coat (plant seed) with soluble nutritive and protective substances to facilitate handling and promote growth.
1936 L. M. T. BELL *Making & Moulding of Plastics* xi. 185 For convenience and ease in the handling of the powdered compounds.., the compounds are frequently pelleted cold prior to moulding. **1944** *Sugar Beet Jrnl.* Jan. 41 A process of 'pelleting' sugar beet seed segments ..has been developed. The new process coats the rough segments with a water-soluble layer of beneficial and inert material, making the seed pieces smooth, spherical, and about the size of small seed peas. **1949** *Chem. Abstr.* XLIII. 2154 The app[aratus] is particularly adapted to pelletting Pb alloys into uniform fine shot. **1950** J. H. PERRY *Chem. Engineers' Handbk.* (ed. 3) 1189/1 Although originally designed for pelleting animal feeds, it is now being adapted to the handling of many other products. **1958** *Times* 24 Nov. 15/3 These low seed rates can be achieved..in the case of timothy, by using seed pelleted with basic slag. **1970** *Country Life* 17–24 Dec. 1187/1 Pelletting hay has been tried without more than local acceptance. **1973** *Daily Tel.* 30 June 8/5 (Advt.), Seed pelleter with sufficient Seedex Plant Food Compound to pellet hundreds of seeds. **1974** *Nature* 22 Nov. 327/1 After

incubation for 30 min at 37°, the microsomes were pelleted by centrifugation and the DNA reisolated and purified.

Hence **pe·lleting** *vbl. sb.* and *ppl. a.*

1936 L. M. T. BELL *Making & Moulding of Plastics* xi. 185 Figure 36 shows a crank pelleting machine..with the powder hopper removed. **1944** *Business Week* 26 Aug. 52/2 Western companies still regard the process as experimental, one question being whether the pelleting material, which easily melts from around the seed in damp midwestern soils, and thus permits emergence of the seedling, may not have more restraint in the dry western soils. **1945** A. T. BIRKBY *Phenolic Plastics* vii. 78 In the Plas[t]ics industry the term tabletting means the compression of moulding powder into a variety of small, easily-handled blocks, each of a pre-determined weight. Two other terms often used for this process are 'preforming' and 'pelletting'. **1950** J. H. PERRY *Chem. Engineers' Handbk.* (ed. 3) 1189/1 Pelleting of dusts, fumes,..and the like can be accomplished in a rotating-drum device known as the Dwight-Lloyd Segregating Pelletizer. **1963** P. FINN-KELCEY in A. N. Duckham *Farming* III. xi. 404 Pelleting machines introduced in recent years are already proving popular with farmers who compound their own stock rations.

pelletable (pe·lėtăb'l), *a.* [f. PELLET *v.* + -ABLE.] Capable of being formed into pellets. Hence **pelletabi·lity.**

1970 *Mikroskopie* XXIV. 296 (*heading*) A simplified protocol for electron microscopy processing of 'pelletable' material. **1973** *Biol. Abstr.* LV. 2932/2 Bull sperm of 296 animals was tested for pelletability. **1976** *Nature* 29 Jan. 324/2 Unknown amounts may have been associated with organelles or plastid fragments of a lower pelletability than intact etioplasts. *Ibid.* 325/1 The pelletable phytochrome investigated by many other workers seems to bind to membranous material only in the Pfr form.

pelleted, *ppl. a.* Add: **2.** Formed into or supplied as pellets.

1943 *Los Angeles Times* 25 Nov. 13/5 Tests being conducted here with newly developed 'pelleted' seed show that complete seed control can be obtained and expensive hand labor..eliminated in favor of mechanical thinners or thinning eliminated altogether. **1951** *Sci. News Let.* 28 Apr. 269/2 One of the most valuable aids to the blind gardener..is the recent development of pelleted seeds. **1961** *Listener* 7 Dec. 992/3 Slugs are controlled with the aid of pelleted metaldehyde. **1970** *Nature* 10 Oct. 178/2 Six lambs..were fed daily a pelleted diet of chopped lucerne hay and oats. **1973** *Guardian* 17 Mar. 8/5 Every effort should be made to sow the seed thinly. Pelleted seeds, of course, make this much easier. **1975** *N.Z. Jrnl. Agric.* Sept. 69/1 They were all fed to three weeks of age on a pelleted starter diet.

pelleter[3]. [f. PELLET *v.* + -ER[1].] An apparatus for pelleting.

1960 *Times Rev. Industry* July 51/1 BIPEL now sells much of its production outside the plastics industry. This includes pelleters for explosives, punch presses for metal work, [etc.]. **1963** P. FINN-KELCEY in A. N. Duckham *Farming* III. xi. 405 Whether an installation is to consist of a mill only, a mill and a mixer or the full layout of mill, mixer and pelleter.., considerable thought must be given to the positioning of each. **1973** [see *PELLET *v.*].

pelletization (pelėtəizēi·ʃən). [f. next + -ATION.] The action or process of forming into pellets.

1959 *Jrnl. Iron & Steel Inst.* CXCIII. 75/3 The article deals with determining the optimum conditions for making use of 'cold' agglomeration, i.e. pelletisation in which the fine material is transformed into small spheres by mechanical rolling. **1966** KIRK & OTHMER *Encycl. Chem. Technol.* (ed. 2) IX. 435 One of the more interesting developments which originated with fluidized calcination is the technique of pelletization. **1971** *Physics Bull.* Mar. 136/2 Major cooperative projects under consideration included an iron mine and an iron ore pelletization plant in the USSR. **1977** *Jrnl. R. Soc. Arts* CXXV. 388/1 Taconite ores..are more amenable to pelletization than higher grade Mesabi-type, deposits.

pelletize (pe·lėtəiz), *v.* [f. PELLET *sb.*[1] + -IZE.] *trans.* To form or shape into pellets. Cf. PELLET *v.* a in Dict. and Suppl.

1952 KIRK & OTHMER *Encycl. Chem. Technol.* IX. 900 The peat is excavated, macerated, pelletized in a long drum, and dried. **1963** *Engineering* 1 Feb. 180 The wood pulp will be pelletized for shipment to the Australian mainland. **1964** *Economist* 23 May 855/1 In America ore preparation is mainly in the form of 'pelletising' the burden. **1973** R. D. PEHLKE *Unit Processes Extractive Metall.* ii. 19 The final temperatures during induration reach 2300–2400°F, depending upon the concentrate being pelletized.

So **pe·lletized** *ppl. a.* = *PELLETED *ppl. a.* 2; **pe·lletizing** *vbl. sb.* and *ppl. a.*

1951 *Industr. & Engin. Chem.* June 1390/1 It is not possible to use pelletized [carbon] black directly for making aqueous carbon black slurries. **1951** *Engineering* 22 June 761/2 During a recent visit to the United States, he had been most impressed with what was being done in regard to the pelletising treatment of iron ores. **1964** *Economist* 25 July 356/1 This pelletised fuel is contained in stainless steel tubes. **1968** *Sci. Jrnl.* Oct. 23/3 Bentonite is used..as an agent for the pelletizing of iron ore. **1969** *Times* 2 May (Mining Suppl.) p. iv/7 Savage River produces magnetite from a relatively low grade deposit, grinds and concentrates this to a high grade pellet feed and pipes it 53 miles to the pelletizing plant at the port. **1970** *Times* 24 Aug. 15/6 Kawasaki is working on a system using oxygen and crude oil or liquefied natural gas combined with pre-treated, pelletized iron ore. **1977** *Cork Examiner* 4 June 17/4 The pellets will get harder with time... At no time was it considered that metal ground.. would be included in the pelletised mix. **1977** *Jrnl. R. Soc. Arts* CXXV. 394/1 Attempts to encourage the industry to construct at least some processing plants near to its raw materials have been most successful in the case of iron ore pelletizing plants.

pelletizer (pe·lėtəizəɹ). [f. prec. + -ER[1].] = *PELLETER[3].

1942 *Ann. Rep. Progr. Rubber Technol. 1941* V. 120 After discharge from the internal mixer the stock passes through a 'Hale Pelletizer' and the pellets are conveyed to storage bins. **1950** [see *PELLETING *vbl. sb.*]. **1961** *Engineering* 9 June 788/2 Pan pelletizers are used for granulating materials in the chemical and fertiliser industries. **1970** *Materials & Technol.* III. iii. 143 The grate-kiln pelletizer.

Pellian, *a.* Add: (Earlier and later examples.) Also *absol.*

[**1767** EULER in *Novi Commentarii Acad. Sci. Imp. Petropolitanæ* XI. 28 (*heading*) De usu novi algorithmi in problemate Pelliano solvendo. *Ibid.* 31, $pp = lqq + 1$... Atque hoc est illud problema olim quidem maxime celebratum a solutionis ingeniosissimae auctore Pellianum vocatum.] **1862** *Rep. Brit. Assoc. Adv. Sci. 1861* I. 314 There does not seem to be any ground for attributing either the problem or its solution to Pell... Nevertheless the equation $T^2 - DU^2 = 1$ is often called the Pellian equation after him, probably upon Euler's authority. **1911** *Encycl. Brit.* XIX. 853/1 This is usually called the Pellian equation, though it should properly be associated with Fermat, who first perceived its importance. **1974** *Sci. Amer.* July 118/3 The Pellian for square hexes is $3x^2 + 1 = y^2$, which is solved by finding the convergents of the continued fraction for the square root of 3.

pellotine (pe·lǒtīn). *Chem.* [ad. G. *pellotin* (A. Heffter 1894, in *Ber. d. Deut. Chem. Ges.* XXVII. 2977), f. Mexican *pellote* *PEYOTE: see -INE[5].] An alkaloid, $C_{13}H_{19}NO_3$, obtained from peyote and formerly used as a hypnotic; 1,2,3,4-tetrahydro-8-hydroxy-6,7-dimethoxy-1,2-dimethylisoquinoline.

1895 *Jrnl. Chem. Soc.* LXVIII. I. 120 Pellotine,..so called from the Mexican name 'pellote', of *Anhalonium Williamsi*, crystallises in colourless, transparent, anhydrous plates, and melts at 110°. **1900** A. R. CUSHNY *Text-bk. Pharmacol. & Therapeutics* II. iii. 220 Pellotine.. has been introduced as a hypnotic, and has been favorably commented on. **1972** *Science* 9 June 1132/3 Tetrazotized benzidine spray..aided in the identification of the four major components [from the Mexican cactus *Pelecyphora aselliformis* Ehrenberg] as hordenine.., pellotine.., anhalidine.., and an unknown alkaloid.

Pelman (pe·lmăn). The name of Christopher Louis *Pelman*, founder (in 1899) of the Pelman Institute for the Scientific Development of Mind, Memory and Personality in London, used *attrib.* to designate the system of memory training taught by this Institute.

1900 *Phonetic Jrnl.* 15 Dec. 790/2, I may say that I speak of the Pelman system from intimate personal knowledge. **1939** R. CAMPBELL *Flowering Rifle* IV. 113 All his Pelman course and monkey's glands With which the Charlie intellect expands. **1972** *Listener* 17 Aug. 210/3, I did a Pelman course, which hasn't done very much good because I've got the worst memory of anybody.

So **Pe·lmanism,** the system taught by the Pelman Institute; also *transf.*; a card game in which the cards lie face down and pairs must be selected from memory as successive cards are turned up; **Pe·lmanist, Pe·lmanite,** a student or advocate of Pelmanism; **Pe·lmanize** *v. intr.* and *trans.*, to practise Pelmanism; to teach (someone) Pelmanism.

1919 *Honey Pot* I. 4 (Advt.), Lots of our fellows are Pelmanising out here. **1920** *Pelman Pie* 25 (Advt.), A very large proportion of its readers are 'Pelmanists'. **1920** *Blackw. Mag.* Nov. 561/2, I fear I must be suffering from what the Pelmanites call 'mind-wandering'. **1921** *Chambers's Jrnl.* Mar. 176/1 In some Oriental way he had Pelmanised his memory. **1922** E. WALLACE *Flying Fifty-Five* xxvi. 154 Bill had begun, as he described it, to Pelmanize his horses. He was super-imposing upon the memory of one evil whistle another which had a more kindly association. **1923** *Hoyle's Games Modernized* 230 Pelmanism is..a splendid exercise for the memory, besides a source of amusement to the players—of whom there may be any number. **1931** R. CAMPBELL *Georgiad* II. 17 Broadcast your love and Pelmanise your Passion. **1934** 'E. M. DELAFIELD' *Provincial Lady in Amer.* 90 Short exercise in Pelmanism enables me to connect wave in her hair with first name, which is Marcella. **1934** *Brit. Weekly* 11 Jan. 319/3 (Advt.), Pelmanise for promotion, for progress, for success. *Ibid.*, There are in the world to-day more than half a million men and women who have become Pelmanists. **1950** *Oxf. Jun. Encycl.* IX. 114/1 In Pelmanism, a memory game, the cards are spread face downwards on the table. The players turn up two at a time, trying to find pairs. Cards which do not make pairs are turned down again, and the players must remember where they are. **1958** R. GODDEN *Greengage Summer* vii. 80 We stayed on at our table, playing cards with old packs from the bar, Racing Demon or Pelmanism or Snap. **1963** R. M. HARE *Freedom & Reason* iv. 60 Ought I not rather to take a course in Pelmanism to correct my absent-mindedness? **1972** *Guardian* 15 Nov. 10/6 There is a kind of common ground here between pulp fiction, science fiction pop mysticism, and a new sort of Pelmanism that goes beyond mere self-improvement and proposes the ways and means of self-transcendence. **1975** *Daily Tel.* 11 July 11/3 Between games of ping-pong or pelmanism they spend the night reminiscing about old times over a continuous supply of drinks.

‖ **pelmeny** (pelme·ni), *sb. pl.* Also **-ni.** [a. Russ. *pel'méni.*] In Russian cookery, small pastry cases stuffed with meat, etc.

1943 E. M. ALMEDINGEN *Frossia* x. 376 A whole mound of *pelmeny*, little lumps of specially made pastry stuffed with meat and onions and boiled in water. **1958** N. & G. J. FROUD *Home Bk. Russian Cookery* 23 Left-over pel'meni are delicious fried in a little butter. **1962** K. PETROVSKAYA *Secrets of Russian Cooking* 163 The best, real way of preparing Siberian pelmeny is to use two kinds of meat for stuffing—beef and pork or veal and pork—and plenty of seasoning. **1972** *Times* 12 Apr. 9/2 Such Russian specialities as *Pelmeny* (a kind of ravioli).

pelmet (pe·lmėt). [Prob. ad. F. *palmette* (see PALMETTE), formerly a conventional ornament on window cornices.] A valance or horizontal strip of curtain, wood or other material, fitted across the top of a door or window, usu. to conceal curtain fittings. Hence **pe·lmeted** *a.*, fitted with a pelmet.

1904 P. N. HASLUCK *Upholstery* 149 This pelmet is fixed to a wood lath screwed underneath the door casing. **1908** *Ladies' Field* 24 Oct. 318/2 (*caption*) Window Treatment: Pelmet and Curtains in Shadow Damask. **1922** *Daily Mail* 21 Nov. 14 If a pelmet is used it should be straight-edged. **1925** PENDEREL-BRODHURST & LAYTON *Gloss. Eng. Furnit.* 123 *Pelmet*, a word used by upholsterers and sometimes by art dealers, who prefer the word 'palmette', to denote the horizontal stiff curtains or valance hiding the rod, rings and headings of the hanging curtain decorating a door, window, bed, etc. **1932** G. B. STERN *Little Red Horses* IV. xxxix. 540 [He] had tried to picture a long-ago scene of Uncle Arthur plucking his bride back from the pelmet. **1940** C. G. TORMLEY *Furnishing your Home* xvi. 109 Pelmets well done are an improvement to most windows. **1964** *McCall's Sewing* xvi. 286 The depth of the pelmet depends on the height of the window, usually one-sixth to one-ninth the length of the curtain. **1970** *Kay & Co.* (Worcester) *Catal.* 1970–71 Autumn/Winter 544 Plywood pelmet. Available in seven lengths. Easily painted. **1974** M. CECIL *Heroines in Love* viii. 189 These magazines ..gave them [*sc.* readers] the latest way with pelmets, and casseroles for winter evenings. **1974** D. FRANCIS *Knock Down* v. 59 Padded and pelmeted curtains and silk lampshades..spoke of enough money.

pelo-. Add: **pelobatid** (example); **pe·lophile** *Ecol.* [a. F. *pélophile* (J. Thurmann *Essai de Phytostatique* (1849) I. xiii. 268): see -PHIL], a plant growing on mud or clay; **pelophilous** *a.* (later example).

1956 *Nature* 18 Feb. 342/2 I have examined tadpoles of the pelobatid *Megophrys major*. **1905** B. D. JACKSON *Gloss. Bot. Terms* (ed. 2) 345/1 Pelophile.., a clay-loving plant. **1960** N. POLUNIN *Introd. Plant Geogr.* xvi. 528 It is also possible..to categorize marine Algae according to..the nature of their substratum (such as epiliths attached to rocks, or pelophiles growing on mud.) **1909** E. WARMING *Oecol. Plants* lviii. 230 (*heading*) Pelophilous halophytes.

peloid (pī·loid). [f. Gr. πηλ-ός clay, mud + -OID.] **1.** (See quots.)

1933 S. J. LEWIS in *Arch. Med. Hydrol.* XI. 181 (*heading*) Semi-solid bath media or 'peloids'. *Ibid.* 265/1 The word Peloid (Greek, πηλος) should be used as a generic name for all forms of muds, moors, etc.. Artificial preparations might be described as artificial peloids. **1953** W. KOSMATH *Brit. Pat.* 695,916 This invention relates to a method for the manufacture of therapeutically effective agents for peloids, which term is here intended to mean bog peat, organic slimes, muds, clays formed by weathering, marl and the like.

2. *Geol.* A particle of microcrystalline or cryptocrystalline carbonate.

1963 E. MCKEE *Prof. Papers U.S. Geol. Survey* No. 475-C. 21/2 Grains within the limestone range in size from fine to very coarse and consist of both bioclasts and peloids (intraformational clastic particles), commonly in an aphanitic calcite matrix. **1969** —— & GUTSCHICK in *Mem. Geol. Soc. Amer.* CXIV. 24 Peloids are defined as ovoid particles of microcrystalline or cryptocrystalline material. *Ibid.* 555 Beds of peloids that seem to be the result of lime-mud deposits having been disturbed and broken up into particles are common. **1972** *Nature* 25 Feb. p. ix/1 (Advt.), Petrography of carbonate grains: oöids, pisolites, peloids and other micritic fabrics. **1976** R. C. SELLEY *Introd. Sedimentology* v. 117 Studies of modern carbonate sediments show that peloids form by a variety of processes. *Ibid.*, In..lagoons and sheltered embayments, peloids are sufficiently abundant to be a dominant rock builder.

Hence **peloi·dal** *a.*

1933 S. J. LEWIS in *Arch. Med. Hydrol.* XI. 182/1 Peloid..is applicable in all languages in the same way as colloid or alkaloid, giving plurals and adjectives (e.g. 'peloidal') to the same models. **1969** MCKEE & GUTSCHICK in *Mem. Geol. Soc. Amer.* CXIV. 555 Peloidal limestone is defined as rock composed dominantly of particles of cryptocrystalline or microcrystalline material, commonly ovoid in shape. **1976** *Nature* 20 May 221/2 A thin oncolitic iron formation is interbedded with peloidal and oolitic ferruginous chert.

pelong (pīlǫ·ŋ). [Derivation uncertain: perh. ad. Malay *pĕlang* striped.] A kind of material used for gowns worn in southern India.

1687 *Charter to Fort St. George* (E. India Co.) f. 5v The said mayor and aldermen may always upon such solemn occasions wear scarlet serge gowns all made after one form or fashion..and that all the burgesses may upon such solemn occasions wear white pelong or other white silk gowns after one form or fashion to be agreed. **1798** *Acct.*

Interview Teshoo Lama & Capt. Samuel Turner 6, I advanced, and, as is the custom, presented a white pelong handkerchief. **1922** C. ILBERT *Govt. of India* 23 The burgesses are, on these occasions, to wear white 'pelong', or other silk gowns. **1924** E. SITWELL *Sleeping Beauty* i. 11 Pelongs, bulchauls, pallampores. **1928** —— *Five Poems* 15 Panōpe..Sees Asia, Parthenope, Eunomia, Euphrosyne, Urania, Ausonia In feathered head-dresses as bright as sleep,..In pelongs, chelloes, and great palampores.

peloothered (pelū·pəɹd). *rare*⁻¹. [Fanciful formation.] Drunk.

1914 JOYCE *Dubliners* 197 It happened that you were peloothered, Tom.

Peloponnesian (pelǒpǫnī·ziăn), *sb.* and *a.* Also 6–8 **Peloponesian.** [f. Gr. *Πελοπόννησ-ος*, L. *Peloponnes-us* Peloponnesus + -IAN.] **A.** *sb.* A native or inhabitant of the Peloponnesus (or Peloponnese), a peninsula forming the southernmost part of the Greek mainland. **B.** *adj.* Of or pertaining to the Peloponnesus or its inhabitants. *Peloponnesian war*, a war fought between Athens and Sparta from 431 to 404 B.C., in which Sparta and its Peloponnesian allies were victorious.

a **1490** J. SKELTON tr. *Diodorus Siculus' Bibliotheca Historica* (1956) I. IV. 275 Oonly the Boecians and the Peloponnesians, and non other, be permytted and licenced to take away of this golde with theym. **1550** T. NICOLLS tr. Thucydides (*title*) The hystory..of the warre, whiche was betwene the Peloponesians and the Athenyans. **1579** NORTH tr. *Plutarch's Lives* 184 Pericles..was thought the only original cause & author of the Peloponnesian warres. **1629** HOBBES tr. *Thucydides' Eight Bks. Pelop. War* I. 14 This Warre, which began from the time that the Athenians and Peloponnesians brake the League. **1709** I. LITTLEBURY tr. *Herodotus' Hist.* II. IX. 370 When the Lacedemonians were advanc'd to the Isthmus, and encamp'd with their Army; the other Peloponesians..thought they could not stay behind without Disgrace. **1752** HUME *Polit. Discourses* x. 226 When they were all chas'd into town, by the invasion of their territory during the Peloponnesian war, the city was not able to contain them. **1808** W. MITFORD *Hist. Greece* II. xv. 95 The Athenians..a little before the beginning of the Peloponnesian war, sent Phormion with thirty triremes to their assistance. **1827** J. R. MAJOR *Questions Mitford's Hist. Greece* 277 The answer of the Pythoness was understood to import that the Peloponnesians would be victorious. **1890** C. W. C. OMAN *Hist. Greece* xxvii. 293 Great battles on shore were very rare during the Peloponnesian war. **1911** *Encycl. Brit.* XXI. 73/2 In 429 the Peloponnesians were deterred by the plague from invading Attica. **1959** N. G. L. HAMMOND *Hist. Greece* 167 Modern scholars have called it [*sc.* the Spartan Alliance], rather misleadingly, 'the Peloponnesian League'. **1960** A. R. BURN *Lyric Age Greece* ix. 176 The Peloponnesian Argives defeated Sparta on the field of Hysiai. **1969** C. M. WOODHOUSE *Philhellenes* iv. 115 Stanhope..adopted the idea of organising a grand conference of national unity... He..visited the seat of the provisional government at Nauplia, to persuade the Peloponnesian leaders to take part... But all was in vain. The Peloponnesians would not come. **1972** D. DAKIN *Unification of Greece* x. 143 Deliyannis..had become the eloquent and popular leader of the disgruntled Peloponnesian peasants. **1972** R. MEIGGS *Athenian Empire* x. 181 Peace..was to be made with the Peloponnesians. **1976** *Classical Q.* XXVI. 233 It is doubtful whether the Peloponnesian detachment was dispatched during the actual celebration of the Olympic games. *Ibid.* 247 The Peloponnesians began construction of the Isthmian wall immediately upon hearing of the outcome of Thermopylae.

pelorus (pělōə·rǔs). Also **Pelorus.** [Name of the supposed pilot of Hannibal when he left Italy.] A compass rose equipped with one or two sighting arms, used for taking the relative bearings of sighted objects.

1854 FRIEND & BROWNING *Brit. Pat. 2652* This invention has for its object the construction and use of an instrument or apparatus which we denominate a pelorus, for determining the amount of magnetic aberration occasioned by local attraction in ships or vessels of every description,..and by the use of which..the true course..may be from time to time accurately ascertained. **1881** S. T. S. LECKY *'Wrinkles' in Pract. Navig.* x. 67 Having a Pelorus, the first thing to do is to provide suitable stands for it in various parts of the ship, so that it may be moved from one to the other as may be found convenient. **1904** WILSON-BARKER & ALLINGHAM *Navigation* (ed. 2) iii. 17 For the purpose of obtaining bearings when the object is not visible from the standard compass..a Pelorus is very useful. **1934** J. IRVING *Navig. Small Yachts* 284 As the ship's head is steadied on a point by the steering compass the bearing of the distant object is noted by the 'pelorus', and this bearing angle (from right ahead) is applied to the compass direction of ship's head. **1943** REDPATH & COBURN *Air Transport Navig.* iv. 63 A pelorus (a dummy compass rose equipped with sighting vanes) is usually mounted on top of the hatch above the cockpit in the airplane. **1973** *Country Life* 27 Nov. (Suppl.) 66/2 Mid 18th century French brass Pelorus... With original travelling case.

pelosity, *rare* var. PILOSITY.

1922 JOYCE *Ulysses* 687 To Bloom: the problems of irritability, tumescence, rigidity, reactivity, dimension, sanitariness, pelosity.

pelota. (Earlier and later examples.)

1844 *Colburn's United Service Mag.* Apr. 492 To see a Spaniard at a festival, a bull-fight, or the rustic game of *pelota*, no one would conceive him given to melancholy. **1929** C. CONNOLLY *Let.* in *Romantic Friendship* (1975) 332 She wants to build a modern Corbusier house with a flat roof which can be used as a pelota court. **1934** R. MACAULAY *Going Abroad* xxix. 251 He was showing Hero how to hold a pelota racquet. **1974** *Spain* (Michelin Tyre Co.) 108 The overriding Basque passion..is *pelota*... There is even a Pelota University.

pelotherapy (pīlǫþe·răpi). *Med.* [f. PELO- + THERAPY.] The application of mud to the body as a therapeutic measure.

1933 S. J. LEWIS in *Arch. Med. Hydrol.* XI. 178/1 The Greek word *Pelos*..would combine with terms of Greek origin forming derivations such as Pelotherapy. *Ibid.* 182/1 'Pelotherapy' would be the medical treatment by Peloids. **1970** *Telegraph* (Brisbane) 12 June 5/1 The mud treatment—or pelotherapy—is claimed to heal body ailments.

‖ **pelouse** (pelūz). [Fr.] An area of grass, a lawn; *spec.* a public enclosure at a French racecourse. Also *transf.*

1923 E. HEMINGWAY *Three Stories and Ten Poems* 36 The procession of them went around on the other side past the pelouse. **1928** *Observer* 11 Mar. 13/3 The Longchamp tote..will unify the betting in all three parts of the course—paddock, pavilion and pélouse. **1953** E. E. CLARK *Indian Legends* 222 A large area of land in south-eastern Washington [State] thought to have been called *pelouse*, 'the grass lands' by French-Canadian voyageurs. **1957** *N. & Q.* June 270/1 On the *pelouse* of open race-courses in and near Paris. **1967** *Punch* 27 Sept. 464/3 A troutstream flows east to west towards the chateau through beautiful Dornford Yatesian pelouses.

pelt, *v.*¹ Add: **3. b.** Also of missiles.

1916 'BOYD CABLE' *Action Front* 210 Maxim and rifle bullets were still pelting from somewhere in half enfilade at long range.

5. (Further example.)

1916 'BOYD CABLE' *Action Front* 116 A heavy rifle and machine-gun fire which was pelted across from the opposite parts of the British line.

pelt, *v.*² **a.** Delete '*Obs.* exc. *dial.*' and add later examples.

1919 W. T. GRENFELL *Labrador Doctor* ix. 176 Then having killed, 'sculped', and 'pelted' the seal, the exciting return to the vessel. **1936** D. MCCOWAN *Animals Canad. Rockies* xxiv. 211 In Canada alone in the first decade of this century, ten millions of the animals [*sc.* mink] were pelted for the sake of the satiny fur. **1948** A. L. RAND *Mammals E. Rockies* 116 It [*sc.* a wolf] is a large, awkward animal to pelt on the trap-line. **1950** *N.Z. Jrnl. Agric.* Sept. 256 (*caption*) Pelting skins on the killing chain. **1972** 'M. YORKE' *Silent Witness* iii. 51 The Derringtons had a mink farm. 'We pelt them in November.'

pelta. Add: **3.** *Archit.* An ornamental shield motif (see quots.).

1928 A. W. CLAPHAM in *Archaeologia* XXVII. 227 The *Pelta Ornament*..consists essentially of pairs of half-circles set back to back in such a way that the combination forms a series of figures like a double-headed axe or an Amazon-shield. **1936** —— *Romanesque Archit.* iii. 61 Of much less frequent occurrence is the Carolingian pelta-ornament, used as a diaper on roll-mouldings at Piacenza, Modena, Cremona, and Ferrara Cathedrals. **1942** *Oxoniensia* VII. 70 The eye is at once attracted to the small field of decoration on the head allotted to an engraved and enamelled pelta-scroll flung haphazard on the surface. **1954** M. RICKERT *Painting in Brit.: Middle Ages* 230 *Pelta*, a classical ornamental motif formed by two converging curves joined by another line. The ancestor of the trumpet pattern. **1967** *Antiquaries Jrnl.* XLVII. 167 On the extreme right is a border of black and white composed of small alternating semicircular forms producing the effect of a pelta pattern. **1965** R. KRAUTHEIMER *Early Christian & Byzantine Archit.* 362 *Pelta*, a shield-shaped design composed of a convex curve joined to two concave curves.

pelter, *sb.*¹ For †*Obs.* read *rare* and add later example.

1922 JOYCE *Ulysses* 130 That old pelters [*sic*], the editor said.

pelter, *sb.*² Add: **1. c.** (Earlier and later examples.)

1791 J. BYNG *Torrington Diaries* (1935) II. 360 Tho' it rain'd all the way, so as to hurry me, yet it was not a pelter. **1816** JANE AUSTEN *Let.* 9 July (1952) 459 We were obliged to turn back..but not soon enough to avoid a Pelter all the way home. **1966** T. H. RADDALL *Hangman's Beach* I. vi. 83 Boats' crews and carpenters..came out in the cold pelter to McNab's island.

d. Phr. *in a pelter*: in a hurry; at speed.

c **1889** 'F. LESLIE' *Let.* in W. T. Vincent *Recoll. Fred Leslie* (1894) II. xxiii. 97 Dear, dear! I have wasted time and ought to have been at work on our burlesque. Now I am determined to go in a pelter.

e. An old or slow horse. *U.S. colloq.*

This may belong to PELTER *sb.*¹: see *Dict. Amer.*

1856 *Knickerbocker* XLVIII. 314 When his earthly tenement yields his soul no shelter, May it animate the corpse of an ancient pelter. **1896** ADE *Artie* i. 4 It's like hitchin' up a four-time winner 'longside of a pelter. **1902** H. F. DAY *Pine Tree Ballads* 147 He'd..take a wheezy old pelter with a hopity gait and he'd make you believe..there were all kinds of pedigrees tied up in him. **1931** D. RUNYON in *Hearst's International* Sept. 84/1 Mahogany..is..not such a bad old pelter.

3. Something exceptionally large. *dial.*

c **1780** M. LONSDALE in S. Gilpin *Popular Poetry of Cumberland* (1875) 61 An' dall! but it's a pelter. **1892** E. J. MILLIKEN *'Arry Ballads* 70/1 Their ain't nothink the nobs is fair nuts on but wot these 'ere bellerers ban. Wy, they're down upon Sport, now, a pelter. Perposterous, ain't it, old man?

pelter, *v.* Add: **1.** (Later example of *intr.* use.)

1939 DYLAN THOMAS *Map of Love* 12 Chimes cheat the prison spire, pelter In time like outlaw rains on that priest, water, Time for the swimmers' hands, music for silver lock And mouth.

2. *intr.* To run with rapid steps; = PELT *v.*¹ 7.

1906 W. S. MAUGHAM *Bishop's Apron* xix. 297 The strange spectacle of a comely young woman and an ecclesiastical dignitary..peltering towards the Achilles Statue as fast as they could go. **1923** *Chambers's Jrnl.* Apr. 240/2 Rawlins..peltered up on deck to recover his composure.

Hence (in sense 1) **pe·ltering** *ppl. a.*

1858 [in Dict.]. **1927** *Glasgow Herald* 27 Aug. 8 The peltering rains (which were certainly general) made the grass so wet that the..cow ate far too much juice.

Peltier (pe·ltie). *Physics.* The name of J. C. A. *Peltier* (1785–1845), French amateur scientist, used *attrib.* with reference to an effect he discovered in 1834, whereby heat is given out, or absorbed, when an electric current passes across a junction between two materials; *Peltier coefficient*, (*a*) the quantity of heat liberated or absorbed at a junction between two conductors when unit charge passes between them; (*b*) of a material, the quantity of heat liberated or absorbed when unit electric charge traverses a junction between that material and a reference conductor.

1856 *Proc. R. Soc.* VII. 54, I hope also to be able to make determinations in absolute measure of the amount of the Peltier effect for a given strength of current between various pairs of metals. **1896** FOSTER & ATKINSON *Elem. Treat. Electr. & Magn.* xiv. 135 This coefficient, known as the Peltier coefficient,..represents for a junction of any two metals the amount of energy converted into or produced from heat per second when a current of unit strength traverses the junction. **1904** J. S. AMES *Text-bk. Gen. Physics* xliv. 681 These forces at the surface of contact of two substances are called 'Peltier electro-motive forces', having been first discovered by him. **1916** F. B. PIDDUCK *Treat. Electr.* vi. 210 In addition to the Peltier heat there is the usual heat developed by the mere passage of the current through the wires. **1958** CONDON & ODISHAW *Handbk. Physics* IV. vi. 84/2 The Peltier coefficient for a junction AB is representable as the difference of two intrinsic Peltier coefficients characteristic of each material separately. **1966** *McGraw-Hill Encycl. Sci. & Technol.* XIII. 581/2 If 1 coulomb of positive charge moves slowly around the circuit, there will be Peltier cooling in its passage from Bi to Cu at T and Peltier heating at T_0. **1972** R. W. URE in Willardson & Beer *Semiconductors & Semimetals* VIII. ii. 68 The Peltier effect at the junction between the liquid and solid phases has been used to remove the latent heat of crystallization in crystal growth.

Pelton (pe·ltən). Also **pelton.** The name of L. A. *Pelton* (1829–1908), U.S. engineer, used *attrib.* to designate an undershot water-wheel he invented that has divided buckets fixed to the rim, which deflect a jet of water directed at them.

1885 *Engineering* 30 Oct. 433 The Pelton wheel is said to have used 162·98 cubic feet of water a minute, and to have given 107·49 horse-power, showing an efficiency of 90·2 per cent. **1916** J. PARK *Text-bk. Pract. Hydraulics* xiv. 242 A Pelton water-wheel 3 feet in diameter, formed of a solid steel disc with phosphor-bronze buckets riveted to the rim, is working in California under a head of 2100 feet. **1962** *Times* 21 May (Commonwealth Chambers of Commerce Suppl.) p. xii/5 (Advt.), Cast steel runners and pelton wheels for hydro-electric plants. **1972** J. M. K. DAKE *Essent. Engin. Hydraulics* vi. 163 It is possible to have more than one jet operating on a Pelton wheel and two jets are quite common.

pelure². Add: **2.** *pelure d'oignon* (dǫnyǫ̃n) [lit. 'onion-skin'], a tawny colour in wines; a wine of this colour; *spec.* the name of a wine produced in the Jura region of France; also *attrib.*

1935 SCHOONMAKER & MARVEL *Compl. Wine Bk.* i. 46 The red and *pelure d'oignon* wines of Arbois were among the many life-long favourites of that..lover of charming ladies and good wines—Henri IV. *Ibid.* viii. 188 A good red wine is red, a deep crimson when young,..a rather more delicate red when old, with that faint but unmistakable brownish tinge which the French call '*pelure d'oignon*'. **1951** H. W. ALLEN *Natural Red Wines* vii. 263 The depth and brightness of its divine reds, purples and browns, the perfect example of the *pelure d'oignon* hue. **1952** A. LICHINE *Wines of France* xiii. 175 When old, the red Hermitages are enormously rich in aroma and aftertaste... Instead of having the complete red spectrum, the wines have a brownish tinge, which the French call *pelure d'oignon*, or onion skin. **1962** *Harper's Bazaar* Oct. 159/2 You will also find some unexpected Rhône wines..and Pelure d'Oignon (onion skin colour). **1965** A. SICHEL *Penguin Bk. Wines* III. 160 The best red wine of the Jura..is light in colour and is often referred to as '*pelure d'oignon*'—onion skin. **1965** O. A. MENDELSOHN *Dict. Drink* 255 *Pelure d'oignon*,..used to denote the characteristic shiny brown hue that aged red wines may acquire. **1967** P. PURSER *Twentymen* xxvii. 187 The day's third bottle of Pelure d'Oignon, beaded with condensation from the refrigerator. **1971** *Guardian* 12 Nov. 9/3 The Montrichard..is a pale pink—nearer the rosy yellow of pelure d'oignon than red. **1976** 'J. FRASER' *Who steals my Name?* xvi. 188 Aveyard examined his crystal glass appreciatively, then replenished it with the delicious Pelure d'Oignon Rosé wine.

pelurious (pėliū·riəs), *a. rare*—[1]. [f. PELURE[1] + -IOUS.] Furred, hairy.

1922 JOYCE *Ulysses* 289 Sieves of gooseberries, pulpy and pelurious.

pelvic, *a.* Add: **1. b.** *pelvic thrust*: the repeated thrusting movement of the pelvis during sexual intercourse.

1953 A. C. KINSEY et al. *Sexual Behav. Human Female* xv. 618 The..rhythmic pelvic thrusts during sexual activity are among the distinctive characteristics of the class Mammalia. **1966** MASTERS & JOHNSON *Human Sexual Response* xviii. 297 Male pelvic thrust and female pelvic accommodation initially are voluntary muscular attempts at sex tension increment. **1969** W. B. POMEROY *Girls & Sex* vii. 105 Intercourse continues with a series of pelvic thrusts. **1969** D. R. REUBEN *Everything you always wanted to know about Sex* (1970) vi. 90 A reasonable yardstick for male potency is the ability to continue intercourse for five to ten minutes. During that time a normally potent male will deliver from fifty to one hundred pelvic thrusts.

† **pelvigraph** (pe·lvigraf). *Obs.* [f. PELVI(S + -GRAPH.] An instrument for recording measurements of the pelvis. So † **pelvi·graphy,** the use of the pelvigraph.

1890 BILLINGS *Med. Dict.* II. 306/1 *Pelvigraphy*, obtaining a contour of the wall of the pelvis. **1892** F. P. FOSTER *Med. Dict.* IV. 2540/1 *Pelvigraph*, a device adopted by Pinard for recording automatically the measurements of dried pelves. **1903** J. C. EDGAR *Pract. Obstetr.* II. 184 The principle involved in the construction and application of the pelvigraph is that of the parallel rulers, one number representing a palpator for the localization of points within the pelvis, while the other is provided with a water-level and a dial index. **1904** *Lancet* 18 June 1728/1 A description is given of pelvigraphy or the method of taking a series of measurements of certain pelvic diameters and thus plotting out the size of the various pelvic planes. **1913** *Jrnl. Obstetr. & Gynæcol.* XXIV. 257 Martin's pelvigraph, introduced in 1827, was..intended for use in the dry pelvis.

pelycosaur (pe·likosǭɹ). Also **pelycosaurian.** [f. mod.L. name of order *Pelycosauria* (E. D. Cope 1878, in *Proc. Amer. Philos. Soc.* XVII. 511), f. Gk. πέλυξ, πέλυκ- bowl, cup + σαῦρος lizard.] A fossil reptile of the order Pelycosauria, known from Permian remains, and sometimes distinguished by bony spines developed from some of the vertebrae. Also *attrib.* or as *adj.*

1880 [in Dict. s.v. PELYCO-]. **1930** H. H. SWINNERTON *Outl. Palæont.* (ed. 2) xii. 334 *Dimetrodon* was a typical Pelycosaurian. **1933** A. S. ROMER *Vertebr. Paleont.* xi. 222 The neural arches of pelycosaurs were (as in most reptiles) narrower than those of the cotylosaurs. *Ibid.*, The pelycosaur palate was constructed on a primitive pattern. **1954** W. E. SWINTON *Fossil Amphibians & Reptiles* vi. 29 A group of very important reptiles, the Therapsida, are descended from the *Dimetrodon*-like Pelycosaurs. **1968** A. S. ROMER *Procession of Life* xiv. 235 The central types among the therapsids were carnivores, continuing the flesh-eating tradition of the main pelycosaur stock. **1973** *Nature* 16 Mar. 203/2 *Dimetrodon grandis* was the end form of an evolutionary series of pelycosaurs that had tended to develop increasingly large sails. **1977** A. HALLAM *Planet Earth* 212 A bizarre characteristic of a number of the pelycosaurs was the development of a huge sail-like structure adorning the back.

Pembroke. **Pembroke table** (later examples).

1853 [see *conversation card]. **1925** *Scribner's Mag.* July 94/1 A Pembroke table with unusual stretchers was in the wood-shed. **1973** [see *HAREWOOD]. **1975** J. SYMONS *Three Pipe Problem* xviii. 181 She sold..a damaged Pembroke table skilfully repaired by Fritz to a woman who was actually looking for a brass fender.

pemoline (pe·molīn). *Pharm.* [Perh. f. P(H)E(NYL + *I)M(INO(-) + *OXAZ)OL(ID)INE, elements in its chemical name.] 2-Imino-4-oxo-5-phenyloxazolidine, $C_9H_8N_2O_2$, a white, crystalline, tasteless powder that is a stimulant of the central nervous system.

1961 *MIMS Monthly Index* Jan. 44 Kethamed Medo-Chemicals Pemoline: 20 MG. tablets. Fatigue, convalescence, etc. **1968** *Sunday Times* 27 Oct. 3 Pemoline has been known sometime to be a mild brain stimulant, midway between Amphetamine and coffee. **1973** *Lancet* 10 Nov. 1091/1 Six amphetamine users who have been taking large doses of pemoline..have become aggressive, excited and disorganised.

pemphis (pe·mfis). [mod.L. (J. R. & J. G. A. Forster *Characteres Generum Plantarum* (1776) 67), f. Gr. πεμφίς cloud.] A small tree of the genus so called, esp. *Pemphis acidula*, belonging to the family Lythraceæ, and found in coastal, tropical areas of Africa and Southern Asia.

1911 *Trans. Linn. Soc.* (*Zool.*) XIV. 403 Throughout the northern section [of Aldabra] the *Pemphis* jungle continues. *Ibid.* 404 Near the sea the trees were all much stunted by the prevalent winds, even the hardy *Pemphis* trees being dwarfed into a low thick scrub. **1919** *Nature* 9 Oct. 118/2 The vegetation [of Aldabra] consists of four types:— (1) Mangrove swamp... (2) Pemphis bush, a dense growth of the hard-wooded *Pemphis acidula* (Lythraceae), a widely distributed sea-coast plant. **1958** *Times* 4 Nov. 12/6 The island [*sc.* Aldabra] rises only some 15 ft. above the sea and is for the most part clothed with a terrible tangle of pemphis bush. **1971** *Phil. Trans. R. Soc.* B. CCLX. 359 Isolated *Scaevola* and *Pemphis* trees have browse lines. *Ibid.* 476 One of them [*sc.* a Malagasy bulbul] was in a *Pemphis* bush.

pempidine (pe·mpidīn). *Pharm.* [f. PE(NTA- + M(ETHYL + PI(PERI)DINE.] An alkaline liquid, $C_{10}H_{21}N$, which has been used (usu. in the form of its hydrogen tartrate, a white, crystalline powder), as a ganglion-blocking agent in the treatment of severe hypertension; 1,2,2,6,6-pentamethylpiperidine.

1958 *Nature* 21 June 1717/2 In the simple..tertiary amine, 1:2:2:6:6-pentamethylpiperidine.., for which the common name pempidine has been suggested, we have a potent ganglion-blocking drug. **1960** *Lancet* 21 Jan. 143/2 In 1958 a new ganglion-blocking agent, pempidine tartrate, was made available under the trade names of 'Perolysen' and 'Tenormal'. **1961** *Ibid.* 12 Aug. 334/2 A Jamaican..was admitted to hospital and stabilised on pempidine and chlorothiazide. **1974** *Prescribers Jrnl.* XIV 47 Ganglion blocking drugs, such as pentolinium..and pempidine.., have been omitted from this short review because in the drug treatment of hypertension they have now been largely superseded.

pen, *sb.*[1] Add: **1. c.** *spec.* A division in a sheep-shearing shed. Also, the work associated with a sheep-shearing pen. *Austral.* and *N.Z.*

1891 R. WALLACE *Rural Econ. Austral. & N.Z.* xxix. 381 On the outside of the smaller pens, and near to the outer side-walls the shearers are placed. **1900** H. LAWSON *Verses, Pop. & Humorous* 168 The shearers squint along the pens, they squint along the 'shoots'. **1905** —— *When I was King* 38 The shed was cooled by electric fans that was over every shoot; The pens was of polished ma-ho-gany. **1933** L. G. D. ACLAND in *Press* (Christchurch, N.Z.) 11 Nov. 15/7 *Pen.* (1) A small yard; a division in the sheep-holding part of a wool-shed. (2) Shearers catch out of a p[en], and when they apply for work they ask for a p[en]. 'Will you keep me a p[en] for next year, boss?' is often their farewell. **1945** BAKER *Austral. Lang.* iii. 65 A shearer gets a *cut* (it is also called a *stand* or *pen*) when he is employed. **1965** *Austral. Encycl.* VIII. 86/2 Shearing became the work of a nomadic band of men who travelled..from shearing shed to shearing shed... The fortunate ones 'got their pen' at the commencement of a shearing whilst the others moved on in the hope of getting work at some other station. **1966** G. W. TURNER *Eng. Lang. Austral. & N.Z.* iii. 48 An Australian instance of this [*sc.* metonymy] is the shearer's request for a *pen*, i.e. work, some sheep to shear.

2. c. A prison; a cell in a prison. orig. *U.S.* (cf. *BULL-PEN 1 a)

Often indistinguishable from *PEN *sb.*[5].

1845 W. G. SIMMS *Wigwam & Cabin* (1846) 2nd Ser. 93 Laughter..ceased on my part, as I got in sight of the 'pen' in which I was to be kept secure. **1853** F. W. THOMAS *John Randolph* 286 If I had not caught him in Baltimore ..and put him in the pen there for debt, I never should have got the money. **1867** W. L. GOSS *Soldier's Story* 144 Every batch of prisoners sent into the 'pen' were accompanied by a spy in U.S. blue. **1904** *N.Y. Even. Jrnl.* 10 May 2 A panic was caused among the prisoners in the pen of the Ewen Street Police Court jail. **1948** PARTRIDGE *Dict. Forces' Slang* 139 *Pen*, a prisoner-of-war cage. (Mostly Army.)

e. A covered dock forming a berth for a naval vessel, esp. for a submarine.

1917 W. S. CHURCHILL *Second World War* (1949) II. I. xii. 216 A..harbour..with regular pens for the destroyers and submarines. **1932** A. R. BRADSHAW *Eng.–French Naval Terms* v. 76 *Destroyer pens*, les appontements. **1942** *R.A.F. Jrnl.* 16 May 19 (*caption*) These..photographs illustrate the constructional development of a possible new Naval Base and set of Submarine Pens. **1944** *Hutchinson's Pict. Hist. War* 12 Apr.–26 Sept. 229 Aircraft of Bomber Command launched a heavy attack on the 8-ft. thick E-boat pens at Le Havre. **1946** *War Report* (B.B.C.) 111 When the famous submarine pens of Cherbourg were inspected they revealed a twenty-foot thickness of reinforced concrete, designed to be absolutely impregnable to air bombardment. **1959** *Economist* 30 May 816/1 Russia does possess a foothold (complete with submarine pens) on the Mediterranean shore. **1961** F. H. BURGESS *Dict. Sailing* 158 *Pen, penns*, the spaces between a series of piers, so built that vessels may berth four to six deep between them. **1974** *Sci. Amer.* Mar. 117/1 The waste and the sorrow glow too hot to be concealed yet, even under the 5.5-meter reinforced-concrete slab over the submarine pens at Doenitz' headquarters port of Brest. **1975** *Ibid.* Oct. 6/1 There are a number of hard military targets other than missile silos, such as buried command posts, nuclear-weapons storage facilities and submarine pens that nuclear weapons may not be effective against unless they are accurate.

4. pen-mate *Austral.* and *N.Z. slang*, a shearer who catches sheep out of the same pen (as another shearer).

1933 L. G. D. ACLAND in *Press* (Christchurch, N.Z.) 11 Nov. 15/7 Two shearers usually catch out of one p[en] and are called p[en]-mates. **1965** J. S. GUNN *Terminol. Shearing Industry* II. 3 'Pen mates' catch their sheep out of the same pen.

pen, *sb.*[2] Add: **4. c.** (Later example.)

1922 JOYCE *Ulysses* 134 Gallaher, that was pressman for you. That was a pen.

7. a. *pen-line, -painting, set, -spray, -stalk, -stand, -stroke* (further examples). **c.** *pen-nibber.* **d.** *pen-painted* adj.

1895 E. M. THOMPSON *Eng. Illum. MSS.* ii. 38 The features of the human face are indicated by very light pen-lines alone without any attempt at modelling. **1978** *Times* 2 June 13/4 White [wall]papers with a thin pen line stripe of bright green or pink or blue. **1823** *Trans. Soc. Arts* XL. 252 This operation..may be performed still more accurately by the Pen-nibber here represented. **1902** *Chambers's Jrnl.* Nov. 692/2 He had in everyday use: (1) wash-hand tray..(13) pen-nibber, (14) ruler. **1929** E. BOWEN *Last Sept.* II. ix. 104 Cushions with pen-painted sprays. **1862** TROLLOPE *Let.* 28 June (1951) 115 The character of Romola..is the perfection of pen painting. **1934** M. ALLINGHAM *Death of Ghost* xi. 130 The shop..which sold her pen paintings 'phoned her..and she spent a busy hour..getting off a consignment of table centres. **1963** L. DEIGHTON *Horse under Water* xvii. 69 On da Cunha's simple mahogany desk was a porcelain-and-gold pen set. **1977** R. LUDLUM *Chancellor Manuscript* ix. 105 Quinn..sat down behind his desk...His eyes fell on..his pen set. **1905** J. W. BRADLEY *Illum. MSS.* II. iii. 142 The greater part of this volume is in the.. 'Berry' style, *i.e.* the fine pen-sprays of ivy leaf of burnished gold. But the first grand border is..transitional, consisting of the pen-sprays of golden ivy leaf alternating with sprays of natural flowers. **1907** K. D. WIGGIN *New Chron. Rebecca* iii. 78 Last night I dreamed that the river was ink and I kept dipping into it and writing with a penstalk made of a young pine tree. **1933** D. GASCOYNE *Opening Day* i. 12 On the flap of the desk were bottles of inks, a pen-stand in red and white mottled marble..and a profuse litter of papers. **1969** E. H. PINTO *Treen* 260/2 Horizontal tiered pen stands, as opposed to vertical pen holders, only became practical when the straight steel-nibbed pen replaced the curved feathered quill. **1928** O. E. SAUNDERS *Eng. Illumination* I. 66 The shading on the draperies is executed by penstrokes, one thick line being regularly bordered by two thin ones. **1977** *Times Lit. Suppl.* 25 Mar. 365/1 In the animation process, where the energy-charge of single penstrokes is naturally sacrificed to the blur of movement.

8. pen-form, the shape of hand-written letters, esp. those influenced by the writing instrument or the way it is used; so **pen-formed** *a.*; **pen-picture** (later example); **pen recorder,** an instrument for producing a continuous graphical record of a variable measured quantity by means of a pen; so **pen-recorded** *a.*, **pen recording; pen-trial,** something written by a scribe on a manuscript to test his pen.

1906 E. JOHNSTON *Writing & Illuminating* iii. 63 For the practical study of pen-forms use a cane or a reed pen. *Ibid.* xiv. 238 The Pen-formed letters are more easily practised. **1955** J. R. R. TOLKIEN *Return of King* 397 They [*sc.* dwarfs] adhered to the Cirth, and developed written pen-forms from them. **1973** *Times* 15 Dec. 4/2 Later the pupils were asked to rate the instructor on such things as intelligence, likableness, popularity and honesty, and give a short pen picture of him. **1973** *Nature* 27 Apr. 601/1 The pen-recorded chart appears in Fig. 1. **1947** *Canad. Jrnl. Res.* B. XXV. 397 In conjunction with a linear direct current amplifier and a Leeds and Northrup Speedomax pen recorder, this unit allows rapid and accurate recording of a given mass spectrum. **1964** *Listener* 27 Feb. 344/2 The radiations from Jupiter.. may also be recorded as a trace, using a pen-recorder, though great care has to be taken with identification. **1972** *Physics Bull.* Jan. 24/3 A permanent record of any defects can be obtained on a chart, the motion of which is synchronized with the position of the transducer.., if the output signal is fed to a pen recorder. **1942** *Rev. Sci. Instruments* XIII. 218 (*heading*) Direct pen recording of galvanometer deflections. **1945** *Ibid.* XVI. 70/2 It was felt to be desirable to employ a pen recording system. **1953** K. SISAM *Stud. Hist. Old Eng. Lit.* vii. 109 At the extreme top of folios 119*a*, 121*a*, 123*a*, 126*a*..is a prayer at the beginning of the sitting..; but it is also, I think, an inconspicuous pen-trial to make sure that pen and ink will go smoothly. **1978** *N. & Q.* Oct. 405/1 Additions to..the manuscript include the clarification of texts, pen trials, [etc.].

pen (pen), *sb.*[5] *U.S.* Abbrev. of PENITENTIARY *sb.* 7, with allusion to *PEN *sb.*[1] 2 c (from which some early uses are indistinguishable).

1884 'C. E. CRADDOCK' *In Tennessee Mts.* 68 He b'lieved the Pen could claim it ez convict labor. **1889** *Provo* (Utah) *Amer.* 28 Mar. 1/4 What John got was eighteen months in the pen. **1908** [see *COLD *a.* 1 e]. **1910** 'O. HENRY' *Whirligigs* xvii. 202 One year after I got to the pen, my daughter died. **1924** W. M. RAINE *Troubled Waters* xxvii. 273 He escaped from the pen four days ago. **1939** J. STEINBECK *Grapes of Wrath* x. 123 I'm a-gonna tell you somepin about bein' in the pen. **1940** R. CHANDLER *Farewell, my Lovely* vi. 43 We got a wire from Oregon State Pen on him. **1956** B. HOLIDAY *Lady sings Blues* (1973) xix. 159 This was the first time I met anybody from the federal pen. **1960** *Times Lit. Suppl.* 16 Sept. 589/4 A junkie..who was..busted by the nailers and after a stretch in the pen cold turkeyed. **1967** *Punch* 22 Nov. 796/2 Semple makes a pass at Carole, is rebuffed, strangles her in a demented fit, and does eighteen years in the pen for it. **1972** 'H. HOWARD' *Nice Day for Funeral* iii. 40 He was her meal-ticket. Why should she want him sent to the pen? **1973** M. CAMPBELL *Halfbreed* xviii. 123, I had only been in Vancouver a few days when I met a guy just out of the Pen. **1975** *High Times* Dec. 9/1 Right now I'm in east Tennessee facing a five-to-15 year term in the state pen for something I haven't done—mainly for selling a schedule-one drug to a narc. **1977** *Time* 20 June 33/1 Another escape try from Missouri state pen, on March 10, 1966.

pen, *v.*[3] Add: **c.** *intr.* To use a pen; to write.

1904 HARDY *Dynasts* I. II. ii. 64 He pens in fits, with pallid restlessness. **1939** JOYCE *Finnegans Wake* 301 He would pen for her, he would pine for her.

penal, *a.* Add: **1. c.** *ellipt.* as *sb.* (*a*) (a sentence or period of) imprisonment; (*b*) a school punishment.

1867 [see *CAPER *sb.*[2] 1c]. **1892** *Daily News* 17 Nov. 6/6, I was speaking to a youth who had undergone two penals ..for picking pockets. **1906** D. COKE *Bending of Twig* xii. 200 He can write lines, or 'penals' instead of going to detentions. **1908** *Outlook* 26 Dec. 901/2 The very interesting article on the Milton tercentenary..reminds me of a public school where some years ago boys had 'penals' selected from 'Paradise Lost'. **1927** W. E. COLLINSON *Contemp. Eng.* 77 A convict doing penal or doing time i.e. sentenced to penal servitude, is sometimes called a lag. **1937** J. M. WEST *Shrewsbury* vi. 71 It was at this time that 'penals' came to be written from Milton's *Paradise Lost*. **1938** F. D. SHARPE *Sharpe of Flying Squad* xvii. 191 Nickname got four years' penal and his companion eighteen months' hard.

e. (Further examples.)

1908 A. DE HORSEY in *Times* 15 Aug. 14/3 It is bad enough that the Isle of Wight at Parkhurst should have been selected as a penal station for the convicts of other parts of England. **1963** T. & P. MORRIS *Pentonville* xi. 225 Their reference group remains very firmly their 'own' prison, which some of the older men still refer to as their 'penal station'.

2. Delete †*Obs.* and add later examples. Now usu. of taxation and other financial burdens.

1953 'M. INNES' *Christmas at Candleshoe* i. 14 His father..declares that penal taxation is ephemeral, and that of the really big English properties the ownership has not changed. **1957** *Sunday Times* 14 July 13/6 The motor and aeroplane, cinema, radio and television, penal taxation of large incomes and compulsory social services have transformed life. **1958** *Spectator* 15 Aug. 234/1 We have had to struggle with..a penal Bank rate.

penalty. Add: **2. b.** (Further examples.)

1972 *Lebende Sprachen* XVII. 134/2 Increases in strength or stiffness have always brought a weight penalty. *Ibid.* 135/1 The aircraft will accept bulky cargo with little penalty in payload.

c. (Further examples.) *spec.* in *Football,* (the award of) a free kick at goal (see also sense 5 in Dict.).

1897 *Encycl. Sport* I. 434/2 Within the twelve yards line, a referee must enforce law 13, and has no power to mitigate the penalty. **1898** A. E. T. WATSON *Turf* 249 When any race is in dispute, both the horse that came in first and any horse claiming the race shall be liable to all the penalties attaching to the winner of that race till the matter be decided. **1899** A. BUDD *Football* (*Rugby*) 53 Free-kicks by way of penalties shall be awarded on claims by the opposite side. **1951** E. RICKMAN *Come racing with Me* ii. 12 The weights are varied in individual cases by 'penalties' (extra weight) for previous wins. **1969** B. JAMES *England v Scotland* x. 229 Mr Skranko awarded no fewer than 55 free kicks and three penalties. **1972** G. GREEN *Great Moments in Sport: Soccer* v. 66 Dorsett shot the penalty home like a thunderbolt. **1974** *Rules of Game* 260/4 Condition (or allowance) races, in which a basic weight allowance for age and sex of horse is varied by added weight penalties for past successes (measured in prize money terms). **1977** *Horse & Hound* 14 Jan. 7/4 Early Spring..was making an 8 lb penalty look very ordinary indeed.

e. *Bridge.* A number of points added to the opponents' score when the declarer fails to make his contract, or to the declarer's score when his call is doubled and he makes his contract.

1908 R. F. FOSTER *Auction Bridge* 37, 50 points penalty for each of the two tricks by which the bidder failed. **1935** *Encycl. Sports* 174/1 Penalties reasonably incurred may be cheaper than allowing your opponents to make game. **1964** *Official Encycl. Bridge* 417/2 *Penalty.* (1) An obligation or restriction imposed upon a side for violation of the Laws of Bridge... (2) An amount scored above the line by the declarer's opponents when the declarer fails to make a contract. **1976** *Field* 30 Dec. 1293/2 He again doubled, but, of course, this time for a penalty.

5. (from sense 2c) *penalty bully, corner, flick, goal, kick* (further examples), *point, stroke, trick, try*; **penalty area,** the area in front of the goal on football and other pitches within which offences can incur the award of a penalty; **penalty bench,** in ice-hockey, seating for match officials and penalized players; also **penalty box,** (*a*) the area taken up by a penalty bench; (*b*) = *penalty area*; **penalty card** *Bridge* (see quot. 1964); **penalty carrier** *Golf,* a player who has a number of strokes added to his total as a handicap; **penalty clause,** a clause in a contract stipulating a penalty for failure to fulfil any of its obligations; **penalty double** *Bridge,* a double made to increase a score if an opponent's contract is defeated; **penalty envelope** *U.S.,* an official envelope which may only be used for its designated purpose, under penalty of a fine stated on it; **penalty killer,** in ice-hockey, a player responsible for preventing the opposing side from scoring while his own team's strength is reduced through penalties; hence **penalty killing** *ppl. a.* and *vbl. sb.*; **penalty line,** a line marking a penalty area on a football pitch; **penalty pass** *Bridge* (see quot. 1964); **penalty rate** *Austral.,* an increased rate of pay for overtime; **penalty spot,** the spot from which penalty shots or kicks are taken.

1905 P. WALKER *How to Play Assoc. Football* 12 Lines shall be marked 18 yards from each goal-post at right angles to the goal-lines for a distance of 18 yards, and these shall be connected with each other by a line parallel to the goal-lines; the space within these lines shall be the penalty area. **1910** *Encycl. Brit.* X. 621/2 If such infringement take place within the penalty area on the part of a player on the side then defending the goal,..a 'penalty kick' is awarded to the attacking side. **1929** *Daily Express* 7 Nov. 19/1 The full-backs were often guilty of dribbling the ball in their own penalty area. **1970** A. WADE *Coach Yourself Assoc. Football* 14 When he reaches the penalty area attacker A can only shoot or pass to B. **1972** G. GREEN *Great Moments in Sport: Soccer* i. 25 Again Mortensen reached a spot right of the penalty area. **1934** WEBSTER, Penalty bench. **1962** *Amer. Speech* XXXVII. 126 Stammbach goes to the penalty bench for two minutes on account of a check. **1974** *Rules of Game* 188/1 Penalty bench with space for eight players and extra seating for timekeepers, scorer, and announcer. **1931** *Vancouver Province* 17 Jan. 7/1 Two Vancouver players [were] in the penalty box. **1954** F. C. AVIS *Soccer Reference Dict.* 90 *Penalty Box*: see Penalty Area. **1963** *Calgary Herald* 11 Nov. 9/2 Alex Faulkner was in the penalty box serving a major penalty for high-sticking Montreal's Ralph Backstrom and drawing blood. **1972** 'E. LATHEN' *Murder without Icing* vi. 62 Paul Imrie fought for the sheer joy of it. He was a constant occupant of the penalty box, he was always being thrown out of games. **1976** E. DUNPHY *Only a Game?* ii. 39 Both goals were breakaways, starting from their own penalty box. **1897** *Encycl. Sport* I. 516/2 A penalty bully is given for deliberately unfair play by the defending side in their own circle. **1909** *Westm. Gaz.* 12 Oct. 12/2 It is rarely that a penalty-bully is given in first-class hockey. **1935** *Encycl. Sports* 347/2 If necessary, time of play shall be extended to admit of a penalty bully being played, or completed. **1974** *Rules of Game* 183/5 Extra time is allowed to take a penalty bully if half or full time is already completed. **1958** *Listener* 25 Dec. 1094/2 The card would have been a penalty card as well. **1959** *Ibid.* 30 Apr. 765/3 Declarer can, in fact, treat the remaining cards of *either* defender as penalty cards. **1963** *Ibid.* 24 Jan. 186/2 Declarer could have..treated the card led as a penalty card. **1964** *Official Encycl. Bridge* 418/1 *Penalty card,* a card that has been prematurely exposed by a defender, and must be left face up on the table until legally played or permitted to be picked up. **1908** *Westm. Gaz.* 12 June 9/3 Mr. Hunter is the only surviving 'penalty-carrier'. His handicap is plus 2, while Mr. Scrutton has an allowance of fourteen strokes. **1935** WODEHOUSE *Luck of Bodkins* xv. 170 The first thing she would do, if she was a sensible kid, would be to go to her lawyer and have a contract drawn up and signed, with penalty clauses. **1967** S. WOODGATE in Wills & Yearsley *Handbk. Managem. Technol.* 74 Some costs increase as the project duration increases, e.g. overheads, penalty clauses, lost revenue, etc. **1969** K. GILES *Death cracks Bottle* i. 13 The new part was accomplished in one cyclonic burst—five months from a standing start with penalty clauses. **1976** E. WARD *Hanged Man* xxviii. 179 The main contractors had a big penalty clause on me and hired Dieter to frighten off skilled labour so they could collect. **1935** *Encycl. Sports* 347/1 Rule 16 shall also apply to a penalty corner. **1967** J. POTTER *Foul Play* xiii. 152 The defence conceded one goal, after the opposition had been awarded a much deserved penalty corner. **1974** *Rules of Game* 183/5 Penalty corners are awarded against defenders for deliberately playing the ball over the goal line [etc.]. **1977** *Guardian* 10 Mar. 27/5 Manchester will consider themselves unlucky to have been denied a penalty stroke when the score stood at 1–1. **1959** *Listener* 30 July 190/1 The theory of the responsive double is that the hand on which one would want to make a penalty double..is of much lower frequency than the hand..when one might prefer to give a picture of general values. **1964** *Official Encycl. Bridge* 135/2 The two main categories [of doubles] are penalty doubles and take-out doubles. **1879** *Postal Laws U.S.* §147 Requisitions for postage-stamps, stamped-envelopes,..and official penalty-envelopes are required to be made upon printed forms. **1903** *N.Y. Times* 29 Aug. 5/1 The officials of the District Government were not entitled to the use of the mails like other Federal officials who use penalty envelopes. **1917** J. A. MOSS *Officers' Manual* (ed. 6) xxv. 272 Official letters are mailed in penalty envelopes. **1967** J. POTTER *Foul Play* ii. 25 One of the umpires..: the one, in fact, who had awarded a short corner instead of a penalty flick. **1977** *Cleethorpes News* 6 May 32/2 Skegness..lost..on penalty flicks to Scunthorpe last year. **1951** *Sport* 27 Apr.–3 May 4/1 The Oakwell Reds would have welcomed the compensation of a penalty-goal in their 6–0 setback at Maine Road. **1979** *Times* 12 Dec. 9/6 Penalty goals rather than tries continue to decide most matches. **1897** *Encycl. Sport* I. 434/1 The referee shall award the opposing side a penalty kick. **1925** [see *EQUALIZE *v.* 4b]. **1960** E. S. & W. J. HIGHAM *High Speed Rugby* 180 There may come a stage in a game when taking a penalty kick at goal is waste of time. **1971** *Referees' Chart* (Football Assoc.) 30 When a penalty-kick is being taken the Referee must not give the signal for the restart until the players have taken up the position ordered by the Law. **1974** *Rules of Game* 159/4 The penalty kick is taken from or behind where the offense occurred. **1962** *Kingston* (Ontario) *Whig-Standard* 14 Dec. 10/1 Not only was Westfall one of the best defencemen in the league, a good point man on the power play and a penalty killer of the first order, but he took over a left wing position just before his departure. **1966** *Hockey News* 1 Jan. 13/2 He is an accomplished man on the power play and is among the top penalty killers in the league. **1968** *Globe & Mail* (Toronto) 15 Jan. 21/1 Three seasons I spent in the National Hockey League exclusively as a penalty killer. **1963** *Kingston* (Ontario) *Whig-Standard* 6 May 11/4 Winger Bill Glashan stepped up from his penalty-killing role to score twice for Flyers. **1963** *Hockey Illustr.* Dec. 38/2 If I took him off penalty killing and put him on the power play he'd score 40 goals a year. **1970** *Globe & Mail* (Toronto) 26 Sept. 35/1 He is the centre on a checking line, a headliner on the penalty-killing unit. **1975** *Cleveland* (Ohio) *Plain Dealer* 6 Apr. 10-C/1 Their power play, keyed by Gordie, is one of the best in the league and the penalty killing, once again led by Howe, is one of the best in the league. **1929** *Evening News* 18 Nov. 13/3 The penalty lines and the touch lines were not visible. **1959** *Listener* 2 Apr. 613/3 He would not consider a penalty pass as his trick-taking capacity was far too slender. **1964** *Official Encycl. Bridge* 420/1 *Penalty pass,* a pass by a player after a take-out double from his partner and a pass by right-hand opponent. **1974** *Rules of Game* 49/2 The competition is won by the finalist with the least penalty points. **1977** *New Yorker* 10 Oct. 150/2 The umpire could have assessed him a penalty point for unsportsmanlike conduct. **1956** S. HOPE *Diggers' Paradise* 98 All workers when they 'work back'—do overtime—come on to 'penalty rates' as they are called. **1973** *Bulletin* (Sydney) 25 Aug. 3/3 We will expect to be dealt with on exactly the same basis as any other Commonwealth public servant, i.e. a 36½-hour-week, penalty rates for overtime, annual leave, sick leave, [etc.]. **1937** F. N. S. CREEK *Assoc. Football* vi. 166 Penalty Spot. **1948** B. STEEL *How to play Football* xvii. 144 As he strode back to take up position for the kick, the wind blew the ball from the penalty spot. **1960** G. GREEN in Fabian & Green *Assoc. Football* III. VIII. 55 Goalkeepers now have to remain stationary on their line until the ball is actually struck from the penalty spot. **1974** *Rules of Game* 183/3 It [*sc.* a penalty stroke in hockey] is taken from the penalty spot by an attacker. **1975** *Evening News* (Edinburgh) (Sports Final ed.) 15 Mar. 10/1 Fairley netted from the penalty spot. **1977** *Daily Mirror* 12 Apr. 28/5 Masson had scored from the penalty spot after Coventry's Brian Roberts and Alan Dugdale combined to push Peter Eastoe to the ground. **1895** W. T. LINSKILL *Golf* (ed. 3) 45 A penalty stroke shall not be counted the stroke of a player, and shall not affect the rotation of play. **1970** H. TAYLOR *Golf Dict.* 153 *Penalty stroke,* an additional stroke debited to a player (e.g. for unauthorized touching of the ball). **1974** *Rules of Game* 183/4 If the ball halts outside the circle or passes out of it, the penalty stroke is ended. **1977** *Sunday Times* 9 Jan. 30/6 England..gave away two silly goals, and were then denied an obvious penalty stroke. **1909** *Westm. Gaz.* 20 Mar. 14/2 Penalty trick scores incurred during the play of a rubber are not irretrievably gone. **1923** P. TREVOR *Rugby Union Football* xi. 149 The awarding of a penalty try is an occasional happening. **1936** H. B. T. WAKELAM *Rugby Football* i. 4 The only other means by which the score can be increased is the very rare penalty try, awarded only under very exceptional circumstances by the referee, upon his deciding that a proper try would have been put on had it not been for some exceptionally flagrant breach of the laws by the opposition. **1959** in V. JENKINS *Lions Down Under* (1960) xiv. 206 A penalty-try,..the first (as far as is known) ever awarded to a touring team visiting New Zealand. **1960** Penalty-try [see *IN-GOAL]. **1976** W. REYBURN *All about Rugby Football* vii. 109 *Penalty try,* awarded when, in the opinion of the referee, a player would have scored had he not been obstructed by a defender; most commonly when both are chasing a ball kicked over the goal line. Conversion of a penalty try is taken from in front of the posts, no matter where it is awarded.

pen and ink, pen-and-ink, *phr.* Add: **A.** as *sb.* **2.** (Earlier and later examples.)

1860 D. G. ROSSETTI *Let.* 28 Sept. (1965) I. 375 Now one of his commissions is for a £50 pen-and-ink. **1976** *National Observer* (U.S.) 10 Apr. 16/2 Mrs. Fisher had once done us a pen and ink of the Poplar Branch landing.

3. A stink. *Rhyming slang.*

1859 HOTTEN *Dict. Slang* 145 *Pen and ink,* a stink. **1935** A. J. POLLOCK *Underworld Speaks* 86/2 *Pen and ink,*..a stink. **1972** G. F. NEWMAN *You Nice Bastard* 347 *Pen* (*and ink*), stink.

B. as *adj.* **1.** Delete 'Now *rare* or *Obs.*' and add later examples.

1967 A. L. LLOYD *Folk Song in England* 14 When [Cecil] Sharp was..in search of song..a wide gulf separated the pen-and-ink man from the man with bowyangs of binder twine. **1972** [see *lensman* s.v. *LENS *sb.* 3].

C. as *vb.* **2.** To stink. *Rhyming slang.* Also *ellipt.,* as *pen.*

1892 *Sporting Times* 29 Oct. 1/2 The air began With his language to pen and ink. **1972** G. F. NEWMAN *You Nice Bastard* iv. 137 'I don't mind, provided he takes a bath.' 'Yeah, he does pen a bit.'

pen and inkery, *phr. nonce-use.* [f. prec. + -ERY.] The use of pen and ink; an author's business.

c **1909** W. DE MORGAN in A. M. W. Stirling *W. De Morgan & his Wife* (1922) xiv. 328, I do wish I had paid more attention to them [*sc.* birds, flowers, and trees] in my time—they would come in so useful in these later days of pen-and-inkery.

‖**penanggalan** (pĕnæ·ŋgălăn). Also **penangalan.** [Malay.] A female vampire (see quots.). Cf. *LANGSUIR.

1839 T. J. NEWBOLD *Pol. & Statistical Acct. Straits of Malacca* II. xii. 191 The Penangalan takes up its abode in the forms of females, and afflicts them with an unnatural craving for human blood. **1900** W. W. SKEAT *Malay Magic* vi. 320 The Pĕnanggalan..is believed to resemble a trunkless human head with the sac of the stomach attached to it, and which flies about seeking for an opportunity of sucking the blood of infants. **1972** *Daily Tel.* (Colour Suppl.) 12 May 58/3 The Malayan vampire family includes..the flamboyant Penanggalan, a monstrous vampire which also sucks at children's blood.

penatin (pe·nătin). *Biochem.* [f. the L. generic name PEN(ICILLIUM + the L. specific epithet *not-at-um* (see *NOTATIN) + -IN[1].] = *NOTATIN (*PENICILLIN 2).

1942 W. KOCHOLATY in *Jrnl. Bacteriol.* XLIV. 143/1 'Penatin' (a newly discovered antibacterial substance produced by *Penicillium notatum*). *Ibid.*, While penicillin ..has only very weak antibacterial properties against *Brucella abortus*, and practically none against *Escherichia coli*, penatin is highly bacteriostatic and bactericidal against those two organisms. **1949, 1963** [see *NOTATIN].

Penbritin (penbri·tin, pe·nbritin). *Pharm.* A proprietary name for ampicillin, $C_{16}H_{19}O_4S$, a semi-synthetic penicillin that resembles penicillin G (benzylpenicillin) in its action against Gram-positive organisms but is more effective against Gram-negative ones, and is used esp. in treating infections of the urinary and the respiratory tracts.

1959 *Trade Marks Jrnl.* 18 Nov. 1197/1 Penbritin... Antibiotic preparations and substances... Beecham Research Laboratories Limited,..Brentford, Middlesex; manufacturers. **1960** *Official Gaz.* (U.S. Patent Office) 26 July TM131/1 Beecham Research Laboratories Limited, Brentford, England. Filed Mar. 25, 1960. Penbritin. For antibiotic preparations and substances. **1961** *Daily Tel.* 21 July 24/5 A new synthetic penicillin, Penbritin, promises to be more active against some strains of bacteria so far immune to previous penicillins and to be of increased potency against others. **1968** J. H. BURN *Lect. Notes Pharmacol.* (ed. 9) 108 Broad spectrum penicillins; one of these is ampicillin (Penbritin). **1968** *Economist* 6 July 66 The product responsible more than any other for more than doubling profits over the last four years is Beecham's penicillin mutant, Penbritin, which took a decade to develop. **1975** D. FISHLOCK *Business of Sci.* viii. 112 The scheme..set Beecham firmly on the path to its big semi-synthetic penicillins of the 1960s: Celbenin.., Orbenin and Penbritin.

pence. b. Applied *colloq.* as *sing.*, orig. to a 'new penny' of the decimal currency introduced in 1971 (see *PENNY 1), and hence *gen.*

1971 *Record* (Oxf. Univ. Press) Dec. 10/2 The computer was found to be rounding up to the nearest pence the Bank Code Numbers on the Wages Slips. **1973** *Daily Tel.* 24 Oct. 16 In our village shop a customer asked for some small change but the shopkeeper was unable to oblige as she was very short of 'two pences and one pences'. **1974** *Ibid.* 19 Dec. 12 In shops and elsewhere I often hear the ungrammatical term 'one pence'. I presume this is because the occurrence of a single penny is becoming a thing of the past. **1975** M. BRADBURY *History Man* i. 3 She leads her daily deputation to the manager with comparative, up-to-the-minute lists showing how Fine Fare, on lard, is one pence up on Sainsbury's, or vice versa. **1977** *Times Lit. Suppl.* 29 Apr. 528/3 The new and the supplemented lexical entries equally reflect the times, with..*p* (but not the singular use of *pence*) for *new penny*. **1979** *Daily Tel.* 11 Apr. 2/1 A taxi passenger who refused to pay an extra charge of one pence on his fare..was killed by the driver, police said in Manila.

pencil, *sb.* Add: **I. 2. d.** *to have the pencil put on one* (Criminals' slang), to be reported to the prison authorities.

1929 *Sat. Even. Post* 13 Apr. 50/3 A prisoner who is reported for some violation is written up or had the pencil put on him. **1934** H. N. ROSE *Thes. Slang* 34/2 Reported for Violation of Rules..*to be written up; have the pencil put on; have the number taken.*

II. 4. (Examples referring to radiation other than light.)

1913 *Phil. Mag.* XXV. 604 A narrow pencil of α particles fell on a zinc sulphide screen. **1938** R. W. LAWSON tr. *Hevesy & Paneth's Man. Radioactivity* (ed. 2) 291 With this apparatus pencils of many micro-amperes of deuterons..have been obtained. **1967** *Listener* 30 Mar. 429/3 The picture is positioned, and a tiny pencil of X-rays is emitted at the spot where we want to analyse a pigment.

6. d. The penis. *slang.*

1937 PARTRIDGE *Dict. Slang* 616/2 *Pencil*, the male member. **1942** BERREY & VAN DEN BARK *Amer. Thes. Slang* § 121/39 Male pudendum..pencil, pencil and tassel. **1967** D. FRANCIS *Blood Sport* v. 58 That Purple Emperor strain is as soft as an old man's pencil.

e. Phr. *lead in one's pencil*: see *LEAD *sb.*[1] 3.

III. 7. a. *pencil-mark* (earlier and later examples as *sb.*); see also sense 7b below; *pencil-slim, -thin* adjs. Also with sense 'resembling a pencil in shape', as *pencil flash(light), microphone, pants, skirt, stripe, torch.*

1929 'E. QUEEN' *Roman Hat Mystery* IV. xxii. 307 Barry examined them..by the same pencil flashlight—a tiny streak of illumination. **1935** R. CHANDLER in *Black Mask* Jan. 15/1, I tried throwing the beam of my pencil flash along the floor. **1824** J. S. MILL in *Westm. Rev.* II. 399 Hume was not..without authority, for Mr. Brodie saw his pencil marks opposite to this story, in the copy of Perinchief belonging to the Advocate's library. **1855** D. G. ROSSETTI *Let.* 25 June (1965) I. 257 Ruskin has been reading those translations since you, and says he could wish no better than to ink your pencil-marks as his criticisms. **1962** A. NISBETT *Technique Sound Studio* ii. 36 A 'pencil' microphone just peeping out of a well in the centre of the table. **1973** P. EVANS *Bodyguard Man* xix. 120 Her right hand was..holding a pencil-microphone. **1960** *News Chron.* 26 Sept. 9 This one is equally good with pencil pants. **1952** C. W. CUNNINGTON *Eng. Women's Clothing* ii. 245 Coatees... Worn with plain pencil skirt. **1960** [see *kick-pleat* s.v. *KICK *sb.*[1] 8]. **1974** P. HAINES *Tea at Gunter's* ix. 96 She was wearing a pencil skirt so tight she could barely walk. **1949** *Women's Wear Daily* 24 Jan. 6/5 Jacqueline Vienne features..long double-breasted jacket over pencil slim skirts. **1976** 'J. ROSS' *I know what it's like to Die* xxii. 144 A pencil-slim ochre-coloured cigar. **1897** *Sears, Roebuck Catal.* 181/2 Boys' two-piece wash goods suit, made of heavy navy blue with pencil stripe. **1960** *House & Garden* June 21/1 (Advt.), Alternating bands of closely spaced pencil stripes. **1970** *New Yorker* 17 Oct. 170 (Advt.), Pencil stripes, yes. Bankers pencil stripes, no. **1962** K. ORVIS *Damned & Destroyed* i. 12 A..pencil-thin Frenchman. **1963** *Times* 25 Feb. (Canada Suppl.) p. vii/4 The huge, pencil-thin Great Lakes ships. **1978** T. GIFFORD *Glendower Legacy* (1979) 298 He came down the stairs, Dapper and pencil-thin. **1937** M. ALLINGHAM *Dancers in Mourning* iv. 59 He had a pencil-torch in his pocket. **1948** M. GILBERT *They never looked Inside* i. 7 A glow-worm came and went ten feet away, and Rod guessed that 'Gunner' was using his pencil-torch with discretion. **1964** 'E. PETERS' *Flight of Witch* x. 166 One of those thin pencil-torches that clip in a breast pocket. **1976** 'Z. STONE' *Modigliani Scandal* IV. iv. 182 He..shone a pencil torch inside.

b. pencil-arm, the arm of a pair of compasses that carries the pencil; **pencil beam,** a narrow, nearly parallel beam; *spec.* in *Radar*, one which in addition has an approximately circular cross-section; **pencil beard** (see quot.); **pencil box,** a box for holding pencils; **pencil cedar,** add: esp. *Juniperus virginiana*; also, any of several Australian trees resembling these kinds of juniper or yielding wood suitable for making pencils; (further examples); **pencil flower** (earlier and later examples); **pencil knife,** a knife for sharpening pencils; **pencil-line,** a line drawn with a pencil or resembling one so drawn; also *attrib.*, esp. in **pencil-line moustache** (see quot. 1966); **pencil mark** = *PENCILLING *vbl. sb.* 1; **pencil moustache** = *pencil-line moustache* above; **pencil pusher** *U.S.*, a derogatory term for one whose occupation involves much writing with a pencil; **pencil tablet,** a notebook of rough paper suitable for writing in pencil but not in pen.

1892 E. ROWE *Hints on Chip-Carving* i. 9 Do not use the left hand to move the pencil-arm of the compasses. **1946** *Jrnl. Inst. Electr. Engin.* XCIII. IIIA. 25/2 A Yagi aerial.. presents the possibility of obtaining a 'pencil' beam of radiation, narrow in two perpendicular planes, from an end-fire array of comparatively small dimensions. **1955** *Sci. Amer.* Mar. 38/1 This antenna has a pencil beam which at a wavelength of 65 centimeters is five degrees wide. **1965** A. NICOL *Truly Married Woman* 98 Bradshaw.. turned quickly down the road, his headlights two pencil beams in the darkness. **1966** J. S. COX *Illustr. Dict. Hairdressing* 110/1 *Pencil beard*, a narrow strip of beard from the lower lip to the chin. **1907** *Yesterday's Shopping* (1969) 132/2 Pencil Box..9 by 2½ in., 1/0. **1912** 'C. F. BENTON' *Fairs & Fetes* 118 School-supplies also may find a place here—slates and pencils..pencil-boxes and rulers. **1935** 'R. CROMPTON' *William—the Detective* xi. 235 Ties an' books an' pencil boxes. **1969** E. H. PINTO *Treen* 422 The Bavarian manufacturers of children's pencil boxes certainly knew how to bring joy to the hearts of late-Victorian and Edwardian school boys and girls. **1977** D. CLARK *Gimmel Flask* vii. 134 Remember the old pencil-boxes with sliding lids and sections inside? **1884** A. NILSON *Timber Trees New South Wales* 53 D[ysoxylon] *Muelleri*.—Pencil Cedar... *D. rufum*.—Bastard Pencil Cedar. *Ibid.* 110 P[odocarpus] *elata*.—Colonial Deal; White Pine; Pencil Cedar. **1908** E. J. BANFIELD *Confessions of Beachcomber* I. v. 184 A huge log of pencil cedar had been cast among the boulders. **1932** R. H. ANDERSON *Trees New South Wales* 89 Bermuda Pencil Cedar..often makes a fine tree. *Ibid.* 143 Red Bean (*Dysoxylum Muelleri*)..is also sometimes known as 'Pencil Cedar'. **1965** *Austral. Encycl.* I. 222/1 *Tieghemopanax elegans* (syn. *Panax elegans*), the black pencil cedar, is an ornamental tree with large, divided leaves, and a soft, light wood. *Ibid.* VII. 106/1 *Glochidion Ferdinandii* (variously known as white beech, pencil cedar, rain tree and 'towwar')..is a medium-sized, rain-forest tree. **1968** W. E. WILLIS *Timber* i. 6 Virginian Pencil Cedar is a species of Juniper and a favourite wood for the manufacture of pencils. **1817** A. EATON *Man. Bot.* 85 *Stylosanthes...elatior* (pencil-flower). **1901** C. T. MOHR *Plant Life Alabama* 570 Stylosanthes... Pencil flower. **1926** E. O'NEILL *Great God Brown* III. iii. 81 Waving his pencil knife with grotesque flourishes. **1905** Pencil-line [listed in Dict., sense 7a]. **1957** R. HOGGART *Uses of Literacy* ix. 235 A neat moustache in dark thin pencil line. **1966** J. S. COX *Illustr. Dict. Hairdressing* 110/1 *Pencil Line Moustache.* (1) A moustache consisting of a very thin line of hairs... (2) A thin line moustache drawn on the upper lip with a coloured cosmetic. **1968** R. C. GALWAY *Assignment Gaolbreak* ix. 88 He had..a vicious-looking pencil-line moustache. **1971** B. MALAMUD *Tenants* 98 Jacob..had uneasy eyes and a pencil-line mustache. **1976** *New Yorker* 15 Nov. 23/2 Greta Garbo, with pencil-line eyebrows above sex-drugged lids, plays a bored, sensual, wicked woman. **1880** H. DALZIEL *Brit. Dogs* II. 332 Feet tanned, but the knuckles with a clear black line, called the 'pencil mark', up the ridge. **1931** A. C. SMITH *About our Dogs* xvi. 245 The standard of the Black-and-Tan Terrier Club:..the forelegs tanned up to the knees, with black lines (pencil marks) up each toe. **1961** W. BROWN *Bedeviled* 77 He was a tall, thin youth with slicked-down, black hair, a pencil moustache and shaggy sideburns. **1965** P. ROBINSON *Pakistani Agent* ii. 8 Parulekar was..in his late twenties, with a pencil moustache. **1973** H. GILBERT *Hotels with Empty Rooms* xv. 128 A cinematographical convention, like crooks with pencil-moustaches. **1881** *Harvard Lampoon* 20 Apr. 42/2 After various chilling repulses, our pencil-pusher discovered a man smaller than himself. **1917** F. D. O'SULLIVAN *Enemies of Underworld* xcvi. 666/1 *Pencil pusher*, clerk. **1926** MAINES & GRANT *Wise-Crack Dict.* 12/2 *Pencil-pusher*, office employe. **1952** in Wentworth & Flexner *Dict. Amer. Slang* (1960) 382/1 The number of pencil pushers and typists has increased in the past 25 years out of proportion to the increase in factory workers. **1959** *Amer. Speech* XXXIV. 79 *Pencil pusher*, a camp book-keeper. **1961** B. JAMES *Night of Kill* ix. 120 He'd be damned if he was going to be a mid-watch pencil-pusher just to please his ulcerated pro-tem captain. **1895** *Montgomery Ward Catal.* Spring & Summer (Index), Pencil Tablets. **1944** T. D. CLARK *Pills, Petticoats & Plows* 45 Across the way there was an assortment of school-books, pencil tablets,..and epsom salts.

pencil, *v.* Add: **2. c.** *to pencil in* (fig.), to note, register, or arrange provisionally or tentatively.

1942 BERREY & VAN DEN BARK *Amer. Thes. Slang* § 628/5 Be penciled in, to be tentatively, but not finally hired. **1959** *Times* 22 June 4/2 He is a name to pencil in for the future. **1967** *Punch* 31 May 783/1 We may have pencilled in an arrangement to throw open our houses to one another, I'm not sure. **1971** WODEHOUSE *Much Obliged, Jeeves* xii.128 You and I, regarding Florence coolly, pencil her in as too bossy for human consumption. **1977** *Daily Mirror* 10 May 31/1 The MCC team to play Australia at Lord's from May 25–27, due to be announced later this week and traditionally a Test trial, might still be very different to the one originally pencilled in.

pencil and paper, pencil-and-paper, *phr.* Usu. *attrib.* or as *adj.* Requiring (only) pencil and paper.

1930 J. B. PRIESTLEY *Angel Pavement* viii. 385 You had to pretend you were having a marvellous time because you were wearing hats from crackers and playing pencil and paper games ('Let me see, a river beginning with "V"?'). **1952** J. B. PICK *Phoenix Dict. Games* 295 (*heading*) Pencil and paper games. **1957** L. FOX *Numerical Solution Two-Point Boundary Probl.* p. v, I have included most of the worthwhile methods known to me which are suitable for pencil-and-paper and desk-machine computation. **1973** *Nature* 27 Apr. 594/2 Table 4.1 only lists some values of a simple function..which is perfectly amenable to pencil-and-paper arithmetic.

pencil-case. Add: **b.** *Bookbinding.* (See quot.)

1885 W. J. E. CRANE *Bookbinding* xvi. 132 This [pressing in at the joint] is very necessary, or the [end] paper may not properly 'go home' and adhere here, and..an unsightly protuberance of loose paper at the joint will be the result, which is generally termed a 'pencil case', and is a clear mark of bad bookbinding.

pencilling, *vbl. sb.* Add: **1.** (Further *transf.* examples.) Also, natural marking on animals.

1909 W. BATESON *Mendel's Princ. Heredity* ii. 42 Pencilling [in fowls] is a dominant to its absence. **1936** C. L. MORGAN *Sparkenbroke* VI. vii. 551 He saw a pencilling of light shine under her door. **1948** C. L. B. HUBBARD *Dogs in Brit.* xx. 309 Colour [of the Manchester terrier] is jet black, with rich mahogany tan markings..('pencillings' on the toes to be black). **1971** F. HAMILTON *World Encycl. Dogs* 659/1 Pencilling: Dark lines divided by strips of tan on feet of Manchester Terrier.

2. (Earlier and further examples.)

1803 *Lett. Miss Riversdale* I. 325 The friction of his pocket had so completely defaced the pencilling. **1835** N. P. WILLIS (*title*) Pencillings by the way. **1845** GEO. ELIOT *Lett.* (1954) I. 187 Thank you for the pencillings... I see that many are obvious and important emendations. **1923** J. M. MURRY (*title*) Pencillings: little essays on literature.

pendeloque. Add to def.: *spec.* a gemstone esp. a diamond cut in the shape of a drop and used as a pendant. Also *attrib.* (Further examples.)

1945, 1949 [see *NAVETTE]. **1955** M. GILBERT *Sky High* ii. 25 A pair of pendeloque-cut diamond earrings set in platinum filigree. **1959** *Times* 24 Feb. 18/7 A large fancy golden pendeloque diamond. **1960** H. HAYWARD *Antique Coll.* 214/2 *Pendeloque*, a gemstone of drop-shape, faceted and used as a pendant. **1973** *Times* 25 Aug. 17/2 There are nine well-recognized styles of lapidary work upon the diamond: brilliant-cut, step-cut, emerald-cut, rose-cut, marquise, briolette, baguette, cabochon and pendeloque. **1974** *Encycl. Brit. Macropædia* VII. 979/2 Noteworthy among the gemstones are an 86-carat pendeloque diamond, as well as large emeralds and red spinels.

pendency. 1. (Later examples.)

1850 E. S. SEYMOUR *Sk. Minnesota* xii. 208 Out of this arose one or two unsuccessful arbitrations. During their pendency the mills came into the possession of the Boston Company. **1972** *N.Y. Law Jrnl.* 22 Aug. 6/1 Section 1830.12 Petitions; content; pendency of prior proceeding. **1979** 'A. HAILEY' *Overload* II. iii. 119 During the pendency of the case, surely there were backstage discussions with commission staff?

pendente lite. (Earlier and later examples.)

1726 J. AYLIFFE *Parergon Juris Canonici Anglicani* 235 Because he came in *Pendente lite.* **1964** R. W. HANSEN in A. E. Wilkerson *Rights of Children* (1973) 240 This conflict may be revealed at the pre-trial hearing before the Family Court commissioner on *pendente lite* support orders, or at the time of trial before the court. **1972** *N.Y. Law Jrnl.* 10 Oct. 1/7 Judge Motley also refused to enjoin the defendant..pendente lite from distributing its similarly designed loudspeakers. **1973**

Ibid. 31 Aug. 18/3 The cross motion for an order for renewal of plaintiff's motion for alimony pendente lite is denied, no sufficiently persuasive ground in support of same having been demonstrated.

pending, *ppl. a.* and *prep.* Add: **A.** *ppl. a.* **1.** (Later examples); so *pending basket, tray*: a basket or tray for correspondence or other papers awaiting attention or decision.

1946 R. GRAVES *Poems 1938–45* 30 World patents pending; tested in the shops. **1955** E. WAUGH *Officers & Gentlemen* I. viii. 102 Guy turned over the papers in the 'pending' tray. **1957** M. SUMMERTON *Sunset Hour* i. 18, I threw the folder into my pending basket. **1961** 'T. HINDE' *For Good of Company* i. 18 Out-tray to his right, in- and pending-trays to his left. **1973** J. WAINWRIGHT *Pride of Pigs* 50 The day clerks..booked it in—this avalanche of paper—and..tossed it into a series of 'pending' trays. The night clerks *dealt* with it. **1975** *Times* 5 Dec. 2/1 An extradition warrant..was in a tray marked 'pending'.

Pendleton (pe·nd'ltǫn). Orig. and chiefly *U.S.* The name of the *Pendleton* Woolen Mills (named after Pendleton, a town in Oregon) used to denote garments made by them, esp. a brightly coloured checked sports shirt. Also *attrib.*

1940 *Esquire* Dec. 204/1 (Advt.), Wear a Pendleton—then you'll know why Pendleton shirts have been a religion with sportsmen. **1947** E. S. GARDNER in *Amer. Mag.* Aug. 152/2 Our party is a man thirty-eight years old, bronzed, wears cowboy boots, a five-gallon hat, leather jacket, Pendleton trousers, rather chunky, and has a wide firm mouth. **1948** *Official Gaz.* (U.S. Patent Office) 28 Dec. 966/2 Pendleton [Trade Mark]. For outer shirts, lounge robes, trousers and slacks, Jackets and blazers, and men's coats. No. 535,993. **1960** *Sports Illustr.* 5 Sept. 22 (Advt.), On campus, a man worth watching will have at least one Pendleton. **1961** 'A. A. FAIR' *Shills can't cash Chips* iii. 71 The guy looked like a tall Texan. He was wearing Pendletons and cowboy boots. **1963** *Pix* 28 Sept. 62/3 *Pendletons*, bright plaid wool shirts one size too big. One point. **1977** *Guardian Weekly* 9 Oct. 16/2 She had a long, red Pendleton, a wool lumberjack shirt still smoke-musty from camping trips in the North Woods.

‖ **pendopo** (pendǭu·po). Also **mendopo, pendapa.** [ad. Javanese *peṇḍåpå.*] In Java: a large, covered porch or veranda in front of a house.

1927 H. S. BANNER *Romantic Java* iv. 56 Its [*sc.* the residence's] most arresting feature is the *Mendopo*, a huge, open-sided verandah in the front. **1958** H. FORSTER *Flowering Lotus* iii. 41 We entered the *pendopo*, skirted the piled desks and reached the 'common room'. **1961** H. GEERTZ *Javanese Family* i. 7 The greater portion of this building is the *pendapa*, a kind of oversized summer-house about a hundred feet square and always cool, dark, and dignified looking. **1971** *Nat. Geographic* Jan. 27/1 Within its gates are large, low, and lovely buildings, perfectly adapted to the hot and humid climate. The best of these are the *pendopos*, huge open-sided structures covered by four-sided roofs, supported above gleaming marble floors by columns of carved teak.

Pendred (pe·ndred). *Path.* [The name of Vaughan *Pendred* (1869–1946), English physician who described the condition in 1896 (*Lancet* 22 Aug. 532).] *Pendred('s) syndrome*: a recessively inherited condition in which an enzyme deficiency leads to goitre and usu. to deafness.

1960 G. R. FRASER *Deafness with Goitre* (*Syndrome of Pendred*) (Ph.D. thesis, Univ. of London) 3 The name Pendred is suggested as a suitable eponym for this syndrome... A..study of sixty-two cases of Pendred's syndrome in forty-one sibships is described. **1966** J. B. STANBURY et al. *Metabolic Basis of Inherited Dis.* (ed. 2) x. 234/2 The patients with the Pendred syndrome do not have large goiters. **1970** J. F. SOTOS in R. M. Goodman *Genetic Disorders Man* xvi. 666/1 In a few reports thyroid disease without deafness has occurred in relatives of patients with the Pendred syndrome. **1964** J. D. MAYNARD in R. M. Kirk et al. *Surgery* xii. 250 Affected children are goitrous, hypothyroid, and sometimes deaf (Pendred's syndrome after the general practitioner who reported the first family in County Durham).

† **pendulation** (pendiŭlēi·ʃən). *Obs.* [f. L. *pendul-us* PENDULOUS *a.* + -ATION.] An oscillatory motion formerly ascribed to the poles of the earth.

1909 *Westm. Gaz.* 1 May 12/3 According to Professor Simroth, pendulation, which is the periodical oscillation of the earth's axes,..explains nearly every observed fact in the development and distribution of all animals. **1924** J. G. A. SKERL tr. *Wegener's Orig. Continents & Oceans* vi. 95 Unfortunately, Reibisch clothed his ideas..in the singular straight-jacket of a strict 'pendulation' of the poles in an 'orbit of swings', which is probably false.

pendule, *sb.* Add: **2. b.** *Mountaineering.* = *PENDULUM *sb.* 1 d.

1957 E. A. WRANGHAM *Sel. Climbs Range Mont Blanc* 170 Rappel down from the summit on the Verte side, go over a gendarme by a small *pendule* on the Charpoua side. **1967** COLLOMB & CREW *Sel. Climbs Mont Blanc Range* I. 180 Traverse L across a very steep ice couloir to a thin and high rock island and continue the traverse by a pendule from a peg high on this island. **1973** C. BONINGTON *Next Horizon* xvi. 232 We had a spectacular pendule by Tom Patey, as he swung out from the base of the overhanging rock. **1973** J. BUNTING *Climbing* 90 *Pendule*, a horizontal *abseil* effected by a sideways swing.

pendule (pe·ndiŭl), *v. Mountaineering.* [f. the sb.] *intr.* To swing to and fro like a pendulum. Also *refl.*

1883 G. MACDONALD *Princess & Curdie* xvi. 128 He dropped himself a little below its level, gave the rope a swing by pushing his feet against the side of the cleft, and so penduled himself into it. **1973** C. BONINGTON *Next Horizon* x. 148 He was now sixty feet up. He paused,.. let out some rope and penduled back and forth across the face, trying to work out the best line.

pendulize (pe·ndiŭləiz), *v.* [f. as PENDULOUS *a.* + -IZE.] *intr.* To poise oneself or hover in the air; to be pendant.

1869 E. NEWMAN *Illustr. Nat. Hist. Brit. Moths* 12 He who has not seen this fairy creature pendulizing over a purple patch of the common bugle..has a delight yet to come.

pendulum, *sb.* Add: **1. c.** Used of similar bodies that oscillate but are not similarly suspended: **horizontal pendulum,** an approximately horizontal rod having a heavy weight at one end and pivoted at the other so that it can swing freely in an approximately horizontal plane, supported by a thread or wire passing from the weighted end to a fixed point almost vertically above the pivot; **inverted pendulum,** a vertical rod having a heavy weight at its upper end and resting on a bearing at the other, and held in position by springs which allow it to oscillate in a vertical plane.

1844 *Trans. R. Soc. Edin.* XV. 219 The elegant inverted Pendulum or Noddy contrived by the late Mr Hardy. **1872** F. ZÖLLNER in *Phil. Mag.* XLIII. 491, I explained the principles of such a method and its practicability in an apparatus for which I proposed the name of 'Horizontal Pendulum', in order to distinguish it from other pendulum-like instruments, also suspended by two threads. **1908** C. G. KNOTT *Physics Earthquake Phenomena* iv. 61 The nearer the point of attachment to a truly vertical position above the pivot the more delicate and the less stable will the horizontal pendulum be, and the better fitted for recording small motions. **1937** D. KENNEDY tr. *Imamura's Theoret. & Appl. Seismol.* xi. 254 The form most extensively used is one that weighs a ton. It is shown in Fig. 119. The heavy bob is an inverted pendulum. Its lower point, the end of the supporting rod, rests in a socket, but as it is unstable in this condition, an arm..extends laterally from the upper end of the pendulum, and connects with a steel spring. **1972** R. B. GORDON *Physics of Earth* vi. 124 An instrument suitable for recording horizontal ground motion is the horizontal pendulum.

d. *Mountaineering.* A swinging movement like that of a pendulum, often used as a deliberate move by a climber using his momentum to swing to a new position. Also *attrib.*

1945 G. W. YOUNG *Mountain Craft* (ed. 4) v. 179 The second [artificial aid] is the *pendulum*. Like most modern technical devices, it is a perfecting of an old alpine fashion... By attaching a rope to the highest point convenient upon our first line, we..can swing across upon it, and reach the new set of holds. **1949** A. ROCH *Climbs of my Youth* xiv. 115 The pendulum was definitely unpleasant, and a few stones fell loose. **1965** A. BLACKSHAW *Mountaineering* ix. 268 If there is no suitable transverse crack it will be necessary to do a pendulum or a horizontal rappel. The former involves abseiling..from a piton and swinging over to the desired new position. **1971** C. BONINGTON *Annapurna South Face* x. 120 He therefore had to climb without any protection from pitons, though if he had fallen off he would have had a punishing pendulum back into the gully. **1972** D. HASTON *In High Places* x. 110 There are some devious pendulums to reach the start of the main crack system. A pendulum is an exciting move, very common to Yosemite climbing. When one line of cracks runs out and there is blank wall before another can be reached, often this gap can be filled in by fixing a piton as high as possible, going down for some way hanging on the rope, then running back and forth to get up enough momentum to make a swing into the next crack system.

4. b. pendulum position *Billiards*, a position of the two object balls beside the cushions on either side of a corner pocket which makes a large number of cannons possible; **pendulum saw** (see quot. 1958); **pendulum swing,** a swing or swinging movement like that of a pendulum; also *fig.*

1927 *Daily Express* 26 Apr. 9/4 Reece..made a record break of 1,151, including 568 cannons by what is known as the 'pendulum position'. **1957** Pendulum saw [see *goose saw* s.v. *GOOSE *sb.* 8]. **1958** *N.Z. Timber Jrnl.* Jan. 46/1 *Pendulum saw*, a machine cross-cut saw that is drawn across the stationary wood in the process of cutting by swinging from the point of suspension like a pendulum. **1926** *Amer. Speech* I. 632/2 *Pendulum swing*, applied to a type of putting stroke. **1947** C. DAY LEWIS *Colloq. Element Eng. Poetry* 9 The verse of the Romance poets, of the early Elizabethan lyricists,..and of the Pre-Raphaelite poets represents a series of pendulum-swings towards the formal, esoteric ideal of poetic diction. **1968** J. WINEARLS *Mod. Dance* (ed. 2) ii. 57 The principle of the outside fall and pick up of a Pendulum Swing can be used in isolated leg and trunk movements.

pe·ndulum, *v.* [f. the sb.] *intr.* To hang or swing like a pendulum. Also *fig.*

1885 W. F. CRAFTS *Sabbath for Man* vi. 458 The Sabbath of our fathers..was far better than the extreme of laxity to which we have pendulumed. **1949** A. ROCH *Climbs of my Youth* xiv. 115 We had to drive a piton into a slab and then pendulum across over the ice of the couloir. **1969** J. ELLIOT *Duel* I. iv. 79 A stop-watch on a long black string pendulummed from her neck. **1971** C. BONINGTON *Annapurna South Face* xii. 145 My progress had dropped to a single push of my jumar clamps at a time; my feet slipped on the snow steps, and I pendulumed clumsily across the arête into the gully. **1973** —— *Next Horizon* x. 146 But what if..you miss the other side and go penduluming back against the sheer ice wall, to be left hanging in the void? **1974** H. MACINNES *Climb to Lost World* xii. 212 'I'll belay you from here,' said Don. 'Then, if the stone comes away, at least you'll pendulum over to this side and shouldn't hurt yourself too much.'

pene-. Delete **penecontemporaneous** and **peneplain,** qq.v. as main entries below. Add: **penesei·smic** *a.* [ad. F. *pénéséismique* (De Montessus de Ballore *La Geogr. Séismologique* (ed. 2, 1906) 11)] (see quot.).

1921 C. DAVISON *Man. Seismol.* x. 161 Peneseismic countries, in which earthquakes are severe, but fall short of destructive power.

pe:necontempora·neous, *a. Geol.* [f. PENE- + CONTEMPORANEOUS *a.*] (See quot. 1972.)

1901 [in Dict. s.v. PENE-]. **1939** W. H. TWENHOFEL *Princ. Sedimentation* x. 375 The present trend of opinion considers that much chert and flint were deposited contemporaneously with the enclosing rocks. The views of origin may be placed in three classes of contemporaneous (syngenetic), penecontemporaneous, and subsequent (epigenetic). **1963** *Jrnl. Sedimentary Petrology* XXXIII. 64 Geologic data allow an assignment of possible penecontemporaneous (early diagenetic) origin to the dolomites of this group. **1969** *Nature* 22 Nov. 821/2 There is evidence of post-depositional weathering penecontemporaneous with deposition. **1972** *Gloss. Geol.* (Amer. Geol. Inst.) 525/2 *Penecontemporaneous*, said of a geologic process, or resultant structure or mineral, occurring immediately after deposition but before consolidation of the enclosing rock.

Hence **pe:necontemporane·ity,** the fact of being penecontemporaneous; **pe:necontempora·neously** *adv.*

1933 P. G. H. BOSWELL *On Mineral. Sedimentary Rocks* i. 1 The mode of formation of matrices and minerals that have developed penecontemporaneously or subsequently in the rocks. **1958** *Q. Jrnl. Geol. Soc.* CXIV. 45 The speaker had been unable to detect any sign of overprinting between these two fold systems..; this was interpreted as proof of penecontemporaneity of the folding. **1964** *Sedimentology* III. 136 The observations of uniform directions in certain penecontemporaneously slumped beds. **1979** *Nature* 7 June 485/1 The Entrance and the Exit Quarries, where sedimentation occurred penecontemporaneously in two separate depositories.

Penelope. Add: **3.** *attrib.* **Penelope canvas,** a double-thread canvas used for needle tapestry work. Also *absol.*

1882 CAULFEILD & SAWARD *Dict. Needlework* 387/2 *Penelope canvas*, a description of cotton canvas made for Berlin woolwork, in which the strands run in couples, vertically and horizontally, thus forming squares containing four threads each. **1895** *Montgomery Ward Catal.* 124/3 Java Canvas... Penelope Canvas. **1926–7** *Army & Navy Stores Catal.* 663/3 Canvas for wool work and embroidery... White 'Penelope'. **1975** *Islander* (Victoria, B.C.) 9 Mar. 7/2 The other type of needlepoint canvas is known as Penelope which is made up of two pairs of vertical and horizontal threads.

penelopize, *v.* Delete (*nonce-wd.*) and add earlier and later examples.

1841 *Congress. Globe* 27th Congress 1 Sess. App. 43/2 Diplomacy was still drawing out its lengthened thread—still weaving its long and dilatory web—still Penelopizing. **1956** 'H. MACDIARMID' *Stony Limits* 39 Nor twissel-tongued can we penelopise.

peneplain [pĭ·niplēⁱn), *sb. Geomorphol.* Also **-plane.** [f. PENE- + PLAIN *sb.*¹] A low, nearly featureless tract of land of undulating relief, esp. one held to be the product of long-continued subaerial erosion of land undisturbed by crustal movement and to represent the penultimate stage in the cycle of erosion in a humid climate; also, a former surface of this kind as it exists today (e.g. after uplift and dissection, or buried as an unconformity).

1889 W. M. DAVIS in *Amer. Jrnl. Sci.* XXXVII. 430 Given time enough, and the faulted ridges of Connecticut must be reduced to a low base-level plain. I believe that time enough has already been allowed, and that the strong Jurassic topography was really worn out somewhere in Cretaceous time, when all this part of the country was reduced to a nearly featureless plain, a 'peneplain', as I would call it, at a low level. **1893** *Bull. Dept. Geol. Univ. Calif.* I. iv. 158 The tilting of the Sierra Nevada peneplane was also a post-Pliocene event. **1933** *Geogr. Jrnl.* LXXXI. 331 These 'residual mountains' rise from a peneplain, that is, a plain of erosion produced during a stable period interrupting an upward movement. **1934** C. R. LONGWELL et al. *Outl. Physical Geol.* xv. 309 The highest ridges of the present Appalachians are remnants of a former peneplane. **1946** L. D. STAMP *Britain's Struct.* xiii. 150 The magnificent modern sea-cliffs are where the peneplanes of the past meet the seas of to-day. **1954** W. D. THORNBURY *Princ. Geomorphol.* viii. 178 Although the peneplain still remains an important concept with most geomorphologists, it is now recognised that many topographic surfaces have been erroneously called peneplains. **1960** B. W. SPARKS *Geomorphol.* xv. 335 Good examples of peneplains are extremely rare and some would say that they do not exist. **1968** J. ARNOLD *Shell Bk. Country Crafts* xxi. 255 The greater part of the many miles of walls [in Pembrokeshire] is composed of small boulders from the peneplain, which is mainly Cambrian. **1970** R. J. SMALL *Study of Landforms* v. 164 Most peneplains in the British Isles take the form of 'hill-top surfaces', and are so fragmented that they are by no means easy to identify. **1977** A. HALLAM *Planet Earth* 301 He assumed a standard life-cycle for a river valley, marked by youth (steep-sided valleys), maturity (flood-plain floors), and old age as the river valley was worn lower and lower into a 'peneplain'. *fig.* **1964** *Listener* 27 Feb. 353/2 In the eyes of a stray bitch Ribbed with hunger, heavy with young, I saw the peneplain of all imagined Misery.

peneplain (pī·niplēⁱn), *v.* *Geomorphol.* Also **-plane.** [f. prec. (after PLANE *v.*[1]), or a back-formation from next.] *trans.* To erode to a peneplain.

1923 [see *KRATOGEN]. **1931** N. M. FENNEMAN *Physiogr. Western U.S.* iv. 172 The original folds of all these mountains were approximately peneplaned. **1969** BENNISON & WRIGHT *Geol. Hist. Brit. Isles* viii. 181 The Old Red Sandstone of south-western Ireland rests on an irregular erosion surface which had not been peneplaned so that the beds are of variable thickness. **1970** R. J. SMALL *Study of Landforms* v. 164 The English Chalk country..may well have been effectively peneplained during the Pliocene period.

peneplained (pī·niplēⁱnd), *a.* *Geomorphol.* Also **-planed.** [f. *PENEPLAIN *sb.* + -ED[2].] Made into a peneplain.

1904 CHAMBERLIN & SALISBURY *Geol.* (1905) I. iii. 85 (*caption*) A peneplaned surface where the elevations are small but steep-sided. **1922** *Bull. U.S. Geol. Survey* No. 730. 2 The older peneplaned surface was elevated, tilted, and dissected. **1963** D. W. & E. E. HUMPHRIES tr. *Termier's Erosion & Sedimentation* ii. 34 (*caption*) Both figures show the Natal monocline, where most of the peneplaned surfaces are dated by marine beds which they cut across near the coast. **1965** G. J. WILLIAMS *Econ. Geol. N.Z.* i. 2/2 The peneplained basement was deeply weathered under podozolising influences. **1978** *Nature* 13 July 131/2 Middle Jurassic sandstones were here laid down directly on the peneplaned Caledonian basement.

peneplanation (pī:niplǎnēⁱ·ʃən). *Geomorphol.* [f. PENE- + *PLANATION.] Erosion to a peneplain.

1899 W. M. DAVIS in *Amer. Geologist* XXIII. 210 The unevenness of the uplands of to-day is a natural result of imperfect peneplanation followed by submature dissection. **1912** *Proc. Amer. Philos. Soc.* LI. 513 Peneplanation of the bituminous region had become far advanced. **1936** *Geogr. Jrnl.* LXXXVII. 22 A complicated history of peneplanation, uparching, faulting, and erosion. **1970** R. J. SMALL *Study of Landforms* v. 163 In an area such as the British Isles, perfectly preserved surfaces of peneplanation do not exist at or near present sea-level.

penetralium (penǐtrēⁱ·liəm). [erron. back-formation from PENETRALIA *sb. pl.*] The interior of a building. Also *fig.*

1817 KEATS *Lett.* (1958) I. 194 Coleridge..would let go by a fine isolated verisimilitude caught from the Penetralium of mystery, from being incapable of remaining content with half knowledge. **1847** E. BRONTË *Wuthering Heights* I. i. 5, I had no desire to aggravate his impatience, previous to inspecting the penetralium.

penetrameter (penǐtræ·mǐtəɹ). *Radiography.* Formerly also **penetrometer.** [f. PENETRA(TION + -METER.] An instrument for determining the wavelength, intensity, or total received dose of X-rays by measuring photographically their transmission through layers of metal of known thickness.

1907 M. K. KASSABIAN *Röntgen Rays & Electro-Therapeutics* iii. iv. 431 (*heading*) Skiameters and penetrometers. **1912** J. M. MARTIN *Pract. Electro-Therapeutics* xiv. 242 Holzknecht's chromoradiometer, Walter's or Benoist's skiameter or penetrameter will be of service in determining the amount of radiance given off from the tube. **1923** GLAZEBROOK *Dict. Appl. Physics* IV. 607/2 Among medical men Benoist's radiochromometer or penetrometer enjoys extensive use as a measurer of hardness. **1950** *Engineering* 7 Apr. 373/2 A penetrameter in steps of 0·010 in., with holes in each step, to calibrate the X-ray film. **1966** *McGraw-Hill Encycl. Sci. & Technol.* XI. 304*b*/2 When the smallest hole in this penetrameter can be seen in the radiograph, the penetrameter sensitivity is 2%. **1975** *Physics Bull.* Feb. 80/2 (Advt.), This issue also reports on ..theoretical aspects of measuring kilovoltage by penetrameter.

penetrance. Restrict † *Obs. rare*[—1] to sense in Dict. and add: **2.** *Genetics.* [ad. G. *penetranz* (O. Vogt 1926, in *Zeitschr. f. ges. Neurol. und Psychiatrie* CI. 809).] The extent to which a particular gene or set of genes is represented in the phenotypes of individuals possessing it, measured by the proportion of carriers having the phenotype characteristic of the gene.

1934 [see *EXPRESSIVITY b]. **1946** R. R. GATES *Human Genetics* I. ii. 15 Lack of penetrance..has become a very important principle in human genetics... The gene is present in the germplasm, as shown by its transmission to the next generation, but for some reason it has completely failed to express itself in the soma. **1965** *Punch* 10 Nov. 689/2 The second complication is known as penetrance. When a gene affects every individual who carries it equally it is said to have 100 per cent penetrance. **1973** *Nature* 2 Mar. 64/2 An hereditary disease controlled by an autosomal Mendelian recessive gene with full penetrance. **1973** B. J. WILLIAMS *Evolution & Human Origins* ii. 30/1 Environmental differences may cause one carrier of a gene to pass this threshold and show the trait whereas another carrier of the same gene does not. This is referred to as incomplete penetrance.

penetrant, *a.* (*sb.*) Add: **A.** *adj.* **3.** *Genetics.* Producing in the phenotype the characteristic effect of the gene or combination of genes.

1955 R. B. GOLDSCHMIDT *Theoret. Genetics* III. v. 379 An incompletely penetrant effect is often based upon a system of multiple factors. **1973** B. J. WILLIAMS *Evolution & Human Origins* ii. 30/1 Genes are spoken of as fully penetrant or incompletely penetrant, but this is, in fact, as much a property of the environment as of the gene. **1978** *Nature* 27 Apr. 755/1 Gajdusek originally suggested that transmission was due to an autosomal dominant gene, fully penetrant in heterozygous females, but rarely penetrant in males unless they were homozygous.

B. *sb.* **2.** A penetrating coloured or fluorescent liquid used in a technique for detecting surface defects, in which the liquid is applied to the surface, excess removed, and developer applied to bring out the liquid left in the cracks and pores. Freq. *attrib.*, as *penetrant inspection, testing.*

1951 *Materials & Methods* Feb. 92/2 Fluorescent penetrant inspection makes use of a water-washable penetrant of high fluorescence and unusual wetting or penetrating properties. **1958** H. ETHERINGTON *Nucl. Engin. Handbk.* x. 152 Penetrant-inspection methods are applicable to all metals as well as glazed ceramics, plastics, and other nonporous materials. *Ibid.*, The penetrant is drawn into surface discontinuities by capillary action. **1959** J. F. HINSLEY *Non-Destructive Testing* xiv. 323 (*caption*) Crack in casting flange revealed by fluorescent penetrant. **1973** A. PARRISH *Mech. Engineer's Ref. Bk.* VIII. 13 Penetrant testing is the modern version of the old oil and whiting technique and is applicable to all metals and many non-metallic materials. **1975** BRAM & DOWNS *Manuf. Technol.* ii. 67 Inspection with penetrant is probably the oldest of the major non-destructive testing methods in use today. *Ibid.*, The surface of the component is examined in order to locate the penetrant indications which have been formed in the developer coating. **1977** *Hot Car* Oct. 58/2 One wheel per batch is pressure tested and a percentage of the batch is checked by a penetrant dye for porosity.

penetrate, *v.* Add: **1. c.** To insert the penis into the vagina of (a woman). Also *absol.*

1953 H. M. PARSHLEY tr. *S. de Beauvoir's Second Sex* IV. iii. 377 Woman, once penetrated, has no such sense of danger; but in return she feels trespassed upon in her flesh. **1960** J. RODNEY *Handbk. Sex Knowledge* iv. 55 Deep penetration must not be aimed at for a number of sessions, and when the woman is ready for it she will move her body in such a way that the penis will penetrate deeply. **1963** M. MCCARTHY *Group* i. 24 Kay had had an awful time with Harald; five times, she insisted, before she was penetrated. *Ibid.* vi. 123 My mother..told me that a gentleman never penetrated his bride on the first night. **1975** *Times Lit. Suppl.* 21 Mar. 293/1 A character.. endeavours in the course of one week to penetrate the female offspring of the entire Cabinet.

d. To infiltrate (an organization, esp. an enemy espionage network) as a spy.

1962 L. DEIGHTON *Ipcress File* 221 He organized a train-wrecking group until it was penetrated and the survivors fled. **1967** L. JAMES *Chameleon File* (1968) xvi. 201 We have penetrated the Cuban g-2, Mr. Wilson. We shall know if you do not do as we have asked. **1972** H. MACINNES *Message from Malaga* xix. 261 Are you forgetting my job? It is to penetrate the Lucas set up. **1977** C. MCCARRY *Secret Lovers* xix. 270 Did you arrange for him to double her, give him the illusion that he was penetrating your network?

4. b. Also, to be understood or fully realized.

1955 E. COXHEAD *Figure in Mist* iv. 134 'You're the most frightful woman I've ever met.' 'All right, it's penetrated.' **1973** G. MOFFAT *Deviant Death* vii. 109 We didn't notice that the gates were open..it wasn't till we came back hours later that it really penetrated.

penetrating, *ppl. a.* Add: **1. b.** Passing readily through matter.

1902 *Nature* 31 July 318/1 Villard..first drew attention to the existence of some very penetrating rays from radium non-deviable by a magnetic field. **1928** [see *COSMIC *a.* 3c]. **1938** R. W. LAWSON tr. *Hevesy & Paneth's Man. Radioactivity* (ed. 2) xxv. 280 A penetrating particle had traversed both counters and the Wilson chamber. **1947** *Radiology* XLIX. 358/2 The malignant response elicited by penetrating radiations, irrespective of type, consisted of hemopoietic tissue tumors. **1968** M. S. LIVINGSTON *Particle Physics* iv. 74 Muons are the 'penetrating' component of the ionizing particles in cosmic radiation observed beneath great layers of earth in salt mines.

penetration. Add: **1. c.** The insertion of the penis into the vagina in copulation.

1613 J. CHAMBERLAIN *Let.* 9 Sept. (1939) I. 475 What would you say yf you shold heare a churchman in open audience demaund of him..whether he had affection, erection, application, penetration, ejaculation. **1729** G. JACOB *New Law-Dict.* s.v. *Rape of women*, There must be Penetration and Emission, to make this Crime. **1848** WHARTON *Law Lexicon* 569/2 In Scotland..the following facts are necessary to be proved on a charge of rape: 1, penetration..; 2, actual force in the consummation. **1957** L. DURRELL *Justine* III. 185 The whole portentous scrimmage of sex itself, the act of penetration. **1960** [see *PENETRATE *v.* 1c] **1963** A. HERON *Towards Quaker View of Sex* 65 'Frigidity'..implies more than failure to have orgasm: it is the inability to enjoy love-making and penetration.

d. The infiltration of a country, organization, etc., by political, financial, etc., means in order to gain influence, power, or information. Also used as a marketing term.

1931 F. L. ALLEN *Only Yesterday* vii. 176 In general the country extended its empire not by military conquest or political dictation, but by financial penetration. **1951** E. E. CUMMINGS *Let.* 3 Aug. (1969) 214 You should glimpse a huge map..to show the Soviet penetration of Greece—all but a little strip in the middle. **1964** L. DEIGHTON *Funeral in Berlin* 257 The detection and penetration of intelligence. **1971** I. DEUTSCHER *Marxism in our Time* 155 The fall in the ideological level of most of the militants..had facilitated to a certain extent the penetration of police agents into the Party. **1976** *National Observer* (U.S.) 21 Feb. 1/2 The relative decline in circulation of daily newspapers and their absolute decline in 'household penetration', has been accompanied by a growth of other printed media that duplicate one of the local daily's functions, but often better.

4. penetration agent, a spy sent to penetrate an enemy organization; **penetration aid,** an object released from a missile as a decoy to draw off any attacking missiles; **penetration twin** *Cryst.*, a twin crystal that presents the appearance of two interpenetrating crystals; so *penetration twinning.*

1966 'A. HALL' *9th Directive* ii. 22 This is a police job. I'm a penetration agent..they've made a mistake. **1976** P. HENISSART *Winter Quarry* III. xxvi. 270 As soon as I learned of McGuire's existence, I mistrusted him—a shiftless contract-agent for the CIA... I know your taste for penetration agents. **1966** *N.Y. Times Mag.* 20 Mar. 59 The decoys—'penetration aids' in the missilemen's jargon—would range from dummy warheads to metalized-plastic warhead shapes. **1967** *Electronics* 6 Mar. 50/2 It is researching the key problem: how to distinguish the lethal reentry vehicle from the penetration aids. **1868** J. D. DANA *Syst. Min.* (ed. 5) 191 Penetration-twins, the forms not corresponding to a regular revolution, but to an irregular interpenetration of unlike parts of the crystal. **1971** C. S. HURLBUT *Dana's Man. Min.* (ed. 18) ii. 97 Twin crystals are usually designated as either contact twins or penetration twins... Penetration twins are made up of interpenetrating individuals having an irregular composition surface, and the twin law is usually defined by a twin axis. **1953** F. H. POUGH *Field Guide Rocks & Minerals* I. iv. 53 We also find attractive penetration twinning in phenakite.

penetrometer (penǐtrǫ·mǐtəɹ). [f. PENETR(ATION + -OMETER.] **1.** An instrument for determining the consistency or hardness of a substance (as asphalt, soil or snow) by measuring the depth or rate of penetration of a rod or needle driven by a known force.

1905 C. RICHARDSON *Mod. Asphalt Pavement* IX. xxvi. 533 (*heading*) New York testing laboratory penetrometer. **1913** BLANCHARD & DROWNE *Text-bk. Highway Engin.* x. 293 Penetrometer to be used in accordance with standard method on materials solid at above temperatures. **1930** *Engineering* 18 July 61/3 The penetrometer is simply a ½-in. square bar fitted loosely in guides and loaded with weights giving steps of about ½ ton per square foot. **1966** C. FRASER *Avalanche Enigma* iv. 71 The first measurement taken is a penetrometer profile. **1971** B. BUCK tr. *Ludewig's Polyester Fibres* iv. 124 In order to determine the melting point, a grain of the polyester is placed into the container of the penetrometer and the needle is centred on the surface of [*printed* on] the substance under test. **1975** D. BAGLEY *Snow Tiger* iv. 49 This is a penetrometer... It measures the resistance of the snow.

2. Obs. var. *PENETRAMETER.

penfieldite (pe·nfīldəit). *Min.* [f. the name of Samuel L. *Penfield* (1856–1906), U.S. mineralogist + -ITE[1].] A basic lead chloride, Pb_2Cl_3OH, occurring as very small, usu. prismatic crystals that are colourless and transparent when pure.

1892 F. A. GENTH in *Amer. Jrnl. Sci.* CXLIV. 260 While examining a lot of minerals, formed by the action of sea water on ancient slags which Mr. Geo. L. English collected at Laurion, Greece, I noticed a *very few* hexagonal crystals which proved to be a new species, for which I propose the name: Penfieldite, in honor to Prof. Sam'l L. Penfield the indefatigable worker in mineralogy and crystallography. **1954** *Mineral Abstr.* XII. 453 The stocks..of two Roman anchors recovered from the Mediterranean are covered with a crust of small crystals of anglesite, phosgenite, penfieldite, with less cerussite, hydrocerussite, and specks of metallic copper and copper stains. **1969** *Ibid.* XX. 144/2 Penfieldite,..from Laurium, Greece, and from Sierra Gorda, Chile, has *a* 11·28, *c* 48·65 Å.

pen-friend (pe·nfrend). [f. PEN *sb.*[2] + FRIEND *sb.*] A friend or contact with whom a regular correspondence is conducted. (See also *PEN-PAL.) Hence **pen-friendship,** the relationship existing between pen-friends.

1933 *Boy's Mag.* XLVII. 106/1 Any reader at home or abroad who would like to correspond with a 'pen-friend' in another land is invited to send his name, address, and age to the Editor. **1943** F. Thompson *Candleford Green* iv. 65 The correspondence languished, then ceased, in the usual manner of such pen-friendships. **1945** 'O. Malet' *My Bird Sings* I. ii. 18 She had returned to England..but none the less they had kept up one of those rambling pen-friendships. **1957** R. Mason *World of Suzie Wong* I. ii. 15 It had caused my predecessor, a Pole, to propose through the post to a pen-friend in Glasgow whom he had never met. **1960** *Woman's Own* 19 Mar. 77/4, I cannot help you to find pen-friends, but..I will send you the name of a pen-friendship organisation. **1974** *Times* 2 Jan. 24/4 (Advt.), Elderly person desiring a pen friend please reply to Box 2901 B, The Times. **1975** *Bangladesh Times* 27 July 7/7, I am a boy of 18 and studying in the 2nd year Commerce. I am very interested in establishing Pen-friendship with boys and girls from all over the world, including Bangladesh. **1977** *Navy News* June 26/4 Readers seeking penfriends in the Royal Navy are listed here.

‖ **penghulu** (pĕŋghū·lu). Also **panghulu, pengulu.** [Malay.] In Malaysia, a head-man or chief.

1821 J. Leyden tr. *Malay Annals* 49 Under the bandahara immediately was the panghulu bandahari. **1894** N. B. Dennys *Descr. Dict. Brit. Malaya* 285 The Penghulus are elected by the neighbours and confirmed by the Government. **1900** W. W. Skeat *Malay Magic* v. 232 After my arrival with the *Pĕnghulu* the ceremony began. **1906** —— & Blagden *Pagan Races Malay Peninsula* I. 500 When a village migrates, the Penghulu conducts the migration. **1927** H. M. Tomlinson *Gallions Reach* xxvii. 219 Norrie addressed himself to the penghulu; the chief answered him with gentle explicitness. **1928** L. R. Wheeler *Mod. Malay* v. i. 194 The peasant class has various grades, from the 'penghulu' type, accustomed to exercise authority on a limited scale in his neighbourhood, to the backward natives. **1971** *Lady* 15 July 88/3 The Pengulu, the Headman, shook us by the hand and welcomed us to his domain. **1972** A. Amin tr. *Ahmad's No Harvest but Thorn* viii. 85 Jeha remembered how Lahuma had asked her to go to the *Penghulu*'s house. **1977** P. Theroux *Consul's File* 131 The *penghulu*, the headman, pointed out that..the rice was planted.

penglima, var. *panglima.

pengo (pe·ŋgō). Pl. **pengo, -oes.** [Hungarian *pengö*, lit. 'ringing'.] The basic monetary unit of Hungary from 1927 to 1946.

1926 *Glasgow Herald* 4 Jan. 12/2 To-day the new Hungarian currency, the pengo, is quoted for the first time. **1927** *Times* 28 Feb. 11/7 The Hungarian government has assigned a sum of 322,820 pengoes..for..a new Hungarian Legation building in London. **1930** *Observer* 23 Feb. 11/2 He earns twenty pengo a week. **1932** *Daily Express* 2 July 12/1 The amounts due to bondholders will be deposited in pengoes in the Hungarian National Bank. **1947** *Whitaker's Almanack* 917/1 The *Pengo* (of 100 *Filler*) was superseded in August, 1946, by a new currency, the *gulder*.

penguin. Add: **2. b.** A machine like an aeroplane but incapable of flight, used in the early stages of an airman's training. Also, a non-flying member of an air force. *Air Force slang.*

1915 G. Bacon *All about Flying* vi. 104 A 'penguin'—a machine with engine not powerful enough to raise it from the ground. **1917** J. R. McConnell *Flying for France* 143 The student is put on..a low-powered machine with very small wings... It could not leave the ground. The apparatus is jokingly and universally known as a Penguin. **1918** *Everybody's Mag.* Jan. 113/2 An officer of flying status, but who for some reason does not fly, is called a 'penguin'. **1918** *Sphere* 4 May 76/2 The three official corps familiarly known as the Waacs, the Wrens, and the Penguins. **1919** *Athenæum* 11 July 582/2 Members of the W.R.A.F. were called 'Penguins' because they were 'flappers' who did not fly. **1925** Fraser & Gibbons *Soldier & Sailor Words* 221 Penguin was also a name for a type of low-powered aeroplane with small planes or wings, used for instructional purposes. **1942** *Gen* 1 Sept. 14/2 No flier spares his contempt for the 'penguins', the nonflying administrative officers in the RAF. **1944** G. Gibson *Enemy Coast Ahead* (1946) vi. 96 In the average Bomber Officers' Mess,..while penguins sing loudly in the mornings as they get up to shave, it was rather hard for the boys who had been up all night to get a good day's rest. **1950** Partridge *Here, There & Everywhere* 53 When an airman refers to himself as a *penguin*, he is resorting to the specialized slang of the Air Force; all he means is that he is a member of the ground staff and therefore does not fly.

c. (With capital initial.) The proprietary name of Longman Penguin Limited, formerly Penguin Books Limited (1936–1966) and The Penguin Publishing Company Limited (1966–1972), used *attrib.* and *absol.* to designate paper-backed books or series of books published by this company. Also (*rare*) as *v. trans.*, to publish as a Penguin book.

1935 *Times Lit. Suppl.* 1 Aug. 491/1 We shall look forward to more Penguin Books, and we wish the experiment—a bold one—all success. **1938** 'G. Orwell' *Homage to Catalonia* x. 177, I..spent hours reading a succession of Penguin Library books. **1939** *Trade Marks Jrnl.* 13 Dec. 1630/1 Penguin... Printed publications, stationery and bookbinding, but not including publications on birds, or shaped sheets of paper for display purposes. Penguin Books Limited,..West Drayton, Middlesex; manufacturers and publishers. **1940** Graves & Hodge *Long Week-End* xxv. 426 Penguins were first published in 1936. **1948** J. Betjeman *Sel. Poems* 84 Whether we like to sit with Penguin books In sheltered alcoves farther up the cliff. **1950** D. E. Stevenson *Music in Hills* vi. 50 Miss Douglas..appeared from behind a large bookcase with two Penguins in her hand. **1950** W. Stevens *Let.* 15 Aug. (1967) 687 At the moment I am reading a Penguin Classic. **1951** R. Macaulay *Lett. to Friend* (1961) 209 *Mary Lavelle* is Penguin'd. **1956** J. Symons *Paper Chase* x. 69 Hedda Pont was at a table reading a Penguin thriller. **1959** J. Braine *Vodi* i. 11 You can have those Penguins in the bottom of the clothes locker. **1962** I. Murdoch *Unofficial Rose* v. 51 There were a few Penguin novels, but they looked dull English tea-party stuff. **1974** *Times Lit. Suppl.* 11 Dec. 22/4 With the publication of *Barnaby Rudge* all but two of Dickens's novels..are now Penguined. **1976** *New Yorker* 15 Nov. 187/1 Michael Hamburger, introducing the Penguin anthology of Enzensberger in translation, writes of the poet's 'moral purpose at variance with his personal needs and perceptions'.

d. A man wearing evening dress (cf. *penguin suit* (*a*) in sense 3 below). *rare.*

1967 *Melody Maker* 1 Apr. 9 Good Music had the sort of melody and clipping beat that even Victor Sylvester didn't have to alter so that the Brylcreemed penguins and their sequined partners could jig about in the ballrooms. **1976** B. Bova *Multiple Man* (1977) v. 56 These stuffed penguins and their bejeweled ladies.

3. penguin suit, (*a*) evening dress; (*b*) a type of suit worn by astronauts.

1967 Partridge *Dict. Slang* Suppl. 1289/1 *Penguin suit*, a dinner jacket. **1968** R. Jeffries *Traitor's Crime* iv. 46 Some smooth bastard in a penguin suit. **1971** *N.Y. Times* 10 June 18 The astronauts donned the tight-fitting overalls, known as a penguin suit, in which tension is produced by several layers of rubberized material. **1971** *Daily Tel.* 1 July 30/5 During the Soyuz 9 and 11 flights, Russian cosmonauts..wore special suits, called 'penguin' suits. **1979** K. M. Peyton *Marion's Angels* vi. 101 Geoff'd better go home for his penguin suit. I'll go up and get my tails.

penguinery. Add: Also **penguinry.** (Later examples.)

1921 H. G. Ponting *Gt. White South* 55 The Adélie penguinry was but a mile or two away. **1979** *Nature* 11 Jan. 88/2 The Adelie and chinstrap penguins feed mainly on krill, but they take different sized prey, either by active selection or by the Adelie feeding further from the rookery (or penguinery).

pengulu, var. *penghulu.

pen-gun. Add: **1.** (Earlier example.)

1807 T. Campbell *Let.* 3 Oct. in W. Beattie *Life & Lett. T. Campbell* (1849) II. v. 121 We crack'd, as the Scotch say, like pen-guns.

2. A small cylindrical gas bomb (see quot. 1965[2]).

Registered in the U.S. as a proprietary name.

1962 *N.Y. Times* 26 May 27/8 Miss Dunsmore told him that the pen-gun had dropped from her pocket-book and a pellet had ruptured, releasing the tear gas. **1965** *Official Gaz.* (U.S. Patent Office) 4 May tm42/1 Penguin Associates, Inc., Malvern, Pa... *Pengun.* For Tear Gas Projectors and Distress and Highway Flare Projectors. First use January 1961. **1965** *Consumer Bull.* Sept. 18/2 The *Pengun* itself is a stainless steel cylinder encased in a gold-anodized aluminum tube about 4 inches long with an interior diameter of ⅜ inch. The 'cartridge' of gas fits into the tube and is released by a firing pin or plunger. **1973** J. Di Mona *Last Man at Arlington* viii. 73 Before he could say another word, she got him with a pen gun filled with mace. 'Ah Christ,' he yelled, bending over, rubbing his eyes. **1978** P. Niesewand *Underground Connection* 24 A pen gun which fired bursts of paralysing gas.

penholder. Add: **2.** Used attrib. to denote a grip in table tennis in which the bat is held between thumb and forefinger.

1935 M. A. Symons *Table Tennis* ii. 14 There are still a large number of players who favour the 'Pen-holder' style of grip. *Ibid.*, Even top-class 'Pen-holder' grip players foozle such a shot. **1959** *Sunday Times* 5 Apr. 36/8 An aggressive opponent who smashed strongly with a pen-holder grip. **1973** *Advocate-News* (Barbados) 11 Dec. 13/3 The Chinese main armoury proved to be not their unorthodox 'pen-holder' style..but their service.

-penia (pī·niă), repr. Gr. πενία poverty, need, is used in *Med.* to denote a deficiency, esp. of a constituent of the blood, as in *granulocytopenia, *pancytopenia* s.v. *pan- 2. Also (*erron.*) **-pœnia.**

1971 *Lancet* 10 July 108/1 May I add *-penia* to the list of alternatives to *hypo-* suggested by Dr. Ell? In Greek it meant 'poverty' and it is currently used in such words as granulocytopenia and thrombocytopenia.

penicillamine (penisi·lămīn). *Chem.* and *Pharm.* [f. *penicill(in + amine.] An amino-acid, $(CH_3)_2C(SH)CH(NH_2)COOH$, produced by the hydrolysis of penicillins and used pharmacologically as a chelating agent; 2-amino-3-methyl-3-mercaptobutanoic acid.

1943 E. P. Abraham et al. in *Nature* 23 Jan. 107/1 The properties of this substance, which we propose to term penicillamine, show that it represents a novel type of naturally occurring base. *Ibid.*, Penicillamine is obtained by hydrolysing barium penicillin..at 100°C. for one hour by means of *N*/10 sulphuric acid. **1947** *Sci. News* IV. 70 The synthesis of penicillin G starts with a benzyl oxazolone and with penicillamine, and attempts to recombine them. **1969** [see *hypogeusia* s.v. *hypo- II]. **1977** *Davidson's Princ. & Pract. Med.* (ed. 12) 733 This disorder [*sc.* Wilson's disease]..can now be arrested by giving copper-binding drugs (chelating agents)... The most valuable of these is penicillamine.

penicillanic (penisilæ·nik), *a. Chem.* [f. as prec. + *-an-* + -ic.] *penicillanic acid*: an acid, $C_8H_{11}NO_3S$, whose molecular structure is the nucleus of the various penicillins and consists of a β-lactam ring fused to a molecule of 5,5-dimethylthiazolidine-4-carboxylic acid.

1953 J. C. Sheehan et al. in *Jrnl. Amer. Chem. Soc.* LXXV. 3293 By a cyclization procedure we have synthesized a β-lactamthiazolidine (VI)... We have chosen to call this compound methyl phthalimidopenicillanate. [*Note*] As a convenience in naming VI and similar analogs of the penicillins we suggest the terms 'penam' and 'penicillanic acid' for the following ring system and substituted ring system. **1959** *Times* 27 Oct. 6/7 The new penicillin, which is the potassium salt of 6-(-α-phenoxypropionamido)penicillanic acid, has the same range of antibacterial activity as previous penicillins. **1969** *Adv. Appl. Microbiol.* XI. 26 (*heading*) Antistaphylococcal activity of 6-substituted penicillanic acid derivatives.

penicillin (penisi·lin). *Pharm.* [f. Penicil-l(ium + -in[1].] **1.** Orig., the antibiotic agent obtained from cultures of the mould *Penicillium notatum*; hence, any of a group of antibiotics that are all derivatives of 6-amino-penicillanic acid in which a radical replaces one of the amino hydrogen atoms, some being acids produced naturally by the growth of various moulds of the genera *Penicillium* and *Aspergillus*, whilst others are acids, salts, or esters prepared synthetically from these; they are active against many kinds of bacteria but virtually harmless to persons not allergic to them.

1929 A. Fleming in *Brit. Jrnl. Exper. Path.* X. 227 In the rest of this article allusion will constantly be made to experiments with filtrates of a broth culture of this mould, so for convenience and to avoid the repetition of the rather cumbersome phrase 'Mould broth filtrate', the name 'penicillin' will be used. This will denote the filtrate of a broth culture of the particular penicillium with which we are concerned. **1941** H. W. Florey et al. in *Lancet* 16 Apr. 188/2 Enough evidence has now been assembled to show that penicillin is a new and effective type of chemotherapeutic agent, and possesses some properties unknown in any antibacterial substance hitherto described. **1947** *Sci. News* IV. 69 There are a number of naturally occurring penicillins, with somewhat different medical effectiveness. **1951** A. Grollman *Pharmacol. & Therapeutics* xxii. 445 The amorphous preparations of penicillin are yellow powders with a characteristic odor and bitter taste. The crystalline pure preparations are white, odorless and practically tasteless. **1953** J. Ramsbottom *Mushrooms & Toadstools* xxiii. 287 Soon after the chemical study was begun it was unexpectedly found that there was more than one kind of penicillin. The first two to be recognised were called Penicillin I and Penicillin II in this country, Penicillin F and Penicillin G in America... Later Penicillin III (X) and Penicillin IV (K) were recognised as being produced in greater or lesser amounts depending on cultural conditions. *Ibid.*, There are now five known 'natural' penicillins. All are dipeptides with the formula $C_9H_{11}O_4N_2S\ R$—the difference between them being in the constitution of the side chain..represented by *R*. **1958** *Listener* 9 Oct. 552/1 For our modern accomplishments are genuine, from the early work we achieved in the realm of atomic science, to the discovery of penicillin and modern progress on jet-propelled aircraft. **1970** Passmore & Robson *Compan. Med. Stud.* II. xx. 12/2 A method has been devised to use these natural penicillins as a source of a new range of compounds which can be made by chemical synthesis.., the new or semi-synthetic penicillins. *Ibid.* 13/1 These semi-synthetic penicillins have a range of novel properties which make them a major addition to the armoury of antibacterial agents. **1973** M. Amis *Rachel Papers* 93 Just two jabs of penicillin up the bum and much humiliation at the local clinic. **1974** M. C. Gerald *Pharmacol.* xxvii. 465 The penicillins were the first antibiotics discovered and remain today the second most widely used class of drugs for the treatment of bacterial infections. *Ibid.*, The most important natural penicillin is benzylpenicillin, which is more commonly designated penicillin G. Although penicillin G is the most potent of all penicillin derivatives, it suffers from several major disadvantages.

2. *penicillin A* or *B*: disused names for *notatin (*penatin), which is chemically unrelated to the penicillins proper.

1941 C. E. Coulthard et al. *Brit. Pat.* 552,619 A substance having bacteriostatic activity, which is hereinafter termed 'Penicillin A',..is produced by selecting a strain of Penicillium notatum which possesses the property..when grown on a suitable culture medium,..of maintaining the pH of the culture medium on the acid side for a considerable period. **1942** [see *notatin]. **1943** E. C. Roberts et al. in *Jrnl. Biol. Chem.* CXLVII. 47 We wish to report an antibacterial substance, penicillin B, produced by *Penicillium notatum*, which is insoluble in lipid solvents but readily separated from the culture medium by adsorption on benzoic acid. *Ibid.*, We shall refer to our product as penicillin B to differentiate it from the product obtained by Abraham *et al.*..which we shall call penicillin A. Although penicillin B may be similar to 'penatin'.., the absence of a discussion of its chemical properties prevents a comparison of the two products. **1949, 1963** [see *notatin].

3. *attrib.* and *Comb.*, as *penicillin-insensitive, -like, -resistant, -sensitive* adjs.; **penicillin unit,** a unit of penicillin which since 1944 has been the amount having the same antibiotic activity as a certain quantity (very nearly, and orig. exactly, 0.6 microgramme) of a standard preparation of the sodium salt of benzylpenicillin (penicillin G), and which is approximately equivalent to the Oxford unit that it superseded.

1929 *Brit. Jrnl. Exper. Path.* X. 234 In some [cultures] there were a few diphtheroid bacilli which were always penicillin sensitive, and in others there were Gram-negative bacilli which were penicillin insensitive. **1953** J. RAMSBOTTOM *Mushrooms & Toadstools* xxiii. 284 *Penicillium notatum* grows best in nearly neutral media, which are equally favourable for penicillin-insensitive organisms..which produce the enzyme penicillinase. **1946** *Nature* 28 Sept. 446/1 Penicillin-like antibiotics are produced by a number of moulds besides *Penicillium notatum*. **1942** *Proc. Soc. Exper. Biol. & Med.* LI. 387 (*heading*) Development of penicillin resistant strains of *Staphylococcus aureus in vitro*. **1971** *Nature* 4 June 284/1 Penicillin-resistant strains of staphylococci emerged in the 1950s. **1929** Penicillin-sensitive [see *penicillin-insensitive* above]. **1959** *Times* 6 Mar. 13/7 The proportion of penicillin-sensitive individuals is small. **1943** *Jrnl. Bacteriol.* XLVI. 189 To eliminate the day-to-day deviation, the Oxford group introduced the concept of the penicillin unit and the use of a standard penicillin preparation. **1947** *Jrnl. Biol. Chem.* CLXVII. 554 In the Casamino acid medium, maximum yields were obtained upon addition of 200 penicillin units per ml. of medium initially. **1953** HEILBRON & BUNBURY *Dict. Org. Compounds* (rev. ed.) IV. 51/2 Penicillin-F... Antibiotic activity: 1,490 Penicillin units per mg.

penicillinase (penisi·linē͡iz, -s). *Biochem.* [f. prec. + *-ASE.] Any of the enzymes (produced by certain bacteria) which cause the breaking up of the carbon–nitrogen bond in the lactam ring of some penicillins (so rendering them ineffective as antibiotics). Cf. *LACTAMASE.

1940 ABRAHAM & CHAIN in *Nature* 28 Dec. 837/1 The activity of the enzyme, which we term penicillinase, is slight at pH5, but increases considerably towards the alkaline range of pH. **1958** *Ann. Rev. Biochem.* XXVII. 176 Cephalosporin-C possesses the interesting property of being resistant to the action of some penicillinases including that produced by penicillin resistant staphylococci. **1971** [see *LACTAMASE]. **1974** M. C. GERALD *Pharmacol.* iv. 72 Recent research has made available new penicillins that are resistant to acid hydrolysis and penicillinase attack. **1975** *Nature* 12 June 526/1 Penicillinases, or as they are now known, β-lactamases, are enzymes which specifically deactivate penicillin by hydrolysis of the β-lactam ring.

penicilloic (penisilōᵘ·ik), *a. Biochem.* [f. *PENICILL(IN + *OIC.] *penicilloic acid*: any of the acids produced when a penicillin is hydrolysed (as by a penicillinase) and the C–N bond of the lactam ring broken.

1945 *Science* 21 Dec. 628/2 The dicarboxylic acid obtained by hydrolysis of penicillin at the site of the potential carboxyl is termed penicilloic acid. This acid is produced in the form of salts by treatment of penicillin with alkalies and is presumably the product of the action of the enzyme penicillinase on penicillin. **1949** MOZINGO & FOLKERS in H. T. Clarke et al. *Chem. of Penicillin* xviii. 542/1 Many of the penicilloic acids..were made in order to study their reactions with various reagents in the interest of their dehydration to the penicillins. **1959** *Observer* 11 Jan. 14/7 It [*sc.* penicillinase] acts by rapidly breaking down penicillin to penicilloic acid, which has no antibiotic activity. **1970** *New Eng. Jrnl. Med.* 16 July 119/1 Penicilloic acid appears to have an important role in some of the allergic reactions caused by penicillins.

Hence **penicillo·ate** [-ATE[1]], a salt or ester of a penicilloic acid.

1946 *Industr. & Engin. Chem.* (*Analytical Ed.*) Oct. 619/1, 8·97 equivalents of iodine per mole..is in reasonably good agreement with the range given..for penicilloates (8·5 to 8·9). **1969** MANHAS & BOSE *Synthesis of Penicillin, Cephalosporin C & Analogs* iii. 38 When this route..met with only limited success the cyclization of penicilloates that could not form oxazolones was investigated.

peninsula·tion. [f. PENINSULATE *v.*] The process of making into a peninsula; the condition of being peninsulated; peninsularity. (In quots. *fig.*)

1923 G. BARKER in Drinkwater & Orpen *Outl. Lit. & Art* (1924) I. x. 194/1 From this peninsulation of the stage several things follow. **1959** *Times* 5 Sept. 9/6 It is the prospect..the isolation or peninsulation.

penis. Delete ‖ and add: Also with pl. **peni** (*erron.*), **penises**. (Earlier and later examples.)

1676 T. BROWNE *Let.* 14 June in *Wks.* (1964) IV. 61 You may observe..the flattish heart, the Lungs,..the penis, the multiple stomack &c. **1926** F. Z. SNOOP *Reproduction & Sexual Evolution* 83 Havelock Ellis quotes other cases, even butterflies (if insects may be here included) who possess excrescences on their penes, which of necessity must cause pain, or something very like pain, during coition. **1929** D. H. LAWRENCE *Paintings*, What do you paint with, Maitre?—With my penis, and be damned! **1933** R. L. DICKINSON *Human Sex Anatomy* vi. 74/2 The long penises are in general narrow and the short broad. **1943** *Amer. Jrnl. Dis. Children* LXV. 541 The penis is primarily an organ of copulation, so that its true physiologic size would be gauged by measurement of the erect phallus. *Ibid.*, The length of the fully stretched penis is practically identical with the length of the erect phallus. **1962** E. L. COCKRUM *Introd. Mammalogy* iii. 76 According to Asdell (1946), Slijper has studied the structure of the penis in its relation to the duration of coitus and developed the following classification of morphological types of peni. **1965** E. W. JOHNSON *Love & Sex in Plain Lang.* ii. 8 A man's most obvious sexual organ is his penis. **1970** H. W. & L. R. LEVI tr. *Kaestner's Invertebr. Zool.* III. v. 130 The paired penes are introduced deep into the posterior opening between the valves, reach the copulatory openings, and mating is accomplished in several minutes. **1972** *Times Lit. Suppl.* 29 Sept. 1156/4 Sexologists now make a clear distinction between 'penis' and 'phallus'; the former being used to define the flaccid organ and the latter the erect organ. **1973** C. PINCHER *Sex in our Time* viii. 92 Just as there are men with large or small penises so there are women with large or small vaginas. **1975** M. SEYMOUR-SMITH *Sex & Society* x. 282 The phallus is the *image* of the *erect* (never flaccid) penis. **1975** FRETTER & GRAHAM *Functional Anat. Invertebr.* (1976) xi. 352 In these sessile forms [*sc.* barnacles] the sperm are filiform and motile and transferred from one individual to the next by a long flexible penis.

b. *penis-cover, -extender, holder, -sheath*; **penis-envy** *Psychoanalysis*, an envy of the male's possession of a penis, postulated by Freud to occur in girls and possibly resulting in a castration-complex (see *CASTRATION 1) or in the adoption of masculine behaviour; **penis gourd** (see quot.).

1966 *New Statesman* 22 Apr. 589/2 Even more remarkable are the penis-covers made of narrow gourds a foot or more in length. [**1920** B. LOW tr. *Freud's Psychogenesis of Case of Female Homosexuality* in *Internat. Jrnl. Psycho-Anal.* I. 146 She had..developed a pronounced envy of the penis.] **1924** *Internat. Jrnl. Psycho-Anal.* V. 58 Its relation to the 'penis-envy' complex is twofold. **1946** *Mind* LV. 354 A girl's penis-envy might also be very much hidden. **1964** A. BOROWIK *How Many Miles to Babylon?* xv. 96 When I hear a guy talking to me about penis envy..I feel an overpowering urge to laugh. **1972** F. WARNER *Lying Figures* III. 20 You'd find penis-envy in a peach. **1973** K. VONNEGUT *Breakfast of Champions* xv. 147 One time Dwayne Hoover got an advertisement through the mail for a penis-extender, made out of rubber. **1971** *World Archaeol.* III. 136 The traditional male dress is the penis gourd: a piece of the stem end of the gourd, varying in length from about three to more than twelve inches, into which the penis is inserted, leaving the scrotum exposed. **1976** *Times* 31 May 7/8 Went native in 1681 living with the Cuna Indians, coated in vegetable dies [*sic*] and clothed only in a conical silver penis holder suspended from the waist by a thong. **1925** C. K. MEEK *Northern Tribes Nigeria* II. 116 Among those people who wear the penis-sheath, the sheath is usually removed before the body is laid in the grave. **1978** *Sunday Times* (Colour Suppl.) 18 June 40/1 Their chief Manuel, denied access to Government chambers in Brasilia for not wearing a suit, has forbidden any Brazilian deputy to set foot on Xavante land unless wearing a penis sheath, hair feathers and body paint.

penitent, *a.* and *sb.* Add: **B.** *sb.* **4*.** *Geogr.* [See quot. 1954[1].] A spike or pinnacle of compact snow or ice which results from differential ablation of a snow or ice field exposed to the sun, occurring esp. in high mountain ranges and freq. in large groups containing specimens of similar size and orientation. Freq. *attrib.* or as *adj.*

[**1910** *Geogr. Jrnl.* XXXV. 125 Among the variety of views that have been advanced, observers have practically agreed that one factor essential to the production of penitentes,..is the unequal melting of *névé* under the application of heat in some form, principally that of the sun.] **1922** WRIGHT & PRIESTLEY *Glaciology* viii. 288 Plate CXCV shows an example of penitent-ice from the Ferrar glacier. **1936** G. SELIGMAN *Snow Struct.* vi. 131 It has been postulated..that the ablative effect in penitent snow has been intensified by the presence of solid matter to absorb the sun's heat. **1941** *Amer. Jrnl. Sci.* CCXXXIX. 382 'Penitent' ice-forms, modelled in some degree by evaporation processes and associated with the same structures, have been described from Antarctica. **1954** *Jrnl. Glaciology* II. 331 We venture to translate the words used by Chileans and Argentinians into English: *penitentes* (noun), *campo de penitentes* (field of penitents). *Nieve penitente* is not used, and *nieve de los penitentes* means 'snow from the penitents'. Both expressions have been introduced into international literature by..glaciologists who did not know Spanish very thoroughly. *Ibid.* 336 When the snow field lies directly upon the ground, the channels between the penitents often succeed in reaching the ground, and the penitents, detaching themselves from one another, assume the vague appearance of an Easter procession of white-cowled Spanish penitents. **1954** W. NOYCE *South Col* v. 83 The ice..had ribbed and wrinkled into bigger honeycomb, more like the ice pinnacles called 'penitents'. **1959** R. E. HUSCHKE *Gloss. Meteorol.* 416 Penitent ice is most developed on low-latitude mountains, especially the Chilean Andes, but has been found even in polar regions. **1972** *Cambridge Mountaineering* 38 An additional reason for travelling to Afghanistan had been to study certain snow formations, called penitents. *Ibid.* 39 Our 'penitents'..were spread all over the place both on the snowfields and sometimes also on the rock surfaces... Their only use turned out to be on steep snow slopes where they provided useful handholds—provided one didn't put too much trust in them.

5. penitent-form (earlier examples).

1865 *Wesleyan-Methodist Mag.* Nov. 484 She was the first to come to the penitent form. **1881** *Doctrines & Discipline Salvation Army* §28 Bring them out to the penitent form before the people, and so test them further, and pledge them publicly.

penk (peŋk), *v. rare.* [? var. PANK *v.*] *intr.* To palpitate; to throb or heave violently or rapidly.

1890 KIPLING *Barrack-Room Ballads* (1892) 27 Wot makes the soldier's 'eart to penk, wot makes 'im to perspire? **1898** —— *Stalky* in *Land & Sea Tales* (1923) 137 They bullocks drove like that—all heavin' an' penkin' an' hotted!

pe·nlight, pen-light. [f. PEN *sb.*[2] + LIGHT *sb.*] An electric torch shaped like a fountain-pen.

1958 *Practical Wireless* XXXIV. 58/2 (Advt.), Uses only one small 8d. penlight battery. **1962** E. AMBLER *Light of Day* x. 210 Miller had a pen-light in his hand and was looking at his watch. **1969** *New Yorker* 12 Apr. 78/2 There are pockets in unlikely places, such as at the ankles and shoulders, for things like scissors, penlights, and checklists. **1971** D. BAGLEY *Freedom Trap* ix. 206, I took out a pen-light and risked a flash. **1972** J. HURTT et al. *Compr. Rev. Orthoptics & Ocular Motility* xviii. 182 The patient is instructed to fixate a wall light at 20 feet while a penlight is held directly in front of his nose. **1977** 'E. MCBAIN' *Long Time no See* ii. 18 Carella took a small penlight from his coat pocket and flashed it over the mailboxes.

penman. Add: **1. c.** *Criminals' slang.* One who commits forgery.

1865 *Sessions Papers* 11 Apr. 519 For being concerned with, *Jemmy the Penman*, and others, now in custody, [etc.]. **1887** J. HAWTHORNE (*title*) An American penman: from the diary of Inspector Byrnes. **1938** F. D. SHARPE *Sharpe of Flying Squad* xxix. 297 As soon as they get some cheques or 'kites', as they call them, these are rushed off to the 'penman' or 'scribe', whose task is that of taking out crosses on them, enlarging the figures and preparing suitable letters to the bank asking them to cash the cheques. **1974** H. MCLEAVE *Only Gentlemen can Play* (1975) II. 97 You'll need a passport... I've got a penman who can doctor it.

pennant[1]. Add: **2. c.** *N. Amer. sport.* A flag symbolizing a league championship; hence, the championship itself. Also *attrib.*

1880 N. BROOKS *Fairport Nine* 188 Billy Hetherington ..was entrusted with the championship pennant. **1886** *Outing* Aug. 572/2 Questions by the dozen come in..in regard to the probable issue of the pennant races in the professional arena. **1915** *Lit. Digest* 21 Aug. 360/3 The Cincinnati Reds..have never yet won a pennant. *Ibid.*, The New York Giants..are not often far from the pennant class. **1924** [see *CINCH *v.* 2 b]. **1947** *Partisan Rev.* XIV. 258 The funeral was the most serious event of Samuel's life,..but this did not prevent him from getting the evening paper when the family returned from the cemetery and studying the final scores in the major league pennant races. **1967** W. S. AVIS et al. *Dict. Canad. Eng., Senior Dict.* 821/2 Pennant... **2** any flag taken as emblem of superiority or success, especially in an athletic contest. **1971** L. KOPPETT *N.Y. Times Guide Spectator Sports* i. 35 The pennant winner in each league turned out to be the team with the best regular-season record. **1975** *New Yorker* 22 Sept. 98/2 The Los Angeles Dodgers have won five pennants and three World Series since their relocation.

pennantite (pe·nāntəit). *Min.* [f. the name of Thomas *Pennant* (1726–98), Welsh zoologist and mineralogist + -ITE[1].] A basic aluminosilicate of manganese, approximately $Mn_9Al_6Si_5O_{20}(OH)_{16}$, most specimens of which are pleochroic and orange in thin section.

1946 W. C. SMITH et al. in *Mineral. Mag.* XXVII. 217 (*heading*) Pennantite, a new manganese-rich chlorite from Benallt mine, Rhiw, Carnarvonshire. *Ibid.* 220 The names manganchlorite (Hamberg) and manganese-chlorite (Eckermann) have been applied to chlorites containing only a low percentage (1·02–2·28) MnO, so it is desirable to avoid the use of either of these names for a chlorite so rich in manganese as the mineral here described, and we therefore propose for it a new name, *pennantite*. **1954** *Ibid.* XXX. 280 The manganese-bearing chlorites include the remarkable species pennantite, chemically a klementite with the magnesium almost wholly replaced by manganese. **1970** *Mineral Abstr.* XXI. 249/2 (*heading*) The ferruginous and magnesium varieties of pennantite from the Atasui deposits in Central Kazakhstan. *Ibid.*, Fe-pennantite occurs in the Ushatan I deposit in veinlets with pyrosmalite and calcite. It is dark green. *Ibid.*, Magnesium pennantite in the Zhumast deposit occurs in marbles and in carbonate layers in braunite ore... Pleochroism α orange pink, γ light orange.

penned, *a.* **2. a.** (Later example.)

1968 B. HINES *Kestrel for Knave* 79, I started training Kes after I'd had her about a fortnight, when she was hard penned, that means her tail feathers and wing feathers had gone hard at their bases.

penner[4] (pe·nəɪ). [f. PEN *v.*[1] + -ER[1].] One who pens cattle; also (*Austral.* and *N.Z.*) **penner-up**, one who pens sheep ready for the shearers in a shearing shed.

1897 D. MCK. WRIGHT *Station Ballads* 101 The penner-up is cursing at the back, The boss is looking savage at a long Australian card. **1904** *Daily News* 2 Dec. 5/1 There are 42 different men in this gang—'penners', 'shacklers', 'hoisters', 'gutters', and so on. **1911** J. COLLIER *Pastoral Age in Australasia* xxix. 216 Besides the shearers, there are penners-up, wool-rollers, pickers-up. **1940** E. C. STUDHOLME *Te Waimate* (1954) xv. 130 The 'sheep-oh' (penner-up)..in addition to filling up the catching-pens.. weighed the bales and recorded them..in the wool book. **1952** [see *DAGGER *sb.*[2] b]. **1955** *People* (Austral.) 30 Nov. 20/1 The penner-up bustles more sheep up the race. **1965** J. S. GUNN *Terminol. Shearing Industry* II. 8 *Penner-up*. This shedhand keeps the sheep moving into the shed and is ready to fill the catching pen when a shearer calls sheep-oh'. One man would be full-time 'penner-up' in sheds of six or more shearing stands. **1972** E. Hargreaves *Fair Green Weed* ii. 24, I had to go down to the cow-pen... One of the penners has had an accident... His mule shied.

penni (pe·ni). Pl. **penni, penniä** (-iā). [Finn.] **a.** A Finnish monetary unit, equal to $\frac{1}{100}$ markka. **b.** The name of the coin equal to this amount.

1893 W. C. Hazlitt *Coinage of European Continent* 222 *Penni*, pl. *pennia*, a Russian copper coin struck for Finland = a French centime. **1903** [see *Markka]. **1957** *Whitaker's Almanack 1958* 964 Finland... *Markka* of 100 *Penni*. **1970** R. A. G. Carson *Coins* (ed. 2) 397 In the later nineteenth century a distinctive coinage began to be issued by the czars of Russia as grand-dukes of Finland. The monetary unit was the silver mark, divided into 100 pennia... A monetary reform in 1963 introduced a new markka equivalent to 100 old markkaa. The types of the former 1 and 5 markkaa coins have been retained for the new 1 and 2 pennia pieces in bronze. **1974** *Encycl. Brit. Macropædia* VII. 306/2 The markkaa (made up of 100 pennia) was devaluated in 1949, 1957, and 1967.

pennif (pe·nif). *slang* (*rare*). [Back-slang f. Finnip.] = Finnip; hence, any bank-note.

1862 [see *Jug *sb.*[2] 2 b]. **1891** 'F. W. Carew' *No. 747* xxxv. 416, I gets clean off with the scawfer and 'bout 'er thirty quid in single-pennifs and silver.

pennill. Add: The correct pl. is **penillion** (quot. 1898, sense b). (Further examples.)

1894 *Wales* Aug. 170/2 As he was so famous a poet, I thought he must be either a writer of hymns or of *penillion* to be sung with the harp. **1938** *Oxf. Compan. Mus.* 1009/2 A certain limited group of harp tunes are habitually used for Penillion performances. **1962** *Times* 31 Jan. (Wales Suppl.) p. xi/6 Penillion Singing (lit., 'singing of verses') to harp accompaniment. **1962** *Listener* 26 Apr. 740/3 The *englynion*, the *penillion telyn*.

Pennsylvania (pensilvē^i^·niă). One of the middle Atlantic states of the United States, named after Admiral Sir William Penn (1621–70), in 1681. Used *attrib.* to denote articles, inhabitants, products, or varieties of plants characteristic of, or growing in, Pennsylvania, as *Pennsylvania anemone, ash, cap, corn, division, dwarf mountain maple, mountain laurel, salve, wagon, wind flower*; **Pennsylvania German** *sb.* and *a.* = *Pennsylvania Dutch *sb.* and *a.*

1900 B. B. Smyth *Plants & Flowers Kansas* ii. 54 On the low prairies may be found plenty of Pennsylvania anemone, a plant with..numerous branches, each terminated by a flower with five broad white sepals. **1810** P. Wakefield *Excursions N. Amer.* (ed. 2) xxviii. 191 The black fir, the Weymouth pine, the red cedar, the common fir, the red maple, the Pennsylvania ash..are also common. **1971** M. Tak *Truck Talk* 116 *Pennsylvania caps*, recapped tires with an unbroken tread line. **1739** in *Colonial Rec. Georgia* (1905) III. 429 We all were disappointed by..planting the yellow Pensilvania Corn. **1929** *Papers Mich. Acad. Sci., Arts & Lett.* X. 314/1 *Pennsylvania Division*, the Twenty-eighth Division. **1785** H. Marshall *Arbustrum Amer.* 2 *Acer pennsylvanicum*, ..Pennsylvania Dwarf Mountain Maple. **1869** *Nation* (N.Y.) 30 Dec. 583/2 The Pennsylvania German is a South German dialect. *Ibid.* 584/1 Divine service among the Pennsylvania Germans is held in High German. **1875** A. R. Horne (*title*) Pennsylvania German manual. **1956** *Publ. Amer. Dial. Soc.* xxvi. 30 The Norwegian spoken among the immigrants showed the same combination of archaism and levelling as other American languages, though the relatively brief period of its life has not permitted the kind of consolidation found in Pennsylvania German or the colonial languages proper. **1970** *Globe & Mail* (Toronto) 25 Sept. T3/3 Mennonite and Pennsylvania-German societies will be in attendance [at a festival]. **1972** H. Kurath *Stud. Area Linguistics* 105 This divergence between Pennsylvania German (essentially a Rhine Frankish folk dialect of west central Germany) and Standard German..would tend to keep the two apart. **1785** H. Marshall *Arbustrum Amer.* 127 *Rhododendrum maximum*, Pennsylvania Mountain Laurel. **1899** 'J. Flynt' *Tramping with Tramps* iv. 396 *Pennsylvania salve*, apple-butter. **1810** M. Dwight *Journey to Ohio* (1912) 39 This line is the shape of a Pennsylvania waggon. **1869** J. G. Fuller *Uncle John's Flower-Gatherers* 28 [The anemone] blooms later, in May and June, and is called the Pennsylvania Wind Flower.

Pennsylvania Dutch, *sb.* and *a.* **A.** *sb.* **a.** *pl.* [Dutch *sb.* 3 a.] The descendants of the original German settlers in Pennsylvania. **b.** [see Dutch *sb.* 1.] A Pennsylvanian dialect derived from the High German of a great number of the early settlers, with a considerable admixture of English elements. **B.** *adj.* [Dutch *a.* 1.] Of or pertaining to the Pennsylvania Dutch or their dialect. So **Pennsylvania Dutchman.**

a **1824** J. Guild in *Proc. Vermont Hist. Soc.* (1937) V. 293, I came across a Pennsylvania Dutch man, and I made a bargain with him. **1831** *Canad. Freeman* (Toronto) 19 May 2/3 Let Mackenzie stick to the Central Committee, the Saddlebags, & the Pennsylvania Dutch of the Home District. **1856** *Spirit of Times* 4 Oct. 71/1 But *revenons a mouton*, which, in plain Pennsylvania Dutch means how Fogie Antique caught..catfish. **1868** H. W. Beecher *Norwood* 468 Them Pennsylvania Dutch think more of their horses than they do of themselves. **1882** P. H. Gibbons *Pennsylvania Dutch* (ed. 3) 401 A 'Pennsylvania Dutch' remedy for whooping-cough. **1943** *Amer. Speech* XVIII. 112 The diphthong *oi* [ɔi] in the Pennsylvania Dutch dialects is interesting both phonemically and historically because of its infrequent occurrence. **1948** W. Stevens *Let.* 1 Dec. (1967) 624 A true Pennsylvania Dutchman. **1974** E. McGirr *Murderous Journey* 98 He lapsed into Pennsylvania Dutch. The quaint idioms and all. **1976** *New Yorker* 16 Feb. 58/2 The sort of packaging that makes pancake-mix pancakes served in a Pennsylvania hotel 'Pennsylvania Dutch pancakes' instead of just pancakes. **1976** R. Condon *Whisper of Axe* I. xvii. 103 He was served *schnitz un knepp*: apples, dumplings, and ham from the Pennsylvania Dutch.

Pennsylva·nian, *sb.* and *a.* [f. *Pennsylvania + -an.] **A.** *sb.* **1.** A native or inhabitant of Pennsylvania.

1685 [see Quakeristical *a.*]. **1747** G. Whitefield *Let.* 6 May in *Wks.* (1771) II. 94 The Pensylvanians I am sure will soon regret the loss of you. **1755** in S. M. Hamilton *Lett. to Washington* (1898) I. 99 The Road upon which the Pennsylvaneans were Employ'd. **1782** 'J. H. St. John de Crèvecœur' *Lett. from Amer. Farmer* 58 Europeans.. become..either Pennsylvanians, Virginians, or provincials, under some other name. **1838** *Southern Lit. Messenger* IV. 165/1 Mr. Ingersoll, being a Pennsylvanian, stands impartial between the two extremes of the Union. **1862** *Evening Post* (N.Y.) 21 May 1/2 Words of warm congratulation were sent to the dashing Pennsylvanian by the Commanding General. **1910** *Harper's Mag.* Aug. 473/1 Georg Shock..is a Pennsylvanian. **1939** [see *insomniac]. **1953** W. Moore *Bring Jubilee* (1955) xx. 194 It was the Fourth of July, and a day of victory and rejoicing for all Pennsylvanians. **1967** *National Observer* (U.S.) 3 July 12/2 True to tradition, the Pennsylvanians are the best shots in the brigade. **1974** *Encycl. Brit. Macropædia* XIV. 28/2 Pennsylvanians still tend toward the Republican Party in state elections. **1976** *Billings* (Montana) *Gaz.* 1 July 3–B/2 Schapp urged all Pennsylvanians to listen to their message with an open mind.

2. *Geol.* The Pennsylvanian period or system.

1906 Chamberlin & Salisbury *Geol.* II. x. 556 In the arctic regions of America, the Mississippian and Pennsylvanian are not differentiated. **1960** J. M. Weller *Stratigr. Princ. & Pract.* xii. 441 Fossils are rare and of little service in separating the Mississippian from the Pennsylvanian. **1969** [see *Mississippian *sb.* and *a.* A. 2]. **1977** A. Hallam *Planet Earth* 207 The Pennsylvanian started with a new transgression of the sea over the low land of the central North American continent.

B. *adj.* **1.** Of, pertaining to, or characteristic of Pennsylvania or its people.

1698 G. Thomas *Hist. & Geogr. Acct. Pensilvania & W. New-Jersey* 2 They (as the Pensilvanian Indians) observe the New Moons with great Devotion. **1785** H. Marshall *Arbustrum Amer.* 51 Pennsylvanian Sharp-keyed Ash (*Fraxinus pennsylvanica*). **1853** A. Bunn *Old Eng. & New Eng.* I. viii. 167 Mr. Nicholas Biddle..issued the notorious Pennsylvanian bonds. **1959** *Chambers's Encycl.* X. 536/2 Pennsylvanian oil production is relatively much less important although quality is high.

2. *Geol.* Of, pertaining to, or designating a period and system of the Palæozoic Era in North America that succeeded the Mississippian and preceded the Permian, and corresponds more or less to the Upper Carboniferous in Europe.

1891 *Bull. U.S. Geol. Survey* No. 80. 5 The Coal Measures or Pennsylvanian series. **1906** Chamberlin & Salisbury *Geology: Earth History* II. x. 539 (*heading*) The Pennsylvanian (coal measures, Carboniferous proper) period. *Ibid.*, The need of a name to distinguish this system of rocks from those which have been described under the name Mississippian has long been felt, and the name Pennsylvanian, which has recently come into wide use in this country, was adopted because the system is well developed and well known in Pennsylvania. **1933** [see *Mississippian *sb.* and *a.* B. 2]. **1945** *Bull. Amer. Assoc. Petroleum Geologists* XXIX. 128 The coal, oil, gas, ceramic clays, and other minerals found in rocks of Pennsylvanian age greatly exceed the value of the mineral resources found in any other system. **1960** J. M. Weller *Stratigr. Princ. & Pract.* vi. 176 Pennsylvanian coal up to nearly 100 feet thick has been mined from several ancient Missouri sink holes of moderate or small size.

penny. Add: **I. 1.** Since 15 Feb. 1971 of the value of $\frac{1}{100}$ of a pound, and for a while known as the *new penny* (see *New *a.* 4). Denoted (after a numeral) by *p* (see *P II, *Pee *sb.*[6]). (Further example.)

1971 *Daily Tel.* 8 Mar. 12 He partly pre-empted his Budget last autumn..by promising six old pennies off the income tax.

2. b. (Earlier and later examples of U.S. usage.) Also Canad. *colloq.*, a Canadian cent.

1831 *Constellation* 12 Mar. 133/4 He meant cents, but they call em pennies in New York. **1902** 'R. Connor' *Glengarry School Days* 166 'Six pennies and two dimes', was Hughie's disconsolate reply. **1925** E. Glasgow *Barren Ground* xi. 303 The price had seemed extravagant, for selling directly to her customer she had asked thirty cents a pound, while butter in Pedlar's store was never higher than ninepence in summer and a shilling in winter, measured in the old English terms which were still commonly used in Queen Elizabeth County. **1966** *New Statesman* 16 Dec. 896/3 Florin..is only used, like the American 'penny', to describe the actual lump of metal. **1971** *Daily Colonist* (Victoria, B.C.) 28 Dec. 7/4 Persons posting first class letters will be nicked another penny starting Jan. 1. **1974** H. McCloy *Minotaur Country* (1975) xvi. 186 You recall the penny that was found..? And the dimes found ..after the fire?

IV. 9. a. So *penny for them* (*'em*); also *ellipt.* as *penny*. **f.** (Further examples.) **l.** *pennies from heaven*: money acquired without effort or risk; also *sing.*, a windfall, a godsend. **m.** *to spend a penny*: to visit a lavatory, to urinate (from the former price of admission to public lavatories). **n.** *the penny has dropped*: a situation or statement has belatedly been comprehended; one has reacted belatedly. (With allusion to the mechanism of a penny-in-the-slot machine). **o.** *two* (also *ten*) *a penny*: commonplace, easily obtainable, occurring frequently.

a. 1900 H. G. Wells *Love & Mr. Lewisham* xxv. 242 'Penny,' she said after an interval. Lewisham started and looked up. '*Eh?*' **1914** C. Mackenzie *Sinister St.* II. iv. iii. 895 'You're very silent, kiddie,' she said. 'I'll give you a penny for them.' **1921** N. Kent *Quest M. Harland* II. iv. 169 'Penny for 'em, old man,' said Dickie presently, after Michael had eaten in silence for nearly five minutes. 'My thoughts?' Michael started and laughed. **1959** J. Braine *Vodi* xiv. 190 Harry's voice broke into her thoughts. 'Penny for 'em, old girl.' **1965** L. Meynell *Double Fault* II. v. 175 'Penny,' Lucian said. She laughed... 'Far too rich and rare for a penny to buy them.' **1973** J. Thomson *Death Cap* x. 142 Finch was sitting looking thoughtfully at the report... 'Penny for them?' suggested the Sergeant.

f. *c* **1882** W. S. Gilbert *Iolanthe* II. 33 In for a penny, in for a pound—It's love that makes the world go round! **1906** L. Strachey in *Lit. Ess.* (1948) 142 The emendator is on an inclined plane which leads him inevitably from readjustments of punctuation to corrections of grammar, and from corrections of grammar to alterations of rhythm; if he is in for a penny, he is in for a pound. **1976** 'J. Fraser' *Who steals my Name?* xii. 149 He seemed to be having some kind of inner conflict which resolved itself. 'All right,' he said, 'in for a penny in for a pound!' **1977** *Transatlantic Rev.* LX. 189 The cabbie steamed up to Notting Hill Gate with an In for a penny, In for a pound expression on his face.

l. 1936 J. Burke (*song-title*) Pennies from heaven. **1965** J. D. MacDonald *Bright Orange for Shroud* xvi. 191 'Sweetie,' I said, 'you are a penny from heaven.' **1971** P. Dickinson *Sleep & his Brother* v. 117 Hard money is what your hospital pays you... Soft money is pennies from heaven, some dirty big company deciding to earn a bit of tax relief by financing medical research. **1972** 'W. Haggard' *Protectors* xiii. 154 He hadn't planned it that way... But when the pennies from heaven fell down he'd seize them.

m. 1945 H. Lewis *Strange Story* iv. 27 'Us girls,' she said, 'are going to spend a penny!' **1955** J. Cannan *Long Shadows* iii. 59, I wasn't sure that Trudy [a dog] had spent her penny. *Ibid.* vii. 127 We'll go indoors and pay for tea and spend a penny. **1960** M. Cecil *Something in Common* xxii. 239 It's tricky about the bathroom, but it's amazing how one can train oneself to spend a minimum of pennies. **1973** *People's Jrnl.* (Inverness & Northern Counties ed.) 28 July 10/1 Anyone on the Islands..after that time who wants to 'spend a penny' must make a 10-minute walk.. to the public toilets.

n. [**1942** N. Balchin *Darkness falls from Air* iv. 70 The penny seems to have stuck in the machine that time. The proper answer to that is, 'I'm flattered.'] **1951** —— *Way through Wood* xv. 214, I sat and thought for a moment and then the penny dropped. **1959** *Sunday Express* 13 Dec. 1/4, I had seen Vivienne before, but the penny didn't drop until I met her that night. **1961** S. Chaplin *Day of Sardine* viii. 174 It took a second or two for the penny to drop. I gave myself a shake and made over to the maybe Old Man. **1973** *Times* 1 Dec. 14 The penny had begun to drop even before the present fuel crisis.

o. 1960 *Times* 11 Jan. 17/1 Penalties were two a penny at Upper Park on Saturday. **1961** New Eng. Bible *Matt.* x. 29 Are not sparrows two a penny? **1966** *Listener* 27 Oct. 612/3 He found in India that subalterns were two a penny and invited nowhere. **1973** *Nature* 20 Apr. 492/2 Recommendations on the so-called energy crisis are by now two a penny. **1973** A. Mann *Tiara* iv. 34 Hunches are two a penny in this business. **1973** C. L. Barnhart et al. *Dict. New Eng.* 355/2 *Ten a penny* is also used in England.

V. 11. a. *penny arcade, awful, bazaar, bun* (earlier example), *club* (later example), *dreadful* (further examples; also, with hyphen, *attrib.*), *ice* (also *comb.*), *magazine, nap* (examples), *novel, novelette, press* (earlier and later examples), *reading* (further examples), *steamboat, steamer* (earlier and later examples), *toy, whistle* (further examples).

1908 C. E. Griffin *Four Years in Europe* ix. 87 The numerous penny arcades and moving picture shows.. were another new wrinkle in American showmanship. **1961** Getlein & Gardiner *Movies, Morals, & Art* I. iv. 48 The penny arcade..can still be found in such urban areas as Times Square. **1889** E. Dowson *Let.* 15 Mar. (1967) 49 It is very bad, very long, & distinctly 'penny awful' not 'shilling shocking'. **1897** H. James *Spoils of Poynton* xiii. 154 An assortment of pen-wipers and ash-trays, a harvest he had gathered in from penny bazaars. **1966** *Guardian* 29 Aug. 4/4 The Shields tram.. full of early homecomers. They got off at the Penny Bazaar. **1976** *Times* 8 Nov. 14/5 If the Church wants..the responsibility for the appointment of its chief pastors it must do much better than this. We are in danger of reducing a great institution to the level of a penny bazaar. **1824** E. Weeton *Jrnl.* 21 July (1969) II. 309 Having had no dinner..but some curds and one or two penny buns. **1844** C. M. Yonge *Abbeychurch* xiii. 278 Elizabeth..went to the school to receive the penny-club money. **1884** *World* 20 Aug. 9/2 The wicked noblemen of the transpontine melodrama or of penny dreadfuls. **1906** M. Corelli *Treasure of Heaven* 55 The proper way for him to behave at this juncture..would be that he should take her tenderly in his arms and murmur, after the penny-dreadful style of elderly hero, 'My darling'. **1925** T. DREISER *Amer. Trag.* II. III. xix. 222 By him sold to a penny-dreadful publisher of Binghamton. **1941** V. NABOKOV *Real Life S. Knight* x. 91 He did not mind in the least 'penny dreadfuls' because he wasn't concerned with ordinary morals. **1963** *Times* 18 Feb. 5/3 He was perfectly happy with a 'penny dreadful', a warm fire, a friendly dog, and a good meal inside him. **1872** B. JERROLD *London* xv. 127 We have found the penny ice-man doing a brisk trade. *Ibid.*, The penny ice has proved too strong for the ancient ginger-beer bottle. **1896** G. B. SHAW *Our Theatres in Nineties* (1932) II. 133 Some appalling tenor from I know not what limbo of street-piano padrones, penny-icemen, and broken choristers. **1914** —— *Fanny's First Play* 169 You should be eating penny ices and enjoying yourself. **1835** DICKENS *Sk. Boz* (1837) 2nd Ser. 145 When penny magazines shall have superseded penny yards of song. **1852** Penny magazine [see *penny lecture* s.v. PENNY 11]. **1889** J. K. JEROME *Three Men in Boat* xix. 306 We played penny nap after supper. **1950** *Hoyle's Games Modernized* (ed. 20) I. 138 If a man calls three at 'penny Nap', he receives 3d. **1861** *Punch* 5 Jan. 3/1 A weakness for..reading penny novels. **1896** G. B. SHAW *Our Theatres in Nineties* (1932) II. 213 You would never dream of asking why Morris did not read penny novelettes, or hang his rooms with Christmas-number chromolithographs. **1840** *Picayune* (New Orleans) 15 Sept. 2/2 The six-penny journals have latterly grown wise enough to drop the naughty habit in which they used to indulge of swearing at the penny press. **1843** *North Amer. Rev.* Jan. 227 They [*sc.* Dickens's *American Notes*] have been scattered all over the country by the penny press. **1932** T. S. ELIOT *Sel. Essays* VI. 341 Those sections about which readers of the penny press are most ready to excite themselves. **1871** F. KILVERT *Diary* 3 Feb. (1938) I. 301 This evening we had our 4th Penny Reading. The room was fuller than ever. **1907** A. HUXLEY *Let.* 17 Nov. (1969) 26 Mr. Taylor wants to know for his *penny reading*. **1969** *Telegraph* (Brisbane) 25 Mar. 8/4 The provisional school was used for monthly 'penny readings'..at that period. **1976** *Trans. Yorks. Dial. Soc.* LXXVI. 33 Traditions which must go back to 'Sir Gawain' and even 'Beowulf' when the 'oral literature' of 600 A.D. and Victorian 'Penny Readings' may seem to be not all that far apart. **1859** G. A. SALA *Twice round Clock* 11 The river glideth in peace, undisturbed by penny steamboats. **1862** A. J. MUNBY *Diary* 7 May in D. Hudson *Munby* (1972) 121 His enjoyment of the Thames from the deck of a penny steamer. **1933** *Radio Times* 14 Apr. 72/3 The 'penny-steamers', those cheerful launches that trail along behind the [Boat Race] umpires and the B.B.C. **1905** *Daily Chron.* 18 Dec. 4/5 The first gutter penny-toy merchant. **1955** *Times* 11 May 12/4 Penny toys (how many of them could be bought for that coin today?). **1931** N. DOUGLAS *London Street Games* (ed. 2) 29, I went down the lane to buy a penny whistle, A copper came by and pinch my penny whistle. **1967** W. SOYINKA *Kongi's Harvest* 64 Penny whistles blow to the tune of the Carpenter's Song. **1978** W. HJORTSBERG *Falling Angel* (1979) vi. 71 Someone played a pennywhistle. Shrill, piping notes.

12. a. *penny-cautious, -conscious, -grubbing, picking* adjs. **c. penny ante** *U.S.*, the game of poker when the ante is fixed at one penny or a similarly insignificant stake; also *attrib.* or as *adj.*, contemptible, trivial; **penny black,** (a specimen of) the first one-penny postage stamp issued in the United Kingdom, on 6 May 1840; also *fig.*; **penny-boy** *slang* (see quot. 1902); (in quot. 1914, a term of mild contempt); **penny-daisy,** prob. = *ox-eye daisy* (OX-EYE 3b); **penny-in-the-slot** *a.* (earlier and later examples); also *ellipt.* as *sb.*; **penny loafer, pennyloafer** *N. Amer.*, a type of casual shoe with a slot in which coins can be placed; **penny number,** (*a*) a cheap periodical; (*b*) *pl.* insignificant quantities (*colloq.*); **penny packet,** (*a*) = *penny steamer* s.v. PENNY 11; (*b*) a small number of persons or things; (*c*) (with hyphen) *attrib.*, contemptible, insignificant; **penny pawn** (see quot.); **penny-peeler,** an avaricious or niggardly person; **penny-piece** (further examples); **penny-pincher,** a niggardly person; **penny-pinching** *a.* (*colloq.*), niggardly, parsimonious; also as *vbl. sb.*; hence (as a back-formation) *penny-pinch* vb. trans. and intr.; *penny-pinched* adj.; **penny plain** *a.*, plain and unpretentious; hence **penny-plainness; penny stock** *U.S.*, a common stock of value less than one dollar, and therefore highly speculative.

1855 'Q. K. P. DOESTICKS' *Doesticks, what he Says* 259 Napoleon spends most of his time playing penny 'ante' with the three Graces. **1935** A. J. POLLOCK *Underworld Speaks* 87/1 *Penny ante league*, small town racketeers. **1936** L. HELLMAN *Days to Come* III. 88 We always used to play penny-ante there. **1946** *Negro Digest* Aug. 48/1 Compared to the man Bilbo, 63-year-old John Rankin is strictly penny ante and colorless. **1976** M. MACHLIN *Pipeline* v. 63 Prices were offered that made Royal American's earlier bids seem like penny ante. **1976** M. MAGUIRE *Scratchproof* ix. 140 I'm not a penny-ante hood. [**1920** E. D. BACON *Line-Engraved Postage Stamps Gt. Brit.* I. 167 In 1864 an application was made to the Board of Inland Revenue for specimens of the One Penny black.] **1922** A. B. CREEKE in C. Nissen *Plating of Penny Black Postage Stamp* p. i, The cult of the 'Penny Black'—and no true British philatelist is so pedantic as to call the first postage stamp the 'Black Penny'!—has..spread amongst..many collectors. **1936** [see *BLACK *sb.* 7e]. **1972** *Daily Tel.* Colour Suppl.) 12 May 62/1 These are so rare that they are referred to as the Penny Blacks of the cigarette card world. **1973** R. HILL *Ruling Passion* II. ii. 99 'What about the stamps?'..'No penny blacks, I'm afraid.' **1977** *Western Mail* (Cardiff) 5 Mar. (Rugby Suppl.) 7/1 Still, the days when English rugby victories were as rare as the Penny Black seem over. **1902** FARMER & HENLEY *Slang* V. 168/1 *Penny-boy* (old), a boy who haunted the cattle markets on the chance of driving beasts to the slaughter-house. **1914** JOYCE *Dubliners* 273 He saw himself as a ludicrous figure, acting as a pennyboy for his aunts. **1939** DYLAN THOMAS *Let.* July (1966) 233 People forced..to be so penny-cautious. **1964** *Economist* 27 June 1481/2 The penny-conscious President. **1920** D. H. LAWRENCE *Lost Girl* i. 24 Big penny-daisies grew in tufts on the brink of the yellow clay. **1942** *New Statesman* 11 July 25/1 The Jews of Poland, on the whole, I have found penny-grubbing, cunning, and given to circumlocution. **1891** KIPLING *Light that Failed* xiv. 281 They've got one of them penny-in-the-slot cash-machines. **1922** D. H. LAWRENCE *England, my England* 255 I'll just put it aside o' the penny-in-the-slot. **1948** *Training of Doctor* (B.M.A.) xv. 74 The fault lies as frequently with the harried and harassed physician seeking a 'penny in the slot' diagnosis. **1954** L. FAIRFIELD *Epilepsy* i. 23 In spite of the brilliant contributions made by encephalographers to the study of epilepsy, it would be wholly wrong to give the impression that they can provide a 'penny in the slot' diagnosis. **1970** *Daily Tel.* 21 May 6/5 Hoisted on his brother's shoulder, he watches a striptease in a penny-in-the-slot machine at a fair. **1970** *Globe Mag.* (Toronto) 26 Sept. 5/3 Chicks..who aren't really hippie, wear really good jeans... Some have penny loafers. **1973** *Maclean's Mag.* (Toronto) Feb. 28/1 They're classic: he's wearing checkered pants and brogues, she's got a skirt and pennyloafers. **1976** T. GIFFORD *Cavanaugh Quest* (1977) i. 15 Two highly polished penny loafers with virgin tan soles. **1901** G. B. SHAW *Capt. Brassbound's Conversion* III. 297 He got his romantic nonsense out of his penny numbers. **1958** *Listener* 5 June 937/1 Pupils arrive from the depot in penny numbers. **1972** *Shooting Times & Country Mag.* 27 May 12/1 The beats of Spey near Grantown were either returning penny numbers of fish or blanks for hard fishing. *c***1846** J. R. PLANCHÉ *Invisible Prince* I. ii. 14 Fierce whiskered gents, as ever in pea jackets, Smoked bad cigars, on board the penny packets. **1943** HUNT & PRINGLE *Service Slang* 51 *Penny packets*, small parties of soldiers, less than a platoon, as seen from the air. **1961** *Daily Tel.* 21 Apr. 17 Lord Bridges, chairman of the Royal Fine Art Commission, yesterday condemned piecemeal, penny-packet planning of new towns and replanning of older ones. **1979** G. C. PEDEN *Brit. Rearmament* 119 The Treasury principle of locating the Air Force centrally instead of in penny packets around the Empire was observed. **1907** *Westm. Gaz.* 16 Dec. 10/1 What are known as 'penny pawns' abound in the district. A broker who keeps one of these can purchase an article of any value from a penny upwards. He is compelled to keep it for seven full days. **1925** J. GREGORY *Bab of Backwoods* xxi. 269 Willoughby, skinflint, penny-peeler and nickel grabber that he was, smelled a deal and asked them five thousand dollars for ten acres! **1920** D. H. LAWRENCE *Lost Girl* vi. 99 This grubby penny-picking England. **1938** M. K. RAWLINGS *Yearling* ii. 17 Why, you leetle ol' penny piece, you. You're good money, a'right, but hit jest don't come no smaller. Leetle ol' Penny Baxter. **1963** *Times* 25 Apr. 17/1 Coyle, he maintained, did not receive 'a penny piece' in the transactions and his only motive in disposing of the bicycles was to please his immediate superiors. **1975** E. PAGE *Element of Chance* vi. 66 In another three years..you can divorce her without her consent... I very much doubt that..you'd have to pay her a penny piece. **1961** J. YAFFE in *Webster* s.v. *penny-pinch*, A sinister but fascinating kind of joy in..penny-pinching his own family. **1961** S. N. BEHRMAN in *Ibid.*, Penny-pinched himself out of..millions of dollars. **1977** P. G. WINSLOW *Witch Hill Murder* II. v. 92 He penny-pinched on the candles..so the servants had to spend their few hours off in practically pitch darkness. **1979** *Jrnl. R. Soc. Arts* CXXVII. 126/1 The dismally penny-pinched equipment compared with foreign institutions. **1934** WEBSTER, *Penny pincher*, a niggardly or parsimonious person. **1956** F. CASTLE *Violent Hours* (1966) xviii. 174 If Forhaan had really been a penny-pincher, he would never have offered so quickly to pay for Hazel's care. **1967** *Guardian* 22 Feb. 4/7 A sparkling dialectic arose between the risk takers on the boards and the penny pinchers. **1973** 'D. SHANNON' *Spring of Violence* (1974) ix. 150 Typical of the penny-pincher miser. **1905** Penny-pinching [listed in Dict.]. **1920** S. LEWIS *Main St.* xi. 144 The penny-pinching old land-thief. **1951** *Ann. Reg. 1950* 192 Mr Johnson had come under heavy fire as the man whose 'penny-pinching' with military expenditures had paved the way for the reverses in Korea. **1953** C. S. FORESTER *Hornblower & Atropos* xiii. 190 The penny-pinching clerks of a penurious government at home would scrutinize those expenditures in time. **1960** *Guardian* 20 July 6/6 Penny-pinching on new roads is inexcusable. **1971** *Ibid.* 7 Aug. 10/1 Mr Rowley's decision is both penny-pinching and short-sighted. **1973** E. BERCKMAN *Victorian Album* 34 The better-off the woman was, the more apt she'd be to play those penny-pinching tricks. **1977** *Time* 30 May 24/2 Under increasing criticism—from liberals, who regard him as too much of a pennypinching conservative,..Carter took to the hustings again by making a whirlwind, campaign-style tour of California. **1859** G. A. SALA *Twice round Clock* 253 The Scala..with its rabbit-hutch-like private boxes, whose doors are scrawled over with the penny plain and twopence coloured-like coats of arms of the..Lombardian nobility. **1884** R. L. STEVENSON in *Mag. of Art* Apr. 227 (*title*) A penny plain and twopence coloured. **1920** 'O. DOUGLAS' *Penny Plain* vi. 60 Having been all her life so very 'twopence coloured' she wants the 'penny plain' for a change. **1974** 'S. WOODS' *Done to Death* 71 A track led to a penny-plain stone cottage. **1920** 'O. DOUGLAS' *Penny Plain* vi. 60 There is no mistake about our 'penny-plainness'—it jumps to the eye! **1932** C. M. ALSAGER *Dict. Business Terms* 261 *Penny stocks*, a term applied to stocks that sell below one dollar per share and that are usually quoted in cents, not in fractions of a dollar, on an exchange or over the counter. **1935** *Sun* (Baltimore) 25 Oct. 22/1 More often than not..an increased turnover in what Wall Street calls the 'penny stocks' has been a sign that the market is heading toward a reaction. **1942** *Richmond* (Virginia) *Times-Dispatch* 29 Dec. 18/1 Turnover of 1,201,522 shares, propped by belated tax offerings in sizable blocks of 'penny' stocks, was the second largest of the year to date. **1967** *Economist* 28 Oct. 419/1 This is a peculiarly American worry...nowhere else are there so many thousands of 'penny' stocks ripe for speculation.

penny-a-line, *a.* (Later example.)

1930 *Argosy* Apr. 15/2 It's my last bit of freedom before I sink into eternal penny-a-line slavedom.

penny-a-line, *v.* Add: Also *intr.*

1851 MRS. GASKELL *Lett.* (1966) 172, I swore I would penny-a-line and have nothing to do with publishers never no more.

So **pe·nny-a-li·ning** *vbl. sb.* and *ppl. a.*

1850 *Punch* 28 Sept. 140/1 (*heading*) Penny-a-lining under difficulties. **1874** GEO. ELIOT *Let.* 2 Nov. (1956) VI. 87 A penny-a-lining literary affair. *a* **1941** V. WOOLF *Captain's Death Bed* (1950) 10 Penny-a-lining came into fashion. **1946** 'G. ORWELL' *Crit. Ess.* 169 In France, all kinds of petty rats—police officials, penny-a-lining journalists, women who have slept with German soldiers—are hunted down.

pe:nny-a-li·neism. [f. PENNY-A-LINE *a.* + -ISM.] The practice of writing in the inflated style of a penny-a-liner; an instance of such writing.

1854 *Punch* 25 Nov. 208/2 That renowned traveller and Protestant champion [*sc.* the Editor of the *Morning Advertiser*] has accepted the appointment of Regius Professor of Penny-a-lineism. **1890** W. JAMES *Princ. Psychol.* I. ix. 263 The whole genus of penny-a-line-isms and newspaper-reporter's flourishes give illustrations of this.

penny-a-liner. (Further examples.)

1871 [see *CENTURY 3b]. **1889** E. SAMPSON *Tales of Fancy* 22 These effusions were usually written by 'Old Willey', printer, penny-a-liner, and pugilistic scribe. **1930** E. WEEKLEY *Saxo Grammaticus* 12 That type of journalist who used to be rudely called a penny-a-liner. **1947** W. S. MAUGHAM *Creatures of Circumstance* 9 He wouldn't have liked it if some damned penny-a-liner had made fun of Evie's effort in one of the papers.

pe·nny-a-wee·k, *a.* [The phrase (*a*) *penny a week* used attrib.] That collects, receives, or subscribes a penny a week.

1895 G. B. SHAW *Let.* 15 Dec. (1965) I. 576 Penny-a-week men enrolled on the spur of the moment. **1914** JOYCE *Dubliners* 206 Many a good man went to the penny-a-week school. **1943** *Times* (Weekly ed.) 19 May 3 The Red Cross and St. John Fund has exceeded £20,000,000... More than one fourth has been contributed through the penny-a-week committee. **1972** *Evening Telegram* (St. John's, Newfoundland) 5 Aug. 6/5 A school in the upstairs flat, the famed 'Penny-a-week' school.

penny farthing, *a.* and *sb.* **A.** *adj.* Ineffective; insignificant.

1887 KIPLING *Plain Tales from Hills* (1888) 78 It was pleasant to watch her unhappiness, and the penny-farthing attempts she made to hide it. **1967** S. BECKETT *Eh Joe* 17 You know that penny farthing hell you call your mind. *a***1974** R. CROSSMAN *Diaries* (1976) II. 60 Harold Wilson's penny-farthing report on the scandals of Party organization had come out long before the 1959 election. **1977** J. WAINWRIGHT *Day of Peppercorn Kill* 68, I.. kicked hell out of every penny-farthing crook I could lay my hands on.

B. *sb.* An early form of bicycle having a large front wheel and a small rear one. Also *attrib.*

This kind of bicycle was introduced in the 1860s and was known by various names, including *ordinary* (see ORDINARY *sb.* 17b), *bone-shaker* (see BONE *sb.* 17) for the wooden-wheeled machine, and BICYCLE for the wire-spoke machine. The name *penny farthing* does not seem to have been used until the 1920s, by which time this type of bicycle was obsolete.

1927 LD. BIRKENHEAD in *Sunday Express* 6 Nov. 11/6, I once rode more or less continuously on a high bicycle (called a 'penny farthing') from my native town of Birkenhead to Edinburgh. **1932** G. M. BOUMPHREY *Story of Wheel* xxiv. 89 These improvements had turned the bone-shaker into what was sometimes called the 'penny-farthing'. **1963** *Times* 20 May 11/1 To do without it would be like giving up our helicopters and going back to penny-farthings. **1976** *Country Life* 27 May 1385/1 Nostalgia for a world..of Norfolk jackets, muttonchop whiskers, penny-farthing bicycles.

pe·nnyweighter. *U.S. criminal slang.* Also **penny weighter, penny-weighter.** [f. PENNYWEIGHT + -ER[1].] One who steals jewellery or precious stones or metals.

1899 'J. FLYNT' *Tramping with Tramps* IV. 396 *Pennyweighters*, jewelry thieves. **1905** *Daily News* 26 July 9 In the American description of her she was said to be a 'penny weighter'... That is, one who goes into a jeweller's shop, inspects jewellery, and by means of some sticky substance on the fingers, manages to palm an article, and deposits it beneath the counter for a confederate to pick up. **1916** [see *HEEL *sb.*[3]]. **1935** *Amer. Speech* X. 19/1 *Pennyweighter*, one who steals gold or silver plate. Still survives in mining camps to designate one who steals very small quantities of gold, as opposed to a high-grader who appropriates any big nuggets which he sees in the sluice boxes. Present usage restricts it to a jewel thief, or a jeweler who substitutes paste gems for genuine ones. **1950** H. E. GOLDIN *Dict. Amer. Underworld Lingo* 155/1 *Penny-weighter*, a thief who specializes in stealing uncut and unset diamonds.

So **pe·nny-weighting** *vbl. sb.*
1903 H. HAPGOOD *Autobiogr. Thief* iii. 56 Penny-weighting is very 'slick' graft... A man..enters a jewelry store and looks at some diamond rings... Then he goes to a fauny shop (imitation jewelry) and buys a few diamonds which match the real ones he has noted. Then he and his pal, usually a woman, enter the jewelry store and..one of them..substitutes the bogus diamonds for the good ones. **1924** G. S. DOUGHERTY *Criminal as Human Being* iii. 89 Such a performance is sometimes staged in 'penny-weighting', but..only a single article can be taken by substitution.

pennywinkle, dial. var. PERIWINKLE².

Penobscot (penǫ·bskǫt), *sb.* and *a.* Also **Penobscote.** [Native name: see F. W. Hodge *Handbk. Amer. Indians North of Mexico* II. 226.] **A.** *sb.* An Algonquian Indian people of the valley of the Penobscot River in Maine, U.S.A.; also, a member of this people.
[**1616** J. SMITH *Descr. New Eng.* 8 The principall habitation Northward we were at, was Pennobscot.. though most [Indian peoples] be Lords of themselues, yet they hold the Bashabes of Pennobscot, the chiefe and greatest amongst them.] **1624** —— *Gen. Hist. Virginia* VI. 240 The Masachusets call their great God Kiehtan, and their Kings there abouts Sachems: The Penobscotes their greatest power Tantum, and their Kings Sagomos. **1713** in *Maine Hist. Soc. Coll.* (1859) VI. 253 In Witness whereof, We,..by name, Kireberuit, Iteansis, and Jackoit, for Penobscot,..have hereunto set our hands & seals. **1910** F. W. HODGE *Handbk. Amer. Indians* II. 226/2 The Penobscot took an active part in all the wars on the New England frontier up to 1749, when they made a treaty of peace, and have remained quiet ever since. **1942** *Fading Trails* (U.S. Dept. Interior Nat. Park Service) vii. 59 Many an aged Penobscot..still wistfully awaits the day when the..peculiar 'click-click' of caribou's feet will resound once more in the frosty air of the muskeg. **1959** E. TUNIS *Indians* 25/2 The Penobscots kept certain of their young men in strict training for running down deer! **1965** *Canad. Jrnl. Linguistics* Spring 135 There are some Algonquian Indians still living along the New England coast,..but except for a few older Penobscot, all speak English. **1974** *Encycl. Brit. Micropædia* VII. 855/1 The Penobscot assisted the French against the English in all the wars on the New England frontier until 1749, when they made peace with the English.
b. The language spoken by the Penobscot people.
1891 J. C. PILLING *Bibliogr. Algonquian Lang.* 110/2 A short catechism in Penobscot begins on page 47. *Ibid.* 199/1 Comparative vocabulary..in the..Penobscot. **1902** [see *ANIMATE *ppl. a.* 4 b]. **1933** L. BLOOMFIELD *Language* 72 The *Algonquian* family..includes the languages..of New England (*Penobscot*..). **1972** *Regional Lang. Stud.—Newfoundland* IV. 2 Penobscot, a dialect closely related to Abenaki.
B. *adj.* Of or pertaining to the Penobscot people or their language.
1727 J. HEATH *Let.* 7 July in *Maine Hist. Soc. Coll.* (1853) III. 409 If Capt. Gyles..can steer the Penobscot Indians to Falmouth, it seems as though these may follow. **1779** S. LOVELL *Orig. Jrnl. Penobscot Exped.* (1881) 97 We are visited by some Penobscot Indians who are determined to proceed with us. **1819** *N. Amer. Rev.* IX. 185 A specimen of the Penobscot dialect (which we obtained from a friend in the District of Maine). **1831** *Boston Even. Transcript* 7 Oct. 1/2 Last week, a wretched and destitute Penobscot Indian was seen traversing our streets. **1854** THOREAU *Walden* 32, I have seen Penobscot Indians, in this town, living in tents of thin cotton cloth. **1893** *Chicago Tribune* 3 July 1/3 The Penobscot tribe of Indians is represented now by ten members from Old Town, Maine. **1973** A. H. WHITEFORD *N. Amer. Indian Arts* 91 Northeastern beadwork is lacy, as shown by the Penobscot collar. **1976** *Time* 27 Dec. 25/2 In Maine, the Passamaquoddy and Penobscot tribes have laid claim to 2.5 million acres of land—two-thirds of the state.

pen-pal (pe·npæl). orig. *U.S.* [f. PEN *sb.*² + PAL *sb.*¹] = *PEN-FRIEND. Hence **penpalmanship, penpalship,** the relationship existing between pen-pals.
1938 *Educational Method* Nov. 83/1 Mary Jones of Portland, Maine, has just requested the Student Letter Exchange of Waseca, Minnesota, to supply her with the name of a 'pen pal' in Mexico City. *Ibid.*, Since its inception in July, 1936, the Student Letter Exchange has provided hundreds of thousands of 'pen pals' around the world. **1941** J. C. FURNAS *How Amer. Lives* 272 Pen-pals are not the only piece of news for the writer in the Kriebel boys' mail. **1960** *20th Cent.* June 517 There are some rather elaborate plans for forming relationships with individual Alphas, on the lines of the children's pen palships in the twentieth-century newspapers. *Ibid.*, You need to be young and so does your pen pal for this type of correspondence. **1962** J. KIRKUP tr. *Brunner's Trouble in Brusada* iii. 26 The girls..had written..to a school class in Zurich with which they regularly corresponded, and..their pen-pals would help them to bear the cost. **1966** *Guardian* 9 June 8/1 The affair was carried on entirely by correspondence... Their penpalmanship had already begun. **1967** *Boston Herald* 1 Apr. 22/6 The children at the Dedham Country Day School are pen pals of children in Dedham, England. They've exchanged Christmas presents and a few have even visited families over there. **1972** M. MEAD *Blackberry Winter* vii. 81, I also had two pen pals whose names I got through *St. Nicholas Magazine.* **1972** C. SHORT *Naked Skier* xxii. 123 Maybe we could be pen-pals... I'll send you a postcard from New York. **1974** 'P. B. YUILL' *Hazell plays Solomon* ii. 25 'Why pay top money for information and a photograph of a child whose surname they don't know?' 'Perhaps they want a penpal?'

pen-pusher (pe·npuːʃəɪ). [f. PEN *sb.*² + PUSHER.] One who is engaged in writing or desk work; a clerk; a writer (freq. derogatory).
1911 *Busy Man's Mag.* Jan. 65/2 That fellow was a pen-pusher in a dough joint—I mean a bank clerk. **1930** *Time & Tide* 24 May 663/2 Clerking! My God, any tuppenny ha'penny pen-pusher can be a clerk. **1940** *Manch. Guardian Weekly* 22 Mar. 228 From his point of view it is much better to be a pen-pusher in..obscurity than a corpse. **1948** 'N. SHUTE' *No Highway* vii. 173 Who the hell are you, anyway? Just a bloody penpusher. **1952** A. GRIMBLE *Pattern of Islands* 177, I do not suppose that George was particularly interested in Stevenson as a writing man—he never had much time for pen-pushers, as he called them. **1954** WODEHOUSE *Jeeves & Feudal Spirit* ix. 80 Florence tells me that La Morehead is one of the more costly of our female pen-pushers and has to have purses of gold flung to her in great profusion before she will sign on the dotted line. **1957** J. BRAINE *Room at Top* iii. 31, I saw myself, compared with him, as the Town Hall Clerk, the subordinate pen-pusher, halfway to being a zombie, and I tasted the sourness of envy. **1972** *Guardian* 23 Oct. 9/3 The more assiduous pen-pushers among London Transport's 6,000 administrative, technical, clerical and control staff.
So **pe·n-pushing** *vbl. sb.*, writing by hand.
1936 'G. ORWELL' *Keep Aspidistra Flying* iii. 61 He dreaded..going to work... Pen-pushing in some filthy office—God! **1952** A. GRIMBLE *Pattern of Islands* 179, I knew that Charles Workman would have made a better job of the pen-pushing than I did. **1972** W. A. PANTIN *Oxf. Life* iv. 53 These volumes represent a great mass of praiseworthy industry.., whether pen-pushing or type-writer-bashing.

penroseite (pe·nrōᵘzəit). *Min.* [f. the name of Richard A. F. *Penrose*, Jr. (1863–1931), U.S. mining geologist + -ITE¹.] A selenide of nickel, ideally $NiSe_2$, which usu. also contains copper, lead, or silver, probably as impurities, and occurs in grey reniform masses.
1926 S. G. GORDON in *Proc. Acad. Nat. Sci. Philadelphia* LXXVII. 317 Penroseite was obtained in a small collection of minerals which the writer purchased from a local merchant at Colquechaca, Bolivia. *Ibid.* 321 It is a pleasure to name this new mineral in honor of Dr. Richard A. F. Penrose, Jr. **1937** *Amer. Mineralogist* XXII. 322 The minerals most likely to be intergrown with penroseite and blockite are cubic in symmetry, such as clausthalite,.., naumannite.., and argentiferous galena. *Ibid.*, Penroseite and blockite may therefore be regarded as identical minerals and the latter name may be discarded. **1968** I. KOSTOV *Mineral.* 124 Penroseite usually contains some copper and cobalt.

‖**pensiero** (pensiē·ro). Pl. **pensieri.** [It.] A thought, an idea; an anxiety. *spec.* in Art, a sketch.
1909 JOYCE *Let.* 7 Sept. (1966) II. 231, I am dreadfully nervous from all the worry and *pensieri* I have had, very very nervous indeed. **1959** *Times* 2 Oct. 5/6 Most of the drawings are *pensieri.* **1961** M. LEVY *Studio Dict. Art Terms* 85 *Pensiero*, an alternative term for a Sketch. **1975** *Times Lit. Suppl.* 4 Apr. 378/5 Each artist was supplied with a design, or *pensiero*, which laid down the pose, proportions and drapery pattern of the statue.

pension, *sb.* Add: **9.** (sense 4) *pension act, benefit, book* (later examples), *fund, law* (example), *money* (later examples), *plan, right, roll* (further examples), *scheme.*
The pl. form *pensions* also occurs in some of the above expressions.
1839 *Southern Lit. Messenger* V. 314/1 A few tardy pension acts..are all the tributes their worth has received. **1968** G. D. GILLING-SMITH *Compl. Guide Pensions* (ed. 2) i. 16 The 1908 Old Age Pensions Act provided a small amount for those who were already old and unable to provide for themselves. **1945** *Release & Resettlement* (H.M. Govt.) xii. 40 Pensions benefits comprise pensions for widows..and orphans, and old age pensions. **1966** *Listener* 17 Mar. 391/2 One result of having this new unified social security administration will be that the pensions book and the National Assistance book..will become one book. **1968** 'C. AIRD' *Henrietta Who?* ix. 77 Did you ever see your mother's pension book? **1974** *Times* 6 Mar. 4/3 A child's printing outfit was used in a scheme to cash stolen pension books with a face value of more than £750,000. **1869** *Bradshaw's Railway Manual* XXI. 361 Donation to the pension fund, 18,573*l.* **1907** G. B. SHAW *Major Barbara* III. 269 Have you gone into the insurance fund, the pension fund, the building society, the various applications of co-operation!? **1965** H. I. ANSOFF *Corporate Strategy* (1968) vi. 104 At the other extreme from a fully integrated firm is a company which primarily buys and sells. This may be an investment trust, a pension fund. **1973** A. BEHREND *Samarai Affair* iv. 51 'Will the Company look after him?' 'I suppose so. Their pension fund's all right.' **1976** *New Yorker* 15 Nov. 176/2 In addition to making contract concessions, the union members, through their pension funds..have become the city's bankers, lending it nearly two billion dollars in the past year. **1838** *Southern Lit. Messenger* IV. 766 When the revolutionary pension-law was enacted, a majority of the war-worn veterans had travelled..beyond the reach of human reward. **1749** *New Hamps. Probate Rec.* (1916) III. 733, I give..all my Waidges Prize money Pention money [etc.]. **1854** B. P. SHILLABER *Life & Sayings Mrs. Partington* 190 The old lady had presented a check for a quarter's pension-money. **1953** *Stroud's Judicial Dict.* (ed. 3) III. 2143 Pension money reduced into possession by the pensioner or his agent loses its character of pension. **1957** CLARK & GOTTFRIED *Dict. Business & Finance* 262/1 *Pension plan*, in business, a plan established and maintained by an employer to provide in a systematic manner for the payment of regular pension amounts to retired or disabled employees. **1961** *Factory* Nov. 101/1 Choose carefully between contributory or non-contributory pension plans. **1973** *N.Y. Law Jrnl.* 31 Aug. 2/4 (Advt.), Metropolitan Life can help you set up a pension plan that will entitle you to the same Federal Income Tax deductions available to other corporations. **1956** G. A. HOSKING *Pension Schemes* xli. 283 The existence of a pension scheme acts as a deterrent when withdrawal means loss of pension rights. **1974** O. MANNING *Rain Forest* I. vi. 87 Temporary and without pension rights, the appointment carried a special salary. **1828** A. SHERBURNE *Mem.* vi. 239 This gentleman..forwarded to me certificates of the continuation of my name on the pension roll. **1907** *Westm. Gaz.* 5 Apr. 10/1 Miss Robb..was the posthumous child of Captain Robb, ..and was put on the State pension-roll at birth. **1892** C. S. LOCH *Old Age Pensions & Pauperism* 3 The returns of pauperism in England and Wales are frequently quoted as absolute evidence in favour of some kind of National Pension Scheme. **1928** ROBERTSON & SAMUELS *Pension & Superannuation Funds* viii. 79 Pension schemes are growing up not only in industry proper; many institutions..have their own schemes of superannuating those in their service. **1969** T. PARKER *Twisting Lane* 16, I was in a good pension scheme too. **1973** L. HOLCOMBE *Victorian Ladies at Work* iii. 39 The government in 1875 revived its original teacher's pension scheme, established in 1846 but abolished in 1861. **1977** W. MCILVANNEY *Laidlaw* xxx. 140 He's worried about his family... They don't have a great pension-scheme for house-breakers.

pension, *v.* Add: **2.** *to pension off* (earlier and later examples). Also *fig.* So *pensioned-off* ppl. a.
1848 GEO. ELIOT *Let.* 8 Mar. (1954) I. 254 Certainly our decayed monarchs should be pensioned off. **1880** G. MEREDITH *Let.* 27 Apr. (1970) II. 595 Owing to the attack I suffered under last year, I have been pensioned off all work of any worth of late. **1898** G. B. SHAW *Let.* 1 Sept. (1972) II. 60 My mother and I had to pension off and get rid of a relative of hers—a woman who was an incorrigible drunkard. **1916** —— *Androcles & Lion* Pref. p. lxvi, Poor people are cancers in the commonwealth, costing far more than if they were handsomely pensioned off as incurables. *a* **1953** E. O'NEILL *More Stately Mansions* (1965) III. i. 154 We'll pension off your mother, and give her the house to live alone in. **1965** D. FRANCIS *Odds Against* xi. 154, I..asked him to lend me his hack, a pensioned-off old steeplechaser. **1968** *Listener* 5 Sept. 290 The convention system..is an old and cunning harridan, as irrelevant as Mayor Daley, and should be pensioned off. **1973** C. BONINGTON *Next Horizon* ix. 131 Gone was the crusty old pensioned-off guide, who lived in a little cubby-hole at the end of the..living room. **1973** *Times* 14 July 8/8 What the BBC publication seems to me to need is the attention of a first-class design consultant who might suggest for example that the rule which, like a rectangular noose, strangles each page, should be pensioned off. **1974** J. CLEARY *Peter's Pence* v. 144 Cork had had no gangsters, just some pensioned-off IRA boys. **1977** *R.A.F. News* 11–24 May 18/5 This is my last match report before being pensioned off.

pensionable, *a.* Add: **a.** (Further examples.)
1906 *Westm. Gaz.* 25 Jan. 4/2 There is nothing radically pensionable about old age; grey hairs are not in themselves a claim on society. **1920** *Act* 10 & 11 *Geo. V* c. 67 Sched. VIII. 4 This provision shall apply to the pensionable assistants of the petty sessions clerks at Cork and Belfast.
b. (Further examples.)
1908 *Daily Chron.* 9 Jan. 6/7 They will have the ultimate prospect..of appointment to permanent and pensionable establishments of the Protectorate. **1945** *Release & Resettlement* (H.M. Govt.) xiii. 45 If..you require..treatment on account of the pensionable disablement, such treatment will be provided. **1955** *Times* 13 Aug. 6/6 The Civil Service is to offer pensionable jobs to men and women aged between 40 and 60. **1976** *Ulverston* (Cumbria) *News* 3 Dec. 9/4 (Advt.), The post is pensionable with promotion prospects to Executive Officer grades and above.
c. Related to, connected with, or affecting a person's pension.
1909 *Westm. Gaz.* 8 Feb. 8/3 Saturday's deputation asked for the recognition of colour service in the Forces for pensionable purposes when they reached the age of sixty. **1920** *Act* 10 & 11 *Geo. V* c. 67 Sched. IX, The allowance awarded..shall in no case exceed two-thirds of his actual pensionable salary. **1970** *Money Which?* Mar. 55/1 If, as well as being self-employed, you have an additional job in which you are employed (i.e. one providing you with some pensionable earnings) the £750 limit will be reduced.
Hence **pensionabi·lity**, entitlement to a pension.
1930 *Times Educ. Suppl.* 24 May 235/4 Sick leave privileges, and pensionability. *a*1966 'M. NA GOPALEEN' *Best of Myles* (1968) 300 Pensionability of entire local populations in respect of military service, notwithstanding international convention as to non-combatancy of juveniles, children and women.

‖**pensione** (pensiō·ne). [It.] In Italy, a small hotel or boarding house.
1938 E. AMBLER *Cause for Alarm* v. 85, I must make a real effort to find a *pensione.* **1957** R. MACAULAY *Last Lett. to Friend* (1962) 252 We stayed in a small and pleasant *pensione* on the Giudecca Canal. **1967** R. SAWKINS *Snow in Paradise* ii. 23 He lived for a while at a *pensione* round the corner. **1969** R. AIRTH *Snatch!* iv. 30 We got to this *pensione* off Via Margutta. **1975** C. MOTT-RADCLYFFE *Foreign Body* ii. 27 They lived in a *pensione* nearby.

pensioneer (pe:nʃənīə·ɹ), *v.* [f. PENSION *sb.* + -EER, after ELECTIONEER *v.*] To bid for votes in an election by promising higher pensions. Hence **pe:nsionee·ring** *vbl. sb.*

1959 *Daily Tel.* 9 June 17/4 The word 'pensioneering'.. has recently been added to the political vocabulary... 'Pensioner, you can't trust the Labour Party. They are simply pensioneering, trying to buy your votes on a promise of 10s.' **1960** *Times* 24 Oct. (Financial Rev.) p. xiii/3 That the paradox of comparative insecurity in the midst of affluence is a disturbing thing..has become apparent in the political field..in the shape of competitive 'pensioneering'. **1963** *Times* 23 Jan. 11/7 As the number of pensioners who could not recover financially from the great depression of the 1930's falls away, what *The Times* called 'pensioneering' becomes politically less productive. *a* **1974** R. CROSSMAN *Diaries* (1975) I. 276 Under cross-examination they got into a horrible mess and confirmed my fear that the whole strategy of our pensioneering, worked out for years before the election, had been jettisoned almost without noticing it by the Minister under the *diktat* of Douglas Houghton.

pensionless, *a.* (Later examples.)

1969 *Guardian* 22 Oct. 10/6 If your husband dies before you are 50, and you have no children, you are thrown pensionless into a hard world. **1974** 'R. TATE' *Birds of Bloodied Feather* iii. 74 Pensionless, I looked round for a job.

‖**pensionnat** (pãńsyona). [Fr.] **a.** In France and other European countries, a boarding-school. **b.** = PENSION *sb.* 6b.

1840 J. R. HOPE-SCOTT in R. Ornsby *Mem.* (1884) I. xiii. 247 Their pupils [in Germany] might come to their classes, but at night they go home, and in their pensionnats..it was impossible to prevent the parents coming every fifteen days or so. **1853** C. BRONTË *Villette* I. vii. 121 As I spoke English, she concluded I was a foreign teacher come on business connected with the Pensionnat. **1867** J. A. SYMONDS *Let.* 26 Sept. (1967) I. 761 We do not see very much of other Pensionnats. They are formed chiefly of Germans, Russians & Americans. **1896** C. SHORTER *C. Brontë & her Circle* iv. 100 The girls were day boarders at the Pensionnat. **1933** *Times Lit. Suppl.* 28 Sept. 653/1 A mildly amusing story in mildly bad taste about a *pensionnat* in Switzerland. **1963** *Listener* 10 Jan. 73/1 There are increasing numbers of hotels..called *pensionnats*. These differ from regular hotels in providing only the bare facilities of rooms and meals. **1967** R. PETRIE *Foreign Bodies* ii. 27 'Then this house is a *pension*? A boarding establishment?.. And not, definitely not, a *pensionnat*?'.. 'Ah, Monsieur..we are a boarding-house, not a boarding-school.' **1972** A. CHRISTIE *Elephants can Remember* v. 78 They had children... A boy at school in England and a girl at a *pensionnat* in Switzerland.

penstock[1]. Add: **2.** For *U.S.* read 'Orig. and chiefly *U.S.*' and add earlier and later examples.

1799 *Trans. Amer. Philos. Soc.* IV. 349 Let ABCD Fig. 1 represent a large cistern or penstock, and MKLN an orifice made in one of its sides. **1933** *Discovery* Apr. 110/2 The station is several miles below Niagara Falls, the water being led to the 'pen-stocks' (the tubes which guide the water to the turbines) by means of a concrete canal from a point above the falls. **1955** *Times* 14 May 13/1 With the expected completion in 1955 of a modern wood-handling system and major repairs to its older penstocks, the company will have reached the end of the rehabilitation programme. **1963** *Weekly News* (Auckland) 21 Aug. 27 Six parallel penstocks made from prestressed concrete will carry the water from Lake Benmore. **1965** E. L. MYLES *Emperor of Peace River* I. xiii. 135 They whip-sawed lumber for the roof and the penstock flue [of a water mill].

penta-. Add: **pe:ntachlor(o)e·thane** *Chem.*, a colourless liquid, C_2HCl_5, that is an intermediate in the industrial production of certain chlorinated hydrocarbons and is used as a solvent; **pe:ntachlor(o)phe·nate** *Chem.*, a salt of pentachlorophenol, esp. sodium pentachlorophenate, C_6Cl_5ONa, a white crystalline solid; **pe:ntachlor(o)phe·nol** *Chem.*, a colourless, crystalline solid with acidic properties, C_6Cl_5OH, which is widely used (often as its sodium salt) in insecticides, fungicides, weed-killers, wood preservatives, etc.; **pentacyclic** *a.*, (*b*) *Chem.*, containing five rings in the molecule; **pentaga·strin** *Pharm.*, a synthetic pentapeptide having the same action as the hormone gastrin; **pentahy·drate,** a hydrate that contains five molecules of water in each molecule; so **pe:ntahydra·ted** *a.*; **pentahy·dric** *a. Chem.*, containing five hydroxyl groups in a molecule; **pentahy·drite** *Min.*, native magnesium sulphate pentahydrate, $MgSO_45H_2O$; **pe:ntahydrobo·rite** *Min.* [ad. Russ. *pentagidroborit* (S. V. Malinko 1961, in *Zapiski Vsesoyuz. Min. Obshchesvta* XC. 673)], a hydrated calcium borate, $CaB_2O_4.5H_2O$, occurring as small, colourless triclinic crystals; **pe:ntahydroca·lcite** *Min.* [ad. Russ. *pentagidrokal'tsit"* (P. N. Chirvinskiĭ 1906, in *Ezhegodnik" po Geol. i Mineral. Rossīi* VIII. 241)], a pentahydrate of calcium carbonate, $CaCO_3.5H_2O$, the natural occurrence of which is uncertain; **pe·ntamer** *Chem.* [*-MER], a polymeric unit or molecule made up of five monomers; hence **pentame·ric** *a.*; † **penta·meride** *Chem.* [after ISOMERIDE] = **pentamer*; **pentame·thylene** *Chem.*, (*a*) a cyclic hydrocarbon, C_5H_{10}, usu. called cyclopentane, which is a colourless volatile liquid found in petroleum; (*b*) the bivalent straight chain radical $—(CH_2)_5—$; **pentame:thylenediamine** (-dəiˌæ·mīn) *Chem.*, a syrupy, fuming liquid, $H_2N(CH_2)_5NH_2$, now usu. called cadaverine, which is a product of the putrefaction of animal proteins; **pentanu·cleotide** *Biochem.*, an oligonucleotide in which the number of nucleotides is five; **pentape·ptide** *Biochem.*, an oligopeptide in which there are five amino-acid residues in the molecule.

1872 *Jrnl. Chem. Soc.* XXV 232 (*heading*) Action of bromine on pentachlorethane. **1930** T. H. DURRANS *Solvents* vii. 119 The following azeotropic mixture is known: Pentachlorethane 85%, glycol 15%, B.P. 154.5°. **1975** *Internat. Jrnl. Chem. Kinetics* VII. 331 The rate of the inhibited pyrolysis of pentachloroethane was studied over the temperature range of 820 to 865°K using the toluene-carrier technique in a stirred-flow reactor. **1938** *Jrnl. Rubber Res. Inst. Malaya* VIII. 325 The material used in the trials..consists of sodium pentachlorphenate and is known by the trade names of 'Santophen 20 S' or 'Santobrite'. **1959** *Times* 24 Sept. 7/2 (Advt.), The most effective chemical for preventing sapstain is Santobrite, Monsanto's sodium pentachlorophenate. **1971** F. C. FORD-ROBERTSON *Terminol. Forest Sci.* 190/1 Its sodium salt (Na pentachlor(o)phenate) is water soluble and is used for preventing fungal stain and surface mould in unseasoned timber and in eradicating dry rot from buildings. **1879** *Jrnl. Chem. Soc.* XXXVI. 463 When heated at 230° with alcohol it [*sc.* perchlorophenol chloride, C_6Cl_7OH] yields pentachlorophenol, C_6Cl_5OH (m.p. 183–184°). **1960** E. L. DELMAR-MORGAN *Cruising Yacht Equipment & Navigation* xxiv. 231 Rotproofing... Lauryl pentachlor phenol..is colourless, odourless, and very effective, and is available in an emulsion or solution form. **1972** *Timber Trades Jrnl.* 3 June 44/1 The formulation is based upon the independently established fungicides tributyl tin oxide and pentachlorophenol. **1977** *Time* 4 Apr. 56/3 They discovered that cattle in his herd, and those on at least seven other farms in the state, have been ingesting a wood preservative called pentachlorophenol (PCP)—probably when the animals licked the sides of their feed bins. **1899** *Jrnl. Chem. Soc.* LXXVI. I. 742 It is one of the first cases observed of the conversion of a pentacyclic into a hexacyclic carbon compound. **1972** *Science* 16 June 1230/1 *Tetrahymena*..contains a pentacyclic triterpenoid which has not been found in other animals. **1967** *Lancet* 11 Feb. 291/1 (*heading*) Pentagastrin as a stimulant of maximal gastric acid response in man. **1970** PASSMORE & ROBSON *Compan. Med. Stud.* II. x. 3/1 For gastric function studies, pentagastrin has the important advantage over histamine in having no circulatory effects. **1974** *Nature* 15 Mar. 238/2 Because changes in fundic mucosal cGMP could result from release of the hormone gastrin from the antrum in response to vagal stimulation, the effect of pentagastrin in concentration sufficient to produce acid secretion.. was tested. **1916** *Amer. Jrnl. Sci.* CXCI. 493 It is claimed that crystals of hydrated carbonate have been found in wells and pumps. [*Note*] F. Pfeiffer..who considered them to be pentahydrate. **1975** *Nature* 28 Aug. 718/2 Hydrated offretite..contains a K ion in each cancrinite cage, a pentahydrate of Mg in each gmelinite cage, and hydrated Ca ions in the main channels. **1851** H. WATTS tr. *Gmelin's Hand-bk. Chem.* V. 430 Penta-hydrated.—The ordinary form of cupric sulphate. **1951** C. PALACHE et al. *Dana's Syst. Min.* (ed. 7) II. 487 Chalcanthite and the not well-established minerals pentahydrite and siderotil are isostructural with a number of artificial salts variously including the pentahydrated sulfates and selenates of Mn, Co, Cu, Zn. **1892** *Jrnl. Chem. Soc.* LXII. 29 Xylitol is..an open-chain pentahydric alcohol, of which xylose is the aldehyde. **1952** J. K. N. JONES in E. H. Rodd *Chem. Carbon Compounds* IB. xix. 1197 Two pentahydric alcohols, adonitol (ribitol) and D-arabitol occur in nature. **1968** J. A. MONICK *Alcohols* v. 426 Ribitol..is a crystalline, 5-carbon pentahydric alcohol. **1951** C. PALACHE et al. *Dana's Syst. Min.* (ed. 7) II. 492 Pentahydrite *Frondel* (priv. comm., 1948). **1972** *Acta Crystallogr.* XXVIII. B. 1448/2 Magnesium sulfate pentahydrate has even been reported..to occur as a mineral (pentahydrite). **1962** *Amer. Mineralogist* XLVII. 1482 (*heading*) New boron minerals—uralborite and pentahydroborite. **1971** [see *NIFONTOVITE]. **1973** *Soviet Physics: Doklady* XVIII. 102/1 Pentahydroborite is the final member in the series of natural water-containing metaborates of calcium, all members of which are characterized by a constant ratio of $CaO:B_2O_3$ = 1:1 with the water content increasing from korzhinskite to pentahydroborite. **1910** *Mineral. Mag.* XV. 427 Pentahydrocalcite... Hydrated calcium carbonate, $CaCO_3.5H_2O$, occurring as a mould-like encrustation on chalk-marl near Nova-Alexandria, govt. Lublin, Russian Poland. **1928** *Ann. Rep. Progr. Chem.* XXIV. 308 The minerals hydroconite, hydrocalcite (trihydrocalcite, pentahydrocalcite), and lublinite periodically come to be regarded as doubtful minerals, because when re-examined on museum material they are found to be merely calcite. **1957** G. E. HUTCHINSON *Treat. Limnol.* I. x. 660 The deposition of hydrates, supposedly $CaCO_3.3H_2O$, trihydrocalcite, and $CaCO_3.5H_2O$, pentahydrocalcite, in nature has been recorded. **1968** I. KOSTOV *Mineral.* 531 Trihydrocalcite..and pentahydrocalcite..are unstable and easily change into calcite. **1929** *Chem. Abstr.* XXIII. 3213 From the MeOH ppt. were obtained another 2 g. of the pentamer and 6, 4, and 6g. of the hexa-, hepta- and octamers resp. **1955** *Jrnl. Polymer Sci.* XVI. 455 The ACA monomer, a considerable part of the linear oligomers up to approximately the pentamer..and a small portion of the sparingly soluble cyclic oligomers dissolve. **1971** *Nature* 30 July 297/3 Thus electron microscopy has shown macroglobulin (immunoglobulin M) to consist of a cyclic pentamer of γG-like (7S) subunits. **1940** Pentameric [see *hexameric* adj. s.v. *HEXA-]. **1971** *Nature* 11 June 361/1 Only the monomer 'IgMs' could be detected inside the cell and only pentameric IgM outside. **1940** *Jrnl. Chem. Soc.* 1171 When the proportion of sulphuric acid in the Bertram-Walbaum reagent was 1–1·8% the yield of polymerides was: dimeride, 29·0; trimeride, 19·5; tetrameride, 18·4; pentameride, 15; higher polymerides, 17%. **1887** *Ibid.* LI. 241 This acid is the orthodicarboxylic acid of pentamethylene, corresponding with phthalic acid of the benzene series. **1909** C. A. KEANE *Mod. Org. Chem* v. 63 The simplest cyclic compounds containing four and five carbon atoms are the hydrocarbons tetramethylene, C_4C_8, and pentamethylene, C_5H_{10}. **1929** I. W. D. HACKH *Chem. Dict.* (1930) 538/1 *Pentamethylene*, the bivalent radical $—CH_2(CH_2)_3CH_2—$. **1946** E. G. ROCHOW *Introd. Chem. Silicones* iii. 48 Those pentamethylene groups which are joined to two different silicon atoms form organosilicon polymers resembling those obtained with phenylene groups. **1951** I. L. FINAR *Org. Chem.* I. xi. 203 Pentamethylene glycol (pentane-1:5-diol), $CH_2OH·(CH_2)_3·CH_2OH$,..can be obtained from pentamethylene bromide. **1958** *Nomencl. Org. Chem.* (I.U.P.A.C.) A. 16 Pentamethylene $—CH_2—CH_2—CH_2—CH_2—CH_2—$. **1883** *Jrnl. Chem. Soc.* XLIV. 910 Pentamethylenediamine, $C_5H_{10}(NH_2)_2$ is produced by the action of zinc and hydrochloric acid on an ethereal solution of trimethylene dicyanide. **1964** N. G. CLARK *Mod. Org. Chem.* xii. 247 Some [aliphatic diamines] occur in nature as a result of bacterial decomposition of proteins; for example,.. cadaverine (pentamethylenediamine). **1931** LEVENE & BASS *Nucleic Acids* x. 303 On warming a solution of the supposed pentanucleotide in 2 per cent solution of sodium hydroxide.., Feulgen split the substance into the two component parts. **1975** *Nature* 6 Mar. 83/2 Statistical considerations indicate that coincidence among oligonucleotides of length six or more (pentanucleotides are marginal) provides strong evidence for primary structural homology in a sequence of 1,600 nucleotides. **1907** *Jrnl. Chem. Soc.* XCII. I. 901 Characteristic of this pentapeptide and of the preceding tripeptide is the property of being precipitated from aqueous solution by ammonium sulphate. **1946** *Biochem. Jrnl.* XL. p. xliv, Their results are only compatible with the presence in the crystals studied either of a simple pentapeptide molecule or of a decapeptide which has crystallographic two-fold symmetry. **1960** *Ibid.* LXXVI. 16P/2 Appreciable hydrolysis..took place yielding, as one of the products, a pentapeptide containing arginine, proline, glycine, and phenylalanine. **1975** *Nature* 2 Oct. 415/1 It probably does not permeate lysosomal membranes, as might be expected for a pentapeptide.

pentad. Add: **2. a.** (Further example.)

1978 *Nature* 26 Jan. 322/2 South of lat 45° S, however, they conclude that average annual temperatures increased between the 1960–64 and 1970–74 pentads.

b. *Meteorol.* A period of five days.

1906 W. MARRIOTT *Hints to Meteorol. Observers* (ed. 6) 67/2 *Pentad*, a period of five days. **1935** *Nature* 12 Oct. 614/1 There has been great discussion of the relative advantages of the 5-day period, or pentad, and the week, with the result that both units have received international approval. **1959** R. E. HUSCHKE *Gloss. Meteorol.* 416 *Pentad*, a group of five. In climatology, it is applied to a period of five consecutive days. It often is preferred to the week for climatological purposes since it is an exact factor of the 365-day year.

pentaerythritol (pe:ntăˌeri·þritǫl). *Chem.* Formerly also **penta-erythritol, penterythritol.** [ad. G. *penta-erythrit* (Tollens & Wigand 1892, in *Ann. d. Chem.* CCLXV. 316): see PENTA- and *ERYTHRITOL.] A white, crystalline, tetrahydric alcohol, $C(CH_2OH)_4$, that is prepared by the condensation of acetaldehyde and formaldehyde and is widely used in the manufacture of paints and varnishes.

1892 *Jrnl. Chem. Soc.* LXII. I. 127 (*heading*) Penterythritol: a tetrahydric alcohol obtained from formaldehyde and acetaldehyde. **1912** *Ibid.* CI. 2091 The condensation between pentaerythritol and aldehydes in general takes place readily in the presence of sulphuric acid of from 30 to 50 per cent. concentration. **1947** WINDING & HASCHE *Plastics* III. 78 The ester of penta-erythritol has become an important resin within the last few years. **1958** *Times Rev. Industry* Feb. 19/3 A large plant has been erected at Dumfries for the production of.. pentaerythritol, a material for which there is an increasing demand in the field of paints. **1972** *Materials & Technol.* IV. x. 364 Acrolein is also used for preparing resins such as the glass-clear polymer obtained when acrolein is condensed with pentaerythritol.

b. pentaerythritol tetranitrate, a white crystalline solid, $C(CH_2NO_3)_4$, used as an explosive and also as a vasodilator in the treatment of coronary ailments.

1923 *Jrnl. Chem. Soc.* CXXIII. 75 Pentaerythritol tetranitrate. **1958** A. GROLLMAN *Pharmacol. & Therapeutics* (ed. 3) xx. 456 Pentaerythritol tetranitrate, N.N.R.., although of no value for the immediate relief of anginal attacks, may by its more prolonged action reduce the number or severity of the attacks. **1972** *Materials & Technol.* IV. viii. 301 The most important [reaction]..is the esterification with nitric acid, which gives PETN or pentaerythritol tetranitrate, a very powerful detonating agent, exploding when shocked or exposed to heat.

pentagon, *a.* and *sb.* Add: **B.** *sb.* **2.** (With capital initial.) The name given to a pentagonal building in Washington, D.C., the headquarters of the U.S. Department of Defense. Hence used allusively for the U.S. military leadership.

1945 *Amer. N. & Q.* July 54/1 (*heading*) Pentagon pip: an affliction common among Army officers and enlisted men stationed in Washington; brought on by an Army order proposing overseas duty for men whose war work has kept them heretofore in the United States. **1951** *Business Week* 29 Dec. 40 To help answer this recurring question the Pentagon set up its own watchdog—the Industrial Relations Division of Assistant Secretary Anna Rosenberg's office. **1952** *Brewer's Dict. Phr. & Fable* (rev. ed.) 697/2 *Pentagon..*, a vast five-sided building erected in Washington, D.C., to house government officials. It is said to be so great that newcomers who leave their offices never find them again. **1952** *Observer* 30 Nov. 5/4 The Pentagon, that immense monument to modern man's subservience to the desk. **1957** *Listener* 24 Oct. 664/3 The Pentagon hoped that Seato would produce a maximum morale-building effect with minimum demands on the American armed forces. **1959** *Ibid.* 4 June 972/2 The converting of Iran into a United States rocket ordnance depot is an integral part of the Pentagon plan. **1964** M. McLuhan *Understanding Media* v. 51 Life at the Pentagon has been greatly complicated by jet travel. **1972** A. Price *Col. Butler's Wolf* xiii. 142 The students didn't approve of the Kremlin any more than the Pentagon. **1974** *Jrnl. Politics* XXXVI. 82 In cases where appropriations had been provided to cover broad categories, the Defense Department should keep faith with the committee and with Congress by adhering to the detailed justifications presented in support of the Pentagon's budget. **1976** H. MacInnes *Agent in Place* ix. 85 The Pentagon might start investigating its own security.

Pentagonese (pe:ntăgŏnī·z). [f. prec. + -ESE.] (See quot. 1961.)

1951 *Collier's* 24 Nov. 33/3 The great virtue of Pentagonese is the facility it provides in conveying meanings briefly. **1961** *Guardian* 20 Mar. 1/4 Pentagonese—the Defence Department's penchant for turning nouns into verbs by the addition of a suffix. **1977** P. Howard *New Worlds for Old* 58 *Low profile* is Pentagonese, or American defence jargon.

pentagram. Add: **2.** A series of five letters or characters.

1972 *Computer Jrnl.* XV. 260/2 The peak frequencies are steadily reduced, from one occurrence of the space symbol in seven characters in the case of single characters, to a maximum frequency of approximately 600 in 1,000 documents in the case of the most frequent pentagram, TION∇. **1974** *Sci. Amer.* Jan. 108/3 Rows 1, 2, 3, 4 and 5, in 32 parts, give the 32 pentagrams.

pentagrid (pe·ntăgrid). *Electronics.* [f. PENTA- + GRID.] A thermionic valve having five grids; a heptode. Freq. *attrib.* or as *adj.*

1933 *Wireless World* 12 May 347/1 The Pentagrid Converter..has been recently developed in America. *Ibid.* 347/3 With the Pentagrid..the necessary coupling occurs within the valve and, by virtue of the screening, is entirely electronic in nature. **1950** P. Parker *Electronics* xiv. 549 Occasionally a frequency-changing valve ..has a suppressor grid; it is then called a heptode or pentagrid. **1953** A. H. W. Beck *Thermionic Valves* x. 308 In the pentagrid mixer, the local oscillation is generated by a separate valve. **1966** H. J. Reich et al. *Theory & Applications Active Devices* vii. 165 Another useful tube structure is the five-grid or pentagrid tube, in which the five grids of helical construction are mounted between the cathode and the plate. This tube affords considerable flexibility in design of certain electronic circuits. Perhaps the most frequent application..has been in the mixer-oscillator section of radio receivers.

pen-tail (pe·ntēil). [f. PEN *sb.*[2] + TAIL *sb.*[1]] In full, **pen-tail(ed) tree-shrew.** A species of tree-shrew, *Ptilocercus lowii*, found in Malaysia, Sumatra, and Borneo, and distinguished by rows of long, stiff hairs fringing the end part of its tail.

[**1848** J. E. Gray in *Proc. Zool. Soc.* XVI. 23 Mr. Low brought with him from Borneo some mammalia and reptiles in spirits; amongst them..was 'a rat-like animal with a pennated tail'.] **1883** *Encycl. Brit.* XV. 402/1 Pen-tail (Ptilocercus lowii). **1910** *Ibid.* XIV. 639/2 In the pen-tailed tree-shrew..the fringes of long hair are confined to the terminal third of the tail. **1926** *Proc. Zool. Soc.* 1179 The Pen-tailed Tree-shrew, *Ptilocercus*, has not been hitherto described except for its general appearance. **1927** *Glasgow Herald* 14 May 4/2 The probability is that the pen-tail and tupaia represent two successive phases in the evolution of a Lemurid. **1967** *Jrnl. Zool.* CLII. 375 The Pentail tree-shrews..are more insectivorous although meat is occasionally eaten. **1968** E. P. Walker et al. *Mammals of World* (ed. 2) I. 400/1 Pen-tailed tree shrews probably feed mainly on insects and fruit. **1969** Ld. Medway *Wild Mammals Malaya* 47/2 (*heading*) Pentail Treeshrew. *Ibid.*, Unlike other treeshrews, the Pentail is nocturnal; it is also largely arboreal.

pentamery (pentæ·mĕri). *Biol.* [f. PENTA- + Gr. μέρος part + -Y[3].] A condition in which structures are present in groups of five.

1902 *Encycl. Brit.* XXV. 433/2 In the pentamery and dimery of Dicotyledons there is usually a posterior sepal with a pair of lateral prophylls. **1962** D. Nichols *Echinoderms* i. 14 The adult members [*sc.* echinoderms] show a body pattern having structures present in fives (pentamery).

pentamidine (pentæ·midīn). *Pharm.* [f. PENT(ANE + *amidine* (f. AMID(E + -INE[5]).] A diamidine that is used, usu. in the form of its isethionate (a white, hygroscopic, crystalline solid), for the prevention and treatment of certain tropical diseases, esp. sleeping sickness; 1,5-di(4-amidinophenoxy)pentane, $(H_2N)(HN)C{\cdot}C_6H_4{\cdot}O{\cdot}(CH_2)_5{\cdot}O{\cdot}C_6H_4{\cdot}C(NH){\cdot}(NH_2)$.

1941 Fulton & Yorke in *Ann. Trop. Med. & Parasitol.* XXXV. 229 The name 'stilbamidine' has been given to 4:4′-diamidino stilbene, 'propamidine' to 4:4′-diamidino diphenoxy propane, 'pentamidine' to 4:4′-diamidino diphenoxy pentane, and 'phenamidine' to 4:4′-diamidino diphenyl ether. **1951** A. Grollman *Pharmacol. & Therapeutics* xx. 417 This led to the trial of other diamidine derivatives of which stilbamidine, propamidine and pentamidine are most widely used. **1974** *Jrnl. Protozool.* XXI. 324/2 Gutteridge..found that *C. fasciculata* mitochondrial respiration was inhibited 71% by 1 mM pentamidine. **1977** *Lancet* 3 Sept. 510/2 A man of 66 with non-Hodgkin's lymphoma was suspected of having *Pneumocystis carinii* infection, and pentamidine was given for 5 days.

pentane. Add: Also **pentano·ic** *a.*, in *pentanoic acid*, valeric acid; **pe·ntanol,** amyl (pentyl) alcohol.

[**1899** *Jrnl. Chem. Soc.* LXXVI. I. 742, 2-Chlorocyclopentanol, $C_5H_8Cl{\cdot}OH$. *Ibid.* II. 1135/1 (Index), *cyclo*-Pentanol.] **1927** Pentanoic acid [see *HEXANOIC *a.*]. **1937** F. C. Whitmore *Org. Chem.* I. 129 Pentanol-2, made by either of these methods, always contained pentanol-3. *Ibid.* 298 *n*-Valeric acid, *n*-valerianic acid, pentanoic acid, *n*-propylacetic acid, $CH_3CH_2CH_2CH_2CO_2H$, is made by the oxidation of *n*-amyl alcohol. **1951** I. L. Finar *Org. Chem.* I. vi. 105 Three amyl alcohols, *viz.*, *n*-pentanol, *iso*pentanol and 'active' amyl alcohol, have been isolated from fusel oil. **1964** N. G. Clark *Mod. Org. Chem.* viii. 139 A mixture of higher-boiling alcohols ('fusel oil') is obtained as a by-product and forms a useful source of pentanols (amyl alcohols), $C_5H_{11}{\cdot}OH$. **1965** *Nomencl. Org. Chem.* (I.U.P.A.C.) C. 112 Saturated aliphatic monocarboxylic acids... Pentanoic. [*Note*] The trivial name is normally preferred.

pentaploid (pe·ntăploid), *a.* and *sb. Biol.* [f. PENTA- + *-PLOID.] (Made up of somatic cells) containing five sets of chromosomes. Also as *sb.*, a pentaploid organism.

1921 *Ann. Bot.* XXXV. 185 Among the roses examined were diploid, tetraploid, pentaploid, and hexaploid forms. **1921** [see *HEXAPLOID *a.* and *sb.*]. **1946** *Nature* 19 Oct. 536/1 The cytology of species of *Magnolia* has proved the existence of diploids.., tetraploids.., and pentaploids. **1968** *Canad. Jrnl. Genetics & Cytol.* X. 910 Of the progeny obtained by backcrossing the pentaploid hybrid (AABBD) from the synthetic wheat to its tetraploid *T*[*riticum*] *durum* parent as male 49% had 28 chromosomes and 28% had 29 or 30.

pentaprism (pe·ntăpriz'm). Also **penta prism, penta-prism.** [f. PENTA(GONAL *a.* (*sb.*)+ PRISM.] A prism whose cross-section is a pentagon with one right angle and three angles of $112\frac{1}{2}°$, so that with silvered reflecting surfaces any ray entering it through one of the faces forming the right angle is deflected through 90°.

1937 *Magneto-theodolite* (Ordnance Survey) 5 The telescope is eccentrically mounted and the change over from theodolite generation to magnetometer operation.. takes place in one second by throwing into the line of sight inside the telescope tube a penta-prism which reflects through 270° rays from the illuminated diaphragm of the eyepiece. **1943** D. H. Jacobs *Fund. Optical Engin.* xi. 160 The penta prism..makes possible the modern high-precision rangefinder. This prism has the unique property of deviating a beam exactly 90° in the plane of the rays shown..even if the beam should not strike the end faces exactly normal. **1954** *Amat. Photographer* 19 May 628/2 The Rectaflex is..a..miniature of the eye-level reflex type, the camera having a manually raised 45-deg. mirror..and brilliant-type screen viewed via a pentaprism. **1977** J. Hedgecoe *Photographer's Handbk.* 11 During the past twenty years..the dominant design trend has been the single lens reflex. This includes both the universally popular 35 mm pentaprism types and roll-film versions.

pentastome. Substitute for first part of etym.: [ad. mod.L. generic name *Pentastoma* (C. A. Rudolphi *Entozoorum Synopsis Mantissa* (1819) 123) or *Pentastomum* (F. C. H. Creplin *Novæ Observationes de Entozois* (1829) 76).] Delete 'an aberrant group of Arachnida'. (Later examples.)

1937 Craig & Faust *Clin. Parasitol.* III. xxxi. 511 (*heading*) 'Tongue worms', Pentastomes (Linguatulida). **1956** T. W. M. Cameron *Parasites* 149 Pentastomes or 'tongue-worms' were until recently regarded as aberrant arachnids.

pentastomid (pentăstō͡u·mid), *sb.* and *a.* [f. mod.L. name of class *Pentastomida*, f. generic name *Pentastoma*: see prec. in Dict. and Suppl. and -ID[3].] A parasitic worm-like arthropod of the class Pentastomida; = *tongue-worm* (*b*) s.v. TONGUE *sb.* 16. Also as *adj.*, of or pertaining to a parasite of this kind. Cf. *LINGUATULID.

1909 A. E. Shipley in *Cambr. Nat. Hist.* IV. xx. 488 Pentastomids are unpleasant-looking, fluke-like or worm-like animals. **1943** *Trans. Amer. Microsc. Soc.* LXII. 194 (*title*) Observations on the pentastomid *Kiricephalus coarctatus*. **1957** *Jrnl. Parasitol.* XLIII. 195 Several pentastomids were removed from a series of mammals and reptiles. **1964** T. C. Cheng *Biol. Animal Parasites* xx. 549/1 Adult pentastomids are usually parasitic in the respiratory tract and lungs of vertebrates. *Ibid.* 552/2 When pentastomid eggs are fed to albino rats,..seven immature stages can be identified within the intermediate host. **1978** *Nature* 2 Mar. 93/1 The remaining 23 chapters deal with metazoan parasites (ten on the platyhelminthes,..and a chapter each on the..pentastomids and parasitic crustacea).

pentathlete. Add: **b.** A competitor in a modern penthathlon (see next). Hence **pentathle·tical** *a.*

1968 *Guardian* 19 Mar. 16/6 Athletes, pentathletes and weightlifters had taken advantage of grants..for altitude training. **1973** *Country Life* 10 May 1296/3 The heartening recruitment of pentathletes from the pony club. **1975** *Times Lit. Suppl.* 12 Dec. 1487/1 These figures [of Burne-Jones] are almost always pentathletical types: imposingly tall, long in the thigh, slim and gradual of hip, and very firmly fleshed. **1976** *Field* 26 Aug. 426/3 In saluting the modern pentathletes on 29 July for their Olympic victory, I remarked the difficulties of a team dividing a single solid prize.

pentathlon. Add: **b.** In modern times, a series of five athletic or sporting events imitative of the ancient pentathlon, *spec.* (*a*) (in full *modern pentathlon*) a competition consisting of fencing, shooting, swimming, riding, and cross-country running; (*b*) a competition for women, consisting of sprinting, hurdling, long jump, high jump, and putting the shot. Also *attrib.*

1905 *Olympic Games Athens* 3 *Pentathlum*, consisting of the five following events: 1) Flat race one Olympic Stade..2) Broad jump..3) Throwing the discus..4) Hurling the javelin..5) Wrestling. **1912** *Olympic Games Stockholm* 10/2 *Modern pentathlon*, duel-pistol shooting.. swimming..fencing..riding..cross-country race. **1929** F. A. M. Webster *Athletics of To-day* vii. 107 Eighty events were decided..including a pentathlon contest and several of the field events. **1932** *New Yorker* 23 July 8/3 The Hungarian swimming and pentathlon teams arrived. **1948** E. A. Bland *Olympic Story* xxii. 140 In 1912, when the Swedish Olympic Committee was deliberating upon the programme of events for the Vth Olympiad, they sought a test which would produce the best all-round sportsman in the world... The contest known as the Modern Pentathlon was the result. **1961** C. Willock *Death in Covert* x. 189 An Olympic Pentathlon..[is] a kind of marathon in which the competitors run, ride, shoot and so on without a break. **1964** M. Watman *Encycl. Athletics* 130/1 The pentathlon is a five-event test of all-round ability... The penthathlon has long been a most popular women's event, and was introduced into the Olympic schedule in 1964. **1970** B. Tulloh *World Athletics Handbk.* vi. 99 With the pentathlon being omitted..the 1928 Games..reached much the same form for the men's events as it has today. **1976** *Gazette* (Montreal) 19 July 0-8/4 Bromont—Thirteen riders of 47 scored a perfect 1,100 points on the modern pentathlon equestrian course. **1979** *Daily Tel.* 2 Oct. 19/4 Pentathlon is a comparatively new sport for women.

Pentathol, var. *PENTOTHAL.

pentatonic, *a.* Add: Also as *sb.*, a scale with five different notes to the octave.

1909 F. R. Burton *Amer. Primitive Mus.* ii. 41 This scale is not what is generally known as the pentatonic, although it consists of the same tones. **1921** H. A. Popley *Mus. India* iii. 28 The pentatonic was the more primitive scale among all peoples. **1928** *Grove's Dict. Mus.* (ed. 3) IV. 100/2 If we continue..to call them gaps, we may notice that they always occur at the interval of a fourth, (or fifth); and that is the distinguishing mark of the true pentatonic. **1936** E. Blom et al. tr. *Einstein's Short Hist. Mus.* 5 In China the development from the non-semitonal to the seven-note scale is certainly traceable, even though the old pentatonic always remained the foundation of its music. **1962** [see *HETEROPHONY].

Hence **pentato·nically** *adv.*, according to a pentatonic scale.

1965 *New Statesman* 17 Dec. 980/3 The almost complete disintegration of traditional controls in those pentatonically whirling winds, those parallel-third woodwinds that are sighing trees. **1967** H. Porter in *Coast to Coast 1965–66* 174 'Good af-ter-noon, Mis-ter Pel-lot,' melodiously and pentatonically in duet chanted the Misses Wee.

pentazocine (pentæ·zosīn). *Pharm.* [f. PENT(ANE + AZ(O- + *-ocine* (f. OC(TA- + -INE[5]).] A tricyclic heterocyclic compound that is a non-addictive analgesic, given as the hydrochloride in tablet form or as the lactate by injection; 1,2,3,4,5,6-hexahydro-8-hydroxy-6,11-dimethyl-3-(3-methyl-2-butenyl)-2,6-methano-3-benzazocine, $C_{19}H_{27}NO$.

1964 *Jrnl. Pharmacol. & Exper. Therap.* CXLIII. 142/1 (*caption*) Compound II has been assigned the generic name 'pentazocine' and Compound IV, 'cyclazocine'. **1967** *Observer* 5 Mar. 13/1 Pentazocine, which in pain-killing potency falls between morphine and pethidine, becomes available in an injectable form (under the name Fortral) on 5 April. **1974** M. C. Gerald *Pharmacol.* xiii. 248 Pentazocine is an effective analgesic agent that also possesses modest narcotic antagonistic properties. **1977** *Sci. Amer.* Mar. 47/2 The prototype is pentazocine (Talwin), which is widely used in the U.S. and is the only powerful opiate analgesic that is not subject to stringent 'dangerous drug' regulations.

Pentecost. 2. Delete '*arch.* or *Hist.*' and add later examples.

1889 H. M. Luckock *Divine Liturgy* xlix. 394 He mentions Epiphany as one of the three days, and omits Pentecost. **1953** A. A. McArthur *Evolution of Christian Year* iv. 165 What does the following of the year actually mean in practice in the periods after Epiphany and Pentecost? **1957** *Oxf. Dict. Chr. Ch.* 1483/1 In the RC Church the Sundays from Pentecost to Advent are usually numbered 'after Pentecost' but in the Anglican Church they are reckoned..'after Trinity', i.e. the Sunday after Pentecost. **1969** *Calendar & Lessons* (Church of England Liturgical Comm.) 5 Trinity Sunday is historically a late feast, exceptional as proclaiming a doctrine rather than commemorating an event. It is only in northern Europe that the Sundays of the unorganized second half of the Church's year have been dated from it, the octave of Pentecost, instead of from Pentecost itself. The calendar proposes that they should be called Sundays after Pentecost. **1976** B. Barker *When Queen was Crowned* 4 Many of the acts, words and anthems in Westminster Abbey in 1953 were seen and heard on the feast of Pentecost in St Peter's church at Bath in 973 when King Edgar was crowned. **1978** P. G. Cobb in C. Jones et al. *Study of Liturgy* vi. i. 418 Pentecost is given a new prominence by becoming a third focus of the Christian Year.

4. The particular day that the Christian feast of Pentecost commemorates, when the Holy Spirit descended upon the apostles (Acts ii).

1882 G. Smeaton *Doctrine of Holy Spirit* ii. 48 The Pentecost was the great day of the Holy Ghost, the opening of the river of the water of life. **1913** W. H. G. Thomas *Holy Spirit of God* i. v. 42 To the disciples the gift of the Holy Spirit at Pentecost may be said to be analogous to the descent of the Holy Spirit on Christ at his baptism. **1925** Chesterton *Everlasting Man* ii. iv. 250 This learned scholar says that Pentecost was the occasion for the first founding of an ecclesiastical, dogmatic and despotic Church utterly alien to the simple ideals of Jesus of Nazareth. **1938** *Doctrine in C. of E.* 161 They would lay stress upon the idea of the Spirit as guiding the Church into all truth, and as therein revealing more fully after Pentecost the significance of what our Lord did at the Last Supper. **1977** *Christian* IV. 33 Jesus' appointment of the twelve, and their special consecration at Pentecost, are not functional devices, otherwise irrelevant to the preaching of the Kingdom.

Pentecostal, *sb.* and *a.* Add: **A.** *sb.* **b.** = *Pentecostalist *sb.*

1904 in C. R. Paige *Alma White's Evangelism* (1939) I. 81 The Pentecostals refrain even from circulating an insinuating hat. **1946** in S. H. Frodsham *With Signs Following* xxiv. 273 The Pentecostals today are receiving the same kind of treatment that the Brethren received in those early days... I have heard as clear a presentation of the gospel in Pentecostal meetings as I ever heard among the Brethren. **1958** E. P. Paulk *Your Pentecostal Neighbor* 7 Pentecostals have spread..until today they compose a major portion of the Christian body. **1969** K. & D. Ranaghan *Catholic Pentecostals* vii. 247 There is no discord between the charismatic movement and the liturgy... There has been no tendency on the part of Catholic pentecostals to substitute prayer meetings or any of the gifts for the sacramental life of the Church. **1971** D. Gelpi *Pentecostalism* v. 132 Non-Pentecostals find it [*sc.* glossolalia] strange and exotic. **1972** S. Durasoff *Bright Wind of Spirit* (1973) xi. 190 In the past Catholics have been looked on with favor only as a fertile field of evangelism by many Pentecostals. **1974** *Encycl. Brit. Micropædia* VII. 858/1 Pentecostals thus hold that a Spirit-baptized believer may receive one or more of the supernatural gifts that were known in the early Church. **1975** *Christian Order* XVI. 419 For the proverbial mess of pottage, the Pentecostals claim, the Church sold her soul to Caesar.

B. *adj.* **b.** Resembling the mixture of nationalities in Jerusalem at Pentecost (Acts ii. 9–11); heterogeneous.

1896 Kipling *Five Nations* (1903) 90, I have watched them in their tantrums, all that pentecostal crew, French, Italian, Arab, Spaniard, Dutch and Greek, and Russ and Jew.

c. Pertaining to or designating Christian sects, movements, and individuals who emphasize the gifts of the Holy Spirit as recorded in Acts ii, seek to express their religious feelings uninhibitedly (e.g. clapping, shouting, and speaking with tongues) and often are fundamentalist in outlook and maintain that a 'baptism in the Spirit' manifested by speaking with tongues is to be sought by all Christians; freq. (with capital initial) forming part of the name of a sect.

1904 *Daily Graphic* 8 Dec. 4/1 Camberwell has received this new form of worship with mingled feelings of tolerance, indifference and hostility, but the Pentecostal Dancers..have maintained their steadfast resolution of dancing themselves into the hearts of their audiences—with but little success so far. **1906** *Apostolic Faith* Oct. 1/1 The waves of Pentecostal salvation are still rolling in at Azusa Street Mission. **1910** *Latter Rain Evangel* Oct. 12/1 A Pentecostal convention will be held..God willing, November 18 to Dec. 4 1910. **1924** *Ibid.* Oct. 10/1 As usual in a real Pentecostal camp meeting, it was harder to stop than to start. **1928** *Amer. Mercury* Oct. 184/2 The Pentecostal Nazarenes have largely duplicated the Methodist system of government by district conferences. **1932** M. Mead *Changing Culture of Indian Tribe* 108 Most of the poor whites go to the Pentecostal Church. **1946** S. H. Frodsham *With Signs Following* (rev. ed.) v. 41 This Pentecostal visitation became so universal in 'The Holiness Church' that it had to be renamed. It is now known as 'The Pentecostal Holiness Church'. **1958** [see *holiness 4b]. **1966** *Listener* 26 May 754/1 Let us consider the West Indian Pentecostal sects. **1970** P. Oliver *Savannah Syncopators* 56 The hand-clapping.. remained a familiar characteristic of the services of the 'Sanctified' and 'Pentecostal' churches. **1974** *Amer. Speech 1971* XLVI. 70 It is too soon to know..whether or not the term [*sc.* jackleg preacher] is used in other urban areas where the storefront pentecostal-and-holiness churches abide. **1974** *Observer* (Colour Suppl.) 17 Nov. 34/1 There are the various 'pentecostal' movements which go in for fervent, excited forms of worship.

Pentecostalism (pentĭkǫ·stăliz'm). [f. prec. + -ism.] The beliefs and practices of the Pentecostal movement or Pentecostal sects.

1932 F. C. Martin *Holy Ghost versus Mod. Tongues* xix. 159 God forbid that modern Pentecostalism with the tongues deception be allowed to continue. **1936** H. J. Stolee *Pentecostalism* ii. 11 Modern pentecostalism also has its type in the problems of the early Church. **1946** C. B. Nervig *Christian Truth & Relig. Delusions* v. 75 Pentecostalism does teach the great essentials of the Christian religion. **1958** *Eternity* Apr. 9/3 In some ways, Pentecostalism..has moderated its extremes in the past fifty years. **1961** B. R. Wilson *Sects & Society* 8 Some expressions of early Pentecostalism. **1966** *Listener* 26 May 754/2, I am thinking of a movement something like the Black Muslims, which is logically possible as an alternative, or in addition to, Pentecostalism. **1971** D. Gelpi *Pentecostalism* i. 5 Catholic Pentecostalism has spread through wide segments of the American Church.

Pentecostalist (pentĭkǫ·stălist), *sb.* and *a.* [f. as prec. + -ist.] **A.** *sb.* A member of any Pentecostal sect; an adherent of the Pentecostal movement. **B.** *adj.* Of or pertaining to Pentecostalism.

1925 *Forum* (N.Y.) Feb. 152 'Pentecostalists' brought to light our partial neglect of the Holy Ghost. **1928** *Amer. Mercury* Oct. 190/1 The epic case of Holy Roller healing is that of the Rev. David Wesley Myland of the Latter Rain Pentecostalists. **1956** *Gordon Rev.* Dec. 131 The Pentecostalists assert that deliverance from physical sickness is provided for in the Atonement. **1958** M. Argyle *Relig. Behaviour* iv. 34 The Baptists and other Evangelical groups were rather similar in 1850 to the Pentecostalists of today. *Ibid.* ix. 110 Boisen gives a case-study of a Pentecostalist leader who was an epileptic. **1961** B. R. Wilson *Sects & Society* i. i. 18 Pentecostalist stress on the Pauline declarations. **1965** *Guardian* 8 Sept. 4/3 The West Indian Pentecostalist sect drew most of its members from the lowest group of Jamaican working class. **1966** *Listener* 26 May 754/2 If Pentecostalists improve their position and become house owners or landlords, will they leave to join a middle-class denomination, or will they restructure their Pentecostalist beliefs, so that a sect becomes a denomination? **1979** R. Blythe *View in Winter* ix. 300 I'm waiting [on God] not listening. Listening is Pentecostalist, and I find it very hard to do.

Pentel (pe·ntĕl). Also **pentel.** The proprietary name of a type of felt-tip pen.

1964 *Observer* 8 Nov. 40/3 What is the particular fascination of a Pentel? It's the new kind of thick-flowing pen—something between a felt marker and a ball-point. **1965** *Guardian* 4 Jan. 5/6 The Japanese 'Pentel' pen, has gained a foothold in British markets... The secret of the 'Pentel' is its tip... The 'Pentel'..will write on anything including glass. **1966** *Trade Marks Jrnl.* 30 Mar. 418/2 Pentel..writing instruments, drawing instruments, marking instruments, chalks,..crayons and artists' brushes. Dainihon-Bungu Kabushiki Kaisha.., Tokyo, Japan; manufacturers and merchants. **1969** 'V. Packer' *Don't rely on Gemini* (1970) ix. 76 Gamble was..making notes with a Pentel. **1976** L. Deighton *Twinkle, Twinkle Little Spy* vi. 51 Several of the hi-fi magazines were marked with a red pentel.

penthouse, *sb.* Add: **B. 1. d.** A separate flat, apartment, etc., situated on the roof of a tall building.

1921 *Country Life* Apr. 65/1 Two of the elevators were designed to run to the roof, where a pent-house..was being built. **1937** *Sunday Dispatch* 28 Feb. 2/7 You all know from American lyric writers that a pent-house is a thing stuck on a roof. It may comprise one or two floors. **1945** E. Waugh *Brideshead Revisited* i. viii. 194 They're going to build a block of flats, and..Rex wanted to take what he called a 'penthouse' at the top. **1948** *National Home Monthly* Feb. 21/2 Back in London in 1932..they built London's first penthouse. **1955** A. Huxley *Let.* 18 Mar. (1969) 738 After that expect to be in NYC until mid-June, when I am to be lent a pent-house on Park Avenue. **1956** 'N. Shute' *Beyond Black Stump* ii. 52 They live in lovely sort of flats called penthouses on the top of skyscrapers. **1958** *Times Lit. Suppl.* 4 July 371/3 After years of travel they built in 1936 what the author calls a 'penthouse' in Park Lane. It was eighty feet above street level. **1978** *Country Life* 3 Aug. (Suppl.) 29/1 A Penthouse with magnificent Thames views..to be sold on a 995 years lease at the rental of one Red Rose on Midsummer Day.

2. b. (Further examples.)

1911 *Encycl. Brit.* XXVI. 626/2 [Royal tennis] is now played in a walled and roofed court, 110 ft. by 38 ft. 8 in., the floor, however, measuring but 96 ft. by 31 ft. 8 in., the difference being the width of a roofed corridor, the 'penthouse', which runs along the two end walls and one of the side walls. **1935** *Encycl. Sports* 619/1 This sloping roof is called the 'penthouse', and is, perhaps, the most characteristic feature of a tennis court. **1963** *Times* 25 May 4/5 Those first four games had cost Aberdare and Warburg the first set, but they were now going well, with Aberdare the best of the four on the floor and Warburg, although he put too much on the penthouse, setting up a powerful attack.

3*. (Properly with capital initial.) The name of a theatre at the University of Washington, used *attrib.* to denote a style of theatre production in which the audience sits in a circular formation around a central acting area. (Cf. *arena 5.)

1940 *Nation's Schools* Nov. 19/1 The penthouse style was first employed by us in the autumn of 1932. *Ibid.* 20/3 Modern comedy and farce, preferably with a single interior setting, are the most successful plays for a penthouse theatre. *Ibid.* 21/3 Without the aid of scenic background and conventional stage atmosphere..the ordinary amateur is not an effective instrument and in penthouse productions he must be effective. **1942** G. Hughes *Penthouse Theatre* iii. 17 Plays which could not very well be done Penthouse style. *Ibid.* viii. 53 We designed a Penthouse Theatre because we had created a tradition of arena production. **1959** W. C. Lounsbury *Backstage from A to Z* 5 *Arena stage...* Also known as arena staging, circular staging, theatre in the round, central staging, Penthouse staging, etc.

4. *penthouse apartment, flat, suite*; fig. *penthouse eyebrow, nab.*

1935 A. Squire *Sing Sing Doctor* v. 59 He developed a taste for lavish penthouse apartments. **1948** *Sun* (N.Y.) 30 Dec. 8 (*caption*) Construction view of the eighteen-story and penthouse apartment building being erected by Samuel Rudin on the former Temple Beth-El site at the south corner of Fifth avenue and 76th street. **1947** Auden *Age of Anxiety* iii. 95 Peasants with penthouse eyebrows. **1972** K. Bonfiglioli *Don't point that Thing at Me* vii. 61 Fifth-floor penthouse flats in Upper Brook Street. **1977** *Wandsworth Borough News* 16 Sept. 15/2 Planning Proposals... Star and Garter Mansions, Lower Richmond-road—erection of penthouse flat on the roof of the building situated between two existing false gables. **1699** B. E. *New Dict. Canting Crew*, *Pentice Nab*, a very broad-brimd Hat. **1785** Grose *Dict. Vulgar T.*, *Penthouse nab*, a broad-brimmed hat. **1948** *Time* 8 Nov. 6/1 The eleventh-floor penthouse suite. **1973** *Times* 5 Dec. 18/1 Sir Lew Grade..is occupying the penthouse suite of the plush Century Plaza hotel.

‖ **pentimento** (pentime·nto). Also **pe·ntiment.** Pl. **pentime·nti.** [It. *pentimento*, repentance.] In a painting (particularly in oils), a trace of an earlier composition or of alterations that has become visible with the passage of time. Also *transf.*

1903 R. Fry *Let.* 6 Mar. (1972) I. 204 What looks like a retouch above the man's left shoulder turns out on closer inspection to be an original *pentimento.* **1933** *Burlington Mag.* May 212/1 Holbein's portraits of the 1530's; a pentimento indicates that originally the *décolleté* was narrower. **1935** *Ibid.* June 259/2 There are signs of *pentimenti* on the heads and hands. **1939** *Ibid.* Sept. 96/1 The pentimenti confirm that we are dealing with an original work of the master. **1945** *Ibid.* Apr. 82/2 A striking *pentimento* is visible, in the form of a segment of a circle, over the red dress under the hands of the Virgin. **1951** R. Mayer *Artist's Handbk.* ii. 100 In galleries one may frequently find a picture in which, by reason of changes wrought by time, oxidation, etc., the refractive index of the oil film has changed and a thin coat of paint.. has become sufficiently transparent to allow underpainting or drawing to show through. The effect is called pentimento. **1961** L. G. G. Ramsey *Connoisseur New Guide Antique Eng. Pott., Porc. & Glass* 26 On this somewhat rough base the painter has to carry out his designs without benefit of rubbings-out or *pentimenti.* **1962** *Sunday Times* (Colour Suppl.) 8 Apr. 20 A pentiment in the muzzle of the greyhound who looks back over his shoulder shows that the design of the Cleveland picture was followed at first in Mr. Getty's by an assistant, and then changed by Rubens. **1966** *Listener* 9 June 845/1 X-rays reveal *pentimenti*—those first thoughts—in both edges of the ruff, between the right forearm and the chair and, above all, in her right hand, which was originally both higher up and further to the right. **1971** *Guardian* 23 Aug. 5 One of the things that distinguish an original from a copy is the existence of *pentimenti* alterations.. done while the work was being painted. **1973** L. Hellman *Pentimento* (1974) 3 Old paint on canvas, as it ages, sometimes becomes transparent. When that happens it is possible, in some pictures, to see the original lines... This is called pentimento because the painter 'repented', changed his mind. **1975** *Times Lit. Suppl.* 31 Oct. 1278/5 He [*sc.* an Italian writer] has recently announced that, after completing all six volumes, he intends to begin all over again with a revised edition to include any *pentimenti* where he has changed his mind.

pentitol (pe·ntitǫl). *Chem.* [f. Pent(ose: see *-itol.] A pentahydric alcohol.

1907 J. B. Cohen *Org. Chem. Adv. Students* I. viii. 310 (*table*) Pentitol. **1954** S. S. Cohen in D. M. Greenberg *Chem. Pathways of Metabolism* I. v. 211 Two naturally occurring pentitols, D-arabitol and ribitol (adonitol), are known. Both appear to be quite rare but are encountered in plant tissues. **1966** *New Phytologist* LXV. 219 Carbon fixed by *Xanthoria aureola* in photosynthesis appears at first mainly in the pentitol. **1971** J. F. Stoddart *Stereochem. Carbohydrates* ii. 20 There are four pentitols.

Pentland (pe·ntlănd). The name of the Pentland Hills, in Midlothian, Scotland, used *attrib.* in **Pentland Crown, Dell,** etc., to designate varieties of potato developed at the Scottish Plant Breeding Station, which is located there.

1959 *Rep. Scottish Plant Breeding Station* 11 (*heading*) Potatoes.—The Registration Trials conducted by the Department of Agriculture for Scotland in 1958 contained thirteen of the Station's seedlings... One..was registered as a new variety suitable for commercial cultivation. It has been named Pentland Crown. **1961** *Ibid.* 16 As a result of its performance in the Merit Trials conducted by the Department of Agriculture and Fisheries for Scotland the [potato] Seedling 2319(a)3 has received 'Commendation'. It has been named 'Pentland Dell', a name that will be registered in compliance with the provisions of the International Code of Nomenclature. *Ibid.* 18 A red variant has been selected from the cultivar 'Pentland Beauty' and as a preliminary to giving it the name 'Red Pentland Beauty' this variant has been entered for the Wart Immunity and Identity Tests. **1962** *Ibid.* 17 An early maturing [potato] seedling, Reference No. 2299 (10), has successfully completed the Merit Trials conducted by the Department of Agriculture and Fisheries for Scotland and..has been named 'Pentland Envoy' a name that will be registered by the National Registration Authority. **1969** *Dict. Gardening* (R. Hort. Soc.) *Suppl.* 150/1 Pentland Beauty. Oval with pale lemon flesh. *Ibid.* 150/2 Pentland Crown. White oval shape. White flesh. Pentland Dell. Shapely white kidney—shows considerable resistance to Blight. **1971** *Arable Farmer* Feb. 3/1 Our variety was Pentland Crown planted in 30″ rows. **1973** *Times* 16 Oct. 6/6 Britain's plant breeders.. are striving to keep their brand names in Europe. To our grain growers Maris means another winner from the Plant Breeding Institute at Cambridge, Pentland a good Scottish potato, and Malling an outstanding new fruit. **1976** *Cumberland News* 3 Dec. 34/4 (Advt.), Pentland Crown seed potatoes for sale, once grown from Scotch seed, blight free, excellent quality.

pentobarbital (pentobā·ɹbităl). *Pharm.* The equivalent in the U.S. Pharmacopeia of *PENTOBARBITONE. Also *pentobarbital sodium, sodium pentobarbital.*

1931 *Jrnl. Amer. Med. Assoc.* 30 May 1871/1 Pentobarbital-sodium is a nonproprietary name given to the mono-sodium salt of ethyl-(1-methylbutyl)barbituric acid. **1935** *Proc. Mayo Clinic* X. 536 The next step forward was the use of the isomer..of amytal, which was first called 'embutal'. The sodium salt was called 'nembutal' and finally, 'pentobarbital sodium'. **1955** *Sci. News Let.* 2 Apr. 219/2 The Boston doctors tested the effects of morphine, heroin, amphetamine, the sleeping medicine pentobarbital and as a control, sodium chloride, or salt. **1962** *Times* 20 Dec. 9/7 Pentobarbital anaesthesia in lions has been studied with special reference to pre-anaesthetic medication. **1965** *Pharmacopeia U.S.* (ed. 17) 633 Sodium pentobarbital. [*In ed.* 16 *as* pentobarbital sodium.] **1974** M. C. GERALD *Pharmacol.* xi. 204 Deep sedation is induced by the intravenous injection of amobarbital (Amytal) or pentobarbital (Nembutal).

pentobarbitone (pentobā·ɹbitōᵘn). *Pharm.* [f. PENT(ANE + -O + *BARBITONE.] The synthetic compound 5-ethyl-5-(1-methylbutyl)-barbituric acid, which is widely used as a sedative-hypnotic and anticonvulsant drug, usu. in the form of its sodium salt, $C_{11}H_{17}N_2O_3Na$, a white crystalline powder often known by the proprietary name *NEMBUTAL; = *PENTOBARBITAL. So *pentobarbitone sodium, sodium pentobarbitone.*

1938 S. ALSTEAD *Poulsson's Text-bk. Pharmacol. & Therapeutics* (ed. 2) i. 41 Nembutal, pentobarbitone, sodium ethyl-methyl-butyl barbiturate. **1950** *Brit. Med. Jrnl.* 25 Mar. 706/1 The child is premedicated with atropine.. and pentobarbitone. **1960** *Times* 6 Jan. 9/5 Once the rhino is dazed, two more rangers will move in with syringes to pump 600 c.c. of pentobarbitone sodium into the hide. **1962** *Lancet* 29 Dec. 1379/1 Progressive fall in temperature down to cardiac arrest, seen in two rabbits subjected to surface cooling in a deep-freeze at 0°C while under pentobarbitone anæsthesia. **1971** *Nature* 21 May 182/1 The dog was anaesthetized with pentobarbitone and heparin was used as an anticoagulant. **1975** *Ibid.* 4 Sept. 62/1 Each rat was killed with an overdose of sodium pentobarbitone.

pentode (pe·ntōᵘd). *Electronics.* [f. PENT(A- + *-ODE.] A thermionic valve having five electrodes. Also *pentode valve.*

1919 W. H. ECCLES in *Electrician* 18 Apr. 475/2 To be systematic I suggest 'tetrode' and 'pentode' for vacuum tubes with four or five electrodes. **1928** *Daily Express* 14 Dec. 5 One pentode valve will do the work of two ordinary valves, but it will be a heavy drain on dry batteries. **1932** E. V. APPLETON *Thermionic Vacuum Tubes* ix. 111 The five electrode tube or pentode possesses a screen grid as does the tetrode, but also has an additional grid situated between the anode and the screen grid. **1965** *IEEE Trans. Electron Devices* XII. 350/2 Conventional beam pentodes can be designed on the computer to have uniform cathode current density. **1973** WHITTLE & YARWOOD *Exper. Physics* xi. 296 The values recorded..are for a pentode valve used for audio-frequency operation, generally as the output stage of an audio-frequency amplifier.

pentolinium (pentoli·niǝm). *Pharm.* [f. *pent(amethylene* (s.v. *PENTA-) + *PYRR)OL-(ID)IN(E + *-IUM b.] A white, crystalline powder which has been used as a ganglion-blocking agent in the treatment of severe hypertension; pentamethylenebis(1-methylpyrrolidinium hydrogen tartrate), $C_{23}H_{42}N_2O_2$; also called *pentolinium tartrate.*

1954 *Lancet* 27 Nov. 1097/2 The preparation used was 'Ansolysen' (M. & B. 2050A),..termed pentolinium tartrate by the British Pharmacopœia Commission in 1954. **1958** J. H. BURN *Lect. Notes Pharmacol.* (ed. 5) 20 Pentolinium (Ansolysen) is similar in action to hexamethonium, but it is more powerful. **1974** [see *PEMPIDINE].

Pentomic, pentomic (pentǫ·mik), *a. Mil.* [f. PENTA- + *ATOMIC *a.*] Divided into five battle groups armed with nuclear weapons.

1956 *Washington Post* 28 Dec. 1/8 The Army announced last night that it will begin reducing the manpower of its divisions early next year and revamp them into new-style 'Pentomic' units geared for atomic warfare. **1958** *Times* 4 Nov. 9/3 The plans are based on the American concept of 'pentomic' divisions. **1959** *New Statesman* 29 Aug. 238/1 Two and possibly more of the US divisions are now Pentomic (i.e. nuclear-armed), but the process of training the first British regiment of nuclear artillery has only just begun. **1961** *Observer* 4 June 10/2 Orders have been given to break up the so-called 'Pentomic' divisions in the United States Army in Europe, in which nuclear weapons have been integrated with conventional arms. **1963** *Times* 10 Jan. 11/7 The Australian Army had adapted for its own use the American 'pentomic' formation. **1972** [see *low-yield* adj. s.v. *LOW *a.* 23]. **1972** *Sat. Rev.* (U.S.) 6 May 30/3 It was considered necessary to shrink the [US] army combat division from a force of three regiments containing three battalions of five companies each to a 'Pentomic' force of five battle groups of four companies.

pentomino (pentǫ·mino). [f. PENT(A- + D)OMINO by deliberately false analogy: see quot. 1961.] Any of the twelve distinct planar shapes that can be formed by joining five identical squares by their edges.

In the U.S. the pl. *Pentominoes* is registered as the proprietary name of a board game involving these shapes.

1954 S. W. GOLOMB in *Amer. Math. Monthly* LXI. 681 There are twelve distinct pentominoes. **1961** *New Scientist* 2 Nov. 316/2 A domino is formed from two adjacent squares: he [*sc.* Golomb] argues that practical needs and false etymology will justify our calling a square a monomino—whence we have a series monomino, domino, tromino, tetromino,..., and Maestro pieces then become pentominoes. **1964** *Listener* 11 June 975/3 The jigsaw pattern is made from a set of twelve pentominoes. **1965** S. W. GOLOMB *Polyominoes* 13, I learned of the true antiquity of pentominoes, one kind of polyomino. Although the name was coined in my lecture of 1953, the first pentomino *problem* was published in 1907. **1975** *Official Gaz.* (U.S. Patent Office) 21 Jan. TM279/2 Solomon W. Golomb, La Canada, Calif. Filed Sept. 13, 1972. *Pentominoes.* For equipment, consisting of the twelve distinct five-celled square figures and a playing board, for use in various combinatorial puzzles and in competitive board games... First used November 1953. **1975** A. C. CLARKE *Imperial Earth* xxiv. 173 He replaced the titanite cross in its setting between the F, N, U and V pentominoes.

penton (pe·ntǫn). *Biol.* [f. PENT(A- + *-ON[1] 2.] A capsomere which occupies any of the twelve vertices of the icosahedral capsid of an adenovirus.

1966 H. S. GINSBERG et al. in *Virology* XXVIII. 782/2 The unit at the twelve corners of the icosahedron should then be termed a penton because each has 5 neighbouring units (hexons). The penton corresponds to the B or cell-detaching antigen; thus the soluble antigen should be called the penton antigen. **1970** *Nature* 17 Jan. 226/2 Adenovirus has a more complex capsid containing 240 hexons and twelve pentons each with a molecular weight of about 400,000. **1972** *Ibid.* 14 Apr. 348/1 The DNA-specific endonuclease associated with the penton bases of the virion may affect the host genome in an apparently random manner.

pentosan (pe·ntosæn). *Biochem.* Also †**-ane.** [a. G. *pentosan* (Schulze & Tollens 1892, in *Ann. d. Chem.* CCLXIX. 55), after *glucosan, hexosan,* etc.: see *PENTOSE.] Any of the class of polysaccharides, occurring widely in plants, of which the constituent monosaccharides are pentoses.

1892 *Jrnl. Chem. Soc.* LXII. 1420 (*heading*) The pentosans of woody vegetable fibre. **1913** HAAS & HILL *Introd. Chem. Plant Products* II. 51 Gums: (*a*) Natural gums and pentosanes $(C_5H_8O_4)n$. (*b*) Mucilages and pectic bodies. **1931** E. C. MILLER *Plant Physiol.* viii. 420 The pentosans have the general formula $(C_5H_8O_4)_n$ and occur, for the most part, in the cell walls of various plant parts. **1938** [see *ARABAN]. **1963** R. R. A. HIGHAM *Handbk. Papermaking* ii. 34 The presence of pentosans in wood pulps helps to produce increased fibre bonding in paper. **1973** R. W. BAILEY in Butler & Bailey *Chem. & Biochem. Herbage* I. iv. 165 Hemicelluloses may be divided into two broad classes; pentosans, based largely on pentoses and non-cellulose hexosans which are pentose-free.

pentose. Add: Any of the monosaccharides with the formula $C_5H_{10}O_5$, among which are ribose and several other naturally occurring sugars. (Earlier and later examples.) [First formed as G. *pentose* (E. Fischer 1890, in *Ber. d. Deut. Chem. Ges.* XXIII. 934).]

1890 [see *heptose* s.v. *HEPTA-]. **1916** A. P. MATHEWS *Physiol. Chem.* ii. 30 The pentoses generally occur in nature in gums and..polysaccharides. **1927** *Jrnl. Biol. Chem.* LXXIII. 18 Any method of pentose estimation.. must prove to be efficacious, not only for xylose and arabinose, but especially for *d*-ribose, for it is as ribose compounds that one finds pentose in the body. **1953** FRUTON & SIMMONDS *Gen. Biochem.* xvii. 381 A number of pentoses have been found in nature; perhaps the most important of these is D-ribose,..a constituent of nucleic acids and of several nucleotides (ATP, DPN, etc.). **1973** R. G. KRUEGER et al. *Introd. Microbiol.* viii. 263/2 Pentoses (five-carbon sugars) are carbon and energy sources for many microorganisms.

2. Special combs.: **pentose nucleic acid,** a nucleic acid in which the sugar is a pentose; (effectively synonymous with *ribonucleic acid,* RNA); **pentose phosphate cycle, pathway,** or **shunt,** a cyclic pathway in the body and in higher plants by which glucose phosphate is converted to a pentose phosphate with the reduction of NADP, the pentose phosphate being afterwards converted into phosphates of a hexose and a triose or else incorporated into nucleotides.

1934 *Biochem. Jrnl.* XXVIII. 2108 The pentose nucleic acid of the pancreas gland. **1947** *Thorpe's Dict. Appl. Chem.* (ed. 4) VIII. 622/1 The idea has arisen that deoxypentose nucleic acid is present in the nucleus, pentose nucleic acid in the cytoplasm. **1953** FRUTON & SIMMONDS *Gen. Biochem.* vii. 184 Although it was once thought that the pentose nucleic acids were characteristic of plant tissues whereas the deoxypentose nucleic acids were confined to animal cells, this separation has been shown to be incorrect. **1968** I. L. FINAR *Org. Chem.* (ed. 4) II. xvi. 724 The nucleic acids are classified according to the nature of the sugar present: the pentose nucleic acids or ribonucleic acids (R.N.A.), and the deoxypentose nucleic acids or deoxyribonucleic acids (D.N.A.). **1960** *McGraw-Hill Encycl. Sci. & Technol.* II. 40/1 The pentose phosphate pathway of glucose decomposition involves hexose monophosphates and pentose monophosphates. **1963** C. H. DOERING tr. *Karlson's Introd. Mod. Biochem.* xv. 269 (*heading*) Glucose oxidation through the pentose phosphate cycle. **1964** W. G. SMITH *Allergy & Tissue Metabolism* viii. 85 Supplies of $NADPH_2$ can be made available by shunting some of the available glucose-6-phosphate into reactions which form ribulose-5-phosphate. This in turn can be converted back to glucose-6-phosphate... The whole process is sometimes referred to as the pentose phosphate shunt. **1970** R. W. MCGILVERY *Biochem.* xxiii. 568 The adrenal cortex has an active pentose phosphate pathway that can provide NADPH in the cytosol by oxidizing glucose-6-phosphate.

pentoside (pe·ntosəid). *Chem.* [f. PENTOS(E, after GLUCOSIDE.] A glycoside which yields a pentose on hydrolysis.

The pentosides of most interest are now referred to as nucleosides.

[**1909**: see *GUANOSINE]. **1910** [see *GLUCOSIDE]. **1916** A. P. MATHEWS *Physiol. Chem.* iv. 171 Guanosine is, therefore, a pentoside. *Ibid.* 172 From yeast another pentoside was isolated, an adenine pentoside called adenosine.

pentosuria (pentosiūə·riă). *Med.* [mod.L., ad. G. *pentosurie* (E. Salkowski 1895, in *Berl. klin. Wochenschr.* 29 Apr. 364): see PENTOSE and -URIA.] The presence of an excess of pentoses in the urine.

1902 *Med. Rev.* V. 94/2 (*heading*) The clinical importance of chronic pentosuria. **1936** *Nature* 7 Nov. 805/2 There are known to be at least two types of the rare chronic pentosuria, differing in the nature of the pentose sugar found, one being optically inactive *dl*-arabinose and the other *l*-xyloketose. **1970** PASSMORE & ROBSON *Compan. Med. Stud.* II. xxxi. 9/1 [Garrod] suggested that in alkaptonuria, albinism, cystinuria and pentosuria there was a block in a metabolic process due to an inherited deficiency of a specific enzyme.

Hence **pentosu·ric** *a.*, of, pertaining to, or having pentosuria; *sb.*, an individual with pentosuria.

1906 J. L. SALINGER tr. F. Blumenthal in R. C. Cabot *Mod. Clin. Med.* 267 The researches..have..made it appear unlikely that pentoses are formed in the pentosuric patient by an imperfect nuclein decomposition. *Ibid.* 271 Have pentosurics..a special liability to become diabetics? **1933** CAMERON & GILMOUR *Biochem. of Med.* vi. 91 Diabetic treatment is unsuitable to the pentosuric. **1964** D. Y. HSIA in G. A. Duncan *Dis. Metabolism* (ed. 5) v. 349 In the 1950's, Lasker reported that she had identified L-xylulose in all 72 pentosuric urines that she had tested. **1968** MARKS & SAMOLS in F. Dickens et al. *Carbohydrate Metabolism* II. xiii. 351 The existence of this pathway of glucose metabolism was first recognised as a result of studies on the biosynthesis of L-ascorbic acid in animals and of L-xylulose in pentosurics.

Pentothal (pe·ntoþæl). *Pharm.* Also (*erron.*) Pentathol, and with small initial. [Refash. of *THIOPENTAL.] A proprietary name for thiopentone sodium; also called *Pentothal sodium, sodium Pentothal.*

1935 *Proc. Mayo Clinic* X. 744 Sodium ethyl 1-methyl butyl thiobarbituric acid (thionembutal or pentothal sodium) and sodium allyl secondary butyl thiobarbituric acid (thiosebutal) induce a satisfactorily deep but relatively transitory anesthesia. **1936** *Official Gaz.* (U.S. Patent Office) 11 Feb. 238/2 Abbott Laboratories, North Chicago, Ill. Filed Dec. 6, 1935... Pentothal... For pharmaceutical product having hypnotic, sedative and anesthetic properties. Claims use since Nov. 15, 1935. **1936** *Trade Marks Jrnl.* 28 Oct. 1326/1 Pentothal... Chemical substances prepared for use in medicine and pharmacy. Abbott Laboratories.., City of North Chicago,..State of Illinois, United States of America; manufacturers of pharmaceutical products. **1940** *N. & Q.* 22 June 448/2, I observe in the press mention of two drugs to induce sleep with new names, Evipan and Pentothal. **1946** M. DICKENS *Happy Prisoner* viii. 153 Elizabeth..suggested Pentathol therapy. **1967** *Punch* 1 Mar. 321/3 One could only ask—..after the mystics, the ESP experts and the computing machines, after the sodium pentathol examinations and the lie detector tests..—after all that was he to turn out to be this nondescript house-painter and handyman who killed at random? **1969** *Daily Tel.* 16 Dec. 15/1 Interviewed under the truth drug pentathol, he told doctors he did not realise he had done the baby any harm. **1973** G. GREENE *Honorary Consul* v. iii. 273

Dying is a wonderfully effective truth drug, better than pentathol. **1974** M. C. GERALD *Pharmacol.* xi. 195 Nonvolatile anesthetics include the intravenously administered barbiturate thiopental (Pentothal).

pentryl (pe·ntril). [f. PENTA-, after *TETRYL 2 (prob. from there being five rather than four nitro groups in the molecule).] A crystalline compound similar to tetryl in chemical structure, explosive power, and sensitivity to detonation; $C_6H_2(NO_2)_3{\cdot}N(NO_2)CH_2CH_2ONO_2$.

1933 L. V. CLARK in *Industr. & Engin. Chem.* Dec. 1385/1 In this paper the writer presents the results of an investigation of *sym*-trinitrophenylnitraminoethyl nitrate, hereafter termed 'pentryl'. *Ibid.* 1386/1 Pentryl detonates when struck a sharp blow. **1967** M. JURECKI tr. *Urbański's Chem. & Technol. Explosives* III. iii. 71 Pentryl is remarkable for its high explosive power which, according to various authors, is equal to or slightly higher than that of tetryl.

penuche, var. *PANOCHE.

penumbral, *a.* (Further *fig.* examples.)

a **1922** T. S. ELIOT *Waste Land Drafts* (1971) 37 Within this penumbral consciousness. **1965** *Mod. Law Rev.* XXVIII. 510 The American concern with the judicial process and the creative element in the common law is particularly appropriate in analysing the role of appeal courts, for appeal courts..are primarily concerned with penumbral issues.

penumbrous, *a.* For *rare*—1 read *rare* and add further examples.

1959 *Times* 16 May 8/6 To proceed to some stygian cellar,..and from the penumbrous interior gathering them [*sc.* mushrooms] by the hundredweight, is not, of course, sport. **1964** *Listener* 19 Mar. 484/2 He's more readable than Grimm, and much more concerned to give a solid idea of those contradictory, penumbrous figures.

Penutian (pĕnū·ʃən, -tiăn), *sb.* and *a.* Also Penuti. [f. Maiduan *pen* two + Miwokan and Costanoan *uti* two + -AN.] **A.** *sb.* **a.** A North American Indian language stock comprising the Miwokan, Costanoan, Wintuan, Maiduan, and Yokutsan families of California. Also, a proposed language phylum comprising the Penutian stock (distinguished as *California Penutian*), the Oregon Penutian and Plateau Penutian stocks, the Chinookan and Tsimshian families, and (in the usage of some scholars) certain other language groupings of North and Central America. **B.** *adj.* Of or pertaining to Penutian.

1912 DIXON & KROEBER in *Amer. Anthropologist* XIV. 692 The new larger families and their components are: *Penutian*, comprising the groups formerly known as Maidu, Wintun, Miwok, Costanoan, and Yokuts. [Etc.] **1914** *Ibid.* XV. 649 There is available enough information on the structure of the five Penutian languages to prove their genetic affinity beyond a doubt. **1932** W. L. GRAFF *Lang.* 431 The most important North American branches: Eskimo..Penutian. **1959** *Chambers's Encycl.* VIII. 360/1 The 22 language-families of North American are: Algonquin,..Penuti, [etc.]. **1965** *Canad. Jrnl. Linguistics* Spring 78 Suggestions of affiliation with ..Penutian. **1968** R. W. LANGACKER *Lang. & its Struct.* viii. 232 Continuing north, we find Takelman..Chinookan, and Plateau Penutian (including Klamath, Modoc, Nez Percé, Cayuse, and Yakima). **1972** *Language* XLVIII. 378 Chinook Jargon, once the means of communication among the (as yet) unrelated Indo-European, Athapaskan, Salishan, Penutian, and Wakashan-speaking peoples of the Pacific North-west. **1973** H. LANDAR in *Current Trends in Linguistics* X. 1294 California Penutian. Rubruz for Yokuts, Maidu, Miwok-Costanoan, and Wintun. **1974** *Encycl. Brit. Micropædia* VII. 859/2 The Penutian languages are sometimes grouped into a yet larger stock, called either Penutian or Macro-Penutian, that includes several Meso-American Indian languages. **1977** C. F. & F. M. VOEGELIN *Classification & Index World's Lang.* 287 Their [*sc.* Dixon and Kroeber's] grouping did not extend Penutian beyond the so-called California Penutian. *Ibid.*, A dozen separate language families beside nine different language isolates..are said to be remotely related to each other within the Penutian phylum.

Hence **Penu·tianist**, a student of Penutian.

1965 *Language* XLI. 173 Sapir's influence extends also to Penutianists.

penwiper. Add: **a.** (Earlier examples.)

1826 E. BROWN *Let.* in C. Oman *Ayot Rectory* (1965) iv. 90 Brown holland pockets containing housewives,..pencils, penwipers, knives. **1838** DICKENS *Diary* 2 Jan. in *Lett.* (1965) I. 629, I wrote to Mrs. Hogarth yesterday,..sending as a New Years' token a pen-wiper of poor Mary's. **1840** —— *Sk. Young Couples* 88 All manner of presents, such as pocket-books, pencil-cases, pen-wipers. **1841** C. RIDLEY *Let.* Nov. in *Cecilia* (1958) vi. 74, I want to know whether you like penwipers with white linen inside? They are all so here and the housekeeper renews them now and then.

b. A handkerchief. *slang.*

1902 FARMER & HENLEY *Slang* V. 170/1 *Penwiper*..a handkerchief. **1942** BERREY & VAN DEN BARK *Amer. Thes. Slang* §88/4 Handkerchief..penwiper.

pe·nwork. Also with hyphen and as two words. [PEN *sb.*2] **a.** Work done with a pen; writing. **b.** The decoration and ornamental lettering of illuminated books and manuscripts done with a pen; also, decoration drawn with a pen on the surface of furniture. Also *attrib.*

1644, etc. [in Dict. s.v. PEN *sb.*2 7]. **1844** H. N. HUMPHREYS *Illum. Bks. Middle Ages* 6/1 The letters..terminating in the margin in long tails,..only, instead of being solid, they are formed of light lines slightly enriched with simple and delicate penwork. **1901** J. W. BRADLEY *Illum. Lett. & Borders* iv. 49 The execution [of Celtic illumination] chiefly consists in pen work in black or coloured inks. **1906** E. JOHNSTON *Writing & Illuminating* xiii. 218 Many of the most beautiful MSS. were made in pen-work throughout. And it is well that the penman should stick to his pen as much as is possible. **1928** O. E. SAUNDERS *Eng. Illumination* I. 110 What distinguishes these borders especially from earlier work are the feathery sprays, indicated by pen-work lightly touched with green and ending in flourishes like the tendrils of a vine. **1969** N. R. KER *Medieval MSS. in Brit. Libraries* I. p. xiii, The terms 'decoration'..and 'ornament'..have been used in describing the surrounds of initials to make the important distinction between work with a brush and penwork flourishings. **1973** *Times* 13 Apr. 18/6 The curiosity of the sale was a monumental Empire ebonized secretaire-cabinet, the top shaped as a temple supported on lightly draped female figures and the whole lavishly applied with classical ormolu motifs and penwork. **1976** *Codicologica* I. 78 Practically no research has been done on the history of decoration of the medieval manuscript and of the numerous elements included in that word: initials,..penwork flourishes on initials or paragraph signs, [etc.]. **1978** *Bodl. Libr. Rec.* IX. 326 Their simple penwork interlace is frequently enlivened by the inclusion of a bird or monster head, a flower or a peascod.

Hence **pe·nworker**, one who works with a pen; **pe·nworked** *a.* (in sense b).

1901 Penworker [in Dict. s.v. PEN *sb.*2 7]. **1965** *Harper's Bazaar* June 76/3 A Regency working-table with an exquisite black pen-worked top..£70.

Penzance (penzæ·ns). The title of James Plaisted Wilde, Lord *Penzance* (1816–99), English lawyer and amateur horticulturist, used *attrib.* in **Penzance briar, rose,** to designate a rose belonging to a group of hybrids developed by him from the sweet briar, *Rosa rubiginosa*, and distinguished by scented foliage and single flowers.

[**1891** *Jrnl. R. Hort. Soc.* XIII. p. cxviii, One of the most interesting features in the exhibition was a stand of seedling Sweet Briar hybrids raised by the Right Hon. Lord Penzance... In the case of Lady Penzance the perfume of the leaves was retained in conjunction with small single flowers of a rosy-salmon hue.] **1902** A. FOSTER-MELLIAR *Bk. of Rose* (ed. 2) ii. 20 It is a great mistake to plant these 'Penzance' or any other Sweet-briars in Rose-beds; for they are very strong growers. **1907** *Gardeners' Chron.* 15 June 382/3 Rambler, Wichuraiana, and Penzance Roses will all submit to gentle forcing. **1912** E. WILLMOTT *Genus Rosa* II. 455 With the introduction of the Penzance Briars a new race of roses came into being. **1935** N. MITCHISON *We have been Warned* II. 196 There were Penzance briars and species roses growing unpruned. **1956** B. PARK *Collins' Guide to Roses* xi. 195 Lord Penzance produced by hybridizing many distinct seedling varieties at the end of the XIXth century which he called Penzance Briars; they represent a distinct series. **1969** C. LLOYD *Gardening on Chalk & Lime* vi. 60, I should avoid the Penzance briars... They are victims of black spot.

peola (pī,ōu·lă). *U.S. Black slang.* [Etym. unknown.] A light-complexioned Black person, esp. a girl.

1942 Z. N. HURSTON in A. Dundes *Mother Wit* (1973) 224/2 Dat broad I seen you with wasn't no pe-ola. **1944** C. CALLOWAY *Hepsters Dict.*, *Peola*, a light person, almost white. **1970** C. MAJOR *Dict. Afro-Amer. Slang* 90 *Peola*, a light-skinned Afro-American girl.

peon. Add: **1.** Also in Bangladesh, Sri Lanka (Ceylon), and Malaysia. **c.** Also, a person who does minor work in an office.

1913 L. WOOLF *Village in Jungle* vii. 211 The peon and the interpreter told Babu to hold his tongue. **1927** R. J. H. SIDNEY *In Brit. Malaya To-Day* 136 Postmen, Government *peons* (messengers), prisoners themselves, all wear materials either made or made-up in Singapore prison. **1931** *Times* 17 Feb. 13/5 Five postal *peons* [servants] were injured while on duty, and the City Post Office was closed for three days... Instead of deliveries by *peons* people are asked to inquire at the post office for letters. **1969** [see *DURZEE]. **1969** *Pioneer* (Lucknow) 13 Aug. 6/2 A peon in the office of the regional transport authority in Bombay attends office in his own car daily. **1971** *Ceylon Observer* (Mag. ed.) 19 Sept. 7/5 A peon has to come to the rescue of the official. **1972** *Straits Times* 26 Apr. 7/6 F and N workers have been picketing the factory..in support of a claim for free shoes for three peons. **1973** *Archivum Linguisticum* IV. 91 Peons, low-caste strangers, and their wives. **1975** *Bangladesh Times* 23 July 1/1 Six persons including a professor, a B.Sc examinee and a college peon, were arrested by the Lalbagh police on Tuesday on charge of adopting unfair means in the examination and abetment of the crime.

2. Also in extended use. (Further examples and earlier *attrib.* example).

1826 W. B. DEWEES *Lett. from Early Settler Texas* (1852) 56 The Peons, or lower class—are a sort of slaves, who are employed by the aristocracy. **1826** [see *ARRIERO]. **1847** W. S. HENRY *Campaign Sk. War with Mexico* xii. 134 This 'peone' system is fully equal to our slavery. **1945** J. L. MARSHALL *Santa Fe* 9 In 1850 New Mexico came into the Union as a free soil territory—and went on buying and selling slaves as of old, calling them *peons* and *peonas*. **1962** N. MAXWELL *Witch-Doctor's Apprentice* vii. 81 They weren't Cotos, only a white man named Rodríguez, his partner, Juan Gómez, and five peons. **1970** S. L. BARRACLOUGH in I. L. Horowitz *Masses in Lat. Amer.* iv. 125 On some traditional Andean haciendas, peons still kneel to kiss the corner of the 'patron's' poncho to show respect. **1972** P. DANIEL *Shadow of Slavery* ix. 177 In New Orleans a couple..took the peons in, gave them directions on how to proceed to..Chicago. Perhaps thirty persons escaped on this modern version of the underground railroad. **1977** *Time* 6 June 42/2 He [*sc.* Elvis Presley] periodically tossed a sweat-stained scarf to the peons below.

‖**3.** *pl.* peones. = BANDERILLERO.

1932 [see *BANDERILLERO]. **1957** A. MACNAB *Bulls of Iberia* v. 50 Each matador's team consists of five assistants: two picadors, mounted, and three peones or capemen on foot—also called *banderilleros* because they plant the sticks called *banderillas*. **1967** MCCORMICK & MASCAREÑAS *Compl. Aficionado* ii. 52 The senior matador who knows and likes this breed, has told his peones not to show a cape until he gives the signal. **1976** E. P. BENSON *Bulls of Ronda* iv. 26 Navarro's peon played the bull for a few minutes before El Zorro gave the bull to Navarro. The boy began a series of passes with his cape.

peonage. Add: **1.** (Further examples). Also, in parts of southern U.S., an arrangement whereby convicts are leased to contractors. Also *transf.* and *attrib.*

1850 *Ex. Doc. 31st U.S. Congress 1 Sess. Senate* No. 64. 49 From this cause, and the miserable system of 'peonage' that prevails, the products of agriculture are barely sufficient to support the inhabitants [north of El Paso]. *a* **1889** J. J. WEBB *Adventures Santa Fé Trade* (1931) 101 The system of peonage, or voluntary servitude, was a fixed institution. **1903** *Nation* (N.Y.) 3 Dec. 436/3 More peonage revelations in various portions of the South must be opening the eyes of those editors who criticised us last spring for believing that the Alabama cases were other than sporadic and unparalleled happenings. **1934** A. WOOLLCOTT *While Rome Burns* 291 The Guild must often wonder why..it should ask..a company to enter into so benumbing a peonage. **1969** A. G. FRANK *Latin Amer.* xix. 302 After the French intervention and under the thirty-year reign of Porfirio Díaz, peonage returned in full force and concentration of landownership became worse than ever. **1972** P. DANIEL *Shadow of Slavery* ii. 33 The root of the peonage problem was anchored in the long-practiced abuse of black laborers. **1972** 'E. LATHEN' *Murder without Icing* (1973) xi. 107 The player..contended that, if he could be forced to..work for another team at the whim of his employer, he had been reduced to an unconstitutional state of peonage. **1972** *National Observer* (U.S.) 27 May 7/4 Federal Judge J. Robert Martin, Jr., had told the jury that Federal law required that proof of 'peonage' must be based on evidence of indebtedness. **1973** L. G. FORER in A. E. Wilkerson *Rights of Children* 31 Legality of the commitment would then be the issue—not the procedures by which he was committed or the quantum of care that he received or the existence of institutional peonage.

peonidin (pīǫ·nidin). *Chem.* [ad. G. *päonidin* (Willstätter & Nolan 1915, in *Ann. d. Chem.* CDVIII. 136), f. *päonin* *PEONIN: see *-IDIN.] An anthocyanidin (usu. isolated as the reddish brown chloride, $C_{16}H_{13}O_6Cl$) that is the aglycone of peonin.

1915 *Chem. Abstr.* IX. 1307 Hydrolyzed by boiling 2·5 min. with 20% HCl, peonin gives 2 mols. glucose and peonidin chloride. **1956** I. L. FINAR *Org. Chem.* II. xv. 587 Peonidin is the monomethyl ether of cyanidin. **1965** J. B. HARBONE in Bonner & Varner *Plant Biochem.* xxiv. 624 While over a hundred different flavonoid aglycons have been isolated from plants, only eleven of these occur at all commonly... Six are anthocyanidins: the scarlet pelargonidin, the crimson cyanidin, the mauve delphinidin, and the three simply derived methyl ethers, peonidin, petunidin, and malvidin.

peonin (pī·ŏnin). *Chem.* [ad. G. *päonin* (Willstätter & Nolan, 1915, in *Ann. d. Chem.* CDVIII. 136), f. *päonie* PEONY: see -IN1.] An anthocyanin (usu. isolated as the reddish violet chloride, $C_{28}H_{33}O_{16}Cl$) that is the colouring matter of red peonies and on hydrolysis gives peonidin and glucose.

1915 *Chem. Abstr.* IX. 1307 The deep violet-red peony meal contains 3–3·5% peonin. **1946** *Nature* 7 Sept. 342/1 An acid aqueous extract of the yellow 'Hofmann's Glory' added to synthetic peonin or malvin makes the red solutions much bluer, and they then simulate the appropriate flower extracts. **1956** I. L. FINAR *Org. Chem.* II. xv. 687 Peonidin chloride..is produced..when peonin chloride is hydrolysed with hydrochloric acid.

peonism. (Examples.)

1851 D. WEBSTER *Wks.* V. 351, I suppose there is no slavery of that description in California now. I understand that *peonism*, a sort of penal servitude, exists there, or rather a sort of voluntary sale of a man and his offspring for debt. **1857** W. W. H. DAVIS *El Gringo* ix. 231 Another peculiar feature of New Mexico is the system of domestic servitude called peonism, that has existed, and still exists, in all the Spanish American colonies.

peony. Add: **2. b.** *peony-flowered* (later examples), *-pink*, *-red* adjs.

1813 M. EDGEWORTH *Let.* 19 Apr. (1971) 21 Her color is less of the peony red than it used to be. **1905** *Daily Chron.* 15 May 3/3 A pretty hat.., made in soft Manilla straw, in the natural colouring, and trimmed with one large pink peony, in soft satin and chiffon, and folded draperies of Louisine silk ribbon, in peony-pink shot with white. 1906 *Ibid.* 4 Oct. 6/5 A new variety of peony-flowered, or art dahlia, in crimson and pink, is shown. 1907 *Ibid.* 18 Sept. 3/5 Some very fine examples of the new peony-flowered variety of dahlia. 1927 *Eaton's News Weekly* 12 Mar. 20 This pretty..frock..comes also in gooseberry green and palmetto green, or in peony red tones. 1957 T. R. H. Lebar *Dahlias for Everyone* ii. 19 The peony flowered varieties..had comparatively flat petals. 1976 W. E. Shewell-Cooper *Basic Bk. Dahlia Growing* ii. 16 Paeony-flowered Dahlias have blooms with two or more rings of generally flattened ray florets, the centre forming a disc.

people, *sb.* Add: **1. c.** *Peoples of the Sea*: name given in Egyptian records of the 19th and 20th Dynasties to various sea-borne migrant peoples who invaded and settled parts of Egypt, Syria, and Palestine. See also *Sea Peoples* s.v. *sea *sb.* 23.

1906 J. H. Breasted *Hist. Egypt* vi. xxiii. 477 The restless and turbulent peoples of the northern Mediterranean, whom the Egyptians designated the 'peoples of the sea', were showing themselves in ever increasing numbers in the south. 1950 H. L. Lorimer *Homer & Monuments* v. 150 On the monuments of Ramses III the most conspicuous of the Peoples of the Sea, the Shardana and Pulesati, are uniformly represented with round shields with single hand-grips. 1973 K. A. Kitchen in D. J. Wiseman *Peoples Old Testament Times* iii. 57 The Lukka..appear as raiders in the Amarna letters *c.* 1370 B.C., as Hittite allies against Ramesses II at Kadesh *c.* 1286 B.C., and then in Libya with Libyans and others in the first attack by 'Peoples of the Sea' on Egypt, repulsed by Merenptah *c.* 1220 B.C.

2. c. *People of the Book*: a body or community whose religion entails adherence to a book of divine revelation, *spec.* [tr. Arab. *Ahl al-Kitāb*] Jews and Christians as regarded in Muslim thought.

1834 A. Burnes *Bokhara* I. x. 313 The Vizier took a cup, and said, 'You must drink with us; for you are people of the book, better than the Russians.' 1861 J. M. Rodwell tr. *Koran* 635 O people of the Book! now hath our Apostle come to you to clear up to you The cessation of Apostles. 1885 T. P. Hughes *Dict. Islam* 280/2 *Kitabi*, a term used for one of the *Ahlu 'l-Kitāb*, 'the people of the Book', or those in possession of the inspired word of God, as Jews or Christians. 1900 'Odysseus' *Turkey in Europe* v. 178 According to strict [Muslim] theology, Jews and Christians are called 'People of the Book' (Ehlu-'l-kitab), and enjoy a position superior to that of heathen polytheists. *a* 1936 Kipling *Something of Myself* (1937) viii. 224 It is true the Children of Israel are 'people of the Book', and in the second Surah of the Koran Allah is made to say: 'High above mankind have I raised you.' 1959 [see *Kitab]. 1967 *Guardian* 19 June 8/3 It..pains me, as it pains most Jews, when 'the people of the book' are compelled to wield the sword. 1976 Y. Menuhin in D. Villiers *Next Year in Jerusalem* 334 A love of improvisation..has never been lost to the people of the Book. 1977 B. Gascoigne *Christians* v. 106 Jews, Christians, Muslims.. are all, in the powerful phrase of the Koran, 'people of the book'.

3. c. (Further examples.)

1822 C. Lamb *Let.* 23 Dec. (1935) II. 356, I rather grudge that S[outhe]y has taken up the History of your People. 1886 *Hist. Sk. Foreign Missions Seventh-Day Adventists* 20/1 Eld. Lindermann after a time became estranged not only from our people but also from a large share of those whom he had been instrumental in leading to the observance of the Sabbath. 1900 F. von Hügel *Let.* 7 July (1931) 86 But, as to the Preface, he says he would, on the one hand, even selfishly like to do so, to prevent the book seeming to appear without any support or knowledge of any of our people. 1916 A. Huxley *Let.* 7 Aug. (1969) 109 I've arranged to be with my people in the country during August. 1971 'M. Innes' *Awkward Lie* viii. 133 You know about my wife's people. 1977 *Belfast Tel.* 28 Feb. 3/7 She used to collect it [*sc.* silver paper] for the Multiple Sclerosis people, but they don't take it now.

4. a. (Later examples.) Cf. *man of the people* s.v. *man *sb.*[1] 18.

1953 E. Simon *Past Masters* iv. ii. 229 Which of them is the scion of the upper classes and which the son of the people? 1969 A. G. Frank *Latin Amer.* xx. 328 The bourgeoisie develops at the cost of exploiting the people. 1973 *Freedomways* XIII. 11 In China, India, the Soviet Union, even in the pre-Nazi Germany of 1932 Robeson traveled, acted and sang and everywhere he met with the people. 1973 *Black Panther* 17 Nov. 9/3 If the people (and when I say 'the people' I mean the oppressed people) control Malcolm X University, if they control it without reservation or without having to answer for what is done there or who speaks there, then Malcolm X University is progressive. 1976 M. J. Lasky *Utopia & Revolution* (1977) xiv. 496 One of the essential preconditions of the establishment..of a revolutionary tradition and its associated components of utopian hope and militant temper is the creation of 'The People' as a political factor. 1977 *Private Eye* 13 May 14/3 It..won't encourage the people to work any harder.

c. (Usu. with capital initial.) The prosecution in a law case as designated in certain States of the U.S.A., the equivalent of the Crown in a British law case.

1801 *Cases of Pract. Supreme Court New-York, 1791–1800* 34 Ludlow *ads.* The People. 1810 *Rep. Cases Supreme Court New-York* II. 301 The People *against* Olcott. 1849 *New York Superior Court Rep.* III. 193 J. McGay for the defendant, cited *The People v. Koeber.* 1898 *Misc. Rep. Courts of Record New York* XXV. 599 The People of the State of New York, Respondent *v.* Irving Mulkins, Appellant. 1926 *Michigan Rep.* CCXXX. 485 People v. Lorde. The people's testimony tends to show that..the defendant..went to the store of one John Kay. 1936 E. S. Gardner *Case of Stuttering Bishop* xiv. 210 You may proceed..with the testimony in the preliminary hearing in the case of People versus Julia Branner. 1960 *California Reporter 1959* I. 245/1 People of the State of California, Plaintiff and Appellant, v. One 1952 Mercury 2-door Sedan..Defendant, Gregorio H. Nunez, sole owner of the above described vehicle, Respondent. 1973 *N.Y. Law Jrnl.* 4 Sept. 4/7 The prosecutor mentioned that he had provided defense counsel with pre-trial statements made by the People's witnesses.

5. Also used in the possessive (*spec.* in the terminology of Communism and Socialism) to designate institutions and concepts which are regarded as belonging to, derived from, or benefiting the people considered as the source of power or the basis of society. See also sense 9 below.

1811 *Weekly Reg.* 7 Sept. 9/2, I will attach myself, as an editor, to no party but the People's Party, whose wish is '*peace, liberty and safety*'. 1834 J. J. Strang *Diary* 3 Mar. in M. M. Quaife *Kingdom of St. James* (1930) 218, I find myself nominated on what is called the people's ticket for constable. 1854 C. Fox *Let.* 21 Nov. in *Jrnls.* (1972) 217 F. Maurice was much cheered by the good beginning of his People's College. 1896 *Rep. on Labor Movement U.S.A. to Internat. Socialist & T.U. Congr.* 2/2 The Socialist Labor party is steadily advancing, the so-called 'People's party'..is not less steadily passing out of sight. 1900 [in Dict., sense 4.]. 1927 H. Dobbs in *Lett. Gertrude Bell* II. 558 On the part of the Opposition, now definitely constituted under the name of the People's Party, with Yasin Pasha as leader, doubts were expressed as to the advantage to Iraq of the extension of the 1922 Treaty for 25 years. 1942 *Ann. Reg. 1941* 16 A number of pacifists, including leading Communists, announced that they were organising a 'People's Convention' to demand 'a People's Government' which should bring the war to an end. 1953 *Encounter* Nov. 69/1 Looking over into East Berlin, one could see only a group of six People's Police in their new grey uniforms. 1958 *Listener* 30 Oct. 682/2 The policy of adventure and provocation of People's China. 1958 *Ibid.* 25 Sept. 452/1 Lloyd George was forty-six when he introduced his 'People's' Budget. 1958 [see *co-operative B. 2 b]. 1959 *Exchange* (N.Y. Stock Exchange) Aug. 2/1 Today we have 12,490,000 [shareholders] plus an estimated 1.4 million owners of private corporations. We have the most broadly owned, most dynamic people's capitalism ever seen on the face of the earth. 1961 *Sunday Bull.* (Philadelphia) 15 Jan. 1. 5/1 Pianist Svyatoslav Richter..has been given the Soviet Union's top artistic award: 'People's Artist'. 1966 R. E. Pickering *Himself Again* xxii. 162 This must be Bratislava. I had escaped from Hungary into Czechoslovakia... Already I imagined my stubborn silence in a windowless room with the People's Police. 1966 'H. MacDiarmid' *Company I've Kept* v. 148 Gaeldom, but for the English, gave good promise many centuries ago of evolving an ideal 'people's state'. 1969 C. Davidson in Cockburn & Blackburn *Student Power* 331 The classless society of America's 'people's capitalism'. 1972 *Buenos Aires Herald* 4 Feb. 9/4 In Buenos Aires, police continued the hunt for the 'People's Revolutionary Army' (ERP) extremists who staged the record robbery of over 400 million old pesos at the National Development Bank. 1973 *Black Panther* 21 July 7/1 Elaine Brown,..the first, genuine People's Artist America has produced. 1974 L. Deighton *Spy Story* xviii. 197 It took a long time before the Russians would let the D.D.R. have submarines. But the People's Navy are all ten-year men. 1974 tr. *Sniečkus's Soviet Lithuania* 108 In recent years, an important form of ideological education—the people's universities—has become widespread. 1975 *New Yorker* 28 Apr. 99/1 When I asked one economist what models the Chinese revolution might provide for Vietnam, the man stared at me for a few moments.., and then said, 'Well, what would *you* suggest? The Cultural Revolution? People's Communes?' 1977 K. Benton *Red Hen Conspiracy* xviii. 143 He'd have to set up..what we call a people's prison to hold the Sheikh safely.

6. In phr. *of all people*, an expression suggesting that no one more surprising could be involved.

1851 S. Spencer *Let.* 1 May (1912) 410 The *Times* yesterday contained some fine tho' rather enthusiastically loyal verses about the opening of the Exhibition by Thackeray of all people. 1922 Chesterton *Man who knew too Much* Why should you, of all people, be so passionate about it? 1965 *Radio Times* 2 May 15/2 Stan and Ollie..cause some hilarious surprises when Stan becomes Lord Paddington with Ollie of all people as his manservant.

e. An individual, a person. *U.S. colloq.*

1926 J. Black *You can't Win* ix. 105 He's good people and I want to get him fixed up for a cell with the right folks. 1934 *Detective Fiction Weekly* 28 Apr. 113/1 'Stick yer four-bits in yer shoe', he snorted, 'I'm people.' 1949 'N. R. Nash' *Young & Fair* I. ii. 14, I guess she's people of good heart. 1956 B. Holiday *Lady sings Blues* (1973) x. 98 A lot of creeps have been dogging Orson Welles ever since but they can't touch him. He's a fine cat... And a talented cat. But more than that, he's fine people.

8. *people-centred, -oriented* adjs.; **people mover**, any of several means of conveying people from one place to another; **people sniffer**, a device that can detect the presence of a person by chemical analysis of the air around him (see also quot. 1977).

1968 *Guardian* 5 Aug. 6/6 The interests of Africa will be best served..by a people-centred system, and African socialism is that system. 1970 *Ibid.* 23 Dec. 7/4 There is such a gulf between books that are system-centred and those that are people-centred. 1971 J. P. Romualdi in *Science Year 1972* 375 A 'people mover', a vehicle smaller than a streetcar..will provide continuous service between the old campus in town and the new campus in the suburbs. 1972 *N.Y. Times* 1 June 30/1 Henry Ford 2d announced yesterday that the Ford Motor Company would build rapid-transit systems based on its driverless, rubber-tired people mover system being demonstrated at the Transpo '72 exhibition here. 1974 *Times* 22 Mar. (Buses Suppl.) p. i/2 Magnetic levitation, vacuum tubes, vertical take-off aircraft, and small-scale automatic and semi-automatic 'people-movers' of all kinds for urban situations. 1970 *New Society* 5 Mar. 392/2 They exhibited the familiar people-oriented value-pattern detected many times among prospective teachers. 1975 *Nature* 27 Nov. 286/1 What more logical project for a rebuilt people-oriented science programme than to attempt to predict earthquakes. 1965 *Daily Tel.* 5 Oct. 22/8 A person being examined is placed in a 'people sniffer', a glass cylinder, and an analysis of the outgoing air discloses the chemical make-up of the subject. 1968 *N.Y. Times* 18 Aug. 1. 3 United States troops refer to the gadget as the 'people sniffer'. It leads American officers here in the Mekong delta to enemy hide-outs by 'sniffing out' the kind of ammonia odors given off by the human body. 1973 *Times* 24 Jan. 8/6 There has been use of the Manpack Personnel Detector, or 'people-sniffer'—picking up the enemy by the smell of his sweat. 1977 *Time* 2 May 44/1 Their principal piece of equipment is a 'people sniffer', an electronic sensing device developed to catch the prowling Viet Cong. Despite its name, the instrument actually detects the minute seismic vibrations caused by a person walking.

9. Special combs. with *people's* (chiefly in sense *5): **people's army**, (*a*) an army organized on egalitarian or communist principles; (*b*) an army composed of the common people; **people's car**, an inexpensive motor car designed for popular sale; **people's choice**, a popular favourite; **People's Court**, (*a*) a court set up by the Nazi regime in Germany to deal with political offences; (*b*) a court in the Soviet and similar legal systems; also *transf.*; **people's democracy**, a political system in which power is regarded as being invested in the people, *spec.* a Communist state, esp. in Eastern Europe; **People's front** = *Popular Front; **People's Palace**, a centre for the recreation and entertainment of the people, *spec.* a former East London institution with library, theatre, educational classes, etc., opened in 1887; also *fig.*; **people's park**, a park intended to be used by all members of a community; **people's republic**, name assumed by a number of left-wing or Communist states, as *People's Republic of China*; also in gen. allusive use; **people's theatre**, a theatre run on socialist lines for the use of the community; **people's war**, (*a*) a war in which the people are regarded as fighting against the ruling classes or foreign aggression; (*b*) a war in which all members of the community are involved, a total war.

1937 E. Snow *Red Star over China* vi. i. 211 The Kuominchun, the 'People's Army' of General Feng Yu'-hsiang. 1941 'G. Orwell' *Coll. Ess.* (1968) II. 116 The Home Guard is..a sort of People's Army officered by Blimps. 1969 A. G. Frank *Latin Amer.* xxiv 366 Nowhere does Debray suggest how the guerrilla band is later to develop into the people's army. 1970 A. Sinclair *Guevara* iii. 37 The regular army must be disbanded and a people's army created..of peasants and workers and soldiers. 1938 *Sun* (Baltimore) 7 Sept. 1/1 Award winners are Prof. Ferdinand Porsche, designer of the 'Volkswagen', Germany's new 'people's car'. 1939 *War Illustr.* 4 Nov. p. iii/1 A scheme by which German artisans paid in advance by weekly instalments for their long-promised 'people's car' would appear to have fallen through, for the great works at Fallersleben, the supposed factory for these cars, are now stated to be turning out munitions. 1958 [see *bubble *sb.* 2 c]. 1972 *Buenos Aires Herald* 2 Feb. 7/6 The rise of nationalism has brought demands for inexpensive 'people's cars' in Chile, Peru and Venezuela. 1953 Wodehouse *Performing Flea* 205 In Dormitory 309 the People's Choice was good old George Travers. 1961 —— *Service with Smile* (1962) v. 80 'Why is he the people's choice?' 'Because she's got the goods on him.' 1934 H. Griffith *People's Court* 9 Comrade Chernov only turned up just in time yesterday not to make the People's Court look ridiculous in the eyes of its clients. 1935 *Ann. Reg. 1934* 1. 191 A law of May 3 constituted a new and extraordinary Court of Justice, the so-called People's Court, for all political offences. This tribunal as well as the old regular courts in numerous cases passed excessively severe sentences on opponents of the Government. 1938 *Ann. Reg. 1937* 181 In April the People's Court sentenced several Catholic priests to long periods of detention. 1946 *Ann. Reg. 1945* 205 Twenty-four People's Courts were established by Decree in Bohemia and Moravia. 1970 H. Trevelyan *Middle East in Revolution* 145 The notorious Colonel Medhawi, a cousin of Qasim, presided over the People's Court [in Iraq]. 1972 *N.Y. Law Jrnl.* 10 Oct. 1/5 The three-level federal system which emerged was composed of People's Courts with jurisdiction in rural areas; Regional Courts which are courts of first and second instance with appellate jurisdiction; and the Supreme Courts which are divided on a territorial basis into Supreme Courts of the autonomous republics, Union Republics and the U.S.S.R. 1977 *Listener* 15 Dec. 779/1 The Provisionals are now attempting to develop 'People's Courts'. 1947 *New Times* 3 Dec. 3 (*heading*) The people's democracies—a fresh breach in the imperialist system. *Ibid.* 4/2 In the people's democracies, power has passed from the hands of the exploiting classes—the landlords and bourgeoisie—into the hands of the people. 1958

F. W. Neal *Titoism in Action* i. 1 The Communist leadership which came to power in Yugoslavia in 1945 organized the country along the lines prescribed by the Soviet Union for an Eastern European 'people's democracy'. **1974** *Times* 22 Jan. 14/2 Mr Jack Jones.. made an unfortunate remark about his desire to see Britain become a People's Democracy, which is the title given to those Eastern European states which have nothing to do with the people and are not democratic; but it turned out that he meant, not a People's Democracy but a people's democracy, which is not at all the same thing and better hadn't be. **1977** P. Johnson *Enemies of Society* viii. 109 Social democrat means a Right-wing anti-Communist politician of the centre; a People's Democracy or a People's Democratic Republic is a form of Communist totalitarian state. **1937** 'G. Orwell' *Coll. Ess.* (1968) I. 271 The worker and the bourgeois.. are fighting side by side. This uneasy alliance is known as the Popular Front (or, in the Communist press, to give it a spuriously democratic appeal, People's Front). **1937** E. Snow *Red Star over China* III. iii. 99 If the Chinese People's Front is powerfully homogeneous..the war will be short. **1958** *Spectator* 13 June 777/3 Mr. Grant's badly camouflaged appeal for a new People's Front. **1854** *Punch* 24 June 266/1 The People's Palace will become a misnomer if the people are so confined in workshops [etc.]..that none but the comparatively idle can visit what is expressly designed for the appreciation of the industrious. **1889** G. B. Shaw *London Music 1888–89* (1937) 210 Covent Garden is a people's palace compared with Bayreuth. **1890** Hardy *Let.* 13 Mar. (1978) I. 210 We cannot do better than what you propose—purchase a library of fiction for the People's Palace. **1892** [in Dict., sense 4]. **1964** D. Owen *Eng. Philanthropy* (1965) III. x. 293 In the early 1930's the original People's Palace was destroyed by fire. It was rebuilt and since 1954 has formed a part of Queen Mary College of London University. **1967** *Guardian* 29 July 12/4 Sir John Wardlaw-Milne..has left £100,000 to the State of Jersey..to build a 'people's palace' where tourists with children can shelter on wet days. **1970** E. J. Hirst *Seeing Glasgow* 41 The Old Glasgow Museum, People's Palace, Glasgow Green, provides a visual record of the development of Glasgow. The City's history is shown in pictures and prints. **1971** P. J. Keating *Working Classes in Victorian Fiction* iv. 96 The People's Palace was built in Whitechapel... In May 1887 the Queen travelled to the Mile End Road to declare the Palace officially open. **1975** *Scottish Field* Mar. 44/1 (*caption*) A bowl traditionally attributed to the old Delftfield pottery, now in the People's Palace Museum, Glasgow. *Ibid.* 45/1 It could mean more interest being taken in the People's Palace exhibit. **1863** Dickens *Uncomm. Trav.* (1866) xxiii. 163/1 The People's Park near Birmingham..was crowded with people from the Black Country. **1873** C. M. Yonge *Pillars of House* III. xxiv. 8 One of the brothers took her out in the street, or to the 'People's Park'. **1963** *Guardian* 19 Nov. 9/7 Rumford..suggested..in 1789 the laying-out of a great 'people's park' along the Isar. **1970** *Time* 23 Nov. 81 Last year he [*sc.* the chancellor of Berkeley] was unfairly blamed for the way police handled student demands that one of the university's empty lots be turned into a 'people's park'. **1976** *Times* 4 Sept. 10/5 In Bremen's 'people's park' the food is tasty. **1949** *Times* 8 Apr. 5/3 Mr. Rákosi..said..that 'the Hungarian Republic must be developed into a People's Republic'. **1972** J. Poyer *Chinese Agenda* (1973) vi. 63 The khaki uniforms and green collar tabs of the Army of the People's Republic of China. **1974** *Encycl. Brit. Micropædia* III. 80/2 Congo (Brazzaville) *Official name*: République Populaire du Congo (People's Republic of the Congo). **1975** *Bangladesh Times* 18 July 2/6 The Magura Journalists Association in a meeting held recently at Magura hailed the Government of the People's Republic of Bangladesh for creating the new district of Magura. **1978** Ld. Hailsham *Dilemma of Democracy* xxii. 148 Probably our own monarch would not survive the institution in Britain of..a people's republic. **1920** D. H. Lawrence *Touch & Go* 5 A nice phrase: 'A People's Theatre'. But what about it? There's no such thing in existence as a People's Theatre. **1929** S. W. Cheney *Theatre* xxii. 506 In Germany a real 'democratic' theatre was developed before the war, and today functions as a 'people's theatre' of a unique sort. It is, perhaps, historically important as a step toward a theatre for a new Socialistic time. The *Volksbühne* in Berlin is owned by its audiences. **1904** L. Hale (*title*) The 'People's War' in France 1870–1871. **1942** E. Waugh *Put out More Flags* i. 86 This is all that anyone talks about, thought Ambrose; jobs and the kind of war it is going to be..people's war, total war, indivisible war, war infinite, war incomprehensible. **1947** J. Bertram *Shadow of War* 9 'How about China's United Front?' I tried to tell them of what I had seen of this people's war. **1968** K. Martin *Editor* xv. 301 It was not until after Dunkirk that the idea of a People's War began to be understood. **1972** P. Black *Biggest Aspidistra* II. v. 133 The broadcasts did not cheat; the voices and sentiments were those of the people's war. **1976** M. Green *Children of Sun* viii. 311 Official propaganda presented this as a 'people's war', and emphasised the proletarian ordinariness of its heroes.

peo·plehood. [f. People *sb.* + -hood.] The condition or state of being a people; the consciousness or awareness of being a people.

1909 in Webster. **1969** V. Ferdinand in A. Chapman *New Black Voices* (1972) 379 We the young birds of blk poetics throw our songs brilliant Against the beautiful black sky of an emerging peoplehood & with the love of us..in our hearts. **1971** *Jrnl. Ecumenical Stud.* VIII. i. 53 This need not..lead to a kind of reductionism which limits the significance of attempts to find historical embodiment for the biblical notion of peoplehood. **1973** *Black World* Mar. 71 For Gwen Brooks, peoplehood or race is not limited to continental boundaries. *Ibid.* Apr. 87 A sense of peoplehood is growing. **1977** *Guardian Weekly* 31 July 7/2 The mini-State, as the Palestinians conceive it, is not just a matter of territory. It is a recognition..of their peoplehood.

pep (pep), *sb. colloq.* (orig. *U.S.*). [Abbrev. Pepper *sb.*] Vigour, energy, spirit, forcefulness.

1912 *Collier's* 13 Apr. 19/1 'Sure, the good old pep,' interposed Callahan. **1916** *Daily Colonist* (Victoria, B.C.) 19 July 9/4 (Advt.), This newest Overland Four has more power, pep, punch, and speed than any other low priced..car. **1923** Wodehouse *Inimitable Jeeves* xv. 187 That seems to be all the poor fish is able to do, dash it. He can chafe all right, but there he stops. He's lost his pep. He's got no dash. **1930** R. Macaulay *Staying with Relations* iv. 56 What a family!.. They don't have any *pep*. Only little Meg has pep and *she* won't be let grow up with it. **1930** E. Pound *XXX Cantos* xi. 51 And came back with no pep in him. **1931** E. F. Benson *Mapp & Lucia* ix. 234 A new hanging committee..full of pep and pop and vim. **1972** *Jrnl. Social Psychol.* LXXXVIII. 279 Lively, active, full-of-pep, energetic, peppy, vigorous, activated.

2. *attrib.* and *comb.*, as **pep rally** *U.S.*, a meeting to inspire enthusiasm, esp. before a sporting event; **pep speech** = *pep talk. See also *pep pill, *pep talk.

1945 *Boulder* (Colorado) *Daily Camera* 24 Nov. 4/2 Speaking at a pep rally..Dr. Allen told his audience.. other schools are spending money for players. **1974** *State* (Columbia, S. Carolina) 15 Feb. 3-B/1 University of South Carolina cheerleaders will conduct a pre-game pep rally in Carolina Coliseum Saturday beginning 12:15 as a prelude to the USC-Notre Dame battle. **1977** *New Yorker* 27 June 35/1 Some activity at the college—a pep rally, a football game, a dance. **1946** D. Hamson *We fell among Greeks* vi. 73, I thought of all the 'pep' speeches we would have to deliver.

pep, *v. colloq.* [f. the sb.] (Const. *up.*) *trans.* To fill or inspire with energy or vigour, to enliven, invigorate, excite, cheer up. Also (*rare*) *intr.*, to improve, to find new life. So **pe·pped-up** *ppl. a.*; **pepper-u·p, pepper-u·pper,** someone who or something which enlivens or stimulates; **pepping-u·p** *vbl. sb.*

1925 H. L. Foster *Trop. Tramp with Tourists* 56 'Just leave them to me,' said the Social Manager. 'I'll get them started, and all pepped up, and the rest will be easy.' **1928** *Daily Express* 30 Nov. 19 University athletics are undergoing a strenuous process of 'pepping up', on strictly scientific lines. **1929** J. P. McEvoy *Hollywood Girl* ii. 28, I was all pepped up about going out there [*sc.* to Hollywood] until I met you the other night. **1931** W. Holtby *Poor Caroline* vi. 202 Keep it vivid. Pep it up with a bit o' farce. **1936** 'P. Quentin' *Puzzle for Fools* iv. 24 We all had our daily treatments and mine consisted of a thorough pepping up. **1936** *Scrutiny* V. III. 270 Our ears are periodically offended by the ghastly and blasphemous harmonic monstrosities perpetrated by the popular peppers-up of Ye Olde Englysshe Folke Musicke. **1937** *N.Y. Post* 29 Jan. 24/3 (Advt.), Pepperupper. **1938** in Mencken *Amer. Lang.* Suppl. (1945) I. 259 A *cocktail* was therefore what I suppose today would be called a *pepper-upper*. **1945** [see *hot rod]. **1959** *Encounter* Sept. 13/1 A kind of forced jollity of a pepped-up Government White Paper. **1965** Leitner & Lanen *Dict. French & Eng. Slang* 98/1 *Pepper-upper*, stimulant. **1967** N. Freeling *Strike Out* 71 You're looking a bit peaked, old chap... Have a drink to pep you up. **1971** *Daily Tel.* 19 Oct. 15/2 These 'insert' tiles are the newest idea to pep up a block of solid colour. **1972** W. P. McGivern *Caprifoil* (1973) iii. 62 A chemical intoxication that stemmed from pepped-up endocrines. **1976** *Time* 20 Dec. 40/1 To pep up sluggish sales, American Motors Corp. is offering a $253 rebate to customers who purchase its 1977 compact Pacer.

peperite (pe·pərəit). *Geol.* [ad. F. *pépérite* (P. L. A. Cordier *Mémoire sur les Substances minérales dites 'en Masse'* (1815) ix. 66), prob. f. *pépér*(*ine* Peperino + *-ite* -ite[1].] A brecciated volcanic material consisting of fragments of lava and sedimentary rock, regarded by some as formed by the intrusion of lava into wet sediment, freq. under water, and by others as a product of the mixing of volcanic ejectamenta with such sediments. Cf. Peperino.

1839 *Civil Engin. & Arch. Jrnl.* II. 195/1 The geological structure of Mr. Hamilton's line of route is simple, being composed of only schistose rocks,..tertiary sandstones and limestones, granite, peperite, trachyte, basalt, and other igneous rocks. **1903** A. Geikie *Text-bk. Geol.* (ed. 4) II. 1254 These intercalations of tuff from the 'Peperites' of Auvergne, regarding which so much difference of opinion has been expressed. **1953** *Prof. Papers U.S. Geol. Survey* No. 454-B. 4/2 On Unalaska, pillows are separated from each other by peperite, fragmental igneous rock, argillite, or crustified chalcedony and quartz... Peperite is a mottled light-gray to pale-green breccia of mixed sedimentary and primary igneous debris. **1969** *Proc. Geologists' Assoc.* LXXX. 177 It is concluded that the peperites [of the Auvergne] are the product of explosive projection of basaltic ejectamenta into steadily accumulating lime-mud.

peperoni, var. *pepperoni.

pepful (pe·pful), *a. colloq.* [f. *pep *sb.* + -ful.] Full of life or verve, vigorous.

1923 *Weekly Dispatch* 22 Apr. 5 The film is..an American conception of the novel, with Richard Dix as a 'pep-ful' parson hero. **1933** *Punch* 29 Mar. 359/2 Mr. Joe Hayman's all-too-brief appearance as the hustling pepful American manager was, as usual, delightful.

pepino (pepī·no). *Physical Geogr.* [Sp., = 'cucumber'.] A small, conical hill characteristic of tropical and subtropical karstic regions, esp. one of those in Puerto Rico. Also *pepino hill.* Cf. *hum *sb.*[4], *mogote.

1899 *Nat. Geogr. Mag.* Mar. 100 Along their inner border these [hills] are of remarkable pointed character,.. and are appropriately termed by the natives 'Pepinos' or cucumbers. **1915** *Ann. N.Y. Acad. Sci.* XXVI. 16 This type of topography is represented by the small level tract surrounded or dotted over with small hills, called 'pepino hills' locally, standing like haystacks above the plain. **1934** *Jrnl. Geol.* XLII. 545 The development of pepino topography is characteristic of limestones in humid tropical countries. **1954** [see *mogote]. **1968** R. W. Fairbridge *Encycl. Geomorphol.* 161/2 Also known as 'haystack hills', or 'tit hills', the Pepino hills are a characteristic feature of a mature karst landscape in tropical to subtropical latitudes.

pepless (pe·plės), *a. colloq.* [f. *pep *sb.* + -less.] Without energy or spirit.

1926 Wood & Goddard *Dict. Amer. Slang* 15 *Dud*,..a failure; a pepless person. *Ibid.* 17 *Fish*, *poor*, pepless creature. **1942** Berrey & Van den Bark *Amer. Thes. Slang* §99/12 Nonalcoholic,..pepless. *Ibid.* 249/2 Lazy, indolent,..pepless. *Ibid.* 276/8 Dull, spiritless,..pepless. **1967** *Observer* 30 Apr. 11/3 The 'vice' in Saigon..has a pepless *Playboy* flavour.

peplum. Add: **2.** (Earlier and later examples.) Also, that part of a long jacket or tunic which hangs below the waist, covering the skirt; hence, a jacket or tunic of this design; also *attrib.* Hence **peplumed** (pe·plŏmd) *a.*

1866 *Queen* 28 Apr. 330/1 No dressy afternoon toilette is now considered complete without a peplum. **1906** *Daily Chron.* 5 Apr. 8/1 A pointed tunic of peplum shape in soft white chiffon hemmed with..mirror velvet. **1930** *Morning Post* 8 Aug. 6 Some dresses have peplums or pleated basques. **1970** *Daily Tel.* 23 Feb. 13 The midi suit which doesn't have either a short cropped waist-length jacket or peplum is likely to be long..and belted. **1972** *Daily Tel.* 29 June 7/7 Or you can play it in strictly neat little Ginger Rogers suits, with flaring skirts, peplumed jackets. **1973** *Times* 15 May 20/5 Big-sleeved black seersucker blouse, the one that belts into a tight waist and then flares into a peplum over a full, long-tiered skirt. **1977** *New Yorker* 11 July 84/1 We see nothing of the longer, fuller skirt, the wasp waist, the peplum. **1977** *Time* 8 Aug. 37/1 Over these dresses or satin pants are worn gargantuan wraps—a peplum coat sewn with real gold thread cloth.

pepper, *sb.* Add: **2. b.** esp. the sweet pepper, *Capsicum annuum*, originally native to tropical America but now widely cultivated elsewhere, and its red, green, or yellow bell-shaped fruits; cf. Capsicum.

[**1728** R. Bradley *Dictionarium Botanicum* I. s.v. *Capsicum siliqua olivaria propendens*, This Pepper hath small and long round Cods.] **1884** tr. *A. de Candolle's Orig. Cultivated Plants* II. iv. 289 It [*sc. Capsicum annuum*] was one of the peppers that Piso and Marcgraf saw grown in Brazil. **1923** H. C. Thompson *Vegetable Crops* xxv. 399 Peppers are grown in very much the same way as egg-plants and tomatoes. *Ibid.* 400 Of the large-fruited, sweet peppers, Ruby King, Bell or Bullnose,..and Golden Queen are well-known varieties. **1949** *Nat. Geogr. Mag.* Aug. 166/2 When we say 'peppers' without any qualifying word, we usually mean sweet or nonpungent kinds that are eaten as a vegetable, either cooked or raw in salads. **1963** L. Phillips *Recipes from Guardian* 124 Crisp red and yellow pepper rings dressed with lemon juice and olive oil and seasoned well make a good salad. *Ibid.*, Scrambled eggs take on a new look if small pieces of different coloured peppers are added. **1972** Y. Lovelock *Vegetable Bk.* III. 320 Capsicums, or peppers, are the various-sized seed-pods of a solanaceous plant, having nothing in common with the true peppers (Piperaceae) except the hot quality of some, but by no means all, of them. **1975** I. & A. Mancinelli tr. *Bianchini & Corbetta's Fruits of Earth* 94 Peppers originated in South America, probably Brazil.

4. (Further examples.)

1922 Joyce *Ulysses* 171 And here's himself and pepper on him, Nosey Flynn said. **1960** *Encounter* Feb. 34/1 'Pepper', that characteristically American streak of free-wheeling, urban critical scepticism. **1966** C. Achebe *Man of People* vii. 81 If you insult me again I will show you pepper. **1973** J. Wainwright *Touch of Malice* 136 'Are you calling me a liar, constable?' Ripley sprinkled pepper on his voice.

4*. Used *ellipt.* for Pepper-pot.

1897 *Sears, Roebuck Catal.* 439/1 Silver plated Pepper or Salt. **1908** *Ibid.* 360/3 Handsome Salt sand Peppers, hand decorated. **1966** J. Douglas *How to Collect* ii. 9 A plain Queen Anne or early Georgian silver pepper can cost you a great deal. **1976** 'D. Halliday' *Dolly & Nanny Bird* ii. 30 He turfed out my things on to the table. The sugar... A miniature pepper and salt. A pack of fruit gums.

4.** In skipping, the speed at which the rope is turned as quickly as possible.

1901 R. C. Maclagan *Games Argyleshire* 229 The skipping may be done rapidly or slowly... In Kintyre slow skipping is called 'salt'; quick skipping, 'pepper'. **1948** *Jrnl. Amer. Folk-Lore* LXI. 65 In Pennsylvania the term 'pepper' means a very rapid, strenuous rhythm. In most other places it is called 'hot pepper' or 'hot peas'. **1972** F. B. Maynard *Raisins & Almonds* 56 Sometimes they skipped to the tune..with the spinning rope. (Hazel did pepper faster than anybody I knew).

5. *pepper-coloured* adj.; **pepper-dulse,** correct the date of quot. 1778 to 1777, and add further examples; **pepper gas**, an anti-personnel 'gas' that produces irritation of the throat and nasal passages; also as *vb. trans.*, to attack with pepper gas; **pepper-mill** (examples); **pepper shaker** *N. Amer.* = PEPPER-CASTOR, -CASTER 1; **pepper soup**, a West African soup made with red pepper and other hot spices; **pepper steak** (see quot. 1970).

1962 I. MURDOCH *Unofficial Rose* x. 99 Mildred..patted her fluffy pepper-coloured hair into place. **1978** H. JOBSON *To die a Little* v. 89, I picked up a pepper-coloured jacket. **1849** D. LANDSBOROUGH *Pop. Hist. Brit. Seaweeds* 254 It is called pepper-dulse, and it certainly has, especially when young, a very pungent smell and peppery taste... It was formerly eaten in Scotland. **1931** L. NEWTON *Handbk. Brit. Seaweeds* 340 This species [sc. *Laurencia pinnatifida*] often has a hot biting taste, and was formerly eaten in Scotland under the name of Pepper Dulse. **1972** Y. LOVELOCK *Vegetable Bk.* I. 209 Pepper dulse (*Laurencia pinnatifolia*) was once eaten in Scotland but never gained great popularity. The name refers to the fact that it has often (though not always) a hot biting taste. **1970** *Times* 9 July 5 About 225 State and city policemen, armed with pepper gas, submachine guns, rifles and shotguns, repelled the mob. **1973** R. HAYES *Hungarian Game* xlvi. 281 When Michael didn't open the door, they began filling the room with pepper gas. **1973** *Black Panther* 17 Nov. 5/4 The 38 have been beaten, peppergassed, maced, isolated, harrassed and now intimidated. **1976** *New Yorker* 26 Jan. 74/2 The police dispersed the demonstrators with tear gas and pepper gas. **1884** G. MEREDITH *Let.* 13 May (1970) II. 735 My table is the richer for a pepper-mill. **1907** *Yesterday's Shopping* (1969) 210/2 Pepper Mills for Table. Walnut..1/3... Ivory—12/11. **1972** J. BURMEISTER *Running Scared* iv. 63, I feel like smoked salmon with four hefty winds on the pepper mill. **1895** *Montgomery Ward Catal.* Spring & Summer 543/3 Salt and pepper shakers, made of crystal blown glass, extra large capacity, and well adapted for kitchen as well as table use. Specify salt or pepper when ordering. **1911** *Daily Colonist* (Victoria, B.C.) 22 Apr. 2/1 (Advt.), Table Necessities..Pepper Shakers of Cut Glass, sterling silver tops. **1977** *Transatlantic Rev.* LX. 89 We divide up nine individual packets of sugar, six of ketchup, three rippled pepper shakers. **1964** J. P. CLARK *Masquerade* in *Three Plays* 76 Why, Only this morning I opened my fishbasket To have stock for our pepper soup. **1966** C. ACHEBE *Man of People* xii. 148 My father was..eating pounded yams and pepper soup. **1951** E. DAVID *French Country Cooking* 114 *Pepper steaks*... Score the steaks..rub them with garlic and then with a thin coating of pounded peppercorns. **1965** K. GILES *Some Beasts no More* v. 125, I had something to eat, they still do a good pepper steak. **1970** SIMON & HOWE *Dict. Gastron.* 297/1 *Pepper steak*, beef steak rubbed liberally with freshly-ground black pepper before cooking. **1976** K. THACKERAY *Crownbird* v. 91 The barbecue area where an African was cooking pepper steaks and kebabs.

pepper, *v.* Add: **3.** Also *intr.* in same sense.

1857 [see *GEEWHILLIKINS *int.*]. **1945** C. MANN in Murdoch & Drake-Brockman *Austral. Short Stories* (1951) 263 They would be routed..by the driven sand and salt peppering into their eyes. **1947** W. DE LA MARE *Coll. Stories for Children* 14 A few hollow cockled-up bean seeds peppered down from out of their dry shucks.

4. b. Const. *away* (earlier example).

1884 'MARK TWAIN' *Huck. Finn* xviii. 167 The Grangerfords..peppered away at him.

pepper-and-salt. Add: **1.** (Further examples.) Hence, someone wearing pepper-and-salt clothes.

1845 *Ainsworth's Mag.* VII. 370 [The boy] is..installed *in* the usual pepper-and-salts, with the black velveteens for Sundays. **1900** E. GLYN *Visits of Elizabeth* 236 At dinner I sat between Charlie and one of the pepper-and-salts... They are going to shoot partridges tomorrow. **1907** *Westm. Gaz.* 11 Oct. 3/2 Husband small, fussy,..violent-tempered, pepper-and-salt-check-trousered, and something..in the City. **1915** W. S. MAUGHAM *Of Human Bondage* xxvi. 107 Very neat in his black coat and pepper-and-salt trousers. **1934** G. B. SHAW *Village Wooing* 129 At this A sits writing. He wears pepper-and-salt trousers of country cut, with an apron. **1978** N. MARSH *Grave Mistake* i. 16 The trousers were unmistakable: pepper-and-salt, shapeless, earthy.

b. *transf.* Used of greying hair, a moustache, or of objects resembling pepper-and-salt cloth in colour. Also, *pepper-salt*.

1853 MRS. GASKELL *Ruth* II. vi. 124 My hair is nearly white. The last time I looked it was only pepper-and-salt. **1909** *Dialect Notes* III. 414 *Pepper and salt*,..painted with white spatters over a darker background. **1930** [see *LAW *sb.*[1] 16a]. **1934** E. BOWEN *Cat Jumps* 83 Matthew had fluffy pepper-and-salt hair. **1951** T. CAPOTE *Grass Harp* (1952) i. 3 A whip-thin, handsome woman with shingled pepper-salt hair. **1955** J. THOMAS *No Banners* xix. 174 A scowling Militiaman with an enormous pepper-and-salt moustache walked up. **1957** E. HYAMS *Into Dream* 128 Clear grey eyes, pepper-and-salt hair worn in the kind of bob which was fashionable about 1925. **1976** A. PRICE *War Game* II. 219 Nayler's lankiness had aged into an acceptable scholarly stoop to which his thick pepper-and-salt thatch added distinction.

3. *fig.*

1887 *Lantern* (New Orleans) 9 July 2/2 But let me commence my assault on the offending ones and give them pepper and salt. **1958** *Times* 24 Oct. 15/4 In Prokofiev's work Mr. Kroll emphasised the lyrical element rather more than the composer's characteristic pepper and salt.

4. pepper-and-salt fundus, a symptom of congenital syphilis, the fundus of the eye having a speckled appearance.

1940 S. DUKE-ELDER *Text-bk. Ophthalm.* III. iii. 2273 The finely pigmented or pepper-and-salt fundus, a picture characteristic of hereditary lues, wherein the entire fundus is dusted with innumerable small bluish pigmented spots between which lie round depigmented areas of a yellowish-red colour. **1975** MARTIN-DOYLE & KEMP *Synopsis Ophthalm.* (ed. 5) vi. 76 Syphilitic Retinitis...In congenital cases a form of peripheral pigmentation known as 'pepper and salt' fundus is common.

5. Forming various nonce-wds.: **pepper-and-salted** *a.*, wearing pepper-and-salt clothing; **pepper-and-saltiness**, pepper-and-salt colour; **pepper-and-salty** *a.*, pepper-and-salt coloured.

1846 R. FORD *Gatherings from Spain* xxiii. 331 This pepper-and-salted Amphion. **1880** R. BROUGHTON *Second Thoughts* I. I. vi. 83 Snow..speckled with blacks into an ugly pepper-and-saltiness. **1952** 'W. COOPER' *Struggles of Albert Woods* I. iii. 34 Dibdin's hair was the colour that is first called sandy and later pepper-and-salty.

pepper-box. Add: **2. b.** The name given to an early type of revolver in which five or six barrels revolve round a central axis; freq. *attrib.*

1861 *Richmond* (Va.) *Examiner* 7 Dec. 3/2 The pistol is one of the old-fashioned pepper-box sort—self-cocking, and..is regarded as dangerous at either end. **1872** 'MARK TWAIN' *Roughing It* ii. 4 An old original 'Allen' revolver, such as irreverent people called a 'pepper-box'. **1887** [see *coffee-mill* s.v. *COFFEE *sb.* 5 b]. **1901** W. CHURCHILL *Crisis* II. xviii. 280 Out of his pocket hung the curved butt of a big pepper-box revolver. **1915** W. B. YEATS *Reveries* (1916) 48 An old pepper-box revolver. **1920** C. W. SAWYER *Our Rifles* 65 The rifle was made about 1855, when pepper-box pistols were in everyday use. **1969** *Canad. Antiques Collector* Feb. 29/1 An early (1851) English 'Improved Revolver' which is part revolver and part pepperbox.

5. (Earlier and later examples.)

1771 T. PENNANT *Tour in Scotl.* 1769 203 A slender square tower with a pepper-box top. **1948** J. R. FIRTH in E. P. Hamp et al. *Readings in Linguistics II* (1966) 178 The Romans and the English managed to dispense with those written signs called 'accents' and avoided pepperbox spelling.

peppercorn. 2. b. Substitute for def.: used *attrib.* or as *adj.* to designate the tufted style in which Hottentots and Bushmen wear their hair; also *transf.*

1868 J. CHAPMAN *Trav. S. Afr.* I. i. 16 Bushmen with peppercorn heads. **1893** [in Dict.]. **1935** L. G. GREEN *Great Afr. Mysteries* x. 121 Reconstructions of these bones suggested that the Strandloopers were never more than five feet in height. Some authorities declare they had peppercorn hair. **1948** H. V. MORTON *In Search of S. Afr.* viii. 251, I could see the road running ahead, disappearing for a while and emerging again upon the face of the greyish-brown plain, which was dotted with small peppercorn bushes like a Hottentot's hair. **1958** L. VAN DER POST *Lost World of Kalahari* i. 12 His [*sc.* the Bushman's] hair was black and grew in thick round clusters which my countrymen called, with that aptitude for scornful metaphor they unfailingly exercised on his behalf, 'pepper-corn hair'. **1959** J. D. CLARK *Prehist. S. Afr.* i. 17 The Hottentot closely resembles the Bushman except in stature. He..has black hair which grows in spirals and is known as 'pepper-corn hair'.

3. peppercorn shrub, tree = PEPPER-TREE in Dict. and Suppl.

[**1830** *Hobart Town Almanack* 65 A thick grove of the pepper-shrub..grows in a close thicket to the height of from six to ten feet.] **1901** M. FRANKLIN *My Brilliant Career* i. 1 The stringybark roof of the salt-shed..peeped out picturesquely from the musk and peppercorn shrubs. **1954** *Coast to Coast 1953–54* 76 Who do you think we see sittin' under a pepper-corn tree but this old sundowner. **1973** *Bulletin* (Sydney) 25 Aug. 43/3 Dejected peppercorn trees by the station. **1978** O. WHITE *Silent Reach* ix. 104 A line of scrawny peppercorn trees.

peppered, *ppl. a.* **b.** *peppered moth*, substitute for def.: the popular name of the geometrid moth, *Biston betularia*, which is usually light-coloured with darker flecks. (Further examples.)

1903 F. E. HULME *Butterflies & Moths* vi. 225 The insect we have represented..is..called the Peppered Moth, or, in the words of some old entomologists, the Pepper and Salt. **1915, 1970** [see *MELANIC *a.* 2]. **1972** *Countryman* LXXVII. II. 131 Bernard Kettlewell's classic study of the peppered moth as an example of natural selection in action is finding its way into the text books. **1975** *Sci. Amer.* Jan. 90/1 Of more than 700 species of larger moths found throughout the British Isles, the peppered moth (*Biston betularia*) is surely the best-known to students of evolution.

c. *peppered steak* = **pepper steak*.

1960 J. DONON *Classic French Cuisine* v. 130 (*heading*) Steak au Poivre (Peppered Steak). **1973** D. MACKENZIE *Postscript to Dead Let.* 30 A Czech couple who serve the best peppered steak in town. **1978** *Times* 4 Mar. 11/5 Stars in Soho..does a good peppered steak (£3·25).

pepperet (pepərə·t). Also **pepperette.** [f. PEPPER *sb.* + -ET.] *rare.* A pepper-pot.

1927 W. DEEPING *Kitty* i. 11 Regency salt-cellars, mustard-pots and pepperets. **1975** *Country Life* 20 Feb. 427/1 A condiment set..mustard pot with liner, a salt-cellar and two pepperettes. **1977** *Times* 26 July 9/7 (Advt.), This pug-dog pepperette..London, 1881.. realised £105.

pepperidge. Add: **2.** esp. *Nyssa sylvatica* (cf. *NYSSA). Also *attrib.* (Earlier and later examples.)

1689 *Huntington* (N.Y.) *Town Rec.* (1888) II. 56 A piperage tree marked faceing eastward and southward. **1743** J. HEMPSTEAD *Diary* 22 Feb. (1901) 406 Wee Sawed of a pr Peperage wheels for my Stone Cart. [**1810** F. A. MICHAUX *Hist. Arbres Forestiers de l'Amérique Septentrionale* I. 30 *Peperidge* fréquemment usitée par les Hollandois du New Jersey.] **1821** J. F. COOPER *Spy* I. ix. 133 A lieutenant of cavalry..whose captain is as tough as a peperage log. **1876** *Field & Forest* I. 66 This parasitic shrub [*sc.* American mistletoe] has been found growing on several Pepperidge or Sour-gum trees. **1900** J. DE F. SHELTON *Salt-Box House* ix. 67 A certain tract of land,.. beginning at the highway near my present house..to a pepperidge tree. **1969** T. H. EVERETT *Living Trees of World* 257/2 The pepperidge, black gum, or tupelo (*N. sylvatica*) of eastern North America ranges from Maine to Michigan, Florida and Texas. Up to 100 feet in height, it forms a flat-topped columnar or pyramidal head of usually somewhat pendulous branches and has blunt, obovate or elliptic, lustrous leaves that turn brilliant cellar and two pepperettes. **1977** *Times* 26 July 9/2 (Advt.), This pug-dog pepperette..London, 1881.. realised £105.

pepperina (pe:pərī·nă). *Austral.* [f. PEPPER(-TREE + *-ina*, as in CASUARINA.] = PEPPER-TREE in Dict. and Suppl. Also *attrib.*

1930 V. PALMER *Men are Human* xviii. 166 Nothing grew save the drooping pepperina that trailed its sheeny leaves over the kitchen roof. **1941** *Coast to Coast* 145 There was a pepperina-tree in the corner of the adjacent yard. **1967** *Southerly* XXVII. 204 Guinea-hens..roosting at night in the pepperina tree beside the back door.

peppermint. Add: **2. b.** (Earlier examples). Also, any peppermint-flavoured sweetmeat.

1829 G. GRIFFIN *Collegians* I. iii. 56 'He gave me an O'Dell-cake when he was last here,' said one. 'And me a stick of peppermint.' **1835** J. TODD *Student's Man.* (ed. 2) 281 A handful of hot peppermints. **1883** *Harper's Mag.* Sept. 534/2 The windows were decorated..with.. glass jars in which were sticks of striped candy, the half-moist peppermint, and the brown sugary squares.

c. Used as a flavouring in drinks: hence, the name of a cordial, and of a liqueur (= *crème de menthe* s.v. *CRÈME 1b).

c **1770** in de Vries & Fryer *Venus Unmasked* (1967) 31 She allows gin and peppermint in the room. **1825** P. EGAN *Life of Actor* ii. 54 Now to avail me of the Friar's hint, He bade me take it in some peppermint. *c* **1863** T. TAYLOR *Ticket-of-Leave Man* I. 8 Four penn'orth of brandy,..and a little peppermint..(*stirring and sipping his brandy and peppermint*). **1865** E. H. GREENHOW in E. R. Pike *Human Documents Victorian Golden Age* (1967) 203 Wine, gin, peppermint, and other stimulants are.. often given.., their actual effect being..to stupefy the child. **1870** D. J. KIRWAN *Palace & Hovel* xxxv. 516 Glass o' nice peppermint! this cold morning—ha'penny a glass! **1900** E. GLYN *Visits of Elizabeth* 77, I could bear most of it, if it wasn't for the peppermint glasses at the end, which the men have. **1963** A. L. SIMON *Guide Good Food & Wines* 742 The highly scented leaves of *Mint* are used in the making of liqueurs usually sold under the name of *Crème de Menthe* or *Peppermint*. **1972** C. DRUMMOND *Death at Bar* i. 32 A little drop of peppermint with a dash of lemonade. **1972** M. GILBERT *Body of Girl* xii. 107 Make it a gin and peppermint and I might join you.

d. Used as the name of various colours (esp. green) associated with peppermint-flavoured drinks or sweets.

1868 D. G. ROSSETTI *Let.* 17 Nov. (1965) II. 676, I wonder has Scotus's peppermint-and-mud tint been applied yet to the wall surrounding the Topsaic tapestries. **1934** A. HUXLEY *Beyond Mexique Bay* 23 The buttery glossiness of acetate silk shone, yellow, or peppermint green. **1963** A. CHRISTIE *Clocks* xiii. 113 The door was opened by an elderly woman with..a black skirt and a rather unexpected peppermint-striped jumper. **1965** R. GOULART in H. Waugh *Merchants of Menace* (1971) (*title*) Peppermint-striped goodbye. *Ibid.* 143 They drove around in an old ice-cream wagon they'd painted with peppermint stripes. **1973** *Observer* (Colour Suppl.) 30 Dec. 29/2 (*caption*) Peppermint washable satin nightdress.., £24. **1976** *Milton Keynes Express* 28 May 48/2 (Advt.), 1976 Moskvitch Estate, peppermint green..£475. **1976** N. THORNBURG *Cutter & Bone* i. 4 Bone slipped into his peppermint-stripe shirt.

3. (Later examples.) Also, *peppermint gum*.

1911 E. M. CLOWES *On Wallaby* ix. 249 In the Wombat Forest..is found messmate, peppermint, and swamp-gum. **1936** F. CLUNE *Roaming round Darling* vi. 51 He found the poor thief by the sight of his boots poking out between two stones that made him a house under a peppermint tree. **1963** W. BLUNT *Of Flowers & Village* 94 The Australian peppermint tree (*Eucalyptus amygdalina*) is the tallest of all trees. **1966** *Southerly* XXVI. 107 The stringybarks and peppermint gums at the edges of the encircling scrub. **1967** T. KENEALLY *Bring Larks* xxv. 189 A half-uprooted peppermint hung over them.

4. peppermint cake = *mint cake* (b) s.v. MINT *sb.*[2] 3; **peppermint cordial**, a cordial flavoured with peppermint; **peppermint cream**, a cream sweet flavoured with peppermint and often covered with chocolate; **peppermint-drop** (earlier examples); **peppermint geranium**, a variety of *Pelargonium tomentosum*, with downy, scented leaves and white flowers; **peppermint gum**: see sense 3 above; **peppermint lump**, a type of sweet flavoured with peppermint; **peppermint oil** (examples);

peppermint-scented *a.*, with a scent of peppermint; *spec.* **peppermint-scented geranium** = **peppermint geranium*; **peppermint-water** (further example).

1863 MRS. GASKELL *Sylvia's Lovers* II. xii. 220 Here's a bit o' peppermint cake; he's main and fond on it. **1917** *Harrods Gen. Catal.* 1293 Schweppes cordials... Peppermint cordial 1/6. **1974** *Guardian* 24 Jan. 6/8 Dr McGill later celebrated his acquittal with peppermint cordial. **1907** *Yesterday's Shopping* (1969) 49/2 Peppermint Creams. **1940** 'R. CROMPTON' *William & Evacuees* ii. 49 'Thank you, dear,' said Mrs. Brown, selecting a peppermint cream. **1976** P. FERRIS *Detective* i. 3 His wife..asked him if he would buy a box of peppermint creams. **1799** F. BOSCAWEN *Let.* 10 Jan. in C. Aspinall-Oglander *Admiral's Widow* (1942) 177, I shall be glad..if you could send me 3 ounces of pepper mint drops such as I am used to have. **1818** [see *DROP *sb.* 10 e]. **1849** DICKENS *Dav. Copp.* (1850) vii. 68 He was so kind as to..dissolve a peppermint drop in it. **1922** A. L. JEKYLL *Kitchen Ess.* iv. 36 Make a quart of good lemon jelly... Whilst warm add a handful of those large green peppermint geranium leaves, thick as a fairy's blanket, soft as a vicuna robe, and to be found in most old-fashioned gardens. **1931** E. S. ROHDE *Scented Garden* vii. 177 The leaves of this kind were large and soft... I know it now for *Pelargonium tomentosum*, usually called the peppermint geranium. **1966** G. B. FOSTER *Herbs for every Garden* iv. 123 Peppermint geranium, with its velvety, grape-like leaves and small white blossoms is *P[elargonium] tomentosum*. **1926–7** *Army & Navy Stores Catal.* 55/2 Sweets... Peppermint lumps. **1932** H. H. PRICE *Perception* viii. 230 The taste of a peppermint lump may linger on when the lump itself is no longer tactually present in our mouth. **1892** *Analyst* XVII. 14 Commercial samples of peppermint oil differ in quality as well as composition. **1966** *McGraw-Hill Encycl. Sci. & Technol.* VIII. 227/2 *l*-Menthol, found as the main constituent..in peppermint oil. **1823** R. SWEET *Geraniaceæ* II. 168 This plant, often known by the name of Peppermint-scented Geranium, is an old inhabitant of our greenhouses. **1907** *Westm. Gaz.* 3 Dec. 2/1 To return to the peppermint-scented schoolroom. **1946** M. FREE *All about House Plants* xvii. 165 *P[elargonium] tomentosum* has long-stalked, Peppermint-scented leaves. **1960** R. HEMPHILL *Fragrance & Flavour* 89 Pick and wash a bunch of peppermint-scented geranium leaves. **1820** *Pharmacopœia U.S.* 85 In the same manner are prepared peppermint water,.. spearmint water,..rose water. **1907** *Yesterday's Shopping* (1969) 516/2 Peppermint Water..8 oz. bot 0/5. *a* **1976** A. CHRISTIE *Autobiogr.* (1977) v. 251, I did..give her an extra dollop of peppermint water.

pepperoni (pepərōu·ni). Also **peperoni.** [ad. It. *peperone* chilli.] Beef and pork sausage seasoned with pepper.

1934 in WEBSTER. **1960** A. E. BENDER *Dict. Nutrition* 113/1 Pepperoni [etc.]..are slowly dried to a hard condition. **1967** *Boston Sunday Globe* 23 Apr. (Advt. section) 7/2 Pepperoni is another ready-to-eat of pork and beef with ground red pepper and the usual dry sausage seasonings. It is a little under 2 inches in diameter. **1969** R. & D. DE SOLA *Dict. Cooking* 172/2 *Peperoni*, highly seasoned Italian sausage. **1971** C. CLAIBORNE *N.Y. Times Internat. Cookbook* 440/2 Dot the surface of the pizza with one sliced peperoni sausage. **1974** *Time Out* 27 Sept. 33 It's still Fellini, which has become an identifiable substance like salami or pepperoni that can be sliced into at any point. **1976** *Times* 26 June 12/5 Pizza..with generous topping of good tomato sauce, Mozzarella cheese, peperoni and fresh mushrooms. **1977** *Custom Car* Nov. 67/3 The only action required is a wink, and wham! out comes his pepperoni!

pepper-pot. Add: **2. a.** (Further examples.) Also *attrib.* in *pepperpot soup*.

1698 E. WARD *Trip to Jamaica* 15 They make a rare Soop they call Pepper-Pot. **1899** [see *FOO-FOO]. **1949** *Caribbean Q.* I. i. 20 Pepper pot..is..the method devised by the aboriginal South American Indians to conserve the food they have got by hunting or fishing. **1958** R. HOWE *Cooking from Commonwealth* 387 (*heading*) Jamaica. Pepperpot soup. **1961** F. G. CASSIDY *Jamaica Talk* xvi. 336 Cassava liquor—once known as *casareep* and the basis of the traditional *pepperpot* soup—is not however favoured. **1965** 'LAUCHMONEN' *Old Thom's Harvest* vi. 81, I can smell pepper-pot and peas. **1970** SIMON & HOWE *Dict. Gastron.* 296/2 Jamaican pepperpot soup is thickened with yam or coconut. **1970** M. SLATER *Caribbean Cooking* 10 *Coalpots*..used in the country, and for traditional stews and pepperpots requiring prolonged cooking. **1971** *Advocate-News* (Barbados) 17 Sept. (Guyana Suppl.) p. i/1 *Casareep*, syrup-like substance left after poison has been boiled out of juice of bitter cassava, used to prepare pepperpot. **1973** *Ibid.* 29 June 7/3 (Advt.), From the choicest Continental cuisine to the spicy Barbadian—from the generous cut of prime sirloin to the traditional Barbadian pepperpot soup—the food is the best.

b. (Examples.)

1794 *Massachusetts Spy* 13 Mar. 1 A wag in my neighbourhood, a lover of pepper pots. **1800** C. MACPHERSON *Mem.* 205 'And what have you got for dinner..?'—'Me have got peppa pot, Massa.' **1825** J. K. PAULDING *John Bull in Amer.* xiv. 231 Whose principal trade consists in the exportation of Toughy and Pepper Pot. **1930** J. WILLIAMSON *Amer. Hotel* 217 A..list..of American culinary creations..would include such concoctions as.. Philadelphia pepper-pot. **1946** S. HIBBEN *Amer. Regional Cookery* 25 Lay in Dumplings for Pepperpot and cook as directed.

pepper-tree. b. Substitute for def.: Either of two Australasian evergreen trees, *Drimys aromatica* or *Pseudowintera axillaris* (*HOROPITO), both belonging to the family Magnoliaceæ, and bearing small dark fruits once used as a substitute for pepper. (Further examples of both senses.)

1857 B. I. HAYES *Pioneer Notes* (1929) 183 When I was at San Bernardino last, I obtained two small fir trees and two pepper trees. **1882** W. D. HAY *Brighter Britain!* II. vi. 195 The Horopito, or 'Pepper-tree' (*Drimys axillaris*) yields also an ornamental timber. **1911** C. E. W. BEAN *'Dreadnought' of Darling* xv. 141 The thick shady wilga—rather like a pepper tree in the distance. **1939** W. FAULKNER *Wild Palms* 192 The pepper trees had been green all winter. **1949** W. HERTRICH *Huntington Bot. Gardens* 4 Where the widening of Huntington Drive was necessary, it was a great misfortune to have to eliminate all of these pepper trees. **1950** G. BRENAN *Face of Spain* iv. 92 The smooth-trunked rubber trees spread out their glossy leaves, the pepper trees trail their feathery tendrils. **1971** *Southerly* XXXI. 5 The impressions that will remain, transfigured, in his memory: the pepper tree breaking into light in the Duffield's yard. **1977** *Austral. House & Garden* Jan. 17/1 Check these and spray them too if necessary: Gardenia,..Chinese tallow tree, Pepper tree (schinus), [etc.]. **1978** 'M. M. KAYE' *Far Pavilions* x. 163 He..kissed her behind a kindly screen of pepper trees.

pepper-up(per): see *PEP *v.*

pepperwood. (Examples.)

1856 *U.S. Naut. Mag. & Naval Jrnl.* V. 228 The timber used..is pepperwood, and was cut from the land close by the prison [*sc.* San Quentin, California]. **1858** C. E. DE LONE *Jrnl.* 5 Mar. in *Calif. Hist. Soc. Q.* (1930) IX. 253 Noticed the beautie's of the peper [*sic*] wood tree. **1882** *Humboldt Times* (Eureka, Calif.) 7 Jan. 1/4 The schooner Alaska, lying in the bay ready for sea, has on board 50,000 feet of pepperwood, commonly called California laurel. **1894** R. B. HOUGH *Amer. Woods* V. 30 *Xanthoxylum Clava-Herculis*, L. Prickly Ash, Sea Ash, Toothache Tree, Pepperwood. **1949** *Natural Hist.* Mar. 130/2 Under a pepperwood tree they did find a pile of glass flakings.

peppery, *a.* Add: **2. c.** In extended uses: unpleasant, objectionable; strong, powerful.

1829 P. EGAN *Boxiana* 2nd Ser. II. 189 This was a short round, but *peppery*. **1901** M. FRANKLIN *My Brilliant Career* ix. 71 Gertie, the boys, and myself had to perform our morning ablutions in a leaky tin dish on a stool outside the kitchen door, which on cold frosty mornings was a pretty peppery performance. **1946** KOESTLER *Thieves in Night* 128 'We even have to hire the tractor of the Hebrews at two pounds and a half per dunum.' 'A peppery price, by Mohammed.' **1958** P. GAMMOND *Decca Bk. Jazz* iv. 55 What was then known as 'The Original Dixieland Jass Band—Untuneful Harmonists Playing Peppery Melodies'. **1958** *Which?* I. ii. 25/1 The overhead-valve engine..is small in displacement, but peppery for its size.

d. Pepper-coloured.

1962 I. MURDOCH *Unofficial Rose* xxxvi. 343 Her soft peppery hair..was cut short in a neat yet raffish style about her beaming countenance.

pep-pill (pe·p,pil). *colloq.* (orig. *U.S.*). [f. *PEP *sb.* + PILL *sb.*[2]] A stimulant drug dispensed in the form of a pill.

1937 *Time* 10 May 45/1 (*heading*) Pep-pill poisoning. The use by college students of a new, powerful but poisonous brain stimulant called Benzedrine last week kept college directors of health in dithers of worry. *Ibid.*, Students who, while cramming for final examinations, collapse,..are under suspicion of using the substance. They call it 'pepper-up', 'pep pills'. **1955** [see *AMPHETAMINE]. **1955** *Sci. News Let.* 2 Apr. 219/2 Amphetamine, or Benzedrine, known as 'pep pills',..is most likely to produce pleasant sensations in normal persons. **1959** *Times* 29 May 14/6 The performance of athletes may be improved through 'pep pills' by as much as 4 per cent. **1959** *Guardian* 16 Nov. 1/4 They had..tomato sandwiches, with coffee and tea, but no 'pep' pills. **1960** *Times Lit. Suppl.* 20 May 323/2 The managerial class gets its kicks from pep pills instead of art. **1960** *Spectator* 22 July 120 The campaign then being waged by some newspapers against the pep-pill Preludin. **1965** *New Scientist* 29 July 261/2 Amphetamines and barbiturates, variously called stimulants and depressants, pep pills and 'goof balls'. **1967** *Spectator* 30 June 758/1 The Rolling Stone Mick Jagger, was found guilty of possessing pep pills. **1974** E. AMBLER *Dr. Frigo* II. 98 As for that movie star, how do you know he isn't on pep pills?

peppy (pe·pi), *a.* orig. *U.S.* [f. *PEP *sb.* + -Y[1].] Full of pep or vigour; spirited, energetic, lively, forceful.

1922 S. LEWIS *Babbitt* vi. 86 Wouldn't it be a good idea if I could go off to China or some peppy place, and study engineering or something by mail? **1922** E. E. CUMMINGS *Let.* 3 May (1969) 84 Thru being more or less true to the peppy thesis.. I feel: more pep, pleasure in living. **1924** WODEHOUSE *Bill the Conqueror* xx. 303, I said it was the peppiest scheme of the age, a lallapaloosa. **1926** *Picture-Play Mag.* July 3/2 (Advt.), How I used to envy..Billy jazzing up a party with his peppy banjo! **1927** *Melody Maker* Sept. 883/1 They have a red 'hot' peppy dance rhythm and are thoroughly bright and interesting. **1930** E. WAUGH *Vile Bodies* vii. 129, I like your page. It's peppy. **1932** T. S. ELIOT *Sel. Essays* III. 197 There is nothing in the play to which could be applied the term appropriately used in the advertisements of some films; the 'peppy situation'. **1934** J. O'HARA *Appointment in Samarra* (1935) 15 Everyone from out of town thought it was the peppiest place in the country at Christmas. **1939** *Melody Maker* 10 June 5/3 This peppy, blonde, stage-and-concert-party artist. **1956** M. STEARNS *Story of Jazz* (1957) xvi. 180 Most of these bands recorded a novelty now and then that might be called 'peppy'. **1969** *New Yorker* 10 May 33/2 He did a peppy foxtrot. **1974** J. HELLER *Something Happened* 14 She was peppy and direct, always laughing and teasing. **1977** *Time* 14 Feb. 39/3 A.M.C...will give the Pacer a peppier engine. **1977** *Rolling Stone* 7 Apr. 69/3 It's an interesting combination and forces all the songs on *Blondie* to work on at least two levels: as peppy but rough pop, and as distanced, artless avant-rock.

Pepsi-Cola (pe·psi,kou·lă). orig. *U.S.* Also in shortened form **Pepsi.** The proprietary names of a popular soft drink, and of the syrup preparations from which it is made.

1903 *New Bern* (N. Carolina) *Jrnl.* 25 Feb. (Advt.), Pepsi-Cola. At Soda Fountains... Aids Digestion. **1903** *Official Gaz.* (U.S. Patent Office) 16 June 1891/2 Flavoring-syrup for soda-water. Caleb D. Bradham, Newbern, N.C. Filed Sept. 23, 1902 Pepsi-Cola. **1906** *Ibid.* 12 June 2342/2 Tonic Beverage. Caleb D. Bradham, New Bern, N.C. Pepsi-Cola. Filed Apr. 15, 1905. **1916** *Ibid.* 9 May 676/1 The Pepsi-Cola Co., Newbern, N.C. Filed Mar. 19, 1915. Pepsi..A Flavoring-syrup for soda water. *Claims use* since Nov. 21, 1911. **1940** *Life* 7 Oct. 79/1 (*caption*) They [*sc.* A. B. Kent and A. H. C. C. Johnson]..are best known for these immortal lines which have even been translated into Yiddish. They are basically a swing version of *John Peel*: Pepsi-Cola hits the spot! Twelve full ounces, that's a lot, Twice as much for a nickel too—Pepsi-Cola is the drink for you! **1949** N. STREATFEILD *Painted Garden* xiv. 156 He gave her a pepsi-cola. **1953** *Trade Marks Jrnl.* 13 May 417/2 Pepsi-Cola... Non-alcoholic drinks and preparations for making such drinks, all containing cola extract..Pepsi-Cola Limited, Pepsi-Cola Factory,..Brentford, Middlesex; manufacturers and bottlers. **1957** C. MACINNES *City of Spades* I. 107 'Some orange juice or Coke?' 'Ta, Guv, I'll have a Pepsi.' **1959** *Encounter* Sept. 50/2 Mugs bearing Shakespeare's image and sold over the counter with root beer and pepsi cola. **1960** *Trade Marks Jrnl.* 17 Aug. 998/1 Pepsi... Non-alcoholic drinks and preparations for making such drinks, all containing cola extract..Pepsi-Cola Limited,..Feltham, Middlesex; manufacturers and bottlers. **1961** *Western Folklore* XX. 182 Pepsi Cola hits the spot Turn the rope and give her hot. **1966** P. WILLMOTT *Adolescent Boys E. London* 207 We went back to the club and had a drink of Pepsi and a game of darts. **1973** *Sat. Rev. World* (U.S.) 25 Sept. 22/1 She smokes a cigarette, sips a Pepsi. **1976** *National Observer* (U.S.) 21 Feb. 5/5 All that *detente* brings the United States, Reagan says, is 'the right to sell Pepsi-Cola in Siberia'.

pep talk (pe·p tǭk). [f. *PEP *sb.* + TALK *sb.*] A speech or address intended to revive morale or promote energy or enthusiasm in its hearers. So **pep talker,** one who delivers a pep talk.

1926 B. REYNOLDS *Cocktail Continentale* xiv. 107 Where the great Cicero propounded his philosophy to the ages and from which our 'Pep' talks of to-day are copied. **1931** K. K. ROCKNE *Coaching* (rev. ed.) xxii. 256 One coach I know has his football team, before a game, gather in a room which is painted red, for their so-called 'pep-talk'. **1934** J. O'HARA *Appointment in Samarra* (1935) iv. 92 'Let's get through these holidays without any more mess... I don't want to give you a pep talk—' 'I know you don't. I don't blame you.' **1935** WODEHOUSE *Luck of Bodkins* vi. 66 I've seen that expression on her face a hundred times when she was giving us a pep talk before a match. **1940** R. CHANDLER *Farewell, my Lovely* xxxvi. 169 'I'm afraid of dying, of being nothing, of not finding a man named Brunette.' He chuckled... 'You sure give yourself a pep talk'. **1943** J. B. PRIESTLEY *Daylight on Saturday* xxx. 243 I'm wondering if we couldn't invite him to lunch and ask him to give the workers a pep talk in the canteen. **1945** [see *FLANNEL *sb.* 1 f]. **1951** in M. McLuhan *Mech. Bride* (1967) 36/1 Dr. Starch does not merely point out..essential qualities of executive leadership. He does not preach or deliver 'pep' talks! **1957** J. BRAINE *Room at Top* v. 47 Worse still, there were what he called Pep Talks which were made specially gruesome by the fact that, since he seemed to be able to speak and scarcely open his lips, his..voice seemed to come from nowhere. **1969** J. WAINWRIGHT *Take-Over Men* vii. 121 Forget the fancy trappings the politicians and pep-talkers hide it behind. **1971** S. HILL *Strange Meeting* iii. 167 Every now and again Coulter gives us his pep talk, about how we are going to 'go out there and show 'em'. **1973** J. WAINWRIGHT *Pride of Pigs* 120 Which was what he was supposed to be doing..taking chances. The reason..for Harris's pep talk. **1976** *New Yorker* 15 Nov. 137/2 The students were given pep talks to build up their confidence and strengthen their 'will'.

peptic, *a.* and *sb.* Add: **A.** *adj.* **1.** *peptic ulcer*, an ulcer that is situated in a part of the alimentary tract bathed by the gastric juice, or that is attributed to its digestive action; so *peptic ulceration*.

1900 DORLAND *Med. Dict.* 726/1 Peptic u[lcer]. **1903** tr. *Riegel's Dis. Stomach* II. 543 Round ulcer of the stomach. Syn.—Ulcus ventriculi simplex,..peptic ulcer, perforating gastric ulcer. **1929** HURST & STEWART *Gastric & Duodenal Ulcer* x. 496 Other forms of œsophageal ulcer.. must be excluded before a diagnosis of peptic ulcer can be made. *Ibid.*, Peptic ulceration of the œsophagus. **1955** *Sci. News Let.* 30 July 3 A child's peptic ulcer may be confused with abdominal migraine, food allergy or other intestinal conditions. **1974** H. J. DWORKEN *Alimentary Tract* vi. 88 Certain other elements determine the ability to withstand formation of peptic ulcers, although the mechanism for their action is not known. Susceptibility to gastric ulcer increases with age; duodenal ulcers are more common in men than in women. *Ibid.*, People who live in the north of England..or at high altitudes such as in the Peruvian Andes show increased frequencies of peptic ulceration.

peptidase (pe·ptidēiz, -s). *Biochem.* [f. *PEPTID(E + *-ASE.] Orig., an enzyme which hydrolyses peptides; now usu. restricted to enzymes (exopeptidases) which hydrolyse the terminal peptide bonds of peptides, liberating amino-acids.

1918 *Jrnl. Infectious Dis.* XXII. 148 Normal human serum contains peptidase and maintains a relatively uniform titer. **1923** *Jrnl. Chem. Soc.* CXXIV. I. 496 The proteases can be provisionally classified as follows. A. True proteases which break down protein to the peptide stage... B. Peptidases or ereptases which only split peptides or peptones. **1936** [see *endopeptidase* s.v. *ENDO-]. **1958** DIXON & WEBB *Enzymes* v. 228 By no means all peptide links are hydrolysed by all peptidases. **1970** R. W. MCGILVERY *Biochem.* xv. 307 They [*sc.* lysosomes] are particulate structures in the cell..loaded with a battery of hydrolytic enzymes: peptidases to attack proteins, esterases to attack lipids, [etc.]. *Ibid.* xxvii. 658 Exopeptidases, sometimes simply called peptidases without a clarifying prefix,..attack terminal peptide bonds.

peptide (pe·ptəid). *Biochem.* [ad. G. *peptid*, back-formation from *di-*, *tripeptid*, etc. (E. Fischer 1902, in *Chemiker-Zeitung* XXVI. 940/2), *polypeptid* (E. Fischer 1903): see *POLYPEPTIDE.] **1.** Any compound in which two or more amino-acids are linked together by peptide bonds (see sense 2 below); according to the number of amino-acid residues such compounds are dipeptides, tripeptides, etc., oligopeptides, or polypeptides. Also *attrib.* or as *adj.*

1906 *Jrnl. Chem. Soc.* XC. II. 293 (*heading*) The fate of certain amino-acids and peptides in the organism of the dog. **1927** HALDANE & HUXLEY *Animal Biol.* iv. 107 We can make..a sugar or peptide (part of a protein molecule) which only differs from the natural variety in that its molecules are related to the natural molecules as a left hand to a right. **1949** ABRAHAM & FLOREY in H. W. Florey et al. *Antibiotics* I. vii. 331 The tomato-wilting agent produced by *Fusarium lycopersici* Sacc. was isolated by Plattner and Clauson-Kaas.., who later..showed that it was a peptide and named it lyco-marasmine. **1953** FRUTON & SIMMONDS *Gen. Biochem.* v. 135 Various strains of microorganisms elaborate substances of peptide nature which have antibacterial activity for other microorganisms. **1972** F. M. MENGER et al. *Org. Chem.* xiv. 359 The distinction between proteins and peptides is arbitrary. Compounds which have molecular weights greater than 10,000 are generally referred to as proteins. **1976** *Sci. Amer.* Feb. 32/1 There are two large classes of hormones, the peptides and the steroids. *Ibid.* 32/2 A typical peptide hormone is insulin.., human insulin consists of 51 amino acid units. **1977** *Time* 21 Nov. 40/3 Drs. Frank Ervin of U.C.L.A.'s Neuropsychiatric Institute and Roberta Palmour of the University of California at Berkeley described the substance as a variant of a peptide—a short chain of amino acids—that belongs to a family of newly discovered opiate-like brain hormones called endorphins.

2. Special comb.: **peptide bond**, a carbon–nitrogen bond of the type —CO·NH— in an organic molecule; *spec.* one between the carboxyl group of one amino-acid residue and the amino group of another; **peptide chain**, a linear sequence of amino-acid residues joined by peptide bonds; **peptide linkage** = **peptide bond*.

1935 *Jrnl. Biol. Chem.* CXI. 249 Aminopeptidase, carboxypeptidase, and dipeptidase need in addition to a peptide bond a free amino group or a free carboxyl group. **1960** *New Biol.* XXXI. 12 There are twenty main different kinds of amino acid involved in protein make-up, though they are basically alike enough to be all connected to each other by the same kind of chemical link (the peptide bond) to form the chain. **1964** N. G. CLARK *Mod. Org. Chem.* xiii. 252 Many important natural products contain the 'amide-linkage' or peptide bond, —CO·NH—; thus, the peptides and proteins..are long-chain polyamides. **1931** *Nature* 2 May 664/2 There is a strong probability that..many proteins will be based on a roughly constant weight of peptide chain. **1935** *Jrnl. Biol. Chem.* CXI. 245 Lysine is coupled in the long peptide chains of proteins with its α-amino and carboxyl groups. **1970** R. W. MCGILVERY *Biochem.* ii. 9 A protein may be only a single, long, peptide chain, but most proteins are made of several peptide chains associated together. **1925** *Proc. R. Soc.* B. XCVIII. 59 This procedure was adopted in order to bring about the scission of the peptide linkages as rapidly as possible. **1964** N. G. CLARK *Mod. Org. Chem.* xvii. 349 Proteins and polypeptides consist of chains of amino-acids linked via amide formation between the carbonyl group of one acid and the α-amino group of the next (the typical linkage, —CO·NH—, is often called a peptide-linkage or -bond).

peptidic (pepti·dik), *a. Biochem.* [f. *PEPTID(E + -IC.] Of, pertaining to, or being a peptide. Hence **pepti·dically** *adv.*, by means of a peptide bond.

1949 F. LIPMANN in *Federation Proc.* VIII. 597/1 To simplify the following discussion, the term 'peptidic link' is introduced as generic name for a —NH·CO-link between any amino or carboxyl group. The term 'peptide link' is then reserved for the 1-carboxyl, 2-amino-link between two alpha amino acids as it occurs in protein. **1964** *Adv. Enzymol.* XXVI. 212 Muropeptides, depending on the murein type, are known to differ by containing either Lys or one or more of the DAP stereoisomers to provide the free NH_2 group for peptidic linking. *Ibid.*, One enzyme..found..in *E. coli* cells..disconnects two C6 units tied peptidically into a C3 molecule. **1973** *Nature* 12 Oct. 288/1 G. Sterba..suggested that peptidic neurohormones might be involved in the generation of emotions by effects in the limbic system.

peptidoglycan (peptəi:dogləi·kæn). *Biochem.* [f. *PEPTID(E + -O + *GLYC(O- + -AN.] = *MUREIN; also, the mucopolysaccharide which forms the strands of this.

1966 *Biochem.* V. 82/1 The biosynthesis of peptidoglycan (mucopeptide) in cell-free extracts of Staphylococcus aureus..has been described by Chatterjee and Park. *Ibid.* 3091 The mechanical strength of the peptidoglycan polymer which forms the rigid network of all bacterial cell walls depends on a high degree of cross-linking between peptide and polysaccharide chains. **1968** A. WHITE et al. *Princ. Biochem.* (ed. 4) xli. 910 Murein synthesis.. may be regarded as proceeding in three stages: synthesis of the precursor units, synthesis of the linear peptidoglycan strands, and cross-linking. **1969** *New Scientist* 10 July 64/1 A major component of the cortex layer [of a bacterial spore] is the polymer murein (or peptidoglycan). **1975** *Nature* 10 Apr. 482/2 The walls of all penicillin-sensitive organisms contain a structural component called peptidoglycan, which consists of glycan chains of alternating residues of N-acetylglucosamine and its 3-*O*-D-lactyl ether..and D-amino acids.

peptidolysis (pe:ptəidǫ·lisis). *Biochem.* [f. *PEPTID(E + -O + *-LYSIS.] The degradation of a polypeptide into smaller peptides or amino-acids. Cf. *PEPTOLYSIS. So **pe:ptidoly·tic** *a.*

1970 *Nature* 25 July 337/2 Studies on the mechanism of action of peptidolytic enzymes..have made much use of their ability to hydrolyse esters as well as amides. **1971** *Ibid.* 25 June 495/2 Both sets of workers compared these data with kinetic results from peptidolytic reactions. **1972** *Biochim. & Biophys. Acta* CCLXV. 70 Cleavage, for example, of a 50 000-dalton peptide into fragments of 44 000 and 6000 daltons, respectively, can clearly be detected... Such peptidolysis can be observed only after dissolution of the protein by the detergent, since separated peptide fragments otherwise tend to remain associated through hydrophobic interactions.

peptization (peptəizēi·ʃən). *Chem.* [f. PEPT(ONE + -IZATION.] The transformation of a solid or semi-solid colloid into a fluid form by chemical means.

1864 T. GRAHAM in *Proc. R. Soc.* XIII. 340 Liquid silicic acid may be represented as the 'peptone' of gelatinous silicic acid; and the liquefaction of the latter by a trace of alkali may be spoken of as the peptization of the jelly. **1916** E. F. BURTON *Physical Prop. Colloidal Solutions* ii. 24 The large number of colloidal solutions prepared by the method known as peptization are examples of the resolution of a moist coagulum. **1934** *Industr. & Engin. Chem.* Nov. 1190/2 (*heading*) Peptization of lightly vulcanised rubber. **1948** A. LANE *Greek Pott.* i. 5 The coagulation can..be broken down by a process known as 'peptization', by the disintegrating action on the clay of certain chemicals. **1960** R. G. HAGGAR *Conc. Encycl. Cont. Pott. & Porc.* 210/2 Modern scholars have..demonstrated the understanding which they [*sc.* the Greeks] had of clay processes, of oxydising and reducing firing techniques, and what to-day are called 'protective colloids' and 'peptization'. **1963** D. W. & E. E. HUMPHRIES tr. *Termier's Erosion & Sedimentation* vi. 135 The peptization of colloidal ferric hydroxide occurs at pH 6·6, under the influence of humus and colloidal silica which is present in the soil. **1972** MOELLER & O'CONNOR *Ions in Aqueous Syst.* v. 113 Conversion of precipitate into a colloidal suspension is called 'peptization'.

peptize (pe·ptəiz), *v. Chem.* [f. PEPT(ONE + -IZE.] *trans.* To convert into a sol; to cause to undergo peptization.

1864 T. GRAHAM in *Proc. R. Soc.* XIII. 340 The pure jellies of alumina, peroxide of iron, and titanic acid, prepared by dialysis, are assimilated more closely to albumen, being peptized by minute quantities of hydrochloric acid. **1934** H. N. HOLMES *Introd. Colloid Chem.* iii. 26 Glue, gelatin, soap, gum arabic, and dextrin are said to be soluble in water. In reality they are merely peptized by water—they are subdivided into particles far larger than molecules. **1939** [see *DISPERSE *v.* 9]. **1955** R. K. ILER *Colloid Chem. Silica & Silicates* v. 92 Various processes have been described which involve making silica gel from acid and silicate, washing out the salts, and peptizing the wet gel by heating it under pressure in the presence of a small amount of alkali. **1972** MOELLER & O'CONNOR *Ions in Aqueous Syst.* v. 116 Freshly prepared and washed precipitates can be peptized in many cases by adding water and a little of the original precipitating reagent.

Hence **pe·ptized, pe·ptizing** *ppl. adjs.* Also **pe:ptizabi·lity, pepti·zable** *a.*

1921 W. D. BANCROFT *Appl. Colloid Chem.* v. 167 We may have peptization by a liquid, by a non-electrolyte, by an adsorbed ion, by a salt, or by a peptized colloid. *Ibid.* 170 Water-peptizable colloids like gelatine, gum arabic, dextrine, [etc.]..will peptize many precipitates. **1925** tr. J. M. van Bemmelen in E. Hatschek *Foundations Colloid Chem.* 129 The peptizing agent may be removed from the solution and the colloid remains dissolved. **1934** *Industr. & Engin. Chem.* Nov. 1190 Rubber which has been lightly vulcanized with sulfur can be dissolved in benzene with the help of peptizing agents... The action of soluble zinc compounds on peptized rubber sulfur causes a gelling action. **1938** *Proc. Rubber Technol. Conf.* 289 Rubber 'softeners'..are commonly used to increase the plasticity of rubber, and it is often assumed that they act through some lubrication, swelling, or 'peptising' action on the rubber. **1963** *Ceylon Vet. Jrnl.* XI. 42 The solubility of the protein of groundnut meals has been determined by the salt-peptizability of its nitrogen.

peptizer (pe·ptəizəɹ). *Chem.* [f. *PEPTIZ(E *v.* + -ER¹.] A substance which causes peptization, or which serves to prevent the coagulation of a colloid suspension; *spec.* a catalyst which facilitates the process of mastication or vulcanization of rubber, by preventing the recombination of broken polymer chains.

1931 E. S. HEDGES *Colloids* iii. 16 If the freshly precipitated ferric hydroxide is treated with..ferric chloride solution it disperses immediately to form a dark reddish-brown colloidal solution. We call..ferric chloride the peptizer or peptizing agent. **1946** *Shell Aviation News* No. 100. 15/3 These [*sc.* additives in oil]..may act as 'peptizers' which help to keep in suspension in the oil any insolubles which are formed. **1961** *New Scientist* 2 Mar. 549/1 Other substances, so called 'peptisers', can be added [to rubber] to ensure this simple form of stabilizing the reactive ends of the broken chains. **1963** H. VAN OLPHEN *Introd. Clay Colloid Chem.* viii. 109 When a small amount of peptizer is added to a pure clay gel, the yield stress decreases drastically. **1972** *Materials & Technol.* V. xiv. 474 Effective peptizers [of rubber] are hydrazine derivatives and organic sulphur compounds like thio-β-naphthol, pentachlor thiophenol, dibenzoyl disulphide.

peptolysis (peptǫ·lisis). *Biochem.* [f. PEPTO(NE + *-LYSIS.] The degradation of a peptone or polypeptide into smaller peptides or amino-acids. Cf. *PEPTIDOLYSIS.

1904 S. H. VINES in *Ann. Bot.* XVIII. 290 Accepting this connotation of 'proteolysis', the successive stages of the process may, I would suggest, be conveniently distinguished as—(*a*) peptonization, the conversion of the higher proteins into albumoses and peptones; and (*b*) peptolysis, the decomposition of peptones into nitrogenous but non-proteid substances. **1949** H. TAUBER *Chem. & Technol. Enzymes* vi. 130 The end products of peptolysis are mostly proteoses and peptones and small quantities of amino acids.

Hence **peptoly·tic** *a.*, **peptoly·tically** *adv.*

1904 *Ann. Bot.* XVIII. 290 Trypsin..forms tryptophane as one of the products of its peptolytic activity. *Ibid.* 299 It was ascertained that a filtered watery extract of yeast was always peptolytically active, however short the period of extraction might be. **1915** *Chem. Abstr.* IX. 2910 The formaldehyde titration for free amino groups in polypeptides and their hydrolytic products is a method practically adapted to the study of the action of peptolytic ferments on polypeptides. **1949** H. W. FLOREY et al. *Antibiotics* I. i. 47 Gram positive proteolytic bacteria such as..staphylococci when grown with gram positive peptolytic bacteria..in a nitrogen-free medium secreted a bacteriolytic substance which dissolved the latter, thus making their nitrogen available.

Pepysian (pī·psiăn), *a.* [f. the name of Samuel *Pepys*, diarist (1633–1703) + -IAN.] Of, pertaining to, or characteristic of Pepys, his writings, his library, or the age in which he lived. So **Pepysia·na** *sb. pl.*

1786 in *Wks. James I of Scotl.* 98 Dr Percy informs us, that this poem is preserved in the Pepysian Library, at Magdalen College, Cambridge. **1847** E. F. RIMBAULT *Nursery Rhymes* p. viii, The popular rhyme 'Three Children sliding on the Ice'..is part of a ballad preserved in the Pepysian collection. **1899** H. B. WHEATLEY *Diary of Samuel Pepys: Suppl. Vol.* (*title*) Pepysiana. **1920** *Glasgow Herald* 21 Sept. 8 Amid the distractions of business he cultivated his early literary bent and kept a diary wherein, with Pepysian frankness,..he chronicled his doings. **1927** W. DEEPING *Kitty* xxx. 385 He was a Pepysian soul and kept a diary. **1927** J. S. HUXLEY *Relig. without Revelation* iv. 119 The Pepysian interest in complete record of all facts centring on self. **1927** W. H. WHITEAR (*title*) More Pepysiana: being notes on the Diary of Samuel Pepys and on the genealogy of the family, with corrected pedigrees. **1934** *Punch* 19 Dec. 699/3 Builders' models of the Pepysian and later periods, rigged models of Dutch Indiamen,..reconstructed models by present-day experts, all find a place in this fascinating gallery.

Pequot (pī·kwǫt), *sb.* and *a.* Also **Pecoate, Pequod, Pequoitt.** [prob. f. native word *paquatanog* destroyers.] **A.** *sb.* **a.** An Indian of an Algonquian tribe of southern New England. **b.** The language spoken by the Pequots. **B.** *adj.* Of or pertaining to the Pequot Indians, or the language spoken by them.

1631 in *New Hampsh. Hist. Soc. Coll.* (1834) IV. 226 Wee heare their numbers exceed any but the Pecoates and Nawagansets. **1637** *Public Rec. Colony of Connecticut* (1850) I. 10 To parle w[i]th the bay aboute o[u]r settinge downe in the Pequoitt Countrey. **1654** E. JOHNSON *Hist. New-England* II. vi. 109 The English sought by all means to keepe these [fighting men] at least from confederating with the Pequods. **1714** S. SEWALL *Diary* (1882) III. 12 Commissioners met to give Govr. Sattonstall an Opportunity to vindicate himself relating to the Pequot and Mohegan Indians. **1849** O. W. HOLMES *Poems* 256 He heard the Pequot's ringing whoop. **1851** H. MELVILLE *Moby Dick* I. xvi. 110 Pequod..was the name of a celebrated tribe of Massachusetts Indians, now extinct as the ancient Medes. **1871** C. M. YONGE *Pioneers & Founders* i. 6 The Pequot Indians, a tall, well-proportioned, and active tribe, belonging to the great Iroquois nation. *Ibid.* 8 The Pequots were..at war with the Dutch. **1903** PRINCE & SPECK in *Amer. Anthropologist* V. 195 Their language, of course, remained Pequot, a dialect which shows a..striking kinship..with the present speech of the Canadian Abenakis. **1945** C. M. WEBSTER *Town Meeting Country* 11 The Pequots were probably the bravest and most ferocious of all the New England tribes. **1979** *Arizona Daily Star* 1 Apr. A 2/2 Among their guests is to be John Hamilton, Chief Rolling Cloud of the Mohegan and Pequot American Indian tribes.

per, *prep.* Add: **I. 4. per contra. a.** (Further examples.)

1903 R. FRY *Let.* 16 Mar. (1972) I. 206 The article won't do the magazine much good, but *per contra* it won't do anyone..any harm. **1919** J. STEPHENSON *Princ. & Pract. Commerc. Corr.* III. iii. 181 Your cash remittance of £1,000 of the 1st inst. came duly to hand and per contra we have purchased Frs. 25,000 French Gold Rente, which we send you enclosed. **1924** A. HUXLEY *Let.* 9 Aug. (1969) 231 The people who have deliberately set out to put great thoughts into verse have generally been the worst poets on record. But, per contra, the best poets have generally implied or directly expressed great thoughts. **1940** G. F.-H. & J. BERKELEY *Italy in Making* III. iii. 52 The Sicilians had only one great enthusiasm—to free their island from the hated Neapolitans... *Per contra*, the Neapolitans' first aim was to maintain their hold on Sicily. **1976** *Listener* 12 Aug. 172/1 Writers from this centre of England..suggest a centrality of English experience... *Per contra*, some explorers..have found a too-muchness in this green country.

b. Also as *adj.*

1972 *Times* 11 May (Spain Suppl.) p. iv/3 A similar list prepared by the *The Banker*, but based on deposits less *per contra* accounts, of world bank groups included two Spanish banks only.

5. per diem. a. (Later examples.)

1906 *Arch. Roentgen Ray* XI. 18/2 When the method of treatment by fractional doses is carried out—for instance, ½X to 1X per diem—the quantimetric method alone is impossible. **1920** A. HUXLEY *Let.* 23 Dec. (1969) 193, I have to go to at least two and sometimes three theatres per diem and write about them afterwards. **1979** C. DEXTER *Service of All Dead* xxxiii. 194 We're all ageing at the standard rate of twenty-four hours *per diem.*

b. (Earlier and later examples.) Also as *adj.*

1809 *Deb. Congress U.S.* 13 Feb. (1853) 350 Officers of the United States..have received..the per diem allowance fixed by law. **1812** *Weekly Reg.* 18 Jan. 361/2 The *per diem* of the members has been raised to *four* dollars. **1839** *Congress. Globe* 25th Congress 3 Sess. App. 66/1 In that case, had he asked for his mileage and per diem, all would have considered it an insult. **1846** T. L. MCKENNEY *Mem.* I. ix. 192, I referred to him the making up of my account for my per diem allowance. **1946** E. HODGINS *Mr. Blandings builds his Dream House* xiii. 195 He would..happily replace the tubs at a per diem rate. **1973** R. HAYES *Hungarian Game* xxxviii. 228 If I made the flight I could crib another twenty dollars on my per diem. **1974** R. THOMAS *Porkchoppers* v. 39 He got another $10,000 a year from the union in per diem and expenses. **1977** D. JAMES *Spy at Evening* iv. 21, I liked the job. I accepted. 'A *per diem* of fifty pounds—travel expenses in addition.'

6. per mensem. (Later examples.)

1886 KIPLING *Departmental Ditties* (ed. 2) 3 A nice retaining fee Supplied, of course, *per mensem*, by the Indian Treasury. **1916** 'TAFFRAIL' *Pincher Martin* vi. 88 The sum of ten shillings *per mensem* was supposed..to suffice for the midshipmen's needs in the way of extras. **1965** *New Statesman* 24 Sept. 466/3 (Advt.), The amounts mentioned below refer to Malayan dollars (per mensem) and their approximate sterling equivalent. **1974** *Nature* 30 Aug. p. xxvii/1 (Advt.), This scholarship carries a stipend of M$700 per mensem for the first 12 months followed by M$800 per mensem beyond that period.

10. per aliud, by or in another entity; extrinsically; with reference to anything else; **per anum**, by the anus, applied esp. to anal sexual intercourse; **per capita**, (*b*) = **per caput*; **per caput**, per person or head (of population); also as *adj. phr.*; **per curiam** (*Law*), 'by action of the court', applied to a judgement, of concise and peremptory character, formulated by the whole bench; freq. *attrib.*; **per impossible** (*Logic*), 'as is impossible', a qualification governing a proposition which can never be true; **per incuriam** (*Law*), 'by carelessness', applied to a judicial decision evidently contrary to the law or facts; also *transf.*; **per mil, per mille**, in every thousand; **per primam** *Med.*, in full **per primam intentionem**, 'by first intention' (see INTENTION 10 b).

1890 W. JAMES *Princ. Psychol.* II. xvii. 42 To say that we feel a sensation's seat to be 'in the brain' or 'against the eye' or 'under the skin' is to say as much *about* it and to deal with it in as non-primitive a way as to say that it is a mile off. These are all secondary perceptions, ways of defining the sensation's seat *per aliud.* **1948** *Mind* LVII. 127 St. Thomas's proof [is] that the existence of finite beings, since it is *per aliud*, must be derived from something that exists *per se.* **1838** *Guy's Hosp. Rep.* III. 340 The constant symptom..was the passing of blood per anum. **1972** P. GREEN *Shadow of Parthenon* 160 Their liking for intercourse *per anum*, perhaps to preserve their virginity for the marriage market. **1972** *Mod. Law Rev.* XXXV. 107 Sexual intercourse *per anum.* **1926** FOWLER *Mod. Eng. Usage* 428/2 *The entire production of opium in India is two grammes per capita yearly.* This use is a modern blunder, encouraged in some recent dictionaries. **1941** WYNDHAM LEWIS *Let.* 9 Nov. (1963) 306 It [*sc.* Canada] reads less per capita than any other known civilised population. **1942** J. S. HUXLEY in *Harper's Mag.* Sept. 340/2 The U.S.S.R., in spite of its low per capita wealth, [etc.]. **1952** [see *GROWTH[1] 1 c]. **1955** *Times* 6 July 8/4 Saving *per capita* varies considerably from territory to territory, and in each territory from year to year, according to the study. **1965** *New Statesman* 30 Apr. 672/3 For the bulk of humanity per capita consumption remains the same. **1974** *Times* 25 Apr. 17/7 Let us have..an electoral system that secures proper proportionate representation both *per capita* and by party. **1975** 'D. JORDAN' *Black Account* 246 Geneva Airport, I always feel, is the richest airport in the world..in terms of *per capita* elegance, tailoring, luggage, comfort. **1975** *Sci. Amer.* Nov. 56/1 Per capita incomes have declined in recent years. **1919** W. T. GRENFELL *Labrador Doctor* (1920) iii. 60 By special arrangement with the railway and other friends, and by very simple living, the per caput charges were so much reduced that many of the boys not only paid their own expenses, but even helped their friends. **1962** *Times* 21 May (Commonw. Chambers of Commerce Suppl.) p. v/5 India plans to..raise the present *per caput* income in the country. **1970** K. J. PARKER in G. G. Birch et al. *Glucose Syrups* v. 77 The current total *per caput* consumption of refined sugar is higher in Britain (112 lb) than in the USA (99·7 lb). **1976** *Lancet* 13 Nov. 1050/2 It may be argued that the per-caput cigarette consumption is not a good measure of the cigarette consumption in young women. **1978** *Jrnl. R. Soc. Arts* CXXVI. 651/2 The Harbin Transistor Plant was achieving very high *per caput* sales. **1890** *Cent. Dict.*, *Per curiam*, in *law*, by the court: a phrase prefixed to judicial opinions indicating the sanction of the court to the statements therein, as distinguished from the individual opinions of a particular judge. **1955** *Bull. Atomic Sci.* Oct. 309/2 It was a brief per curiam decision in a case which involved no contested issue. **1959** JOWITT *Dict. Eng. Law* II. 1327/2 *Per curiam, per cur.*, by the court. **1972** *N.Y. Law Jrnl.* 24 Oct. 2/1 Per curiam: Order reversed, with..costs and defendant's motion..granted. **1973** *Ibid.* 20 Feb. 4/4 If a court writes a per curiam opinion like this, what justification is there for demanding better writing from attorneys? **1847** A. DE MORGAN *Formal Logic* vii. 132 The moods *Baroko* and *Bokardo* do not admit of reduction to the first figure, by any fair use of the phrase: but the logicians were determined that they should do so, and they accordingly hit upon the following plan, which they called reduction *per impossibile.* **1883** F. H. BRADLEY *Princ. Logic* 217 If, I say, *per impossibile* this phantom could be real—..the above chance of irregularity would vanish. **1896** L. T. HOBHOUSE *Theory of Knowl.* 199 It was a onesided error to suggest that the immediate object of vision is colour or rows of coloured points from which, *per impossibile*, extension was conceived as removed. **1912** A. LANG *Shakespeare, Bacon & Gt. Unknown* xii. 267 If he knew that the author was Bacon, and knew it under pledge of secrecy, and was asked (*per impossibile*) 'Who wrote these plays?' he had only to say, 'Look at the title-page.' **1923** H. W. B. JOSEPH *Labour Theory of Value in Karl Marx* vi. 145 And supposing the equilibrium in an equal exchange were *per impossibile* between satisfaction on one side and sacrifice on the other, such equilibrium could only be said to exist in single exchanges independently. **1935** *Mind* XLIV. 237 Butler's 'let it be allowed' that virtue could not be justified if (*per impossibile*) it were contrary to self-interest. **1963** J. LYONS *Structural Semantics* iii. 42 Suppose, *per impossibile*, that we were transported as investigating linguists to Athens of the fifth century B.C. **1972** *Times Lit. Suppl.* 22 Dec. 1550/4 Have you for the moment forgotten *per impossibile* in which opera the chorus 'Upon our sea-girt land' occurs. **1867** WHARTON *Law Lexicon* (ed. 4) 709/1 *Per incuriam*, through want of care. **1925** F. NEWBOLT *Out of Court* iii. 162 To attain this object you should first succeed in life, and have your portrait, or *per incuriam* that of a confusing namesake, inserted in a good picture paper. **1963** *Times* 24 Apr. 5/2 Mr. Puntan now appealed against that order; and his Lordship was afraid that the Divisional Court had acted *per incuriam* in making the order they did. **1970** *Internat. & Compar. Law Q.* XIX. 340 Parts of the judgement must be regarded as given *per incuriam*, and cannot be relied upon. **1976** *Phipson's Law of Evidence* (ed. 12) xxix. 677 A document omitted *per incuriam* was allowed to be put in by the prosecution during the reply. **1902** *Encycl. Brit.* XXXI. 404/2 The bottom waters have almost uniformly a salinity of 34·8 per mille, corresponding closely with the bottom waters of the south Atlantic. **1957** A. GRIMBLE *Return to Islands* 102 Perhaps five or six per mil of his parishioners at most. **1957** L. F. R. WILLIAMS *State of Israel* 189 Infant mortality among the Arab community has fallen steadily to about 60 per mille of live births. **1972** *Nature* 25 Feb. 417/1 The seasonal amplitude is reduced to around 2 per mille. **1972** *Science* 22 Sept. 1099/3 The sulfur isotopic values on the west side averaged around 5·3 per mil. **1907** *Practitioner* Sept. 335 The wound healed *per primam*, except at the drain opening, and this was quite closed on the eighteenth day. *Ibid.* 336 Union *per primam* without any trouble. **1957** H. N. HARKINS in J. G. Allen et al. *Surgery* ii. 9/1 Healing of wounds can be divided into 3 types: (1) Healing by first intention (per primam intensionum [*sic*]: primary union).

III. 1. (Later examples.) *per margin*: (earlier example); (*as*) *per usual* (later examples); also with ellipsis of *usual*. Also, other humorous and extended uses.

1782 *Town & Country Mag.* Dec. 669/1, I stood with the squadron, as per margin, to the southward, all that night. **1922** JOYCE *Ulysses* 343 As per usual somebody's nose was out of joint. **1923** 'K. MANSFIELD' *Bad Idea* in *Doves' Nest* 146 So I took her up a cup of tea..as per usual on her headache days. **1938** J. PHELAN *Lifer* xxi. 212 That's right,..no grounds, as per. **1959** N. MARSH *False Scent* (1960) i. 12 He'll be bringing his present later on, as per usual. **1960** S. BARSTOW *Kind of Loving* II. vii. 263, I reckon after tonight we can't carry on as per. **1960** 'B. MATHER' *Pass beyond Kashmir* xviii. 240 It'll have to be per boot again—and across country at that. **1966** 'J. HACKSTON' *Father clears Out* 115 The Butler boys returned home (as per precedent) from breaking-in up north. **1966** *Rev. Mod. Physics* XXXVIII. 221/2 Look at one of the product tableaux obtained as per previous instructions with the markings 1, or 2,..or *N* in the various squares inserted. **1972** 'A. ARMSTRONG' *One Jump Ahead* i. 13, I came back as per usual about five o'clock. **1972** *Mod. Law Rev.* XXXV. 58 It cannot make a bare declaration (see *per* Lord Hailsham L.C., H.L.Deb., Vol. 318, col. 936). **1977** J. BINGHAM *Marriage Bureau Murders* i. 9 I'll stay in a pub... As per usual.

2. Also with ellipsis of *cent, head, hour, week*, etc.

1899 G. W. PECK *Uncle Ike* iii. 31 Listened to a heavenly choir that is paid a hundred dollars per. **1901** *Hide & Leather* 24 Aug. 30/2 He now sits in the Usher's box near the entrance to the jobbing house and draws $10 per. **1903** 'J. FLYNT' *Rise of R. Clowd* iii. 111 The percentage that Ruderick was to receive excited the liveliest interest... 'I wouldn't give any kid more'n twenty-five per.' *a* **1911** D. G. PHILLIPS *Susan Lenox* (1917) II. iv. 86 We'll get married as soon as he has a raise to twelve per. **1911** J. LONDON *Let.* 18 Oct. (1966) 353 To exploit the mediocre for the consumption of mediocrity at so much exultantly per. **1935** J. N. CHANCE *Wheels in Forest* viii. 153 The road is clear at eleven ten, and Lombard is here at eleven nineteen. That's nine minutes; an average of eighty miles per. **1946** [see *BEEF *sb.* 6]. **1973** E. MCGIRR *Bardel's Murder* ii. 52 '[He] thinks his two daughters have been got at by the chauffeur.'.. 'I phoned up old Sir Omicron Pie, who kicks us back fifty per on the surgery.' **1976** *New Yorker* 23 Feb. 28/2 Many of the chain hotels are run by managing directors who have wives who think they are interior decorators and get on the payroll at twenty-five thousand per.

peracarid (perăkæ·rid), *sb.* (and *a.*) [f. mod.L. name of division *Peracarida* (W. T. Calman 1904, in *Ann. & Mag. Nat. Hist.* 7th Ser. XIII. 150), f. Gr. πήρα pouch + καρίς shrimp, prawn: see -ID[3].] A crustacean belonging to the division of the subclass Malacostraca so called, including sand-hoppers and woodlice possessing brood pouches. Also as *adj.* So **peraca·ridan, peracari·dean** *a.*

1931 W. SCHMITT *Crustaceans* in *Shelled Invertebr. of Past & Present* II. iii. 156 The two final orders comprising the peracarids. **1961** H. SCHÖNE in T. H. Waterman *Physiol. Crustacea* II. xiii. 486 Female peracaridans carry eggs and young in a marsupium between their legs. **1965** B. E. FREEMAN tr. *Vandel's Biospeleol.* ix. 117 *Spelaeogriphus* is most certainly the last relict of a primitive peracarid type. **1965** W. SCHMITT *Crustaceans* iii. 88 This [*sc.* Spelaeogriphacea] is one of the most recently established of the six peracaridean orders. *Ibid.* 89 The Spelaeogriphacea differ from all other peracaridans in having vesicular, oval gills. **1967** *Oceanogr. & Marine Biol.* V. 518 The first group includes the peracarids *Gnatha oxyurea*, *Eriopisia elongata*..and also many (better known) decapods.

peracetate. *Chem.* Restrict †*Obs.* to sense in Dict. and add: **2.** An ester or related derivative of peracetic acid.

1901 *Jrnl. Chem. Soc.* LXXX. I. 308 Acetic anhydride furnishes an oily product, probably ethyl peracetate. **1949** *Chem. Rev.* XLV. 8 Ethyl peracetate has been reported... This compound cannot be classed as a derivative of peracetic acid and ethyl alcohol, but rather as a derivative of acetic acid and ethyl hydroperoxide. **1967** L. F. & M. A. FIESER *Reagents for Org. Synthesis* I. 790. The reaction may proceed through the hemiacetal peracetate.

peracetic (pərăsī·tik), *a.* *Chem.* [f. PER-[1] 5 b + ACETIC *a.*] *peracetic acid*: $CH_3CO{\cdot}O{\cdot}OH$, a colourless, corrosive, pungent liquid that is explosive when hot and is widely used, usu. dissolved in acetic acid, as an oxidizing agent in synthesis, as a bleach and as a sterilizing agent, etc.

1903 *Jrnl. Chem. Soc.* LXXXIV. I. 398 The aqueous solution gradually suffers hydrolysis with formation of molecular proportions of acetic and peracetic acids. **1938** [see *EPOXIDE]. **1965** *Economist* 20 Feb. 780/1 The new process for the oxidation of cyclohexanone to caprolactone with peracetic acid. **1970** *New Scientist* 15 Jan. 102/1 Peracetic acid is a powerful oxidizing agent that readily kills bacterial spores. **1972** NORMAN & WADDINGTON *Mod. Org. Chem.* xxi. 321 It [*sc.* nylon] can be bleached with a dilute solution of peracetic acid.

peracid (pəræ·sid). *Chem.* Also **per-acid.** [f. PER-[1] + ACID *sb.*, as tr. G. *persäure* (von Baeyer & Villiger 1900, in *Ber. d. Deut. Chem. Ges.* XXXIII. 2480).] An acid which contains a peroxide group, esp. (in *Org. Chem.*) the group —CO·O·OH.

1900 *Jrnl. Chem. Soc.* LXXVIII. I. 626 The authors suggest that hydrogen peroxide, its acyl derivatives, and their peroxides should be called 'hydroperoxide', 'per-acids' and 'peroxides' respectively. **1922** J. W. MELLOR *Comprehensive Treat. Inorg. & Theoret. Chem.* I. xiv. 959 The true peracids are either formed by the action of hydrogen peroxide on ordinary acids or their derivatives, or else they furnish hydrogen peroxide when hydrolyzed with dilute sulphuric acid. **1950** N. V. SIDGWICK *Chem. Elements* II. 871 Other compounds with the O—O link are numerous per-acids (or peroxy-acids), such as persulphuric, perboric, percarbonic, pertitanic, perchromic, etc. **1972** *Materials & Technol.* IV. xiii. 477 All preparations of, and reactions with, organic peroxide and peracids should be conducted behind safety shields, because a reaction occasionally proceeds with uncontrollable violence.

peracute *a.* Delete 'Now *rare*' and substitute 'Now chiefly *Vet. Med.*'. Add later examples.

1963 *Daily Tel.* 3 Dec. 23/1 A highland steer which went down with peracute pneumonia early yesterday recovered sufficiently to win a first prize in its class later in the morning. **1970** W. H. PARKER *Health & Dis. in*

Farm Animals ix. 102 The word subacute is used to describe a condition between acute and chronic while a disease which kills very quickly..is called peracute.

perahera (perăhe·ră). Also **perahar, perahära.** [Sinhalese *perahera* protection, safety.] In Sri Lanka: a procession, orig. of a religious (Hindu, later also Buddhist) character, of praise or thanksgiving, or of intercession.

1681 R. Knox *Hist. Relation Ceylon* III. iv. 78 That they may..honour these Gods, and procure their aid and assistance, they do yearly in the Month of June or July, at a New Moon, observe a solemn feast and general Meeting, called Perahar. **1817** in R. Pieris *Sinhalese Social Organization* (1956) III. 135 *Perhära*..is a very ancient ceremony in commemoration of the birth of the god Vishnu. *Ibid.* 136 Five days having expired, another ceremony, an important and essential part of the *perahära*, commences..which lasts five days more. *Ibid.* 137 The ceremony of *perahära* is continued up to the day of the full moon... On the night of the full moon..the shrine is carried in the procession. **1913** L. Woolf *Village in Jungle* v. 113 Last night we took him in the perahera, and called upon the god to hear us. **1923** D. H. Lawrence *Birds, Beasts & Flowers* 170 But the best is the Pera-hera, at midnight, under the tropical stars..the Pera-hera procession, flambeaux aloft in the tropical night. **1971** *Ceylon Daily News* 17 Sept. 1/3 He will be taken in a perahera to the avasa where a felicitation meeting is to be held. **1974** *Oxf. Jun. Encycl.* (rev. ed.) I. 102/2 The principal occasion is the Perahera, a great annual pageant in Kandy, when a relic, reputed to be a tooth of Gautama Buddha, is carried about the town in grand procession on the back of a gorgeously caparisoned elephant.

‖**perahu,** var. Proa.

1939 A. Keith *Land below Wind* III. xi. 186 The river travel would be accomplished in small native canoes known as *perahus.* **1958** J. Slimming *Temiar Jungle* ii. 19 The kit was..stowed away in the boat—a thirty-five-foot *perahu* with a thirty-horse-power engine. **1965** R. McKie *Company of Animals* i. 1 The Malay perahu..was thirty feet long with a four-foot beam, a thin slice with a stern flattened just enough to hold an outboard motor, and a bow so sharp that it parted the river like a comb. **1966** *Festival Malaysia 1966: Calendar of Events* 6/2 The intricate carvings that decorate the racing perahu can be seen.

peralkalic (pəræ·lkălik), *a. Petrol.* [f. Ped-[1] 4 + Alkalic *a.*] = next.

1902 W. Cross et al. in *Jrnl. Geol.* X. 592 The divisions in classes I, II, and III are fivefold: Rang 1:

$$\frac{K_2O' + Na_2O'}{CaO'} > \frac{7}{1}, \text{ peralkalic.}$$

1976 *Nature* 10 June 482/1 The Saint Francois Mountains form a distinctive unmetamorphosed igneous complex comprising chiefly alkalic to peralkalic rhyolite and granite.

peralkaline (pəræ·lkăləin), *a. Petrol.* [f. Per-[1] 4 + Alkaline *a.*] Of a rock: containing a high proportion of soda and potash; now *spec.* (see quot. 1931).

1913 A. N. Winchell in *Jrnl. Geol.* XXI. 210 Along this co-ordinate igneous rocks are classified as normal or alkali-calcic.., alkaline, and peralkaline. *Ibid.* 211 Peralkaline rocks are characterized mineralogically by the presence of feldspathoids (or lenads)... Chemically they are distinguished by insufficient silica to combine with the abundant alkalies to form feldspars after saturation of other available bases as orthosilicates. **1927** S. J. Shand *Eruptive Rocks* vii. 128 The following groups of rocks stand out as chemically distinct:— (a) A peraluminous group, characterised by primary muscovite, biotite, corundum, tourmaline, topaz, almandine, or spessartite. (b) A peralkaline group, characterised by soda-pyroxenes or soda-amphiboles,.. and by the virtual absence of anorthite... (c) A group characterised by common pyroxenes, amphiboles, olivine, [etc]. **1931** —— *Study of Rocks* iv. 52 Peraluminous rocks... The molecular proportion of alumina exceeds the molecular proportions of soda, potash and lime combined... Peralkaline rocks... The molecular proportion of alumina is less than that of soda and potash combined. **1950** *Rep. 18th Internat. Geol. Congr. 1948* II. 129 Peralkaline rocks..only occur in stable parts of the earth's crust, outside active orogenic zones. **1974** *Nature* 24 May 315/1 Alkaline and peralkaline igneous rocks were intruded and extruded in distinct nodes. **1974** [see *peraluminous *a.*].

Hence **pe:ralkali·nity,** the state of being peralkaline.

1969 *Amer. Jrnl. Sci.* CCLXVII. 242 A quadrilateral diagram in which molecular alumina is plotted against soda/potash ratio can then be employed to show the variation in alkali ratio in whole rocks..with changes in silica content and peralkalinity. **1974** Bowden & Turner in H. Sørensen *Alkaline Rocks* iv. viii. 334/2 The variation in the coloured mineral content is dependent on the peralkalinity of the granites.

peraluminous (pərăl*iu*·minəs), *a. Petrol.* [f. Per-[1] 4 + Aluminous *a.*] Of a rock: (see quots. 1974[1] (and 1931), 1972).

1927, 1931 [see *peralkaline *a.*]. **1964** *Mineral. Abstr.* XVI. 488/2 A peraluminous granite stock and related pegmatites..have been emplaced in pelitic and quartzo-feldspathic schists. **1972** *Gloss. Geol.* (Amer. Geol. Inst.) 527/1 *Peraluminous*, said of an igneous rock in which the molecular proportion of aluminum oxide is greater than that of sodium and potassium oxide combined. **1974** I. S. E. Carmichael et al. *Igneous Petrology* ii. 31 This leads to four more classes of rocks, each independent of silica saturation: 1. Peraluminous rocks, in which the molecular proportion of Al_2O_3 exceeds (CaO + Na_2O + K_2O)... 4. Peralkaline rocks, in which Al_2O_3 < (Na_2O + K_2O). **1974** W. C. Luth in H. Sørensen *Alkaline Rocks* vi. vi. 506/1 Several key factors provide limiting conditions. These include..the relatively large amounts of the peraluminous hydrates required.

perambulate, *v.* Add: **3. a.** *intr.* Of a (light) vehicle: to be in motion, to move about. *rare.* **b.** *trans.* To wheel, convey, or conduct (*about*) in or as in a perambulator (sense 3); to travel on or traverse in a perambulator.

1856 *Chambers's Jrnl.* 23 Aug. 116/2 The young brother.. can hardly reach to the bar, but nevertheless the light crrriage perambulates obediently under his guidance. **1865** P. H. Gosse *Year at Shore* iv. 87 The open gate of a villa reveals a little girl 'perambulating' a baby. **1902** *To-Day* 30 Apr. 8/1 Babies..are not allowed to 'perambulate' the pavement two or three abreast. **1909** M. B. Saunders *Litany Lane* xxii. 295 The Princess Max, having opened the affair, was being perambulated about as usual. **1922** J. A. Dunn *Man Trap* i. 9 Jovial of mouth and eyes despite the handicap that reduced him to being perambulated. **1929** P. Gibbs *Hidden City* xi. 50 Four acres of garden in which some neat nursemaids were perambulating the pink-cheeked babies of the well-to-do.

perambulating, *ppl. a.* (Further examples.)

1926 W. J. Locke *Stories Near & Far* 280 Then he walked round his perambulating property [*sc.* a caravan]. A big-boned brown horse ceased his munching as he approached. **1938** P. W. Sergeant *Championship Chess* i. 26 There is little to be said for perambulating chess matches —except that they bring in more money. **1949** E. Coxhead *Wind in West* vi. 165 We're..all products of what Rory calls the book-learning. We're his perambulating text-books.

perambulator. 1. a. For Now *rare* or *Obs.* read *rare* and add further examples. Also *fig.*

1870 Hazlewood & Williams *Leave it to Me* 3 Joe's a perambulator;..a perambulating greengrocer, called by vulgar people a costermonger. **1925** J. Bone (*title*) The London perambulator. **1930** R. Campbell *Adamastor* 64 Speed, motion, flight!..Perambulator of the Bored And ambulance of broken hearts! **1971** *Daily Tel.* 18 Oct. 10 (Advt.), Dickens was a determined perambulator of London, either in search of material..or simply wandering the streets.

2. Delete †*Obs.* and add later examples.

1855 J. Butler *Trav. & Adventures Assam* i. v. 56 Some idea may be formed of the impassable nature of the country we travelled over this day, when I state that we only came eight miles one furlong, by the perambulator, in eight hours. *a* **1877** [see *delineator 3]. **1913** Close & Cox *Text Bk. Topogr. & Geogr. Surveying* (ed. 2) iv. 76 A perambulator should not be used over very rough ground, and both it and the cyclometer should be checked over known measured distances. **1964** D. Greenhood *Mapping* ix. 262/2 For doing the same kind of measuring on the ground itself, there are various makes of distance meters, sometimes called 'perambulators', which are wheels that you push by a handle, like a roller toy. They register distances up to 10,000 ft. **1969** Tooley & Bricker *Hist. Cartogr.* 42 (*caption*) Colles's map..was probably made with compass, plane table, and perambulator.

3. (Earlier and later examples.) Also *attrib.*, *Comb.*, and *fig.*

1856 *Chambers's Jrnl.* 23 Aug. 116/2 The *Perambulator*.. has given us children, looking on with their grave smooth faces at the business of life,..as they lean back philosophically in their carriages. **1856** *Punch* 22 Mar. 118/2 (*caption*) I shan't play no more with that Matilda Jenkins. —'Er doll ain't got no Perambylatur. **1861** *Temple Bar* I. 539 These creatures [*sc.* kangaroos]..have the power of carrying their delicate, prematurely born young about with them wherever they go. They have this condition, viz. a soft, warm, well-lined portable nursery-pocket, or 'perambulator'. **1866** *Leisure Hour* XV. 347/2 Certain ill-tempered bachelors did indeed protest against them, complaining that perambulator-drivers did occasionally drive their new-fangled machines against their shins. **1936** P. M. Clark *Autobiogr. Old Drifter* iv. 47 Some time after this I was on my way to Rondebosch to meet a married cousin whom I had not seen since my perambulator days. **1972** *Daily Tel.* 3 June 32/4 They came with shopping bags, picnic baskets, babies in perambulators and pushchairs, babies in arms.

perambulatory, *sb.* **a.** (Later example.)

1843 *Knickerbocker* XXII. 85 Let..the temperance-halls and root-beer perambulatories make answer.

perbenzoic (pəɹbenzōu·ik), *a. Chem.* [f. Per-[1] 5 b + Benzoic *a.*] *perbenzoic acid*: a colourless crystalline solid, $C_6H_5CO{\cdot}O{\cdot}OH$, which is a widely used oxidizing agent, esp. for epoxidation reactions.

1903 *Jrnl. Chem. Soc.* LXXXIV. i. 397 Benzoic acetic peroxide undergoes hydrolysis in aqueous solution with production of perbenzoic and acetic acids, together with benzoic peroxide. **1938** *Thorpe's Dict. Appl. Chem.* (ed. 4) II. 373/1 Benzoyl peroxide is comparatively inert, but treatment with alcoholic sodium ethoxide yields the reactive perbenzoic acid,..which is used very widely for oxidising ethylenic compounds. **1967** L. F. & M. A. Fieser *Reagents for Org. Synthesis* I. 791 The reaction of perbenzoic acid with an olefin usually proceeds smoothly at a low temperature (0–25°) and affords an epoxide in high yield.

perborate (pəɹbōə·rēit). *Chem.* [a. F. *perborate* (A. Étard 1880, in *Compt. Rend.* XCI. 932): see Per-[1] 5 and Borate.] Any of a number of strongly oxidizing derivatives of boric acid which contain peroxo-anions, and are usu. prepared by the action of hydrogen peroxide on borates; *esp.* the sodium salt, a white crystalline solid of empirical formula $NaBO_3{\cdot}4H_2O$, which is widely used as a bleach and is a constituent of washing powders.

1881 *Chem. News* 14 Jan. 25/2 He [*sc.* A. Étard] has obtained barium perborate,—$Bo_2O_7BaH_4$ + H_2O, a white amorphous insoluble salt. **1898** *Jrnl. Chem. Soc.* LXXIV. ii. 427 The heat of decomposition by sulphuric acid was determined in the case of sodium perborate and ammonium perborate. **1916** *Chem. Abstr.* X. 2803 Heretofore bleaching with persalts, such as perborate, has been more costly than bleaching with chloride of lime. **1959** *Observer* 6 Sept. 18/4 Perborate bleach works only at high temperatures. **1959** *Guardian* 28 Sept. 3/6 The woollen cardigan..had..changed colour..due to the perborate (a stain-removing bleach) added..to a soap powder. **1967** E. L. Muetterties *Chem. Boron & its Compounds* iii. 192 The X-ray crystal structure determination of 'sodium perborate'..reveals a dimeric tetrahedral configuration with dihedral angle equal to 64°:..and the anionic formula $B_2(O_2)_2(OH)_4{}^{2-}{\cdot}2Na^+{\cdot}6H_2O$. **1974** *Sci. Amer.* Jan. 125/2 Sodium perborate is the cheapest and safest of all peroxy salts and is much used in detergents, particularly for very-hot-water washing.

perboric (pəɹbōə·rik), *a. Chem.* [ad F. *perborique* (A. Étard 1880, in *Compt. Rend.* XCI. 931), f. *per-* Per-[1] 5 b + *borique* Boric *a.*] *perboric acid*: the supposed parent acid of perborates, which was formerly thought to have the formula HBO_3 and is only known in acidic solutions containing perborate anions.

1881 *Chem. News* 14 Jan. 25/2 Whilst an equimolar mixture of magnesium sulphate, ammonium chloride, and ammonia is not rendered turbid either by oxygenated water or by boric acid, a mixture of the two precipitate it abundantly, acting as perboric acid. **1924** J. W. Mellor *Comprehensive Treat. Inorg. & Theoret. Chem.* V. xxxii. 116 Perboric acid itself has not been made... In ethereal soln. and an excess of hydrogen peroxide, the partition coeff. of boric acid increases a little corresponding with the formation of free perboric acid in the etheral soln. **1973** N. N. Greenwood *Chem. Boron* (1975) vi. 887 Reaction of orthoboric acid with hydrogen peroxide gives perboric (peroxoboric) acid solutions which probably contain the monoperborate anion $[HOOB(OH)_3]^-$.

perbromic (pəɹbrōu·mik), *a. Chem.* [f. Per-[1] 5 b + Bromic *a.*] *perbromic acid*: $HBrO_4$, a strong acid with oxidizing properties that was first prepared in 1968. Hence **perbro·mate**, a salt of this acid.

Claims for the preparation of the acid and its salts in the 19th c. proved to be mistaken.

1864 *Chem. News* 30 Apr. 205/2 Perbromic acid has been fruitlessly investigated by many chemists, but M. Kaemmerer has obtained it in the most simple manner by treating perchloric acid with bromine. *Ibid.* Perbromate of potash is more soluble than the perchlorate, and less so than the bromate. **1866** [in Dict. s.v. Per-[1] 5 b]. **1912** *Chem. News* 2 Aug. 50/1 It seems that it must be finally concluded that perbromic acid and its salts are incapable of existence. **1968** *Jrnl. Amer. Chem. Soc.* XC. 1900/2 These results indicated the formation of a relatively unreactive perbromate ion and suggested that a determined effort might lead to the preparation of macro amounts of perbromates. *Ibid.* 1901/2 As expected, the volatility of perbromic acid is less than that of perchloric acid. **1973** Downs & Adams in J. C. Bailar et al. *Comprehensive Inorg. Chem.* II. xxvi. 1451 First obtained in studies of the β-decay of $^{83}SeO_4{}^{2-}$, perbromates are also formed in the γ-radiolysis of crystalline bromates. *Ibid.* 1452 On very rapid evaporation, crystallization of perbromic acid solutions occurs (possibly to give $HBrO_4$, $2H_2O$) just before decomposition sets in.

Perbunan (pəɹbiu·năn). Also **perbunan.** [a. G. *Perbunan*, f. *per-* + *buna* *Buna + *N*, chem. symbol for nitrogen.] A proprietary name for a nitrile rubber first made in Germany and originally called Buna-N.

1938 *Trade Marks Jrnl.* 4 May 551/2 Perbunan... Compositions consisting mainly of reaction products obtained by the polymerisation of butadiene hydrocarbons, sold in the form of sheets, blocks, tubes, [etc.]... I. G. Farbenindustrie Aktiengesellschaft.., Frankfort-on-Main, Germany; manufacturers. **1938** *Chem. Abstr.* XXXII. 3663 The mech. and elec. properties of Buna-S and Perbunan (formerly Buna-N,..),..are described... The elec. properties of both are excellent, and Buna-S is less permeable to water than are Perbunan and natural rubber. **1940** *Jrnl. R. Aeronaut. Soc.* XLIV. 159 A cable consisting of rubber covered with a thin perbunan sheath and an oil varnished ozone-resisting braid would probably give the best results. **1959** *Times* 27 Apr. (Rubber Industry Suppl.) p. ii/4 These basic synthetic rubbers, buna S, neoprene and perbunan, developed in the 1930s, were the forerunners of the main synthetic rubbers we use to-day. **1959** *Official Gaz.* (U.S. Patent Office) 18 Aug. TM 82/1 Farbenfabriken Bayer Aktiengesellschaft, Leverkusen-Bayerwerk, Germany. Filed Feb. 12, 1959. Perbunan... For rubber and rubber substitute materials. **1973** *Nature* 14 Sept. 93/1, I have carried out some measurements on an alkaline perbunan latex dispersion.

perc, var. *perk *sb.*[3], *perk *v.*[3]

perceived, *ppl. a.* **2.** (Later examples, esp. in sense of *perception 9.)

1943 M. FARBER *Found. Phenomenology* xii. 335 If the eruption is therefore to be critically judged as a deception,..illusion, etc., then the perceived, seen color of the object also does not exist. **1971** *Nature* 19 Feb. 518/1 Mr Stein's apparently innocent bill to limit noise at New York airports to 108 perceived noise decibels by July.. could be..a serious threat to the viability of Concorde. **1973** *Jrnl. Genetic Psychol.* CXXII. 269 The study of perceived (subjective) age changes. **1976** *Times Lit. Suppl.* 3 Sept. 1080/2 In all these instances the KKE was reacting to actual or perceived efforts to destroy it.

perceivedness. (Later example.)
1967 S. BECKETT *Film* 32 Anguish of perceivedness.

perceiver, *sb.* **1.** (Later examples.)
1947 G. MURPHY *Personality* xiv. 331 (*heading*) The perceiver. **1971** *Jrnl. Gen. Psychol.* LXXXIV. 158 The history of the gestalt psychology is filled with many other instances in which missing parts are ignored by the perceiver. **1972** *Sci. Amer.* Nov. 85/1 The students who were three-dimensional perceivers spent more time looking at the ambiguous trident. **1973** *Nature* 14 Dec. 434/2 He stresses that painters and sculptors, like poets, expect the perceiver to do at least half the work.

per cent, *phr.* (*sb.*) Add: Now freq. without full-stop, and as one word. **A.** *Phrase.* **a.** Also with preceding numeral as an approximate estimate of extent in unquantifiable contexts. *a* or *one hundred per cent*: see *HUNDRED *sb.* and *a.* 2c.
1939 F. PRATT *Secret & Urgent* 258 It will be noted that more than fifty per cent of all English words end in E, S, D or T. **1961** *Information & Control* IV. 65 The study of this particular data collection showed that over 95 percent of the vocabulary could be represented by 13 characters. **1973** *Times* 21 Dec. 14/6 This trouble's cut my social life by about 35 per cent. **1973** [see *PERCENTAGE b]. **1975** *Sci. Amer.* Feb. 15/3 The two reasons most often given for emigrating are 'Better training in the U.S.' (69 percent) and 'Political factors' (8 percent). **1976** *Ibid.* May 108/3 Io is particularly red, and its colour, together with its high reflectivity (about 62 percent, roughly equivalent to white sand), make it a unique object in the solar system. **1976** *Daily Tel.* 20 July 1/5 Average earnings in May were 19·4 per cent. up on the previous year, compared with a 15·4 per cent. rise in retail prices.
c. As quasi-*sb.* Percentage; one per cent.
1905 G. W. ROLFE *Polariscope* 96 The per cent of sucrose in the sample. **1934** *Jrnl. Sedimentary Petrology* IV. 68/2 In setting up a histogram, we are in effect setting up a series of separate 'bins', each of which contains a certain per cent of the grains. **1960** *Anatomical Rec.* CXXXVIII. 395/2 The statistical significance..was calculated by determining the median for the combined population and comparing the percent of the animals that had cataracts in each group. **1966** T. PYNCHON *Crying of Lot 49* v. 122 Always just that little percent on the wrong side of breaking even... Why don't I quit? **1970** *Nature* 7 Nov. 546/2 If the relative abundances of ^{15}N and ^{17}O in the sample are found to be a few tenths of a percent higher than normal, [etc.]. **1971** *Daily Tel.* 27 Oct. 1/3 The retail price index has risen by only three-quarters of a per cent. in the three months since June. **1972** *Science* 12 May 595/2 The magnitude of the effect is again a few tenths of a percent. **1977** *Daily Tel.* 23 Dec. 2/7 Those provincial journalists whose immediate settlement hopes have foundered over ·56 of a per cent.

percentably (pəɪse·ntăbli), *adv. rare.* [f. PER CENT *phr.* (*sb.*) + -ABLY.] By an appreciable percentage.
1928 *Sunday Dispatch* 2 Sept. 10 Men..who are bent on reducing the moufflon population percentably.

percentage. Add: **a.** (Later *attrib.* examples.) Freq. equivalent to 'per cent' qualifying the sb., as *percentage error* (= error per cent), *point* (= point per cent), etc.
1906 *Westm. Gaz.* 25 Jan. 8/1 Both first- and third-class passengers showed a percentage increase. **1920** H. CRANE *Let.* 30 July (1965) 41 A drawing account at the bank..in addition to a good percentage commission on everything I sell. **1928** *Britain's Industr. Future* (Liberal Industr. Inquiry) v. xxxi. 444 The choice in particular cases between block grants and percentage grants. **1941** J. S. HUXLEY *Uniqueness of Man* v. 144 It warns us not to be too hasty in drawing conclusions as to intelligence from *percentage* brain-weight, or as to the efficiency of circulation from *percentage* heart-weight. **1948** MENCKEN *Amer. Lang.* Suppl. II. 766 Percentage man. A news photographer who makes a large number of exposures, hoping that chance will give him a few good pictures. **1961** C. C. T. BAKER *Dict. Math.* 233 Percentage error = true error/actual error × 100. **1964** *Economist* 18 Jan. 182/2 The common American practice of 'percentage rents'—gearing rents and ground rents over the initial period to a percentage of turnover. **1969** 'R. CRAWFORD' *Cockleburr* I. vii. 71 I'm a percentage man... He's paying me ten per cent to get him clear with the money. **1971** *Gloss. Electrotechnical, Power Terms (B.S.I.)* I. iv. 7 *Percentage error*, the relative error multiplied by 100. **1971** *Times* 3 Sept. 13/1 Yesterday's action by the Bank of England in cutting Bank rate by a full percentage point. **1972** *Fremdsprachen* XVI. 61/2 Percentage point, full—*ein ganzes Prozent*. **1973** *Computers & Humanities* VII. 134 Q measures the percentage improvement, in terms of the function F. **1974** 'A. GARVE' *File on Lester* xxxvi. 129 The poll figures..were shattering—a big percentage lead for the Government. **1974** *News & Press* (Darlington, S. Carolina) 25 Apr. 16/2 Primary metal industries showed the greatest percentage increase (267 percent) over 1967.

b. *fig.* Advantage, gain; probability of successful outcome (*in* a situation, course of action, etc.). *colloq.* (orig. *U.S.*).
1862 B. HARTE *Notes 'by Flood & Field'* in *Golden Era* 14 Sept. 5/3 What's the per centage—workin' on shares, eh? **1911** *Chicago Daily News* 2 Mar. 6/6 Johnny Coulon is unable to see the percentage in taking on Frankie Conley for another pummelling in the adjacent future. **1925** *College Humor* Aug. 117/2 No percentage in staying on in this house. Darn thing's too big. **1938** D. RUNYON *Furthermore* xiii. 255 There is no percentage in hanging around brokers [*sc.* people who are broke]. **1940** *Woman* (U.S.) Sept. 69/1 Marge was courageous and a straight shooter but there was no more percentage in taking her out than one of the other guys. **1950** R. MOORE *Candlemas Bay* VI. 302, I don't see how you figure that what peas you can shell with one thumb makes any percentage to me. **1952** B. MALAMUD *Natural* 90 He decided there might be some percentage to all these comparisons. **1952** H. WAUGH *Last seen Wearing* (1953) 71 Well, hell, she turned down my dates and..there's no percentage in that. **1960** C. HATTON in *Pick of Today's Short Stories* XI. 151 Roxy..could be relied on to stir up trouble anywhere even if there was no percentage in it for Roxy. **1966** J. PORTER *Sour Cream* xii. 162 There was no percentage in hanging around the airport terminus. I had to get away. **1973** E. MCGIRR *Bardel's Murder* i. 27 He plays better bridge than ninety-eight per cent of the population... He doesn't cheat: he doesn't have to because he's got the percentage. **1976** A. PRICE *War Game* I. 123 There was no percentage in rushing him.
c. Slang phr. *to play the percentages*: to play safely or methodically with regard to the odds in favour of success.
1964 A. WYKES *Gambling* i. 22 A considerable number of women gamblers take a strictly 'professional' approach. Ignoring 'intuition', they attack with expertise; if their game is horse racing, they are vastly knowledgeable about horses' and jockeys' past records. Others may 'play the percentages' in casinos. **1973** *Daily Pennsylvanian* 9 Oct. 6 Houston knows the game and its angles thoroughly and plays the percentages to perfection. **1977** *Tennis World* Sept. 17/3 To 'out-steady' someone is to play a superior defensive game, and 'playing the percentages' is the art of going for shots that are cheap and clean, rather than costly and glorious. Statistically it pays off better than 'going for broke'—risking everything on breath-taking winners.

perce·ntage-wise, *adv.* Also **percentagewise.** [WISE *sb.*[1] II.] (Expressed) as a percentage; also more generally, (regarded) relatively.
1912 F. SODDY *Matter & Energy* ii. 53 Quite a large number of commonly occurring compounds had been analysed by chemists and the composition expressed percentage-wise as above. **1944** *Sun* (Baltimore) 5 Apr. 10/2 In that State the number of Negroes is, percentage-wise, even smaller than the number of Negroes in Maryland. Here Negroes vote regularly. **1945** NELSON & WRIGHT *Tomorrow's House* vi. 72/1 Very few families, percentagewise, have ever been able to afford hired help. **1955** J. A. WHEELER in W. Pauli *Niels Bohr* 176 Z^2/A does not have to change much percentage-wise to carry fission half lives from values too long to observe to values too short for reasonable stability. **1960** *Guardian* 8 Mar. 1/2 The number of deaths percentagewise is far less than other deaths..by other heating means. **1967** E. S. GARDNER *Case of Queenly Contestant* (1973) xiii. 151 She told me..I could inherit a very substantial sum of money and asked me what it would be worth to me percentage-wise if [etc.]. **1972** *Amer. Speech 1968* XLIII. 211 On January 15, 1967, during the..telecast of the Super Bowl Game.., the announcer..said, 'Bart Starr has had a terrific year, percentagewise, as well as touchdownwise.'

percental (pəɪse·ntăl), *a.* Also **per cental.** [f. PER CENT *phr.* (*sb.*) + -AL I.] Reckoned by the hundred; calculated as a percentage.
1895 *Daily News* 18 Dec. 9/5 In wheat a fair extent of business was put through at ½d per cental decline. **1897** *Geogr. Jrnl.* IX. 319 A map showing, by means of six colours distinguishing different percental proportions, the distribution of German-speaking people in the lands of the Hungarian crown.

percenter. Also **per center, per-center.** [f. PER CENT *phr.* (*sb.*) + -ER[1].] Following a number (occas. with hyphen): that on (or from) which a percentage (specified by the number) is reckoned; a chance, situation, etc., the value of which is reckoned as a specified percentage. Also, one who lends or deals in money involving a certain rate of interest or commission.
c **1863** T. TAYLOR *Ticket-of-Leave Man* III. 52 *Moss* (*at the counter, getting out his bills*)... For two hundred at two months—drawn by Captain Crabbs—accepted the Honourable Augustus Greenway: that's a thirty per center. **1897** [in Dict. s.v. PER CENT *phr.* (*sb.*).] **1949** [see **influence pedlar*]. **1950** E. HEMINGWAY *Across River* xxxiii. 208 The brown-nosers, the five and ten and twenty percenters and all the jerks. **1959** *Punch* 10 June 781/1 We are tempted to deduce that her age bracket..is a sure hundred percenter. **1960** *Times* 5 Feb. 16/5 One explanation was the rush by the public to buy the new five percenter Treasury bonds. **1976** 'Z. STONE' *Modigliani Scandal* IV. i. 154 Louis was 99 per cent sure the caller was a nutcase: but it was by following up the one-percenters that great exclusives were found.

percentile, *a.* and *sb.* (Later examples.)
1956 W. H. WHYTE *Organization Man* (1957) 407 Don't strive to get yourself in the 70th or 80th percentile for extroversion. **1957** G. E. HUTCHINSON *Treat. Limnol.* I. vi. 384 (*caption*) Mean percentile absorption at different wave lengths. **1970** *Jrnl. Gen. Psychol.* LXXXIII. 154 The high dependency groups consisted of those 13 Ss whose autonomy minus deference scale percentile ranks score was 20 or above.

percentual (pəɪse·ntiuăl), *a.* [irreg. f. PER CENT *phr.* (*sb.*) + -*ual*, after *accentual*, *eventual*, etc.]
1937 H. TINGSTEN *Political Behavior* iii. 147 The voting frequency of a group increases with the percentual strength of the group in question. **1949** KOESTLER *Promise & Fulfilment* I. iii. 31 The striking percentual increases in the statistics quoted.
Hence **perce·ntually** *adv.*
1942 L. B. NAMIER *Conflicts* 73 'Janus' in *The Spectator* of March 7, 1941, shows that percentually the losses of the last war do not justify the talk about a 'missing generation'.

percept. Add: Also *Psychol.* **1.** (Further examples.)
1964 M. CRITCHLEY *Developmental Dyslexia* xiii. 78 Not only is it a matter of defective perception, but it is also one of inadequate association of lexical percepts. *Ibid.*, This process of linking one percept with another is where the principal fault may lie. **1973** *Nature* 6 July 54/2 The Necker cube has been viewed as an ambiguous figure whose configuration and accompanying instructions usually limit the number of percepts to two. **1974** *Sci. Amer.* Jan. 126/3 No one else smelled it [*sc.* poison gas], she was assured. Her enemy was so ingenious, she retorted, that his gas was odorless! Her experience was thus no percept at all, but a projection from internal ideas. **1976** SMYTHIES & CORBETT *Psychiatry* v. 55 This man had a normal percept but attached a special, personal meaning to it which was quite false.
2. (Later examples.)
1949 *Mind* LVIII. 450 William James sometimes used the word 'percept' to refer to the content of consciousness during perception; it is this fact which has made the name 'Percept Theory' seem to me appropriate for the particular theory of perceptual consciousness which he himself supported. **1970** *Jrnl. Gen. Psychol.* LXXXIII. 66 Sex responses are numerous... The number of human percepts is low. **1972** *Sci. Amer.* Sept. 47/2 It is along this pathway that the visual image formed on the retina by light rays entering the eye is transformed into a visual percept, on the basis of which appropriate commands to the muscles are issued. **1976** *Word 1971* XXVII. 226 Each physical stimulus, after interpretation by the mental processes, will result in a percept.

perception. Add: **6.** (Further examples.)
1943 M. FARBER *Found. Phenomenology* xiii. 396 The perception realizes the possibility of the development of the *intending-this* with its definite relation to the object. **1962** MACQUARRIE & ROBINSON tr. *Heidegger's Being & Time* I. iii. 130 When the experience of hardness is Interpreted this way, the kind of Being which belongs to sensory perception is obliterated, and so is any possibility that the entities encountered in such perception should be grasped in their Being. **1965** *New Statesman* 3 Sept. 327/4 He [*sc.* Merleau-Ponty] held..that the higher forms of human behaviour—art, science, political life—could only be understood in their genesis from original perception.
9. *Psychol.* The neurophysiological processes, including memory, by which an organism becomes aware of and interprets external stimuli or sensations (closely related to PERCEPTION 4 and 6). So *attrib.* and *comb.*, as **perception psychology,** that branch of psychology which is concerned with the study of perception.
1875 A. J. ELLIS tr. *Helmholtz's On Sensations of Tone* I. iv. 99 There are several much more complicated cases in which many sensations must concur to furnish the foundation of a very simple perception. **1913** A. A. BRILL tr. *Freud's Interpr. of Dreams* vii. 426 We assume that a first system of apparatus takes up the stimuli of perception, but retains nothing from them—that is, it has no memory. **1949** D. O. HEBB *Organization of Behavior* i. 16 According to these ideas, perception does depend on exciting specific parts of the receptor surface. **1951** LICKLIDER & MILLER in S. S. Stevens *Handbk. Exper. Psychol.* 1040/1 Although the perception of speech is a psychological problem, it remained for telephone engineers..to develop procedures for the quantitative investigation of speech perception. **1956** J. R. SMYTHIES *Anal. of Perception* p. ix, In order to construct a comprehensive theory of perception..it would be necessary to have at least a good working knowledge of epistemology and the philosophy of sense perception, neurology, neuroanatomy and neurophysiology, psychiatry and psychopathology with particular reference to the effects produced by the hallucinogenic drugs, anthropology, physics and experimental psychology. **1958** M. E. SPIRO *Children of Kibbutz* VI. xvi. 435 Assumptions derived from an adaptation of psychoanalytic, learning, and perception theories. **1964** M. A. K. HALLIDAY et al. *Linguistic Sci.* iii. 60 Psychological phonetics..has arisen out of modern developments in perception psychology. **1968** R. N. HABER *Contemp. Theory & Res. Visual Perception* (1970) p. vi, While it will be clear throughout this book that memory and what is traditionally known as perception cannot be distinguished by any but the most arbitrary of rules. **1974** *Drive* Autumn 3/1 At least one perception expert considers they could, indeed, be doing far more in teaching distance assessment in a following situation at speeds over 30mph. *Ibid.* 29/2 The university's department of perception-psychology aims to produce a lighting system that gives clearer warning of a car's presence to pedestrians and oncoming traffic.

perce·ptionalist, *a. rare.* [f. PERCEPTION + -AL I + -IST.] Of or pertaining to philosophical theories of knowledge that are based on perception.
1847 J. D. MORELL *Hist. View Philos.* (ed. 2) I. i. 130 On this perceptionalist controversy, consult Sir W. Hamilton's admirable article.

perceptron (pəɹse·ptrǫn). [f. PERCEPT *sb.* + *-TRON.] A model or machine devised to represent or simulate the ability of the brain to recognize and discriminate, orig. based on statistical concepts.
1958 F. ROSENBLATT in *Psychol. Rev.* LXV. 386 (*heading*) The perceptron: a probabilistic model for information storage and organization in the brain. *Ibid.* 387/2 The theory has been developed for a hypothetical nervous system, or machine, called a perceptron. The perceptron is designed to illustrate some of the fundamental properties of intelligent systems in general, without becoming enmeshed in the special..conditions which hold for particular biological organisms. **1962** W. S. HOLMES in G. L. Fischer et al. *Optical Character Recognition* 213 A program of pattern recognition research based on early concepts of Dr. Frank Rosenblatt..has turned toward the application of perceptrons to useful tasks such as the recognition of printed characters. **1966** Y. BAR-HILLEL in *Automatic Transl. of Lang.* (NATO Summer School, Venice 1962) 22 Though certain electronic devices (such as perceptrons) have been built which can be 'trained' to perform certain tasks..and though computers have been programmed to do certain things..it would be disastrous to extrapolate from these primitive exhibitions of artificial intelligence to something like translation. **1971** *New Scientist* 2 Sept. 525/2 There are some 50 approaches to neuron modelling and machines were constructed based on some of these models. Perhaps the most famous..was the Perceptron device built at the Cornell Aeronautical Laboratory. **1978** A. BUNDY et al. *Artificial Intelligence* v. 184 The important point about a perceptron is that it makes a global decision about a figure by weighing only local evidence.

perceptual, *a.* Add: (Earlier and later examples.) *perceptual defence*, a raising of the threshold of perception when the stimulus is emotionally charged in an unfavourable way; *perceptual-motor* adj., involving motor behaviour as guided by or dependent on perception.
1878 S. H. HODGSON *Philos. of Reflection* I. 315 The conceptual order being the obverse aspect of the perceptual. **1948** L. POSTMAN in *Jrnl. Abnormal Psychol.* XLIII. 152/1 Value orientation may..raise thresholds for unacceptable stimulus objects. We shall refer to this mechanism as perceptual defense. **1950** *Jrnl. Personality* XIX. 85 These data were interpreted as indicative of a perceptual defense to emotional stimuli originating at a level which precedes full conscious awareness. **1951** *U.S. Human Resources Research Center Research Bull.* No. 51–7 (*title*) The influence of types of instructions on the performance of a perceptual-motor task. **1955** [see *MECLOZINE]. **1962** J. G. TAYLOR *Behavioral Basis of Perception* vi. 130 It is no more possible for one person to make comparisons with another person's perceptual field than it is to describe the dimensions of personality in terms of centimeters, grams, and seconds. **1968** J. B. OXENDINE *Psychol. of Motor Learning* i. 14 A forehand stroke in tennis would be classified as a perceptual-motor skill, and swimming would not. **1969** FREEMAN & GIOVANNONI in Lindzey & Aronson *Handbk. Social Psychol.* (ed. 2) V. 688 Studies of schizophrenics indicate that perceptual thresholds and estimation of size are dependent on the emotional concomitants of the visual stimuli. **1970** M. J. MELDMAN *Dis. Attention & Perception* v. 95 The phenomenon of perceptual defense and the relationship of emotion to perception. **1972** *Village Voice* (N.Y.) 1 June 36/5 Dr. Krippner told me just a few of the non-drugging approaches that could and should be used with children whose classroom behavior is 'divergent'—vitamin therapy, perceptual-motor therapy, [etc.]. **1976** *Classical Q.* XXVI. 39, I shall be illustrating the perceptual case, so let me simply note here a few examples from the case of pleasure and pain. **1977** *Times Lit. Suppl.* 29 Apr. 529/2 We do not observe the seventeenth-century butcher directly vivid though the picture is; we see him through the perceptual schemata of the artist and his patron.

Hence **perce·ptualize** *v.*, to express in perceptual terms; **perce:ptualiza·tion.**
1896 W. CALDWELL *Schopenhauer's Syst.* iii. 167 A highly interesting feature..is his pronounced tendency to *perceptualise intellection*, to assimilate all real knowledge to the type of perception and immediate apprehension. **1968** P. MCKELLAR *Experience & Behaviour* iv. 121 This hallucination represents an instance of a perceptualization of the man's realization of what had happened to him.

perceptually (pəɹse·ptiuăli), *adv.* [f. PERCEPTUAL *a.* + -LY[2].] In a perceptual manner.
1878 S. H. HODGSON *Philos. of Reflection* I. 394 We might pick out those differents which are most strongly contrasted perceptually. **1909** W. M. URBAN *Valuation* xiv. 394 When the object is neither perceptually verifiable nor continuous with other truth judgments, a re-adjustment of reality-meanings takes place. **1922** A. G. HOGG *Redemption from this World* vi. 197 Thus miracles..render perceptually obvious both the personality and the infinitude of the Divine will. **1932** H. H. PRICE *Perception* vi. 164 We attribute a characteristic to some material thing which is now being perceptually accepted. **1972** *Science* 9 June 1149/2 We reported this ability to perceptually synthesize missing phonemes.

perceptum (pəɹse·ptɒm). Pl. percepta. [L. *perceptum* (a thing) perceived, neut. of pa. pple. of *percipĕre* to PERCEIVE.] = PERCEPT 1.
1887 S. H. HODGSON *Let.* 10 Dec. in R. B. Perry *Tht. & Char. of W. James* (1935) II. 82 An immediate perception of spatial extension as part..of the visual perceptum. **1913** *Mind* XXII. 14 To instinctive action there corresponded a *perceptum* or percept which was its object. **1920** S. ALEXANDER *Space, Time & Deity* II. 92 The perceived object or thing, the perceptum, is a contemplated synthesis. **1929** A. N. WHITEHEAD *Process & Reality* 22 When science deals with emotions, the emotions in question are percepta. **1936** W. F. R. HARDIE *Study in Plato* ii. 12 Plainly its plausibility will depend on what characteristics of *percepta* are held to preclude their being known.

perceptuo- (pəɹse·ptiŭo), combining form of L. *perceptu-s*, pa. pple. of *percipĕre* to perceive, as *perceptuo-motor* adj., = *perceptual-motor* adj. s.v. *PERCEPTUAL *a.*
1973 K. WEDELL (*title*) Learning and perceptuo-motor disabilities in children. **1974** *Nature* 8 Nov. 121/1 A series of experiments in perceptuo-motor adaptation that provide fairly direct evidence favouring the existence of such a mechanism. *Ibid.* 122/2 Perceptuo-motor effects were found for the voiceless stop consonants but not for their voiced counterparts.

perch, *sb.*[1] Add: **3. perch-hole**, a hole in which perch are found.
1906 *Macm. Mag.* June 574 Agatha by the side of the perch-hole, very erect, with a still more erect fishing-rod, surprised by the..angler.

perch, *sb.*[2] Add: **2. c.** *Theatr.* A platform from which lights are directed on to the front of the stage; *pl.*, the lights placed on this platform.
1933 P. GODFREY *Back-Stage* i. 18 The stops controlling the amber circuits in No. 1 batten, floats, and P. and O.P. perches slide up to full. *Ibid.* vii. 90 'What's in your perches?' 'Ambers, sir.' **1934** A. P. HERBERT *Holy Deadlock* 215 From time to time he gave a quiet order to an invisible person called Joe about Batten Number One, about a border or a perch, a flat or the floats. **1957** *Oxf. Compan. Theatre* (ed. 2) 472/2 The mobility of the bridge is allied in control with the 'perches' or ladder-type boomerangs, which can be moved on or off stage according to the width of the scene. *Ibid.* 474/2 The spot batten and perches will, when a cyclorama is used, illuminate adequately the acting area to within a certain distance of the cyclorama. **1959** RAE & SOUTHERN *Internat. Vocab. Techn. Theatre Terms* 58 *Perch*, platform for tormentor spot. **1967** *Punch* 16 Aug. 242/3 For *Figaro* and Verdi's *Macbeth*.., John Christie had to bring in a lighting bridge and sixty floods and perches from Glyndebourne.

3. e. *to knock off one's perch*: also in weakened senses: to disconcert, humiliate, snub; *to come* (or *get*) *off one's perch*: to climb down, to adopt a less arrogant or condescending manner.
1896 *Dialect Notes* I. 421 'Come off your perch,' stop being fresh. **1900** 'FLYNT' & 'WALTON' *Powers that Prey* 238 'It's up to you to do the talking... All I've got to do is just to sit quiet.'.. 'Sure! I'll say it fast enough. But you can come off your perch just the same.' **1915** MRS. BELLOC LOWNDES *Diary* 24 Mar. (1971) 60 The American said: 'What you've first got to do is to come off your perch—and listen to what we want...' The great man gave in and got off his perch. *a* **1916** 'SAKI' in *Coll. Short Stories* (1930) 316 Mrs. Quabari, to use a colloquial expression, was knocked off her perch. **1923** G. MCKNIGHT *Eng. Words* iv. 65 *Stop crowing* becomes *come off the perch.* **1931** M. ALLINGHAM *Look to Lady* xv. 156 For Gawd's sake come off yer perch and listen to this seriously. **1936** S. SASSOON *Sherston's Progress* III. 151 Tells Hooper to come off his perch and put the kettle on, which isn't well received by the golden-haired one. **1976** D. CLARK *Dread & Water* v. 104, I reckon..that he's been knocked off his perch by our form of investigation.

4. Also, a horizontal bar used in softening leather.
1898 *Hide & Leather* 24 Sept. 21/3 After drying they [*sc.* skins] are softened, dry, over a perch with a moon-knife. **1902** *Mod. Amer. Tanning* I. 201 When the pelt is about half dry, it must be worked over what is called a perch. **1903** H. R. PROCTER *Princ. Leather Manuf.* 188 'Perching'..[consists] in fixing the skins on a horizontal pole (the 'perch'), and working them with..a tool formed somewhat like a small shovel with a semicircular blade. **1909** H. G. BENNETT *Manuf. Leather* 359 In perching the mechanical treatment is less violent, the goods being fixed on a 'perch'—a horizontal pole about 5 feet above the ground—and scraped by means of the 'moon-knife'. **1940** [see *PERCHING *vbl. sb.*[1]].

perched, *ppl. a.*[1] **1.** Add: (Further examples.) In *Geol.* also applied to blocks left in such a position by other causes; more generally, having an elevation that is exceptionally high in relation to the immediate locality; applied esp. to ground water separated from an underlying saturated zone by an intervening unsaturated zone.
1900 H. JAMES *Little Tour in France* (ed. 2) vi. 62 In the matter of position Amboise is certainly supreme in the list of perched places. **1901** *Bull. Mus. Compar. Zoöl.* XXXVIII. 134 (*heading*) Perched boulders. **1906** A. C. VEATCH et al. in *Prof. Papers U.S. Geol. Survey* No. 44. 57 There are..a number of more or less limited areas of saturated beds above the main one. These perched ground-water tables are for the most part confined to the moraine. **1923** *Water-Supply Papers U.S. Geol. Survey*, No. 494. 42 If water poured into the well all drains out the well evidently ends in an unsaturated bed and the overlying ground water is perched. *Ibid.* 57 The term *perched* may be applied to streams in the same way as it is applied to ground water. **1956** W. EDWARDS in D. L. Linton *Sheffield* i. 8 All the igneous rocks are basaltic... Their clayey tops support 'perched' water-tables in parts of the limestone uplands. **1968** R. W. FAIRBRIDGE *Encycl. Geomorphol.* 740/1 'Cirques'..are formed at the heads of glaciers both large and small—including a great many perched, or hanging, glaciers of small dimensions. *Ibid.* 823/2 (*caption*) Perched block of Bluff Sandstone.., due to slumping, followed by slope retreat. **1972** J. G. CRUICKSHANK *Soil Geogr.* iii. 84 Any cemented or compacted horizon..can function in the same way and support a perched water table with accumulating soil water.

percher[1]. Add: **8.** *Cricket.* A ball that 'perches' or hangs in the air; *spec.* = *BOUNCER 6.
1913 *Cricket* 14 June 305/2 Every bowler pitches short sometimes, and..the resultant 'rib-roaster', 'percher', 'flier', 'bouncer',..is no more than an ordinary risk. **1961** *Times* 23 June 4/1 As big a percher as can ever have been missed in a match between England and Australia.

perching, *vbl. sb.*[1] Add: **2.** A process for softening skins in leather-making; cf. *PERCH *sb.*[2] 4. Freq. *attrib.*
1897 C. T. DAVIS *Manuf. Leather* (ed. 2) 361 There are.. above the perching room.., two large logwood tanks. *Ibid.* 362, 12 Slocomb perching machines. These perching machines take the place of hand work. **1903, 1909** [see *PERCH *sb.*[2] 4]. **1940** *Chambers's Techn. Dict.* 625/2 *Perching* (*leather*), a process for stretching and softening a skin by working over it with a crutch stake, on the flesh side, while it is fixed to a horizontal pole (*perch*).

perchist (pə̄·ɹtʃist). *poet. nonce-wd.* [f. PERCH *sb.*[2] + -IST.] A trapeze artist.
1938 L. MACNEICE *Earth Compels* 18 *Perchists*... They rise into the tent's Top like deep-sea divers... Hang by their teeth Beneath the cone of canvas.

perchloroethylene (pəɹklōᵊ:rōᵘe·þilīn). *Chem.* Also **perchlorethylene.** [ad. G. *perchloräthylen*, f. *per-* PER-[1] 5 + *chlor-* CHLORO- + *äthylen* ETHYLENE.] A colourless, non-flammable, toxic liquid, C_2Cl_4, which is widely used as a solvent, esp. in dry cleaning fluid, and medicinally for the treatment of worm infestations; = *TETRACHLOROETHYLENE.
1873 *Jrnl. Chem. Soc.* XXVI. 866 The action of sodium ethylate on perchloroethylene has been studied by Fischer and Geuther. **1875** *Ibid.* XXVIII. 746 The distillate which comes over slowly consists of perchlorethylene holding in solution aniline and carbon sesquichloride. **1954** A. K. DOOLITTLE *Technol. Solvents & Plasticizers* xii. 720 Perchloroethylene finds use as a dry-cleaning, metal-degreasing, and rubber solvent, and as an anthelmintic. **1963** *Economist* 12 Jan. 115/2 The customer can watch her clothes tumbling through a solvent (perchlorethylene). **1971** *Daily Tel.* 10 June 1/4 Perchloroethylene can cause drowsiness, coma and death if taken in sufficient quantities. **1976** *Sci. Amer.* May 52/2 The apparatus ..basically consists of a tank of 100,000 gallons of the common dry-cleaning fluid perchloroethylene.

percipient. B. *sb.* **b.** (Later examples.)
1955 *Sci. Amer.* Oct. 116/3 As a result of extensive tests, mainly involving two extraordinarily gifted 'percipients' in the business of card guessing, Soal and his co-worker Bateman were converted from doubt to ardent belief. **1966** K. R. RAO *Exper. Parapsychol.* i. 6 The hypothesis that the *percipient*, not the agent, is the likely initiator of the psi experience. **1974** *Listener* 3 Jan. 22/2 Some of the target images were lantern-slides... The guessers or 'percipients' were asked to try to draw the image.

percolate, *v.* Add: **1. b.** (Later examples.)
1970 P. LAURIE *Scotland Yard* iv. 92 Churchill's funeral was ten years' planning, and it probably contained, percolated through a succession of intermediate heroes, elements of Nelson's. **1978** *Time* 6 Nov. 28/2 Connecticut's Ella Grasso, the first woman to win a governorship in her own right, says these victories will percolate women into office in a few years.

c. To prepare (coffee) in a percolator.
1966 *New Statesman* 3 June 819/1 First found percolating stale morning coffee in his office. **1974** 'J. Ross' *Burning of Billy Toober* xiv. 127 Rogers made the mortuary in twenty minutes, not stopping to shave or percolate coffee. **1978** N. J. CRISP *London Deal* v. 72 The man-servant was percolating coffee.

2. b. (Later examples.)
1934 C. LAMBERT *Music Ho!* III. 185 Oriental influences..have percolated naturally through these racial frontiers. **1935** B. MALINOWSKI *Coral Gardens* II. VI. 244 The magic percolates,..so that practically everybody in the village knows it. **1977** P. D. JAMES *Death of Expert Witness* III. 128 News percolated through a village community by a process of verbal osmosis.

3. (Later *fig.* example.)
1965 *New Statesman* 7 May 737/2 One reason why this has so slowly percolated British consciousness..is British reporting.

4. *intr.* To walk, to stroll. *U.S. slang.*
1942 Z. N. HURSTON in A. Dundes *Mother Wit* (1973) 223/1 Then he would..percolate on down the Avenue. **1945** L. SHELLY *Jive Talk Dict.* 15/2 *Percolate*, to meander.

percolater, var. PERCOLATOR.
1861 MRS. BEETON *Bk. Househ. Managem.* 875 Let the coffee be freshly ground..; put it into a percolater, or

filter, . . and pour *slowly* over it . . boiling water. **1958** *Times* 6 Nov. 12/6 If we wanted a pint of essence of ginger, we just put 10 oz. of powdered Jamaica ginger into a percolater, and allowed sufficient rectified spirit to pass through to collect a pint.

percolating, *vbl. sb.* Add: *percolating filter*, a type of filter used in the treatment of sewage, usu. after the removal of suspended solids, consisting of a bed of inert, porous material such as crushed rock through which the sewage is allowed to percolate, so that noxious organic matter is removed by aerobic micro-organisms.

1901 S. BARWISE *Bacterial Purification of Sewage* iv. 37 The Commissioners in their Report speak of two artificial filtration processes—Contact Beds and Continuous Filtration. In this book I have adopted the phrase 'Percolating Filters', instead of that of 'Continuous Filters', because some of the continuous filters are worked intermittently, and intermittent continuous filtration is a verbal contradiction. **1936** [see *BACTERIUM 2]. **1972** *Water Research* VI. 781 In the United Kingdom conventional sewage treatment by sedimentation plus secondary treatment by percolating filters or activated sludge plants is not normally adequate to provide an effluent acceptable for re-use.

percolator. Add: **b.** (*a*) (Earlier and later examples.) Also *attrib.*

1845 E. ACTON *Mod. Cookery* xxvii. 647 It will be stronger if slowly filtered in what is called a percolator, or coffee-biggin, than if it be boiled. **1869** *Pattern Bk. Copper, etc., Ware* (H. Loveridge & Co.) 103 Coffee Percolators. **1963** *B.S.I. News* May 35 Electric coffee percolators. **1978** L. DEIGHTON *SS-GB* xv. 126 She tipped the coffee into the percolator top, closed the lid and set it on the heat.

c. *fig.* (*a*) A carburettor; (*b*) a house-rent party (*HOUSE *sb.*[1] 23); loosely, any party. *U.S. slang.*

1942 BERREY & VAN DEN BARK *Amer. Thes. Slang* §82/4 *Carburetor*, carb, jug, juicer, juice pot, mixer, percolator, pot, sifter. **1946** R. BLESH *Shining Trumpets* xiii. 303 The great South Side institution of 'rent party' (locally known as 'skiffle', 'spice', or 'percolator'). **1956** S. LONGSTREET *Real Jazz* xvi. 126 You could always . . get together . . and charge a few coins and have . . a percolator. **1967** PARTRIDGE *Dict. Slang* Suppl. 1289/2 '*To have a shake, rave or percolator* . . to have a party' (Anderson): beatniks': since ca. 1959. **1971** M. TAK *Truck Talk* 117 *Percolator*, the carburetor. **1974** H. L. FOSTER *Ribbin'* iv. 141 In Chicago, these parties were called a 'parlour social', 'gouge', 'struggle', 'percolator', 'too terrible party', or the 'skiffle'.

percussion, *sb.* Add: **2. a.** Also *concr.*, a percussion gun.

1821 P. EGAN *Real Life in London* I. i. 8 My new patent double-barrelled percussion.

c. (Earlier example of *collect.* use.)

1889 G. B. SHAW *How to become Mus. Critic* (1960) 164 Brass and percussion [are] behind the wood wind and under the stage.

e. *bulb of percussion*: see *BULB *sb.* 4 b.

5. percussion lock (earlier U.S. example).

1829 in *Reg. Deb. Congress U.S.* (1831) 21st Congress 2 Sess. App. p. xcii/2 I have used the percussion locks but little, but believe them admirably well constructed for general use.

percussionist (in Dict. s.v. PERCUSSION *sb.*). Restrict † (*obs.*) to sense in Dict. and add: **b.** A player of a percussion instrument.

1950 WEBSTER Add. p. cxix, *Percussionist*, one skilled in the playing of percussion instruments. **1955** L. FEATHER *Encycl. Jazz* 256/1 His use of the top cymbal . . was imitated by countless other percussionists. **1962** *Times* 18 Apr. 7/6 In the course of the piece everybody is a percussionist. **1969** *Daily Tel.* 15 Feb. 15/1 A truly professional percussionist rather than just another polished, expert drummer. **1977** *Listener* 18 Aug. 216/1 In the second programme they had Tristram Fry, the percussionist.

percussiveness (in Dict. s.v. PERCUSSIVE *a.*). (Later examples in *Mus.*)

1958 *Times* 9 Oct. 7/1 The tense percussiveness of Bartok's concerto. **1970** *Daily Tel.* 16 June 14/2 He lets unfold . . a veritable rhapsody of percussiveness (by no means just Brahms's in E flat) and reveals the soul in staccato. **1976** *Gramophone* Sept. 424/1 Queffélec, however, never plays with the almost brutal percussiveness of Bernstein.

Percy (pə·ɹsi). The masculine Christian name used, freq. with connotations of weakness or effeminacy, as a representative name for **a.** a conscientious objector; **b.** (see quot. 1932); **c.** in the armed services, an officer or an educated man.

1916 G. B. SHAW in *Nation* 27 May 258/2 Mobbed and pilloried and photographed in the 'Daily Sketch' as 'Percy' (all Percies are now—shade of Hotspur!—supposed to be cowards). **1932** E. WEEKLEY *Words & Names* 91 *Percy* . . is still used in the United States of the typical young Englishman. **1961** PARTRIDGE *Dict. Slang* Suppl. 1217/2 *Percy*, in the Royal Navy, has, since ca. 1925, meant an effeminate man; but since ca. 1940, also and esp. a studious, quiet, educated man as opposed to an uncouth 'tough'. **1974** 'B. MATHER' *White Dacoit* xxi. 216 Most of the young Percies in our mob had to take their boots off to count up to twenty. *Ibid.* xxiii. 237 There's a young Percy in charge . . . The Percy says to one of them, 'What's your unit, my man?'

percylite. (Further example.)

1974 *Mineral. Rec.* V. 286 We believe that type percylite has been shown to be a mixture [of boleite and pseudoboleite] and that the same is true of percylites from other major localities.

perdure, *v.* Delete 'Now *rare*' and add later examples.

1963 J. WIESENFARTH *Henry James* iv. 91 The romp of Aggie and Petherton perdures through the conversation. **1973** BOILÈS & HORCASITAS tr. *M. León-Portilla's Time & Reality in Thought of Maya* ii. 33 For longer than a millennium and a half, not a little of Maya symbolism has perdured. **1979** *Nature* 22 Mar. 348/1 Thus enough maternal gene products (mRNAs or proteins) may perdure in embryonic cells to allow normal segmentation and cuticular differentiation.

perduring *ppl. a.* (Further examples).

1951 C. KLUCKHORN et al. in Parsons & Shils *Toward Gen. Theory Action* iv. 399 A value or values restrain or canalize impulses in terms of wider and more perduring goals. **1977** *Dædalus* Summer 63 The assignment and re-assignment of meaning must be investigated as processes in the domain of resilience possessed by each population recognizing itself to be culturally perduring.

‖ **père** (pɛ̄r). Also **pere.** [Fr., = father.] **1.** Applied as a prefix to the name of a French priest; = FATHER *sb.* 6 e.

1619 J. CHAMBERLAIN *Let.* 30 Oct. (1939) II. 270 The Jesuites hold a chapter of theyre order at Rome whether Pere Coton is sent out of France. **1699** M. LISTER *Journey to Paris* 96, I bought the works of Pere Pezaron, a Bernadin, now Abbot de Charmoyse near Rheims. **1777** P. THICKNESSE *Year's Journey* I. xx. 174 Nor did the whole community afford but a single member (pere tender, a Fleming) who could speak French. **1879** R. L. STEVENSON *Trav. with Donkey* 119 There was Père Apollinaire hauling his barrow. **1978** *Times* 3 Nov. 7/1 (Advt.), The Sayings of Père Patriarche . . . 'To buy wine with uncertainty lacks any amusement.'

2. The father, senior: appended to a name to distinguish between a father and son of the same name. Cf. *FILS.

1802 M. EDGEWORTH *Let.* 8 Dec. (1979) 58 M. Delessert père at a card table with another gentleman. **1858** O. W. HOLMES *Autocrat of Breakfast-Table* 28, I have not taken the trouble to date them, as Raspail, *père*, used to date every proof he sent to the printer. **1893** E. DOWSON *Let.* c 28 Nov. (1967) 299, I am dining with Horne & Horne Père at the Constitutional tonight. **1907** 'ELIZABETH' *Fraulein Schmidt & Mr. Anstruther* xxxiii. 120 Collins *père* is a person who makes nails in Manchester. **1948** E. S. TURNER *Boys will be Boys* v. 80 It will be seen that there was a Harkaway *père* and a Harkaway *fils.* **1964** *Guardian* 18 June 9/3 Everything about Tabarly père gives a kind of ageless impression of the sea . . . All this is highly relevant in considering Tabarly fils. **1972** J. WAIN in Cox & Dyson *20th-Cent. Mind* I. xi. 364 Yeats *père* moved his household many times, and William was educated in London or Dublin by fits and starts. **1977** *N.Y. Rev. Bks.* 10 Nov. 10/2 Zola père was a Venetian of distinguished family.

3. In phrases *père de famille* (də famiy) [see *FAMILLE], father of a family, family man; *père et fils* (e fīs) [see *FILS], father and son.

1820 M. EDGEWORTH *Let.* 14 May (1979) 124, I could not see in either his figure or face any hint of the young père de famille. **1853** *Thackeray Let.* in *Lett. A. T. Ritchie* (1924) iv. 52 The quantity of acquaintances and ½ acquaintances that as père de famille I did not care to make whole acquaintances. **1862** —— *Philip* II. ii. 33, I am secretly of the disposition of the time-honoured *père de famille* in the comedies. **1871** D. G. ROSSETTI *Let.* ? Aug. (1967) III. 963 Constant calls on Urizen père et fils . . in the nature of supplications. **1962** *Observer* 1 July 19/4 Through this gate came Agamemnon the victim and Orestes the avenger, prototypes of the two Hamlets, *père et fils.* **1964** *Ibid.* 27 Sept. 24/6 A rather stuffy English *père de famille.* **1964** *House & Garden* Oct. 111/1 In this dual promotion *père et fils* certainly succeeded. **1973** I. BUTLER *Eldest Brother* viii. 78 The rôle of '*père de famille*' and respectable bourgeois. **1978** N. MARSH *Grave Mistake* iv. 113 You should hear the Rattisbons, *père et fils*, on the subject.

Père David (pɛ̄r davī·d). The name of Armand *David* (1826–1900), French missionary naturalist, used *attrib.*, in the possessive, or *absol.*, in **Père David('s) deer** to designate *Elaphurus davidianus*, a large, long-tailed deer discovered by him in China in 1865, named after him by A. Milne-Edwards in 1866, and now extinct in the wild in its native land, although it survives in zoological gardens and parks, esp. in a large herd at Woburn Abbey, Bedfordshire, established by the 11th Duke of Bedford soon after 1900.

[**1871** P. L. SCLATER in *Trans. Zool. Soc.* VII. 333 This fine animal is one of the many zoological discoveries which are due to the researches of M. le Père Armand David, Missionary of the Congregation of Lazarists at Pekin.] **1898** R. LYDEKKER *Deer of all Lands* 237 The general appearance of Père David's deer, when roaming in the park at Woburn Abbey, being quite unlike that of any other member of the group. **1927** G. JENNISON *Nat. Hist.: Animals* 290 It is known to Europeans as the Père David Deer from the Naturalist Missionary who discovered it in 1865. **1955** *Times* 11 May 12/7 Chief among them [*sc.* the Woburn deer] is the herd of 300 Père David's deer—a species now extinct in its native China and existing only at Woburn and in a few small offshoots (for example, at Whipsnade) from the Woburn herd. **1973** G. DURRELL *Beasts in my Belfry* v. 96 Undoubtedly the rarest animals in our care, a pair of young Père David deer. *Ibid.* 100 An outbreak of foot-and-mouth disease . . could have exterminated the Père David very successfully. **1975** *New Yorker* 24 Mar. 34/2 The Père David deer, six hundred and forty extant, twenty-seven in the Bronx.

peregrinatory, *a.* (Later example.)

1906 *Chambers's Jrnl.* Feb. 150/1 One sees in the streets . . peregrinatory makers of sugar puppets.

peregrine, *sb.* Add: **4.** Usu. with initial capital. A red-skinned variety of peach with white flesh, developed and introduced by the Rivers nursery in 1903.

1903 *Jrnl. R. Hort. Soc.* XXVIII. p. cxcii, Award of Merit . . . To Peach 'Peregrine' . . from Messrs. Rivers, Sawbridgeworth. **1907** *Daily Chron.* 13 June 6/4 A specimen peregrine peach tree grown in quite a small flower-pot is seven feet high, and bears much fruit. **1929** E. A. BUNYARD *Anat. Dessert* 89 In mid-August we have Peregrine, that finest of recent peaches, combining flavour, appearance, and good crop in a manner rarely found. **1958** *Listener* 20 Nov. 853/3 The most outstanding variety of peach is Peregrine. **1971** G. E. WHITEHEAD *Grow Fruit in your Greenhouse* viii. 94 The peach 'Peregrine' and the nectarine, 'Pine Apple', make an ideal pair.

pereiopod. (Further examples using this spelling, which is now the usual one.)

1932 J. S. HUXLEY *Probl. Relative Growth* iii. 87 Those pereiopods which are used as walking legs . . have a definite but slight growth-gradient. **1964** *Oceanogr. & Marine Biol.* II. 467 In these displays, serving a threat function, the crab stands higher on its pereiopods. **1970** *Nature* 16 May 661/2 The pereiopods of *M*[*erguia*] *rhizophorae* are more robust than in most marine shrimps.

perennate, *v.* Restrict *rare* to sense a and add further examples in *Bot.* of sense b. Hence **pere·nnating** *ppl. a.*; **perennation** (further example).

1905 I. B. BALFOUR tr. *C. E. von Goebel's Organogr. Plants* II. 689/1 Perennating, geophilous shoot. **1913** [see *chamæphyte* s.v. *CHAMÆ-]. **1926** TANSLEY & CHIPP *Study of Vegetation* ii. 21 The perennating buds . . continue the growth of the plant from season to season. **1927** *Forestry* I. 108 Besides overwintering in the buds, the fungus perennates on dead oak-leaves. **1969** F. E. ROUND *Introd. Lower Plants* xiii. 153 Vegetative propagation of the gametophyte from gemma-like outgrowths is common in some genera [of ferns] and in a few these even become thickened and act as perennating organs. **1971** *Country Life* 16 Dec. 1736/3, I nearly always get a casual crop of mushrooms, though where the spawn comes from is a mystery. Perhaps it perennates in the ground below the [compost] heap. **1977** J. L. HARPER *Population Biol. of Plants* iii. 62 For perennial plants the seed is an alternative means of perennation. *Ibid.* xxi. 651 In most plants the seed is a perennating organ.

perennial, *a.* Add: **2. a.** *perennial philosophy* = *PHILOSOPHIA PERENNIS.

1933 W. R. INGE *God & Astronomers* i. 13 The perennial philosophy . . is the only system which will be found ultimately satisfying. **1945** A. HUXLEY (*title*) The perennial philosophy. *Ibid.* p. vii, Rudiments of the Perennial Philosophy may be found among the traditionary lore of primitive peoples in every region of the world, and in its fully developed forms it has a place in every one of the higher religions. **1962** E. WYNNE-TYSON *Philos. of Compassion* 3 The most fundamental difference between the teachings of the western religions and those of the perennial philosophy and of the original Creed of Christ. **1974** R. C. ZAEHNER *Our Savage God* 12 'All is One, and One is All . .', seems to have been . . what Aldous Huxley considered to be the kernel of . . the 'perennial philosophy'.

perenniality. (Further example.)

1977 J. L. HARPER *Population Biol. of Plants* xviii. 543 It is often possible to extend the perenniality of a biennial by continually preventing seed formation.

perentie (pĕre·nti). *Austral.* Also **parenti, perenty.** [Aboriginal name.] A large, burrowing, monitor lizard, *Varanus giganteus*, which may be as much as eight feet long and is found in desert areas of central and northern Australia. Also *attrib.*

a **1928** E. R. WAITE *Reptiles or Amphibians S. Austral.* (1929) v. 125 Perentie or Sjonba . . . The discovery of the gigantic goana on the Komodo Islands illustrates the inadvisability of naming specimens by comparative measurements. The Perentie is, however, the largest Australian species. **1942** C. BARRETT *On Wallaby* iii. 43 Perenties three yards long were said to exist in the ranges. **1944** *Living off Land* ii. 24 The large Parenti lizard provides about the best food supply of the reptiles. **1963** E. WORRELL *Reptiles Austral.* 83 Perenty . . . Length to 8 feet. This is Australia's largest monitor. **1968** V. SERVENTY *Wildlife Austral.* v. 126 The goannas range from the short-tailed goanna, a seven-inch long sprite, to the eight-foot giant of the inland, the perentie. **1973** *Panorama* (Austral.) Oct. 5/3 (*caption*) Dick Lang with a perentie he chased and caught.

perequation. Delete *rare*$^{-0}$ and add later examples.

1920 *Times* 4 Aug. 4/3 This price we pay for English coal has obliged us to force up the interior price for our own coal, by a 'perequation', so as not to handicap those.. who are obliged by geographical reasons to burn English coal only. **1954** *Economist* 19 June 983 A perequation levy is collected from coal sold by countries where the average costs of production are lower than the weighted average. **1973** H. Trevelyan *Diplomatic Channels* ix. 132 It was egalitarianism run mad, the doctrine of the perequation of misery.

perequitate, *v.* For *rare*—¹ read *rare* and add later example.

1957 P. M. Kendall *Warwick Kingmaker* iii. vi. 158 A poor clerk of Evreux, leaving the royal cavalcade to take a message to his Chapter and immediately setting forth with their reply, had to ride for sixty-six days before he caught up with his perequitating sovereign [*sc.* Louis XI].

perester (pərə·stəɹ). *Chem.* [f. Per-¹ 5 + *ester.] An ester of a peracid.

1933 *Jrnl. Amer. Chem. Soc.* LV. 351 The perester on standing at room temperature..hydrolyzes to yield methyl hydroperoxide and the original monomethyl ester of camphoric acid. **1946** *Ibid.* LXVIII. 642/1 Organic peresters cannot be classified as derivatives of organic peracids and alcohols, but rather as derivatives of organic acids and hydroperoxides. **1975** *Org. Reaction Mechanisms 1973* iii. 80 Induced decompositions of peresters have been brought about by trialkyltin radicals.

perfect, *a.* Add: **B. 4. d.** *a perfect day* (*colloq.*), a day of which every part has been enjoyable; *esp.* in phr. *the end of a perfect day.*

1910 C. Jacobs-Bond *Perfect Day* (song) 6 For mem'ry has painted this perfect day With colors that never fade, And we find at the end of a perfect day The soul of a friend we've made. **1923** *Liverpool Echo* 13 Sept. 6/3 (*heading*) The boy and the balloon. The sad end of a perfect day. **1976** S. Kaufman *Master & Other Stories* (1977) 193 Nothing crossed her mind as she floated, a thing made of air, and dreamily listened to the carrying voices from shore, except the one thought: What a perfect day.

5. c. (Further examples.) Also in phrases *perfect gentleman, lady.*

1807 Wordsworth *Poems* I. 15 A perfect woman; nobly plann'd, To warn, to comfort, and command. **1818** Byron *Beppo* xxxii. 17 In short, he was a perfect cavaliero, And to his very valet seem'd a hero. **1834** G. Crabbe Jun. in *Poet. Wks. G. Crabbe* I. vi. 147 Miss Waldron.. could sing a jovial song like a fox-hunter,.. and yet there was such an air of high *ton*, and such intellect mingled with these manners, that the perfect lady was not veiled for a moment. **1856** C. M. Yonge *Daisy Chain* i. xxiii. 245 Her instinct showed her that she was talking to a man of high ability. A perfect gentleman she saw him to be. **1872** Geo. Eliot *Middlem.* I. ii. xvi. 299 Rosamond.. was active..in being from morning till night her own standard of a perfect lady. **1903** G. B. Shaw *Revolutionist's Handbk.* i, in *Man & Superman* 182 This..is a great advance on the popular demand for a perfect gentleman and a perfect lady. **1949** E. Coxhead *Wind in West* i. 25 You'll like the Fletchers—Hermia is a wonder, the perfect wife. **1967** A. Wilson *No Laughing Matter* iii. 320 All perfect ladies..eat messily, don't they? **1972** J. Porter *Meddler & her Murder* iv. 49, I never knew old Adam was a womanizer! Must say, he's always behaved like a perfect gentleman with me. **1978** H. MacInnes *Prelude to Terror* iv. 34 The perfect hostess..a woman putting a guest at ease with food and drink.

f. Complete, utter (referring to a person in neutral or favourable contexts).

1903 G. B. Shaw *Man & Superman* i. 40 You seem to understand all the things I dont understand; but you are a perfect baby in the things I do understand. **1919** T. K. Holmes *Man from Tall Timber* xxiv. 292 That Anabelle Whitman is a perfect scream. **1927** C. Connolly *Let.* 27 Jan. in *Romantic Friendship* (1975) 231 Thou art heavenly he a 'perfect scream'. **1931** T. E. Lawrence *Lett.* (1938) 713 The Coroner was a perfect pet. **1959** *Listener* 4 June 998/2 He [*sc.* Harry Secombe] is indeed a Perfect Scream in both senses of that noun. **1961** Parks & Leighton *My Thirty Years backstairs at White House* xiii. 190 Rob Roy was a perfect angel with the First Family.

8. (Later examples.)

1901 *Ann. Math.* II. 103 By a perfect number is meant a number which is equal to the sum of those of its divisors which are less than the number. Thus 6 = 1 + 2 + 3 is a perfect number. *Ibid.* 104 His [*sc.* Sylvester's] proof of the non-existence of odd perfect numbers. **1958** R. V. Andree *Sel. Mod. Abstr. Algebra* i. 30 The first four perfect numbers were discovered by the end of the first century. By 1870, only four more had been found. Between 1870 and 1950, four additional even perfect numbers were discovered... Since then, five more perfect numbers have been found. **1971** *Sci. Amer.* June 56/2 Whether or not there are any odd perfect numbers is still undecided.

10. e. *perfect pitch*, the ability to judge pitch absolutely, and hence recognize the pitch of any individual note. (Cf. *absolute pitch* (b) s.v. *absolute *a.* 16.)

1949 F. Towers *Tea with Mr. Rochester* 19 She is very musical, and has perfect pitch. **1958** *Gramophone* Oct. 17 Listeners with perfect pitch are warned that, this being the Schnitger organ at Cappel, all the works here sound a semitone higher than usual. **1971** *Nature* 2 Apr. 337/1 Few people possess 'perfect pitch' and it is not known whether it is learned or inherited. **1975** *Sunday Times* (Colour Suppl.) 13 July 47/4 Although he does not sight read he has perfect pitch. **1976** *Gramophone* Aug. 318/3 Listeners with perfect pitch should be warned that the present issue sounds a semitone lower than normal.

15. Also applied to sheets that have been printed on both sides.

1841 W. Savage *Dict. Art of Printing* 701 The reader, in revising the second form, then sees the sheet perfect, which is necessary to ascertain that the matter follows. **1960** G. A. Glaister *Gloss. Bk.* 303/2 In edition binding the printed sheets are said to be perfect as soon as some or all of the sheets (and plates) have been printed.

16. *Bot.* Applied to the stage in the life cycle of a fungus at which sexual spores are produced, and to a fungus in that state.

1891 G. Massee *Brit. Fungi* 32 The incomplete form is considered as belonging to the same genus as the perfect form. **1909** *Mycologia* I. 115 A single boll [of cotton].. was examined in the laboratory and found to be covered with the perfect stage of the *Colletotrichum.* **1945** G. R. Bisby *Introd. Taxon. & Nomencl. Fungi* xvi. 87 The perfect state is that which ends in the ascus stage in the *Ascomycetes*, in the basidium in the *Basidiomycetes*, in the teleutospore or its equivalent in the *Uredinales*, and in the spore in the *Ustilaginales.* **1950** E. A. Bessey *Morphol. & Taxon. Fungi* i. 18 In fungi with several stages of development to which different names have been given, the species epithet that is to be retained is the one applied to the 'perfect' stage of the fungus. **1967** M. E. Hale *Biol. Lichens* iii. 45 The parasymbiont *Abrothallus suecicus* is the perfect stage of the imperfect fungus *Phoma.* **1971** [see *imperfect *a.* 8 b.]

17. Applied to a form of bookbinding in which the single leaves of a book are attached individually to the spine by an adhesive, instead of the printed sheets being folded and sewn.

1893 *Amer. Bookbinder* July 86 (*heading*) Perfect library binding. *Ibid.*, Mr. Crawford is the inventor of what is known as the 'perfect library binding'. **1910** G. A. Stephen *Commerc. Bookbinding* 9/2 A revolution in the method of binding monthly magazines was inaugurated by the invention of the Sheridan 'Perfect Binder'. **1926** *Amazing Stories* July 359/1 We..took immediate ways and means to do away with the old-fashioned binding, and you now hold in your hand a magazine bound with the so-called 'Perfect' binding. **1956** H. Williamson *Methods Bk. Design* xix. 332 Sewing, rounding, backing, and lining can all be dispensed with in the unsewn or 'perfect' methods of binding. **1960** *Times Lit. Suppl.* 3 June 360/3 The so-called 'perfect' binding, in which, the backs of the quires having been guillotined away, the resultant single leaves are held hopefully together by adhesive. **1977** *Ibid.* 28 Jan. 104/2 The pages are now smaller, the paper thinner,.. and the binding is perfect (i e, imperfect). **1977** *Special Libraries* Feb. 6A/2 Perfect bound ('newspeak' for 'unsewn') bindings on books have caused librarians grief and libraries money (for rebinding) since they fall apart so readily... I urge publishers not to utilize this type of binding until they have really perfected the process.

18. *Econ.* Designating (notional or actual) ideal market conditions in which adverse factors are removed; *perfect competition*, competition in which all elements of monopoly are absent and the market price of a commodity is beyond the control of individual buyers and sellers.

1897 *Q. Jrnl. Econ.* XII. 125 In passing from the study of perfect monopoly to that of perfect competition, Cournot considers also the intermediate case of a few, say two, competitors. **1906** *Ibid.* XX. 211 Perfect competition is the fundamental hypothesis of economics in the sense that perfect competition is postulated in nearly every argument as to economic equilibrium. **1922** H. A. Silverman *Substance Econ.* vi. 72 Perfect competition..is not usually realized in practice. **1939** Lyness & Emmet *Introd. Econ.* iv. 38 The characteristics of a perfect market are, firstly, full information... Secondly, complete accessibility... Thirdly, full freedom of choice. **1944** A. Cairncross *Introd. Econ.* xiv. 180 The first requirement of perfect competition..is that the market..should be perfect; a perfect market being one in which buyers have no preferences as between the different units of the commodity offered for sale, sellers are quite indifferent to whom they sell, and both buyers and sellers have full knowledge of prices in other parts of the market. **1969** D. C. Hague *Managerial Econ.* iii. 59 There is an established market where all buyers and sellers can keep in close touch with each other, and have become used to doing so. Economists sometimes say that there is then a *perfect market.* **1971** I. Deutscher *Marxism in our Time* (1972) xii. 259 Even when, for the sake of argument, he [*sc.* Marx] assumed perfect competition, he did it only in order to prove that that competition was necessarily self-destructive. **1974** M. B. Brown *Econ. of Imperialism* ii. 30 The classical vision of an economy where there is perfect competition reaches its apogee in the Theory of Free Trade. **1976** *Economist* 16 Oct. 21/2 Foreign exchange markets do not quite match up to the ideal of perfect competition described by theory.

19. *Math.* **a.** Of a set of points: closed, and such that every neighbourhood of each point of the set contains at least one other point of the set.

1906 *Q. Jrnl. Math.* XXXVII. 23 *P* is a rim point, so that the rim is closed, and, being dense in itself, is perfect. **1926** J. E. Littlewood *Elem. of Theory of Real Functions* (ed. 2) iv. 50 A perfect set is an existent set which is closed and dense-in-itself. **1957** J. R. Aumann et al. tr. *Hausdorff's Set Theory* vi. 133 The null set is everything: isolated, dense-in-itself, closed, perfect. **1970** C. A. Rogers *Hausdorff Measures* ii. 61 A set is perfect if it is closed, non-empty and dense in itself.

b. Of a group: such that the subgroup generated by the set of commutators of the group is the group itself.

1898 *Amer. Jrnl. Math.* XX. 277 Since a perfect group is identical with its derivatives, it cannot be isomorphic to any Abelian group whose order exceeds unity. **1908** H. Hilton *Introd. Theory Groups of Finite Order* x. 134 Every simple group is perfect. **1940** D. E. Littlewood *Theory of Group Characters* x. 174 A group is perfect if it is identical with its commutator subgroup. Hence the condition that a group is perfect is that it possesses no character satisfying $\chi_0 = 1$ save that character which is unity for every operation. **1959** J. S. Lomont *Applications of Finite Groups* ii. 2 Let us call a group (of order > 1) perfect if it is identical with its commutator subgroup. Every perfect group is then insolvable.

D. 4. [tr. med.L. *perfectus* in the same sense (also used).] Among the Catharist heresy of the Albigenses in the 12th and 13th centuries, one who had received the *consolamentum or spiritual baptism, thereby accepting all the precepts of Albigensian doctrine.

1742 L. Brown tr. *Bossuet's Hist. Variations Protestant Churches* II. xi. cxl. 156 In regard of those four thousand *Cathari*,..none were understood by that name but the *perfect* of the Sect... When the Sect was weaken'd, tho' there were but four thousand perfect *Cathari*, yet..the multitude..of simple *Believers*, was then infinite. **1826** in J. C. L. S. de Sismondi *Hist. Crusades against Albigenses* p. xvii, They were divided into two classes, the *perfect* and the *believers.* **1832** S. R. Maitland *Albigenses & Waldenses* x. 271 Those men who assert that they alone are good christians whom the most Holy Roman Church persecuted, and condemns, and calls *perfecti*, or *consolati* (more properly *desolati*) heretics. **1888** H. C. Lea *Hist. Inquisition Middle Ages* I. ii. 84 The Perfects would die rather than violate the precept. *Ibid.* iii. 103 If the Perfect is exhorted by the God in whom he believes to tell all about his life, he will faithfully detail it without falsehood. **1926** A. L. Maycock *Inquisition* ii. 40 The 'Perfect' were forbidden to eat meat, eggs, cheese or anything that was the result of sexual procreation. **1957** N. Cohn *Pursuit of Millennium* (1970) viii. 140 The Catharist *perfecti* dominated the religious life of a large part of southern France for half a century or more. **1961** [see *endura]. **1970** [see *consolamentum]. **1975** *Times* 24 Feb. 15/5 Fox had resembled a Perfectus, with no sense of sin... Penn represents another type of Cathar.

perfect, *v.* Add: Now usu. with pronunc. (pəɹfe·kt). **1. b.** (Later examples.)

1899 J. Southward *Mod. Printing* III. xii. 117 Rotary web machines also perfect the paper..before it is delivered. **1927** R. B. McKerrow *Introd. Bibliogr.* i. ii. 21 It is often evident..that the printer printed the whole number of impressions on one side before starting to perfect. *Ibid.* iii. i. 261 It is possible that a sheet may be perfected from a wrong forme. **1964** F. Bowers *Bibliogr. & Textual Criticism* iii. i. 71 The specific example of *Match Me in London* and its sheet that was perfected out of phase. **1972** P. Gaskell *New Introd. Bibliogr.* 132 The sixteenth-century account of Le Roy suggests that the heap was normally printed as white paper in the morning, turned at the midday break, and perfected in the afternoon.

perfecta (pəɹfe·ktă). orig. *U.S.* [abbrev. Amer. Sp. *quiniela perfecta* perfect quinella.] A method of betting in which the bettor must pick the first and second finishers of a race in the correct order. Also *attrib.*

1971 *New Yorker* 20 Feb. 107 For horseplayers who hopefully bet on exactas, perfectas, quinellas, doubles, and such, I can report that..an exacta paid $25,257. **1971** L. Koppett *N.Y. Times Guide Spectator Sports* x. 184 In the 'perfecta'..you must pick the first two [finishers] in the correct order. **1972** *Telegraph* (Brisbane) 17 June 18/3 His target was to fix races which were the subject of 'perfecta betting'. **1974** *Cleveland* (Ohio) *Plain Dealer* 26 Oct. 8-D/4 He also had the $13·80 perfecta in the seventh. **1975** *Ibid.* 6 Apr. 13-C/1 A new ruling allows Northfield four (instead of three) perfecta races nightly, which will be raced as the third, fifth, seventh and tenth races. To pick a winning perfecta combination, you must pick the first two horses that finish a race, in order.

perfectability, var. Perfectibility.

1872 [see Perfectibility 2]. **1970** *Sci. Jrnl.* Apr. 4/1 The US places more reliance on technological solutions and has more faith in human perfectability than any other nation today. **1975** *Christian* II. 229 The potential for perfectability.

perfecting, *vbl. sb.* Add: **a.** (Later examples, in sense 1 b of the vb.)

1951 S. Jennett *Making of Bks.* vii. 101 The printing of the second side of the sheet is known as perfecting. **1972** P. Gaskell *New Introd. Bibliogr.* 133 It appears to coincide with the practice of consecutive perfecting at different presses.

b. perfecting cylinder, machine (later examples), **press** (later examples).

1967 V. Strauss *Printing Industry* vi. 298/2 A third cylinder..is denoted as the 'perfecting cylinder' because of its paramount importance to the perfecting operation. **1880** F. J. F. Wilson *Typogr. Printing Machines* xi. 61 Perfecting machines are of three kinds—1. The Web. 2. The Drop-bar. 3. The Gripper. The above terms signify the manner by which white paper is conveyed into the tapes. **1973** J. Moran *Printing Presses* ix. 133 Between 1836–63 Napier made at least eighty-seven perfecting machines. **1902** R. Hoe *Short Hist. Printing Press* 17 In 1814 Koenig patented a continuously revolving Cylinder Press... This press, termed a 'perfecting press', was afterwards improved by Applegath and Cowper. **1967** V. Strauss *Printing Industry* vi. 279/1 Perfecting presses, or perfectors..print both sides of the sheet in one color in one pass through the press.

perfectionism. Add: **2.** Refusal to accept any standard short of perfection.

1937 *Nation* (N.Y.) 30 Oct. 465/2 Labor..cannot afford perfectionism. **1945** F. D. ROOSEVELT *Public Papers & Addresses 1944–5* (1950) 498 Perfectionism, no less than isolationism or imperialism or power politics, may obstruct the paths to international peace. **1957** *Listener* 24 Oct. 642/1 Sir Lewis Namier once gave up writing a book he had planned because some manuscripts in private hands were not made available to him. This was a fine example of scientific perfectionism. **1968** P. B. AUSTIN *On Being Swedish* iii. 21 Perfectionism always implies, at a deeper level, its opposite.

perfectionist. Add: **2. a.** One who is only satisfied with the highest standards.

1934 in WEBSTER. **1951** 'J. TEY' *Daughter of Time* ii. 28 A worrier: perhaps a perfectionist. A man..anxious over details. **1969** 'R. GORDON' *Facts of Life* ii. 14, I hated performing anything badly... Like so many women doctors, I was a perfectionist. **1978** *Vogue* 1 Mar. 114/1 Bette Davis's misfortune is to be a perfectionist in an industry run by opportunists.

b. as *adj.* Demanding perfection or perfectionism (sense *2).

1958 *Times Rev. Industry* Aug. 50/3 The extreme sensitivity of the Talysurf and its companion instrument aroused some resistance among engineers at first. They claimed that the methods were too perfectionist for everyday practical purposes. **1977** *Listener* 17 Mar. 332/2 Let us not be élitist, perfectionist... Singapore does provide its people with a decent..existence. **1978** P. BOARDMAN *Worlds of Patrick Geddes* vii. 226 P. G. certainly could be called a perfectionist parent. He urged them from early years to take notes.

perfectionistic, *a.* Add: **b.** Tending towards perfectionism (sense *2).

1968 P. B. AUSTIN *On Being Swedish* xvii. 124 In its heaviness of spirit, a bleakness of insight so intense that all its perfectionistic arrangements can obviously only be oil on the stormy waters. **1977** W. J. BATE *Samuel Johnson* II. viii. 117 Johnson's fears of insanity..[were] a fanciful delusion resulting from a perfectionistic notion of 'sanity'.

perfectivation (pəɹfektivēⁱ·ʃən). [f. PERFECTIVE *a.* + -ATION.] The action of rendering a verb perfective.

1926 G. W. S. FRIEDRICHSEN *Gothic Version of Gospels* vii. 100 This is an instance of the colourlessness of verbal prefixes when used as an instrument of perfectivation. **1954** PEI & GAYNOR *Dict. Linguistics* 163 *Perfectivation*, the transformation of an imperfective verb into a perfective one by a morphological change. **1962** R. W. ZANDVOORT in F. Behre *Contrib. Eng. Syntax* 15 Mossé.. believes in perfectivation in O.E. by means of the prefix *ge-*.

perfective, *a.* (*sb.*) For 'Now *rare*' read 'Now *rare* except in *Gram.*' and add: **3.** (Further examples.)

1889 [see *DURATIVE *a.*]. **1924** [see *ASPECT *sb.* 9 b]. **1968** J. LYONS *Introd. Theoret. Linguistics* viii. 396 The English 'perfect with *have*'..was at first restricted to transitive verbs, and thus preserved its relationship with the perfective passive without *have* (still current in such sentences as *The work is done, The house is built*). **1975** *Language* LI. 444 The tenses were divided into an imperfective and a perfective set with three tenses in each.

B. *sb.* **2.** (Further examples.)

1949 *Archivum Linguisticum* I. 176 Perfectives are not always easy to recognize formally. **1968** J. LYONS *Introd. Theoret. Linguistics* vii. 314 Many perfectives [in Russian] are derived by prefixation of the corresponding imperfectives. **1970** B. M. H. STRANG *Hist. English* II. i. 100 The tendency to regularise verb-forms also appears in the use of *has*, etc. to form perfectives.

perfectiveness. (Later example.)

1964 *Philos. Rev.* LXXIII. 20 Ryle..was perhaps led to this opinion partly by the perfectiveness of 'to see'.

perfe·ctivizing, *ppl. a.* Rendering perfective.

1908 *Expositor* July 91 The function of the perfectivising preposition is to supply a present answering to the past ἔσχον. **1949** *Archivum Linguisticum* I. 7 Let us suppose that we have a set of distinct prepositions each identical with a perfectivising prefix. **1961** *Brno Studies in English* III. 99 The function the Czech perfectivizing verbal prefix may play.

perfecto (pəɹfe·kto). orig. *U.S.* Also **Perfecto, Perfectos.** [Sp. *perfecto* perfect.] A type of cigar, thick in the centre and tapering at each end.

Also used in the names of various brands of cigar and cigarette.

1894 *Harper's Weekly* 5 May 429/2 A minute later two of the raggedest-looking tramps you ever saw were trudging westward through the rain, each smoking a Carolina Perfecto costing thirty-five cents apiece. **1897** *Sears, Roebuck Catal.* 24/2 La Flor de Portuondo, Perfectos. A 5 inch cigar. **1898** H. E. HAMBLEN *Gen. Manager's Story* 3 The old gentleman..blowing the smoke from his 'perfecto' out into the cool starlight. **1904** 'O. HENRY' *Four Million* (1906) 74 He always..handed out real perfectos to the delighted boys. **1931** E. S. GARDNER in *Detective Fiction Weekly* 14 Mar. 302/2 He took a box of perfectos..and selected one. **1944** S. BELLOW *Dangling Man* (1946) 149, I sucked tranquilly at my Perfecto Queen and said to myself, 'It's in the bag.' **1953** *Trade Marks Jrnl.* 5 Aug. 707/2 Perfectos Finos... Cigarettes for export. British-American Tobacco Company, Limited, Westminster House, 7, Millbank, London, S.W.1; Tobacco Manufacturers. **1960** R. K. HEIMANN *Tobacco & Americans* 248/2 Where fat perfectos and 'banker' sizes had once ruled the glassed counters, slim panetelas and palmas moved to the front row. **1961** C. WILLOCK *Death in Covert* iv. 78 Crumbe-Howard took a Perfectos Finos from a gold case. **1968** D. MACKENZIE *Three minus Two* 85 Smith chose a Perfecto and lit it. **1973** 'D. JORDAN' *Nile Green* xiii. 54, I took a Perfectos from the silver box and tried to light a match on my thumbnail.

perfector. Add: **2.** *Printing.* Also **perfecter.** = *perfecting machine, press* s.v. PERFECTING *vbl. sb.* b in Dict. and Suppl.

1899 J. SOUTHWARD *Mod. Printing* III. xii. 124 (*caption*) Dawsons' Patent Fast Gripper Perfecter. **1940** *Chambers's Techn. Dict.* 626/1 *Perfector*, a type of machine which prints both sides of the paper before delivery. **1951** S. JENNETT *Making of Bks.* vii. 101 These machines are in effect two presess combined in one, printing one side of the sheet first and the other side immediately afterwards. They are called perfecters. **1975** *Bookseller* 6 Dec. 2590/3 Paper of 100 per cent recycled content can now be used for printing on offset litho perfectors.

perfervidly (pəɹfɜ·ɹvidli), *adv.* [f. PERFERVID *a.* + -LY².] In a perfervid manner.

1906 *Macm. Mag.* Oct. 884 The General was gripping de Pellotin's hand perfervidly. **1922** JOYCE *Ulysses* 709 Symposium of incoordinately abstract, perfervidly concrete mercantile coexreligionist excompatriots.

‖ **perfide** (pę̄rfīd), *a.* [Fr., = treacherous.] In phr. *perfide Albion*, with reference to the Fr. phr. *la perfide Albion*, 'perfidious Albion' (see *ALBION).

1846 [see *ALBION]. **1899** BEERBOHM *Around Theatres* (1924) I. 52 Had Mr. Kipling been born a Frenchman.. he..would..be known to us only as a..fulminator against '*perfide Albion*'. **1926** GALSWORTHY *Silver Spoon* II. iv. 142 *Perfide Albion!* Heh! We always wait till the last moment to declare our policy... Gives the impression that we serve time. **1947** H. NICOLSON *Diary* 2 Jan. (1968) 88 We always go through these stages of being beastly to our friends because we are frightened of our enemies. It is this that has earned us the reputation of *perfide Albion*. **1972** R. MAYNE *Europeans* v. 119 The phrase '*la perfide Angleterre*', later to become '*perfide Albion*', may have been coined by Jacques Bérigne Bossuet in a sermon on New Year's Day, 1654.

perfidiousness. (Later examples.)

1935 E. R. EDDISON *Mistress of Mistresses* iii. 54 Perfidiousness is a common waiter in most princes' courts. **1963** *Times* 30 Jan. 9/4 Mr. Macmillan's journey to Moscow..resurrected in Dr. Adenauer's mind all repressed fears of the perfidiousness of Albion.

perfidity. Delete †*Obs.* and add later example.

1903 J. KELMAN *Honour towards God* iii. 22 Instances are only too common in which Pagan and Mohammedan honour has shamed the perfidity of so-called Christians.

perfluorinated (pəɹflū·ŏrinēⁱtėd), *ppl. a.* *Chem.* [f. PER-¹ 5 + *FLUORINATED *ppl. a.*] Applied to a (usu. organic) compound, radical, etc., in which fluorine has replaced hydrogen to the maximum extent short of altering the characteristic functional groups of the species.

1947 *Chem. Rev.* XL. 52 This method cannot in general be used successfully..to prepare fluorocarbons or other perfluorinated compounds which are of much significance. **1972** *Materials & Technol.* IV. vii. 237 A number of perfluorinated aromatic and heteroaromatic compounds have been synthesized in recent years. **1974** *Physics Bull.* June 226/2 Electrolytic generation from water has made progress with the use of solid electrolytes such as perfluorinated sulphonic acid, which could allow efficiencies of up to 95% for the conversion from electrical energy to energy stored in the form of hydrogen.

perfluoro- (pəɹflū·ŏro), *pref.* *Chem.* [f. PER-¹ 5 + FLUOR- + -O.] Used to designate organic compounds, radicals, etc., in which hydrogen has been replaced by fluorine to the maximum extent short of altering the characteristic functional groups of the species.

1947 *Industr. & Engin. Chem.* Mar. 236/2 Perchlorobenzene is a high melting solid, whereas perfluorobenzene is a liquid boiling at about the same temperature as benzene... Also, the boiling points of the perfluoroalkanes having more than five carbon atoms are actually lower than those of the hydrocarbons. *Ibid.* 241/1 The members of the panel..made the recommendation that the prefix 'perfluoro' be used to denote complete substitution by fluorine of all positions attached to the carbon skeleton. **1951** I. L. FINAR *Org. Chem.* I. v. 89 When catalysts other than copper..are used,..perfluorocompounds are obtained, e.g. *n*-heptane gives perfluoroheptane. **1962** P. J. & B. DURRANT *Introd. Adv. Inorg. Chem.* xxiii. 913 Perfluoroethylene polymerises under pressure in contact with an aqueous solution of a persulphate to yield the polymer teflon. **1971** *Nomencl. Org. Chem.* (I.U.P.A.C.) (ed. 2) C. 145 Halogen-containing compounds or radicals in which all hydrogen atoms, except those whose replacement would affect the nature of characteristic groups..present, have been replaced by halogen atoms of the same kind may be named by adding the prefixes 'perfluoro-', 'perchloro-',..[etc.] to the name of the corresponding non-halogenated compound or radical. **1972** *Materials & Technol.* IV. vii. 252 The excellent electrical properties of perfluoropolymers, which have been known for many years, are shared by the simple fluorocarbons. **1976** *Nature* 4 Mar. 8/1 Perfluoropropane, C_3F_8, appears to be an ideal refrigerant.

Hence **perflu:oroca·rbon**, any binary compound of carbon and fluorine, analogous to a hydrocarbon.

1947 *Industr. & Engin. Chem.* Mar. 292/1 Until October 1941 no practical general method for the synthesis of perfluorocarbons had been reported in the literature. **1961** G. H. BEAVEN et al. *Molecular Spectrosc.* I. iii. 101 Organic solvents for use down to 200 mμ are limited, in practice, to the saturated hydrocarbons and the aliphatic alcohols and ethers, although perfluorocarbons may be used more, as they become more readily available. **1972** *Materials & Technol.* IV. vii. 231 The perfluorocarbons are synthesized either by direct fluorination using elemental fluorine or by vapour phase fluorination techniques using hydrogen fluoride and a suitable catalyst. *Ibid.* 251 One of the most successful ways to coat a surface is to incorporate the fluorochemical in a polymer in which the perfluorocarbon chains constitute a series of side chains.

perforable, *a.* (Further example.)

1926 J. M. ROBERTSON *Mr. Shaw & 'The Maid'* v. 46 The real question is simply whether his shield is perforable.

perforated, *ppl. a.* Add: **1.** *perforated tape*, tape in which data are recorded by means of the pattern of holes punched in it; cf. TAPE *sb.*¹ 2b, *paper tape* s.v. *PAPER *sb.* 12, *punched tape* s.v. *PUNCHED *ppl. a.* 2.

1890 *Electrician* 4 July 235/1 The key-board no longer gives direct electric contacts, but produces mechanically a perforated tape on which the signs are represented by holes at their respective places. **1964** N. N. BISWAS *Princ. Telegr.* iv. 93 Transmission on the line may be made either from the keyboard or by a perforated tape on the tape transmitter. **1973** GOACHER & DENNY *Teleprinter Handbk.* ii. 35/2 The perforated tape forms a permanent record of all the code signals involved in a particular message in a form suitable for storage.

perforation. Add: **4. perforation plate** *Bot.* (see quot. 1933).

1933 *Tropical Woods* XXXVI. 7 *Perforation plate*, a term of convenience for the area of the wall (originally imperforate) involved in the coalescence of two members of a vessel. **1953** K. ESAU *Plant Anat.* xi. 223 The perforations of vessel members commonly occur on the end walls, but they may be present on the lateral walls too. The wall bearing the perforation is called the perforation plate. *Ibid.* 233 A pitted wall part became a scalariform perforation plate, which changed into a simple perforation plate. **1975** S. CARLQUIST *Ecol. Strategies of Xylem Evol.* i. 13 There are even dicotyledons with simple perforation plates and scalariform lateral-wall pitting.

perform, *v.* Add: **7. e.** *intr.* To display extreme anger or bad temper; to swear loudly; to make a great fuss. *Austral. slang.*

1901 M. FRANKLIN *My Brilliant Career* xix. 163 Badtempered is a tame name for it. You should have seen the dust he raised the other day with old Benson. He just did pefrorm. **1911** L. STONE *Jonah* v. 45 Ow'l Chook perform, if 'e ain't at Ada's? **1959** BAKER *Drum* (1960) ix. 68 We say that a man *performs* when he is indulging in a frenzy of anger or vituperation.

performability (pəɹfǭ·ɹmăbi·lĭti). [f. PERFORMABLE *a.* + -ILITY.] The capability of being performed.

1947 A. EINSTEIN *Mus. Romantic Era* xv. 222 He [*sc.* Alkan] lost his sense of proportion, with regard to both the performability and the dimensions of his piano works. **1962** H. C. WESTON *Sight, Light & Work* (ed. 2) vi. 185 Levels of illumination which are supposed to give equal visibility or 'performability' for widely differing visual tasks.

performance. Add: **2. a.** (Further examples.) *spec.* the capabilities of a machine or device, now esp. those of a motor vehicle or aircraft measured under test and expressed in a specification. Also used *attrib.* to designate a motor vehicle with very good performance.

Cf. quots. 1766, 1825 in Dict.

1832 *Mechanics' Mag.* 30 June 224/2 Extraordinary railway performances... On two occasions, a load amounting to 100 tons was drawn by one engine..a distance of above 30 miles, in an hour and a half. **1840** *Min. Proc. Inst. Civil Engin.* 34 The paper is accompanied by..tabular statements of their performances during the year 1839, showing the number of miles traversed by each engine, the weight conveyed, [etc.]. **1883** W. H. MAW *Recent Pract. Marine Engin.* I. 216/1 On the first regular journey from Queensborough to Flushing, the Prinses Marie made the journey of 101½ knots in 372 minutes, giving a mean speed of 17·12 knots..and the coal consumption..being 1·92 lb. per indicated horse-power per hour, an excellent performance considering that the cylinders are not steam jacketted. **1907** *Proc. Incorporated Inst. Automobile Engineers* I. 235 A formula of this kind..is most useful in comparing the performance of small engines with large. **1931** R. N. LIPTROT in *Handbk. Aeronautics* (R. Aeronaut. Soc.) ii. 98 The top speeds and best rates of climb are now plotted against altitude, giving the required performance of the aircraft. **1952** W. W. BALDING in *Bk. of Motor Car* 98/2 If one carefully studies the reports of technical performance.., one quickly recognises the importance attached to vehicle-acceleration. **1961** *Times* 7 Nov. 19/1 In Britain a thriving business has grown up in tuning and modifying the engines of existing models to give more performance. **1968** MILLER & SAWERS *Technical Devel. Mod. Aviation* vi. 173 The superior performance offered by the first bombers with swept-back wings won them the orders. **1969** *Daily Tel.* 1 Oct. 16/8 Performance: Acceleration: 0–60 mph 12·3 seconds; 50–70 mph in top gear 13 seconds. Speed in gears, 1st 30 mph, 2nd 48 mph, 3rd 75 mph... Fuel consumption: 26·3 mpg (overall); 30·6 mpg (touring). **1976** *Ibid.* 18 Feb. 10 (Advt.), Today we give you details of a high-performance FM tuner. **1976** *Daily Mail* (Hull) 30 Sept. 11/3 A performance car with a top speed in excess of 100 mph, it runs at over 30 mpg on two-star petrol. **1977** P. HARCOURT *At High Risk* i. 90 If you're interested in performance cars, as I am, you're also mildly interested in the people who drive them.

d. *Psychol.* The observable or measurable behaviour of a person or animal in a particular, usu. experimental, situation.

1898 E. L. THORNDIKE in *Psychol. Rev. Monogr. Suppl.* II. IV. 39 The best interpretation of even the most extraordinary performances of animals has been that they were the result of accident and association or imitation. **1901** *Psychol. Rev. Monogr. Suppl.* III. VI. 2 All human performances, when objectified in units of space, time, etc., seem to follow certain laws of variability. **1912** *Psychol. Rev.* XIX. 73 (*title*) The influence of caffein on the speed and quality of performance in typewriting. **1938** R. S. WOODWORTH *Exper. Psychol.* vi. 138 Several varieties of performance preferential have been discovered. **1949** STOUFFER & DEVINNEY in S. A. Stouffer et al. *Amer. Soldier* I. iii. 85 Morale is presumed to be an important element in performance. **1951** *Mind* LX. 2 The performance or non-performance of a certain act.. we shall call performance-values. **1959** E. GINZBERG et al. *Patterns of Performance* xiii. 272 We did not choose the concept of performance potential because of its predictive value. **1964** COFER & APPLEY *Motivation* xi. 520 This distinction between learning and performance and the effects of drive on performance constitute the second problem.

e. *Linguistics.* (See quots.) Opp. *competence.*

1963 N. CHOMSKY in R. D. Luce et al. *Handbk. Math. Psychol.* II. 326 A generative grammar..can be regarded as a partial theory of what the mature speaker of the language knows. It in no sense purports to be a description of his actual performance. **1964** —— in *Proc. 9th Internat. Congr. Linguists* 915 Clearly the description of linguistic competence provided by the grammar is not to be confused with an account of actual performance. **1964** *Harvard Educ. Rev.* XXXIV. 263 The distinction between competence and performance or language and speech is quite crucial for understanding at least three goals related to linguistic descriptions proper. **1966, 1969** [see *COMPETENCE 4f]. **1971** B. L. LILES *Introd. Transformational Gram.* i. 8 Another way of stating this is to say that he is interested in the speaker's competence, or knowledge of the language, rather than in his performance, or actual use of it. **1976** *Word 1971* XXVII. 144 He simply recalls our linguistic habits, our performances, as Chomsky would say.

3. d. A display of temperament, anger, or exaggerated behaviour; a fuss or 'scene'; a difficult or annoying action or procedure. *colloq.*

1936 G. B. SHAW *Six of Calais* 94 They tear a piece of linen from the back of his shirt, and bind his mouth with it. He barks to the last moment. John of Gaunt laughs ecstatically at this performance, and sets off some of the soldiers. *Ibid.* 100 *Peter* (growling in his face like a dog) Grrrr!!! *The King* (returning the growl chin to chin) Grrrr!!!!!! They repeat this performance, to the great scandal of the Queen, until it develops into a startling imitation of a dog fight. **1962** A. NISBETT *Technique Sound Studio* x. 176 Dialling is rather more of a performance than being on the receiving end of a phone call. **1964** J. SYMONS *End of Solomon Grundy* III. iii. 180 For Christ's sake don't let's make a performance out of it. **1971** A. PRICE *Alamut Ambush* i. 16 He had to come here and tell you all about it and make a great performance of it.

5. *attrib.* and *Comb.*, as **performance art**, a form of visual art in which the activity of the artist forms a central feature, combining static elements with dramatic performance; so **performance artist**; **performance bond**, a bond issued by a bank or other financial concern, guaranteeing the fulfilment of a particular contract; **performance test**, (*a*) *Psychol.* (in sense *2 d), a non-verbal test of capability or intelligence based on the performance of certain manual tasks; (*b*) the measurement of weight gain, food conversion, and other heritable characteristics of farm animals, as a guide to selective breeding; also **performance testing**; so **performance-tested** *a.*, having had heritable qualities evaluated.

1971 *Rolling Stone* 24 June 37 *Performance art* is basically an extension of art into the theater, often involving more or less set programs at specified times and places... A..work of performance art was staged by..cars whose drivers all sounded their horns according to a prearranged score, and the noise was broadcast by a local radio station. **1976** *National Observer* (U.S.) 7 Feb. 20/2 Not quite the same as theater or dance, though it combines elements of both, performance art grew out of *avant-garde* movements, particularly in poetry and painting, that swept Europe early this century. **1978** *Times* 23 Nov. 18/1 Three fine arts graduates were discovered walking around East Anglia with a pole on their heads, supported by a council grant for a work of performance art. **1976** *Observer* 11 Apr. 2/3 Despite his outlandish name, P-Orridge..is one of Britain's leading young 'performance' artists, a type of art in which the artist includes himself in his work. **1976** *Loughborough Monitor* 26 Nov. 7/4 Mr. Richards, who describes himself as a performance artist and lives in Nottingham, had applied for a grant for his Christmas show. **1979** *Listener* 22 Feb. 293/2 There were performances by three performance artists... Kevin Atherton stripped off all his clothes on the gallery steps. **1938** *Sun* (Baltimore) 3 June 4/3 It is.. a general practice that the solicitor writing the 'bid bonds' also writes the 'performance bond' of the same contractor if his bid is accepted. **1965** PERRY & RYDER *Thomson's Dict. Banking* (ed. 11) 436/1 Perhaps the most common type of performance bond is that given on behalf of a customer who is entering upon a housing contract for a local authority. **1970** *Globe & Mail* (Toronto) 26 Sept. B1/7 A performance bond with the amount of $10-million issued by the Commercial Union Insurance Co. in favor of Prince Albert [Pulp] is in existence. **1977** *Offshore Engineer* Apr. 18/1 Venezuelan conditions included a 25% performance bond and no progress payments. **1917** PINTNER & PATERSON (*title*) A scale of performance tests. *Ibid.* p. v, The work grew directly out of the psychological examination of deaf children... This work was begun in 1914 with the standardization of a few performance tests. **1921** R. S. WOODWORTH *Psychol.* (1922) xii. 275 Language plays little part in a performance test. **1932** J. L. LUSH in *Proc. Soc. Animal Production* XXIV. 52 The swine Record of Performance test is regarded as a progeny test of the sire and dam rather than as a performance test of the individual pigs which are fattened and slaughtered. **1954** *Jrnl. Animal Sci.* XIII. 215 Few sheep breeders have the necessary assistance, time and facilities to conduct a progeny and performance testing programme. **1959** *Ibid.* XVIII. 1464 Seven years' data..were analyzed to determine the effectiveness of using final weight as a criterion in the selection of performance tested bulls. *Ibid.* 1465 Fifteen bulls and twenty-three heifers were placed on experiment to compare three systems of performance testing. **1970** PRESTON & WILLIS *Intensive Beef Production* iii. 132 Performance testing involves the measurement of traits in the live animal... The major advantage of performance testing is that it permits evaluation of the animal at a much earlier age than is possible with progeny testing. *Ibid.* 137 Bulls on performance test should not be given hormone treatment. *Ibid.*, The object of any system of performance testing must be to evaluate.. genetic differences between animals in terms of their phenotypic expression. **1971** *Farmer & Stockbreeder* 23 Feb. 13/3 Co-operative breeding schemes, designed to get the most impressive, performance-tested bulls widely used. **1972** *Encycl. Psychol.* II. 379/2 Performance tests are especially useful for subjects with some speech disability. **1977** *N.Z. Herald* 8 Jan. 2–8/7 (Advt.), Modern methods of management are being used to produce performance-tested rams and bulls for the department's other blocks throughout the province.

performative (pəɹfǭ·ɹmǎtiv), *a.* and *sb.* [f. PERFORM *v.* + -ATIVE, as in *imperative.*] **A.** *adj.* Of or pertaining to performance; *spec.* designating or pertaining to an utterance that effects an action by being spoken or written or by means of which the speaker performs a particular act. **B.** *sb.* Such an utterance. Hence **perfo·rmatively** *adv.*, **perfo·rmativeness.**

1955 J. L. AUSTIN *How to do Things with Words* (1962) i. 6 What are we to call a sentence or an utterance of this type? I propose to call it a performative sentence or a performative utterance, or, for short, 'a performative'. **1955** A. J. AYER in B. I. Evans *Stud. in Communication* 27 There are very many uses of language, prescriptive, ritualistic, playful, or performative, which are not fact-stating. **1956** J. HOLLANDER in *Jrnl. Aesthetics* XV. 239 A *performative* system of scansion..would present a series of rules governing a locutionary reading of a particular poem, before a real or implied audience. It would end up by *describing* not the poem itself, but the unstated canons of taste behind the rules. Performative systems of scansion, disguised as descriptive ones, have composed all but a few of the metrical studies of the past. **1960** *Proc. Aristotelian Soc.* LX. p. v, The most famous of his [*sc.* J. L. Austin's] discoveries in this field was of the element of performativeness that enters into many kinds of utterance ordinarily classified as statements. **1963** J. LYONS *Structural Semantics* ii. 33 The philosophers have accustomed us to the wide variety of uses which the verb *know* can have... Among them they distinguish what has been called a 'performative' use. **1964** R. H. ROBINS *Gen. Linguistics* 23 It is best to regard knowledge of the meaning or meanings of a word as a performative knowledge (like knowing how to ride a bicycle). **1970** *Language* XLVI. 35 It is probable that the notion of the declarative sentence can be defined in terms of performatives. *Ibid.* 100 *For* clauses..provide important evidence for the performative analysis. **1973** *Archivum Linguisticum* IV. 82 Being an imperative construction, it would presumably require the postulation of an underlying performative. **1973** *Times Lit. Suppl.* 5 Oct. 1161/5 Illocutionary acts of *x*-ing could be made explicit..by use of the 'performative' first-person present-indicative form 'I *x*'—e.g. acts of asking by prefacing the question by the phrase 'I ask you:..'. **1973** G. W. TURNER *Stylistics* vii. 208 A performative utterance has validity if the speaker's social position entitles him to make it; it is therefore often part of an occupational language. **1976** *Archivum Linguisticum* VII. 69 The same applies to the everyday use (as opposed to the analysis) of speech act labels, whether these are used performatively or not. **1976** P. DONOVAN *Relig. Lang.* vii. 80 Performative words are used, for instance, when we vote for a motion by saying 'Aye', bid in an auction by shouting 'Fifty pounds', or adjourn a meeting with the words 'The meeting is adjourned'. **1978** *Listener* 30 Mar. 396/3 When I say, 'I promise', or 'I bet' or 'I apologise' or 'Thanks'..these he called 'performatives'.

performatory (pəɹfǭ·ɹmǎtəri), *a.* and *sb.* [f. as prec.: see -ORY².] = prec. Hence **perfo·rmatorily** *adv.*

1949 *Mind* LVIII. 359 To make a promise is to perform an *act* in which language is involved as an integral part... Mr. J. L. Austin distinguishes this as the 'performatory' use of language. I am indebted to him for this point. **1949** *Philosophy* XXIV. 90 There are..performatory sentences like 'I name this ship Shamrock'. **1951** *Aristotelian Soc. Suppl. Vol.* XXV. 207 Group I [*sc.* the verbs 'advise', 'order', 'command', 'tell'] can be used performatorily, but Group II [*sc.* the verbs 'persuade', 'induce', 'cause', 'get'] cannot; thus I can say 'I advise you to make yourself scarce before he comes', but not 'I persuade you to make yourself scarce before he comes'. **1955** J. L. AUSTIN *How to do Things with Words* (1962) i. 6 Formerly I used 'performatory': but 'performative' is to be preferred. *Ibid.* ii. 12 A few simple utterances of the kind known as performatories or performatives. **1966** L. J. COHEN *Diversity of Meaning* (ed. 2) i. 1 Their arguments have often relied on such distinctions as those between customary and indirect meaning, logical words and object words,..or performatory and non-performatory verb-uses. **1967** *Listener* 2 Feb. 162/1 The listener.. may have expected a more substantial work than was due to be played... If he perseveres with it, what sounded prefatory can come to sound performatory.

performer. Add: **2. b.** One who 'performs' (see *PERFORM *v.* 7e); one who causes trouble or disturbance. *slang* (chiefly *Naut.*).

1937 PARTRIDGE *Dict. Slang* 619/1 *Performer*,..one who is apt to make a great fuss or noise. **1946** *Seafarers' Log* 6 Dec. 10/5 You get a performer aboard a ship who makes it bad not only for himself but for the crew and the Union. **1958** E. S. LAND *Winning War with Ships* xiv. 193 In the early months of World War II unions were battling against a threat of the Navy taking over merchant marine personnel because of reported incidents of drunkenness, insubordination and trouble making by individuals whom the unions called 'performers'.

performing *vbl. sb.* Add: **4. performing art,** an art (such as the dance, drama, etc.) involving public performance (chiefly *pl.*); **performing right,** add: usu. *pl.* (further examples).

1929 J. B. PRIESTLEY *Good Companions* III. iii. 534 Performing rights, sheet music, gramophone records... There's bags of money in it. **1946** *N.Y. Times* 7 June 21/5 The High School of the Performing Arts will differ from other vocational or academic schools in several important details. **1961** V. KREPELA in *Webster* s.v. performing adj., Project an image of the U.S. through displays, films, publications, fine arts, and the performing arts. **1967** CHUJOY & MANCHESTER *Dance Encycl.* 719/2 The function of Performing Arts School is not to create artists, but rather to prepare competent craftsmen. **1968** *Listener* 8 Aug. 177/3 When I did my first film..someone said: 'It may not be so much money they are paying you down, but you get an income from it for performing rights.' **1971** *Times* 22 Feb. (Canada Suppl.) p. vii/3 It is much more comfortable politically to subsidize the performing arts (where results can be seen and enjoyed by large numbers of voters) than to support the creative individuals. **1974** *Times* 9 Oct. 18/1 All that is best in our performing arts depends for its survival on money. **1976** *National Observer* (U.S.) 23 Oct. 15/2 You'll find some kind of alliance developing among performing-arts centers in cities like Washington, Denver, Los Angeles. **1977** *Rolling Stone* 7 Apr. 35/2 The performing-rights organization negotiates license fees with *commercial* users (nonprofit organizations, such as churches and schools, are exempt from paying for use of copyrighted material).

performing, *ppl. a.* Add: **2.** (Earlier and later examples.) Esp. designating a flea trained to perform tricks; also *fig.*

1854 DICKENS *Hard T.* I. iii. 14 Signor Jupe was that afternoon to 'elucidate the diverting accomplishments of his highly trained performing dog Merrylegs'. **1889** G. B. SHAW *London Music 1888–89* (1937) 205 The only artist who never gets accustomed to his part is the performing flea who fires a cannon. **1922** E. WALLACE *Flying Fifty-Five* vii. 45 Your last stable was a stable of performing fleas, for I swear you know nothing about horses. **1953** WODEHOUSE (*title*) Performing flea: a self-portrait in letters. **1966** M. WOODHOUSE *Tree Frog* xviii. 134 Driver came me a look as though I were a performing seal. **1973** 'E. PETERS' *City of Gold & Shadows* ii. 29 The secret of success with performing fleas..is to synchronise your orders with their hops. **1978** D. BLOODWORTH *Crosstalk* xxi. 167 I'm a cop. I run a team of performing dogs—the best in the business.

perfume, *sb.* Add: **3.** *perfume atomizer, spray*; *perfume-sprayed* adj.

1897 *Sears, Roebuck Catal.* 329/1 A fine imitation cut glass perfume atomizer. **1942** E. PAUL *Narrow St.* xxviii. 254 He began to throw Jeanne's toilet articles at her, perfume atomizer, box of powder, lipstick, mirror. **1973** M. & G. GORDON *Informant* xxxvi. 142 Out spilled a wallet, lipstick,..a perfume atomizer, nail file. **1898** *Illustr. London News* 22 Jan. 126 (Advt.), These concentrated perfume sprays give a delightful refreshing coolness. **1926–7** *Army & Navy Stores Catal.* 498/2 Perfume sprays. **1975** D. BEATY *Electric Train* 42 Daphne was sitting at the dressing-table, her perfume spray in her hand. **1922** JOYCE *Ulysses* 523 As they are now, so will you be, wigged, singed, perfumesprayed, ricepowdered, with smoothshaven armpits.

perfusate (pəɹfiū·zēit). *Med.* [f. PERFUS(E *v.* + *-ate*, after *filtrate, precipitate*, etc.] Any fluid used for perfusion.

1915 *Amer. Jrnl. Physiol.* XXXVIII. 201 Winterstein perfused new-born rabbits with saline solution..and concluded that the hydrogen-ion concentration of the perfusate governed the function of the respiratory center. **1938** *Nature* 29 Oct. 800/2 The frog's liver perfused with a saline solution can secrete natural and artificial pigments in concentrations many hundred times those in the perfusate. **1961** *Jrnl. Clin. Invest.* XL. 1079/2 Solutions pumped into the oral end of the tube entered the intestine at a known site; 15 cm distally the perfusate was aspirated and collected from the anal end of the tube. **1968** *Sci. Jrnl.* Nov. 63/3 The use of balanced salt solution perfusates without red cells (solutions having a composition similar to extra-cellular fluid). *Ibid.* 64/2 Blood and a variety of other perfusates were studied.

perfuse, *v.* Add: **3.** *Med.* To supply (an organ, tissue, or body) with a fluid artificially by circulating it through blood vessels or other natural channels; to pass a fluid through (a hollow organ).

1903 *Jrnl. Physiol.* XXIX. 266 The method of examining the physiological action of an organ or tissue by perfusing it by blood after its removal from the body has already proved of great value. **1920** *Amer. Jrnl. Physiol.* LII. 101 Using a mixture of red cells and whole serum or diluted serum or modified Locke's solution, the investigator should be able to perfuse satisfactorily the various organs or combinations of organs and tissues. **1962** *Lancet* 6 Jan. 13/2 Radiography will then reveal whether anastomoses exist, by showing the radio-opaque material in arteries which were not perfused. **1965** *Gut* VI. 387/2 After perfusing the intestine for 30 minutes a steady state is reached, and intraluminal contents are then aspirated through a hole. **1966** *Maclean's Mag.* 2 Apr. 18/3 The current belief is that before freezing the body should be perfused—that is, the blood should be replaced with a chemical that would prevent, or at least minimize, cellular damage during freezing. **1971** *Jrnl. Physiol.* CCXVI. 735 The lumen was perfused with a raffinose-electrolyte solution having a low sodium concentration.

Hence **perfu·sed** *ppl. a.*, (of an organ, etc.) kept supplied with a flow of fluid; (of a fluid) supplied as a substitute for blood; **perfu·sing** *vbl. sb.*

1903 *Jrnl. Physiol.* XXIX. 271 Difficulties in the way of obtaining a sufficiently rapid rate of flow through the perfused organ. **1906** *Ibid.* XXXV. 54 The amount of oxygen in the perfused liquid and the rate of perfusion were as far as possible controlled. **1916** *Amer. Jrnl. Physiol.* XL. 516 With the perfusing fluid running..a cannula is passed into the popliteal below the nutrient artery. **1962** *Lancet* 6 Jan. 13/2 Another unreported source of error is the perfusing of hearts still affected by rigor mortis.

perfusion. Add: **d.** *Med.* The process of passing through an organ or tissue a fluid, esp. treated blood or a substitute for blood; the treatment of a patient by a continuous transfusion of prepared blood. Freq. *attrib.*

1903 *Jrnl. Physiol.* XXIX. 266 Special arrangements were provided for quantitatively determining the changes of the blood gases in the perfusion. **1910** *Ibid.* XL. 297 Perfusion experiments with tortoise hearts were made by Gaskell in 1883, his perfusion liquid being a mixture of 1 part of sheep's blood and 2 of saline. **1940** C. S. Sherrington *Man on his Nature* iii. 87 The perfusion-fluid itself is chemical nutriment for all the cells of the body, supporting their energy-needs. **1963** *Gastroenterology* XLIV. 134/2 Absorption was studied by transintestinal intubation with polyvinyl tubing..with a perfusion technique. **1969** *Jrnl. Physiol.* CCIV. 22P In order to show that it was the ionic composition of the perfusion fluid which produced the changes..rather than the experimental procedure, perfusion of both vasa deferentia with Krebs-Ringer preceded perfusion of one vas deferens with the test solution. **1972** *Brit. Med. Jrnl.* 1 Jan. 23/1 Two patients in deep hepatic coma due to fulminant viral hepatitis were treated by extracorporeal baboon liver perfusion. *Ibid.* 23/2 The liver was aseptically removed from healthy baboons..; it was immediately cooled by perfusion with a chilled electrolyte solution..and then taken to the perfusion apparatus in the patient's room. Perfusion was started after 30–40 minutes of cold ischaemia and was maintained for a period of 13–16 hours.

perfusionist (pəɹfiū·ʒənist). *Med.* [f. prec. + -ist.] The member of a surgical team responsible for the perfusion of a patient while his circulation is interrupted.

1964 *Sunday Mail Mag.* (Brisbane) 25 Oct. 2/3 The doctor who assembles the machine is a perfusionist. He will operate the machine during the operation. **1975** *Islander* (Victoria, B.C.) 21 Sept. 3/4 Although there are five anaesthetists, Mr. Kemna is the only perfusionist and assists at every open heart operation.

Pergamene (pɜ̄·ɹgămīn), *sb.* and *a.* Also **Pergame·nian** (6 **Pargamenian,** 9 **-onian**), **Pergame·nic.** [f. L. *Pergamum*, Gr. *Πέργαμος, -ον* city and capital of an ancient kingdom in Asia Minor.] **A.** *sb.* An inhabitant of Pergamum. **B.** *adj.* Of or pertaining to Pergamum, the school of sculpture that flourished there in the third and second centuries B.C., or the Church founded there in the first century after Christ.

1579 North tr. *Plutarch's Lives* 1056 He wrote vnto the Pargamenians in this sorte. [**1608** Topsell *Serpents* 122 Wee doe read that the Pergameni did buy..certaine peeces of a Cockatrice.] **1774** T. Reid in Ld. Kames *Sk. Hist. Man* II. iii. 168 He [*sc.* Aristotle] was the first we know, says Strabo, who composed a library. And in this the Egyptian and Pergamenian kings, copied his example. *a* **1823** R. Culbertson *Lect. Revelation* (1826) I. xvi. 214 Pergamos..together with all that territory over which the Pergamonian princes bore rule, was bequeathed by Attalus..to the Romans. **1865** J. B. Lightfoot *Galatians* 5 The Pergamene prince Attalus the first effectually curbed their power. **1867** C. M. Yonge *Pupils of St. John* vi. 87 The sharp piercing two-edged sword of the Word of God..was held up threateningly to warn the Pergamenes. **1896** *Pall Mall Gaz.* 19 May 3/2 A victorious king..is to be met by a troop of priests, and conducted to the Pergamenic altar. **1903** *Westm. Gaz.* 23 Sept. 3/2 Visitors..will be delighted to recognise the Pergamenian type of the so-called 'Dying Alexander'. **1904** W. M. Ramsay in *Expositor* June 407 The honourable history and the steadfast loyalty of the Pergamenian Church..had been tarnished by the error of a small part of the congregation. *Ibid.* 409 We shall find that both in the Thyatiran and in the Pergamenian letter St. John exalts the dignity, authority and power that shall fall to the lot of the victorious Christian. **1926** *Chambers's Jrnl.* 11 Sept. 649/1 It is this temple..which is referred to as 'Satan's throne' in St John's letter to the Pergamene Church. **1947** E. V. Hansen *Attalids of Pergamon* vi. 157 Five envoys were sent by the Pergamenes to both cities to obtain..the evidence of the contending parties. *Ibid.* viii. 277 Another sculptor who had a long career at the court of the Attalids was a native Pergamene, Epigonus the son of Charius. **1960** R. Carpenter *Greek Sculpture* vii. 191 The Pergamenian rulers conceived the ambition to bring that golden period to life. **1968** G. E. Bean *Turkey's Southern Shore* vi. 81 The figure of Nike, goddess of victory, which appears on..coins of Side may commemorate a victory won by the city against the Pergamenes. **1972** P. M. Fraser *Ptolemaic Alexandria* I. iii. 98 A Pergamene inscription tells us that the supreme magistrates of the city..were appointed by the King at least on one occasion. **1972** 'M. Innes' *Open House* xiv. 138 This revolting masterpiece of the Pergamene school.

pergelisol (pɜ̄·ɹdʒe·lisǫl). *Geomorphol.* [f. Per-[1] + L. *gel-āre* to freeze + -i- + *-sol.] = *permafrost.

1946 K. Bryan in *Amer. Jrnl. Sci.* CCXLIV. 635 It is impossible to make a verb or a verbal noun from 'permafrost' as 'permafrosting' and 'permafrosted' imply that a permanent surface or coating has been applied... Further, the term cannot be easily converted into other European languages. These various objections can be met by a new term... Such a word is 'pergelisol'. **1963** *Geomorphol. Abstr.* 38 Canada, in the opinion of Dr. Hamelin, can be divided into eleven periglacial 'provinces'. The first four provinces: Elizabeth, Victoria, Keewatin and Innuit are closely associated with continuous pergelisol. **1968** R. W. Fairbridge *Encycl. Geomorphol.* 1185/1 The south- to west-facing slopes thaw earlier and more deeply than the opposite ones, where the pergelisol remains near the surface. **1972** Sparks & West *Ice Age in Brit.* iv. 99 With this wholly admirable intensification of study [of periglacial phenomena] has come a wholly regrettable spate of jargon, not all of which fortunately has found favour. Thus, most people still speak of frost shattering rather than congelifraction, active layer rather than mollisol, permafrost rather than pergelisol.

perhapser (pəɹhæ·psəɹ). *slang.* [f. Perhaps *adv.* (*sb.*) + -er[1].] A risky stroke in cricket.

1954 J. Fingleton *Ashes crown Year* xxiii. 247 Morris somewhat luckily got Bedser fine for 4... It was what cricketers know as a 'perhapser'. **1957** D. Stivens *Scholarly Mouse* (1958) 86 Did you ever see such a p'rapser—he pushed a yorker away for four!

perhexiline (pəɹhe·ksilīn). *Pharm.* [Arbitrary blend of Pi)peridine and Hexyl.] A white crystalline solid which is a vasodilator, tablets of the maleate of which are given for the relief of angina pectoris; 2-(2,2-dicyclohexylethyl)piperidine, $C_{19}H_{35}N$.

1969 *Current Therapeutic Res.* XI. 99 A clinical study was undertaken to explore the effectiveness of perhexiline in relief of angina pectoris. **1970** *Chest* LVIII. 579/2 There was slowing of the heart rate as a result of the infusion of perhexiline. **1977** *Lancet* 30 July 260/1 The Committee on Safety of Medicines has circulated an adverse-reactions warning about perhexiline maleate ('Pexid'). *Ibid.* 12 Nov. 1028/1 During treatment with perhexiline maleate hypoglycæmia, hyperlipidæmia, and liver dysfunction have been reported.

peri-, *prefix.* Add: **1. a. perianal** (examples); **peria·pical,** situated or occurring around the apex of the root of a tooth; **pe:riaquedu·ctal,** situated around the aqueduct of the midbrain; **pericapi·llary,** around a capillary blood vessel; **periceme·ntal,** of or pertaining to the pericementum; **perico·lic,** situated or occurring around the colon; **perige·nital,** situated in the area around the genitals; **perigona·dial,** situated around a gonad; **perihæ·mal** *Zool.* [ad. G. *perihämal* (H. Ludwig 1877, in *Zeitschr. f. Wissensch. Zool.* XXX. 123)], used to designate certain vessels and cavities in echinoderms and other invertebrates (see quots.); **periodontal:** hence **periodo·ntally** *adv.*; **pe:riurete·ric,** around one or both ureters.

1890 Billings *Med. Dict.* II. 311/1 Perianal. **1897** *Q. Jrnl. Microsc. Sci.* XL. 291 [In the larval form of *Phoronis*] there are three prominent ciliated bands... Of the three the perianal band is the most prominent. **1971** G. H. Bourne *Ape People* xi. 246 Goodall suggests that the function of the swollen perianal region of the sexually receptive chimpanzee..is to signal to males..that the female is in fact in estrus. **1977** *Lancet* 20 Aug. 403/2 The perioral and perianal zones are bright and red. **1920** Endelman & Wagner *Gen. & Dental Path.* xxxi. 422 The periapical tissues may be invaded by bacteria which from the start give rise to chronic symptoms. **1974** H. P. Hitchcock *Orthodontics for Undergraduates* xxviii. 480 Periapical lesion around a replanted tooth. **1950** *Physiol. Rev.* XXX. 460 Excitable foci may be followed caudalward..through the periaqueductal grey. **1973** *Nature* 26 Oct. 447/2 Binding in the periaqueductal area of the midbrain was about the same as that of the posterior amygdala. **1928** *Anatomical Rec.* XXXIX. 45 The impression seems to be general..that there is but one type of pericapillary cell. **1953** *Jrnl. Appl. Physics* XXIV. 1424/1 They [*sc.* the endothelial cells] possess..a large number of vesicles concentrated immediately under the cell membranes facing both the capillary lumen and the pericapillary spaces. **1977** *Lancet* 25 June 1364/2 The basal ganglia, thalamus, corpus callosum, and cerebral white-matter are peppered with innumerable pericapillary and periarteriolar microinfarcts, which sometimes coalesce into larger areas of softening. **1886** Pericemental [see *implantation 5 b]. **1940** H. K. Box *Twelve Periodontal Studies* v. 84 The formation, in the pericementum, of a new tissue..changes the normal arrangement of the pericemental structures, and..replaces the bone substance of the alveolar process. **1907** *Allbutt's Syst. Med.* (ed. 2) III. 1015 Pericolic inflammation may be excited by external violence. **1939** *Times* 20 Feb. 12/7 Lieutenant-Colonel Anderson I.M.S., successfully operated on Lord Brabourne, the Governor of Bengal, at Government House yesterday for pericolic inflammation. **1965** *Arch. Surg.* XCI. 407/2 The final diagnosis was pericolic abscess surrounding a solitary diverticulum of the ascending colon. **1962** *Science Survey* III. 261 The perianal and perigenital glands of the *Mustelidae* like the stoat, skunk, civet, and others..play an important part in the sexual and social life of their carriers. **1971** *Nature* 7 May 50/1 These results clearly established a sex difference in the development of perigenital adipose tissue. **1888** *Ibid.* 22 Mar. 498/2 The perigonadial spaces (so-called generative glands) and the pericardial space..are, then, the cœlom of the mollusca... In Cephalopods..the pericardial and perigonadial cœlomic remnants are continuous, and form one cavity. **1942** Grove & Newell *Animal Biol.* xiv. 220 Each gonad then acquires a cavity—the primary gonadial cavity—and becomes almost completely surrounded by a secondary or perigonadial cavity (gonocoel). **1881** *Q. Jrnl. Microsc. Sci.* XXI. 171 The space..between the water-vessel above and the ambulacral epithelium below, which is traversed by the perforated longitudinal septum, was named by Ludwig the 'perihæmal canal'. It had been previously called the nerve-vessel or nerve-canal, and was supposed to form an integral part of the blood-vascular system. Now, however, it is regarded by Ludwig merely as a derivate of the body-cavity. **1897** *Ibid.* XL. 321 The front dorsal part of the trunk cœlom is produced into a pair of perihæmal spaces, embracing the dorsal blood-vessel. **1962** D. Nichols *Echinoderms* ii. 27 Perihaemal system. As its name suggests, this system normally surrounds the haemal complex, though some recent authors prefer to call it the hyponeural sinus system, referring to its relation to one part of the nervous system. **1955** J. Osborne *Dental Mech.* (ed. 4) ix. 148 Periodontally diseased teeth. **1975** H. Thomson *Occlusion* xi. 215 Periodontally disturbed abutment teeth..may have to be crowned and splinted to sound adjacent teeth. **1900** Dorland *Med. Dict.* 496/1 *Periureteric*, about the ureter. **1962** *Lancet* 6 Jan. 31/2 The causes of hydronephrosis included prostatic hypertrophy, bladderneck obstruction, periureteric fibrosis, and aberrant renal vessels.

b. pericementum (earlier and later examples); **periodontium,** add: in mod. use, all the tissues surrounding a tooth, including the alveolar process, the cementum, and the gingiva, as well as the periodontal membrane; (examples); (*periodontum* is now *Obs.*).

1879 C. F. W. Bödecker in *Dental Cosmos* XXI. 593 The pericementum (root membrane, or alveolo-dental periosteum, etc., as it has been termed by former writers) is a formation of connective tissue, identical with the periosteum which covers all bones. **1940** Pericementum [see *pericemental* above]. **1881** T. E. Satterthwaite *Man. Histol.* viii. 108 The development of the cement takes place precisely as bone is produced, viz., from the periosteum, or..from the fibrous tissue of the tooth-sac, the periodontium. **1922** K. H. Thoma *Oral Roentgenol.* (ed. 2) iv. 196 *Periodontium*, the pericementum and all investing structures of the teeth. **1927** O. E. Inglis *Burchard's Text-bk. Dental Path. & Therapeutics* (ed. 7) xvi. 536 All those tissues which invest the teeth including the pericementum.., the alveolar process and the gingivae, particularly the marginal and cemental gingivae are now generally understood as included in the term periodontium. **1940** H. K. Box *Twelve Periodontal Studies* ii. 29 In 1920, the writer first used the term 'periodontium' to designate the supporting tissues of the teeth, and to embrace as the three essential tissue-components, the gingivae, the periodontal membrane, and alveolar process. As the word 'periodontium' was occasionally used to denote the periodontal membrane, it was felt that the usage of the term in this new sense would make for exactness in terminology. **1969** *Gloss. Terms Dentistry* (*B.S.I.*) 67 *Periodontium*, the collective term for the tissues immediately surrounding the teeth.

c. periarteritis, add: [coined in Ger. as *periarteritis nodosa* (Kussmaul & Maier 1866, in *Deutsch. Arch. f. klin. Med.* I. 484)]; = *polyarteritis* s.v. *poly- 1; *periarteritis nodosa* (nodō·ză) [L. *nōdōsus* knotty, f. *nōdus* a knot], an often fatal form of periarteritis characterized by the formation of aneurysms; (earlier and later examples); **pe:ricementi·tis,** inflammation of the pericementum of a tooth.

1876 Dunglison *Dict. Med. Sci.* (rev. ed.) 773/2 *Periarteritis*, inflammation of the sheath of an artery. **1892** F. P. Foster *Med. Dict.* IV. 2547/1 *P*[*eriarteritis*] *nodosa*, a thickening of the intima and infiltration of the adventitia of an artery, producing a nodular prominence. **1933** *Practitioners Libr. Med. & Surg.* III. cxii. 1136 Periarteritis nodosa is a rare disease affecting medium-sized arteries in any portion of the body, most commonly in males between the ages of twenty and forty. **1961** R. D. Baker *Essent. Path.* viii. 136 The interaction of antigen and antibody may produce lesions in the heart, liver and kidneys resembling those of periarteritis nodosa. **1974** R. M. KIRK et al. *Surgery* ii. 9 Generalised diseases such as infections, uraemia, diabetes, scurvy, periarteritis..nodosa..and food allergies may be associated with frailty of the capillary walls. **1882** *Dental Rec.* II. 441 A little sensitiveness becomes noticeable..indicating a beginning of pericementitis. **1969** LUEBKE & MULLANEY in Morris & Bohannan *Dental Specialities in Gen. Practice* viii. 357/2 Pericementitis..sometimes follows overinstrumentation or overmedication of a noninfected canal.

periapsis (periˌæ·psis). *Astr.* [f. PERI- + APSIS, after PERIGEE, PERIHELION, etc.] That point in the path of a natural or artificial satellite at which it is closest to a primary.

1964 J. L. NAYLER *Dict. Astronautics* 194 *Periastron* (*periapsis*), the nearest point on the orbit of a stellar satellite to the star, or in a binary star the point at which the companion is nearest to the primary. **1971** *Nature* 26 Nov. 168/3 The manoeuvre, which changed the orbit of the spacecraft so that periapsis (closest approach to Mars) is now 868 miles. **1972** *Daily Colonist* (Victoria, B.C.) 25 Feb. 5/2 Pioneer will be close to Jupiter for about four days (100 hours) and will see the planet in full sunlight 50 hours before periapsis, or the closest point of the fly-by. **1976** *Sci. Amer.* June 59/1 Those commands will..place the spacecraft in an elliptical orbit around Mars that will vary in altitude from 33,000 kilometers at apoapsis down to 1,500 kilometers at periapsis.

periauger. Read: Var. PIRAGUA 2.

1898 *Rudder* Dec. 407/2 Let go our hook just ahead of a large periauger-rigged sharpie, called the Pirate. **1899** *Ibid.* Feb. 53/1 Her rig is that of a perianger [*sic*]—or, as some call it, a double cat—having two masts with a boom and gaff sail on each.

pericardium. Add: Hence also **pe:ricard(i)e·ctomy** [*-ECTOMY], surgical removal of all or part of the pericardium; **perica:rdiocente·sis** [Gr. κέντησις pricking], surgical puncturing of the pericardium.

[**1900** DORLAND *Med. Dict.* 491/2 Pericardicentesis.] **1913** STEDMAN *Med. Dict.* (ed. 2) 672/2 Pericardectomy... Pericardiectomy. **1938** M. THOREK *Mod. Surg. Technic* II. xxxi. 1206 Technic of pericardiocentesis. *Ibid.* 1212 (*heading*) Pericardiectomy in the treatment of the Pick syndrome. **1956** W. P. CLELAND in Bailey & Love *Short Pract. Surg.* (ed. 10) xliii. 892 At operation (pericardectomy) it is essential to remove the thickened pericardium from the ventricles. **1967** S. TAYLOR et al. *Short Textbk. Surg.* xvi. 223 Constrictive pericarditis... Pericardiectomy is the treatment of choice, and is best done through a vertical incision splitting the sternum, which affords excellent exposure. **1977** *Lancet* 6 Aug. 301/2, 15 underwent pericardiocenteses (with recurrent of effusion afterwards) before definitive therapy by pericardial drainage and local steroid instillation. *Ibid.* 15 Oct. 817/1, 3 of these 17 had tamponade which was successfully treated by pericardectomy.

pericentric, *a.* Add: **2.** *Cytology.* [cf. *-CENTRIC 2.] Involving parts of a chromosome at both sides of the centromere. Opp. *PARACENTRIC *a.*

1938 [see *PARACENTRIC *a.*]. **1962** *Lancet* 6 Jan. 21/2 Chromosome analyses in a girl with mongolism and in her parents have disclosed abnormalities which we attribute to pericentric inversion of a maternal 21st chromosome. **1973** *Nature* 3 Aug. 260/2 The very fact that some X chromosomes, such as that of the mouse are acrocentrics reveals that pericentric inversions did occasionally occur. **1977** *Ibid.* 6 Jan. 65/2 The aberrant chromosome was interpreted as an aneusomic recombinant from the father who was heterozygous for a pericentric inversion of chromosome 4.

periclinal, *a.* (*sb.*) Add: **2.** (Further examples.) More widely, occupying or occurring in a layer parallel to the surface of an organ.

1965 BELL & COOMBE tr. *Strasburger's Textbk. Bot.* 69 (*caption*) Each segment becomes divided by a periclinal wall..into an inner and an outer (cortical) cell. **1965** K. ESAU *Plant Anat.* (ed. 2) iv. 76 The lateral meristems are particularly distinguished by divisions parallel with the nearest surface of the organ (periclinal divisions). **1975** M. E. MCCULLY in Torrey & Clarkson *Devel. & Function of Roots* vi. 111 The daughter cells of these periclinal divisions lack the intense basophilia of the parent epidermal cells.

b. Applied to a type of chimæra (see quot. 1968). Also as *sb.*, a periclinal chimæra. [ad. G. *periklinalchimäre* (E. Baur 1909, in *Zeitschr. f. induktive Abstammungs- u. Vererbungslehre* I. 344).]

1916 *Jrnl. Genetics* VI. 78 Proof that a plant is a periclinal chimaera may..be obtained from adventitious buds arising in internodes of the stem, as well as from those formed on roots. **1925** *Ibid.* XVI. 44 Simple white-over-green periclinals would presumably..give only white seedlings. **1959** *New Biol.* XXX. 39 In periclinal chimeras there is often great variation in the pigment distribution pattern. **1963** *Heredity* XVIII. 270 The striped varieties of *Commelina, Tradescantia* and *Zebrina* have also been shown to be periclinal chimeras with a rather specialised development. **1968** R. RIEGER et al. *Gloss. Genetics & Cytogenetics* 59 Chimeras..in plants may be classified..according to their structure into a) sectorial (different tissues grow side by side and occupy distinct sectors of varying size), b) periclinal (different tissues are disposed one with the other..), c) mericlinal (actually an interrupted periclinal..).

periclinally *adv.*, (*b*) *Bot.*, in the manner of a periclinal division or chimæra.

1916 *Jrnl. Genetics* VI. 79 Plants in which the variegation affected the skin periclinally. **1963** *Heredity* XVIII. 281, L I which does not divide periclinally in the apex may do so frequently during leaf development. **1975** M. E. MCCULLY in Torrey & Clarkson *Devel. & Function of Roots* vi. 111 When the young primordium is about one-third of the way across the cortex a few epidermal cells at its tip divide periclinally and thus produce the root cap initials.

periculous, *a.* Delete †*Obs.* and add later examples.

1932 W. E. D. ALLEN *Hist. Georgian People* iii. 27 The land is poor and snowbound, craggy and periculous. **1959** A. A. MACGREGOR *Phantom Footsteps* iii. 70 The mountain's precipitous upper slopes at the time were treacherously encased in ice, its ravines deceptively filled with periculous snow.

pericyclic (perisəi·klik), *a. Chem.* [f. PERI- + CYCLIC *a.*] Of a reaction: involving a concerted rearrangement of bonding in which all the bonds broken or formed in the reaction lie on a closed ring, whether or not a cyclic molecule is involved.

1969 WOODWARD & HOFFMANN in *Angewandte Chemie* (Internat. Ed.) VIII. 848/1 In our development of the theme of orbital symmetry control of concerted chemical changes, we have laid the basis for a general consideration of all pericyclic reactions—that is, reactions in which all first-order changes in bonding relationships take place in concert on a closed curve. **1974** GILL & WILLIS *Pericyclic Reactions* iv. 99 The basic tenet of the Woodward-Hoffmann theory is that orbital symmetry is conserved in concerted pericyclic reactions. *Ibid.* vi. 162 The six-electron cyclo-addition and reversion processes are by far the most common of all pericyclic changes... Within this category falls the well-known Diels-Alder reaction. **1975** W. R. DOLBIER in Buncel & Lee *Isotopes in Org. Chem.* I. ii. 27 The class of reactions which are presently known as pericyclic or multi-centered reactions..include cycloadditions, electrocyclic reactions and sigmatropic processes.

pericynthion (perisi·nþiǫn). *Astr.* [f. PERI- + Gr. Κύνθιον, neut. of Κύνθιος, adj. designating Mt. Kynthos on Delos, the birthplace of Artemis, goddess freq. associated with the moon.] That point at which a spacecraft in lunar orbit is closest to the moon's centre: applied esp. if the spacecraft was not launched from the moon.

1959 SPITZ & GAYNOR *Dict. Astron. & Astronautics* 295 *Pericynthion*, that point in the orbit of a moon rocket which is closest to the moon. **1969** *Times* 17 May 8/6 Then the descent engines of the L.M. will be fired..to propel it into an orbit in which it will swing around the moon in an elliptical orbit. At its nearest (pericynthion) it will be eight nautical miles from the surface.

pericyte (pe·risəit). *Histology.* [ad. G. *pericyt* (K. W. Zimmerman 1923, in *Zeitschr. f. Anat. und Entwicklungsgeschichte* LXVIII. 67): see PERI- and -CYTE.] One of many flattened branching cells found around capillary blood vessels.

1925 *Amer. Jrnl. Anat.* XXXV. 257 The 'pericytes' of mammals which Zimmerman has described. **1928** *Anatomical Rec.* XXXIX. 45 The designations Rouget cells, adventitial cells, and pericytes are used indiscriminately on the assumption that they connote the same structures. **1965** HAM & LEESON *Histol.* (ed. 5) xxii. 592 Opinion soon changed, and it was generally conceded that such cells as could be seen just outside the endothelium of the capillaries and the venules of most of the bodies of mammals were not contractile. Moreover, the noncontractile cells in this location came to be known by the terms of perivascular cells or pericytes. **1976** W. J. CLIFF *Blood Vessels* iv. 68 Pericytes are non-contractile cells which have well-developed phagocytic powers. *Ibid.* 71 Pericytes have primarily a mechanical supporting function within the walls of minute blood vessels.

peridinian (peridi·niăn). *Biol.* Also **peridinean, peridiniean.** [f. mod.L. generic name *Peridinium* (C. G. Ehrenberg *Organisation, Systematik und geographisches Verhältniss der Infusionsthierchen* (1832) II. 74/2), f. Gr. περιδινής whirled round: see -AN.] A dinoflagellate, usually from a marine habitat, belonging to the order Peridinales. Also *attrib.* or as *adj.*

1912 MURRAY & HJORT *Depths of Ocean* x. 674 Among plants the peridineans..are noted for their power of emitting light. **1928** RUSSELL & YONGE *Seas* i. 25 The Peridinians..can be considered either plants or animals as they have certain characteristics of both. **1935** F. E. FRITSCH *Struct. & Reprod. Algae* I. 664 The Peridiniean flora of warmer zones..differs very markedly from that of colder seas. **1963** D. W. & E. E. HUMPHRIES tr. *Termier's Erosion & Sedimentation* xi. 236 Most of the flagellates giving rise to 'waterbloom' are Peridineans. **1976** P. BOUGIS *Marine Plankton Ecol.* i. 11 Generally, a peridinian has chlorophyll and is autotrophic. *Ibid.* 12 *Noctiluca* is now placed in the Peridiniales... Its spores are of the peridinian type.

peridotic, *a.* (Examples.)

1880 *Mineral. Mag.* III. p. ix (*heading*) On some peridotic rocks from the island of St. Paul's. **1891** MURRAY & RENARD in *Rep. Sci. Results Voy. H.M.S. Challenger: Deep-Sea Deposits* vi. 374 Manganese is rarer in these rocks, but is found as a constituent of pyroxenic, amphibolic, and peridotic minerals.

peridotite. For *Min.* read *Petrogr.* and substitute for def.: Any of the group of plutonic rocks containing little or no feldspar but substantial olivine, usu. with pyroxene, amphibole, or other mafic minerals. [In this sense ad. G. *peridotit* (H. Rosenbusch *Mikrosk. Physiogr.* (1877) II. 522; previously F. *péridotite* had been used for an olivine-basalt (Cordier & d'Orbigny *Descr. des Roches* (1868) II. 118).]

1878 J. D. DANA *Man. Mineral. & Lithol.* (ed. 3) 451 Doleryte... There are two series: A. Ordinary, B. Chrysolitic, and for the latter the name Peridotyte has been used. **1882** A. GEIKIE *Text-bk. Geol.* 151 A series of crystalline rocks composed essentially of olivine, with usually one or two other magnesium silicates..has been classed by Rosenbusch under the general name of Peridotites. **1931** S. J. SHAND *Study of Rocks* vii. 114 Kimberlite.., the matrix of all African diamonds.., is a highly serpentinised peridotite. **1950** E. E. WAHLSTROM *Introd. Theoret. Igneous Petrol.* xiii. 291 Dunite, a variety of peridotite, is almost 100 per cent olivine. **1963** [see *melanocratic* adj. s.v. *MELANO-]. **1972** *Mineral. Mag.* XXXVIII. 437 The peridotite consists dominantly of coarse-grained (2 mm) olivine with minor interstitial clinopyroxene and amphibole of similar grain size.

Hence **peridoti·tic** *a.*, containing, consisting of, or resembling peridotite.

1886 J. J. H. TEALL *Brit. Petrogr.* iv. 68 Peridotitic, hornblendic, and augitic rocks have been serpentinised. **1935** BRANSON & TARR *Introd. Geol.* iii. 13 Magmas occurring to depths of 10 miles are of one type, those that are 10 to 40 miles (the maximum thickness of the crust) down are of another type, and those in the layer (approximately 900 miles thick) next below the crust are of still another. These three regions of the earth's body are known as the granitic, gabbroid or basaltic, and peridotitic zones. **1971** *Nature* 22 Oct. 522/2 The general hypothesis of sea-floor spreading envisages the upwelling of peridotitic mantle material beneath mid-oceanic ridges. **1974** *Mineral. Mag.* XXXIX. 798 Peridotitic rocks in the Massif du Sud..have suffered about 30% serpentinization.

perifoveal (perifōᵘ·vĭăl), *a. Anat.* [f. PERI- + FOVEA.] Applied to the part of the retina regarded as the periphery of its central region, surrounding the parafovea.

1926 *Brit. Jrnl. Ophthalm.* X. 229 (*heading*) The perifoveal circulation. **1941** S. L. POLYAK *Retina* xv. 196 From the axial center to the anterior retinal boundary there are..seven regions: the central area, composed of (*I*) central fovea, (*II*) parafoveal region, and (*III*) perifoveal region or areal periphery; and the extra-areal periphery, composed of (*IV*) near periphery, (*V*) middle periphery, (*VI*) far periphery, and (*VII*) extreme periphery. *Ibid.* xvi. 213 The perifoveal region or the periphery of the central area is its most outward belt... Inwardly it begins at points where the ganglion cell layer still contains four rows of cells. Outwardly it ends where the ganglion layer becomes reduced to a single row of closely packed cells. **1966** *Jrnl. Physiol.* CLXXXVII. 456 There is considerable antagonistic interaction between rod and cone signals at the ganglion cell layer in the perifoveal retina of dark-adapted monkeys.

Hence (as a back-formation) **perifo·vea,** the perifoveal region.

1963 H. DAVSON *Physiol. of Eye* (ed. 2) II. i. 86 (*heading*) Parafovea and perifovea. **1964** J. Z. YOUNG *Model of Brain* ix. 160 The larger parasol bipolars and garland and giant ganglion cells make contact with hundreds or thousands of bipolars and thus cones (and rods) of the fovea and perifovea. **1975** *Nature* 6 Feb. 406/2 When fovea and perifovea are stimulated together (as in everyday life) foveal responses are relatively depressed suggesting that different retinal regions interact abnormally.

perifusate (perifiū·zē¹t). *Med.* [f. next + *-ate*, after *PERFUSATE.] The liquid that results from perifusion.

1969 *Lancet* 25 Oct. 883/1 In the perifusion system, 4–6% of the total pancreatic I.R.I. leaked into the perifusate during the initial 'washing' of the freshly cut tissue. **1978** *Nature* 19 Jan. 272/2, 6 mM L-glucose was added to a perifusate containing 3 mM D-glucose without significantly changing the rate of $^{42}K^+$ efflux as compared with controls maintained in 3 mM D-glucose alone.

perifuse (pe·rifiūz), *v. Med.* [f. PERI- after *PERFUSE *v.* 3.] *trans.* To subject to an enveloping flow of liquid. So **pe·rifused** *ppl. a.*

1969 *Lancet* 25 Oct. 882/1 (*heading*) Dynamic aspects of proinsulin release from perifused rat pancreas. **1972** *Diabetes* XXI. 989/2 The islets were perifused with glucose (1·0 mg./ml.). **1974** [see *PERIFUSION]. **1975** *Nature* 1 May 71/1 Cycloheximide (5 μM) was added to the medium used to perifuse one group of halved pituitaries whereas the other group received only the control medium. **1978** *Ibid.* 19 Jan. 272/1 (*caption*) Effect of D-glucose on potassium efflux.., and insulin release..from perifused rat islets.

perifusion (perifiū·ʒən). *Med.* [f. PERI- after *PERFUSION d.] The action or process of perifusing.

1969 *Lancet* 25 Oct. 882/1 We used a perifusion system in which small pieces of pancreas are washed by a continuous flow of buffer. Although, unlike perfusion systems, this method does not utilise an intact vascular bed it has the advantage of permitting simultaneous control and test experiments to be done on the same pancreas. **1974** *Jrnl. Endocrinol.* LXIII. 23P The glands were perifused with KRBGA only for a period of 1 to 2 h and then challenged by 5 min perifusion with hypothalamic extract in KRBGA. **1978** *Nature* 19 Jan. 272/2 A perifusion system was used to monitor continuously the dynamics of $^{42}K^+$ efflux from preloaded isolated rat islets.

perigee. Add: **1.** Also used with reference to artificial satellites. (Further examples.)

1962 J. Glenn in *Into Orbit* 142 We planned for an apogee, or high point, of about 145 miles and a perigee or low point, of about 85 miles. **1966** *Electronics* 3 Oct. 179 It will orbit out to an apogee of 138,000 miles for the interplanetary readings and then dip back to a perigee of 120 miles.

periglacial (periglē·siăl, -ʃăl, -ʃiăl), *a. Geomorphol.* [ad. G. *periglazial* (W. Łoziński 1909, in *Bull. internat. de l'Acad. des Sci. de Cracovie: Classe des Sci. math. et nat.* I. 16): see Peri-¹ and Glacial *a.*] Characteristic of or being a region where the influence of an adjacent ice sheet or glacier, or of frost action, is important in forming or modifying the landscape.

1928 *Amer. Jrnl. Sci.* XVI. 163 The complete realization that continental glaciation implies that a zone of periglacial climate borders the ice should lead to interesting and fruitful studies of the zone immediately south of our extensive glacial boundary. **1936** *Proc. Prehist. Soc.* II. 61 Although the Thames Valley was not actually invaded by ice..it was subject to peri-glacial phenomena. **1954** *Sci. News* XXXIII. 67 The processes of earth sculpture operating in periglacial conditions, perhaps a considerable distance from the ice-front, produce deposits and landforms of a special type. **1967** *Jrnl. Glaciol.* VI. 551 The limited earlier work in Southern Africa suggested that the Pleistocene climate was too dry for glaciation to have occurred, but the existence of oversteepened slopes, solifluction slumps and cirques is indicative of a periglacial environment. **1973** *Boreas* II. 9 Bonafide 'periglacial' forms and deposits of late Pleistocene age are present in the Drakensberg and adjacent parts of the northeastern Cape Province.

Hence **perigla·cially** *adv.*, in or by a periglacial environment.

1941 *Trans. R. Soc. Edin.* LX. 406 The Thames lay periglacially to the ice-sheets of East Anglia. **1962** *Proc. Yorkshire Geol. Soc.* XXXIII. 336 Dartmoor..preserves the finest set of periglacially formed tors in Britain. **1972** *Trans. Norfolk & Norwich Naturalists' Soc.* XXII. 229 (*heading*) Periglacially modified chalk and chalk ridge-diapirs from Norwich, Norfolk.

pe:riglacia·tion. *Geomorphol.* [f. Peri- + Glaciation, after prec.] The state of being subject to a periglacial climate; periglacial processes collectively.

1957 M. T. te Punga in *Tijdschr. Koninklijk Nederlandsch. Aardijkskundig Genootschap* LXXIV. 408 Wind-worked pebbles and boulders..are well known as relics of periglaciation in many parts of the world. **1963** *Geomorphol. Abstr.* 38 (*heading*) Periglaciation of Canada. **1968** *Geogr. Abstr.* A. 30 The scarp..was formed during the Quaternary when the region underwent severe periglaciation with immense frost riving and modification of plateau valleys. **1970** R. J. Small *Study of Landforms* i. 2 Our knowledge of the vital role of periglaciation in shaping the landscapes of present-day temperate areas is based almost wholly on analysis by geomorphologists of the distribution and character of solifluxion gravels, 'head', 'coombe rock' and the like.

Périgordian (perigōə·ɹdiăn), *a. Archæol.* Also **Perigordian.** [tr. F. *Périgordien* (D. Peyrony 1933, in *Bull. Soc. Préhist. Française* XXX. 558), f. the place-name *Périgord* (see Périgord) + -ian.] A name given to an Upper Palaeolithic culture represented by flint tools of the kind found at Laugerie-Haute in the Périgord region of Dordogne (see quot. 1938). Also *absol.* as *sb.*

1938 *Proc. Prehist. Soc.* IV. 4 Peyrony..has found at Laugerie Haute an industry of blunted-back blades... He concludes that in the Chatelperron–Laugerie Haute–La Gravette succession we are dealing with a culture totally different from the so-called Middle Aurignacian,..and he proposes to group all those industries characterised by the blunted-back blade under the title of Perigordian. **1941** *Ann. Reg. 1940* 342 A remarkable painted cave of Perigordian art was found at Lascaux in the Dordogne. **1949** M. C. Burkitt *Old Stone Age* (ed. 2) iv. 64 The *Audi* and *Châtelperron* knife blades form an evolving series characteristic of the Périgordian element in the early Aurignacian. **1956** H. Read *Art of Sculpture* ii. 34 There can be little doubt that the so-called *Venus* of Laussel attributed by the Abbé Breuil to the Périgordian period, is such a cult object. **1970** Bray & Trump *Dict. Archaeol.* 174/1 *Périgordian*, French terminology for a series of Upper Palaeolithic flint industries which are thought to represent a continuing technological tradition. *Ibid.* 174/2 No known site has a complete and unbroken 'Périgordian' sequence. **1977** D. K. Bhattacharya *Palaeolithic Europe* iv. 168 In 1933, Dr. Peyrony declared that what was earlier thought to be lower and upper Aurignacian, is in reality a tradition different from Aurignacian and he named this Perigordian.

Périgordine. Add: **B.** *adj.* Of or pertaining to Périgord, esp. to the gastronomic specialities of the region.

1931 A. de Croze *What to eat & drink in France* 230 Sanguète périgourdine..blood of chicken browned in goose dripping with garlic, shallots, and verjuice. **1951** E. David *French Country Cooking* 192 A kind of soufflé eaten cold, a Périgordine speciality. **1959** *Times* 7 Feb. 9/1 The food..tends to be lighter, though quite as delicious as the famed Périgourdine fare farther west. **1973** *Times* 22 Mar. 15/8 (Advt.), Lovely Perigourdine house XVIIIth century.

perigraphe. Restrict *Obs.* to sense a and add: **b.** (Later example in *poet.* use.)

1956 'H. MacDiarmid' *Stony Limits* 38 We turn in vain This way and that and but changing perigraphs gain.

Périgueux (pe·rigö). *Cookery.* The name of a city in the Périgord region of south-west France used *attrib.* to designate a type of sauce made with truffles.

1846 A. Soyer *Gastronomic Regenerator* 25 *Sauce Perigeux.* Put four middling-sized truffles..into a stewpan with a glass of sherry. **1877** E. S. Dallas *Kettner's Bk. of Table* 340 Perigueux sauce..is the best brown sauce, with a glass of sherry or Marsala added to it, and a quantity of chopped truffles. **1937** X. M. Boulestin *Finer Cooking* II. 84 For the Sauce Périgueux.—Chop the trimmings of the truffles finely and cook them in a small saucepan with a glass of Madeira. **1956** C. Brown et al. *Four-in-One Bk. Continental Cookery* 337 Dish up, and serve with Périgueux Sauce. **1972** G. A. Browne *11 Harrowhouse St.* (1973) v. 51 Next came Tournedos Rossini. Filets of beef..covered with Périgueux sauce.

perikaryon (perikæ·riǫn). *Anat.* Pl. **-karya.** [f. Peri- + Gr. κάρυον nut, kernel.] The cell-body of a neurone; that part of a nerve cell which contains the nucleus.

1897 M. Foster *Text Bk. Physiol.* (ed. 7) III. i. 928 It will be convenient to distinguish by a separate name between the processes whether axon or dendrite, and the part from which these processes start, namely the body of the cell surrounding the nucleus; the latter might be called the perikaryon. **1961** *New Scientist* 12 Oct. 117/3 In the invertebrates the [nerve] fibre is not so long and does not usually end on a blood vessel; the perikaryon instead provides more or less all the available storage space. **1975** *Nature* 25 Dec. 746/2 Brain tissue..after this treatment exhibits only weak nonspecific fluorescence with some bright yellow autofluorescent granules in large neuronal perikarya. **1977** P. B. & J. S. Medawar *Life Sci.* xv. 122 The most obviously cell-like part of the neurone is called the cell-body or perikaryon, and this houses the nucleus.

peril, *sb.* Add: **5. peril point** *U.S. Econ.* (see quot. 1965).

1948 *Congress. Rec.* 26 May 6503/2 No foreign trade agreement could be entered into until the Tariff Commission reports to the President its findings as to the so-called peril-point below which tariffs may not be cut. **1949** *Sun* (Baltimore) 11 July 10/2 The main innovation in the Republican program is the so-called 'peril-point' report which must be made to the President by the Tariff Commission. **1949** *Economist* 17 Sept., *Peril Points.* This year's battle over American tariff policy opened just as the Administration was assuring Sir Stafford Cripps and Mr Bevin that the United States would pursue policies appropriate to a great creditor nation. **1961** *Ibid.* 9 Dec. 1025/2 The President's authority to lower tariffs being renewed grudgingly but limited by 'peril points' and 'escape clauses'. **1965** *McGraw-Hill Dict. Mod. Econ.* 376 *Peril point*, the maximum cut in a U.S. import duty which could be made for a given commodity without causing serious injury to domestic producers or to a similar commodity.

perilune (perilū·n). *Astr.* [f. Peri- + L. *lūna* moon; cf. Perigee, Perihelion, etc.] That point at which a spacecraft in lunar orbit is closest to the moon's centre: applied esp. if the spacecraft was launched from the moon.

1960 *Aeroplane* XCIX. 638/2 Lunar gravity should draw the probe into an orbit which has a period of about 10 hr., an apolune (farthest distance from the Moon) of approximately 3,000 miles and a perilune (closest distance) of 1,500 miles. **1968** *Sci. Jrnl.* Oct. 5/2 The orbital velocity at perilune—altitude 100 km, 2°N latitude—was about 7200 km/hour relative to the Moon. **1969** *Nature* 12 July 129/2 Choosing the major axis of the orbit to pass through the mascon..is equally effective in nullifying the orbital instability represented by cumulatively increasing displacements of perilune and apolune.

perimenopausal (pe:rimenǒpǭ·zăl), *a. Med.* [f. Peri- + *menopausal *a.*] Occurring at around the time of the menopause.

1961 J. K. Frost in Novak & Jones *Textbk. Gynecol.* (ed 6) xxxvi. 774 Except postpartum, the parabasal type cell does not exfoliate normally until the later years of the reproductive period, or the perimenopausal period. **1961** *Obstetr. & Gynecol.* XVII. 331/1 Many of our colleagues use ovarian hormones, especially estrogens, for the control of the perimenopausal syndrome. **1970** Te Linde & Mattingly *Oper. Gynecol.* (ed. 4) xxxvi. 795/2 With the current liberal use of estrogen and progesterones in the perimenopausal age group for pregnancy protection and menopausal symptoms, the physician must be particularly alert to the camouflaged symptoms of endometrial carcinoma in patients using steroid hormones. **1977** *Lancet* 8 Oct. 762/2 There was a 6% ($P < 0{\cdot}001$) excess of left-sided tumours, primarily at perimenopausal and postmenopausal ages.

So **perime·nopause,** the perimenopausal period.

1962 J. K. Frost in Novak & Woodruff *Gynecol. & Obstetr. Path.* (ed. 5) xxxv. 608/2 Following the initial period of endocrine adjustment in the establishment of menses (perimenarche) and extending into the disruption of endocrine interplay (perimenopause), the hormonal pattern varies widely within each lunar cycle. **1969** *Obstetr. & Gynecol.* XXXIII. 581/2 More than 120 women ..were seen initially for, and found to have problems relating to, the perimenopause or menopause.

perimeter. Add: **1. c.** *Mil.* A defended boundary of a troop position. Also *transf.*, the boundary of an airfield or civil airport.

1943 J. Duffy *Australians in Malaya* 41 Possibly this was true of an attack from the sea, but on the northern perimeter were no adequate defences. **1958** *Spectator* 11 July 52/3 A can tell you what really happened in the fighting round the perimeter. **1967** *Boston Herald* 1 Apr. 14/6 The enemy opened up with mortar and howitzer fire, hitting American troops who had pulled back into defensive perimeters. **1974** *Guardian* 1 Aug. 1/7 Soldiers.. moved on to the airport perimeter. **1977** *Times* 9 Sept. 15/7 After six hours without food in a plane on the perimeter at Heathrow the flight was cancelled.

3. *attrib.* and *comb.*, as (sense *1c) *perimeter fence, road*; **perimeter track,** a runway round an airfield. See also sense 2 in Dict.

1974 A. Price *Other Paths to Glory* III. i. 249 Soldiers.. patrolling the perimeter fence. **1976** *Scottish Daily Express* 27 Dec. 1/2 Two wolves were shot dead only yards from the perimeter fence by zoo director Roger Wheater. **1974** *Times* 7 Jan. 1/4 There were five road blocks of troops and police on the airport perimeter road where it passes close to runways. **1946** *Happy Landings* (Air Ministry) July 10/1 The Spitfire was taxying out for take-off, along the perimeter track. **1959** J. L. Nayler *Dict. Aeronaut. Engin.* 187 *Perimeter track*, a taxi track round the perimeter of an airfield for the use of aircraft and motor vehicles.

perimetral, *a.* (Later example.)

1971 J. Needham *Sci. & Civilisation in China* IV. III. xxviii. 94 (*caption*) Diagrams to elucidate Chinese and Western building construction... Comparison of the fundamental Chinese building design with that of Greek and Gothic building... Normally the Greek gable covered the perimetral colonnade.

perinatal (perinē·tăl), *a. Med.* [f. Peri- + Natal *a.*¹ and *sb.*] Of or pertaining to the period comprising the latter part of fœtal life and the early postnatal period (commonly taken as ending either one week or four weeks after birth: see quots.).

1952 *Amer. Jrnl. Publ. Health* XLII. 505/2 Such conditions as birth injury, congenital malformation, cerebral palsy, and epilepsy..may possibly be traceable to perinatal causes. **1958** *Economist* 22 Feb. 654/2 The phrase perinatal mortality has been coined to describe the combined death rate of babies born dead and those who die in the first week of life. **1966** *Ann. Rev. Med.* XVII. 213 The perinatal period extends from the completion of embryonic differentiation into recognizable organ structures to the end of the first month of postnatal extra-uterine existence. **1973** *Where* Apr. 102/3 If they smoke after the third month of their pregnancy there is an excess of peri-natal deaths of about 30 per cent. **1976** *Lancet* 30 Oct. 941/1 The French Government aimed to reduce the burden of handicap caused by conditions arising in the perinatal period (defined as the period from 28th week of gestation to the end of the first week of life). In 1968 40 000 French children who had survived the first year of life were judged to have a handicap of perinatal origin. **1977** *Ibid.* 25 June 1357/2 The W.H.O. recommendation reads: 'It is recommended that national perinatal statistics should include all fetuses and infants delivered weighing at least 500 g (or, when birthweight is unavailable, the corresponding gestational age (22 weeks) or body length (25 cm crown-heel)), whether alive or dead.

period, *sb.* Add: **I. 3. b.** Also *sing.* and *attrib.*

1891 I. Ellis *Essentials of Conception* 28 (Advt.), Ladies' 'period' towels. **1922** Joyce *Ulysses* 368 Some women for instance warn you off when they have their period. **1939** M. Spring Rice *Working-Class Wives* vi. 145 She suffers from 'period pains'. **1953** H. Miller *Plexus* (1963) iii. 112 Between times I wondered what was eating her. Maybe her period coming on. **1956** R. M. Lester *Towards Hereafter* x. 123 In January 1952 I missed a period and with high hopes I went to see my G.P. and told him the glad news. **1970** G. Greer *Female Eunuch* 52 The genteel..'I've got my period'. **1976** W. H. Canaway *Willow-Pattern War* xv. 156 She'd cried off at the last minute with a period pain.

4. c. *spec.* (*a*) a portion of an artist's life characterized by a particular style; (*b*) freq. with poss. adj.: the particular historical or cultural portion of time with which one is concerned.

1891 O. Wilde *Pict. Dorian Gray* xix. 319 What has become of that wonderful portrait he did of you?.. It belonged to Basil's best period. **1921** W. S. Maugham *Circle* I. 13, I want you to look at this chair I've just got. .. About 1750, I should say... It's exactly my period. **1925** R. Fry *Let.* 1 May (1972) II. 568 Lady Cunard.. wanted a Picasso of the blue period. **1952** 'W. Cooper' *Struggles of Albert Woods* II. iv. 100, I hardly know Picasso's rose period from his blue. **1958** M. Kelly *Christmas Egg* I. 29 He had been at a loss for the date of the battle of Agincourt, and had excused himself with the plea that it was outside his period. *a* **1966** M. Allingham *Cargo of Eagles* (1968) i. 16 I'm certain there's an early fortress..just waiting to be uncovered... That's not my period and so is not my province. **1973** M. Mackintosh *King & Two Queens* ii. 27 The Picasso Museum..has very good examples of his pink and blue periods? **1978** J. Hansen *Man Everybody was Afraid Of* xii. 93 She handed Dave one of the mugs. 'From my potting period.'

d. (Earlier and later examples.) Also *out of period*: anachronistic.

1859 A. J. Munby *Diary* 19 July in D. Hudson *Munby* (1972) 39 An Englishman of the period, smoking a cigar; his dress is 'civilized'—he wears gloves. **1902** G. B. Shaw *Mrs. Warren's Profession* Pref. p. xv, Both plots conform to the strictest rules of the period. **1933** E. O'Neill *Ah, Wilderness!* I. 15 Scene—Sitting room of the Miller home in a large small-town in Connecticut—about 7:30 in the morning of July 4th, 1906. The room is..furnished with the scrupulous medium-priced tastelessness of the period. **1961** C. Willock *Death in Covert* iii. 66 A serving-wench.. asked him: 'Sack, mulled claret, or Madeira?' Mr Goss felt that two at least of these were out of period. **1969** Y. Carter *Mr. Campion's Farthing* ii. 15, I hate getting out of period but sometimes one has to be modern. **1976** *Listener* 20 May 647/4 Wesley..had the imaginative and technical powers to transcend the humdrum idiom of so much church music of the period without, at the same time, discarding its essential nature.

e. *Educ.* A portion of time set aside for a lesson or other activity; cf. *free period* s.v. *free *a.* D. 2.

1876 C. M. Yonge *Womankind* xiii. 92 Most people's breakfast hour coincides with this only period permitted [in National Schools] for religious teaching. **1930** *Times Educ. Suppl.* 18 Jan. 21/2 The pupil has five periods a week..for French. **1948** 'N. Shute' *No Highway* vi. 167 'What about the school?' 'I've only got one period tomorrow.' **1955** E. Blishen *Roaring Boys* I. 30, I had an odd period of history with one of the first-year classes. **1966** J. Partridge *Middle School* i. 24 Nearly every class has a 'library period'. **1974** H. L. Foster *Ribbin'* i. 8 Hey, Teach, we work a period, read comics a period, and then take off the last period—OK?

f. One of the intervals into which the playing time of a sporting fixture is divided.

1898 *Encycl. Sport* II. 128/2 The duration of play in a match shall be one hour, divided into three periods of twenty minutes. **1935** *Encycl. Sports* 359/2 Two timekeepers..inform the referee..that the end of each period or rest has arrived. **1968** *Globe & Mail* (Toronto) 5 Feb. 17/2 Pit Martin also scored for a three-goal first period for Chicago and Wayne Maki tallied early in the second. **1974** *State* (Columbia, S. Carolina) 3 Mar. 1-D/1 The Paladins opened 11-point leads on three occasions in the final period.

III. 11. b. Also added to a statement to emphasize a place where there is or should be a full stop, freq. (*colloq.*) with the implication 'and that is all there is to say about it', 'and it is as simple as that'.

1934 J. O'Hara *Appointment in Samarra* (1935) viii. 248 'An unscrupulous woman can make a man—' 'Period.' **1946** *Sun* (Baltimore) 2 Oct. 8 (Advt.), A cigarette is supposed to give you *pleasure*. Period. **1947** *Mind* LVI. 65 The empirical evidence suggests the generalisation and supports it. If it does, it does. Period. **1948** H. Lawrence *Death of Doll* i. 21 'Lucky Monny to have her own pocket.' 'Stop that. Lucky Monny, period.' **1951** C. Armstrong *Black-Eyed Stranger* (1952) xvii. 150, I don't want to think you are a romantic young thing, period. **1956** J. L. Austin in *Proc. Brit. Acad.* XLII. 113 It does *not* follow either that 'I panted whether or not I ran' or that 'I panted' period. **1958** Rice & 'McBain' *April Robin Murders* (1959) xxii. 245 But Browne doesn't care... He wants the money, period. **1960** 'M. Cronin' *Begin with Gun* xii. 141 'You know how nosy I am about unsolved crimes.' 'Nosy. Period.' **1964** V. Nabokov *Defence* x. 156, I can't abandon him. And I won't. Period. **1972** *Science* 12 May 638/1 Don't know, but we have exceeded it: 7. Don't know, period: 10. **1974** H. L. Foster *Ribbin'* vi. 285 It is wrong for any teacher to have an affair with a student, period. **1976** *Shooting Times & Country Mag.* 16–22 Dec. 18/1 So far as the Spey was concerned this year, however, the fish did not arrive—period! **1977** *Language* LIII. 409 If this is the view R got from 'On generative semantics', he is illiterate, period.

15. *Chem.* A horizontal row in the periodic table of the elements; the set of elements occupying such a row, usu. comprising an alkali metal and those elements of greater atomic number up to and including the next noble gas. Cf. *group *sb.* 3 c (ii).

1879 *Chem. News* 5 Dec. 268/1 In the first [table] the elements are placed in large periods, with their atomic weights. In the second they are arranged in groups and series, that is to say, in small periods, in such a manner that the differences between the odd and even series become very apparent. *Ibid.* 19 Dec. 291/1 We see..that the members at the beginning of the large periods (as well as the small periods commencing with Na and Li) are metals of a very strongly pronounced alkaline nature. **1946** [see *lanthanide 1]. **1965** Phillips & Williams *Inorg. Chem.* I. ii. 40 (*caption*) The series of elements from Li to Ne will be referred to as the first row or the first short period, and similarly the series Rb to Xe as the fourth row or the second long period. **1974** D. M. Adams *Inorg. Solids* ii. 37 Across each period of the Periodic Table, ionic radii decrease with increasing charge and atomic number.

IV. 16. *attrib.* or as *adj.* in sense 'belonging to, characteristic, imitative, or representative of, a particular (past) period' esp. in style or design in architecture, dress, furniture, literature, etc.

Freq. in inexact or euphemistic use.

1905 (*title*) Borgia: a period play. **1906** G. Kobbé *How to appreciate Music* 47 A pianoforte has no business in a 'period' room. If the person is rich enough to afford 'period' rooms, he also can afford a music room. **1908** *Westm. Gaz.* 17 Dec. 4/1 Some of them..may be said to be striving to create a 'period' type of carriage for themselves. **1914** Eberlein & McClure (*title*) The practical book of period furniture. **1920** W. R. Lethaby in *Form in Civilization* (1922) 12 That which now professes to be designed in a style, or, as the still more disgusting slang runs, to be 'period work', has not the essence of life. **1925** in F. Madan *Oxford outside Guide-Bks.* (ed. 2) 202 (Advt.), Write for new illustrated Catalogue containing fullest particulars of Minty Bookcases, including various 'period' styles at moderate prices. **1927** *Times* 28 Oct. 17/3 The bride..wore a period gown of cream chiffon velvet, trimmed with seed pearls. **1928** *Daily Sketch* 2 Aug. 15 (*caption*) 'Period' pages... The little pages wore replicas of the old-time uniform of the Queen's Bays. **1931** *Times Lit. Suppl.* 26 Mar. 249/2 The contrast between these two volumes makes an interesting study. Neither is 'period-printing'; but the Chapman is properly 'spacious' for an Elizabethan work; and the Pope [etc.]. **1935** N. Mitchison *We have been Warned* II. 154 'You'll be saying you like the "Idylls of the King" next.' 'Oh, but I do. They're so deliciously period.' **1937** D. L. Sayers *Busman's Honeymoon* xviii. 346, I was going to.. have the spit turned by electricity. And an electric cooker for the days when we didn't feel so period. **1940** L. MacNeice *Last Ditch* 18 Cranks, hacks, poverty-stricken scholars, In pince-nez, period hats or romantic beards. **1958** B. Nichols *Sweet & Twenties* 79 The word 'treasure' is charmingly period. In the upper classes it implied the perfect Jeeves or the ideal nanny. **1960** R. A. Knox *Occasional Sermons* xl. 331 It is all quite convincing, and beautifully period. Why is it so period? **1965** *Listener* 25 Nov. 869/3 A series of Edith Wharton's novels are being reprinted..; great period interest, and well worth re-examination. **1967** E. Short *Embroidery & Fabric Collage* iii. 74 The heavy curtains associated with the period four-poster. **1974** *Listener* 10 Jan. 59/3 *Whose body?*..one of Dorothy Sayers's Lord Peter Wimsey stories..is period stuff, thick with now discarded or at least unfashionable snobberies. **1976** *Liverpool Echo* 24 Nov. 5/4 The undeniable pleasure of watching sport, natural history, travel, ballet, period dramas and even the news is taken for granted. **1977** *N.Y. Rev. Bks.* 29 Sept. 12/4 Baum was a handsome young man with gray eyes, straight nose, dark brown hair, and a period mustache that looked to be glued on. **1977** *Radio Times* 12 Nov. 4/3 It was great fun but it was 'period' and we wanted to get back to the present.

b. Special Combs., as **period–luminosity** *a. Astr.*, relating the period of a variable star, esp. a Cepheid, to its luminosity; **period-piece**, a work of art, furniture, literature, etc., considered from the aspect of its associations with or evocativeness of a past period of time; contemptuously, such a work possessing interest only from such associations or evocativeness.

1918 H. Shapley in *Contrib. Mt. Wilson Solar Observatory* No. 153. 2 For parallaxes obtained with the period-luminosity curve the accuracy appears to surpass that of direct measures on any object for which the parallax is less than 0″·01, and is essentially independent of distance. **1950** *Sci. News* XV. 46 We can..get from the [light] curve the mean apparent magnitude and the period. From the period-luminosity relation we then find the absolute magnitude, and so, knowing both *m* and M we can find the distance. **1964** *Listener* 21 May 831/2 It was by studying the short-period variables in the Small Cloud, fifty years ago, that Miss Henrietta Leavitt, at Harvard..made the discoveries that led on to the 'period-luminosity law' of Cepheid stars. **1927** S. Ertz *Now East, Now West* iii. 32 She saw she would have the pleasure of buying certain things—period pieces—that she could either sell at the end of their stay or take back to America. **1931** *Times Lit. Suppl.* 24 Dec. 1033/2 Spenser supported the remote splendour of his mythical heroes with deliberately archaic language, turning his poem into a period piece. **1934** C. Lambert *Music Ho!* III. 172 The English folk song..is nothing more than a very pretty period piece. **1943** H. Pearson *Conan Doyle* v. 81 Nowadays we can see that the facile saga of Sherlock Holmes is far more valuable even as a 'period piece' than the diligent epic of Edward the Third. **1957** *Essays & Stud.* X. 54 But I am here concerned with Robert Elsmere not primarily as a work of art but as a symbol or symptom of a certain phase of liberal religious thought in the later nineteenth century—as a 'period piece' if you will, only that I prefer not to use a phrase which might suggest (wrongly, as I think) that the book is a mere antique. **1961** L. Mumford *City in Hist.* xiii. 408 Washington..might have been a miracle of the solo town planner's art: a final period-piece to close the epoch. **1972** S. Hynes *Edwardian Occasions* xv. 188 The essays..are belles-lettres of the most inoffensive kind..period pieces even when [Maurice] Hewlett wrote them. **1975** M. Drabble *Realms of Gold* iv. 269 Mays Cottage was a period piece, completely unrestored, which in these days seemed to be an asset.

periodate, per-iodate. Add: *periodic acid–Schiff* (Biol.), phr. used *attrib.* and *absol.* to designate a procedure for the detection of carbohydrates by first oxidizing them to polyaldehydes with periodic acid and then staining with Schiff's reagent.

1947 *Jrnl. Laboratory & Clin. Med.* XXXII. 911 McManus reported the use of a periodic acid–Schiff technique for the demonstration of mucin. **1956** *Nature* 3 Mar. 432/2 Secretory inclusions which are positive to the periodic-acid–Schiff test are conspicuous in the non-ciliated iodine-binding cells of the endostyle of *Ciona*. **1960** E. Gurr *Encycl. Microsc. Stains* I. 274 The author describes..results obtained with silver staining and periodic acid–Schiff. **1974** H. C. Cook *Man. Histol. Demonstr. Techniques* i. 16 They [*sc.* basement membranes] may be demonstrated..by the periodic acid–Schiff (PAS) technique and a variant of this, the Allochrome method.

periodic, *a.*[1] Add: **2.** (Earlier example in *Math.*) *periodic classification* or *system* (Chem.): an arrangement or classification of the chemical elements according to the periodic law; *periodic law* (Chem.): add to def.: now recognized to be a function of atomic number rather than of atomic weight, thus removing certain discrepancies in the original scheme; (examples); *periodic table* (Chem.): a table of the elements arranged according to the periodic law; *spec.* one in which they are arranged in order of atomic number, usu. in rows, such that groups of elements possessing analogous electronic structures, and hence exhibiting similar properties, form vertical columns ('groups') of the table.

1850 J. F. W. Herschel in *Phil. Trans. R. Soc.* CXL. 400 If A_x, B_x, &c. be simply constant, the function may be termed a periodic one, since it assumes in periodic and constantly recurring succession the values A, B, C..N, A, B, &c. *ad infinitum*. **1872** *Phil. Mag.* XLIII. 251 The regular progression in physical and chemical properties observable in members of the same family..are either consequences of, or closely related to, these 'periodic laws'. **1875** *Chem. News* 24 Dec. 293/1 The periodic law indicates the gaps which still exist in the system of the known elements, and enables us to predict the properties of the unknown elements. *Ibid.* 294/1 These characters of [gallium]..have been obtained..by considering its place in the periodic system of the elements. **1881** *Ibid.* 14 Jan. 16/1 The criticism of Prof. Wurtz upon the periodic classification. **1895** Thomson & Bloxam *Bloxam's Chem.* (ed. 8) 278 The Periodic Table has found a twofold application. **1913** Periodic system [see *atomic number* s.v. *atomic *a.* 1] **1919** *Jrnl. Chem. Soc.* CXV. 11 The occupant of a separate place in the periodic table of elements. **1930** *Engineering* 21 Mar. 372/2 The sequence of the elements in the old periodic table with its eight groups and seven periods. **1957** Periodic table [see *lanthanide 1]. **1969** J. W. van Spronsen (*title*) The periodic system of chemical elements. **1974** *Encycl. Brit. Macropædia* IV. 116/2 The periodic classification places elements with similar electron arrangements in vertical columns. **1974** Goldberg & Dillard *College Chem.* ii. 38 The periodic law..states that the properties of the elements are periodic functions of their atomic numbers.

4. (Further example.)

1930 H. G. Wells *Autocracy of Mr. Parham* II. iv. 128 The need of a stronger and clearer guidance in our periodic literature.

6. as *sb. pl.* = *periodical *sb.* 3.

1920 C. E. Mulford *Johnny Nelson* xvii. 222 That's th' worst of them periodics! You can't never tell when they'll start.

periodical, *sb.* Add: **1.** Also *attrib.*

1878 *Harper's Mag.* Jan. 192 He used to look into the windows of the periodical stores. **1910** A. E. Bostwick *Amer. Publ. Library* 282 In some New York branches periodical reading rooms may be used as assembly rooms. **1938** L. M. Harrod *Librarians' Gloss.* 99 *Magazine case*, a cover for periodicals, usually having some contrivance for holding the magazine-cord, rod, etc. Also called 'Periodical case' and 'Reading case'. **1961** T. Landau *Encycl. Librarianship* (ed. 2) 275/2 *Periodical stack*, a stack constructed to display periodicals, with space on lower shelves for storage of back numbers.

3. *pl.* *U.S. slang.* Recurring drinking bouts or sprees.

1890 in Barrère & Leland *Dict. Slang* II. 124/1 Are you in the book business?.. Ma and pa were talking last night about your having your little periodicals. **1902** H. L. Wilson *Spenders* x. 107 They telegraphed the Butte National to wire his description, and the answer was 'tall and drunk'. Well, son, his periodicals wa'n't all.

periodicity. Add: **1. b.** *Chem.* The complex periodic variation of the properties of the chemical elements with increasing atomic number.

1879 Roscoe & Schorlemmer *Treat. Chem.* II. II. 506 The law of periodicity was afterwards further developed by Meyer and Mendelejeff. **1907** *Westm. Gaz.* 4 Feb. 6/3 Gallium, scandium, and germanium, all subsequently discovered, did fit into the scale of 'periodicity'. **1969** A. J. Ihde in J. W. Van Spronsen *Periodic Syst. Chem. Elem.* p. x, The periodic table reached its final forms before atomic structure revealed the basis for periodicity.

c. The frequency of a periodic phenomenon, esp. an alternating current.

1900 *Jrnl. Soc. Arts* XLVIII. 848/2 The other carrying about 20 amperes with a periodicity of 60 cycles per second. **1913** *Chambers's Jrnl.* Jan. 102/1 The electricity used for wireless telegraphy is..used under different conditions as to pressure and periodicity. **1938** *Times* 13 Oct. 8/3 The periodicities of the front and back springs are arranged at a predetermined variance so that coincidence should not occur. **1943** *Gloss. Terms Electr. Engin.* (*B.S.I.*) 11 *Frequency* (*periodicity*, deprecated), the number of cycles per second. The reciprocal of the period.

periodiza·tion. [f. Periodize *v.* + -ation.] Division into periods of time; *spec.* the grouping of historical and cultural events in chronological periods (see Period *sb.* 4 c in Dict. and Suppl.) for the purposes of discussion and evaluation.

1938 [see *CONCEPT *sb.* 2 b]. **1952** K. R. POPPER *Open Society* (ed. 2) II. xii. 59 No doubt, his [*sc.* Hegel's] vast historicist generalizations, periodizations, and interpretations fascinated some historians. **1957** K. A. WITTFOGEL *Oriental Despotism* ix. 395 This periodization appeared again in an article in 1916. **1963** R. M. GRANT *Hist. Introd. New Testament* i. 14 The question of periodization arose in the second century... Generally speaking, historians have differentiated three periods. **1967** L. DEUEL *Conquistadors without Swords* xxi. 285 Uaxactún yielded a continuous series of pottery which made it possible to establish a complete overall Maya stratigraphy and periodization. **1970** B. BREWSTER tr. *Althusser & Balibar's Reading Capital* (1975) II. iv. 94 On this level, then, the whole problem of the science of history would consist of the division of this continuum according to a *periodization* corresponding to the succession of one dialectal totality after another. **1973** *Times Lit. Suppl.* 16 Nov. 1386/1 Accepting the traditional periodization of world history according to the days of creation. **1974** J. WHITE tr. *Poulantzas's Fascism & Dictatorship* IV. 233 The general line which was progressively dominant in the USSR and in the Comintern can allow us to make a relatively clear periodization of the Comintern, a periodization which can also be very useful for the history of the USSR. **1976** *Brit. Jrnl. Sociol.* XXVII. 301 In as far as sociology defines its object of investigation as 'society', 'the social system' or some such general unspecified synonym, it denies itself any rigorous principle of historical periodization.

periodize, *v.* Restrict †*Obs.* to sense in Dict. and add: **2.** To divide (a portion of time) into periods; to assign (historical and cultural events) to specified periods. Cf. prec. So (*rare*) **pe·riodizer,** one who periodizes in this way; **pe·riodizing** *vbl. sb.*

a **1943** R. G. COLLINGWOOD *Idea of Hist.* (1946) II. 54, I will take a single example of medieval periodizing. In the twelfth century Joachim of Floris divided history into three periods. **1959** *Listener* 20 Aug. 291/2 The fifteenth century has been a favourite hunting ground for the periodizers of history. **1965** K. CHARLTON *Educ. Renaissance Eng.* ii. 40 The dangers of periodizing history and of ignoring the carry-over of medieval ideas alongside and within humanistic thought have already been mentioned. **1970** B. BREWSTER tr. *Althusser & Balibar's Reading Capital* (1975) II. iv. 103 This is antipodal to the empirically visible history in which the time of all histories is the simple time of continuity and in which the 'content' is the vacuity of events that occur in it which one later tries to determine with dividing procedures in order to 'periodize' that continuity. **1972** *Language* XLVIII. 423 Lyons' manner of 'periodizing' Chomsky's intellectual history has its justification, but a somewhat different distribution of emphasis might be fairer to the histories of both linguistics and rationalism. **1973** *Sci. Amer.* Sept. 194/2 The bulk of the text summarizes and criticizes the theories for Bode's law in the context of an overall view of the origin of the solar system, an event that Nieto broadly periodizes along the lines of Sir Fred Hoyle's nebular-plus-magnetic theory.

periodogram (pīəriǫ·dŏgræm). [f. PERIOD *sb.* + -O + -GRAM.] A diagram or method of graphical representation which is designed to detect or display any periodicity (usu. with time) in a set of measurements of a quantity; *spec.* one in which the results of harmonic analysis of the data, performed on the assumption in turn of different periods of variation, are plotted as a function of the period. Freq. *attrib.*, as **periodogram analysis,** the analysis of data by means of a periodogram.

1898 A. SCHUSTER in *Terrestr. Magn.* III. 24 It is convenient to have a word for some representation of a variable quantity which shall correspond to the 'spectrum' of a luminous radiation. I propose the word *periodogram*. *Ibid.* 25 The periodogram of the sound emitted by an organ pipe or a violin string consists of a series of equidistant 'lines'. **1906** *Proc. R. Soc.* A. LXXVII. 141 The periodogram..is the diagram representing the intensity of periodic variations as determined from the sum of the squares of the two Fourier coefficients belonging to each assumed period. **1919** *Nature* 26 June 338/1 A periodogram analysis of the Greenwich temperature records. **1939** J. A. SCHUMPETER *Business Cycles* I. iv. 165 This is the most successful application so far made of the periodogram analysis to economic data. **1957** G. E. HUTCHINSON *Treat. Limnol.* I. v. 334 Olson (1950) examined the matter by means of periodogram analysis and found no evidence of a period near 12 hours. **1974** *Nature* 8 Feb. 339/3 The apparently erratic optical fluctuations have been analysed by various investigators using power spectra and the so-called periodogram techniques.

periodograph (pīəriǫ·dŏgrɑf). [f. PERIOD *sb.* + -O + -GRAPH.] **1.** A periodogram; orig. *spec.* a curve drawn in a periodogram.

1899 A. SCHUSTER in *Trans. Cambr. Philos. Soc.* XVIII. 108 With T as abscissa and S^2 as ordinate, draw a curve, which may be called the 'Periodograph'... It will be seen that the 'Periodograph' corresponds exactly to the curve which represents the distribution of energy in the spectrum. **1936** *Rev. Econ. Statistics* XVIII. 63/2 Like the Fourier periodogram, this periodograph will show distinct peaks in the vicinity of real periodicities. **1950** CONRAD & POLLAK *Methods in Climatol.* (ed. 2) xi. 370 The name 'periodograph' is no longer used and Schuster's 'periodograph' is now called a 'periodogram'.

2. An instrument for automatically making a periodogram analysis or Fourier analysis of a curve by optical means.

1930 G. A. R. FOSTER in *Jrnl. Textile Inst.* XXI. T18 The grating periodograph now described is an instrument which has been..designed for the examination of the irregularities in cotton spinning products... The periodograph is simply a method of carrying out automatically the periodogram analysis..of series of observations for hidden periodicities. **1946** *Suppl. Jrnl. R. Statistical Soc.* VIII. 44 In the correlation periodograph, due to Martindale, the grating of the grating periodograph is replaced by a replica of the curve on a reduced scale. **1973** *Physics Bull.* Mar. 154/2 The 'Periodograph' was never applied to the analysis of electron micrographs until Warren (1972) had the ingenious idea of replacing the grating by a series of point sources such as flashlamp bulbs and interposing a micrograph between the bulbs and the final screen.

periodontia (peri,ŏdǫ·ntiă). *Dentistry.* orig. *U.S.* [f. *periodont(ium* s.v. PERI- 1 b + -IA[1].] = *PERIODONTICS.

1914 *Items of Interest* July 429 We..deem it for the best interests of the public and the profession that a society should be formed, to the end that those especially interested may meet and work together..for the scientific investigation of periodontoclasia and caries, and that the practice of oral prophylaxis and periodontia as an exclusive speciality may be encouraged. **1924** *Glasgow Herald* 5 Mar. 9/4 Harold Box..holds the position of Professor of Dental Pathology and Periodontia at the Royal College of Dental Surgeons at Toronto, Canada. **1960** S. SORRIN *Pract. of Periodontia* p. vii/1 The treatment for periodontal disease is of interest not only to the specialist in periodontia but also to the general practitioner of dentistry. **1960** *Times* 27 July 3/2 (Advt.), Applications are invited for the appointment of Head of Department of Periodontia.

Hence **periodo·ntic** *a.* = *periodontal* adj. s.v. PERI- 1 a.

1926 R. J. E. SCOTT *Gould's Med. Dict.* 984/1 *Periodontic*, same as periodontal. **1978** *N.Y. Times* 30 Mar. B18/2 (Advt.), Dentist. Experienced for general practice. .. Crown and bridge, periodontic, endodontic, pedodontic.

periodontics (peri,ŏdǫ·ntiks), *sb. pl.* (const. as sing.). *Dentistry.* [f. as prec.: see -IC 2.] The branch of dentistry concerned with periodontal tissue, disorders, etc.

1948 L. I. GROSSMAN *Handbk. Dental Pract.* v. 83/1 Periodontics is that branch of dentistry which deals with the science and treatment of periodontal disease. **1960** S. SORRIN *Pract. of Periodontia* i. 1 The practice of periodontics is based on an understanding and recognition of the healthy periodontium. **1969** BOHANNAN & SAXE in Morris & Bohannan *Dental Specialities* vii. 260/1 Time devoted to periodontics in the traditional dental educational program has been woefully inadequate. **1975** J. E. CHASTEEN *Essent. Clin. Dental Assisting* xi. 200/1 Periodontics is the branch of dentistry that deals with the diagnosis and treatment of diseases which destroy the supporting tissues of the teeth.

periodontist (peri,ŏdǫ·ntist). *Dentistry.* [f. *PERIODONT(IA + -IST.] A specialist or expert in periodontics.

1920 STEDMAN *Med. Dict.* (ed. 6) 755/2 *Periodontist*, a dentist who specializes in periodontia. **1954** *Sydney Morning Herald* 26 Oct. 1/3 The judges were an orthodontist (for straightness), a periodontist (for condition of the gums), and a children's dental specialist. **1963** E. B. WHITE *Let.* 6 May (1976) 500 A periodontist.. proposes to remove a small section of my gum. **1965** J. C. MUHLER *Fifty-Two Pearls* ix. 93 In most cases the family dentist will..refer the patient to a periodontist (a dental specialist who treats diseased gingiva or bone). **1969** BOHANNAN & SAXE in Morris & Bohannan *Dental Specialities* vii. 259/2 There are..not enough practicing periodontists to treat all periodontal disease. **1978** *Detroit Free Press* 16 Apr. 14c/4 (Advt.), A local Don Juan periodontist is murdered.

periodontoclasia (pe:ri,ŏdǫntoklæ·siă). *Dentistry.* [f. as *PERIODONTIA + Gr. κλάσ-ις breaking (f. κλάειν to break) + -IA[1].] Destruction or degeneration of periodontal tissue.

1914 [see *PERIODONTIA]. **1960** S. SORRIN *Pract. of Periodontia* iv. 128/2 Pulpal disease may invade the periodontal space, producing inflammation and periodontoclasia.

periodontology (pe:ri,ŏdǫntǫ·lŏdʒi). *Dentistry.* orig. *U.S.* [f. as *PERIODONTIA + -OLOGY.] = *PERIODONTICS.

1914 *Items of Interest* July 529 (*heading*) A statement to the profession. From the American Academy of Oral Prophylaxis and Periodontology. **1920** *Jrnl. National Dental Assoc.* Feb. 159 (*heading*) Fundamentals of periodontology. **1960** S. SORRIN *Pract. of Periodontia* p. vii, Constant ferment of research and practical application is vital to progress in the art and science of periodontology. **1962** R. BRADLAW in Blake & Trott *Periodontology* p. v, Periodontology has not had the emphasis in dental education that it should have had. **1972** *Science* 2 June 1033/1 Department of Periodontology, Harvard School of Dental Medicine, Boston, Massachusetts.

periodontosis (pe:ri,odǫntōu·sis). *Dentistry.* [f. as *PERIODONTIA + -OSIS.] A periodontal disorder; *spec.* one in which there is a loss of alveolar bone, leading to displacement or loosening of teeth, without inflammation.

1936 DUNNING & DAVENPORT *Dict. Dental Sci.* 422/2 *Periodontosis*, a diseased condition of the periodontal membrane. **1942** ORBAN & WEINMANN in *Jrnl. Periodontology* XIII. 31 (*heading*) Diffuse atrophy of the alveolar bone (periodontosis). **1962** BLAKE & TROTT *Periodontology* iii. 28 Incidence of periodontal associated with alveolar bone destruction and pocket formation. This type of disease has been divided into chronic periodontitis.., which is inflammatory, and periodontosis .., which is principally degenerative. Periodontosis is often complicated by inflammation and the condition is then called periodontitis complex. **1975** J. D. MANSON *Periodontics* (ed. 3) xviii. 222 (*heading*) Juvenile periodontitis ('periodontosis'). *Ibid.*, Orban and Weinmann (1942) coined the term 'periodontosis' believing that the condition represented a degeneration of the periodontal ligament. However, there is no evidence for that belief.

periost (pe·ri,ǫst). *Anat.* [f. mod.L. PERIOST(EUM.] = PERIOSTEUM.

1900 in DORLAND *Med. Dict.* **1902** *Proc. Zool. Soc.* I. 212 The perisclerium is continuous with the periost of the pedicle portion [of the horn]. **1927** HALDANE & HUXLEY *Animal Biol.* ix. 185 The basal joint..was removed and a piece of healthy bone with its bone-forming membrane (periost) grafted in from another situation. **1959** *Jrnl. Exper. Zool.* CXLII. 631 Both the periost and hypertrophied areas show a strong black deposit of cobalt sulphide. **1973** *Biol. Abstr.* LVI. 719/1 In the periost, described were fibroblasts, precursor cells, [etc.].

peripediment (pe·ripedimĕnt, peripe·dimĕnt). *Geomorphol.* [f. PERI- + PEDIMENT[1].] A broad, gently sloping surface that is the top of a thickness of detrital alluvium and either extends outwards from a mountain-foot in an arid or semi-arid region or else smoothly continues the line of an intervening pediment.

1942 A. D. HOWARD in *Jrnl. Geomorphol.* V. 11 The term peripediment is suggested for a pediplane which levels an earlier basin fill. If both elements of the pediplane are present, the peripediment is always beyond and peripheral to the pediment. **1970** R. J. SMALL *Study of Landforms* ix. 308 The smaller and steeper bajadas tend to mask only the upper part of the rock pediment, burying the piedmont angle, but the larger and more gently sloping fans may be so extensive as to grade into the alluvial deposits of the peripediment. **1975** *Nature* 7 Aug. 468/1 This gravel..seems to have been deposited as a series of large confluent fans derived from the escarpment, which form an extensive..peripediment.

peripeteia, peripety. Add: (Further examples.) Also, according to the theory of Jung, the third stage, culmination, or turning point of a dream.

1911 BEERBOHM *Zuleika D.* ix. 151 For him to fall in love was a violent peripety, bound to produce a violent upheaval. **1942** K. W. BASH tr. *Jacobi's Psychol. C. G. Jung* iii. 79 *Peripetie*, which forms the 'backbone' of every dream, the weaving of the plot. The intensification of events to a crisis or to a transformation, which may also consist in a catastrophe. **1950** *Brit. Jrnl. Psychol.* XL. 236 Jung goes on to discuss the structure of dreams... He distinguishes..the culmination or peripety, and..the final lysis or solution. **1960** R. F. C. HULL tr. *Jung's On Nature of Dreams* in *Coll. Wks.* VIII. 295 The third phase brings the culmination or *peripeteia*. Here something decisive happens or something changes completely. **1964** M. MCLUHAN *Understanding Media* x. 103 So sudden an upsurge of academic training into the marketplace has in it the quality of classical peripety or reversal. **1976** S. HYNES *Auden Generation* vii. 193 In that pattern, 1936 is the peripeteia, the point where the action turned.

peripheral, *a.* Add: (Further examples.) In *Anat.* also with especial reference to the circulation, as *peripheral resistance*. Also *fig.*, marginal, superficial, on the fringe.

1877 M. FOSTER *Text Bk. Physiol.* I. iv. 92 It is this peripheral resistance (in the minute arteries and capillaries)..which gives the circulation of the blood its peculiar features. **1909** *Jrnl. Physiol.* XXXVIII. 237 Peripheral reference is the earliest phenomenon of recovery. **1915** W. M. BAYLISS *Princ. Gen. Physiol.* viii. 242 The peripheral resistance of the arterial system, resulting from the division into small arterioles, is due entirely to the internal friction of the blood, not to friction against the walls of the vessels. **1949** E. A. NIDA *Morphol.* (ed. 2) 84 A peripheral morpheme never consists of a root and is always structurally 'outside' of the nuclear constituent. *Ibid.*, Note, however, that infixes and some replacives are 'peripheral' even though they are formally included within the nuclear constituent. **1956** D. L. ABRAMSON *Diagnosis & Treatm. Peripheral Vascular Disorders* p. xiii, The physiology of the peripheral circulation. **1962** *Lancet* 27 Jan. 193/2 Chromosome analysis of peripheral-blood leucocytes grown in tissue culture. **1962** *Listener* 29 Mar. 542/2 We must distinguish between the kinds of conventional forces useful in Europe and those that might be used in the peripheral areas. *Ibid.* 10 May 825/2 Dr O'Leary mentions it in his conclusion, but it is peripheral to his main interest. **1965** M. MORSE *Unattached* i. 44 He said little and was essentially peripheral, mildly amused, and always following. **1972** R. HARTENSTEIN *Princ. Physiol.* ix. 421 Peripheral resistance and the force and rate of cardiac contractions are the major overall factors that determine blood pressure, velocity of flow, and the distribution of blood. **1973** *Word 1970* XXVI. 101 Discussion of the ultimate phonetic output of /S/ (or /z/) is peripheral to the core of this paper. **1976** *Vancouver Province* 18 June 21/2 Canadian cultural expression will remain peripheral to Canadians—unless we tackle the economics.

2. *Computers.* Applied to equipment that is used in conjunction with a computer without being an integral or necessary part of it, and to operations involving such equipment.

1956 *Proc. Eastern Joint Computer Conf. 1955* 67/2 An important current trend is toward peripheral equipment with corresponding flexibility. **1962** *Gloss. Terms Auto-*

matic Data Processing (*B.S.I.*) 25 *Peripheral transfer*, the process of transferring a block of data between peripheral equipment and a store or between two units of peripheral equipment. **1963** A. M. HILTON *Logic, Computing Machines, & Automation* vi. 256 Electric typewriters and machines to perforate paper tape are among the most widely used items of peripheral equipment, particularly for small computing-machine systems. **1967** *Times* 6 May 17/1 Many vital pieces of equipment that go into a computer installation are not made in Europe. These units, which come under the heading of peripheral equipment, are becoming more and more important. **1970** *Sci. Amer.* Oct. 102 East Germany will probably supply peripheral equipment; Hungary, magnetic memories and software (programs).

B. *sb.* *Computers.* A peripheral device. Usu. *pl.*

1966 *Economist* 10 Sept. 1048/1 It just has not got the sort of money needed to develop and market a complete line of data processing equipment and the associated 'peripherals'. **1970** *Physics Bull.* July 306/2 External storage is made up of a variety of bulk or file storage units of very large capacity, which are operated as peripherals to the central processor. **1971** B. DE FERRANTI *Living with Computer* 89 To prevent the CPU from slowing to the speed of a peripheral, a buffer may be used so that the peripheral transfers information to the buffer at its own speed while the CPU does other work. **1973** T. ALLBEURY *Choice of Enemies* xii. 53 Computer peripherals,..the bits and pieces you hang on and plug into computers. **1977** D. BAGLEY *Enemy* xii. 81 A small computer with a variety of input and output peripherals including an X-Y plotter.

peri:pheriza·tion. *rare.* [f. PERIPHER(Y + -IZATION.] Obscurity or indirectness of expression.

1926 E. POUND *Let.* 15 Nov. (1971) 202 Ms. arrived this A.M... I will have another go at it, but up to present I make nothing of it whatever. Nothing..short of divine vision or a new cure for the clapp can possibly be worth all the circumambient peripherization.

periphonic (perifǫ·nik), *a.* [f. PERI- + PHONIC *a.*] Such as to reproduce the vertical as well as the horizontal distribution of sound that has been recorded, by means of one or more loudspeakers above the level of the listener in addition to ones around him at his own level.

Whether this is the sense in quot. 1970[1] is uncertain.

1970 *Times* 25 June 7/2 The French pieces were almost as uneventful, even with benefit of this excellent multi-channel, so-called periphonic, sound. **1970** M. GERZON in *Studio Sound* Aug. 338/1 The second part of this article is devoted to the use of these considerations in obtaining a system of Periphonic (Greek: *peri-*, around) sound reproduction, i.e. the reproduction of sound in all spatial directions. **1974** *Nature* 13 Dec. 537/1 A minimum of four loudspeakers are geometrically necessary to surround the listener in three dimensions and give periphonic reproduction. **1976** *Gramophone* Feb. 1398/1 The real potential of four channels lies in periphonic reproduction using at least six loudspeakers. *Ibid.*, Although four channels are in a sense ideal for periphonic reproduction, it can be realised using only three channels.

Hence **peri·phony**, periphonic reproduction.

1970 M. GERZON in *Studio Sound* Sept. 380/1 While Granville Cooper has recently described a system of periphony called 'tetrahedral ambiophony', this is only one of many possible periphonic techniques. **1974** *Nature* 13 Dec. 537/1 To satisfy the psycho-acoustic criteria sufficiently well, however, the practical minimum is..six [loudspeakers] for periphony.

periplasm. Add: **2.** *Microbiology.* The region of a bacterial or other cell immediately within the cell wall, outside the plasma membrane. Hence **peripla·smic** *a.*

1961 P. MITCHELL in Goodwin & Lindberg *Biol. Struct. & Function* II. 590 Observations forced us to the conclusion that the glucose-6-phosphatase of intact *Escherichia coli* is enclosed in a region between the cell wall and the surface of the osmotic barrier component which we might appropriately call the 'periplasm'. **1967** *Science* 16 June 1453/3 Some time ago Mitchell proposed that glucose-6-phosphatase activity is located in such a 'periplasmic space'. **1974** *Jrnl. Bacteriol.* CXIX. 243/2 To determine whether the Hg(II)-reducing activity is present in the cytoplasm, the periplasm, or both. *Ibid.* 244/1 Alkaline phosphatase is one of the periplasmic enzymes. **1978** *Sci. Amer.* Oct. 74/2 The rat proinsulin would then 'hitch-hike' with the bacterial penicillinase into the periplasmic space, from which it could be extracted and then assayed with an antibody technique.

periplum (pe·riplʋm). [L., neut. f. PERIPLUS.] In the poetry of E. Pound (see quot. 1940).

1940 E. POUND *Cantos* lix. 83 Periplum, not as land looks on a map But as sea bord seen by men sailing. **1948** —— *Pisan Cantos* (1949) lxxiv. 7 The great periplum brings in the stars to our shore. *Ibid.* 13 Under the grey cliff in periplum. *Ibid.* lxxxii. 118 Three solemn half notes Their white downy chests black-rimmed On the middle wire Periplum.

Perique (perī·k). Also **perique.** [Louisiana F. (see quot. 1931).] In full *Perique tobacco.* A strong, dark, Louisiana tobacco.

1882 *Congress. Rec.* 6 Apr. 2642/2 Perique tobacco may be sold by the manufacturer or producer..in the form of carottes..without the payment of tax. **1885** E. CUSTER *Boots & Saddles* 84 The officers gave this chief tobacco—Perique I think it is called. **1931** W. A. READ *Louisiana-French* 57 *Perique* is said to have been the popular pseudonym of Pierre Chenet, an Acadian who first produced this variety of tobacco. **1941** E. P. O'DONNELL *Great Big Doorstep* iv. 63 Evvie's composition dealt with Louisiana products... 'Rice, cotton, perique tobacco, and fur.' **1949** *Tobacco* 7 Apr. 15/1 Perique is the only tobacco steeped in its own juice, and has a mildly fermented smell, like wine. **1976** *National Observer* (U.S.) 12 June 17-A/5 (Advt.), It's Perique, a zesty, dark and aromatic tobacco.

periscope. Add: **II. 3.** Also, a similar kind of tube-and-mirror or -prism apparatus used on land, as in trench warfare. See **trench-periscope.*

1917 A. G. EMPEY *Over Top* 303 *Periscope*, a thing in the trenches which you look through. **1951** 'M. INNES' *Operation Pax* v. xiii. 251 Remnant was fiddling with a long forceps and a couple of mirror-like stainless-steel plates. 'First-rate periscope,' he said. **1976** *Sci. Amer.* Dec. 32/3 The crane operator, protected by heavy shielding and observing his tasks through a periscope, could remove and install any of the equipment by using impact wrenches to manipulate the connectors at the ends of the jumpers.

4. *attrib.* and *Comb.*, as *periscope-wise* adv.; **periscope depth** (see quot. 1928); **periscope level** = **periscope depth.*

1928 C. F. S. GAMBLE *Story N. Sea Air Station* xviii. 309 German submarines, when travelling awash, could reach 'periscope depth' (that is, the depth at which the fully extended periscope just reaches to the surface—normally 45 feet) in 1½ minutes. **1974** L. DEIGHTON *Spy Story* xviii. 194 'Periscope depth', said Ferdy... The Captain..took us up to periscope level. **1923** J. S. HUXLEY *Ess. Biologist* iii. 116 It [*sc.* the grebe] lifts its head and neck above the water, periscope-wise, to assure itself of its direction.

pe·riscope, *v.* *poet.* [f. the sb.] *intr.* To look as if through a periscope.

1934 DYLAN THOMAS *18 Poems* 12 Where fishes' food is fed the shades Who periscope through flowers to the sky.

perish, *v.* Add: **1.** Jocose phr. *or perish in the attempt.*

1861 T. HUGHES *Tom Brown at Oxf.* I. ii 23 However, he addressed himself manfully to his task; savage indeed, and longing to drive a hole in the bottom of the old tub, but as resolved as ever to get to Sandford and back before hall time, or perish in the attempt. **1870** L. M. ALCOTT *Old-Fashioned Girl* xvii. 337 He..sternly resolved to be an honor to his family, or perish in the attempt. **1978** *Country Life* 30 Nov. 1915/4 Too often publishers are determined to illustrate or perish in the attempt.

c. Esp. of rubber.

1884 *Queen* 29 Mar. (Advt.), A flat elastic section (which, unlike rubber elastic, will not heat the person or perish in wear). **1910** *Bradshaw's Railway Guide* Apr. facing p. xv (Advt.), Self-filling fountain pen... No rubber to perish. **1971** C. M. BLOW *Rubber Technol. Manuf.* ii. 36 Familiar to all is the liability of rubber to 'perish', to harden and crack or soften to a sticky residue.

e. Now only in phr. *perish the thought.*

[**1700** C. CIBBER *King Richard III* 52 Perish that thought!] **1893** H. JAMES *Let.* in C. Mackenzie *My Life & Times* (1963) II. 317, I don't in the least pretend that any scenario I can send you..is..my *last word.* Perish the thought—it isn't the way I work. **1926** W. S. MAUGHAM *Constant Wife* III. 150 Perish the thought. I've worked like a dog..and last night..I downed tools. **1953** R. MACAULAY *Let.* 23 Jan. in *Last Lett. to Friend* (1962) 75 Which disposes of your notion that I should ever write to Miss Prescott. Perish the thought! **1961** *New Left Rev.* Mar.–Apr. 59/1 Had he, perish the thought, been privately soaking? **1974** 'D. FLETCHER' *Lovable Man* II. 120 Oh, one wouldn't go as far as that. Perish the thought.

2. Also in *pres. pple.* with the auxiliary *be* (now the more usual form with reference to exposure to (cold) weather).

1885 A. EDWARDES *Girton Girl* III. i. 11 You have given me hot coffee when I was perishing with cold. **1930** W. S. MAUGHAM *Cakes & Ale* viii. 96 Isn't it awful, the weather? You must be perishing.

3. (Further example.)

1898 W. P. RIDGE *Mord Em'ly* xv. 228 Chrise, I'll perish you, if you ain't careful.

perish, *sb.* Restrict *rare*—¹ to sense in Dict. and add: **2.** *Austral.* A state of near starvation, great thirst, or any kind of deprivation or destitution; esp. in phr. *to do a perish*: to come to such a state. Also trivially (see quot. 1941).

1894 *Argus* (Melbourne) 28 Mar. 5/4 When a man or party has nearly died through want of water he is said to have 'done a perish'. **1903** R. BEDFORD *True Eyes* 312 If Xavier Quinn hadn't found this show three months ago ye'd have done a perish. **1924** *Truth* (Sydney) 27 Apr. 6 *Perish, doing a*, to shiver; to be cold. **1929** K. S. PRICHARD *Coonardoo* v. 60 But we near done a perish for water, You. **1935** H. H. FINLAYSON *Red Centre* iii. 28 The constant struggle out of one 'perish' into another. **1941** BAKER *Dict. Austral. Slang* 53 *Do a perish*, suffer greatly from thirst, hunger or destitution. 'In a city, to sleep out in parks, to be homeless.' **1942** 'M. INNES' *Daffodil Affair* II. v. 64 'He didn't die,' said Hudspith. 'He perished.' 'He did a perish,' said Appleby corroboratively and idiomatically. **1944** F. CLUNE *Red Heart* 19, I did a thousand miles in eleven weeks on camel-back to find Lasseter's track, and follow it into the country where he did a perish. **1953** D. STIVENS *Gambling Ghost* 3 You'll do a perish, mate, and no mistake. You're two hundred miles as the crow flies from anywhere. **1959** H. P. TRITTON *Time means Tucker* 15/1 The train-crew who had made us do a perish on the Galathera Plain. **1969** 'A. GARVE' *Boomerang* ii. 71 His intention was to enjoy this trip..not to 'do a perish' in the Never Never.

perishable, *a.* (*sb.*) **1.** (Further examples.)

1810 E. WEETON *Jrnl.* Apr. (1969) I. 257 He will sometimes order such quantities of perishable household articles, that one half are sometimes wasted. **1929** F. C. BOWEN *Sea Slang* 102 *Perishable Cargo.* In the 18th century, slaves or fruit. **1958** M. ROBERTS *Gustavus Adolphus* II. i. 43 Gustav Vasa..discharged his debt to Lübeck in goods, and sometimes in goods of a dangerously perishable nature: at least one instalment was paid in butter.

perished, *ppl. a.* (Further examples.)

1747 H. GLASSE *Art of Cookery* xxi. 161 If any soft or perished Place appear on the Outside [of cheese], try how deep it goes. *a* **1922** T. S. ELIOT *Waste Land Drafts* (1971) 75 Over perished plains, stumbling in cracked earth. **1922** H. P. STEVENS in S. Morgan *Prep. Plantation Rubber* xxi. 306 After a time, vulcanised rubber tends to harden, cracks appear on the surface when the article is bent or stretched, and eventually the rubber becomes rotten and 'perished'. **1923** B. D. W. LUFF *Chem. of Rubber* vii. 86 Spiller found that the unvulcanised rubber coating on a piece of fabric after six years had lost its original properties and had become hard and brittle, or 'perished', to use the term now applied to such a change. **1950** J. CANNAN *Murder Included* vii. 158 A perished washer might account for the dripping. **1964** R. PETRIE *Murder by Precedent* iii. 39 The half-perished suspenders and wrinkled stockings. **1965** D. FRANCIS *Odds Against* xiii. 178 Weather forecasts are as reliable as a perished hot-water bottle. **1967** LEYLAND & WATTS in J. A. Brydson *Devel. with Natural Rubber* v. 67 If this were so, then under the more severe running conditions.., casing compounds based conventionally on natural rubber would reach a perished condition in a relatively short time. **1978** *Country Life* 30 Nov. 1915/3 Old nylon stockings.. infinitely superior to perished rubber releasing corroded wire.

perisher. Add: **a.** Also, more generally used of persons, with an overtone of pity. Also (*little*) *perishers* pl., children.

1908 A. N. LYONS *Arthur's* II. i. 106 Poor ole perisher's 'fraid to come in, 'e is. **1924** R. KEABLE *Recompence* i. 9 But we can't hear of a soul, or, if we do, the perisher funks this place. **1935** WODEHOUSE *Luck of Bodkins* xv. 181 If you ask me, they don't learn the little perishers nothing. **1942** —— *Money in Bank* (1946) xi. 85 Most modern young men are squirts and perishers. **1957** R. PARK *One-a-Pecker* (1958) xi. 199 He had no name. In the thaw they buried him in the pass, and his epitaph was *Some Poor Bloody Perisher.* 1864. **1979** *Guardian* 30 Apr. 13/2, I taught the whole school..about Palm Sunday... Not one of the little perishers knew.

b. *Austral.* = *PERISH *sb.* 2.

1903 R. BEDFORD *True Eyes* 292 Of course that country we went to on the Peak was a shicer. Just's well you didn't come—we near did a perisher there. **1903** 'T. COLLINS' *Such is Life* I. 7 You will understand that the bullock drivers' choice of accommodation lay between the selection, the ram-paddock, and a perisher on the plain... A perisher on the plain is seldom hard to find in a bad season, when the country is stocked for good seasons. **1936** A. RUSSELL *Gone Nomad* vi. 44 Where one flood will leave behind a well-filled waterhole..the next, probably, will fill the hole with sand. And that is precisely what had happened here... It looked as if we were in for what the Inlander calls a 'perisher'.

c. *Naval slang.* A periscope. Hence in extended uses (see quot. 1962).

1925 FRASER & GIBBONS *Soldier & Sailor Words* 221 *Perisher*, periscope. **1948** PARTRIDGE *Dict. Forces' Slang* 139 *The Perisher*, the C.O.'s course for submarine commanders. **1952** E. YOUNG *One of our Submarines* viii. 115 At one time the course on which we were embarked had been called the Periscope School; hence the grimly humorous contraction 'Perisher'. Now it was officially the C.O.Q.C., or Commanding Officers' Qualifying Course, but, by tradition we were still known as the perishers. *Ibid.* 125 Ours happened to be the first perisher course to have Teddy Woodward for instructor. **1962** GRANVILLE *Dict. Sailors' Slang* 87/2 *Perisher, the*, periscope course for officers selected to command submarines. A 'perishing' difficult examination. 2. An officer undergoing this course, which is officially styled *the Commanding Officers Qualifying Course.* **1973** D. REEMAN *Go in & Sink!* i. 16 We did our *Perisher* together, and even when I got *Tristram* he was given *Tryphon.*

perishing, *vbl. sb.* Add: **c.** *spec.* of rubber.

1913 B. D. PORRITT *Chem. of Rubber* i. 12 The oxidation of rubber..is technically known as 'perishing'. **1935** DAWSON & PORRITT *Rubber* 602/1 *Perishing*, the final stage in the ageing of vulcanised rubber which becomes oxidised with the formation of resinous materials, losing its characteristic elastic properties. **1954** H. J. STERN *Rubber* v. 152 The 'perishing' of rubber, particularly of manufactured rubber articles, has been a source of trouble to all concerned from the time of Hancock down to the present day. **1961** D. W. HUKE *Introd. Natural & Synthetic Rubbers* v. 80 One of the most important problems a rubber compounder has to face is the perishing—usually referred to as the ageing—of rubber.

perishing, *ppl. a.* Add: **2.** Also *Austral.*, with reference to *PERISH *sb.* 2.

1941 I. L. IDRIESS *Great Boomerang* xvii. 124 Sixty miles to water, along a perishing track on a perishing day.

3. *colloq.* Applied disparagingly to anything: insignificant; troublesome; also as an intensive and as a filler.

1847 E. BRONTË *Wuthering Heights* II. xiii. 266 Do you imagine..that healthy, hearty girl, will tie herself to a little perishing monkey like you? **1903** KIPLING *Five*

Nations 196 We were sugared about by the old men (Panicky, perishin' old men). **1916** 'TAFFRAIL' *Pincher Martin* iii. 32 A long coaling in the winter is the 'perishin' limit', as some one put it. **1918** [see *BLIGHTY, BLIGHTY *sb.* c]. **1930** [see *flat spin* s.v. *FLAT *a.* 15]. **1952** M. ALLINGHAM *Tiger in Smoke* iv. 75 These perishing crooks, who do they think they are all of a sudden?

4. as *adv.* Excessively, perishingly.

1888 E. MARSHALL *Bristol Diamonds* ix. 106 It is perishing cold to-day. **1906** *Westm. Gaz.* 26 Feb. 4/2 I'm perishing hungry. I feel as if I should drop. **1933** M. LOWRY *Ultramarine* ii. 63 You've been a perishing long time with that coffee! **1945** G. MILLAR *Maquis* i. 21 They all say it's perishing cold in the aircraft.

b. Used as a mere intensive.

1959 M. GILBERT *Blood & Judgement* v. 54 He..turns right at the top, because it's the only way he perishing well can turn.

perishless (pe·riʃlės), *a.* [f. PERISH *v.* + -LESS.] That cannot perish; imperishable.

1605 SYLVESTER tr. *Du Bartas's Weekes & Workes* 628 We must, to make vs blest,..propose our selues that perfect, perish-les, That true vnfained good, that good all danger-les From th'vniust spoile of theeues. **1885** J. BEVERIDGE *Poets of Clackmannanshire* 144 Wallace of perishless renown. **1915** *Times* 31 Mar. 9/3 The perishless faith of the lover takes their spears of rebellion into its own wounds to hide them.

peristeronic, *a.* Add: Also, suggestive of pigeons.

1931 J. CANNAN *High Table* 21 A discourse..which Anne and Cecilia punctuated with polite little peristeronic sounds.

peritectic (perite·ktik), *a.* and *sb.* [ad. G. *peritektisch* (W. Guertler *Metallographie* (1912) I. vi. 278), f. Gr. περί around, about + τηκτικ-ός able to dissolve (f. τήκειν to melt): cf. EUTECTIC *a.* and *sb.* in Dict. and Suppl.] **A.** *adj.* Of, pertaining to, or designating a reaction that occurs between the solid phase and the liquid phase during the cooling of a mixture, with the formation of a new solid phase; *peritectic point*, the state at which all three phases coexist in equilibrium, the composition being such that a fall in temperature results in the disappearance of the two phases that exist above that temperature; also, the point representing this state in a constitutional diagram.

1924 JEFFRIES & ARCHER *Sci. of Metals* ix. 323 There are different solid phases in equilibrium with the melt above and below the peritectic temperature. During the peritectic reaction there are three phases (two solid and one liquid) in equilibrium, so that the temperature must remain constant until at least one of the phases disappears. **1936** *Nature* 18 Apr. 657/2 Preliminary results from an X-ray study of the peritectic reaction α + liquid $\rightarrow \beta$ in the Cu-Zn system prove that the orientations assumed by the β-phase are definitely related to the orientation of the α-phase. **1965** PHILLIPS & WILLIAMS *Inorg. Chem.* I. viii. 302 The cases in which there is one or more eutectic or peritectic points..reflect rather an unfavourable interaction between A and B which may well be caused by size differences in the atom. **1967** A. H. COTTRELL *Introd. Metall.* xv. 230 The composition at *r*..is the peritectic composition and the isothermal line *pq* marks the peritectic temperature. Just above this temperature there is no β-phase in any alloy; just below, all alloys from *p* to *q* contain some β. The silver-platinum system has a simple peritectic diagram. **1968** B. BAYLY *Introd. Petrol.* 330 If we knew that all Hawaiian rocks were generated from one homogeneous initial magma pool, we would conclude that there was necessarily a peritectic relation. **1973** J. G. TWEEDDALE *Materials Technol.* I. vi. 163 The reverse type of change to a eutectic reaction called a peritectic reaction can occur in many materials—this cannot be used to induce supersaturation but may be a means for producing a stable solid solution structure.

B. *sb.* A peritectic point or temperature.

1929 *Jrnl. Iron & Steel Inst.* CXIX. 337 In carbon steels, between the temperature of freezing and that of the peritectic, iron containing a maximum of 0·07 per cent. of carbon is the only solid to separate. **1975** *Nature* 20 Nov. 220/2 Any model of the igneous processes which produced the eucrites must account for this preferential generation of liquids at peritectic *A* (Fig. 1).

Hence **perite·ctically** *adv.*, by a peritectic reaction.

1935 G. E. DOAN *Princ. Physical Metall.* iv. 158 At 1500° the melt and δ crystals react peritectically to form γ-iron solid-solution crystals. **1967** A. H. COTTRELL *Introd. Metall.* xv. 233 Fig. 15.12 shows an example in which the γ primary solution also forms peritectically.

peritectoid (perite·ktoid), *a.* [f. prec. + -OID, after *EUTECTOID *a.* and *sb.*] Of, pertaining to, or designating a reaction analogous to a peritectic reaction but involving three solid phases.

1936 H. L. ALLING *Interpretative Petrol. Igneous Rocks* viii. 97 The diagram shows that hedenbergite, $CaFeSi_2O_6$ on heating dissociates before reaching the solidus, forming a solid solution. I suggest this may be called a 'peritectoid' reaction. **1967** A. H. COTTRELL *Introd. Metall.* xv. 235 Eutectoid and peritectoid changes occur in the solid state which are the exact analogues of the eutectic and peritectic forms of the liquid-solid change. **1973** J. G. TWEEDDALE *Materials Technol.* I. vi. 163 There is also a form of reaction in the solid state, called the peritectoid reaction which is similar to the peritectic reaction.

peritoneoscopy (peritonĭ·ǫ̆skǫpi, pe:ritoni,ǫ·-skǫ̆pi). *Med.* [f. PERITONEO- + *-SCOPY.] Visual examination of the peritoneal contents by means of a narrow instrument passed through a small incision in the peritoneum.

1936 in STEDMAN *Med. Dict.* (ed. 13). **1959** BAILEY & LOVE *Short Pract. Surg.* (ed. 11) xxiv. 501 For many years peritoneoscopy has been advocated for inspecting intraperitoneal organs without the necessity of laparatomy, but comparatively few surgeons employ it. **1974** R. M. KIRK et al. *Surgery* vi. 108 The diagnosis may be confirmed by needle biopsy, surgical biopsy, or at peritoneoscopy using an endoscope inserted through a small abdominal incision.

peri-urban (pe·ri,ǝ̄rbăn), *a.* [f. PERI- + URBAN *a.* and *sb.*] Esp. in Africa: immediately adjoining a city or conurbation.

1948 *Rep. Native Laws Comm., 1946–48* (Dept. Native Affairs, S. Afr.) 5/1 Johannesburg is still grappling desperately with its problem of peri-urban squatters, of whom over 50,000 have already been collected in the controlled squatters' camps of Moroka and Jabavu. **1952** L. MARQUARD *Peoples & Policies S. Afr.* 51 In 1947 the Department of Native Affairs estimated that 154,000 urban and peri-urban houses were required for Africans. **1961** *Times* 25 July 8/3 The fashionable peri-urban district some 11 miles from Johannesburg. **1971** *E. Afr. Standard* (Nairobi) 13 Apr. 9/8 Patients from the rural and peri-urban areas. **1971** E. JONES in J. Spencer *Eng. Lang. W. Afr.* 67 These figures are for Freetown only; there were for example 1,216 persons in Regent Town, one of the several peri-urban settlements. **1974** *Times* 17 Sept. 15/5 Unified Family Courts have been set up in peri-urban areas of Vancouver. **1976** *Nature* 1–8 Jan. 40/1 Thirty-six peri-urban Kikuyu infants..participated in the study.

periwinkle[1]. Add: **3. b.** A blue colour like that of the periwinkle flower. Also *attrib.* and as *adj.*

1902 [in Dict., sense 4]. **1922** *Daily Mail* 20 Dec. 1 (Advt.), *Lingerie crepe*... In a full range of charming colours, including Pink, Sky, Jade, Flesh, Shrimp, Saxe,..Fawn, Periwinkle and Cham. **1973** L. COOPER *Tea on Sunday* i. 22 His waisted periwinkle coat. **1977** C. STORR *Tales Psychiatrist's Couch* 83 'Plenty of time to think of getting married later, that's what I say,' Liz said, fixing me with those bulging periwinkle eyes.

perk, *sb.*[2] For *slang* read *colloq.* and add earlier and later examples.

1824 J. MACTAGGART *Scottish Gallovidian Encycl.* 383 *Pirkuz*, any kind of perquisite. **1869** J. GREENWOOD *Seven Curses of London* ix. 169 The species of dishonesty alluded to..is called by the cant name of 'perks', which is a convenient abbreviation of the word 'perquisites', and in the hands of the users of it, it shows itself a word of amazing flexibility. It applies to such unconsidered trifles as wax candle ends, and may be stretched so as to cover the larcenous abstraction by our man-servant of forgotten coats and vests. **1876** *Punch's Almanack for 1877* 12/3 Christmas Carol (By a Poor Expectant of Perks)... When other Govs. for other clerks Shall 'strike upon the bell', And proffer..The 'tips' they love so well... Then, *Yule*, remember me! **1897** A. BENNETT *Jrnl.* 16 Dec. (1932) I. 66 'My missis,' he said, 'has extraction money and toothpowder money for 'er perks.' **1939** J. MASEFIELD *Live & Kicking Ned* 147 It's the Old Man's perk to order some damned silly thing. **1941** J. CARY *Herself Surprised* lxiv. 160 But she would do her own housekeeping. 'For I hate waste,' she said, 'and I never allow perks.' **1957** A. GRIMBLE *Return to Islands* 7, I began bargaining for better pay and perks than she had mentioned. **1959** *News Chron.* 20 Oct. 6/1 The post [of Speaker] was in danger of becoming a Tory perk. **1961** H. S. TURNER *Something Extraordinary* v. 116 The child allowance..is regarded as a perk for the parents. **1970** G. F. NEWMAN *Sir, You Bastard* 11 Perks were part of the profession. **1976** *Daily Mirror* 16 July 9/6 British Rail are cutting back on travel perks for their top managers following last year's £500 million loss. **1977** *Times* 8 Feb. 17/1 The philistines would be foolish to regard aid for the arts merely as a perk provided by all for the esoteric pursuits of the few.

perk, *sb.*[3] Also **perc.** [Abbrev. of PERCOLATOR.] **a.** A coffee percolator. **b.** Coffee made in a percolator.

1934 F. E. BAILY *Fleet St. Girl* iii. 59 Amazing coffee Charles makes in that electric perc. **1941** J. SMILEY *Hash House Lingo* 42 *Perk*, coffee. **1945** BAKER *Austral. Lang.* xv. 264 *Perc* from percolator. **1956** H. GOLD *Man who was not with It* (1965) xxx. 277 But don't try to use the perc, you're too stupid. **1960** WENTWORTH & FLEXNER *Dict. Amer. Slang* 384/1 *Perk, perc* n., percolated coffee, as opposed to that boiled in a pan. Orig. cowboy use; later hobo use.

perk, *v.*[1] Add: **I. 1.** (Further example.)

1957 M. SPARK *Comforters* viii. 197 Her whole body seemed to perk with delight.

f. For *dial.* read *colloq.* (Further examples.)

1936 WODEHOUSE *Laughing Gas* iii. 31 As the days went along, I found myself perking up a bit. I seemed to be making progress. **1936** M. MITCHELL *Gone with Wind* vii. 132 Dr. Fontaine admitted that he was puzzled, after his tonic of sulphur, molasses and herbs failed to perk her up. **1957** M. SPARK *Comforters* i. 18 Then she perked up. **1957** E. EAGER *Magic by Lake* iv. 89 It seemed to do him good. For he perked up noticeably, and the flush of health began to appear on his wan cheek. **1962** *Listener* 20 Dec. 1041/1 The rate of growth dropped to 3 per cent. between 1958 and 1961. It is only in the past year or so that it has perked up. **1977** *Time* 10 Jan. 44/2 The Christmas results constituted fresh evidence that consumers are starting to spend again and the sluggish economy is perking up. **1977** *Lancet* 6 Aug. 291/2 Within days of stopping propranolol the patient perked up and became once more his old self.

II. 2. b. To enliven; elevate; stimulate interest in. Usu. with *up*.

1965 *Amer. Speech* XL. 287 The plentiful examples.. are often entertaining enough..to perk up the laziest student. **1968** *Globe & Mail* (Toronto) 17 Feb. 9/3 The election so perked up spirits that many people began talking of new possibilities of cooperation and solidarity among the 22 active member states of the OAS. **1973** *Publishers Weekly* 1 Jan. 53/1 His hardnosed critique of modern capitalism..and his incisive study of the New Left's shortcomings..are sufficiently pragmatic to perk the interest of a good many readers concerned with change. **1976** *Scotsman* 15 Dec. 20/4 In the last week nearly £1 million—in theory at any rate—has changed hands down south as clubs attempt to perk up ailing sides with that most obvious of remedies. **1976** *Time* 20 Dec. 32/2 After 34 years of perking up Washington as a White House reporter..Auntie Mameish Liz Carpenter is heading home to Austin, Texas.

c. To say or comment in a brisk, lively, or self-assertive manner. *rare.*

1940 W. EMPSON *Gathering Storm* 15 Small lar that sunned itself in Mercury And perked one word there that made space ends meet. **1973** C. HIMES *Black on Black* 135 'Maybe it's some scoff from the government's thing for the poor folks,' she perked hopefully.

perk, *v.*[3] *colloq.* (orig. *U.S.*). Also **perc.** [Abbrev. of PERCOLATE *v.*] **a.** *trans.* To make (coffee) in a percolator; to boil (coffee) *up*. Also *absol.* **b.** *intr.* Of coffee: to percolate, bubble, or boil (also said of the vessel). Also *transf.* and *fig.* Hence **perked** *ppl. a.*, **pe·rking** *vbl. sb.*

In *fig.* uses not easily distinguished from *PERK *v.*[1] 1f.

1934 in WEBSTER. **1936** MENCKEN *Amer. Lang.* (ed. 4) v. 192 To *perc* (to make coffee in a *percolator*). **1939** C. MORLEY *Kitty Foyle* 330 We..flopped ourselves down and perked some coffee. **1940** C. MCCULLERS *Heart is Lonely Hunter* (1943) I. iv. 46 An electric coffee-pot was perking on the table. **1943** in Simmons & Meyer *This is your Amer.* III. 33 This unit will toast the bread..perk the coffee. **1948** F. BROWN *Murder can be Fun* (1951) vii. 102 I'll start some coffee perking. **1952** G. W. BRACE *Spire* (1953) xx. 202, I always perked the stuff... We thought the perking was as good as magic. *Ibid.*, I decided the perked stuff was too thin. **1960** 'E. MCBAIN' *Give Boys Great Big Hand* vi. 54, I think the coffee's perking. **1964** *Which?* Feb. 47/2 All the percolators were allowed to 'perc' for 10 minutes. **1972** *Newsweek* 10 Jan. 19 By summer, so the calculations go, the economy will be perking quite nicely, and the President will go to the people as the agent of newfound prosperity. **1972** *Daily Colonist* (Victoria, B.C.) 25 June 7/4 They are designed to boost employment and get slow-growth areas of Canada perking from a new-industry point of view. **1973** K. GILES *File on Death* iii. 78 Come in, sport, and take some coffee. I was just perking some up. **1976** D. HEFFRON *Crusty Crossed* ix. 72 She showed us how to perk the coffee and conquer the toaster. **1977** P. HARCOURT *At High Risk* i. 37 While I waited for the coffee to perc, I made my bed.

Perkin[3] (pǝ̄·ɹkin). *Chem.* [The name of Sir William *Perkin* (1838–1907), English chemist.] **a.** *Perkin's mauve*, †*purple*, or *violet*, a dye that was first prepared by Perkin in 1856 by oxidizing crude aniline with potassium dichromate, and was the first synthetic dye to be used commercially; = MAUVE *sb.*

1860 *Chem. News* 21 Jan. 74/2 Notices of some of the patents taken out for the preparation and use of the new purple dyes generally known as the 'mauve or Perkins' [*sic*] Purple', [etc.]. **1886** ROSCOE & SCHORLEMMER *Treat. Chem.* III. III. 319 Other patents were soon taken out for this colour, and it came into the market under different names, such as Tyrian purple, Aniline violet, Perkin's violet, [etc.]. **1908** *Jrnl. Chem. Soc.* XCIII. 2247 Many of the products obtained by these inventors could not have been Perkin's mauve at all, and,..not one of these rival processes was enabled to compete successfully with the original 'bichromate' method. **1964** N. G. CLARK *Mod. Org. Chem.* xxii. 454 Perkin's Mauve, as the substance was called, became the first synthetic dye. **1971** E. GURR *Synthetic Dyes* 123 Mauveine (mauve; Perkin's violet) is a basic dye of the azine group... Mauveine has been obsolete for several decades past.

b. *Perkin('s) reaction* or *synthesis*, any of a number of types of reaction discovered by Perkin, esp. that in which, typically, an arylacrylic acid is formed by the condensation of an aromatic aldehyde with the anhydride of an aliphatic acid, in the presence of the sodium salt of the latter.

1882 *Jrnl. Chem. Soc.* XLII. 190 (*heading*) Interpretation of syntheses by Perkin's reaction. **1908** *Ibid.* XCIII. 2226 About 1867 he [*sc.* Perkin] must have commenced these researches..which..culminated in that beautiful method of synthesising unsaturated acids now known as the 'Perkin synthesis'. **1960** GOWAN & WHEELER *Name Index Org. Reactions* (ed. 2) 189 Perkin synthesis of alicyclic compounds. Compounds containing active methylene groups react with polymethylene dihalides in the presence of a base..to yield alicyclic compounds. **1972** *Materials & Technol.* IV. xiii. 462 Acetic anhydride is the most applicable reagent in the Perkin reaction. **1973** B. J. HAZZARD tr. *Organicum* 479 In the Perkin synthesis, aldehydes or ketones are treated with anhydrides of aliphatic carboxylic acids, giving rise to α, β-unsaturated carboxylic acids.

perk test (pə̄·ɹk test). *U.S.* [f. PERC(OLATION + TEST *sb.*[1]] The act of percolating water through earth as a test of suitability for a septic tank. Hence **pe·rk-tested** *ppl. a.*

1974 *State* (Columbia, S. Carolina) 1 Apr. 9-B/6 (Advt.), Near Hilton, 158′ on water, 208′ in depth, 161′ on rear, water system & perk test approved (restricted). **1976** *Washington Post* 19 Apr. C20/3 (Advt.), Surveyed, staked, recorded & 'perk' tested. **1976** *Billings* (Montana) *Gaz.* 30 June 7-D/2 (Advt.), Beautiful view, live stream, good road, perk test, soil samples comp. Protective restrictions. Ready to build on.

perlative (pə̄·ɹlătiv). *Linguistics.* [f. L. *perlatus*, *pa. pple.* of *perferre*, to carry through, convey + -IVE.] A grammatical case signifying movement alongside or means of transportation.

1953 *Trans. Philol. Soc. 1952* 72 The use of the perlative case..is of some interest. *Ibid.*, The perlative would seem to indicate going 'alongside' so as to be 'at'. **1966** G. S. LANE in Birnbaum & Puhvel *Anc. Indo-European Dial.* 217 A distinguishes formally between an instrumental in *-yo* and a so-called perlative in *-ā*.

perleau (pə̄·ɹlōu). *U.S. dial.* Also perlo. = PILAU.

1933 in *Amer. Speech* VIII. III. 40/2 A month later I went down to Uncle Rich's hunting cabin for a perleau supper. **1935** Z. N. HURSTON *Mules & Men* I. i. 31 There was plenty of chicken perleau and baked chicken. **1955** *This Week* 25 Sept. 32/1 Perlo in local parlance [north Florida] is a chicken pilau.

perlemoen (pɛ̄rləmu·n). *S. Afr.* Also **paarlmoer.** [Afrikaans, f. Du. *parelmoer* mother of pearl.] = *KLIPKOUS.

1853 L. PAPPE *Synopsis Edible Fishes Cape Good Hope* 12 Amongst the mollusca, none are more eagerly caught, and none have such a deserved reputation as *Haliotis Midae Lin.* (Klipkous; Sea-ear), and a species of *Stomatia* (Paarlmoer). **1911** J. D. F. GILCHRIST *S. Afr. Zool.* ix. 192 The transposition of the organs [of unequal-sided molluscs]..may be so complete that the visceral loop is pulled into the form of the figure 8. Forms in which this occur..are the ordinary Limpet.., the Perlemoen or Klipkoes of South African Seas.., and the common periwinkle. **1947** [see *KLIPKOUS]. **1950** *Cape Times* 5 July 14/3, I have already mentioned having enjoyed a *perlemoen* dish out at Blaauwberg. **1958** L. G. GREEN *S. Afr. Beachcomber* xi. 127 South Africans are compensated for the scarcity of scallops by an abundance of *perlemoen.* This is the abalone of America and the *ormer* of the Channel Islands. They grow up to nine inches, and one of that size makes a rich meal indeed. **1966** [see *KLIPKOUS]. **1970** G. CROUDACE *Scarlet Bikini* ii. 14 Perlemoen was said to have the effect of oysters upon the human libido.

perlite. Add: *spec.* Fine or coarse grains of this mineral used, with appropriate nutrient solutions, as a medium for the growth of plants.

1956 T. M. MORRISON in *N.Z. Jrnl. Agric.* XCIII. 503/1 The coarse grade of expanded perlite now on the market in New Zealand is ideal for plant growth. *Ibid.* 503/3 Perlite is cheap enough to be thrown out after several crops have been raised in it. **1971** 'D. HALLIDAY' *Dolly & Doctor Bird* viii. 106 We saw the trucks going by from the big netted nursery... Trucks full of potted plants, and bags of horticultural perlite, and Canadian sphagnum peat moss. **1976** A. C. BUNT *Mod. Potting Composts* ii. 38 Perlite is an alumino-silicate of volcanic origin and is widely used in the USA and New Zealand, both countries having large natural deposits of this mineral.

perlo, var. *PERLEAU.

perlocution (pə̄ɹlokiū·ʃən). Restrict † *Obs. rare* to sense in Dict. and add: **b.** *Philos.* A speech act, such as persuading or convincing, that may or may not be successfully achieved by an illocutionary act such as entreating or arguing. Also *attrib.* So **perlocu·tionary** *a.*

1955 J. L. AUSTIN *How to do Things with Words* (1962) viii. 101 Act (C. *a*) or Perlocution. He persuaded me to shoot her. *Ibid.* 102 We can similarly distinguish the locutionary act 'he said that..' from the illocutionary act 'he argued that..' and the perlocutionary act 'he convinced me that..'. **1969** J. KAMINSKY *Lang. & Ontology* viii. 111 It could be said to have perlocutionary act potential in that it is clearly meant to have an effect on Jones. **1973** *Times Lit. Suppl.* 5 Oct. 1161/5 Austin called a speaker's act perlocutionary so far as, by saying something, the speaker produced some intended or unintended effect on the feelings, thoughts or actions of someone. **1976** *Archivum Linguisticum* VII. 67 Perlocutionary effects have to do with whether or not one actually succeeds in apologizing, persuading, or whatever, over and above communicating the fact that one is attempting to do this. **1977** *Language* LIII. 197 Both getting the officer to evict them and getting them to leave are perlocutionary *sequels* to the illocutionary act of asking the question.

Perlon (pə̄·ɹlǫn). Also **perlon.** A proprietary name (first used in Germany) for nylon 6, a type of nylon produced by the polymerization of caprolactam.

1941 *Chem. Abstr.* XXXV. 7200 In Germany the polymer is known as Igamide, the fiber as Perlon. **1954** *Brit. Rayon & Synthetic Fibres Man.* i. 45 Perlon (nylon 6) is a polyamide chemically resembling nylon 66 very closely. **1958** *Official Gaz.* (U.S. Patent Office) 28 Jan. TM 110/1 Perlon-Warenzeichenverband E.V., Frankfurt (Main), Germany. Filed Nov. 21, 1955... Perlon... For nylon fibers, filaments, strands, [etc.]. **1958** *Trade Marks Jrnl.* 12 Mar. 265/2 Perlon... synthetic textile fibres. Perlon-Warenzeichenverband Eingetragener Verein.., Frankfurt/Main, Germany; merchants. **1960** *Vogue Pattern Bk.* Autumn 45 Girdle in lightweight Perlon elastic with a Perlon tafetta front panel. **1973** C. BONINGTON *Next Horizon* xii. 168 Economising on weight, we had used 7 mm perlon,..with a breaking strain of 2,000 lb. **1976** M. & G. GORDON *Ordeal* (1977) xvii. 181 They carried pitons, nuts, stoppers, braided perlon cord..and other mountain-climbing equipment.

perlustration. Delete *Obs.* exc. in techn. use and add later examples.

1946 L. P. HARTLEY *Sixth Heaven* v. 98 The interest of seeing whether he was before or behind his schedule.. helped..the process of perlustration. **1967** *Times* 15 Mar. 6/5 Mr. Hugh Fraser..asked the Prime Minister whether cables and radio telegrams sent by M.P.s were privileged from perlustration by the security services. *Ibid.*, Perlustration was in common use in the secret police of the Tsarist regime. **1972** *Oxf. Univ. Gaz.* CII. Suppl. No. 8. 47 The Curators conducted a perlustration of the Library on 29 May—the first ever at Rhodes House.

perm (pə̄ɹm), *sb.*[1] *colloq.* Abbrev. of *permanent wave* s.v. *PERMANENT *a.* (*sb.*) 1 d.

1927 *Home Chat* 22 Oct. 200 How long does a 'perm' last? **1929** N. ROYDE-SMITH *Summer Holiday* 113 The old girl's had a perm. Look at the waves. **1932** *Modern Weekly* 30 Apr. 136 You can have a 'perm.', or you may find a tong wave best. **1937** G. FRANKAU *More of Us* xv. 162 All perfume, perm and pearls and prominent teeth. **1943** J. B. PRIESTLEY *Daylight on Saturday* vii. 43 There was a girl called Elsie, who was a fake blonde, had a terrific perm. **1954** WODEHOUSE *Jeeves & Feudal Spirit* xii. 109 This aunt who sat before me clutching feverishly at her perm. **1960** M. SPARK *Ballad of Peckham Rye* iii. 45 She moved her hand across her perm, nipping each brown wave in turn between her third and index fingers. **1976** *National Observer* (U.S.) 31 Jan. 8/2 After carrying around a headful of perfectly straight hair, I now sport a crown of exotic, wavy, fluffy, jaunty, tousled, perky, spirally, bouncy curls. I have a perm.

perm, *sb.*[2] *colloq.* Abbrev. of *PERMUTATION 4*.

1956 *News Chron.* 1 Nov. 10/8 Perms and plain paper bets accepted. **1958** L. GIBBS *Gowns & Satyr's Legs* xix. 128 He studied it [*sc.* a printed paper] intently, being in the process of constructing what..he called a 'perm'. **1958** *Punch* 27 Aug. 265/3 No pools investor of quality would seek advice from hacks who write:..Middlesbrough rate high in homes perm. **1971** *E. Afr. Standard* (Nairobi) 10 Apr. 2/7 (Advt.), See our collector for coupons, plans and perms. **1973** *Weekly News* (Glasgow) (Football Suppl.) 11 Aug. 3/1 And perm fans especially welcome the chance to cover more matches that the lower stakes give. **1974** *Guardian* 26 Nov. 27/2 Littlewoods have introduced a new perm—the £½ plan—using 12 selections which gives tight cover for only 50p. One is guaranteed 24 points if any nine matches result as score draws, and there are several other combinations which would provide a first dividend with only eight.

perm, *v.*[1] *colloq.* [f. *PERM *sb.*[1]] *trans.* To give a permanent wave to (the hair). So **permed** *ppl. a.*, having a permanent wave.

1928 *Daily Express* 17 Mar. 9/5 These girls took their chairs at 7.30 p.m... Three hours later they rose 'permed', as one says in the profession. **1931** S. HOLME in *Repertory* 6 June 10/2 Thea spent nearly all day at the hairdresser's having her hair 'permed'. **1936** A. CHRISTIE *ABC Murders* xi. 83 Her hair had evidently recently been permed, it stood out from her head in a mass of rather frizzy curls. **1952** *News Chron.* 8 July 4/1 Children's hair differs from adults in that it is finer in texture and less elastic. Meaning that what perms Mother won't necessarily perm daughter. **1956** I. MURDOCH *Flight from Enchanter* 192 Her elaborately permed hair. **1959** *News Chron.* 11 Aug. 6/2 There is a growing tendency for British mothers to perm children's hair. **1960** F. RAPHAEL *Limits of Love* III. v. 328 Newly permed brown hair. **1970** 'D. HALLIDAY' *Dolly & Cookie Bird* iv. 52 His golden, permed sideburns glistened. **1973** J. THOMSON *Death Cap* v. 75 She had her brother's..gingerish, greying hair, although hers was permed into a lot of little waves.

perm, *v.*[2] *colloq.* [Abbrev. PERMUTE *v.* or f. *PERM *sb.*[2]] To make a selection of (so many) from a larger number; to make a permutation of (*PERMUTATION 3 b).

1959 *Times* 9 Mar. 11/4 One trusting citizen, having duly filled in a complex formula 'perming' a number of matches, looked upon his labour as a guarantee that dividends would automatically come pouring in. **1968** *Guardian* 11 July 9/7 Perm any six of these reasons to find out why an aircraft..crashed last week. **1972** *Ibid.* 3 Apr. 9/3 He went about it..composing 50 horoscopes in a single night... Then daily he permed any 12 from 50 so that 'conflict within the home' would befall Leos one week and Scorpios another. **1973** *Milestones* Summer 21/1 There are 12 all told, if you perm the alternatives of 2- or 4-door body shells and four engine sizes (of which two are also available in hotted up 'Sport Special' form). **1976** J. SNOW *Cricket Rebel* 51 At the start he would 'perm' any two from three with the new ball, each bowler taking a turn at bowling with the wind at his back. **1976** *Shooting Mag.* Dec. 18/1 Gilstone Manor—I dare not use its real name—sits on the edge of a National Park (perm any one from nine) and is a hybrid i.e. a cross between Cold Comfort Farm and 'Upstairs Downstairs'. **1976** *Sunday Mail* (Glasgow) 26 Dec. 35/3 Pools Guide... Perm any 3 from 6 in first and second columns with any 2 from 3 in third column—20 × 20 × 3—1200 lines at 1/8p per line = £1.50 staked.

permafrost (pə̄·ɹmăfrǫst). [f. PERMA(NENT *a.* (*sb.*) + FROST *sb.*] Subsoil or other underground material that is at a temperature of less than 0°C throughout the year, as in Arctic regions; permanently frozen ground.

1943 S. W. MULLER *Permafrost or Permanently Frozen Ground* 3 The expression 'permanently frozen ground'..is too long and cumbersome and for this reason a shorter term '*permafrost*' is proposed as an alternative. **1952** *Sci. News Let.* 2 Aug. 70/3 Currently it is studying permafrost, permanently frozen ground that creates many problems in construction work. **1955** PETERSON & FISHER *Wild Amer.* (1956) xxxiii. 357 Here on the tundra the permafrost forbids any digging and the Eskimos bury their dead above the ground. **1958** *New Biol.* XXVI. 90 In the subarctic the peat has a permafrost layer, that is a layer, usually a foot or two below the surface, which remains frozen for the whole year round, and acts as an impermeable layer. **1968** R. W. FAIRBRIDGE *Encycl. Geomorphol.* 838/1 Many other engineering problems result from changes in the mechanical properties of permafrost caused by thawing or freezing of its moisture beneath such structures as roadways or heated buildings. **1971** *New Scientist* 8 Apr. 70/1 The heated pipeline would be laid for several hundred miles over or through a peaty soil where the permafrost may reach as much as 500 metres depth. **1974** T. P. WHITNEY tr. *Solzhenitsyn's Gulag Archipel.* I. I. ii. 24 This wave poured forth, sank down into the permafrost, and even our most active minds recall hardly a thing about it. **1975** *Nature* 1 May 27/1 A possible reason is that the increasing permafrost in the soil forced the late Vikings to change their burial customs. **1977** *New Yorker* 9 May 95/2 There is ice under the tundra, mixed with soil as permafrost, in some places two thousand feet deep.

permalloy (pə̄·ɹmăloi). [f. PERM(EABILITY + ALLOY *sb.*] Any of a series of alloys consisting chiefly of nickel and iron, which have very high magnetic permeability and are widely used in electrical equipment, esp. in telecommunications.

1923 ARNOLD & ELMEN in *Jrnl. Franklin Inst.* CXCV. 621 For convenience we call these peculiarly magnetic alloys by the general name 'permalloy', which serves at the same time to recall their characteristic capability of attaining high initial permeability. **1925** *Chambers's Jrnl.* Apr. 220/1 The conductor of this distortionless cable is composed of a special alloy, known as permalloy. **1926** *Glasgow Herald* 9 Sept. 8/4 The Western Union Telegraph Company announce that the laying of the new permalloy cable between England and New York was successfully completed on Sunday last. **1932** [see *MU-METAL]. **1946** [see *nickel-iron* s.v. *NICKEL *sb.* 3 b]. **1965** *Wireless World* Sept. 431/1 The auto-transformer core should be of magnetically soft material such as permalloy, mumetal, H.C.R. alloy or some similar grade. **1969** E. N. SIMON *Dict. Alloys* 127 Permalloy 45 contains basically 45 nickel, 55 iron, per cent. *Ibid.*, Permalloy 4-79 contains basically 79 nickel, 4 molybdenum, the balance iron, per cent...and is used for audio coils, transformers and magnetic shields.

permanent, *a.* (*sb.*) Add: **1. d.** *permanent blue* (examples); *permanent dye*, a long-lasting dye used in hairdressing; *permanent hardness*, hardness of water that is not removable by boiling; *permanent magnet* (earlier example); so *permanent magnetism*; *permanent pasture*, land left unploughed for a long period, used for growing grass; *permanent press*, a process designed to produce lasting creases in materials for clothing; the fabric treated in this way; *permanent revolution*, a concept orig. attributed to L. D. Trotsky (1879–1940) which envisaged the dependence of Russia's bourgeois and proletarian revolution on a continuing process of European revolutions; also *transf.*; *permanent secretary*, a senior grade of the civil service, now normally denoting a permanent administrative officer of the highest grade in a Department of State; *permanent set* (Mech.), a deformation that remains after the removal of the stress that produced it; *permanent tint* = *permanent dye* above; *permanent under-secretary*, (*a*) a senior permanent adviser to a minister who is a Secretary of State; (*b*) a senior grade of the civil service below that of a permanent secretary and normally applied to the head of a division within a Department of State; *permanent wave*, a special process designed to produce a lasting wave in the hair (also as *vb.*); the wave so produced; so *permanent waver*, *waving*; *permanent way* (earlier and later examples); also *attrib.*; *permanent white* (later examples).

1886 H. C. STANDAGE *Artists' Man. Pigments* iii. 32 Permanent Blue is a pale ultramarine with a cobalt hue. **1895** *Montgomery Ward Catal.* Spring & Summer 252/3 Artists Tube Oil Colors... Permanent Blue. **1939–40**

Army & Navy Stores Catal. 372/2 Moist water colours.. Permanent mauve..Permanent blue. **1966** J. S. Cox *Illustr. Dict. Hairdressing* 110/2 *Permanent dye*, a dye in which the susceptibility to lose colour under normal conditions has been reduced to a minimum. **1888** *Encycl. Brit.* XXIV. 409/1 The remaining or permanent hardness consists of sulphate of lime and other soluble salts. **1969** H. T. Evans tr. *Hägg's Gen. & Inorg. Chem.* xxvi. 666 Carbonate precipitation on boiling causes the water to lose its carbonate hardness or temporary hardness while a permanent hardness remains. **1828** F. Watkins *Pop. Sk. Electro-Magnetism* 12 If a steel needle be inserted in a coil and removed again immediately, it will become a permanent magnet. **1827** J. Cumming *Man. Electro Dynamics* 259 If it be possible to give permanent magnetism to steel by this species of electricity. **1965** A. H. Morrish *Physical Princ. Magn.* i. 1 Permanent and induced magnetism represent two of man's earliest scientific discoveries. **1861** M. H. Sutton in *Jrnl. R. Agric. Soc.* XXII. 416 *(title)* Laying down land to permanent pasture. *Ibid.* 421 We offer the foregoing hints, on laying down permanent pastures, &c., founded on our own experience and observation during full thirty years. **1897** W. S. Everitt *Pract. Notes Grass & Grass Growing E. Anglia* iii. 44 First select the land which is suitable for a permanent pasture. **1924** W. J. Malden *Grassland Farming* viii. 101 If permanent pasture seeds are sown in the spring without a corn crop, they may or may not.. make growth which will be valuable to feed during the first summer. **1968** F. W. Gould *Grass Systematics* i. 5 Geese feed extensively on rice.. and also take significant amounts of forage from temporary and permanent pastures of the Gulf Coastal Prairie. **1964** *Mod. Textiles Mag.* Dec. 55 *(heading)* Garments with permanent press finishes. *Ibid.* 55/2 The concept of *permanent press finish*. ..is being widely..exploited in the men's and boys' casual and work slacks market. *Ibid.* 59/1 There are a number of competing processes now being offered..with claims of permanent creasing, permanent pressing, permanent shape retention, etc. **1965** *Observer* 10 Apr. 3/4 This new material..is generally known as 'permanent-press', a description which applies to a new process for treating cotton-and-Dacron goods so that they will never lose their shape or pleating. **1967** *Family Herald* 6 July 35/1 Permanent press involves treating the fabric chemically with a resin compound and then setting or 'curing' it by high heat in an oven. **1969** *Time* 18 Apr. 61 Foreign competition is most severe in man-made-fiber textiles, the most rapidly growing segment of the industry since advancing technology gave the world wash-'n'-wear shirts and permanent-press pants. **1978** *N.Y. Times* 30 Mar. A6/1 (Advt.), Made just for us by this top maker, a handsome selection of short sleeve shirts in solids, stripes, plaids and patterns. All in easy care permanent press polyester and cotton. **1928** Permanent revolution [see *Menshevism]. **1942** S. Neumann *(title)* Permanent revolution. **1964** I. Deutscher in *Trotsky's Age of Permanent Revolution* 18 Trotsky is deeply committed to one element in classical Marxism, its quintessential element: permanent revolution. **1972** D. Bloodworth *Any Number can Play* xx. 206 My fidelity to the Maoist theory of permanent revolution is absolute. **1975** *Guardian* 22 Jan. 10/1 Trotsky was the hero..and the notion of 'permanent revolution' was the great hope. **1867** E. E. Bridges *Treasury* (1964) 233 My Lords are of opinion that the office should now be given a more substantive character than that of Assistant Secretary and they are pleased to direct that its title shall be that of 'Permanent Secretary to the Treasury'. *a* **1974** R. Crossman *Diaries* (1975) I. 25 She continued the war, capturing Fred Willey and putting him in a room by himself in our Ministry while she got hold of his new Permanent Secretary, Mr Bishop, and lectured him. **1976** H. Wilson *Governance of Britain* iv. 99 The Treasury took the lead in setting up official inter-departmental committees, some at permanent-secretary level. **1822** T. Tredgold *Pract. Ess. Strength of Cast Iron* ii. 24 The second table..is intended to show the greatest weight a beam of cast iron will bear in the middle of its length, when it is loaded with as much as it will bear, so as to recover its natural form when the load is removed. If a beam be loaded beyond that point, the equilibrium of its parts is destroyed, and it takes a permanent set. **1888** Permanent set [see Set *sb.*[1] 16]. **1935** *Jrnl. R. Aeronaut. Soc.* XXXIX. 554 The highest stress in service should be below the true elastic limit of the material in order to avoid 'permanent set'. **1972** E. N. Simons *Testing of Metals* i. 21 The proof stress..is the load or stress that, applied for a minimum period of 15 min, gives a plastic extension or permanent set of 0·1% (or 0·5% with certain alloys). **1966** J. S. Cox *Illustr. Dict. Hairdressing* 110/2 *Permanent tint*, a cuphemism for Permanent Dye. **1968** J. Ironside *Fashion Alphabet* 191 One very rarely hears the word 'dyeing' nowadays; it is always 'tinting'. There are permanent tints (which last through the life of the hair); semi-permanent tints [etc.]. **1904** *Rep. War Office (Reconstruction) Comm.* ii. 9 in *Parl. Papers* (Cd. 1932) VIII. 101 The Council should consist of seven members—four military and three civil—with the Permanent Under-Secretary as Secretary. **1917** G. Bell *Let.* 20 July (1927) II. 420, I wish you would go and see Sir A. Hirtzel, the Permanent Under-Secretary. **1959** P. Fleming *Siege at Peking* vii. 106 The fullest account of what they did do is contained in a confidential letter written on 4 September by Sir Claude MacDonald to Mr Bertie, the Permanent Under-Secretary of State at the Foreign Office. **1974** P. Gore-Booth *With Great Truth & Respect* 324 The Permanent Under-Secretary of any department of Government is the senior official or civil servant in that department. The word 'permanent' is accurate in the sense that, if there is a change of government or of Secretary of State, you do not have to move out or even go through a formal process of resignation and reappointment. **1978** *Illustr. London News* Nov. 134/3 He certainly was an extraordinary figure—the last of the permanent under secretaries (PUS in professional jargon) to spend the whole of his effective career in Whitehall. **1909** *Hairdresser* June 6/1 Children who have undergone the X-ray treatment for ringworm are growing curly hair... Would it be possible for a lady who desires to secure a permanent wave to undergo the treatment? **1919** *Honey Pot* I. ii. 1 (Advt.), Permanent waves... T. Vasco Ltd. **1922** U. Sinclair *They call me Carpenter* ix. 27 Would you like to see how we make eet—the permanent wave? **1925** *Scribner's Mag.* July 20 (Advt.), You will enjoy your permanent wave at Nestle's. **1928** *Daily Express* 23 Aug. 3/6 The curling irons and the tentacles of the permanent waver will be busier than ever in the autumn season. **1928** R. Macaulay *Keeping up Appearances* viii. 70, I want a permanent wave at twelve o'clock to-day. **1932** *Woman's Pictorial* 12 Mar. 14/2 What is a permanent wave? Answer (so far as my experience goes): a wave that is anything but permanent. **1946** *Mod. Beauty Shop* Dec. 128/2 Some hair which I permanent waved did not take the permanent. **1964** N. G. Clark *Mod. Org. Chem.* xvi. 352 If these linkages are broken (by reducing agents), the fibres bent to an artificial shape, and new disulphide linkages formed (by oxidizing agents), the fibres retain their new shape. This is the basis of 'permanent-waving' hair. **1967** O. Wynd *Walk Softly* v. 70 The Katsugis, celebrated for having dyed their long black hair bright orange, then permanent-waving it. **1968** J. Ironside *Fashion Alphabet* 196 At first permanent waving tended to give tight waves and curls, but over the past twenty years or so the tendency has been for a softer more natural looking permanent. **1975** *Times* 26 Aug. 12/8 Beauty salons..in the hectic flush of the permanent wave boom. **1838** *Mechanics' Mag.* 13 Oct. 32/2 The permanent way between Deptford High-street and the Greenwich terminus, is in a very forward state. This portion of the line is laid on longitudinal wooden sleepers, with three-feet bearing. **1869** *Bradshaw's Railway Manual* XXI. 392 Upwards of 4,000,000 *L.* was expended in England for permanent way materials, locomotives, stores, &c., sent out from that country. **1879** E. J. Simmons *Mem. Station Master* (1974) iii. 37 The station and line were occasionally enveloped in a very thick fog. On these occasions, we were allowed to employ one of the permanent-way men to stand all night on the line beyond the signals with his hand lamp. **1906** *Daily Chron.* 31 Jan. 4/5 Instructions had been issued to the permanent-way staff to adhere..to the regulations. **1926** T. E. Lawrence *Seven Pillars* vi. lxxviii. 409 It was impossible to leave them joined up to the exploder in the proper way, since the spot was evident to the permanent-way patrols as they made their rounds. **1957** J. Bledlow *Cotswolds in Colour* 47 Work was being done on the permanent way. **1967** G. F. Fiennes *I tried to run a Railway* iv. 40 They took Ticket Inspector Whipp at Liverpool Street and threw him off the platform on to the permanent way. **1973** *Railway Mag.* Mar. 129/2 Five of these engines were kept for permanent-way and shunting duties at Neasden. **1854** Permanent white [see *Constant *a.* 4 f]. **1860** C. M. Yonge *Hopes & Fears* I. i. iv. 108 The front was all over scaffolds and cement, in all stages of colour, from rich brown to permanent white. **1934** H. Hiler *Notes Technique Painting* ii. 89 Permanent white (a special preparation of oxide of zinc prepared for oil painting).

3. d. = *permanent wave* above.

1926 *Hairdressing* 10 Sept. 241/1 This can only be done by superior work; namely, excellent setting of the finished permanent. **1932** *New Yorker* 4 June 64/3 (Advt.), A deep-wave marcel permanent styled for you alone in the modern manner. **1939** A. Huxley *After Many a Summer* ii. i. 6 Facials, Permanents, Manicures... Next door to the beauty shoppe was a Western Union office. **1941** J. C. Furnas *How Amer. Lives* 324 Twice a year she goes to a beauty shop to have a new 'permanent'. **1948** E. Waugh *Loved One* 78 Permanents, facials, wax—everything you get in a beauty parlour. **1951** E. Paul *Springtime in Paris* v. 117 Is there anything wrong with Yvette's beauty parlour..? I'm going there this afternoon—for a permanent. I hope it lasts a week. **1974** *New Yorker* 3 June 90/2 It is not uncommon for a woman to be receiving a permanent in one barber chair while a man is shaved in the other. **1976** N. Thornburg *Cutter & Bone* xii. 283 Their women were..constantly fussing with yesterday's permanents.

permanentize (pəˑɹmǽnĕntəiz), *v.* [f. Permanent *a.* (*sb.*) + -ize.] To make permanent. So **peˑrmanentizing** *vbl. sb.*

A word of little value and rarely found in serious writing.—Ed.

1961 *Guardian* 20 Mar. 1/4 The latest word to be added to Pentagonese..is 'permanentise'. **1963** *Punch* 6 Nov. 665/1 The Ferrets have set about permanentising their idyll. **1966** *Ibid.* 21 Dec. 911/3 Meanwhile jeopardising our chance of permanentising the Sino-Soviet *détente*, and welding the Communist bloc more dangerously together. **1975** M. Bradbury *History Man* ii. 20 Society's technique for permanentizing the inherent contingency of relationships..that is to say, they got married.

permanently, *adv.* (Further examples.)

1885 *Geol. Mag.* Decade III. II. 516 On the depth of the permanently frozen stratum of soil in British North America. **1903** G. B. Shaw *Man & Superman* iii. 103 With such a majority as mine I cannot be kept permanently out of office. **1921** *Daily Colonist* (Victoria) 18 Mar. 9/4 (Advt.), Ladies come and have your hair permanently waved... We have the latest machines and are expert in the art. **1929** A. Noyes *Return of Scare-Crow* i. 11 There were pictures of permanently waved young women, with carefully arranged flowers in their hair. **1930** J. Cannan *No Walls of Jasper* 192 She stood..with..the sun in her eyes, and the wind in her permanently-waved hair. **1959** *Housewife* June 46 Shirt and permanently-pleated skirt. **1962** *Guardian* 15 Jan. 4/4 Drip-dry, uncrushable, and permanently pleatable cottons. **1969** *Jane's Freight Containers 1968–69* 105 A new permanently-coupled articulated flat car developed by Union Pacific. **1975** G. Howell *In Vogue* 208/2 Nylon transformed the fifties wardrobe..the fake furs and the permanently pleated nightdresses.

permansive (pəɹmæˑnsiv), *a. Gram.* [f. L. *permans-um* supine of *permanēre* to remain (see Permanent *a.* (*sb.*)) + -ive.] Applied to a tense in certain languages which is used to denote a more or less permanent state.

1866 E. Hincks in *Jrnl. R. Asiatic Soc.* Dec. 485 The verbal forms belonging to each conjugation may be divided into two great classes, which I call permansive and mutative. The former denotes continuance in the state which the verb signifies in that conjugation; the latter denotes change into that state. **1872** A. H. Sayce *Assyrian Gram.* 52 The Assyrian verb is rich in tenses. It possesses a Permansive, or Perfect as it is generally called in Semitic grammars, of comparatively rare occurrence in the historic inscriptions, but sufficiently common in the tablets; besides four more other tenses. **1924** O. Jespersen *Philos. Gram.* xx. 269 It [*sc.* the perfect tense] is a present, but a permansive present: it represents the present state as the outcome of past events, and may therefore be called a retrospective variety of the present. **1939** L. H. Gray *Foundations of Lang.* 359 In the historic period, Semitic possesses..two aspects (telic and atelic, commonly called perfect and imperfect..), to which Akkadian adds a permansive. **1972** Hartmann & Stork *Dict. Lang. & Linguistics* 21/1 Permansive aspect expressing a permanent state as a result of a completed action etc.

permeability. Add: Also, the degree to which a solid allows the passage of fluid through it, measured by the *coefficient of permeability* (or *permeability coefficient*), the volume of fluid flowing through unit cross-section in unit time under a unit (pressure or concentration gradient).

1902 *Sci. Abstr.* V. 856 *(heading)* Permeability of animal membranes. *Ibid.* 857 Inactive membranes..offer but little resistance to the passage of the different ions, and the permeability does not alter by contact with the solution. **1917** *Rep. & Mem. Advisory Comm. Aeronaut.* No. 317. 4 This permeameter is readily adapted to the determination of temperature coefficients of permeability. **1920** *Ibid.* No. 360. 4 The average permeability of rubbered airship fabrics..is not usually much less than 10 litres per sq. metre per day. **1931** *Jrnl. Gen. Physiol.* XIV. 408 This definition of permeability is seen to possess a definite physical meaning *viz.*, the number of cubic micra of water entering the cell per minute per unit area of membrane, per atmosphere of difference in osmotic pressure between interior and external medium. **1960** *Ibid.* XLIII. 523 *(heading)* Experimental study of the independence of diffusion and hydrodynamic permeability coefficients in collodion membranes. **1962** R. C. S. Walters *Dam Geol.* xiv. 67 The permeability [of the Oxford clay] ranged from 12×10^{-6} to $4{\cdot}1 \times 10^{-6}$ cm per sec. **1966** *McGraw-Hill Encycl. Sci. & Technol.* XII. 453/2 The permeability coefficient varies from 100 cm/sec for clean gravel to 10^{-9} cm/sec for heavy clay.

b. (*magnetic*) *permeability*, also, one of the physical parameters of a medium, equal to the ratio of the magnetic induction B to the magnetic field strength H at any point in it; also (more fully *relative permeability*), the ratio of the permeability of a medium to the permeability of free space; *permeability of free space*, a constant μ_0 which in the C.G.S. electromagnetic system of units is unity and in the International System of Units is defined as a base quantity with the value 4π (12·57) $\times 10^{-7}$ henry per metre. (Further examples.)

Of the different permeabilities mentioned in quot. 1872 in Dict., the magnetic kind is the only one that gained currency.

1892 J. A. Ewing *Magn. Induction* ii. 56 Prof. Knott has proposed to call this quantity the 'differential susceptibility'; similarly $d\mathbf{B}/d\mathbf{H}$ may be called the differential permeability. **1939** L. F. Bates *Mod. Man.* ii. 67 Pure iron has an initial permeability of about 250. **1942** *Phil. Mag.* XXXIII. 488 The universal constant $1/\mathbf{a}c^2$ occurring in (12.2) has the value..$1/10^7$ ohm sec./m... and is called the permeability of empty space. Consistency practically compels us to call the constant $\mu/\mathbf{a}c^2$ in (12.3) the permeability of the medium. **1944** [see *permittivity]. **1962** Corson & Lorrain *Introd. Electromagn. Fields* v. 177 The constant μ_0 is called the permeability of free space and is arbitrarily taken to be exactly $4\pi \times 10^{-7}$ newton/ampere[2] in rationalized m.k.s. units. *Ibid.* vii. 284 Figure 7-17 shows magnetization data for several different kinds of iron, with lines of constant relative permeability indicated. The detailed shape of the magnetization curve and the maximum permeability achieved with a given sample of iron depend on the purity, the method of annealing, and on the thickness of the sheets. **1971** *Nature* 16 July 208/2 The indiscriminate use of the symbol μ..both for the permeability of free space and that of ferromagnetic materials may temporarily confuse the unwary.

2. Special Comb.: **permeability tuning** *Electronics*, tuning in which the resonant frequency of a circuit is changed by moving a magnetic core into or out of a coil forming part of it, so as to change its inductance.

1933 W. J. Polydoroff in *Proc. IRE* XXI. 694 The apparent inductance is increased to tune to lower frequencies by introducing a magnetic core into the field of the coil. As the core is inserted into the coil, more lines of the magnetic field are intercepted by the core, and, in effect, the average apparent permeability of the medium surrounding the coil increases from 1 (for air) to a certain maximum... For this reason, and for other reasons.., it is appropriate to describe this method as 'Permeability Tuning'. **1968** *Radio Communication Handbk.* (ed. 4) iv. 35/2 Although permeability tuning has been most successfully used for many years by one major American company, the mechanical and electrical complications involved in band-switched receivers have resulted in little progress in this field by amateur constructors.

permeabilize (pɔ̄·ɹmiˌăbiləiz), *v. Biol.* [f. L. *permeābil-is* PERMEABLE *a.* + -IZE.] *trans.* To make permeable. So **pe·rmeabilized** *ppl. a.*

1971 *Nature* 3 Dec. p. ix/2 DNA synthesis—Observation in permeabilized yeast mutants. **1973** *Developmental Biol.* XXXV. 382/2 A technique..to permeabilize eggs for cytochemical and metabolic studies. *Ibid.* 384/1 The permeabilized eggs were..very sensitive to the composition of the incubation medium. **1974** *Jrnl. Bacteriol.* CXVIII. 1186/1 Several techniques have been used to permeabilize bacterial cells.

Hence **pe:rmeabiliza·tion**, the action of permeabilizing.

1973 *Nature New Biol.* 2 May 18/1 The synthesis observed is due to the growth of newly initiated chains, not merely the extension of chains initiated during normal growth before permeabilization. **1973** *Developmental Biol.* XXXV. 386/2 The permeabilization of the vitelline membrane of *Drosophila* eggs with octane offers the opportunity to study the influence of different substances on development and facilitates cytochemical investigations of the egg. **1974** *Jrnl. Bacteriol.* CXVIII. 1186 A cell permeabilization procedure is described that reduces viability less than 10%.

permeameter (pɔ̄ɹmiˌæ·mĭtəɹ). [f. PERMEA(BILITY + -METER.] **1.** An instrument for measuring the magnetic permeability of a substance or object.

1890 S. P. THOMPSON in *Jrnl. Soc. Arts* 12 Sept. 885/2 *Permeameter Method*, this is a method which I have myself devised for the purpose of testing specimens of iron... For carrying it out a simple instrument is needed, which I venture to denominate as a permeameter. **1931** *Bureau of Standards Jrnl. Res.* (U.S.) VI. 355 The permeameters in general use for commercial magnetic testing have an upper limit of about 300 gilberts per centimeter. **1936** C. E. WEBB in Vigoureux & Webb *Princ. Electr. & Magn. Measurements* II. xii. 309 The average magnetic properties of a non-uniform specimen may often be found more accurately in the Fahy permeameter than in permeameters dependent on the production of equality of flux or of magnetic potential at a limited number of points in the magnetic circuit. **1969** *IEEE Trans. Magnetics* V. 662/1 Straight magnetic samples are usually tested on hand compensated permeameters.

2. An instrument for measuring the permeability of a substance, esp. soil, to fluids.

1917 G. A. SHAKESPEAR in *Rep. & Mem. Advisory Comm. Aeronaut.* No. 317. 3 The following is a brief account of a permeability tester which was designed for the rapid testing of balloon and airship fabrics... The apparatus (called a 'permeameter' for short) consists of a shallow cylindrical vessel of cast iron, about 13 cm. in diameter [etc.]. **1941** D. P. KRYNINE *Soil Mech.* iii. 54 The general idea of permeameters or apparatus to determine the coefficient of permeability *k* in the laboratory is (*a*) to create a flow of water through a sample of a thickness *L* and having a definite cross section *A* [etc.]. **1971** B. F. CURTIS in R. E. Carver *Procedures Sedimentary Petrol.* xiv. 353 Although liquid permeameters are used when thought necessary, it is far more common to measure permeabilities using gas as the moving fluid. **1974** A. KÉZDI *Handbk. Soil Mech.* I. vi. 129/1 Constant head permeameters are particularly suited to the testing of highly pervious coarse grained soils. For soils with medium to low permeability, the falling head permeameters are used.

permease (pɔ̄·ɹmiˌeiz, -s). *Biochem.* [ad. F. *perméase* (H. V. Rickenberg et al. 1956, in *Ann. de l'Inst. Pasteur* XCI. 843), f. *permé(able* PERMEABLE *a.*: see *-ASE.] Any enzyme which assists the passage of a substrate into a cell through the cell wall.

1957 *Bacteriol. Rev.* XXI. 169/1 During the past few years, however, definite proof of the existence, in bacteria, of stereospecific permeation systems, functionally specialized and distinct from metabolic enzymes, has been obtained... The generic name 'permeases' has been suggested for these systems. **1970** *New Scientist* 1 Jan. 8/1 This so-called 'permease' has since been found to be a protein, located in the cell membrane, which somehow transfers lactose from the outside of the cell to the interior. **1975** D. V. PARKE *Enzyme Induction* i. 7 Maltase and maltose permease are induced together by maltose in yeast.

permeator (pɔ̄·ɹmiˌēitəɹ). [a. L. *permeator*, f. *permeāre* (see PERMEATE *v.*).] **1.** One who or that which permeates; in quot. 1944, ? an infiltrator.

1944 G. B. SHAW *Everybody's Pol. What's What?* xxxi. 271, I, a Fabian permeator, knew the questions and had doctrinaire answers ready for some of them. **1969** *Ann. Rev. Plant Physiol.* XX. 602 Wartiovaara..compared the permeability constants of homologue series of permeators (e.g., alcohols..) and concluded that two parallel and alternative pathways for permeation of molecules through the protoplasm did not exist. *Ibid.*, The breaking of hydrogen bonds between permeator molecule and water during the passage of the permeator through the membrane is considered to be the important feature.

2. A vessel divided into two by a semi-permeable membrane, used in the large-scale removal of solutes from a liquid by reverse osmosis.

1975 M. J. HAMMER *Water & Waste-Water Technol.* vii. 266 In addition to the permeators, a basic reverse osmosis system consists of pretreatment pumps.., tanks and appurtenances for cleaning and flushing, and a disposal system for waste brine. *Ibid.* (*caption*) A module of 24 reverse-osmosis permeator units used to desalt a municipal ground-water supply. **1977** *Design Engin.* July 6/3 A new high-capacity permeator..can convert thousands of gallons of seawater into potable water every day.

Permian, *a.* (*sb.*) Add: **2.** The name of the people of Perm and the language spoken by them.

1886 [see *Cis-Uralian* adj. s.v. *CIS- I.]. **1908** T. G. TUCKER *Introd. Nat. Hist. Lang.* 132 Permian, embracing Permian proper, Siryenian and Votiak. These are spoken by sparse populations near the Urals in the E.N.E. of European Russia. **1932** W. L. GRAFF *Lang.* 405 Permian, with its two varieties Zyrian and Votyak. **1933** L. BLOOMFIELD *Lang.* 68 Four further branches of the Finno-Ugrian stock... Permian, consisting of Votyak and Zyrian. **1961** L. F. BROSNAHAN *Sounds of Lang.* viii. 177 The languages of this family.., Permian, Votyak.

Permic (pɔ̄·ɹmik), *a.* [f. as prec. + -IC.] = PERMIAN *a.* (*sb.*) in Dict. and Suppl.

Permian is the more usual term.

1921 A. W. GRABAU *Textbk. Geol.* II. xxxviii. 506 (*heading*) The Permian or Permic system. **1964** *Language* XL. 96 Komi..and Udmurt..comprise the Permic group of the Uralic family. **1967** *Ural-Altaische Jahrbücher* XXXIX. 163 (*title*) Split, shift and merger in the Permic vowels.

permillage. Delete *rare* and add further examples.

1900 *Fortn. Rev.* Jan. 62 It should, perhaps, be remarked that I have reduced Dr. Galton's results to permillages. **1960** *Amer. Mineralogist* XLV. 6 (*caption*) The structure of perrierite projected on (010). The numbers give the *y*-parameters as permillage of the *b*-length. **1967** *Oceanogr. & Marine Biol.* V. 152 See Table VII, in which enrichment of ^{18}O is expressed in terms of δ^{18}O, the permillage enrichment relative to Standard Mean Ocean Water.

permineralization (pəɹmi:nĕrăləizēi·ʃən). *Geol.* [f. PER-[1] + MINERALIZATION.] The action or result of fossilization by the deposition of minerals from solution in the interstices of hard tissue. Hence **permi·neralize** *v. trans.*, **-mi·neralized** *ppl. a.*

1893 C. A. WHITE in *Rep. U.S. Nat. Museum 1892* 264 There are seven different natural conditions in which fossil remains are recognizable, three of which relate to substance, three to form, and one to both. To those relating to substance I have applied the terms permineralization, histometabasis, and carbonization... The term permineralization applies to that condition of fossil remains of animals which differ least from their original condition as parts of living animals. **1915** C. SCHUCHERT *Text-bk. Geol.* II. xvii. 436 The great majority of fossil specimens preserve more or less of the original hard or mineral substance of the individual plant or animal, and to this may have been added in the organic interstices more or less of other mineral substances during the process of fossilization, forming the permineralized fossils. **1952** R. C. MOORE et al. *Invertebr. Fossils* i. 4/1 Shells and bones, which are somewhat porous, may be made more dense by deposition of mineral substances by ground water. Hard parts altered in this way are permineralized; the process of alteration is termed permineralization or petrifaction. **1958** C. L. & M. A. FENTON *Fossil Bk.* i. 5 This process [*sc.* petrification].. takes place in two related ways. The simpler, termed permineralization, takes place when fat and other organic substances decay while water containing dissolved mineral matter soaks into every cavity and pore of hard—especially limy—structures. *Ibid.* 7 (*caption*) Permineralized corals that preserve both shape and structure. **1979** *Nature* 19 Oct. 640/2 Microfossils detected in the upper Brioverian dolomitic limestones..are permineralised in carbonate rather than silica.

perminvar (pɔ̄·ɹminvāɹ). Also **Perminvar.** [f. PERM(EABILITY + INVAR(IABLE *a.* (*sb.*).] Any of a series of alloys containing nickel, iron, and cobalt which have an approximately constant magnetic permeability over a range of field strengths.

The name is proprietary in the U.S.

1928 *Official Gaz.* (U.S. Patent Office) 12 June 277/1 Western Electric Company..N.Y. Filed Nov. 8, 1927. Perminvar..For ferromagnetic alloys comprising nickel, iron, and cobalt. Claims use since Aug. 23, 1927. **1928** G. W. ELMEN in *Jrnl. Franklin Inst.* CCVI. 318 We have chosen 'perminvar' as the name for alloys in the iron-cobalt-nickel series, which are characterized, when properly heat treated, by constancy of permeability for a considerable range of the lower part of the magnetization curve. **1939** *Chem. Abstr.* XXXIII. 6775 Rapidly cooled Perminvar (45% Ni, 30% Fe, 25% Co) exhibits a clear increase in specific heat over a rather broad temp. range. **1962** N. H. CODLING in G. A. T. Burdett *Automatic Control Handbk.* viii. 21 Perminvar, comprising nickel, cobalt and iron, subjected to heat treatment, has nearly constant permeability for inductions below 1000 G. **1968** S. J. ROSENBERG *Nickel & its Alloys* 131/2 Useful alloys in the Perminvar class include the nickel-iron-alloys Conpernik (50% Ni) and Isoperm (40% Ni).

‖ **permis de séjour** (pĕ̄rmi də seʒūr). [Fr.] Permission to stay in a country; a permit allowing this, a residence permit. Also *fig.*

1884 A. FORBES *Chinese Gordon* iv. 130 All persons residing in Darjour must have a *permis de séjour*. **1885** W. JAMES *Lit. Remains H. James* 14 The ordinary empirical ethics of evolutionary naturalism can find a perfect *permis de séjour* under the system's wings. **1923** *Michelin Guide Gt. Brit.* (ed. 7) 861 Passengers not of French nationality must present themselves to the local authorities to obtain a 'Permis de séjour' if staying in France over 14 days. **1951** E. AMBLER *Judgment on Deltchev* xviii. 219, I propose to have your visa and *permis de séjour* cancelled. **1960** O. MANNING *Great Fortune* xxiv. 256 Should his *permis de séjour* be cancelled, Foxy or Fitzsimon would see that it was renewed. **1972** J. AIKEN *Butterfly Picnic* iv. 65, I will see that your *permis de séjour* is extended.

permissible, *a.* Add: *permissible dose* (see quot. 1954).

1954 *Brit. Jrnl. Radiol.* XXVII. 245/2 Permissible dose is defined as that dose of ionizing radiation that, in the light of present knowledge, is not expected to cause appreciable bodily injury to a person at any time during his lifetime. **1960** *Lebende Sprachen* V. 163/2 The pilots who fly the modern airplane are subjected to a rather heavy dose (very close to the permissible dose) from the self-illuminating control-instruments.

permissive, *a.* **1.** Add to def.: Freq. in modern use in the sense 'tolerant, liberal, allowing freedom, *spec.* in sexual matters'; freq. in phr. *permissive society*. Hence as *sb.*, a permissive person. (Add later examples.)

1934 *Sun* (Baltimore) 25 May 6/2 All he asked was that the 'permissive' features of the pay-off provisions be made 'directive'. Later he explained that this would mean simply that the FDIC be 'authorized and directed' instead of 'authorized and empowered' to appraise the assets of the closed banks. **1946** *Amer. Psychologist* I. 416/2 If the counselor creates a warm and permissive atmosphere in which the individual is free to bring out any attitudes and feelings which he may have [etc.]. **1956** C. A. TONSOR in *Clearing House* XXX. v. 289, I realize that in the face of the permissive tendencies of the age, there is not much respect for rules. **1967** *Punch* 15 Mar. 372/2 If, in the nineteenth century, sadists in mortar-boards, and often in dog-collars also, belaboured little Johnny's bottom in order to knock Latin grammar into his head, some of today's jeans-and-gimmicks permissives may go too far the other way. **1968** *Listener* 4 Jan. 18/3 This dreadful dilemma of the puritan in a permissive society. **1970** *Times* 5 Feb. 9 It [*sc.* a proposal for a world-wide cricket tour] also irritates the extreme cricket-establishment people, some of whom seem to relish the thought of the tour, barbed wire and truncheons and all, to show that they are not going to be dictated to by the long-haired permissives. **1970** G. GREER *Female Eunuch* 45 The permissive society has done much to neutralize sexual drives by containing them. **1971** *Publ. Amer. Dial. Soc. 1969* LII. 14 Americans tend to be permissive in matters of pronunciation and vocabulary. **1971** J. WAINWRIGHT *Last Buccaneer* II. 106 He was nineteen years old and there are few nineteen-year-old male virgins in the permissive age. **1972** *Guardian* 6 July 14/1 The charge against the permissive society is that the controls have slipped: things are being permitted that ought not to be permitted. **1976** U. HOLDEN *String Horses* ix. 106 My kiddies all have their Daddies. My Herb belongs to Jim. I'm not permissive. **1976** F. ZWEIG *New Acquisitive Society* I. v. 47 The prevailing ethic of today is the ethos of the permissive society. **1977** *Time* 10 Oct. 24/3 Neither a cajoling arm twister like Lyndon Johnson nor a permissive parent like mild-mannered Mike Mansfield, Byrd is distinguished by his ability to gauge correctly what a majority of the Senate wants.

2. *permissive waste* (later example).

1971 *Mod. Law Rev.* XXXI. 698 A student who uses a conventional law textbook may be excused if he gains the impression that much of his professional career will be spent in advising about perpetuities, permissive waste and the principal mansion house.

3. Expressing permission or exhortation: applied to the verbal mood which expresses permission or an exhortation. Also as quasi-*sb.*

1845 [see *ADHORTATIVE *a.*]. **1892** H. SWEET *New Eng. Gram.* I. 108 The combination of *may* and its preterite *might* with the infinitive (*may see, might see*) is called the permissive mood, as in *may you be happy!* **1898** *Ibid.* II. 116 Thus the present permissive is used in independent sentences to express wish: *may you succeed!* **1924** O. JESPERSEN *Philos. Gram.* xxiii. 320 As a tentative scheme of the purely notional ideas expressed more or less vaguely by the verbal moods and auxiliaries of various languages we might perhaps give the following list... I. Containing an element of will... Permissive: you may go if you like. **1955** J. L. AUSTIN *How to do Things with Words* (1962) xii. 158 In the special case of permissives we might ask whether they should be classified as exercitives or as commissives. **1976** J. S. GRUBER *Lexical Struct. Syntax & Semantics* I. vi. 167 *Let* can be used as a fairly general Permissive Agent of Motion.

permissiveness. Add: (Later examples.) Cf. prec.

1946 *Amer. Psychologist* I. 420/2 When genuine acceptance and permissiveness are your tools it requires nothing less than the whole complete personality. **1958** B. SPOCK *Baby & Child Care* (new ed.) 56 *Strictness or permissiveness?*.. This looms as a big question for many new parents. **1966** *Listener* 6 Oct. 492/2 Permissiveness can rarely have gone further than it does today, and it may be..that we shall soon be due for a reaction, and a return to stricter standards. **1969** J. MANDER *Static Society* ix. 303 The *permissiveness* of Brazilian society is an important element in her reputation for tolerance in racial and social matters. **1971** *Daily Tel.* 21 July 14 Perhaps it is time.. for Parliament to have another look at the whole subject of abortion, family planning and perhaps permissiveness in general. **1973** M. AMIS *Rachel Papers* 130 The so-called new philosophy, 'permissiveness' if you like, seen from the right perspective, is only a new puritanism, whereby you're accused of being repressed or unenlightened if you happen to object to infidelity, promiscuity, and so on. **1974** F. WARNER *Meeting Ends* II. i. 35 With the new laws I suppose we've priced ourselves out of the marriage market. With 'permissiveness' a man can have it all, so why should he take on a bloodsucking estate as well?

permissivism (pəɹmi·siviz'm). [f. PERMISSIV(E *a.* + -ISM.] Attitudes or beliefs that are regarded as excessively tolerant or permissive.

1968 *Manch. Guardian Weekly* 17 Oct. 3 But the most impressive tributes to 'the high priest of permissivism', as he [*sc.* Benjamin Spock] once described himself, were casual. Not a single baby cried during the 90 minutes of protest. **1972** *Sat. Rev.* (U.S.) 20 May 30/2 Permissivism —i.e., the notion that all art is good art, etc.

permissivist (pəɹmi·sivist). [f. PERMISSIV(E *a.* + -IST.] A person considered excessively indulgent toward generally unacceptable or unconventional behaviour or attitudes, *spec.* in sexual matters.

1966 *Times* 16 Feb. 13 Theatrical permissivists should ask themselves whether, if there must be censorship, it is not better from their point of view that it should remain with a rationally indefensible institution, which is in no position to enforce for long unpopular or unjustifiable standards. **1970** [see *PABLUM]. **1972** *Daily Tel.* 13 Apr. 8/6 Since sex is a mere function away from all feeling it may be discussed, say the permissivists, in whatever detail, without anyone suffering any harm. **1973** *Church Times* 16 Nov. 9 The permissivists meanwhile demand.. evidence, confident that it is..unobtainable.

permit, *v.* Add: **3.** *spec.* in phr. *weather permitting*, if the weather permits or allows, and in similar phrases.

1840 C. BROWN in H. E. Rollins *Lett. J. Keats* (1958) I. i. 422 'Weather permitting', unless of the bad and excessive kind, was not of much force in our agreement. **1922** JOYCE *Ulysses* 611 It was not so dear, purse permitting, a few guineas at the outside, considering the fare to Mullingar where he figured on going was five and six there and back. **1957** R. W. ZANDVOORT *Handbk. Eng. Gram.* I. ii. 36 Compare also the phrase *weather permitting*, where the meaning implied is one of condition. [*Note*] Also *funds permitting*, and similar combinations. **1978** T. ALLBEURY *Lantern Network* iii. 32 Arms..will be dropped to your instructions, weather permitting.

permit, *sb.* Add: **1.** (Further *attrib.* examples.) Also *Comb.*

1774 in *14th Rep. R. Comm. Hist. Manuscripts* App. x. 393 in *Parl. Papers 1895* (C. 7883) LIX. 1 Have coaxed the people to part with their money and give paper in return to keep up armies of placemen, permit men, custom house officers, pensioners and soldiers. **1921** *Daily Colonist* (Victoria, B.C.) 11 Mar. 4/1 It will be a method of checking bootlegging, and preventing those who are not permit-holders from coming into possession of liquor. **1926** T. E. LAWRENCE *Seven Pillars* v. lvii. 300 A mixed body of Egyptian and British military police came round the train... It was proper to make war on permit-men, so I replied crisply. **1933** *Brit. Birds* XXVII. 138 Last year and again this year, this colony was wiped out,.. and so permit-holders visited the colonies on the gravel bed instead. **1945** *Seafarers' Log* 13 Apr. 7/1 To members in full standing, who bring in their friends for permit cards, study the last weeks LOG on the Agents Conference pertaining to permit men. **1977** *Evening Gaz.* (Middlesbrough) 11 Jan. 14/5 But it will not affect last year's winner, Tsuru, one of two representatives for Somerset permit-holder and wholesale butcher Tony Cobden who has also declared Rio.

permittance. (Later example.)

1912 *Housemaster's Lett.* 124 The wilful misuse of them or the callous permittance of them to go blunt and to rust.

† **2.** *Physics.* = *CAPACITANCE. *Obs.*

1887 O. HEAVISIDE in *Electrician* 3 June 79/2 A telegraph circuit, when reduced to its simplest elements,.. still has no less than four electrical constants, which may be most conveniently reckoned per unit length of circuit—viz., its resistance, inductance, permittance, or electrostatic capacity, and leakage conductance. **1890** [see *ELASTANCE]. **1908** *Jrnl. Inst. Electr. Engin.* XL. 58 Dr. Heaviside's permittivity..is measured in terms of the permittance of unit volume.

permitted, *ppl. a.* Add: **b.** *permitted hours*: the hours during which the sale of intoxicating liquor is legal.

1923 W. B. CAPPER *Licensed Houses* III. lxxii. 211 In Wales and Monmouthshire, however, there are no permitted hours for licensed premises on Sundays. **1946** H. DUGDALE *Managem. of Public-House* x. 67 Occasionally, the permitted hours applicable to a public-house do not sufficiently meet the requirements of the neighbourhood wherein the 'house' is situated. **1964** V. HEATON *Pub of your Own* xvi. 115 Though licensed premises may not sell intoxicating liquor after the permitted hours, nor may it be consumed later than ten minutes after permitted hours, there is no compulsion either to close the premises or to hide any display of liquor.

permittivity (pə̄ɹmiti·vĭti). *Physics.* [f. PERMIT *v.* + -IVITY.] One of the physical parameters of a medium, equal to the ratio of the electric displacement D to the electric field strength E at any point in it; also (more fully *relative permittivity*), the ratio of the permittivity of a medium to the permittivity of free space: = **dielectric constant*; *permittivity of free space*, a constant ϵ_0 which in the C.G.S. electrostatic system of units is unity and in the International System of Units is $1/\mu_0 c^2$ ($= 8{\cdot}854 \times 10^{-12}$) farad per metre, where μ_0 is the permeability of free space and c is the speed of light.

1887 O. HEAVISIDE in *Electrician* 17 June 124/1 Nomenclature Scheme... Permittance. Permittivity. **1890** [see *ELASTANCE]. **1938** G. P. HARNWELL *Princ. Electr. & Electromagn.* i. 12 If the charges are measured in coulombs and if **r** is in meters and **F** in newtons, the constant κ_0 has the value $\kappa_0 = ..8{\cdot}85 \times 10^{-12}$ farads/meter... This constant..is known as the permittivity of free space. **1944** *Phil. Mag.* XXXV. 83 Guggenheim has suggested the term *permittivity* for the fundamental quantity and *specific inductive capacity* or *dielectric constant* for the derived quantity. In conformity with the other suggestions in this paper it would be more uniform to adopt *permittivity* and *relative permittivity*... Similarly in the magnetic case we have *permeability* and *relative permeability*. **1946** *Nature* 6 July 33/2 The paper contains a description of apparatus used for measurements at frequencies of about 3,000 Mc./s...and a statement of typical experimental results obtained with a specimen of polythene, which at the above frequency had a permittivity of 2·27. **1962** CORSON & LORRAIN *Introd. Electromagn. Fields* ix. 317 The permittivity of free space ϵ_0 can..be determined directly from measurements involving electrostatic phenomena. **1971** *Engineering* Apr. 44/1 The capacitance C (microfarads) of a parallel plate capacitor..is..proportional to the relative permittivity ϵ_r of the dielectric medium. **1974** HARVEY & BOHLMAN *Stereo F.M. Radio Handbk.* vii. 148 Because of the presence of water vapour in particular, the permittivity of the air in the troposphere is greater than unity.

Permocarboniferous, *a.* Add: Also, pertaining to or including the Permian and the Carboniferous systems or periods. Also *absol.* Usu. written **Permo-Carboniferous.** (Earlier and later examples.)

1874 *Q. Jrnl. Geol. Soc.* XXX. 217 Taking into consideration the great thickness of the Carboniferous in Nova Scotia and the large development of this Upper Permo-Carboniferous member, it would not be surprising that in this last we may have a chronological equivalent of part at least of the European Permian. **1897** *Trans. Manchester Geol. Soc.* XXV. 207 (*heading*) On the Permo-Carboniferous boundary. **1928** C. DAWSON *Age of Gods* i. 5 The vast glaciation of Permo-Carboniferous times..marks the end of the Primary Palæozoic world. **1955** G. G. WOODFORD tr. *Gignoux's Stratigr. Geol.* v. 156 The great variety of facies of the Permo-Carboniferous in Europe and the harmonious way in which they can be grouped make of this system, seen as a whole, a magnificent illustration of stratigraphic synthesis. **1971** A. G. SMITH in I. G. Gass et al. *Understanding Earth* xv. 224/1 The distribution of Permo-Carboniferous tillites.

Pe:rmo-Pennsylva·nian, *a.* *Geol.* [f. as next + *PENNSYLVANIAN *sb.* and *a.*] Belonging either to the lowest Permian or the uppermost Pennsylvanian. Also *absol.*

The equivalent in the U.S. of prec.

1937 *Bull. Amer. Assoc. Petroleum Geologists* XXI. 1252 Late Pennsylvanian and Permo-Pennsylvanian. Figure 2 represents a composite of late Pennsylvanian and early Permian time. **1965** *Ibid.* XLIX. 1572/2 An early sequence of Permo-Pennsylvanian sediments accumulated in this bay.

Permo-Triassic (pə̄:ɹmotrəiˌæ·sik), *a.* *Geol.* [f. *Permo-*, used as comb. form of PERMIAN *a.* (*sb.*) + TRIASSIC *a.*] Of or pertaining to the Permian and the Triassic systems or periods. Also *absol.*

1876 [see SILURIAN *a.* 2 a]. **1903** J. LE CONTE *Elements Geol.* (ed. 5) III. v. 619 Some indications of glaciation have been reported from other horizons than the Permo-Triassic. **1926** *Proc. Geologists' Assoc.* XXXVII. 11 By the close of Permo-Triassic times the climate would have altered considerably from that at the commencement of the period. **1956** W. EDWARDS in D. L. Linton *Sheffield* i. 3 They are being exploited, for oil as well as for coal, below the 'cover' of Permo-Triassic rocks. **1969** BENNISON & WRIGHT *Geol. Hist. Brit. Isles* xii. 272 The drawing of the Permo-Triassic boundary is fraught with difficulties. **1977** *Offshore Engineer* May 51/1 Effective basement in the Gulf of Valencia area appears to be hard Carboniferous sandstones and clays, overlain in some areas by Permo-Triassic sands and evaporites.

So **Permo-Tri·as**, the Permo-Triassic system or period.

1926 *Proc. Geologists' Assoc.* XXXVII. 1, I am convinced that the divisions of the Permo-Trias, in Britain, are not time-divisions, but represent, to a considerable extent, merely different conditions of deposition. *Ibid.*, In Britain the Permo-Trias formations are always unconformable to and rest upon an uneven surface of the rocks below. **1969** BENNISON & WRIGHT *Geol. Hist. Brit. Isles* xi. 255 Strata of continental facies were laid down over wide areas in the succeeding Permian and Triassic Periods... Frequently considered together as the Permo-Trias, there are however significant palaeontological differences.

perm. s(ec)., permsec, abbrevs. of 'permanent secretary' (esp. in an African country)

1942 PARTRIDGE *Dict. Abbrev.* 78/2 *P.S.*..Permanent Secretary. Also *Perm.S.* **1975** J. WYLLIE *Butterfly Flood* xxii. 95 The Perm. Sec's. house was..much pillared and porticoed. **1976** *Daily Times* (Lagos) 8 July 5/3 (*heading*) Permsec files counter-claim. *Ibid.* 16 Oct. 19/1 (*heading*) Why retired permsec's daughter stole in London.

permselective (pə̄ɹmsĭle·ktiv), *a.* *Chem.* [f. PERM(EABLE *a.* + SELECTIVE *a.*] Of an ion-exchange membrane: permeable to anions but not to cations, or *vice versa*; more generally, selectively permeable to certain molecules or ions. Hence **pe:rmselecti·vity.**

1953 A. G. WINGER et al. in *Jrnl. Electrochem. Soc.* C. 178/2 For the purpose of this paper, an ideal permselective membrane will be defined to be a membrane which, when subjected to a potential gradient, permits passage of cations to the exclusion of anions, or vice versa. *Ibid.* 179/1 In any electrolytic process ion concentrations are appreciable and perfect permselectivity is an idealized situation of little practical interest. **1962** S. B. TUWINER *Diffusion & Membrane Technol.* ix. 177 The most important factor which affects permselectivity for a given membrane is the concentration of the electrolyte. **1968** *Encycl. Polymer Sci. & Technol.* VIII. 636 The ability of an ion-exchange membrane to discriminate between ions of different sign is called its permselectivity. **1969** W. R. R. PARK *Plastics Film Technol.* viii. 197 A process which may come to have the universal utility of distillation is the use of permselective membranes for the separation of mixtures of liquids or gases. **1971** A. F. STANCELL in Tobolsky & Mark *Polymer Sci. & Materials* xii. 263 The preferred permeation of one molecule through a polymer with respect to other diffusing molecules is termed membrane permselectivity.

permutate, *v.* Delete *rare* and add: **2.** (Later examples.) Also *absol.*

Probably regarded by those who use it as a back-formation from *permutation*.

1969 *Daily Tel.* 5 May 14/3 One gets the impression that..three basic dress designs were drawn up and three basic jacket patterns, and ever since designers have been ..endlessly permutating these like resigned pools punters. **1971** *Ibid.* 18 June 22 If your baldness cure is a mixture of known ingredients, however you permutate their quantities, it won't get patent protection. **1975** *Times Lit. Suppl.* 18 Apr. 416/3 The plot, involving revelations about hitherto unsuspected relationships and passions permutating with unforeseen power. **1978** *Gramophone* Jan. 1321/2 Coleman really did reject the old package of chords; but what Coltrane did was to find a new way of permutating them, running through the scales they suggested.

permutated (pə̄·ɹmiutēˈited), *ppl. a.* [f. PERMUTAT(ION + -ED[1].] In *Football Pools*: subjected to permutation.

1947 [see *BANKER[2] 5].

permutation. Add: **2. c.** *Logic.* A form of immediate inference from a proposition by negating it and substituting a contradictory predicate; obversion.

1851 W. H. KARSLAKE *Aids Study Logic* I. 64 The third form of Immediate Inference which we have to speak of is, what may be called *Permutation*. **1906** H. W. B. JOSEPH *Introd. Logic* 214 In Permutation, or (as it has been also called) Obversion, there is no transposition of terms, but the quality of the proposition is changed. **1931** R. M. EATON *Gen. Logic* 206 Obversion, also known as permutation differs from conversion in that the subject and predicate do not change places.

4. b. In the semantic theories of Nils Gustaf Stern: see quot. 1931.

1931 G. STERN *Meaning & Change of Meaning* xiii. 361 Permutations are unintentional sense-changes in which the subjective apprehension of a detail—denoted by a separate word—in a larger total changes, and the changed apprehension (the changed notion) is substituted for the previous meaning of the word. **1933** *Mod. Lang. Notes* XLVIII. 386 The linguistically conditioned changes are.. analyzed into shifts of..'permutation' and 'adequation'. **1965** *Eng. Stud.* XLVI. 405 The type of semantic change involved is that called by Gustaf Stern 'permutation'.

4*. *Football Pools.* A system whereby any combination of a specified number of entries drawn from a larger, selected, number of chances may be considered for a dividend.

1952 *Times* 16 May 7/5 The whole business of forecasting, study of form, permutations, and all the rest of it is, in fact, pure nonsense. **1954** M. CROFT *Spare the Rod* III. v. 198 Football pools—that's the safest bet... Once you've worked up an interest in permutations you can sit down and leave them alone for a whole day. **1959** *Listener* 19 Feb. 347/3 The complications of this revenge put as much strain on one's attention as does the filling of a 'Pools' coupon with recommended permutations. **1960** *Comp* 20 Feb. 7/2 Find the straightforward permutation of allowing for any 3 from 8.

permute, *v.* Add: **2. a.** (Later example.)

1846 *Proc. Philos. Soc.* III. 1 In certain cases a letter may have been permuted, that is, changed to some kindred letter.

b. *Logic.* To submit to the process of permutation or obversion.

1906 H. W. B. JOSEPH *Introd. Logic* 215 The process of permuting and then converting is called Conversion by Negation.

3. Also in *Linguistics.*

1967 D. G. HAYS *Introd. Computational Linguistics* 153 We may be required to permute those elements. **1968** *Language* XLIV. 31 To account for the fairly flexible ordering of major constituents in a German sentence.., we must have a number of optional rules that permute the subject, object, and adverbials. **1975** N. CHOMSKY *Logical Struct. Linguistic Theory* x. 422 In actually formulating $\Phi_2{}^p$ as a grammatical transformation we must be careful to indicate that the element K..and the following verb are not permuted when K belongs to the preceding noun phrase.

permuted (pəɹmiū·tėd), *ppl. a.* [f. PERMUTE *v.* + -ED[1].] Subjected to permutation; transposed.

1846 *Proc. Philol. Soc.* III. 2 In Irish orthography, the permuted letter instead of being displaced by its substitute is merely preceded, or as the Irish grammarians express it, eclipsed by it. **1970** O. DOPPING *Computers & Data Processing* xxiii. 373 Provided that the titles of the material one wishes to register are sufficiently descriptive, the permuted title systems have many advantages. **1971** *Computers & Humanities* V. 309 Scope of present study: to produce permuted indices. **1971** D. I. SLOBIN in W. O. Dingwall *Survey Linguistic Sci.* 352 Structures requiring permutation of elements will first appear in non-permuted form. **1976** *Gloss. Documentation Terms* (*B.S.I.*) 47 *Permuted title*, a title in which the significant words have been rearranged, so that they can be used in indexing.

permutite (pə̄·ɹmiūtəit, pəɹmiū·təit). [ad. G. *permutit*, f. L. *permūt-āre* to exchange + *-it* -ITE[1].] **a.** Any of a class of artificial zeolites which are widely employed as ion-exchangers, esp. for the softening of water. **b.** Written **Permutit** or **permutit** (-it). A proprietary name for ion-exchange materials and equipment utilizing such zeolites. Also *attrib.*, as *permutit(e) process*, the softening of water by treatment with any of these substances.

1907 *Chem. Abstr.* I. 2755 He [*sc.* A. Feldoff] reports the use of Permutite (after Gans) in the refinery at Glogau where much better yields of sugar were obtained by its use than without it. **1910** *Trade Marks Jrnl.* 12 Jan. 44 Permutit... Chemical substances..being artificially prepared compounds for the purification of water, molasses and saccharine juices. *Ibid.* 53 Permutit... Filters and engineering and building contrivances for supplying and distributing water,.. J. D. Riedel Aktiengesellschaft,.. Berlin, Germany; manufacturers. **1911** *Chambers's Jrnl.* 29 Apr. 352/1 For the removal of iron and manganese and for the destruction of germ-life, manganese permutit is used in place of the sodium permutit. **1913** *Official Gaz.* (U.S. Patent Office) 4 Nov. 266/2 The Permutit Company, New York, N.Y. Filed Aug. 19, 1913. Permutit. ..water purifying and treating materials. **1917** A. SMITH *Introd. Inorg. Chem.* (ed. 3) xxxv. 724 In the permutite process the water is simply filtered through sodium silico-aluminate. **1925** *Glasgow Herald* 13 Feb. 6/2 Under the head of artificial silicates mention should be made of glass, Portland cement, water glass, and the permutites. **1943** *Thorpe's Dict. Appl. Chem.* (ed. 4) VI. 276/2 After partition between 70% alcohol and hexane the alcoholic layer is filtered through 'permutite' to remove adrenalin. **1963** R. R. A. HIGHAM *Handbk. Papermaking* x. 245 This process [*sc.* base exchange] relies on the exchange of sodium ions for those of calcium and magnesium and is referred to as the Zeolite or Permutit method of water softening. **1974** D. M. ADAMS *Inorg. Solids* vii. 255 This process [*sc.* cation exchange] forms the basis of the Permutit water-softening process in which Ca^{2+} is removed from 'hard' water by exchange for sodium. **1974** D. W. BRECK *Zeolite Molecular Sieves* i. 11 The accepted term for synthetic aluminosilicates which are crystallographically amorphous and are prepared for the ion exchange properties is 'permutite'... The chemical composition of most permutites is represented by an empirical formula in terms of the oxides: $Na_2O{\cdot}Al_2O_3{\cdot}xSiO_2{\cdot}yH_2O$ in which x often has a value of 5–6.

pern, perne, varr. PIRN *sb.*[2]

pern (pə̄ɹn), *v.*[3] Also **perne.** [f. *pern* var. PIRN *sb.*[2]] *intr.* In the poetry of W. B. Yeats: to move with a winding motion.

It has been suggested (1961 *N. & Q.* Jan. 9/1) that PERN *v.*[2] is the same word.

1920 W. B. YEATS *Michael Robartes* (1921) 17 Though I had long perned in the gyre, Between my hatred and desire, I saw my freedom won And all laugh in the sun. **1920** [see *GYRE *v.* 3]. **1928** [see *GYRE *sb.* 1]. **1938** W. B. YEATS *New Poems* 34 Those new dead That come into my soul and escape Confusion of the bed, Or those begotten or unbegotten Perning in a band.

Pernambuco (pə̄ɹnæmbu·kō). Also **Fernambuk.** The name of a state in Brazil, used *attrib.* and *absol.* to designate the hard, reddish timber of the tree *Cæsalpinia echinata*, of the family Leguminosæ, which is used for dyeing as well as decorative woodwork. Cf. BRAZIL[1] 1.

1794 H. BARHAM *Hortus Americanus* 23 The true Brasil is called Pernambuca, being the place from whence they come in Brasil. **1829** C. SEALSFIELD *Tokeah* II. 124 The carriage whirled along the levee, through oyster and orange shops; mountains of Pernambuco logs and bricks. **1870** J. YEATS *Nat. Hist. Commerce* II. 219 Brazil wood is imported principally from Pernambuco, and is also known by the name of Fernambuk wood in allusion to the place of importation. **1902** G. S. BOULGER *Wood* II. 271 Peachwood (*Cæsalpinia echinata* Lam: Order *Leguminosæ*). Central and South America. Known also as 'Lima, Nicaragua or Pernambuco-wood'. **1920** A. L. HOWARD *Man. Timbers of World* 40 Used as a dye-wood..there is nothing that will yield the same result as the Pernambuco or brazil-wood. **1943** RECORD & HESS *Timbers of New World* 275/2 The principal foreign demand for the timber at present is..for the manufacture of violin bows and in this trade it is known as Pernambuco, taking its name from the Brazilian state where the best grades originate. **1976** *Early Music* Oct. 521/1 (Advt.), Suppliers of wood for stringed and wind instruments: Poplar, Lime, Maple, Fruitwood, Ebony, Box, Rosewood, Walnut, Beech, Holly, Oak, Ash, Mahogany... African Blackwood and Pernambuco.

pernettya (pəɹne·tiă). Also **pernettia.** [mod.L. (C. Gaudichaud-Beaupré 1825, in *Ann. Sci. Nat.* V. 102), f. the name of A. J. *Pernetty* (1716–1801), French explorer.] A small evergreen shrub of the genus so called, belonging to the family Ericaceæ, native to South America, New Zealand, or Tasmania, and bearing leathery leaves and white or pink flowers, followed by white, red, or purplish berries.

1835 *Edwards's Bot. Reg.* XX. 1675 (*heading*) Pointed-leaved Pernettia. **1840** *Ibid.* XXVI. 63 (*heading*) Narrow-leaved Pernettya. **1888** *Garden* 4 Feb. 106/2 Where cut flowers are needed sprays of the Pernettyas are very useful. **1916** L. H. BAILEY *Stand. Cycl. Hort.* V. 2555/1 The pernettyas are low much-branched shrubs with dense and small evergreen leaves and small nodding flowers, followed by very decorative berries varying in color from white to purplish black. **1962** *Listener* 6 Sept. 370/3 If you..want one of the heaviest berried shrubs I know, get some pernettya seedlings. **1973** C. D. BRICKELL in A. Gemmell *Sunday Gardener* iii. 85 *Pernettya* has already been mentioned for winter use, but the berries are well coloured by October.

pernicious, *a.*[1] Add: *pernicious anæmia*: this is now susceptible to treatment; (earlier and later examples): [tr. G. *perniciöse* (now *perniziöse*) *anämie* (A. Biermer 1868: see *Correspondenzblatt für schweiz. Aerzte* (1872) 1 Jan. 15).]; *pernicious contrary*, in paper-making, a substance difficult to detect in the raw material, which inhibits the pulping process. Cf. *CONTRARY *sb.* 3 d.

1874 *Med. Times & Gaz.* 21 Nov. 581/2 (*heading*) Pernicious anæmia: a new disease. *Ibid.* 582/1 Under the name of 'Progressive Pernicious Anæmia', Dr. Biermer, of Zürich, has described an affection which differs from ordinary simple anæmia in a marked manner, and which ..appears to be a disease *sui generis*. **1936** *Discovery* Apr. 123/1 Pernicious anaemia, a disease which was reckoned incurable until 1926, and which, since then, it has been found possible to keep under control by large and frequent doses of fresh liver. **1961** [see *CONTRARY *sb.* 3d]. **1963** R. R. A. HIGHAM *Handbk. Papermaking* ii. 50 (*heading*) Pernicious contraries in waste paper. **1968** PASSMORE & ROBSON *Compan. Med. Stud.* I. v. 15/2 The patient with pernicious anaemia formerly died, because he was unable to transport one-millionth of a gram of the vitamin [*sc.* B_{12}] daily across one or two millimetres of the gut wall. Nowadays he receives an injection of the vitamin at fortnightly or monthly intervals. With this, he is in every respect a normal healthy person. **1972** *Listener* 21 Sept. 383/2 Some 5 per cent or so of waste paper is tainted by what the industry calls 'pernicious contraries' —substances like the bitumen used to waterproof paper or board.

pernio (pə̄·ɹnio). *Med.* Pl. **perniones** (pə̄ɹniō̆u·nīz). [a. L. *pernio, perniōn-* chilblain (f. *perna* haunch or ham).] A chilblain.

1676 R. WISEMAN *Several Chirurgicall Treat.* I. xiii. 62 Pernio is a peculiar Inflammation, and belongeth to Bloud; it raiseth a thick red Swelling with itching pain in the Hands and Feet. Those affecting the Hands are generally called Chilblanes... When they affect the Feet they are called Kibes. **1822** J. M. GOOD *Study of Med.* II. 313 That the pernio or chilblain belongs to the genus erythema is perfectly obvious. **1885** in tr. *H. von Ziemssen's Handbk. Dis. Skin* 169 Such is the mode in which chilblains (perniones) make their appearance. **1941** J. MASEFIELD *Gautama* 19 Cures for all from pernio to spasms. **1959** H. L. DUVRIES *Surg. of Foot* v. 103 Repeated mild frostbite produces vasomotor instability resulting in chilblains, or perniones. **1974** *Arch. Dermatol.* CIX. 57/1 Our cases best fit into the classification of acute pernio or chilblains.

perniosis (pə̄ɹniˌō̆u·sis). *Med.* [mod.L., f. prec. + -OSIS.] A chilblained condition of the skin.

1896 N. WALKER tr. *Unna's Histopath. of Dis. of Skin* I. 20 In rare cases the point of the nose..is the seat of a perniosis. **1952** M. K. POLANO *Skin Therapeutics* iii. 97 A good cream in perniosis. **1968** R. J. CAIRNS et al. in A. J. Rook et al. *Textbk. Dermatol.* I. xv. 337/1 Papular perniosis may closely mimic erythema multiforme. **1974** PASSMORE & ROBSON *Compan. Med. Stud.* III. I. xvii. 27/1 (*heading*) Perniosis (chilblains).

pernoctate, *v.* Delete † *Obs. rare*—[0] and add examples.

1923 *Blackw. Mag.* Aug. 250/1 Families of Oriental pilgrims, pernoctating within the Church, will squat down in front of the Tomb of Christ. **1975** *Wadham Coll. Gaz.* I. I. 6 The second event that demands to be recorded is the arrival of the first women undergraduates. The first to pernoctate as a member of the college came from Kingston, Ontario, to read law. **1978** 'M. INNES' *Ampersand Papers* iii. 28 A bedroom..and sitting-room were in permanent readiness for him should he be minded to pernoctate at Treskinnick.

Pernod (pẹ̄rno, pə̄ɹno). Also **pernod.** The proprietary name of a drink manufactured by the firm of *Pernod* Fils and used as an aperitif; a glass of Pernod. Also *attrib.*

Before 1918 the name referred to a brand of absinthe.

[**1876** *Trade Marks Jrnl.* 11 Oct. 574 Pernod Fils... Louis Pernod, on behalf of self and partner, Fritz Pernod, trading as Pernod, Fils, Pontarlier, Doubs, France; manufacturers of absinthe.] **1908** C. E. GRIFFIN *Four Years in Europe* vi. 58 Men and women sit day and night, sipping their wine or *pernod* (absinthe). **1914** *Blast* June 13 Oh blast France... Blast aperitifs (Pernots, Amers picon) Bad change Naively seductive Houri salon-picture Cocottes. **1919** *Century Mag.* Aug. 446/2 He.. poured a glass of Pernod. **1928** J. RHYS *Postures* xvi. 163 Then she would drink a couple of Pernods..to deaden the hurt. **1931** *Daily Express* 23 Sept. 9/3 There are small cafés, with men and women drinking the yellow-greenish pernod, the near-absinthe, now that the manufacture of absinthe is forbidden, but as like absinthe as one pea is like another. **1936** BENTLEY & ALLEN *Trent's Own Case* xi. 130 Trent called for a Pernod. **1942** 'N. SHUTE' *Pied Piper* i. 19 He would take a little glass of Pernod with Madame? **1958** E. DUNDY *Dud Avocado* I. i. 9 Glancing down at my Pernod, I discovered..that I'd already finished it. **1964** *Sun-Herald* (Sydney) 21 June 11/2 Five men unconscious on the floor of the hold and five empty pernod bottles. **1967** S. BECKETT *Stories & Texts for Nothing* VII. 110 But what is this I see..at pernod time. **1975** *Times* 29 July 5/8 Fendi shapes Pernod coloured mink..into trench coats. **1976** J. VAN DE WETERING *Corpse on Dike* vi. 72 The first French I read here was on the label of the Pernod bottle.

peroba (pĕrō̆u·bă). [Pg., f. Tupi.] Any of several Brazilian hardwood trees, esp. *Aspidosperma peroba* and other members of this genus, belonging to the family Apocynaceæ, or *Paratecoma peroba*, of the family Bignoniaceæ; also, the wood of these trees.

1875 T. LASLETT *Timber & Timber Trees* xxv. 184 Peroba is stronger than teak, but not so heavy. **1920** A. L. HOWARD *Man. Timbers of World* 209 Peroba Branca... The wood is light greyish-yellow in colour, close and fine in the grain. *Ibid.* 210 Peroba Rosa... This wood is of a pale rose colour with some darker streaks. **1936** *Nature* 9 May 790/2 First Class restaurant [of the Queen Mary]: Peroba, with feature panels in selected maple burr. **1956** *Handbk. Hardwoods* (Forest Prod. Res. Lab.) 185 Red peroba (Great Britain). The name peroba rosa is applied to a group of species of *Aspidosperma*, of which the principal one is *A. peroba*. **1971** F. H. TITMUSS *Commerc. Timbers of World* (ed. 4) 236 White Peroba is essentially a timber for high-quality furniture, panelling and veneers. **1978** *Sunday Times* (Colour Suppl.) 18 June 47/1 Once lush rain forest, ablaze with jacaranda and peroba trees, settlement is rapidly turning into a wasteland.

perofskite. Add to def.: and usu. containing lanthanides or alkali metals in place of much of the calcium and often niobium in place of some of the titanium; also, a particular variety or specimen of this mineral, or (more widely) any mineral having the same crystal structure. Freq. *attrib.*, with reference to its structure. (The usual form is now *perovskite.*) (Earlier and further examples.)

1840 *Edin. New Philos. Jrnl.* XXIX. 418 (*heading*) Perowskite, a new mineral species. *Ibid.* It is named Perowskite, in honour of M. von Perowski, an intelligent Russian mineralogist. **1906** J. P. IDDINGS *Rock Minerals* 463 Perovskite occurs in basic igneous rocks, peridotite, melilite-basalt, alnöite, and in nephelite- and leucite-bearing rocks, that is, in titaniferous rocks low or comparatively low in silica. **1939** R. C. EVANS *Introd. Crystal Chem.* viii. 204 The structure of perovskite corresponds to the composition ABO_3 and has the cubic or pseudo-cubic unit cell shown in Fig. 46. *A* ions are situated at the corners of the cell and a *B* ion at its centre, while the faces are centred by oxygen. *Ibid.* 205 The appearance of KIO_3 and $RbIO_3$ among the compounds with the perovskite structure is of particular interest. **1955** *Physical Rev.* XCVIII. 1201/2 $KNbO_3$ and $KTaO_3$ are ferroelectrics of the perovskite type. **1956** *Electronic Engin.* XXVIII. 132 The remarkable and technically important properties of $BaTiO_3$ and other perovskite-type ceramics. **1962** W. A. DEER et al. *Rock-Forming Min.* V. 50 Hevesy *et al.* (1929) reported that for a number of perovskites the ratio Ti : Nb was about 3,000 : 1 and Ti : Ta 7,000 : 1. **1970** *Mineral. Abstr.* XXI. 155/1 The composition of synthetic complex perovskites can be expressed in terms of simpler formula units... E.g. $Pb(W_{1/4}Fe_{1/4}Li_{1/4})O_3 = \frac{3}{8}[Pb(W_{1/3}Fe_{2/3})O_3] + \frac{5}{8}[Pb(W_{3/5}Li_{2/5})O_3]$.

Peronism (pe·rọniz'm). [ad. Sp. *Peronismo* (also used), or f. the name *Perón* (see below) + ISM.] The political ideology of Juan Domingo Perón (1895–1974), president of Argentina from 1946 to 1955 and from 1973 to 1974, advocating nationalism and the organization of labour in the interests of social progress; the political movement supporting Perón or his policies.

1946 *Times* 4 June 5/6 Although the Labour Party is the left wing and the Peronista Radicals are the right wing of Peronismo, the schism is more a struggle for the fruits of office than a conflict of ideology. **1953** G. I. BLANKSTEN *Perón's Argentina* III. xii. 281 Peronism.. was not naziism. It was not fascism. It was not communism... It was *justicialismo*, or the 'Third Position'. **1957** *Economist* 21 Dec. 1063/2 Peronism is near its end as an organized movement. General Perón has suffered two or three severe defeats since he was overthrown. **1962** *Listener* 28 June 1102/2 The late Frondizi government encouraged a revival of Peronism. **1964** G. GERMANI in I. L. Horowitz *New Sociol.* 408 A comparative analysis of fascism and peronism..may be found in Gino Germani, *La integración política de las masas y el totalitarismo*. **1964** J. R. SCOBIE *Argentina* ix. 233 'Peronismo', a doctrine and a political movement which emphasized the importance of the working man. **1972** *Buenos Aires Herald* 1 Feb. 7/2 Members of the youth movement charged..that death of militant member Enrique Castro was due to groups in Peronism that followed the moderate line of former party chief Jorge Daniel Paladino. **1975** *New Yorker* 28 Apr. 18/1 (Advt.), A didactic, explosive, semi-documentary on Peronism and the necessity to create national consciousness in Argentina and other Latin-American countries. **1977** *Time* 11 Apr. 37/2 We are not ready for elections until Peronism is dismantled and forgotten.

Peronist (pe·rǫnist), *a.* [ad. Sp. *Peronista* (also used), or f. as prec. + -IST.] Of, pertaining to, or advocating Peronism. Also as *sb.*, a supporter of Perón or of Peronism.

1946 [see prec.]. **1955** *Times* 7 May 7/4 A group of 10 Peronista deputies belonging to the General Confederation of Labour submitted a Bill yesterday in the Argentine Congress. **1958** *New Statesman* 8 Mar. 291/2 Though Frondizi's victory was won with the help of the Communist and Peronist parties, he would have won even without their support. **1960** *Economist* 15 Oct. 243/2 The xenophobia of the Peronist years. **1963** *Times* 26 Feb. 11/6 The Peronists, despite their internal bickerings, retained their fundamental unity. **1969** J. MANDER *Static Society* viii. 245 Borges never concealed his contempt for the *peronista* régime. **1970** G. GERMANI in I. L. Horowitz *Masses in Lat. Amer.* xvi. 595 The basis of the new political movement was provided by..Perónist penetration of the older unions. **1971** *Guardian* 17 Apr. 10/3, I was only 12 when Peron fell in 1955, but I have always been a Peronist. **1974** *Times* 15 Oct. 9/3 Three car loads of men..shot up the headquarters of the Peronist youth organization.

peroperative (pərǫ·pĕrĕtiv), *a. Surg.* [f. PER-[1] 1 + OPERATIVE *a.* and *sb.*] Given, performed, or occurring during the course of an operation. Hence **pero·peratively** *adv.*

1976 *Lancet* 14 Aug. 325/2 (*heading*) Single-dose peroperative antibiotic prophylaxis in gastrointestinal surgery. **1977** *Ibid.* 2 July 6/1 None of the four patients with preoperative or peroperative peritoneal soiling had post-operative infection. *Ibid.* 6 Aug. 304/2 There are several papers demonstrating the efficacy of a combination of lincomycin and gentamicin (or tobramycin) given in one or two doses peroperatively.

peroral (pərōə·răl), *a.* [f. PER-[1] + ORAL *a.* (*sb.*)] Occurring or carried out by way of the mouth.

1908 *Lancet* 18 Apr. 1183/2 Sauerbruch's low-pressure apparatus, Brauer's high-pressure apparatus, and Kühn's method of producing high pressure by per-oral tubage had now made the way for the surgeon an easy one. **1974** *Jrnl. Infectious Dis.* CXXX. 225 The susceptibility of the newborn mouse to peroral infection with a group B coxsackievirus (B_5) was compared with susceptibility to parenteral infection with this agent.

So **pero·rally** *adv.*

1934 in WEBSTER. **1969** *Canad. Jrnl. Physiol. & Pharmacol.* XLVII. 841/2 The rats were administered water perorally. **1976** *Lancet* 18 Dec. 1320/1 Jejunal-biopsy specimens were taken perorally with the Crosby capsule.

perorative (pe·roreitiv), *a.* [f. PERORAT(ION + -IVE.] Appropriate to or suggestive of a peroration.

1921 *Glasgow Herald* 29 Oct. 4 Messrs. Hart (said Cleland in a perorative phrase..) are of that class in society who have found their way to philosophy without the aid of regular tuition.

peroratorical (pe:rŏrătǫ·rikăl), *a.* [f. PERORATOR after ORATORICAL *a.*] Characteristic of a peroration; perorational.

1927 C. E. MONTAGUE *Right off Map* vi. 56 His voice was taking on the peroratorical note.

perosis (pĕrōu·sis). *Vet. Sci.* [ad. Gr. πήρωσις maiming, f. πηροῦν to maim.] A disease of poultry (see quot. 1937).

1931 *Science* 4 Sept. 249/2 Several of the stations reported that when the 'uniform diet' was fed to chicks kept in confinement a high percentage of them became afflicted with perosis (deforming leg weakness). **1937** *Jrnl. Nutrition* XIV. 155 Perosis..is an anatomical deformity of the leg bones of young chickens, turkeys, pheasants, grouse and quail... The symptoms generally found are gross enlargement of the tibial-metatarsal joint, twisting or bending of the distal end of the tibia and of the proximal end of the metatarsus, and slipping of the gastrocnemius tendon from its condyles. **1950** *New Biol.* VIII. 104 There is some evidence that the disease in hens known as perosis may be due to manganese deficiency. **1970** *Poultry Sci.* XLIX. 1753/1 Perosis is an extremely complex condition that can be produced experimentally by an inadequate intake of several different nutrients.

perosmate (pəɹǫ·zmēit). *Chem.* [f. PER-[1] 5 + OSMATE.] A salt of osmium containing the anion $[OsO_4(OH)_2]^{2-}$, in which osmium has an oxidation state of 8. Formerly represented as $M_2O.OsO_4$ (where M is an alkali metal) and called osmiates (see OSMIATE in Dict. and Suppl.).

The passage in ed. 7 (1890) of *Bloxham's Chem.* corresponding to quot. 1895 occurs s.v. *OSMIATE.

1895 THOMSON & BLOXAM *Bloxam's Chem.* (ed. 8) 470 By dissolving perosmic anhydride in potash, potassium perosmate is supposed to be formed, but this has not been isolated. **1949** *Thorpe's Dict. Appl. Chem.* (ed. 4) IX. 134/1 Addition of alcohol to the clear solution and washings precipitates the ruthenium..and reduces the perosmate to violet osmate. **1973** S. E. LIVINGSTONE in J. C. Bailar et al. *Comprehensive Inorg. Chem.* III. xliii. 1232 Potassium osmate $K_2[OsO_2(OH)_4]$..is best prepared by reduction with alcohol of potassium perosmate $K_2[OsO_4(OH)_2]$, which can be prepared by treating OsO_4 with cold KOH. *Ibid.*, The octavalent state..occurs in the tetroxide OsO_4, the perosmate $[OsO_4(OH)_2]^{2-}$, [etc.].

perovskia (perǫ·vskiă). Also **perowskia, perowskya.** [mod.L. (G. Karelin 1841, in *Bull. Soc. Imp. des Naturalistes de Moscou* 15), f. the name of V. A. *Perovski* (1794–1857), once governor of the Russian province of Orenburg.] A herb or sub-shrub of the genus so called, belonging to the family Labiatæ, native to temperate regions of west and central Asia, and bearing panicles of deep blue flowers.

1907 *Gardeners' Chron.* 21 Dec. 426/1 In the case of Perovskia there is added charm in the pretty inflorescences late in autumn. **1961** *Amat. Gardening* 25 Nov. 8/3 It is best not to cut down the long stems of perowskia until the spring. **1973** C. D. BRICKELL in A. Gemmell *Sunday Gardener* iii. 85 *Perovskia*, with tall upright growths with grey-green aromatic leaves, will reach four feet, with long sprays of lavender-blue in September.

perovskite, var. PEROFSKITE in Dict. and Suppl.

peroxidase (pərǫ·ksidēiz, -s). *Biochem.* Formerly also **peroxydase.** [a. F. *peroxydase* (G. Linossier 1898, in *Compt. Rend. des Séances de la Soc. de Biol.* L. 373), f. *peroxyde* PEROXIDE: see *-ASE.] Any of a large class of iron-containing enzymes found esp. in plants which catalyse the oxidation of a substrate by peroxides, usu. hydrogen peroxide.

1903 *Jrnl. Chem. Soc.* LXXXIV. I. 378 The substance is a very powerful peroxydase, and renders hydrogen peroxide..very active towards pyrogallol, gallic acid, aniline, [etc.]. **1907** J. B. COHEN *Org. Chem. Adv. Students* I. ix. 357 Many other vegetable oxidases have been described, including the so-called 'peroxidases' which activate hydrogen peroxide and possibly other peroxides. **1925** *Jrnl. Chem. Soc.* CXXVIII. I. 615 Peroxydases are found to be present in abundance in most common dried seeds in the resting condition. **1956** *New Biol.* XXI. 46 The same haem is shared by all haemoglobins and myoglobins, as well as..other compounds of biological importance, notably the enzymes catalase and peroxidase. **1971** *New Scientist* 25 Feb. 411/2 The presence of ethylene in a young pea cell causes an increase in the level of the enzyme peroxidase which is capable of tacking the OH group onto proline.

Hence **peroxida·tic** *a.*, characteristic of a peroxidase.

1945 *Biochem. Jrnl.* XXXIX. 300/2 It is conceivable that in addition to alcohols catalase may promote a peroxidatic oxidation of other biologically important substances. **1954** A. WHITE et al. *Princ. Biochem.* xvi. 368 The catalytic splitting of hydrogen peroxide to water becomes merely a special case of a peroxidatic reaction, where hydrogen peroxide serves both as substrate and as acceptor. *Ibid.*, Catalase also exhibits peroxidatic activity. **1972** I. YAMAZAKI et al. in Åkeson & Ehrenberg *Struct. & Function Oxidation-Reduction Enzymes* 326 Peroxidatic reactions are catalyzed in the presence of various non-specific catalysts, such as transition metal ions and their coordination complexes.

peroxide. Add to def.: Now usu. restricted to those oxides which have at least one pair of oxygen atoms bonded to each other in the molecule, or which contain the anion O_2^{2-}. **b.** Any organic compound containing two linked oxygen atoms in its molecule. (Further examples.)

1858 B. C. BRODIE in *Proc. R. Soc.* IX. 362, I have to add a new term to this series, of which hitherto no analogue has existed. This term is the peroxide of the organic radical,—the body which in the series of acetyl corresponds to the peroxide of hydrogen or barium in the series of the metal. **1881** *Chem. News* 20 May 233/1 The peroxide of ethyl remains as a dense syrupy liquid, miscible with water. **1922** H. G. DENHAM *Inorg. Chem.* xiii. 198 True peroxides are held to possess the linking present in hydrogen peroxide, —O—O—. **1950** N. V. SIDGWICK *Chem. Elements* II. 871 From hydrogen peroxide are derived a large number of compounds containing the O—O link; not only organic derivatives such as the alkyl and acyl peroxides, the percarboxylic acids.. but also many inorganic derivatives, in which one or more oxygen atoms of a basic or inorganic oxide, or an oxy-acid, are replaced by O—O groups. The binary inorganic compounds are commonly known as peroxides: this name should be confined to O—O compounds, but is often extended to include any metallic oxides with an unusually large amount of oxygen, such as PbO_2 and MnO_2. **1971** *Nomencl. Org. Chem.* (I.U.P.A.C.) (ed. 2) C. 161 Ethyl phenyl peroxide $C_6H_5O—OC_2H_5$. **1973** E. A. V. EBSWORTH et al. in J. C. Bailar et al. *Comprehensive Inorg. Chem.* II. xxii. 783 Organic peroxides decompose readily to give free radicals. *Ibid.* 784 Many transition metal peroxides are dangerously explosive.

2. Short for **peroxide blonde.* colloq.

1918 G. FRANKAU *Poetical Wks.* (1923) II. 108 Thy merchant-princes, whose week-end peroxides Hastened, safe-screened in many a Triplex-glass car. **1919** E. JORDAN *Girl in Mirror* (1925) ii. 45 'She's probably a peroxide,' he said. 'Even if she isn't, she can't hold a candle to your sister.'

3. Special Combs., as **peroxide blonde** *colloq.*, a woman with peroxided hair; **peroxide bond,** a single bond between two oxygen atoms in a molecule; **peroxide group,** the divalent group —O—O—; **peroxide hair,** hair bleached with hydrogen peroxide; **peroxide shampoo** (see quot.).

1920 S. LEWIS *Main St.* 314 Have you heard about this awful woman that's supposed to have come here to do dressmaking—a Mrs. Swiftwaite—awful peroxide blonde? **1927** A. CHRISTIE *Big Four* xiv. 187 (*title*) The peroxide blonde. **1947** N. MARSH *Final Curtain* vi. 90 An old man ..doting on a peroxide blonde. **1974** *Times* 26 Oct. 8/8 The corny peroxide blondes with their plucked eyebrows. **1949** *Chem. Rev.* XLV. 399 Whether the decomposition of a given hydroperoxide involves radical or cationic intermediates probably depends on the amount of polarization of the peroxide bond. **1961** A. G. DAVIES *Org. Peroxides* x. 143 Familiarity with the homolysis of the peroxide bond delayed the recognition that the above reaction is often heterolytic. **1899** *Jrnl. Chem. Soc.* LXXVI. II. 659 The authors have obtained two new series of compounds which contain the peroxide group. **1939** F. A. PHILBRICK *Inorg. Chem.* xvii. 274 In structure the true peroxides are distinguished by containing in the molecule one or more peroxide groups, —O—O—, such as are present in hydrogen peroxide. **1968** *Jrnl. Chem. Soc.* A. 397/1 The great majority of transition-metal peroxide complexes involve a co-ordinated bidentate peroxide group, but a few are known in which the peroxide functions as a bridging ligand. **1937** W. S. MAUGHAM *Theatre* i. 2 Notwithstanding her cropped peroxide hair and her heavily-painted lips she had the neutral look that marks the perfect secretary. **1966** J. S. COX *Illustr. Dict. Hairdressing* 111/1 *Peroxide shampoo*, a soft soap shampoo incorporating a small quantity of 20 vol. peroxide of hydrogen and two or three drops of ·880 ammonium hydroxide.

Hence **peroxi·dic** *a.*, having the properties of a peroxide; containing or forming part of a peroxide group.

1945 *Jrnl. Org. Chem.* X. 416 This liberation of iodine indicated that peroxidic compounds had been formed in these solvents during ozonization. **1949** *Chem. Rev.* XLV. 385 In the decomposition of organic peroxides, rupture of the bond between the two peroxidic oxygens is often accompanied by cleavage of an adjacent carbon-to-carbon bond. **1956** *Nature* 21 Jan. 129/2 The first product is probably the hydroperoxide.., and indeed very labile, strongly peroxidic, solids have been detected, but isolation has not been possible. **1961** A. G. DAVIES *Org. Peroxides* iii. 56 Peroxylauric acid..loses about 15 per cent of its peroxidic oxygen after 1 week at 25°.

pero·xided, *ppl. a.* [f. PEROXIDE + -ED[1].] **a.** Treated with (hydrogen) peroxide. **b.** Having bleached hair. Also *absol.*

1906 B. VON HÜTTEN *What became of Pam* x. 71 Miss Vesey had highly peroxided hair and a manner of suspicious dignity. **1910** BARONESS ORCZY *Lady Molly* ix. 234 An over-dressed, much behatted, peroxided young woman. **1930** *Observer* 18 May 15/3 Simon, and Sylvia whom he loved, and Sylvia's peroxided mamma were agreeable company. **1946** WODEHOUSE *Joy in Morning* iv. 29 What was it? Blackmail? Does he want you to pinch damaging correspondence from the peroxided? Has some quick-thinking adventuress got him in her toils? **1947** D. M. DAVIN *Gorse blooms Pale* 205 The hair, peroxided it was. **1976** *Times* 5 Mar. 9/5 Two tanned and peroxided matrons in their fifties.

peroxisome (pərǫ·ksisōum). *Cytology.* [f. PEROXI(DE + *-SOME[4].] An organelle present in the cytoplasm of many kinds of cell which contains the reducing enzyme catalase and usu. some oxidases that produce hydrogen peroxide.

1965 C. DE DUVE in *Jrnl. Cell Biol.* XXVII. 25A The name *peroxisome* is proposed for the microbodies of rat liver and for the particles of similar biochemical nature existing in kidney and in *Tetrahymena pyriformis*. The peroxisomes contain large amounts of catalase and several hydrogen peroxide-producing oxidases. **1970** *Sci. Amer.* Sept. 113/3 Recently the cells of higher organisms have been found to contain organelles called peroxisomes, whose major function is thought to be the protection of cells from oxygen. **1975** *Science* 21 Nov. 787/1 Peroxisomes (microbodies), cytoplasmic constituents characterized morphologically by a single limiting membrane and a finely granular or homogeneous matrix, have recently been recognized as ubiquitous structures in animal and plant cells.

Hence **peroxiso·mal** *a.*

1969 *Jrnl. Protozool.* XVI. 430/2 The 6 acid hydrolases studied have almost identical distribution patterns, differing clearly from those of the mitochondrial malate dehydrogenase, peroxisomal catalase and urate oxidase. **1972** *McGraw-Hill Yearbk. Sci. & Technol.* 321/1 Although peroxisomal respiration will be considered primarily, the entire process of photorespiration involves the mitochondrion. **1975** *Science* 21 Nov. 789/1 Recent studies.. failed to demonstrate the presence of peroxisomal oxidases in these catalase-containing particles isolated from Harder's gland.

peroxo(-) (pərǫ·kso), *prefix* and quasi-*adj. Chem.* [f. PER-[1] 5 + *OXO(-): cf. PEROXIDE.] **A.** *prefix.* Used in inorganic chemistry in the names of compounds, complexes, etc., that contain a peroxide group. **B.** Hence as quasi-*adj.*: containing or being a peroxide group. Cf. *PEROXY(-).

*PEROXY(-) is the usual form in organic chemistry.

1910 *Jrnl. Chem. Soc.* XCVIII. II. 858 Tetraethylenediamine-μ-ammoniumperoxocobalticobalte salts. *Ibid.* 869 On heating with concentrated sulphuric acid, it is decomposed with evolution of oxygen and nitrogen, the volumes of these gases obtained showing that the compound contains a peroxo-group and tervalent and quadrivalent cobalt. **1930** *Chem. Abstr.* XXIV. 2672 In the presence of air and light, peroxo compds. possessing unusual oxidizing powers are produced in addn. to the usual Fe^{+++} and Fe^{++} complex ions. **1943** THORNE & ROBERTS tr. *Ephraim's Inorg. Chem.* (ed. 4) xi. 321 The simplest..of the multinucleate cobaltammines are the peroxo-salts $[(NH_3)_5Co—O—O—Co(NH_3)_5]X_4$. **1959** R. S. CAHN *Introd. Chem. Nomencl.* 19 Peroxoacids, in which —O— is replaced by —O·O—, are similarly distinguished by the prefix peroxo- (peroxy- or simply per- have frequently been used in the past), as, for example, in HNO_4 peroxonitric acid. **1960** HESLOP & ROBINSON *Inorg. Chem.* xxxvii. 527 There are two peroxo-acids of sulphur, $H_2S_2O_8$, peroxodisulphuric acid, and H_2SO_5, peroxomonosulphuric acid. **1966** COTTON & WILKINSON *Adv. Inorg. Chem.* (ed. 2) xiii. 376 The peroxo acids are useful oxidants and sources of free radicals. **1971** *Nomencl. Inorg. Chem.* (I.U.P.A.C.) (ed. 2) 33 The prefix peroxo-, when used in conjunction with the trivial names of acids, indicates substitution of —O— by —O—O—. **1973** [see *PERBORIC *a.*].

peroxy(-) (pərǫ·ksi), *prefix* and quasi-*adj. Chem.* [f. PER-[1] 5 + OXY-: cf. PEROXIDE.] **A.** *prefix.* Orig. used in the names of compounds containing a larger proportion of oxygen than the parent compound, now in the names of compounds, radicals, etc., that contain a peroxide group. **B.** Hence as quasi-*adj.*: Containing or being a peroxide group. Cf. *PEROXO(-).

*PEROXO(-) is now the usual form in inorganic chemistry.

1878 *Jrnl. Chem. Soc.* XXXIV. 237 The relation between hæmatin and peroxyhæmoglobin must be sought by investigating the bearing of the albumin. **1900** *Chem. News* 16 Feb. 83/2 We thus obtain a microcrystalline compound, the peroxysulphate of silver, which is decomposed by warm water. **1912** *Jrnl. Chem. Soc.* CII. II. 156 The reaction may be considered a general one for differentiating between three peroxy-salts and hydrogen peroxide additive products. **1956** *Nature* 28 Jan. 182/1 Hydrogen in and on the metal now becomes anodic, and by reaction with oxygen doubtless goes into transient peroxy compounds. **1961** A. G. DAVIES *Org. Peroxides* iii. 55 There are three important types of acyl peroxides—the peroxyacids.., the peroxyesters.., and the diacyl peroxides. **1961** E. G. E. HAWKINS *Org. Peroxides* p. xii, Peroxy ($RO_2·$) radicals,..give substitution products with many reactive molecules. **1964** *Economist* 25 July 356/2 A virulent family of pollutants known as peroxyacylnitrates (PANs). **1971** *Nomencl. Inorg. Chem.* (I.U.P.A.C.) (ed. 2) 41 In conformity with the practice of organic nomenclature, the forms peroxy [etc.]..are also used but are not recommended. **1973** E. A. V. EBSWORTH et al. in J. C. Bailar et al. *Comprehensive Inorg. Chem.* II. xxii. 780 The peroxy-group may replace an oxygen atom as a bridge between two other groups, giving compounds such as $Me_3SnOOSnMe_3$. **1975** J. O. SCHRECK *Org. Chem.* iii. 60 Acyl radicals are precursors of peroxyacyl nitrates, which are lacrimators often associated with smog.

Perp, perp. (pə̄rp), abbrev. PERPENDICULAR *a.* 3. Now freq. in colloq. allusive use. Also *ellipt.*

1867 *Murray's Handbk. Trav. Yorkshire* 116/1 The great features of the exterior..are the North Porch, and the West Front... Both of these are Perp... The West Front..is as fine an example of a Perp. composition. **1894** K. BAEDEKER *Gt. Brit.* (ed. 3) 407 The most striking features of the exterior [of York Minster] are the noble *W. Façade* (Dec.; towers, 201 ft. high, Perp.) [etc.]. **1933** J. E. MORRIS *Northumberland* (ed. 3) 247 Much of the other work is modern and misleading,..the 'Perp.' W. window of the S. aisle, *c.* 1832. **1937** A. CHRISTIE *Dumb Witness* vii. 68 Though an attractive specimen of what the guidebook calls Early Perp. it [*sc.* a church] had been so conscientiously restored in Victorian vandal days that little of interest remained. **1945** J. BETJEMAN *New Bats in Old Belfries* 46 Grey-blue of granite in the small arcade (Late Perp). **1951** N. PEVSNER *Middlesex* 143 The tomb in the aisle chapel is purely Perp. **1957** 'J. WYNDHAM' *Midwich Cuckoos* I. 10 The church is mostly perp. and dec., but with a Norman west doorway and font. **1967** 'M. HUNTER' *Cambridgeshire Disaster* ix. 60 The usual slab of village with a nice old Perp. church. **1974** SHERWOOD & PEVSNER *Oxfordshire* 118 The wall-shafts of the nave [of Christ Church Cathedral] have Perp. shafts with concave-sided capitals. **1974** *Times* 10 Jan. 16/7 His love of Gothic architecture made him befriend cathedrals, abbeys and churches, particularly the Perp and Dec so abundant in East Anglia.

perpend, *v.* **1. a.** (Later examples.)

1930 J. BUCHAN *Castle Gay* xi. 172 He retired to the inn ..to write out his notes and perpend the situation. **1939** JOYCE *Finnegans Wake* I. 187 Perpending that Putterick O'Purcell pulls the coald stoane out of Winterwater's and Silder Seas sing for Harreng our Keng. **1966** 'H. MACDIARMID' *Company I've Kept* vii. 172 The chapters in Professor Hofrichter's book..should be carefully perpended by those who fail even yet to see the full significance of Ezra Pound's great slogan: 'Make it new!'

perpension. Delete †*Obs.* and add later example.

1890 R. L. STEVENSON *Let.* 13 July (1911) III. 165 Upon these points, perpend, and give me the results of your perpensions.

perpetual, *a.* (*adv.* and *sb.*) Add: **1.** Phr. *perpetual student* (also *perpetual scholar*): used of one who stays on as a student at a university or similar institution far beyond the normal period.

1924 G. CALDERON tr. *Tchekhof's Cherry Orchard* I. 132 Yes, I expect I shall be a perpetual student. *Ibid.*, The 'Perpetual Student' has become a common type in Russia during the last fifteen or twenty years. **1960** G. BUTLER *Death lives Next Door* i. 10 The perpetual scholar; the man who is always proceeding to the next and then the next degree. **1967** E. GRIERSON *Crime of one's Own* xix. 154 He looked a little on the young side..to spend his life in lending libraries. The perpetual student? **1975** 'J. BELL' *Victim* vi. 71 The real university-type fanatics and loud-mouthed perpetual students.

c. *perpetual calendar,* substitute for def.: (*a*) a calendar which can be adjusted to show any combination of day, date, and month; (*b*) a set of tables from which the day of the week can be reckoned for any date; (*c*) (in full *perpetual calendar clock*) a clock which indicates the date and automatically takes account of the length of each month.

1895 *Montgomery Ward Catal.* 254/3 Perpetual Calendar, made of celluloid and..imitation silver..silk ribbons with dates, etc. **1960** H. HAYWARD *Antique Coll.* 215/1 *Perpetual calendar clock,* clock including a calendar, which corrects itself for the short months... The mechanism consists of a slotted wheel revolving once a year..with slots of varying length which control the movement of a lever, allowing it to pass one or more teeth of the calendar wheel at a time. **1962** E. BRUTON *Dict. Clocks & Watches* 130 *Perpetual calendar,* calendar worked by a clock which corrects for months of different lengths (and sometimes for leap years also). **1971** L. P. DAVIES *Shadow Before* iii. 30 A perpetual calendar confirmed his earlier estimate. **1973** W. J. BURLEY *Death in Salubrious Place* v. 105 The perpetual calendar said Wednesday August 25th. Clarissa had changed it that morning.

f. Of an investment: irredeemable. Also *ellipt.* or as *sb.* Cf. ANNUITY 3.

1869 *Bradshaw's Railway Manual* XXI. 30 Perpetual 4 per cent. stock... Present terminable 4½ per cent. stocks. **1882** R. BITHELL *Counting-House Dict.* 224 Consols—commonly called Bank Annuities—are perpetual. **1948** G. CROWTHER *Outl. Money* (rev. ed.) ii. 75 The mediums, the longs and the perpetuals are liquid at a price. **1965** PERRY & RYDER *Thomson's Dict. Banking* (ed. 11) 436/2 *Perpetual annuity*... The purchaser cannot obtain the principal back, but he can sell his right to the annual payment to someone else.

2. c. *perpetual check*: in Chess and related games, a situation in which one player cannot prevent the other from making an unlimited sequence of checking moves (and thus obtaining a draw). Also ellipt. as *perpetual.*

1820 J. S. BINGHAM tr. *E. Dal Rio's Incomparable Game of Chess* 44 At the end of the game..the Rook sometimes draws the game against the Queen, and is admirable in making a drawn game by perpetual check. **1856** C. TOMLINSON *Chess Player's Ann.* 120 'You might have drawn the game,' said he, 'by perpetual check.' **1960** R. C. BELL *Board & Table Games* I. ii. 60 [Shatranj.] *Perpetual check* was considered a drawn game. **1973** *Correspondence Chess* Spring 385/2 Black either has to take a perpetual or allow White to queen a P with a dangerous check.

d. *perpetual-flowering carnation,* a variety of carnation with a long flowering season, usually grown in a cool greenhouse, as it is not hardy out of doors.

1885 T. BAINES *Greenhouse & Stove Plants* 93/2 Carnation (Perpetual Flowering)... With a sufficient number of plants they may be had in bloom all the year round. **1900** J. DOUGLAS in W. D. Drury *Bk. Gardening* iii. 55 Perpetual-Flowering Carnations are generally propagated by slips. **1926** M. C. ALLWOOD *Carnations* viii. 55 The Perpetual-flowering Carnation can be planted in May. **1960** *Times* 29 June 17/3 Perpetual-flowering carnations and pinks form a very attractive exhibit. **1971** S. BAILEY *Perpetual-Flowering Carnations* (rev. ed.) 18 The perpetual-flowering carnation owes its origin to at least two *Dianthus* species, namely *D. caryophyllus* and *D. sinensis.*

perpetualism (pəɹpe·tiu̦ăliz'm). [f. PERPETUAL *a.* + -ISM.] Lasting, perpetual, or universal quality, *spec.* as a doctrine in political science or religion.

1885 *Encycl. Brit.* XIX. 391/1 Cosmopolitanism..and what has been called perpetualism, or the assumption of a system applicable to every social stage, were alike discredited. **1905** *Westm. Gaz.* 31 July 6/7 Perpetualism abolishes both hell and heaven. **1931** *Observer* 8 Nov. 24 The hybridist who can develop even a slight measure of perpetualism in this plant will sweep the horticultural board of its best cups and medals.

perpetuana. For † *Obs.* read *Hist.* and add later example.

1972 A. PLUMMER *London Weavers' Company 1600–1970* xiv. 292 Indian wrought silks and painted and dyed calicoes became extremely fashionable, taking the place of English silks, half-silks, slight silks, worsted stuffs, says and perpetuanas.

perpetuant. Add: **2.** = PERPETUANA.

1753 E. BOWEN *Map of Devon*, The chief Manufactures [of Devon] are Kerseys, Serges, Druggets, Perpetuants, fine and coarse Cloths, and Lace, in all which many Families are employd.

perpetuate, *v.* Add: Also *absol.*

1894 E. FAWCETT *New Nero* ii. 26 That soulless and mysterious will-to-live, which for ever creates, protects, and perpetuates, though blindly and dumbly, unconscious that she does either.

perpetuative (pəɹpe·tiu̦ătiv), *a.* [f. PERPETUATE *v.* + -IVE.] Having a tendency or inclination to perpetuate.

1957 P. WORSLEY *Trumpet shall Sound* 273 Such movements can be either revivalistic—stressing the readoption of customs fallen into desuetude—or perpetuative—seeking to maintain the existing order. **1977** *Dædalus* Summer 61 My personal view is that anthropology is shifting from a stress on concepts such as structure, equilibrium, function, system to process, indeterminacy, reflexivity..but with a tender perpetuative regard for the marvellous findings of those who, teachers of the present generation, committed themselves to the discoveries of 'systems' of social relations and cultural 'items' and 'complexes'.

‖ **perpetuum mobile** (pə̄ɹpe·tuŏm mōu·bilī, -um mōu·bile). [f. L. *perpetu-us* continuous + *mobil-is* movable, after PRIMUM MOBILE.] **1.** = *perpetual motion* s.v. PERPETUAL *a.* 1 b. Freq. in allusive use.

a **1688** CUDWORTH *Treatise Freewill* (1838) 28 This is an ever bubbling fountain in the centre of the soul, an elater or spring of motion, both a *primum* and a *perpetuum mobile* in us, the first wheel that sets all the other wheels in motion, and an everlasting and incessant mover. **1904** B. RUSSELL in *Mind* XIII. 337 'There is no *perpetuum mobile*' does not mean 'whatever exists differs from the *perpetuum mobile*'. **1933** J. N. FINDLAY *Meinong's Theory of Objects* iii. 89 That China is a Republic, that there is no *perpetuum mobile*, that dirigible airships exist, all these may indifferently be called circumstances or states of affairs. **1953** R. F. C. HULL tr. *Jung's Psychol. & Alchemy* in *Coll. Wks.* XII. II. iii. 172 This theme was already hinted at in dream g, with its pendulum clock, a *perpetuum mobile*. **1964** V. NABOKOV *Defence* x. 162 The passionate chess player is just as ridiculous as the madman inventing a *perpetuum mobile*.

2. *Mus.* = *moto perpetuo* s.v. *MOTO.

1893 J. S. SHEDLOCK tr. *Riemann's Dict. Music* 588/2 *Perpetuum mobile*..the name given to pieces written from beginning to end in notes of equal, and short value. **1938** *Oxf. Compan. Mus.* 708/2 *Perpetuum mobile*,..a rapid instrumental composition that proceeds throughout in notes of the same value. **1969** W. S. NEWMAN *Sonata since Beethoven* xii. 508 The rondo is a virtual *perpetuum mobile*. **1972** H. TISCHLER tr. *Apel's Hist. Keyboard Music to 1700* xix. 664 One of the four pieces..is a kind of *perpetuum mobile* in 12/8. **1978** *Times* 6 Apr. 16/8 Ravel asked Enesco if he would mind running through the whole sonata with him. They played it through, including the punishing perpetuum mobile.

perphenazine (pəɹfe·năzīn). *Pharm.* [f. PI)PER(IDINE + PHEN(YL + *AZINE, constituent parts of the systematic name.] A whitish powder that is a derivative of phenothiazine and has actions and uses similar to, but stronger than, those of chlorpromazine, being used as a sedative and anti-emetic and in the treatment of alcoholism; 2-chloro-10-{3-[4-(2-hydroxyethyl)piperazin-1-yl]propyl}-phenothiazine, $C_{21}H_{26}N_3OClS$.

1957 *Jrnl. Pharmacol. & Exper. Therap.* CXX. 376 Sch3940 is now known by the generic name of perphenazine and is marketed under the trade name, Trilafon. **1971** P. K. BRIDGES *Psychiatric Emergencies* vi. 158 Chlorpromazine.., trifluoperazine..and perphenazine (Fentazin, Trilafon) are commonly given to patients with neurotic illnesses. **1978** *Nature* 23 Mar. 331/2 Chlorpromazine and perphenazine were found..to be as effective as conventional tricyclic antidepressant drugs in the treatment of certain forms of depression.

perrhenic (pəɹ,rī·nik), *a. Chem.* [f. PER-[1] 5 b + *RHEN(IUM + -IC.] *perrhenic acid,* a strong acid, $HReO_4$, which is known only as a colourless aqueous solution and is an oxidizing agent.

1929 *Chem. Abstr.* XXIII. 1833 Yellow oxide, Re_2O_7,..is water sol[uble], hygroscopic, forming a strong acid, perrhenic acid. **1962** P. J. & B. DURRANT *Introd. Adv. Inorg. Chem.* xxiv. 1019 Rhenium heptoxide dissolves freely in water to form perrhenic acid. *Ibid.*, Many salts of perrhenic acid are known. **1973** R. D. PEACOCK in J. C. Bailar et al. *Comprehensive Inorg. Chem.* III. xxxix. 946 Perrhenic acid is a strong acid; this is shown by the pH of its aqueous solution, its attack upon metals, [etc.].

Hence **perrhe·nate** [-ATE[4]], a salt of this acid; the anion ReO_4^-.

1929 *Chem. Abstr.* XXIII. 4632 Perrhenates of non-volatile bases can be ignited in O_2 without decompn. **1950** N. V. SIDGWICK *Chem. Elements* II. 1295 Perrhenates are formed with great ease by the action of oxidizing agents..on metallic rhenium or its lower oxides and their derivatives. **1962** COTTON & WILKINSON *Adv. Inorg. Chem.* xxx. 801 After concentration, the perrhenate is precipitated by addition of potassium chloride as the sparingly soluble salt, $KReO_4$. **1972** *Inorg. Syntheses* XIII. 219 This difficulty has been overcome for $ReHg^{2-}$ by a synthesis of the disodium salt in which an ethanol solution of sodium perrhenate is reduced with sodium metal to give the hydride in *ca.* 35% yield.

Perrier[2] (pe·rie). The proprietary name of an effervescent natural mineral water from the South of France.

1907 *Trade Marks Jrnl.* 30 Oct. 1928 Perrier... Natural mineral water obtained from the spring known as 'Source Perrier' situated at Vergeze in France. St. John Harmsworth, trading as Perrier,..London,..merchant. **1907** *Yesterday's Shopping* (1969) 27 Mineral waters (natural). ..Perrier..Table water. **1928** A. Huxley *Point Counter Point* xiii. 244 If only Grace could be bottled like Perrier water. **1957** [see *Italian *sb.* 6]. **1960** I. Fleming *For your Eyes Only* 14 He always stipulated Perrier, for in his opinion expensive soda water was the cheapest way to improve a poor drink. **1973** D. Mackenzie *Postscript to Dead Let.* 173 Tully was drinking beer. There was a bottle of Perrier in front of Misty. **1975** *New Yorker* 30 June 33/3 She measures his orange juice and Perrier water as carefully as if it were a Martini. **1977** *Rolling Stone* 30 June 73/4 At the Caffe Tartufo, while I lunch, she orders a Perrier water and tosses a carefully rolled stick of Doublemint into her mouth.

perrierite (pe·riərəit). *Min.* [a. It. *perrierite* (Bonatti & Gottardi 1950, in *Atti d. Accad. naz. d. Lincei: Rendiconti. Classe di Sci. fis.*, etc. IX. 361), f. the name of Carlo *Perrier* (1886–1948), Italian mineralogist: see -ite[1].] A silicate of lanthanides, titanium, iron, and other elements, occurring as black or reddish brown, prismatic, monoclinic crystals.

1951 *Chem. Abstr.* XLV. 7923 (*heading*) Perrierite, a new mineral. **1962** *Mineral. Mag.* XXXIII. 45 These experiments..suggest that perrierite is probably an oxidized form of chevkinite. **1966** *Amer. Mineralogist* LI. 1394 Recent *x*-ray studies of metamict minerals which occur in Virginia have shown that some of the materials heretofore reported as allanite or chevkinite are actually perrierite. **1971** *Ibid.* LVI. 308 Chevkinite and perrierite exhibit thermal polymorphism only within certain compositional ranges.

Perrier-Jouët (pe·rie,ʒue). The proprietary name of the champagne produced by the firm of Perrier-Jouët of Epernay.

1891 in C. Ray *Compleat Imbiber* (1967) IX. 122 All Brands of Champagne in stock..Pommery Greno, Perrier Jouet, Heidsieck, Giesler. **1899** O. Wilde *Importance of being Earnest* iii. 136 He drank..an entire pint bottle of my Perrier-Jouet, Brut, '89. **1914** C. Mackenzie *Sinister St.* II. iii. xii. 745 Forty Good Eggs drank forty-eight bottles of Perrier Jouet '93. **1920** G. Saintsbury *Notes on Cellar-Bk.* v. 71 The very best [champagne] I ever had was a Perrier-Jouet. **1971** J. Doxat *Drinks & Drinking* 165 *Perrier Jouet*, this champagne has a fine 1961 extra dry *cuvée reserve*. **1975** N. Freeling *What are Bugles blowing For?* xvi. 93 The waiter had brought a 'Belle Epoque' bottle of Perrier-Jouet.

perryite (pe·ri,əit). *Min.* [f. the name of Stuart H. *Perry* (1874–1957), U.S. mineralogist + -ite[1].] A nickel-rich mineral also containing silicon and phosphorus that is reported to have been found in several meteorites.

1965 Fredriksson & Henderson in *Trans. Amer. Geophysical Union* XLVI. 121/2 The Horse Creek, Baca County, Colorado, iron meteorite, found in 1937, is unique for four reasons:..(4) this iron contains about 3% of Perryite, nickel silicide, a new mineral... The approximate chemical composition of Perryite is Ni 81%, Si 12%, Fe 3% and P 5%. **1968** *Mineral. Mag.* XXXVI. 852 The South Oman enstatite chondrite also contains perryite, but its abundance is much less than in Kota-Kota... In this meteorite, perryite occurs as small laths, usually associated with kamacite. **1970** *Geochim. et Cosmochim. Acta* XXXIV. 169 Electron-microprobe analysis of Si, P and Ni in the metal grains and associated schreibersite and perryite of eight enstatite achondrites shows that the compositions of these phases are relatively constant within a given meteorite, but show substantial variations between meteorites.

persecution. Add: **1. d.** *Psychol.* The irrational sense of being victimized by malign forces which features in many forms of mental disorder and is now commonly considered paranoid.

1881 *Jrnl. Nerv. & Mental Dis.* VIII. 28 We may have delusions of persecution which are systematized and such which are unsystematized. **1883** T. S. Clouston *Clin. Lect. Mental Dis.* vi. 255 The third great class of delusional cases are those of suspicion and persecution. **1926** W. McDougall *Outl. Abnormal Psychol.* xx. 337 The two forms of delusion mentioned.., delusions of persecution and of grandeur, are the fundamental and most frequent. **1970** Hinsie & Campbell *Psychiatric Dict.* (ed. 4) 542/1 A form of paranoia characterized by more or less incessant quarrelsomeness due to alleged persecution.

4. (esp. in sense *1 d) *persecution complex, fantasy*; **persecution mania** (earlier and later examples); also *transf.* and in extended uses; hence **persecution maniac,** a person of unbalanced mind suffering from delusions of persecution.

1961 J. Heller *Catch-22* (1962) xxvii. 294 You've got a bad persecution complex. You think people are trying to harm you. **1966** 'H. MacDiarmid' *Company I've Kept* v. 139 The delusions of a man unbalanced by a persecution-complex. **1971** *Rand Daily Mail* 3 Apr. 5/8 We shall develop a persecution complex and go round moaning that we are misunderstood. **1950** T. Wiesengrund-Adorno et al. *Authoritarian Personality* iv. 615 The persecution fantasy of what the Jews *might* do to her, is used..as a justification of the genocide committed by the Nazis. **1892** D. H. Tuke *Dict. Psychol. Med.* II. 934/2 From a medico-legal point of view, cases of persecution-mania afford matter for consideration of the greatest importance. **1903** R. Fry *Let.* 21 Jan. (1972) I. 200 Langton Douglas..has the persecution mania..and I need hardly say B.B. looms large. **1934** *Punch* 7 Mar. 278/1 The present [Russian] régime's..persecution-mania, misrepresentation of the outside world and progressive debasement of the arts are..set-backs to the advantage of what Miss Hamilton..calls 'the Insect State'. **1942** E. Waugh *Put out More Flags* iii. 203 He had left his persecution mania downstairs with his hat and umbrella. **1968** C. Rycroft *Crit. Dict. Psychoanal.* 115 Persecution mania is an obsolete term for paranoia. **1978** I. Murdoch *Sea* 69, I have never gone in for persecution mania and do not propose to start now. **1943** J. S. Huxley *Evolutionary Ethics* iii. 19 Unable to bear the condemnation of his super-ego, the persecution-maniac projects this into society, thus..being able to accuse the world of cruelty or oppression. **1955** Koestler *Trail of Dinosaur* i. 19 The persecution-maniacs in the West who still lived on the Red Scare had by that time become a dwindling, reactionary minority.

persecutory, *a.* **1. a.** (Later examples.) **b.** (Later examples.) Now used esp. with reference to *persecution 1 d.

1881 *Jrnl. Nerv. & Mental Dis.* VIII. 33 We have such [*sc.* delusions] of a depressive erotic character, usually persecutory. **1936** W. S. Sadler *Theory & Pract. Psychiatry* xix. 334 The child can very early acquire a 'persecutory complex' built up out of his memory feelings of being many times unjustly treated. **1952** *Brit. Jrnl. Psychol.* XLIII. 81 Religion is a form of psychotherapy which promotes a belief in the existence of idealized good objects as a defence against persecutory and depressive guilt. **1962** *Lancet* 19 May 1065/1 He soon developed persecutory ideas and was admitted to hospital. **1963** *Observer* 2 June 18/6 Cameras planted all over the place like persecutory eyes.

perseverate (pəɪse·vərēit), *v. Psychol.* [Back-formation from Perseverat(ion; cf. L. *persevērāre* to persevere.] *intr.* To repeat a response after the cessation of the original stimulus, in various senses of *perseveration 2.

1915 *Brit. Jrnl. Psychol.* VII. 388 The varying degree in which their ideas after disappearing from consciousness continue to 'perseverate' unconsciously. **1927** C. Spearman *Abilities of Man* xvii. 293 They seem not even to have cared to inquire whether..he who perseverates in one kind of operation may be expected to do so..in others. *Ibid.* 306 A tendency for mental processes to have a certain lag or inertia and in this meaning to 'perseverate'. **1968** P. McKellar *Experience & Behaviour* xii. 324 One subject started to draw an analogy with a gramophone record, and perseverated. **1976** Smythies & Corbett *Psychiatry* vii. 105 He may be talkative but difficult to understand, and perseverates—that is replies to questions with responses appropriate to previous questions. **1977** *Word 1972* XXVIII. 214 Often, the archiunit is one which was used appropriately some time ago in the conversation. It then pops up again and again—both in the patient's own speech and in his misunderstanding of the speech which he hears. In the latter case, the patient is said to *perseverate* on the archiunit.

Hence **perse·verating** *ppl. a.*; **perse·verative** *a.*; **perse·verator,** one who perseverates.

1915 *Brit. Jrnl. Psychol.* VII. 389 This inhibition of a succeeding by the effect of a preceding experience must also be expected to reveal itself in the relative slowness of the perseverator. **1923** E. Jones *Papers on Psycho-Anal.* (ed. 3) xxxiii. 445 The perseverating influence of this last reaction is also to be noticed in the next succeeding one. **1924** R. M. Ogden tr. *Koffka's Growth of Mind* iv. § 5. 178 This 'perseverative tendency' of certain methods deserves special consideration. **1927** C. Spearman *Abilities of Man* xvii. 292 The perseverator has been assumed to be stable in his emotions and steadfast in his purposes. **1943** H. Read *Educ. through Art* v. 150 On the other hand we have slight ability to direct attention, inclination to concentrate on colour to the neglect of form, perseverative talent—all symptoms of the tetanoid type. **1964** M. Critchley *Developmental Dyslexia* vi. 23 Words may be repeated in a perseverating fashion, e.g. *The cat the cat.* **1972** *Science* 16 June 1227/1 Attempts to reproduce such effects [*sc.* of medial temporal lesions] in animals have been largely fruitless; perseverative or disinhibitory effects have been the most frequent outcome. **1977** *Lancet* 10 Dec. 1227/2 She had a generalised memory disorder, momentary confusion, and mental and motor inertia and perseverative responses.

perseveration. 1. Delete † *Obs.* and add later examples.

1915 *Brit. Jrnl. Psychol.* VII. 388 The 'Perseveration'-qualities of character, *i.e.* perseverance or persistency of will. **1971** *Where* Nov. 333/2 The *Pinky and Perky* annual shows this nauseating little pair in stories, pictures, strip cartoons, puzzles, crosswords and as objects to paint. Faced by this merciless perseveration, an adult reader can be excused for thinking longingly of an efficient bacon-slicer.

2. *Psychol.* **a.** The tendency for an activity to be persevered with or repeated after the cessation of the stimulus to which it originally responded, studied as an aspect of behaviour.

[**1901** *Brain* XXIV. 620 G. E. Müller and Pilzecker have shown that an image..that has occupied consciousness tends to rise again to consciousness spontaneously,.. a tendency to which they give the name 'Perseverationtendenz'.] **1915** *Brit. Jrnl. Psychol.* VII. 388 Is Perseveration a general factor,—comparable with General Ability, influencing the entire range of mental activity? **1916** A. A. Brill tr. *Freud's Leonardo da Vinci* v. 96 We call such a repetition a perseveration. It is an excellent means to indicate the affective accentuation. **1927** C. Spearman *Abilities of Man* iv. 42 He [*sc.* Müller] writes: 'Consistency of thought and action that extends beyond the immediately given is based to an essential degree upon perseveration.' *Ibid.* 52 As most fundamental of all concepts involved, we may pick out that of 'perseveration'. **1951** J. C. Flugel *Hundred Yrs. Psychol.* (ed. 2) xi. 322 One of the most remarkable [general characteristics] concerns a factor known as *p* ('perseveration'), manifesting itself as a general inertia, which..makes it difficult for the subject to pass rapidly from one kind of mental operation to another. **1963** T. Alcock *Rorschach in Pract.* xi. 172 He is also showing some perseveration of theme on winged objects, whether creatures or emblems. **1973** P. E. Vernon in J. R. Royce *Multivariate Anal. & Psychol. Theory* 127 Tests of different kinds of perseveration, inertia or rigidity, often showed little or no correlation with one another.

b. The mechanical and involuntary repetition of a motor or verbal response, despite a change of stimulus, as a result of brain damage or organic malfunction; usu. distinguished from the stereotypy associated with schizophrenia.

1910 *Lippincott's New Med. Dict.* 715/1 *Perseveration*, the senseless repetition of a word just pronounced or an act accomplished: either a functional or an exhaustion psychosis. **1937** *Jrnl. Mental Sci.* LXXXIII. 144 Perseveration, an extremely common symptom of organic disease..can be present in various degrees, and may extend to words, phrases, actions or to the total behaviour. **1961** W. R. Brain *Speech Disorders* v. 62 Perseveration may lead to difficulties, the whole or part of a previous word being repeated and thus persisting to contaminate the new word which should be evoked. **1966** I. B. Weiner *Psychodiagnosis in Schizophrenia* iv. 36 In 'fixed concept' perseveration a response that accurately corresponds to a blot when first given is repeated on subsequent blots without regard for actual blot qualities. **1976** M. Hamilton *Fish's Schizophrenia* (ed. 2) iii. 58 Perseveration consists in continuing to carry out a goal-directed activity after the need for this activity has ceased. It..is different from a stereotypy because it has been initiated by a goal-directed activity.

Persian, *a.* and *sb.* Add: **A.** *adj.* **1.** Also, of or pertaining to a Persian cat.

1889 H. Weir *Our Cats* 28 Tabby is not a Persian colour. **1972** Ing & Pond *Champion Cats of World* ii. 73 When the two varieties [*sc.* the Angora and the Persian] were mated together by the early fanciers it was found that the Persian characteristics were dominant, so gradually all the Longhairs were classified as 'Persian'.

2. *Persian carpet* (earlier and later examples), (*flower*) *pattern*; **Persian cat,** a long-haired cat, formerly one belonging to a variety introduced from Persia, distinguished by broad, round heads, small ears, stocky bodies, and thick, rather woolly fur; (earlier and later examples); **Persian cord** (earlier example); **Persian lamb,** the skin or pelt of the karakul lamb, which has a silky, tightly-curled appearance; a coat made from this fur; **Persian lilac,** a shrub, *Syringa persica*, of the family Oleaceæ, bearing panicles of fragrant, mauve or white flowers; **Persian sheep,** a southern African breed of sheep, kept for the meat it produces; also called the blackhead Persian; **Persian ware** (examples); **Persian wheel** (later example); **Persian Yellow (rose),** a variety of the Austrian briar, *Rosa foetida* var. *persiana*, which bears fragrant, double, yellow flowers and was brought back to England from Persia by Sir Henry Willock in 1837.

1616 T. Roe *Jrnl.* 11 Mar. in *Embassy to Court of Gt. Mogul* (1899) I. 143 Vnder foote it is layd with good Persian Carpetts of great lardgnes. **1621** J. Chamberlain *Let.* 10 Nov. in *Mem. Amer. Philos. Soc.* (1939) XII. ii. 406 The Moscovie ambassador..brought divers presents of ermins, sables, blacke foxe, Persian carpetts wrought with gold..besides a faire Persian tent. **1844** A. W. Kinglake *Eothen* xxvii. 394 A few Persian carpets (which ought to be called Persian rugs, for that is the word which indicates their shape and dimension,) are sometimes thrown about near the divan. **1969** *Times* 12 Dec. (Kenya Suppl.) p. viii/3 A friend..drove all the way to Rhodesia, with her savings invested in a dozen Persian carpets supporting three dogs in the back of a station wagon. **1978** *Times* 22 Nov. 2/1 Public auction sale of genuinely rare and valuable Persian Carpets on behalf of foreign creditors. **1821** Byron *Don Juan* iii. xviii. 157 Two parrots, with a Persian cat and kittens, He chose from several animals he saw. **1824** M. R. Mitford *Our Village* I. 289 The white kitten..has succeeded to his lamented grandfather, our beautiful Persian cat. **1889** H. Weir *Our Cats* 24 The Persian cat..differs somewhat from the Angora. **1903** F. Simpson *Bk. of Cat* vii. 98/1 In classing all long-haired cats as Persians I may be wrong, but the distinctions between Angoras and Persians are of so fine a nature that I must be pardoned if I ignore the cat commonly called Angora, which seems gradually to have disappeared from our midst... It is my intention to confine my division of cats to long-haired or Persian cats, and short-haired or English and foreign cats. **1935** E. B. Simmons *Cats* xxvii. 133 In the beginning there were Persian cats..and Angora cats... Interbreeding has made the two one. **1972** Ing & Pond *Champion Cats of World* ii. 72 Eventually all Angora and Persian cats were referred to as Longhairs. **1873** *Young Englishwoman* June 312/1 Two good merinos, one Russell or Persian cord. **1889** Persian lamb [see Lamb *sb.* 5 b]. **1892, 1899** [see *broad-tail]. **1937** J. Laver *Taste & Fashion* xv. 215 All kinds of combinations of furs were tried: squirrel collared with fox, Persian lamb trimmed with mink kolinsky. **1959** J. LUDWIG in *Tamarack Rev.* Summer 6 She..walks.. not in her Persian lamb..but in that worn cloth coat. **1972** C. DRUMMOND *Death at Bar* v. 123 Mrs. Gaukroger, wearing a purple pyjama suit under her Persian lamb coat. **1640** J. PARKINSON *Theatrum Botanicum* 1468 This Persian Iasmine (or Persian Lilac, whether you will) is a shrub, or shrubby plant. **1712** [see LILAC 1 b]. **1800** *Curtis's Bot. Mag.* XIV. 486 The Persian Lilac is a shrub of much humbler growth than the common sort. **1847** F. A. KEMBLE *Let.* 12 Dec. in *Rec. Later Life* (1882) III. 301 Her maid has been with me this morning, with..a bunch of delicious Persian lilac. **1861** [see LILAC 1 b]. **1959** A. MOOREHEAD *No Room in Ark* ii. 62 The incredibly sweet scent of Persian lilac hung in the air. **1975** V. NABOKOV *Tyrants Destroyed* 47 A bright breeze ruffled the Persian lilacs. **1870** D. ROCK *Textile Fabrics* p. lxvi, Though there be seen the 'homa', the 'cheetah', and other elements of Persian patterns, still the discordant two-handled vase..betrays the textile to be not Persian, but Syrian. **1895** *Montgomery Ward Catal.* Spring & Summer 37/2 Ladies' Shirt Waists... New fancy Persian patterns. **1971** *Guardian* 30 Mar. 9/2 Printed Crimplene sweaters in a Persian flower pattern. **1912** R. LYDEKKER *Sheep & its Cousins* x. 209 The Persian fat-rumped sheep..is a well-known breed, which has been carried to Cape Colony and Rhodesia, where it is now bred to a considerable extent. **1932** S. ZUCKERMAN *Social Life Monkeys* xii. 206, I have seen Chacma baboons playing about and foraging in the midst of a flock of Persian sheep. **1966** E. PALMER *Plains of Camdeboo* xvi. 256 'I guess it is a black-head Persian from the Karoo.' 'You're right,' replied Sir Abe [Bailey] with delight. 'It is Karoo Persian.' When he travelled he took with him live Persian sheep from the Karoo to be slaughtered when he needed them. **1903** M. L. SOLON *Hist. Old French Faïence* iv. 52 This..bears a distant likeness to the Persian ware. **1971** L. A. BOGER *Dict. World Pott. & Porc.* 165/1 The earliest extant examples of Persian underglaze blue and white wares date from the 15th century. **1972** H. HODGES *Pottery* 53 Throughout the twelfth century the larger part of Byzantine polychrome pottery is best seen as a poor copy of Persian wares. **1864** J. A. GRANT *Walk across Afr.* xvii. 403 The Persian wheel, with its hanging earthen jars, overhangs the river [Nile] and..raises the water to the heights of the fields and gardens. **1843** *Gardeners' Chron.* 25 Feb. 121/1 The new Persian Double Yellow Rose..is an entirely different variety from *Rosa Harrisonii*; it is very like the old double yellow. **1848** W. PAUL *Rose Garden* 97 Persian Yellow; flowers of the deepest yellow, large and full; form, globular... Introduced from Persia by Sir H. Willock in 1837. **1898** M. A. VON ARNIM *Elizabeth & her German Garden* 17 The Persian Yellows look as though they intended to be big bushes. **1911** E. WILLMOTT *Genus Rosa* II. 271 It is easy to understand the popularity of the beautiful Persian Yellow Rose. **1971** 'L. BLACK' *Death has Green Fingers* iv. 37 Two other strains of roses were added to the family tree, one species called the Persian Yellow.

b. In names of colours associated with Persia or its products, e.g. *Persian blue, green, red.*

1869 *Bradshaw's Railway Manual* XXI. 460/2 (Advt.), Reds..Persian Red..Venetian Red. **1873** *Young Englishwoman* Aug. 390/1 Bright but delicate shades, such as sky blue, Persian green, and blush rose. **1886** H. C. STANDAGE *Artists' Man. Pigments* v. 51 Besides the Persian red obtained from the ochres, there is another which is a chromate of lead. **1903** M. L. SOLON *Hist. Old French Faïence* ix. 139 Some of the earliest pieces are painted upon Persian blue ground. **1934** H. HILER *Notes Technique Painting* ii. 116 *Persian green*, synonym for emerald green. **1951** R. MAYER *Artist's Handbk.* ii. 57 *Persian orange*, lake made of aniline colour on a barytes or blanc fixe base. Not permanent. **1963** tr. *Kornerup & Wanscher's Handbk. Colour* 177/1 *Persian blue*, the colour of Persian porcelain... Before about 1912, this name referred to the colour of certain Persian fabrics dyed with indigo blue. *Ibid. Persian orange*, this name probably corresponds to Persian yellow, a pigment derived from a compound of arsenic and sulphur.

B. *sb.* **4.** Insert 'usu.' before 'used' and add further examples.

1818 M. EDGEWORTH *Let.* 8 Sept. (1971) 85 Little Lady Louisa flying about with her green persian sash floating. **1853** MRS. GASKELL *Ruth* I. ii. 39 Miss Hilton! where have you put the blue Persian?

6. = *Persian cat* in sense A. 2 in Dict. and Suppl.

1871 *Graphic* 22 July 75/3 A Persian, direct from Persia,..'a very amiable beast'. **1879** M. E. BRADDON *Vixen* III. i. 52, I have a Persian who has been my attached companion for the last ten years. **1902** A. BENNETT *Anna of Five Towns* vii. 152 The Persian with one ear met them in the lobby, his tail flying. **1921** C. VAN VECHTEN *Tiger in House* i. 15 Jessie Pickens had a very remarkable brown tabby Persian. **1934** M. V. HUGHES *London Child of Seventies* x. 113 The parlour cats were Persians, sat on laps and best chairs. **1956** G. DURRELL *My Family* ix. 116 The consul was a great cat-lover, and he possessed three large and well-fed Persians to prove it. **1972** ING & POND *Champion Cats of World* II. 72 The fur texture also differed, that of the Angoras being soft, fine and silky, while the Persians were more woolly.

7. Other misc. ellipt. or substantival uses, esp. = *Persian carpet* in sense *A. 2.

1897 [see *FLORAL *sb.* 2]. **1903** W. D. ELLWANGER *Oriental Rug* (1904) ii. 15 The Persians came first, and perhaps in the following order of excellence: Kirman, Sehna, [etc.]. **1905** *Daily Chron.* 9 Sept. 3/2 'Persians' and other East Indian skins are stripped of their original tannage, and then finished as morocco. **1915** J. WEBSTER *Dear Enemy* 43 New rugs on the floor (my own prized Persians). **1957** M. MCCARTHY *Memories Catholic Girlhood* viii. 197 In the winter, she would have on her mink or her Persian or her squirrel or her broadtail. **1960** *News Chron.* 12 Sept. 6/4 Persians can be geometric or floral. **1964** *House & Garden* Dec. 42/3 The rugs are Persians and Kelims **1970** *Times* 12 May 11/8 The design of the print is a combination of paisley and persian.

Persianization (pə̄ːɹʃănəizēⁱ·ʃən). [f. PERSIAN *a.* + -IZATION.] The process of making Persian in appearance, structure, or other attributes.

1910 *Encycl. Brit.* XIII. 479/2 This extreme Persianization of Urdu was due rather to Hindu than to Persian influence. **1916** G. A. GRIERSON *Linguistic Survey India* IX. I. 45 This extreme Persianisation of Hindōstānī is not ..the work of conquerors ignorant of the tongue of the people. *Ibid.*, Like Urdū it [*sc.* Dakhinī] is written in the Persian character, but is much more free from Persianisation. **1924** P. BROWN *Indian Painting under Mughals* 18 The earlier Mughal emperors..introduced the art of miniature painting into Hindustan from Persia. Their action..represents..only one comparatively small item in a fairly wide movement. From the nature of this movement it may be termed the 'Persianization' of Northern India. **1937** *Scrutiny* V. 446 Mr. Chib..attributes the Persianization of Urdu and the Sanskritization of Hindi to communal jealousy. **1948** D. DIRINGER *Alphabet* II. vi. 362 *Hindi* is the modern development of Hindustani which is free from Persianization.

persicary. Delete *Obs.* and add later examples.

1938 M. HADFIELD *Everyman's Wild Flowers & Trees* 131 Spotted Persicary, *Polygonum Persicaria*... A branching annual up to 2 ft. high... Pale persicary..is a very similar plant. **1952** *Common Farm Weeds Illustr.* (Plant Protection Ltd.) I. 60 Willow-weed (*Polygonum persicaria*). Other names: Redshank, Persicary. **1972** R. ADAMS *Watership Down* xlv. 375 The weeds of harvest —knot-grass and pimpernel..heartsease and persicary.

persimmon. Add: **3.** (Further U.S. examples.) Phr. *to be a huckleberry to* (or *over*) *someone's persimmon*: see *HUCKLEBERRY 4.

1841 *Spirit of Times* 18 Dec. 499 They had not forgotten that the game little mare had put Sarah up to 7:45–7:40, in March last, and it seemed as if it was now their turn to 'shake down the persimmons'. **1844** in Sperber & Trittschuh *Amer. Pol. Terms* (1962) 313/2 David Tod should go there and repeat that original remark of his about the longest pole knocking down the persimmons. **1845** *Knickerbocker* XXV. 425 Wall now, that are's a jump above my tallest persimmons. **1857** *Call* (San Francisco) 3 Apr. 4/2 He will deal himself four aces and his opponent four queens, so that your honor will perceive he must 'rake the persimmons'. **1861** in W. H. Russell *My Diary North & South* (1863) II. iii. 62 Let both parties meet where there will be no interruption at the scalping business, and the longest pole will knock the persimmon. **1900** F. P. DUNNE *Mr. Dooley's Philos.* 68 'I'll jus' move me music back a mile,' he says, 'an' peg away, an' th' longest gun takes th' persimmons,' he says. **1946** *California Folklore Q.* July 240 That's the ripe persimmon. That is just right, or taken at the best moment.

3*. *U.S.* **a.** The colour of persimmon fruit, yellow to red-orange. **b.** The colour of persimmon wood, reddish brown. Also *attrib.* and *Comb.*

1928 S. V. BENÉT *John Brown's Body* 150 Grievin' yaller gals always does all right. Next time I'se gwine to git me a coal-black gal. I'se tired of persimmon-skins. **1975** *Vogue* Dec. 103 Persimmon lipstick. **1977** *Time* 27 June 50/1 The thickly painted figures with features eroded by light, the sharp eupeptic color—emerald, persimmon, rust, ultramarine. **1977** *New Yorker* 10 Oct. 132/2 They looked forward eagerly to sporting their persimmon outfit, say, in the first round of the club championship.

4. *persimmon-beer* (earlier and later examples), *-bush*.

1737 J. BRICKELL *Nat. Hist. N. Carolina* 38 The following are made in the Country, *viz.* Cyder, Persimon-Beer, made of the Fruit of that Tree, [etc.]. *a* **1941** P. B. BARRINGER *Natural Bent* (1949) xxvi. 189 In the early seventies alcohol was everywhere in the South, and cut glass decanters stood on every sideboard... Beer was just coming, unless we except 'persimmon beer' and 'locust beer' made on every plantation and in many village homes. **1950** *Publ. Amer. Dial. Soc.* XIV. 51 *Persimmon beer*, a beverage made from ripe persimmons. **1786** G. WASHINGTON *Diary* 8 Aug. (1925) III. 102 A parcel of small Persimon bushes. **1944** G. WILSON *Passing Institutions* 177 Many an upland field not good for cultivation formerly had its flock of sheep, browsing among the sassafras and persimmon bushes.

persistence. Add: **2. b.** *persistence of an impression* (also simply *persistence*): used chiefly with reference to vision (so *persistence of vision*). (Further examples.)

1902 *Encycl. Brit.* XXVII. 95/1 Cinematograph... This apparatus shows in rapid sequence a series of views representing closely successive phases of a moving object, and persistence of vision creates the illusion that the object is in motion. **1924** J. P. C. SOUTHALL tr. *H. von Helmholtz's Treat. Physiol. Optics* II. 228 The best way to realize this persistence of the impression is to turn the eye to a perfectly dark field after it has been gazing at bright objects. **1944** R. W. MONCRIEFF *Chem. Senses* iii. 56 Although it has not been measured the persistence of odour must be short like that of taste. **1952** PIRENNE & ABBOTT tr. *Piéron's Sensations* IV. iii. 283 It is generally stated that visual sensations have a persistence of a tenth of a second. **1966** C. W. WILMAN *Seeing & Perceiving* vi. 52 Persistence of vision is one reason..why a series of pictures presented at short intervals produces a satisfactory effect in the cinema.

c. (The duration of) the emission of light by a luminescent substance after the cause of the luminescence has ceased; *persistence characteristic* (see quot. 1950[1]).

1917 *Physical Rev.* IX. 297 It appears that the persistence of luminescence is due to the consistency of the substance and disappears as the fluidity increases. **1935** *Proc. IRE* XXIII. 1325 Slight changes in either the screen material or the method of manufacture may result in large changes..in the persistence with which the light continues to emanate from the excited portion of the screen after the electron beam has been removed. *Ibid.*, Screens which have a short persistence are desired for recording on moving film. *Ibid.* 1341 The persistence characteristic is taken by the use of some form of stroboscopic apparatus by means of which one is able to measure the relative brilliance of the screen at definite times after excitation. **1950** RIDER & USLAN *Encycl. Cathode-Ray Oscilloscopes* vii. 157/1 A plot of the brightness.. versus the decay time of the phosphorescence is termed the persistence characteristic of the screen. **1950** H. W. LEVERENZ *Introd. Luminescence of Solids* v. 150 For (conventional) luminescence emissions, all persistences longer than about 10^{-8} sec are called phosphorescence to indicate an abnormal delay. **1967** *Electronics* 6 Mar. 127/1 In the 710B, the top scope is coated with P7 phosphor for good persistence.

persister. Restrict *rare* to sense in Dict. and add: **b.** *Biol.* A bacterium which continues to live in the presence of enough antibiotic to kill almost all members of its species.

1944 J. W. BIGGER in *Lancet* 14 Oct. 498/1 These abnormal cocci have been termed 'persisters', to denote their power of surviving in the presence of sufficient penicillin to be lethal for the normal forms. **1949** E. CHAIN et al. in H. W. Florey et al. *Antibiotics* II. xxxv. 1143 The proportion of persisters in cultures of staphylococci is not constant, and the factors governing their numbers are not yet fully understood. **1970** *Jrnl. Med. Microbiol.* III. 669 Another type of persister is a cell in a non-replicating phase on which the antibiotic cannot act because of the absence of cell-wall synthesis. **1977** *Lancet* 15 Oct. 822/2 Electron microscopy was the only technique to demonstrate successfully the presence of small numbers of bacterial persisters in the vegetations of this treated case of streptococcal endocarditis.

persnickety (pəɹsni·kėti), *a.* (*adv.*) *U.S. colloq.* Also **persni·kity.** varr. PERNICKETY *a.* Hence **persni·cketiness.**

1905 *Dialect Notes* III. 63 *Persnickety*,..disagreeable, or snippy. 'They acted mighty *persnickety*.' **1915** *Ibid.* IV. 215 Fern is more persnikity about her clothes than either of the other girls. **1922** W. STEVENS *Let.* 5 May (1967) 227, I have no desire to be persnickety about the arrangement of the group. **1940** *Sat. Even. Post* 10 Feb. 25 Dad was too old to begin being what he called 'persnickety'. **1960** WENTWORTH & FLEXNER *Dict. Amer. Slang* 384/1 *Persnickety, pernickety* adj., fussy; fastidious; punctilious; snobbish. Since *c.* 1890. 'Pernickety' is now obs.; 'persnickety', once dial., is now colloq. **1967** R. STEIN *Great Cars* 222/1 That archetype of persnickety Yankee toolmakers. **1977** *Time* 17 Oct. 48/2 Billy compensates for his brother's sweet-eyed psalm-singing and persnicketiness.

person, *sb.* Add: **I. 1.** Also, *persons of the drama* [tr. DRAMATIS PERSONÆ]. *lit.* or *fig.*

1895 G. B. SHAW *Our Theatres in Nineties* (1932) I. 39 The persons of the drama belong rather to the world of imagination than of reality. **1948** M. SHARP *Flowering Thorn* II. iii. 72 Thus admitted, so to speak, among the persons of the drama, the young American rose to his feet.

II. 2. d. Also, of a woman.

1935 *Punch* 18 Dec. 678 This Pearl person has neglected to say whether [etc.]. **1939** *Punch* 23 Aug. 198/1 She was a sort of secretary person down at the works.

f. Used (*a*) as a substitute for MAN *sb.*[1] (esp. sense 4p: also for BOY *sb.*[1], etc.) as second element in numerous *Combs.* relating to offices which may be held by a member of either sex, as *chairperson, salesperson*; (*b*) with preceding defining word, as *marketing person*, and in other fanciful formations of this type, as *henchperson*.

In practice usually employed to avoid alleged sexual discrimination and widely regarded as having amusing connotations.

1971 *Sci. News* 11 Sept. 166 A group of women psychologists thanked the board for using the word 'chairperson' rather than 'chairman'. **1971** *Sci. Amer.* Dec. 37/1 (Advt.), If there is any doubt at the counter, let him show the salesperson this ad. **1972** *Listener* 24 Aug. 232/1 Two young black women will almost certainly join Representative Shirley Chisholm in Congress..putting up the number of black 'Congresspersons' to at least 14. *Ibid.*, Yvonne Brathwaite Burke..the stunning and extremely saucy 'Vice-Chairperson'. **1973** *Ibid.* 1 Mar. 286/3 Chairperson Mitchell and her henchpersons looked at the way education brainwashes girls. **1974** *Black Panther* 23 Feb. 9/2 Brother Malcolm Kelley, chairperson for the Committee for Justice for Tyrone Guyton. **1976** 'L. BLACK' *Healthy Way to Die* ii. 19 You're a newspaperwoman—or, as we have to say in these days of female emancipation, a newspaper person. **1976** *Publishers Weekly* 16 Feb. 81/1 The author [*sc.* Jeanne Wilson] is a solid craftsperson who tells her old-fashioned story in a winning manner. **1976** *Oxford Times* 23 July 32 (Advt.), Builders' merchants require yardperson. **1976** *Jrnl. R. Soc. Arts* CXXIV. 510/1 The exercise known amongst marketing men, or should I say marketing persons, as market segmentation. **1977** *Times Lit. Suppl.* 29 Apr. 506/5 A pair of homosexual network anchorpersons. **1977** C. SAGAN *Dragons of Eden* ii. 41 A group of literary Englishpersons, immobilized in the Alps by inclement weather. **1978** *Amat. Photographer* 29 Nov. 119/3 We saw nothing in cine to rival the spectacular application of high-technology design to still cameras for everyman (sorry, everyperson).

IV. 6. b. Euphemistically, the genitals.

1824 *Act 5 Geo. IV* c. 83 §4 Every Person wilfully, openly, lewdly and obscenely exposing his Person in any Street, Road or public Highway, or in View thereof, or in any place of public Resort, with intent to insult any Female.., shall be deemed a Rogue and Vagabond within the true Intent and Meaning of this Act. **1853** MR. JUSTICE MAULE in *Law Jrnl. Rep.* XXXI. III. 123/1 What do you mean in law by exposing his *person*? The indictment should have been for exposing his *private parts*. **1911** *Straits Times* (Singapore) 13 June 7/3 He let go my arms, held me round the waist with his right arm and used his left hand. He stooped to do it. He put his hand on my person. **1973** R. E. MEGARRY *Second Miscellany-at-Law* ii. 165 Few readers of the newspapers can be unaware of the curious convention whereby for many years past the word 'person' was used anatomically in prosecutions for indecency.

8. (Later examples.)

c **1850** [see APOCOPATE *ppl. a.*]. **1905** [see THOU *pers. pron.* 2 b]. **1951** V. NABOKOV *Speak, Memory* i. 17 In addressing me, a small boy, he used the plural of the second person. **1962** J. G. BENNETT *Witness* xxv. 333 She never said 'I', but always referred to herself in the third person as 'Madame' or even 'she'. **1966** J. DERRICK *Teaching Eng. to Immigrants* ii. 89 The teacher must proceed slowly and patiently, and again has good reason for confining questions to 1st and 2nd person forms only at first.

VIII. 14. *Comb.* **person-object** (*a*) *Gram.*, a personal object of a verb; (*b*) in psychoanalytic theory, the choice of a person as the object of one's libidinal energy; also *attrib.*; **person-oriented** *a.*, of that in which interest or concern is centred on the person as contrasted with (by implication) a theory or thing; **person-perception,** perception which leads to or constitutes awareness and understanding of another person or persons.

1928 H. POUTSMA *Gram. Late Mod. Eng.* (ed. 2) I. I. iii. 176 It will, therefore, often be useful to distinguish person-objects and thing-objects. Even when both objects, considered apart from the context, are the names of things, one of them more or less distinctly suggests, through its connexions, thoughts of personal qualities. **1949** M. MEAD *Male & Female* vii. 154 The distinction between mother's body and the own body..in person-object terms, is an important one. **1954** *Essays in Crit.* IV. 316 The pre-Hellenic nature cults are accused..of failing to own that the person-to-person drive must push on past the person-object situation to find a response which plays back. **1964** E. BECKER in I. L. Horowitz *New Sociol.* 123 The schizophrenic is..someone who has been accustomed to relating to symbol-objects rather than to person-objects. **1972** *Encycl. Psychol.* II. 336/1 An object of experience, especially a 'person-object'. **1967** M. L. KING JR. in *Freedomways* VII. 114 We must rapidly begin the shift from a 'thing-oriented' society to a 'person-oriented' society. **1972** *Jrnl. Social Psychol.* LXXXVI. 135 The concept of dependency has been used..to describe person-oriented behavior. **1973** J. LYONS *Experience* IV. viii. 241 Its major practitioners [*sc.* of encountering], who are likely to be ex-theologians, teachers, counselors, actors..—whatever field can furnish perceptive, person-oriented leaders—rather than formally trained psychotherapists. **1958** TAGIURI & PETRULLO (*title*) Person perception and interpersonal behaviour. *Ibid.* p. x, We propose using the term *person perception* whenever the perceiver regards the object as having the potential of representation and intentionality. **1964** M. ARGYLE *Psychol. & Social Probl.* iii. 36 Person perception has been made the object of considerable research. **1972** *Jrnl. Social Psychol.* LXXXVI. 23 Accurate person perception is repeatedly identified as an essential component of effectiveness in the research literature concerned with interpersonal functioning.

b. With a period of time, as *person-day, -month*, units equivalent to one day, month, of one person's work or life. Cf. *MAN *sb.*[1] 20 b.

1970 *Sci. Amer.* Feb. 91 In that year people in California spent some 235 million person-days in specified outdoor recreational activities, primarily swimming, picnicking, fishing and boating. **1975** *Nature* 30 Oct. 733/2 Under an agreement signed recently in Stockholm, scientists and experts from the two countries will exchange visits of 10 person-months a year.

persona. Add: **1. persona grata** (examples). Also **persona non grata** (pl. **personæ non gratæ**), an unacceptable or unwelcome person.

1882 *Standard* 20 Dec. 5 At a supper of criminals in full work in their profession he might be welcomed as a *persona grata*. **1884** E. W. HAMILTON *Diary* 2 Sept. (1972) II. 679 Malet did well at Versailles and is a *persona grata* to Bismarck, who was intimate with Malet's mother. **1904** CONRAD *Nostromo* I. vi. 86 See that, Mr. Gould? *Persona non grata*. That's the reason our government is never properly informed. **1928** 'BRENT OF BIN BIN' *Up Country* iv. 52 He was admirably suited to his calling at that time, and his education and personality made him *persona grata* to all his superiors, from the Surveyor-General downwards. **1928** D. L. SAYERS *Lord Peter views Body* vi. 151 Oh, I'll keep out of it... I shan't be exactly persona grata, don't you know. **1935** H. EDIB *Clown & his Daughter* xlii. 238 The fact that he is his father's son makes him *persona grata* in the Sultan's eyes. **1958** *Oxford Mail* 15 Feb. 1/2 The BMC management should have known that the introduction of two or three people who are persona non grata with the other 350 men in the shop would create difficulty. **1964** M. GOWING *Britain & Atomic Energy, 1939–1945* v. 172 He made it clear that Mr Akers was *persona non grata* to the Americans on account of his industrial connections with I.C.I. **1965** C. D. EBY *Siege of Alcázar* (1966) i. 30 At such times Army officers were *personae non gratae*. **1968** *Listener* 7 Nov. 603/3 Gandhi was..always *persona grata* with the high-ups. **1972** *Daily Tel.* 2 June 3/3 Your recent book has.. caused a lot of annoyance here, and you would not be *persona grata* at Eton on the Fourth of June. **1973** *Times* 15 Feb. 7/8 In view of Pakistan's 'violation', the spokesman added, the Iraq Government had decided to retaliate by declaring the Pakistan Ambassador and a Second Secretary as *personae non gratae* and warning them against returning to Iraq. **1974** *Times* 23 Jan. 15/1 Moscow intercepts a Peking-bound Chinese diplomat.. claims he is carrying espionage material, and declares him persona non grata. **1976** A. GREY *Bulgarian Exclusive* xvi. 109 With half a dozen telephone calls..you will be *persona non grata*..throughout Eastern Europe.

3. *persona designata* [Law L.], a specified person; one who is individually denominated, as opp. one who is included in a legal category or class consisting of several persons.

1875 *Law Rep. Chancery Appeal Cases* X. 359 The legatees in this case, although described as a class, are in fact *personæ designatæ* as much as if they were mentioned by name. **1876** H. S. THEOBALD *Conc. Treat. Construction of Wills* xiii. 114 My nephew Joseph is clearly *persona designata*, and the question then is whom did the testator mean to point out? **1955** *Times* 4 May 4/3 It was against him as the person designated to carry out certain functions prescribed by Act of Parliament of laying before each House of Parliament a draft scheme, and that was done as a *persona designata*. **1973** *Deb. Senate Canada* 19 June 4889/1 There have been examples of an appeal court challenging the actions of an appellate court judge when he was acting *persona designata*.

4. Pl. **personæ, personas. a.** A character deliberately assumed by an author in his writing; also *transf.*

1909 E. POUND (*title*) Personae. **1958** *Times Lit. Suppl.* 20 June 345/1 To this extent, Lewis Eliot is, as it were, a convenient and comfortable persona for his author. **1962** W. NOWOTTNY *Lang. Poets Use* ii. 42 So far as a particular kind of *persona* is necessary to the poem, the poet's diction must create it. **1963** AUDEN *Dyer's Hand* 401 The more closely his [*sc.* Byron's] poetic *persona* comes to resemble the epistolary *persona* of his letters to his male friends..the more authentic his poetry seems. **1976** *Gramophone* Dec. 965/3 George Logan and Patric Fyffe in the *personae* of Dr Evadne Hinge and Dame Hilda Bracket are on EMI One-Up OU2125 (7/76).

b. In Jungian psychology, the set of attitudes adopted by an individual to fit himself for the social role which he sees as his; the personality an individual presents to the world; also *loosely*. Opp. *ANIMA.

1917 C. E. LONG tr. *Jung's Coll. Papers Analytical Psychol.* (ed. 2) xv. 466 The persona is always identical with a *typical* attitude, in which *one* psychological function dominates, *e.g.* feeling, or thought, or intuition. **1923** [see *ANIMA]. **1931** H. G. WELLS *Work, Wealth & Happiness of Mankind* (1932) viii. 298 A man's guiding and satisfying idea of himself is what Jung calls his '*persona*'. *Ibid.* xii. 617 There was nothing in their personas to prevent it. **1935** *Trans. Philol. Soc.* 66 We are born individuals. But to satisfy our needs we have to become social persons, and every social person is a bundle of rôles or *personæ*. **1936** 'M. INNES' *Death at President's Lodging* iii. 51 In the Dean's *persona* the episcopal idea had of late been rapidly developing. **1940** H. G. WELLS *Babes in Darkling Wood* IV. ii. 333 Some austerer element in his make-up was putting his *persona* on trial. **1966** COX & ROLFE tr. *Herzog's Psyche & Death* xv. 193 The dreamer has to answer for himself in his own right—he cannot claim the protection of the persona of his office. **1972** *Observer* 30 Jan. 9/6 He can be a pompous, contentious man, yet his private persona sometimes contrasts sharply with his more abrasive public image... He has also kept his dignity, consistently refusing to exploit or trivialise his public persona in the lucrative entertainment field.

personal, *a.* (*sb.*) Add: **1. a.** Also, *personal friend, hygiene.*

1782 LD. AUCKLAND *Let.* 22 Aug. (1861) I. 29 Lord North, too, could on *very easy* terms answer for thirty or forty, quite as personal friends and followers. *a* **1794** GIBBON *Mem.* (1796) I. 71 Mr. Allamand, Minister at Bex, was my personal friend. **1853** C. BRONTË *Villette* I. xv. 304 Had that audience numbered as many personal friends and acquaintance for me, as for him, I know not how it might have been. **1915** T. F. A. SMITH *Soul of Germany* 54 Opponents are often personal friends, but that makes no difference. **1938** AUDEN & ISHERWOOD *On Frontier* I. i. 24 The Valerian School..will educate your dear little kiddies in Patriotism and Personal Hygiene. **1970** *Guardian* 17 Aug. 7/5 Much propaganda about 'personal hygiene' is on the wrong track... Why the obsession with stopping *fresh* perspiration? **1979** D. ATTENBOROUGH *Life on Earth* xi. 248 The sloth..pays such little attention to its personal hygiene that green algae grow on its coarse hair.

c. Designating an official or employee attached to one's person in a subordinate capacity, as *personal assistant, maid,* etc.

1928 *Radio Times* 2 Nov. 301/3 My personal maid.. [was] sent to service at 11 years. **1941** in G. Howell *In Vogue* (1975) 162 A personal maid..is absent, on munitions. **1956** *Times* 21 Jan. 7/5 An adequate type of skilled secretarial assistant could be ensured by certain responsible bodies..holding examinations for executive secretaries/personal assistants (as opposed to company secretaries). **1958** P. SCOTT *Mark of Warrior* I. 21 'These chaps are your personal servants,' the receiving officer explained. **1964** M. LASKI in S. Nowell-Smith *Edwardian Eng.* iv. 144 Personal servants at least must wait up until their masters and mistresses chose to go to bed. **1972** T. P. MCMAHON *Issue of Bishop's Blood* iv. 44 Frank Velandi..three arrests for assault... Said at one time to be Streppelli's personal bodyguard. **1977** A. SCHOLEFIELD *Venom* v. 198 M. Michel Blanchet, the hotel millionaire wanted a personal maid for his new wife. **1978** W. GARNER *Möbius Trip* i. 21 Hand over the mouthpiece she called 'Prime Minister's personal assistant'.

4. e. Of newspaper advertisements: small, on private matters (see also quot. 1902); esp. in *personal column.*

1888 W. WHITMAN *Daybks. & Notebks.* (1978) II. 448 Letter from J. G. Bennett, N.Y. Herald, ask'g me to write for 'Personal' col Herald. **1902** *Encycl. Brit.* XXXI. 173/2 'Personal journalism', *i.e.*, paragraphs about the private life or personal appearance of individuals..of note or notoriety in society or public affairs, has become far more marked. **1936** *Discovery* Dec. 386/1 The 18th century 'personal' advertisement, dealing with such wants as wives, lost umbrellas, or menservants 'of black complexion and sound principles'. **1948** *Chicago Daily News* 30 Aug. 19/3 German newspapers have 'personal' columns filled with advertisements for mates. **1966** *Listener* 6 Jan. 14/2 Most of its members were gathered by putting an advertisement in the personal column of a daily newspaper. **1978** J. WAINWRIGHT *Ripple of Murders* 11 A small ad. in the Personal Column ..will read 'J.D. Message received'.

f. Of a letter or other communication: intended for the attention of a particular recipient.

1934 G. B. SHAW *Too True to be Good* II. 50 Is this a personal letter to be sent on to him, or is it a dispatch? **1940** R. S. LAMBERT *Ariel & all his Quality* ix. 244 A letter was delivered..addressed 'H. Brown, Esq., Broadcasting House'. It was not marked 'Personal' or 'Private'. **1973** 'D. JORDAN' *Nile Green* i. 9 A stack of letters was open on my desk including..two which must have been marked 'Personal' on the envelope. **1978** J. SYMONS *Blackheath Poisonings* v. 241 The rectangular package was addressed..to Mr George Collard, and marked *Personal*.

g. Of a (transistor) radio or television: small (see quot. 1962).

1962 *Which?* Feb. 36/1 The two main categories are: personal radios, which will slip into a pocket—or are just too large to do so—and portable radios, which have to be carried. **1973** *Philadelphia Inquirer* 7 Oct. 16 (Advt.), Personal size 16″ diagonal screen.

6. c. *personal representative* (earlier and later examples).

1796 A. ANSTRUTHER *Reports* I. 131 The personal representative is *in general* considered as trustee of the property devised from the testator, undisposed of, *as belonging to him*. **1832** RUSSELL & MYLNE *Rep. Cases Chancery* 1829–30 I. 589 The ordinary sense of the words 'personal representatives' is, executors and administrators. **1967** E. RUDINGER *Wills & Probate* 40 The people who deal with what you own when you die are called your personal representatives.

10. Special collocations, as *personal appearance*, (*a*) the appearance or presence of an individual (esp. a celebrity) in person; (*b*) the visual aspect or looks of a person, considered in terms of dress, grooming, and expression; *personal bill*, a private bill (BILL *sb.*[3] 3) usu. introduced in the House of Lords, relating to the estate, status, or other personal concern of an individual (see also quot. 1844); *personal call*, a telephone call in which the caller specifies to the operator the person to whom he wishes to speak, and only the time so spent is charged for (in addition to a fixed service charge); *personal caller*, a prospective client who establishes personal contact with a business; *personal explanation*, a statement made by a Member of the House of Commons in explanation or mitigation of recent conduct; *personal god*, a god possessing personal attributes; *personal government*, autocratic rule in which effective power is vested in the person of a monarch (commonly associated with the reign of George III); *personal idealism*, philosophical idealism which emphasizes the essential role of the conscious person in relation to perception of external reality and, usu., also in relation to God as supreme Person; akin to *PERSONALISM b; hence *personal idealist*; *personal loan*, a loan made to an individual for his private requirements by a finance company or bank; *personal name*, the name by which an individual (occas. a thing) is distinguished or identified; *personal shopper*, one who shops in person, as opposed to by mail-order; *personal touch*, a personal element introduced into something otherwise institutional or impersonal.

1610 S. RID *Martin Mark-all* sig. A 3, They presently send to the Beadle of the Hall to make his personal appearance at the Swan with five necks in Kings Streete. **1736** M. W. MONTAGU *Let.* Dec. (1966) II. 111 Halfe those aspirations to the B.V. would deserve her personal appearance to encourrage so sincere a Votary. **1842** DICKENS *Amer. Notes* I. viii. 277 Comparing notes on my personal appearance with as much indifference as if I were a stuffed figure. **1883** [see APPEARANCE 2]. **1914** G. B. SHAW *Fanny's First Play* 152 Mr Trotter.. assisted the make-up by which Mr Claude King so successfully simulated his personal appearance. **1951** S. J. PERELMAN in *New Yorker* 2 June 26/3, I caught your personal appearance at the Mastbaum in Philly. **1962** L. Deighton *Ipcress File* xvi. 92 A cinema where a nineteen-year-old rock-an'-roll singer was making a personal appearance for £600. **1972** *N.Y. Law Jrnl.* 22 Aug. 8/1 *Personal Appearances*..Ping Keun Chu v. Jade Fountain of Paramus, Inc. [etc.]. **1976** T. Heald *Let Sleeping Dogs Die* i. 7 She had little time for clothes and cared nothing for her personal appearance. [**1683** Personal bill: see Personal *a.* 1 a.] **1844** T. E. May *Treat. Parliament* xxviii. 457 All private bills, during their progress in the commons, are known by the general denomination of private bills; but in the lords the term 'private' is applied *technically* to estate bills only, all other bills being distinguished as 'local' or 'personal', although in the standing orders no such distinction is expressed. **1929** G. F. M. Campion *Introd. Proc. House of Commons* ix. 274 Personal Bills, *i.e.* Estate, Divorce, Naturalisation, Restitution and Name Bills..always originate in the Lords. **1973** *Jrnl. House of Lords* (1974) 14 Nov. CCVI. 29/2 Personal Bills: Select Comee appointed. **1930** *Telegr. & Telephone Jrnl.* XVI. 70/2 Another important event of the past year was the introduction of the 'personal' call system in the Inland and Anglo-Continental trunk services. **1947** Auden *Age of Anxiety* (1948) ii. 43 To be held waiting in A packed lounge for a Personal Call From Long Distance. **1960** [see *person-to-person *adj.* (and *adv.*) *phr.* a]. **1967** E. Lemarchand *Death of Old Girl* ii. 21 There's a phone call for you... A personal call from London. **1978** F. Durbridge *Tim Frazer gets Message* iv. 61 Can Miss Thackery take a personal call? **1966** *Listener* 25 Aug. 291 (Advt.), Send now for a free copy... For personal callers—235 Grand Buildings, Trafalgar Sq., W.C.2. Tel.: WHItehall 8377. **1976** *Norwich Mercury* 19 Nov. 12/5 (Advt.), Personal callers will be welcomed by a receptionist at Prospect House. **1844** T. E. May *Treat. Parliament* xi. 195 (*heading*) Personal explanation. **1857** *Sat. Rev.* 14 Feb. 152/2 That green oasis in the desert of legislation—that dainty morsel in the sessional banquet—a personal explanation, which, in Mr. Disraeli's hands, was pretty sure to include also a personal attack. **1886** J. Bailey *Let.* 11 Apr. (1935) 24, I might say a good deal on this subject but as the House of Commons has lately made personal explanations vulgar, I don't think I will. **1974** *House of Commons Man. Procedure Publ. Business* (ed. 11) viii. 116 By the indulgence of the House, a Member may make a personal explanation, although there is no question before the House, but in this case no debatable matter may be brought forward, and no debate can arise. **1860** Personal God [in Dict., sense 5 b]. *a* **1902** S. Butler *Way of All Flesh* (1903) xlix. 225 There is not one of you here who doubts the existence of a Personal God. **1921** G. B. Shaw *Back to Methuselah* p. xlii, We had been so oppressed by the notion that everything that happened in the world was the arbitrary personal act of an arbitrary personal god of dangerously jealous and cruel personal character, so that even the relief of the pains of childbed and the operating table by chloroform was objected to as interference with his arrangements which he would probably resent, that we just jumped at Darwin. **1963** J. A. T. Robinson *Honest to God* iii. 48 The difference..can perhaps best be expressed by asking what is meant by speaking of a *personal* God. Theism..understands by this a supreme Person, a self-existent subject.., who enters into a relationship with us comparable with that of one human personality with another. **1976** P. Hill *Hunters* vi. 73 An allegedly all-powerful and personal God. **1909** W. Toynbee *Glimpses of Twenties* i. 1 George the Third..ascended the throne with a fixed determination to re-establish 'personal government', which quickly aroused the misgivings of even his best-affected subjects. **1954** *Proc. Brit. Acad.* XXXVIII. 225 We no longer believe that George III's system of personal government came to an end in 1784, and that power was then transferred from the King to the Prime Minister. **1901** G. H. Howison (*title*) The limits of evolution, and other essays illustrating the metaphysical theory of personal idealism. **1921** *Encycl. Relig. & Ethics* XII. 229/2 Where personal idealism means spiritual pluralism of a theistic type, the concept of purpose applied to the interpretation of the universe yields a conclusion that satisfies. **1966** F. Copleston *Hist. Philos.* VIII. iii. xiii. 296 It is so often religiously minded people who are attracted in the first instance to personal idealism. **1902** H. Sturt *Personal Idealism* p. vi, Naturalism and Absolutism, then, are the adversaries against whom the personal idealist has to strive. **1966** F. Copleston *Hist. Philos.* VIII. iii. xiii. 296 Unless the personal idealist equates ultimate reality with the system of finite selves, as McTaggart did, he must be a theist. **1914** *Laws State of N.Y.* II. 1435 When authorized by the superintendent of banks..three or more persons.. may form a corporation to be known as a personal loan company. **1957** D. Karp *Leave me Alone* v. 80 Individual enterprisers offered..dry cleaning, baked goods..personal loans. **1958** *Times* 29 Aug. 8/7 Barclays are after all to be the first of the banks to bring a personal loans scheme into operation. **1961** *Which?* May 103/1 The banks have started 'Personal Loan' schemes, whereby you can borrow money from a bank without providing security. **1979** *Guardian* 5 Feb. 15/4 Basically the clearing banks offer three kinds of packages: overdraft facilities; loan accounts, and personal loans. **1748** B. Martin *Institutions of Lang.* 27 Of nouns or names there are three sorts, common, proper or personal, and relative... Proper or personal names are such as denote the individuals of each species; as Cæsar,..London, Paris, &c. **1871** E. B. Tylor *Primitive Culture* I. viii. 276 Up from this savage level the same childlike habit of giving personal names to lifeless objects may be traced, as we read of Thor's hammer, Miölnir. **1911** J. G. Frazer *Golden Bough: Taboo* (ed. 3) vi. 318 (*heading*) Personal names tabooed. **1925** O. Jespersen *Mankind, Nation & Individual* ix. 172 The Araukans carefully conceal their personal-name from strangers. **1950** *Funk's Stand. Dict. Folklore* II. 782/2 It is believed that if one is sick one's name is possibly not agreeing with one, hence the name is 'washed off', and a new personal name given. **1972** *Harrods Christmas Catal.* 58/1 *Fresh pâté de foie gras*... For personal shoppers only. **1976** *Field* 18 Nov. 1023/2 (Advt.), Send SAE for descriptive leaflet of our full range including a How-to-find-us map for personal shoppers. **1887** S. A. Barnett *Let.* 12 Oct. in H. Barnett *Canon Barnett* (1918) II. xxxiii. 63 We talked of how workmen could be made at home in Toynbee. I am sure that attractions won't bring them, but only the personal touch. **1936** A. Christie *ABC Murders* i. 11, I had various affairs to see to in England that I felt could only be successful if a personal touch was introduced. **1967** A. Hunter *Gently Continental* vi. 75 We try to make people feel they belong here. The personal touch, you know. **1976** 'O. Jacks' *Assassination Day* iii. 48 Butcher hadn't overplayed his hand. He'd been crafty, relying on the personal touch.

B. *sb.* **2. c.** For def. read: An item in a newspaper about a person or group of persons; a classified advertisement addressed to an individual person. orig. *U.S.*

1861 in A. Sterling *Belle of Fifties* (1904) 238, I inclose you a 'personal' from Brother Clement, published in yesterday's *Enquirer.* **1873** F. Hudson *Journalism in U.S.* 472 Take the 'personals' of the *Herald* any day, and they will set one to thinking. **1875** J. G. Holland *Sevenoaks* viii. 103 Returning..to look over the papers, his eye was attracted, among the 'personals', to an item [etc.]. **1888** [in Dict.]. **1901** *Daily Colonist* (Victoria, B.C.) 16 Oct. 7/1 (*heading*) Personals. **1913** *Collier's* 1 Feb. 17/3 He inserts a 'personal' in a New York newspaper under her initials. **1968** L. Durrell *Tunc* iii. 166 He had invented what he called the mnemon which he insisted was a literary form... *Times* Personals of a slightly surrealist tinge. **1977** R. E. Harrington *Quintain* viii. 76 The classified section was his favorite part of the paper. He enjoyed reading the disguised, plaintive little cries for help in the Personals.

5. A personal friend. *colloq.*

1961 *Listener* 21 Dec. 814/3 Reynard La Spoon, the choreographer—he's a close personal, ent he, Jule?

6. *Basketball.* A foul involving bodily contact with an opponent.

1961 in Webster. **1969** *Eugene* (Oregon) *Register-Guard* 3 Dec. 1D/3 Love played only the first eight or nine minutes of the first half before collecting his third personal. **1974** *State* (Columbia, S. Carolina) 3 Mar. 2-D/1 He fouled out in the game's final minute after playing almost 13 minutes with four personals.

personalia (pɜ̄rsənēɪ·liă), *sb. pl.* [ad. L. *personālia*, neut. pl. of *personālis* personal.] Personal matters; personal allusions; personal mementoes.

1903 'Sigma' (*title*) Personalia: political, social, and various. **1909** H. G. Wells *Tono-Bungay* iii. ii. 314 My aunt received these personalia cheerfully. **1920** *Glasgow Herald* 27 Mar. 8 His speech on Wednesday contained some quite superfluous personalia. **1928** J. Bailey *Let.* 26 Oct. (1935) 292 The best letters of you, as of other masters of the art epistolary, are the ones full of personalia—*from you to me, etc.* **1969** *Daily Tel.* 25 Oct. 8/1 On the theme of Ruskin and Venice this exhibition includes watercolours and drawings by him, various editions of his works and personalia. **1974** M. Z. Lewin *Enemies Within* xxxi. 140 That lovely desk, which I would have filled to the brim with personalia. **1974** *Nature* 3 May 6/1 With pieces of original equipment..and personalia including Marconi's swordstick.

personalism. Add: **b.** A philosophical view, usually theistic and positing God as supreme Person, that reality has meaning only through the conscious minds of persons; a view of social organization that places primary emphasis on the person and his involvement in it rather than on the material means necessary for achieving such organization.

1908 B. P. Bowne (*title*) Personalism. *Ibid.* iii. 111 We have now to consider the phenomenality of the physical world. This is the next step in the establishment of personalism. **1917** *Encycl. Relig. & Ethics* IX. 771/2 Aristotle laid the foundation for personalism by affirming self-consciousness as the highest being. **1938** tr. *Mounier's Personalist Manifesto* i. 1 Personalism is for us at present a sort of general pass-word. We are using it as an inclusive term for various doctrines that in our present historical situation can be made to agree upon the elementary physical and metaphysical conditions of a new civilization. **1947** *Partisan Rev.* XIV. 396 Berdyaev developed into one of the outstanding religious writers of our time, preaching a synthesis of socialism, personalism, and corporate Christianity. **1957** M. P. Fogarty *Christian Democracy* iii. 29 Personalism, as distinct from individualism, is held by Christian Democrats to imply a certain 'solidarist' conception of the individual's responsibility to and for the society around him. **1959** *Pacific Affairs* XXXII. 77 Since 1956 the Ngo brothers and officials high and low in the government have referred to Personalism (and humanism) as the philosophical basis of the national revolution. **1966** F. Copleston *Hist. Philos.* VIII. iii. xiii. 296 The basic tenet of personalism has been stated as the principle that reality has no meaning except in relation to persons; that the real is only in, of or for persons. **1971** A. R. Caponigri *Hist. Western Philos.* V. vi. v. 349 He [*sc.* the person] finds the plenitude of his self-affirmation and of the affirmation of his vertical relation to God in the recognition of, and cooperation with, other persons. This has been called the social dimension of Stefanini's personalism.

c. Allegiance to a person, esp. a political leader, rather than to a party or ideology.

1937 *Times* 4 Sept. 11/6 Personalism is a characteristic of Argentine politics. A party is the personal following of a man. **1964** M. C. Needler *Polit. Syst. Lat. Amer.* xxi. 518 Personalism stands in inverse relation to permanence of party organization, the extreme case of personalism being found in the party organized solely to support the candidacy of one individual. **1970** N. A. Victoria in I. L. Horowitz *Masses in Lat. Amer.* xv. 557 One of the conditions which may favor the emergence of such leadership is an element of 'personalism', or the extraordinary extension of the personal and emotional sphere. **1976** *Encounter* June 79 General Franco instinctively sensed something of the communal dangers inherent in Spanish personalism ('individualism' is the conventional term, but it fails to convey the whole meaning).

‖ **personalismo** (pĕrsonalizmo). [Sp. and Pg.] = *personalism c.

1962 G. Blanksten in M. A. Kaplan *Revolution in World Politics* iii. v. 120 *Personalismo* may be regarded as the custom of following or opposing a political leader on the basis of his personality rather than on ideological grounds. **1964** L. B. Lott in M. C. Needler *Polit. Syst. Lat. Amer.* xii. 244 A strong tendency on their [*sc.* the people's] part to associate themselves with powerful personalities rather than with programs and issues. This tendency we may label *personalismo.* **1969** *Language* XLV. 464 Joshua Fishman's comparison of those two categories in terms of cross-cultural indices reveals a most interesting association between linguistically heterogeneous polities and 'personalismo' or 'charisma' in follower–leader relationships. **1969** J. Mander *Static Society* i. 66 Mexico has cast off the incubus of *personalismo.*

personalist. Add: **b.** Further examples, esp. with reference to *personalism b and c. Also *attrib.*

1917 *Encycl. Relig. & Ethics* IX. 771/2 In this sense Eucken, Howison, Bergson, James.., and others of the modern school may be called personalists. **1937** *Times* 4 Sept. 11/6 The Radicals who remained faithful to the 'Chief' were known as Personalist or Irigoyenist Radicals. **1938** tr. *Mounier's Personalist Manifesto* i. 1 We shall apply the term *personalist* to any doctrine or any civilization that affirms the primacy of the human person over material necessities and over the whole complex of implements man needs for the development of his person. **1938** G. Reavey tr. *Berdyaev's Solitude & Society* 33 Personalist philosophy, as I understand it, has nothing in common with the subjectivist, individualist, empirical or nominalist currents of to-day. **1962** S. E. Finer *Man on Horseback* ix. 131 Paraguay..the parties—Colorados and Azules—are personalist cliques. **1970** B. Brewster tr. *Althusser & Balibar's Reading Capital* (1975) ii. viii. 172 This is a stumbling-block for all the interpretations of Marxism as a 'philosophy of labour', whether ethical, personalist or existentialist. **1970** D. Goldrich et al. in I. L. Horowitz *Masses in Lat. Amer.* v. 190 APRA..the personalist party of former dictator General Odría. **1976** H. A. Williams *Tensions* vi. 99 Personalist pastors, perhaps more than public campaigners, sometimes try (unsuccessfully) to impose a totalitarian tyranny upon scholars and thinkers.

Hence **personali·stic** *a.*, of or pertaining to a person considered as different and separate from other people, esp. of the psychological study of the individual in relation to his personal experience (see quots.). Also occas. **personali·stics** *sb. pl.* (treated as *sing.*).

1929 H. Klüver in G. Murphy *Hist. Introd. Mod. Psychol.* xxv. 424 But returning..to personalistic theory, some further implications of the 'psychophysical neutrality' of 'person' should be considered. **1936** *Mind* XLV. 247 The 'personalistic' Psychologists go so far as to insist on the uniqueness of every combination of dispositions. **1938** H. D. Spoerl tr. *Stern's Gen. Psychol. from Personalistic Standpoint* p. vii, In spite of this basic concern with the whole fabric of psychological specialties, our book will maintain a thoroughly distinctive and novel point of view... This is the *personalistic* point of view, which here finds its first occasion to demonstrate its fitness to formulate and interpret a particular empirical science. *Ibid.* xxvii. 494 The author..points to this personalistic basis of transfer without knowing anything about personalistics. **1939** *Brit. Jrnl. Psychol.* XXIX. 411 Stephenson.. proposed to substitute a modified system of his own, which, he maintains, should lead to 'an entirely new branch of psychometry, for which the term Personalistics may be coined'. *Ibid.* XXX. 65 The roots of 'personalistics' clearly go back to the classical researches embodied in the *Differentielle Psychologie.* **1956** *Jrnl. Theol. Stud.* VII. 165 He [*sc.* Luther] maintains a thoroughly personalistic idea of grace, which is received by faith alone. **1969** C. Davidson in Cockburn & Blackburn *Student Power* 359 The hippy movement has served to make many of our people withdraw into a personalistic, passive cult of consumption.

personality. Add: **2. a.** (Further *fig.* examples.) Also in phr. *to have personality*, to have qualities or traits of character to an unusual or noteworthy degree.

1902 W. D. Howells *Lit. & Life* 249 How many houses now have character—personality? **1934** C. Fox in *Proc. 1st Internat. Congr. Prehist. & Protohist. Sci.* 27 Position, outline, and structure..; the climate resulting from position, and the soil derived from structure, determine the vegetable life which she nourishes and the animal life which she harbours. The whole represents Man's environment, and Britain's 'Personality'. **1940** R. S. Lambert *Ariel & all his Quality* iv. 116 To attract a solid core of permanent readers to any literary paper presupposes that that paper shall have a 'personality' to distinguish it from others of its kind. *a* **1960** E. M. Forster *Maurice* (1971) xxxiv. 155 So he was in a way, but evidently he had personality. **1973** *Times* 31 Jan. (Mediterranean Suppl.) p. i/3 The Mediterranean islands could easily lose their personality in a short time.

c. *Psychol.* and *Sociol.* The unique combination of psychophysical qualities or traits, inherent and acquired, that make up each person as observable in his reactions to the environment or to the social group; also, psychological study concerned with such aspects of the person, and with the similarities and differences that exist between persons.

1879 H. Maudsley *Path. of Mind* (ed. 3) i. 12 It is this physiological unity of organic functions, which is something deeper than consciousness and constitutes our fundamental personality. **1906** M. Prince (*title*) The dissociation of a personality. *Ibid.* i. 3 A more correct term is *disintegrated* personality, for each secondary personality is a part only of a normal whole self. **1921** Park & Burgess *Introd. Sci. of Sociol.* ii. 144 In sociology, personality is studied, not only from the subjective standpoint of its organization, but even more in its objective aspects and with reference to the rôle of the person in the group. **1930** *Psychol. Bull.* XXVII. 677 The methods and problems of contemporary research in personality. **1947** G. Murphy *Personality* p. x, The approach to personality is made chiefly in terms of origins and modes of development on the one hand, interrelations or structural problems on the other. **1949** Kluckhohn & Murray *Personality* i. 6 In trying to remedy these failures, there emerged the first comprehensive dynamic theory of personality—psychoanalysis. **1950** E. Frenkel-Brunswick in T. Wiesengrund-Adorno et al. *Authoritarian Personality* ix. 291 (*heading*) An approach to the prejudiced personality. **1964** J. Strachey et al. tr. *Freud's New Introd. Lect.* xxxi, in *Compl. Psychol. Wks.* XXII. 57 (*title*) The dissection of the psychical personality. **1969** J. W. Getzels in Lindzey & Aronson *Handbk. Social Psychol.* (ed. 2) V. xlii. 463 A social psychology of education is concerned with the interaction of role and personality in the school or classroom. **1975** J. Plamenatz *K. Marx's Philos. of Man* xiv. 401 There are ideas of love and freedom common to liberal 'bourgeois' society and to its Utopian critics which differ from these older ties and forms. There are ideas of personality, of personal relationships, and of their social conditions, peculiar to this society and to its critics.

3. b. A person who stands out from others either by virtue of strong or unusual character or because his position makes him a focus for some form of public interest.

1889 G. B. Shaw in *Church Reformer* Mar. 68/1 Individuality is concentrated, fixed, gripped in one exceptionally gifted man, who is consequently what we call a personality, a man pre-eminently himself, impossible to disguise. **1919** V. Woolf *Night & Day* iv. 46 I've only seen her once or twice, but she seems to me to be what one calls a 'personality'. **1933** *Radio Times* 14 Apr. 82/3, I apply what may seem a whimsical test to broadcasting personalities. I ask myself if I would care to meet and talk with them in the flesh. **1947** *Sat. Rev. Lit.* (U.S.) 26 Apr. 4/1 In Elizabeth Ann McMurray, John McGinnir, Jimmie Albright, and Lon Tinkle, it harbors four of the outstanding personalities in the American book world. **1959** *Language Learning* IX. iv. 79 It is used with the greatest aplomb and ease by radio and T.V. personalities. **1962** *Listener* 22 Mar. 503/1 He is a local councillor in a small town, and one of its prominent personalities. **1973** *Birmingham* (Alabama) *News* 10 June E-7/4 More recently she has tried, fairly unsuccessfully, for a career as television personality. **1973** D. Miller *Chinese Jade Affair* xviii. 176 The woes of being a secret policeman during the visits of V.I.P. personalities. **1976** *National Observer* (U.S.) 13 Nov. 1/1 'In movies they buy personalities,' says Billy Dee.

7. *attrib.* and *Comb.*, as *personality assessment, clash, defect, disorder, problem, test, theory*; **personality cult**, devotion to a leader that is deliberately fostered by the emphasis placed on certain aspects of his personality; **personality dynamics**, a term used for the active, though not necessarily conscious, adaptation effected by a person of his personality to his environment; **personality factor**, a trait considered as sufficiently distinct and general in the study of personality to be measurable by factor analysis; **personality integration** (see quot. 1970); **personality inventory**, a questionnaire designed to assess personality traits; **personality pattern**, the pattern of personality that is formed by the inherited and acquired traits of an individual; **personality structure**, the combination of traits that make up a personality; **personality system**, a sociological term for individual personality in its dynamic social context; **personality trait**, a particular feature or characteristic that can be considered as relatively stable in an individual personality; **personality type**, a classification of personality according to the preponderant features or traits found either in a person or in a society; **personality variable** = **personality factor*.

1956 G. G. Stern et al. (*title*) Methods in personality assessment. **1964** *Eng. Stud.* XLV. 50 The intellectual and personality assessment of boys. **1969** *Playboy* July 102/1 These range from personality clashes..to on-the-job incompetence. **1956** *Canadian Forum* May 25/1 The spread of the 'personality cult' diminished the role of collective leadership within the party and sometimes led to serious defects in our work. **1957** *Economist* 21 Sept. 912/2 The election campaign was marked by a personality cult, but its inspiration and techniques owed infinitely more to Madison Avenue than to Dr Goebbels. **1959** *Encounter* July 80/2 The emphatic condemnation of the 'personality cult' at the 20th Congress of the CPSU by Mr. Krushchev. **1960** *20th Cent.* Apr. 342 A big factor in the sale of the more popular 'name' records is the personality cult. **1971** *Black Scholar* Apr.–May 7/2 We must be careful to avoid the tendency of building personality cults around specific individuals. **1971** I. Deutscher *Marxism in our Time* (1972) xv. 290 The crudities and cruelties of the 'personality cult' must have made him shudder more than once. **1973** *Times* 4 Dec. 16/7 Signs of new trouble in the Kremlin are evident in the rapid growth of the Brezhnev personality cult. **1927** *New Republic* 21 Sept. 129/1 The understanding thus gained spreads to all the slighter estrangements, the problems of discipline,..the normalization of those with personality deficits or defects. **1936** W. S. Sadler *Theory & Pract. Psychiatry* xxiv. 393 About one-quarter of all school children carry definite personality defects. **1970** 'T. Coe' *Wax Apple* (1973) vii. 56 A naturally offensive man who had found a way..to turn a personality defect to advantage. **1938** L. P. Thorpe *Psychol. Found. Personality* viii. 338 Investigators..have attempted to ascertain the degree of relationship obtaining between glandular disturbances and personality disorders. **1969** *Guardian* 22 July 11/7 The 11-year old girl.. sentenced to life detention..for strangling two small boys ..suffers from..a severe personality disorder, for which there is no organic cause. **1976** Smythies & Corbett *Psychiatry* xvii. 290 Some patients who ask his help.. suffer from a different kind of illness—a personality disorder. **1954** B. R. Sappenfield (*title*) Personality dynamics: an integrative psychology of adjustment. **1958** M. Argyle *Relig. Behaviour* v. 48 M. B. Smith and others (1956) distinguish those people whose attitudes are primarily an adjustment to group standards from those whose attitudes are based more on internal personality dynamics. **1960** J. C. Coleman (*title*) Personality dynamics and effective behavior. **1932** P. M. Symonds *Diagnosing Personality & Conduct* xi. 438 The creatinine concentration of the urine was also found by Rich to be associated with personality factors. **1957** R. B. Cattell *Personality & Motivation* ix. 335 A personality factor will have a series of predictive validities against specific cultural performances. **1971** Lanyon & Goodstein *Personality Assessment* iv. 89 A system of five relatively orthogonal (independent) and easily interpreted personality factors. **1938** L. P. Thorpe *Psychol. Found. Personality* ix. 434 (*heading*) Definition and nature of personality integration. **1970** G. A. & A. G. Theodorson *Mod. Dict. Sociol.* 297 *Personality integration*, the harmonious coordination of the various aspects of the personality with each other, and of the personality as a whole with its environment... Perfect personality integration is.. certainly not normal for persons in social interaction. **1932** P. M. Symonds *Diagnosing Personality & Conduct* v. 208 An integration of these various questionnaires designed to measure adjustment has been effected in a 'Personality Inventory' constructed by Bernreuter. **1933** *Jrnl. Social Psychol.* IV. 389 The test which was constructed has been entitled the Personality Inventory and is referred to herein as the P-I test. **1950** E. A. Suchman in S. A. Stouffer *Measurement & Prediction* v. 162 Evidence of the quasi-scale pattern in the case of personality inventories, information tests, and measures of intensity of feeling. **1968** Blum & Naylor *Industr. Psychol.* iv. 113 Numerous reasons have been suggested to account for the general lack of success in industrial situations of personality inventories. **1971** 'D. Halliday' *Dolly & Doctor Bird* xiii. 193 I've done an Eysenck personality inventory on you both... You wouldn't suit. **1949** C. E. Thompson *Thematic Apperception Test: Manual* 3 When cultural prejudices or antagonisms are part of the personality pattern of the Negro they are likely to reduce the subject's identification with the white figures of the TAT. **1960** R. F. Peck et al. *Psychol. of Character Devel.* iv. 89 There are distinct personality patterns which characterize each type group, and which differentiate one group from another. **1973** E. B. Hurlock *Personality Devel.* (1974) ii. 19 The personality pattern is not the product of learning exclusively or of heredity exclusively..it comes from an interaction of the two. **1963** A. Heron *Towards Quaker View of Sex* 51 Symptoms of deeper personality problems. **1939** R. Linton in A. Kardiner *Individual & his Society* p. vi, Basic personality structure, as the term is used here, represents the constellation of personality characteristics which would appear to be congenial with the total range of institutions comprised within a given culture. It..is, therefore, an abstraction of the same order as culture itself. **1947** G. Murphy *Personality* xxviii. 664 Problems of generality of the conditioned response being interwoven with problems of personality structure in the true sense. **1957** R. B. Cattell *Personality & Motivation* viii. 281 A comparatively new world of personality structure..has become visible to psychologists... On this foundation of measurable functions, the psychology of the second half of the twentieth century may proceed to build its laws and theories of personality. **1972** *Jrnl. Social Psychol.* LXXXVI. 151 Individuals will be encouraged to hold attitudes of intolerance largely irrespective of their basic personality structure. **1951** Parsons & Shils *Toward Gen. Theory Action* ii. i. 55 A personality system is a system of action... Social systems, personality systems, and cultural systems are critical subject matter for the theory of action. **1961** L. Thompson *Toward Sci. of Mankind* i. iv. 68 The personality system and the core values function as covert connecting links between the other four systems. **1971** F. Hollis in Roberts & Nee *Theories Social Casework* 59 This means attention to both the interpersonal system—parent–child, husband–wife, family—and to the personality systems of the individuals who compose the interpersonal system. **1927** *Psychol. Bull.* XXIV. 419 A battery containing a mixture of intelligence and personality tests was used by Gallup. **1964** M. Argyle *Psychol. & Social Probl.* xi. 139 The contribution of psychology.. has been to devise various objective tests and measures which are better able to select those who are good at the job. These include intelligence tests, personality tests, [etc.]. **1957** Hall & Lindzey *Theories of Personality* xiv. 538 It seems appropriate..to pause and attempt to identify general trends which exist in spite of the tremendous differences among personality theories. **1977** R. Holland *Self & Social Context* v. 131 The emergence of new personality theories is accompanied by ambivalence towards predecessors as the new theorists filter out what they need from the past and construct around it a new position. **1921** F. H. & G. W. Allport in *Jrnl. Abnormal Psychol.* XVI. 6 (*title*) Personality traits: their classification and measurement. **1931** T. H. Pear *Voice & Personality* ii. 18 In the speech of some persons, there are sounds which really symbolise personality-traits. **1948** *Mind* LVII. 511 The gesture in question is a personality trait of a given individual if it is performed by him, say, six out of every ten times when he might have performed it. **1972** *Jrnl. Social Psychol.* LXXXVI. 30 We deduced that the personality traits of leaders would be more varied in the nonconformity than in the conformity situation. **1919** *Psychol. Rev.* XXVI. 374 Personality-type A..is an individual rated as especially intelligent, prompt, persistent,..sensitive, not at all loquacious. **1936** W. S. Sadler *Theory & Pract. Psychiatry* liv. 845 The most important etiologic factor..is to be found in the personality type of these patients. **1949** MacIver & Page *Society* iii. 58 These studies have rather convincingly demonstrated..that each culture tends to create and is supported by a 'basic personality type'. **1966** *Philosophy* XLI. 299 Different social norms result in different modal personality-types. **1968** A. Etzioni *Active Society* xxi. 627 Most studies of efforts to affect 'deep' personality variables—especially psychoanalysis, 'brainwashing', and psychological experiments—show these efforts to have little effect. **1972** *Encycl. Psychol.* II. 385/1 Such personality variables as aggression, anxiety or authoritarianism. **1972** *Jrnl. Social Psychol.* LXXXVI. 121 Choosing groups dichotomized along some single personality variable, such as aggression, would allow far too many sources of variance.

personalization. (Further examples.)

1911 W. W. Fowler *Relig. Experience Roman People* vii. 149 It is not..*a priori* probable that the process of personalisation (if I may coin the word) should have proceeded..so far as to ascribe to these named deities..the characteristics of human beings. **1957** R. Hoggart *Uses of Literacy* vi. 163 The quite unusual degree of 'personalisation' in the newspapers designed particularly for working-class people. **1968** S. Brittan *Left or Right* viii. 172 The personalisation of politics round the leaders. **1973** *Times* 24 Jan. (Security Printing Suppl.) p. i/9 A developing sphere of operation for the security printer is in the realm of cheque printing and personalization. The latter is the process whereby the account holder's name and initials are printed on to the cheque.

personalize, *v.* Add to def.: to make (some impersonal object or thing) more obviously related to, or identifiable as belonging to, a particular individual; also *fig.*

1935 *Advt. for Mohawk Sheets* (Miller & Rhoads, Richmond, Va.), Now personalized with smart needlecrest initials. **1947** *Amer. Speech* XXII. 71/1 Personalize your luggage, personalized stationery. **1961** *Daily Tel.* 28 Feb. 24/6 He [*sc.* Mr. Gaitskell] probably appreciates that any further move towards 'personalising' the defence issue would merely play into Mr Crossman's hands. **1966** *Electronics* 31 Oct. 42/3 In the CP and EP, the memory is a plug-in unit that can be replaced in a few minutes, so that the design of either model can be quickly personalized for a special application. **1967** *Autocar* 27 Dec. 9/2 All the multitude of accessories offered (and bought) for the embellishment of ordinary cars is enough to show that many buyers want, in the American phrase, to 'personalize' their transport. **1970** *Daily Tel.* (Colour Suppl.) 13 Nov. 21 (*caption*) Dealer delegate is chatted up by an oil executive... Moments like these help to 'personalise' a giant company with the employees. **1972** *Daily Tel.* 24 Nov. 6/7 Outstandingly clever children often pass through school unnoticed by their teachers... 'One major reason is the failure in schools to personalise the learning environments which they provide.' **1977** *New Yorker* 9 May 143/2 Crossman blames the mass media for personalizing politics.

personalized, *ppl. a.* (Further examples.)

1947 *Forum* (Johannesburg) 26 Apr. 46/1 (Advt.), Fare is inclusive of personalised steward service throughout journey. **1959** *Economist* 4 Apr. 68/1 A 'personalised' cheque, one that carries an identifying account number and so can be used only by the owner of the account. **1974** *Times* 14 Dec. 24/6 Personalized crystal glasses, initials, names, dates, crests, etc., hand engraved to your requirements. **1976** *National Observer* (U.S.) 13 Mar. 11/2 (Advt.), Personalized attention, experienced tutors, relaxed atmosphere. **1977** *Theology* LXXX. 191 The man Jesus Christ as the personalized instrument..of the self-expressive activity of God. **1978** *Bull. Amer. Acad. Arts & Sci.* Jan. 10 Scholars with no prior knowledge of computers will be able to obtain a personalized index to the material most relevant to their particular researches.

personalizing, *vbl. sb.* and *ppl. a.* (Further examples.)

1957 R. Hoggart *Uses of Literacy* vi. 165 As the 'personalising' technique becomes yearly more machine-tooled, so a good instinct is pulled out of shape. **1961** *Daily Tel.* 28 Feb. 24/6 (*heading*) No witch hunt. Against 'Personalising'. **1977** *Theology* LXXX. 191 Such a union would be marked by *eudokia*, or divine good-pleasure, and by *synapheia* or true and personalizing relationship. *a* **1977** *Harrison Mayer Ltd. Catal.* 39/3 The Cerama-pen is a fibre tip pen filled with precious metal ink. Ideal for thin line decorating and personalising work.

personhood. [f. Person *sb.* + -hood.] The quality or condition of being an individual person.

1959 *Times Lit. Suppl.* 3 Apr. 197/3 From there he proceeds to the machine-like properties of animals and so on up to responsible human personhood. **1971** *Time* 13 Dec. 36 The United Church of Christ has in hand a statement written by six Christian education executives which maintains that sex is moral if the partners are committed to the 'fulfilling of each other's personhood'—pointedly omitting marriage as a prerequisite. **1973** *Austral.*

Humanist XXVI. 10/1 The locus of power needs to move from institutionalization towards man in his personhood, thus freeing man to respond to life with his own body, his own thinking, feeling and acting, expressing his abilities by working creatively with his human, natural and material environments. **1973** *Black World* Mar. 71 'Collage' defines her Black womanhood first in relation to her personhood, selfhood, or humanness and then in relation to her femininity. **1974** K. MILLETT *Flying* (1975) I. 34 There is something healing in her talk: its religious care for personhood. **1976** *Church Times* 12 Nov. 9/1 My unreflective believers have been denied the home atmosphere which encourages them to find their own personhood and value it.

personless, *a.* [f. PERSON *sb.* + -LESS.] **a.** Unrecognized as a person; denied individuality. **b.** Making no distinction of persons.

1909 E. HILL in Hill & Shafer *Gt. Suffragists* 11 The slaves of ancient empires, like women of to-day, were not recognised as 'persons', but they built the hanging gardens of Babylon and her mammoth buildings, and the material glory of Athens, just as the 'personless persons' of to-day weave the great moral fabric of the universe and, departing, bequeath their ideals to the willing souls ready to receive them. **1932** H. S. WALPOLE *Fortress* IV. ii. 607 He was by temperament intensely cautious and by training suspicious, and, mingled with these two strains, there was an odd element of personless, rather noble philanthropy.

personnel. Delete ‖ and add: Now almost invariably with pronunc. (pɜ̄ɹsǒne·l). (Earlier and later examples.)

1837 J. S. MILL in *Westm. Rev.* XXVIII. 25 In moments of general enthusiasm it is enough that a party carries the favourite banner; but in the intervals between those moments, its importance depends upon the confidence inspired by its *personnel*. **1899** H. JAMES *Awkward Age* x. xxxvii. 397 The *personnel*, as the newspapers say, of the saloon will shift and change. **1943** *R.A.F. Jrnl.* Aug. 3 The new basis of distribution is one copy to every twenty-five personnel. **1944** *Return to Attack* (Army Board, N.Z.) 15/1 British forces then rushed the landing ground..capturing nineteen aircraft together with a number of somewhat bewildered air-force personnel. **1969** [see *JAWAN]. **1972** J. MOSEDALE *Football* v. 56 Sammy Baugh of the Washington Redskins, playing with inferior personnel overall, lasted 16 years.

b. *spec.* The members of an orchestra, band, etc.

1956 *Gramophone* June 25/1 The sleeve [of a record] gives personnels. **1962** *Oxford Mail* 19 Feb. 6/5 The personnel of the nine bands on this important release includes many of the most famous names in jazz. **1967** *Melody Maker* 16 Dec. 10/5 It is certainly a very good band with above average solo strength and a personnel which includes a mass of arranging talent. **1968** *Blues Unlimited* Nov. 10 It is owing to him that personnels and dates for so many blues/gospel recordings by this company are now wellknown. **1973** *Melody Maker* 4 Aug. 50/6 When the Humphrey Lyttelton Band makes an appearance at the Lancastrian Hall, Swinton, Manchester, ..the personnel will include Kathy Stobart (tenor), [etc.].

c. (Usu. with capital initial.) = **personnel department*.

1960 M. SPARK *Ballad of Peckham Rye* v. 86 I'm just mentioning a factor that Personnel keep stressing. **1970** 'D. CRAIG' *Young Men may Die* xviii. 127, I rang Personnel at the office and asked for Stephen's full name. **1973** *Clarendonian* XXVII. I. 21 It was not therefore surprising that when a vacancy occurred, J.L.A. asked for her in Personnel.

2. Personal appearance. *rare.*

1861 T. MCWEENEY in D. Crow *Theresa* (1966) xvi. 182 Mrs Yelverton is still in the possession of an exceedingly agreeable personnel, and, without being positively handsome, she is most prepossessing and ladylike. **1909** W. DE MORGAN *It never can happen Again* I. x. 139 Contrast it with the dowdy personnel and awkward manners of the political gentleman's wife.

3. *attrib.* and *Comb.*, as *personnel audit, car, carrier, department, management, manager, officer, policy, procurement, secretary, transfer capsule; personnel-designating* adj.; *personnelwise* advb.

1967 COULTHARD & SMITH in Wills & Yearsley *Handbk. Managem. Technol.* 211 *Personnel audit*—in the same way that a firm's accounts are audited, or the stockrooms checked periodically, it is desirable to maintain an accurate analysis of the company's personnel needs—in managerial, clerical, sales, and manufacturing areas—together with an assessment of its strengths, as made up by the individuals concerned. **1914** *Illustr. London News* 17 Oct. 540/2 The personnel-car of the Schneider guntrain. **1945** *Finito! Po Valley Campaign* (15th Army Group) 51 A German convoy of two 170 mm cannon pulled by prime movers and followed by personnel carriers swung out of a side road. **1975** *N.Y. Times* 8 Sept. 2/2 A modern armored personnel carrier is one of Israel's obvious military needs. **1976** *Globe & Mail* (Toronto) 24 Sept. 9/1 The Post Office says there are now 908 'mailmobiles' or 'personnel carriers' operating across Canada. **1977** *Time* 25 July 37/1 A wave of Soviet tanks and armored personnel carriers rolls across the northern German plain. **1943** J. B. PRIESTLEY *Daylight on Saturday* vi. 32 Mr. Cheviot..was very keen on the personnel department and welfare generally. **1962** S. E. GODFREY *Retail Selling & Organization* vii. 55 The personnel department is also responsible for keeping detailed records of each employee and for authorizing salary payments. **1973** E. PACE *Any War will Do* (1974) i. 15 All the famous benefits the personnel department was always talking about. **1963** F. G. LOUNSBURY in S. Koch *Psychol.* VI. 570 Lexical units in kinship terminologies can differ, as between different societies, in two aspects of their meanings: the 'personnel-designating' aspect and the 'role-symbolizing' aspect. **1957** CLARK & GOTTFRIED *University Dict. Business & Finance* 265/1 *Personnel management*, the branch of business management concerned with the administration and direction of all of the relations between a company and its employees. **1959** *Cambr. Rev.* 6 June 575/1, I have heard personnel management described as a career that the liberal-minded, not unintellectual arts graduate of this university can take up without being accused of selling himself to mammon. **1973** 'M. UNDERWOOD' *Reward for Defector* v. 38 He would need a bread and butter job... He mentioned personnel management. **1926** M. S. LEUCK *Fields of Work for Women* vii. 74 (*heading*) Personnel manager. **1951** J. B. PRIESTLEY *Festival at Farbridge* I. i. 21, I have a friend..who's now the personnel manager at Whatmore's. **1973** Personnel manager [see *labour relations* s.v. *LABOUR *sb.* 8]. **1957** C. SMITH *Case of Torches* xi. 132 The women's personnel officer was tall, smart and superior. **1958** A. WILSON *Middle Age of Mrs Eliot* III. 430 Old Shuffler suggested that I got a job as secretary to a personnel officer at some big works in the London area. **1976** M. HINXMAN *End of Good Woman* x. 139 'Work your way up, lad,' the personnel officer told him. **1949** M. MEAD *Male & Female* xvii. 349 The personnel policy is protecting the firm, not the married men and women. **1950** *N.Y. Times* 20 Apr. 1/3 Donald Dawson, an administrative assistant responsible for personnel procurement, who has the never-ending task of seeking and investigating candidates for important vacancies. **1923** H. CRANE *Let.* 10 June (1965) 136, I don't know many at the office yet..but I've already been invited out to tea by the personnel secretary. **1965** *Tuscaloosa* (Alabama) *News* 11 Sept. 8/1 Doctors say a swift rise to the surface would probably be fatal. So the aquanauts will enter a special personnel transfer capsule that will take them to the surface where they will enter a decompression chamber on the mother ship's deck. **1975** *Offshore* Aug. 54/3 The personnel transfer capsule (PTC) was launched from the YDT to carry out open sea dives to 1,000 ft. **1963** R. I. MCDAVID *Mencken's Amer. Lang.* 250 The practice [of forming adverbs from nouns by adding *-wise*] quickly spread from the admen to the bureaucrats and the educationists and soon yielded *curriculumwise*,.. *personnelwise* and *weatherwise*.

personology (pɜ̄ɹsǒnǫ·lǒdʒi). *Psychol.* [f. PERSON *sb.* + -OLOGY.] A term sometimes used for the study of personality. So **persono·logical** *a.*; **persono·logist**, one who studies personality.

1926 J. C. SMUTS *Holism & Evolution* x. 262 Personality is, in fact, largely an unexplored subject and requires a discipline to itself as a real factor in the universe. 'Characterology' has been suggested as a name for the new discipline, but there are objections to it, and Personology is suggested as a better name. The 'Person' is a concept of the Roman law, not of Greek philosophy, and the hybrid is therefore justified. **1938** H. A. MURRAY *Explorations in Personality* i. 4 The branch of psychology which principally concerns itself with the study of human lives and the factors that influence their course, which investigates individual differences and types of personality, may be termed 'personology' instead of 'the psychology of personality' a clumsy and tautological expression. *Ibid.* 8 Since the latter [*sc.* psychic impulses] are intangible, personologists must imagine them. **1951** J. S. BRUNER in Blake & Ramsey *Perception* v. 121 The perception-centered approach takes as its primary focus of interest the variables of perception and studies the way these are affected by various learnings, motivational states, personological structures, etc. **1957** HALL & LINDZEY *Theories of Personality* v. 157 The focus of this theory is upon the individual in all his complexity and this point of view is highlighted by the term 'personology'. **1967** R. R. HOLT in Lazarus & Opton *Personality* 48 Personologists have increasingly begun to recognize that all the error-terms of standard psychological equations are their own happy hunting grounds. *Ibid.* (*heading*), The logic of the Romantic point of view in personology. **1980** *Underground Grammarian* Mar., Since personology must be too subtle a science for the likes of us, we cannot explain how 'personological' variables might be different from differences in persons.

person-to-pe·rson, *adj.* (and *adv.*) *phr.* **a.** Designating a personal telephone call: see *personal call* s.v. *PERSONAL *a.* 10. orig. and chiefly *U.S.*

1919 *N.Y. City Telephone Directory* 20/2 A Person-to-Person Toll Call is one made by name for a particular person reached through a telephone which is located outside the local service area and at a point to which there is a person-to-person toll rate. **1933** *Sat. Even. Post* 11 Feb. 57 There are two classes of Long Distance calls: station-to-station and person-to-person... When the caller asks the operator for a specific individual, the person-to-person rate applies. **1960** C. FITZ GIBBON *When Kissing had to Stop* viii. 128 I've put through a personal call, what they call a person-to-person call over there. **1973** C. EGLETON *Seven Days to Killing* xx. 222 They stopped by the call-box..and Tarrant got the operator to put through a person-to-person call. **1973** *Sat. Rev. Society* (U.S.) Mar. 70/2 Person-to-person calls are, of course, more expensive than station-to-station calls. **1977** *Transatlantic Rev.* LX. 50 A representative of the Columbus Police Department placed a person-to-person call to Dr. Edward Hudson in Padananim.

b. Taking place directly between individuals; interpersonal.

1951 R. FIRTH *Elem. Social Organiz.* i. 30 Some anthropologists have argued that a social structure is the network of all person-to-person relations in a society. **1954** [see *high-potential* s.v. *HIGH *a.* 22 a]. **1960** *Times* 12 Feb. 4/6 Person-to-person communication between specialists is much less satisfactory in applied science. **1965** H. KAHN *On Escalation* xiii. 248 The person-to-person meeting of Khrushchev and Kennedy. **1970** *Hospital Tribune* 26 Jan., Person-to-person spread probably accounted for the introduction of new cases into communities. **1977** *Proc. R. Soc. Med.* LXX. 553/1 Leukaemia and Hodgkin's disease are unusual among neoplastic disorders in man in often having aroused suspicion of person-to-person transmission or an infective aetiology.

As *adv. phr.* (usu. without hyphens).

1971 G. CUTTLE in B. de Ferranti *Living with Computer* i. 4 This does not mean that in future all contact will be person-to-person over the telephone and viewing screen. **1977** B. LUCAS tr. *C. De Foucauld's Lett. from Desert* vii. 128 Apostolic work..as I envisage it consists in talking person to person with infidels.

persorption (pəɹsǭ·ɹpʃən). *Chem.* [f. PER-(MEATION + *SORPTION.] Sorption in which molecules of a gas enter pores in a solid that are only a little larger than themselves.

1930 MCBAIN & BRITTON in *Jrnl. Amer. Chem. Soc.* LII. 2220 The sorbed molecules of nitrogen must be so intimately surrounded by the atoms of carbon with which they are in contact that the designation 'adsorption', which implies a surface, becomes a misnomer. There is very little difference in such a case between adsorption and absorption; and if a precise word to describe sorption by charcoal were required, the new term 'persorption' might be coined. **1948** GLASSTONE *Textbk. Physical Chem.* (ed. 2) xiv. 1204 It is probable that persorption is operative in the highly active charcoals, and perhaps to some extent in silica gel; the occlusion of hydrogen by palladium..may well be an extreme case of combined activated adsorption and persorption. **1960** A. W. ADAMSON *Physical Chem. of Surfaces* xi. 523 What might be considered to be a limiting or extreme case of persorption is the formation of clathrate compounds.

persp. (pɜ̄ɹsp). Also **persp** (without full point). Colloq. abbrev. of PERSPIRATION 4.

1923 WODEHOUSE *Inimitable Jeeves* ii. 24 The good old persp. was bedewing my forehead by this time in a pretty lavish manner. **1966** —— *Plum Pie* i. 19 It was with quite a few beads of persp bedewing the brow that I went back to the dining room. **1974** —— *Aunts aren't Gentlemen* ii. 12 He said 'Phew' and removed a bead of persp. from the brow.

perspectival (pəɹspe·ktivăl), *a.* [f. PERSPECTIV(E *sb.* + -AL.] Of or pertaining to perspective, esp. in a *fig.* sense of a mental perspective. Hence **perspe·ctivally** *adv.*

a **1866** J. GROTE *Exploratio Philosophica* (1900) II. xii. 121 The '*perspectival*' fact (so to call it) of foreshortening..is opposed to his argument in one respect. **1932** H. H. PRICE *Perception* vii. 196 The group would be a *series* of shapes having a certain limit... The series will consist primarily of perspectival distortions. **1957** *Scottish Jrnl. Theol.* X. 126 It is now clear that all historiography is perspectival, originating from some given point in the economic, political, cultural and moral structures of society and in the course of history itself. **1967** *Philos. Rev.* LXXVI. 193 Seeming to behold our universe(s) *from a place*, perspectivally. **1970** TODES & DREYFUS in J. M. Edie et al. *Patterns of Life-World* xviii. 363 Corresponding to each of these ideas of truth is a certain degree of awareness that knowledge is 'perspectival', i.e., that what we know reflects our ways and means of knowing it. **1977** *Dædalus* Summer 75 The perspectival view from the infrastructure may be at least as false as any superstructural cosmology.

perspective, *sb.* Add: **3. d.** Hence the point of view itself; a way of regarding (something).

1907 H. ADAMS *Educ. Henry Adams* ii. 20 Time and experience, which alter all perspectives. **1934** M. BODKIN *Archetypal Patterns in Poetry* 307 Writing from the psychological standpoint, I intend this statement less as criticism than as recognition of the limitations of the vital perspective present in these essays. **1949** R. K. MERTON *Social Theory* III. ix. 262 Mannheim's inconsistency..stems from an indefinite distinction between incorrectness (invalidity) and perspective ('onesidedness'). **1963** J. T. WATERMAN (*title*) Perspectives in linguistics. **1964** GOULD & KOLB *Dict. Social Sci.* 262/1 There has been much discussion from many perspectives as to the origins and 'causes' of fascism.

e. An apparent spatial distribution or extent in perceived sound. Freq. preceded by a qualifying word, as *auditory, sound*, etc.

1934 STEINBERG & SNOW in *Electrical Engineering* (N.Y.) Jan. 12/1 An audience..senses the spatial relations of the instruments of the orchestra. This spatial character of the sounds gives to the music a sense of depth and of extensiveness, and for perfect reproduction should be preserved. In other words, the sounds should be reproduced in true auditory perspective. **1949** FRAYNE & WOLFE *Elem. Sound Recording* xxxii. 674 Adjustment of the gain of the individual channels also helps in preserving the acoustic perspective. **1961** G. MILLERSON *Technique Television Production* i. 17 He can warn boom operators against dipping into shot..while assisting them in achieving sound perspective to suit the transmitted picture. **1963** *Times* 12 Jan. 11/3 The sound is all too full and forward, and badly lacking in aural perspective.

5. b. (Later example.)

1965 *Economist* 6 Mar. 989/2 Only a general negotiation can offer the perspective of a return to peace and a real independence.

8. *perspective control; perspective-free, -suggesting* adjs.; **perspectiveless** *a.* (*lit.* example).

1971 C. BONINGTON *Annapurna South Face* App. F. 285, I used 2 Nikon bodies, with 24-mm. and 35-mm. perspective-control lenses, [etc.]. **1966** R. L. GREGORY *Eye & Brain* ix. 163 It would be interesting to bring animals up in a perspective-free environment. **1970**

Nature 4 July 93/1 From the perspectiveless drawing of the Ancient Egyptians to the deliberate mixing of contradictory signs of depth by Hogarth and later artists. **1880** W. JAMES *Let.* 12 Dec. in R. B. Perry *Tht. & Char. W. James* (1935) I. 727 Metaphors and epigrams which, witty and striking and perspective-suggesting as they often are,..may be in danger of having the changes rung on them too long.

Hence **perspe·ctive** *v.*, to set in perspective. Also *intr.*, to draw a plan of the perspective of a drawing, etc. Hence **perspe·ctived** *ppl. a.*

1812 B. R. HAYDON *Jrnl.* 4 Apr. in *Autobiogr.* (1853) I. x. 171 Began my picture—perspectived the greater part of the day—felt a sort of check in imagination at the difficulties I saw coming. **1908** *Westm. Gaz.* 8 Aug. 4/1 A certain aimlessness, casualness almost, has suddenly been perspectived into purpose and plan. **1949** BROOKS & WARREN *Mod. Rhetoric* xiii. 442 It is the prose of a mind which is arranging its world, by delicate adjustments and careful discriminations, into a perspectived pattern. **1978** *Gramophone* July 181/1 These arrangements even make more comfortable and perspectived listening than the harpsichord originals.

perspective, *a.* Add: **2.** (Later examples.)

1852 THACKERAY *Esmond* II. x. 174 We have but to change the point of view, and the greatest action looks mean; as we turn the perspective-glass, and a giant appears a pigmy. **1859** DICKENS *T. Two Cities* v. 59 If a girl..swoons within a yard or two of a man's nose, he can see it without a perspective-glass. **1867** *Atlantic Almanac 1868* 9 So thought Lonson Nash,..who saw it [*sc.* a sea-serpent] through a perspective-glass in the year 1817.

3. (Further examples.)

1777 P. THICKNESSE *Year's Journey* I. p. xiii, I might raise..money sufficient to pay for engraving a perspective view of Montserrat. **1911** *Encycl. Brit.* XX. 470/2 A fresco of 'The Flood' at Florence is even more naive in its parade of the painter's [*sc.* Uccello's] newly won skill in perspective science. *Ibid.* XXI. 257/2 A horizontal plane on which we suppose the objects to rest of which a perspective drawing is to be made. **1935** *Burlington Mag.* Apr. 200/1 This artist's work, including his portraits, perspective pieces and genre subjects. **1942** D. D. RUNES *Dict. Philos.* 230/2 In epistemology: the perspective predicament, the limited though real viewpoint of the individual; the plight of being confined to the experience of only part of actuality. **1959** W. C. LOUNSBURY *Backstage from A to Z* 34 Perspective drawings of sets executed to dimension can be of great value, but avoid misleading, haphazard drawings which merely confuse. **1959** P. & L. MURRAY *Dict. Art & Artists* 236 The basic assumption of all perspective systems is that parallel lines never meet, but that they appear to do so. **1961** *Architect & Building News* 21 June 822/2 The perspective drawing realistically illustrates this interesting feature of the design. **1961** G. MILLERSON *Technique Television Production* iii. 31 (*caption*) Viewing from too close or too far makes its perspective look unnatural. This is termed perspective distortion. **1970** *Oxf. Compan. Art* 843/1 Shortly after Brunelleschi made his perspective demonstrations his fellow architect Alberti devised a perspective construction for the special use of painters, which he described in detail in his famous treatise *On Painting* (1436)... This is the first known written account of a fully scientific perspective construction. **1972** *Jrnl. Social Psychol.* LXXXVII. 143 The average number of illusion supporting responses was scored for each of five geometric illusions... Muller-Lyer..; Sander parallelogram..; perspective drawing.

perspectivic (pəɹspe·ktivik), *a. rare.* [f. PERSPECTIV(E *sb.* + -IC.] = PERSPECTIVE *a.* 3.

1949 KOESTLER *Insight & Outlook* xxii. 315 The laws of perspectivic geometry make the painter *see* differently.

perspectivism (pəɹspe·ktiviz'm). [f. PERSPECTIV(E *sb.*+-ISM.] **1.** *Philos.* The theory that knowledge of a subject is inevitably partial and limited by the individual perspective from which it is viewed; also, the partiality and limitation inherent in knowledge on this view.

1910 T. COMMON tr. *Nietzsche's Joyful Wisdom* 299 Fundamentally our actions are in an incomparable manner altogether personal, unique and absolutely individual—..but as soon as we translate them into consciousness, they do not appear so any longer... This is the proper phenomenalism and perspectivism as I understand it. **1949** R. K. MERTON *Social Theory* ix. 261 Mannheim's conception of 'perspectivism' is substantially the same as the Rickert-Weber conception of *Wertbeziehung* (which holds that values are relevant to formulation of the scientific problem and choice of materials but are not relevant to the validity of the results). **1954** A. HUXLEY *Let.* 17 Jan. (1969) 693 Von Bertalannfy..calls it 'Perspectivism', and points out that the unity of science is to be sought..in the isomorphy of explanatory laws in the different fields and disciplines of science. **1965** A. DANTO *Nietzsche* iii. 80 Does Perspectivism entail that Perspectivism itself is but a perspective, so that the truth of this doctrine entails that it is false? **1969** C. O. SCHRAG *Experience & Being* viii. 276 Is it possible for a philosophy of experience..to proceed beyond the perspectivism of point of view philosophizing? **1973** J. P. STERN *On Realism* v. 64 This perspectivism to which all experience is subject.

2. The practice of regarding and analysing a situation, work of art, etc., from different points of view and on different levels.

1948 L. SPITZER *Linguistics & Lit. Hist.* ii. 50 We may assume that the linguistic perspectivism of Cervantes is reflected in his invention of plot and characters... Cervantes' perspectivism, linguistic and otherwise, would allow him qua artist to stand above, and sometimes aloof from, the misconceptions of his characters. **1949** WELLEK & WARREN *Theory of Lit.* xii. 158 The unsound thesis of absolutism and the equally unsound antithesis of relativism must be superseded and harmonized in a new synthesis which makes the scale of values itself dynamic, but does not surrender it as such. 'Perspectivism', as we have termed such a conception, does not mean an anarchy of values, a glorification of individual caprice, but a process of getting to know the object from different points of view which may be defined and criticized in their turn. **1962** M. MCLUHAN *Gutenberg Galaxy* 125 The habit of a fixed..'point of view'..gave popular extension to the avant-garde perspectivism of the fifteenth century.

perspectivist (pəɹspe·ktivist). [f. PERSPECTIV(E *sb.* + -IST.] An artist who specializes in perspective effects; one who studies the principles of perspective.

1942 *Burlington Mag.* Jan. 24/2 In the case of Fouquet the traditional methods of the master of the Bedford Hours..gives way to the influence of Fra Angelico, of Jacopo Bellini and of the Florentine perspectivists. **1955** H. READ *Icon & Idea* 149 The 'Commentaries' of Ghiberti.., which are a kind of commonplace book in which we find all the ancient texts and recorded observations that occupied the minds of these fifteenth-century perspectivists, depend a good deal on Arabic sources. **1958** R. MYERSCOUGH-WALKER *Perspectivist* i. 7 A perspectivist never, under any condition, begins with an image behind the transparency. *Ibid.* 11 There are very few professional perspectivists in England at this moment. **1970** M. H. PIRENNE *Optics, Painting & Photogr.* vii. 85 On 'perspectivists', that is artists who made such illusionistic paintings [*sc.* painted ceilings], see Maffei... This interesting article..does not refer to the works of perspectivists extant in Great Britain.

perspectivistic (pəɹspe:ktivi·stik), *a.* [f. PERSPECTIV(E *sb.* + -ISTIC.] Of or pertaining to perspectivism.

1948 L. SPITZER *Linguistics & Lit. Hist.* 67 We are offered basically the same perspectivistic pattern that we have noted in the case of the *baciyelmo*. **1950** J. MESERVE tr. E. Auerbach in *Partisan Rev.* May–June 416 And so the excursus does not begin until two lines later, when Eurycleia has discovered the scar—the possibility for a perspectivistic connection no longer exists, and the story of the wound becomes an independent and exclusive present.

perspectivity (pəɹspekti·viti). [f. PERSPECTIV(E *sb.* + -ITY.] The quality or condition of being limited by or confined to a particular perspective or point of view.

1910 A. M. LUDOVICI tr. *Nietzsche's Will to Power* II. 20 (*heading*) Biology of the instinct of knowledge. Perspectivity. **1930** A. O. LOVEJOY *Revolt against Dualism* iii. 92 The necessary diversity of the characters experienced by percipients having different standpoints, we may call 'perspectivity'. **1933** *Jrnl. Philos.* XXX. 63 Such perspectivity is what the organism escapes to the extent that it becomes aware of..the logical dimension of nature. **1969** C. O. SCHRAG *Experience & Being* viii. 276 In becoming clear about the meaning of perspectivity, a rather firmly entrenched prejudice needs to be suspended.

Perspex (pə·ɹspeks). Also **perspex.** [Irreg. f. L. *perspect-*, ppl. stem of *perspicere* to look through (1st pers. perfect *perspexi*), f. PER *prep.* + *specere* to look (at).] A proprietary name for polymerized methyl methacrylate, a tough transparent thermoplastic that is much lighter than glass and does not splinter. Freq. *attrib.* and in *Comb.*

In the U.S. sold under the names of *PLEXIGLAS and *LUCITE.

1935 *Trade Marks Jrnl.* 9 Jan. 48/2 Perspex... Synthetic resins sold in the form of sheets, rods, tubes and shaped pieces, and as moulding powders. I.C.I. (Fertilizer & Synthetic Products) Limited, London,..manufacturers. **1937** *Nature* 20 Feb. 336/1 The lenses..were made of a particular form of the plastic material known by the trade name of 'Perspex'. **1943** L. CHESHIRE *Bomber Pilot* i. 9, I asked Percy to dim his light; it reflected on the perspex in front and I couldn't see out. **1946** *Electronic Engin.* XVIII. 224 The needle holder is in the form of a small perspex block. **1951** *Official Gaz.* (U.S. Patent Office) 13 Nov. 336/1 Imperial Chemical Industries Limited, London... Perspex... Claims use since 1934; and since November 1949 in commerce between Great Britain and the United States. **1957** *Times* 21 Dec. 9/7 The sculpture is dominated by..designs for a fountain and a triptych in Perspex. **1959** G. FREEMAN *Jack would be Gent.* i. 13 There were two large, ornate chandeliers made of wrought iron and bits of Perspex. **1960** *Practical Wireless* XXXVI. 397/1 Behind a small sheet of perspex screwed to the front above the speaker aperture. **1961** *Lancet* 23 Sept. 680/2 After infection, groups of mice were kept in airtight 'Perspex' boxes. **1963** *Times* 11 May 4/7 The perspex windscreen is faired down almost to the driver's seat. **1975** N. LUARD *Travelling Horseman* iii. 81 A damn great Perspex-faced wall map of London.

persuade, *v.* Add: **2.** Also const. *away from* (a belief, etc.), *down to* (a place, etc.), *off* (an intention, place, etc.).

1777 C. REEVE *Champion of Virtue* 30 Let it be kept from my two cousins.., if they offer to be of the party I will persuade them off it. **1895** 'G. MORTIMER' *Like Stars that Fall* ii. 17, I wish you'd just try to persuade Lou off a silly idea she's just got hold of. **1941** A. L. ROWSE *Tudor Cornwall* xiv. 348 The object of which was to persuade him away from his stand for catholicism. **1959** M. SHADBOLT *New Zealanders* 12 He..persuaded his brother off the waterfront to look after the herd for six months. *Ibid.* 218 I've been trying to persuade Izzy down to the city for the last five years.

persuader. Add: **b.** (Further examples.)

1862 *N.Y. Tribune* 3 June 3/5 In the South heavy guns are called persuaders. **1884** W. L. REDE *Sixteen String Jack* II. iv. 14/2 It's no use resisting, 'cause ve has the persuaders. *Ibid.*, Dick, out vith your persuader! (Draggle puts a pistol to his head.) **1900** ADE *More Fables* 54 The Colonel arose and pulled his Persuader, expecting to make it a Case of Justifiable Homicide. **1925** FRASER & GIBBONS *Soldier & Sailor Words* 221 *Persuader*, a nickname for the club, or knob-kerry, carried by trench raiders. Also, bayonet. **1930** *Detective Fiction Weekly* 10 May 48/1 Papers..held down by what crooks call a 'sap' or a 'persuader'. **1935** A. J. POLLOCK *Underworld Speaks* 87/1 *Persuader*, a pistol. **1964** L. DEIGHTON *Funeral in Berlin* xlii. 258 'Do you have a pistol or a knife or a persuader?' 'I have a persuader... Two hundred dollars in singles.' **1974** P. CAVE *Mama* (new ed.) xiv. 113 'How the hell are you gonna persuade the guy to pull off the road?' asked Ethel... 'I've thought of that,' answered Mama coldly. 'And that's one of the little changes... I'm gonna have to take along a little persuader.'

c. *Printing.* A tool used as a lever by a compositor when type matter and furniture is being fitted into a chase.

1898 J. SOUTHWARD *Mod. Printing* I. xli. 257 Fit the quoins, using the 'persuader' to squeeze in the pages, and tap up all round. The 'persuader' is usually a tool made by the compositor himself... The tool is a lever whereby the space between the type matter and the chase can be expanded.

d. *Television.* An electrode in the image orthicon camera tube which deflects the returning beam of scanning electrons into the electron multiplier. Freq. *attrib.*

1946 *RCA Rev.* VII. 361 The persuader electrode is tied electrically to the first stage. *Ibid.* 362 There is no need to adjust the persuader voltage for controlling uniformity of gain. **1953** AMOS & BIRKINSHAW *Television Engin.* I. 108 The persuader potential can be set to any value up to +300 volts. **1967** H. A. COLE *Basic Television* I. 56 When they get near the electron gun, the returning electrons are diverted on to the first dynode of the electron multiplier by an electrode aptly named the persuader grid.

pert, *a.* Add: **2. b.** (Later example.)

1952 W. G. HARDY *Unfulfilled* III. v. 246 Actually, as he looked her over, she was rather cute—slim young body and pert young breasts.

4. b. (Further examples.)

1898 G. B. SHAW *Candida* I. 82 In a black merino skirt and a blouse, rather pert and quick of speech, and not very civil in her manner. **1924** —— *St. Joan* vi. 87 We are not so foolish as you think us. Try to resist the temptation to make pert replies to us.

6. (Further examples.)

a. 1565, etc. [see PEARMONGER]. **1859** W. WARNER *Albion's Eng.* II. xxxi. 135 As peart as bird. **1774** P. V. FITHIAN *Jrnl.* (1900) 241 Ben seems a little more pert today. **1832** W. IRVING *Jrnl.* 10 Nov. (1919) III. 171 My horse goes quite peart. **1873** A. J. MUNBY *Diary* 11 July in D. Hudson *Munby* (1972) 335 Sir Arthur Helps with his bristling white hair and 'peart' white face, so like Mazzini. **1891** L. T. MEADE *Sweet Girl Graduate* xxii. 187 I'll be glad to lie down... I'll be as pert as a cricket in the morning. **1943** *Amer. Speech* XVIII. 67/2 *Peart* (lively, in good health, especially of older people).

b. 1772 in *Maryland Hist. Mag.* (1919) XIV. 272 The Corn looks pert & green.

C. *adv.* (Later examples.)

1902 W. N. HARBEN *Abner Daniel* 230 Well, I'm glad I won't have to go furder'n Darley... By ridin' peert I can let you out before sundown. **1972** *News & Observer* (Raleigh, N. Carolina) 30 Dec. 4/3 We aren't journey proud, and few of us get the big head or act pert.

Perthes(') disease (pə̄·ɹtəz). *Med.* [Named after Georg Clemens *Perthes* (1869–1927), German surgeon, who described the condition in 1910.] A disease of the hip occurring in children, probably owing to an interrupted blood supply, in which necrosis of part of the head of the femur leads to progressive deformity of the joint.

1915 *Amer. Jrnl. Orthopedic Surg.* XII. 557, I shall try to reproduce these features which give a character of its own to Perthes disease, and to describe it as a new and typical disease of the hip. *Ibid.* 564 One must conclude that Perthes disease has a tendency to spontaneous reparation and that all treatment is useless. **1958** *Jrnl. Bone & Joint Surg.* XL-B. 173 Stigmata of pre-existing Perthes' disease: a large [femoral] head, decreased height of the epiphysis, slight subluxation, shortening or broadening of the femoral neck. **1974** *Israel Jrnl. Med. Sci.* X. 230 The results may indicate that the deformity of the acetabulum in Perthes disease, generally recognized as secondary to femoral head deformity, may in fact develop in the initial stages of the disease.

perthitic, *a.* Add: (Examples.) Hence **perthi·tically** *adv.*, in the manner of perthite.

1906 J. P. IDDINGS *Rock Minerals* II. 236 Perthitic intergrowth. **1930** PEACH & HORNE *Geol. Scotl.* 112 The alkali-felspar includes both orthoclase and albite, which may be present separately, perthitically intergrown. **1949** *Econ. Geol.* XLIV. 174 In the diorite facies the microcline is generally only slightly perthitic..whereas in the syenitic rock it is ordinarily highly perthitic. *Ibid.* 179 The sodic solutions soaked into the microcline and replaced it perthitically by albite and then by grains along margins and fractures. **1965** G. J. WILLIAMS *Econ. Geol. N.Z.* xiii. 208/2 A radioactive biotite-granite with quartz, perthitic orthoclase, microcline and 20 per cent of dark minerals was also found in the Big River area.

perturb, *v.* Add: **2.** (Later example of absol. use.)

1902 *Daily Chron.* 23 Apr. 3/3 It is the unexpected that perturbs.

3. *Physics* and *Math.* To subject (a physical system, or a set of equations, or its solution) to a perturbation (sense *4).

1901, etc. [implied in *PERTURBED *ppl. a.* 2]. **1931** *Physical Rev.* XXXVIII. 875 The $^3P_2{}^0$ sequence is perturbed by $X^3P_2{}^0$. **1973** *Nature* 17 Aug. 416/1 If the initial potential is that of a hard sphere, this can be 'perturbed' into a realistic form by adding an attractive term and softening the repulsion.

perturbation. Add: **2. b.** (Further example.)

1946 H. & B. S. JEFFREYS *Methods Math. Physics* xvi. 464 Without the disturbance due to other planets, the motion of any planet would be an ellipse, specified by six constants... To allow for perturbations these constants are taken as variables.

4. *Physics* and *Math.* A slight alteration of a physical system, esp. of the conditions which a solution of Schrödinger's equation must satisfy, or of a set of equations, from a relatively simple form to one which is to be studied by comparison with the simpler form. Freq. *attrib.*, as *perturbation calculation, expansion, method, series*; **perturbation theory,** the method of investigating solutions of equations of state by relating them to solutions of similar but simpler equations which can be solved directly.

[**1868** *Phil. Mag.* XXXVI. 135 The motions [of molecules] are, however, not altogether free from perturbation.] **1899** *Q. Jrnl. Math.* XXX. 47 In this paper it is proposed to follow the theory of perturbations in the problems of mechanics in the order of its historical development from Lagrange to Lie. **1926** *Proc. R. Soc.* A. CXI. 301 If the [magnetic] field is weak we may use perturbation theory, according to which the change of energy of the stationary states is given, to the first order, by the constant term in the Fourier expansion of the energy of the perturbation in terms of the uniformising variables for the undisturbed system. **1937** E. C. KEMBLE *Fund. Princ. Quantum Mech.* xi. 380 In quantum mechanics, as in the Bohr theory, perturbation methods are of fundamental importance due to the fact that so few problems can be rigorously solved by direct methods. *Ibid.* xiv. 526 The usual method of approach to the problem of the many-electron atom is through a perturbation calculation in which the unperturbed problem..is of the central-field type. **1956** R. H. ATKIN *Math. & Wave Mech.* xi. 241 The method of perturbations is a practical technique for approximating to such solution. **1957** *Technology* Apr. 73/2 Perturbation theory and electron spin are studied, and used to explain the periodic table of elements and chemical bonds. **1961** POWELL & CRASEMANN *Quantum Mech.* xi. 381 We shall begin by deriving..the result of Section 5–8, giving the effect of a small perturbation on the energy levels of a system with discrete stationary states. *Ibid.* 403 A system subject to a weak time-dependent perturbation can be described approximately by a Hamiltonian of the form $H = H^0 + V(t)$. *Ibid.*, Since the perturbation is time-dependent, the system does not, in general, have stationary states. **1968** FOX & MAYERS *Computing Methods for Scientists & Engineers* ii. 17 We accept the 'solution'..and try to find a 'neighbouring' problem, a 'perturbation' of the given problem. **1972** G. E. BROWN *Many-Body Probl.* ii. 25 The two types of perturbation theory most commonly used are the Brillouin-Wigner perturbation expansion and the Rayleigh-Schrödinger one. **1973** ALONSO & VALK *Quantum Mech.* v. 202 Expressions (5.8–19) through (5.8–23) constitute the Rayleigh–Schroedinger perturbation series.

Hence **perturbation-theoretic, -theoretical** *adjs.*, of, pertaining to, or involving perturbation theory.

1964 *Physical Rev.* CXXXIII. A1070 (*heading*) Perturbation theoretic calculation of polaron mobility. **1968** C. G. KUPER *Introd. Theory Superconductivity* i. 2 Early attempts to construct a perturbation-theoretical model based on Fröhlich's interaction encountered severe mathematical difficulties.

perturbative, *a.* (Examples in *Physics.*)

1971 *Ann. Physics* LXIV. 383 The change in the initial set of site amplitudes is sufficiently small so that a perturbative solution of the set of equation[s] remains valid. **1973** *Physics Bull.* Dec. 734 A perturbative approach to the valence charge density in tetrahedrally bonded semiconductors.

Hence **pe·rturbatively** (or *perturba·tively*) *adv.*

1977 *Nature* 21 July 205/2 Since α is about 1/127, things may be calculated perturbatively.

perturbed, *ppl. a.* Add: **2.** *Physics* and *Math.* Subjected to a perturbation (sense *4).

1901 *Phil. Mag.* II. 268 By a kinematical analysis he (Stoney) shows that such perturbed elliptic motion may be regarded as resultant of two or more circular motions of different amplitudes and frequencies. **1927** *Proc. R. Soc.* A. CXIII. 639 The wave equation of the perturbed system. **1937** E. C. KEMBLE *Fund. Princ. Quantum Mech.* xi. 380 We designate the problems based on the two operators H_0 and H as the unperturbed and the perturbed problems, respectively. **1949** *Q. Jrnl. Math.* XX. 155 (*heading*) Perturbed functional equations. **1968** FOX & MAYERS *Computing Methods for Scientists & Engineers* ii. 17 We can often say that we have obtained an *exact* solution of the perturbed problem.

perturber. Add: **2.** *Physics.* A particle which interacts with a radiating atom or ion, affecting the wavelength of the emitted radiation.

1932 *Physical Rev.* XL. 401 R_1 means, crudely speaking, the distance of closest approach between the excited Hg-atom and its perturber. **1962** M. BARANGER in D. R. Bates *Atomic & Molecular Processes* xiii. 505 It often happens that the interaction of the perturbers with the atom in the lower state of a given line is much weaker than their interaction with the upper state. **1974** H. R. GRIEM *Spectral Line Broadening by Plasmas* ii. 72 The principal difference between the broadening of neutral-atom and positive-ion lines lies in the presence of the long range Coulomb interactions between radiators and charged perturbers.

Perugian (pĕrū·dʒiăn), *sb.* and *a.* [f. *Perugia* the name of a city and province in central Italy + -AN.] **A.** *sb.* A native or inhabitant of Perugia. **B.** *adj.* Of or pertaining to Perugia; *spec.* of or relating to a division of the Umbrian school of painting having Perugia as its centre.

1759 A. BUTLER *Lives Saints* IV. 62 He with several others was carried away prisoner by the Perugians. *c* **1863** MRS. GASKELL *Lett.* (1966) 934 The first thing..[is] to tell you how capitally our Perugian journey answered. **1864** CROWE & CAVALCASELLE *New Hist. Painting Italy* II. vii. 187 The fragment of a recovered fresco..explains the rise and progress of the Perugian school out of that of Gubbio. **1885** *Encycl. Brit.* XVIII. 680/1 In the centre rises the great marble fountain constructed about 1277 by Bevignate, Frate Alberto (both Perugians), and Boninsegna (a Venetian). **1887** A. H. LAYARD *Kugler's Handbk. Painting: Italian Schools* (ed. 5) I. vii. 212 That branch of the Umbrian school which we may term the 'Perugian', was developed at a later period..it culminated in *Raphael.* **1914** BROWN & RANKIN *Short Hist. Italian Painting* II. 155 Pleasing as is this early phase of Perugian painting, it is chiefly valuable as a factor in the education of less local men. **1934** E. BOWEN *Cat Jumps* 193 Over the bed hung a panel of leafy Perugian damask. **1936** G. F.-H. & J. BERKELEY *Italy in Making* II. vii. 108 Dr. Luigi Masi..was a young Perugian. **1970** A. P. OPPÉ *Raphael* ii. 29 The irregularity of Raphael's advance is shown in the two pictures of the Madonna which alone give certain evidence of the characteristics of his Perugian period.

Peruginesque (pĕrūdʒĭne·sk), *a.* [f. *Perugino* (see below) + -ESQUE.] Resembling the style of the Italian painter Pietro Vannucci (*c* 1450–1523), known as Pietro *Perugino* after the town Perugia.

1842 tr. *Kugler's Handbk. Hist. Painting* I. IV. iv. 172 The figures are beautiful and dignified, but without constraint or Peruginesque mannerism. **1863** G. M. HOPKINS *Let.* 10 July (1956) 202 There are the most deliciously graceful Giottesque ashes..here—I do not mean Giottesque though, Peruginesque, Fra-Angelical(!), in Raphael's earlier manner. **1874** E. EASTLAKE tr. *Kugler's Handbk. Painting: Italian Schools* (ed. 4) I. IV. ii. 297 Various pictures, more or less weak, of a Peruginesque class, bear his name. *Ibid.*, His [*sc.* Lo Spagna's] style is a mixture of the Peruginesque and Raphaelesque. **1936** *Burlington Mag.* Sept. 130/1 The two saints..have indeed something Umbrian, even late Peruginesque, in them. **1956** K. CLARK *Nude* vi. 232 Drawings in a Peruginesque style, which show the holy women weeping over the stretched-out body of the dead Christ.

peruke-maker. (Later examples.)

1905 T. AUDEN *Shrewsbury* viii. 201 Brought up at Manchester as a barber and peruke-maker, he adopted the Jacobite principles. **1966** J. S. COX *Illustr. Dict. Hairdressing* 111/2 s.v. Peruke 'Riot', As the distressed peruke-makers marched through the streets it was seen that most of them were without wigs themselves.

peruse, *v.* Add: **5.** Also *absol.* or *intr.*

1886 HARDY *Mayor Casterbr.* II. xviii. 254, I have tried to peruse and learn all my life; but the more I try to know the more ignorant I seem. **1909** H. G. WELLS *Ann Veronica* i. 25 Her father..appeared not to observe her entry. 'Sit down,' he said, and perused..for some moments.

Peruvian, *a.* (*sb.*) Add: **a.** *Peruvian lily* = *ALSTRŒMERIA.

1883 W. ROBINSON *Eng. Flower Garden* 10/1 Alstrœmeria (Peruvian Lily)... One or two kinds..are hardy and charming as any flowers on warm soil. **1931** M. E. STEBBING *Hardy Flower Gardening* v. 100 *Alstrœmerias*, called 'Peruvian Lilies', do curiously well in Scotland, considering they come from such a warm climate. **1970** *Sunday Tel.* 3 May 19/2 Among many plants which can be grown out of doors for cut flowers, excitement has been aroused by the new Peruvian lilies, or alstroemerias, bred in Holland.

c. *Peruvian Jew* = sense B. 2 below.

1899 in C. Pettman *Africanderisms* (1913) 370 Peddling Peruvian Jews were mulcted in sums from £10 downwards ..and compelled to contribute to the Pretorian warchest.

B. *sb.* **2.** [Prob. f. acronym *P.R.U.* Polish and Russian Union.] In South Africa, a contemptuous name for a Jew, esp. from Central or Eastern Europe.

1898 L. SEARELLE *Tales of Transvaal* 4 A 'Peruvian' standing by, whose name was Schadrach Levi. **1900** *Rand Daily Mail* (Pettman), Behold one of the most striking types of Johannesburg life—the Peruvian. **1936** 'IDLER' *Rolling Home* 385 He called me one day to a little Jew of the worst type which comes from Eastern Europe—the type of 'Peruvian' in South Africa. **1956** H. M. BATE *S. Afr. without Prejudice* iii. 59 Kruger and other equally stubborn of his advisers saw in this a deliberate move by Rhodes to dominate the polls with mine employees and, as they so ungallantly added, 'Peruvians' (a term of contempt which is applied to Jews of low class). **1972** E. ROSENTHAL *Let.* 23 May in *Voorloper* (1976) 638 According to Max Sonnenburg, the expression originated in the early days of Kimberley, where a body was set up, called 'The Polish and Russian Union', the initials of which 'P.R.U.', gave rise to the word 'Peruvian'.

perv (pɔ̄ɹv), *v.* *Austral. slang.* Also **perve.** [f. PERVERT *sb.*] *intr.* To act as or like a sexual pervert; to indulge in eroticism. Phr. *to perv at, on*: to look at with sexual or erotic interest. Hence **pe·rving** *vbl. sb.*

1941 BAKER *Dict. Austral. Slang* 53 *Perve, to,* to act as a sexual pervert. **1944** L. GLASSOP *We were Rats* xxxiii. 183 'Doing a bit of perving again?' I asked, looking at the gallery of nudes he had gathered from all sorts of magazines. **1959** BAKER *Drum* 134 *To perve at* (a girl), to extract pleasure from looking at her, esp. if she is scantily dressed as on a beach. **1964** B. HESLING *Dinkumization* vi. 116 What they get you for, perving? **1966** BAKER *Austral. Lang.* (ed. 2) vii. 154 *Perve on,* to contemplate with erotic interest. **1969** *Truth* (Melbourne) 18 Oct. 2/3 They caught me perving on the nurses at the Austin Hospital. **1972** I. HAMILTON *Thrill Machine* iii. 17 She's a cheap thrill machine for the boys to stare at and perve on. **1973** A. BROINOWSKI *Take One Ambassador* iii. 30 'Paper'd fold without me.' 'Yeah, I'll bet. Nothing for old Hastings to perve at.' **1974** K. COOK *Bloodhouse* 65 The little poofter perving on her hand ought to have his balls kicked in.

perv (pɔ̄ɹv), *sb.* *Austral. slang.* Also **perve.** [Shortened from PERVERT *sb.*] A sexual pervert. Also *attrib.* or as *adj.*

1944 L. GLASSOP *We were Rats* xxxi. 177 Bluey brought a perv book back from Cairo with him. **1949** R. PARK *Poor Man's Orange* (1950) v. 51 That dirty old cow, always making up to kids... Merv, Merv, the rotten old perv. **1959** E. LAMBERT *Glory Thrown In* 18 He was a perv. Special attention given to small boys. **1964** B. HESLING *Dinkumization* vi. 116 Two cops, according to the inquiry, booked nearly two hundred 'pervs' a year. **1967** H. STOREY in *Coast to Coast 1965–66* 203 It's that bloody old perve from next door. **1968** D. IRELAND *Chantic Bird* x. 101 He might have been a perve or a copper's nark. **1973** A. BROINOWSKI *Take One Ambassador* x. 163 My god, the number of pervs there must be in this country.

2. Someone given to 'perving'; the act of 'perving'.

1963 J. CANTWELL *No Stranger to Flame* 15 'Never even saw him. Might have been a spook.' She did up the top button on the green blouse. 'Even spooks like a bit of a perv.' **1974** STACKPOLE & TRENGROVE *Not just for Openers* 38 After the next bowl had been bowled, the blokes' heads would turn around unobtrusively so they could have a 'perv' at a bird in a mini-skirt walking down the aisle.

pervaginal (pəɹvădʒəi·năl), *a.* [f. PER-[1] + VAGINAL *a.* and *sb.*] Done or performed along the vagina.

1922 JOYCE *Ulysses* 483, I have made a pervaginal examination and..I declare him to be *virgo intacta.*

pervaporation (pəɹvæpŏrēi·ʃən). *Chem.* [f. PER(MEATION + E)VAPORATION.] The evaporation of a liquid through a semi-permeable membrane with which it is in contact.

1917 P. A. KOBER in *Jrnl. Amer. Chem. Soc.* XXXIX. 944 My assistant..called my attention to the fact that a liquid in a collodion bag, which was suspended in the air, evaporated, although the bag was tightly closed... Further experiments..soon forced us to the conclusion that the aqueous vapor is given off through the membrane, as though the water were suspended as a solid without any membrane present. This phenomenon we have named pervaporation. **1934** H. N. HOLMES *Introd. Colloid Chem.* ii. 19 Dilute hydrochloric acid solutions were concentrated by pervaporation to the acid of constant boiling point. **1956** *Science* 13 July 77/2 We have used pervaporation to dehydrate mashed potatoes. **1964** *New Scientist* 26 Nov. 591/1 For the separation of mixtures of non-ionic liquids considerable interest is being shown in what is called the method of 'pervaporation' using thin polymer films. **1968** *Encycl. Polymer Sci. & Technol.* VIII. 629 In pervaporation a mixture of liquids, often heated, on the upstream side of a membrane is driven through the film by a vacuum applied to the downstream side.

Hence **perva·porate** *v. trans.* and *intr.*, to evaporate in this way; **perva·porated, perva·porating** *ppl. adjs.*

1917 *Jrnl. Amer. Chem. Soc.* XXXIX. 944 After fanning these containers with an ordinary office fan for 24 hours the aqueous layer had pervaporated to dryness. *Ibid.* 945 The pervaporating surface decreased with the sinking of the water level. *Ibid.* 947 A similar container was filled with..sodium chloride solution and pervaporated. **1934** H. N. HOLMES *Introd. Colloid Chem.* ii. 18 A protein digestion residue containing strong hydrochloric acid, histidine, and enough humin to make it black was pervaporated. **1956** *Science* 13 July 77/3 The filtrate from a mixture of mashed potato, ethanol, and water was pervaporated... In pervaporating solutions containing class-I solutes, the percentage of water in the pervaporated vapor varied somewhat.

perveance (pɔ̄·ɹviăns). *Electronics.* [Perh. f. the sound of PERVIOUS *a.* + -ANCE (after *resistance, conductance, permittance*, etc.).] A valve parameter which in the case of a diode is equal to the anode current divided by the three-halves power of the anode voltage.

1928 Y. KUSUNOSE in *Res. Electrotechn. Lab.* (Japan) No. 237. 3 The constant *G* which is called 'perveance' may be determined from the electrode configurations. **1951** D. V. GEPPERT *Basic Electron Tubes* iv. 155 The perveance of a parallel-plane tetrode is equal to the perveance of the triode portion of the tube considering the screen grid as the plate. **1962** C. SUSSKIND *Encycl. Electronics* 229/2 It is convenient to classify electron guns in terms of their perveance, a parameter that remains invariant when the gun is geometrically scaled. **1973** FERRARI & JONSCHER *Probl. Physical Electronics* i. 20 It is interesting to note that the ratio $\Delta V/V_0$..depends upon the beam perveance $P = I_0 V_0^{-3/2}$ but not upon the beam radices, suggesting that the quantity *P* is the deciding factor as to whether a beam will be perturbed by its own space charge, independently of any particular beam geometry.

pervenche (pervã·nʃ). [Fr., = PERIWINKLE[1].] **1.** A shade of light blue, resembling the colour of the flowers of the periwinkle. Also *attrib.* or as *adj.*

1899 *Westm. Gaz.* 30 Mar. 3/1 Pervenche and navy are the opposite points of the cold tone of blue. **1909** *Daily Chron.* 6 July 4/5 She wore a beautiful dress of blue embroidered net in a shade of pervenche blue. **1923** *Daily Mail* 26 Apr. 9 The Queen wore a gown of pervenche blue.

2. = PERIWINKLE[1] I.

1948 E. POUND *Pisan Cantos* (1949) lxxvi. 44 And in spite of hoi barbaroi Pervenche and a sort of dwarf morning-glory.

perversion. Add: **1. b.** *Psychol.* A disorder of sexual behaviour in which satisfaction is sought through channels other than those of normal heterosexual intercourse.

1892 D. H. TUKE *Dict. Psychol. Med.* II. 1156/2 *Sexual perversion*, an innate perversion or 'inversion' of the sexual feelings with consciousness of its morbid nature... A passion for the sex to which the sufferer belongs, instead of the normal inclination to the opposite sex. **1894** H. ELLIS *Man & Woman* xvi. 365 Sexual perversions, again, are more common in men than in women. **1937** J. S. PLANT *Personality* II. viii. 223 A perversion in sexual expression has nothing at all to do with the form of the act but only with its purpose. **1948** A. C. KINSEY et al. *Sexual Behavior Human Male* viii. 264 Perversions are defined as unnatural acts, acts contrary to nature, bestial, abominable, and detestable. Such laws are interpretable only in accordance with the ancient tradition of the English common law which..is committed to the doctrine that no sexual activity is justifiable unless its objective is procreation. **1949** J. STRACHEY tr. *Freud's Three Ess. Theory of Sexuality* i. 28 Even in the most normal sexual process we may detect rudiments which, if they had developed, would have led to the deviations described as 'perversions'. *Ibid.* 37 Extreme cases of masochistic perversion. **1967** BRUSSEL & CANTZLAAR *Chambers's Dict. Psychiatry* 88 Exhibitionism, a form of sexual perversion in which erotic gratification is obtained from the exposure of parts of the body that have sexual significance. **1968** C. RYCROFT *Crit. Dict. Psychoanal.* 88 Masochism, sexual perversion in which the subject claims to get erotic pleasure from having pain inflicted upon himself. **1973** I. SINGER *Goals of Human Sexuality* 156 It would be erroneous to assume that the so-called perversions are merely alternative attitudes, as desirable as any other sexual possibility.

pervert, *sb.* Add: **2.** *Psychol.* One who suffers from a perversion of the sexual instinct.

1897 H. ELLIS *Stud. Psychol. Sex* I. i. 11 A pervert whom I can trust told me that he had made advances to upwards of one hundred men. **1906** *Jrnl. Abnormal Psychol.* Apr. 28 Subconscious feelings which represent, in embryo, the grosser manifestations of the most abandoned sexual perverts. **1924** D. BRYAN tr. *Freud's Hysterical Phantasies* in *Coll. Papers* II. v. 51 The strange conditions under which certain perverts carry out their sexual gratifications—either in imagination or in reality. **1972** *Encycl. Psychol.* II. 388/1 In psychoanalytic theory it is postulated that the child shows perversions or is a 'polymorphous pervert'. **1977** *Gay News* 24 Mar. 27/1 The word 'pervert' hardly seems apt to describe Douglas, in the light of such facts.

pervicacious, *a.* Delete 'Now *rare*' and add further examples.

1973 *Daily Tel.* 16 Apr. 13/4 Are audiences the only thing wrong with the theatre?.. At once funky and firm, a pervicacious horde of floating voters, they rush confidently to support the worst candidate on offer. **1973** *N.Y. Law Jrnl.* 7 Aug. 4 The language of the bureaucrats and administrators must needs be recognized as an outgrowth of legal parlance. There is no other way to explain its pervading, pervicacious and pernicious meanderings. **1978** W. M. SPACKMAN *Armful of Warm Girl* 37 Must she like a pervicacious angel think that because he loved her with every beat of his heart, [etc.].

pervy (pɜ̄·ɹvi), *a. slang.* [f. PERV(ERTED *ppl. a.* + -Y[1].] Sexually perverted; erotic.

1944 L. GLASSOP *We were Rats* xxxi. 178 Listen to this. ..'He buried his head in the warm fragrance of her bosom.' So-and-so, so-and-so. It gets pervy again here. 'His hungry kisses were returned with passionate abandon.' **1970** G. F. NEWMAN *Sir, You Bastard* viii. 223 Twenty maximum security, the lights never out, pervy screws watching every movement.

perylene (pe·rilīn). *Chem.* [ad. G. *perylen* (R. Scholl et al. 1910, in *Ber. d. Deut. Chem. Ges.* XLIII. 2202), f. *per(i-di-naphth)ylen*, f. *peri-* PERI- (used in a spec. chemical sense) + *di-* DI-[2] + *naphthylen* NAPHTHALENE.] A yellow, crystalline hydrocarbon, $C_{20}H_{12}$, consisting of five fused aromatic rings, which occurs in coal tar and from which certain organic pigments are derived.

1910 *Jrnl. Chem. Soc.* XCVIII. I. 616 To establish the constitution as a *peri*-derivative, 1:8-naphthalenediamine was converted into the azimide, this into 8-iodo-α-naphthylamine, and further into 1:8-di-iodonaphthalene, which last when heated with copper powder yielded..peri-dinaphthalene, which it is proposed to term perylene. **1946** *Nature* 10 Aug. 209/2 It has also been found that the position and number of fluorescence bands of anthracene, perylene, phenanthrene and naphthacene in benzene are independent of the wave-length of the exciting radiation. **1966** *New Scientist* 29 Dec. 735/3 An electron donor such as perylene (which consists of a series of fused benzene rings) is combined with an electron acceptor such as iodine. **1974** *Environmental Sci.* IX. 352/2 A one-year study of the amount of..benzo(*a*)pyrene, benzo(*k*)fluoranthrene, and perylene, was carried out for the particulate matter collected at the York [Ontario] sampling station.

‖ **Pesach** (pe·saχ). [Heb.] = PASSOVER I.

1613 PURCHAS *Pilgrimage* II. xviii. 173 From the second night of their Pesach they number to their Pentecost fifty daies inclusively. **1887** [see *HAGGADAH 2]. **1893** I. ZANGWILL *Ghetto Tragedies* 94 'Passover is over,' she said... 'Is *Pesach* over?' he said mournfully. **1905** [see *MAROR]. **1928** *Daily Express* 9 Apr. 10 Passover, or 'Pesach', is the most interesting ceremony in the Jewish calendar. **1950** M. HAY *Foot of Pride* iii. 77 The date of Easter corresponded approximately to the period of the Jewish *Pesach* when Jews were obliged by their law to eat unleavened bread. **1960** *Jewish Chron.* 8 Apr. 35/1 The Rev. S. Black..told the boys and girls of Pesach and its meaning. **1970** I. SIEFF *Mem.* ii. 20 On the eve of this great day, the most cherished of Jewish holidays, called the *Pesach*, a great family *Seder* is held. **1972** [see *MAROR]. **1973** *Jewish Chron.* 19 Jan. 43/3 (Advt.), Book now for Pesach & Summer season.

Pesaro (pesā·ro). The name of a city in northern Italy, used *attrib.* to designate majolica made there in the fifteenth and sixteenth centuries, and the potters who made it.

1856 O. JONES *Gram. Ornament* xvii. 12 *Renaissance ornament*. As early as 1486 the Pesaro ware was considered so superior to all other Italian ware, that a protection was granted to it by the lord of Pesaro. **1885** [see *GUBBIO]. **1960** R. G. HAGGAR *Conc. Encycl. Cont. Pott. & Porc.* 345/1 A Pesaro potter, Jacomo de Pesaro, was working in Venice in 1542.

pesewa (pesī·wǎ). [Fante *pesewa* penny.] A monetary unit of Ghana, equivalent to one hundredth of a cedi.

1965, 1970 [see *CEDI]. **1976** M. BIRMINGHAM *Heat of Sun* iv. 52, I paid him the few pesewas he asked.

peskily, *adv.* (In Dict. s.v. PESKY *a.*). (Further examples.)

1834 C. A. DAVIS *Lett. J. Downing* 139 The Post Office accounts was the next bother; and that puzzled all on us peskily. **1877** *Atlantic Monthly* July 77/2 It does rile him peskily.

pesky, *a.* Add: (Further examples.) Also *U.K. colloq.*

1775 S. DEANE in *Connecticut Hist. Soc. Coll.* (1870) II. 224 What reply, think ye, these heroes of five companies of the invincible Royal Irish, gave to this pesky Yankey? **1830** *Massachusetts Spy* 13 Oct. 4/1 I'm plagu'd most to death with these ere pesky sore eyes. **1860** HOTTEN *Dict. Slang* (ed. 2) 189 *Pesky*, an intensive expression, implying annoyance. **1901** M. FRANKLIN *My Brilliant Career* xiii. 113 He had always considered Harold as too sensible to neglect his business to stand grinning at a pesky youngster in short skirts and a pigtail. **1909** L. M. MONTGOMERY *Anne of Avonlea* xxvii. 318 Them pesky hens are in my pansy bed again. **1942** E. PAUL *Narrow St.* xxiii. 193 Sometimes I wish he would take over this pesky garden and let me manage the restaurant. **1956** D. KARP *All Honorable Men* 252 Just stay away from reporters. And if you can't—you have no comment. If they get real pesky, tell them to talk to me. **1959** I. & P. OPIE *Lore & Lang. Schoolch.* ix. 161 Juvenile repugnance continues to be expressed by the old standbys:..pesky [etc.]. **1974** *Times* 23 Jan. 1/8 Dr Benjamin Spock..says that an inability to be firm with their children is the commonest problem of parents in America today, and that it can lead to a child's personality becoming 'balkier and peskier' as the months and years go by. **1974** *Sunday Express* 30 June 6/4 The pesky thing didn't come anywhere near to working. **1977** *Time* 8 Aug. 39/2 But a pesky psychological climate is overhanging the securities markets.

b. (Later examples.)

1901 *Harper's Mag.* Dec. 228 Pesky few Democrats ever I see. **1939** L. M. MONTGOMERY *Anne of Ingleside* xxii. 153 O' course I don't believe in fairies... I've heard they were pesky mischievous.

pessary. Add: **3.** A contraceptive device which is placed in the vagina, now *esp.* a suppository.

1886 H. A. ALLBUTT *Wife's Handbk.* (ed. 2) vii. 48 Dr. Mensinga, of Flensburg, has invented a preventive pessary, to be worn by the woman, which..will,.. properly adjusted, be a real preventive of conception. **1922** *Brit. Med. Jrnl.* 19 Aug. 327/2 In cases unable to maintain themselves or their children the woman should be temporarily sterilized by compulsion..—for example, by the insertion of the spring wish-bone pessary. **1935** H. B. WHITEHOUSE *Eden & Lockyer's Gynæcol.* (ed. 4) 211 Of mechanical devices to prevent conception three are in common use to-day, the male sheath or condom.., the female vaginal occlusive pessary.., and the cervical cap pessary. **1957** T. N. A. JEFFCOATE *Princ. Gynaecol.* xxxviii. 583 Some pessaries dissolve to form a 'foam' which creates a mechanical barrier between the spermatozoa and the cervix. **1973** B. LAW *Family Planning in Nursing* ii. 44 Pessaries, vagitories and foaming tablets are other forms in which spermicides are presented.

pessimum (pe·simŏm). [neut. sing. of L. *pessimus* worst.] The most unfavourable condition in the habitat of an animal or plant. Also *attrib.* and *transf.*

1931 R. N. CHAPMAN *Animal Ecol.* viii. 189 It is possible..to conceive of survival potential as representing the actual position on the temperature scale where a species would experience its optimum and pessimum conditions. **1937** *Nature* 16 Oct. 663/2 The first part [of the Russian book under review] contains..a clear presentation of basic ecological principles, namely, factors of existence, ecological valency, optimum and pessimum, habitat concept, biological types (life-forms) and biocœnoses. **1947** N. BALCHIN *Lord, I was Afraid* 180 Assume that the radius of effectiveness..is 100 feet for a two-ton bomb—which is in many ways the pessimum hypothesis. **1976** *Nature* 19 Feb. 537/2 Above ~10 Ci s (4 rad to 1 kg) there is a '*pessimum*' number of particles.

pest. Add: **3.** *pest control*; *pest-free* adj.; **pest officer**, one who is responsible for the control or extermination of animal pests.

1931 J. S. HUXLEY *What dare I Think?* i. 30 Dr Tillyard, now in charge of pest control. **1947** *Nature* 4 Jan. 32/1 The use of a highly refined petroleum oil for application to orchard trees..is firmly established as a valuable pest-control treatment with citrus. **1978** A. HUXLEY *Illustr. Hist. Gardening* v. 179 Pest control by chemicals is often called warfare. **1944** J. S. HUXLEY *On Living in Revolution* x. 111 Once more the goal is in sight.., the goal of pest-free stores and stored materials. **1950** *Mind* LIX. 161 An apple..of pleasing taste, high vitamin content and pest-free. **1963** *Times* 9 Mar. 12/4 The hunting of deer was likely to be a more economic and efficient way of controlling them if the hounds were followed only by a small number of qualified foresters or pest officers. **1976** A. PRICE *War Game* I. vi. 115 He was..a cross between a high class refuse collector and the municipal pest officer.

pesta (pe·stǎ). [Malay, f. Pg. *festa* feast.] In Malaysia, a festive gathering, a festival.

1964 K. G. TREGONNING *Hist. Mod. Malaya* xiv. 298 The dominant Malay element..was gathered together in a highly successful three day *Pesta* or Festival. **1972** S. BACKHOUSE *Singapore* iv. 95 In 1966 the first *Pesta Sukan*, the festival of sport took place, and now accompanies the National Day celebrations held in August. *Ibid.* 96 The *Pesta Sukan* holds two chess tournaments. **1972** *Malay Mail* (Kuala Lumpur) 27 May 2/5 The pesta will have 50 games stalls run by the various societies in the university. **1972** M. SHEPPARD *Taman Indera* 93 The Cultural Festival, or 'Pesta', organized in Kuala Lumpur in 1956.., gave a fresh stimulus to older dance forms.

Pestalozzi (pestălǫ·tsi). The name of Jean Henri *Pestalozzi* (see PESTALOZZIAN *a.*) used *attrib.* in *Pestalozzi (children's) village* to designate any of several communities of refugee and homeless children established on Pestalozzian principles in Switzerland and elsewhere in Europe after the war of 1939–45.

1947 *Internat. Child Welfare Rev.* I. 253 Pro Juventute.. on two occasions made collections in favour of the Pestalozzi Village. **1949** D. MACARDLE *Children of Europe* xv. 219 The most lasting of Swiss projects for child victims of the war was initiated in 1946 and opened in October in Trogen... The Pestalozzi Children's Village is a great experiment in education for peace. **1950** T. BROSSE *Homeless Children* i. 5 In Switzerland,.. in the Canton of Appenzell, a Children's Village was built in 1946, on the initiative of Walter Robert Corti. *Ibid.* ii. 16 The Pestalozzi School-Town was founded in January 1945 [in Florence]. **1969** *Guardian* 8 Mar. 5/3 The 20 Tibetan children from the Pestalozzi village in Sussex came to dance in traditional style. **1974** *Radio Times* 14 Mar. 25/4 *Down Your Way*. Brian Johnston recently visited Pestalozzi Children's Village, Sedlescombe, Sussex.

peste, *v.* Restrict *rare* to sense in Dict. and add: also used as a curse or exclamation of annoyance (*arch.*).

1768 STERNE *Sentimental Journey* I. 143 La Fleur.. began to search for the letter..*Diable!*—then sought every pocket..not forgetting his fob—*Peste!*—then La Fleur emptied them upon the floor. **1858** THACKERAY *Virginians* I. ii. 15 Peste! I don't know why my father gave up such a property. **1896** G. A. HENTY *Through Russian Snows* x. 193 *Peste!* these Russians are obstinate brigands. **1898** S. WEYMAN *Shrewsbury* xlv. 393 '*Peste!*' he said, taking snuff with a droll expression of chagrin. 'Will anyone else ask a question.' **1932** G. HEYER *Devil's Cub* xv. 240 'But I do not know!' cried madame... 'Oh, *peste!*' said Léonie impatiently.

pester (pe·stəɹ), *v.*[2] [ad. Romany *pessa* to pay.] To pay. So **pe·stering** *vbl. sb.*

1936 J. CURTIS *Gilt Kid* v. 53 She had to pester up herself out of the pound you give her. *Ibid.* viii. 88 Tell him to go out and get me a new shirt... Tell him to pester about seven and six for it. *Ibid.* xi. 116 'It's his flat. He pays the rent.' 'Sure. I know he does the pestering.'

pestersome (pe·stəɹsǝm), *a.* [f. PESTER *v.* & *sb.* + -SOME^1.] Annoying, troublesome.

1843 *Amer. Pioneer* II. 439 All innocent enquiries, by infants and children..should be indulged and encouraged, how pestersome soever they may seem. **1906** *Dialect Notes* III. 150 *Pestersome*, bothersome, annoying.

pesticide (pe·stisəid). [f. PEST + -I- + -CIDE 1.] A substance for destroying pests, esp. insects.

1939 *70th Ann. Rep. Entomol. Soc. Ontario* 16 A special committee..known as the Pesticide Supply Committee is being set up. **1943** *Farm Jrnl. & Farmer's Wife* Sept. 71/1 A new word, 'pesticide', has crept into garden literature this year. **1947** *Times* 9 May 10/1 The demand for 'Gammexane', a pesticide which we discovered, has grown rapidly. **1955** *Sci. News Let.* 24 Sept. 197/3 A pesticide that kills injurious plant mites, but leaves beneficial honeybees and other insects alive has been developed. **1958** *Manch. Guardian* 13 Sept. 2/5 Chemical weed-killers should generally be regarded only as elements in a management programme, not as specific pesticides to to be used when weeds became a nuisance. **1964** *Daily Tel.* 3 Jan. 19/2 Pesticide residues in the fat of birds, animals and human beings were absorbed into the body and gradually built up in the body fat. **1969** *Times* 8 May 12/7 The chief threat to birds of prey is the use of pesticides. **1971** *Power Farming* Mar. 5/1 Shell, like most other companies in this field, recognize that the indiscriminate use of pesticides is highly undesirable. **1978** *Dædalus* Spring 43 The development of a specific sweetener, pesticide, or weapon could be prevented with little generalized effect.

Hence **pestici·dal** *a.*

1950 in WEBSTER Add. **1956** *Nature* 25 Feb. 350/1 The United States Department of Agriculture has a list of thirty thousand pesticidal formulations. **1971** *Ibid.* 3 Sept. 72/1 The properties, functions, utility and contributions of pesticidal chemicals to human welfare.

pesto (pe·sto). [a. It. *pesto*, contracted form of *pestato*, pa. pple. of *pestare* to pound, to crush.] A pasta sauce of crushed herbs, garlic, and olive oil.

1937 M. MORPHY *Good Food from Italy* 166 When used with pastes, such as macaroni,..the *pesto* is diluted with 3 or 4 tablespoons of boiling water. **1953** R. HOWE *Italian Cooking* 61 Prepare a vegetable soup..just before it is ready stir into it a garlic paste or *pesto*. There are several recipes for making *pesto*. **1954** E. DAVID *Italian Food* 288 (*heading*) Pesto. *Ibid.*, 1 large bunch of fresh basil, garlic, 1 handful of pine nuts, 1 handful of grated Sardo or Parmesan cheese, 1½–2 oz. of olive oil... When the *pesto* is a thick purée start adding the olive oil. **1962** M. SOPER *Encycl. European Cooking* 398 Pesto is a sauce of Genoese origin... Any left-over pesto may be placed in a small jar, covered with olive oil and kept for some days. **1976** R. CONDON *Whisper of Axe* I. x. 59 Enid grew basil for making *pesto*. **1976** *Times* 6 Mar. 12/3 Home-made pesto followed by aïoli garni at the Carved Angel in Dartmouth. **1976** *Publishers Weekly* 20 Sept. 83/1 Sauces such as pesto, aioli, mayonnaise.

pestology (pestǫ·lǒdʒi). [f. L. *pest-is* PEST + -OLOGY.] The scientific study of pests and methods of dealing with them. Hence **pesto-lo·gical** *a.*, of or pertaining to pestology; **pesto·logist**, an expert or specialist in pestology.

1921 *Glasgow Herald* 26 Nov. 6 Lieut.-Colonel Nathan Raw, M.P., has become President of the newly formed Institute of Applied Pestology. **1927** *Daily Express* 23 Sept. 3/3 The pestological exhibition and conferences.. opened yesterday... There were insect powders, sprays, pastes and—this will show you how far a pestologist goes —automatic fire-arms. **1927** *Times* 27 Sept. 12/5 An exhibition organized by the College of Pestology..was opened on Thursday. **1971** *New Scientist* 3 June 554/2 Our war-weary pestologists may perhaps become disenchanted with the scientific approach.

pesty (pe·sti), *a. U.S. colloq.* [f. PEST + -Y^1.] Obnoxious, troublesome, annoying.

1962 E. LACY *Freeloaders* iv. 65 My last pesty question —can you spare a hundred bucks? **1974** *Spartanburg* (S. Carolina) *Herald* 24 Apr. (Sky City Advt. Suppl.) 5 Twin flaming torches $3^{99} pr... Kills pesty bugs and mosquitoes. For outdoor lighting, everywhere. **1976** B. BOVA *Multiple Man* (1977) xiii. 139 Our pesty friend here..has found out.

pet, *sb.*^{1} Add: **2. b.** Also, a sweet or obliging person. † Also as a name for a favourite boxer (*obs.*). Phr. *teacher's pet*: a derogatory term for a teacher's favourite pupil; also *transf.*

1841 DICKENS *Let.* 9 Feb. (1969) II. 208 'The Pet of the Fancy', or 'the Slashing Sailor Boy', or 'Young Sawdust'. **1848** THACKERAY *Van. Fair* xxxiv. 303 James Crawley had met the Tutbury Pet, who was coming to Brighton to make a match with the Rottingdean Fibber; and enchanted by the Pet's conversation, had passed the evening in company with that..man. **1859** J. BLACKWOOD *Let.* 8 July in *Geo. Eliot Lett.* (1954) III. 113 A dive kept.. by Dick Curtis the pet of the Fancy. **1914** B. TARKINGTON *Penrod* xii. 89 'Teacher's pet!' whispered Penrod hoarsely. He had nothing but contempt for Georgie Bassett. **1922** WODEHOUSE *Girl on Boat* iv. 82 Do be a pet and go and talk to Jane Hubbard. I'm sure she must be feeling lonely. **1930** J. DOS PASSOS *42nd Parallel* III. 237 The other employees in the department hated her and nicknamed her Teacher's Pet. **1952** S. KAUFFMANN *Philanderer* (1953) xii. 199 He was not only the 'teacher's pet', he was the 'rich kid'. He was doubly isolated. **1957** J. KIRKUP *Only Child* xi. 139 So immediately after lessons were over, I would not linger in the classroom 'sucking up to teacher' as the 'teacher's pets' did. **1968** *Guardian* 16 Mar. 11/5 The anxious child was usually the conventional teacher's pet, always well dressed and obedient. **1976** T. HEALD *Let Sleeping Dogs Die* ix. 184 Be a pet and fetch me a Tom Collins. **1976** H. WILSON *Governance of Britain* i. 12 It [*sc.* the phrase 'prime minister'] was used to denote 'court favourite', with connotations similar to 'teacher's pet'.

d. Used as a term of endearment or familiar vocative.

1849 J. RUSKIN *Let.* 24 Apr. in M. Lutyens *Ruskins & Grays* (1972) xxi. 185 Do you know, pet, it seems almost a dream to me that we have been married. **1939** L. M. MONTGOMERY *Anne of Ingleside* xxxvii. 293 There is a parcel I want to send up to Thomasine Fair... Will you run up with it this afternoon, pet? **1972** G. SERENY *Case M. Bell* I. ii. 33 Mary smiled and asked to see Martin. I said, 'No, pet, Martin is dead.' **1975** J. WAINWRIGHT *Square Dance* 186 He..spoke to the policewoman on duty... 'Now then, pet—can you help me?' **1977** *Daily Mirror* 22 Mar. 24 Sounds like just the job for you, pet, eh?

3. b. (Earlier and later examples.) *pet aversion* (earlier example); also, *pet hate*; *pet peeve*: see *PEEVE *sb.*

1826 *Blackw. Mag.* XX. 53/1 Men of the most different habits and characters in other respects, resemble each other in the practice of nursing in secret some pet superstition. **1880** 'MARK TWAIN' *Tramp Abroad* xxvi. 262 For years my pet aversion had been the cuckoo clock. **1920** [see *ASSASSINATE *v.* 3]. **1939** *Sun* (Baltimore) 21 Apr. 28/2 Hill-passers, he said, were one of his 'pet hates'. **1949** *Proc. Inst. Electr. Engin.* XCVI. II. 629/1 Engineers will always have their pet ideas and want their special sizes of cables. **1969** *Morning Star* 19 Nov. 4 Many of you will have your own pet dishes... With your help we could give the cookery column a real international flavour. **1974** 'R. TATE' *Birds of Bloodied Feather* vi. 118 No doubt you have one of your pet theories. **1977** *National Observer* (U.S.) 22 Jan. 12/2 Another pet hate is the 'News Flash' that breaks into a program with total disregard for its distracting impact on the show.

c. Also **pet-form**, an adaptation of a name used as a pet-name.

1932 E. WEEKLEY *Words & Names* X. 138 *Christopher* may have implied stupidity, as its German pet-form *Stoffel* is synonymous with blockhead. **1956** *Archivum Linguisticum* VIII. 70 *Ned* and *Nanny* are..mere pet-forms like *Ted*. **1960** P. H. REANEY *Orig. Eng. Place-Names* i. 8 We must believe..that *Brihtling* was a pet-form for *Brihtric*.

d. *pet-vendor*; **pet cemetery** = **pets' cemetery*; **pet-day** (further example); **pet-food**, food for pet animals; **pets' cemetery**, a burial-ground for domestic pets; **pets' corner**, a part of a display, zoo, etc., reserved for the display of animals normally kept as pets or suitable for keeping as pets; **pet-shop**, a shop selling animals to be kept as pets.

1967 A. LEWIN *Unaltered Cat* II. viii. 180 He telephoned the pet-cemetery... Mr Carpenter agreed to pick up the cat-corpse. **1973** *Post-Herald* (Birmingham, Alabama) C1/1 The Los Angeles Pet Cemetery has a small 'slumber room' where owners may view their pet lying in state on a blue satin covered stand. **1939** L. M. MONTGOMERY *Anne of Ingleside* ii. 14 Such a lovely day... I'm afraid it's a pet day though—there'll be rain to-morrow. **1961** A. WILSON *Old Men at Zoo* i. 48 If I'd been made Director, Beard would be getting a thumping great subsidy from some of those big pet food people. **1968** *Observer* (Colour Suppl.) 25 Feb. 35/1 Pet foods come sixth in the consumer top ten. Baby food lags way behind. **1973** R. HILL *Ruling Passion* II. vi. 132 A man was unloading trays of meat and made-up pet food from a blue van. **1908** HARDY *Let.* 23 Dec. in *One Rare Fair Woman* (1972) 138 Our very old cat 'Comfy' died two days ago... He is buried in our pets' cemetery. **1948** E. WAUGH *Loved One* 27 He took a job at the pets' cemetery. **1940** Pets' corner [see *DUMB *a.* 1 b]. **1961** *Guardian* 5 May 15/4 In the children's corner [of the park] there is..a pets' corner. **1968** J. RATHBONE *Hand Out* xiv. 113 Gee, Elmer, it's better'n pets' corner back home. **1976** *Star* (Sheffield) 29 Oct. 14/6 Now he is hoping to open a pet's corner and leisure centre there, with a pride of lions as the star attraction. **1928** KIPLING *Limits & Renewals* (1932) 47 Mr. Wilham's fashionable West End pet-shop. **1942** D. POWELL *Time to be Born* (1943) xii. 295 In front of the pet-shop window a man stood watching half a dozen infant Siamese kittens. **1976** W. GREATOREX *Crossover* 35 He called at the pet shop... There were whining puppies and mewing kittens. **1924** *Glasgow Herald* 21 Nov. 10/7 A London pet-vendor has had about 2,500 snakes through his hands within the last few months.

pet, *v.*^{1} Add: **b.** *intr.* To have erotic physical contact with another person by kissing, caressing, and sexual stimulation. orig. *U.S.*

1924 P. MARKS *Plastic Age* vi. 53 I'm a bad egg. I drink and gamble and pet. I haven't gone the limit yet.. —but I will. **1953** A. C. KINSEY et al. *Sexual Behav. Human Female* ix. 389 The most responsive females may be the ones who most often pet to orgasm before marriage. **1959** N. MAILER *Advts. for Myself* (1961) 230 The game she cherished was to play the bobby-soxer who petted with a date in the living room and was finally seduced. **1969** E. M. BRECHER *Sex Researchers* (1970) v. 113 Some lower-level boys also occasionally pet. **1977** C. STORR *Tales Psychiatrist's Couch* 84 Haven't you ever reached a climax when you've been out with a boy? When you'd be petting?

peta- (pe·tă), *prefix*. [Said to be f. PE(N)TA-, the mode of formation having been suggested by *TERA-/TETRA-.] Prefixed to the names of units to form the names of units 10^{15} times larger (symbol P).

1975 *Physics Bull.* Mar. 105/1 The Committee [*sc.* the International Committee of Weights and Measures (CIPM)] also agreed to recommend that the 15th and 18th powers of 10 be assigned the names 'peta' (symbol P) and 'exa' (symbol E) respectively. **1975** *B.S.I. News* Dec. 13/3 The Conference [*sc.* the General Conference of Weights and Measures (CGPM)]..adopted the name peta, symbol P, for 10^{15} and exa, symbol E, for 10^{18}.

petal, *sb.* Add: **3.** *petal-shower*, *-tambourine*; *petal-soft* adj.; **petal collar**, a collar on a woman's garment cut in the shape of petals; **petal ware**, a type of pottery (see quot. 1960).

1957 M. B. PICKEN *Fashion Dict.* 74/1 *Petal collar*, collar made of overlapping petals of fabric. **1969** *Times* 24 Mar. 13/8 (Advt.), A button-through coat dress for Spring into Summer. Short sleeves, petal collar. *a* **1918** W. OWEN *Coll. Poems* (1963) 117 Stirs Of leaflets in the gloom; soft petal-showers. **1945** P. LARKIN *North Ship* 4 Whose every hall The light as music fills, and on your face Shines petal-soft. **1947** *Sun* (Baltimore) 6 Aug. 9 (Advt.), Generously cut to the new hem lengths..and pretty as you please, Colony Club's pettiskirt... In petal-soft Bur-Mil rayon crepe, white, pink or black. **1922** BLUNDEN *Shepherd* 26 And petal-tambourines shall earn A largess this May morn. **1930** D. T. RICE *Byzantine Glazed Pott.* 9 In dealing with the Constantinople finds,..six main groups were distinguished; plain glazed ware; stamped ware; white inscribed or sgraffito ware; 'petal' ware [etc.]. **1952** —— *Eng. Art 871–1100* viii. 248 The glazes, however, are of a type not so far known from Germany, and suggest, rather Byzantine prototypes; one group, indeed, where the glaze is thick and dark, and where a decoration of blobs has been added, is extremely close to a Byzantine group, usually classed as 'petal' ware. **1960** R. G. HAGGAR *Conc. Encycl. Cont. Pott. & Porc.* 345/2 *'Petal' ware*, ware found at Constantinople, characterized by the addition of horizontal bands of lumps of clay, pressed firmly to the body at one end but left free at the other, which resemble crude petals, hence the name.

petal (pe·tăl), *v. poet.* [f. the sb.] *trans.* To provide or scatter with petals. Also *fig.*

1907 *Westm. Gaz.* 3 June 2/3 Sigh, little wind.., Winnow the lilacs pink and white, Petal the shining grass. **1930** E. POUND *XXX Cantos* iv. 17 Saffron sandal so petals the narrow foot. **1955** —— *Section: Rock-Drill* (1957) xci. 76 The water-bug's mittens petal the rock beneath.

petalled, petaled, *a.* Add: Also, formed like or resembling a petal or petals.

1862 G. M. HOPKINS *Vision of Mermaids* (1929), Betwixt ten thousand petall'd lips. **1929** G. C. ALLEN *Oxf. Poetry* 1 Let's pick the petals of all joy apart, And launch them uncontrolled on the wind-stream With gleam of petalled gold. **1937** BLUNDEN *Elegy* 74 The petalled cloud and the blue brook aflow. **1975** G. HOWELL *In Vogue* 30 Delysia looking curious in a petalled evening dress.

petalodic (petălǫ·dik), *a. Bot.* [f. Gr. πεταλώδ-ης leaf-like (cf. PETALODY) + -IC.] Exhibiting petalody.

1909 W. BATESON *Mendel's Princ. Heredity* xi. 198 In the hose-in-hose *Campanula*, which has the sepals petaloid, the well-formed anthers contain plenty of pollen (some may be petalodic).

‖**pétanque** (petañk). [Fr.] A game, resembling bowls, played orig. and chiefly in southern France. Also *attrib.* Cf. *BOULE^4 2.

1955 *Times* 8 Aug. 8/7 No longer the fraternal glass of pastis..no longer..the earnest game of *pétanque*, that travesty of bowls. **1956** N. RYAN tr. *Simenon's My Friend Maigret* vii. 112 Two old men were playing bowls, *pétanque* style, that is without sending the jack more than a few yards from their feet. **1963** N. FREELING *Because of Cats* vii. 105 Cunning little French butane stoves and the chi-chi of le camping, huge rubber water-wings, *pétanque* sets and elaborate German beach toys. **1967** G. BELLAIRS *Single Ticket to Death* i. 7 Littlejohn and Dorange were playing *pétanque*... The players, with a twist of the wrist, hurled their steel balls at the small wooden jack. **1972** A.H. HAYNES *Story of Bowls* i. 7 In..Petanque..a small marker ball is thrown a distance of up to ten yards; occasionally the distance is doubled and in this event, remarkable skill is demonstrated by the players in putting top and side spin on the heavy steel balls bowled underarm towards the marker ball. **1977** *Times* 25 Apr. 16/7 The finals of the London pétanque championship.

petara(h, varr. PITARAH.

petasma (petæ·zmă). *Zool.* [a. Gr. πέτασμα something spread out.] In prawns of the family *Penæidea*, a membranous appendage attached to the first pair of pleopods.

1888 C. S. BATE in *Rep. Sci. Results Voy. H.M.S. Challenger: Zool.* XXIV. 230 The pleopods [of *Penæus*] are large and powerful, terminating in two foliaceous branches in every pair except the first, which in the male carries attached to the base a large membranous appendage that I call 'petasma'. **1909** A. E. SHIPLEY in A. Sedgwick *Student's Text-bk. Zool.* III. v. 527 In *Penæus*, *Leucifer* and *Sergestes* a lobe projects inwards from the base of the first pleopods in the male, and may unite with its fellow to form the petasma (or curtain). **1966** *McGraw-Hill Encycl. Sci. & Technol.* V. 105/1 The male [genital] system [of Eumalocostraca] consists of the testis, vas deferens, ductus ejaculatorius, and sometimes a penis, modified thoracic limbs (pleopods), or petasma.

Pete, pete (pīt). [Dimin. of the name *Peter* (see PETER *sb.*).] **1.** *slang.* (With small initial.) **a.** A safe. Cf. *PETER *sb.*[1] 6 b.

1911 G. BRONSON-HOWARD *Enemy to Society* iv. 73 All the time a man equipped with burglar's tools would be kneeling behind the safe and drilling it open; those 'petes'—as cracksmen call them—in people's houses are generally very easy to open. **1932** WODEHOUSE *Hot Water* i. 32 Show me the pete I can't open with my eye-teeth and a pin, and I'll eat it. **1938** D. RUNYON *Furthermore* viii. 153 This is a very soft pete. It is old-fashioned, and you can open it with a toothpick. **1951** WODEHOUSE *Old Reliable* x. 129 You think I'm scared to bust that pete?

b. Nitroglycerine, as used for safe-breaking.

1931 D. W. MAURER in *Writer's Digest* Oct. 29/2 *Soup*, nitroglycerine or 'pete'. **1948** MENCKEN *Amer. Lang.* Suppl. II. 668 Among the cant terms of the *jug-heavies* are..*soup* or *pete*, nitroglycerine.

c. *attrib.* and *Comb.*, as **pete box** = sense *1 a; **pete-man** = *PETERMAN 3 c.

1931 D. RUNYON *Guys & Dolls* (1932) iv. 77 Nobody opens pete boxes for a living any more. They make the boxes too good, and they are all wired up with alarms. **1911** G. BRONSON-HOWARD *Enemy to Society* v. 105 You've already caught four 'pete-men' who attempted to drill the safe. **1931** *Everyman* 21 May 522/1 All my safe-blower pals used..'pete-men'.

2. (With capital initial.) Used in various mild exclamations and phrases expressive of exasperation or annoyance; esp. in phr. *for Pete's sake.*

1924 *Dialect Notes* V. 274 For the love of Pete, for Pete's sake. **1942** N. BALCHIN *Darkness falls from Air* ix. 170 Why in the name of Pete didn't you say so? **1949** N. MARSH *Swing, Brother, Swing* iv. 59 Carlisle heard Mr. Bellairs whisper under his breath: 'For the love of Pete!' **1959** W. GOLDING *Free Fall* vi. 129 Marry me, Taffy, for Pete's sake marry me. **1973** 'B. MATHER' *Snowline* xviii. 223 For Pete's sake don't ask bloody fool questions. **1975** *Listener* 24 July 115/1 For Pete's sake when will so-called 'experts'..get it into their noddles that rising wages and prices *are* inflation.

Peter, *sb.*[1] Add: **1. b.** [Imitative.] The cry of various tits.

1874 C. M. YONGE *Lady Hester* ii. 28 The tomtits were calling 'peter' in the trees. **1892** —— *Old Woman's Outlook* ii. 37 Sunshine, setting the thrushes and robins to sing, and the ox-eyes to cry Peter.

2. (Later examples.)

1926 *Times* 7 Jan. 9/6 Martin and Martin had been in low water for a long time and had recourse to the method of robbing Peter to pay Paul. **1961** D. WOODWARD tr. *Simenon's Premier* iii. 84 After the diastrous experiments made by previous governments, which had lived from day to day, robbing Peter to pay Paul, the only solution was a large-scale devaluation. **1976** *Star* (Sheffield) 29 Oct. 13/7 A Sheffield man who tried to set up a travel agency business was accused of 'robbing Peter to pay Paul', at Sheffield Bankruptcy Court.

6. a. Now also *Taxi-drivers' slang.* (Further examples.)

1930 'A. ARMSTRONG' *Taxi* xii. 164 'Peters' are pieces of luggage,—a threepenny extra for the driver. **1939** H. HODGE *Cab, Sir?* III. xv. 221 The driver calls each package a 'Peter'.

b. *Criminals' slang.* A safe or cash-box; a cash register, a till.

1859 G. W. MATSELL *Vocabulum* 66 *Peter*, a portmanteau; a travelling-bag; a trunk; an iron chest; a cash-box. **1862** [see *peter-cutter*, sense 8 a]. **1868** [see *peter-screwing*, sense *8 a]. **1869** *Macm. Mag.* Oct. 506/1 After we left the course, we..got a peter (cashbox) with very near a century of quids in it. **1889** CLARKSON & RICHARDSON *Police!* xxv. 351 In order to 'ready' these places, they watch the shops at closing time, to learn if the swag is placed in the 'Peter', or safe. **1935** A. J. POLLOCK *Underworld Speaks* 87/1 *Peter*, a cash drawer; a money box; cash register. **1936** J. CURTIS *Gilt Kid* xvii. 171 There was no safe. 'There ain't no peter.' 'No.' **1943** *Penguin New Writing* XVII. 66 He pushed me over one more double gin which he only pretended to ring up on the peter, but there wasn't a chance to talk. **1945** BAKER *Austral. Lang.* viii. 140 *To tickle the peter*, to rob a till. **1958** F. NORMAN *Bang to Rights* III. 121 If some poor unsuspecting manageing [*sic*] director left his peter open well, I ask you? **1965** M. SHADBOLT *Among Cinders* xvi. 143 'Did he tickle the peter?'.. 'To the tune of two thousand quid.' **1967** K. GILES *Death & Mr Prettyman* v. 98 But level, old boy, was Prettyman tickling the peter? **1970** G. F. NEWMAN *Sir, You Bastard* viii. 211 There was s'posed to be some dough in the Peter. **1978** *Daily Mail* 25 Jan. 12/2 While most of the country's police call the safe a 'peter', in London it's a 'gas'.

c. *slang.* A cell in a prison, a police station, a court of law, etc.; a lock-up. orig. *Austral.*

1890 BARRÈRE & LELAND *Dict. Slang* II. 125/1 *Peter*.. (Australian prison), punishment cell. **1953** K. TENNANT *Joyful Condemned* vi. 55 The doors of the peters just crash open at the name of McGarty. **1955** D. NILAND *Shiralee* 69 They could throw you in the peter stone-cold sober. **1958** F. NORMAN *Bang to Rights* I. 9, I turned and walked down the stairs to the peter under the court. **1960** C. HATTON in *Pick of Today's Short Stories* XI. 147 He snapped up any likely bloke just as soon as he..had come out of the peter. **1965** *Guardian* 10 Oct. 21/6 'Hurry up and slop out'—'Get back in your f— Peter'. **1973** 'J. PATRICK' *Glasgow Gang Observed* ix. 81 He..had spent the first night in a police cell (or 'peter' as they call it).

d. *U.S. slang.* A stupefying drug.

1899 'J. FLYNT' *Tramping with Tramps* IV. 396 'Knock-out drops' are also 'peter'. **1933** *Amer. Speech* VIII. II. 27/1 Among the addicts dope in general is known as *gow, junk*, or *peter* (any kind of *knockout drops*). **1971** E. E. LANDY *Underground Dict.* 148 *Peter*..Chloral hydrate.

e. *slang.* The penis.

1902 FARMER & HENLEY *Slang* V. 177/1 *Peter*... 4. (venery).—The *penis:* also *St. Peter.* **1928** *Dialect Notes* VI. 61 The proper name *Peter*..is so universally used by children and facetious adults as a name for the penis that it never quite loses this significance. Very few natives of the Ozarks will consider naming a boy *Peter.* **1940** C. MCCULLERS *Heart is Lonely Hunter* I. ii. 18 There was one fellow who had had his peter and his left leg blown off in a boiler explosion. **1970** R. D. ABRAHAMS *Positively Black* ii. 41, I fuck your mammy on a red hot heater; I miss her pussy and burn my peter. **1975** M. KENYON *Mr Big* v. 48 In New Jersey peter was childhood slang for penis, equivalent to willie and john thomas. **1977** J. WAMBAUGH *Black Marble* (1978) vi. 75 If you look very closely you can see a gerbil's dick, but not a parakeet's peter.

7. Also (*Naut.*) simply *Peter.* In *Bridge,* = *ECHO *sb.* 8.

1891 KIPLING *Barrack-Room Ballads* (1892) 205 See the shaking funnels roar, with the Peter at the fore. **1939** [see *ECHO *sb.* 8]. **1945** PHILLIPS & REESE *How to play Bridge* III. xiii. 115 East's play of the 8 is the commencement of what is known as a 'peter'. **1959** *Listener* 27 Aug. 334/2 There are those who advocate the peter to indicate length at virtually all times in defence. **1966** *Sunday Tel.* 14 Aug. 9/6 Every bridge player knows the principle of high-low defence as a signal of encouragement. Generally known as the 'peter' in Britain and the 'echo' or 'come-on' in America, it is most frequently used against an opponent's trump contract to indicate strength or a doubleton. **1974** *Country Life* 28 Mar. 750/3 South played a Diamond to the King, East starting a peter.

8. a. Peter Grievous (also **Peter Grievance**), one who complains; a whining child; freq. *attrib.* or as *adj.*, complaining, fretful, miserable (*dial.* and *slang*); (sense 6) *peter-ringer*; (sense *6 b) *peter-popping, -screwing* (see quots.).

[**1724** (*title of play*) Valentine and Orson, with the comical whining humours of Peter Pitiful.] **1774** F. HOPKINSON (*title*) A pretty story written in the year of Our Lord 2774. By Peter Grievous, Esq. **1777** H. L. THRALE in *Thraliana* (1942) I. 155 Cradocke had written a Tragedy a very *deep* one they said..We'll call it *Peter* said he—the scene was in Russia, at least said I let it be *Peter Grievous.* **1875** W. D. PARISH *Dict. Sussex Dial.* 86 *Peter-grievous*, fretful; whining. 'What a peter-grievous child you are! Whatever is the matter?' **1894** *Southward Ho!* I. 338 (E.D.D.), A peter-grievous wot shrapes an makes a rookery, an a ranky chimley be pettigues fer to send a feller in de crazy-house. **1896** G. F. NORTHALL *Warwickshire Word-bk.* 172 *Peter Grievous, sb.* A grumbler: a grievance-monger. Oxf. (*Peter Grievance*, a cross, fretful child). The word is used as an adjective also, as 'He's a regular peter-grievous fellow.' Glouc., Worc. **1932** E. WEEKLEY *Words & Names* vii. 90 *Peter grievous*, a lachrymose individual, belongs to the class of *simple Simon.* **1960** *Observer* 24 Jan. 5/2 The expertise of peter-popping consists in knowing just how much gelignite to use on the safe in question. **1863** *Once a Week* 7 Nov. 555/2 Well, my friend, a Peter-ringer is one who tries to get his living by stealing carpet-bags. **1868** *Temple Bar* XXIV. 537 'What do you mean by 'lob-sneaking', and 'Peter-screwing'?' 'Why, 'lob' means the till, and 'Peter' means a safe. Stealing the till and opening the safe is what we call 'lob-sneaking' and 'Peter-screwing'.'

Peter (pī·tər), *sb.*[2] The name of Dr. Laurence Johnston *Peter* (b. 1919), Canadian-born U.S. educationalist and author, used *attrib.* in *Peter principle* (see quot. 1968). Also *Peter's principle.*

1968 L. J. PETER *Peter Principle* (1969) i. 25 My analysis of hundreds of cases of occupational incompetence led me on to formulate *The Peter Principle*: In a Hierarchy Every Employee Tends to Rise to His Level of Incompetence. **1969** *Sunday Times* (Colour Suppl.) 21 Dec. 30/2 What is now called the Peter Principle: the system by which a man is always promoted until he reaches a job which he cannot do. **1970** *Guardian Weekly* 25 July 6 Much blame must attach to the administrative system,.. which religiously follows the Peter Principle of promoting mediocrities. **1976** *Publishers Weekly* 15 Mar. 58/3 Most flibbertigibbet corporate president (maybe the Peter Principle applies here). **1978** *Jrnl. R. Soc. Arts* CXXVI. 273/2 In in-company situations, assessment centres can hopefully help avoid Peter's principle, whereby everyone is promoted to his level of incompetence. **1980** *Observer* 27 Jan. 4/3 There is a school of Westminster and Belfast thought which sees Mr Atkins as a classic example of the Peter Principle—promoted above his level of competence.

peter, *v.*[2] Add: **2.** Also simply *peter.* (Earlier and later examples.) Hence **pe·tering-out** *vbl. sb.*

1846 *Quincy* (Illinois) *Whig* 6 Jan. 1/4 When my mineral petered why they all Petered *me.* If so be I gets a lead, why I'm Mr. Tiff again. **1854** H. H. RILEY *Puddleford* vi. 84 He 'hoped this 'spectable meeting war n't going to Peter-out'. **1923** R. MACAULAY *Told by Idiot* III. 221 The year and the government petered towards their end. **1926** E. F. SPANNER *Naviators* 100 Lucky your engine petered out, Sterne. **1944** F. CLUNE *Red Heart* 6 The fabulous silver-lead wealth..has enticed a city of 15,000 inhabitants to arise in the desert wastes—and there they will continue to dwell until the lode peters. **1949** 'J. TEY' *Brat Farrar* xix. 170 The..petering-out of the poorer suburbs. **1955** *Times* 28 June 3/3 With the end of this partnership, however, the innings virtually petered out. **1976** *Quoddy Tides* (Eastport, Maine) 13 Aug. 4/4 Hurricane 'Belle'..petered out before reaching the Quoddy area.

b. *trans.* To exhaust; to cause or allow to peter out; const. *away*, to squander. Freq. as ppl. adj.

1869 *Overland Monthly* III. 127 After a long desert journey the oxen become much 'petered'. **1878** C. HALLOCK *Amer. Club List & Sportsman's Gloss.* p. viii/1 *Peter-out*, to fail; to exhaust; to collapse. **1943** *Amer. Speech* XVIII. 67/2 *Petered out* (exhausted), S.C., N.C., Tenn., La., Tex. **1956** B. HOLIDAY *Lady sings Blues* (1973) vi. 58 He wouldn't give us nothing but a lecture on how he saved his money and how we petered ours away. **1971** 'D. HALLIDAY' *Dolly & Doctor Bird* xvi. 228 It was another petered-out trail.

3. *intr. Whist* and *Bridge.* To play a high card followed by a low one. Cf. PETER *sb.*[1] 7 in Dict. and Suppl.

1887 *N. & Q.* 29 Oct. 356/1 The Blue Peter..is..used when a ship is about to start... Calling for trumps at whist or 'petering' is derived from this source. **1901** C. J. MELROSE *Bridge Whist* 38 Another whist convention, which may occasionally be employed with advantage in Bridge..is known variously as 'Petering', the 'trump signal' or the 'call for trumps'. **1939** N. DE V. HART *Bridge Players' Bedside Bk.* 141 At one time..a player petered to show two cards only of a suit. **1961** *Times* 7 June 8/3 My partner had not petered in hearts. **1976** *Country Life* 22 Jan. 202/1 West started by cashing two top diamonds, on which East petered.

4. *slang.* **a.** *intr.* (See quot. 1925.) **b.** *trans.* To blow open (a safe).

1925 *Flynn's* 7 Mar. 192/1 *Peter, v.*, to use knock-out drops; to use nitroglycerine. **1962** B. KNOX *Little Drops of Blood* iii. 65 The Dolman boys are going to peter a pawnshop safe tonight.

Peterborough[1] (pī·təɹ,bɒrŏ). Also **Peterboro.** *N. Amer.* The name of a town in Ontario used *attrib.* and *ellipt.* to designate a type of canoe (orig. built there), made entirely of wood.

1882 *Forest & Stream* 2 Nov. 277/1 There is the open Peterboro' canoe, so familiar to the Canadian eye. **1895** *Rudder* Sept. 215 Eleven paddling canoes—eight Peterboro's and three Rushton—and the Cruiser, complete the fleet. **1897** J. W. TYRRELL *Across Sub-Arctics of Canada* ii. 20 We launched our handsome 'Peterboroughs' in the great stream. **1901** *Daily Colonist* (Victoria, B.C.) 30 Oct. 6/2 We portaged around it on the way up by packing our Peterboro up a hill one hundred feet high, taking us a whole day. **1966** *Canad. Geogr. Jrnl.* Sept. 78/3 John Stephenson..later came up with the excellent cedar rib craft known the world over as the Peterborough Canoe. **1973** D. ANDERSEN *Ways Harsh & Wild* iii. 86, I set a net in an eddy and later paddled Ted's Peterborough canoe down to check.

Peterborough[2] (pī·təɹ,bɒrŏ). The name of a town in eastern England, site of a phase of the Neolithic Age: used to denote the type of civilization of that period, and the materials or people associated with its culture.

1910 *Archaeologia* LXII. 346 The characteristic decoration of the drinking-cup or beaker is well known, and full justice has been done to the Peterborough series by our Fellow, Mr. Praetorius. **1922** *Antiquaries Jrnl.* II. 231 The Peterborough pottery seems to bear all the signs of its makers advancing in ceramic skill by gradual stages. **1935** HUXLEY & HADDON *We Europeans* vii. 237 The 'Peterborough' ware was brought from the Baltic by long-headed people who buried their dead in long barrows. **1939** V. G. CHILDE *Dawn European Civilization* (ed. 3) xviii. 306 In Norfolk and even Wiltshire Peterborough folk..were associated with its exploitation. *Ibid.* 317 Skara Brae and Peterborough traditions survived. **1943** J. & C. HAWKES *Prehist. Brit.* ii. 47 These are the Peterborough people, largely descendants of the old Mesolithic inhabitants of Britain, who, while adopting certain Neolithic accomplishments such as potting, herding and simple husbandry, continued to follow the old mode of life as hunters and fishers. **1947** V. G. CHILDE *Dawn European Civilization* (ed. 4) xviii. 323 In the standard Peterborough ware the rims are thickened and the shallow bowls are richly decorated. **1951** *Proc. Prehist. Soc.* XVII. 119 The associations and chronology of these Group VI factories and their products are firmly fixed in the Neolithic with emphasis in favour of the Peterborough phase. **1954** S. PIGGOTT *Neolithic Cultures* xi. 303 We can now see that Peterborough pottery is distinctive of only one variant within a group of Secondary Neolithic cultures. *Ibid.* 312 (*heading*) Relationships of the Peterborough culture. **1967** *Antiquaries Jrnl.* XLVII. 201 Its sharply formed tripartite upper half, and the decoration of this so lavishly by whipped-cord impression, support those traits in strongly recalling Neolithic antecedents, among the Mortlake bowls..of British 'Peterborough' ware.

peterman. Add: **3. b.** (See quots.) *slang.*

1897 ELDRIDGE & WATTS *Our Rival* xi. 289 The rogue's name for the professional users of 'knockout drops' is Peter-men or Peter-players. **1904** 'No. 1500' *Life in Sing Sing* 256/2 *Peter man*,..person who administers a drug for the purpose of robbery. **1908** *Sun* (N.Y.) 2 Mar. 2/2 A peterman is one who uses knockout drops as an aid to robbery.

c. A safe-blower. *slang.*

1900 'FLYNT' & 'WALTON' *Powers that Prey* 176 Sliger's record, both as 'peter-man' and convict, was produced. **1936** J. G. BRANDON *Pawnshop Murder* i. 5 Your flash 'peterman' is as gentle-natured as the average curate. **1950** R. CHANDLER *Let.* 18 May in *R. Chandler Speaking* (1966) 80 Opening a good safe (without a time lock) requires expensive and heavy tools, the finest drills either to drill out the lock or to get in the nitro if he is a peterman. **1960** *Observer* 24 Jan. 5/1 Gelignite in plastic sticks..was the British peterman's basic material. **1968** P. N. WALKER *Carnaby & Gaolbreakers* i. 13 Well, you'd never be a peter man, or a breaker in a month of Sundays. **1973** 'B. GRAEME' *Two & Two make Five* vii. 68 The wall safe..would [not] have presented much difficulty to an expert peterman. **1977** J. WAINWRIGHT *Nest of Rats* I. vii. 46 The genuine peterman—the safe-breaker who takes a personal pride in pitting his wits against those of the safe-makers.

Peter Pan. [The name of the boy hero of J. M. Barrie's play *Peter Pan, the boy who wouldn't grow up* (1904).] **1.** Used *attrib.* to designate various styles of clothing, esp. **Peter Pan collar** (also with lower-case initials), a flat collar with rounded ends, often white or light-coloured.

1908 S. FORD *Side-Stepping with Shorty* iv. 60 She was sportin' a Peter Pan peekaboo that would have made Comstock gasp. **1909** *Westm. Gaz.* 10 July 15/1 The collars and cuffs are what we call 'Peter Pan'.., edged with Valenciennes. **1923** *Daily Mail* 12 June 1 (Advt.), Can also be had with Robespierre or Peter Pan collar. **1933** M. LUTYENS *Forthcoming Marriages* 204 She was wearing a white Peter Pan collar over a little blue cape. **1948** 'J. TEY' *Franchise Affair* xiv. 148 Miss Tuff had worn peter-pan collars over her dark frock for twenty years. **1958** *Vogue* Sept. 133 Clothes for children with puff sleeves, peter pan collars. **1960** *Times* 15 Jan. 14/3 A white silk shirt with a frilled Peter Pan collar. **1975** *Listener* 10 July 46/1 The maids, they used to wear what we call their print dresses in the mornings. In the afternoon they changed into blue alpaca or black, with white Peter Pan collar and little cuffs.

2. Used allusively for an immature adult (usu. a man); one who is emotionally (occas. physically) retarded. Also *attrib.*

1914 G. B. SHAW *What I really wrote about War* (1930) ii. 109 It is frightful to think of the powers which Europe ..left in the hands of this Peter Pan [*sc.* the Kaiser]. **1927** A. HUXLEY *Proper Stud.* 163 An electorate composed in a great part of mental Peter Pans. **1931** J. S. HUXLEY *What dare I Think?* ii. 62 The Peter Pan type of semi-dwarf who, though perfectly proportioned, never grows up fully. **1956** I. BROMIGE *Enchanted Garden* II. iii. 99 'Fiona..has the wide-eyed simplicity of eternal youth.' 'A Peter Pan.' **1958** *Sunday Express* 15 June 15/2 Bogarde has still got his hooks into the Peter Pan racket... He is still prowling the screen, demanding mother love from his millions of female fans. **1971** *Guardian* 21 Oct. 6/4 Professor Desmond Pond... Professor of psychiatry at the London Hospital,..told of highly-educated students who became 'Peter Pans' and never managed to leave adolescence. **1976** J. WAINWRIGHT *Bastard* v. 76 He is something of a museum-piece..Peter Pan, in person. The fink who never grew up..never acknowledged the responsibilities of adulthood. **1978** *Time* 3 July 48/2 Warren's conquests of women are not totally successful... But the Peter Pan quality in Warren is very attractive to some. He teaches them to fly, and they have extraordinary experiences with him. Then they grow up and go on, and he keeps flying. Like Peter Pan, he always comes back to another little girl who's ready to fly off with him to never-never land.

Hence **Peter Pa·nic** (*nonce*) [joc. f. PANIC *sb.*[2]], confused, childish behaviour; also as *adj.* [-IC], characteristic of a Peter Pan; **Peter Pa·n(n)ish** *a.* [-ISH[1]] = **Peter Panic* adj.; hence *Peter Pan(n)ishness*; **Peter Pa·nnery, peter-pannery**, immaturity; childish quality or behaviour; **Peter Pa·nning** (see quot. 1974).

1914 'I. HAY' *Knight on Wheels* (ed. 2) xiv. 143 Mr. Mablethorpe remained as incorrigibly Peter Pannish as ever. Although his hair was whitening..he declined to grow up. **1928** F. E. BAILY *Golden Vanity* xvi. 252 They were all in the early twenties except Joe, and he had an eternal Peter Pan-ish-ness which made the passage of time as marked by the calendar quite immaterial in his case. **1934** R. CAMPBELL *Broken Record* 160 Though not predisposed to this Peter Panic, I had considerable time to see it at work at first hand. **1937** *Times Lit. Suppl.* 10 July 502/3 If we are seeking to know what gives a thinness to much of his fiction..it was not 'Peter Pannishness' in the sense of shrinking from adult reality. **1958** *Listener* 12 June 987/3 The Peter-Panish English is not entirely the fault of the translator. **1960** *Spectator* 2 Sept. 345 An occasional embarrassing lapse into peter-pannery. **1962** A. HUXLEY *Island* ix. 152 A year in jail won't cure a Peter Pan of his endocrine disbalance... For Peter Panic delinquency, what you need is early diagnosis. **1962** *John o'London's* 2 Aug. 115/3 General air of Peter Pannery. **1974** *Daily Tel.* 12 Mar. 3/2 So many people have invented fictitious children to evade income tax that Inland Revenue officials have introduced their own catch phrase for it 'Peter Panning'. **1975** *Listener* 9 Oct. 464/3 To use one's children's slang is Peter Pannish. **1978** *Radio Times* 28 Jan. 13/4 You could say that Lewis was a latter-day Lewis Carroll... There is a Peter Panishness to his heroes and echoes of Ratty and Badger in his anthropomorphics.

Petersen grab (pī·təɪsən). *Marine Biol.* [Named after its inventor, Carl Georg Johan *Petersen* (1860–1928), Danish marine biologist, who first described it in 1911 (*Rep. Danish Biol. Station* XX. 47).] A kind of grab for obtaining a sample of the bed of a body of water, consisting of two jaws semicircular in vertical cross-section and hinged along the top, arranged so as to close automatically on contact with the bottom.

1923 *Sci. Investigations, 1922* (Fishery Board Scotland) III. 1 (*title*) Preliminary survey of the Scottish waters of the North Sea by the Petersen grab. **1950** *Biol. Rev.* XXV. 309 The Petersen grab will only produce reliable results on the softer bottoms. **1970** tr. *J. Schwoerbel's Methods Hydrobiol.* iv. 118 In larger rivers the Petersen grab can be used... The grab weighs 40 kg.

Petersen graph (pī·təɪsən). *Math.* [Named after Julius *Petersen* (1839–1910), Danish mathematician, who first devised it (*L'Intermédiaire des Mathématiciens* (1898) V. 227).] A graph having ten vertices and fifteen lines, which may be drawn as a pentagram disposed symmetrically within a pentagon, each vertex of the latter being joined by a line to the nearest vertex of the former.

1947 *Proc. Camb. Philos. Soc.* XLIII. 460 The 5-cage is the 'Petersen graph'. **1962** O. ORE *Theory of Graphs* xv. 240 The so-called Petersen graph has the form indicated in Figure 15.1.3. It is regular of degree 3 and order 10. It was first introduced by Petersen as an illustration of a graph with $\rho = 3$ which is not the sum of 3 subgraphs of first degree. **1976** *Sci. Amer.* Apr. 127/1 The other class of uncolorable trivalent maps Tait missed are all nonplanar (impossible to draw on the plane without at least one intersecting edge). The simplest example, known as the Petersen graph, is shown in the upper illustration at the right.

Petersham. Add: **b.** (Examples.)

1873 *Young Englishwoman* Mar. 147/2 Waistband *Petersham*, and all the odds and ends of needlework. **1930** V. SACKVILLE-WEST *Edwardians* ii. 62 Miss Wace..affected a dress of heliotrope serge with a stiff petersham belt. **1957** *Terms & Definitions* (Textile Inst.) (ed. 3) 82 *Petersham ribbon* (*millinery*), a ribbon usually with silk or rayon warp and having single picks of relatively coarse weft. *Ibid.*, *Petersham ribbon* (*skirt*), a narrow-fabric having a pronounced rib weft-way composed of one or more picks per rib and having lateral stiffness. **1972** *Daily Tel.* 18 May 9/2 The jacket was edged in navy petersham and fastened with navy and gold buttons.

c. A style of hat.

1825 H. WILSON *Mem.* III. 65 His little Petersham hat seemed to have been remit de nouveau, for the third time, at least.

Petertide (pī·təɪtəid). [f. PETER *sb.*[1] + TIDE *sb.*] The 29th of June (the feast of St. Peter in the Church of England and of St. Peter and St. Paul in the Roman Catholic Church), or the period round about it.

1912 C. MACKENZIE *Carnival* xxxiv. 349 Well, being in the city, I suppose we must follow city manners, but darn 'ee, I never thought to go gazing at dancing like maidens at Petertide. **1974** *Daily Tel.* 3 July 16 Southwark..has worked out a fair system. This accounts for the large number of ordination candidates over Petertide. **1975** *Church Times* 7 Mar. 12/5, I look forward to my ordination at Petertide conscious of the numerous people who have made it possible.

pethidine (pe·þidīn). *Pharm.* [f. P(IPER)IDINE with insertion of *eth* from ETHYL, METHYL.] A narcotic analgesic (usu. given, orally or intramuscularly, as the hydrochloride, a colourless crystalline compound) which has actions similar to those of morphine but of shorter duration and is less addictive; ethyl 1-methyl-4-phenylpiperidine-4-carboxylate, $C_{15}H_{21}NO_2$.

1942 *Lancet* 22 Aug. 234/2 Pethidine hydrochloride, a synthetic compound closely allied to morphine in composition, and combining the analgesic effect of morphine with the spasmolytic effect of the atropine group and papaverine, is issued by Roche Products. **1942** *Ibid.* 24 Oct. 487 Fairly recent..is the carboxylic acid ethyl ester of 1-methyl-4-phenylpiperidine, officially named pethidine by the GMC a year ago and known on the continent as 'Dolantin' and in the United States as 'Demerol'. **1947** *Daily Tel.* 1 Mar. 3/4 Several bottles found in the man's room were marked 'pethidine'. **1955** *Times* 2 July 4/3 The annual Government report to the United Nations.. estimates that there are 317 known drug addicts... Heroin and pethidine were used by 17 per cent. and 16 per cent. respectively. **1962** [see *MEPERIDINE]. **1972** *Nature* 15 Dec. 411/2 Hysterotomy patients received pethidine 100 mg postoperatively for analgesia. **1974** M. C. GERALD *Pharmacol.* xiii. 247 Meperidine or pethidine, as this drug is more commonly called outside the United States, was fortuitously discovered in 1939 as the result of a search for atropine-like agents possessing antispasmodic activity. This compound was the first totally synthetic narcotic analgesic agent.

‖ **pétillant** (petiyaṅ), *a.* [Fr.] Crackling, sparkling, lively; *spec.* of semi-sparkling wine (see quot. 1965).

1881 C. C. HARRISON *Woman's Handiwork* III. 215 Permit your wood-fire to sink into the *pétillant* stage upon the tiled hearth. **1902** G. MEREDITH *Let.* 19 Apr. (1970) III. 1440, I wish I were about in the world to give you communications more *pétillantes*. **1938** *Times Lit. Suppl.* 15 Jan. 43/1 Her spirit is..more fiery, its flame richer, more consuming and far less *pétillant* than before. The sparkle, which made her such an entertaining, quick-witted.. character on her first appearance has now almost vanished. **1955** A. LICHINE *Wines of France* (ed. 2) 214 Mousseux and pétillant wines are rarely imported into the United States, largely because these lesser wines carry the same high duty as fine Champagnes, and the resulting prices make them poor value. **1959** *Times* 14 Nov. 9/7 The light pétillant white wines of Neuchâtel are famous. **1960** *House & Garden* Aug. 71/3 It [*sc.* a wine] has a slight prickle—it is what the French call *pétillant*. **1965** O. A. MENDELSOHN *Dict. Drink* 257 *Pétillant*, French term, meaning crackling or sparkling, applied to slightly sparkling wines, much less heavily charged than mousseux. **1971** *Homes & Gardens* Aug. 102/1 These pétillant wines are now all the rage in France. **1974** *Times* 16 Feb. 15/4 The only successful *pétillant* (semi-sparkling) wine so far produced in the Eastern Mediterranean is Bellapais.

So **pétilla·nce** *sb.*

1951 R. POSTGATE *Plain Man's Guide to Wine* iv. 87 *Pétillance* occurs when the wine in bottle is still working, and produces some natural gas. **1974** *Times* 18 May (Summer Drinking Suppl.) p. i/2 A good muscadet..with its faint *pétillance*, more felt than seen. **1975** *Times* 28 June 13/3 A deliciously fragrant rosé... There is a slight liveliness, verging on *pétillance*.

petit, *a.* (*sb.*) Add: **5. petit battement (sur le cou-de-pied, sur le talon)**, (see quots. 1957); **petit beurre**, a sweet butter biscuit; **petit bleu**, a telegram in France, esp. one sent by the pneumatic post in Paris; **petit déjeuner**, breakfast in France, and by extension, elsewhere; **petit four**, a small fancy cake, biscuit, or sweet, usu. served with the dessert course of a meal; also *fig.*; **petit nègre** (see quots.); **petit nom**, a pet-name; **petit pain**, a small bread roll; **petits paquets**, name of a game of some kind; **petit poussin**, a young chicken; **petits** (erron. **petit**) **pois**, young sweet green peas; **petits soins**, small attentions or services [*lit.* small cares]; **petit suisse**, a cream cheese (see quot. 1966); **petit tranchet** (*Archæol.*), a small stone artefact whose blade is produced by transverse-flaking; **petit verre** (earlier and later examples).

1914 Petit battement [see *pas de chat* s.v. *PAS 2]. **1930** CRASKE & BEAUMONT *Theory & Pract. Allegro in Classical Ballet* 66 Bring the *right* foot *sur le cou de pied devant* and execute four *petite battements devants* (that is, beaten without passing). **1957** G. B. L. WILSON *Dict. Ballet* 48 *Petit Battement sur le Talon*, lit. small beating on the heel, a movement in which the danseuse, on the point and supported by her partner, lightly beats the heel of the supporting foot with the sole of the working foot. *Ibid.*, *Petit Battement sur le Cou-de-pied*, an exercise at the bar in which the dancer beats lightly with the working foot, which may be fully extended or partially relaxed, to the front and back of the cou-de-pied of the supporting leg. **1906** *Mrs. Beeton's Bk. Househ. Managem.* facing p. 1432 Biscuits... Cream Toast... Wine... Petit Beurre. **1913** C. MACKENZIE *Sinister St.* I. I. ix. 130 They all sat down at midnight,..not at all too much tired to sip grenadine sucrée and to crunch Petit Beurre biscuits. **1937** J. BETJEMAN *Continual Dew* 22 He gives his Ovaltine a stir And nibbles at a 'petit beurre'. **1958** I. MURDOCH *Bell* ii. 39 She indicated a large biscuit tin... 'No more Petit Beurre,' Peter Topglass was saying meditatively to himself. **1967** V. NABOKOV *Speak, Memory* (rev. ed.) ii. 46 A couple of broken Petit-Beurre biscuits she had found on a plate. **1975** *Times* 13 Mar. 14/7 An expensive-looking parcel..revealed a pound of *petit beurre* biscuits. **1908** W. S. MAUGHAM *Magician* x. 171 The note..was a *petit bleu* sent off from the Gare du Nord. **1920** D. H. LAWRENCE *Touch & Go* 7 It may be that coal-owners are like the *petit bleu* arrangement, a system of vacuum tubes for whooshing Bradburys about from one to the other. **1924** W. J. LOCKE *Coming of Amos* xvi. 204 She had just finished dressing when a *petit-bleu*—a letter sent by pneumatic post, was delivered. **1933** 'G. ORWELL' *Down & Out* vi. 44 An agency..sent me a *petit bleu.* **1978** R. GRAYSON *Murders at Impasse Louvain* xvi. 113 He had sent her..a 'petit bleu' or message by the pneumatic telegraph. **1895** E. DOWSON *Let.* 9 Dec. (1967) 326 After a petit déjeuner at the Crémerie I get hungry again. **1909** W. J. LOCKE *Septimus* iii. 37, I skip afternoon tea and dinner and supper, and *petit déjeuner*. **1914** R. BROOKE *Lett.* (1968) 561 Up at 6 and bathe. *Petit déjeuner* of coffee and fruit 6.45. **1926** F. W. CROFTS *Inspector French & Cheyne Mystery* xv. 213 The 4.50 fr. for *petit dejeuner* suggested a fairly good hotel. **1936** J. BUCHAN *Island of Sheep* xii. 228 The fashion of the household was for a skimpy *petit déjeuner* and then an elaborate midday meal. **1963** N. MARSH *Dead Water* (1964) v. 125, I took my *petit dejeuner* in my room. **1972** L. BACHMANN *Ultimate Act* v. 39 Your *petit déjeuner* is waiting. **1884** L. TROUBRIDGE *Life amongst Troubridges* (1966) 172 We all went to Charbonnel..for iced coffees and *petits fours*. **1898** H. A. DE SALIS *Housewife's Referee* 266 *Petits Fours*, small fancy biscuits. **1904** H. JAMES *Golden Bowl* II. xlii. 367 Amerigo..selected for presentation to the other visitor a plate of *petits fours*. **1908** [see *CRYSTALLIZED *ppl. a.* 3]. **1948** *Good Housek. Cookery Bk.* 59 *Petits fours*, very small fancy cakes, iced cakes and biscuits served at the end of the formal dinner. Crystallised fruits, and caramellised and fondant-coated fruits are often included in the petits fours. **1961** [see *KUGELHUPF]. **1970** *New Yorker* 19 Sept. 31/1 The French served champagne and *petits fours*. **1974** *Publishers Weekly* 25 Mar. 55/2 Reichler's little prose petit fours accompanying the book's 100-plus photos..are toothsome and on-the-nose. **1964** E. PALMER tr. *Martinet's Elem. Gen. Linguistics* v. 156 '*Petit nègre*' is the nearest equivalent in French to pidgin. **1972** J. L. DILLARD *Black English* i. 22 Pidgin versions of French (still represented in West Africa by *Petit Nègre*) and English began developing in the factories. *Ibid.* iii. 78 Pidgin French (called *Petit Nègre*)..came to the New World at about the same time. **1974** *Times* 7 Jan. 16/3 Many [immigrants] get by on a pidgin language which the French call 'petit negre'. **1867** O. LOGAN in *Galaxy* Aug. 442 'Well, you see,' replied he, referring to her familiarly by her *petit nom*, 'Leo hates the leg business as much as anybody but, bless you, nothing else pays now-a-days; so what can she do?' **1939** W. FORTESCUE *There's Rosemary* lxxi. 368 After dinner she said gaily: 'And now for your important business with B.D. (her *petit nom* for General Long).' **1841** THACKERAY in *Fraser's Mag.* June 718/2 I..swallow..the greater portion of my petit pain, too, before my second dish arrives. **1924** A. D. SEDGWICK *Little French Girl* I. i. 3 The long buttered *petits pains.* **1963** J. CREASEY *Depths* vi. 47 Sitting on the terrace, eating croissants or *petits pains.* **1977** E. AMBLER *Send no more Roses* vii. 141, I had one of the petits-pains just delivered by the village bakery. **1821** M. EDGEWORTH *Let.* 19 Dec. (1971) 298 Went to the *hall of the marble table* and there played at *petits paquets* (not time to describe) a great deal of running and laughing among pretty men and pretty maids. **1874** L. TROUBRIDGE *Life amongst Troubridges* (1966) 88 After tea we..played at Petit Pacquet in the field outside. **1902** Petit poussin [see *milk chicken* s.v. *MILK *sb.* 10]. **1926–7** *Army & Navy Stores Catal.* 69/1 Poultry..Petit Poussin (English)—each 3/-. **1927** *Daily Express* 1 Apr. 5, English poultry is dear, but there are spring chicken and petits poussins, ducklings and plovers' eggs. **1961** *Harrods Food News* 16/2 Poultry..English Petit Poussin. **1820** M. EDGEWORTH *Let.* 4 June (1979) 144, I give you one dinner..2d service—œufs au jus—petits pois (stewed)—lettuce (ditto). **1855** F. DUBERLY *Jrnl.* 21 Mar. in E. E. P. Tisdall *Mrs. Duberly's Campaigns* (1963) v. 134 We made purchases of chickens, carrots, *petits pois verts* and various other necessaries. **1916** A. BENNETT *Lion's Share* xi. 87, I shall like very much to hear the details of this story of *petits pois.* **1951** *Good Housek. Home Encycl.* 591/1 Peas vary in size from the small 'petit pois' to large ones. **1952** A. GRIMBLE *Pattern of Islands* 81 An exquisite little shoulder of frozen lamb, *and* some onions, *and* potatoes, AND a tin of real French petits pois. **1961** J. CREASEY *Follow Toff* xx. 171 He served the duck..the *petit pois,* tiny new potatoes. **1820** A. OPIE *Tales of Heart* IV. 292 Melville dined at home that day, and paid her voluntarily all those *petits soins* which she had demanded of Arthur. **1825** H. WILSON *Mem.* III. 50, I never..heard of one.. who was so eternally au [*sic*] petits soins, and paid a woman the unremitting attention which I received from Worcester. **1847** F. A. KEMBLE *Let.* 17 Dec. in *Rec. Later Life* (1882) III. 318 The 'small attentions', *les petits soins* of affection. **1857** C. KINGSLEY *Two Yrs. Ago* II. iii. 59 Elsley showed Lucia no *petits soins.* **1959** *Times* 31 Oct. 7/4 All the barometer ever gets in the way of *petits soins* is this allegedly deleterious tapping. *c* **1906** A. JOHN *Let.* in *Listener* (1972) 6 July 10/1 He is always asking for petits-suisses which are unheard of in this country. **1951** [see *GERVAIS]. **1962** J. BRAINE *Life at Top* iii. 53 He selected a piece of Gorgonzola, then..pointed out a *petit Suisse.* **1966** P. V. PRICE *France: Food & Wine Guide* 284 *Petit Suisse,* a small, round, fresh cream cheese, evolved by a farmer's wife..near Gournay, about the middle of the nineteenth century. **1979** H. MCCLOY *Smoking Mirror* ii. 12 A delicious cream cheese called *petit suisse.* **1939** W. B. WRIGHT *Tools & Man* ix. 76 The microliths are predominantly trapezes or *petits tranchets* for use as arrow heads. **1949** *Proc. Prehist. Soc.* XV. 127 A flint assemblage including petit-tranchet derivative arrowheads and one leaf-arrowhead. **1954** S. PIGGOTT *Neolithic Cultures* ii. 44 An arrowhead of the 'derived *petit-tranchet*' type. **1963** H. N. SAVORY in Foster & Alcock *Culture & Environment* iii. 33 In South Wales, the main overlap of this new element was with the Western Neolithic rather than the Beaker Culture, as is shown by the regular appearance of *petit-tranchet* derivatives in surface collections where leaf arrowheads predominate. *a* **1855** C. BRONTË *Professor* (1857) I. viii. 141 They proposed a 'petit verre', I declined. **1860** *Once a Week* 23 June 606/2 He must be an unfortunate Frenchman indeed who cannot contrive to get a *bouillon* and a *petit verre* at the railway station. **1939** AUDEN & ISHERWOOD *Journey to War* 292 Self-confident among the laughter and the *petits verres.*

‖ **petit bourgeois** (pəti būɪʒwa). Also fem. **petite bourgeoise**; pl. **petits bourgeois**; fem. **petites bourgeoises.** [Fr., lit. 'little citizen': see BOURGEOIS *sb.*[1] and *a.*] A member of the middle or commercial classes in a society; freq. in derogatory use, one judged to have conventional or conservative political and social attitudes. Also *fig.* and (freq. with hyphen) *attrib.* or as *adj.* See also *PETTY BOURGEOIS.

1853 C. BRONTË *Villette* III. xliii. 338 Should you object to beginning with three petite bourgeoises, the Demoiselles Miret? **1859** M. ARNOLD *England & Italian Question* iii. 16 How indignant he was with the townspeople, the *petits bourgeois.* **1887** F. ENGELS in Moore & Aveling tr. *Marx's Capital* I. i. 39 It is, of course, highly desirable in the eyes of the petit bourgeois, for whom the production of commodities is the ne plus ultra of human freedom and individual independence, that the inconveniences resulting from this character of commodities not being directly exchangeable, should be removed. *Ibid.* ii. 59 We may form an estimate of the shrewdness of the petit-bourgeois socialism, which, while perpetuating the production of commodities, aims at abolishing the 'antagonism' between money and commodities, and consequently,.. at abolishing money itself: We might just as well try to retain Catholicism without the Pope. **1897** G. B. SHAW *Our Theatres in Nineties* (1932) III. 79 She suddenly drops from an Egyptian warrior queen into a naughty English *petite bourgeoise.* **1931** *Times Lit. Suppl.* 1 Oct. 755/1 'Elise Hermann'..takes the reader into a *petit bourgeois* world. **1939** S. SPENDER tr. *Toller's Pastor Hall* II. 82 We called freedom a petit bourgeois phrase, so little did we know what slavery is. **1942** E. WAUGH *Put out More Flags* iii. 216 The provincial *petit-bourgeois* youth floundering and groping in the gloom of Teutonic adolescence. **1943** C. GRAY *Contingencies* (1947) i. 11 Arthur Rimbaud..sought refuge in the existence of a typical French *petit bourgeois* from the terrible and terrifying realities which confronted him. **1958** *Times Lit. Suppl.* 19 Sept. 525/3 Comrade Nemeth is an ambitious bureaucrat, anxious to allay the guilt of his *petit bourgeois* birth by utter conformity to proletarian party standards. **1959** N. MAILER *Advts. for Myself* (1961) 163 Sam and Eleanor do not think of themselves as really belonging to a class, and they feel that the Sperbers and Rossmans are petit-bourgeois. **1973** *Sat. Rev.* (U.S.) 25 Sept. 22/3 The children of an ideology dominated by *petit bourgeois* sexual repression. *a* **1974** R. CROSSMAN *Diaries* (1976) II. 160 His [*sc.* Harold Wilson's] natural modesty has remained unchanged. So have his modest tastes, his simple liking of high tea, his completely unaffected petit-bourgeois habits. **1975** A. BEEVOR *Violent Brink* iii. 56 She was a fraud; a *petit* [sic] *bourgeoise* in revolt..for emotional reasons. **1976** J. M. BROWNJOHN tr. *Kirst's Time for Payment* iii. 58 You're putting a petit bourgeois cat among the pigeons.

Hence **petite** (erron. **petit**) **bourgeoisie** (pətīt būɪʒwazī), the middle classes collectively (see BOURGEOISIE, *PETTY BOURGEOISIE).

1916 A. E. GALLATIN *Certain Contemporaries* 53 In all his studies of bohemians, vagabonds and the *petite bourgeoisie,* there exists only tenderness and sympathy. **1928** F. STARK *Let.* 26 Oct. (1974) I. 179 They are all good—Scotch of the very petite bourgeoisie—city folk. **1930** *N. & Q.* 10 May 325/1 The intellectual man is.. frequently drawn from the peasantry or the *petite bourgeoisie.* **1949** N. MARSH *Swing, Brother, Swing* xi. 250 He..and our Mr. Eton-and-Oxford Detective-Sergeant Salis got into a discussion about the *petit bourgeoisie.* **1950** A. L. ROWSE *England of Elizabeth* v. 174 The petite-bourgeoisie were a strong element in Cromwell's support. **1970** *Times* 11 Mar. 11/2 There is today a strong Conservative government in power, to which the petite bourgeoisie naturally looks. **1976** *Brit. Jrnl. Sociol.* XXVII. 50 It is a good idea to bear in mind Rosenberg's taunt: 'Amateur sociologists have generally concluded that the petit-bourgeoisie was that mysterious class with the aid of which Hitler and Mussolini won their victory.'

petite, *a.* Add: **2.** (Further examples.) Also used *absol.*

1901 [see *JAPANESEY, JAPANESY *a.*] **1935** H. EDIB *Clown & his Daughter* vii. 33 Durnev Hanim did come in, a *petite* person with large innocent brown eyes and very black eyebrows. **1958** *Times Lit. Suppl.* 10 Oct. 573/3 Being American, of course, fifteen-year-old Franzie, petite and bouncy, has begun her sentimental education long before she meets the 'surf-bums' on Malibu beach. **1960** *News Chron.* 12 Sept. 6/1 The dress is from a newish range for the petite. **1972** M. KAYE *Lively Game of Death* ii. 9 Some men would probably dismiss her as 'small'... 'Petite' is *le mot juste.*

2. b. Used of small sizes in women's clothing. Also used *absol.*

1929 *Radio Times* 8 Nov. 439/2 This Stylish Coat.. From Petite to Matrons' Sizes. **1960** *Harper's Bazaar* Oct. 5 Afternoon dress..in 'petite' sizes for the 5′2″ and under. **1974** *Times* 26 Apr. 7/7 The tights..are in three sizes—Petite, Medium or Large. **1978** *N.Y. Times* 29 Mar. A6 (Advt.), You'll find whatever you're looking for in misses (6 to 18), petites (6 to 16), juniors (5 to 13) and women's ($16\frac{1}{2}$ to $24\frac{1}{2}$) in the brightest spring colors.

3. petite amie (see quot. 1966); **petite culture,** small farming; **petite marmite,** soup of meat and vegetables served in a marmite; **petite noblesse,** the lesser nobility in France; **petite vitesse,** slow train.

1848 MILL *Pol. Econ.* I. I. ix. 179 The working of the *petite culture* cannot be fairly judged where the small cultivator is merely a tenant. **1883** C. M. YONGE *Stray Pearls* I. iv. 32 He had only known of two ladies who had followed their husbands to the wars, and both of them only belonged to the *petite noblesse.* **1887** F. ENGELS in Moore & Aveling tr. *Marx's Capital* II. xxvi. 739 The labourers of the towns [in Northern Italy] were driven *en masse* into the country, and gave an impulse..to the *petite culture,* carried on in the form of gardening. *Ibid.* xxvii. 741 Japan, with its purely feudal organisation of landed property and its developed *petite culture,* gives a much truer picture of the European middle class than all our history books. **1896** E. DOWSON *Let.* c 24 Apr. (1967) 355 Here, I have no petites Amies. **1905** *Spectator* 7 Jan. 13/2 France is notoriously a country of *petite culture.* **1906** A. FILIPPINI *Internat. Cook Bk.* 250 Petite Marmite. .. It is very important that during the two and a half hours it should simmer exceedingly slowly. **1913** T. E. LAWRENCE *Home Lett.* (1954) 277 On a railway with one train a day in four hours should take three days and *petite vitesse* ten days is a mystery. **1921** BEERBOHM *Lett. to R. Turner* (1964) 258, I..told him that you had ordered the book for me, and that I expected it had been sent by *petite vitesse.* **1923** A. HUXLEY *Let.* 2 Sept. (1969) 219 The bulk of the luggage..is still on its way from England, coming by *petite vitesse* which appears to be extremely petite. **1924** Petite noblesse [see *HAUTE BOURGEOISIE]. **1945** A. L. SIMON *Conc. Encycl. Gastron.* VII. 93 *Petite marmite,* the name given in restaurants to a *consommé*.. served in the earthenware pot in which it was made. **1966** A. J. BLISS *Dict. Foreign Words & Phrases* 279 *Petite amie*.., the female friend of a middle-aged man. 20c. Always with the implication that the friendship is not wholly Platonic. **1972** R. MAYNE *Europeans* v. 102 Gay Paree..home of the *grisette,* the *petite amie,* the bedroom farce. **1978** W. GARNER *Möbius Trip* v. 111 His *petite amie*..had raised the subject of marriage. **1978** G. VIDAL *Kalki* viii. 191, I narrowly avoided a lapful of petite marmite as one bemused agent's ladle missed the soup plate.

4. *Biol.* Used, freq. as *sb.,* to designate certain variant strains of yeast that are characterized by the cytoplasmically heritable lack of mitochondrial constituents and tend to form small colonies. [The sense is due to B. Ephrussi et al., who used F. *petite colonie* (*Annales de l'Inst. Pasteur* (1949) LXXVII. 64).]

1951 *Genetics* XXXVI. 572 In many strains of yeast apparently non-genetic, cytochrome-deficient variants exhibiting a single strong alpha absorption band at 550 mu occur frequently ('petites'). **1968** *Jrnl. Molecular Biol.* XXXVII. 493 In cytoplasmic petite mutants no changes were observed in the major band. **1971** D. J. COVE *Genetics* viii. 115 It is possible to get mutant strains of yeast which are incapable of metabolising sugars oxidatively; such strains grow almost as well as the wild type on glucose, which they ferment, but on carbon sources such as acetate, which can only be metabolised oxidatively by the tricarboxylic acid cycle, they are unable to grow. These strains, called petite, can often be shown to be abnormal in their mitochondrial constituents. Some have certain mitochondrial enzymes and cytochromes absent, and others have the relative proportions of these components altered. **1978** *Nature* 23 Feb. 750/2 Cytoplasmically inherited respiratory deficient mutants termed *petites,* were first described in baker's yeast over 20 years ago.

petitionable (pĭti·ʃənăb'l), *a.* [f. PETITION *sb.* + -ABLE.] That allows, justifies, or involves, the making of a petition.

1898 *Westm. Gaz.* 14 Mar. 2/1 A few suggestions for amending the Bankruptcy Act... 1. Reduce the petitionable amount from fifty pounds to five.

petitionary, *a.* Add: **2.** (Earlier example.)

1604 MARSTON *Malcontent* I. v. sig. B4 Petitionarie vassailes licking the pauement with their slauish knees.

petitive (pe·titiv), *a.* [f. L. *pĕtītus* pa. pple. of *pĕtĕre* to ask: see -IVE.] Of, relating to, or expressing a prayer or request; = PRECATIVE *a.*

1923 J. S. HUXLEY *Ess. Biologist* vii. 297 Although the value of prayer persists in so far as it is meditative and a self-purification of the mind, yet its commonly accepted petitive value must fall to the ground. **1964** E. A. NIDA *Toward Sci. Transl.* ix. 201 Mode (or mood), which defines the psychological background of the action, involves principally such categories as possibility..necessity.. and desire (desiderative, optative, and petitive). **1977** *Maledicta* Summer 33 The more active attitude of seeking or desiring we call *petitive.*

petit-maître. Add: (Further examples.) Also as *adj.*

1883 C. M. YONGE *Stray Pearls* I. x. 115 He would be ashamed to count kindred with that effeminate *petite maître*! *c* **1905** E. NEWMAN in H. Van Thal *Fanfare for E. Newman* (1955) x. 145 It is the *petit-maître* Mozart, tripping along with his manneristic little elegancies of walk and gesture but scarcely conscious of the bigness of the world around him or of the real nature of the humanity that strives in it. **1939** 'A. BRIDGE' *Four-Part Setting* vi. 63 His manners were slightly *petit-maître.* **1948** D. CECIL *Two Quiet Lives* 88 At moments..one is tempted to dismiss him [*sc.* Horace Walpole] as an affected petit-maître who happened to be gifted with a talent for letter writing.

2. A 'minor master' with reference to musicians, writers, etc. (usu. derog.).

1856 J. B. WARING in O. Jones *Gram. Ornament* (1865) xviii. 132 As regards another main feature in Elizabethan ornament, viz. the complicated and fanciful interlaced bands, we must seek its origin in the..designs of the class of engravers known as the 'petits maîtres' of Germany and the Netherlands. **1934** C. LAMBERT *Music Ho!* III. 168 Liadoff, a real petit-maître, produced at rare intervals a few miniatures of extraordinary felicity. **1960** *Times* 8 Mar. 4/7 Michel is accounted a *petit-maître* and in French comparison does not reach the same height as Théodore Rousseau. **1963** *Listener* 3 Jan. 45/3 He [*sc.* Puccini] was a musician of great artistic integrity who clearly recognized his limitations... But such awareness does not make him a *petit maître* any more than it did Chopin, Bizet, Ravel. **1975** *Daily Tel.* 10 June 11/4 Pierre Prins is one of those French petits maitres whom, if we only saw their best work, we would rate rightly.

petit mal. Add: There is only momentary confusion or unconsciousness without general convulsions or other major manifestations. (Earlier and later examples.)

[**1842**: see *GRAND MAL.] **1874** J. CUNNINGHAM *New Theory of Knowing* 173 Some persons afflicted with the *petit mal* continue their work..after they have sunk into unconsciousness. **1879,** etc. [see *GRAND MAL]. **1927** *Daily Express* 6 Aug. 7/6 She was suffering from a disease known as petit mal, which occasionally makes persons unconscious of their surroundings, and they then perform normal actions. **1957** L. DURRELL *Justine* III. 160 An occasional headache only proved him to be a victim of *petit mal*—or some other such customary disease of the rich and idle. **1974** *Daily Tel.* (Colour Suppl.) 18 Jan. 19/1 In a 'Petit Mal' a child looking out of the window may see the nose of a passing bus come into his line of vision and then, straight away, the disappearing tail of the same bus. The only ill effect is that he probably gets ticked off for daydreaming.

‖ **petits chevaux** (pəti ʃəvō). [Fr., lit. little horses.] A gambling game in which bets are placed on the performance of mechanically operated horses made to spin round a flag placed at the centre of a specially prepared circular table.

1891 *Clown* 9 June 13/2 Some of the most naughty of us will go and tempt fortune with the 'petit[s] chevaux'—at Dieppe. **1905** W. J. LOCKE *Morals M. Ordeyne* xii. 147 She has a consuming passion for *petits chevaux.* I speak sagely of the evils of gambling. **1911** [see *BOULE[4] 1]. **1912** 'SAKI' *Chron. Clovis* 181 It was just before *petits chevaux* had been supplanted by *boule.* **1929** R. ALDINGTON *Death of Hero* III. vi. 330 He disapproved of baccarat, roulette, and *petits chevaux.* **1964** C. MACKENZIE *My Life & Times* III. i. 22, I do not know what the rules are to-day for *petits chevaux* but in 1900 horse number 5 of the 9 horses meant that the bank won. **1964** A. WYKES

Gambling ix. 211 Other variations of roulette..*Petits chevaux*—which still flourishes in Northern France and Ireland.

pe·t-name, *v.* [f. *pet name* s.v. PET *sb.*[1] 3 c.] *trans.* To give (a person) a pet-name; to call by a pet-name.

1915 E. CORRI *30 Yrs. Boxing Ref.* 183 Men of the most human type are usually pet-named by the public in some way. **1942** C. MORLEY *Thorofare* (1943) xix. 66 He had pet-named the two funnels for his twin daughters, Alma and Sophie. **1973** *Times Lit. Suppl.* 1 June 608/3 His young bride Nadia petnamed him Klop (which is Russian for 'bug').

‖**peto** (pe·to). [Sp.] A padded or stuffed protective covering for a picador's horse.

1957 A. MACNAB *Bulls of Iberia* v. 52 The number of pics is not rigid..for with the *peto* the contact may last some time, and not be broken at once as in the pre-*peto* days. **1967** MCCORMICK & MASCAREÑAS *Compl. Aficionado* ii. 35 Before 1928, when the peto was introduced, the work of the picador was more prominent than it is in the modern corrida. **1968** *Economist* 17 Feb. 32/1 It was she [*sc.* Queen Victoria Eugenia] who insisted on the use of the *peto*, the ugly mattress-like covering that protects picadors' horses, though not infallibly, from disembowelment.

petrean, *a.* Restrict *rare.* ? *Obs.* to sense in Dict. and add: Also **petræan. 1.** (Later example.)

1849 J. FORBES *Physician's Holiday* xx. 294 The same petræan desert continues beyond Swarenbach.

2. (With capital initial.) Of or pertaining to Petra, a city in ancient Arabia Petræa. Also as *sb.*, an inhabitant of Petra.

1852 E. A. ANDREWS *Copious Latin-Eng. Lex.* 1133/2 *Pĕtra*,.. a city in Arabia Petraea, now the ruins of Wadi Musa... Hence..*Pĕtreus*, a, um, adj., Petrean. **1923** A. FORDER *Petra: Perea: Phœnicia* 10 One would gather from Bible records that the Petreans were always a proud and turbulent people. *Ibid.* 20 A feasible explanation..was given to me by a modern Petrean. **1925** A. B. W. KENNEDY *Petra* iii. 34 Very little is known about the religion of the Nabataeans as a nation, and even less, perhaps, about the religion of those of the nationality whom we may call particularly Petraeans, and who are responsible for the monuments of Petra. *Ibid.* 35 We know from the dated tombs at Madaïn Salih that the most complex and highly developed of the Petraean designs were already in existence before the commencement of our era. **1957** *Encycl. Brit.* XVII. 652/2 The chief god of Petra was Dhūsharā..he was worshipped under the form of a black rectangular stone, a sort of Petraean Ka'ba. **1965** N. GLUECK *Deities & Dolphins* (1966) x. 331 The Petraean feminine figure on a sea animal could.. be identified with an Atargatis or Aphrodite mounted on a fish-tailed Capricornus.

petrefact (pe·trĭfækt). Also **petrifact.** [f. L. *petra* rock, stone after *artefact.*] An object made of stone; also *fig.*, something that has become hardened or fixed.

1911 BEERBOHM *And Even Now* (1920) 39 He..does strive, by day and by night, poor petrefact, to rip off these fell and clownish integuments... He forgets that after all he is only a statue. **1932** *Brit. Jrnl. Psychol.* Apr. 313 Those in whom space perception is still of the early, plastic form frequent among children, in whom the later 'petrefacts' have not yet been crystallized out.. should be primary colour perceptors. **1975** *Encounter* Sept. 86 In Germany, in any case, he destroyed numerous outdated structures, did away with old classes, smashed to pieces revered petrifacts.

Petri (pe·tri, pī·tri). Also **petri.** [Name of R. J. *Petri* (1852–1922), German bacteriologist, who first proposed the use of such a dish (*Centralbl. f. Bacteriol. und Parasitenkunde* (1887) I. 279).] *Petri* (or † *Petri's*) *dish*: a shallow, circular, flat-bottomed glass (or plastic) dish with vertical sides and with a cover of the same shape but slightly larger, which is used particularly for growing cultures of bacteria or the like. Also *fig.*

1892 A. C. ABBOTT *Princ. Bacteriol.* viii. 87 Petri's dishes are flat, double dishes of glass. *Ibid.* xx. 212 Place the tissue in a sterilized Petri dish. **1897** MUIR & RITCHIE *Man. Bacteriol.* 57 The latter are known as Petri's dishes. **1903** *Univ. Nebraska Stud.* Oct. 2 The hydroids were cut.. into the desired lengths and placed in watch glasses, petri-dishes, finger bowls, etc. **1946** F. SCHNEIDER *Qualitative Organic Microanalysis* vii. 187 Stopper the flask with a small cork, place the side arm in the petri dish, and fill the latter with alkaline permanganate solution. **1973** J. GOODFIELD *Courier to Peking* xv. 211 I've got a test I want to do. Get me a Petri dish smeared with gelatine and the following serums. **1976** *Nature* 24 June 701/1 Both cell types were plated on plastic Petri dishes (5 cm diameter).

petrichor (pe·trikǫɹ). [f. PETR(O- + ICHOR.] A pleasant, distinctive smell that frequently accompanies the first rain after a long period of warm, dry weather in certain regions; in quot. 1975, applied to an oily substance obtained from the ground in which this smell was concentrated.

1964 BEAR & THOMAS in *Nature* 7 Mar. 993/2 The diverse nature of the host materials has led us to propose the name 'petrichor' for this apparently unique odour which can be regarded as an 'ichor' or 'tenuous essence' derived from rock or stone. This name, unlike the general term 'argillaceous odour', avoids the unwarranted implication that the phenomenon is restricted to clays or argillaceous materials; it does not imply that petrichor is necessarily a fixed chemical entity but rather it denotes an integral odour. **1971** *Listener* 4 Nov. 612/3 No matter what kind of rock or earth was used, the oily essence always possessed the aroma of petrichor—the smell of rain falling on dry ground. **1975** *Sunday Mail* (Brisbane) 2 Nov. 32/2 CSIROs Melbourne mineral chemistry division discovered that it was not fungi or dead vegetation which produced the smell, but small yellowish-gold oily globules. The globules, nicknamed 'petrichor' or 'essence of rock' by the researchers, contained at least 50 different compounds, not unlike a perfume and were absorbed into the ground from the air.

petrified, *ppl. a.* Add: Esp. in phr. *petrified forest.* (Further examples.)

1830 *Illinois Monthly Mag.* Oct. 31 The earth's surface is literally covered with stumps, roots and limbs of petrified trees; presenting the appearance of a 'Petrified Forest'. **1873** S. W. COZZENS *Marvellous Country* 76 We came upon the remains of a petrified forest,..converted by some chemical process into specimens of variegated jasper. **1937** M. HUXLEY *Let.* 13 Oct. in *Lett. A. Huxley* (1969) 425 We drove through all the view places and the petrified forests and the grand-canyons. **1969** E. H. PINTO *Treen* 196 Petrified wood. The most interesting and highly prized results of wood transformed into rock, are examples from the several petrified forests which exist in various parts of the world. *Ibid.* 197 Two of the most famous of the petrified forests are situated in the U.S.A.—one at the Yellowstone National Park.., the other in Chalcedony Park, Arizona.

2. Add to def.: terrified, extremely frightened; also const. *of.* (Further examples.)

1869 'MARK TWAIN' *Innoc. Abr.* xlvi. 481 A great herd of curious-looking Syrian goats and sheep were gratefully eating gravel. I do not state this as a petrified fact. I only *suppose* they were eating gravel, because there did not appear to be any thing else for them to eat. **1875** —— *Sk. New & Old* 219 Here, here, you petrified fool. **1963** R. WOLFF *I, Keturah* (1964) II. xvii. 229, I was petrified of all the gadgets. **1968** *Observer* 7 Jan. 28/6 [They] *think* they want the foreign flavour; but actually couldn't be more petrified of it. **1974** W. J. BURLEY *Death in Stanley St.* xi. 186 He was trying to get at the gun... I was petrified!

Petrine, *a.* Add: **1.** *Petrine claims* (example).

1930 tr. *F. von Hügel's Some Notes on Petrine Claims* vii. 30 Four contentions which make up the Catholic Petrine claims.

2. Of, pertaining to, or characteristic of Peter I the Great (1672–1725), tsar and emperor of Russia.

1908 R. N. BAIN in *Cambr. Mod. Hist.* V. xvii. 549 At least half the Senate (though that was a purely Petrine institution). **1927** E. M. ALMEDINGEN in *Magnificat* Mar. 235/2 No really great men of letters lived in Peter's time: Theophanus..and Prince Kantemir..were the two men who left any mark at all in the annals of Petrine literature. **1956** E. MUNZER *Solovyev* iii. 41 It was he [*sc.* the Patriarch Nikon] who paved the way to the Petrine perversion, or pseudomorphosis, of the Russian soul. **1964** *Listener* 5 Mar. 392/1 [Alexis] Tolstoy's Peter the Great modifies the Petrine myth in accordance with an up-to-date and almost professional conception of history. **1974** *Times Lit. Suppl.* 13 Sept. 984/3 No extracts on eastern Europe;.. none on Russia, where the Petrine reforms were nothing if not military.

Petrinist (pī·trinist). [f. PETRINE *a.* + -IST.] A follower of St. Peter; a student of Petrine theology.

1922 JACKSON & LAKE *Beginn. Christianity* II. I. v. 123 Gfrörer thought that the compiler of Acts..used a collection of unhistorical legends arranged by a zealous Petrinist.

‖**pétrissage** (petrisāʒ). [Fr., f. *pétrir* to knead.] A kneading process used in massage.

1886 W. MURRELL *Massage* iii. 11 Next [after *effleurage*] comes *pétrissage* which is more important and is by no means easy to acquire. **1906** *Practitioner* Dec. 769 *Pétrissage* is performed by grasping the tissues to be operated on, lifting the mass thus seized, and alternately loosening and tightening the grasp. **1957** *Encycl. Brit.* XV. 32/1 Pétrissage..consists of a seizure by the hands of muscles or other tissues which are then subjected to a process of kneading. **1961** [see *MALAXATION c].

petro-[2] (pe·tro), combining form of PETROLEUM, in recent formations as *petro-politics, -power, -resources, -wealth*; freq. with ref. to revenue, esp. foreign exchange, deriving from petroleum exports, as *petro-billion, -naira, -pound.* Also *PETRODOLLAR. Cf. *PETROCHEMISTRY 2.

1973 *Time* 3 Dec. 44/1 The energy crisis..may have been artificially imposed, but its implications stretch far beyond petropolitics. **1974** *Newsweek* 7 Oct. 52/3 Top Arab leaders have now decided not to put their petrobillions into U.S. Treasury bonds..but to invest in American industry instead. **1975** *Publishers Weekly* 19 May 99/1, I understand they're rolling in petropounds since oil was discovered in the North Sea. **1976** *Ibid.* 5 Jan. 60/1 An Arab emirate saturated with petro-resources. **1976** *Daily Times* (Lagos) 5 May 7/1 As the tenth largest oil producer in the league, Nigeria has every reason to tout her petro-wealth. **1976** *Daily Colonist* (Victoria, B.C.) 20 June 35/1 'There are two kinds of power,' he said, 'petropower and agripower.' **1976** *Daily Times* (Lagos) 20 July 7/1 Nigeria's foreign exchange reserve zoomed to N2,047 million through oil boom, thus projecting an over-sized petro-naira bubble which beclouded the vision of some former military rulers. **1977** *Time* 11 July 36/3 The Saudis can be expected to wield their petropower prudently.

petrochemical (petroke·mikăl), *a.* and *sb.* Also **petro-chemical.** [f. next, after *chemistry, chemical.*] **A.** *adj.* **a.** Of or pertaining to petrochemistry (sense *1).

1913 *Chem. Abstr.* VII. 3949 (*heading*) Petrochemical studies. **1952** *Geochim. et Cosmochim. Acta* II. 283 (*heading*) A petrochemical study of the Tertiary lavas of northeast Ireland. **1960** *Internat. Geol. Rev.* II. 273 (*heading*) Petrochemical study of the Cenozoic basaltic rocks in eastern China. **1975** *Nature* 27 Feb. 691/1 Another study of the intrusion was initiated in the hope that new geophysical and petrochemical techniques might provide the added insight needed to resolve some of these questions.

b. Of or pertaining to petrochemistry (sense *2) or petrochemicals.

1942 *Oil & Gas Jrnl.* 30 Apr. 47 The long experience of the Badger Company..enables it..to meet the requirements of the rapidly expanding Petro-Chemical Industry. **1947** *Chem. & Engin. News* 8 Dec. 3634/1 Increasing demands for organic chemicals..have led to rapid development of the petrochemical industry. **1959** *Times Rev. Industry* Sept. 99/3 The Monsanto Chemical Company..will build a petro-chemical factory..to produce styrene monomer from which polystyrene plastics are made. **1961** G. R. CHOPPIN *Exper. Nucl. Chem.* xi. 185 Further reduction is effected by using solvents of petrochemical origin. **1969** *Times* 30 Apr. 23/2 (Advt.), Dutch-American firm, specialising in design and fabrication of unusual petrochemical heat transfer equipment,..seeks experienced man. *a* **1974** R. CROSSMAN *Diaries* (1976) II. 290 There was a likelihood of petro-chemical and associated development in the Invergordon area.

B. *sb.* Any chemical compound or element obtained or derived industrially from petroleum or natural gas. Freq. *attrib.* in *pl.*

1942 *Oil & Gas Jrnl.* 25 June 180 (Advt.), Typical 'petro-chemicals' already in production: alcohols, butadiene, benzol, [etc.]. **1950** *N.Y. Times* 19 Nov. 1F/3 Petrochemicals which are derived from the vast supplies of petroleum and natural gas available in the South, are the bellwether of the country's economy. **1959** *Engineering* 2 Jan. 24/1 The new petrochemicals plant at the Fawley refinery of Esso. **1967** *New Scientist* 16 Feb. 385/3 Chemical engineering has now advanced to the point whereby the idea of using this gas [*sc.* carbon monoxide] as the key building block for petrochemicals—such as plastics and pesticides..—is no longer a pipe-dream. **1972** HARKER & ALLEN *Fuel Sci.* iii. 35 Crude oil also provides the source of raw material for the rapidly growing petrochemicals industry. **1975** *Petroleum Rev.* XXIX. 381/2 (*caption*) 65,000 tons of petrochemicals..are stored under an inert blanket.

Hence **petroche·mically** *adv.*

1952 *Trans. Edin. Geol. Soc.* XV. 82 Ophitic texture is the result of delayed crystallisation of augite from magma characterised petrochemically by marked undersaturation in the pyroxene-components. **1963** *Economist* 28 Sept. 1140, 60 per cent of world nitrogen is petrochemically derived. **1973** *Nature* 27 Apr. 566/1 'Petrographically' the dredged lavas are typically submarine fine grained, vesicular and porphyritic basalts... 'Petrochemically' the basalts are classified as tholeiites according to the Yoder and Tilley normative scheme.

petrochemistry (petroke·mistri). [f. PETRO- (in sense 2 repr. *petroleum*: cf. *PETRO-[2]) + CHEMISTRY.] **1.** *Geol.* The chemistry of the composition and formation of rocks (as distinct from minerals, ore deposits, etc.), esp. igneous and metamorphic ones.

1937 *Bull. Volcanologique* I. 59 (*heading*) Petrochemistry of the Scottish Carboniferous-Permian igneous rocks. **1958** *Q. Jrnl. Geol. Soc.* CXIII. 393 (*heading*) The petrochemistry of the Ardara aureole. **1971** *Internat. Geol. Rev.* XIII. 561/2 In petrochemistry we are often required to compare associations of rocks of different regions and assign them to definite petrographic groups. **1974** *Nature* 18 Oct. 581/2 There is, as yet, insufficient documentation of the relationship between precisely measured Sr isotope ratios and the petrochemistry of Icelandic rocks.

2. The chemistry of petroleum and natural gas, and of their refining and processing.

1942 *Oil & Gas Jrnl.* 18 June 96/1 The section in next week's Journal devoted to petro-chemistry is something you'll not want to miss. **1954** *Chem. & Engin. News* 20 Sept. 3719/3 Entrance of one company into field of petrochemistry in 1925 was followed by dozens of others. **1959** *Ibid.* 22 June 41 (Advt.), Exciting new products through petro-chemistry.

petrodollar (pe·trŏˌdǫləɹ). [f. *PETRO-[2] + DOLLAR.] A notional unit of currency available in a petroleum-exporting country. Freq. *attrib.* of the surplus of petroleum exports over imports of all other goods, and in *pl.*

1974 *Globe & Mail* (Toronto) 27 Aug. 7/1 What emerged in Washington..was a growing concern over the swiftly accelerating petrodollar holdings of the Arabs. (Petrodollars are defined as the excess foreign-exchange assets of the oil-producing countries)... There simply isn't sufficient data on the flow of petrodollars. *Ibid.* 7/6 Still, the question of petrodollars and their potential recycling into U.S. industries..is something officials and analysts are studying. **1974** LD. GLADWYN in *Hansard Lords* 5 Nov. 310 The loan to Italy, the sugar deal, which they approved; the beginning of petro-dollar recycling are all instances in point. **1974** *Financial Times*

21 Nov. 23/3 The size of the 'petrodollar' surplus—defined as the current earnings of the OPEC countries over and above what they can spend on imports—has been estimated at about $60 bn. [*sc.* thousand million] this year. **1975** *Times* 8 Jan. 1/6 Two suggested schemes for recycling surplus petrodollars to deficit countries. **1976** *Time* 27 Dec. 21/1 Problems of inflation, devaluation and petrodollars intimately bind our economy and that of other nations into a common system. **1977** *Time* 18 July 39/1 In Aspen, Colo. the Empress..danced away the Fourth of July at a local night-spot and dropped some petrodollars in Aspen shops.

petrofabrics (petrofæ·briks), *sb. pl. Geol.* [f. PETRO- + FABRIC *sb.*: see -IC 2.] The texture and microscopic structure of a rock or rocks, or the study of these, esp. as guides to the movements to which they have been subjected. Cf. *PETROTECTONICS *sb. pl.*

1934 B. SANDER in *Amer. Jrnl. Sci.* XXVIII. 37 (*heading*) Petrofabrics (Gefügekunde der Gesteine) and orogenesis. *Ibid.*, Petrofabrics denotes the study of the internal space relations of a rock. **1949** *Q. Jrnl. Geol. Soc.* CV. 111 The greatest contribution of the Sander–Schmidt school of petrofabrics has been its emphasis on the movements influencing fabric rather than on the forces responsible for the movements. **1960** *Liverpool & Manch. Geol. Jrnl.* II. 503 (*heading*) New work on petrofabrics. **1974** *Nature* 12 Apr. 621/3 Papers on..the petrofabrics of the peridotite suite xenoliths.

So **petrofa·bric** *a.*

1934 B. SANDER in *Amer. Jrnl. Sci.* XXVIII. 38 Petrofabric analysis is..important for purely petrographic investigations that seek only descriptive characteristics of rocks. **1942** M. P. BILLINGS *Structural Geol.* xviii. 341 Many petrofabric diagrams show the attitude of the cleavage rather than the orientation of the optic axes. **1956** E. W. HEINRICH *Microsc. Petrogr.* vii. 208 Petrofabric studies reveal that the optic axes of the quartz grains usually are well oriented in one of several patterns. **1968** B. BAYLY *Introd. Petrol.* xxv. 303 There is..a large field known as petrofabric analysis, in which the orientation of many individual grains is studied.

Petro-Forge (pe·trofɔ̄ədʒ). Also **-forge.** [f. PETRO- (taken as repr. PETROL) + FORGE *sb.*] A forging machine powered by a petrol engine.

1964 *Engineering* 2 Oct. 438/2 A session at the fifth MTDRC was devoted entirely to high energy rate forming... The paper read last: 'Petro-Forge Mk I-DRD',..gave evidence of industry's keen interest in the development of a method of high energy operation which uses the internal combustion process for its power source. **1965** *Economist* 18 Dec. 1354/3 The Petro-Forge has been sufficiently developed (it started under a DSIR grant in 1962) to show that even when working at slow speeds it will be cheaper and better than existing forging machinery. **1970** DAVIES & AUSTIN *Devel. High Speed Metal Forming* II. i. 54 Multi-blow operation at one second intervals is..possible and enables the Petro-Forge to be used for large volume production of components. **1973** E. C. ROLLASON *Metall. for Engineers* (ed. 4) vii. 129 In the Petro-forge the energy is derived from the combustion of a fuel/air mixture in the cylinder of an internal combustion engine.

petrogenesis (petrŏdʒe·nĕsis). *Petrol.* [f. PETRO- + -GENESIS. Cf. G. *petrogenese* (R. Th. Simler *Ueber die Petrogenese* (1862)); *petrogenesis* was used by F. Zirkel (*Lehrb. der Petrogr.* (1866) I. 159).] (The study of) the formation of rocks, esp. igneous and metamorphic rocks.

1901 *Q. Jrnl. Geol. Soc.* LVII. p. lxv, Hutton was in advance of his time on matters relating to petrogenesis. **1911** *Geol. Mag.* Decade V. VIII. 248 (*heading*) The fundamental problems of petrogenesis, or the origin of the igneous rocks. **1956** *Nature* 14 Jan. 68/1 He has achieved high distinction for his researches on petrogenesis, notably on rock transformations in the granitic suite. **1960** *Times* 13 Feb. 8/4 Lyell Medal to Dr. Doris Reynolds for her work on the rocks of Northern Ireland and her contributions to petrogenesis. **1971** *Nature* 24 Sept. 260/1 Romey..suggests that theories of lunar petrogenesis are developing too fast. **1977** A. HALLAM *Planet Earth* 313 *Petrogenesis*, an envelope term embracing all aspects and features of the formation of rocks.

Hence **pe:trogene·tic** *a.*, **-gene·tically** *adv.*

1911 *Geol. Mag.* Decade V. VIII. 251 Such a conception exists, but we can oppose to it several geological data and petrogenetic considerations. **1950** A. K. WELLS in F. H. Hatch et al. *Petrol. Igneous Rocks* (ed. 10) 5 The modern tendency to explain many petrogenetic problems in terms of emanations, ionic migration and 'granitization'. **1954** *Jrnl. Geol.* LXII. 172 (*heading*) The trace elements of the plutonic complex of Loch Doon..and their petrogenetic significance. **1970** *Mineral. Abstr.* XXI. 77/1 Petrogenetically it is suggested that a basalt differentiated to produce an olivine-augite peridotite which subsequently assimilated a potassic granite.

petrogeny (petrǫ·dʒĕni). *Petrol.* [f. PETRO- + -GENY.] = *PETROGENESIS. Chiefly in *petrogeny's residua system.*

1937 N. L. BOWEN in *Amer. Jrnl. Sci.* CCXXXIII. 1 It is concluded..that in mixtures containing all of these (SiO_2, Al_2O_3, iron oxide, CaO, MgO, Na_2O and K_2O) the residual liquid from fractional crystallization will show this same character of great enrichment in alkali-alumina silicate. Since the oxides listed above make up some 97 per cent of the composition of the average igneous rock the alkali-alumina silicate system ($NaAlSiO_4$–$KAlSiO_4$–SiO_2) is here referred to as petrogeny's 'residua system'. **1948** [see *MAGMATISM a]. **1950** E. E. WAHLSTROM *Introd. Theoret. Igneous Petrol.* i. 3 Petrogeny places emphasis on the manner of origin or genesis of rocks. **1966** *Jrnl. Petrol.* VII. 115 It is necessary to know something of the residual liquids that might be produced in the course of crystallization of silicate melts, and a considerable part of the efforts of experimental petrology has been directed to this end. The classic system in this regard is 'petrogeny's residua system', $NaAlSiO_4$–$KAlSiO_4$–SiO_2..but..even this is a residua system only for liquids in which the alkali/alumina ratio [*printed* ration] is unity.

So **petroge·nic** *a.* = *PETROGENETIC *a.*

1908 *Amer. Jrnl. Sci.* CLXXVI. 45 In a fully represented petrogenic cycle at a batholithic area..the oldest intrusion should be a rock of gabbroid (basaltic) composition. **1947** A. KNOPF *Pirsson's Rocks & Rock Minerals* (ed. 3) vi. 144 A period in which a genetically related series of igneous rocks was formed is called a petrogenic epoch, and as this concept is more definite than 'petrographic province', it is supplanting the older idea. **1971** I. G. GASS et al. *Understanding Earth* 12 The rise of understanding of rocks, and particularly of petrogenic processes, was initially highly dependent on the way in which microscopy assisted in the study of the constituent minerals.

petroglyph. (Further examples.)

1952 V. G. CHILDE *New Light Most Anc. East* ii. 23 Petroglyphs, like microliths, attest hunting over many areas now uninhabitable. **1955** *Sci. News Let.* 9 July 31/2 The crescent is not a common figure among petroglyphs and pictographs of northern Arizona. **1958** E. A. ARMSTRONG *Folklore of Birds* i. 10 In the Californian deserts I have seen petroglyphs made by Red Indian initiands. **1972** *Sci. Amer.* June 91/1 The use of a line to depict a contour may well have been one of the earliest developments in art, as exemplified by the 'line drawings' in the pictographs and petroglyphs of prehistoric artists. **1974** *Environmental Conservation* I. 8/2 The desert is dotted with..fossil remains..of domestic animals whose present range lies well outside the areas of the petroglyphs.

petrographic, *a.* Add: *petrographic province*: see *PROVINCE 6 b.

petrographical, *a.* Add: *petrographical province*: see *PROVINCE 6 b.

petroil (pe·troil). [f. PETR(OL + OIL *sb.*[1]] = *MIXTURE 3 e. Freq. *attrib.*

1927 A. W. JUDGE *Mod. Motor Engineer* III. vi. 164 In the case of two-stroke engines using the 'petroil' (i.e. petrol and oil mixture) system of lubrication, it is important to keep the float chamber and filter clean. **1959** *Motor* 21 Oct. 344/1 The petroil system of lubrication has been so refined that only one pint of oil need be added to each 5 gallons of petrol. **1967** P. E. IRVING *Two-Stroke Power Units* vii. 129 With crankcase compression, it is manifestly impossible to have large quantities of oil splashing around inside the engine... The most generally accepted way out of this situation is to dissolve a small amount of oil in the fuel, the resulting mixture being termed 'petroil' (in England, anyway). **1972** J. STEVENS *Scooter* iv. 98 Another cut in running costs comes from the scooters which run on a petroil mixture containing only 2% of oil. **1977** *Good Motoring* Oct. 8/1 Mixed a gallon of petroil to fill the tank of a two-stroke motor cycle.

petrol. Add: Now only with pronunc. (pe·trǫl). **3.** (Earlier example.)

For an attribution of the Eng. word to Frederick Simms, 1893, see E. Liveing *Pioneers of Petrol* (1959) 42. However *pétrole* was current in Fr. by 1892 (cf. G. Richard *Les nouveaux Moteurs à Gaz et à Pétrole* (1892)).

1895 F. R. SIMMS in *Sat. Rev.* 3 Aug. 144/1 The Daimler carriage can easily take a gradient of 1 in 10... The fuel used is rectified petroleum or petrol or benzoline, of a specific gravity of 0·680 to 0·705, which has many advantages over common petroleum, and is obtainable almost anywhere.

3. b. *petrol adjustment, bowser* [*BOWSER[2]], *bus, can,* † *car, consumption, costs, engine* (further examples), *feed, -filler, fumes, lamp, motor, ration, rationing, tank, tanker, tap, tin, vapour*; *petrol-driven, -engined, -propelled* adjs.; **petrol attendant,** one who attends to the petrol pumps at a petrol station; **petrol blue,** a shade of blue similar to the colour of petrol; **petrol coupon,** a petrol rationing coupon; **petrol-electric** *a.*, (*a*) driven by electric motors powered by current from a generator, which in turn is driven by a petrol engine (cf. **diesel-electric* adj.); (*b*) applied to a petrol-driven electricity generator; **petrol gauge,** a meter indicating the quantity of petrol in a tank; **petrol injection,** fuel injection, where the fuel is petrol; **petrol lighter,** a cigarette lighter employing petrol; **petrol pump,** (*a*) a pump at a petrol station for supplying motor vehicles with petrol; (*b*) a pump which delivers petrol from the petrol tank of a motor vehicle or aircraft to the engine; **petrol sniffer,** one who inhales petrol fumes for a narcotic effect; hence **petrol-sniffing,** the activity of a petrol-sniffer; **petrol station** = *filling station* s.v. *FILLING *vbl. sb.* 4.

1920 Petrol adjustment [see *IDLE *v.* 4 a]. **1963** M. LEVINSON *Taxi!* iv. 47 He can very easily get a part-time job..as a petrol attendant. **1975** *Evening Herald* (Dublin) 8 May 12/3 (Advt.), Petrol attendants required. **1949** *Dict. Colours Interior Decoration* (Brit. Colour Council) III. 21/1 *Petrol blue*, a colour name introduced into seasonal ranges by B.C.C. in 1943. **1971** *Sunday Mirror* 21 Mar. 15/1 You can't sell them bright or pastel colours. In summer they just want petrol blue, bottle green or navy. **1973** *Guardian* 10 Apr. 13/3 (*caption*) Chunky petrol blue mohair cardigan. **1943** T. R. ST. GEORGE *C/o Postmaster* 58 We learned, presently, that it wasn't a gas station at all, for that matter, but a 'petrol bowser'. **1943** P. BRENNAN et al. *Spitfires over Malta* 24 A petrol bowser on the perimeter track caught fire..and blazed fiercely. **1911** *Chambers's Jrnl.* Jan. 77/1 The electrically propelled vehicle..is smoother in running, more silent, and more convenient to handle than the petrol-bus. **1966** M. WOODHOUSE *Tree Frog* xxii. 159 The jeep bounced... Yancy cursed the petrol cans fluently. **1975** M. RUSSELL *Murder by Mile* xiv. 151 The petrol cans that she's just been emptying. **1900** Petrol car [in Dict., sense 3 a]. **1902** A. C. HARMSWORTH et al. *Motors* x. 183 (*heading*) The petrol car. **1908** *Westm. Gaz.* 16 June 4/2 Petrol-consumption is a factor which is taken into serious consideration by purchasers of cars nowadays. **1936** 'N. BLAKE' *Thou Shell of Death* ii. 37 Your defence planes of the future..must, above all, have a very low petrol consumption. **1974** A. ROSS *Bradford Business* 15 We covered the hundred and seventy miles..at an average speed of 91·5 miles an hour... The petrol consumption was..sixteen imperial gallons. **1955** *Times* 10 May 6/3 Their petrol costs, according to a branch official, are being met by some of the voluntary miners' funds. **1939** *Times* 14 Oct. 5/3 (*heading*) Supplementary petrol coupons. **1963** D. HUGHES in Sissons & French *Age of Austerity* IV. 86 Forged petrol coupons changed hands at half a crown a time. **1971** A. DIMENT *Think Inc.* iv. 59 This man concerned himself with rough copies of ration books and petrol coupons. **1973** T. ALLBEURY *Choice of Enemies* viii. 35 Bring..your car—we'll see you get enough petrol coupons. **1905** *Westm. Gaz.* 2 Jan. 2/1 Purely petrol-driven auto-cars on exactly the same principle as a road automobile. **1937** BLUNDEN *Elegy* 50 The televisionary world to come, The petrol-driven world already made. **1960** *Farmer & Stockbreeder* 22 Mar. (Suppl.) 8/1 You can pay as little as 33gs for a 14in petrol-driven mower. **1964** J. J. WALSH *Understanding Paraplegia* xvi. 113 Popularity of the fast and more powerful petrol-driven tricycle. **1905** *Westm. Gaz.* 2 Jan. 2/1 The North-Eastern, Great Northern, and Brighton Railways. The first-named has some petrol-electric coaches. **1909** *Installation News* III. 117/2 The petrol electric set..is increasing in popularity every day; at the moment however the danger does not present itself..as a source of loss to the Central Station. **1930** *Times* 25 Mar. 25/1 With regard to the replacement of our motor omnibuses,.. the petrol-electric machine..has given us very good service. **1940** *Chambers's Techn. Dict.* 631/1 *Petrol-electric generating set* (Elec. Eng.), a small generating plant using a petrol engine as the prime-mover. **1902** R. J. MECREDY in A. C. Harmsworth *Motors* vii. 105 'Petrol Engine' is a slang term for an engine driven by a series of explosions of a mixture of the vapour of a light spirit of petroleum with air. **1916** A. GARRARD (*title*) Gas, oil, and petrol engines. **1933** Petrol engine [see *INJECTION 1 b]. **1974** *Country Life* 3 Oct. 948/1 Daimler's petrol engine was used in vehicles constructed between 1885 and 1888. **1906** *Daily Chron.* 27 June 3/5 The invention of a petrol-engined torpedo-boat. **1936** *Discovery* Sept. 289/1 The new L.M.S. 'Coventry' petrol-engined railcar. **1971** *Daily Tel.* 28 Jan. 3/1 A regulation requiring new petrol-engined vehicles to be fitted with means to prevent fumes escaping from the crank-case is to be laid before Parliament. **1913** *Autocar Handbk.* (ed. 5) iii. 67 (*caption*) Exhaust pressure petrol feed. **1928** *Manch. Guardian Weekly* 10 Aug. 107/4 They experienced trouble with the petrol feed and turned back. **1935** C. DAY LEWIS *Time to Dance* 34 They..rose and flew on to Paris, and there Trivially were delayed—a defective petrol feed—Three days. **1977** J. CLEARY *High Road to China* v. 145 One of the petrol feed pipes had been dented... Fuel had been getting to the engine only in a trickle. **1907** *Westm. Gaz.* 22 Nov. 10/1 The latest thing in petrol-fillers, horns and sirens. **1970** *Country Life* 31 Dec. 1278/2 A conical petrol-filler with a spout that he got from a local garage. **1908** *Lancet* 29 Feb. 658/2 He was only able to find in the literature one other case relating to the toxic effects of petrol fumes. **1912** KIPLING *Let.* 10 Dec. in C. E. Carrington *Rudyard Kipling* (1955) xvi. 420 A rather shrill stink..like chlorine gas on top of petrol fumes... That's the stink of the aeroplane. *a* **1930** D. H. LAWRENCE *Last Poems* (1932) 32 The weather in town is always benzine, or else petrol fumes. **1974** N. FREELING *Dressing of Diamond* 45 The summer night..was still tainted with petrol fumes. **1976** M. HINXMAN *End of Good Woman* vii. 94 She had stood on traffic intersections..inhaling petrol fumes. **1913** *Autocar Handbk.* (ed. 5) iii. 66 As the tank is arranged near the occupants a simple form of petrol gauge can be fitted. **1938** N. MARSH *Artists in Crime* xiii. 198 The petrol gauge ..registered only two gallons. **1974** D. KYLE *Raft of Swords* xiv. 156 He glanced down at the petrol gauge, saw the tank was roughly half empty. **1940** *Chambers's Techn. Dict.* 249/2 *Direct petrol injection* (I.C. Engs.), a method of operating a petrol engine by injecting liquid petrol directly into the induction pipe or cylinder during the suction-stroke, thus dispensing with a carburettor; in aero engines it avoids carburettor freezing troubles. **1972** K. NEWTON et al. *Motor Vehicle* (ed. 9) xvii. 379 Even in the U.S.A., where..very high-powered vehicles are the rule, petrol injection seems to make little headway. **1977** *Economist* 3 Sept. 51/1 (Advt.), Petrol injection makes for cleaner..combustion than the conventional carburettor. **1917** W. OWEN *Let.* 9 Feb. (1967) 432 Last night I burnt a petrol lamp under my bed! **1957** L. DURRELL *Justine* I. 14 The boys stir uneasily at their backgammon under the petrol-lamps. **1978** G. SIMS *Rex Mundi* vii. 45 We sped with..straining sails and hissing petrol lamps. **1926–7** *Army & Navy Stores Catal.* 88/1 Automatic 'Petrol' Lighter..With Nickel Case—each 1/3. **1930** SAYERS & 'EUSTACE' *Documents in Case* I. 151, I hunted through my pockets for a petrol lighter. **1978** D. BLOODWORTH *Crosstalk* iv. 35 The end of his cigarette trembling in the tiny spluttering flame of an almost extinct petrol lighter. **1904** T. H. WHITE (*title*) Petrol motors and motor cars: a handbook for engineers, designers and draughtsmen. **1912** *Motor Manual* (ed. 14) i. 1 The modern motorcar has been a gradual development since the introduction of the petrol motor or light internal-combustion engine by Benz, Levassor and Daimler. **1907** *Westm. Gaz.* 9 July 4/2

Wright's breakdown in the race..was variously ascribed to a broken valve, a seized piston, a choked petrol-pipe. **1925** *Morris Owner's Manual* ii. 33 Clean petrol filter and petrol pipe. **1963** R. F. WEBB *Motorists' Dict.* 170 *Petrol pipe*, the flexible or copper tube carrying petrol from the petrol tank to the petrol pump or carburettor. **1908** *Westm. Gaz.* 14 Apr. 4/2 Both the Wolseley and Thornycroft motors are masterpieces of engineering skill and ingenuity, and are taking us along as fast as applied science will admit towards the petrol-propelled battleship. **1922** JOYCE *Ulysses* 703 A scheme for the development of Irish tourist traffic in and around Dublin by means of petrolpropelled riverboats. **1928** *Manch. Guardian Weekly* 19 Oct. 301/2 A hideous outbreak of advertisement hoardings, petrol pumps..and gaunt new motor-tracks. **1932** J. BUCHAN *Gap in Curtain* ii. 96 They had to make a forced landing..on the skirts of Ruwenzori, where they found that something had gone wrong with the petrol pump and that some of the propeller and cylinder bolts had worked loose. *Ibid.* iv. 210 We want to get past the garages and petrol pumps and county council cottages to the ancient rustic England. **1963** R. F. WEBB *Motorists' Dict.* 170 When the float chamber of the carburettor is filled, the petrol pump encounters pressure and this opens a valve which stops further supplies of fuel being pumped up to the carburettor until the level of the reserve has dropped slightly. **1970** 'D. HALLIDAY' *Dolly & Cookie Bird* iv. 48 A black and white petrol-pump sign. **1976** 'W. TREVOR' *Children of Dynmouth* i. 16 His sister was..employed as a petrol-pump attendant on the forecourt of the Smiling Service Filling Station. **1939** *Times* 14 Oct. 5/3 Owners of vehicles and industrial plant who have been issued with only one month's additional petrol ration from the divisional petroleum office, should now apply for a further allowance for the second month if this is needed for essential purposes. **1948** G. V. GALWEY *Lift & Drop* v. 107 He's very scrupulous about his petrol ration being for professional purposes only. **1973** *Country Life* 6 Dec. 1892/1 Last week..motorists were beginning to queue for their petrol-ration books. **1948** M. LASKI *Tony Heaven* iv. 59, I take it..that there's no petrol rationing for A's? **1973** *Times* 4 Dec. 10/7 One or two people involved in industry said they were not worried about petrol rationing.. they would..buy one or two more cars, draw the coupons, and sell the cars when rationing ended. **1958** W. SANSOM *Cautious Heart* 53 Do you know what a petrol-sniffer is?.. It's quite serious really, it's an addiction to the smell of petrol—like any other narcotic. People who work among petrol fumes get the habit. **1973** *Black World* June 47/2 The..escapism..is 'petrol-sniffing', which produces a coma-like state. **1926** *Times* 6 May 1/4 (Advt.), Wanted, hard, ambitious, and independent worker with £750, to erect and operate new petrol station under exceptionally favourable supply contract. **1954** *Coast to Coast 1953–54* 145 A petrol-station at the far end. **1969** *Listener* 15 May 669/3, I suspect that Penguins and other paperbacks wouldn't sell at all well at petrol stations. **1972** 'J. & E. BONETT' *No Time to Kill* v. 52 He was approaching a petrol station... He drew up beside a row of pumps. **1902** KIPLING *Traffics & Discov.* (1904) 189 At Pigginfold, after ten minutes, we refilled our petrol tank and lavishly oiled our engines. **1973** J. LEASOR *Host of Extras* viii. 142 Drugs in spare tyres, dummy petrol tanks..windscreen washer tanks. **1974** *Country Life* 21 Nov. 1579/2 The petrol-tank capacity of 9·9 gallons was small for such a car. **1975** J. RATHBONE *Kill Cure* I. i. 7 His eyes returned to the road and the back of the large petrol tanker. **1908** *Autocar Handbk.* (ed. 2) xix. 148 The petrol tap having been turned on, the float may be agitated so as to flood the carburetter. **1925** *Morris Owner's Manual* i. 9 The petrol tap is at the bottom of the tank, under the dashboard. **1916** J. BUCHAN *Greenmantle* xvi. 217, I got out the petrol tins and spare tyres and cached them among some rocks on the hillside. **1940** 'GUN BUSTER' *Return via Dunkirk* I. x. 76 First name out of the petrol tin was Turner's. **1966** M. WOODHOUSE *Tree Frog* vi. 49 Petrol vapour clawed its way harshly into my lungs. **1974** J. DYSON *P.M.'s Boat is Missing* xl. 209 He could smell the strong petrol vapour.

4. = **petrol blue*.

1927 *Daily Express* 22 Feb. 6 (Advt.), White, Phlox, Cardinal, Red, Black, Brown, Navy, Bois de Rose, Lavender, Petrol, New Blue, Grey. **1971** *Vogue* 15 Sept. 129/1 Coat..sizes 10–16; colours: black, purple, green, brown, petrol. **1971** *Guardian* 18 Sept. 11/1 Dress and coat..Brown..Petrol, Grotto or Tomato.

Hence **pe·trolless** *a.*, having no petrol.

1908 *Daily Chron.* 31 July 4/3 The foolish virgins, with their oilless lamps, have found a latter-day analogue in the petrolless taxi-cabby. **1944** DYLAN THOMAS *Let.* 27 July (1966) 265 The well-off people were dry and thin and grieved over their petrolless motorcars.

petrolatum. Add to def.: = **petroleum jelly*. (Further examples.)

1959 *Industr. Wood Processes* VII. 15 (*heading*) The effect of petrolatum on the strength of glued joints. **1972** *Materials & Technol.* V. xiv. 520 Other plasticizers derived from petroleum are: petrolatum, paraffin waxes, ..and asphalts. **1976** *Lebende Sprachen* XXI. 151/2 Lubricate sparingly with petrolatum/white petroleum before destructive testing.

petrol bomb. [f. PETROL + *BOMB *sb.* 2.] A bomb, usu. home-made and thrown by hand, consisting of a petrol-filled bottle and a wick; a Molotov cocktail.

1958 [see *flick-knife* s.v. *FLICK *sb.*[1] 4]. **1963** *Times* 20 Feb. 11/3 It will be imposed where petrol bombs or inflammatory liquid or explosives are used against persons. **1969** *Guardian* 13 Aug. 1/1 The rioters threw petrol bombs. **1971** *Peace News* 10 Sept. 7/1 The effects of petrol bombs, CS gas and searchings were tragically obvious in the children. **1976** P. FERRIS *Detective* ii. 24 A petrol bomb was thrown.

Hence **pe·trol-bomb** *v. trans.*, to throw a petrol bomb at; to destroy or damage with a petrol bomb; **pe·trol bomber**, one who throws a petrol bomb; **pe·trol-bombing** *vbl. sb.*, throwing of a petrol bomb.

1963 *Times* 23 Feb. 7/4 Sir Edgar Whitehead, said that unless the Government dropped the provision making the death sentence for petrol bombing compulsory, the Opposition 'with all the constitutional means at our disposal will fight this Bill clause by clause to the bitter end'. **1969** *Guardian* 16 Aug. 9/1 The Catholics who were petrol-bombed out of their homes. **1971** *Daily Tel.* 4 Jan. 7/6 Other odd areas [of Paris] that are patrolled include the Chad Embassy (petrol-bombed a year ago). **1974** J. MITCHELL *Death & Bright Water* vii. 60 All he had to worry about now was the petrol bombers he'd seen. **1976** *Times* 23 Dec. 10/5 The dockyard boys had petrol-bombed the rent office.

petroleum. Add: Also in extended use (see quots.).

1938 A. W. NASH in A. E. Dunstan et al. *Sci. of Petroleum* I. I. 12/1 Petroleum may contain, or be composed of, ..compounds in the gaseous, liquid, and/or solid state, depending on the nature of these compounds and the existent conditions of temperature and pressure. **1960** J. W. AMYX et al. *Petroleum Reservoir Engin.* i. 1 Virtually all petroleum is produced from the earth in either liquid or gaseous form. **1960** C. GATLIN *Petroleum Engin.* i. 1/1 Petroleum may be defined as a naturally occurring mixture of hydrocarbons which may be either gas, liquid, or solid. *Ibid.* 4/2 (*heading*) Gaseous petroleum (natural gas). **1967** J. R. HUGHES *Storage & Handling Petroleum Liquids* 3 Petroleum, by legal definition (Petroleum (Consolidation) Act, 1928) 'includes crude petroleum, oil made from petroleum, or from coal, shale, peat or other bituminous substances, and other products of petroleum'. .. The term may also include natural gas found in petroleum-bearing formations.

b. *petroleum-bearing* adj.; **petroleum coke**, the solid, non-volatile residue left after the distillation and cracking of petroleum; **petroleum geology**, the branch of geology concerned with the search for oil and natural gas and with their formation, occurrence, and exploitation; so **petroleum geologist**; **petroleum jelly**, a soft, greasy, semi-solid mixture of hydrocarbons obtained from petroleum, used as an ointment and lubricant; cf. PETROLATUM, VASELINE.

1882 E. O'DONOVAN *Merv Oasis* I. ii. 37 Proprietors of large tracts of petroleum-bearing ground. **1963** D. W. & E. E. HUMPHRIES tr. *Termier's Erosion & Sedimentation* xi. 231 The evolution of petroleum-bearing sediments is brought to its final stages by diagenetic processes. **1881** *Jrnl. Chem. Soc.* XL. 239 (*heading*) Products from petroleum coke. **1971** *Materials & Technol.* II. x. 638 Since 1920 petroleum coke has become a plentiful by-product of petroleum cracking. *Ibid.* xi. 655 The high graphitizability of the petroleum coke results from the formation of large polycyclic aromatic molecules, which assists carbon crystallite alignment during the coking operation. **1917** *Bull. Geol. Soc. Amer.* XXVIII. 157 Petroleum geology is..a new profession. *Ibid.*, (*heading*) Ethics of the petroleum geologist. **1928** E. R. LILLEY *Geol. Petroleum & Nat. Gas* i. 8 The main work of the petroleum geologist until recently was that of locating areas in which anticlinal folds showed in the outcropping strata. **1973** R. E. CHAPMAN *Petroleum Geol.* ii. 22 A study of petroleum geology suggests that the construction of boreholes in the 20th century has not contributed sufficiently to modern geological thought, and that some of the difficulties..are due to the extension of the concepts developed from surface geology to the subsurface. *Ibid.* 27 The chemistry of petroleum..is low on the petroleum geologists' list of priorities. **1897** *Sears, Roebuck Catal.* 27/2 Petroleum Jelly. This is another name for the preparations called Vaseline, Cosmoline, etc., all made from Petroleum. **1906** T. E. HERBERT *Telegraphy* xxii. 782 As the cable passes into the pipe it is heavily anointed with petroleum jelly. **1922** D. T. DAY *Handbk. Petroleum Industry* II. 360 The official petrolatum of the United States Pharmacopœia, otherwise known as petroleum jelly, or 'Vaseline'. **1966** J. S. COX *Illustr. Dict. Hairdressing* 112/1 *Petroleum jelly*, (Petrolatum, Vaseline, Paraffin Jelly), a purified mixture of semi-solid hydrocarbons, chiefly of the Methane series.

petrolization (pe:trǒləizē^i·ʃən). [f. PETROLIZ(E *v.* + -ATION.] The oiling of water in order to kill mosquito larvæ.

1901 L. O. HOWARD *Mosquitoes* 193 The petrolization of mosquito-breeding pools is one of the most important measures to be taken in the warfare against mosquitoes. **1930** [see next].

petrolize, *v.* Add: **3.** = *OIL *v.* 1 c. So **pe·trolizing** *vbl. sb.*

1901 L. O. HOWARD *Mosquitoes* 193 To the Italians we are indebted for a useful expression, which we might just as well adopt, namely to 'petrolize', meaning to treat waters with kerosene. **1903** *Boston Even. Transcript* 28 Apr. 9/2 All the breeding places [of the mosquito] treated last year will again be petrolized this year. **1906** *Westm. Gaz.* 21 Apr. 16/1 Marshes are drained; ponds are petrolised or stocked with fish. **1930** I. J. KLIGLER *Epidemiology & Control of Malaria in Palestine* vii. 144 Petrolization and petrolizing mixtures.—One of the most important and useful methods of antilarval control is the oiling of the surface of breeding-places.

petrology. Add: **b.** The petrological features *of* something or somewhere.

1880 [in Dict.]. **1954** *Geol. Mag.* XCI. 44 (*heading*) Further data on the petrology of the pelitic hornfelses of the Carn Chuinneag-Inchbae region, Ross-shire. **1975** *Sci. Amer.* Jan. 29/1 The mineralogy, the content of trace elements and gas, the petrology and so on of literally hundreds of different meteorites have been measured.

petrologic *a.* (examples); chiefly *U.S.*

1936 H. L. ALLING *Interpretative Petrol. Igneous Rocks* p. vii, The portions of the book devoted to petrologic history. **1972** *Science* 3 Nov. 497/1 Approximately one-third of the book is devoted to mineralogic and petrologic attributes of sandstones.

Petronella (petrǒne·lă). Also with lower-case initial. [? the feminine name *Petronella*.] A Scottish country dance.

1897 *Ball Room* Nov. 11/1 The country dances of twenty-five or thirty years ago were being quite forgotten. 'Sir Roger', 'Triumph', 'Pettonella' [*sic*], the 'Saraband', [etc.]. **1905** F. H. NORMAN *Compl. Dance Instructor* 50 Petronella. **1907** N. MUNRO *Daft Days* xxx. 251 Our dances at the inn are not like city routs: Petronella, La Tempête, and the reel have still an honoured place in them. **1924** *Glasgow Herald* 1 Sept. 8 Despite the grumbles of old-timers who lament the passing of the schottisch, the lancers, and the polka—not to speak of petronella and 'La Va'—the dancing world is eminently conservative. **1935** N. MITCHISON *We have been Warned* I. i. 17 You and I danced Strip the Willow and Petronella. **1978** A. DUNNETT *No Thanks to Duke* xii. 175 We danced the whole night..Petronella, Strip the Willow,..Foursome Reel.

petrophysics (petrofi·ziks), *sb. pl.* (const. as *sing.*). *Geol.* [f. PETRO- + PHYSICS.] The study of the physical properties and behaviour of rocks.

1950 G. E. ARCHIE in *Bull. Amer. Assoc. Petroleum Geologists* XXXIV. 942 'Petrophysics' is suggested as the term pertaining to the physics of particular rock types, whereas geophysics pertains to the physics of larger rock systems composing the earth. The petrophysics of reservoir rocks is discussed here. **1959** *Times* 28 July 2/6 (Advt.), They [*sc.* applicants] should also be fully conversant with modern petrophysics methods. **1976** *Nature* 19 Feb. 607/2 Esoteric accounts of palaeotemperature analysis, coal metamorphism, petrography of volcanic rocks, petrophysics of chalk, and intimate analyses of stratigraphic boundaries.

So **petrophy·sical** *a.*; **petrophy·sicist**, a specialist or expert in petrophysics.

1950 G. E. ARCHIE in *Bull. Amer. Assoc. Petroleum Geologists* XXXIV. 961 A tentative petrophysical system ..is presented. **1956** *Geol. Mag.* XCIII. 112 The petrophysical characteristics of sedimentary and igneous rocks are important..in..deformation. **1972** *Bull. Amer. Assoc. Petroleum Geologists* LVI. 1906/2 Petrophysical analysis utilizing digital-log information has recently become a recognized tool in the search for oil and gas. **1975** G. ANDERSON *Coring* vii. 128 Most discussions on wireline logs define shale as a nonporous rock as compared to porous reservoir rocks, a point worth remembering in geological discussions with petrophysicists and the like.

petrosal, *a.* Add: Also applied to some branches derived from the facial and glossopharyngeal nerves that pass through the petrosal bone, and to the inferior ganglion of the glossopharyngeal nerve, situated in a notch in this bone. (Further examples.)

1881 A. L. RANNEY *Appl. Anat. Nervous Syst.* II. 179 (*caption*) A diagram of the branches of the facial nerve... 3, orifice of aqueduct of Fallopius; 4, large petrosal nerve; 5, small petrosal nerve; 6, external petrosal nerve. **1888** W. R. GOWERS *Man. Dis. Nervous Syst.* II. 250 The tympanic nerve of Jacobson (arising from the enlargement on the glosso-pharyngeal, termed the 'petrosal ganglion'), forms, with the sympathetic, the tympanic plexus in the wall of the middle ear. **1934** L. B. AREY *Developmental Anat.* (ed. 3) xvi. 438 The sensory fibres of the glossopharyngeal nerve arise from two ganglia, the superior ganglion closer to the brain and the petrosal ganglion farther peripherad on the trunk. **1972** M. L. BARR *Human Nervous Syst.* viii. 128/2 The sensory fibres in question [*sc.* those for taste] leave the facial nerve in the greater petrosal branch at the level of the geniculate ganglion.

petrotectonics (pe:trotektǫ·niks), *sb. pl.* (const. as *sing.*). *Geol.* [f. PETRO- + TECTONICS, repr. G. *petrographische tektonische analyse*.] The study of the structure of rocks, esp. as a guide to the movements to which they have been subjected. Cf. *PETROFABRICS *sb. pl.*

1933 *Amer. Jrnl. Sci.* XXV. 433 (*heading*) Petrotectonics. *Ibid.* 439 Sander uses the word petrotectonics to express the branch of the investigation that deals with the relation of the oriented microscopic fabric of deformed rocks to their tectonic history. **1937** *Q. Jrnl. Geol. Soc.* XCIII. 581 The science of *Gefügekunde*, variously translated as petrofabrics, petrotectonics, or structural petrology, is understood to comprise a study of all the spatial data, macroscopic and microscopic, which go to form a complete vector-picture so far as this is legible in the make-up of the rock. **1974** *Nature* 10 May 107/3 Evidence supporting the composite nature of Asia has been adduced from palaeomagnetism, palaeontology, geology and petrotectonics.

So **pe:trotecto·nic** *a.*

1933 *Amer. Jrnl. Sci.* XXV. 470 The ultimate test..will be the study by petrotectonic methods of material that has been deformed under known stress conditions. **1970** *Internat. Geol. Rev.* XII. 361/2 The internal petrotectonic structure of the intrusive body, which was established by systematic study of the orientations of the planar and linear parallelism, primary jointing, chromite and durite segregations and so forth, is folded and..corresponds to the folding of the host rocks.

pe-tsai (pe,tsai·). Also **Pe-Tsai.** [Older transliteration of Chinese *báicài*, f. *bái* white + *cài* vegetable; cf. *PAK-CHOI.] A Chinese species of cabbage, *Brassica pekinensis.* Also *attrib.*

1795 W. WINTERBOTHAM *Hist., Geogr., & Philos. View Chinese Empire* v. 221 The Chinese make provision of *pe-tsai* for winter; pickling of it, and mixing it with their rice. **1845** *Encycl. Metrop.* XVI. 588/1 The *Pe-tsai*, or white herb, a kind of mustard,..is cultivated in large fields, and eaten either fresh or pickled, like the German *Sauer-kraut.* **1885** [see *Chinese cabbage* s.v. *CHINESE *a.* 2]. **1900** L. H. BAILEY *Cycl. Amer. Hort.* I. 178/2 Pe-tsai cabbage. *Ibid.*, The Pe-tsai, or Chinese cabbage, is no longer a novelty in American gardens, though it does not appear to be well known, and its merits are not understood. **1960** *Farmer & Stockbreeder* 8 Mar. (Suppl.) 11/2 The celery-cabbage (Pe-Tsai) is worth trying, too. The heads are crisp and tender. **1969** *Oxf. Bk. Food Plants* 154/1 Pe-Tsai (*Brassica pekinensis*) is grown mostly for use as an autumn and winter vegetable... Pe-tsai has soft green, prominently veined leaves... The rather loose, elongated head bears some resemblance to a cos lettuce. **1972** *Homes & Gardens* Aug. 104/1 Chinese cabbage, or pe-tsai, is a new vegetable to this country. It comes from Israel and looks like a cross between a very pale whitish-green cos lettuce and a head of celery, although it is larger and considerably heavier than both. **1972** *Country Life* 14 Dec. 1676/3 Last autumn's drought delayed the growth of Chinese Pe-Tsai cabbage, sown in August, so..they are being cooked now.

petsywetsy (pe:tsiwe·tsi). *Nonce-wd.* [f. PET *sb.*^{1}: see -SY.] A fanciful extension of PET *sb.*^{1} 2.

1928 D. H. LAWRENCE *Lady Chatterley* xvii. 305 I'm not content to be any man's little petsywetsy.

pettable (pe·tăb'l), *a.* [f. PET *v.*^{1} + -ABLE.] Suitable for petting. Hence **pettabi·lity.**

1934 WEBSTER, Pettable. **1962** *Times* 17 Sept. 15/3 There is scarcely a 'pettable' creature that has not been adopted by my family. **1963** F. E. SPARSHOTT *Structure of Aesthetics* iii. 74 'Handsome'..is applied to things whose appearance stirs the imagination—but by suggestions of vigour rather than of pettability. **1978** *Chicago* June 50/2 In the large Children's Zoo, youngsters can walk into a petting area and be surrounded by pettable domestic animals.

petter, *sb.* Add: **2.** One who pets (*PET *v.* b); one who engages in petting (*PETTING *vbl. sb.* 2).

1925 *College Humor* Aug. 77/1 Have a nice evening? Jean's some high-type petter, isn't she? **1930** F. DELL *Love in Machine Age* ix. 170 Science's adjuration to the petters is only: 'You really *must* get *some* food and sleep, my dears!' **1931** F. L. ALLEN *Only Yesterday* v. 101 The vendors of another picture promised 'neckers, petters, white kisses, red kisses, pleasure-mad daughters, sensation-craving mothers'. **1931** *Brit. Jrnl. Psychol.* Oct. 183 One finds oneself extremely dubious about this contention that the modern adolescent 'petter' and 'demi-vierge' have discovered for themselves a satisfactory way of acquiring the adequate pre-marital emotional education. **1942** BERREY & VAN DEN BARK *Amer. Thes. Slang* § 443/13 Heavy necker *or* petter.

petti- (pe·ti). Combining form of PETTI(COAT *sb.*, designating garments having some of the characteristics or functions of a petticoat.

1922 JOYCE *Ulysses* 360 He could see her other things too, nainsook knickers, the fabric that caresses the skin, better than those other pettiwidth, the green, four and eleven, on account of being white. *Ibid.* 544 Lifting up her pettigown and folding a half sovereign into the top of her stocking. **1923** *Dialect Notes* V. 246 *Pettibockers*, n. pl. A loose garment for girls, worn under skirts: contamination of *petticoat* and *knickerbockers.* **1939** JOYCE *Finnegans Wake* IV. 611 His yellow saffron pettikilt. **1942** BERREY & VAN DEN BARK *Amer. Thes. Slang.* § 87/27 *Pettibockers*, women's old-fashioned knickerbockers. **1960** *Harper's Bazaar* Apr. 11 Nightdresses, slips, pettiskirts, panties. **1963** *Seventeen* Aug. 32 A new word in lingerie. Pettisets (a petti-top matched with petti-pants as well as a petticoat). **1964** *N.Y. Post* 7 Oct. 13 Perfect under your swinging skirts, pettipants fashioned with a divided skirt. **1968** J. IRONSIDE *Fashion Alphabet* 71 *Pettipants*, petticoat and pants combined. **1970** N. ARMSTRONG et al. *First on Moon* vi. 126 They found a present for Jan's friend—pettipants edged with green lace. **1972** *Daily Tel.* (Colour Suppl.) 13 Oct. 16/1 On top of this I wore a petti-blouse (which is a blouse and a petticoat).

Petticoat Lane. A popular name given to Middlesex Street (formerly Hog Lane) in the City of London, where dealers in second-hand clothes and other commodities congregate. Also *attrib.*

1602 in *Calendar of Cecil MSS.* 168 in *Parl. Papers 1910* (Cd. 5291) XXXIV. 1, I understand by Udall that Eccleston is a gentleman dwelling near Knowsely, but has left his habitation, and abides altogether in London, in Peticote Lane. **1631** B. JONSON *Devil an Ass* I. i. 60 We will suruay the Suburbs, and make forth our sallyes, Downe Petticoate-lane, and vp the Smock-allies, To Shoreditch, Whitechappell, and so to Saint Katharnes. **1909** W. W. HUTCHINGS *London Town* II. xc. 967/1 This street formerly Petticoat Lane, and in yet earlier days Hog Lane, has of late years been rebuilt, but it is still largely inhabited by dealers in second-hand clothes, and still on Sundays it is thronged by those who come to buy other people's cast-off garments. **1967** M. WADDELL *Otley Pursued* xii. 109 It was 6.42 by my Petticoat Lane watch, give or take ten minutes or so. **1972** *Police Rev.* 17 Nov. 1495/3 The man who had been given the licence had described the street..as 'Petticoat Lane'. Section 21(1) required that the particular street must be named, and Petticoat Lane has become Middlesex Street. **1976** *Oadby & Wigston Advertiser* 26 Nov. 10/1 Glen Parva Borstal was like a 'small Petticoat Lane' with items being offered for sale all the time, Rutland magistrates heard on Monday.

petting, *vbl. sb.* (in Dict. s.v. PET *v.*^{1}) Add: **2.** In the sense of *PET *v.*^{1} b: the action of amatory caressing and fondling; non-coital sexual activity. Also *attrib.* See also *heavy petting* s.v. *HEAVY *a.*^{1} 13.

1920 [see sense 3 below]. **1922** S. LEWIS *Babbitt* xviii. 228 Babbitt had heard stories of what the Athletic Club called 'goings-on' at young parties; of girls 'parking' their corsets in the dressing-room, of 'cuddling' and 'petting', and a presumable increase in what was known as Immorality. **1928** J. P. MCEVOY *Show Girl* 11 They have no time to perfect their petting technique. **1929** B. RUSSELL *Marriage & Morals* xii. 126 There is so much 'petting' and 'necking' that the absence of complete intercourse can only be viewed as a perversion. **1933** AUDEN *Dance of Death* 25 Gay girl to whom petting Matters so much Poor kid, the reason's You're out of touch With flowers and such. **1947** *Partisan Rev.* XIV. 273 When the couple finally reached the stage of mild petting in the living room, Ruth in the kitchen listened with a mixture of pleasure and distaste. **1948** A. C. KINSEY et al. *Sexual Behavior in Human Male* xvi. 531 This behavior is known to the younger generation as petting, although certain other terms are applied to certain types of contacts. Those which are confined to latitudes not lower than the neck are sometimes known as necking, and petting is distinguished from the heavy petting which involves a deliberate stimulation of the female breast, or of the male or female genitalia. *Ibid.*, In the present volume the term 'petting' has been applied to any sort of physical contact which does not involve a union of genitalia but in which there is a deliberate attempt to effect erotic arousal. **1956** S. ERTZ *Charmed Circle* 62 Indulging in a pastime that was highly popular with the young... They had been 'necking' or 'petting'. **1958** M. ARGYLE *Relig. Behaviour* x. 123 '*Petting to climax*' was as common among Kinsey's devout men as for the non-religious. A smaller proportion of Kinsey's devout female sample reported this, but Chesser's devout women reported as much 'petting' as the others. **1960,** etc. [see *HEAVY *a.*^{1} 13]. **1971** A. F. GUTTMACHER *Understanding Sex* iv. 52 There are many degrees of petting, from holding each other in your arms to mutually manipulating the genitals..without actually having sexual intercourse. **1976** *N.Y. Rev. Bks.* 13 May 20/4 Since the time of Kinsey there have been some important changes:..a decline in petting..and an increase in copulation.

3. *Comb.*, as **petting party,** a social gathering at which petting is the principal activity.

1920 F. SCOTT FITZGERALD *This Side of Paradise* I. ii. 64 That great current American phenomenon, the 'petting party'. **1926** A. HUXLEY *Jesting Pilate* IV. 265 Hymns and the movies and Irving Berlin. Petting Parties and the First Free United Episcopal Methodist Church. Jazz it up! **1934** R. CHANDLER in *Black Mask* Oct. 28/1 The prowl car takes a slant down it [*sc.* the old road] now and then looking for petting parties. **1946** [see *half-virgin* s.v. *HALF- II n]. **1973** A. MACVICAR *Painted Doll Affair* viii. 91 Drinking parties, drug parties, petting parties. Mostly youngsters.

petto. Add: *in petto*, ¶ (*b*) by confusion with PETTY *a.* (*sb.*^{1}): in short, in miniature, on a small scale.

1838 EMERSON *Jrnl.* 19 Sept. (1911) V. 53 Such ostentation *in petto* I never did see. **1844** DISRAELI *Coningsby* I. II. ii. 185 He commenced a discourse, which was in fact, one of his 'slashing' articles in petto on Church Reform. *a* **1846** B. HAYDON *Autobiogr.* (1853) I. 247 Away we marched, my little guide wearing a red night-cap..till we came in sight of the height, when my grenadier in petto turned round. **1894** W. S. HADLEY *Euripides' Hecuba* p. x, The effect thus produced within the compass of a single play is comparable to that brought about on a larger scale by the older trilogy... This trilogy *in petto* may be regarded as an experiment made by the youngest of the three great tragedians. **1901** KIPLING *Kim* xiii. 341 He represents *in petto* India in transition—the monstrous hybridism of East and West. **1924** T. E. LAWRENCE *Let.* 1 Jan. (1938) 450 Yes, it will be revised, but only in petto. No good cuts or noble changes, no re-writing: just punctuation and insect-blemishes removed. **1937** L. BROMFIELD *Rains Came* II. ii. 258 Mr. Bannerjee's house and garden were a kind of India *in petto*, overcrowded, confused, swarming with noisy life. **1979** *Country Life* 29 Mar. 947/4 In small (or, as people now cheerfully and wrongly say, *in petto*).

petty, *a.* (*sb.*^{1}) Add: **A.** *adj.* **5. petty apartheid,** apartheid as exercised in everyday life; racial segregation in its trivial applications (see *APARTHEID); **petty cash** (further example); also *attrib.*; **petty cash book** (examples).

1966 *Cape Argus* 8 Apr. 14 While separate development proceeds so slowly, the Government, for home consumption, makes demonstrations of strength on the petty apartheid front. **1971** *Rand Daily Mail* 10 June 12 You can just imagine what it feels like when you have to use a lift which is marked 'Goods only'; when you have to wait for the train in a cage-like sort of place, packed like sardines; when you have to buy food at a snack bar only through a window at the back. I think all these are what a sound mind can classify as petty apartheid. **1974** *Black Panther* 9 Feb. 15/4 Last week the Johannesburg City Council announced measures to eliminate what is called here 'petty apartheid'. These are practices of discrimination against the city's Blacks and coloreds not imposed by national law. **1977** *Time* 27 June 20/1 There have been some changes in 'petty apartheid'. Whites boast that 'international' hotels have been opened to blacks, and that blacks now participate in white sports, which has great symbolic meaning. **1839** DICKENS *Let. c* 18 Feb. (1965) I. 509 He was not quite correct in the facts of the 'petty cash' story, the realities of which are far more honorable to the noble fellows concerned. **1886** A. W. THOMSON *Text-bk. Princ. & Pract. Bk.-Keeping* iii. 37 When a number of small payments need to be made..a separate book called the Petty Cash Book is kept for recording such payments. **1922** JOYCE *Ulysses* 171 He went towards the window and, taking up the petty cash book, scanned its pages. **1974** *Terminol. Managem. & Financial Accountancy* (Inst. Cost and Managem. Accountants) 57 *Petty cash book*, a separate record of small cash receipts and payments.

B. *sb.*^{1} **1.** Restrict † *Obs.* to sense in Dict. and add: **b.** A school or class for small boys.

c **1810** W. HICKEY *Mem.* (1913) I. ii. 13, I however soon got out of that disgraceful and ignorant form, passed with rapidity and *eclat* the under and upper petty, and entered into the upper first. **1961** R. WILLIAMS *Long Revolution* 133 The 'petties' or 'ABCs' were proper schools.

2. (Examples.)

1848 M. J. STANLEY *Let.* 27 Sept. in N. Mitford *Ladies of Alderley* (1938) 206 If these houses had been built by his Lordship every one would have had his *petty*, at all events dividing the odour. **1961** E. WILLIAMS *George* I. vii. 87 It was a nice little cottage.., with a lot of neglected garden and a tumbledown petty. *Ibid.* II. xi. 151 Mam.. hated the petty for being attached to next door's.

petty (pe·ti), *sb.*^{2} Familiar abbrev. of PETTICOAT *sb.*

1915 T. BURKE *Nights in Town* 63 There..was young Beryl, superintending her aunt's feverish struggles with paint and powder-jars, frocks, petties,..and wraps. **1939** JOYCE *Finnegans Wake* I. 87 The litigants..were egged on by their supporters in the shape of betterwomen with bowstrung hair of Carrothagenuine ruddiness, waving crimson petties and screaming from Isod's towertop. **1971** *Guardian* 24 Aug. 9/1 The language of lingeries..petties and pretties, and frillies.

petty bou·rgeois. [f. PETTY *a.* (*sb.*^{1}) as anglicization of Fr. *petit* + BOURGEOIS *sb.*^{1} and *a.*] = *PETIT BOURGEOIS. Also (occas. with hyphen) *attrib.* or as *adj.*

1888 S. MOORE tr. *Marx & Engels's Manifesto of Communist Party* 24 In countries where modern civilization has become fully developed, a new class of petty bourgeois has been formed. *Ibid.* 26 German Socialism recognised.. its own calling as the bombastic representative of the petty bourgeois socialism. **1904** in R. C. K. Ensor *Mod. Socialism* xx. 289, I reckon, the life of the petty bourgeois, ..is an unhappy one. **1906** E. M. AVELING tr. *Plechanoff's Anarchism & Socialism* iii. 26 His [*sc.* Max Stirner's] 'League of Egoists' is only the Utopia of a petty bourgeois in revolt. *Ibid.* iv. 35 Proudhon was the most typical representative of petty bourgeois socialism. **1931** *Times Lit. Suppl.* 26 Feb. 141/3 It is for its intellectual critics, whom it first degrades by the question-begging epithet 'petty-bourgeois', that Bolshevism reserves its cruellest penalties. **1936** 'M. INNES' *Death at President's Lodging* vii. 133 Our Inspector's petty-bourgeois passion for the till. **1943** H. READ *Politics of Unpolitical* 15 According to Dr. Fromm, Hitler succeeded so well because he was able to combine the qualities of a resentful petty-bourgeois.. with those of an opportunist ready to serve the interests of the German industrialists and Junkers. **1951** C. W. MILLS *White Collar* I. ii. 30 It is..a feature of such petty-bourgeois life that extreme repression is often exercised in its patriarchal orbit. **1954** KOESTLER *Invis. Writing* 25 Revulsion against this code was a sign of sentimental *petit-bourgeois* prejudice. **1958** I. MURDOCH in N. Mackenzie *Conviction* 230 This mass is now quiescent, its manner of life largely suburban and its outlook 'petty bourgeois'. **1960** D. LESSING *In Pursuit of English* i. 13 These are not the real working-class. They are the lumpen-proletariat, tainted by petty-bourgeois ideology. **1974** J. WHITE tr. *Poulantzas's Fascism & Dictatorship* III. ii. 111 The Nazi Party was filling the whole State apparatus..with members of petty-bourgeois origin and with their own quite specific petty-bourgeois ideology. **1977** *Time* 24 Jan. 14/3 Italian Communist Party.. spokesmen have denounced the leftists as 'petty bourgeois' hoodlums. **1978** *Encounter* Feb. 36/2 The 'people' is what the petty bourgeois of the spirit transform all men and women into.

pe·tty bourgeoisie·. [f. as prec. + BOURGEOISIE.] = *PETIT BOURGEOISIE.

1850 *Red Republican* 16 Nov. 171/1 The petty Bourgeoisie, the inferior ranks of the middle-class, the small manufacturers, merchants, tradesmen, and farmers, tend to become Proletarians. **1920** F. E. GREEN *Hist. Eng. Agric. Labourer 1870–1920* v. 125 The farmers and the petty bourgeoisie took possession of the Parish and the Rural District Councils. **1924** G. B. SHAW *Saint Joan* Pref. p. xiii, In short, much more of a young lady, and even of an intellectual, than most of the daughters of our petty bourgeoisie. **1930** tr. *Marx & Engels's Communist Manifesto* iii. 56 In the countries where modern civilization flourishes, a new petty bourgeoisie has come into being. This class hovers between the proletariat and the bourgeoisie. **1956** C. W. MILLS *Power Elite* xiv. 329 Classic conservatism has required the spell of tradition among such surviving elements of pre-industrial societies as an aristocracy of noble men, a peasantry, a petty-bourgeoisie with guild inheritances. **1957** R. N. C. HUNT *Guide to Communist Jargon* 118 Generally speaking, Marx and Engels understood by the petty-bourgeoisie the small traders who, they contended, were being driven down into the proletariat by the monopolist capitalists. **1969** A. G. FRANK *Latin Amer.* xix. 312 The next layer may be termed the middle class or petty bourgeoisie. It comprises a large variety of economic walks of life—small landowner, professional, merchant, clergy, government and white collar worker, small politician—but it affords considerable lateral mobility within it, from one occupation to another. **1975** *Times Lit. Suppl.* 14 Mar. 270/4 In Havana in 1827,..a higher proportion of coloureds were legitimately married than of whites. This black 'petty bourgeoisie' was, however, dispersed..in the repression of 1844 and the terms of the racial stratification system were redefined to the advantage of the whites.

petty-mi·nded, *a.* [MINDED *ppl. a.* III.] Having or characteristic of a mind that dwells on the trivial and ignores what is important. So **petty-mi·ndedness.**

1909 *Daily Chron.* 10 June 7/4 Weakness and petty-mindedness were fostered by the narrow sphere and limited outlook that..such tasks necessitated. **1927** V. WOOLF in *Forum* (N.Y.) May 707 It was all so paltry, weak-blooded, and petty-minded to care so much at her age. **1954** T. S. ELIOT *Confid. Clerk* I. 25 He's not petty-minded—though nothing escapes him. **1963** W. SOYINKA *Dance of Forests* 57 Is the nation to ignore the challenge of greatness because of the petty-mindedness of a few cowards and traitors. **1978** *Times* 24 Jan. 14/5 This.. petty-minded change of policy.

petulate (pe·tiul*ē*it), *v. rare*[−1]. [f. PETUL(ANT *a.* + -ATE[3].] *trans.* To make petulant or peevish. In quot. as *ppl. adj.*

1897 [see *HYPERSENSITIZE *v.*].

Peulh (pəl), *sb.* and *a.* Also 8 **Pholey,** 9 **Pul(ah), Púl(l)o,** 9-**Peul, Pul(l)o; Peuhl.** [Native name; prop. the sing. of *FULAH.] = *FULAH *sb.* and *a.*

[**1611** BIBLE *Isaiah* lxvi. 19, I will send those that escape of them unto the nations, to Tarshish, Pul and Lud.] **1799** M. PARK *Trav. Afr.* (ed. 2) ii. 17 The Foulahs (or Pholeys)..are chiefly of a tawny complexion, with soft silky hair, and pleasing features. **1858** H. BARTH *Trav. N. & Cent. Afr.* II. xxxiv. 414 A Mohammedan kingdom engrafted upon a mixed stock of pagan tribes,—the conquest of the valorous and fanatic Púllo chieftain, A'dama, over the great pagan kingdom of Fúmbiná. *Ibid.* IV. lvii. 143 If any African tribe deserves the full attention of the learned European, it is that of the Fúlbe (*sing.* Púllo), or Fula, as they are called by the Mandingoes. **1876** G. A. L. REICHARDT *Gram. Fulde Lang.* p. xiii, (*heading*) Introduction to a grammar of the Pul language... The proper and indigenous name for the Fulahs, as we have called them, is Pulo. *Ibid.* p. xiv, we find a strong Pulo empire in a northwesterly direction, from the upper course of the Jaliba. **1883** R. N. CUST *Mod. Lang. Afr.* I. x. 158 This language..is known by many names, Fula,..Púlo, Pulah,..; its meaning is said to be 'light brown', as opposed to that of the neighbouring people, Wolof or 'black'. **1898** A. J. BUTLER tr. *Ratzel's Hist. Mankind* III. v. xi. 296 Fulbe or Fulah (sing. Pullo, Peul) is the Mandingo name, Fellani the Houssa... These names seem to indicate the lighter colour of their skin. **1915** A. WERNER *Lang. Families Afr.* vi. 100 We have.. referred to the Fula language... The people who speak it call themselves Ful-be (in the singular, Pulo). **1921** F. W. TAYLOR *First Gram. Adamawa Dial. of Fulani Lang.* 6 The people whose language is the subject of this book call themselves Pullo in the singular and Fulbe in the plural. **1931** W. B. SEABROOK *Jungle Ways* III. ii. 199 Women walked in groups, with long black robes and faces of pale ivory, cameo-cut... These special women, notoriously beautiful as a race,..were Peuhls. **1932** W. L. GRAFF *Lang.* 154 Peul, Wolof, and Serere, three languages of the above-mentioned African group. **1935** G. GOVER *Africa Dances* II. 159 The Peulh women were remarkable for their lighter skin and sharper features. **1959** *Encounter* Sept. 36/1 M. Diallo belongs to the Peulhs, a fascinating people..spread throughout the sub-Saharan regions of Africa. **1973** *Guardian* 19 June 18/1 The Tuareg and Peul nomads have..watched the bulk of their scrawny animals die.

pew, *sb.*[1] Add: **2. d.** Loosely, a seat, esp. in phr. *take a pew.*

1898 BELLOC *Mod. Traveller* i. 5 Be seated; take a pew. **1903** WODEHOUSE *Prefect's Uncle* xvi. 230 The genial 'take a pew' of one's equal inspires confidence. **1914** C. MACKENZIE *Sinister St.* II. III. vii. 652 Come in, you chaps... I don't know any of your names, but take pews, take pews. **1926** I. MACKAY *Blencarrow* xiii. 116 'Have a pew?' he offered, making himself as small as possible on the red plush car seat. **1939** R. LEHMANN *No More Music* 90 Colonel: (drawing up a chair) Take a pew. **1958** B. HAMILTON *Too Much of Water* xi. 232 Have the pew. I'll squat on the bed. **1974** K. ROYCE *Trap Spider* ii. 30 Sit down, Spider. Take a pew.

4. *pew-door* (later examples); **pew group** *Pottery,* figures on a high-backed bench, usu. in salt-glazed stoneware.

1803 G. COLMAN *John Bull* I. i. 4 Troth! and myself.. was brought up to the church... I opened all the pew doors at Belfast. **1842** Pew-door [see UNACCOMMODATED *ppl. a.*]. **1906** G. W. & F. A. RHEAD *Staffs. Pots* xiv. 170 The British Museum 'pew group'..is one of four known pieces of the kind, all evidently by the same hand. **1942** *Burlington Mag.* Oct. 260/1 Most dangerous are the increasingly skilful fakes of Astbury and Whieldon figures, first betrayed by the marks of Wedgwood on a pew group and Ralph Wood on a figure of similar origin. **1961** L. G. G. RAMSEY *Connoisseur New Guide Antique Eng. Pott., Porc. & Glass* 39 Aaron Wood (1717–85), to whom have been attributed also the vigorous and amusing salt-glaze 'Pew Groups', modelled in the round and representing a man and woman courting, a pair of musicians, etc. **1976** *Country Life* 5 Feb. 278/1 These..Staffordshire salt-glaze groups are still referred to as pew groups, where everyone by now is aware that these people..are not seated in church..but are on a wooden settle.

pewful. (Later example.)

1938 M. MUGGERIDGE *In Valley* iv. 23 The congregation, a few pewfuls, nodded to his words.

pewing, *vbl. sb.* (In Dict. s.v. PEW *v.*[1]) (Further *concr.* examples.)

1840 W. DYOTT *Diary* 31 July (1907) II. 322, I visited the old church at Ashbourne to admire the new pewing and other highly ornamental improvements. **1970** H. BRAUN *Parish Churches* i. 20 The Victorian church,.. packed with pewing and comfortably behassocked.

pewter. Add: **1. c.** The colour of the alloy, a bluish or silver grey.

1971 *Vogue* Nov. 81/1 One size tights in palest pewter. **1979** *Guardian* 28 Apr. 32/2 Single-leg stocking tights... Colours: Dark Tan, Mink, American Tan, Pewter, Black.

2. c. (Earlier example.)

1829 P. EGAN *Boxiana* 2nd Ser. II. 90 The exertions of *Jack's* fists and his tongue were both rewarded by a shower of *browns,* and also a little *pewter* into the bargain.

5. b. Of the colour of pewter.

1922 JOYCE *Ulysses* 46 Galleys of the Lochlanns ran here to beach,.. their bloodbeaked prows riding low on a molten pewter surf. **1972** 'H. BUCKMASTER' *Walking Trip* 135 They stood silently looking at the pewter water and pewter sky. **1975** B. GARFIELD *Death Sentence* (1976) xxix. 137 The sky had thickened and gone pewter.

6. pewter grey = sense *1 c.

1973 J. ROSSITER *Manipulators* xiii. 134 Lampett Street was long..its pewter-grey length made residential by the planting of trees. **1975** 'D. JORDAN' *Black Account* xxxviii. 193 The White Nile is no longer white but pewter grey.

pewterer. (Later examples.)

1930 *Aberdeen Press & Jrnl.* 14 Oct. 6 Pewterers nowadays are making their articles tougher and more shock-resisting. **1955** *Times* 16 June 9/6 The pewterer's craft is a peculiarly English one. **1976** *New Yorker* 15 Nov. 73/2 (Advt.), Our attention to detail and unexcelled workmanship have earned us a Royal Title—a distinction no other pewterer in the world can claim.

-pexy (peksi), terminal element repr. Gr. -πηξια, πῆξις a fixing or putting together (f. πηγνύναι to join or fix), used in the names of surgical operations for fixing organs in position; as *hysteropexy* (s.v. HYSTERO-[1]), *orchidopexy* (s.v. *ORCHIDO-).

Peyerian, *a.* (Examples of *Peyer's patches* (rarely in *sing.*).)

1858 R. G. MAYNE *Expos. Lex. Med. Sci.* (1860) 924/1 Peyer's glands, Peyer's patches. **1870** *Trans. Path. Soc.* XXI. 391 There were no leuchæmic nodules in the liver or kidneys, and the tonsils, like Peyer's patches, were remarkably inconspicuous. **1886** C. H. FAGGE *Princ. & Pract. Med.* I. 183 If in a Peyer's patch, it is usually elongated in the direction of the axis of the intestine. **1955** *Sci. News Let.* 23 July 51/1 Polio antibodies in the blood.. build up their response to polio while the virus is still multiplying in the tonsils and the Peyer's patches of the small intestine. **1974** PASSMORE & ROBSON *Compan. Med. Stud.* III. xii. 46/1 Enteric or typhoid fevers... Hyperplasia and mononuclear infiltration lead to swelling of the intestinal lymphoid tissue, especially the Peyer's patches of the lower ileum.

peyote (pey*ō*u·te). Also **payote, pellote, pelotte, peyoti, peyotl,** etc. [Amer. Sp. *peyote,* a. Nahuatl *peyotl.*] **1.** = *MESCAL 3 a.

[**1859** BARTLETT *Dict. Amer.* (ed. 2) 509 *Whiskey-root,* a plant of the Cactus species possessing intoxicating properties, which is thus described by a correspondent of the New Orleans Picayune: 'It is what the Indians call Pie-o-ke.'] **1885** *Proc. U.S. Nat. Museum* VIII. 521 It is principally as an intoxicant that the Peyote has become noted, being often added to 'tizwin' or other mild fermented native drink to render it more inebriating. **1898** J. MOONEY in *17th Ann. Rep. U.S. Bureau Amer. Ethnol. 1895–96* I. 238 The worship of the peyote..is comparatively modern with the Kiowa. **1911,** etc. [see *MESCAL 3 a]. **1927** *Daily News* 28 Sept. 8/7 M. R. Desille..said that a herb..known as peyotl 'produced remarkable hallucinations of undoubted psychic value'. **1955** *Sci. News Let.* 2 July 4/1 Mescaline is extracted from the Mexican plant better known as peyote. **1969** D. WENIGER *Cacti of Southwest* 95/2 The insignificant members of this genus [sc. *Lophophora*]..are the sacred plants of the Indians best known by the ancient Indian name, *peyotl,* which has become the peyote of modern usage. **1977** LEWIS & ELVIN-LEWIS *Med. Bot.* xviii. 405/2 Peyote is usually eaten as mescal buttons, the dried, brown pieces of the above-ground part of the cactus. Occasionally fresh green pieces are used. *Ibid.* 407/1 Peyote is also brewed and the tea drunk.

2. = *MESCAL 3 b.

1849 J. W. AUDUBON *Western Jrnl.* (1906) 186 Out of these acorns the Indians make their 'payote', a kind of paste. **1913** [see **mescal button*]. **1915** *Jrnl. Heredity* VI. 295/2 The majority from the *peyote* and the wine were unable to utilize their legs. **1916** *Jrnl. Amer. Med. Assoc.* 15 Jan. 194/2 Among the menaces..to which some of the American Indians are said to be exposed..is the use of a natural product variously known as mescal buttons, peyote or pellote. **1953** [see *HIGH *sb.* 1 h]. **1975** *High Times* Dec. 49/3 Many natural hallucinogens—peyote is a good example—are supposed to trigger nausea by their direct pharmacological actions.

3. *attrib.* and *Comb.,* as *peyote cactus, high;* **peyote button** = **mescal button*; **peyote cult** = *PEYOTISM.

1921 M. R. HARRINGTON *Relig. & Ceremonies of Lenape* viii. 185 (*caption*) Peyote 'Button'. Diameter 1·9 in. **1966** G. BAXT *Queer Kind of Death* (1967) xiv. 204 The stupid bastard must have cut himself a peyoti button. **1975** 'S. MARLOWE' *Cawthorn Journals* (1976) II. xi. 88 Have you ever eaten peyote buttons? **1953** A. HUXLEY *Let.* 21 June (1969) 678 The most extraordinary fact about mescaline—the active principle in the peyotl cactus used by the North American Indians..—is that it is almost completely non-toxic. **1974** M. C. GERALD *Pharmacol.* xvii. 327 Among the plants the Spanish conquistadors observed to be worshipped by the Mexican natives was the peyote cactus. **1920** *Univ. Calif. Publ. Amer. Archaeol. & Ethnol.* XVI. 437 It was quite customary to eat peyote during the day in the early days of the peyote cult. **1970** *Times Lit. Suppl.* 18 Dec. 1480/5 Now coca..became the basis of a kind of peyote cult. **1953** Peyote high [see *HIGH *sb.* 1 h].

peyotism (pē·yǒ̄tiz'm). [f. *PEYOT(E + -ISM.] A religious cult of American Indians in which peyote is taken sacramentally. Hence **peyo·tist,** one who practises this religion.

1934 V. PETRULLO (*title*) The diabolic root: a study of peyotism, the new Indian religion, among the Delawares. *Ibid.* II. 126 The original Peyote people claim that one cannot be a Christian and a Peyotist at the same time. **1953** A. HUXLEY *Let.* 17 Aug. (1969) 683 No craving.. even among people who have been peyotists for forty or fifty years. **1957** P. WORSLEY *Trumpet shall Sound* 223 Henceforth the Indians turned..to pacific cults like peyotism. **1971** E. SHORRIS *Death of Great Spirit* iii. 34 God may change the peyotist, but the peyotist..has no hope of changing God. *Ibid.* 38 Apologists for peyotism say, 'It is the only thing we have left that is Indian.'

Peyronie's disease (pē[i]rǒni). *Path.* [Named after François de La *Peyronie* (1678–1747), French physician, who described the condition in 1743 (*Mém. Acad. r. de Chirurgie* I. 425).] (See quot. 1974.)

1903 *Boston Med. & Surg. Jrnl.* CXLVIII. 245/1 (*heading*) Peyronie's disease. **1949** H. C. ROLNICK *Pract. Urol.* I. xi. 173 In Peyronie's disease or plastic induration of the corpora cavernosa the incurvation becomes noticeable on erection. **1974** PASSMORE & ROBSON *Compan. Med. Stud.* III. xxvii. 13/1 Fibrous cavernositis (Peyronie's disease) is a condition in which fibrous plaques develop near the glans or on the dorsum of the penis, and cause curvation, swelling, pain on erection and interference with coitus.

pezazz, var. *PIZZAZZ.

Pfalzian (pfæ·ltsiăn), *a.* (*sb.*) *Geol.* Also **Pfälzian.** [ad. G. *Pfälzische* (F. Kühne 1922, in *Jahrb. Preuss. Geol. Landesanst.* XLIII. 433), f. *Pfalz,* the (Rhineland) Palatinate (ult. f. L. *palatium* imperial residence: see PALACE *sb.*[1]): see -IAN.] Pertaining to or designating a minor orogenic episode in Europe which is believed to have occurred in the Permian period, later than the *SAALIAN. Also *ellipt.* as *sb.*

1931 GREGORY & BARRETT *Gen. Stratigr.* 19 Pfalzian. Between Trias and Permian. **1932** T. W. E. DAVID *Explan. Notes to accompany New Geol. Map Austral.* 73 While the epi-Permian movement as a whole seems nearly to correspond with the Pfalzian of Europe and the Appalachian of U.S.A., it would seem that in eastern Australia it continued, in places, for some little time after Pfalzian and Appalachian disturbance had ended. **1937** A. L. DU TOIT *Our Wandering Continents* viii. 164 At the close of the Permian, during the Pfalzian Phase, the central plateau of France and the Saar region were upheaved along an E.–W. axis. **1974** [see *SAALIAN *a.*].

‖ **Pfannkuchen** (pfa·nkuχĕn). Also **pfannekuchen.** [G.] In Germany and other German-speaking areas, a pancake.

1877 [see *KRAPFEN]. **1906** *Cosmopolitan* XLII. 547/1 Do you sometimes haf *pfannekuchen* for supper? **1964** L. DEIGHTON *Funeral in Berlin* xl. 242 'You got rid of your tail?'..'He got a lapful of *Pfannkuchen* and scalding coffee.'

‖ **Pfefferkuchen** (pfe·fərkuχĕn). Also **pfeffer-kuchen.** [G., lit. 'pepper cake'.] In Germany and other German-speaking areas, a spiced cake, gingerbread.

1870 *Western Monthly* Jan. 29/1 One long room..being gay with bright Christmas trees loaded with nuts, apples, sugar-plums, and all sorts of jolly-looking figures in honey-cake and *pfeffer-kuchen.* **1961** J. HELLER *Catch-22* (1962) xxiv. 249 Pumpernickel and *Pfefferkuchen* from Berlin. **1977** G. BUTLER *Brides of Friedberg* v. 136 Underneath I put little dishes of Pfefferkuchen, Nüsse and Stolle.

Pfeiffer (pfəi·fəɹ). *Bacteriol.* The name of Richard *Pfeiffer* (1858–1945), German bacteriologist, used in the possessive and *attrib.* to designate: **a.** The specific lysis of the cholera vibrio in the presence of antibody and complement as described by him (in *Zeitschr. für Hygiene und Infektionskrankh.* (1893) XIV. 59).

[**1895** E. METCHNIKOFF in *Ann. de L'Inst. Pasteur* IX. 438 La découverte de la destruction extracellulaire des microbes dans le liquid péritonéal, ou de ce qu'on peut appeler le 'phenomène de Pfeiffer', suggère toute une série de questions touchant le problème général de l'immunité.] **1897** MUIR & RITCHIE *Man. Bacteriol.*

xvii. 393 A striking change is observed microscopically in the vibrios when injected along with the protective serum into the peritoneal cavity of another guinea-pig—Pfeiffer's reaction. **1929** TOPLEY & WILSON *Princ. Bacteriol. & Immunity* II. lxi. 905 Pfeiffer's phenomenon is of great value in the identification of the cholera vibrio. **1970** *Science* 3 Apr. 141/2 (*heading*) A new application of he Pfeiffer phenomenon.

b. A species of bacterium, *Hæmophilus influenzæ*, described by him (in *Deutsch. med. Wochenschr.* (1892) 14 Jan. 28) as the causal agent of influenza, but now known not to be. **1900** H. J. CURTIS *Essent. Pract. Bacteriol.* 287/1 (Index), Pfeiffer's influenza bacillus. **1910** HISS & ZINSSER *Text-bk. Bacteriol.* xxxvii. 528 The bacillus of influenza (Pfeiffer bacillus) is an extremely small organism, about 0·5 micron long. **1936** *Lancet* 12 Dec. 1383/1 The illness produced by introducing virulent cultures of Pfeiffer's bacillus into a healthy person is not genuine epidemic influenza. **1953** J. RAMSBOTTOM *Mushrooms & Toadstools* xxiii. 278 The insensitive Pfeiffer's bacillus.. in the respiratory tract is usually associated with organisms highly sensitive to penicillin.

pfella (Pfe·la). Also **pfeller.** Repr. Austral. Aborigines' pronunc. of FELLOW *sb.* Cf. *FELLA, FELLAH. In Austral. Pidgin often used as a marker of an adjective, demonstrative, or numeral. **1908** 'G. SEAGRAM' *Bushmen All* 310 Now you go longa Warrego an' big pfella pleeseman hang you longa rope. **1921** A. B. PATERSON *Man from Snowy River* (new ed.) 74 What parson tellin' you, Ole Mister Dodd, Tell you in Sunday-school? Big pfeller God! **1936** M. FRANKLIN *All that Swagger* iii. 38 That one sit down longa white pfella—all same as white pfella. *Ibid.* iv. 46 Danny had established himself as a superman, a big pfella chief. *Ibid.* vii. 65 Minetinkit, that pfella budgery! **1936** I. L. IDRIESS *Cattle King* xxix. 257 How much would you want to make a big pfella flood, Paddy?

pfennig, -ing. Add: Also *Comb.* **1909** *Daily Chron.* 15 July 4/7, I have an actual pfennig-piece before me as I write, which was coined in 1894. **1979** R. COX *Auction* iii. 75 Pouring pfennig pieces into a coinbox.

pfft (f't, pf't). Also **pfft, phfft, phtt,** etc. [Echoic.] = *PHUT *int.* (*adv.*, *sb.*). **1923** KIPLING *Irish Guards in Gt. War* I. 5 One..rifle-bullet landed with a *phtt* in the chalk between two officers. **1934** *Amer. Speech* IX. 313/2 Then it all goes pfft. **1942** BERREY & VAN DEN BARK *Amer. Thes. Slang* §360/2 *Divorce*,..go pfft, — pffft *or* phut,..pfft, phffft, phut. **1954** WODEHOUSE *Jeeves & Feudal Spirit* iii. 29 It wouldn't take much to make the Stilton–Florence axis go p'fft again. **1972** F. WARNER *Lying Figures* I. 6 Commuters' corset till sixty-five, then pppfft! the six by four. **1975** *Washington Post* 10 Mar. B1 A voice..said 'Thank you, Barbra' and, phffft! The hour was over. **1977** *Ibid.* 13 Jan. C1/3 Senatorial marriages of 5, 23 and 35 years were going pfffffff, as the Hollywood columnists used to write. **1977** *Rolling Stone* 16 June 11/2 Nothin' serious; $500 in bail, phffffftttt.

Hence **pfft** *v. intr.* (*U.S. journalists' slang*), to come to an abrupt end, to collapse; of a couple, to become estranged, to separate, to divorce; also *transf.* and as *ppl. adj.* **1930** *Vanity Fair* (N.Y.) Jan. 48/3 Mr. Walter Winchell ..exercises a tremendous power for mischief with impassive diablerie: 'the so-and-sos have phfft!' **1938** W. WINCHELL in *Baltimore News-Post* 16 Mar. 16/2 Have Lionel Stander and the films phfft? **1938** —— in *Ibid.* 21 Mar. 10/1 Burton Rascoe and Dorothy Parker have phffft! **1939** *Time* 28 Aug. 13 Gossip columnists took this as renewed notice that the Franklin D. Jrs. are not *phphpht* as gossiped. **1940** *New Yorker* 13 July 22/3 International Politics, March 29, 1937. 'Adolf and Benito have phffft! The break will be announced soon enough.' **1946** J. T. SHIPLEY in W. S. Knickerbocker *20th Cent. English* 136 To indicate the collapse of a project..the columnist declares that it has pfft. **1957** *Chicago Amer.* 9 Feb. 17/8 Alan and Joanne Rio, who were dating, have pffft.

pfui (fu·i, ‖ pfu·i), *int.* [G.: cf. PHOO *int.*, *PHOOEY *int.* (*sb.*).] (Orig. in Germany or among German-speaking people) an exclamation of contempt or disgust.

Hence **pfuiteufel** (pfŭ·i,toifĕl) [G. *teufel* devil], emphatically in same sense. **1866** C. M. YONGE *Dove in Eagle's Nest* I. x. 206 Christina heard Friedel say..'I think I shall be a priest, Ebbo.' To which Ebbo only answered, 'Pfui!' **1871** GEO. ELIOT in *Macm. Mag.* July 185 Pfui! The time was, I drank that home-brewed wine. **1920** D. H. LAWRENCE *Touch & Go* 6 The plays are good... What about your *good* plays? Whose good? *Pfui* to your goodness! **1922** JOYCE *Ulysses* 184 Out on't! *Pfuiteufel!* **1934** R. MACAULAY *Going Abroad* xxxiii. 281 Pfui, my poor Pierre, you are a fool. **1935** C. ISHERWOOD *Mr. Norris changes Trains* iv. 52 You men are all alike; from seventeen to seventy... *Pfui!* I'm surprised at you. **1937** WYNDHAM LEWIS *Blasting & Bombardiering* 100 Why should one be asked to meet such people? It is absurd that a Bennett should be referred to, for anything except the time of a train or the cost of a bicycle lamp! Pfui! **1943** E. M. ALMEDINGEN *Frossia* ii. 107, 'I trusted you. Pfui,' he spat on the paper-strewn floor. **1949** R. STOUT *Second Confession* xiii. 134 'I didn't get him to. As it says, he wrote and signed it of his own free will.' 'Pfui. I know what it says. But why should I believe that when I don't believe anything in it?' **1966** —— *Death of Doxy* (1967) vi. 71 Pfui. A prodigy on a treadmill. Take him off. **1972** *Human World* May 96 Brutal to give a little girl a doll? Brutal to bring children up? Pfui! Not all the madmen are in the madhouses. **1974** WODEHOUSE *Aunts aren't Gentlemen* ix. 163, I don't mind criticism, but I will not endure vulgar abuse. 'Pfui,' I said. It is an expression I don't often use, but Nero Wolfe is always saying it with excellent results.

Pfund (funt). *Physics.* The name of A. Herman *Pfund* (1879–1949), U.S. physicist, used *attrib.* to designate a series of lines in the infra-red part of the spectrum of atomic hydrogen, with wave numbers represented by $R(1/5^2 - 1/m^2)$ (where R is the Rydberg constant and m = 6, 7, ...), of which the first line has a wavelength of 74·61 micrometres and the series limit is at 22·80 micrometres. **1934** H. L. BROSE tr. *Sommerfeld's Atomic Struct. & Spectral Lines* (ed. 3) ii. 73 A. H. Pfund found an infra-red line belonging to hydrogen at $\lambda = 7{\cdot}40\mu$, which is the first member of a 'Pfund series' and corresponds to $n = 5$, $m = 6$. **1970** D. W. TENQUIST et al. *University Optics* II. ii. 43 Lines in the infra-red part of the spectrum are caused by transitions terminating at $n = 3$ (Paschen series), $n = 4$ (Brackett series) and $n = 5$ (Pfund series).

pH (pī,ē·tʃ). Formerly also p_H, **PH.** [Introduced (in Ger.) as p_H. by S. P. L. Sörensen 1909, in *Biochem. Zeitschr.* XXI. 134, the *p* repr. G. *potenz* power and H· the hydrogen ion.] A measure of the acidity or alkalinity of a solution, equal to the logarithm to the base 10 of the reciprocal of the effective concentration (activity) of hydrogen ions (in moles per litre).

A pH of 7 corresponds to a neutral solution, one less than 7 to an acidic solution, and one greater than 7 to an alkaline solution.

1909 *Jrnl. Chem. Soc.* XCVI. 861 The optimal concentration was p_H = 4·4 to 4·6. **1920** W. M. CLARK *Determination Hydrogen Ions* i. 26 As a matter of typographical convenience we shall adopt pH in place of P_{H+}. **1921** *Jrnl. Nat. Dental Assoc.* VIII. 653/1 He uses agar with a PH value of 8·1 as a basis for blood agar. **1935** W. A. KOEHLER *Princ. & Applic. Electro-Chem.* II. xiv. 359 The bulb dips into the solution of unknown P_H. **1937** PIERCE & HAENISCH *Quantitative Analysis* viii. 121 Acid-base indicators are highly colored organic dyes which exhibit a change in color when the *p*H of a solution is changed. **1952** C. E. L. PHILLIPS *Small Garden* iii. 25 For general garden purposes in this country best results come from a neutral or slightly acid *p*H reading. **1970** *Pure & Appl. Chem.* XXI. 33 In all existing national standards the definition of pH is an operational one. *Ibid.*, The difference between the pH of two solutions having been defined as above, the definition of pH can be completed by assigning a value of pH at each temperature to one or more chosen solutions designated as standards. **1974** P. SVENDSEN *Introd. Animal Physiol.* xiii. 143 The maximum acidity of the wine is about pH 4·5.

2. *attrib.* and *Comb.*, as *pH meter, scale, value; pH-dependent* adj.; **pH-stat**, a device for automatically maintaining a solution at constant pH. **1960** *Jrnl. Bacteriol.* LXXIX. 734 (*heading*) Temperature and pH-dependent changes of electrophoretic mobility of *Pasteurella pestis*. **1972** *Brit. Jrnl. Nutrition* XXVIII. 389 The pH-dependent rearrangements have also to be borne in mind when performing administration experiments with formylfolates in metabolic studies. **1940** REILLY & RAE *Physico-Chem. Methods* (ed. 3) xii. 493 The Beckman *p*H meter..uses the principle of the potentiometer system in which the voltage of the electrode system is balanced against that of a standard cell. **1968** PASSMORE & ROBSON *Compan. Med. Stud.* I. vi. 3/1 The pH measured electrometrically by a glass electrode and a pH meter is not in fact a precise measure of actual hydrogen ion concentration. **1920** W. M. CLARK *Determination Hydrogen Ions* ii. 41 It is advantageous to show the position of the several indicators on the pH scale. **1973** F. G. SHINSKEY *pH & pIon Control in Process & Waste Streams* iii. 57 The pH scale is not bound to the limits of 0 to 14. **1957** *Methods Biochem. Anal.* IV. 174 A pH-stat consists of an appropriate cell..connected with a suitable pH-meter which in turn is connected with an adjustable controlling device. **1974** SAWYER & ROBERTS *Exper. Electrochem. for Chemists* ix. 417 In general autotitrators that work with a preset endpoint lend themselves to application as pH-stats. **1920** W. M. CLARK *Determination Hydrogen Ions* ii. 38 To a series of test tubes are added, seriatim, 10 cc. of each of a series of standard solutions whose pH values are known. **1932** T. P. FRANCIS *Mod. Sewage Treatm.* 252 The pH values for filter effluents should not differ by more than ·6. **1946** J. W. DAY *Harvest Adventure* iii. 44 Every acre of arable land has had a dressing of chalk. In all..some 30,000 tons have been put down, the idea being to maintain a *p*H-value of 5. **1974** *Encycl. Brit. Macropædia* X. 606/1 Some volcanic lakes are extremely acid, however, with pH values below 4, and some lakes with very high pH values, such as Lake Nakuru, Kenya, also occur in nature.

phacelia (fasī·liă). [mod.L. (A. L. Jussieu *Genera Plantarum* (1789) 129), f. Gr. φάκελος bundle, in reference to the clustered flowers.] An annual herb of the genus so called, belonging to the family Hydrophyllaceæ, usually native to western North America and bearing clusters of blue, violet, or white flowers. **1818** A. EATON *Man. Bot.* (ed. 2) II. 354 *Phacelia.. bipinnatifida* (phacelia..). **1835** *Edwards's Bot. Reg.* XX. 1696 (*heading*) Tansy-leaved Phacelia. **1898** A. M. DAVIDSON *California Plants* 119 There are many kinds of Phacelias; the flowers vary very much in size and in color and form, but they always grow in clusters that last a long time. **1903** M. AUSTIN *Land of Little Rain* 145 Larkspur in the *coleogyne*, and for every spinosa the purpling coils of phacelia. **1911** A. E. SPEER *Annual & Biennial Garden Plants* 206 The Phacelias are a family of hardy annuals useful for edgings or groups, and are all natives of either California, Texas, or Mexico. **1935** *Times Educ. Suppl.* 9 Mar. (Home and Classroom Suppl.) p. iv/3 Phacelia is a lovely little plant of which the colour rivals that of the Gentians. **1962** *Amat. Gardening* 24 Mar. 9/2 My own favourite hardy annuals are..phacelia,..eschscholtzia.

phacoanaphylaxis (fæ:ko,ænăfilæ·ksis). *Ophthalm.* Also **phako-.** [Mod.L., f. Gr. φακό-ς lentil + *ANAPHYLAXIS.] Allergic reaction to protein released from the crystalline lens of the eye. [**1922** VERHOEFF & LEMOINE in *Trans. Internat. Congr. Ophthalm.* 274 Certain individuals are hypersensitive to lens protein... When in such individuals rupture of the lens capsule takes place through injury or operation or spontaneously, a characteristic inflammatory reaction may properly be termed endopthalmitis phacoanaphylactica.] **1948** *Amer. Jrnl. Ophthalm.* XXXI. 1006/2 Verhoeff and Lemoine conceived the idea of phacoanaphylaxis in order to explain the postoperative inflammatory reaction of the eyes with extracapsular extraction. **1962** D. G. COGAN in A. Pirie *Lens Metabolism Rel. Cataract* 291 The lens..becomes invaded by polymorphonuclear cells, especially in the immunological reactions known as phakoanaphylaxis. **1964** *Arch. Ophthalm.* LXXII. 14/2 Sympathetic ophthalmia and phacoanaphylaxis are both manifestations of autoimmune reactions, the former to uveal pigment and the latter to lens protein.

So **pha:coanaphyla·ctic** *a.*, of, pertaining to, or involving phacoanaphylaxis. **1922** *Trans. Internat. Congr. Ophthalm.* 280 Intraocular inflammation resulting from rupture of a Morcagnian cataract is not usually phacoanaphylactic in nature. **1966** *Amer. Jrnl. Ophthalm.* LXI. 1431/1 The phacoanaphylactic reaction was seen in full bloom.

phacoidal (făkoi·dăl), *a.* *Petrogr.* [f. as PHACOID *a.* + -AL.] **a.** Lens-shaped, lenticular. **b.** Characterized by the presence of lenticular inclusions. **1901** *Rep. Brit. Assoc. Adv. Sci.* 617 The basic dykes.. appear frequently as phacoidal masses amid the re-constructed gneiss. **1920** [see *EYE *sb.*[1] 12 e]. **1956** E. W. HEINRICH *Microsc. Petrogr.* vii. 185 In phacoidal rocks the characteristic textural feature consists of ellipsoidal or lensoid units in a finer-grained matrix that is brecciated and sheared. *Ibid.* 186 Some mechanically metamorphosed conglomerates also possess the phacoidal texture. **1959** W. W. MOORHOUSE *Study of Rocks in Thin Section* xxviii. 463 Granites, syenites, and granodiorites show some foliation and a lenticular, 'phacoidal' form of quartz and feldspar grains.

phacolite (fæ·kolait). *Geol.* [f. Gr. φακός lentil: see -LITE.] = next. **1909** A. HARKER *Nat. Hist. Igneous Rocks* iii. 77 A concurrent influx of molten magma will..find its way along the crests and troughs of the wave-like folds. Intrusive bodies corresponding more or less closely with this ideal case are common in folded districts. Since some distinctive name seems to be needed, we may call them phacolites... The intrusions..are not, like true laccolites, the cause of the attendant folding, but rather a consequence of it. **1937** WOOLDRIDGE & MORGAN *Physical Basis Geogr.* viii. 109 Phacolites are lens-shaped masses of rock occupying the saddles of anticlines or the heels of synclines, places where rigid rock sheets naturally gape apart in the folding process. **1946** [see *LACCOLITE].

phacolith (fæ·koliþ). *Geol.* [Alteration of prec.: see -LITH.] An intrusive mass of igneous rocks situated between consecutive strata at the top of an anticline or the bottom of a syncline. **1910** LAKE & RASTALL *Text-bk. Geol.* xiii. 225 These long narrow intrusions are called by Mr. Harker phacolites (more correctly phacoliths). **1947** S. J. SHAND *Study of Rocks* (ed. 2) ii. 16 The phacolith might be described as a saddle-shaped laccolith;..but there is this important difference between a laccolith and a phacolith that the former is the cause of the folding of its country rocks while the latter is a consequence of folding. [*Ed.* 1 (1931): phacolite, laccolite.] **1971** B. W. SPARKS *Rocks & Relief* iii. 93 Laccoliths are approximately circular, but phacoliths are not, except in the rare case of their being formed in a dome. Usually they are elongated in the direction of the axes of the folds. **1977** A. HALLAM *Planet Earth* 68 Phacoliths are curved sill-like intrusions emplaced in the crests and troughs of folded rocks.

phænogamic, phænogamous, *adjs.* (Earlier example.) **1808** S. F. GRAY in *Monthly Mag.* XXIV. 612 Phœnogamic [*sic*], or phænogamous, is a word much used by the German botanists in contradistinction to cryptogamic, and from its convenience begins to be adopted here.

phænotype, obs. var. *PHENOTYPE.

phæochrome (fī·okrōum), *a.* *Histology.* Also **pheo-.** [f. Gr. φαιός dusky + χρῶμα colour.] = *CHROMAFFIN *a.* **1909** BAILEY & MILLER *Text-Bk. Embryol.* xv. 43 The medulla is composed of irregularly arranged sympathetic ganglion cells and other granular cells which, after treatment with chrome salts, acquire a peculiar brownish color. The brown cells are known as chromaffin (or phæochrome) cells and their granules as chromaffin (or phæochrome) granules. **1929** M. A. GOLDZIEHER *Adrenals* v. 223 The phæochrome tumors produce an excessive amount of adrenalin. **1941** R. G. HOSKINS *Endocrinol.* ii. 51 A tumor made up of pheochrome cells..may be situated in either the adrenal medulla or in one of the paraganglia. **1956** ROBSON & KEELE *Recent Adv. Pharmacol.* (ed. 2) i. 29 Phæochrome tumours..are benign in nearly 90 per cent of cases.

phæochromocyte (fīˌokrōᵘ·mosəit). *Med.* Also **pheo-**. [ad. G. *phäochromocyte* (H. Poll 1906, in O. Hertwig *Handb. d. vergleich und exper. Entwickelungslehre d. Wirbeltiere* III. 460), f. *phäochrom* *PHÆOCHROME: see -CYTE.] A chromaffin cell, esp. one in the adrenal medulla.

1929 *Arch. Path.* VII. 229 The final stage of differentiation brings forth the mature pheochromocytes, which are large, irregular or polyhedral cells, with each a round or ovoid vesicular nucleus, containing a loose chromatin network, and a well formed nucleolus. *Ibid.* 230 The pheochromocytes have the peculiar property of staining brown with chromic salts. **1948** MARTIN & HYNES *Clin. Endocrinol.* vii. 144 Phæochromocytomata... The tumours consist of mature phæochromocytes and 90 per cent are benign. **1975** *Nature* 27 Nov. 342/1 Pheochromocytoma cells exhibit properties of both pheochromocytes and neurones as a manifestation of neoplasia.

phæ:ochromocyto·ma. *Path.* Also **pheo-**. Pl. **-omas, -omata.** [mod.L., ad. G. *phäochromocytom* (L. Pick 1912, in *Berlin. klin. Wochenschr.* 1 Jan. 21/2): see prec. and *-OMA.] A tumour arising from chromaffin cells of the adrenal medulla. Cf. *PARAGANGLIOMA.

1929 *Arch. Path.* VII. 228 (*heading*) Chromaffin cell tumor of the suprarenal medulla (pheochromocytoma). **1929** *Trans. Assoc. Amer. Physicians* XLIV. 298 Pheochromocytomas are a rare tumor. **1931** W. BOYD *Path. Internal Dis.* ix. 482 Chromaffin cell tumor..is also known as a paraganglioma, a pheochromocytoma and a chromaffinoma. **1943** J. M. BEATTIE et al. *Textbk. Path.* (ed. 4) xxiv. 847 The chromaphil (or so-called 'chromaffine') tumour or phæochromocytoma is a growth affecting especially adults and is usually benign, although malignant varieties are recorded. **1944** *Surg. Clinics N. Amer.* Aug. 932 The terms 'chromaffinoma' and 'pheochromocytoma' have by common consent been used to describe supra-renal tumors of this type insomuch as they almost exclusively produce the clinical phenomena of hyperadrenalism. The term 'paraganglionoma' is reserved for extra-adrenal chromaffinomas, such as tumors of the carotid body. **1948, 1956** [see *PARAGANGLIOMA]. **1974** PASSMORE & ROBSON *Compan. Med. Stud.* III. xxiii. 55/2 Histologically phaeochromocytomata closely resemble normal chromaffin tissue.

phæophorbide (fīofǭ·ɹbəid). *Biochem.* Also **pheo-**. [ad. G. *phäophorbid* (Willstätter & Stoll 1911, in *Ann. d. Chem.* CCCLXXVIII. 25), f. as next + Gr. φορβή pasture, food: see -IDE.] Either of two compounds (orig. not distinguished) formed by the action of a strong acid on chlorophyll or phæophytin, having the structure of the latter except for the replacement of the phytol group by a hydrogen atom: phæophorbide *a*, HOOC·-$C_{32}H_{32}N_4O$·$COOCH_3$, or phæophorbide *b*, HOOC·$C_{32}H_{30}N_4O_2$·$COOCH_3$. Also, an ester of one of these compounds (as phæophytin).

1911 *Chem. Abstr.* V. 873 The following nomenclature is now adopted: for the free tricarboxylic acid, the basis of chlorophyll, the name chlorophyllin is retained, the monomethyl ester is called chlorophyllide and the deriv. free from Mg, pheophorbide. **1950** J. BONNER *Plant Biochem.* xxx. 470 Hydrolysis of pheophytin with stronger acid removes the phytol group to yield pheophorbides *a* and *b*, which are both monocarboxylic acids and which can be esterified..to yield the alkyl pheophorbides. **1956** I. L. FINAR *Org. Chem.* II. xix. 697 These phytyl phæophorbides are also known as phæophytins *a* and *b*. *Ibid.* 702 When phytyl phæophorbide-*a*..is hydrolysed with acid, the phytyl group is removed to form phæophorbide-*a*. **1963** R. P. DALES *Annelids* ii. 56 The intestine..is apparently absorptive. It is this region that has a deep green colour, just as that of Chaetopterus has, and for the same reason, for in both the colour is due to phæophorbides—breakdown products of chlorophylls presumably derived from the food. **1975** *Nature* 24 Jan. 241/1 Sudden heating [of leaf juice] inactivates chlorophyllase and so prevents the formation of phaeophorbide.

phæophytin (fīofəi·tin). *Biochem.* Also **pheo-**. [a. G. *phaeophytin* (now *phäo-*) (Willstätter & Hocheder 1907, in *Ann. d. Chem.* CCCLIV. 207), f. Gr. φαιός dusky + φυτόν plant: see -IN¹.] Either of two brownish compounds (orig. not distinguished) formed by the action of a weak acid on chlorophyll, having the structure of the latter except that the magnesium atom is replaced by two hydrogen atoms; a phytyl ester of phæophorbide: phæophytin *a*, $C_{20}H_{39}OOC$·$C_{32}H_{32}N_4$-O·$COOCH_3$, or phæophytin *b*, $C_{20}H_{39}OOC$·-$C_{32}H_{30}N_4O_2$·$COOCH_3$.

1907 [see *PHYTOL]. **1950, 1956** [see prec.]. **1967** *Oceanogr. & Marine Biol.* V. 269 The increase of the pigment ratio in deep water has to be ascribed in part to the persistence of yellow pigments and phaeophytin in decomposing plankton and in excrements.

† **phæoplast** (fī·ŏplast, -plæst). *Obs. Bot.* [a. G. *phaeoplast* (now *phäo-*) (A. F. W. Schimper 1885, in *Jahrb. für wissensch. Bot.* XVI. 34), f. Gr. φαιός dusky + πλαστ-ός formed, moulded; cf. *CHLOROPLAST.] A chromoplast of a brown alga.

1886 *Jrnl. R. Microsc. Soc.* VI. 640 For the chromoplasts of the Phæophyceæ the author proposes the term phæoplasts. **1904** *Amer. Naturalist* XXXVIII. 378 The chromatophores of the higher brown Algæ (Phæophyceæ)..have the discoid form characteristic of chloroplasts. They might be called phæoplasts..if one wished to classify plastids according to their color.

phage (fēⁱdʒ). *Biol.* [Shortening of *BACTERIOPHAGE.] A virus which attacks bacteria, entering the cell and either multiplying at its expense until the cell is lysed and the phage particles released, or becoming attached to the bacterial genome as a prophage and replicating synchronously with it; = *BACTERIOPHAGE. Also *collect.*

[**1925** *Lancet* 1 Aug. 234/2 The musical comedy spirit which reduces 'bacteriophage' to its final syllable.] **1926** *Encycl. Brit.* I. 302/1 If a tube of suitable diluted phage, inoculated with *B. dysenteriae*, is incubated for three hours, and a loop of it then inoculated on agar, confluent growth of the bacteria may be obtained with a number of small, round, clear areas where no growth of bacteria has occurred. **1936** TOPLEY & WILSON *Princ. Bacteriol. & Immunity* (ed. 2) x. 238 Phages acting on one or other of the normal or pathogenic intestinal bacteria can almost always be isolated from fæces, from sewage, or from polluted water supplies. **1939** *Nature* 24 June 1073 Lowering of virulence can..be induced by incubating phage with bacteria in media containing neither calcium nor magnesium salts. **1949** ABRAHAM & HEATLEY in H. W. Florey et al. *Antibiotics* I. ii. 89 A thin layer of agar containing an organism susceptible to lysis by the phage was spread on the plate and incubation was continued. **1960** *New Biol.* XXXI. 77 Like other viruses, phages multiply by causing the host cells to synthesize the components of the virus. **1968** H. HARRIS *Nucleus & Cytoplasm* ii. 22 Infection of *E. coli* with phage λ, however, allows β-galactosidase synthesis to continue almost until the time of lysis. **1972** *Nature* 21 Jan. 129/1 Carcinogens.. were tested for mutagenic activity in conventional assay systems, involving the use of bacteria or phage as target organisms. **1975** E. NNOCHIRI *Med. Microbiol. in Tropics* xi. 306/2 Temperate phages..fail to lyse the cells they infect but continue, nevertheless, to reproduce synchronously with the bacterial host for many generations.

b. *attrib.* and *Comb.*, as *phage genome, particle, replication*; *phage-infected, -related, -resistant, -specific* adjs.; **phage type** *sb.*, a division of a bacterial species characterized by a common susceptibility to a particular group of phages; so **phage-typing** *vbl. sb.* the determination of the phage type of a bacterium; **phage-type** *v. trans.*

1969 A. M. CAMPBELL *Episomes* i. 5 We conclude that a phage genome can indeed multiply in two different states. **1964** G. H. HAGGIS et al. *Introd. Molecular Biol.* xii. 315 Although these first experiments were made on phage-infected, evidence has also been found in normal bacteria for an RNA fraction with rapid turnover. **1957** C. E. CLIFTON *Introd. Bacterial Physiol.* 380 The number of phage particles adsorbed per bacterium can vary with experimental conditions. **1957** *Virology* II. 256 (*heading*) Production of phage-related structures during multiplication of phages T2 and T4. **1968** J. D. WATSON *Double Helix* xvii. 121 André [Lwoff] was very keen about the role of divalent metals in phage replication. **1951** WHITBY & HYNES *Med. Bacteriol.* (ed. 5) xxiv. 436 Phage-resistant mutants of undiminished virulence may replace the originally susceptible bacteria. **1973** R. G. KRUEGER et al. *Introd. Microbiol.* xviii. 479/2 The bacterial cell wall contains phage-specific receptor sites that undergo chemical union with the attachment apparatus of the virus. **1942** *Jrnl. Infectious Dis.* LXXI. 165/2 A series of mouse passage tests resulted in cultures of the same phage type as the original strains. **1961** *Lancet* 29 July 248/1 The second distinctive feature in Australia is an apparently great prevalence of antibiotic-resistant staphylococci, including phage-types 47 and 80. **1975** E. NNOCHIRI *Med. Microbiol. in Tropics* xi. 307/1 If a particular phage-type of *Salmonella typhi* is the cause of an outbreak of typhoid infection, a search is made for carriers of organisms of the same phage-type. **1938** *Canad. Publ. Health Jrnl.* XXIX. 493 (*heading*) The limitations of phage typing *B. typhosus*. **1949** *Brit. Med. Jrnl.* 10 Sept. 565/2 Staphylococci isolated from a series of 100 cases of infection occurring in this hospital have all been tested for penicillin sensitivity and phage-typed to see if the two could be correlated. **1961** *Lancet* 2 Sept. 506/2 All strains of *Staph. aureus* were tested for sensitivity to eight antibiotics, and a small number were phage-typed. **1942** *Jrnl. Infectious Dis.* LXXI. 161/1 Phage typing of typhoid culture has been employed quite extensively in Canada as an aid in tracing the origin of typhoid fever outbreaks. **1970** PASSMORE & ROBSON *Compan. Med. Stud.* II. xviii. 70/2 There are a number of phages with specific affinities for different staphylococci and it is therefore possible to identify strains of staphylococci by their phage-sensitivity patterns. This is the basis of phage-typing which is of great use in the investigation of outbreaks of staphylococcal sepsis.

phagocytable (fæ·gŏsəităb'l), *a. Biol.* [f. *PHAGOCYT(E *v.* + -ABLE.] Susceptible to phagocytosis. Hence **pha:gocytabi·lity.**

1911 *Jrnl. Amer. Med. Assoc.* 11 Nov. 1579/2 Pneumonic leukocytes would take up more easily phagocytable pneumococci than normal leukocytes. **1915** THOMAS & IVY *Appl. Immunol.* i. 15 An ingenious..laboratory method was devised whereby the measure of the ratio of phagocytability could be determined and this was styled the 'opsonic index'. **1921** WRIGHT & COLEBROOK *Technique Teat & Capillary Glass Tube* (ed. 2) ix. 208 (*heading*) Requirements in the matter of the number and phagocytability of the microbes employed in opsonic testing. **1927** *Jrnl. Bacteriol.* XIII. 40 Microbic dissociation *in vivo* would serve to transform a virulent but non-phagocytable organism into a non-virulent but phagocytable organism. *Ibid.*, The frequent correlation between S type culture, high virulence and non-phagocytability on the one hand, and, on the other, the correlation between R type culture, non-virulence and phagocytability, are emphasized.

phagocyte. Add: More widely, any cell in the body that phagocytoses bacteria or foreign particles. (Further examples.)

1939 F. A. KNOTT *Clin. Bacteriol.* iii. 45 The lining cells of the hepatic spaces (Küpffer cells) and the reticular cells of the cells of the spleen and lymph glands and the septal cells lining the pulmonary alveoli..can all be shown..to be active phagocytes and capable of ingesting pathogenic bacteria. **1972** R. HARTENSTEIN *Princ. Physiol.* xi. 494 Reticular cells differentiate into various forms of phagocytes including the fixed dust cells of vertebrate lungs, cellular linings of sinuses within glands, fixed Kupffer cells in the capillary sinusoids of liver.

phagocytic *a.*, add: so *phagocytic index*, any of various indices of phagocytic activity; hence **phagocy·tically** *adv.*; **phagocytosis,** substitute for def.: the process by which a cell engulfs or absorbs bacteria or foreign particles so as to isolate or destroy them; (further examples).

1904 WRIGHT & DOUGLAS in *Proc. R. Soc.* LXXIII. 129 The phagocytic index given below..represents in each case the average number of bacteria ingested by the individual P.W.B.C. The number of polynuclear white blood corpuscles which have furnished the index is in each case inserted in brackets. **1908** R. W. ALLEN *Vaccine Therapy* (ed. 2) xii. 199 The phagocytic index appears to be depressed for three to six weeks after commencing treatment. **1911** *Jrnl. Amer. Med. Assoc.* 11 Nov. 1580/1 So far as staphylococci are concerned, the cells with one nucleus are more active phagocytically and those with four least active. **1937** E. E. HEWER *Text-bk. Histol.* 7 This property of phagocytosis is shown by the blood leukocytes, osteoclasts, and all the histiocyte cells scattered throughout the body. **1963** R. P. DALES *Annelids* ii. 55 Kermack also found that food particles in the stomach were taken up phagocytically by certain epithelial cells. **1970** *Times Lit. Suppl.* 23 Oct. 1221/2 Amoebocytes..tend to be of variable shape and to engulf particles in their environment by the process of phagocytosis. **1971** HERBERT & WILKINSON *Dict. Immunol.* 139 *Phagocytic index*, a measure of the activity of the reticulo-endothelial system of the body. It is usually represented by a constant K that characterizes the rate of carbon clearance..from the blood and is inversely proportional to the dose of carbon injected. **1972** F. SPENCER *Aspects Human Biol.* iv. 112 As performed by such primitive cells as the protozoon amoeba, phagocytosis or engulfment represents a normal feeding mechanism. In the higher animals..phagocytosis is a highly developed activity, as exemplified by the granular leucocytes, and the cells of the reticulo-endothelial system. **1974** *Brit. Jrnl. Haematol.* XXVIII. 542 The phagocytic index was the average number of particles per neutrophil. **1977** P. B. & J. S. MEDAWAR *Life Sci.* xiii. 100 *Phagocytosis*, a process in which antigenic particles are engulfed into and very often digested by, or in any case rendered harmless by, 'macrophages' and 'polymorphs'.

phagocyte (fæ·gŏsəit), *v. Biol.* [f. the sb.] *trans.* = *PHAGOCYTOSE *v.* So **pha·gocyting** *ppl. a.*

1906 *Jrnl. Exper. Med.* VIII. 676 With a dilution of 1:20 not more than four or five staphylococci are taken up by the phagocyting cells. *Ibid.*, This possibility that a second substance besides the opsonins may determine the number of organisms phagocyted, also exists in the case of normal blood serum. **1933** M. FERNÁN-NÚÑEZ tr. *S. Ramón y Cajal's Histol.* xxi. 547 The Kupffer cells.. phagocyte senile and injured erythrocytes. **1961** H. CHANTRENNE *Biosynthesis of Proteins* iii. 88 The low residual incorporation observed in enucleate *Amoeba proteus* is due to the activity of micro-organisms recently phagocyted by the *Amoeba*.

phagocytize (fægŏsəi·təiz), *v. Biol.* [f. PHAGOCYT(E *v.* + -IZE.] *trans.* = *PHAGOCYTOSE *v.*

1925 *Physiol. Rev.* V. 195 The ink particles so carried into the liver were readily phagocytized by the Kupffer cells of that organ. **1956** *Arch. Path.* LXI. 165/2 Many of the spores were phagocytized early in the normal rabbit. **1973** R. G. KRUEGER et al. *Introd. Microbiol.* xxiii. 582/1 This cell type [*sc.* the macrophage] is characterized by its large size, ability to migrate, and its ability to phagocytize foreign materials.

So **pha·gocytized, -izing** *ppl. adjs.*, **pha·go-cyti:zable** *a.*

1923 *Johns Hopkins Hosp. Bull.* XXXIV. 328/1 The Kupffer cells..were filled with phagocytized ink particles. **1924** *Physiol. Rev.* IV. 559 No evidence..of the true endothelium of the blood- and lymph-vessels and the heart..producing wandering, phagocytizing cells in inflammation. **1948** *Biol. Skrift. K. Danske Videnskabernes Selskab* IV. VII. 82 In histological sections from animals which have received injections of phagocytizable material, such as India ink, some of the sinusoid lining cells contain ink and some do not.

phagocytose (fægǒsəi·tōᵘz, -s), *v. Biol.* Also **-oze.** [Back-formation from PHAGOCYTOSIS.] *trans.* To engulf or absorb (a cell or particle) like a phagocyte, so as to isolate or destroy it.

1912 R. W. ALLEN *Vaccine Therapy* (ed. 4) i. 32 The number of bacteria phagocytozed in a certain number of corpuscles were counted. **1943** PAPANICOLAOU & TRAUT *Diagnosis Uterine Cancer by Vaginal Smear* iii. 16 Endometrial cells which are being phagocytized by histiocytes. **1973** *Nature* 21 Sept. 50/2 These cells phagocytosed 'Zymosan' particles for at least 6 weeks. **1973** R. G. KRUEGER et al. *Introd. Microbiol.* xxiii. 582/1 The neutrophil..is capable of actively phagocytozing foreign material.

Hence **pha·gocytosed, pha·gocyto:sing** *ppl. adjs.*

1912 R. W. ALLEN *Vaccine Therapy* (ed. 4) i. 42 The phagocytosed bacteria should stain clearly. **1958** J. K. FROST in E. & E. R. Novak *Gynecol. & Obstetr. Path.* (ed. 4) xxxv. 626 (*heading*) Hypersecretory vacuoles filled with phagocytosing neutrophils. **1970** *Nature* 1 Aug. 511/1 These cells did not contain any phagocytosed particles, such as aluminium phosphate. **1972** *Science* 2 June 1040/1 [They] have reported that phagocytosing leukocytes take up inorganic iodide.

phagolysis (fægǫ·lisis). *Med.* [mod.L., ad. F. *phagolyse* (E. Metchnikoff 1895, in *Ann. de l'Inst. Pasteur* IX. 441), f. *phagocyte* PHAGOCYTE: see *-LYSIS.] **a.** Lysis of phagocytes. **b.** Lysis by phagocytes.

1898 W. S. L. BARLOW *Man. Gen. Path.* ix. 403 Attack directed from the German schools and advancing knowledge have obliged Metchnikoff to assume that under certain circumstances the phagocytes become dissolved (phagolysis) in the body fluids. *Ibid.*, The phagocytes, chiefly by phagocytosis, but partly by phagolysis, are responsible for immunity, natural and acquired. **1905** F. G. BINNIE tr. *Metchnikoff's Immunity in Infective Dis.* x. 534 Phagolysis (so I termed this transitory damage to the phagocytes) is indispensable for the manifestation of Pfeiffer's phenomenon in the peritoneal fluid. **1963** *Antibiotiki* VIII. 465 (*heading*) Effect of Levomycetin..on phagolysis of Flexner dysentery bacteria resistant to this antibiotic.

phagolysosome (fægoləi·sosōᵘm). *Biol.* [f. next + *LYSOSOME.] A structure formed in the cytoplasm of a cell by the fusion of a phagosome and a lysosome, in which the foreign particle is digested.

1963 W. STRAUS in de Reuck & Cameron *Lysosomes* 166 The term 'phagosomes' was used to characterize the segregating ability of granules; the term 'lysosomes' was used to indicate the contents of hydrolytic enzymes in the granules.., and the terms 'lyso-phagosomes' or 'phago-lysosomes' were used when both these properties were described for the same granules. **1964** *Jrnl. Histochem. & Cytochem.* XII. 470/2 The foreign protein..was segregated in small and large 'phagosomes'. These later fused with pre-existing lysosomes. The gradual digestion of the injected protein in the 'phago-lysosomes'..could be followed by double staining. **1973** R. G. KRUEGER et al. *Introd. Microbiol.* xxiii. 584/1 The phagolysosome, containing the remains of the foreign object is then either eliminated from the cell or is left in the cytoplasm. **1977** *Lancet* 29 Oct. 929/2 These organelles are probably secondary lysosomes (phagolysosomes), common in actively feeding cells.

Hence **pha:golysoso·mal** *a.*

1975 *Nature* 3 July 48/2 The phagolysosomal membrane was invariably applied closely to the surface of the enclosed yeast cell.

phagosome (fæ·gosōᵘm). *Biol.* [f. PHAGOCYTE + *-SOME[4].] A vacuole formed in the cytoplasm of a cell when a particle is phagocytosed and enclosed within a part of the cell membrane.

1958 W. STRAUS in *Jrnl. Biophysical & Biochem. Cytol.* IV. 548 The uptake of proteins is probably the function of certain intracellular granules related to the droplets of kidney cells. The term 'phagosomes' is suggested for these granules. (If these granules, characterized by segregating ability, are found to be identical with the 'lysosomes', the latter term can be used as a common nomenclature.) **1974** *Nature* 22 Nov. 305/2 If these processes engage in phagocytosis, phagosomes containing groups of cone disks should be observed within their cytoplasm.

Hence **phagoso·mal** *a.*

1975 *Nature* 17 Apr. 600/2 Possibly the living bacteria produce a factor which inhibits fusion between phagosomal and lysosomal membranes and thereby prevent the discharge of putatively bactericidal lysosomal contents into the bacterial environment.

phakellite, var. *FACELLITE.

phakic (fē̆ⁱ·kik), *a. Ophthalm.* [f. Gr. φακ-ός lentil + -IC.] Of an eye: having a crystalline lens (as in the normal organ). Cf. *APHAKIC *a.*

1918 J. H. PARSONS *Dis. Eye* (ed. 3) xxiv. 495 It is easy to calculate the amount of axial myopia of a phakic eye which is 31 mm. long. **1961** *Lancet* 22 July 169/1 Two perforating grafts have been performed in phakic eyes, and although the appearance of the cornea has improved the results are not as good as in the aphakic cases. **1975** R. N. SHAFFER in D. R. Anderson et al. *Symposium on Glaucoma* xiv. 250 In the phakic eye pupillary block is caused by apposition of the iris to the lens.

phakoanaphylaxis, var. *PHACOANAPHYLAXIS.

Phalangist[2] (fa·landʒist). [ad. Sp. *falange*: see *FALANGE.] **1.** A member of the Spanish *FALANGE. Also *attrib.* or as *adj.*

1936 *Times* 17 Aug. 10/1 The main attack was delivered by a force of some 3,000 men, including the Foreign Legion, Moroccan troops, and 'Phalangists' or insurgent militia, divided into two columns. **1937** KOESTLER *Spanish Testament* i. 20 He [*sc.* a foreigner in Vigo] notes, during his hour's walk through the town, that it is chock-full of troops—Legionaries, Carlists, Phalangists, but no Moors. **1938** *Ann. Reg. 1937* 240 It was substantially the Phalangist programme which was adopted as the basis of the proposed Constitution for 'Nationalist' Spain. **1938** [see * FALANGE].

2. *transf.* A member of a right-wing, mainly Christian party in Lebanon. Also *attrib.* or as *adj.*

1972 *Daily Tel.* 20 June 4/3 Leaders of the mainly Christian Phalangist party are calling for an end to the 1969 Cairo agreement providing a Lebanese sanctuary for the commandos. **1975** *Times* 28 June 4/5 The Prime Minister-designate..is trying to reconcile differences between the mainly Christian Phalangists and..the influential socialist leader. **1977** *Time* 8 Aug. 29/1 The results were clearly joyous to a crowd including Israeli border police and flag-bearing Lebanese Christian Phalangist soldiers allowed on Israeli territory for the occasion. **1979** *Guardian* 9 Apr. 7/5 Iran's young Guerillas..find themselves increasingly out of step with the..'Phalangists' as the Left-wing has dubbed the country's new theocracy.

phalangitis (fælǣndʒəi·tis). *Path.* [f. *phalanges*, pl. of PHALANX (sense 3) + -ITIS.] Inflammation of the phalanges.

1877 J. D. HOOKER in L. Huxley *Life J. D. Hooker* (1918) II. 142 [I get home] with a crick in my shoulder and 'phalangitis' from pump-handling some 500 people. **1903** *Lancet* 30 May 1526/1 He regarded the case as one of phalangitis of syphilitic origin.

phalanstery. (Earlier and later examples.)

1846 *Knickerbocker* XXVIII. 16 And are all your slaves productive workers? This is contemplated, I believe, in all the *Phalansteries* of Unitative Associationists. **1963** V. NABOKOV *Gift* iv. 235 Let us dream of the phalanstery living in a palace: 1,800 souls—and all happy!

phalaris (fæ·lăris). [L., f. Gr. φαλαρίς, Pliny's name for a similar grass; adopted by Linnæus in his *Hortus Cliffortianus* (1737) 23 as the name of a genus.] A grass of the genus so called, which includes canary-grass and some species useful for grazing.

1911 *Agric. Gaz. N.S.W.* XXII. 407 *Phalaris* and Kentucky Blue are spreading well. **1942** *Austral. Vet. Jrnl.* XVIII. 182 In three districts in South Australia the grazing of stock on pastures consisting almost exclusively of *Phalaris* has resulted in the occurrence of a 'staggers' syndrome. **1946** *Ibid.* XXII. 92/1 The general technique has been to select..areas of pasture in which phalaris was dominant. **1956** *Brit. Vet. Jrnl.* CXII. 390 When the disease is noticed early the sheep are moved to a fresh pasture containing no phalaris and the nervous condition soon improves. **1966** *New Scientist* 25 Aug. 412/1 Nervous disfunction of sheep grazing phalaris has been recognized for many years. **1977** *Weekly Times* (Melbourne) 19 Jan. 10/5 Some stands of the sub clover and phalaris have been harvested for seed.

2. phalaris staggers, a nervous disorder of sheep and cattle caused by the consumption of the perennial grass, *Phalaris tuberosa.*

1946 I. W. MCDONALD in *Austral. Vet. Jrnl.* XXII. 91/2 A disease of sheep and cattle characterized by profound nervous symptoms and degenerative changes in the central nervous system was described. The disease was associated with the consumption of the perennial grass *Phalaris tuberosa* and thus had become colloquially known as 'phalaris staggers'. **1966** *Ibid.* XLII. 279/1 Neurological disorders of sheep grazing *Phalaris tuberosa* have hitherto been grouped under the term 'phalaris staggers'. **1970** JUBB & KENNEDY *Path. Domestic Animals* (ed. 2) II. vii. 387/2 The lesser syndrome, known as phalaris staggers, occurs when the plant is in lush growth and in 3–10 days after animals are given access to such pasture. Affected sheep appear normal when quiet, but, when disturbed, they show stiffness, incoordination, a staggering gait, and a tendency to fall.

phallic, *a.* Add: (Further examples.) Also in spec. collocations as *phallic stage* Psychoanal., *phallic symbol*; and in adj. phr. as *phallic-centred, -shaped.*

1907 G. B. SHAW *John Bull's Other Island* II. 38 The view that the Round Towers are phallic symbols. **1923** *Internat. Jrnl. Psycho-Anal.* IV. 383 Charlie Chaplin as phallic symbol. **1927** *Ibid.* VIII. 468 Freud postulated a 'phallic' stage in female development corresponding with that in the male. **1928** D. H. LAWRENCE *Let.* 15 Mar. (1962) II. 1046 It is a nice and tender phallic novel. **1949** J. STRACHEY tr. *Freud's Three Ess. Theory of Sexuality* ii. 77 This phase..is differentiated from the final organization of sexual maturity... For it knows only one kind of genital: the male one. For that reason I have named it the 'phallic' stage of organization. **1952** C. THOMPSON *Psychoanal.* iii. 69 A phallic character comes from sublimation of the phallic stage. Such a person is..insolent, domineering, and aggressive. **1959** E. POUND *Thrones* xcix. 49 That man's phallic heart is from heaven a clear spring of rightness. **1963** A. HERON *Towards Quaker View of Sex* iii. 23 Males are very phallic-centred. **1964** P. F. ANSON *Bishops at Large* ix. 358 The 'forces' and 'vibrations' within this phallic-shaped building. **1968** R. & G. BLANCK *Marriage & Pers. Devel.* ii. 9 The anal character is greedy; the anal character is stubborn and parsimonious; the phallic character is exhibitionistic and competitive. **1968** M. ELLMAN *Thinking about Women* ii. 46 It is through this identification that phallic criticism regularly and rapidly shifts from writing by women, which can be dismissed as innocuous, to their vicious influence upon writing by men. **1972** C. SHORT *Naked Skier* xxiv. 137, I switched my mind to contemplation of the Eiffel Tower. It too was a phallic symbol. **1975** C. REGISTER in J. Donovan *Feminist Lit. Crit.* 9 A second exercise in Phallic Criticism is to admit grudgingly to the literary value of works by women, and then to deny that it is consciously attained. **1977** *Spare Rib* Sept. 13/2 Now we [*sc.* women] can have the phallic freedoms to screw where and when we want. **1978** *Amer. Poetry Rev.* July/Aug. 19/1 If you riffle the pages from back to front you will see one block of pattern divide, while another phallic-shaped pattern slowly enters it.

phallically (fæ·likăli), *adv.* Also **phallicly.** [f. PHALLIC, PHALLICAL *adjs.*: see -ICALLY.] In a manner resembling a phallus.

1967 E. GRIERSON *Crime of one's Own* i. 9 In the distance Brunelleschi's dome and Giotto's tower rose phallically towards the Tuscan sky. **1971** *Daily Tel.* (Colour Suppl. 11 June 27/4 *Bomb Release*, Dennis's own work that lights up and changes colour while it erects phallicly. **1978** J. UPDIKE *Coup* (1979) iii. 102 Abrasive ointments phallically packaged and chemically fortified.

phallicist. (Example.)

1924 *Jrnl. R. Anthrop. Inst.* LIV. 49 The phallicists of the seventies, Burton, Fergusson,..and Westropp.

phallin (fæ·lin). *Chem.* Also **-ine.** [a. G. *phallin* (R. Kobert 1891, in *St. Petersb. med. Wochenschr.* XVI. 472/2), f. mod.L. *phalloides* (see *PHALLOIDIN): see -IN[1], -INE[5].] A haemolytic substance present in the death cap toadstool, *Amanita phalloides*, and formerly thought to be its poisonous principle.

1897 *Trans. Brit. Mycol. Soc.* I. 27 Professor Kobert.. has given the name of phalline to the poisonous substance present in *Amanita phalloides*, Fries. *Ibid.* 28 Phalline is a very powerful agent..in causing the dissolution of the red corpuscles of the blood. **1930** *Lancet* 1 Feb. 228/1 The toxin of tetanus is checked by La Bourboule water and not by Mont Dore, phallin poison by Mont Dore water and not by La Bourboule. **1965** BELL & COOMBE tr. *Strasburger's Textbk. Bot.* 508 Familiar Agaricaceae:.. *Amanita phalloides*.., deadly poisonous with toxic glucosides (phallin) and peptides (phalloidin, amanitin). **1972** T. & O. WIELAND in S. J. Ajl et al. *Microbial Toxins* VIII. x. 252 A hemolytic agent..was obtained from *A. phalloides* as early as 1891 by Kobert and was called 'phallin'. It has recently been reinvestigated by Fiume (1967), who..stated that, in addition to a hemolytic action, a cytotoxic effect on cultures of cells of KB line and of human amnion cells occurred. This substance, whose chemical nature has not yet been established, is presumably destroyed in the gastrointestinal tract and, therefore, cannot be responsible for lethality of the mushroom.

phallism. (Later examples.)

1928 A. HUXLEY *Point Counter Point* x. 165 Civilized lasciviousness is the same as the healthy—what shall I call it?—phallism..of the ancients... Worshipping with the body—that's the genuine phallism. **1950** *Funk's Stand. Dict. Folklore* II. 863/2 Among some ethnic groups phallism, also often called sex worship, is the worship of the male sexual organ.

phallocentric (fælose·ntrik), *a.* [f. Gr. φαλλός penis + *-CENTRIC.] Centred on the phallus. Hence **phallocentri·city, phalloce·ntrism.**

1927 *Internat. Jrnl. Psycho-Anal.* VIII. 459 There is a healthy suspicion growing that men analysts have been led to adopt an unduly phallo-centric view of the problems in question. **1951** *Brit. Jrnl. Psychol.* XLII. 382 The phallocentric tendencies of early psychology. **1970** G. GREER *Female Eunuch* 48 The enormous hoo-ha about the strange impalpable results of vasectomy..results from..phallocentricity. **1977** *Spare Rib* June 46/4 She capitulates, without too much struggle, to an individual solution of phallocentric romantic love. **1977** A. SHERIDAN tr. *Lacan's Écrits* vi. 198 The phallocentrism produced by this dialectic is all that need concern us here. **1977** R. HOLLAND *Self & Social Context* viii. 254 Wilden's critique of Lacan, whose valuable exposition of the Imaginary does not allow him to escape its vicissitudes, as can be seen by his phallocentrism and his elitist conceptual violence.

phallocrat (fæ·lǒkræt). [f. as prec. + -CRAT: cf. Fr. *phallocrate.*] One who advocates or assumes the existence of a male-dominated society; a man who argues his superiority over women because of his masculinity. Also *attrib.* or as *adj.* So **phallo·cracy, phallocra·tic** *a.*

1977 *Gay News* 24 Mar. 11/3 The march was backed up by members of the Groupe de Liberation Homosexuel.. shouting the slogan 'with women against phallocracy'. **1977** *Times Lit. Suppl.* 10 June 699/3 That feeble tyrant, the reincarnation of her father—the 'phallocrat' male.

1977 *Radical Philos.* Summer 9/2 It would be a mystery how the jury of 1971 could have escaped the effects of this phallocratic unconscious. *Ibid.*, Her phallocrat of a husband or lover letting her deal with all the domestic chores. **1977** *Ibid.* Autumn 1, I do myself think that the style of at least some of those 'great texts' is indeed phallocratic. **1978** *Times Lit. Suppl.* 24 Mar. 342/5 By a species of reification no more excusable than that dictated by the phallocrats, they have consecrated a ready-made caricature of Woman which serves to reduce all women to an absolute type.

phalloid, *a.* (Example.)
1967 A. Edwardes in R. E. L. Masters *Sexual Self-Stimulation* 308 Arab and Israeli girls of prepubertal age.. masturbate..with fingers or some phalloid object.

phalloidin (fæ̆loi·din). *Chem.* Also **-ine.** [a. G. *phalloidin*, given its present meaning by U. Wieland 1938 (*Ann. d. Chem.* DIII. 100) following its coinage as F. *phalloïdine* by A. Gubler 1877 (*Bull. de l'Acad. de Méd.* VI. 879) to denote an 'amorphous toxic principle' obtained from *A. phalloides* by P. C. Oré; f. mod.L. *phalloides*, specific epithet (f. Gr. φαλλός penis: see -oid): see -in[1], -ine[5].] The principal phallotoxin, $C_{35}H_{48}N_8O_{11}S$.
1938 *Chem. Abstr.* XXXII. 3456 Toxin II has been crystd. (needles) and is designated as phalloidin. **1955** *Sci. News Let.* 23 Apr. 265/2 The two amanitines and phalloidine in mushrooms affect the liver, kidney and heart. **1961** *Lancet* 16 Sept. 630/2 More than a century of investigation, mainly in Germany and France, has led to the isolation of five crystalline toxins from *Amanita phalloides* (α, β, and γ amanitin, phalloin, and phalloidin). **1972** *Science* 1 Sept. 808/1 The principal phallotoxin is phalloidin. **1977** R. Jeffries *Troubled Deaths* xiii. 101 The normal symptoms of phalloidine poisoning.

phalloin (fæ·lo,in). *Chem.* [a. G. *phalloin* (Wieland & Mannes 1957, in *Angewandte Chem.* LXIX. 389/1), f. mod.L. *phallo-ides* (see prec.) + -in[1].] One of the phallotoxins, $C_{35}H_{48}N_8O_{10}S$.
1959 *Chem. Abstr.* LIII. 18880 Chromatographic sepn. of the enriched poison mixt. of the amanita mushroom on neutral Al_2O_3 in H_2O-satd. BuOH + 10% EtOH mixt. gave another toxin, called phalloin. **1961** [see *phalloidin]. **1968** [see *phallotoxin].

phallophoria (fælofǫ·riă). [f. Gr. φαλλοφορ-εῖν to bear a phallus + -ia[1] or ad. Gr. φαλληφόρια (see Phallephoric *a.*) influenced by the root φαλλό-ς.] The carrying of a phallus, esp. as part of a festival of Dionysus in ancient Greece. Hence **phallopho·ric** *a.*, = Phallephoric *a.*
The Gr. word φαλληφόρια is a neuter plural, but the English form *phallophoria* is usu. const. as a sing.
1903 J. E. Harrison in *Jrnl. Hellenic Stud.* XXIII. 322 We have established..that a phallophoria formed a part of Dionysiac mysteries. **1950** *Funk's Stand. Dict Folklore* II. 864/1 The carrying of phalli in public processions (*phallophoria*). **1964** *New Statesman* 13 Mar. 398/1 The puppets looked more phallophoric than the Beatles themselves. As the taped Beatle music rose to a pitch, the jiggling became an almost indecent enactment of sexual rhythm. **1967** A. L. Lloyd *Folk Song in England* ii. 93 The randy animal-guiser song of the 'Derby Ram'.. a song that is the lyrical equivalent of those phallophoric dances that survive in farming communities in Europe, intended to celebrate and stimulate the powers of reproduction.

phallophorus (fælofǫ·rǒs). Also **-phoros.** Pl. **-phori, -phoroi.** [ad. Gr. φαλλοφόρος bearing a phallus.] One who carries a phallus, esp. as part of a festival of Dionysus in ancient Greece.
1854 C. D. Yonge tr. *Athenæus' Deipnosophists* III. xiv. 992 Semos the Delian says in his book about Pæans... 'And those,..who are called Ithyphalli, wear a mask representing the face of a drunken man... And the Phallophori..wear no masks, but they put on a sort of veil of wild thyme... The Phallophorus..marched straight on, covered with soot and dirt'. **1885** H. M. Westropp *Primitive Symbolism* 54 The periphallia.. carried long poles with phalli hung at the end of them: they were crowned with violets and ivy... These men were called phallophori. **1909** L. R. Farnell *Cults Gk. States* V. v. 210 It may be that Semos of Delos is describing something that happened in the later Attic festival when—according to Athenaeus—he speaks of 'the ithyphalloi'..and of the phallophoroi without masks entering through the central doors of the theatre. **1927** A. W. Pickard-Cambridge *Dithyramb Tragedy & Comedy* iii. 234 The phallophorus proper had his face disguised with soot. (Probably he carried, but did not wear, the phallus). *Ibid.* 235 Possibly the ceremony of the phallophori was of a common type, differing little from town to town. **1931** A. Nicoll *Masks, Mimes & Miracles* i. 26 Bethe thinks that the *phallophoroi* were Delians; for this there is no proof.

‖**phallos** (fæ·lǫ̆s). Pl. **-oi.** [Gr. φαλλός penis.] = Phallus. Also *attrib.* and *Comb.*
1928 D. H. Lawrence *Lady Chatterley* x. 161 The man dwindled to a..mere phallos-bearer, to be torn to pieces when his service was performed. **1950** *Funk's Stand. Dict. Folklore* II. 862/1 The Greek satyrs of the Dionysiac *orgia* stamped and capered with gigantic phalloi and artificial breasts—a symbol of self-fructification. **1963** Auden *Dyer's Hand* III. 102 If all round hills were suddenly to turn into breasts, all caves into wombs, all towers into phalloi, we should not be pleased..we should be bored. **1972** *Times Lit. Suppl.* 19 May 565/3 Golden phalloi of superb craftsmanship and considerable avoirdupois. **1978** K. J. Dover *Greek Homosexuality* III. 133 The 'phallos-bird', which has the legs, body and wings of a bird but a neck and head in the form of a curved penis with the foreskin rolled back and an eye on the glans.

phallotoxin (fælotǫ·ksin). *Chem.* [f. mod.L. *phallo-ides* (see *phalloidin) + Toxin.] Any of several closely related poisonous peptides present in the death cap toadstool, *Amanita phalloides*, all of which have the same ring structure of seven amino-acids bridged by a sulphur atom.
1968 *Science* 1 Mar. 949/1 The phallotoxins include phalloidin, phalloin, [etc.]. **1972** *Ibid.* 1 Sept. 808/1 The rapidly acting phallotoxins..are responsible for the gastrointestinal phase of the poisoning. **1975** *Sci. Amer.* Mar. 95/1 In the phallotoxins the cyclopeptide ring has seven amino acids; in the amatoxins it has eight.

phallus. Add: **1. b.** The male generative organ, often in the context of its symbolical significance; in psychoanalysis, in the context of the pre-genital phase of sexual development.
By some writers used in the specific sense 'erect penis'.
1924 J. Riviere tr. *Freud's Infantile Genital Organization* in *Coll. Papers* II. 245 The primacy reached is..not a primacy of the *genital*, but of the *phallus*. *Ibid.* 247 The significance of the castration complex can only be rightly appreciated when its origin in the phase of the primacy of the phallus is also taken into account. **1935** M. Balint *Primary Love & Psycho-Anal. Technique* (1952) iii. 56 The same is true of the phenomena of the phallic period: belief in the non-existence of the female genital organs.. or in the existence of mothers with a phallus. **1935** R. V. Storer *Sexual Technique* xxi. 274 Effective virility therefore depends on erectile capacity; that is, the penis must be able to become a phallus (as the erect male organ in action is called). **1951** Ford & Beach *Patterns of Sexual Behavior* ii. 22 The bodily adjustments that give rise to these sensations involve merely insertion of the phallus followed by piston-like thrusts within the vagina. **1960** J. Rodney *Handbk. Sex Knowledge* iv. 45 In its simplest—and crudest—form, copulation consists of the entrance of the erect penis or phallus into the vagina, followed by certain movements which produce an ejaculation of male semen into the vaginal cavity. **1961** C. & W. M. S. Russell *Human Behaviour* vi. 271 A welter of key stimuli independent of the individual's personality, of breasts and phalluses, hands and feet. **1963** A. Heron *Towards Quaker View of Sex* iii. 35 The experience is thus phallus-centred and produces excitement without deep commitment. **1972** *Times Lit. Suppl.* 29 Sept. 1156/5 A phallus is a prerequisite of intercourse and, being so, has a social significance..whereas a penis can never have more than a biological significance. **1974** H. S. Kaplan *New Sex Therapy* i. 21 The female sexual response transforms the tight, dry vaginal potential space into a well-lubricated, open receptacle for the phallus. **1977** *Times* 18 Feb. 11/7 Fat villains sporting Old Comedy phalli.
2. (Later examples.)
1953 J. Ramsbottom *Mushrooms & Toadstools* xvi. 182 A violet-scented *Phallus* would certainly be exceptional. **1976** G. C. Ainsworth *Introd. Hist. Mycology* iii. 38 There is a figure of the stink-horn (both 'egg' and fruit-body) which in 1562 had been described and illustrated by the Dutch physician Adriaen Jonghe (H. Junius) who gave the name 'Phallus' to it in the first independently published mycological monograph.
3. *phallus-worship* (earlier example).
1850 Carlyle *Hudson's Statue* in *Latter-Day Pamphlets* vii. 43 Kings and Papas flying like detected coiners; and in their stead Icaria, Red Republic,..Literature of Desperation curiously conjoined with Phallus-Worship, too clearly heralding centuries of bottomless Anarchy.

Phanar. Add: (Earlier and later examples.) Also, the seat of the Patriarch of Constantinople after the Ottoman conquest. Also *transf.*
The more common spelling in the 19th century was *Fanar.
1897 R. Davey *Sultan & his Subjects* II. iii. 112 The noble Greek families which returned after the siege and settled in that quarter of Constantinople, known as the Phanar. **1900** 'Odysseus' *Turkey in Europe* vi. 276 One small Slavonic Church, however, that of Montenegro, resisted Hellenism and the Phanar as successfully as the Government withstood the Turks. **1911** E. Pears *Turkey & its People* vii. 118 The patriarch of Constantinople..resides at the Phanar, a district in Constantinople... As there was much intrigue and bribery..under the sultans, Phanariot came to be a synonym for a man of unscrupulous political intrigue. **1936** H. Luke *Making of Mod. Turkey* iv. 97 It was only in 1850 that the Phanar, reluctantly and under Russian pressure, recognized the Church of the Greek kingdom as independent. **1961** D. Attwater *Christian Churches of East* II. iii. 22 In 1766 the Phanar obtained from the sultan Mustafa III an order for the suppression of the Serbian independent church. **1964** P. F. Anson *Bishops at Large* viii. 281 No Christian Church would be able to offer such..ceremonial as this new one with its '*phanar*' or '*curia*' in Holloway.

phanatron, var. *phanotron.

phanerophyte (fæ·nĕrofəit). *Bot.* [ad. Da. *fanerofyt* (C. Raunkiaer 1904, in *Bot. Tidsskr.* XXVI. p. xiv), f. Phanero- + -phyte.] A plant which bears its dormant buds well above the surface of the ground.
1913 W. G. Smith in *Jrnl. Ecol.* I. 17 Phanerophytes have their dormant buds on branches which project freely into the air; they are the trees and shrubs. **1932** Fuller & Conard tr. *Braun-Blanquet's Plant Sociol.* xii. 295 The more northern phanerophytes are characterized by special bud protection. **1934** H. Gilbert-Carter tr. *Raunkiaer's Life Forms of Plants* ii. 19 By Phanerophytes I mean plants whose buds and apical shoots destined to survive the unfavourable period of the year project into the air on stems which live for several, often for many, years. **1952** [see *chamæphyte* s.v. *chamæ-]. **1976** Bell & Coombe tr. *Strasburger's Textbk. Bot.* (rev. ed.) 191 Phanerophytes..bear their resting buds more than 50 cm above the soil surface.

phanerozoic (fæ:nĕrozōu·ik), *a.* [f. Phanero- + Gr. ζωή life + -ic.] **1.** *Ecol.* Describing those animals living in exposed conditions above the surface of the ground. Cf. *cryptozoic *a.* 1.
1896 A. Dendy in *Natural Sci.* July 8 Cryptozoic fauna imperceptibly blends with what by way of contrast may be called the 'phanerozoic'. **1911** A. Willey *Convergence in Evolution* iii. 23 Phanerozoic or diurnal animals are positively heliotropic. **1922** Flattely & Walton *Biol. of Sea-Shore* i. 7 We thus have two great sub-realms: the phanerozoic and the cryptozoic.
2. *Geol.* (With capital initial.) Of, pertaining to, or designating the whole of the geological time since the beginning of the Cambrian period, as contrasted with the Pre-Cambrian (Cryptozoic); (so named in allusion to its abundant evidence of life). Also *absol.*
1930 G. H. Chadwick in *Bull. Geol. Soc. Amer.* XLI. 48 The following classificatory scheme is offered for criticism. ..Phanerozoic or Phanerobiotic 45%... Cryptozoic or Cryptobiotic (Precambrian) 55%. **1958** R. C. Moore *Introd. Hist. Geol.* (ed. 2) iv. 59/2 It is convenient also to designate the Cryptozoic rocks as Precambrian, a commonly used term indicating age older than the Cambrian Period, first division of the Paleozoic Era and of the Phanerozoic Eon. **1963** *Q. Jrnl. Geol. Soc.* CXIX. 137 The rocks concerned range in age from 1055 to 1700 m.y. (radiometric dating), spanning more time than the whole of the Phanerozoic. **1971** *Nature* 25 June 498/1 All stratigraphic methods of correlation..that are used for Phanerozoic rocks should be extended as far as possible in the Pre-Cambrian part of the stratigraphic column. **1974** *Ibid.* 18 Oct. 568/2 It is no coincidence that the three faunally defined eras of Phanerozoic time, the Palaeozoic, Mesozoic and Cainozoic, are divided by these two so-called crises in the history of life. **1977** A. Hallam *Planet Earth* 189 The later Proterozoic Grenville belt of southern Canada..is a linear belt with more similarities to the younger mountain belts of the Phanerozoic.

phanerozonate (fænĕrozōu·nēit), *a. Zool.* [f. mod.L. order name *Phanerozonia* (W. P. Sladen in Thomson & Murray *Rep. Sci. Results Voy. H.M.S. Challenger: Zool.* (1889) XXX. p. xxvi), f. Phanero- + Gr. ζώνη girdle + -ia[2]: see -ate[2].] Characteristic of or comprising certain starfishes grouped in the order Phanerozonia, distinguished by conspicuous marginal plates.
1889 W. P. Sladen in *Rep. Sci. Results Voy. H.M.S. Challenger: Zool.* XXX. p. xxvi, I consider that the Phanerozonate group is older than the Cryptozonate. **1906** E. W. MacBride in *Cambr. Nat. Hist.* I. xvi. 454 In a very large number of Asteroidea the supero- and inferomarginal ossicles are represented by squarish plates even when the rest of the skeleton is reticulate; this is the so-called 'phanerozonate' structure. **1923** *Nature* 13 Jan. 47/1 What these specialists are impressed by is the 'phanerozonate' character of the Astropectinidae, that is, the edging of the arms with a series of broad plates termed the 'marginals'. **1966** J. W. Durham et al. in R. C. Moore *Treat. Invertebr. Paleont.* U. I. u36/2 Some Cryptozonia have a phanerozonate stage in ontogeny.

phanerozone (fæ·nĕrozōun), *a.* (*sb.*) *Zool.* [see prec.] = prec. Also as *sb.*
1962 D. Nichols *Echinoderms* iii. 51 *Petraster* is a true phanerozone starfish. *Ibid.* 53 There is a thick aboral membrane for protection instead of the paxillate condition normally associated with the phanerozones. **1964** *Oceanogr. & Marine Biol.* II. 394 Spencer..describes the transition from the early somasteroid stock to the phanerozone asteroids.

phanopœia (fæ:nopī·yă). [f. Gr. φανό-ς light, bright, f. φαίνειν to shine, give light + ποι-εῖν to make, after Melopœia: see -ia[1].] (See quot. 1929.)
1929 E. Pound in *N.Y. Herald-Tribune* 20 Jan. xi. 5/4 There are three 'kinds of poetry': Melopoeia... Phanopoeia, which is a casting of images upon the visual imagination... Logopoeia. *Ibid.* 6/1 In phanopoeia we find the greatest drive toward utter precision of word. **1934, 1957** [see *logopœia]. **1961** [see *modernist 5].

phanotron (fæ·nǒtrǫn). *Electronics.* Also **phanatron.** [f. *phano-* (? f. Gr. φαίνειν to bring to light, cause to appear) + *-tron.] A thermionic diode rectifier utilizing an arc discharge in mercury vapour or gas at very low pressure.
Formerly a proprietary name in the U.S.
1931 *Thomas' Reg. Amer. Manuf.*, *1931–32* (ed. 22) *Leading Trade Names* 447 Phanotron vacuum tubes, General Electric Co., Schenectady, N.Y. **1933** J. H. Morecroft *Electron Tubes* viii. 193 In the Phanotron a

low temperature filament must be used, because the mercury vapor has not enough density to prevent the evaporation of the filament. **1939** H. J. REICH *Theory & Applications Electron Tubes* xii. 430 The construction of the type FG-166 phanatron. **1966** *McGraw-Hill Encycl. Sci. & Technol.* VI. 62/1 Typical phanotrons have average current ratings from 1·25–10 amperes and peak inverse voltage ratings of 10,000–22,000 volts. **1975** YEAGER & GOURLEY *Introd. Electron & Electromech. Devices* (1976) xiv. 283 We will discuss two types of gaseous discharge: arc discharge and glow discharge... Arc discharge tubes are commonly called thermionic gas tubes; for example the gas diode (phanotron) and the gas triode (thyratron).

phanta·smically, *adv.* [f. PHANTASMICAL *a.* + -LY².] = PHANTASMALLY *adv.*

1906 *Daily News* 2 Jan. 6 If I stretch out my hand to a touch, will it not surely melt under my fingers?—melt and form again phantasmically.

phantastica (fæ̆ntæ·stikă). [f. *phantastic*, var. FANTASTIC *a.* and *sb.* + *-a* (cf. -A 4).] Hallucinogenic drugs collectively; ¶ also, one such drug.

1931 L. LEWIN *Phantastica, Narcotic & Stimulating Drugs* 31 Phantastica; hallucinating substances. This series comprises a number of substances of vegetable origin, varying greatly in their chemical constitution, and to these belongs in its proper sense the name Phantastica, or Drugs of Illusion. *Ibid.* 92, I mean the action of chemical substances capable of evoking such transitory states without any physical inconvenience for a certain time in persons of perfectly normal mentality who are partly or fully conscious of the action of the drug. Substances of this nature I call Phantastica. They..influence particularly the visual and auditory spheres as well as the general sensibility. **1958** *Sci. News* XLVII. 31 The two groups of drugs on which most attention has been focused recently have been: (*a*) those that tend to make normal people appear to be psychotic (hallucinogens, psychotomimetic drugs or phantastica), and (*b*) those that are mostly intended to have the opposite effect. **1967** M. M. GLATT et al. *Drug Scene* i. 9 The three principal drugs in this group are mescaline, psilocybin, and lysergic acid diethylamide (LSD 25 or LSD). These drugs are also designated as phantastica, psychedelic, and psychotomimetic drugs. **1968** J. BLACKBURN *Young Man from Lima* v. 51 Marcus tried to remember what he knew about modern hallucinogenics... Lysergine..was probably the most powerful phantastica known to man.

phantastikon (fæ̆ntæ·stikǫn). *poet.* [f. Gr. φανταστικόν imaginative faculty, neut. of φανταστικός (see FANTASTIC *a.* and *sb.*).] Imagination.

1917 E. POUND *Lustra* 187 Shall I claim; Confuse my own phantastikon Or say the filmy shell that circumscribes me Contains the actual sun. **1933** —— *Let.* 15 Jan. (1971) 243 As fer yr. final pp., that is about the kind of mess that has been trespassin on my phantastikon for several weeks.

phantastron (fæntæ·strǫn). *Electronics.* [f. alteration of FANTASTIC *a.* and *sb.*: see *-TRON.] A circuit in which a brief triggering pulse produces at one electrode a longer pulse whose duration is proportional to an applied control voltage, and at another electrode a linear sweep voltage of the same duration (which can then be used to generate another pulse that will occur at a definite interval after the triggering pulse).

1943 (*title*) An adaptation of the phantastron delay multivibrator circuit to the 6SA7 tube. (M.I.T. Radiation Laboratory Rep. 63-21.) **1947** L. J. HAWORTH in L. N. Ridenour *Radar Syst. Engin.* xiii. 500 The phantastron of Fig. 13·17 is a flip-flop..which serves as a timing circuit maintaining its calibration to about one per cent. **1953** *Electronic Engin.* XXV. 143/1 The position of the selector pulse in the time scale depends on the delay produced by the phantastron and is controlled by R_{13}. **1964** R. BLITZER *Basic Pulse Circuits* vi. 215 A linear sawtooth voltage generator similar to the Miller sweep circuits of Sec. 6·11 is called the phantastron... Besides the sawtooth waveshape being used as a sweep, the phantastron is also often used as a delay circuit.

phantastry, the more usual form of FANTASTRY.

Not *Obs.* in this spelling.

1656, etc. (in Dict. s.v. FANTASTRY]. **1870** *Contemp. Rev.* XIII. 1 It [*sc.* the Church] must have its pomp and phantastry, its tributes and taxes. **1922** HARDY *Late Lyrics* 72 So white her drape..I could not guess what phantastry it meant.

phantom, *sb.* Add: **5. c.** *Telegr.* and *Teleph.* An additional circuit obtained by using each of two other circuits as one of its two conductors, the two wires of each of the other circuits being effectively in parallel. Usu. *attrib.*

1883 G. BLACK in *Operator & Electr. World* 3 Feb. 71/1 The method of telephonic transmission was discovered by myself in 1878, while experimenting to get rid of telegraphic induction in telephones. I found that my apparatus gave me a new 'phantom' circuit over a telegraph wire. **1920** J. G. HILL *Telephonic Transmission* ix. 192 If one of the side circuits in a phantom circuit is out of order, the phantom necessarily fails with it. **1924** W. AITKEN *Automatic Telephone Syst.* II. xlviii. 229 In using phantom or superimposed circuits on automatic systems great care must be exercised to prevent impulse and other currents in one physical circuit affecting the mate physical circuit by way of the phantom loop. **1943** A. L. ALBERT *Fund. Telephony* x. 258 A phantom circuit is obtained by repeating coils..installed at each end of two pairs of wires constituting the phantom group. This arrangement gives three telephone channels: one over each side circuit and one channel over the phantom circuit. **1957** W. FRASER *Telecommunications* v. 123 The additional circuits may be provided by utilising pairs of phantom circuits to produce other phantom circuits.

d. *Radiology.* A life-size model of part of the body made of material which absorbs radiation in a similar way, used in investigations into the character and absorption of a beam of radiation.

1922 tr. *Kroenig & Friedrich's Princ. Physics & Biol. Radiation Therapy* i. 33 Perthes had to employ a solid substance, namely aluminium, as phantom material... These aluminium phantoms have general use in practice on account of their convenience. **1950** WALTER & MILLER *Short Textbk. Radiotherapy* iv. 99 Water is not always an ideal medium in which to insert small ionization chambers... A suitable phantom can be made of layers of pressed wood fibre which can be obtained of unit density. Suitable holes..enable the ionization chamber to be inserted. **1974** RAFLA & ROTMAN *Introd. Radiotherapy* iii. 35/1 A plastic material.., which simulates water (and soft tissues), has been described. If such a material is placed around a bony skeleton, then a phantom that simulates the body with its bones more accurately than water alone can be built.

6. (Further examples.) Also in more general use: imaginary; false; devised by way of pretence, imitation, or deceit.

1885 KIPLING *Phantom 'Rickshaw* (1889) 25 The phantom 'rickshaw and I went side by side along the Chota Simla road in silence. **1897** W. B. YEATS *Let.* 24 Dec. (1954) 293 He did not come because of the phantom sore throat. **1909** *Westm. Gaz.* 19 Aug. 8/1 There was more phantom work on the Downs yesterday. **1927** H. CRANE *Let.* 7 Jan. (1965) 283 The 'ships' [in a poem] should meet and pass in line and type—as well as in wind and memory, if you get my rather unique formal intentions in this phantom regatta seen from Brooklyn Bridge. **1931** *Daily Express* 28 Apr. 11/4 The ball was centred, and the eleven men, playing a phantom team, swept down the pitch to the unguarded goal. **1934** *Sun* (Baltimore) 5 Apr. 1/3 The steel industry was indulging in a monopolistic form of price boosting and price fixing which included the writing into its price structure of so-called 'phantom' freight rates which the consumer pays, but which find their way into the manufacturers' coffers and not those of the railroads. **1951** M. MCLUHAN *Mech. Bride* (1967) 143/2 They are not rooted in any concept of civilized society but are merely a blind drive toward the phantom security of subrational collectivism. **1952** *Times* 12 Dec. 12/3 Lot 90 was not a phantom beaver coat, or indeed a beaver coat at all, but a phantom racoon coat. **1958** *Times* 29 Sept. 13/1 The duvetyn coat with a phantom beaver collar. **1976** *National Observer* (U.S.) 29 May 9/2 A 'phantom', or dummy, fluorescent tube that reduces the amount of electricity used by standard two-tube fixtures.

7. a. *phantom-life*; **b.** Also objective, as *phantom-chaser*; also *phantom-wise* adv.

1954 KOESTLER *Invisible Writing* ii. 34 The phantom-chaser..who discovers Helen's image in each beloved face. **1907** *Folk-Lore* June 147 Cuchulain was recalled to phantom-life on one occasion by St. Patrick. **1871** 'L. CARROLL' *Through Looking-Glass* 223 Still she haunts me, phantomwise.

8. phantom limb, a sensation of the presence of an amputated limb; so **phantom pain,** pain perceived as in a phantom limb.

[**1872** S. W. MITCHELL *Injuries of Nerves* xiv. 349, I recently faradised a case of disarticulated shoulder... As the current affected the brachial plexus of nerves, he suddenly cried aloud, 'Oh, the hand, the hand!' and attempted to seize the missing member. The phantom I had conjured up swiftly disappeared.] **1879** G. H. LEWES *Probl. Life & Mind* (ser. 3) II. 336 The 'phantom limb', of which Weir Mitchell speaks, is only one detail in the general picture mentally formed of the body. **1937** *Lancet* 8 Aug. 314/1 After amputation it was usual for the patient to experience sensations as if his limb were still present. These phantom limbs might be painless or painful. **1955** *Sci. News Let.* 13 Aug. 104/3 Phantom limb pains, a troublesome affliction in amputation cases, and pains in amputation stumps can be relieved in many cases by ultrasound treatment. **1974** *Nature* 26 Apr. 731/1 Phantom limbs occur in 95 to 100% of all people who have had a limb or part of a limb amputated. **1960** I. A. STANTON *Dict. for Med. Secretaries* 115/2 Phantom pain. **1964** *N.Y. State Jrnl. Med.* LXIV. 2907/2 Many theories have been advanced to explain the mechanism of phantom pain. **1973** *Daily Colonist* (Victoria, B.C.) 11 Apr. 34/7 It's pretty weird to have a pain in a foot that has been amputated... The person [is] suffering from 'phantom pains' as they are called.

pharaoh. Add: **4. Pharaoh hound,** a short-coated, tan-coloured hunting dog with large, pointed ears, belonging to the breed so called; **Pharaoh's ant** (examples).

1967 R. GLYN *Champion Dogs of World* 191/2 The Ibizan Hound. Also known as the Pharaoh Hound. **1969** V. CANNING *Queen's Pawn* xiii. 240 Raikes sat..reading an article about the revival of interest in Pharaoh hounds from Malta. **1974** A. G.-I. BROWNE *Hamlyn Guide to Dogs* 180 Pharaoh Hound... Although in the opinion of many people they belong to one and the same breed, the FCI [*sc.* Fédération Cynologique Internationale] recognizes the Pharaoh Hound as well as the Podenco Ibicenco [or Ibizan hound]... It is supposed that the Pharaoh Phoenicians. **1910** W. M. WHEELER *Ants* i. 10 Some of them [*sc.* tropical ants], like Pharaoh's ant.., have been carried by commerce to all the inhabited regions of the globe. **1939** METCALF & FLINT *Destructive & Useful Insects* (ed. 2) xxi. 770 Pharaoh's ant, *Monomorium pharaonis*... This tiny, slender, yellowish-red ant..generally nests in inaccessible places about the foundations and in the walls of buildings, from which it forages indoors the year round in search of food. **1978** *Times* 24 Apr. 2/2 Ministry of Agriculture scientists have devised a way to get rid of one of the more serious modern hospital pests, the Pharaoh's ant.

pharaonic, *a.* (Later examples.)

1958 L. DURRELL *Mountolive* i. 17 Forgotten Pharaonic frescoes of light and darkness. **1972** *Nature* 14 Apr. 324/1 A travelling exhibition of works of art dating from both Pharaonic and Islamic times. **1976** *Sci. Amer.* Aug. 38/2 It is interesting to note that in the earliest Pharaonic era, that of the Old Kingdom, the Egyptians showed a lively interest in domesticating local animals.

pharate (fæ·rēit), *a. Ent.* [f. Gr. φᾶρ-ος cloak + -ATE².] (See quot. 1946.)

1946 H. E. HINTON in *Nature* 27 Apr. 553/1 The term 'pharate'..is proposed to designate the place of an instar which is enclosed within the cuticle of the previous instar. **1957** RICHARDS & DAVIES *Imms's Gen. Textbk. Entomol.* (ed. 9) 222 There may be an appreciable interval between the two events, during which the instar within the old cuticle is known as the pharate instar. **1971** *Nature* 12 Feb. 490/1 The developing adult inside the pupal cuticle (the pharate adult) can also move the spiracles. **1973** W. S. ROMOSER *Sci. of Entomol.* viii. 242 The pharate condition..is where the adult is fully formed but is still within the confines of the pupal cuticle.

Pharisaist (fæ·risе͵ist), *a.* [After PHARISAISM, f. PHARISEE *sb.* + -IST.] = PHARISAIC *a.*

1918 P. T. FORSYTH *This Life & Next* xi. 112 Its idea of resurrection means something very much more than the repristination of the old life under happier circumstances. That..is but Jewish, and Pharisaist, and Moslem.

Pharisee, *sb.* Add: **2*.** Usu. in *pl.*: app. a dialectal alteration of *fairies*, pl. of FAIRY *sb.*

[**1807** SOUTHEY *Lett. from Eng.* III. liv. 37 The man observed..that the fairies were never seen now, as they used to be in old times... The man persisted [to the priest], —'It is no longer ago than last Sunday you read about the Scribes and *Pharisees*.'] **1850** H. ELLIS *Brand's Observations on Pop. Antiquities* (ed. 4) II. 504 The calf is rid every night by the *farisees*. **1852** J. ALLIES *Antiquities & Folk-Lore Worcestershire* (ed. 2) xii. 418 According to tradition,..Oseberrow..Rock..was a favourite haunt of the fairies (*vulgo* pharises). **1854** M. A. LOWER *Contributions to Lit.* 157 It's very hard to say how them rings do come, if it isn't the Pharisees that makes 'em. **1884** *Contemp. Rev.* Aug. 329 Among the peasants of the South Downs a belief in the existence of fairies, or, as they call them, 'Pharisees', has not died out. **1906** KIPLING *Puck of Pook's Hill* 264 'Pharisees,' cried Una. 'Fairies? Oh, *I* see!' **1930** M. ALLINGHAM *Mystery Mile* iv. 49 Seven Whistlers... No one knows if they be ghosts or Pharisees—that be fairies. **1947** E. MEYNELL *Sussex* ix. 243 The belief in fairies—though few of the old Sussex people would dream of using such an 'outland' word, it is as pharisees they are known—also continued late in the county. **1948** L. SPENCE *Fairy Tradition in Brit.* iv. 82 'Pharisees', a term used to denote the fairies in Suffolk.

pharmaceutic, *a.* and *sb.* Add: **B.** *sb.* (Further examples.) Also *concr.*, a medicinal drug; = PHARMACEUTICAL *sb.*

1927 *Daily Express* 11 May 11/4 The agreement will later be extended to include artificial silk,..fertilisers, pharmaceutics, and many other products. **1974** *Nature* 6 Sept. p. xi/1 (Advt.), Applications are invited for the post of Senior Lecturer in the Department of Pharmaceutics commencing January 1, 1975.

pharmaceutical, *a.* (*sb.*) **B.** *sb.* (Further examples.)

1955 T. STERLING *Evil of Day* iv. 39 The night-table.. was prominently littered with pharmaceuticals. **1958** *Times* 5 Dec. 3/3 An international company manufacturing surgical and orthopaedic dressings, pharmaceuticals and proprietary medical products.

pharmaco-. Add: **pharmacodynamic** *a.* (examples); hence **pha:rmacodyna·mically** *adv.*; **pharmacodynamics** *sb. pl.* (further examples); **pharmaco·gnosist,** an expert in pharmacognosy; **pha:rmacogno·stic** *a.*, of or pertaining to pharmacognosy; **pha:rmacokine·tics** *sb. pl.* (const. as *sing.*), the branch of pharmacology concerned with the movement of drugs within the body; so **pha:rmacokine·tic** *a.*, **-kine·tically** *adv.*

1906 *Jrnl. Infectious Dis.* III. 572 (*heading*) Pharmacodynamic action due to ions. **1951** A. BURGER *Medicinal Chem.* I. xxi. 386 Certain cholinergic agents (Doryl) can add to the analgetic effect produced by injected epinephrine. The pharmacodynamic mechanism..is as yet uncertain; it may be that the para-sympathomimetic drug stimulates the output of epinephrine by the adrenal gland which can then enhance the peripheral adrenergic vasoconstrictor effect. **1929** MITCHELL & HAMILTON *Biochem. Amino Acids* vii. 363 It is a fact of great significance that histidine, a substance entirely indifferent pharmacodynamically, should be transformable by simple decarboxylation into such an active substance as histamine. **1959** K. H. BEYER in Waife & Shapiro *Clin. Eval. New Drugs* ii. 19 Some compounds are so active that no chemical or isotopic method may be suitable to follow them at pharmacodynamically effective dosages. **1867** R. E. SCORESBY-JACKSON *Note-Bk. Materia Med.* i. 3

Pharmacology..is divided into General Pharmacology and Special Pharmacology, and is subdivided into Pharmacognosy, Pharmacy, and Pharmacodynamics. **1925** E. Novak in *Gynecol. & Obstetr. Monogr.: Appendix* 22 The study of the pharmacodynamics of the various forms of ovarian extract has until recent years yielded unimpressive results as regards the generative system. **1974** M. C. Gerald *Pharmacol.* i. 9 Pharmacodynamics, a basic experimental science, is a study of where a drug acts in the body..and how it acts (what is its mechanism of action in physiological and/or biological terms). **1934** Webster, Pharmacognosist. **1939** *Nature* 1 Apr. 540/2 The complete pharmacognosist is a man of many parts. His preliminary training in botany, zoology, chemistry and physics furnishes him with a foundation on which to build experience in the technique of microscopy, histology, morphology, [etc.]. **1972** *Ibid.* 21 Jan. 134/1 Some people may have thought of pharmacognosists as witch doctors in that their methods of selection of plants for study have relied to some extent on folklore and ancient custom. **1961** Webster, Pharmacognostic. **1974** *Nature* 13 Sept. 169/1 While familiarising himself with the natural history of the islands, Linnaeus was instructed particularly to look for plants..with pharmacognostic value. **1964** *Antibiotica et Chemotherapia* XII. p. viii/1 A list of symbols for the use in pharmacokinetic models. **1976** *Lancet* 9 Oct. 808/1 Pharmacokinetic analysis indicates that binding is unlikely to be a major problem in vivo when less than 75–85% of the drug is bound. **1972** *Nature* 28 Apr. 434/2 The leaching of DDT from fatty tissue after exposure to abnormally large controlled doses of DDT appears to be pharmacokinetically similar to the uptake process. **1960** *Jrnl. Amer. Pharmaceutical Assoc.* XLIX. 311 (*heading*) Dosage schedule and pharmacokinetics in chemotherapy. **1971** R. E. Notari *Biopharmaceutics & Pharmacokinetics* i. 4 Since the movement of drug from the site of administration to the site of action requires time, the overall process may best be analyzed by what is called pharmacokinetics. **1973** *Nature* 22 June p. xvi (Advt.), A graduate with experience in pharmacokinetics and drug metabolism.

pha:rmacogene·tics, *sb. pl.* (const. as *sing.*). *Pharm.* [ad. G. *pharmakogenetik* sb. (F. Vogel 1959, in *Ergebnisse d. inneren Med. und Kinderheilkunde* XII. 117): see Pharmaco-, Genetic *a.*, and -ic 2.] The study of the effect of genetic factors on reactions to drugs.

1960 *Times* 11 Nov. 17/2 This development of pharmaco-genetics may affect quite considerably our methods of treating patients. **1962** W. Kalow (*title*) Pharmacogenetics: heredity and the response to drugs. **1965** Fingl & Woodbury in Goodman & Gilman *Pharmacol. Basis Therapeutics* (ed. 3) i. 25/2 The objectives of pharmacogenetics include not only identification of differences in drug effects that have a genetic basis but also development of simple methods by which susceptible individuals can be recognized before the drug is administered. **1974** M. C. Gerald *Pharmacol.* iii. 58 Among the newest subdivisions of pharmacology is that of pharmacogenetics which is the study of the influence of genetic factors on the drug response.

Hence **pha:rmacogene·tic** *a.*, **-gene·ticist.**

1962 *Pharmaceutical Jrnl.* CLXXXIX. 282/3 Pharmacogenetic studies. **1970** Passmore & Robson *Compan. Med. Stud.* II. xxxi. 11/1 Not all pharmacogenetic studies are prompted by the occurrence of adverse effects. **1971** *Sci. News* 26 June 439 Some pharmacogeneticists advocate screening individuals who are to receive succinylcholine before surgery for their pseudocholinesterase activity. **1974** M. C. Gerald *Pharmacol.* iii. 59 Pharmacogenetic differences, in part, account for the development of resistant strains of bacteria and insects.

pharmacology. Add: Hence **pha:rmacolo·gic** *a.* (chiefly *U.S.*) = Pharmacological *a.*

1901 T. Sollmann *Text-bk. Pharmacol.* 8 The organic poisons..often require pharmacologic experience for their recognition. **1973** *Sci. Amer.* Sept. 123/3 Psychiatry ..has two faces, one represented by treatment at the psychosocial level and the other by treatment at the pharmacologic level.

‖ **pharmakos** (fā·ɹmăkǫs). Pl. **pharmakoi.** [Gr. φαρμακός scapegoat.] In ancient Greece, a scapegoat chosen in atonement for a crime or misfortune. Also *transf.* in allusive use.

1903 J. E. Harrison *Proleg. Study Greek Relig.* iii. 104 The pharmakos is killed then, not because his death is a vicarious sacrifice, but because he is so infected and tabooed that his life is a practical impossibility. **1923** A. Le Marchant *Greek Relig. to Time of Hesiod* iv. 25 A ceremony in which two men called Pharmakoi, decked with branches, were led out of the city. **1926** J. Buchan *Dancing Floor* ii. 42 You have your purgation herbs like buckthorn and agnus castus, and you have your *pharmakos*, your scapegoat, who carries away all impurities. **1957** N. Frye *Anat. Crit.* 41 The figure of a typical or random victim begins to crystallize in domestic tragedy as it deepens in ironic tone. We may call this typical victim the *pharmakos* or scapegoat.

pharyngal or **pharyngeal,** *a.* (*sb.*) Add: **A.** *adj. spec.* of speech-sounds: (see Pharyngal *a.* (*sb.*)); also applied to consonantal sounds articulated with obstruction of the air-stream at the pharynx.

1925 W. H. T. Gairdner *Phonetics of Arabic* iv. 27 [ħ].. is a pharyngal unvoiced fricative. **1931** G. Noël-Armfield *Gen. Phonetics* (ed. 4) xviii. 107 Two very difficult plosive sounds for English people..are the Arabic (or Hebrew) *qaf* and its voiced correspondent. They are somewhat similar to [k] and [g] respectively... These consonants, though usually termed uvular, would be better regarded as pharyngal. **1950** D. Jones *Phoneme* p. xiii, ħ, breathed pharyngal fricative. **1964** *Language* XL. 501 A series of pharyngal stops, plain and labialized, aspirated and glottalized. **1968** Chomsky & Halle *Sound Pattern Eng.* 305 Ubykh, a Caucasian language, distinguishes pharyngeal, uvular, velar, and perhaps also palatal obstruents. **1978** *Studies in Eng. Lit.: Eng. Number* (Tokyo) 159 Part III consists of two chapters, the first of which is concerned with the phonological characterisation of pharyngeal consonants.

B. *sb.* **2.** *spec.* designating speech-sounds: (see Pharyngal *a.* (*sb.*)); also, a pharyngeal consonant.

1925 W. H. T. Gairdner *Phonetics of Arabic* iv. 27 We are faced with two difficulties in regard to the two pharyngals ħ and ʕ. **1968** Chomsky & Halle *Sound Pattern Eng.* 305 The consonants where the primary constriction is formed with the body of the tongue..: the palatals, velars, uvulars, and pharyngeals. **1976** *Archivum Linguisticum* VII. 91 Nor is it [*sc.* preaspiration] necessarily a pharyngeal..but may be realized as a spirant formed at some other point of articulation.

Hence **phary·ng(e)alization,** obstruction of the air-stream at the pharynx; modification into a pharyngeal sound; **phary·ng(e)alized** *ppl. a.*, produced by pharyngealization.

1931 G. Noël-Armfield *Gen. Phonetics* (ed. 4) 186 (Index), Pharyngalised consonants. **1947** K. L. Pike *Phonemics* xvi. 219 Pharyngealized consonants which are phonemically distinct from nonpharyngealized consonants would..need a special symbol. **1949** *Trans. Philol. Soc. 1948* 148 All the *gh* spellings..are realized as long slightly pharyngalized vowels. **1964** R. Kingdon in D. Abercrombie et al. *Daniel Jones* 115 Secondary articulations such as..pharyngalization. **1968** Chomsky & Halle *Sound Pattern Eng.* 309 We know of no languages that exhibit parallel variations in degree of narrowing concomitant with palatalization or pharyngealization. **1968** P. M. Postal *Aspects Phonol. Theory* iv. 82 Consonants are normally non-Pharyngealized. Hence there are no languages with only Pharyngealized consonants. **1977** J. C. Catford *Fund. Probl. Phonetics* ix. 182 Pharyngealized vowels involve a compression of the pharynx simultaneously with a primary vowel articulation... Such vowels occur in several Caucasian languages of Dagestan.

pharyngo-. Add: **phary:ngoconju·nctival** *a.*, epithet of a syndrome that is characterized by conjunctivitis, pharyngitis, and fever and occurs chiefly in epidemics among children; **pharyngo-nasal** *a.* (examples); now *rare* or *obs.* (cf. *nasopharyngeal* adj. s.v. *naso-).

1955 J. A. Bell et al. in *Jrnl. Amer. Med. Assoc.* 26 Mar. 1092/2 Study of the clinical, etiological, and epidemiological attributes of a newly recognized communicable disease entity has appeared to differentiate one disease entity from the poorly defined mass of undifferentiated respiratory illnesses generally known as the common cold, catarrhal fever, nonstreptococcic sore throat, or acute respiratory disease. We suggest that this disease entity be named pharyngoconjunctival fever. **1974** Passmore & Robson *Compan. Med. Stud.* III. xii. 18/1 (*heading*) Pharyngo-conjunctival syndrome. **1976** *Lancet* 6 Nov. 990/2 Respiratory illness and pharyngoconjunctival fever are commonly associated with adenovirus infections. **1861** G. D. Gibb tr. *Czermak's On Laryngoscope* iii. 25 The principle of the laryngoscopic method could be equally applied to the inspection of..the superior parts of the pharynx (pharyngo-nasal vault). **1894** J. W. Downie *Clin. Man. Study Dis. Throat* i. 29 These growths..may attain to such a size as to completely block the pharyngo-nasal cavity, thereby hindering nasal respiration.

phase, *sb.* Add: **2.** Esp. in phr. *phase one* (or *two*, etc.): the first (or second, etc.) planned stage of a process, series of events, etc.

1957 *Economist* 5 Oct. 24/2 There was little..to suggest that the government expects Britain to be a very active combatant in 'Phase Two' of another war. Mr Butler's emphasis was solely on Phase One. **1974** *Times* 1 Apr. 21/1 A contract..for phase one of a new district general hospital. **1977** *Whitaker's Almanack 1978* 580/1 The Chancellor of the Exchequer, other ministers, and the T.U.C. economic committee opened negotiations for a Phase 3 pay policy.

b. *Zool.* A particular period of an animal's life, distinguished by a characteristic form, colour, or type of behaviour. Also *attrib.*

1873 [see *form-genus* (*form *sb.* 22)]. **1921** B. P. Uvarov in *Bull. Entomol. Res.* XII. 153 We are yet far from knowing whether the transformation of one form [of locust] into the other is due to some immediate external influence or to some yet unknown internal cause; I think therefore, that the term 'phase'..suggested to me by Dr. G. A. K. Marshall is more appropriate [than 'morpha']. *Ibid.* 155 The swarming phases [of locusts] enable the species to extend at one stroke its area of distribution. **1937** *Ann. Reg. 1936* 54 Phase variation was found in grasshoppers. **1947** *New Biol.* III. 10 It is now a recognised fact that all true locusts occur in two phases—the solitary and the swarming, or gregarious as it is usually called. **1956** *Nature* 28 Jan. 167/2 Dr. M. L. Roonwal's work has been concerned..with phase-transformation and population dynamics of the desert locust. **1964** L. S. Crandall *Managem. Wild Mammals in Captivity* 368 It [*sc.* the jaguarundi]..occurs in two color phases, dark gray and reddish brown. **1966** B. P. Uvarov *Grasshoppers & Locusts* I. 386 The ideas behind the phase theory are being followed by workers on other insects. **1973** *Nature* 24 Aug. 484/1 Phase transformation in locusts refers to the changes induced when solitary hoppers (juvenile locusts) become gregarious. **1977** *Times* 18 Aug. 14/5 A slate-black falcon..was agreed to have all the field-clues of the dark phase of Eleanora's falcon, one of Europe's rarest predators.

c. A temporarily difficult or unhappy period or stage of development, esp. of adolescents; freq. in *to go* (or *pass*) *through a phase.*

1913 W. J. Locke *Stella Maris* xix. 258 'What's the matter with her, for pity's sake?' asked Herold... 'Perhaps it's a phase. Young girls often pass through it.' **1932** R. Lehmann *Invitation to Waltz* i. ii. 27 Mrs. Curtis was silent: a pregnant silence. Kate was going through a phase. Best not to take too much notice. **1960** *Times* 28 May 7/4 'It's only a phase', we say uncertainly when our children sulk, fight, or burst into tears for no reason. **1971** [see *crowd *sb.*[3] 2 c]. **1971** H. McCloy *Question of Time* i. iii. 36 Whenever Pel or Mél get into trouble, Mrs Heron always says: 'It's just a phase they're going through.'

3. Add to def.: Considered in relation to a particular reference position or time. Also *transf.* *in phase*, in the same phase; having the same phase at the same time; const. *with*; *out of phase*, not in phase. (Earlier and further examples.)

1861 *Phil. Mag.* XXI. 163 Two series of undulations traversing the same space do not combine into one resultant as two attractions do, but produce an effect depending on relations of *phase* as well as intensity. **1863** E. Atkinson tr. *Ganot's Elem. Treat. Physics* vii. viii. 474 Fig. 362 represents two waves issuing from the same source of light, and meeting at *a*, under a very acute angle in the same phases [*ed.* 2 (1866): in the same phase], while fig. 363 represents the coincidence of two waves in opposite phases of undulation. **1891** J. W. Urquhart *Dynamo Construction* xvi. 239 If switched when not 'in phase', the fresh machine would..be quickly pulled into unison. **1903** T. Sewell *Elem. Electr. Engin.* (ed. 2) xvii. 337 The current flowing in the circuit, whether it be in or out of phase with the e.m.f., is indicated by the ammeter. **1931** Moyer & Wostrel *Radio Handbk.* ii. 74 In a circuit containing only non-inductive resistance the current and voltage are in phase. **1936** L. S. Palmer *Wireless Engin.* x. 403 The plate and outer grid may be indirectly connected by any device..which changes the phase of the output with respect to the input by 180°. **1953** *Economist* 14 Nov. 505/2 To keep the supply of raw materials in phase with productive capacity. **1973** *Sci. Amer.* June 47 The light is reflected from a system of mirrors and arrives either in phase or out of phase at the second Kerr cell, depending on the length of the light path between the cells.

c. *Electr. Engin.* Each of the windings of a polyphase machine.

1904 M. B. Field in M. Maclean *Mod. Electr. Pract.* II. i. vi. 28 If one of the phases of a Δ-connected system is disconnected, the remaining two can still supply a three-phase current, but with a diminished efficiency. **1931** G. C. Blalock *Princ. Electr. Engin.* xviii. 243 The power in any polyphase circuit must of necessity be the sum of the powers in the component phases. It is usually more convenient, however, to determine polyphase power in terms of line voltage and current. **1962** *Newnes Conc. Encycl. Electr. Engin.* 787/2 The phases are interlinked in star connection. **1972** Smith & Hosie *Basic Electr. Engin. Sci.* ix. 244 Symmetrical delta-connected systems... The power developed in the generator, when supplying a balanced load, is three times that developed in each phase. *Ibid.* 254 Each phase of a 3-ph star-connected load is a coil of resistance 20 Ω.

4. A physically distinct and homogeneous form of matter that may be present in a system, characterized by its composition and state and when present separated by a bounding surface from other forms.

1875 J. W. Gibbs in *Trans. Connecticut Acad.* III. 152 We may call such bodies as differ in composition or state, different phases of the matter considered, regarding all bodies which differ only in quantity and form as different examples of the same phase. **1916** C. A. Edwards *Physico-Chem. Properties of Steel* iv. 47 From the phase rule we know that three phases can coexist in equilibrium, in a binary system, only at one temperature. At the Ar_1 point there are three phases—namely, α-iron, carbide of iron, and the solid solution of the eutectoid composition. **1931** Maass & Steacie *Introd. Princ. Physical Chem.* ix. 135 Every liquid has a vapour pressure and will evaporate and enter the gas phase. **1967** J. Wilks *Properties of Liquid & Solid Helium* i. 6 Both solid ^{3}He and ^{4}He exist in three phases with different crystal structures. **1971** I. G. Gass et al. *Understanding Earth* iii. 55/1 These two phases, sand and clay, are very effectively separated from each other by deposition or sedimentation from water.

5. *attrib.* and *Comb.*, as (sense 3) *phase difference*, *relation(ship)*, *reversal*; *phase-sensitive* adj.; (sense *4) *phase boundary*; **phase advancer** *Electr. Engin.*, a device for improving the power factor of an induction motor by generating a magnetizing current in the rotor circuit which leads the main rotor current in phase; **phase change,** a change in the phase of a wave (Phase 3) or of a substance (*phase *sb.* 4); **phase changer** *Electr. Engin.* = **phase converter*; **phase contrast,** the technique in microscopy of introducing a phase difference between parts of the light supplied by the condenser so that interference causes the outlines of the sample, or the boundaries between parts of differing optical density, to appear more prominent; usu. *attrib.*, esp. in *phase-contrast microscope, microscopy*; **phase converter, convertor** *Electr. Engin.*, a device which converts an alternating current into one having a different number of phases but the same frequency; **phase dia-**

gram *Chem.*, a diagram which represents the limits of stability of the various phases of a chemical system at equilibrium with respect to two or more variables (commonly composition and temperature); an equilibrium diagram; **phase displacement** *Electr.*, a difference in phase; **phase distortion,** distortion of a waveform caused by components of different frequencies being propagated at different speeds, so that their phase relations are altered; **phase inverter, invertor** *Electr.*, a phase splitter which produces two signals 180 degrees out of phase; **phase-lock** *sb. Electronics*, the stabilization of the frequency of an oscillator with respect to that of another, stable, oscillator of lower frequency, by means of a circuit in which any variation in the higher frequency generates a phase difference which produces an automatic correction to that oscillation; freq. *attrib.*; so **phase-lock** *v. trans.*, to stabilize (an oscillation or a device) in this way; **phase-locked** *ppl. a.*, **-locking** *vbl. sb.*; **phase microscope** *Biol.*, a phase-contrast microscope; so **phase microscopy; phase modulation** *Telecommunications*, modulation of a wave by variation of its phase; hence **phase-modulated** *ppl. a.*, (as a back-formation) **phase-modulate** *v. trans.*; **phase reaction** *Chem.*, a chemical or physical change which involves the transfer of material between phases, or the appearance or disappearance of a phase; **phase rotation** *Electr. Engin.* = *PHASE SEQUENCE 1; **phase rule, Phase Rule** *Physical Chem.* (see quots. 1913, 1966); **phase separation** *Physical Chem.*, the separation of one phase into two, esp. the separation of a mixture by partition between two phases, or the coacervation of a colloidal solution; **phase shift,** a change in the phase of a waveform; **phase-shifter** *Electr.*, a circuit or device which introduces a change in the phase of an oscillation; orig. *spec.* a transformer which alters the power factor in an a.c. circuit by changing the phase relationship of voltage and current; so **phase-shifted, -shifting,** *ppl. adjs.*; **phase space** *Physics*, a multi-dimensional space in which each axis corresponds to one of the co-ordinates (spatial or other) required to specify the state of a physical system, all the co-ordinates being thus represented so that a point in the space corresponds to a state of the system; **phase-splitter** *Electr.*, a circuit or device which splits a single-phase voltage into two or more voltages differing in phase; so **phase-splitting** *ppl. a.* and *vbl. sb.*; **phase transition,** a change in the phase of a substance (*PHASE *sb.* 4); **phase velocity,** the speed of propagation of a sine wave or a sinusoidal component of a complex wave, equal to the product of its wavelength and frequency (cf. **group velocity*); **phase-wound** *a. Electr. Engin.*, having a secondary in the form of windings rather than a squirrel-cage.

1909 M. WALKER in *Jrnl. Inst. Electr. Engin.* XLII. 611 The author believes that it is possible to devise a new type of machine to act as an exciter in the manner proposed by M. Leblanc... Such a machine might be called a 'phase advancer'. **1920** *Whittaker's Electr. Engineer's Pocket-bk.* (ed. 4) 521 Should the speed be increased above synchronism, the reactance attains a negative value (*i.e.* the phase-advancer acts as a capacity), with the result that the current is advanced and the leading component of it compensates for the magnetizing current of the induction motor, thereby relieving the system. **1962** *Newnes Conc. Encycl. Electr. Engin.* 596/1 Many different types of phase advancer have been developed but they are only rarely used because of the high maintenance required. **1952** *New Biol.* XII. 99 The adsorption of simple organic molecules from the atmosphere or from solutions at the surface of phase boundaries may have been of far greater importance. Suitable phase boundaries occur..at the surface of crystals of inorganic minerals. **1914** *Physical Rev.* III. 126 At high pressures we are concerned with phase changes of only two types, from the fluid to the solid (or crystalline) phase, and from one solid phase to another. *Ibid.* 354 Methods..for determining the phase change produced by reflection from the surfaces of metals. **1956** *Nature* 4 Feb. 240/1 The rate of diffusion in the plane of the layers for each phase-change is equal in all directions. **1962** A. NISBETT *Technique Sound Studio* 254 Noise..is strongly discriminated against [by frequency modulation], though it does produce phase-change effects which cannot be eradicated. **1974** *Times* 4 Feb. 14 It was once thought that deep earthquakes marked the simultaneous collapse of many cubic kilometres of rock from one atomic structure to another—a so-called phase change. **1900** *Jrnl. Electr., Power & Gas* Oct. 81/2 (*heading*) An induction motor phase changer. **1935** *Discovery* Nov. 326/1 Phase changers and automatic regulators have worked perfectly [in locomotives of Hungarian railways]. **1934** F. ZERNIKE in *Monthly Notices R. Astron. Soc.* XCIV. 377 (*heading*) Diffraction theory of the knife-edge test and its improved form, the phase-contrast method. **1942** *Jrnl. Sci. Instrum.* XIX. 71 (*heading*) Phase-contrast microscopy. **1947** *Nature* 21 June 829/2 Mr. Taylor has made and described a new phase-contrast microscope in which a controlled variable amplitude for the 'direct-light' component is obtained. **1961** M. FRANÇON *Progress in Microsc.* ii. 65 Originally used by its inventor [*sc.* Zernike] for inspecting telescope mirrors, the phase contrast technique was applied to microscopy shortly afterwards. **1966** *McGraw-Hill Encycl. Sci. & Technol.* VIII. 399/2 The phase contrast microscope is the routine instrument for the examination of living cells. **1970** E. M. SLAYTER *Optical Methods in Biol.* xiii. 288 The phase contrast microscope is a device which renders differences in refractive index between regions of a specimen visible as differences in intensity. **1971** *Nature* 17 Sept. 198/1 Parasitaemia was estimated by examination of fresh blood preparations by phase contrast microscopy..every 2–3 days. *Ibid.* 26 Nov. 227/2 Cytological characters and chromosomal behaviour during mitosis were studied in live cultures under phase contrast. **1916** *Trans. Amer. Inst. Electr. Engin.* XXXV. 1318 No. 4 is in general respects the same as No. 2 with the addition of a relatively new development known as the 'phase converter' which preserves the balance of the system even when large blocks of single-phase power are taken from the system. **1935** *Discovery* Nov. 326/1 The phase converter is usually regarded as the most complicated part of the locomotive. **1967** C. V. JONES *Unified Theory Electr. Machines* xviii. 241 As a final example of induction motor performance, its operation as a phase converter will be briefly considered. **1911** *Chem. Abstr.* V. 1219 (*heading*) Phase diagram of silver iodide. **1926** *Jrnl. Iron & Steel Inst.* CXIII. 655 The phase diagram is characterised by a solid solution of tin in iron with a maximum of 18 per cent tin, and by two compounds. **1972** *McGraw-Hill Yearbk. Sci. & Technol.* 350/2 The most apparent departure from conventional behavior is seen in the phase diagram of solid He^3 shown in Fig. 2. **1889** J. A. FLEMING *Alternate Current Transformer* I. iv. 291 θ is the angle of phase difference of the currents. **1962** *Symp. Zool. Soc.* No. 7. 10 It has been generally supposed until recently that for man..phase differences are of no account. But we now realize that if changes of phase of particular components occur at a sufficiently rapid state, then differences of sound-quality are in fact heard. **1907** H. H. NORRIS *Introd. Study Electr. Engin.* iv. 120 (*heading*) Phase displacement of alternating quantities. **1933** Phase displacement [see *BALANCED *ppl. a.* 6]. **1928** *Bell Syst. Techn. Jrnl.* VII. 195 For relatively short distances the deleterious effects of phase distortion are not appreciable. **1961** G. MILLERSON *Technique Television Production* iii. 43 Certain video distortions, from phase-distortion to signal reflections, can also be the reason for poor definition in a picture. **1970** J. EARL *Tuners & Amplifiers* ii. 43 For high quality all the significant sideband signals must be handled by the i.f. channel to avoid phase distortion and treble attenuation. **1942** A. HUND *Frequency Modulation* xi. 178 Figure 49 shows a balanced reactance-tube modulator where a phase inverter replaces the push-pull input transformer. **1951** *Electronic Engin.* XXIII. 64 Phase-invertors using resistance-loaded triode valves are well known. **1960** E. N. LURCH *Fund. Electronics* xv. 353 A circuit arrangement to produce balanced voltages which are 180° out of phase for the grids of the push-pull stage is termed a phase inverter. **1953** W. A. EDSON *Vacuum-Tube Oscillators* xiv. 342 The question of time delay or phase lock arises in all methods of frequency composition. **1957** *Electronic & Radio Engineer* XXXIV. 141/2 The simple phase-lock loop is effectively a position control servo-mechanism operated by a d.c. error voltage from the phase-sensitive detector. **1973** *Wireless World* Dec. 605/1 The device contains a phase-locked loop which I have found suitable for demodulating teleprinter f.s.k. signals because it requires only a small input signal for phase lock. **1974** HARVEY & BOHLMAN *Stereo F.M. Radio Handbk.* iv. 65 When 'phase-lock' is achieved the in-phase detector registers this by providing a d.c. output. **1955** *Proc. IRE* XLIII. 869/1 A circuit has been developed with which microwave oscillators may be phase-locked to weak but stable reference signals. **1967** *Electronics* 6 Mar. 6/2 (Advt.), The generator frequency can be phaselocked to an external standard frequency. **1959** *Proc. IRE* XLVII. 1137/2 A phase-locked oscillator can serve as a filter of arbitrarily narrow bandwidth. **1976** *Gramophone* Aug. 354/2 A quartz crystal controlled phase-locked servo circuit holds speed drift within 0.002% and is independent of any changes in line voltage or frequency. **1955** *Proc. IRE* XLIII. 872/2 This phase-locking circuitry may also be used to make a divider of particular use in the microwave region where no other kind exists. **1963** *Electronics* 19 Apr. 45/2 Because phase-locking is used, the offset between channels is affected only by the frequencies assigned to the i-f reference oscillators. **1977** *Proc. R. Soc. Med.* LXX. 379/2 Temporal information depends on phase-locking; the nerves fire at a particular phase of the stimulating wave-form so that for sinusoids the time intervals between firings are approximately integral multiples of the period of the wave-form. **1946** *Trans. Amer. Microsc. Soc.* LXV. 129 (*heading*) Phase microscopy. *Ibid.*, The Phase Microscope reveals detail in transparent materials having regions of slightly differing absorption or with different indices of refraction. **1949** *World-Herald* (Omaha, Nebraska) 4 Dec. 19-A, The phase microscope can see the interior of a cell in bright or dark contrast to bring hidden parts into view. **1964** N. S. COHN *Elem. Cytol.* ii. 22 The observation of living cells has been greatly facilitated by the development of phase microscopy and related optical systems. **1970** O. W. RICHARDS in J. E. Blair et al. *Man. Clin. Microbiol.* 24/1 The phase microscope has an annular stop in the condenser to limit the lighting to a symmetrical hollow cone. **1930** *Proc. IRE* XVIII. 633 (*heading*) The effect of frequency or 'phase' modulation upon signal quality. **1936** Phase-modulated [see *FREQUENCY-MODULATED *ppl. a.*]. **1941** *Electronic Engin.* XIV. 537/3 Phase modulation possesses much the same advantages as frequency modulation. Signal-to-noise ratio is greater than for amplitude modulation..though it is less than for frequency modulation since the triangular noise spectrum effect is absent because noise itself phase modulates the carrier. **1962** J. H. & P. J. REYNER *Radio Communication* iii. 140 Whereas with phase modulation the modulation index *m* is simply proportional to the amplitude of the modulating signal, with frequency modulation it is *also* inversely proportional to the modulation frequency. **1968** B. P. LATHI *Communication Syst.* iv. 213 If we integrate the modulatory signal $f(t)$ first and then allow it to phase-modulate the carrier, we obtain a frequency-modulated carrier. **1974** HARVEY & BOHLMAN *Stereo F.M. Radio Handbk.* ii. 36 It is a characteristic of phase modulation that the amount of frequency swing introduced is proportional not only to the amplitude of the modulating signal but also to its frequency. **1976** *Sci. Amer.* June 62/3 The antenna transmits a phase-modulated radio signal that carries scientific and engineering data from the spacecraft to the radio tracking stations on the earth. **1920** D. A. CLIBBENS *Princ. Phase Theory* i. 3 If the temperature is raised,..a transference of material from one phase to another will, in general, occur; such a transference is known as a phase reaction. **1923** A. C. D. RIVETT *Phase Rule* iv. 72 Until the temperature reaches that of x_1,..cooling does not bring about any phase reaction. **1938** S. T. BOWDEN *Phase Rule & Phase Reactions* i. 6 A phase reaction is a physical or chemical change which involves the appearance or disappearance of a phase. **1878** *Proc. R. Soc. Edin.* IX. 604 They may be so related in phase that at one of the instants of maximum pressure of one of the constituents there is also maximum pressure of the other constituent. The same phase-relation, if the harmonic numbers of the constituent tones be odd, will give also coincident minimums. **1896** S. P. THOMPSON *Dynamo-Electr. Machinery* (ed. 5) xxvi. 708 (*heading*) Phase-relations in transformers. **1962** A. NISBETT *Technique Sound Studio* xii. 218 The phase relationship between the sounds. **1898** Phase reversal [in Dict., sense 3 b]. **1938** *Science* 4 Mar. 213/2 [They] misinterpret the situation still more by referring to..the setting of gelatine as involving phase-reversal. **1957** *Practical Wireless* XXXIII. 539/2 There is a phase reversal across the common emitter circuit. **1962** A. NISBETT *Technique Sound Studio* 244 *Cardioid microphone*, microphone with a heart-shaped polar diagram (arrived at by adding omnidirectional and figure-of-eight responses together, taking into account the phase reversal at the back of the latter). **1918** K. EDGCUMBE *Industr. Electr. Measuring Instruments* (ed. 2) 254 The direction of phase rotation of the secondary pressures and currents may conveniently be checked by a phase rotation indicator. **1922** [see *PHASED *ppl. a.* 1]. **1962** *Newnes Conc. Encycl. Electr. Engin.* 572/2 A simple portable instrument to indicate phase rotation. **1896** *Jrnl. Chem. Soc.* LXX. II. 415 Only at some one definite temperature would all four salts tend to coexist in an unchanged condition. This point is, in the case of solutions of the salts, a sextuple point in the sense of the phase rule. **1904** [in Dict., sense 3 b]. **1913** BLOXAM & LEWIS *Bloxam's Chem.* (ed. 10) 338 The Phase Rule of Willard Gibbs..is expressed in the equation P+F=C+2,..where P is the number of phases, F the number of degrees of freedom, and C the number of components. **1935** *Discovery* Sept. 258/2 A system so complex as to baffle the most ardent exponent of the phase rule. **1966** *McGraw-Hill Encycl. Sci. & Technol.* V. 55/1 If a system consists of *P* phases and *C* distinguishable components, there are $C+2$ thermodynamic variables (*C* chemical potentials μ_i, plus the temperature and pressure) which are interrelated by an equation for each phase. Since there are *P* independent equations relating the $C+2$ variables, one needs to fix only $F=C+2-P$ variables to define completely the state of the system at equilibrium; the other variables are then beyond control. This relation for the number of degrees of freedom *F*, or variance, is called the Phase Rule and was first derived by Willard Gibbs in 1873. **1957** Phase-sensitive [see *phase-lock* sb. above]. **1963** B. FOZARD *Instrumentation Nucl. Reactors* xi. 135 This requires the provision of a phase-sensitive rectifier at the output. **1941** *Nature* 27 Sept. 373/1 We have sought to replace the customary phase separation of 'crude carotene' and xanthophylls by using the same chromatographic technique for the removal of xanthophylls as well as of non-carotene chromogens from the petrol ether solution. **1947** *Jrnl. Polymer Sci.* II. 90 The phase separation in solutions of high polymers in the same solvent (technically known as incompatibility) has been studied for fourteen high polymers..dissolved in thirteen solvents. **1948** [see *HÆM, HEME b]. **1960** P. A. ALBERTSSON *Partition of Cell Particles* ii. 13 Bungenberg de Jong & Kruyt..coined the term 'coacervation' for the general phenomenon of phase separation of colloid mixtures. **1970** [see *COACERVATION 3]. **1971** *Materials & Technol.* II. vi. 340 Devitrification of glass is the formation of crystals (phase separation) in a glass. **1927** *Wireless World* 1 June 686/2 In order to give a high-grade telephone line such an extended characteristic, special equipment for the equalisation of attenuation and of phase shift had to be devised. **1929** J. A. RATCLIFFE *Physical Princ. Wireless* iii. 37 If a beam of light is focussed on to a point and then allowed to spread out on the other side of the focus, the total phase-shift is π. **1960** *Practical Wireless* XXXVI. 411/2 While a simple phase-shift oscillator..may be used coupled into a suitable amplifier installation, a neater method is to build the complete practice set together with power supply, speaker and controls into a self-contained unit. **1976** *Gramophone* Feb. 1398/1 Either we must accept some loss of loudness of rearward sources in mono playback, or a certain amount of phase-shift between the signals coming from the two loudspeakers in stereo. **1965** *Wireless World* Aug. 396/2 If the gate voltage is phase-shifted with respect to the anode voltage, the firing point is delayed by the appropriate time. **1908** *Electrician* 11 Dec. 341/2 In Fig. 1, which shows diagrammatically a phase shifter for a two-phase supply, AB and CD are the terminals of the two phases. **1951** *Engineering* 23 Feb. 221/2 The first method enables the point in each cycle at which the anodes become conducting to be delayed..by a double-wound phase-shifter. **1959** K. HENNEY *Radio Engin. Handbk.* (ed. 5) xiv. 16 In the microwave region, a matched transmission line or slotted line may be used as a phase shifter. **1908** *Electrician* 11 Dec. 341/1 (*heading*) The use of a phase-shifting transformer for wattmeter and supply meter testing. **1929** *Phil. Mag.* VIII. 168 Thus the artificial line has zero attenuation at all frequencies, and is a pure phase-shifting network. **1965** *Wireless World* July 332/1 Thin film circuits..may be more useful where passive networks only are required—for attenuators, RC phase shifting networks, etc. **1927** R. C. TOLMAN *Statistical Mech.* iii. 32 To follow the behavior of such a system..it is very convenient to think of its phase as given by the position of a representative point..in a 2*m*-dimensional space (phase space) corresponding to the 2*m* coordinates and momenta whose values are to be specified. **1970** G. K. WOODGATE *Elem. Atomic Struct.* vi. 98 The exclusion principle states, in this context, that not more than two electrons are allowed in each volume of size h^3 in phase space. **1974** G. REECE tr. *Hund's Hist. Quantum Theory* vi. 80 Ehrenfest attempted to interpret the radiation formulae by means of a weight function in phase space. **1896** D. C. & J. P. JACKSON *Alternating Currents* 652 Special starting devices must be included in the design and construction [of single-phase induction motors]. As a rule, this takes the form of what is called a Phase Splitter. **1965** *Wireless World* Aug. 72 (Advt.), A pentode triode ideally suited for use as a voltage amplifier and phase splitter. **1970** J. EARL *Tuners & Amplifiers* ii. 54 The collector and emitter outputs..are equal in amplitude but opposite in phase, rather like the signals from a simple valve phase-splitter circuit. **1895** S. P. THOMPSON *Polyphase Electric Currents* iv. 99 (*caption*) Phase-splitting device. **1947** *Wireless World* Aug. 274/1 The advantages of resistance-capacitance circuits for phase-splitting in push-pull amplifiers are now well recognized. **1969** R. W. SMEATON *Motor Applic. & Maintenance Handbk.* xviii. 14 A simple phase-splitting device could be rigged up..so that the motors could be used on 120 volts, 60 cycles, single-phase. **1975** G. J. KING *Audio Handbk.* iv. 84 Some form of 'phase-splitting' stage is necessary to drive common-pair output stages. **1939** *Jrnl. Chem. Physics* VII. 1019/1 A first-order phase transition. **1968** R. A. LYTTLETON *Mysteries Solar Syst.* ii. 71 *L* is the energy per unit mass required for the phase-transition from solid to liquid. **1977** A. HALLAM *Planet Earth* 11 Such a phase transition does not involve differences in chemical composition but only a spatial rearrangement of the atoms in the silicate structure. **1932** LADNER & STONER *Short Wave Wireless Communication* iii. 34 For the case of a group of waves passing through an ionised medium, therefore, the phase velocity will be greater than *c*, the velocity of light in a pure dielectric,..but the group velocity will be less than *c*. **1968** M. S. LIVINGSTON *Particle Physics* iii. 49 Consider a pulse of water waves originating from the point where a stone strikes the water, and focus on a particular wave crest... The velocity with which the general disturbance moves is the group velocity; the velocity of the wave crest relative to the water is the phase velocity. **1907** H. H. NORRIS *Introd. Study Electr. Engin.* x. 290 The phase-wound motor has very satisfactory starting qualities and draws little excess starting current.

phase (fēiz), *v.* [f. the sb.] **I. 1.** *trans.* To adjust the phase of; to bring into phase, synchronize.

1938 A. E. GREENLEES *Amplification & Distribution of Sound* x. 154 Wherever two or more loudspeakers are used, these must be properly phased so that all the diaphragms move in the same direction at the same time. **1951** S. DEUTSCH *Theory & Design Television Receivers* xvi. 502 A phasing control is needed in order to phase the oscilloscope sweep so that the beam goes from left to right when the sweep frequency goes from its lowest to highest extremes. **1967** *Electronics* 6 Mar. 67/2 Researchers have succeeded in phasing the lasers. **1970** J. EARL *Tuners & Amplifiers* vi. 131 The two speakers of a stereo pair..can be correctly phased initially with little danger of the phasing being upset subsequently. **1974** *Sci. Amer.* Jan. 118/2 One can also 'phase' the drum and the mirror by interrupting the circuit of the drum motor momentarily.

2. *trans.* To organize or carry out gradually in planned stages or instalments.

1949 [implied in *PHASED *ppl. a.* 2]. **1955** *Bull. Atomic Sci.* Jan. 9/3 The British-French proposals were directed primarily to the problem of phasing the controls. **1963** *Ann. Reg. 1962* 97 The British members of the Commission preferred a merger phased over five years. **1969** *Daily Tel.* 8 Jan. 22/7 New tenants will face rent increases of as much as £1 a week, while increases will be phased over three years for existing tenants.

II. With adverbs: **3. phase down:** to reduce or decrease (something) gradually or in planned stages.

1970 *Times* 6 Nov. 8 The secretary said that the programme to phase down American operations in Indo-China..'is solidly based'. **1972** *Physics Bull.* Feb. 76/1 If the innovation manager is truly perceptive, he can phase down his work *without* human suffering. **1974** *Daily Tel.* 11 Feb. 2/8 Production had been cut to 60 per cent of normal. It would be phased down further for two months, when virtually no steel would be produced.

4. phase in. a. *intr.* To come into phase. *rare.*

1929 *Proc. IRE* XVII. 1787 The separate multiple echoes from a given set of pulses phase in and out at different rates... Part of the observed phasing must be due to changes in optical path.

b. *trans.* To introduce or incorporate (something) gradually or in planned stages. Also *intr.*, to be so introduced.

1955 *Bull. Atomic Sci.* Feb. 57 New weapons must be 'phased in' gradually to our existing weapons systems. **1959** *Time* 9 Feb. 11 It would be dangerous to phase out obsolescent weapons too slowly. But it would be exceedingly wasteful to phase in too heavily the newer weapons. **1971** *Farmer & Stockbreeder* 23 Feb. 7/3 The levies should be phased in over a one-year period. **1972** [see sense 5 d below]. *a* **1974** R. CROSSMAN *Diaries* (1976) II. 472 As for national superannuation, we shouldn't try and bring it forward but phase it in in 1975, when a large number of existing pensioners will be dying off.

5. phase out. † **a.** *Electr. Engin.* To eliminate phase differences between (parts of polyphase equipment that are to be connected together). *Obs.*

1921 W. S. IBBETSON *Motor & Dynamo Control* viii. 283 The synchronising of two- and three-phase generators may be performed by connecting the synchronising lamps across one phase only, provided the alternators are correctly connected up to the bus bars. To phase out such connections before a machine may be paralleled the following operations may be performed. **1939** —— *Electric Power Engineers' Handbk.* vi. 151 If the leads were not correctly phased out so that the phases of all the machines were in the same sequence, interchange of current between the alternators would occur.

b. To eliminate by adjustments of phase. *nonce-use.*

1921 *Wireless World* 6 Aug. 287/2 The interfering note can be completely 'phased out' by adjusting bellows and tube to equal length.

c. *intr.* To become out of phase. *rare.*

1929 [see 4 a above].

d. *trans.* To remove, eliminate, or take out *of* gradually or in planned stages. Also *intr.*, to disappear gradually.

1954 *Quartermaster Rev.* July–Aug. 159/1 We in Defense are phasing out the support of basic research for the general welfare. **1955** *Sun* (Baltimore) (B ed.) 25 Apr. 8/5 The old propellor-driven Mustangs..will be 'phased out' on August 1—which means that replacement parts will have become so scarce that they cannot longer be operated in safety. **1959** [see sense 4 b above]. **1959** *New Scientist* 17 Sept. 446/2 Finding a way to phase out the jet lift as forward speed generates lift in the wings. **1967** *Guardian* 9 Jan. 6/4 We could safely decide to phase out the carrier fleet by 1970. **1969** J. GARDNER *Compl. State of Death* ix. 172 It's been a tricky job phasing out these people. **1969** *Daily Tel.* 13 Dec. 13/1 While he was 'phasing out' from the public view, he said, he was not shirking his duties as an MP. **1970** *Ibid.* 30 Sept. 1/6 The Jaguar 420G range of cars is to be gradually phased out of production. **1971** *Nature* 1 Oct. 299/1 Five top level scientific committees.. have recommended that the pesticide be phased out of domestic use. **1972** *Lebende Sprachen* XVII. 135/1 In a research organization projects do phase in and phase out all the time. **1975** *Times* 22 Sept. 3/3 The Government wants to phase out pay beds. **1977** B. PYM *Quartet in Autumn* xii. 102 The whole department was being phased out and only being kept on until the men working in it reached retirement age. **1979** *Time* 2 Apr. 59/1 It has been generally thought that Ford would start phasing out after Sept. 4, 1980, when he turns 63.

† **6. phase up** *Electr. Engin.*: to synchronize, bring into phase. *Obs. rare.*

1904 W. R. BOWKER *Dynamo, Motor & Switchboard Circuits* v. 99 In connecting two-phase generators for parallel running it is necessary to synchronise both phases the first time the machines are paralleled. After they have once been 'phased-up' synchronising one phase is sufficient. Fig. 101 shows the connections for properly 'phasing up' two two-phase generators.

phase angle. [f. PHASE + ANGLE *sb.*[2]] **1.** An angle representing a difference in phase, 360 degrees (2π radians) corresponding to one complete cycle.

1889 J. A. FLEMING *Alternate Current Transformer* I. iii. 110, OP..is called the amplitude or maximum value, and POM the phase angle of the motion. **1936** *Discovery* Mar. 80/2 By phase-angle changes so produced..any of our mean amplitudes may be much reduced and the real importance of a periodicity [in the weather] accordingly masked proportionately. **1947** R. LEE *Electronic Transformers & Circuits* v. 127 These waves indicate that the phase angle encountered in audio transformers does not of itself introduce much distortion in a lightly loaded triode. **1966** BROSAN & HAYDEN *Adv. Electr. Power & Machines* vii. 279 The voltage will be alternating, and..in general, $e = E_m \sin \omega t$. If the coil is connected to an external circuit, a current will flow, given by $i = I_m \sin (\omega t - \psi)$ where ψ is the internal phase angle.

2. *Astr.* The angle between the lines joining a given planet to the sun and to the earth.

1926 H. N. RUSSELL et al. *Astron.* I. ix. 234 How much of the illuminated hemisphere can be seen from the earth depends upon the angle at the planet between lines to the earth and to the sun. Where this phase angle is always very small, as it is from the most distant planets, there is never any perceptible deviation from a circular disk. **1974** R. H. STOY *Everyman's Astron.* vi. 203 The apparent brightness of any minor planet varies inversely both as the square of its distance from the Earth and as the square of its distance from the Sun. It also depends on the phase angle, that is on the angle between the lines joining the minor planet to the Sun and to the Earth.

phased (fēizd), *ppl. a.* [f. *PHASE *v.* + -ED[1].] **1.** Synchronized; adjusted to be in phase.

1922 GLAZEBROOK *Dict. Appl. Physics* II. 936/2 If these two readings give zero reading, the transformers are correctly phased... If readings are obtained across EE′ and FF′ then polarity or phase rotation is incorrect. **1929** *Photoplay* (Chicago) Apr. 31/2 *Phased*, or *interlocked*, all motors of sound and picture recording equipment lined up in readiness to start out in perfect step together. **1951** S. DEUTSCH *Theory & Design Television Receivers* xiii. 435 When the sync pulse is near the center of the saw-tooth retrace, there can be no doubt that the picture is correctly phased with respect to the horizontal sweep. **1958** *Listener* 9 Oct. 558/1 Zoning, road classification, phased traffic lights. **1969** *Focal Encycl. Film & Television Techniques* 544/1 The associated synchronizing pulse trains are locked together and correctly phased. **1971** *Hi-Fi Sound* Feb. 71/2 It can be difficult for the newcomer to hi-fi to know whether the loudspeakers are correctly phased or not.

b. *phased array*: an array of aerials that is made to transmit or receive at a variable angle by delaying the signals to or from each one by an amount depending on its position in relation to the others.

1938 *Television* XI. 644/3 None of these changes..affect the description of the phased array. **1960** *Proc. IRE* XLVIII. 1715 Phased arrays can provide scanning patterns and scanning rates which are impossible to attain with mechanically scanned antennas. **1966** *Electronics* 3 Oct. 173 The satellite transponder will receive signals on 149.2 Mhz with an 8-element phased array. **1970** *New Scientist* 10 Sept. 534/1 The beams formed by phased arrays can be steered electronically, and can be scanned up to several hundred million times a second.

2. Planned or carried out in stages or by degrees.

1949 *Archit. Rev.* CV. 225/2 A phased building programme for all developments proposed for the accommodation of population and industry from London. **1953** *Manch. Guardian* 12 May 1/3 Mr Dulles issued a statement that the United States Government favours a 'phased' withdrawal of British troops from the Canal Zone. **1956** *Sun* (Baltimore) (B ed.) 30 Nov. 1/6 Lord Salisbury..declared: 'Our policy is that of a phased withdrawal.' This supposedly means a step by step withdrawal..rather than a quick overall pullout. **1967** D. WILSON in Wills & Yearsley *Handbk. Managem. Technol.* iii. 49 The phased implementation of new procedures. **1972** *Daily Tel.* 4 Mar. 32/6 A policy to end imprisonment without trial by a phased programme of releases of every detainee and internee. **1976** *Glasgow Herald* 26 Nov. 3 The council who are planning 800 phased redundancies in the department next year. **1976** *Broadcast* Dec. 1/1 There will have to be a phased introduction of any changes that are agreed in pay structures and conditions of service.

phase-down (fēi·zdaun). [f. *PHASE *v.* 3.] A gradual reduction or planned decrease.

1968 *Times* 12 Feb. 17 The best scope for achieving economies in clerical staff will probably come on the female side, where the turnover is rapid and any required phasedown can thus be acquired easily in a relatively short time. **1972** *Lebende Sprachen* XVII. 135/1 The systems division has reported the phase-down of its program office. **1973** *Times* 10 Oct. 19/8 An employee has a progressively shorter working year (the phase-down being at the rate of one, two or perhaps three weeks per annum).

phasemeter (fē·zmītəɹ). *Electr.* [ad. G. *phasenmeter*, † *phasometer* (M. von Dolivo-Dobrowolsky 1894, in *Elektrotechnische Zeitschr.* XV. 351): see PHASE and METER *sb.*[3]] An instrument which measures the phase difference between two oscillations having the same frequency, esp. that between an alternating current and the corresponding voltage (hence giving the power factor).

1894 *Electrician* 21 Sept. 610/1 The phasemeter here described is essentially an ampere meter measuring the idle current. **1903** G. D. A. PARR *Electr. Engin. Measuring Instruments* vii. 194 The phasemeter now under consideration, made by the Electrical Co., Ltd., of London, is an instrument for measuring directly the value of the wattless current in an inductive alternating-current circuit. **1974** *Physics Bull.* Oct. 477/1 The circuitry of the phasemeter has been designed to reduce the effects of errors introduced by crossover distortion and noise in the input signal, which are the most common sources of inaccuracy.

phaseolin (fǣsī·olin). *Biochem.* [f. L. *phaseolus* kidney-bean; see -IN[1].] **a.** A crystalline globulin found in the seeds of the kidney bean.

1893 T. B. OSBORNE in *17th Ann. Rep. Connecticut Agric. Exper. Station* IV. 187, I have been able to identify and obtain in a state of comparative purity, two distinct proteids, one, the most abundant, having quite the properties of a globulin, which I shall designate phaseolin. **1921** *Nature* 21 July 666/2 Little or no cystines in a protein has also an effect upon the growth of rats. This has been most clearly demonstrated in the case of the protein, phaseolin, of the navy bean. **1964** *Chem. Abstr.* LXI. 10938 The enzymic hydrolysis of phaseolin with trypsin was affected by addn. of the azo dye, amaranth, at pH 8.

† **b.** = next. *Obs.*

1963 CRUICKSHANK & PERRIN in *Life Sci.* II. 680 The isolation is now reported of a further phytoalexin of the *Leguminosae*, sub-family *Papillionaceae*. This substance, for which we propose the trivial name, phaseolin, has been obtained by inoculation of detached, opened pods of the French bean, *Phaseolus vulgaris* L., using a spore suspension of [the fungus] *Monilinia fructicola* (Wint.). **1964** [see next].

phaseollin (fǣsī·olin). *Biochem.* [f. prec. with inserted *l*: see quot. 1964[1].] A fungitoxic phytoalexin produced by the kidney bean plant, which has been isolated as a white, crystalline heterocyclic compound, $C_{20}H_{18}O_4$.

1964 D. R. PERRIN in *Tetrahedron Lett.* VIII. 438 The author's attention has been drawn to the prior use of the term phaseolin to denote a protein from *Phaseolus vulgaris*. Accordingly the name of the phytoalexin from *P. vulgaris* is now changed to phaseollin. **1964** CRUICKSHANK & PERRIN in J. B. Harborne *Biochem. Phenolic Compounds* xiii. 530 Phaseollin is similar in its biological properties to pisatin. **1967** R. K. S. WOOD *Physiol. Plant Path.* xiv. 497 Another phytoalexin, closely related to pisatin and called phaseollin has now been obtained from pods of French bean (*Phaseolus vulgaris*) inoculated with conidia of *S[clerotinia] fructicola*. **1973** *Nature* 20 Apr. 533/1 The phytoalexin phaseollin does accumulate in hypersensitive responses in leaves of French bean.. caused by avirulent bacteria but this substance has little or no effect on growth of bacteria.

phase-out (fēi·zaut). [f. *PHASE *v.* 5 d.] A gradual removal or planned elimination. Also *attrib.*

1958 *Time* (Atlantic ed.) 6 Oct. 26 The Moroccans countered a request for a three-year phase-out. **1960** *Economist* 8 Oct. 126/1 Britain has thus given *de facto* recognition to the Norwegian twelve-mile limit, but the ten year phase-out period for fishing in the outer six miles will do something to cushion the blow to Hull and Grimsby. **1961** *Ann. Reg. 1960* 298 There was a planned phase-out in the field of economic aid. **1969** *New Scientist* 28 Aug. 421/1 The RAF..is to assign more strike aircraft to cover Britain's seaward approaches as the phase-out of the Navy's carriers proceeds. **1972** *Science* 12 May 618/3 In 1971 Shell announced the phase-out of the Emeryville station. **1975** *Daily Tel.* 7 May 8/5 Unless the Government abandoned some [Bills], there seemed little chance of beginning the pay-beds phase-out until 1976 at the earliest.

phase sequence. [f. PHASE *sb.* + SEQUENCE.] **1.** *Electr. Engin.* The sequence in which the different lines of a polyphase system attain their maximum voltage.

1918 K. EDGCUMBE *Industr. Electr. Measuring Instruments* (ed. 2) 257 A simple method of determining phase sequence when a rotation indicator is not available has been described. **1971** A. SYMONDS *Electr. Power Equipment* vi. 91 There are three essential conditions to be met before two transformers can be connected in parallel: (a) Secondaries must have the same phase sequence. This can be checked by a phase-sequence indicator.

2. *Psychol.* A hypothetical sequence of cellular activity in the brain initiated by a sensory stimulus, suggested by D. O. Hebb as an explanation of motivated behaviour.

1946 D. O. HEBB in *Psychol. Rev.* LIII. 269/1 Let us designate the specific pattern of cellular activity throughout the thalamo-cortical system, at any one moment, as a 'phase'. Behavior is directly correlated with a phase sequence which is temporally organized. **1954** *Brit. Jrnl. Psychol.* XLV. 189 Hebb (1949) expresses the belief that the mental processes corresponding to cortical processes ('phase-sequences') will be most rewarding..when the phase-sequences are in the course of being built up. **1964** COFER & APPLEY *Motivation* viii. 407 The theory presented..was essentially..that nerve cells in the brain when more or less simultaneously excited constitute assemblies of mutually facilitating, and to some extent stimulating, elements, a series of such cell assemblages acting one after another constitute a 'phase sequence'. **1970** C. TAYLOR in Borger & Cioffi *Explanation in Behavioural Sci.* 77 Hebb..presents mechanisms, the 'cell assembly' and 'phase sequence', which although expressed in neurological terms are not based on any direct supporting neurological evidence.

phasic, *a.* Add: (Further examples.)

1947 *Sci. News* V. 24 Gjessing concluded that the phasic disturbance of nitrogen metabolism constituted the fundamental pathology of the disorder, the mental changes being merely the outward symptoms. **1975** *Nature* 6 Nov. 81/1 Action potential firing of individual endocrine cells falls into two principal categories: most fire continuously and randomly at 1–2 spikes s^{-1}, while the rest have a phasic pattern of firing, periods of bursting activity alternating over 10–60 s with periods of silence.

2. *Physiol.* Responding to a change in environment, rather than to a constant stimulus.

1906 C. S. SHERRINGTON *Integrative Action Nervous Syst.* viii. 302 The very muscles that to the observer are most obviously under excitation by the *tonic* system are those most obviously inhibited by the *phasic* reflex system. **1956** *Jrnl. Physiol.* CXXXIV. 48 A temperature receptor..has..a high coefficient of phasic discharge to temperature change or a high coefficient of tonic discharge to maintained temperatures. **1973** *Sci. Amer.* May 97/1 Many human receptors, such as the ones that sense pressure on the skin, are phasic; if they were not, one would be constantly conscious of such things as a wristwatch or a shirt.

Hence **pha·sically** *adv.*

1975 *Nature* 6 Nov. 81/1 We found that, during bilateral occlusion of the common carotid arteries, supraoptic neurones are excited and that this activation is confined almost exclusively to phasically active neurones.

phasing (fēi·ziŋ), *vbl. sb.* [f. PHASE *sb.* or *PHASE *v.* + -ING[1].] **1.** The action of adjusting or eliminating a phase difference.

1896 *Trans. Amer. Inst. Electr. Engin.* XII. 514 The condenser in this combination fills two very important functions, first assists in the phasing, and second prevents the lag upon the line. **1922** GLAZEBROOK *Dict. Appl. Physics* II. 935/2 Before connecting any two polyphase transformers in parallel it is necessary to ensure that the phase rotation is correct, and this can only be done by phasing out. The term 'phasing out' is applied to the procedure adopted for determining the correct junction of the terminals of two or more transformers. **1940** *Amat. Radio Handbk.* (ed. 2) v. 72/2 Let it be assumed that the parallel capacity C_4 has been balanced by the phasing condenser K. **1949** FRAYNE & WOLFE *Elem. Sound Recording* xxx. 627 The process of choosing the optimum position is known as the phasing of the speakers. **1959** R. L. SHRADER *Electronic Communication* xvi. 525 Another entirely different method of producing a single-sideband suppressed-carrier emission is to use 90° phasing networks. **1960** *Times* 12 Jan. 15/6 Pedestrians are ignored in the phasing of traffic lights at many T-junctions. **1978** *Hi-Fi News* Sept. 179/1 Phasing is.. produced by mixing a direct signal with the same signal when passed through a phase-shift network.

b. The relationship between the phases of two or more periodic phenomena having the same frequency.

1929 [see *PHASE *v.* 4 a]. **1938** A. E. GREENLEES *Amplification & Distribution of Sound* x. 154 Each loud-speaker should have one terminal marked..so that when all these are connected to one line wire and the remaining terminals connected to the other, correct phasing is assured. **1951** S. DEUTSCH *Theory & Design Television Receivers* xiii. 435 Incorrect phasing is illustrated in Fig. 13-7, where the picture signal begins before the horizontal sweep has ended. **1962** A. NISBETT *Technique Sound Studio* 264 Correct phasing of speakers is..vital to true stereo reproduction. **1968** *Radio Communication Handbk.* (ed. 4) xiii. 61/1 If two such aerials are erected horizontally in the form of a *V*.., and if the phasing between them is correct, the two pairs of lobes will add fore and aft. **1970** [see *PHASE *v.* 1].

2. The action of *PHASE *v.* 2. Chiefly in *phasing in, out,* a gradual planned introduction or elimination (cf. *PHASE *v.* 4 b, 5 d).

1955 *Sun* (Baltimore) (B ed.) 25 Apr. 8/5 The 'phasing out' will end the official approval for even this operation. **1962** *Times* 8 Dec. 5/4 The phasing-out schedule for Thor..ballistic missiles. **1964** *Ann. Reg. 1963* 1 Whitehall was still preoccupied with..the phasing-in of British farm subsidies into the European system. **1964** G. L. COHEN *What's Wrong with Hospitals?* iii. 45 There exist new hospitals of greater efficiency than this one (for the Government's 'phasing' policy has entailed some incredible botching). **1967** *Boston Sunday Globe* 23 Apr. 20/4 The report recommends a gradual phasing out of these incinerators by 1985. **1969** *Daily Tel.* 18 Nov. 16 In Zambia the currency went decimal..overnight without any phasing-in of coins over two years. **1971** *Guardian* 7 June 11/4 The French..want to discuss the phasing out of sterling as a reserve currency. **1971** *Daily Tel.* 14 Aug. 13/7 The phasing of the new plants depends on the CEGB's planning timetable. **1977** *Air Mail* Spring 27/1 The Command is now coming to the end of another extensive re-equipment programme which will have seen the introduction of the Jaguar and the phasing out of the Lightning. **1977** *Time* 30 May 24/3 Carter said that he was 'committed to the phasing-in of a national health insurance system' and would send the legislation to Congress early next year.

phasitron (fēi·zitrǫn). *Electronics.* [f. PHAS(E + -I- + *-TRON.] An electron tube suitable for phase-modulating a wave by large amounts, in which a pattern of beams emitted radially from a central cathode passes through a slotted cylindrical anode to a coaxial second anode, the pattern of beams being both rotated at a steady rate by a three-phase supply and modulated by a varying axial magnetic field that advances and retards the beams and thereby also the phase of the current at the second anode.

1946 *Electronics* Oct. 108/2 The carrier frequency.., after one stage of amplification, is used to drive a phase-splitting network to provide three-phase voltages for the input deflector grids of a 'Phasitron' tube. *Ibid.* 111/2 Since the Phasitron is modulated by a magnetic field, fields other than those produced by the audio input will cause noise modulation of the carrier. **1966** *McGraw-Hill Encycl. Sci. & Technol.* V. 514/1 An improvement in the phase-modulation method is provided by a special tube called the phasitron, which is capable of increasing the amount of phase shift.

phasor (fēi·zər). *Electr.* [f. PHAS(E + *-or,* after VECTOR.] A line whose length and direction represent a complex electrical quantity with no spatial extension. Freq. *attrib.*

1944 *Proc. IRE* XXXII. 181/3 The instantaneous angular velocity of the voltage phasor may, in a special case of particular interest, be of the form $\omega_t = \omega + \Delta\omega \cos \Omega t$, where Ω is the angular velocity of the frequency deviation. **1958** W. D. COCKRELL *Industr. Electronics Hand-bk.* I. 249 The term 'phasor' is in the process of replacing the time-honored term 'vector'. **1962** F. DE LA C. CHARD *Power Syst. Engin.* i. 4 Phasor impedance can be shown on phasor diagrams and treated mathematically as a true complex quantity, but it differs from phasor voltage and current in the important respect that its value is invariable with time. **1973** M. R. WARD *Electr. Engin. Princ.* iii. 47. The phasors are drawn of length proportional to the r.m.s. **1975** R. F. W. COATES *Mod. Communication Syst.* i. 2 The phasor conveys the essential information regarding amplitude and phase of a fixed frequency sinusoid.

phatic (fæ·tik), *a.* [f. Gr. φατός spoken, or φατικ-ός assertory, f. φάναι to say: see -IC.] Of or pertaining to speech or verbal expression; *spec.* in *phatic communion*, a term applied by B. Malinowski (see *MALINOWSKIAN *a.*) to speech communication as used to establish social relationships rather than to impart information. Hence used *gen.* to denote formal or trivial verbal contact.

1923 B. MALINOWSKI in Ogden & Richards *Meaning of Meaning* 478 There can be no doubt that we have here a new type of linguistic use—*phatic communion* I am tempted to call it, actuated by the demon of terminological invention—a type of speech in which ties of union are created by a mere exchange of words. **1929** I. A. RICHARDS *Pract. Crit.* IV. i. 318 It would be an excellent thing if all the critical chitchat..were universally recognised to be what it is, social gesture, 'phatic communion'. **1942** T. C. POLLOCK *Nature of Lit.* ix. 167 Phatic communion is one of the important ways in which men use language. **1954** W. LA BARRE *Human Animal* xv. 306 A surprisingly large part of every culture is merely the phatic sharing of common emotional burdens, and has no relevance at all to the outside world. **1959** *20th Cent.* Nov. 379 The magic words of phatic chat that fell from my falsely smiling lips. **1964** *Listener* 15 Oct. 603/3 How many of the youthful roarers of Parry's *Jerusalem* know that Blake's 'dark satanic mills' are not factories but churches?.. But the whole evening was warmly phatic, providing an image of British teenagers as less delinquent than jingoistic. **1971** J. SPENCER *Eng. Lang. W. Afr.* 29 Phatic expressions and greeting and leave-taking formulae never precisely match across cultural borders. **1972** *Scholarly Publishing* Apr. 282/2 The reader on a committee who blandly and thoughtlessly says, 'You really ought to get this study published' (in the same phatic way he says, 'Good morning'). **1976** *Archivum Linguisticum* VII. 86 Those illocutionary acts for which there might seem, on the face of it, to be no propositional content at all: 'greet' for example..or 'phatic communion' of various sorts. **1977** *Time* 21 Mar. 67/1 Many Western ears will find it hard to tell whether Merwin is being vatic or phatic.

pheasant. Add: **1. b.** In South Africa, applied to certain francolins, esp. *Francolinus capensis,* and other birds belonging to the family Phasianidæ.

1785 G. FORSTER tr. *Sparrman's Voy. Cape Good Hope* I. iv. 153, I found here two new species of the genus of *tetrao*, one of which is called *partridge* and the other *pheasant*: either sort being nearly of the size of our partridges. **1837** N. POLSON *Subaltern's Sick Leave* v. 119 There is also a bird, general all over the Colony, styled 'pheasant', though about as like a pheasant of England as a Dutch Boer is to a Bond-street exquisite. **1896** R. WALLACE *Farming Industries Cape Colony* i. 15 No true pheasant..is found in Africa... Several species of francolins belonging to the same family..are known as pheasants. **1970** *Stand. Encycl. S. Afr.* II. 345/1 Most of the birds of the open veld are well camouflaged, for example the pheasants, partridges and quails, the bustards and korhaans.

3. pheasant-coucal (examples).

1873 [see *COUCAL]. **1908** E. J. BANFIELD *Confessions of Beachcomber* I. iii. 103 The swamp pheasant, or pheasant coucal..is also an early bird. **1935** [see *COUCAL]. **1944** A. RUSSELL *Bush Ways* ii. 17 The cuckoos, with the single exception of the pheasant-coucal, build no nests of their own. **1965** *Austral. Encycl.* VII. 90/2 Pheasant, a name formerly applied in Australia to the lyrebird and still in general use for the pheasant-coucal or swamp pheasant (*Centropus phasianinus*).

phellem (fe·lĕm). *Bot.* [a. G. *phellem* (F. von Höhnel 1877, in *Sitzungsber. Math.-Naturw. Classe K. Akad. Wissenschaften (Wien)* LXXVI. 600), f. Gr. φελλ-ός cork + *-em* as in *phloem.*] = CORK *sb.*[1] 5.

1887 W. HILLHOUSE tr. *Strasburger's Handbk. Pract. Bot.* xiv. 153 A meniscus..produces externally colourless cells, which become rounded..and internally cork-cells, or Phellem. **1925** EAMES & MACDANIELS *Introd. Plant Anat.* ix. 206 The cells constituting phellem, commonly known as cork cells, are for the most part uniform in shape. **1953** K. ESAU *Plant Anat.* xiv. 327 The type of phellem used for bottle cork consists of thin-walled, air-filled cells. **1971** A. CRONQUIST *Introd. Bot.* (ed. 2) xxiv. 455/2 Cork is also called phellem.

pheme (fīm). [ad. Gr. φήμη words, speech.] A term used by the American philosopher, C. S. Peirce (1839–1914), for words in an utterance as they make up a grammatical unit in language, contrasted with words used in speech to convey sense (see *RHEME, *SEME).

1906 C. S. PEIRCE in *Monist* XVI. 506 By a *Pheme* I mean a Sign which is equivalent to a grammatical sentence, whether it be Interrogative, Imperative, or Assertory... Such a Sign is intended to have some sort of compulsive effect on the interpreter of it. **1923** OGDEN & RICHARDS *Meaning of Meaning* 438 We are introduced to Semes, Phemes, and Delomes. **1931** G. STERN *Meaning & Change of Meaning* iii. 31 Meaning is a property peculiar not only to what we traditionally call words, but also to parts of words, *e.g.* the genitive ending in *man's*... As a comprehensive term..Vendryes..has proposed *sémantème*, and C. S. Peirce, quoted by Ogden–Richards..has *seme* and *pheme*. **1955** J. L. AUSTIN *How to do Things with Words* (1962) viii. 97 The same pheme (token of the same type) may be used on different occasions of utterance with a different sense or reference, and so be a different rheme... The pheme is a unit of *language*... But the rheme is a unit of *speech*.

phememe (fī·mīm). *Linguistics.* [f. prec.: see *-EME.] A term used by Leonard Bloomfield for the smallest linguistic unit.

1933 L. BLOOMFIELD *Language* xvi. 264 The parallelism of lexical and grammatical features can be exhibited in a set of terms like the following: (1) Smallest and meaningless unit of linguistic signaling: *phememe*; (a) lexical: *phoneme*; (b) grammatical: *taxeme*. **1936** J. R. KANTOR *Objective Psychol. Gram.* xi. 149 The reader will notice the three hierarchical steps or classes: phememe, glosseme, and linguistic form. **1955** J. L. AUSTIN *How to do Things with Words* (1962) vii. 92 A 'pheme' (as distinct from the phememe of linguistic theory).

phen-, pheno-. Add: **phenetol** [a. G. *phenetol* (A. Cahours 1850, in *Ann. d. Chem. u. Pharm.* LXXIV. 314)]; now usu. written **phenetole**; (earlier and later examples).

1850 *Q. Jrnl. Chem. Soc.* III. 78 Phenetol is a colourless, very mobile liquid, lighter than water; and having an agreeable, aromatic odour. **1972** *Materials & Technol.* IV. 306 Reaction [of phenol] with dimethyl or diethyl sulphate in a weakly alkaline solution gives anisole,..or phenetole, $C_6H_5OC_2H_5$ respectively.

phenacaine (fe·năkēin). *Pharm.* Formerly also **phenocain(e.** [f. PHEN- + *-a* + *-caine* after COCAINE.] Holocaine.

1907 *Brit. Pharmaceutical Codex* 260 Many synthetic substitutes for cocaine have been suggested for use as local anæsthetics, including..phenacaine (Holocaine). **1911** *Ibid.* 312 Phenocaine. **1920** MARTINDALE & WESTCOTT *Extra Pharmacopœia* (ed. 17) I. 331 Holocain Hydrochloride... *Syn.* Phenocain. **1946** *Brit. Jrnl. Pharmacol.* I. 99 Pethidine, phenacaine and papaverine possess both aromatic and basic groups and have a quinidine-like action. **1968** [see *HOLOCAINE].

phenagle, var. *FINAGLE *v.*

phenakistoscope. Add: (Later examples.) Also **phenakistiscope.** Hence **phenakistosco·pic** *a.*, resembling or reminiscent of a phenakistoscope.

1934 V. M. YEATES *Winged Victory* 162 It was gone, and beyond a phenakistoscopic veil he saw the flying moons and spheres caught in webs and dragged away. **1955** *Times* 18 July 3/4 The exhibition takes us back to beyond the origins of the cinema proper, to Plateau's Phénakistiscope, in which pictures, mounted on the inside of a circular revolving drum and viewed through slits, first created the illusion of continuous movement. **1961** *Glasgow Herald* 13 July 6/4 The thaumatrope, the phenakistiscope, the zoetrope, and the tachyscope..are the steps by which the modern cinema climbed to its present perfection. **1978** *Radio Times* 4–10 Mar. 4/4 A phenakistoscope and other Victorian toys.

phenanthroline (fĭnæ·nþrŏlīn). *Chem.* [ad. G. *phenanthrolin* (Z. H. Skraup 1882, in *Ber. d. Deut. Chem. Ges.* XV. 895), f. *phenanthr-en* phenanthrene (s.v. PHEN-, PHENO-) + *chinoline* CHINOLINE, QUINOLINE.] An organic compound, $C_{12}H_8N_2$, whose molecule is a tricyclic phenanthrene ring system in which one CH group in each of the two outer rings is replaced by a nitrogen atom, and the *ortho* isomer of which is used esp. as an indicator for iron, with which it forms a red-orange complex.

1882 *Jrnl. Chem. Soc.* XLII. 1111 Phenanthroline,.. obtained by the action of glycerol and sulphuric acid on metadiamidobenzene, crystallises in transparent plates (m.p. 79°). **1909** *Chem. Abstr.* III. 2571 The terms *o-*, *m-* and *p-phenanthroline* are suggested in place of isophenanthroline, phenanthroline and pseudophenanthroline. **1935** *Chem. Rev.* XVI. 113 The development of the use of *o*-phenanthroline-ferrous complex..constitutes one of the most outstanding advances of recent years in the field of analytical chemistry. Its application to many new procedures of analytical chemistry immediately followed. **1966** *McGraw-Hill Encycl. Sci. & Technol.* IV. 273/1 Certain organic compounds, such as 1,10-phenanthroline, also catalyze the drying of oils and have been used for this purpose. **1978** *Sci. Amer.* July 120/2 After the bromine color disappears mix in one milliliter of ·025-molar phenanthroline ferrous sulfate (a dye sometimes called ferroin).

phencyclidine (fensəi·klidīn). *Pharm.* [f. PHEN- + CYCL(O- + PIPER)IDINE, constituent parts of the systematic name.] A powerful analgesic and anæsthetic whose use is now chiefly restricted to veterinary medicine on account of its hallucinogenic effects; 1-(1-phenylcyclohexyl)piperidine hydrochloride, $C_{17}H_{25}N.HCl$. Abbrev. PCP.

1959 *Antibiotic Med.* VI. 84 Phencyclidine, when given to patients with anxiety symptoms, appeared to be most effective in mild to moderately severe reactions. **1963** *Lancet* 16 Feb. 392/2 Phencyclidine was used to relieve the pain of multiple rib fractures in a 57-year-old male who had bronchitis. **1973** *Daily Tel.* 20 Dec. 3 A new drug called 'angel dust' which causes people to believe they have been reduced to the size of Tom Thumb is to be brought to the attention of the authorities... The drug, known as phencyclidine or PCP, was not covered by the Dangerous Drugs Act. **1974** M. C. GERALD *Pharmacol.* xvii. 330 Phencyclidine (Sernyl) is employed therapeutically as a veterinary anesthetic agent. *Ibid.*, Compounds purported to be mescaline, LSD, psilocybin, and THC..have often been chemically identified as phencyclidine. **1979** *Tucson* (Arizona) *Citizen* 20 Sept. 7c/1 Seven men have been charged by a federal grand jury with conspiracy to manufacture and distribute phencyclidine, and for possession of the drug.

phenelzine (fĕne·lzīn). *Pharm.* [f. the systematic name 2-*phen*ethyl*hydrazine*, f. PHEN- + ETHYL + HYDRAZINE.] A monoamine oxidase inhibitor that is used as an antidepressant, usu. in the form of the sulphate, $C_6H_5CH_2CH_2NHNH_2.H_2SO_4$, a white crystalline solid with a pungent odour.

1959 *Amer. Jrnl. Psychiatry* CXVI. 64/1 Twenty-five patients with depression who entered this hospital on the female service were assigned alternately to Phenelzine and ECT. **1961** *Lancet* 16 Sept. 622/2 A housewife, aged 56, with depression, had for five months been taking phenelzine..when she suddenly got pruritis, pain behind the eyes, and anorexia, and noticed that she was becoming yellow. **1965** [see *PARNATE]. **1971** G. G. LUCE *Body Time* iii. 85 Other drugs sometimes used to combat depression, such as phenelzine, have an opposite effect and shorten the sleep cycle.

Phenergan (fe·nəɹgăn). *Pharm.* Also **phenergan.** A proprietary name for promethazine.

1947 (Sept. 16) [registered in Canada as a trade mark, no. 112/28759]. **1948** *Canad. Med. Assoc. Jrnl.* LIX. 322/2 The name phenergan (3,277 R.P.) has been given to the N-dimethylaminopropyl derivative of phenothiazine. **1949** *Trade Marks Jrnl.* 8 June 499/1 Phenergan... Pharmaceutical preparations consisting of or containing benzine or its derivatives for human use and veterinary use. May & Baker Limited, Dagenham, Essex; manufacturing chemists. **1956** *Jrnl. Amer. Med. Assoc.* 3 Mar. 755/1 From these studies, several drugs have emerged that provide significant protection against motion sickness. These..include..promethazine (Phenergan) hydrochloride. **1958** A. HUXLEY *Let.* 4 Jan. (1969) 841 He has been experimenting with..a mixture of aspirin, chlorpromazine and phenergen [*sic*] compounded a year or so ago by some French physicians and used for producing a form of hibernation. **1977** *Detroit Free Press* 11 Dec. 18-B/2 It takes down about 10 percent of the cold-remedy business with its Dristan and Phenergan lines.

phenethicillin (fĕne:þĭsi·lin). *Pharm.* [f. PHEN- + ETH(YL + *PEN)ICILLIN.] The compound 6-(2-phenoxypropionamido)penicillanic acid, $C_{17}H_{20}N_2O_5S$, which is a semi-synthetic penicillin active when given by mouth and is usu. employed in the form of the white, crystalline, potassium salt.

1960 *Brit. Med. Jrnl.* 1 Oct. 994/2 When phenethicillin (6-(α-phenoxypropionamido)penicillanic acid) was marketed as 'broxil', it was claimed that this preparation would give blood levels at least equal to those after intramuscular injection of corresponding doses of penicillin G. **1965** G. T. STEWART *Penicillin Group of Drugs* iii. 25 In scientific medical circles, the advent of phenethicillin as the first offspring of the new biosyntheses was something of an anticlimax. *Ibid.* iv. 34 As prepared at present, phenethicillin is a racemic mixture containing 55–75% of the L-isomer and 25–45% of the D-isomer. **1970** *Daily Tel.* 23 Oct. 13/3 The first semi-synthetic penicillin, phenethicillin, introduced in 1959, became widely used for the infections treated by family doctors.

phenetic (fĕne·tik), *a. Taxonomy.* [f. Gr. φαίν-ειν to appear + *-etic* as in PHYLETIC *a.*] (See quot. 1960.) So **phene·tically** *adv.*, showing similar characteristics; **phene·ticism,** taxonomy that stresses classifications based on obvious resemblances; **phene·ticist,** a taxonomist using classifications of this type.

1960 CAIN & HARRISON in *Proc. Zool. Soc.* CXXXV. 3 Following a suggestion made by Mr. H. K. Pusey, we shall refer to the arrangement by overall similarity, based on all available characters without any weighting as phenetic, since it employs all observable characters (including of course genetic data when available). *Ibid.*, When a good fossil record is available..the whole evolutionary dendrite can be worked out for that group simply by putting those forms together that are most alike phenetically. **1963** DAVIS & HEYWOOD *Princ. Angiosperm Taxon.* iv. 112 The separation of phenetic and phylogenetic classifications is not generally accepted today. **1968** *Nature* 9 Nov. 547/1 The school of the pheneticists, one of the branches of numerical taxonomy. They deliberately set out to 'make' taxa on the basis of calculated overall similarity. *Ibid.*, The phenetic approach has been most useful when applied to groups with immature classifications..and to those with numerous non-redundant characters. **1971** *Virology* XLV. 357/2 To be useful, a classification of viruses..must be based on many characters, not few... This will give a classification based on the general resemblance of the phenotypic characters of the viruses (a 'phenetic classification'). **1972** *Nature* 21 Apr. 412/2 Extreme pheneticism is equally criticized.

phenformin (fenfǭ·ɹmin). *Pharm.* [f. PHEN- + FORM(ALDEHYDE + *IMINO(-), constituent parts of the alternative name *phen*ethyl-*form*amidinyl*imino*urea.] A white crystalline solid, 1-phenethylbiguanide hydrochloride, $C_{10}H_{15}N_5.HCl$, which is used in the oral treatment of diabetes. Also *phenformin hydrochloride.*

1959 *Canad. Med. Assoc. Jrnl.* LXXX. 773/1 In 1957 Ungar, Freedman and Shapiro reported that hypoglycæmic properties had been discovered in a synthetic diguanide compound, N′-β-phenethylformaminyliminourea hydrochloride, subsequently designated DB1 or phenformin. **1960** [see *BIGUANIDE]. **1961** *Lancet* 9 Sept. 566/1 Phenformin is clearly a potent hypoglycæmic substance effective in most diabetics we have tested. **1967** *Martindale's Extra Pharmacopoeia* (ed. 25) 675/2 Phenformin hydrochloride is contra-indicated in acidosis, coma, infections, [etc.]. **1974** M. C. GERALD *Pharmacol.* xxv. 441 It appears that phenformin may act by accelerating the intracellular oxidation of glucose, a process which is depressed in the absence of insulin. Phenformin is used alone for the treatment of maturity-onset diabetes and in combination with insulin in juvenile diabetes. **1977** *Lancet* 22 Jan. 191/2 Metformin is replacing phenformin as the biguanide of choice in the treatment of obese maturity-onset diabetics because of the association between phenformin therapy and lacticacidosis.

phenindione (fenindəi·ōᵘn). *Pharm.* [f. PHEN- + IN(DO-[2] + *-DIONE.] A white crystalline solid, 2-phenylindan-1,3-dione, $C_{15}H_{10}O_2$, which is a vitamin K analogue used as an anticoagulant, esp. in the treatment of thrombosis.

1955 *Proc. Soc. Exper. Biol. & Med.* LXXXIX. 81/1 In an investigation of the effect of phenindione (PID) on the coagulation mechanism.., it was discovered that patients who had received this anticoagulant for more than about 30 days developed a distinctly prolonged glass clotting time. **1962** *Lancet* 13 Jan. 104/2 Treatment with heparin and phenindione was begun, but after six hours the patient suddenly became unconscious and pulseless, though slow voluntary respirations persisted. **1974** R. H. HAMMER in W. O. Foye *Princ. Med. Chem.* xviii. 409/1 Phenindione is the most commonly used 1,3-indandione anticoagulant... The chief disadvantage of phenindione is its toxic side effects.

pheniprazine (fĕni·prăzīn). *Pharm.* [f. PHEN- + I(SO- + PR(OPYL + HYDR)AZINE.] The compound 1-phenyl-2-hydrazinopropane, $C_9H_{14}N_2$, which was formerly used (as the hydrochloride) for the treatment of depression, angina, and hypertension.

1960 *Jrnl. Amer. Med. Assoc.* 2 Apr. 1554/1 Mackinnon and co-workers used pheniprazine to treat a series of 28 patients with the anginal syndrome. **1961** *Lancet* 16 Sept. 622/2 It seems probable that pheniprazine was the cause of the jaundice; the total dose was 560 mg. given over sixty days. **1971** L. E. HOLLISTER in Melmon & Morrelli *Clin. Pharmacol.* (1972) xi. 459/1 The first hydrazide drug was iproniazid... A later member of the series was pheniprazine (Catron). Both have subsequently been removed from the market because of intolerable toxicity.

phenmetrazine (fenme·trăzīn). *Pharm.* [f. PHEN(YL + *-metr-* (f. MET(HYL + HYD)R(O-) + *AZINE, constituent parts of the systematic name *2-phenyl-3-methyl-tetrahydro-1,4-oxazine.*] 3-Methyl-2-phenylmorpholine, $C_{11}H_{15}NO$, the hydrochloride of which, a white powder, has been used as an appetite suppressant and is a stimulant of the central nervous system similar to (though weaker than) amphetamine, to which it is chemically related.

1956 *Amer. Jrnl. Digestive Dis.* I. 155 Phenmetrazine has been used clinically in Germany in the management of obesity. **1959** *Lancet* 22 Aug. 152/1 Phenmetrazine ('Preludin'), a sympathomimetic drug discovered by Thomae and Wick, was first used in 1954 in the treatment of obesity. Since then it has been given in asthma, in parkinsonism, and as a euphoriant. **1962** [see *HERNIATION]. **1970** [see *PRELUDIN].

pheno (fī·no), colloq. abbrev. of *PHENOBARBITAL, *PHENOBARBITONE.

1966 J. PEARL *Crucifixion P. McCabe* (1967) viii. 118 Take a couple of my phenos and sack in early. **1968** 'E. TREVOR' *Place for Wicked* vi. 82 She'd just managed to catch the chemist open for some phenos:..after the plane journey she wouldn't be able to sleep properly. **1971** *Where* Dec. 360/2 He agreed that she did not need such a heavy dose and suggested a quarter grain of pheno twice a day only if she was under the weather.

phenobarb (fīnobā·ɹb). Also **pheno barb** and with final point. Abbrev. of *PHENOBARBITAL, *PHENOBARBITONE, used *colloq.* and in *Pharm.*

1956 M. MCMINNIES *Flying Fox* III. iv. 223 Whatever next? Not with all that phenobarb inside you. **1961** *Lancet* 22 July 205/2 Finally my colleague pleaded: 'If you won't take that phenobarb. yourself, for Heaven's sake dish it out to the rest of us.' **1971** *Where* Dec. 360/1 When Sarah got her sight back..she came back to us on a dose of one grain of pheno barb twice a day. **1972** J. MANN *Mrs. Knox's Profession* x. 82 She picked up a small bottle and said, 'Phenobarb?' **1977** N. ADAM *Triplehip Cracksman* xii. 125 The phenobarb and the adrenalin, the swallowed capsule and the upcoming junket.

phenobarbital (fīnŏ-, fenŏbā·ɹbităl). *Pharm.* [f. PHENO- + *BARBITAL.] The equivalent in the U.S. Pharmacopeia of *PHENOBARBITONE; also, a tablet of this.

[**1918** *New & Nonofficial Remedies* (Amer. Med. Assoc.) p. vi, In accordance with the action of the Federal Trade Commission, New and Nonofficial Remedies recognizes.. Phenylbarbital as the official name for the product first introduced as luminal.] **1919** *Ibid.* 84 Phenobarbital is claimed to be a useful hypnotic in nervous insomnia. **1938** [see *AMPHETAMINE]. **1950** M. LOWRY *Let.* Jan. (1967) 189, I must have had one too many phenobarbital. **1974** M. C. GERALD *Pharmacol.* ii. 18 Barbiturates, such as phenobarbital, cause depression. *Ibid.* xi. 202 Barbital was widely used for about a decade until the introduction of phenobarbital (Luminal) in 1912.

phenobarbitone (fīnŏ-, fenŏbā·ɹbitōᵘn). *Pharm.* [f. PHENO- + *BARBITONE.] A white crystalline compound, 5-ethyl-5-phenylbarbituric acid, $C_{12}H_{12}N_2O_3$, which is widely used as a sedative, hypnotic, and anticonvulsant, often in the form of its sodium salt. So *phenobarbitone sodium*. Cf. *LUMINAL *sb.*

1932 *Brit. Pharmacopœia* 330 Phenobarbitone is 5-phenyl-5-ethylbarbituric acid, and may be obtained by the condensation of ethyl phenylethylmalonate with urea. **1943**, etc. [see *ANTI-CONVULSANT *a.* and *sb.*]. **1954** *Newsweek* 12 Apr. 90/2 To 'keep their interest up', he [*sc.* a rowing coach]..reportedly prescribed phenobarbitone pills for a good night's sleep on the eve of the race. **1970** 'D. HALLIDAY' *Dolly & Cookie Bird* vi. 85 She has an Attitude to Life which would drive a phenobarbitone pill up the wall. **1975** CAWSON & SPECTOR *Clin. Pharmacol. in Dentistry* vi. 106 The main disadvantage of phenobarbitone is that as well as anti-anxiety (anxiolytic) properties, it is strongly sedative.

phenocain(e), obs. varr. *PHENACAINE.

phenocopy (fī·nokǫpi). *Biol.* [ad. G. *phänokopie* (R. Goldschmidt 1935, in *Zeitschr. für induktive Abstammungs- und Vererbungslehre* LXIX. 46): see PHEN-, PHENO- and COPY sb.] An individual showing features characteristic of a genotype other than its own, but induced by a modified environment.

1938 R. GOLDSCHMIDT *Physiol. Genetics* ii. 14 The production of phenocopies in Drosophila succeeded only if the temperature shock was applied at a definite time in development, the sensitive period. **1957** *Amer. Naturalist* XCI. 86 The production of phenocopies succeeded more readily in organisms which were heterozygous for a recessive mutant gene with homologous morphological effects. **1971** D. J. COVE *Genetics* xii. 172 A wild-type organism which has been subjected to such a heat treatment may develop so that it resembles closely an organism with a particular mutation. These environmentally induced abnormal organisms are called phenocopies.

phenogenetics (fī:nodʒĕne·tiks), *sb. pl.* (const. as *sing.*). *Biol.* [ad. G. *phänogenetik* (V. Haecker *Entwicklungsgeschichtliche Eigenschaftsanalyse* (1918) i. 4): see PHEN-, PHENO-, GENETIC *a.*, and -IC 2. Cf. next.

Haecker previously called it *phänogenese* (*Zeitschr. f. induktive Abstammungs- und Vererbungslehre* (1915) XIV. 260).]

(See quots.)

1938 R. GOLDSCHMIDT *Physiol. Genetics* ii. 23 It becomes imperative to know the details of development that distinguish the mutant types from the wild type. Studies of this type have been called..phenogenetics, a term that is not necessary but is sometimes useful. **1962** I. H. HERSKOWITZ *Genetics* xxx. 262/2 How does the mutant change normal development to produce the new morphological result? The answer to the latter question deals with learning how phenotypes (of any type) come into being via gene action, and is the subject of phenogenetics, a study which is of broader scope than developmental genetics. *Ibid.* 269 Phenogenetics starts out as a study of the developmental genetics of morphology.

phenol. Add: **b.** (Examples of sing. use.)

1868 JONES & WATTS *Fownes' Man. Elem. Chem.* (ed. 10) III. 646 A xylylic phenol is mentioned by Hugo Müller as occurring in coal-tar. **1952** L. N. FERGUSON *Electron Struct. Org. Molecules* viii. 189 For the same type of dissociation of a phenol..the large increase in dissociation constant can be attributed largely to the effects of resonance. **1964** N. G. CLARK *Mod. Org. Chem.* xxi. 431 The acidity of a phenol is increased by a nitro group located *ortho* and/or *para* to the functional group.

c. phenol-formaldehyde, used *attrib.* and *absol.* to designate plastics, resins, etc., made by condensation of phenols with formaldehyde; **phenol oxidase, phenolo·xidase** *Biol.* [ad. G. *phenoloxydase* (Battelli & Stern 1912, in *Biochem. Zeitschr.* XLVI. 396): see *OXIDASE], = *PHENOLASE; **phenol red** = *phenolsulphonphthalein* in sense *d; **phenol resin,** a phenolic resin (see *PHENOLIC *a.* b).

1912 *Jrnl. Industr. & Engin. Chem.* IV. 737/2 (*heading*) Phenol-formaldehyde condensation products. **1933** *Archit. Rev.* LXXIII. 1 The most modern and significant group consists of the synthetic plastics of which the two best known and most fully developed are the Phenol-formaldehyde and the Urea-formaldehyde types. **1965** *Wireless World* Sept. 32 (Advt.), New 10 pin (Decal) based valves type B10B, moulded in polypropylene and phenol formaldehyde. **1972** *Materials & Technol.* V. 95 All types of phenol formaldehyde glue are resistant to organic solvents, bacteria and fungi. *Ibid.* 96 The largest use of phenol formaldehyde resin adhesives is in gluing wood. **1913** *Chem. Abstr.* VII. 796 The authors [*sc.* Battelli & Stern] recommend that the term phenolase be dropped and the term phenoloxidase be used instead. **1920** *Biochem. Jrnl.* XIV. 539 The oxidase (synonymous with laccase, phenoloxidase and phenolase) of the pear and potato. **1931** E. C. MILLER *Plant Physiol.* xiii. 769 Substances which give the same or similar reactions as laccase toward the phenol compounds..have been named collectively the 'laccases', the 'phenol oxidases', or the 'phenolases'. **1971** I. ZELITCH *Photosynthesis* v. 136 Phenol oxidase activity is responsible for the familiar 'browning' observed in plant cells after injury. **1916** CLARK & LUBS in *Jrnl. Washington Acad. Sci.* VI. 488 Phenol red and cresol red are undoubtedly the most reliable indicators of the series. **1956** WHITBY & HYNES *Med. Bacteriol.* (ed. 6) xi. 151 Collect the supernatant fluid, add a drop of phenol red solution, neutralize with N NaOH, and centrifuge. **1974** D. H. KAY in W. O. Foye *Princ. Med. Chem.* xxxvii. 816/2 This dye is also known as phenol red and is official as phenolsulfonphthalein (U.S.P.). **1912** J. W. AYLSWORTH *U.S. Pat. 1,020,593* The fusible anhydrous resinous condensation product.. (hereinafter termed a 'phenol resin') is first prepared by causing a reaction between suitable amounts of phenol and formaldehyde. **1923** *Industr. & Engin. Chem.* July 677/1 The phenol resins continue to find wider applications in the industries on account of their physical and chemical properties. **1947** R. NAUTH *Chem. & Technol. Plastics* ii. 16 (*caption*) The dark rings which look like grain are..an effect produced by the phenol resin between the laminated veneers. **1973** *Materials & Technol.* VI. viii. 591 Phenol resins are widely used in the furniture and woodworking industries.

d. phe:nolcarbo·xylic (or **phenol carboxylic**) **acid,** any acid which contains a carboxyl group and a hydroxyl group bonded to the same benzene ring; **phe:nolsulphonphtha·lein** [SULPHON(E + PHTHALEIN], a red crystalline solid $C_{19}H_{14}O_5S$, which is used as an indicator in the pH range 6·7 (yellow) to 8·3 (red), and in medicine is given intravenously as a test of kidney function.

1899 *Collective Index Trans. & Abstr. Chem. Soc. 1873–82* II. 471/1 Phenolcarboxylic acid. *See* Hydroxybenzoic acids and Salicylic acid. **1946** *Thorpe's Dict. Appl. Chem.* (ed. 4) VII. 285/1 All the compounds of this sub-series have been shown to be phenol carboxylic acid derivatives.., and the majority belong to the depsides. **1956** [see *DEPSIDE]. **1975** D. JARVIS tr. *Hess's Plant Physiol.* 128 Phenol carboxylic acids, such as protocatechnic acid and gallic acid, occur widely. **1898** M. D. SOHON in *Amer. Chem. Jrnl.* XX. 263 Phenolsulphonphthalein, $C_{19}H_{14}SO_5$..was obtained as a bright red crystalline powder, somewhat soluble in water. **1960** I. A. STANTON *Dict. for Med. Secretaries* 116/1 Phenolsulphonphthalein is injected intramuscularly or intravenously and should normally appear in the urine in 10 or 15 minutes. **1974** [see *phenol red* in *c].

phenolase (fī·nǫlēiz, -s). *Biol.* [a. G. *phenolase* (F. Czapek 1906, in *Jahrb. f. wissensch. Bot.* XLIII. 380), f. *phenol* PHENOL: see *-ASE.] Any of a class of copper-containing enzymes found esp. in plants, which oxidize phenols to quinones; = *phenol oxidase* s.v. *PHENOL c.

1911 *Jrnl. Chem. Soc.* C. I. 824 The phenolase was prepared from *Lactarius vellerius*. **1931** E. C. MILLER *Plant Physiol.* xiii. 768 The oxidases of plants that have been studied have been grouped into two main classes according to the substances upon which they act. These are the laccases or phenolases and the tyrosinases. **1956** *Nature* 14 Jan. 79/1 The phenolase complex, widely distributed throughout the phylogenetic scale, consists of two enzymic activities, phenol *o*-hydroxylase..and *o*-diphenol dehydrogenase. **1964** *Oceanogr. & Marine Biol.* II. 408 Isolation of the amoebocytes from the fluid brings about more rapid oxidation, suggesting that an inhibitor to phenolase activity may exist in the coelomic fluid. **1975** D. JARVIS tr. *Hess's Plant Physiol.* 83 Cytochrome oxidase a_3 makes direct contact with oxygen and is therefore known, together with a few other enzymes, (peroxidases, catalases, and phenolases), as a 'direct' oxidase.

phenolate (fī·nǫlēit). *Chem.* [f. PHENOL + -ATE[1].] = *PHENOXIDE.

1885 I. REMSEN *Introd. Study Compounds of Carbon* xv. 270 Potassium phenolate, C_6H_5.OK, made by dissolving potassium in phenol, and by treating phenol with caustic potash. **1913** A. R. WARNES *Coal Tar Distill.* viii. 79 Owing to the pressure of the C_6H_5 radicle the ·OH group (hydroxyl) possesses slight acid properties.., and..reacts with the caustic alkalies, forming salts known as phenolates. **1963** F. G. BORDWELL *Org. Chem.* v. 159 (*caption*) Resonance in the phenolate ion. **1974** R. S. CAHN *Introd. Chem. Nomencl.* (ed. 4) vi. 95 Salts of alcohols and phenols should receive the ending -olate, as in sodium methanolate.., sodium phenolate.., but names such as..the abbreviated methoxide,..and phenoxide are extremely common.

phenolic, *a.* Substitute for def.: Of the nature of, belonging to, derived from, or containing a phenol; *esp.* containing or being a hydroxyl group bonded directly to a benzene ring. (Further examples.)

1932 *Ann. Rep. Chem. Soc.* XXVIII. 236 Marrian had identified the substance $C_{18}H_{24}O_3$ as a trihydric alcohol with one phenolic hydroxyl. **1951** I. L. FINAR *Org. Chem.* I. xxvii. 533 Phenolic aldehydes..are very important compounds, and contain an aldehyde group and one or more hydroxyl groups directly attached to the nucleus. *Ibid.* xxviii. 557 It should be noted that only half the phenol is converted into the phenolic acid. **1964** N. G. CLARK *Mod. Org. Chem.* xxi. 430 The crude oily phenolic layer is separated from the aqueous liquor, and purified by distillation. *Ibid.* 431 The formation of simple ethers in this manner is a convenient way of 'protecting' a phenolic group. **1970** *Watsonia* VIII. 3 Chromatographic investigation..into the intraspecific variation of phenolic and other compounds is proving to have interesting results. **1973** *Nature* 20 July 132/1 A serine hydroxyl.. makes a hydrogen bond to a phenolic hydroxyl hydrogen, the oxygen of which bonds to another phenolic hydroxyl.

b. Designating a large class of usu. thermosetting polymeric materials that have wide industrial applications as plastics or resins and are prepared from phenols by condensation with aldehydes in the presence of acid or base catalysts; as *phenolic plastic* or *resin*.

1910 J. W. AYLSWORTH *U.S. Pat. 1,020,593*, I..have made a certain new and useful Invention in Phenolic Condensation Products and Methods of Preparing Same. **1917** *Chem. Abstr.* XI. 693 (*heading*) Insoluble phenolic resins. **1931** *Product Engin.* Nov. 503/2 Cast phenolic plastics are softer than the ordinary phenolic materials. **1944** *Electronic Engin.* XVII. 35/1 A skilful combination of a polyvinyl acetal resin..with a thermo-setting phenolic resin has enabled 'Thermex' enamel to be produced from wholly synthetic sources. **1963** *House & Garden* Feb. 8/2 (*caption*) Mural panel in polished copper and black phenolic resin. **1968** *Wall St. Jrnl.* 26 July 28/1 Prices of phenolic molding compounds, among the more widely used plastics, will be raised one cent a pound by Union Carbide Corp. **1973** *Materials & Technol.* VI. viii. 589 The starting materials for the manufacture of phenolic plastics are mainly phenols and formaldehyde.

B. *sb.* **a.** Phenolic plastic or resin.

1935 *Industr. & Engin. Chem.* Oct. 1141/1 Certain plastics, particularly the cast phenolics, have unusual qualities for the passage and reflection of light. **1946** H. A. TAYLER *Plastics Explained* iv. 90 Cast phenolics are resistant to moisture, weak acids, oils and organic solvents. **1960** *Times Rev. Industry* Mar. 57/1 British plastics production..total was divided as: thermosetting materials 195,000 tons (alkyds 50,000 tons; aminoplastics 55,000 tons; phenolics 75,000 tons) and thermoplastics 300,000 tons. **1968** *Wall St. Jrnl.* 26 July 28/1 (*heading*) Phenolics price boost is planned by Union Carbide. **1973** *Sci. Amer.* July 42/3 The matrix in glass-reinforced composites may be either a thermoset plastic, such as polyester, phenolic or epoxy, or any of a number of thermoplastic resins, such as nylon, polyethylene or polystyrene.

b. Chiefly *Biochem.* Any compound containing a hydroxyl group bonded directly to a benzene ring, esp. one that occurs in plants.

1956 *Chem. & Industry* 9 June 478/2 Ellagic acid occurs in 43 families of dicotyledons, and is usually accompanied by the other vicinal-trihydroxy phenolics myricetin and leucodelphinidin. **1960** A. H. WILLIAMS in J. B. Pridham *Phenolics in Plants* I. 3 Phloridzin, the principal phenolic of apple leaf and bark is absent from the flesh of the fruit. **1970** J. VAN BUREN in A. C. Hulme *Biochem. Fruits* I. xi. 298 Varieties of fruits high in phenolics are more astringent than varieties low in phenolics. **1976** *Which?* Aug. 185/2 The household disinfectants you'll usually find in your shop will be either phenolics or hypochlorites.

phenolized (fī·n-, fe·nǫləizd), *ppl. a.* Chiefly *Med.* [f. PHENOL + -IZ(E + -ED[1].] Treated with phenol; *spec.* (of vaccines, cell samples, etc.) suspended in a dilute solution of phenol. So **phenoliza·tion.**

1921 DORLAND *Med. Dict.* (ed. 11) 791/1 *Phenolization*, treatment of infected wounds by subjecting them to the energetic action of strong carbolic acid. **1922** *Jrnl. Amer. Vet. Med. Assoc.* LXI. 40 The vaccination consists of a single injection of a large dose of phenolized fixed virus. **1949** RHODES & VAN ROOYEN *Textbk. Virol.* xxv. 226 The most popular method [of reducing the potency of rabies vaccine] is the use of phenolized virus... A common practice is to issue a vaccine consisting of a 4 to 5 per cent suspension of infected nervous tissue with 0·5 per cent phenol. **1961** *Amer. Jrnl. Med.* XXX. 804/2 Phenolized and acetone-extracted vaccines were ineffective in preventing clinical disease but probably modified the course of illness. **1975** *Nature* 24 July 277/1 Pure MS2 A-protein was obtained by isolation of the A-protein—RNA complex.., phenolisation, chromatography..and further separation. **1976** *Lancet* 9 Oct. 764/2 Granulomas were not transmitted by either frozen (−25°C) or phenolised sarcoid or Crohn's tissue homogenates.

phenological, *a.* Add: So **phenolo·gic** *a.*

1947 [see *ISOPHANE, ISOPHENE]. **1974** *Nature* 1 Mar. 42/1 This proposed sequence of major volcanic eruptions followed by several years of cold summers and then by glacial advance is supported by historic and phenologic data.

† phenoloid (fī·no-, fe·noloid), *sb.* and *a.* *Obs.* [f. PHENOL + -OID.] **A.** *sb.* A phenoloid substance, *spec.* phenoloid oil. **B.** *adj.* Of the nature of, containing, or resembling phenols; *phenoloid oil*, a form of creosote obtained from the distillation of coal, esp. as a by-product from blast-furnace gases.

1907 V. B. LEWES *Liquid & Gaseous Fuels* 99 The oil obtained from blast furnaces is also sometimes used locally for fuel purposes under the name of 'Phenoloid', or blast furnace oil. **1911** *Med. Ann.* 758 Phenoloid Disinfectant. —This contains 66 per cent phenoloid, with high carbolic acid coefficient. **1913** V. B. LEWES *Oil Fuel* 129 Another variety of oil is obtained from blast furnaces, and is known as blast furnace oil, or 'phenoloid oil'. **1920** J. M. FORTESCUE-BRICKDALE *Text Bk. Pharmacol.* ix. 74 Phenoloids are bodies having similar properties [to cresols], and are obtained from the distillation of coke. Cyllin, izal, and kerol are mainly composed of phenoloids. **1929** *Encycl. Brit.* VI. 668/2 The mixture of phenol and phenoloid substances derived..from coal, wood, blast furnace, and other tars. *Ibid.* 669/1 Blast-furnace creosote, sometimes known also as phenoloid' resembles vertical-retort tar. **1961** *Brit. Med. Dict.* 1092/1 *Phenoloid*..a term, now becoming obsolete, describing substances of phenolic character such as cresols and xylenols.

phenolphthalein. Substitute for def. (in Dict. s.v. PHENOL d): A whitish or yellowish crystalline solid,

$$(HO{\cdot}C_6H_4{\cdot})_2C{\cdot}C_6H_4{\cdot}CO,\ \text{with O bridging C and CO}$$

which is used in alcoholic solution as an indicator in the pH range 8 to 10, in which it changes from colourless to red, and is also used medically as a laxative.

1875 *Jrnl. Chem. Soc.* XXVIII. 67 When phenol is gently warmed with phthalic anhydride and sulphuric acid the mixture assumes a brownish yellow colour, from the formation of phenol-phthalein. **1881** J. ATTFIELD *Chem.* (ed. 9) 658 In delicate experiments turmeric, 'eosin', 'phenolphthalein', etc., may be used instead of litmus. **1893** [in Dict. s.v. PHENOL d]. **1946** *Nature* 23 Nov. 744/2 Back titration of the solution immediately after the substance had dissolved, using phenolphthalein as an indicator, indicated an apparent equivalent weight of 325. **1951** R. MAYER *Artist's Handbk.* ii. 97 Acids and alkalis are detected by the use of litmus, phenolphthalein, or other indicators. **1974** M. C. GERALD *Pharmacol.* ii. 31 In some laxatives, such as Ex-Lax and Feen-A-Mint, the active ingredient is phenolphthalein.

phenomena: as erron. sing. form (see PHENOMENON 1 *β* in Dict. and Suppl.).

phenomenal, *a.* Add: **1. a.** *Psychol.* Of or relating to a phenomenon as it is directly perceived or sensed, esp. as compared with its objective reality; also in spec. collocations, as *phenomenal regression*, the tendency for a shape, esp. a perspective, to be perceived as nearer to the shape of a related and known object than it actually is.

1922 K. KOFFKA in *Psychol. Bull.* XIX. 569 A field, reflecting a certain amount and quality of light, depends for its phenomenal color-quality upon the ground on which it appears. **1931** R. H. THOULESS in *Brit. Jrnl. Psychol.* XXI. 340 The shape reported by the subject as seen by him may be called the 'apparent shape' or 'phenomenal shape'. *Ibid.* 344 As a general name for this tendency, in whatever kind of perceptual character it is found, we may use the term *phenomenal regression to the 'real' object* or, more shortly, *phenomenal regression.* **1948** *Jrnl. R. Aeronaut. Soc.* LII. 467/1 The factor of phenomenal regression was a quantity differing widely among different people. **1951** G. R. WENDT in S. S. Stevens *Handbk. Exper. Psychol.* xxxi. 1208/2 We lack words in our language to distinguish phenomenal motion from the physical event. **1969** C. O. SCHRAG *Experience & Being* I. i. 19 The phenomenal field, according to Merleau-Ponty, is neither an 'outer world' of objectively reconstituted properties..nor is it an abstracted 'inner world'.

phenomenalism. Add: **phenomenalist,** also as *adj.*, of or pertaining to phenomenalism or a phenomenalist; **phenomenalistic** *a.* (later examples); **phenomenali·stically** *adv.*, as regards or in terms of phenomenalism. Also **phenomenalistically-minded** adj.

1885 W. JAMES *Coll. Ess. & Rev.* (1920) 277 Modern thinkers..for the most part obey a common drift.. towards a phenomenalistic or idealistic creed. **1904** Phenomenalistic [see *ANTE REM]. **1909** WEBSTER, Phenomenalistically. **1914** C. D. BROAD *Perception* iii. 166 Berkeley, whose argument is properly phenomenalistic. *Ibid.* 171 The phenomenalist position has to be stated as follows. **1934** A. C. EWING *Idealism* vii. 294 A sense which cannot..be analysed phenomenalistically. **1943** *Mind* LII. 340 But surely it ought to worry a phenomenalistically-minded philosopher; and Mr. Smith does not seem to be sufficiently worried by it. **1956** E. H. HUTTEN *Lang. Mod. Physics* ii. 64 It is..said that a thing-language, or a phenomenalist language, e.g. one taking sense-data as a key-concept, represents an empiricist language. **1963** Phenomenalistic [see **direct realism*]. **1975** *New Left Rev.* Nov.–Dec. 33 Knowledge is restricted to what is known for certain; it is then shown, in a phenomenalistic analysis of perception, that what is known in perception is certain; only perception gives knowledge of things (principle of empiricism); hence knowledge must be what is given in perception.

phenomenality. Delete *rare* and add further examples.

1884 W. JAMES in R. B. Perry *Tht. & Char. W. James* (1935) I. 580 To see whether the object thus given be itself only more subjectivity, more phenomenality, more experience than the instant. **1917** A. S. PRINGLE-PATTISON *Idea of God* xi. 211 This organic point of view delivers us..from the difficulties which so sorely afflict modern philosophy as to the relativity, or subjectivity, or phenomenality, of knowledge. **1933** *Jrnl. Theol. Stud.* XXXIV. 314 The notion that all phenomenality including the self is illusory..finally became..the foundation of Sankara's philosophy. **1969** T. F. TORRANCE *Theol. Sci.* i. 21 Modern philosophy in its preoccupation with phenomenality.

phenomenalize, *v.* (Earlier example.) **phenomenalization.** (Later example.)

1878 S. H. HODGSON *Philos. of Reflection* I. 213 What *was* the Thing-in-itself has been phenomenalised and relegated to this possible world. **1921** HANNAY & COLLINGWOOD tr. *G. de Ruggiero's Mod. Philos.* III. ii. 274 Bradley..fails to see that the true absolute is..appearance itself, in so far as it is the absolute process of appearing, the phenomenalization of the absolute.

phenomenist. Add: Also *attrib.* or as *adj.*

1871 *Dublin Rev.* Oct. 309 No one will doubt, either that the phenomenist school professes the general doctrine we have ascribed to it, or that Mr. Mill habitually identifies himself with this school.

phenomenistic, *a.* (Earlier example.)

1871 *Dublin Rev.* Oct. 309 The phenomenistic doctrine is such as this: that an ascertained truth, means a truth experienced or inferred from experience.

phenomenological, *a.* (In Dict. s.v. PHENOMENOLOGY.) Add to def.: dealing with the description and classification of phenomena, not with their explanation or cause; *phenomenological method*, the method outlined by Husserl for the description and analysis of phenomena as they are directly experienced (cf. *PHENOMENOLOGY b).

1923 OGDEN & RICHARDS *Meaning of Meaning* 419 It is important for the understanding of Husserl's terminology to realise that everything he writes is developed out of the 'Phenomenological Method and Phenomenological Philosophy'. **1931** W. R. B. GIBSON tr. *Husserl's Ideas* 14 There..grows up, on the pure basis of inner intuition, of the intuition of the soul's own essence, a phenomenological psychology. **1956** A. A. TOWNSEND *Struct. Turbulent Shear Flow* iii. 33 The success of this approach has led to the present tendency to approach the problem of turbulence by examining the dynamics of the turbulent motion itself in preference to using phenomenological theories which do not attempt to describe the turbulent motion but only its effects on the mean flow. **1963** J. WILD in A. L. Fisher tr. *Merleau-Ponty's Struct. Behaviour* (1965) p. xvi, The phenomenological thinking of this book cuts through the traditional oppositions between..body and soul, sense and reason, and subjectivism and objectivism. **1965** *Math. in Biol. & Med.* (Med. Res. Council) IV. 131 These difficulties..may be largely responsible for the fact that neurophysiologists..have often been hesitant to go beyond reporting raw data in a somewhat phenomenological manner. **1968** C. G. KUPER *Introd. Theory Superconductivity* i. 4 Long before the physics of superconductivity was understood, a number of phenomenological theories had been proposed. **1976** T. EAGLETON *Crit. & Ideology* i. 24 He rejected, naturally, the political consequences..but the phenomenological basis of that criticism was of peculiarly direct relevance to him. **1977** *Dædalus* Summer 63 Processual analysis has undoubtedly gained from the phenomenological critique of positivist anthropology.

pheno:menolo·gically, *adv.* [f. prec. + -LY[2].] In terms of, or as regards, phenomena or phenomenology.

1891 M. E. LOWNDES tr. *Höffding's Outl. Psychol.* ii. 63 Phenomenologically, he [*sc.* Lotze] thus places himself at the standpoint of the natural interaction. **1909** W. M. URBAN *Valuation* i. 18 Ideals of a supernatural character are the product, phenomenologically speaking, of individual and racial appreciative constructions. **1942** *Amer. Jrnl. Physiol.* CXXXV. 736 Phenomenologically, the muscular reactions during a tonic-clonic response to electrical stimulation of the motor cortex have for a long time been recognized as analogous to those in Jacksonian or in grand-mal epilepsy. **1958** *Times Lit. Suppl.* 23 May p. xii/3 These images can be observed and described phenomenologically and by the means of psychology. **1975** *Sci. Amer.* June 56/3 If the collision yields an electron-positron pair, the annihilation and rebirth of such a pair is phenomenologically indistinguishable from the mere elastic scattering of the incident electron and positron. **1977** P. JOHNSON *Enemies of Society* xvii. 227 When we enter a cathedral, and examine its various axial tendencies and its symmetrical, and asymmetrical forms, we perceive it phenomenologically; the approach to music is, in all essentials, the same.

phenomenologist (fĭnǫmenǫ·lŏdʒist). [f. PHENOMENOLOG(Y + -IST.] One who makes a study of, or adheres to the doctrines of phenomenology, esp. a philosopher or psychologist. Also *attrib.*

1865 J. H. STIRLING *Secret of Hegel* I. i. 19 He who shall make it his business to watch the gathering of the materials for the seething..will be the Phaenomenologist or Historian of the Seething. **1910** *Mind* XIX. 287 Another line of derivation from Kant leads..to Nelson and to the phenomenologists (Gomperz). **1951** *Scottish Jrnl. Theol.* IV. 175 Most modern Existentialists are phenomenologists. They do not however totally deny the existence of external reality. **1957** H. WHITEHALL in N. Frye *Sound & Poetry* 135 The Polish critic-philosopher, Roman Ingarden, using the phenomenologist techniques of Husserl, banished the form–content dichotomy. **1967** J. F. CORSO *Exper. Psychol. Sensory Behavior* i. 9 Those psychologists who emphasize the importance of experience in psychology and use subjective..terms to describe experience are called phenomenologists. **1975** *Listener* 25 Dec.–1 Jan. 857/2, I regard myself as a phenomenologist—that is, someone who is studying the phenomena of the human mind in an existential way. **1977** *Dædalus* Summer 63 The phenomenologists, notably Schutz, insisted that the social world is in many important respects a cultural construct, an organized universe of meaning in the form of what Harold Garfinkel calls a series of 'typifications' of the objects within it.

phenomenology. Add: **b.** *Philos.* The theory, put forward by the German philosopher Edmund Husserl (1859–1938) and his followers, to the effect that the pure and transcendental nature and meaning of phenomena, and hence their real and ultimate significance, can only be apprehended subjectively; the method of reduction, based by Husserl on Descartes's method, whereby all factual knowledge and reasoned assumptions about the phenomenon as object and the experiencing 'ego' are set aside so that pure intuition of the essence of the phenomenon may be rigorously analysed and studied.

1914 *Mind* XXIII. 588 Phenomenology, then, if I have understood it right, is the science of the essential connexions of vital experiences, as rooted in their nature or their character; not, for example, of their causal connexions as events in time. **1931** W. R. B. GIBSON tr. E. Husserl (*title*) Ideas: general introduction to pure phenomenology. *Ibid.* 11 Under the title 'A Pure or Transcendental Phenomenology', the work here presented seeks to found a new science..a science covering a new field of experience, exclusively its own, that of 'Transcendent Subjectivity'. **1938** G. REAVEY tr. *Berdyaev's Solitude & Society* 57 For this reason Husserl's Phenomenology fails to be an Existential philosophy although it exercised a considerable influence on Heidegger. **1949** H. F. MINS tr. G. Lukács in R. W. Sellars et al. *Philos. for Future* 572 Modern phenomenology is one of the..philosophical methods which seek to rise above both idealism and materialism by discovering a philosophical 'third way', by making intuition the true source of knowledge. **1957** H. E. BARNES tr. *Sartre's Being & Nothingness* p. xlvi, Phenomenology is anything but a nominalism. **1974** D. CARR *Phenomenology & Probl. of Hist.* I. 33 The 'common' subject matter of phenomenology and psychology, consciousness, is subjected in phenomenology to an essential rather than a factual consideration.

c. *Psychol.* The methods of description and analysis developed from philosophical phenomenology applied to the subjective experiencing of phenomena and to consciousness, esp. in the fields of Gestalt psychology, existential analysis and psychiatry.

1930 W. B. WOLFE tr. *Wexberg's Individual Psychol.* 8 Phenomenology prepared the way for the decisive step toward a comparative and contextual point of view in psychology. **1935** K. KOFFKA *Princ. Gestalt Psychol.* iii. 73 For us phenomenology means as naïve and full a description of direct experience as possible. **1958** H. F. ELLENBERGER in R. May et al. *Existence* I. iii. 92 There is a wide gap between the philosophical phenomenology of Husserl and the psychiatric phenomenology of Minkowski. *Ibid.* 101 Phenomenology can also use a 'categorical' frame of reference... The two basic categories of inner experiences are considered to be time ('temporality') and space ('spatiality'). **1959** A. W. LEVI *Philos. & Mod. World* II. x. 405 The phenomenology of the human condition..in which inescapable situations constitute the historical determination in its four forms of death, suffering, conflict, and guilt. **1969** C. O. SCHRAG *Experience & Being* I. ii. 65 Psychiatric phenomenology has contributed interesting and revealing studies on the nature of psychological space and..time in their pathological expressions.

phenomenon. 1. *β.* (Further examples.)

1783 J. WOODFORDE *Diary* 8 Jan. (1926) II. 54, I went ..to see a wonderful Phœnomena in Nature a Heifer 3 years old with two distinct Heads. **1947** GERTH & MILLS *From M. Weber: Ess. in Sociol.* iii. 73 In this conception of freedom as a historically developed phenomena,.. Weber represents humanist and cultural liberalism rather than economic liberalism. **1969** *Daily Progress* (Charlottesville, Va.) 5 Feb. 1/7 'They have an image now,' said Dr. Granville C. Fisher, University of Miami psychologist, 'and many others will follow the same route. It is a phenomena that will keep spreading.' **1970** *Nature* 31 Oct. 405/2 His work is fundamental to the concept of 'frozen' lines of magnetic force being held inside a plasma, a phenomena of great importance to any understanding of the processes occurring in the magnetosphere. **1972** *Real Estate Rev.* Winter 6/1 In some of our major cities, the abandonment phenomena to be witnessed is unlike anything that can be found in the United States outside the ghost towns of the old West.

phenon (fe·non). [f. Gk. φαίνειν to appear + *-on*.] **a.** *Biol.* A group of apparently similar plants or animals.

1943 CAMP & GILLY in *Brittonia* IV. 335 Phenon: a species which is phenotypically homogeneous and whose individuals are sexually reproductive, but which is composed of intersterile segments. **1969** E. MAYR *Princ. Systematic Zool.* i. 5 There is no generally accepted technical term for a phenotypically reasonably uniform sample, but it may be designated as a phenon. *Ibid.* 10 A phenon is not necessarily a population in the biological sense.

b. *Taxonomy.* A grouping of plants or animals established by techniques of numerical analysis.

1962 SNEATH & SOKAL in *Nature* 3 Mar. 860/1 How should we name the groups which are established by numerical taxonomy?.. We call the groups simply 'phenons'. **1963** DAVIS & HEYWOOD *Princ. Angiosperm Taxon.* iv. 136 Sneath & Sokal have introduced the concept of a phenon for the definition of groups obtained by cluster analysis... In practice a phenon defines groups by drawing lines horizontally across the dendrograms. **1963** SOKAL & SNEATH *Princ. Numerical Taxon.* ix. 251 The phenon nomenclature... Phenons are groups which approach natural taxa more or less closely, and..they can be of any hierarchic rank or of indeterminate rank. **1966** *New Scientist* 20 Jan. 151/3 These groups are called *phenons*... If the original taxa are species each of the three new phenon taxa might represent a sub-genus or genus. **1973** SNEATH & SOKAL *Numerical Taxon.* v. 294 The term phenon is intended to be general, to cover the groups produced by any form of cluster analysis.

phenosafranine (fīnŏsæ·frănīn, -in). *Chem.* Formerly also **-in.** [ad. G. *phenosafranin* (O. N. Witt: see R. Nietzki in *Ber. d. Deut. Chem. Ges.* (1883) XVI. 466), f. *pheno-* PHENO- + *safranin* SAFRANIN.] A synthetic red dye, $C_{18}H_{15}N_4Cl$, which is used in photography as a desensitizer; also, any of the derivatives of this compound.

1883 *Jrnl. Chem. Soc.* XLIV. 731 Phenosafranine,.. obtained by Witt by oxidising a mixture of aniline (2 mols.) and paraphenylenediamine (1 mol.).., forms beautifully crystalline salts. **1921** [see *DESENSITIZE *v.*].

1937 *Thorpe's Dict. Appl. Chem.* (ed. 4) I. 571/2 Nietzki showed that the same phenosafranine may be obtained (*a*) by condensing phenyl-*m*-phenylenediamine with phenyl-*p*-phenylenediamine, or (*b*) from diphenyl-*m*-phenylenediamine..and *p*-phenylenediamine. **1970** *Amat. Photographer* 11 Mar. 63/3 The phenosafranines and allied desensitising dyes are not suitable for papers as they stain badly.

phenothiazine (fīno-, fenoþəi·ăzīn). *Pharm.* Formerly also **phenthiazine.** [f. PHENO- + THI(O- + *AZINE.] **a.** A green, crystalline, heterocyclic compound, $C_{12}H_9NS$, which is used in veterinary medicine in the treatment of parasitic infestations. **b.** Any of various derivatives of this, which constitute an important class of tranquillizing drugs used esp. in the treatment of mental illnesses.

1894 G. M'GOWAN tr. *Bernthsen's Text-bk. Org. Chem.* (ed. 2) 539 Nile Blue springs from naphtho-phenoxazine; and the thionine dyes from phen-thiazine. **1917** *Chem. Abstr.* XI. 3903 (Index), Phenothiazine. **1926** H. G. RULE tr. *J. Schmidt's Text-bk. Org. Chem.* 709 Phenthiazine, thio-diphenylamine,..is also the parent compound of a number of dye-stuffs. **1940** *Nature* 17 Aug. 232/2 Since phenothiazine is a new and valuable vermifuge, its effect on animal tissues is of some general interest. **1959** *Times* 14 Sept. 19/4 The nodula worm of sheep has been completely eliminated..by the use of pheno-thiazine during the period of winter housing. **1969** *Daily Tel.* 1 Nov. 2/7 Large doses of phenothiazines induce a Zombi-like rigidity. **1974** M. C. GERALD *Pharmacol.* iv. 71 The phenothiazine nucleus has proved..a rather versatile progenitor of pharmacologically useful compounds. *Ibid.* xvi. 301 Chlorpromazine (Thorazine), the most commonly employed phenothiazine.

phenotype (fī·notəip). *Biol.* Also †**phæno-type.** [ad. G. *phaenotypus* (W. Johannsen *Elem. der exakten Erblichkeitslehre* (1909) vii. 123): see PHEN-, PHENO- and -TYPE.] A type of organism distinguishable from others by observable features; the sum total of the observable features of an individual, regarded as the consequence of the interaction of its genotype with its environment. Cf. *GENOTYPE *sb.*[2]

1911 W. JOHANNSEN in *Amer. Naturalist* XLV. 132, I have proposed the terms 'gene' and 'genotype' and some further terms, as 'phenotype' and 'biotype', to be used in the science of genetics. *Ibid.* 134 All 'types' of organisms, distinguishable by direct inspection or only by finer methods of measuring or description may be characterized as 'phenotypes'. **1931** S. J. HOLMES *Life & Evolution* xiv. 277 A study of our checkerboard indicates that there are four phaenotypes. **1958** *Antiquity* XXXII. 207 The Neolithic people were mostly of a different phenotype. **1964** G. H. HAGGIS et al. *Introd. Molecular Biol.* vii. 193 In this scheme the bodily characteristics, or phenotype, are jointly determined by the environment on the one hand and by the inherited chromosomal complement, or genotype, on the other. **1969** *Times Lit. Suppl.* 20 Nov. 1341 Darwinian selection acts on phenotypes. **1971** D. J. COVE *Genetics* iv. 45 It is usual to refer to the genetic constitution of a strain as its genotype, and to its appearance as its phenotype. **1973** *Listener* 28 June 851/1 Whether or not the average phenotypes of such races can be shown to differ significantly in IQ is beside the point. **1976** SMYTHIES & CORBETT *Psychiatry* iv. 36 A number of different subgroups based on different biochemical lesions..all..end up with a similar clinical picture. In other words many different genotypes can end up with a very similar phenotype.

Hence **phenoty·pic, phenoty·pical** *adjs.*, of or pertaining to the observable features of, or differences between, organisms (often used with the implication 'not genotypic'); **phenoty·pically** *adv.*

1911 *Amer. Naturalist* XLV. 148 The phenotypically distinct and even diversely localized 'characters' convey easily the impression that they are the reactions of different genes. *Ibid.* 156 The merely phenotypical phenomena of alternative variability first pointed out by De Vries. **1929** R. R. GATES *Heredity in Man* ii. 26 There are cases where two or more factors combined to produce a single phenotypic character. **1930** *Biol. Bull.* LVIII. 85 (*heading*) Phenotypical variation in body and cell size of *Drosophila melanogaster.* **1935** *Proc. Nat. Acad. Sci.* XXI. 22 A rare phenomenon—the recurrence of phaenotypically the same scute mutation. **1942** *Endeavour* I. 18/2 Many geneticists have..attempted to discover the processes involved in the mechanism by which the genes of the genotype bring about phenotypic effects. **1964** M. CRITCHLEY *Developmental Dyslexia* x. 64 His present study lent no support to the hypothesis that specific dyslexia, mental deficiency,..and speech defects were different phenotypical manifestations of the same hereditary taint. **1964** *Punch* 28 Oct. 652/2 Earlier [sheep] breeders..chose their stock phenotypically, that is, by the look of them. **1970** *Sci. Amer.* Feb. 62/3 It seems likely that the highlanders have derived their special qualities from acclimatization—in short, that their response to their environment is phenotypic rather than genotypic. **1977** J. L. HARPER *Population Biol. of Plants* viii. 239 Parts of a clone or shoots on a tree will differ phenotypically, e.g. in age and size.

phenotyping (fī·nŏtəipiŋ), *vbl. sb.* [f. prec. + -ING[1].] Allocation to a phenotype.

1964 *Jrnl. Dairy Sci.* XLVII. 1262/1 That agreement in phenotyping exists is valuable in..establishing a uniform nomenclature of the genetic variants. **1977** *Lancet* 8 Jan. 82/1 The variants so recognised are labelled alphabetically in the protease-inhibitor (Pi) phenotyping system.

phenoxide (fīnǫ·ksəid). *Chem.* [f. PHEN-, PHENO- + OXIDE *sb.*] A salt of phenol, containing the anion $C_6H_5O^-$; = PHENATE, *PHENOLATE.

1888 *Jrnl. Chem. Soc.* LIV. 586 (*heading*) Compounds of phenoxides with cuprous and mercurous chlorides. **1906** J. J. SUDBOROUGH *Bernthsen's Org. Chem.* (rev. ed.) xxiv. 405 The phenols possess the character of weak acids, and they form salts with alkalis..known as phenates or phenoxides. **1936** L. J. DESHA *Org. Chem.* 185 Phenoxides, sometimes called phenates, are formed from phenols either by the action of the strongly positive free metals such as sodium or by dissolving in aqueous alkalies such as solutions of sodium hydroxide. **1966** RAKOFF & ROSE *Org. Chem.* xviii. 594 Phenols..are stronger acids than water; they will react with sodium hydroxide to form water and sodium phenoxide. **1974** [see *PHENOLATE].

phenoxy(-) (fīnǫ·ksi), *prefix* and *a.* (*sb.*). *Chem.* and *Pharm.* [f. PHEN- + OXY-.] **A.** (Before a vowel formerly also **phenox-.**) An inseparable formative element in names of compounds which contain the group —$O{\cdot}C_6H_5$, as in **pheno:xyace·tic** (or †*phenoxacetic*) **acid**, a colourless, crystalline solid, $C_6H_5O{\cdot}CH_2COOH$; also, any of the chlorinated derivatives of this, which are widely used as weedkillers; **pheno:xymethylpeni-ci·llin** a white powder, 6-phenoxyacetamido-penicillanic acid, $C_{16}H_{18}N_2O_5S$, which is a semisynthetic penicillin.

1879 *Jrnl. Chem. Soc.* XXXVI. 322 The author [*sc.* P. Fritzsche]..has undertaken the investigation of oxy-phenylacetic acid,..which was discovered and described by Heintz.., and named by him phenoxacetic acid. *Ibid.* 642 (*heading*) Phenoxypropionic acid. **1880** *Ibid.* XXXVII. 318 The preparation of phenoxyacetic acid is described at length. **1900** E. F. SMITH tr. *V. von Richter's Org. Chem.* (ed. 3) II. 146 Phenoxyacetone,..$C_6H_5O.CH_2.CO.CH_3$, boiling at 230°, is condensed by concentrated sulphuric acid to methyl cumarone. **1926** D. W. MACARDLE *Use of Solvents in Synthetic Org. Chem.* iv. 62 Marvel and Tanenbaum found that if in the preparation of phenoxybutyl alcohol, ethyl alcohol dried over lime was used as solvent, yields of not over 45% were obtained. **1946** LONG & BRENCHLEY *Suppression of Weeds* (ed. 2) xiii. 62 As a result of the work carried out..at Jealott's Hill Research Station a range of phenoxyacetic acid products were discovered, of which Methoxone (4-chlor-2-methylphenoxyacetic acid) was finally chosen as being a most efficient weed killer with selective properties. **1948** O. K. BEHRENS et al. in *Jrnl. Biol. Chem.* CLXXV. 798 Phenoxymethylpenicillin—N - (2 - Hydroxyethyl) - phenoxyacetamide (150 mg. per liter)..was used as the precursor for this penicillin. **1954** W. J. HICKINBOTTOM in E. H. Rodd *Chem. Carbon Compounds* IIIA. viii. 426 By the action of alcoholic potash, phenoxyacetylene is formed, an unstable oil. **1959** *Jrnl. Exper. Bot.* X. 33 (*heading*) Factors controlling the uptake of phenoxyacetic acids by *Lemna minor.* **1959** *Times* 6 Mar. 13/6 A preparation of penicillin—penicillin V, or phenoxymethyl-penicillin—was produced which was not destroyed by the acid contents of the stomach. **1969** *New Scientist* 9 Jan. 61/2 Even the relatively innocuous phenoxyacetic acid compounds..have already caused significant ecological damage by destroying natural mangrove associations. **1970** HOOVER & STEDMAN in A. Burger *Medicinal Chem.* (ed. 3) I. xviii. 382/1 Phenoxymethylpenicillin (penicillin V) is now the only important biosynthetic penicillin in use.

B. In Combs. in which *phenoxy* may be used *attrib.* (without hyphen) or joined by a hyphen to the second element. **1.** Containing or being the group —$O{\cdot}C_6H_5$.

1896 *Jrnl. Chem. Soc.* LXIX. 161 (*heading*) On γ-phenoxy-derivatives of malonic acid and acetic acid. **1923** *Chem. Abstr.* XVII. 3864 (*heading*) Phenoxy derivatives of propane. **1926** *Jrnl. Amer. Chem. Soc.* XLVIII. 2748 The method chosen for the synthesis of these compounds was first to prepare the phenoxy alcohols and then to convert them into the chlorides. **1926** *Biochem. Jrnl.* XX. 1083 Replacement of the two phenoxy-groups by bromine. **1928** *Chem. Abstr.* XXII. 769 (*heading*) Influence of the phenoxy group and its derivatives upon the halochromism of known chromogens. **1964** L. J. AUDUS *Physiol. & Biochem. Herbicides* v. 195 The effects of the halogenated aliphatic acids on total soil populations are as diverse as those of the phenoxy herbicides. **1964** W. A. WATERS *Mechanisms Oxidation Org. Compounds* ix. 139 In aqueous solution the phenoxy radical itself has a mean lifetime of about 10^{-3} second. **1974** *McGraw-Hill Yearbk. Sci. & Technol.* 330/2 The phenoxy herbicides (2,4-D and 2,4-T), aminotriazole.., and pidoram are frequently used in forestry.

2. Designating thermoplastics characterized by a linear molecule containing recurring phenoxy groups, which are usu. made by condensation of epoxides, esp. epichlorhydrin, with certain phenols. Also as *sb.*

1962 *Mod. Plastics* Nov. 169 (*heading*) Phenoxy—a new thermoplastic. *Ibid.*, Phenoxy materials are a new family of thermoplastic resins that can be chemically cross-linked to impart thermosetting properties. **1963** *Aeroplane* 21 Feb. 29/2 Ventilating ducts in the Boeing 727 are fabricated from self-extinguishing phenoxy resin. **1967** *Times Rev. Industry* May 76/2 There has also been progress in the currently lower tonnage plastics such as nylon and polyester in film laminates for packaging processed foods, phenoxy polymer in blown bottles, and polycarbonate for sterilizable containers. **1969** L. S. MOUNTS in W. R. R. Park *Plastics Film Technol.* v. 141 Phenoxy films are rigid transparent films with high impact strength. **1970** W. G. POTTER *Epoxide Resins* ii. 19 The 'phenoxies' are in fact to be regarded as high-M thermoplastic materials and have been used either as surface-coating binder resins.., or as thermoplastics for blow moulding, injection moulding, [etc.].

phenthiazine, obs. var. *PHENOTHIAZINE.

phentolamine (fentǫ·lămīn). *Pharm.* [f. PHEN-, PHENO- + TOL(YL + AMINE.] A white or cream-coloured heterocyclic solid, $C_{17}H_{19}N_3O$, which is used (in the form of its salt) as a vasodilator, esp. in the treatment of hypertension caused by phæochromocytoma.

1953 *Jrnl. Amer. Med. Assoc.* 15 Aug. 1533/2 Phentolamine hydrochloride, a salt of phentolamine base, is suitable for oral administration and acts as a potent adrenergic blocking agent, producing adrenolytic and sympatholytic effects. **1961** L. MARTIN *Clin. Endocrinol.* (ed. 3) vi. 182 Phentolamine is the most reliable of the adrenolytic substances both for diagnosis of phæochromocytoma and for use during its removal. **1968** J. H. BURN *Lect. Notes Pharmacol.* (ed. 9) 8 Patients with a high blood pressure may suffer from an adrenal medullary tumour which secretes noradrenaline and adrenaline into the blood. This can be diagnosed by injecting phentolamine intravenously. **1972** *Materials & Technol.* V. xxi. 810 Alpha receptor blockers such as tolazoline may be used in the treatment of peripheral blood vessel spasm, while phentolamine is used to treat hypertensive (high blood pressure) crises.

phenyl. Now also with pronunc. (fī·nəil). Add: **2 b. phe:nylarso·nic** *a.* [ARSONIC *a.*], in *phenylarsonic acid*, a colourless, toxic, crystalline solid, $C_6H_5AsO(OH)_2$, which is used as a trypanocide; also, any derivative of this; **phenylhy·drazone** [ad. G. *phenylhydrazon* (O. Rudolph 1888, in *Ann. d. Chem. u. Pharm.* CCXLVIII. 99): see *HYDRAZONE], any of a class of compounds formed by condensation of an aldehyde or ketone with phenylhydrazine, which are usu. crystalline solids and are used to characterize the parent aldehyde or ketone; **phenylme·rcury**, used *attrib.* or *absol.* to denote compounds which contain a phenyl group bonded directly to a mercury atom; so **phe:nylmercu·ric** *a.*, as *phenylmercuric acetate*, a white crystalline solid, $CH_3COOHgC_6H_5$, used mainly as a fungicide and herbicide; *phenylmercuric nitrate*, a white crystalline solid, $C_6H_5HgNO_3.C_6H_5HgOH$, used mainly as a fungicide and disinfectant; **phe:nyl-pyru·vic** *a.*, *phenylpyruvic acid*, a colourless crystalline solid, $C_6H_5CH_2CO{\cdot}COOH$, which in phenylketonuria is produced by the metabolism of phenylalanine and excreted in the urine; hence **phe:nylpyru·vate**, a salt or the anion of this acid; **phe:nylthi:oca·rbamide**, a white, crystalline solid, $NH_2{\cdot}CS{\cdot}NH{\cdot}C_6H_5$, which has a bitter taste to persons possessing a certain dominant gene and is tasteless to those lacking it; **phe:nylthiourea** (-þəi:o,yurī·ă) = *phenylthiocarbamide* above.

1905 *Amer. Chem. Jrnl.* XXXIII. 104 The reduction takes place with equal ease in the aromatic series, monophenyl arsine..being obtained from phenyl arsonic acid. **1937** *Thorpe's Dict. Appl. Chem.* (ed. 4) I. 488/1 The introduction of an amino group into the para-position in phenylarsonic acid decreases its toxicity and increases its trypanocidal activity. **1959** *Times* 7 Dec. (Agric. Suppl.) p. vii/1 So far as arsenicals are concerned, two phenyl-arsonic acids have received attention [as growth stimulants for poultry]. **1889** *Jrnl. Chem. Soc.* LVI. 251 (*heading*) Phenylhydrazones. **1938** [see *HYDRAZONE]. **1966** *McGraw-Hill Encycl. Sci. & Technol.* VII. 62/2 When the starting material is the phenylhydrazone of acetone, the product is 2-methylindole. **1920** *Chem. Abstr.* XIV. 2181 There at once sep. leaflets of phenylmercuric chloride, PhHgCl, m. 250°. **1921** F. C. WHITMORE *Org. Compounds Mercury* iii. 65 Phenyl mercuric acetate reacts with ammonium hydroxide giving a substance $(C_6H_5Hg)_2NH_2OAc$. *Ibid.* ix. 177 Phenylmercuric nitrate forms rhombic tablets, insoluble in cold water. **1951** A. GROLLMAN *Pharmacol. & Therapeutics* xxv. 510 The first of these compounds used as an antiseptic was phenyl-mercuric chloride but..this was supplanted by the more soluble basic phenylmercuric nitrate. **1966** *McGraw-Hill Encycl. Sci. & Technol.* I. 483/1 The most important of the organic mercurials are phenylmercuric nitrate and acetate. **1972** Phenylmercuric [see *phenylmercury* below]. **1931** *Jrnl. Infectious Dis.* XLIX. 440 Phenyl-mercury-nitrate was first prepared by Otto in 1870, but its biologic characteristics have..never been studied. **1955** G. J. ROSE *Crop Protection* vi. 103 Bacterial canker of cherries has been controlled by applications of a formulation containing the phenyl mercury salt of naphthyl methane sulphonic acid. **1969** JOHNELS & WESTERMARK in Miller & Berg *Chem. Fallout* x. 224 There is no indication..that the use of..phenylmercury from 1930 to 1940 has caused an increase in the mercury content of these terrestrial bird species. **1971** *Nature* 20 Aug. 535/1 The death of birds in Sweden was traced to the use of phenylmercury compounds in the pulp and paper industry. **1972** F. MATSUMURA *Environmental Toxicol. Pesticides* 532 In the U.S. the source of contamination of many rivers has been suspected to be by phenylmercuries, because of the extensive use of phenylmercuric acetate as a slime treatment agent in paper mills. **1932** *Jrnl. Biol. Chem.* XCVI. 628 In one experiment, after 2·5 gm. of sodium phenylpyruvate had been fed for 2 successive days, it was possible to isolate from the urine 0·4 gm. of phenaceturic acid. **1970** R. W. McGilvery *Biochem.* xvii. 387 People with phenylketonuria also excrete some other aromatic compounds.., representing aberrations of the normal process of metabolism due to the high concentration of phenylpyruvate. **1887** *Jrnl. Chem. Soc.* LII. 142 The author..advances the view that the compound is probably phenylpyruvic acid. **1935** [see *phenylketonuria]. **1968** Passmore & Robson *Compan. Med. Stud.* I. xi. 24/2 Presence of phenylpyruvic acid in the blood leads to mental retardation. Arrangements to test the urine of every child soon after birth for phenylpyruvic acid have been made in many places. **1879** *Jrnl. Chem. Soc.* XXXVI. 804 Mono- and di-phenylthiocarbamide..are soluble in caustic soda or potash. **1932** [see PTC s.v. *P II]. **1976** *Nature* 20 May 223/2 This report concerns two dermatoglyphic traits, fingerprint pattern index and total ridge-count, both strongly heritable. In addition, phenylthiocarbamide (PTC) taster ability..and skin colour were studied. **1896** *Jrnl. Chem. Soc.* LXIX. 857 If dilute hydrochloric acid be now added to the clear solution, a white solid at once separates, which..forms white prisms..consisting of phenylthiourea. **1959** *Listener* 3 Dec. 968/2 People who can taste phenylthiourea seem to be slightly more liable to get one form of thyroid disease and slightly less liable to get another. **1971** J. Z. Young *Introd. Study Man* xxxviii. 553 A minimal yet striking example [of genetic variation of the nervous system] is the inheritance of the capacity to taste the substance phenylthiourea.

phenylalanine (fe·nil-, fīnəilæ·lănīn). *Biochem.* [ad. G. *phenylalanin* (Erlenmeyer & Lipp 1883, in *Ann. d. Chem. u. Pharm.* CCXIX. 186), f. *phenyl* Phenyl + *alanin* Alanine.] A colourless, crystalline amino-acid, $C_6H_5CH_2{\cdot}CH(NH_2)COOH$, which, in its lævorotatory form, is widely distributed in plant proteins and is an essential constituent of the human diet.

1883 *Jrnl. Chem. Soc.* XLIV. 992 Phenyl-α-amidoproprionic acid (phenylalanine),..obtained as a hydrochloride by pouring the crude product of the action of ammonia on phenylethylidine cyanhydrin into hydrochloric acid, and boiling the mixture. **1934** *Times Lit. Suppl.* 1 Nov. 758/3 Whether this represents a real ability to synthesize the amino-acid for all purposes, or simply a power to use dietary phenylalanine, remains an open question. **1955** *Sci. News Let.* 22 Jan. 52/1 Since phenylalanine poisoning caused the mental deficiency, Dr. Woolf decided to try devising a diet that would not contain this amino acid. **1956** [see *dopa]. **1970** *Observer* 12 Apr. 25/4 Because he lacks a single pair of genes out of all those thousands, his liver cannot convert a chemical in his diet, called phenylalinine, into another chemical, tyrosine, and soon after birth he will start sliding down into severe mental retardation unless his diet is strictly controlled. **1970** [see *phenylketonuria].

phenylbutazone (fenil-, fīnəilbiū·tăzōun). *Pharm.* [f. Phenyl + But(yl + Az(o- + -one.] A white or cream-coloured crystalline solid which is used as an analgesic, esp. for the relief of rheumatic pain, and as an antipyretic; 4-butyl-3,5-dioxo-1,2-diphenylpyrazolidine, $C_{19}H_{20}N_2O_2$.

1952 *Jrnl. Amer. Med. Assoc.* 21 June 729/1 Phenylbutazone..is one of a group of pyrazole derivatives developed by the chemists of the J. R. Geigy Co., of Basel, Switzerland. **1963** *Lancet* 5 Jan. 21/2 She was given phenylbutazone ('Butazolidin') for five days, with immediate relief of her joints. **1974** *Daily Colonist* (Victoria, B.C.) 1 June 1/3 The U.S. tests on the hard, round, black pills have apparently shown the presence of aminopyrine and phenylbutazone, two drugs legally available in Canada only on prescription. **1974** M. C. Gerald *Pharmacol.* xiv. 273 Phenylbutazone is a potent analgesic, antipyretic, and anti-inflammatory agent.

phenylene (s.v. Phenyl). Add: **phenylene blue,** a blue dye (see *indamine); **phenylene brown** = **Bismarck brown* (s.v. *Bismarck 1), Vesuvin; **phe:nylenedi·amine,** any of three isomeric, toxic, crystalline solids, $C_6H_4(NH_2)_2$, or their alkylated derivatives, which are widely used in the dye industry, as photographic developers, and (in the case of the *para* isomer) as an additive in rubber to prevent oxidation.

1889 G. M'Gowan tr. *Bernthsen's Text-bk. Org. Chem.* 356 The simplest member of this class is the indamine 'Phenylene Blue', $C_{12}H_{11}N_3$,..which results from the oxidation of a mixture of aniline and *p*-phenylenediamine. **1903** [see *indamine]. **1952** K. Venkataraman *Chem. Synthetic Dyes* II. xxv. 762 The indamines (e.g., Phenylene Blue) are obtained by oxidizing a neutral solution of..a *p*-diamine.., and..a monamine (e.g. aniline) having a free *p*-position. **1867** *Chem. News* 12 July 24/2 The phenylene-brown consists chiefly of a new base of the composition $C_{12}H_{13}N_5$. **1885** [see *Bismarck 1]. **1922** A. Clarke *Coal-Tar Colours in Decorative Industries* iii. 43 The colours most suitable for this method are:– On White Earth—..Phenylene Brown, Crystal Violet and Methyl Violet. **1862** A. W. Hofmann in *Proc. R. Soc.* XI. 519 The idea very naturally suggested itself, to look to dinitrobenzol as the source from which phenylene-diamine might reasonably be expected to arise. **1918** *Jrnl. Chem. Soc.* CXIV. ii. 69 The authors have investigated the..binary systems formed between phenol ..and the three phenylenediamines. **1972** *Materials & Technol.* V. xiv. 522 Only the..*p*-phenylene diamines and dihydroquinolines give good ozone protection [to rubber]. **1973** D. A. Spencer *Focal Dict. Photogr. Technol.* 440 *Phenylenediamines*, generic name for compounds derived from ortho-phenylenediamine and para-phenylenediamine which act as photographic developing agents.

phenylephrine (fenil-, fīnəile·frin, -īn). *Pharm.* [f. Phenyl + *epin)ephrine.] The lævorotatory form of 1-(*m*-hydroxyphenyl)-2-methylaminoethanol, $HO{\cdot}C_6H_4{\cdot}CH_2OH{\cdot}{\cdot}NH{\cdot}CH_3$, which is used (usu. as the hydrochloride) as an anti-hypotensive agent and nasal decongestant. Cf. *Neo-Synephrine.

1947 *New & Non-Official Remedies* 225 Phenylephrine hydrochloride is a vasoconstrictor and is active as a vasopressor when administered orally. **1950** *Jrnl. Amer. Pharmaceut. Assoc.* XXXIX. 50/1 Phenylephrine N.N.R. (Neo-Synephrine) is a sympathomimetic amine in general use. **1963** *Lancet* 19 Jan. 138/2 Our experience and published reports suggest that, of the vasoconstrictors, phenylephrine and noradrenaline are probably the most satisfactory. **1974** [see *Neo-Synephrine]. **1975** *Sci. Amer.* Nov. 117/1 On one of her visits she had her pupils artificially dilated with the drug phenylephrine hydrochloride. **1976** [see *phenylpropanolamine].

phenylketonuria (fe:nil-, fī:nəilkītoniuə·riă). *Path.* [f. Phenyl + *ketonuria.] An inherited inability to metabolize phenylalanine normally, which if untreated in children leads to mental deficiency.

1935 *Lancet* 27 July 192/2 Phenylpyruvic amentia, more conveniently termed phenylketonuria. *Ibid.* 193/1 Dr. J. H. Quastel..suggested the name phenylketonuria. **1958** *Observer* 23 Mar. 9/8 An estimated 30 babies are born every year with an unsuspected 'metabolic' disorder called phenylketonuria. **1958** *New Biol.* XXV. 22 Phenylketonuria is a chemically definable character inherited as a Mendelian recessive, and accounting for perhaps 1 per cent of certifiable mental defect. **1965** *New Statesman* 10 Dec. 922/1 The classic examples here are phenylketonuria and galactosaemia, in which the lack of a single gene means that the body cannot use or break down normal substances in the diet..so that toxic products accumulate and poison the brain. **1970** Passmore & Robson *Compan. Med. Stud.* II. xxv. 40 In phenylketonuria the hereditary deficiency of the enzyme phenylalanine hydroxylase in the liver cells retards or deletes the normal oxidation of phenylalanine to tyrosine. **1977** *Jrnl. R. Soc. Arts* CXXV. 186/2 The 'inborn error of metabolism', phenylketonuria..is a simply inherited defect which causes mental retardation, due to accumulation of toxic products from birth onwards.

Hence **phe:nylketonu·ric** *sb.*, an individual with phenylketonuria; *a.*, affected with or pertaining to this disorder.

1937 *Biochem. Jrnl.* XXXI. 270 Experiments were carried out..to determine the effects of feeding phenylalanine to a phenylketonuric on a low protein diet. **1961** *Lancet* 26 Aug. 465/2 This suggests that there is no biochemical reason why any phenylketonuric woman should not have normal children. *Ibid.*, Exposure to a phenylketonuric environment while in utero. **1975** *Nature* 4 Dec. 462/3 Even if an observed difference is genetic it does not mean that a trait cannot be altered substantially by an appropriate environmental change. An example is the treatment of phenylketonurics.

phenylpropanolamine (fī:nəil-, fe:nil-prōupăno̧·lămīn). *Pharm.* [f. Phenyl + *propanol + Amine.] = *norephedrine* s.v. *nor- 1a.

1947 Lorhan & Mosser in *Ann. Surg.* CXXV. 171 (*heading*) Phenylpropanolamine hydrochloride: a vasopressor drug, for maintaining blood pressure during spinal anesthesia. **1968** W. C. Bowman et al. *Textbk. Pharmacol.* xxix. 750 Phenylpropanolamine, or norephedrine, is known commercially as Propadrine. **1969** [see *cold *sb.* 5c]. **1976** *Which?* Mar. 53/1 Some pills and capsules are intended to help your nose feel less blocked up (they contain phenylephrine or phenylpropanolamine for this).

phenytoin (fe·nito,in). *Pharm.* [f. Pheny(l + Hydan)toïn.] 5,5-Diphenylhydantoin, $C_{15}H_{12}N_2O_2$, an anticonvulsant widely used in the treatment of epilepsy (usu. in the form of its sodium salt, a white powder).

1942 *Jrnl. Amer. Med. Assoc.* 4 Apr. 1209/2 White phenytoin sodium (sodium diphenyl hydrantoinate, or dilantin sodium) was effective in protecting animals from electrically induced convulsions it produced little sedative effect. **1952** A. H. Douthwaite *Hale-White's Materia Medica* (ed. 29) 193 When grand mal and petit mal occur in the same patient phenobarbitone and troxidone should be used together: phenytoin must not be employed. **1961** *Lancet* 23 Sept. 683/2 Since then, she has had post-encephalic epilepsy which is controlled by phenobarbitone and phenytoin sodium. **1969** *New Scientist* 10 July 57/3 Patients who had received phenobarbitone or phenytoin showed a dramatic reduction in DDE levels. **1973** [see *Mysoline].

pheophorbide, -phytin, varr. *phæophorbide, -phytin.

‖ **pheran** (fē̜·răn, pē̜·răn). [Kashmiri, prob. ad. Pers. *pairáhan* a shirt.] (See quots.)

1882 *Encycl. Brit.* XIV. 12/1 The Kashmíris, both men and women, wear commonly a kind of loose gown with sleeves, called *phéran* (Pers., *pairáhan*, 'a robe'). **1895** W. R. Lawrence *Valley of Kashmir* xix. 464/2 Tunic worn by all Kashmíris..*Pheran.* **1922** *Chambers's Jrnl.* Nov. 760/2 He is robed in the national Kashmiri dress—the pheran—a loose, flowing garment of white lawn or silk. **1953** R. Godden *Kingfishers catch Fire* ii. 18 He wore a grey *pheran*—the loose robe that most Kashmiri men and women wore. **1976** R. Kalapesi *Catal. Pageant of Indian Costumes* 29 In Kashmir, the long pant is called the 'salwar' and is worn with a loose shirt, called the 'pheran', with its typical embroidered Sassanian neckline and square armholes.

pheromone (fe·romōun). *Biol.* [f. Gr. φέρ-ειν to convey + -o + ὁρμῶν, pres. pple. of ὁρμᾶν to set in motion, urge on (after *hormone*).] Any substance that is secreted and released by an animal (usu. in minute amounts) and causes a specific response when detected by another animal of the same (or a closely related) species.

1959 Karlson & Lüscher in *Nature* 3 Jan. 55/2 We propose..the designation 'pheromone' for this group of active substances... Pheromones are defined as substances which are secreted to the outside by an individual and received by a second individual of the same species, in which they release a specific reaction, for example, a definite behaviour or a developmental process... Having stated that pheromones act on individuals of the same species, they must be differentiated from other stimulating substances, like..scents of flowers and insect repellents... Strict species-specificity is not required; certain overlaps between closely related species may occur. **1962** *New Scientist* 19 Apr. 86/2 The queen substance of honeybees, which inhibits ovary development and profoundly affects behaviour in workers, is a pheromone; and pheromones of various kinds are supposed to affect caste differentiation and colony structure in termites. **1965** *Listener* 14 Jan. 57/2 Our observation of ant colonies.. has led us to believe that as few as ten pheromones, transmitted singly or in combination, might suffice for the total organization of ant society. **1971** *Nature* 17 Dec. 415/2 We now describe a case in which male attraction to females of the same species is inhibited by a pheromone emitted from females of a closely related species. Our tests were conducted with the Indian meal moth *Plodia interpunctella* (Hübner) and the almond moth *Cadra cautella* (Walker), both phycitid species. **1973** H. O. Box *Organisation in Animal Communities* viii. 200 Examples.. include the blocking of pregnancy in the females of some strains of mice by a pheromone in the urine of a strange male mouse. **1975** D. S. Hill *Agric. Insect Pests of Tropics* iii. 23 Behavioural control with several types of pheromone may be possible, but attention has been focused on pheromones causing aggregation for mating, feeding or oviposition. **1977** *Sci. Amer.* May 104/3 It now appears that certain insects take chemicals from the plants they eat, store the chemicals and later emit them for defense, as 'aggregation pheromones' or perhaps as sex attractants.

Hence **pheromo·nal** *a.*, of, pertaining to, or being a pheromone or pheromones.

1959 *Ann. Rev. Entomol.* IV. 39 Pheromonal secretion need not occur in definite glands (though that is the case normally). **1971** *New Scientist* 25 Feb. 413/1 Much of this would be speculation alone if research had not produced an intriguing instance of human communication which might just possibly prove to be pheromonal. Recently, Dr Martha McClintock of Harvard..has investigated the menstrual cycles of women students in a hall of residence... Her investigation threw up the bizarre observation that, precisely as in mice, the cycles of close friends..fall into synchrony. **1971** *Nature* 16 Apr. 432/1 Odour fingerprinting techniques and gas chromatography now make the detection and preparation of human pheromonal agents feasible if they exist. **1975** *Sci. Amer.* May 59/1 The physiological causes, possibly pheromonal ones, for the synchrony of births remain to be determined, and it will not be easy to determine them with lions in the wild.

phi (fəi). [The name of ϕ, Φ, the 21st letter of the Greek alphabet (in Gr. called φεῖ).] **1.** *Petrol.* The negative of the logarithm to base 2 of the diameter in millimetres of a particle. Freq. *attrib.*, as *phi scale*, and written as ϕ.

1934 W. C. Krumbein in *Jrnl. Sedimentary Petrol.* IV. 76, ξ is the numerical value of the diameter... The substitution $\phi = -\log_2 \xi$, or $\xi = (\frac{1}{2})^{\phi}$, is made in part for typographical convenience, but also to introduce a convenient symbol that may be used for expressing grain diameters. **1936** —— in *Ibid.* VI. 38/1 One immediately apparent advantage accruing from the ϕ-scale is the elimination of unwieldy fractions or decimals, such as 1/1024 mm. (0·00098 mm.). *Ibid.* 45/1 The use of ϕ as the new independent variable..makes available a series of statistical measures based on the moments of the distributions. **1949** *Ibid.* XIX. 76/1 The sieve interval of one phi unit is too large to make the true and nominal mean diameters reasonably equal for all size fractions. **1961** *Ibid.* XXXI. 205/2 Comparison of the mean diameters of each pair of beach-dune samples..shows that there is little difference between the two. In these comparisons, 48 are within 0·2 phi of each other. **1971** E. F. McBride in R. E. Carver *Procedures Sedimentary Petrol.* vi. 110 The Phi scale is now used almost exclusively for computation and is gradually replacing the millimeter scale. **1978** *Nature* 14 Sept. 100/2 The sediments..have mean sizes of 1·6–0·125 mm (—0·7 to 3·0 phi: very coarse to fine sand)... These sands exhibit good sorting, with standard deviations that are generally less than 0·8 phi units.

2. *phi coefficient* (Statistics): A synonym for the product-moment coefficient of correlation (see *product *sb.*[1]) used when each of the observed variables has only two possible values.

[**1904** K. PEARSON in *Drapers' Co. Res. Mem.: Biometric Ser.* I. 6, I shall call $\phi^2 = \chi/N$ the mean square contingency. **1913** *Biometrika* IX. 214 We do not agree with him, but it is singular that if he thinks so, he should not have rejected the use of ϕ, the 'theoretical value of the correlation'.] **1950** S. A. STOUFFER *Measurement & Prediction* x. 410 [This] is the Pearson *r* or the so-called phi-coefficient of the latent fourfold table, which appears here as a mere algebraic byproduct. **1968** BLUMLER & MCQUAIL *Television in Politics* iv. 75 All the phi coefficients of ·30 or higher (a level which is most unlikely to be reached by chance) were picked out. **1975** MOREHOUSE & STULL *Statistical Princ. Physical Educ.* xi. 235 The phi coefficient is also related to chi-square... $\phi = \sqrt{(\chi^2/N)}$, where N = number of observations. *Ibid.* 237 The phi coefficient is often recommended for use in the analysis of test items in which the items are scored as correct or incorrect, pass or fail.

3. *Nuclear Physics.* In full *phi meson.* A neutral meson that has the same quantum numbers as the omega meson (*OMEGA 2* b), is observed as a resonance, has a mass of 1019 MeV (1995 times that of the electron), and on decaying usu. produces two kaons or three pions. Freq. written ϕ.

1962 J. J. SAKURAI in *Physical Rev. Lett.* IX. 472/1 In a recent issue of this journal a Brookhaven–Syracuse group reports the possible presence of a narrow resonance ($\Gamma \approx 20$ MeV) in the $K\bar{K}$ system with mass ≈ 1020 MeV in the reactions $K^- + p \rightarrow K^+ + K^- + \Lambda$, $K^0 + \bar{K}^0 + \Lambda$. In discussing the quantum numbers of the resonating $K\bar{K}$ pair, which we tentatively refer to as the ϕ meson, [etc.]. *Ibid.* 474/1 We would like to suggest that this discrepancy is due to mixing between ω and ϕ arising from the fact that the ω and ϕ have the same quantum numbers as far as spin-parity, isospin, and *G*-parity are concerned. **1968** J. BERNSTEIN *Elem. Particles* vi. 86 Since these objects, the ρ, ω^0, ϕ^0, are very short-lived ($\tau \sim 10^{-23}$ sec), it is not really correct, in a rigorous sense, to treat them as if they were stable particles. **1971** *Sci. Amer.* July 100/2 Three vector mesons with zero strangeness are currently known: the rho, the omega and the phi. **1974** *Nature* 6 Dec. 438/2 Another well established meson, called the phi, also has electromagnetic decays to e^+e^-. **1975** *Sci. Amer.* Oct. 48/2 Zweig's rule was formulated to explain the decay of the phi meson, which is made up of a strange quark and a strange antiquark and has a mass of about 1 GeV. The two particles are closely analogous, but the decay of the *J* is appreciably slower than that of the phi.

Phi Beta Kappa (fəi bī·tă (or bē·tă) kæ·pă). *U.S.* [f. the initials of Gr. φιλοσοφία βίου κυβερνήτης philosophy (the) guide of life.] An honorary society to which distinguished undergraduate, and occas. graduate, scholars may be elected; a member of this society. Also *attrib.*

[**1776** in *William & Mary College Q.* (1896) Apr. 214 A list of Members who have been Initiated into the S.P. *alias ΦBK* Society.] **1831** *N.Y. Mirror* 3 Sept. 71/2 Chancellor Kent will deliver an oration before the Phi Beta Kappa Society, at the annual commencement of Yale College. **1894** *Harper's Mag.* June 34/1 I've got to read the Phi Beta Kappa poem at Harvard next week. **1912** M. NICHOLSON *Hoosier Chron.* 278 Sylvia..just walked through everything and would be chosen for the Phi Beta Kappa. **1929** *Chicagoan* 17 Aug. 21/3 Harvard University Phi Beta Kappa conventions. **1932** W. FAULKNER *Light in August* xix. 419 A Harvard graduate, a Phi Beta Kappa. **1949** *Newsweek* 5 Dec. 54/2 Selby won a Phi Beta Kappa key at Northwestern. **1954** W. STEVENS *Let.* 29 Jan. (1967) 816, I am going to read a Phi Beta Kappa poem..at Columbia. **1968** *Wall St. Jrnl.* 19 Feb. 1/1 Mr. Kahn, a Phi Beta Kappa member in his junior year. **1974** 'I. DRUMMOND' *Power of Bug* x. 144 The other was collegiate too, but not an athlete, a Phi Beta Kappa. **1976** *National Observer* (U.S.) 10 July 11/1 Phi Beta Kappa was founded as a secret society at the College of William and Mary on Dec. 5, 1776, and it featured, along with an oath of secrecy, mottoes in Latin and Greek, a code of laws, elaborate initiation rites, a badge, a seal, and a special handclasp. **1978** *Detroit Free Press* 16 Apr. 23A/1, I notice you wearing your Phi Beta Kappa Key from Barnard.

Phil (fil), colloq. abbrev. PHILHARMONIC *sb.* b (in Dict. and Suppl.). Also *attrib.*

1949 E. COXHEAD *Wind in West* iii. 84 Alan was a violinist. He played in the Northern Phil. **1963** *Times* 25 Jan. 14/7 The 'Phil' audience, as regular and loyal as any in London. **1977** *Listener* 28 Apr. 564/3 A 'great' orchestra such as the New York Phil or the Concertgebouw. **1978** J. GALLWAY *Autobiogr.* xiv. 162, I thought the fellows in the Berlin Phil a marvellous bunch.

-phil, -phile. Add: *spec.* in *Biol.* and *Med.* in the sense 'having an affinity for (a certain substance or class of substances)', as in *EOSINOPHIL *a.* and *sb.*, *neutrophil(e* adj. and sb. (s.v. NEUTRO- in Dict. and Suppl.).

phil (fil), *a. rare.* [The suffix -PHIL used as a separate word.] Having a love or leaning (towards something).

1915 [see *PHOBE *a.*].

Philadelphia (filăde·lfiă). The name of the city in Pennsylvania, U.S.A., used *attrib.* in **Philadelphia chromosome,** an abnormal small chromosome sometimes found in the leukocytes of patients suffering from leukæmia, esp. chronic granulocytic leukæmia; **Philadelphia lawyer,** a lawyer of great ability, esp. one expert in the exploitation of legal technicalities; a shrewd or unscrupulous lawyer.

[**1961** I. S. TOUGH et al. in *Lancet* 25 Feb. 411/2 In this paper the abnormal chromosome, for the sake of brevity, is referred to by the symbol Ph¹. This is chosen as it indicates the geographical location, Philadelphia in the United States, of the laboratories in which the chromosome was first noted, and thus it accords with the recommendations on the nomenclature of abnormal chromosomes of the Denver conference.] **1963** WALTER & ISRAEL *Gen. Path.* iii. 45 Some of the leucocytes show replacement of one of their small autosomes by a minute chromosome (the 'Philadelphia chromosome'). This is generally assumed to be 21. **1977** R. B. THOMPSON *Disorders of Blood* xxxv. 566/1 The Philadelphia chromosome usually arises by a translocation from G22 to C9. **1788** *Columbian Mag.* Apr. 182 They have a proverb here [in London], which I do not know how to account for;—in speaking of a difficult point, they say, *it would puzzle a Philadelphia lawyer.* **1803** *Balance* (Hudson, N.Y.) 15 Nov. 363/1 It would (to use a Yankee phrase) *puzzle a dozen Philadelphia lawyers* to unriddle the conduct of the democrats. **1834** W. G. SIMMS *Guy Rivers* II. i. 23 You would have made a prime counsellor..worthy of the Philadelphia lawyers. **1896** *N.Y. Weekly Witness* 30 Dec. 13/1 Not even a Philadelphia lawyer would have been able to pick the winners [in an election contest]. **1901** *Daily Tel.* 6 Nov. 5/4 What entertainment is afforded by a horse-race run 'in camera', only a Philadelphia lawyer would be able to explain. **1909** L. M. MONTGOMERY *Anne of Avonlea* xxvi. 306, I won't undertake to answer Davy's questions... I'm not an encyclopedia, neither am I a Philadelphia lawyer. **1947** *Daily Times* (Chicago) 28 Nov. 14/3 The new violation ticket will be in quadruplicate, and traffic officials say it takes a 'Philadelphia lawyer' to fix it. **1977** *Washington Post* 25 Mar. D18/2 President Carter has made it clear that he understands how complex the income tax laws are. To head IRS, he has picked a Philadelphia lawyer.

Philadelphian, *a.* and *sb.* Add: **A.** *adj.* **3.** (Examples referring to the city in Pennsylvania.)

1775 *Short View of Lord High Admiral's Jurisdiction* 35 A Philadelphian ship might be tried with a fairer chance of condemnation at Halifax than at Philadelphia. **1855** H. A. MURRAY *Lands of Slave & Free* I. xiv. 360 The only peculiarity in the Philadelphian mint is a frame-work for counting the number of pieces coined. **1930** R. MACAULAY *Staying with Relations* i. 14 She loved her little Philadelphian aunt. **1975** *Country Life* 2 Jan. 21/3 Rococco mirrors and girandoles attributed to the Philadelphia craftsman James Reynolds... The majority of the other pieces in the house are also Philadelphian.

B. *sb.* **3. a.** A native or inhabitant of the ancient city of Philadelphia in Asia Minor.

1725 E. COMTE tr. *Huet's Weakness of Human Understanding* 117 Herodotus, the Tutor of Sextus Chaeronensis, was a Philadelphian. **1904** W. M. RAMSAY *Lett. Seven Churches* xviii. 249 The writer seems not to have loved the Ephesians as he did the Smyrnaeans and Philadelphians.

b. A native or inhabitant of the city of Philadelphia in Pennsylvania.

1744 A. HAMILTON *Itinerarium* (1907) 164, I dined with Mr. Fletcher in the company of two Philadelphians. **1789** J. MORSE *Amer. Geogr.* 332 The Philadelphians have exerted their endeavours..to prevent the intemperate use of spirituous liquors. **1803** *Lit. Mag.* (Philadelphia) Dec. 170 A Philadelphian..told us, he could not, after repeated trials, find a chaise. **1841** J. S. BUCKINGHAM *America* II. 84 The Philadelphians have the reputation of being cold, formal, and difficult of approach. **1891** L. J. JENNINGS *Philadelphian* I. i. 11 The reputation of Mr. Snapper for integrity stood deservedly high, and in entrusting his capital to the hands of the Philadelphian, Pendleton incurred no more than the ordinary and legitimate risks of commercial affairs. **1901** *Chambers's Jrnl.* Jan. 31/2 One enterprising Philadelphian has been trying to form a Snake Trust. **1947** *Harper's Mag.* Sept. 200/2 The Proper Bostonian is a very well-defined type—more so..than the Proper Baltimorean, the Proper Philadelphian, or the Proper person of any other city. **1976** *Amer. Speech 1974* XLIX. 213 The Philadelphian is also judged the richest and least friendly of the group and seventh in politeness. **1977** *Sci. Amer.* Nov. 30/2 Redheffer took his device to New York (but only after the ingenious Philadelphians had made up and showed him their own perpetual-motion machine).

philadelphus (filăde·lfŏs). [mod.L. (C. Bauhin *Πιναξ Theatri Botanici* (1623) 398, adopted by Linnæus in *Systema Naturæ* (1735) as a generic name), f. Gr. φιλάδελφος loving one's brother, used as a plant name.] A shrub of the genus so called, belonging to the family Saxifragaceæ, native to southern Europe, North America, or Asia, and generally bearing white or cream flowers, often fragrant; also called mock orange or syringa.

1783 [see SYRINGA]. **1797** *Bot. Mag.* XI. 391 *(heading)* Philadelphus Coronarius. Common Philadelphus, or Mock-Orange. **1899** G. JEKYLL *Wood & Garden* iii. 22 How extremely dense and hard is the wood of Philadelphus! as close-grained as Box. **1938** M. HAWORTH-BOOTH *Flowering Shrub Garden* xvi. 158 When a Philadelphus.. is grown in the open, say as a specimen set in the turf, such [drastic] pruning is unnecessary. **1970** *Times* 14 July 10/7 Notcutts nurseries show large flowered philadelphus. **1975** C. NESBITT *Little Love & Good Company* xvii. 220, I used to think the lilac tree had the sweetest scent, till the philadelphus came with summer and was still sweeter.

philander, *sb.* Add: **1. b.** A love-making or philandering.

1898 G. B. SHAW *Philanderer* I. 78 It was nothing but a philander with Julia—nothing else in the world, I assure you.

philanthropically, *adv.* Add: Also *Comb.*

1976 'D. FLETCHER' *Don't whistle 'Macbeth'* 20 Various philanthropically-minded and prestige-seeking business and industrial concerns. **1980** J. ROSE *Elizabeth Fry* vi. 105 A number of philanthropically-minded ladies.

philanthropoid (filæ·nþrŏpoid). orig. *U.S.* [f. PHILANTHROP(IST + -OID, joc. after ANTHROPOID *a.* and *sb.*] A professional philanthropist, a worker for a charitable or grant-awarding institution. Also *attrib.* or as *adj.* Hence **philan:thropoi·dal** *a.*; **philan:thropoi·dally** *adv.*

1949 *Harper's Mag.* Mar. 9/1 Edwin R. Embree..calls himself a 'philanthropoid', a term which he and Frederick Keppel of the Carnegie Corporation coined some years ago to describe a person who gives away other people's money. **1957** *Britannica Bk. of Year* 512/1 Coinages with a more colloquial or individualistic ring were..*philanthropoid,* one who disburses the money of a philanthropic institution or foundation. The adjectival and adverbial forms *philanthropoidal* and *philanthropoidally* also occurred. **1959** *Fortune* May 110/2 Philanthropoid is what Jonathan King cheerfully calls himself. King has spent most of his adult life giving away money. **1966** *Economist* 31 Dec. 1391/3 All of this brings a danger that there will be in-breeding of ideas, grants going round in circles... Representatives of the best foundations try to avoid this... Indeed, most of these complaints about 'philanthropoid man' are well on the way to being out of date. **1977** *Daily Tel.* 13 Jan. 17/3 I'm not playing the role of the hard-headed tycoon who thinks all philanthropoids are Socialists and all university professors are Communists.

philately. Add: **b.** Stamps collectively.

1930 *19th Cent.* Dec. 785 The small-bourgeois quality of English philately remained untarnished with sham elegance.

philautian (filǭ·tiăn), *a. rare*—¹. [f. as PHILAUTY + -AN.] Selfish.

1811 SHELLEY *Let.* 25 July (1964) I. 98 This is entirely a *philautian* argument.

philetism: see *PHYLETISM.

Philharmonic, *a.* and *sb.* Add: **A.** *adj.* Also used characteristically in the names of symphony orchestras.

[**1895** G. B. SHAW in *Daily Chron.* 6 Nov. 6/5 Every violoncellist in the Philharmonic orchestra [*sc.* the Philharmonic Society orchestra] used to dread the trio of the third movement.] **1898** STAINER & BARRETT *Dict. Mus. Terms* 362/1 The pitch of Costa's Philharmonic Orchestra..was A. 452·5. **1923** *Gramophone* Apr. 14/1, I prefer the old rendering [of Beethoven's C minor Symphony] conducted by Nikisch with the Berlin Philharmonic Orchestra. **1937** N. SLONIMSKY *Music since 1900* I. 371, 1934... German State Philharmonic Orchestra of the German Soviet Republic of the Volga basin is established. .. *Fifth Symphony* of Arnold Bax is performed..by the London Philharmonic Orchestra. **1940** GRANT & HETTINGER *America's Symphony Orchestras* iii. 70 The New York Philharmonic, Philadelphia, and Boston symphony orchestras..have been grouped together as Group I. **1944** B. GEISSMAR *Baton & Jackboot* 25 The Berlin Philharmonic Orchestra unanimously voted for Furtwängler. **1961** *N.Y. Times* 17 Nov. 38 In recent years Anna Xydis has played with the New York Philharmonic. **1974** *Encycl. Brit. Micropædia* I. 927/1 Beecham..founded the Royal Philharmonic Orchestra in London (1947).

B. *sb.* (Earlier example of sense *Philharmonic Society.*) Also, short for *Philharmonic Orchestra.*

1855 GEO. ELIOT in *Fraser's Mag.* July 51/1 When a symphony of Beethoven's was first played at the Philharmonic, there was a general titter among the musicians in the orchestra. **1897** [see PERFORMING *vbl. sb.* 4 b]. **1931** *Gramophone* Apr. 526/2 Even the famous New York Philharmonic..must, I think, take second place. **1933** M. BAUER *20th Cent. Music* iv. 40 Spohr..was the first to conduct an orchestra, the London Philharmonic (1820) with a baton and without the aid of a piano. **1944** B. GEISSMAR *Baton & Jackboot* 24 Arthur Nikisch..had been permanent conductor..of the Hamburg Concerts with the Berlin Philharmonic since 1897. **1951** J. H. MUELLER *Amer. Symphony Orchestra* iii. 63 A century of uninterrupted orchestral programs of the New York Philharmonic affords an extraordinary view of changes in musical taste. **1961** J. WILLIAMS *Forger* i. 12 The artist is like a fragment of a mosaic—no, he is more than that, a virtuoso performer in some vast philharmonic. **1977** *Time* 10 Oct. 17/3 Her orchestral works have been performed by the Philadelphia Orchestra and the Los Angeles and New York Philharmonics.

‖**philia** (fi·liă). [ad. Gr. φιλία friendship.] Amity, friendship, liking.

1953 J. A. K. THOMSON *Ethics of Aristotle* VIII. 202 The subject of the eighth and ninth books is *Philia,* the feeling which friends have for one another. *Ibid.*, Without this discussion of *Philia* the *Ethics* would have nothing to say on the subject of love. **1960** C. S. LEWIS *Four Loves* iv. 69 The very tone of the admission, and the sort of acquaintanceships which those who make it would describe as 'friendships', show clearly that what they are talking about has very little to do with that *Philia* which Aristotle classified among the virtues. **1963** AUDEN *Dyer's Hand* 143 From that moment on his relationship with Passepartout ceases to be impersonal; *philia* is felt by both. **1977** *Christian* IV. 137 For everybody, whatever his or her sexual orientation.., life can include all the elements of love: eros, philia, and agape. *Ibid.*, Philia, affection, as we have seen, is not easily expressed in public in our society, and it is most difficult for gay men.

-philia (fi·liă), ad. Gr. φιλία friendship, fondness, forming abstract sbs. (usu. corresp. to an adj. in -PHIL, -PHILE, *-PHILIC, or -PHILOUS), with the senses 'affinity for' (as in *EOSINOPHILIA), 'undue inclination towards' (as in HÆMOPHILIA, *SPASMOPHILIA), 'love of or liking for' (as in *ANGLOPHILIA, *necrophilia* s.v. *NECRO-).

-philic (fi·lik), f. -PHIL, -PHILE + -IC (cf. Gr. φιλικός), used to form adjs. with the sense 'having an affinity for, attracted by, liking', as in *LYOPHILIC, *mesophilic* s.v. *MESO-, *neutrophilic* s.v. *NEUTRO-. Cf. -PHILOUS.

philippina, philopœna. (Earlier and later examples.)

1839 C. F. BRIGGS *Adventures H. Franco* II. xiv. 143 There would be..scandal by the wholesale, besides sugar kisses, and phillippinas [at the party]. **1917** H. H. RICHARDSON *Fortunes R. Mahony* III. v. 213 She had won a pair of gloves in a philippine with Mr. Urquhart.

Philippine (fi·lipīn), *a.*[1] and *sb.* Also **Filippine,** and *sb. pl.* in It. form **Philippini.** [f. the name of St. *Philip* Neri (1515–95), founder of the Congregation of the Fathers of the Oratory at Rome + -INE[1].] Of, pertaining to, or characteristic of the Oratorians or the Oratory of St. Philip Neri (ORATORY *sb.*[1] 5). **B.** *sb.* A father or priest of this Oratory; also, a female novice (see quot. 1773).

1773 *Encycl. Brit.* III. 476/2 *Philippines*, a religious society of young women, at Rome; so called from their taking St. Philip de Neri for their protector: they consist of an hundred poor girls, who are brought up till they are of age to be married, or become nuns. **1848** F. W. FABER *Let.* 17 Feb. in J. E. Bowden *Life & Lett. F. W. Faber* (1869) viii. 337 Father Superior has now left us, all in our Philippine habits with turndown collars, like so many good boys brought in after dinner. **1852** —— *Let.* 14 Jan. in M. Trevor *Newman: Pillar of Cloud* (1962) 578 F. Rossi..declares..that he has acted in a manner unworthy of a Filippine *in re Achilli.* **1856** J. H. NEWMAN *Let.* 2 Jan. in M. Trevor *Newman: Light in Winter* (1962) 99 The Philippine house is one large vault. *Ibid.* 7 Jan. 101 The brief half-hour we had for going to the Philippini. **1863** —— *Let.* 27 Dec. in W. Ward *Life J. H. Newman* (1912) I. xix. 612 Since 1846 or 1847,.. since I went to Propaganda and came back a Philippine. **1959** J. C. CHAPIN tr. *Giovannetti's We have Pope* v. 111 Patriarch Roncalli thought it proper to cede to the Filippine Institutes (now run by the Brethren of the Christian Schools) the splendid Villa Fietta.

Philippine (fi·lipīn), *a.*[2] [ad. Sp. *Filipino*: see *FILIPINO *sb.* and *a.*] Of or pertaining to a Filipino, or to the Philippine islands (now the Republic of the Philippines). Also *Comb.*

1812 W. MARSDEN *Gram. Malayan Lang.* p. xxi, The dictionaries of *Tagala, Bisaya, Pampagna*, and other Philippine languages are voluminous. **1815** J. F. STEPHENS in G. Shaw *Gen. Zool.* IX. I. 190 Philippine Woodpecker... About eleven inches in length... It is said to make a great noise with its beak. **1832** R. BAIRD *View of Valley of Mississippi* xxiv. 287 The Philippine or ribband cane is rapidly supplanting this species of cane. **1899** W. JAMES *Talks to Teachers* x. 98 What a help is our Philippine war at present in teaching geography! **1932** W. L. GRAFF *Language* 423 The Philippine–Formosa group [of languages]. **1941** *Sun* (Baltimore) 12 Aug. 17/2 A considerable quantity of Philippine mahogany also will be used in the construction of the hulls. **1945** C. L. B. HUBBARD *Observer's Bk. Dogs* 115 Though not recognized by The American Kennel Club, Philippine Dogs are generally bred to a type. **1947** J. C. RICH *Materials & Methods Sculpture* x. 292 Philippine mahogany is not a true mahogany. The name is applied to at least a half-dozen species of the dipterocarp family. Most of the woods referred to as Philippine mahogany are fairly soft and carve well. **1948** F. H. TITMUSS *Conc. Encycl. World Timbers* 72 Lauan..is sometimes exported under the title of Philippine Mahogany, but is not a member of the true Mahogany family. **1964** P. F. ANSON *Bishops at Large* xi. 530 Only one Philippine-born priest, a *mestico*, was raised to the episcopate. **1976** E. S. GRUSON *Checklist Birds of World* 77 *Picoides maculatus* Philippine Pygmy Woodpecker. **1977** *Time* 12 Dec. 27/1 Manila-born Emerson Coseteng, by contrast, is a 46-year-old naturalized Philippine citizen and a major stockholder in the Mariwasa group of companies.

philippinite (filipī·nəit). *Geol.* [f. prec. + -ITE[1].] Any tektite from the tektite field of the Philippine Islands.

1951 H. E. SUESS in *Geochim et Cosmochim. Acta* II. 76 So-called 'gas-rich' philippinites, tektites from the Philippines, which are exceptionally rich in bubbles of various sizes. **1961, 1964** [see *JAVAITE]. **1969** *New Scientist* 30 Oct. 237/1 We find ages of indochinites and philippinites to lie between 0·6 and 0·7 m.y.

Philips, var. *PHILLIPS[1].

philism (fi·liz'm). *rare.* [The termination of such words as NEGROPHILISM and *ANGLOPHILISM, used as a noun.] A feeling of friendliness towards another race or nation.

1917 *Edin. Rev.* July 127 Germany is the home of such movements..and many other 'philisms' and 'phobisms'. **1923** *Contemp. Rev.* Sept. 325 Tzankoff..is not credited with 'philism' or 'phobism' toward any particular country.

Phillips[1] (fi·lips). Also **Philips.** [The name of Henry F. *Phillips*, of Portland, Oregon.] A proprietary name used *attrib.* to designate screws having a slot in the form of an equal-armed cross, and corresponding screwdrivers.

1935 *Iron Age* 7 Nov. 42/3 American Screw Co., Providence, R.I., announces a line of case-hardened sheet metal screws featuring a new 'Phillips' recessed, self-centering head in place of the conventional screw-slot. *Ibid.*, The geometric pattern of the Phillips head provides that the screw shall hold to the taper point of the driver and may be brought into position with one hand. **1938** *Official Gaz.* (U.S. Patent Office) 18 Oct. 517/2 Henry F. Phillips, Portland, Oreg... Phillips Recessed Head. For screws. Claims use since Dec. 15, 1934. **1952** *Trade Marks Jrnl.* 20 Feb. 159/1 Phillips Recess... Screws of common metal. Guest, Keen & Nettlefolds Limited,.. Smethwick; manufacturers. *Ibid.* 161/1 Phillips Recess... Screwdrivers. Guest, Keen & Nettlefolds Limited,.. Smethwick; manufacturers. **1956** A. P. MORGAN *Woodworking Tools* ii. 37 Phillips head screws require a Phillips screwdriver. **1962** E. AMBLER *Light of Day* viii. 172 He had used an ordinary screwdriver on the Phillips heads. **1966** *Official Gaz.* (U.S. Patent Office) 18 Oct. TM119/1 Phillips Screw Company, Natick, Mass. Filed April 14, 1966. Phillips... For screws and allied fasteners. First use 1933. **1972** *Practical Motorist* Oct. 209/3 For Philips screws, you may be able to get by with one screwdriver but it's better to buy a large and a small one. **1976** *Practical Householder* Nov. 55/1 The kit comprises the Impact Driver, bit holder, two cross points for Philips screws, two ordinary screw-driver bits for slotted screws and instructions for use, all packed in a strong metal case.

Phi·llips[2]. The name of A. W. H. Phillips (1914–75), New Zealand economist, used *attrib.* or in the possessive in *Phillips* (or *Phillips') curve*, a supposed inverse relationship between the level of unemployment and the rate of inflation.

1969 *Times* 5 May (Wall St. Suppl.) p. i/4 The Phillips curve was mentioned frequently during last year's presidential campaign, usually with the assumption that a Nixon Administration would tolerate a higher level of unemployment and thereby bring about a lower rate of inflation than would the opposition party. **1974** *Times* 23 Mar. 13/1 Many have come to doubt whether any such choice—between unemployment and inflation as expressed in the traditional Phillips's curve—exists at all. **1977** *Dædalus* CVI. IV. 90 The observation that prices start to rise long before the real GNP reaches full employment levels led to the Phillips curve hypothesis.

phillumenist (filiū-, filū·mĕnist). Also **philumenist.** [f. PHIL- + L. *lūmen* light + -IST.] A collector of match-box or match-book labels. Hence **phillu·meny,** the collecting of such labels.

Quot. 1943, supplied by a private correspondent, is from an unverifiable source.—Ed.

1943 M. S. EVANS in *Floyd's Label Rev.* May 4, I have been wondering..if we could not have a better name than 'labelists'... Under luminary in the dictionary I found the Latin word Lumen (light) and under philately the Greek word Philos (loving), also came across the Latin word Lucus (light). These suggest Phillumenist and Philucist. **1949** *This Week* 23 Oct. 24/2 Phillumenists (the word properly fits those who collect labels from wooden-match boxes, but also is applied to the paper-book fans) are outnumbered among hobbyists only by stamp collectors. **1951** *Britannica Bk. of Year* 686/2 *Phillumeny*, the hobby of collecting match-box covers. **1960** *News Chron.* 18 Feb. 4/5 Are phillumeny, meadopholy, tegestology and fromology as popular as they were? **1960** W. MILLER *Russians as People* 178 Some matchbox designs, among the hundreds which now make Russia a philumenist's paradise, have a charming simplicity suited to their size. **1967** *Listener* 13 Apr. 493/3 Little did John Walker foresee that his invention would become a great blessing to mankind, or that it would give rise to a popular hobby—phillumeny. **1976** *Weekend Mag.* (Montreal) 18 Dec. 8/1 Phillumenists go weak in the knees at the prospect of a rare matchbook cover.

Philly (fi·li). Also **Phillie.** U.S. slang abbrev. *Philadelphia* (see *PHILADELPHIA and PHILADELPHIAN *a.* 3 in Dict. and Suppl.).

1891 W. DE VERE *Tramp Poems of West* 79 Draw up a chair 'thatch', I'll tell you a story, That happened in 'Philly' some twenty years since. **1899** 'J. FLYNT' *Tramping with Tramps* IV. 396 *Phillie*, Philadelphia. **1930** *Sat. Even. Post* 5 Apr. 46/2, I hope and trust that you do all right for yourself in Philly. **1961** *Rogue* May 14/3 After a while, Kitty murmured something to Cappy, and he held her close, answering, 'We'll just have to wait till we pull into Philly, honey.' **1971** *Black World* Apr. 65 To what hospital you goin?.. Back down in Philly. **1972** L. NEAL in A. Chapman *New Black Voices* 308 Remembering the time in Philly/the cops crashing the hotel room. **1976** 'D. HALLIDAY' *Dolly & Nanny Bird* vii. 90 Philly socialites. **1977** *Time* 31 Jan. 52/1 Nicky..has shot a bookie and is holed up in a fleabag Philly hotel, going crazy.

philo-. Add: *phil-athlete, -athletic* (further examples), *-irenist; phil-Athenian* (examples); *philo-African* (earlier example); **philo-Se·mite,** one who is favourable to or who supports the Jews; also as *adj.*; so **philo-Semi·tic** *a.*; **philo-Se·mitism,** theory, action, or practice directed in favour of the Jews; **philothe·rian** *a.* and *sb.* [Gr. θήρ wild beast], (a person) that loves wild animals; so **philothe·rianism,** love of wild animals.

1908 *Westm. Gaz.* 19 Aug. 4/3 Are we to suspect a phil-Athenian bias in the story? **1922** S. LESLIE *Oppidan* xi. 133 The Philathlete and the Philistine. **1905** *Blackw. Mag.* Dec. 811/2 Pick out an untrained but philathletic young Englishman. **1922** S. LESLIE *Oppidan* iii. 42 In an anti-musical philathletic school he was always anxious to impress the new boys. **1929** *Observer* 17 Nov. 11/2 The Sixth Form cricket ground and the Philathletic field of the School have been zoned as residential areas. **1922** JOYCE *Ulysses* 574 Modern philirenists, notably the tsar and the King of England, have invented arbitration. **1865** W. WHITMAN *November Boughs* (1888) 106 He will not countenance at all the demand of the extreme Philo-African element of the North. **1946** KOESTLER *Thieves in Night* 275 If the Jews were as the philosemites describe them, there would be no reason for this Return. **1948** WYNDHAM LEWIS *Let.* 25 Oct. (1963) 467, I am not philosemite. **1976** C. BERMANT *Coming Home* I. ii. 28 All *goyim* were presumed to be *antisemitten* unless they showed definite proof to the contrary, whereupon they were pronounced *Judenfreint*—philosemites. **1962** *Observer* 27 May 28/2 Philo-semitic authors can be no whit less tedious than anti. **1977** *Daily Tel.* 31 May 16 Both Jews and philo-Semitic people have been made aware of the ghastly similarities between the 'old' form of anti-Semitism and its 'modern' euphemism [*sc.* 'anti-Zionism']. **1965** *New Statesman* 16 Apr. 617/3 He calls attention to the scale and cohesion of the philo-semitism now current in the cultural life of America. **1976** M. J. LASKY *Utopia & Revolution* (1977) viii. 301 Philo-Semitism was a natural by-product of the enthusiasm with which the Puritan generation returned to the old books of the Bible for inspired guidance. **1906** *Times* 24 Aug. 1/2 The terrible cruelties practised on quadrupeds..have been.. denounced by..that noble and devoted philotherian. **1909** *Athenæum* 23 Oct. 494/3 An indulgence having been accorded to persons..purchasing, perusing, or subscribing to any philotherian publication. *Ibid.* 495/1, I ask myself why the practice of charity, in the shape of philotherianism, should be left out of sight.

philology. Add: **1.** (Further examples.) Still the usual sense in the U.S.

1922 O. JESPERSEN *Language* iii. 64 In this book I shall use the word 'philology' in its continental sense, which is often rendered in English by the vague word 'scholarship', meaning thereby the study of the specific culture of one nation. **1925** L. BLOOMFIELD in *Language* I. 4 That noblest of sciences, philology, the study of national culture is..greater than a misfit combination of language plus literature... The British use of 'philology' for linguistics leaves no name for the former subject. **1931** J. W. SPARGO tr. *Pedersen's Linguistic Sci. 19th Cent.* iv. 79 One may define philology briefly as a study whose task is the interpretation of the literary monuments in which the spiritual life of a given period has found expression. *Ibid.* 80 The use of 'philology' as a mere synonym for 'linguistics' is to be avoided. **1939** L. H. GRAY *Foundations of Lang.* 3 A more serious objection to the term [*sc.* comparative philology] lies in the fact that 'philology', strictly speaking, denotes not only the study of language, but also of literature and of all the civilisational phenomena of a people. *a* **1941** B. L. WHORF in *Ann. Rep. Board of Regents Smithsonian Inst. 1941* (1942) 502 As the major linguistic difficulties are conquered, the study becomes more and more philological; that is to say, subject matter, cultural data, and history play an increasing role... This is philology. But at the base of philology we must have linguistics. **1947** E. H. STURTEVANT *Introd. Linguistic Sci.* i. 7 Philology is a word with a wide range of meaning. I use it here to designate the study of written documents. **1954** F. G. CASSIDY *Robertson's Devel. Mod. Eng.* (ed. 2) 424 *Philology*, the study of thought and culture as embodied in literary monuments; in a narrower sense, the study of language (but for this sense, the term linguistics is now preferred). **1964** R. H. ROBINS *Gen. Linguistics* i. 6 In German,.. *Philologie* refers more to the scholarly study of literary texts, and more generally to the study of culture and civilization through literary documents... This meaning..is matched by..the use of *philology* in American learned circles. **1980** *Yale Rev.* Winter 312 Philology meant, and still ought to mean, the general study of literature.

3. (This sense has never been current in the U.S.) In Britain, now usu. restricted to the study of the development of specific languages or language families, esp. research into phonological and morphological history based on written documents. (Later examples.)

Linguistics is now the more usual term for the study of the structure of language, and, with qualifying adjective or adjective phrase, is replacing *philology* even in the restricted sense.

1964 R. H. ROBINS *Gen. Linguistics* i. 6 In British usage philology is generally equivalent to comparative philology, an older and still quite common term for what linguists technically refer to as comparative and historical linguistics. **1968** J. LYONS *Introd. Theoret. Linguistics* i. 22 The term 'comparative philology', which I shall use to refer to this period of linguistics [*sc.* the nineteenth century].., though less commonly used these days by linguists themselves (who tend to prefer 'comparative and historical linguistics'), is not infrequently met in general books on language and, like many other unsuitable terms, has been perpetuated in the titles of university chairs and departments and of prescribed courses of study. **1974** R. QUIRK *Linguist & Eng. Lang.* v. 84 'Developmental' and 'general' philology—or, as we would usually call them today, historical and general linguistics.

philomath. Delete 'Now *rare*' and add later examples.

1927 A. HUXLEY *Proper Stud.* 132 It is precisely for the philomaths that universities ought to cater. **1955** *Sci. Amer.* May 114/3 John Whiblin, the carpenter and 'philomath' who was 'ingenious at models'. **1977** R. V. HUDSON in Bond & McLeod *Newslett. to Newspaper* II. 120 The philomath responsible for it..was selected to receive the shafts of Franklin's wit.

philosoph, -ophe. Add: (Earlier and later examples as Fr. form in sense of PHILOSOPHIST 2.) Also *attrib.* or as *adj.* and *transf.*

[**1774** H. WALPOLE *Let.* 28 Sept. (1904) IX. 59 Madame du Deffand hates *les philosophes*.] **1779** —— *Let.* 7 July (1904) X. 441 The *philosophes*, except Buffon, are solemn, arrogant, dictatorial coxcombs. **1830** J. P. COBBETT *Jrnl. Tour in Italy* 286 Guard us ye powers..against all that calls itself '*liberal*' or '*philosophe*'! **1840** J. S. MILL in *London & Westm. Rev.* Mar. 270 Those writers were as much cried down among the *philosophes* themselves. **1932** *Scrutiny* I. 122 Two things appeared to Bentham's *philosophe* mind to be necessary. **1961** *Times* 25 Mar. 3/7 He [*sc.* Raymond Williams] is not a politician so much as a prophet really, a sort of English *philosophe*. **1969** *Listener* 9 Jan. 37/2 All the *philosophes*, all the Encyclopedists, shared the Baconian belief that science could save mankind. **1977** *N.Y. Rev. Bks.* 13 Oct. 8/3 Despite his genuine and profound erudition, Gibbon was a *philosophe* far more than a philosopher, though he hankered after being a philosopher of history.

philosopher. Add: **1. c.** A member of a class called 'Philosophers' in certain Jesuit schools and colleges.

1711 in E. H. Burton *Life Bishop Challoner* (1909) I. iii. 32 Ye Superiors had inculcated..ye two pair of beads to be said every week by one of ye Philosophers. **1712** in *Ushaw Mag.* (1904) Mar. 20 Ye Littanies of ye Saints, every night our Ladyes wch are solemnly sung every Saturday, ye two pair of beads to be said every week by one of ye Philosophers, ye fasting before our Ladyes dayes and ye like. **1809** in *Edmundian* (1948) Summer 9 The boys in the higher classes viz. Philosophers and Rhetoricians have separate rooms. **1915** *Ushaw Mag.* Dec. 292 The new furniture..is to be arranged and then the Divines and Philosophers can take possession.

5. *philosopher-king* (examples), *-scientist*.

1923 A. HUXLEY *Let.* 12 Nov. (1969) 222 One determined Poincaré can defeat..ten philosopher-kings. **1962** *Listener* 25 Jan. 163/1 It is doubtful whether Socrates and the philosopher-kings of the Republic could have lived peaceably together. **1979** *Guardian* 3 Sept. 10/1 The TUC's last philosopher-king, George Woodcock. *a* **1937** J. L. STOCKS *Reason & Intuition* (1939) v. 68 The philosopher-scientist of the nineteenth century had certainly no place for chance. **1945** R. G. COLLINGWOOD *Idea of Nature* II. iii. 128 A philosopher-scientist like Whitehead can restate Hegel's theory (not knowing that it is Hegel's, for he does not appear to have read Hegel).

b. philosopher's philosopher [after *poet's poet* s.v. *POET 1c], a philosopher whose works appeal, or are intelligible, primarily to another philosopher.

1937 A. H. MURRAY *Philos. of James Ward* ii. 45 Bradley may have been a philosopher's philosopher, but much of what he describes and analyses in the tendency to unity inherent in thought is part of the direct experience of thinkers—and of other people. **1957** J. PASSMORE *100 Yrs. Philos.* iv. 81 McTaggart was a philosopher's philosopher, if ever there has been one. **1971** *Classical Rev.* XXI. 224 Aristotle, a philosopher's philosopher. **1974** A. W. LEVI *Philos. as Social Expression* v. 298 That *déformation professionnelle*..has produced the doctor's doctor, the lawyer's lawyer, and the philosopher's philosopher.

‖ **philosophia perennis** (filǫsǫ·fiă pĕre·nis). [L., = perennial philosophy.] An alleged central core of philosophical truths that are generally accepted regardless of time or place, usu. taken to be exemplified by Aristotle and St. Thomas Aquinas.

[**1540** A. STEUCHUS (*title*) De perenni philosophia.] **1858** A. C. FRASER *Rational Philos.* ii. 116 The long line of what an old writer calls *philosophia perennis*. **1933** W. R. INGE *God & Astronomers* i. 13 The classical tradition of Christian philosophy, which Roman Catholic scholars call the *philosophia perennis*. **1941** *Mind* L. 166 The tradition of Nominalism, Naturalism, Materialism, which has always haunted the *Philosophia Perennis* like a shadow. **1960** H. KRAEMER *World Cultures & World Relig.* vi. 150 A..career of proclaiming in America, England and Europe the glorious universality of Vedanta as the philosophia perennis. **1965** *Listener* 1 July 14/1 Like the *philosophia perennis* which it reflects, his [*sc.* Dante's] poem just goes on applying to the human situation year after year.

‖ **philosophia prima** (filǫsǫ·fia prī·mă). [L., = first philosophy.] The study of the most general and universal truths of all science, (so called by Aristotle, followed by Francis Bacon and others); also, more specifically, the study of the divine and eternal.

1605 BACON *Adv. Learning* II. fol. 20v Therefore it is good, before wee enter into the former distribution, to erect & constitute one vniuersal Science by the name of *Philosophia Prima, Primitive* or *Svmmarie Philosophie*, as the Maine and common way, before we come where the waies part. [**1641** DESCARTES (*title*) Meditationes de prima philosophia, in qua Dei existentia, & animæ immortalitas demonstratur.] **1651** HOBBES *Leviathan* IV. xlvi. 371 There is a certain *Philosophia prima*, on which all other Philosophy ought to depend; and consisteth principally, in right limiting of the significations of such Appellations, or Names, as are of all others the most Universall. **1865** J. S. MILL *Exam. Hamilton's Philos.* xxiv. 464 What is inappropriately termed the Philosophia Prima..would be more properly called *ultima*, since it consists of the widest generalizations respecting the laws of Existence and Activity. **1890** G. T. LADD *Introd. Philos.* (1891) 14 Yet a *prima philosophia* is in some sort recognized, which is nothing more than a mixture of definitions of the more fundamental conceptions. **1945** *Mind* LIV. 209 An author who calls himself a positivist had better show cause that he is in earnest when he protests his concern for *philosophia prima*.

philosophic, *a.* (*sb.*) Add: **3.** (Later examples.)

1816 JANE AUSTEN *Emma* II. xvi. 304 The philosophic composure of her brother on hearing his fate. **1822** DE QUINCEY *Confess.* 110 The poor are far more philosophic than the rich... They show a more ready and cheerful submission to what they consider as irremediable evils. **1927** E. O'NEILL *Marco Millions* II. i. 85 The expression has grown mask-like, full of philosophic calm. *a* **1953** —— *Touch of Poet* (1957) II. 86, I flatter myself I have preserved a philosophic poise. **1977** D. AITKIN *Second Chair* xxiv. 227 She was composed and philosophic, aware that I did not blame her.

4. *philosophic radical* (also with capital initials) = **philosophical radical*; hence *philosophic radicalism*.

1834 J. S. MILL in *Monthly Repos.* VIII. 309 Few of the results of the Reform Bill have fallen more short of our hopes, than the conduct of the little band of enlightened and philosophic Radicals. **1837** —— in *Westm. Rev.* XXVII. 67 Those whom..we call philosophic radicals, are those who in politics observe the common practice of philosophers—that is, who, when they are discussing means, begin by considering the end, and when they desire to produce effects, think of causes. *a* **1854** —— *Early Draft Autobiogr.* (1961) 114 Almost every debate was a bataille rangée between the philosophic radicals & the Tory lawyers. *Ibid.* 157 The foundation of a periodical organ of philosophic radicalism. **1882** A. BAIN *John Stuart Mill* iv. 124 In the days when he was heading the philosophic radicals, he was conscious of the weakness of his position in not being himself in the House of Commons. **1911** *Encycl. Brit.* XVI. 661/1 In April 1835 he [*sc.* William Molesworth] founded, in conjunction with Roebuck, the *London Review*, as an organ of the 'Philosophic Radicals'. **1969** D. BEALES *From Castlereagh to Gladstone* I. iv. 68 Bentham..was the most productive..of a group which was of great importance in that it had some influence on public opinion at large, more on political leaders, and more still..on practical administration. They were known as the Philosophic Radicals.

philosophical, *a.* (*sb.*) Add: **4.** *philosophical logic*, logic pertaining to philosophy (opp. **mathematical logic*); *philosophical radical* (also with capital initials), a member of a group of early 19th-century radicals whose advocacy of reform was based on the utilitarian theories of Bentham and James Mill; hence *philosophical radicalism*.

1903 B. RUSSELL *Princ. Math.* ii. 32 It remains a question for philosophical logic whether there is not a quite different notion of the disjunction of individuals. **1921** C. K. OGDEN *Let.* 5 Nov. in B. Russell *Autobiogr.* (1968) II. ii. 121, I am still a little uneasy about the title [of Wittgenstein's *Tractatus*] and don't want to feel that we decided in a hurry on *Philosophical Logic*. **1952** *Mind* LXI. 57 That philosophical logic is concerned with form is the traditional and still prevalent view. **1967** P. STRAWSON *Philos. Logic* 1 Wittgenstein's suggestion does not itself belong to formal logic. It belongs to philosophical logic. **1834** J. S. MILL in *Monthly Repos.* VIII. 174 Those who aspire to be..distinguished as the instructed and philosophical Radicals. **1855** in T. Woollcombe *Notices of Late Sir W. Molesworth* (1857) 36 They were generally known by the rather ambitious title of philosophical radicals. **1873** H. GROTE *Personal Life G. Grote* vi. 56 The 'Philosophical Radicals' as the followers of Bentham were designated. **1885** W. HARRIS *Hist. Radical Party* vii. 130 The so-called Philosophical Radicals, following the methods and sharing the conclusions of Bentham, performed the duty of proving that the political reforms..were not the mere creations of disaffected ignorance, but were founded on great moral and social laws. **1945** B. RUSSELL *Hist. Western Philos.* (1946) III. xxi. 746 The romantic revolt.. passes on, somewhat softened, to the philosophical radicals in England. **1974** *Encycl. Brit. Macropædia* XII. 197/2 The *Westminster Review*..was the organ of the philosophical radicals. **1910** *Ibid.* V. 351/2 Carlyle had some expectation of the editorship of the *London Review*.., an organ of philosophical radicalism. **1935** A. HUXLEY *Let.* 13 Jan. (1969) 390 Bertrand Russell's book on 19th century history..was excellent if regarded as a series of essays on different aspects of the time—Marxism, Philosophical Radicalism and so forth. **1966** F. COPLESTON *Hist. Philos.* VIII. I. i. 3 The philosophical radicalism which is associated with the name of Jeremy Bentham and which had already been expressed by him in the closing decades of the eighteenth century.

philosophically, *adv.* Add: (Earlier and later examples corresponding to PHILOSOPHICAL *a.* 3.)

1873 HARDY *Pair of Blue Eyes* III. iii. 75 The practical husbands and wives who take things philosophically are very humdrum, are they not? **1898** G. B. SHAW *Widowers' Houses* (rev. ed.) II. 46 Trench..tries to take his disenchantment philosophically. **1933** E. O'NEILL *Ah, Wilderness!* I. 43 *Mrs. Miller.* (stares after him worriedly—then sighs philosophically). **1971** *Countryman* Autumn 112 Suddenly the third member of the brood swooped down from its perch in a nearby spruce and flew back to the tree with the worm in its beak. The hen [blackbird] philosophically started again. **1977** K. O'HARA *Ghost of T. Penry* xi. 97 He..switched off Joe's lamp. Philosophically coiling down the cord, Joe said 'Exactly.'

b. *Comb.*, as *philosophically-minded* adj.

1942 R. G. COLLINGWOOD *New Leviathan* xliii. 365 We know too much about the Bogomils to be content with a Gibbonesque, eighteenth-century picture of them as simple, philosophically minded innocents. **1955** *Sci. Amer.* July 73/1 Only a few scientists had been philosophically minded, but today physicists are almost all philosophers.

philosophico-. Add: *philosophico-lexicological, -linguistic, -religious, -scientific* adjs.

1924 C. K. OGDEN tr. *Vaihinger's Philos. of 'As If'* 140 We will not embark here on a philosophico-lexicological excursus. **1967** C. L. WRENN *Word & Symbol* 2 A creative fundamental philosophico-linguistic re-assessment. **1934** WEBSTER, Philosophicoreligious. **1960** PARTRIDGE *Charm of Words* 96 Rosenkreuz..founder..of a philosophico-religious secret society. **1977** *Times Lit. Suppl.* 18 Feb. 190/1 The problem of 'life'..is so fraught with philosophico-religious profundities. **1847** W. SMITH tr. *Fichte's Characteristics Present Age* 242 The Philosophico-scientific character of the Third Age has been already set forth.

philosophize, *v.* Add: **2.** Also, to say or comment philosophically.

1922 JOYCE *Ulysses* 203 The will to live, John Eglinton philosophised, for poor Ann, Will's widow, is the will to die. **1977** J. WAINWRIGHT *Do Nothin'* vi. 97 'It takes all sorts,' I philosophise.

philosophy, *sb.* Add: **7.** (Further examples.)

1823 SCOTT *Let.* 5 Oct. (1935) VIII. 104, I would defer to the very last what is always taught first namely the philosophy as it has been termd [*sic*] of history. **1835** J. S. MILL in *London Rev.* I. I. 106 The evidence of history.. leaves the philosophy of society in exactly the state in which physical science was, before the method of experiment was introduced. **1843** —— *Logic* I. I. v. 119 The notion..seems to me one of the most fatal errors ever introduced into the philosophy of Logic. **1847** J. D. MORELL *Hist. View Philos.* (ed. 2) II. v. 15 We have already shown in the case of Reid, that the philosophy of perception was well commenced, but not fully completed. **1852** *Westm. Rev.* Oct. 435 (*heading*) The philosophy of style. **1853** LYTTON *My Novel* IV. xxxv. 283 Levy is a man who has admitted the fiercer passions into his philosophy of life. **1865** J. S. MILL *Auguste Comte* 54 The philosophy of science consists of two principal parts; the methods of investigation, and the requisites of proof. **1890** W. JAMES *Princ. Psychol.* I. xiv. 585 We see in the philosophy of desire and pleasure, that such nascent excitements..may become potent mental stimuli and determinants of desire. **1896** W. CALDWELL *Schopenhauer's Syst.* iii. 162 A philosophy of life must make some broad assertion about reality as a whole. **1919** G. B. SHAW *Heartbreak House* p. xxvii, It is impossible to estimate what proportion of us..grasped the war and its political antecedents as a whole in the light of any philosophy of history or knowledge of what war is. **1940** F. J. E. WOODBRIDGE *Essay on Nature* i. 53 Expressions like 'philosophy of science', 'philosophy of history', 'philosophy of government', 'philosophy of law', 'philosophy of religion', and so forth creep into the language, indicating that after scientists, historians, statesmen, jurists, priests, and the rest have said all they have to say, there is still need of a special kind of knowledge to inform us what it is all about. **1957** G. RYLE in C. A. Mace *Brit. Philos. in Mid-Cent.* 243 We do systematically construe 'name' on the model of 'proper name'. The assumption of the truth of this equation has been responsible for a large number of radical absurdities in philosophy in general and the philosophy of logic in particular. **1960** H. L. BOND *Lit. Art E. Gibbon* vii. 138 Gibbon's well-defined manner of speaking and the details of his style reflect..his whole philosophy of life. **1966** J. J. KATZ *Philos. Lang.* i. 4 Philosophy of language is an area in the philosophical investigation of conceptual knowledge, rather than one of the several branches of contemporary philosophy such as philosophy of science, philosophy of mathematics, philosophy of art, and so forth. **1976** *Hiroshima Stud. Eng. Lang. & Lit.* XXI. 60 This is a study of D. H. Lawrence's *The Man Who Loved Islands* with a view to locating the spot it occupies in a series of works descriptive of his unique philosophy of life. **1977** P. A. FRENCH et al. (*title*) Studies in the philosophy of language.

8. (Further examples.) Also, more generally, a set of opinions, ideas, or principles; a basic theory; a view or outlook.

1898 G. B. SHAW *Plays Unpleasant* p. xix, It is quite possible for a piece to enjoy the most sensational success on the basis of a complete misunderstanding of its philosophy. **1899** O. WILDE *Ideal Husband* I. 12 *Mrs. Cheveley.* I don't know that women are always rewarded for being charming. I think they are usually punished for it! Certainly, more women grow old nowadays through the faithfulness of their admirers than through anything else! At least that is the only way I can account for the terribly haggard look of most of your pretty women in London! *Sir Robert Chiltern.* What an appalling philosophy that sounds! **1901** G. B. SHAW *Three Plays for Puritans* p. xxxii, It is the philosophy, the outlook on life, that changes, not the craft of the playwright. *Ibid.*, Such men must rewrite all the old plays in terms of their own philosophy. **1903** —— *Man & Superman* p. v, Here is your play!..Its profits, like its labor, belong to me: its morals, its manners, its philosophy, its influence on the young, are for you to justify. *Ibid.* III. 126 Yes, Juan: we know the libertine's philosophy. Always ignore the consequences to the woman. **1922** JOYCE *Ulysses* 629 You have every bit as much right to live by your pen in pursuit of your philosophy as the peasant has. **1946** E. O'NEILL *Iceman Cometh* (1947) I. 45 You pretend a bitter, cynic philosophy, but in your heart you are the kindest man among us. **1959** *Economist* 12 Sept. 836/1 Rival policies—or at least rival philosophies, for they barely reached the stage of practical policies—were very much in the centre of public attention. **1962** G. COOPER in *Into Orbit* 30 The entire philosophy had to be revised once we got involved with manned flights. **1973** *B.S.I. News* Dec. 32/2 Philosophy of control assignment on keyboards... Outlines the general philosophy for the positioning of areas for control keys, in relation to 'graphic' areas, of..keyboards for office machines. **1975** J. PLAMENATZ *K. Marx's Philos. of Man* i. 4 It is not surprising, then, that these ideas, derived from philosophies alien to them, should be less interesting to Marxists and students of Marxism outside the West. Even if they have similar ideas in their native philosophies, they are ideas differently expressed, and so such similarities as there may be go unrecognized.

philothion (filǫþəi·ən). *Biochem. Obs.* exc. *Hist.* [a. F. *philothion* (J. de Rey-Pailhade 1888, in *Compt. Rend.* CVI. 1684), f. Gr. φιλο- (see PHILO-) + θεῖον sulphur.] = *GLUTATHIONE.

1888 *Jrnl. Chem. Soc.* LIV. 1101 It follows that the substance, to which the author gives the name *philothion*, exists in animal tissues in a form different from that in which it exists in yeast. It stands to sulphur in the same physiological relation as hæmoglobin to oxygen, that is to say, it renders it soluble and assimilable. **1900** [see *HYDROGENASE]. **1921** [see *GLUTATHIONE]. **1954** T. WIELAND in S. Colowick et al. *Glutathione* 45 In 1888 de Rey-Pailhade..described a substance containing sulfur which he had been able to isolate from yeast in an impure state and which he called 'philothion'.

-philous. Add: **b.** In *Biol.* forming adjs. with the sense 'having an affinity for or thriving in (a particular kind of habitat or environment)', as in *dendrophilous* s.v. DENDRO-, HYDROPHILOUS, *hygrophilous* s.v. HYGRO-.

phizgig (fi·zgig). *Austral. slang.* Also **phizzgig.** = *FIZGIG 6. Hence as *v. intr.*, to act as an informer.

1941 in BAKER *Dict. Austral. Slang.* **1955** V. KELLY *Shadow* i. 10 The boys suspect he's been phizgigging. *Ibid.* iv. 45 Prior passed the word along to phizgigs that the police would appreciate information about the identity of the counterfeiters. **1973** *Nation Rev.* (Melbourne) III. No. 49. 2/2 Lenny..was described in his biog as a former 'phizzgig' (police informer).

phizog (fi·zǫg). *joc. colloq.* Also **fizzog, phisog, physog, phyzog.** [f. as PHIZ.] = PHIZ. Cf. PHYSIOG.

1811 *F. Grose's Lexicon Balatronicum, Physog*, the face. A vulgar abbreviation of physiognomy. **1829** P. EGAN *Boxiana* 2nd Ser. II. 706 A certain melancholy cast was taking possession of Tom's *phisog*. **1846** *Swell's Night Guide* 127/2 *Phizog*, the face. **1850** C. KINGSLEY *Alton Locke* II. iii. 37 He had received an anonymous letter, 'a'thegither o' a Belgravian cast o' phizog,' containing a bank-note for twenty pounds. **1912** W. OWEN *Let.* 12 Jan. (1967) 110 Unable to get out and see anything better in the way of physogs. **1922** JOYCE *Ulysses* 297, I saw his physog do a peep in and then slidder off again. **1939** *Airman's Gaz.* Dec., One observer 'snapped' Adolph's phisog. **1946** B. MARSHALL *George Brown's Schooldays* iv. 16 The prefect shuts the door in their physogs. **1959** I. & P. OPIE *Lore & Lang. Schoolch.* x. 194 'Shut yer face'—'fizzog'—'flycatcher'—or, 'gate'. **1980** *Radio Times* 5–11 Jan. 15/1 The phizog is definitely familiar... 'I get recognised wherever I go,' he says.

phlebo-. Add: **phlebogram, -graphy** (see main entries below); **phlebothrombosis** (examples); add to def.: in mod. use a venous thrombosis in which inflammation of the vein is absent or of only secondary significance.

1939 A. OCHSUER in *Surgery* VI. 129 In considering intravascular clotting, it is important to distinguish between those lesions which are associated with an inflammatory process in the vessel wall, a true thrombophlebitis, and those in which there is intravascular clotting without the associated inflammatory lesion which can be termed a 'phlebothrombosis'. **1956** P. MARTIN et al. *Peripheral Vascular Disorders* xx. 628 Phlebothrombosis occurs frequently in both legs yet one side only may progress to thrombophlebitis. **1974** PASSMORE & ROBSON *Compan. Med. Stud.* III. xvii. 33/1 There are two types of venous thrombosis depending upon whether the wall of the vein is inflamed (thrombophlebitis) or not inflamed (phlebothrombosis).

phlebogram. Add: (Examples.) Now *rare.*

1885 W. STIRLING tr. *Landois's Text-bk. Human Physiol.* I. II. 194 In order to interpret the various events of the phlebogram it is most important to record simultaneously the events that take place in the heart. **1923** W. D. REID *Heart in Mod. Pract.* iii. 59 The nodal extrasystole is not common. It gives rise to an exaggerated wave in the phlebogram. **1964** HOCHSTEIN & RUBIN *Physical Diagnosis* xix. 266 The *c* wave, although inscribed on a phlebogram, is not seen by clinical inspection of the neck veins, either because it is an artifact of the phlebogram due to the adjacent carotid pulse, or because the *c* wave of the right atrial pressure pulse is too small in magnitude to be reflected visually in the jugular pulse.

2. *Med.* An X-ray photograph of a vein.

1933 *Lancet* 18 Nov. 1144/2 The speed of circulation is very different in the brain as compared with other parts of the head... We have ascertained this fact by studying the arteriograms and phlebograms of diverse cases. **1969** D. SUTTON *Textbk. Radiol.* xxxi. 602 (*caption*) Adrenal vein phlebogram showing small Conn's tumour in the adrenal. Other investigations including angiography and air insufflation had failed to show the lesion. **1977** *Lancet* 1 Jan. 49/2 Evidence for a 50% frequency of a minor degree of iliac-vein compression was based on phlebograms.

phlebography. Add: **2.** *Med.* The recording of the pulse in a vein. *rare.*

1915 DORLAND *Med. Dict.* (ed. 8) 731/2 *Phlebography*, the graphic recording of the venous pulse. **1966** R. B. REES in H. F. Conn et al. *Current Diagnosis* XII. 521/2 The Trendelenburg test, Perthes's test, phlebography and other tests of venous competence are sometimes useful in determining whether vein surgery is indicated.

3. *Med.* Radiography of a vein, carried out after the introduction into it of a contrast medium.

1937 L. J. FRIEDMAN *Text-bk. Diagnostic Roentgenol.* 612/2 (Index), Phlebography (see Angiography). **1946** E. V. ALLEN et al. *Peripheral Vascular Dis.* xxv. 619 Theoretically the amount and location of organic obstruction to the veins in the limb can be determined with great accuracy by means of indirect phlebography (intra-arterial injection). The technic of this procedure, however, is rather difficult and..it is not advisable to attempt it during the acute stage of thrombophlebitis. The technic of direct phlebography is much simpler, but with this procedure only a portion of the venous tree can be visualized. **1972** *Lancet* 27 May 1134/2 A small-calf-vein thrombosis confirmed by phlebography.

phlebotomist. Add: In mod. use, someone trained to take blood from a person for subsequent examination or transfusion.

1974 N. M. ABELSON *Topics in Blood Banking* vi. 124 The skill of the phlebotomist. **1976** I. CHANARIN et al. *Blood & its Dis.* ix. 78 Venous blood samples are required. These may be collected by either laboratory staff, medical staff, nursing staff or phlebotomists. **1977** *Age & Ageing* VI. 85 Blood was taken, usually by a phlebotomist, after the skin had been prepared.

phlizz (fliz). [Fanciful.] In Lewis Carroll's book *Sylvie and Bruno*, a fruit or flower that has no real substance; hence, allusively, anything without meaning or value, a mere name.

1889 'L. CARROLL' *Sylvie & Bruno* vi. 75 Bruno.. picked a fruit... 'It hasn't got no taste at all!' he complained. 'It was a *Phlizz*,' Sylvie gravely replied. *Ibid.* xx. 294 They *will* be sorry when they find them [*sc.* flowers] gone!.. The nosegay was only a *Phlizz*. **1899** *Johnson Club Papers* 188 We crown the musicians with flowers that, like poor Bruno's in the fairy tale, are but a phlizz. **1926** GALSWORTHY *Silver Spoon* II. ix. 187 What was his image of her but a phlizz, but a fraud? *Ibid.* xii. 218 Was Foggartism a phlizz? **1931** —— *Maid in Waiting* iv. 20 The thing's a phlizz. Just a low type of Homo Sapiens.

phloem. Substitute for first part of etym.: [a. G. *phloëm* (C. W. Nägeli *Beiträge zur wiss. Bot.* (1858) I. 9).] (Later examples.) Also *phloem-island, -strand.*

1889 Phloem-island, -strand [see *interxylary* adj. s.v. *INTER- 6]. **1891** *Ann. Bot.* V. 178 The phloëm-islands are produced centrifugally by the cambium. **1914** M. DRUMMOND tr. *Haberlandt's Physiol. Plant Anat.* xiv. 656 The various tissues that are comprised in the general category of secondary phloem are usually arranged in more or less distinct tangential layers. **1951** MCLEAN & IVIMEY-COOK *Textbk. Theoret. Bot.* I. xxi. 922 Phloem Islands..are formed by the enclosure of portions of the normal phloem by short arcs of secondary cambium. **1953** K. ESAU *Plant Anat.* xii. 265 The phloem is the principal food-conducting tissue of the vascular plants. **1969** [see *interxylary* adj. s.v. *INTER- 6]. **1975** J. D. HAYNES *Botany* xx. 314 The vascular tissue is the transport tissue of the plant, and is composed of two major issue types, the xylem and the phloem. **1978** J. UPDIKE *Coup* (1979) iii. 95 Some substratum in the phloem or xylem savored smartly of those little glossy red American candies.

phlomis (flǫ·mis). [mod. L. (J. P. de Tournefort *Institutiones Rei Herbariæ* (1700) I. 178), a. Gr. φλομίς a name used by Dioscorides.] A shrub or herb of the large genus so called, belonging to the family Labiatæ, and native to temperate parts of Asia and southern Europe, esp. *Phlomis fruticosa*, the Jerusalem sage, which has pale green leaves with white, hairy undersides, and whorls of deep yellow flowers.

1706 [see PHLOME]. **1789** W. AITON *Hortus Kewensis* II. 307 Broad-leav'd shrubby Phlomis, or Jerusalem Sage. **1908** G. JEKYLL *Colour in Flower Garden* ix. 80 Further back among the flowers are..some grey bushes of Phlomis and a silvery leaved Willow. **1961** *Times* 25 Nov. 11/4 Phlomis, verbascums, and many more, can be brought into service for such [dry, sunny] positions. **1974** *Country Life* 21 Mar. 627/3, I particularly like the bold groups of golden foliage..and woolly, silvery phlomis with the purple nut. **1976** *Daily Tel.* 9 Oct. 6/2 Here..I would grow the pink-flowered Italian phlomis, which has come into garden centres in recent seasons, as well as the old Jerusalem one,.. which..has yellow flowers, in addition to the silvery, woolly leaves characteristic of the group.

phlorizin. For 'Also †**phlori·dzin(e**' read: Also **phlo(r)rhizin, phlori·dzin** († -ine). [First formed as G. *phloridzin* (L. de Koninck 1835, in *Ann. der Pharm.* XV. 76; *phlorrhizin* suggested there by the editor as the proper form of the word.] (Add earlier and further examples.)

1835 *Amer. Jrnl. Sci.* XXVIII. 383 (*heading*) Phloridzin, a new substance. **1867** BLOXAM *Chem.* 478 Phloridzine..is extracted from the bark of the apple, pear, plum, and cherry tree. **1900** *Amer. Jrnl. Physiol.* IV. p. xi, If a well fed milch goat be made to fast two days and phlorhizin be administered three times daily during the two days, the milk flow stops entirely. **1927** M. BODANSKY *Introd. Physiol. Chem.* ix. 232 The experimental production of this condition [*sc.* renal diabetes] was accomplished in 1886 by von Mering upon injecting into animals phlorizin, a glucoside which is found in the root bark of the cherry, apple, pear and plum tree. **1947** E. BALDWIN *Dynamic Aspects Biochem.* vii. 199 Both phlorrhizin and iodoacetate are known to be powerful inhibitors of fermentation and glycolysis. **1968** PASSMORE & ROBSON *Compan. Med. Stud.* I. xi. 21/1 Phlorizin poisons the renal tubules. **1969** DATTA & OTTAWAY *Biochem.* (ed. 2) viii. 154 Active absorption of sugars can be inhibited specifically by low concentrations of phlorrhizin. **1970** A. L. LEHNINGER *Biochem.* xxii. 491 Such a net conversion of tricarboxylic cycle intermediates is also observed in animals treated with the toxic glycoside phloridzin. **1970** R. W. MCGILVERY *Biochem.* xvii. 399 Phlorhizin is a polyphenolic glycoside.

phlorizinized (florəi·zinəizd), *ppl. a.* Forms: see prec. [f. prec. + -IZE + -ED[1].] That has been given phlorizin. So **phlori·zinize** *v. trans.*

1900 *Amer. Jrnl. Physiol.* IV. p. x, A well phlorhizinized muscle begins to go into rigor within five minutes after death. **1912** A. E. TAYLOR *Digestion & Metabolism* vi. 393 In the phloridzinized dog, it is assumed that no sugar is burned and that neither sugar nor nitrogen is stored. **1927** M. BODANSKY *Introd. Physiol. Chem.* ix. 220 Mandel and Lusk gave phlorizinized dogs lactic acid and recovered it as extra glucose in the urine. **1954** CANTAROW & SCHEPARTZ *Biochem.* xvii. 434 Under ordinary dietary conditions, the body stores of carbohydrate are never depleted to the point where fat and protein catabolism are significantly increased, as they are in the phlorizinized animal. **1965** DATTA & OTTAWAY *Biochem.* xi. 199 It was observed many years ago that when single amino acids were fed to diabetic or phlorrhizinized animals, some caused the excretion of extra glucose in the urine, others the excretion of extra ketone bodies.

Also **phlori:ziniza·tion,** the action of making, or state of being, phlorizinized.

1917 *Amer. Jrnl. Med. Sci.* CLIII. 330 Maximal phloridzin poisoning with feeding of nothing but fat, or the longest possible phloridzination on diet free from carbohydrate and high in fat, has failed to produce in dogs anything resembling diabetic lipemia. **1959** W. B. WHALLEY in J. W. Fairbairn *Pharmacol. Plant Phenolics* 30 The glucosuria in phlorizinisation is to be attributed to the rapid loss of glucose through the kidney.

phloro-. Add: **phloroglucin, -glucinol.** *phloroglucinol* is the only name now current; (examples).

1879 *Jrnl. Chem. Soc.* XXXVI. 633 By this synthesis, the aromatic nature of phloroglucinol is definitely established. **1949** E. CHAIN in H. W. Florey et al. *Antibiotics* II. xix. 758 They also tested a large number of chemicals for their ability to stimulate the production of penicillin... Among the ineffective substances were sodium azide,.. phloroglucinol, naphthol, [etc.]. **1963** [see *FILICIC *a.*].

phloxin. Add: Now usu. **phloxine.** (Further examples.)

1954 MARTIN & HYNES *Clin. Endocrinol.* (ed. 2) i. 10 A preliminary eosinophil count is made by the method of Randolph. [*Note*] By Randolph's method blood is diluted in a white cell pipette with a fluid composed of phloxine and methylene blue dissolved in equal parts of propylene glycol and water. The eosinophils are counted directly per c.mm. on a counting chamber. **1956** KIRK & OTHMER *Encycl. Chem. Technol.* XV. 141 The Phloxines are chlorinated derivatives of Eosine. *Ibid.*, The two Phloxines are used interchangeably as biological stains and have also been used in lake and pigment manufacture. **1967** KARCH & BUBER *Offset Processes* vii. 269 Phloxine or eosine lakes are brilliant reds with a 'bluish' or 'purplish' cast or undertones not fast to light.

pho, phoh, *int.* (Later examples.)

1908 S. WEYMAN *Wild Geese* xx. 304 Pho! Take my word for it, he's no man to bear malice! **1942** BERREY & VAN DEN BARK *Amer. Thes. Slang* §151/11 *Nonsense!; it is ridiculous!..pho!*

phobe (fōᵘb), *a. rare.* [The suffix -PHOBE used as a separate word.] Having a hatred or aversion (towards someone or something).

1915 *Times* 5 Apr. 5/6 The Italian people is not, and cannot be at this moment, either phil or phobe regarding any other people.

phobia. Add to def.: In *Psychol.*, an abnormal and irrational fear or dread which is caused by a particular object or circumstance. (Earlier and further examples.)

1786 *Columbian Mag.* Nov. 110/1, I shall begin, by defining Phobia in the present instance, to be a fear of an imaginary evil, or an undue fear of a real one. **1897** tr. *T. Ribot's Psychol. of Emotions* II. ii. 215 We can easily see that many phobias come under this category. **1907** S. A. K. WILSON tr. *Meige & Feindel's Tics* iv. 88 Prominent among the mental anomalies of the subjects of tic are found different sorts of phobia. **1909** A. A. BRILL tr. *Freud's Sel. Papers on Hysteria* v. 123 Thus far the processes are the same in hysteria, in phobias and obsessions, but from now on their ways part. *Ibid.* 127 Thus..freed anxiety, the sexual origin of which can not be recalled, attaches itself to the common primary phobias of man. **1954** R. F. C. HULL tr. *Jung's Devel. of Personality* in *Coll. Wks.* XVII. iv. 74 The latter [*sc.* the mother] projected all her phobias onto the child. **1974** E. B. MCNEIL *Psychol. of being Human* ix. 232 Phobias are symptoms issuing from unacceptable basic urges that have been repressed from consciousness. When repression is effective, phobia symptoms need not exist. **1978** *New York* 3 Apr. 85/2 (Advt.), Swim-o-phobia? Cure it forever. Our private lessons by professional instructors will have you phobia-free and swimming in no time.

phobic (fōᵘ·bik), *a.* and *sb.* [f. PHOB(IA + -IC.] **A.** *adj.* Pertaining to, or characterized by a phobia. **B.** *sb.* A person suffering from a phobia.

1897 tr. *T. Ribot's Psychol. of Emotions* II. ii. 215 For 'phobic' subjects it is (at least potentially) a permanent state, ready to arise when suggested by some association. **1930** *Brit. Jrnl. Med. Psychol.* X. 46 (*heading*) A phobic case. *Ibid.* 66 Recall and reunion may simply give the phobic mechanism a chance to dominate the normal system. **1964** GOULD & KOLB *Dict. Social Sci.* 466/2 Hysteria, obsession-compulsion, and phobic reactions.. tend to restrict the scope of the neurotic's behaviour. **1968** *N.Y. Rev. Bks.* 29 Feb. 32/4 She has small regard for the population of South Vietnam which she sees as an unpleasant amalgam of cynical self-seekers, stooges, and phobics (i.e., people who fear Communism). **1970** *Daily Tel.* (Colour Suppl.) 4 Sept. 11/4, I..learned that phobics all over the country were undergoing such unlikely cures as yoga, hypnosis, acupuncture and shock treatment. *Ibid.* 12/2 'Desensitisation' thus involves a simple-sounding cure: the phobic patient is taught right habits again. **1976** J. PAYNE *All in Mind* 47/1 A bird phobic would initially be talked to by therapist about phobia, then about birds, then (with a relaxing injection if necessary) pictures of birds would be introduced... It is a very gradual process by which the phobic is helped to overcome the object of irrational fear.

phobism (fōᵘ·biz'm). *rare.* [f. as PHOBIA + -ISM.] A morbid fear of or aversion to anything.

1917, 1923 [see *PHILISM].

phoby (fōᵘ·bi), colloq. shortening of HYDROPHOBIA 2 (*rare*).

1843 DICKENS *Mart. Chuz.* (1844) xvii. 223 A jug and ewer, that might have been mistaken for a milk-pot and slop-basin... 'They've certainly got a touch of the 'phoby, sir.'

Phocæan (fōᵘsī·ăn), *sb.* and *a.* Also 7 **Phocean.** [f. Gr. Φώκαι-α, the place-name Phocæa, or L. *Phocaei* Phocæans + -AN.] **A.** *sb.* A native or inhabitant of the ancient city of Phocæa, the most northern of the Ionian cities on the west coast of Asia Minor.

1600 HOLLAND tr. *Livy's Romane Hist.* XXXVIII. 1007 The Phocæans had both their owne lands restored unto them.., and also libertie to live under their auncient lawes. **1784** W. MITFORD *Hist. Greece* I. vii. 297 The Phocæans, hard pressed, obtained a truce for a day. **1797** *Encycl. Brit.* XIV. 613/1 The Phocaeans were expert mariners. **1899** R. MUNRO *Prehistoric Scotl.* i. 2 At a subsequent date (600 B.C.) the Phocæans founded Massilia. **1909** W. W. FOWLER *Social Life at Rome* i. 9 At a later time of deep depression Horace could fancifully suggest that the Romans should leave their ancient home like the Phocaeans of old. **1962** J. M. COOK *Greeks in Ionia & East* iv. 59 Phocaea lacked good arable land... But the Phocaeans had the benefit of a magnificent harbour.

B. *adj.* Of or relating to Phocæa or its inhabitants.

1614 A. GORGES tr. *Lucan's Pharsalia* v. 168 And to Massilians (Cæsars spoyle) They freely gave the Phocean soyle. **1797** *Encycl. Brit.* XIV. 613/2 The Massilienses, a Phocaean colony, interposed, and with much difficulty, assuaged the anger of the senate. **1929** CARY & WARMINGTON *Anc. Explorers* ii. 22 The last stage of the Phocaean track was marked by a colony at Maenace. **1957** E. HYAMS *Speaking Garden* 163 Italy and France could have had wine and vines from one or both of two sources: Phœnician.., or Greek, by way of the Phocaean colony in Marseilles. **1966** G. E. BEAN *Aegean Turkey* v. 119 The Phocaean adventurers arrived hoping to establish a city.

Phocian (fōᵘ·siăn), *sb.* and *a.* Also 5 **Phocean,** 6 **Phocayan.** [f. Gr. Φωκί-ς the place-name Phocis, or L. *Phocii* Phocians + -AN.] **A.** *sb.* A native or inhabitant of the ancient region of Phocis in central Greece.

a **1490** J. SKELTON tr. *Diodorus Siculus' Bibliotheca Historica* (1956) I. I. 57 In Boecia the streme callyd Cifissus that cometh fro the Phoceans [*Note*] MS.: Thophoceans. **1567** A. GOLDING tr. *Ovid's Metamorphoses* XI. 141 Commes ronning thither all in haste and almost out of breth Anætor the Phocayan who was Pelyes herdman. **1612** SELDEN *Illustr. Drayton's Poly-olb.* x. 168 A colony of Phocians. **1774** GOLDSMITH *Grecian Hist.* II. ii. 55 The first cause of the rupture, (which was afterwards called the Sacred War) arose from the Phocians having ploughed up a piece of ground belonging to the temple of Apollo at Delphos. **1797** *Encycl. Brit.* XIV. 615/1 The Phocians afterwards formed themselves into a commonwealth. **1845** *Encycl. Metrop.* IX. 617/2 The Amphictyonic council..found themselves induced to impose on the Phocians a heavy fine for their impiety. **1951** J. B. BURY *Hist. Greece* (ed. 3) ix. 357 At the same time the Phocians entered into the alliance of Athens. **1967** H. W. PARKE *Oracles of Zeus* vii. 139 The Phocians had just occupied the Delphic sanctuary. **1968** V. EHRENBERG *From Solon to Socrates* 419 The Phocians heard the rustling of the leaves under the feet of the Persians before they could see them.

B. *adj.* Of or relating to Phocis or its inhabitants.

1614 A. GORGES tr. *Lucan's Pharsalia* v. 174 A garland greene of Laurell dight, With Phocian vaile of lawne pure white. **1774** GOLDSMITH *Grecian Hist.* II. ii. 72 Philip.. went on, according to his agreement with the Thebans, to put an end to the Phocian war. **1790** W. MITFORD *Hist. Greece* II. xiv. 160 Not only Delphi was again brought under Lacedæmonian influence, but the Phocian people were gained to the Lacedæmonian interest. **1845** *Encycl. Metrop.* IX. 618/2 Philomelus, the Phocian general, was succeeded by Onomarchus. **1911** *Encycl. Brit.* XXI. 448/2 The Dorian population of Delphi constantly strove to establish its independence and about 590 B.C. induced a coalition of Greek states to proclaim a 'Sacred War' and free the oracle from Phocian supervision. **1970** *Oxf. Classical Dict.* (ed. 2) 943/2 The *Second Sacred War* was precipitated by a Phocian seizure of Delphi.

phocid. Add to etym. after *phōca*: adopted as the name of a genus by Linnæus in his *Systema Naturæ* (ed. 10, 1758) I. 37. Also as *adj.*, of or pertaining to the family Phocidæ; (examples). **phocine** *a.* (later example).

1880 J. A. ALLEN *Hist. N. Amer. Pinnipeds* (U.S. Geol. Survey Misc. Publ. No. 12) 421 All the Phocids or Earless Seals known to systematic writers were referred to the common seal. *Ibid.* 470 Some supposed Phocine remains were described. *Ibid.* 740 It [*sc.* the hooded seal] is commonly described as the most courageous and combative of the Phocids. **1930** A. B. HOWELL *Aquatic Mammals* ii. 34 The otariids have descended from the bears and the phocids from the otters. *Ibid.* xi. 283 No great significance can be attached to details of the phocid tarsal bones. **1958** V. B. SCHEFFER *Seals, Sea Lions & Walruses* v. 87 Thirteen genera of phocids are recognized. **1970** *Sci. Jrnl.* Apr. 69/2 The so-called 'true' or phocid seals (which lack external ears and have small pectoral flippers) are not such rapid swimmers but can dive for longer times. **1976** H. L. GUNDERSON *Mammalogy* v. 122 The otariids and the phocids may have a common ancestor.

phocomelia (fōᵘkomī·liă). *Med.* Also **phokomelia.** [mod.L., f. Gr. φώκ-η seal + -o + μέλ-ος a limb + -IA¹.] A congenital defect of the limbs (see quot. 1892).

1892 F. P. FOSTER *Med. Dict.* IV. 2567/2 *Phocomelia*, a monstrosity in which one or both of the hands or feet, or all four of those members, or rudimentary semblances of them, are attached to the trunk like flippers, with little or no intervening structures. **1932** H. CUMMINS in *Practitioners Libr. Med. & Surg.* I. i. 20 In phocomelia the extremity is abbreviated, through reduction or absence of the proximal and intermediate segments, the hands and feet approaching normal. **1947** *Arch. Path.* XLIV. 521 The majority of the homozygous Creeper embryos die on the fourth day... Those which survive have phokomelia. **1968** *Brit. Med. Bull.* XXIV. 207/1 The demonstration of an association between phocomelia and thalidomide. **1974** *Jrnl. Embryol. & Exper. Morphol.* XXXI. 732 Embryos showing almost the complete absence of humerus, radius, and ulna, described previously as phocomelia. **1978** *Sci. Amer.* Oct. 130/3 The drug thalidomide could cause phocomelia..in a fetus when it was taken by a pregnant woman.

Hence **phocome·lic** *a.*, exhibiting or characteristic of phocomelia; also *ellipt.* as *sb.*

1942 *Jrnl. Exper. Zool.* LXXXIX. 104 These transplants differentiated into 'phocomelic' limbs. **1947** *Arch. Path.* XLIV. 521 In eyes of homozygous Creeper embryos transplanted to the flanks of normal embryos colobomas develop similar to those of phokomelic embryos. **1959** *Jrnl. Exper. Zool.* CXLII. 635 The lethal period of phocomelics. **1962** *Lancet* 1 Dec. 1155/2 No firm rule should guide schooling for phocomelic children. **1978** *Time* 20 Feb. 69/3 Children who are born legless or armless, their limbs amputated by a tangled umbilical cord, are sometimes hard to tell from true phocomelics, or seal-children, with vestigial hands and feet attached directly to the torso.

Phœbe¹. Restrict *poet.* to sense in Dict. and add: **2.** *attrib.* and *Comb.*, as **Phœbe lamp** *N. Amer. Hist.* (see quots. 1935 and 1970).

1935 *Colony of Connecticut* (Conn. Board Educ.) (Senate Doc. 53, 74th Congr., 1st Sess.) 15 Phoebe lamps: .. These were similar to Betty lamps in shape... Some had double wicks from a nose on either side. **1970** G. PAYTON *Webster's Dict. Proper Names* 525/2 *Phoebe lamp*, American pioneers' name for a primitive tallow-and-wick lamp of the type used down the ages, e.g. by the Ancient Greeks. **1972** F. VAN W. MASON *Roads to Liberty* 182 Betty..lit a Phoebe lamp with a splinter from the fire.

phœbe². Add: Also **phebe.** Substitute for def.: A small North American flycatcher of the genus *Sayornis*, esp. *S. phœbe*, which is common in the eastern part of the continent. (Earlier and later examples.)

1700 J. GREEN *Jrnl.* 4 Mar. In *Essex Inst. Hist. Coll.* (1866) VIII. 216 Cloudy & rainy. heard a Phebe and other birds sing. **1782** 'J. H. ST. JOHN DE CRÈVECŒUR' *Lett. from Amer. Farmer* ii. 40 That [*sc.* a nest] of a swallow was affixed in the corner next to the house; that of a phebe in the other. **1947** E. B. WHITE *Lett.* (1976) 284, I haven't been doing much of anything—just..watching phoebes through binoculars, and mixing drinks. **1961** O. L. AUSTIN *Birds of World* (1962) 209/1 Another flycatcher that announces itself is the Phoebe, the pert olive-grey bird that plasters its mud and moss nest under bridges over country streams.

Phœnician, *sb.* **2.** (Further examples.)

1836 N. WISEMAN *Twelve Lect. on Connexion betw. Sci. & Revealed Relig.* I. i. 53 Cadiz, or *Gadir*, as it was originally called, must no longer signify, as the word does graphically in Phenician, *the island* or *peninsula.* **1861** *Dublin Rev.* Feb. 400 Joseph Scaliger demonstrated that the well-known passage of the Pœnulus of Plautus was a fragment of genuine Phœnician. **1948** E. POUND *Pisan Cantos* (1949) lxxix. 76 'Prepare to go on a journey.' Or to count sheep in Phoenician. **1965** *Illustr. London News* 13 Feb. 22/3 Three thin rectangular sheets of gold leaf... One of them is inscribed in Phoenician, the other two in Etruscan.

phœnix¹, phenix. Add: **5.** (*a*) *phœnix riddle*; also passing into adj. (= phœnix-like; as of a phœnix), as *phœnix-birth, -fuel, -life, -moon, -pyre, -resurrection, -tinder, -world.*

1946 R. CAMPBELL *Talking Bronco* 69 The proud Alcazar caught the fire Which gave that splendour phoenix-birth. **1977** *Listener* 10 Nov. 617/1 His radio ballads, combining actuality voices, music and sound effects were a phoenix birth at a dark hour. **1936** R. CAMPBELL *Mithraic Emblems* 50 True phoenix-fuel whom no burning mars. *a* **1957** —— tr. *Quevedo's On Lisi's Golden Hair* in *Coll. Poems* (1960) III. 83 Out of their ash to fan new phoenix-lives. **1934** L. B. LYON *White Hare* 29 The phoenix moon with molten breast. **1930** R. CAMPBELL *Adamastor* 78 And now from the wet earth reborn, All Africa his phoenix pyre. **1963** L. TRILLING in N. Frye *Romanticism Reconsidered* 88 When he [*sc.* Keats] is 'consumed in the fire', they will contrive his Phoenix-resurrection. *a* **1631** DONNE *Canonization* in *Poems* (1633) 203 The Phoenix ridle hath more wit By us, we two being one, are it. **1939** R. CAMPBELL *Flowering Rifle* III. 74 So their black chaos is but welcome fuel And phoenix-tinder to this fierce renewal. **1944** W. TEMPLE *Let.* 22 Feb. (1963) 147 The reforms necessary for the arising of that brave new phoenix-world on which we have set our hearts.

phokomelia, var. *PHOCOMELIA.

Pholey, var. *PEULH *sb.* and *a.*

phon (fǫn). [a. G. *phon* (H. Barkhausen 1926, in *Zeitschr. für techn. Physik* VII. 601/1), f. Gr. φωνή sound.] A unit of loudness (strictly, loudness level), defined so that the loudness in phons of any sound is numerically equal to the intensity in decibels of a pure 1000 Hz tone judged to be equally loud. Formerly = *DECIBEL.

1932 *B.B.C. Techn. Tables & Gloss.* 63/2 Two noises may be compared in strength in sensation units or phons by comparing the attenuations necessary to reduce each to the threshold of audibility. **1932** *Engineering* 9 Sept. 314/3 For quantitative measurements we turn to a unit called the decibel. [*Note*] Called the 'phon' in Germany. **1935** *Sunday Times* 13 Oct. 18/3 Now a machine exists which measures units of noise in 'phons', and no vehicle will be allowed after a certain date to make more than 90 phons of noise at a speed of 30 m.p.h. **1937** A. H. DAVIS *Noise* iv. 46 Originally a 'phon' had been used in Germany as a four-fold power ratio. Later it was employed as an equivalent of the decibel. *Ibid.*, Limitation of the decibel to intensity ratios and the phon to loudness scales has been adoped by the British Standards Institution. **1942** *Wireless World* June 132/2 The magnitude of these upper intensity levels in terms of loudness can be expressed by writing phons for decibels, since they are equal, in the range here considered. **1959** G. R. PARTRIDGE *Princ. Electronic Instruments* xvi. 303 A loudness of 70 phons requires 80 db intensity at 70 cycles. **1962** A. NISBETT *Technique Sound Studio* 264 Phons equal decibels at 1000 c/s, and at other frequencies are related to this scale by contours of equal loudness. **1963** JERRARD & MCNEILL *Dict. Sci. Units* 104 The loudness of a jet aircraft engine is about 140 phon, whereas the noise of a steam railway locomotive is less than 100 phon. **1974** *Daily Colonist* (Victoria, B.C.) 22 Nov. 16/5 Tokyo metropolitan government standards set permissible noise levels at 40 phon (sound measurement) in the morning and evening and at 45 phon during the day.

phonæstheme (fōᵘ·nĕsþīm). *Linguistics.* Also **phonaestheme, phonestheme.** [f. PHONE *sb.*¹ + ÆSTH(ETIC *a.* and *sb.* + *-EME.] A phoneme or group of phonemes with recognizable semantic associations due to recurrent appearance in words of similar meaning.

1930 J. R. FIRTH *Speech* vi. 50 The *slack* etymeme belongs to a much bigger group of habits we may call the *sl* phonæstheme. *Ibid.* vi. 53 The habit background of *wirl*..probably includes the *tw* and *irl*, *-url* phonæsthemes. **1946** *Word* II. 83 Phonestheme is defined as a phoneme or cluster of phonemes shared by a group of words which also have in common some element of meaning or function, tho [*sic*] the words may be etymologically unrelated. **1957** *Gen. Linguistics* II. 55 Previous studies have erred in attempting to separate the long consonant phonesthemes from the other phonesthemes of the language. **1969** *Language* XLV. 284 The term 'phonaestheme' has been used, but it seems to mean different things for those who have used it. **1972** M. L. Samuels *Linguistic Evol.* iii. 46 The phonaestheme /sl-/ may be assigned the values 'slippery' or 'falling' in *slide, slip, slime, slush*..; and it may also be assigned the closely related values 'inactive', 'degenerate' or 'morally worthless' in *slow, sloth, sleep(y), slumber, slack, slouch,* [etc.]. **1974** *Amer. Speech 1971* XLVI. 129 The word-initiating segments *sn-* and *sl-* (as in *snit* and *slit*), which, because they are not readily identifiable as morphemes or other grammatical units, are often referred to as 'phonesthemes'. **1977** *Word 1972* XXVIII. 305 Phonesthemes are considered to have meaning through their occurrence in words of a particular meaning.

Hence **phonæsthesia** (fōᵘnēsþī·siă, -ziă) [*Æsthesia], **phonæsthesis** (fōᵘnēsþī·sis, -zis) [Æsthesis], sound symbolism; the use of phonæsthemes; **phonæsthetic** (fōᵘnēsþe·tik) [Æsthetic *a.*] *a.*, of or pertaining to phonæsthemes; **phonæsthe·tically** *adv.*

1930 J. R. Firth *Speech* vi. 52 The phonæsthetic habits..are much more than 'blends'..and are of general importance in speech. *Ibid.* 54 Play on phonæsthetic habits gives much of the pleasure of alliteration, assonance, and rhyme. **1950** *Archivum Linguisticum* II. 97 Phonaesthesia or sound symbolism. **1965** *Language* XLI. 347 Morphophonemics, phonesthesis, and paralanguage she wholly ignores. **1971** *Archivum Linguisticum* New Ser. II. 43 Some verbs, for example, do not occur without aspectival..or directional..extension; *shamble*, for instance, requires the 'complementation' of *off, on, up, down, across*, etc., a fact to which its phonaesthetic overtones of *amble, shuffle*,.. may or may not relate. **1972** M. L. Samuels *Linguistic Evol.* iii. 48 The growth of phonaesthetic patterns is of importance as a special type of linguistic change. *Ibid.* xiii. 161 In some verbs where a short vowel had been developed phonetically, it was phonaesthetically suited for the expression of point-action. **1977** *Maledicta* Summer 65 (*heading*) Phonesthesis and scatology.

phonation. Add: Also *spec.* the process or act of producing voice (Voice *sb.* 1 g). (Further examples.)

1931 *Musical Times* Jan. 18/2 The simplest act of speech involves the co-ordination of three very complicated sets of muscles: those of inspiration and expiration; those of phonation (the intra- and extra-laryngeal muscles); and those of articulation. **1935** *Jrnl. Mental Sci.* LXXXI. 837 The muscles of respiration, phonation, and articulation. **1956** J. Whatmough *Language* ix. 157 It [*sc.* language] is now articulated (i.e. jointed) phonation, though originally simple and reflex. **1959** E. Pulgram *Introd. Spectrogr. of Speech* iv. 43 Many experiments have been performed..to measure subglottic pressure during phonation. *Ibid.* xviii. 140 *Fig. 30* illustrates four phonations of the vowel [i]. **1962** A. C. Gimson *Introd. Pronunc. Eng.* ii. 9 The action of the vocal cords which is most characteristically a function of speech consists in their role as a *vibrator* set in motion by lung air—the production of *voice*, or *phonation*. **1964** J. C. Catford in D. Abercrombie et al. *Daniel Jones* 28 Various components of speech-sound pronunciation, including phonation-types. **1970** *Language* LXVI. 313 The human larynx is so constructed that the fundamental frequency of phonation is a function of both the transglottal air pressure drop and the tensions of the laryngeal muscles. **1976** *Canad. Jrnl. Linguistics* XXI. i. 118 A most informative explanation of air-stream mechanisms and phonation times, including voice-onset-time.

Hence **phona·tional** *a.*, = Phonatory *a.*

1939 L. H. Gray *Foundations of Lang.* i. 5 Persons whose phonational and auditory apparatus are normal. *Ibid.* ii. 18 This condition..is the auditory counterpart of the pathological forms of the phonational soliloquy. **1947** *Word* III. 2 The phonational act..gives rise, in the hearer, to an acoustic image which is distinct from the physical sound.

phone, *sb.*[1] Add: (Earlier and later examples.) Also = *Allophone.

a **1866** J. Grote in *Jrnl. Philol.* (1872) IV. 55 When I mean words as sounded I shall use the term *phone* (like *zone*, φωνή, ζώνη). **1924** H. E. Palmer *Gram. Spoken Eng.* i. 1 A phone may be a simple sound, such as [f]..or it may be an intimate combination of simple sounds, such as [tʃ]... On the other hand, sounds such as non-significant glides are not phones. **1942** *Language* XVIII. 8 A phone is a member of a phoneme. **1950** *Ibid.* XXVI. 90 In the latter meaning, the term 'phone' is a shorter equivalent of 'allophone'. **1957** [see *Allophone]. **1959** E. Pulgram *Introd. Spectrogr. of Speech* xix. 145 All those phones, that is, events of articulation, which are linguistically identifiable with one another though not acoustically identical with one another, belong to the same class, which we call phoneme. **1961** W. R. Brain *Speech Disorders* 9 A phone is the name for a single isolable sound made in the course of speech by a speaker. **1964** [see *Allophone]. **1971** D. Crystal *Linguistics* iv. 178 The term 'phoneme' had been used in the nineteenth century, but it referred to a unit of sound (that is, a phonetic unit—what we would usually these days call a 'phone'), and not to any abstract notion involving contrastivity. **1975** L. M. Hyman *Phonology* 8 The units of phonetic description are sound segments (or *phones*), while the units of phonological description are *phonemes*. **1976** *Language* LII. 317 In the early distinctive-feature model, phonemes are redundancy-free versions of the corresponding phones.

2. Special Combs., as **phone-type,** a speech-sound considered as a purely phonetic event.

1961 F. W. Householder in Saporta & Bastian *Psycholinguistics* 19/2 Biuniqueness..means that to any given phone-type in a given environment there must correspond only one possible phoneme, and to any phoneme in a given string there must correspond only one phone-type. *Ibid.*, It is frequently simpler and more elegant to have units so chosen that a given phone-type in one environment may be an allophone of one such phoneme, but in another an allophone (or the only allophone) of a different one. **1965** R. L. Kellogg in Bessinger & Creed *Medieval & Linguistic Stud.* 67 We might add that the fixed formula is to the abstract pattern of which it is a manifestation as the phonetype is to the phoneme.

phone (fōᵘn), *sb.*[2] Add: Also **'phone. 1.** (Further examples.) Also, a telephone call.

1922 J. Reith *Diary* 6 Nov. (1975) i. 87 Many phones from the National Liberal Headquarters asking for speakers. **1942** Berrey & Van den Bark *Amer. Thes. Slang* § 808/5 *Telephone call*,.. phone. **1943** J. Thurber *Men, Women & Dogs* 105 If I called the wrong number, why did you answer the phone? **1949** N. Spain *Death goes on Skis* iii. viii. 186 For an intellectual she seems to be quite illiterate..saying 'phone for telephone. **1960** K. Amis *Take Girl like You* xxvii. 306 A telephone was ringing... 'Jenny, someone on the phone for you.' **1974** M. Spark *Abbess of Crewe* i. 30 Mildred treads softly over the green carpet..and answers the phone. **1976** *Daily Tel.* 13 Nov. 17/3 A 19-year-old youth made an estimated 1,000 fraudulent telephone calls..and was on the 'phone for 63 hours.

2. Colloq. abbrev. of *ear-phone* s.v. *Ear *sb.*[1] 16, *Head-phone. Usu. *pl.*

1913 *Wireless World* May p. v (Advt.), High resistance 'phones. **1926** R. Macaulay *Lett. to Sister* (1964) 27 No longer..does the husband have to sit in the evenings and listen to inanities from his wife..; he and she can now both sit in silence, with the phones on their ears. **1948** *Electronics* Aug. 88/2 A person listening to sound through a binaural system has the illusion that the sound originates in the room rather than in the phones. **1962** A. Nisbett *Technique Sound Studio* 256 Some degree of control of volume can be achieved with telephone receiver type phones by moving them a little off the ear. **1970** J. Earl *Tuners & Amplifiers* iii. 76 It also pays for the amplifier etc. to carry a loudspeaker switch to cut the speakers when listening on 'phones. **1977** *Rolling Stone* 24 Mar. 79/2 Played back over the phones part of the system..the sense of space and realism of sound is unbelievable.

3. *attrib.* and *Comb.* (in sense 1), as *phone bell, call, caller, exchange* [*Exchange *sb.* 10 c], *installation, jack* [*Jack *sb.*[1] 15 d], *kiosk, message, operator* [*Operator 5 a], *order, receiver, wire*; *phone-answering* ppl. adj. and vbl. sb.; **phone bill,** an account for the cost of hire of a telephone and of calls made from it; **phone book,** a telephone directory; **phone booth, box,** a box-like kiosk in which a public telephone is installed; **phone number,** the identifying call-number assigned to a telephone, line, etc.; **phone patch** [*Patch *sb.*[1] 6 f], a temporary radio link made to establish communication between a radio operator and a telephone user; **phone-tapping** *vbl. sb.* = **telephone-tapping* vbl. sb.; so **phone-tap** *sb.* and *v. trans.*; **phone-tapper.**

1976 *New Yorker* 23 Feb. 30/2 The Silverstein headquarters..has a phone-answering machine that will deliver a tape-recorded message from the candidate. **1977** E. Ambler *Send no more Roses* v. 111 Business accommodation services which provided mail-forwarding and phone-answering. **1937** M. Allingham *Dancers in Mourning* xxv. 300 The 'phone bell alone was silent and everyone..was waiting for that shrill, familiar alarum. **1950** T. Walsh *Nightmare in Manhattan* (1951) iii. 86 The phone bell had given him a first intuitive comprehension. **1972** 'H. Howard' *Nice Day for Funeral* v. 82 It was the phone bell that prodded me awake. **1965** N. Freeling *Criminal Conversation* i. ix. 63 Sounds like your night for collecting a phone bill. Why not do this in the office—then you wouldn't have to pay for them? **1972** *Guardian* 24 Aug. 20/5 He..had to sell his camera to pay his phone bill. **1925** F. Scott Fitzgerald *Great Gatsby* (1926) ix. 198 Meyer Wolfsheim's name wasn't in the phone book. **1963** 'E. McBain' *Ten Plus One* (1964) ii. 23 Carella picked up the phone book and looked up the number. **1977** G. Scott *Hot Pursuit* vi. 56 Give us a ring. We're in the phone book. **1927** W. R. James *Cow Country* vii. 199 He came back in the hotel and went in the phone-booth and there he proceeded to call them up, one after another. **1952** S. Kauffmann *Philanderer* (1953) xi. 186 He had to fret away three or four minutes outside the busy phone booth. **1976** 'M. Delving' *China Expert* vi. 72 One of the phone booths across the street. **1954** M. Stewart *Madam, will you Talk?* xvi. 127 There's a phone box a mile or so along the road. **1968** 'R. Raine' *Night of Hawk* xiv. 75 Henry made an anonymous call to the police from a near-by phone box. **1977** D. James *Spy at Evening* ix. 61, I left the hot-house atmosphere of the phone box. **1929** D. Hammett *Dain Curse* (1930) xv. 166, I wasn't convinced that my phone call was of any importance. **1959** N. Mailer *Advts. for Myself* (1961) 198 About a month later, this letter was followed by a phone call. **1977** W. McIlvanney *Laidlaw* xxxviii. 179 There had been a funny phone-call for me when I got back.. checking that I could still be reached here. **1972** J. Philips *Vanishing Senator* (1973) ii. ii. 67 Some of those letter writers and phone callers might be willing to help. **1939** R. Campbell *Flowering Rifle* v. 131 In the munition-works, the 'phone-exchange. **1924** H. Crane *Let.* 29 Jan. (1965) 173 Putting down money for a phone installation. **1946** P. Carter in *Astounding Sci. Fict.* Aug. 49/2 He pulled out the phone jack, plugged it in elsewhere. **1973** *New Yorker* 14 Apr. 32/2 It will have phone jacks, so the staff will be able to answer queries without going back to a central desk. **1976** M. Machlin *Pipeline* ii. 31 There was a phone jack just behind his chair in the dining room. **1968** R. V. Beste *Repeat Instructions* xv. 154 He..went out to the phone kiosk and arranged to see King. **1977** G. Markstein *Chance Awakening* lv. 169 That silent street corner by the 'phone kiosk. **1930** M. Allingham *Mystery Mile* xxiii. 217 He overheard a 'phone message. **1955** *Times* 23 July 4/4 Norbury knows nothing about this. In all the 'phone messages I have impersonated him. **1978** M. Birmingham *Sleep in Ditch* 117 He has no address now, just gets a phone message once a month telling him where to send a money order. **1911** G. Stratton-Porter *Harvester* xvii. 393, I want Dr. Frank Harmon... I don't know the 'phone number. **1960** C. MacInnes *Mr. Love & Justice* 51 I'm a seaman... I've got stacks of foreign phone numbers in my diary. **1971** R. Rendell *One Across* vi. 51 One day he'd walk in..to find the lot of them gone and a note on the table with a Chigwell phone number on it. **1973** E. Hyams *Final Agenda* vi. 82 Call that phone operator and make sure she knows English, French or German. **1932** *New Yorker* 4 June 7 (Advt.), Mail and phone orders filled. **1975** *Ibid.* 20 Oct. 38/1 Martin finds phone-patch relays difficult; he forgets to say 'Over' when it's time for his father to speak, and he can't get used to the idea of not being able to interrupt. **1976** Perkowski & Stral *Joy of CB* xii. 142 A phone patch links a mobile rig to a land line through a base station. The mobile user contacts a base station with a phone patch. The base station operator then places the call, and connects the land line to the base's rig, placing the telephone handset in a cradle device or otherwise establishing an electrical connection with the rig. Once the connection is made, a voice-operated transmitter relay or a switch operated by the base station operator transmits the voice of the land-line party through the base transmitter. **1970** R. Lowell *Notebk.* 191 He's trying to part his hair on the phone-receiver. **1959** *Daily Tel.* 10 Dec. 1/8 Motion of censure on 'phone tap'. **1966** 'G. Black' *You want to die, Johnny?* vii. 130, I didn't think he'd known about the phone tap. **1973** J. Wainwright *Pride of Pigs* 169 No sweat, princess. They don't phone-tap too easily in this country, so we're okay. **1976** W. Greatorex *Crossover* 193 Meade had just told him of the phone-tap report. *Ibid.* 191 She said it in Russian knowing that the phone tappers would have to send the tape to the linguists. **1957** *Times* 12 June 9/5 We are thus, it seems, to have phone-tapping on suspicion. **1976** R. Perry *One Good Death* v. 68 Phone-tapping had become one of the essential props of modern government. **1951** Phone wire [see *Phonevision]. **1964** L. Deighton *Funeral in Berlin* xxxvii. 227 Two G.P.O. phone wires had been brought in..and could be attached to the handset. **1978** R. Hill *Pinch of Snuff* v. 44 The phone wire was cut.

phone (fōᵘn), *v. colloq.* Also **'phone.** [Abbrev. Telephone *v.*] **a.** *trans.* = Telephone *v.* 1 c. Also const. *up* and with advbs.

1889 *Telephone* 1 Feb. 56/1 The expression 'I telephoned So-and-So', is often rendered 'I phoned So-and-So.' **1900,** **1901** [in Dict.]. **1909** *Daily Chron.* 10 Dec. 7/2 He could 'phone up Scotland Yard for a detective. **1910** 'W. Lawton' *Boy Aviators on Secret Service* ii. 22 Wait a minute while I go to 'phone my resignation. **1962** I. Murdoch *Unofficial Rose* xvi. 159 Was it really necessary to phone me? **1963** L. Deighton *Horse under Water* xliv. 181, I couldn't have Charley phoning up the police. **1974** A. Ross *Bradford Business* 146 [He] offered me a tuppenny piece... 'Take it,' he said testily, 'and phone her back.' **1976** *Daily Tel.* 2 Nov. 17/2, I 'phoned Paris, and explained what had happened.

b. *intr.* = Telephone *v.* 1 a. Freq. with particle as phrasal verb or with advbs.

1925 F. Scott Fitzgerald *Great Gatsby* viii. 193 Gatsby..left word with the butler that if any one phoned word was to be brought to him at the pool. **1926** E. O'Neill *Great God Brown* iii. i. 73 Shall I phone for a doctor? **1927** *Rev. Eng. Stud.* Oct. 433 Phrases like *e.g. phone through* and *come across* no more represent 'degradation' than do *give up, give in, ring up, send off, think out*. **1932** T. S. Eliot *Sweeney Agonistes* 13 She says will you ring up on Monday... All right, Monday you'll phone through. **1946** E. O'Neill *Iceman Cometh* iv. 231 It was Hickman himself phoned in and said we'd find him here around two. **1955** *Times* 11 June 4/3 If you will 'phone for an appointment when the strike is over, I will try to fix a convenient date. **1959** I. Jefferies *Thirteen Days* viii. 105 He phoned around and..within an hour I had a motley but effective army. **1962** L. Deighton *Ipcress File* xvii. 101 Phone in this time tomorrow. **1972** C. Fremlin *Appointment with Yesterday* vii. 56 You've hardly been in the place two hours, and she has to phone up. **1977** F. Branston *Up & Coming Man* xiii. 147 Andy and I took turns to phone round... Nearly every news desk called back.

c. *trans.* Const. *in.* = Telephone *v.* 1 b.

1972 *Radio Times* 28 Dec. 53/1 Parents phone in their questions on the three Rs to Miss Edith Biggs..and Ronald Palmer. **1973** *Black World* Mar. 15 (*caption*) Tell him to hurry up—I've got to phone in a bomb threat. **1977** *Gay News* 24 Mar. 20/1 We have many flats and bedsits with understanding landlords available now. (Landlords, please phone in your vacancies!)

Hence **pho·ner** = Telephoner; also *phoner-in*; **pho·ning** *vbl. sb.* = Telephoning *vbl. sb.*

1908 *Daily Chron.* 10 Aug. 7/1 So graphically had Enid done her bit of descriptive 'phoning that he was under no illusions as to what he had to do. **1942** Berrey & Van den Bark *Amer. Thes. Slang* § 808/3 *Telephoner*, phoner. **1957** 'A. Garve' *Narrow Search* iii. 80 I'll have to do a bit of phoning in the morning. **1972** *Listener* 27 Jan. 124/1 An excellent job of training phoners to that programme by classic reward and punishment methods. **1975** *Times* 26 Apr. 8/5 Radio 4's *The Forbidden Subject* was..a phone-in... The phoners-in, with two exceptions, were all women. **1977** *Belfast Tel.* 24 Jan. 3/5, I hope that phoners-in are not an accurate cross-section of the population. **1977** *Times* 12 Feb. 12/1 This is your late night phone-in programme... Mr Jenkins..says you phoners are ignorant, pathetic and moronic.

-phone (fōᵘn), ad. Gr. φων-ή voice, φῶν-ος sounding. **1.** Used in the sense 'sound' in the names of various instruments (scientific and musical), as GRAMOPHONE, MAGNETOPHONE, MEGAPHONE, *MELLOPHONE, MICROPHONE, *VIBRAPHONE.

2. Used in the sense 'speaker of' or '-speaking' in the formation of nouns and adjectives from Latinate combining forms of names of peoples and languages, as *Anglophone, Bulgarophone,* *FRANCOPHONE *sb.* and *a.*, *Turcophone.*

1900 Anglophone [see *FRANCOPHONE *sb.* and *a.*]. **1937** Bulgarophone [see *EXARCHIST]. **1977** *Times Lit. Suppl.* 18 Mar. 295/5 His description of Turcophones in Iran (of whom he is one) as a 'nation'.

phone [reak, var. *PHONE PHREAK *sb.* and *v.*

phone-in (fōᵘ·nin). [f. phr. *to phone in,* f. *PHONE *v.* + IN *adv.*; for sense 1 see also *-IN[3].] **1.** A protest in the form of mass telephone calls of complaint.

1967 *New Statesman* 17 Mar. 356/3 In San Francisco.. Mrs. Whitehouse has perfected the phone-in. **1973** *Times* 8 Feb. 6/1 Actress Dame Peggy Ashcroft plans to join a massive 'phone-in'..aimed at jamming the switchboard of the Department of the Environment.

2. A 'live broadcast' radio or television programme during which listeners telephone the studios to ask questions or express their views. Also, this type of broadcasting. Also *attrib.*

1968 *Time* 29 Mar. 16 He proposed reducing transit fares for San Franciscans over 65 to 5¢ and, on a subsequent TV 'phone-in', said he would try to get buses closer to the curb at pickup. **1971** *Listener* 30 Dec. 915 One of the most exciting potentials this year has been the phone-in. **1972** *Guardian* 13 Mar. 11/2 Duke Miller of St Petersburg asked him on a phone-in show..how voters were expected to forgive him for his part in the escalation of the war. **1974** *Daily Tel.* 30 Jan. 13/1 The arrival of phone-in conveniently coincided with the fashion for public 'participation and access' in broadcasting. *Ibid.* 11 Feb. 5/5 There will be a daily 55-minute 'phone-in' on Radio 4 to 13 leading figures from the main Parties. **1977** B. PYM *Quartet in Autumn* xiv. 118 Listening to a phone-in programme on the radio she had heard a question about holidays for people on their own.

phonematic (fōᵘnėmæ·tik), *a.* and *sb. Linguistics.* [f. Gr. φωνήματ- stem of φώνημα sound made + -IC.] **A.** *adj.* **a.** = *PHONEMIC *a.*

1936 *Proc. 2nd Internat. Congr. Phonetic Sci.* 50, Z, considered as a phonematic unit, has a value very different from the value it has when considered as a grammatical unit. **1936** *Language* XII. 311 Professor J. Vendryes..announced that competent legal opinion indicated the desirability of organizing separate national groups..for the advancement of phonological (phonematic) studies. **1949** *Trans. Philol. Soc. 1948* 129 We may speak of a five-vowel or seven-vowel phonematic system. **1952** A. COHEN *Phonemes of Eng.* i. 12 An implication is the replacing of one phoneme by another under definite phonematic conditions. **1956** J. WHATMOUGH *Language* v. 84 The strange words that a language adopts are adapted to its own phonematic and other patterns. **1958** *Proc. 8th Internat. Congr. Linguists* 763 Quechua, a language with a phonematic system of 3 vowels only. **1962** P. S. RAY in F. A. Rice *Study of Role of Second Lang. in Asia, Afr. & Lat. Amer.* 101 Even one who prefers to write 'phonemic' rather than 'phonematic' is doing a bit of prescriptive intervention. **1977** A. SHERIDAN tr. *Lacan's Écrits* iv. 126 The elements of the language (*langue*) at its different levels, from the phonematic pair of oppositions to the compound expressions to disengage the stable forms of which is the task of the most modern research.

b. In 'prosodic analysis', designating a segmental element of vowel or consonant features which combines with prosodies (see *PROSODY 2*).

1949 [see *PROSODY 2*]. **1964** R. H. ROBINS *Gen. Linguistics* iv. 159 *Prosodic analysis,* as it is usually called, is a brief title for a method of phonological analysis that employs as fundamental concepts two types of element, not reducible to a common type, prosodies and phonematic units. **1968** J. LYONS *Introd. Theoret. Linguistics* iii. 129 The sequence of phonematic units constitutes the segmental 'infrastructure' of the word, whereas the prosodies form its 'superstructure'. **1972** HARTMANN & STORK *Dict. Lang. & Linguistics* 187/2 At first sight phonematic units and prosodies seem to be equivalent to segmental and suprasegmental phonemes of the traditional phonemic analysis, but in a prosodic analysis, features which would be assigned to segmental phonemes in a phonemic analysis are sometimes assigned to prosodies, e.g. such features as palatalisation, nasalisation or lip rounding.

B. *sb. pl.* [see -IC 2.] **a.** Phonemics.

1936 *Proc. 2nd Internat. Congr. Phonetic Sci.* 49 By *phonematics* I understand a science which treats phonemes exclusively as elements of language. **1939** L. H. GRAY *Foundations of Lang.* iii. 62 The phoneme..is..regarded as..a point in the linguistic (grammatical) pattern ('phonematics'). **1949** *Amer. Speech* XXIV. 54 It [*sc.* the term *phonemics*] has replaced in American usage the terms *phonology* and *phonematics.* **1953** W. J. ENTWISTLE *Aspects of Lang.* iii. 94 The chapter-heading *Sounds* is used to cover..questions affecting the pattern (phonematics, not the ungrammatical 'phonemics'). **1960** J. VACHEK *Dict. de Linguistique de l'École de Prague* 61/1 *Phonologie* (Phonemics; less frequently, Phonematics/Phonology..). **1961** *Brno Studies in English* III. 55 In his well-known compendium of diachronistic phonematics, ..A. Martinet rightly insists on the presence in any language of two opposed forces. **1964** E. PALMER tr. *Martinet's Elem. Gen. Linguistics* i. 30 They form a chapter entitled prosody distinct from phonematics, which treats of the units of the second articulation.

b. That part of 'prosodic analysis' which deals with phonematic units.

1971 *Archivum Linguisticum* New Ser. II. 68 'Phonematics' (a term which bears only etymological resemblance to 'phonemics').

So **phonema·tically** *adv.*, in relation to phonemes or phonematic units; according to the theory of phonemes or phonematic units; **phonematiza·tion,** advancement from allophonic to phonemic status; **phonemato·logy,** phonemics, phonematics (sense *a).

1949 *Archivum Linguisticum* I. 41 There is, further, a well-known problem in English phonematology. **1950** *Ibid.* II. 181 The book [*sc.* D. Jones's *The Phoneme*] is.. essentially a hand-book of phonematology. **1951** S. ULLMANN *Princ. Semantics* ii. 47 With reference to phonematically constituted word-engrams. **1956** *Trans. Philol. Soc.* 34 There are distinctions in the written language which are phonematically motivated. **1956** J. WHATMOUGH *Language* i. 11 If you hear *pwivate* 'private' from a few speakers [w] is a variant, phonematically speaking, of [r]. **1958** A. S. C. Ross *Etym.* i. 24 Phonematology has one extremely practical application, that is, the construction of alphabets for languages hitherto unwritten. **1962** *Canad. Jrnl. Linguistics* VII. ii. 79 When such adaptations become loanwords, however, they sometimes are phonematically homophonous with native words. **1964** *Amer. Speech* XXXIX. 70 Phonematization of /ü/ in eastern dialects of Basque resulted from changes [o] → [u], [u] → [ü]. **1971** *Archivum Linguisticum* New Ser. II. 85 With the exception of the 3 sg. general tense ending.., all the endings can be analyzed phonematically as the same for each person regardless of tense. **1977** *Word 1972* XXVIII. 250 Automatic nasalization of vowels in contact with nasal consonants is a general characteristic of languages in which there are no phonematically nasalized vowels. **1978** *Language* LIV. 231 Phonematization relies on the examination of contrasts.

phoneme. Restrict *rare* to sense in Dict. and add: Now with pronunc. (fōᵘ·nīm). **1. b.** A phonological unit of language that cannot be analysed into smaller linear units and that in any particular language is realized in non-contrastive variants. Also *attrib.* See *ALLOPHONE.

Although its exact nature is disputed, and the existence of an abstract phonemic level (and hence the abstract phoneme as a constituent of morphemes) is controversial in phonological theory, the phoneme remains a standard taxonomic unit in the description of speech. The phoneme of structural linguistics is sometimes called the *autonomous* or *taxonomic phoneme* by generative phonologists, and distinguished from the *systematic phoneme.*

1896 R. J. LLOYD in *Die Neueren Sprachen* III. 615 There are a few of these terms which the author [*sc.* J. Baudouin de Courtenay] still thinks valuable and retains. One of these is the term *phoneme,* invented by Kruszewski. .. I take it that the various sounds which are accepted as identical by any speaking community are one *phoneme,* though they may differ considerably in actual sound. **1917** D. JONES in *Trans. Philol. Soc. 1917–20* (1932) 99 The Sechuana language appears to contain twenty-eight phonemes, i.e. twenty-eight sounds or small families of sounds which are capable of distinguishing one word from another. **1928** I. C. WARD *Phonetics of English* 61 Care must be taken not to confuse the various members of the phoneme with the different pronunciations heard from different people. The latter may be termed *variant pronunciations*; the different sounds constituting a phoneme occur in *one* person's pronunciation. **1933** L. BLOOMFIELD *Language* v. 80 The phonemes of a language are not sounds, but merely features of sound which the speakers have been trained to produce and recognize in the current of actual speech-sound. **1935** G. K. ZIPF *Psycho-Biol. of Lang.* i. 20 A word may consist of a single phoneme..or it may represent a phoneme-sequence of considerable magnitude. **1936** *Amer. Speech* XI. 109 When in a given language two sounds occur in the same phonological conditions and neither of the two sounds may be substituted for the other without changing the meanings of the words, the two sounds are capable of differentiating two words and are realizations of two different phonemes. **1939** L. H. GRAY *Foundations of Lang.* iii. 61 The exact nature of the phoneme is disputed. It is variously regarded as 1) a mere grouping of sounds..2) as a point in the psychological pattern (..Sapir and the Prague School); or 3) as a point in the linguistic (grammatical) pattern. **1950** D. JONES *Phoneme* ii. 10 A phoneme is a family of sounds in a given language which are related in character and are used in such a way that no one member ever occurs in a word in the same phonetic context as any other member. *Ibid.* 12 Some phoneticians have employed the term phoneme to mean anything that may serve to effect a minimal distinction..between one word and another. **1958** K. AMIS *I like it Here* i. 6 To cut Sinatra off in mid-phoneme was not such uproarious fun. **1961** W. R. BRAIN *Speech Disorders* i. 10 The letters of an alphabet transcribe with more or less precision the phonemes of speech, of which standard English has about thirty-two. **1962** A. C. GIMSON *Introd. Pronunc. Eng.* v. 44 It is possible to establish the phonemes of a language by means of a process of commutation or the discovery of *minimal pairs,* i.e. pairs of words which are different in respect of only one sound segment. **1968** R. T. HARMS *Introd. Phonological Theory* 14 In this presentation the term 'phoneme' is used in the sense of systematic phoneme. **1968** *Language* XLIV. 723 A consideration of the taxonomic phonemes of a language may..be of use in determining the orthographic peculiarities of a scribe. **1970** F. BRENGELMAN *Eng. Lang.* p. viii, The concept of the phoneme is used here because the author believes that the English spelling system can be described best with reference to a segmented representation. **1971** D. CRYSTAL *Linguistics* iv. 183, I have spent so much space on the phoneme concept because of its unequalled status as a concept for organizing people's thinking in the first half of this century. **1975** *Jrnl. Linguistics* XI. 1. 40 This phonologically motivated structure is given in terms of systematic phonemes. **1975** L. M. HYMAN *Phonology* 82 It would be worthwhile to briefly examine the kind of argument given against what has come to be known as the 'autonomous' or 'taxonomic' phoneme. **1977** *Language* LIII. 241 He rejects the orthodox neo-Bloomfieldian motto 'Once a phoneme, always a phoneme'. **1978** *Ibid.* LIV. 173 With one of his main points (that the taxonomic phoneme is not dead), I would naturally agree.

2. *Psychol.* [ad. G. *phonem* (C. Wernicke *Grundriss der Psychiatrie* (1896) II. 126).] (See quot. 1911.)

1905 A. J. ROSANOFF tr. *J. Rogues de Fursac's Man. Psychiatry* i. ii. 44 Phonemes (the verbal auditory hallucinations of Séglas) have..a special significance, inasmuch as they consist of 'words representing ideas'. **1911** W. A. WHITE *Outl. Psychiatry* (ed. 3) vi. 47 The more complicated hallucinations which are conceived by the patient to be 'voices'—verbal auditory hallucinations—are known as phonemes.

Hence **pho:nemiza·tion** = **phonemicization.*

1959 E. PULGRAM *Introd. Spectrogr. of Speech* xi. 78 (*heading*) Phonemization. **1960** *Amer. Speech* XXXV. 218 The Middle English phonemization of the Old English allophones of the postdental spirant.

phonemic (fonī·mik), *a.* and *sb. Linguistics.* [f. *PHONEME 1 b + -IC.] **A.** *adj.* Of or pertaining to phonemes or phoneme theory; analysable in terms of phoneme theory.

1933 L. BLOOMFIELD *Language* v. 85 The laboratory phonetician usually knows, from other sources, the phonemic character of the speech-sounds he is studying. **1933** E. SAPIR in *Encycl. Social Sci.* IX. 155/2 Not only are all languages phonetic in character; they are also 'phonemic'. *Ibid.*, Languages differ very widely in their phonemic structure. **1942** BLOCH & TRAGER *Outl. Linguistic Analysis* ii. 36 For nearly all purposes it is better to use a *Phonemic* transcription, which represents the sounds of the language organized into a few dozen distinctive units. **1947** E. H. STURTEVANT *Introd. Linguistic Sci.* xi. 122 No scholar has a right to demand.. that we discard the familiar and convenient word *phonemic* for the reason that if an ancient Greek had coined an adjective from the noun *phōnēma* he would probably have produced *phōnēmaticos.* **1950** R. A. HALL *Linguistics & Your Lang.* vi. 96 Then, when he has gotten the best phonetic and phonemic analysis possible for the language he is working on, the linguist is ready to go ahead and analyze its grammatical structure. **1950** D. JONES *Phoneme* ii. 9 The more general use of the term [*sc.* language] covers the speech of people who speak in ways differing considerably from each other—who use different sounds, or who use sounds in such a way that a different phonemic classification is called for. **1955** *Q. Jrnl. Speech* XLI. 254/1 The variation is non-significant, of course, but belongs on the morphemic rather than the phonemic level. **1958** *Times Lit. Suppl.* 13 June 334/5 The earlier lessons, which offer a phonemic transcription with the ordinary spelling of words, ask for hard work both in the classroom and outside. **1964** M. A. K. HALLIDAY et al. *Linguistic Sci.* 300 Transformation grammar has thus taken over, but reversed, the hierarchical relation among levels that is characteristic of phonemic–morphemic theory. **1965** CHOMSKY & HALLE in *Jrnl. Linguistics* I. 98 We suggested the names *systematic phonemic and systematic phonetic* for these levels of representation. *Ibid.*, We called these *taxonomic phonemic theories* so as to bring out their reliance on procedures of segmentation and classification and their essential independence of 'higher levels'. **1967** *Ibid.* III. 3 The advantage of introducing a systematic phonemic level is that it enables us to generalize the phonological description beyond the limits of one speaker. *Ibid.* 25 Given a taxonomic phonemic system, it can always be 'translated' into distinctive feature terms. **1968** CHOMSKY & HALLE *Sound Pattern Eng.* 11 We will make no further mention of 'phonemic analysis' or 'phonemes' in this study and will also avoid terms such as 'morphophonemic' which imply the existence of a phonemic level. **1968** P. M. POSTAL *Aspects Phonol. Theory* iv. 90 It is natural to view autonomous phonemic representations as being exactly like phonetic representations except that certain 'redundant', 'predictable', 'noncontrastive', etc., features of the phonetic representation have been eliminated. **1971** *Language* XLVII. 503 Some of the theoretical discussions dealing with generative phonology have been concerned with demonstrating that a *phonemic* level of representation could not be motivated within phonological descriptions and that the only relevant levels were the morphophonemic and the phonetic. **1972** M. L. SAMUELS *Linguistic Evol.* iii. 31 Phonemic shifts are..often extensive and involve a large part of the vocalic or consonantal systems. **1973** A. H. SOMMERSTEIN *Sound Pattern Anc. Greek* i. 2 An autonomous phonemic description of classical Attic. **1974** tr. *Wertheim's Evolution & Revolution* iii. 74 At present China could lead the way in introducing 'phonemic spelling'.

B. *sb. pl.* (const. as *sing.*) [See -IC 2.] The study of phonemes and phoneme systems; phonemic analysis.

1936 W. F. TWADDELL in *Language* XII. 294 These [t]s, in the practice of every writer on phonemics, are considered as one phoneme. **1940** *Ibid.* XVI. 247 In English we have the incomparably superior term *phonemics,* which leaves us free to use *phonology* in its old and widely established usage as a general term for all the phenomena concerned with the production and use of sounds. **1949** G. L. TRAGER *Field of Linguistics* 5 The description of the phonemes of a language, and of their occurrence and arrangement, is the phonemics of that language. **1952** A. COHEN *Phonemes of Eng.* i. 4 Phonemics..must concern itself with studying distinctive oppositions existing between sounds or sound features. **1957** N. CHOMSKY *Syntactic Struct.* i. 11 A linguistic level, such as phonemics, morphology, phrase structure, is essentially a set of descriptive devices that are made available for the construction of grammars. **1964** —— *Current Issues in Linguistic Theory* 74 It seems necessary to conclude that systematic phonemics and systematic phonetics are the only two levels of representation that appear in structural descriptions provided by the phonological component. *Ibid.* 75 Let us coin the term 'taxonomic phonemics' to refer to this body of doctrine. **1968** P. M. POSTAL *Aspects Phonol. Theory* iv. 89 Traditional autonomous phonemics was able to maintain a natural relation between phonetic and phonemic organization in the absence of any universal rules of the type required by systematic phonemics simply because its phonemic and phonetic systems were so close. **1968** *Language* XLIV. 723 The concept of taxonomic phonemics in linguistics..arose in part as a result of traditional orthographic practices. **1972** M. L. SAMUELS *Linguistic Evol.* i. 4 There has been justifiable insistence, in recent decades, that graphetics and graphemics must in the first instance be studied separately, before their relationship with phonetics and phonemics can be considered. **1975** L. M. HYMAN *Phonology* 82 Systematic phonemics..goes beyond proposing an abstract morphophonemic level.

Hence **phone·mically** *adv.*, with regard to phonemes; in terms of phoneme theory; **phonemicist** (fonī·misist), a specialist in or student of phonemics.

1934 *Language* X. 123 If a set of phonemic elements only occur together, they constitute a phonemically unitary complex; thus, the stop and the aspiration in English initial f. **1935** *Ibid.* XI. 97 The technique of analyzing phonemically the structure of a dialect. **1942** BLOCH & TRAGER *Outl. Linguistic Analysis* iii. 46 If a language has only five vowel phonemes, the best way of representing them phonemically—regardless of their phonetic nature—is by the letters *a, e, i, o, u*. *Ibid.* 49 The affricates in *chain* and *Jane* are treated by many phonemicists as unit phonemes, often written /č, ǰ/. **1951** *Language* XXVII. 219 The English affricates *ch* and *j* have generally been regarded as double sounds by phoneticians; but phonemicists have vacillated back and forth. **1966** N. CHOMSKY in *Current Trends in Linguistics* III. 49 The notion of 'complementary distribution'.. permits analyses that are not acceptable to the taxonomic phonemicist (or to anyone else). **1967** C. L. WRENN *Word & Symbol* 5 The multifarious and phonemically divergent regional dialects spoken in the Chinese Republic. **1975** *Amer. Speech 1972* XLVII. 246 We list all the contrasting ways of beginning an English stressed syllable (in utterance-initial) that every classical phonemicist would have agreed must be a 'cluster' rather than a single 'segmental phoneme'.

phonemicize (fonī·misəiz), *v. Linguistics.* [f. *PHONEMIC *a.* and *sb.* + -IZE.] **1.** *trans.* To classify, analyse, or describe in terms of phoneme theory. Also *absol.* or *intr.*

1940 *Language* XVI. 354 Lorimer made no attempt to phonemicize here. **1951** *Ibid.* XXVII. 340 We are forced to phonemicize as /patadak/ and /padatak/. **1953** *Ibid.* XXIX. 81 It is difficult to explain to a communications engineer what we mean by phonemicizing. **1953** *Internat. Jrnl. Amer. Linguistics* XIX. 166 Each long nucleus has been phonemicized as a cluster of two phonemes. **1957** *Publ. Amer. Dial. Soc. 1956* XXVI. 46 In these terms learning the sound system of another language could be described as a phonemicizing of diaphones. **1960** *Amer. Speech* XXXV. 234 Would lead to a rapid collection of vast body of contemporary speech by uniform procedures yielding easily phonemicized data. **1960** Z. S. HARRIS *Structural Linguistics* vii. 71 Such is the question of how to phonemicize long vowels. **1963** F. G. LOUNSBURY in S. Koch *Psychol.* VI. 567 This process is called 'phonemicizing' the transcription. **1965** *Language* XLI. 480 It would seem possible to phonemicize [nt·] as a cluster *nht. **1972** H. KURATH *Stud. Area Linguistics* 31 When two or more plans of phonemicizing the data seem feasible, preference is given to the one that facilitates the comparison of the dialects. **1975** *Amer. Speech 1972* XLVII. 240 Does 'phonemically different' imply 'different phonemes'? This is a catch-question I put to my students at a certain point as they are learning to 'phonemicize'. **1976** *Language* LII. 307 Once the surface redundancy has been lost, the forms which violate the lost constraint may be phonemicized as having the impermissible sequence.

2. a. *trans.* To advance from allophonic to phonemic status.

1972 M. L. SAMUELS *Linguistic Evol.* iii. 35 The split of one phoneme into two is clearly mechanical in origin: what are at first allophones of a single phoneme are 'phonemicised', or attain the status of separate phonemes. **1976** *Archivum Linguisticum* VII. 184 One could postulate..another old series of labials and dentals which changed *u to o and which then joined with the other dentals and labials, 'phonemicizing' the old allophone.

b. *intr.* To attain phonemic status.

1973 J. M. ANDERSON *Struct. Aspects Lang. Change* 142 The reduction of the labiovelars allowed these fronted allophones to phonemicize.

Hence **phone:miciza·tion**, (*a*) classification into phonemes, description in terms of phoneme theory; phonemic transcription or an instance of this; (*b*) development from allophonic to phonemic status.

1942 C. F. HOCKETT in *Language* XVIII. 20 Grammatical work is carried on, of course, in cases where phonological information is incomplete... But many of the gaps and ambiguities in such grammar have their source directly in the lack of complete phonemicization. **1948** —— in *Ibid.* XXIV. 123 He should make his phonemic interpretation clearly recognizable..by including for every form cited..a possible phonemicization. **1957** *Trans. Philol. Soc.* 22 There is no difficulty about the phonemicization, since there is contrast in such pairs as ker..and kar,..pe·r-..and pa·r. **1972** M. L. SAMUELS *Linguistic Evol.* iii. 37 It is still possible to argue that what appears to us as coincidental is in fact nothing of the sort, and that the functional pressures towards phonemicisation are more important than the mechanical. **1975** N. CHOMSKY *Logical Struct. Linguistic Theory* vi. 163 There is no need to think of phonemes as literally occurring in sequence, each with its distinctive physical properties, in the stream of speech. Any attempt to maintain such a view will lead to very artificial phonemicization.

phone phreak (fōᵘ·n frīk), *sb.* and *v.* Also **phone freak.** [f. *PHONE *sb.*² + *PHREAK *sb.* and *v.*] **A.** *sb.* (See quot. 1972².)

1972 *Daily Tel.* 15 Apr. 3 The Post Office are trying to break up a ring of 'phone phreaks' who are cheating the telephone service. *Ibid.* 9 Oct. 13/6 Detectives and Post Office officials investigating 'phone phreaks'—people who make free telephone calls all over the world by using an electronic device—raided a flat in Hammersmith. **1973** *New Scientist* 5 Apr. 23 The challenge of beating the telephone system to get long distance calls for the 2p price of a local call is not restricted to the so-called 'phonephreaks'. **1973** *Guardian* 1 June 10/1 Andy first heard the news of Edie Sedgwick's death from a fellow phone-freak on the West Coast. **1976** 'O. BLEECK' *No Questions Asked* xiv. 156 He's a monster phone freak... He knows all the phone company jargon.

B. *v. intr.* To use an electronic device to make telephone calls without payment. Only as **pho·ne phreaking** *vbl. sb.*

1972 *Daily Tel.* 9 Oct. 13/6 Scotland Yard and the Post Office have been investigating phone phreaking since January. **1973** *Guardian* 22 Jan. 5/3 'Phone phreaking' —making free calls with the use of electronic gadgets— is a growing international problem. **1974** W. GARNER *Big enough Wreath* xiii. 197 'What is it? Some kind of calculator?' Bip began with technicalities, ended with a complete exposition of phone freaking. **1976** *Computing Europe* 2 Sept. 5/2 There are a lot of Post Office employees and the recent 'phone phreaking' cases have shown that at least some of them can have criminal inclinations.

phonetic, *a.* Add: **2. c.** *Comb.* (= PHONETICO-), as *phonetic-linguistic, -morphological, -phonemic, -semantic* adjs.

1961 L. F. BROSNAHAN *Sounds of Language* v. 101 The criteria..are of phonetic-linguistic nature. **1921** E. SAPIR *Language* viii. 185 In other words, on this particular point it took German at least three hundred years to catch up with a phonetic-morphological drift that had long been under way in English. **1966** M. PEI *Gloss. Linguistic Terminol.* p. ix, A specialist in descriptive linguistics and phonetic-phonemic description. **1931** L. BLOOMFIELD in *Language* VII. 205 Some linguistic forms bear no partial phonetic-semantic resemblance to other forms. **1966** M. PEI *Gloss. Linguistic Terminol.* 204 There is a partial phonetic-semantic resemblance in all forms containing a particular phonestheme.

B. *sb.* An element of a Chinese character which is itself the character for another word, adopted as part of the new character because of the words' identity or similarity of sound. = *PRIMITIVE *sb.* 6.

1842 J.-M. CALLERY *Encycl. Chinese Lang.* 3 The phonetic is in itself one of the characters of primitive formation, which cannot be annexed to any of the preceding orders, and which must therefore be looked on as indivisible. **1874** S. W. WILLIAMS *Syllabic Dict. Chinese Lang.* p. lvi/1 That part of a character which is not the radical, has no name among the Chinese, but foreigners have termed it the *primitive* or *phonetic*. **1907** W. HILLIER *Chinese Lang.* i. 6 It is possible..by learning these phonetics, or primitives as they are sometimes called, to make a very close guess at the sound of any Chinese character. **1948** R. A. D. FORREST *Chinese Lang.* ii. 38 In many cases the connection of the phonetic element, whether in sound or shape, with a word still existing independently, or with the same phonetic in other characters, has become much more obscure through changes in sound or in written form. **1968** P. KRATOCHVÍL *Chinese Lang. Today* v. 151 The former was the borrowed phonetic..and the latter the radical added as an indication that the whole form was borrowed and denoting something connected with manual action. **1973** *Sci. Amer.* Feb. 54/2 There are characters that are not pronounced like their phonetic, often for reasons of historical change.

Hence **phonetician** (further examples); **phoneticism** (examples); (*b*) phonetic spelling; an example of this; (*c*) use of the criterion of phonetic similarity to determine the phonemes of a language; **phoneticist,** (*b*) = *phonetician*; **phoneticization** (-səizē·ʃən), phonetic spelling; an example of this; (greater) correlation of symbol and sound (in a writing system).

1933 L. BLOOMFIELD *Language* v. 75 The phonetician can study either the sound-producing movements of the speaker..or the resulting sound-waves. **1964** D. ABERCROMBIE *Eng. Phonetic Texts* 14 It is not, in the nature of things, possible for a 'standard' mode of transcription of English, suitable for all purposes and all audiences, to be agreed on by phoneticians. **1975** *Amer. Speech 1973* XLVIII. 111 To do so is perfectly sound phonemically, though Phoneticians use a modified symbol (with hook) for the *r*-colored vowel. **1885** G. L. GOMME *Hist. T. Hickathrift* p. iv, There are too few phoneticisms and dialect words to make it probable that the print in the Pepysian collection is the one directly derived from popular tradition. **1938** *Better English* Nov. 44/1 Phoneticism is not a noble progressive movement. It is only an annoying attack on a superior language which will never give up its proud fundamental structure. **1939** *Amer. Speech* XIV. 148/1 The author condemns phoneticism as contrary to language structure. **1952** A. COHEN *Phonemes of Eng.* ii. 24 The same objection to phoneticism in phonemic analysis can be raised against Trubetzkoy's handling of the problem how to decide whether we have to do with one or more phonemes. **1977** *Daily Tel.* 24 Feb. 18 Probably the most bizarre example of phoneticism I have ever come across was an 11-year-old's spelling of the word 'usual'—'yousyouall'. **1932** G. K. ZIPF *Sel. Stud. Princ. Relative Frequency in Lang.* 1. 4 All phoneticists agree about it; it is at once evident to anyone listening to a native of Peking speak. **1935** —— *Psycho-Biol. of Lang.* (1936) 96 The highly important work of the experimental phoneticist. **1954** PEI & GAYNOR *Dict. Linguistics* 168 *Phoneticist*, a person who studies or is skilled in phonetics. **1915** *Spectator* 21 Aug. 235/1 To turn the Russian genitive plural termination into 'off', as is sometimes done, is to go in for an exaggerated phoneticization. **1959** *Brno Studies in English* I. 14 Voices demanding reforms of traditional spellings usually regard 'phoneticization' of such spellings as the only effective remedy. **1970** *Language* XLVI. 959 For a primitive logographic system can develop into a full system of writing only if it succeeds in attaching to a sign a phonetic value independent of the meaning which this sign has as a 'word'; this is phoneticization. **1975** *Daily Colonist* (Victoria, B.C.) 22 Aug. 5/1 The common direction of phoneticization for all written languages in the world must be followed.

phonetico-. Add: **phonetico-ideogra·phic** *a.*, of or pertaining to ideographs having a phonetic value; **phonetico-phone·mic** *a.*, employing both phonetic and phonemic criteria.

1891 C. LOMBROSO *Man of Genius* III. ii. 189 This mixture of letters, hieroglyphics, and figurative signs, constitutes a kind of writing recalling the phonetico-ideographic stage through which primitive peoples (the Mexicans and Chinese certainly) passed, before the discovery of alphabetic writing. **1952** A. COHEN *Phonemes of Eng.* iv. 85 M. Swadesh..distinguished between the two categories [*sc.* long and short vowels] on a mixed phonetico-phonemic basis.

phonetics, *sb. pl.* Add: Now usu. restricted to the study of speech sounds as physical phenomena, and distinguished from *phonology*. (Further examples.)

1924 O. JESPERSEN *Philos. Gram.* ii. 35 It would, perhaps, be advisable to restrict the word 'phonetics' to universal or general phonetics and to use the word *phonology* of the phenomena peculiar to a particular language (e.g. 'English Phonology'), but this question of terminology is not very important. Some writers would discriminate between the two words by using 'phonetics' of descriptive (static), and 'phonology' of historical (dynamic) 'lautlehre', but this terminology is reversed by some (de Saussure, Sechehaye). **1937** J. ORR tr. *Iordan's Introd. Romance Linguistics* 287 Generally, 'phonetics' is used to designate the physiology of sounds, and 'phonology' the history of sounds. Saussure reverses the use of the two terms. **1953** J. B. CARROLL *Study of Lang.* ii. 25 General phonetics, in fact, is virtually a science in its own right, with two chief branches, *motor phonetics* (or *articulatory phonetics*) and *acoustic phonetics*. **1962** A. C. GIMSON *Introd. Pronunc. Eng.* I. i. 2 Our primary concern will be the production, transmission, and reception of the sounds of English—in other words, the *phonetics* of English. **1964** P. STREVENS in D. Abercrombie et al. *Daniel Jones* 120 There seem to be two main kinds of use of the term... 'Phonetics' for some means 'making sounds', while for others it refers to a component of the discipline of linguistics. **1970** G. C. LEPSCHY *Survey Structural Linguistics* iii. 59 Trubeckoj mentions a number of linguists who preceded him..in distinguishing between sound and phoneme, and thus between phonetics and phonology.

phonetist. 1. Delete 'a phonologist' from def.

phonetization. Add: Also = *PHONETICIZATION. (Further examples.)

1952 I. J. GELB *Study of Writing* iii. 66 The need for indicating grammatical elements was of no great importance in the origin of phonetization. *Ibid.* 67 Phonetization..arose from the need to express words and sounds which could not be adequately indicated by pictures or combinations of pictures. **1976** *Visible Language* Winter 20 Phonetization of the alphabet and other writing systems is a province of orthoepy.

Phonevision (fōᵘ·nviʒən). [f. *PHONE *v.* + VISION *sb.*] The proprietary name of a pay-as-you-view television system (see quot. 1951).

1950 *N.Y. Times* 10 Feb. 42/3 The Zenith plan involves the use of so-called 'phonevision'. By this method, special programs are televised in scrambled form so they cannot be picked up on any ordinary receiver. A subscriber, however, can receive the program by telephoning his local exchange and establishing a connection between the television set and the telephone system. **1951** *Life* 5 Feb. 43/1 Phonevision, or PV,.. offers a way of bringing movies straight into the family parlor. Under PV, a television set owner learns that a certain movie is being scheduled at a given time. It goes out over a TV channel and shows on his set as a confusion of blurs. If he calls the Phonevision switchboard, an unscrambling device on his set, which is hooked up to the phone wires, is turned on and the blurs become a clear picture. **1953** *Official Gaz.* (U.S. Patent Office) 8 Sept. 281 Zenith Radio Corporation—Phonevision. For Radio and Television Transmitting and Receiving Operations and Parts Thereof. Claims use since June 13, 1947. **1975** *New Trends in Cable Television* (Com Quest Corp.) iii. 51 Zenith Radio Corporation developed the first commercially used pay-television/broadcasting equipment under the tradename

Phonevision. **1978** *CATV Market* (Frost & Sullivan, Inc.) iv. 65 This Phonevision service was offered under a special permit from the F.C.C.

phoney, phony (fōu·ni), *a.* and *sb.* orig. *U.S.* [Of uncertain origin.] **A.** *adj.* That has no real existence; fake, sham, counterfeit; false; insincere.

1900 Ade *More Fables* 138 'Overlook all the Phoney Acting by the Little Lady, Bud,' said the Fireman. **1916** C. Sandburg *Chicago Poems* 63 You're only shoving out a phoney imitation of the goods. **1924** *Scribner's Mag.* Aug. 204/1 Hope you didn't mind when I gave you a phony name. **1933** *Sun* (Baltimore) 2 May 8/7 A line of argument..which I have long suspected is quite phoney. **1935** C. Day Lewis *Time to Dance* 60 You funny old, phoney old bogus man! **1949** *Chicago Tribune* 17 Sept. III. 18/3 Stop moaning about that phony blonde and her phonier lawsuit. **1951** J. D. Salinger *Catcher in Rye* ii. 19 They had this headmaster, Mr. Haas, that was the phoniest bastard I ever met in my life. **1956** W. Slim *Defeat into Victory* ix. 181 On our side we had the somewhat phoney propaganda that followed Wingate's raid and the more solid influence of General Giffard's character. **1970** *Daily Tel.* 10 Nov. 12/4 Like his singing, he is gentlemanly: no long hair, exaggerated clothes, or phony emotionalism. **1974** E. Brawley *Rap* (1975) I. x. 169 My parole officer violated me on another phony beef.

b. Special collocations, as **phoney war**, the period of comparative inaction at the beginning of the war of 1939–45; also *transf.* and *fig.*; so *phoney peace.*

1940 *Times* 19 Apr. 7/2 When the Allies seemed slow at getting off the mark,..it was whispered to the American public that this was a 'phoney' war. **1940** *Manch. Guardian Weekly* 12 July 25 During the eight months of the 'phoney' war everything seemed to be running smoothly between Great Britain and France. **1940** G. Greene *Lost Childhood* (1951) 115 This can never at any time have been a 'phoney' war: from the word go, these famous individuals were on the job. **1944** J. S. Huxley *On Living in Revolution* 9 The inadequacy of British production and planning during the Chamberlain 'phony war' period. **1947** *Partisan Rev.* XIV. 347 Within each state the necessary psychological atmosphere would be kept up by complete severance from the outer world, and by a continuous phony war against rival states. **1954** N. Coward *Future Indefinite* III. 114 The Germans invaded Norway and Denmark... The reaction of the Americans to the break-up of what they themselves had christened the 'Phoney War' would be interesting to observe. **1960** O. Manning *Great Fortune* xv. 199 This sort of phoney war can't go on for ever. Someone's going to move some time and we'll be trapped. **1964** *New Statesman* 4 Sept. 301/2 The electoral phoney war is almost over. **1972** *Daily Tel.* 29 Mar. 2/6 A curious 'phoney war' atmosphere has pervaded Ulster during the past few days. **1977** *Guardian Weekly* 27 Feb. 9/2 At this stage of phoney peace, the Americans are being careful to say or do nothing that might alarm Israel.

B. as *sb.* A phoney person or thing.

1902 C. L. Cullen *Six Ex-Tank Tales* 99 If youse tinks f'r a minnit dat youse is goin' t' git away wit' a phony like dat wit' me youse is got hay in y'r hemp, dat's wot. **1916** *San Francisco Call & Post* 28 Nov. 12 'Don't Mr. Jenks know a lot of people?' 'They're all phonies.' **1938** E. Ambler *Cause for Alarm* xi. 170 He's probably gone to the trouble to check the first lot and found that they're phoneys. **1952** S. C. Armstrong *Black-Eyed Stranger* i. 5 Lynch is no international jewel thief. He's a tired old phony. **1958** K. Amis *I like it Here* xvi. 200 The kind of prancing, posturing phoney who'd say he was better than Fielding. **1971** F. Forsyth *Day of Jackal* II. xv. 262 'Leave the others to continue checking the remainder, just in case there is another phoney among the bunch,' instructed Thomas. **1971** S. E. Morison *European Discovery Amer.: Northern Voy.* iii. 79 Adolf Rieth..tells of European false runic inscriptions and other famous phonies, one of which, the 'turkey frieze' in Schleswig Cathedral, pertains to America. **1977** *New Yorker* 27 June 79/1 This simple test—a way of telling the phonies from the truly committed.

Hence **pho·neyness, phoniness**, the state or quality of being phoney; deceitfulness, unreality, insincerity; **pho·nily** *adv.*, in a phoney manner; falsely; insincerely.

1942 Berrey & Van den Bark *Amer. Thes. Slang* §315/1 Fakeness, phoniness. **1947** D. M. Davin *Gorse blooms Pale* 212 You felt a sort of phoneyness in your power. **1949** D. Smith *I capture Castle* ix. 139 Am I just trying to rationalize my phoniness? **1959** *Times Lit. Suppl.* 17 Apr. 224/4 A racket is phoneyness organized. **1961** C. J. Rolo in *Webster* s.v., Phonily flamboyant amours and impossible deeds of derring-do. **1961** W. C. Booth *Rhetoric of Fiction* II. vii. 193 Though attracted by youth and freshness, he can see the phoniness of the American worship of Hollywood's idea of youthfulness. **1976** T. Gifford *Cavanaugh Quest* (1977) iii. 51 Tim didn't have any phoniness about him; he was what we used to call a regular guy. **1976** *Economist* 16 Oct. 15/2 Name another [parliamentary democracy] that could pass through the past 18 months and still have a parliament doing business phonily as usual. **1978** P. McCutchan *Blackmail North* iv. 38 He brightened rather phonily. 'It could have been worse.'

phoney, phony, *v. slang* (chiefly *U.S.*). [f. the adj.] *trans.* and *intr.* To counterfeit, falsify, make *up*. (See also quot. 1950.)

1942 Berrey & Van den Bark *Amer. Thes. Slang* §207/12 *Disguised,..* phonied up. **1950** H. E. Goldin *Dict. Amer. Underworld Lingo* 156/1 *Phony up*, to counterfeit; to set up an impressive front or agency for purposes of swindling; to alter the amount of money indicated on a check; to change the serial number of a stolen bond or commit any similar criminal act; to turn traitor to the underworld. 'I got a chill on (doubt the courage of) this dude we're working with. He might phony up on a drop (under police pressure coincident with arrest).' **1952** *New Yorker* 26 July 43, I ain't phoneying them woids. **1963** 'E. McBain' *Ten plus One* (1964) xv. 173 I'll phony it up, stall him. **1968** 'G. Bagby' *Another Day* iii. 53 He..made no effort to phony up an excuse. **1972** B. F. Conners *Don't embarrass Bureau* (1973) II. 200 It's tough for a cop to stay completely honest... It's like an agent who won't phoney his overtime. **1977** *Daily Tel.* 8 Dec. 3/7 Furs are often not clearly labelled. Cat skins could be passed off as 'bunny'. You can phoney anything up.

phoniatric (fōuniæ·trik), *a. Med.* [f. Gr. φων-ή voice + ἰατρικ-ός of or for a doctor.] Of or pertaining to phoniatrics (logopedics).

1938 *Jrnl. Speech & Hearing Disorders* III. 286 (*heading*) Phoniatric aspects of unilateral recurrent paralysis. **1947** *Folia Phoniatrica* I. 14 Patients often receive wrongly and unsuccessfully treatment for chronic laryngitis, whereas, only phoniatric treatment..is promising. **1960** F. Trojan *Current Probl. Phoniatrics & Logopedics* I. 53 Further research will enable this problem to be solved both from the surgical and the phoniatric point of view.

Hence **phoniatri·cian, phoni·atrist** (fonəi·ătrist), an expert or specialist in phoniatrics; **phonia·trics** *sb. pl.* (const. as *sing.*), **phoni·atry** (fonəi·ătri) = *logopedics *sb. pl.*

1947 *Folia Phoniatrica* I. 5 Phoniatry deals with the.. sciences of the voice, speech and speech training, the problem of the deaf and dumb and musical problems and technique. **1950** *Ibid.* II. 175 Phoniatrics is practically inexistent. *Ibid.* 182 There exists no preparation or control for the Phoniatrist's profession. **1950** S. Potter *Our Language* 186 Ward is more concerned with phoniatry and the rectification of faulty pronunciation in the speech of English children. **1959** *Amer. Speech* XXXIV. 55 Conscientious report on the articulatory organs, functions, and theories as they would interest the phoniatrician rather than the phonetician. **1960** F. Trojan *Current Probl. Phoniatrics & Logopedics* I. 67 The relation of phoniatry to laryngeal surgery has two aspects. *Ibid.*, Surgical operations upon professional voice users should be undertaken by the phoniatrist. **1961** L. F. Brosnahan *Sounds of Language* vi. 144 Speech therapists and phoniatricians. **1962** *Folia Phoniatrica* XIV. 81 If we accept that phoniatrics means the 'medicine and medical art of phonation' it is clear that we limit ourselves to the medical aspects of impaired phonation.

phonic, *a.* (*sb.*) Add: **1.** *phonic wheel* [tr. F. *roue phonique* (P. Lacour 1878, in *Compt. Rend.* LXXXVII. 500)], a toothed disc or rotor of magnetic material which is caused to rotate at a constant speed by an electromagnet energized by alternating, or interrupted direct, current (orig. derived from a tuning fork vibrating against a contact and sustained by another electromagnet); also *phonic motor.*

1878 *Telegraphic Jrnl.* VI. 476/2 M. Paul la Cour has succeeded in causing a phonic wheel to maintain its uniform rate of rotation when acted upon by an accelerating or retarding force of one kilogramme-metre-minute. **1906** T. E. Herbert *Telegraphy* 838 Fig. 493 is a general view of the transmitter. At the back may be seen the rectangular frame of a La Cour phonic wheel motor that drives the transmitter. **1924** *Jrnl. Sci. Instruments* I. 162 By making use of a device known as a phonic motor—invented by the late Lord Rayleigh—a wheel is constrained to rotate at a constant speed controlled by an electromagnetically maintained tuning-fork. **1930** A. B. Wood *Textbk. Sound* II. 129 The phonic motor provides a very convenient and accurate method of determining the frequencies of electrically-maintained forks. **1956** *IRE Trans. Electronic Computers* V. 159/1 The clock frequency is 50 kc, obtained from a phonic wheel on the drum.

2. (Further examples.) *phonic method*, a method of teaching reading by correlating alphabetic symbols and sounds (= *phonics *sb. pl.* 4).

1875 G. C. Mast *Primer of Phonic Method* p. iv, For years it had been his [*sc.* the Author's] wish to introduce in this country the German, or Phonic method of teaching reading and writing simultaneously. **1928** Ward & Roscoe *Approach to Teaching* ix. 110 The Phonic Method..has the undoubted advantage that the children, if properly taught, are from the first not afraid to attack new words. **1954** *Language* (Ministry of Educ.) v. 56 The alphabetic method was superseded generally in British schools by the *phonic* method. **1966** J. Derrick *Teaching Eng. to Immigrants* v. 184 English is not a 'phonic' language—the sounds represented by certain letters or groups of letters do not all fit neatly into readily observed and easily learnt patterns (like those of Italian, or Welsh, for instance). **1968** J. Lyons *Introd. Theoret. Linguistics* ii. 62 Whatever other factors may have influenced the development of human speech, it is clear that phonic substance (that range of sound which can be produced by the human speech organs and falls within the normal range of human hearing) satisfies the conditions of availability and convenience fairly well. **1973** D. Rockey *Phonetic Lexicon* ii. 36 For many years reading theories have been polarised between two extremes—the phonic method and the so-called 'Look-and-Say'. **1976** *Amer. Speech 1974* XLIX. 12 As understood here, a *phonic transcription* includes the broad phonetic transcription presently favored by European phoneticians, the unsystematic simplification of phonetic forms often used by American dialectologists under the term *diaphone*, and the systematic broad phonics of Bloch and Trager.. that is called 'classical phonemics' by generative apologists.

Hence **pho·nically** *adv.*, in respect of vocal sound; in the form of speech sounds.

1959 *Brno Studies in English* I. 12 The spoken norm of language is a system of phonically manifestable language elements. **1962** S. R. Levin *Linguistic Struct. in Poetry* v. 50 The occurrence of phonically or semantically equivalent forms in equivalent positions, either syntagmatically or conventionally defined. **1965** [see *high *a.* 4 b]. **1977** *Word 1972* XXVIII. 310 The values assigned to the sequences may be analyzed with exclusive regard to the semantic qualities associated with these phonically polar vowels.

phonics, *sb. pl.* Delete ? *Obs.* and add: **2.** (Later examples.)

1961 *Amer. Speech* XXXVI. 93 (*title*) Phonemics and phonics in historical phonology. **1976** [see *phonic *a.* (*sb.*) 2].

4. The correlations between sound and symbol in an alphabetic writing system; used *spec.* with reference to a method of teaching reading by associating letters or groups of letters with particular sounds (cf. *phonic method* s.v. *phonic *a.* (*sb.*) 2).

1908 E. B. Huey *Psychol. & Pedagogy of Reading* III. xiv. 280 Too often the line between phonics and reading is not drawn. **1960** J. R. Newton *Reading in your School* iv. 63 Phonics is that part of phonetics which is used in reading and spelling. **1966** K. De Hirsch et al. *Predicting Reading Failure* viii. 82 Five auditorily gifted children who read well had been intensively trained in phonics. **1966** *New Statesman* 30 Dec. 962/3 *Look and Say, Phonics* and *The Sentence Method* are all at the moment acting as smokescreens which obscure a simple fact known to most mothers but few reading research experts. The most important thing in a reading beginner's life is a willing listener. **1973** *Daily Tel.* 10 Apr. 18, I believe that most teachers of remedial reading would agree that more attention to phonics when teaching children to read would be an excellent thing. **1976** *Sci. Amer.* July 8/2 They replaced the teaching of reading by phonics with the 'look-see' method.

phonily, phoniness: see *phoney, phony *a.* and *sb.*

phono-. Add: **pho:no-electroca·rdioscope** *Med.*, an instrument for registering simultaneously the sounds and the electrical changes caused by the heart, or one of these together with the pulse; **phono-lary·ngoscope** (-dʒoskōup), an apparatus for observing the operation of the larynx in the production of speech sounds; so **phonolaryngosco·pic** *a.*; **pho:nophoto·graphy,** photographic recording of the physical parameters of speech or singing; hence **pho:nophotogra·phic** *a.*; **pho:no-photogra·phically** *adv.*; **pho·noreception** *Biol.*, perception of sound by a living organism; hearing; so **pho·noreceptor,** a sensory receptor for sound; † **pho·novision,** a system of television in which the signals were stored on gramophone records to be reproduced at will.

1942 *Lancet* 26 Dec. 759/2 In what he calls by the rather cumbersome name of a phono-electrocardioscope, G. E. Donovan has introduced an instrument which holds out high promise of useful service to the clinician. *Ibid.*, The most obvious application of the phono-electrocardioscope is in the teaching of auscultation. **1943** G. E. Donovan in *Jrnl. Inst. Electr. Engin.* XC. III. 39/1 The present apparatus incorporates a double-beam cathode-ray oscilloscope with a fluorescent screen of long afterglow. This permits the simultaneous direct visual observation of two phenomena such as the phonocardiogram and electrocardiogram, or sphygmogram and phonocardiogram, etc., at the patient's bedside. The amplified heart sounds can be heard at the same time. The instrument is called a phono-electrocardioscope. **1950** *Electronic Engin.* XXII. 90/2 In order to time accurately the events of the cardiac cycle, an electrocardiogram occurring simultaneously should accompany a phonocardiogram, and his [*sc.* Donovan's] apparatus, the phonoelectrocardioscope, is designed on these principles. **1953** L. F. Brosnahan *Some Old Eng. Sound Changes* 11 The production of each of the Dutch vowels, as observed with Russell's 'phono-laryngoscope'. **1934** *Amer. Speech* IX. 226/2 A phonolaryngoscopic examination of the position and function of the various organs of the larynx. **1928** M. Metfessel *Phonophotogr. in Folk Music* 22 All the twists, quavers, trills, breaks in the voice, quick slurs, erratic tempi and other similar features..are..what phonophotography will reveal. *Ibid.* 19 There was no simple ready-made phonophotographic camera, nor had there ever been any studies which required the detailed reading of the sound wave photographs. **1931** T. H. Pear *Voice & Personality* 17 Dr. Milton Metfessel..has recorded 'phonophotographically' the turns..of the 'Jubilee voice' of the negro. **1933** *Brit. Jrnl. Psychol.* Apr. 408 Seashore's claim..that his phonophotographic methods constitute an objective approach to the study of the beautiful,..in the performance of vocal music. **1935** *Amer. Speech* X. 312/2 By means of phonophotography the readings of several distinguished poets were analyzed for pitch, loudness and duration in an effort to solve some of the fundamental problems of verse. **1939** *Ibid.* XIV. 228/1 The application for the first time of phono-photographic technics to study of melody in isolated southern districts of the United States. **1968** P. Oliver *Screening Blues* 10 Phonophotography and voice-prints may give an accurate translation of certain characteristics of the voice in graphic form. **1940** *Biol. Rev.* XV. 108 The substitution of the term 'phonoreception' for hearing evades the real issue. **1960** *Neurology* X. 662/1 Photoreception and phonoreception provide the principal means of association between the individual and his external environment. **1968** D. W. Wood *Princ. Animal Physiol.* ix. 188 Phonoreception is really a specialized case of mechano-reception, and it is not always easy to distinguish between the two. *Ibid.*, It is probably simpler to include vibration reception in phonoreception and to define the latter as the perception of any mechanical disturbance external to the animal that involves regular repetition. **1961** Webster, Phonoreceptor. **1968** D. W. Wood *Princ. Animal Physiol.* ix. 191 The most primitive phonoreceptor in vertebrates is the lateral line organ-system of fishes and a few amphibians. **1927** *Punch* 7 Sept. 253/3 Mr. J. L. Baird, the inventor of television and phonovision, is reported as saying that some faces sound like a gargle. **1935** *Times* 16 May 9/3 The new system of 'Phonovision' demonstrated some years ago in which wax-disk records of television signals were employed in much the same way.

phono (fōᵘ·no), colloq. abbrev. of Phonograph *sb.* (sense 3). Chiefly *U.S.*, exc. as applied to a type of plug (and the corresponding socket) used with audio equipment, in which one conductor is cylindrical and the other is a central prong that extends beyond it. Freq. *attrib.* and in *Comb.*

1948 F. Brown *Dead Ringer* 9 You can play the phono. **1956** C. Fowler *High Fidelity* x. 203 Interconnections to and from preamp-control units are made via so-called 'phono plugs'. *Ibid.*, Hum is almost inevitable when the control unit is switched to the phono channel and the bass tone control is fully advanced. **1970** J. Earl *Tuners & Amplifiers* iii. 70 American 'phono' sockets are commonly used for the tape signals. **1971** *Computers & Humanities* VI. 95 Such multi-media materials as broadsides, films, filmstrips, and phono-records. **1973** *Washington Post* 13 Jan. H7/5 (Advt.), Automatic portable phono. **1975** *Hi-Fi Answers* Feb. 74/3 Some amplifiers do not have a DIN socket for tape recording, there being only phono types. **1975** *Physics Bull.* May 229/1 These can be substituted for permanent magnets in phonocartridges. **1976** *Gramophone* May 1835/1 The controls on the front panel are a large selector knob for phono, tuner, auxiliary, tape 1 and tape 2. [Etc.] **1978** *N.Y. Times* 30 Mar. C10/1 Mounting a phono cartridge in a tone arm.. invariably makes me think I'm in the wrong trade.

phonocardiogram (fōᵘnokā·ɹdiˌogræm). *Med.* [f. Phono- + *cardiogram* s.v. *Cardio-.] A tracing of the sounds made by the heart.

1912 *Heart* IV. 161 In many of our phonocardiograms it is very possible that we should have discovered initial vibrations. **1942** *Lancet* 26 Dec. 759/2 Permanent photographic records can be obtained of the phonocardiogram, electrocardiogram or sphygmogram. **1974** *Physics Bull.* Feb. 70/2 Incompatibility between echo signals and phonocardiograms.

phonocardiograph (fōᵘnokā·ɹdiˌograf). *Med.* [f. Phono- + *cardiograph* s.v. Cardio-.] An apparatus used for registering phonocardiograms.

1926 *Amer. Heart Jrnl.* I. 721 (*caption*) Phonocardiograph record of human heart. **1943** *Jrnl. Inst. Electr. Engin.* XC. III. 43/1 The phonocardiograph employed by Einthoven possessed a simple but crude sort of high-pass acoustic filter. **1977** *Lancet* 19 Mar. 646/1 Records of the beat can be taken with an apex-cardiograph/phonocardiograph transducer attached to a commercial electrocardiograph.

phonocardiography (fōᵘ:nokāɹdiˌǫ·grăfi). *Med.* [f. Phono- + *cardiography* s.v. Cardio-.] The investigation and interpretation by means of a phonocardiograph of the sounds made by the heart.

1921 *Jrnl. Amer. Med. Assoc.* 12 Feb. 434/1 Such a conception will explain a murmur of regurgitation in early systole... The first sound, as has been observed in phonocardiography, is held to be present, but its initial components may be masked by the murmur. **1926** *Amer. Heart Jrnl.* I. 717 (*heading*) Phonocardiography of the human fetus. **1961** *Lancet* 16 Sept. 644/1 Lewis et al. have shown by intracardiac phonocardiography that a similar murmur can be recorded in the main pulmonary artery of all healthy subjects. **1971** *Nature* 25 June 542/3 The basic principles of auscultation and phonocardiography are dealt with in the first chapter.

Hence **pho:nocardio·grapher**, one who operates a phonocardiograph or is expert in phonocardiography; **pho:nocardiogra·phic, -gra·phical** *adjs.*, of, pertaining to, or involving phonocardiography; **pho:nocardiogra·phically** *adv.*

1935 *Amer. Heart Jrnl.* X. 458 We suggest that further phonocardiographic studies be performed along these lines. **1943** *Jrnl. Inst. Electr. Engin.* XC. III. 52/1 Certain frequency components..which are met with in routine phonocardiographical clinical work. **1967** M. E. Tavel *Clin. Phonocardiography* i. 15 The phonocardiographer..is usually presented with a complex array of sounds, murmurs, and pulses. **1973** *Brit. Heart Jrnl.* XXXV. 1276/1 Both major components of the first sound were demonstrated phonocardiographically. **1974** *Circulation* XLIX. 5/2 Phonocardiographers are often faced with the difficult problem of telling the auscultator what he is hearing. *Ibid.* 434/1 We have delineated the phonocardiographic.. characteristics of the mitral prosthesis.

phonofiddle (fōᵘ·nofid'l). *Mus.* Also **Phono-fiddle.** [f. Phono- + Fiddle *sb.*] A type of violin in which the usual body of the instrument is replaced by a mechanism connected with an amplifying horn. Also *attrib.*

1923 *Ashore & Afloat* Aug. (Advt.), Zither Banjos, Houson Phonofiddles, Strohviols, One String Fiddles. **1930** *Stage* 3 Apr. 9/4 A string of merry jokes and just sufficient phono-fiddle work to add to their appeal. **1955** *Oxf. Compan. Mus.* (ed. 9) 995/2 The Phonofiddle is sometimes played with a plectrum. **1977** *Early Music* Apr. 265/3 Susan Baker plays and talks about the.. phonofiddle, [etc.].

phonofilm (fōᵘ·nofilm). *Obs.* exc. *Hist.* Also **Phonofilm.** [f. Phono- + Film *sb.*] A cinema film having a sound-track.

Orig. a proprietary name in the U.S.

1921 *Official Gaz.* (U.S. Patent Office) 8 Nov. 391/2 Phonofilm... Claims use since Jan. 1, 1921. **1922** *Radio Broadcast* Dec. 96 De Forest's Phono-film. **1923** *Weekly Dispatch* 13 May 5 In so far as it eliminates the use of a gramophone..the new phono-film..would appear to mark a decided step forward. **1928** *Manch. Guardian Weekly* 17 Aug. 134/4 The Prime Minister for a quarter of an hour delivered to an audience of half a dozen people and two phonofilm cameras a farewell address. **1930** A. B. Wood *Textbk. Sound* v. 495 A somewhat similar process is used in the production of phonofilms or 'speaking pictures'. **1973** *Listener* 7 June 744/3 There we were, south of San Francisco... Just down the road, De Forest had invented the radio valve and the phonofilm.

phonogenic (fōᵘnodʒe·nik, -dʒī·nik), *a.* [f. Phono- + *-genic b.] With pleasing voice qualities; well suited to mechanical reproduction of sound; of or pertaining to pleasing recorded sound.

1945 *Office Economist* June 10 (*heading*) Are you Phonogenic? **1947** *Red Barrel* Feb. 22 She shows how to be phonogenic by what not to do. **1957** Manvell & Huntley *Technique Film Music* v. 205 Roman Vlad..claims that he prefers to use a chamber music orchestra for what he calls 'phonogenic' reasons..('the possibilities of obtaining a clearer sound are superior'). **1977** *Gramophone* Jan. 1131/2 Perhaps hers is not a 'phonogenic' voice; the vibrations which are part of its appeal in a large house might appear too prominently in recording.

phonogram. Add: **2.** (Earlier and later examples.)

1879 *Telegraphic Jrnl.* VII. 233/1 M. Delecheneau has succeeded in getting phonograms on zinc and brass cyclinders. **1967** A. L. Lloyd *Folk Song in England* i. 65 Dr. Walker Fewkes made phonogram recordings among North American Indians in 1889. **1976** *Daily Tel.* 10 July 4/8 To celebrate the centenary of sound recording next year major record companies in more than 60 countries are to present a programme of events... This was announced yesterday by the International Federation of Producers of Phonograms and Videograms. **1977** *Gramophone* Apr. 1527/2 It is not a laughing matter that it has taken so long and so much effort to establish the recording, the phonogram, as a serious creative art form in its own right.

3. A telegram that the sender dictates over the telephone. Freq. *attrib.*

1911 D. Murray in *Jrnl. Inst. Electr. Engin.* Aug. 451 Economic necessity will..lead to a great increase in telephone-telegrams, or, as the British Post Office already calls them, 'phonograms'. **1932** *Telegraph & Telephone Jrnl.* Oct. 2/1 Any telephone subscriber can hand over and receive his telegrams by telephone (phonogram service). **1968** E. H. Jolley *Introd. Telephony & Telegr.* i. 16/2 Nowadays small offices generally dictate their telegrams over the telephone to an appointed office. The appointed office receives the traffic from a group of minor offices..and is provided with special phonogram equipment designed to facilitate the handling of calls from the various offices. **1969** *West Australian* 5 July 66/2 (Advt.), Postmaster-General's Department has vacancies for phonogram operator (Perth). **1976** R. N. Renton *Telegraphy* ix. 246/1 As far as the method is reversible, a telegram is delivered to the recipient over the same medium used for handing in, e.g. via phonograms, printergrams or leased teleprinter circuit. **1976** *Sydney Telephone Directory*, Phonograms. To save time, telephone your telegrams. The usual telegram charges will be debited to your telephone account.

phonograph, *sb.* Add: **3.** In Britain the word is retained only for early cylinder machines, but in N. Amer. it has become synonymous with *record player*, *record deck*, etc., corresponding to the British *gramophone*. (Further examples.) Also *attrib.*

1878 G. B. Prescott *Speaking Telephone* x. 305 Having provided thus for the durability of the phonograph plate, it will be very easy [etc.]. *Ibid.* 430/2 (Index), The talking phonograph record. **1909** *Jrnl. Industr. & Engin. Chem.* Mar. 157/2 Phonograph records have been made with it [*sc.* Bakelite]. **1913** [see *Gramophone]. **1927** *Jrnl. Abnormal Psychol.* XXII. 13 Several of the major phonograph companies maintain 'race record' departments. **1929** E. Wilson *I thought of Daisy* i. 15 Somebody turned on the phonograph which began jigging a popular fox-trot. **1946** *Fortune* Oct. 158/2 Home phonographs rarely compare in precision with professional studio equipment. **1949** *Reader's Digest* Dec. 139/1 Sixteen million American phonograph owners are bewildered and unhappy. **1952** [see *Gramophone]. **1956** C. Fowler *High Fidelity* i. 9 Time was when a phonograph made by one of the big companies was automatically considered low-fidelity. **1960** C. Hansen in A. Dundes *Mother Wit* (1973) 507 The advertisements of..phonograph record companies. **1967** A. L. Lloyd *Folk Song in England* i. 65 Singers..whom Percy Grainger recorded on phonograph cylinders as early as 1904. **1975** *Daily Tel.* 17 Jan. 8/6 An Edison phonograph of about 1905 obtained £240. It was sold with 38 cylinder records. **1975** *New Yorker* 29 Sept. 64/2 Mrs. Santana turned off the TV, turned on the phonograph to its top volume, and went into the kitchen.

phonographic, *a.* **3.** (Further examples.)

1878 G. B. Prescott *Speaking Telephone* x. 303 (*heading*) Tracings from phonographic records. **1898** H. G. Wells *Let.* 22 Jan. in *G. Gissing & H. G. Wells* (1961) 79 A beautiful phonographic newspaper with a leathery flat voice. **1976** *Times* 2 Nov. 5/2 The British phonographic industry.

phonographical, *a.* For *rare*⁻⁰ read *rare* and add example.

1974 *Country Life* 12 Dec. 1857/3 The two-volume CBS Astaire solo anthology..are transfers of old Brunswick 78s and therefore more satisfying in purely phonographical terms.

phonology. Add 'No longer equated with *phonetics*' and substitute for first part of def. in modern use: That branch of linguistics which deals with sound systems, or with sound systems and phonetics; the study of the sound system of a particular language. (Further examples.)

The domain of phonology is variously limited by different linguists and linguistic schools of thought. In the writings of the Prague school it is used to mean phonemics.

1924, etc. [see *Phonetics *sb. pl.*]. **1933** L. Bloomfield *Language* viii. 138 The description of a language, then, begins with phonology, which defines each phoneme and states what combinations occur. **1937** J. Orr tr. *Iordan's Introd. Romance Linguistics* iv. 287 The great majority of linguists and all the phoneticians..use 'phonetics' for the physiology of sounds, and although all do not adopt the term 'phonology' for their historical study, those who use the term 'phonetics' for the latter avoid confusion by speaking of 'historical phonetics'. *Ibid.* 288 This matter of terminology has become complicated still further by the special meaning given to 'phonology' by the Prague philologists. **1939** *Language* XV. 1 We use the term phonology to refer to alternations (synchronic phonology) or changes (historical, diachronic phonology) in sounds, rather than for the theory of the nature and permutations of the sounds. The latter we call phonemics. Those who use 'phonology' in this sense.. deprive themselves of a convenient means of distinguishing two fundamentally distinct subjects. **1949** G. L. Trager *Field of Linguistics* 5 The phonetics and phonemics of a language are its phonological systems, its phonology. **1953** J. B. Carroll *Study of Lang.* ii. 43 Some languages have only a limited number of phonemes, while some others appear to possess extremely complex phonologies, offering a large number of finely differentiated phonemes. **1962** E. F. Haden et al. *Resonance-Theory for Linguistics* iii. 29 Phonology is the true-structure whose contributing members are phonemics and phonotactics. **1968** Chomsky & Halle *Sound Pattern Eng.* p. vii, In the course of this detailed investigation of English sound patterns and their underlying structure, certain rules of English phonology are developed. **1972** M. L. Samuels *Linguistic Evol.* i. 3 For some, at present, phonology is less important than grammar or lexis.

phonologic *a.*, delete 'phonetic' from def. and add further examples; **phonological** *a.* (earlier example); **phonologically** *adv.*, delete 'phonetically'; **phonologist**, delete 'a phonetist' and add earlier example; **phonologiza·tion,** (*a*) shift to phonemic status; (*b*) development (of a phonetic feature) to the status of the distinguishing feature in a phonemic opposition.

1936 *Amer. Speech* XI. 110 A 'phonologic system' is defined as the ensemble of phonologic oppositions proper to a given language. **1955** [see *Minimal *a.* b (*a*)]. **1970** *Language* XLVI. 312 Some phonologic features are closely related to an articulatory maneuver that involves a specific muscle. **1977** *Archivum Linguisticum* VIII. 50 'Generative grammar' in the second sense is concerned with the description of rules for sentence-structures which include the phonologic level as well as the semantic one. **1818** *Trans. Amer. Philos. Soc.* I. 246 These modifications ..may be distinguished in a phonological alphabet by particular signs. *Ibid.* 241 This *Sheva*, the English phonologists (if I may be allowed to use the name) have almost uniformly represented by *u* short. **1936** *Proc. 2nd Internat. Congr. Phonetic Sci.* 63 The phonologization of Middle English voiced spirants is an isolated process in the development of Germanic languages. **1964** B. Trnka in D. Abercrombie et al. *Daniel Jones* 190 The phonologization of voice of spirants. **1976** *Archivum Linguisticum* VII. 95 Preaspiration..was consequently inadmissible in *kampur*, etc., but since it had been distinctive its loss was accompanied by phonologization of the devoicing of the sonant.

phonometric, *a.* (Examples.)

1895 E. B. Titchener tr. *Külpe's Outl. Psychol.* I. iii. 156 The phonometric determination of sound intensity in psychophysical experiments is..usually carried out upon a principle similar to that employed in photometry. **1938** *Amer. Speech* XIII. 278 This typical example of phonometric technique has clearly a considerable bearing upon both phonology and dynamic philology. **1965** *Jrnl. Appl. Physiol.* XX. 302/2 Pressure determinations were made at the same time as the phonometric ones.

Hence **phonome·trically** *adv.*, using the methods of phonometry.

1938 *Amer. Speech* XIII. 282 Taking the long vowels of German which, merely for the sake of illustration, we shall assume are a phonometrically unclassifiable residue.

phonometrics (fōᵘnǫme·triks), *sb. pl.* (const. as *sing.*) [f. PHONOMETRIC *a.*: see -IC 2.] The study and practice of phonometry.

1957 H. J. ULDALL in Hjelmslev & Uldall *Outl. Glossematics* I. 16 In linguistics, phonometrics, experimental phonetics, and word counting. **1970** H. BLUEHME tr. *E. & K. Zwirner's Princ. Phonometrics* 4 Phonometrics is based on the assumption that the description and the synchronic or diachronic comparison of languages can be extended beyond what would be possible on the basis of the mere mastery of language by speaking, listening, or writing. **1972** HARTMANN & STORK *Dict. Lang. & Linguistics* 175 *Phonometrics*, the analysis and description of the spoken language by phonological (linguistic) and phonetic (instrumental) as well as statistical means.

phonometry (fonǫ·mėtri). [ad. G. *phonometrie* (E. & K. Zwirner, *Grundfragen der Phonometrie* (1936)).] A method of investigating language by the statistical analysis of instrumentally measured speech sounds and informants' responses to the same data.

1936 *Amer. Speech* XI. 358 The first volume..seeks to provide the historical and the theoretical bases for the methods of 'Phonometry'. The *raison d'être* of this venture is the conviction that the problems of comparative and historical linguistics are susceptible of further solution than has yet been achieved if one applies to these problems the technique known in biology as the statistics of variations. **1938** *Ibid.* XIII. 275 The chief concern of phonometry to date has been the empirical study of the variation of speech sounds, or, more precisely stated, the attributes of speech sounds, such as, for example, that of the duration of vowels. **1964** *Phonetica* XI. 151 Phonometry always works with recordings of connected speech.

phonon (fōᵘ·nǫn). [f. PHONO- + *-ON¹.] **1.** *Physics.* A quantum or quasiparticle associated with compressional waves, such as sound or those in a crystal lattice.

1932 J. FRENKEL *Wave Mech.* vi. 267 It is possible to associate the acoustical waves with certain particles which we shall call 'phonons', and to replace the study of the heat oscillations forming these waves by the study of the motion of the corresponding 'phonons'. [*Note*] It is not in the least intended to convey hereby the impression that such phonons have a real existence. **1953** C. KITTEL *Introd. Solid State Physics* v. 82 If the forces between atoms were purely harmonic, there would be no mechanism for collisions between different phonons, and the mean free path would be limited solely by collisions of a phonon with the crystal boundary, and by lattice imperfections. **1968** C. G. KUPER *Introd. Theory Superconductivity* i. 2 In field-theoretical language the mechanism responsible for electrical resistance is scattering of electrons, with associated emission or absorption of quanta ('phonons') of the acoustic vibration field of the medium. **1969** *New Scientist* 2 Jan. 32/3 They calculated that 100 W of the light were converted into coherent phonons. **1974** H. E. HALL *Solid State Physics* ii. 67 It is often convenient to treat lattice vibrations in an analogous way, and introduce the idea of phonons of energy $\hbar\omega$ as quanta of excitation of the lattice. Our normal modes are plane waves extending throughout the crystal lattice, and correspondingly the phonons are not localized particles. *Ibid.*, Like photons, phonons are bosons and are not conserved.

2. *Linguistics.* In stratificational grammar, a phonetic feature which is capable of distinguishing phonemes. Cf. *distinctive-feature* s.v. *DISTINCTIVE *a.* 1 b. Hence **phono·nic** *a.*

1964 S. M. LAMB in Romney & Andrade *Transcultural Stud. in Cognition* (Amer. Anthropologist: special publication) 60 The elementary units of which the phoneme, the morpheme, the lexeme, and the sememe are composed may be called the *phonon*, the *morphon*, the *lexon*, and the *semon* respectively. **1965** *Language* XLI. 200 Units that Lamb calls 'phonons' but that I shall call distinctive features. **1966** S. M. LAMB *Outl. Stratificational Gram.* ii. 29 The phononic alternation pattern specifies alternations involving phonological components. *Ibid.* iii. 57 The following symbols..may be used for hypophonemic signs, hypophonemes, and phonons. **1967** C. F. HOCKETT *Lang., Math. & Linguistics* 83 The pair 'pit' and 'bit' attests to a minimal difference,..but that difference is between voicelessness and voicing, not between /p/ and /b/. We shall follow Lamb in calling the terms of such minimal differences *phonons*. **1969** *Language* XLV. 300 The use of phonons in stratificational phonology is compared with the use of marked vs. unmarked features by transformationalists. **1975** *Amer. Speech 1972* XLVII. 248 In many, most, or all languages there are recurrent bundles of phonons which it is convenient to represent in a linear rotation by single letters.

phonostylistics (fōᵘnostəili·stiks), *sb. pl.* (const. as *sing.*) [f. PHONO- + STYLISTIC *sb.*] **a.** The study of the stylistic implications of phonetic variation. **b.** (See quot. 1972¹.) Hence **phonostyli·stic** *a.*

1968 M. SHAPIRO *Russian Phonetic Variants & Phonostylistics* p. vii, Phonetic free variation in Russian is treated in the present monograph not only for itself but as the material of a new subdiscipline of phonology which I have called phonostylistics after Trubetzkoy. *Ibid.* ii. 9 For the purposes of a special investigation, be it phonostylistic or otherwise, one cannot adopt the uneconomical view. **1969** *Computers & Humanities* III. 252 Linguistic features of style may be classified under *phono-stylistics* (meter, rhyme), *morphostylistics*,..and *syntactostylistics*. **1972** HARTMANN & STORK *Dict. Lang. & Linguistics* 175/2 *Phonostylistics*, that branch of stylistics which investigates the expressive function of sounds, e.g. the use of onomatopoeia in poetry. **1972** *Language* XLVIII. 350 It is of interest to note the phonostylistic correlates of these alternate pronunciations.

phonotactics (fōᵘnotæ·ktiks), *sb. pl.* (const. as *sing.*) *Linguistics.* [f. PHONO- + TACTICS.] That part of phonology which comprises or deals with the rules governing the possible phoneme sequences in a language. So **phonota·ctic, phonota·ctical** *adjs.*; **phonota·ctically** *adv.*

1956 E. HAUGEN in M. Halle et al. *For Roman Jakobson* 216 The key to our understanding of the syllable lies in the development of phonotactics, or the study of phonemic distribution. **1958** [see *MORPHOTACTICS *sb. pl.*]. **1958** A. A. HILL *Introd. Linguistic Struct.* viii. 116 Such a form reaches the maximum sequence which is pronounceable without breaking English phonotactic sequences. **1962** E. F. HADEN et al. *Resonance-Theory for Linguistics* iii. 24 Phonotactics..deals with the order of phonic entities. The field of phonotactics is phonemes-in-sequence. **1964** E. BACH *Introd. Transformational Gram.* ii. 23 A restatement of the rules in which there is a clean break between phonotactic and allophonic rules will require a longer description. **1965** W. WINTER *Evidence for Laryngeals* 210 We do not yet know enough about the phonotactics of Proto-Tocharian to rule out the possibility that..**ssk* and **tsk* were reduced to *sk* and *tk*. **1967** D. STEIBLE *Conc. Handbk. Linguistics* 96 Phonotactical description defines the phoneme classes which occur in a language. **1970** *Language* XLVI. 211 Young Binis..pronounce the word *epich*, deliberately violating Bini phonotactic rules (which forbid closed syllables). **1972** *Ibid.* XLVIII. 465 Prenasalized stops are found in many languages, and are not usually subject to such stringent phonotactical restrictions; in Albanian, for example, they occur both initially and as first members of clusters. **1973** D. ROCKEY *Phonetic Lexicon* ii. 28 Tests for phoneme recognition should be designed with the aim of determining whether the patient has grasped the phonotactic rules of the language, that is, whether he knows the phonemes and their combinations. **1973** *Word 1970* XXVI. 108 Monosyllabic nonsense forms, phonotactically Russian. **1975** *Canad. Jrnl. Linguistics* XX. I. 61 Portuguese phonotactics generally does not tolerate word-final stops. **1976** *Ibid.* XXI. I. 38 Many of the morphological rules which are proposed by linguists, whether morphophonemic or phonotactic in presumed character, are posited primarily, if not solely, in order to capture certain kinds of supposed 'lexical redundancies'. **1977** *Ibid.* XXII. I. 45 R2 and R3 are phonotactically motivated P-rules; they 'conspire' to prevent occurrences of *ss*-sequences on the surface.

phonus-bolonus (fōᵘ·nǒs bǫlōᵘ·nǒs). *U.S. slang.* Also **phonus bolognus.** [f. *PHON(EY, PHON(Y *a.* and *BALON(EY, BOLON(EY + the meaningless syllable *-us*.] Nonsense, exaggeration, ostentation, an insincere statement; fraud, trickery; goods not up to specification; a swindling transaction. Also as *adj.*

1929 D. RUNYON in *Hearst's International* July 58/1 Of course this message is nothing but the phonus bolonus. **1936** WODEHOUSE *Laughing Gas* xviii. 202 Sure. It was just a bit of phonus-bolonus. I was stringing you along so's I could get hold of that notebook. I'd be a fine sap giving you money. **1947** —— *Full Moon* vi. 115 His little friend had scouted the idea that there was any phonus-bolonus afoot between Veronica Wedge and this prominent Anglo-American snake. **1948** in Wentworth & Flexner *Dict. Amer. Slang* (1960) 386/1 The phonus-bolonus which gums up the average backstage musical. **1950** R. STARNES *Another Mug for Bier* xviii. 121 Who was ..the one who engineered the phonus-bolonus deal? **1955** *Sun* (Baltimore) 3 Feb. 3/1 'Phonus Bolognus!' whipped back Charles Hess.

phony: see *PHONEY *a.* and *sb.*, *v.*

phoo, *int.* Add: (Later examples.) Also used to express cursory dismissal (of a proposition, idea, etc.) or reproach, and to express discomfort or weariness (cf. PHEW *int.*).

1814 JANE AUSTEN *Mansf. Park* I. xv. 305 Phoo! Phoo! Do not be so shamefaced. **1840** HOOD *Up Rhine* 46, I.. enquired how the untoward event had originated. 'Originated!—*phoo, phoo*—no such thing, it was done on purpose.' *c* **1874** D. BOUCICAULT in M. R. Booth *Eng. Plays of 19th Cent.* (1969) II. 171 Phoo! How my arms ache! **1960** J. STROUD *Shorn Lamb* xviii. 201 I'm fed up o' lodgings...Feet orf my sofa, no smokin' in front o' children—phoo! **1978** 'J. LYMINGTON' *Waking of Stone* i. 26 She..dropped on the seat and went, 'Phooo!'

Hence **pho(o)-pho(o)** *v. trans.*, to ridicule, = POOH-POOH *v.* Also *absol.*

1865 *Cornh. Mag.* June 755 He pho-pho'd the poor ghost. **1866** *Ibid.* Aug. 141 It is easy to blame and to phoo-phoo.

phooey (fū·i), *int.* (*sb.*) orig. *U.S.* Also **phooie.** [f. PHOO *int.* + -Y⁶, or ad. *PFUI *int.*] An expression of strong disagreement with or disapproval of something said. Also as *sb.*, applied to the thing said: nonsense, 'baloney'.

1929 *Sun* (Baltimore) 11 July 11/1 Girls are described as weenies, janes, dames and broads. A mad-man is phooey, crackers or blooey. **1936** O. NASH *Primrose Path* 185 And I'll say, 'Phooie!' or something of the sort. **1940** R. CHANDLER *Farewell, my Lovely* xix. 95 'Ten o'clock at The Belvedere Club,' I said. Somebody said: 'Phooey'. **1946** —— *Let.* 29 Jan. in *R. Chandler Speaking* (1966) 45 So let's not have any more of that phooey about 'as literature my stuff still stinks'. **1951** J. B. PRIESTLEY *Festival at Farbridge* I. ii. 55 Oh phooey, Benny... This don't count as a drink. **1957** J. BRAINE *Room at Top* x. 94 'Keep right on believing that, and it won't be long before I see your name in the Sunday papers.' 'Phooey,' I said. 'It's a simple straightforward transaction.' **1967** *Boston Globe* 30 Mar. 18/2 The governor's advisers, spoilsports, have said 'Phooey' to the technicalities. **1972** R. LOCKRIDGE *Something up Sleeve* (1973) x. 135 The answer to that was simple. It was 'Phooey!' **1975** A. PRICE *Our Man in Camelot* v. 94 'Oh—phooey.' She scowled at him.

phorate (fǭ·rēᶦt). [f. phos*phor*odithio*ate*, f. PHOSPHORO- + DI-² + THIO- + -ATE¹.] A systemic and soil insecticide that is effective against a wide range of insects and is also poisonous to man on contact or ingestion; *O,O*-diethyl-*S*-(ethylthio)methylphosphorodithioate, $(C_2H_5O)_2PS{\cdot}S{\cdot}CH_2SC_2H_5$.

1959 *Jrnl. Econ. Entomol.* LII. 1032 Changes in common names of insecticides... Name to be used..phorate. **1962** *New Scientist* 7 June 508/3 Disyston (thiodemeton) and Thimet (phorate)..gave the best control of aphids and the most improved yield. **1973** *Pesticide Sci.* IV. 90 Phorate has been effective for the control of two-spotted spider mite. *Ibid.* 97 Foliar application of phorate results in moderate initial residues on mint hay which disappear rapidly.

phorbol (fǭ·ɹbǫl). *Chem.* [a. G. *phorbol* (Flaschenträger & Boehm 1927, in *Ber. über die ges. Physiol. und exper. Pharmakol.* XLII. 585), f. Gr. φορβή fodder, forage (f. φέρβειν to feed): see -OL.] A tetracyclic compound, $C_{20}H_{28}O_6$, some of the esters of which are cocarcinogens and are present in croton oil.

1935 *Chem. Abstr.* XXIX. 2533 Phorbol ($C_{20}H_{28}O_6$ or $C_{20}H_{30}O_6$) with very dilute H_2SO_4 in N_2 gives 38% crotophorbolon. **1939** *Thorpe's Dict. Appl. Chem.* (ed. 4) III. 434/2 Phorbol and the product of its benzoylation are physiologically inactive, but the (?tetra-)acetate is highly toxic. **1967** *Chem. & Engin. News* 16 Oct. 42/1 A possible absolute configuration of phorbol, polyfunctional parent alcohol of tumor-promoting compounds in croton oil, has been determined. **1978** *Nature* 17 Aug. 640/2 The most powerful known tumour promoters are the phorbol esters, which are not carcinogenic in themselves but can induce tumour growth after a subthreshold dose of carcinogen.

phoresis (forī·sis). *Med.* Now *rare* or *Obs.* [ad. Gr. φόρησις being carried; cf. *CATAPHORESIS, *ELECTROPHORESIS.] = *CATAPHORESIS a.

1902 HERDMAN & WILLEY in *Jrnl. Physical Therapeutics* III. 125 In view of this fact that certain substances are actuated to seek the anode while others are moved toward the cathode when a difference of potential is established in the liquid in which they are dissolved, or suspended, it would seem that a generic term, as *phoresis*, should be chosen to designate the therapeutic employment of this physical action of a direct electric current, a term which would comprehend in its meaning the moving power of the current in whatever direction upon particles suspended in it or held in solution by it, while the specific terms, *cataphoresis* and *anaphoresis* would, as now, indicate the direction taken by certain of these substances. **1911** C. S. POTTS *Electr.* (1912) ii. 50 The [ionic] migration will take place even through a porous barrier or membrane, in which case it is known as electric osmosis or phoresis. **1936** H. H. U. CROSS *Electr. in Therapeutics* vii. 184 The essential distinction between the modern ionic medication and the older cataphoresis (or simply phoresis).

-phoresis (-forī·sis), *suffix* [f. as prec.], forming sbs. which describe the movement of small particles by some agency, as *CATA-, *ELECTRO-, *IONO-, *IONTO-, *PHOTOPHORESIS.

phoresy (forī·si, fǫ·rəsi). Also **phoresis.** [a. F. *phorésie* (P. Lesne 1896, in *Bull. Soc. Ent. France* 164), f. Gr. φόρησις being carried.] An association in which one organism is carried by another, without being a parasite upon it. Hence **phore·tic** *a.*, of or pertaining to an association of this type.

1923 L. O. HOWARD in *Entomol. News* XXXIV. 90 (*heading*) An interesting new case of phoresie. **1927** —— in *Ibid.* XXXVIII. 145 In 1896 P. Lesne..proposed the name *phorésie*..to describe the carriage of small insects by larger insects without the actual feeding of the smaller upon the larger in the adult stage... It is proposed to give it the English form, *phoresy*. Apparently, in this form it has not occurred in the English language, although the word *phoresis* is used by electricians to express the conduction of substances dissolved in a liquid through a membrane by means of a current. **1942** E. O. ESSIG *College Entomol.* xxxiv. 663 The remarkable phenomenon of phoresy occurs in the case of *Rielia manticida* Kieffer, the adult females of which attach themselves to the body of the praying mantid. **1962** J. D. SMYTH *Introd. Animal Parasitol.* i. 3 Phoresis. This term is used for a particular type of association in which one organism merely provides shelter, support or transport for another organism of a different species. *Ibid.*, In phoresis..there is no metabolic dependence of either of the associates on the other. **1965** B. E. FREEMAN tr. *Vandel's Biospeleol.* xv. 245 Phoresy or epizoism, that is to say the fixation of a plant or animal species on to the surface of another organism without the first living at the expense of the second. *Ibid.* 248 The ciliates may be divided into internal parasites, and epizoic or phoretic types which do not live at the expense of their hosts. **1969** R. F. CHAPMAN *Insects* xvii. 327 An association in which an animal of one species provides transport for another species is known as phoresy.

-phoria (fǭ·riă), comb. form f. Gr. φόρος bearing (f. φέρειν to bear: see -IA[1]), used in *Ophthalm.* to form terms denoting a tendency to squint, as *ESOPHORIA, *heterophoria* s.v. *HETERO-.

phoria (fǭ·riă). *Ophthalm.* [f. prec.] A tendency for the eyes to be directed towards different points in the absence of a visual stimulus.

1891 *Trans. Amer. Ophthalm. Soc.* VI. 136, I..then record the 'phoria' or 'heterophoria' found. **1937** *Times* 23 July 18/5 Every discovered phoria with a history of flying trouble was not for certain the absolute root cause. **1975** *Nature* 20 Nov. 202/2 Now phorias, or tendencies to strabismus, are common in infancy.

phormium. Substitute for etym. and def.: [mod.L. (J. R. & G. Forster *Characteres Generum Plantarum* (1776) 47), f. Gr. φορμίον, dim. of φορμός mat, basket, in reference to the use made of the fibres of the leaves.] An evergreen plant of the genus so called, belonging to the family Liliaceæ, native to New Zealand, and distinguished by long, tough leaves in tufts at the base and large, erect panicles of dull red or yellow flowers; = *New Zealand flax* s.v. *NEW ZEALAND 1. (Earlier and later examples.)

1821 J. YULE in *Edin. Philos. Jrnl.* V. 345 The following results..manifest the comparative superiority in strength of the fibres of the Phormium. **1905** [see *MILLABLE *a.*]. **1933** W. J. BEAN *Trees & Shrubs Hardy in Brit. Isles* III. 274 Strictly speaking, the phormiums are, I suppose, 'herbs', but they are genuinely evergreen. **1955** *Sci. News Let.* 2 Apr. 213/2 Four fiber crops also under study for use on American farms are ramie, kenaf, sanseveria, and phormium. **1972** S. EMBERTON *Year in Shrub Garden* III. 150 The tall, snow-trapping evergreen leaf blades of the phormiums (New Zealand Flax) never regain their poise once their stiff backs have been broken by the weight of snow. **1976** *Country Life* 26 Feb. 478/1 Shrubs like..phormiums, variegated osmanthus, carefully chosen hebes.

phorometer (forǫ·mĭtəɪ). *Ophthalm.* [f. Gr. -φόρος bearing, f. φέρ-ειν to bear + -METER.] Any instrument for measuring the degree to which the eyes tend to be differently directed.

1888 G. T. STEVENS in *Med. Rec.* 5 May 511/1 New instruments. A phorometer... This instrument is designed to assist in the determination of the visual lines to each other. *Ibid.* 511/2, I have now used the phorometer during several months past. **1941** *Arch. Ophthalm.* XXV. 483 As a part of the flight surgeon's equipment there is a phorometer trial frame with an adjustable bracket and a tripod stand, a rather complex and impressive piece of equipment. **1970** *Jrnl. Gen. Psychol.* LXXXII. 111 The apparatus consisted of..(*b*) a head rest, (*c*) American Optical phorometer, [etc.].

Phosfon (fǫ·sfǫn). Also Phosphon and with small initial. A proprietary name for an organophosphorus compound used to retard the growth of chrysanthemums and certain other garden plants. Also *Phosfon-D.*

1961 *Official Gaz.* (U.S. Patent Office) 22 Aug. TM104/2 Virginia–Carolina Chemical Corporation, Richmond, Va. Filed June 1, 1960. Phosfon-D for chemical height-retardant for chrysanthemums. First use Feb. 25, 1960. **1962** *Economist* 21 Apr. 248/2 The size of plants can be regulated by two new chemicals (one of which, phosfon-D, is already on the market) so that lilliputian Easter lilies and dwarf hydrangeas are possible. **1962** *Official Gaz.* (U.S. Patent Office) 2 Oct. TM7/1 Virginia–Carolina Chemical Corporation, Richmond, Va. Filed Feb. 8, 1962. Phosfon... For chemical height retardant for garden chrysanthemums. First use Jan. 1, 1962. **1968** *New Scientist* 10 Oct. 84/2 Studies in Israel have shown that another retardant, 2-4-dichlorobenzyltributyl phosphonium chloride (Phosfon) gives better control of the Oleander aphid. **1969** *Trade Marks Jrnl.* 23 Dec. 2098/2 Phosfon... Chemical substances..for use in agriculture and horticulture, being or containing compounds of phosphorus. Mobil Oil Corporation.., New York City.., United States of America; manufacturers and merchants. **1975** *Adv. Agronomy* XXVII. 116 Other chemicals which reduce stomatal aperture such as phosphon-D..tend to protect against smog injury.

phosgene. Add: Used as a poison gas in the war of 1914–18, and now as an intermediate in the manufacture of some synthetic resins and organic chemicals. (Further examples.)

1918 M. PLOWMAN *Right to Live* 3 They have been poisoned with phosgene. **1919** C. P. THOMPSON *Cocktails* 26 The laboratory where the Corps chemists pored over the latest phials of German phosgene. **1938** *Encycl. Brit. Bk. of Year* 144/1 Phosgene has a faint smell of musty hay; and it tends to work its way down into cellars and 'dug-outs'. **1953** KIRK & OTHMER *Encycl. Chem. Technol.* X. 397 Throughout 1917, phosgene was the gas used in largest tonnage by all belligerents. However, mustard gas was introduced by the Germans in 1917 and gradually supplanted phosgene. **1967** SIMONDS & CHURCH *Encycl. Basic Materials for Plastics* 432/1 Both sodium hydroxide and sodium promote the bisphenol A–phosgene reaction to form polyacrylcarbonates. Phosgene is produced catalytically from chlorine and carbon monoxide. **1978** A. PRICE *'44 Vintage* i. 12 His father..had been with him in the trenches and came back with a lungful of phosgene.

phosphagen (fǫ·sfădʒĕn). *Biochem.* [f. PHOSPHA(TE + -GEN.] An organic phosphate in muscle tissue (in vertebrates, creatine phosphate) whose phosphate group is readily released and transferred to adenosine diphosphate, thereby forming the triphosphate needed for muscular contraction.

1927 P. & M. G. EGGLETON in *Nature* 5 Feb. 194/2 There appears to be in muscle tissue an organic phosphorus compound which, by reason of its great instability in acid solution, has been confused hitherto with inorganic phosphate... The confusion is increased by the fact that this substance, the organic phosphorus compound which we have designated 'phosphagen', is intimately connected with the chemical mechanism of contraction. **1937** BEST & TAYLOR *Physiol. Basis Med. Pract.* liii. 971 In the presence of oxygen the phosphoric acid and creatine are resynthesized to phosphagen. **1965** *New Scientist* 18 Feb. 445/1 So far, animal tissues have been found to contain organic compounds, N-phosphorylated guanidines, whereas plants and microorganisms contain only inorganic polyphosphates. This clear distinction between the two characteristic types of 'phosphagen' seems to offer a basis for deciding whether a particular organism is a plant or an animal. **1972** J. A. WILSON *Princ. Animal Physiol.* v. 141/1 Several other phosphagens have been found in the annelids.

phosphatæmia (fǫsfætī·miă). *Physiol.* Also **phosphatemia.** [f. PHOSPHAT(E + Gr. αἷμα blood: see -IA[1].] The concentration of phosphates (and other compounds of phosphorus) in the blood. Less commonly = *hyperphosphatæmia* s.v. *HYPER- IV.

1926 *Jrnl. Amer. Med. Assoc.* 6 Feb. 451/1 Phosphatemia and fibroma.—Dalsace and Guillaumin noted an exaggerated amount of phosphorus in the blood of women with a fibroma. **1928** *Q. Cumulative Index Medicus* III. 163/1 Glycemia and phosphatemia following intravenous injection of defibrinated blood. **1961** *Lancet* 22 July 215/1 In a control group of 20 normal adult men the average value for serum-phosphate was 3·43 mg. per 100 ml.,.. so we can take 2·6 mg. per 100 ml. as the lower limit of normal phosphataemia. **1973** *Ann. d'Endocrinol.* XXXIV. 621 (*heading*) Role of the fœtal parathyroids in the regulation of calcemia and phosphatemia of the rat fœtus.

phosphatase (fǫ·sfătēiz, -s). *Biochem.* [f. PHOSPHAT(E + *-ASE.] **a.** Any enzyme which catalyses the synthesis or hydrolysis of an ester of phosphoric acid.

H. Euler (in *Zeitschr. für physiol. Chem.* (1911) LXXVII. 14) coined the G. *phosphatese*, having proposed that the termination *-ase* be restricted to enzymes which decompose substrates, and *-ese* be used for enzymes which synthesize. Hence quot. 1911.

[**1911** *Jrnl. Chem. Soc.* C. I. 1051 There is no evidence that the enzyme which synthesises carbohydrate phosphoric acid esters has any splitting action. The term *phosphatese* is suggested.] **1912** *Chem. Abstr.* VI. 2084 Expts. with pepsin, trypsin, and animal organ exts. failed to show conclusively the presence of phosphatase. **1931** *Times Lit. Suppl.* 2 Apr. 274/3 There are two mechanisms at work in calcification: (*a*) a phosphatase mechanism which produces in the matrix fluid, by hydrolysis of phosphoric ester, a condition of supersaturation with respect to the bone phosphate. **1951** WEST & TODD *Textbk. Biochem.* xiv. 471 The acid and the alkaline phosphatases of serum are so called because of optimum activity at an acid and at an alkaline pH respectively. **1968** [see *ISOENZYME]. **1973** B. J. WILLIAMS *Evolution & Human Origins* iv. 67/1 Red cell acid phosphatase provides a good illustration of the fact that alleles at a single locus can produce a 'continuous' trait in the manner described.

b. phosphatase test, a test applied to dairy products to find whether they have been adequately pasteurized.

1933 KAY & GRAHAM in *Jrnl. Dairy Res.* V. 70 If..the cream was pasteurised, its phosphatase content was completely or almost completely destroyed. This suggested to us the possibility that the phosphatase test might also be used for determining whether a given sample of butter had been made from fresh or from pasteurised cream. **1960** JUDKINS & KEENER *Milk Production & Processing* xiv. 256 The phosphatase test is very sensitive and will show very small variations in the time and temperature of pasteurization. As little as 0·1 per cent raw milk in pasteurized milk is also easily detected by this test. **1975** J. W. G. PORTER *Milk & Dairy Foods* xi. 55 The phosphatase test shows whether the proper temperature has been reached during pasteurization.

phosphate. Add: An ester or other organic derivative of a phosphoric acid; esp. in *Biochem.*, any of these derivatives of sugars, nucleosides, etc., which occur widely in living organisms. Also, a radical or group derived from a phosphoric acid. Also *attrib.* (Further examples.)

1895 *Jrnl. Chem. Soc.* LXVIII. I. 639 The liquid separates into two layers, the upper of which seems to contain triallylic phosphate. **1930** CAVEN & LANDER *Systematic Inorg. Chem.* ix. 237 Soluble phosphates, e.g. those of sodium,.. show marked hydrolysis in solution. **1953** *Nature* 25 Apr. 737/1 The bases are on the inside of the helix and the phosphates on the outside. *Ibid.* 741/2 The phosphate groups lie on the outside of the structural unit, on a helix of diameter about 20 A. **1953** FRUTON & SIMMONDS *Gen. Biochem.* xix. 422 In the formulae for the sugar phosphates, the phosphoric acid residue is written in the undissociated form. **1954** A. WHITE et al. *Princ. Biochem.* xvi. 381 Enzymes which catalyze transfer of phosphate from ATP to an acceptor are designated kinases. **1957** *Encycl. Brit.* XVII. 780/2 Considerable tonnages of other phosphates such as $(NH_4)H_2PO_4$ and $(NH_4)_2HPO_4$ are also used in the fertilizer industry. **1964** N. G. CLARK *Mod. Org. Chem.* xxi. 433 Triphenyl phosphate ..is used as a plasticizer for various cellulose and vinyl plastics. **1968** A. WHITE et al. *Princ. Biochem.* (ed. 4) xv. 315 Three classes of high-energy phosphate compounds are known: acid anhydrides, phosphate esters of enols, and derivatives of phosphamic acid R—NH—PO_3H. **1972** FARAGO & LAGNADO *Life in Action* v. 129 The starting material, glucose, is converted into phosphate derivatives which then go through a series of molecular gyrations, and are finally broken down to three-carbon units. **1976** *Nature* 1 July 45/1 Adsorption of phosphate on hydrous metal oxides is of considerable importance in soil fertility and eutrophication studies.

b. Add to def.: Also to that of lime (calcium) as a mineral; also *sing.*, esp. when *attrib.*

1849 *Q. Jrnl. Geol. Soc.* V. p. lxxxiv, We find such phosphates surrounding some fossils, such as crustaceans from the London clay, leading us to infer a connexion between the animal matter and this substance. **1891** F. WYATT *Phosphates of Amer.* iii. 28 The principal phosphate mines of Canada have been located on those positions of the pyroxenite belt in which, at the surface, the apatite has shown signs of predominating. **1892** *Amer. Jrnl. Sci.* XLIII. 403 The South Carolina phosphates are nodular in form. **1936** J. C. BROWN *India's Mineral Wealth* (ed. 2) x. 225 The problem of the utilization of Indian rock phosphates demands more research than it appears yet to have received. **1954** K. B. CUMBERLAND *Southwest Pacific* ii. 42 In the central Pacific province the only mining is that of phosphate. **1976** *Nature* 10 June 452/3 If Abbott's Booby were found nesting in the group, this could be of crucial importance for the species, which is now reduced to about 2,000 pairs threatened by phosphate mining on Christmas Island. **1977** *Radio Times* 1 Jan. 54/4 The Banabans of Ocean Island.. claim that they have been exploited..for 76 years because their island turned out to be full of phosphate.

2. Special Comb.: **phosphate bond** *Biochem.*, a bond between a phosphate group and another part of a molecule, esp. such a bond in an adenosine phosphate which is hydrolysed to provide energy in living organisms; **phosphate glass,** a glass of which the major constituent is phosphorus pentoxide or a phosphate; **phosphate island,** an island consisting largely of phosphate rock; **phosphate rock,** rock containing a substantial amount of calcium phosphate (usu. in the form of apatite).

1940 *Jrnl. Biol. Chem.* CXXXIV. 463 Since pyruvic acid was found to promote adenylic acid phosphorylation, any such intermediate must contain an energy-rich phosphate bond. **1953** FRUTON & SIMMONDS *Gen. Biochem.* xv. 355 It has become the custom to refer to phosphate bonds whose hydrolysis is accompanied by the liberation of 8000 to 16,000 cal per mole..as 'high-energy' phosphate bonds.., whereas the ester phosphate bonds (as in glucose-6-phosphate) are termed 'low-energy' phosphate bonds. **1962** I. ASIMOV *Life & Energy* xxi. 291 The two phosphate groups at the end away from the adenosine portion are more easily hydrolyzed than phosphate bonds generally are. **1977** *Sci. Amer.* Mar. 147/2 It now seems that fast direct-energy release by the splitting of high-energy phosphate bonds supplies our initial power, up to half of the overall oxygen debt. **1937** *Glass* XIV. 519/1 This work originated from the observation that a phosphate glass..turns red on exposure to soft X-rays. **1950** J. E. STANWORTH *Physical Properties Glass* i. 8 It has long been known that phosphate glasses may be made which resist the attack of hydrofluoric acid solution or gas. **1959** W. A. WEYL *Coloured Glasses* i. 36 Phosphate glasses..offer certain unique features when used as a base for coloured glasses. **1925** *Econ. Geol.* XX. 276 The next change is when a phosphate island is elevated by earth movements. **1936** *Discovery* Aug. 260/1 He [sc. A. F. Ellis] 'discovered' Nauru as a phosphate island. **1870** F. S. HOLMES *Phosphate Rocks S. Carolina* 87 The Ashley Phosphate-rock is used in the manufacture of their fertilizer. **1915** W. S. BAYLEY *Minerals & Rocks* I. ii. 71 Phosphate rock is a mixture of apatite, phosphorite and various hydrated phosphates. **1923** A. B. SEARLE *Sands & Crushed Rocks* I. iv. 199 Coprolite and Phosphorite are natural phosphate rocks which are produced by the accumulation of organic remains. **1965** E. T. DEGENS *Geochem. Sediments* iii. 149 Phosphate rocks owe some of their rare metals to co-existing organic matter and sulfides rather than to phosphates themselves.

phosphate (fǫ·sfēit), *v.* [f. the sb. Cf. PHOSPHATED *a.*] *trans.* = *PHOSPHATIZE *v.* 2.

1939 BURNS & SCHUH *Protective Coatings for Metals* xvi. 374 'Coslettizing' was..used in England for phosphating the steel parts of bicycles. **1963** H. R. CLAUSER *Encycl. Engin. Materials* 477/1 The fabricated parts are cleaned.., phosphated and rinsed thoroughly.

Hence **pho·sphating** *vbl. sb.*

1948 H. SILMAN *Chem. & Electro-Plated Finishes* v. 166 In the presence of accelerators the phosphating process is completed rapidly. **1940** J. C. HUDSON *Corrosion of Iron & Steel* vi. 136 The proprietary phosphating processes, such as Parkerising and Bonderising. **1956** WERNICK & PINNER *Surface Treatm. & Finishing of Aluminium & Alloys* vi. 213 As distinct from chemical oxidation, phosphating is carried out on a clean surface, and the work is therefore degreased before immersing..

in the phosphating solution. **1976** J. A. von Fraunhofer *Basic Metal Finishing* xiii. 146 The simplest phosphating treatment is immersion in hot dilute orthophosphoric acid solution for up to 30 min. but many proprietary solutions and commercial processes are in use.

phosphatide (fǫ·sfătəid). *Biochem.* Also † -id. [f. Phosphat(e + -ide.] Formerly = *phospholipid; now *esp.* a fatty acid ester of glycerol phosphate in which a nitrogen base is linked to the phosphate group.

1884 J. L. W. Thudichum *Treat. Chem. Constitution Brain* i. 4 According to the result of this revision the phosphorised substances [in the brain] are not glycerides at all, as commonly defined, and have nothing in common with fats considered as glycerides, except that some of them contain fatty acids also present in fats... In accordance with this new knowledge, I have termed the phosphorised substances phosphatides, that is to say, substances which are similar to (but not by any means identical with) phosphates, on the assumption that their basal or principal joining radicle is that of phosphoric acid and that in this acid one, two, or three molec[u]les of hydroxyl may be replaced by radicles of alcohols, acids, or bases. **1910** [see *phospholipin]. **1918** [see *heparin]. **1921** B. Harrow *Vitamines* 43 A number of very complicated substances—the phosphatids—are found in larger quantities in the brain than in other parts of the body. **1927** [see *phospholipin]. **1944** L. F. & M. Fieser *Org. Chem.* xix. 490 In the more active tissues (brain, liver, kidney, etc.) they [*sc.* fats] usually occur in a form more complex than depot fats, which are mainly glycerides... These fats can be divided into two classes, phosphatides and cerebrosides. The former on hydrolysis yield fatty acids, a nitrogenous base, phosphoric acid, and usually glycerol. **1951** H. J. Deuel *Lipids* I. i. 4 Phospholipids or Phosphatides. The former term is most generally employed in the United States while the latter one is favored in English and German literature. **1953** Fruton & Simmonds *Gen. Biochem.* xxii. 509 Evidence has been presented for the occurrence, in the..brain, of a phosphatide that contains inositol. **1954** A. White et al. *Princ. Biochem.* v. 87 The next large class of lipids..is the phospholipids, more usually called phosphatides... The members of this group all contain a nitrogenous base. **1968** *Ibid.* (ed. 4) iv. 69 The larger groups of naturally occurring phospholipids are termed phosphatides.

phosphatidic (fǫsfătəi·dik, -ti·dik), *a. Biochem.* [f. prec. + -ic.] *phosphatidic acid*: any of the esterified derivatives of glycerol phosphate in which the hydrogen atoms in both hydroxyl groups are replaced by fatty acid radicals.

1927 Channon & Chibnall in *Biochem. Jrnl.* XXI. 1115 It seems to us preferable to keep to Thudichum's original definitions [of *phosphatide* and *cerebroside*]. If this is done the diglyceridephosphoric acid and its salts are phosphatides. Since the acid is chemically the parent acid of the two more commonly occurring phosphatides lecithin and kephalin, we propose to call it phosphatidic acid. **1954** A. White et al. *Princ. Biochem.* v. 88 The phosphatides of known structure which contain one atom of N per atom of P may be regarded as derivatives of phosphatidic acid. **1964** W. G. Smith *Allergy & Tissue Metabolism* viii. 87 Once these fatty acids are converted to fatty acyl CoA they could be incorporated immediately into diglyceride formed from 1-glycerophosphate via phosphatidic acid. **1967** [see *phosphoglyceride* s.v. *phospho-]. **1979** *Sci. Amer.* Jan. 49/1 Two molecules of a fatty acid..are transferred from a donor to a molecule of glycerol phosphate, forming the most primitive phospholipid, phosphatidic acid.

Hence **phosphatidyl** (fǫsfătəi·dəil, -il, fǫsfæ·tidəil, -il), the univalent radical of phosphatidic acid formed by the loss of a hydrogen atom from the phosphate group; usu. *attrib.* or in *Comb.* in the names of esters (phospholipids), as *phosphatidyl choline, ethanolamine, serine.*

1941 J. Folch in *Jrnl. Biol. Chem.* CXXXIX. 973 In a recent paper it was shown that cephalin prepared in the usual manner..did not contain..all of its nitrogen in the form of ethanolamine, but that from 40 to 70 per cent was in the form of a β-hydroxyamino acid... The cephalin fraction containing the amino acid has now been isolated, and the amino acid crystallized as..*l*(+)-serine. We shall call this phosphatide 'phosphatidyl serine'. **1942** —— in *Ibid.* CXLVI. 35 Cephalin prepared from brain by the classical methods has..been separated into three fractions: (*a*) phosphatidyl ethanolamine so called because it has its nitrogen as ethanolamine and its P as glycerophosphoric acid, [etc.]. **1954** A. White et al. *Princ. Biochem.* v. 88 Phosphatidyl choline, or lecithin, has the following formula. **1964** *Oceanogr. & Marine Biol.* II. 173 Among the phospholipids of vertebrates is a class known as plasmalogens. These are closely related to the classical lecithin (phosphatidyl choline) and cephalin (phosphatidyl ethanolamine). **1967** *Information Bull. Internat. Union Pure & Appl. Chem.* XXX. 23 The term 'lecithin' is permitted but not recommended to designate a 1,2-diacyl-*sn*-glycero-3-phosphorylcholine. The recommended generic term for such compounds is 3-*sn*-phosphatidylcholine. **1971** M. F. Mallette et al. *Introd. Biochem.* ix. 324 Phosphatidylserine..is another phospholipid isolated from plant and animal sources.

phosphatize, *v.* Add further example and substitute for def.: To convert into a phosphate. Usu. as *phosphatized *ppl. a.*

1885 *Q. Jrnl. Geol. Soc.* XLI. 80 There this process of phosphatizing the coral has been in operation on a most extensive scale.

2. *trans.* To treat with a phosphate; to coat (metal) with a phosphate to protect it against corrosion.

1939 *Metal Treatment* IV. 172 A modern phosphatising process for sheet steel work comprises the following steps:—1. degrease, 2 phosphatise, 3 chromate rinse, 4 dry off. **1961** *Engineering* 23 June 855/2 The skin which forms protects it from sprays used to clean and phosphatise the panels.

Hence **pho·sphatizing** *ppl. a.* and *vbl. sb.*; **phosphatization** (earlier and later examples).

1875 *Q. Jrnl. Geol. Soc.* XXXI. 362 At the Berwyn mine this process of phosphatization is most complete. **1900** *Proc. Geologists' Assoc.* XVI. 385 The 'rock phosphates' are phosphatised portions of the underlying Eocene and Miocene limestones... What was the nature of the phosphatising agent? **1939** *Automobile Engineer* XXIX. 460/1 Phosphatisation converts the work surfaces to a porous but adherent coating of iron phosphate. *Ibid.* 460/3 Specimens having the full treatment of phosphatising and chromate rinse showed markedly superior performance. **1965** G. J. Williams *Econ. Geol. N.Z.* xvi. 262/2 Reed believed the phosphatization to have occurred during the deposition of the Miocene beds. **1976** J. R. Duncan tr. *Bartoň's Protection against Atmospheric Corrosion* v. 114 Chemical pre-treatment methods have come into use as an answer to the problem of finding methods for rust stabilization... Phosphatizing is the most frequently used of these methods. **1977** A. Hallam *Planet Earth* 173 The phosphatization produced nodules and pellets up to 2 cm..in diameter.

phosphatized (fǫ·sfătəizd), *ppl. a.* [f. Phosphate + -ize + -ed[1].] **1.** Converted into a phosphate; = Phosphated *a.*

1875 *Q. Jrnl. Geol. Soc.* XXXI. 361 The shales..are rich in organic remains. These..are all more or less phosphatized. **1935** *Jrnl. R. Anthrop. Inst.* LXV. 345 It was much sought after years ago for its contained rolled lumps of phosphatized clay—the so-called 'coprolites'. **1976** *Nature* 12 Feb. 473/2 They are characterised by..phosphatised fish debris and faecal pellets.

2. Treated or coated with a phosphate.

1939 *Metal Treatment* IV. 170 Phosphatised work, when successfully effected, was superior to work having the protective coating alone. **1976** J. R. Duncan tr. *Bartoň's Protection against Atmospheric Corrosion* v. 114 There is greater resistance to under-rusting of phosphatized substrates under cracked or mechanically damaged layers.

phosphazene (fǫ·sfăzīn). *Chem.* Also **-ine.** [ad. G. *phosphazin* (Staudinger & Meyer 1919, in *Helv. Chim. Acta* II. 619), f. *phosph-in* Phosphine + *azin* *azine.] Any compound containing the group —N=P<, esp. as a repeating unit of a ring or chain in which two substituents are attached to each phosphorus atom. Cf. *phosphonitrile, *phosphonitrilic *a.*

1920 *Jrnl. Chem. Soc.* CXVIII. 105 Tertiary phosphines combine more or less readily with the most varied aliphatic diazo-compounds, yielding derivatives, for which the name phosphazines is proposed, in accordance with the scheme CR_2:N:N + PR_3 → R_2C:N—N:PR_3. **1958** J. R. Van Wazer *Phosphorus & its Compounds* I. vi. 341 The compound $(C_6H_5)_3$PNN=C$(C_6H_5)_2$, a typical phosphazine, is a yellow, stable solid with slightly basic properties. **1961** *Inorganic Polymers* (Chem. Soc. Special Publ. No. 15) 115 The family of polymers, which are called variously phosphinic nitrides, phosphonitriles, and phosphazenes. These names all describe a bonding system characterized by the repeating unit —PR_2=N—. **1970** *New Scientist* 5 Nov. 275/1 The cyclic nitrogen and phosphorus compounds known as phosphazenes will make life easier for textiles manufacturers in the UK and the US... Phosphazenes, which are incorporated into viscous rayon during the spinning process,..are ideal for flame proofing. **1974** *Nature* 29 Nov. 427/3 A simple survey of the structural chemistry of the phosphazines.

phosphite. Add: Also, an ester of this acid. (Further examples.)

1890 *Jrnl. Chem. Soc.* LVIII. 858 Ethyl phosphite, P(OEt)$_3$, is obtained,..when phosphorus trichloride is gradually added to finely divided sodium ethoxide, covered with ether. **1966** J. Cason *Princ. Mod. Org. Chem.* xxxiii. 603 Phosphorus trichloride reacts with alcohols to give phosphite esters... Only the tri-esters of phosphorous acid are known. **1970** *Encycl. Polymer Sci. & Technol.* XII. 748 Tertiary phosphites are among the most efficient groups of materials which have been used as poly(vinyl chloride) stabilizing agents.

phospho-. Add: † **pho:sphocozy·mase** *Biochem.* [*cozymase] = NAD(P) s.v. *N II. 1; **phosphocre·atine** *Biochem.*, creatine phosphate, HOOC·CH_2·N(CH_3)·C(NH)·NH·PO(OH)$_2$, the phosphagen of vertebrate muscle; **pho:sphodiester** (-dəi͵e·stəɪ) *Biochem.*, used *attrib.* to designate a bond of the kind joining successive sugar molecules in a polynucleotide or oligonucleotide, in which a molecule of phosphoric acid links a hydroxyl group in one molecule to a hydroxyl group in the next with the loss of two molecules of water (giving the sequence —O·PO(OH)·O— between carbon atoms); **pho:sphodiesterase** (-dəi͵e·stərēⁱz, -s) *Biochem.* [a. G. *phosphodiesterase* (S. Uzawa 1932, in *Jrnl. Biochem.* (Japan) XV. 22)], any enzyme that breaks a phosphodiester bond in an oligonucleotide; **pho:sphoe:nolpyru·vate** *Biochem.*, the anion CH_2:C(O·PO(OH)$_2$)·COO$^-$ derived from the phosphate ester of the enol of pyruvic acid; **phosphofe·rrite** *Min.* [ad. G. *phosphoferrit* (Laubmann & Steinmetz 1920, in *Zeitschr. für Kryst. und Min.* LV. 569)], a hydrated phosphate of ferrous iron and bivalent manganese (the former predominating), (Fe,Mn)$_3$(PO$_4$)$_2$.3H_2O, which forms an isomorphous series with reddingite and occurs as pale green, translucent or transparent, orthorhombic crystals; **pho:sphofru:ctoki·nase** *Biochem.*, an enzyme that catalyses the phosphorylation of fructose phosphate to fructose diphosphate; **pho:sphoglu:comu·tase** *Biochem.*, an enzyme that catalyses the transfer of a phosphate group between the first and the sixth carbon atoms of a molecule of glucose phosphate; **phosphogly·ceride** *Biochem.*, any phospholipid with a structure based on glycerol phosphate; **phosphoino·sitide** *Biochem.*, any phospholipid in which inositol is linked to the phosphate group; **phosphoki·nase** *Biochem.* = *kinase b; **pho:sphomonoesterase** (-mǫno͵e·stərēⁱz, -s) *Biochem.* [a. G. *phosphomonoesterase* (S. Uzawa 1932, in *Jrnl. Biochem.* (Japan) XV. 20)], any enzyme that removes a terminal phosphate group from an oligonucleotide or a mononucleotide; **phosphophy·llite** *Min.* [ad. G. *phosphophyllit* (Laubmann & Steinmetz 1920, in *Zeitschr. für Kryst. und Min.* LV. 566), f. Gr. φύλλον leaf, in allusion to its perfect cleavage], a brittle, almost colourless secondary mineral that is a hydrated phosphate of zinc, iron, and manganese, Zn_2(Fe,Mn)(PO$_4$)$_2$.4H_2O, and occurs as tabular, monoclinic crystals; **phosphopro·tein** *Biochem.*, any protein that contains phosphorus other than in a nucleic acid or a phospholipid; **phosphosi·licate**, any substance which contains phosphate and silicate anions, or consists largely of the corresponding oxides; freq. *attrib.*

1946 *Nature* 24 Aug. 275/2 It was found with a preparation of cozymase and phosphocozymase received from Prof. Otto Warburg that only one pentose was found for two phosphorus atoms. **1964** Phosphocozymase [see *cozymase]. **1927** Fiske & Subbarow in *Science* 22 Apr. 402/2 Our main evidence for the existence of 'phosphocreatine' in muscle is of a quite different nature. **1950** G. A. Baitsell *Human Biol.* (ed. 2) xiv. 243 The energy for the resynthesis of phosphocreatine, following contraction, comes indirectly from the oxidation of glucose in the muscle cells. **1969** J. I. Routh et al. *Essent. Gen., Org. & Biochem.* xxxiv. 666 Creatine..is especially abundant in muscle tissue, where it is combined with phosphoric acid as phosphocreatine, or creatine phosphate. **1953** Fruton & Simmonds *Gen. Biochem.* vii. 190 The products obtained from PNA preparations have been shown to be chains of nucleosides linked by 3′,5′- (or 2′,5′-)phosphodiester bonds. **1975** *Sci. Amer.* July 25/3 A DNA strand is a chain of nucleotides... The individual nucleotide building blocks are connected by phosphodiester bonds between the carbon atom at position No. 3 on one sugar and the carbon atom at position No. 5 on the adjacent sugar. [**1932** *Chem. Abstr.* XXVI. 2994 (*heading*) The phosphormonoesterase and the phosphordiesterase.] **1937** *Ibid.* XXXI. 10078/1 Phosphodiesterase. *See* Phosphatases. **1967** *Biochim. & Biophys. Acta* CXLII. 111 (*heading*) The action of snake venom phosphodiesterase on liver ribosomal ribonucleic acids. **1968** J. H. Burn *Lect. Notes Pharmacol.* (ed. 9) 65 Cyclic AMP is broken down by phosphodiesterase to the inactive 5-AMP. **1968** Phosphodiesterase [see *phosphomonoesterase* below]. **1956** W. F. H. M. Mommaerts in O. H. Gaebler *Enzymes* xiv. 319 The system consists..of a hydrolyzing enzyme (actomyosin), a common substrate (ATP), a resynthesizing enzyme (pyruvate kinase), and a reservoir substrate (phosphoenol pyruvate or PEP). **1970** *New Scientist* 23 Apr. 168/1 The last step in the glycolytic pathway, from phosphoenolpyruvate to pyruvate, is effectively irreversible... But in liver and kidney there is a carboxylation reaction which reverses the step. **1921** *Mineral. Abstr.* I. 125 *Phosphoferrite* from Hagendorf, as cloudy-white or greenish, crystalline masses with greasy lustre; H. 4–5, sp. gr. 3·156. **1955** *Ibid.* XII. 562 Phosphoferrite (Fe,Mn)$_3$(PO$_4$)$_2$.3H_2O and reddingite (Mn, Fe)$_3$(PO$_4$)$_2$.3H_2O have recently been found in the south pegmatite quarry at Hagendorf, Bavaria, as hydrothermal alteration products of triphylite. They are orthorhombic and isomorphous, the former..of cubo-octahedral or tabular (on 001) habit. **1974** *Nature* 27 Sept. 305/2 The evidence clearly points to a complete solid solution series between Fe_3^{2+}(H_2O)$_3$[PO$_4$]$_2$ (phosphoferrite) and Fe_3^{3+}(OH)$_3$[PO$_4$]$_2$ (kryzhanovskite). **1947** *Federation Proc.* VI. 297 (*heading*) The purification of phosphofructokinase from rabbit muscle. **1970** Ambrose & Easty *Cell Biol.* xiii. 246 Fructose-6-phosphate is phosphorylated by ATP to form fructose-1,6-diphosphate in a reaction catalyzed by a specific phosphofructokinase. .. This phosphorylation is also essentially irreversible and is an important control point in metabolism. **1938** G. T. Cori et al. in *Jrnl. Biol. Chem.* CXXIV. 543 A study of the enzyme which causes a migration of the phosphate group from carbon atom 1 to the spacially [*sic*] adjacent carbon atom 6; the enzyme will be referred to as phosphoglucomutase. **1964** A. White et al. *Princ. Biochem.* (ed. 3) xxi. 403 The best-studied mutase is phosphoglucomutase, which has been obtained in pure form from rabbit muscle, yeast, and several bacterial species. **1954** A. White et al. *Princ. Biochem.* xxxii. 800 These phosphatides include phosphoglycerides, phosphosphingosides, and the phosphoinositides. **1967** *Information Bull. Internat. Union Pure & Applied Chem.* XXX. 22 The term 'phosphoglyceride' signifies any derivative of glycerophosphoric acid that contains at least one *O*-acyl, or *O*-alkyl, or *O*-alk-1′-en-1′-yl group attached to the glycerol residue... The term 'phosphatidic acid' signifies a derivative of glycerophosphoric acid in which both remaining hydroxyl groups of glycerol are esterified with fatty acids. **1970** A. L. Lehninger *Biochem.* x. 195 The most abundant phosphoglycerides in higher plants and animals are phosphatidyl ethanolamine and phosphatidyl choline. **1954** Phosphoinositide [see *phosphoglyceride* above]. **1961** West & Todd *Textbk. Biochem.* (ed. 3) vi. 154 Two different types of phosphoinositides have been described which are differentiated by the inositol derivatives yielded upon hydrolysis. One type found in heart, liver, soybean, and wheat germ yields inositol monophosphate, fatty acids, and α-glycerol phosphate..; it..is phosphatidyl inositol... Another type of phosphoinositide found in brain..yields inositol-m-diphosphate, glycerol, and fatty acids. **1971** D. G. Bishop in Johnson & Davenport *Biochem. Lipids* xx. 411 Although phosphoinositides have been recognized as important constituents of brain lipids for some time, their occurrence in nature is now known to be widespread. **1946** Dixon & Needham in *Nature* 28 Sept. 435/1 Needham has given reasons for believing that the component of the pyruvate oxidase system which is inhibited may be a phosphate-transferring enzyme belonging to the same group as hexokinase. We suggested the name 'phosphokinase' for this small but important group of enzymes. **1953** *Brit. Med. Bull.* IX. 110/2 The phosphokinases all seem to have the common property that they require the presence of Mg^{++} for their activity. **1962, 1964** Phosphokinase [see *kinase b]. [**1932** Phosphomonoesterase: see *phosphodiesterase* above.] **1933** *Chem. Abstr.* XXVII. 1020 (*heading*) Phosphomonoesterase of animal organs and especially of the blood. **1968** Passmore & Robson *Compan. Med. Stud.* I. xii. 25/1 The combined action of the depolymerases, phosphodiesterases and phosphomonoesterases is to degrade RNA and DNA to the state of nucleosides. **1921** *Mineral. Abstr.* I. 125 *Phosphophyllite* from Hagendorf, colourless to pale-blue, well-developed, monoclinic crystals,..with perfect micaceous cleavage and lamellar twinning both parallel to *c* (001); H. 3–4, sp. gr. 3·081. **1968** *Mineral. Mag.* XXXVI. 624 In both phosphophyllite and hopeite ..the P—O tetrahedron shares one oxygen with six-coordinated zinc (Zn^{VI}) and three with four-coordinated zinc (Zn^{IV}). **1908** *Jrnl. Biol. Chem.* IV. p. l, Joint Recommendations of the Physiological and Biochemical Committees on Protein Nomenclature... *Phosphoproteins.* Compounds of the protein molecule with some, as yet undefined, phosphorus containing substance other than a nucleic acid or lecithin. **1929** R. A. Gortner *Outl. Biochem.* xvi. 391 Casein of milk and vitellin of egg yolk are the two most important phosphoproteins. **1968** H. Harris *Nucleus & Cytoplasm* i. 14 Synthesis of a specific plasma phosphoprotein induced in male chickens by the administration of diethylstilboestrol. **1964** *IBM Jrnl. Res. & Devel.* VIII. 378/2 The importance of the phosphosilicate layer for transistor stabilization has also been shown by the examination of production transistors after life tests. **1966** *Solid-State Electronics* IX. 1009 An i.r. spectrophotometer..detects accurately the presence of the phosphosilicate layer. **1975** *Physics Bull.* Jan. 14/1 A team at Southampton University has also achieved very low losses with a new type of fibre—a phosphosilicate (P_2O_5/SiO_2) glass core contained in a pure silica cladding. **1975** *Nature* 27 Feb. 722/2 Except for the chemical analysis of minerals such as viseite and wilkeite, few systematic studies of phosphosilicates have been made.

phospholipase (fǫsfoli·pēiz, -s). *Biochem.* [a. G. *phospholipase* (H. Udagawa 1935, in *Jrnl. Biochem.* (Japan) XXII. 324): see next and *-ase.] Any enzyme that hydrolyses lecithin (phosphatidyl choline) and similar phospholipids; = *lecithinase.

1945 *Jrnl. Biol. Chem.* CLVII. 643 A method is described for following the partial hydrolysis of phospholipids by the phospholipase of moccasin venom. **1965** Hanahan & Brockerhoff in Florkin & Stotz *Comprehensive Biochem.* VI. iii. 91 Through the use of quite specific enzymes, called the phospholipases (or lecithinases), the phosphatidyl choline (lecithin) molecule can be effectively degraded in a stepwise manner... The enzyme, phospholipase A, is found in high concentration in many species of snake venom... Phospholipase C has been found in high concentration in plant tissues, such as carrots, spinach and cabbage leaves whereas phospholipase D occurs mainly in bacteria. **1974** Dunn & Bondy *Functional Chem. of Brain* iv. 84 Lecithin (phosphatidylcholine) may be hydrolyzed by phospholipase A to lysolecithin (lecithin lacking its β-fatty acid).

phospholipid (fǫsfoli·pid). *Biochem.* Also **-ide** (now *rare*). [f. Phospho- + *lipid.] Any compound whose products of hydrolysis include fatty acids, phosphoric acid, and (with some writers) a nitrogen base; *esp.* one that is an ester of glycerol phosphate; in recent use applied more widely to any lipid containing phosphoric acid, esp. ones having a structure based on glycerol phosphate.

1928 *Industr. & Engin. Chem.* (*News Ed.*) 10 Sept. 3 The Commission [on the Reform of Biological Chemical Nomenclature]..proposes the following classification of the group lipides... The term *phosphatides* is abolished. It is replaced by the terms *phospholipides* and *phosphoaminolipides*. Phospholipides are the lipides which contain phosphorus (in the form of the phosphoric radical). Phosphoaminolipides are the lipides which contain both phosphorus..and nitrogen. **1929** *Jrnl. Biol. Chem.* LXXXII. 117 (*heading*) The rôle of the phospholipids of the intestinal mucosa in fat absorption. **1946** *Nature* 27 July 119/2 These results indicated strongly that the vaccinia and ectromelia hæmagglutinins were composed of a virus antigen plus a phospholipid component, the latter being responsible for union with the surface of the cell. **1951** [see *phosphatide]. **1951** E. A. Zeller in Sumner & Myrbäck *Enzymes* I. xxx. 987 The fact that the hemolysis caused by many animal poisons is connected with the breakdown of lecithin considerably stimulated the investigation of the metabolism of phospholipides. **1953** Fruton & Simmonds *Gen. Biochem.* xxii. 511 In the plasma of mammals..nearly all the phospholipid contains choline, and is therefore largely composed of lecithins and sphingomyelins. **1967** I. L. Finar *Org. Chem.* (ed. 5) I. xi. 292 One subgroup of the phospholipids is the phosphatides... Another group of phospholipids is the sphingolipids. These are not glycerides... Sphingolipids are also known as sphingomyelins. **1967** *Information Bull. Internat. Union Pure & Appl. Chem.* XXX. 26 The term 'phospholipid' may be used for any lipid containing a radical derived from phosphoric acid. **1971** M. F. Mallette et al. *Introd. Biochem.* ix. 321 The phospholipids can be defined as those lipids which contain phosphate esters of acylated glycerol..or sphingosine. **1972** D. J. Hanahan in F. Snyder *Ether Lipids* ii. 27 Structure (7) is the unusual diether phospholipid found in an extremely halophilic bacterium. **1973** S. J. Edelstein *Introd. Biochem.* xii. 210 Phospholipids are composed of fatty acids linked to a glycerol backbone. **1976** *Daily Colonist* (Victoria, B.C.) 31 Mar. 18/4 Liposomes are balls made from fatty substances called phospholipids, found in the membranes of animal cells.

† **phospholipin** (fǫsfoli·pin). *Biochem. Obs.* [f. Phospho- + *lipin.] = prec.

1910 J. B. Leathes *Fats* i. 41 Compounds of fatty acids containing phosphorus and nitrogen... Thudichum gave the name 'phosphatides' to a number of such substances... The indefinite nature of the term has led to its application frequently to substances that are not compounds of fatty acids at all. And it is indeed impossible to say what kind of substances should be regarded as phosphatides... In these pages, therefore, for the compounds of fatty acids containing phosphorus and nitrogen the term phospholipine will..be used. **1915** *Jrnl. Biol. Chem.* XX. 404 Preparations of phospholipins, *i.e.*, lecithin, the alcohol-soluble compound, and kephalin, the alcohol-insoluble compound, were made. **1927** M. Bodansky *Introd. Physiol. Chem.* iii. 55 The phosphatides (also called phospholipins) are present in every animal and vegetable cell and are especially abundant in the brain, heart, muscles, liver, and eggs. On hydrolysis these substances yield fatty acids, a nitrogenous base, phosphoric acid, and usually glycerol. **1948** *New Biol.* V. 38 Their [*sc.* microsomes'] principal constituents are phospholipins (complex fatty molecules containing phosphoric acid and organic acids and bases) and nucleoproteins.

Phosphon: see *Phosfon.

phosphonitrile (fǫsfonəi·trəil). *Chem.* [f. Phospho- + Nitrile.] = *phosphazene.

1921 J. R. Partington *Text-bk. Inorg. Chem.* xxxi. 625 At 175–200°, ammonia and phosphorus pentachloride form a mixture of six phosphonitrile chlorides: $(PNCl_2)_3$, $(PNCl_2)_4$, [etc.]. **1943** *Chem. Rev.* XXXII. 102 Most investigators have accepted the designation phosphonitrile for the PN group, since it is looked upon as a group resembling the CN or nitrile radical. **1961** [see *phosphazene]. **1972** H. R. Allcock *Phosphorus–Nitrogen Compounds* i. 3 The cyclo- or polyphosphazenes (phosphonitriles) are probably the best known and most intensively studied phosphorus–nitrogen derivatives.

phosphonitrilic (fǫ:sfonəitri·lik), *a.* *Chem.* [f. as prec. + -ic.] Containing the phosphonitrile group, —N=P<—. Cf. *phosphazene.

1895 H. N. Stokes in *Amer. Chem. Jrnl.* XVII. 278, (*d*) is a polymer of an acid N≡P(OH)$_2$, which we may call phosphonitrilic acid. **1943** *Chem. Rev.* XXXII. 119 The phosphonitrilic chlorides form as complete a polyhomologous series as is known in the realm of chemistry. *Ibid.* 122 The phosphonitrilic halides undergo reactions of hydrolysis to yield partially and completely hydroxylated products—the latter being known as the phosphonitrilic acids. **1956** H. H. Sisler in Sneed & Brasted *Comprehensive Inorg. Chem.* V. i. ii. 134 All the phosphonitrilic chlorides, when heated to about 300°C, are converted to an elastic product, possessing many of the properties of rubber. **1974** D. E. C. Corbridge *Struct. Chem. Phosphorus* xii. 333 Phosphonitrilic compounds, or phosphazenes, are characterized by the presence of the group P=N—.

phosphor, *sb.* (*a.*) **2.** Delete †*Obs.* and add: In mod. use [after G. *phosphor* (Lenard & Klatt 1904, in *Ann. der Physik* XV. 226)], any substance exhibiting phosphorescence or fluorescence, esp. one that is an artificially prepared solid. Also *attrib.* and *Comb.*

The more restricted meaning in quot. 1950 is not usual.

1910 *Sci. Abstr.* A. XIII. 269 Different phosphores consisting of an alkaline earth sulphide and heavy metal. **1914** *Chem. Abstr.* VIII. 3751 For Sa-Ca-'phosphor'.. the rate of decay of the phosphorescence increases with increasing temp. **1943** *Endeavour* Jan. 25/1 Phosphors are principally used for the fluorescence which they exhibit. **1950** H. W. Leverenz *Introd. Luminescence of Solids* v. 147 The generic term *luminophor* is subclassified into fluorophors..(fluorescent materials) and phosphors (phosphorescent materials). **1960** Chalmers & Quarrell *Physical Examination of Metals* (ed. 2) xvi. 777 Sodium iodide, activated with a trace of thallium..combines a number of properties which make it one of the most important tracer scintillation phosphors. **1961** G. Millerson *Technique Television Production* ii. 21 By applying the video signal to regulate the picture-tube's beam, a pattern of light and shade can be built up on the screen's phosphor, corresponding to the light distribution in the studio scene. **1971** D. Potter *Brit. Eliz. Stamps* ii. 25 Phosphor bands are practically invisible in normal light. **1975** *New Yorker* 5 May 51/3 Television pictures are produced by a flow of electrons moving in straight lines across the phosphorcoated surface of a cathode-ray tube.

phosphorane. Restrict † to sense in Dict. and add: **2.** *Chem.* [after *methane*, *ethane*, etc. (-ane 2 b).] Any compound that is regarded as a derivative of PH_5, the phosphorus having five covalencies.

1952 *Chem. & Engin. News* 2 June 2336/2 PH_5 is phosphorane (not phosphane, as the latter name is used in the series diphosphane, triphosphane, and so on..). **1963** *Q. Rev. Chem. Soc.* XVII. 411 Stable phosphoranes of the formula Ph_3P:CXY (X,Y = CN, CO_2R, COR) can be obtained. **1970** *Nature* 25 July 335/2 Examples of the utility of phosphoranes in the Wittig olefin synthesis were numerous. **1971** P. A. T. Hoye in *Mellor's Comprehensive Treat. Inorg. & Theoret. Chem.* VIII. Suppl. III. xxxiii. 881 Pentaphenylphosphorane was first obtained by Wittig and Rieber by the reaction of tetraphenylphosphonium iodide with phenyl lithium... The phosphoranes $(C_6H_5)_4PC(C_6H_5)_3$ and p-$CH_3 \cdot C_6H_4P(C_6H_5)_4$ are prepared similarly.

phosphorescence. Add: In scientific use now distinguished from fluorescence on techn. grounds (see quots.); (the various definitions are all broadly equivalent).

1949 P. Pringsheim *Fluorescence & Phosphorescence* 5 A photoluminescence process of this type, involving the passage through a metastable level, is called phosphorescence. *Ibid.*, It is no longer possible to define some arbitrary duration of the emission process as the boundary between fluorescence and phosphorescence. *Ibid.* iv. 292 The duration of a fluorescence process is essentially independent of external conditions insofar as this duration is determined by internal transition probabilities... The duration of a real phosphorescence is fundamentally a function of temperature. **1950** H. W. Leverenz *Introd. Luminescence of Solids* iv. 124 If the excitation and emission process occurs in times approximating the natural lifetimes of excited nonmetastable isolated atoms (about 10^{-8} sec for optical transitions), the process is called fluorescence, whereas longer-duration processes are called phosphorescence. **1954** C. Zwikker *Physical Prop. Solid Materials* xiii. 228 Fluorescence is the process in which the radiating electron falls back from the same energy level to which it was raised by the impinging photon..; phosphorescence is that in which the electron, after being raised to a higher energy level, first moves to a metastable level from where it can only be moved by external interference. **1971** *Physics Bull.* Oct. 577/2 The terms fluorescence and phosphorescence denote allowed and partially forbidden transitions respectively, though the practical distinction based on lifetimes is largely arbitrary. **1973** *Sci. Amer.* June 51/3 Today the definition is more technical, fluorescence corresponding to 'spin-allowed' electric dipole transitions and phosphorescence to 'spin-disallowed' transitions.

phosphoric, *a.* Add: **1.** (Further *fig.* example.)

1929 A. E. Coppard in *Legion Bk.* 61 Baxter and Brabazon..had been subjected to some phosphoric comments by the magistrate.

2. *phosphoric acid.* Add to def.: = *orthophosphoric acid* s.v. Ortho- 2 a; also applied *loosely* to phosphorus pentoxide, P_2O_5, as a constituent of minerals and fertilizers, and (freq. in *pl.*) to any of the common acids (meta-, ortho-, and pyrophosphoric acid) which contain pentavalent phosphorus. (Further examples.)

1912 J. W. Mellor *Mod. Inorg. Chem.* xxx. 597 The three phosphoric acids and their salts are distinguished by the difference in their behaviour towards silver nitrate. **1941** *Thorpe's Dict. Appl. Chem.* (ed. 4) V. 69/2 These phosphates have a range of from about 25–32% of phosphoric acid (P_2O_5). **1950** N. V. Sidgwick *Chem. Elements* I. 745 Esters of all three types of phosphoric acid are known. **1952** W. H. Waggaman *Phosphoric Acid, Phosphates & Phosphatic Fertilizers* (ed. 2) i. 13 The term phosphoric acid..has been, and still is used very loosely... In the fertilizer industry the term phosphoric acid refers to phosphorus pentoxide... To the chemical manufacturer and distributor phosphoric acid means orthophosphoric acid.

phosphorolysis (fǫsfǒrǫ·lisis). *Biochem.* [f. Phosphor(us or *phosphor(ylation + Hydr)olysis.] A form of hydrolysis in which a bond in an organic molecule is broken and an inorganic phosphate group becomes attached to one of the atoms previously linked.

1937 *Enzymologia* II. 160 Phosphorolysis is an enzymic process. **1946** *Nature* 23 Nov. 746/2 It was suggested that the coenzyme in muscle, while taking up two hydrogen atoms in the pyridine nucleus through the addition of free phosphate, undergoes a phosphorolysis and is split into pyridin[e] nucleotide and adenosine diphosphoric or triphosphoric acid. **1970** R. W. McGilvery *Biochem.* xv. 296 Glycogen is mainly degraded by a simple phosphorolysis of the 1 → 4 glucosidic bonds to form glucose-1-

phosphate... The primary reaction is catalyzed by the enzyme, phosphorylase.

Hence **pho:sphoroly·tic** *a.*

1937 *Enzymologia* II. 154 Phosphorolytic decomposition of glycogen. **1970** A. L. LEHNINGER *Biochem.* xv. 328 *(caption)* Phosphorolytic removal of a glucose residue from the nonreducing end of a glycogen chain by phosphorylase.

phosphor-roesslerite (fǫsfǫ̈rō·slərəit). *Min.* Also **phosphorrösslerite.** [ad. G. *phosphorrösslerit* (Friedrich & Robitsch 1939, in *Zentralbl. für Min., Geol., und Paläont.* A. 143), f. *phosphor* PHOSPHORUS: see *ROESSLERITE.] A hydrated acid phosphate of magnesium, $MgH(PO_4).7H_2O$, that is isomorphous with rösslerite and occurs as monoclinic crystals that are usually discoloured by impurities and that lose water on exposure to air.

1939 *Mineral. Abstr.* VII. 316 Mud in old workings in the gold mines at Schellgaden (in Salzburg) shows glistening crystals of the new mineral phosphorrösslerite... The water-clear crystals, usually yellow from iron staining, are monoclinic. **1951** C. PALACHE et al. *Dana's Syst. Min.* (ed. 7) II. 713 Phosphorroesslerite.

phosphoryl (fǫ·sfǒril, -əil). *Chem.* [f. PHOSPHOR(US + -YL.] **a.** The usu. trivalent radical PO. **b.** The univalent phosphate radical, $—PO(OH)_2$.

1871 *Jrnl. Chem. Soc.* XXIV. 1161 In the first case, ordinary phosphoryl trichloride is produced: $P_2O_3Cl_4 + PCl_5 = 3POCl_3$. **1912** J. W. MELLOR *Mod. Inorg. Chem.* xxx. 586 Phosphoryl fluoride, POF_3, as well as the other phosphoryl compounds can be made by the action of phosphorus pentoxide, P_2O_5, on the halogen acid. **1962** S. G. WALEY in A. Pirie *Lens Metabolism Rel. Cataract* 360 In the enzymatic reaction, there is a direct transfer of the phosphoryl $\left(O{=}P\begin{smallmatrix}\diagup OH\\ \diagdown OH\end{smallmatrix}\right)$ group from phosphoenolpyruvate to ATP. **1964** N. G. CLARK *Mod. Org. Chem.* 553 Phosphoryl chloride ('phosphorus oxychloride'), $POCl_3$, is a colourless liquid..which reacts slowly with water giving phosphoric acid. **1964** W. G. SMITH *Allergy & Tissue Metabolism* viii. 82 Thus the synthesis of glycerophosphatide is dependent on the availability of these phosphoryl bases as well as diglyceride. **1979** *Science* 7 Dec. 1151/1 Figure 7, from this work, represents a hypothetical example in which phosphoryl is conducted from ATP on the left to a substrate S on the right.

phosphorylase (fǫsfǫ·rilẽⁱz, -s, fǫ·sfǒrilẽⁱz, -s). *Biochem.* [f. prec. + *-ASE.] An enzyme that introduces a phosphate group into an organic compound.

1939 G. T. CORI et al. in *Jrnl. Biol. Chem.* CXXVII. 771 Various mammalian tissues..contain an enzyme which can be extracted with water and which forms glucose-1-phosphoric ester..from glycogen and inorganic phosphate... This enzyme, which will be referred to as phosphorylase, initiates the degradation of glycogen. **1955** *Sci. News Let.* 7 May 297/1 Use of muscle to do work and its recovery depends upon the chemical action of an enzyme, phosphorylase, which is found in muscle. **1970** [see *PHOSPHOROLYSIS]. **1971** *Nature* 19 Feb. 529/1 The breakdown of glycogen, in accordance with instantaneous energy requirements, is controlled by the activity of glycogen phosphorylase. This enzyme exists in two states: phosphorylase *b*..is a form of low concentration... Under the action of phosphorylase kinase it is phosphorylated at one serine residue in each of the four subunits, to give the highly active phosphorylase *a*.

phosphorylation (fǫ:sfǫrilẽⁱ·ʃən). *Biochem.* [f. as prec. + -ATION.] The introduction of a phosphate group into an organic molecule.

1925 *Chem. Abstr.* XIX. 3278 Dry yeast..did cause the formation of phosphoric ester with glucose. Slight phosphorylation occurred with yeast ext. **1931** [see *DEPHOSPHORYLATION]. **1960** *Radio Times* 22 Jan. 38/4 From the latest work it appears that the capacity to transform the light energy absorbed by chlorophyll into the energy of phosphate bonds (photosynthetic phosphorylation) is its unique feature. **1962** H. A. KREBS in A. Pirie *Lens Metabolism Rel. Cataract* 351 Owing to the obligatory coupling between the electron transport from substrate to oxygen and oxidative phosphorylation, oxidations cannot take place unless ADP and phosphate are available. **1973** R. G. KRUEGER et al. *Introd. Microbiol.* viii. 254/2 Let us..consider the mechanism of the electron transport system and of oxidative phosphorylation. The cell uses these mechanisms to capture energy from reduced coenzymes (NADH and NADPH) to store in ATP.

So **phospho·rylate** *v. trans.*, to introduce a phosphate group into; **phospho·rylated, phospho·rylating** *ppl. adjs.*

1931 *Jrnl. Biol. Chem.* XCII. 765 Phosphorylated sugars. **1937** *Nature* 20 Feb. 309/2 Prof. Verzár attributes these observations to the fact that glucose is rapidly phosphorylated in the cells of the living mucous membrane. **1937** *Biochem. Jrnl.* XXXI. 329 *(heading)* Competition between phosphorylating enzymes in muscle extract. **1962** R. VAN HEYNINGEN in A. Pirie *Lens Metabolism Rel. Cataract* 399 In general, carbohydrate metabolism in animal tissues proceeds by way of phosphorylated intermediates. **1970** R. W. MCGILVERY *Biochem.* x. 197 Racker has..suggested that the nonheme iron, that is, iron not associated with porphyrins,..may also be associated with the phosphorylating complex rather than with the electron transfer system. **1971** [see *PHOSPHORYLASE].

phot (fōᵘt). *Physics.* [a. F. *phot*, f. Gr. φῶς, φωτ- light.] † **a.** A unit of the product of illumination and duration, equal to one lux maintained for one second. *Obs.*

1894 tr. A. Blondel in *Electrician* 28 Sept. 634/2 Some years ago the photographers..established under the presidency of eminent *savants* (MM. Abney, Cornu, Janssen, Sébert, Violle, &c.), a unit of time-illumination (*illumination*) specially applicable to photography, the 'phot'.

b. A unit of illumination equal to one lumen per square centimetre (equivalent to 10,000 lux).

1917 *Trans. Illuminating Engin. Soc.* (U.S.) XII. 440 Using the centimeter as the unit of length, the unit of illumination is one lumen per square centimeter, for which Blondel has proposed the name 'phot'. One millilumen per square centimeter (milliphot) is more useful as a practical unit. **1939** [see *metre-candle* s.v. *METRE sb.*[2] b]. **1953** AMOS & BIRKINSHAW *Television Engin.* I. 280 The phot is rather a large unit, and its submultiple the milliphot (equal to 10^{-3} phot) is frequently used.

Photian (fōᵘ·ʃǎn), *sb.* and *a.* [f. *Photius*, the name of a ninth-century Patriarch of Constantinople + -IAN.] **A.** *sb.* A follower or supporter of Photius. **B.** *adj.* Of or pertaining to Photius or the schism in which he took a part. Hence **Pho·tianism; Pho·tianist** *a.* and *sb.*

1849 D. ROCK *Church of our Fathers* I. I. ii. 90 Not only the united or orthodox Greeks..but the Photians or separated Greeks, and the other sects in the East living apart, by schism and heresy, from Rome, entirely agree with her and the Latins upon Transubstantiation. **1850** Æ. McD. DAWSON tr. *J. M. de Maistre's The Pope* IV. iii. 307 The Photian churches are preserved in the midst of Mahometanism, as an insect is preserved in amber. *Ibid.* x. 340 Among the Photians, on the contrary, as among all other Protestants, there is no unity. **1854** J. H. NEWMAN *Lect. Hist. Turks* III. ii. 183 The unhappy city..which had been successively the seat of Arianism, of Nestorianism, of Photianism. **1864** in E. S. Purcell *Life & Lett. A. P. de Lisle* (1900) I. xv. 388 Photianism and Anglicanism are two forms of the same true Christian religion. **1907** *Catholic Encycl.* II. 45/1 The mutual bitterness which was evinced in Constantinople by the contending parties of Photians and Anti-Photians was reflected here in Athens... Sabbas, who succeeded Anastasios, was likewise a Photian. **1948** F. DVORNIK *Photian Schism* I. i. 27 The Fathers had listened to the Photianist bishops Zachary and Theophilus. *Ibid.* ii. 46 The anti-Photianist Collection...contains all the documents against Photius and served the extreme Ignatians as an armoury in their struggle against the Photianists. **1967** *New Catholic Encycl.* XI. 328/2 We have only..an extract in Greek, preserved in the anti-Photianist collection. *Ibid.*, The Photian legend grew in the West, picturing the patriarch as the father of schism and the archenemy of papal primacy.

photic, *a.* Delete *rare* and add further examples.

No reference is now implied to any 'fluid' of light.

1919 *Jrnl. Exper. Zool.* XXIX. 254 Tactile receptors, photic receptors, and chemoreceptors [of chitons] are physiologically distinct. **1957** G. E. HUTCHINSON *Treat. Limnol.* I. xiii. 757 The rather feeble photic requirements of the purple bacteria. **1971** *Nature* 30 Apr. 579/2 The clam has just been placed on its side and, in response to both tactile and photic disturbance (a shadow cast on the exposed tissues), has tightly closed its valves. **1973** *Black Panther* 18 Aug. 8/3 The photic driver..uses flashing infrared light and pulsing ultrasonic noise to pull brain waves from their normal frequency. The subjected individual sees and hears nothing, becomes lethargic, dizzy, perhaps nauseous, and may suffer epileptic fits.

b. Applied to the parts of the oceans penetrated by sufficient sunlight for the growth of plants.

1903 W. R. FISHER tr. *Schimper's Plant-Geogr.* 782 Three chief stages of brightness may be distinguished: 1. The photic or bright region, in which the intensity of light is sufficient for the normal development of macrophytes. **1972** A. LAURIE *Living Oceans* iv. 88 For small, slow-moving animals the twilight zone is also a safer habitat than the photic zone, which is the home of many active predators, especially fast-moving fish. *Ibid.* vi. 126 The photic zone of the oceans reaches down to a depth of 650 feet below the surface, which is deeper than the continental shelf. The entire shelf sea lies within the photic zone.

Hence **pho·tically** *adv.*, by light.

1960 *Recent Adv. Biol. Psychiatry* II. 181 Photically evoked cerebral patterns have been studied. **1971** *Jrnl. Gen. Psychol.* LXXXIV. 22 Later components of the photically evoked cortical potential.

photism. (Earlier example.)

1892 D. H. TUKE *Dict. Psychol. Med.* II. 1126/1 Most sound photisms are projected on externality.

photo. Add: **1. A.** *sb.* (Earlier examples.)

1860 QUEEN VICTORIA *Let.* 24 Oct. in R. Fulford *Dearest Child* (1964) 275 She is waiting to know..about the photo. *Ibid.* 28 Nov. 286, I send you (*to look at only*) a wonderful photo: of the Queen of Naples. **1861** D. G. ROSSETTI *Let.* 11 July (1965) II. 411 The only way I know about Scott's photos, is to send you a set I have.

b. = *PHOTO-FINISH. Also *attrib.*

1937 *N.Y. Times* 3 Jan. S7/3 Kindred Spirit survived a hair-raising finish to take a photo decision at 18-1 under Jimmy Start. **1946** *Sun* (Baltimore) 2 Oct. 15 War Trophy..closed with a belated rush..to earn the photo. **1950** *Ibid.* 1 June 21/8 *(heading)* Tar wins in photo. **1976** *Scottish Daily Express* 23 Dec. 10/6 Brigadier General Preston Gilbride's ex-Irish colt..collared Gambling Prince..smoothly in the closing stages to win by four lengths..with the photo showing Bronson to have held O'Conna out of third spot.

B. *vb.* (Earlier and later examples.)

1868 D. G. ROSSETTI *Let.* 21 Feb. (1965) II. 653, I shall be anxious to have a set of his admirable photo'd drawings. **1928** A. HUXLEY *Let.* 12 Dec. (1969) 304 The type is photoed on to sheets of jelly..and printed from the jelly. **1973** A. BEHREND *Samarai Affair* xi. 109 O.K. sarge. Do we..wait till you've had him photoed?

photo-. Add: **1. photoabso·rbing** *ppl. a.*, that absorbs light; capable of absorbing a photon; **photoabso·rption,** absorption of a photon; **photoact** (fōᵘ·toˌækt) *Biochem.* = next; **pho·toaction** *Biochem.*, a molecular event caused by light; **photoa·ctivate** *v. trans.*, to induce a change in or render active by means of light; hence **photoa·ctivated** *ppl. a.*; **pho:to-activa·tion,** activation by means of light; **photoa·ctive** *a.*, capable of or involving a chemical or physical change in response to illumination; hence **pho:toacti·vity,** the degree to which a substance or system is photoactive; **photoaffi·nity** *a. Biochem.*, applied to a technique of labelling large molecules (esp. proteins) at specific sites by means of molecules which initially form loose complexes at the active sites and are then photochemically converted *in situ* to reactive forms which immediately bond more permanently; so *photoaffinity label* sb. and vb. trans.; **photo-a·llergy,** an allergy brought about by light; hence **photo-alle·rgic** *a.*; **pho:toassimila·tion** *Biol.*, photo-synthetic assimilation; so **photo-assi·milate** *v. trans.*; **pho:toautotro·phic** *a. Bot.* [after G. *photoautotrophie* sb. (E. G. Pringsheim 1932, in *Naturwiss.* XX. 479/1)], autotrophic and obtaining energy from light; so **photoau·totroph,** a photoautotrophic organism; **photobio·logy,** the study of the effects of light on living things; so **pho:tobiolo·gical** *a.*, **photobio·logist; photoblea·ching,** a loss of colour when illuminated; **pho:toconve·rsion** *Biochem.*, any reversible chemical change effected by light, esp. that of one form of phytochrome to the other; hence **pho:to-conve·rt** *v. trans.*, to change by photoconversion; **pho:toconve·rtible** *a.*, capable of undergoing photoconversion; **pho·tocurrent,** an electric current induced by illumination; **pho·todamage,** damage caused by (esp. ultraviolet) light; **pho:todensito·meter,** an instrument for measuring the density of a photographic negative or the opacity of a fluid; hence **pho:todensito·metry; photodestru·ction,** destruction brought about by light; **photode-ta·chment** *Physics*, detachment *of* an electron from an atom caused by an incident photon; **pho·todetector,** a device that responds to incident light, esp. one whose operation depends on the electrical effect of individual photons; so **pho:todete·ction; pho:todisinte-gra·tion** *Nuclear Physics*, the breaking up of a nucleus by the action of a gamma ray; **pho·to-effect** *Physics*, a photoelectric effect, esp. the emission of an electron from an atom or of a nucleon from a nucleus by the action of a photon; **photoeje·ction,** ejection (of an electron from an atom) as a result of the absorption of a photon; **pho:toelectroche·mical** *a.*, of, pertaining to, or designating an electrochemical cell in which the electrode potential or the current flowing depends upon the degree of illumination of the cell; **pho:toelectromagne·tic** *a. Physics* = *photomagnetoelectric* adj. below; **pho·toenvi:ronment,** the environment formed by light; **photoenzyme** (fōᵘ·toˌenzəim) *Biol.*, an enzyme that catalyses a photochemical reaction; hence **pho:toenzyma·tic** *a.*, **-enzyma·tically** *adv.*; **photo-equilibrium** (examples); **pho:to-excita·tion** *Physics*, excitation (sense *5) caused by light or by a photon: so **pho:toexci·ted** *ppl. a*; **pho·tofabrica:tion,** the manufacture of integrated circuits by photolithography; **pho·tofission** *Nuclear Physics*, fission of an atomic nucleus caused by a gamma-ray photon; **pho·toformer** *Electronics*, an apparatus for generating a voltage corresponding to a given curve, incorporating a cathode-ray tube, a photo-electric cell, and an intervening opaque mask with an edge cut to the shape of the curve; **pho:to-heterotro·phic** *a. Bot.* [after G. *photoheterotrophie* sb. (E. G. Pringsheim 1932, in *Naturwiss.* XX. 479/1)], heterotrophic and obtaining energy from light; hence **pho:toheterotro·phically** *adv.*; also **photohe·terotroph,** a photoheterotrophic organism; **pho:toinactiva·tion** *Biochem.*, destruction by light of the biological activity of an enzyme or other substance; **photola·bile** *a.*, unstable in the presence of light; opp. *photostable* adj. below; hence **photolabi·lity; photoli·thotrophy** *Bot.* [Gr. λίθος stone + τροφή nourishment], a form of nutrition in which energy is obtained photosynthetically from inorganic compounds; so **pho:tolithotro·phic** *a.*, characterized by photolithotrophy; **photoli·thotroph,** a photolithotrophic organism; **photomagnetic** *a.*, add: (*b*) = next; **pho:tomagne:toele·ctric** *a. Physics*, of, pertaining to, or designating an effect observed in some solids, whereby illumination of a solid subjected to a magnetic field parallel to its surface gives rise to a voltage at right angles to both the direction of the field and that of the illumination; **pho·tomask** *Electronics*, in the manufacture of microcircuits, a photographic pattern through which a photoresist is irradiated with ultraviolet light in order to transfer the pattern on to it; **photome·son** *Nuclear Physics*, a meson emitted from a nucleus as a result of the interaction of a gamma-ray photon with it; hence **photome·sic** *a.*, **pho·tomixer** *Physics*, a device that acts as a mixer (*MIXER 2c) for light waves; so **pho·tomixing** *vbl. sb.*, the mixing of light waves in a heterodyne or homodyne process; **photoneu·tral** *a.*, unaffected in some respect by light; **photoneu·tron** *Nuclear Physics*, a neutron released from a nucleus by the action of a gamma-ray photon; **photonu·clear** *Nuclear Physics*, of or pertaining to the interaction of a photon with an atomic nucleus; **pho:toorgano·trophy** *Bot.* [Gr. τροφή nourishment], a form of nutrition in which energy is obtained photosynthetically from organic compounds; so **pho:toorganotro·phic** *a.*, characterized by photoorganotrophy; **pho:to-organotro·phically** *adv.*; **pho:toorga·notroph,** a photoorganotrophic organism; **photophil** (also **-phile**) *a.*, add to def.: thriving best in abundant light; *spec.* [after G. *photophil* (E. Bünning 1944, in *Flora* CXXXVIII. 95)], applied to a phase of the circadian cycle of a plant or animal during which light tends to stimulate reproductive activity; (further examples); **photophi·lic** *a. Biol.* = next; **photo·philous** *a. Biol.*, light-loving; thriving best in abundant light; **photo·phily,** the state of being photophilous; **photophysical** *a.* (further examples); so **photophy·sics** *sb. pl.* (const. as *sing.*); **pho·topigment** *Biol.*, a pigment (e.g. in the eye) whose chemical state depends on its degree of illumination; **photopolarimeter,** substitute for def.: † (*a*) [ad. F. *photopolarimètre* (A. Cornu in *Compt. Rend. Assoc. Française pour l'Avancement des Sci. 1882* 253)], an apparatus for measuring the proportion of polarized light in a given beam; *rare*⁻⁰; (*b*) a telescopic apparatus for photographing distant objects (as planets) and measuring the polarization of light from them; hence **pho:topolarime·tric** *a.*, **-polari·metry; pho·to-potential,** an electric potential generated by light; **pho·toprocess,** a (biological or chemical) process involving light; **pho·toproduct,** a product of the chemical action of light; **pho·toproduction,** production by light or by a single incident photon; so **pho·toproduced** *ppl. a.*; **photopro·tein** *Biol.*, any protein active in the emission of light by a living creature; **photopro·ton** *Nuclear Physics*, a proton released from a nucleus by the action of a gamma-ray photon; **pho·to-reaction,** a photochemical reaction; **photo-reco·very** *Biol.* = *PHOTOREACTIVATION; **photore·gulate** *v. trans.*, to regulate (a biological process) by means of light; so **photore·gulated** *ppl. a.*; **pho:toregula·tion,** the act of photoregulating; **photore·gulator,** a biological mechanism that regulates a process according to the duration, intensity, etc., of the light which it detects; **pho·torepair** *Biol.*, repair of tissue brought about by the action of (visible or ultraviolet) light; so **photorepai·rable** *a.*; **pho:toresi·stance** *Physics*, (an) electrical resistance that is light-dependent; also, a photoresistor; **pho:toresi·stive** *a.*, exhibiting photoresistance; **pho·toresistor,** a resistor whose resistance varies according to its degree of illumination; **pho·toresponse,** a response to light; *esp.* a response of a plant mediated otherwise than through photosynthesis; so **photorespo·nsive** *a.*, **-respo·nsiveness; photoreve·rsal,** reversal of a (biological) process by the action of light; **photoreve·rsible** *a. Biol.*, capable of being reversed by the action of light; (of a substance) changing from one form into another and back again as the degree of illumination increases and decreases; hence **pho:toreversibi·lity; photose·nsor,** a sensor that responds to light; **photose·nsory** *a. Biol.*, pertaining to or involving the perception of light; **pho·to-shock** *Psychiatry* [ad. F. *photo-choc* (Cossa & Gastaut 1949, in *Ann. Médico-Psychologiques* CVII. 187)], a flash or series of flashes of light given as part of shock therapy; **photosta·ble** *a.*, stable in the presence of light; opp. *photolabile* adj. above; so **photostabi·lity; photosta·tionary** *Chem.*, applied to a state of equilibrium in a photochemical reaction in which the rate of dissociation of the reactants equals their rate of recombination; **pho:to-stimula·tion,** stimulation by means of light; so **photosti·mulate** *v. trans.*, **photosti·mulated** *ppl. a.*, **-sti·mulating** *vbl. sb.*; also **photosti·mulator,** an apparatus used for photostimulation; **pho:tostimula·tory** *a.*, pertaining to or involving photostimulation; **pho·tosurface** *Electr.*, a surface which emits electrons when illuminated; **phototelegraphy** (examples); in mod. use, a system of facsimile telegraphy in which variations of tone are adequately preserved; hence **pho:totelegra·phic** *a.*; also **photote·legram,** a telegram sent by phototelegraphy; **photote·legraph,** an apparatus used for phototelegraphy; **phototoxi·city,** the property of causing a harmful reaction to sunlight; so **phototo·xic** *a.*; **pho:totransforma·tion,** a transformation (of a chemical compound) effected by light; **phototra·nsient** *Chem.*, a short-lived molecular species produced by irradiation; **pho·totroph** *Bot.*, a phototrophic organism; **pho·totrophy** *Bot.* [Gr. τροφή nourishment], nutrition in which sunlight is utilized as a source of energy; so **photo-tro·phic** *a.*, characterized by phototrophy; **phototro·phically** *adv.*; **photovoltaic** *a.*, substitute for def.: pertaining to, exhibiting, or utilizing the generation of an e.m.f. by light incident on an interface between certain pairs of substances; (examples); hence **photo-volta·ically** *adv.*; **photovolta·ics** *sb. pl.* (const. as *sing.*), the branch of science and technology concerned with photovoltaic effects and devices.

1966 PHILLIPS & WILLIAMS *Inorg. Chem.* II. xx. 87 A biological system obtains energy from the oxidation of organic substrates or from the action of light on its photo-absorbing pigments. **1977** I. M. CAMPBELL *Energy & Atmosphere* viii. 252 (*heading*) The generation of the photoabsorbing species and their relative significance. **1966** *Physical Rev.* CXLIX. 55/1 (*caption*) Charge distribution of ions resulting from photoabsorption primarily in the 3*d* shell of krypton. **1976** *Physics Bull.* Dec. 544/2 The continuum states of two electron atoms and ions can be studied by electron scattering or by photoabsorption. **1971** *Nature* 5 Feb. 372/1 The second possibility is that the mechanism of photosynthesis switches from a reaction involving two photosystems to a simpler form involving but one photoact. **1971** R. GREGORY *Biochem. of Photosynthesis* ii. 36 Eight separate 'photoacts' are involved, so that we should expect 2500/8, say 300 chlorophyll molecules to be associated with each reaction centre. **1957** *Plant Physiol.* XXXII. 397/2 Since the most probable photoreceptor is the oxidized form of the flavoprotein, the photoactions are effective in its return to the reduced form. **1965** HENDRICKS & BORTHWICK in T. W. Goodwin *Chem. & Biochem. Plant Pigments* xv. 409 Reversibility of light action..indicates that the photoactions are conversions of molecular configuration. **1926** *Ann. Rep. Progr. Chem.* XXII. 340 In the case of chlorine,..W. Taylor draws the conclusion that only absorption within the continuous absorption band will photoactivate the gas. **1959** *Mycologia* LI. 87 Pigmentation was photo-activated. Light of wave lengths between 390 and 513 mμ stimulated the production of colour. **1926** *Ann. Rep. Progr. Chem.* XXII. 360 In general, the 'electron-loosening' mechanism of Stark..describes the state of a photo-activated molecule better than the other conceptions put forward by photochemists. **1954** *Jrnl. Res. Nat. Bureau of Standards* (U.S.) LIII. 125 (*heading*) Catalytic photoactivated polymerization of tetrafluoroethylene. **1925** *Phil. Mag.* XLIX. 1116 (*heading*) A note on the photo-activation of chlorine. **1974** *Physiologia Plantarum* XXXII. 228 (*heading*) Action spectrum for photoactivation of the water-splitting system in plastids of intermittently illuminated wheat leaves. **1908** *Physical Rev.* XXVI. 541 A study of photo-active effects produced by illuminating one electrode only, no external electromotive force being applied. **1951** *Sci. News* XXII. 75 Perhaps indeed the carotenoids were the primaeval photoactive pigments which in the course of evolution of green plants and algae have been functionally although not physically replaced by..chlorophyll. **1975** *Nature* 10 Apr. 507/2 The properties of an organic photovoltaic cell in which the photoactive material is microcrystalline chlorophyll-*a*. **1915** *Physical Rev.* V. 45 This value of current was used in comparing the photo-activity of solutions. **1970** *Biochim. & Biophys. Acta* CCXXIII. 444 The photoactivity was measured by observation of the blue-shift. **1970** *Proc. Nat. Acad. Sci.* LXVII. 1694 Binding sites of similar specificities in the same membrane preparation..may be photo-affinity labeled by the same reagents. **1976** *Nature* 29 Apr. 802/1 Without irradiation the photoaffinity label reversibly inhibited the potassium conductance..whereas the sodium conductance was not affected. **1970** H. KIEFER et al. in *Proc. Nat. Acad. Sci.* LXVII. 1688 The method of affinity labeling is in widespread use for the attachment of covalent labels at the active sites of protein molecules. The usual affinity-labeling reagent has the structure R—X, where R is the portion of the molecule that binds specifically and reversibly to the active site under study, and X is a chemically reactive group, such as diazonium or haloacyl... In photo-affinity labeling, a reagent R—P is used, where P is a group that is ordinarily unreactive, but which can be converted by photolysis to an exceedingly reactive intermediate P*. Those molecules of R—P that are reversibly bound to the active sites react instantaneously upon conversion to R—P* before they can dissociate from the site. **1978** *Nature* 12 Jan. 157/1 The modified pheromone is radioactively labelled, and since the carbene is generated photolytically, the process is called photoaffinity labelling. **1939** *Jrnl. Investigative Dermatol.* II. 45 (*heading*) Mechanism of the photoallergic reaction. **1968** HJORTH & FREGERT in A. J. Rook et al. *Textbk. Dermatol.* I. 300/1 Photo-allergic reactions can resemble sunburn. **1976** *Lancet* 20 Nov. 1116/1 Chloroquine..is also used in..photoallergic reactions. **1939** S. EPSTEIN in *Jrnl. Investigative Dermatol.* II. 45 These experiments demonstrate a true allergic type of photosensitivity (photoallergy). As far as I can see, this is the first report of this particular type of photosensitization and the first experimental proof of the allergic nature of this form of light sensitivity. **1976** *Arch. Dermatol.* CXII. 1124/1 The diphenhydramine photoallergy was elicited by long-wave ultraviolet light. **1922** *Jrnl. Soc. Dyers & Colourists* XXXVIII. 8/1 The green pigment chlorophyll has been shown by Willstätter to be an equilibrium mixture of chlorophyll A and chlorophyll B... This equilibrium is not appreciably altered when photo-assimilation of CO_2 is taking place. **1975** *Nature* 9 Oct. 490/2 The ability of the cyanobacterium to photoassimilate CO_2 in reactions driven by photosystem I alone and using Na_2S was demonstrated..; no photoassimilation was observed in the absence of sulphide or light. **1951** J. W. FOSTER in Werkman & Wilson *Bacterial Physiol.* 363 Photoautotrophs are those which utilize light. **1974** *Encycl. Brit. Macropædia* X. 896/1 A green plant is a typical example of a photoautotroph. **1943** *Physiol. Rev.* XXIII. 350 This..implies that the organism so operating must be capable of carrying out conversions of organic compounds. Theoretically it should even be able to grow heterotrophically on the proper organic substrates. Many of the photo-autotrophic organisms have yielded to this treatment. **1975** *Nature* 25 Dec. 715/1 Manganese is required for the photoautotrophic growth of O_2-evolving organisms. **1977** A. HALLAM *Planet Earth* 189 This may bear some relation to the rapid evolution of photoautotrophic organisms such as blue-green algae. **1907** *Chem. Abstr.* I. 190 (*heading*) The photobiological sensitizers and their proteid compounds. **1976** *Sci. Amer.* Feb. 119/1 The results of the experiment..also rule out for the wasp any model of a clock in which light induces, or starts, diapause or development by photobiological means other than mere entrainment. **1958** *Plant Physiol.* XXXIII. 447/1 Robert Bruce Withrow died on April 8, 1958... With his passing this country lost one of its prominent photobiologists. **1973** *Nature* 6 July 37/1 Wald has therefore suggested that photobiologists should plot spectral functions on a frequency scale. **1935** *Science* 31 May 526/2 The cure of rickets by ultra-violet light constitutes one of the most interesting chapters in photo-biology. **1941** H. F. BLUM *Photo-dynamic Action* i. 3 Although.. the phenomenon has been found to have a more limited significance in photobiology, the name photodynamic action has persisted. **1968** *New Scientist* 5 Dec. 579/2 This Penguin survey is a valuable guide to the present knowledge and research work in photobiology. **1937** *Ann. Rep. Progr. Chem.* XXXIII. 426 Considerations of the photobleaching of fluorescent dyes in an oxygen-free atmosphere by the action of ferrous salts. **1974** *McGraw-Hill Yearbk. Sci. & Technol.* 127/2 Light conversion in photoactive chlorophyll is accompanied by photobleaching and by the simultaneous appearance of a free or unpaired electron. **1952** *Jrnl. Chem. Soc.* 4524 The photoconversion of (I) and (III) into coloured forms does not occur with light of wave-lengths greater than about 540 mμ. **1964** *Photochem. & Photobiol.* III. 521 The absorption spectra of the two forms of phytochrome show, in addition to the major absorption bands in the red and far-red regions, minor bands in the blue and near u.v. which are also effective in the photoconversions of phytochrome, $P_R \leftrightarrows P_{FR}$. **1971** *Nature* 27 Aug. 602/1 The implication is that acetylcholine is involved in electrical changes in the plant which presumably follow the photoconversion of phytochrome. **1962** *Jrnl. Physical Chem.* LXVI. 2476/1 Any X formed from B being immediately photoconverted into A. **1970** *Nature* 15 Aug. 666/1 The axis of orientation of the chromophores is parallel to the plasmalemma surface in the P_R form, but is changed to an orientation at 90° to the surface of the plasmalemma when photoconverted to P_{FR}. **1962** *Jrnl. Physical Chem.* LXVI. 2469/2 Only this isomer is photoconvertible into the spiropyran by visible light. **1913** H. S. Allen *Photo-Electricity* x. 127 The proportionality factor between light absorption and photocurrent is only independent of the angle of incidence ϕ for an electric vector..vibrating at right angles to the plane of incidence. **1913** *Physical Rev.* I. 74 The photocurrent-potential curve was almost identical with that furnished by the mercury lamp. **1936** *Discovery* May 151/2 This type of light-sensitive cell..requires no battery to obtain the photo-current. **1974** *Nature* 26 Apr. 804/1 Light-induced release of protons might thus provide an alternative mechanism for generation of the photocurrents. **1973** *Nature* 12 Jan. 133/1 This demonstrates the potential importance of the excited states of tryptophan as intermediates in lens photodamage. **1977** I. M. Campbell *Energy & Atmosphere* ix. 348 The link between DNA photodamage in living tissue cells and carcinogenesis by radiation is somewhat empirical. **1928** *Jrnl. Optical Soc. Amer.* XVI. 222 A self-registering photodensitometer has been described in which the direct-reading method and a thermocouple are employed. **1949** *Jrnl. Appl. Physics* XX. 129/2 The specimen containing the diffused Na^{24} was placed directly on the emulsion for one-half hour... The plate was then developed and analyzed in a photo-densitometer. **1971** *Nature* 19 Feb. 572/1 For most plant shoots, however, the change in methylene blue concentration is far too small to be accurately measured using standard photodensitometers. **1971** *Ibid.* 16 July 185/1 The haloes were also evident in a photodensitometer profile across a cloud bank image, and extended 1 km from the cloud edge. **1965** *Biochemistry* (Easton, Pa.) IV. 1653/2 Sometimes absorption optics are used on the ultracentrifuge, and in this event concentrations are measured by photodensitometry. **1964** *Jrnl. Cell Biol.* XXII. 448/2 The most conspicuous structural change in the plastids during the 1 to 3 hours of photodestruction of the pigments is the formation of stacked lamellar structures. **1977** I. M. Campbell *Energy & Atmosphere* ix. 371 The minimum in the altitude concentration profile of nitric oxide with altitude near to 70 km is evidently a reflection more of the variation of production rate with altitude than of the variation of the photodestruction rate. **1943** *Phil. Trans. R. Soc.* A. CCXXXIX. 278 (*heading*) Photodetachment of electrons from normal O^- ions. **1973** *Nature* 26 Oct. 450/2 The profiles..confirmed the hypothesis that the daytime D region of the ionosphere below 80 km may be formed by photo-detachment of electrons. **1959** *Rev. Sci. Instruments* XXX. 593/1 The application of the parametric amplifier principle to photodetection. **1972** S. S. Charschan *Lasers in Industry* ix. 523 In direct photodetection, all optical frequency and phase information is lost. **1947** *Proc. Nat. Electronics Conf. 1946* 171 (*heading*) Photodetectors for ultraviolet, visible and infrared radiation. **1959** *Proc. IRE* XLVII. 1475/1 Until the early 1950's, the development of infrared photodetectors revolved principally around polycrystalline films of PbS, PbSe, or PbTe. **1967** *New Scientist* 16 Nov. 416/1 The infrared radiation falls on the photodetector and produces visible radiation from the photoemitter. **1972** S. S. Charschan *Lasers in Industry* ix. 529 Quantum or photodetectors depend on the action of light quanta on a single electron rather than on the absorption and distribution of energy over an entire macroscopic body. **1935** *Proc. R. Soc.* A. CLI. 481 The next point of interest is the probability of the 'photo'-disintegration. *Ibid.* 482 The effect of the γ-rays of radium in producing the photo-disintegration was also examined. **1942** J. D. Stranathan *'Particles' of Mod. Physics* xi. 444 Another illustration of photodisintegration is that of ${}_4Be^9$. This reaction is ${}_4Be^9 + h\nu \rightarrow {}_4Be^8 + {}_0n^1$. **1968** D. D. Clayton *Princ. Stellar Evolution & Nucleosynthesis* vii. 519 What happens then, as the temperature rises, may be described as a redistribution of loosely bound nucleons into more tightly bound states. We choose to call this process..photodisintegration rearrangement. **1903** *Encycl. Brit.* XXXV. 729/4 (Index), Photo-effect. **1913** H. S. Allen *Photo-Electricity* i. 8 For substances which show only a 'normal' photo-effect the specific photo-electric activity increases continuously as the wave-length diminishes. **1938** R. W. Lawson tr. *Hevesy & Paneth's Man. Radioactivity* (ed. 2) x. 123 These [γ-]rays are able to bring about nuclear photo-effects by the ejection of neutrons from the nuclei of various elements. **1960** R. H. Bube *Photoconductivity of Solids* i. 2 Two new photoeffects were discovered in the early 1930s. In 1931, Dember..reported that a potential difference was developed in cuprous oxide in the direction of the light. **1974** *Encycl. Brit. Macropædia* XV. 439/2 The photoeffect probability goes as approximately the fifth power of the atomic number of the absorbing material. **1966** *Physical Rev.* CXLIX. 55/1 Photoejection of a 4*d* electron. **1977** I. M. Campbell *Energy & Atmosphere* i. 2 The photoejection of electrons from a metal surface irradiated with monochromatic..light. **1972** *Nature* 7 July 37/2 If the energy of light is used effectively in an electrochemical system, it should be possible to decompose water with visible light. Here we describe a novel type of photo-electrochemical cell which decomposes water in this way. **1976** *Ibid.* 9 Sept. 100/1 Better and cheaper means of storing electricity..remain desirable, and hence the practical importance of photoelectrochemical decomposition of water into hydrogen and oxygen. **1953** *Proc. Physical Soc.* B. LXVI. 743 If the slab [of germanium] is placed in a magnetic field perpendicular to the direction of illumination, a voltage is produced at right angles to both field and illumination (photoelectromagnetic effect). **1965** K. F. Hulme in C. A. Hogarth *Materials used in Semiconductor Devices* vi. 153 The theory and the constructional details and performance of a practical room-temperature photoelectromagnetic detector have been given. **1965** M. Evenari in E. J. Bowen *Recent Progress in Photobiol.* v. 161 The ocean of light which constitutes the photoenvironment. **1973** *Nature* 6 July 37/1 The adrenal cortex, thyroid and pineal of birds are affected by the photoenvironment. **1962** *Jrnl. Gen. Physiol.* XLV. 703 (*heading*) Photoenzymatic repair of ultraviolet damage in DNA. **1975** *Nature* 17 Apr. 627/1 If ultraviolet biological damage can be reversed by true photoenzymatic repair, then dimers have a major role in the production of that damage. **1966** *Adv. Radiation Biol.* II. 23 A photoenzymatically reversible competitive inhibition of transforming DNA repair *in vitro*. **1960** Photoenzyme [see *photoreactivating *ppl. a.*]. **1966** *Adv. Radiation Biol.* II. 19 This type of PR [*sc.* photoreactivation] does not result from the same type of photoenzyme. **1924** H. S. Taylor *Treat. Physical Chem.* II. xviii. 1239 With constant illumination, between reaction temperatures of 50 and 800° C., the photo-equilibrium is the same, regardless of the gas temperature. This indicates that the temperature coefficient of the two photo-processes is the same. **1962** *Jrnl. Physical Chem.* LXVI. 2472/2 In reversible photoisomerizations photoequilibrium is established when the rates of the two opposing photoreactions $A \rightleftarrows B$ under the action of the particular photoactive light used, are equal. **1974** *Chem. Soc. Rev.* III. 332 As the sensitizer energy is reduced the efficiency of sensitization of the *cis*-isomer falls below that of the *trans*. As a result there is a region where the *trans*-isomer is selectively excited and the proportion of *cis*-isomer at photoequilibrium is greater. **1918** *Physical Rev.* XI. 485 Having followed the kathodo phosphorescence for 300 seconds by the usual well-known method of a single excitation and determined the form of the curve of decay, the relation of this curve to that obtained by photoexcitation is of importance. **1946** *Nature* 2 Nov. 603/2 In the large gap region it was necessary to increase the stress above that calculated, to provide the required photoexcitation. **1975** *McGraw-Hill Yearbk. Sci. & Technol.* 357/1 In photoconductors the carriers can be generated internally by photoexcitation. **1954** *Ann. Rev. Plant Physiol.* V. 277 In basic solvents like pyridine, photoexcited chlorophyll can be reduced by ascorbate. **1970** *Physics Bull.* Nov. 488/2 The migration of photoexcited electrons out of regions of high optical excitation to be entrapped in regions of low optical excitation. **1967** *Sci. Amer.* Apr. 47 Photofabrication starts with drawings and by chemistry and optics transforms them into the objects, usually with a linear reduction in scale. **1968** *Physics Bull.* Dec. 423/1 The application of holography to ..the photofabrication of microcircuits. **1939** *Physical Rev.* LVI. 449/2 We can form an estimate of the cross section for photo-fission by comparison with the yields of photoneutrons. **1974** *Encycl. Brit. Macropædia* XIV. 299/2 More complicated [photonuclear] interactions involve either the emission of heavier particles.., many particles, or photofission. **1949** *Electronics* Feb. 100/1 The Photoformer, as it is called since it generates waveshapes through the use of a cathode-ray tube and phototube, is fed with a sawtooth voltage of the desired frequency. **1965** *Math. in Biol. & Med.* (Med. Res. Council) i. 38 Figure 3 shows how an analogue computer is used to resolve such a curve into its components... A voltage generated from the curve by a photoformer is compared with the sum of exponentials generated in the computer. **1951** J. W. Foster in Werkman & Wilson *Bacterial Physiol.* 364 The above two classes of autotrophs have their counterparts in the heterotrophic bacteria. Thus there are chemoheterotrophs and photoheterotrophs... The latter are a specialized photosynthetic group which is capable of using for growth both radiant energy and preformed organic matter. **1963** *Studies on Microalgae & Photosynthetic Bacteria* (Jap. Soc. Plant Physiologists) 465 Two characteristic facultative photoheterotrophs.. have been examined for response to nitrate under various conditions of growth. **1945** E. I. Rabinowitch *Photosynthesis* I. v. 106 The metabolism of the 'photoheterotrophic' bacteria—that is, bacteria which require light for the assimilation of organic nutrients, seemed at first to be quite different from that of the 'photautotrophic' bacteria. **1975** *Nature* 18 Dec. 631/1 Typical purple bacteria produce large quantities of molecular hydrogen during photoheterotrophic growth on organic acids. **1972** *Science* 27 Oct. 404/3 Under anaerobic conditions in the light, cultures [of flexibacteria] grow photoheterotrophically. **1938** *Recueil des Travaux bot. Néerlandais* XXXV. 12 The decrease of the curvature with auxin-a by light must be ascribed to the photo-inactivation of the auxin-a-lactone. **1973** *Biochemistry* (Easton, Pa.) XII. 2540/2 Studies..on the photoinactivation of a purified bovine kidney mutarotase were undertaken. **1937** *Nature* 25 Sept. 545/1 In the chicken retina, which contains principally cones, attempts to identify photo-labile pigments heretofore have failed. **1975** *Ibid.* 31 Jan. 316/2 Some photolabile metabolite accumulates until a threshold concentration is reached. **1961** Webster, Photolability. **1968** *Arch. Biochem. & Biophysics* CXXIII. 109 (*heading*) Formation and photolability of a methyl cobalamin enzyme. **1958** R. Y. Stanier et al. *Gen. Microbiol.* 669 The most familiar examples of the photolithotrophs are the green plants, which use water as a hydrogen donor in photosynthesis. **1971** J. S. Poindexter *Microbiol.* xxi. 473 Ectotrophic mycorrhizae are found in many forest trees... Generally, these trees are photolithotrophs as adults, and their seeds contain sufficient organic nutrients to provide the energy for germination and development of photosynthetic capacity. **1976** *Nature* 18 Mar. 200/2 Photolithotrophs such as *Thiorhodaceae* or purple sulphur bacteria and *Chlorobacteriaceae* or green sulphur bacteria, learned, through photochemical promotion, to use inorganic reductants as electron donors. **1958** R. Y. Stanier et al. *Gen. Microbiol.* xiv. 292 For the enrichment of chemolithotrophic and photolithotrophic organisms, organic compounds must be omitted from the medium, and CO_2 or bicarbonate must be used as the only source of carbon. **1972** Goodwin & Mercer *Introd. Plant Biochem.* i. 3 The phototrophic bacteria are subdivided into photolithotrophic bacteria (e.g. green and purple sulphur bacteria) whose growth is dependent on exogenous inorganic hydrogen donors..and photoorganotrophic bacteria (e.g. purple, non-sulphur bacteria) whose growth is dependent on exogenous organic hydrogen donors. The biochemistry of photolithotrophic bacteria is related to that of green plants. **1947** *Cold Spring Harbor Symp. Quant. Biol.* XI. 302 The following terminology is hereby proposed to characterize nutritional types [of microorganism]... A. *Phototrophy.* Energy chiefly provided by photochemical reaction. 1. Photolithotrophy. Growth dependent on exogenous inorganic H-donors. 2. Photoorganotrophy. Growth dependent on exogenous organic H-donors. B. *Chemotrophy.* Energy provided entirely by dark chemical reaction. **1969** F. E. Round *Introd. Lower Plants* i. 2 Photolithotrophy is the common photosynthesis of plants possessing chlorophyll a and using water as the hydrogen donor. **1959** R. A. Smith *Semiconductors* viii. 315 From equations (309) and (328) we may obtain an expression for the ratio of the photo-magnetic current per unit magnetic field to the photo-conductive current per unit electric field. **1975** *Physics Bull.* Jan. 15/1 The materials in which such 'photomagnetic' phenomena have been observed so far are magnetic insulators or semiconductors. **1934** *Physik. Zeitschr. der Sowjetunion* V. 597 (*heading*) On the explanation of the photomagnetoelectric effect in semi-conductors. **1967** R. H. Bube in Willardson & Beer *Semiconductors & Semimetals* III. xi. 473 The photomagnetoelectric (PME) effect provides a technique for the determination of minority-carrier lifetimes. **1965** W. R. Runyan *Silicon Semiconductor Technol.* iv. 76 Silicon dioxide is very convenient to use as a mask since it can be easily delineated by standard photomask techniques. **1977** *Sci. Amer.* Sept. 114/3 Thus each photomask, typically a glass plate about five inches on a side, has a single pattern repeated many times over its surface. **1952** R. E. Marshak *Meson Physics* iii. 104 The photomesic production process probably leads, in the majority of cases, to excited states of the final nucleus having smaller spins than 4. **1974** (*title*) Photomesic and photonuclear reactions and investigation methods with synchrotrons. **1950** A. S. Bishop *Photoproduction of Mesons from Hydrogen* (Univ. of Calif. Radiation Lab., UCRL-874) 40 By definition, $\sigma(E_{ph})$, the excitation function at 90° for photo-meson production from protons, constitutes the probability that a photon of energy E_{ph}, interacting with a proton, will produce a meson at 90° in the laboratory system. **1951** *Physical Rev.* LXXXI. 189/1 The angular dependence of the nuclear cross section for photo-meson production..yields fairly direct information concerning the momentum distribution with[in] the nucleus. **1954** *Ibid.* XCV. 592/2 (*heading*) Negative-to-positive ratio of photomesons from deuterium. **1955** *Ibid.* XCIX. 1694/2 It is in the photoelectric mixing tube, or photomixer,.. that the beat frequency is generated. **1975** *Nature* 13 Feb. 515/1 We have built a heterodyne spectrometer using..a HgCdTe photodiode as a photomixer. **1962** *Appl. Optics* I. 51/1 This paper reports the observation of microwave signals produced by photomixing of near-neighbour axial mode components in the output spectrum of a ruby optical maser. **1966** M. Ross *Laser Receivers* iv. 125 Photomixing has been successfully achieved under laboratory conditions. However, no operational receiver incorporating photomixing has yet been announced. **1950** Curtis & Clark *Introd. Plant Physiol.* xx. 630 Some plants are evidently highly indifferent to the photoperiod with respect to their flowering behavior and will flower over almost any photoperiod ranging from a 5-hr daily exposure to a 24-hr, or continuous, exposure. Some of the plants that fall into this indeterminate, or photoneutral, group are buckwheat, sunflower, tomato, cotton, and dandelion. **1975** *Nature* 25 Dec. 712/2 Natural populations of *D. melanogaster* and *D. pseudoobscura* are photoneutral in general, but respond rapidly to selection for positive or negative phototactic behaviour. **1935** *Proc. R. Soc.* A. CLI. 488 The angular distribution of the photo-neutrons from beryllium was investigated. **1975** K. G. McNeill et al. in Jochim & Ziegler *Interaction Stud. in Nuclei* 451 Predictions have been made of the angular distributions of the photoprotons emitted from ${}^{40}Ca$ and going to the ground state of ${}^{39}K$..and of the distribution of ground state photoneutrons. **1949** *Science* 2 Dec. 579/1 There is an appreciable background of photonuclear stars and proton tracks. **1959** Deutsch & Kofoed-Hansen in E. Segrè *Exper. Nucl. Physics* III. x. ii. 305 Photonuclear reactions are sometimes used for the detection of high-energy gamma-rays and for the measurement of their energies. **1973** *Physics Bull.* Nov. 694/3 The program will cover effective interactions in light nuclei, photonuclear reactions, neutron scattering below 15 MeV, [etc.]. **1965** A. H. Rose *Chem. Microbiol.* iii. 40 Thus we arrive at the following four nutritional categories of micro-organisms based on their energy-yielding metabolism: photolithotrophs, photoorganotrophs, chemolithotrophs and chemoorganotrophs. **1976** *Nature* 18 Mar. 200/2 Photo-organotrophs such as purple non-sulphur bacteria use as electron donors in the light, in anaerobic conditions, those organic electron donors which were used by fermenters in the dark. **1958** R. Y. Stanier et al. *Gen. Microbiol.* xiv. 292 Since the photoorganotrophic bacteria require various growth factors, a small amount of yeast extract is generally added to the enrichment medium. **1972** Photoorganotrophic [see *photolithotrophic* adj. above]. **1971** J. S. Poindexter *Microbiol.* xiii. 154 The few types of algae that can grow photoorganotrophically are aerobes. **1947** Photoorganotrophy [see *photolithotrophy* above]. **1952** *Physiologia Plantarum* V. 81 Bünning concluded that light is favourable to flowering during the 'rising' or photophile phase of the leaf movement, and inhibiting during the falling or scotophile phase. **1964** E. Bünning *Physiol. Clock* xiv. 122 During the long dark period the plants endogenously reach a second 'photophil' state. **1965** *Plant Physiol.* XL. 873/1 Light during the photophil phases may stimulate flowering to such an extent that..nearly every bud on the plant responds. **1975** D. Vince-Prue *Photoperiodism in Plants* v. 170 He [*sc.* Bünning] proposed that photoperiodism involves a regular oscillation of phases or half-cycles with different sensitivity to light, and postulated that transfer to light sets in motion a *photophile* (or light-loving) phase, which is followed about twelve hours later by a *skotophile* (dark-loving) phase, also of twelve hours duration. **1900** A. J. Ewart tr. *Pfeffer's Physiol. Plants* I. vii. 358 Even for light-loving (photophilic) plants bright diffuse daylight seems as a general rule to be preferable to strong sunlight. **1967** M. E. Hale *Biol. Lichens* v. 72 Photophilic algae as *Pleurococcus*, when lichenized would be inhibited by reduced light. **1905** I. B. Balfour tr. *C. E. von Goebel's Organogr. Plants* II. 463 They [*sc.* geophilous shoots]..are united by many intermediate stages with 'photophilous' shoots. **1967** M. E. Hale *Biol. Lichens* vii. 87 The photophilous (light-loving) characteristics of most lichens. **1934** Webster, Photophily. **1960** *Cold Spring Harbor Symp. Quantitative Biol.* XXV. 241/1 The phase of strongest responsiveness to temperature in both types coincides with maximum responsiveness to light..: with maximum photophily in long-day plants and maximum scotophily in short-day plants. **1974** *Biol. Abstr.* LVII. 762/1 An ecological scale of photophily was developed. **1914** S. E. SHEPPARD *Photo-Chem.* p. vii, There exists..some difference of opinion as to the desirability of incorporating a discussion of photo-physical and radiation phenomena and laws in a work on photo-chemistry. **1971** *Physics Bull.* Sept. 546/1 (Advt.), A comprehensive treatment is given of the interactions of low energy electrons with atoms and molecules, and photophysical processes. **1976** *Nature* 15 Apr. 654/2 Two chapters deal with photophysical processes: the first is a brief survey of the electronic spectroscopy of complexes. **1961** M. CALVIN in McElroy & Glass *Symposium on Light & Life* 317 A discussion of some of the photochemistry and photophysics of porphyrins. **1970** J. B. BIRKS *Photophysics of Aromatic Molecules* p. vii, There are six related subjects concerned with the interaction of radiation with molecular systems: photophysics, photochemistry and photobiology, which deal with optical non-ionizing radiation; and radiation physics, radiation chemistry and radiation biology, which deal with ionizing radiation. Photophysics is the keystone of the structure, since it is an integral constituent of each of the other five subjects. **1937** *Nature* 25 Sept. 545/2 The familiar Purkinje effect, for which clearly the extracted photo-pigments form an adequate chemical basis. **1964** S. DUKE-ELDER *Parsons' Dis. Eye* (ed. 14) xxiv. 364 It [*sc.* colour blindness] is an inherited condition,..and is probably due to the absence of one of the two photopigments normally found in the foveal cones. **1970** HAND & DAVENPORT in P. Halldal *Photobiol. of Microorganisms* ix. 278 The photopigment responsible for phototaxis and photokinesis is probably flavin. **1971** *Time* 15 Mar. 46 Light measurements by Pioneer's imaging photo-polarimeter will enable computers on earth to construct about ten pictures of the planet [*sc.* Jupiter] that will show features as small as 250 miles across. **1972** *Daily Colonist* (Victoria, B.C.) 25 Feb. 5/2 In the last 20 hours before closest approach, the spacecraft's imaging photopolarimeter will take 100 pictures of the planet. **1974** *Nature* 6 Sept. 18/1 The imaging photopolarimeter of Gehrels *et al.* contained a 2·5 cm telescope which made maps of Jupiter. **1971** *Icarus* XV. 454 (*heading*) Photopolarimetric observations of the minor planet Flora. **1974** *Sci. Amer.* Feb. 43/1 More detailed knowledge of the planet's atmosphere awaits analysis of photopolarimetry measurements. **1914** *Physical Rev.* IV. 229 The results as a whole confirm the point of view adopted by Richardson and Compton in regard to the relation between photo- and contact potentials. **1924** *Jrnl. Physical Chem.* XXVIII. 333 Becquerel was the first to observe that the photo-potential of the silver iodide electrode: electrolyte cell was not always positive. **1976** *Nature* 9 Sept. 99/2 If we want to use a semiconductor with an optical bandgap, so as to give optimal utilisation of solar radiation.., the maximum photopotential attainable will be ~0·4 eV. **1924** Photoprocess [see *photo-equilibrium* above]. **1926** *Trans. Faraday Soc.* XXI. 560 Weigert sees in the photosensitisation of ozone decomposition by chlorine, the simplest possible photoprocess. **1959** W. H. KLEIN in R. B. Withrow *Photoperiodism* III. 207 (*heading*) Interaction of growth factors with photoprocess in seedling growth. **1974** *Photochem. & Photobiol.* XIX. 441/2 The versatility of flavins as photosensitizers in numerous photoprocesses. **1953** *Physical Rev.* XCI. 480/2 The cross section obtained in this way is modified principally by the presence of terms describing the multiple scattering of the photo produced mesons. **1973** *Physics Bull.* July 431/1 Modulation excitation (ME) spectrophotometry is a technique to measure the absorption spectra of short lived photoproduced transients, such as excited states of molecules. **1926** E. MAYER *Clin. Applic. Sunlight* iii. 30 This action of small doses of radiant energy may be due to toxic 'photo-product'. **1941** *Brit. Jrnl. Psychol.* XXXII. 79 The rate of dark adaptation is supposed..to be determined by the concentration of photoproduct present at each moment. **1977** *Nature* 17 Feb. 660/2 Comparison of spectra taken before and after prolonged irradiation..showed no change in the relative position or intensity of the shoulder, eliminating a permanent photoproduct generated by the high intensity pulse as the species responsible for the shoulder. **1950** *Federation Proc.* IX. 544/1 (*caption*) Photoproduction of H_2 from succinate by *Rhodopseudomonas gelatinosa.* **1950** A. S. BISHOP *Photoproduction of Mesons from Hydrogen* (Univ. of Calif. Radiation Lab., UCRL-874) 5 From the measured energy distribution of the mesons at 90°..it is possible to determine the excitation function for photoproduction of mesons at 90°. **1961** *Nature* 13 May 602/1 Photoproduction of hydrogen gas by photosynthetic cells was first observed..in the green alga *Scenedesmus.* **1974** FRAUENFELDER & HENLEY *Subatomic Physics* xii. 326 (*caption*) Total cross sections for the photoproduction of neutral and charged pions from hydrogen, as a function of the incident photon energy. **1966** SHIMOMURA & JOHNSON in Johnson & Haneda *Bioluminescence in Progress* 495 Solutions of the protein, for which the general term 'photoprotein' is suggested, show a fluorescence maximum at 458 mμ when excited at 350 mμ. *Ibid.* 497 As a convenient, general designation of the active component in the hydromedusan and *Chaetopterus* type of system, to which the terms 'luciferin' and 'luciferase' do not apply in their usual meaning, we propose the term 'photoprotein'. **1975** *Nature* 17 July 236/2 The photoprotein aequorin (molecular weight about 30,000) isolated from the bioluminescent jellyfish *Aequorea aequorea* emits blue light. **1935** CHADWICK & GOLDHABER in *Proc. R. Soc.* A. CLI. 480 The experimental arrangement for the detection of the protons released from deuterium, which we may for convenience call 'photo'-protons, was as follows. *Ibid.*, An estimate of the energy of the photoprotons can be deduced from the measurement of the size of the oscillograph kicks. **1975** Photoproton [see *photoneutron* above]. **1909** *Jrnl. Chem. Soc.* XCV. 442 That most remarkable photo-reaction which Marckwald..has named phototropy. **1925** H. S. ALLEN *Photo-Electricity* (ed. 2) xiv. 235 Perrin has developed..the view that 'ordinary' chemical reactions may be regarded as due to radiation, *i.e.* they are photo-reactions. **1975** D. VINCE-PRUE *Photoperiodism in Plants* iv. 146 The photoreactions which control the induction of flowering in LDP [*sc.* long-day plants] and SDP [*sc.* short-day plants] are remarkably similar. **1950** *Proc. Nat. Acad. Sci.* XXXVI. 626 The photorecovery after ultra-violet radiation, manifested by the *Arbacia* egg, seems in all ways parallel to the 'photoreactivation' in fungi and bacteria. **1974** *Encycl. Brit. Macropædia* XV. 390/1 It is probable that photorecovery mechanisms are continually operative in some plants exposed to direct action of sunlight. **1969** *Proc. Nat. Acad. Sci.* LXIV. 1103 The enzymic activity of acetylcholinesterase can be photoregulated through the mediation of photochromic inhibitors of the enzyme. **1957** *Bot. Gaz.* CXVIII. 207/2 Flowering, seed germination, and certain other photoregulated phenomena. **1970** *Proc. Nat. Acad. Sci.* LXVI. 853 A systematic study of the interaction of naturally occurring carotenoids with various enzyme systems might provide information useful for an understanding of photoregulated processes found in nature. **1968** *Science* 27 Dec. 1487 (*heading*) Photoregulation of an enzymic process by means of a light-sensitive ligand. **1970** *Proc. Nat. Acad. Sci.* LXVI. 850 A possible role in photoregulation is suggested for naturally occurring carotenoids. **1959** R. J. DOWNS in R. B. Withrow *Photoperiodism* ii. 129 The woody plant thus appears to be running two different systems with the same photoregulator. **1970** *Nature* 22 Aug. 778/1 Bieth *et al.* conjecture that carotenoids of animals and plants..might function as photoregulators, controlling diurnal and seasonal changes in metabolic levels. **1967** *Mutation Res.* IV. 22 The impossibility of attaining complete photorepair of lethal and mutagenic damage raises the important question of whether there is a qualitative difference between damage which is photoreactivable and damage which is not. **1978** *Nature* 31 Aug. 891/1 Forward mutations at a variety of loci in *rad* 1–1 yeast are also subject to photorepair. **1966** *Adv. Radiation Biol.* II. 49 The number of photorepairable lethal lesions in..DNA. **1978** *Nature* 31 Aug. 890/2 As many as 80% of the extra *lys*+ revertants are photorepairable and therefore dimer-associated in origin. **1925** *Astrophysical Jrnl.* LXII. 317 (*heading*) Apparent photoresistance effects. **1957** *Chem. Abstr.* LI. 7134 At low levels of ionizing radiation CdS photoresistances exhibited considerable inertness. **1970** *New Scientist* 14 May 335/1 The rate at which the charge of any photo-element leaks away between sweeps depends upon the value of the photo-resistance. **1978** *Nature* 23 Mar. 315/1 The light rays impinged on the photoresistances L_1 and L_2, which formed a bridge circuit with the variable resistances R_1 and R_2. **1933** *Jrnl. Inst. Electr. Engin.* LXXIII. 437/1 The first step towards the conversion of the picture into electrical energy was taken by May in 1873, with his discovery of the photo-resistive property of selenium. **1973** *Sci. Amer.* Jan. 116/3 Selenium and cadmium photocells are more sensitive, but they are of the photoresistive type and require an external source of power. **1959** *Chem. Abstr.* LIII. 13793 (*heading*) Germanium photoresistors. **1965** LINDMAYER & WRIGLEY *Fund. Semiconductor Devices* x. 384 Photoresistors made from nearly intrinsic polycrystalline thin films are very sensitive detectors for the average intensity of a wide source spectrum. **1969** *New Scientist* 18 Sept. 568/3 Shamer and Fox observed no fringe shift using..sensitive photoresisters to detect the fringe positions. **1977** J. HEDGECOE *Photographer's Handbk.* 21 (*in figure*) Cds photo-resistor cell. **1950** *Ann. Rev. Plant Physiol.* I. 43 The photoresponses of plants at different ages or stages of development may be opposite. **1955** HENDRICKS & BORTHWICK in *Proc. 1st Internat. Photobiol. Congr.* i. 23 Photoresponses controlling etiolation of plants and germination of seeds are also examples [of photoperiodism]. **1971** *Jrnl. Appl. Physics* XLII. 568/2 Additional silver increases the photoresponse. **1976** *Nature* 19 Aug. 680/2 For photoresponse spectra, electrodes were illuminated by 400-Hz chopped, monochromatic radiation. **1955** HENDRICKS & BORTHWICK in *Proc. 1st Internat. Photobiol. Congr.* i. 31 Flowering in photo-responsive plants can be controlled through a single leaf in the presence of other leaves. **1974** *Nature* 26 Apr. 800/2 If the cells of *D. discoideum* are broken gently in a Dounce homogenizer, the photoresponsive pigment sediments with the mitochondrial fraction collected by differential centrifugation between 6,000 and 10,000 g. **1972** *Science* 27 Oct. 421/2 Severance of the optic nerve in immature male ducks decreased the photoresponsiveness to one-fifth of the normal. **1954** *Bot. Gaz.* CXV. 216/2 (*heading*) Photoreversal of promotion and inhibition of germination of Grand Rapids lettuce seed at 20°C. after irradiation at 26° and 6°–8°. **1966** *Adv. Radiation Biol.* II. 20 The direct nonenzymatic photoreversal of UV damage to DNA. **1954** HENDRICKS & BORTHWICK in D. Rudnick *Aspects of Synthesis & Order in Growth* vii. 159 Some further details about the several photoreversibilities. **1955** *Plant Physiol.* XXX. 468 (*heading*) Photoreversibility of leaf and hypocotyl elongation of dark grown red kidney bean seedlings. **1975** D. VINCE-PRUE *Photoperiodism in Plants* iv. 108 Extracts of leaves of several species have been found to show photoreversibility. **1954** HENDRICKS & BORTHWICK in D. Rudnick *Aspects of Synthesis & Order in Growth* vii. 154 The cuticle coloration response..is photoreversible. **1966** *Adv. Radiation Biol.* II. 21 The photoreversible effects of UV on cytoplasmic entities of cells..formerly suggested RNA damages. **1972** W. SHROPSHIRE in Mitrakos & Shropshire *Phytochrome* p. v, Phytochrome is a photoreversible pigment which can exist in two principal forms. **1962** *Instrument Pract.* XVI. 1519/2 (*heading*) Subminiature photosensors. **1964** *New Scientist* 4 June 594/2 The photo-sensor is simply a detector which changes light into an electrical signal... Several types exist, such as photo-emissive cells, photo-conductors, photo-voltaic cells, and photo-transistors. **1975** *Physics Bull.* Feb. 82/3 The solid state cameras..replace the bulky Vidicon tube normally used by an array of 10^4 photosensors, which have a broad spectral response. **1919** *Jrnl. Gen. Physiol.* I. 556 The photosensory responses of an animal like *Mya.* **1972** *Internat. Jrnl. Neurosci.* III. 145 (*heading*) Photosensory cell of the flatworm ocellus. **1953** *Amer. Jrnl. Psychiatry* CIX. 744/1 Although the method for producing convulsions (photoshock) presented here may be considered similar to that of Metrazol shock, it is our impression that this modified procedure has several possible advantages. **1955** *Sci. News Let.* 21 May 325/1 Instead of electric current, a flashing light is used for 'photo-shock' treatment. **1936** *Jrnl. Gen. Physiol.* XX. 52 The ammoniacal retina bleaches more slowly than the neutral tissue. This difference cannot be ascribed to induced photostability in the visual purple itself. **1965** J. B. THOMAS *Primary Photoprocesses in Biol.* iv. 85 The acid-resistance as well as the photostability of suspensions of such native chlorophyll are much higher than those of dissolved chlorophyll. **1977** *Protecting World's Crops* (Shell Internat. Petroleum Co.) 2 Recently, however, compounds have been synthesized which combine with photostability remarkable activity against insects. **1921** *Jrnl. Gen. Physiol.* III. 380 The filters are quite photostable. But in order to avoid any possible bleaching effect, a shutter is placed between the light source and the filter. **1973** Photostable [see *photocatalysed* ppl. adj. s.v. *PHOTOCATALYSE *v.*]. **1924** *Trans. Faraday Soc.* XX. 112 The decomposition of sulphur dioxide gas under the action of light radiated from a uviol mercury lamp has been investigated, and the resulting photostationary state, characteristic of a given set of conditions, determined, using a number of different light filters. **1972** W. HAUPT in Mitrakos & Shropshire *Phytochrome* xxi. 561 Whenever a randomly distributed population of phytochrome molecules is irradiated, light is absorbed by P_r and P_{fr} to different extents... This difference leads to a photostationary state of P_{fr}/P which depends only on the wavelength and which can therefore be predicted precisely. **1956** *Nature* 21 Jan. 143/1 Attempts to photostimulate tropical birds have been rare, and the results confusing. **1971** *New Scientist* 29 July 255/1 Since it seems that the timing of a light stimulus rather than its duration might be important it is conceivable that a bird could be photostimulated with even very small daily doses of light that would normally be non-stimulatory. **1959** D. S. FARNER in R. B. Withrow *Photoperiodism* x. 729 In domestic ducks..both ocular and encephalic receptors are involved in photostimulated testicular development. **1970** *Proc. Nat. Acad. Sci.* LXVI. 850 (*caption*) Photostimulated *cis-trans* isomerism. **1967** *Ibid.* LVIII. 2129 The initial photostimulating step..is postulated as being followed at some stage by release of a 'hormone', the hypothetical 'florigen'. **1937** *Jrnl. Exper. Biol.* XIV. 86 Many shallow-water teleosts,..when blinded, show a pigmentary response to photostimulation. **1955** *Sci. News Let.* 21 May 325/1 The flashing light shock is given after patients have had injected into their veins the drug, Azozol... Results were compared with..another group given less intensive 'photostimulation', in which smaller quantities of the drug were used and the light flashes were interrupted oftener. **1959** D. S. FARNER in R. B. Withrow *Photoperiodism* x. 724 These investigations suggest that photostimulation of gonadal development does not involve entirely the same receptors as are involved in vision. **1967** *Psychol. Abstr.* XLI. 1499/1 The role of intermediary structures of the brain in the formation of certain functional relationships in the human CNS was studied, employing single, rhythmic, and interrupted photostimulation in Ss with lesions of the diencephalic region and brain stem. **1971** *Nature* 18 June 465/1 The lamp of the photo-stimulator was above and behind an animal's head at 110 cm from the centre of the hemisphere. **1976** *Ibid.* 3 June 423/2 Photostimulatory cues..influence the hypothalamic input to the pars intermedia. **1939** *Jrnl. Inst. Electr. Engin.* LXXXV. 472/2 The optical picture to be transmitted is focused on a continuous transparent photo-surface. **1952** *Electronic Engin.* XXIV. 302/1 The spectral response curves of these photosurfaces are compared. **1970** *Proc. IEEE* LVIII. 1794/1 The AgOCs photocathode, the only photosurface to give appreciable response beyond 1 micron until recently. **1929** *Telegraph & Telephone Jrnl.* XVI. 3/2 Photo-telegrams will have to be charged by space measurement instead of the number of words. **1948** *Post Office Guide* 283 A reply voucher issued with a phototelegram may be used to prepay an ordinary telegram. **1968** *Guardian* 10 Apr. 8/3 To quote the bleak prose of Her Majesty's Post Office, 'Telex—no service. Phototelegrams—no service. Telephone—no service.' **1909** *Electrical Mag.* XII. 249/1 (*heading*) The Sémat phototelegraph. **1949** *Post Office Electr. Engineers' Jrnl.* XLI. 189 (*heading*) The Post Office phototelegraph service to Europe. **1959** J. W. FREEBODY *Telegr.* xiii. 538/2 (*heading*) The Muirhead-Jarvis photo-telegraph equipment. **1909** *Electrical Mag.* XI. 57/1 New York, Chicago, and other cities are now about to commence photo-telegraphic trials. **1940** *Wireless World* Sept. 398/3 The clarity of reception, at a distance of 12,000 miles, of photographs transmitted from the West Base of the U.S. Navy Antarctic Expedition, is attributed to the use of a recently developed phototelegraphic technique to counteract selective fading of the carrier frequency. **1886** W. GEMMILL *Brit. Pat. 4841* 6 It will be seen that the system of photo-telegraphy opens up an entirely new field in telegraphy, namely the actual reproduction of photographs through the medium of electrically conducting wires. **1930** *Post Office Electr. Engineers' Jrnl.* XXIII. 1/2 British newspapers using photo-telegraphy transmit to and from London and their provincial offices using 'Four-Wire' telephone circuits. **1976** R. N. RENTON *Telegr.* iv. 60/1 Telephone circuits are used as the 'bearer' circuits for multiplex telegraph systems and for phototelegraphy. **1942** S. EPSTEIN in *Jrnl. Investigative Dermatol.* V. 290, I propose the term 'phototoxicity' for the primary, non-allergic photosensitivity, and 'phototoxic reaction' for the effect produced by this mechanism... Phototoxic reactions apply indiscriminately to all individuals. **1974** M. C. GERALD *Pharmacol.* xxvii. 471 Demeclocycline has been shown to cause phototoxicity in some patients, where severe burns develop when susceptible patients are exposed to sunlight. **1976** *Arch. Dermatol.* CXII. 327/1 The duration of methoxsalen's phototoxic potentiality, after its application to skin, varied in direct proportion to chemical concentration. **1962** *Jrnl. Physical Chem.* LXVI. 2470 The results indicate the occurrence of consecutive and concurrent phototransformations and thermal interconversions between stereoisomers of the colored modification. **1975** D. VINCE-PRUE *Photoperiodism in Plants* vi. 215 The general conclusion..is that the phototransformation of phytochrome may very rapidly lead to an alteration of membrane properties. **1973** *Physics Bull.* July 431/1 It is obvious that for light induced species with large lifetimes, a simple DC method would suffice to measure their absorption. However, with the short lifetimes associated with excited states, the changes occurring in DC current by the absorption of the phototransient will be much smaller than the noise. **1975** *Nature* 25 Dec. 767/2 Evidence was obtained that this phenomenon is a consequence of an overlap from a shorter lived phototransient (maximum about 530 nm) which is the precursor of the 410-nm species. **1941** R. P. Hall in Calkins & Summers *Protozoa in Biol. Res.* ix. 477 Some [chlorophyll-bearing protozoa] appear to be obligate phototrophs. **1965** A. H. Rose *Chem. Microbiol.* iii. 39 Only a minority of micro-organisms including algae and photosynthetic bacteria and protozoa are able to utilize directly the energy of solar radiation. These organisms are described as phototrophs to distinguish them from chemotrophs. **1975** *Nature* 7 Aug. 463/2 This versatility would give it a clear advantage over other blue-green algae (mostly obligate phototrophs) as well as over bacteria. **1939** H. W. Harvey in P. D. Trask *Recent Marine Sediments* II. 145 Although plants are occasionally found down to considerable depths, they can only grow and increase down to a depth to which sufficient light penetrates. In clear blue-green water of temperate regions this phototrophic zone may extend down to 30 or 50 meters in summer time. **1965** Pelczar & Reid *Microbiol.* (ed. 2) vi. 496/2 Phototrophic organisms are regarded as the most important plankton organisms since they are the primary producers of organic matter via photosynthesis. **1972** Phototrophic [see *photolithotrophic* adj. above]. **1973** *Biochim. & Biophys. Acta* CCCXXX. 80 (*heading*) Membrane differentiation in phototrophically growing *Rhodospirillum rubrum* during transition from low to high light intensity. **1947** [see *photolithotrophy* above]. **1959** Lamanna & Mallette *Basic Bacteriol.* (ed. 2) xi. 467 (*heading*) Phototrophy. **1923** *Jrnl. Physical Chem.* XXVII. 601 The terms 'Becquerel effect' and 'photo-voltaic effect' have been used to distinguish between the light-sensitive systems of the electrode-electrolyte type and the well known 'Hallwachs effect' or 'photo-electric effect'. Cells having one or more light-sensitive electrodes of the former type are able to convert radiant energy into electrical energy and have been called 'photo-voltaic cells'. **1943** D. H. Jacobs *Fund. Optical Engin.* xxiii. 377 Some problems in instrument design call for vacuum or gas-filled photo-emissive cells, and some call for photovoltaic cells. **1953** Amos & Birkinshaw *Television Engin.* I. iii. 41 An electrode may, however, be sensitive to light in other ways; for example, it may be photo-voltaic, i.e., develop e.m.f.s when illuminated. **1957** *Proc. Inst. Electr. Engin.* CIV. B. 467/1 In 1839 Becquerel had found that, when light fell on two metal electrodes immersed in an electrolyte, a potential difference was established between them; this is now known as the photo-voltaic effect. **1964** *Oceanogr. & Marine Biol.* II. 359 Clark (1933) demonstrated the correlation between diurnal migration of plankton and changes in submarine irradiation by means of a photo-voltaic cell. **1977** *Undercurrents* June–July 8/2 A comparison of fast breeder reactor technology with photo-voltaic (solar cell) technology neatly illustrates the two poles of opinion. **1978** *Solar Energy* (Shell Internat. Petroleum Co.) 5 A second way of using sunlight is photovoltaically—the direct conversion of sunlight into electricity. **1973** *Physics Bull.* Jan. 53/3 Papers are invited on the following areas: photovoltaics, thermo-electrics, electrochemical conversion, [etc.]. **1978** *Telegraph* (Brisbane) 16 May 6/2 Photovoltaics is the dream form of solar power—a single cell without moving parts, silent, reliable and pollution free. **1978** *Nature* 13 July 117/1 The United States administration is clearly determined to make a success of photovoltaics.

2. **pho·to-call**, a summoning (cf. Call *sb.* 6 h) of theatrical performers or the like to be photographed; the session at which they are photographed; **pho·tocha:rger**, a device for photographically recording details of books loaned from a library; so **pho·tocha:rging** *vbl. sb.*; **pho:toclino·metry** [Clino-], the process of deriving topographical information about a region from measurements of the brightness distribution in aerial photographs of it; **pho·to-e:ssay**, an essay or short biography consisting of text matter and (numerous) photographs; **pho·to-e:tcher**, one who employs a photographic process in etching; **photofacsi·mile**, facsimile in which the likeness is reproduced in photographic form; usu. *attrib.*; **photoflu·orogram**, a photograph of a fluoroscopic X-ray image; **photoflu·orograph** *sb.* = prec.; *v. trans.*, to examine by photofluorography; **pho:tofluoro·graphy**, photography of a fluoroscopic X-ray image; hence **pho:tofluorogra·phic** *a.*, **pho:tofluorogra·phically** *adv.*; **photoflu·oroscope**, an instrument for taking photofluorograms; **pho:tofluoro·scopy** = *photofluorography* above; **pho:togonio·meter**, (*a*) an instrument for measuring angles indirectly from photographs of an area; (*b*) an instrument for photographically recording the X-rays diffracted at known angles by a crystal or substance; hence **pho:togoniome·tric** *a.*, **-gonio·metry**; **pho:to-interpreta·tion**, the interpretation of aerial photographs; so **photo-inte·rpreter**; **photo-inte·rpretative**, **-inte·rpretive** *adjs.*; **photojou·rnalism**, the use of photographs in journalism; so **photojou·rnalist**; **pho·to-magazine**, a magazine containing many photographs; **pho·tomap**, a map consisting of or drawn on a photograph or photomosaic of the area concerned; **photomosa·ic** = *Mosaic *sb.* 3 d; **photomu·ral**, a mural consisting of a photograph or photographs; **photony·mograph** *Cartography* [Aeolic Gr. ὄνυμ-α name], an instrument used in map production for producing printed names photographically; **pho·toplate**, a photographic plate (Plate *sb.* 5 c); **photora·diogram**, a picture, diagram, or the like transmitted by radio; (formerly a proprietary name in the U.S.); **pho·to-re:cce**, colloq. abbrev. of next; **photo-reco·nnaissance**, reconnaissance by means of aerial photography; **pho:to-reporta·ge** = *photojournalism* above; also, a report that uses photographs; so **pho·to-reporting; pho·to-scanning** *vbl. sb. Med.*, photography of the pattern of radiation from the body following the internal administration of a radio-isotope (e.g. to locate tumours); so **pho·toscan**, a photograph so obtained; **pho·toscanner**, an apparatus for taking such photographs; **photoste·reogram**, a stereophotograph; **photo-ste·reograph**, an instrument for the observation, measurement, and interpretation of pairs of stereophotographs for surveying purposes; so **pho:tostereogra·phic** *a.*; **pho·to-sto:ry**, a story with accompanying photographs; **pho·to-ti:mer**, (*a*) (see quot. 1942); (*b*) (see quot. 1949).

1958 L. Vining in *Newnes Compl. Amat. Photogr.* xx. 182 Theatre photography can be divided into two classes—photo calls when you have control of the actors and lights, and photographing from the stalls during the performance, when you have no control of anything. **1966** 'S. Harvester' *Treacherous Road* i. 22 A string of camels kept motionless against the burnt yellow sky, well-trained as pop singers on a photo-call. **1971** *Times* 8 Sept. 3 Sir Bernard, who plays Iago, promised that the official photocall next week would reveal all of Miss Stevenson, and a very lyrical and beautiful sight it would be. **1977** J. Hedgecoe *Photographer's Handbk.* 93 Most photography of theatrical productions takes place under one of two distinct sets of conditions—during an actual public performance, or during a dress rehearsal or specially staged 'photo-call'. **1959** L. M. Harrod *Librarians' Gloss.* (ed. 2) 208 *Photo-charger*, an electrical machine for recording the loan of books on microfilm. **1967** L. V. Paulin in W. L. Saunders *Librarianship in Brit. Today* i. 4 The introduction of more photochargers. **1955** W. Ashworth *Handbk. Special Librarianship* xii. 319 Such devices as audio-charging..and photo-charging..have been used in America in public libraries. **1967** C. R. Eastwood *Mobile Libraries* ix. 94 Photocharging is widely used on American mobile libraries but not in Britain. **1967** *Surveyor III* (U.S. Nat. Aeronaut. & Space Admin. SP-146) iii. 16 (*caption*) Photoclinometric profiles of the Surveyor III landing site. Profiles were calculated from photometric measurements of Lunar Orbiter III photograph H154..(photoclinometry by H. E. Holt and S. G. Priebe). **1974** *Nature* 10 May 132/1 The development of inferred topography on the basis of the brightness distribution in the image of a surface exhibiting diffuse reflection, and a knowledge of the quantitative law of light scattering for the kind of surface under scrutiny, has been called photoclinometry by common agreement over the past few years. (The word 'photoclinometry' is due to J. F. McCauley...) An operational photoclinometric theory adapted to light scattering properties peculiar to the Moon was worked out..several years ago. **1975** *Times* 18 June 2/2 A group..specializing in lunar and planetry sciences at Lancaster University..is using a method known as photoclinometry to measure the profiles and heights of hills, craters, ridges and cliffs [on Mercury]; the process depends on assessing subtle changes in brightness of the ground and rocks on the pictures. **1976** *Publishers Weekly* 2 Aug. 104/1 Mexican landscape architect Luis Barragán..in a major book... Seven of his most characteristic works—each briefly prefaced and explored at length in a photo-essay. *Ibid.* 4 Oct. 65/3 Seven sumptuous photo-essays (more than 300 pictures, many in color). **1977** C. McFadden *Serial* (1978) ix. 24/2 Michael Bry would..do this photo essay on her. **1889** *Year Bk. Photogr.* 158 One difficulty which photo-etchers have to contend against in the City is the vibration caused by the incessant traffic. **1959** K. Henney *Radio Engin. Handbk.* (ed. 5) xxiii. 1 Photofacsimile systems reproduce the subject copy on photographic papers or films. **1971** *Science* 6 Aug. 529/2 These transmissions, known as the DRIR (direct readout infrared) data, can be displayed on a photofacsimile recorder, which produces a continuous strip image. **1973** *Nature* 16 Feb. 434/2 His youthful German collaborator made a fair copy of Copernicus's precious autograph (now splendidly reproduced in photofacsimile). **1942** *Radiology* XXXVIII. 453/2 The initial scrutiny of routine photofluorograms by the staff radiologist will provide him with an objective means of determining which of all patients..should be referred for searching x-ray examination of the chest. **1975** B. W. Gayler in E. J. Potchen *Current Concepts in Radiol.* II. vii. 131 For many years, mass survey and screening chest radiographs were taken as 70 mm photofluorograms. **1941** *Med. Jrnl. Austral.* I. 267/2 The method of focusing is to make photofluorographs of a wire mesh mounted immediately in front of the fluorescent screen holder. **1972** *Science* 16 June 1186/3 The American public would be exposed to hundreds of thousands of unnecessary chest photofluorographs each year. **1945** *Amer. Jrnl. Roentgenology* L. 405/2 A subject 20 cm. in thickness photofluorographed with the roentgen machine operating at 90 kv. **1957** *Ibid.* LXXVII. 1079/1, 101 persons were photofluorographed. **1941** *Med. Jrnl. Austral.* I. 267/2 The four inches by five inches photo-fluorographic unit incorporates a special 14 inches by 17 inches fluorescent screen. **1954** *Brit. Jrnl. Radiol.* XXVII. 459/1 An attempt to reduce cost of routine examinations..by employing the photofluorographic method. **1972** J. E. Cullinan *Illustr. Guide X-Ray Technics* i. 24/1 A photofluorographic unit is a quick, efficient way to accomplish mass survey chest radiography. **1949** *Amer. Jrnl. Roentgenology* LXI. 186/1 All patients above the age of forty..will be examined photo-fluorographically. **1941** *Med. Jrnl. Austral.* I. 266/1 Photofluorography opens up a new avenue of examination to the wage-earning class. **1974** *Encycl. Brit. Macropædia* XV. 462/2 Photofluorography and television observation can take place simultaneously by means of separate apertures, and thus observation of what is being photographed is achieved. **1896** J. M. Bleyer in *N.Y. Med. Jrnl.* LXIII. 540/1 The photo-fluoroscope is an instrument which differs from all other fluoroscopes in the fact that it allows a direct shadow picture to be taken from the screen on the fluoroscope, after it is focused through the screen, and the image is seen on the ground glass in the photographic focusing box. **1933** O. Glasser *Sci. of Radiol.* i. 10 J. M. Bleyer of New York built his photofluoroscope which was destined to become the predecessor of the roentgen moving picture camera. **1955** G. L. Clark *Appl. X-Rays* (ed. 4) ix. 197 (*heading*) Photofluoroscopy (indirect radiography). **1966** *McGraw-Hill Encycl. Sci. & Technol.* XI. 302/2 The photography of the fluorescent image, as in mass chest examinations, is called photofluoroscopy. **1926** A. W. Judge *Stereoscopic Photogr.* xviii. 218 The effect of tilting and swinging the plate in the photogoniometer is such as to render the angular measurements..the same as if the view had been taken on a vertical plate. **1927** *Jrnl. Sci. Instruments* IV. 273 (*heading*) A universal X-ray photogoniometer... Combining: apparatus for single crystal rotation photographs—Laue photographs—X-ray spectrometry—powder photographs—photographs of crystal aggregates, metals, materials, etc. **1933** A. R. Hinks *Maps & Survey* (ed. 3) xii. 243 The machines which have been developed during the last few years all utilise..the principle of the *Bildmesstheodolit*, otherwise called the Photogoniometer, in which the plates are viewed through objectives identical with those which took them. **1939** *Geogr. Jrnl.* XCIII. 150 The American Geographical Society first of all made a photogoniometer (*Bild-Theodolit*) on a somewhat novel principle. **1970** *Chem. Abstr.* LXXIII. 305/2 A single-circle universal photogoniometer with vertical crystal-bearing attachment,.. was devised. **1939** *Geogr. Jrnl.* XCIII. 242 The first extensive photographic survey was that of the stars, made by Kapteyn..with a photogoniometric machine he built about 1890. **1968** *Chem. Abstr.* LXIX. 6626/2 (*heading*) Photogoniometric investigation of a crystal surface. *Ibid.*, A goniometric study of crystals is rarely made because labs. often have no goniometer. The goniometric method in many cases can be replaced by photogoniometry. **1939** B. B. Talley *Engin. Applic. Aerial & Terrestr. Photogrammetry* ii. 9 (*caption*) Photogoniometry by the method of Porro and Koppe. **1923** *Photogrammetric Engin.* VIII. 27 The..function of exploiting and developing the intelligence from the aerial photos falls within the sphere of photo interpretation units. **1959** *Proc. Geologists' Assoc.* LXX. 144 It may be necessary.. to complete a preliminary photo-interpretation before planning ground traverses. **1966** *Daily Tel.* 20 Aug. 14/5 These pictures will form stereo-pairs and can be analysed by standard techniques of photo-interpretation to give maximum information about the terrain on which American astronauts may land. **1973** *Sci. Amer.* Feb. 21/2 The cost of hardware and manpower for photo-interpretation..will remain high. **1959** *Proc. Geologists' Assoc.* LXX. 144 The best practice is a judicious combination of photo-interpretative methods and geological field mapping. **1942** *Photogrammetric Engin.* VIII. 26 While the aerial camera sees all, it is the photo interpreter who must know all and tell all. **1957** *Ibid.* XXIII. 933 A mathematical proof is presented for the statement that differential parallaxes smaller than 0·001 inch cannot be detected by average photo-interpreters. **1977** *Sci. Amer.* Sept. 57/1 Only the wide curve it must make on slopes betrays it to the photointerpreter. **1967** *Boston Sunday Herald* 26 Mar. (Comic Section), I subjected the film to the usual photo-interpretive analysis. **1944** K. Hubschmann in A. Kraszna-Krausz *Photogr. as Career* 118 My friend proved an excellent teacher of the essentials of photo-journalism. **1958** M. F. Harker in *Newnes Compl. Amat. Photogr.* xiii. 140 The present trend of photo-journalism which attempts to put over human stories in pictures rather than words. **1976** *National Observer* (U.S.) 11 Sept. 20/1 This colorful chap is Nelson Wadsworth, who teaches photojournalism, magazine writing, and investigative reporting at Brigham Young University in Utah. **1977** *Time* 12 Dec. 60/2 World War II was the longest-running story in the history of *Life*, the magazine that practically invented photojournalism. **1959** C. B. Neblette *Photogr. Lens Manual* ii. 25 After the 50 mm, the 35 mm medium wide-angle, or wide-field lens is undoubtedly the most useful to..the photojournalist. **1963** A. E. Woolley *Creative 35mm Techniques* III. 113/2 At all times a photojournalist is aware of the maximum emotion or conflict of the subject of the story. **1974** *Nat. Geographic* Aug. 252 At last I am here in North Korea, the first American photojournalist to gain entry into a country cloistered from the non-Communist world for a quarter of a century. **1978** *New York* 3 Apr. 32/3 Micha Bar Am/Harold Edgerton/Frank Rinehart—Begin and Sadat by this Mid-East photojournalist. **1960** *News Chron.* 10 Oct. 4/1 Paris-Match, the most powerful photo-magazine in Europe. **1969** *Amat. Photographer* 28 May 26/3 Few of the present-day casual photographers and snapshotters do their own processing. The photographic trade and the photo-magazines do not encourage it. **1939** B. B. Talley *Engin. Applic. Aerial & Terrestr. Photogrammetry* xix. 521 When this becomes economically feasible encouragement should be given to the development of 'photo-maps' to which may be added contours. **1955** *Times* 1 Aug. 6/1 The first 200 photographic sky charts..are being sent to observatories all over the world, and when the atlas is completed in 1956 it will include 1,758 such 'photomaps'. **1969** *Nature* 16 Aug. 668/1 (*caption*) Satellite photomap of the Tucson, Arizona, area with transport network superimposed. The map is based on a photograph taken..from Gemini V. **1958** *New Scientist* 13 Nov. 1247/3 The photomosaic is being assembled now. **1962** *Times* 17 May 10/3 The leading aircraft, navigating on a photo-mosaic. **1973** *Sci. Amer.* Dec. 132/3 This is the planet Mars, drawn from *Mariner 9* photomosaics. **1977** *Time* 17 Oct. 45/1 Among the pictures released by NASA: a photomosaic of the planet's north pole, showing a concentric pattern of striations in the ice cap. **1935** W. D. MORGAN et al. *Leica Manual* 469 (*caption*) Photomurals with the Leica. **1937** *Archit. Rev.* LXXXI. 86 The true photo-mural... This new process of mural decoration, which can now be said to have passed the experimental stage, has its chief virtue in that the design is projected direct on to the wall surface. The surface is first sprayed with photo-sensitive emulsion, and the photograph printed on it much in the same way as an ordinary camera enlargement. **1960** *House & Garden* Oct. 65/1 For ease of hanging, these photomurals are printed on lightweight white base paper. **1976** *National Observer* (U.S.) 24 Apr. 24/2 Once inside, the visitor encounters giant photomurals, three-quarter mock-ups of building exteriors, [etc.]. **1933** J. S. A. SALT *Simple Method Surveying from Air Photogr.* xi. 130 The names.. are printed photographically in a Photonymograph... Names may be printed in a variety of sizes and styles on a strip of sensitized paper. The alphabet..and any other signs..are contained on a master-disc. With the disc in position, each letter in turn is brought into position and an exposure made... The strips are developed and fixed ..and then show a series of names in various sizes and styles. **1963** *Record* (Oxf. Univ. Press) Dec. 2/3 The Drawing Office has installed a 'photonymograph' (a device whose development was in fact sponsored by the Cartographic section) to produce its lettering and so free draughtsmen for drawing. **1971** MONKHOUSE & WILKINSON *Maps & Diagrams* (ed. 3) i. 64 The new model..of the Photonymograph (developed from a machine which appeared in its earliest form over thirty years ago) is made by Barr and Stroud, Ltd. **1918** *Physical Rev.* XI. 137 (*heading*) Images on silvered photo-plate. **1974** *Nature* 20 Dec. 698/2 Organochlorine compounds may be identified at low concentrations in crude extracts of natural samples by a high resolution mass spectrometric method involving photoplate detection. **1924** *Glasgow Herald* 13 Dec. 9 The signature was that of Sir Robert Kindersley, whose photo-radiogram read—'My warmest greetings.—R. M. Kindersley.' The message and signature accompanied a radio photo of Sir Robert. **1925** *Official Gaz.* (U.S. Patent Office) 26 May 803/1 Radio-corporation of America, New York, N.Y. Filed Jan. 13, 1925. *Photoradiogram*... Pictures, drawings, and facsimiles transmitted by radio. Claims use since Nov. 30, 1924. **1926** *Daily News* 1 May 5/6 Most of the photo-radiograms sent from this side during the night will appear in American newspapers today. **1927** *Daily Express* 16 Dec. 1, December 21 is the latest date for handing in Christmas photo-radiograms at Marconi offices. **1946** *War Report* (B.B.C.) vi. 149 Then on Sunday evening one of our photo-recce Spitfires was shot down in German territory. **1971** *N.Y. Times* 13 June IV. 37 We have a high priority requirement for night photorecce of key motorable routes in Laos. **1944** *Sci. News Let.* 19 Aug. 117/3 Photo reconnaissance supplies information regarding the strength of enemy troops. **1951** A. C. CLARKE *Sands of Mars* xvi. 209 I'm going to suggest a photo-reconnaissance of all the..forests. **1973** *Sci. Amer.* Feb. 14/2 The main restrictions imposed by both of the SALT I agreements can be..monitored largely by means of sensors carried on board such orbiting photoreconnaissance systems. **1960** *Spectator* 17 June 886 The great photo-reportage magazines have now..largely relinquished their commanding position to television. **1960** L. DURRELL *Spirit of Place* (1969) 162, I remember seeing a photo-reportage in *Life* magazine once which dealt with the extraordinary changes in physique which immigrants to the U.S.A. underwent. **1966** *Punch* 6 Apr. 498/1 One of the many technical hazards which are endemic in photo-reportage are bound to materialise in full force. **1957** T. L. J. BENTLEY *Man. Miniature Camera* (ed. 5) iv. 41 The few models which incorporate a motor drive create totally new possibilities of rapid-sequence pictures which may be quite invaluable in..records of sporting events and photo-reporting for journalistic purposes. **1956** *Radiol.* LXVI. 737/2 (*heading*) Photoscan (superimposed on roentgenogram) shows lesion to be thyroid tissue rather than metastasis from breast. **1974** *Cancer Res.* XXXIV. 1/1 The photoscans showed an increased uptake of radioactivity over the tumors. **1959** *Internat. Jrnl. Appl. Radiation & Isotopes* IV. 154 (*heading*) A versatile, high-contrast photoscanner for the localization of human tumors with radioisotopes. **1966** *Sci. News* 12 Nov. 400 The gamma rays coming from the abnormal portions of bone are detected by a photoscanner that is passed externally over the body. Any portion of bone that gives off gamma rays is considered diseased. X-rays, in contrast, work by showing changes in bone density. **1956** *Internat. Jrnl. Appl. Radiation & Isotopes* I. 137/1 A photo scanning device has been devised which presents a 150% increase in picture density as the result of a 10% increase in count rate. **1967** *Times* 19 Sept. 9 Photo-scanning using radioactive isotopes can tell us if cancer is present in such organs as the thyroid gland, the liver and the brain. **1974** *Cancer Res.* XXXIV. 1/1 Radiolabeled nonantibody components of heterospecific IgG can be localized in certain tumors and normal tissues by photo-scanning. **1913** *Chem. Abstr.* VII. 3862 App[aratus] for copying the surface of a solid body from a photostereogram. **1939** B. B. TALLEY *Engin. Applic. Aerial & Terrestr. Photogrammetry* xix. 526 (*caption*) The Nistri photostereograph. **1963** W. K. KILFORD *Elem. Air Survey* xi. 265 (*caption*) The photostereograph (Beta/2) coupled with coordinate computer on the left and plotting table and coordinate plotter on right. **1933** A. R. HINKS *Maps & Survey* (ed. 3) xii. 243 (*heading*) Recent developments in photostereographic surveying. **1940** *War Illustr.* 19 Jan. 627 (*heading*) Photo-story of the life and death of a U-boat. **1972** *Guardian* 24 Mar. 12/6 The photo-story in 7 Days left one with a powerful impression. **1973** D. MATIAS tr. C. Metz in *Screen* Spring/Summer 197 Image-languages..figurative drawing,..television, photography, the photo-story etc. **1942** *Amer. Jrnl. Roentgenology* XLVIII. 220/1 A new instrument, a photoelectric timing mechanism, capable of regulating automatically the length of roentgenographic exposure time has been developed... The photoelectric timing mechanism, or phototimer, is a modification of the roentgenographic exposure meter. **1949** *Britannica Bk. of Year* 687/2 *Photo-timer*, an electrical device which photographs the finish of a race and supplies the elapsed time from start to finish. **1958** *Times* 22 Aug. 4/1 The race..should be started farther back from the bend, in spite of the cost of moving the electrical photo-timer.

3. pho:todegrada·tion, degradation of a substance caused by light; so **photodegra·dable** *a.*; **photodi·mer** *Chem.*, a dimer formed by photochemical action; so **photodime·ric** *a.*; also **pho:todimeriza·tion**, the formation of, or conversion into, a photodimer; **photodi·merize** *v. trans.* and *intr.*, to dimerize by the action of light; **pho:todissocia·tion** *Chem.*, dissociation of a chemical compound by the action of light; so **photodisso·ciate** *v. trans.*, to dissociate by means of light; **photo-oxidation** (further examples); also **photo-o·xidative** *a.*, involving or characterized by photo-oxidation; **photo-o·xidize** *v. trans.*, to oxidize photochemically; hence **photo-o·xidizable** *a.*, **-o·xidized** *ppl. a.*; **pho:tophosphoryla·tion** *Biochem.*, the process by which light energy is utilized by a plant or micro-organism to convert adenosine diphosphate to adenosine triphosphate without the reduction of oxygen to water that occurs in oxidative phosphorylation; **photopo·lymer**, a polymer produced photochemically; **pho:topolymeriza·tion** *Chem.*, polymerization brought about by the action of light; so **photopo·lymerize** *v. trans.*, to polymerize photochemically; **photopo·lymerized** *ppl. a.*; also **photopo·lymerizable** *a.*, capable of being photopolymerized; **pho:topolymerizabi·lity.**

1972 *New Scientist* 5 Oct. 41/2 (*heading*) Photo-degradable plastic carriers. **1975** RÅNBY & RABEK *Photodegradation* ix. 361 The development of methods for making plastics which are photodegradable to form harmless and biologically useful chemical compounds is of great interest. **1962** J. T. MARSH *Self-Smoothing Fabrics* xviii. 303 The resin exerts a considerable protective influence even in presence of those vat dyes whose action accelerates photo-degradation of cellulose. **1975** *Physics Bull.* Apr. 164/1 (Advt.), The fundamental photochemical reactions involved in photodegradation of polymers. **1936** *Trans. Faraday Soc.* XXXII. 521 The photodimer of thiophosgene. **1970** J. B. BIRKS *Photophysics of Aromatic Molecules* vii. 322 If..photodimers of other anthracene derivatives are irradiated with ultraviolet photons of sufficient energy..photolysis occurs and the dimer reverts to the original pair of individual molecules. **1952** *Chem. Rev.* LI. 19 The non-occurrence of the photodimeric products of the previously mentioned anthracene derivatives is probably due to their thermolability. **1936** *Trans. Faraday Soc.* XXXII. 517 A photodimerisation of 9-10-diphenyl anthracene has not yet been observed. **1972** DEPUY & CHAPMAN *Molec. Reactions & Photochem.* iv. 65 Naphthalenes, anthracenes, and polyacenes in general undergo photodimerization. **1955** *Jrnl. Chem. Soc.* 315, 3-Bromothionaphthen 1:1-dioxide was photodimerised in order to ascertain whether angular..or linear dimerisation was favoured. **1969** *Organic Photochem.* II. 75 Acyclic α,β-unsaturated ketones photodimerize when substituted with an aromatic group in the beta position. **1970** J. B. BIRKS *Photophysics of Aromatic Molecules* vii. 321 There are a large group of other 9-substituted and 9,10-disubstituted anthracenes which also photodimerize. **1962** F. I. ORDWAY et al. *Basic Astronautics* vi. 249 Water vapor is constantly being photodissociated by the action of sunlight. **1969** *Nature* 22 Nov. 756/2 NH_3, H_2O and H_2CO can all be photodissociated by ultraviolet photons of $E < 13{\cdot}6$ eV. **1925** *Phil. Mag.* XLIX. 1166 It becomes of interest..to investigate the relation between the activation, and the frequency of the illumination;.. only recently has a similar investigation been made on the photo-dissociation of sulphur dioxide. **1974** *Sci. Amer.* June 29/1 Atomic iodine is prepared in the proper excited state by the photodissociation of gaseous compounds such as iodotrifluoromethane (CF_3I) with xenon flash lamps. **1977** *Jrnl. R. Soc. Arts* CXXV. 766/2 The high spectral brightness of lasers can be used resonantly to obtain selective photodissociation. **1941** *Jrnl. Gen. Physiol.* XXV. 309 The ultimate cause of the extra oxygen absorption after or during irradiation consists of photoxidation processes sensitized mainly by chlorophyll. **1956** *Nature* 17 Mar. 513/2 The Bituminous Binder Research Unit has completed a preliminary investigation of photo-oxidation in the weathering of binders on the road. **1971** *Jrnl. Oil & Colour Chemists' Assoc.* LIV. 846 Bleaching by sunlight may be due to photo-oxidation of double bonds. **1937** *Ann. Rep. Progr. Chem.* XXXIII. 431 There is little doubt that this element [*sc.* manganese] can affect the chlorophyll content of leaves, and probably also its photo-oxidative properties. **1976** *Nature* 13 May 169/2 A film exposed under high vacuum showed a dose response almost identical to that of one exposed in air, and indicates the photolytic rather than the photo-oxidative nature of the process. **1949** *Chem. Abstr.* XLIII. 5391 (*heading*) Photoöxidizable derivatives of helianthrene. **1974** *Photochem. & Photobiol.* XIX. 35/1 Dye-sensitized photo-oxidation.. permitting preferential destruction of the photo-oxidizable amino-acid residues of proteins. **1941** *Adv. Enzymol.* I. 232 Artificially added substances whose oxidation products can be recognized by their color are actually photo-oxidized in plants. **1975** *Nature* 9 Oct. 490/2 It seems that *O. limnetica* photo-oxidises S^{2-} quantitatively to S^0. **1973** *Biochem.* XII. 2540/2 The tryptophan content of the native and the photooxidized enzyme was measured. [**1954** D. I. ARNON et al. in *Nature* 28 Aug. 394/1 Evidence has now been obtained that whole chloroplasts..have the ability to carry out..photosynthetic phosphorylation, a term which we use for the conversion of light energy into the high-energy phosphate bonds of adenosine triphosphate (ATP), without the participation of respiration.] **1956** *Plant Physiol.* XXXI. p. xxx/2 (*heading*) The mechanism of cell-free, bacterial photophosphorylation. **1956** *Federation Proc.* XV. 260/2 Photophosphorylation depends upon an inductive reduction. **1971** M. F. MALLETTE et al. *Introd. Biochem.* xviii. 646 Photosystem 1, the longer wave length photosystem, has been associated with the reduction of $NADP^+$ and with photophosphorylation. Photosystem 2 is related to dissociation of water and the evolution of oxygen. **1973** R. G. KRUEGER et al. *Introd. Microbiol.* viii. 271/1 Photophosphorylation occurs in the reduction of cytochrome c with the generation of ATP from ADP and inorganic phosphate. The electron initially emitted from chlorophyll is ultimately returned to chlorophyll in a cyclic fashion; hence, the entire process of converting light energy to ATP (chemical energy) is termed cyclic phosphorylation... In plants and algae, a noncyclic type of photophosphorylation also occurs. **1932** *Canad. Jrnl. Res.* VII. 479 The photo-polymer of vinyl butyl ether was purified. **1953** *Jrnl. Res. Nat. Bureau of Standards* (U.S.) LI. 327 Teflon and tetrafluoroethylene photopolymers, on pyrolysis in a vacuum at 423·5° to 513·0 °C, yield almost 100 percent of monomer. **1961** *Printing News* 16 Feb. 10 The first complete 4-colour magazine to be produced from 'Dycril' photo-polymer (light-sensitive plastic) printing plates. **1974** *Clarendonian* XXVIII. 1. 41 There are plans afoot to convert other letterpress 'classics' to this type of plate should photopolymers prove the equal of our now traditional hot-moulded plastic plates. **1932** *Canad. Jrnl. Res.* VII. 473 The photo-polymerizability is practically the same as that of the butyl ether. *Ibid.*, Comparison with the closely related vinyl esters.. shows that, in the absence of catalysts, the latter are much more readily photo- and thermo-polymerizable. **1973** *Materials & Technol.* VI. ix. 664 The photopolymerisable amide-compositions are used for the production of letterpress printing plates. **1920** *Chem. Abstr.* XIV. 4427/1 (Index), Photopolymerization. **1924** *Jrnl. Amer. Chem. Soc.* XLVI. 1614 It is concluded that in the photopolymerization of anthracene, a single molecule is activated by absorption of blue light and then proceeds to react with an unactivated molecule to form the polymer. **1970** H. L. NEEDLES in R. F. Reinisch *Photochem. Macromolecules* 129 Both oxygen and hydrogen donors effect riboflavin-sensitized photopolymerizations of aqueous acrylamide. **1921** *Jrnl. Chem. Soc.* CXIX. 1028 Whether the same explanation does not apply to all carbohydrates and to chlorophyll, namely, that under the influence of light of very short wave-length they are decomposed to carbon dioxide, which is photosynthesised to formaldehyde, and this in its turn photopolymerised to sugars. **1933** *Jrnl. Amer. Chem. Soc.* LV. 577 Ethyl acetate does not react with Wijs solution; nor does the polymerized product, since..solid photopolymerized vinyl acetate gave iodine values as low as 9·5 and 6·3, corresponding to 96 and 98% polymerized. **1974** *Sci. Amer.* Oct. 119/2 They are made by first crystallizing the molecules of an appropriate monomer and then photopolymerizing the monomer crystal with ultra-violet light or gamma rays.

photoabsorbing to **photoautotrophic**: see *PHOTO- 1.

pho:tobio·graphy. [f. PHOTO- 2 + BIOGRAPHY.] A person's life shown in a series of photographs.

1944 *Spectator* 3 Mar. 188/1 A 'photobiography', consisting of 250 scenes from Woodrow Wilson's life, with 150 pages of letterpress..is in an advanced stage of preparation. **1951** C. BEATON (*title*) Photobiography. **1952** *N.Y. Times Bk. Rev.* 1 June 12 A 'photobiography' that does not seem likely to lose the general votes in the future.

photobiological to **-bleaching**: see *PHOTO- 1.

photoblepharon (fō^u^toble·fărǫn). [mod.L. (M. Weber *Siboga Expeditie* (1902) I. 108), f. PHOTO- 1 + Gr. βλέφαρον eye.] A small luminous fish of the genus so called, found in the Red Sea and the Indian Ocean.

1920 E. N. HARVEY *Nature Animal Light* i. 18 Leaving out of account..the use for bait, in fishing, of the luminous organ of a fish, *Photoblepharon*, by the Banda islanders, we find that luminous bacteria are of value for certain purposes in the laboratory. **1928** C. M. YONGE in Russell & Yonge *Seas* viii. 193 Light organs are apparently commonest in fish which live in the upper 500 metres of the warmer seas, although there are notable exceptions, for example, a..fish..called Photoblepharon found in pools of fresh water in quarries and the craters of extinct volcanoes in Malaya. **1964** *Oceanogr. & Marine Biol.* II. 356 In *Photoblepharon* the glow may be hidden by an opaque screen. **1978** *Nat. Geogr. Mag.* Nov. 722 Despite its name, *Photoblepharon* has no real eyelid.

photo-call: see *PHOTO- 2.

photocatalyse (fō^u^tokæ·tăləiz), *v. Chem.* Also (*U.S.*) **-yze.** [f. PHOTO-1 + *CATALYSE *v.*] *trans.* To subject to photocatalysis.

1921 *Jrnl. Chem. Soc.* CXIX. 1034 The photosynthesis of formaldehyde from carbon dioxide and water can be photocatalysed by certain coloured basic substances...

The photosynthesis then takes place in visible light. *c* **1955** *Proc. 1st Internat. Photobiol. Congr. 1954* ii. 137 Ferric chloride photocatalyses the reduction of..methylene blue by citrate in water. **1970** *Nature* 22 Aug. 832/2 The decomposition of N_2O photocatalysed both by metal free and Cu-phthalocyanine.

Hence **photoca·talysed** *ppl. a.*

c **1955** *Proc. 1st Internat. Photobiol. Congr. 1954* ii. 135 The observed total reaction consists of a photocatalysed reaction between leucoindophenol and air plus a dark reaction between leucoindophenol and peroxide. **1973** *Biochem.* XII. 4154/1 Although sensitive to photocatalyzed degradation, these reagents readily react with thiol compounds..yielding photostable covalent derivatives.

photocatalysis (fōutokătæ·lisis). *Chem.* †Also with hyphen. [f. PHOTO- 1 + CATALYSIS. The words of this group originated with the Ger. adj. (see below).] The acceleration of a reaction by light; the catalysis of a photochemical reaction.

1913 *Jrnl. Chem. Soc.* CIV. II. 653 (*heading*) Photocatalysis. **1916** W. C. McC. LEWIS *Syst. Physical Chem.* II. III. i. 420 Another instance of photo-catalysis in solution is the decomposition of aqueous sodium hypochlorite. **1970** *Nature* 22 Aug. 832/2 (*heading*) Homogeneous photocatalysis by organic dyes in the liquid phase.

So **pho:tocataly·tic** *a.* [ad. G. *photokatalytisch* (J. Plotnikow *Photochemie* (1910) II. 72)], pertaining to or exhibiting photocatalysis; **pho:tocataly·tically** *adv.*; **photoca·talyst**, †**-ca·talyser**, a substance that acts as a catalyst in a photochemical reaction.

1913 H. S. ALLEN *Photo-Electricity* xiv. 198 We may conveniently divide..photo-chemical reactions into three main classes. To the first class may be assigned the so-called photokatalytic reactions, in which light only accelerates an irreversible process. **1914** S. E. SHEPPARD *Photo-Chem.* vii. 293 The kations Fe, Mn, Ce were peculiarly effective photo-catalysts for the reaction. **1923** *Jrnl. Chem. Soc.* CXXIII. 189 The synthesis takes place photocatalytically by the influence of visible light when the carbonic acid is in loose combination with a coloured base, such as malachite green. **1926** E. MAYER *Clin. Applic. Sunlight* viii. 160 Metallic compounds, especially iron salts, act as photocatalyzers. For example, benzoic acid under the influence of light will change very quickly to salicylic acid if an iron salt be present. **1945** E. I. RABINOWITCH *Photosynthesis* I. iii. 56 Chlorophyll is a photocatalyst, since no decrease in the concentration of chlorophyll in leaves has been observed after intense photosynthesis. **1959** *Ann. Rev. Plant Physiol.* X. 56 (*heading*) Photocatalytic activities of bacterial chromatophores. **1971** E. GURR *Synthetic Dyes* 108 Crystal violet is one of the dyes used by Binding (1970) as a photocatalyst. **1978** *Nature* 3 Aug. 508/1 The concentration of Ru (about 8×10^{-6} M) changed by less than 5%, so the complex was acting as a photocatalytic agent.

photocathode (fōutokæ·pōud). *Electronics.* Also **photo-cathode**, †**-kathode**. [a. G. *photokathode* (P. Selényi 1929, in *Physik. Zeitschr.* XXX. 933/1): see PHOTO- 1 and CATHODE.] A cathode which emits electrons when illuminated, thereby allowing an electric current to pass.

1930 *Sci. Abstr.* A. XXXIII. 525 (*heading*) Red-sensitive sodium photo-kathodes (photo-electric cells). **1931** *Physics* I. 343 If a silver surface is first oxidized in an electrical discharge, and then baked in the presence of caesium vapor, it may be converted into a photo-cathode of remarkable sensitivity. **1957** *Proc. Inst. Electr. Engin.* CIV. B. 470/2 The photo-electric surface developed by Koller in 1929, consisting of a complex mixture of silver, oxygen and caesium, was the first of the really efficient modern photo-cathodes and it is still in use, especially when red or infra-red sensitivity is required. **1969** *New Scientist* 10 July 21/1 An image tube consists of a photocathode which emits electrons in direct proportion to the amount of light falling on it.

photocell (fōu·tosel). Also **photo-cell, photo cell.** [f. PHOTO- 1 + CELL *sb.*[1]] A device which generates an electric current or voltage dependent on its degree of illumination.

1891 *Phil. Mag.* XXXI. 232 The effect of this connexion with the Daniell is to develop between the poles of the photo cell a difference of potential opposed in sign to that which light produces. **1913** *Physical Rev.* I. 74 When.. the spark gap was pulled six feet away from the photocell the positive potential slowly fell to 1·6 volts. **1932** *Discovery* Apr. 112/1 By passing the film between a light and..a photocell the film can be turned into speech again. **1938** G. H. SEWELL *Amateur Film-Making* ii. 21 The photo-cell meter is recognized as the most accurate light-measuring device normally available. **1958** *New Statesman* 23 Aug. 214/2 There will be a system of photo-cells, which, sensitive to infra-red and visible rays, will scan the hidden side of the moon, as the rocket-probe spins on its axis. **1973** *Daily Tel.* 10 Dec. 7/3 When fog distorts the light path, it alters the pattern being received by the photocell, which is then electronically translated into distance of visibility.

photocharger, -charging: see *PHOTO- 2.

photochemical, *a.* Add: *photochemical smog*, a condition of the atmosphere attributed to the action of sunlight on hydrocarbons and nitrogen in it and characterized by the presence of aerosols and increased ozone and nitrogen oxides and by effects that include irritation of the eyes, damage to plants, and visibility reduced to a mile or less.

1957 *Rep. Air Pollution Foundation* (U.S.) No. 21. 1 It is now realized that Los Angeles' smog is primarily a reaction between organic matter and nitrogen oxides in the presence of sunlight. The need for irradiation to produce the reaction has led to the designation 'photochemical' smog. **1972** *Daily Colonist* (Victoria, B.C.) 13 Feb. 27/5 His studies of animals show that Vitamin E serves as an antioxidant to protect lung tissue from damage by the ozone in photochemical smog. **1972** *Nature* 18 Feb. 360/1 There is no doubt that motor vehicles are the principal outlets for photochemical smog in large cities. **1976** *New Yorker* 16 Feb. 74/2 Los Angeles is perhaps the best-known victim of the bus and the automobile; photochemical smog, the distinctive pollutant of these vehicles, made its first recorded appearance in Los Angeles in 1943.

photochemically *adv.* (earlier and later examples); **photochemist** (examples); **photochemistry** (later examples).

1881 *Phil. Mag.* XII. 21 The impression of an electromotive force upon a film possessing, as do all photochemically active bodies, electrolytic conductivity, will tend to produce at least partial electrolysis. **1926** *Trans. Faraday Soc.* XXI. 438 Stark's views undoubtedly did not receive from photochemists the attention they deserved. **1941** S. H. BARTLEY *Vision* i. 5 The photochemist has given increasing attention to the cycle of changes that occur in the eye in response to light. **1961** G. R. CHOPPIN *Exper. Nucl. Chem.* xii. 194 It is tempting to seek to relate photochemistry and radiation chemistry by considering that ionization is the ultimate state of excitation. **1967** MARGERISON & EAST *Introd. Polymer Chem.* iv. 184 The process is started by the decomposition of an initiator induced thermally, photochemically or by admixture of another substance. **1972** DEPUY & CHAPMAN *Molec. Reactions & Photochem.* i. 6 Photochemistry is the study of the chemistry of electronically excited molecules produced by the absorption of electromagnetic radiation. **1973** *Sci. Amer.* Apr. 68/2 Photochemists have measured the probability that ultraviolet photons will destroy particular molecules. **1978** *Nature* 23 Feb. 733/1 Photochemically produced sulphate aerosols can, in certain circumstances, account for a large proportion of total particulate mass in the 0·1–1·0 μm size range.

photochromic (fōutokrōu·mik), *a.* and *sb.* [f. as next + -IC.] **A.** *adj.* Of, pertaining to, or displaying photochromism.

1953 *Jrnl. Chem. Physics* XXI. 1619/2 In those compounds which exhibit both thermochromism and photochromism the thermochromic and the photochromic colors are in each case spectroscopically identical. **1965** *New Scientist* 29 Apr. 291/3 Silver halide particles dispersed through this sheet of 'photochromic' glass.. cause the glass to darken on exposure to light, and clear again within minutes. **1971** H. MEIER in K. Venkataraman *Chem. Synthetic Dyes* IV. vii. 427 The photochromic reaction of aqueous solutions of the leucosulfite of parafuchsine could be used as a UV dosimeter for the measurement of the UV radiation of sky light. **1974** *Observer* (Colour Suppl.) 13 Oct. 18/4 Photochromic lenses that automatically change the darkness of their tint to match the prevailing brightness.

B. *sb.* A photochromic substance.

1965 *Guardian* 13 Apr. 14/5 Sunglasses which are clear in ordinary daylight but which darken progressively in increasing sunlight, were among the practical applications of photochromics described in London yesterday. **1970** *Physics Bull.* Nov. 487/1 Two other classes of material which have been developed recently as promising photochromics..are the alkaline earth fluorides and titanates.

Hence **pho:tochromi·city** = *PHOTOCHROMISM.

1966 *Applied Optics* V. 946/2 The size of the silver halide microcrystals embedded in the glass matrix determines not only the photochromicity but also the character of the unexposed material (transparent, translucent, and opaque).

photochromism (fōutokrou·miz'm). [f. as next + -ISM.] The phenomenon whereby certain substances undergo a reversible change of colour or shade when illuminated with light of appropriate wavelength.

1951 *Physics Abstr.* A. LIV. 204/2 (*heading*) Photochromism in the bianthrone series. **1953** [see *PHOTOCHROMIC *a.*]. **1960** *New Scientist* 2 June 1424/1 This new kind of reversible colour change in organic compounds was first described by me [*sc.* Yehuda Hirshberg] in 1950, and I called it 'photochromism'. *Ibid.* 1425/3 Another recent development in photochromism is the discovery that many compounds which undergo reversible colour changes by exposure to ultraviolet light show the same effect when subjected to high-energy electrons or to any ionizing radiation. **1972** *Nature* 31 Mar. 245/2 Photochromism is an effect associated with compounds which reversibly change their absorption spectra on illumination with light.

photochromy (in Dict. s.v. PHOTOCHROMATIC *a.*). Add: **c.** [ad. F. *photochromie.*] = *PHOTOCHROMISM.

1951 *Chem. Abstr.* XLV. 10059 (*heading*) Photochromy in the bianthrone series. **1963** *Adv. Photochem.* I. 282 Photochromy and thermochromy are mutually exclusive properties in crystalline salicylidine-anilines.

photoclinometry: see *PHOTO- 2.

pho:tocoagula·tion. *Ophthalm.* [f. PHOTO- 1 + COAGULATION.] The surgical technique of using an intense beam of light to coagulate small areas of tissue, esp. of the retina.

1961 *Times* 16 Jan. 11/7 Today by surgery and the use of electro or photo-coagulation successful reposition..is achieved. **1971** G. N. WISE et al. *Retinal Circulation* xv. 446/1 Photocoagulation is an effective method of destroying individual features of proliferative diabetic retinopathy. **1972** T. N. WAUBKE in Michaelson & Berman *Causes & Prevention of Blindness* 313/1 Most of our patients did not realize the defects in the visual field which occur after photocoagulation.

Hence **pho:tocoa·gulate** *v. trans.*, to treat by this technique; **pho:tocoa·gulating** *ppl. a.*; **pho:tocoa·gulator**, an apparatus which produces the light beam used for photocoagulation.

1967 *New Scientist* 30 Mar. 679/3 The sharply focused beam caused only minimal scars to surrounding tissue. Ultimately they hope to develop more versatile laser photocoagulators. **1969** *Sci. Jrnl.* July 16 When the retina is subjected to a photocoagulating laser pulse..the transient pressure waves which reverberate through the eyeball resemble the seismic records following an earthquake. **1972** L. M. AIELLO in Michaelson & Berman *Causes & Prevention of Blindness* 317/2 A ruby laser photocoagulator. *Ibid.* 318/2 Control studies are important..in order ..to control our eagerness to photocoagulate every eye of all diabetics.

photocomposing (fōu:tokǫ̆mpōu·ziŋ), *vbl. sb.* *Printing.* Also with hyphen. [f. PHOTO- 2 + COMPOSING *vbl. sb.*] **1.** The setting of text by the projection of images of letters or symbols on to photographic film, which is then used in the preparation of the printing surface; filmsetting. Freq. *attrib.*

1929 *N.Y. Times* 30 Jan. 11/1 There is another great revolution coming in the printing industry... That is the use of photo-composing instead of metal composing. Instead of producing a column of metal type, we will have a machine which produces a strip of film. **1929** *Times* 29 Oct. (Printing Suppl.) p. xii/7 The Typary machine..though not strictly a photo-composing machine, was directly inspired by the desire to abolish typesetting. **1948** *Sci. News Let.* 4 Dec. 362/1 Several photocomposing machines are in experimental use. **1955** *Times* 5 July 6/5 This is the first time that..photocomposing machines have been on view at Olympia as working exhibits. **1961** *Spectator* 14 Apr. 509/3 Technical advances, particularly in photo-composing and the printing of matter from film, rather than metal, are reaching a stage where their place in the British industry must be decided. **1973** S. JENNETT *Making of Bks.* (ed. 5) v. 83 All three hot-metal composing-machine companies in Britain, and others abroad, have introduced photocomposing machines.

2. The manufacture of printing plates directly from photographic images for the production of multiple copies of illustrations, designs, etc.

1929 W. C. HUEBNER in *Trans. Amer. Soc. Mech. Engin.* L. PI. 21/2 Photo composing or photo-mechanical imposition is..the art of making printing plates wherein original designs are photographed directly on the press plate. **1953** *Composition Manual* (Printing Industry of Amer.) VIII. 296/1 It [*sc.* photo-typesetting] should not be confused with 'photo-composing' because the latter has been definitely applied, for a number of years, to machines that are used for the multiple-printing of photographic images in offset lithography and other process work... The word 'photo-composition', sometimes used in current writing to denote photo-typesetting, has likewise been a source of some confusion.

So **pho:tocompo·se** *v. trans.*, **-compo·sed** *ppl. a.*; **pho:tocompo·ser**, a machine for carrying out photocomposition.

1929 W. C. HUEBNER in *Trans. Amer. Soc. Mech. Engin.* L. PI. 21/2 The results attained by photo-composed plates indicate the wide range of work that can be done economically. *Ibid.* 22/1 All sizes of work..are photo-composed successfully. *Ibid.* 23/1 The photocomposer can do it [*sc.* produce several copies of a plate] better. **1948** *Sci. News Let.* 4 Dec. 362/1 One company known for typesetting machinery has its photocomposer in day-by-day use. **1965** *Economist* 22 May (Press Ahead Suppl.) p. xvi/2 Two photocomposers were installed. **1969** *Physics Bull.* Jan. 24/1 The *Current Papers* will be photocomposed for printing under computer control. **1970** A. CAMERON et al. *Computers & Old Eng. Concordances* 7 Photo-composed pages can look very handsome indeed. **1972** *Computers & Humanities* VI. 153 Computerized photocomposers may be divided into three stages of development or three generations of machine in use today.

photocomposition (fōu:tokǫ̆mpǫ̆zi·ʃən). *Printing.* [f. PHOTO- 2 + COMPOSITION.] = *PHOTOCOMPOSING *vbl. sb.* Also *attrib.*

1929 *N.Y. Times* 30 Jan. 11/1 (*heading*) Publisher.. tells of a photo-composition machine that will do away with metal composition. **1949** H. O. SMITH *Rotophoto Process* 5 With the commercial advent of mechanical photocomposition the future will undoubtedly see more print changing over to photographic methods of reproduction. **1953** [see *PHOTOCOMPOSING *vbl. sb.* 2]. **1957** E. LINKLATER *Private Angelo* 238 (*colophon*) Of this book, first published by Jonathan Cape in 1946, two thousand copies were printed at Christmas 1957 for Sir Allen Lane and Richard Lane... The book was composed entirely without metal type: it is the first to have been produced in Great Britain by means of photocomposition. **1967** D. G. HAYS *Introd. Computational Linguistics* iv. 67 Early photocomposition devices..used photosensitive stock and stored negative images of characters. **1968** A. BLUHM *Photosetting* i. 3 These two terms [*sc.* photosetting and filmsetting], and also photocomposition and phototypesetting, are all currently used to mean exactly the same thing, namely the composition of letters and symbols by photographic exposure from a set of transparent master characters for subsequent reproduction by any printing process. **1975** *Times* 4 Sept. 1/1 The printing unions were told..that labour-saving photocomposition techniques would be introduced. **1977** *Times* 14 May 1/2 The plans also involve..Fleet Street production by the new technology of photocomposition.

pho:tocondu·ctance. *Physics.* [f. PHOTO- 1 + *CONDUCTANCE.] = *PHOTOCONDUCTIVITY.

1939 *Jrnl. Chem. Physics* VII. 426/2 Photovoltaic experiments indicate the release of photoconductance electrons. **1959** *Bell Syst. Techn. Jrnl.* XXXVIII. 750 Measurements..of work function, photoconductance, surface conductivity and field effect have indicated that there is a large density of surface states.

pho:tocondu·cting, *ppl. a. Physics.* Also with hyphen. [f. PHOTO- 1 + CONDUCTING *ppl. a.*] Exhibiting or utilizing a decrease in electrical resistance when illuminated.

1929 *Sci. Abstr.* A. XXXII. 638 (*heading*) Thallium photo-conducting cells. **1932** HUGHES & DUBRIDGE *Photoelectric Phenomena* viii. 329 Cuprous oxide..was found to be photoconducting. **1974** *Encycl. Brit. Macropædia* XI. 184/2 Zinc sulfide phosphors..are photoconducting, which means that many excited electrons are lifted to the conduction band.

pho:tocondu·ction. *Physics.* Also with hyphen. [f. PHOTO- 1 + CONDUCTION.] = *PHOTOCONDUCTIVITY.

1929 CAMPBELL & RITCHIE *Photoelectric Cells* ii. 20 Our present knowledge of photo-conduction is largely due to the work of Gudden and Pohl. **1955** *Proc. IRE* XLIII. 1819 (*heading*) Photoconduction in germanium and silicon. **1965** PHILLIPS & WILLIAMS *Inorg. Chem.* I. vi. 209 Excitation of electrons in semiconductors can also be brought about by absorption of light, the phenomenon of photo-conduction. **1971** SMITH & THOMSON *Optics* xxiii. 334 In another type of television camera tube, the basic effect is photoconduction instead of photo-emission.

pho:tocondu·ctive, *a. Physics.* Also with hyphen. [f. PHOTO- 1 + CONDUCTIVE *a.*] Photoconducting; of or pertaining to the property of being photoconducting.

1929 CAMPBELL & RITCHIE *Photoelectric Cells* i. 1 Selenium cells might be termed photo-conductive. **1933** *Product Engin.* Aug. 289/1 With each of the three general types of cells, photo-voltaic, photo-emissive and photo-conductive, it is possible to use a wide variety of auxiliary equipment. **1957** *Proc. Inst. Electr. Engin.* CIV. B. 467/1 In 1873, Smith discovered the change in conductivity of selenium when sunlight fell upon it—the photo-conductive effect. **1960** *Times* 8 Mar. 2/3 The effects of light, X and gamma radiation on photoconductive materials. **1971** *Sci. Amer.* June 13/3 (Advt.), An advantage of photovoltaic detectors is that no external power supply is required to produce the photosignal, whereas photoconductive detectors must be activated.

Hence **pho:toconducti·vity**, the property of being photoconductive.

1929 CAMPBELL & RITCHIE *Photoelectric Cells* ii. 20 The effect of the radiation appears as an increase of conductivity of the material rather than as a current flowing from it. This is the ultimate principle of selenium and other photo-conductivity devices. **1932** HUGHES & DUBRIDGE *Photoelectric Phenomena* viii. 329 Coblentz studied the photoconductivity of the halides of thallium, lead, and silver. **1974** *Encycl. Brit. Macropædia* XIII. 817/2 The most outstanding physical property of crystalline selenium is its photoconductivity: on illumination, the electrical conductivity increases more than 1,000-fold.

pho:tocondu·ctor. *Physics.* Also with hyphen. [f. PHOTO- 1 + CONDUCTOR.] A photoconducting substance or device.

1929 *Sci. Abstr.* A. XXXII. 638 Detailed instructions for constructing photo-conductors. **1947** *Sun* (Baltimore) 1 Jan. 6/2 A newly developed photoconductor cell, the size of a peanut, has already spotted things never seen before on Venus and Saturn. **1967** E. CHAMBERS *Photolitho-Offset* xiv. 203 The two most common photoconductors used are selenium and zinc oxide. **1973** *Focal Dict. Photogr. Technol.* 445 Photoconductors are available whose respective sensitivities cover between them all wavelengths from 450 to 7,000 nm.

photocontro·l. [f. PHOTO- 1, 2 + CONTROL *sb.*] **1.** Control by light.

1954 *Bot. Gaz.* CXV. 360 (*heading*) Oxygen consumption of lettuce seed in relation to photocontrol of germination. **1975** *Nature* 10 Apr. 512/2 Many aspects of plant development are subject to photocontrol by way of the chromoprotein photoreceptor phytochrome.

2. *Surveying.* (Also as two words.) A control (i.e. a system of precisely surveyed points in terms of which subordinate local surveys are carried out) consisting of points that can be identified on aerial photographs.

1956 *Nature* 3 Mar. 419/1 Good progress was made with geodetic surveys, and the triangulation and photo-control work over twenty thousand square miles..was completed. **1967** F. H. MOFFITT *Photogrammetry* (ed. 2) v. 126 The rigid requirements for precision photo control for analytic control extension, for cadastral surveys, and for certain types of highway design mapping, make it necessary to pre-mark a great deal of the control points. **1974** P. R. WOLF *Elem. Photogrammetry* xi. 223 According to this rule, a map being plotted with a contour interval of 10 feet requires vertical photo control accurate to within ±2·0 feet.

photoconversion to **-convertible:** see *PHOTO- 1.

photocopier (fōu·tokǫpi,əɹ). Also (*rare*) **-copyer.** [f. next + -ER¹.] **a.** An apparatus for making photocopies.

1934 in WEBSTER. **1959** *Economist* 21 Mar. 1087/1 For more than 20 to 25 copies it will prove cheaper to use some kind of duplicator than even the cheapest type of photocopyer. **1964** D. FRANCIS *Nerve* xvi. 210, I made ten copies of this statement and then on the photocopier printed ten copies each of the statements. **1973** *Daily Colonist* (Victoria, B.C.) 29 July 4/5 They're electioneering day by day with their photocopiers reeling out these miles of guff. **1978** 'L. BLACK' *Foursome* xi. 104 There was a public photo-copier in the main post office..coin-operated, 5p per one copy of one sheet.

b. One who operates a photocopying machine.

1977 *Daily Tel.* 26 Nov. 15/2 A fourth man,..who had worked at Somerset House as a photocopier, was jailed for nine months.

photocopy (fōu·tokǫpi), *v.* [f. PHOTO- 2 + COPY *v.*¹

In quot. 1924 the formation is prob. *photo* + *copying machine* rather than *photocopy* + *-ing* + *machine.*]

trans. To make a photocopy of. So **pho·to-copied** *ppl. a.*, **pho·tocopying** *vbl. sb.* and *ppl. a.*

1924 C. W. HACKLEMAN *Commerc. Engraving & Printing* (rev. ed.) 792 Photo copying machines. In Fig. 2015 is shown a machine for making copies of records, drawings,..flat merchandise, etc., by a simplified method of photography, the copies being made in enlarged, reduced or natural size directly upon sensitized paper. *Ibid.* 793 (*caption*) Prints as made with a photo copying machine. **1942** H. H. FUSSLER *Photogr. Reproduction for Libraries* xi. 192 Less expensive papers can be used in many instances for enlargement printing than are required in the original photocopying machines. **1948** *Library Assoc. Rec.* Feb. 37/1 There are private photo-copying firms in most cities. **1952** I. GRAHAM *Encycl. Advertising* 350/1 The original subject may be photo-copied in actual, enlarged, or reduced size; the finished photocopy may be black on a white background (called a 'positive') or white on a black background (called a 'negative'). **1958** S. HYLAND *Who goes Hang?* xxxix. 184 Neat files of photo-copied documents. **1958** H. R. VERRY *Document Copying* vii. 40 Photocopying processes are..able to copy material which cannot be reproduced on the typewriter, such as drawings, half-tone and line illustrations. **1966** *McGraw-Hill Encycl. Sci. & Technol.* X. 142/2 Photocopying processes may be somewhat arbitrarily divided into seven classes: silver halide photocopying, transfer processes, thermography.., plan copying, electrostatic processes, the electrolytic process, and microfilming. **1968** *Brit. Med. Bull.* XXIV. 222/1 Many laboratories..have used photocopying or laboratory record cards as a means of reporting their results. **1972** A. PRICE *Col. Butler's Wolf* vi. 55 He passed the sheets to Butler. Anonymous, greyish photocopying paper; the reproduction of a letter. **1973** *Nature* 16 Mar. 147/2 Advance copies of the technical report are available in photocopied form. **1976** P. HILL *Hunters* v. 47 Here's the questionnaire, get it photocopied.

photocopy (fōu·tokǫpi), *sb.* [f. prec. or f. PHOTO- 2 + COPY *sb.*] A copy of documentary material made by any of various processes (usu. involving the chemical or electrical action of light on a specially prepared surface) in a copying machine and usu. the same size as the original.

1934 in WEBSTER. **1952** [see prec.]. **1958** S. HYLAND *Who goes Hang?* xxii. 97 A simple photo-copy, in black and white, of a..drawing. **1966** *Lancet* 24 Dec. 1414/1, I was flattered enough to have some photocopies made of my modest contribution. **1971** *Physics Bull.* Nov. 682/1 In the USA, theses are readily available either on micro-film or as photocopies. **1973** 'C. AIRD' *His Burial Too* xiv. 130 The photocopy..had been folded neatly inside a telephone directory.

photocurrent, -damage: see *PHOTO- 1; **photodegradable, -degradation:** see *PHOTO- 3; **photodensitometer** to **-detector:** see *PHOTO- 1; **photodimer** to **-dimerize:** see *PHOTO- 3.

photodiode (fōutodəi·ōud). *Electronics.* Also with hyphen. [f. PHOTO- 1 + DIODE *a.*, *sb.*] A semiconductor diode which generates a potential difference or changes its electrical resistance when illuminated.

1945 S. BENZER *Photoelectric Effects in Germanium* (U.S. Dept. of Commerce, Office of Publication Board PB 28644) 3 In exploring germanium samples for their rectification at different points, uncommon current-voltage characteristics are sometimes observed. There are two types which are of particular interest because of their sensitivity to light... K. Lark-Horovitz has given the descriptive names 'photodiode' and 'photopeak' to these characteristics. *Ibid.* 4 Even in the most highly saturated photodiodes, the current continues to rise somewhat as the voltage is raised. **1959** [see *PHOTO-TRANSISTOR]. **1962** *Jrnl. Optical Soc. Amer.* LII. 1237/1 Large-area photodiodes have been in use for a number of years as solar cells for the conversion of solar radiation to electrical power. **1971** *Nature* 20 Aug. 540/1 The photometers are protected from excessive light levels by protective photodiodes which disconnect the high voltage supply at times when the light level is above a minimum value. **1975** D. G. FINK *Electronics Engineers' Handbk.* xi. 67 Figure 11-55 is a cross-sectional diagram of a metal semiconductor (Schottky barrier) photodiode. **1978** *Gramophone* Jan. 1322/2 A light beam from a helium-neon laser scans the track and the reflected light is directed towards a photodiode which converts the light variations into a corresponding electrical signal for decoding and relaying to the aerial socket of a standard TV set for viewing and listening.

photodisintegration: see *PHOTO- 1; **photo-dissociate, -dissociation:** see *PHOTO- 3.

photodynamic, *a.* (in Dict. s.v. PHOTO- 1). Add: **b.** [after G. *photodynamisch* (H. von Tappeiner 1904, in *Münch. med. Wochenschr.* 19 Apr. 714/1)]. Involving or causing a toxic response to light, esp. ultraviolet light.

1909 *Jrnl. Chem. Soc.* XCVI. II. 925 Extracts in methyl alcohol of various etiolated plants invariably showed a distinct photodynamic action on suspensions of red-blood corpuscles. **1937** *Ann. Reg. 1936* 59 Advance was made in the understanding of the photodynamic inactivation of viruses and bacteria. **1965** SELIGER & MCELROY *Light* v. 327 Calcutt (1954) found a large group of carcinogens, other than the polycyclic hydrocarbons, that was also photodynamic. **1973** *Daily Colonist* (Victoria, B.C.) 16 Nov. 5/5 The 'photodynamic therapy' may provide a new approach to treating several human cancers. **1974** *Nature* 9 Aug. 504/1 Light of wavelengths between 400 nm or 500–600 nm causes lesions through photodynamic action of porphyrin in the skin. **1977** *Ibid.* 3 Nov. 15/3 The use of dye photosensitisers in research on the so-called photodynamic effect is an area in which an important role for $^1\Delta_gO_2$ is beyond dispute.

Hence **pho:todyna·mically** *adv.*

1926 E. MAYER *Clin. Applic. Sunlight* v. 87 With the exception of toluene-red and indigo-carmine, all dyes which stained staphylococci well, and were not toxic for them, were photodynamically active. **1954** *Jrnl. Bacteriol.* LXVIII. 125/2 Photodynamically inactivated phage. **1967** J. M. HOSKINS *Virol. Procedures* xiii. 181 Neutral red is a photodynamically active dyestuff, and infected cells incubated in its presence in the light fail to yield normal plaques.

photo-effect, -ejection: see *PHOTO- 1.

photoelastic (fōuto,ǐlæ·stik), *a.* Also with hyphen. [f. PHOTO- 1 + ELASTIC *a.* and *sb.*] Employing or exhibiting the property of becoming birefringent when mechanically stressed, so that polarized light passed through such a substance gives rise to interference fringes that display the stress patterns in it.

1911 E. G. COKER in *Trans. Inst. Naval Archit.* LIII. 265 (*heading*) The determination, by photo-elastic methods, of the distribution of stress in plates of variable section, with some applications to ships' plating. **1920** *Flight* XII. 399/1 On arrival..they were welcomed by the Superintendent, and later attended the lecture of Professor Coker on his photo-elastic method of measuring stresses in materials. **1936** *Jrnl. R. Aeronaut. Soc.* XL. 472 To analyse quick variations of internal stresses, *e.g.*, in vibrating specimens or in impact phenomena, kinematography or [*read* of] photo-elastic fringes at very high speeds was devised. **1953** FAIRMAN & CUTSHALL *Mech. of Materials* xiii. 372 A third method of experimental stress analysis involves the transmission of polarized light through transparent models and is known as the photoelastic method. **1958** *New Scientist* 2 Oct. 953/2 The 'photo-elastic technique'..enables the movements of stresses inside the gear teeth under load to be seen. **1965** HAWKES & HOLISTER in Zienkiewicz & Holister *Stress Anal.* xii. 267 In the photoelastic coating technique, sheets of birefringent plastic are bonded, using a reflective cement, to the surface of the body being studied. When the body is strained under load, the strain is conveyed through the cement to the coating where isoclinic and isochromatic fringes appear, when the coating is viewed through a reflection polariscope. **1970** *New Scientist* 3 Dec. 377/2 The photoelastic plastic generally indicated higher stresses than did the strain gauges.

So **pho:toelasti·city**, the photoelastic method (of stress analysis).

1911 E. G. COKER in *Engineering* 6 Jan. 1/1 (*heading*) Photo-elasticity. **1950** DOLAN & MURRAY in M. Hetényi *Handbk. Exper. Stress Anal.* xvii. 829 His [*sc.* E. G. Coker's] introduction of celluloid for models and the use of monochromatic light have led to the modern laboratory methods which make photoelasticity a powerful engineering tool. **1959** R. R. ARCHER et al. *Introd. Mech. of Solids* iv. 157 The three most widely used methods of measuring strain are 1. Photoelasticity. 2. Brittle coatings. 3. Wire or foil strain gages.

photo-electric, *a.* Now usu. written as one word. **c.** Add to def.: pertaining to or employing a photoelectric effect; *photoelectric absorption,* the absorption of light by an atom which then emits an electron; *photoelectric cell* = *PHOTOCELL; *photoelectric effect* (see quot. 1973); *photoelectric emission,* the emission of electrons by an illuminated surface.

1891 *Phil. Mag.* XXXI. 231 The seleno-aluminium cells differ from all other photoelectric cells that I have constructed in their great sensitiveness to all parts of the spectrum. **1892** *Photogr. Ann.* II. 113 As a rule a much greater photo-electric effect is produced by the more refrangible rays than by the less refrangible. **1912** *Physical Rev.* XXXIV. 475 Photoelectric cells containing sodium or potassium..give a current on illumination which is strictly proportional to the intensity of the exciting light. **1921** *Jrnl. R. Soc. Arts* 16 Dec. 85/1 The electrons so detached are called photoelectrons and the action photoelectric. **1949** *Jrnl. Brit. Interplanetary Soc.* VIII. 115 The photo-electric telescope, which can amplify faint images. **1955** *Sci. News Let.* 12 Mar. 168/3 The instrument, known as a photoelectric polarimeter, measures polarization of skylight with the aid of polarizing prisms. **1958** W. K. MANSFIELD *Elem. Nucl. Physics* i. 10 The electrons can gain this energy by absorbing electromagnetic radiation which gives rise to photoelectric emission of electrons. *Ibid.* v. 44 In photoelectric absorption the γ-ray interacts with an atom as a whole, ejecting an electron. **1960** R. W. MARKS *Dymaxion World of B. Fuller* 25/1 In 1927, seeking photo-electric cells and relay-actuated devices, he wrote to his brother. **1961** G. R. CHOPPIN *Exper. Nucl. Chem.* iii. 30 The photoelectric effect is the predominant mode of interaction in aluminium for gamma rays below 60 kev. **1970** O. DOPPING *Computers & Data Processing* xi. 161 In the photo-electric reader, a lamp sends light beams onto a number of photo cells through the holes in the tape. **1973** J. YARWOOD *Electricity & Magnetism* xv. 594 There are three main photoelectric effects: (*a*) the photoemissive effect or surface photoemission, in which electrons are emitted from the surface of a material when radiation falls upon it; (*b*) the photoconductive effect, concerned when the incident radiation causes electrons to be released within the material (a non-metallic solid) and so increase its conductivity; (*c*) the photovoltaic effect, in which the radiation absorbed in a device causes an e.m.f. to be set up at a discontinuity..at a barrier between two different materials.

photo-electrical *a.* (examples); so **pho:to-ele·ctrically** *adv.*

1888 A. RIGHI in *Phil. Mag.* XXV. 315 The system of the two metals, when receiving the radiation, behaves then as a voltaic cell, and can be called a photoelectrical cell. **1911** *Physical Rev.* XXXII. 631 A platinum cathode film on glass is photo-electrically active even when of the utmost tenuity. **1923** GLAZEBROOK *Dict. Appl. Physics* IV. 563/2 One of the most interesting phases of the inquiry into the laws and constants of radiation is the confirmatory data which one obtains from a consideration ..of photo-electrical action. **1941** MILLMAN & SEELY *Electronics* iii. 101 The number of electrons released photoelectrically from any part of the photocathode depends upon the intensity of the light at that point. **1974** *Physics Bull.* May 204/1 The work functions of polycrystalline films of aluminium..were measured photoelectrically.

photoelectrochemical, -electromagnetic: see *PHOTO- 1.

photoelectron (fōu·to,ĭlektrǫn). *Physics.* Also with hyphen. [f. PHOTO- 1 + *ELECTRON[2].] An electron released from an atom by the interaction of a photon with it; *esp.* one emitted from a solid surface by the action of light.

1912 *Phil. Trans. R. Soc.* A. CCXII. 206 The law connecting the maximum emission velocity of the photo-electrons with the wave-length has been investigated by Ladenburg for Cu, Zu and Pt, and by Kunz for Na-K alloy and Cs. **1934** [see *COMPTON]. **1962** H. D. BUSH *Atomic & Nucl. Physics* ix. 209 An electron bound in an atom may absorb the whole of the energy of an incident γ-ray photon, being ejected from the atom as a photo-electron. *Ibid.* 210 The photoelectrons..will have a short range in the absorbing material, and so unless the material is very thin they are likely to be reabsorbed. **1965** *Wireless World* Sept. 442/1 The process by which the energy of the particles is converted first into photons and then into photo-electrons at the cathode of a photo-multiplier tube is very inefficient. **1975** J. R. LAMARSH *Introd. Nuclear Engin.* iii. 76 The kinetic energy of the ejected photoelectron is equal..to the energy of the photon less the binding energy of the electron to the atom.

Hence **pho:toelectro·nic** *a.*, of or pertaining to a photoelectron, or the interaction of light with electrons; **pho:toelectro·nics** *sb. pl.* (const. as *sing.*), the study of photoelectronic phenomena.

1922 *Physical Rev.* XX. 195 (*heading*) Symmetry of emergent and incident photoelectronic velocities. **1940** *Chambers's Techn. Dict.* 638/1 Photo-electronics. **1947** *Jrnl. Optical Soc. Amer.* XXXVII. 430/1 The lower limit of usable voltage or gain in the photomultiplier tube in a pulse-counting application is reached when the photo-electronic output pulse becomes reduced..to the point where there is confusion from the tube noise and the thermal noise of the coupling resistor. **1957** *Proc. Inst. Electr. Engin.* CIV. B. 480/1 The photo-electric effect is the fundamental basis of the generation of television signals, since this depends on the conversion of light energy into electrical energy. A detailed account of this branch of photo-electronics is beyond the scope of this review. **1963** *Adv. Photochem.* I. 276 The second fundamental photo-electronic mechanism often producing photochromism is charge transfer (photoionization). **1966** N. S. KAPANY *Fiber Optics* (1967) viii. 206 One important application of fiber optics in photoelectronics lies in the coupling of image intensifier stages. **1970** *Sci. Jrnl.* Aug. 90/1 Modern photoelectronic devices can detect or produce radiations over the whole electromagnetic spectrum. **1977** *Gramophone* Apr. 1629/1 The auto-stop and pickup return at the end of a record is sensed by photo-electronic means, involving no side pressures.

photoemission (fōu·to,ĭmiʃən). *Physics.* Also with hyphen and † as two words. [f. PHOTO- 1 + EMISSION.] The emission of electrons from a surface by the action of light incident on it.

1916 *Physical Rev.* VII. 383 (*heading*) Theories of photo emission. **1923** *Ibid.* XXII. 578 It is evident..that the gases given off by the copper-oxide cylinder during the baking out of the tube and the glowing of the filament, have a pronounced effect upon the photo-emission. **1961** G. R. CHOPPIN *Exper. Nucl. Chem.* iii. 35 Tertiary electrons may be produced by photoemission resulting from the photons of the secondary ionization process. **1971** SMITH & THOMSON *Optics* xxiii. 334 In another type of television camera tube, the vidicon, the basic effect is photoconduction instead of photoemission.

So **pho·toemitted, -emitting** *ppl. adjs.*; **photoemi·ssive** *a.*, exhibiting, employing, or pertaining to photoemission; **pho·toemitter,** a photoemissive body or substance.

1932 *Electronics* Jan. 19/2 The necessary condition arises to develop a photoemissive surface which..gives satisfactory emission. **1933** *Jrnl. Inst. Electr. Engin.* LXXIII. 439/1 The equilibrium potential of the element is defined by (*a*) the velocity of the beam [of electrons] and (*b*) the secondary emission from the photo-emitting substance due to bombardment by the electrons. **1957** *Ibid.* CIV. B. 467/1 Hertz discovered the photo-emissive effect—the loss of negative electric charges from metal surfaces which are illuminated. **1957** *Proc. Inst. Electr. Engin.* CIV. B. 468/2 The earliest photo-emitters were common metal surfaces. **1959** *Control* Feb. 92/2 The spectral response of photoemissive cells depends on the cathode coating. **1970** *Nature* 3 Oct. 6/1 Two new spectroscopes using synchroton radiation and photoemitted electrons are singled out for special mention. **1971** SMITH & THOMSON *Optics* xxiii. 333 Semiconductors are widely used as photoemitting surfaces. **1973** [see *PHOTOELECTRIC *a.* c]. **1975** *Physics Bull.* Feb. 65/2 For the first time in a commercial instrument the simultaneous measurement of the energy and angular distribution of photoemitted or secondary electrons can be made.

photoenvironment to **-fabrication:** see *PHOTO- 1; **photo-essay** to **-facsimile:** see *PHOTO- 2.

photo-fi·nish. Also photo finish. [f. PHOTO- 2 + FINISH *sb.*] The finish of a race in which competitors are so close that the result has to be determined by reference to a photograph of the situation. Also *attrib.* and *fig.*

1936 *N.Y. Times* 1 July 36/6 New..tests will be made tomorrow at Pimlico on the photo finish device. *Ibid.* 2 July 16/8 At Belmont Park thirty pictures were called for. Of this number the photo finish awarded the decision to sixteen horses racing on the outside, with fourteen on the inside. **1938** D. RUNYON *Take it Easy* xv. 283, I will take a chance on Nicely-Nicely against anything on four legs, except maybe an elephant, and at that he may give the elephant a photo finish. **1940** *Sun* (Baltimore) 22 Nov. 1/2 Gov. Payne H. Ratner..emerged a photo-finish leader tonight in the complete unofficial count of ballots cast sixteen days ago. **1944** J. H. FULLARTON *Troop Target* 160 'We've got to choose between security and progress.' 'Personally,' said MacVaughan, 'I'm for security—but it's a photo finish.' **1951** *Sport* 7–13 Jan. 4/2 Combination 'B' looks like proving a photo-finish between Plymouth and Chelsea, with Charlton holding an outside chance. **1961** *Times* 22 July 3/2 Jones.. snatched second place through a photo-finish from Radford. **1973** D. FRANCIS *Slay-Ride* iv. 55 Sixteen hundred metres for staying two-year-olds... There was a photo-finish. **1974** *Times* 6 May 1/3 A photo finish was predicted by the last two public opinion polls. The final one showed M Mitterrand..winning on the second ballot by a short head. **1976** *Guardian Weekly* 19 Sept. 7/2 The Zia coup was a photofinish affair just four days after another army putsch that is popularly supposed to have been backed by India. **1976** *Norwich Mercury* 19 Nov. 10/1 A number of very close contests took place in Division Two, but Thetford British Legion B and Saints E were involved in a 'photo-finish' which the Legion won by a whisker.

photofission: see *PHOTO- 1.

photofit (fōu·tofit). Also **Photo-Fit.** [f. PHOTO- 2 + FIT *sb.*[4]] Name of a method of building up an identikit picture (cf. *IDENTIKIT) by assembling a number of photographs of individual facial features; a picture so formed. Freq. *attrib.*

1970 *Guardian* 23 Apr. 6/4 The Home Office believes it has a 'promising development' at its disposal with the introduction of a new system of criminal identification—the Photo-Fit. By using photographs instead of line drawings, the new technique will enable the police to build up..many..composite faces. *Ibid.* 6/5 Photo-Fit is a product of the invention of Mr Jacques Penry..and the manufacturing facilities of John Waddington Ltd. of Leeds. **1971** *Daily Tel.* 5 Mar. 2/8 Photo-Fit and Identikit pictures have been issued to police throughout London. **1973** *Oxf. Times* 10 Aug. 1/9 Thames Valley Police have issued a photofit picture and a description of a man they wish to interview. **1974** J. GARDNER *Corner Men* xiv. 233 They showed..a straight and recent picture of Peppe, together with some photofits put together to show the [Mafia] don in a permutation of disguises. **1976** *Daily Record* (Glasgow) 4 Dec. 13/2 Police are so anxious to capture him that they applied for special permission from the Lord Advocate to issue this photofit picture.

photoflash (fōu·toflæʃ). Also with hyphen. [f. PHOTO- 2 + FLASH *sb.*[2]] A flash of light produced to enable a photograph to be taken; a device for producing such a flash. Freq *attrib.*

1930 *N.Y. Times* 24 Oct. 21/2 Noiseless and smokeless photoflash lamp devised. **1946** L. E. O. CHARLTON *R.A.F. & U.S.A.A.F. July 1943 to Sept. 1944* vii. 156 (*caption*) This night photograph shows huge volumes of smoke pouring from targets bombed at Duesseldorf which have been illuminated by a photo flash bomb. **1946** *R.A.F. Jrnl.* May 170 (*caption*) A Lancaster Master-Bomber on a night raid dropping a photo-flash. **1956** A. H. COMPTON *Atomic Quest* I. 58 The question is one of straightforward thermodynamics, which I had myself used several years before in calculating..the forces that cause bursting of photoflash bulbs. **1964** L. DEIGHTON *Funeral in Berlin* vii. 46 Photo-flashes sliced instants from eternity. **1972** *Gloss. Electrotechnical, Power Terms* (*B.S.I.*) IV. iii. 15 *Photoflash lamp,* lamp giving..a single high light output for a very brief period, for lighting objects to be photographed. **1975** N. FREELING *What are Bugles blowing For?* iv. 17 An expressionless face for the photo-flash.

photoflood (fōu·toflʌd). [f. PHOTO- 2 + FLOOD *sb.*] A very bright flood-light used in photography and cinematography. Freq. *attrib.*

1933 *Pop. Sci. Monthly* Feb. 76/1 The ordinary bulb in the reading light was removed and a photoflood bulb substituted... The photoflood is so strong that it will give the proper effect during the brief time the shutter is open for the flash. **1937** *Discovery* Feb. 57/2 A photoflood bulb gives an intensity of the same order at close range. **1962** *Which?* May 133/2 The Type A photoflood version of Kodachrome. **1972** *Amat. Photographer* 12 Jan. 38 A most popular light source with amateur photographers, photofloods have a colour temperature of 3,400°K and a very high light output. **1977** J. HEDGECOE *Photographer's Handbk.* 34 A larger 'No. 2' photoflood bulb..offers longer life but is more expensive.

photofluorogram to **-fluoroscopy:** see *PHOTO- 2; **photoformer:** see *PHOTO- 1.

photog (fotǫ·g). Also fotog. N. Amer. colloq. abbrev. of PHOTOGRAPHER.

1913 *Technical World* XIX. 385/1 The elements of the air..and a dozen other things may make the newspaper 'fotog' ready to throw up the sponge. **1934** H. N. ROSE *Thes. Slang* 51/2 Photographer: *a photog.* **1952** *Daily News* (N.Y.) 21 Aug. c4 The Swedish fotogs were actually saving film. **1968** *Globe & Mail* (Toronto) 17 Feb. 35 (Advt.), A photog's delight! **1973** R. PARKES *Guardians* vi. 104 You'll like that fashion photog of ours—what's her name.

photo-galvanic, *a.* Add: Now usu. written **photogalvanic. 2.** *Physics.* Designating or utilizing the generation of a potential difference between two electrodes by a photo-chemical reaction in the electrolyte containing them.

1940 E. RABINOWITCH in *Jrnl. Chem. Physics* VIII. 551/1 The term 'photogalvanic effect' is used in the present series of papers to denote a special case of the so-called Becquerel effect, in which the influence of light on the electrode potential is due to a photochemical process in the body of the electrolyte (as distinct from photochemical or photoelectric processes in the surface layer of the electrode..). *Ibid.* 553/2 The top curve shows *L* [*sc.* the intensity of illumination] as a function of time... The lower curve represents the simultaneous changes in the potential of a Pt-electrode placed in the solution—the 'photogalvanic effect'. *Ibid.* 560 The oxidation-reduction system thionine-iron..provides an extremely sensitive photogalvanic cell. **1956** *Nature* 21 Jan. 110/2 Electrical processes for the direct conversion of radiation to electricity, including thermoelectric generators, photovoltaic cells and *p-n* junctions and photogalvanic cells. **1976** *Interdisciplinary Sci. Rev.* I. 132/2 The irradiation of an electrode/electrolyte system produces a change in the electrode potential (on open circuit) or in the current flowing (on closed circuit). The cause of this may be a photochemical reaction in bulk solution, the products of which are electroactive, in which case the cell is commonly called a photogalvanic cell.

photogenic, *a.* Add: Also with pronunc. (-dʒī·nik).

1. Delete *rare* and add further examples.

1954 *Brain* LXXVII. 234 Photic excitation has been subjected to intense study in electroencephalographic laboratories... Yet clinical descriptions of photogenic epilepsy are few. **1962** *Times* 30 June 12/2 Self-induced photogenic epilepsy in children. **1972** NAQUET & MELDRUM in D. P. Purpura et al. *Exper. Models of Epilepsy* xv. 373 (*heading*) Photogenic seizures in baboon.

2. For *Obs.* read '*Obs.* exc. *Hist.*' and add later example.

1973 *Times* 22 May 28/5 (Advt.), Early photographs and related material, including..calotypes by William Henry Fox Talbot; early photogenic drawings; [etc.].

4. Of a person or thing: that is a good subject for photography; that shows to good advantage in a photograph or film. Also in Fr. form *photogénique*. orig. *U.S.*

1928 *Reflex* June 91/1 The mere doll-face, the photogenic type which thrived on 'fan' adulation, will be a thing of the past. **1931** S. GOLDWYN in *Sat. Rev.* 14 Feb. 220/1 An actor may be 'photogenic' and have personality and appearance, but that is not enough. **1931** *Daily Express* 13 Mar. 19/4 Look at..Pamela Nickalls, with her perfect oval face and high, photogenic forehead. **1935** *Times Lit. Suppl.* 10 Oct. 631/4 Spain is very probably the most *photogénique* country in Europe. **1940** *New Statesman* 19 Oct. 379 The thrills in *Foreign Correspondent* are massive and photogenic to a degree. **1948** E. WAUGH *Loved One* 5 Her legs were never *photogénique*. **1958** *Newnes Compl. Amat. Photogr.* 143 Take two common 'photogenic' subjects, a scene of hills and sky, and a child playing in a flower garden. *Ibid.* 150 It is a fact that very few faces are symmetrical, regular or photogenic. **1974** M. HASTINGS *Dragon Island* viii. 74 She was a good-looking girl; photogenic..and with the right bone structure.

photogenically *adv.* (examples relating to sense *4 above).

1959 *Times* 23 Feb. 10/6 There were nets drying photogenically in the sun. **1974** *Daily Tel.* 9 Aug. 13/2 The director..does score photogenically in the action scenes.

photogeology (fōᵘtodʒiˌǫ·lǒdʒi). Also with hyphen. [f. PHOTO- 2 + GEOLOGY.] (See quot. 1941.)

1941 H. C. REA in *Bull. Amer. Assoc. Petroleum Geologists* XXV. 1796 For this little known branch of geology the writer suggests the term 'photogeology', which is defined as the geologic interpretation of aerial photographs. **1970** *Nature* 24 Jan. 322/1 The long range aim is to establish an absolute lunar time scale directly related to relative ages obtained by photogeology over the whole lunar surface. **1976** *Jrnl. R. Soc. Arts* CXXIV. 639/2 British scientists [in the Antarctic] possess an impressive array of modern techniques: airborne magnetometry,..satellite photogeology, [etc.].

Hence **pho:togeolo·gic, -lo·gical** *adjs.*, of or pertaining to photogeology; **pho:togeolo·gically** *adv.*, by photogeological means; **photogeo·logist,** an expert or specialist in photogeology.

1941 *Bull. Amer. Assoc. Petroleum Geologists* XXV. 1796 A photogeologic map would be a map produced from a stereoscopic study of the aerial photos. *Ibid.* 1797 It proved that a trained photogeologist could produce a map which would agree very favorably with actual field observations. **1949** *Ibid.* XXXIII. 1251 During 1947, more than 110,000 square miles in the Rocky Mountain region were covered photogeologically. **1950** *Ibid.* XXXIV. 2285 Mutual checking of photogeological and field work should be just as apt to lead to corrections of the one as the other whenever discrepancies are found. **1962** F. I. ORDWAY et al. *Basic Astronautics* v. 206 The first remotely conducted photogeologic experiment of another world was remarkably successful. **1966** E. BURGESS *Assault on Moon* ii. 43 The Army Map Service produced a general photogeologic map of the Moon in the late 1950s. **1967** *Q. Jrnl. Geol. Soc.* CXXIII. 255 It is possible to define the geometry of photogeologically observed large folds by plotting..dip and strike values on a stereographic net. **1972** *Science* 2 June 976/3 Deposits of basin ejecta concentric about Imbrium are termed the Fra Mauro Formation by photogeologists. **1977** A. HALLAM *Planet Earth* 111 Photogeological interpretation assists rapid production of geological maps from aerial photographs.

photogoniometer to **-metry:** see *PHOTO- 2.

photogram. Add: (Further examples.) (Still *rare.*)

1935 *Amer. Mineral.* XX. 476 Montmorillonite was *x*-rayed..and its lines..agree with the powder spectrum photograms of other investigators. **1961** (*title of periodical*) New photograms.

†**2.** A photograph, picture, diagram, or other facsimile transmitted by wireless or ordinary telegraphy. *Obs.* (Now called a phototelegram (see *PHOTO- 1).)

1928 *Observer* 24 June 23 The wireless photogram service..has been extended. **1928** *Times* 6 Sept. 11/6 The Postal Telegraph Company put into commercial operation to-day a new telephoto and facsimile message service, which it calls photograms. **1929** *Telegraph & Telephone Jrnl.* XVI. 4/1 Suppose that transmissions of photo-grams by modified television apparatus can take place at the rate of 30 per second.

3. A photographic picture made without a camera (see quots.). Also † *photogramme.*

1934 *Archit. Rev.* LXXV. 12/2 As a photographer he [*sc.* Moholy-Nagy] has been a pioneer in the photogramme (the cameraless photography which he regards as the art-form of the future). **1948** J. H. GABLE *Compl. Introd. Photogr.* III. xvii. 209 The first photogram was probably made by Fox Talbot by placing lace on a sheet of his calotype paper and exposing it to light. **1958** *Newnes Comp. Amat. Photogr.* III. xxvii. 241 Photograms can also be made with the aid of a torch bulb. **1972** *Sci. Amer.* Dec. 115/1 A photogram is made without a camera by exposing photographic paper to a point light source, the leaf or the fruit being placed directly on the paper. **1978** J. H. COOTE *Focalguide to Cibachrome* 175 You can easily make photograms in colour, directly from leaves, flowers and any other translucent objects.

photogrammetry. Add: More widely, the technique of using photographs to ascertain measurements relating to what is photographed. (Further examples.)

1933 *Jrnl. R. Aeronaut. Soc.* XXXVII. 386 Most of the continental plotting machines..were designed originally for terrestrial photogrammetry, where each goniometer in the plotter can be set to a known orientation. **1934** *Ibid.* XXXVIII. 257 (*heading*) Photogrammetry of landing speeds. **1948** *Sci. News* VII. Pl. 25, After the church had been destroyed..the essential dimensions were deduced from a pre-war snapshot... The science of deducing dimensions from photographs is called Photogrammetry. **1959** F. H. MOFFITT *Photogrammetry* i. 1 The term *aerial photogrammetry* denotes that branch of photogrammetry wherein photographs of the terrain..are taken by a precision camera mounted in an aircraft... The term *terrestrial photogrammetry* denotes that branch..wherein photographs are taken from a fixed, and usually known, position on or near the ground and with the camera axis horizontal or nearly so. *Ibid.* 2 Terrestrial photogrammetry embraces also the use of cameras at ground stations in known positions for the following purposes: To reproduce plan and elevation views of buildings and structures... By means of motion-picture photography, to make measurements involving transitory phenomena such as wave motion,..moving machinery, [etc.]. **1965** *New Scientist* 18 Nov. 507/1 Photogrammetry is now being explored for use on large microwave aerials, to check the accuracy of construction, and to measure deformations under wind loads. **1978** *Jrnl. R. Soc. Arts* CXXVI. 473/1 Ankara, particularly at the Middle East Technical University, was early in the field in the use of photogrammetry for mass recording.

Hence **photogramme·tric** *a.*, **photogramme·trically** *adv.*; **photogra·mmetrist,** an expert or specialist in photogrammetry; **photogrammetrical** *a.* (later example).

1906 J. A. FLEMER *Elem. Treat. Phototopogr. Methods* i. 5 The theoretical principles upon which photogrammetric methods are primarily based were known to J. H. Lambert.., who published a work on perspective in 1759. *Ibid.* xii. 397 If differences in the elevations of points of the terrene are to be deduced photogrammetrically within a limit of error not exceeding one meter, the pictured length..of a meter..should not appear shorter than 0·1 mm. **1939** B. B. TALLEY *Engin. Applic. Aerial & Terrestr. Photogrammetry* i. 6 For photogrammetrical purposes photographs may be classified as either aerial or terrestrial, depending on whether the taking camera was borne aloft or..on the surface of the earth. *Ibid.*, Photogrammetry..should never be considered as an end in itself. Such consideration is the stumbling block of photogrammetrists. **1950** *Antiquity* XXIV. 85 With the use of Photogrammetric Tables, extreme accuracy was possible in determining and measuring the exact position on the ground of crop-mark sites visible in the air photographs. **1957** *Oxf. Mag.* 21 Nov. 131/1 The search for oil today requires the organisation of teams of specialists: surveyors, palaeontologists, photogrammetrists, geophysicists and geochemists. **1970** J. A. HOWARD *Aerial Photo-Ecol.* ix. 98 Vertical photographs are simple to use photogrammetrically, as a minimum of mathematical correction is required. **1975** *Sci. Amer.* Jan. 130/3 In 1962..he organized a modern aerial photogrammetric survey of the site from 4,000 feet.

photograph, *sb.* Add: **c.** *photograph album* (examples), *book* (examples), *frame* (example), *gallery.*

1858 F. J. COOK *Let.* 19 Sept. in F. G. Bascom *Lett. Ticonderoga Farmer* (1946) 46, I..visited..Brady's celebrated photograph gallery. **1870** O. LOGAN *Before Footlights* 258 The only thing worth carrying away was a decent sort of photograph album. **1872** E. WORDSWORTH in E. Romanes *C. M. Yonge* (1908) ix. 150, I found her armed with a large photograph-book of friends and relations. **1873** *Young Englishwoman* Feb. 94/2 Photograph frame in leather work. **1888** MRS. H. WARD *R. Elsmere* I. iii. 76 Mrs. Seaton was severely turning over a photograph book. **1940** T. S. ELIOT *East Coker* v. 14 The evening with the photograph album. **1949** *Chicago Tribune* 18 Sept. 27/4 Andrew Burgess..bought and operated Brady's national photograf gallery in Washington.

photograph, *v.* Add: **1. b.** (Earlier example.)

1857 C. KINGSLEY *Two Yrs. Ago* III. i. 37 If any one will ensure me a poor two thousand a year, I will promise to photograph no more.

c. (Further examples.)

1919 *Conquest* Nov. 24/1 The red leaves of autumn photograph as black. **1931** F. L. ALLEN *Only Yesterday* vi. 126 He photographed well and the pictures of him in the rotogravure sections won him affection and respect. **1949** E. COXHEAD *Wind in West* i. 10 A creamily handsome young woman..Hedy Lamarr type, would photograph, summed up Tony at a glance. **1965** *Listener* 18 Nov. 817/2 Wales photographs beautifully: the short, slated roofs, the coal-tips and the valleys, the terraced houses on grey streets—none of them loses much in black and white reproduction. **1974** 'E. LATHEN' *Sweet & Low* xix. 183, I don't like the way he photographs. Yours is the face I want.

photographable, *a.* (Further examples.)

1939 [see *ABSORPTIOMETER 2]. **1962** C. WALSH *From Utopia to Nightmare* i. 20 Some artists..have created.. nothing remotely photographable. **1973** 'E. MCBAIN' *Hail to Chief* i. 13 A blush which, if not quite kissable, is at least photographable.

† **photogra·pheme.** *Obs. rare.* [f. PHOTOGRAPH *sb.* + *-eme* as if f. Gr. -ημα (cf. *-EME).] A photograph.

1864 G. M. HOPKINS *Further Lett.* (1956) 211 She *comprehood* who I was by my photographeme which you strangely said was not like me. **1888** *Ibid.* 291 It is not altogether as I should wish it either as a portrait or as a.. photograph, photogram, photographeme, φωτογράφημα, a work of the photographic camera.

photographic, *a.* Add: **c.** *photographic memory*: a memory that records visual perceptions with the accuracy of a photograph.

1940 in *Chambers's Techn. Dict.* 638/1. **1948** 'J. TEY' *Franchise Affair* vii. 73 She has a photographic memory... She would remember what she saw. **1964** M. CRITCHLEY *Developmental Dyslexia* ix. 62 He is perhaps a person weak in visual imagery and visual memory of all types, the opposite of the person with eidetic imagery and photographic memory. **1974** A. MORICE *Killing with Kindness* iv. 37 I've got what they call a photographic memory and I don't visualise her wearing a wedding ring.

photographica (fōᵘtogræ·fikǎ), *sb. pl.* [f. PHOTOGRAPHIC *a.*: see -A 4]. Books, albums, or collections of photographs; items connected with photography.

1973 *Country Life* 20 Sept. (Suppl.) 76 (Advt.), Photographs and Photographica. **1976** *Times Lit. Suppl.* 25 June 804/3 Photographica, which until recently accounted for a minute part of each year's offerings at book auctions in the United States, was the subject of no less than three large sales this spring. **1976** *National Observer* (U.S.) 4 Dec. 20/3 There can be no doubt that this is one of the most remarkable collections of American photographica.

photographically, *adv.* (Earlier and later examples of literal use.)

1842 J. F. W. HERSCHEL in *Phil. Trans. R. Soc.* CXXXII. 194 The retina itself may be *photographically* impressible by strong lights. **1968** R. A. LYTTLETON *Mysteries Solar Syst.* iv. 119 Comet Borelly showed photographically as many as nine tails.

photoheterotroph to **-inactivation:** see *PHOTO- 1.

photoinduce (fōᵘ:toˌindiū·s), *v.* Also with hyphen. [f. PHOTO- 1 + INDUCE *v.*] *trans.* To induce by the action of light; esp. in *Plant Physiol.*, to induce reproductive behaviour in a plant by an appropriate sequence of light and darkness (used with the behaviour or the plant as obj.).

1949 *Bot. Gaz.* CX. 495/1 If one part of the plant was kept completely in the dark and some other part above it was photoinduced to flower, then the part in the dark also flowered. **1952** *Ann. Rev. Plant Physiol.* III. 269 If a plant is photoinduced and then is grafted on to an individual kept on the noninductive conditions, the latter plant will also initiate flowers. **1974** *Photochem. & Photobiol.* XIX. 163/1 It is..of importance to determine if an electron transfer reaction of this type can be photoinduced in a model system.

So **photoindu·ced** *ppl. a.*, induced by the action of light; also **photoindu·cible** *a.*, capable of being photoinduced.

1947 *Bot. Gaz.* CIX. 121/1 Buds develop and flower only on the photoinduced portion or one node beyond. **1961** *Jrnl. Appl. Physics* XXXII. 1901/2 The photoinduced current..is equal to the diode current with the bias voltage zero. **1970** DORION & WIEBE *Photocromism* i. 9 The reversible or self-bleaching feature distinguishes photochromism from the well-known irreversible photoinduced reactions. **1970** GRESSEL & GALUN in G. Bernier *Cellular & Molecular Aspects Floral Induction* x. 154 Some fungal systems are reported to be photoinducible by ultraviolet light as short as 230 mμ with no sporulation beyond 340 mμ. **1974** *Nature* 26 Apr. 801/1 We have not obtained a cell-free system from *P*[*hycomyces*] *blakesleeanus* which shows the photoinducible changes. **1977** I. M. CAMPBELL *Energy & Atmosphere* ix. 344 It is generally considered that erythema is the least serious of a series of photoinduced skin complaints.

photoinduction (fōᵘtoˌindɒ·kʃən). [f. PHOTO- 1 + INDUCTION.] The action or process of induction by light, esp. of reproductive behaviour in plants.

1947 *Bot. Gaz.* CIX. 131/2 A reduction in total reproductive activity in relation to reduced photoinduction. **1971** *New Scientist* 9 Sept. 558/1 Flowering..occurred about 20 days after this photoinduction. **1975** D. VINCE-PRUE *Photoperiodism in Plants* vi. 229 Endogenous cytokinins may..be involved in the process of photoinduction.

photoinductive (fōᵘtoˌindɒ·ktiv), *a. Bot.* [f. PHOTO- 1 + INDUCTIVE *a.*] Tending to induce flowering or other activity in plants by means of a regime of alternating periods of light and darkness; *photoinductive cycle*, a circadian cycle of one period of light and one of darkness.

1940 *Bot. Gaz.* CI. 667 (*caption*) Effect of duration and intensity of light during seven photoinductive cycles on subsequent initiation of floral primordia by Biloxi soybean. **1956** *Plant Physiol.* XXXI. 280/2 A measure of the amount of stimulation afforded by photoinductive treatments. **1971** *New Scientist* 9 Sept. 558/2 Flowering was..enhanced if the plants got a drenching during the photoinductive period. **1975** D. VINCE-PRUE *Photoperiodism in Plants* i. 42 In the SD [*sc.* short-day] grass, *Rottboellia exaltata*..a minimum of six photoinductive cycles are necessary for flowering.

photo-interpretation to **-interpretive:** see *PHOTO- 2.

photo-ionization (fōᵘ:toˌəiǒnəizēⁱ·ʃən). *Physics.* Also without hyphen. [f. PHOTO- 1 + *IONIZATION².] Ionization produced by electromagnetic radiation.

1914 S. E. SHEPPARD *Photo-Chem.* ix. 356 (*heading*) Photo-ionization of gases. **1955** *Jrnl. Brit. Interplanetary Soc.* XIV. 18 From its effect in lowering the D layer, H. Friedman deduced that the intensity of the sun's radiation in the Lyman alpha wave-length must increase a thousand fold during solar flares. He added that it creates the D region by photo-ionization of nitrous oxide. **1975** D. H. BURRIN in Williams & Wilson *Biologist's Guide to Princ. & Techniques Pract. Biochem.* v. 166 Alternatively, strong electric fields..or ultraviolet light (photoionization) may be employed to ionize the sample.

So **photoi·onize** *v. trans.*, to ionize by means of electromagnetic radiation; **photoi·onized, -i·onizing** *ppl. adjs.*

1953 MEEK & CRAGGS *Electr. Breakdown of Gases* i. 15 Photoionizing radiations. **1962** *Jrnl. Optical Soc. Amer.* LII. 1241/1 Different responses at short wavelengths result from the different thicknesses of the surface layer from which the photo-ionized carriers must diffuse before recombination. **1974** *Rev. Sci. Instruments* XLV. 662/2 The approach consists of photoionizing some species in a field-free region and extracting a portion of the photo-electrons thus produced into a beam. **1977** *Jrnl. R. Soc. Arts* CXXV. 767/1 A second laser beam was..used to photoionize the excited magnesium atoms.

photoisomer (fōu͡tǫ,əi·sǒmə.ɪ). *Chem.* [f. PHOTO- 1 + ISOMER.] An isomer formed by irradiation of a different, often more stable, form of a compound.

1960 *Jrnl. Amer. Chem. Soc.* LXXXII. 3642/2 Colchicine..on prolonged exposure to sunlight gave three photoisomers. **1965** SELIGER & MCELROY *Light* v. 307 The temperature..of the solution affected the stability of the various photoisomers that were formed upon initial irradiation of the room-temperature stable material. **1973** *Tetrahedron* XXIX. 3869/1 This new photoisomer is formed from heptachlor epoxide exposed to sunlight on bean leaves only in the presence of a photosensitizer.

Hence **pho:toisome·ric** *a.*, of or pertaining to a photoisomer or photoisomers; **pho:to-iso·merism**, the fact of being or having a photoisomer.

1955 *Jrnl. Chem. Physics* XXIII. 1367/1 The final photoisomeric equilibrium was always independent of the isomeric composition before irradiation. **1965** SELIGER & MCELROY *Light* ii. 144 The photoisomerism of 11-*cis* retinene.

photoisomeriza·tion (fōu͡tǫ,əis-). *Chem.* [f. PHOTO- 1 + *ISOMERIZATION.] The formation of a photoisomer.

1926 H. A. SPOEHR *Photosynthesis* v. 285 They tried to detect the photoisomerization of the chlorophyll-carbonic acid complex. **1956** H. A. BORTHWICK et al. in A. Hollaender *Radiation Biol.* III. x. 494 The relative biological response, such as internode elongation, seed germination, or flowering, is limited by the photoisomerization of the pigment. **1965** SELIGER & MCELROY *Light* v. 305 When rhodopsin in the retina is exposed to white light, the result is a photoisomerization to the yellow-colored all-*trans* form through several intermediate steps. **1976** H. CAMPION et al. in B. E. C. Nordin *Calcium, Phosphate & Magnesium Metabolism* xii. 452 Ergocalciferol itself can, under prolonged irradiation, undergo irreversible photoisomerization.

So **pho:toiso·merize** *v. intr.*, to undergo photoisomerization.

1963 *Adv. Photochem.* I. 325 Simple tropolones also photoisomerize. γ-Tropolone methyl ether..gives the bicyclic photoisomer..on irradiation in aqueous solution.

photojournalism, -ist: see *PHOTO- 2.

photokinesis (fōu:tokəinī·sis, -kĭnī·sis). *Biol.* [mod.L., ad. G. *photokinese* (T. W. Engelmann 1883, in *Archiv. f. ges. Physiol.* XXX. 95): see PHOTO- 1 and *KINESIS.] An undirected movement of an organism in response to the effect of light.

1905 [see *KINESIS 2]. **1940** *Jrnl. Compar. Psychol.* XXIX. 448 Photokinesis (the activating effect of light) is particularly a function of the visual receptor. This characteristic accounts for the excitation of the ants at daybreak. **1967** *Oceanogr. & Marine Biol.* V. 361 Aggregation [of polyzoan larvae] in a shaded area may..perhaps best be explained in terms of low photokinesis. **1970** W. NULTSCH in P. Halldal *Photobiol. of Microorganisms* viii. 219 The photokinetic action of light absorbed by photosynthetic pigments has led to the conclusion that photokinesis may be linked with photosynthesis.

Hence **photokine·tic** *a.*, pertaining to or exhibiting photokinesis; **photokine·tically** *adv.*

1900 *Amer. Jrnl. Physiol.* III. 291 Light may cause gatherings of animals... By a reaction of the animal to sudden changes in the intensity of illumination... Such animals Loeb calls 'Unterschiedsempfindlich', photokinetic. **1907** *Jrnl. Exper. Zool.* V. 72 The purpose..is to consider the phototactic movement of planarians, as distinct from their photokinetic behavior. **1957** G. E. HUTCHINSON *Treat. Limnol.* I. ix. 617 Oxygen uptake in the clear bottles is actually higher than in the black... This is presumably due to a photokinetic effect on the zooplankton in the bottles. **1967** *Oceanogr. & Marine Biol.* V. 361 It seems probable that polyzoan larvae display photokinetic responses. **1970** W. NULTSCH in P. Halldal *Photobiol. of Microorganisms* viii. 218 As the ultraviolet region of the spectrum is photokinetically effective, too, this effectiveness must be due to another photoreceptor of unknown chemical structure.

photolabile, -lability: see *PHOTO- 1.

photolitho. Add: Also **photo-litho.** Also abbrev. of PHOTOLITHOGRAPH, PHOTOLITHOGRAPHY.

1896 *Photographic Jrnl.* XX. 278 In photo-litho in line a perfect transfer must be as follows, the lines must be perfectly firm and free from rottenness, the ink forming the image must be hard... For photo-litho transfers in half-tone the smooth gradations of the photograph must be broken up by the discriminating reticulation of gelatine. **1907** C. SALTER tr. *Andés' Treatment of Paper* xvii. 191 Ordinary transfer paper for photolitho work is liable to stretch in the press. **1921** *Brit. Printer* Nov. 163/1 From an economic aspect photo-litho easily holds its own when compared with letterpress printing. **1946** *Nature* 28 Dec. 929/1 This volume..is published in photo-litho. **1960** G. A. GLAISTER *Gloss. Bk.* 306/1 Various methods were attempted to produce workable photo-lithos by copying direct on stone. *Ibid.*, Photo-lithography at the end of the 19th century was dominated by Eugen Albert's photo-litho paper. **1973** S. JENNETT *Making of Bks.* (ed. 5) x. 162 Like letterpress..photo-litho can print only an even film of ink.

2. photo-litho offset (see quot. 1934).

1931 A. ESDAILE *Student's Man. Bibliogr.* v. 170 Photo-litho-offset in various processes is now largely used for the cheap production of unaltered reprints of books. **1934** H. CURWEN *Processes of Graphic Reproduction in Printing* I. 64 Under offset printing must be mentioned the very wide use made of 'photo litho offset'. As the name implies, this is printing by lithography via a rubber blanket, from printing surfaces prepared by photographic methods. **1948** H. MISSINGHAM *Student's Guide Commercial Art* II. 129 Photo-litho offset..is a method of printing by lithography, in which the design is photographed on to zinc plate. **1960** G. A. GLAISTER *Gloss. Bk.* 306/1 The negative is copied on to a photo-lithographic plate from which printing is done by photo-litho offset.

photolithographic, *a.* (Earlier and later examples.) So **photolithogra·phically** *adv.*

1862 *Rep. Juries Internat. Exhib.* Class XIV. 5. The following may be considered as a classification of photo lithographic processes. **1945** H. BARRON *Mod. Plastics* xxv. 523 Photolithographic printing plates are now being made with surfaces based on polyvinyl alcohol. **1965** *Wireless World* July 338/2 The original pattern to be photolithographically reproduced was formed by.. winding plastics strip round pegs. **1972** *Physics Bull.* Dec. 743/2 By employing photolithographic techniques.. IRD has produced simple arrays of detectors. **1977** *Sci. Amer.* Sept. 76/1 Areas to be doped..are defined photolithographically.

photolithography. Add: Esp. a planographic printing process using plates prepared from photographic negatives, usually printed by offset methods.

1929 *Times* 29 Oct. (Printing Suppl.) p. xii/7 The process of photo-lithography through the growing importance of the offset process directed fresh attention to the subject [of composing textual matter without the use of type]. **1948** *Science News* VII. 100 Photographic prints on metal are the basis of another major industry—photo-lithography—and here again war-time researches have made possible considerable simplifications in the working procedures. **1966** *Listener* 22 Sept. 422/3 The two [books].. have now reappeared, beautifully reproduced by modern photo-lithography. **1972** *Guardian* 25 Nov. 14/3 Photo-lithography is ousting other methods [of making prints] in the commercial market.

photolithotroph to **-trophy:** see *PHOTO- 1.

pho:tolumine·scence. *Physics.* † Also with hyphen. [ad. G. *photolumineszenz* (E. Wiedemann 1888, in *Ann. d. Physik und Chem.* XXXIV. 447): see PHOTO- 1 and LUMINESCENCE.] Luminescence caused by visible light or by infra-red or ultraviolet radiation.

1889 tr. E. Wiedemann in *Phil. Mag.* XXVIII. 151 According to the mode of excitation I distinguish Photo-, Electro-, Chemi-, and Tribo-luminescence. In particular, photo-luminescence, including fluorescence and a number of cases of phosphorescence, is defined as those phenomena in which the incident light excites vibrations within the molecule of a body which produce directly an emission of light. **1913** H. S. ALLEN *Photo-Electricity* xi. 147 By means of this hypothesis [*sc.* of light quanta] Einstein sought to explain such phenomena as the photo-electric effect, the ionisation of gases by ultra-violet light, photo-luminescence, and the theory of specific heat. **1930** *Times Lit. Suppl.* 6 Mar. 195/2 A masterly account.. including the theory of atomic and molecular structure and spectra, and photoluminescence. **1968** *McGraw-Hill Yearbk. Sci. & Technol.* 345/1 Little effort has been put into using semiconductors in powder phosphor applications for photoluminescence and cathodoluminescence, because efficient powder phosphors are already available to cover the entire visible spectrum.

Hence **pho:tolumine·scent** *a.*

1909 in *Cent. Dict.* Suppl. **1958** *Sci. News* XLVII. 14 The difference between photoluminescent materials, e.g., those used in fluorescent lamps, and most electroluminescent phosphors is thus primarily a difference in the mode of electron excitation. **1968** H. T. MINDEN in S. L. Marshall *Laser Technol. & Applic.* v. 102 Before describing the GaAs injection electroluminescent spectra, it is instructive to study the more conventional photoluminescent spectrum.

photolyse (fōu·tǒləiz), *v.* Also (chiefly *U.S.*) **-lyze.** [f. next, after *analysis, analyse.*] **a.** *trans.* To decompose or dissociate by irradiation with light. **b.** *intr.* To undergo photolysis.

1956 *Jrnl. Amer. Chem. Soc.* LXXVIII. 6229/1 Pure liquid ethyl iodide was photolyzed at several light intensities and for varying times. **1970** *Nature* 7 Mar. 928/2 In our experiments the Xe lamp not only photolysed ICN but also excited it to the $B^2\Sigma$ state. **1978** *Ibid.* 21 Sept. p. xv/2 The detector senses any halogen-containing compound which will photolyse in the presence of UV light.

Hence **pho·tolysed** *ppl. a.*

1960 *Jrnl. Chem. Soc.* 977 No electron-spin resonance absorption could be detected with the photolysed glasses. **1973** *Nature* 6 July 49/2 A washed and concentrated suspension of bacteria (for example, *Proteus mirabilis*) caused a conversion of photolysed rhodopsin to isorhodopsin.

photolysis (s.v. PHOTO- 1). Add: **2.** *Chem.* Decomposition or dissociation of molecules by the action of light; *flash photolysis*: see *FLASH *sb.*[2] 14 b.

1911 *Chem. Abstr.* V. 1705 When the action is prolonged the decomp[osition] products may also undergo a partial photolysis. **1938** *Phil. Trans. R. Soc.* A. CLXIV. 151 (*heading*) The theory of the photolysis of silver bromide and the photographic latent image. **1955** *Jrnl. Amer. Chem. Soc.* LXXVII. 6457/2 Most of the photolyses were carried out at room temperature. **1965** *New Scientist* 29 Apr. 291/1 Fission of the molecule (photolysis) occurs. **1972** R. A. JACKSON *Mechanism* iv. 61 Radicals may be introduced into reaction systems by photolysis or pyrolysis of a suitable molecule.

Hence **photoly·tic** *a.*, produced by or being photolysis; **photoly·tically** *adv.*

1934 WEBSTER, Photolytic. **1938** *Phil. Trans. R. Soc.* A. CLXIV. 151 (*heading*) Direct photolytic reduction of silver halides. **1946** *Nature* 7 Sept. 345/1 Both the reducing hydrogen and the hydroxyl radicals were supposed to be photolytic products of water. **1951** *Sci. News* XXII. 78 Carbon dioxide is not directly reduced to formaldehyde by the photolytically produced hydrogen. **1970** *Photochem. & Photobiol.* XII. 228 One is led to the conclusion that the chemically reactive intermediate in these photolytic systems is $^3SO_2$. **1977** I. M. CAMPBELL *Energy & Atmosphere* viii. 227 It..allows nitrogen dioxide to be photolytically dissociated within the troposphere.

photomacrography (fōu:tomæ̆krǫ·grăfi). [f. PHOTO- 2 + μακρός large + PHOTO)GRAPHY.] = *MACROPHOTOGRAPHY.

1936 J. DESCHIN *New Ways in Photogr.* xiv. 208 A type of photography..which has recently gained..general favor among hobbyists is that known as photomacrography. **1942** *Ilford Man. Photogr.* (ed. 2) xxiii. 407 These are low-power magnifications mainly concerned with the surface detail of opaque objects and to this type of work the term photomacrography is applied. **1967** [see *MACROPHOTOGRAPHY]. **1972** *Sci. Amer.* Jan. 68 (Advt.), Photomacrography at magnifications in the vicinity of 2-3× with conventional equipment has been practically impossible. **1976** *Publishers Weekly* 27 Sept. 82/2 'Photomacrography'—a photo technique obtaining an image the size of the object photographed, or larger.

So **photoma·crograph** = *MACROPHOTOGRAPH; **pho:tomacrogra·phic** *a.*

1948 J. H. GABLE *Compl. Introd. Photogr.* II. xi. 117 Photomacrography is a method whereby this image can be made many times larger than the object, and a picture so made is called a photomacrograph. **1961** WEBSTER, Photomacrographic. **1966** A. FEININGER *Compl. Photographer* VIII. 309 A photograph in which the subject is rendered in natural or larger than natural size on the film..is called a 'photomacrograph'. **1972** *Sci. Amer.* Jan. 68 (Advt.), It makes superb large-format, widefield photomacrographs all the way from 40× down to 1/3×. **1978** *Nature* 21 Sept. p. xii/3 The Polaroid MP-4 camera is a copy, photomacrographic and photomicrographic recording system.

photo-magazine, -map: see *PHOTO- 2; **photo-magnetic** to **-mask:** see *PHOTO- 1.

Photomaton (fōu͡tǫ-mătǫn). orig. *U.S.* [f. PHOTO- 2 + AUTO)MATON.] The proprietary name of a machine that takes photographs automatically; a photograph taken by such a machine. Also abbrev. as *Pho·tomat.*

1927 *N.Y. Times* 28 Mar. 1/3 Henry Morgenthau.. and a group of business associates announced yesterday that they had purchased the control of the Photomaton—the quarter-in-the slot automatic photographing device which has been in use in this city since last September. **1927** *Bulletin* (Glasgow) 28 Mar. 3/3 Anatol Josephs, the inventor of the Photomaton machine, sold the rights yesterday to a syndicate..for 1,000,000 dollars. **1928** *Daily Express* 22 Feb. 11/5 Mr. O'Connor..tried his luck with the 1s. in the slot Photomaton with successful results. **1936** G. GREENE *Gun for Sale* iii. 104 I'll wire home for a better likeness. I've got a whole strip of Photomatons at home. Her face from every angle. You couldn't have a better lot of photos for newspaper purposes. **1963** *Trade Marks Jrnl.* 22 May 691/1 Photomaton... Photographic apparatus and parts thereof.. Cyril Astor Photomaton (London) Limited,..Rhyl,.. North Wales; manufacturers and merchants. **1966** L. COHEN *Beautiful Losers* (1970) III. 237 The Photomat was broken; it accepted quarters but returned neither flashes nor pictures. **1966** J. BETJEMAN *High & Low* 48 The enlarged Photomaton—that's the latest. **1973** M. A. SINCLAIR tr. *Simenon's Maigret & M. Charles* iv. 92 A small passport photograph taken in a Photomat.

Hence **photo·maton** *v. trans.*, to photograph (someone) by means of a Photomaton.

1933 V. WOOLF *Let.* 19 Feb. (1979) V. 161 I've got to be photomatoned tomorrow.

photomesic, -meson: see *PHOTO- 1.

photometer. Add: **2.** Special Combs.: **photometer bench**, an apparatus similar to an optical bench for the support of a photometer and light sources; cf. **photometric bench*; **photometer head**, the part of a photometer by means of which the comparison or measurement is effected.

1900 W. M. STINE *Photometrical Measurements* iii. 104 The Reichanstalt photometer bench is commonly made for a maximum working distance between the light sources of either 200 or 250 centimetres. **1966** LARGE & WILMAN in Hewitt & Vause *Lamps & Lighting* vii. 89 An appropriate calibrated lamp is..mounted on the photometer bench. **1907** SHEPPARD & MEES *Investigations Theory Photogr. Process* I. ii. 27 Simmance and Abady's new flicker photometer possibly forms the best of the bench photometer heads. **1966** LARGE & WILMAN in Hewitt & Vause *Lamps & Lighting* vii. 89 Distance between the photometer head and lamps may be adjusted and accurately measured. *Ibid.*, The photometer head may consist of either a photocell or a visual device such as the Lummer-Brodhun Contrast Head. **1973** W. THOMAS *SPSE Handbk. Photographic Sci. & Engin.* ii. 153 Photometer heads are used in conjunction with some means for varying the luminance of one or both surfaces in a known manner so that a photometric balance may be obtained.

photo·meter, *v.* [f. the sb.] *trans.* To measure the brightness of (a light source or an illuminated surface) by means of a photometer. Hence **photo·metered** *ppl. a.*, **photo·metering** *vbl. sb.*

1900 *Jrnl. Franklin Inst.* CXLIX. 291 The leading makers now photometer each and every lamp, and the practice of photometering a few and picking out the remainder by the eye is past. **1917** *Physical Rev.* X. 695 The photographs taken thus far are not suitable for photometering, but arrangements are complete for taking such photographs, and for measuring the intensity of the lines. **1923** *Amer. Jrnl. Sci.* CCV. 459 The films were photometered with a microphotometer at the Bureau of Standards. *Ibid.* 460 No high precision was sought in the photometering. *Ibid.* 461 The photometered maximum in the mixture lies between the positions of the two simple maxima. **1966** D. G. BRANDON *Mod. Techniques Metallogr.* iii. 127 The minimum area that can be photometered is principally limited by the size of the diffraction image of the spot selected for photometry.

photometric, *a.* Add: *photometric bench* = **photometer bench.*

1894 G. W. & M. R. PATTERSON tr. *Palaz's Treat. Industr. Photometry* iv. 178 The photometric bench is an optical bench strongly and carefully constructed. **1966** LARGE & WILMAN in Hewitt & Vause *Lamps & Lighting* vii. 89 Where measurements involving direction and distance are concerned a photometric bench is required.

photomicrographer. Add: (Earlier and later examples.) Also **photomicro·graphist.**

1887 *Jrnl. R. Microsc. Soc.* VII. 358 As an evidence of progress in another direction, perhaps equally important to the photomicrographer, the negatives which accompany the *Amphipleura* specimens may not be without interest. **1937** *Discovery* Sept. 283/1 (*heading*) Dufaycolor for the photo-micrographist. **1958** *Newnes Compl. Amat. Photogr.* 6 Nowadays the photographer can take his camera underwater, and record the life of the seabed; amateur photomicrographists can explore the world of nature. **1971** *Sci. Amer.* Dec. 37/1 (Advt.), The complaints will now cease that when we speeded up Kodachrome Film we robbed the photomicrographer of some of his resolving power.

photomixer, -mixing: see *PHOTO- 1.

photomontage (fōu:to,mǫntā·ʒ). Also with hyphen. [f. PHOTO- 2 + *MONTAGE.] Montage (*MONTAGE 2) using photographs or photographic negatives; a picture made by this method.

1931 *Times Lit. Suppl.* 25 June (Arts Suppl.) p. iv/3 'Photomontage', the use of stripped negatives in futurist compositions to convey the effect of simultaneous ideas, .. made its first success in the U.S.S.R. **1936** [see COLLAGE]. **1944** K. VAUGHAN in *Penguin New Writing* XXII. 153 Attempts at combining modern type faces with drawing and photomontage..have more often been made by certain branches of publicity. **1958** N. MARSH *Singing in Shrouds* (1959) ii. 19 They could see her reflection in the window-pane, like a photomontage richly floating across street lamps and the façades of darkened buildings. **1971** P. GRESSWELL *Environment* 231 A series of photo-montages should be prepared. **1972** *Daily Tel.* 8 Mar. 16 Not all the illustrations, which range from drawings to photomontage, come from people known primarily as artists. **1975** *Times Lit. Suppl.* 9 May 519/3 Ingeniously chosen illustrations and designs—notably the surrealistic photomontages of Benjamin Palencia. **1978** *Nature* 26 Jan. 359/1 (*caption*) Superimposed photomontages from serial frontal sections of Procion yellow-stained horizontal cells contrasting sharply against the autofluorescing background tissue.

pho:tomorphoge·nesis. *Bot.* [f. PHOTO- 1 + MORPHOGENESIS.] (See quots. 1964.)

1959 A. W. GALSTON in R. B. Withrow *Photoperiodism* ii. 139 Further knowledge of this substance..will help elucidate the details of photomorphogenesis. **1964** *Biol. Rev.* XXXIX. 87 By the term *photomorphogenesis* we designate the control which may be exerted by visible radiation over growth, development and differentiation of a plant, independently of photosynthesis. *Ibid.* 506 Photomorphogenesis concerns the regulation of plant growth and morphology by light. **1975** *Nature* 10 Jan. 94/2 Profound changes in the activity of many plant enzymes occur during photomorphogenesis, the response of dark-grown plants to light.

So **pho:tomo:rphogene·tic, -ge·nic** *adjs.*, of or pertaining to the effects of light on plants; **pho:tomo:rphogene·tically, -ge·nically** *advs.*

1956 *Plant Physiol.* XXXI. 279/1 This same reversible photoreaction was also established for the control of flower initiation of Xanthium..and photomorphogenic effects such as leaf expansion. **1959** A. W. GALSTON in R. B. Withrow *Photoperiodism* ii. 139 We have been concerned with the photomorphogenic reaction and auxin metabolism. *Ibid.* 153 Certain experiments have suggested that the cofactor is transformed, by photomorphogenically active light, into the inhibitor. **1960** *Chem. Abstr.* LIV. 25090 Some expts. indicated that *V*.. is converted to *I* by photomorphogenetically active light. **1962** *Plant Physiol.* XXXVII. 142 (*heading*) Photomorphogenetic responses of sporelings of *Marsilea vestita.* **1971** *Nature* 27 Aug. 602/1 Acetylcholine, when given to dark grown seedlings, mimicked the effect of red light in certain photomorphogenic responses. **1975** D. VINCE-PRUE *Photoperiodism in Plants* iv. 119 Some experiments suggest that..the photomorphogenetic response occurs because P_{fr} operates *via* a threshold type of mechanism.

photomosaic: see *PHOTO- 2.

photomu·ltiplier. Also with hyphen. [f. PHOTO- 1 + MULTIPLIER.] Also *photomultiplier tube.* A phototube in which the small current from the photocathode is multiplied by a succession of secondary electrodes, so that light of very low intensity can be detected.

1940 *Rev. Sci. Instruments* XI. 226/1 In the photomultiplier the original electron current is supplied by a photo-cathode. **1955** *Sci. News* XXXVI. 21 A photomultiplier, in which an initial small pulse of light is converted into a cascade of electrons. **1961** G. R. CHOPPIN *Exper. Nucl. Chem.* vii. 93 Normally, in scintillation systems it is not the phosphor or photomultiplier tube that determines the resolving time, but rather it is the electronic system. **1968** *Brit. Med. Bull.* XXIV. 261/1 Light from the spot is imaged onto the specimen.., and a photomultiplier positioned so as to read the intensity of the transmitted light. **1975** D. H. BURRIN in Williams & Wilson *Biologist's Guide to Princ. & Techniques Pract. Biochem.* v. 137 Photomultiplier tubes are more sensitive than simple photocells. **1977** *Dædalus* Fall 42 Photomultipliers convert the light pulses into electric pulses.

photomural: see *PHOTO- 2.

photon[1] (fōu·tǫn). *Physics.* [f. PHOTO- 1 + *-ON[1].

In senses 1 and 2 the ending *-on* may be merely arbitrary.]

† **1.** = *TROLAND. *Obs.*

1916 L. T. TROLAND in *Trans. Illuminating Engin. Soc.* (U.S.) XI. 950, I have..found it very convenient to express all intensity measures in terms of a unit of retinal illumination which I have called the photon. **1929** *Bureau of Standards Jrnl. Res.* (U.S.) II. 445 If the rods initiate the nerve activity responsible for the blue arcs a pure spectral stimulus of wave length, say, 640 mμ, would have to be at a much higher illumination (measured in photons..) than a stimulus of wave length less than, say 550 mμ. **1934** *Jrnl. Gen. Physiol.* XVII. 241 With the present apparatus, which has a pupil area of 2·54 sq. mm. the maximal retinal illumination available in the central test area when it is not interrupted is very nearly 6000 photons. **1944** [see *TROLAND]. **1949** J. H. PRINCE *Visual Devel.* I. vi. 85 Feldman..has estimated that, whereas a rod requires only 0·00025 photons to stimulate it, a cone requires 0·025 photons. **1953** H. H. EMSLEY *Visual Optics* (ed. 5) II. xviii. 232 A surface of luminance one millilambert observed through a 4 mm. diameter pupil gives a retinal illumination of $2{\cdot}5 \times 4^2 = 40$ photons.

† **2.** (See quot.) *Obs. rare.*

1921 J. JOLY in *Proc. R. Soc.* B. XCII. 226 In the foregoing pages..the unit light stimulus discharged by a single visual fibre is frequently referred to. It represents a very small amount of energy... It must not be confused with the quantum of energy... I propose to designate it a photon. *Ibid.* 228 The stimulus value of the three colour sensations in such proportions as to give white light is nine photons.

3. A quantum of light or other electromagnetic radiation, the energy of which is proportional to the frequency of the radiation.

1926 G. N. LEWIS in *Nature* 18 Dec. 874/1, I therefore take the liberty of proposing for this hypothetical new atom, which is not light but plays an essential part in every process of radiation, the name *photon.* **1929** *Jrnl. Amer. Chem. Soc.* LI. 2850 In 1906, Einstein showed that the photo-electric effect and many photochemical reactions could be explained in terms of the Quantum Theory if light itself consisted of discrete particles of energy or quanta, now usually called photons. **1934** *Discovery* May 125/1 Photons (quanta or packets of electro-magnetic energy) are in general more efficient in bringing about atomic changes than particles of corresponding energy. **1942** J. D. STRANATHAN '*Particles' of Mod. Physics* viii. 357 The ejection of a β particle might leave the new nucleus in an excited state. In this case one would expect the disintegration to be followed by the radiation of a γ-ray photon having an energy equal to the excitation energy. **1948** *Sci. News* VI. 75 In the quantum theory a light signal cannot be sub-divided indefinitely, but consists of finite units, so-called light quanta, or 'photons', each carrying an amount of energy proportional to the frequency of the light wave of which they form part. **1959** [see *COMPTON]. **1968** M. S. LIVINGSTON *Particle Physics* v. 96 In particle physics, the individual photons entering or emerging from interactions are treated as particles with zero rest mass, velocity *c*, energy $E = h\nu$, and momentum $p = E/c$. **1971** *Nature* 2 July 67/2 The dark-adapted human eye is capable of detecting a pulse of less than a hundred photons. **1977** *Dædalus* Summer 26 On the subnuclear level the gluons are the analogues of the photons or quanta of the electromagnetic field for atomic processes.

4. Special Comb.: **photon rocket**, a rocket propelled by the backward ejection of photons.

1949 *Jrnl. Brit. Interplanetary Soc.* VIII. 242 Two possible schemes for utilizing nuclear energy are then considered, the first using a nuclear 'boiler' to heat a working fluid which is then expanded through a nozzle in the normal way and the second using the energy direct in a 'photon' rocket. **1958** C. C. ADAMS et al. *Space Flight* 347 Others ponder photon rockets driven by parallel beams formed by properly designed reflectors.

Hence **photo·nic** *a.*

1938 R. W. LAWSON tr. *Hevesy & Paneth's Man. Radioactivity* (ed. 2) v. 61 In the production of the former the whole of the energy of the γ-quantum or photon..is transmitted to the electron, whereas in the production of recoil electrons only a fraction of the photonic energy is handed over to the recoil electron. **1952** R. E. MARSHAK *Meson Physics* iii. 98 The first observations on the photonic production of charged π mesons were made in 1949. **1952** *Jrnl. Brit. Interplanetary Soc.* XI. 59 Whether the 'jet propulsion engine' concerned is of a type that consumes air, burns chemical propellants, utilizes nuclear power, or represents some form of electronic or photonic drive. **1958** C. C. ADAMS et al. *Space Flight* 348 The best we can do is to base our calculations on highly developed systems using atomic, ionic, or photonic particles. **1969** AUDEN *City without Walls* 97 His light is felt as a friendly presence not a photonic bombardment. **1970** *Science* 30 Jan. 618/2 The rocks were analyzed by photonic microscopy (transmitted and reflected light).

Photon[2] (fōu·tǫn). [f. PHOTO- 2 + *-n.*] The proprietary name of a range of photo-composing equipment (see quot. 1958). Also *attrib.*

1953 *Publishers' Weekly* 7 Feb. 756/2 'The Wonderful World of Insects' is the first volume to be composed with the revolutionary Higgonet-Moyroud [*sic*] photographic type-composing machine, more commonly called Photon. **1953** *Newsweek* 16 Feb. 82/3 Last week the Photon made its formal debut... Dr. Bush presented..the first Photon-composed book, 'The Wonderful World of Insects'. **1958** *Times Lit. Suppl.* 11 Apr. 200/2 This apparatus was invented in 1944 by two French engineers, MM. Higonnet and Moyroud, who sold their plans to the Graphic Arts Foundation of Cambridge, Mass., which has developed their invention since 1949 under the name of Photon. The machine prints letters on to film by stroboscopic flashes of light which pass through a continuously revolving disc, upon which are carried sixteen founts of ninety letters each. *Ibid.* 200/3 The first Photon book was *The Wonderful World of Insects*, by Albro Gaul, published by Rinehart & Company Inc. in New York in 1953. **1967** C. J. DUNCAN in Cox & Grose *Organiz. Bibliogr. Rec. by Computer* II. 45 In the Photon 540 or the Intertype, the characters are held on a disc.

photonegative (fōutone·gătiv), *a.* Also with hyphen. [f. PHOTO- 1 + NEGATIVE *a.*] **1.** *Zool.* Of an animal: tending to move away from light.

1914 S. O. MAST in *Biol. Zentralblatt* XXXIV. 662 In place of positively or negatively phototropic, geotropic, etc., we might use photo-, geo-, negative or positive, etc. **1923** *Jrnl. Exper. Zool.* XXVIII. 120 Insects with one eye blinded usually turn, in non-directive light, toward the functional eye if they are photopositive and toward the blinded eye if they are photonegative. **1945** T. H. SAVORY *Spiders Brit. Isles* (ed. 2) 143 They [*sc.* harvestmen spiders] are strongly photonegative and collect in the darkest corner of their cage. **1975** *Nature* 25 Dec. 712/2 Flies entering the maze..receive phototactic scores ranging from 1·0 (highly photonegative) to 16·0 (highly photopositive).

2. *Physics.* Pertaining to or exhibiting a decrease in electrical conductivity when illuminated.

1915 *Physical Rev.* V. 62 For certain regions of the spectrum these cells were photo-negative, while for longer wave-lengths they were photo-positive. **1925** H. S. ALLEN *Photo-Electricity* (ed. 2) vi. 95 In some instances an apparent *rise* in resistance has been observed on exposure to light. This type of response is said to be 'photo-negative'. **1932** [see *PHOTOPOSITIVE *a.* 2].

Hence **pho:tonegati·vity.**

1962 *Jrnl. Insect Physiol.* VIII. 253 There is a less pronounced shift towards photonegativity in the later instars. **1974** *Marine Biol.* XXV. 313/2 Photokinesis and phototaxis were deliberately confounded in this measure, since there was no way to predict which behavioural element might respond to selection for photonegativity in the tidal pool.

photoneutral, -neutron: see *PHOTO- 1.

photonics (fotǫ·niks), *sb. pl.* [f. *PHOTON: see -IC 2.] The study of the applications of the particle properties of light.

1952 *Jrnl. Brit. Interplanetary Soc.* XI. 58 From the fundamental domains of photonics, electronics, nuclear physics, atomic physics and physical chemistry, our interest passes without interruption, via thermodynamics and gas kinetics, to aerodynamics and the physics of solid bodies. **1976** *Physics Bull.* Mar. 126/1 The term 'photonics', by analogy with electronics, describes the application of the photon to the transmission of information, and includes such topics as photon beam production waveguiding, deflection, modulation, amplification, image processing, storage and detection. **1978** *Daily Tel.* 11 Mar. 10/6 According to the commentary..we can expect the new science of photonics to be comparable to electronics. We shall be making telephone calls by laser and watching three dimensional films on television.

photonuclear: see *PHOTO- 1; **photonymograph:** see *PHOTO- 2.

photo-offset (fōu:to,ǫ·fset). [f. PHOTO(LITHOGRAPHY + OFFSET.] A planographic printing process in which a photographic negative is used as the basis of the printing surface; also called *photolitho offset*. Also *attrib.* Cf. *OFFSET *sb.* 10 b.

1926 F. B. WIBORG *Printing Ink* ix. 122 During the last few years a number of photo-offset processes have been perfected... By means of some of these processes it is now possible to photograph a design directly upon the surface of a prepared metal plate, and then to mechanically etch the plate for printing. **1947** R. MESSNER *Selling Printing & Direct Advertising* vi. 140 Both the simplest black-and-white pieces and the most elaborate productions in many colors may thus be 'photo' 'offset' lithography. **1957** *Times Lit. Suppl.* 20 Dec. 780/3 The time is surely ripe for general agreement upon a standard set of [bibliographical] terms designed to cover modern processes, including the now commonly used method of photo-offset reproduction. **1970** O. DOPPING *Computers & Data Processing* xxiii. 377 Multiple copies can be produced by means of carbon, stencil, offset, or photo offset. **1976** *Sat. Rev.* (U.S.) 4 Sept. 7/1 The Folio Society..does not mass-produce huge editions by photo-offset.

photoorganotroph to **-organotrophy:** see *PHOTO- 1; **photo-oxidation** to **-oxidized:** see *PHOTO- 3.

photoperiod (fōu·topiə̄riǒd). *Biol.* [f. PHOTO- 1 + PERIOD *sb.*] The period of daily illumination which an organism receives; also, the value of this period which optimally stimulates reproduction or some other function.

1920 GARNER & ALLARD in *Jrnl. Agric. Res.* XVIII. 603 The term *photoperiod* is suggested to designate the favorable length of day for each organism, and *photoperiodism* is suggested to designate the response of the organism to the relative length of day and night. **1932** FULLER & CONARD tr. *Braun-Blanquet's Plant Sociol.* v. 102 Photoperiod affects growth as well as flowering of plants. **1937** *Ann. Reg. 1936* 58 The photoperiod of a plant can be modified by temperature. **1957** *New Biol.* XXIII. 10 The profound importance which the daily photoperiod may have in controlling the time of transition from vegetative growth to flowering was discovered more than forty years ago. **1972** *Sci. Amer.* Aug. 27/1 It is likely..that temperature rather than photoperiod directly influences the duration of incubation [of mallard eggs]. **1976** *Nature* 1–8 Jan. 41/1 The fish were maintained in aquaria at 22–24°C, on a light–dark (LD) 12:12 photoperiod.

Hence **pho:toperio·dic** *a.*, of, pertaining to, or influenced by photoperiods; **pho:toperio·dically** *adv.*, by means of or with regard to photoperiods; **pho:toperiodi·city** = *PHOTOPERIODISM (see quot. 1945[1]).

1923 *Jrnl. Agric. Res.* XXIII. 873 The wide extent and great variety in form of the photoperiodic response verifies..the modern view..that environment through its action on internal conditions governs the form of expression in the plant. **1936** *Q. Rev. Biol.* XI. 373/2 It is open to question whether they are true cases of sexual photoperiodicity. **1940** *Bot. Gaz.* CI. 815 These differences.. indicated that young leaves were photoperiodically more effective than old ones. **1945** *Science* 6 Apr. 353/2 Botanists refer to this phenomenon as 'photoperiodism', while most zoologists use the term 'photoperiodicity'. *Ibid.* 354/1 'Photoperiodicity'..has now come to include any periodic or rhythmic process controlled by photoperiods. It is not only reproduction controlled photoperiodically, but includes pelt cycles, plumage cycles in birds and migrations also. **1971** *Canad. Jrnl. Zool.* XLIX. 109 Two morphological variations of *Davainea tetraoensis* were found... Changes in diet and changes in photoperiodicity do not seem to effect any change from one form to the other. **1972** *Country Life* 16 Mar. 630/4 Wild rock doves are photoperiodic..and cease to breed when day lengths become shortened in winter. **1974** *Nature* 10 May 183/2 The data showed that different strains produced F1 hybrids photoperiodically intermediate between the parents. **1976** *Sci. Amer.* Feb. 114/2 It has..been demonstrated that the insect's eye is not involved in its photoperiodic response.

photoperiodism (fōutopiə̄·riǒdiz'm). *Biol.* [f. prec. + -ISM.] The phenomenon whereby many plants and animals are stimulated or inhibited in breeding and other functions by the lengths of the daily periods of light and darkness to which they are subjected. Cf. *PHOTOPERIODICITY.

1920 [see *PHOTOPERIOD]. **1929** WEAVER & CLEMENTS *Plant Ecol.* xiii. 328 Knowledge of photoperiodism, as these responses to length of day are called, should aid the plant breeder. **1971** *Country Life* 30 Dec. 1854/1 The commercial production of chrysanthemums has been revolutionized by the application of the principles of photo-periodism. **1976** *Sci. Amer.* Feb. 114/2 Most of the early investigations of photoperiodism in insects were concerned with the nature and location of the photoreceptors and the effector system.

photophil to **-philous:** see *PHOTO- 1.

photophore. 2. (Further examples.)

1934 *Bull. N.Y. Zool. Soc.* XXXVII. 193/1, I [*sc.* W. Beebe] suddenly saw the amazing beauty of the photophores [of the constellation fish, *Bathysidus pentagrammus*]. There were five rows of these. **1963** P. H. GREENWOOD *Norman's Hist. Fishes* (ed. 2) x. 168 There are typically two rows of organs, or photophores, on either side of the fish [*sc.* a wide-mouth]. **1964** *Oceanogr. & Marine Biol.* II. 354 In each of these groups of prawns the pattern of the photophores is similar. **1974** *Nature* 18 Jan. 155/2 The ventral photophores of some mesopelagic fishes in the upper regions of the sea may produce bioluminescence.

photophoresis (fōutofori·sis). *Physics.* Also with hyphen. [ad. G. *photophorese* (F. Ehrenhaft 1918, in *Ann. der Physik* LVI. 93): see PHOTO- 1 and *-PHORESIS.] The motion of small particles under the influence of a beam of light.

1919 *Sci. Abstr.* A. XXII. 275 (*heading*) Mechanical and osmotic actions of radiation on the media passed through. Theory of photophoresis. **1950** *Engineering* 14 Apr. 407/1 The generation of such heat would probably introduce difficulties due to thermal currents and photo-phoresis effects. **1972** *Sci. Amer.* Feb. 64/3 In the case of photophoresis single particles would be heated asymmetrically by the light and would as a result move through the surrounding medium.

Hence **photophoretic** (-fore·tik) *a.*, of or pertaining to photophoresis.

1924 *Sci. Abstr.* A. XXVII. 397 Especially through it [*sc.* this hypothesis] is the fact of the small dependence of the photophoretic force on pressure made understandable. **1941** *Physical Rev.* LX. 169/2 The possibility of finding an explanation of the cause of the Earth's magnetism in terms of the photophoretic influence will be discussed. **1976** *Chem. Abstr.* 23 Feb. 404/2 Est[imatio]n of the value and direction of photophoretic velocity was made.

photophosphorylation: see *PHOTO- 3.

photophthalmia (fōu:tǫfþæ·lmiă). *Ophthalm.* [f. PHOTO- 1 + OPHTHALMIA.] Inflammation of the cornea produced by ultraviolet light, causing blindness or defective vision.

1907 J. H. PARSONS *Dis. Eye* x. 211 Electric Light Ophthalmia (Photophthalmia).—The ultraviolet rays of the electric light, especially of the arc lamp, may cause extreme burning pain, lacrymation, photophobia, blepharospasm, and swelling of the palpebral conjunctiva and retrotarsal folds, coming on a few hours later. **1916** *Proc. Amer. Acad. Arts & Sci.* LI. 641 An ordinary case of photophthalmia completely disappears in less than a week and repair is going on all through this period. **1947** *Med. Jrnl. Austral.* 26 Apr. 524/2 Solar photophthalmia occurred in summer months among convoy drivers in the Northern Territory. **1969** *Amer. Jrnl. Optometry* XLVI. 569 The radiation below 305 nm required to produce marked photophthalmia was approximately 2×10^6 ergs/cm^2.

Hence **pho:tophtha·lmic** *a.*, of or pertaining to photophthalmia.

1913 *17th Internat. Congr. Med.* IX. i. 204 The flash of a short circuit is extremely rich in ultra-violet rays, and to these are to be attributed the photophthalmic symptoms. **1947** *Med. Jrnl. Austral.* 26 Apr. 524/2 Duke Elder considers the name 'snow blindness'..as thoroughly unsatisfactory, since the photophthalmic symptoms are not caused by snow, but by solar energy partly reflected by snow.

photophysical, -physics: see *PHOTO- 1.

photopic (fotǫ·pik, fotōu·pik), *a.* *Physiol.* [f. PHOT(O- 1 + *-OPIA + -IC.] Of or pertaining to vision in levels of illumination similar to daylight, believed to involve chiefly the cones of the retina.

1915 J. H. PARSONS *Introd. Study of Colour Vision* ii. 17 If the eye has been exposed to bright light it is said to be light-adapted. I shall speak of vision under these circumstances as photopia, and the light-adapted eye as a photopic eye. **1921** *Phil. Mag.* XLI. 298 The entire luminosity curve of photopic vision will be shifted towards the red end of the spectrum. *Ibid.*, The photopic luminosity curve does not quite coincide with the scotopic luminosity curve. **1960** *Electronic Engin.* XXXII. 145/1 For the comparison of camera versus visual estimates of relative luminance, it is convenient to have inscribed on the graticule to photopic curve. **1965** J. E. CROUCH *Functional Human Anat.* xix. 597/1 The cones are photopic or discriminative and enable us to see details of form, structure, and color. **1975** J. P. THOMAS in Carterette & Friedman *Handbk. Perception* V. vii. 238 At photopic levels of illumination, acuity is highest when the target is viewed with the center of the fovea and decreases rapidly as the image of the target is displaced toward the periphery.

photopigment: see *PHOTO- 1; **photoplate:** see *PHOTO- 2.

photoplay (fōu·to,plēi). orig. *N. Amer.* Also **photo-play.** [f. PHOTO- 2 + PLAY *sb.*] A cinematic representation of a play or drama; a motion picture. Also *attrib.* and *Comb.*

1910 *Moving Picture World* 12 Nov. 1103/2 (*heading*) The Barnstormer in the photoplay. **1911** *Daily Colonist* (Victoria, B.C.) 1 Apr. 11/1 (Advt.), Romano Photoplay Theatre. The Aristocrat of Picturedom. Continuous performances daily from noon to 11 p.m. **1912** *Everybody's Mag.* Oct. 505/2 The clever photoplays that dramatize the hard, dry facts into living stories. **1913** [see *film studio* s.v. *FILM *sb.* 7 c]. **1914** [see *CREDIT *sb.* 13 f]. **1918** V. O. FREEBURG (*title*) The art of photoplay making. *Ibid.* 57 The filming and projection of a photoplay. **1920** *Chambers's Jrnl.* Mar. 188/1 Los Angeles.. is the scene of many well-known and popular photo-plays. **1930** *Times Educ. Suppl.* 22 Feb. 81/1 The historical accuracy of the photoplays is vouched for by specialists. **1950** BLESH & JANIS *They all played Ragtime* iii. 59 The ragtimers' repertory, finally, included descriptive overtures. These prefigured the early photoplay interpretation of the nickelodeon pianos. **1975** *Language for Life* (Dept. Educ. & Sci.) xxii. 319 Some [children] have made photoplays to illustrate a story or give a visual interpretation of a piece of music.

photopolarimeter to **-metry:** see *PHOTO- 1; **photopolymer** to **-polymerized:** see *PHOTO- 3.

photopositive (fōutopǫ·zitiv), *a.* Also with hyphen. [f. PHOTO- 1 + POSITIVE *a.* and *sb.*]

1. *Zool.* Of an animal: tending to move towards light.

1914 [see *PHOTONEGATIVE *a.* 1]. **1923** *Jrnl. Exper. Zool.* XXXVIII. 194 The photopositive reactions of insects under normal conditions usually result in their escape from places of danger. **1964** *Oceanogr. & Marine Biol.* II. 482 The larvae [of *Spirorbis*] may settle or may resume their pelagic existence, again becoming photopositive for a short time. **1975** [see *PHOTONEGATIVE *a.* 1].

2. *Physics.* Pertaining to or exhibiting an increase in electrical conductivity when illuminated.

1915 [see *PHOTONEGATIVE *a.* 2]. **1932** HUGHES & DUBRIDGE *Photoelectric Phenomena* viii. 328 The effect of light [on photoconducting substances] is usually to increase the conductivity (the photopositive effect..), but occasionally it is found that light apparently diminishes the conductivity (the photonegative effect..). The photonegative effect occurs above a critical voltage whose value depends on the temperature.

Hence **photopo·sitively** *adv.*; **pho:topositi·vity.**

1946 *Nature* 13 July 58/2 When behaving photopositively *Hydra* orientates itself klinokinetically. **1962** *Jrnl. Insect Physiol.* VIII. 251 Photopositivity declines continuously within each instar, but shows an increase after each moult.

photopotential to **-production:** see *PHOTO- 1.

photoprote·ction. *Biol.* [f. PHOTO- 1 + PROTECTION.] The process whereby illumination of living matter with visible light can protect it from being harmed by subsequent ultraviolet irradiation.

1958 J. JAGGER in *Bacteriol. Rev.* XXII. 100/1 'Post-UV-photoprevention' would describe completely what is here called photoreactivation. In addition, this term would distinguish the present effect from photoprotection ('pre-UV-photoprevention'). **1962** *Photochem. & Photobiol.* I. 256 Photoprotection is found to require, at an ultraviolet survival level of 2 per cent, about three times as much radiation energy as photoreactivation. **1975** *Nature* 17 Apr. 628/1 We..conclude that photoprotection does not contribute to the increased survival of HSV in Jay Tim cells treated with photoreactivating light.

photoprote·ctive, *a.* [f. PHOTO- 1 + PROTECTIVE *a.* (*sb.*).] **a.** Of or pertaining to protection conferred by light (as in photoprotection). **b.** Of or pertaining to protection against harmful effects of light.

1961 *Jrnl. Bacteriol.* LXXXI. 526/2 Visible light irradiation of *Nocardia corallina* was found to render the culture more resistant to subsequent X irradiation... The results appear to be attributable only to a photoprotective action. **1975** *Sci. Amer.* July 73/1 Patients with the disease complain at first of a burning sensation in areas of the skin that are exposed to sunlight... The symptoms of the disease can be ameliorated by administering photoprotective agents such as carotenoids. **1976** *Nature* 12 Feb. 507/1 The melanosome has long been considered a passive cellular organelle. Its considered role as a photoprotective agent in the skin and other illuminated areas, could not explain its presence and function in the non-illuminated areas (for example, the midbrain).

photoprotein, -proton: see *PHOTO- 1.

photoptic (fotǫ·ptik), *a.* *Physiol.* [f. PHOT(O- 1 + Gr. ὀπτικ-ός OPTIC *a.*] = *PHOTOPIC *a.*

1949 *Amer. Jrnl. Bot.* XXXVI. 198/2 The scattered red light was just on the threshold of photoptic vision for the dark-adapted eye. **1955** C. W. ALLEN *Astrophysical Quantities* v. 103 (*heading*) Relative visibility K_λ for normal brightness.., the photoptic curve (International) (cone vision at fovea).

photoradiogram, -reaction: see *PHOTO- 2, 1.

photorea·ctivate, *v.* *Biol.* [f. PHOTO- 1 + *REACTIVATE *v.*] *trans.* To repair by photoreactivation.

1954 *Biochim. & Biophys. Acta* XV. 471 They [*sc.* the systems studied] are then photoreactivated and the reactivated complexes are again exposed to UV in order to determine their UV sensitivity. **1975** *Nature* 13 Mar. 160/1 Even though cells of the higher plants can photoreactivate ultraviolet damage.., the absence of dark-repair capability could be a significant disadvantage.

So **photorea·ctivated, -rea·ctivating** *ppl. adjs.; photoreactivating enzyme*, any enzyme which catalyses photoreactivation. Also **pho:toreactivabi·lity**, the potential for photoreactivation; **photorea·ctivable** *a.*, (of a biological system) capable of displaying photoreactivation; (of damage caused by ultraviolet irradiation) capable of being photoreactivated.

1953 *Jrnl. Bacteriol.* LXV. 252 (*heading*) Growth, respiration and nucleic acid synthesis in ultraviolet-irradiated and in photoreactivated *Escherichia coli*. **1958** *Jrnl. Gen. Physiol.* XLI. 463 (*heading*) Subcellular nature of the photoreactivating system. **1960** *Ibid.* XLIII. 592 This photoreactivating enzyme (PRE) is interesting for two reasons. First, it is a photoenzyme, and few enzymes involved in photochemical reactions are known at present. Second, it acts on DNA *in vitro* without depolymerizing it. **1961** J. A. Schiff et al. in Christensen & Buchmann *Progress in Photobiol.* vi. 290 Photoreactivability of the cells falls off rapidly when the cells are permitted to divide. Under non-dividing conditions, the cells remain completely photoreactivable indefinitely. **1965** J. Jagger in E. J. Bowen *Recent Progress in Photobiol.* ii. 61 Evidence for the photoreactivability of RNA. **1975** *Nature* 13 Mar. 160/1 Some types of excisable ultraviolet-induced DNA damage are not photoreactivable. **1975** [see *photoreactivation].

pho:toreactiva·tion. *Biol.* [f. Photo- 1 + *reactivation.] The process whereby illumination of living matter with visible light can counteract the destructive effects of previous ultraviolet irradiation.

1949 A. Kelner in *Jrnl. Bacteriol.* LVIII. 511 The effect of reactivating light will be referred to in this paper as *photoreactivation*. [*Note.*] The use of this term was suggested by Dr. Max Delbrück. **1962** [see *photoprotection]. **1966** *Adv. Radiation Biol.* II. 21 These photoreactivations may result from DNA inactivations repairable by the mechanisms already described here. **1969** A. C. Giese in F. Urbach *Biol. Effects Ultraviolet Radiation* 63 With protozoans..even UV radiation as well as blue-violet visible light are effective for photoreactivation, while yellow visible light during or after UV exposure is ineffective. **1975** *Nature* 11 Sept. 133/1 Photoreactivation is a DNA repair process in which the photoreactivating enzyme (PRE) monomerises pyrimidine dimers induced by ultraviolet light.

photorealism (fōu·torī·ăliz'm). *Art.* Also **Photorealism, Photo-Realism.** [f. Photo- (in *photographic*, etc.) + Realism.] Detailed and unidealized representation in art, characteristically of the banal, vulgar, or sordid aspects of life. So **pho:to-re·alist** *a.* and *sb.*

1961 J. Williams *Forger* i. 6 A gigantic exhibition that will span everything..from extreme abstract expressionism to extreme photorealism. **1973** *Art Internat.* Mar. 49/1 Curators, critics, teachers, and writers all over the world, who come to it looking for women's art of every sort from photo-realist to conceptual. **1973** *Guardian* 11 Apr. 10 There's something a bit pompous..about the claims made for Photorealism, the kick-off show at the Serpentine... Photorealist sculpture is there too. **1975** *New Yorker* 19 May 11/3 (Advt.), The paintings, done in an authoritative Photo-Realist style, dramatically illustrate Photo-Realism's strange ability to invest ordinary, ugly, even disgusting objects of our Pop culture with an appearance of home truth that borders on beauty. **1976** *Ibid.* 26 Apr. 137/1 There are Abstract Expressionist, Conceptual, and even Photo-Realist photographs being made. **1977** *It* June 5/4 About a foot away from it..hover a ghastly mob of poofs, lesbians, photo realists and deviants of every conceivable kind. **1977** *Jrnl. R. Soc. Arts* CXXV. 272/1 America, which Hockney visited towards the end of the '60s, brought him to some of his major paintings. In these he had used extensive photographic material for a variety of purposes—for information, for realistic detail, for inspiration, the result yielding a new photo-realism of strictly integrated design.

photo-recce: see *photo- 2.

photoreceptor (fōu·torīseptǫ̈ɪ). *Biol.* Also with hyphen. [f. Photo- 1 + Receptor.] Any living structure which responds to incident light, esp. a cell in which light is absorbed and converted to a nervous or other signal.

1906 C. S. Sherrington *Integrative Action Nervous Syst.* ix. 334 The free-swimming Ascidia with fin-like motor organs and semi-rigid aerial notochord..bears at its anterior end a well-formed photo-receptor organ (eye) and a well-formed otocyst (head proprio-ceptor). **1944** *Electronic Engin.* XVII. 189/3 The retina consists of ten layers, in the third of which are embedded the photoreceptors. **1964** [see below]. **1969** F. E. Round *Introd. Lower Plants* ii. 14 The locomotory flagellum [of the alga *Euglena*]. It has a..swelling, the 'photoreceptor', near its entry into the cell. **1974** *Photochem. & Photobiol.* XIX. 435/1 The question as to the identity of the photoreceptor pigment (carotenoids or flavins) for phototropism in higher plants has not been resolved.

So **pho·toreception,** the process of absorption, and esp. of detection, of light by an animal or plant; **pho·toreceptive** *a.*, able to respond to light; of or pertaining to photoreception.

1906 C. S. Sherrington *Integrative Action Nervous Syst.* ix. 334 The elaborateness of the photo-receptive organs of the flying Insecta corresponds with the great power of these forms to traverse space. **1908** *Amer. Jrnl. Physiol.* XXI. 198 The immediate results following the destruction of photo-reception in one eye are: (1) The production of rapid rotations..on the longitudinal axis of the body, [etc.]. **1943** *Vitamins & Hormones* I. 211 Ordinarily these organisms contain a structure which appears to be specifically concerned with photoreception, the stigma or eye-spot. **1964** *Ann. N.Y. Acad. Sci.* CXVII. 211 Red rays can penetrate to the hypothalamus with a sufficient intensity to activate the deeper photoreceptive structures. **1964** *Oceanogr. & Marine Biol.* II. 403 The photoreceptor pigment is unknown... That in *Diadema*..has an absorption maximum in its acid form at 462/63 mμ, but whether it is involved in the photoreceptive process is as yet unknown. **1973** J. J. Wolken in L. P. Miller *Phytochem.* I. ii. 26 Experimental observations..indicated that the photosynthetic process was not a simple photoreception sensitized by chlorophyll.

photo-reconnaissance, -recovery: see *photo- 2, 1.

pho:toredu·ction. Also with hyphen. [f. Photo- 3 + Reduction.] **1.** Chemical reduction effected by light; in *Bot.*, such a reduction of carbon dioxide in which water is formed (rather than oxygen, as in ordinary photosynthesis).

1888 [in Dict. s.v. Photo- 3]. **1939** *Jrnl. Cellular & Compar. Physiol.* XIII. 333 For the photo-reduction of one mole of carbon dioxide in the photosynthetic purple bacteria Streptococcus varians at high light intensity 2·6 moles of gaseous hydrogen are used. **1940** H. Gaffron in *Amer. Jrnl. Bot.* XXVII. 282/2 Such a..conception of photosynthesis in green plants and bacteria allows us to group the light metabolism of the bacteria and the 'anaerobic light respiration' of the plants under one term: 'anaerobic photosynthesis' or, shorter, 'photoreduction'. This leaves 'aerobic photosynthesis' or 'photosynthesis' proper for the assimilation of carbon dioxide with the liberation of molecular oxygen. **1957** *Jrnl. Amer. Chem. Soc.* LXXIX. 294/1 Acriflavine and fluorescein-type dyes in solution undergo photoreduction in the presence of mild reducing agents. **1970** C. A. Price *Molec. Approaches to Plant Physiol.* ii. 115 A number of algae show 'photoreduction',..in which no O_2 is evolved. **1972** DePuy & Chapman *Molec. Reactions & Photochem.* iv. 48 Photoreduction of ketones is one of the oldest and most thoroughly investigated photochemical processes.

2. Reduction in size effected photographically.

1967 E. R. Lannon in Cox & Grose *Organiz. Bibliogr. Rec. by Computer* iv. 95 This latter version is printed..on 17″ × 22″ pages, suitable for 50% photoreduction and subsequent publication by offset press. **1968** *Bodl. Libr. Rec.* VIII. 64 The flexowriter produced a text in double column..from which, after 30 per cent photo-reduction, offset-litho plates were made. **1972** *Sci. Amer.* Dec. 15/1 All the equipment for integrated-circuit work, including the photoreduction microscope and the ultrasonic bonder, was of Chinese manufacture.

So **photoredu·ce** *v. trans.*, to reduce photochemically; **photoredu·ced, -redu·cing** *ppl. adjs.*

1957 G. Oster in H. Gaffron et al. *Res. Photosynthesis* I. 53 Acriflavine under conditions where it is not photoreduced in the unbound state, is readily photoreduced when bound to polymeric acids. **1959** —— in R. B. Withrow *Photoperiodism* i. 7 In my opinion..intermediate colored forms of photoreduced porphyrins are obtainable. **1965** *Biochim. & Biophys. Acta* XCIX. 159 The lost NADP photoreducing activities of the sonicated chloroplasts..are fully restored on addition of plastocyanin. **1968** *Plant Physiol.* XLIII. 606/1 All the mutants appeared to have the enzymes needed for the reduction of carbon dioxide..but..they photoreduced little or no CO_2.

photoregulate to **-repairable:** see *photo- 1; **photo-reportage, -reporting:** see *photo- 2.

photoresist (fōutorīzi·st). Also **photo-resist.** [f. Photo- 1 + Resist *sb.*] A photosensitive resist which when exposed to (usu. ultraviolet) light loses either its resistance or its susceptibility to attack by an etchant or solvent.

1953 *Printing Mag.* Oct. 56/1 The Kodak Photo-Resist, developed by Eastman Kodak Co., has great possibilities. It is the result of an extensive study and seems to possess ideal properties for a photoresist. **1960** *Times Rev. Industry* Aug. 46/1 The copper-clad phenolic panels..are sprayed with a photo-resist. **1965** D. I. Gaffee in L. Holland *Thin Film Microelectronics* vi. 261 Kodak Photo-resist was originally designed for making letter-press printing plates and lithographic plates. **1969** *R. & E. Coordinator* (Res. & Engin. Council Graphic Arts Industry) Apr. 10/1 The new photoresist can be used in chemical milling of copper, copper alloys, and stainless steel, provided only acid solution etchants are used. **1972** *Daily Tel.* 23 Mar. 30 (Advt.), The Applications Laboratory requires a technologist to work on new and improved Kodak lithographic printing plates... The person filling the post will probably have had experience with similar plates.., including some knowledge of photoresists. **1973** *Sci. Amer.* Apr. 70/1 (*caption*) High-performance MOSFET is made in these steps. Light admitted through a mask sensitizes a 'photoresist' protecting a silicon oxide layer grown on a silicon wafer... Unprotected silicon oxide is etched away and phosphorus atoms are diffused into them to produce 'source' and 'drain' areas.

photoresistance to **-resistor:** see *photo- 1.

pho:torespira·tion. *Bot.* [f. Photo- 1 + Respiration.] A respiratory process in many higher plants by which they take up oxygen in the light and give out some carbon dioxide, contrary to the general pattern of photosynthesis.

1945 E. I. Rabinowitch *Photosynthesis* I. xx. 569 We now come to the problem of 'photorespiration' proper, that is, a direct photochemical acceleration of normal respiration which disappears in the dark as instantaneously as does photosynthesis. *Ibid.* 570 None of the experiments described above provides a final proof of the nonexistence of true 'photorespiration'. **1966** *Physiologia Plantarum* XIX. 732 Evolution of carbon dioxide in light, or photorespiration, was affected by oxygen... Oxygen had no effect on dark respiration. This discrepancy..can best be explained by an assumption that photorespiration and dark respiration are two different processes. **1972** [see *peroxisomal *a.*]. **1977** I. M. Campbell *Energy & Atmosphere* iv. 76 Plants with high rates of photorespiration such as wheat.

Hence **photorespi·re** *v. intr.*, to carry out photorespiration; **photorespi·red** *ppl. a.*, evolved by photorespiration; **photorespi·ring** *ppl. a.*; **photorespi·ratory** *a.*, of, pertaining to, or evolved by photorespiration.

1968 *Plant Physiol.* XLIII. 1840/1 Glycolate oxidation appears to be responsible for much of the photorespiratory CO_2. *Ibid.* 1843/2 At high concentrations of CO_2 the synthesis of the photorespiratory substrate, glycolate, is severely inhibited. **1969** *Proc. Nat. Acad. Sci.* LXIII. 668 Species of the first group also photorespire, evolving CO_2 into the atmosphere in light. **1970** *Nature* 14 Nov. 687/2 Such plants may not photorespire, or alternatively may be capable of refixing all the photorespired CO_2 by an unusually efficient photosynthetic mechanism. *Ibid.* 688/1 Glycollate seems to be the primary substrate for photorespiration, and it does not normally accumulate in photorespiring tissue. **1974** H. Fock et al. in *Bull. R. Soc. N.Z.* XII. 235 (*heading*) Estimation of carbon fluxes through photosynthetic and photorespiratory pathways. *Ibid.* 237 At 400 ppm CO_2 most or all of the photorespired carbon dioxide from intact leaves..may be derived from ^{14}C-labelled early products of photosynthesis.

photoresponse to **-reversible:** see *photo- 1; **photoscan** to **-scanning:** see *photo- 2.

photoscopic, *a.* Add: **c.** *Computers.* Applied to a photographic method of storing digital information.

1955 *Sci. Amer.* June 100/3 Gilbert W. King..has undertaken to exploit the great density of information storage that is possible through the use of high-resolution photographic emulsions. With his 'photoscopic' technique information can be stored at densities more than a hundred times as great as those possible in magnetic media. **1970** O. Dopping *Computers & Data Processing* x. 151 One example of photographic film memories is the photoscopic memory, which has been used for dictionaries in mechanical translation from one natural language to another. The medium is a continuously rotating disk of transparent plastic carrying a photographic layer upon which a pattern corresponding to zeroes and ones has been recorded.

photosensitive (fōutose·nsitiv), *a.* [f. Photo- 1 + Sensitive *a.* and *sb.*] Responding to light in some way (biologically, chemically, electrically, etc.).

1886 *Jrnl. R. Microsc. Soc.* VI. 596 [In the Elateridæ] the photosensitive reflex action has its seat in the cerebroid ganglia. **1918** *Science* 23 Aug. 199/2 Decomposition of the photosensitive material by light, presupposes the formation of this substance within the sense organ. **1925** *Jrnl. Chem. Soc.* CXXVII. I. 787 (*heading*) The photosensitive formation of water from its elements in the presence of chlorine. **1957** G. E. Hutchinson *Treat. Limnol.* I. vi. 399 The study of the transmission of light by means of suitably photosensitive instruments. **1967** D. G. Hays *Introd. Computational Linguistics* iv. 68 Another mirror is used to position the beam at the desired place on the photosensitive stock. **1977** 'E. Trevor' *Theta Syndrome* v. 64 Mancini was lying down with dark glasses on... He was photo-sensitive.

Hence **photose·nsitiveness** (*rare*), **pho:tosensiti·vity.**

1889 R. Mendola *Chem. of Photography* i. 13 The photo-sensitiveness of ferric compounds has long been known. **1914** *Physical Rev.* IV. 228 The plan..was to observe the time changes in contact potential differences and photosensitiveness of photo-electrically or mechanically treated surfaces. **1918** *Science* 23 Aug. 198/2 (*heading*) Adaptation in the photosensitivity of *Ciona intestinalis*. **1939** *Jrnl. Inst. Electr. Engin.* LXXXIV. 473/1 In the normal Emitron the photo-sensitivity is limited to about 12 μA/lumen. **1947** *New Biol.* III. 93 Many other urodeles, *i.e.*, tailed Amphibia, retain their photosensitivity and continue to move away from light after their eyes have been removed. **1961** *Lancet* 26 Aug. 450/2 His clinical photosensitivity showed fluctuations of intensity which corresponded with quantitative changes in his erythrocyte and fæcal porphyrins; hence it seems justifiable to conclude that the porphyrins produced in his body are responsible for his photosensitisation. **1970** R. A. & B. M. Maier *Compar. Animal Behavior* xvii. 365 Photosensitivity seems to have evolved from a general sensitivity to chemical stimulation.

pho:tosensitiza·tion. [f. PHOTO- 1 + SENSITIZATION.] **a.** *Chem.* The initiation of a reaction by light acting on a suitable photosensitizer.

1924 H. S. TAYLOR *Treat. Physical Chem.* II. xviii. 1241 Uranium salts are positive catalysts for the photoreaction, presumably by photo-sensitization. **1933** *Jrnl. Amer. Chem. Soc.* LV. 587 A maximum of twenty per cent. photosensitization to visible light was found for the polymerization among seventy organic substances tried. **1974** D. R. ARNOLD et al. *Photochem.* vi. 133 Photosensitization involves the absorption of radiation by a strongly absorbing substance, the photosensitizer and its collisional transfer to another substance which is non-absorbing at the same wavelength.

b. (The production of) a condition in which light of certain wavelengths is harmful to an individual, usu. owing to the presence in the body of a photodynamic substance.

1926 E. MAYER *Clin. Applic. Sunlight* v. 86 (*heading*) Photosensitization. **1927** K. M. L. GAMGEE *Artificial Light Treatm. Children* xii. 108 Experimental photosensitization in animals and human beings is known to follow the administration of certain substances, such as eosin and haematoporphyrin, and death may result on exposure to light. **1941** H. F. BLUM *Photodynamic Action* xv. 159 Mathews..finds part of the symptoms which follow feeding on *Agave lechuguilla*, found in the arid regions of New Mexico, Mexico and Texas, to result from photosensitization. **1961** *Lancet* 26 Aug. 450/2 In cases of porphyria with photosensitisation, it is often uroporphyrin which is present in greatest excess, and the response to irradiation is by erythema and itching followed by slowly developing œdema. **1973** STOUT & SCHULTES in L. P. Miller *Phytochem.* III. xiv. 384 These last [*sc.* photodynamic toxins] may act either by sensitizing the animal directly..or by causing liver damage, which then leads to photosensitization as a secondary consequence.

photosensitize (fōutose·nsitəiz), *v.* [f. PHOTO- 1 + SENSITIZE *v.*] *trans.* **a.** *Chem.* Of a substance: to initiate (a chemical change) by absorbing light energy and transferring it to a reactant.

1927 *Jrnl. Amer. Chem. Soc.* XLIX. 2763 (*heading*) Hydrogen peroxide formation photosensitized by mercury vapor. **1928** *Proc. R. Soc.* A. CXXI. 297 Uranyl ion has..been found to photosensitize the decomposition of glucose in solution. **1951** *Symp. Soc. Exper. Biol.* V. 142 Photolysis of water can be accomplished with much less energy if the process is suitably 'photosensitized', for instance, if water is irradiated in the presence of suitable ions. **1966** GUCKER & SEIFERT *Physical Chem.* (1967) xxiii. 722 The dissociation of hydrogen molecules into atoms requires..a quantum of wavelength 2770 Å. Hydrogen molecules do not absorb light of this wavelength, but mercury atoms, which absorb light at 2536·52 Å, have plenty of energy to photosensitize the formation of hydrogen atoms.

b. To make photosensitive.

1933 *Jrnl. Inst. Electr. Engin.* LXXIII. 441/2 The mosaic..is composed of a very large number of minute silver globules, each of which is photo-sensitized by cæsium through utilization of a special process. **1941** *Nature* 10 May 581/2 Carcinogenic hydrocarbons in very low concentration are able to photosensitize Paramecia. **1977** J. L. HARPER *Population Biol. of Plants* xvii. 503 The plant is a serious weed..because it photosensitizes the skin of white-skinned animals.

Hence **photose·nsitized** *ppl. a.*, **-se·nsitizing** *vbl. sb.* and *ppl. a.*

1914 S. E. SHEPPARD *Photo-Chem.* xi. 435 The photochemical sensitiveness of dye-stuffs..depends in part upon the formation of a specific adsorption-complex of the dye with the substance sensitized. This photosensitizing is of considerable interest. **1931** R. G. W. NORRISH in *Photochem. Processes* (Faraday Soc.) II. 461 (*heading*) The photosensitised formation of hydrogen peroxide in the system hydrogen-oxygen chlorine. **1935** *Discovery* Sept. 278/1 The mosaic screen is made up of millions of isolated photo-sensitised elements upon a mica sheet. **1964** *Oceanogr. & Marine Biol.* II. 406 There are indications that urchins can be induced to cover by injecting photo-sensitizing dyes. **1974** *Photochem. & Photobiol.* XIX. 35/1 Some amino acids..are sensitive to photosensitized oxidation.

photosensitizer (fōutose·nsitəizəɹ). [f. PHOTO- 1 + SENSITIZER.] **a.** *Chem.* A substance capable of photosensitizing a reaction.

1914 S. E. SHEPPARD *Photo-Chem.* vii. 293 Winther succeeded in showing that the chlorine water was not a true photo-sensitizer since it had the same effect in darkness upon the precipitation of calomel. **1928** *Proc. R. Soc.* A. CXXI. 296 It is not to be supposed that only fluorescent substances will act as photosensitizers; substances capable of absorbing radiation of the appropriate frequency may be effective, whether fluorescent or not. **1957** G. E. HUTCHINSON *Treat. Limnol.* I. xvi. 865 In addition to ultraviolet light certain oxides must be present as photosensitizers. **1974** *Photochem. & Photobiol.* XIX. 441/2 The versatility of flavins as photosensitizers in numerous photoprocesses.

b. A photodynamic substance.

1925 *Practitioner* Aug. 103 The visible rays, however, have this effect when the irradiated cells are incorporated with photosensitizers, such as eosin and hæmatoporphyrin. **1946** *Nature* 14 Dec. 877/2 They found that the cancerogenic substances had a stronger effect than the non-cancerogenic photosensitizers. **1967** M. E. HALE *Biol. Lichens* xi. 161 The possibilities that uric acid may be a photosensitizer and a cause of respiratory allergy are also being explored. **1975** *Sci. Amer.* July 72/3 A number of widely prescribed drugs (such as the tetracyclines) and constituents of foods (such as riboflavins) are potential photosensitizers.

photosensor(y): see *PHOTO- 1.

photosetting (fōu·tose:tiŋ), *vbl. sb. Printing.* [f. PHOTO- 2 + SETTING *vbl. sb.*] = *PHOTOCOMPOSING *vbl. sb.* 1. So **pho·toset** *v. trans.*; **pho·toset** *ppl. a.*; **pho·tose:tter,** a photocomposing machine.

1957 *Americana Ann.* 330/1 Tabular matter can be photoset in the same manner as ordinary typewriting. **1958** *Ibid.* 243/1 An electric combination photosetting and photocomposing machine was developed. **1959** *Times* 14 Jan. 12/4 Photosetting machines are unlikely to replace all these [hot-metal typesetting machines]. **1959** in E. Fitzgerald tr. *Hils's Toy* 4 Printed in England from photoset typematter. **1961** *Printing News* 30 Mar. 6/5 One American printer is currently producing upwards of 100 photoset books a year. **1968** A. BLUHM *Photosetting* i. 6 The beginning of the 'modern' period of photosetting may be conveniently dated at 1955, when prototypes..of several current machines for text setting were shown at the IPEX exhibition in London. **1970** *Brit. Printer* Dec. 72/2 A new photosetter in what is described as the moderate price range has been introduced. **1974** *Times* 14 Oct. (Sheffield Suppl.) p. iv/8 Both papers..have..an ambitious reorganization scheme... It includes changing to photo-setting instead of the traditional typesetting.

photoshock to **-stable:** see *PHOTO- 1.

Photostat (fōu·tostæt). orig. *U.S.* Also **photostat.** [f. PHOTO- 2 + -STAT.] **a.** The proprietary name of a kind of photocopying machine. **b.** A copy made on such a machine; *loosely*, any photocopy. Also *attrib.*

1911 *Trade Marks Jrnl.* 24 May 761 Photostat... Photographic cameras for making photographic copies of the pages of books, drawings, applications for life insurance and the like. Commercial Camera Company.., Providence, Rhode Island, United States of America; manufacturers. **1912** *Chambers's Jrnl.* June 414/2 By means of the photostat a new filing method is possible. **1927** *Glasgow Herald* 26 May 9 The reference to a subterranean photostat room is quite in accord with the general cinematographic nature of the raid... Such photostats exist nowadays in most large commercial undertakings. **1928** P. S. ALLEN *Let.* 27 July (1939) 258, I should be glad to have the photostats (where does the word come from?) quickly. **1931** *Times Lit. Suppl.* 17 Dec. 1028/1 The number of manuscripts known has increased..to eighty-four, of which photostats are now at the University of Chicago. **1932** [see *book-page* s.v. *BOOK *sb.* 18]. **1940** *Chambers's Techn. Dict.* 639/1 *Photostat*, trade-name for photographic apparatus (also for any print made by it) designed for rapidly copying, to the required size, flat originals on sensitised paper, and giving a negative image. **1959** T. S. ELIOT *Elder Statesman* II. 57 I'm afraid I can't show you the originals; They're in my lawyer's safe. But I have photostats Which are quite as good, I'm told. **1961** T. LANDAU *Encycl. Librarianship* (ed. 2) 121/1 The 'Photostat' has after many years become a household word among librarians and readers, and is indiscriminately used in describing any photographic reproduction of a document. It is in fact a trade name, and a 'Photostat' copy of a document is one produced by the 'Photostat' apparatus. **1964** 'R. MACDONALD' in *Manhunt* May 142/1, I pulled out my photostat and slapped it down on the desk. **1975** *Guardian* 25 Feb. 5/7 Inside the envelope there were simply photostats of correspondence. **1976** *Gloss. Documentation Terms* (*B.S.I.*) 48 *Photostat*, a trade mark of Kodak Ltd. for photocopying cameras, chemicals and sensitive materials, the optical copies produced being right-reading.

Hence **pho·tostat** *v. trans.*, to photocopy; so **pho·tostat(t)ed** *ppl. a.*, **pho·tostat(t)ing** *vbl. sb.*; also **photosta·tic** *a.*, of, pertaining to, or produced by a Photostat or other photocopying machine.

1914 *Amer. Machinist* 9 Apr. 642/1 A prism is used to 'turn the corner', making it more convenient than if the book or other object being 'photostated' had to be set up on edge. **1925** M. R. RINEHART *Red Lamp* 139 One of the evening newspapers to-night prints a photostatic copy of the cipher found in our garage. **1932** *N. & Q.* 5 Nov. 328/1 In corresponding about having the letter photostated we were informed of still another letter. **1937** MRS. P. CAMPBELL *Let.* 25 Aug. in *B. Shaw & Mrs. Campbell* (1952) 314 He doesn't know I have had two photostated copies made of them. **1947** [see *EAGER *a.* 6]. **1957** *Amer. Speech* XXXII. 57 Libraries quickly learned the uses they could make of photostatic machines. **1959** H. HAMILTON *Answer in Negative* i. 8 All our printing, and photo-statting of cuttings, is done by the *Echo's* dark-room. **1967** N. FREELING *Strike Out* 141 They weren't going to open an embassy safe and photostat the contents. **1973** R. HILL *Ruling Passion* III. iii. 179 He passed out some photostatted sheets. **1976** T. ALLBEURY *Only Good German* ix. 59 A photostated copy of an item in *The Times*. **1978** *Daily Tel.* 5 May 14/6 Some might feel that for a rather smaller price the 'Compact' DNB, the full work with minute, photostated text,..might be a better buy.

photostationary to **-surface:** see *PHOTO- 1; **photostereogram** to **-story:** see *PHOTO- 2.

photosynthate (fōutosi·nþēit). *Bot.* [f. next + *-ate*, after *filtrate, precipitate.*] A substance formed by photosynthesis.

1913 W. F. GANONG *Living Plant* ii. 24 The process being one of formation, or synthesis, under action of light, is called scientifically photosynthesis, while the substance made is the photosynthate. **1938** WEAVER & CLEMENTS *Plant Ecol.* (ed. 2) xiv. 395 Many species of evergreens are known to make photosynthate in winter in sufficiently large amounts to balance that oxidized in respiration. **1978** *Nature* 5 Jan. 93/2 A conifer manufactures photosynthates at all times of the year except when climatic conditions are unsuitable, due for example to low temperatures or drought stress.

photosynthesis (fōutosi·nþĭsis). *Bot.* [ad. G. *photosynthese*: see PHOTO- 1 + SYNTHESIS.] The process by which carbon dioxide is converted into organic matter in the presence of the chlorophyll of plants under the influence of light, which in all plants except some bacteria involves the production of oxygen from water; also, any photochemical synthesis of a chemical compound.

1898 *Botanisches Zentralblatt* LXXVI. 258 It is not important whether photosyntax or photosynthesis, or some other word, finally comes into general use to describe the manufacture of carbohydrates by green tissues under the action of light. **1902** *Encycl. Brit.* XXXI. 760/1 The course of photosynthesis has been with tolerable certainty found to lead to the construction of sugar. **1914** S. E. SHEPPARD *Photo-Chem.* vii. 295 The photo-synthesis of phosgene ($COCl_2$) from chlorine and carbon monoxide.. has been studied by several observers. **1924** *Industr. & Engin. Chem.* Oct. 1018/1 The optimum experimental conditions having been determined, it has been found possible to carry out the photosynthesis on a larger scale than in the test tube. **1927** *Proc. R. Soc.* A. CXVI. 203 The photosynthesis of complex organic substances takes place when carbonic acid in the presence of a surface is exposed to ultra-violet light. **1932** FULLER & CONARD tr. *Braun-Blanquet's Plant Sociol.* v. 97 There is a limited amount of photosynthesis in the invisible infra-red and ultra-violet. **1952** P. W. RICHARDS *Trop. Rain Forest* vii. 180 Even at the low light intensities found in the shade of the Tropical Rain forest, a high carbon dioxide concentration would probably allow a rate of photosynthesis considerably higher than that at normal concentration. **1957** *Times* 11 Sept. 6/2 Recent studies using radiocarbon indicated that the yield of photosynthesis by the plankton of the oceans was at least equal to that of the land flora, and might be several times greater. **1958** R. Y. STANIER et al. *Gen. Microbiol.* xi. 213 In bacterial photosyntheses, there is also a light-driven reduction of CO_2 to cell material, but oxygen is never produced because water cannot serve as the ultimate hydrogen donor. Instead, the reduction of CO_2 is coupled with the oxidation of externally supplied organic or inorganic hydrogen donors. **1964** E. J. H. CORNER *Life of Plants* iii. 38 There are chromoplast colours that work together with chlorophyll in photosynthesis. **1975** H. SMITH *Photochrome & Photomorphogenesis* ii. 15 Photosynthesis presents an excellent example of light and dark reactions acting sequentially.

Hence **pho:tosynthe·tic** *a.*, of, pertaining to, produced by, or involved in photosynthesis; *photosynthetic quotient* or *ratio*, the rate of evolution of oxygen by photosynthesizing tissue divided by its rate of consumption of carbon dioxide, or the reciprocal of this; **pho:tosynthe·tically** *adv.*

1900 A. J. EWART tr. *Pfeffer's Physiol. Plants* I. vii. 293 The photosynthetic assimilation in the chloroplastid only provides the organic food, which in green and non-green plants, and in animals also, has the same function to perform. *Ibid.* 326 With the exception of carbon dioxide, no carbon compounds are known which can be photosynthetically assimilated. **1913** W. F. GANONG *Living Plant* ii. 27 The photosynthetic sugar and starch which appear in lighted green leaves. **1926** H. A. SPOEHR *Photosynthesis* ii. 92 The photosynthetic quotient may yield some information relative to the first product formed in photosynthesis. **1931** E. C. MILLER *Plant Physiol.* viii. 431 The determination of the photosynthetic ratio is difficult, because the process of respiration is proceeding at the same time and in the opposite direction [to that of photosynthesis]. **1945** E. I. RABINOWITCH *Photosynthesis* I. iii. 31 The 'photosynthetic quotient', $Q_P : Q_P = \Delta O_2/-\Delta CO_2$. (The term 'photosynthetic quotient' has been used by many authors.. to designate the inverse ratio, $-\Delta CO_2/\Delta O_2$; this difference calls for care in the quotation of numerical results.) **1962** *Listener* 3 May 768/2 Some scientists believe that free oxygen is entirely biological in origin and that it arose *after* the emergence of photosynthetic life. **1971** *Sci. Amer.* Sept. 92/3 Plants reflect about 8 percent of photosynthetically active wavelengths. **1971** I. ZELITCH *Photosynthesis* v. 129 At the high O_2 concentrations, *Amaranthus* leaves had a photosynthetic quotient of 0·50 and bean leaves 0·33. **1974** A. HUXLEY *Plant & Planet* iii. 22 It was probably not the seaweeds that gave rise to land plants but, from their similar photosynthetic pigments and photosynthetic mechanism, the green algae.

photosynthesize (fōutosi·nþĭsəiz), *v. Bot.* [f. prec. + -IZE.] **a.** *trans.* To create by photosynthesis. **b.** *intr.* To carry out photosynthesis.

1921 *Jrnl. Chem. Soc.* CXIX. 1029 Carbohydrates can be photosynthesised from carbon dioxide and water in two stages. **1927** *Proc. R. Soc.* A. CXVI. 212 These [results] convinced us that it is possible by the use of coloured powders to photosynthesise organic compounds from carbonic acid with the help of visible light. **1951** *Symp. Soc. Exper. Biol.* V. 300 When algae or barley leaves photosynthesize..in $C^{14}O_2$ for 30 sec. [etc.]. **1974** A. HUXLEY *Plant & Planet* iii. 18 Some bacteria..can either photosynthesize or, if in the dark, gain energy from decomposing organic matter.

Hence **photosy·nthesized, photosy·nthesizing** *ppl. adjs.*; also **photosy·nthesizer,** an organism which carries out photosynthesis.

1910 F. KEEBLE *Plant-Animals* iii. 79 From the photosynthesised carbohydrate are derived the cellulose substances. **1927** *Proc. R. Soc.* A. CXVI. 213 The photosynthesised compounds are very similar in appearance to those described in the previous paper. **1937** *Enzymologia* IV. 254 (*heading*) On the fluorescence of photosynthesizing cells. **1958** *Sci. News* XLIX. 25 Animals, fungi, and most of the bacteria..only shuffle..the materials the photosynthesizers have made. **1970** L. MARGULIS *Origin of Eukaryotic Cells* iv. 94 This gas [*sc.* hydrogen sulphide] was utilized by anaerobic photosynthesizers as hydrogen donors in photosynthesis. **1973** *Sci. Amer.* Oct. 83/3 They supplied carbon dioxide labeled with carbon 14 to photosynthesizing sugarcane plants.

pho·tosystem. *Bot.* [f. *PHOTO(SYNTHETIC *a.* + SYSTEM.] Either of the two biochemical mechanisms in plants by which light is converted into useful energy.

1965 *Biochim. & Biophys. Acta* CIX. 349 Photoreduction of substrate V by photosystem I. **1973** J. J. WOLKEN in L. P. Miller *Phytochem.* I. ii. 26 This phenomenon termed the 'red drop' is interpreted, at present, as due to a special form of 'long wavelength absorbing' chlorophyll belonging to a Photosystem I. *Ibid.*, The low efficiency of the far-red (beyond 680 nm) would require another pigment-complex absorbing below 680 nm, which has been designated as Photosystem II. **1974** *Nature* 4 Jan. 4/1 There now seems to be no doubt that KCN inhibits photosynthesis by specifically blocking electron flow through photosystem one (S1).

phototactic, *a.* Substitute for def.: Exhibiting or characterized by phototaxis. (Earlier and later examples.) [ad. G. *phototaktisch* (E. Strasburger 1878: see *PHOTOTAXIS).]

1882 S. H. VINES tr. *F. G. J. von Sachs's Text-bk. Bot.* III. iii. 752 Zoogonidia which exhibit these phenomena are said, by Strasburger, to be phototactic. **1907** *Jrnl. Exper. Zool.* V. 72 Any organism is said to be positively phototactic when it moves towards the source of light and negatively phototactic when it goes in the opposite direction. **1969** F. E. ROUND *Introd. Lower Plants* ii. 15 Euglenoids are positively phototactic. **1976** *Sci. Amer.* June 42/1, I had noticed a phototactic response in *H. halobium*; the cells reversed their direction of swimming when the intensity of illumination was decreased in the red part of the spectrum.

Hence **photota·ctically** *adv.*

1914 [see *KINETIC *a.* 2 b].

phototaxis. Substitute for entry:

phototaxis (fōutǫtæ·ksis). *Biol.* Pl. **-taxes** (-tæ·ksīz). [mod.L., coined in Ger. (E. Strasburger 1878, in *Jenaische Zeitschr. f. Naturwissensch.* XII. 587): see PHOTO- I and TAXIS.] The innate movement in a definite direction of an organism or part of one in response to the stimulus of light; *esp.* the bodily movement or orientation of a freely motile organism (see quot. 1960 and cf. *PHOTOTROPISM).

1893 *Athenæum* 16 Sept. 375/3 Phototaxis and chemiotaxis are the last instances of physiological adaptation cited [by J. S. B. Sanderson]. **1894** J. S. B. SANDERSON in *Rep. Brit. Assoc. Adv. Sci. 1893* 24 A single instance.. must suffice to illustrate the influence of light in directing the movements of freely moving cells, or, as it is termed, phototaxis. **1902** *Jrnl. R. Microsc. Soc.* 31 Phototaxis is the peculiarity displayed by free-swimming organisms of orienting the body so as to place its long axis in a definite relation to the direction of the rays. **1911** A. WILLEY *Convergence in Evolution* iii. 25 The vegetable kingdom as a whole exhibits positive phototaxis. **1954** *New Biol.* XVII. 49 Several workers have found negative phototaxis (movement away from light) in a number of species [of woodlice]. **1960** THIMANN & CURRY in Florkin & Mason *Compar. Biochem.* I. vi. 244 In all these organisms the response to light is a free movement of the whole body directed towards or away from the light, and this is defined as phototaxis. In fungi and higher plants, as also in the colonial hydroids, the body is anchored at one end and the response to light is shown by a curvature. It is this which is phototropism properly speaking... Zoologists have, it is true, used the term phototropism for free movements of animals, while botanists have been more precise in preserving the distinction, but the distinction is a valuable and even essential one to make... In Phototaxis the light influences the organs of movement,.. while in Phototropism it influences the growth of the organism. **1975** *Nature* 3 Jan. 43/2 It would seem that the light intensity dependent behaviour in these two examples could be divided into retinally evoked phototaxes and an extraretinally evoked kinesis which cannot be separated in sighted larvae. *Ibid.* 4 Sept. 44/2 The internal parts of the maze were of clear Perspex which allowed the flies to be attracted through the maze by phototaxis.

phototelegram to **-telegraphy:** see *PHOTO- I; **photo-timer:** see *PHOTO- 2.

pho:totopo·graphy. Also with hyphen. [f. PHOTO- 2 + TOPOGRAPHY.] A system of surveying which employs photography as well as the usual methods.

The word has largely given way to *photogrammetry*.

1893 *Geogr. Jrnl.* I. 89 Photo-topography. **1895** *Rep. U.S. Coast & Geodetic Survey 1893* II. 42 During the Franco-Prussian war phototopography was called into service by the German army. **1922** *Geogr. Jrnl.* LIX. 274 The methods of Phototopography developed by Laussedat in France and by Deville in Canada..depend on the measurement of identical points on pairs of plates taken on determined azimuths at trigonometrical points. **1970** *Canad. Cartographer* VII. 19/2 The ground photo-topography continued in the mountains of British Columbia.

Hence **pho:totopo·grapher,** one who is skilled in phototopography; **pho:totopogra·phic, -ical** *adjs.*, of, pertaining to, or using phototopography; **pho totopogra·phically** *adv.*

1895 *Rep. U.S. Coast & Geodetic Survey 1893* II. 45 A phototopographic survey of the Oasis Gassr Dachel in the Libyan desert. **1902** *Encycl. Brit.* XXXIII. 95/2 The field work of a photo-topographic party consists primarily in execution of a triangulation by the usual methods. *Ibid.*, The photo-topographical survey. **1906** J. A. FLEMER *Elem. Treat. Phototopogr. Methods* xii. 387 The phototopographer..can in a few good days, cover a larger territory than is possible with any other surveying method. *Ibid.* 390 A large territory may be reconnoitered phototopographically in a comparatively short time. **1926** A. L. HIGGINS *Phototopography* ii. 42 Phototopographical instruments. **1970** *Canad. Cartographer* VII. 18/1 During the development of the photo-topographic work it became the practice to rule a perspective grid onto the print of the photograph to assist..in positioning horizontal detail.

phototoxic to **-transient:** see *PHOTO- I.

phototransistor (fōu:totrɑnzi·stəɹ). *Electronics.* Also with hyphen. [f. PHOTO- I + *TRANSISTOR.] A junction transistor which responds to incident light by generating and amplifying an electric current.

1950 J. N. SHIVE in *Bell Lab. Rec.* XXVIII. 337/2 Experiments have resulted in the production of a new photoconductivity cell, called the 'Phototransistor'. **1959** *Control* Feb. 95/2 It is a logical step from the photodiode to the *p-n-p* phototransistor, in which the amplifying action of the transistor is applied to the photocurrent. *Ibid.*, The Mullard OCP71 phototransistor is enclosed in a glass bulb 5·9 mm in diameter and 15 mm in length. **1959** *Electronic Engin.* XXXI. 36 The advent of the commercially produced junction photo-transistor has brought with it the possibility of operating a relay directly from the light sensitive element. **1962** P. M. WILLIAMS in G. A. T. Burdett *Automatic Control Handbk.* ix. 52 Phototransistors can be made which are sensitive to X-rays, ultra violet and infra red. **1970** *New Scientist* 24 Dec. 554/1 The new reading head is only a few centimetres across and contains a matrix of 144 bipolar phototransistors on a silicon chip 3 × 5 mm in size.

phototroph to **-trophy:** see *PHOTO- I.

phototropic, *a.* For *Bot.* read *Biol.* and add pronunc. (fōutotrōu·pik). Substitute for def.: Exhibiting or characterized by phototropism. (Further examples.) **phototropically** *adv.* (further examples).

1903 *Mark Anniversary Vol.* xxiii. 455 Loeb maintained that butterflies as well as moths are positively phototropic. *Ibid.* 457 When feeding or near food the butterflies do not respond phototropically. **1943** *Vitamins & Hormones* I. 211 In some structures also (*Avena, Pilobolus, Phycomyces*) carotenoid pigmentation has been shown to be concentrated in or restricted to the phototropically sensitive zones. **1972** *Plant Physiol.* XLIX. 993/1 Etiolated plants are known to be more sensitive phototropically than are green ones. **1976** BELL & COOMBE tr. *Strasburger's Textbk. Bot.* (rev. ed.) 350 Phototropic behaviour is not confined to the higher plants; it occurs also in fungi and algae.

2. = *PHOTOCHROMIC *a.*

1900 *Jrnl. Chem. Soc.* LXXVIII. II. 125 Benzilosazone, salicylosazone, and vanillylosazone are, however, not phototropic. **1929** *Chem. Rev.* VI. 220 Most phototropic substances exhibit phototropy only in the solid state. **1960** *New Scientist* 2 June 1423/2 In the same family of substances some derivatives are phototropic while others, which resemble them closely, do not show the effect. **1971** *Materials & Technol.* II. vi. 410 Phototropic glass is made by melting an alkali-alumino-borosilicate glass containing some lead and small amounts of silver, chloride, bromide, and iodide, forming the glass in the normal way, and then submitting the article to a heat treatment for several hours.

phototropism (fotǫ·trŏpiz'm, fōutotrōu·piz'm). [f. PHOTO- I + TROPISM.] **1.** *Biol.* [ad G. *phototropie* (F. Oltmanns 1892, in *Flora* LXXV. 214).] The innate movement in a definite direction of an organism or part of one in response to the stimulus of light; *esp.* the directional bending or growth of a plant or sessile animal (see quot. 1960 and cf. *PHOTOTAXIS).

[**1892** *Jrnl. R. Microsc. Soc.* 513 The phenomena of phototropy—i.e. positive or negative heliotropic movements.] **1899, 1900** [in Dict. s.v. PHOTOTROPIC *a.*]. **1902** *Jrnl. R. Microsc. Soc.* 31 He [*sc.* W. A. Nagel] applies the term phototropism to the peculiarity displayed by many sedentary organisms or special organs, of taking up a fixed position in regard to light, by means of bending movements, movements of growth or of torsion. **1907** T. H. MORGAN *Exper. Zoöl.* xvi. 265 Growth toward the Light; Phototropism... Some animals that are fixed turn toward the light. **1924** R. M. OGDEN tr. *Koffka's Growth of Mind* iii. 111 A cockroach possesses a negative phototropism. **1947** *Biol. Bull.* XCII. 127 The terms, phototropism and phototaxis, will be used synonymously in this paper. **1960** [see *PHOTOTAXIS]. **1965** B. E. FREEMAN tr. *Vandel's Biospeleol.* xxv. 400 Light very frequently attracts or repels animals and these conditions are given the names of positive and of negative phototropism. **1976** G. C. AINSWORTH *Introd. Hist. Mycol.* vii. 198 Phototropism has been much studied in the Mucorales.

fig. **1923** R. GRAVES *Whipperginny* 38 Watch the blind Phototropisms of my fluttering mind.

2. = *PHOTOCHROMISM.

1921 *Jrnl. Amer. Chem. Soc.* XLIII. 333 (*heading*) Studies on phototropism in solution. **1952** K. VENKATARAMAN *Chem. Synthetic Dyes* II. xl. 1217 A review of phototropism in solution and on dyed textiles. **1962** J. T. MARSH *Self-Smoothing Fabrics* xviii. 298 Phototropism is the change in shade which occurs on exposure to strong light, followed by a gradual return to the original shade when the light is removed. **1974** RATTEE & BREUER *Physical Chem. of Dye Adsorption* vii. 229 Three dyes..were all found to exhibit phototropism on cellulose acetate film.

phototropy (fōutǫ·trŏpi). [ad. G. *phototropie* (W. Marckwald 1899, in *Zeitschr. f. physik. Chem.* XXX. 140), f. Gr. φωτο- (see PHOTO-) + -τροπία turning.] = *PHOTOCHROMISM, *PHOTOTROPISM 2.

1900 *Sci. Amer.* 24 Feb. 123/2 To these phenomena the experimenter gives the name of phototropy. **1929** [see *PHOTOTROPIC *a.* 2]. **1949** *Thorpe's Dict. Appl. Chem.* (ed. 4) IX. 585/2 There is evidence..that phototropy is not a purely physical phenomenon. **1954** *Jrnl. Amer. Chem. Soc.* LXXVI. 3846/1 Observations on the phenomenon of phototropy in alkaline earth titanates. **1971** R. L. M. ALLEN *Colour Chem.* iii. 23 The stereoisomerism of azo dyes is of practical importance..in that it gives rise to the phenomenon of phototropy.

phototube (fōu·totiūb). [f. PHOTO- I + TUBE *sb.*] A photocell in the form of a vacuum tube or gas-filled tube with a photoemissive cathode and an anode.

1930 *Electronics* I. 418/1 (*heading*) Phototube voltage supervisor. An aid to tube production. **1953** [see *MARK *sb.*[1] 13 e]. **1964** *Oceanogr. & Marine Biol.* II. 358 It is only since the adoption by biologists of the multiplier phototube..that more precise measurements of the spectral composition of luminescence,..and rates of flashing, have become feasible. **1973** *Nature* 12 Jan. 132/2 The emission was observed at right angles..and detected photoelectrically with a '1P28' phototube.

phototypesetting (fōutotəi·pˌsetiŋ), *vbl. sb. Printing.* [f. PHOTO- 2 + *type-setting* s.v. TYPE *sb.*[1] 10.] = *PHOTOCOMPOSING *vbl. sb.* I. Also *attrib.* So **phototy·peset** *ppl. a.*; **phototy·pesetter,** a photocomposing machine.

1931 *A.S.M.E. News* 7 Apr. 3/3 Louis Flader..described the Uher photo-typesetting machine, having recently inspected it in Germany. **1949** E. THIRKETTLE in H. O. Smith *Rotophoto Process* 3 Technical improvements in lithographic printing presses are conveniently keeping in line with phototypesetting developments. **1955** *Times* 5 July 6/5 Outstanding among the advances of the last two decades has been the development known as phototypesetting. **1966** N. S. M. COX et al. *Computer & Library* v. 74 The phototypesetter can produce 'graphic arts quality' printing. **1970** *Brit. Printer* Dec. 43 Massive trade typesetting operations based on computers (the one in question was a Fototronic, the highest speed phototypesetter at present available) can be assimilated. **1971** *Penrose Ann.* LXIV. 176 Many more phototypesetting devices will come on to the market over the next few years. *Ibid.*, Throughout 1970, technical innovation flowed on unabated, with ten new phototypesetters announced. **1973** *Physics Bull.* Dec. 743/1 The World Patents Index..is computer generated and will publish the information in a phototypeset gazette. **1976** *Nature* 24 June 664/2 CSIRO's computer with its microfilm output equipment (a COMp 80 phototypesetter) is now being used to produce camera-ready copy.

photovisual (fōutovi·ʒiuăl), *a.* (*sb.*) Also **photo-visual.** [f. PHOTO- 2 + VISUAL *a.* and *sb.*] **1.** Of a lens or an optical instrument: bringing both visible and actinic, non-visible rays to the same focus. Also as *sb.*, such a lens or telescope.

1909 in *Cent. Dict.* Suppl. **1922** L. BELL *Telescope* iv. 89 The..objective..carries the name of 'photo-visual' since the exactness of corrections is carried well into the violet, so that one can see and photograph at the same focus. **1955** J. B. SIDGWICK *Amateur Astronomer's Hand-bk.* xxiii. 422 For photography a reflector is to be preferred, unless a photovisual is available. **1958** J. STRONG *Concepts of Classical Optics* xiv. 323 Three different glasses, properly chosen for their partial dispersions, can be combined in components to yield a composite lens... Fig. 14-14 gives a tabulation..for the three glasses used in the Cooke photo-visual triplet lens. **1964** *Yearbk. Astron. 1965* 191 The main instruments at present are a 13-inch reflector, a 10-inch refractor, a 6-inch photovisual refractor, a 16 centimetre transit telescope and various cameras. **1977** *Sci. Amer.* Sept. 29/2 (Advt.), Sixth, the design must be photovisual so that he could record on film whatever these superior optics would present to the eye.

2. *Astr.* Applied to stellar magnitudes determined in terms of the spectral response of the eye by photographic or photoelectric means.

1914 *Carnegie Inst. Yearbk. 1913* 214 The comparison of these 'photovisual' results with the ordinary photographic magnitudes shows an increase in the color index as the variable approaches its minimum. **1927** H. N. RUSSELL et al. *Astron.* II. xviii. 620 With isochromatic plates and a 'color filter' to cut off the blue and violet light and let through the green and yellow, magnitudes may be obtained which agree very closely with the visual scale. These are called photo-visual magnitudes. **1958** C. C. ADAMS et al. *Space Flight* 132 At this time it is expected to be of the fifth photovisual magnitude, which is about the same brightness as the faintest star that, under reasonably good observing conditions, can be seen with the naked eye. **1963** C. W. ALLEN *Astrophysical Quantities* (ed. 2) x. 195 The effective wavelengths of a colour index system change with the colour itself. The U.B.V. system..has replaced the international photographic and photovisual systems.

photovoltaic: see *PHOTO- 1.

Photronic (fōu·trǫ·nik). Also photronic. [f. PHOT(O- 1 + *ELEC)TRONIC *a.*] An American proprietary name for a kind of photovoltaic cell. Also *attrib.* or as *adj.*

The word is registered in the U.S. as a proprietary term for several other devices also.

1932 *Official Gaz.* (U.S. Patent Office) 15 Mar. 554/1 Weston Electrical Instrument Corporation, Newark, N.J. Filed Oct. 1, 1931. Photronic. For light sensitive cells. Claims use since Sept. 25, 1931. **1938** G. H. SEWELL *Amateur Film-Making* ii. 21 The light intensity is received by a photronic type of cell. **1948** *Electronic Engin.* XX. 136/2 A method is described by which it is possible to check the balance of the printer instantly by means of tricolour readings with a photronic cell.

photy (fōu·ti). *colloq.* (chiefly *Sc.*). [f. PHOT(OGRAPH *sb.* + -Y⁶.] A photograph.

1973 *Sunday Post* (Glasgow) 5 Aug. 17/3 *Wannysee wurphoties?*—Are you prepared for an hour of utter boredom?..*Attaka noffiphoty*—Photographs never flatter me. **1974** *Weekly News* (Glasgow) 31 Aug. 11/5 'Maist o' yer photies seems tae be of Edwina,' Wee Sadie remarked.

phragmites (frægmai·tīz). [mod.L. (C. B. Trinius *Fundamenta Agrostographiæ* (1820) 134), f. Gr. φραγμίτης growing in hedges.] = REED *sb.*[1] 4. Also *attrib.*

1920 *Blackw. Mag.* May 650/1 It may be necessary to cleave a passage..—cutting through papyrus, tearing at the tangling *Phragmites*, severing the long stems of the water-convolvulus. **1946** F. E. ZEUNER *Dating Past* iii. 56 Peats growing under or at the water level: *Phragmites* peat (peat formed by the Common Reed and similar plants growing in shallow water). **1957** E. E. EVANS *Irish Folk Ways* xv. 217 Large lake rushes provided materials for caulking..and phragmites stems for winding yarn in the shuttle. **1959** J. D. CLARK *Prehist. S. Afr.* viii. 201 Phragmites reeds cut transversely and possibly left over from making arrow shafts,..abound in the upper layers of the cave. **1965** P. WAYRE *Wind in Reeds* xi. 156 Little pockets of phragmites had sprung up in the odd corners and shallow bays all round the main [gravel] pit. **1977** *New Yorker* 5 Sept. 23/2 An impenetrable marsh of phragmites..and other plants clogs the length of the channel.

phragmoplast (fræ·gmoplast). *Bot.* [a. G. *phragmoplast* (L. Errera 1888, in *Bot. Centralbl.* XXXIV. 397), f. Gr. φράγμ-α fence, screen: see -O and -PLAST.] A set of fibrils which appears during mitosis in some plant cells as a barrel-shaped structure joining the two sets of chromosomes after their separation to the poles and which lasts until the formation of the cell plate.

1912 W. H. LANG tr. *Strasburger's Text-bk. Bot.* (ed. 4) 89 A barrel-shaped figure, the phragmoplast, is formed, which either separates entirely from the developing daughter nuclei, or remains in connection with them by means of a peripheral sheath. **1941** *Amer. Jrnl. Bot.* XXVIII. 227/2 In late anaphase or during telophase the phragmoplast extends laterally and a cell plate is formed across the cell. **1976** A. W. DAVIDSON in M. M. Yeoman *Cell Division in Higher Plants* xii. 419 The phragmoplast, which heralds cell plate formation, appears at the equator of the mitotic spindle and moves centrifugally outwards along the phragmosome.

Hence **phragmopla·stic** *a.*

1952 A. HUGHES *Mitotic Cycle* iv. 147 This form of cytokinesis..is really a variety of the phragmoplastic method. **1953** K. ESAU *Plant Anat.* iii. 62 Phragmoplastic fibers appearing at the margins of the cell plate.

phragmosome (fræ·gmosōum). *Bot.* [f. as prec. + *-SOME⁴.] **a.** A layer of darker cytoplasm which forms during mitosis in some plant cells at the site of the future cell plate. **b.** One of the large number of small particles that form this layer.

1940 SINNOTT & BLOCH in *Proc. Nat. Acad. Sci.* XXVI. 226 This cytoplasm..tends to become aggregated into a series of strands..which occupies the position of the future wall and which thus indicates..where the plane of the division is to be. For this plate of cytoplasm the writers propose the term phragmosome. **1960** *Proc. 4th Internat. Conf. Electron Microscopy* 505 Other structures of the cytoplasm are consistently associated with the plate... The more obvious of these bodies (phragmosomes) tend to be a uniform distance from the cell plate. *Ibid.*, How these phragmosomes contribute to plate formation is not very clear. **1965** FREY-WYSSLING & MÜHLETHALER *Ultrastruct. Plant Cytol.* 279 During and after the formation of the cell plate osmiophilic particles become evident in the phragmoplast, which can reach light microscopic dimensions and which are known as phragmosomes. **1971** *Canad. Jrnl. Bot.* XLIX. 927 RNA was concentrated in phragmosomes and at the newly formed cell plates. **1976** A. W. DAVIDSON in M. M. Yeoman *Cell Division in Higher Plants* xii. 414 It is changes that occur within this limiting membrane [*sc.* the plasmalemma] which determine the point at which the phragmosome is formed and hence the position of the new cell wall.

phrasal, *a.* Add: **a.** Used in *Gram.* in collocations qualifying the name of a part of speech to denote phrases which have the function of that part of speech, esp. *phrasal verb*, an idiomatic verbal phrase consisting of a verb and adverb or a verb and preposition. (Further examples.)

1879 J. EARLE *Philol. Eng. Tongue* (ed. 3) x. 553 Modern English has made a new phrasal verb, and one that yet waits for a name. In this new verb the pronoun *it*, referring to no noun, acts as an objective accompaniment, and runs next after the verb. **1925** L. P. SMITH *Words & Idioms* v. 172 Even more numerous are the idiomatic collocations of verbs followed by prepositions, or by prepositions used as adverbs. Collocations of this kind, 'phrasal verbs' we may call them, like 'keep down', 'set up', 'put through', and thousands of others. [*Note*] The term 'phrasal verbs' was suggested to me by the late Dr. Bradley. **1954** E. GOWERS *Compl. Plain Words* vi. 71 There is today a tendency to form phrasal verbs to express a meaning no different from that of the verb without the particle... *Drown out, sound out, lose out, rest up, miss out on*, are other examples of phrasal verbs which I am told are used in America in senses no different from that of the unadorned verb. **1959** M. SCHLAUCH *Eng. Lang.* 310 (Index), Phrasal adjectives. **1961** R. B. LONG *Sentence & its Parts* ix. 218 In units such as *three-year-old*, whether used as phrasal nouns (as in *the three-year-old next door*) or as prepositive modifiers (as in *any three-year-old child*), the construction is different but obviously related. *Ibid.* x. 235 Units such as *tomorrow afternoon*..are syntactically much like phrasal-proper-name units such as Earlham College. **1973** *Word 1970* XXVI. 116 The following contain phrasal verbs: *You will have to look out for yourself*; *He did away with himself.*

b. *Mus.* Of or belonging to a phrase (in sense 5 of the sb.).

1946 R. BLESH *Shining Trumpets* v. 106 This solo puts the semitonally flatted third and fifth in phrasal conjunction.

phra·sally, *adv.* [f. PHRASAL *a.* + -LY².] In or by phrases; as a phrase.

1934 in WEBSTER. **1971** *Archivum Linguisticum* II. 61 The fact that *black bird* is labelled phrasally reflects, it seems, a combination of conventional practice, analytical convenience, and the ascribing of special semantic significance to this particular type of structural relationship. **1973** *Ibid.* IV. 47 A given 'place' may..be occupied by more than one phrasally contributing form.

phrase, *sb.* Add: **2. d.** *transf.*

1908 G. JEKYLL *Colour in Flower Garden* 15 While the wide-stretching shadow-lengths throw the woodland shades into woodland *phrases* of broadened mass. **1922** [see *CHOREOGRAPHICALLY *adv.*].

7. *phrase-family, -form, -formative, -meaning, -tag*; *phrase-final, -internal* adjs.; **phrase-book** (earlier and later examples); also *attrib.*; **phrase-maker** (later examples); also, a composer of musical phrases; hence **phrase-making** *vbl. sb.* (also in literal sense); **phrase-marker** *Linguistics*, a diagrammatic or formulaic representation of the constituent structure of a sentence; abbrev. *P-marker* s.v. *P III 5; **phrase-structure,** a group of words that constitutes a phrase; in *Gram.*, the structure of a sentence in terms of its constituent phrases (also *attrib.*); hence *phrase-structurally* adv.; **phrase-word** (see quot. 1933).

1594 NASHE *Unfortunate Traveller* sig. F1, In emptying their phrase bookes, the ayre emptied his intrailes. **1905** G. MEREDITH *Let.* 7 May (1970) III. 1522 A pocket Italian-English phrase-book should be taken. **1963** L. DEIGHTON *Horse under Water* xiv. 60 He had used pompous phrase-book Portuguese. **1968** *Listener* 27 June 827/3 Pack one of those old-fashioned and much-mocked phrase books. **1907** 'MARK TWAIN' *Christian Sci.* II. vii. 163 These great officials are of the phrase-family of the Church-Without-a-Creed..that is to say, of the family of Large-Names-Which-Mean-Nothing. **1949** E. A. NIDA *Morphol.* (ed. 2) v. 126 In phrase-final position. **1968** *Language* XLIV. 80 The glide on the short nucleus may be phonetically long, particularly in phrase-final position. **1911** BRERETON & ROTHWELL tr. *Bergson's Laughter* ii. 114 Sometimes, too, the effect is a complicated one. Instead of one commonplace phrase-form, there are two or three which are dovetailed into each other. **1926** L. BLOOMFIELD in *Language* II. 156 The possessive [z] in *the man I saw yesterday's daughter*... Such a bound form is a *phrase-formative*. **1964** E. BACH *Introd. Transformational Gram.* vi. 137 The rules begin with a string of forms..which are bracketed by numbered boundaries of two kinds: phrase-internal and compound-internal boundaries. **1924** P. C. BUCK *Scope of Music* 39 There will come a time when the phrase-maker desires to extend his tune beyond the limits of one breath. **1967** *Listener* 22 June 835/3 Certainly 'the dramatization of the significant' (what phrasemakers these Americans are!) is a worthy aim. **1977** *Rolling Stone* 7 Apr. 63/1 He knows how to 'use' television, he's a phrasemaker, he's good-looking and has a deep voice. **1867** W. D. WHITNEY *Lang. & Stud. Lang.* 116 All word-making by combination..is closely analogous with phrase-making. **1905** *Athenæum* 25 Nov. 717/3 Phrase-making is not style.., nor is rhetoric the sole canon of speech. **1926** V. WOOLF *Writer's Diary* (1953) 96 No power of phrase-making. Difficulty in writing. **1929** C. DAY LEWIS *Transitional Poem* I. 17 Phrase-making, dress-making—Distinction's hard to find; For thought must play the mannequin. **1963** CHOMSKY & MILLER in R. D. Luce et al. *Handbk. Math. Psychol.* II. 288 We assume that such a tree graph must be a part of the structural description of any sentence; we refer to it as a *phrase-marker* (P-marker). **1965** N. CHOMSKY *Aspects of Theory of Syntax* i. 17 The *base* of the syntactic component is a system of rules that generate a highly restricted (perhaps finite) set of *basic strings*, each with an associated structural description called a *base Phrase-marker*. These base Phrase-markers are the elementary units of which deep structures are constituted. **1968** J. LYONS *Introd. Theoret. Linguistics* vi. 259 A labelled-bracketing of a string is referred to, technically, as a *phrase-marker*. Phrase-markers may also be represented by means of a tree-diagram with labelled nodes. **1971** *Archivum Linguisticum* II. 129 Removing all sequences of morphemes which can be referred to embedded phrase-markers, we are still left with complicated strings which obviously demand an ingenious transformational explanation of a kind which has not yet been offered. **1973** *Studies in Eng. Lit.: Eng. Number* (Tokyo) 52 Irrelevant structural details will hereafter be omitted from our phrase markers. **1931** G. STERN *Meaning & Change of Meaning* 2 Phrase-meanings and word-meanings. **1965** *Language* XLI. 277 A constituent string, which is always marked phrase-structurally for terminal fade. **1975** *Studies in Eng. Lit.: Eng. Number* (Tokyo) 69 They suggest..that *Jane and Bill* be generated phrase-structurally. **1957** N. CHOMSKY *Syntactic Struct.* iv. 28 The determination of the phrase structure (constituent analysis) of the derived sentence. **1960** J. B. CARROLL in Saporta & Bastian *Psycholinguistics* (1961) 337/2 In the latter part of the babbling period..there are the *first* evidences of..phrase-structures on the part of the child. **1967** D. G. HAYS *Introd. Computational Linguistics* viii. 147 A comparatively simple phrase-structure grammar produces deep structures with associated terminal strings. **1976** *Word 1971* XXVII. 257 Phrase-structure rules generate the deep-structure b-sequence from which the well-formed a-sequence is derived by transformation rules. **1957** N. FRYE *Anat. Crit.* 103 The fixed epithets and phrase-tags of medieval romance and ballad. **1933** L. BLOOMFIELD *Language* xi. 180 The forms of the type *devil-may-care* are classed as words (phrase-words) because..as a phrase *devil-may-care* would be an actor-action form, but as a phrase-word it fills the position of an adjective. **1979** *Dictionaries* I. 78 Other phrase words were very late innovations, stemming mostly from New High German times.

phrase, *v.* Add: **6. a.** (Earlier *absol.* and later *trans.* examples.)

1876 STAINER & BARRETT *Dict. Mus. Terms* 348 s.v. *Phrasing*, A performer who brings into due prominence the grouping of sounds into figures, sentences, &c., is said to *phrase* well. **1877** G. B. SHAW *How to become Mus. Critic* (1960) 29 It is easy to say that a singer 'phrases' well, because so few know what phrasing means. **1962** *Times* 15 June 13/7 All thrushes (not only those in this neck of the Glyndebourne woods) sooner or later sing the tune of the first subject of Mozart's G minor Symphony (K. 550)—and, what's more, phrase it a sight better than most conductors. **1976** *Gramophone* Oct. 611/1 He has rather a sour tone and does not phrase the music as elegantly as his rivals.

b. *Dance.* To link (movements) in a single choreographic sequence, or part of a sequence.

1959 *Times* 22 Jan. 3/4 Miss Georgina Parkinson, who phrases travelling movements with much smoothness.

phraselet (frēi·zlėt). *rare.* [-LET.] A short phrase (in music).

1925 P. A. SCHOLES *Second Bk. Gramophone Rec.* 86 The Clarinet repeats its last phraselet.

phrasial (frēi·ziăl), *a. rare.* [f. PHRAS(E *sb.* + -IAL.] Of or pertaining to (musical) phrases.

1918 *Proc. Musical Assoc.* Apr. 135 The phrasial formalities..engender a monotony.

phrasing, *vbl. sb.* Add: **2. a.** (Earlier and later examples.)

1877 [see *PHRASE *v.* 6 a]. **1921** A. RIVARDE *Violin & its Technique* i. 11 Many violinists..are constantly blustering with long bows, very often spoiling the phrasing and making violinistic rather than musical effects. **1966** *Crescendo* Feb. 35/3 To hear drum phrasing at its very best. **1976** *Gramophone* Apr. 1611/3 Though individual soloists are naturally as fine as one expects of the LSO, the style of phrasing in ensembles is stiffer than it might be.

b. in sense *6 b of the verb.

1978 *Daily Tel.* 22 Aug. 9/1 In the pas de trois,..in spite of some uncertainty over supported pirouettes, there was splendidly crisp phrasing from Kenneth McCombe and his partners.

3. *transf.*

1949 M. MEAD *Male & Female* iii. 65 All these themes are present in every cultural phrasing of the mother-child relationship. **1967** W. W. NEWCOMBE in F. Kirkland *Rock Art of Texas Indians* iv. 40/2 Certainly the two cultural complexes are phrasings of a single basic culture.

phreak (frīk), *sb.* and *v.* [Modified spelling of FREAK *sb.*[1], *v.*, under influence of *PHONE *sb.*[2], *v.*] **A.** *sb.* = *PHONE PHREAK *sb.* **B.** *vb. trans.* and *intr.* To use an electronic device to obtain (a telephone call) without payment. So **phrea·king** *vbl. sb.*

1972 *Daily Tel.* 15 Apr. 3/2 The craze started in America and there are said to be 150 'phreaks' in this country who swop information and have equipment and dialling codes which give them free use of the world's telephone system. **1972** *Oxford Times* 9 June 7/5 Used telephone codes and his expert knowledge to 'phreak' phone calls... 23 attempts at 'phreaking', of which seven were successful.

phreatic, *a.* Substitute for def.: Of, pertaining to, or designating water below the water-table, esp. that which is capable of movement. [ad. F. *phréatique* (G. A. Daubrée *Les Eaux Souterraines* (1887) I. ii. 19).] (Earlier and further examples.)

1891 R. J. HINTON *Irrigation in U.S.: Progress Rep. for 1890* (U.S. 51st Congress, 2nd Sess. Senate Ex. Doc. No. 53) 42 At the point at which most of them leave the mountain ranges there commences an enormous phreatic absorption of the volume of flow that has descended from the summit above. **1892** R. HAY *Final Geol. Rep.* (U.S. 52nd Congress, 1st Sess. Senate Ex. Doc. No. 41) III. 8 Prof. Hill has given definitions of the technical words used by him, and to his list may be added the new word *phreatic*, which is a very convenient term for underground waters which can be, or which it is hoped may be, reached by wells or other sub-ground works. [*Note*] This word was first used in American hydro-geologic investigation by the Artesian and Underflow Office in 1890. **1917** *Econ. Geol.* XII. 494 Daubrée (1887, p. 19) invented 'phreatic' from a Greek expression for 'well'... Originally..the word meant seepage water and particularly that below the water-table. It was so used by Hay (1892, p. 8) and McGee (1894, pp. 16, 42)... Suess (1909, p. 655) appears to have included in 'phreatic water' that of connate origin as well as seepage water... The writer believes that the history of the word and practical expediency should make 'phreatic' mean the infiltered waters which are bounded above by the water-table. **1954** *Times Lit. Suppl.* 5 Feb. 93/2 Theories of their [*sc.* caves'] formation are classed as 'vadose' or 'phreatic' according as it is held that caves are formed above the water-table or below it. **1966** DAVIS & DEWIEST *Hydrogeol.* ii. 42 The zone of phreatic water merges at depth into a zone of dense rock with some water in pores, although the pores are not interconnected so that water will not migrate. **1973** *Nature* 9 Nov. 77/2 After the solutional formation of a cavity beneath the water table, incision and reduction of local base level produced lowering of the phreatic surface. **1977** A. HALLAM *Planet Earth* 108 Where the top of the zone of saturation of an aquifer is a free-water surface it is known as the water table (or phreatic surface).

2. Of, pertaining to, or designating a volcanic explosion caused by the sudden heating and volatilization of underground water when it comes into contact with hot magma or rock.

1909 H. B. C. & W. J. SOLLAS tr. *Suess's Face of Earth* IV. xvi. 568 Phreatic explosions. When juvenile hydrogen encounters an unlimited quantity of vadose water, we witness a spectacle such as was presented by Krakatoa in 1883... In this case the effect may have been due to phreatic water in the neighbourhood of the sea, but when phreatic water is confined in the fissures of a limestone formation, the explosion shatters the limestone. **1926** R. A. DALY *Our Mobile Earth* iv. 158 Not all explosions are due to the pressure of magmatic gas... In the year 1888 the side of the Japanese cone, Bandai-San, was ripped out... The cavity, technically called a 'phreatic caldera', is about two miles long. *Ibid.*, The 1924 explosion at Kilauea was of phreatic character. **1964** *New Scientist* 5 Mar. 585/2 The co-existence and maintenance of such 'phreatic' activity (here ascribable to sea water suddenly flashed into steam by contact with hot lava in a vent) with the contrasting fire-fountains, characteristic of 'Strombolian' volcanic activity.., calls for somewhat unusual conditions. **1975** FIELDER & WILSON *Volcanoes of Earth, Moon & Mars* iv. 53/2 In a phreatic eruption, horizontal surges carry low density loads outwards from the eruptive centre. **1976** P. FRANCIS *Volcanoes* iv. 143 This steam sometimes blasts its way up to the surface through the lava, causing what is known as a phreatic explosion.

phreatophyte (fri,æ·tofəit). [f. Gr. φρέαρ, φρεατ- tank, cistern + -PHYTE.] A plant with a deep root system that draws its water supply from near the water-table.

1920 *Bull. Geol. Soc. Amer.* XXXI. 333 In arid regions plants of certain species habitually utilize water from the zone of saturation. For such plants the name *phreatophyte* (meaning a well-plant) has been proposed... Willow trees are among the most common phreatophytes in the arid West. **1928** *Ecology* IX. 474 The phreatophytes or 'well plants' which derive their water supply from the ground water and are more or less independent of local rainfall. **1963** D. W. & E. E. HUMPHRIES tr. *Termier's Erosion & Sedimentation* vi. 136 Most other plants in dry regions need roots long enough to reach down to the water table, or at least to its capillary fringe; these are the phreatophytes. **1965** R. G. KAZMANN *Mod. Hydrol.* v. 144 The most widespread of the desert phreatophytes in the United States are salt grass, greasewood, mesquite, and salt cedar. **1974** *Internat. Gloss. Hydrol.* 171/2 *Phreatophytes*, water-loving plants that grow mainly along stream courses and/or where their roots reach the capillary fringe.

phrenicectomy (frenise·ktŏmi). *Surg.* [f. as next + *-ECTOMY.] Surgical removal or destruction of a section of a phrenic nerve, formerly carried out as an alternative to phrenicotomy.

1929 *Surg., Gynecol. & Obstetr.* XLVIII. 274/1 The indications for phrenicectomy are lesions which may be benefited by partial compression and immobilization of a lung. **1943** B. M. DICK in C. F. W. Illingworth *Textbk. Surg. Treatm.* xxviii. 381 Phrenicectomy is used as an adjuvant to other types of collapse therapy—as an independent measure where artificial pneumothorax has failed owing to adhesions, and as a palliative for hæmoptysis, harassing cough, vomiting, or pain due to diaphragmatic adhesions. **1957** E. H. HUDSON in F. R. G. Heaf *Symposium of Tuberculosis* vii. 381 Stuertz of Cologne is credited as the first to perform phrenicectomy as a therapeutic measure in the treatment of brochiectosis of the lower lobe of the lung in 1911.

phrenicotomy (freniko̢·tŏmi). *Surg.* [f. PHRENIC *a.* (*sb.*) + -O + -TOMY.] Surgical cutting of a phrenic nerve, so as to paralyse the diaphragm on the same side.

1913 *Internat. Abstr. Surg.* XVII. 417/2 Oehlecker.. performed the phrenicostomy [*sic*] in three cases. **1926** *Encycl. Brit.* III. 691/1 Phrenicotomy (division of the phrenic nerve in the neck) is said to paralyse the corresponding half of the diaphragm; it is sometimes practised in conjunction with other means of putting one lung at rest. **1950** J. K. BERMAN *Princ. & Pract. Surg.* viii. 231 Compression of the lung is best secured by the subperiosteal resection of ribs over the affected side. Should symptoms persist after pneumothorax and phrenicotomy, thoracoplasty may be used. **1974** *Jrnl. Appl. Physiol.* XXXVII. 315/1 Tracings of pleural pressure on the intercostal and diaphragmatic surfaces under normal conditions and after complete bilateral phrenicotomy are shown in Fig. 5.

phreno-. Add: **phrenotro·pic** *a.* = *PSYCHOTROPIC *a.*

1956 [see *PSYCHOTROPIC *a.*]. **1957** *Ann. N.Y. Acad. Sci.* LXVI. 765 Ibogaine began to be of interest to us in connection with its possible phrenotropic activity.

Phrygian, *a.* (*sb.*) Add: **B.** *sb.* **a.** (Earlier and later examples.)

a **1490** J. SKELTON tr. *Diodorus Siculus' Bibliotheca Historica* (1956) I. IV. 293 Than went she downe throughout by all the lande of the Phirigians vnto the grete see. **1963** *Times* 12 Jan. 9/6 It sounded like an Aesop's fable (and it occurred suddenly to me that Aesop, a Phrygian, had lived near Sivrihisar). **1966** G. E. BEAN *Aegean Turkey* v. 125 This was a time of good relations between the Phrygians and the Greeks, when King Midas was the first barbarian to make an offering at Delphi.

c. The Indo-European language of the ancient Phrygians.

1791 W. JONES in *Asiatick Researches* (1792) III. 14 A drum is called *dindima* both in Sanscrit and Phrygian. **1888** J. WRIGHT tr. *Brugmann's Elem. Compar. Gram. Indo-Gmc. Lang.* I. 3 Of others we have only very scanty fragments left,..as of Phrygian. **1933** C. D. BUCK *Compar. Gram. Greek & Latin* 13 Phrygian is known, apart from proper names and glosses, from a few old inscriptions in an archaic Greek alphabet and some others of Christian times. **1967** M. SCHLAUCH *Language* ii. 28 Among the Indo-European languages no longer spoken, some are known to us from inscriptions (for instance, Thracian and Phrygian). **1972** W. B. LOCKWOOD *Panorama Indo-European Lang.* 174 Early or Old Phrygian survives in nearly 25 short inscriptions of doubtful date (perhaps eighth to six centuries B.C.) written in an alphabet of an archaic Greek type. A more recent form of the language, Late or New Phrygian, is found in about a hundred inscriptions in the Greek alphabet dating from the first three centuries A.D.

phthalaldehyde (fþæ̆læ·ldĭhəid). *Chem.* [f. PHTHAL(IC *a.* + ALDEHYDE.] Any of three isomeric compounds of formula $C_8H_6O_2$ having two formyl groups bonded directly to a benzene ring; *spec.* the *ortho* isomer, a yellow crystalline solid.

1886 *Jrnl. Chem. Soc.* L. 455 By the oxidation of phthalic alcohol with chromic mixture, a thick, viscid oil is obtained containing phthalaldehyde, phthalide, and unaltered phthalic alcohol. All attempts to isolate phthalaldehyde from this mixture were fruitless. **1942** *Jrnl. Amer. Chem. Soc.* LXIV. 315 (*heading*) A new synthesis of phthalaldehydes. **1951** I. L. FINAR *Org. Chem.* I. xxix. 586 When treated with ozone, naphthalene forms the diozonide and this, on treatment with water, gives phthalaldehyde. **1967** L. F. & M. FIESER *Reagents for Org. Synthesis* I. 740, *o*-Phthalaldehyde reacts with nitromethane in alcoholic alkali to give, after acidification yellow 2-nitro-3-hydroxyindene.

phthalazine (fþæ·lăzīn). *Chem.* [ad. G. *phtalazin* (C. Liebermann 1886, in *Ber. d. Deut. Chem. Ges.* XIX. 766), f. *phtal-* (cf. *phthal-* s.v. PHTHALIC *a.*) + *azin* *AZINE.] A colourless, crystalline, heterocyclic base, $C_8H_6N_2$; also, any derivative of this.

1893 *Jrnl. Chem. Soc.* LXIV. I. 347 The bye-product obtained in methylating phthalazine is very similar to the last compound. **1929** [see *CINNOLINE]. **1947** *Nature* 11 Jan. 53/2 Phthalazine derivatives are formed by the action of excess sodium hydroxide on the diazosulphonate derived from diazotized *p*-nitro-aniline and β-naphthol-l-sulphonic acid. **1956** I. L. FINAR *Org. Chem.* II. xii. 468 Phthalazines are formed by heating the benzoyl derivative of benzaldehyde hydrazones. *Ibid.* xix. 706 Thus there are probably four $C_8H_4N_2$ units, each having an *iso*indole structure,..or a phthalazine structure. **1970** W. F. BEECH *Fibre-Reactive Dyes* v. 175 Phthalazines. In this series also only one compound has so far become of importance for making reactive dyes, viz 1,4-dichlorophthalazine-6-carbonyl chloride.

phthalic, *a.* Add: *phthalic anhydride*, the anhydride of phthalic acid, a white crystalline solid, $C_8H_4O_3$, which is made industrially by the catalytic oxidation of naphthalene or *o*-xylene, and is widely used in the manufacture of plastics, resins, dyes, etc.

1855 W. ODLING tr. *Laurent's Chem. Method* 53 Thus we can obtain in a direct manner the..tartaric, camphoric, succinic, phthalic, &c., anhydrides. **1859** H. WATTS tr. *Gmelin's Hand-bk. Chem.* XIII. 15 Phthalic anhydride forms long white needles having the lustre of silk and united in feathery groups. **1913** THORPE *Dict. Appl. Chem.* (ed. 2) IV. 251/2 Owing to the extensive use of phthalic anhydride in the manufacture of synthetic indigo..a cheap technical process for its preparation in large quantities was essential. **1945** H. BARRON *Mod. Plastics* xxvii. 559 Glycerine and phthalic anhydride are the two most important constituents for alkyd resins. **1966** R. M. STEPHENSON *Introd. Chem. Process Industries* xvi. 329 About 459 million pounds of phthalic anhydride were produced in the United States in 1963.

phthalocyanine (fþælosəi·ănīn). *Chem.* [f. PHTHAL(IC *a.* + -O + CYANINE.] **a.** A greenish-blue crystalline porphyrin, $C_{32}H_{18}N_8$, or any of its substituted derivatives. **b.** Any of the metal chelate complexes of these, which form a large and important class of pigments and dyes ranging in colour from green to blue.

1933 R. P. LINSTEAD in *Rep. Brit. Assoc. Adv. Sci.* 465 When phthalimide is heated with certain metals,..in a current of ammonia, a complex reaction occurs with the formation of highly coloured substances of a novel type. These have been named phthalocyanines from their origin and deep-blue colour,.. The metal may be eliminated from the magnesium compound..to yield phthalocyanine, the parent substance of the group. **1942** *Endeavour* I. 80/2 Phthalocyanines, themselves entirely products of the chemist's skill, have resemblances to two important substances which occur abundantly in nature. **1961** COCKETT & HILTON *Dyeing of Cellulosic Fibres* v. 207 Copper phthalocyanine is the important pigment Monastral Blue BS, the lead compound being Monastral Green. **1972** RYS & ZOLLINGER *Fund. Chem. & Applic. Dyes* vii. 97 Because of their good fastness properties phthalocyanines are suitable for almost all processes in which pigments are used.

b. phthalocyanine blue (also with capital initials), copper phthalocyanine, an important blue pigment; **phthalocyanine green** (also with capital initials), a chlorinated (or brominated) derivative of copper phthalocyanine, important as a green pigment.

1942 E. R. ALLEN in J. J. Mattiello *Protective & Decorative Coatings* II. viii. 261 Likewise phthalocyanine green shows a somewhat similar relationship to orthodox pigments. **1947** L. S. PRATT *Chem. & Physics Org. Pigments* ii. 8 Other pigments which also contributed to this change were..very recently the benzidine yellows and phthalocyanine blues and greens. **1967** V. STRAUSS *Printing Industry* ix. 592/2 The development of phthalocyanine blue, perhaps better known under its duPont trade-mark as Monastral blue, was one of the greatest achievements in the field of pigments. **1968** KIRK & OTHMER *Encycl. Chem. Technol.* (ed. 2) XV. 491 Phthalocyanine green (Pigment Green 7, CI 74260) is a polychlorinated copper phthalocyanine containing about fourteen atoms of chlorine. The most usual shade is the G type although there are several shades in the G range, representing slight variations in degree of chlorination or particle size and shape. *Ibid.*, Two yellower shades of green are available as Phthalocyanine Green 27... In these types, part of the chlorine has been replaced by bromine. **1970** [see *MONASTRAL]. **1972** *Materials & Technol.* V. xi. 359 Phthalocyanine blues are intense blues which are not used in full colour because bronzing develops... Two forms are used, beta phthalocyanine blue of relatively green shade,..and the less stable alpha phthalocyanine blue, of a redder shade.

phthalylsulphathiazole (fþæ:lil,sɒlfăþəi-ă-zōul). *Pharm.* Also (*U.S.*) **-sulfa-.** [f. PHTHALYL + *SULPHATHIAZOLE.] A sulphonamide drug, $HOOC{\cdot}C_6H_4{\cdot}CONH{\cdot}C_6H_4{\cdot}SO_2NH{\cdot}C_3H_2NS$, that is a whitish powder and is used to suppress bacteria in the gastro-intestinal tract.

1943 POTH & ROSS in *Federation Proc.* II. 89/2 An extension of the studies on acylated sulfonamides as intestinal antiseptics..has uncovered another effective derivative of this series of drugs, phthalylsulfathiazole. **1961** M. HYNES *Med. Bacteriol.* (ed. 7) x. 138 Inabsorbable compounds (e.g., phthalyl-sulphathiazole) are available for oral treatment of intestinal infections. **1970** PASSMORE & ROBSON *Compan. Med. Stud.* II. xx. 25/1 Succinylsulphathiazole and p[h]thalylsulphathiazole are both poorly absorbed from the gastrointestinal tract and have been advocated for the treatment of intestinal infections and for prophylactic use in elective operations on the colon. **1977** *Proc. R. Soc. Med.* LXX. 482/1 The preliminary results of this study have shown that a combination of oral phthalylsulphathiazole and metronidazole for preparation of the bowel for surgery reduces the incidence of postoperative infection compared with phthalylsulphathiazole alone.

phthiocol (fþəi·ŏko̢l). *Biochem.* [f. PHTHI(SIS + -O + *-col* (perh. f. alco*hol*).] A yellow crystalline pigment, 3-hydroxy-2-methyl-1,4-naphthoquinone, $C_{11}H_8O_3$, originally isolated from tubercle bacilli, which has the action of vitamin K.

1933 ANDERSON & NEWMAN in *Jrnl. Biol. Chem.* CIII. 197 In order to indicate its origin, we propose to designate the pigment by the name phthiocol. **1954** H. J. ALMquist in Sebrell & Harris *Vitamins* II. ix. 393 Synthetic phthiocol tested with vitamin K-deficient chicks was found to be distinctly active in restoring normal blood-clotting time and thus became the first completely identified form of vitamin K. **1960** A. E. Bender *Dict. Nutrition* 133/2 Natural vitamin K chemically is a phylloquinone... The synthetic materials, menadione..and phthiocol (2-methyl-3-hydroxy-1:4-naphthoquinone), are more active than the naturally occurring vitamins. **1964** Asselineau & Lederer in V. C. Barry *Chemotherapy of Tuberculosis* i. 21 Phthiocol..isolated..after saponification of mycobacterial fat, is an artefact, produced from a vitamin K-like polyisoprenoid naphthoquinone.

phthioic (fþəi·ŏ,ik), *a. Biochem.* [f. Phthi(sis + *-oic.] *phthioic acid*: a yellowish oil, now known to be a mixture of fatty acids, which was orig. obtained from tubercle bacilli and is capable of inducing the symptoms of tuberculosis; hence, any of these constituent acids or their synthetic derivatives.

1929 R. J. Anderson in *Jrnl. Biol. Chem.* LXXXIII. 171 In order to indicate the relation of this acid to tuberculosis we wish to designate it by the name phthioic acid. **1946** *Nature* 5 Oct. 489/1 Phthioic acid $C_{26}H_{52}O_2$, is a liquid saturated fatty acid isolated from the lipoids of tubercle bacilli. **1951** *Chem. & Industry* 11 Aug. 685/1 Recent work on the fatty acids of the lipins of tubercle bacilli has shown that Anderson's phthioic acid was a mixture. **1964** W. Pagel et al. *Pulmonary Tuberculosis* (ed. 4) ii. 31 Phthioic acids synthetized [*sic*] by Robinson (1946) were shown to produce necrosis and granulomata in guinea-pigs.

† **phthisiatry.** *Med. Obs. rare*$^{-1}$. [f. Phthisi(s + Gr. ἰατρεία healing, medical treatment, f. ἰατρός healer.] = *phthisiotherapy.

1928 *Amer. Rev. Tuberculosis* XVIII. 105 The method can give genuinely beneficial results, and its possibilities should always be valuable in phthisiatry.

† **phthisiogenesis** (fþ-, þiziodʒe·nėsis). *Med. Obs.* [f. Phthisi(s + -o + Genesis.] The causation and development of phthisis. Hence † **phthi:siogene·tic** *a.*, causing or pertaining to the development of phthisis.

1904 C. Bolduan tr. *E. von Behring's Suppression of Tuberculosis* 45 Observations concerning the study of phthisiogenesis in man and animals. *Ibid.* 46 Improbability, so far as importance as a phthisiogenetic factor is concerned, of a primary bronchial..Tb infection. **1924** *Amer. Rev. Tuberculosis: Abstr. Tuberculosis* X. 24/2 Experimental studies on phthisiogenesis.—Inoculation of human tubercle bacilli into the tonsils or soft palate in rabbits of different ages resulted in a tuberculosis running the course of pulmonary phthisis. **1936** *Univ. Durham Coll. of Medicine Gaz.* XXXVI. 128 The study of phthisiogenesis involves the reconciliation of..much discordant data.

phthisiology. Add: (Examples.) Hence **phthisiolo·gical** *a.*; **phthisio·logist,** a specialist in phthisiology.

1913 *Q. Jrnl. Med.* VI. 259 Artificial pneumothorax has become the topic of the day in phthisiological literature. **1928** *Amer. Rev. Tuberculosis* XVIII. 110 The general conclusions..were not accepted at once by phthisiologists. **1946** H. T. Hyman *Integrated Pract. Med.* III. civ. 2208 The indications for inducing an artificial pneumothorax are best discussed by the practitioner with the consultant phthisiologist. **1947** *Ibid.* IV. clxxxii. 3901 In the larger medical communities and fully staffed institutions, internal medicine is subdivided... Thus there are established departments of gastro-enterology, hematology,..phthisiology, metabolism, [etc.]. **1953** *Tubercle* XXXIV. 237/1 It is most deplorable that phthisiologists ever applied and accepted so wrong and unfitting a term [*sc.* therapeutic 'collapse'] to a condition which in fact is no 'collapse' at all. **1957** F. R. G. Heaf *Symposium of Tuberculosis* p. xv, The amount of disablement caused by bone and joint tuberculosis in oversea countries is very great, so the chapter dealing with this subject should be of value to the general physician and surgeon, as well as the specialist in phthisiology.

phthisiophobia (fþ-, þizioföu·biă). *Med.* [f. as next + -phobia.] An unjustified or exaggerated fear of tuberculosis.

1906 J. B. Huber *Consumption* xi. 445 It is really deplorable to consider the degree of cruelty and selfishness to which this phthisiophobia has driven people. **1948** F. M. Pottenger *Tuberculosis* xxxvi. 579 If we frighten people into believing that tuberculosis is a highly infectious disease.., we create an unnecessary and harmful phthisiophobia, which reacts against the patient.

† **phthisiotherapy** (fþ-, þizioþe·răpi). *Med. Obs.* [f. Phthisi(s + -o + Therapy.] The medical treatment of phthisis. Also **phthi:siotherapeu·tics** *sb. pl.*

1899 S. A. Knopf *Pulmonary Tuberculosis* xix. 284 Modern phthisio-therapeutics, as carried out in well-equipped sanatoria, must be practically studied. **1900** Dorland *Med. Dict.* 505/1 Phthisiotherapy. **1903** *Med. Rec.* (N.Y.) 2 May 719/1 There is abundant evidence..of his deep interest in phthisiotherapy. **1934** *Amer. Rev. Tuberculosis* XXX. 188 The maintenance by each sizeable sanatorium of a resident thoracic surgeon whose special training in phthisiotherapy can be relied upon to aid in careful selection of suitable cases for surgical collapse.

Hence **phthi:siotherapeu·tist, phthisiothe·rapist,** a specialist in or practitioner of phthisiotherapy.

1899 S. A. Knopf *Pulmonary Tuberculosis* xix. 285 The peculiar psychological state of nearly all phthisical patients..makes it necessary for the true phthisiotherapeutist..to be..his best and most confidential friend. **1907** *Med. Rec.* (N.Y.) 9 Nov. 758/2 The pneumatic cabinet..although long since discarded by most phthisio-therapists, has been persistently used by a few. **1929** *Amer. Rev. Tuberculosis* XIX. 76 There are some phthisiotherapists..who advocate rib-resection in lieu of pneumothorax. **1933** *Jrnl. Amer. Med. Assoc.* 4 Feb. 313/1 Collapse therapy is considered by the majority of expert phthisiotherapists to have created a revolution in the treatment of pulmonary tuberculosis. **1939** *Amer. Rev. Tuberculosis* XXXIX. 162 The value of artificial pneumothorax in closing open cavities is admitted by every phthisiotherapeutist.

phugh, var. Phew *int.*

1889 E. Dowson *Let.* 30 June (1967) 88, I think it is possible for the feminine nature to be reasonably candid & simplex, up to the age of 8 or 9. Afterwards—phugh! **1892** [see Phew *int.*].

phugoid (fiū·goid), *a.* and *sb.* [f. Gr. φυγή flight (*sb.*[2] in Dict.: erron. taken for Flight *sb.*[1]) + -oid.] **A.** *adj.* Of or pertaining to the longitudinal stability of an aircraft flying a nominally horizontal course in a vertical plane; applied *spec.* to a slow fore-and-aft oscillation in which the flight path assumes the form of a series of shallow waves and the aircraft undergoes synchronous increases and decreases of speed.

1908 F. W. Lanchester *Aerodonetics* ii. 37 The Phugoid theory deals with the longitudinal stability, and the form and equations of the flight path of an aerodone. *Ibid.* 40 This is the general equation to the curves of flight or the phugoid equation. *Ibid.* iii. 59 The plotting of the phugoid curves forming a complete series, from the straight line representing the path of uniform gliding, to the tumbler type of curve with constants varying to any desired degree, may be termed a phugoid chart. **1920** *Flight* XII. 817/1 They would talk of bumps and pitching when, of course, they merely meant anabatics or katabatics, or peradventure nothing more serious than a phugoid oscillation. **1965** G. Sutton *Mastery of Air* v. 125 The enhanced speed brings about an increase in lift, which ultimately stops the descent and causes the machine to climb again. At the top of the climb the machine has insufficient lift to maintain itself and if left alone will fall again and so on. This is the phugoid oscillation, consisting of a wave-like path or a series of loops. **1974** H. Ashley *Engin. Anal. Flight Vehicles* iii. 62 The latter situation arises..during the higher portion of the entry trajectory of a lifting glider. The long-period or phugoid longitudinal mode may then have a period as great as half the total interval required for entry.

B. *sb.* A phugoid oscillation.

1908 F. W. Lanchester *Aerodonetics* ii. 42 With these two equations we are in a position to investigate the general characteristics and particular forms of the curves of flight or Phugoids, as they may be appropriately termed. **1945** *Jrnl. R. Aeronaut. Soc.* XLIX. 346/1 He became so interested in a phugoid that he allowed it to develop beyond control, and he found himself spinning inverted at 33,000 feet. **1948** L. M. Milne-Thomson *Theoret. Aerodynamics* xvi. 309 A phugoid is the path of a particle which moves under gravity in a vertical plane and which is acted upon by a force L normal to the path and proportional to V^2, the square of the speed. **1975** L. J. Clancy *Aerodynamics* xvi. 485 The consequence of the disturbance is an oscillation in which the aircraft successively gains and loses height, while losing and gaining forward speed. This oscillation is known as a phugoid.

phulkari. For '*East Ind.*' read '*N. India*'. (Earlier and later examples.)

1872 B. H. Baden-Powell *Hand-bk. Econ. Products of Punjab* II. ix. 100/1 'Phúlkárí' (*lit.* 'flower work') scarf, value Rs. 11. *Ibid.* x. 106 Over the head is thrown a 'chádar' of coarse cloth, prettily embroidered in many colored silks, called 'phulkári'. **1887** H. G. H. Blackwood *Jrnl.* 1 Dec. in *Our Viceregal Life in India* (1889) II. xiii. 224 They were collected in a small inner court, which was hung with the pretty phulcarries they make here. **1888** Mrs. F. A. Steel in *Jrnl. Indian Art* II. 72 Intending purchasers..should remember that *phulkari* work is a true art. *Ibid.*, *Phulkaris* are still a necessary part of a Hindu and Sikh bride's trousseau. **1893** G. Birdwood in *Catal. Loan Exhib. Embroidery by Indian Women* (Soc. Encouragement Indian Art) 15, I did not know of any needlework being produced by the women of India for sale, excepting the *phul-kāri* (*i.e.*, 'flower-work'). **1969** *Eve's Weekly* (Bombay) 20 Dec. 43/1 Another in magenta white and saffron phulkari against brown is styled on the same lines. **1969** *Femina* (Bombay) 26 Dec. 8/4 She had revived an old art like the 'phulkari'... The applique work was bold and mirror work pretty. **1971** *Sunday Australian* 8 Aug. 46 Phulkari embroidery is the traditional work used on all the linen items in a girl's glory box.

Phurnacite (fʊ̄·ɹnăsəit). Also **phurnacite.** A proprietary name for a kind of smokeless fuel made by carbonizing briquettes at relatively low temperatures.

1937 *Trade Marks Jrnl.* 10 Feb. 150/1 Phurnacite... Powell Duffryn Associated Collieries, Limited,..London, ..colliery owners. **1951** *Good Housek. Home Encycl.* 32/1 Smokeless fuel, the bulk of which is known as Phurnacite. **1952** *Economist* 1 Nov. 332/2 The favourite small coals of the domestic consumer—anthracite and the best briquettes—remain scarce. The board [*sc.* the National Coal Board] still has only one—now considerably enlarged—plant making 'phurnacite', which is an excellent but expensive carbonised briquette. **1955** *Times* 4 July 5/5 Welsh coals..and 'Phurnacite', a member of the manufactured fuel group, are still restricted, but coke, 'Coalite', and 'Rexo' are said to be freely available. **1976** *Guardian* 10 Apr. 10/8 The coalman poured the sack of phurnacite into the bunker.

phut. Substitute for entry:

phut (fɒt), *int.* (*adv.*, *sb.*). Also **fut.** [Echoic, but cf. Hindi and Urdu *phatnā* to split or burst.] An imitation of a dull, abrupt sound, esp. that of a firearm. Also as *sb.*, the sound of something 'going phut'. Phr. *to go phut*: to come to a sudden end; to break down, cease to function.

1888 Kipling *Story of Gadsbys* (1889) 55 The whole thing went *phut*. She wrote to say that there had been a mistake. **1892** —— & Balestier *Naulahka* 259 The hospital has all gone *phut*. **1898** [see *fut]. **1898, 1905** [in Dict.]. **1908** A. S. M. Hutchinson *Once aboard Lugger* III. iii. 150 The plans..have all gone fut. **1917** 'Contact' *Airman's Outings* 242 He will sometimes hear the rattle of a mysterious machine-gun, or even the phut of a bullet. **1917** W. J. Locke *Red Planet* xiii. 156 There's a limit to the power of bearing strain. As soon as you feel you're likely to go *fut*, throw it all up and come and see me. **1918** A. Quiller-Couch *Foe-Farrell* 47 'It's a lie!' Foe was on his legs, and he fairly shouted it. Shell-shock? Phut!—It exploded right at our feet below the platform. **1919** G. Page *Veldt Trail* i. 10 The carburetter went *fut* yesterday. **1921** *Punch* 30 Nov. 429/1 Send me a subject with a bit more pep in it or the Club will go phut. **1923** *Daily Mail* 22 Jan. 8 He stood to lose some enormous number of millions of marks if Germany went *phut*. **1926** S. Horler *Order of Octopus* 238 Now that this pet stunt.. had gone phut. **1931** E. F. Benson *Mapp & Lucia* x. 270 She'd still have been terribly interested in life till she went phut. **1972** *Daily Tel.* (Colour Suppl.) 24 Nov. 7/3 The kids had broken a window, and the colour television had gone phut. **1973** H. Carvic *Miss Seeton Sings* (1974) 72 The trigger pulled and—*phut*, the enemy dropped dead. *Ibid.* 83 Never before had this place been used for target practice, with things that went *phut*. **1978** D. Bloodworth *Crosstalk* xxi. 164 It was a bomb... But when it went off it was only like some kind of firecracker, just, you know—phut!—and that was it.

Hence **phut** *v. intr.*, to land with an abrupt sound; to 'go phut', to cease to function.

1901 [see *fut *v.*]. **1916** G. Frankau *Guns* 26 Waking, they know the instant foe, the bullets phutting by. **1959** J. Verney *Friday's Tunnel* xxvii. 250 He and Robin.. got inside last night, only the torch phutted.

phut-phut, *sb.* and *v.* [Reduplication of prec.] = *put-put *sb.*, *v.*

1951 M. R. Anand *Seven Summers* 78 The sahibs who came on bicycles or 'phut-phuties'. **1952** R. Finlayson *Schooner came to Atia* 144 Phut-phut goes the exhaust. **1956** 'J. Wyndham' *Seeds of Time* 39 He listened to the phut-phutting of the old engine. **1958** J. Carew *Black Midas* vi. 103 The motor sputtered, then settled down to a steady phut-phutting. **1958** *Spectator* 10 Oct. 479/2 People on the outskirts would receive less noise from a vtol airliner than from a clip-on phut-phut passing along the road outside their houses. *a* **1966** M. Allingham *Cargo of Eagles* (1968) xi. 129, I dropped over on my phut-phut about half past eight. **1971** *Guardian* 14 May 11/1 Phutt-phutting around London on her three-wheeled scooter. **1977** P. Harcourt *At High Risk* i. 93 The schoolkids were streaming out of the *lycée* and tearing up the street on their phut-phutting *quarante-neufs*.

phwat, repr. an Ir. pronunc. of What *pron.*, etc.

1898 J. D. Brayshaw *Slum Silhouettes* ii. 12 Oh, murther aloive! Phwat did ye do that for? **1914** R. Brooke *Let.* Nov. (1968) 630 'How many handkerchiefs have you?'..'How many phwat, sorr?' **1920** 'Sapper' *Bull-Dog Drummond* vi. 154 And phwat the divil has that got to do with it, at all? **1936** M. Franklin *All that Swagger* xvii. 164 But seeing phwat has happened, I can do no other.

phy (fəi), slang abbrev. of *physeptone.

1971 *Guardian* 30 Mar. 11/6 There is thus now a completely new group [of drug addicts in Britain] on methadone, or 'phy' (physeptone is the British word for which the World Health Organisation title, methadone, is being substituted). **1973** *Times* 22 Mar. 6/2 She said to him: 'Do you want some phy (Physeptone)?' and made it quite clear that she meant the drug.

phyco-. Add: **phycolo·gical** *a.*, of, pertaining to, or dealing with, phycology; **phycologist** (later examples); **phycology** (earlier and later examples); **phy·coplast** *Cytology* [-plast], an array of microtubules found between pairs of nuclei in algal cells after mitosis (see quot. 1972).

1892 (*title*) Phycological memoirs, being researches made in the Botanical Department of the British Museum. Edited by George Murray. **1895** J. D. Hooker *Let.* 9 June in L. Huxley *Life J. D. Hooker* (1918) II. xli. 294, I have this morning received..a notice published in the 'Phycological Memoirs' of *Pachytheca*, which is enough to turn your hair grey—if it were not so already! **1954** *Nature* 14 Aug. 294/1 The botanical world, and more especially the phycological section of it, has suffered grievous loss in the passing of Prof. Fritsch. **1973** J. R. Stein (*title*) Handbook of phycological methods. **1951** G. W. Prescott in G. M. Smith *Man. Phycology* i. 4 The marine phycologist Harvey..established many genera. **1969** *Brit. Phycological Jrnl.* IV. 141 Virtually the whole of his [*sc.* Hustedt's] career as a phycologist was devoted to diatoms. **1847** J. LINDLEY *Elem. Bot.* (ed. 5) p. lxx/2 Phycology. That part of Botany which treats of Sea-weeds. **1935** J. E. TILDEN *Algae* p. v, Phycology offers an enormously stimulating field for research. **1951** G. W. PRESCOTT in G. M. Smith *Man. Phycology* i. 1 The history of phycology is as old as the history of botany. **1976** *Biol. Abstr.* LXI. 6112/1 The history of marine phycology in New England (USA) is summarized, followed by citations emphasizing recent research dealing with the local marine algal vegetation. **1972** J. D. PICKETT-HEAPS in *Cytobios* V. 63 Since this disposition of microtubules is so common in algae, I have coined the term 'phycoplast' to describe it. This implies that it can to some extent be considered an analogue of the higher plant cell phragmoplast, but its main distinguishing feature is the orientation of its constituent microtubules in the plane of cytoplasmic cleavage. **1975** *Nature* 6 Nov. 32/1 The unicellular condition, the possession of basal bodies, flagella, a closed centric spindle, a phycoplast and cell division by furrowing, are deemed to be primitive features.

phycobilin (fəikobəi·lin). *Bot.* [a. G. *phycobilin* (R. Lemberg 1929, in *Naturwissenschaften* XVII. 541/2): see PHYCO- and BILIN.] **a.** Any of a group of compounds that are present in some algæ as prosthetic groups of chromoproteins such as phycocyanin and phycoerythrin. **b.** Also *phycobilin pigment.* Any of these chromoproteins.

1945 E. I. RABINOWITCH *Photosynthesis* I. xv. 417 The separation of the chromophoric groups from the carrier protein was achieved by Lemberg (1929), who introduced the name 'phycobilins' because of the similarity between these chromophores and the bile pigments. **1950** *Jrnl. Gen. Physiol.* XXXIII. 418 Light absorbed by the phycobilin pigments (phycoerythrin and phycocyanin) is utilized with good efficiency. **1962** C. Ó hEOCHA in R. A. Lewin *Physiol. & Biochem. of Algae* xxv. 421 Photosynthetically active red and blue biliproteins, called phycoerythrins and phycocyanins, respectively, have been isolated only from algae. Their prosthetic groups or chromophores are tetrapyrroles known as phycobilins. Unlike the chlorophylls, phycobilins are not readily released from associated proteins. **1965** BELL & COOMBE tr. *Strasburger's Textbk. Bot.* 466 Rhodophyceae, red algae... Chlorophyll and the associated carotinoids..are masked by a red, strongly fluorescent, water-soluble pigment, phycoerythrin (a phycobilin..with absorption-bands differing from those in the Cyanophyceae). **1971** *Nature* 26 Nov. 232/1 One of the first obvious effects of nitrogen starvation in blue-green algae is the disappearance of phycobilin pigments, which normally constitute about 15% of the dry weight.

phycobiliprotein (fəi:kobəiliprōu·tīn). *Bot.* [f. prec. + PROTEIN.] Any chromoprotein having a phycobilin as the prosthetic group; a phycocyanin or a phycoerythrin.

1966 *Brookhaven Symp. Biol.* XIX. 402 The blue-green algae have predominantly phycocyanin as the major phycobiliprotein. **1975** *Nature* 24 Jan. 285/2 The chlorophylls, carotenoids and phycobiliproteins of the blue-green algae are particularly similar to those of the red algae.

phycobilisome (fəikobəi·lisōum). *Bot.* [f. as prec. + *-SOME[4].] In certain algæ, a photosynthetic granule containing phycobiliprotein.

1966 GANTT & CONTI in *Brookhaven Symp. Biol.* XIX. 404 The following are the reasons for considering these chloroplast granules of *P[orphyridium] cruentum* as sites of phycobilin aggregation... For these granules we propose the name phycobilisomes. **1971** *Jrnl. Cell Biol.* XLVIII. 285/2 Whereas it is true that phycobilisomes have not yet been found in every species of red and blue-green algae, they are believed to exist in all photosynthetic species of these two groups. **1976** *Nature* 24 June 697/2 Those [algal cells] from *Diploısoma virens*.. show no evidence of phycobilisomes on the thylakoids.

phycobiont (fəikobəi·ǫnt). *Bot.* [f. PHYCO- + Gr. βιουντ-, pr. pple. stem of βιοῦν to live, f. βίος life.] The algal component of a lichen; any alga which is associated with a fungus to form a lichen.

1957 G. D. SCOTT in *Nature* 2 Mar. 486/2 Three new terms are here proposed... They are: (1) 'phycobiont', applicable to an alga in association with a fungus in the formation of a lichen; [etc.]. **1962** *New Scientist* 28 June 719/1 Efforts have previously been made to investigate the exact nature of the relationship between the algal partner (sometimes called the phycobiont) and the fungus. **1969, 1973** [see *MYCOBIONT]. **1976** G. C. AINSWORTH *Introd. Hist. Mycol.* iv. 98 The phycobiont frequently shows no apparent differences from its free-living counterpart.

phycomycete (fəi·koməisīt). *Bot.* [sing. of mod.L. *Phycomycetes* (A. de Bary *Morphol. & Physiol. der Pilze* (1866) p. vi), f. PHYCO- + MYCETES.] A fungus belonging to one of the primitive groups formerly included in the class Phycomycetes, nearly always characterized by a vegetative thallus without septa and either asexual reproduction by means of sporangiospores or conidia or sexual reproduction by means of oospores or zygospores. Also *attrib.* Cf. *phycomycetous* adj. s.v. PHYCO-.

[**1887** H. E. F. GARNSEY tr. *A. de Bary's Compar. Morphol. & Biol. Fungi* iv. 132 Groups 1–4 [of the Ascomycete series] have been brought together under the name of Phycomycetes on account of their close approximation to the Algae.] **1932** *Bot. Gaz.* XCIII. 427 The attachment of the flagellum or flagella of the phycomycete zoospore is usually posterior or lateral. **1933** *Trans. Brit. Mycol. Soc.* XVIII. 199 (*heading*) *Azygozygum chlamydosporum* Nov. gen. et sp. A phycomycete associated with a diseased condition of *Antirrhinum majus*. *Ibid.* 201 The Phycomycete was isolated from several varieties of *Antirrhinum*. **1936** *Forestry* X. 14 All three species showed mycorrhizal infection of the well-known 'phycomycete type'. **1976** G. C. AINSWORTH *Introd. Hist. Mycol.* ix. 236 The most important [aquatic fungi] taxonomically were the phycomycetes.

phycomycosis (fəi:koməikōu·sis). *Path.* Pl. **-mycoses.** [f. *PHYCOMYC(ETE + -OSIS.] Infection with or a disease caused by phycomycetes, esp. the genera *Mucor*, *Rhizopus*, or *Absidia*; mucormycosis.

1959 LIE-KIAN-JOE et al. in *Amer. Jrnl. Clin. Path.* XXXII. 62/1 We use the name phycomycosis to designate a fungous infection caused by a member of the Phycomycetes. It is proposed in order to avoid the more restricted connotations of mucormycosis, and includes infections caused by Mucor, Absidia, Rhizopus, Mortierella, Basidiobolus, and similar Phycomycetes. The name is useful, too, for mycoses in which no culture was obtained but in which sections of involved tissues reveal the presence of a fungus with the morphology usually associated with a Phycomycete. **1965** [see *MUCORMYCOSIS]. **1972** *Radiology* CIII. 332/2 Craniofacial phycomycosis appears to originate by invasion of the nasal mucosa.

phylactology (fəi:læktǫ·lŏdʒi). *nonce-wd.* [f. Gr. φυλακτ-ός or -ήριος vbl. adjs. f. φυλάσσειν to guard + -OLOGY.] The science or business of counter-espionage. Hence **phylactolo·gical** *a.*; **phylacto·logist.**

1966 K. AMIS *Anti-Death League* I. 18 Apparently what's called the philosophy of phylactology—spy-catching to you—has been transformed. *Ibid.* 108, I had no idea you were practised in phylactological thought. *Ibid.* III. 269 This mere technician, this electrical eavesdropper, seemed to imagine he was on a level with a qualified phylactologist like himself.

† **phylaxis** (filæ·ksis). *Path. Obs.* [ad. Gr. φύλαξις watching, guarding; cf. *ANAPHYLAXIS.] The protection of a cell or organism against the effects of a toxin, esp. a neurotoxin, by the action of an artificially introduced substance which prevents its uptake by cells. Hence **phyla·ctic** *a.*

1913 [see *ANAPHYLAXIS]. **1919** A. E. WRIGHT in *Lancet* 29 Mar. 490/1 To combat bacterial infection the organism must have defensive powers. That power of guarding itself against infection we may—the suggestion is Lord Moulton's—call phylactic power. The leucocytes and the bacteriotropic substances in the blood fluid we may call phylactic agents. **1931** H. GAINSBOROUGH tr. *Billard's Phylaxis* i. 11 After a discussion with G. Ramon and in agreement with him..I adopted a new term—phylaxis. *Ibid.* iii. 29 (*heading*) Phylaxis by certain mineral waters against certain neurotoxins. *Ibid.* 40 As regards the phylactic action of sparteine I have insisted at some length on the particular affinity of the neurotoxins for the lipoids. **1931** *Times Lit. Suppl.* 3 Dec. 985/4 Phylaxis is a conception mainly due to Professor Billard's experiments.

phyletic, *a.* Insert at beginning of etym.: [a. G. *phyletisch* (E. Haeckel *Generelle Morphologie der Organismen* (1866) II. xx. 299).] Substitute for def.: Of or pertaining to the development of a species or other taxonomic group. (Later examples.)

1928 *Brit. Jrnl. Med. Psychol.* VIII. 59 It is my essential position that what we call mental is itself physiological when viewed in a social or phyletic as well as in an individual or ontogenetic sense. **1933** *Proc. Linn. Soc.* CXLV. 155 He does not claim that his analysis necessarily represents the true phyletic position of the various species. **1943** [see *group-analysis* s.v. *GROUP *sb.* 6 b]. **1944** G. G. SIMPSON *Tempo & Mode in Evolution* vii. 205 Phyletic evolution goes on continuously ..in populations of all sizes and kinds. **1951** G. H. M. LAWRENCE *Taxon. Vascular Plants* ii. 96 Some phylogenists have given too little attention to the phyletic significance of pollen grain and starch grain morphology. **1963** DAVIS & HEYWOOD *Princ. Angiosperm Taxon.* ii. 44 Both *phyletic* and *phylogenetic* refer to the course of evolution and are virtually interchangeable. **1969** E. MAYR *Princ. Systematic Zool.* x. 251 Species living at the present time are the current end points of innumerable phyletic lines. **1972** *Sci. Amer.* Jan. 98/3 Individuals representing nothing more than successive stages of a single phyletic line have in a number of cases been assigned distinctive taxonomic names, as if they had actually been contemporaries and neighbors. **1973** A. J. POMERANS tr. *Piaget & Inhelder's Memory & Intelligence* 2 Our first problem, then, is to distinguish between the acquired memory (or the memory proper) and the phyletic memory or conservation and utilization of hereditary information.

phyletically, *adv.* Add: Also, regarding a common evolutionary descent. (Further examples.)

1930 *Psyche* XI. ii. 10 After all, the whole field of man's unconscious life..must be regarded phyletically as man's inattention in the immediate moment. **1933** *Proc. Linn. Soc.* CXLV. 162 A and B may be the nearest allies phyletically. **1950** [see **intention movement*]. **1951** G. H. M. LAWRENCE *Taxon. Vascular Plants* v. 99 The Magnoliales are phyletically old. **1965** ZUCKERKANDL & PAULING in Bryson & Vogel *Evolving Genes & Proteins* III. 164 Any variants within a given type of tertiary structure and function seem to have a much greater chance to be phyletically related than unrelated. **1976** *Nature* 24 June 694/1 Many species will evolve phyletically with no change in size.

phyletism (fəi·lĕtiz'm, fī-). Also erron. **philetism** (perh. infl. by PHILO-). [f. Gr. φυλέτ-ης fellow tribesman, f. φυλή tribe: see -ISM.] In the Orthodox Church, an excessive emphasis on the principle of nationalism in the organization of church affairs; a policy which attaches greater importance to ethnic identity than to bonds of faith and worship.

The term is applied chiefly in hist. use to the claim of the Bulgarian Church to jurisdiction over Bulgarian nationals in all parts of the world, leading in 1872 to the condemnation passed by the Synod of the Ecumenical Patriarchate in Constantinople and to a schism between the Greek-speaking Orthodox churches and the Bulgarian Church which lasted until 1945.

1900 'ODYSSEUS' *Turkey in Europe* 285 The Patriarchate..stigmatised by the name of Phyletism the doctrine that persons of a particular race..are entitled to a separate ecclesiastical administration. **1907** A. FORTESCUE *Orthodox Eastern Church* IV. x. 278 He finds Philetism to be a deadly heresy. Poor Patriarch!.. Shall he denounce Philetism, stand out for the old rights of the hierarchy and of the chief sees, preach unity and ancient councils? **1923** R. L. LANGFORD-JAMES *Dict. Eastern Orthodox Church* 99/1 Phyletism is the error of the undue exaltation of the necessary independence of National Churches, so that Nationalism in religion overshadows Catholicism. **1927** B. J. KIDD *Churches of Eastern Christendom* xii. 301 This last phase of shrinkage and retreat, ending..in the emancipation of the Balkan nations, had encouraged Philetism and diminished the range of the Patriarch's authority by the creation of National Churches. **1957** tr. *V. Lossky's Mystical Theol. Eastern Church* i. 15 The view which would base the unity of a local church on a political, racial or cultural principle is considered by the Orthodox Church as a heresy, specially known by the name of *philetism*. **1961** D. ATTWATER *Christian Churches of East* II. 248 *Phyletism*.., the name by which the patriarch of Constantinople condemned a form of nationalism in the Orthodox Church in 1872. **1974** *Encycl. Brit. Macropædia* VI. 159/1 The council [of 1872] condemned 'phyletism'—the national or ethnic principle in church organization—and excommunicated the Bulgarians, who were certainly not alone guilty of 'phyletism'.

phylic (fəi·lik), *a.*[1] [f. Gr. φυλ-ή tribe + -IC.] Of or pertaining to a Greek phyle or tribe.

1891 *Jrnl. Hellenic Stud.* XII. 30 The increase of the *Phylae* involved changes in the institutions based upon the phylic system. **1908** J. L. MYRES in R. R. Marett *Anthropol. & Classics* 142 The solidarity of the Greek phylic institutions.

phylic (fəi·lik), *a.*[2] *Psychol.* [f. PHYL(UM + -IC.] Of or relating to the phylum (sense *b). Also *absol.*

1949 T. BURROW *Neurosis of Man* vii. 169 As an outgrowth of this phylic principle of integration, the individual remains always an integral element within the organism of man as a unit. **1952** W. J. H. SPROTT *Social Psychol.* 246 The fault lies mainly in our individualism, or, rather, in our isolationism. We have over-developed the 'private' and lost touch with the 'phylic'. **1953** T. BURROW *Sci. & Man's Behavior* vi. 74 The term 'species'..has no adjectival form. In order to fill this breach, I adopted 'phylic', from *phylum*, which in its original Greek had the meaning of 'tribe'.

phyllo-. Add: **phy·llomorph** [Gr. μορφή form], the representation of a plant in art; **phy·llosphere**, the surface area of the leaves, or, more generally, of all the parts of a plant above ground.

1889 *Trans. Lancs. & Cheshire Antiquarian Soc.* VII. 166 The forms of ornament demonstrably due to structure require a name... Those taken from animals are called zoomorphs, and those from plants phyllomorphs. **1895** A. C. HADDON *Evol. Art* 126 The terms 'zoomorph' and 'phyllomorph' have been employed for the representation in art of plants and animals. **1955** F. T. LAST in *Trans. Brit. Mycol. Soc.* XXXVIII. 221 It is suggested that, as with roots and the 'rhizosphere', leaves have a 'phyllosphere', with a characteristic micro-flora that may contain many species. **1956** J. RUINEN in *Nature* 4 Feb. 221/2 These observations suggested the existence of a characteristic milieu which is conditioned by the leaf, and may be called, in analogy with the rhizosphere, the 'phyllosphere'. **1972** J. G. CRUICKSHANK *Soil Geogr.* vi. 175 On the surface of living aerial parts of plants, particularly on the leaves—the phyllosphere.

phyllocarid (filokæ·rid). *Zool.* [a. mod.L. name of division *Phyllocarida* (A. S. Packard 1879, in *Amer. Naturalist* XIII. 128), f. PHYLLO- + Gr. καρίς shrimp, prawn.] A crustacean belonging to a group of the subclass Branchiopoda, which includes those types distinguished by the broad, flat limbs known as phyllopodia. Also *attrib.* Hence **phylloca·ridan** *a.*

1882 A. S. Packard in *Amer. Naturalist* XVI. 870 He [*sc.* Claus] failed to appreciate the independent, synthetic nature of the Phyllocaridan type. **1896** *Proc. Geol. Soc.* LII. p. xcvi, We have here..a passage upward from the more ancient Phyllocarid type..to the more modern Cumacea. **1902** *54th Ann. Rep. N.Y. State Mus. Nat. Hist. 1900* I. 98 The museum record of localities now bears the following entries at which species of these phyllocarids have been obtained. **1911** *Geol. Mag.* VIII. 64 In the black shales we succeeded in finding organic remains, including..a bivalve phyllocarid crustacean. *Ibid.*, A few specimens of a bivalve phyllocarid allied to *Caryocaris* and *Lingulocaris.* **1935** Twenhofel & Shrock *Inverteb. Paleontol.* x. 444 Nebaliacea—A heterogeneous group of living and fossil phyllocarids. **1973** P. Tasch *Paleobiol. of Invertebr.* xi. 600/2 There have been several finds of fossil phyllocarids with appendages preserved.

phyllopodium (filopōu·diǒm). [f. Phyllo- + Podium.] **1.** *Bot.* The base of a leaf stalk, or the main axis of a leaf.

1884 F. O. Bower in *Phil. Trans. R. Soc.* CLXXV. 569, I therefore propose the term phyllopodium to express the whole of the main axis of the leaf, exclusive of its branches. **1923** —— *Ferns* I. v. 82 The branches are then arranged in two longitudinal rows, one on either side of a central stalk or rachis, which is continuous below into the stipe or petiole, often of considerable length. The whole of this, including petiole and rachis, may be styled the Phyllopodium. **1951** McLean & Ivimey-Cook *Textbk. Theoret. Bot.* I. xvi. 653 Delpino..described the stem as a pseudaxis or phyllopodium. *Ibid.* xxii. 978 The mature leaf consists of three portions, the lamina, the petiole, and the leaf base or phyllopodium. *Ibid.* 979 (*caption*) Development of the phyllopodium as a leaf sheath.

2. *Zool.* (See quot. 1967.)

1926 L. A. Borradaile in *Ann. & Mag. Nat. Hist.* XVII. 194, I have..argued in support of the view that all the post-antennulary limbs of the primitive crustacean were alike, and that they were flat structures with endites and exites. It is convenient to call such appendages 'phyllopod limbs' or phyllopodia, whether they occur in the Phyllopoda (Branchiopoda) or elsewhere. *Ibid.*, The phyllopodium has all the essentials of a biramous limb. **1967** P. A. Meglitsch *Invertebr. Zool.* xviii. 755/1 An unusual feature of the branchiopods is the soft, flattened type of trunk appendage characteristic of most of the groups. Covered with a delicate cuticle, they are flexible enough to move freely without segmentation. This type of appendage is known as [a] phyllopodium.

phylloquinone (filokwi·nōun). *Biochem.* [ad. G. *phyllochinon* (Karrer & Geiger, at the suggestion of H. Dam, in *Helv. Chim. Acta* (1939) XXII. 946), f. Gr. φύλλον leaf + G. *chinon* quinone (cf. China[3] 2).] Vitamin K_1, a yellow, fat-soluble oil that is present in green leafy vegetables and is important in blood clotting; 2-methyl-3-phytyl-1,4-naphthoquinone, $C_{31}H_{46}O_2$.

1939 *Chem. Abstr.* XXXIII. 8191 The light yellow vitamin K_1 from alfalfa, named by Dam..'α-phylloquinone', (I) crystallizes at low temp. **1953** Fruton & Simmonds *Gen. Biochem.* xxxviii. 908 Vitamin K_2 (2-methyl-3-difarnesyl-1,4-naphthoquinone), which is formed by some bacteria.., differs from phylloquinone only in the substituent in the 3 position of the naphthoquinone ring. **1970** R. W. McGilvery *Biochem.* xxvi. 651 (*caption*) Phylloquinones from plants are absorbed to some extent as such, and they have vitamin K activity. However, the side chain is removed from most of the ingested compounds by intestinal bacteria; the resultant menadione is absorbed and a new side chain is constructed to create menaquinone, the principal form of vitamin K found in animals. **1972** *Materials & Technol.* V. xix. 692 Menadione, phylloquinone and the menaquinones can all be obtained synthetically, but only menadione is produced in any quantity.

phyllosilicate (filosi·likēit). *Min.* [a. G. *phyllosilikat* (H. Strunz 1938, in *Zeitschr. für ges. Naturwiss.* IV. 185), f. as prec.: see Silicate.] Any of the group of silicates characterized by SiO_4 tetrahedra linked in sheets of indefinite extent in which the ratio of silicon and aluminium to oxygen is 2:5.

1947 *Mineral. Abstr.* X. 52 The different types of SiO_4 bonding give at last a systematic classification of silicates into nesosilicates.., sorosilicates.., inosilicates.., phyllosilicates.., and tectosilicates. **1966** *McGraw-Hill Encycl. Sci. & Technol.* XII. 312/1 The phyllosilicates as a group typically have a platy crystal habit, with a cleavage parallel to the plane of layering of the structure, and are optically negative with rather high birefringence. **1972** *Nature* 1 Sept. 7/1 Phyllosilicates are the most common material in carbonaceous meteorites.

phylo-. Add: **phyloana·lysis** *Psychol.*, analysis of an individual that takes account of him as part of a phylum (sense *b); hence **phyloa·nalyst; phyloanaly·tic** *a.*; **phylogero·ntism,** phylogerontic character or condition.

1930 T. Burrow in *Psyche* XI. II. 67 (*heading*) Physiological behavior-reactions in the individual and the community: a study in phyloanalysis. **1940** Hinsie & Shatzky *Psychiatric Dict.* 418/2 Phyloanalysis regards the symptoms of the individual and of society as but outer aspects of impaired tensional processes which affect the balance of the organism's internal reaction as a whole. **1949** T. Burrow *Neurosis of Man* vii. 168 Phyloanalysis set out with the attempt to analyse the affecto-symbolic 'I'-persona and its special prerogative as commonly assumed by social man; and it undertook to differentiate this pseudo-entity from the organism's biological basis of integration and behaviour. **1933** W. Galt *Phyloanalysis* II. i. 113 The phyloanalyst does not at all credit the obvious manifestation. **1932** T. Burrow *Struct. Insanity* vi. 66 The aim, therefore, of the phyloanalytic method is the application of a technique that will enable the patient to acquire a facility for rendering his own physiological tensions objectively perceptible to him. **1902** *Amer. Naturalist* XXXVI. 940 In the majority of specialized gastropods phylogerontism is expressed, not in the non-coiling of the last portion of the spire, but in its expansion and wrapping about the earlier whorls.

phylogenesis. Add to etym.: [coined in Ger. (E. Haeckel *Generelle Morphologie der Organismen* (1866) II. xx. 299).] (Later examples.) Also *transf.*

1926 W. McDougall *Introd. Social Psychol.* (ed. 20) 402 The psychologist may legitimately speculate on the problems of phylogenesis; but he is under no obligation to offer any phylogenetic theory. **1940** Hinsie & Shatzky *Psychiatric Dict.* 418/2 The biological concept of phylogenesis has been used in different ways for analytical analogies in the psychological sphere, in order to emphasize the role of racial elements in the manifestations of the psyche. **1957** *Times Lit. Suppl.* 1 Nov. 659/1 He [*sc.* Jung] claimed that the doctrine which asserts that ontogenesis is a repetition of phylogenesis was also true of psychic life. **1966** Davis & Zangerl tr. *Hennig's Phylogenetic Systematics* iii. 199 Phylogenesis is the origin of groups of species from a stem species and its descendants by progressive splitting. **1977** P. Johnson *Enemies of Society* xvii. 226 Since the phylogenesis of music is communication, it must have a structure.

phylogeneticist (fəi:lo,dʒĕne·tisist). [f. Phylogenetic *a.* + -ist.] = Phylogenist.

1968 R. D. Martin tr. *Wickler's Mimicry in Plants & Animals* iii. 39 The famous phylogeneticist George Gaylord Simpson called for a detailed investigation.

phylogenetics (fəi:lo,dʒĕne·tiks), *sb. pl.* [f. Phylogenetic *a.*: see -ic 2.] The study of phylogeny, esp. the factors influencing its course. (Usu. const. as *sing.*)

1937 K. Faegri in *Bot. Rev.* III. 400 (*heading*) Some fundamental problems of taxonomy and phylogenetics. *Ibid.* 422 Phylogenetics: the science of the tribal history and descent (phylogeny) of plants and animals. **1966** Davis & Zangerl tr. *Hennig's Phylogenetic Systematics* iii. 201 Determining the significance of individual factors in the total evolutionary process is the unique task of phylogenetics. **1975** *Nature* 18 Dec. 641/2 Palaeogenetics ..as well as protein phylogenetics..assume that comparative analyses of amino acid sequence data..yield a realistic image of evolution.

phyloge·nically, *adv.* [f. Phylogenic *a.*: see -ically.] = Phylogenetically *adv.*

1975 *Nature* 5 June 483/1 So far the only studies on the teratogenic effects of this virus have been in the chick embryo and rodents, animals phylogenically distant from *Homo sapiens.*

phylogeny. Add coinage details to etym.: [(E. Haeckel *Generelle Morphologie der Organismen* (1866) I. iii. 57).] **1.** Also, the evolutionary development of particular organs or other components of a plant or an animal. (Further examples.)

1897 *Bot. Gaz.* XXIV. 172 We are warranted in strenuously urging a conformity of taxonomy with phylogeny. **1901** *Trans. Linn. Soc.* (*Zool.*) VIII. 270 The Plates attached to this paper represent with approximate accuracy the phylogeny of the intestinal tract in birds. **1940** J. S. Huxley *New Systematics* 19 Phylogeny may be almost hopelessly obscured by parallel or convergent evolution. **1953** E. Mayr et al. *Methods & Princ. Systematic Zool.* iii. 42 It is the avowed aim of a modern classification to reflect phylogeny. **1971** J. Z. Young *Introd. Study Man* xxxv. 486 We cannot measure the development of the frontal lobes in phylogeny accurately.

2. (Earlier example.)

1872 [see *bathmic *a.*].

phylum. Add: Also *transf.* and *fig.*

1945 Auden *Coll. Poetry* 162 Whole phyla of resentments every day Give status to the wild men of the world Who rule the absent-minded. **1971** *New Scientist* 25 Mar. 682/1 We have to regard science as a 'phylum' (as the term is used by Pierre Teilhard de Chardin)—that is, as an expanding movement within the four-dimensional space-time continuum of the social system. **1973** *Sci. Amer.* Apr. 121/1 Computers are no longer individuals with names but a phylum of many species, rapidly evolving under selection pressures.

b. *Psychol.* The human race or group as it is relevant to the development of the individual.

1927 T. Burrow in *Brit. Jrnl. Med. Psychol.* VII. 199 The social group or phylum. *Ibid.* 202 In a comprehensive view of our human phylum there remains no other conclusion than that the social mind..comprises a systematization of social images. **1930** —— in *Psyche* XI. II. 69 Medicine, then, became a science when the symptoms of the individual ceased to be the focus of interest and when interest became focussed instead upon the pathological germ or cause of definite alterations of tissue and their characteristic symptoms, as these..were observed within the organism of man..as a species or phylum. **1940** H. G. Baynes *Mythol. of Soul* I. xii. 460 The concept of individuality as a self-contained, self-regulating organism has no validity unless it also embraces this backward extension of the ancestral phylum. **1953** T. Burrow *Sci. & Man's Behavior* vi. 73 Some of my colleagues commented upon the unusual sense in which I use the term 'phylum'... By this term I do not mean to separate man from the rest of the vertebrates. I am merely trying to discuss man, with his social needs and interests, as a biological organism.

2. *Linguistics.* A group of languages related, or believed to be related, less closely than those of a family or stock.

1958 H. Hoijer in R. H. Thompson *Migrations in New World Culture Hist.* 59 There is no indication that the families of a phylum, or the phyla of a macro-phylum, need be connected by clearly statable phonetic correspondences. **1965** *Canad. Jrnl. Linguistics* X. 142 The reconstruction (by comparative method linguistics) is systematic... The reconstruction (in phylum linguistics) is illustrative and restricted to a relatively small set of cognates and typological samenesses which point to an earlier phylum parent language in the prehistoric era. **1973** A. P. Sorensen in D. R. Gross *Peoples & Cultures of Native S. Amer.* 333 Two of them represent the comparative method linguistics approach..; the other two represent the phylum linguistics approach. **1973** *Language* XLIX. 239 Tarascan, like Zuni, is a one-language phylum.

-phyre (fəiᵊɹ), comb. form of Porphyry used in names of porphyritic rocks, as Granophyre, *keratophyre.

physaliferous (fəisăli·fĕrəs), *a. Biol.* [f. Gr. φυσαλλ-ίς bladder + -iferous.] = *physaliphorous *a.*

1954 G. L. Fite tr. R. Virchow in *Amer. Jrnl. Leprosy* XXII. 209 They [*sc.* the cells] have one characteristic that is especially noteworthy, i.e., their tendency to form a sort of vacuole, apparently from taking up water, so that under the circumstances they acquire a wholly physaliferous appearance. **1977** *Proc. R. Soc. Med.* LXX. 276/2 A large number of the cells had a vacuolated cytoplasm with hyperchromatic nuclei, the pattern being that of 'physaliferous' cells characteristic of a chordoma.

physaliphore. Add: (Earlier example.)

1860 F. Chance tr. *R. Virchow's Cellular Path.* xviii. 401 (*caption*) Endogenous new formation; cells containing vesicles (physaliphores).

Hence **physali·phorous** *a.*, that contains vesicles; cf. *physaliferous *a.*

1964 D. F. Cappell *Muir's Textbk. Path.* (ed. 8) xvii. 701/2 The tumour tissue [of a chordoma] consists of lobules of rounded or polyhedral cells arranged in alveoli or cords: some of these cells contain numerous intracytoplasmic vacuoles of mucin, 'physaliphorous cells'.

physalis (fəi·sălis, fəisēi·lis). [mod.L. (Linnæus *Hortus Cliffortianus* (1738) 62), f. Gr. φυσαλλίς bladder, in reference to the inflated calyx.] An annual or perennial herb of the genus so called, belonging to the family Solanaceæ, mostly native to North or Central America, and bearing white, yellow, or purple flowers and, in some species, edible red or purplish berries; cf. Alkekengi, *Cape gooseberry* s.v. Cape *sb.*[3] 4 in Dict. and Suppl., *Chinese lantern* (*plant*) s.v. *Chinese *a.* 2, *ground-cherry* b s.v. Ground *sb.* 18c, Winter cherry 1 a.

1807 *Curtis's Bot. Mag.* XXVII. 1068 (*heading*) Eatable Physalis or Cape Gooseberry. **1907** T. W. Sanders *Flower Garden* 196 The Physalises belong to the Nightshade order. **1930** *Times Educ. Suppl.* 18 Oct. 431/2 The windows of the florists are bright just now with the fruits of physalis, the winter cherry. **1961** *Amat. Gardening* 30 Sept. 7/2 'Lanterns' of physalis..can be skeletonised. **1968** S. C. Emberton *Garden Foliage* ix. 219 Mustard yellow achillea and orange 'lanterns' of physalis teamed up with bulrushes.

Phys. Ed., phys. ed., colloq. abbrev. of **physical education.* Also *attrib.*

1955 *Amer. Speech* XXX. 304 *Phys ed major*, mannish female. **1957** O. Nash *You can't get there from Here* 84 Get them interested in hotel management and phys. ed. **1968** A. Holden *Death after School* iv. 31 There's the Phys Ed man. **1972** P. Marks *Collector's Choice* ii. 82 A converted basement of the Phys Ed building. **1977** *Time* 9 May 50/3, I was very poor on the parallel bars, and my phys.-ed class came at the damn wrong hour.

Physeptone (fəise·ptōun). *Pharm.* Also **physeptone.** A proprietary name for methadone hydrochloride. Cf. *phy.

1947 *Lancet* 6 Sept. 370/2 (*heading*) Miadone (Physeptone) in obstetrics. **1948** *Trade Marks Jrnl.* 15 Sept. 743/1 Physeptone... All goods included in class 5 [*sc.* pharmaceutical, veterinary and sanitary substances, etc.]. The Wellcome Foundation Limited,..London,.. manufacturing chemists. **1951** *Pharmaceutical Jrnl.* CXII. 52/1 An inquest was held at Coventry on a three-year-old boy who died from an overdose of Physeptone linctus. **1969** *Daily Tel.* 3 Feb. 22/6 Physeptone, a narcotic drug first used in America for the gradual withdrawal of drug addicts from heroin, is proving successful in 'weaning' British addicts off hard drugs. **1971** [see *phy]. **1972** J. Brown *Chancer* ii. 30 She was on 5 and 3 at the time—five one-sixth grains of heroin and three ten-milligram ampoules of physeptone. **1976** H. Ferguson *Confessions Long Distance Acid Head* 7 Apart from cannabis, I have used barbiturates, amphetamines,.. the synthetic opiate physeptone, morphine, cocaine,.. even apomorphine once.

physic, *sb.* Add: **6. physic-box** (later Austral. example).

1900 H. Lawson *On Track* 55 An' if yer don't get yer physic-box an' come wi' me, by the great God I'll—.

physical, *a.* Add: **I. 1.** (Earlier example of *physical cause*.)

1605 Bacon *Adv. Learning* ii. 29 For the handling of finall causes mixed with the rest in Phisicall enquiries, hath intercepted the seuere and diligent enquirie of all reall and phisicall causes.

3. c. as *sb.* A medical examination to determine physical fitness.

1934 N. Sainsbury *Gridiron Grit* in *Stirring Football Stories* (1941) 77 He found that everybody had had the same idea about physicals and that there were at least forty candidates..ahead of him. **1944** H. McCloy *Panic* 131 If you imagine he didn't try to get in the Army, you're mistaken... I saw him each time he got back from his physical. **1968** *Guardian* 28 Dec. 1/5 A day of medical tests—which will go far beyond the 'complete physical' that an ordinary citizen knows. **1973** W. McCarthy *Detail* i. 66 Doctor Miller will see you..for a short physical. **1978** N. Freeling *Night Lords* xix. 89 No cop got sent to investigate his own appartment block... It was..like a doctor being asked to give his own wife a physical.

d. Characterized by or suggestive of bodily (as distinct from mental or psychological) activities or attributes. Of a person or activity: inclined to be bodily aggressive or violent.

1970 J. G. Vermandel *Dine with Devil* xii. 77 He's obviously one of these tremendously *magnetic* types. And you Scorpios are so *physical*, aren't you? **1972** J. Mosedale *Football* vii. 100 Facing the very physical Philadelphia team. **1974** 'J. Le Carré' *Tinker, Tailor* viii. 59, I was feeling pretty physical. Frustrated, you could almost say. **1975** J. Mitchell *Smear Job* xiii. 104 It's up to you. Either you belt up or I'll get physical. **1976** *Ilkeston Advertiser* 10 Dec. 16/3 Morton became involved and there was 'some physical horseplay'. **1978** *Rugby World* Apr. 8/3 Rugby is a physical game.

II. 7. physical anthropology, the study of the evolution of man and animals closely related to him, involving the observation or measurement of anatomical features, growth rates, genetic mechanisms, etc.; so **physical-anthropological** *a.*; **physical anthropologist; physical astronomy** (earlier example); **physical chemistry,** substitute for def.: the application of the techniques and theories of physics to the study of chemical systems; the study of the interrelation of chemical and physical properties; (earlier and later examples); so *physical-chemical* adj. (= physico-chemical), *physical chemist*; **physical culture,** the development of the body by exercise; hence **physical culturist,** an advocate or exponent of physical culture; **physical drill,** physical exercises; **physical education,** regular instruction in bodily exercise and games, esp. in schools; **physical geography** (earlier example); **physical jerks**: see *jerk *sb.*[1] 2 d; **physical metallurgy,** the science dealing with the structure and physical properties of metals; **physical object** *Philos.*, an object that exists in space and time and that can be perceived; also *attrib.*; **physical therapy** = *physiotherapy; hence **physical therapist,** a physiotherapist; **physical torture** *slang*, physical training; **physical training,** the systematic use of exercises to promote physical fitness.

1958 G. Daniel *Megalith Builders of W. Europe* i. 25 The word race is used..in its strict physical-anthropological connotation of a group of people with heritable physical characteristics in common. **1878** *Jrnl. Anthrop. Inst.* VII. 540 The physical anthropologist often regards the prehistoric worker as an antiquarian only, whilst the former is sometimes simply looked upon in the light of a demonstrative anatomist. **1936** R. Linton *Study of Man* ii. 23 The first physical anthropologists..believed that every species and variety was the result of a separate act of creation and was therefore fixed and unchangeable. **1974** *Times* 8 Nov. 12/4 The leprous bones were identified by..a physical anthropologist (an expert with skeletons). **1873** A. L. Fox in *Jrnl. Anthrop. Inst.* II. 361 The two expeditions which have lately left this country for Central Africa..have been furnished with detailed notes and queries on general anthropology, physical anthropology, religions, myths, customs, [etc.]. **1904** W. L. H. Duckworth *Morphol. & Anthropol.* ii. 14 This application of the principles of Morphology to the special case of Man constitutes the essence of Physical Anthropology. **1923** A. L. Kroeber *Anthropol.* i. 5 Biological or physical anthropology—'Somatology' it is sometimes called in Anglo-Saxon countries, and simply 'anthropology' in continental Europe—has in part constituted a sort of specialization or sharpening of general biology. **1951** E. E. Evans-Pritchard *Social Anthropol.* i. 3 Physical anthropology..is a branch of human biology and comprises such interests as heredity, nutrition, sex differences, the comparative anatomy and physiology of races, and the theory of human evolution. **1976** *Ann. Rev. Anthropol.* V. 5 Hrdlicka was the founding father of American Physical Anthropology. **1834** *Penny Cycl.* II. 529/2 The third department of astronomy..is that which goes under the name of *physical astronomy*, and consists in the combination of the various phenomena as actually observed, in order to find out what are their physical causes, and according to what laws those causes act. **1964** *Economist* 29 Feb. 790/1 The Humboldt university, of whose physical-chemical institute he is the director. **1967** *Oceanogr. & Marine Biol.* V. 63 It shows itself essentially in the form of a dome structure..which can be detected in all the physical-chemical properties of the water. **1971** *Who's Who* 331/1 *Bowen*, Edmund John... Papers on physical chemical subjects in scientific journals. **1929** *Amer. Jrnl. Physiol.* LXXXIX. 171 Physical chemists.. have criticized methods which make use of tubes of small diameter. **1935** *Discovery* Apr. 98/2 A problem for a physical chemist, assisted by a bio-chemist. **1893** I. Remsen *Princ. Theoret. Chem.* (ed. 4) p. v, I have been tempted to change the book fundamentally and give it a character more in keeping with the recent tendencies of work in the field of Physical or General Chemistry. **1898** C. L. Speyers *Text-bk. Physical Chem.* i. 1 Physical Chemistry is the science which has for its object the investigation of chemical changes by physical methods. **1940** Glasstone *Text-bk. Physical Chem.* p. xi, Obviously, atomic combination involves atomic forces, and it is one of the objects of physical chemistry to see how far the chemical interactions observed between atoms and molecules can be interpreted by means of the forces existing within and between atoms. **1966** *McGraw-Hill Encycl. Sci. & Technol.* X. 203/1 There are three different approaches to the study and use of physical chemistry: thermodynamics,..kinetics,..and molecular structure. **1867** S. D. Kehoe *Indian Club Exercise* 18 Having discoursed..on the important benefits to be derived from physical culture..we will now describe some of the special means of exercise. **1893** *Harper's Mag.* Apr. 668/2 In the high-school department,..further instruction is given in.. physical culture. **1912** V. L. Whitechurch *Thrilling Stories of Railway* 11 He was a strong faddist on food and 'physical culture'. **1963** D. Webster *Compl. Physique Bk.* ii. 9 In all the systems of physical culture existing throughout the world non-apparatus work plays a most important part. **1904** C. L. Neil *Mod. Physical Culture* xviii. 115 (*heading*) The physical culturist's library. **1936** *Discovery* Nov. 362/2 The concluding chapter deals with the athlete, and it is of great value to the physical trainer and culturist. **1960** J. Hewitt *Yoga* iii. 56 A large number of the exercises popular with physical-culturists in the West are taken from Yoga. **1915** W. Owen *Let.* 30 Oct. (1967) 362 This morning we had 'Physical Drill' under a special Gymnastic Instructor. **1838** S. Smiles *Physical Education* 10 Here we may state what is the scope and object of a proper physical education. **1858** *Southern Cultivator* XVI. 32/1 The subject of physical education is beginning to attract attention. **1895** W. Maclaren in A. Maclaren *Physical Educ.* (rev. ed.) p. v, It is now more than thirty years since the demand for systematized Physical Education began to make itself heard in this country. **1926** *Encycl. Brit.* III. 141/2 Physical education..includes systematic and graded exercises chosen for their physiological and corrective results, folk-dancing, swimming, organized games and sports. **1960** *Where* No. 3. 16 *Physical Education* (*PE*), the current term for what most parents remember as 'gym' or PT. **1977** E. W. Hildick *Loop* ix. 54 A Physical Education teacher. **1808** J. Playfair *Syst. Geogr.* I. p. ccv, To narrate the appearances which nature exhibits to our view, and to give an idea of what is movable and immovable upon, and under the surface of the earth, is the province of *Physical Geography*. **1914** Physical metallurgy [see *metallurgy]. **1935** Williams & Homerberg *Princ. Metallogr.* (ed. 3) i. 1 Metallography is commonly subdivided into..(1) production metallurgy..and (2) physical metallurgy. **1956** A. W. Chapman in D. L. Linton *Sheffield* x. 212 The faculty includes a postgraduate School of Physical Metallurgy in which the teaching is specially adapted to provide men from industry with instruction. **1965** R. W. Cahn *Physical Metallurgy* p. v, Physical metallurgy..is the root from which the modern science of materials has principally sprung. **1912** B. Russell *Probl. Philos.* i. 18 The real table, if it exists, we will call a 'physical object'. Thus we have to consider the relation of sense-data to physical objects. **1952** *Mind* LXI. 505 His only irrefutable position is to reduce his physical object claim to an announcement concerning his own sensations. **1954** A. J. Ayer *Philos. Ess.* iv. 88 This procedure..serves to clarify the meaning of statements about physical objects by relating them to statements of a different logical form. **1973** —— *Cent. Questions Philos.* iii. 62 What Hume calls the philosophical account of physical objects differs from the vulgar account in that it distinguishes them from perceptions. **1954** Physical therapist [see *crash *sb.*[1] 7 b]. **1922** *Lancet* 2 Dec. 1175/1 The first edition of this book appeared in 1910. Notable advances in physical therapy have now necessitated the preparation of a second edition. **1973** R. Kraus *Therapeutic Recreation Service* i. 19/1 In the fields of occupational therapy or physical therapy, professional training is carried on in close cooperation with medical authorities or educators. **1900** *Dialect Notes* II. 48 *Physical torture*, physical culture. **1920** *331st Field Artillery* (U.S.) 417 The officers,..knowing that boat drills were something of a bore, attempted to make them more interesting..by giving us 'physical torture' at these times. **1959** I. & P. Opie *Lore & Lang. Schoolch.* ix. 173 One feels Lewis Carroll would have liked the current terms Physical Torture (for P.T.) and Religious Destruction or Ridiculous Kapers (for R.K.). **1968** W. C. Anderson *Gooney Bird* iii. 35 The physical torture program..started promptly at 0630 every morning at Eglin Air Force Base. **1889** *Infantry Drill* 11 *Physical training*. In order to expand his chest, and develop his muscles, the soldier will be practised in the following exercises. **1910** Street & Gooderson *Handbk. Physical Training* i. 12 Physical training at schools should provide for the stimulation of the physiologic functions of the body. **1926** *Encycl. Brit.* III. 141/2 The model course, which originally consisted largely of military drill, has developed into the present Syllabus of Physical Training, based on the Swedish system. **1974** *Oxf. Jun. Encycl.* (rev. ed.) IX. 270/2 In the forces and in club work the aim is to train performers in set exercises and vaults which.. are the result of physical training as opposed to physical education.

physicalism (fi·zikăliz'm). *Philos.* [f. Physical *a.* 2 + -ism.] A term originally used by members of the Vienna Circle for the theory that all science must eventually be capable of being expressed in the language of physics.

1931 O. Neurath in *Monist* XLI. 618 (*title*) Physicalism: the philosophy of the Viennese Circle. *Ibid.* 620 In a sense unified science is physics in its largest aspect, a tissue of laws expressing time-space linkages—let us call it: Physicalism. **1936** L. Bloomfield in *Language* XII. 93 The testing of this hypothesis of *physicalism* will be a task of the next generations, and linguists will have to perform an important part of the work. **1940** B. Russell *Inquiry into Meaning & Truth* 93 The thesis which Carnap calls 'physicalism', which maintains that all science can be expressed in the language of physics. **1965** *Language* XLI. 196 He [*sc.* Bloomfield]..recommended a policy known first as 'mechanism' or 'antimentalism', later as 'physicalism' which..amounted to the emancipation of linguistics from irrelevant psychologizing... Bloomfield himself was not able to pursue this policy with complete success. **1972** *Science* 16 June 1204/3 Science has been..historically associated with a philosophy of physicalism, the belief that reality is all reducible to certain kinds of physical entities. **1975** *Jrnl. Philos.* LXXII. 565 Physicalism does not entail reductionism, at least if we follow Hellman and Thompson in taking reductionism to mean explicit definability.

physicalist. Add: *Philos.* **2.** One who adheres to the theory of physicalism. Also as *adj.*, of or pertaining to such a theory.

1934 *Times Lit. Suppl.* 5 July 479/1 The paper now translated was first published in 1932..under the title of 'Physicalist language as the Universal Language of Science'. **1937** J. R. Firth *Tongues of Men* ix. 119 Let us turn to the 'physicalists' or 'methodical materialists' of the Vienna Circle. **1956** A. J. Ayer *Probl. Knowl.* 214 To apply the physicalist thesis to one's own experiences, is, as it were, to pretend to be anaesthetized. **1959** H. Kuhn in P. A. Schilpp *Philos. C. D. Broad* xx. 606 The German *Geisteswissenschaft* and Phenomenology..have labored to rouse modern thought from its dogmatic physicalist slumber. **1972** R. Plant in Cox & Dyson *20th-Cent. Mind* III. iii. 69 The relationship [between behaviour and pain] is not an external, contingent one as the dualist would suggest, nor is it a necessary one as the behaviourist or physicalist would claim. **1973** A. J. Ayer *Cent. Questions Philos.* vi. 126 Materialists, or physicalists as they are now more often called, who deny the existence of mental as opposed to physical events.

physicalistic (fizikăli·stik), *a.* [f. Physicalist + -ic.] Pertaining to or characterized by physicalism. Hence **physicali·stically** *adv.*

1934 M. Black tr. *Carnap's Unity of Sci.* 95 For the sake of precision we might supplement or replace 'physical language' by the term '*physicalistic language*'; denoting by the latter the universal language which contains not only physical terms (in the narrow sense) but also all the various special terminologies (of Biology,..etc.) understood as reduced by definitions to their basis in physical determinations. **1949** M. Schlick in Feigl & Sellars *Readings in Philos. Analysis* 407 The validity of the physicalistic assertion would be ever more restricted. **1954** Webster Add., Physicalistically. **1956** A. J. Ayer *Probl. Knowl.* v. 210 It is only if such statements [about thoughts, feelings] are interpreted 'physicalistically' that they can convey any information from one person to another. **1972** *Science* 16 June 1204/3 To physicalistic philosophy they [*sc.* altered states of consciousness] are epiphenomena. **1978** P. Pettit in Hookway & Pettit *Action & Interpretation* 51 Something as deep as the physicalistic prejudices of natural science or the postulates of rational man theory.

physicality (in Dict. s.v. Physical *a.*). Add: (Later examples.)

1944 M. Weitz in P. A. Schilpp *Philos. B. Russell* 73 Here Russell objects because..some entities, the unperceived entities of physics, even though they are neutral—i.e., have no first-order property of mentality or physicality—cannot be brought into psychological causal laws. **1948** *Mind* LVII. 8 Ayer chooses to call the commonly accepted criteria of physicality (the various meanings attached to the word 'physical world') 'assumptions'. **1953** *Mind* LXII. 26 Ontological assumptions concerning the nature of physicality.

2. The quality that pertains to physical sensation or to the body as distinct from the mind.

1849 J. S. Mill *Lett.* (1910) I. 143 Take again all the delicacies respecting bodily physicalities which savages have not a vestige of. **1930** E. Sitwell *Coll. Poems* 126 This bestial consciousness that is desire Is the hot muscles' vast fluidity, Muscular life, not physicality. **1964** *Listener* 27 Aug. 317/1 The climax is Thornhill's visit to a bullfight. The terse physicality of Mr Scott's style, his ability to evoke place and register action, avoids much suggestion of the derivative. **1972** C. L. Cooper in W. King *Black Short Story Anthol.* 218 The trunk of her, he saw self-consciously, with a tiny tickle of physicality, was full to bursting with youth under the plain dress. **1977** *N.Y. Rev. Bks.* 24 Nov. 42/4 Dancing, because of its immediate physicality, its shift in time and space, has a fluid plausibility which is apparently undemanding.

phy·sicalize, *v.* [f. PHYSICAL *a.* + -IZE.] *trans.* To express or represent by physical means, *spec.* in the theatre, to represent (an idea) in physical terms, as the movements of the body of an actor. So **physicaliza·tion,** the representation of an idea by physical means.

1947 E. KAZAN in Cole & Chinoy *Directing Play* (1953) 297 An effort to put poetic names on scenes to edge me into stylizations and physicalizations. Try to keep each scene in terms of Blanche. *Ibid.* 308 Stanley..is completely self-absorbed to the point of fascination. To physicalize this: he has a most annoying way of being preoccupied—or of busying himself with something else while people are talking with him. **1972** *Village Voice* (N.Y.) 1 June 54/4 Its publicized aim: 'to explore various means of physicalization to test the theory that theatre should be a hieroglyphic of speaking icons'. **1977** *Rolling Stone* 7 Apr. 14/3 Lily is particularly taken with Rick at the moment, partly because when she did him on the 'friends of Lily Tomlin' videotape, when she 'physicalized' him by wearing a moustache, sideburns and leather jacket, strutting and tugging at his/her crotch, hardly anyone recognized that the stud was her.

physico-. Add: **phy·sicomorph,** a representation in art of an inanimate object or phenomenon of the physical world; **physico-philosophical** *a.* (example); **phy:sico-psycholo·gical** *a.*, pertaining both to the physical and the psychological.

1895 A. C. HADDON *Evol. Art* 118 Under the term of 'physicomorph' I propose to describe any representation of an object or operation in the physical world. **1977** M. COHEN *Sensible Words* 145 The restrictiveness of Ong's view can be estimated by his determination to turn Swift into a stubborn, and unhappy, physicophilosophical writer. **1927** A. HUXLEY *Proper Stud.* 34 It is..only in the abstract that we can discuss the varieties of intelligence without considering the varieties in the other constituents of the physico-psychological personality.

physico-chemical, *a.* Add: (Later examples.) So **phy:sico-che·mically** *adv.*; **physico-chemist** (later examples); **phy:sico-che·mistry.**

1885 I. B. YEO tr. *Oertel's Respiratory Therapeutics* II. 731 It has been thought that the diminution of air pressure acts physico-chemically in another sense. **1909** *Jrnl. Industr. & Engin. Chem.* Mar. 158/2 Unless my friends, the physico-chemists, will..discover some way for establishing some optical properties or other physical constants, we are very much at a loss to establish the molecular size of my product. **1934** *Current Res. Anesthesia & Analgesia* XIII. 86 (*heading*) The physico-chemistry concerned in the action of anesthesia on blood colloids in relation to the safer handling of surgical and anesthetic risks. **1953** S. E. LURIA *Gen. Virol.* iv. 82 Their tendency to lengthwise and sidewise aggregation has rendered their study by hydrodynamic methods a most perplexing problem for the physicochemist. **1958** *Times Lit. Suppl.* 10 Jan. 14/4 He looks forward to the day when psychological changes can be correlated convincingly with physico-chemical processes. **1966** *Mineral Abstr.* XVII. 739/2 The physicochemistry and origin of the deposits are discussed. **1969** *Listener* 20 Mar. 389/1 Goldmann believes that the social sciences cannot be conducted on the model of what he calls the 'physico-chemical' sciences. **1970** AMBROSE & EASTY *Cell Biol.* viii. 258 Studies of the permeability of membranes to gases, water, non-electrolytes, and ions were interpreted physico-chemically. **1971** I. G. GASS et al. *Understanding Earth* viii. 120/1 The physico-chemical conditions within the meteorite parent bodies. **1972** *Nature* 3 Mar. 44/1 The physico-chemistry of fibrous proteins. **1973** *Ibid.* 21–28 Dec. 528/1 The crystals were identified physico-chemically by their solubility in HCl, by the Meingen reaction, by infrared spectroscopy, and by petrographic microscopy. **1977** *Dædalus* Summer 66 The neurological and physicochemical bases of human behavior are clearly not exhausted by genetically fixed enduring neuronal pathways.

† physicotherapy (fizikoþe·răpi). *Obs.* [f. PHYSICO- + THERAPY.] = *PHYSIOTHERAPY.

1903 *Med. Rec.* (N.Y.) LXIII. 881/2 Dr. J. Rivière of Paris advocated the employment of physicotherapy, or the combined action of electricity, heat, and light, in the treatment of uterine fibromata.

Hence **† phy:sicotherapeu·tic** *a.*, physiotherapeutic.

1904 *Nature* 21 Jan. 280/1 The results achieved..in the treatment of inoperable malignant growths by physicotherapeutic means.

physio-. Add: **physioplastic** *a.* (further examples); **phy:sio-psycho·logy,** physiological psychology; so **phy:sio-psycholo·gic, -lo·gical** *adjs.*

1943 Physioplastic [see *IDEOPLASTIC *a.*]. **1939** *Burlington Mag.* June 300/2 The familiar opposition between geometrical and 'vital' forms, impressionist and expressionist art, 'ideoplastic' and 'physioplastic', and so on, is shown to possess a concrete sanction in the aesthetic attitudes of blind artists. **1932** G. BLUMER in *Practitioners Libr. Med. & Surg.* I. ix. 698 Constitution, which includes physiopsychologic factors, may change considerably during life. **1874** J. CUNNINGHAM *New Theory of Knowing* 155 Every one..knows what is meant by getting a 'start', though the physio-psychological explanation of it is not so clear. **1875** C. WRIGHT *Let.* 12 July in R. B. Perry *Tht. & Char. W. James* (1935) I. 530 The other is in a book-notice by him [*sc.* William James]..of Wundt's physio-psychology. **1903** *Amer. Anthropologist* V. 586 In a general way, comparative physio-psychology has aided us in the search for the key to this great problem [of various intellectual endowment].

physio (fi·zio). Colloq. abbrev. of *PHYSIOTHERAPIST or *PHYSIOTHERAPY.

1962 *Times* 3 July 5/3 They should, like the orthopaedic physiotherapists, also be nurses... I tell my physios: 'Keep your hands off, keep your minds on.' **1967** PARTRIDGE *Dict. Slang* Suppl. 1291 *Physio*, physiotherapy. **1968** M. WOODHOUSE *Rock Baby* iii. 21 Don't have him doing full knee bends... Reminds me, I must get in the physios chop-chop. **1971** 'J. BELL' *Hole in Ground* iv. 59 Dr Colthorp wants her to have physio after the plaster comes off. **1973** *Times* 7 Feb. 15/3, I remember we didn't have a physio of our own, so we had to go to the athletics one. **1977** *Lancet* 5 Feb. 301/2 His details are entered in the book for the agreed date, with comments such as 'very fat' or 'needs pre-op physio'.

physiognomic, *a.* (*sb.*) Add: **3.** *Ecol.* Of or pertaining to the physiognomy of a plant community (*PHYSIOGNOMY 4b).

1911 BEVIS & JEFFERY *Brit. Plants* ii. 16 The physiognomic groups into which we have divided the vegetation (woodland, grassland, heath, etc.) are only in part associated with definite types of climate. **1926** TANSLEY & CHIPP *Study of Vegetation* x. 204 It is..by the physiognomic characters of the vegetation, especially when correlated with some topographic feature, that the traveller will find it easiest to recognise and record the chief types of vegetation in the course of his journey. **1951** *Ecology* XXXII. 279/2 The practical aspects of the physiognomic method are reflected in its use by foresters. **1959** *New Scientist* 29 Oct. 803/2 When the change in climatic pattern is gradual, the change in physiognomic type is correspondingly slow and *vice versa.* **1971** *Nature* 18 June 430/1 The Radforth muskeg classification system..is based on physiognomic characteristics.

physiognomy. Add: **B. II. 4. b.** *spec.* in *Ecol.* The general appearance, form, or characteristics of a community of plants.

1909 GROOM & BALFOUR tr. *Warming's Oecol. Plants* vi. 25 The temperature and length of the vegetative season affect the physiognomy of the individual plant and the whole vegetation. **1926** TANSLEY & CHIPP *Study of Vegetation* ii. 11 The physiognomy or 'look' of an association is primarily determined by the life form of its dominant species. **1951** *Ecology* XXXII. 278/2 Gillman.. produced an excellent map of the physiognomy of the vegetation of Tanganyika. **1973** W. B. CLAPHAM *Nat. Ecosystems* vii. 230 Many of the basic variables of the microhabitat, such as temperature, humidity, and the like, are functions of the physiognomy of the climax community.

physiographic, *a.* Add: *physiographic province*: see *PROVINCE 6c.

physiographically (fiziogræ·fikăli), *adv.* [f. PHYSIOGRAPHICAL *a.* + -LY².] From a physiographical point of view.

1902 in *Encycl. Dict.* Suppl. **1908** *Westm. Gaz.* 24 Mar. 12/1 This church stands nearly 1,450 feet above sea-level, and is considered the 'highest'—not ecclesiastically, but physiographically—in Great Britain. **1928** V. G. CHILDE *Most Anc. East* ii. 22 Physiographically the last-named chains constitute a more real dividing line than the inland sea. **1973** *Nature* 1 June 277/2 Somewhat older deltas exist which receive little or no drainage today and are therefore harder to distinguish physiographically.

physiological, *a.* Add: **2.** (Further examples.) *physiological psychologist*, a specialist in physiological psychology.

1875 G. H. LEWES *Probl. Life & Mind* (ser. 1) II. 482 The common error of mistaking ideal separations for real separations..leads the physiological psychologist to the conclusion that the objective aspect of the phenomenon..is the cause of the subjective aspect. **1899** W. JAMES *Talks to Teachers* xii. 119 If we remember because of our associations, and if these are (as the physiological psychologists believe) due to our organized brain-paths, we easily see how the law of recency and repetition should prevail. **1904** E. B. TITCHENER tr. *Wundt's Princ. Physiol. Psychol.* p. vi, I have here sought to give this important chapter of physiological psychology at any rate a tentative systematic setting. **1933** Physiological phonetics [see **acoustic phonetics*]. **1950** *Sci. News* XV. 9 These facts caused Thomas Young, who has since been called 'the father of physiological optics' to propose, a century and a half ago, the three-colour theory of vision which bears his name. **1960** C. WINICK *Dict. Anthropol.* 411/2 Physiological phonetics is part of laboratory or experimental phonetics. **1967** R. F. THOMPSON *Found. Physiol. Psychol.* p. xxvii, Physiological psychology is concerned with the physiological bases of behavior. In the last analysis this means the organization and functions of the brain. **1973** DEWSBURY & RETHLINGSHAFER *Compar. Psychol.* 10 Lashley was a teacher of several men who became outstanding in the revitalization of comparative and physiological psychology that occurred after World War II.

b. *Med.* = *NORMAL *a.* 2f.

1896 *Jrnl. Physiol.* XX. 145 (*heading*) On the initial rate of osmosis of blood-serum with reference to the composition of 'physiological saline solution' in mammals. **1923** P. H. MITCHELL *Text Bk. Gen. Physiol.* vi. 148 Physiological salt solutions do not have irritating effects when in contact with open wounds. **1952** *Sci. News* XXIV. 27 Minced animal tissues were extracted with physiological saline (0·85% NaCl). **1969** J. H. GREEN *Basic Clin. Physiol.* vi. 37/1 The sodium chloride is present in plasma to the extent of 0·9 g. per 100 ml. A solution containing this amount of sodium chloride in water is termed normal isotonic or physiological saline, and it has the same electrolyte strength as blood.

physiologue (fi·ziolǫg). *rare.* [ad. L. *physiologus*: see PHYSIOLOGER.] = PHYSIOLOGIST.

1877 J. D. HOOKER in L. Huxley *Life J. D. Hooker* (1918) II. 236, I think *Gnetum* is quite overlooked by the Physiologues in removing Gymnosperms from Dicots. **1923** A. HUXLEY *Antic Hay* v. 70, I have with me..a physiologue, a pedagogue and a priapagogue.

physiopathological (fi:ziopæþolǫ·dʒikăl), *a.* *Med.* Also **physio-** (with hyphen). [f. PHYSIO- + PATHOLOGICAL *a.*] Of or pertaining to physiopathology. Also **phy:siopatholo·gic** *a.*

1867 ROBERTSON & RUTHERFORD tr. *Griesinger's Mental Path. & Therapeutics* I. iii. 23 (*heading*) Preliminary physio-pathological observations on mental phenomena. **1930** *Brit. Med. Jrnl.* 8 Feb. 234/2 Endarteritis obliterans is a special localization of athero-sclerosis. In fact, in athero-sclerosis the same constellation of etiological factors, and the same physio-pathological conditions (proliferation of the intima, disturbances in cholesterol metabolism, etc.), are found. **1938** *Arch. Neurol. & Psychiatry* (Chicago) XL. 1126 (*heading*) Physiopathologic and pathoanatomic aspects of major trigeminal neuralgia. **1968** E. KELEMEN *Physiopath. & Therapy Human Blood Dis.* (1969) p. xv, Contemporary physiopathological research..is, at least to some extent, very liable..to lose sight of the ultimate aim of the project.

physiopathology (fi:ziopăþǫ·lŏdʒi). *Med.* Also **physio-** (with hyphen). [f. PHYSIO- + PATHOLOGY.] (See quot. 1904.) Also, the physiology of a diseased organism. So **phy:siopatho·logist.**

1904 STEDMAN *Dunglison's Dict. Med. Sci.* (ed. 23) 875/2 *Physiopathology*, study of function as modified by disease. **1930** *Brit. Med. Jrnl.* 8 Feb. 234/1 The frequency of the occurrence of this morbid condition raises important problems as to its physio-pathology and its treatment. **1953** HOMBURGER & FISHMAN (*title*) The physiopathology of cancer. **1954** *Acta Physiol. Scand.* XXXI. 359 A study has been made of the physiopathology of the asphyxiated human fetus in order to improve the results of resuscitation. **1972** GALLO & SANTAMARIA *Res. Progress Org.-Biol. & Med. Chem.* III. I. p. vi, The discovery of the photodynamic phenomenon helps the physiopathologists to characterize diseases which were once joined together under general terms of skin disorders. **1974** *Nature* 29 Mar. 371/2 Fifty laboratories provide facilities for basic and applied research into bacteriology, virology, physiopathology, [etc.].

physiophonetics (fi:ziofǫ̆ne·tiks), *sb. pl.* (const. as *sing.*) *Linguistics.* [f. PHYSIO- + PHONETICS *sb. pl.*] (See quot. 1950.) Hence **phy:siophone·tic** *a.*

1936 J. R. KANTOR *Objective Psychol. Gram.* xii. 162 It was Baudouin de Courtenay, according to Troubetzkoy, who first made a genuine separation between physical and physiological sounds and psychological phonic images—in other words gave the term *phoneme* what Troubetzkoy calls its present meaning—namely, the element of psychological language—and placed it within the field of psychophonetics instead of physiophonetics. **1950** D. JONES *Phoneme* xxix. 213 Professor Baudouin de Courtenay..defined phonemes as 'mental images', and accordingly distinguished two kinds of phonetics which he called 'physiophonetics' and 'psychophonetics' respectively. He applied the term 'physiophonetics' to the study of sounds actually uttered, and used the term 'psychophonetics' to denote the study of the 'mental images' which uttered sounds are intended to represent. **1956** Physiophonetic [see *PSYCHOPHONETICS *sb. pl.*].

physiotherapist (fizioþe·răpist). [f. next + -IST.] One skilled or trained in physiotherapy.

1923 C. M. SAMPSON *Physiotherapy Technic* xxvi. 409 Lucky is the physiotherapist who can plan his department in a new building. **1944** *Times* 24 Jan. 5/5 A Chartered Physiotherapist to-day is trained not only in massage and gymnastics but also in electrical and all forms of ray therapy. **1958** *Times* 7 July 22/4 The role of physiotherapy is still large, and the supply of physiotherapists on the whole well maintained. **1972** D. HASTON *In High Places* ii. 20 My physiotherapist was very sympathetic. I worked really hard on exercises, and the wasted arm became stronger.

physiotherapy (fizioþe·răpi). [f. PHYSIO- + THERAPY.] The treatment of disease, injury, or deformity by physical methods, such as massage, exercise, and the application of heat, light, fresh air, and other external influences.

1905 *Brit. Med. Jrnl.* 15 July 126/2 The first congress of physiotherapy will be held at Liége on August 12th. **1928** *Sunday Dispatch* 16 Dec. 1/1 Two new specialists, both experts in radiology and massage, and in the treatment generally known as physio-therapy, were called to Buckingham Palace yesterday. **1958** *Times Lit. Suppl.* 4 Apr. 187/2 Full details are given of methods of physiotherapy that can be carried out in the home. **1958** [see *PHYSIOTHERAPIST]. **1975** SCRUTTON & GILBERTSON *Physiotherapy in Paediatric Pract.* 1 Physiotherapy involves the modification of the patient's physical external environment, either generally or topically, so as to promote healing or otherwise improve the body's efficiency.

Hence **phy:siotherapeu·tic** *a.*, of, pertaining to, or involving physiotherapy.

1905 *Brit. Med. Jrnl.* 15 July 126/2 The abuses caused by 'healers' who pretend to treat by physiotherapeutic procedures. **1926** *Encycl. Brit.* III. 686/1 As convalescence goes on, physiotherapeutic measures..are employed to hasten recovery. **1957** M. SPARK *Comforters* viii. 196 He is receiving physiotherapeutic treatment.

1976 NICHOLS & HAMILTON *Rehabilitation Med.* ii. 21 There are innumeralbe reports in the medical and physiotherapeutic literature extolling the virtues of specific techniques.

physiqued (fizī·kt), *a.* [f. PHYSIQUE + -ED[1].] Having a physique of a specified character.

1926 *Contemp. Rev.* June 690 These ill-fed, ill-housed, wretchedly physiqued and noisy communist agitators.

physisorb (fi·zisǭɹb), *v. Chem.* [Back-formation from next.] *trans.* and *intr.* To collect by physisorption. So **phy·sisorbed, phy·sisorbing** *ppl. adjs.*

1966 *Surface Sci.* IV. 103 (*heading*) Ordered physisorbed layers on graphite. **1967** *Ibid.* VI. 1 It has been argued that due to the weakness of physisorbing forces, the electron beam of the instrument would disturb the molecules significantly. *Ibid.* 2 Materials highly volatile at room temperature could not be physisorbed to concentrations approaching a monolayer. *Ibid.*, A substance with a vapor pressure of 1×10^{-2} Torr or more will not physisorb on graphite in quantities approaching a monolayer if its ambient pressure over the graphite is 1×10^{-4} Torr or less. **1970** C. OKKERSE in B. G. Linsen *Physical & Chem. Aspects Adsorbents & Catalysts* v. 253 Wirzing suggested the use of the combination band of water at 5265 cm^{-1} for the quantitative determination of physisorbed water. **1971** *Sci. Amer.* Dec. 51/1 A physisorbed species retains substantially its original structure.

physisorption (fizisǭ·ɹpʃən). *Chem.* [f. PHYSI(CAL *a.* + AD)SORPTION.] Adsorption which does not involve the formation of chemical bonds. Cf. *CHEMISORPTION.

1965 *Progress Solid State Chem.* II. 94 At higher pressures and lower temperatures (−78°C) physisorption without formation of ordered structures was observed. **1973** *Sci. Amer.* May 34/2 There have been several more recent electron-diffraction studies of physisorption with other gases and other substrates. **1976** *Physics Bull.* May 218 This book..is extremely timely in marshalling ideas on physisorption because there is now an increasing interest in the more difficult process of chemisorption.

physog, var. *PHIZOG.

physogastrism (fəisogæ·striz'm). *Ent.* [ad. G. *physogastre* (E. Wasmann *Kritisches Verzeichniss d. Myrmekophilen u. Termitophilen Arthropoden* (1894) 87), f. PHYSO- + Gr. γαστ(ε)ρ-, γαστήρ, belly: see -ISM.] In certain insects, a condition in which the abdomen becomes distended by the growth of fat bodies or other organs. Also **phy·sogastry** in the same sense. So **physoga·stric** *a.*, exhibiting this condition.

1903 *Nature* 12 Feb. 351/1 They [*sc.* symphilous beetles] also show certain modifications of the mouth-organs.., as well as 'physogastrism', accompanied by excessive development of the fat-bodies, or sexual glands. **1914** *Ann. Natal Museum* III. 103 Dr. Trägårdh examined many nests of termites in Natal, but no other physogastric Staphylinids were discovered. **1920** *Ibid.* IV. 326 In the female there is no excessive amount of fat-body. The physogastrism is mainly due to the great bulk of the genital organs and of the mid-gut. **1922** W. M. WHEELER *Social Life Insects* vi. 273 Many [termitophiles]..have acquired peculiar characters, the most characteristic of which is physogastry, or excessive enlargement of the abdomen. *Ibid.* 277 Probably this is also the case with other physogastric termitophiles. **1952** ROTHSCHILD & CLAY *Fleas, Flukes & Cuckoos* xi. 222 The abdomen becomes enormously distended owing to the abnormal growth of the fatty tissues. This curious condition is known as physogastry and it is usually developed by flies or beetles which are parasitic or symbiotic in ants' or termites' nests. **1971** R. R. ASKEW *Parasitic Insects* v. 73 The abdomen [of *Ascodipteron*] becomes bloated (physogastric) as the fly takes in blood from the host. *Ibid.* 311/2 Physogastry.

physostegia (fəi:søste·dʒiă). [mod.L. (G. Bentham 1829, in *Bot. Reg.* XV. 1289), f. Gr. φῦσα bladder + στέγη roof + -IA[1], in reference to the inflated calyx.] A perennial herb of the genus so called, belonging to the family Labiatæ, native to North America, and bearing spikes of pink or white flowers; also called the obedient plant or false dragonhead.

1830 J. C. LOUDON *Hortus Britannicus* 483 *Physostegia* Berth. [English name] Physostegia. **1835** *Curtis's Bot. Mag.* LXII. 3386 (*heading*) Imbricated Physostegia. **1905** E. V. BOYCE in M. T. Earle et al. *Garden Colour* 70 The habit of the Physostegia's little pale pinkish flower to stay fixed and still in whatever position it may be turned, was thought to be caused by coma. **1962** *Amat. Gardening* 17 Mar. 4/1 Among a number of self-supporting plants may be included..physostegias. **1971** J. RAVEN *Botanist's Garden* xi. 201 The typical form of the Physostegia..is of my least favourite shade somewhere between pink and mauve.

physostigmine (fəisosti·gmīn). *Chem.* and *Pharm.* Also † **-in.** [ad. G. *physostigmin* (Jobst & Hesse 1864, in *Ann. d. Chem. u. Pharm.* CXXIX. 118): see PHYSOSTIGMA and -INE[5].] A colourless or pale yellow crystalline tricyclic alkaloid, $C_{15}H_{21}N_3O_2$, which is the active principle of the calabar bean and is used medicinally (esp. as a miotic) on account of its anticholinesterase activity.

1864 *Chem. News* 5 Mar. 109/1 The physiological properties of the Calabar bean have been well studied in this country, but the authors above named are..the first who have isolated the alkaloid to which it owes its activity, and to which they have given the name Physostigmine. **1865, 1896** [in Dict. s.v. PHYSOSTIGMA]. **1907** J. H. PARSONS *Dis. Eye* iv. 74 Eserin or physostigmin, the most powerful miotic we possess, acts by stimulating the third nerve endings in the sphincter and in the ciliary muscle. **1938** *Thorpe's Dict. Appl. Chem.* (ed. 4) II. 200/1 The physiological action of physostigmine depends on its inhibition of the hydrolysis of acetyl choline by cholinesterase. **1970** *Nature* 4 Apr. 21/2 Drugs which..increase the concentration [in the brain] of acetylcholine (for example, physostigmine) exacerbate Parkinsonism. **1974** M. C. GERALD *Pharmacol.* vii. 128 Many very common drugs are alkaloids, some of which include..physostigmine.

phytal (fəi·tăl), *a. Ecol.* [f. PHYT- + -AL.] Of, pertaining to, or designating those parts of a body of water which are shallow enough to permit the growth of rooted green plants.

1918 R. A. MUTTKOWSKI in *Trans. Wisconsin Acad. Sci., Arts & Lett.* XIX. 378 The lake as a whole may be divided into three general regions,—the littoral, or phytal region; the aphytal region; and pelagic region. **1926** A. S. PEARSE *Animal Ecol.* vi. 210 Muttkowski uses 'littoral' as synonymous with 'phytal'.., but in very turbid lakes the phytal zone may be thinner than that of wave action, and in clear, small lakes it may be thicker. **1958** W. D. R. HUNTER in Miller & Tivy *Glasgow Region* 107 (*caption*) Map of Loch Lomond showing the extent of water (less than 13 feet deep), which is shallow enough to permit the growth of rooted green plants, *i.e.* the potential phytal zone. **1973** *Nature* 8 June 342/1 Marine grasses would also have provided new sources of food for the macrofauna and microfauna and new means of dispersal for benthonic and phytal organisms.

phytane (fəi·tēⁱn). *Chem.* [ad. G. *phytan* (Willstätter & Hocheder 1907, in *Ann. d. Chem.* CCCLIV. 208): see PHYT- and -ANE.] A colourless liquid hydrocarbon, 3,7,11,15-tetramethylhexadecane, $C_{20}H_{42}$, that is the paraffin corresponding to phytol.

1907 [see *PHYTOL]. **1911** *Chem. Abstr.* V. 874 Phytane, $C_{20}H_{42}$, obtained by the reduction of phytol,..crystallizes in liquid air. **1965** *New Scientist* 6 May 378/1 Certain hydrocarbons, such as the branched-chain compounds phytane and pristane, can if found [in rocks] be taken to be definite evidence of life. **1971** *Sci. Amer.* May 38/3 The chemical analysis of organic material from the Gunflint cherts in several laboratories reveals the presence of the hydrocarbons pristane and phytane: two 'chemical fossils' that can most reasonably be regarded as being breakdown products of chlorophyll.

phytase (fəi·tēⁱz, -s). *Biol.* [a. G. *phytase* (U. Suzuki et al. 1907, in *Bull. College Agric.* (Tokyo Imperial Univ.) VII. 503): see PHYT- and *-ASE.] Any of a class of enzymes found esp. in cereals and yeast which convert phytic acid to *myo*-inositol and phosphoric acid.

1908 *Jrnl. Chem. Soc.* XCIV. I. 236 The change is shown to be due, not to putrefaction, but to an enzyme, phytase, which was isolated from rice bran and wheat bran. **1931** E. C. MILLER *Plant Physiol.* xi. 632 The glucoside phytin is decomposed into phosphoric acid and inosite, $C_6H_{12}O_6$, by the action of the enzyme phytase. **1947** *Nature* 18 Jan. 99/2, 25 ml. of the solution correspond to the phytase activity of about 15gm. barley. **1966** NOWAKOWSKI & CLARKE tr. *Kretovich's Princ. Plant Biochem.* vi. 215 The phytases of yeasts and flour split much of the inositol-phosphoric acid during fermentation of dough. **1975** *Science* 7 Feb. 432/3 A phytase which we extracted and purified from wheat bran.

phytic (fəi·tik), *a. Biochem.* [f. *PHYT(IN + -IC.] *phytic acid*: a phosphoric acid ester, $C_6H_6(OPO_3H_2)_6$, of *myo*-inositol which is found (often as salts) in plants, esp. in the seeds of cereals.

1908 *Jrnl. Biol. Chem.* IV. 497 Wheat bran, which contains 1½ per cent of phosphorus, was found to be essentially free from inorganic phosphates, the whole of the phosphorus being present as salts of phytic acid. **1943** *Endeavour* II. 75/2 One important dietary constituent, phytic acid (inositol hexaphosphoric acid),..interferes with calcification by precipitating calcium in the gut and making it unavailable. **1966** *McGraw-Hill Encycl. Sci. & Technol.* VII. 121/2 The phytic acid of whole wheat is of nutritional importance because it combines with dietary calcium, decreasing its availability. **1978** R. MITCHISON *Life in Scotland* ii. 71 Recent work on nutrition has shown that..some foodstuffs contain inhibitors.., for instance, phytic acid.

Hence **phy·tate**, a salt, or the anion, of phytic acid.

1908 *Jrnl. Biol. Chem.* IV. 498 In all cases blank determinations were made on the tissue extract alone and on a solution of sodium phytate which were digested in a similar manner. **1961** *Lancet* 26 Aug. 483/1 In dietary deficiency of vitamin B_{12}, serum-iron has been found to fall... This is thought to be due to ingestion of excessive amounts of phytate in wholemeal flour and bread. **1968** *New Scientist* 28 Nov. 512/2 The staple article of the typical village diet [in Iran] is wheat bread, which contains a chemical called phytate. This chemical renders zinc and possibly iron unavailable. **1976** *Sci. Amer.* Sept. 57/1 Ferrous iron, however, is absorbed less efficiently when it is ingested in combination with phytates and oxalates, which are found in leafy green vegetables and the whole-grain, unleavened bread of North Africa and the Middle East.

phytin (fəi·tin). *Biol.* and *Med.* [a. G. *phytin* (S. Posternak 1904, in *Schweiz. Wochenschr. f. Chem. u. Pharm.* XLII. 405): see PHYT- and -IN[1].] **a.** An insoluble salt of phytic acid with calcium and magnesium, which is found in plants, esp. cereals; also, *loosely*, the acid itself. **b.** Also **Phytin,** † **-ine.** A proprietary name for tonic preparations containing this.

1905 *Brit. Med. Jrnl.* 14 Jan. 81/1 Phytin has hitherto been simply described as a compound prepared from various seeds which contain phosphorus in combination... Phytin is claimed to be of use in all cases where invigorating treatment is indicated and to possess a specific action against impotence. **1905** *Official Gaz.* (U.S. Patent Office) 28 Feb. 2375/2 Certain named pharmaceutical products. Society of Chemical Industry in Basle, Basle, Switzerland. Filed Nov. 29, 1904. Phytine...used since February, 1903. **1906** *Amer. Jrnl. Physiol.* XVII. 76 Commercial phytin has lately been introduced into medical practice with somewhat extravagant claims. **1934** *Brit. Pharmaceutical Codex* 1656 *Phytin*, calcium and magnesium salt of inositol hexaphosphoric acid. **1936** [see *INOSITOL]. **1938** E. C. MILLER *Plant Physiol.* (ed. 2) viii. 545 When chlorophyll is treated with dilute acids, the magnesium is removed and replaced with two hydrogen ions without otherwise changing the molecule. A series of decomposition products result [*sic*] which are called 'phytins' and which correspond to the alkali decomposition products of chlorophyll, except that the magnesium is lacking. **1947** *Dispensatory U.S.A.* (ed. 24) 1489/1 The calcium-magnesium salt of inositol hexaphosphate is available under the name *Phytin* (Ciba) in tablets containing 0·25 gm. **1957** G. E. HUTCHINSON *Treat. Limnol.* I. xii. 735 Chu (1946) found that *Nitzschia palea* could use phytin (magnesium inositol hexaphosphate) and glycerophosphoric acid as phosphorus sources. **1969** N. W. PIRIE *Food Resources* vii. 164 The old-fashioned method of making porridge..destroys phytin which would otherwise make the calcium in the food less easy to absorb.

phyto-. Add: **phytobe·nthos** [*BENTHOS], the aquatic flora of the region at or near the bottom of the sea; **phytochemical** *a.* (examples); hence **phytoche·mically** *adv.*; also **phytoche·mist**, an expert or specialist in phytochemistry; **phytochemistry** (earlier and further examples); **phytoe·cdysone** *Biol.* [*ECDYSONE; prob. first formed in Jap.], any substance that occurs in a plant and causes moulting in insects; **phytofla·gellate** [*FLAGELLATE *sb.*], a plant-like flagellate belonging to the subclass Phytoflagellata or Phytomastigophore; **phytomi·togen**, a mitogen derived from a plant; **phytomo·nad** [a. mod.L. order name *Phytomonadina*, f. generic name *Phytomonas* (C. Donovan 1909, in *Lancet* 20 Nov. 1496/2) + MONAD 4], a phytoflagellate belonging to the order Phytomonadina; **phytopathology**, delete sense (*b*) and add examples of sense (*a*); **phytopathological** *a.* (examples); **phytopathologist** (further examples).

1931 R. N. CHAPMAN *Animal Ecol.* xvi. 333 The phytobenthos is along the shore or in the littoral region. **1964** *Oceanogr. & Marine Biol.* II. 127 (*caption*) Other organisms listed included zooplankton, phytobenthos, zoobenthos, and fishes. **1973** *Nature* 6 Apr. 415/2 The rates of ..photosyntheses of phytoplankton and phytobenthos.. have been made [*sic*] using carbon-14. **1877** *Chem. News* 4 May 185/1 (*heading*) On phyto-chemical processes. **1921** *Experiment Station Rec.* XLIII. 820 (*heading*) Phytochemical investigations on indigenous and naturalized plants. **1972** *Nature* 21 Jan. 134/1 The joint meeting of the Phytochemical Society and the Pharmaceutical Society of Great Britain on plant constituents of pharmacological interest. **1972** *Science* 9 June 1131/2 Schultes has repeatedly suggested that these additional 'peyote' cacti be examined phytochemically. **1969** H. ERDTMAN in Harborne & Swain *Perspectives in Phytochem.* v. 109 That symposium was important because it brought together scientists of different specializations, botanical taxonomists, phytochemists and chemists interested in biosynthetic problems. **1972** *Nature* 28 Apr. 469/2 The contributors are leading specialists in umbellifer taxonomy..together with many other scarcely less eminent systematists and phytochemists. **1837** *Phil. Mag.* X. 247 (*heading*) A report of the progress of phytochemistry in the year 1835. **1912** *Carnegie Inst. Year Bk.* 49 The chief problems of the Department have been taken to lie in the domain of phyto-chemistry, in the water-relations of plants, and in the environic reactions of organisms. **1968** *Jrnl. Chromatogr.* XXXVI. 22 Methods for the separation and identification of microquantities of phenolic glycosides are of great importance for work in phytochemistry, pharmacognosy and chemotaxonomy. **1968** *Tetrahedron Lett.* July 3883 Four additional phytoecdysones have now been isolated from the leaves [of *Podocarpus macrophyllus*]. Interestingly, these new phytoecdysones..have steroid skeletons with 28 and 29 carbon atoms. **1974** HIKINO & TAKEMOTO in W. J. Burdette *Invertebr. Endocrinol.* II. 187 The occurrence of phytoecdysones in plants raises the question whether they have any beneficial or adverse effects on the plants themselves or on the phytophagous animals in their natural habitat... The leaves of *Morus* species and *Podocarpus macrophyllus* which are known to contain considerable amounts of phytoecdysones, are food of the larvae of the moths, *Bombyx mori* and *Milionia vasalis pryeri*, respectively. **1978** *Nature* 9 Mar. 122/1 The generic term 'phytoecdysones' should be abandoned. **1947** *Palestine Jrnl. Bot.* IV. 14 *Prymnesium parvum* Carter is a phytoflagellate belonging to the order of the Chrysomonadales, differing from other members of this order in the presence of an immobile spine-like third flagellum, a feature unique among phytoflagellates. **1951** HUTNER & PROVASOLI in A. Lwoff et al. *Biochem. & Physiol. Protozoa* I. 29 The phytoflagellates are a heterogeneous group occupying a systematic position at intersections of plant and animal lines of descent. **1957** *New Biol.* XXIII. 93 This phytoflagellate [sc. *Prymnesium parvum*] was first blamed for mass fish mortality in Holland and later in Denmark. **1973** M. A. SLEIGH *Biol. Protozoa* i. 2 The cell possesses the basic components of a phytoflagellate, including flagella, nucleus, plastid,..and other..inclusions. **1961** MARSHALL & CAPON in *Lancet* 8 July 104/1 We suggest that until more is known about their structure, factors extracted from plants which exhibit mitogenic activity, be referred to as phytomitogens. **1964** *Ibid.* 21 Nov. 1101/1 These observations suggest that the distribution of 'phytomitogens' in the plant kingdom may be more widespread than is recognised. **1974** *Jrnl. Exper. Med.* CXXXIX. 1553 The lymphocyte response to phytomitogens is generally considered to be nonspecific. **1926** G. N. CALKINS *Biol. Protozoa* v. 279 Phytomonads with a bivalve shell, or at least a membrane which splits easily to form two lens-like halves, as in *Phacotus lenticularis*. **1953** R. P. HALL *Protozool.* iv. 151 Lipids, although usually not abundant, are stored by many phytomonads. **1961** R. D. MANWELL *Introd. Protozool.* xiv. 174 Most of the phytomonads are rather small, roundish forms. **1889** *Cent. Dict.*, Phytopathological. **1909** B. M. DUGGAR *Fungous Dis. Plants* 4 The foundations were laid for a more careful study of the fungi from a phytopathological point of view. **1959** *Ann. Rev. Microbiol.* XIII. 224 The term 'toxin', in the phytopathological literature, is used in the general sense of a poisonous substance generated by the pathogen regardless of its chemical nature. **1962** W. CARTER *Insects in Relation to Plant Dis.* p. vii, There.. has been a growing awareness of the toxicogenic insect as a phytopathological agent. **1917** J. W. HARSHBERGER *Text-bk. Mycol. & Plant Path.* xxiii. 271 A study of phytopathology..presupposes that the would-be phytopathologist is acquainted with plant morphology, systematic botany..histology, cytology, embryology, genetics, physiology, [etc.]. **1958** *Austral. Jrnl. Biol. Sci.* XI. 275 The problem of disease resistance in plants has exercised the minds of phytopathologists for more than half a century. **1891** *Vet. Jrnl.* XXXII. 253 Phytopathology afforded many instances of local death of a part produced by the parasite. **1911** *Encycl. Brit.* XXI. 754/2 'Phytopathology' or plant pathology..comprises our knowledge of the symptoms, course, causes and remedies of the maladies which threaten the life of plants, or which result in abnormalities of structure that are regarded, whether directly injurious or not to life, as unsightly or undesirable... As a branch of botanical study it is of recent date. **1976** *Nature* 12 Feb. 449/1 A large proportion of the money devoted to agricultural research in the UK is spent on phytopathology and crop protection and has enabled the production of virus-free and disease-resistant crops.

phytoagglutinin (fəito,ægl'ū·tinin). *Biochem.* [f. PHYTO- + *agglutinin* s.v. *AGGLUTINATE *v.*] Any plant protein that is an agglutinin.

1959 *Archiwum Immunologii i Terapii Doświadczalnej* VII. 793, 214 plant species from various botanic families were examined for the presence of phytoagglutinins; they have been found in seed extracts of 50 plant species. **1971** *Proc. Nat. Acad. Sci.* LXVIII. 1818/2 The *C[olletotrichum] lindemuthianum* polygalacturonase inhibitor isolated from Red Kidney bean hypocotyls has several properties which suggest that it is one of the glycoproteins commonly referred to as phytoagglutinins. **1974** A. HUXLEY *Plant & Planet* xxv. 285 Many plants.. contain antibiotic substances which help to repel fungus invasions... These substances, which are possibly based on proteins known as phytoagglutins [*sic*], remind one of antibodies in animals.

phytoalexin (fəi:to,ăle·ksin). *Bot.* [a. G. *phytoalexin* (Müller & Börger 1941, in *Arb. aus der biol. Reichsanstalt Land- und Forstwirtschaft* XXIII. 223): see PHYTO- and *ALEXIN.] Any substance that is produced by plant tissues in response to contact with a parasite and specifically inhibits the growth of that parasite.

The term was orig. defined with regard to fungal parasites only, but in 1956 Müller extended the meaning to cover all parasites.

1949 *Nature* 26 Mar. 498/2 The necrosis of the affected tissues must be accompanied by the formation or activation of a principle ('phytoalexin') which exercises a retarding influence on the penetrating parasite. **1956** K. O. MÜLLER in *Phytopath. Zeitschr.* XXVII. 254 'Phytoalexines' [*sic*] are defined as antibiotics which are the result of an interaction of two different metabolic systems, the host and the parasite, and which inhibit the growth of microorganisms pathogenic to plants. **1964** CRUICKSHANK & PERRIN in J. B. Harborne *Biochem. Phenolic Compounds* xiii. 534 Susceptibility [to fungal attack] may be due to the inability of the infecting fungus to stimulate the formation of the phytoalexin or to its capacity to tolerate the phytoalexin produced. **1975** *Sci. Amer.* Jan. 88/3 Plants do not produce antibodies but some of them do produce phytoalexins. **1977** *Observer* 4 Sept. 4/2 Dr. David Smith..told a meeting of the British Association for the Advancement of Science last week that chemicals called phytoalexins—substances produced by plants when they are attacked by disease—merited a major investigation.

phytochrome (in Dict. s.v. PHYTO-). Add: **2.** *Bot.* A blue-green chromoprotein which regulates many aspects of development in higher plants according to the nature and timing of the light which it absorbs.

1960 BORTHWICK & HENDRICKS in *Science* 28 Oct. 1223/1 This control of flowering..implies a time-measuring system that distinguishes between light and darkness through mediation of a pigment... The pigment, now called phytochrome, is a blue or a bluish-green protein that exists in two forms interconvertible by light,..with 660 and 730 mμ the absorption maxima of the two forms. **1962** *Amat. Gardening* 20 Jan. 12 Phytochrome has been isolated, and shown to be sensitive even to very short periods of light. **1971** *New Scientist* 18 Feb. 365/1 One of the 'states' of phytochrome is physiologically active and plays a part in controlling many processes ranging from seed germination..to the onset of reproductive behaviour. **1977** J. L. HARPER *Population Biol. Plants* v. 144 The phytochrome system which controls the light sensitivity of germination in many species involves an interconversion of two forms of phytochrome.

phytocidal (fəitosəi·dăl), *a.* [f. PHYTO- + -CIDE + -AL.] Lethal or injurious to plants.

1934 *Ann. Rep. East Malling Res. Station 1933* 157 The immediate problem to be solved by this field spraying trial was whether..lime-sulphur could be used in conjunction with nicotine or with derris with satisfactory fungicidal, insecticidal and phytocidal results. [*Note*] This term is now being used in reference to the effect of sprays on the tree. **1936** H. MARTIN *Sci. Princ. Plant Protection* (ed. 2) vi. 110 It is convenient in describing phytocidal activity to distinguish between acute injury, characterized by the localized killing of plant tissue (necrosis) and popularly termed 'scorch' or 'burn', and chronic injury which involves deep-seated physiological changes and causes, for example, the stunting and premature drop of fruit and leaves. **1946** *Nature* 21 Sept. 417/2 One other point regarding phytocidal action may be mentioned. Unnecessarily heavy dressings of B.H.C. do not appear to have a hurtful action on the carrot, whereas with the Brassicæ even moderate dressings may seriously affect the stem at the point where contact is made. **1970** *Weed Res.* X. 367 (*heading*) The correlation of the phytocidal effect of 3-amino-1,2,4-triazole with the growth stage of oat plants.

So **phy·tocide**, a phytocidal agent.

1936 *Ann. Rep. East Malling Res. Station 1935* 198 Cuprous cyanide..[etc.] were retained for further phytocide tests. **1961** *New Scientist* 21 Dec. 724/3 Treatment with selective phytocides such as copper sulphate.

phytoclimate (fəi·tokləimĕt). *Bot.* [ad. Da. *fanerofytklimaet, kryptofytklimaet* (C. Raunkiaer 1908, in *Bot. Tidsskr.* XXIX. 54): see PHYTO- and CLIMATE *sb.*] Local climate in its ecological aspects.

1950 *Bot. Rev.* XVI. 1 (*heading*) Life-forms and phytoclimate. *Ibid.* 16 We have here only a general correlation between Raunkiaer's hemicryptophytic phytoclimate and Köppen's C and D climates which are based on physical data. **1968** J. M. MACLENNAN tr. *Sukachev & Dylis's Fund. Forest Biogeocoenol.* i. 31 Inter-crown and intra-crown breaking of twigs.., by increasing the distance between trees and lessening the depth and density of the canopy, causes substantial changes in the phytoclimate, litter, and soil processes. **1975** *Lesovedenie* vi. 36 (*heading*) Alteration of phytoclimate in stem pests nidus.

So **phytoclima·tic** *a.*, of or pertaining to phytoclimate.

1913 *Jrnl. Ecol.* I. 18 In Table I we give a few of Raunkiaer's analyses for various types of climate; the locality is indicated, also the total species actually analysed, while in the later columns the results are given as percentages according to the grouping given above. Such an analysis for any region is termed a biological or phyto-climatic spectrum. **1976** *Biol. Abstr.* LXI. 5689/1 The following parameters are given for each provenance: .., phytoclimatic zone according to Pavari and soil.

phytocœnose (fəitosī·nōuz). *Ecol.* [f. PHYTO- + Gr. κοίνωσις mingling.] A community of plants; all of the plant species found at a particular site.

1930 G. E. DU RIETZ in *Svensk Bot. Tidskr.* XXIV. 489 Only of the phytocoenoses, or 'complete plant-communities', all units of higher and lower rank have been included. **1955** *Jrnl. Ecol.* XLIII. 650 It is always possible to list the species in a phytocoenose (i.e. the vegetation occupying a definite area of ground). **1964** *Bot. Zhurnal* XLIX. 74 The study of the sward structure in a phytocoenose reveals the fact that the latter consists of layers.

phytoene (fəi·to,īn). *Chem.* [f. PHYTO- + -ENE.] A colourless viscous liquid, $C_{40}H_{64}$, which is a polyunsaturated branched-chain hydrocarbon and a precursor in the biological synthesis of carotenoids.

1950 PORTER & LINCOLN in *Arch. Biochem.* XXVII. 391 The name phytoene is given to a compound reported by Porter and Zscheile... It has previously been called a colorless, nonfluorescent polyene. **1966** *McGraw-Hill Encycl. Sci. & Technol.* II. 54/2 The synthesis of carotenoids leads..to the colorless compound, phytoene, which has the branched, 40-carbon chain characteristic of the carotenoid skeleton. **1978** *Sci. Amer.* Sept. 94/1 Carotenoids are derived from the 40-carbon compound phytoene.

phytogeography. Add: (Earlier and later examples.)

1847 H. C. WATSON *Cybele Britannica* I. 2 This study has been variously denominated 'Phyto-Geography', 'Botanical Geography', 'Geographical Botany', and 'Geographical Distribution of Plants'. **1859** *Ibid.* IV. x. 373 Phytogeography traces out the history and distribution of plants in connexion with the geographical position. **1933** *Geogr. Jrnl.* LXXXI. 462 A further problem remains, far more serious in the case of zoogeography than with phytogeography. Can the essentials be put..without assuming a knowledge of taxonomy beyond the reach of the average geographer? **1956** H. GODWIN (*title*) The history of the British flora: a factual basis for phytogeography. **1960** N. POLUNIN *Introd. Plant Geogr.* i. 2 Plant geography, also called phytogeography..deals with the plant cover of the world—with its composition, its local productivity, and particularly its distribution. **1976** *Conservation News* Sept./Oct. 3/1 The Library is one of the richest of its kind in the world, being particularly strong in plant taxonomy, phytogeography and related fields.

phytogeographer (earlier and later examples); **phytogeographical** *a.* (earlier and later examples).

1859 H. C. WATSON *Cybele Britannica* IV. x. 375 The ultimate objects to be sought by phyto-geographical investigations, are neither the countries of plants nor the plants of countries. *Ibid.* 441 A first call on the phytogeographer is to ascertain where the plants are now distributed. **1951** *Geografiska Annaler* XXXIII. 149 The vegetative highland areas consist mainly of bogs, mostly of the type which in Icelandic is called *flá*. Phytogeographers are using *flá* as a phytogeographical concept. **1977** *Jrnl. R. Soc. Arts* CXXV. 225/1 The Swiss phytogeographer Alphonse de Candolle.

phytograph (fəi·tograf). *Ecol.* [f. PHYTO- + Gr. -γρα-ος: see -GRAPH.] A diagram showing several quantifiable criteria of the ecological status of a (usu. silvan) species within an association.

1930 H. J. LUTZ in *Ecology* XI. 9 The term phytograph is proposed to designate a chart of this kind when used to characterize plant relationships. **1950** *Forestry Abstr.* XI. 580/2 Jack pine stands of equal age subjected to different degrees of thinning might be represented for purposes of comparison by phytographs constructed on 5 axes on which are shown their respective:—(1) average spacing of stems, [etc.]. **1971** F. C. FORD-ROBERTSON *Terminol. Forest Sci.* 194/1 Phytograph... A polygonal figure depicting the role of a species in a plant community.

phytohæmagglutinin (fəi:to,hīmăgl'ū·tinin). *Hæmatol.* Also (chiefly *U.S.*) **-hem-.** [f. PHYTO- + *HÆMAGGLUTININ, HEM-.] Any plant protein that is a hæmagglutinin.

1949 *Blood* IV. 673 We rediscovered this phytohemagglutinin accidentally and independently. **1951** *Amer. Jrnl. Med.* X. 776/2 The phytohemagglutinin of red beans (Phaseolus vulgaris) was recently isolated in pure form. **1955** *Jrnl. Biol. Chem.* CCXII. 615 This phytohemagglutinin, in either the mucoprotein or the protein form, is a non-toxic, powerful hemagglutinin of all types of human erythrocytes, and those of the horse, pig, [etc.]. **1960** *Cancer Res.* XX. 462 The mucoprotein plant extract, phytohemagglutinin (PHA), employed originally as a means of separating the leukocytes from whole blood in preparing the cultures, was found to be a specific initiator of mitotic activity: in its presence, cell division occurred; in its absence, no mitoses appeared. **1977** I. M. ROITT *Essent. Immunol.* (ed. 3) vi. 180 Comparable changes can be induced in lymphocytes by certain plant mitogens of which the best known are phytohaemagglutinin (PHA) and concanavalin A (conA). These..react with the cell surface non-specifically (i.e. not as an antigen) and produce the same series of cellular events as does antigen locking on to its specific surface receptor.

phytohormone (fəito,hǭ·ɹmōun). *Bot.* [ad. G. *phytohormon* (Kögl & Smit 1931, in *K. Akad. von Wetenschoppen te Amsterdam: Proc. Sect. Sci.* XXXIV. 1416): see PHYTO- and *HORMONE.] Any substance which has a hormonal effect on a plant; = *HORMONE 2.

1933 *Chem. Abstr.* XXVII. 1645 (*heading*) Vegetable growth substances... A phytohormone of cell extension. **1940** W. R. FEARON *Introd. Biochem.* (ed. 2) xxiv. 446 The effect of the phytohormones is non-specific as regards species. **1952** [see *HORMONE 2]. **1959** L. J. AUDUS *Plant Growth Substances* (ed. 2) i. 16 In the past a rigid distinction has been made between..'synthetic growth-regulating substances' and 'natural phytohormones'. **1971** *Nature* 4 June 332/1 Jump suggested that a phytohormone produced by *A[ureobasidium] pullulans* (*Dematium pullulans*) may have been responsible for forking in red pine.

phytol (fəi·tǫl). *Biochem.* [a. G. *phytol* (Willstätter & Hocheder 1907, in *Ann. d. Chem.* CCCLIV. 207): see PHYT- and -OL.] A colourless oil whose molecule forms part of that of chlorophyll and vitamins E and K, and which is an acyclic terpenoid alcohol; 3,7,11,15-tetramethyl-2-hexadecenol, $C_{20}H_{40}O$.

1907 *Jrnl. Chem. Soc.* XCII. i. 784 The authors have been able..to remove the magnesium quantitatively and to obtain for the first time an ashless compound closely related to chlorophyll. This derivative is an ester, termed phaeophytin, and is hydrolysed readily by alkalis, yielding an unsaturated alcohol, phytol, $C_{20}H_{40}O$, which is formed also by the action of alkalis on chlorophyll. For the hypothetical saturated hydrocarbon, corresponding with this alcohol, the authors propose the name phytane. **1911**

[see *PHYTANE]. **1950** [see *PHÆOPHORBIDE]. **1974** *Sci. Amer.* Dec. 73/1 Attached to the porphyrin ring in chlorophyll is a long hydrocarbon 'tail', the phytol chain. It consists of carbon atoms linked together, but only one of the bonds is double. **1977** *Nature* 18 Aug. 621/2 The precursors of these hydrocarbons are unknown, but it is surmised that they result from the diagenesis of phytol, a moiety widely distributed among plant pigments.

Hence **phy·tyl** (-il, -əil), the univalent radical derived from phytol by the loss of a hydrogen atom.

1911 *Jrnl. Chem. Soc.* C. I. 145 Phytyl hydrogen phthalates, $CO_2H{\cdot}C_6H_4{\cdot}CO_2{\cdot}C_{20}H_{39}$, are formed when the phytol and phthalic anhydride are boiled for five hours with benzene. **1956** [see *PHÆOPHORBIDE]. **1973** *Nature* 20 July 155/1 Although other contributors, such as vitamin K_1, α-tocopherol and phospholipids from..bacteria and algae which have been shown to possess a phytyl side chain, are also possible, the most obvious source for the ketone is phytol.

phytolith. Restrict † *Obs.* to sense in Dict. and add: **2.** A minute mineral particle formed inside a plant.

1958 *Jrnl. Soil Sci.* IX. 154 *Nardus stricta*..contains phytoliths which could not be mistaken for those from any other of the grasses encountered. **1960** *Proc. R. Soc. Victoria* LXXII. 21 Phytoliths are important, if not abundant, constituents of dust in Australia. The common varieties are opal-phytoliths, but calcite-phytoliths and quartz-phytoliths have also been detected. **1964** *Ann. Bot.* XXVIII. 181 In some grasses..the absence or almost complete absence of phytoliths may be a characteristic of the species. **1975** *Nature* 17 Apr. 588/2 The abundance of opal phytoliths in the midden further indicate that there was then no scarcity of grass and reeds in the immediate vicinity of the site.

phytometer (fəitǫ·mĭtəɹ). *Bot.* [f. PHYTO- + -METER.] A plant or group of plants used to indicate, by its health and rate of growth, the physical properties of its surroundings.

1919 F. E. CLEMENTS et al. in *Carnegie Inst. Year Bk. 1918* 288 An endeavor has been made to devise a biological method of measuring habitats by means of standard plants. Batteries of such plants, for which the term 'phytometer' is suggested, have been installed at the various factor stations, and three series have been measured during the summer. **1929** WEAVER & CLEMENTS *Plant Ecol.* xiv. 330 Since phytometers are often placed in habitats that make extreme demands upon the plants, it is best to use species that are as hardy and vigorous as possible. **1954** *Austral. Jrnl. Bot.* II. 322 There is much to be said for the view that the complexes of environmental factors determining plant distribution can be indicated and measured better indirectly, through the plants themselves, than by direct physical measurements; this is, of course, the idea behind the use of 'phytometers' in agricultural meteorology. **1977** J. L. HARPER *Population Biol. Plants* xi. 361 It would be of immense interest to use standard plant units (phytometers), either pots freely supplied with water and nutrients or small water culture vessels with a test plant in each, and to place these units in transects across vegetation through open land, grassland, scrub and woodland.

phytopathogen (fəi:to,pæ·þodʒĕn). *Biol.* [f. PHYTO- + PATHOGEN.] Any micro-organism which produces disease in plants.

1934 in WEBSTER. **1943** *Phytopathology* XXXIII. 314 Experiments were performed to determine for the growth of the bacterial phytopathogens the suitability of a medium containing asparagin as the sole source of both carbon and nitrogen. **1959** *Ann. Rev. Microbiol.* XIII. 225 Pectinolytic enzymes are commonly formed by bacterial phytopathogens. **1976** *Nature* 15 Apr. 604/1 The ecological success of bracken is partly a result of its extensive rhizome system, and because of its ability to synthesise various secondary compounds which deter predators and phytopathogens.

phytopathogenic (fəi:to,pæþodʒe·nik), *a. Biol.* [f. PHYTO- + PATHOGENIC *a.*] Producing disease in plants. Hence **phy:topathogeni·city**, the property of being phytopathogenic.

1925 *Jrnl. Path. & Bacteriol.* XXVIII. 203 (*heading*) The investigation of phytopathogenic bacteria by serological and biochemical methods. *Ibid.*, An extensive literature has developed..with regard to the morphology and pathogenicity of various organisms isolated from phytopathogenic lesions. **1959** *Ann. Rev. Microbiol.* XIII. 224 Considerable effort has been expended in recent years in relating phytopathogenicity to discrete bacterial substances ('toxins') which induce disease symptoms in the host plant. *Ibid.* 225 Certain polysaccharides produced by phytopathogenic bacteria *in vitro* possess wilt-inducing properties. **1973** *Nature* 9 Mar. 87/3 Previous studies..postulated a symbiotic or parasitic relationship between phytopathogenic bacteria and insect 'hosts'.

phytophthora (fəitǫ·fþŏră). [mod.L., f. PHYTO- + Gr. φθορά destruction.] A fungus of the genus so called, belonging to the order Peronosporales and including several parasitic species which damage plants, esp. *Phytophthora infestans*, the cause of potato blight. Also *attrib.*

[**1876** A. DE BARY in *Jrnl. Bot.* XIV. 106 The characters..divide the..*Peronosporeæ* generally into two, perhaps better into three, genera, *Cystopus, Peronospora*, and a third, which may be called *Phytophthera.*] *Ibid.* 109 Up to this time the sexual organs have not been observed in *Phytophthora*, the Potato-fungus. **1925** *Jrnl. Agric. Res.* XXX. 463/2 Practically all of the fruit on the ground showed the typical symptoms of Phytophthora rot. **1930** *Phytopathology* XX. 209 Oospores had been reported previously in these two Phytophthoras. **1961** A. SCHOENFELD tr. *Stapp's Bacterial Plant Pathogens* II. 127 Together with *phytophthora* rot and leaf curl disease, it [*sc.* bacterial ring-rot] is..one of the three most severe potato diseases in the U.S.A. **1969** HAWKES & HJARTING *Potatoes of Argentina, Brazil, Paraguay, & Uruguay* II. 266 It may therefore be possible to transfer valuable qualities of *Phytophthora* resistance from these Mexican series.

phytoplankter (fəi·to,plæŋktəɹ). *Biol.* [f. PHYTO- + *PLANKTER.] A phytoplanktonic individual or species.

1957 G. E. HUTCHINSON *Treat. Limnol.* I. xiv. 798 Apart from diatoms, a few phytoplankters use silica. **1960** N. POLUNIN *Introd. Plant Geogr.* xvi. 517 The rate of sinking of a body heavier than water, as most phytoplankters (phytoplanktonic individuals) are, depends upon the ratio of surplus weight to friction. **1967** *New Scientist* 2 Feb. 276/3 The zoologist studies the nutritional requirements and efficiencies of food conversion of marine animals (zooplankters) feeding on marine phytoplankters or other small animals. **1972** *Science* 5 May 535/1 These substances are rapidly absorbed from water by organisms, including phytoplankters. **1976** *Nature* 17 June 584/1 *Gonyaulax*, a marine phytoplankter, is normally grown in a medium of approximately 500 mM salt.

phytoplankton (fəi·to,plæŋktǫn). *Biol.* [f. PHYTO- + PLANKTON.] The microscopic plants forming part of the plankton. Also *attrib.* So **phytoplankto·nic** *a.*

1897 P. T. CLEVE (*title*) A treatise on the phytoplankton of the Atlantic. **1900** *Geogr. Jrnl.* XV. 336 In the spring months there is a great development of bacteria and other Phytoplankton, which render the water less transparent than at other times of the year. **1909** E. WARMING *Oecol. Plants* xxxvii. 155 Phytoplankton..always consists of minute plants. *Ibid.*, Phytoplankton-organisms are all minute. **1928** *Daily Express* 28 May 10/7 Miss S. M. Marshall..is described technically as the 'phytoplankton worker'. **1944** *Jrnl. Marine Biol. Assoc.* XXVI. 285 Phytoplanktonic diatoms may utilize ammonium nitrogen in preference to nitrate nitrogen. **1956** *Nature* 3 Mar. 438/1 Smaller phytoplankton elements which will pass through the finest nets are of great importance in the productivity of the oceans. **1957** G. E. HUTCHINSON *Treat. Limnol.* I. xi. 714 These forms of iron may be assimilable by diatoms and perhaps by other phytoplanktonic organisms. **1964** *Oceanogr. & Marine Biol.* II. 137 Possibly fallout from a phytoplankton bloom would sometimes cause the immediate surface organisms to multiply. *Ibid.* 149 The amino acid compositions of phytoplankton and pure cultures of phytoplanktonic species have been determined. **1973** *Nature* 3 Aug. 307/1 The crustaceans in turn feed at least partially on the phytoplankton. **1977** P. B. & J. S. MEDAWAR *Life Sci.* i. 17 The most important—because they are the most abundant—organisms involved in the capture of carbon dioxide and the liberation of oxygen are forest trees and minute plants carried in the surface layers of the sea—'phytoplankton'.

phytosanitary (fəi:to,sæ·nitări), *a.* [f. PHYTO- + SANITARY *a.*] Pertaining to the health of plants; applied *spec.* to a certificate stating a plant is free from infectious diseases.

1949 L. LING *Digest of Plant Quarantine Regulations* (U.N. Food & Agric. Organization) July 5 Importation into Belgian Congo requires a special permit in accordance with the prescribed conditions: the presentation of a phytosanitary certificate of origin. *Ibid.* 35 Shipments of plant materials must be accompanied by certificates indicating origin and phyto-sanitary conditions. **1960** E. GRAM in Horsfall & Dimond *Plant Path.* III. ix. 332 Countries with no phytosanitary service..are the happy hunting grounds of botanists and geneticists. **1976** *Nature* 12 Feb. 449/2 Much of this material is accompanied by phytosanitary certificates of the exporting countries which are not necessarily the countries of origin.

phytosociology (fəi:to,sōᵘʃiǫ·lŏdʒi, -sōᵘsiǫ·l-). [ad. Russ. *fitosotsiologiya*: see PHYTO- and SOCIOLOGY.] The study of plant communities, their composition and structure. So **phytosociolo·gical** *a.*, **phytosociolo·gically** *adv.*; **phytosocio·logist**, one engaged in this study.

1928 K. D. GLINKA in *Proc. & Papers 1st Internat. Congr. Soil Sci.* I. 129 These ideas of Dokuchaiev could not but have the greatest influence on Russian works referring to..botanical geography, phytosociology, forestry. *Ibid.*, The present day phytosociologist begins to pay an increasing attention to the geography and topography of soils. **1928** *Jrnl. Ecol.* XVI. 18 The establishment of ecological series of spruce communities gives us a clear idea of the phytosociological and genetical relations between these communities. **1932** FULLER & CONARD tr. *Braun-Blanquet's Plant Sociol.* p. vii, Phytosociology, the study of vegetation, has had a very rapid development. **1955** *Jrnl. Ecol.* XLIII. 226 (*heading*) The use of phytosociological methods in ecological investigations. *Ibid.* 227 Plant sociology (or phytosociology) is defined as the discipline which concerns itself with the study of vegetation as such, with its floristic composition, structure, development and distribution. **1967** M. E. HALE *Biol. Lichens* vii. 87 Phytosociology is probably the most thoroughly investigated aspect of lichen biology. **1969** *Nature* 19 Apr. 242/2 Specialized communities..are phytosociologically distinct. **1970** *Watsonia* VIII. 172 The phytosociological classification of the vegetation of the limestone dales. **1973** *Nature* 30 Mar. 354/2 In the chapter dealing with the phytosociology of heathlands, the reader might be forgiven for gaining the impression that..the southern limit of heathland is France. *Ibid.* 21–28 Dec. 537/1 Continental phytosociologists may feel that some of their carefully defined association binomials have been applied a little loosely. **1974** *Ibid.* 24 May 307/3 Bushmeat species are remarkably resistant to infections that kill domestic stock, and they seldom destroy the phytosociological structure of their habitats. **1976** *Jrnl. R. Soc. Arts* CXXIV. 640/2 Between 1960 and 1973 botanical surveys and collections of plants were made throughout the maritime Antarctic and South Georgia. From these, descriptive floras together with ecological and phytosociological accounts have been produced. **1977** *Dædalus* Fall 130 In some of its branches, such as biogeography and phytosociology, the systems of classification and quantitative description reached phantasmagoric extremes.

phytosterol (fəitǫ·stērǫl). *Biochem.* [f. PHYTO- + *-STEROL.] Any of a large class of sterols which are found in plants; orig. *spec.* = *phytosterin* s.v. PHYTO-.

1898 *Jrnl. Chem. Soc.* LXXIV. I. 598 The soluble fat, which is dark green, consists principally of the ethereal salts of phytosterol, $C_{26}H_{44}O + H_2O$ (melting at 137°), and oleic and palmitic acids. **1906** *Ibid.* XC. II. 311 The author has submitted a number of cholesterols and phytosterols to Neuberg and Rauchwerger's colour test. **1915** J. LONDON *Jacket* v. 34 Professor Schleimer had similarly been collaborating with me in the detection of phytosterol in mixtures of animal and vegetable fats. **1939** MEYER & ANDERSON *Plant Physiol.* xxiii. 396 Cholesterol is not known to occur in the higher plants, but a number of similar compounds, known as the phytosterols, have been isolated from plant tissues. **1975** D. JARVIS tr. *Hess's Plant Physiol.* 108 The biosynthesis of the phytosterols..is not completely understood.

phytotoxic (fəito,tǫ·ksik), *a.* [f. PHYTO- + TOXIC *a.*] Poisonous or injurious to plants.

1933 *Proc. Nat. Acad. Sci.* XIX. 487 Macht showed that the blood of leprosy patients also gives a specific phytotoxic reaction. **1953** *Phytopathology* XLIII. 663/1 Ethylene..arises from plant tissue injured by such phytotoxic compounds as endothal. **1963** *Ann. Rev. Microbiol.* XVII. 223 The injurious effects of phytotoxic materials traditionally have been treated as plant diseases. **1976** *Weed Abstr.* XXV. 108/1 No treatment was phytotoxic to the blueberries.

Hence **phy:totoxi·city**, the property of being phytotoxic.

1945 J. G. HORSFALL *Fungicides* xvi. 172 Phytotoxicity is a term to describe the injuriousness of fungicides to host plants. **1958** *Times* 4 Dec. 1/5 (Advt.), Agricultural Research Council require a Plant Physiologist..to work on fundamental aspects of phytotoxicity. **1974** *Nature* 8 Feb. 337/3 Fungicides..must be selected and timed so that disease control is achieved with minimal phytotoxicity.

phytotoxicant (fəito,tǫ·ksikănt). [f. PHYTO- + TOXICANT *a.* and *sb.*] A substance poisonous or injurious to plants; *esp.* one present in the air. Also *attrib.* or as *adj.*

1959 *Internat. Jrnl. Air Pollution* I. 160 The decreased damage at the higher olefin concentration can be explained by the more rapid consumption of ozone to form the phytotoxicant which then partly decomposes before reaching the plants. **1961** *Ann. Rev. Plant Physiol.* XII. 431 The principal phytotoxicants recognized several decades ago were fairly specific, simple molecules, such as ethylene, fluorides, hydrogen sulfide, and sulfur dioxide. **1971** *McGraw-Hill Yearbk. Sci. & Technol.* 91/2, O_3 has been recognized as a phytotoxicant for at least 100 years. **1977** I. M. CAMPBELL *Energy & Atmosphere* viii. 248 The level of sophistication which has now been attained has resulted in the identification of single phytotoxicant species, together with the development..of computer simulation procedures for photochemical smog formation.

phytotoxin (fəito,tǫ·ksin). [f. PHYTO- + TOXIN.] **1.** Any toxin derived from a plant.

1909 R. J. M. BUCHANAN *Blood in Health & Dis.* xii. 289 Of chemical agents causing hæmorrhage, bacterial products take a prominent place, but many poisons, phytotoxins (plant poisons), zootoxins (animal poisons).. are especially effective. **1924** *Chem. Abstr.* XVIII. 1857 (*heading*) The protein phytotoxins, with special reference to the new 'modeccin'. **1974** *Nature* 18 Oct. 628/1 Very low concentrations of phytotoxins can kill mammalian cells, and some of them..have been reported to suppress protein synthesis in cells and cell-free systems.

2. A substance poisonous or injurious to plants, esp. one produced by a parasite.

1962 *Phytopathology* LII. 586/1 (*heading*) Production of a phytotoxin by *Rhizoctonia solani*. **1963** *Ann. Rev. Microbiol.* XVII. 224 The term 'phytotoxin' will be used for all products of living organisms toxic to plants. The designation, phytotoxin, does not imply that such a material plays any role whatever in relation to any disease caused by a pathogen. **1970** STROBEL & MATHRE *Outl. Plant Path.* xxii. 318 Phytotoxins induce few or none of the symptoms usually caused by the pathogen from which they originate. Compounds such as lycomarasmin, altemaric acid, and numerous smaller molecular weight organic acids fall into this category.

phytotron (fəi·tŏtrǫn). [f. PHYTO- + *-TRON: see quot. 1949.] A laboratory where plants can be maintained and studied under a wide range of controlled conditions.

1949 *Plant Physiol.* XXIV. 553 The word phytotron was coined for the new laboratory by Dr. R. A. Millikan..who feels that it will play the same role in plant physiology and the applied plant sciences..as the cyclotron has already had in pure and applied physics. **1958** *Observer* 7 Sept. 8/4 The Australian Government is to spend £500,000 on a new type of phytotron. **1974** *Telegraph* (Brisbane) 23 Sept. 6/6 The phytotron would enable scientists to grow four crops of rice a year and thus speed up research. **1976** *Sci. Amer.* Mar. 129/2 A phytotron is a combination of temperature-controlled greenhouses and artificially lighted rooms; here temperature, light and humidity can be controlled at will for the purpose of studying the response of plants to their environment.

phytyl: see *PHYTOL.

phyzog, var. *PHIZOG.

pi, *sb.* Add: **2.** *Electr.* Applied to a four-terminal set of three circuit elements in which one element is in series between two in parallel. Usu. written as π or Π.

1924 K. S. JOHNSON *Transmission Circuits for Teleph. Communication* xi. 124 If the structure shown in Fig. 1 is considered to be made up of Π sections.., each section may be regarded as terminating in a mid-shunt iterative impedance. **1930** DANNATT & DALGLEISH *Electr. Power Transmission* v. 118 This network is frequently used as an equivalent circuit for a transmission line, and is referred to as a π-circuit. **1930** [see *ladder network* s.v. *LADDER *sb.* 6]. **1950** [see *LATTICE *sb.* 2 d]. **1961** *Amat. Radio Handbk.* (ed. 3) vi. 175/1 The pi-network coupler is often used for delivering power to an aerial feeder. **1972** R. H. WARRING *Ham Radio* v. 68 The adoption of a pi-network tank circuit does not automatically ensure that no harmonics are radiated which may show up..on near-by television receivers, when a transmitter is being worked on the various amateur bands.

3. *Physics* and *Chem.* [After *P III. 2.] Used to designate electrons, orbitals, molecular states, etc., possessing one unit of angular momentum about an internuclear axis; *pi-* (or π-)*bond*, a bond formed by a π-orbital.

Usu. written π when it refers to one electron or orbital and Π when it refers to a molecule as a whole.

1929 R. S. MULLIKEN in *Chem. Rev.* VI. 532 The molecule contains two $1s\sigma$ electrons ($1s\sigma^2$)..and two $3s\sigma$ electrons, and (in NO and O_2) one or two $3p\pi$ electrons... The second (Greek) letter gives the value of a quantum number λ which does not exist for the atom, (σ, π, δ,... mean λ = 0, 1, 2,...). *Ibid.* 534 Two σ electrons of any one kind.., or four π, or δ, electrons of any one kind.. constitute a closed shell for a diatomic molecule. **1930** —— in *Physical Rev.* XXXVI. 616 The use of the symbols Σ, Π, Δ, Φ, Γ, H,..to indicate Λ = 0, 1, 2, 3, 4, 5,.. is recommended. **1939** J. W. T. SPINKS tr. *Herzberg's Molecular Spectra* I. v. 291 Examples of $^2\Sigma-^2\Pi$ transitions are the ultraviolet OH bands. **1947** *Q. Rev. Chem. Soc.* I. 157 A double bond is normally a σ-bond and a π-bond together. **1952** L. N. FERGUSON *Electron Struct. Org. Molecules* ii. 19 The π electrons are bound less firmly and can be more easily polarized (that is, attracted to either end of the molecular orbital) than σ electrons, so the former are commonly referred to as mobile electrons, whereas the σ electrons are said to be localized. **1954** G. I. BROWN *Introd. Electronic Theories Org. Chem.* iv. 49 Two atoms linked by a σ-bond can rotate freely about the bond, unless there is some steric interference.., but free rotation is prevented when two atoms are linked by a π-bond. **1964** D. F. EGGERS et al. *Physical Chem.* xvi. 630 Since many molecular properties seem to be governed largely by the pi electrons, most theoretical calculations for such molecules are carried out for the pi electrons only. **1966** *New Scientist* 29 Dec. 735/2 So-called pi-bonded systems containing alternating sequences of single and double bonds. **1972** J. C. SCHUG *Introd. Quantum Chem.* xi. 263 The remaining six valence electrons [in the benzene molecule] occupy the unhybridized p orbitals of the carbon atoms, which are perpendicular to the plane of the molecule... Each of these so-called pi electrons can be paired with a pi electron on a neighboring atom to form three additional pi-type bonds, as in ethylene. **1973** A. W. ADAMSON *Textbk. Physical Chem.* xvii. 838 Pi bonding is considered not so much as providing the primary bonding holding a molecule together as supplementing an already present sigma bond. **1975** H. W. KROTO *Molecular Rotation Spectra* x. 224 The $^2\Pi$ ground state of NO..has both orbital and spin angular momentum.

pi, *a.* (*sb.*) Add: (Later examples as *adj.*) See also PIE *a.*[1] in Dict. and Suppl.

1916 [see *FIT *a.* 5 b]. **1968** J. R. ACKERLEY *My Father & Myself* viii. 79 He invited the two of us into the billiard-room..for a 'jaw', which could hardly be called 'pi' and which he himself described as 'man to man'. **1972** *South China Morning Post* (Hong Kong) 20 Nov. 16/4 The subject emerges, I believe falsely, as a kind of overgrown school-prefect, bossy, frustrated and a bit pi. **1975** J. HITCHMAN *Such Strange Lady* ii. 27 'That were only sparrers... They aren't good for nothing.' 'God made them,' retorted the clergyman's daughter, 'so they must be good for something.' All very pi' of course. **1978** *Broadcast* 3 Apr. 42/2 'Blue Peter', though never pi or holier than thou, is always on the side of the.. decencies.

piaculative (pəiˌæ·kiŭlătiv), *a.* *rare.* [f. L. *piāculum* PIACLE + -ATIVE.] = PIACULAR *a.* I.

1919 T. S. ELIOT *Poems*, The young are red and pustular Clutching piaculative pence.

Piagetian (piăʒī·ʃən), *a.* [f. the name of Jean *Piaget* (1896–1980) + -IAN.] Of or pertaining to the theories or methods of Piaget, Swiss educational child psychologist. Also **Piagetan** (piā·ʒeˌăn).

1960 *Jrnl. Child Psychol.* I. 191 (*heading*) Some points of Piagetian theory in the light of experimental criticism. **1973** *Jrnl. Genetic Psychol.* CXXII. 27 This study has as its point of departure the Piagetan conceptions of the nature and development of logical structures. *Ibid.* CXXIII. 277 The large number of investigations that have tried to establish normative data in the area of Piagetian conservations. **1974** *Nature* 30 Aug. 713/2 The Piagetian tests, which are intended to reflect changes in mental maturity, are sensitive to age differences. **1977** *Language* LIII. 483 Arguing from a Piagetian perspective of cognitive development, B concludes that children know very little about syntax prior to the use of two-word utterances.

piai: see PEAI *sb.*

Pian (pəi·ăn), *a.* [f. L. *Pius* (see PIOUS *a.*), a name adopted by several Popes + -AN.] Of or pertaining to Pius; *spec.* of or pertaining to the pontificate or liturgical reforms of Pope Pius V or Pope Pius X.

1916 *Month* Sept. 258 The publication of the Pian Breviary in 1568. **1959** N. ABERCROMBIE *Life & Work Edmund Bishop* v. ix. 353 Converts of Leo XIII's time must learn to curb themselves, and accommodate themselves to 'Pian days'. **1960** *Duckett's Reg.* Mar. 32/2 It was surely the intention of these 'Neo-Gallicans' to rid themselves..of all that savoured of Trent and the Pian liturgical revision. **1971** *Tablet* 16 Jan. 65/2 Paul VI..explains..why the Pian document and Missal of 1570 give way to the Pauline rite.

pianette. Add: (Further example.) Also **pianet.**

1894 G. B. SHAW *How to become Mus. Critic* (1960) 222 Excellent French pianets. **1897** A. BEARDSLEY *Let.* 7 Jan. (1971) 240 Don't feel bound in any way about the pianette. I'm afraid you expected a larger affair. Of course it is quite a small instrument. **1908** G. B. SHAW *Pen Portraits* (1932) 80 Has Chesterton ever spent his last half-crown on an opera by Meyerbeer or Verdi, and sat down at a crazy pianet to roar it and thrash it through?

pianism. Add: **a.** (Further examples.) **b.** The art of composing for the piano, *spec.* the particular skill or characteristic style of a composer of music for the piano; the action or art of arranging a musical composition for performance on the piano.

1889 *Cent. Dict.*, *Pianism*,..the adaptation of a piece of music to effective performance on the pianoforte. **1892** G. B. SHAW *Music in London 1890–94* (1931) II. 37 Her fault now is that her pianism has outstripped her musicianship. **1934** S. R. NELSON *All about Jazz* ii. 41 The diatonic and chromatic figurations that occur..in ordinary piano compositions..have no counterpart in dance pianism. **1946** R. BLESH *Shining Trumpets* (1949) II. xiii. 299 George Zack is as successful at this underworld pianism as any. **1960** [see *HAUTE ÉCOLE]. **1961** *Listener* 19 Oct. 627/1 Liszt's pianism (his writing for the instrument as well as the style of performance) is perhaps the least problematic. **1964** *Ibid.* 27 Feb. 373/1 It is worth noting that pure pianism as such came into its own in the Romantic age, and that mastery of the new technical resources of Chopin and Liszt does not necessarily benefit the performance of earlier music. **1971** *Daily Tel.* 8 Mar. 10/2 Mr Lill's pianism was admirable, but its very virtues underlined the absence of a lively interpreting personality. **1971** [see *PIANISTICALLY *adv.*]. **1977** *Listener* 17 Nov. 655/1 Young Sorabji seems to have been a composer..who thought in terms of the most stratospheric achievements of transcendental pianism.

pianist. Add: **c.** in appositive *Combs.*, as *pianist-arranger*, *-composer*, *-conductor*, *-leader*.

1955 KEEPNEWS & GRAUER *Pict. Hist. Jazz* xx. 264 Pianist-arranger George Handy..turned..to the work of such as Bartok and Stravinsky. **1958** M. WHITE in P. Gammond *Decca Bk. Jazz* xviii. 220 Lew Stone..had been working as pianist-arranger for Roy Fox's band. **1928** E. BLOM *Romance of Piano* 156 The most accomplished amongst the earliest pianist-composers. **1942** —— *Music in Eng.* vii. 116 Thus arose the new race of pianist-composers which so conspicuously helps to people the musical history of this period, and to which even Mozart and Beethoven in a sense belong. **1959** 'F. NEWTON' *Jazz Scene* ii. 34 A wayward and notable pianist-composer. **1960** *Times* 22 Sept. 16/4 Rachmaninov the pianist-composer. **1934** S. R. NELSON *All about Jazz* v. 105 Claude Lapham..began his career as a pianist, and appeared as pianist-conductor at such well-known New York theatres as Ziegfeld's. **1955** L. FEATHER *Encycl. Jazz* 185 Rose to prominence as pianist leader of a band that made its bow..in 1924. **1958** C. Fox in P. Gammond *Decca Bk. Jazz* vii. 97 Another pianist-leader, though not quite of Hines' calibre, was Claude Hopkins.

pianistic, *a.* Add: Also, pertaining to or suitable for performance on the piano; of, pertaining to, or characteristic of pianism.

1921 I. SCHARRER in L. Ronald *Music Lovers' Portfolio* III. p. ix/1, First of all, I would emphasise the fact that it is perfect piano music; nothing before or since has been more absolutely pianistic, more thoroughly suited to the instrument. **1931** G. JACOB *Orchestral Technique* v. 50 Note the way in which the pianistic idiom..has been translated into its orchestral equivalent. **1942** E. PAUL *Narrow St.* xxiii. 203 Only one pupil..had such pianistic genius. **1950** *Chambers's Encycl.* VIII. 67/1 The same 12-bar pattern..serves as a basis for the 'Boogie Woogie', a typically pianistic species. **1955** *Times* 4 July 12/4 Two pieces by his mother, Teresa de Rogatis, demonstrated the pianistic fluency of both mother and son. **1958** *Listener* 21 Aug. 285/1 Leonard Borwick's exquisitely pianistic version of Debussy's 'L'Après midi d'un faune'. **1975** *Ibid.* 18 Sept. 378/1 The most outstanding pianistic feat..Dmitry Alexeev's playing of Prokofiev.

B. *sb. pl.* The art of playing the piano, *spec.* skilful technique in piano-playing.

1950 BLESH & JANIS *They all played Ragtime* viii. 149 The formidable eight-to-the-bar pianistics of Meade Lux Lewis, Albert Ammons of Chicago, and Pete Johnson of Kansas City. **1958** P. GAMMOND *Decca Bk. Jazz* xv. 184 His dazzling and immensely skilful display of pianistics.

Hence **piani·stically** *adv.*, in a pianistic manner; from a pianistic point of view.

1926 W. C. HANDY *Blues* 20 Instrumentally and in particular pianistically, the mode was backward. **1928** *Daily Tel.* 5 June 9/5 She would have approached nearer to the real Bach if she had thought less pianistically in the matter of tone-colour. **1946** R. BLESH *Shining Trumpets* (1949) xiii. 317 Pianistically, it has passages of great beauty but it is not completely Negroid. **1971** *Daily Tel.* 6 Apr. 12/7 The most remarkable work of the evening pianistically—and pianism was this programme's concern—was the Grand Concert Fantasy on Themes from Bellini's 'Sonnambula'. **1977** *Gramophone* June 63/1 Berman's playing here has a child-like directness allied to playing which is, pianistically, very complex with all manner of material in the inner parts coming interestingly and engagingly through.

piano, *a.* (*adv.*) *sb.*[1] Add: **1. a.** *adj.* (Examples of *fig.* use.)

a **1817** JANE AUSTEN *Persuasion* (1818) IV. vi. 120 James Benwick is rather too piano for me. **1900** E. GLYN *Visits of Elizabeth* 188 The Marquis..looked thoroughly worn out and as *piano* as a beaten dog. **1922** A. HUXLEY *Let.* 9 Sept. (1969) 209 Aunt Nettie is with us: but happily she is in a very calm and piano mood so that she is quite an agreeable companion. **1941** [see *EXALTÉ *a.*]. **1953** E. M. FORSTER *Hill of Devi* 138 Very piano and tired, poor dear.

piano, *sb.*[2] Add: **1. b.** Piano-playing.

1946 J. CARY *Moonlight* viii. 55, I was looking forward to some real old romantic piano, with the genuine macassar flavour. **1950** BLESH & JANIS *They all played Ragtime* iii. 55 Turpin, who had pioneered syncopated piano in the Missouri metropolis. **1968** *Blues Unlimited* Sept. 10, I heard..some straggling piano. **1975** *Listener* 11 Dec. 796/2 A boy with a musical ear, who had picked up piano from an old black man in a city dive. **1978** *Gramophone* July 178/1 He then went on to study piano and finally, almost by accident, conducting.

c. Chiefly *U.S. slang.* = SPARE-RIB.

1911 J. W. HORSLEY *I Remember* xi. 254 Ingenuity and humour are sometimes the parents of slang terms..I was reminded by..'piano' for ribs of beef. **1942** Z. N. HURSTON in *Amer. Mercury* July 96/1 *Piano*, spare ribs (white rib-bones suggest piano keys).

2. a. *piano bench*, *-case* (examples), *concerto*, *-lamp*, *piece*, *recital*, *recording*, *rehearsal*, *solo*, *sonata*, *-stool* (examples); **b.** *piano-player* (later examples), *-playing* (earlier and later examples), *-thumping* vbl. sb. and ppl. adj., *-tuner* (examples), *-tuning* vbl. sb. and ppl. adj.; **d. piano-accordion** (see *ACCORDION); **piano-conductor**, a musician who conducts a band while playing the piano part; **piano part**, the part assigned to the piano in concerted music; **piano quartet** = *pianoforte quartet* s.v. *PIANOFORTE b; **piano quintet** = *pianoforte quintet* s.v. *PIANOFORTE b; **piano rag**, a rag for performance on the piano (see *RAG *sb.*[5] 2); **piano reduction**, an arrangement of orchestral music for performance on the piano (see *REDUCTION 11 d; **piano roll** = *music-roll* (*b*) s.v *MUSIC *sb.* 12 d; also (with hyphen) *attrib.*; **piano score**, a pianoforte score, *spec.* a condensed version of a full score for performance on the piano; **piano trio** = *pianoforte trio* s.v. *PIANOFORTE b; **piano wire**, a special kind of strong steel wire used for the strings of pianos (see quot. 1956); a length of this; cf. **pianoforte wire*; **piano-writing**, composing for the piano.

1914 G. B. SHAW *Pygmalion* (1916) II. 137 Higgins.. takes refuge on the piano bench. **1977** *New Yorker* 19 Sept. 62/3 She picked up the score from the piano bench. **1850** *Rep. Comm. Patents 1849* (U.S.) I. 300 What I claim..is a piano case or trunk lock. **1876** J. S. INGRAM *Centenn. Exposition* x. 334 Another very creditable piece of work was a rosewood piano-case. **1908** *Sears, Roebuck Catal.* 210/2 Every Beckwith piano case..is double veneered inside and outside. **1879** GROVE *Dict. Mus.* I. 387/2 In the whole of his piano concertos..we find an allegro, a slow movement, and a finale in quick time. **1934** A. L. BACHARACH *Mus. Compan.* iv. 598 There are far greater depths in the two piano concertos of Brahms. **1975** *Times* 22 Mar. 11/3 With 18 versions of Schumann's piano concerto already available, an immediate reaction to HMV's latest could well be 'why another?' **1934** S. R. NELSON *All about Jazz* ii. 43 The piano-conductor part of a commercial orchestration is very similar. **1957** MANVELL & HUNTLEY *Technique Film Music* i. 21 A series of scenes involving Lynch and Colonel Cameron, occupying two pages of the piano-conductor score. **1896** *Whims* Apr. 72 Ushered in, he found Margaret doing fancy-work under a large piano-lamp in the parlor. **1897** *McClure's Mag.* Nov. 57 The soft, yellow light from the shaded piano-lamp fell about her. **1909** *Cent. Dict.* Suppl. 996/3 *Piano-lamp*, a lamp intended for use with a piano: usually one with a firm tripod or other base and an adjustable standard by which it can be raised or lowered. **1934** A. L. Bacharach *Mus. Compan.* v. 482 There are..modern chamber works weighted with piano parts that make as heavy demands on virtuosity as any concerto. **1955** G. Abraham in H. Van Thal *Fanfare for E. Newman* 26 Telling touches were added..notably the sharpening of the D in the piano-part. **1969** *Listener* 2 Jan. 25/1 Another [friend] was forbidden to have his new work performed unless he omitted some offending clusters from the piano part. **1897** *Sears, Roebuck Catal.* 538/1 Easy and medium piano pieces..just the collection for home. **1935** E. Farjeon *Nursery in Nineties* 283 We drew up a programme.. a group of Harry's last piano-pieces, a Solo by Joe. **1977** K. O'Hara *Ghost of T. Penry* iv. 32 Faintly..came the sound of the same piano piece. **1906** *Chambers's Jrnl.* 31 Mar. 286/2 Anything in the nature of a mechanical piano-player uncontrolled by the taste and discretion of some guiding mind..is naturally abhorrent. Yet the instrument under review is..absolutely automatic. **1907** *Westm. Gaz.* 17 Sept. 10/1 The most rapid growth has been in mechanical piano-players and piano-playing attachments. **1933** H. S. Walpole *Vanessa* III. iv. 558 A typist whom Alfred had engaged actually owned a mechanical piano-player, bought of course on hire-purchase. **1964** L. Deighton *Funeral in Berlin* x. 64 The piano-player did a fancy cadenza. **1857** C. G. Leland in *Graham's Illustr. Mag.* May 458/1 Hans Breitmann gife a barty—dey had biano-blayin. **1859** Geo. Eliot *Let.* 7 Oct. (1954) III. 172, I had abundant time and opportunity for hours of piano-playing. **1956** 'C. Blackstock' *Dewey Death* vii. 169 She persistently told the world about..her piano playing and her temperament. **1977** *Times* 15 Nov. 17/5 The idiosyncrasy of his piano-playing. **1934** A. L. Bacharach *Mus. Compan.* viii. 488 During the same four years he wrote also a piano trio..and the first of his piano quartets. **1975** *Radio Times* 15 May 32/3 Dvořák... Piano Quartet in D major, Op. 23: Beaux Arts Trio with Walter Trampler (viola). **1925** E. Sackville-West *Piano Quintet* i. 1 A piano quintet, they were to start in a month's time upon a professional tour on the Continent. **1934** A. L. Bacharach *Mus. Compan.* viii. 488 There are many who regard this work as the direct ancestor of the great piano quintets of Schumann and Brahms. **1959** *Collins Mus. Encycl.* 525/2 The combination of piano with string quartet is called a piano quintet. **1972** *Jazz & Blues* Oct. 32/1 (Advt.), Joshua Rifkin's first Nonesuch album of piano rags. **1974** *Melody Maker* 20 Apr. 46 The first piano rag publication was 'Mississippi Rag' in 1897 by William H. Kvell. **1881** *Harper's Mag.* May 814/1 Piano and organ recitals have long been fashionable. **1950** L. Salter *Going to Concert* 99 At everything but piano recitals, there is a second person involved who has it.. in his power to turn the whole affair into a success or a failure. **1972** E. Greenfield *Penguin Guide to Bargain Records* No. 3. 297 As a popular piano recital this seems wholly successful. **1962** Piano recording [see *piano-stool* below]. **1975** *Hi-Fi News* Feb. 131/3 One of the most unspectacularly natural piano recordings I have heard for a long time. [**1944** W. Apel *Harvard Dict. Mus.* (1946) 631/2 *Réduction*, Fr., arrangement. *Piano réduction*, arrangement for piano.] **1966** *Listener* 29 Dec. 976/2 Autograph or copyist's manuscripts are still turning up. To mention one striking find of recent years, a copyist's manuscript of a piano reduction of the second Prologue of *Romeo and Juliet*. **1979** E. Wilkins et al. tr. *Sel. Lett. Gustav Mahler* 209, I hope you have received the piano reduction. **1966** *Listener* 10 Nov. 704/3, I had coached most of the singers..and I also played for his piano rehearsals. **1926** Whiteman & McBride *Jazz* viii. 170 The mechanical royalties arising from phonograph and piano roll records are usually protected in the contract. **1956** M. Stearns *Story of Jazz* (1957) xiii. 143 Most piano-roll companies employed a hack who could 'rag' any tune for issue on a piano roll. **1965** *Listener* 1 Apr. 501/2 They did make a considerable number of piano-rolls, but with the ascendancy of the gramophone in the twenties, these perforated screeds of paper were relegated to the lumber-room of the past. **1973** *Guardian* 7 Mar. 10 'Maple Leaf Rag' underwrote [Scott] Joplin's reputation... His own piano rolls, cut late in his career when his health was failing, hardly do him justice. **1929** H. Crane *Let.* 26 Feb. (1965) 339 They've promised to publish *The Bridge*—on sheets as large as a piano score. **1938** *Oxf. Compan. Mus.* 851/2 A Piano Score is the reduction of an orchestral score to a piano version. **1964** D. Francis *Nerve* ii. 16 My mother's grand piano lay inches deep in piano scores. **1977** R. Barnard *Death on High C's* xviii. 185 The piano score of *Rigoletto*. **1923** J. Reith *Diary* 19 Mar. (1975) 131 There was no piano solo so I..got him to play Schubert's 'Marche Militaire'. **1943** L. Abbott *Approach to Music* iv. 74 Schubert composed his 'Serenade' as a song, but Liszt transcribed it for piano solo. **1977** *Listener* 17 Feb. 215/3 The atmospheric 'Slow Drag'..includes a delicate piano solo by Kenny Kersey. **1859** A. J. Munby *Diary* 25 May in D. Hudson *Munby* (1972) 33 Songs, serious & comic: piano-sonatas, and duets and trios with violin and violoncello. **1924** M. Kennedy *Constant Nymph* xvi. 214 A piano sonata which Sebastian was to play at a concert. **1975** *Gramophone* Mar. 1629/1 She could play a piano sonata by ear as a child. **1847** C. Brontë *Jane Eyre* II. iii. 82 She turned round on the piano-stool. **1877** E. S. Ward *Story of Avis* 335 Barbara Allen sat on the piano-stool. **1930** G. Greene *Two Witnesses* 34 We would finish up the evening sitting on either side of him on the piano-stool while he played and sang, in his funny husky tenor voice. **1962** A. Nisbett *Technique Sound Studio* 38 A piano-stool squeak can spoil a piano recording. **1906** *Westm. Gaz.* 11 Aug. 4/3 In these days of universal piano-thumping. *c* **1909** D. H. Lawrence *Collier's Friday Night* (1934) II. 30 I'll bet it was a thump! Pomp! Pomp! (*Makes a piano-thumping gesture.*) **1934** A. L. Bacharach *Mus. Compan.* vii. 486 The majority of his numerous piano trios belong to this early period. **1977** *Listener* 20 Jan. 94/2 Detailed analyses of the piano trios, piano sonatas, string quartets and symphonies. **1858** *Boyd's Philad. City Business Directory* 223 (*heading*) Piano Tuners. **1900** H. A. Jones *Mrs. Dane's Defence* I. 17 A young piano-tuner. **1973** A. Christie *Postern of Fate* II. iii. 80 It's the gentleman what's come to do the piano... You said I'd have to get a piano tuner. **1897** *Sears, Roebuck Catal.* 538/1 *Piano tuning hammer*... Long Rosewood handle, double head with oblong holes, and single head with star hole. **1974** *Times* 21 Oct. 24/3 (Advt.), Piano tuning and repairs. **1975** *Times* 2 Jan. 3/4 Total of piano-tuning trainees trebled. **1870** *English Mechanic* XII. 215/3 Piano wire..—What are the different sizes of wire as now used for a 7 octave cottage piano? **1938** J. Williamson *Surveying & Field Work* (ed. 2) xvii. 430 Two heavy weights are suspended by five piano wires from an overhead frame. **1955** W. Gaddis *Recognitions* I. iv. 161 All you got to do is get them dumb cops on their motorcycles, and string a good piece of piano wire across the road. **1956** A. K. Osborne *Encycl. Iron & Steel Industry* 317/1 *Piano wire*, wire made from the best-quality plain carbon steel, with a carbon content of about 0·80% to 0·95%. It is usually drawn to a tensile stress of more than 120 tons per sq. in. **1973** R. Busby *Pattern of Violence* viii. 122 Black hostile faces confronted him in an atmosphere as taut as a piano-wire. **1977** *Sci. Amer.* Oct. 74/3 These light-weight gliders gave MacCready the idea of using an aluminum-tube skeleton braced with piano wire. **1946** E. Lockspeiser in A. L. Bacharach *Brit. Music* xv. 196 There is often clumsiness in the piano-writing, too monotonous an insistence on pattern, or a lack of finish in the way he handles a phrase. **1959** D. Cooke *Lang. Mus.* i. 6 Comparisons such as those of piano-writing with black-and-white drawing, of orchestration with colour.

pianoforte. Add: **b.** *pianoforte concerto*, *-player* (earlier and later examples), *recital*, *solo*, *sonata*, *-tuner* (examples); **pianoforte jump, obstacle,** a jump or obstacle in a steeplechase whose shape resembles that of a pianoforte; **pianoforte quartet,** a quartet for violin, viola, cello, and pianoforte; **pianoforte quintet,** a quintet for pianoforte and string quartet; **pianoforte score** (see quot. 1876); **pianoforte trio,** a trio for violin, cello, and pianoforte; † **pianoforte wire** = *piano wire* s.v. *piano *sb.*[2] 2 d.

1932 *Radio Times* 29 July 269/2 Hilda Bor and orchestra—pianoforte concerto in D minor—*Mozart*. **1934** A. L. Bacharach *Mus. Compan.* iv. 591 The pianoforte concertos of the modern repertory begin with J. S. Bach, who arranged sixteen violin concertos of Vivaldi for the clavier. **1962** G. Moore *Am I too Loud?* v. 52 Many people in different parts of the world have given it as their opinion that he [*sc.* Solomon] is the finest player of a pianoforte concerto they have ever heard. **1908** *Daily Chron.* 9 June 3/5 Some of the Italian officers will give a display of what is known as the Pianoforte jump. **1909** *Westm. Gaz.* 8 Mar. 6/4 The 'pianoforte' obstacle will consist of four feet of water, followed by a sloping bank of turf with a three-foot wall at the end of it. **1836** Dickens *Sk. Boz* II. 271 The pianoforte player.. fainted away. **1849** Mrs. Gaskell *Let.* 13 May (1966) 829 Benedict the great piano-forte player. **1887** C. H. H. Parry *Stud. Gt. Composers* iv. 108 Haydn is said to have persisted in regarding Beethoven as a pianoforte player, and not as a composer. **1883** Grove *Dict. Mus.* III. 58/2 Next to the string quartet ranks the pianoforte quartet, which, however, is built on quite a different principle. **1954** *Ibid.* (ed. 5) I. 878/1 There is a precedent in the slow movement of Schumann's pianoforte Quartet. **1828** E. Holmes *Ramble among Musicians of Germany* 282 M. Herder played a pianoforte quintet in E flat of his composition. **1954** *Grove's Dict. Mus.* (ed. 5) I. 877/1 The pianoforte Quintet in F minor..was originally composed, but not published, as a string Quintet with two cellos. **1914** G. B. Shaw *Misalliance* 56 How many of them could be bribed to attend a pianoforte recital by a great player? **1876** Stainer & Barrett *Dict. Mus. Terms* 353/2 *Pianoforte score*, a score of a vocal or instrumental composition, under which is written in two lines a condensed form of the harmonies for the use of a pianoforte. **1912** W. Owen *Let.* 11 Jan. (1967) 108, I shall substitute for it a pianoforte solo. **1954** *Grove's Dict. Mus.* (ed. 5) V. 946/2 Of other works for pianoforte solo the Fantasy in C minor..is of special importance. **1883** *Ibid.* (ed. 1) III. 577/1 The slow movements of both are very well known; that of the Pianoforte Sonata being the Funeral March. **1954** *Ibid.* (ed. 5) V. 947/2 It was in fact Mozart's own work in that form and was intended to become part..of a complete pianoforte sonata. **1889** *Ibid.* (ed. 1) IV. 172/1 Pianoforte trios, as they are called, caused all others to retire into the background. **1954** *Ibid.* (ed. 5) V. 947/2 The pianoforte trios were mainly written for performance at private music meetings. **1801** Busby *Dict. Mus.* s.v. *Tuning fork*. This instrument [*sc.* a tuning-fork] is chiefly used by harpischord and piano-forte tuners. **1861** Dickens *Gt. Expect.* I. xi. 183 At the pianoforte-tuner's across the street. **1838** *Osborne's Guide Grand Junction Railway* (Advt. section) 113 Piano Forte Wires and Roman Strings. **1870** *English Mechanic* 30 Sept. 35/2 Pianoforte wire.—What weights it will support, etc. **1902** *Chambers's Jrnl.* June 413/2 This kite is of the box or Hargreave pattern... Its 'string' consists of four miles of pianoforte-wire.

Pianola. Add: Also, a piano which incorporates such a mechanism, a player-piano. Also *attrib.* (Further examples.)

1908 *Daily Chron.* 31 July 5/4 The ingenious contrivance of an Australian engineer who claims to have invented an accurate recording target... The figures are printed on paper, which runs at the required speed on two rollers on what may be described as the pianola principle. **1912** *Collier's* 26 Oct. 23/1 It's usually one of the White Light hits to begin with—and it's odd how exquisite they are on the Pianola. **1916** *Proc. Musical Assoc.* *1915–16* 16 The Press have adopted the term 'Pianola' as a generic name for all mechanical piano-player devices. **1943** J. B. Priestley *Daylight on Saturday* xii. 78 We'll find out.. we're not making planes any more but sewing machines and pianolas. **1947** *Sat. Rev. Lit.* (U.S.) 25 Oct. 65/2 Unlike vaudeville, the pianola is not dead. **1953** Dylan Thomas *Under Milk Wood* (1954) 10 He sold the pianola. **1962** *Trade Marks Jrnl.* 26 Sept. 1315/2 Pianola... Player-pianos. Aeolian American Corporation.., New York,.. United States of America; manufacturers and merchants. **1978** F. Weldon *Praxis* xii. 82 Mrs. Allbright played the pianola with too many stops out. **1980** L. Lewis *Private Life of Country House* iv. 47 A large walnut Steck piano with pianola player incorporated.

b. = *pianola hand* below.

1974 *Country Life* 9 May 1155/3 With everything right, the [bridge] contract is a pianola.

c. *Comb.*, as *pianola-like* adj.; **pianola hand** *Cards*, a hand that is easy to play; **pianola roll** = *music-roll* (*b*) s.v. *music *sb.* 12d.

1913 F. Irwin *Auction High-Lights* ii. 22 Which do you like better, a 'pianola' hand or a hand where you have to tussle and fight for every point? **1945** E. Bowen *Demon Lover* 134 The pianola-like play of the conversation did not drown the nervousness round the table. **1915** *Chicago Daily News Almanac 1916* 615/2 The Coe music collection..[contains] 560 pianola rolls. **1959** 'F. Newton' *Jazz Scene* ii. 33 Old pianola rolls by the leading composer-players of this earliest jazz style.

pianolaed (pīˌănōu·lăd), *a.* [f. Pianola + -ed[1].] Rendered by a pianola.

1926 A. B. Smith *Studies & Caprices* 176 The pauses.. are not, as in the pianolaed performance, the mere passing of time.

pianoless (piˌæ·nolės), *a.* [f. Piano *sb.*[2] + -less.] Without a piano, esp. designating an ensemble of musicians which does not include a pianist.

1955 L. Feather *Encycl. Jazz* 66 Gerry Mulligan and others experimented with pianoless units. **1956** M. Stearns *Story of Jazz* (1957) xviii. 240 Pacific Jazz recorded the pianoless quartet of Chet Baker and Gerry Mulligan. **1973** *Black World* Oct. 48/1 His preferred instrumental format for his own recordings is with pianoless groups.

pianolist (pĭˌănōu·list). [f. Pianola + -ist.] A person who plays a Pianola.

1908 G. Kobbé (*title*) The pianolist: a guide for pianola players. *Ibid.* 8 Another purpose..is to furnish pianolists with a guide to the music which they play, or might play. **1916** *Proc. Musical Assoc.* *1915–16* 24 There are many pianolists so keen that they will cut their own music in unique single copies. **1927** *Observer* 23 Oct. 14 The player seems to have the same sort of relation to his instrument as the pianolist to his.

‖ **piano nobile** (pyā·no nōu·bile). *Archit.* [It., f. *piano* floor, storey + *nobile* noble, great.] The main storey of a large house, usually on the first floor, of lofty structure, and containing the principal apartments.

1909 in *Cent. Dict.* Suppl., s.v. *piano*[3]. **1910** *Encycl. Brit.* X. 527/1 The principal floor is the storey which contains the chief apartments whether on the ground- or first-floor; in Italy they are always on the latter and known as the 'piano nobile'. **1922** F. G. Ellerton *Let.* 14 Apr. in J. Bailey *Lett. & Diaries* (1935) 216 The great windows of the *piano nobile* and the fine ones of the second floor where the Strozzi still live after *four hundred and fifty years*! **1928** A. Huxley *Point Counter Point* iii. 37 Two flights up, between the *piano nobile* and the servants' quarters under the roof. **1939** J. D. S. Pendlebury *Archaeol. Crete* iv. 186 The South Propylaeum, from which access was obtained to the 'piano nobile'. **1955** L. Woolley *Alalakh* iii. 94 The upper floor, the *piano nobile*, no longer exists, but its principal room, the *grand salon*, can safely be reconstructed. **1965** B. Sweet-Escott *Baker St. Irreg.* vi. 180 On the *piano nobile* was a large room in which Mr Bertram Mills himself had sat. **1970** *Guardian* 16 Sept. 11/1 The 'piano nobile', entered through a colonnaded portico and up a curving flight of carpeted marble. **1974** K. Clark *Another Part of Wood* vi. 238 The whole *piano nobile*, with beautiful 'Adam' rooms, marble chimney pieces and painted ceilings, was completely unnecessary. **1976** J. Lees-Milne *W. Beckford* v. 70 The Octagon Cabinet..and the Crimson Breakfast Parlour..bring the apartments of the *piano nobile* of the Abbey to an end.

piano-organ. Add: So **pia:no-o·rganist.**

1885 W. S. Gilbert *Mikado* I. 9 The piano organist—I've got him on the list! **1955** L. Feather *Encycl. Jazz* 123 Her husband, piano-organist Jesse Crump, worked and recorded with her.

piano piano. (Later example.)

1925 D. H. Lawrence *Let.* 25 Nov. (1962) II. 867 But it's no good: we've got to go *piano-piano*.

piassaba. Add: Also, the tropical African palm, *Raphia vinifera*, or the fibre obtained from it. (*Piassava* is now the usu. form.) (Later examples.)

1889 G. S. Boulger *Uses of Plants* VI. 171 Pará Piassaba, of which the ramenta are used for brushes. **1922** W. Schlich *Man. Forestry* (ed. 4) I. 309 The valuable 'piassava fibre' is prepared from the leaves of the bamboo palm. **1936** *Nature* 28 Mar. 528/1 The Hard Fibres Section of the British Empire Producers' Organisation has arranged a comprehensive group of exhibits of sisal and sisal manufacturers... Other stands display.. West African piassava. **1957** M. Banton *W. Afr. City* iii. 43 Kola-nuts are grown in the south,..piassava along the southern coast. **1964** J. P. Clarke *Three Plays* 21 Let's Sing of souls tied down with ropes Of piassava so strong. *Ibid.* 74 What single harm Have I done that this poison more catching Than fruit from the piassava palm should..be bailed into the stream Of my blood. **1966**

E. J. H. CORNER *Nat. Hist. Palms* iii. 65 The thick brown coating of leaf-base fibres of the piassába or chiquichiqui palm *Leopoldinia piassaba*..are made into ropes. *Ibid.* xiv. 331 Piassava, or African bass, is derived from the vascular bundles of the leaf-stalk and sheath [of *Raphia vinifera*]. **1969** E. H. PINTO *Treen* 194 Piassava fibre.. has been used in bass brooms for many centuries.

Piastraccia (pyastrā·tʃia), the name of a quarry near Seravezza, between Carrara and Lucca in N. Italy, used to designate a variety of white marble with slender grey veins quarried there.

1909 *Westm. Gaz.* 9 June 11/3 The entrance hall and corridor walls are faced with polished Piastraccia and Swedish green marble. **1955** W. GADDIS *Recognitions* III. i. 726 In response to the darkening sky, the sea changed its surface from glass to marble, the Breche rose marble of Italy reflecting the broken color of the sun, and losing that, to the gray-white Piastraccia, reflecting light from nowhere, veined with shadows.

piastre, piaster. Add: **3.** (In form *piastre.*) The name of a unit of currency introduced in Indo-China under French rule in 1885.

1908 *Whitaker's Almanack 1909* 618/1 The financial and political unity of Indo-China was finally established in 1898... The revenue, about 51,850,000 piastres, is derived mainly from customs, excise, and other indirect taxes. **1955** [see *KIP *sb.*[8]]. **1968** R. WEST *Sk. Vietnam* i. 22 The street hawkers who offer you two hundred and fifty piastres a dollar. **1970** *Daily Tel.* 22 July 14 In Saigon, prices are sky high. The piastre, officially worth 118 to the dollar, is traded by black marketeers at nearly 400 to the dollar. **1977** *Private Eye* 1 Apr. 20/2 (Advt.), 100 piastre (£70 face value) South Vietnamese note.

Piat (pī·ăt). [Acronym f. the initials of *p*rojector *i*nfantry *a*nti-*t*ank.] A weapon used by infantry against tanks in the war of 1939–45.

1944 *Hutchinson's Pict. Hist. War* 27 Oct. 1943–11 Apr. 1944. 321 The powerful new P.I.A.T. (projector, infantry, anti-tank) loaded and in position for firing... In this demonstration test of the 'Piat', a German tank has received a direct hit. **1948** PARTRIDGE *Dict. Forces' Slang* 140 *Piat*, Projector *I*nfantry *A*nti-*T*ank. A mortar type of projector designed to destroy tanks at close range... It had a complement of two men, but could be easily handled by one. **1964** A. MCKEE *Caen* vii. 101 Small parties of infantry, with Piats,.. began to stalk the Tigers. **1974** C. RYAN *Bridge too Far* III. xiv. 206 Frost could hear the crash of Vlasto's Piat bombs smashing into the pillbox.

piazza. Add: Now usu. with pronunc. (-ts-). Pl. **piazze** (-tse). **1.** (Later examples in extended and *transf.* uses.)

1942 *Country Life* 9 Oct. 694/3 (*caption*) Piccadilly Circus..a new building repeats that at present facing down Lower Regent Street. Between them a 'piazza' for pedestrians is formed. **1959** *Listener* 3 Dec. 962/2 The idea of enlarging the present underground booking-hall to create a vast below-street-level shopping piazza. **1962** *Ibid.* 19 Apr. 689/3 Among the features of the scheme is a paved piazza. **1967** C. SETON-WATSON *Italy from Liberalism to Fascism* xi. 425 Many were appalled by the irruption of the *piazza* and the press into delicate questions of international diplomacy. **1976** *Times* 20 Feb. 12/5 George Street [in Edinburgh] still has the Georgian Assembly Rooms midway between the two great *piazze* of St Andrew Square and Charlotte Square. **1977** *New Yorker* 26 Sept. 32/2 Moulmein was reading..on his piazza when I got home. **1978** J. MCNEIL *Consultant* i. 21 He could see the City [of London], far below..the small *piazza* he had crossed.

2. b. (Earlier and *attrib.* examples.)

1724 H. JONES *Present State Virginia* 26 It is a lofty Pile of Brick Building adorn'd with a Cupola... There is a spacious Piazza on the West Side, from one Wing to the other. **1771** J. S. COPLEY *Let.* 3 Aug. (1914) 137 You see I have Drawn the Chinea Clossit Store Room in the east piaza. **1876** A. D. WHITNEY *Sights & Insights* I. 8 There were settees, and regular piazza chairs. *a* **1916** H. JAMES *Ivory Tower* (1917) I. ii. 18 Shaking his little foot from the depths of a piazza chair,.. where..the cool spreading verandah, commanded the low green cliff. **1977** MCDAVID & O'CAIN in S. Greenbaum *Acceptability in Lang.* viii. 112 The uncultivated almost unanimously characterize *porch* as modern and *piazza* as old-fashioned.

piazzetta. (Later examples.) *spec.* (with cap. initial), the *Piazzetta di San Marco* in Venice.

1824 W. IRVING *Tales of Traveller* I. I. 106 They crossed the Piazzetta, but paused in the middle of it to enjoy the scene. **1869** GEO. ELIOT *Jrnl.* in J. W. Cross *George Eliot's Life* (1885) III. 45 Even landing on the Piazzetta, one has a sense..of being in an entirely novel scene. **1888** H. JAMES *Aspern Papers* I. v. 84 The sea-breeze passed between the twin columns of the Piazzetta. **1906** *Edin. Rev.* July 194 To cross its bridges and its piazzette and to pass under its gateways. **1910** H. G. WELLS *New Machiavelli* (1911) II. iii. 246 We would stroll on the Piazzetta, or go out into the sunset in a gondola. **1931** C. BAX *Venetian* I. i. 5 The main part of the stage represents a piazzetta or flagged yard. **1942** A. L. ROWSE *Cornish Childhood* i. 22 It played the part of the back-alley in East End life, if not of the piazzetta in a little Italian town. **1966** *Listener* 20 Jan. 105/2 In little back alleys and piazzettas water will pour from a spout into a marble basin or stone trough. **1977** P. D. JAMES *Death of Expert Witness* I. vi. 28 To see..that incomparable view of San Marco from the western end of the Piazza... To stand together on the Piazzetta..and look across the shimmering water.

pi·bble-pa:bble, pibble-babble, alterations of BIBBLE-BABBLE.

1599 SHAKES. *Hen. V* IV. i. 72 There is no tiddle tadle nor pibble bable in Pompeyes Campe. **1953** *Essays & Stud.* VI. 112 Our South Wales dialect in English, a pibble-pabble inadequate to the demands of a full and varied literature. **1959** *20th Cent.* June, He was the main topic of the pibble-pabble in the forum last month.

pibcorn. For *Obs.* read '*Obs.* exc. *Hist.*' and add later examples.

a **1953** [see *CRWTH]. **1968** J. ARNOLD *Shell Bk. Country Crafts* 316 The Pibcorn, of Wales, dating from the eighteenth century, was a pastoral hornpipe.

piblokto (piblǫ·kto). Also **piblockto, piblok-toq.** [Eskimo.] **a.** = *Arctic hysteria* s.v. *ARCTIC *a.* 1 c. **b.** A form of hysterical illness prevalent among Eskimo dogs.

1898 *Geogr. Jrnl.* XI. 228, I pushed on until the 'piblockto', or Greenland dog madness, induced by the continued exposure, got such a hold of my dogs as to make it absolutely impracticable for me to go further. **1910** R. E. PEARY *North Pole* xviii. 156 The adults are subject to a peculiar nervous affection which they call *piblokto*... The attack usually ends in a fit of weeping; and when the patient quiets down, the eyes are bloodshot, the pulse high, and the whole body trembles for an hour or so afterward. **1921** A. B. READER tr. *Tremblay's Cruise of Minnie Maud* vi. 125 The adult Eskimo are often subject to a peculiar nervous affection, a form of hysteria, which they call piblokto... Eskimo dogs and foxes suffer also from piblokto. **1945** C. L. B. HUBBARD *Observer's Bk. Dogs* 207 The dread Arctic disease, piblockto (a devastating form of distemper). **1959** *Camsell Arrow* (C. Camsell Hospital, Edmonton, Alberta) Jan.–Feb. 74/1 There is a strange Eskimo madness—piblokto. Men and women are seized with uncontrollable frenzies during which they do all sorts of weird and violent things. **1969** *Daily Tel.* 8 Feb. 16/3 Eskimos have been known to have seizures of *Pibloktoq*, in which they undergo periods of depression followed by wild excitement, then convulsions and stupor, possibly due to the biological effects of the loss of a human time-structure.

pi-bond: see *PI *sb.* 3.

pic[3] (pik), U.S. colloq. abbrev. of PICAYUNE *sb.*

1839 *Spirit of Times* 18 May 129/1 The gentleman of the bar..set back the bottle and popped the 'pic' in the drawer. **1841** E. R. STEELE *Summer Journey in West* 159 In paying for them I found a new currency here, my shillings and sixpences being transformed into *bits* and *pics* or picayunes. **1846** E. W. FARNHAM *Life in Prairie Land* II. i. 291 'How much does the muskito-bar cost a yard?' 'Two bits and a pic, or three bits.' **1850** 'M. TENSAS' *Odd Leaves Life Louisiana Swamp Doctor* 51 The animal didn't mind him a pic. **1855** 'Q. K. P. DOESTICKS' *Doesticks, What he Says* xxiii. 202 A stranger must disburse an avalanche of 'bits', 'pics', and 'levys', before he can get even a plate of cold victuals. **1859** P. H. GOSSE *Lett. from Alabama* 103 The negroes ferried me over the romantic river, for which I paid a '*pic*' (*i.e.* a picayune, the sixteenth of a dollar, or half a 'bit'), the smallest silver coin current.

pic[4] (pik), colloq. abbrev. of PICTURE *sb.* in Dict. and Suppl. Cf. *PICCY. **a.** In sense 2 b.

1884 RUSKIN *Let.* 16 Nov. in S. Birkenhead *Illustrious Friends* (1965) xxxiii. 304, I am so very sorry I cant 'reprieve'—as you call it—the 'pics'. **1891** KIPLING *Light that Failed* v. 82, I must see your pics first. **1910** C. E. MONTAGUE *Hind let Loose* v. 81 He was sent off to see some pics; an'..he saw..just what the men were about that had painted them. **1948** L. DURRELL *Spirit of Place* (1969) 98 I've suggested to Tambi that *Runciman* might do a small Patmos book to go with your pics? **1952** M. ALLINGHAM *Tiger in Smoke* i. 17 The pics themselves are covered with fingerprints. **1971** *Petticoat* 17 July 3/2 They're sold with ready-cut pics. **1976** *Sunday Post* (Glasgow) 26 Dec. 13/3 I sent £7.22 to photographer in Wembley for two coloured photos of a show jumping event in Warwickshire. When no pics came I wrote.

b. In sense *2 i.

1936 *Esquire* Sept. 160/4 Raft's next pic is *Proud Rider.* **1970** Y. CARTER *Mr. Campion's Falcon* iii. 26 The Hag is out for the evening—gone off..to the pics. **1973** 'A. BLAISDELL' *Crime by Chance* (1974) vii. 125 All of a sudden, Latin romances sort of passé... Everybody doing the big war pics.

pic[5] (pik). *colloq.* [Abbrev. PICADOR or Sp. *pica* lance.] **a.** A picador. **b.** A picador's lance, or the thrust made by it. Also as *v. trans.* and *intr.*

1925–6 E. HEMINGWAY in *This Quarter* Autumn–Winter 206 'How about picadors?'.. 'I've got to have one good pic.' **1926** —— *Sun also Rises* II. xv. 173 Watching the picador place the point of his pic. **1927** [see *CUT *v.* 53 h]. **1932** R. CAMPBELL *Taurine Provence* 38 From the beginning of the 18th century we know almost every pass, pic, or estocada that has been performed up to the present day. **1934** —— *Broken Record* 195, I pic'd better than any of the professionals. **1957** A. MACNAB *Bulls of Iberia* vi. 63 The picador rides slowly forward towards the bull, it charges, and just as it arrives he jabs the pic down on the top of its shoulders behind the neck muscle. *Ibid.* 65 The sight of a brave, powerful bull being pic'd honourably ..is a fine one. **1967** MCCORMICK & MASCAREÑAS *Compl. Aficionado* ii. 30 If the toro refuses to take the pic, he is supposed to be returned to the corrals. **1976** E. P. BENSON *Bulls of Ronda* iv. 26 The bull..felt the picador plunge the steel pic into its tossing muscle... Navarro distracted the bull and prepared him for another picing.

1978 M. WALKER *Infiltrator* i. 11, I want to watch the pics.

Picard (pi·kā̆ɹd, ‖pikar), *sb.*[2] and *a.* Also 7 **Picardin.** [a. F. *picard* in the same sense.] **A.** *sb.* **a.** A native or inhabitant of Picardy, a region and former province centred on Amiens in northern France, now the departments of Somme, Aisne, and Oise. **b.** The dialect of French spoken there.

a **1400** [see *BRETON *sb.* and *a.*]. **1598** J. STOW *Survey of London* 116 Iohn Mutas (a Picarde) or Frenchman. *a* **1666** EVELYN *Diary* an. 1644 (1955) II. 138 The University [of Orleans] is..divided now..into that of 4 Nations French, High-dutch, Normans and Picardins. **1900** H. BELLOC *Paris* i. 6 Here Calvin the Picard preached his Batavian theory. **1903** *Knowledge* Dec. 267/2 The dialect of the Isle of France supplanted Picard, Burgundian, and Norman, and became the French language. **1924** G. B. SHAW *Saint Joan* iv. 40 Are these Burgundians and Bretons and Picards and Gascons beginning to call themselves Frenchmen? **1932** W. L. GRAFF *Lang.* 377 French group, with its subdivisions:..Norman, Picard, [etc.]. **1968** E. HYAMS *Mischief Makers* ix. 165 His name was Waché and he was, I think, from the north, a Picard. **1976** N. ROBERTS *Face of France* iv. 49 There are usually witnesses who have seen 'a sallow man..of North African type' near the scene of the crime, of which, later, a blond Norman or Picard may be convicted

B. *adj.* Of or pertaining to Picardy or its inhabitants.

1650 J. HOWELL in *Cotgrave's Fr.-Eng. Dict.* sig. a4, The French toung hath divers dialects, the Picard, that of Iersey and Guernsay..the Provensall, the Gascon. **1833** MACAULAY in *Friendship's Offering 1833* 17 On that famed Picard field, Bohemia's plume, and Genoa's bow, and Caesar's eagle shield. **1954** W. FAULKNER *Fable* 60 One of those sweating stone courtyards which for a thousand years the French have been dotting about the Picard and Artois and Flanders countryside. **1972** R. COBB *Reactions to French Revolution* iii. 93 The apprentice is set upon by a group of big Picard servants.

picarel (pi·kărel). [Fr: cf. PICKEREL[1].] A small marine fish belonging to the family Centracanthidæ (Mæna), found in the eastern Atlantic, the Mediterranean, and the Indian Ocean; esp. the Mediterranean species, *Mæna smaris.*

1905 D. S. JORDAN *Guide to Study of Fishes* II. xix. 347 The Mænidæ, or Picarels, are elongate, gracefully formed fishes. **1972** A. DAVIDSON *Mediterranean Seafood* 107 In Venice you could insult someone by calling him a picarel-eater; and at Port Vendres and some other places in France the fish is known as mata-soldat, or kill-soldier... The picarel can be quite good fried.

picaresque. Add: **a.** (Later examples in *transf.* and extended uses.) Also as *sb.*

1918 A. G. GARDINER *Leaves in Wind* 245 Near by lives a distinguished lady of romantic picaresque tastes, who dotes on street pianos. **1955** *Times* 9 Aug. 9/7 The Russians are paying a price for the energetic imposing of rigid form..on a nation which is in character essentially picaresque. **1958** *Listener* 19 June 1011/1 The first of a trilogy, it is more accessible than its companions, and more lively; a kind of psychological picaresque. **1959** J. M. S. TOMPKINS *Art R. Kipling* i. 29 There is some likeness in the broad, general plan of the two stories [*sc. Kim* and *Huckleberry Finn*]. They are picaresque narratives, with boys as travellers. **1965** *Times Lit. Suppl.* 25 Nov. 1035/4 There is a strong school of black picaresque. **1976** *Ibid.* 23 Apr. 481/5 The central character of this contemporary picaresque of the mind [*sc.* a novel].

¶ **b.** Of a situation: transitory, impermanent. Of a person: drifting, peregrinatory.

An erron. usage from an inference that the picaresque hero is a vagrant or wanderer.

1959 *Manch. Guardian* 28 July 6/5 The boys are attracted by the picaresque nature of working with a private building or decorating firm. **1960** *Observer* 17 Apr. 20/7 One is beginning to dread that word 'picaresque'... He dashes his suburban hero all over the place. **1978** *Country Life* 6 July 57/4 Kyril Bonfigliole..has now produced.. an historical picaresque—picaresque in both the popular sense of roaming far afield and in the strict sense of being..about a rogue.

picarian, *a.* Insert in etym. after '*Picariæ*': (C. L. Nitzsch 1820, in *Deutsches Archiv für Physiol.* VI. 255). (Examples.)

1908 E. J. BANFIELD *Confessions of Beachcomber* I. iii. 96 Picarian Birds. Large-tailed Nightjar... Blue Kingfisher... Bronze Cuckoo. **1955** [see *HONEY-GUIDE 1].

picaro. For *Obs.* read 'Now *arch.*' and add later examples.

1749 SMOLLETT tr. *Le Sage's Gil Blas* IV. x. xii. 115 If Scipio in his childhood was a real Picaro, he has corrected his conduct so well since that time, that he is now the model of a perfect servant. **1966** *New Statesman* 21 Jan. 96/2 The rude and cynical picaro, the philandering gambling tailor or tailoring gambler, finds himself so deeply fascinated by a wealthy young American college girl that he puts on a black roll-neck jersey, poses as a writer, and hopefully takes her to Italy. **1972** M. BRADBURY in Cox & Dyson *20th-Cent. Mind* III. xii. 343 Jack Donaghue in [Iris Murdoch's] *Under the Net* may seem a typical fifties *picaro*; but he is a novelist, facing the problem of the possible collapse into contingency of language and the fascinations of silence. **1977** *Times Lit. Suppl.* 20 May 605/2 Picaresque grants an author licence to switch his tones about as the picaro speeds from adventure to adventure.

picaroon, *sb.*[1] Add: **1.** (Later examples.)

1904 BURGESS & IRWIN (*title*) The picaroons, a San Francisco night's entertainment. **1924** H. LANDON (*title*) The elusive picaroon. **1935** A. J. POLLOCK *Underworld Speaks* 87/2 *Picaroon*, thief who preys on tourists.

3. b. (With reference to BARRACOON.) A slave-ship.

1893 KIPLING *Seven Seas* (1896) 23 Then said the souls of the slaves that men threw overboard: 'Kennelled in the picaroon a weary band were we.'

picaroon, *sb.*[2] For *Canada* read *N. Amer.* and substitute for def.: A long pole fitted with a spike or hook, used in logging and fishing. (Add examples.)

1837 *North Amer. Rev.* Apr. 354 The rafters..[make] use of a picaroon, or pole with a spike in the end of it, which is..driven into the boards, taking out perhaps a piece at each time. **1850** S. JUDD *R. Edney* 42 Richard, armed with a picaroon, descended the slip..to the basin, where the logs lay in the water ready to be drawn in. **1905** *Bull. Bureau of Forestry* (U.S. Dept. Agric.) No. 61, 43 *Pickaroon*, a piked pole fitted with a curved hook, used in holding boats to jams in driving, and for pulling logs from brush and eddies out into the current. **1949** N. C. BROWN *Logging* II. v. 101 Pickaroons are short poles 35″ to 40″ long with a recurved pike or hook used in drawing or pulling small products such as cross ties, 4′ pulpwood, fuel wood, chemical wood, cooperage, and bolts down steep slopes. **1972** F. FORD *Atush Inlet* viii. 78 The crew worked with picaroons spiking the fish into the scow.

Picassian (pikæ·siăn), *a.* [f. the maternal name of Pablo (Ruiz y) *Picasso* (1881–1973), Spanish painter: see -IAN.] Of, pertaining to, or characteristic of Picasso or his style of painting. Also **Picassoe·sque.**

1940 L. ADAM *Primitive Art* xvii. 115 Picasso's primitiveness is quite definitely his own 'Picassian primitiveness'. **1959** *Times* 21 Sept. 5/6 They have none of the Parisian flair, except for Mr Roque A. Riera Rojas, whose shadowy 'Bullfighter' with the piquant, Picassian features and costume of silver grey looming from the shadows is a thoroughly suave, skilful performance. **1968** *Time* 27 Dec. 30/1 *Yellow Submarine* combines every trick and treat of film animation with a dazzle of takeoffs on schools and styles of art. Picassoesque monsters compete with gentle grotesques. **1972** Y. YADIN *Hazor* II. vii. 82 It depicts in a schematic manner the naked body of a woman. Only half of her features are accentuated: one eye, half the nose and mouth, one breast, and half of the vulva. This Picassoesque figurine seems to represent 'life and death' or the 'born and unborn'. **1978** *Listener* 13 July 56/3 The Picassoesque line..is a reminder of something he [*sc.* Henry Moore] learned from both Picasso and Matisse.

picathartes (pikăþā·ɹtīz). *Ornith.* [mod.L. (R. P. Lesson *Manuel d'Ornithologie* (1828) I. 374), f. L. *pīca* magpie + *Cathartes*, generic name of certain American vultures, f. Gr. καθαρτής cleanser (f. καθαίρειν to cleanse).] A bare-headed West African bird of the genus so called, belonging to the babbler family or Timaliidæ; also called the bald crow or rock-fowl.

1931 *Discovery* May 140/1 Looking at this bird, named misleadingly the white-necked bald crow, one's mind instinctively reverts to prehistoric times, for..the Picathartes is a most extraordinary looking object. **1938** *Ibis* II. 255 An investigation of the stomach-contents of the rare West African bird *Picathartes* reveals the fact that insect fragments predominate. **1960** G. DURRELL *Zoo in Luggage* ii. 57 The *Picathartes* was about the size of a jackdaw, but its body had the plump, sleek lines of a blackbird. **1972** *Daily Colonist* (Victoria, B.C.) 30 July 27/3 The picathartes, a rare bald-headed bird..will fetch £100.

picayune, *sb.* and *a.* Add: Also **piccayune, picharoon, pickayune. A.** *sb.* (Earlier and later examples.)

1804 J. F. WATSON *Jrnl.* 4 Nov. in *Amer. Pioneer* (1843) II. 228 One can't buy anything [at New Orleans] for less than a six cent piece, called a *picayune*. **1832** R. BAIRD *View of Valley of Mississippi* xxii. 264 [In Louisiana] the words 'piccayune' (6 1–4 cents) and bit—(12 1–2 cents) fall upon the ear at every step. **1839** J. K. TOWNSEND *Narr. Journey Rocky Mts.* i. 17 We gave him a *pickayune* for his trouble, and went on. **1904** *N.Y. Even. Post* 25 Jan. 6 It doesn't matter a picayune whether the justices or the members of the diplomatic corps were presented first. **1948** *Reader's Digest* Dec. 148/1 Don't care a picayune how you waste that boy's time, do you? **1979** M. G. EBERHART *Bayou Road* xxi. 288 His life wouldn't be worth a picayune.

B. *adj.* (Earlier and later examples.) Also *absol.*

1813 *Cramer's Pittsburgh Almanac 1814* 60 The incessant hum of the blabbering (coloured) market women, seated on the ground..by the side of their picharoon (six cent) piles of vegetables. **1837** *Congress. Globe* 25th Congress 2 Sess. App. 19 The hon. Senator from Kentucky..by way of ridicule, calls this a 'picayune bill'. **1915** *New Republic* 31 July 336/1 They instinctively regard the critic as puny and picayune. **1936** *Delineator* Nov. 11/2 No picayune place like this could pay that man. **1955** E. POUND *Classic Anthol.* II. 104 Your picayune in-laws in fat government jobs. **1965** H. MITCHELL *Underground War against Revolutionary France* iv. 46 Overlooking the serious divisions between the pure and constitutional royalists, Grenville naïvely expected them to bury their picayune differences in a sudden glow of friendship. **1967–8** *Bahamas Handbk. & Businessmen's Ann.* (ed. 7) 77 A picayune mongrel comes from its midday torpor. **1973** *Listener* 20 Dec. 849/3 His projects at that point were getting picayune. He was no longer a great baseball-player. **1974** [see *NITPICKER]. **1975** *Encounter* Feb. 44/2 Most of the snags and pratfalls he cites seem to me picayune matters.

picayunity (pikăyū·nĭti). [f. PICAYUNE *sb.* and *a.* + -ITY.] Insignificance, triviality.

1948 O. NASH in *New Yorker* 13 Nov. 32 In this imponderable world I lose no opportunity To ponder on picayunity. **1977** *Ibid.* 2 May 54/1 To the point of picayunity the state's road system is limited.

Piccadilly (pikădi·li). The name of a street and circus (sense 7) in London (see note s.v. PICCADILL, PICKADILL), used *attrib.* in *Piccadilly weeper(s)*, long drooping side whiskers, sometimes extending below the chin, worn without a beard; loosely, = *Dundreary whiskers* s.v. *DUNDREARY; *Piccadilly window* (slang), a monocle.

1874 HOTTEN *Slang Dict.* 252 *Piccadilly weepers*, long carefully combed-out whiskers of the Dundreary fashion. **1894** Piccadilly weeper [see *DUNDREARY]. **1897** E. GRAHAM *Golden Dustman* (song), Nah I'm goin' to be a reg'lar toff... A Piccadilly winder in my eye. **1907** [see *BURNSIDE, BURNSIDE]. **1909** J. R. WARE *Passing Eng.* 195/2 *Piccadilly window (street*, '90's), single eye-glass worn by some men of fashion—hence the Piccadilly. **1936** P. M. CLARK *Autobiogr. Old Drifter* xiii. 177 'It' was a regular Ha-ha Johnnie with a 'Piccadilly window' in his eye. **1960** C. W. CUNNINGTON et al. *Dict. Eng. Costume* 163/1 *Piccadilly weepers.* 1870's and 1880's. (M.) Long combed-out whiskers fashionable in those decades. **1973** J. FLEMING *You won't let me Finish* ii. 19 A fragile moustache that drooped right down past his mouth, the kind of moustache that used to be called a 'Piccadilly weeper'.

piccaninny, pickaninny, *sb.* (*a.*) Add: Also **picanini, piccin, piccinini, piccney, picken, pickini, pickinny, pickne, pickney, picknie, pickny, picny.**

The term now often gives offence when applied to children by people of European extraction.

a. In the speech of West Indian Blacks freq. with uninflected pl. (Further examples.)

1790 J. B. MORETON *Manners & Customs West India Islands* 152 The women..are obliged to..take their pickinnies (*i.e.* children) on their backs, to which they are tied with handkerchiefs. **1847** *Knickerbocker* XXX. 216 It might be very pleasant to be surrounded by half-a-dozen negro waiting-women, with their picaninnies. **1868** T. RUSSELL *Etym. Jamaica Gram.* 2 Pickne. *Ibid.* 6 Pickini—A child. African. **1907** W. JEKYLL *Jamaican Song & Story* 40 Now Toad have twenty picny. **1937** R. MACAULAY *I would be Private* II. i. 147 That naked piccney. **1958** J. CAREW *Wild Coast* viii. 117 All you is, is a maugre, skin-and-bone pickny. **1969** S. M. SADEEK *Windswept & Other Stories* 37 'I was working for the estate, until..' 'Until alyou get busy making picknie.' **1974** *Practitioner* CCXIII. 845 To 'give pickney' or to 'breed' [in Jamaica] is to get a woman with child. **1977** *Westindian World* 3–9 June 4/1 It has been made very plain that quite a number of teachers in schools up and down de country are in many cases more dunce than de pickney dem teach themselves.

b. (Further examples.) Also, the offspring of an animal.

1841 R. HOWITT *Impressions Australia Felix* (1845) 103 Two women, one with a piccaniny at her back. **1855** in J. W. Colenso *Ten Weeks in Natal* Add. p. 3 What will the poor little piccaninnies do, Boy? **1911** *East London* (Cape Province) *Dispatch* 24 Nov. 7 (Pettman), Mothers nursing their picaninies and maidens listening to lovers rude. **1925** *Brit. Weekly* 31 Dec. 340/2 A mother..crooned gently to her 'piccin' not more than a few weeks old. **1926** *Ibid.* 27 May 158/1 A mischievous picannin..was weeding the vegetable garden. **1936** I. L. IDRIESS *Cattle King* xxviii. 245 He met numerous blackfellow friends, they and their lubras and piccaninnies, all in fat good humour. **1953** G. DURRELL *Overloaded Ark* iii. 59 Na catar beef, sah, and 'e get picken for 'e back. **1961** G. GREENE *Burnt-Out Case* IV. i. 100 The piccin that stole sugar from the white man's cupboard. **1963** *Sydney Morning Herald* 19 Nov. 6/4 The use of such words as 'boy', 'lubra' and..'piccaninny' to describe aborigines has been banned to Northern Territory welfare officers. **1966** C. SWEENEY *Scurrying Bush* xiv. 199 He guided me about half a mile up the road, the rest of the piccannins scampering behind. **1979** P. NIESEWAND *Member of Club* ii. 21 The bantu we've chosen..is a piccanin called Elias.

B. *adj.* spec. *piccaninny dawn, daylight*, earliest dawn, first light (chiefly *Austral.*). (Earlier and later examples.)

1707 H. SLOANE *Voy. Jamaica* I. p. lii, They have..Christmas Holidays, Easter call'd little or Piganinny, Christmas, and some other great Feasts. **1835** R. R. MADDEN *Twelvemonth's Residence W. Indies* II. 153 To..spend piccanini Christmas (Easter) dancing. **1848** W. WESTGARTH *Australia Felix* viii. 104 The hut would be attacked before 'piccinini sun'. **1870** in 'Mark Twain' *Screamers* (1871) xxv. 132 A pickaninny,..mud-turtle-shaped craft of a schooner. **1910** ANDERSON & CUNDALL *Jamaica Anancy Stories* 37 Go a pickney mumma yard an' you sure fe get somet'ing. *a* **1912** 'T. COLLINS' *Buln-Buln & Brolga* (1948) 107 Blackfellers mostly goes in for a piccaninny fire—jist three sticks, with the ends kep' together. **1936** M. FRANKLIN *All that Swagger* xvi. 153 At piccaninny dawn, the billy with the lid off was found rolling on the floor. **1953** G. DURRELL *Overloaded Ark* iv. 78 'Eh.. aehh!' he shouted, 'napicken bushcat here for inside.' **1970** 'E. LINDALL' *Gathering of Eagles* viii. 101 The piccaninny dawn, that false lightening of the sky that fades to darkness before the sun finally makes its presence known. **1971** *Courier-Mail* (Brisbane) 12 July 2/6 Before piccaninny daylight on June 14, Vernon Boundy..was standing on the southern bank of Tallebudgera's tidal estuary. **1974** *Sunday Mail Mag.* (Brisbane) 15 Sept. 3/3 In the chilly piccaninny dawn we drove out to the Wyloo strip with kangaroos bounding along beside and in front of the truck.

piccolo. Add: **4.** A boy who assists a waiter at a hotel, restaurant, etc.; a page at a hotel.

1910 'SAKI' *Reginald in Russia* 71 Watching the amount that I gave to the piccolo. **1926** R. HALL *Adam's Breed* I. x. 94 He had six enormous aprons... He had been very generously equipped for his duties as 'piccolo'. **1927** *Observer* 19 June 12 [German hotels] Head waiter..; elder page,.. younger page,.. 'piccolo', or very small page,.. still smaller 'piccolo', just beginning career. **1960** O. MANNING *Great Fortune* iii. 31 The piccolo arrived, a scrap of a boy, laden with bottles, glasses and plates. **1972** L. P. BACHMANN *Ultimate Act* i. 9 In his early teens he began work as a piccolo in hotels and restaurants.

5. = **juke-box. U.S. slang.*

1938 *N.Y. Amsterdam News* 12 Mar. 17 The Harlem Hamfats grind out the tune on myriad Harlem piccolos. **1946** E. BISHOP *North & South* 50 He's drinking in the warm pink glow To th' accompaniment of the piccolo. **1950** *Publ. Amer. Dial. Soc.* XIV. 52 [S. Carolina] *Piccolo*, an automatic music box, worked by a nickel slot machine. Origin undetermined. **1970** C. MAJOR *Dict. Afro-Amer. Slang* 91 *Piccolo*,.. juke box.

Picco pipe (pi·ko). *Mus.* Also with lower-case initial. [f. the name of *Picco* or *Picchi*, 'the Sardinian minstrel', who performed on this instrument with great virtuosity and was heard in London in 1856.] (See quot. 1876.)

1876 STAINER & BARRETT *Dict. Mus. Terms* 354/1 *Picco pipe*, a small pipe having two ventages above and one below. It is blown by means of a mouthpiece like a *flûte à bec* or whistle; and in playing, the little finger is used for varying the pitch by being inserted in the end. **1920** U. DAUBENY *Orchestral Wind Instruments* iii. 27 An instrument..was revived about the middle of last century by a blind Italian peasant named Picco, who gave remarkable performances on the 'Picco pipe'. **1939** A. CARSE *Mus. Wind Instruments* x. 119 Probably the smallest of all whistle-flutes is the Picco pipe, a tiny shrill whistle about 3½ inches long. **1960** L. G. LANGWILL *Index Wind-Instrument Makers* 90 A young blind Sardinian shepherd, Angelo Picchi appeared in..London (1856), playing on a small pipe (Zuffolo) which was named after him, Picco Pipe. **1977** *Early Music* Oct. 555/2 Amongst woodwind were items such as a picco pipe (£165),..and a two-keyed oboe.

piccy (pi·ki), colloq. abbrev. of PICTURE *sb.* 2 b. Cf. *PIC[4], *PICKY.

1889 KIPLING *Let.* in C. E. Carrington *Rudyard Kipling* (1955) vi. 143 It's mighty curious to see behind an R.A.'s piccy and note the bits of things it is made up of. **1968** A. DIMENT *Bang Bang Birds* I. v. 75 They popped my piccy into a dud passport. **1977** *Hot Car* Oct. 75/1 The end result of fitting these packages on your Ford can be, if the piccies are anything to go by, rather on the eye-catching side.

pice: see also *PAISA.

picein (pi·-, pəi·sĭ,in). [f. L. *pice-us* pitchy (f. *pix* PITCH *sb.*[1]) + -IN[1].] **1.** *Chem.* [ad. F. *picéine* (Ch. Tanret 1894, in *Compt. Rend.* CXIX. 80).] A glucoside present in various trees, notably willows and conifers; *p*-hydroxyacetophenone-β-glucoside, $CH_3 \cdot CO \cdot C_6H_4 \cdot O \cdot C_6H_{11}O_5$.

1894 *Jrnl. Chem. Soc.* LXVI. I. 616 Picein, $C_{14}H_{18}O_7$, whether anhydrous or hydrated, crystallises in silky, prismatic needles, with a bitter taste. **1934** C. C. STEELE *Introd. Plant Biochem.* xi. 118 Picein, $C_{14}H_{18}O_7$, salinigrin, or salicinerin, occurs in several species of *Salix* and *Populus*. **1968** *Jrnl. Chromatogr.* XXXVI. 28 The collected fraction of pure trimethylsilyl picein also gave a satisfactory infrared spectrum.

2. Also *picein wax*, and with capital initial. An inert thermoplastic substance composed of hydrocarbons from rubber, shellac, and bitumen and used for sealing joints against air.

1927 G. W. C. KAYE *High Vacua* v. 69 Khotinsky cement..is widely used in the States for vacuum work, while Picein finds extensive application on the Continent. **1936** *Discovery* Sept. 286/1 A plug of picein wax in the capillary is thereby melted and seals up the tube. **1968** *Chem. Abstr.* LXIX. 6796/1 An elec.-insulating material was developed which permitted one to apply fields of up to 2×10^6 w./cm. The material consisted of varying amts. of quartz powder in picein. **1974** L. HOLLAND et al. *Vacuum Manual* i. 65 Picein. This is a classical vacuum wax—sticks well to metal and glass, is resistant to dilute acid and alkalies, is thermoplastic and made from bituminous substances. **1975** *Sci. Amer.* Feb. 110/3 Only prices are missing from this admirable guide to a world of high-technology commerce. String and sealing wax are gone (although not picein wax, quite).

Picene (pəi·sīn), *a.* and *sb.* [f. L. *Picen-us* Picene: see -IAN.] **A.** *adj.* Of or pertaining to ancient Picenum, a region in eastern central Italy, or the pre-Roman iron-age culture associated with it. **B.** *sb.* A native or inhabitant of Picenum; the pre-Sabellian language attested there. Also **Pice·nian.**

1600 HOLLAND tr. *Livy's Romane Hist.* XXII. 437 He [*sc.* Hannibal] turned another way into the Picene countrie. **1601** —— tr. *Pliny's Nat. Hist.* XVIII. xi. 567 The Picenes in times past invented a way by themselves of making bread. **1863** W. P. DICKSON tr. *Mommsen's Hist. Rome* III. IV. ix. 332 The corps of Picenian volunteers soon grew to three legions. **1924** D. RANDALL-MACIVER *Villanovans & Early Etruscans* ii. 5 The burial rite of the Villanovans..opposes them to the Etruscans and the Picenes. *Ibid.* iv. 75 It is natural to suppose that *all* the inhumations in the Forum are of the Picene race. **1933** R. S. CONWAY et al. *Prae-Italic Dial. Italy* II. iv. 213 This Picene culture extends along the Adriatic coast southwards from Rimini at least as far as the river Sangro. **1939** L. H. GRAY *Foundations of Lang.* xi. 335 A language sometimes called Pre-Sabellian, Liburnian, or Picenian. **1948** D. DIRINGER *Alphabet* II. ix. 498 The Picenian alphabet is..very old. **1949** L. R. TAYLOR *Party Politics in Age of Caesar* ii. 45 In the elder Pompey's bodyguard.. was a group of young Picene officers. **1959** *Chambers's Encycl.* V. 461/2 In the east the Fossa peoples were supplemented by another Illyrian-speaking group, known as Picene, between Rimini and the Abruzzi. **1974** E. S. GRUEN *Last Generation of Roman Republic* ii. 63 Pompey's following went beyond..the old aristocracy. From his father he inherited..a virtual barony in Picenum. Some of his adherents, from lesser families, seem to possess Picene origins. *Ibid.* iii. 118 Q. Numerius Rufus was probably a Picene.

Picentine (pike·ntəin, pəis-), *a.* and *sb.* Also 8 **Pycentine.** [f. L. *Picentin-us* Picentine: see -INE[1].] **A.** *adj.* = *PICENE *a. Picentine bread*, a kind of bread made in ancient Picenum (with reference to Pliny, *Nat. Hist.* XVIII. xxvii: see quot. 1958). **B.** *sb.* = *PICENE *sb.*

1708 W. KING *Art of Cookery* 147 The first Chapter contains the admirable Receipt of a Salacacaby of Apicus. Bruise in a Mortar Parsley Seed, dry'd Peneryal, ..Raisons ston'd, Honey, ..Oyl and Wine, put 'em into a Cacabulum, three crusts of Pycentine Bread, the Flesh of a Pullet,..pour a soup over it, garnish it with Snow. **1855** BOSTOCK & RILEY tr. *Pliny's Nat. Hist.* I. III. xviii. 235 The fifth region is that of Picenum, once remarkable for the denseness of its population; 360,000 Picentines took the oaths of fidelity to the Roman people. **1863** W. P. DICKSON tr. *Mommsen's Hist. Rome* III. IV. vii. 228 The Latin could remind the Picentine that they were both in like manner 'subject to the fasces'. **1888** [see *MARRUCINIAN *sb.* and *a.*]. **1933** R. S. CONWAY et al. *Prae-Italic Dial. Italy* II. iv. 209 The insc. on the Osimo statuette.. resembles more closely than any of the rest the Italic dialects proper..whether its language be described as 'Picentine' or as 'Umbrian'. **1939** A. J. TOYNBEE *Study of Hist.* IV. 312 The new foundation was called into existence by the..'civilization' (in the literal sense) of the indigenous population, as when..the Romans organized..a Picentine village into a *forum* or *conciliabulum.* **1958** FLOWER & ROSENBAUM *Roman Cookery Bk.* IV. 93 Picentine bread. According to Pliny..this bread—invented by the people of Picenum—was made of spelt-grits. The spelt-grits were left to soak for nine days, and on the tenth day were made into dough by mixing them with raisin juice. The dough was put into earthenware pots and baked hard in the oven. **1974** E. S. GRUEN *Last Generation of Roman Republic* iii. 110 The trustworthy Picentine L. Afranius.

picey (pəi·si), *a. slang.* [Prob. f. PICE + -Y[1].] Mean, niggardly.

1937 PARTRIDGE *Dict. Slang* 624/1 *Picey*, adj., mean: Regular Army: late C. 19–20. **1965** P. ROBINSON *Pakistani Agent* v. 61 She deserved better than that, the miller would be too *picey.*

pick, *sb.*[1] Add: **1. c.** *Archæol.* A prehistoric implement used for breaking up rocks, soil, etc.

1949 W. F. ALBRIGHT *Archaeol. of Palestine* iii. 59 Among large flint artifacts the most noteworthy are sickle-blades and 'picks', which point to the agricultural character of Natufian culture... Some of the so-called picks are rather hoes, used to break up the ground before sowing grain. **1959** J. D. CLARK *Prehist. S. Afr.* vi. 157 Small, nearly parallel-sided picks.

5. c. *Mus.* A plectrum. Cf. PICK *v.*[1] 12. orig. *U.S.*

1895 *Montgomery Ward Catal.* Spring & Summer 243/2 Mandolin picks, made of celluloid, imitation tortoise shell, oval pattern. **1973** *Advocate-News* (Barbados) 24 Feb. 3/6 (Advt.), Attention all musicians... Just arrived:.. Picks Finger Picks Thumb Picks. **1976** D. MUNROW *Instruments Middle Ages & Renaissance* 25/4 The long stem of the quill is shown held between the third and index finger (as a modern guitarist holds a flat pick).

8. *pick-handle* (examples); **pick-pole** *U.S.* = PICAROON *sb.*[2]

1850 N. KINGSLEY *Diary* 1 Nov. (1914) 156 Tinkered a little at Pick handles, putting door in the tent, [etc.]. **1873** J. MILLER *Life amongst Modocs* v. 64 A long white pole, perhaps a sort of pick-handle. **1908** *Sears, Roebuck Catal.* 522/2 Drifting pick handles, 34 inches long. **1979** D. LOWDEN *Boudapesti 3* xiii. 68 The man who'd hit him four times with the pickhandle. **1837** *North Amer. Rev.* Apr. 353 The persons who undertake it [*sc.* breaking a log-jam] must go on to the mass of logs, work some out with their pickpoles, [etc.]. **1972** *Christian Science Monitor* 28 Sept. 16/3 The river-drivers could stay on a pitching, twisting log long log, keeping balance with a pick-pole.

pick, *sb.*[3] Add: **10.** In basketball, a permissible block (see quot. 1961).

1951 *Sun* (Baltimore) 24 Dec. 13/2 There is no consistency among officials on calling picks and screens. **1961** J. S. SALAK *Dict. Amer. Sports* 325 To set a pick, the offensive player is entitled to take up a position in front of a defensive opponent provided such maneuver does not hinder the 'normal movement' of the defensive man. **1976** A. CROSS *Question of Max* iv. 43 Kate..had become someting of a basketball aficionado... To her..regret, she could never recognize when someone had set a 'pick', and she tended to admire the wrong members of any team.

pick, *v.*[1] Add: **IV. 7. a.** Also colloq. phr. *to pick them*: in emphatic contexts, to make a wise choice, *spec.* in personal relationships (freq. *ironical*).

1945 A. MARSHALL in *Coast to Coast 1944* 84 He greeted Olive cheerfully, then turned to me with simulated surprise. 'Well, you can certainly pick 'em,' he said. **1953** A. CHRISTIE *Pocket Full of Rye* x. 62 My stepmother was there... The old boy certainly knew how to pick them. **1966** H. WAUGH *Pure Poison* (1967) ii. 11 Fred, glancing ..to the young face of his daughter-in-law to be, had to admit that Larry could pick 'em. **1973** G. SCOTT *Water Horse* (1974) vii. 44 An art student, Polly? You do pick them, don't you. **1976** P. HENISSART *Winter Quarry* xv. 150 'Christ, she really picks them,' muttered McGuire. 'Does she know who he is?' **1978** L. MEYNELL *Papersnake* iii. 53 Baa-Lamb came home..at the very agreeable odds of twelve to one... 'What did I tell you, cobber?.. If you can pick 'em, you can pick 'em.'

f. *ellipt.* for *to pick one's way.*

1865 R. D. BLACKMORE *Cradock Nowell* (1866) I. xvi. 153 Hogstaff tottered along before him, picking uneasily over the stones. **1878** HARDY *Ret. Native* I. iii. 66 The track is rough, but if you've got a light your horses may pick along wi' care. **1961** 'G. HOLDEN' *Deadlier than Male* xiv. 102 This time the search took twice as long, cutting down on his extra reading, for he had to pick through several columns of one- and two-line social notes in each issue.

g. *trans.* To guess, deduce; to predict. *Austral.* and *N.Z. colloq.*

c **1926** 'MIXER' *Transport Workers' Song Bk.* 128 I'm picking we'll soon have a row. **1943** N. MARSH *Colour Scheme* vi. 100 There's a bit of a shelf above the cliff... I picked that was where he'd go. **1959** D. NILAND *Big Smoke* vi. 145 He looked up at the boy with a pleased, questioning expression. 'I pick it right?'

VII. 14. *to pick at* ——. **b.** Also *Austral.*

1916 C. J. DENNIS *Songs Sentimental Bloke* 127 *Pick at*, to chaff; to annoy. **1941** BAKER *Dict. Austral. Slang.* 54 *Pick at*, to blame, chaff, irritate.

15. *to pick on, upon* ——. Delete 'Now *U.S. dial.*' and add further examples. Also, to single out for attention or adverse criticism; to victimize.

1875 W. D. PARISH *Dict. Sussex Dial.* 87 They always pick upon my boy coming home from school. **1888** in Farmer *Americanisms* (1889) 419/1 Joseph White..slept for five days and nights, and then jawed his wife for waking him up. He said she was always picking on him when she saw him taking comfort. *c* **1910** D. H. LAWRENCE *Phoenix II* (1968) 26 You always pick on the Gordons—you're always on to us—! **1919** WODEHOUSE *Coming of Bill* (1920) II. iii. 141 That wouldn't make no difference.—She'd pick on me just the same. **1929** J. BUCHAN *Courts of Morning* III. ii. 331 Looks as if you folk had been picking on my poor little country. **1930** J. B. PRIESTLEY *Angel Pavement* vi. 297 They begin picking on her and she stands up for herself. **1930** S. JEPSON *I met Murder* ii. 27 Have you any idea why the Inspector should have picked on you first? **1947** 'N. SHUTE' *Chequer Board* 73 Last night they was picking on the coloured boys—saying nasty things about niggers in their hearing. **1959** G. FREEMAN *Jack would be Gent.* 140 Don't keep picking on him, please, Mum. **1961** [see *BACK *sb.*[1] 23 d]. **1975** *Times* 15/4 Why pick on the present Government? Has any government..in the past 30 years ever..done anything to encourage that aim?

VIII. 18. pick off. c. *Baseball.* To put out (a runner) at a base.

1948 *Sun* (Baltimore) 1 Dec. 17/4 The play in question came when Bobby Feller, Cleveland pitcher, whirled and threw to Manager Lou Boudreau in an effort to pick off Masi, Boston catcher. **1974** *Spartanburg* (S. Carolina) *Herald* 23 Apr. A6/4 Dancy was picked off by catcher Luis Rosado as he inexcusably wandered too far off third.

19*. pick over. To sort; to select the best from (a group or collection); to pick off dead flowers from.

1917 *Dialect Notes* IV. 397 She is picking over blackberries. **1924** A. D. SEDGWICK *Little French Girl* i. 6 She.. picked over the herbs that were to be dried for *tisane.* **1946** D. C. PEATTIE *Road of Naturalist* iii. 40 The supplies were picked over and over. One necessity after another was thrown away, as the owner remembered that he might have to carry it, if the oxen died. **1971** *Vogue* Dec. 48/3 The geraniums had flowered once, and needed to be picked over to induce a second flowering. **1972** D. WESTHEIMER *Over Edge* (1974) ii. 20 Karen..could spend hours happily picking over rejects in a surplus store. **1973** E. PAGE *Fortnight by Sea* i. 8, I don't think there'll be any strawberries left... The beds were picked over pretty thoroughly a couple of days ago. **1978** *Lancashire Life* Apr. 78/2 Though the summer suns are not yet exactly at the glowing stage, wise girls will buy their summer clothes now, rather than wait till the best things have been picked over.

20. pick up. b. Also *spec.* (*a*) *trans.* to gather (a shorn fleece) from the floor of the shearing shed, carry it to a table, and throw it out flat so that it can be skirted, rolled, and classed, also *absol. Austral.* and *N.Z.* (*b*) *absol.* in game-shooting, to make a retrieval, esp. to collect unretrieved game after a shooting party.

a. 1862 J. G. WALKER *Jrnl.* 10 Nov. (typescript) 24 My job at first was picking up fleeces. **1926** J. DEVANNY *Butcher Shop* 11 The naked feet of the brown women 'picking up' from the shining greasy floor. **1940** F. SARGESON *Man & Wife* (1944) 47 It was early summer, shearing time. Tom and me went into the country and we got a job picking up fleeces in a big shed. **1967** J. MORRISON in *Coast to Coast 1965–66* 157 He'd been away picking-up in the shearing sheds.

b. 1888 W. B. LEFFINGWELL *Wild Fowl Shooting* xxxvi. 364 After the pup has gotten to understand your orders of picking up, and bringing the glove to you from short distances, throw it farther. **1897** *Encycl. Sport* I. 442/1 The keeper..must be careful to judge accurately when to start the next drive, after one is over, so as to give reasonable time for picking up. **1976** *Shooting Times & Country Mag.* 16–22 Dec. 20/2 My immediate neighbours ..did help pick up and I am happy to say the count, if nothing else, was quite gratifying.

e. *spec.* To form an acquaintance with (a person) casually or informally, esp. with the intention of having a sexual relationship.

1698 [in Dict.]. **1698** J. COLLIER *Short View Immorality Eng. Stage* vi. 238 Nothing being more common than to see Beauty surpriz'd, Women debauch'd, and Wenches Pick'd up at these Diversions. **1734** *Select Trials 1720–1724* 59/1 The Prosecutor pick'd me up and went with me to my Lodgings..where he would have lain with me. **1785** COWPER *Let.* 4 June in *Corr.* (1904) II. 325 He was seen by Mr. Shepherd..leading a female companion into a wood.., whom he saw him pick up as he went. **1812** J. H. VAUX *Vocab. Flash Lang.* in *Mem.* (1964) 257 To pick up a cull, is a term used by blowers in their vocation of street-walking. **1893** G. B. SHAW *Widowers' Houses* I. viii. 29 'I have made the acquaintance of'—or you may say 'picked up', or 'come across', if you think that would suit your friend's style better. **1921** *Sat. Even. Post* 1 Oct. 18/2 You are right in thinking there must be something wrong with girls who try to 'pick up' strange men as no girl with self respect would do such a thing. **1932** E. BOWEN *To North* iv. 34 She wished she had not picked Markie up in the train and given him her address. **1933** *Times Lit. Suppl.* 30 Mar. 223/3 One evening Sam 'picks up' a young woman at an open-air concert. **1942** E. PAUL *Narrow St.* xvii. 135 The wife of one of the officers.. formed the habit of picking up rich gentlemen in department stores. **1961** J. DOS PASSOS *Midcentury* 94 Eileen got to dancing..and trying to pick up strange men. **1975** *Evening Standard* 14 May 5/3 It is not difficult to learn.. that it is possible to obtain money, food or a bed for the night by being 'picked up'. **1976** D. MARLOWE *Nightshade* xii. 143 Who was that old man?.. He was trying to pick you up.

f. Also, to succeed in seeing, hearing, detecting, receiving, etc., by means of an appropriate instrument or apparatus.

1888 *Electrician* 2 Nov. 833/1 For researches of this description it is necessary to employ as sensitive an instrument as it is possible to obtain, to pick up, so to speak, such minute currents. **1908** *Rep. Brit. Assoc. Adv. Sci. 1907* 621 The receiving apparatus..would pick up a number of disturbances from other stations. **1908** *Westm. Gaz.* 23 Oct. 5/3 The following notes will enable it [*sc.* a comet] to be 'picked up' with the aid of an opera-glass and a star-map. **1913** *Pop. Mag.* 1 May 79/2 The only signals which it was picking up now were..those of the enemy. **1921** [see *GET *v.* 22 b]. **1922** *Encycl. Brit.* XXX. 88/2 Presently the airship was 'picked up', and immediately from all quarters of the defences searchlights could be seen moving across to get on to it. **1929** S. ERTZ *Galaxy* xvii. 365 She and the General thoroughly enjoyed their wireless in the evening, and it was amusing to pick up Paris or Berlin. **1941** [see *ATMOSPHERE *sb.* 4 b]. **1948** F. P. SHEPARD *Submarine Geol.* ii. 16 The radar screen will pick up land objects and will show the position of islands, capes and mountain peaks, giving their direction and distance. **1960** *McGraw-Hill Encycl. Sci. & Technol.* XIII. 462/1 Television camera tubes are designed primarily to pick up live programs, indoors and outdoors, as well as to reproduce motion pictures. **1973** *Guardian* 20 June 13/1 BBC Monitoring Service reports that the only Moscow Radio commentaries on Watergate picked up so far in any language were in Quechua. **1977** *Lancet* 4 June 1187/2 Clinically, cerebral blood-flow is measured after intra-arterial injection of xenon-133; gamma radiation is picked up by two detectors and the scintillation-counts are fed into a laboratory digital computer. **1978** *Nature* 6 Apr. 481/2 This detection capability has improved roughly threefold; explosions of yields of 1 or 2 kilotons in hard rock in most parts of the Northern Hemisphere would now most likely be picked up.

g. *to pick up the pieces* (fig.): to (try to) redeem some advantage or compensation from an apparently hopeless situation.

1912 KIPLING *Divers. Creatures* (1917) 17, I should have said it was half a night. Now, shall we go down and pick up the pieces? **1938** M. ALLINGHAM *Fashion in Shrouds* vi. 92 It'll come to a quiet, uncomfortable end and you'll have to stand by and pick up the pieces. **1951** J. C. FENNESSY *Sonnet in Bottle* v. iv. 163 Injy was very good at taking things as they came. But he generally found it was his job to pick up the pieces afterwards. **1970** A. TOFFLER *Future Shock* (1971) xvii. 391 By proliferating enclaves of the past, living museums as it were, we increase the chances that someone will be there to pick up the pieces in case of massive calamity. **1973** A. BROINOWSKI *Take One Ambassador* vii. 97 We could see them [*sc.* the Japanese] picking up the pieces in Indo-China after the Americans. **1977** R. PERRY *Dead End* i. 12 If anything does go wrong it'll be nice having you around to pick up the pieces.

j. *trans.* and *intr.* To steal, rob, pilfer; to cheat, swindle. *slang.*

c **1770** R. KING *Frauds of London Detected* 39 [Highwaymen] have various schemes for carrying on their business, such as seeing ostlers, bribing landlords, on the road, for intelligence of *who is worth picking up*. **1829** H. WIDOWSON *Pres. State Van Diemen's Land* 73 There are always a number of loose characters lurking about, on the look-out for strangers, to 'pick them up', as they term it, which, in other words, means to rob them. *a***1876** E. LEIGH *Gloss. Words Dial. Cheshire* (1877) 154 *Picking up*, a term for picking a pocket. **1903** *Mark of Broad Arrow* vii. 108 Within twenty-four hours of that man's release the three prison-made thieves were looking round the town to see what they could 'pick up'—in plain language, to see what they could thieve. **1928** *Detective Fiction Weekly* 8 Sept. 565/2 Gentleman George..would mark down his traveler, knowing him to be in possession of jewelry or other valuables, and tirelessly follow him until the opportunity arose to 'pick-up' his all-important bag.

k. *trans.* To find fault with, call to account; to detect (a person) in a mistake; to show up. *colloq.*

1846 S. F. SMITH *Theatr. Apprenticeship* 149 The bystanders..were crowding around the table in great numbers to see the fun—all considering me most undoubtedly 'picked up'. **1878** B. HARTE in *Scribner's Monthly* Dec. 184/1 When we were coming down the valley you picked me up twice..*contradicted* me, that's what I mean. **1922** *Daily Mail* 5 Dec. 11, I am picked up for saying that the initiative in the Steamer case should have come from the stewards.

l. In *Cricket*, to succeed in hitting (a ball, esp. one that pitches close to the ground).

1851 J. PYCROFT *Cricket Field* vii. 153 If you reach far enough, even a shooter may be picked up. **1862** —— *Cricket Tutor* 8 The old bat used to be heavy at the point —very requisite for picking up a Grounder. **1959** *Times* 29 May 4/1 He could not have picked up the ball off his legs so crisply.

m. *trans.* To cause (a person) to revive; to serve as a 'pick-me-up' for (someone).

1857 DICKENS & COLLINS *Lazy Tour* v, in *Househ. Words* 31 Oct. 412/1 Several..look in at the chemist's..to be 'picked up'. **1889** [in Dict., sense 20 g]. **1914** G. B. SHAW *Misalliance* 80 Have you had your tea?.. A cup of tea will pick you up. **1978** J. CARROLL *Mortal Friends* I. ii. 22 'You know me, Colman. Tea anytime.' 'Indeed, Father. It picks a body up.'

n. *trans.* and *intr.* To tidy or clean up; to put in order. *colloq.* (chiefly *U.S.*).

1861 *Trans. Illinois Agric. Soc.* IV. 204 We did not find 'things picked up in it'—no air of comfort about it. **1874** E. S. WARD *Trotty's Wedding Tour* 214 It had taken all day to 'pick up' after the departed travellers. **1888** N. PERRY *Flock of Girls* 81 She mends these little bits of things and 'picks up' after you, as you call it. **1889** [in Dict., sense 20 g]. **1966** J. BALL *Cool Cottontail* (1967) v. 44 'The room isn't properly picked up yet,' the woman said. 'When you have five kids..you can't get everything done.' **1973** *Sunday Bull.* (Philadelphia) 7 Oct. (Parade Suppl.) F5/4 Ask your children for their ideas. It's the best way to enlist their help in keeping their rooms 'picked-up'.

o. *trans.* To arrest, apprehend. Cf. sense 20 d in Dict. *slang* (orig. *U.S.*).

1871 *Congress. Globe* 5 Jan. 317/2 They are picked up for taking horses or sheep or anything of that sort. **1887** *Lantern* (New Orleans) 11 June 2/2 I'll have the police pick him up for blackmail. **1934** J. T. FARRELL *Young Manhood* xii. 192 He gazed around the church to see if any of the boys were present. Seeing none of them, he guessed that they must all have been picked up, and were enjoying Christmas Day in the can. **1938** F. D. SHARPE *Sharpe of Flying Squad* xiv. 157, I picked them up for stealing a man's wallet. *Ibid.* xvi. 183, I picked Billy up, knowing that he was 'wanted' for a job. **1946** F. SARGESON *That Summer* 102 We all had to stand there with a crowd of jacks in plain clothes standing round, and one in uniform called out our names and said what we'd been picked up for. **1956** H. GOLD *Man who was not with It* (1965) xxii. 202 You want to be able to tell the fuzz the truth if we're picked up? **1961** *Confidential* Jan. 39/2 When Farouk was overthrown, police picked up his personal pimp, Pulley Bey. **1976** 'TREVANIAN' *Main* x. 213 Things start to go badly for him. His boys..get picked up for every minor charge in the book. **1979** *Massachusetts Daily Collegian* 30 Apr. 14/4 He said he was not drunk when picked up on East Pleasant St. on March 29.

p. *to pick up on*: (*a*) to draw near, begin to overtake (a person) in a race; (*b*) *U.S. slang*, to understand, appreciate, or obtain.

1908 *Daily Chron.* 27 Nov. 7/6 At the fifth lap.. Dorando held him, and then began to pick up on him. **1944** D. BURLEY *Orig. Handbk. Harlem Jive* 15 Let me boot you to my play [*sc.* inform you of my plan] and, maybe, you can pick up on the issue. **1946** MEZZROW & WOLFE *Really Blues* 377 *Pick up on*, get, take, learn. *Ibid.*, *Pick up on what's going down*, understand what's happening. **1956** B. HOLIDAY *Lady sings Blues* (1973) i. 8 In Baltimore, places like Alice Dean's were the only joints fancy enough to have a victrola and for real enough to pick up on the best records. **1972** *Jazz & Blues* Feb. 19/1 They came to gig in their own clubs before white people picked up on them. **1977** MCKNIGHT & TOBLER *Bob Marley* iii. 46 Paul McCartney was noted as having 'picked up on reggae'.

q. *intr.* and *trans.* Of a vehicle, aircraft, etc.: to gain speed after being slow-moving or stationary; to recover (speed). Cf. sense 20 h in Dict.

1922 S. LEWIS *Babbitt* v. 53 He noted how quickly his car picked up. **1932** C. ISHERWOOD *Memorial* III. i. 181 'That's a damn fine bus,' said Farncombe earnestly. 'My Christ, Gerald, you should see the way she picks up.' **1939** *War Illustr.* 29 Dec. 539/3 However, as we got down to five hundred feet the engines began to pick up.

r. *trans.* To pay (a bill, account, etc.); esp. in phr. *to pick up the bill, check, tab*, etc.; also *fig. colloq.* (orig. *U.S.*).

1945 *Sun* (Baltimore) 23 Oct. 4 (*heading*) 'Lobbyist' said to have picked up check for Truman outing. **1947** *Ibid.* 12 May 2/5 Some United States diplomats have entertained each other with the taxpayers picking up the check. **1956** S. BELLOW *Seize the Day* ii. 26 His father might have offered to pick up his hotel tab. **1956** B. HOLIDAY *Lady sings Blues* (1973) xxiii. 196 Americans used to make fun of the British health system, where sick people could go to doctors and hospitals for free and the government picked up the tab. **1961** R. BLOCH *Blood runs Cold* 215 I'm permitted to attend a party..when they go out to eat because I always pick up the check. **1964** WODEHOUSE *Frozen Assets* ii. 32 'Coffee's out, I'm afraid.' 'Nonsense. I'll pick up the tab.' **1966** M. BREWER *Man against Fear* vii. 77 Tonight we pick up her bill. **1967** *Canad. Ann. Rev. 1966* 65 Ottawa would pick up a $14 million tab for a system already in operation. **1976** *S. Wales Echo* 27 Nov. 2/2 Mr. Gray asked if the college should be expected to 'pick up the tab' for even greater expenditure if grants to the theatre were cut. **1978** *Daily Tel.* 13 Feb. 6/5 Ratepayers would have to pick up the bill if important jobs were transferred from the county councils to some of the larger districts.

pick-. Add: **pick-and-gad** *a.* (see quot.); **pick-and-shovel** *a.*, that uses a pick and shovel; also *fig.*; **pickbrain** *a. poet.*, that picks one's brains; **pick-proof** *a.*, secure against picking.

1883 *Encycl. Brit.* XVI. 444/2 The so-called 'pick and gad' work consists in breaking away the easy ground with the point of the pick, wedging off pieces with the gad, [etc.]. **1895** F. REMINGTON *Pony Tracks* 193 They are all cavalry..and are not hindered by..pick-and-shovel work. **1907** *Westm. Gaz.* 11 Mar. 9/3 You don't look much like pick-and-shovel men. **1911** *Chambers's Jrnl.* Mar. 167/2 The ordinary pick-and-shovel man earns..one shilling and eightpence per day. **1930** BLUNDEN *De Bello Germanico* 42 Taking pick-and-shovel troops forward. **1953** *Sun* (Baltimore) 24 Nov. 40/1 Chief Magistrate Sherr yesterday called the search for motorists who have ignored a series of tickets a 'pick and shovel job', in contrast to the 'machine age system' he saw in action during a trip to New York city. **1934** DYLAN THOMAS *18 Poems* 25 My pickbrain masters morsing on the stone Despair of blood, faith in the maiden's slime. **1950** *Sun* (Baltimore) 4 Mar. 2/7 A new electric 'pickproof' motor car lock..is being manufactured. **1976** *National Observer* (U.S.) 29 May 9/2 Eastside tailor seeks design for pick-proof man's hip pocket. **1977** H. GREENE *FSO-1* vii. 63 He had a love for the pick-and-shovel people, the working stiffs behind the men..who wielded power.

pick-a-back, *adv. phr.* (*a.*, *sb.*) Add: The dominant form (except in sense *c) is now **piggy-back.** **b.** (Further examples.) Also in reference to a thing; *spec.* (*a*) an aircraft, rocket, or the like, to which is attached another aircraft, etc., usu. for launching in mid-air; (*b*) a flat railway car on which a truck, container, or the like is carried.

1901 *Punch* 2 Oct. 247/1 Oh, Mr. Green,..Effie..is so miserable because she hasn't had her donkey ride. Would you mind giving her a pick-a-back? **1931** R. CAMPBELL *Georgiad* I. 21 The garden path—a sort of Rotten Row Where oft a merry pick-a-back they go. **1936** [see *mother plane* s.v. *MOTHER *sb.*[1] 16 a]. **1936** L. A. G. STRONG *Last Enemy* iii. 203 Ann came up. 'Piggy-back, please,' she said. 'You mustn't worry poor Mr. Boyle. It's too hot.'.. Ann, hoisted on Denis's back, turned to her. **1944** *Sun* (Baltimore) 13 July 9/2 Two Liberator crewmen with only one parachute between them made a 'piggyback' leap recently from a burning bomber. **1946** L. E. O. CHARLTON *Britain at War: R.A.F. & U.S.A.A.F., July 1943–Sept. 1944* 306 The 'pick-a-back' consisting of an Me 109 fighter mounted on the back of a Ju 88... When approaching its target the Ju 88 was released and guided by remote control towards its objective. **1953** *Evening Jrnl.* (Lincoln, Nebraska) 3 Nov. 6 No sooner had 'piggy back railroading' (hauling truck trailers on flat cars) been hailed by various railroads and one automotive manufacturer as a strikingly simple idea for abating highway congestion and cutting the high price of trucking, than the organized truck operators rose to denounce it. **1954** *Economist* 13 Mar. 779/1 These 'piggy-backs' or 'trailers-on-flat-cars (TOFC)'..have now become a major preoccupation of the railways. **1954** *Railway Age* 26 July 3/2 Further expansion of piggyback by the Chicago & North Western took effect on July 15. **1954** *Times* (Seattle) 21 Sept. 16/1 Railroads throughout the country are studying or instituting limited pickaback service. **1956** *Sun* (Baltimore) 29 Feb. 7/3 A 'piggyback' experiment in which vacationists' automobiles will accompany them on train trips in Germany is planned for next summer. **1959** H. PINTER *Birthday Party* II. 37 Maybe I played piggy-back with you. **1960** *Daily Tel.* 23 June 1/4 (*heading*) U.S. 'pick-a-back' spheres over Russia every 101 min. *Ibid.*, Two 'pick-a-back' satellites were launched by the same rocket from Cape Canaveral, Florida, early today. **1961** *Flight* LXXIX. 827/1 Under the heading 'aerodynamic efficiency' an interesting 'piggyback' vehicle was exhibited. **1965** *Listener* 1 July 6/1 A series of pick-a-back rockets called the Precious Stones are the most important outcome. **1969** [see *MANIFEST *sb.* 3]. **1969** I. & P. OPIE *Children's Games* vi. 185 Riding on people's backs ('Horse Race', 'Piggyback Race'). *Ibid.* vii. 217 The craze at our school is piggy-back fighting. **1969** *Sat. Rev.* (U.S.) 28 June 18/3 Railways are currently taking pride in their new innovation, 'piggyback' service, in which highway trailers..can travel across long distances hitching rides on various railroads. **1973** *Kingston* (Ontario) *Whig-Standard* 21 Sept. 9/6 The CPR diesels still thunder through the hamlet with their cargoes of 'piggy backs', but the little station has been gone for many years now. **1974** W. FOLEY *Child in Forest* I. 25 Our usual practice of running to meet him for pick-a-backs up the garden path. **1977** *Time* 14 Feb. 54/3 The orbiter will be 'mated' to a carrier plane, a Boeing 747 with special mounts on top... The piggyback pair will first run up and down the Edwards runway to test for vibration and stability.

c. *Comb.*, as **pick-a-back plant**, a perennial herb, *Tolmiea menziesii*, of the family Saxifragaceæ, native to western North America and distinguished by cordate leaves that appear to grow one on top of another.

1946 M. FREE *All about House Plants* xviii. 275 The Picka-back Plant has come very much to the fore as a house plant. **1973** J. L. FAUST *N.Y. Times Bk. House Plants* 135 Piggyback plant (*Tolmiea menziesii*) has somewhat fuzzy leaves. **1973** HITCHCOCK & CRONQUIST *Flora Pacific Northwest* 199 *Tolmiea*... Youth-on-Age; Pig-a-Back-Plant; Thousand Mothers.

d. as *v. intr.* and *trans.* To ride piggy-back; to attach on the back of; to carry or transport by means of a piggy-back method. Also *fig.* So **pi·ggy-backing** *vbl. sb.*

1959 *Wall St. Jrnl.* 29 Jan. 1/1 A number of railroad and truck equipment makers have jumped into the manufacture of rail cars and trailers especially designed for piggybacking. **1960** *Economist* 3 Sept. 894/2 The haulage industry is threatened by the rapid spread of the practice of 'piggy-backing'—transporting a loaded lorry or trailer on a railway wagon. **1967** *Freight Management* Jan. 48/2 Piggybacking must not be left out of any argument about future inter-modal methods of transportation. **1968** *Wall St. Jrnl.* 25 Mar. 14/3 To the degree heroin does piggyback on marijuana, it seems more due to the law than to the pushers. **1968** A. DIMENT *Gt. Spy Race* iv. 56 Mr Spont would have to piggy-back me all the way to get a commission. **1973** T. H. WHITE *Making of President 1972* (1974) v. 123 They're tired of Humphrey, he's been around too long... But we have to piggyback him on local campaigns. Wherever we back a local candidate in the primary, we'll pack Hubert in on top. **1975** C. BEECK in *Proc. 25th Electronic Components Conf.* 158/1 Selecting a shaft diameter which would accommodate a coaxial shaft inside it in case another control had to be piggy-backed to the knob. **1975** *Time* (Canada ed.) 17 Mar. 7/1 Arctic Gas argues that the only economical way to bring Canadian gas south is by 'piggybacking' on a line largely given over, at first, to carrying more abundant Alaskan gas. **1976** *Billings* (Montana) *Gaz.* 7 July 4-B/1 The women are content to let the men set the standards and then piggy-back on our efforts. **1977** *Offshore Engineer* May 97/3 A free-standing well-protector jacket platform is attached or 'piggybacked' to the mobile platform at the dock before tow-out. **1977** C. MCCULLOUGH *Thorn Birds* ii. 21 Come on, Meggy, I'll piggyback you the rest of the way. **1979** *Economist* 17 Nov. 79/2 Why not piggyback a federal sales tax on to the levies which people are used to paying and collecting?

pickable, *a.* (Further examples.)

1966 C. SWEENEY *Scurrying Bush* x. 142 This little bird is supposed to enter the mouths of crocodiles to pick their teeth, but..the teeth of a crocodile..are widely spaced so that they are not really pickable—no particles of food being likely to remain. **1969** K. BENTON *24th Level* iv. 59 Black people..going downwards to the city and jobs and suckers with pickable pockets.

picked, *ppl. a.* Add: **5.** *picked-over*, from which the best has already been selected.

1839 *Congress. Globe* 25th Congr. 3 Sess. App. 47/2 All the emigrants went on to the new lands, where they could get first choices at $1.25 per acre, because they could not give that sum for picked-over lands in the old counties. **1886** N. SHEPPARD *Before Audience* viii. 124 Audiences in England outside of the Established Church are weeded. To an American lecturer or preacher they have a picked-over appearance. The church takes the cream, the chapel the milk of society. **1979** A. PARKER *Country Recipe Notebk.* iii. 60 Fill up with well-picked-over berries.

‖ **pickelhaube** (pikəlhau·bə). Also **pickel-haube** (with hyphen) and with capital initial. Pl. **pickel-hauben, pickelhaubes.** [G.] A German spiked helmet of a type worn esp. before and during the earlier part of the war of 1914–18. Also, by metonymy, a German soldier.

1875 *Encycl. Brit.* II. 596/2 The [Prussian] uniform is a dark blue tunic, grey trousers with red stripe, helmet of black leather with brass ornaments and spike (*Pickelhaube*). **1880** G. A. SALA *Amer. Revisited* 213/2 The brutal jest of the cynical master of so many thousands of stolid men with needle-guns and *pickelhaubes* [*sc.* Bismarck] could turn all into mockery and contempt! **1887** *Athenæum* 1 Jan. 16/1 Here is represented the old Empire with powder and wigs, while in Julius Grosse's novel..we find the new Empire with its *Pickelhaube*. **1890** *Times* (Weekly ed.) 28 Feb. 16/1 A dragoon regiment with *pickelhaube* helmet. **1901** *Scotsman* 29 Nov. 5/4 Germany is defied in a manner fitted to stiffen the pickelhauben of the General Staff. **1927** *Bulletin* (Glasgow) 4 Oct. 12/2 A German officer's silver-plated pickel-haube. **1931** E. LINKLATER *Juan in Amer.* II. xvii. 181 Prussian wombs bore pickelhaubes. **1969** G. COPPARD *With Machine Gun to Cambrai* xxi. 89 A dozen Jerry soldiers... The *pickelhaubes* on their heads made them look a leering bunch of devils. **1972** M. GLENNY tr. *Solzhenitsyn's August 1914* xxv. 260 Even when the *Pickelhauben* were no more than a hundred yards away, the Russians showed no fear. **1976** *Leicester Chron.* 26 Nov. 14/5 The first distinctive German steel helmets were introduced in 1916 as a replacement for the pickelhaube, and other armies quickly followed suit.

picker[1]**.** Add: **1. g.** One who picks (PICK *v.*[1] 12) or plucks the strings of a musical instrument such as the banjo or guitar; usu. with the name of the instrument prefixed.

1923 in *John Edwards Mem. Foundation Q.* (1969) V. II. 62 Old fiddlers and banjo pickers. **1934** S. R. NELSON *All about Jazz* vi. 126 The modern method of picking and slapping on the bass was found to be much more rhythmic. So a race of pickers and slappers..sprang into being. **1951, 1959** [see *guitar-picker* s.v. *GUITAR *sb.* b]. **1964** *Amer. Folk Music Occasional* I. 43, I know a banjo picker who hasn't performed for anyone except his wife for the last three years. **1969** N. COHN *A WopBopaLooBop* (1970) viii. 77 A strange city, filled to overflowing with guitar pickers by the thousand. **1976** *National Observer* (U.S.) 23 Oct. 20/3 It's not a novel story. Country music is rife with legend about pickers hitting Lower Broad with a nickel and a song.

4. For 'in Australia' read 'in Australia and New Zealand'. (Earlier and further examples.)

1761 STERNE *Tr. Shandy* III. xxxiv. 159 Indissolubly annex'd by the picker up, to the thing pick'd up. **1881** A. BATHGATE *Waitaruna* xii. 172 The 'pickers-up' were busy gathering the fleeces as they fell from the bereft sheep and carrying them to the sorting table. **1913** —— *Sodger Sandy's Bairn* 57 The pickers-up gathered the fleeces as they fell intact from the shears and bore them to the sorting table, where they were quickly 'skirted' and 'classed'. **1940** *Essays & Stud.* XXV. 111 The picker-up of unconsidered historical trifles. **1956** S. HOPE *Diggers' Paradise* 99 A sixteen-year-old lad could earn £17 a week as a 'picker-up' in the wool-shed. **1959** H. P. TRITTON *Time means Tucker* iii. 26/2 Pickers-up took the fleece as it fell on the board and spread it skin-side down on the wool-tables. **1977** *Shooting Times & Country Mag.* 13–19 Jan. 22/1 There are plenty of pickers-up on this shoot, and little is lost.

b. picker-upper, one who, or that which, picks up.

1936 *Esquire* Sept. 162/2 *Variety* maintains a news staff—not a bunch of press-release picker-uppers. **1942** *Amer. Speech* XVII. 104/1 *Picker upper*, service car with crane. **1944** *N.Y. Times* 3 Sept. S2/6 Her devoted spouse is an avid picker-upper of any hairpins he can find. **1947** *Philadelphia Bull.* 28 July 8 (Advt.), Energy picker-upper..chocolate cookies. **1961** *Times* 19 Aug. 6/7 A mechanical means of gathering up lumps of oil..has been built. It is described as a 'picker-upper', which might be drawn by a tractor.

pickerel frog. *U.S.* [PICKEREL¹.] A common North American frog, *Rana palustris.*

1839 D. H. STORER in Storer & Peabody *Rep. Fishes, Reptiles & Birds Mass.* 238 The pickerel frog..is..met with about the margins of fresh water brooks and ponds. **1906** M. C. DICKERSON *Frog Bk.* 189 The brook and the fields and meadows near make the home of the Pickerel Frogs. **1961** D. M. COCHRAN *Living Amphibians of World* 107/1 The entire skin of the North American pickerel frog, *Rana palustris*, secretes a substance which is lethal to frogs of other species.

Pickering (pi·kəriŋ). *Physics.* The name of Edward Charles *Pickering* (1846–1919), U.S. astronomer, used, usu. *attrib.*, with reference to a series of lines in the spectrum of ionized helium with wave numbers represented by $4R(1/4^2 - 1/m^2)$ (where R is the Rydberg constant and $m = 5, 6, \ldots$), of which the first line has a wavelength of 1012 nanometres and the series limit is at 364 nanometres; (observed by Pickering in 1896 (*Astrophysical Jrnl.* IV. 369, V. 92)).

1922 A. D. UDDEN tr. *Bohr's Theory of Spectra* I. 3 Recently however the question has been reopened and Fowler (1912) has succeeded in observing the Pickering lines in ordinary laboratory experiments. **1923** H. L. BROSE tr. *Sommerfeld's Atomic Struct. & Spectral Lines* iv. 208 Pickering's series (7) includes only one-half of the lines represented by (7a), namely, those for which *k* is odd. *Ibid.*, It is..unjustifiable and arbitrary to detach one-half as the Pickering series and to ascribe it to hydrogen. The other half was overlooked earlier only because it could not be separated from the neighbouring true hydrogen lines. **1942** J. D. STRANATHAN *'Particles' of Mod. Physics* vi. 222 Alternate lines of the Pickering series of helium coincide almost exactly with the Balmer lines of hydrogen. But..the Pickering lines fall at slightly shorter wave lengths. **1967** W. R. HINDMARSH *Atomic Spectra* ii. 5 It was first believed that the Pickering series arose from a special form of hydrogen but it is now known to be due to ionized helium.

picket, *sb.*¹ Add: **I. 1. c.** Also, a triangular or arrow-shaped mark cut in turf or placed on masonry, used in making measurements.

II. 4. d. Short for *picket duty*.

1775 J. HALLAM *Let.* 10 Dec. in H. P. Johnston *Nathan Hale* (1901) 158 Your being on Picquet is a sufficient excuse that you wrote no more. **1834** *Chambers's Edin. Jrnl.* III. 167/2 For three weeks I have been on picquet every night. **1861** O. W. NORTON *Army Lett.* (1903) 34, I have just returned from picket. **1944** J. S. PENNELL *Hist. Rome Hanks* 41 You're on picket, aren't you?

5. For 'men' read 'people'. Also, applied to a person or group conducting a demonstration at particular premises, a particular installation, etc. Also collective sing. Also, the conduct or activity of pickets; an instance of picketing.

1938 *Sun* (Baltimore) 7 Sept. 2/2 Patient parish pickets, determined to retain the Rev. Simon Borkowski as pastor of St. Barbara's Catholic Church, kept their vigil today as they have for more than three weeks to prevent him from fulfilling a transfer order. **1973** *Freedom* 12 May 4/4 (Advt.), Stop the French tests. Regular picket, and London–Paris walk 14th May–3rd June. **1977** *New Society* 30 June 655/2 The picket's mood turned restive, apprehensive. *Ibid.* 657/1 Comment on the picket has almost entirely missed the point by concentrating on how the law might be changed to reconcile heavy strike-breaking vehicles and mass pickets.

IV. 7. *picket duty* (earlier example), *fence* (earlier and later examples), *fort*, *rope* (examples), *tent*, *work*; **picket-boat** (earlier and later examples); **picket line** (*b*) (earlier and later examples); **picket-pin (gopher)** *U.S.*, a ground squirrel of the genus *Citellus*, esp. *C. richardsoni*, found in parts of western North America.

1866 *Oregon State Jrnl.* 13 Jan. 1/4 For the capture of the Albermarle [*sic*], by Lieu[t]. Cushing's picket-boats, the crew netted $100 per man. **1942** *R.A.F. Jrnl.* 13 June 28 On the far side of the harbour, was the dockyard, with its cranes and bustling tugs and picket boats. **1975** *Times Lit. Suppl.* 22 Aug. 936/2 As a fifteen-year-old midshipman in HMS Bacchante, he commanded a picket boat during and after the landings [at Gallipoli in 1915]. **1862** O. W. NORTON *Army Lett.* (1903) 112 Very little drill or other duty, no picket duty or trenching. [**1800** *Carpenters' Rules of Work* (Boston) 32 Plain picket open fence.] **1817** S. R. BROWN *Western Gazetteer* 66 A garden..with high, substantial picket fences to prevent the thefts of the Indians. **1946** D. C. PEATTIE *Road of Naturalist* iii. 36 At home, in fertile Illinois, with the clean snow on the picket fences of Galena, they would be cooking goose. **1951** J. FRAME *Lagoon* 126 We were sitting in little brown summer-houses, and touching the brown picket-fences. **1972** *Evening Telegram* (St. John's, Newfoundland) 24 June 9/6 Grand Beach is..a clean place with picket fences. **1775** in *Mass. Hist. Soc. Coll.* (1814) 2nd Ser II. 230 This fort consists of two large block houses, and a large barrack, which is enclosed with a picket fort. **1846** T. L. MCKENNEY *Mem.* I. vi. 127 The old picket fort standing on the plain..quite a ruin. **1856** R. GLISAN *Jrnl. Army Life* (1874) xx. 277 Indians broke through the picket line. **1945** A. HUXLEY *Let.* 13 Oct. (1969) 536 Matthew was fortunately absent when the violence broke out on the picket line, but he got arrested. **1973** *Guardian* 11 June 13/8 The manual workers at Salford will hold a mass meeting to decide if they will cross the picket line. **1978** *Guardian Weekly* 29 Jan. 17/2 It violates the basic military axiom of not putting the main body of troops on the picket line. Crowding the bulk of NATO's troops along the front line shows the Soviets where the alliance is strong and where it is weak. [**1893** V. BAILEY *Prairie Ground Squirrels* 32 Striped Prairie Spermophile... The little Striped Spermophile..is seen standing upright on its hind feet, straight and motionless as a stick... At a little distance it is impossible to distinguish it from an old picket pin or tent stake.] **1901** E. T. SETON *Lives of Hunted* 214 The darling ambition of his life..was to catch one of the Picket-pin Gophers... These little animals have a trick of sitting bolt upright on their hind legs, with their paws held close in, so that at a distance they look exactly like picket-pins. **1936** *Univ. Arizona Gen. Bull.* III. 79 Last of the ground squirrels to be mentioned are the small ones..variously known over the West as spermophiles, picket-pin gophers, or simply ground squirrels. **1947** V. H. CAHALANE *Mammals N. Amer.* 342 They spend a great deal of time sitting straight up on their haunches, their backs and necks as straight as ramrods. For this reason they are often called 'picket pins'. **1962** W. STEGNER *Wolf Willow* II. i. 41 The earth was densely peopled with small creatures as with large—prairie dogs, picket-pin gophers, field mice. **1967** D. L. ALLEN *Life of Prairies* 78 Overlapping the prairie country..is the realm of a truly abundant grassland rodent, the Richardson's ground squirrel. Sometimes we count dozens or even hundreds to the acre as each squirrel stands high on its hind feet beside a mound of fresh earth. It is evident why this creature will be called 'picket pin'. **1834** in *New Mexico Hist. Rev.* (1927) II. 298 The Acting Asst. Qr Master will have prepared a suitable number of wooden posts for the support of the Picket rope. **1946** *Sierra Club Bull.* (San Francisco) Dec. 4 We had carried with us all of our pack and picket ropes that could be spared. **1961** C. FARRELL *Trail of Tattered Star* xvi. 171 Mike ran down the line, slashing picket ropes with the bayonet. **1862** O. W. NORTON *Army Lett.* (1903) 59 We pitched our picket tents..on the ground lately occupied by a *secesh* regiment. **1804** LEWIS & CLARK *Orig. Jrnls. Lewis & Clark Expedition* (1904) I. 208 The [Mandan] Village..containes houses in a kind of Picket work.

picket, *v.* Add: **4. a.** (Further examples.) **b.** (Later example.)

1941 B. SCHULBERG *What makes Sammy Run?* viii. 156 Wilson ought to picket in front of Sammy's office... Sammy Glick Is Unfair to Organized Double-Crossers! **1972** *Daily Tel.* 25 Jan. 6/2 The power station is being picketed by miners attempting to stop oil supplies used to ignite coal in its boilers. **1977** *Times* 27 June 2/5 Six strikers..were picketing near the main gates.

picketed, *ppl. a.* (Earlier and further examples.)

1758 *Essex Inst. Hist. Coll.* (1881) XVIII. 102 Two Piquitted Forts or Garisons and a Hospetle. **1817** S. R. BROWN *Western Gazetteer* 27 Almost every house has a spacious picketed garden in its rear. **1890** KIPLING *Barrack-Room Ballads* (1892) 97 The picketed ponies, shag and wild, Strained at their ropes as the feed was piled. **1905** H. COHEN *Law Strikes & Lock-Outs* 16 He was watching the employed coming from the picketed works.

picketer. For 'a man' read 'a person' and add: Also, one engaged in a demonstration at particular premises, etc. (Further examples.)

1930 *Times Educ. Suppl.* 19 July 325/4 The picketers broke a barrier on the stairway. **1972** W. P. MCGIVERN *Caprifoil* (1973) i. 8 They are vocal liberals. Marchers, picketers, demonstrators. **1975** *Time Out* 17 Oct. 5/1 Many of the morning's picketers had lined up behind the main banners. **1978** S. BRILL *Teamsters* v. 181 The truck sped wildly toward the gate, with the picketers in full view.

picketing, *vbl. sb.* Add: **b.** secondary picketing: see *SECONDARY *a.*

c. *concr.* A fence or palisade made of pickets; picket-work. *U.S.*

1755 in *New Hampsh. Hist. Soc. Coll.* (1837) V. 254 Seven men..who were out..getting a few poles to complete the new picketing of the fort. **1860** J. F. H. CLAIBORNE *Life & Times Gen. Sam. Dale* 25 These forts were merely a number of log cabins built round a small square,..the whole surrounded by a rough picketing.

pickey, var. *PICKIE.

Pickford (pi·kfǒɹd). The name of a firm engaged in the removal of furniture, used *ellipt.* or in the possessive to denote a van used by Pickfords to remove furniture, or the firm itself. Also *fig.* and *attrib.*

[**1833** C. MATHEWS *Let.* 8 Oct. in A. Mathews *Mem. Charles Mathews* (1839) IV. 205 It will be lighter for posting than any travelling carriage now in his yard. It cannot be called *a Pickford*, at any rate.] **1864** *Chambers's Jrnl.* 5 Mar. 152 The ubiquitous Pickford breaks the street-lamps, by going too near to the pavement. **1865** DICKENS *Mut. Fr.* II. IV. xii. 263 The sanctuary was..a kind of criminal Pickford's. The lower passions and vices were regularly ticked off in the books, warehoused in the cells, carted away. **1873** D. G. ROSSETTI *Let.* 18 Dec. (1967) III. 1250 Pickfords must be mad if they really took it to the wrong station. **1901** *Daily Tel.* 14 Nov. 4/5, I have seen a pair-horse Pickford tip coming up London Bridge. **1907** G. B. SHAW *John Bull's Other Island* p. xv, We cannot crush England as a Pickford's van might crush a perambulator. We are the perambulator and England the Pickford. **1975** J. HONE *Sixth Directorate* III. 94 What he isn't taking is being stored. Pickfords are coming tomorrow. **1980** R. MCCRUM *In Strange State* ix. 74 'Keys to the boot, please, sir.'.. Another constable.. rummaged about among his books, papers and clothes. 'A regular Pickfords.'

pickie (pi·ki). *Sc.* and *Ir. local.* Also **pickey.** [f. PICK *sb.*⁴ + -Y⁶, -IE.] Hopscotch. Also pl. (const. sing.). Also *comb.*

1885 'J. STRATHESK' *More Bits from Blinkbonny* ii. 33 The 'pickies' (or the 'beds', or the 'Pall-all'), played with a flat stone on the pavement. **1906** Pickie [used in def. s.v. PICK *sb.*⁴ 3]. **1922** JOYCE *Ulysses* 76 With careful tread he passed over a hopscotch court with its forgotten pickeystone.

picking, *vbl. sb.*¹ Add: **1. a.** (Further examples corresponding to PICK *v.*¹ 12.)

1934 [see *PICKER¹ 1 g]. **1956** [see *guitar-picking* s.v. *GUITAR *sb.* b]. **1973** *Time Out* 2–8 Mar. 21/1 The audience whoop away like madmen, and there's some marvellous pickin' and fiddlin'.

b. (Earlier and further examples.)

1618 H. WOTTON *Let.* in L. P. Smith *Life & Lett. Sir H. Wotton* (1907) II. 159 Remarkable how the divine justice, in a casual picking out of the foresaid number, from a 150 tumultuary men, did direct the man employed about this choice. **1846** G. DODD *Brit. Manuf.* 6th Ser. v. 131 The part of the coach-painter's work which requires the largest amount of care and neatness is that of 'picking-out', or painting fine lines, scrolls, &c. of one colour on a groundwork of a different colour. **1863** *Once a Week* 14 Nov. 569/2 There is one infamous method of thieving in the streets..which is called 'picking up'... This 'picking-up' system abounds in every large town... A woman is always the principal actor in these cases, and she is called the 'picking-up moll'. **1868** L. M. ALCOTT *Little Women* I. xi. 169 They [*sc.* plates of fruit] dwindled sadly after the picking over. **1869** F. HENDERSON *Six Yrs. in Prisons Eng.* vii. 76 'I heard a bloke talking about a "picking-up moll" he used to live with. What did he mean by that?' 'O! that's a very common racket. He meant a "flash-tail", or prostitute who goes about the streets at nights trying to pick up "toffs".' **1889** [see *cosher* s.v. *COSH *sb.*³]. **1925** *Times* 23 May 9/3 The picking-up power of an aërial varies as the square of the effective height. **1976** *West Lancs. Evening Gaz.* 8 Dec. 8/3 If a train leaving Blackpool early on Saturday morning for London is full by the time it leaves its last picking-up point at Wigan, it will have 500 people aboard helping a scout effort. **1977** *Gay News* 24 Mar. 15/4 Glasgow SMG is still suffering from the bad image—'a closetted picking-up place'—of the early years. **1979** P. COSGRAVE *Three Colonels* 189 That greatest of vices of warriors after a battle, the picking over..of memories.

2. f. *Basket-weaving.* (See quot.)

1912 T. OKEY *Introd. Art of Basket-Making* 153 Picking, cutting off the projecting ends of rods when the work is partially or wholly finished.

5. *picking-time* (examples); (sense *2 f) *picking-knife*; **picking-bee** *N. Amer.* (see BEE¹ 4); **picking-belt,** a travelling belt on which coal is picked.

1828 in *Dict. Americanisms* (1951) s.v. *picking bee*, Mother went to a picking Bee to pick wool. **1905** M. G. SHERK *Pen Pict. Early Pioneer Life Upper Canada* 177 The wool was then picked over by the women and girls, to get out any burs or lumps of dirt that might have adhered to it, 'pickin'' bees being frequently made for this purpose. **1943** S. MENEFEE *Assignment: U.S.A.* 48 In 1943 the townspeople were prepared to turn out for a picking-bee lasting most of the season, if necessary, to save the crop. **1901** *Chambers's Jrnl.* May 312/2 The excellent condition in which the coal was shipped,..was in great part due to the use of an appliance known as a 'picking' belt. **1921** *Spectator* 28 May 680/1 Girls on a picking-belt or in a colliery brick-works were earning similarly inflated wages. **1912** T. OKEY *Introd. Art of Basket-Making* vi. 28 The ends of the bottom-sticks are now cut off by the shears and the projecting tops and butts neatly picked off with the picking knife. **1960** E. LEGG *Country Baskets* 57 The last operation is the trimming off of all ends of canes and rods, 'picking the basket' as the craftsman calls it, for which he uses a special picking knife. **1835** J. H. INGRAHAM *South-West* II. 285 'Picking time'..continues where full crops are made until the first of December. **1848** [see *KNOCK *v.* 7*]. **1949** C. S. MURRAY *This our Land* 87 Picking time begins about August 20.

pickle, *sb.*[1] Add: **4.** (Further examples.)

1926 H. CRANE *Let.* 29 Mar. (1965) 243 I'm in no particular pickle at present. **1943** E. CALDWELL *Georgia Boy* ii. 21 I've got that marriage ceremony to perform in less than half an hour. It's too late for me to hunt up anybody else to ring the bell, and if you don't ring it for me, I'll be in a pretty pickle. **1955** *Times* 24 May 4/7 Leicestershire would have been in a pretty pickle without their captain, C. H. Palmer, in their current match with Surrey at Leicester. **1960** M. SPARK *Bachelors* ii. 19 You're going to leave Alice in a nice pickle if the case goes against you. *Ibid.* viii. 115 You've got us in a pickle. **1961** B. FERGUSSON *Watery Maze* x. 245 This landing had got into a pickle partly because of the bad weather, which had impeded the rate of build-up. **1967** G. F. FIENNES *I tried to run Railway* iv. 40 In a matter of days we were in a rare pickle. **1977** *Jersey Even. Post* 26 July 8/6 Don't leave jobs unfinished in order to start on something new, or you'll end up in a right old pickle.

c. *pl.* Nonsense, something worthless, an absurd statement. Also as *int. slang.* (No longer current.)

1846 *Swell's Night Guide* 34 'Pickles,' as the swell draper would say, 'but they frizzle and mangle music like bricks.' **1859** H. J. BYRON *Maid & Magpie* v. 31 If you and your minion Indulge that opinion, Ten pounds to an onion it's pickles, I bet. **1889** J. HATTON *Reminisc. J. L. Toole* II. v. 150 Or, the advance being ordered, had he exclaimed, 'Oh, Pickles!' before seeking convenient shelter from the foe? **1898** L. MERRICK *Actor-Manager* v. 66 The rent they ask is a hundred and fifty, but that's all pickles!

5. c. A woman with a sour disposition; an unattractive woman. *slang.*

1950 [see *LEMON *sb.*[1] 1 b]. **1970** *Women Speaking* Apr. 5/1 If a man doesn't like a girl's looks or personality, she's a..pickle, prune, [etc.].

6. *pickle-bottle* (earlier and later examples), *-jar* (earlier and later examples), *-pot* (later example).

1852 DICKENS *Bleak Ho.* (1853) v. 35 Pickle bottles, wine bottles, ink bottles. **1945** *Coast to Coast 1944* 140 Davie always had a pickle bottle for staging heroic contests between red-joes and black-joes. **1836** DICKENS *Sk. Boz* 1st Ser. I. 237 Some pickle-jars; some surgeons' ditto. **1952** *Coast to Coast 1951–52* 29 The farmer carried a glass pickle-jar with a screw-top lid. **1977** G. MARTON *Alarum* 49 The Russians re-ordered the smoked salmon—ate the garnish of pickles around the salmon and..wanted the whole pickle jar. **1903** *Nature* 19 Nov. 68/2 After Watt's patent, Newcomen engines were made with separate condensers without air-pumps, the air being discharged through a snifting-valve. Such condensers were known as 'pickle-pots'.

pickle, *v.*[1] Add: **1. c.** *intr.* To undergo the process of pickling.

1904 G. PARKER *Ladder of Swords* ix. 110 You have prepared your own brine, monsieur; in it you shall pickle.

5. *trans.* (See quot. 1970.) *U.S.A.F. slang.*

1966 *Time* 20 May 36/3 'I broke to the right,' recalled Dudley after last week's action, 'and pickled (dropped) my fuel tanks.' **1970** *Word Watching* Apr. 7/1 *Pickle*, to drop extra fuel tanks or equipment: to drop bombs.

pickled, *ppl. a.*[1] Add: **1.** (Further examples.)

1629 [see *DAN(T)ZIG]. **1739** E. SMITH *Compl. Housewife* (ed. 9) 43 Strow upon your Cutlets pickled walnuts in quarters. **1747** H. GLASSE *Art of Cookery* ii. 22 Put to it some pickled Gerkins chopp'd and boil'd Chesnuts. **1837** DICKENS *Pickw.* xlviii. 519 Demanding a mutton chop and a pickled walnut instantly. **1843** —— *Mart. Chuz.* (1844) vi. 66, I remember thinking.., in the days of my childhood, that pickled onions grew on trees. **1849** B. S. ELY *There she Blows* i. 9 An Irishman..wanted some pork to make 'pickled oysters'. This dish was made by cutting raw pork up fine, and covering it with pepper sauce and black pepper. **1877** E. S. DALLAS *Kettner's Bk. of Table* 423 *Shalot Sauce* is the same as what is called Sharp Sauce or Sauce Piquante, with this only difference—that to the latter there is added pickled gherkins. **1945** *Sun* (Baltimore) 22 Oct. 4/1 Hot-rolled pickled and cold rolled sheet deliveries run late into the second quarter next year. **1967** K. GILES *Death & Mr Prettyman* iv. 87, I put out a bit of ham..and some pickled walnuts. **1969** T. C. THORSTENSEN *Pract. Leather Technol.* v. 76 In the manufacture of garment suede leather the raw materials are primarily the pickled sheep skins based on New Zealand lamb and sheep. **1970** C. KERSH *Aggravations M. Ashe* iii. 45, I have terrible dreams if I eat pickled cucumbers. **1974** J. STUBBS *Painted Face* i. 23 Trying..to banish the cheese and pickled onions from the table. **1977** G. SCOTT *Hot Pursuit* iii. 25 Pickled eggs like lumps of coal.

2. *spec.* Drunk. *slang.*

1842 [in Dict.]. **1900** ADE *More Fables* 171 'It may be that I was a mite Polluted,' he suggested. 'You were a teeny bit Pickled about Two..,' said Mr. Byrd. **1919** WODEHOUSE *Damsel in Distress* xx. 236 On that occasion a most rummy and extraordinary thing happened. I got pickled to the eyebrows. **1926** WOOD & GODDARD *Dict. Amer. Slang* 20 *Gills, pickled to the*, soused; drunk. **1933** WODEHOUSE *Heavy Weather* vii. 95 The ink was still wet on a paragraph where, searching like some Flaubert for the *mot juste*, he had run his pen through the word 'intoxicated' and substituted for it the more colourful 'pickled to the gills'. **1939** [see *BIRD *sb.* 1 e]. *a* **1953** DYLAN THOMAS *Prospect of Sea* (1955) 128 On Sundays, and when pickled, he sang high tenor, and had won many cups. **1959** P. MOYES *Dead Men don't Ski* vii. 86 He gets the most extraordinary ideas sometimes, and he's pretty pickled, anyhow.

pickler[2]. Add: **3.** A vessel in which vegetables can be pickled.

1862 *Illustr. Catal. Internat. Exhib., Industr. Dept., Brit. Div.* II. No. 6870, Bottles, filters, jars, foot-warmers, jugs, picklers, casks, jelly-cans.

pickling, *vbl. sb.*[1] **b.** (Further examples.)

1906 *Daily Chron.* 31 Oct. 8/4 At Southwold the pickling-plots..will be just at the back of the landing wharves. **1958** *Times Rev. Industry* June 50/3 To produce stainless [steel] strip..required..the installation of ..a pickling line.

picklock, *sb.*[1] **1.** (Later fig. example.)

1929 R. BRIDGES *Testament of Beauty* I. 21 This picklock Reason is still a-fumbling at the wards.

pick-me-up. Add: **2.** A woman who readily allows herself to be picked up; a prostitute. Cf. *PICK-UP *sb.* c.

1922 JOYCE *Ulysses* 49 She lives in Leeson park, with a grief and kickshaws, a lady of letters. Talk that to some else, Stevie: a pickmeup. **1941** J. SMILEY *Hash House Lingo* 42 *Pick me up*, loose woman.

pi·ck-off. Also **pickoff, pick off.** [f. vbl. phr. *to pick off* s.v. PICK *v.*[1] 18.] **1.** Chiefly *Aeronaut.* In an automatic control or guidance system, any device which produces or alters a pneumatic or an electrical output in response to a change in motion.

1938 P. V. H. WEEMS *Air Navigation* (ed. 2) xiv. 243 If the aircraft changes attitude laterally, one of the ports ..of the air pick off is opened fully and the other closed. **1938** A. JORDANOFF *Through Overcast* xiv. 180 Whenever you wish to fly in a certain direction under automatic control, you must be sure to set the air pick-offs at neutral at the time your plane points in the direction which gives the desired reading on the directional gyro. **1940** E. MOLLOY *Aeroplane Maintenance & Operation* II. I. 12 In actual practice the air pick-off consists of a disc attached to the gyro element, with knife edges which intercept the air flow at two nozzles on the supporting frame. **1958** J. G. TRUXAL *Control Engineers' Handbk.* xvii. 49 The displacement gyro is continually being torqued by the coupling of the motion of the base through the gimbal gearing friction and pickoff loading to the wheel. **1962** F. I. ORDWAY et al. *Basic Astronautics* ix. 377 The precession..is sensed by a pickoff that sends a signal to the servo amplifier.

2. In baseball: the act of catching a runner off base by means of the pitcher or catcher suddenly throwing the ball at that base. Freq. *attrib.*

1939 G. S. COCHRANE *Baseball* iv. 76 The danger of a throw to first for the pickoff is that the runner has overrun first not only too far to get back but far enough to make a break for second. **1948** *Sun* (Baltimore) 19 July 12 (*caption*) Bill Martin gets back in time as Eddie Shokes..tries to complete pickoff attempt in opener. **1968** *Washington Post* 4 July C 2/4 Wills moved to second when Ryan's attempted pickoff throw went wide. **1968** *Globe & Mail* (Toronto) 10 July 26/6 Killebrew.. said Tiant's pickoff throw on Mays, which opened the gates for the winning run, was behind the runner. **1974** *Spartanburg* (S. Carolina) *Herald* 23 Apr. A6/4 Bill Dancy of Spartanburg singled with one out in the fourth, moved to second on an errant pickoff attempt and went to third on Mark Ammons' infield hit. **1976** *Washington Post* 19 Apr. D2/2 Manning scored the only run Cleveland needed in the first inning when he..came home when Busby threw away a pickoff throw.

3. Used *attrib.* to designate auxiliary parts of a machine positioned so as to be easily selected or brought into use when required.

1949 *Tool Engineers Handbk.* (Amer. Soc. Tool Engineers) xxxv. 602 A secondary operation may be eliminated by the use of a pick-off attachment, which is an independently driven spindle and collet arrangement mounted in the cutoff position. **1950** J. A. OATES in A. W. Judge *Machine Tools & Operations* III. i. 30 These 'pick-off' gears are arranged under a cover..in some easily accessible position, and it is only a matter of two or three minutes to change over to a new speed or feed.

pickpocketing. (Earlier and later examples.)

1789 G. PARKER *Life's Painter* xv. 176 Going upon the knuckle is going a thieving, pickpocketing, &c. **1818** J. MILNER in F. C. Husenbeth *Life J. Milner* (1862) xx. 353 Not only an affront of a real diabolical nature, but also a serious pick-pocketing roguery. **1957** MANVELL & HUNTLEY *Technique Film Music* 232 The 'Juggler's Waltz' is a period piece for a music-hall act which takes place in a Paris café during an incident in which the visiting Inspector of Police witnesses a pick-pocketing attempt. **1977** *New Society* 7 July 5/2 Their game has confused pickpocketing with bag snatching and mugging.

Pick's disease (piks dizi·z). **1.** [f. the name of Friedel *Pick* (1867–1926), Austrian physician.] A form of multiple serositis characterized by constrictive pericarditis, hepatomegaly, and ascites.

1900 DUNGLISON *Dict. Med. Sci.* (ed. 22) App. 1314/2 *Pick's disease*, pseudocirrhosis of the liver, sometimes accompanying adhesive pericarditis. **1935** *Lancet* 14 Sept. 602/1 The prognosis of Pick's disease without surgical treatment is unfavourable for health and in some cases for life. **1940** E. ROSENTHAL *Dis. Digestive Syst.* iii. 278 Such a perihepatitis may be the result of liver disease or may accompany 'pericarditic pseudocirrhosis' (Pick's disease). **1959** BAILEY & LOVE *Short Pract. Surg.* (ed. 11) xx. 376 The best example of perisplenitis occurs in association with multiple serositis (Pick's disease).

2. [f. the name of Arnold *Pick* (1851–1924), Austrian psychiatrist and neurologist.] A condition, chiefly afflicting persons in late middle age, which is characterized by deterioration of intellect and judgement, speech disturbance and eventual dementia, and is caused by progressive atrophy of the frontal and temporal lobes of the brain.

1931 *Lancet* 20 June 1331/2 Pick's disease is a slowly progressive dementia starting usually in the sixth decade and accompanied by focal manifestations. **1935** *Jrnl. Nervous & Mental Dis.* LXXXII. 71 High blood pressure and arteriosclerosis are peculiarly absent in Pick's disease. **1955** H. H. MERRITT *Textbk. Neurol.* vi. 417 The cardinal symptoms of both Pick's and Alzheimer's disease are progressive dementia and disturbances in the speech. **1974** PASSMORE & ROBSON *Compan. Med. Stud.* III. xxxv. 76/1 The underlying cerebral atrophy..is restricted to the frontal and temporal lobes in Pick's disease. **1976** SMYTHIES & CORBETT *Psychiatry* vii. 126 Pick's disease is marked by a rapid and profound blunting of social judgement.

pick-up, *sb.* (*a.*) Add: Also **pickup. a.** (ii) [*PICK *v.*[1] 20 b (*b*).] The collection of unretrieved game after a shooting party; the quantity of game so collected.

1897 *Encycl. Sport* I. 443/1 Too large a 'pick up' means that the work was not properly done on the day itself. **1939** *Country Life* 11 Feb. 153/1, I wish all hosts would provide themselves with those little cards that tell you the total bag together with the pick-up and the names of the guns. **1976** *Shooting Times & Country Mag.* 16–22 Dec. 16/2 At the end of the pick-up a smile at last creased the face of keeper Bunny Spicer for the total bag was 253 pheasants, a record!

(iii) [*PICK *v.*[1] 20 o.] The act of apprehending or arresting. orig. *U.S.* Also, *pick-up van* (S. Afr.), a police van.

1908 J. M. SULLIVAN *Criminal Slang* 18 *Pickup*, an arrest followed by no charge of crime. **1934** L. BERG *Revelations Prison Doctor* viii. 109 Rao..called his arrests 'pickups' and inferred that the charges were too trivial to be worthy of notice. **1942** P. ABRAHAMS *Dark Testament* I. xii. 63 They all turn, and see a group of policemen jumping out of the moving pick-up van and running towards them. **1946** *Sun* (Baltimore) 8 Nov. 6/2 The Kansas sheriff responded with a request for a 'pick-up' on another man in the case. **1948** O. WALKER *Kaffirs are Lively* xi. 173 There comes the big van... They call it the *pick-up van*. **1953** P. LANHAM *Blanket Boy's Moon* I. vi. 50 'Police! Police! The pick-up van's coming.' Even as he shouted the warning, the police arrived in their closed van with a squealing of brakes. **1970** G. JACKSON *Let.* 10 June in *Soledad Brother* (1971) 34, I..started getting 'picked up' by the pigs more often. .. These pick-ups were mainly for 'suspicion of' or because I was in the wrong part of town.

(iv) [PICK *v.*[1] 20 h.] Recovery, improvement.

a **1916** H. JAMES *Ivory Tower* (1917) I. iii. 69 'It's one of Mr. Betterman's [nurses] taking a joy-ride in honour of his recovery!'.. 'His pick-up *will* be a sell,' [Davey] ruefully added. **1922** H. TITUS *Timber* xxxii. 279 During all those years there will be a steady pick-up in quality. **1933** *Sun* (Baltimore) 10 Nov. 14/1 It is idle to suggest..that this newest relief scheme will help to tide the jobless over until 'the spring pick-up begins'. **1958** *Times Rev. Industry* Sept. 50/2 Export orders continue to be small, and there is little hope, with the American recession affecting steel-using industries on the Continent, of any pick-up in the near future. **1961** *Wall St. Jrnl.* 4 Oct. 1 Farm machinery dealer Bob Houtz tilts back in a battered chair and tells of a sharp pickup in sales. **1970** *Daily Tel.* 3 Feb. 19/2 Car sales showed their expected pick-up last month.

(v) [PICK *v.*[1] 20 f in Dict. and Suppl.] Reception of signals by electrical apparatus; *spec.* interference; also, a received radio or television programme.

1923 *Electrical Communication* I. IV. 25/1 A portable amplifier for use with the 'pick-up' microphones..made it possible to pick up speeches or music at any desired point ..and distribute the output to sound projectors. **1925** *Scribner's Mag.* Oct. 90 (Advt.), Low-loss doughnut coils.. conquer 'pick-up' of unwanted stations. **1937** *Discovery* Nov. 330/2 To provide the subject matter for transmission, direct pick-up, artists in the studio, or previously photographed sound-film may be used. **1943** *Electronic Engin.* XV. 521/3 Although the balanced input circuit minimises the pick-up it is sometimes essential to enclose the patient in a screened cubicle. **1948** *Sun* (Baltimore) 3 Jan. 2/2 It was a thirty-minute radio network program with pick-ups from scattered points in the United States and abroad. **1949** FRAYNE & WOLFE *Elem. Sound Recording* xxxii. 674 Microphone placement is less exacting in the stereophonic pickup of orchestral music. **1956** *Electronics* Feb. 170/2 A series of measurements was made on the cross pickup of pulses in a 100-foot length of ..communication cable. **1965** *Wireless World* Aug. 383/2 When ferrite aerials are close to the inverter transformers, inductive pick-up can result. **1971** *Sci. Amer.* Oct. 28/1 With a community wired from one or more terminal points to individual homes the local pickup would not be limited to the channels of the commercial television networks; instead participants could receive through the satellite a number of services to meet individual tastes. **1976** *Broadcast* 29 Nov. 18/1 The camera has to be blimped to prevent noise pick-up from microphones.

(vi) [Cf. *PICK *v.*^{1} 20 j.] Robbery, theft. Freq. *attrib. slang.*

1928, etc. [see **pick-up man* (sense B. a)]. **1938** F. D. Sharpe *Sharpe of Flying Squad* i. 14 Lower down come the suit-case thieves, the pick-up merchants, small time smash-and-grabbers, [etc.]. *Ibid.* xxiii. 240 He had been persuaded to try his hand at 'the pick up' (stealing from unattended motor cars). **1962** *Gross's Criminal Investigation* (ed. 5) viii. 206 *At the pick-up*, suitcase stealing.

(vii) [Cf. Pick *v.*^{1} 20 e.] Collection and transportation by means of an aircraft, motor vehicle, ship, etc. Freq. *attrib.*

1938 W. L. G. Cowan *Loud Report* III. 220 We usually kip in the afternoon and push on at night. There's a better chance of a pick-up. **1940** *Mech. Engin.* Apr. 283/1 The record is not clear as to exactly when the first pickup in flight was made. *Ibid.* 285/2 The pickup system..makes possible the picking up of heavier loads. **1943** *Jrnl. R. Aeronaut. Soc.* XLVII. (Abstr. from Sci. & Techn. Press) 72 The Air Mail Pick-up service was started by the American Post Office Department in 1939. *Ibid.*, Since short hauls seem to offer the best field for cargo glider operation, a similar method of pick-up becomes most attractive. **1952** E. F. Davies *Illyrian Venture* iv. 68 The American pilot signalled Cairo that it was possible to rescue them by air pick-up from Gjinokaster airfield. **1960** R. Williams *Border Country* iv. 94 'Where's the pickup then?' 'Signalled now.'.. Rees..crossed the line and walked down..to the siding. **1960** R. W. Marks *Dymaxion World of B. Fuller* 22/1 Fuller's toilets.. consisted of a splashless hermetic and waterproof packaging system which mechanically packed, stored, and gross-cartoned wastes for eventual pickup for processing by chemical industries. **1971** P. O'Donnell *Impossible Virgin* xii. 238, I fixed for the 'copter to stand by for a pick-up at eighteen 'undred hours. *Ibid.* xiv. 275 They rested beside..a triangle of flat stony ground... This was the pick-up area Willie had arranged. **1972** 'G. Black' *Bitter Tea* (1973) vii. 100 The *Kao Ming* hasn't been converted for carrying..steel containers, serving out her now very limited time on the copra pick-up routes. **1974** L. Deighton *Spy Story* xis. 208 That radio signal obliges us to continue with the pick-up, even if we were certain it's phoney. **1976** *National Observer* (U.S.) 11 Dec. 4/3 Ankeny, Iowa, saved $9,000 by opening dump sites to the public for two weekend clean-ups a year and abolished curbside pickups. **1977** *Chicago Tribune* 2 Oct. XII. 2/2 The garbage just piled up all summer. No pickup. **1978** J. Krantz *Scruples* ix. 259 Billy also established a delivery service in a town where multimillionaire customers have to do their own pickups in every boutique.

(viii) *Nuclear Physics.* A reaction in which an incident particle such as a proton or deuteron captures one or more nucleons from an atomic nucleus. Usu. *attrib.*

1950 *Physical Rev.* LXXVII. 470 It is proposed that the fast deuterons observed among the products of high energy nuclear reactions are to be understood in terms of a 'pick-up' or sudden rearrangement process. *Ibid.*, The pick-up process must not be thought of as taking place within the nucleus. **1970** I. E. McCarthy *Nuclear Reactions* I. v. 95 If one of these interactions seems more plausible than the other to the reader, he need only consider the time-reversed situation (pick-up). **1971** W. M. Gibson *Nuclear Reactions* vii. 108 A pick-up reaction in a nucleus with an odd neutron outside a closed inner shell can provide useful information about the state of the odd neutron..which is directly relevant to the shell model of the nucleus. **1975** *Nature* 6 Mar. 19/3 The spectroscopic factors for stripping and pickup reactions on the same nucleus can be related to each other.

b. (Further examples.)

1972 M. Glenny tr. *Solzhenitsyn's August 1914* xlii. 419 Trams passed, clanging, their pick-ups hissing along the wires. **1974** *Physics Bull.* Apr. 154/3 The dangers caused by power failure in magnetic hoists are avoided in a new design from Mullard. For the pickup is a permanent magnet rather than the usual ferroelectric magnet.

(ii) (*a*) A sensor or transducer.

1943 D. G. Fink *Television Standards & Pract.* iv. 91 Specifications to be placed on the spectral response of each of the three color-sensitive elements of the pickup. **1957** R. A. Heinlein *Door into Summer* v. 79, I suppose it was a stethoscope he used although it looked like a miniaturized hearing aid... The pick-up he pushed against me was as cold and hard as ever. **1961** *Engineering* 8 Sept. 309/1 Phototransistor pickups, focused on rotating black and white discs, provide signals for the phase meter. **1962** F. I. Ordway et al. *Basic Astronautics* vii. 316 By placing temperature pickups at various points on the model flame deflector it was possible to determine the approximate temperatures encountered..in an actual firing. **1978** J. Gores *Gone* (1979) iii. 24 He was at the corner where he knew the concealed pickup was.

(*b*) *spec.* = *cartridge 1 e, *head *sb.* 11 g, *pick-up arm* in sense B. a below.

1926 *Glasgow Herald* 5 Oct. 5 Instead of the conventional sound-box an electrical device known as a magnetic 'pick-up' is guided over the record, converting the mechanical vibrations imparted to the needle into electrical vibrations. **1926** *Gramophone* Dec. 294/1 Instead of a sound-box there is what is known as a 'pick-up'. **1938** *Times* 25 Aug. 8/2 It has been specially designed as a supplementary unit for existing radio receivers having pick-up terminals. **1940** *Gramophone* Sept. 93/1 The output is very much less than that given by the average moving iron or piezo electric types of pick-up. **1941** [see *cartridge 1 e]. **1946** *Newsweek* 13 May 23 (Advt.), Your Victrola's jewel-point pickup floats like a feather on water. **1951** [see *head *sb.* 11 g]. **1959** *New Scientist* 31 July 517/2 The whole pick-up must be able to do the manœuvres required of it without giving rise to excessive pressures which would damage the record. **1963** *Which?* Jan. 8/2 The pick up is composed of two parts—an arm, and at the end of the arm..a head. **1975** G. J. King *Audio Handbk.* viii. 170 The modern pickup consists of an arm and a cartridge. **1976** 'J. Fraser' *Who steals my Name?* ix. 107 The needle on the pick-up of his record player..had a beard on it... His room was filthy.

(*c*) *spec.* A device that produces an electrical signal corresponding to the displacement, speed, or acceleration of a vibrating body.

1950 P. G. Andres *Survey Mod. Electronics* viii. 346 Electronic comparator gauges use a pickup that operates on the principle of displacing an armature..to generate a corresponding voltage. *Ibid.* 363 Since the pickup responds to the acceleration of the vibratory motion, integrating networks convert its output..into readings proportional to velocity or displacement. **1966** *McGraw-Hill Encycl. Sci. & Technol.* VIII. 667/1 A vibration pickup can be used to generate an electrical signal directly from the vibration of a string; this is the case in the electric guitar and electric piano. **1968** *Melody Maker* 6 Apr. 5 (Advt.), Take our pickups... To get sound from a metal guitar string, all you have to do is wind wire around a magnetic core and place it near that string. **1970** R. H. Wallace *Understanding & measuring Vibration* iv. 40 Because the aircraft structure is such that low frequencies under, say, 10 Hz are readily transmitted,.. it will be vital to use pickups and read-out equipment going down to zero frequency, or near. **1972** M. P. Blake in Blake & Mitchell *Vibration & Acoustic Measurement Handbk.* xx. 422 The proximity pickup is likely to become increasingly popular for monitoring the shafts of high-speed, large, powerful drives, such as turbines, reading directly in displacement which, in this application, is usually the parameter of most interest. *Ibid.*, A growing tendency among those who measure vibration favors the acceleration pickup.

(iii) In full, *pick-up truck* or *van*. A small truck or van used for carrying light loads (see also sense a (iii) above). So *pick-up body*, a small, detachable body for use on various types of light trucks.

1932 *Kansas City* (Missouri) *Times* 21 Jan. 22 There was a delivery car with a pick-up body on it in King City. **1939** *Sun* (Baltimore) 18 Jan. 7/2 Dairies' pickup trucks were subject to commission regulation. **1944** *Democrat* 29 June 1/4 This includes all operators of trucks and pickups whose gasoline rations are not controlled. **1948** *Southern Sierran* (Los Angeles) Apr. 4/1 The work will be made lighter if someone will provide the use of a pick-up truck for removing the dirt. **1959** F. Stark *Riding to Tigris* 96 A piece of the bull-dozer was extracted and loaded on the pick-up, which looked like a bright orange lorry. **1973** A. Ross *Dunfermline Affair* 45 He must be going out in the pick-up. *Ibid.* 48 There were still plenty of motor cars in the car park, but no small grey pick-up truck. **1977** *Cork Examiner* 8 June 14/3 (Advt.), 30 cwt. pick-up truck and driver available. **1977** *Western Morning News* 30 Aug. 2/2 (Advt.), J.4 Pick-up J registered.. long M.O.T.

c. (Further examples.) *spec.* A person whose acquaintance is formed with the intention of having a sexual relationship; a prostitute or street-walker; also, the act of forming such an acquaintanceship.

1848 Trollope *Kellys & O'Kellys* III. xi. 269 The pick-up on the Derby is about four thousand. **1871** L. H. Bagg *4 Years at Yale* 46 *Pick-up*,..a street-walker, of the less disreputable sort. **1927** Dunning & Abbott *Broadway* xvi. 158 'Dan McCorn out there?' enquired Porky. Steve nodded. 'He's talking to one of the pick-ups.' **1930** *San Antonio* (Texas) *Light* 31 Jan. 14/7 (Advt.), A real pickup for someone: 50 feet on Broadway... An exceptional site. **1930** J. B. Priestley *Angel Pavement* iv. 170 The big teashops..were always crowded with girls and always offered a chance of a pick-up. **1935** G. Greene *England made Me* IV. 169 She might be meeting her lover and not a pick-up in Gothenburg. **1944** M. Laski *Love on Supertax* iv. 52 And what about you, Clarissa? Who's your latest pickup? **1957** 'M. Yourcenar' *Coup de Grâce* 66 She was fairly throbbing against me, and no previous feminine encounter, whether with a chance pick-up, or with an avowed prostitute, had prepared me for that sudden, terrifying sweetness. **1970** [see *fille de joie]. **1974** T. Allbeury *Snowball* ix. 48 The pick-up lacked grace and she made it clear she was bored. **1977** *New Yorker* 22 Aug. 66/3 Paolo..accedes with wearied eyelids to the blandishments of yet another of his pickups.

d. (Examples.)

1905 *Daily Chron.* 31 Aug. 3/1 If one accidentally pulled a ball in a school pick-up. **1917** A. Waugh *Loom of Youth* I. ii. 31 Even a desultory Pick-Up woke into excitement when the shrill, piping voice of a full-back came in with, 'The Bull's coming.'

f. = Pick-me-up.

1881 Hardy *Laodicean* III. v. iii. 36 Every sip you took of your pick-up as you sat there showed me something was wrong. **1921** D. Marquis *Old Soak* 10, I took mine straight for the most part, except when I needed some special kind of a pick-up in the morning. **1936** *N.Y. Herald-Tribune* 25 Aug. 8 Mix it with orange, lemon, grapefruit, pineapple juices or with ginger ale for a zesty pick-up. **1949** *Sun* (Baltimore) 9 Nov. 15/4 Investigation of methods to improve your morning pickup [*sc.* coffee].

g. [Cf. *pick *v.*^{1} 20 q.] The capacity of an engine for recovering speed; acceleration.

1909 *Times* 27 Apr. 4/1 The flexibility and 'pick up' of the engine were such that the merest novice could handle the car with ease. **1923** *Daily Mail* 16 Mar. 10 (Advt.), An engine of great power, exceptional pick-up and flexibility, of notable smoothness and quietness. **1930** *Engineering* 12 Sept. 326/1 Apart from these factors, a smooth pick up, absence of vibration, and uniform torque are of great value. **1934** W. Nelson *Seaplane Design* vi. 53 The form of the underwater portion of the float must be such that water resistance does not hinder a quick pick-up to planing attitude. **1963** *Lebende Sprachen* VIII. 108/1 The car has good pick-up.

h. *Mus.* A series of introductory notes leading to the opening of a tune or portion of a tune.

1934 S. R. Nelson *All about Jazz* iii. 65 After a short passage of one or two bars, as a 'pick up', the ensemble will then take the last chorus and coda. **1949** L. Feather *Inside Be-Bop* 62 The last phrase starts with a three-beat pickup into an on-the-beat quarter note on the first beat of bar 7. **1956** O. Duke *Sideman* xii. 150 Bert played a piano intro and Bernie took pickups into *Laura* and then just sang it.

i. Tendency to pick up or absorb.

1938 *World Petroleum* Apr. 45/3 The flow through the main part of the furnace is in four parallel paths, each designed to have the same heat pick-up. **1955** Mondolfo & Zmeskal *Engineering Metall.* viii. 181 Pickup is the inclusion of foreign particles, especially scale, on the surface of the rolled product. **1955** *Jrnl. Soc. Dyers & Colourists* LXXI. 896/2 Although high pick-up is generally desirable, some fabrics need to be well squeezed. *Ibid.* 899/1 The padding temperature was 50°c. and the pick-up of the medium-weight rayon-staple fabric to be dyed was 100%. *a* **1977** *Harrison Mayer Ltd. Catal.* 67/1 The batts and props we supply are designed to have a low glaze pick up.

B. *attrib.* or as *adj.* **a. pick-up arm,** in a record-player or record deck, an arm carrying the stylus at one end and usu. counter-balanced at the other so as to be able to swing horizontally over the turntable and vertically; **pick-up baler,** a machine that picks up hay, etc., and bales it; **pick-up man** *colloq.*, (*a*) a thief, esp. of luggage; (*b*) *U.S.*, one who collects money wagered with bookmakers; (*c*) at a rodeo: see quot. 1961; **pick-up tube** *Television*, a vacuum tube that produces an electrical signal corresponding to an optical image formed in or on it; a camera tube.

1937 Pick-up arm [see *overhang *sb.* d]. **1946** [see *cartridge 1 e]. **1976** *Gramophone* July 237/2 Installing the QDC-1e cartridge in an SME 3009/II pickup arm with Thorens TD125/II turntable presented no problems. **1946** *Agricultural Progress* XXI. I. 34 The increasing use of the one-man, twine tying, pick-up baler. **1951** *Engineering* 26 Jan. 92/1 Imports from the United Kingdom were to include 6,000 wheeled tractors..; imports from the United States..pick-up balers and combine harvesters. **1928** *Detective Fiction Weekly* 8 Sept. 564/2 (*heading*) International crooks I have known; No. 6—'Gentleman George', pick-up man. **1944** C. Himes *Black on Black* (1973) 244 The pickup man took his book one day, and he told Clara, 'We should have been on the other end.' **1961** *Times* 14 Nov. 12/7 From the moment that he leaves the chute, the cowboy must remain in the saddle for 10 seconds. Then, on a whistle signal, two mounted 'pick-up' men converge on the buckhorse and the cowboy dismounts as best he can. The 'pick-up' men gallop after the riderless horse. One of them grabs the rein or head collar, and forces him out of the arena through a gate into a collecting ring. This in itself is often a thrilling spectacle, as it is a point of honour for the 'pick-up' men to take out the bucking animal at full gallop. **1964** A. Wykes *Gambling* iv. 92 These agents are known as 'pickup men' or 'writers'; they collect and pay out on behalf of the bookmakers, who pay them 10 per cent of their net winnings. **1966** *Sunday Mail Mag.* (Brisbane) 9 Jan. 1/3 As soon as a gong had clanged the all-clear, pick-up men..tore after them on horses. **1933** *Jrnl. Inst. Electr. Engin.* LXXIII. 438/2 The development of the pick-up tube was pushed on, and the results..soon surpassed those of mechanical scanning. **1965** *Wireless World* Sept. 461/2 A small television camera which uses a solid-state image sensing panel in place of the conventional electron-beam pick-up tube. **1978** *Broadcast* 21 Aug. 12/3 An Ikegami CT2-2400 three-tube colour camera, with Saticon pick-up tubes, and synchronised to a broadcast sync pulse generator.

b. (Examples.)

1909 *Q. Rev.* Oct. 618 The rest of the administration was arranged on the principle which governs 'pick-up' sides in a school-match. **1936** *Rhythm* Apr. 28/1 The ensemble is good, allowing for the difficulties surrounding the formation of a pick-up nine-piece band. **1938** D. Baker *Young Man with Horn* IV. iii. 220 He..made records with who knows how many pick-up bands. **1956** D. Flower tr. *Panassié & Gautier's Dict. Jazz* 197 *Pick-up band*, a band formed of musicians who regularly play elsewhere, but who come together for a special purpose, e.g. a recording date, a broadcast, a concert, a short nightclub engagement. **1959** 'F. Newton' *Jazz Scene* iv. 65 These were mostly small groups playing in odd night-clubs, or pick-up bands for recordings. **1962** *Sunday Times* (Colour Suppl.) 10 June 3 His strength is as the lead of pick-up groups of first-rate players. **1972** J. Mosedale *Football* iv. 47 He suffered a leg injury in a pick-up basketball game. **1977** *Gramophone* Apr. 1618/1 Lester headed a pick-up group containing trumpeter Billy Butterfield and pianist Johnny Guarnieri. **1977** *Tennis World* Sept. 17/3 A 'pick-up' doubles team is a scratch combination. **1977** *Transatlantic Rev.* LX. 120 Every Sunday morning he and his friends had a pick-up game over on Wentbridge Common.

c. pick-up camper (see quots.).

1973 *Country Life* 15 Nov. 1568/3 The 'pick-up' camper..is the coachbuilt caravan in demountable form on a pick-up truck... On arrival on site, it is jacked clear of the vehicle. **1974** *Trailer Life* Nov. 92 Some trailerists, concluding it was easier to drive a truck than hitch and unhitch a trailer, had their trailers mounted on a truck bed. This was practical. But since the trailers had not been designed for their new purpose, it proved unattractive. And so the pickup camper came into being, followed by a more stable and spacious chassis-mount.

Pickwickian, *a.* Add: (Earlier and further examples, without ref. to language.)

1836 DICKENS *Let.* 18 Feb. (1965) I. 132 Believe me (in Pickwickian haste) Faithfully Yours Charles Dickens. **1899** [see PRUSSIAN *a.* 2 b]. **1953** 'N. BLAKE' *Dreadful Hollow* 147 Blount, whose Pickwickian exterior camouflaged a mind as ruthlessly purposeful as a guided missile. **1975** J. SYMONS *Three Pipe Problem* xvii. 173 Johnson's Pickwickian features were unusually solemn.

2. *Med.* Also **pickwickian.** [Named in allusion to the fat boy Joe in *Posthumous Papers of the Pickwick Club.*] Having or being a syndrome occurring in some obese adults (rarely in obese children) characterized by somnolence, respiratory abnormalities, and bulimia.

1956 C. S. BURWELL et al. in *Amer. Jrnl. Med.* XXI. 812/1 Figure 1 represents Thomas Nast's drawing of Mr. Wardle's boy, Joe. This masterful description by Charles Dickens of a patient with marked obesity and somnolence is the first complete description of this syndrome that we have been able to find in the literature. For this reason we have called it the Pickwickian syndrome. **1965** *Progress Brain Res.* XVIII. 157 The short diurnal periods of light sleep (10–12 sec duration) in Pickwickian patients are characterized by apnea, increased cyanosis and muscular relaxation. **1977** *Lancet* 7 May 993/1 There are many other conditions, usually clinically obvious such as the pickwickian syndrome, in which there is both a respiratory and sleep abnormality.

B. *sb.* **1.** A member of the Pickwick Club.

1836 DICKENS *Pickw.* (1837) i. 1 A proposal, emanating from the aforesaid Samuel Pickwick..and three other Pickwickians..for forming a new branch of United Pickwickians. *Ibid.* ii. 7 The intelligence of the Pickwickians being informers was spread among them. **1905** *Daily Graphic* 1 Feb. 9/4 The minds of many of the lovers of Dickens who were present at the Dickens Character Ball..reverted to another ball-room—still in existence—where one of the most famous of the incidents in the 'Pickwick Papers' occurred—that of the Bull Inn at Rochester. And that ball, too, like this one, wherein not only the Pickwickians but many other characters which sprang from the brain of their creator were incarnated, was a charity ball. **1909** [see *BATHLESSNESS].

2. *Med.* A person with the Pickwickian syndrome.

1965 *Progress Brain Res.* XVIII. 156 Most obese people..present no diurnal sleeping syndrome, and so far as is known no nocturnal apnea, so that the Pickwickian should have some central disturbance of respiration and arousal. **1975** *Electroencephalogr. & Clin. Neurophysiol.* XXXIX. 579/2 The data obtained were compared with those observed in a group of 59 hypersomnolent patients aged between 19 and 83.., 18 of whom were Pickwickians.

Hence **Pickwickia·na,** publications about the *Posthumous Papers of the Pickwick Club.*

1899 J. GREGO (*title*) Pictorial Pickwickiana.

picky (pi·ki), *a.* [f. PICK *v.*[1] + -Y[1].] Fastidious, finicky, 'choosey' (see also quot. 1867). Hence **pi·ckiness.**

1867 W. DICKINSON *Gloss. Words & Phrases Cumberland* (Suppl.) 28 *Picky*, of weak appetite. **1900** DICKINSON & PREVOST *Gloss. Dial. Cumberland* (rev. ed.) 243/1 T'barn 's nut weel, it 's too picky by far. **1917** in *Dialect Notes* (1918) V. 12 Not an ugly picky thing in all she has to say. **1932** *New Yorker* 11 June 50/2 People who are picky about their food on shipboard..will be glad to know that the Clyde-Mallory Lines now allow you to buy a ticket for transportation only and order meals à la carte. **1957** 'R. TRAVER' *Anat. Murder* (1958) I. xv. 101, I don't want to seem picky, Lieutenant, but I happen to consider your particular doctor professionally on a par with Amos Crocker. **1966** *New Statesman* 29 Apr. 618/2 A hesitant, picky account of Mississippi's economic and electoral.. history. **1971** D. BAGLEY *Freedom Trap* iii. 62 This is a very exclusive mob; very picky and choosy. **1974** D. SCANNELL *Mother knew Best* iii. 27, I was always 'gastric' and Mother would get different meals for me as she thought me a 'picky' eater and needed tempting. **1977** *Sci. Amer.* Apr. 145/1 He was meticulous, even picky, about expense accounts. **1977** *Verbatim* May 6/1 And if you are willing to discard mere pickiness, you know what *taken for granite* and *scuenting* mean, too.

picky, var. *PICCY.

1931 E. F. BENSON *Mapp & Lucia* iii. 64 Go on with your picky, as if I was not here. How well you've got the perspective!

picloram (pi·klǒræm). [f. PIC(OLINE + CH)LOR-[2] + AM(INE.] A white crystalline compound, 4-amino-3,5,6-trichloropicolinic acid, $C_6H_3Cl_3N_2O_2$, which is used as a herbicide and defoliant against deep-rooted weeds and woody plants.

1965 *Proc. Northeast. Weed Control Conf.* XIX. 140 Effective control [of mugwort]..was obtained with.. 4-amino-3,5,6-trichloropicolinic acid (picloram). **1965** *B.S.I. News* May 24 The following new names have been approved by the Pest Control Products Industry Standards Committee for eventual inclusion in B.S. 1831... picloram... 4-amino-3,5,6-trichloropicolinic acid. **1969** *Sci. Jrnl.* Feb. 10/1 According to one estimate, no less than 2250 tonnes of picloram have been dumped on South Vietnam in 1968. **1970** *Guardian Weekly* 21 Feb. 6/4 The recently introduced chemical, picloram, is one of the longest-lived pesticides. **1974** *Sci. Amer.* Apr. 49/2 The herbicides sprayed over Vietnam were chemicals that are routinely applied for weed control: 2,4-D and 2,4,5-T, picloram and cacodylic acid.

picnic, *sb.* Add: **1. b.** (Earlier example of the *sb.*)

1825 H. WILSON *Mem.* II. 248, I sate down to consider the plan of a book, in the style of the Spectator, a kind of pic nic, where every wiseacre might contribute his mite of knowledge.

c. (Earlier and further examples.) Now usu. something straightforward or agreeable; a lively time; a treat; *no picnic, not a picnic*, not an easy task; a formidable undertaking.

1818 KEATS *Let.* Dec. (1958) II. 13 Perhaps as you were fond of giving me sketches of character you may like a little pic nic of scandal. **1886** *Lantern* (New Orleans) 27 Oct. 6/1 Hanley sparred with a smile on his face much as to say, 'What a picnic I've got with this kid.' **1888** KIPLING *Wee Willie Winkie* 84 'Taint no bloomin' picnic in those parts I can tell you. **1890** —— *Life's Handicap* (1891) 125 A knot of furious brother officers demanding the court-martial of Tommy Dodd for 'spoiling the picnic'. **1901** W. CHURCHILL *Crisis* II. iii. 136 This isn't any picnic. **1909** 'O. HENRY' *Roads of Destiny* xxii. 315 It was a picnic for the census takers. They just counted the marshal's posse that it took to subdue us, and there was your population. **1914** A. BENNETT *Price of Love* xii. 248 'But doesn't it *hurt?*' 'Depends what you call hurt. It ain't a picnic.' **1916** [see *EMBUSQUÉ]. **1919** *Mr. Punch's Hist. Gt. War* 114 It is not a picnic for the men in our front line. **1926** GALSWORTHY *Escape* II. iv. 50 If you want to get thin. It's a top-hole cure for adipose. An escape's no picnic. **1947** *Richmond* (Virginia) *Times-Dispatch* 4 May 26/5 The war memorial..was rejected as 'morbid': those who object to the ban on this work argue that the war was no picnic. **1961** B. FERGUSSON *Watery Maze* xvi. 394 It was going to be no picnic co-ordinating land, sea and air forces from so many different points of departure at so many different speeds. **1965** *Listener* 3 June 835/3 It can have been no picnic to be a poet in the age of Eliot. **1971** S. HILL *Strange Meeting* i. 10 Think yourself lucky you got off a bit early. It's no picnic now. **1974** J. STUBBS *Painted Face* xxiii. 286 What do *you* know of prison? This here's a picnic compared to what it will be.

d. *Austral.* and *N.Z.* Used ironically of an awkward situation or a difficult or unpleasant experience.

1896 in MORRIS *Austral Eng.* (1898) 351/1 If a man's horse is awkward and gives him trouble, he will say, 'I had a picnic with that horse,' and so of any misadventure or disagreeable experience in travelling. **1939** N. MARSH *Overture to Death* xiii. 125 I'm sorry to have neglected you like this; but we're in for a picnic, and no mistake, with this case up at Moorton Park. **1941** BAKER *Dict. Austral. Slang* 54 *Picnic*, any unpleasant experience, a disagreeable and complicated task. **1945** *Coast to Coast 1944* 125 What a mess, what a picnic! **1955** D. NILAND *Shiralee* 38 All I know is I'm going to have one helluva picnic if she doesn't find it. **1959** BAKER *Drum* (1960) 68 We call a wild confusion or a particularly difficult task a picnic.

e. *U.S.* = *picnic ham* below.

1910 L. D. HALL *Market Classes Meat* 281 *Picnics* or *calas* (formerly termed California hams) are cut 2-½ ribs wide... They..are sold almost entirely as sweet-pickled, smoked and boiled meats. **1949** *New Harmony* (Indiana) *Times* 5 Aug. 6/2 (Advt.), Smoked Picnics, 3 to 5 lb. average lb. 45c. **1974** *Columbia* (S. Carolina) *Record* 24 Apr. 21-B (Advt.), Sliced picnic 1.89. **1976** *Washington Post* 19 Apr. A19/1 (Advt.), Smoked picnics.

3. (Further examples.) Also: *picnic basket, hamper, pie, shelter, site, spot, stove, tea*; **picnic area,** a piece of ground designated as suitable for picnics; **picnic chair,** a (usu. collapsible) chair for use on a picnic; **picnic ground** = **picnic area*; **picnic ham** *U.S.*, a small cut of shoulder bacon in the form of a ham; **picnic lunch,** a packed lunch, *spec.* one provided by a hotel in place of a regular meal; **picnic meal,** a meal eaten as a picnic; also, a quick meal eaten indoors; **picnic plate,** a plastic or paper plate suitable for use on a picnic; **picnic race meeting, races** *Austral.* and *N.Z.*, a race meeting held in a country area, accompanied by other social events; **picnic table,** a table suitable for use on a picnic; a small hinged table in a car.

1959 Picnic area [see *PIPED *ppl. a.*[1] 3 c]. **1968** *Guardian* 5 July 3/2 The NCB will restore the landscape and provide access roads, car parks, picnic areas, a hard standing and slipway for boats. **1968** [see *camp-ground* s.v. *CAMP *sb.*[2] VII. b]. **1973** V. CANNING *Flight of Grey Goose* i. 9 A large picnic area on the edge of a wood. **1885** *List of Subscribers, Classified* (United Telephone Co.) (ed. 6) 125 (*heading*) Luncheon and picnic basket manufacturers. **1931** *N. & Q.* 11 Apr. 258/2 The car was packed with bathing things, camp-stools and picnic basket. **1955** A. HUXLEY *Let.* 4 Apr. (1969) 739 Yes, by all means let us take a picnic basket so that we can be independent of restaurants. **1972** D. E. WESTLAKE *Cops & Robbers* (1973) xvi. 239 Macy's has a wicker picnic basket. It costs around eighteen bucks, with the tax. **1975** 'A. HALL' *Mandarin Cypher* xvii. 233 One narrow bunk..cheap cardtable and picnic chair. **1977** M. JANCATH *Seatag* I. vii. 41 Emrich was surprised to see a wooden picnic table and chairs. **1926** *Daily Colonist* (Victoria, B.C.) 2 July 5/3 The streets were almost deserted save for those hastening toward some of these attractive picnic grounds. **1947** E. S. GARDNER in *Amer. Mag.* Aug. 148/3 You can see the camp and the picnic grounds from here. **1969** H. MACINNES *Salzburg Connection* ii. 33 He began walking down towards the picnic ground. **1974** *Country Life* 3 Oct. 930/3 A 14-acre picnic ground has been cleared. **1897** *Sears, Roebuck Catal.* 13/3 Meats... Picnic Hams. **1944** *Chicago Daily News* 13 July 21/2 A picnic ham may be boned, rolled and tied before roasting to make carving easier. **1973** *Black Panther* 25 Aug. 3/3 Picnic ham at 97 cents or salt pork at 99 cents a pound? **1862** W. COLLINS *No Name* I. 332 We have a picnic hamper with us..and away we drive on a pleasure trip. **1896** E. TURNER *Little Larrikin* xviii. 208 Several picnic hampers and a case of champagne. **1966** B. COOPER *Drown him Deep* vi. 52 He went to the back of the car, and began to pull out the picnic hamper. **1972** R. HILL *Fairly Dangerous Thing* II. vi. 179 We.. took our picnic-hamper with us into a wood. **1917** D. CANFIELD *Understood Betsy* (1922) x. 189 They were to meet the Wendells in the shadow of Industrial Hall and eat their picnic lunch together. **1933** E. O'NEILL *Ah, Wilderness!* (1934) I. 18 We're going to have a picnic lunch on Strawberry Island. **1971** J. TYNDALL *Death in Lebanon* vii. 105 Let's ask the hotel for a picnic lunch and get off as soon as we can. **1972** *Guardian* 22 July 7/3, I continued along the D94..but soon stopped for a picnic lunch. **1876** GEO. ELIOT *Dan. Der.* I. II. xiv. 264 The coachful of servants with provisions had to prepare the picnic meal. **1889** Picnic meal [in Dict.]. **1911** A. BENNETT *Hilda Lessways* II. iii. 161 They had been very busy in Hilda's house..and had eaten only a picnic meal. **1929** S. ERTZ *Galaxy* xiii. 294 They had a picnic meal of bread and cheese and fruit and California wine. **1972** 'G. NORTH' *Sgt. Cluff rings True* x. 78 Discards from picnic meals defaced verges. **1849** H. C. ROBINSON *Diary* 22 June (1967) 255 A picnic party had been formed..to take tea on the top of the hill. **1977** R. BARNARD *Blood Brotherhood* vi. 61 The thought of some fearsome affray..came upon him with all the welcomeness of a thunderclap on a picnic party. **1865** TROLLOPE *Can you forgive Her?* II. xxx. 234 Cold chickens, picnic-pies, and the flying of champagne corks. **1911** G. STRATTON-PORTER *Harvester* xvi. 371 Big, fancy brick and frame things..gay as frosted picnic pie. **1926–7** *Army & Navy Stores Catal.* 378B/4 Picnic plates. **1933** E. A. ROBERTSON *Ordinary Families* i. 16 The boats were only old cardboard picnic plates. **1896** N. GOULD *Town & Bush* xiv. 225 The owners of the horses running at picnic races are generally men of means. **1911** C. E. W. BEAN '*Dreadnought*' *of Darling* xxxiv. 294 If a town has picnic races or a polo week, it is 'alive'. **1928** 'BRENT OF BIN BIN' *Up Country* xiii. 202 Here took place the first picnic races of the district, which affairs, so informally started among neighbours, in later days command special trains and viceregality. **1955** P. WHITE *Tree of Man* (1956) II. ix. 132 Always in demand,.. and above all at picnic races. **1964** D. HORNE *Lucky Country* 52 One of the most rigid institutional manifestations of this difference [between landed family and town] appears at the annual picnic races. **1972** *Sunday Tel.* (Sydney) 15 Oct. 132 Everyone, but everyone, is getting ready for the Bong Bong Picnic Races next Saturday. **1978** O. WHITE *Silent Reach* xvi. 160 He's a pansy and goes for the public school jackeroos at the picnic races. *Ibid.* xxi. 219 The Fitzroy Crossing picnic race meeting. **1943** J. S. HUXLEY *TVA* ix. 61 Picnic shelters are included in the parks and campgrounds. **1959** *Canad. Geogr. Jrnl.* Feb. 55/1 Picnic shelters have been constructed for the convenience of picnickers during inclement weather and thirty-two of these are now in use. **1976** *Billings* (Montana) *Gaz.* 28 June 1-B/1 The state Board of Examiners this week approved expenditure of $398,565 for building of picnic shelters and other recreation facilities, landscaping and construction of restrooms at the park. **1971** P. GRESSWELL *Environment* 187 Picnic sites need to be considered in relation to planning policy. **1972** *Country Life* 7 Dec. 1581/1 Somerset County Council has decided to spend some money this year on..picnic sites. **1959** I. & P. OPIE *Lore & Lang. Schoolch.* xii. 253 On Easter Day we usually pack a picnic lunch, including a hard boiled egg. When we reach the picnic spot we sit down and play at games. **1977** B. PYM *Quartet in Autumn* v. 43 When they arrived at the picnic spot, Marjorie produced two folding canvas chairs from the boot of the car. **1963** *Which?* Mar. 89/2 A solid fuel for picnic stoves. **1974** *Janet Frazer Catal.* Spring/Summer 458/2 Camping Gaz International picnic stove... Boils water quickly. **1926–7** *Army & Navy Stores Catal.* 225/1 The 'picnic' table... Folds perfectly flat. **1963** 'H. CALVIN' *It's Different Abroad* ii. 16 Between them was a folding picnic-table. **1970** *Times* 16 Apr. 3/3 (Advt.), We don't forget power assisted steering, adjustable steering column, reclining seats and picnic tables. **1976** *Norwich Mercury* 17 Dec. 9/6 Two picnic tables with bench seats were officially handed over. **1976** N. THORNBURG *Cutter & Bone* ix. 219 It was a small park, not much more than a few acres of grass fringed with eucalyptus trees and three or four picnic tables. **1900** C. M. YONGE *Mod. Broods* xvi. 153 My mother wants you all to come up to picnic tea to see the foxgloves in the dell. **1907** R. FRY *Let.* 24 Sept. (1972) I. 291 This afternoon we are to drive out to a picnic tea at Blackwell. **1932** 'E. M. DELAFIELD' *Thank Heaven Fasting* III. ii. 262 Monica and the vistor set out..taking with them a picnic tea. **1955** A. SINCLAIR in *Granta* 26 Nov. 10/1 We'll say we want a picnic tea.

picnickish (pi·knikiʃ), *a. rare.* [f. PICNIC *sb.* + -ISH[1].] Suitable for or suggestive of picnics.

1852 'G. GREENWOOD' *Haps & Mishaps Tour in Europe* (1854) v. 101 It is a pretty, picturesque, and picnickish place.

pico, var. *PIKAU *sb.*

pico- (pī·ko, pəi·ko), *prefix.* [f. Sp. *pico* beak, peak, (in phrases) little bit.] Prefixed to the names of units to form the names of units 10^{12} times smaller, i.e. one million-millionth part of them (symbol p), as *picoamp* (so *picoammeter*), *-curie, -farad, -gramme, -litre, -volt* (so *-voltmeter*), *-watt.* Also *PICOSECOND.

1915 W. H. ECCLES *Wireless Telegr.* 18 Symbols for multiples and sub-multiples... 10^{-12}... Pico-... p or $\mu\mu$. **1947** *Compt. Rend. de la 14me Conf.* (Union Internat. de Chimie) 115 The following prefixes to abbreviations for the names of units should be used to indicate the specified multiples or sub-multiples of these units:..p pico- 10^{-12} ×.

1952 *Wireless World* Jan. 19/2 The suggestions to adopt new prefixes, 'nano' and 'pico' for small capacitance values, would permit any value to be expressed as a whole number. **1952** [see *NANO-]. **1975** *Physics Bull.* Feb. 67/1 A range of stabilized high voltage power supplies and picoammeters manufactured by V G Electronics Ltd will also be shown. *Ibid.* June 249/2 (Advt.), Sensitivities down to 1 microvolt, 10 picoamps, and 1 milliohm are founded on Keithley's lifetime of expertise in designing and building low-level instrumentation. **1963** *Times* 15 Feb. 8/1 The level of 150 picocuries over a three-month period is considered by scientists to be the tolerable limit for humanity. **1976** *Globe & Mail* (Toronto) 16 Jan. 1/3 The readings in 30 of these, however, are less than three picocuries of radon for each litre of air, the exposure level that Government standards allow the public. For workers in atomic plants, the standard is 30 picocuries a litre. **1926** *Gloss. Terms Electr. Engin.* (Brit. Engin. Stand. Assoc.) 26 *Picofarad*, a unit of electrostatic capacity equal to 10^{-12} farad. Symbol: $\mu\mu$F. **1945** *Electronic Engin.* XVII. 473/2 At a working frequency of ½ Mc/s., a difference of about 1/10 picofarad can be readily observed. **1976** *Gramophone* Jan. 1283/1 A slight platform rise of up to about 2 dB from 12 kHz upwards was measured which I take to be a result of the Dual's low capacitance cable, whereas Shure recommend 400 to 500 pico-farads per channel. **1951** Picogram [see *nanogramme* s.v. *NANO-]. **1967** *Oceanogr. & Marine Biol.* V. 271 If carbon content is compared with the surface area of [plankton] cells, the range of variation is smaller, 0·11 to 0·66 picograms/μ^2. **1975** WILLIAMS & WILSON *Biologist's Guide to Princ. & Techniques Pract. Biochem.* iii. 72 It has very high sensitivity and can detect as little as one picogramme of these compounds. **1973** *Sci. Amer.* Sept. 160/2 (Advt.), For electron probe sampling, hundreds of picoliter fluid droplets are positioned automatically under an electron beam. **1971** *Physics Bull.* Nov. 678/2 The picovolt measuring system permits the detection of small voltages from sources at low temperatures which would be overwhelmed by thermal voltages in the leads to a room temperature instrument. *Ibid.* 678/3 The picovoltmeter will be useful for the measurement of low temperatures by means of thermocouples. **1967** D. H. HAMSHER *Communication Syst. Engin. Handbk.* xvi. 10 The noise power measurement without any weighting of the frequency response of the instrument is expressed usually in picowatts (10^{-12} watt = pw). **1977** *Sci. Amer.* Feb. 62/2 At the earth station the 30-metre dish antenna collects a scant three picowatts of energy and feeds it into a low-noise receiver.

picolinic (pikǫlī·nik), *a. Chem.* [f. PICOLIN(E + -IC.] *picolinic acid*: a colourless crystalline acid, pyridine-2-carboxylic acid, C_5H_4N-(COOH), which is derived from picoline by oxidation of the methyl group.

1880 *Jrnl. Chem. Soc.* XXXVIII. 268 Picolinic Acid, $C_6H_5NO_2$..Crystallises in prismatic needles..which are easily soluble in alcohol and in water. **1946** A. A. MORTON *Chem. Heterocyclic Compounds* viii. 213 Picolinic acid..is obtained in 50 to 51 per cent yield from α-picolin. **1968** *Listener* 21 Mar. 376/1 A second class of compounds being used [as defoliants, etc.] are derivatives of picolinic acid.

Picon (pīkoṅ). [Fr., f. *Amer Picon*, f. *amer* bitter + *Picon* et Cie, the manufacturers.] In full, *Amer Picon*. The proprietary name of an aperitif of bitters (see quot. 1967).

1914 [see *PERNOD]. [**1917** *Bull. Offic. Marques de Fabrique* 25 Jan. 54/1 *Amer Picon*. M.p. désigner un amer, déposée..par MM. Picon et Cie.] **1934** H. MILLER *Tropic of Cancer* (1961) 21 Paris..shutters going up with a bang..*Amer Picon* in huge scarlet letters. **1936** BENTLEY & ALLEN *Trent's Own Case* xi. 133 Sipping his Amer Picon—that formidable brown drink of which..a single undiluted drop will burn a neat round hole in a shirt cuff. **1939** L. MACNEICE *Autumn Jrnl.* 22 Something out of the usual, a Pimm's Number One, a Picon. **1950** D. AMES *Corpse Diplomatique* i. 11 He ordered a *Pernod* and an *Amer Picon*. **1962** N. FREELING *Love in Amsterdam* I. 48 Herman had raw *schinken* with kümmel in it, and a bottle of Picon. **1967** A. LICHINE *Encycl. Wines* 71/1 *Amer Picon*, a proprietary French bitters used as an aperitif, made with a wine and brandy base to which has been added quinine (to impart a bitter taste), orange peel, and innumerable herbs. It is drunk with ice, diluted with water, and usually sweetened with grenadine or cassis.

picong (pi·kǫŋ). [ad. Sp. *picón*.] In Trinidad and some other parts of the Caribbean: verbal insult or ridicule; facetious raillery; taunting; esp. in phr. *to give picong*. Cf. *to play* (*the*) *dozens* s.v. *PLAY *v.* 16 e.

1956 *Caribbean Q.* IV. III–IV. 198 The Congos..carried on 'picong' or 'fatigues', elaborate ribbing of each other and the bystanders. **1960** *Tamarack Rev.* XIV. 19 Then again, the boys might start to give Frederick picong, when Bat beg them to ease up. **1974** *Sunday Guardian* (Port-of-Spain) 28 July 8/2 They [*sc.* students] were screaming and laughing and giving picong to all kinds of rhythms, on the edge of Grand Etang. *Ibid.* 12/4 The humour here is not at all picong, but more humour for its own sake.

picornavirus (pikǭ·ɹnăvəiᵊrv̆s). *Microbiol.* [f. *PICO-, taken to mean 'very small' + *RNA + VIRUS.] Any of a group of very small animal viruses consisting of single-stranded RNA in an unenveloped icosahedral capsid, which includes enteroviruses, rhinoviruses, and the virus of foot-and-mouth disease.

1962 *Adv. Virus Res.* IX. 296 At a meeting of the Virus Subcommittee of the International Nomenclature Committee, held in Montreal in August 1962, the following decisions were made: (1) The proposed name nanivirus is to be replaced by Picornavirus. **1963** *Internat. Bull. Bacteriol. Nomencl. & Taxon.* XIII. 218 It was agreed that a name was needed for the small ether-resistant RNA viruses of which enteroviruses form an important part. The name 'Nanivirus'..was discarded in favour of 'Picornavirus'. The prefix Pico- implies very small size, and RNA of course indicates nucleic-acid composition. (The initial letters of Picornavirus may be taken to refer to Poliomyelitis, insensitivity to ether, Coxsackie, orphan and Rhinovirus.) **1974** L. LEVINTOW in Fraenkel-Conrat & Wagner *Comprehensive Virology* II. iii. 154 Picornaviruses are the agents of a number of other important diseases of man and animals which remain to be controlled, including the common cold. **1976** FENNER & WHITE *Med. Virology* (ed. 2) xviii. 333 There are no antigenic relationships between most of the picornaviruses.

picosecond (pī·ko-, pəi·kosekənd). [f. *PICO- + SECOND *sb.*[1]] A unit of time equal to one million-millionth of a second.

1966 in *Random House Dict.* **1967** *Electronics* 6 Mar. 60/2 The..circuits..have switching speeds of 350 picoseconds. **1972** *Sci. Amer.* Dec. 16/2 A sampling oscilloscope with a rise time..of 44 picoseconds. **1974** *Nature* 15 Mar. 222/2 A complete formalism now exists to do the complete physics of the first picoseconds of the big-bang origin of the universe. **1975** *Daily Colonist* (Victoria, B.C.) 9 July 5/8 By using lasers capable of picosecond, or trillionth of a second, bursts of light and using ultra fast 'streak' cameras, researchers are now able to measure the conversion of light to other forms of energy in plants.

picot (pī·ko), *v.* [f. the sb.] *trans.* To ornament (cloth) with picots. So **picoted** (pī·kōᵘd) *ppl. a.*; **picoting** (pī·koˌiŋ) *vbl. sb.*

1927 *Daily Express* 7 Mar. 5/5 Flowers were cut out of sheet metal..even the picotted [*sic*] edges of certain varieties of carnation being faithfully rendered. **1928** *Ibid.* 11 May 5/3 Buy a square of plain or flowered.. georgette, and have it picoted all round by machine. The picoting is really machine hemstitching cut through the middle.

picral (pi·kræl). *Metallurgy.* Also **Picral.** [f. PICR(IC *a.* + AL(COHOL.] An etchant consisting of about 2 to 5 per cent of picric acid in ethyl alcohol.

1928 WILLIAMS & HOMERBERG *Princ. Metallogr.* (ed. 2) 237 The term *picral* is frequently applied to any solution of picric acid in alcohol. **1936** [see *NITAL]. **1963** C. H. SAMANS *Metallic Materials in Engin.* vi. 267 The action of picral is similar, except that it etches fine pearlite much more uniformly than nital does. However, it does not etch ferrite so rapidly as nital, and does not indicate the ferrite grain boundaries clearly.

picrite. Delete entry in Dict. and substitute: **picrite** (pi·krəit). [f. Gr. πικρ-ός bitter: see -ITE[1].] † **1.** *Min.* [a. G. *picrite*(*s*) (J. F. Blumenbach *Handb. der Naturgeschichte* (ed. 5, 1797) xii. 584).] = DOLOMITE. *Obs. rare.*

1814 [in Dict.]. **1836** T. THOMSON *Outl. Min., Geol.* I. 181 Calcareo-carbonate of Magnesia. Dolomite—conite— ..muricalcite—pearl spar—picrite [etc.]. **1896** [in Dict.].

2. *Petrogr.* Also 9 **picryte, pikrite.** [ad. G. *pikrit* (G. Tschermak 1866, in *Sitzungsber. der K. Akad. der Wissensch.* (*Math.-naturw. Classe*) LIII. 262).] A dark ultrabasic igneous rock, commonly hypabyssal, containing a substantial amount of olivine together with augite and other ferromagnesian minerals and a small amount of plagioclase.

1868 J. D. DANA *Syst. Min.* (ed. 5) 258 A chrysolite rock occurring at L. Lherz, consisting largely of chrysolite, has been called Lherzolyte... Another similar rock from Moravia, called picryte, consists half of chrysolite, along with feldspar, diallage, hornblende, and magnetite. **1879** [in Dict.]. **1882** A. GEIKIE *Text-bk. Geol.* 151 Olivine Rocks... The following are the more important species:— Pikrite, a rock rich in olivine, usually more or less serpentinized, with augite, magnetite, or ilmenite, and a little brown biotite, hornblende, or apatite; [etc.]. **1931** S. J. SHAND *Study of Rocks* vii. 112 Picrites with forty to seventy-five per cent. of olivine have been described in Skye. The picrite of Tabankulu, South Africa, is composed to the extent of one-third to two-thirds of well-shaped crystals of olivine which are enclosed in larger crystals of pyroxene and felspar. **1976** *Mineral. Mag.* XL. 683 Exposures of baked siltstone occur on top of the ridge with picrite exposed only on the scarp face... The picrite averages 50% olivine, 35% plagioclase, and 15% pyroxene with a maximum grain size of 6 mm.

Hence **picri·tic** *a.*

1931 *Amer. Jrnl. Sci.* CCXXI. 403 Even a picritic subbasalt..exhibits some interstitial quartz. **1958** *Trans. R. Soc. Edin.* LXIII. 459 In this paper it is proposed to use the term 'picritic' to denote, in minor intrusions and lavas, an amount of forsteritic olivine considerably beyond that which normally crystallizes in basaltic magma. This amount of olivine varies between 25 and 60 per cent. **1965** *Carnegie Inst. Year Bk. 1964* 126/2 In general, picritic lavas and hypabyssal intrusives are few in number and restricted to the lower parts of both oceanic and continental volcanic columns. **1974** P. G. HARRIS in H. Sørensen *Alkaline Rocks* vi. 430/1 At pressures of about 30–40 kbar, i.e. depths below 90–100 km, the mantle mineralogy will be that of a garnet lherzolite, and there is a marked change in the first-formed liquid which is now picritic or ultrabasic.

picro-. Add: **picrochro·mite** *Min.*, a chromite of magnesium, $MgCr_2O_4$, which in its pure form is known only as an artificial product (see quots. 1939) and which in nature is a brittle black mineral that contains a substantial amount of ferrous iron replacing magnesium; **picroilmenite** (pikroˌi·lmĕnəit) *Min.* [ad. G. *pikroïlmenit* (P. Groth *Tabellarische Übersicht der Mineralien* (ed. 4, 1898) ix. 143)], a magnesian variety of ilmenite.

1920 E. S. SIMPSON in *Mineral. Mag.* XIX. 100 Dealing with the minerals of the spinel–chromite series.., the four variables, which constitute two pairs, are MgO, FeO, Al_2O_3, Cr_2O_3. Four mineral species are possible, the pure forms of which are (1) $MgO.Al_2O_3$ spinel, (2) $MgO.Cr_2O_3$ picrochromite, (3) $FeO.Al_2O_3$ hercynite, and (4) $FeO.Cr_2O_3$ chromite. [*Note*] New name required to complete the series and to designate already known minerals. *Ibid.* 104 At least three previously described minerals, viz. chrompicotite of Dun Mt., New Zealand; magnesiochromite of New Caledonia; and 'chromite' of Lake Memphremagog in Quebec, are members of a new species for which the author proposes the name picrochromite. **1939** *Special Rep. Iron & Steel Inst.* No. 26. 202 Picrochromite was prepared in a manner similar to that used for spinel but employing equivalent amounts of magnesia and chromic oxide. *Ibid.* 204 Picrochromite was green in daylight and reddish-grey in artificial light..when viewed in mass. It occurred as aggregates of minute crystals which were practically colourless and presented occasional octahedral faces. **1970** *Mineral. Abstr.* XXI. 314/2 (*heading*) Determination of the fusion temperature of picrochromite. **1900** *Mineral. Mag.* XII. 389 Picroilmenite... The same as picrotitanite, a variety of ilmenite rich in magnesium. **1906** *Ibid.* XIV. 166 It is advisable to divide the ferro-magnesian titanates into ilmenites and geikielites, and to regard picroilmenite as the middle member of the series. **1972** *Mineral. Abstr.* XXIII. 338/1 Picroilmenite occurs, associated with diamond, in the kimberlites and in the Carboniferous, Jurassic, and Cretaceous formations [in the Anabar area, western Yakutia]. Its hardness ranges from 450 to 750 kg/mm²; it is anisotropic, optically negative, and has a weak bireflectance.

picrolichenic (pikrolǝi·kĕnik), *a. Biochem.* [f. next + -IC.] *picrolichenic acid*: a very bitter, crystalline, polycyclic acid, $C_{25}H_{30}O_7$, isolated from the lichen *Pertusaria amara*; = next.

1902 *Jrnl. Chem. Soc.* LXXXII. I. 465 The name *picrolichenic acid* is suggested for picrolichenin. **1957** *Chem. & Industry* 27 July 1042/2 Picrolichenic acid, a constituent of the common crustose lichen *Pertusaria amara* Ach...is responsible for the well known, very bitter, quinine-like taste of this lichen. **1959** *New Biol.* XXIX. 86 Picrolichenic acid..is a previously undescribed type of lichen acid in which the ring structures in the molecule are joined by a direct carbon to carbon link rather than by an oxygen atom as is the case in depsidones. **1973** S. HUNECK in Ahmadjian & Hale *Lichens* xv. 511 The only hitherto known depsone from lichens is picrolichenic acid.

picrolichenin (pikrolǝi·kĕnin). *Biochem.* [a. G. *picrolichenin* (A. Alms 1832, in *Ann. d. Pharm.* I. 62), f. *picro-* PICRO- + *lichenin* LICHENIN.] = prec.

1862 H. WATTS tr. *Gmelin's Hand-bk. Chem.* XV. 56 A pound of the lichen yields half an ounce of picrolichenin. **1901** *Jrnl. Chem. Soc.* LXXX. I. 88 The author has isolated salazinic acid and picrolichenin from *Pertusaria amara.* **1958** *Svensk Kem. Tidskr.* LXX. 129 The bitter principle isolated by Alms from this lichen—'Picrolichenin'—was claimed to be useful as a remedy in the treatment of malaria, and this is now being checked.

picryl. Now also with pronunc. (pi·krəil). Delete '(See quot.)' and substitute: † **1.** Also **picril, picryle.** [a. F. *picryle* (A. Laurent 1844, in *Rev. sci. et industr.* XVIII. 201).] (See quot. 1866 in Dict.) *Obs.* (Earlier examples.)

1847 W. GREGORY *Outl. Chem.* (ed. 2) 546 *Picrine*, Syn. *Picryle*, $C_{42}H_{15}NO_4$, is formed when the mass produced by acting on oil of bitter almonds by sulphuret of ammonium is distilled. **1858** H. WATTS tr. *Gmelin's Hand-bk. Chem.* XII. 188 Picril dissolves very readily in ether.

2. The 2,4,6-trinitrophenyl group, —$C_6H_2(NO_2)_3$, contained in picric acid.

1866 [in Dict.]. **1875** *Jrnl. Chem. Soc.* XXVIII. 165 Metanitraniline and picryl chloride act on one another when dissolved in boiling absolute alcohol. **1877** *Ibid.* XXXII. 758 It is..very possible that in one of the resulting compounds the two picryl groups may be identical. **1889** G. M'GOWAN tr. *Bernthsen's Text-bk. Org. Chem.* xxiii. 385 Picryl chloride, $C_6H_2(NO_2)_3Cl$.., resembles the acid chlorides..in behaviour. **1937** F. C. WHITMORE *Org. Chem.* 737 Picryl iodide is a stable yellow crystalline product obtainable from the chloride and KI. **1964** J. W. LINNETT *Electronic Struct. Molecules* vii. 107 The reason why the diphenyl picryl compound is more stable than the triphenyl compound is presumably that the picryl group relieves the adjacent nitrogen atom of some of the negative charge. **1975** *Nature* 3 Jan. 72/2 The lymph node cells of mice rendered unresponsive by the injection of picryl sulphonic acid (PSA) depress the passive transfer of contact senstivity.

Pictish, *a.* Add: Also, of or pertaining to the language (or languages) of the Picts.

1710 R. SIBBALD *Hist. Fife & Kinross* I. ii. 3 Both in Bertius his excellent Edition and the late Map of Gale, it [*sc.* Votadini] is read Vacomagi, and the Greek in both these answer to Vacomagi, which by the by..doth much confirm Mr. Robert Maule his Ratio nominis Veach, Pictus, since in Veach here, and in Wauchopdale in the South..the Pictish Veach appears to be the rise of both these Words. **1840** *Penny Cycl.* XVIII. 148/2 Their language appears to have nearly resembled the Welsh.

One Pictish word only has been expressly mentioned by any old writer, *Peanvahel*. **1868** W. F. SKENE *Four Ancient Bks. of Wales* I. viii. 130 In the fifth, the Pictish *duiper* and the Gaelic *saoibher* are the same word. **1892** J. RHYS in *Proc. Soc. Antiquaries Scotl.* XXVI. 310 Lastly, Pictish *enn* is to be found in some instances where the Celtic stem is usually made to end..in *on*. **1946** T. F. O'RAHILLY *Early Irish Hist. & Mythol.* 369 Compare Celt. *vroiko-* giving Pictish **vrŏg*, whence..Sc. *frŏg*, 'a fen'. **1955** K. H. JACKSON in F. T. Wainwright *Probl. Picts* vi. 142 *Forcus* at St Vigeans is the exact Gaelic equivalent of Pictish *Uurguist*.

B. *sb.* The language (or languages) of the Picts.

Pictish is evidenced only in a few proper names, inscriptions, and glosses, and its affiliations have been much disputed. The view most widely accepted now is that expressed by K. H. Jackson in F. T. Wainwright *The Problem of the Picts* (1955) 152: 'There were at least two languages current in northern Scotland before the coming of the Irish Gaels in the fifth century. One of them was a Gallo-Brittonic dialect not identical with the British spoken south of the Antonine Wall, though related to it. The other was not Celtic at all, nor apparently even Indo-European, but was presumably the speech of some very early set of inhabitants of Scotland.'

1857 W. REEVES *Life St. Columba* 62/2 This case saves that recorded in ii. 32, *infra*, from being 'a solitary allusion to the diversity of Gaelic and Pictish'. **1868** W. F. SKENE *Four Ancient Bks. of Wales* I. viii. 138, I consider, therefore, that Pictish was a low Gaelic dialect... Old Scottish..was the high Gaelic dialect, and Pictish the low Gaelic dialect. **1891** W. STOKES in *Trans. Philol. Soc. 1888–90* 417 The foregoing list of names and other words contains much that is still obscure; but on the whole it shows that Pictish, so far as regards its vocabulary, is an Indo-European and especially Celtic speech. Its phonetics, so far as we can ascertain them, resemble those of Welsh rather than of Irish. **1892** J. RHYS in *Proc. Soc. Antiquaries Scotl.* XXVI. 307 Pictish being, as I take it, a non-Aryan language. **1923** J. FRASER *Hist. & Etym.* 15 Rhys's view that Pictish was a non-Indogermanic language involves the same fallacy as the view that it was Goidelic or Brythonic. **1946** T. F. O'RAHILLY *Early Irish Hist. & Mythol.* 353 The preponderant opinion of modern scholarship is that Pictish was a Celtic language, different from both British and Goidelic, but decidedly more akin to the former than to the latter. **1955** K. H. JACKSON in F. T. Wainwright *Probl. Picts* vi. 134 We seem to find it implied or clearly stated by contemporary and almost contemporary writers that Pictish was a separate speech of its own, identical neither with the Gaelic of Scotland and Ireland nor with Brittonic. **1963** N. K. CHADWICK *Celtic Brit.* i. 20 In Scotland the royal Pictish families seem to have spoken Pictish as late as the ninth century. **1976** C. F. & F. M. VOEGELIN *Classification World's Lang.* (1977) 104 [Goidelic = Q-Celtic] Pictish. Formerly spoken in Scotland but not necessarily as a Celtic language.

pictogram (pi·ktŏgræm). [f. L. *pict-us* painted + -GRAM.] = PICTOGRAPH in Dict. and Suppl.

1910 *Encycl. Relig. & Ethics* III. 549/2 The primitive characters or 'pictograms'..afford unmistakable evidence as to the ideas which existed long anterior to the time of Confucius. **1936** V. G. CHILDE *Man makes Himself* viii. 208 Even the picture-signs, though much more realistic than Sumerian pictograms, conform to a social convention. **1939** *Trans. Philol. Soc.* 76 K. Haag.. worked out a scheme of pictograms, based partly on the fundamental space relations and supplemented by the use of symbols like the heart for emotion. **1952** G. SARTON *Hist. Sci.* I. ii. 20 We may assume that the Egyptians began by using pictograms (images) representing things or ideas rather than words. **1960** E. H. GOMBRICH *Art & Illusion* viii. 280 They see the picture still as a flat surface covered with a pictogram. **1965** H. K. COMPTON *Gloss. Purchasing & Supplies Managem. Terms* 101 *Pictogram*, diagrams drawn in different sizes more or less to scale to demonstrate relative sizes of statistical batches which are illustrated, often by pictures depicting the subject matter. **1970** *Which?* Nov. 352/2 The use of pictograms (eg '?' to show an information desk) is increasing. **1971** *Nature* 16 July 148/3 At the top there are pictograms of a sword, a shield and two crosses and a triangle. **1973** J. M. ANDERSON *Struct. Aspects Lang. Change* 14 Pictograms can be read..with varying choice of words in any language. **1977** *New Yorker* 2 May 135/3 Occasionally he resorts to dance pictograms.

pictograph. Add: (Further examples.) Also *attrib.*

1937 *Discovery* Aug. 249/1 The Lachish dagger with pictograph inscription. **1955** *Bull. Atomic Sci.* Mar. 91/2 An Indian pictograph enthusiast..noticed carnotite stain on a cliff face in the Edgemont, S. D., area. **1955** *Sci. News Let.* 9 July 31/2 The crescent is not a common figure among petroglyphs and pictographs of northern Arizona. **1971** N. SMITH *Hist. Dams* i. 23 In ancient Egypt..the hieroglyph for a 'province' is a pictograph of an irrigation system. **1973** *Nature* 26 Oct. 422/2 He sees close parallels with the Juxtlahuaca Cave paintings, as well as the earlier pictographs at Chalcacingo, and attempts to define the symbolic elements common to all of them. **1978** *New York* 3 Apr. 32/3 Pictographs from the Warlis, an East Indian tribe.

b. A pictorial representation of statistical data.

1937 R. MODLEY *How to use Pictorial Statistics* iii. 19 The chief variation is that the bar chart can indicate the diversity in subject only in its printed legend, while the pictograph expresses the subject by the character of the symbols which make up each 'bar'. In other words the bar chart is an abstract presentation of facts; the pictograph is concrete. **1954** D. HUFF *How to lie with Statistics* vi. 66 The daddy of the pictorial chart, or pictograph, is the ordinary bar chart.

pictographic *a.* (further examples).

1895 [see *ETEOCRETAN *a.* and *sb.*]. **1932** [see *ACROPHONIC *a.*]. **1952** G. SARTON *Hist. Sci.* I. ii. 20 Words containing the same sounds, especially proper names or abstract words, which were not susceptible of pictographic representation. **1971** *Nature* 30 Apr. 552/1 The signs on these three small baked clay plaques were accepted..as representing a script closely resembling the pictographic writing seen on the 'protoliterate' tablets from Uruk in Mesopotamia.

pictorial, *a.* (*sb.*) Add: **3.** (Further examples.) *pictorial paper* = sense B in Dict. and Suppl.

1873 'MARK TWAIN' & WARNER *Gilded Age* xliii. 394 The pictorial papers caricatured its friends. **1897** *Pearson's Mag.* IV. 405 It is a wonderful invention—this pictorial postcard craze. **1933** *Burlington Mag.* Sept. 140/2 The student who has not an extensive library might like to have possessed a pictorial record. **1935** *Discovery* Dec. 365/2 Sets of pictorial postcards of the park and its inhabitants. **1937** J. R. HUNT (*title*) Pictorial journalism. **1948** C. ABEL *Business of Photogr.* v. 37 Another offshoot of commercial photography..is the growing field of pictorial journalism. **1968** G. JONES *Hist. Vikings* III. ii. 188 From the Gotland pictorial stones it appears that sail could be effectively shortened by the use of reefing lines.

B. (Earlier and later examples.)

1844 *Knickerbocker* XXIII. 197 'The Columbian'..is to run a brisk competition..with the other pictorials. **1851** C. CIST *Sk. Cincinnati in 1851* iv. 77 Illustrated Western World... Oncken's Western Scenery... These two last are pictorials. **1934** G. B. SHAW *Too True to be Good* I. 43 In her lily hand was a copy of The Lady's Pictorial. It contained an illustrated account of your jewels.

2. A postage stamp on which a picture or scene is printed, usu. to commemorate a particular anniversary or event.

1934 in WEBSTER. **1939** P. HAMILTON *Hundred Years of Postage Stamps* v. 74 Pictorials are a characteristic feature of the second half of our hundred years of postage stamps. **1953** HARRISON & ARMSTRONG *New Approach to Stamp Collecting* xi. 173 The rocky finances of certain Central and South American states were the healthier for some really splendid 'pictorials'. **1973** *Daily Tel.* 8 Jan. 9/3 The islands' first pictorials, showing views of the various islands, were issued in 1942-43. **1974** W. FINLAY *Illustr. Hist. Stamp Design* ix. 119/1 The issues of the six Australian states..included a fair number of pictorials.

pictorialist (later examples).

1971 *Amat. Photographer* 3 Mar. 6/2 The panel..does not have the dynamic impact of new pictures or of the more forceful avant-garde work of some modern pictorialists. **1979** G. MACDONALD *Camera* xii. 169/1 The aping of the avant garde by some of the pictorialists.

pi:cturabi·lity. [f. PICTURABLE *a.*: see -ILITY.] The state or quality of being picturable; capacity for visual representation.

1934 in WEBSTER. **1957** R. W. BROWN in Saporta & Bastian *Psycholinguistics* (1961) 505/1 The concrete noun with the smaller denotation is likely to be more picturable than its superordinate, and picturability is another common sense of 'concrete'. **1968** M. JAMMER in R. Klibansky *Contemp. Philos.* II. 349 The shackles of intuitive picturability ('*Anschaulichkeit*').

picture, *sb.* Add: **2. e.** (Earlier examples.)

1802 T. HOLCROFT *Tale of Mystery* 30 Enter Malvoglio. He stops in the middle of the stage: the company start up... The peasants, alarmed and watching: the whole, during a short pause, forming a picture. *c***1825** J. POOLE *Paul Pry* I. ii. 13 There is a general shout of '*Paul Pry*'. *Picture, and act closes.*

f. (Further examples.)

1915 *Wireless World* June 193/1 A picture, constant as long as the cells are under the influence of the original picture, is thus obtained on the receiving screen. **1928**, etc. [see *FRAME *sb.* 12 c]. **1934** J. H. REYNER *Television* iii. 33 Fig. 14 shows the number of pictures per second at which flicker can just be detected, in terms of illumination. **1943**, etc. [see *FIELD *sb.* 16 d]. **1953** AMOS & BIRKINSHAW *Television Engin.* I. i. 14 This time must be short to enable pictures to be transmitted in quick succession, as in cinema film projection. **1956** *B.B.C. Handbk.* 1957 215 The television services of the two countries use different standards, the English system based on a 405-line picture and the French on one of 819 lines. **1960** J. STROUD *Shorn Lamb* xxii. 240 Some well-intentioned hostesses obligingly turned off the sound but not the picture. **1972** G. WHITE *Video Recording* iii. 17 The definition of the reproduced picture depends upon the frequency response of the signal system. **1976** *Daily Tel.* 30 June 2/6 Pictures sent back so far show that areas previously believed to be smooth channels..are pock marked with craters. **1977** J. FRENCH *Small Craft Radar* iii. 86 The radar picture is built up by displaying on a time-related sweep line the instantaneous point of arrival of the echo.

g. (Later examples.)

a **1817** JANE AUSTEN *Northanger Abbey* (1818) I. iv. 49 'How excessively like her brother Miss Morland is!' 'The very picture of him, indeed!' **1877** G. MACDONALD *Marquis of Lossie* III. iv. 81 Isna his mere 'at they ca' Kelpie jist the pictur' o' the deil's ain horse. **1896** P. A. GRAHAM *Red Scaur* 271 You're the verra pictur' o' awd Mr. Selwyn.

h. (Examples.) See also *pretty as a picture* s.v. *PRETTY *a.* II. 4a.

1815 *Sporting Mag.* XLVII. 135/2 She looked a perfect picture. **1827** J. CONSTABLE *Let.* 4 Oct. in *Corr.* (1962) I. 234 Minna looks so nice in her pelisse—the blew band or what it is called was a picture. **1842** C. BRONTË *Let.* 20 Jan. in W. Gérin *C. Brontë* (1967) xii. 179 He sits opposite to Anne at Church sighing softly..and Anne is so quiet.. they are a picture. **1848** DICKENS *Dombey* lvii. 575 He has been working..to make his cabin what the Captain calls 'a picter', to surprise his little wife. **1871** G. MEREDITH *Let.* 15 Feb. (1970) I. 439 The French..have many a noble turning, and are always a picture, good for study. **1937** A. CHRISTIE *Dumb Witness* vii. 65 The gardens are a picture. **1961** *Guardian* 9 June 12/1 The bride was, as they say, 'a picture'. **1977** *Daily News* (Perth, Austral.) 19 Jan. 50/5 The rain this week won't have hurt. All it has done is make the grass greener. The court looks a picture.

i. A representation (of a scene) on a cinematographic film; the film produced or its projection on a screen, = *FILM *sb.* 3 c. Freq. in *pl.*, (*a*) cinematographic productions collectively; (*b*) usu. with *the*, the showing of a film in a cinema, a picture-show.

1896 [see *PROJECT *v.* 9 d]. **1912** *Home Chat* 25 May 391/1 In order to get a picture of the sacking of a village, an actual village was some time ago purchased and fired. **1913** *Ibid.* 20 Sept. 530/1 The pictures one sees nowadays are..in much better taste than those of a few years ago. **1915** *Kinematograph & Lantern Weekly* 1 July 61/2 During his very successful career in 'pictures' he has appeared in some..thrilling productions. **1915** T. BURKE *Nights in Town* 110 Mother and Father..go to the pictures at the Palladium near Balham Station. **1916** *Variety* 27 Oct. 12/2 His bride was in the Kellermann picture, 'A Daughter of the Gods'. **1923** WODEHOUSE *Inimitable Jeeves* xii. 129 Charlotte is coming to the Zoo with me this afternoon. Alone. And later on to the pictures. **1937** D. L. SAYERS *Busman's Honeymoon* x. 225 Off to them pictures again. **1947** A. HUXLEY *Let.* 27 July (1969) 573 The ticklish situation on the set made it impossible to come to New York for Claire's wedding. But we hope and intend to make the trip after the picture is finished. **1960** M. STARK *Ballad of Peckham Rye* viii. 187 They came out of the pictures at eight o'clock. **1974** *Sat. Rev. World* (U.S.) 19 Oct. 56/2 My son had gone to the movies... I asked him, 'How was the picture?' **1977** I. SHAW *Beggarman, Thief* III. xi. 354 The picture was not scheduled to start for another ten minutes. **1978** P. GRACE *Mutuwhenua* iii. 11, I went to the pictures or a social with my cousins.

j. Phr. *every picture tells a story*, orig. popularized by an advertising slogan (see quot. 1927); also in extended uses.

[**1847** C. BRONTË *Jane Eyre* I. i. 5 The letter-press..I cared little for... Each picture told a story.] **1906** *S. A. News Weekly* 26 Sept. 23/3 (Advt.), Every picture tells a story... At the first sign of kidney disease..take Doan's Backache Kidney Pills. **1923** A. HUXLEY *Antic Hay* xxi. 290 'I'm very ill,' she went on expiringly. 'Look at me,' she pointed to herself, 'and me again.' She waved her hand towards the sizzling brilliance of the portrait. 'Before and after. Like the advertisements, you know. Every picture tells a story.' **1927** W. E. COLLINSON *Contemp. Eng.* 65 The wording accompanying..the distressing pictures of human suffering, amenable to treatment by Doan's Backache Kidney Pills, supplies us with the useful Every picture tells a story!—often used derisively of anecdotal paintings. **1976** *Radio Times* 25 Sept. 5 (*caption*) Every picture tells a story: Rod Stewart, the working-class boy who has become a working-class hero.

k. *one picture is worth ten thousand words* and varr.

[**1921** *Printer's Ink* 8 Dec. 96 (*heading*) One look is worth a thousand words.] **1927** *Ibid.* 10 Mar. 114 (*caption*) Chinese proverb. One picture is worth ten thousand words. **1954** R. HAYDN *Jrnl. Edwin Carp* 90 'One picture speaks louder than ten thousand words.' Mr. Bovey repeated the adage this morning when..he handed me my finished portrait. **1979** *Daily Tel.* 14 Aug. 11 If proof was ever needed that a few good pictures are worth more than a thousand statistics it came with bludgeoning force in last night's account of *The Voyage of Rainbow Warrior* (BBC-2) in the 'Inside Story' series.

3. b. *Med.* The sum of the clinical or histological features present in a particular state of the body.

1897 [in Dict., sense 3]. **1931** *Jrnl. Exper. Med.* LIV. 244 The clinical picture of 'mad itch' is very suggestive of pseudorabies. **1940** *Endocrinology* XXVII. 127 The histological pictures of the hypertrophied uteri after vitamin E administration and after mechanical stimulation of the cervix uteri were identical. **1966** WRIGHT & SYMMERS *Systemic Path.* II. xxxix. 1475/1 The histological picture of psoriasis is distinctive but not pathognomic. **1977** *Lancet* 30 July 241/1 Another renal biopsy on March 31 revealed a hyperacute picture (diffuse small and medium arteriolar fibrin thrombi, infarction, and glomerular necrosis).

c. In extended uses, a set of circumstances or state of affairs, esp. in phrs. *to be in the picture*, to understand or be involved in a particular situation or activity, to be in harmony with one's surroundings; similarly *to be out of the picture*, to be uninvolved, inactive, or out of place; *to get the picture*, to grasp or become aware of certain circumstances or facts; *to put* (someone) *in the picture*, to inform (that person) of particular circumstances or facts.

1900 BEERBOHM *Around Theatres* (1924) I. 165 His performance is, strictly, more 'in the picture' than was Mr. Robertson's. **1902** C. MORRIS *Stage Confidences* 202 Oh, well, I feel that I am in the picture, when I wear black during Lent. **1918** LD. DERBY in R. S. Churchill *Lord Derby* (1959) xv. 337 He [*sc.* a new ambassador in Paris]..would..by entertaining be able to bring the British Embassy more, what I may call, 'into the picture' than it is at the present moment. **1923** T. E. LAWRENCE *Let.* 19 Mar. (1938) 411, I said to one 'They're the sort who instinctively fling stones at cats'..and he said 'Why what do you throw?' You perceive that I'm not yet in the picture. **1923** Wodehouse *Good Morning, Bill!* I. 24 'And what's the matter with taking me along?' 'I don't think you would be quite in the picture.' **1926** Maines & Grant *Wise-Crack Dict.* 11/2 *Out of the picture*, in the wrong company. **1936** R. Lehmann *Weather in Streets* III. iv. 320 Think of me as out of the picture..for ever. Unless, of course, you should wish to see me. **1937** L. Bromfield *Rains Came* I. xlv. 190 She should never have come out to India. She doesn't fit into the picture. **1938** [see *chin *sb.*[1] 1 d]. **1939** L. M. Montgomery *Anne of Ingleside* xlii. 327 Christine took possession of the whole room... Anne felt as if she were not in the picture at all. **1942** E. Waugh *Put out More Flags* ii. 150 'Put these men in the picture, Smallwood,' he said, and there had followed a tedious and barely credible narrative about the unprovoked aggression of Southland against Northland. **1950** N. Streatfeild *Mothering Sunday* 144 You keep calling me a criminal, darling, but that's where you aren't in the picture. **1959** P. McCutchan *Storm South* xvii. 239, I would have to be kept right out of the picture so far as the Australian public eye and the police..are concerned. **1960** C. S. Lewis *Studies in Words* v. 128 The attitude of any slave-owning society is and ought to be repellent to us, but it is worth while suppressing that repulsion in order to get the picture as Aristotle saw it. **1961** T. Coffin *Not to the Swift* xviii. 201 Do you get the picture of the kind of fellow he was? **1963** A. Huxley *Let.* 17 Nov. (1969) 964 Under what conditions is this being done and where do I come into the picture? **1966** 'A Hall' *9th Directive* i. 14 At this time..the South-east Asian picture is confused and threatening. **1970** G. Greer *Female Eunuch* 128 Nurses are skilled menials, and as such they fall into line with the dominant pattern of female employment. Salesgirls..waitresses..tea ladies, fill out the picture. **1971** K. Amis *Girl, 20* iv. 129 I'm sorry I've been out of the picture, but I've been up to my neck... Haven't had a bloody minute. **1973** A. Behrend *Samarai Affair* xiii. 136 Come over here soon as possible and I'll put you in the picture. **1975** N. Luard *Travelling Horseman* viii. 198, I explained all this... He seems to get the picture. **1977** *New Yorker* 15 Aug. 36/2, I suppose you were trying to make me jealous—jealous and not jealous. Tearing poor Ann down but letting me know she was in the picture.

4. b. *Philos.* In the study of meaning, the mental image that is assumed to correspond to a fact; also *attrib.*

1922 tr. *Wittgenstein's Tractatus* 39 We make to ourselves pictures of facts. *Ibid.*, The picture presents the facts in logical space, the existence and non-existence of atomic facts. **1940** B. Russell *Inquiry into Meaning & Truth* xiii. 230, I can make a picture of Brutus killing Caesar..but I cannot make a picture, either real or imagined, of quadruplicity killing procrastination. **1946** *Mind* LV. 47 With their use of 'the picture gallery method', and with their insistence on the marginal case, the W[ittgensteinia]ns should be the first persons to admit..this possibility. **1956** J. O. Urmson *Philos. Analysis* v. 54 The relation of language and the world, or picture of fact and fact. **1970** D. M. Taylor *Explanation & Meaning* xi. 132 (*heading*) The picture theory of meaning. **1975** Hargreaves & White tr. *Wittgenstein's Philos. Remarks* iii. 63 The essential difference between the picture conception [of intention] and the conception of Russell, Ogden and Richards, is that it regards recognition as seeing an internal relation. *Ibid.*, The intention never resides in the picture itself. **1977** G. Hallett *Compan. to Wittgenstein's 'Philos. Investigations'* 41 The direction Wittgenstein's thinking took momentarily when he pondered the implications of the picture theory.

6. a. *picture-cycle, frock, gown, library, newspaper, -paper* (earlier and later examples), *story* (later and *attrib.* examples), *-strip, -thought*; (in sense *2 i) *picture-house, -palace, -play, -playhouse, theatre.* **b.** *picture-cleaning* (examples), *-going, -making* (later examples); *picture-cleaner* (earlier and later examples), *-dealer* (later examples), *-framer, -goer, -maker* (later and *fig.* examples), *-taker.* **c.** *picture-thinking* (earlier and later examples).

1763 H. Walpole *Let.* 1 July in *Corr.* (1941) X. 84 Gilders, carvers, upholsterers and picture-cleaners are labouring at their several forges. **1902** *Chambers's Jrnl.* July 433/2, I entrusted the panel to the most expert picture-cleaner of my acquaintance, from whose hands it came out perfect. **1978** *P.O. Telephone Directory: Yellow Pages Classified: London (North)* Apr. 294/3 Picture cleaners and restorers. **1871** D. G. Rossetti *Let.* 4 Aug. (1967) III. 966, I (like most artists) am quite ignorant about picture cleaning. **1937** *Burlington Mag.* May p. xxxiv/1 The picture-cleaning controversy at the National Gallery. **1968** *Medium Ævum* XXXVII. 56 This picture-cycle must have been in existence by 1215. **1971** *Amer. N. & Q.* Sept. 14/2 The whole vast field of early Biblical picture-cycles. **1847** A. Brontë *Agnes Grey* i. 14 What do you say to doing a few more pictures.. getting them framed..and trying to dispose of them to some liberal picture-dealer? **1950** E. H. Gombrich *Story of Art* xx. 311 He had..to rely on middlemen, picture dealers. **1933** *New Yorker* 1 Apr. 37/3, I..hurried around to the nearest picture-framer. **1972** *Times* 30 Sept. 11/1 Pass the picture framer's on the right. **1905** in C. W. Cunnington *Eng. Women's Clothing* (1952) ii. 67 The rage for the picture frock for evening, of the Greuze or Romney style. **1930** *Daily Express* 8 Sept. 3/6 There must be curls..to harmonise with the long Victorian dresses and picture frocks. **1975** G. Howell *In Vogue* 92 (*caption*) This picture frock of pale blue taffeta. **1922** *Moving Picture Stories* 30 June 23/3 The millions who are regular picture-goers. **1947** *Landfall* I. 294 The contemporary cinema, as it is seen by the New Zealand picture-goer. **1976** *Cumberland & Westmorland Herald* 4 Dec. 3/4 Picturegoers may remember the woman who used to turn and smile from the screen as the hallmark of Gainsborough productions. **1976** 'G. Black' *Moon for Killers* i. 19, I always watch the movie. I really catch up on my picture-going in airplanes. **1922** *Liberty Dresses* (Catal.) Spring 25 Picture gown, adapted from a 17th-Century design. **1949** A. Christie *Crooked House* xiv. 107 Magda, the Duchess of Three Gables, in a picture gown of taffetas. **1975** G. Howell *In Vogue* 147 (*caption*) Picture gown of black tulle. **1908** *Variety* 23 May 12 Hundreds seated in a picture house who..watch with cooling brows the reels run off. **1913** *Punch* 31 Dec. 543/3 Scene outside an Islington Picture-house. **1939** [see *fried *ppl. a.* b]. **1975** *Country Life* 6 Feb. 326/1 In 1928, the publisher..laid out £4,000 promoting a song..sending lantern slides..to every picture house in the country. **1958** *Times* 31 July 4/6 B.B.C. buy picture library. The B.B.C. have bought the Hulton picture library from Hulton Press Ltd., it was announced yesterday. The library, which was originally called the Picture Post library.. will be known as Radio Times Hulton picture library. **1975** N. Luard *Travelling Horseman* vi. 167, I got back ..from the picture library about 5.30. **1853** Dickens *Bleak Ho.* xxxiii. 329 There comes the artist of a picture newspaper. **1979** G. Macdonald *Camera* x. 148/2 The development of picture magazines and newspapers. **1894** A. Macdonell *Thomas Hardy* x. 232 Story-teller, picture-maker, humourist, it is entertainment he offers us. **1926** V. Woolf *Captain's Death Bed* (1950) 167 The picture-makers seem dissatisfied with such obvious sources of interest. *Ibid.* 169 The picture-making power. **1961** J. McCabe *Mr. Laurel & Mr. Hardy* (1962) viii. 159 The trouble with modern picture-making is the lack of time for preparation. **1908** *Stage Year Bk.* 48 There are now indications that before long these picture 'palaces' will be a feature of London and the larger provincial towns. **1937** D. L. Sayers *Busman's Honeymoon* iv. 85 The neighbourhood boasted a picture palace. **1973** *Listener* 26 July 124/3 A secure world of..visits to the pie-and-mash, and Tuesdays at the Carlton picture-palace. **1867** *Harper's Mag.* 2 Feb. 80/1 I'm sure, Dear, the Picture Papers can not make Frights of us now! **1959** T. S. Eliot *Elder Statesman* II. 43 I'll feel more confidence after a fortnight..Of people not staring Or offering picture papers. **1911** *Chambers's Jrnl.* Sept. 621/1 Many of the leading dramatists now devote their energies seriously to the elaboration of scenarios for picture-plays. **1923** Picture play [see *picture magazine* s.v. sense 6 d below]. **1919** *Honey Pot* I. iv. 1 (Advt.), The New Gallery Kinema, Society's Picture Playhouse. **1966** J. Derrick *Teaching Eng. to Immigrants* vii. 224 There are in fact several wall charts and picture-story picture sets especially printed for language teachers. **1968** *Tamarack Rev.* Spring 18 Somebody passed Jake the issue of *Life* magazine with the lead picture story on Israel. **1949** Koestler *Insight & Outlook* xxiv. 345 Transitions from primitive picture-strip language to more abstract forms of expression. **1959** I. & P. Opie *Lore & Lang. Schoolch.* ix. 172 Few people now are nicknamed 'Giglamps'.., although derivatives persist in the picture strips. **1966** J. Derrick *Teaching Eng. to Immigrants* v. 183 Picture-strip stories, in which a little episode is told in pictures as in comic strips. **1979** 'S. Kemp' *Goodbye, Pussy* ix. 115 Just like a picture-strip, isn't it? **1909** *Westm. Gaz.* 10 July 14/2 Two out of three men..neglect their apparatus and drift out of the ranks of the picture-takers. **1969** *Amat. Photographer* 28 May 53 (Advt.), The sort of picture-taker who winds the film on the wrong way. **1976** *Daily Progress* (Charlottesville, Va.) 27 Apr. (Advt.), CB spoken here..*Picture taker*, radar unit. **1908** *Variety* 16 May 11 A new picture theatre will be opened at 276 State Street. **1970** *Southerly* XXX. 124 The town which could offer them a pub, picture theatre, souvenir shops, milk bars. **1976** *Times* 13 Mar. 9/1 All the Continental towns they visited had moving picture theatres while Ireland had none. **1874** W. Wallace tr. *Hegel's Logic* 30 Conception or picture-thinking works with materials from the same sensuous source. **1945** R. A. Knox *God & Atom* vii. 90 One will depend more on picture-thinking, on crude, unanalysed notions, than another. *a* **1963** C. S. Lewis *Poems* (1964) 78 Film, broadcast, propaganda, picture-thinking. **1874** W. Wallace tr. *Hegel's Logic* 53 The predicates by which the object is to be determined are supplied from the resources of picture-thought.

d. picture black *Television*, the light level of the darkest element of a television picture, or the picture signal voltage corresponding to this; **picture-book** (earlier and later examples); also *attrib.* or as *adj.*, characteristic or suggestive of a picture-book; excessively or sentimentally pretty; **picture-card** (earlier and later examples); also *fig.*, and used of any card bearing a picture; **picture element** *Television*, any of the minute areas of uniform illumination of which a television image is composed and which are produced successively by the scanning beam; **picture-frame**, also *Theatr.*, used *attrib.* and *absol.* to designate the stage or stage setting regarded as a picture enclosed by a frame; also *transf.*; **picture frequency** *Television*, † (*a*) (the frequency of) the picture signal; (*b*) the number of times per second a complete television image is scanned or transmitted; **picture-frustration** *Psychol.*, used *attrib.* to designate personality tests that aim to assess a subject's prejudices or personality traits through his reactions to pictures that show potentially frustrating incidents; **picture gallery** (further examples); also *fig.*; **picture hat** (later examples); hence **picture-hatted** *a.*; **picture magazine**, an illustrated magazine; **picture monitor** *Television*, a television screen which is used to provide an immediate display of the image being received by a television camera; **picture-plane**, an imaginary plane on which the perspective of a painting or the like meets the eye of the viewer; **picture postcard**, also *fig.*, a scene, etc., reminiscent of or suitable for a picture postcard; freq. *attrib.* or as *adj.*, conventionally attractive or pretty, in the manner of a picture postcard; so **picture-postcardish** *a.*; **picture show**, (*a*) an exhibition of pictures; (*b*) a cinema performance, a film show; **picture signal** *Television*, the component of the video signal which carries the information relating to the brightness of the picture elements; **picture-space**, a painted canvas considered as a whole in relation to parts of the painting; **picture stage**, a picture-frame stage; **picture telegraphy**, the telegraphic transmission of still pictures, now usu. called *facsimile telegraphy*; cf. *phototelegraphy* s.v. Photo- 1 in Dict. and Suppl.; **picture-telephone** = *videophone; **picture tie**, a neck-tie with a representational design; **picture tube** *Television*, a cathode-ray tube of the kind used for forming the picture in a television set; **picture window**, a large window consisting of a single pane of glass; also *transf.* and *fig.*; hence **picture-windowed** *a.*; **picture-wire**, wire of the kind used for hanging pictures.

1938 *Jrnl. Inst. Electr. Engin.* LXXXIII. 770/1 The insertion of the d.c. component into a train of picture signals implies that the signal corresponding to picture black is established at a definite potential. **1961** G. Millerson *Technique Television Production* iii. 51 Picture black may not be constant. The darkness of the blackest tones in the picture may vary from shot to shot, with picture content. **1972** G. J. King *Beginner's Guide Television* (ed. 5) ii. 43 In television parlance, below-picture black level is called blacker than black. **1847** Thackeray *Van. Fair* (1848) xxxvii. 338 Rawdon bought the boy plenty of picture-books, and crammed his nursery with toys. **1922** A. Huxley *Mortal Coils* 201 It's one of those picture-book German towns. **1926** T. E. Lawrence *Seven Pillars* (1935) xxxiv. 199 A tiny, picture-book train rolled slowly into view across the hollow sounding bridge. **1965** *Eng. Stud.* XLVI. 370 A..human figure which looks half like..a picture-book goddess. **1974** *Sat. Rev. World* (U.S.) 2 Nov. 9/3 Kyrenia..gave promise..of a picture-book port. **1976** H. Kemelman *Wednesday the Rabbi got Wet* xlix. 272 A lovely sunny day with a blue sky and picture-book clouds. **1979** *Jrnl. R. Soc. Arts* CXXVII. 662/2 The book succeeds in being an attractive picture book. **1837** Dickens *Pickw.* xliv. 479 Keep quiet, do,.. there never vos such a old picter-card born. **1908** R. Fry *Let.* 11 July (1972) I. 304 I've sent picture cards to the dear ones. **1932** H. Crane *Let.* 13 Aug. (1965) 409, I must write him a picture card at least in answer; but I'm damned if I want to continue any correspondence of that kind. **1959** I. & P. Opie *Lore & Lang. Schoolch.* ix. 166 Bubble gum,..with its tempting picture card in each packet, is known as 'beetle fat'. **1966** J. Derrick *Teaching Eng. to Immigrants* 239 The work cards, picture-cards, wall pictures and flashcards which accompany the course, are also recommended. **1927** *Wireless World* 1 June 684/2 The mosaic of dots, or picture elements, would be a jumble..if there was an error of 1-90,000th part of a second in the synchronisation between the sending and receiving apparatus. **1940** D.G. Fink *Princ. Television Engin.* ii. 25 The transmission of television images..is accomplished by analyzing the scene into its picture elements, which are selected from the picture area in the orderly sequence of scanning and transmitted one after the other. **1976** *Science* 27 Aug. 792 (*caption*) At this resolution an object 6 m in size subtends one picture element at the nominal horizon. **1928** J. Dolman *Art of Play Production* iii. 43 There are many who are ruthlessly condemning the modern theatre for its illusion, its 'peep-hole' realism, its 'picture-frame' stage. **1936** P. Rotha *Documentary Film* II. i. 76 Guidance of the actors in speech and gesture, composition of the separate scenes within the picture-frame. **1959** *News Chron.* 29 Dec. 4/2 By the late 'sixties the flat 30 in. picture-frame sets hanging discreetly on our walls, masked during non-viewing periods by..a Constable or a Breughel, will be giving us a reasonably good colour picture. **1966** J. R. Taylor *Penguin Dict. Theatre* 254 By the middle of the nineteenth century the picture-frame stage, in which the whole stage was framed by the proscenium with virtually no forestage at all, had become general. **1978** *Listener* 8 June 740/3 The cast..will be holding their breaths to squeeze on to the little picture-frame stage. **1926** *Wireless World* 5 May 645/1 The same wavelength carries both the picture frequency, from which the received photograph is built up, and the synchronism frequency which controls the motors. **1930** *Electronics* Aug. 236/2 The Bell 50-line system, 17·7 repetition rate and theoretical maximum picture frequency of 22,125 cycles. **1935** *Discovery* Sept. 277/2 They [*sc.* T.V. pictures] are bright, steady (having regard to picture frequency). **1953** Amos & Birkinshaw *Television Engin.* I. i. 15 The number of complete pictures transmitted per second is known as the picture frequency and must be high enough to give the impression of natural movement and to minimise flicker. **1967** H. A. Cole *Basic Television* I. 32 The number of complete pictures presented in every second is called the picture frequency. **1945** *Jrnl. Abnormal Psychol.* XL. 200/1 The Picture-Frustration Study is a limited projective technique for assessing an individual's characteristic modes of reaction. **1949** S. Rosenzweig *Psychodiagnosis* vii. 167 The Picture-Frustration (P-F) Study, or—by its full name—the Picture-Association Study for Assessing Reactions to Frustration, is a limited projective procedure for disclosing patterns of response to everyday stress. **1968** *Jrnl. Abnormal Psychol.* LXXIII. 381 (*heading*) Coronary artery disease and response to the Rosenzweig picture-frustration study. **1842** W. P. Hawes

Sporting Scenes I. 178 [Wild geese are] willing to wait for the wooden devices which we have anchored in the shallow feeding-grounds, as a picture-gallery of their uncles, cousins, and sweet-hearts. **1850** C. Fox *Jrnl.* 1 Apr. (1972) 196 This evening Clara Balfour's picture-gallery included Christina of Sweden, Anne of England [etc.]. **1931** *Amer. Mercury* Nov. 353/2 *Picture gallery*, the tattooed man. **1941** F. Thompson *Over to Candleford* x. 152 One of these new fancy bazaars..was to be held in the picture gallery. **1979** R. Cox *Auction* i. 23 The museum's picture gallery. **1928** Mrs. Belloc Lowndes *Diary* 20 Feb. (1971) 112 A black lace frock with a large picture hat trimmed with roses. **1958** L. Durrell *Balthazar* ix. 178 Inside the cupboard I found an immense, old-fashioned picture-hat of the 1912 variety. **1975** G. Howell *In Vogue* 112/2 Dressed by Norman Hartnell, she wore..a picture hat and a long full dress for receptions. **1977** *Jersey Even. Post.* 26 July 10/1 Her matching picture hat was decorated with white tulle and flowers. **1922** W. J. Locke *Tale of Triona* vii. 71 Her exquisitely picture-hatted head. **1959** Picture-hatted [see *goose pimples* s.v. *goose *sb.* 8]. **1923** Ade *Let.* 26 Jan. (1973) 91 Two or three weeks ago I picked up a picture magazine and read the outline of the new picture play called 'Fury'. **1967** G. Steiner *Lang. & Silence* 417 He is as remote, or more so, than is the modern picture-magazine and paper-back from the chained, leather-bound folio of the late medieval scholar. **1979** J. Scott *Clutch of Vipers* vii. 120 She was..reading a picture magazine designed for semi-literate young ladies. **1933** *Proc. IRE* XXI. 1690 The picture monitor may be connected to either the output of the picture amplifier or to a radio receiver, which makes possible the monitoring of the radiated signals. **1961** G. Millerson *Technique Television Production* i. 15 The [production control] room's dominating feature is the row of picture monitors. **1975** A. Bermingham et al. *Small Television Studio* 60 A picture monitor is, to all appearances, a high grade TV set without sound. **1797** *Encycl. Brit.* XIV. 182/1 If BA be drawn in the ground plan, and EV be drawn parallel to it, meeting the picture-plane or perspective-plane in V, [etc.]. **1934** *Burlington Mag.* Aug. 91/2 The projection of the three dimensions of nature on to the two dimensions of the picture-plane. **1959** P. & L. Murray *Dict. Art & Artists* 240 *Picture plane*, the extreme front edge of the imaginary space in the picture. It lies immediately behind the glass of the frame and is the plane at which the world of the spectator and of the picture make contact. **1972** E. Lucie-Smith *Eroticism in Western Art* iii. 63 Her hips seem to swell towards us out of the picture-plane. **1907** R. Brooke *Let.* 23 Aug. (1968) 100, I shall be looking at them [*sc.* antiquities] when you & Arthur Watts are staring at picture-postcard skies & snow. *a* **1930** D. H. Lawrence *Phoenix II* (1968) 285 As a picture of Sicily in the middle of the last century, it is marvellous. But it is a picture done from the inside. There are no picture-postcard effects... There is nothing showy. **1936** A. Huxley *Eyeless in Gaza* xli. 491 Against a picture postcard of sunset the immoderately tall thin palms were the emblems of a resigned hopelessness. **1957** J. Braine *Room at Top* xi. 113 Her picture-postcard face with the dyed red bubble-curls and the Lily Langtry nose and chin. **1959** *Sunday Express* 22 Mar. 9/8 The picture-postcard village of Finchingfield. **1973** V. Canning *Flight of Grey Goose* v. 90 You're like all summer tourists. All you see is a nice picture-postcard sort of place. **1977** *Time* 24 Oct. 55/2 Bibi Andersson is pallid by comparison, a picture-postcard beauty. **1969** *Daily Tel.* 14 Mar. 16/4 Bavaria and the Vorarlberg, through which they travel in spring-time, look very picture-postcardish in Robert Paynter's colour photography. **1869** D. G. Rossetti *Let.* 24 Dec. (1965) II. 781 Nor indeed do I ever go to any picture shows whatever now. **1912** *Home Chat* 20 Apr. 148/1 She takes me to theatres and picture shows. **1921** R. Macaulay *Dangerous Ages* ii. 47 I'll go to theatres and picture shows and concerts and meetings. **1940** R. Chandler *Farewell, My Lovely* xxx. 227 Folks took me to the picture show. **1948** E. Pound *Pisan Cantos* (1949) lxxx. 94 And he said to Yeats at a vorticist picture show: 'You also of the brotherhood?' **1976** J. M. Brownjohn tr. *Kirst's Time for Payment* vi. 137 Let's inspect the results of our picture show. **1927** Secor & Kraus *Television* iii. 15 As the incoming picture signals are passed through an electromagnet or solenoid, it is caused to open and close a light shutter made of a small piece of aluminum and a spring. **1953** Amos & Birkinshaw *Television Engin.* I. i. 17 The picture signal voltage at any point in a television system varies between two limits, one representing the maximum brightness it is intended to transmit and known as white level and the other representing zero tonal value or black and known as black level. **1972** G. J. King *Beginner's Guide Television* (ed. 5) ii. 43 The picture signal controls the brightness of the scanning spot. **1925** Picture-space [see *imaginally *adv.*]. **1937** *Burlington Mag.* Apr. 183/1 The balance between the figures and the picture-space as a whole is roughly identical. **1959** H. Read *Conc. Hist. Mod. Painting* v. 156 The arrangement of the elements within the picture-space remains intuitive. **1951** C. B. Purdom *Producing Plays* (ed. 3) viii. 113 There can be no doubt that the picture stage is doomed and that stages in new theatres should not be constructed on that principle. **1961** R. Williams *Long Revolution* ii. vi. 254 The modern picture-stage. **1913** *Wireless World* Sept. 354/2 Just as with picture-telegraphy with conductors, we can distinguish between a black and white method..and a half-tone method. **1934** *Discovery* Dec. 336/2 Partly owing to..the..lack of general realisation of the existence of picture telegraphy services, these have not yet been nearly as freely used as they might be. **1976** Picture telegraphy [see *private *a.* 4 d (i)]. **1968** *Listener* 1 Aug. 155/3 Picture-telephones are not only going to be embarrassing to live with, they are going to drain a lot more magic out of life. **1969** *Sci. Jrnl.* May 36/3 This summer the Swedish L. M. Ericsson concern..is to install and test a picture-telephone connection between Stockholm and Gothenburg. **1969** P. West *Words for Deaf Daughter* vi. 151 Will you zoom off into a future which..brings shopping by picture-telephone? **1957** R. Mason *World of Suzie Wong* ii. iv. 151, I thought how quietly dressed you were for an American. I mean, you weren't wearing a picture-tie, or anything like that. **1963** 'D. Rutherford' *Creeping Flesh* i. 63 That black man with the blue suit and silk picture tie. **1940** D. G. Fink *Princ. Television Engin.* i. 19 The image-reproducing tube ('picture' tube)..is a funnel-shaped glass structure in the narrow end of which is contained an electrode structure capable of producing a narrow beam of electrons. **1966** H. Nielsen *After Midnight* (1967) v. 77 My picture tube blew at ten-thirty and I went straight to bed. **1976** *Guardian* 21 Apr. 19/1 Picture tubes account for 40 per cent of the cost of the components in a set. **1938** *Amer. Home* Nov. 20/2 If you have a large picture window, we suggest sill-length casement drawn curtains. **1942** *Pencil Points* Nov. 65/1 Extensive fenestration makes it possible to bring the outdoors into the house (note the plate glass, stationary picture windows). **1945** Nelson & Wright *Tomorrow's House* vi. 75/2 Storage cupboards have been grouped in such a way that picture windows could be used. **1958** J. Cannan *And be a Villain* iv. 79 It was a fairly recent erection with 'picture' windows. **1960** *Chicago Rev.* Autumn–Winter 117 Everett Knight is all for bringing intellectuals down from their tower. The question is whether he himself has actually come out of it or simply ordered some picture windows installed. **1969** *New Yorker* 12 Apr. 90/3 For twenty-one days, the astronauts may look out of a huge picture window, tinted brown against the Texas sun. **1972** J. Mann *Mrs. Knox's Profession* x. 78 The local style was for picture windows.. affording a good view of the modern furniture drawn up around the television set. **1977** *Time* 25 July 9/2 He staked out the eighth-floor penthouse, with picture windows offering a panoramic view of Lake Geneva and the Alps, as his personal pad. **1969** R. Blythe *Akenfield* 16 The 'young marrieds' go less and less for the converted cottage and more for picture-windowed bungalows. **1978** G. Mitchell *Mingled with Venom* vi. 63 Dame Beatrice.. took him into the dimly-lit lounge, out through the picture-windowed bar. **1895** *Montgomery Ward Catal.* Spring & Summer 352/3 Braided picture wire..2½ yards. **1923** Kipling *Land & Sea Tales* 88 Carpenter was off in pursuit of rabbits, with a pocket full of fine picture-wire. **1973** R. Hayes *Hungarian Game* ii. 22 He took the guy out with a two-foot length of picture wire and sweet *Jesus* it was great.

picture, *v.* **4.** (Further example in sense of *picture *sb.* 4 b.)

1923 *Mind* XXXII. 467 It is not asserted that the picture must have the same logical form as what it pictures, but that all pictures must have *the* logical form.

picturedom (pi·ktʃəɹdəm). [f. Picture *sb.* + -dom.] Pictures or moving pictures collectively.

1902 *Strand Mag.* Apr. 440/1 One who knows him says that 'Zim' is the 'Mark Twain' of picturedom. **1920** *Chambers's Jrnl.* 21 Feb. 188/1 It was at the same ranch [near Los Angeles] that many of the most terrible battles in picturedom were fought and filmed. **1945** *Sun* (Baltimore) 2 Oct. 5/7 (Advt.), True antiques of picturedom.

picturedrome (pi·ktʃəɹdrōᵘm). [f. *picture *sb.* 2 i + *-drome, after *hippodrome *sb.* 3.] A building intended for picture shows; a cinema.

1914 *Durham Advertiser* 19 June 8 Arrangements are being made..for the 'Varsity students' 'rag'..to be shown at the Assembly Rooms Picturedrome. **1918** A. Quiller-Couch *Foe Farrell* 116, I dragged him and Petunia back into the shadow under the side-wall of the Picturedrome. **1927** *Punch* 27 July 97/3 Give us more dance saloons, More epileptic tunes, More syncopating coons, More Picture-dromes. **1933** P. MacDonald *Mystery of Dead Police* i. 2 The colossal Pantheon Picturedrome—all Ionic pillars and organ solo. **1945** *Gen* 5 May 24/2 A cinema owner can extol the modernity of his 'Picture-drome'.

picturegraph (pi·ktʃəɹgrɑf). [f. Picture *sb.* + -graph.] A symbol representing a picture or image; a pictograph. Also *fig.*

1926 G. Murray in *Pioneer of Reformed Spelling* Apr. 2 You could communicate ideas by making certain signs or marks on some material—from that you get, first picturegraphs, and eventually alphabetical writing. *a* **1930** D. H. Lawrence *Apocalypse* (1931) ix. 127 Every image fulfils its own little circle of action and meaning, then is superseded by another image... Every image is a picture-graph, and the connection between the images will be made..differently by every reader. **1962** *Punch* 11 Apr. 570/2 There was..Diplodocus Carnegii,..alive, in his own era—a rare picturegraph in those days.

Picturephone (pi·ktʃəɹfōᵘn). Also with lower-case initial. [f. Picture *sb.* + Phone *sb.*[2]] A videophone. Cf. *picture-telephone* s.v. *picture *sb.* 6 d.

A proprietary name in the U.S.

1964 *N.Y. Times* 21 Apr. 31/2 The Picturephone was demonstrated yesterday with a see-as-you-talk call between the World's Fair and Anaheim, Calif. **1965** *Punch* 23 June 912 The picturephone is not yet domesticated. There is an experimental commercial hook-up between New York, Chicago and Washington. **1966** *Official Gaz.* (U.S. Patent Office) 27 Sept. TM192/2 American Telephone and Telegraph Co., New York. Filed April 13, 1965. Picturephone. For: See-while-you-talk, sometimes known as visual telephone, services. First use at least as early as April 20, 1964. **1970** *Nature* 25 July 331/1 The first commercial picturephone service was opened recently by the Bell Telephone Service. **1970** *New Scientist* 24 Dec. 565 As befits an executive in a communications company,.. Thomas has a Picturephone on his desk, and takes part in conferences by TV. **1974** *Times Lit. Suppl.* 1 Nov. 1216/1 Set in the near future (though the only concession to documentary detail is the picturephone over which leading political figures are apt to receive 'blank-screen calls').

picturesque, *a.* Add: **1. b.** (Earlier examples.)

a **1763** [see *landscape-gardening* s.v. *landscape *sb.* 5]. **1783** W. Burgh in W. Mason *Eng. Garden* 236 There is nothing in picturesque Gardening which should not have its archetype in unadorned Nature.

4. (Earlier examples.)

1789 W. Gilpin *Observations Rel. Picturesque Beauty* I. viii. 72 Let the picturesque traveller watch for these effects. *Ibid.* xiv. 139 The picturesque eye regrets the loss of it's towers.

5. (Earlier and later examples.)

1749 D. Hartley *Observations on Man* I. 427 The Nature of the Caricatura, Burlesque, Grotesque, Picturesque, &c. may be understood from what is delivered.. concerning Laughter, Wit, Humour, the Marvellous, Absurd, &c. to which they correspond. **1782** W. Gilpin *Observations on River Wye* 93 Col. Mitford..is well-versed in the theory of the picturesque. **1927** C. Hussey *Picturesque* iii. 66 The Picturesque was to be a practical aesthetic for gardeners, tourists, and sketchers. **1955** N. Nicholson *Lakers* iii. 46 In the Picturesque, the only creative act is that of man himself, a small, mean, self-satisfied manipulation of an abstract landscape. **1961** *Amer. Q.* Winter 529 The outlook for the amateur..is usually dependent on his fondness for local history or for the picturesque.

2. A picturesque landscape. *rare.*

1889 G. Meredith *Let.* 20 May (1970) II. 959 We had here a young and promising Bostonian..fresh from a ride over the picturesques of Greece.

picturesqueness. Add: (Further examples.) Also *transf.* and *fig.*

1867 [see *featureliness]. **1907** 'Mark Twain' *Christian Sci.* ii. iii. 130 Repetition of pet poetic picturesquenesses.

picturesquerie (piktʃəre·skəri). [f. Picturesque *a.*, after Grotesquerie.] The picturesque; picturesqueness.

1962 *Punch* 12 Sept. 392/3 Miscegenation and picturesquerie on beaches. **1963** *Punch* 20 Mar. 396/2 An endless stream of..picturesquerie, from Maundy Money to the Royal Enclosure. **1968** *Listener* 12 Sept. 322/1 Soon, we were back with French TV's old faults of inconsequential folklore and half-conscious chauvinism. Shock and protest gave place to a routine rag-bag of patriotic picturesquerie. **1978** 'M. Delving' *No Sign of Life* i. 5, I hadn't much time for prettiness and picturesquerie.

picture-writing. Add: **3.** Language or writing that is graphic or vivid. *rare.*

1942 Blunden *Romantic Poetry & Fine Arts* 19 Such picture-writing as Tennyson's 'Palace of Art'; of which I remember my old headmaster saying..'very much like paintings'.

picturing, *vbl. sb.* **b.** (Further examples esp. in sense of *picture *sb.* 4 b.)

1956 J. O. Urmson *Philos. Analysis* v. 76 By no means all the atomists used the terminology of 'picturing'. **1963** W. Sellars *Sci., Perception & Reality* vi. 211 But what if, instead of construing 'picturing' as a relationship between *facts*, we construe it as a relationship between linguistic and nonlinguistic *objects*? **1970** R. Rhees *Discussions of Wittgenstein* i. 5 Well, how do you know? How do you know there is any such picturing? **1971** F. W. Garforth *Scope of Philos.* xii. 237 Nor is 'picturing' an adequate account of what language is and does.

picturization (pi:ktʃərəizēⁱ·ʃən). [f. next.] Representation by means of a picture or pictures (in the various senses of the sb.).

1917 *N.Y. Times* 12 Mar. 9/2 A picturization of 'A Tale of Two Cities' was the new offering at the Academy of Music. **1918** *Dialect Notes* V. 9 'The Little American' is a stirring picturization of events in France during the great war. **1920** [see *cinematograph *sb.*]. **1925** *Lit. Digest* 4 July 30/2 The public does not demand picturizations which truly mirror American life. **1938** I. Kuhn *Assigned to Adventure* vi. 71 He made the stories inspirational and romantic by vivid picturization of human beings at a dramatic time in their lives. **1951** G. Humphrey *Thinking* ix. 286 The hindrance to thought that comes from..picturization or fitting the images into a consistent picture. **1957** V. J. Kehoe *Technique Film & Television Make-Up* viii. 97 There are a number of differences between film and television picturizations.

picturize (pi·ktʃərəiz), *v.* [f. Picture *sb.* + -ize.] *trans.* To represent by or adorn with a picture or pictures (in the various senses of the sb.). Hence **pi·cturized** *ppl. a.*; **pi·cturizing** *vbl. sb.*

1846 in J. E. Worcester *Universal & Crit. Dict. Eng. Lang.* **1918** *Dialect Notes* V. 13 The Common Law, by R. W. Chambers, is soon to be picturized by one of the leading film companies. **1918** *N.Y. Times* 11 Nov. 13/3 William A. Brady as producer, Harley Knowles as director, and all others concerned have done a good piece of work in the so-called 'picturizing' of 'Little Women', which was shown yesterday at the Strand Theatre. **1920** *Ibid.* 24 May 20 The photoplay, however, remains simply a picturized reproduction of the stage play. **1923** *Westm. Gaz.* 26 July 8/6 It is..not an attempt..to picturise the whole of scientific theory on the subject. **1930** *Publishers' Weekly* 1 Mar. 1127 (Advt.), The new Encyclopædia Britannica humanized and picturized. **1952** N. V. Peale *Power of Positive Thinking* iv. 49 When either failure or success is picturized it strongly tends to actualize in terms equivalent to the mental image pictured. **1967** Singha & Massey *Indian Dances* iii. 46 The really expert dancer appears to picturize the music with her arms and body.

picuda (piku·dă). [Amer. Sp., f. Sp. *picudo, -a* pointed, sharp.] The great barracuda, *Sphyræna barracuda,* of the family Sphyrænidæ, a large marine fish found in oceans bordering eastern central America, from Florida to Brazil.

1931 B. MIALL tr. *Guenther's Naturalist in Brazil* ii. 48 There is also, on the coast of north-eastern Brazil, a fish of the Mullet family, the Picuda, which is sometimes as much as six feet in length. **1963** H. ULRICH *America's Best Deep-Sea Fishing* II. 102 Barracuda... Other Names: Great barracuda, common barracuda, picuda, sea tiger, cuda. **1975** FELTON & FOWLER *Best, Worst & most Unusual* 234 The men work two or three short days a week fishing for picuda.

piddle, *v.* **1. a.** Delete 'now *rare*' and add later examples. Freq. with *about, around.*

1938 M. K. RAWLINGS *Yearling* iii. 25 Don't you and your Pa be gone too long now, follerin' that fool hound. I'm o' no mind to set around waitin' breakfast and you two piddlin' around in the woods. **1957** R. A. HEINLEIN *Door into Summer* (1960) ii. 32, I piddled along with the help of the shop mechanics until I had *Frank* looking less like a three-car crash. **1961** I. JEFFERIES *It wasn't Me!* iv. 56 We piddled about with ballistics too, but mostly talk. **1973** *N.Y. Times* 10 June VII. 22/3 Since the whole family piddled with archery, we had our gear with us. **1977** *Sounds* 9 July 22/3 He returned to New York and 'piddled around' doing Public Relations.

d. (Later examples.)

1942 BERREY & VAN DEN BARK *Amer. Thes. Slang* §239/3 *Waste*,..piddle away. **1958** 'E. McBAIN' *Killer's Payoff* (1960) xvii. 160 Ruther had inherited money which..he'd piddled away. **1965** [see *INTERFACE 2 a]. **1978** D. A. STANWOOD *Memory of Eva Ryker* ii. 15, I was patrolling Kapiolani Boulevard, piddling away the final moments of my ungodly long shift.

2. (Earlier and later *fig.* and later *lit.* examples.)

1814 W. SCOTT *Let.* 10 Nov. (1932) III. 515 The last act is ill contrived. He piddles (so to speak) through a cullender, and divides the whole horrors of the catastrophe ..into a kind of drippity-droppity of four or five scenes. **1931** R. CAMPBELL *Georgiad* II. 21 Across the lawn they [*sc.* dogs] shank it on all fours, To argue, fight, and copulate, and piddle Around the sacred lamp-post in the middle. **1947** M. LOWRY *Let.* May (1967) 142 Meantime we have been here quietly piddling in our pants with suspense. **1951** H. BENNETT *We never called him Henry* iii. 18 Mr. Ford..would tell me, 'So-and-so was piddling in my ear'. That was a favourite expression of his. **1974** R. ADAMS *Shardik* xxv. 205, I have no idea what portents he employs—possibly the bear piddles on the floor and he observes portents in the steaming what-not. **1976** *Listener* 15 July 55/3 To greet the crowd meeting him, he openly piddles on the platform.

piddle (pi·d'l), *sb. colloq.* [f. the vb.] **1.** Urine; an act of urinating. Also *fig.*

1901 in Farmer & Henley *Slang* V. 191/1. **1937** PARTRIDGE *Dict. Slang* 625/2 *Piddle*, urine; occ. the act of making water. **1959** E. BURGESS *Divided we Fall* x. 115 Take the poodle for its piddle. **1962** M. DUFFY *That's how it Was* xii. 105, I envied him his ability to tie his little soft winkle into a knot at the end and blow it out like a balloon with unshed piddle. **1972** D. BLOODWORTH *Any Number can Play* x. 77 How could these red-haired brutes eat that filthy muck, not to mention the piddle and milk they called tea?

2. A trifle; nonsense.

1910 R. BROOKE *Let.* 2 Mar. (1968) 223 It's the alteration of the little words that makes all the difference between Poetry & piddle.

piddler. (Later example.)

1911 R. D. SAUNDERS *Col. Todhunter* ii. 25, I ain't never seen no piddler at meal times that was fit to do a man's work.

piddling, *ppl. a.* Add: **1.** (Later examples.)

1902 W. E. HENLEY *Views & Reviews: Art* 10 *The Castle of Otranto* is a piddling piece of super-nature. **1936** [see *DOLESS *a.*]. **1948** [see *GOUGER c]. **1966** *Electronics* 31 Oct. 149 The European market for IC's is still piddling. **1971** *Maclean's Mag.* Sept. 4/1 In plain words, I found out what my job was. No piddling assignment either. What it amounted to was saving the country. **1972** V. CANNING *Rainbird Pattern* i. 2 Use other people's..piddling fears about their own status, and the world is at your feet. **1976** 'D. FLETCHER' *Don't whistle 'Macbeth'* 47 You'd never drown... Not in that piddling little stream.

2. Making water, urinating.

1968 *Listener* 2 May 579/3 Far and away the best.. is *Thinking Girl.* Some may be inclined to poke fun by retitling Miss Meacock's book *Piddling Girl*, after counting the number of times the characters are glimpsed in lavatories.

piddly (pi·dli), *a.* [f. *PIDDLE *sb.* + -LY[1].] = PIDDLING *ppl. a.* 1.

1946 B. MARSHALL *George Brown's Schooldays* xv. 72 Filthy little funks, skittering away down a piddly little track like that.

pidgin, pigeon. Add: **a.** (Earlier examples.)

1826 B. HALL *Acct. Voy. Corea* (rev. ed.) vi. 287, I come to see about your pigeon. *Ibid.* 288, I afterwards learned that..'pigeon', in the strange jargon spoken at Canton by way of English, means business. **1845** J. R. PETERS *Misc. Remarks upon Chinese* vii. 73 Pidgeon, is the common Chinese pronunciation of business.

b. A language as spoken in a simplified or altered form by non-natives, *spec.* as a means of communication between people not sharing a common language. Freq. *attrib.* or in *Comb.* Also *fig.*

1891 [in Dict.]. **1921** H. E. PALMER *Princ. Language-Study* 107 Pidgin or pidgin-speech may be defined as that variety of a language which is used exclusively by foreigners. **1943** R. A. HALL *Melanesian Pidgin Eng.* 8 The phonetics of Melanesian Pidgin are basically those of a slightly sub-standard English. *Ibid.* 9 In the absence of native speakers, Pidgin does not present the same constant features of pronunciation and grammatical usage as do major languages. **1955** P. STREVENS *Papers in Lang.* (1965) ix. 120 Esperanto is, in fact, a kind of glorified Pidgin Indo-European. **1962** *Listener* 27 Sept. 467/2 Pidgin exists in India and Africa as well—but the context is very different from that of Pidgin in New Guinea. **1964** *Ibid.* 5 Mar. 388/2 At Layer Marney the old is all. The Renaissance motifs are handled awkwardly. This is trying to speak Italian without command of grammar, syntax, or vocabulary... It is the pidgin-Italian spoken by the sturdy Englishman of the Perpendicular. **1968** W. J. SAMARIN in J. A. Fishman *Readings Sociol. of Lang.* 667 In the fifteenth century there developed a pidgin Portuguese which may have originated in the first contacts with the Africans, but ultimately spread to the ports of the Far East. *Ibid.* 671 The ease with which Korean Bamboo English developed leads one to imagine the inevitability of pidgins in the world. **1968** *Economist* 14 Dec. 4/1 The Soviet graduates, to whom you refer, are as little satisfied with pidgin marxism as young opinion in the British 1930s was with Mr Neville Chamberlain. **1974** *Florida FL Reporter* XIII. 17/1 While agreeing with Nida and Fehdereau that pidgin-using and koine-forming situations are strongly analogous, I cannot agree that the 'Sabir Pidgins'..at least are special formations. **1975** *Language* LI. 684 The use of morphemes borrowed by a pidgin or creole language..from a European language often diverges widely from the use of the source morpheme in the source language. **1978** *Verbatim* Feb. 10/1 Both authors hold to..the Creolist theory, which traces the present-day Black English vernacular to a Plantation Creole, to a plantation-maritime pidgin, to an African origin.

c. Phr. (*to be*) *someone's pigeon*: to be (that person's) concern, affair, etc.

1904 KIPLING *Traffics & Discov.* 293 'What about their musketry average?' I went on. 'Not my pidgin,' said Bayley. **1919** B. RUCK *Disturbing Charm* II. x. 248 It was not Jack's pidgin to do anything until then. **1924** G. L. MALLORY *Let.* 11 May in E. F. Norton *Fight for Everest: 1924* (1925) II. 233 Geoffrey Bruce whose 'pigeon' it is to deal with the porters. **1929** C. MACKENZIE *Gallipoli Memories* xiii. 237 'Nothing known of this man here.' 'Pass to N.T.O. K beach.' 'From M.L.O. Lancashire Landing to A.P.M. K beach. This is your pigeon, I think.' **1929** J. MASEFIELD *Hawbucks* 164 This is my pidgin; none of yours at all. **1935** *Punch* 30 Jan. 136/1 'There's trouble in Paraguay,' said the man from Geneva. 'Then leave it there,' said I. 'It's not my pigeon.' **1957** 'J. WYNDHAM' *Midwich Cuckoos* iii. 26 'Not our kind of job,' he said, with the air of one recalling a useful Union decision. 'More like the fire chaps' pigeon, I'd say.' **1959** *Times* 6 Mar. 11/7 If it is the fur (not our pigeon) that makes Mr. Page furious, maybe the answer is mothballs. **1961** L. P. HARTLEY *Two for River* 45 Well, you do something, Thomas Henry, it's your pigeon. **1977** B. PYM *Quartet in Autumn* xviii. 160 Janice wondered whether anyone else had been to see Marcia... She was Janice's special pigeon, if you could put it like that.

pidginize (pi·dʒinəiz), *v.* [f. *PIDGIN b + -IZE.] To produce a simplified or pidgin form of (a language). So **pidginiza·tion**, the fact or process of pidginizing; a pidginized language; **pi·dginized** *ppl. a.*

1934 PRIEBSCH & COLLINSON *German Lang.* I. ii. 35 This 'pidginization' [in Afrikaans] is thought to be due to sudden contact with a Creolized language, in this case a blend called Malayo-Portuguese. **1937** J. R. FIRTH *Tongues of Men* vi. 80 If English were to be pidginized the simplification of pronunciation would have to be based on those differences between sounds which most men could hear..without expert tuition. **1949** [see *CREOLIZED *ppl. a.* 2]. **1956** J. LOTZ in Saporta & Bastian *Psycholinguistics* (1961) 14/1 Various attempts at an international language like Esperanto or Basic English either end up as incomplete replicas of natural languages or as primitive pidginizations. **1962** *Listener* 27 Sept. 467/1 The more pidginised the language becomes, obviously the less useful English can be as a world language. **1972** J. L. DILLARD *Black English* iii. 135 Theoretically, any language can be pidginized, although historically not all have been. **1974** L. TODD *Pidgins & Creoles* i. 5 Pidginization and creolization may have been much more prevalent in language change than linguists have hitherto acknowledged. **1977** *Language* LIII. 495/1 First he discusses borrowings from American Indian languages, particularly the pidginized forms that underwent various semantic shifts and are still current, such as *bury the hatchet* and *Great White Father.*

pi-dog, var. PYE-DOG in Dict. and Suppl.

1920 *Blackw. Mag.* Oct. 525/2 Later still at night.. would come droves of pi-dogs sweeping..through the compound. **1927** *Daily Express* 30 May 7/5 They were hounds running with a good cry, not pi-dogs barking. **1959** *Times* 12 June 14/6 A mangy pi-dog shared his humble abode. **1972** 'M. RENAULT' *Persian Boy* xxii. 287 It was so quiet, you could hear..the pi-dogs bickering. **1978** J. UPDIKE *Coup* (1979) i. 29 His woman whispered to me that he was a rascal without a tribe, who had never had so much as a pet pi-dog to his name.

pie, *sb.*[2] Add: **1. c.** (Further examples.) Also in more general allusive use, an affair, concern, etc., regarded in terms of one's possible involvement in it. Phrs. *to cut a pie* (U.S.), to become involved in a particular matter; *to put a finger into* (*another's*) *pie* (and variants)' to meddle in (someone else's) business.

1843 T. C. HALIBURTON *Attaché* 1st Ser. I. xi. 180 By gosh Aunty,..you had better not cut that pie: you will find it rather sour in the apple sarse, and tough in the paste. **1868** 'MARK TWAIN' *Let.* 6 Feb. (1920) 85 They want to send me abroad, as a Consul or a Minister. I said I didn't want any of the pie. **1871** J. O. BROOKFIELD *Influence* II. 12, I don't see what excuse she has for putting her finger into everybody's pie as she does. **1879** *London Society* Christmas Number 87/2 If you keep straight yourself you'll have quite enough to do, without putting your fingers into other folks' pies. **1921** L. STRACHEY *Queen Victoria* iii. 93 Her uncle Leopold had apparently determined..that her cousin Albert ought to be her husband. That was very like her uncle Leopold, who wanted to have a finger in every pie. **1924** A. CHRISTIE *Poirot Investigates* i. 19 What I do now is for my own satisfaction—the satisfaction of Hercule Poirot! Decidedly, I must have a finger in this pie. **1940** N. MITFORD *Pigeon Pie* iii. 57 Aristocrats are inclined to prefer Nazis while Jews prefer Bolshies. An old bourgeois like yourself ..should keep your fingers out of both their pies. **1970** G. JACKSON *Let.* 17 Apr. in *Soledad Brother* (1971) 224 We don't want their culture. We *don't* want a piece of that pie. **1979** *Homes & Gardens* June 90/2 One of the many pies he keeps a finger in is the Color Association of the USA.

d. Assets, proceeds, wealth, etc., considered as something to be apportioned or shared out (cf. *CAKE *sb.* 7 b).

1967 *Boston Sunday Herald* 7 May III. 14/4 The result of an Appellate Court victory..which cut Weymouth's total property valuation by $40 million to give the town a bigger slice of the sales tax pie. **1971** *Ink* 12 June 7/4 The thousands of workers..are searching for ways to fight not only for a bigger portion of the capitalist pie but for a freer and more dignified life. **1978** *Washington Post* 29 July D30/2 Although more than 50 million watches will be sold in the United States this year, there is no consensus on what piece of the pie digitals will get.

2. (Earlier and later examples of *bran-pie.*)

1877 *Cassell's Family Mag.* May 377/1 In the last division of the tent we had..a bran-pie... The bran-pie was an oblong washing-tub..filled with bran, in which were hidden..small articles. **1889** *Peel City Guardian* 28 Dec. 7/4 Sometimes what is termed a 'bran pie' is employed..for storing the presents in. **1902** *Little Folks* Jan. 54/2 Every single thing was bought, including the packets in the bran-pie. **1916** *Daily Colonist* (Victoria, B.C.) 4 July 4/4 All sorts of seasonable refreshments will be served and the blue ribbon girls will have an attraction in the form of a bran pie. **1931** V. WOOLF *Waves* 236, I think more disinterestedly that I could when I was young and must dig furiously like a child rummaging in a bran-pie to discover myself.

3. b. *Austral.* (See quot. 1960[1].)

1960 *Times Rev. Industry* Jan. 103/1 A pie is a combination of wool buyers who do not bid against one another at wool sales, then divide the wool purchased by members of the group. **1960** *Sydney Morning Herald* 25 Mar. 7 He said he had known since 1945 that 'pies' were operating. **1966** BAKER *Austral. Lang.* (ed. 2) iii. 58 The Australian public became aware in 1958 that wool-buying was not always a straightforward operation... Some buyers were combining into *pies* (also called *rings*) to bid and then share purchases, so that competition was reduced.

4. a. (Earlier and later examples.) Also used in comparative phrases: (*as*) *good* (*nice, sweet,* etc.) *as pie.*

1857 'DOW JR.' *Dow's Patent Sermons* 1st Ser. 21 Let her alone and in five minutes the storm will be over, and she as good as pie again. **1884** 'MARK TWAIN' *Huck. Finn* ii. 15 You're always as polite as pie to them. *Ibid.* v. 34 So he took him to his own house, and dressed him up clean and nice,..and was just old pie to him, so to speak. **1887** R. T. COOKE *Happy Dodd* xvii. 178 We've been awful good; good as pie, hain't we? **1888** W. F. CODY *Story of Wild West* 531, I wanted to reach Fort Larned before daylight, in order to avoid if possible the Indians, to whom it would have been 'pie' to have caught me there on foot. **1891** *Harper's Mag.* Sept. 579/1 Ain't he as polite as pie to her? **1922** JOYCE *Ulysses* 309 See him of a Sunday with his little concubine of a wife, and she wagging her tail up the aisle of the chapel,..nice as pie, doing the little lady. **1933** E. O'NEILL *Ah, Wilderness!* IV. iii. 151, I ran into him upstreet this afternoon and he was meek as pie. **1939** J. STEINBECK *Grapes of Wrath* vi. 65 Well, the guy that come aroun' talked nice as pie. **1952** M. LASKI *Village* vi. 109 She was as sweet as pie, said she was awfully sorry. **1958** *Listener* 11 Sept. 388/3 When foreign dignitaries come from all corners of the world to pay their respects to me..I am as nice as pie. **1974** P. DE VRIES *Glory of Hummingbird* (1975) xviii. 265 People were wonderful, nice as pie, glad to see me fallen. **1978** F. WELDON *Praxis* xxiv. 256 She's very stubborn. Sweet as pie just so long as she's doing exactly what she wants.

b. Political favour or patronage. *U.S. slang.*

1910 *Richmond* (Virginia) *Weekly Times-Dispatch* 17 Aug. 10 Representative Slemp was looked upon as the dispenser of the patronage in Virginia because of the promise of the President that he would allow the pie to be handed out by the men who did the fighting. **1916** *N.Y. Times* 12 May 10/4 Take your tribute, but buy national defense with it, don't waste it in 'pork' and 'pie' and Populist lunacies!

c. Something easily accomplished or dealt with, a 'cinch'; *spec.* in phr. *easy* (*simple,* etc.) *as pie. slang* (orig. *U.S.*). Cf. *PIE IN THE SKY.

In some uses not clearly distinguishable from sense 4 a (in Dict. and Suppl.).

1889 *Outing* Nov. 151/2, I thought it would just be pie for me to buy him, and take him through the 'bushes'... (The 'bushes', you know, means the country fairs.) **1905** N. DAVIS *Northerner* 93 It will be just—what was it you said—pie?—pie for them, won't it. **1919** WODEHOUSE *Coming of Bill* (1920) I. v. 54 This Kid Mitchell was looked on as a coming champ in those days... I guess I looked pie to him. **1923** E. WALLACE *Missing Million* xx. 161 Murder was cream pie to Tod. **1925** WODEHOUSE *Sam the Sudden* xix. 156 'How do you propose to make your entry?'..'Easy as pie. Odd-job man... They always want odd-job men.' **1937** D. L. SAYERS *Busman's Honeymoon* xii. 210 He's knocked out... Simple as pie. No cutting or stealing keys or hiding blunt instruments or telling lies. **1948** J. B. PRIESTLEY *Linden Tree* I. 39 It's as simple as pie. **1959** C. BUSH *Case of Careless Thief* vii. 87 It's in the bag... Everything we wanted and easy as pie. **1967** G. F. FIENNES *I tried to run a Railway* iii. 26 In the current work York was pie compared with Cambridge. **1972** WODEHOUSE *Pearls, Girls & Monty Bodkin* iv. 53 Interesting Llewellyn in Silver River would be pie, but I'd also have to interest her, and she's not the right woman for that.

5. *pie-fork, -knife, -plate* (earlier and later examples), *shell*; **pie-biter,** (*a*) *U.S.*, one who has a fondness for pies; *fig.* (in sense *4 b), one who takes part in political patronage; (*b*) *Austral. slang*, = **pie-eater* (b); **pie-card** *U.S. slang*, (*a*) a meal ticket; one who begs for a meal; (*b*) a union-card; the holder of a union-card; also *attrib.*; **pie-cart** *N.Z.* (see quot. 1922); **pie chart** = **pie diagram*; **pie-counter** *U.S.*, a counter at which pies are sold; *fig.*, a source of grants or favours (see sense *4 b); **pie diagram,** a circle divided by radii into sectors whose areas are proportional to the relative magnitudes or frequencies of a set of items; **pie-eater,** (*a*) someone who eats pies; (*b*) *Austral. slang*, someone of no importance, a 'small-timer'; also, a fool or simpleton; so *pie-eating* ppl. a.; **pie-funnel,** a support for a pie-crust during cooking; **pie-melon,** †(*a*) *U.S.*, a melon used for pies (*obs.*); (*b*) *Austral.*, a variety of watermelon, *Citrullus lanatus*; **pie-plant** (earlier and later examples); also *attrib.*; **pie-wagon** *U.S. slang* (see quot. 1960).

1868 *Daily Territorial Enterprise* (Virginia City, Nevada) 2 Apr. 3/1 Through these same [April fool] doughnuts many a lunch-eater and pie-biter came to grief. **1902** O. WISTER *Virginian* ix. 104 He held out to his pony a slice of bread matted with sardines, which the pony expertly accepted. 'You're a plumb pie-biter, you Monte,' he continued. **1908** in W. R. Hunt *North of 53°* (1974) xxvi. 225 Persons interested in other points, and paid knockers and piebiters may pound and hammer until their auditors are deafened. **1911** E. DYSON *Benno* 144 He was that angry with the South pie-biters, he didn't care what 'appened to 'em. **1938** K. DOUTHITT *Romance & Dim Trails* 106 [He was] better known over the northwest and in camp life as Pie Biter, because he was very fond of pie. **1909** W. G. DAVENPORT *Butte & Montana beneath X-Ray* 56 Say, on the dead level, Andy, couldn't you let me have a lonely ten spot?..Say, Andy, you've just got to jar loose with five bucks for my pie card is so full of holes it looks like a piece of mosquito bar. **1929** *Amer. Speech* IV. 343 *Pie card*, a union card used to obtain food or lodging. **1931** 'D. STIFF' *Milk & Honey Route* 211 *Pie card*, one who hangs around and lives on a remittance man or some other person with money. **1945** *Seafarers' Log* 25 May 2/1 The Commie stooges and pie-cards kick us around. **1948** MENCKEN *Amer. Lang.* Suppl. II. 678 *Pie-card*, a union card used as a credential in begging. **1960** *New Left Rev.* 26 Sept. 41/1 The retired.. comfortably fixed pie-card artists of every lost..cause of the labour and radical movements. **1973** C. RUBIN *Log* 64 All of them phony, pie-card officials who sit on their big fat asses and twiddle their thumbs. **1922** C. G. TURNER *Happy Wanderer* 37 We drifted down..to the pie-cart (coffee-stall, in your speech). **1949** D. M. DAVIN *Roads from Home* 70 Somebody having a feed at the pie-cart. **1954** *Numbers* Nov. 23 A poky..kind of joint, just one degree better than a pie-cart. **1963** *Weekly News* (Auckland) 5 June 37/2 The Mussons..were many years in the piecart business in Christchurch. **1973** A. HOLDEN *Girl on Beach* 160 We went down town to the all-night pie-cart and bought masses of pies and chips..and drove up to the top of Mount Victoria. **1922** A. C. HASKELL *Graphic Charts in Business* xiv. 75 Because the circle, divided..into sections, resembles a pie which has been cut in the usual manner, the Circular Percentage Chart is sometimes referred to as the 'pie chart'. **1972** Pie chart [see *line graph* s.v. *LINE *sb.*[2] 32]. **1977** *Lancet* 17 Dec. 1264/2 There is neither graph nor histogram nor pie chart to help the reader. **1903** *N.Y. Times* 16 Dec. 3 When his constituents asked him why he could not secure more routes [for free postal delivery] the only reply he could make was that he could not get up to the pie counter. **1912** M. NICHOLSON *Hoosier Chron.* 470 I'm in the ranks of the patriots and not looking for the pie counter. **1921** H. SECRIST *Statistics in Business* v. 65 Pie-diagram showing the distribution of the total stock of hams, bacon and shoulders, reported August 31, 1917. **1954** *Brit. Jrnl. Psychol.* XLV. 149 The book is..well produced with numerous pie-diagrams, bar diagrams and other pictographic devices. **1979** *Jrnl. R. Soc. Arts* July 493/2 Whether they be dancers, writers, poets, actresses, painters or musicians they are largely unproductive of material which can be categorized, computed, stored, programmed, evaluated or turned into pie diagrams. **1904** Pie-eater [in Dict.]. **1953** BAKER *Australia Speaks* 134 *Pie-eater*.., a small-time crook. **1953** K. TENNANT *Joyful Condemned* xviii. 166 He's one of those big he-men that go sneaking around the park waiting to snitch some chromo's handbag. Just a pie-eater. **1966** *Sunday Tel.* (Sydney) 22 May 25/2 The Australian appetite for pies has even added to our slang with the term 'pie eater'. Once meaning a small time crook, it is now used as a derogatory expression, close in meaning to 'a dill'. **1975** *Sun* (Sydney) 10 Jan. 52/7 A bunch of pie-eaters. Excuse me if I find an expression from my old mate, the late Siddie Barnes, but that's what the English team has turned out to be. **1949** L. GLASSOP *Lucky Palmer* 96 The trouble is, Mr. Hughes, you're too good for the pie-eating bookmakers round these parts. You bet too well for them, Mr. Hughes. **1887** C. B. GEORGE *40 Yrs. on Rail* ix. 187 An exquisite set of pie forks, of English make, and valued at seventy-five dollars. **1910–11** *Junior Army & Navy Stores Catal.* 1304 Pie funnel. **1926** S. E. NASH *Cooking Craft* xx. 186 Pile [meat] up in the centre to support the pastry, if there is not sufficient meat use an egg cup or pie funnel. **1960** *Woman* 23 Apr. 3/3 Use an empty salt cellar... It works as well as a proper pie funnel. **1875** MRS. STOWE *We & our Neighbors* liii. 474 Of course the reader knows that there were the usual amount of berry-spoons, and pie-knives, and crumb-scrapers. **1860** *Trans. Mich. Agric. Soc. 1859* X. 623 Best pie melon, H. J. Young..$0.50. **1882** W. D. HAY *Brighter Britain!* I. vii. 223 We grow large quantities of melons—..rock-melons, Spanish melons, pie-melons and so on. **1945** [see *CHOKO]. **1965** *Austral. Encycl.* III. 140/1 Some introduced cucurbits have become troublesome weeds, notably the..pie melon (*Citrullus vulgaris*); colocynth.. and squirting cucumber. **1978** J. A. MICHENER *Chesapeake* 833 A pie-melon was a kind of gourd raised along the edges of cornfields, and..it produced one of the world's great pies. **1838** *Youth's Mag.* (N.Y.) July 91 Half a dozen roots of the pie-plant (rhubarb) will furnish abundant materials for pies and tarts. **1884** E. W. NYE *Baled Hay* 207 Afterward pulverize and spread over the pie plant bed. **1894** *Harper's Mag.* May 931/2 There is one old soul who especially loves rhubarb pies,..and it is she who remembers me and my row of pie-plant. **1952** J. STEINBECK *East of Eden* xvii. 159 He..chatted about the pieplant roots. **1976** *Hortus Third* (L. H. Bailey Hortorium) 967/2 Rhubarb is a strong, hardy, Old World perennial grown for the thick leaf stalks, which are cooked fresh in early spring for their agreeable acid flavor. It is also known as pie plant. **1598** FLORIO *Worlde of Wordes* 394/2 *Statccia* [sic], a cake, a tarte. Also any flat thing or pye plate. **1653** R. VERNEY *Let.* May in M. M. Verney *Mem.* (1894) III. iv. 113, I presume there are dishes, pyplates, candlesticks. **1895** *Montgomery Ward & Co. Catal.* Spring & Summer 431/3, Agate iron pie plates. **1948** *Good Housek. Cookery Bk.* 410 Place the round of pastry neatly and evenly on a flat pie plate. **1978** E. TIDYMAN *Table Stakes* II. iii. 187 A broad Irish face as open as a pie plate. **1935** *Motion Picture* Nov. 79/2 Pour into baked pie shell. **1976** TURGEON & BIRMINGHAM *All Amer. Cookbk.* (1977) 206/2 Put the pie shell in the refrigerator while rolling out the top crust. **1898** Pie-wagon [see *moving-van* s.v. *MOVING *vbl. sb.* 5]. **1904** 'No. 1500' *Life in Sing Sing* 257/1 *Pie wagon*, patrol wagon. **1960** WENTWORTH & FLEXNER *Dict. Amer. Slang* 388/2 *Pie wagon*, a police truck used to transport arrested persons to jail; a Black Maria.

pie, *a.*[1] Delete *Obs. rare*[-1] and add later examples.

In occasional use as a variant of PI *a.* in Dict. and Suppl. **1932** C. S. LEWIS in *Essays & Stud.* XVII. 71 She is an admirable person. The only trouble is that she is rather *pie*. **1957** M. A. JEEVES *St. Thomas Becket* i. 13 Some of the more lugubrious sects' offsprings from the Reformation are also responsible for the eulogizing of 'pie' types of people.

pie (pəi), *a.*[2] *N.Z. slang.* [ad. Maori *pai* good.] (See quots.) Cf. *HALF-PIE *a.*

1941 BAKER *N.Z.Slang* vi. 56 *To be pie at* (or *on*), to be expert or efficient at something, is another phrase of wide use in this country. It has been derived from the Maori *pai*, good. **1943** *Amer. Speech* XVIII. 93 'To be pie on' (= to be very good at) seems to be derived from the Maori *pai ana*.

piece, *sb.* Add: **I. 1. a.** *spec.* One of the irregular sections of a jig-saw puzzle. Freq. *fig.*

1911 *Encycl. Brit.* XXII. 675/1 The commonest of all puzzles are coloured maps, pictures ('jig-saw') or designs, dissected into numerous variously shaped pieces, to be fitted together to form the complete design. **1925** E. WALLACE *Fellowship of Frog* xix. 144 She's only another little bit of the jigsaw puzzle that will fall into place when we fix the piece that's shaped like a Frog. **1935,** etc. [see *JIG-SAW *sb.* b]. **1935** W. G. HARDY *Father Abraham* 140 Quite suddenly the pieces seemed to fit together. **1955** H. KURNITZ *Invasion of Privacy* (1956) ix. 67 Mr. Fenn think[s] that there might be something about this case he doesn't understand, a missing piece somewhere. It spoils the picture for him. **1963** A. HERON *Towards Quaker View of Sex* i. 5 The study of homosexuality and its moral problems could not be divorced from a survey of the whole field of sexual activity: a few pieces of the jigsaw-puzzle could not be identified without the whole picture. **1973** G. SCOTT *Water Horse* (1974) xxii. 152 If Oliver were really involved in this organization, then certain jigsaw pieces could fall more satisfactorily into place. **1977** P. COSGRAVE *Cheyney's Law* vii. 65 He had a name... If pieces were not exactly falling into place, there was at least movement.

c. (Further examples.)

1667 PEPYS *Diary* 29 Aug. (1974) VIII. 406 The Court is at this day all to pieces, every man of a faction of one sort or another. **1700** CONGREVE *Way of World* I. 6 She once us'd me with that Insolence, that in Revenge I took her to pieces. **1892** 'MARK TWAIN' *Amer. Claimant* xvii. 173 The hackman will just go all to pieces when he sees that. **1923** H. CRANE *Let.* 21 July (1965) 140 The center of such pain as would tear me to pieces to tell you about. **1925** W. S. MAUGHAM *Painted Veil* xiv. 47 When he has bad cards he goes all to pieces. **1933** J. HILTON *Lost Horizon* ix. 196 You were so damned good in that Baskul affair that I can hardly believe you're the same man. You seem to have gone all to pieces. **1957** A. MACNAB *Bulls of Iberia* ii. 26 Once a grand herd under the old Duke, now gone all to pieces. **1976** *Daily Record* (Glasgow) 22 Nov. 27/1 How can a team perform so well, score a goal, then go to pieces?

d. *all to pieces*: completely, through and through, from beginning to end. *dial.* and *U.S.*

1839 C. F. BRIGGS *Adventures H. Franco* I. iv. 27 'Do you know the name of that individual who helped you to steak?' 'I know him all to pieces,' replied the gentleman. **1840** C. F. HOFFMAN *Greyslaer* I. I. x. 114, I know the ground here all to pieces. **1892** W. G. LYTTLE in *Eng. Dial. Dict.* (1903) IV. 491/2 She wud a pleesed ye a' tae pieces, an' wud a been charmed tae a haen a minister fur a son-in-law. **1925** *Dialect Notes* V. 325, I knows un all to pieces.

e. *to fall to pieces* (fig.): to give birth to a child. *dial.* and *Austral. slang.*

1881 S. EVANS *Evans's Leicestershire Words* (new ed.) 212 Anybody can say what's the matter wi' yew wi' 'af a oy. Ye'r a-gooin' to fall to paces. **1941** BAKER *Dict. Austral. Slang* 28 *Fall to pieces*,..to undergo confinement, to give birth to a child.

f. *to pick up the pieces*: see *PICK *v.*[1] 20 g.

2. d. (Further examples.)

1838 DICKENS *Let.* 25 Oct. (1965) I. 445 Kate boasts.. of having told you 'a piece of her mind'. **1914** W. OWEN *Let.* 24 May (1967) 256 Now it is Wednes. and I have had with delight your news. I shall hope to have an important piece of your mind on Sunday. **1930** G. B. SHAW *Apple Cart* I. 5 He is coming here today to give the King a piece of his mind..about the crisis. **1946** E. S. GARDNER *Case of Borrowed Brunette* (1951) ii. 21 He said I could wear what I had on, no matter where I went. And I certainly gave him a piece of my mind about that. **1956** E. WILSON (*title*) A piece of my mind: reflections at sixty. **1979** D. SANDERS *Queen sends for Mrs. Chadwick* 14 I'm going to give a few people a piece of my mind.

3. d. *piece of goods* (further example); *piece of ass, tail*, etc. (U.S. coarse slang), a person, esp. a woman, regarded as an object of sexual gratification; hence, sexual intercourse; also *ellipt.* as *piece*.

1922 JOYCE *Ulysses* 66 A wild piece of goods. Her slim legs running up the staircase. **1942** BERREY & VAN DEN BARK *Amer. Thes. Slang* § 362/1 *Copulation*,..piece, piece *or* hunk of tail, -skirt, -ass *or* butt. **1950** 'D. DIVINE' *King of Fassarai* xxviii. 252 Them guys from the merchant ships will do anything for a piece of tail. **1953** T. MORRISON *Stones of House* v. iii. 243 You couldn't put up a memorial to a boy whose younger brother had just given the family and the college a bad name, not even sneaking off to a house somewhere if he wanted a piece. **1957** G. GREENE *Quiet American* (new ed.) I. iii. 28 Get me another drink. And then let's go and find a girl. You've got a piece of tail. I want a piece of tail too. **1968** E. LOVELACE *Schoolmaster* xii. 191 Boy, go and getta pieca ass, then go in your bed. **1972** G. V. HIGGINS *Friends E. Coyle* xix. 119 Him and four buddies want a little dough to get a high class piece of tail. **1972** *Screw* 12 June 21/2 Several revolutionary leaders and a host of government figures all stop by for a piece of ass. **1974** H. L. FOSTER *Ribbin'* v. 208 He said he fucked your baby sister and poked your baby niece And when he sees your little brother he's going to ask him for a piece. **1978** J. KRANTZ *Scruples* ii. 21 He..thought she was a flaming, fabulous piece of ass.

f. With *of.* A share in; a financial interest in (a business, project, etc.); freq. in phr. *a piece of the action.* (*U.S. slang.*)

1929 *Theatre Mag.* June 33/3 *Piece*, share. As 'A piece of the show', a financial share in the production. **1930** *Amer. Mercury* Dec. 457/1 He muscles in for a piece of the cleaners' racket. **1940** J. O'HARA *Pal Joey* 66 He owns a piece of the room [*sc.* nightclub] where I sing in. **1950** *Democrat & Chron.* (Rochester, N.Y.) 13 Jan. 22/1 Offered to let me buy a small piece of 'As You Like It'. **1972** 'E. LATHEN' *Murder without Icing* ii. 18 'I've had a piece of the Huskies for a long time now.'..'I figure your interest is worth twice what you paid.' *Ibid.* 21 What's it got to do with her if you sell your piece of action? **1973** C. ALVERSON *Fighting Back* (1978) i. 2 This is a very pretty little bar you've got here... I want a piece of it. I think you could use a partner. **1976** C. FRICK in *6,000 Words* 156 They were..managers and agents and producers and all the others that had a piece of the action. **1978** R. LEWIS *Uncertain Sound* iii. 78 Manson would be wanting a 'piece of the action'.

g. *a piece of cake*: see *CAKE *sb.* 7 c.

6. b. A member of an orchestra or band. In isolation usu. pl. Freq. (sing.) with prefixed numeral forming an attrib. phrase (see sense *24 b); also *absol.*

1912 J. WEBSTER in *Ladies' Home Jrnl.* May 70/2 We had..a band consisting of fourteen pieces (three mouth organs and eleven combs). **1922** S. LEWIS *Babbitt* xii. 156 Their favorite motion-picture theater..had an orchestra of fifty pieces. **1925** F. SCOTT FITZGERALD *Great Gatsby* (1926) iii. 48 The orchestra has arrived, no thin five-piece affair, but a whole pitful of oboes and trombones and saxophones. **1938** *Melody Maker* 27 Aug. 11/4 Billy will use his 14-piece stage band. **1959** P. CAPON *Amongst those Missing* 221 It was like shouting against a ninety-piece orchestra. **1965** *New Yorker* 2 Jan. 40/1 The only band we had trouble with..was the Savoy Sultans, the house group at the Savoy Ballroom in Harlem. They only had eight pieces, but they could swing you into bad health. **1966** *Crescendo* Apr. 12/1 A Saturday night last August. A ten-piece required a little way out of town. **1975** *New Yorker* 21 Apr. 7/3 On Monday: Dave Matthews' twelve-piece band, made up of studio musicians.

7. *piece of work*: **c.** Applied, usu. contemptuously, to a person.

1928, etc. [see *NASTY *a.* 7]. **1936** 'N. BLAKE' *Thou Shell of Death* vii. 122 She..had been Fergus's mistress. She *is* a pretty grand piece of work. **1965** A. NICOL *Truly Married Woman* 109 Jolson..looking at Newi's heavy square mahogany face..thought what an obstinate and unpleasant piece of work the fellow was.

II. 9. Restrict *arch.* and *dial.* to sense a.

a. (Later example.)

1918 L. STRACHEY *Eminent Victorians* 63, I hate that man, he is such a forward piece.

b. (Further examples.)

Now mostly of a woman or girl regarded as a sexual object.

1846 *Swell's Night Guide* 86 She is a charming piece. **1854** M. J. HOLMES *Tempest & Sunshine* iv. 57 Dr. Lacey laughed heartily at this speech and called her an 'original little piece'. **1873** J. MILLER *Life amongst Modocs* xv. 194 Rather a good-looking piece you got here now, ain't she? **1908** Z. GALE *Friendship Village* 251 [When] Zorah had took sick..this little piece here had up an' offered [to dance in the carnival]. **1939** W. FAULKNER *Wild Palms* 334 'Woman. It was a fellow's wife.' 'You mean you had been toting one piece up and down the country day and night for over a month and now..you got to get in trouble over another one?' **1946** K. TENNANT *Lost Haven* (1947) x. 160 You speak to him, Alec... Gallivanting around with that peroxided piece. **1966** K. AMIS *Anti-Death League* 329 Those two pieces in leather who served you your coffee. **1972** F. VAN W. MASON *Roads to Liberty* 18 Katie wouldn't be a bad-looking piece..if she'd half take care of her appearance. **1978** I. B. SINGER *Shosha* xiii. 232 He was allegedly going to divorce his wife, who was a common piece.

11. b. Now chiefly *U.S. slang.* (Further examples.)

1930 *Amer. Speech* V. 392 *Piece*, a firearm of any kind, including a pistol. **1956** 'E. MCBAIN' *Cop Hater* (1958) x. 91 In this neighbourhood, you don't carry a knife or a piece, you're dead. **1970** L. SANDERS *Anderson Tapes* xxxi. 82 You're a good shot... But you've never carried a piece on a job... If this campaign goes through, you'll have to pack a piece. **1973** *Black World* July 55/2, I slid the piece from under my shirt. **1976** *Times Lit. Suppl.* 6 Aug. 998/2 A high-class, good burglar..who has never carried a piece in his life.

14. a. (Further examples.)

1897 KIPLING *Capt. Cour.* viii. 165 We'll fish a piece till the thing lifts. **1937** G. HEYER *They found him Dead* iv. 68, I wouldn't run the risk of bumping off an old man who had a valvular disease of the heart. Guess I'd wait a piece for Nature to do its work.

c. Also in occas. wider use. (Further examples.)

1873 E. B. TUTTLE *Boy's Bk. Indians* 134 Major Gordon descended the ridge..and carrying the body of Stambaugh a piece, hid it away in some bushes. **1908** L. M. MONTGOMERY *Anne of Green Gables* ii. 18 We've got to drive a long piece, haven't we? Mrs. Spencer said it was eight miles. **1931** *Amer. Speech* VII. 20 *Piece*, a short walk. 'I will go a piece with you.' **1940** BRYANT & AIKEN *Psychol. of Eng.* 84 Come and walk a piece with me. **1956** B. HOLIDAY *Lady sings Blues* (1973) x. 98, I thought we were stranded until I saw a car down the road a piece. **1971** *Sunday Express* (Johannesburg) 28 Mar. (Homefinder section) 3/3 (Advt.), Fabulous fishing, Superb surfing. Nearby golf courses, Not forgetting swinging Margate..just up the road a piece. **1978** G. MITCHELL *Wraiths & Changelings* i. 11 He's in a bad way..on the floor of my cottage. It's just a piece down the road.

15. b. Also used sporadically elsewhere. (Further examples.)

1834 *Chambers's Edin. Jrnl.* III. 254/2 Receiving each a piece and jelly on 't from granny, because they were guid bairns. **1878** C. HALLOCK *Sportsman's Gazetteer* (ed. 4) 696 *Piece*, a lunch, a snack (Pennsylvania). **1911** E. M. CLOWES *On Wallaby* vi. 164 The children..wander..in and out of the kitchen, with incessant demands for what is known as 'a piece'—a liberal slice of bread, butter, and jam. **1949** 'J. TEY' *Brat Farrar* xix. 175 Saturday afternoon was a holiday for the Ashby children and they were accustomed..to take a 'piece' with them and pursue their various interests in the countryside until it was time to come home to their evening meal. **1962** M. DUFFY *That's how it Was* x. 85 'Gi's a piece, our mam,' and they would run off with a doorstep of bread and jam. **1973** 'J. PATRICK' *Glasgow Gang Observed* 234 *Piece*, sandwich. **1978** *Jrnl. Lancs. Dial. Soc.* Jan. 15/2 [Edinburgh] *Piece*, sandwich. E.g. *jeely piece* (one containing cheap jam).

h. pl. *pieces.* The oddments of wool which are detached from the skirtings of a fleece; also, the skirtings themselves. Chiefly *Austral.* and *N.Z.*

1881 A. BATHGATE *Waitaruna* 173 The 'pickers up' were..carrying [the fleeces] to the sorting table, where they were stripped of the 'pieces', which were thrown aside. **1891** R. WALLACE *Rural Econ. Austral. & N.Z.* xxix. 384 The washing of wool, either before or after shearing, is, with the exception of locks and pieces, which are generally scoured, almost entirely given up. **1951** [see *fleece-wool* s.v. *FLEECE *sb.* 6]. **1965** [see *piece picker*, sense *23]. **1971** J. S. GUNN *Distrib. Shearing Terms N.S.W.* 20 The south was the only area where..there was a preference for *pieces* rather than *skirtings*.

i. A quantity of a drug (esp. morphine or heroin) approximately equal to one ounce. *U.S. slang.*

1935 A. J. POLLOCK *Underworld Speaks* 2/2 *Piece, a*, an ounce of morphine, cocaine or heroin. **1945** W. J. SPILLARD *Needle in Haystack* viii. 77 'I hava da pieces—pure stuff.' Pieces was an underworld term for ounces. **1963** *U.S. Supreme Court Reports* 371 U.S. 474 Johnny kept about a piece of heroin [*Note*] A 'piece' is approximately one ounce. **1965** *Reader's Digest* June 228 He buys heroin in 'pieces' (ounces) cuts it, and bags it.

16. *spec.* In the N. Amer. fur trade, a package of goods or furs weighing about ninety pounds. *Hist.*

The exact weight of the pound referred to is not certain.

1774 [see *PACK *sb.*[1] 2]. **1809** A. HENRY *Trav. & Adventures Canada* II. ii. 15 The freight of a canoe.. consists in sixty *pieces*, or packages, of merchandize, of the weight of from ninety to a hundred pounds each. **1836** G. BACK *Narr. Arctic Land Expedition* i. 32 Every package had been reduced or augmented to a 'piece' of 90 lbs. weight. **1931** G. L. NUTE *Voyageur* 38 Each package, or piece, was made up to weigh ninety pounds, and two ears were left at the top by which the voyageur could lift it easily in the manner of a modern flour bag. **1949** *World-Herald* (Omaha) 19 June III. 5/2 In the north, 80 pounds is considered a 'piece'... In the days of the early fur traders that was considered a proper load of skins for a man. **1972** T. MCHUGH *Time of Buffalo* viii. 89 A single sack, weighing about ninety pounds, was known as a 'piece' of pemmican, and made a convenient parcel for back-packing or portaging.

17. Delete '*Obs.* in general sense' and add later examples.

1904 H. JAMES *Golden Bowl* I. vii. 141 Representative precious objects, great ancient pictures..fine eminent 'pieces' in gold, in silver..had for a number of years.. multiplied themselves round him. **1976** *National Observer* (U.S.) 6 Nov., 'Orders are pouring in like gangbusters,' says Bob Koppang, a Hopkins, Minn., novelty dealer. 'Last week alone we sold nearly 29,000 pieces.' **1978** I. MURDOCH *Sea* 31 The big oval mirror in the hall ..is perhaps the best 'piece' in the house. **1979** *Country Life* 12 Apr. 1142/1 Special-occasion pieces..help these self-supporting artists. . A piece of jewellery by a contemporary artist is a wonderfully exciting thing to own.

c. Delete † *Obs.* and add later examples.

1950 D. GASCOYNE *Vagrant* 13 A hand-high Rodin piece. **1961** C. P. FITZGERALD in *Webster* s.v., Images of the Buddha are made to certain conventional patterns and there is often great difficulty in determining the origin of any piece on stylistic grounds. **1979** *Country Life* 12 Apr. 1142/1 Sculptor Peter Lyon['s] pendant.. is very reminiscent of his full-scale work..for example ..a piece in the central gardens of Park Town, Oxford.

d. Also, an article for a newspaper, journal, or other publication.

1936 D. POWELL *Turn, Magic Wheel* I. 36 That..fellow who was always after him to write a 'piece' for the weekly he ran. **1961** *Noble Savage* Oct. 10 A period in which he ..had a small piece in *Partisan Review*. **1974** 'D. CRAIG' *Dead Liberty* xxi. 124 Dravier worked on two features for the paper,..a piece about price stability in East Germany..and..a Youth article. **1976** *Gramophone* June 32/3 In the same month came Beethoven's Symphony No. 9 on seventeen sides, to which WRA [*sc.* the reviewer] devoted a page and a half..; one of WRA's most perceptive pieces.

g. A short discourse; a passage for recitation (*dial.* and *U.S.*). Also colloq. phr. *to say* (or *speak*) *one's piece*: to express one's opinion or judgement on a subject or question; to have one's say.

1845 C. M. KIRKLAND *Western Clearings* 158 Some of the best speakers mount the platform, and 'speak a piece'. **1865** C. F. BROWNE *A. Ward: his Travels* II. i. 128, I have spoken my piece about the Ariel. **1879** *Congress. Rec.* 16 May 1380/2, I expect to read tomorrow [in the papers] that I spoke a piece, that is the way they print it sometimes, in favor of slavery. **1882** NODAL & MILNER *Gloss. Lancs. Dial.* 212 We're gooin' a-sayin' pieces at schoo'. **1886** R. HOLLAND *Gloss. Words County of Chester* 258 In the country schools when children recite poetry it is always called 'saying their pieces'. **1890** *Harper's Mag.* Dec. 139/2 Don't you want to hear me speak my piece? **1895** 'ROSEMARY' *Under Chilterns* 83 All the 'pieces' that the children learnt to repeat at school they taught to her. **1896** *Leeds Mercury Suppl.* 26 May, Ahr Louisa wor allus a gooid un at sayin pieces. Hes ta le'nt that piece yut? **1902** MRS. G. M. MARTIN *Emmy Lou* 115 Emmy Lou had to learn a piece for Friday. It was poetry, but you called it a piece. **1941** U. ORANGE *Tom Tiddler's Ground* vi. 117 Lady Cameron was simply furious with me after that concert-party episode, when I just flatly refused to say my piece. **1942** [see *DRIFT *v.* 1 c]. **1949** *North Dakota Hist.* Jan. 23 He didn't like recitations, and would rather hunt rabbits than speak pieces. **1949** G. B. SHAW *Buoyant Billions* IV. 54 Dick, I will say that you are wonderful when you speak your piece, though I never understand a word. **1973** J. PORTER *It's Murder with Dover* xi. 115 'You didn't speak to Marsh again?' 'No. I'd said my piece.' **1976** A. MILLER *Inside Outside* xi. 181 A structured or unstructured group where all were free to say their piece.

III. 19. Also *on piece.*

1903 [see *LINOTYPE]. **1911** *Rep. Labour & Social Conditions in Germany* (Tariff Reform League) III. 96 Those on 'piece' earn from 49s. to 58s. 9d. per week. All the men are on 'piece', and work 53 hours per week.

20. Also *fig.*, whole, without injury or loss.

1929 D. HAMMETT *Dain Curse* (1930) xiii. 141, I returned to the ravine..reaching the bottom all in one piece with nothing more serious the matter with me than torn fingers. **1968** W. GARNER *Deep, Deep Freeze* xxxi. 256 My orders are just to get him to London in one piece. After that, he's someone else's worry. **1973** 'D. JORDAN' *Nile Green* vi. 29, I thought I'd come and see you through Customs in one piece. **1976** P. & W. PROCTOR *Women in Pulpit* v. 88 When I arrived at a church, I was glad to be there in one piece, and the people were just as glad to see me.

21. (Earlier and later examples.) Also *all-of-a-piece* attrib. phr.; hence *all-of-a-pieceness.*

1612 CHAPMAN *Widow's Tears* sig. I, O happy starres. And now pardon, Ladie; me thinks these [kisses] are all of a peece. **1912** GALSWORTHY *Sheaf* (1916) 21 Odd how all of a piece taste is! **1914** G. B. SHAW *Misalliance* 71 It's all of a piece here. The men effeminate, the women unsexed. **1924** GALSWORTHY *Forest* II. i. 35 An expedition like this has to be all of a piece, in the leader's hand. **1938** W. S. MAUGHAN *Summing Up* xvii. 58, I think what has chiefly struck me in human beings is their lack of consistency. I have never seen people all of a piece. **1956** A. WILSON *Anglo-Saxon Att.* II. ii. 318 Goodness isn't all of a piece..any more than badness. **1958** *New Statesman* 20 Dec. 881/1 What is remarkable about this remarkable musical is its all-of-a-pieceness. **1960** *Times* 1 Nov. 16/1 He is a convincing all-of-a-piece characterization. **1962** *Times* 6 Apr. 20/1 A corresponding all-of-a-piece protein.

b. (Later examples.)

1916 GALSWORTHY *Caravan* (1925) 579 Mr. Bosengate looked at this peach with sorrow rather than disgust. The perfection of it was of a piece with all that had gone before this new and sudden feeling. **1957** G. RYLE in C. A. Mace *Brit. Philos. in Mid-Cent.* 258 The assumption that doing philosophy..is of a piece with doing natural science. **1977** G. BUTLER *Brides of Friedberg* iii. 59 How like the innocent Empress Frederick to lease such a place for me. But it was entirely of a piece with all one knew of her.

IV. 23. piece-bag, box *U.S.*, a bag or box for holding pieces of cloth; **piece-bright** *a.* (*poet. nonce use*), ? bright here and there; **piece-dye** *v. trans.*, to dye (cloth) after it is woven; **piece hand** = *piece-compositor*; **piece picker** = *fleece picker* s.v. *FLEECE *sb.* 6; **piece-rate**, also *attrib.*; **pieceways** *U.S. dial.* = PIECE *sb.* 14c.

1869 L. M. ALCOTT *Little Women* II. i. 11 So rich a supply of dusters, holders, and piece-bags. **1900** E. A. DIX *Deacon Bradbury* 251 Mr. Bradbury..sought his wife, who was upstairs sorting over her piece-bag. **1898** M. DELAND *Old Chester Tales* 272 It has been lying there in my piece-box for six years. **1877** G. M. HOPKINS *Poems* (1967) 67 This piece-bright paling shuts the spouse Christ home. **1931** E. MIDGLEY *Technical Terms Textile Trade* I. 10 The cloth is woven in a white or undyed condition and piece-dyed black for wool, so that the cotton fibres remain their natural colour. **1962** W. J. ONIONS *Wool* xi. 253 Interesting coloured effects may also be obtained by piece-dyeing cloth already made up of white and coloured yarn. **1978** *Country Life* 9 Nov. 1494/2 The fabric..is now finished and piece-dyed in Huddersfield. **1890** in E. HOWE *London Compositor* (1947) 316 The rapid growth of the 'stab system has rendered the condition of the piece hand in many instances almost unbearable. **1947** E. HOWE *Ibid.* 60 The piece-hand could reckon to earn more [than the establishment wage], by the exercise of both energy and skill. **1965** J. S. GUNN *Terminol. Shearing Industry* II. 8 *Piece picker*, sometimes called the 'fleece picker' or 'fleecy', his main job is to take the skirting from the roller and to divide it into lines defined by the classer, for example 'broken wool', 'first pieces'..and 'pieces'. **1954** J. A. C. BROWN *Social Psychol. of Industry* vi. 181 Workers..who are paid on an individual piece-rate basis. **1955** *Times* 3 May 10/1 The men allege that the piece-rate schedules are out of date and demand a revision. **1976** *Ilkeston Advertiser* 10 Dec. 2/2 Why is a factory worker who fiddles a 25p piece-rate coupon sacked on the spot, whereas his factory manager who fiddles his expense accounts to the tune of several pounds each week gets away with it? **1932** W. FAULKNER *Light in August* i. 9, I was trying to get up the road a pieceways before dark.

24. b. With prefixed numeral, forming attributive phrases, as *one-piece, three-piece*, etc.: see the first element.

piece, *v.* Add: **II. 3*. piece down.** *trans.* and *intr.* To increase the length or width of (a garment) by the insertion of a piece of material.

1870 J. P. SMITH *Widow Goldsmith's Daughter* vi. 80 Mrs. Goldsmith's economy would not permit her to cast aside any garment that could be pieced down. **1903** K. D. WIGGIN *Rebecca* xvii. 176 The limit of letting down and piecing down was reached.

pièce. Add: **a.** (Later examples.)

1882 A. J. MUNBY *Diary* 5 Apr. in D. Hudson *Munby* (1972) 405 Some day I may publish some of these—*pieces* [sic] *justificatives*, as the phrase is. **1917** N. DOUGLAS *South Wind* xxxiv. 412 The various *pièces justificatives* were lying in their sealed envelopes. **1954** W. K. HANCOCK *Country & Calling* viii. 227 The historian, although he may employ analysis and its technical language in his preliminary studies or his *pièces justificatives*, remains just as deeply committed as Herodotus and Thucydides were to narrative and the language of narrative. **1975** *Listener* 7 Aug. 186/1 Laud wanted to publish the Greek and oriental manuscripts which..were *pièces justificatives* of the continuous, independent Church of England.

c. *pièce de conviction* (pyęs də koṅviksyoṅ): an object produced as evidence in a criminal case, an exhibit; also *fig.*, the conclusive argument which decides a question.

1877 [see *Black Museum* s.v. *BLACK *a.* 19]. **1894** G. B. SHAW *Let.* 6 Dec. (1965) I. 469 Perhaps it may a little disappoint you, after the fantastic solution of Peer Gynt, and the no-solution of Rosmersholm, that a real solution is only found in something that brings the great Ibsen into line with Monsieur Tout-le-monde; but that, in my view, is the final *pièce de conviction*.

d. *pièce d'occasion* (pyęs dokāzyoṅ): a play or other literary work, or a musical composition, written for a special occasion.

1883 E. B. BAX *Kant's Prolegomena & Metaphysical Found. Nat. Sci.* p. xxvii, Kant believed himself to have no special bent for the professorate in question, which would have involved the criticism of all *pièces d'occasion*, as well as the composition of such on academic festivals. **1891** G. B. SHAW *Quintessence of Ibsenism* p. vi, I had laid it aside as a *pièce d'occasion* which had served its turn. **1914** —— *Dark Lady of Sonnets* 103 This little *pièce d'occasion*, written for a performance in aid of the funds of the project for establishing a National Theatre as a memorial to Shakespear. **1934** C. LAMBERT *Music Ho!* II. 63 These mild pièces d'occasion no more affected the main course of music than an Olde Worlde Bunne Shoppe affects..architectural experiments. **1955** *Times* 29 Aug. 10/6 The result may not be homogeneous enough in style to ensure the work a place in the regular orchestral repertory, but it is certainly a splendid *pièce d'occasion* for this orchestra, who played it with tremendous verve and finish [at their Prom début]. **1971** *Nature* 25 June 537/1 His Presidential Address of 1951..is..an attempt to condense the history of chemistry in a single *pièce d'occasion.* **1979** *Jrnl. R. Soc. Arts* CXXVII. 181/2 This book is a *pièce d'occasion*—a collection of essays published to coincide with the exhibition of Cézanne's late work, held in New York and Houston in 1977 and in Paris in 1978.

e. *pièce de circonstance* (pyęs də sirkoṅstaṅs): a literary composition, theory, etc., having its genesis in a particular situation.

1926 R. H. TAWNEY *Relig. & Rise of Capitalism* ii. 89 His sermons and pamphlets..were *pièces de circonstance,* thrown off in the storm of a revolution. **1972** R. PLANT in Cox & Dyson *20th-Cent. Mind* II. iv. 68 The fact that the historical circumstances which gave rise to [social] theories no longer obtain does not thereby entail that they have become outmoded. Such theories, far from being mere *pièces de circonstance,* rather embody an element which transcends the particular problems which generated them.

f. *pièce noire* (pyęs nwār): a play or a film with a tragic or macabre theme.

1958 *Times* 17 Apr. 3/4 *Payment Deferred* or *The Postman Always Rings Twice* are good *pièces noirs* [sic] because their characters are motivated by passions so intensely conveyed that the subsequent developments are inescapable. **1959** *Oxf. Compan. French Lit.* 22/2 [Anouilh's] *Pièces roses*..and *Pièces noires*..like Shaw's *Plays Pleasant and Unpleasant*..deal with the lighter or the darker side of life. **1963** *Punch* 20 Nov. 754/3 As black a *pièce noire* as can be.

g. *pièce rose* (pyęs rōᵘz): a play or a film having a theme which is pleasantly entertaining; a comedy.

1959 [see *pièce noire* above]. **1963** *Times* 18 May 5/1 It is what Anouilh calls a *pièce rose* and lightly tosses around such ideas familiar to the playwright as innocence and faith, illusion and reality. **1968** *Punch* 6 Nov. 668/3 Eighteen years (and *Look Back in Anger*) later Anouilh's *pièce rose* seems pathetically pale and withered around the edges.

h. *pièce à thèse* (pyęs a tęz): = *thesis-play* s.v. THESIS 6.

1961 *Times* 17 Oct. 16/5 In most hands this [television play] could turn into a mechanical *pièce à thèse.* **1974** *Independent Broadcasting* Aug. 5/2 How far the *pièce à thèse,* the play with a social or political message, is permissible within the impartiality rule.

piecemeal, *v.* Add: Also const. *out.* (Later example.)

1975 *Washington Post* 6 Sept. A2/4 To announce even the topic of the hearings would result in 'prematurely piecemealing the information out',—he said.

piece-wise, *adv.* (In Dict. s.v. PIECE *sb.*). Also **piecewise.** Delete '*rare* or *nonce-wd.*' and add: *spec.* in *Math.,* throughout each of a finite number of separate parts or regions but not necessarily throughout the whole. (Later examples.)

1933 H. B. PHILLIPS *Vector Anal.* v. 101 Vectors which are only piecewise differentiable. **1939** *Mind* XLVIII. 366 They have to proceed piece-wise, measuring every little line and bend. **1953** L. V. AHLFORS *Complex Anal.* ii. 65 We shall say that the arc is differentiable if $z'(t)$ exists and is continuous... An arc is piecewise differentiable..if the same conditions hold except for a finite number of values *t.* **1962** ALLEY & ATWOOD *Electronic Engin.* xvi. 546 This method is known as the piecewise-linear method, since the tube or transistor is assumed to be linear over certain regions of operation. **1966** SCOTT & TIMS *Math. Anal.* vi. 209 It is useful also to consider functions which, while not continuous in a whole interval, are nevertheless made up of a *finite* number of continuous pieces. Such functions are called piecewise continuous. **1979** *Nature* 12 Apr. 623/1 Their major effect is to re-order, piecewise, the fibre map of the eye circumference laid out across the *t* axis of the ribbon.

piece-work. Add: Also **piecework.** (Earlier and further examples.)

1549 *Coventry Leet Bk.* (1909) III. 792 No persone of the Craft of Cappers shall put owt eny pece-woork, but to suche of the same Craft as the maisters..shall agree & consent vnto. **1770** J. WEDGWOOD *Let.* 12 May (1965) 91 You will certainly do right in bringing the painting to piece work. **1817** H. L. PIOZZI *Let.* 14 Apr. in A. Hayward *Autobiogr. Mrs. Piozzi* (1861) II. 200 A gentleman.. called fifteen of his principal people..and told them he was no longer able to give them piece-work. **1885** G. B. SHAW *Let.* 29 Dec. (1965) I. 149 Paquito has not the remotest idea of what it is to be exploited on the piecework system by newspapers. **1894** [see *FELLER¹ 4]. **1911** *Rep. Labour & Social Conditions in Germany* (Tariff Reform League) III. 31 He also informed us that most of the joiners worked piecework. *Ibid.* 186 There was a lock-out in the building trade, owing to a grievance in the piecework system. **1967** M. ARGYLE *Psychol. Interpersonal Behaviour* iv. 73 Under competition hostile attitudes will develop; an example of this is the payment of salesgirls by individual piece-work, leading to their fighting over the more desirable customers. **1970** T. LUPTON *Managem. & Social Sci.* (ed. 2) iii. 63 Pitting wits against management on piecework rates.

2. = PATCHWORK 4 b.

1842 C. M. KIRKLAND *Forest Life* I. 90 No gorgeous piece-work bed-quilts exhibiting stars of all magnitudes and moons in all quarters. **1935** M. M. ATWATER *Murder in Midsummer* viii. 71 You'll find a piecework spread in the bottom drawer.

piecrust. Add: **c.** Applied to a table having an ornamental edge suggestive of the crust of a pie, as *pie-crust table, top.*

1902 L. V. LOCKWOOD *Colonial Furnit. Amer.* 232 The handsomest of the Dutch tea-tables were what are popularly known as 'pie-crust tables'. **1914** R. & E. SHACKLETON *Charm of Antique* iii. 49 The most sought-for and rarest of little tables is the 'pie-crust' tip-table, so named from its apparently finger-dented pie-crust-like margin of regular irregularity. **1923** W. DEEPING *Secret Sanct.* xx. 210 She had closed the lid of her work-basket and placed it on the 'pie-crust' table by the window. **1951** *Good Housek. Home Encycl.* 106/1 Tripod tables..with 'pie-crust' tops. **1969** A. NEGUS *Going for Song* 120 So on original pie-crust tables there are no joins at all round the pie-crust edge. **1973** A. BEHREND *Samarai Affair* iv. 53 The glossy telephone on the antique piecrust table.

pied, *ppl. a.*¹ Add: **d. pied crow,** the black and white crow, *Corvus albus,* found in most parts of Africa south of the Sahara; **pied flycatcher,** substitute for def.: a black and white flycatcher, *Muscicapa* (or *Ficedula*) *hypoleuca,* found in Europe and north and west Africa; (examples); **pied kingfisher** (examples); **pied wagtail,** substitute for def.: a western European wagtail, *Motacilla alba yarrelli;* (later examples).

1930 W. L. SCLATER *Systema Avium Ethiopicarum* II. 650 Pied Crow... Throughout the Ethiopian Region. **1958** G. DURRELL *Encounters with Animals* III. 109 A pied crow from West Africa..suddenly decided that I was the only person in the world for him. **1967** W. CONDRY *Birds & Wild Afr.* iv. 65 In one palm a pair of pied crows were courting. **1776** T. PENNANT *Brit. Zool.* (ed. 4) I. 351 (*heading*) Pied fly-catcher. **1843** W. YARRELL *Hist. Brit. Birds* I. 169 The Pied Flycatcher..is a rare bird in England. **1882** [see FLY-CATCHER 2]. **1894** C. DIXON *Nests & Eggs Brit. Birds* 157 The Pied Flycatcher arrives in our islands during the latter half of April. **1971** *Country Life* 25 Mar. 705/2 Other garden birds [in West Berlin] include redstarts and pied flycatchers. **1865** *Ibis* 2nd Ser. I. 408 Pied Kingfisher. Appears to be the common species of Lower Bengal. **1924** W. L. SCLATER *Systema Avium Æthiopicarum* I. 211 Pied Kingfisher... The Greek Islands, Cyprus, Asia Minor and Egypt to the Persian Gulf. **1953** G. DURRELL *Overloaded Ark* xiii. 221 There were Pied kingfishers, vivid black and white. **1971** *Country Life* 28 Oct. 1127/2 The much larger pied kingfishers hovered like kestrels, then plunged into the water from a height. **1894** C. DIXON *Nests & Eggs Brit. Birds* 64 The White Wagtail does not differ in its habits.. from the Pied Wagtail. **1964** G. B. SCHALLER *Year of Gorilla* (1965) i. 39 Pied wagtails flitted around the huts. **1975** E. SIMMS *Birds of Town & Suburb* i. 25 The trodden grass swards may be visited by an occasional pied wagtail.

e*. *Pied Piper*: in a German legend (the subject of Browning's poem *The Pied Piper of Hamelin* (1845)), a piper in parti-colour dress who rid the town of Hameln (Hamelin) of a plague of rats by charming them to follow him into the river Weser, and who, on being refused the promised reward, led away the children of the town: used allusively.

1942 'N. SHUTE' (*title*) Pied piper. **1946** KOESTLER *Thieves in Night* 154 There was a horra in the Square with Mendl doing his Pied Piper act. **1966** *Listener* 27 Oct. 631/3 There was something very unpleasant about this Pied Piper of adolescent religious feelings [*sc.* David Wilkerson, an American evangelist]. **1972** T. P. MCMAHON *Issue of Bishop's Blood* (1973) i. 15 The pathetic thousands who trek endlessly after the Pied Pipers of the cancer cures. **1976** *Western Producer* (Saskatoon, Saskatchewan) 24 June 7/4 In Ottawa..Bobby Gimby, Canada's pied piper, will sail along Rideau Canal followed by a flotilla of canoes filled with youngsters singing his pop Canadian hit 'Canada'. **1977** S. BRETT *Star Trap* xiii. 144 Charles could not help admiring the Pied Piper strength of the man's personality. The company was carried along on the wave of his vitality. **1979** *Guardian* 2 May 10/7 I'm the Pied Piper and every toddler is..singing 'Vote vote vote for Mr Ashton'.

pied, *ppl. a.*² (Later examples.)

1904 'MARK TWAIN' in *Harper's Weekly* 10 Dec. 12/2 A thing that gets pied is dead,..its chance of seeing print is gone. **1956** J. WHATMOUGH *Language* i. 9 A haphazard jumble of symbols, say a pied text, is a..nightmare.

‖ **pied à terre** (pyetatęr'). Pl. **pieds à terre.** [Fr., lit. 'foot on the ground'.] A small town house, flat, or room used for short periods of residence; a 'home base'.

1829 CARLYLE in *Foreign Rev.* III. VI. 445 She is perpetually travelling: a peaceful philosopher is lugged over the world, to Cirey, to Lunéville, to that *pied à terre* in Paris. **1838** J. PARDOE *Beauties of Bosphorus* 20 The Greek emperor..acceded to the desire of Mahomet to possess a *pied-à-terre* on the European edge of the channel. **1870** D. G. ROSSETTI *Let.* 15 Mar. (1965) II. 815, I have not yet written to thank you for a much more independent and promising *pied-à-terre* than I could have found in the tents of the stranger. **1901** 'L. MALET' *Hist. R. Calmady* v. i. 383 Richard Calmady had taken her husband's villa at Naples on lease, it offering, as he said, a convenient *pied à terre* to him while yachting along the adjacent coasts. **1926** [see *METROLAND]. **1927** C. CONNOLLY *Let.* Dec. in *Romantic Friendship* (1975) 316 It might help you to have a *pied-à-terre.* **1936** F. CLUNE *Roaming round Darling* i. 7 Australia is still a land of change and Australians, generally, are a restless race, preferring a mere *pied-à-terre* before a taxable home-fire. **1958** [see *accommodation address* s.v. *ACCOMMODATION 6 b]. **1964** C. WILLOCK *Enormous Zoo* vii. 114 They had given us a room in their own house which we were free to use as a *pied-à-terre.* **1977** *Wandsworth Borough News* 7 Oct. 23/2 (Advt.), Ideal pied-a-terre—very reasonably priced studio flat in a detached Victorian property.

‖ **pied d'éléphant** (pyedelefaṅ). [Fr., lit. 'elephant's foot'.] A padded sack used to protect the lower part of the body on a bivouac in mountaineering and rock climbing.

1956 C. EVANS *On Climbing* viii. 120 For alpine bivouacs, it is customary to make the sleeping bag as it were a part of your clothing using..a sawn-off sleeping-bag, the 'pied d'elephant', to cover the legs. **1963** P. NOCK *Rock Climbing* ix. 81 One addition which is sometimes carried is a 'pied d'elephant'. This is like the bottom half of a sleeping bag of minimum weight. **1966** C. BONINGTON *I chose to Climb* xvi. 188, I was once again fully equipped with borrowed duvet, pied d'éléphant, [etc]. **1968** P. CREW *Encycl. Dict. Mountaineering* 91/1 *Pied d'Elephant,*..a waist length bag for protecting the lower part of the body on bivouacs. **1973** C. BONINGTON *Next Horizon* x. 149, I managed to pull my boots off, slipped them in my rucksack and then pulled the pied d'éléphant over my legs, ending up with my feet in my rucksack.

piedmont (pī·dmǫnt). [Orig. (in sense 1) *Piemont,* after It. *Piemonte,* lit. 'mountain foot', name of a region of N. Italy, f. *piede* foot (:—L. *ped-, pēs*) + *monte* mountain (:—L. *mont-, mons*).] **1.** Also **Piedmont.** The name of a fertile upland region of the U.S. between the Blue Ridge and Appalachian Mountains to the west and the Atlantic coastal plain to the east, and extending from near New York to Alabama. Freq. *attrib.*

1755 L. EVANS *Geogr. Ess.* 7 Between the South Mountain and the hither Chain of the Endless Mountains..is the most considerable Quantity of valuable Land that the English are possest of; and runs through New-Jersey, Pensilvania, Mariland and Virginia. It has yet obtained no general Name, but may properly be called Piemont, from its Situation. **1855** *Southern Lit. Messenger* XXI. 672/2 The next breadth of country, known in several of the States as the Piedmont district, was more salubrious in its atmosphere. **1857** 'PORTE CRAYON' *Virginia Illustr.* 235 The soil of this [*sc.* Amherst Co., Va.], in common with many other of the piedmont counties, is of a bright red in many places. **1905** W. H. NORTON *Elem. Geol.* iii. 87 The surface of the Piedmont is gently rolling. **1927** H. C. GROOME *Fauquier during Proprietorship* i. 1 A contour line through the falls of these rivers marks the boundary between Tidewater Virginia and that region which rolling upward to the foothills of the Appalachians is today known as the Piedmont Plateau. **1929** J. BUCHAN *Courts of Morning* II. xi. 257 A rambling country-house high up in the South Carolina piedmont, with the blue, forested hills behind. **1951** TRAGER & SMITH *Outl. Eng. Struct.* I. 25 In the Southeast of the United States, in both the Coastal and Piedmont speech. **1968** R. W. FAIRBRIDGE *Encycl. Geomorphol.* 844/2 The Piedmont Province..is the older part of the Appalachians... Rocks of the piedmont..are of early Paleozoic to Precambrian age. **1972** H. KURATH *Stud. Area Linguistics* viii. 128 From 1790 to 1860 Negro slaves outnumbered the Whites in the piedmont of Virginia. **1976** *Scottish Rev.* Summer 5 After the failure of the Forty-Five, many Highland families moved to the pine barrens and hills of piedmont North Carolina.

2. Any region or area at the foot of a mountain or mountain range.

1860 MAYNE REID *Odd People* 430 Having reached the *piedmont* of the Andes, you still find yourself on a plain, but one which is elevated 3,000 feet above the point from which you started. **1944** A. HOLMES *Princ. Physical Geol.* xi. 201 Where closely spaced streams discharge from a mountainous area across a piedmont (a mountain-foot lowland), their deposits coalesce to form a piedmont alluvial plain. **1960** [see *BAJADA]. **1962** *Times* 2 June 11/6 Those along the northern piedmont consider themselves Bughtis and owe their allegiance to the Nawab in the remote tribal capital of Dera Bughti. **1974** *Encycl. Brit. Micropædia* I. 741/3 A bajada is usually composed of gravelly alluvium... In humid climates, landforms of this nature are usually referred to as piedmonts.

3. (See quot. 1905¹.)

1905 H. T. FERRAR in R. F. Scott *Voy. 'Discovery'* II. 461 Large areas of ice which lie at the foot of high land and which have no obvious single source may be described as 'piedmonts'. *Ibid.,* Piedmonts afloat are by far the most important. **1914** [see *ice-shelf* s.v. *ICE *sb.* 8].

4. *attrib.* or as *adj.* Situated or occurring at the foot of a mountain or mountain range.

1891 I. C. RUSSELL in *Nat. Geogr. Mag.* May 122 The Malaspina glacier belongs to a class of ice bodies not previously recognized, which are formed at the bases of mountains by the union of several glaciers from above. Their position suggests the name of *Piedmont glaciers* for the type. **1905** W. H. NORTON *Elem. Geol.* iv. 99 Mountain streams may build their confluent fans into widespread piedmont (foot of the mountain) alluvial plains. **1907** *Bull. Geol. Soc. Amer.* XVIII. 355 On leaving the mountains the Tarim river enters the great plain which forms the floor of the Lop, or Tarim basin... At the lower ends of many small streams which now wither to nothing in the piedmont gravel or sand of the basin floor, there are old channels and strips of vegetation. **1936** P. FLEMING *News from Tartary* 334 It brought us to Igiz Yar, a little oasis on a rolling slope of piedmont gravel. **1942** [see *PEDIPLANE]. **1957** G. E. HUTCHINSON *Treat. Limnol.* I. i. 57 The numerous and remarkable large lakes produced in piedmont regions. **1962** *Times* 2 June 11/6 The piedmont zone of hill slopes has long formed the ethnic frontier between the plundering hill men and the peaceful Sindhi cultivators. **1965** [see *OUED]. **1974** *Nature* 29 Nov. 373/1 The United States Range where piedmont glaciers descend southwards along the northern edge of the Hazen Plateau. **1976** R. C. SELLEY *Introd. Sedimentol.* viii. 257 Between mountains and adjacent lowlands it is often possible to define a distinct belt known as the piedmont zone.

Piedmontese (pīdmǫntī·z), *sb.* and *a.* Also 7 Piemontese. [f. *Piedmont* (see prec.) + -ESE.] **A.** *sb.* **a.** The dialect of Piedmont in Italy. **b.** A native or inhabitant of Piedmont. **B.** *adj.* Of or pertaining to Piedmont, its inhabitants, or the dialect spoken by them.

1642 [see *MILANESE *sb.* 3]. **1655** MILTON *Poems* (1925) I. 236 Slain by the bloody Piemontese. **1673** J. RAY *Observations Journey Low-Countries* 249 The Piemontese are generally well to live. **1768** STERNE *Sentimental Journey* II. 200 The lady was a Piedmontese of about thirty. **1770** [see COURIER 3]. **1776** LADY A. MILLER *Lett. from Italy* I. 90 The Spanish army..had not failed to guard all the passes they knew of, in order that no communication should be kept up between the Savoyards, the Piedmontese, and Swiss army. **1846** DICKENS *Let.* 22 June (1977) IV. 568 It [*sc.* Lausanne] contains only one Roman Catholic church, which is mainly for the use of the Savoyards and Piedmontese. **1858** A. GALLENGA *Country Life in Piedmont* 31 There is hardly an instance of a Piedmontese mountaineer settling permanently abroad. *Ibid.* 128, I have tried to convince the Piedmontese Press that [etc.]. **1878, 1880** [see *EMILIAN *a.* and *sb.*]. **1902** *Encycl. Brit.* XXXI. 769/2 The Piedmontese dialect has been rather strongly influenced by French. **1927,** etc. [see *LIGURIAN *sb.*]. **1931** *Times Lit. Suppl.* 15 Oct. 787/2 The young Prince.. was made commandant of the Piedmontese artillery. **1932** G. F.-H. BERKELEY *Italy in Making* I. xi. 160 Of course Gioberti was a Piedmontese, and in Piedmont the people were satisfied. **1968** D. M. SMITH *Mod. Sicily* xlviii. 446 Observers remarked on a tremendous feeling against everything which smacked of Piedmontese. **1974** *Times* 1 Feb. 18/4 After his death the secretaryship passed on [to] Luigi Longo, a dour Piedmontese. **1977** *Canad. Jrnl. Linguistics* XXII. I. 17 *The Sermoni Subalpini*..is the first extant Piedmontese document.

piedmontite. Add: Now freq. called *PIEMONTITE. The spelling *piedmontite* was an alteration of J. D. Dana's. (Further examples.)

1933 *Mineral. Mag.* XXIII. 417 The pleochroic colours shown by the mineral in thin section closely resemble those of piedmontite from Japan and from South Mountain, Pennsylvania. **1961** *Current Sci.* XXX. 223/1 (*heading*) Some observations on piedmontite from Goldongri Manganese Mine.

‖**pied noir** (pye nwār). Pl. **pieds noirs.** [Fr., = black foot.] A name given to people of French origin living in Algeria during French rule, and to those who returned to Europe after the granting of independence to Algeria in 1962.

The name was applied formerly to Algerian stokers who worked bare-footed on French cargo-boats, and by extension, to Algerians generally.

1961 *Times* 6 May 9/6 They are the *pieds noirs*, fiercely proud of this pejorative nickname given them by the metropolitan French. **1962** *Economist* 28 Apr. 344/3 Returned conscripts [from Algeria] and vacationing *pieds noirs*..played an important part in informing the public. **1963** *Times Lit. Suppl.* 31 May 384/3 These two large monographs are devoted to painters—both dead—..the one Flemish, the other a *pied noir* from Constantine. **1965** *Economist* 27 Mar. 1365/1 Marseilles, a sprawling city with an ethnically mixed-up population—Greek, Armenian, Italian, Corsican, and now *pied-noir* from North Africa—has a certain charm. **1969** *Listener* 27 Mar. 417/2 M. Fabre was an elderly colon, one of the original French families in Algeria—a *pied noir*, as they like to be called. **1972** D. LEES *Zodiac* 9 This one..was called Daria-Daria Massenet, which made her a Pied Noir. **1977** *Time* 21 Nov. 12/1 Unlike the white settlers of Rhodesia or the French *pieds-noirs* of Algeria, the Afrikaners have no ties to a European motherland.

pie-eyed (pəiˌəi·d), *a. slang* (orig. *U.S.*). [f. PIE *sb.*[2] + EYED *ppl. a.*] Intoxicated to such an extent that vision is affected; drunk.

1904 ADE *True Bills* 41 They put him down at a Table and sat around him and inhaled the Scotch until they were all Pie-Eyed. **1910** S. E. WHITE *Rules of Game* I. xvii. 103 'Oh, *he's* in town..' 'Drunk, eh?' 'Spifflicated, pie-eyed, loaded, soshed.' **1924** *T. P.'s & Cassell's Weekly* 6 Sept. 631/1 He is partial to a 'shot of gin', and on occasion will drink till he is 'pie-eyed'. **1924** WODEHOUSE *Ukridge* x. 256 What they put in that stuff..I don't know, but the fact remains that the bird almost instantly became perfectly pie-eyed. **1932** —— *Hot Water* iii. 89 It is our great fancy costume carnival... Everybody puts on funny clothes and becomes pie-eyed. **1937** *Daily Express* 27 Jan. 19/1 Personally I didn't care if the whole band was pie-eyed, I wanted them to be busy playing good dance music. **1946** E. O'NEILL *Iceman Cometh* IV. 225 Why the hell don't you get pie-eyed and celebrate? **1957** J. BRAINE *Room at Top* xxx. 255 'You *are* pie-eyed, aren't you?' Eva said. **1959** 'J. CHRISTOPHER' *Scent of White Poppies* iii. 43 He was utterly pie-eyed. He could scarcely talk straight. **1970** *New Yorker* 8 Aug. 34/2 Piet, who is pie-eyed drunk and needs to be helped homeward. **1974** N. FREELING *Dressing of Diamond* 32 You shouldn't be driving at all, you're pie-eyed.

pie-face (pəi·fē[i]s). [f. PIE *sb.*[2] + FACE *sb.* I.] A person of round or blank countenance; a stupid person. (In quot. 1922 used of an effeminate man.)

1922 S. LEWIS *Babbitt* vii. 99 Oh, there's a swell bunch of Lizzie boys and lemon-suckers and pie-faces. **1930** *Amer. Speech* VI. 92 The following expressions belong to colloquialisms and slang, including movie and radio neologisms... *Pie-face.* **1960** WENTWORTH & FLEXNER *Dict. Amer. Slang* 388/2 *Pie-face*, a person with a round face and a blank, funny, or homely expression; a stupid person.

pie-faced, *a.* [f. PIE *sb.*[2] + FACED *ppl.a.*[2]] Of a person, having a round countenance or a blank or solemn facial expression; stupid. Now commonly used as a general term of mild abuse (see also quot. 1939). Also *transf.*

Quot. 1955 may represent PIE *a.* (in Dict. and Suppl.) rather than PIE *sb.*[2]

1912 *Dialect Notes* III. 585 *Pie-faced*,..round-faced; flat-faced. **1923** WODEHOUSE *Inimitable Jeeves* x. 112 Did you put that pie-faced infant up to bally-ragging Mr. Bassington-Bassington? **1935** —— *Luck of Bodkins* xiv. 147 You don't suppose I care what old pie-faced Gertrude thinks of me, do you? **1938** G. HEYER *Blunt Instrument* x. 183 'Pie-faced creature, with a nasty, sly smile.' 'The Mona Lisa!' **1939** J. B. PRIESTLEY *Let People Sing* i. 17 He was disturbed again, this time by..a messy, dribbling, pie-faced urchin. **1955** *Times* 29 Aug. 10/7 They spare us those moments of pie-faced solemnity with which comic dramatists here are wont to becloud their activities.

pie-gow, var. *PAI KAU.

pie in the sky. *colloq.* (orig. *U.S.*). [see PIE *sb.*[2] 4.] A prospect, often illusory, of future happiness, esp. as a reward in heaven for virtue or suffering on earth; an extravagant promise that is unlikely to be fulfilled. Also (with hyphens) *attrib.* Hence **pie-in-the-skyer,** one who puts forward a prospect or promise of this kind.

1911 J. HILL in G. M. Smith *Joe Hill* (1969) i. 20 You'll get pie in the sky when you die. **1926** *Amer. Mercury* Jan. 65/1 *Pie in the sky* is a somewhat cynical reference to the bourgeois heaven. **1939** N. MONSARRAT *This is Schoolroom* IV. xviii. 426 Christianity..would end by backing the guns, blessing the flags, and preaching pie-in-the-sky-when-you-die. **1941** *Archit. Rev.* LXXXIX. 117/1 Utopianism, or wishful-thinking, or pie-in-the-sky, or whatever we care to call it. **1951** [see *JAM *sb.*[2] b]. **1951** R. HOGGART *Auden* vi. 190 He is afraid that God will be just a woozy dream, pie-in-the-sky, to his subjects. **1958** *Times Lit. Suppl.* 26 Dec. 750/4 Rightly mistrusting the idea of 'pie in the sky', he [*sc.* the American] expects to have his reward here. **1959** *Sunday Express* 30 Aug. 12/7 With the election moving remorselessly nearer, pie-in-the-sky days are here again. Everything our hearts could desire is promised us by politicians. **1960** O. MANNING *Great Fortune* vi. 79 Pie in the sky. Accept the condition it has pleased God to put you in. **1962** *Times* 11 Oct. 10/5 General Eisenhower has attacked the Kennedy Administration as a 'pie-in-the-sky' Government. **1971** *Physics Bull.* June 322/1 Is this just pie-in-the-sky dreaming about some utopian future where there will be no more pollution, poverty, malnutrition and similar afflictions? **1973** *Time* 25 June 4/2 Exposing shenanigans, militants, self-servers and pie-in-the-skyers must be done, no matter how or by whom. **1975** *Listener* 16 Jan. 89/1 Pie-in-the-sky wage claims. **1976** E. MACLAREN *Nature of Belief* iv. 34 The point is obvious when the argument for belief is as crude as some traditional pie-in-the-sky promises. **1977** *Undercurrents* June-July 12/1 To expect the NHS to encompass all sorts of fringe or alternative practices whilst even the level of basic medical care that people want is unobtainable in some areas (abortion) is pie in the sky.

pie-jim-jams (pəidʒi·mdʒæmz). A child's name for 'pyjamas'.

1902 *Little Folks* Apr. 265/2 'Why! I'm in my pie-jimjams!' he murmured..with a doubtful look at his bare feet and his pyjamas. **1964** M. LASKI in S. Nowell-Smith *Edwardian England* iv. 204 For bedwear, pyjamas—'pie-jim-jams'—were recommended for boys and girls alike.

pi electron: see *PI *sb.* 3.

piemontite (pī·mǫntəit). *Min.* [ad. G. *piemontit* (G. A. Kenngott *Das Mohs'sche Mineralsystem* (1853) 75): see PIEDMONTITE.] A synonym of PIEDMONTITE, adopted as more in accord with the original Ger. spelling and with European practice.

1892 E. S. DANA *Dana's Syst. Min.* (ed. 6) 1125/3 (Index), Piedmontite 521. Piemontite, 521. **1950** *Årsbok Sveriges Geologiska Undersökning* XLIV. II. 15 In some parts of the limestone,..crystalline masses of piemontite appear in zones measuring many meters in thickness. **1956** *Mineral. Mag.* XXXI. 241 The piemontite from the schist is granular in form, ruby red, and has pearly lustre. **1971** *Ibid.* XXXVIII. 104 Recommendations of the Commission [on New Minerals and Mineral Names of the International Mineralogical Association] on minerals for which more than one name is in common use...Piemontite, not piedmontite. **1973** *Canad. Jrnl. Earth Sci.* X. 1401/1 Most piemontites are the product of metasomatic or low-grade regional metamorphism of manganiferous rocks.

pier, *sb.*[2] Add: **5.** *pier-master* (examples); **pier-mirror** (examples); **pier-stake,** one of the columns or piles on which a pier is supported; **pier-table** (earlier and later examples).

1936 J. GRIERSON *High Failure* ii. 27, I slept in the piermaster's cottage in order to be as near my machine as possible. **1971** *Daily Tel.* 16 July 7/1, I liked the pier-master, pompous but human in nautical beard and gold braid. **1976** *Southern Even. Echo* (Southampton) 11 Nov. (Advt. Suppl.) 12/7 Fairey Yacht Harbours Pier Master required for yacht harbour. **1863** O. W. NORTON *Army Lett.* (1903) 185 Pier mirrors twenty feet high on three sides of the room. **1969** *Sears Catal.* Spring/Summer 1295, 2-piece pier table and mirror set. **1927** JOYCE *On Beach at Fontana* in *Pomes Penyeach*, Wind whines and whines the shingle, The crazy pierstakes groan. **1955** A. ROSS *Australia 55* ix. 122 Watching schools of parrot fish and pike twist among the pier-stakes. **1803** M. WILMOT *Let.* 25 July in *Russ. Jrnls.* (1934) I. 24 A pier table furnish'd with splendid Gilt China cups and saucers 'wisely kept for shew'. **1952** J. GLOAG *Short Dict. Furnit.* 361 (*caption*) Pier glass and pier table, designed as a decorative unit. **1979** W. J. BURLEY *Charles & Elizabeth* v. 81 A pair of carved and gilded pier tables with mirrors above.

pier (pī[ə]ɹ), *v. rare.* [f. PIER[2].] **a.** *trans.* To provide with a pier. **b.** *intr.* To reach *out* like a pier.

1857 *Trans. Mich. Agric. Soc.* VIII. 731 If they can coax Uncle Sam to pier the outlet of that Lake and make it a splendid harbor for navigable purposes. **1951** W. SANSOM *Face of Innocence* iii. 25 Above them the curved glass cupola..that goes piering out over the garden.

pierced, *ppl. a.* Add: **c.** Of silver, plate, china, porcelain, etc.: ornamented with perforations.

1756 in R. W. Read *Reprint of Orig. Catal. Chelsea Porcelain Manuf.* (1880) 6 Four round pierced baskets enamel'd in flowers. *Ibid.* 7 A fine perfume pot pierced, chased and gilt, and enamel'd in birds. **1785** *Daily Universal Reg.* 1 Jan. 3/2 Pierced and engraved oval salts... Pierced and solid headed mustard pots. **1875** E. METEYARD *Wedgwood Handbk.* 338 The high fluted pillar candle-stick, the pierced fruit basket,..and various other articles, all show an infinite variety, beauty, and fitness of outline. **1931** E. WENHAM *Domestic Silver* v. 88 Pierced baskets for bread were also made in the Early Stuart period and.. are the prototypes of the baskets popular in the eighteenth century. **1956** [see *cake-basket* s.v. *CAKE *sb.* 9 a]. **1970** G. SAVAGE *Dict. Antiques* 319/2 In more recent times George Owen (d. 1917) made elaborately pierced or reticulated porcelain for the Royal Worcester Porcelain Company. **1974** A. GRIMWADE *Rococo Silver* iv. 45 An exceptional set of twelve [salt-cellars] by Emick Romer, about 1760, have glass bowls enclosed in pierced cage-work on *chinoiserie* motifs.

2. Special collocations, as **pierced earring** *U.S.*, an earring designed to be worn in a pierced ear; **Pierced-nose** = *NEZ PERCÉ, NEZ PERCE.

1965 *Time* 15 Oct. 70/3 Pierced earrings are by far the most attractive ones available. **1966** *N.Y. Times* 6 June 53 Variation on the pierced earring theme. **1971** *Tuscaloosa* (Alabama) *News* 31 Dec. 8 The package deal includes the purchase of a $6 pair of pierced earrings... The customer may..have her (or his) ears pierced free of charge. **1805** W. CLARK in Lewis & Clark *Orig. Jrnls. Lewis & Clark Expedition* (1905) III. 78 They call themselves the *Cho pun-nish* or Pierced noses. **1831** R. COX *Adventures Columbia River* II. vi. 122 We had many reasons to suspect that the Pierced-noses..were actuated by feelings of hostility. **1837** W. IRVING *Rocky Mountains* I. xviii. 183 A Pierced-nose chief, named Blue John by the whites. **1908** H. J. SPINDEN in *Mem. Amer. Anthropol. Assoc.* II. III. 172 Ross says the people are called Pierced Noses from the custom 'of having their noses bored to hold a certain white shell like the fluke of an anchor'.

piercement (pī[ə]·ɹsmĕnt). *Geol.* [f. PIERCE *v.* + -MENT, tr. G. *durchspiessungs(falten.*] The penetration of overlying strata by a mobile rock core, often of salt. Usu. *attrib.* Cf. *DIAPIR.

1925 D. C. BARTON in *Bull. Amer. Assoc. Petroleum Geologists* IX. 1239 The salt is merely part of the peculiar type of fold called by Mrazec 'diapir' fold, or by Krejci 'piercement' folds (*Durchspiessungsfalten*). **1942** M. P. BILLINGS *Structural Geol.* xiv. 254 Salt domes are classified by some geologists into piercement domes and non-piercement domes, the former being discordant, the latter concordant. **1965** A. HOLMES *Princ. Physical Geol.* (ed. 2) ix. 206 Diapiric folds (also known as piercement folds). **1965** E. LEHNER et al. in G. J. Williams *Econ. Geol. N.Z.* xix. 337/2 It seems improbable that the Tertiary anticlinal structure[s] without piercement cores, or at a long strike distance away from them, could owe their shape solely to hidden diapirism (e.g., upward movement of the clay core without a breakthrough to surface), without at least some help from tangential forces. **1975** *Nature* 29 May 393/2 Because of the circular exposure of evaporite surrounded by younger disturbed rocks, Haughton Dome has been considered a piercement dome.

pier-head. Add: *attrib.* and *Comb.* **pier-head jump,** (*a*) (see quot. 1892); (*b*) an act of leaving a ship as it is about to sail; (*c*) a person who joins a ship as it is leaving the dock; hence *pier-head jumper.*

1892 [in Dict.]. 1927 F. SHAW *Knocking Around* 65 One man was short: he'd done a pierhead jump. 1928 F. P. HARLOW *Making of Sailor* 229 All the other members of the crew had made a pier-head jump during the night. 1931 S. W. RYDER *Blue Water Ventures* iii. 40 At the last minute the scallywags who could not get a ship in the ordinary way had to be accepted; these 'pier-head jumpers' being pushed on board by the boarding-house runners as the steamer was moving out of dock. 1936 B. ADAMS *Ships & Women* xi. 238 Often among pierhead jumps were rattling good sailors. 1938 E. LINKLATER *Child under Sail* 169 There were no pier-head jumpers to be found, and we had to sail a man short. 1945 *Seafarers' Log* 13 July 6/4 Fred took a few minutes to call his family, and then made the tanker on a pierhead jump. 1967 S. WATERS *Indentures Indorsed* 117 He had not passed the doctor, but was a pier-head jump. 1978 *Navy News* Dec. 6/1 The cartoon on page 14 reminded me of a pierhead jump I had from the Defiance in 1940.

b. Designating a type of variety entertainment traditionally associated with summer shows on piers in seaside resorts.

1932 *Statesman* (Calcutta) 2 Aug., There is always a public, and not only a pierhead public, for a thoroughly good pierrot show. 1960 *Times* 2 Mar. 13/2 Here was good old bandsman's pier-head stuff. 1963 *Times* 8 Feb. 14/5 Some ambiguous remarks..—in the best early pierhead manner—suggesting that he is either describing the chassis of a car technically or that of a young woman vulgarly.

pierid (pəi·ərid), *sb.* and *a.* *Ent.* Also **Pierid**, † **-ide.** [f. mod.L. family name *Pieridæ*, f. the generic name *Pieris* (see *PIERIS) + -ID³.] **A.** *sb.* A white or yellow butterfly belonging to the family Pieridæ. **B.** *adj.* Of or pertaining to this family.

1885 W. F. KIRBY *Elem. Text-bk. Entomol.* 155 A white, black-bordered species..could hardly be mistaken for anything but a Pieride. 1905 V. L. KELLOGG *Amer. Insects* xiv. 445 The males of many Pierids give off a pleasing aromatic odor. 1926 *Contemp. Rev.* Sept. 370 Pierids are essentially creatures of the open country. 1932 METCALF & FLINT *Fund. Insect Life* viii. 291 (*caption*) Three common pierid butterflies. 1954 BORROR & DELONG *Introd. Study Insects* xxvi. 494 The pierids are medium-sized to small butterflies, usually white or yellowish in color. 1963 V. NABOKOV *Gift* ii. 109 The long cloud consisting of myriads of white pierids..moves through the sky. 1973 *Nature* 9 Feb. 408/2 Mating behaviour in pierid butterflies is affected by light intensity.

Pierine (pəi·ərīn, -əin), *sb.* and *a.* *Ent.* [f. mod.L. subfamily name *Pierinæ*, f. next + -INE¹.] **A.** *sb.* A white butterfly belonging to the subfamily Pierinæ, which includes the common cabbage white. **B.** *adj.* Of or pertaining to this subfamily.

1898 *Rep. Brit. Assoc. Adv. Sci. 1897* 691 A white butterfly with such a border becomes an extremely conspicuous object, and this appearance of *Mylothris* is mimicked..by species from a number of Pierine genera. 1930 *Proc. Entomol. Soc. London* V. 66 (*heading*) Attacks by a sparrow upon the Pierine butterfly *Aporia bieti*, Oberth., at Tachienlu, Tibet. 1934 *Discovery* July 195/2 It seemed unlikely that certain features in which the Pierines resembled the supposed models were simply adopted from the latter. *Ibid.*, The similar features..were on the whole most distinct and most Pierine-like in those forms that were locally associated with the Pierine *Pereutes* and *Euterpes*.

pieris (pəi·əris). [mod.L., f. L. *Pīeris* a Muse, f. *Pīeria* (see PIERIAN *a.*).] **1.** [Adopted by D. Don 1834, in *Edin. New Philos. Jrnl.* XVII. 159.] An evergreen shrub of the genus so called, belonging to the family Ericaceæ, native to the southern United States, China, and Japan, and bearing panicles of small, bell-shaped white flowers.

1838 J. C. LOUDON *Arboretum* II. 1115 The oval-leaved Pieris..was introduced in 1825. 1909 *Curtis's Bot. Mag.* CXXXV. 8283 The introduction into European gardens of this handsome *Pieris* appears to have taken place upwards of half a century ago. 1935 A. J. SWEET *Trees & Shrubs* xi. 82 Andromeda can be increased by division and cuttings..and Pieris by layering. 1962 R. PAGE *Educ. Gardener* ix. 260 Evergreens, such as rhododendrons, skimmias, pieris, aucuba. 1975 *Country Life* 10 Apr. 891/3 Other ericaceous plants include pieris with its splendid spring leaf colours.

2. [Adopted by F. von P. Schrank 1801, in *Fauna Boica* II. 152.] A white butterfly of the genus so called, which includes the common cabbage whites.

1863 H. W. BATES *Naturalist on River Amazons* I. i. 22 Numbers of fine showy butterflies were seen...A white Pieris (P. Monuste), and two or three species of brimstone and orange-coloured butterflies. 1969 R. F. CHAPMAN *Insects* xvii. 330 Female *Pieris* ready to oviposit are attracted to green surfaces.

Pierrot. Add: **3.** *attrib.* and *Comb.*, as (sense 1) *Pierrot costume, doll, show*; *Pierrot-like* adj.; **Pierrot collar** (see quot. 1957).

1957 M. B. PICKEN *Fashion Dict.* 250/2 *Pierrot collar*, ruff like that worn by French pantomime character. 1977 *Time* 8 Aug. 38/1 Pierrot collars and flounces adorned many of Bohan's dresses, capes and blouses. 1893 A. BEARDSLEY *Let. c.* 15 Feb. (1971) 43 Strange hermaphroditic creatures wandering about in Pierrot costumes or modern dress; quite a new world of my own creation. 1960 Pierrot costume [see *concert-party]. 1935 A. CHRISTIE *Three Act Tragedy* III. ix. 188 A ridiculously elongated pierrot doll [was] lying across the sofa. 1967 A. WILSON *No Laughing Matter* II. 39 Rupert lolling on cushions..aimlessly waving the limp Pierrot doll beside him. 1979 A. BUCHAN *Scrap Screen* viii. 132 Emancipated girls..moved into bedsitters..and filled them with black and orange cushions and Pierrot dolls. 1977 *Rolling Stone* 19 May 73/1, I hadn't quite expected the faultless intonation..of that shining, graceful, Pierrot-like figure. 1951 J. FLEMING *Man who looked Back* i. 14 They saw the pierrot show from comfortable deck-chairs. 1978 M. GILBERT *Empty House* xiii. 107 There's..a pierrot show in the Palais de Dance [*sic*].

Pierrotic (pīĕrǫ·tik), *a.* [f. PIERROT + -IC.] Of, belonging, or pertaining to pierrots.

1927 *Observer* 16 Oct. 15/3 The delightful tenor raptures of Mr. Georges Metaxa are in the best Pierrotic tradition. 1931 *Times Lit. Suppl.* 13 Aug. 614/1 Mr. Nicoll seems to pass lightly over his [*sc.* Punch's] white-bloused, Pierrotic, Neapolitan avatar.

‖ **pietas** (pi,ēi·tās). [L.] An attitude of respect towards an ancestor, scholarship, an institution, a country, etc.

1924 J. BAILEY *Let.* 27 Apr. (1935) 244 Both Llanthony, to which, of course, *pietas* specially draws me, and Llangammarch look very attractive. 1930 *N. & Q.* 22 Feb. 143/1 Yet another Early English Text appears under the editorship of an American scholar, a new proof of *pietas*. 1944 *Horizon* Sept. 188 And yet, with all his *pietas*, when Joyce died..he had not set foot in his native city for over thirty years. 1960 C. DAY LEWIS *Buried Day* i. 26 *Pietas*—a habit of respect for gods, ancestors, parents, country, institutions. 1961 *Times* 30 Nov. 16/2 *Pietas* is the curse of the commissioned biographer. 1965 N. ST. JOHN-STEVAS in *Bagehot's Coll. Wks.* I. 11 The *Economist* ..has supported this undertaking, as..an act of *pietas* to its..most famous editor. 1976 *Church Times* 16 Jan. 15/5 A requiem will be sung for him in St. Oswald's, Durham, with his music—not just as an act of *pietas*, but in gratitude to God for one who, although a man of his age, yet reminds us of several needs in today's Church.

Pietism. Add: **1.** Also in extended use, any similar movement within Protestantism.

1900 tr. *A. Ritschl's Christian Doctrine of Justification & Reconciliation* i. 84 It is..an inversion of the Reformation point of view when Pietism makes the moral power of faith the object which God invests with the value which moral conduct would possess when carried out. 1934 R. N. FLEW *Idea of Perfection in Christian Theol.* xvi. 275 The essential mark of Pietism is its quest for individual holiness. 1958 E. L. MASCALL *Recovery of Unity* i. 9 The word 'pietism'. By this I mean an attitude to Christianity..which, in contrast to the corporate, objective, liturgical and theocentric religion of the primitive Church, is individualistic, subjective, pietistic and Christocentric. 1967 D. T. KAUFFMAN *Dict. Relig. Terms* 354/1 *Pietism*, protestant religious current emphasizing personal devotions, Bible study, evangelism, and the like. 1967 M. J. HEINECKEN in J. Macquarrie *Dict. Christian Ethics* 257/1 Pietism has been and continues to be a valid protest against sterile orthodoxism and false sacramentalism.

piet-my-vrou (pi·tmēⁱfrōᵘ). *S. Afr.* Also **piet-myn-vrouw.** [Afrikaans, lit. 'Peter my wife', echoic, f. the bird's call.] The red-chested cuckoo, *Notococcyx* (or *Cuculus*) *solitarius*; also, occasionally used as a name for the noisy robin-chat, *Cossypha bicolor*, which imitates the call of the red-chested cuckoo.

[1790 E. HELME tr. *Le Vaillant's Trav. Afr.* II. xviii. 367 One of them [*sc.* the Hottentots] named *Pit*, was the first who brought me this bird... He had no sooner shot the hen, than the cock flew after him, repeating several times *Pit me frow*; it must be observed, it is the usual cry of this bird, as I was afterwards convinced, on shooting some of the same kind.] 1835 A. STEEDMAN *Wanderings S. Afr.* I. v. 189 The 'Piet myn vrouw', a bird of which the Hottentots relate many amusing stories. 1923 F. W. FITZSIMONS *Nat. Hist. S. Afr.: Birds* II. 31 (*caption*) Noisy Robin Chat, or Piet-myn-vrouw (*Cossypha bicolor*). An active and efficient policeman of the forests and dense scrub on the eastern side of South Africa. 1937 M. ALSTON *Wanderings of Bird-Lover in Afr.* viii. 50 The Dutch call him [*sc.* the noisy robin-chat] the piet-myn-vrouw because of his imitating the red-chested cuckoo. 1949 *Cape Argus Mag.* 5 Nov. 7/6 The piet-my-vrou and turtle doves make the afternoon drowsy with their calls. 1966 E. PALMER *Plains of Camdeboo* xii. 216 Sometimes in the bush we hear..the Piet-my-vrou, and its call is unmistakable. 1971 *Stand. Encycl. S. Afr.* III. 571/1 The piet-my-vrou or red-chested cuckoo (*Cuculus solitarius*) is a fairly large, brownish cuckoo.

‖ **pietra** (pi,e·trā). Pl. **pietre** (-e). The Italian for 'stone'; occurring in Italian phrases, more or less in current use in the terminology of art, etc.

a. pietra commessa (kǒme·sā), pl. **commesse** (-e) [fem. of *commesso*, pa. pple. of *commettere* to fit together]: mosaic work; an example of this.

a 1666 EVELYN *Diary* an. 1644 (1955) II. 191 Here were divers incomparable tables of Pietra Commessa, which is a marble ground inlayd with severall sorts of marbles & stones of divers colours, in the shapes of flowers, trees, beasts, birds & Landskips like the natural. *a* 1668 R. LASSELS *Voy. Italy* (1670) II. 220 A curious table of *pietre commesse* about 12 foot long & 5 wide. 1766 SMOLLETT *Trav.* II. xxviii. 70 These *pietre commesse* are better calculated for cabinets, than for ornaments to great buildings. 1848 H. R. FORSTER *Stowe Catal.* 287 A box, with slabs of pietre commesse, of birds, fruits, and flowers.

b. pietra dura (du·rā), pl. **dure** (-e) [fem. of *duro* hard]: (see quot. 1962); also (sing. and pl.) mosaic work of such stones; also *attrib.*

1805 P. BECKFORD *Familiar Lett. from Italy* I. 148 The best part of the furniture is the inlaid tables in Pietra Dura, a work of great labour and great expence. 1845 R. FORD *Hand-bk. for Travellers Spain* II. 580/2 Observe the Florentine pulpit of *Pietre dure*. 1901 'L. MALET' *Hist. R. Calmady* III. v. 199 Certain treasures, unique in historic worth, locked in the glass tables and fine Florentine and *piétra dura* cabinets of the Long Gallery. 1942 *Burlington Mag.* Apr. 87/1 The chief piece of furniture mentioned is the enormous cabinet of *pietra dura* that now stands in the ballroom at Badminton. 1961 *Connoisseur* Dec. p. xxxiii, Louis XVI cabinets..inset with panels of pietre dure in the form of flat mosaics of different birds. 1962 R. G. HAGGAR *Dict. Art Terms* 259/1 *Pietra dura*,..those stones which, mainly composed of silicates, are in English generally described as semiprecious stones. *Pietra dura* were much used for altar frontals, table-tops, and the like in the sixteenth century. 1970 *Oxf. Compan. Art* 871/1 *Pietre dure*... A term applied to a particular kind of mosaic work in which coloured stones.. are used to imitate as far as possible the effect of painting. 1976 *Country Life* 27 May (Suppl.) 47 A Florentine pietra dura casket with ormolu mounts.

c. pietra serena (sĕre·nā) [fem. of *sereno* clear]: a bluish sandstone much used for building in Florence and throughout Tuscany; also *attrib.*

1873 S. & J. HORNER *Walks in Florence* II. xxii. 296 The aisles are carried round the nave and transepts by a line of handsome columns, of pietra-serena, with Corinthian capitals. 1888 G. J. OAKESHOTT *Detail & Ornament of Ital. Renaissance* Pl. 37 Examples of Corbels from Florence, Siena etc.. in pietra serena by Donatello in the Bargello. 1927 E. W. ANTHONY *Early Florentine Archit. & Decoration* x. 69 The sculpture of the Gothic period, in general, gives up the decorated backgrounds of the older school, and the reliefs are executed in white marble or *pietra serena*. 1931 R. FRY *Let.* 22 July (1972) II. 661 It's odd that Florence..couldn't make a city and these rather second-rate Bolognese could—it's true they had brick instead of that abominable *pietra-serena*. 1971 F. M. GODFREY *Ital. Archit. up to 1750* iv. 198 The interior differs from the Cappella Pazzi by the stressed corner pilasters in dark *pietra serena*, supporting the arches at the joints. 1975 *Ashmolean Mus. Rep. Visitors 1973–74* 34 The present building with its *pietra serena* pilasters and window frames, so characteristic of Renaissance architecture in Tuscany.

piewipe: see PEEWEEP in Dict. and Suppl.

pie·zo-. Add: Now usu. with pronunc. (pəi,ī·zo). **pie·zo-crystal,** a piezo-electric crystal used in an electrical circuit; **pie:zo-crystalliza·tion** *Geol.* [ad. G. *piezokrystallisation* (E. Weinschenk 1895, in *Abhandl. d. Bayerischen Akad. d. Wissensch.* (*Math.-phys Klasse*) XVIII. 741)], crystallization of a magma, usu. in a distinctive or abnormal manner, under conditions of mechanical stress; (? *obs.*); **piezo-electricity,** delete def. and see main entry below; **pie:zoma·gnetism** [ad. G. *piezomagnetismus* (W. Voigt 1901, in *Nachrichten v. d. K. Ges. d. Wissensch. zu Göttingen* (*Math.-phys. Klasse*) I. 1)], magnetism induced in a crystal by the application of mechanical stress; hence **pie:zomagne·tic** *a.*, of, pertaining to, or exhibiting piezomagnetism; **pie:zoresi·stance, -resisti·vity,** change in the electrical resistance or resistivity of a solid when subjected to mechanical stress; freq. *attrib.*; so **pie:zoresi·stive** *a.*, of, pertaining to, or utilizing this effect.

1928 *Exper. Wireless* July 414/2 (*caption*) Mounting piezo crystals. 1936 *Amer. Speech* XI. 95/2 A piezo-crystal cutter for aluminum discs with which frequencies from 40 to 10,000 cycles can be recorded. 1958 *Engineering* 31 Jan. 160/3 An alternative type of drum is the large sheet of steel with a piezo-crystal fixed to a particular part of it. 1903 A. GEIKIE *Text-bk. Geol.* (ed. 4) II. 718 He [*sc.* Weinschenk] believes that rock to have been part of a normal granitic magma which crystallized under abnormal conditions, and that it owes its mineralogical composition and characteristic foliated structure..to the peculiar relations of tension accompanying the plication of the mountains. To these relations he has given the name of 'piezocrystallization'. 1938 A. JOHANNSEN *Descr. Petrogr. Igneous Rocks* IV. 79 The parallel texture is seen in dynamometamorphosed rocks or in border facies. In the latter case it may be due to piezocrystallization, for the feldspars also are often more or less parallel. 1954 R. L. PARKER tr. *Niggli's Rocks & Min. Deposits* xiv. 523 Effects of stress on partly solidified material. Such effects leave their impression on structures and textures and are responsible for the piezo-crystallization of magmas. 1901 *Sci. Abstr.* A. IV. 1043 The recorded observations determine, for the pyro- and piezo-magnetic excitement, only superior limiting values. 1959 *Physics & Chem. of Solids* XI. 77/2 The piezomagnetic moment will be reversed in sign when the antiferromagnetic sublattice magnetizations are reversed in sign. 1972 *Nature* 8 Dec. 348/2 Both volcanic eruptions and the San Andreas creep increments are very imperfectly understood so that a large scale control experiment which demonstrates quantitatively the role of the piezomagnetic effect in producing local magnetic anomalies is very desirable. **1978** *Ibid.* 9 Mar. 130/1 When a stress is applied to, or removed from, a rock there is a distortion of crystal structure which often gives rise to a small change in the rock's remanent magnetisation. This is known as the piezomagnetic effect and has an obvious application to the prediction of earthquakes. **1901** *Sci. Abstr.* A. IV. 1043 (*heading*) Pyro- and piezo-magnetism of crystals. **1931** S. R. WILLIAMS *Magn. Phenomena* v. 164 With the advent of the electron theory of matter,.. physicists began to inquire as to the possibility of the phenomena of pyro- and piezo-magnetism. **1967** CONDON & ODISHAW *Handbk. Physics* (ed. 2) IV. viii. 143/1 In antiferromagnetic crystals of sufficiently low symmetry, such as CoF_2 and MnF_2, the magnetic analogue of piezo-electricity, piezomagnetism, can occur. **1978** *Nature* 9 Mar. 130/1 In practice, piezomagnetism has been of little use in earthquake prediction. **1954** *Physical Rev.* XCIV. 42/2 The piezoresistance results for germanium and silicon..have been expressed in terms of the pressure coefficient of resistivity and two simple shear coefficients. **1970** *Jrnl. Appl. Physics* XLI. 811/2 (*heading*) Piezo-resistance in SnTe. *Ibid.*, The piezoresistance effect has been used in the past with success in determining the symmetry of the bands in various semiconductors. **1935** J. W. COOKSON in *Physical Rev.* XLVII. 194/2 It is herein meant by the piezo-resistive effect that change in electrical resistance which a homogeneous body undergoes when subjected to mechanical stress. **1963** *Jrnl. Appl. Physics* XXXIV. 684/2 The piezoresistive effect in semi-conductors..is generally a result of the dependence of the electronic energy levels of a crystal on the state of strain in the crystal. **1973** *Physics Bull.* Dec. 743/3 The cartridge consists of an elastic stainless steel cantilever on to which a pair of silicon piezoresistive strain gauges have been fused. **1958** *Solid State Physics* VI. 232 The most important examples of unsymmetrical fourth rank properties are the classical piezooptic effect (photo-elasticity) and the piezoresistivity effect. **1965** *Wireless World* Aug. 380/2 Although carbon has been used as the sensitive element in pressure transducers, piezo-resistivity in ordinary carbon composition resistors appears to have attracted little attention.

piezo (pəiˌī·zo), *a.* = *PIEZOELECTRIC *a.*

1922 GLAZEBROOK *Dict. Appl. Physics* II. 600/1 To demonstrate the piezo effect it is convenient to place a sheet of tinfoil on a slab of tourmaline and connect the foil to an electrometer. **1930** *Proc. IRE* XVIII. 491 A piezo oscillator is the most suitable frequency standard thus far devised. **1946** W. G. CADY *Piezoelectricity* i. 6 Piezo resonators and oscillators have proved useful in many kinds of electrical measurement. **1970** J. EARL *Tuners & Amplifiers* i. 27 Some of the inexpensive systems use a piezo cartridge (crystal or ceramic). **1975** G. J. KING *Audio Handbk.* viii. 174 Early piezo pickups used a natural crystal element..as the signal generator.

piezoelectric (pəiˌī:zoˌīle·ktrik), *a.* and *sb.* Also **piezo-electric.** [f. PIEZO- + ELECTRIC *a.* and *sb.*] **A.** *adj.* Of, pertaining to, exhibiting, or utilizing piezoelectricity.

1883 *Jrnl. Chem. Soc.* XLIV. 412 (*heading*) Actinoelectric and piezoelectric properties of quartz. **1921** *Physical Rev.* XVII. 531 The possibility is discussed of using the piezo-electric resonator for a standard of high frequency. **1947** CROWTHER & WHIDDINGTON *Science at War* iv. 175 Modified quartz piezo-electric hydrophones were used to measure vibrations as low as 1 cycle per second. **1958** N. CUSACK *Electr. & Magn. Prop. Solids* xviii. 410 The piezoelectric properties of Rochelle salt have been widely used in gramophone pick-ups, microphones, loudspeakers, surface roughness analysers, and other electromechanical devices. **1972** *Last Whole Earth Catalog* (Portola Inst.) 88/2 The piezoelectric effect has been observed in a number of organic materials, among them wood, bone, tendon and skin. **1973** M. WOODHOUSE *Blue Bone* xvii. 190 He was talking about some kind of reversed piezoelectric effect. **1977** *Rolling Stone* 7 Apr. 88/1 (Advt.), But only Ovation's six-element piezo-electric pickup captures both top *and* individual string vibration.

B. *sb.* A piezoelectric substance or body.

1913 *Phil. Mag.* XXVI. 1053 These high resistances.. are both cheaper and easier to use than either standard capacities or quartz piezoelectrics. **1971** B. JAFFE et al. *Piezoelectric Ceramics* i. 1 The creation of useful piezo-electrics by treatment of a polycrystalline material depends on ferroelectricity. **1975** *Physics Bull.* May 212/3 For economic and technical reasons the piezoelectrics most commonly used for SAW generation are lithium niobate and quartz.

Hence **pie:zoele·ctrical** *a.* = *PIEZOELECTRIC *a.*; **pie:zoele·ctrically** *adv.*, as regards, or by means of, piezoelectricity.

1923 *Physical Rev.* XXI. 350 Quartz, another piezo-electrically active substance. **1937** *Discovery* Jan. 22/1 One method of producing them [*sc.* ultra-sounds]..is to employ the piezo-electrical effect in quartz. **1969** *Sci. Jrnl.* Aug. 21/2 Current from the voltage source is fed through a superconductive coil which is vibrated by a piezoelectrically driven metal tuning fork. **1976** *Physics Bull.* Feb. 61/3 New techniques include..very high frequency phonon generation..using a far infrared laser on a piezoelectrical crystal.

piezoelectricity (pəiˌī:zoˌīlektri·sĭti). Delete entry s.v. PIEZO- and substitute: Also **piezo-electricity.** [ad. G. *piezoelectricität* (W. G. Hankel 1881, in *Ber. d. K. Sächsischen Ges. d. Wissensch. zu Leipzig* XXXIII. 52).] Electric polarization in a substance resulting from the application of mechanical stress, esp. in certain crystals.

1883 *Jrnl. Chem. Soc.* XLIV. 412 This phenomenon the author proposes to call piezoelectricity. **1895** [in Dict. s.v. PIEZO-]. **1929** J. A. RATCLIFFE *Physical Princ. Wireless* i. 2 The facts of piezo-electricity have been applied in the quartz oscillator. **1956** *Nature* 17 Mar. 537/2 Tests for pyroelectricity and piezoelectricity were negative. **1974** J. KYLE *Electronics Unravelled* (1975) ii. 45 Piezoelectricity is due to an unusual crystal structure found in several materials.

piezometer. Add to sense b: or in an aquifer. (Further examples.)

1904 *Johns Hopkins Hosp. Bull.* XV. 293 (*heading*) The piezometer, an instrument for measuring resistances. *Ibid.* 293/2 There are two ways of using the piezometer for the purpose of outlining an abdominal tumor. **1954** ROE & AYRES *Engin. Agric. Drainage* x. 266 The piezometer is a length of ½- or ¾-inch iron pipe driven into the soil so that there is no leakage into or out from the sides. **1970** *Nature* 4 July 11/1 Piezometers were used to measure water pressures in the rock joints.

Hence **piezome·tric** *a.*; *spec.* in *Hydrology*, of or pertaining to the measurement of hydrostatic pressure in an aquifer; *piezometric surface* (see quot. 1923[2]).

1923 O. E. MEINZER in *Water-Supply Papers U.S. Geol. Survey* No. 494. 6 The expression piezometric surface is obtained from the French. *Ibid.* 38 The piezometric surface of an aquifer is an imaginary surface that everywhere coincides with the static level of the water in the aquifer. It is the surface to which the water from a given aquifer will rise under its full head. **1966** DAVIS & DEWIEST *Hydrogeol.* ii. 48 The elevation to which water will rise in artesian wells, or wells penetrating confined aquifers, defines the piezometric surfaces. *Ibid.* 49 The general direction of ground-water flow can be shown..on piezometric maps. **1973** GREGORY & WALLING *Drainage Basin Form & Process* iii. 113 This data is used to plot lines of equal piezometric head or equipotentials on a vertical cross section of the aquifer... Similarly, equipotentials or piezometric surfaces could be plotted for several horizontal planes at different depths.

Piffer (pi·fəɹ). *slang.* [From the initials of the name of the force + -ER[1].] A member of the Punjab Frontier Force (a military unit raised in 1849 and employed esp. to police the North-West Frontier of India during British rule) or of one of the regiments that succeeded it. Also (*attrib.*), the force itself.

1892 *Pall Mall Gaz.* 24 Oct. 3/1 The Punjab Frontier Force is known in India as 'The Piffers'. **1901** *Blackw. Mag.* June 780/1 A strong garrison of the three arms, all Piffers. *Ibid.* 788/2 One regiment of Piffer infantry could move anywhere in the hills. **1922** *19th Cent.* Jan. 48 The establishment of a British observation corps, similar to the 'Piffers' of later times. **1958** O. CAROE *Pathans* xx. 345 For many years the Piffers served under the Panjab Lieutenant-Governor. **1970** A. J. SMITHERS *Man who Disobeyed* x. 100 The Guides, the Punjab Frontier Force (Piffers), the Sikhs and the Gurkhas, would have allowed no affectations of superiority from any British regiment, household or line.

‖ **pifferaro** (pifera·ro). Pl. **pifferari.** [It.] A performer on the *piffero*.

1854 THACKERAY *Newcomes* I. xxii. 212 A Contadina and a Trasteverino dancing at the door of a Locanda to the music of a Pifferaro. **1860** *Once a Week* 14 July 71/2 Three of the *pifferari* whom you find at Christmas time in such numbers in the Piazza di Spagna at Rome. **1870** QUEEN VICTORIA *Let.* 6 June in R. Fulford *Your Dear Letter* (1971) 281 Imagine our astonishment at seeing in the village [*sc.* Balmoral] this morning an Italian pifferaro ..and two boys dancing. **1920** *Punch* 30 June 510/3 The local condettieri, pifferari, banditti and lazzaroni. **1974** *Times Lit. Suppl.* 8 Mar. 228/4 The charming shepherds who came to the cities from the Abruzzi to play their bagpipes in front of the wayside shrines—the pifferari. **1977** *Gramophone* June 41/3 He also draws a marvellously keen, edgy sound from piccolo and oboe in the Serenade, for all the world like a *pifferaro* squealing on the Abruzzi air.

pi·ffing, *vbl. sb. slang.* [Cf. PIFF *int.*] (See quots.)

1928 *Daily Tel.* 10 Jan. 11/5 Gunnery training is confined for the most part to sub-calibre firing—'piffing', as it is known in service parlance. **1962** GRANVILLE *Dict. Sailors' Slang* 88/1 *Piffing*, sub-calibre firing. Echoic of the sound. (Gunnery term.)

piffle, *sb.* Add: Also used as a derisive retort.

1914 'HIGH JINKS, JR.' *Choice Slang* 16 *Oh piffle*, an exclamation denoting inconsequence of the subject in question. **1920** 'B. L. STANDISH' *Man on First* xviii. 127 'The Hawks have the lead on us, still.' 'Piffle!' said Cady. 'We'll even things up to-morrow.' **1959** *Elizabethan* Apr. 10/1, I gave you a bar of chocolate on the train from London. So piffle!

pifflicated (pi·flikēⁱtĕd), *ppl. a. U.S. slang.* [A fanciful formation of PIFFLE *v.*, infl. by SPIFLICATE *v.*] Drunk, intoxicated.

1905 TAYLOR & GIBSON *Log of Water Wagon* 50 (*caption*) Professor Bunn's patent plugs for pifflicated people. **1934** S. ROBERTSON *Devel. Mod. Eng.* (1936) xi. 465 English (chiefly American) terms for the idea of 'drunk' or 'intoxicated'... *shellacked, soused, piffled, pifflicated, blotto, stinko.*

piffling, *ppl. a.* (In Dict. s.v. PIFFLE *v.*) (Further examples.)

1916 'BOYD CABLE' *Action Front* 17 You don't think a pifflin' little Pip-Squeak shell could go through *his* head? **1927** *Daily Express* 26 July 3/4 The Bench consider that this is a piffling offence, and..that a warning would have been sufficient. **1927** *Observer* 13 Nov. 10/4 The mechanical parts of the moving-pictures are superb, but the imaginative and intellectual parts are piffling. **1963** *Times* 12 June 8/7 The sum involved was piffling compared with the firm's £25m. a year turnover. **1973** J. WAINWRIGHT *Pride of Pigs* 56 The lesser hooks being pulled in for the piffling crimes, while the big boys work the blinders.

pig, *sb.*[1] Add: **I. 1.** Phr. *in pig*, of a sow: pregnant; also *transf.* of a girl or woman (*slang*).

1886 J. LONG *Bk. Pig* iv. 59 They [*sc.* gilts] are less costly than if either tolerably fat or, as it is called, 'in pig', or in farrow. **1917** W. POWELL-OWEN *Pig-Keeping* v. 59 Sows that are in-pig do best when given their liberty. **1937** H. M. RIKARD-BELL *Handk. Mod. Pig Farming* ii. 33 Watch carefully after three weeks have elapsed for fear that the recurrence of their oestrum periods will prove them [*sc.* gilts] to be not in-pig. **1945** N. MITFORD *Pursuit of Love* x. 83, I am in pig, what d'you think of that? **1950**, etc. [see *IN-PIG *a.*]. **1976** 'D. HALLIDAY' *Dolly & Nanny Bird* vii. 86 Since when had her mother paid the slightest attention to anything her darling daughter said or did, except to do her level best to keep her from marrying anything less than a duke, until she had to get herself in pig.

5. (Further examples.)

1927 *Dialect Notes* V. 458 *Pig*, a woman—sottish, surly, disgruntled, stinking—who has sunk to the lowest level of prostitution. The bum who *keeps a pig* rents her out to others. **1931** E. O'NEILL *The Hunted* IV, in *Mourning becomes Electra* 155 That yaller-haired pig with the pink dress on! **1932** J. T. FARRELL in *Story* Mar.–Apr. 47 Jack told of an anecdote about a pig he had picked up once. She was too lousy and scummy to take a chance on. **1960** I. JEFFERIES *Dignity & Purity* v. 83 I'm having a golf lesson from the Advertising pig tomorrow. **1966** *Sunday Times* (Colour Suppl.) 13 Feb. 35/4 *Pig*, an unattractive girl. **1968–70** *Current Slang* (Univ. S. Dakota) III–IV. 91 *Pig*, a girl who is both promiscuous and drunken. **1973** *Daily Californian* 1 Feb. 1/4 The Pentagon Papers..'provide evidence of pig foreign policy. A pig is someone who attacks you and at the same time claims he is the victim', he said. **1976** *National Observer* (U.S.) 21 Feb. 14/6 The quick resort to the phrase 'pig' for the blue-collar, lower-class people who were doing the job they thought they were supposed to do. **1977** P. G. WINSLOW *Witch Hill Murder* II. 227, I had some beautiful birds in London, but I had to stay on the good side of that pig, or she might have noticed more than was good for her. **1979** R. RENDELL *Make Death love Me* i. 16 I'm not demeaning myself to reply to you, pig.

b. Colloq. phr. *to make a pig of oneself*, to gluttonize.

1942 BERREY & VAN DEN BARK *Amer. Thes. Slang* §272/3 *Be greedy or selfish*,..make a pig..of oneself. **1961** F. S. ANTHONY in *Webster* s.v., Not make such a gorging pig of himself. **1979** *Guardian* 22 June 9/5 We had made pigs of ourselves on the bread.

c. Applied contemptuously or opprobriously to a thing.

1975 'W. HAGGARD' *Scorpion's Tail* i. 2 What a summer, he thought—what a perfect pig. The rain and the cold. **1978** *Times* 15 Feb. 8/1 Miller was out in Collinge's second over to a pig of a ball. **1978** F. MULLALLY *Deadly Payoff* xi. 154 Watch for the potholes. It's a pig of a road. **1978** *Hot Car* June 93/4 The car became a pig to start.

6. b. Delete † *obs.* and add earlier and later examples. Now usu. disparaging.

1811 *Lexicon Balatronicum*, s.v. *Pig*, a China street pig; a Bow-street officer. **1874** HOTTEN *Slang Dict.* 253 *Pig*, a policeman; an informer. The word is now almost exclusively applied by London thieves to a plain-clothes man, or a 'nose'. **1967** C. DRUMMOND *Death at Furlong Post* v. 63, I had to give the local P.C. a lift. I dropped the pig at Packenham. **1970** *Times* 7 Aug. 4/7 'Pig' is slang for a policeman—and the defence says that the word 'pig' was scrawled over the doors of the house after the killings. **1973** *Black World* July 56/1 The pigs swooped by, going west, the emergency light blinking green. **1975** D. LODGE *Changing Places* v. 170 Any pig roughs you up, make sure you get his number. **1975** N. LUARD *Travelling Horseman* vi. 146 The police Rover and some motorcycle pigs providing escort. **1977** 'E. CRISPIN' *Glimpses of Moon* xi. 217 'My God, it's the pigs,' said the hunt saboteuse disgustedly.

d. An informer. ? *Obs.*

1874 [see 6 b above]. **1904** 'No. 1500' *Life in Sing Sing* 251/1 *Pig*, prisoner who reports another; stool-pigeon. **1918** *Amer. Law Rev.* LII. 891 A 'prison stool pigeon' is a 'trusty', 'psalm singer' or 'pig'.

e. Any of various forms of transport (see quots.).

1898 *North Amer. Rev.* June 723 Whalebacks, or 'pigs', as the lake sailors call them. **1938** L. BEEBE *High Iron* 223/2 (Gloss.), *Pig*, locomotive. **1946** *Jrnl. R. Aeronaut. Soc.* L. 85 He had made no great contribution publicly to aeronautical science, but the fact that he had taken the first 'pig' (the name sometimes applied to early biplanes—Ed.) into the air. **1961** *Amer. Speech* XXXVI. 273 *Pig*, *n.*, an old truck. **1967** *Evening Standard* 26 July 13/3 'We'll hop in my pig, catch the rays and have a boss time.' ..The latest in American teenage talk... 'The pig' is a car which looks powerful but has a small engine; 'catching the rays' is getting a sun tan; and 'boss' is the same as great. **1971** *Guardian* 27 Aug. 11/7 He did indeed ride with Melbourne's Hell's Angels..garaging his extremely powerful pig (bike) beside his Porsche. *Ibid.*, 22 Nov. 6/1 The soldiers were in a convoy of 'pigs'—armoured personnel carriers, trucks, and Land-Rovers. **1972** *Times* 8 June 16/2 It was only a patrol of one armoured personnel carrier, a great heavy green vehicle, which everyone calls a 'pig' because of its snout shaped bonnet. **1973** *Amer. Speech 1969* XLIV. 207 *Pig*, 1. Trailer transported on a flat car. 2. Tractor with little power. **1978** *Times* 19 Jan. 29/3 The Pig, the armoured vehicle most used in Belfast.

f. *pl.* Used as a derisive retort. Also const. *to*. *Austral. slang.*

1906 E. Dyson *Fact 'ry 'Ands* i. 5 'Pigs to you!' said Benno, with incredible scorn. **1933** N. Lindsay *Saturdee* ix. 165 Peter had to cover his confusion by saying 'Pigs to you' as he went out kicking the door. **1957** 'N. Culotta' *They're a Weird Mob* (1958) iv. 47 'She's worn out.' 'Pigs she is. There's a lot of life in 'er yet.' **1975** L. Ryan *Shearers* 119 'Ar, pigs to you!' 'In your dinger, too!'

g. *blind pig*: see *blind *a.* (and *adv.*) 16.

II. 8. c. (Later examples.)

1943 E. M. Almedingen *Frossia* vi. 240 Some people are like oranges..all divided into neatly separated pigs. **1961** I. Fleming *Thunderball* iv. 38 The orange, carefully sliced into symmetrical pigs. **1974** P. Dickinson *Poison Oracle* v. 133 They were sharing a second orange, putting it pig by pig into each other's mouths.

d. (Further examples: see quots.)

1926 Maines & Grant *Wise-Crack Dict.* 12/2 *Pig in a blanket*, sausage in a roll. **1941** J. Smiley *Hash House Lingo* 43 *Pig in a blanket*, frankfurter sandwich. **1973** *Observer* (Colour Suppl.) 16 Sept. 83/2 The famous savoury angels on horseback. (The Americans call it pigs in blankets.)

8*. A device that fits snugly inside an oil or gas pipeline and can be sent through it, e.g. to clean the inside or to act as a barrier between fluids either side of it.

1949 *Amer. Speech* XXIV. 33 A few field workers apply the term [*sc.* 'rabbit'] to scrapers used in pipelines to remove paraffin, but the most common name for this device is *pig*, because of the grunting noise it makes as it is forced through the line. **1949** *Sun* (Baltimore) 30 Nov. 13/1 In order to make sure that the pipe had no leaks and was free of all foreign matter, a 'pig'—a rubber object headed by a washer the same diameter as the pipe—was sent through by air pressure. **1956** *Ibid.* (B ed.) 27 Oct. 11/6 A 'pig' is a contraption consisting of blades, wheels, and brushes that runs through a pipeline to clean it. **1970** W. G. Roberts *Quest for Oil* xii. 126 (*caption*) Plastic pig used to clean a 30-inch diameter pipeline in Libya. *Ibid.*, A third way of checking what is going on in a pipeline is to insert some solid separator at the interface [between different products], fitting closely enough in the pipe to make sure that it will be pushed along at the same rate as the oil. Such devices are known as 'batching pigs'. **1977** *Time* 27 June 37/1 The moving oil will push the pig through the 48-in.-diameter steel pipe at 1 m.p.h. As it goes, the cylinder will shove out of the pipe any refuse that may be contained (for example, tools left behind by forgetful workmen) and emit beeps indicating its location.

9. *pigs in clover* (earlier examples); *pig* (also *piggy*) *in the middle*, (*a*) a game in which one child is encircled by others and must escape by any of a number of (usu. vigorous) means; (*b*) a chasing game in which players must cross from one side of an open space to the other without being stopped by a child (or children) in the middle; (*c*) a ball game, usu. for three, in which the middle child tries to intercept the ball as it passes between the other two; also, the player in the middle in any of these games; also *transf.* and *fig.*

1889 *Amer. Stationer* 14 Feb. 355/3 'Pigs in Clover' is the taking name of a new game which has just been placed upon the market by the toy house of Selchow & Righter. **1892** 'Mark Twain' *Amer. Claimant* xxiv. 250 A toy puzzle called Pigs in Clover, had come into sudden favor. **1887** *Folk-Lore Jrnl.* V. 50 Some of the games were much rougher such as 'Pig in the middle and can't get out'. **1915** W. S. Maugham *Of Human Bondage* xi. 39 The new boys were told to go into the middle, while the others stationed themselves along opposite walls. They began to play *Pig in the Middle*. The old boys ran from wall to wall while the new boys tried to catch them: when one was seized and the mystic words said—one, two, three, and a pig for me—he became a prisoner and, turning sides, helped to catch those who were still free. **1962** *Guardian* 3 Aug. 4/5 He was..pig-in-the-middle between his sweet, faint, pietistic mother and his impossibly stiff-necked father. **1962** C. Storr *Robin* viii. 37 You're blue with cold... You *will* have to play pig-in-the-middle. **1969** I. & P. Opie *Children's Games* viii. 238 This game (Bull in the ring) seems to be less played today than in the nineteenth century, when it was frequently recorded... 'Pig in the Middle and Can't Get Out'. **1970** *Times* (Saturday *Rev.*) 28 Feb. p. i/6 Dr. Robinson has thus been rudely abused from all sides of the shrinking Kingdom, piggy-in-the-middle of a debate which..is..fought with..bitterness. **1970** N. Fisher *Walk at Steady Pace* iv. 231 They all knew more..than I did. All three were able to use me as pig in the middle. **1973** M. Amis *Rachel Papers* 125 Four boys..stood in a semicircle round a fifth. ..Having looked round for encouragement or approval, one of the boys leaned over and slapped the piggy in the middle quite hard on the face. **1977** W. McIlvanney *Laidlaw* xii. 51 He's not a good *polis*-man... He doesn't know which side he's on. He's pig in the middle. **1977** *Times* 1 Sept. 5/2 You have to take the decisions, and often you are the piggy in the middle; in our case, for example, between pilots and shipowners.

10. f. *to draw pig on* (or *upon*) *pork* (or *bacon*) (Commercial slang): (see quots.); hence *pig-on-bacon*, a bill drawn in this way.

1849 J. W. *Perils Emigrant* ii. 84, I..had exhausted every means of renewal, borrowing, exchanging cheques, drawing 'pig on pork', as it is technically called. **1872** *Porcupine* 16 Nov. 555/2 In Liverpool..issuing a bill on their London branch establishment..in commercial phraseology, is termed drawing 'pig upon bacon'. **1911** W. Thomson *Dict. Banking* 397/1 '*Pig upon bacon.*' In the case of an accommodation bill, where e.g., Brown accepts merely to oblige the drawer, Jones, Brown has no intention of meeting the bill at maturity. He expects that Jones will himself provide the funds necessary to pay the bill when it is due. As Jones in his own mind considers himself practically the acceptor as well as the drawer, Jones on Brown is therefore likened to a bill drawn by 'Pig on Pork' or 'Pig upon Bacon'. **1920** A. C. Pigou *Econ. of Welfare* ii. v. 144 The variety of accommodation bills known as 'pig-on-bacon', where the acceptor is a branch of the drawing house under an *alias*, is..different. **1930** W. Thomson *Dict. Banking* (ed. 7) 548/2 When the drawers and drawees of a bill are the same, as when a foreign branch of a firm draws on its London office, and there are no documents for goods attached to the bill, the firm is said to be drawing 'Pig on Pork'.

g. *in a pig's eye, ear, arse*: used as a derisive retort; freq. as a strong negative or an emphatic.

Most of the examples are *U.S.* or *Austral.*

1872 'P. V. Nasby' *Struggles* cxiii. 315 A poetickal cotashun..which..wuz,—'Kum wun, kim all, this rock shel fly From its firm base—in a pig's eye.' **1919** W. H. Downing *Digger Dial.* 38 *Pig's ear*, a contemptuous ejaculation. **1932** O. R. Cohen *Star of Earth* xxv. 270 'Here I am,' he says: 'I did it..and that means Mary didn't!'..'In a pig's eye it does!' **1942** Berrey & Van den Bark *Amer. Thes. Slang* §166/7 *I don't believe it!*..It is in a pig's eye *or* arse! *Ibid.* §170/8 *You are mistaken*... It is in a pig's eye! *or* arse! *Ibid.* §229/5 *You will not!*..In a pig's eye *or* arse you will! **1951** E. Lambert *Twenty Thousand Thieves* 322 'Pig's arse to that!' another voice cried. 'A jack-up—that's the shot.' **1957** J. Blish *Fallen Star* v. 70 'You'll have to.' 'In a pig's eye,' she said. **1962** *Observer* 21 Jan. 11/7 Immigration from Ireland, said the Prime Minister.., will be included in the general controls. In a pig's eye it will. **1968** W. Garner *Deep, Deep Freeze* ix. 110 'One stops short of probing the private lives of people for whom one has a regard.' 'In a pig's ear!' she said vulgarly. 'If duty called you'd have a man under the bed on my honeymoon.' **1968** H. Waugh *Con Game* v. 53 'He claimed he didn't want to—.' Mrs. Fogarty said, 'In a pig's eye he didn't want to.' **1969** G. Johnston *Clean Straw for Nothing* 307 'That's because she won't face realities.' 'Pig's arse. And anyway who are you to talk?' **1973** J. Wainwright *Pride of Pigs* 83 'Preston,' suggested Harris. 'In a pig's eye!' growled Ripley. **1974** P. Larkin *High Windows* 35 My wife and I have asked a crowd of craps To come and waste their time and ours: perhaps You'd care to join us? In a pig's arse, friend. **1976** *Time* 5 Apr. 23/2 Attorney General Edward Levi let it be known that he considered the matter 'extremely serious'. To officials of the Federal Bureau of Investigation, Levi's comment was a monumental understatement. 'Extremely serious in a pig's eye,' said one. 'It's a disaster.'

h. *on the pig's back* (occas. *the pig's ear*): in a fortunate position; on top of the world; riding high.

1900 *19th Cent.* July 81 [Ireland] 'You're on the pig's back' means prosperity. 'The pig is on your back' indicates misfortune. **1922** Joyce *Ulysses* 177 That'll be two pounds ten... Three Hynes owes me... Five guineas about. On the pig's back. **1930** [see *home *adv.* 2 b]. **1946** C. Mann in *Coast to Coast 1945* 27 We always were lucky. He's home on the pig's ear. **1949** H. Wadman *Life Sentence* i. i. 10 Could anything be nicer? Basil is on the pig's back. **1958** J. Lodwick *Bid Soldiers Shoot* viii. 277 Nixon, who in Crete had suffered horribly from solitude, was now a happy man—on the pig's back, one might say, and the image is appropriate since the grunting of the corralled porkers never ceased. **1962** R. Wallis *Point of Origin* 11 Then aerial topdressing came in and they were on the pig's back. **1966** 'L. Lane' *ABZ of Scouse* ii. 78 *On ther pig's back*, lucky; doing well; in the money.

i. *to make a pig's ear* (*out*) *of*: to make a mess of; to bungle.

1954 E. Hargreaves *Handful of Silver* xii. 183 'I've made a real pig's ear of it, haven't I?' said Basil, with an attempt at lightness. **1973** *Observer* 29 July 14/5 If you are doing something wrong, you will..make a pig's ear of its execution.

11. b. In various phrases and locutions connected with the idea of pigs flying, freq. as a type of the unlikely or untrue.

1616 W. Clerk *Withals's Dict. Eng. & Lat.* (rev. ed.) 583 Pigs fly in the ayre with their tayles forward. **1639** J. Clarke *Paroemiologia Anglo-Latina* 147/1 Pigs fly in the aire with their tailes forward. **1670** J. Ray *Coll. Eng. Proverbs* 189 Pigs fly in the air with their tails forward. *c* **1860** [in Dict.]. **1865** 'L. Carroll' *Alice's Adventures in Wonderland* ix. 155 'I've a right to think,' said Alice sharply... 'Just about as much right,' said the Duchess, 'as pigs have to fly.' *a* **1871** A. De Morgan *Budget of Paradoxes* (1872) 275 There is a proverb which says, A pig may fly, but it isn't a likely bird. [**1871** 'L. Carroll' *Through Looking-Glass* iv. 76 'The time has come,' the Walrus said, 'To talk of many things: Of shoes—and ships—and sealing-wax—Of cabbages—and kings—And why the sea is boiling hot—And whether pigs have wings.'] **1880** C. H. Spurgeon *John Ploughman's Pictures* 32 They say that if pigs fly they always go with their tails forward. **1913** *Punch* 13 Aug. 156/1 'If pigs could fly...' The clumsy brutes can't, of course, while we flies *can* pig—see us in a confectioner's shop. **1937** Partridge *Dict. Slang* 628/2 *Pigs fly, when*, never. **1949** 'J. Tey' *Brat Farrar* x. 81 'I may, some day. I may.' 'Pigs may fly.' **1952** Wodehouse (*title*) Pigs have wings. **1972** 'J. Quartermain' *Rock of Diamond* xxvii. 176 'I'll wait... Perhaps he'll have news...' 'Maybe... And maybe pigs have wings.' **1973** J. Higgins *Prayer for Dying* xii. 165 'Something could come out of that line of enquiry.' 'I know... Pigs might also fly.'

IV. 12. a. *pig bin* (also fig.), *-byre, house* (also fig.), *man* (earlier and later examples; also fig.), *manure, -meat* (earlier and later examples; also fig.), *-pail, -pen* (further examples; also fig.), *-wire*; (sense 6 b in Dict. and Suppl.) *pig car, station.*

1959 I. & P. Opie *Lore & Lang. Schoolch.* ix. 167 They call him [*sc.* a greedy-guts]: dustbin,..pig-bin, [etc.]. **1972** P. Black *Biggest Aspidistra* ii. iv. 124 Outside the houses stood a row of huge bins, one for collecting paper, one for tins, one for bottles, one for kitchen waste. They were known as pigbins, though..the pigs ate only the waste. **1979** 'M. Hebden' *Death set to Music* iii. 29 Pel sniffed at his stew. 'I think they took it from the pig bin,' he observed coldly. **1906** *19th Cent.* June 967 Already half the cottage pig-byres stand empty in our lanes. **1970** G. Jackson *Let.* 10 June in *Soledad Brother* (1971) 36, I sat in the back of the pig car and bled for two hours. **1845** C. Cist *Cincinnati Misc.* I. 186 A stout looking fellow set his gun leaning on a pig house, and jumped in to catch some fowls. **1950** *N.Z. Jrnl. Agric.* Apr. 369/1 In considering the design of pig houses there are two main factors. **1960** *Farmer & Stockbreeder* 9 Feb. 76/2 The value of..good pighouse insulation. **1963** *Amer. Speech* XXXVIII. 173 [Kansas University] A sorority known for its unprepossessing members.. *campus pig house*..*pig house*. **1825** *Whole Proc. Old Bailey* 15 Jan. 116/2, I..saw the prisoner in the kitchen—he said, if I came with any *pigman* he would knock my head off. **1971** *Farmers Weekly* 19 Mar. 75/3 Continental pigmen want hybrid boars. *a* **1975** Wodehouse *Sunset at Blandings* (1977) vii. 52 Clarence's pig man claims to have seen the White Lady of Blandings one Saturday night. **1976** *Eastern Daily Press* (Norwich) 19 Nov. 11/1 (Advt.), Assistant pigman/woman required.. to join staff of five, on 500-sow herd. **1960** *Farmer & Stockbreeder* 1 Mar. 107/1 Future developments include a pig-manure spreading service which will give back to the members the pig manure they would have had if they had reared their pigs on their farms. **1975** J. Wyllie *Butterfly Flood* (1977) xxiii. 105 The compost heap was.. activated by pig manure. **1798** J. Woodforde *Diary* 2 July (1931) V. 125 Pig Meat now is but of little value to what it has been. **1942** Z. N. Hurston in *Amer. Mercury* July 96/1 *Pig meat*, young girl. **1970** G. Greer *Female Eunuch* 265 Perhaps words like *pig, pig-meat* or *dog* are inspired by the sadness which follows unsatisfactory sex. **1971** *Farmers Weekly* (Extra) 19 Mar. 12/2 High beef prices have pushed up demand for fresh pigmeat. **1977** *Times* 8 Feb. 17/3 We break the [EEC] rules by subsidizing pigmeat. **1908** *Westm. Gaz.* 18 Jan. 2/3 The cricket climbed the side of the..pig-pail. **1872** *Harper's Mag.* Apr. 690/2 A one-story wooden structure..became the rallying-place of the tribes. This [room], by reason of its general unsightliness, was denominated by Tammany's political adversaries the 'Pig-Pen'. **1907** J. London *Let.* 25 July (1966) 247 He left his stateroom the filthiest pig-pen I ever saw. **1952** R. P. Bissell *Monongahela* i. 5, I took my paper suitcase out of the pigpen and up to the mates' room, and one thing sure, that mates' room smelled better than the deckhands' bunkroom, and even had a light in the bunk to read by, and a clean blanket with no fuel oil or coal ground into it. **1960** T. Hughes *Lupercal* 38 Toward the pig-pens on his right. **1971** M. Tak *Truck Talk* 118 *Pigpen*, a sloppy, ill-run truck stop. **1978** J. Wainwright *Jury People* xxxv. 106 They carried him to the pig-pens. **1979** R. Gillespie *Crossword Mystery* v. 116 'Did you search his place?' 'Yeah. A pigpen.' **1970** G. Jackson *Let.* 10 June in *Soledad Brother* (1971) 34, I stopped attending school regularly, and started getting 'picked up' by the pigs more often. The pig station, a lecture, and oak-stick therapeutics. **1975** P. Moyes *Black Widower* i. 13 Assemble..outside the Georgetown Pig Station..for a protest march. **1964** *Listener* 19 Mar. 458/1 Scrapping the hedges, replacing them with concrete posts and pigwire. **1971** *Ideal Home* Apr. 119 To restrain dogs and children the cheapest and strongest I know is Smith's (of Bristol) Bulwark fencing—what my father calls pig-wire—a heavy galvanised mesh varying from 6 in. square at the top to 6 in. by 3 in. at the bottom, 32 in. high.

b. *pig-keeper, -netter, -stalker*; *pig-rearing, -stalking*; (sense 7) *pig-breaking.*

1902 *Encycl. Brit.* XXIX. 578/1 A great saving of labour was effected by the introduction of 'pig-breaking' machines. **1906** *Westm. Gaz.* 20 Aug. 10/1 The fact, too, that acorns are a heavy crop will gladden the hearts of pig-keepers. **1971** *Farmers Weekly* (Extra) 19 Mar. 33/2 The slump has hit heavy hog producers hardest of all pig-keepers. **1923** *Blackw. Mag.* Dec. 768/1 They concocted a plan by which the boar should be netted... Professional pig-netters were summoned. **1907** *Westm. Gaz.* 31 July 12/2 Pig-rearing..is on the downward grade. **1960** *Farmer & Stockbreeder* 29 Mar. 88/3 The most important ingredient of pig-rearing success is undoubtedly hard work. **1978** *Dumfries Courier* 13 Oct. 20/1 A sow and seven piglets died early yesterday afternoon when fire raged through a pig-rearing building at Laghall Farm, New Abbey Road, Dumfries. **1908** *Westm. Gaz.* 2 Mar. 5/2 'The indiscriminate offer of rewards in no way tends to the destruction of the real man-eater,' says Mr. Rees, 'while it ensures the extermination of the useful..deer and pig-stalker.' **1867** M. A. Barker *Station Life N.Z.* (1870) xv. 109 We go over the hills pig-stalking.

c. *pig-ploughed*; *pig-jawed* (example), *-snouted*; *pig-ignorant* (hence *pig-ignorance*), *-lucky, -sick, -sober, -sticky, -stupid, -tight* (examples) adjs.

In the last type of use, often merely with the force of an intensifier: extreme(ly), thorough(ly).

1973 H. Miller *Open City* xvii. 187 Boorishness and Glasgow-bred pig-ignorance. **1972** J. Wainwright *Requiem for Loser* iv. 82 I'm not pig-ignorant... But you're pig-*stupid*. **1973** A. Price *October Men* vi. 84 [He] was clearly pig-ignorant of everything that did not concern him. **1976** T. Heald *Let Sleeping Dogs Die* vii. 132

Those press johnnies..would never twig. Too gullible and too pig ignorant. **1942** 'M. Innes' *Daffodil Affair* I. v. 30 'A nice dog,' Appleby said... Mr Gee swung round. 'Dish-faced,' he said... 'And undershot... Pig-jawed, in fact.' **1939** J. Steinbeck *Grapes of Wrath* xvi. 253 'Get her fixed?' 'We was pig lucky,' said Tom. 'Got a part 'fore dark.' **1921** H. Guthrie-Smith *Tutira* xix. 165 These pig-ploughed shreds [of land]. **1948** A. Baron *From City from Plough* i. 9 Wha's up, Sergeant?.. You look pigsick. **1965** A. Prior *Interrogators* xiii. 244 He was pig-sick of talking to the old bastard. **1977** J. Wainwright *Nest of Rats* I. vii. 51, I was pig-sick of Rawle and his devious ways. **1923** E. Sitwell *Bucolic Comedies* 9 And old pig-snouted Darkness grunts and roots in the hovels. **1960** *Times* 29 Sept. (Nigeria Suppl.) p. xxi/5 The weighty pig-snouted aardvark. **1945** Koestler *Twilight Bar* III. 62, I thought so. Pig-sober. **1922** Joyce *Ulysses* 445 Eat it and get all pigsticky. **1972** Pig-stupid [see **pig-ignorant* adj.]. **1859** Pig-tight [see *bull-strong* s.v. *Bull *sb.*[1] 11]. *a* **1930** Pig-tight [see *horse-high* adj. s.v. *Horse *sb.* 27a].

13. pig board *Surfing* (see quots.); **pig-boat** *U.S. slang*, a submarine; **pig-boiling** *Metallurgy*, the puddling of unrefined pig-iron, which is characterized by a period of rapid bubbling of gas from the molten metal; **pig-dog**, add to def.: and New Zealand (further example); (*b*) used as a term of abuse; **pig net**, a type of strong net; **pig-root** *v.*, (*b*) *Austral.*, of a horse or other animal, to kick upwards with the hind legs, the forelegs remaining rigid; **pig-rooting** *vbl. sb.*, (*a*) *N.Z.*, a patch of ground grubbed or rooted up by wild pigs; (*b*) the action of **pig-root* vb. (b); **pig-run**, a tract of land used by (wild) pigs; also, a track made or used by wild pigs in a forest; **pig-sign** *N.Z.*, the droppings of wild pig(s); **pig-washing** *Metallurgy*, the refining of molten pig-iron by treatment with molten iron oxide; **pig-yoke** (*a*) (earlier example).

1965 J. Pollard *Surfrider* ii. 18 Your board can be a 'pigboard'—wide at the stern and tapered to a point at the nose. **1970** *Studies in English* (Univ. Cape Town) I. 28 Older designs include the *pig board*, that is, a board characterized by a narrow nose and a broad tail. **1921** *Periscope* (U.S. Submarine Base, San Pedro, Calif.) Apr. 21/1 The dukes what passes the exam..finally goes to the subs..and they career as a pig bout [*sic*] sailor is started. This of course, means a sub, witch they is also called sea pigs. **1939** *Newsweek* 9 Jan. 20/1 Presumably Germany will now build up to this by constructing ocean-going pigboats. **1974** G. Jenkins *Bridge & Magpies* xiv. 218, I understand now what the pig-boat saying means—'by guess and by God'. **1975** *Redbook* Aug. 118/3 What do you think about Pearl Harbor? The newer boats are there. I'd like to get one of them and avoid the old pig-boats if I can. **1856** J. Hall in *Birmingham Jrnl.* 26 Sept. Suppl. 3/5 As regards the improved apparatus for the refinery, my principle is the *doing away* with the *refinery process* by pig boiling. **1882** [see Wet *a.* 17]. **1928** H. M. Boylston *Introd. Metallurgy Iron & Steel* vi. 187 Hall's process was also known as the 'pig-boiling process' because of the vigorous boiling or bubbling of the molten metal. **1958** A. D. Merriman *Dict. Metallurgy* 244/1 *Pig boiling*, the name used in reference to that stage in the puddling process..when the original pig iron is melted and thoroughly mixed with the oxidising substances... The whole mass..becomes agitated with the escape of carbon monoxide giving the impression of 'boiling'. **1922** Joyce *Ulysses* 460 Pig dog and always was ever since he was pupped! **1961** B. Crump *Hang on a Minute* 18 My mate reckoned he'd never laughed so much since his brother's pig-dogs got loose and followed him into the Waitawheta dance hall! **1977** *N.Z. Herald* 8 Jan. 4-9/6 (Advt.), Pig dog pups, boxer blue merle pointer cross. **1907** *Yesterday's Shopping* (1969) Index p. xlvi/3 Nets...Pig. **1966** D. Francis *Flying Finish* v. 54 A cart with a pig-net over it. **1971** *Country Life* 11 Mar. 533/1 Some chaps got a tiddler [*sc.* a sturgeon], weighed a hunderd pound, in a pig net. **1913** W. K. Harris *Outback in Australia* 27 We had a second horse afflicted with a tendency to buck, and this one could be depended upon to 'pig-root' for at least half a mile as soon as we made a start. **1957** P. White *Voss* x. 276 This caused Turner to curse and kick, and his nag in consequence to sidle and pigroot. **1921** H. Guthrie-Smith *Tutira* xix. 169 It [*sc.* manuka] now began to colonise the paddock..appearing about pig-rootings, along sheep-tracks. **1966** 'J. Hackston' *Father clears Out* 168 Bucking, backbending, side-jumping, leaping, and pig-rooting. **1848** T. Chapman *Jrnl.* 3 Dec. II. 381 (typescript), Thousands of Acres on all sides of you... Here and there little patches are under cultivation—the rest are 'pig-runs'. **1900** *Geogr. Jrnl.* XVI. 174 In dense forest where the pig-runs are the only means of passage. **1950** *N.Z. Jrnl. Agric.* 346/3 This type of utilisation..at the same time allows some rejuvenation of the pasture in the permanent pig runs. **1960** B. Crump *Good Keen Man* 57, I was thoroughly interrogated every evening as to the whereabouts of any fresh pig-sign I had seen that day [in the bush]. **1887** Phillips & Bauerman *Elem. Metallurgy* (ed. 2) 280 A similar process, used for some time by Krupp, was described by the late Mr. A. L. Holley under the name of 'pig-washing'. **1910** *Encycl. Brit.* XIV. 824/2 In the Bell-Krupp or 'pig-washing' process..advantage is taken of the fact that..the phosphorus and silicon of molten cast iron are quickly oxidized and removed by contact with molten iron oxide. **1958** A. D. Merriman *Dict. Metallurgy* 244/2 *Pig-washing process*, a term used in reference to those methods of refining molten pig iron by oxidising treatment at relatively low temperatures. **1845** *Knickerbocker* XXV. 424 Yellow buttons..'and geese', as he said, 'sittin' on a pig-yoke, printed on to 'em.'

b. pig-face, pig's face *Austral.*, add def.: a succulent plant belonging to the family Aizoaceæ, esp. *Disphyma* (formerly *Mesembryanthemum*) *australe*, bearing pink or purplish-red flowers and edible fleshy berries; also, the berries themselves; also *attrib.*; (further examples); **pig-fern** *N.Z.* the hard fern, *Paesia scaberula*, of the family Polypodiaceæ; also called lace-fern, ring-fern, and scented fern; **pig-lily**, for *Richardia æthiopica* substitute *Zantedeschia æthiopica*; (earlier and later examples).

1889 J. H. Maiden *Useful Native Plants Austral.* i. 44 'Pig Faces'... The fleshy fruit is eaten raw by the aborigines. The leaves are eaten baked. **1920** B. Cronin *Timber Wolves* 69 On the crest of a knoll, Heritage paused a moment to admire the royal purple of the pig-face bloom. **1933** *Bulletin* (Sydney) 29 Nov. 21/3 The fleshy leaves of the pigface plant, which grows along the sandy seashores. **1944** [see *Ice-plant]. **1963** Moore & Adams *Plants N.Z. Coast* 59 *Disphyma australe*..ice-plant, pig-face. **1977** J. Galbraith *Field Guide Wild Flowers S.E. Austral.* 114 'Pigface' with large pink flowers. **1926** F. W. Hilgendorf *Weeds N.Z.* ii. 19 Hard fern (*Paesia scaberula*), called also pig fern and silver fern, is abundant in both islands. **1929** W. Martin *N.Z. Nature Bk.* (1930) II. iv. 44 Pig-fern and Lace-fern are local names given to a dwarf species (*Paesia scaberula*), with finely divided leaflets. **1952** G. R. Gilbert *Glass* 59 Struggling through the thick scrub and tangled pig-fern, the brother and sister tramped on towards the mountains. **1848** C. J. F. Bunbury *Jrnl. Residence Cape of Good Hope* viii. 188 *Calla* (*Zantedeschia*) *Æthiopica*... Commonly called at the Cape the Pig Lily. **1870** *Cape Monthly Mag.* Aug. 104 The 'arum'..grows in all the ditches under the title of 'pig-lily'. **1971** U. van der Spuy *Wild Flowers S. Afr. for Garden* 229/2 It [sc. *Zantedeschia æthiopica*] is said to have been given the common name of 'pig-lily' because in the south-western Cape, where it grows prolifically, pigs are said to relish the rootstock.

c. Many of the combinations with *pig's* also occur in phrases (see *10). *pig's fry* (examples); **pig's breakfast**, used as a type of the unappetizing or unattractive; **pig's ear** *Rhyming slang*, beer; **pig's face** (later example); **pig's foot** = *pig-trotter* (chiefly *pl.*); **pig's whisper**, (*a*) (earlier and later examples).

1933 L. G. D. Acland in *Press* (Christchurch, N.Z.) 9 Sept. 15/7 Two may possibly be Canterbury expressions ..(1) As rough as a bag. (2) As rough as a pig's breakfast. **1948** K. M. Wells *Owl Pen Reader* (1969) I. 45 Lucy and I looked unbelievingly at the mess in the kettles. Bits of charred wood, charcoal, old leaves and wood ash floated there in the midst of an uninviting white scum. It looked like poor porridge, a pig's breakfast to us. **1880** D. W. Barrett *Life & Work among Navvies* (ed. 2) ii. 40 'Now, Jack, I'm goin' to get a tiddley wink of pig's ear..'. A tiddley wink of pig's ear!..What does it mean? Simply this... a workman..goes to get a drink of beer. Had our friend wished for something more potent than the pig's ear aforesaid, he would have substituted the phrase.. 'Tommy get out, and let your father in', meaning thereby *gin*. **1936** J. Curtis *Gilt Kid* xx. 199 But the most of the fiver would go in the old pig's ear. **1974** P. Wright *Lang. Brit. Industry* x. 88 In the pub you can ask for a pint of *pig's ear* (beer). **1929** 'M. B. Eldershaw' *House is Built* III. ix. 217 Nothing but a few clumps of pig's face throve in the pockets of earth it provided. **1922** H. Crane *Let.* 23 Jan. (1965) 78 We begin with pigs' feet and sauerkraut. **1968** C. Brown in *Esquire* Apr. 88/1 Certain foods..are associated almost solely with the nigger: collard greens..hog maws, black-eyed peas, pigs' feet. **1788** J. Woodforde *Diary* 7 Nov. (1927) III. 63 We had for Dinner, Some Fish..Giblets, Piggs Fry. **1939** F. Thompson *Lark Rise* i. 13 The first delicious dish of pig's fry sizzling in the frying-pan. **1970** G. E. Evans *Where Beards wag All* xxv. 264, I had a fancy for something tasty, and one night I gave her a pig's fry and asked her to cook it for us for next day. **1821** P. Egan *Real Life in London* I. xi. 189 The lad *nibbled the bait*, and was off in a *pig's whisper*. [Note] *Pig's Whisper*—A very common term for speed. **1963** *Times* 11 Mar. 1/7 If you are unfortunate enough to snore, you are said 'to drive pigs', or perhaps you may do something in a very short time, in which case it is said that you have done it 'in a pig's whisper'.

pig, *v.* Add: **2.** (Further examples.) Also const. *along*, to live from day to day like an animal.

1896 *Pall Mall Gaz.* Sept. 70 She isn't fit to pig along in the way we have to here. **1909** [see *Master-mind *sb.* a]. **1931** *Times Lit. Suppl.* 19 Feb. 131/3 It was not enough for Arthur Phelps 'just to pig along', working to live and living to work. **1939** G. B. Shaw *In Good King Charles's Golden Days* II. 112 Give me a skilled trade and eight or ten shillings a week, and you and I, beloved, would pig along more happily than we have ever been able to do as our majesties. **1930** J. Buchan *Castle Gay* ix. 145 They would have to pig it in a moorland inn. **1964** 'M. Innes' *Money from Holme* xxvi. 171 'Dear me,' Binchy said. 'If it isn't friend Cheel.' He turned to Braunkopf. 'Cheel and I pig together, more or less.' **1977** —— *Honeybath's Haven* iii. 34 He didn't approve of the proposal to pig it in the studio.

pig-bel (pi:gˌbe·l). *Med.* Also **pigbel.** [See quot. 1966.] A severe necrotizing enterocolitis found in Papua New Guinea, caused by *Clostridium welchii* and associated with feasts of pork.

1966 T. G. C. Murrell et al. in *Lancet* 29 Jan. 217/2 It was felt that the syndrome in New Guinea, being ætiologically related to pig-feasting, should be designated by a specific name. 'Pig-bel' has been proposed because this is the 'pidgin English' name used by medical orderlies to describe the abdominal discomfort which follows a large pork meal. **1969** Edington & Gilles *Path. in Tropics* vi. 273 A diffuse sloughing enteritis of the jejunum, ileum, and colon (enteritis necroticans, 'pigbel') has been described in Germany and New Guinea... It is the commonest acute abdominal condition requiring laparotomy in hospital practice in the highlands of New Guinea. The disease in this area, in both epidemic and sporadic forms, is related to pig feasting. **1977** *Lancet* 17 Sept. 617/2 The epidemic forms of necrotising enteritis ('pig-bel' and *Darmbrand* enteritis) have been consistently associated with strains of *C. welchi* producing mainly b [*recte* β] toxin.

pigeon, *sb.* **I. 3. a.** Restrict †*Obs.* to sense 'a coward' and add later examples in senses 'a young woman, a girl; a sweetheart'.

1916 Joyce *Portrait of Artist* iii. 116 Is that you, pigeon? **1940** *Music Makers* May 37/3 *Pigeon*, a young girl. **1970** G. Greer *Female Eunuch* 265 The basic imagery behind terms like..*pigeon* is the imagery of food. **1977** J. Wambaugh *Black Marble* (1978) viii. 125 She accepted it graciously, thinking she must remember to give Philo a bonus for finding a little pigeon with tits big enough to bring old Landon McWhorter back to life.

b. (Further examples.) Also in extended use.

1941 *Sun* (Baltimore) 14 Aug. 13/7 These amateur gamblers are the greatest pigeons I ever knew. **1956** B. Holiday *Lady sings Blues* (1973) xvii. 136 So they handed me a white paper to sign... I signed... The rest was up to them. I was just a pigeon. **1959** [see *Murphy[2] 4]. **1962** J. D. MacDonald *Girl* xi. 150 Anybody steals that much, they're a pigeon for the first people that get to him. **1977** *Tennis World* Sept. 17/3 A 'pigeon' is a frequent victim—that is, until he plays out of his tree. **1978** G. A. Sheehan *Running & Being* xii. 165 Whatever your game, you can always spot a pigeon. When I warm up for a road race I can usually tell at a glance the newcomers to the sport.

d. = *stool-pigeon* s.v. Stool *sb.* 19b.

1849 *National Police Gaz.* (U.S.) 12 May 2/7 The Mayor of Philadelphia having discovered that an old pigeon known as Bill Forebaugh was accustomed to point out his officers to the different knucks who arrived in the city, determined to put a stop to this new lay. **1859** G. W. Matsell *Vocabulum* 66 *Pigeon*, a thief that joins in with other thieves to commit a crime, and then informs the officer, who he pigeons for, and for this service the officer is supposed to be *occasionally* both deaf and blind. **1934** R. Chandler in *Black Mask* Oct. 14/2 Don't come here again—..I don't like—pigeons. **1966** *Sunday Tel.* (Brisbane) 15 May 15/1 In the underworld, this is the mark of the 'copper', 'grass', 'nark', 'pigeon', or 'squealer'. **1971** 'D. Shannon' *Ringer* (1972) ix. 154 A lot of our pigeons offer the info to the other side too. **1976** R. Rosenblum *Sweetheart Deal* i. 11 For years guarding witnesses remained a .. shoestring operation. Rent a hotel room and keep the pigeon under wraps.

II. 5. a. *pigeon loft* (later examples; also fig.); *pigeon-pie* (earlier and later examples).

1891 Kipling *City of Dreadful Night* v. 34 Do you mean that you can from this absurd pigeon-loft locate the wards in the night-time! **1969** *Times* 4 Sept. 3/1 The difference between the sun's time at the pigeon loft, given by the pigeons' internal sense of time, and the time registered by the sun's position at the release site, gives a measure of the difference in longitude between the two points. **1977** *Evening Post* (Nottingham) 27 Jan. 7/7 They also admitted two accusations of jointly entering two pigeons lofts as trespassers. **1655** in M. M. Verney *Mem.* (1894) III. iv. 129 Madcap..brags..that she hath jeer'd you into good pidgeon pies. These were soe good that there is not one left of them. **1779** J. Woodforde *Diary* 15 Apr. (1924) I. 249 We had for dinner..a Pidgeon Pye. **1843** *Ainsworth's Mag.* IV. 13 Swallowing a morsel of *foie gras* as uncognizantly as though it had been pigeon-pie. **1937** *Daily Herald* 8 Feb. 7/4 Pigeon-pie parties, an old-fashioned country custom, will be renewed this week in England and Wales. **1978** K. Bonfiglioli *All Tea in China* xx. 248 The black puddings, râgout of kidneys and pigeon pie..were barely touched.

d. *pigeon-tailed* adj.

1901 W. Churchill *Crisis* II. ix. 202 The red pigeon-tailed coat. **1957** W. Faulkner *Town* iv. 83 Come in a Pullman in striped britches and a gold watch chain big enough to boom logs with and gold eyeglasses and even a gold toothpick and the pigeon-tailed coat.

6. pigeon drop *U.S. criminals' slang*, (*a*) a form of confidence trick which begins with the dropping of a wallet before the victim or 'pigeon'; (*b*) (see quot. 1959); so **pigeon dropper; pigeon dropping** = **pigeon drop* (a); **pigeon-fancier** (earlier and later examples); **pigeon grass**, substitute for def.: a grass of the genus *Setaria*, esp. *S. glauca* or *S. viridis*; (examples); **pigeon millet** = **pigeon grass*; **pigeon-pair** (further examples); also *transf.*; **pigeon-post** (further examples); **pigeon-weed** *U.S.*, the corn gromwell, *Lithospermum arvense*, or the spikenard, *Aralia racemosa*; **pigeon-woodpecker**, substitute for def.: a flicker, *Colaptes aureus*, found in eastern North America; (examples).

1937 E. H. Sutherland *Professional Thief* iii. 67 Among the short-con rackets, dropping the poke (also known as the pigeon-drop) is frequently used. **1959** *Washington Post* 18 Mar. A3/1 In the pigeon drop a confidence man tells his victim he has found a large amount of money and will share it if the victim will kick in some money as a show of good faith. **1961** Harney & Cross *Narcotic Officer's Notebk.* vi. 118 Sometimes it was the 'pigeon-drop'. A purse or billfold containing a considerable amount of money was dropped.

The 'sucker' was allowed to find it right along with a member of the mob. **1979** *Monitor* (McAllen, Texas) 22 July 2F/5 A Houston woman held on attempted theft charges claims to be part of a national 'pigeon drop' confidence ring. **1961** WEBSTER, Pigeon-dropper. **1977** J. WAMBAUGH *Black Marble* (1978) vi. 76 Pigeon droppers, pursepicks, muggers. Don't walk the Boulevard at night. **1850** *Green's St. Louis Directory for 1851* p. xviii, Such practice is immensely more disrespectable than procuring money under false pretenses—no more honorable than veritable pigeon-dropping. **1955** K. SULLIVAN *Girls who go Wrong* (1956) xii. 128 Elmira became the more proficient of the pair at the badger game—flim flam and pigeon dropping. **1970** C. MAJOR *Dict. Afro-Amer. Slang* 91 *Pigeon dropping*, confidence game-playing. **1807** SOUTHEY *Lett. from Eng.* I. xxi. 233 The Columbarians or pigeon-fanciers. **1822** M. EDGEWORTH *Let.* 19 Jan. (1971) 326 He explained to me what is meant by being *in the fancy*—pigeon fanciers—rabbit fanciers &c. **1941** [see *DART *sb.* 1 d]. **1976** *Deeside Advertiser* 9 Dec. 2/3 He was employed at the C.E.G.B. Power Station and a keen pigeon fancier. **1838** H. COLMAN *1st Rep. Agric. Mass.* (Mass. Agric. Survey) 128 There were several patches of black or pigeon grass when the dyke was built. **1901** C. T. MOHR *Plant Life Alabama* 358 Chaetochloa glauca... Pigeon Grass. **1926** F. W. HILGENDORF *Weeds N.Z.* facing p. 17 (*caption*) Pigeon grass (*Setaria glauca*). **1948** A. L. BLOMQUIST *Grasses N. Carolina* 186 One species (*S*[*etaria*] *viridis*) known as 'pigeon millet' or 'foxtail' is an obnoxious weed in cultivated ground in some of the Northern states. **1878** HARDY *Ret. Native* I. II. i. 240 She and Clym Yeobright would make a very pretty pigeon pair—hey? **1954** *Publ. Amer. Dial. Soc.* XXI. 34 *Pigeon pair*, a boy and girl, usually brother and sister, close enough in age to be congenial playmates. **1960** *Woman* 23 Apr. 5/2 A mother there had twins—boy and girl—on February 29, brother and sister for her pigeon pair born on the *previous* Leap Year Day. **1964** D. VARADAY *Gara-Yaka* xx. 178, I recognized Moll [*sc.* a lion] in the harem-nursery with three lively youngsters, while the two older females both appeared to have chipped in with a pigeon-pair each. **1909** *Chambers's Jrnl.* Oct. 661/2 Extensive practice is carried out in..photographing forts and positions of troops, and sending the films by means of pigeon-post to be developed and printed at headquarters. **1963** *Times* 3 May 13/7 It also became, thanks to Julius Reuter and his pigeon post of 1850, a vital link in the network of telegraphic communications. **1975** *Times* 15 Mar. 14/7 It will cost 7p to have a first-class letter delivered... To set up a pigeon post is remarkably cheap and easy. **1785** *Mem. Amer. Acad. Arts & Sci.* I. 431 *Aralia... Berry-Bearing Angelica.* Shot Bush. Pigeon Weed. Blossoms white. Berries black. Common in new plantations. **1851** J. F. W. JOHNSTON *Notes on N. Amer.* I. 305 Richer clover also had come up on another drained spot, and less of the pigeon-weed..with which this clay land is infested. **1889** G. VASEY *Agric. Grasses U.S.* (new ed.) 103 Pigeon-Weed ..grows chiefly in cultivated grounds. **1844** J. E. DEKAY *Zool. N.Y.* II. 192 This species..is called Highhole, Yucker, Flicker, Wake-up and Pigeon Woodpecker..in this State. **1847** THOREAU *Let.* 15 Feb. in *Corr.* (1958) 175, I remember a pigeon-woodpecker's nest in the grove on the east side of the yard. **1870** [see FLICKER *sb.*[4]]. **1917** T. G. PEARSON *Birds Amer.* II. 163 Flicker. *Colaptes auratus auratus*... Clape; Pigeon Woodpecker; Yellowhammer. **1955** *Amer. Speech* XXX. 181 Of bird names given for size, consider:..pigeon woodpecker.

b. pigeon's wing, (*c*) a type of wig worn in the 18th century; also *attrib.*

1753 [see *NEGLIGENT *sb.* 2]. **1966** J. S. COX *Illustr. Dict. Hairdressing* 113/1 *Pigeon's wing periwig*, a man's wig dressed with two horizontal rolls above the ears. The top, sides and back being dressed smooth and plain. This style was worn with different styles of queue.

pigeon: see PIDGIN in Dict. and Suppl.

pigeon-berry. **1.** Substitute for def.: One of several plants whose fruit is attractive to birds, esp. in North America, the pokeweed, *Phytolacca americana*, or a dogwood, *Cornus canadensis* or *C. alternifolia*, and, in the West Indies, *Duranta repens*; also, the fruit of these plants.

1856 W. E. CORMACK *Narr. Journey across Newfoundland* iii. 13 The surface [of the ground] is bespangled ..by..*Cornus canadensis*, bearing a cluster of wholesome red berries, sometimes called pigeon berries. **1868** *Canad. Naturalist* III. 409 Among the most common plants which overspread the burned ground..are..the pigeonberry (*Cornus canadensis*); and the red strawberry. **1885** A. BRASSEY *In Trades, Tropics, & Roaring Forties* xviii. 425 A pretty tree with a large lavender flower, and great orange-coloured clusters of what are called 'pigeon-berries'. **1920** BRITTON & MILLSPAUGH *Bahama Flora* 372 *Duranta repens*... Bermuda; Florida; West Indies and Mexico to northern South America. Pigeon-berry. **1942** W. R. VAN DERSAL *Ornamental Amer. Shrubs* xii. 183 The plant [sc. *Cornus alternifolia*] has a number of common names, including..purple dogwood, pigeonberry, umbrella tree, and pagoda cornel. **1958** J. G. MACGREGOR *North-West of 16* v. 62 The bright red pigeon-berries, and the piles of spruce cones shelled out by the squirrels. **1971** H. M. S. LEWIN in E. L. Wardman *Bermuda Jubilee Garden* v. 90/2 *D*[*uranta*] *repens.* Pigeonberry, Sky-flower, Golden dewdrop. A slender evergreen shrub with drooping sprays of lilac-blue flowers that are followed by clusters of golden yellow berries. **1973** HITCHCOCK & CRONQUIST *Flora Pacific Northwest* 104 *P*[*hytolacca*] *americana* L. Pokeberry, pokeweed, pigeonberry.

2. pigeon-berry ash *Austral.*, an evergreen tree of the genus *Elæocarpus* or *Cryptocarya*; **pigeon-berry bush** = sense 1 above; **pigeon-berry tree** *Austral.*, the native mulberry, *Litsea dealbata*; also = *pigeon-berry ash*.

1785 *Mem. Amer. Acad. Arts & Sci.* I. 411 *Pigeon-Berry Bush...* Pigeons feed on the berries, which has been the occasion of its trivial name. **1832** W. D. WILLIAMSON *Hist. State Maine* I. 115 The pigeon-berry bush is as tall as that of a blackberry, bears an abundance of small purple berries, the chief food of pigeons. **1884** A. NILSON *Timber Trees New South Wales* 55 *E*[*læocarpus*] *obovatus.* —Ash; Pigeon-berry Tree.—A noble tree, attaining sometimes a height of 130 feet. **1889** J. H. MAIDEN *Useful Native Plants Austral.* 563 *Litsea dealbata...* 'Pigeon-berry Tree.' 'Native Mulberry.' 'Black Ash.' **1936** J. W. AUDAS *Native Trees Austral.* 190 Elaeocarpus Baurleni.. grows in New South Wales to the Queensland border, known popularly as Pigeon-Berry Ash. *Ibid.* 192 Elaeocarpus obovatus..is known as Pigeon-berry Ash. *Ibid.* 229 Litsea dealbata... A well-known tree of Queensland and New South Wales called Native Mulberry or Pigeon-Berry Tree. **1965** *Austral. Encycl.* III. 137/1 The rose maple or rose walnut..is most generally known to timber-getters as pigeon-berry ash.

pigeon-breast. (Earlier example.)

1842 DICKENS *Let.* 3 Apr. (1974) III. 180 That valiant general..is an old, old man with..the remains of a pigeon-breast in his military surtout.

pigeoneer (pidʒənīə·ɹ). *U.S.* [f. PIGEON *sb.* + -EER.] **a.** A person who trains or breeds homing pigeons, formerly esp. in the U.S. Army Signal Corps. **b.** (See quot. 1944[1].)

1918 *Boston Evening Rec.* 11 Jan. 9/2 A pigeoneer is an expert handler of homing pigeons. **1918** *Personnel Specifications* (U.S. Signal Corps) 21 Chief Pigeoneer:.. homing pigeon expert..in charge of the training and instruction of the men as pigeoneers. **1940** *Amer. Pigeon Jrnl.* Dec. 420/1 We have hundreds of young men of military age who have had the advantage of the experience and training of the pigeoneers of 1917-1918. **1944** *Sunday Jrnl. & Star* (Lincoln, Nebraska) 30 Apr. 8 Frank Robbins receives calls daily from people who wish pigeons to be exterminated around their homes... Assistant 'pigeoneer' at different times is Detective Captain Eugene Masters who is also an expert shot. **1944** M. B. COTHREN *Pigeon Heroes* i. 7 [The pigeon] dropped abruptly down on the landing board of its loft and walked through the trap door... In a jiffy a pigeoneer pulled out the message.

pigeon-hawk. (Earlier and later examples.)

1731 M. CATESBY *Nat. Hist. Carolina* I. 3 The Pigeon-Hawk..is a very swift and bold Hawk, preying on Pigeons and wild Turkeys while they are young. **1772** J. RUTTY *Ess. Nat. Hist. Co. Dublin* I. 297 The Pigeon Hawk or Goshawk..is said to breed in Ireland's Eye. **1831** J. J. AUDUBON *Ornith. Biogr.* I. 467 The Pigeon Hawk does not, I believe, raise its young within the United States, but somewhere farther to the north. **1913** H. K. SWANN *Dict. Eng. & Folk-Names Brit. Birds* 181 Pigeon Hawk: The Goshawk... also the Sparrow-hawk. **1958** E. T. GILLIARD *Living Birds of World* 111/2 A well-known small species of the Northern Hemisphere, the Pigeon Hawk or Merlin (*Falco columbarius*), is very similar to the Peregrine in general shape and color.

pigeon-hole, *sb.* Add: **2.** (Earlier example of a room.) Also, a small flat.

1777 P. THICKNESSE *Year's Journey* II. li. 151 All the rest of the apartments are pidgeon-holes, filled with fleas, bugs, and dirt. **1869** 'MARK TWAIN' *Innoc. Abr.* viii. 80 You can rent a whole block of these pigeon-holes for fifty dollars a month.

7. (Earlier and later examples.)

1688 LOCKE *Let.* 6 Feb. in B. Rand *Corr. J. Locke & E. Clarke* (1927) 245 Another way may be with pigeon-holes as they call them: at these twenty-four holes, over the first paste an *A*, over the second a *B*, [etc.]. **1972** C. ACHEBE *Girls at War* 99 'Can I see your pigeon-hole?' ..'That's the glove-box. Nothing there.' **1978** *Lancashire Life* Nov. 151/1 Some find it possible to envy those who sit on the official side of counter or pigeonhole.

b. Also for the classification of persons, as by occupations.

1938 [see *ALL-ROUNDER]. **1957** [see *DEFERRAL].

8. (Earlier and later examples.)

1685 LOCKE *Jrnl.* 28 Aug. in P. King *Life Locke* (1829) 167, I saw a boor's house a mile or more from Amsterdam... There were three pigeon-hole beds, after the Dutch fashion. **1968** R. A. LYTTLETON *Mysteries Solar Syst.* iv. 137 On a simple pigeon-hole argument, the probability of the distribution being due to pure chance turns out to be less than 1 in 1000.

pigeon-hole, *v.* Add: **1.** (Earlier and later examples.)

1840 C. CAMPBELL in T. Bland *Bland Papers* I. p. v, The lady..reached down a bundle of letters..from the interstices of the eaves of the porch, where they were nicely pigeon-holed. **1855** *Knickerbocker* XLVI. 95 The bill of the gentlemanly proprietor..was deliberately met by a bill for 'damages to cow-catcher', and pigeon-holed. **1940** WODEHOUSE *Eggs, Beans & Crumpets* 154 Putting the prophet Hosea to one side for the moment and temporarily pigeon-holing the children of Adullam. **1949** *Jrnl. R. Aeronaut. Soc.* LIII. 410/2 Although the flying bomb project was pigeon-holed, out of this early work the Mark 1A Auto-pilot and the Queen Bee target aeroplane emerged. **1955** *Times* 15 June 3/3 Why had the Minister pigeon-holed the Phillips report? **1963** *Ann. Reg. 1962* 205 Tentative plans for an exchange of television appearances by the Soviet and American leaders were also pigeon-holed. **1976** *Milton Keynes Express* 16 July 2/5 One plan that seems to have been pigeon-holed for the time being is the idea of finding another site for the College of Further Education.

2. (Examples with a person as object.)

1950 D. GASCOYNE *Vagrant* 59 Keep your labels for people who need them; I cannot be pigeonholed neatly. **1978** J. B. HILTON *Some run Crooked* v. 41 Why? 'To avoid Cantrell..having already pigeon-holed him as a kerb-crawler.'

3. (Further fig. example.)

1940 [see *DING AN SICH, DING-AN-SICH].

pigeonite (pi·dʒənəit). *Min.* [f. the name of *Pigeon* Point in NE. Minnesota + -ITE[1].] A silicate of magnesium, ferrous iron, and calcium, $(Mg,Fe^{II},Ca)(Mg,Fe^{II})Si_2O_6$, that is a monoclinic calcium-poor pyroxene substantially free of aluminium and ferric iron, and that is found chiefly in basic igneous, esp. volcanic, rocks.

1900 A. N. WINCHELL in *Amer. Geol.* XXVI. 204 Since the anomalous condition was first discovered in the rocks from Pigeon point, it would be appropriate to call pyroxene thus optically abnormal pigeonite. **1931** *Amer. Jrnl. Sci.* CCXXI. 405 The clino-pyroxenes..form a continuous series of mix crystals, from diopside-rich (the phenocrysts are always diopsidic augites) to clino-enstatite- and hypersthene-rich (pigeonites). **1951** *Jrnl. Geol.* LIX. 480/1 Pigeonites under plutonic conditions invert with cooling to orthopyroxenes. **1970** *Nature* 25 Apr. 334/2 Interstitial pigeonite and augite in the lunar gabbroic anorthosite have Cr contents of 0·6 and 6·0 per cent respectively. **1975** J. W. FRONDEL *Lunar Mineral.* ix. 217 Because of their chemical variability, exsolution textures, epitaxy with augite and orthopyroxene,..and relative abundance, lunar pigeonites have played a significant role in a reconstruction of the crystallization histories of mare basalts.

Hence **pigeoni·tic** *a.*

1931 *Amer. Mineralogist* XVI. 207 The groundmass pyroxene is often said to be of the pigeonitic variety (Holmatindur, Eskifjord; Vágsfjord, Faeroes; etc.). **1957** *Mineral. Mag.* XXXI. 540 It is evident that the degree of inversion of the pigeonitic pyroxenes..must, in general, be correlated with the composition of the minerals as well as with their cooling history. **1972** *Contrib. Mineral. & Petrol.* XXXV. 235 (*heading*) Variation of rare earth concentrations in pigeonitic and hypersthenic rock series from Izu-Hakone region, Japan.

pigeon-pea. **1.** Substitute for def.: A leguminous shrub, *Cajanus cajan*, probably native to Africa, but widely cultivated in tropical and subtropical regions; = CAJAN, DAL. (Later examples.)

1907 FREEMAN & CHANDLER *World's Commercial Products* 260 Pigeon Pea or Dhol of commerce..is an erect sub-shrubby plant..widely cultivated in the tropics and sub-tropics of both hemispheres. **1952** S. SELVON *Brighter Sun* v. 85 Is just dat yuh must love de tomatoes and lettuce and pigeon peas. **1969** *Oxf. Bk. Food Plants* 34/1 In the West Indies..pigeon peas provide a useful part of the protein supply in the diet of the poorer people, and a canning industry has been developed. **1972** I. ARNON *Crop Production in Dry Regions* II. vi. 255 The Pigeon-pea (*Cajanus cajan*) is a tropical legume of very ancient cultivation that is grown in tropical and sub-tropical regions of Asia and Africa. **1975** *Sunday Advocate-News* (Barbados) 15 June 8/1 Pigeon peas, rice,..bread and cream of wheat are fairly good nutritional buys.

pigeon's milk. Delete '8', leaving 'Also pigeon milk'. **1.** (Later examples.)

1891 R. WOODS *Pract. Guide Successful Pigeon-Culture* vii. 73 The parent birds..are also provided with an ample supply of veritable pigeon's milk. **1897** PARKER & HASWELL *Text-bk. Zool.* II. xiii. 380 It [*sc.* the young pigeon] is at first covered with fine down, and is fed by the parents with a secretion from the crop, the so-called 'Pigeon's milk'. **1943** T. I. STORER *Gen. Zool.* xxxi. 659 In adult pigeons, while rearing young, the epithelial lining sloughs off as 'pigeon milk' used to nourish squabs in the nest. **1967** D. GOODWIN *Pigeons & Doves of World* 45 The parent takes the squab's soft bill..into his, or her, own mouth and regurgitates pigeons' milk. **1973** *Sci. Amer.* Dec. 142/2 They [*sc.* pigeons] breed fast, and they..feed the young ones in the nest from the protein-rich 'pigeon milk', a curd formed in the parent bird's gut.

pigeon-toed, *a.* **2.** (Further examples.)

1887 *Harper's Mag.* Dec. 71/2 One would have imagined that he would deem it meet that a Kittredge should be pigeon-toed. **1976** A. WHITE *Long Silence* i. 6 It does my heart good to see these lads come here pigeon-toed and flat-chested and go out..holding themselves upright.

pigeon-wing, *sb.* Add: **3.** (Further examples.) Also, a dance; the music for such a dance or dance-step.

1873 B. HARTE *Mrs. Skaggs's Husbands* 166 A light figure..cut a pigeon-wing,..and then advanced to the footlights. **1889** *Century Mag.* Apr. 858/2 A row of cavaliers..cut the pigeon wing in square-toed pumps. **1935** Z. N. HURSTON *Mules & Men* (1970) I. v. 117 Jack was justa dancin' fallin' off de log and cuttin' de pigeon wing—(diddle dip, diddle dip—diddle dip) 'from pine to pine Mr. Pinkney'. **1947** E. H. PAUL *Linden on Saugus Branch* 50 He had..a Chickering grand piano on which he played..all the reels, jigs, pigeon-wings, moriscos, sarabands, [etc.]. **1954** *Publ. Amer. Dial. Soc.* XXI. 34 *Pigeonwing*, a type of dance involving the use of the arms.

pigeon-wing, *v.* Add: **b.** *refl.* To convey or transport (oneself) by or in the manner of one dancing or cutting pigeon-wings.

1839 POE *Devil in Belfry* in *Tales of Grotesque* (1840) 166 The rascal..pigeon-winged himself right up into the belfry of the House of the Town Council.

Piggery[1]. Add: **1.** (Earlier and later examples.)
1781 R. F. GREVILLE *Diary* 9 Aug. (1930) 20 Returned to The Grove after viewing The Farm & well kept Piggery. **1799** *Times* 1 June 4/3 Stabling for 3 horses, chaise-house, piggery, and out-buildings. **1936** *Times Lit. Suppl.* 29 Feb. 182/3 She contrasts the spoilt young things in luxurious homes with the free young things in Chelsea piggeries. **1971** *Farmers Weekly* (Extra) 19 Mar. 5/1 For cleaning and sterilising piggeries, equipment, troughs and machinery, etc. **1972** T. A. BULMAN *Kamloops Cattlemen* xiv. 80 One part of the Grande Prairie layout was designated as the piggery.
2. (Further examples.)
1972 *Daily Tel.* 10 Nov. 15/2 The pin-up is just male chauvinist piggery. **1977** H. GREENE *FSO-1* i. 4 A black citadel of male-chauvinist piggery.

pigging, *vbl. sb.*[1] Add: **2. pigging back** *Metallurgy*, the addition of more pig-iron to the charge in an open-hearth furnace in order to raise its carbon content when this has fallen too much during boiling.
1900 *Jrnl. West of Scotland Iron & Steel Inst.* VII. 128 For quick working, plenty of carbon in the pig in proportion to phosphorus is desirable,..otherwise there is delay by the addition of grey pig for 'pigging back' or..prolonging the boil. **1951** G. R. BASHFORTH *Manuf. Iron & Steel* II. vii. 174 The 'pigging back' of a large furnace to the extent of 20 points of carbon gave very beneficial results.
3. The use of pigs (*PIG *sb.*[1] 8*); cleaning by means of a pig.
1972 L. M. HARRIS *Introd. Deepwater Floating Drilling Operations* xix. 208 A system that permits: pump-down tools; pigging of lines; [etc.]. **1976** *Offshore Engineer* Mar. 52/3 Production manifold, the third subsystem, gives gathering, gas-lift, testing, pigging and through flowline capability.

pi·gging, *vbl. sb.*[3] *U.S.* [f. PIG *sb.*[1]] Hog-tying; only *attrib.* in **pigging string**, a short cord or rope used for hog-tying.
1926 R. SANTEE *Men & Horses* 4 On came the roper.. his 'piggin' string between his teeth. **1971** H. A. SMITH *View from Chivo* ii. 28 He stood for a moment looking at the rope in his hand, reflecting on the fact that it was known as a piggin' string. **1976** 'D. HALLIDAY' *Dolly & Nanny Bird* vii. 98 Hog-tie it! Get the crittur! Where's your pigging-string? Get him down, boys! Throw him!

pi·ggism. *rare.* [f. PIG *sb.*[1] + -ISM.] Piggish behaviour.
1852 MRS. GASKELL *Schah's Eng. Gardener* in *Househ. Words* V. 321/1 They ate their peas and beans unshelled.. a piece of piggism which especially scandalised him. **1979** *Daily Tel.* 10 Feb. 20 Women's Lib and male chauvinist piggism are both based upon the false premise that people are merely bodies instead of free spirits temporarily housed in flesh.

piggle (pi·g'l), *sb. dial.* [f. next.] (see quot. 1889.)
1889 *Cent. Dict.*, *Piggle*.., a many-pronged hook, with a handle like that of a hoe, used in digging potatoes, and in mixing various materials, as clay, mortar, compost, etc. **1922** C. SIDGWICK *Victorian* xxxvii. 278 Impident toad! Comes up to me and sez we aren't agoin' to build this hedge with a foundation! Oh! aren't we? sez I. You get to yer work, my lad, and do a bit with that piggle.

pi·ggle, *v. dial.* [Origin obscure: cf. PIDDLE *v.* 1.] **a.** *trans.* To uproot; to pick at, to pick out. **b.** *intr.* To trifle or toy *with*. So **pi·ggling** *ppl. a.*, petty, paltry, niggling.
1847 J. O. HALLIWELL *Dict. Archaic & Provinc. Words* II. 622/2 *Piggle*, to root up potatoes with the hand. **1877** F. Ross et al. *Gloss. Words Holderness* 107/1 *Piggle*.., to pick out with a pointed instrument. **1911** D. H. LAWRENCE *White Peacock* II. iii. 265 Don't be piggling and mean and Grundyish. **1923** —— *Kangaroo* i. 7 Awful piggling suburban place. *Ibid.* iii. 40, I can't piggle with those draughtsmen dodges. **1976** SCOLLINS & TITFORD *Ey up, mi Duck!* I. 59 *Piggle*, to work away at something with the fingers. A certain spreader of acne.

Piggly-Wiggly (pi:gli,wi·gli). *U.S.* [Fanciful.] A type of self-service store (see quots. 1928, 1953). Also *attrib.* or as *adj.*
'Piggly Wiggly' is a registered service mark in the United States.
1917 *Printer's Ink* 20 Dec. 17/1 Perhaps no chain of stores that has been organized in recent years has been the object of so much curiosity and speculation as the Piggly Wiggly stores, which were started in Memphis, Tenn., in 1916. *Ibid.* 20/1 As an experiment in distribution, Piggly Wiggly is interesting and is worth watching. **1928** *Publishers' Weekly* 10 Nov. 1972/2 The obvious objection to the idea of a Piggly-Wiggly bookshop is that few book stores are adapted to the customary Piggly-Wiggly pattern, with the turn-stile entrances and exits, and all the merchandise set out onto tables in a U-shaped semi-circle. **1953** *Sun* (Baltimore) 17 Oct. 8/1 News comes of the death..of Clarence Saunders, founder of the Piggly Wiggly stores. It is probable that few members of the younger generation know what a Piggly Wiggly was. Certainly they would not regard it as the novelty it was at the time of its creation 36 years ago. For the Piggly Wiggly..was nothing more than a clerkless grocery store in which a customer helped himself to goods off the shelves and paid at the door as he went out. In short, save perhaps for minor details.., the Piggly Wiggly represented a system that since has become standard as the super-market. **1955** 'P. QUENTIN' *Man with Two Wives* xxii. 246 He used to work in the Piggly-Wiggly. That's a kind of store they have out there [in California] like the A. and P. **1971** 'S. WOODS' *Knavish Crows* v. 55 There were houses..a do-it-yourself laundry—a Piggly Wiggly supermarket. **1973** *Guardian* 2 June 11/5 Grants, New Mexico..has 56 garages, 421 motel rooms, a Piggly Wiggly Supermarket.

piggy, piggie, *sb.*[1] Add: **2.** (Earlier and later examples.) Also *attrib.*
1862 C. C. ROBINSON *Dial. Leeds* 384 *Piggy*, a game played by boys with sticks, and a piece of rounded wood, pointed at each end, called the 'piggy', which, when struck at either end, rebounds, similar to the game of 'cat' elsewhere. **1909** *Westm. Gaz.* 10 May 12/1 About 300 spectators attended the Barnsley Queen's Grounds.. on the occasion of a long knock piggy match for £50 and the championship of Yorkshire. **1971** C. BONINGTON *Annapurma South Face* iv. 49 We have..a game of 'Piggy', where you throw a small peg into the air, strike it as far as you can with a stick, and nominate the number of strides a member of the opposing team must take to reach the peg; he can challenge you to meet the nominated number of strides.
3. Special Combs., as **piggy-and-stick** = sense 2; **piggy bank**, a pig-shaped money-box, often made of pottery (see also quot. 1976); also (with hyphen) *attrib.*; **piggy-in-the-middle**: see *PIG *sb.*[1] 9; **piggy-stick** (*a*) *Mil. slang*, the wooden handle of a soldier's entrenching tool; (*b*) = sense 2.
1932 L. GOLDING *Magnolia St.* I. ix. 159 The little Jewboys..started playing ball or piggy-and-stick. **1941** *Butler Brothers Dry Goods, Home Goods, Toys Catal.* Spring 312B/2 Piggy Banks..flesh colored composition. **1951** WODEHOUSE *Old Reliable* x. 129 'Listen, I've busted banks.' 'You mean piggy banks?' **1955** A. HUXLEY *Genius & Goddess* 51 Ruth broke her piggy bank and squandered a year's accumulated savings on a make-up kit and a bottle of cheap perfume. **1972** *Daily Colonist* (Victoria, B.C.) 12 Jan. 28/1 Police said a piggy bank thief entered the house through an unlocked window. **1976** LIEBERMAN & RHODES *Compl. CB Handbk.* i. 20 To identify your own location..look for the nearest landmark. A few examples: the 'piggy bank' (toll booth) you just went through, a milepost, [etc.]. **1977** *New Yorker* 29 Aug. 69/2 The passengers who rode American trams were so honest that they didn't even use tickets—they just dropped the fare in a piggy bank for the driver to collect when he was ready. **1930** BROPHY & PARTRIDGE *Songs and Slang 1914–18* 149 *Piggy-stick*, the wooden helve for the entrenching tool which the infantryman carried next his bayonet... From a child's game, tip-cat. **1968** P. JENNINGS *Living Village* 179 The game which we knew in Coventry as *tip-cap*..was called in Yorkshire *Knur and spel*, in Cumberland *piggy-stick*.

piggy, *a.* Add: (Further examples.) Also, suggestive of pigs; loosely, unpleasant, unreasonable. Also *comb.*
1927 J. MASEFIELD *Midnight Folk* 24 There were seven old witches..at a very good supper... They were very piggy in their eating (picking the bones with their fingers, etc.). **1942** [see *GRABBY *a.*]. **1957** 'N. SHUTE' *On Beach* viii. 264 'Getting a bit piggy, isn't it?'.. 'Everything shut up, and dirty, and stinking.' **1958** —— *Rainbow & Rose* iv. 159, I started back and it began to rain and it got very piggy. *a* **1963** S. PLATH *Crossing Water* (1971) 35 They have a piggy and a fishy air. **1970** *New Yorker* 26 Sept. 39/2 'I don't want you to make love to anyone but me.' 'That's being piggy.' **1976** P. HILL *Hunters* xi. 158 Did she know her husband had lied to cover for Gatwood? Fat piggy-eyed Gatwood.

piggy-back: see PICK-A-BACK *adv. phr.* in Dict. and Suppl.

piggy-wiggy. (Further examples.)
1879 [see *PITTY[2]]. **1929** E. BOWEN *Last Sept.* vi. 62 Your scrumptious Irish teas make a perfect piggy-wig of me. **1957** [see *nursery word* s.v. *NURSERY 8 a].

pi·g-hunting, *vbl. sb.* Chiefly *N.Z. Hist.* [f. PIG. *sb.*[1] + HUNTING *vbl. sb.*] Hunting for wild pigs. Hence **pi·g-hunt** *v.*; **pi·g-hunter**. Also **pi·g-hunt** *sb.*
In quot. 1614 a humorous exaggeration.
1614 JONSON *Barth. Fair* (1631) III. ii. 34 These are Banbury-bloods, o' the sincere stud, come a pigge-hunting. **1845** R. BURROWS *Diary* 1 May (1886) 24 They ..went off to pig-hunt. **1850** C. O. TORLESSE *Torlesse Papers* (1958) vii. 132 We have to cater for ourselves in the way of meat, which involves some pig hunting. **1851** J. R. CLOUGH *Jrnl.* 19 May in J. Deans *Pioneers of Canterbury* (1937) 293 Four pig-hunters came here; stopped all night. **1880** J. C. CRAWFORD *Recoll. Trav. N.Z. & Austral.* 163 Just below Puketapu we met a canoe laden with dogs going on a pig-hunting expedition. *a* **1948** L. G. D. ACLAND *Early Canterbury Runs* (1951) x. 262 In 1878..one of the shepherds, took a pig-hunting contract. **1961** J. REID *Kiwi Laughs* 9 The misfortunes of that pig-hunt which is an almost indispensable episode in fiction or memoirs.

Pig Island. *Austral.* and *N.Z. slang.* Also with lower-case initials and in pl. [PIG *sb.*[1]] New Zealand, so called because of the introduction of pigs (which then went wild) by Captain Cook. Also *attrib.* So **Pig Islander,** a native or inhabitant of New Zealand.
1917 [see *HOOT *sb.*[3]]. **1917** E. MILLER *Camps, Tramps & Trenches* (1939) 65 We Pig Islanders are not nearly so hot-blooded in our manner of speaking [as Australians]. **1927** J. DEVANNY *Old Savage* 278 I'll back one pig island miner against three of the best that ever came out of England. **1933** *Bulletin* (Sydney) 13 Sept. 29/4 The Pig Islanders are due in Britain in 1936. **1938** 'R. HYDE' *Nor Years Condemn* 164 They call us Homies... A lot of people called the New Zealanders Pig Islanders, and the Australians the Aussies. **1945** J. HENDERSON *Gunner Inglorious* 149 Back home in old Pig Island. **1946** L. R. C. MACFARLANE *Amuri* III. 117 *He* returned to the Pig Islands. **1948** in J. Reid *Kiwi Laughs* (1961) 161 The hell with all those soft-brained pig-islanders. They remind me of yahoos. **1952** *Landfall* VI. 262 It [*sc.* his voice] reverts to a rough pig-island twang. **1960** I. CROSS *Backward Sex* v. 103, I felt it, and was made easier by it, being a pig islander. **1967** F. SARGESON *Hangover* vii. 48 'Young man,' he said, 'it is my advice that you get off back to England... Pig Island is no place for the likes of you.' **1970** *N.Z. Listener* 21 Dec. 8/4 Another guy got blackmailed into taking a sheila half-way around Pig Island.

pig-jump, *v.* Add: (Further example.) Hence **pi·g-jump** *sb.*, a jump from all four legs without bringing them together; **pig-jumper** (further example).
1928 *Funk's Stand. Dict.* s.v. *Pig n.*, Pig-jump, n. **1929** K. S. PRICHARD *Coonardoo* 51 Up and down it the colt went, slewing, rooting, pig-jumping. **1943** 'W. HATFIELD' *I find Austral.* iv. 52 Sending it [*sc.* a mule] away in a series of flying pig-jumps while Tim felt for his off stirrup. *Ibid.* xvi. 213 We'll see what you can do on this pig-jumper of ours.

pig Latin. Also **pig latin.** [f. PIG *sb.*[1] + LATIN *sb.*] An invented language formed by systematic distortion of the source language; *spec.* one in which the initial consonant or consonant cluster of each word is transferred to the end of that word and a vocalic syllable (usually (ēi)) added. Also *transf.* and *attrib.*
1937 R. CHANDLER in *Dime Detective Mag.* Nov. 50/1 'Big white father say come now.'..'Don't give me any more of that pig Latin.' **1937** E. LYONS *Assignment in Utopia* (1938) III. xii. 402 Ideological hair-splitting and proletarian pig-Latin. **1938** F. SCOTT FITZGERALD *Let.* Feb. (1964) 22 But when anything, Latin or pig latin, was ever put up to me..I could always rise to meet that. **1944** [see *JIVE *sb.* 3]. **1956** B. CLEARY *Fifteen* (1962) i. 16 *Utpay atthay owndday*..the boy was saying, 'Put that down,' in pig Latin. **1959** 'F. NEWTON' *Jazz Scene* v. 89 The whites, whose slang name, *ofays*—from the pig latin for 'foe'—sufficiently indicates the tension between the races. **1959** I. & P. OPIE *Lore & Lang. Schoolch.* xiv. 321 'Pig Latin'..thus: 'Unejay ithsmay isay igpay' (June Smith is a pig)..has been spoken by children since before the First World War. **1960** C. GEERTZ in J. A. Fishman *Readings Sociol. of Lang.* (1968) 294 A kind of 'pig-latin' form in the higher term involving..various forms of medial or final nasalization. **1965** *Language* XLI. 219 Pig Latin would have infixes where English has suffixes. **1978** R. MOORE *Big Paddle* i. 7 'Fee-a-zuck yee-a-zoo, I'm wee-a-zith ee-a-zit!' Cliff remembered his father's warning about obscenities, but in carney pig-latin it didn't sound too bad.

pig-lead. (Later example.)
1903 J. MASEFIELD *Ballads* 19 With a cargo of Tyne coal, Road-rails, pig-lead.

pigment, *sb.* Add: **3. b. pigment epithelium** or **layer** *Ophthalm.*, the layer of the retina next to the underlying choroid, which consists of a single layer of pigmented cells having processes that extend between the rods and cones of the adjacent layer, and which continues forwards over the posterior surfaces of the ciliary processes and the iris.
1873 tr. M. Schultze in *Stricker's Man. Human & Compar. Histol.* III. xxxvi. 269 Although..not directly continuous with the nerve fibres, the layer of pigment cells, ordinarily termed the pigment epithelium of the choroid, still belongs, both physiologically and morphologically, to the retina. **1892** A. DUANE tr. *Fuchs's Text-bk. Ophthalm.* iv. 247 The inner surface of the uvea is everywhere coated with a layer of pigmented cells, belonging to the retina and having the character of epithelial cells (pigment-epithelium). **1971** T. L. LENTZ *Cell Fine Struct.* 386 The pigment epithelium has traditionally been considered as a layer of the retina. It may more logically, however, belong to the choroid, because the basement lamina..of the pigment epithelium is part of the glassy or Bruch's membrane of the choroid. **1889** J. LEIDY *Elem. Treat. Human Anat.* (ed. 2) xvi. 875 Pigment-layer of the choroidea. **1974** D. SHEPRO et al. *Human Anat. & Physiol.* ix. 251 The pigment layer absorbs extraneous light that might randomly stimulate receptor cells and create a poorer image.

pigment (pi·gmĕnt), *v.* [f. the sb.] *trans.* To colour with or as with a pigment.
1900 *Nature* 1 Mar. 416/1 To pigment the image, a piece of carbon tissue is soaked in a weak solution containing acetic acid, hydroquinone, and ferrous sulphate, squeezed on to the print and allowed to dry. **1908** A. S. M. HUTCHINSON *Once aboard Lugger* v. i. 285 The stain enters the blood and, thence oozing, pigments every part of the being. **1979** G. MACDONALD *Camera* xii. 175 Robert Demachy experimented skilfully with gum prints which allowed him to pigment and work the coatings until the images looked more like drawings than photographs.
Hence **pi·gmenting** *ppl. a.*
1906 *Westm. Gaz.* 1 Dec. 18/2 The effect of the silver image in the bromide print, in conjunction with the 'pigmenting' solution taken up by the plaster, is to render the pigmented compound forming the plaster..insoluble. **1958** *Engineering* 21 Mar. 384/1 The material is a blend

of polymeric materials, solvents, stabilisers, and pigmenting compounds. **1971** *Brit. Poultry Sci.* XII. 206 The purpose..was to evaluate the efficacy of canthaxanthin for the augmentation of naturally occurring pigmenting compounds found in yellow corn and alfalfa for the pigmentation of broilers.

pigmentocracy (pigmĕntǫ·krăsi). [f. PIGMENT + -OCRACY.] A ruling class made up of people of one skin-colour (usu. white); a country or state with such a ruling class.

1952 *Economist* 6 Dec. 702/2 A natural white aristocracy, with aristocratic virtues as well as vices, was already becoming merely a pigmentocracy. **1956** A. SAMPSON *Drum* xv. 210 In the 'pigmentocracy' of South Africa, skin colour was firmly linked with money and success. **1959** *New Statesman* 19 Dec. 874/3 South Africa is a pigmentocracy, dedicated before God and the whole world to the proposition that 'South Africa is the white man's country: it shall never be ruled by Kaffirs, Hottentots and Coolies.'

pig-nut. 3. Substitute for def.: *N. Amer.* The small pear-shaped nut of the broom hickory, *Carya glabra*, or the closely related species, *Carya ovalis*; also, the trees themselves, which belong to the family Juglandaceæ; = HOG-NUT 1. Also *attrib.* (Earlier and later examples.)

1666 *Early Rec. Warwick, Rhode Island* (1926) 323 Upon a straight lyne from the pond to a pignut tree standing upon a hill. **1705** R. BEVERLEY *Hist. Virginia* II. iv. 16 There are also several Sorts of Hickories, call'd Pig-nuts. **1785** H. MARSHALL *Arbustrum Amer.* 68 White, or Pig-nut Hickory [*sic*]... generally grows pretty large. **1832** D. J. BROWNE *Sylva Amer.* 183 The pignut hickory is one of the largest trees of the American forest. **1908** N. L. BRITTON *N. Amer. Trees* 237 Pignut hickory. ..A tree of drier ground than that in which most other hickories grow. **1969** T. H. EVERETT *Living Trees of World* 98/2 The pignut..occurs as a native in dryish soils from New York to Missouri and Florida. *Ibid.*, The closely related sweet pignut..differs in that its leaves have seven leaflets rather than the usual five.

pigskin. Add: *Sporting slang*, (*a*) (further examples); also *attrib.*; (*b*) *U.S.*, a football; also *attrib.*

1894 *University of Chicago Weekly* 11 Oct. 8/2 Roby put the pigskin over the line. **1898** *Sporting Times* 26 Nov. 3/3 He..has again electrified English turf followers by riding rings around their crack knights of the pigskin. **1928** GALSWORTHY *Swan Song* II. i. 105 Val..had picked him up on his retirement from the pig-skin in 1921. **1941** BAKER *Dict. Austral. Slang* 54 *Pigskin artist*, a jockey. **1945** *Richmond* (Virginia) *Times-Dispatch* 25 Oct. 10/6 Our football prophets are unfortunate fellows... I was told by the prophets of the pigskin that Ohio State would romp over poor Purdue. **1970** *New Yorker* 3 Oct. 34/3 A quick-thinking distaff pigskin zealot. **1974** *Anderson* (S. Carolina) *Independent* 24 Apr. 5B/1 He carried the pigskin on the end around 11 times for 73 yards, or an average of 6.6 yards per carry. **1977** *Time* 14 Nov. 49/2 The British-born geologist..may not help his school's pigskin standings, but no matter.

2. *Med.* = *PEAU D'ORANGE.

1898 [see *PEAU D'ORANGE]. **1943** C. F. GESCHICKTER *Dis. Breast* xx. 480 There is no sharp dividing line between the inflammatory change in the skin observed in acute carcinoma and the more common pigskin or lenticular dermatitis observed late in the disease in cases of large infiltrating mammary cancer. **1966** WRIGHT & SYMMERS *Systemic Path.* I. xxviii. 1010/2 Other cutaneous changes are local oedema ('pigskin', *peau d'orange*..) due to tumour cells growing in and blocking the lumen of the lymphatics in the superficial tissue of the breast, [etc.].

pig-stick (pi·gˌstik), *sb.* [f. PIG-STICKING.] A wild-boar hunt; a pig-sticking. Also *fig.*

1906 *Westm. Gaz.* 13 July 2/1 Pickle meanwhile was having a pig-stick on the sands, with Floss in the rôle of pig. **1906** *Daily Chron.* 26 Oct. 3/4 His book..is just a simple account of his every-day life in Algeria, including a bath and a shave, a 'pig-stick', and a visit to a café.

pigsticker. (In Dict. s.v. PIGSTICKING.) Add: **c.** A sharp implement or weapon, as a lance, bayonet, knife, etc. *slang.*

1890 BARRÈRE & LELAND *Dict. Slang* II. 129/1 *Pig-sticker* (army), sabre. **1895** *Funk's Stand. Dict.*, *Pig-sticker*..3. A boar-spear. 4. (Slang.) A large pocket-knife. **1902** FARMER & HENLEY *Slang* V. 198/2 *Pig-sticker*... 2. (common).—A long-bladed pocket-knife; and (3) a sword. **1918** C. J. SWAN *My Company* viii. 129 All this time the steel pigsticker was resting on his rotund stomach with the rifle behind it cocked. **1941** J. SMILEY *Hash House Lingo* 43 *Pig sticker*, carving knife. **1964** G. L. COON *Short End* 242, I had awful visions of somebody clinging to the business end of that pig sticker of mine. **1978** A. MELVILLE-ROSS *Blindfold* xxx. 191 Trelawney crossed to the far wall, yanked the knife from it... 'You'll hand over that pig-sticker and come home with uncle.'

d. A butcher of swine (cf. PIGSTICKING 2). *dial.* and *slang.*

1886 H. BAUMANN *Londinismen* 138/1 *Pig-sticker*.. scherzhaft: Schweineschlächter. **1895** in *Funk's Stand. Dict.* **1939** F. THOMPSON *Lark Rise* i. 12 The travelling pork butcher, or pig-sticker. **1948** *Amer. Speech* XXIII. 317/2 *Pig sticker*, man who bleeds hogs.

pigsticking. Add: **1.** Also *attrib.*

1907 *Yesterday's Shopping* (1969) 666/2 The usual length for pig-sticking lances is:—For use in Bengal Presidency, 6 ft. 6 in. to 7 ft. **1910** *Blackw. Mag.* Apr. 559/1 The Ganges Cup was first run for in 1869 after the pig-sticking season. **1972** *Shooting Times & Country Mag.* 1 July 21/2, I now treat you to a potted picture of a typical pig-sticking run.

pigtail. Add: **1. d.** *Electr.* A short length of flexible conductor; *spec.* one in an electrical machine connecting a brush to its brush-holder; (see also quot. 1971).

1903 HAWKINS & WALLIS *Dynamo* (ed. 3) xix. 606 The flexible copper conductor..forms a twisted pig-tail with enough slack to allow of the normal amount of brush movement. **1949** *Jrnl. Appl. Physics* XX. 805/2 Some cartridges..were fitted with pigtails for convenience in wiring. **1962** C. O. SWANSON in Roberson & Farrior *Guidance & Control* 400 The pigtails, which pass power to and from the floated assembly, are very small in size. **1963** ROSENBLATT & FRIEDMAN *Direct & Alternating Current Machinery* ii. 15 Except in small dynamos, the current is taken from the brush by means of a flexible copper wire embedded in the brush, called the pigtail. **1964** R. F. FICCHI *Electr. Interference* ix. 166 The conductor may be buried in the concrete slab under the equipment with pigtail conductors protruding above the concrete for equipment grounds. **1971** M. TAK *Truck Talk* 118 *Pigtail*, the cable that transmits electricity to the trailer from the tractor.

pigtailed, *a.* Add: **1.** Esp. in the name of the **pigtailed macaque** or **monkey**, *Macaca nemestrina*, native to southern Asia, Sumatra, and Borneo. (Later examples.)

1932 S. ZUCKERMAN *Social Life Monkeys* vi. 90 The cycle in the pig-tailed macaque varies roughly form thirty to forty days. *Ibid.* xi. 188 The pig-tailed monkeys that live on the Island of Singapore are believed to be escaped captives. **1969** *Daily Tel.* 22 Aug. 19/8 A pig-tailed monkey was born at London Zoo on Sunday. The species..is named because of its ability to curl its tail like a pig's. **1977** ROONWAL & MOHNOT *Primates of S. Asia* 177 Owing to the local demand for pig-tailed macaques for food..its numbers are rapidly declining all over its range.

pigweed. Substitute for def.: A name given to many plants used as animal fodder or potherbs, esp. goosefoots belonging to the genus *Chenopodium* and amaranths, esp. *Amaranthus retroflexus*; in Australia, a name for purslane, *Portulaca oleracea*. (Earlier and further examples.)

1806 T. G. FESSENDEN *Orig. Poems* (rev. ed.) 17 The hyacinth and daffodil, With now and then a big weed Of purslain and of pig weed. **1835** J. H. INGRAHAM *South-West* II. 110 A weed not unlike the common pig-weed. **1850** [see **apple-peru*]. **1864** R. HENNING *Let.* 4 Mar. (1966) 157 The Irish family..were so alarmed at the idea of getting scurvy also..that the two little girls..devoted their leisure to picking 'pigweed', rather a nasty wild plant, but supposed to be exceedingly wholesome, either chopped up with vinegar or boiled. **1909** L. M. MONTGOMERY *Anne of Avonlea* xxvii. 319 I've begun to grow like pigweed in the night. **1911** W. R. GUILFOYLE *Austral. Plants* 298 Portulaca oleracea. 'Common Purslane' or 'Pigweed'. **1927** M. M. BENNETT *Christison* xi. 116 It's a hungry place, Lammermoor! Nothing to eat but pigweed and mutton. **1941** I. L. IDRIESS *Great Boomerang* vii. 55 There were creepers too, crowfoot and pigweed, parakelia and geranium. **1943** FERNALD & KINSEY *Edible Wild Plants Eastern N. Amer.* 177 Pigweed, Goosefoot, Lamb's-Quarters, *Chenopodium album* and 14 other species... The common Pigweed, so familiar in rich garden soil, in barnyards, and similar habitats, has always been a popular potherb. **1945** J. M. FOGG *Weeds of Lawn & Garden* 75 The Green Amaranth or Pigweed is the most common species of the genus found as a garden weed. **1965** *Austral. Encycl.* VII. 232/1 The almost cosmopolitan *P[ortulaca] oleracea* (..purslane or pigweed) is used as a green food by Indonesian and Polynesian peoples. **1966** L. J. KING *Weeds of World* i. 12 The grain amaranths are inextricably involved in any history of the non-cultivated or weedy amaranths or 'pigweeds'. **1975** D. MCCLINTOCK *Wild Flowers of Guernsey* 86 Pigweeds [*sc.* species of *Amaranthus*] are unexpectedly rare in Guernsey.

pi-jaw (pəi·dʒǭ), *sb. slang* (now *arch.*). [f. PI *a.* (*sb.*) + JAW *sb.*¹] A pious lecture or exhortation, esp. one addressed to schoolboys or young persons by their teachers or parents. Hence **pi·jaw** *v. trans.*, to lecture or exhort; **pi-·jawing** *vbl. sb.*

1891 R. G. K. WRENCH *Winchester Word-bk.* 31 He pi-jawed me for thoking. **1912** G. W. E. RUSSELL *One Look Back* ii. 25 It was his custom..to call us all together.., and give us what we called a 'Pi-jaw'. **1913** *Pearson's Mag.* June 606/2 There is no suspicion of 'pi-jaw' about it. **1922** A. S. M. HUTCHINSON *This Freedom* IV. iv. 303 You..get me here to pijaw me about my duty to my pretty young wife. **1923** *Blackw. Mag.* Jan. 56/1 He..treated me to the Persian equivalent of a 'pi-jaw'. **1925** M. I. ROGERS in *Inner Life* (ser. 2) xiii. 257 Older children..are more interested in ideas and the way in which things happen. They dislike 'pi-jaw'. **1930** J. DOUGLAS *Down Shoe Lane* 210 It may be that they yawn over pompous pi-jawing and middle-aged platitudinarianism. **1937** G. FRANKAU *More of Us* xi. 121 The tortures of a miserable Upper Pi-jawed beyond the sacred hour of supper. **1945** G. B. GRUNDY *55 Yrs. at Oxf.* 38 What a boy or young man loathes above all is pi-jaw.

pika (pəi·kă, pī·kă). Also **pica**. Substitute for def.: A small herbivorous quadruped belonging to the genus *Ochotona*, closely related to hares and rabbits, distinguished by short, rounded ears, reddish-brown or grey fur, and the lack of a tail, and found in mountainous regions of western North America and north-east and central Asia. (Later examples.)

1851 J. RICHARDSON *Arctic Searching Exped.* I. v. 178 The little Pika, or tail-less hare, occupies the grassy eminences, and lays up a stock of hay for winter use. **1858** J. PALLISER *Jrnl.* 16 Aug. in I. M. Spry *Papers of Palliser Exped. 1857–1860* (1968) 294, I also heard the squeaking note of the little Pica or tailless hare... It is about the size of a small rat, but made exactly like any other rabbit, excepting that it has round open ears. **1925** E. F. NORTON *Fight for Everest: 1924* 173 Our ponies were off after them in a mad gallop down the nullah side, heedless of rocks and pika burrows. **1936** D. MCCOWAN *Animals Canad. Rockies* iv. 36 Pikas feed on grass and the many varieties of small Alpine plants. **1958** L. WHISHAW *As far as You'll take Me* xi. 176, I had the impression that a pika had spotted us. **1964** L. S. CRANDALL *Managem. Wild Mammals in Captivity* 201 The round-eared, nearly tailless pikas (*Ochotona*) are found in rock areas or 'slides', generally at high altitudes. **1971** L. H. MATTHEWS *Life of Mammals* II. v. 138 The genus *Ochotona*, the only one in the Ochotonidæ, contains about twelve species of whistling hares or rock rabbits, generally known as pikas. **1973** P. GEDDES *Ottawa Allegation* vi. 83 A pika is a bunny... When the sun shines he..cuts all the grass he wants for winter and lays it out to dry.

pikau (pī·kau), *sb. N.Z.* Also **peko, pico.** [Maori.] A pack for carrying on the back, a knapsack, a swag. Also *attrib.* Hence **pi·kau** *v. trans.*, to carry (a pack) on the back.

1836 J. A. WILSON *Jrnl.* 23 Aug. in *Missionary Life & Work N.Z.* (1889) III. 48 Our natives weary with their *pikaus*. **1847** G. F. ANGAS *Savage Life* II. i. 3 [The natives] severally carried [our baggage] in their *pikau* or knapsacks, strapped over their shoulders with the leaves of flax. **1848** *McLean Papers* V. 265 (MS.) One of the natives left us at Woons..so we had to put the *pico* on the mule and trudge along. **1851** J. C. RICHMOND *Let.* 25 Mar. in *Richmond–Atkinson Papers* (1960) I. ii. 79 We were 6 in party, ourselves, young Stark & 3 Maoris with 'pikau' burdens. **1874** W. M. BAINES *Narr. E. Crewe* iii. 49 [The pig's] legs [were] tied together so as to make him a handy 'pikau'. **1882** W. D. HAY *Brighter Britain!* II. 94 Both men and women [*sc.* Maoris] are able to pikau (hump, or carry on the back and shoulders) great weights. **1882** T. H. POTTS *Out in Open* 24 A line of women and girls..have just brought away from the potato pits their heavily-laden kits, carried pikau fashion. **1892** E. S. BROOKES *Frontier Life* 148 Most of us were now loaded with heavy pekoes or swags on our backs. **1902** W. SATCHELL *Land of Lost* vii. 50 He..commenced to fill his *pikau*. **1911** *Chambers's Jrnl.* 4 Mar. 223/2 We succeeded almost noiselessly in doing to death a fine young sow, and, having cut up the carcass, started for camp with the meat 'pikaued' (carried as in a knapsack) in sugar-bags on our shoulders. **1950** F. SARGESON in *Landfall* IV. 285 The rest of his [*sc.* a farmer's] luggage would be a *peko* slung on his shoulders. **1958** *Tararua* XII. 27 The gumdiggers used a *pikau*, a bag with shoulder straps, a good deal smaller than the usual tramper's pack. **1960** B. CRUMP *Good Keen Man* 123 To ensure [my dog] Flynn's co-operation I tied him to my belt with the rope off my pikau.

pike, *sb.*¹ Add: **II. 2.** (Later example.)

1976 *New Yorker* 9 Feb. 32/3 Her sleeve catches in the metal pike of the turnstile and Jane picks it out, in the nick of time.

III. 4. b. (Later example.)

1957 [see *BICK].

pike, *sb.*⁶ Add: **2.** (Earlier and later examples.) Also *fig.* Freq. in phr. (N. Amer. colloq.) *to come down the pike*: to appear on the scene; to come to notice. *to hit the pike*: see *HIT *v.* 11a.

1812 M. EDGEWORTH *Absentee* in *Tales Fashionable Life* VI. xvi. 377 Keep the *pike* till you come to the turn at Rotherford, and then you strike off into the by-road to the left. **1899** B. TARKINGTON *Gentleman from Indiana* iv. 44 The roans setting a sharp pace as they turned eastward on the pike toward home and supper. **1903** [see *FLOSSY *a.*]. **1904** [see *HIT *v.* 11 a]. **1907** 'E. C. HALL' *Aunt Jane of Kentucky* v. 107 Horseback riders had been pouring into town over the smooth, graveled pike. **1910** W. M. RAINE *Bucky O'Connor* 73 Cut loose and hit the pike for yourself. **1912** [see *duck soup* s.v. *DUCK *sb.*¹ 12]. **1926** *Flynn's* 16 Jan. 640/2, I also got cases on a couple of flivvers for a getaway, as we were about fourteen kilos from the main pike. **1934** E. LINKLATER *Magnus Merriman* 82 Then I hit the pike for home. **1949** *Sun* (Baltimore) 12 Oct. 12/1 Unfortunately, the State cannot control roadside development on the sections of the pike completed thus far. **1956** E. O'CONNOR *Last Hurrah* v. 101 Your uncle's the ablest politician to come down the pike in these parts in the last fifty years. **1963** [see *defenceman, defenseman* s.v. *DEFENCE *sb.* 9]. **1966** R. S. RUDNER *Philos. Social Sci.* 2 'Normative' itself is not the clearest term to come to us down the philosophical pike. **1968** *Down Beat* 7 Mar. 19/2 Jack thought that Jimmy was just about the greatest 'bone that had ever come down the pike, and Jimmy felt the same way about Jack, putting him above Miff Mole, who also was a tremendous trombone on that scene. **1970** *New Yorker* 28 Feb. 41/1 A big truck went by way up on the pike. **1974** *Anderson* (S. Carolina) *Independent* 24 Apr. 2A/1 The plan is 'halfway down the pike' but much more effort is needed to make its redevelopment a reality. **1976** *New Yorker* 26 Apr. 59/3 You could see how tired she was after a few hours of 'being presentable to every Tom, Dick, and Harry who comes down the pike'.

b. A railway line or system. Also of a model railway. *U.S.*

1940 *Railroad Mag.* XXVII. VI. 69/1 Lake Erie & International..recently highballed its first Limited around the newly completed circuit of main line. The pike boasts one Diesel-electric and one steam loco.., and its rolling stock is steadily growing. *Ibid.*, Metropolitan Society of Model Engineers... tackled three layouts at one time. The first, a small HO pike was recently presented to the Union Station. **1945** F. H. HUBBARD *Railroad Avenue* ii. 9 They knew he [*sc.* Casey Jones] never dawdled at coal chutes, water cranes, or cinder-pit tracks or wasted time along the pike. **1945** *Railroad Mag.* XXXVII. II. 13 The financing of this little pike was an epic in itself... People along the route were so eager to see the rails laid that they donated labor.

3. *pike-road* (earlier example).

1838 'J. PUNKIN' *Downfall of Freemasonry* II. 115 This threw everything into commotion, and as the teamsters say of a drove of cattle on a dirty pike road, 'kicked up a dust'.

pike (pɔik), *sb.*[10] *N. Amer. dial.* [f. *Pike* County, Missouri, whence the first of these persons are said to have come to California.] Term of contempt on the Pacific coast for a person of no means or of migratory habits; a poor white; a thief. Cf. *PIKER[4]. Also as *adj.*

1854 G. H. DERBY in *Pioneer* (San Francisco) June 379 A tall yellow-haired, sun-burned Pike, in the butternut-colored hat, coat and so forths 'of the period'. **1860** C. W. WILSON *Mapping Frontier* (1970) II. 126 There are about 350 inhabitants, miners, gamblers, sharpers, Jews, Pikes, Yankees, loafers & *hoc genus omne.* **1863** *Harper's Mag.* June 25/2 Society in San José is decidedly Pike' in its character. **1872** C. NORDHOFF *California* xi. 138 The true Pike, however, in the Californian sense of the word, is the wandering, gipsy-like southern poor white. **1928** R. W. RITCHIE *Hell Roarin' Forty-Niners* xv. 234 This Pike had an imagination and a devilishly sly humor which would qualify him to-day for one of our highly specialized lines of salesmanship. **1946** *St. Louis* (Missouri) *Globe-Democrat* 17 Nov. E 2/6 The term 'Pike' or 'piker', in the sense of a worthless, lazy, good-for-nothing person arose first in California in the days of the Forty-Niners.

pike (pɔik), *sb.*[11] [Origin obscure.] A position of the body in diving (see quot. 1928); cf. *JACK-KNIFE *sb.* 3. Also, a similar body position in gymnastics. Also *attrib.*

1928 *Daily Express* 13 July 4/4 For a pike dive spring up as for a header, then bend sharply at the waist and touch the toes without bending knees or ankles, then straighten again and enter head first. **1931** *Morning Post* 21 Aug. 14/5 The pike reverse is a combination of the front pike and reverse. **1956** KUNZLE & THOMAS *Freestanding* v. 60 Aim for a rhythmic drop and beat without any intermediate pause, but make sure that the pike is a full one. **1964** *Trampolining* ('Know the Game' Ser.) 11/2 Piked straddle jumping. Similar to the Pike Jump. **1974** *Rules of Game* 203 In pike dives with twist, the twist must follow the pike.

pike, *v.*[3] Add: **2.** (Further examples.) Also, to proceed or go. Also with other adverbs.

1753 [see *LUMBER *sb.*[2] 3]. **1846** *Swell's Night Guide* 127/2 *Pike off*, run away. **1864** 'E. KIRKE' *Down in Tennessee* xiii. 162, I piked off for the ruin. **1886** *Outing* IX. 49/2 Tell ye what, jist climb onto my pony, an' we'll pike fer the spring. **1893** H. FREDERIC *Copperhead* (1894) 191 It looked kind o' curious to me, your pikin off like that. **1900** ADE *More Fables* (1902) 106 When all the Smart Set got ready to pike away for the Heated Term..she would remain at Home. **1902** H. L. WILSON *Spenders* iv. 44 Do me a last favour before you pike off East. **1904** S. E. WHITE *Silent Places* vi. 50 'We'd better pike out, if we don't want to get back with th' squaws,' suggested Dick. **1909** R. A. WASON *Happy Hawkins* xvii. 207, I piked on over to Danders thinkin' I'd get on a train an' go somewhere. **1924** P. MARKS *Plastic Age* 18 Say, I've got to pike along; I've got a date with my faculty adviser. **1927** H. CRANE *Let.* 4 July (1965) 303 My old jack tar friend..was back from his long trip..so I just piked in and saw him.

3. *intr.* To shirk; to hold back; to back *out*; (see also quot. 1889).

1889 FARMER *Americanisms* 420/1 *To pike* (Cant), to play cautiously and for small amounts, never advancing the value of the stake... Those who gamble in this fashion are called *pikers.* **1954** A. FULLERTON *Bury Past* I. iii. 47 Queer fellow—he worked like hell at the office stuff, the routine, the paper-work, and then suddenly when it came to the push, he'd pike, like he'd done tonight. **1959** *Numbers* Feb. 13/1 'No dogs', said Mr Reginald. 'You wouldn't be piking, would you?' Sonny murmured. **1969** *Southerly* XXIX. 287 Ann's heart began to thump with her secret fear. She waited for someone to veto the idea, not daring herself. But no one did. She could not 'pike' out.

pike (pɔik), *v.*[8] *Diving* and *Gymnastics.* [f. *PIKE *sb.*[11]] **a.** *intr.* To adopt a pike position. **b.** *trans.* To move (a part of the body) as for adopting a pike position. Cf. *PIKED *a.*[2]

1956 KUNZLE & THOMAS *Freestanding* iii. 36 When falling backwards with straight legs, first pike, then drop backwards. *Ibid.* 41 Roll over one shoulder with a half turn, tucking in the head and piking at the hips. **1964** G. C. KUNZLE *Parallel Bars* ii. 45 Pike the hips sharply..and press off the bar strongly with the arms.

piked (pɔikt), *a.*[2] *Diving* and *Gymnastics.* [f. *PIKE *sb.*[11] or *v.*[8]] In a pike position; with the body in a pike position.

1951 *Swimming* (Eng. Schools Swimming Assoc.) v. 71 There are three recognized positions in which the body may be held during the execution of a dive... *Piked.* The body is bent forward at the hips, but the legs must remain straight at the knees with toes pointed. **1956** KUNZLE & THOMAS *Freestanding* iii. 34 If it is properly timed, the roll will finish in piked stand... Loose hamstrings are essential to allow sufficient pike at the hips. **1964** *Trampolining* ('Know the Game' Ser.) 11/1 Piked jumping. Keep trunk as erect as possible... Point toes and touch upper insteps. **1974** *Rules of Game* 36 Two or three running steps into forward piked salto, land on one leg *Ibid.* 38 Swing forward over bar with legs piked.

pikelet[1]. Add: (Later example.)

1974 P. WRIGHT *Lang. Brit. Industry* iv. 43 *Pikelet* is used in the West and Midlands for a round teacake with small holes, to be buttered and toasted; but in other districts it seems to be a sticky unsweetened crumpet or else a muffin.

b. Chiefly *Austral.* and *N.Z.* A drop-scone.

Known personally to me in N.Z. in the 1920s.—Ed.

1943 A. L. SIMON *Conc. Encycl. Gastron.* IV. 97/2 *Welsh Pikelets*..flour..sugar..salt..bicarbonate of soda..buttermilk..Take a tablespoon of this batter and fry in a little hot lard..turn when half cooked. **1952** B. NILSON *Penguin Cookery Bk.* xviii. 332 Drop Scones, Pikelets ..or Scotch Pancakes. Cooking time 3-4 minutes each batch. **1963** *Moderna Språk* LVII. I. 4 *Pikelets*, ..This is the name of the most popular teacake in Australia, yet most Englishmen from South England at least, have never heard of it. **1965** S. T. OLLIVIER *Petticoat Farm* vi. 83 'I've brought some pikelets,' she said. **1970** D. M. DAVIN *Not Here, Not Now* II. ix. 119 Then she made pikelets for tea. **1977** *N.Z. Woman's Weekly* 10 Jan. 54/1 It is then easy to slip the ice in sheets from the sides by using the spatula normally used for turning girdle scones or pikelets.

pike-pole. For *U.S.* read *N. Amer.* and add earlier and later examples.

1850 N. KINGSLEY *Diary* (1914) 139 The weeds are put down with a pike pole and the pressure of the water keeps them to their place. **1926** *Daily Colonist* (Victoria, B.C.) 5 Jan. 1/3 Mattatall sighted it [*sc.* a bag] and hauled it up with a pike pole. **1945** D. D. CALVIN *Saga of St. Lawrence* 68 Men..sorted out with their long pike-poles (which were like twenty-foot boat-hooks with a sharp point and hook) the longer, thinner pieces. **1964** *Daily Colonist* (Victoria, B.C.) 27 Sept. 36/2 A powered boom scooter rides herd on logs in the water where the timber used to be shoved around by a man with caulk boots, a pike pole and the agility of a cougar. **1968** R. M. PATTERSON *Finlay's River* 103 Careering downstream, steering their heavy craft by means of long pike-poles, they crashed into one driftpile, sheered out and spun end for end three times.

b. A long pole having a fire-hook at one end.

1949 *Chicago Daily News* 17 Sept. 1/7 Firemen worked with pike pole and shovel in the wreckage. **1969** *Publ. Amer. Dial. Soc.* LII. 34 *Pike pole*, a rake-like device used to pull plaster loose or to clear an area. 'Clear it out with the pike pole.'

piker[3]. Add: **2.** *Austral.* A wild ox living in the bush. Also *transf.*

1887 *All Year Round* 30 July 67 'Pikers' are wild cattle. **1893** K. MACKAY *Out Back* (ed. 2) III. vi. 265 Blowed if this cask ain't harder to round up nor a mallee piker. **1904** 'G. B. LANCASTER' *Sons o' Men* 22 The grunt of broken-winded pikers came clear above the sharp crackle of undergrowth where the boys rode. **1936** I. L. IDRIESS *Cattle King* vii. 62 The boy bought a teamster's cast-off bullock for two pounds. It was an old piker, worked to the very bone. **1941** —— *Great Boomerang* vii. 51 Fine upstanding beasts, the pick of a dozen stations. No old 'pikers' these.

Pi·ker[4]. [f. *PIKE *sb.*[10] + -ER[1].] = *PIKE *sb.*[10]

1859 in L. Hafen *Colorado Gold Rush* (1941) 318 An extra train of [returning] 'Pikers' came in [to Hannibal] about 2 o'clock yesterday afternoon. **1869** R. KEELER *Gloverson & his Silent Partners* 92 He is what we call a 'Piker', you see,..and he stole some of our sheep. **1873** J. H. BEADLE *Undevel. West* xxxv. 763 These old Pikers don't want the country fenced up and the game scared off. **1907** W. E. CONNELLEY *Doniphan's Exped.* 9 Mr. Moore says that in California in the early days Missourians were called 'Pikers' indiscriminately and generally.

piker[5]. *slang* (orig. *U.S.*). [Cf. *PIKE *v.*[3] 3.] **a.** A cautious or timid gambler who makes only small bets; a person who takes no chances; a 'poor sport' or 'poor thing'; a shirker; a lounger. Also *attrib.*

[**1872** E. CRAPSEY *Nether Side N.Y.* 98 A 'piker' is a tolerated collapse who makes a stray bet when he can borrow a 'check'.] **1889** [see *PIKE *v.*[3] 3]. **1901** 'H. McHUGH' *John Henry* 92 She put us wise to the fact that ..Edgar Allen Poe was a piker compared with her. **1910** W. M. RAINE *Bucky O'Connor* 233 Do you think I'm a cheap piker? **1912** R. W. SERVICE *Rhymes of Rolling Stone* (1913) 96 It's the plugging away that will win you the day, So don't be a piker, old pard. **1919** H. L. WILSON *Ma Pettengill* vii. 216 'I says to myself the other day: "I'll bet a cookie he'd like to be like me!"' Homer was a piker, even when he made bets with himself. **1929** J. BUCHAN *Courts of Morning* I. xii. 138, I don't say there mayn't be some pikers at Headquarters. **1935** Z. N. HURSTON *Mules & Men* (1970) 308 The pikers choose a card each from among those turned off to bet on. **1947** *Sat. Even. Post* 15 Mar. 111/3 It is natural that I should have gone far beyond the sort of piker activities which characterize the average soldier. **1947** D. M. DAVIN *Gorse blooms Pale* 207 'Don't be a piker, Mick,' he said. **1957** 'N. CULOTTA' *They're a Weird Mob* (1958) xiii. 203 It [*sc.* bludger] means that you are criminally lazy.. that you are a 'piker'—a mean, contemptible, miserable individual. **1968** M. RICHLER in R. Weaver *Canad. Short Stories* 2nd Ser. 156 The dirty piker he asked her to marry him he hasn't even got a job. **1969** *Southerly* XXIX. 308 Mat saw me coming. He said: 'We've got a piker on our hands. He reckons he hasn't got enough for a feed at La Roma. Pulling out on us he is.' **1971** H. W. TILMAN *In Mischief's Wake* III. x. 112 He is definitely no piker and although only 22 is one of the old school and believes in discipline. **1973** K. GILES *File on Death* ii. 43 'You have that much authority?' 'He is no piker. I run the place... I can roughly do what I like on the business side.'

b. A person who speculates in stocks, esp. with only small sums.

1898 *N.Y. Jrnl.* 12 Aug. 1/7 John Pettit started in as a 'piker'. That's what the downtown brokers call a man who speculates with a few hundreds at a time instead of with thousands. **1901** *McClure's Mag.* June 159/1 In the absence of complaisant lambs, the financial cannibals known as 'room traders' and 'pikers' tried to 'scalp eighths' out of each other for weeks. **1902** H. L. WILSON *Spenders* xxxi. 360 They're used to those fifty and a hundred thousand dollar pikers down in that neighbourhood. *Ibid.* 365 We'll make those Federal Oil pikers think we've gnawed a corner off the subtreasury. **1942** BERREY & VAN DEN BARK *Amer. Thes. Slang* §563/1 *Piker*, a speculator on a small scale.

piker[6]. [Etym. unknown.] Also **pika.** In Guyana, a plover.

1936 J. BOND *Birds W. Indies* 101 South American Ring Plover (*Charadrius collaris*)...Little Ploward; Nit; Pika; Snipe. *Ibid.* 102 Wilson's Plover (*Charadrius wilsonia*)... Snipe; Little Ploward; Nit; Pika. **1958** J. CAREW *Black Midas* x. 200, I saw curlews and pikers.. flying low over a rim of amber foam.

pikey (pɔi·ki). *dial.* or *slang.* Also **piky.** [f. PIKE *sb.*[6] turnpike] = PIKER[3].

1847 J. O. HALLIWELL *Dict. Archaic & Provinc. Words* 623/2 *Piky*, a gipsey. *Kent.* **1874** HOTTEN *Slang Dict.* 253 *Pikey*, a tramp or gipsy. **1887** PARISH & SHAW *Dict. Kentish Dial.* 116 *Piky*,..a turnpike traveller; a vagabond; and so generally a low fellow. **1955** P. WILDEBLOOD *Against Law* 125 My family's all Pikeys, but we ain't on the road no more!

piki (pī·ki). [Hopi.] Bread made from maize-meal, baked in very thin sheets on heated stones by the Hopi Indians of the south western U.S. Also *attrib.*

1889 in *Cent. Dict.* s.v. *peekee, piki.* **1893** T. DONALDSON *Moqui Pueblo Indians* 72 Piki, or corn bread of many colors, is plentiful, and the evidences of a feast are on every hand. **1922** E. S. CURTIS *N. Amer. Indian* XII. 43 The commonest food derived from corn is piki. **1936** A. M. STEPHEN *Hopi Jrnl.* II. 1197 The men quarry out and roughly dress the piki stone to required dimensions, but the women finish and smooth it by rubbing. **1948** *Southwestern Jrnl. Anthropol.* Winter 376 Corn, flour, breadstuffs—especially piki (wafer bread)—melons, chili, and dried fruit were most sought after. **1959** E. TUNIS *Indians* 119/2 The [Hopi] Pueblos knew fifty-two ways of cooking corn. Most of them weren't unlike the ways other Indians cooked it, but the 'paper bread', called piki, belonged to them alone. It was made from a thin batter and was cooked on a flat stone placed over the fire.

piking (pɔi·kiŋ), *vbl. sb.* and *ppl. a. dial.* and *slang.* [? f. *pike*, var. PICK *v.*[1]: cf. PIKER[1].] Cheating; using sharp practices.

1884 in *Western Pennsylvania Hist. Mag.* (1918) I. 97 After considerable deliberation I concluded to try a little 'piking', and had Leslie sell five thousand barrels 'short' at 64. **1955** W. GADDIS *Recognitions* II. v. 490 The Father of His Country was crumpled, folded, and offered in the most piking and meretricious traffic millions of times a day. **1972** *Daily Tel.* 1 Nov. 2/6 An East End publican who referred in his bar to the Tibbs family as 'dirty piking bastards' was attacked in the street by four men with knives and an axe.

pikipiki (pi·kipiki). [Mbuti.] A whistle used by the Mbuti pygmies of Zaïre (see quot. 1933). Also *attrib.*

1933 G. GRIFFIN tr. *Schebesta's Among Congo Pygmies* iii. 78 The pikipiki is..a kind of whistle, about the thickness of a man's finger, and is cut out of a round piece of wood. In both ends holes are..burned, with a red-hot spike. It can then be used as a whistle like a hollow key. Pikipikis often have one hole only, and may be decorated with spiral metal ornamentations... The pikipiki is used for making magic, not only by the huntsmen, but by every member of the pygmy community. **1936** —— tr. *Schebesta's My Pygmy & Negro Hosts* vi. 114 It seems that all the negro tribes believe in the supernatural powers of the 'pikipiki whistle'. **1958** *Listener* 2 Oct. 508/1 The production of shrill notes from their whistles called pikipikis. **1960** *New Scientist* 6 Oct. 903/1 The songs which they sing nightly to the accompaniment of pikipiki whistles all reflect their belief that..the forest is the great provider and eternal refuge of the chosen people, the Ba'mbuti.

piky, var. *PIKEY.

pilau, pilaw, pilaff. Add: Also prepared in certain areas with wheat in place of rice. (Further examples.)

Still spelt in many different ways in various regions.

1930 W. J. Locke *Town of Tombarel* iv. 114 A pilaff of sea-fruits is a succulent dish, composed of rice and as many fruits of the sea as you can imagine. 1935 H. Edib *Clown & his Daughter* xxiv. 130 Who would believe that any city under the sun could produce such crowds, such colour..and above all such colossal quantities of roast lamb and pilaff! 1936 P. Fleming *News from Tartary* 288 We lunched off pilaffe and sour milk. 1938 M. K. Rawlings *Yearling* xxxi. 392 Ma Baxter made a pilau of the squirrels for supper. 1949 B. A. Botkin *Treas. S. Folklore* iv. i. 552 Marylanders grow lyrical over Brunswick stew..South Carolinians, over rice, calibash, and pilaus (pronounced pé-los, púr-loos). 1956 R. Macaulay *Towers of Trebizond* xv. 182 He did not mind me lying on his floor, he fed me with yoghourt and coffee and offered me some rice pilav. 1959 F. Maclean *Back to Bokhara* ii. 88 A veritable mountain of pilav or *plov*—rice cooked in mutton fat. 1967 *Punch* 12 Apr. 543/1 The lobster pilaf, *côtelettes à la Kiev* and *pommes Anna* with which Carlos Lacerda entertained the Gunthers when he was governor of Guanabara. 1971 *Carry Singapore in your Pocket* (Singapore Tourist Promotion Board) (ed. 3) 31 One first-class Kashmiri restaurant..serves..a wide variety of naan and pilau prepared in Kashmiri style. 1971 *Hindustan Times Weekly* (New Delhi) (Suppl.) 4 Apr. p. iv/5 Just heat up some *ghee*, fry the rice as for a *pullao*. 1971 *Illustr. Weekly India* 25 Apr. 57/2 We will have a proper lunch. Pulao, Chapattis, Shreekand, the lot. 1971 R. Russell tr. *Ahmad's Shore & Wave* ix. 118 'Can I get you anything?' he asked. 'Chicken? Pulao?' 1978 *Detroit Free Press* 16 Apr. 6c/1 (Advt.), This Sunday, Monday or Tuesday you can order our thick and juicy prime rib (served with our special rice pilaf).

pile, *sb.*[1] Add: **1. b.** Delete †*Obs.* and add later examples. Now also made of substances other than metal.

1875 *Encycl. Brit.* II. 376/1 Arrows are manufactured generally of red-pine timber,..glued on one end, upon the point of which the iron pile is fixed. 1894 H. Walrond in Longman & Walrond *Archery* xviii. 304 Arrows are..called 'self' or 'footed' according as to whether they are footed or not with hard wood at the pile end. 1939 P. H. Gordon *New Archery* ii. vi. 67 The solid-tipped 'parallel pile' is preferable to hollow-point 'bullet ferrules'. 1958 Wiseman & Brundle *Archery* 83 The piles or tips of arrows are made of brass, steel, aluminium, horn or plastic. 1972 T. Foy *Beginner's Guide Archery* xvi. 124 In the eighteenth-century the Turks were superb Flight Shots, and they invented 'barrelled' arrows which were thicker at the centre than at the nock and pile. 1979 R. Laidlaw *Lion is Rampant* xiii. 104 They were target arrows with conical piles.

5. a. *pile-bridge* (examples). **b.** *pile guide.* **d.** **pile-built** *a.* (earlier example); **pile-cap** (examples).

1899 *Westm. Gaz.* 9 Dec. 5/3 The scarcity of timber or other material suitable for the erection of a trestle or pile bridge. 1940 *Chambers's Techn. Dict.* 643/1 *Pile bridge*, a bridge whose superstructure is carried on piles. 1851 A. O. Hall *Manhattaner* 5 It was a modest commercial plain; pile-built, and earth filled. 1898 C. E. Fowler *Coffer-dam Process for Piers* iv. 49 The small hammer.. is used for sheet pile work by inserting a 'follower' of oak which fits the base or pile cap, and which has a slit in the lower end to fit the sheet pile. 1944 [see *piling *vbl. sb.*[1] 2]. 1975 R. Holmes *Introd. Civil Engin. Construction* iv. 166 Pile caps are usually constructed of concrete to such a depth as will ensure full transfer of load to the piles and, at the same time, resist punching shear. 1974 *People's Jrnl.* (Inverness & Northern Counties ed.) 29 June 22 (*caption*) In one of the biggest lifts ever in the off-shore oil industry a 940-ton pile guide cluster is lifted into position to be fixed to the base of the huge oil rig jacket now being finished at Nigg. 1975 *Offshore* Sept. 11/1 The 'Heerema Steel Structure' consists essentially of a jacket made up of four steel towers which fit into a steel base frame incorporating pile guides.

pile, *sb.*[3] Add: **3. h.** (Further examples.) Also in phr. *to go one's pile*, to stake all one's money on a single chance, to 'go the whole hog'.

1839 *Picayune* (New Orleans) 29 Mar. 2/2 Friends of the Lubber, becoming excited at the unexpected termination of the first heat, were willing to go a 'small pile' somewhere in the neighborhood of even. 1840 *Spirit of Times* X. 498 Considerable sums were laid out..the Georgians 'going their pile' on the Andrew filly. 1865 'Mark Twain' *Celebr. Jumping Frog* (1867) 37 His last acts was to go his pile..when there was a 'flush' out agin him. 1915 J. Buchan *39 Steps* i. 10, I had got my pile—not one of the big ones, but good enough for me. 1915 Wodehouse *Psmith Journalist* xxii. 166 He made a bit of a pile out of the job, and could afford to lie low for a year or two. 1969 *Listener* 24 July 103/2 So many Poles or Ukrainians ..had spent part of their life in the United States, and returned home after making a decent pile. 1973 *Times* 22 Mar. 25/1 This is tough talk from a man who first made his pile as an investment banker. 1977 McKnight & Tobler *Bob Marley* i. 17 The only way to get ahead, make your pile and escape from the overwhelming oppression and depression of poverty.

i. A nuclear reactor.

1942 H. L. Anderson et al. in E. Fermi *Coll. Papers* (1965) II. 129 At the end of September, 1941, a new and taller exponential pile was set up and the accuracy was further increased by using a 2 gram Ra+Be source instead of the original source of about 600 mg. 1945 H. D. Smyth *Gen. Acct. Devel. Atomic Energy Mil. Purposes* v. 48 In a memorandum written to Bush on May 14, 1942.., Conant estimated that there were five separation or production methods that were..likely to succeed: the centrifuge, diffusion, and electromagnetic methods of separating U-235; the uranium-graphite pile and the uranium-heavy-water pile methods of producing plutonium. 1945 *War Illustr.* 9 Nov. 439/1 The natural uranium (U238) is in the shape of rods embedded in a graphite block and contained in an atomic 'pile'. 1945 *Nature* 29 Dec. 768/2 They give..brief accounts..of the construction and testing of the first self-sustaining chain-reacting pile. 1946 *Ann. Reg. 1945* 354 A pile, containing 12,400 lb. of uranium in lumps separated by graphite, set up in Chicago under the direction of Prof. E. Fermi, was first operated on December 2, 1942. 1948 K. K. Darrow *Atomic Energy* iv. 66 When I heard the name in its new meaning and knew that Fermi an Italian had invented the new pile, I took it for granted that he had intentionally chosen the appellation of Volta. Great was my surprise when I learned from Fermi that it was a mere coincidence. He had conferred the name on his device because it was 'such a big pile of graphite and uranium'. 1952 *Nucleonics* Mar. 11/1 In later developments, most of the assemblies bear no resemblance to piles so that the expression nuclear reactor is to be preferred. Some British writers make the distinction that piles imply the use of natural uranium, and reactors, the use of enriched uranium. 1954 C. P. Snow *New Men* vi. 100 'If the pile gets too hot, then they automatically shut the whole thing off,' said Luke. 1955 *Sci. News Let.* 26 Mar. 201/2 Fissionable material to fuel the pile will be obtained from the AEC on an extended loan basis. 1957 *Times* 12 Oct. 6/1 The danger of radioactivity being disseminated from the pile chimney in steam. 1964 M. Gowing *Britain & Atomic Energy, 1939–1945* x. 284 The theoretical physicists also contributed greatly to a whole range of pile theory and pile design problems. 1976 *Sci. Amer.* Dec. 32/2 Barely two and a half years elapsed between the initial chain-reacting pile on December 2, 1942, and the explosion of the first plutonium bomb on July 16, 1945.

pile, *sb.*[5] Add: **1.** Also, the fine undercoat of certain rough-coated dogs, esp. the Old English sheep-dog.

1905 J. Watson *Dog Bk.* v. 386 The under coat [of the bob-tailed sheep dog] should be a waterproof pile. 1938 E. C. Ash *New Bk. Dog* x. 395 Coat [of Old English sheep-dog].—Profuse, and of good hard texture... The undercoat a pile when not removed by grooming. 1971 Dangerfield & Howell *Internat. Encycl. Dogs* 348/1 Pile. Dense undercoat.

c. Red or yellowish markings on white or pale-coloured fowls; a fowl with this coloration. Also *attrib.*

1854 *Poultry Chron.* I. 289 The 'white or pile game'.. were withheld from prizes altogether. 1913 W. Bateson *Mendel's Princ. Heredity* (rev. ed.) 120 The coloration known as 'Pile' in fowls is seldom bred for exhibition from two pile kinds. 1929 E. Brown *Poultry* I. iii. 62 Pile Leghorns were produced by Mr. George Payne, of Woking. *Ibid.* 69 Pile.—This is a purely exhibition fowl, so named from its having the markings of the old variety of Game fowl with the same designation.

pile, *v.*[2] Add: **1. c.** (Earlier example.)

1839 *Civil Engin. & Arch. Jrnl.* II. 17/2 A reverberatory furnace of the common construction employed in 'puddling', 'balling', or 'piling' iron.

e. *to pile up*: to wreck (a ship); to crash (an aircraft, vehicle, etc.).

1899 C. J. C. Hyne *Further Adventures Capt. Kettle* vi. 137 If the bar had shifted, he himself could have put this steamer on the ground as handily as the other man had piled up the branch boat. 1923 *Times Lit. Suppl.* 29 Mar. 218/2 An old battle-cruiser which gets adrift in a gale..[and] is piled up on the rocks. 1925 Fraser & Gibbons *Soldier & Sailor Words* 223 *Pile up one's bus, to*, an airman's expression for coming a 'crash'. 1930 Kipling *Limits & Renewals* (1932) 230 We had a passenger..who wanted to see Caesar. It cost us our ship... He piled up the *Eirene* on his way. 1932 'N. Shute' *Lonely Road* ix. 196 The fellow was so drunk that he'd probably have piled his car up anyway. 1942 N. Streatfeild *I ordered Table for Six* 236 Andrew cautiously steered Claire to the centre of the floor... He was afraid if he talked he might pile her up. 1959 G. Jenkins *Twist of Sand* iv. 78, I hope to God they don't pile that monster up on my runways. 1971 M. Tak *Truck Talk* 119 *Pile up*, to wreck a truck.

2. (Further examples.)

1860 *Baily's Mag.* Sept. 429 The Kent innings was piled up the next day to 152. 1873 *Ibid.* Dec. 287 We fancy there are some batsmen who would pile up the runs rapidly off his leg balls. 1898 J. A. Gibbs *Cotswold Village* xi. 246 Once fairly started on a sequence of big scores, the cricketer goes on day by day piling up runs. 1948 'N. Shute' *No Highway* i. 25 The Reindeers were flying over the Atlantic piling up the hours faster than Mr. Honey's test.

b. (Later example.) Also *to pile it on.*

1852 *Star* (Los Angeles) 3 Apr. 1/5 The wags observed that Caleb was getting exceedingly uneasy, and 'piled it on'. 1876 'Mark Twain' *Old Times Mississippi* viii. 43 'Now I don't want to discourage you, but—' 'Well, pile it on me; I might as well have it now.' 1943 J. B. Priestley *Daylight on Saturday* xxxviii. 297, I fancy you're piling it on too much. There are lots of things you can enjoy, if you set about it properly. 1969 E. Gébler *Shall I eat you Now?* 56 But that was piling it on a bit; she wasn't that daft. *a* 1974 R. Crossman *Diaries* (1976) II. 601, I suppose he will get what he wants at Cabinet but he's piling it on a bit thick. 1976 *West Lancs. Evening Gaz.* 15 Dec. 8/2 And now they want to pile on the agony with rip-roaring monsters going round and round.

3. (Further examples.)

1926 *Scribner's Mag.* Sept. 266/1 'How things did pile up!'..Almost every person Peter particularly dislikes came in for tea and..Feinberg showed up with Sally. 1930 *Morning Post* 14 July 6/7 Vehicles crossing the circus diagonally had to 'pile up' in the centre. 1942 *We speak from Air* 39 Whether you get the Hun or miss him, he frequently piles up on the ground through making his landing in fright. 1947 *John o' London's Weekly* 25 July 502/3 In referring to the traffic 'piling up', did he mean that motor-cars, lorries, bicycles were stacked up in neat heaps on the roadway? 1956 'C. Blackstock' *Dewey Death* vii. 160 The work is just piling up. 1975 *Times* 18 Mar. (Greece Suppl.) 1/4 It is not just the old problems. Each day new ones pile up.

b. To climb *on* or go *into* (a vehicle, building, etc.) so as to form a pile; hence, to enter (a place) in crowds; and simply, to mount, enter, etc. orig. *U.S.*

1841 L. B. Swan *Jrnl. of Trip to Michigan* (1904) 30 Brooks brought up his lumber wagon and we all 'piled in'. 1854 M. J. Holmes *Tempest & Sunshine* iii. 44 Fanny with half a dozen other girls..began piling on to Bill's old sled. 1879 J. Burroughs *Locusts & Wild Honey* (1884) 38 They [*sc.* bees] come piling in till the rain is upon them. 1884 'Mark Twain' *Huck. Finn* xxxvi. 345 Here comes a couple of the hounds in from under Jim's bed; and they kept on piling in till there was eleven of them. 1923 R. D. Paine *Comrades of Rolling Ocean* vii. 114 Judson introduced his four shipmates who piled into the automobile. 1929 R. Graves *Good-Bye to all That* x. 103 There were about three thousand prisoners already there and more piled in every day. 1943 N. Coward *Middle East Diary* (1944) 100 We flagged a passing lorry .., piled into it bag and baggage and whirled off to the airport. 1956 B. Holiday *Lady sings Blues* (1973) viii. 72 We piled into his car and were off. 1972 J. Wambaugh *Blue Knight* (1973) xiii. 231 We jawed..and finally piled into the cars.

c. Hence used of the reverse processes: to climb *down from*, or *off* (a vehicle); to come *out of* (a place), etc., in crowds. orig. *U.S.*

1884 'Mark Twain' *Huck. Finn* xxii. 205 A lot of men begun to pile down off of the benches and swarm toward the ring. 1896 Ade *Artie* xi. 100 We stopped in front of the church and piled out. 1902 S. E. White *Blazed Trail* xx. 150 Then they piled out for the boss. 1908 —— *Riverman* xxii. 195 They piled off the train at Sawyer's. 1921 C. E. Mulford *Bar-20 Three* xvii. 224 Six sleeping men piled from their bunks and..chased the cursing trail-boss. 1972 *Times* 20 Nov. 8/6 Hundreds more piling off every train.

d. *to pile on to* (N. Amer.), to attack vigorously, to assail.

1894 *Outing* XXIV. 417/1 The dog ..[will] never 'pile onto' any more bears. 1906 U. Sinclair *Jungle* xvi. 183 Like as not a dozen [policemen] would pile on to him at once, and pound his face into a pulp. 1970 *Globe & Mail* (Toronto) 25 Sept. 30/1 The Australian tub, Gretel, hit the American scow, Intrepid, below the gunwale the other day, or tugged its saddle blanket, or piled on with unnecessary roughness.

e. To move or advance in a throng.

1925 H. L. Foster *Trop. Tramp with Tourists* 102 The tourists piled towards the exits.

f. *to pile in*: to crash.

1944 G. Netherwood *Desert Squadron* ii. 21 So low did Pilot Officer Weeks fly as he did the Victory Roll, that those watching him made certain that he would 'pile in'.

pilea (pəi·liă). [mod.L. (J. Lindley *Collectanea Botanica* (1821) 4), f. L. *pīleus* cap.] An annual or perennial herb of the genus so called, belonging to the family Urticaceæ, native to many tropical regions, and cultivated elsewhere as a house plant; esp. *Pilea muscosa*, the artillery or gunpowder plant, which discharges clouds of pollen when it is touched.

1918 N. L. Britton *Flora of Bermuda* 105 Large-leaved Pilea, Jamaican, seen in the garden at Mt. Hope in 1914. 1958 *Times* 29 Nov. 9/5 We have the pileas, the tradescantias, and..all the various forms of *Begonia rex.* 1971 *Country Life* 25 Nov. 1443/1 Among the most interesting recent introductions are three pileas. 1974 W. Davidson *All about House Plants* 156/1 On the whole pileas are small, compact plants.

pileated, *a.* **1.** For *Picus pileatus* substitute *Dryocopus pileatus.* (Later examples.)

1928 G. M. Sutton *Introd. Birds Pennsylvania* 81 The call of the Pileated is a high, irregular cackle. *Ibid.*, The food of the Pileated Woodpecker is chiefly grubs. 1956 G. Durrell *Drunken Forest* ix. 169 Pileated jays have long, magpie-like tails of black and white... The feathers on the forehead were black, short, and plushy, and stuck up straight. 1969 R. Lowell *Notebk. 1967–68* 57 A large pileated bird flies up. 1971 W. Hillen *Blackwater River* ix. 80 A pileated woodpecker gave his jungle-like call and flashed his scarlet crest through the trees.

piled, *ppl. a.*[2] Add: **a.** (Later examples with *up.*)

1898 P. Geddes *Let.* Feb. in P. Boardman *Worlds of Patrick Geddes* (1978) vi. 167 The piled-up picturesqueness of Old Edinburgh. 1935 C. S. Forester *African Queen* vi. 109 The *African Queen*..reared up as she hit the piled-up water. 1948 H. Innes *Blue Ice* vii. 191 Mile on ghastly mile of piled-up snow-capped peaks. 1978 'L. Black' *Foursome* i. 7 The piled-up dishes, bowls, plates.

b. With all sails set.

1851 H. Melville *Moby Dick* II. ix. 62 With every mast-head manned, the piled-up craft rolled down before the wind.

c. Crashed, wrecked.

1939 J. Steinbeck *Grapes of Wrath* vi. 61 They ain't whole, out lonely on the road in a piled-up car. They ain't alive no more. 1943 C. H. Ward-Jackson *Piece of Cake* 48 *Piled in* or *up*, crashed.

pi·le-dri:ve, *v.* [Back-formation from PILE-DRIVER.] **a.** *trans.* To construct (something) using a pile-driver; to act as or like a pile-driver on (something).

1894 KIPLING in *Century Mag.* Dec. 295/1 I'll catch 'em by the back o' the neck, an' pile-drive 'em a piece. **1932** *Daily Express* 27 June 9/4 Trotsky may not convince the world that the revolution in which he and Lenin were the giants was a splendid thing, but he pile-drives the contention that it was inevitable in Russia. **1971** 'D. HALLIDAY' *Dolly & Doctor Bird* vii. 94 They're still pile-driving the quayside. **1972** D. HASTON *In High Places* vii. 91 Chris was falling every second turn, pack pile-driving his head into the snow.

b. *intr.* (See quot. 1929.)

1898 *Nautical Mag.* LXVII. 355 After pile-driving off Cape Horn for some days, she squared away..and eventually reached San Francisco. **1929** F. BOWEN *Sea Slang* 103 *Pile Driving*, steaming or sailing into a heavy head sea. **1937** G. S. DOORLY *In Wake* viii. 127 We had been 'pile-driving' heavily through the night.

pile-driver. Add: **2.** *transf.* A very strong or powerful hit, stroke, kick, etc., in various games; something of great strength or power.

1858 A. MAYHEW *Paved with Gold* II. xii. 189 After some sparring, Jack threw out his 'pile-drivers' and caught Ned on the 'sniffer', but the nose didn't suffer much. **1929** *Star* 21 Aug. 17/1 Hammond was let off when 59 from a pile-driver to third man. **1929** *Daily Express* 7 Nov. 19/1 Their inside right put in a couple of pile-drivers that missed the target by inches only. **1952** M. ALLINGHAM *Tiger in Smoke* i. 18 His piledriver personality forced home the suggestion. **1962** [see *back-breaker* s.v. *BACK- B]. **1964** *Guardian* 2 Mar. 7/6 He's using pile-drivers (dropping on the head). **1968** R. WEST *Sk. Vietnam* ii. 60 'The noise of these pile-drivers,' he said with great satisfaction, 'was heard as far as Saigon.' **1973** *Sunday Tel.* 4 Mar. 38/8 Jones picked up a loose clearance from Feltwell, and her pile-driver took the paint off the post. **1973** D. LEES *Rape of Quiet Town* vi. 93 The big boys were dishing out pile-drivers and body-slams, cracking heads and snapping spines.

pile-driving, *sb.* and *a.* Add: (Further examples.) Also *fig.*

1894 'MARK TWAIN' in *Century Mag.* Jan. 335/1 The title came upon them as a kind of pile-driving surprise. **1942** PARTRIDGE *Usage & Abusage* (1947) 126/2 If the point is still not made, let us take a few more of Jespersen's pile-driving examples. **1960** *Farmer & Stockbreeder* 15 Mar. 46/2 This simple pile-driving machine, easily attached to any tractor fitted with P.T.O. and hydraulic lift will reduce fencing costs to a minimum.

Pilentum (pile·ntə̆m). *Hist.* Also **pilentum.** [f. L. *pilentum* an easy chariot used by ladies or for carrying the vessels, etc., for sacred rites.] A type of carriage (see quot. 1961).

1837 W. B. ADAMS *Eng. Pleasure Carriages* xvii. 278 The next attempt in the 'service of the public', was the introduction of a vehicle with the..title of a Four-wheeled Cabriolet. This is a modification of..a Pilentum. **1843** *Ainsworth's Mag.* IV. 100 If I could have built a mother for myself, as one does a Brougham or pilentum. **1849** E. RUSKIN *Let.* 30 Sept. in M. Lutyens *Effie in Venice* (1965) I. 41 We concluded by fixing to take two [carriages], one for John..and an elegant *Pilentum* for Charlotte and me. It is an open carriage but shuts very easily... It is rather heavy..and will require three horses. **1961** M. WATNEY *Elegant Carriage* 60 The Pilentum..was an open carriage with the doorway very near the ground, the driving seat was also low, but it was built in different sizes to carry four or six people, and to be drawn by one or two horses. In appearance, the Pilentum was not unlike a Victoria, although it had doors at the sides. **1974** F. SELWYN *Cracksman on Velvet* II. 76 On its indiarubber bearings..the swan's neck Pilentum seemed to roll in air above the glittering spokes of its wheels.

pi·le-up. [f. vbl. phr. *to pile up*: see PILE *v.*² I a, e in Dict. and Suppl.] **1.** A crash or collision, often involving several vehicles; a vehicle that has been involved in a crash. Also *fig.*

1929 *Papers Mich. Acad. Sci., Arts & Lett.* X. 314 *Pile-up*, a crash; a smash. **1945** *Richmond* (Virginia) *Times-Dispatch* 18 Sept. 15/2 (*heading*) Five harness racers injured in pile-up. **1951** W. SANSOM *Face of Innocence* x. 138 We passed one pile-up with its dead-slumped radiator and its ragged little crowd. **1954** L. KLEMANTASKI tr. *Fraichard's Le Mans Story* v. 46 A tremendous multiple pile-up, which was visible from the grandstands, had eliminated six of the competing cars. **1957** S. MOSS *In Track of Speed* iii. 34 Both of us had escaped a pile-up of about half a dozen cars early in the race. **1968** *New Scientist* 3 Oct. 38/2 A recent pile-up on the M1 in Bedfordshire involving 30 cars has apparently moved the Ministry of Transport to do some thinking. **1973** *Black Panther* 31 Mar. 8/1 When the sky rocketing demands for human rights and the technology of the super-industrial state (U.S.A.) clash head on, there is a bloody social pile-up. **1973** *Times* 1 Aug. 2/8 Three people were killed and three seriously injured in a pile-up involving three lorries and a car on the A17. **1977** *Belfast Tel.* 27 Jan. 1/3 A woman and her nine-year-old son were killed in a traffic pile-up in Dublin today.

2. a. An accumulation; an amassing of tasks, papers, etc. Also *attrib.*

1945 *Sun* (Baltimore) 14 Feb. 6/7 The Marshalls, the mid-Pacific cluster of coral pileups just above the equator. **1946** *Ibid.* 26 Apr. 10/3 Rain slowed air traffic in and around Washington, causing a 'pile-up' of planes over the Washington airport. **1948** M. LASKI *Tory Heaven* viii. 119 Unless one can get each crop of débutantes married off as it comes out, we're only going to get the same pile-up all over again. **1951** C. W. MILLS *White Collar* I. iii. 39 A tangled pile-up of restrictive legislation. **1963** *Times* 5 Feb. 13/3 More people might well be laid off in spite of the pile-up of work waiting for them. **1964** *Amer. Folk Music Occasional* I. 88 An endless 'pile-up song' which begins: I had a hen, and the hen pleased me. **1964** V. J. CHAPMAN *Coastal Vegetation* viii. 194 The 'pile-up' to form our shingle beaches is due to the action of direct onshore waves. **1966** *Word Study* Dec. 2/2 Sentences were talk-built, producing both fragments and pileups. **1968** C. HELMERICKS *Down Wild River North* II. xxiii. 368 We jumped out into the water and struggled to thrust the boat up onto a pileup of logs which was wedged there.

b. *Electronics.* A lack of linearity or resolution in a pulse circuit caused by the pulses arriving too rapidly.

1962 C. SUSSKIND *Encycl. Electronics* 18/2 Pile-up is not necessarily an excursion into a nonlinear region but the result of coupling capacitances not fully discharging after each pulse. **1973** *Nature* 23 Mar. 270/2 This potential source of electronic pile-up background was eliminated by anti-pile-up circuitry allowing detection of the desired gamma rays in the presence of counting rates up to 10^5 s^{-1} below 1 MeV.

pilfer, *sb.* Add: **2.** *Comb.*, as *pilfer-proof* adj.

1959 *Light Metals* Jan. 18/3 Specially designed extrusions..provide a weather- and pilfer-proof seal where the two pivoting roof sections meet axially. **1965** *Economist* 3 July 35/4 Weld mesh cages, fitted to the decks, can be locked before being stowed, thus becoming pilfer-proof. **1969** *Jane's Freight Containers 1968–69* (Advt. section) 21 Because the Freightank is pilferproof insurance premiums are reduced.

pilferage. Add: (Later examples.) Also *Comb.*

1964 *Spectator* 13 Mar. 337/2 An installation with a primary mission of production control can simultaneously be used to promote safety and prevent pilferage. **1969** *Daily Tel.* 22 July 17 (Advt.), We have the only through-pallet service between here and the Far East via the U.S.A...which means much less chance of loss, pilferage, and damage. **1969** *Jane's Freight Containers 1968–69* 482/3 In the side walls there are pilferage-proof ventilation openings. **1971** *Daily Mail* 6 May 24/4 Pilferage last year totalled half of 1p.c. of the..turnover. **1974** *Islander* (Victoria, B.C.) 1 Sept. 11/2 When visitors leave, all their baggage is inspected by police to forestall pilferage.

pilger (pi·lgəɹ), *sb.* and *v.* *Metallurgy.* Also **Pilger.** [a. G. *pilger* pilgrim, in allusion to the alternate feeding in and partial withdrawal of the billet during the operation of the mill, which is said to resemble the steps of pilgrims approaching a shrine.] Used *attrib.* (in *pilger mill, process, roll*, etc.) with reference to a rolling mill for reducing the outside diameter of a tube without changing the inside diameter, its two rollers each having a semicircular groove of decreasing diameter passing round the circumference, so that in conjunction they form a circular hole through which the tube can be forced on a cylindrical mandrel and which decreases gradually and increases suddenly in size during each revolution of the rollers.

1902 *Proc. S. Wales Inst. Engineers* XXII. 351 One of the most interesting..devices is the machine named the Pilger carriage, to which the hollow billet is attached previous to being operated upon in the pilgrim mill. **1905** *Min. Proc. Inst. Civil Engineers* CLIX. 335 A tube produced by means of pilger-rolls frequently possesses a rippled or undulating surface. **1922** *Iron & Coal Trades Rev.* 9 June 849/1 The Pilger mill consists of two..'cam' rolls, fixed in housings, and driven through two-high pinions in practically the same manner as a two-high merchant bar mill, except that the Pilger rolls rotate in an opposite direction. **1954** A. R. BAILEY *Text-bk. Metallurgy* xii. 419 (*caption*) Diagram showing the step-by-step method of rolling in the Pilger process. **1968** R. N. PARKINS *Mech. Treatm. Metals* iv. 263 In the Pilger mill, the tube is deformed over a mandrel between rolls that work the tube during only part of each revolution. **1973** [see below].

So **pi·lger** *v. trans.*, to make in a pilger mill; **pi·lgering** *vbl. sb.*

1902 *Proc. S. Wales Inst. Engineers* XXII. 350 Pilgering or pilgrim mill. This mill derives its name from its peculiar intermittent action upon the hollow billet. **1923** HARBORD & HALL *Metallurgy of Steel* (ed. 7) II. xxiii. 467 Tubes are not usually made by pilgering with walls less than 9 or 10 gauge in thickness. **1945** *Metallurgia* XXXIII. 61/1 If the partly pilgered tube is withdrawn, the shape of the cone between bloom and tube will thus be a projection of the groove that varies around the roll. *Ibid.* 61/3 One company once pilgered a tube 10$\frac{3}{8}$ in. outside diameter × $\frac{3}{16}$ in. thick by no less than 135 ft. 8 in. long. **1973** J. G. TWEEDDALE *Materials Technol.* II. iv. 95 Pilgering is the name given to the second tube-forge-rolling system, which is done in a pilger mill.

pilgrim, *sb.* **5.** (Earlier and later U.S. examples.)

1841 W. L. MACCALLA *Adventures in Texas* 46 After such an address from a citizen of that calumniated country Texas to a shattered old pilgrim, I took the liberty of withdrawing to another apartment. **1867** J. F. MELINE *Two Thousand Miles on Horseback* 22 The term Pilgrims for emigrants first came into use at the period of the heavy Mormon travel—the Mormons styling themselves 'Pilgrims to the promised land of Utah'. **1885** *Rep. Indian Affairs* (U.S.) 120 This, we think, is a very fair crop of calves considering the fact that the cattle were what is called 'pilgrim' cattle (cattle for the States that had never passed through a winter before without being housed and fed). **1942** E. E. DALE *Cow Country* 194 They mingled with 'drift cattle' from Kansas or with the trail herds of 'pilgrim cattle' from Texas. **1943** J. K. HOWARD *Montana* 139 They were for the most part 'pilgrims' who remained and were 'made into hands'.

pilgrimage, *sb.* Add: **3. pilgrimage church, town, village,** etc., a church, town, village, etc., to which pilgrimages are made.

1889 L. T. SMITH tr. *Jusserand's Eng. Wayfaring Life in Middle Ages* III. iii. 348 It was..a town of inns and churches, as pilgrimage towns have generally been. **1908** *Westm. Gaz.* 28 July 8/2 [They] paid a visit to the picturesque pilgrimage village of Sainte Anne de Beaupré. *Ibid.*, His Royal Highness alighted and proceeded to enter the Pilgrimage Church, the steps of which were crowded with cripples and pilgrims. **1935** *Burlington Mag.* Oct. 183/1 The great aisled transept [of Laon cathedral], she derives from the so-called 'pilgrimage churches' of which much has been written in recent years.

pili (pī·li). [Hawaiian.] A Hawaiian name for the perennial grass, *Heteropgon contortus*, formerly used as a thatching material. Also *attrib.*

1888 W. HILLEBRAND *Flora Hawaiian Islands* 508 Common on all islands, the 'Pili' of the natives, very troublesome on account of its awns, which get entangled in the wool of sheep. **1915** W. A. BRYAN *Nat. Hist. Hawaii* v. 59 Should a chief order a house built, certain men would cut the timbers, others gather the pili grass. **1917** *Nature* 20 Sept. 57/2 The grass used for this purpose [*sc.* thatching] is usually pili.., an indigenous grass. **1934** M. D. FREAR *Lowell & Abigail* ii. 94 It was easy to accept the Hawaiian roof of thatch, using..*ti* leaf where *pili* grass was not to be had. **1949** P. H. BUCK *Coming of Maori* II. ii. 119 The Hawaiians used a similar [thatching] technique with *pili* grass. **1965** M. C. NEAL *In Gardens of Hawaii* 80 In Hawaii, *pili* was preferred to other thatch material because of its pleasant odor, brown color, and neat appearance.

piliated (pi·-, pəi·li,ē¹·tėd), *a.* *Bacteriol.* [f. *pili-*, taken as comb. form of *PILUS + -ATE² + -ED¹, or directly f. *PILUS + *-iated* after *fimbriated.*] Bearing pili.

1960 *Biochim. & Biophys. Acta* XLII. 298 Many piliated strains of bacteria can exist in two forms, the completely piliated..or the completely non-piliated. **1973** DOETSCH & COOK *Introd. Bacteria* ii. 28 Bacteria capable of producing pili, when freshly isolated from natural sources, are usually 'piliated'.

piling, *vbl. sb.*¹ **1.** (Later example.)

1973 *Daily Tel.* 3 Apr. 21 (Advt.), Piling has also been completed on the Hutchison House site and construction of the foundation is well in hand. **1975** *BP Shield Internat.* May 2 (*caption*) Piling into sea bed after removal of flotation tanks. **1977** *Daily Times* (Lagos) 25 Feb. 3/4 Mr. Ogundiya recalled that during the initial piling on the site, the management of Leventis wrote to his ministry threatening to claim ₦6 million if there was any damage to their building.

2. (Further examples.)

1939 A. RANSOME *Secret Water* xiv. 170 The wood of the quay was rotting, and water was working in and out through gaps in the piling. **1944** *Sun* (Baltimore) 18 Mar. 6/2 It is claimed that the timber piling is not sufficiently strong to support the structure and the loads it carries; the pile caps and stringers are in poor condition. **1975** *Lamp* (Exxon Corporation) Winter 11/2 When the platform's steel jacket was being emplaced this spring, the pilings struck a patch of sand in the bottom clay and couldn't be driven until larger and more powerful pile-driving equipment was moved to the site. **1977** *New Yorker* 9 May 118/2 They should see Prudhoe Bay. It's so damned clean and neat and sterile—with refrigerated pilings, so the tundra won't melt.

pilkins (pi·lkinz), *sb. pl. local.* [Perh. f. PILCH *v.*: see *N. & Q.* Aug. 1979, p. 305.] = TAILING *vbl. sb.*¹ 2 a.

1859 G. MEREDITH *Ordeal R. Feverel* I. vi. 101 He swears soam o' our chaps steals pilkins. *Ibid.* xii. 177 The Bantam said he had seen Tom secreting pilkins in a sack.

pill, *sb.*² Add: **1. b.** (Further examples.)

1928 L. NORTH *Parasites* 87 There are lots of folks to give you a lift down in the morning... It's getting up that hill at night is the pill. **1931** R. CAMPBELL *Georgiad* II. 38 He..takes his pleasures as a bitter pill Or social duty, much against his will. **1943** J. B. PRIESTLEY *Daylight on Saturday* xxv. 195 Fincham [*sc.* a factory] especially is a pill. We never ought to have allowed ourselves to have been persuaded into using that old mill. **1961** B. FERGUSSON *Watery Maze* ii. 68 Dakar was indeed a bitter pill, both professionally and politically. **1977** *Times* 9 Nov. 15/3 Mrs Williams is well aware of this and her decision to champion parental choice is sugar on the pill of her pledge to support local authorities in the matter of school closures. **1978** P. BAILEY *Leisure & Class in Victorian Eng.* ii. 54 The entertainments..were devised to sugar the pill of instruction.

c. *the pill* or *Pill*: a contraceptive pill.
1957 'C. H. Rolph' *Human Sum* 6 He gives a modestly exciting account of the quest now going on..for what laymen like myself insist on calling 'the Pill'; and by this phrase..I mean the simple and completely reliable contraceptive taken by the mouth. **1958** A. Huxley *Brave New World Revisited* (1959) xii. 156 'The Pill' has not yet been perfected. **1960** *Economist* 22 Oct. 335/1 For about thirty years a campaign has been carried on for the reform of Britain's abortion law... It..looks as if the search for the 'Pill'—a simple, safe contraceptive—may be rewarded first. **1964** 'J. Melville' *Murderers' Houses* vii. 116 Emily knew all about the Bomb and the Pill. **1969** *New Scientist* 22 May 415/2 As contraceptives, IUDs are not as effective as the pill. **1970** *Daily Tel.* 17 July 2/8 Investigations showed that the increased risk of thrombo-embolism declined rapidly after the patient stopped taking the pill. **1975** D. Lodge *Changing Places* i. 20 They went on the Pill and suffered side-effects. **1975** *Woman's Jrnl.* Sept. 110/1 Emma's burgeoning again... It seems she can't remember to take the pill. **1976** [see *on *prep.* 1 k].

d. A pill or tablet of a barbiturate or amphetamine. *slang.*
1963 [see *pill popper* below]. **1967** *Trans-Action* Apr. 7/1 Pills are 'reds' and 'whites'—barbiturates and benzedrine or dexedrine. **1970** *New Statesman* 16 Jan. 90/1 The police were not too hip on drugs, and pills used to be passed out at clubs like ordinary cigarettes. **1972** *Guardian* 5 Dec. 15/3 It's impossible to discover how many adolescents use the more common illicit soft drugs —cannabis, LSD, 'pills' (amphetamines, barbiturates or mixtures of both). **1976** Deakin & Willis *Johnny go Home* ii. 38 The suburban kids' drugs: pills, uppers and downers, bennies and blueies.

2. b. Also, a shell, bomb, or hand grenade; *spec.*, the atom bomb. Hence in *pl.*, ammunition. (Further examples.)
1841 H. J. Mercier *Life in Man of War* 234 A dose of Yankee *pills*..would take her some time to digest. **1883** *United Service* June 652 That serpent was rather hard on the pills... How do you account for that fellow's swallowing those shells so easily? **1917** P. S. Allen *Let.* 24 Mar. (1939) 137 The submarine proceeded to lie on the bottom..but one day they realized they were spotted. 'Pills' kept dropping close to them, and sending the water a-swish all round. **1919** V. Vigorito in Hamilton & Corbin *Echoes from Over There* III. xi. 203 A sergeant..counts out the required number of pills (H.E. grenades). **1921** *Amer. Legion Weekly* 15 Apr. 22 Damn the Boche that threw the pill. **1921** *Flight* XIII. 618/2 Another range-finding bomb was dropped by the next Martin, and then the following machine scored the first hit with its 2,000-lb. 'pill', which struck the deck in the bow. **1927** L. H. Nason *Three Lights from Match* 220 What do they use those pills in? **1939** P. G. Hart *Hist. 135th Aero Squadron* 135 When I got over the town I let my pills go. **1948** Partridge *Dict. Forces' Slang* 142 *Pills*, ammunition. (Army; especially among gunners.) **1957** *Daily News* (N.Y.) 7 Aug. 7 A Jesuit priest who was a survivor of the A-bombing of Hiroshima 12 years ago.. said he was drinking coffee when the big pill came down. **1969** M. Pei *Words in Sheep's Clothing* (1970) vi. 51 Interestingly, 'the Pill' was used around 1957 with reference to the Hiroshima atom bomb.

c. Also in *sing.*, = Ball *sb.*^{1} 4 a.
1908 *Atlantic Monthly* Aug. 224/2 Mr. O'Hooligan, steeped in the lore of the 'spitball',..and aware that the finger-tips, as the 'pill' leaves the hand, endow it with its rotary genius, pays this wizard [*sc.* the pitcher] the homage of a somewhat more enlightened reverence. **1909** P. A. Vaile *Mod. Golf* viii. 110 The ball is microscopic—a veritable, as it is sometimes slangily called, 'pill'. **1916** *Dialect Notes* IV. 279 *Pill*,..golf ball. 'Curses on that *pill*. It won't get off the ground.' **1922** Wodehouse *Clicking of Cuthbert* ix. 203 'I don't mind her missing the pill,' said the young man. 'But I think her attitude toward the game is too light-hearted.' **1946** B. Marshall *George Brown's Schooldays* 6 As a matter of fact, I think that's the dirty cad hacking that footer pill over there. **1977** Scollins & Titford *Ey up, mi Duck!* II. 50 *Pill*, ball: usually a football.

d. A pellet of opium prepared for smoking.
1887 *Lantern* (New Orleans) 21 May 4/2 The longer end of the stem is handed the person opposite and so the pill is consumed by the party drawing in their breath, which some call the 'long draw'. **1926** J. Black *You can't Win* xvii. 238 He feverishly rolled the first 'pill'... Each succeeding pill is smaller, more carefully browned over the lamp, and smoked with increased pleasure. **1935** A. J. Pollock *Underworld Speaks* 88/1 *Pill*, after opium has been cooked for smoking, it takes the form of a round pill, which is placed in the pipe and smoked. **1948** [see *cook *v.*^{1} 2 d]. **1948** *Amer. Speech* XXIII. 247/1 *Pill*, the pellet of opium which has been prepared for smoking. **1955** *U.S. Senate Hearings* (1956) VIII. 4162 The opium pill must be brought to a flaming heat before being placed in position over a hole in the center of the well-heated bowl of the pipe. *Ibid.*, 'Cook a pill', heat opium for smoking.

e. *slang.* A cigarette.
1914 'High Jinks, Jr.' *Choice Slang* 16 *Pill*, a cigarette. **1927** *Amer. Speech* II. 281/2 *Pill*,..cigarette. **1927** D. Hammett in *Black Mask* Feb. 31/2 Those pills you smoke are terrible. **1934** *Amer. Ballads & Folk Songs* 135 Then we rode down the hill, each a-puffin' a pill. **1966** 'L. Lane' *ABZ of Scouse* 82 *Pill*, a cigarette.

f. An animal's dropping. Usu. *pl.*
1926 D. H. Lawrence *David* xii. 89 They have passed, letting fall promises as the goat droppeth pills. *a* **1930** —— *Phoenix* (1936) 10 So we had him [*sc.* a pet rabbit] upstairs, and he dropped his tiny pills on the bed.

g. in *pl. slang.* The testicles; *fig.* nonsense (cf. *ball *sb.*^{1} 15 b).
1935 I. Miller *School Tie* xi. 158, I explained to him about the prayers... 'Awful pills,' I whispered; 'but it can't be helped.' *Ibid.* xiv. 270 'No, it really is true. Not doing much good here, you know.' 'Pills! Bags of pills!' **1937** Partridge *Dict. Slang* 630/2 *Pills*,.. testicles. **1968** A. Diment *Gt. Spy Race* vi. 77, I..wished I had followed up my elbow in the throat with a hefty boot in his peasant pills. One in the balls is worth two in the teeth—a motto of unarmed combat instructors.

h. A small ball of fluff found on the surface of a fabric (see *pill *v.*^{1} 6 c, *pilling *vbl. sb.* 2 b).
1958 *New Scientist* 3 Apr. 17/2 The 'pills' are the little balls of fibre which, in the course of wear, form on the surface of cardigans, jerseys and similar articles. **1963** A. J. Hall *Textile Sci.* v. 273 The formation of a pill is primarily due to a rubbing of the fabric surface to cause a number of fibre ends to protrude and then become entangled. **1969** —— *Stand. Handbk. Textiles* (ed. 7) v. 336 The presence of these pills gives the fabric a highly objectionable appearance... As the material is further worn so do the anchoring fibres gradually wear and weaken until they break and the pill falls off. **1970** [see *pill *v.*^{1} 6 c].

3. (Earlier and later examples.)
1871 L. H. Bagg *4 Years at Yale* 141 The name 'Delta Phi man' is fast becoming a synonym for 'scrub', and 'pill', and even the neutrals regard its members with a sort of pitying contempt. **1880** A. A. Hayes *New Colorado* (1881) v. 64 He was the worst-looking pill you ever saw. **1886** *Galaxy* 1 Oct. 272 Various sorts of contemptible young men are designated as..'pills', 'squirts', [etc.]. **1925** Wodehouse *Carry on, Jeeves!* iii. 61 What's to be done?.. That pill is coming to stay here. **1939** L. M. Montgomery *Anne of Ingleside* xxxiii. 242 That kid is a pill. My, doesn't she think it smart to fool people! **1970** *Women Speaking* Apr. 5/1 If a man doesn't like a girl's looks or personality, she's a..pill. **1977** B. Garfield *Recoil* xi. 120 'Do you love your wife?'.. 'You're a pill. Yes, I love her.'

4. (Further examples.) *spec.*, (a member of) the Royal Army Medical Corps; a medical officer or his orderly.
1866 *Harper's Mag.* July 268/1 One day..the two young 'pills' were arguing some case. **1915** 'Bartimeus' *Tall Ship* ix. 159 They seized the Young Doctor, who was a small man, and deposited him on the deck. 'Couldn't you see I was asleep, Pills?' demanded the other. **1924** 'Nauticus' *Sea Ways & Wangles* ix. 57 In some ships the sick list is so small that one of the young doctors—or 'Pills' as a Surgeon Lieutenant is sometimes called in order to distinguish him from his more venerable senior the P.M.O.—has even found time to take on the keeping of the ward-room wine accounts. *Ibid.* 58 Then again at a ward-room sing-song after dinner 'Pills' will often help matters along by playing the piano. **1925** Fraser & Gibbons *Soldier & Sailor Words* 223 *Pills*,..a nickname for a Medical Officer's orderly. **1929** *Papers Mich. Acad. Sci., Arts & Lett.* X. 314 *Pills*.., the surgeon.

5. pill-bag, a bag in which pills are carried; **pill-bug**, a woodlouse of the genus *Armadillidium*, able to roll itself into a ball; **pill cooker** *slang*, (see quot.); **pill head** *slang*, a drug addict; **pill-millipede**, a millipede belonging to the order Oniscomorpha, esp. the genus *Glomeris*; in quot. 1868 = *pill-bug*; **pill peddler, pusher, roller** *slang*, a doctor or pharmacist; **pill popper** *slang*, one who takes barbiturate or amphetamine pills freely; a barbiturate or amphetamine addict; hence *pill-popping* vbl. sb.; **pill-rolling** *vbl. sb.*, the action of making into pills by rolling (also *fig.*); **pill shooter** *slang*, a doctor; **pill slab** (further examples); **pill-woodlouse** = *pill-bug*.
1852 *Knickerbocker* XL. 470 After procuring his degree, he had not the wherewithal to buy him pill-bags. **1874** E. Eggleston *Circuit Rider* xx. 189 'And you want me to see him,' said the doctor,..seizing his 'pill-bags' and donning his hat. **1930** J. F. Dobie *Coronado's Children* i. 43 James had been educated to medicine in Kentucky.. and riding with his 'pill bags' over the far-stretched hills of the Colorado River satisfied his ambition. **1884** J. S. Kingsley *Stand. Nat. Hist.* II. 72 In common parlance these forms [of terrestrial isopod] are known as 'sow-bugs', 'pill-bugs', and 'wood-lice'. **1915** W. A. Bryan *Nat. Hist. Hawaii* xxxi. 408 The curious oval little silver-gray creature found in large numbers in damp places, under boards and stones, is usually an introduced species known to many as the pill-bug, slater, sow-bug or wood-louse. **1954** *New Biol.* XVII. 41 *Porcellio* and *Armadillidium* (the pill-bug) appear to be able to withstand drier conditions than the rest [of the woodlice]. **1971** E. S. Bakker *Island called California* xii. 191 If you examine such a decaying log, you are likely to find centipedes and pill bugs curled in the dirt. **1929** M. A. Gill *Underworld Slang*, *Pill cooker*, opium smoker. **1965** *Maclean's Mag.* 4 Sept. 31/1 The population totalled..fourteen narcotic addicts, two marijuana smokers and two 'pillheads', including me. **1969** *Courier-Mail* (Brisbane) 2 July B/1 He was all boy, and a drug taker—'A Pill Head' in his own words. **1971** S. Houghton *Current Prison Slang* (MS.) 23 *Pill head*, amphetamine addict. **1973** *Times Lit. Suppl.* 16 Mar. 299/4 (Advt.), His experiences with junkies, pillheads, homosexuals and drop-outs in Soho. **1976** N. Thornburg *Cutter & Bone* x. 244 Oh, she was a pillhead, yeah. And maybe the world's worst housekeeper too. **1868** Bate & Westwood *Hist. Brit. Sessile-Eyed Crustacea* II. 494 It [*sc. Armadillo vulgaris*]..is often seen running about foot-paths, rolling itself up into a ball at the least alarm. This has gained for it the name of Pill millepede [*sic*]. **1899** W. T. Fernie *Animal Simples* 236 Hoglouse, or Pill Millipede... This Hoglouse, or Millipede, was the primitive medicinal pill. **1958** J. L. Cloudsley-Thompson *Spiders, Scorpions, Centipedes & Mites* xi. 17 The family Glomeridae contains the common British pill-millipede. **1967** P. A. Meglitsch *Invertebr. Zool.* xix. 839/1 Order Oniscomorpha. Pill millipedes. Mostly tropical millipedes..; body can be rolled into a ball. **1857** M. J. Holmes *Meadow Brook* v. 78 Why, he's a young pill-peddler, who's taken a shine to Rosa. **1925** S. Lewis *Arrowsmith* xiii. 137 How could old Max have gone over to that damned pill-pedler? **1931** [see *croaker 4]. **1941** J. Smiley *Hash House Lingo* 43 *Pill peddler*, druggist. **1963** *Time* 1 Nov. 74 Can a lonely New Jersey pill popper who sleeps on a board find enduring happiness with an ebullient Hungarian gourmet who sleeps on a rug? **1975** *Publishers Weekly* 27 Jan. 286/3 The author, then a sophomore at a Wisconsin law school, was a pill popper—amphetamine to get her through the days, phenobarbital to get her through the nights. **1972** *Jrnl. Social Psychol.* LXXXVII. 121 The film illustrates the dangerous psychological and physiological effects of pill-popping. **1977** J. Wambaugh *Black Marble* (1978) xii. 304 They have a pill-popping party and she..dies of an overdose. **1909** J. R. Ware *Passing Eng.* 196/2 *Pill-pusher*.., doctor. Fine example of the graphic in phraseology. **1919** H. S. Warren *Ninth Company* 34 *Pill pusher*, member of the medical corps. **1935** A. J. Pollock *Underworld Speaks* 88/1 *Pill pusher*, a doctor. **1961** *Amer. Speech* XXXVI. 147 *Pill pusher*, a specialist in internal medicine, as contrasted with a practitioner of the surgical specialties. Loosely, any M.D. **1969** Linn & Pearl *Masque of Honor* 66 Hell, I'm only a pill-pusher, Lieutenant. **1917** *Editor* 13 Jan. 33 *Pill rollers*, Hospital Corps. **1918** *Yank Talk* 21 'Why?' asked the pill roller. **1930** J. W. Barkley *No Hard Feelings!* 268 He told me to get it on record with the pill-rollers. **1936** J. Curtis *Gilt Kid* viii. 87 He was damned if he let a lousy pill-roller know just how bad he felt. **1942** French & Sliper *Army-Navy Guide* 181 *Pill roller*, an enlisted member of the medical corps. **1968** R. Hooker *MASH* (1969) 175 Let the pill rollers..do it. **1961** R. D. Baker *Essent. Path.* xxii. 597 Parkinsonism.. is a chronic disorder usually of elderly persons characterized by 'pill-rolling' rhythmic movements of the hands. **1972** *Country Life* 9 Mar. 572/3 Such things [*sc.* pill-slabs or -tiles] were used for pill-rolling and also, as in the more elaborate slabs..for hanging up as a sign of the owner's profession. **1928** L. H. Nason *Sergeant Eadie* 337 The gallant pill-shooters won't let us stay in these nice soft beds any longer than they can help. **1938** Partridge *World of Words* III. vii. 196 *Doctor* becomes.. slang *the vet* or..*pill-shooter*. **1941** J. Smiley *Hash House Lingo* 43 *Pill shooter*, physician. **1966** H. Marriott *Cariboo Cowboy* ix. 89 In those years, an average fellow was darn near down-and-out before he headed out to see a pill-shooter. **1960** H. Hayward *Antique Coll.* 218/2 Apothecaries' pill-slabs were made in tin-glazed earthenware at Lambeth. **1972** *Daily Tel.* 19 Jan. 9 A polychrome Delft heart-shaped pill-slab, which was used for rolling pills, was bought by Tilley for £2,800 at Sotheby's yesterday. **1972** *Country Life* 9 Mar. 572/3 The plaque.. which was in the same sale is a pill slab of 1664, also English Delft, and an exceptional rarity. **1863** Pill-woodlouse [see Wood-louse 2]. **1906** *Essex Naturalist* XIV. 53 'The common armadillo'..is the old name for the pill-woodlice now known as *Armadillidium*. **1931** W. T. Calman in W. P. Pycraft *Standard Nat. Hist.* ix. 169 The common Pill Woodlouse, *Armadillidium*, may often be seen crawling actively about on rocks in hot sunshine.

pill, *sb.*^{3} Add: **2.** *Comb.*, as **pill yawl**, a sprit-rigged, three-masted boat used in the Bristol Channel.
1883 *Boats of World* 30 The Bristol Channel, where the Pill Yawls, large or small, decked or undecked, hold their own with any craft of their size. **1929** F. C. Bowen *Sea Slang* 103 *Pill Yawl*, a Bristol Channel pilot boat.

pill, *v.*^{1} Add: **6. c.** To gather into small balls of fluff on the surface of a fabric (said of the fibre, and of the fabric as a whole). Hence **pilled** *ppl. a.*, of or pertaining to fibres that have gathered in this way.
1962 *Which?* Aug. 240/1 One [Orlon cardigan]..was starting to pill after 10 washes. **1970** *Cabinet Maker & Retail Furnisher* 23 Oct. 173/2 Cloth so blended 'pilled'—fluffed, if you prefer it—very badly. *Ibid.*, While most worsted and woollen cloths, like a woollen carpet, tend to pill in the beginning, these pills wear off quickly and never recur. **1970** *Which?* Oct. 301/3 Trousers didn't pill, but as they were knitted some snagged. **1971** *Daily Tel.* 19 Apr. 12/4 That curious pilled wool we wore a few years ago, bumpy as if the wool had come out in a rash. **1971** *New Yorker* 21 Aug. 46/2 (Advt.), An exclusive Hathaway process that keeps the collar from pilling (i.e., fuzzing) throughout the life of the shirt.

pill, *v.*^{2} Add: **3. b.** To fail (a candidate) in an examination. *slang.*
1908 A. S. M. Hutchinson *Once aboard Lugger* I. i. 15 'Your examination?' George half turned away. The bitterest moment of a sad day had come. He growled: 'Pipped.' 'Pipped?' 'Pilled.' 'Pilled?' 'Spun... I failed. I was referred for three months.' **1925** W. Deeping *Sorrell & Son* xxii. 208 Gorringe had a sick face... 'Pilled,' thought Kit, and was not sorry, for Gorringe needed a course of pilling.

pillaloo (pi·lălū, -liū), *sb.* (*int.*) Also **pillilew, pilliloo**, etc. *dial.* [Imit.] **a.** A cry expressing grief or anger. **b.** A name for such a cry; a noise, disturbance, or outcry; a fierce argument. Hence **pillaloo·ing** *vbl. sb.*
1796 *Hull Advertiser* 23 July 4/2 The woman, having prostrated herself on the grave of the deceased, continued some time in silent meditation or prayer; then crying *Pillilew!* after the manner of the Irish at funerals, she sorrowfully departed with her husband. **1811** *Lexicon Balatronicum*, *Pillaloo*, the Irish cry or howl at funerals. **1829** G. Griffin *Collegians* I. v. 101 She got a stitch an' died..an'..Dan made a *pilliloo* an' a *lavo* over her, as if he lost all belongen' to him. *Ibid.* xiv. 303 Jug..began bawling..the mother joined her, and such a pillilu as

they raised between 'em was never known. **1847** *Paddiana* I. 100 Divle such a pillalooing as Lanty made out o' the windy ye never heered! **1851** H. NEWLAND *Erne* xiii. 385 Such a combination of huzzaing and pillalooing as never English ears had heard. **1888** 'Q.' *Troy Town* xi. 120 What wi' the rumpus an' her singin' out 'Pillaloo!'..the Lawyer's sarmon..was clean sp'iled. **1899** S. MACMANUS *In Chimney Corners* 189 Nanny sitting in the chimney corner whillilew-ing and pillillew-ing, crying the very eyes out of her head. **1900** *N. & Q.* 12 May 373/1 To have 'a pillilew' it is not always necessary that there should be a fight, as a wrangle in which a number take part is 'a pillilew'. **1900** *Yorks. Weekly Post* 22 Sept. 11/1 We ran after him wol we collared him, en then we made him sing pillilew.

pillar, *sb.* Add: **2. c.** A metal column in the bodywork of a vehicle separating the front and rear doors, or the front door and windscreen. Also, a thin metal strip dividing the windscreen into two parts.

1907 *Car* 25 Sept. 261/1 The hind pillars were painted white from top to bottom. **1926** *Motor* 26 Oct. 637/1 The roof..slides back as far as the pillars in front of the rear doors. **1937** *Motor* 9 Mar. 219/3 A point..noticeable when sitting in the car is the wide range of vision made possible by extremely narrow pillars. **1938** *Times* 13 Oct. 8/1 Designers are..taking..pains to reduce the width of pillars. **1964** *Which? Car Suppl.* Apr. 47/2 The VW Devonette had its windscreen divided by a pillar which did not help forward vision. **1971** *Sci. Amer.* Oct. 11/3 (Advt.), Deflector fins on the front pillars keep the side windows free from dirt. **1977** *Custom Car* Nov. 19/2 The new Granada shape is clean and very smart, though it has lost the rather pleasant kink by the rear pillar.

3. b. in phr. *pillar of society, of the establishment* (see also 3 c below).

1961 *Ann. Reg. 1960* 445 The melodramas and crime dramas included..*Never Take Sweets from a Stranger*, with Felix Aylmer as a small-town pillar of society responsible for the seduction of small girls. **1961** NEW ENG. BIBLE *Gal.* ii. 9 Those reputed pillars of our society, James, Cephas, and John, accepted Barnabas and myself as partners. **1964** *Ann. Reg. 1963* 32 One by one the pillars of the establishment—Lord Salisbury, Lord Stuart of Findhorn, Lord Eccles among them—deserted a baffled and pleading Lord Chancellor. **1970** *Nature* 26 Sept. 1371/1 Those pillars of the establishment of the 1920s, such as Nancy Astor, Lord Haldane and the editors of *The Times* and *The Observer*. **1979** D. CLARK *Heberden's Seat* iii. 48 Heberden! A pillar of society locally.

c. (Further examples.)

1888 W. ARCHER tr. H. Ibsen (*title*) The pillars of society and other plays. **1902** G. B. SHAW *Mrs. Warren's Profession* Pref. p. vii, Dearer still..is that sense of the sudden earthquake shock to the foundations of morality which sends a pallid crowd of critics into the street shrieking that the pillars of society are cracking and the ruin of the State at hand.

12. pillar clock (see quot. 1962); **pillar drill** or **drilling machine** *Engin.*, a drilling machine incorporating a work-table supported on a column attached to the base of the machine; **pillar letter-box** = PILLAR-BOX; **pillar rose** (earlier and later examples); **pillar (and) scroll (top) clock** (see quot. 1960).

1933 *Burlington Mag.* Aug. p. xvi/1 Mr. Mody..retains the useful terms 'Lantern, Bracket, and Pillar Clocks' to describe the main types. **1962** E. BRUTON *Dict. Clocks & Watches* 131 *Pillar clock*, French drum clock with round movement and dial on four vertical pillars standing on a round base. The pendulum hangs in the middle of the pillars... Also a special form of Japanese clock showing time by a pointer moving along a linear scale, or any clock on a pillar. **1881** E. MATHESON *Aid Bk. Engin. Enterprise* II. xxiii. 313 The self-contained Pillar drill is useful, as there is more room around the machine within which to move the article. **1942** W. STEEDS *Engin. Materials* xiii. 204 The sensitive drilling machines taking drills up to about $\frac{1}{8}$ or $\frac{3}{16}$ in. diameter and the pillar drill up to as much as 2 in. diameter, according to size. **1964** S. CRAWFORD *Basic Engin. Processes* ix. 224 The multi-spindle machines consist of a series of pillar drills mounted over a common table, thus eliminating the constant tool change associated with the single-spindle machine. **1873** C. P. B. SHELLEY *Workshop Appliances* vii. 214 (*heading*) Double-geared pillar drilling machine. **1975** BRAM & DOWNS *Manuf. Technol.* vii. 198 The pillar drilling-machine..is similar in general design to the sensitive drill. **1879** TROLLOPE *Duke's Children* (1880) I. xxiv. 284 'Has it gone?' asked the Countess. 'I put it myself into the pillar letter-box.' **1837** T. RIVERS *Rose Amateur's Guide* 81 Clarissa Harlowe is a pillar-rose, of first-rate excellence. **1856** MRS. STOWE *Dred* II. 129 She was sitting..under the shadow of one of the pillar-roses. **1869** S. R. HOLE *Bk. about Roses* ix. 128 These Pillar Roses are beautiful additions to the Rosarium. **1965** G. S. THOMAS *Climbing Roses* xii. 176 Isolated pillars to take 'pillar' roses can be connected with a wooden beam. **1974** *News & Press* (Darlington, S. Carolina) 25 Apr. 7/4 Pillar roses at the lantern post are not only beautiful by day but have an accent of beauty when the light is turned on at night. **1860** C. JEROME *Hist. Amer. Clock Business* iii. 44, I took about one dozen of the Pillar Scroll Top Clocks, and went to..Wethersfield to sell them. **1912** N. H. MOORE *Old Clock Bk.* caption facing p. 113 Pillar and scroll top clock. **1929** G. H. BAILLIE *Watchmakers & Clockmakers of World* 349/2 They were at first wall clocks, but from 1814 brackets or shelf clocks known as Pillar Scroll Top clocks. **1950** B. PALMER *Bk. Amer. Clocks* 10 The Pillar and Scroll Clock remained the most popular Shelf Clock until about 1825 and survived well into the 1830's. **1960** H. HAYWARD *Antique Coll.* 218/2 *Pillar and scroll clock*, an American shelf or mantel clock. ..The wooden works are housed in a vertical rectangular case with a scrolled-arch top, small, round pillars at the sides, and delicately small feet. **1970** K. D. ROBERTS *Contrib. of Joseph Ives to Connecticut Clock Technol. 1810–1862* iv. 64 (*caption*) Pillar and scroll shelf clock with looking glass by Ives and Lewis.

pillar-box. Add: (Further examples.)

1939 'J. STRUTHER' *Mrs. Miniver* 173 She put on a mackintosh and struggled up the square to the pillar-box. **1978** L. DAVIDSON *Chelsea Murders* xix. 106 This one had been posted in a street pillar box.

b. In full, *pillar-box red*: a shade of red, that of a pillar-box.

1916 *Sphere* 1 July p. iv/1 Some charming *chapeaux* of the new pillar-box red. **1926** *Daily Colonist* (Victoria, B.C.) 21 July 16/4 (Advt.), Attractive Dresses of silk crepe, spun silk and silk broadcloth... Shades include black and white, blue..pillar-box red. **1934** *Archit. Rev.* LXXV. 108/1 It [*sc.* a built-in gramophone fitment]..is made entirely of laminated boarding painted white on the outside and pillar box red on the inside. **1950** 'E. CRISPIN' *Frequent Hearses* i. 44 A wind-machine, painted a minatory pillar-box red. **1959** J. BRAINE *Vodi* i. 16 Dick thought of the shop... It had been redecorated in pillar-box red and white. **1963** *Listener* 10 Jan. 84/2, I don't like the colours, especially the Ribena, pillarbox, scrofula, and sulphur. **1970** *Vogue* Jan. 37/1 (Advt.), Pillar box cotton jersey for the jeans..and cropped T-shirt. **1973** P. EVANS *Bodyguard Man* vi. 50 A small Fiat in pillar-box red swirling round the corner fifty metres away and out of sight.

pillared, *ppl. a.* Add: **1.** (Further examples.)

1924 R. CAMPBELL *Flaming Terrapin* i. 16 In that pillared temple grew a heart. **1924** E. SITWELL *Sleeping Beauty* iii. 21 That pillared avenue Of tall clear-fruited ripe trees. **1953** E. M. FORSTER *Hill of Devi* 129 One passes through a pillared hall on to a terrace. **1961** *N.Y. Times* 3 July 13 The many country mansions..that dot the environs of Vicenza. How far that pedimented and pillared style has shed its influence Mr. Sansom reminds us. **1978** *Morecambe Guardian* 14 Mar. 23/1 (Advt.), The accommodation provides: pillared porch, hall, lounge, [etc.].

2. (Further examples.) Also *fig.*

1727 THOMSON *Summer* 60 Of growling Hills, that shoot the pillar'd Flame. **1864** TENNYSON *Voyage* in *Enoch Arden* 145 How oft we saw the Sun retire, And burn the threshold of the night, Fall from his Ocean-lane of fire, And sleep beneath his pillar'd light! **1924** R. CAMPBELL *Flaming Terrapin* iii. 45 Thick mælstroms propped the dense and sagging shades With pillared thunder. **1929** R. GRAVES *Poems* 20 True to the eagle nose, the pillared neck, (Missed by the intervening generation).

pillarless (pi·lǝ̆ɹlės), *a.* [f. PILLAR *sb.* + -LESS.] Lacking or without pillars.

1889 W. B. YEATS *Wanderings of Oisin* II. 28 And the dome Windowless, pillarless, multitudinous home Of faces, watched me. **1922** *Glasgow Herald* 7 June, The experimental work on 'pillarless' electric safety lamps..has been conducted by the Miners' Lamps Committee. **1977** *Custom Car* Nov. 50/3 And there it sits, in all its glory; four-door pillarless body skulking over a mill of 390 cubic inch displacement.

pill-box. Add: **a.** (Earlier and later examples.)

1730 *Maryland Hist. Mag.* (1924) XIX. 182 From Eyre & Beecher (Druggists)... 12 Papers pill boxes. **1934** G. B. SHAW *Too True to be Good* I. 27 A measuring glass, a pill box, a clinical thermometer in a glass of water. **1977** *Halcyon Days Catal.* 8 A new range of small pillboxes with snap-on enamelled lids.

b. *spec.* A small round concrete emplacement used for housing a machine-gun or similar weapon. Also *transf.* and *fig.* Also, short for *pill-box cap, hat.*

1887 R. D. BLUMENFELD *Diary* 27 June (1930) 17 The pill-box..protects only a small portion of the head and forehead from the sun. **1917** *Scotsman* 13 Sept. 6/4 The strength of these concreted farm cellars and individual pillboxes is amazing. **1923** *Daily Mail* 26 Feb. 7 On reaching shore again he [*sc.* a fox] made for the cliffs and hid in a concrete pill-box, where he was caught and killed. **1929** *Papers Mich. Acad. Sci., Arts & Lett.* X. 314/2 *Pill-boxes*, concrete structures or blockhouses developed by the Germans for use in their 'elastic' defense. They were employed as machine-gun nests. **1930** H. A. TAYLOR *Good-Bye to Battlefields* 136 The Germans, by means of their almost indestructible pill-boxes, have taught the inhabitants the virtues of concrete. **1935** A. J. POLLOCK *Underworld Speaks* 88/1 *Pill box*, enclosure of machine gun on prison wall. **1944** *Daily Progress* (Charlottesville, Va.) 2 Oct. 1/8 The planes dropped hundreds of tons of explosives on Nazi pillboxes and gunposts. **1958** L. DURRELL *Mountolive* viii. 166 Red pill-boxes mounted upon cancelled faces. **1958** *Listener* 4 Dec. 933/2 Is it another pill-box attempt to debunk the shameful Victorians of the middle and upper classes because the contemplation of the shameless purity and austerity of their private lives is galling to the rebellious youth of today? **1968** T. PARKER *People of Streets* 27, I was the lift boy and I had one of those round hats, pill-boxes they used to call them. **1973** *Guardian* 6 Mar. 6 The pillbox on the left is in yellow straw with a white daisy. **1974** *Times* 16 Jan. 2/4 He had led Mr Brook across the fields... They rested in a wartime pillbox and then got a lift to the outskirts of Chelmsford. **1978** J. KRANTZ *Scruples* iv. 99 Billy, about to go for job interviews, took herself to the custom-order millinery salon..in order to have Halston, then Jackie Kennedy's favorite hat designer, make her one perfect pillbox.

c. *pill-box cap* (example), *hat* (further examples).

1910 *Daily Chron.* 18 Apr. 1/7 It is much greater fun to wear the B.-P. hat of the scout than the neat 'pill-box' cap of the Church Lads' Brigade. **1964** MRS. L. B. JOHNSON *White House Diary* 10 Mar. (1970) 82 Archbishop Iakovos..dressed in long, black clerical garb.. and the black pillbox hat from which flowed long black veils. **1974** *Country Life* 3–10 Jan. 54/3 That badge of 1960s elegance, the Jackie Kennedy pillbox hat.

pilling, *vbl. sb.* Restrict '*arch.* or *dial.*' to senses in Dict. and add: **2. b.** The gathering of fibres into small balls of fluff on the surface of a fabric (see *PILL *v.*[1] 6 c).

1958 *New Scientist* 3 Apr. 17/2 In a test cardigan..the treated sleeve showed a remarkable resistance to pilling. **1959** A. J. HALL *Stand. Handbk. Textiles* (ed. 5) v. 314 Pilling has become especially noticeable since the introduction of the synthetic fibres. **1965** *New Scientist* 8 Apr. 95/1 Synthetic fabrics have one common shortcoming: they are highly susceptible to what is known as 'pilling', a tendency to form small tangled knots of fibres. **1968** J. IRONSIDE *Fashion Alphabet* 244 *Pilling*,.. the term used when fibres gather into a ball on the surface. **1970** *Cabinet Maker & Retail Furnisher* 23 Oct. 173/2 The inclusion of nylon in the blend..aggravated the pilling. **1970** *Which?* Oct. 300/2 A few brands suffered slightly from pilling (little balls of fibre on the surface). **1972** *Times* 28 Nov. 19/8 E. Gomme..has encountered problems of 'pilling' in the fabric. **1974** *Amer. Speech 1970* XLV. 179 An antistatic pilling-resistant (resistant to gathering small 'pills' of fuzz) finish.

pillion, *sb.*[1] **a.** Restrict '*Obs.* exc. *Hist.*' to senses in Dict. and add to def.: In modern use, a seat located behind the saddle of a motorcycle, on which a second person may ride. Hence *to go, ride* (cf. RIDE *v.* 1 d), *sit pillion*, to travel on this seat. Also *transf.*

The application in quot. 1878 is unusual, but anticipates use in the modern sense.

1878 *Design & Work* IV. 215/1 To use the electric light on a bicycle is very easy, if you can arrange to place upon a pillion behind you a large steam engine and boiler and a Gramme machine, the whole weighing only about 3 tons. **1911** *Motor Cycle* 27 Apr. 481/1 The pillion or tandem seat is likely to become increasingly popular. **1923** *Weekly Dispatch* 13 May 9 Riding his motor-cycle..with Miss Esther Gwyther, a nurse, on the pillion, he collided [etc]. **1926** T. E. LAWRENCE *Seven Pillars* (1935) IV. xliv. 255 He stopped babbling, and began to wail out his sorrows. I sat him, pillion, on the camel's rump; then stirred her up and mounted. **1927** *Glasgow Herald* 31 Aug. 10 A clerk..on whose machine Miss Paterson was riding pillion. **1934** T. S. ELIOT *Rock* i. 21 But every son would have his motor cycle, And daughters ride away on casual pillions. **1958** J. BETJEMAN *Coll. Poems*, And country girls with lips and nails vermilion Wait, nylon-legged, to straddle on the pillion. **1965** *Listener* 27 May 785/1 They [*sc.* Vietnamese girls] ride bicycles, sit pillion on motor-bicycles, and manage their delightful floating garments with elegance and dignity at all times. **1973** J. WAINWRIGHT *Pride of Pigs* 142, I got rid of my scooter, and started going pillion with Lance. **1979** R. RENDELL *Make Death love Me* iii. 30 Alan had once seen her get off the pillion of a boy's motor-bike.

b. *pillion passenger, ride, rider, -riding* vbl. sb. and ppl. adj., *seat* (modern use); **pillion cloth**, a cloth placed under a pillion; **pillion stick**, a stick fastened in a pillion to hold luggage in place; **pillion stone**, a stone used to facilitate mounting to a pillion seat.

1648 *Public Rec. Colony of Connecticut* (1850) I. 508, 1 sidesaddle and pillion cloath. **1684** *Essex Inst. Hist. Coll.* (1888) XXV. 155 In the Kitchine..a sadle, pillyon and pillyon cloath. **1929** J. DE F. SHELTON *Salt-Box House* iv. 34 Cuffee busied himself making sure that the dark blue pillion-cloth protected her dress from the horse's flank. **1973** J. WAINWRIGHT *Pride of Pigs* 92 The pillion-passenger was thrown clear, but the motor-cyclist was pinned under his machine. **1976** *Deeside Advertiser* 9 Dec. 24/3 A teenage motor cyclist died and his pillion passenger was injured in an accident on a sharp bend on the main Corwen-Chester Road at Treuddyn. **1935** T. E. LAWRENCE *Let.* 31 Jan. (1938) 845 It was a good idea, that pillion ride. **1963** L. DEIGHTON *Horse under Water* xxiv. 107 Giorgio had got a pillion ride..with a two-stroke motor bike. **1920** *Motor Cycle* 24 June 714/2 Motor-cyclists are summoned for having their number plates obscured by any part of a pillion-rider's dress. *a* **1974** R. CROSSMAN *Diaries* (1975) I. 40 We had the most amiable cup of tea before driving home to Prescote through the fog, where I found that another pillion rider had come down with my third red box. **1920** *Motor Cycle* 8 July 45/1 The local authorities have threatened a campaign against pillion riding. **1927** W. E. COLLINSON *Contemp. Eng.* 35 Probably pillion-riding..will also be prohibited and dazzle head lights have to be dimmed. **1932** H. S. WALPOLE *Fortress* I. 83 Many came in pillion-riding as for hundreds of years they had done, while the grander farmers were proud in the 'shandy-carts'. **1970** *R.A.C. Guide & Handbk.* 59/1 Pillion Riding. Only one passenger may be carried on a solo motor cycle, and.. must be seated astride behind the driver on a proper pillion seat. **1911** *Motor Cycle* 27 Apr. 418/2 A pillion seat, if not very sociable, certainly has some advantages. **1973** J. WAINWRIGHT *Pride of Pigs* 88 The youth astride the Road Rocket kicked the starter... His companion settled himself on the pillion-seat. **1784** J. F. D. SMYTH *Tour U.S.A.* II. 248 All these papers were concealed in the mail pillion-sticks on which the servant carried his portmanteau. **1907** *Manch. Guardian* 20 July 7/7 On one side of the porch is a horsing or pillion stone.

pillion (pi·lyǝn), *v.* [f. PILLION *sb.*[1]] **1.** *trans.* To equip (a horse or saddle) with a pillion. Chiefly in pa. pple. or ppl. adj.

1843 *Knickerbocker* XXII. 431 The cozy couple..ride.. side by side upon the pillioned saddle. **1929** J. D. SHEL-

TON *Salt-Box House* iv. 33 Thaddeus's best pacing-mare being duly saddled and pillioned. **1935** W. FORTESCUE *Perfume from Provence* 234 They rode upon pillioned horses decorated with favours.

2. *trans.* To place on a pillion. Chiefly as ppl. adj.

1906 A. NOYES *Drake* I. II. 59 Little the boy remembered of that flight, Pillioned behind his father. **1910** W. DE MORGAN *Affair of Dishonour* iv. 46 A horseman here and there, alone or with a wench pillioned behind. **1958** P. MORTIMER *Daddy's gone a-Hunting* i. 8 A motor cycle turned into the road... She caught sight of..a pillioned girl with hair streaming.

3. *intr.* To ride on the pillion of a motor-cycle. *rare.*

1935 T. E. LAWRENCE *Let.* 31 Jan. (1938) 845 Pretty awful pillioning with a suitcase and masterpiece in one's arms!

pillionaire (pilyənēə·ɹ). Now *rare* or *Obs.* [f. *PILLION *sb.*[1] after MILLIONAIRE.] One, usu. female, who rides on the pillion of a motor-cycle or on a seat at the back of a bicycle.

1931 *Newark Advertiser* 26 Aug. 7/2 'What is a proper pillion seat?' was the question for the wisdom of the Bench at Newark Borough Police Court. Apparently it is a seat occupied by a pillionaire. **1931** *Times* 4 Sept. 6/5 On the back of his bike the defendant had a pillionaire —a female. **1937** PARTRIDGE *Dict. Slang* 630/1 *Pillionaire*, a female occupant of a 'peach-perch' or 'flapper-bracket'.

pillionist (pi·lyənist). *rare.* [f. *PILLION *sb.*[1] + -IST.] One who rides on the pillion of a motor-cycle.

The more usual term is *pillion rider.*

1923 *Motor Cyclist* 26 Sept. 643/1 As a confirmed pillionist I do not add my voice to those who are clamouring for legal abolition of this form of passenger riding.

pillock, pillok. Substitute for entry: **pillock** (pi·lək). *North. dial.* and *slang.* Also †**pillok, pilloch, pilluck.** [Variant of PILLICOCK.] **1.** = PILLICOCK 1.

1535 [see PILLICOCK 1]. **1903** *Eng. Dial. Dict.* IV. 503/1 *Pill,..pilluck* Wm. Yks..., the male organ, the penis.

2. *transf.* A fool, a stupid person; also in weakened sense, a fellow, bloke.

1967 J. BURKE *Till Death us do Part* viii. 135 What are you talking about, you great hairy pilloch? **1968** J. WAINWRIGHT *Darkening Glass* viii. 70 She..glared across the room and said: 'Where's that pilluck with the drinks?' **1976** —— *Bastard* vii. 93 'You always were a pillock,' he says, with feeling. **1978** 'J. GASH' *Gold from Gemini* vii. 70 The pillock mistook my astonishment for awe.

pillow, *sb.* Add: **3. a.** (Later example.)

1895 *Wales* Apr. 179/1 Went to yearly meeting at Hereford with a few others, Molly Lloyd riding on pillow behind him.

5*. *Geol.* A body of rock, esp. lava, likened to a pillow or filled sack in shape and usu. occurring with other similar bodies. Cf. *pillow lava, structure* below.

[**1890** *Q. Jrnl. Geol. Soc.* XLVI. 312 The structure is more commonly irregular, the masses resembling pillows or soft cushions pressed upon and against one another.] **1899** *Summary of Progress Geol. Survey U.K. 1898* 108 It shows the 'pillow' structure already referred to, some of the 'pillows' being a yard or more in diameter. **1944** C. A. COTTON *Volcanoes* xv. 290 Lava pillows are commonly three to four feet in diameter. **1955** LONGWELL & FLINT *Introd. Physical Geol.* v. 72 We conclude that pillows result from immersion of hot lava in water. **1962** E. A. VINCENT tr. *Rittmann's Volcanoes* ii. 71 The freshly formed pillows are in effect bladders filled with still-fluid lava, which roll down..and pile up one above the other. **1971** I. G. GASS et al. *Understanding Earth* xxi. 302/2 Being erupted under water, the lava flows tend to segregate and to form accumulations of sub-cylindrical bodies called pillows.

6. pillow-book, (*a*) a book suitable for reading in bed; freq. an erotic book; (occas. used as the title of such a book); (*b*) in Japan, a type of private journal or diary; **pillow coat** (further examples); **pillow cover** = PILLOW-CASE; **pillow-fight** (earlier and later examples); also as vb.; **pillow lava** *Geol.*, lava exhibiting pillow structure; **pillow mound** *Archæol.* (see quots.); **pillow muff** = MUFF *sb.*[2] 1a; **pillow-sham** (earlier and later examples); **pillow-slip** (further examples); **pillow structure** *Geol.*, a rock structure in which numerous closely fitting 'pillows' are fused together, found in some lavas and attributed to eruption under water; (cf. sense 5* above); **pillow talk,** conversation, usu. of an intimate kind, held in bed; also as vb.; **pillow tank,** a collapsible rubber container used for storing large quantities of liquid.

1906 N. G. R. SMITH (*title*) The Pillow-Book. *Ibid.* Pref., The pillow reader will surely find passages taken and left from the pillow books of his own election. **1907** *Daily Chron.* 5 July 3/4 When one thinks of it, Scott in verse is certainly a good pillow book. **1928** A. WALEY *Pillow-Bk. of Sei Shōnagon* 21 The *Pillow-Book*..consists partly of reminiscences, partly of entries in diary-form. *Ibid.* 24 Shōnagan protests, as do most diarists and makers of journals, that the *Pillow-Book* was intended for herself alone. **1960** *Ibid.* (rev. ed.) 16 To keep some kind of journal was a common practice of the day [*sc.* the 10th century]. The name Pillow-Book, *Makura no Sōshi*, was given at the time to notebooks in which stray impressions were recorded. **1963** 'HAN SUYIN' *Four Faces* 33 'Your blonde..is she a writer?' 'Pillow books.' **1967** *Spectator* 22 Dec. 782/3 Presumably one tries to write as well in a pillow-book as in a novel. **1968** *Guardian* 7 May 6/1 Around the walls were eleventh-century Indian temple sculptures, pillow books from Japan..and too many modern works. **1977** E. J. TRIMMER et al. *Visual Dict. Sex* (1978) xxi. 222 Any erotic books can be pillow books if they have the right effect on the reader. **1651** in *Mayflower Descendant* (1908) X. 39, I give her the bed.. with two pairs of sheets two pillows two paire of pillow coates. **1727** in *Ibid.* 15, I Give to my Granddaughter Mary Bangs A pillow-coat. [**1644** in *Essex County, Mass. Probate Rec.* (1916) I. 41 Two Pilcovrs and two Payer of course sheets, 10s.] **1912** N. L. MCCLUNG *Black Creek Stopping-House* 113 There disappeared at the same time towels, pillow-covers, and a few small tools. **1969** WIDDOWSON & HALPERT in Halpert & Story *Christmas Mumming in Newfoundland* 151 Pillowcovers were also worn, or a large sheet might be draped over the head, with holes cut for eyes, nose, and mouth. **1871** L. M. ALCOTT *Little Men* i. 16 We always allow one pillow-fight Saturday night. **1892** 'MARK TWAIN' *Amer. Claimant* xiii. 119 They generally wound up with a pillow fight, in which they banged each other over the head, and threw the pillows in all directions. **1903** T. ROOSEVELT *Lett. to his Children* (1919) 69 The pillow fight raged up and down the hall. **1939** C. ISHERWOOD *Goodbye to Berlin* 268 Two young men were pillow-fighting with cushions. *a* **1953** E. O'NEILL *More Stately Mansions* (1965) I. iii. 52 We had a pillow fight. **1960** L. HELLMAN *Toys in Attic* III. 66 Shall we have a pillow fight or make fudge? **1976** *Ulverston* (Cumbria) *News* 3 Dec. 4/4 Gary White, of the Barrow Sailing Club was the winner of the pillow fight on the pole. **1903** *Amer. Geologist* XXXII. 67 Immediately above the lava sheet is the pillow lava, proved to be about 60 meters in thickness. **1971** I. G. GASS et al. *Understanding Earth* xxi. 302/2 The presence of such pillow lavas in ancient rock sequences..is unequivocal evidence of sub-aqueous eruption. **1977** A. HALLAM *Planet Earth* 96 Ridges or cones of granular glassy rocks and pillow lavas result from subglacial eruption through fissures or vents respectively. **1928** CRAWFORD & KEILLER *Wessex from Air* 23 At High Beech the rabbits use the pillow-mounds very extensively. **1932** *Field Archæol.* (Ordnance Survey) 5 Low, flat mounds of earth have been noticed. They are called Pillow-mounds, and appear to be of a much later date [than long barrows]. **1963** E. S. WOOD *Collins Field Guide Archaeol.* II. ii. 233 *Pillow mounds*, these are low, oblong mounds..2 to 3 ft. high; most have a shallow ditch round them. **1908** *Westm. Gaz.* 24 Dec. 15/2 Her furs were cinnamon fox with a bunch of violets in the pillow muff. **1871** 'S. MAY' *Prudy keeping House* 43 As she had decided to call herself Mother Hubbard, she made an ample cap, by folding a 'pillow-sham', and putting two of its ruffled edges around her face for a double border. **1914** KIPLING *Lett. Travel* (1920) 244 Our great National Policy of co-educational housekeeping! Ham-frills and pillow-shams. **1926** *Chicago Tribune* 11 Sept. 2/2 Then there was the pillow-sham holder. **1947** *Christian Sci. Monitor* 15 Jan. 6/5 And pillow shams! Like the splashes, they were painstakingly worked in red outline. **1963** G. H. THOMSON *Crocus Country* xvi. 100 The pillow-shams or covers.. were all crisp and white. **1975** *New Yorker* 17 Nov. 134/2 To bring a woman's brass bed into line with her nightshirt, there are antique pillow shams, often copiously trimmed with lace, eyelet, and tucks. **1874** J. A. MAIR *Handbk. Proverbs* 461 *Pillow-slip*, pillow-case. **1920** T. S. ELIOT *Ara Vos Prec* 22 Pushing the framework of the bed And clawing at the pillow slip. [**1897** A. GEIKIE *Anc. Volcanoes G.B.* I. iii. 26 Some basic lavas on flowing into water or into a watery silt have assumed a remarkable spheroidal sack-like or pillow-like structure.] *Ibid.* xiv. 244 Some of the diabase-masses display the pillow-structure and amygdaloidal texture. **1930** PEACH & HORNE *Geol. Scotl.* 142 Pillow-structure is well developed in some of the volcanic rocks, the chilled margins of the pillows and the concentric arrangement of the vesicles being marked features. **1971** I. G. GASS et al. *Understanding Earth* xiii. 165/1 There may be some instances (e.g. pillow structures in lavas) when igneous and metamorphic rocks yield important information. **1977** A. HALLAM *Planet Earth* 188 Similar pillow structures characterize basaltic lavas erupted on the present ocean floors. **1939** JOYCE *Finnegans Wake* I. 57 Mid pillow talk and chithouse chat, on Marlborough Green as through Molesworth Fields. **1971** *Femina* (Bombay) 16 Apr. 7/2 Is your husband out pillow-talking with some bright young doll? **1971** *Daily Tel.* 17 Dec. 9/6 Thanks to a bug under the bed, a man down in the basement..is putting on tape all Ingrid's pillow talk, not to mention her sighs and squeals. **1973** R. THOMAS *If you can't be Good* (1974) xii. 109 She told the senator. Pillow talk, I would think. **1975** *Times* 23 Aug. 4/7 Mrs Ford..makes it plain she gets her views across to Mr Ford in what she calls 'Pillow talk'. **1951** *Sci. News Let.* 10 Feb. 93/1 A new synthetic rubber-nylon 'pillow' tank for gasoline that lies flat on the ground and provides 10,000 gallons of storage in ten minutes will soon be servicing U.S. fighting tanks and trucks at the front. **1959** *Post & Times Herald* (Washington) 5 Aug. B7 (*caption*) The pillow tanks can be used to transport virtually all types of liquid on trucks, railroad cars and barges. When not in use, the collapsible containers can be rolled up and packed in a box. **1962** *Engineering* 26 Jan. 144 An example of the collapsible pillow tank principle, in the transport of water.

pillowing (pi·lōu,iŋ), *a. rare.* [f. PILLOW *sb.* + -ING[2].] Pillow-making.

1924 *Times Trade & Engin. Suppl.* 29 Nov. 247/2 Bleaching fabrics such as pillowing, art, or handkerchief linens.

pillowy, *a.* Add: Also *fig.*

1805–6 WORDSWORTH *Prelude* (1959) III. 99 From these I turned to travel with the shoal Of more unthinking natures, easy minds And pillowy.

pilluck, var. *PILLOCK.

pilo-. Add: **pi·loerection,** the erection or bristling of hair or fur; **pi·loerector,** an agent that causes piloerection; **pilomotor** *a.*, add: more widely, involved in or pertaining to the movement of hair by bodily processes; also as *sb.*, a pilomotor nerve or muscle; (earlier and later examples); **pilonidal** *a.* (earlier and later examples).

1938 J. F. FULTON *Physiol. Nervous Syst.* xiii. 248 The most important mechanisms of heat production and preservation are shivering, mobilization of carbohydrate reserve, vasoconstriction, piloerection, increase in heart rate, and elevation of metabolic activity. **1958** *Jrnl. Investigative Dermatol.* XXX. 107/2 Injection of.. epinephrine regularly produced 'goose-flesh' and pilo-erection. **1974** CARLSON & HSIEH in N. B. Slonim *Environmental Physiol.* iv. 67/2 Fur-bearing animals can greatly increase the insulation of their outer coat by piloerection. **1977** RUMBAUGH & GILL in D. M. Rumbaugh *Language Learning by Chimpanzee* ix. 175 Lana's response was to hoot with apparent agitation; she also displayed piloerection and a furrowed brow. **1946** A. KUNTZ *Autonomic Nervous Syst.* (ed. 3) xv. 327 Intracutaneous administration of acetylcholine..elicits strong fleeting pilo-erector activity. **1965** *Jrnl. Investigative Dermatol.* LXIV. 86/1 The vasoconstrictor and pilot erector effect in man of noradrenaline was compared with those of..dopamine. **1891** LANGLEY & SHERRINGTON in *Jrnl. Physiol.* XII. 278 It will be convenient to have a short name for the nerve-fibres, stimulation of which causes contraction of the erectores pilorum. We shall call them 'pilo-motor' fibres on the analogy of 'vaso-motor' fibres. **1892** *Ibid.* XIII. 701 This class of fibres consists of the eye-fibres of the sympathetic. Langley has shewn this for cat and rabbit, and they often in monkey extend a segment higher than do the pilo-motors for the scalp. **1909** *Ibid.* XXXVIII. 174 The paralysis of the pilo-motor mechanism is one of the.. results of nerve section. **1927** *Ibid.* LXIV. 98 Shallow incisions..through the layers which contain the insertions of the pilomotor muscles into the hair roots. **1932** *Amer. Jrnl. Physiol.* CII. 30 The pilomotors reacted..to single shocks. **1948** A. BRODAL *Neurol. Anat.* xi. 394 The hypothalamus is probably concerned in integrating the activity of the pilomotors with other autonomic functions. **1880** R. M. HODGES in *Boston Med. & Surg. Jrnl.* CIII. 486/1 For the development of this rather singular lesion, to which..I venture to give the name of pilo-nidal (*pilus*, a hair, *nidus*, a nest) sinus, the following elements are necessary:—(1.) The presence of a congenital coccygeal dimple. (2.) Abundant pilous development... (3.) Insufficient attention to cleanliness. **1956** *Lancet* 15 Dec. 1244 An interdigital sinus behaves like a fistula-in-ano or a pilonidal sinus elsewhere... These pilonidal sinuses appear to be acquired and may be caused by loose hairs, foreign bodies, or inspissated secretions being drawn into small abrasions or acne pits in the skin. **1957** S. L. ROBBINS *Textbk. Path.* xxx. 1186/2 Anatomically, these lesions consist sometimes of sinus tracts, pilonidal sinus, communicating with the surface through minute (probe diameter) pores; at other times well developed epidermal-lined cysts, pilonidal cyst, that may or may not communicate with the surface. **1964** D. E. SMITH in L. V. Ackerman *Surg. Path.* xxvi. 1063 In their simplest form pilonidal sinuses or cysts are tracts lined by epidermis that extend beneath the skin toward the dura.

pilón (pilōu·n). *Southwestern U.S.* Also **pilon.** [Mexican Sp., a. Sp. *pilón* sugar-loaf, mortar.] A free gift given when a purchase is made or an account paid; = *LAGNIAPPE. Also *fig.*

1892 *Dialect Notes* I. 251 *Pilón*.., the gratuity given by merchants to customers, whenever accounts are settled. **1932** H. W. BENTLEY *Dict. Spanish Terms in Eng.* 180 *Pilon*,..a favor; a gratuity. Literally the word signifies a small cone-shaped cake of sugar. It may be conjectured that a small *dulce* of this sort constituted the *pilon* originally. **1947** R. BEDICHEK *Adventures with Texas Naturalist* vii. 75 It [*sc.* yaupon]..stands drought, resents coddling, and throws in, as a *pilon* to its domesticator, decorative red berries in the fall and winter. **1962** E. B. ATWOOD *Regional Vocab. Texas* iii. 68 The custom of giving something extra with a purchase (or when a bill is paid) is firmly established in the United States... Most areas lack a specific word for this sort of gift. In the Southwest, the West, and part of Central Texas *pilón* is very well known and widely used. *Ibid.* vii. 124 (*heading*) Lexicographical pilón. *Ibid.* 128 Modern stores are becoming less and less inclined to give pilón.

pilot, *sb.* Add: **1. b.** (Further examples.) Esp. a skilled guide employed on land.

1672 J. PAINE *Jrnl.* in *Publ. Colonial Soc. Mass.* (1917) XVIII. 189 Wee mett with ye Riuor Hosick wch wee Set or corse for by Direction of or Indian Pilate and ther.. wee dismounted. **1710** T. BUCKINGHAM in S. Knight *Jrnls.* (1825) 94 Mr. Christophers and myself, having provided horses and a pilot, set out for Boston. **1847** J. PALMER *Jrnl. Trav. Rocky Mts.* 15 In case the company would elect him pilot, and pay him five hundred dollars, *in advance*, he would bind himself to pilot them to fort Vancouver. **1927** *Dialect Notes* V. 459 *Pilot*, the boy who accompanies a blind beggar. The American 'Lazarillo'. **1936** I. L. IDRIESS *Cattle King* vii. 63 A squatter was overlanding with a big mob of stock, his wagons loaded with a year's supplies. He had taken up country on the 'blind', without ever having seen it... He needed a pilot to show him the waterholes on his own country.

c. (Earlier U.S. example.) Also short for *pilot light.*

1883 F. M. A. ROE *Army Lett.* (1909) 313 It requires two engines to pull even the passenger trains up, and when the divide is reached the 'pilot' is uncoupled and run down ahead. **1964** E. BERCKMAN *Simple Case of Ill-Will* x. 98, I smelled *gas!*.. There's a pilot on your cooker, an open flame. **1973** R. L. SIMON *Big Fix* (1974) vi. 48 All the lights were out except for a couple of pilots beneath the tape decks.

d. One who controls an aircraft, balloon, spacecraft, or the like during flight, usu. a person duly qualified to do so. *automatic pilot*: see *AUTOMATIC *a.* 2.

1848 *Sporting Life* 12 Aug. 289/1 The aëronautic race was conducted by Lieutenant Gale and Professor Gypson, ..the latter acting as the pilot of the Royal Albion. **1851** *Illustr. London News* 13 Sept. 330/2 We..threw out more ballast.., and descended..in a..field. I fell.., and the car over us all; while 'the pilot who had weathered the storm' was thrown with..violence from among the cordage. **1852** *Ibid.* 18 Sept. 224/3 'Sit still, all of you, I say!' roared our pilot, as he saw some one endeavouring to leave the car. *Ibid.*, Indeed, long shall we all remember the pleasant night we passed with the old ethereal pilot on his 500th ascent with the Royal Nassau Balloon. **1899** *English Mechanic* 14 July 480/3 The new machine.. is said to be able to carry in its car as many as six men and travel easily at a rate of 100 miles an hour under the absolute mastery of its engineer and pilot. **1907** *Navigating the Air* (Aero Club Amer.) 247 In order to qualify as a pilot one must make ten ascensions, one of which must be made at night, and two of which must be made alone. **1913**, etc. [see *air pilot* s.v. *AIR *sb.*[1] B. III. 4]. **1916**, etc. [see *FLY *v.*[1] 1 g]. **1936**, etc. [see *bush pilot* s.v. *BUSH *sb.*[1] 11]. **1953** 'N. SHUTE' *In Wet* v. 136 This was the first Ceres that had visited Edmonton, and a small crowd of pilots and R.C.A.F. officers gathered around it on the tarmac. **1962** *Into Orbit* 243 *Backup pilot*, an Astronaut who..may go on the mission himself if the Astronaut named as pilot is unable to make the flight at the last minute. **1974** *Daily Tel.* 14 June 8/4 Among the pilots flying this weekend will be Charles Dollfus, 83-year-old leading French balloonist who has been flying since 1911. **1978** *Dumfries Courier* 13 Oct. 9/1 He..would like other hang-glider 'pilots' in the area to contact him with a view to starting a Dumfriesshire Hang-Gliding Club.

e. *to drop the pilot*: to abandon a trustworthy adviser.

After a cartoon by J. Tenniel in *Punch*, 20 Mar., 1890 depicting the recent dismissal of Bismarck from the Chancellorship of Germany by William II.

1926 G. M. TREVELYAN *Hist. Eng.* IV. vi. 456 In face of these signs Charles decided to 'drop the pilot'. It was indeed tempting to make a scapegoat of Clarendon. **1958** J. RAYMOND *England's on Anvil!* 149 The Kaiser is aged thirty. He has been on the throne a year and is already preparing to 'drop the pilot', get rid of Bismarck. **1979** D. GURR *Troika* vi. 32 Khruschev'll be dropping that pilot before they clear the river.

f. Short for *pilot film, plant, programme*, etc.: see sense 6 b below.

1962 *Listener* 18 Oct. 633/2 A little tighter and tauter and the production would have looked for all the world like a pilot for a new series. **1971** M. BABSON *Cover-up Story* xiv. 153, I came by..to talk over a few points before we started filming the pilot tomorrow. **1971** *Guardian* 26 Feb. 13/4 Sir Lew Grade..gave an uncharacteristically terse 'no comment' when asked if he had made any pilots in the recent past. **1971** *Inside Kenya Today* Mar. 9/1 If this pilot is successful an important export oriented mining enterprise will be established. **1973** *Nation* (Barbados) 16 Dec. 2/2 He has recently signed to be..a star in a pilot for a television series which is being written by Everett Chambers. **1975** *Radio Times* 30 Aug.–5 Sept. 14/3 It was only a pilot which would not be seen by the general public. **1977** *Time Out* 17–23 June 16/2 Thames' fourth telefilm in three days. Repeat of the pilot for a never-made series about a big city newspaper.

g. A jockey.

1976 *Horse & Hound* 10 Dec. 41/1 He was to underline his Epsom misfortune by streaking home in the Irish Sweeps Derby, when his French pilot was replaced by Geoff Lewis. **1976** M. MAGUIRE *Scratchproof* iv. 54 Will Highwayman jump the fence without a pilot?

5*. *Telecommunications.* An unmodulated signal transmitted with another signal for purposes of reference or control. Freq. *attrib.*, as *pilot carrier, tone*, etc.

1935 *Proc. IRE* XXIII. 702 The high degree of frequency stability required for single side-band suppressed-carrier transmissions can be dispensed with by transmitting a pilot frequency over the channel. **1957** D. G. FINK *Television Engin. Handbk.* xviii. 31 The L3 system makes use of six pilots for dynamic regulating and equalizing purposes. These are 308, 556, 2,064, 3,096, 7,266, and 8,320 kc. *Ibid.* xvi. 249 Oscillator-frequency drift causes picture-hue shift by changing the signal location on the phase characteristics of the pilot carrier and sideband circuits. **1962** C. F. BOYCE *Open-Wire Carrier Telephone Transmission* vii. 95 Over the 3-channel carrier range a single pilot can regulate for changes in flat and slope loss. .. In a 12-channel system two pilots, one at each end of the band, are required. **1966** M. SCHWARTZ et al. *Communication Syst. & Techniques* xi. 492 One technique for monitoring the channel state in a digital signaling system would be to transmit a pilot tone (unmodulated tone) along with the information-bearing waveforms. **1974** H. BURSTEIN *Q. & A. about Tape Recording* (1975) xv. 194 The FM stereo broadcast contains a 19 kHz pilot signal. **1974** HARVEY & BOHLMAN *Stereo F.M. Radio Handbk.* ii. 23 The reason for using a 19 kHz oscillator in the signal encoder now becomes clearer, since the oscillator provides a reference between the transmitted 19 kHz pilot tone and the 38 kHz subcarrier feed to the balanced modulator. **1975** *Which?* Sept. 278/3 An FM stereo radio signal has three parts. The main one is a mono signal... The extra information the tuner needs to produce stereo is in the other two parts—a sub-carrier and a pilot tone.

5.** *Electr.* = *pilot wire* in *6.

1940 *Chambers's Techn. Dict.* 644/1 *Pilot*, in power systems, a conductor used for auxiliary purposes, not for the transmission of energy. **1957** M. D. KIPPEN in E. O. Taylor *Power Syst. Communications* i. 6 It has been the policy of many city undertakings when laying power cables to lay protection pilots and, in some cases, telephone pilots in the same trench. **1966** W. J. CHEETHAM in Taylor & Boal *Electr. Power Distribution 415V–33kV* iii. 125 Post-office pilots are much more prone to interference during maintenance work on adjacent communication circuits.

6. *pilot error*; *pilot-balloon* (earlier and later examples), *-engine* (later example), *-locomotive, -tunnel* (examples); **pilot biscuit** *U.S.*, ship's biscuit; **pilot-bread** (earlier and later U.S. examples); **pilot cable** *Electr.* = *pilot wire* below; **pilot chute** or **'chute** (see quot. 1925); **pilot-cloth** (earlier N.Amer. examples); **pilot-coat** (examples); **pilot driver,** an engine-driver who accompanies another over a route with which the latter is unfamiliar; **pilot guard** (see quot. 1921); **pilot-house** (earlier and later examples); also (*U.S.*), a house on land in which a pilot lives or stays; **pilot lamp** = **pilot light* (*c*); **pilot light** (further examples); †(*b*) a small light left permanently on to provide illumination; (*c*) a small electric light used to give an indication or warning rather than illumination; **pilot-man,** a railway official who directs the movement of trains over a section of track being temporarily used as a single line; also, a pilot driver; **pilot officer,** a commissioned rank in the Royal Air Force, equivalent to a second lieutenant in the Army; **pilot parachute** = **pilot chute;* **pilot-snake** (earlier and later examples); **pilot valve** *Engin.*, a small auxiliary valve that is operated in association with a larger valve; **pilot-weed** (earlier and later examples); **pilot-whale** (later examples); **pilot wire** *Electr.*, an auxiliary wire or cable for conveying information about an associated power line or telegraph line or for operating apparatus connected with one.

1802 *Sporting Mag.* XX. 295/1 A Pilot Balloon, as it is called, was first launched. **1924** Pilot balloon [see *BALLON-SONDE]. **1942** *Endeavour* I. 118/2 The information on temperature is obtained from pilot balloons—small balloons carrying a cage of instruments to read temperature, .. at the altitude at which the balloon is set to burst, the cage then falling safely to earth. **1836** T. POWER *Impressions Amer.* I. 21 Lift a piece of pilot biscuit, request some kind soul to shave the under side of the corned round for you, then..fly the place and seek the deck. **1944** *Chicago Daily News* 11 Oct. 25/1 The pilot biscuit—great flat round crackers that may be purchased at the grocer's—were toasted and lightly spread with butter. **1788** *Maryland Jrnl.* 7 Mar. 4/2 (Advt.), The subscriber..has just begun to bake Ship, Pilot, and Cag Bread. **1831** [see **navy bread*]. **1894** *Outing* XXIV. 252/2 He quickly wrapped up some pilot-bread. **1977** *New Yorker* 9 May 112/2 With..six pieces of pilot bread, he got into his single Klepper and bobbed down the river. **1937** H. COTTON *Transmission & Distribution of Electr. Energy* xv. 349 The pilot wires are usually in the form of a three-core cable, which can be buried in the ground in the case of an insulated cable system, or slung from the towers in the case of an overhead system. Apart from the high cost of these pilot cables, [etc.]. **1967** M. F. BUCHAN *Electr. Supply* x. 296 As the two ends of the system may be some distance apart, an information link is required, and this may be a pilot cable, a radio link, or carrier currents superimposed on the system itself. **1925** *Sci. Amer.* Mar. 203/2 The majority of parachutes are equipped with a 'pilot chute' which is a miniature structure made with ribs and spring in umbrella fashion. When the pilot pulls the 'rip cord'.. the 'pilot chute' springs out, catches the air and helps to lead out the main parachute. **1973** 'A. HALL' *Tango Briefing* x. 118 Free fall... Seven, eight, nine. Pull it. Crack of the pilot 'chute. Then the jerk and the drag. **1834** W. F. TOLMIE *Jrnls.* (1963) 262 Have donned pilot cloth vest. **1840** *Knickerbocker* XV. 140 His winter clothing is usually a peet jacket and trowsers, of strong pilot cloth. **1836** DICKENS *Sk. Boz.* (1837) 2nd Ser. 96 Pilot great coats with wooden buttons, have usurped the place of the ponderous laced coats with full skirts. **1840** *Spirit of Times* 9 May 116/2 A young man attired in a pilot coat and velvet stock. **1842** DICKENS *Amer. Notes* I. ii. 41 The captain comes down again, in a sou'-wester hat.. and a pilot-coat. **1858** TROLLOPE *Three Clerks* I. ii. 29 A short bargee's pilot-coat, and a pipe of tobacco, were soon familiar to him. **1884** F. M. CRAWFORD *Amer. Politician* II. ii. 30 Enormous Irishmen in pilot coats..were struggling to keep the drifts from the pavement. **1907** *Westm. Gaz.* 15 Feb. 7/1 Drivers should not be allowed to drive an engine over a road that they were not acquainted with without a pilot driver. **1955** *Railway Mag.* May 302/1 A halt was made at Blarney, to detach the pilot engine. **1975** *Times* 3 Sept. 1/2 Last year the International Air Transport Association said that half of all air accidents were caused by pilot error. **1978** J. GARDNER *Dancing Dodo* xxxii. 252 The thing went wrong...If they wanted accuracy, they needed men to ensure it. What they got was..pilot error, or malfunction. **1881** *Instructions to Census Clerks* (1885) 33, 78 Railway Guard... Pilot Guard. **1921** *Dict. Occup. Terms* (1927) § 702 *Pilot guard*, a guard..who pilots trains over portion of line where single line working is necessitated, or over bridges under repair. **1812** A. STODDARD *Sk. Louisiana* 160 On the south side of the east pass, about three miles from the bar, is the pilot house. **1827** J. L. WILLIAMS *View of West Florida* 18 A small fort and pilot house formerly stood near the west end of the island. **1846** *Spirit of Times* 16 May 133/1 He placed his hand upon a small brass knob at the back of the pilot house. **1863** 'G. HAMILTON' *Gala-Days* 120 An Indian pilot comes on board, and mounts to the pilot-house. **1897** W. B. YEATS *Secret Rose* 207 The disused pilot-house looks out to sea. **1967** *Jane's Surface Skimmer Systems 1967–68* 34/2 Forward of the well..is the pilothouse. **1977** I. SHAW *Beggarman, Thief* I. i. 7 Alone in the pilothouse..stood Wesley Jordache. **1977** *Washington Post* 4 Sept. A12/1 The top tier of this floating cake is the 'pilot house'—what a seagoing sailor would call the 'bridge'. **1884** *Jrnl. Soc. Telegr. Engin.* XIII. 515 As the speed began to increase, the lamp lit up intermittently, but in a few seconds more the machines dropped into step together, and the pilot lamp lit up to full brightness and became perfectly steady. **1906** J. POOLE *Pract. Telephone Handbk.* (ed. 3) xvii. 220 Whenever a call is made on any one of these lines the pilot relay is operated, and causes a specially large lamp, called the 'pilot lamp', to glow. **1918** R. KNOX *Radiogr. & Radio-Therapeutics* II. 437 There is nearly always a pilot lamp on the switchboard by which the tints may be accurately gauged. **1977** 'E. TREVOR' *Theta Syndrome* i. 14 In the main laboratory there were only the pilot lamps going. **1906** *Daily Colonist* (Victoria, B.C.) 26 Jan. 10/1 Pilot lights have also been placed in all the hallways and dark passages of the building. **1907** *Daily Chron.* 16 Apr. 6/7 This is the 'pilot' light, which is never extinguished, which burns night and day from the time a theatre is opened throughout the whole of its existence. **1939** I. BAIRD *Waste Heritage* x. 130 The radio man clicked on the pilot light and grunts and squeals began to come from the little machine. **1964** J. CHEEVER *Wapshot Scandal* vi. 58 The pilot light on the gas range isn't working and the cook has to keep lighting the range with matches. **1970** *Which?* Nov. 332/2 A pilot light goes on while the iron is heating. **1972** *Guardian* 2 Dec. 8/8 People were asked to turn their gas taps to 'off' so that unlit pilot lights..would not allow gas to seep into their homes when the supply was restored. **1907** *Westm. Gaz.* 21 Sept. 12/2 An antique pilot-locomotive slouched out and stopped. **1881** *Instructions to Census Clerks* (1885) 33, 77 Railway Engine Driver... Pilot, Pilot-man. **1921** *Dict. Occup. Terms* (1927) § 701 *Pilotman*.., a guard.. who accompanies a train between given points on single line, other line being temporarily out of use, to advise driver of difficulties of road, special signalling arrangements, etc. **1971** D. J. SMITH *Discovering Railwayana* x. 58 *Pilotman*, driver taking charge of single-line workings, especially when one line of a double track is under repair. **1919** *Monthly Air Force List* Aug. 15 Air Ministry... Directorate of Personnel... Staff Officers, 3rd Class... Dawes, Pilot Officer H., Gunn, Pilot Officer D.B. **1935** T. S. SPRIGG *Royal Air Force* xii. 91 Accepted candidates who have not had previous experience in the Air Force are entered in the Special Reserve with the rank of Pilot Officer on probation. **1965** W. M. W. FOWLER *Countryman's Cooking* p. x, Where the fault lay was obvious even to a very young Pilot Officer. **1975** *Sunday Times* 23 Feb. 19/7 In May, 1943, I was a lowly WAAF serving on a station in Hampshire... My fiancé, Ken, was a pilot officer. **1926** Pilot parachute [see *PACK *sb.*[1] 1 g]. **1942** A. M. LOW *Parachutes* 41 The effect of pulling the rip-cord was first of all to release the pilot parachute packed on the outside of the pack so that this in turn may draw out the main parachute. **1853** R. B. MARCY *Explor. Red River* (1854) 196 The names of Bull, Pine, and Pilot snake are commonly given to different species of this genus [sc. *Pituophis*]. **1946** G. STIMPSON *Bk. about Thousand Things* 480 The pilot snake..gets its name from the curious belief that it precedes rattlesnakes and warns them of the approach of danger. **1956** L. M. KLAUBER *Rattlesnakes* II. xviii. 1244 Another phase of the myth is that pilot snakes are crosses between rattlesnakes and bull snakes. **1891** *Cent. Dict.* (s.v. *tunnel*), *Pilot tunnel*, a device for directing a tunnel in the prescribed grade, consisting of a flanged tube made up of interchangeable plates, which can be bolted to the shield and forced concentrically into the silt in advance of the face of the heading. **1906** *Chambers's Jrnl.* 29 Sept. 701/1 Within the small pilot-tunnel a large number of refrigerating tubes is placed. **1958** *Engineering* 18 Apr. 502/1 Short pilot tunnels were driven out from the shore on both sides of the Channel. **1902** *Internat. Library of Technol.* VII. B. § 39. 13 For high-speed hydraulic elevators..the relief valve is not sufficient to guard against shocks..nor is it possible to regulate the speed readily... This has led to the introduction of the auxiliary, or pilot, valve. *Ibid.* 18 The pilot valve allows a perfect regulation of the speed of the [elevator] car. **1953** E. MOLLOY *Maintenance Engineers' Pocket Bk.* II. 67 In large boilers.. pilot valves are often fitted to the main stop valves, and the pilot valve should be opened to warm up the steam main before the main stop valve is opened, thus avoiding the danger of water hammer. **1971** H. C. TOWN *Design & Construction of Machine Tools* ix. 194 If the reversing valve has to handle large volumes of oil..the reverse valve is better operated by a pilot valve which may be trip operated. **1848** W. H. EMORY *Notes Mil. Reconn.* 11 In the uplands..occasionally is found the wild tea, .. and pilot weed. **1951** *Dict. Gardening* (R. Hort. Soc.) III. 1957/1 Compass Plant, Pilot Weed, Polar Plant. **1901** SHIPLEY & MACBRIDE *Zool.* xix. 527 The Ca'ing or Pilot Whale.., which also feeds chiefly on cuttle-fish, has teeth in both upper and lower jaws. **1921** J. T. JENKINS *Hist. Whale Fisheries* viii. 268 A third whale fishery practised in northern waters..was that for the Grindhval or Pilot Whale. **1962** E. LUCIA *Klondike Kate* ii. 40 At times schools of happy pilot whales followed the vessel. **1974** G. B. CORBET in D. L. Hawksworth *Changing Flora & Fauna of Brit.* xi. 199 Species that are more frequent in the recent period are pilot whale (*Globicephala melaena*) with 46 strandings between 1948 and 1966. **1890** J. W. URQUHART *Electric Light* (ed. 3) x. 321 It is far more important to be informed as to the actual potential of the mains at the various points of consumption. For low tension constant current systems this is usually accomplished by the use of 'pilot wires'. **1930** *Engineering* 12 Sept. 347/1 An examination of the available protective schemes not involving the use of pilot wires had shown that a close approximation to the performance of pilot protective gear could be obtained by the use of distance relays. **1968** P. J. FREEMAN *Electr. Power Transmission & Distribution* x. 275 On long sections the capacitance currents between the pilot wires may be high enough to operate the relay, causing instability.

b. Used *attrib.* or as *adj.* to denote something that serves as a prototype or experimental undertaking prior to full-scale operation, activity, or use; experimental, initial; as *pilot film, plant, programme, project, scheme, study, survey, trial*; so **pilot-scale** *a.*, done on the scale of a pilot scheme. Cf. *pilot-tunnel* above.

1928 *Daily Mail* 13 Aug. 18/2 This company produced 40 tons of tin concentrates with its small pilot mill in the June quarter. **1934** *Planning* I. XVII. 9 Actually research has become specialised not only by subjects but by processes and each process—background, basic, *ad hoc* and pilot, or whatever else they may be termed—is inseparable from the one before it and from the one after it. **1936** *Economist* 1 Feb. 275/1 The dry crushing and roasting plant treated 186,422 tons [of ore] and the pilot flotation plant 5,688 tons. **1938** *Rep. R. Comm. Oil from Coal* §27 in *Parl. Papers 1937–38* (Cmd. 5665) XII. 439 Experimental work started at Billingham early in 1927, and in 1929 it was decided to build a pilot plant there to treat 10 tons of coal per day. **1939** *Nature* 12 Aug. 279/2 The Department of Biochemistry..[has conducted] pilot scale tannery operations to improve the vegetable chrome process. **1944** *Times* 18 Mar. 2/3 The Ministry of Food has recently installed a pilot plant for drying meat near Belfast. **1947** *Yale Law Jrnl.* Dec. 197 They had an opportunity to build a 'pilot model', a spacious though inexpensive cooperative in..a Warsaw suburb. **1951** (*title*) The Haiti Pilot Project: Phase One (UNESCO). **1951** *Chambers's Jrnl.* Oct. 638/1 Two recent American developments, both at present in the pilot or experimental stage, may widen the already versatile uses of glass. **1952** Pilot reactor [see *CRITICALITY 2]. **1952** W. J. H. SPROTT *Social Psychol.* vi. 102 The 'open-end' question may be used in a pilot survey, which helps to determine the multiple-answer question. **1952** *Times* 25 Jan. 3/4 The corporation stated that it did not propose to proceed with a large-scale irrigation scheme for rice cultivation until results on a pilot area had shown this to be economically possible. **1953** *Britannica Bk. of Year* 638/2 *Pilot scheme* (a preliminary to a full scale agricultural or industrial project). **1953** *Ann. Reg. 1952* 416 A new vaccine selected from pilot trials of the previous winter. **1954** A. HUXLEY *Let.* 12 Dec. (1969) 718 The TV decision would not be made until after the production of a pilot film. **1956** *Planning* XXII. 19 In 1954 the Nottingham Book Festival was organised by a committee of the Booksellers Association as a pilot scheme for a national publicity campaign. **1957** *Ann. Reg. 1956* 348 In Russia it appeared that underground gasification of coal was passing from the pilot stage to industrial operation... In Britain..the Coal Board and the Central Electricity Authority decided to proceed with pilot plant for producing electricity from gas made underground from inferior coal. **1957** R. K. MERTON *Social Theory* (rev. ed.) II. x. 387 The initial substantive aim of this pilot study was fourfold. **1959** *Listener* 22 Jan. 173/1 We hoped to do a pilot survey on the reactions of individuals to television programmes. **1961** *Technology* Feb. 34/4 The scheme will start in three pilot areas. **1961** *Harper's Bazaar* Feb. 23 The trend-setters.., the 'pilot' clothes that look ahead. **1964** M. GOWING *Britain & Atomic Energy, 1939–1945* v. 150 The Chicago pilot-scale graphite pile. **1966** T. PYNCHON *Crying of Lot 49* ii. 33 They've done the pilot film of a TV series, in fact, based loosely on my career. **1969** N. W. PIRIE *Food Resources* 13 With less initial obstruction, and a steady increase in the scale of pilot projects, the ultimate acreage aimed at would probably have been reached earlier. **1971** *Brit. Med. Bull.* XXVII. 6/2 Sensitivity and specificity may be assessed from the results of a pilot trial undertaken on a group of individuals similar to those who are to be screened. **1971** *Guardian* 26 Feb. 13/3 US networks are no longer so keen to buy British programmes without seeing a pilot episode. **1971** *Jrnl. Gen. Psychol.* Apr. 191 On the basis of a pilot study..it was predicted that..total list acquisition would not differ as a function of stimulus clustering. **1974** *Nature* 1 Feb. 248/3 Pilot plants started within the next year or two could be working productively within the next five years. **1975** *Radio Times* 30 Aug. 14/2, I saw a pilot programme for the new series. **1975** *Daily Tel.* 3 Oct. 7/2 A pilot plant to 'lock' radioactive wastes inside solid glass is now being commissioned. **1976** *Leicester Chron.* 26 Nov. 2/3 Leslie Crowther presented the pilot show but future commitments prevented him taking it on permanently. **1978** *Jrnl. R. Soc. Arts* Dec. 8/2 Examinations in Communication were offered..on a pilot basis.

pilot, *v.* Add: **1. b.** To act as pilot on (an aeroplane or other aircraft) in the air; to fly (passengers) in an aircraft. Also *absol.*

1852 *Illustr. London News* 18 Sept. 224/3 The veteran aëronaut who had successfully piloted them and some hundred others through the air. **1911** *Daily News* 20 July 2/4 The Dutch aviator has decided to pilot a.. monoplane .. instead of a .. biplane. **1931** F. L. ALLEN *Only Yesterday* viii. 222 If you did not know how to pilot a plane you could still be a passenger. **1946** *Happy Landings* (Air Ministry) July 6/3 These considerations led me to select a Mosquito..and to pilot myself. **1955** *Times* 22 Aug. 5/4 The crowd saw a fly-past of aircraft piloted by men of the R.A.F. **1958** 'CASTLE' & 'HAILEY' *Flight into Danger* viii. 113 The first officer, then the captain were taken sick. Luckily there was a passenger on board who had piloted before and he took over the controls. **1977** *Daily Tel.* 7 Apr. 7/3 An attempt..to become the first woman to pilot a hot air balloon across the English Channel.

2. b. To secure the passage of (a bill) *through* a legislative assembly; to carry. orig. *U.S.*

1929 *Randolph Enterprise* (Elkins, W. Virginia) 21 Mar. 1/4 The bill..piloted..thru the House by Representative Karl Kyle. **1974** *Lebende Sprachen* XIX. 39/2 He piloted through the House the government's elaborate education bill. **1976** *Leicester Mercury* 16 July 4 It now goes to the Lords. It is likely to be piloted there by Liberal Lord Avebury.

c. To use experimentally; to try out, test.

1960 *Sunday Times* 10 Jan. 14/6 Practically all these devices for saving time and labour have been piloted in the fifties. The sixties should see them put into commercial production in sufficient quantity to make them financially feasible. **1965** *New Society* 23 Dec. 15/3 The Rowntree survey (piloted in Harrow, and subsequently carried out in York). **1967** G. WILLS in Wills & Yearsley *Handbk. Managem. Technol.* 186 Always, but always, *pilot* a questionnaire before sending it out into the field. Never try and scorn the researcher who asks for time and money to pilot his work. **1977** *Jrnl. R. Soc. Arts* CXXV. 308/2 Not only does he [*sc.* the skilled question designer] pilot his questionnaire, but periodically he tests his questions to find out how they are actually understood.

pilotage. 1. (Further examples.)

1922 *Encycl. Brit.* XXX. 13/2 Then came pilotage and the elements of commercial flying. **1924** *Air Pilot: Gt. Britain* II. iv. 19 (*heading*) Pilotage Directions. **1932** *Flight* 6 Oct. 949/1 The Air Council have had under consideration the policy regarding training in air pilotage. **1946** *Happy Landings* (Air Ministry) July (verso front cover), The various sciences which together contribute to our present day knowledge of practical pilotage. **1969** *Daily Mail* 16 Jan. 5/6 We had some difficulty on Apollo 8, with 'pilotage', that is, trying to plot our path on the map of the back side of the Moon.

piloted (pəi·lətėd), *ppl. a.* [f. PILOT *v.* + -ED[1].] Controlled or guided by a pilot.

1945 C. MILBURN *Diary* 18 Mar. (1979) 278 Last night piloted enemy planes were over northern England and.. casualties also occurred from V bombs in the south. **1946** *Jrnl. R. Aeronaut. Soc.* July 508/1 The other piloted rocket aircraft was intended to be catapulted at an angle of 75°. **1952** *Ann. Reg. 1951* 411 The next stage [in space travel] would be piloted rockets designed as space stations. **1961** *Shell Aviation News* Dec. 4/1 Already, in certain circumstances 'the one who controls the aeroplane' can equally well be in another aircraft or on the ground. In this new situation the terms 'piloted' and 'pilotless' become confusing anomalies.

piloting, *vbl. sb.* (in Dict. s.v. PILOT *v.*). (Further examples.)

1919 W. H. BERRY *New Traffic* (*Aircraft*) i. 5 Good piloting does not depend on cleverness in tinkering with the engine. **1922** *Encycl. Brit.* XXX. 14/1 Aerial navigation, as distinct from piloting with the ground in view, developed tardily everywhere. **1959** *Manch. Guardian* 6 July 2/4 The hour's piloting round a town that makes up most [driving] lessons. **1977** *Belfast Tel.* 28 Feb. 9/2 (*caption*) Too old for piloting in 1939 he became an air gunner with 235 Squadron Coastal Command.

‖ **pilotis** (pilo*ti*). [Fr.] A series of columns or piles, esp. used to raise the base of a building above ground-level.

1947 *Archit. Rev.* CI. 172/1 Low-growing palms make patterns against the pale pink granite pilotis. **1957** *New Yorker* 5 Oct. 166/2 The most striking feature of the building [*sc.* Le Corbusier's Unity House] is that it is raised twenty-four feet aboveground on a double row of cyclopean, wedge-shaped concrete columns, or *pilotis*, which uphold the hollow canopy of concrete that forms the basement of the building proper. **1971** *Country Life* 25 Nov. 1444/3 The studio stood on *pilotis*, but..it has been converted into a house. **1972** E. LUCIE-SMITH in Cox & Dyson *20th-Cent. Mind* II. xiv. 492 Pure forms achieved by the use of continuous window-strips, glass walls, flat roofs; the lightness which came from raising the structure on *pilotis*.

pilotless, *a.* (s.v. PILOT *sb.*). Add: (Further examples.) Now esp. of aircraft.

1806 SCOTT *Let.* 20 Sept. (1932) I. 317 The pilot-less state in which the political vessel has remained since his [*sc.* Pitt's] death. **1909** *Westm. Gaz.* 22 Oct. 7/2 We only just missed the new spectacle of a pilotless aeroplane. **1922** *Glasgow Herald* 15 Nov. 9 The Army Air Service [U.S.A.] announces that successful tests have been made with automatically controlled pilotless aeroplanes. **1937** *Aeroplane* 16 June 3 (Advt.), A pilotless flyaway plane. **1943** R. V. JONES *Most Secret War* (1978) xxxix. 356 The Germans are installing..a large and important ground organization in Belgium–N. France which is probably concerned with directing an attack on England by rocket-driven pilotless aircraft. **1944** [see *buzz-bomb* s.v. *BUZZ *sb.*[1] 5]. **1945** H. KNIGHT in *Penguin New Writing* XXIII. 47 Pilotless men whose personalities have been disintegrated by concussion and too many action stations. **1961** [see *PILOTED *ppl. a.*]. **1966** M. WOODHOUSE *Tree Frog* v. 35 The curious blind look of all pilotless aircraft which stems from having no cockpit. **1974** *Guardian* 18 Mar. 5/4 The pilotless planes, named Falcons, are designed for taking aerial photographs.

pilpul (pi·lpʊl). [Heb.: see PILPULIST.] Subtle or keen rabbinical investigation or argumentation; an instance of this. Also *transf.*, hair-splitting and unprofitable disputation.

1894 tr. *Graetz's Hist. Jews* IV. xiii. 418 The astonishing facility of ingenious disquisition on the basis of the Talmud (Pilpul), attributed to Polak, which attained its highest perfection in Poland, proceeded from a native of Poland. **1905** J. Z. LAUTERBACH in *Jewish Encycl.* X. 39/2 (*heading*) Pilpul. A method of Talmudic study. The word is derived from the verb 'pilpel' (lit. 'to spice', 'to season', and in a metaphorical sense, 'to dispute violently'..or 'cleverly'..). Since by such disputation the subject is in a way spiced and seasoned, the word has come to mean penetrating investigation, disputation, and drawing of conclusions, and is used especially to designate a method of studying the Law... The essential characteristic of pilpul is that it leads to a clear comprehension of the subject under discussion by penetrating into its essence and by adopting clear distinctions and a strict differentiation of the concepts. **1920** OESTERLEY & BOX *Short Survey Lit. of Rabbinical & Mediæval Judaism* IV. ii. 228 So far from destroying *pilpul*—casuistical discussion—the *Code* or *Mishneh Torah* itself became the object of pilpulistic comment. **1964** H. KEMELMAN *Friday the Rabbi slept Late* (1965) xxi. 156 We read a passage..of the Law... We were adding our own arguments..and twists of logic, the so-called pilpul. **1966** —— *Saturday the Rabbi went Hungry* i. 10 The cantor's chuckle told him he was won over. The rabbi returned to the table. His wife shook her head with a smile. 'That was a terrible pilpul.' **1967** C. POTOK *Chosen* II. v. 107 Pilpul, these discussions are called—empty, nonsensical arguments over minute points of the Talmud. **1968** L. ROSTEN *Joys of Yiddish* 287 *Pilpul*,..unproductive hair-splitting that is employed not so much to advance clarity or reveal meaning as to display one's own cleverness. **1976** *Brit. Jrnl. Sociol.* XXVII. 41 A key difficulty in the concept of alienation is that many of the succeeding theoretical discussions of the idea have taken off from the false leads in Marx, and the Talmudic *pilpul* over dissecting his text has only produced further confusion.

Pils (pilz, pils). [Abbrev. *PILSENER, PILSNER.] A type of beer similar to Pilsener.

1961 *Dude* Sept., I had part of a bottle of French beer called Panther Pils (so help me) then switched to Tuborg. **1962** [see *EXPORT *sb.* 3 b]. **1971** M. SINCLAIR *Sonntag* iii. 22 In..the scruffy *Bierstube* he sat scowling with a thin glass of *Pils*. **1972** P. CLEIFE *Slick & Dead* xx. 157 Normally I never drink when I'm flying but thought.. that a light Belgian Pils would be harmless. **1977** *Grimsby Even. Tel.* 24 May 10/2 (Advt.), Large Quantity of beers... Newcastle Brown, Prize Medal, Carlsberg, Pils in bottles, etc.

Pilsen (pi·lz-, pi·lsən). Also with lower-case initial. [See next.] = next.

It is not certain that quot. 1939 belongs here.

1939 JOYCE *Finnegans Wake* (1964) III. 492 My dodear devere revered mainhirr was confined to guardroom, I hindustand, by my pint of his Filthered pilsens bottle. **1964** L. DEIGHTON *Funeral in Berlin* xxxi. 162 The waiter had brought two tall, ice-cold Pilsen lagers. **1968** *Listener* 25 July 103/3 One continually meets these ironies in Bohemia. Over stew and dumplings and draught Pilsen, he boasted that his son had actually been named in the Moscow press as a dangerous deviationist. **1977** P. SOMERVILLE-LARGE *Eagles near Carcase* iv. 61 The barman..had some tall cold bottles of Pilsen.

Pilsener, Pilsner (pi·lz-, pi·ls(ə)nəɹ). [G., f. *Pilsen* (Czech. *Plzeň*), a province and city in W. Bohemia, Czechoslovakia.] In full *Pils(e)ner beer*. A pale-coloured lager beer with a strong hop flavour. Also *attrib.*

The name now designates type rather than origin. Beer from Plzeň itself is known as *Pils(e)ner Urquell* (G., primary source).

1877 C. SCHREIBER *Jrnl.* 3 Aug. (1911) II. 49 Much rain—no breakfasts in the garden and Pilsner beer luncheons this year! **1890** KIPLING *Life's Handicap* (1891) 161 'Pilsener?'..'Beer's out, I'm sorry to say.' **1894** *Clarion* 3 Nov. 2/4 The elder waiter sent my empty bottle of Pilsener flying. **1909** M. DIVER *Candles in Wind* iii. 35 A glass of Pilsener to ward off regrets next morning. **1920** E. SITWELL *Wooden Pegasus* 67 And sat and drank our Pilsener beer. **1933** *Sun* (Baltimore) 6 Dec. 18/5 (Advt.), Light Pilsner style or dark kulmbacher—as you prefer it. **1964** L. DEIGHTON *Funeral in Berlin* xxxi. 161 Groups of men shouted for slivovice, borovicka or Pilsner Urquell. **1980** *Brit. Med. Jrnl.* 29 Mar. 916/1 It [*sc.* class 2 beer] was available in two strengths—a middle European Pilsner beer..and a somewhat stronger English lager type.

b. Special Combs., as **Pils(e)ner glass, pils(e)ner glass**, a tall beer glass tapered at the bottom.

1966 'E. LATHEN' *Murder makes Wheels go Round* xvi. 130 Waymark pushed his pilsener glass to one side. **1971** J. BALL *First Team* (1972) xxvi. 406 Zalinsky poured out the two drinks in pilsner glasses. **1975** *Times* 18 Jan. 12/1 A..sight of the world..through the bottom of a Pilsner glass.

Piltdown (pi·lt,daun). The name of a village in Sussex, England, used *attrib.* esp. in **Piltdown jaw, man, skull,** with reference to the fossil remains of a skull found there, or the primitive hominid described as *Eoanthropus dawsoni*, to which these remains were attributed; the skull was proved fraudulent in 1953 by J. S. Weiner and K. P. Oakley. Also *absol.*

1912 *Times* 19 Dec. 4/5 He [*sc.* A. S. Woodward] inclined..to the theory that..surviving modern man might have arisen directly from the primitive source of which the Piltdown skull provided the first discovered evidence. **1913** *Q. Jrnl. Geol. Soc.* LXIX. 139 It seems reasonable to interpret the Piltdown skull as exhibiting a closer resemblance to the skulls of the truly ancestral mid-tertiary apes than any fossil human skull hitherto found. **1931** *Times Lit. Suppl.* 23 Apr. 317/1 On comparing her [*sc.* a female hominid] with the Piltdown man he [*sc.* Sir A. Keith] makes amends by describing her as Piltdown refined. **1933** A. S. ROMER *Man & Vertebrates* xi. 246 Can it be that the Piltdown jaw does not belong with the skull? **1953** WEINER & OAKLEY in *Bull. Brit. Mus.* (*Nat. Hist.*), *Geol.* II. III. 145 The iron and chromate staining of the Piltdown jaw seems to us to be explicable only as a necessary part of the deliberate matching of the jaw of a modern ape with the mineralized cranial fragments. **1955** *Bull. Brit. Mus.* (*Nat. Hist.*), *Geol.* III. VI. 228 We are now in a position to give an account of the full extent of the Piltdown hoax.. Not one of the Piltdown finds genuinely came from Piltdown. **1955** J. S. WEINER *Piltdown Forgery* 204 The end of Piltdown man is the end of the most troubled chapter in human palaeontology. **1956** *Proc. R. Inst. Gt. Brit.* XXXVI. 150 The Piltdown forgery was the greatest archaeological hoax of its kind ever perpetrated. **1957** T. STEELE in *Time* 30 Dec. 48/1 Rock with caveman Roll with caveman.. Piltdown poppa sings this song Archaeologist done me wrong The British Museum's got my head Most unfortunate 'cause I ain't dead. **1970** R. LOWELL *Notebk.* 98 The Piltdown Man, first carnivore to laugh. **1973** *Listener* 10 May 605/3 Man..was not put together from the cranium of one primate and the jaw of another—that misconception..only makes a fake like the Piltdown skull.

2. *transf.* and *fig.*

1956 A. WILSON *Anglo-Saxon Att.* I. i. 27 Alas, we historians have so little scandal. We are not palaeontologists to display our Piltdowns. **1961** *Times* 9 Nov. 17/1 We must always be beholden to Evans over whom suspicions of a Piltdown sort hang, darkened now by Professor Palmer's discoveries in the Ashmolean. **1971** N. FLEMING *Hash* i. 12 So there is a brain underneath that thatch-covered Piltdown skull of yours. **1976** *Spectator* 2 Oct. 7/3 Ford..is waiting to be shot full of holes, not only because of his Piltdown Man performance as a congressman, but as the head of a government which is clearly out of administrative control.

So **Pi·ltdowner** = **Piltdown man* (lit. and fig.).

1954 A. HUXLEY in *Encounter* Feb. 11/1 In the tiny Natural History Museum at Idaho Falls, we found ourselves talking to two people from a far remote past.. These were Piltdowners whose reaction to the stuffed grizzly was a remark about sizzling steaks of bear-meat. **1961** C. WILLOCK *Death in Covert* i. 6 A big-boned, shambling man..with the stance of a Piltdowner. **1978** 'J. GASH' *Gold from Gemini* v. 37 He really talks like this, the Piltdowner. No wonder he's thick.

pilule. Add: (Earlier fig. and later lit. examples.) Also (pl.) as an exclamation of outrage or exasperation (*rare*).

1889 E. DOWSON *Let.* c. 10 May (1967) 77 Pilules! What in Heaven's name do they mean? **1890** *Ibid.* 12 Jan. 131 Excuse these pilules—but I warned you that I had absolutely nothing to say. **1907** [see *DROSERA]. **1960** L. P. HARTLEY *Facial Justice* xxx. 250 At the thought of 'then' her throat contracted and would hardly let the pilule pass.

pilus (pəi·lŏs). *Bacteriol.* Pl. **pili.** [L. *pilus* hair.] Any of the several types of filamentous appendages, other than flagella, that are facultatively produced by some bacterial cells.

1959 C. C. BRINTON in *Nature* 21 Mar. 782/2 Pili have been called by several different names: 'fine threads', 'bristles', 'fimbriæ', and 'filaments'. It is felt that the word 'pilus' is the most descriptive term, since the pili usually cover most of the bacterial surface and are continually growing out in a manner quite analogous to hair or fur. **1969** A. M. CAMPBELL *Episomes* iii. 36 Of the various types of pili formed by enteric bacteria, F-pili are distinguishable by the specific adsorption of male-specific bacteriophages to their surfaces. **1975** *Ann. Rev. Microbiol.* XXIX. 104 Once mating pairs were formed, phage f1 failed to interfere with the conjugation event, suggesting the involvement of the pilus..in the transfer of bacterial DNA. **1976** P. COLLARD *Devel. Microbiol.* viii. 108 A number of pilus-specific phages have been discovered.

pily, *a.*[2] Add: esp., in reference to the coat of certain dogs, containing a mixture of short, soft hairs and longer, harder ones. (Later examples.)

1922 R. LEIGHTON *Compl. Bk. Dog* p. xiv, Pily.—A peculiar quality of coat consisting of two kinds of hair, the one soft and woolly, the other long and wiry. **1942** [see *FEATHER *sb.* 11 b]. **1963** S. M. LAMPSON *Country Life Bk. Dogs* 123/2 The coat [of the Dandie Dinmont terrier]..is a mixture of hardish and soft hair, which gives it a pily feeling.

Pima (pī·mă). Also 9 **Pimo.** ['Said to be from a native word meaning "no" incorrectly understood and applied by missionaries. The term prob. was brought into American use from Spanish.' (*D.A.*)] **1.** A North American Indian people living chiefly along the Gila and Salt rivers in Arizona; a member of this people. Also, the Uto-Aztecan language of the Pima and Papago, especially the dialect of the Pima. Also *attrib.* See also *PAPAGO *sb.* and *a.*

[**1775** P. FONT *Diary* 29 Oct. (1913) 16 Muy de mañana se despacharon unos Yndios, â dar aviso de nuestra venida â los Pimas del rio Gila.] **1850** *California Courier* (San Francisco) 3 July 2/3 From the Pecos river in Texas to the Pimos villages on the Gila, roving bands of Apaches are hovering around the emigrants, stealing their animals. **1864** *Harper's Mag.* Dec. 23/2 It was gratifying..to know that the Pimos were rapidly becoming a civilized people. **1884, 1912** [see *HOHOKAM *sb.* and *a.*]. **1918** A. A. BRILL tr. *Freud's Totem & Taboo* (1919) ii. 68 After a Pima Indian had killed an Apache he had to submit himself to severe ceremonies of purification and expiation. **1932** W. L. GRAFF *Lang.* 430 The Uto-Aztec group comprises the three branches of Shoshonean, Pima-Sonoran, and Nahuatl. **1959** C. OGBURN *Marauders* vi. 189 Herman Manuel was a swarthy, squat Pima Indian from Arizona. **1960** C. WINICK *Dict. Anthropol.* 414/2 *Pima-Papago*, a general term used to describe the art of the south-west Indians of the United States. It includes the techniques of several crafts. **1962** D. H. HYMES in J. A. Fishman *Readings Sociol. of Lang.* (1968) 118 The functional load of /p/ in a community cannot be analyzed apart from the nature and use of various channels, as when among the Pima the functional load of /p/ differs between singing and recitation. **1964** S. M. LAMB in *Univ. Calif. Publ. Linguistics* XXXIV. 110 The Papagos speak Pima. **1965** *Canad. Jrnl. Linguistics* X. 141 Daughter languages of the Uto-Aztecan family..(Hopi, Pima-Papago, [etc.]). **1974** *Encycl. Brit. Micropædia* VII. 1009/3 *Piman languages*, Uto-Aztecan language group.., including Papago, Pima, [etc.]. **1979** *Tucson Mag.* Apr. 26/1 Ask a Pima or a Papago Indian—these are people who have been here for hundreds of years.

2. [f. *Pima* County, S. Arizona.] In full *Pima cotton.* A fine quality cotton developed from Egyptian cotton. Also *attrib.*

1936 *Sears Catal.* (ed. 173) 469 Pima is the finest of all American cotton. **1953** *New Biol.* XIV. 59 In Arizona a local selection of Egyptian origin, known as Pima, proved to be long but relatively weak. **1962** A. HUXLEY *Island* ix. 134 A Whisper-Pink Bra in Dacron and Pima Cotton. **1965** J. M. CAIN *Magician's Wife* (1966) xii. 86 She met him downstairs..in dark blue pima suit. **1976** *National Observer* (U.S.) 23 Oct. 9/6 (Advt.), Nothing compares to our handsome, pure pima cotton broadcloth plain collar shirts.

Piman (pī·măn), *a.* and *sb.* [f. prec. + -AN.] **A.** *adj.* Of or pertaining to the Pima and Papago Indians or their language. Also, of or pertaining to any of several ethnic and linguistic groupings of Indians of varying extent, comprising the Pimas, the Papagos, and certain other related peoples. **B.** *sb.* **a.** A Pima or Papago Indian; *pl.* the Pima and Papago Indians considered as a single ethnic and linguistic group. **b.** The Uto-Aztecan language of the Pima and Papago; also called *Papago, Pima, Pima-Papago,* and *Papago-Pima.* Also used of any of several wider groupings (see the adj.).

1891 J. W. POWELL in *7th Ann. Rep. U.S. Bureau Amer. Ethnol. 1885–86* 98 (*heading*) Piman family. **1933** L. BLOOMFIELD *Language* iv. 72 The Piman family (east of the Gulf of California). **1936** B. L. WHORF in *Ess. in Anthropol. presented to A. L. Kroeber* 198 Piman,..one of the groups most unlike the groups with which we began the classification. **1942** CASTETTER & BELL *Pima & Papago Indian Agric.* 1 The Pimans, a name applied to the whole group of Pima-Papago in both Mexico and the United States, anciently extended in irregular distribution from southern Sonora to the Gila River. **1950** J. H. STEWARD *Handbk. S. Amer. Indians* VI. 501 Its major use has been by the *Cáhita* and *Piman* tribes and their neighbors, that is, in the area adjacent to the upper Gulf of California. **1965** *Canad. Jrnl. Linguistics* X. 79 He also includes Nahuatl and Sonoran (Piman). **1969** K. L. HALE in D. & L. Saxton *Dict. Papago & Pima* Introd., The Piman languages, of which Papago-Pima is the northernmost, are of considerable interest for the fact that they constitute a close-knit, well defined subfamily within Uto-Aztecan. **1973** B. L. FONTANA in —— *Legends & Lore Papago & Pima Indians* p. xi, This volume of Papago and Pima literature makes available to readers of both Piman and English an important collection of heretofore widely scattered materials, much of it provided by Piman spokesmen many years ago. **1975** D. M. BAHR *Pima & Papago Ritual Oratory* 1 The hero of Piman (Pima-Papago) ritual oratory is a medicine man. [*Note*] The Pima and Papagos today are separate tribes. This study includes texts from each and considers ideas they have in common. I use the word 'Piman' to represent this common culture. *Ibid.*, Oratory.. must have afforded the Pimans a means of harmonizing these various activities. *Ibid.* 3 A second group interested in this poetry is of course the native speakers of Piman, Pima and Papago Indians of southern Arizona.

pimelea (pimī·liă). Also (erron.) **-ia.** [mod.L. (D. Solander in J. Gaertner *De Fructibus et Seminibus Plantarum* (1788) I. 186), f. Gr. πιμελή fat, in allusion to the oily seeds.] An evergreen shrub of the genus so called, belonging to the family Thymelaeaceæ, native to Australasia, and bearing small terminal clusters of white, pink, or yellow flowers.

[**1793** J. E. SMITH *Specimen Bot. New Holland* 32 Gaertner..adopted the name of *Pimelea* from the manuscripts of Dr. Solander.] **1810** W. AITON *Hortus Kewensis* (ed. 2) I. 25 Flax-leaved Pimelea. Nat[ive] of New South Wales. **1842** W. COLENSO *Let.* 1 Sept. in *Lond. Jrnl. Bot.* (1844) III. 8, I found a handsome *Pimelea* in flower, a shrub of 2–3 feet in height. **1885** T. BAINES *Greenhouse & Stove Plants* 281/1 All the kinds of Pimelea strike readily from cuttings made of the points of the young shoots. **1951** *Dict. Gardening* (R. Hort. Soc.) III. 1572/1 Pimeleas are compact, free-growing plants needing greenhouse conditions. **1966** H. E. & J. BAWDEN *Making Shrub Garden* 216 Some of the pimelias are greenhouse shrubs.. There are other pimelias which grow high up in the mountains.

pimento. Add: **2.** For *Eugenia Pimenta* substitute *Pimenta dioica.* (Later examples.)

1889 G. S. BOULGER *Uses of Plants* i. 66 Allspice, or Pimento, is the dry berry of *Pimenta officinalis* Lindl... a West Indian evergreen-tree. **1969** *Oxf. Bk. Food Plants* 132/2 Allspice (*Pimenta dioica*) is a small tropical tree whose unripe dried berries provide the spice called allspice. .. It is also known as 'pimenta' and 'pimento'.

b. = *PIMIENTO, *PAPRIKA 2.

1918 A. QUILLER-COUCH *Foe-Farrell* 94 What do you say now..to a pig's trotter farced with pimento. **1943** D. WELCH *Maiden Voy.* xvi. 132 The soup..was delicious; pieces of pimento swam about in it like goldfish. **1950** E. DAVID *Bk. Mediterranean Food* 132 Mixed red, green, and yellow pimentos, cooked a few minutes in boiling water, then peeled and sautéd in butter. **1978** *Nagel's Encyl.-Guide: China* 375 *Hu nan* and *Hu bei* are both known for chicken and pimento (*la zi ji*), soy-bean omelettes (*dou pi*) and bread with stuffing.

c. = **pimento red.*

1976 *Northumberland Gaz.* 26 Nov. 16 (Advt.), Triumph Dolomite. Pimento, tan fabric trim. **1977** *Time* 21 Feb. 43/1 A pimento handkerchief-style dress.

3. For the Latin names applied to the tree, substitute *Pimenta dioica.* (Later examples.)

1950 P. BOTTOME *Under Skin* x. 95 You had better stop here under this pimento. *Ibid.* xvi. 137 Pimento trees with their greenish bark and dark glossy leaves. **1958** D. P. STORER *Familiar Trees & Cultivated Plants of Jamaica* 69 The Pimento grows to about 30 ft. in height.

4. pimento berry = sense 2 a; **pimento cheese,** soft cheese flavoured with chopped sweet peppers; **pimento dram,** a Jamaican liqueur made with pimento berries; **pimento red,** an orange-red colour; also *attrib.* or as *adj.*

1893 C. SULLIVAN *Jamaica Cookery Bk.* 104 Pimento Dram... Put four quarts of ripe pimento berries into a jar, and boil till the berries burst... Add two bottles of brandy or good old rum... Then add a thick syrup of loaf sugar. **1907** *Daily Consular & Trade Rep.* (U.S. State Dept.) 5 Oct. 11 Ripe pimento berries are used to make pimento dram, a native drink. **1970** *Nature* 8 Aug. 556/2 Pimento berries are gathered while still green. **1916** *Daily Colonist* (Victoria, B.C.) 1 July 6/5 (Advt.), Cream or Pimento Cheese, each 10¢. **1967** MRS. L. B. JOHNSON *White House Diary* 23 Apr. (1970) 510, I had had a platter of sandwiches put in the refrigerator—roast beef and pimento cheese. **1893, 1907** Pimento dram [see *pimento berry* above]. **1958** D. P. STORER *Familiar Trees & Cultivated Plants of Jamaica* 70 'Pimento-dram' is a delicious Jamaican liqueur made, essentially, by soaking the ripe berries in rum. **1975** *Vogue* Dec. 107 Pimento red Hurel jersey. **1979** U. CURTISS *Menace Within* ix. 90 An abstract painting in pink and pimento red.

pi-meson (pəi:mī·zǫn, -me·zǫn). *Nuclear Physics.* Also **pi meson, pimeson.** [f. PI *sb.* + *MESON[3].] The original name for the *PION. (Freq. written *π-meson.*)

[**1947** LATTES, OCCHIALINI, & POWELL in *Nature* 4 Oct. 455/1 It is convenient to refer to this process..as the *μ*-decay. We represent the primary mesons by the symbol *π*, and the secondary by *μ*.] *Ibid.* 456/1 The restricted range of the *π*-mesons in the emulsion. **1950** D. HALLIDAY *Introd. Nucl. Physics* xii. 455 When negative pi-mesons are absorbed in matter,.. there is a major nuclear disruption. **1953** *Jrnl. Brit. Interplanetary Soc.* XII. 203 The neutral pi-meson dissociates almost immediately into two high energy gamma rays (photons), which initiate the photon-electron cascades that are frequently observed in cosmic ray processes. **1968** *Times* 19 Jan. 13/8 The object..is to see how frequently an electron and a positive electron (or positron) would be converted..into the radio-actively unstable particles of matter called pimesons (or pions). **1972** *Daily Colonist* (Victoria, B.C.) 3 Mar. 16/8 The new technique involves a radioactive beam of sub-atomic particles called pimesons. **1978** *Sci. Amer.* Mar. 57/1 The mass of the muon (106 MeV) is quite close to the mass of the pi meson, or pion (140 MeV).

Hence **pi-me·sic, -meso·nic** *adjs.* = *PIONIC *a.*

1952 *Physical Rev.* LXXXVIII. 134/1 We have found direct evidence for *π*-mesic atom formation with the nuclei of carbon, oxygen, and beryllium. **1953** *Ibid.* XCII. 789/2 Experimental studies of *π*-mesonic x-rays in light elements have been made. **1954** *Ibid.* XCVI. 774 (*heading*) Energy level displacements in pi-mesonic atoms. **1970** LOCK & MEASDAY *Intermediate Energy Nucl. Physics* xi. 276 Because the mass of the π^- (139·6 MeV) is greater than that of the μ^- (105·7 MeV), the energies of the pi-mesic x-rays are about 30% higher than those of the equivalent mu-mesic x-rays.

pimiento (pimie·nto). Also (*rare*) **pimienta.** [Sp.] = *PAPRIKA 2.

1845 [see *GAZPACHO]. **1846** R. FORD *Gatherings from Spain* xi. 131 Add a bit of bacon, onions, garlic, salt, pepper, *pimientos*, a bunch of thyme. **1901** *Daily Colonist* (Victoria, B.C.) 15 Oct. 6/6 (Advt.), Glass Jars Olives (with Pimientos). **1937** A. F. HILL *Econ. Bot.* xx. 476 The paprikas are European varieties [of sweet pepper] with large mild fruits. Spanish paprika..is better known as pimiento. **1960, 1969** [see *PAPRIKA 2]. **1979** L. KALLEN *Introducing C.B. Greenfield* xii. 144 My grocery bag of chicken, shrimp, olives, pimentos.

b. = *PIMENTO 2 c.

1972 J. POTTS *Trouble-Maker* iii. 18 Her living-room—avocado and chocolate brown, pimiento accents.

2. *attrib.* **pimiento cheese** = *pimento cheese* s.v. *PIMENTO 4; **pimiento(-stuffed) olive**, an olive with its stone replaced by a piece of red sweet pepper.

1922 *Hotel World* 15 Apr. 15/1 American or Pimiento cheese. **1972** *Harrods Christmas Catal.* 60/2 Jar Harrods Pimiento Olives. **1974** *Ibid.* 40/1 Jar Pimiento Stuffed Olives.

piminy (pi·mini). *nonce-wd.* [?Shortened f. MIMINY-PIMINY *a.* and *sb.*, NIMINY-PIMINY *a.*] ? Something expressive of affectation.

1819 KEATS *Let.* 22 Sept. (1958) II. 175 Poor thing she little thinks how she is..making her nose quite a piminy.

Pimm's (pimz). Also **Pimms**, (*erron.*) **Pim.** [Proprietary term, f. the name of the proprietor of the restaurant where these drinks were created.] Used to designate any of four spirit-based mixed drinks ('cups'), taken neat or used as a basis for long drinks; also, a drink of one of these. Also *ellipt.*

Where no number is specified, the reference is usually understood to be to *Pimm's Number One Cup*, which is gin-based.

[**1888** *Trade Marks Jrnl.* 20 June 817 Pimms. Poultry. London. Pimms & Co.,..Poultry, London; restaurant proprietors... Wines and spirits, excepting brandy.] **1912** *Ibid.* 27 Nov. 1782 Pimm's No. 1 Cup... An alcoholic beverage. H. D. Davies & Co., Limited,..London,.. wine merchants. **1931** R. H. HEATON *Perfect Hostess* 56 Pim Cup. One wineglass of No. 1 Pim cup mixture [etc.]. **1939** L. MACNEICE *Autumn Jrnl.* v. 22 And this, we say, is on me; Something out of the usual, a Pimm's Number One. **1957** J. BRAINE *Room at Top* xxv. 202 The de-luxe bar and the iced Pimm's. **1960** *20th Cent.* July 73 Exams are over for ever, Pimm's is flowing. **1966** 'K. NICHOLSON' *Hook, Line & Sinker* v. 66 Mrs. Fairchild created a diversion by mixing everyone a Pimms. **1967** A. LICHINE *Encycl. Wines* 404/1 There are four Pimm's Cups, and it is said that they were originated by a bartender at Pimm's Restaurant in London and so delighted the customers that the staff was continually being asked to put some up for people to take home. As a result, they begun to be made commercially. **1972** F. WARNER *Lying Figures* I. 6 Barman! Make it a double Pimms!

Pimo, var. *PIMA.

pimozide (pi·mozəid). *Pharm.* [f. PI(PERIDINE + elements in *benzimidazolin*, part of the systematic name of the compound (see IMIDE and AZO-).] A derivative of piperidine that is a colourless powder used as a tranquillizer in the treatment of schizophrenia and anxiety states.

1968 *Arzneimittel-Forschung* XVIII. 261 (*heading*) Pimozide, a chemically novel, highly potent and orally long-acting neuroleptic drug. **1976** SMYTHIES & CORBETT *Psychiatry* iii. 27 Other effective anti-psychotics..include the butyrophenones and pimozide. **1977** *Lancet* 21 May 1105/1, I have treated a boy of 17..for anorexia nervosa... He received pimozide 4 mg three times a day for a month.

pimp, *sb.*[1] Add: **a.** (Further examples.)

1932 *Evening Sun* (Baltimore) 9 Dec. 31/5 *Pimp*, man who is supported by women. **1961** J. DOS PASSOS *Midcentury* I. vii. 96 I'd thought him a pimp or procurer but he didn't seem to be. **1968–70** *Current Slang* (Univ. S. Dakota) III–IV. 92 *Pimp*, one who solicits women and girls to sell themselves and turn all the money over to him. He, in turn, gives them their salary. **1972** T. KOCHMAN *Rappin' & Stylin' Out* 243 The 'pimp'..a person of considerable status in the street hierarchy.. has acquired a stable of girls to hustle for him and give him money. **1976** *Toronto Star* 21 Aug. B1/2 It's getting busier partly because so many black American hookers and their pimps come and check into a hotel here for the weekend and compete for our territory.

b. (Later examples.)

1962 S. E. FINER *Man on Horseback* xii. 241 Mill recognized the 'necessity' of some despotic régimes; but he saw them..as a *pis aller*. He did not, like today's pimps of tyranny, pretend that the despotism was superior to the system of representative government. **1968** *Listener* 22 Aug. 252/1 Of course, it's cheaper to take on men trained in Fleet Street than to train them yourself, but the BBC should be the custodian of, not the pimp for, popular forms.

b*. In various other uses: (*a*) *Austral.* and *N.Z. slang*, an informer, a tell-tale; (*b*) *Welsh dial.*, one who spies on lovers, a peeping Tom; (*c*) *U.S. slang*, a male prostitute.

a **1885** *Penguin Bk. Austral. Ballads* (1964) 74 Bluecoat imps, Who were laid on to where he slept, By informing peeler's pimps. **1938** X. HERBERT *Capricornia* 567 'I'm not a pimp.' 'What you mean pimp?' 'I'm not a police-informer.' **1940** DYLAN THOMAS *Portrait of Artist as Young Dog* 126, I lay like a pimp in a bush by Tom's side and squinted through to see him round his hands on Norma's breast. **1942** G. CASEY *It's Harder for Girls* 51 'I just say I'm not a pimp,' Brownie insisted, beginning to blubber. **1942** Z. N. HURSTON in A. Dundes *Mother Wit* (1973) 223 In Harlemese, *pimp* has a different meaning than its ordinary definition as a procurer for immoral purposes. The Harlem pimp is a man whose amatory talents are for sale to any woman who will support him... He is actually a male prostitute. **1969** D. NILAND *Dead Men Running* 290 'There's a pimp at work.'..'The same pimp is it, that potted Shannessy and Halloran?' **1974** *Age* (Melbourne) 12 Oct. 12/1 You fat pimp! The standard response to 'I'm going to tell on you'.

pimp, *v.* Add: **1.** (Later examples.)

1975 *New Yorker* 26 May 18/2 His father (Jack Warden) pimps to add to his income as a taxi-driver. **1976** *Ibid.* 1 Mar. 79/1, I also especially enjoyed Roscoe Onman as Pretty Eddie, the 'happy dust' addict who pimps for his girl.

c. *to pimp on*: to scrounge off; to take advantage of. *U.S. slang.*

1942 Z. N. HURSTON in A. Dundes *Mother Wit* (1973) 226/1 'You got any money?' the girl asked... 'Nobody ain't pimping on me. You dig me?'

3. *intr.* To tell tales; to inform *on* someone. *Austral.* and *N.Z. slang.*

1941 BAKER *Dict. Austral. Slang* 54 *Pimp*,.. to inform on. **1945** G. CASEY *Downhill is Easier* 109 This dago bastard pimped on him to Hayes, an' lost him his job. **1949** *Landfall* Mar. 30 He would grope out, head down, afraid to meet someone who would pimp on him. **1957** J. WATEN *Shares in Murder* 155 You made up to me so you could get me to pimp on Charlie for you. **1960** N. HILLIARD *Maori Girl* 229 She's bound to pimp and make trouble.

4. *intr.* To spy on lovers. *Welsh dial.*

1976 R. LEWIS *Witness my Death* i. 13 Dai—Pimping again then, is it?

pimpernel. Add: **3.*** (Chiefly with capital initial.) [The name given to Sir Percy Blakeney, hero of Baroness Orczy's novel *The Scarlet Pimpernel* (1905), who rescues victims of the Terror and smuggles them out of France, characterized (ch. xii) as 'that demmed, elusive Pimpernel'.] **a.** Something elusive or much sought after. **b.** Someone whose exploits are comparable to those of 'The Scarlet Pimpernel'. See also *Scarlet Pimpernel* s.v. *SCARLET *a.* 4 a.

1955 *Times* 10 May 14/1 The elusive pimpernel, the Liberal vote, is being eagerly sought by the two main parties in the Peterborough division. **1961** *House & Garden* Oct. 112/3 Highlanders soon became a band of Pimpernels smuggling their aristocratic whiskies to the Lowlands. **1962** *Guardian* 9 Aug. 7/6 The man who has become known as the 'Black Pimpernel of South Africa'. **1963** *Times Lit. Suppl.* 18 Jan. 40/5 In the hope of being able to function like a modern-day Pimpernel. **1974** 'D. CRAIG' *Dead Liberty* xvii. 81 Hans Lenzlinger, the greatest Pimpernel between East and West ever known.

pimping, *vbl. sb.*[1] (s.v. PIMP *v.*). (Later examples.)

1957 C. MACINNES *City of Spades* II. ix. 165 Ite..put on his tailored duffel coat, and said, 'Now I must get out in the cold and do me pimpin'.'... A little coloured lady for you?' **1967** *Trans-Action* Apr. 8/2 The degree of organization in hustling depends frequently on the kind of hustling. Regular pimping and pushing require many trusted contacts and organization.

pimping, *vbl. sb.*[2] *local.* [f. PIMP *sb.*[2] + -ING[1].] The preparation of bundles of firewood. (In quot. comb.)

1930 V. SACKVILLE-WEST *Edwardians* vi. 251 He looked into the pimping-shed, where old Turnour was chopping faggots.

pimpish (pi·mpiʃ), *a.* [f. PIMP *sb.*[1] + -ISH[1].] Resembling or characteristic of a pimp.

1935 W. EMPSON *Some Versions of Pastoral* 47 The comic characters' experimental wish to satisfy all parties ..has a certain pimpish complacence. **1971** W. BURROUGHS *Wild Boys* 11 Six pimpish young men burst through the door in a reek of brilliantine. **1976** *Daily Tel.* 19 Aug. 11/7 A horde of football fans attempt to lure into their bedrooms a pair of tarts by arrangement with the pimpish day porter.

pimple, *v.* Delete 'Now *rare*' and add: **a.** Also, to cover as with pimples. (Later examples.)

1909 'O. HENRY' *Roads of Destiny* xix. 311 The levee where his freight-car stood was pimpled with dark bulks of merchandise. **1940** L. MACNEICE *Last Ditch* 14 The rain of London pimples The ebony street with white. **1961** *Daily Tel.* 29 Aug. 18/4 Caravans and tents pimpling remote villages and hillsides are causing concern to planning authorities. **1972** K. BONFIGLIOLI *Don't point that Thing at Me* xix. 167 Lurid tents and tasteful pastel caravans pimple the landscape. **1974** P. DICKINSON *Poison Oracle* iv. 98 The dunes along the marsh were pimpled with their tents.

b. Also *transf.*, to develop small bulges.

1940, 1962 [implied in *PIMPLING *vbl. sb.* 2]. **1970** *Motoring Which?* July 93/2 On all three cars, the rear light surrounds were pimpling and the bumpers had begun rusting.

pimpling, *vbl. sb.* (in Dict. s.v. PIMPLE *v.*). Add: **2.** The presence of small bulges on the surface of metal.

1940 J. D. JEVONS *Metall. Deep Drawing & Pressing* viii. 293 A troublesome defect, which is sometimes encountered, particularly when the carbon content is rather high, is that known in the shops as 'pimpling'. **1962** J. C. WRIGHT *Metall. in Nucl. Power Technol.* vi. 106 Examples of workable solutions to pimpling are the use of an aluminium-silicon brazed bond which does not spread significantly with time in the neighbourhood of 300°C, and the provision of anodic coating on the inside of the aluminium tubing.

pimplous (pi·mpləs), *a. rare.* [f. PIMPLE *sb.* + -OUS.] Characterized by pimples; pimply.

1906 W. J. LOCKE *Beloved Vagabond* xii. 152 Cooling medicaments wherewith to mitigate a certain pimplous condition of cheek.

pimply, *a.* Add: Also *fig.*

1958 *Spectator* 22 Aug. 260/1 The man-eating British lion By a pimply age brought down. **1973** M. AMIS *Rachel Papers* 17 It was a month I always think of with a certain pimply lyricism.

pimpmobile (pi·mpˌmobīl). *U.S. slang.* [f. PIMP *sb.*[1] + *AUTO)MOBILE *sb.*] A large, flashy car used by a pimp.

1973 *Washington Post* 21 Apr. D7/1 Features of the luxury pimpmobile—glittering striping, dual spares, elaborate scrollwork and amber sunroofs—are showing up, somewhat toned-down, in stylized automobiles, according to car customizers. **1975** *Daily Mail* 13 Sept. 2/5 The pimpmobiles—the long, long Cadillacs with a Rolls front—no longer cruise everywhere. They are finding it less profitable to keep girls here. **1977** *Rolling Stone* 24 Mar. 71/1 'Norman', the story of a gambler who rides around in a Rambler (a secondhand pimpmobile?), is introduced by a melancholy horn riff with the drummer loping along like a dragging muffler, while Romeo's voice is high and airy.

pin, *sb.*[1] Add: **I. 1. m.** One of the metal projections of a plug, which make the electrical connection when it is inserted into a socket.

1888 [see *PLUG *sb.* 1 c]. **1902** W. C. CLINTON *Electric Wiring* iv. 85 The flexible..terminates in two split pins, which are a spring fit into two tubular sockets. **1945** F. WISEMAN *Penguin Handyman* i. 19 One end is connected to the earth pin in the three-pin plug, whilst the other end is connected to the metal housing or frame of the fire. **1963** *House & Garden* Feb. 8/3 Replace those old-fashioned two-pin plugs with a three-pin, and check the fuse-box. **1972** *Electricity Supply & Safety* (Consumers' Assoc.) 49 You can connect an old type of plug with round pins to a rectangular hole socket with the right adaptor.

n. A metal peg which prevents a hand-grenade from exploding by holding down the activating lever.

1917 C. R. GIBSON *War Inventions* vi. 95 Until the soldier was ready to throw the bomb the little lever was held down by a metal pin. When the soldier withdrew this pin, the lever was still held down by the hand with which he threw the bomb, and not until it left his hand did the fuse begin to burn. **1920** A. R. BOND *Inventions of Gt. War* ii. 29 The Mills hand-grenade..was provided with a lever which was normally strapped down and held by means of a safety-pin. **1952** G. E. THORNTON *Handbk. Weapon Training* ix. 101 With a hand grenade these [techniques] include..the method of removing the safety pin or cap. **1972** 'H. CALVIN' *Take Two Popes* xv. 182 Soldiers..ready to pull out grenade pins with their teeth. **1977** C. FORBES *Avalanche Express* viii. 85 The grenade he would have withdrawn the pin from..if.. faced with imminent arrest.

o. A coupling-pin. Used esp. in phr. *to pull the pin*: to uncouple; also *fig.* (see quots.). *N. Amer. slang.*

1927 *Amer. Speech* II. 391/2 To *bunch*, or to *drag it*, means to quit. To *pull the pin* has the same meaning. This is a railroad term and means to uncouple. **1947** R. O. BOYER *Dark Ship* II. xvii. 227 The teamsters had pulled the pin too early. The strike is being lost. **1955** *Amer. Speech* XXX. 92 *Pull the pin*, to release the pin that connects a semitrailer to a fifth wheel. **1968** *Ibid.* XLIII. 289 *Pull the pin*, to resign, quit, or be fired from a job: 'They pulled the pin on him.' Relates to the switching function in the days of the link-and-pin coupler (long since replaced by the safer automatic coupler) by which a car was uncoupled and released. **1972** J. WAMBAUGH *Blue Knight* (1973) x. 161 An old man that should've pulled the pin years ago. Now he'd been here too long. He couldn't leave or he'd die. **1977** —— *Black Marble* (1978) ix. 168 Twenty-six years on the job when he pulled the pin and went to Arizona.

p. A support of an arch.

1928 *Daily Tel.* 7 Feb. 14/1 The arch is a two 'pin' crescent structure, and the distance from 'pin' to 'pin'.. is 531 ft.

II. 3. Also (*U.S.*), a badge indicating membership of a university or college fraternity, or similar society, etc.

1871 L. H. BAGG *4 Years at Yale* 144 Its original badge was a rectangular gold plate, about the size and shape of the present Beta Xi pin. **1893** W. K. POST *Harvard Stories* 216 Freddy..asked me one day why Sheffield wore that funny little pin all the time. **1910** J. HART *Vigilante Girl* 19 My dear fellow, you may cast aside your Eastern frigidity—in fact, I will call it your Cambridge frigidity, for I see you wear a Harvard pin. **1928** *Amer. Speech* III. 220 *Put out one's pin*, v. phr., to become engaged, to promise marriage. 'Scoop didn't have his pin on Dorothy very long, did he?' **1943** *Ibid.* XVIII. 154/2 *Plant a pin*, the process by which a fraternity man signifies his willingness to wait in the hall for the same girl every time. It consists of presenting her with his pin to wear. **1974** *Marlboro Herald-Advocate* (Bennettsville, S. Carolina) 18 Apr. 7/1 Rupert Kiker, president presented John L. Hargrave with a 20 year membership pin in the Lions International. Roy Easterling, Sr., was presented a 15 year pin. **1977** C. McFadden *Serial* (1978) xviii. 43/2 He still wear his Key Club pin?

b. *two pins* (earlier and later examples). Also, *a row of pins* (in quot. 1896 as a type of similarity).

1891 [see For *prep.* 9]. **1896** Kipling *Seven Seas* 193 When you get to a man in the case, They're like as a row of pins—For the Colonel's Lady an' Judy O'Grady Are sisters under their skins! **1914** W. W. Jacobs *Night Watches* i. 25 'For two pins—' he began. 'For two pins I'll go back 'ome and stay there,' said Mr. Flynn. **1918** A. G. Gardiner *Leaves in Wind* 162 John Burns..does not care two pins who sees him or talks about him. **1920** W. J. Locke *House of Baltazar* i. 16 It doesn't seem to amount to a row of pins compared with my meeting you. **1947** [see *Hide *sb.*¹ 2 c]. **1973** J. Porter *It's Murder with Dover* vii. 64 Her unsupported word isn't worth a row of pins. **1979** *Country Life* 16 Aug. 489/2 This Lord Hertford cared not two pins for society... His single passion was collecting.

d. *pins and needles* (earlier example). *on pins and needles* (earlier and later examples).

1810 J. Poole *Hamlet Travestie* 8 Would it were supper-time... Till then I'm sitting upon pins and needles. **1813** W. Dunlap *Mem. G. F. Cooke* II. xxx. 265 As it was—it was bad enough—my voice—haw!—there are pins and needles—I must send for a physician. **1858** Queen Victoria *Let.* 8 Mar. in R. Fulford *Dearest Child* (1964) 72 All you say..reminds me of what I was always used to as a child. Always on pins and needles, with the whole family hardly on speaking terms. **1944** W. S. Maugham *Razor's Edge* iii. 112 The bishop had been a cavalry officer..and his austere, cadaverous vicar general was always on pins and needles lest he should say something scandalous. **1951** E. Paul *Springtime in Paris* xv. 283 Dr. Thiouville was on pins and needles. **1979** *Country Life* 16 Aug. 489/4 The French were waiting on pins and needles to hear that the great [Wallace] collection would be theirs.

e. *as neat as a* (*new*) *pin.*

1787 *Columbian Mag.* I. 636 [He was] neat as a new pin. **1801** J. Wolcot *Wks.* (1812) V. 35 How neat was Ellen in her dress! As neat as a new pin! **1849** Thackeray *Pendennis* I. xiii. 118 Major Pendennis, whom Miss Costigan declared to be a proper gentleman entirely,.. and as neat as a pin. **1933** L. A. G. Strong *Sea Wall* 245 Sheehan's pride was to have his cottage as neat as a new pin. **1961** *Dog World* Apr. 30 In the morning we leave the room looking as neat as a pin!

f. *to be able to hear a pin drop* (or *fall*), etc.: used to suggest absolute silence or stillness.

[**1775** F. Burney *Diary* 11 June (1907) II. 81 Had a *pin* fallen, I suppose we should have taken it at least for a *thunder-clap*.] **1814** M. B. Smith *Let.* Aug. in G. Hunt *40 Yrs. Washington Society* (1906) 113 It was so still you might have heard a pin drop on the pavement. **1824** S. Ferrier *Inheritance* ii. xiv. 156 You might have heard a pin drop in the house while that was going on. **1831** Macaulay *Let.* 30 Mar. (1974) II. 10 You might have heard a pin drop as Duncannon read the numbers. Then again the shouts broke out. **1870** [in Dict., sense 3]. **1890** [see Drop *v.* 3]. **1914** *Maclean's Mag.* May 9/2 We could have heard a pin drop. **1934** A. Christie *Murder on Orient Express* iii. ix. 246 Every eye was fixed upon him. In the stillness you could have heard a pin drop. **1959** I. & P. Opie *Lore & Lang. Schoolch.* x. 193 'Let's 'ave a bit of shush', 'Let's hear this pin drop',..'Pipe down'. **1977** *Daily Mirror* 15 Mar. 3/3 They screamed, yelled and clapped between numbers, but while he sang you could have heard a pin drop.

g. *to stick pins into* (a person): to incite to action; to irritate or annoy.

1903 A. H. Lewis *Boss* 184 This ain't meant to stick pins into you.

h. A gramophone needle.

1914 Kipling *Lett. of Travel* (1920) 215 They slipped in pin and record.

IV. 7. (Further, including sing., examples.) Also *fig.*

1829 P. Egan *Boxiana* 2nd Ser. II. 10 With all his struggling to right himself, he could not recover the use of his pins. **1880** 'Mark Twain' *Lett. to Publishers* (1967) 125. It saved the company's life and set them high on their pins and free of debt. **1890** *Harper's Mag.* LXXX. 269/2 Glad to hear that he is on his pins yet; he might have pegged out in ten years, you know. **1917** 'H. H. Richardson' *Fortunes R. Mahony* iv. viii. 355 Give your old pin here, and let me poultice it. **1960** [see *Few *a.* 2 f]. **1971** *Petticoat* 17 July 32/1 You need to be healthy too because you're likely to find yourself standing on your two pins all day and every day. **1976** *Daily Mirror* 11 Mar. 24/2 You look a bit wobbly on your pins, pet.

8. Also, a skittle or pin knocked down, as a scoring point. (Later examples.)

1974 *Cleveland* (Ohio) *Plain Dealer* 13 Oct. 8-c/3 Anthony..missed a perfect game by a single pin in the.. finals. *Ibid.* 26 Oct. 5-d/4 A bowling ball can mean the difference of up to 20 pins in a game depending on the surface and balance the ball. **1976** *Burnham-on-Sea Gaz.* 20 Apr. 21/5 Thatchers Arms A, the North Petherton Summer Skittles League champions, lost their first home match of the new season by six pins when Clarence Hotel A came from behind on the last hand. **1976** *Bridgwater Mercury* 21 Dec. 18/2 Brent Knoll Inn put an end to the last 100 per cent record in the first division of the Burnham, Highbridge and District Ladies' Skittles League by gaining a seven-pin away win at White Hart Hotel.

VI. 18. *pin-flag, -heel* (so *-heeled* adj.), *-hook* (also fig.; earlier and later examples); *pin-sharp* adj.; **pinboard,** a panel having an array of identical sockets each connected to some of a set of wires, so that inserting a conducting pin into any of the sockets makes an electrical connection between some of the wires; **pin-bone,** (*a*) (later examples); (*b*) (see quot. 1936); **pin-boy** (see quots.); **pin-brained** *a.*, foolish, stupid; **pin-buttock** (later examples); **pin clover,** also, = *alfilaria; (later examples); **pin connexion** (examples); so **pin-connected** *a.* (cf. **pin-jointed* adj.); **pincord** = *needlecord* s.v. *Needle sb. 14; **pin-curl,** (*b*) a curl held in position during setting by a hairpin or other clip; **pin curler,** a pin or clip for securing pin-curls; **pin dot** (see quot. 1957); **pin-dropping** *a.* = *pin-drop* adj.; also as adv.; **pin-fall** (*a*) the fall of a pin; a trifling incident; (*b*) the number of pins knocked down in a tenpin bowling game; a score in tenpin bowling; **pin-fit** *v. trans.* and *intr.*, in *Sewing*, to pin into position during fitting; **pin-grass** (examples); **pin hinge,** a hinge in which the two leaves are pivoted on a pin passing through a sheath in each; **pin-hooker** *U.S.* (see quot. 1944); **pin joint** (examples); so **pin-jointed** *a.*; **pin-leg,** (*a*) a wooden leg; (*b*) a narrow, spindly leg; hence **pin-legged** *a.*; **pin lever,** used *attrib.* and *absol.* to denote a pin-pallet watch or escapement; **pin-man,** (*b*) a figure of a man appearing as composed of lines without breadth, esp. in a drawing; **pin-mark,** a circular impression on the side of a piece of type, made by part of the mould used in casting; **pin-new** *a.*, brand-new; **pin oak** (earlier and later examples); also *attrib.*; **pin pallet,** add: in an escapement, a pallet in the form of a metal pin or a semi-circular jewel (now used chiefly in cheap escapements); (earlier and later examples); **pin party** *Naut. slang* (see quot. 1946); **pin plate,** *Engin.*, a plate with a hole for the pin that is riveted to a member at the site of a pin joint; **pin-pool,** 'a game played on a billiard-table with three balls, and five small pins' (*Century Dict.* 1889), or any of various related games; **pin screen** *Cinematogr.* (see quot. 1976); also *attrib.*; **pin seal,** the treated skin of young seals; also *attrib.*; **pin-setter,** in tenpin bowling, a person who, or a machine that, rearranges fallen skittles; = **pin-boy*; hence **pin-setting** *vbl. sb.*; freq. *attrib.*; **pin-splitter** *Golfing slang*, (*a*) a crack golfer; (*b*) an accurate shot to the pin or a club which is supposed to aid such a shot; **pin-spot,** (*b*) *Theatr.* (see quots.); **pin spotter** = **pin-setter*; **pin stenter,** a stenter in which cloth is held by means of two rows of pins, one along each edge; **pin-stitch** (see quot. 1936); hence **pin-stitched** *a.*, **pin-stitching; pin-table** = *pin-ball machine* s.v. *Pin-ball 3; **pin valve** = *needle valve* s.v. *Needle *sb.* 14; **pin-worm,** substitute for def.: a parasitic nematode worm of the order Oxyuroidea; also = **tomato pinworm.*

1957 *Electronic Engin.* XXIX. 30 Problems are programmed by plugging step by step operations in columns on the pinboards, a column for each operation, and when a pin is inserted into a hole, connexions are automatically made to carry out the instruction. **1966** R. K. Richards *Electronic Digital Syst.* ix. 553 Like a plugboard, a complete pinboard assembly with its pins can be removed from a system and saved for re-use while other pinboards ..are used for the solution of other problems. **1969** P. B. Jordain *Condensed Computer Encycl.* 383 A 10 × 10 pinboard with 100 holes can connect any of 10 incoming signals (horizontal) to any of 10 outgoing paths (vertical). **1936** *Discovery* Oct. 321/1 Pins had been made by individual craftsmen using a small bone implement, on the flat surface of which was a series of inch-long grooves, deep at one end but tapering at the other. This tool served to file the pins to a point, its formation making it possible to shape several at one time from lengths of wire. Many of these 'pin-bones' still exist. **1945** *ABC of Cookery* (Ministry of Food) ix. 29 Hip or pin bone steak. **1973** R. D. Symons *Where Wagon Led* p. xiii, I learned the cowboy's names, and could speak of pinbones and stifles and croups. **1978** *Sunday Tel.* 17 Sept. 11/3 Do you know, for example, what is called Pope's eye or heuk bone in Scotland, hip bone in the Midlands or pin bone in Wales? It's what many of us call rump. **1892** A. E. Vogell *Bowling* 8 Pin boy, boy who returns the balls cast and resets the pins. **1958** *Wall St. Jrnl.* 9 Dec. 1/4 Automatic pinboys..have played a major role in the bowling boom. **1959** *Listener* 19 Mar. 501/1 The latest development is an automatic pin-boy... An ingenious electrical device will set up the pins and return the balls. **1975** *Oxf. Compan. Sports & Games* 92/1 In the earlier years of the game pin-boys were employed to re-set the pins after each frame. **1964** *Listener* 20 Feb. 313/1 A smug biologist and his pin-brained wife. **1966** B. Kimenye *Kalasanda Revisited* 31 His successor was flirting madly with some pin-brained girl. **1977** 'E. Crispin' *Glimpses of Moon* i. 11 There were several such benches in the bar-room—memorials to a centuries-extinct clientèle of pin-buttocks—but otherwise the furniture was all modern. **1913** W. C. Barnes *Western Grazing Grounds* 39 Alfileria is also known as 'heron's bill' and 'pin clover'. **1925** W. L. Jepson *Man. Flowering Plants Calif.* 592 The term filaree..is, like the names Pin Clover or Pin Grass, indifferently applied to either this species [sc. *Erodium moschatum*] or to no. 5 [sc. *E. cicutarium*]. **1878** *Min. Proc. Inst. Civil Engin.* LIV. 179 All these American bridges are 'pin connected', this style of construction being preferred by American engineers for spans exceeding 100 feet, on account of the mathematical certainty with which the strains can be calculated. **1968** E. H. & C. N. Gaylord *Struct. Engin. Handbk.* vi. 71 The AISC Specification requires that the allowable tensile stress on the net section transverse to the axis of the member be reduced 25 percent at pinholes in pin-connected plates. **1969** *Civil Engin.* (Easton, Pa.) June 45/1 Columns were pin-connected top and bottom to prevent any supplementary stress from differential settlement or rotation of the foundations. **1878** *Min. Proc. Inst. Civil Engin.* LIV. 214 There was undoubtedly a considerable difference in the use of what the Author [sc. T. C. Clarke] called pin-connections as compared with rivet-connections. **1974** *Encycl. Brit. Macropædia* III. 177/2 The first major iron-truss bridge, with pin connections, was built in the United States in 1851. **1977** *New Yorker* 8 Aug. 72/1 (Advt.), Our handsome, lightweight hobby pants in no-iron Dacron/cotton pincord, ideal for travel and leisure. **1979** A. Scholefield *Point of Honour* 142 White pincord slacks. **1931** G. A. Foan *Art & Craft of Hairdressing* 28/1 Pin-curls..may be used as side-pieces to be worn in front of the ears. **1950** E. Hemingway *Across River* xix. 152 You ought to have to sleep in a bed with a girl who has put her hair up in pin curls to be beautiful tomorrow. **1963** D. B. Hughes *Expendable Man* (1964) i. 10 'Don't you need a mirror?'..But she could wind the pin curls without it. *Ibid.* 18 Her hair done up in pin curlers under the dirty scarf. **1957** M. B. Picken *Fashion Dict.* 252/2 *Pin dot*, smallest dot used as fabric design. **1978** *N.Y. Times* 30 Mar. A4/1 (Advt.), A pin-dot tie. **1971** D. Francis *Bonecrack* i. 9 There was a long pin-dropping silence. **1973** *Advocate-News* (Barbados) 29 June 6/6 The lighting..succeeded in transforming the massive stadium through moods of harried excitement to 'pin-dropping' silence. **1977** *New Yorker* 19 Sept. 50/1 The hall was pin-dropping quiet. **1912** W. Deeping *Sincerity* vii. 56 A good lady whose troubles had been so many pinfalls in the closeted selfishness of her little life. **1974** *Cleveland* (Ohio) *Plain Dealer* 27 Oct. 1-c/4 Colwell began the first day of competition in this inaugural event with a 1363 pinfall. **1976** *Billings* (Montana) *Gaz.* 30 June 4-e/2 Here are the top 10 bowlers and their total pinfall after four rounds (26 games) of the $60,000 Portland Open Bowling Tournament. **1964** *McCall's Sewing* ii. 31/1 *Pin-fit*, to pin and adjust the garment to your figure before permanent stitching. *Ibid.* vi. 93/1 When you try on the garment, it is very easy to pin-fit and taper the legs to a becoming width. **1973** *Washington Post* 5 Jan. B5/4 (Advt.), Price includes fabric and labor with choice of skirt, self-cording and pin-fitting in your home. *a* **1916** 'Saki' *Toys of Peace* (1919) 290 To-day we are putting little pin-flags again into maps of the Balkan region. **1957** M. Banton *W. Afr. City* ix. 176, 4,000 pin-flags were brought out of concealment and fastened in the clothing of their comrades. **1847** *Californian* (San Francisco) 10 July 3/1 Quality of Pasture—Bunch Grass; Clover; Wild Oats and Pin Grass, all in abundance. **1888** [see *Alfilaria]. **1914** C. F. Saunders *With Flowers & Trees in Calif.* iii. 55 Still another wild pasture-plant..is the stork's-bill.., commonly known as pingrass or filaree. **1949** E. L. Palmer *Fieldbk. Nat. Hist.* 241/3 Common names [of *Erodium cicutarium*] include wild musk, pin clover, pin grass, pinweed and heron's bill, mostly based on character of fruit. **1958** R. C. Rollins *Fernald & Kinsey's Edible Wild Plants Eastern N. Amer.* (ed. 2) 259 Storksbill, Pin-grass, *Erodium cicutarium.* **1961** R. Longrigg *Daughters of Mulberry* i. 8 Giggles Ballantyne..teetered unhappily on tall pin heels. **1960** C. Storr *Marianne & Mark* iv. 54 A pair of tight pinheeled patent-leather shoes. **1963** *Times* 20 Feb. 14/7 We were joined by a girl in pointed pin-heeled shoes which soon put an end to her enthusiasm. **1940** *Chambers's Techn. Dict.* 644/2 Pin hinge. **1964** W. L. Goodman *Hist. Woodworking Tools* ii. 53 This cupboard door, in a light-brown hardwood, appears to have been the right-hand leaf of a pair, as the pin hinge is slightly longer at the top. **1834** D. Crockett *Narr. Life* 207 In this hunt every..little pin-hook lawyer was engaged. **1840** *Southern Lit. Messenger* VI. 386/2 Ellen used to fish there for minnoes with a pin-hook. **1970** *Country Life* 17–24 Dec. 1199/1 Losing..a string of sausages to..a tramp with a pin-hook on a piece of string. **1942** *Sun* (Baltimore) 23 Sept. 7/2 'Pin hookers', who make small purchases in auction markets and then resell them in the same markets also are exempt from price control. **1944** *Richmond* (Virginia) *Times-Dispatch* 5 Oct. 18 The fixation of prices this year is bad business for the time honored 'pinhooker', the man with relatively small operating capital who, during the more spacious days of tobacco selling when the auctioneer got the green light for a sale from wall to wall, bought tobacco when the market was low and held it until it was high, pocketing the difference. The prices this year are so narrow that the pinhooker's business has been practically squeezed out. **1949** L. Rapport in B. A. Botkin *Treas. S. Folklore* iv. iii. 652 There's Carroll, Jones, and Mallory for the Big Three..buyers from the four large independents who are on this market, and seven or eight pinhookers. **1966** *Publ. Amer. Dial. Soc.* xlv. 19 The pinhooker will attach his sales tag to a lot of tobacco waiting to be received by the warehouse workers. **1886** A. B. W. Kennedy *Mech. of Machinery* xii. 586 The efficiency of a pin joint, or turning pair, is generally very much greater than that of a sliding pair. **1919** Pippard & Pritchard *Aeroplane Struct.* x. 122 An important case occurs when..a pin-joint is made in an aeroplane spar at any place other than near one of the positions of the points of inflection. **1978** J. E. Gordon *Structures* x. 205 The concentration of stress at the pin joints calls for a tough and ductile material, such as wrought iron. **1882** *Min. Proc. Inst. Civil Engin.* LXIX. 111 Of a well-designed pin-jointed structure, all the principal members must be connected directly with the pin. **1908** E. S. Andrews *Theory & Design of Struct.* xvii. 508 Pin-jointed eye bars are not much used in this country for bridge work, and for roof work they are going out of use. **1974** *Nature* 4 Jan. 77/2 It covers the treatment of pin-jointed frameworks, beams, circular sandwich plates, Michell's structural continua and plates loaded in their planes. **1862** *Illustr. Catal. Internat. Exhib., Industr. Dept., Brit. Div.* II. No. 3600 A case with jointed pin-leg, artificial human leg, and others. **1960** S. PLATH *Colossus* (1967) 39 The oracular ghost who dwindles on pin-legs. **1936** DYLAN THOMAS *Twenty-Five Poems* 44 Pin-legged on pole-hills with a black medusa By waste seas where the white bear quoted Virgil. **1939** —— *Let.* Mar. (1966) 226 The English poets now are such a pinlegged..crowd. **1946** in D. de Carle *Pract. Watch Repairing* (prelim. advt.) The new pin lever—seven jewels. **1962** *Which?* June 165/1 In many cheaper watches, there is a pin-pallet (or pin lever) type of escapement, in which the pallets are hardened steel pins instead of jewels. **1976** M. CUTMORE *Watch Collector's Handbk.* ii. 70 In the pin-lever design the impulse pallets on the lever are replaced by steel pins... The escape-wheel teeth supply most of the lift and have steeply sloped faces. **1934** DYLAN THOMAS *Let.* 2 May (1966) 114 And I have, too, a violent desire to draw pin-men. **1953** J. MASTERS *Lotus & Wind* i. 8 The engineer was little more than a pin man in the distance. **1965** J. WADE *Boy with Sling* I. i. 11 He flicked at the ground..with a switch, drawing an elongated pinman. **1975** *Times Lit. Suppl.* 7 Feb. 129/3 The movement of the train, and the view through its windows, reduce what Rhoda sees to a scene of pin-men moving awkwardly and senselessly through an unwelcoming landscape. [**1887** T. B. REED *Hist. Old Eng. Letter Foundries* 26 A more probable explanation seems to be that the head of a small screw or pin, used to fix the side-piece of the mould,..left its mark on the side of the types as they were cast.] **1888** C. T. JACOBI *Printers' Vocab.* 100 Pin mark.—This is the slight mark in the side of a type near the top of the shank made in casting by machinery. **1916** LEGROS & GRANT *Typogr. Printing-Surfaces* iii. 14 The pin-mark, or drag,..only occurs in certain machine-made type. **1922** D. B. UPDIKE *Printing Types* I. ii. 16 The pin-mark is an indentation on the upper part of the body, made by the pin in casting. **1951** S. JENNETT *Making of Bks.* ii. 34 The other [side], in foundry type, bears the pin-mark, or occasionally two pin-marks... The pin-mark is formed by the mechanism that ejects the type from the mould when it is cast. **1967** T. KENEALLY *Bring Larks* xxviii. 222 By the time he sighted the pin-new East Indiaman, it had already ripped through the oyster-shell horizon far out to the south-east. **1976** *New Society* 19 Feb. 373/1 A dozen girls sit in the toy department of a pin-new department store. **1813** H. MUHLENBERG *Catal. Plantarum Americæ Septentrionalis* 87 Swamp or Pin Oak, (*Quercus palustris*). **1847** D. COYNER *Lost Trappers* I. 23 The young trapper was relieved by the arrival of two of the company, one of whom climbed a pin-oak tree. **1857** *Yale Lit. Mag.* XXII. 284 His head is as obtuse and spongy as the butt-end of a pin-oak rail. **1941** P. P. PIRONE *Maintenance of Shade & Ornamental Trees* iv. 45 Pin oaks in alkaline soils often develop yellow or chlorotic leaves. **1975** *Country Life* 16 Jan. 148/3 American woodland in the east..is composed largely of oak, not our oak, but the slim and lofty red oak, white oak, pin oak and chestnut oak. **1860** E. BECKETT *Rudimentary Treat. Clocks* (ed. 4) 103 Pin Pallets. **1903** F. J. GARRARD *Watch Repairing* x. 101 The 'pin-pallet' escapement..has round pins for pallets, and the inclines are on the scape teeth. **1946** D. DE CARLE *Pract. Watch Repairing* vi. 55 Some designs of pin pallets are so made that the arms carrying the pallet pins can be bent quite easily. **1976** M. CUTMORE *Watch Collector's Handbk.* i. 47 The cheap watch had developed independently in Switzerland and in the form which was eventually to become world-wide. Roscopf designed and produced a pin-pallet lever watch in 1867. **1942** *Ark Royal* (Ministry of Information) 18/2 When a squadron is preparing for a reconnaissance, the ground staff bring the aircraft from the hangar to the flight deck... The ranging party..then take over and push the aircraft aft, assisted by a small 'pin party' to spread and secure the wings. **1946** J. IRVING *Royal Navalese* 135 *Pin party*,..the working party, in a Carrier, which prepares aircraft on the flying deck for taking off. **1893** J. B. JOHNSON et al. *Theory & Pract. Mod. Framed Struct.* xxi. 338 The Lengths of Bearing or Pin Plates are determined by the following considerations. **1968** E. H. & C. N. GAYLORD *Struct. Engin. Handbk.* VI. 71 Usually, a pin plate is assumed to transmit a fraction of the main member force proportional to its thickness. *c* **1866** W. B. DICK *Amer. Hoyle* (ed. 3) 428 The game of Pin Pool is played with two white balls and one red, together with five small wooden pins. **1900** ADE *Fables in Slang* 16 The Local Editor..was playing Pin-Pool with the Superintendent. **1915** B. EDWARDS in H. Dempsey *Best of Bob Edwards* (1975) v. 107 Men who blew all their money on whisky and pin pool. **1959** in Halas & Manvell *Technique Film Animation* xxvi. 304 (*heading*) Pin screen animation. *Ibid.*, The pin screen is designed for black-and-white films. **1976** *Oxf. Compan. Film* 11/2 After watching *L'Idée* (1934) in production in 1932 he [*sc.* Alexandre Alexeïeff] experimented with animation techniques and invented the pin screen, a metal surface pierced by about five million tiny holes through which he pressed metal pins which, obliquely lit, created shadows with all possible gradations from black to white according to the length of pin protruding from the screen. **1926–7** *Army & Navy Stores Catal.* 408B/3 *Pochettes*...Pin seal leather, lined silk. **1934** *Times* 29 Nov. 19/3 In black pinseal with the new short handles there is a useful bag with a triple frame. **1961** [see *billfold(er* s.v. *BILL *sb.*[3] II]. **1972** J. MOSHER *Some would call it Adultery* III. xv. 139 Then he took a change purse from an inside pocket. It was black pinseal leather, opening with a snap. **1974** *Country Life* 21 Nov. (Suppl.) 45 Pin seal wallet £30. **1916** H. M. RIDEOUT *Far Cry* xi. 150 Like a pin-setter in a bowling alley, Mace carefully planted his bottles upright on the floor. **1958** *Economist* 20 Dec. 1085/1 In 1954 the American Machine & Foundry Company began large-scale production of an electronic automatic pin-setter, or pin spotter as it is also called. **1958** *Wall St. Jrnl.* 9 Dec. 1/4 In the past seven years they've [*sc.* automatic pinboys have] taken over the pinsetting chores on all but a small minority of the existing lanes. **1964** *Economist* 30 May 1024/3 The introduction of pin-setting machines that speeded the game. **1972** *Mainichi Daily News* (Japan) 7 Nov. 6/4 The company signed a contract with Yungtay Engineering Co. of Taichung to export pin-setting machines for 100 bowling lanes. **1947** W. DE LA MARE *Coll. Stories for Children* 60 He crinkled up his pin-sharp eyes. **1978** *SLR Camera* Aug. 4/1 (Advt.), Pinsharp projection from corner to corner. **1926** *Glasgow Herald* 26 June 8 Their prowess as 'par-beaters' and 'pin-splitters'. **1961** PARTRIDGE *Dict. Slang* Suppl. 1222/1 *Pin-splitter*.. Since ca. 1935, predominantly a golf-shot dead on the pin. **1973** *Country Gentlemen's Mag.* Mar. 181/1 Gents Pinsplitter Golf Clubs. **1947** *Gloss. Technical Theatr. Terms* (Strand Electr. & Engin. Co.) 22 *Pin spot*, any spot lantern so adjusted that its maximum light is focussed into the smallest possible area. **1961** A. BERKMAN *Singers' Gloss. Show Business* 7 *Baby spot*.., a small spotlight used for illuminating any small object on stage; often used for lighting just the face of the performer. (Also called *pin-spot*.) **1958** Pin-spotter [see **pin-setter*]. **1975** *Oxf. Compan. Sports & Games* 90/2 Modern bowling centres, with automatic pin-spotters and score-indicators, have replaced the rough, tough alleys lit by kerosene lamps, which catered for saloon crowds in the early days of the twentieth century. **1947** J. T. MARSH *Introd. Textile Finishing* i. 20 The beater untangles the matted pile, and the fabric then passes into the pin stenter which is equipped with from eight to sixteen rotating cards. **1962** —— *Self-Smoothing Fabrics* xi. 171 Since the advent of the crease-resisting process, with its earlier emphasis on rayon fabric production, there has been a corresponding emphasis on pin stenters compared with the clip stenter. **1936** A. M. MIALL *Everyday Embroidery Bk.* viii. 74 *Punch, Lace, Pin or Turkey-stitch* (it has all these names) is an open-work stitch which is sometimes used in rather elaborate *broderie anglaise*, or in cut-work..as an open-work filling for a flower or motif. **1948** C. CHRISTOPHER *Compl. Bk. Embroidery* viii. 185 Pin Stitch is used to applique motifs of self material on either wrong or right side of fabric. **1972** B. SNOOK *Creative Art of Embroidery* 92 *Pin stitch*. This is used along a hem edge. **1960** S. PLATH *Colossus* (1967) 48 At the price of a pin-stitched skin Fish-tailed girls purchase each white leg. **1935** G. W. FRY *Embroidery & Needlework* viii. 188 As with hemstitching so with pin stitching, the decorative effect may be obtained with nothing more than outlines. **1936** *Archit. Rev.* LXXIX. 135/1 Under one of these, however, peeps out a gay little shop in bright green paint, full of pin-tables, where one can lose one's money in proper Strand fashion. **1957** *Observer* 20 Oct. 16/3 Entirely devoted to a single situation—pin-table saloon proprietors versus local councillor. **1973** 'M. UNDERWOOD' *Reward for Defector* ii. 13 Questions..were flashing through his mind like lights on a pin-table. **1977** *Irish Press* 29 Sept. 16/1 (Advt.), Pool tables, pin tables, fruit machines, etc., on sharing basis. **1903** *Electr. World & Engin.* 18 July 115 The pressure is admitted to or withdrawn from the piston by means of a pin-valve. **1910** K. WINSLOW *Prevention & Treatm. Dis. Domestic Animals* 191 Oxyuris, Whip, Thread or Pin Worm. **1933** *Jrnl. Econ. Entomol.* XXVI. 138 In California, the Pin Worm [*sc.* an insect larva] has done much damage to tomatoes. **1961** E. R. & G. A. NOBLE *Parasitol.* vi. 312 *Oxyuris equi* is the common pinworm in the cecum and colon of horses. *Ibid.* 317 *Enterobius vermicularis* is the pinworm or seat-worm of man. **1974** M. C. GERALD *Pharmacol.* ii. 35 Piperazine (Antepar) and chloroquine..have been quite effective in the cure of..pinworm, and malaria, respectively.

pin, *sb.*[2] Add: **pin-bullock** *Austral.*, one of the pair of bullocks in a team nearest the wagon.

1936 I. L. IDRIESS *Cattle King* viii. 68 They call the two polers the pin bullocks, because they swing the turntable of the wagon! **1959** H. P. TRITTON *Time means Tucker* 36 A bullock-team is made up in four parts: polers, pin, body and leaders... The pin-bullocks take the pull.

pin, *sb.*[3] Add: **1.** (Further examples.)

1911 A. C. WHITE *First Steps Classification Two-Movers* 73 The Black King moves into a triple pin, which is the feature of the problem. **1932** *Times Lit. Suppl.* 8 Dec. 948/3 Forcing the king where he wanted it, and then releasing the 'pin' paved the way for the threatened 26. **1976** *Daily Tel.* 4 Dec. 11/6 Black thinks it time to bring his queen into play and finds an unexpectedly troublesome pin.

2. [f. PIN *v.*[1] 5 a.] **pin-fall** *Wrestling*, a fall in which a wrestler must hold an opponent down for a specified length of time.

1907 *Daily Chron.* 21 Dec. 9/5 These two..wrestlers having agreed to contest the best of three pin falls in the catch-as-catch-can style. **1976** K. BONFIGLIOLI *Something Nasty in Woodshed* iv. 41 He helps the other chap back into the ring..then administers a fearsome forearm smash and the winning pinfall.

pin, *v.*[1] Add: **I. 2. c.** To spread *out* (dough or paste) with a rolling-pin.

1889 R. WELLS *Pastrycook & Confect. Guide* 39 Pin them out not too thick, and cut them into four.

d. *Austral. slang.* To 'do down', to cause trouble for (someone). (See also quot. 1941.)

1934 C. STEAD *Seven Poor Men of Sydney* iv. 122 A poor man..never 'as anything but a poor, miserable, wretched, untidy, un'appy life. They don't let 'im even be honest or 'ave a friend, if some one wants to pin 'im. **1941** BAKER *Dict. Austral. Slang* 54 *To pin someone*, to have someone 'set', to have a grudge against a person.

e. In phrases *to pin someone's ears back* (orig. *U.S.*), to chastise, to rebuke; *to pin one's ears back*, to listen attentively.

In quot. 1977 'lugholes' is colloquially substituted for 'ears'.

1941 H. L. ICKES *Diary* 22 June (1954) III. 546 It certainly was intended to pin my ears back. **1949** WODEHOUSE *Uncle Dynamite* ix. 160 His manner that of a man who has had his ears pinned back. **1961** PARTRIDGE *Dict. Slang* Suppl. 1222/1 *Pin back your ears* of *pin your ears back*, listen carefully. **1962** N. STREATFEILD *Apple Bough* xi. 146 I'd get my ears pinned back if I tried to cut down his practice time. **1966** 'L. BLACK' *Bait* iii. 33, I shall keep eyes open. And ears pinned back. **1977** D. FRANCIS *Risk* xvi. 12 Well, mate, pin back your lugholes. That boat you were on was built at Lymington.

4. For 'Now *rare*' read 'Now *rare* except in sense "to fasten or fix (anything objectionable) *on* a person"'. Also, *on* a thing. (Later examples.)

1924 'W. FABIAN' *Sailors' Wives* 34 Dorrisdale credits me with at least three [lovers], but they've never been able to pin it on me with anyone. **1942** E. PAUL *Narrow St.* xxi. 169 As usual, when anything sinister happened, his enemies tried to pin everything on Caillaux, who cleared himself promptly. **1966** *Listener* 3 Nov. 652/3 Medical research workers have been suspicious that some difficult and resistant diseases..are associated with these same PPLO or mycoplasma, but nobody has been able to pin it on them. **1970** N. FLEMING *Czech Point* ii. 39 No doubt up till now he had never had to cope with a crime more heinous than skiing without due care and attention. He could have pinned that rap on the Australian girl in the PVC outfit any day he cared. **1977** L. MEYNELL *Hooky gets Wooden Spoon* xii. 150 'Can the Law connect her with you?' '..No, they couldn't pin anything on me.'

5. (Earlier and later examples.)

1740 FIELDING in *Champion* 1 Apr., When he is pinned down,..particularly by one large Mastiff, I do not perceive that Readiness to relieve him which hath been formerly shewn. **1945** *Sun* (Baltimore) 21 Feb. 1/7 (*heading*) 4th Division pinned down by mortar fire 17 hours. **1970** *Globe & Mail* (Toronto) 25 Sept. 8/9 The Ambassador and 24 members of his staff..were pinned down in the Embassy since the fighting started. **1977** *Times* 17 Jan. 7/1 Underwood did his usual job pinning the batsmen down with geometrical control.

6. b. With *down*. To manœuvre (a person) into a position where evasion is impossible.

1904 ADE *True Bills* 40 Horace tried to side-step the Questions about Drinking and Smoking, but Uncle pinned him down. **1914** 'HIGH JINKS, JR.' *Choice Slang* 16 (*To*) *pin down*, to corner.

c. With *down*. To define, evaluate, isolate; to restrict *to*.

1951 M. MCLUHAN *Mech. Bride* (1967) 137/1 The kind of spectator participation in baseball..would be hard to pin down. **1955** *Times* 26 July 8/3 It would never be possible to pin down the cause of death to radiation, he added. **1963** T. PARKER *Unknown Citizen* v. 139 There was obviously a good deal more to it underneath, which you could never pin down. **1965** *Listener* 2 Dec. 920/2 This symbolism is far more difficult to pin down than Rublowsky seems to suppose. **1973** *Times* 27 Apr. 1/8 Attempts to pin down the origin of the disease were inconclusive.

piña. Add: **4. piña colada** (kolā·dă) [Sp., lit. 'strained pineapple'], a long drink made with pineapple juice, rum, and coconut.

1975 P. MOYES *Black Widower* xiii. 159 In the bar itself, ice tinkled merrily into tall glasses of rum punch and *piña colada*, and smooth, sun-tanned men and women sipped and chatted. **1977** *N.Y. Times Mag.* 4 Dec. 42/1 She is wearing a long, batik-printed dress and bearing two piña coladas on a tray. **1978** *Chicago* June 172/3 There was gin and piña coladas and talk about Estée Lauder..and money..and clothes.

pinacol (pi·năkǫl). *Chem.* [f. PINAC(ONE + -OL.] = PINACONE in Dict. and Suppl.; **pinacol rearrangement**, a reaction typified by the conversion of pinacol into pinacolone, in which a 1,2-glycol loses water on heating with acid to form a ketone.

1911 *Chem. Abstr.* V. 3561 The solid pinacols have normal mol. wts. in dil. C_6H_6. **1912** *Ibid.* VI. 82 The fraction b. 214° of the products of hydrolysis of crude pinacol by H_2SO_4. **1936** L. J. DESHA *Org. Chem.* 538 The pinacol rearrangement is irreversible in the sense that pinacolins do not change into pinacols. **1938** E. S. WALLIS in H. Gilman *Org. Chem.* I. 723 Numerous examples of this reaction, now known as the pinacol rearrangement, have been found since the time of Fittig's discovery [in 1859]. **1964** N. G. CLARK *Mod. Org. Chem.* x. 180 Acetone is reduced with amalgamated magnesium to pinacol. **1966** *McGraw-Hill Encycl. Sci. & Technol.* III. 375/2 Ketones are converted to tetrasubstituted ethylene glycols (called pinacols) by certain reducing agents. **1966** SMITH & CRISTOL *Org. Chem.* xiii. 289 The pinacol rearrangement is quite general for glycols in which all four groups..are alkyl or aryl groups.

pinacolin. Add: Also **-ine.** [First formed as G. *pinacolin* (R. Fittig 1860, in *Ann. d. Chem. u. Pharm.* CXIV. 58).] Also, any other ketone in which the carbonyl group is bonded to at least one tertiary carbon atom. Now usu. called *PINACOLONE. (Further examples.)

1884 [see *PINACONE]. **1913** T. H. POPE tr. *Molinari's Treat. Org. Chem.* II. 183 When distilled with dilute sulphuric acid, it [*sc.* pinacone] is transformed into pinacoline, $(CH_3)_3C.CO.CH_3$. **1936** [see *PINACOL]. **1973** B. J. HAZZARD tr. *Organicum* 587 In textbooks, the dihydric alcohol here termed pinacol is often called pinacone and the ketone produced by the rearrangement pinacoline.

pinacolone (pi·năkǒlōu:n). *Chem.* [f. *PINACOL + -ONE.] = PINACOLIN in Dict. and Suppl.

1925 *Org. Syntheses* V. 91 The combined pinacolone fraction is dried over calcium chloride, filtered, and fractionally distilled. **1932** *Jrnl. Amer. Chem. Soc.* LIV. 825 Because of the need of large amounts of pinacolone for investigations in progress in this Laboratory, methods for its preparation have been studied. **1940** S. MIALL *New Dict. Chem.* 400/1 When heated with mineral or organic acids, pinacols undergo a molecular rearrangement with loss of water to give ketones known as pinacolones. **1944** *Jrnl. Amer. Chem. Soc.* LXVI. 634/2 It was anticipated that this pinacolone should be 3,3-dianisyl-2-butanone. **1967** L. F. & M. A. FIESER *Reagents for Org. Synthesis* I. 772 On brief exposure to moist air the fluorohydrin is rearranged to pinacolone..and hydrogen fluoride.

pinacone. Add: [First formed as G. *pinakon* (G. Städeler 1859, in *Ann. d. Chem. u. Pharm.* CXI. 279).] Also, any other alcohol having two hydroxyl groups which are bonded to adjacent tertiary carbon atoms. Now usu. called *PINACOL. (Further examples.)

1884 ROSCOE & SCHORLEMMER *Treat. Chem.* III. II. 12 The pinacones decompose very readily into water and the ketones, to which the name of pinacolines is given. **1913** T. H. POPE tr. *Molinari's Treat. Org. Chem.* II. 182 A special group of glycols, the pinacones, containing two adjacent tertiary alcohol groups. **1973** [see *PINACOLIN].

pinafore, *sb.* Add: Also, a low-necked, sleeveless fashion garment worn by women and girls, usu. over a blouse or jumper.

[**1907**: see *pinafore-frock* below.] **1960** *Vogue Pattern Bk.* Autumn 46 Dark grey pinafore tops a gay printed blouse. **1974** *Country Life* 21 Feb. 398/1 Dark brown pinafore in fine corduroy worn with white cotton shirt. **1976** *Vogue* Jan. 44/2 Low-slung pinafore.

c. Also *pinafore dress, frock, gown.*

c **1909** D. H. LAWRENCE *Collier's Friday Night* (1934) ii. 35 She is wearing a dark blue cloth 'pinafore-dress'. **1973** *Times* 15 Nov. 6/3 The bridesmaid, Lady Sarah Armstrong-Jones, wore a pinafore dress. **1907** *Westm. Gaz.* 8 Apr. 13/1 Our grown-up pinafore-frock must confess itself borrowed from the nursery. **1952** C. W. CUNNINGTON *Eng. Women's Clothing* iii. 91 The Pinafore frock is revived [in 1909], worn over a tucked chemisette. **1932** *Mod. Weekly* 30 Apr. 118 Her adorable, black velvet, pinafore gown. The tiny puff-sleeves are of silver tissue. **1952** C. W. CUNNINGTON *Eng. Women's Clothing* ii. 71 *The Pinafore Gown* [in 1906] 'is often allied to the frock with brace over a lace blouse'.

‖**pinard** (pinār). Also **Pinard.** [Fr.] Coarse red wine (orig. that issued to French troops), vin ordinaire; *loosely*, any wine; a glass of this wine.

1922 E. E. CUMMINGS *Enormous Room* iv. 85 A glass apiece of red acrid *pinard.* **1924** *Blackw. Mag.* Oct. 556/2 Some of the adversaries are toasting each other in pinard. **1928** R. HALL *Well of Loneliness* xxxvi. 335 The Unit's rations—cold meat, sardines, bread and sour red Pinard. **1937** PARTRIDGE *Dict. Slang* 631/1 *Pinard,* liquor; wine: Soho (-1935). **1947** M. LOWRY *Let.* Nov. (1967) 160 Wonderful skipper on this ship, engineers, seamen, cats, stewards, pinard. **1950** E. HEMINGWAY *Across River* xii. 112 In a Great Hotel, wine must cost money. You cannot get Pinard at the Ritz. **1969** B. WEIL *Dossier IX* iii. 23 He..drank a *pinard* as if the rough red wine would take away the taste of a probable duplicity.

pinarette (pinăre·t). [f. PINA(FO)RE *sb.* + -ETTE.] A short pinafore (in the senses of Dict. and Suppl.).

1951 *Sunday Pictorial* 21 Jan. 15/6 (Advt.), Pinarette, exclusive design in cotton print. Stock size. Fully cut with perfect finish. **1959** 'H. CARMICHAEL' *Stranglehold* xii. 102 A nondescript girl..wearing a pinarette and a maid's cap. **1962** J. CANNAN *All is Discovered* ii. 30 The gaudy cotton dress, the strong bare legs, the black felt slippers, the homely 'pinarette'. **1966** 'K. NICHOLSON' *Hook, Line & Sinker* ii. 27 She was wearing a floral pinarette over a pink satin blouse.

‖**piñata, pinata** (pinyā·tă, pinā·tă). Also 9 **piñate.** [Sp., jug, pot.] In Mexico and Mexican-influenced areas of the U.S.A., a decorated container (orig. a pottery bowl), filled with sweets or other gifts which is broken by a blindfolded person or otherwise opened at Christmas and on other festive occasions.

1887 F. C. GOOCH *Face to Face with Mexicans* viii. 264 The breaking of the *piñate* is the chief sport of the *posada.* The *piñate* is an oval-shaped earthen jar, handsomely decorated and covered with bright ornaments... There are turkeys, horses, birds, monkeys, [etc.]. *Ibid.* 265 The fun of breaking the *piñate* begins. It is suspended from the ceiling, and each person..blindfolded..proceeds to strike the swinging *piñate.* **1934** E. FERGUSSON *Fiesta in Mexico* xiv. 254 There is a party, with..sweets and paper toys in a huge pottery ball decorated with paper to look like a turkey, Charlie Chaplin,..anything. The littlest child or favored guest pulls the string which releases the shower of candies. This is the piñata, which is in season anytime from the first posada to *Diá de los Reyes,* Twelfth Night. **1947** C. U. STOKER *Under Mexican Skies* 169 The *patio* looked very pretty with its gardens all in bloom. The children had hung a *piñata,* representing the Christmas Star, in the center of the *patio* with room enough for all to strike at it. **1959** C. RAMSDELL *San Antonio* IV. xv. 262/1 The *piñata,* in Texas at least, is now made in a charming variety of shapes. *Ibid.* 262/2 At Christmas or birthday parties the *piñata* is always the climax. Child after child, blindfolded, is whirled about, and turned loose to bat wildly in the supposed direction of the piñata, which dangles at the end of a rope. **1976** *Examiner* (Coolidge, Arizona) 13 May 10 (*heading*) Second graders celebrate Cinco de Mayo... The children learned some Spanish words..and made *pinatas.*

pin-ball. For *U.S.* read 'orig. *U.S.*'. **1.** (Earlier and later examples.)

1803 E. BOWNE *Girl's Life* (1887) 175 We went to a room where they keep their work for sale,—pocket-books, pin balls, [etc.]. **1870** L. M. ALCOTT *Old-Fashioned Girl* vi. 76 Her scissors and pin-ball at her side, and her thimble on. **1963** *Times* 9 Mar. 11/5 Silver-banded pin-balls were then made to hang from the girdle and even Queen Elizabeth herself deigned to accept a New Year gift of a 'pin pillow embrodred'.

3. A game resembling bagatelle, in which small balls are propelled across a sloping surface towards targets which indicate the score when they are hit. Freq. *attrib.*, as *pin-ball arcade, game, machine, table.*

1911 *R. Bliss Illustr. Catal.* in B. Whitton *Bliss Toys & Dollhouses* (1979) 27 Pin ball game...One of our popular marble games. **1935** *Sun* (Baltimore) 2 Apr. 1/7 One of the bills would allow the State..to license claw machine and pinball games. **1936** *N.Y. Times* 5 Feb. 40/3 Justice Rosenman said he was surprised that the pin-ball machines had been licensed in the first place. **1937** *Pop. Mechanics* Feb. 278 (*heading*) Trip 'em; home pin-ball game. **1946** *Sun* (Baltimore) 30 Dec. 2/3 This ordinance also imposes a license fee on claw machines or pinball machines or similar devices for public amusement, operated through the insertion of a coin or token. **1951** J. D. SALINGER *Catcher in Rye* v. 46 We just had..hamburgers and played the pinball machine for a little while. **1959** *Times* 12 Feb. 10/7 To-day the senators were ringed with juke-boxes, pinball tables, 'one-armed bandits', and other coin-operated devices. **1969** N. COHN *Pop from Beginning* xix. 170 Kids..like myself, gave their lives to pinball. **1973** M. AMIS *Rachel Papers* 17 It was a month of plonk and coffee-bars, pinball arcades and party-hunts. **1975** R. L. SIMON *Wild Turkey* (1976) i. 4 Gunther lit up like a pinball machine on twenty replays. **1976** DEAKIN & WILLIS *Johnny go Home* iii. 57 Ernie showed Johnny how to fix the machines in the Amusement Arcades, and together they played the pin-ball tables.

pince-nez. Add: Also **pincenez.** (Earlier and later examples.) Also *attrib.*

1876 GEO. ELIOT *Let.* 3 Feb. (1956) VI. 220 Our young Charles..was slightly short-sighted and used only occasionally a pince-nez. **1904** JOYCE *Let.* 28 Dec. (1966) II. 75, I shall go to an oculist..to get pincenez glasses. **1927** F. B. YOUNG *Portrait of Clare* 26 She brushed the dust from her skirt..her grey eyes swimming behind the lenses of her pincenez. **1941** *Punch* 13 Aug. 148/2 There was a frail creature in pince-nez at the other end of the table. **1974** *Oxf. Jun. Encycl.* (rev. ed.) XI. 422/2 The portrait of Cardinal Ugone in the church of San Nicolo at Treviso shows spectacles in which the two lenses are held together by a joint or hinge which fitted on the nose (an early form of pince-nez).

Hence **pince-nezed,-nez'd** [-ED[2]] *a.*, wearing a pince-nez.

1919 J. C. SNAITH *Love Lane* xi. 51 An important, pince-nezed gentleman. **1922** W. J. LOCKE *Tale of Triona* xv. 170 Mrs. Rowington, thin, angular, pince-nez'd. **1958** B. HAMILTON *Too Much of Water* i. 18 A spare pince-nez'd man with sandy-red hair. **1976** J. CROSBY *Snake* (1977) xxxviii. 232 The doctor was a precise, pince-nezed Spaniard.

pincers, *sb. pl.* Add: **1. b.** *Mil.* = *pincer(s) movement* in sense 3 b below.

1942 T. RATTIGAN *Flare Path* II. i. 38 There wasn't anything fresh, I suppose. No pincers on anything anywhere? **1969** G. MACBETH *War Quartet* 73 Firing turn by turn, Encircling him with pincers..At last..we killed him. **1978** J. A. MICHENER *Chesapeake* 638 [In 1863] southern armies were involved in a stupendous march north in an effort to create a pincers which would curl back to engulf Philadelphia, Baltimore and Washington itself. The end of the war seemed at hand.

3. *pincer-like* adj. (further examples); **pincer-leg** = sense 2.

1909 *Daily Chron.* 20 Aug. 4/4 Note the disparity in the size of the two large pincer-legs. **1941** H. G. WELLS *You can't be too Careful* v. iii. 249 When confronted by a pincer-like movement, a soldier and a gentleman abandons his men and material and bolts home. **1962** D. NICHOLS *Echinoderms* viii. 101 The two living classes with relatively non-flexible exterior surfaces, the echinoids and asteroids, are provided with almost unique pincer-like organs, the pedicellariae.

b. *Mil.* Used *attrib.*, esp. in *pincer(s) movement*, to designate an operation involving the convergence of two forces on an enemy position like the jaws of a pair of pincers; a double envelopment; also *transf.* and *fig.*

1929 *Papers Mich. Acad. Sci., Arts & Lett.* X. 314/2 *Pincer drive*, an enveloping drive launched from two sides of an objective. **1939** AUDEN & ISHERWOOD *Journey to War* ix. 225 The Japs were to be..destroyed by the time-honoured pincer-movement. **1944** S. PUTNAM tr. *E. da Cunha's Rebellion in Backlands* x. 458 As may be seen, it was a vigorous pincers movement which was thus planned. **1954** T. GUNN *Fighting Terms* 34 Planning when you have least supplies or clothing A pincer-move to end in an embrace. **1959** *Listener* 28 May 919/2 At one end of the barrier the Soviet Union is conducting a pincer movement on Persia, from Transcaucasia and Iraq. **1968** *Times* 8 Oct. 7/7 Hardened layers of sediment which accumulated on the bottom of the Tethys Sea and were later thrust up to the surface by the pincer movement of the two continental masses. **1973** *Times* 9 Aug. 17/1 The pincer movement against Unilever—soaring commodity prices..on the one hand, and selling price controls..on the other—is beginning to bite. **1975** D. BAGLEY *Snow Tiger* xiv. 120 Rickman and Lyall are cooking up something... It'll be a pincer movement.

pinch, *sb.* Add: **I. 1. c.** A theft; an act of stealing or plagiarism; something stolen or plagiarized. *slang.*

1757 *London Chron.* 15–17 Mar. 258/1 They have almost reduced Cheating to a Science; and have affixed technical Terms to each Species; three of which are the Pinch, the Turn, and the Mace. **1812** J. H. VAUX *Vocab. Flash Lang.* in *Mem.* (1964) 258 This game is called *the pinch.* **1903** 'J. FLYNT' *Rise of R. Clowd* (1904) i. 64 That was just a pinch that I took. *Ibid.* 66 One night..on his way home..Ruderick..took a 'pinch' too large. **1931** G. IRWIN *Amer. Tramp & Underworld Slang* 146 *Pinch*,.. a small theft. **1965** *New Statesman* 19 Mar. 430/2 The 10-point charter drawn up hurriedly by its 'brains trust' during the much publicised Brighton weekend was almost a complete 'pinch' of the charter circulated in January by the Medical Practitioners' Union. **1966** *Melody Maker* 7 May 13/4 A pleasant selection of Italian-sung numbers—including what sounds like a Latin pinch from Presley.

d. An arrest or charge; imprisonment. Also *transf. slang* (orig. *U.S.*).

1900 'FLYNT' & 'WALTON' *Powers that Prey* 81 Told me to tell you't he'd have to make a pinch if you give the wheel another turn. **1906** E. DYSON *Fact'ry 'Ands* viii. 101 Ther Elder was back in er hour, 'n' had me outer pinch ez quick ez could be. **1926** [see *CAPER *sb.*[2] 1 c]. **1939** J. STEINBECK *Grapes of Wrath* xx. 371 Sheriff gets seventy-five cents a day for each prisoner, an' he feeds 'em for a quarter. If he ain't got prisoners, he don't make no profit... This fella today sure looks like he's out to make a pinch one way or another. **1948** *Sun* (Baltimore) 7 Jan. 13/1 If an official sees a violation, he is duty-bound to make the pinch, you might say. There is no compromise. Either it is a foul or it isn't. **1960** 'H. CARMICHAEL' *Seeds of Hate* xix. 164 Before I make a pinch I like to be reasonably sure that the charge will stick. **1970** E. R. JOHNSON *God Keepers* (1971) ii. 20 Right now you got a goof-ball pinch... Get your coat on. **1978** P. G. WINSLOW *Coppergold* 24 More worried about his clobber than the pinch.

2. Esp. in phr. *to feel the pinch.*

1861 [in Dict.]. **1961** NEW ENG. BIBLE *Luke* xv. 14 He had spent it all, when a severe famine fell upon that country and he began to feel the pinch. **1974** *Nature* 11 Jan. 79/1 The industrialised nations are the first to feel the pinch. **1977** *World of Cricket Monthly* June 46/1 Otago are really feeling the pinch.

4. (Further examples.) Also *in a pinch.*

1821 M. EDGEWORTH *Let.* 9 Nov. (1971) 259 Even her humor would *on a pinch* submit to her sense of duty. **1903** *Booklovers' Mag.* Dec. 582, I have seen her tend bar in a pinch. **1936** C. SANDBURG *People, Yes* 67 People lie in a pinch, hating to do it. **1943** H. READ *Politics of Unpolitical* i. 6 It has always been recognized that a king might easily degenerate into a tyrant, but his natural life is limited and can at a pinch be artificially shortened. **1966** M. R. D. FOOT *SOE in France* iv. 88 It could carry two passengers easily, three at a pinch, or four in a crisis. **1977** *Belfast Tel.* 17 Jan. 13/1 The Beetle cabriolet is a four-seater which can take five at a pinch.

6*. *slang.* Something easy to accomplish or attain; a certainty.

1886–96 in Farmer & Henley *Slang* (1902) V. 205/2 The race would be a pinch, Sir, barring accident or spill. **1899** 'G. G.' *Winkles* vi. 72 Harkaway for the Scurry Handicap at Landown, good, a 'pinch'; go nap on it! **1903** A. M. BINSTEAD *Pitcher in Paradise* xii. 280 Sustained by the conviction that he had made his match a 'pinch' indeed.

II. 9. For 'Now *dial.*' read 'Now chiefly *dial.*, *Austral.*, and *N.Z.*' Also, a steep hill. (Further examples.)

1848 H. W. HAYGARTH *Recoll. Bush Life Austral.* xii. 126 As we approached the end of our journey we came to one or two 'pinches', which is the colonial term for steep hills. **1862** J. S. DOBIE *S. Afr. Jrnl.* (1945) 30 At an ugly pinch of boulders we had another stick up. **1898** *Longman's Mag.* Nov. 51 Shepherd Robbins shambling slowly down the steep 'pinch' of road that led to the farm gate. **1901** M. FRANKLIN *My Brilliant Career* xxvi. 220 Don't push him too quickly up that pinch by Flea Creek, or he might drop dead with you. **1928** 'BRENT OF BIN BIN' *Up Country* xv. 253 She..could carry him up pinches so steep that no amateur could have sat on at such an angle. **1950** *N.Z. Jrnl. Agric.* Aug. 162 [inset] The steep pinches and faces take their toll of injuries and deaths.

10. Also, in *Geol.*, a similar narrowing of any stratum; freq. in phr. *pinch and swell.* Cf. *PINCH-OUT. (Earlier and later examples.)

1873 J. H. BEADLE *Undevel. West* 333 All the strange terms in mining parlance: 'true lodes, fissure-veins, pinches,..variations and sinuosities'. **1916** F. H. LAHEE *Field Geol.* vi. 140 That the country rock was warm and plastic enough to be deformed by the force of intrusion is suggested by the pinch-and-swell form of many pegmatite dikes in schists. **1955** *Jrnl. Geol.* LXIII. 520/1 The pinch-and-swell structure so commonly developed in conformable pegmatites and quartz veins. **1972** L. E. WEISS *Minor Struct. Deformed Rocks* 15 Structures closely related to boudins also formed in progressively extended layers are..'pinch and swell' structures or 'necks'.

10*. *Electronics.* (See quot. 1973.)

1941 A. V. EASTMAN *Fund. Vacuum Tubes* (ed. 2) ii. 22 All the electrodes are supported by wires held in a glass 'pinch' at the base of the tube and by a mica disk at the top. **1954** *Electronic Engin.* XXVI. 16/1 Electrical leakage may be due to..getter on the pinch and micas of the valve. **1973** *Gloss. Electrotechnical, Power Terms* (*B.S.I.*) I. vi. 19 *Pinch*, a flat fused glass seal forming part of the foot through which pass the leads from the electrodes to the pins in the base.

10.** *Physics.* A cylindrical or toroidal plasma confined by the pinch effect.

1951 *Proc. Physical Soc.* B. LXIV. 161 The discharge becomes brighter when it is contracted, and the brightness and sharpness of the 'pinch' increase with decrease in pressure. **1966** F. I. Boley *Plasmas* ii. 38 The kink instability of the plasma pinch..is an example of a large class of instability phenomena that is important to the dynamics of plasma. **1971** *Nature* 16 July 152/2 Research on high beta toroidal confinement is still in an early stage as groups previously working on linear theta pinches move into the field.

11. *with a pinch of salt* (fig.): see *salt *sb.*[1] 2 d.

pinch, *v.* Add: **I. 2. e.** *to pinch off*: *intr.*, to undergo a localized constriction that progresses until separation into two portions occurs; to become separate in this way; also *trans.*, to detach in this way.

1687 [in Dict., sense 2]. **1910** *Jrnl. Morphol.* XXI. 278 (*caption*) Megakaryocyte showing a platelet in process of pinching off from a pseudopod. *Ibid.*, Various phases are shown in the process of pinching off portions of the cytoplasm of the thrombocytes to form blood platelet-like corpuscles. **1952** [see *pinch-off]. **1956** *Essays in Crit.* VI. 10 Science begins to appear in the odd role of being pinched off and occupying the lonely end of a polar opposition to religion. **1956** L. P. Hunter *Handbk. Semiconductor Electronics* iv. 29 If the bias on the gate is high enough, the depletion region of the encircling PN junction becomes thick enough to 'pinch off' the channel through which the working current flows. **1956** *Jrnl. Biophysical & Biochem. Cytol.* II. Suppl. 107 The invaginated membrane is pinched off, resulting in the formation of an intracellular vacuole. **1959** *Bell Syst. Techn. Jrnl.* XXXVIII. 777 If sufficiently high voltage is applied, the channel will 'pinch off' and its current will essentially saturate. **1962** *Science Survey* III. 170 The living endothelial cell has almost nothing in its cytoplasm but masses of tiny smooth vesicles pinching-off and opening at the cell surfaces. **1966** *McGraw-Hill Encycl. Sci. & Technol.* X. 233/1 Once the process starts, the pressure at a narrow neck in the ring of fused metal is able to squeeze out the fluid metal until the neck pinches off completely, cutting off the current. **1979** *Nature* 11 Jan. 91/1 One suggestion has been made that the clathrin physically pinches off a membrane vesicle.

II. 10. b. *to pinch pennies* (or *a penny*): to be penny-pinching or parsimonious.

1942 E. Paul *Narrow St.* xix. 152 The surly Monsieur Salmon..complaining and pinching pennies as he made his purchases. **1962** J. D. MacDonald *Key to Suite* (1968) iii. 40 I'm not about to pinch a penny on a thing like this. **1973** J. Cleary *Ransom* xi. 255 'This city is too expensive for a cop on my pay. Especially when it almost cost me my wife, too.' 'He's always pinching pennies,' said Lisa.

III. 14. Also, in *Geol.*, said of strata generally; also with *down*. Cf. *lens *v.* (Earlier and later examples.)

1867 J. A. Phillips *Mining & Metallurgy Gold & Silver* iv. 56 The lode, which is eight feet wide on the north side of the Eureka, pinches out very rapidly in that direction. **1916** F. H. Lahee *Field Geol.* ix. 240 Sometimes strata are irregularly thinned and thickened so that they 'pinch and swell', as seen in cross section. **1923** *Ibid.* (ed. 2) v. 88 If a stratum continues to thin out in a certain direction,..it may finally 'pinch out' or 'lens out' altogether. **1928** W. A. Chalfont *Outposts of Civilization* 82 High-grade veins were followed as they pinched down, even to half inch seams which were profitably 'spooned out'. **1945** *Bull. Amer. Assoc. Petroleum Geologists* XXIX. 1563 The reservoir bed must pinch out in all updip directions. **1961** *Jrnl. Geol.* LXIX. 339/1 The layered marine sediments pinch out to the south.

15. a. (Earlier and later examples.)

1656 *Witty Rogue Arraigned* xxi. 30 Pinch'd the Cully of a Casket of Jewels. **1900** [see *commandeer *v.* c]. **1930** J. B. Priestley *Angel Pavement* ix. 474 Buying cars that have been pinched like that is a mug's game. **1936** [see *fat *sb.*[2] 2 d]. **1969** *Listener* 24 July 103/2 'This was by car I take it—was there petrol?' 'Well, we somehow managed to pick it up.' 'You mean pinch it?' **1979** 'C. Brand' *Rose in Darkness* xiii. 189 You simply pinched it from a shop.

b. (Earlier and later examples.)

1837 *Sessions Papers Cent. Criminal Court* 4 Dec. 157 D——d if I'm not *pinched* for housebreaking at last. **1925** H. L. Foster *Trop. Tramp with Tourists* 41 A traffic policeman had stopped us. But not to pinch us for speeding. **1932** T. S. Eliot *Sweeney Agonistes* 28 These fellows always get pinched in the end. **1938** [see *guy *v.*[4]]. **1955** *Times* 12 Aug. 5/4 He explained that Heard gave him the tobacco and then put in another officer to 'pinch' him. **1979** N. Hynd *Fake Flags* iv. 25 Nobody knew what night Vassiliev was going to be pinched.

pinch-. Add: **pinch-batter** = **pinch-hitter*; **pinch-bottle** *U.S.*, a bottle with indented sides, *spec.* a whisky bottle; so, by metonymy, whisky; **pinch-face,** a pinch-faced person; **pinch-faced** *a.*, having the features pinched or emaciated; **pinch-fist** (later examples); **pinch-hit** *v. intr.* (orig. *U.S.*), in baseball, to bat as a substitute for another batter, esp. at a critical point in the game; freq. *transf.*, to act as a substitute, esp. in an emergency; to stand in *for* someone; also as *sb.*, a hit made by a substitute batter; so **pinch-hitter, -hitting; pinch-pleat,** one of a cluster of small pleats, used esp. in curtains; hence **pinch-pleated** *a.*; **pinch-point,** (*b*) a point of congestion, confusion, or difficulty; **pinch roll,** (*a*) each of a pair of rolls, usu. hydraulically controlled, which grip the material passing between them; (*b*) = **pinch roller*; **pinch roller,** in a tape recorder or tape deck, a spring-loaded roller which presses the tape against the capstan; **pinch-runner** *N. Amer.* (see quot. 1961); **pinch-waist,** a tightly-fitted waist; also *attrib.*; hence **pinch-waisted** *a.*; **pinch wheel** = **pinch roller*.

1928 *Chicago Tribune* 5 Oct. 26/1 The pinch batter exercised rare judgment and drew a pass. **1974** *Spartanburg* (S. Carolina) *Herald* 22 Apr. B1/2 Franklin walloped five home runs in the six-day series. He started five of the games and was a pinch-batter in the other two. **1939** C. Morley *Kitty Foyle* x. 103 Mr Rittenhouse gave him a lift to the bootlegger's, ordered a whole case of pinchbottle on Pop's recommendation..and invited us down to..dinner. **1940** E. Hemingway *For whom Bell Tolls* xvi. 204 'When we have electricity again, what a lamp we can make of this bottle.' She looked at the pinch-bottle admiringly. **1963** *New Yorker* 8 June 57 We made it [*sc.* men's toiletry] clean-smelling and gutsy and put it up in hefty glass pinch bottles. **1917** W. Owen *Let.* 27 Sept. (1967) 497, I called for the poet—a wizened little pinch-face, about two feet high! **1863** G. M. Hopkins *Let.* 22 Apr. (1956) 73 Woolcomb,..a pinch-faced old man, whom everybody likes as much as they yawn over his divinity lectures. **1943** *Gen* 10 Apr. 23/1 Pinch-faced, thin-limbed, he seemed to be needing a good dinner. **1917** 'H. H. Richardson' *Fortunes R. Mahony* I. ix. 84 They were pinchfists when it came to parting with their money. **1978** *Verbatim* May 1/1 One incurs hostile mutters of *sparethrift* or *sparegood*, *scrapepelf* or *scrapegood*, *pinchfist* or *skinflint*. **1931** *Kansas City* (Missouri) *Star* 17 Dec. 24 John Neilson gave the talk,..but I thought they were just using him to pinch-hit for Bo McMillin. **1948** *Capital-Democrat* (Tishomingo, Okla.) 17 June 5/5 Duggan Smith, pinch hitting for W. C. Whiteley, had sent a high drive out to center. **1957** R. Longrigg *Switchboard* iv. 59 'I wonder if you can help me out of a jam?..I'm supposed to be lunching with a man called Robinson... I now find I can't do it. I've made some kind of nonsense with the dates—' 'Shall I pinch-hit?' **1966** *N.Y. Times* (Internat. ed.) 22 Apr. 12/1 California's Joe Adcock hit a pinch-hit single in the bottom of the eleventh inning. **1973** E. Taylor *Serpent under It* (1974) x. 156 'With no secretary, how do we find out where they are?' 'They've got some old girl from the History Department pinch-hitting.' **1974** *Cleveland* (Ohio) *Plain Dealer* 13 Oct. 14-C/4 If we were ahead by only one run, I would have pinch hit for Rollie in the top of the ninth because Catfish was ready. **1976** *Billings* (Montana) *Gaz.* 24 June 1-D/3. With one out. Kautzmann delivered a pinch-hit single to left field to drive in Art LaGaly with the lead run. **1912** *Lit. Digest* 10 Aug. 238/2 Things did not run very smoothly the famous 'Cub' pinch hitter himself tells us. **1939** Ade *Let.* 7 June (1973) 210, I have tried to get either 'Chick' Evans or 'Red' Grange for the June party but without success. We don't want to miss a month and so..I am offering myself as a pinch-hitter. **1970** *Globe & Mail* (Toronto) 26 Sept. 39/8 Singles, by pinch-hitter Mack Jones, Bob Bailey and pinch-hitter Jim Fairey in the bottom of the ninth produced one run. **1976** *Washington Post* 19 Apr. D4/1 Major league baseball has designated ABC as its pinch hitter for NBC on Monday night television this season. **1931** M. Loeb *Please stand By* I. x. 118 Just because Will Rogers did some pinch-hitting for Fred Stone and got away with it is no reason why you should send some college cub-reporter up here to cover the greatest discovery on the air. **1947** *Los Angeles Times* 6 Oct. 11/7 Brown..kept up his red-hot pinch-hitting when he singled for Phillips in the third. **1974** *Anderson* (S. Carolina) *Independent* 23 Apr. 3A/5 At present, the recreational program is being operated by Assistant Director Benny Burrell, 'who is doing a good job of pinch hitting,' said Evatt. **1958** *Times* 23 June 11/3 For long windows the pinch-pleat treatment in the last small sketch is very effective. **1973** *Guardian* 29 Mar. 13/3 The curtains are backed by Sekers's own make-up service which can provide pinch or pencil pleated or gathered curtains to the customer's own specifications. **1961** *Times* 15 Aug. 10/3 No loading or unloading at all will be permitted at important intersections and other 'pinch points'. **1965** *New Society* 11 Nov. 10/3 Oliver Cox considers heating one of the major 'pinch-points' in building today. **1973** *Country Life* 31 May 1527/3 The bridge is a pinch-point and congestion soon builds up. **1953** *Engineer* 23 Oct. 526/2 The slabs have to be pressure fed into the rolls at a constant rate by pinch or feed rolls. **1958** H. G. M. Spratt *Magnetic Tape Recording* vii. 202 The tape..is held in tight contact with it [*sc.* a roller] by means of a spring-loaded, free-running, rubber or rubber-covered roll generally referred to as the pinch roll. **1960** A. R. Bailey *Text-bk. Metall.* (ed. 2) 402 The steel slabs pass directly from the reheating furnace to a pair of pinch rolls that grip the metal and force it into the mill. **1964** A. A. McWilliams *Tape Recording* viii. 160 The tape is held in firm contact—with a rotating spindle—the capstan—by means of a rubber-tyred pressure roller, or pinch roll. **1969** W. R. R. Park *Plastics Film Technol.* ii. 41 At the same time, the pinch rolls are pulling the film away. **1949** S. J. Begun *Magnetic Recording* vi. 174 An interesting feature of this equipment is the..spindle which acts as a capstan as soon as a rubber-tyred pinch roller sandwiches the tape against it. **1961** G. L. Davies *Magnetic Tape Instrumentation* iv. 79 The pinch roller..is operated by a solenoid. **1974** *Physics Bull.* Apr. 151/1 Another feature is the vacuum buffered, low tension drive which eliminates pinch-rollers and associated mechanical problems. **1961** J. S. Salak *Dict. Amer. Sports* 328 *Pinch runner* (baseball, softball), a substitute runner for a teammate who has reached a base, the original runner being out of the game from that time on. **1970** *Toronto Daily Star* 24 Sept. 17/1 Cash wound up at second and pinch-runner Freddie Patek at third. **1976** *Billings* (Montana) *Gaz.* 20 June 4-E/4 Tim Foli singled off starter Tommy John to open the inning and was replaced by pinch-runner Jim Lyttle. **1969** *Time* 31 Jan. 55 Among the customers for his men's clothes—distinguishable by their long jackets and pinch waists—are movie stars, [etc.]. **1975** M. Bradbury *Hist. Man* i. 11 She wears a white pinch-waist, full-length raincoat. **1977** *Times* 5 Oct. (Fashion Suppl.) p.i/7 The lavishly lapelled, pinch-waisted..caricature..of the Italian style. **1962** H. B. Hadden *High-Quality Sound Production & Reproduction* x. 160 The tape is held in contact with the capstan by the pinch wheel. **1968** C. N. G. Matthews *Tape Recording* iv. 36 The capstan and pinch wheel are disengaged.

pi·nchable, *a.* [f. Pinch *v.* + -able.] That may be pinched; that invites pinching. Hence **pi·nchably** *adv.*

1921 *Public Opinion* 15 July 56/1 The greater the pinchable surface, the sharper the tweak that you will get. **1939** Joyce *Finnegans Wake* (1964) III. 417 As entomate as intimate could pinchably be. **1977** P. Ustinov *Dear Me* ix. 120 This volatile hedonist, with his unending stream of pinchable starlets.

pinch-bug. *U.S.* A stag-beetle belonging to the family Lucanidæ.

1856 'Mark Twain' *Let.* 25 May in *Iowa Jrnl. Hist.* (1929) XXVII. 423 A tenor and bass duet by thirty-two thousand locusts and ninety-seven thousand pinch-bugs was sung. **1870** E. Eggleston *Bk. Queer Stories* ix. 74 We came to a log on which two of that sort of beetles that children call 'pinch-bugs', were fighting. **1876** 'Mark Twain' *Tom Sawyer* v. 47 It was a large black beetle with formidable jaws—a 'pinch-bug' he called it. **1915** W. A. Bryan *Nat. Hist. Hawaii* xxxi. 417 The stag-beetles or pinch bugs, so called on account of their large mandibles. **1959** A. B. & E. B. Klots *Living Insects of World* 132/2 There is little doubt that the 'pinch bug' Tom Sawyer took to church was a stag beetle.

pinched, *ppl. a.* Add: **1.** Also with *in*.

1920 [see *dock-glass* s.v. *dock *sb.*[3] 7]. **1941** *Amer. Speech* XVI. 67/1 Avoid pinched-in-waistlines for teen ages.

e. *Physics.* Confined by the pinch effect.

1907 *Trans. Amer. Electrochem. Soc.* XI. 331, *C* is the column of liquid conductor,..and *P* is one of these pinched contractions. **1951** *Proc. Physical Soc.* B. LXIV. 161 Just after the breakdown the discharge..is observed to contract into a narrow filament; the discharge does not stay 'pinched' but immediately expands again, and proceeds to oscillate. **1959** *Daily Tel.* 23 July 7/8 But, unlike Zeta, the pinched gas will be stable. **1962** *Times* 28 Apr. 8/4 The first photograph of a 'pinched' lightning discharge has been obtained. **1973** Kettani & Hoyaux *Plasma Engin.* vii. 206 Consider a pinched column of fully ionised plasma.

7. Of paper: slightly smaller than the normal size (see quots.).

1893 J. Kay *Paper* 100 Sizes of Papers... Demy.. Post..Pinched Post..Foolscap. **1894** G. Clapperton *Pract. Paper-Making* 193 Sizes of Lined Papers. Pinched for 8vo Expansion by $14\frac{1}{2}$ in. **1926** *Paper Terminol.* (Spalding & Hodge) 20 *Pinched post*, a standard size of writing paper measuring $14\frac{1}{2} \times 18\frac{1}{2}$ in. **1952** E. J. Labarre *Dict. Paper* (ed. 2) 199/1 *Pinched post*, a size of writing paper standardized at $18\frac{1}{2}'' \times 14\frac{1}{2}''$, but with variants still in use, also for drawings... For 'pinched' the same word is used in Dutch: *geknepen*, when a sheet is slightly reduced from the standard or normal dimensions for that size. **1962** F. T. Day *Introd. to Paper* vii. 70 An even greater variety of sizes is covered by these names by the addition of qualifying words—Single or Half, Double or Quad, Small or Large, Extra or Super, Pinched or Reduced. *Ibid.*, Pinched Post..$14\frac{1}{2} \times 18\frac{1}{2}$ in. Pinched Post (Double)..$18\frac{1}{2} \times 29$ in.

pinch effect. [f. Pinch *sb.* + Effect *sb.*]

1. *Physics.* The constriction exhibited by a fluid through which a large electric current is flowing, caused by the attractive force produced by the interaction of the current with its own magnetic field.

[**1907** E. F. Northrup in *Physical Rev.* June 474 Some months ago, my friend, Carl Hering, described to me a surprising and apparently new phenomenon which he had observed. He found, in passing a relatively large alternating current through a non-electrolytic, liquid conductor contained in a trough, that the liquid contracted in cross-section and flowed up hill lengthwise of the trough... Mr. Hering suggested the idea that this contraction was probably due to the elastic action of the lines of magnetic force which encircle the conductor... As the action of the forces on the conductor is to squeeze or pinch it, he jocosely called it the 'pinch phenomenon'. **1907** C. Hering in *Trans. Amer. Electrochem. Soc.* Sept. 331 As the column of liquid looks as though it were being pinched by some mysterious and invisible force, the writer termed it the 'pinch phenomenon'. *Ibid.* 337 If to this field there is added another one, I see no reason why it should not add to the pinching effect.] **1911** G. H. Clamer in *Ibid.* XIX. 264 The heavy current..rapidly brings these columns of metal to the liquid condition, and produces therein the 'pinch' effect. **1956** *Sci. News Let.* 15 Sept. 174/1 Generating the high heat..requires containers that will not melt or be otherwise affected. Using the 'pinch effect' would seem to eliminate the container problem, since the reacting gas column would contract to contain itself, thus not touch any walls.

1958 *Listener* 25 Sept. 454/2 The Americans and Russians independently have developed a principle different from Zeta, although both are working on the Zeta principle of what is known as the pinch effect. **1966** *McGraw-Hill Encycl. Sci. & Technol.* X. 233/1 The force of the pinch effect has..been known to manifest itself by a crushing of tubular conductors exposed to large impulsive currents such as occur in lightning strokes or high-power short circuits. **1972** *Physics Bull.* Feb. 83/2 Flash photolysis features in the Exhibition. Chelsea Instruments is showing its apparatus (based on its Garton flash tube) which utilizes the pinch effect (as in some thermonuclear apparatus) to produce high intensity.

2. The slight narrowing of a record groove caused by the transverse movement of the cutting stylus, resulting in a vertical movement of the stylus at that point during playing.

1935 H. C. Bryson *Gramophone Record* x. 271 Hill and Dale cut records possess great advantages... There is no pinch effect. **1965** J. Walton *Pick-Ups* iii. 40 A mono pick-up (as well as of course the stereo pick-up) should have some vertical compliance and low vertical mass if pinch effect is not to cause damage and excessive 'needle talk'. **1975** G. J. King *Audio Handbk.* viii. 192 Because the groove is cut by a chisel-shaped tool whose face is at right-angles to the motion of the record, the groove width decreases along the sloping sides of the waveform... This, called 'pinch effect', results in vertical oscillation of the replay stylus at a frequency twice that which utilizes the pinch effect (as in some thermonuclear apparatus) to produce high intensity.

pinching, *vbl. sb.* Add: **6. pinching bug** = *PINCH-BUG.

1850 L. H. Garrard *Wah-to-Yah* xix. 253 Noah was so hurried to git the yelaphants, pinchin bugs, an' sich varment aboard. **1877** R. J. Burdette *Rise & Fall of Mustache* 77 That Bilderback boy..put a pinching-bug as big as a postage-stamp down a boy's back. **1928** Metcalf & Flint *Destructive & Useful Insects* i. 16 A certain amount of pain may result from mere mechanical injury by insects as when a boy finds a 'pinching bug' for the first time. **1954** Borror & DeLong *Introd. Study Insects* xxii. 381 These large brownish beetles [*sc.* stag beetles] are sometimes called pinchingbugs because of the large mandibles of the male.

pinch-off. *Electronics.* Also **pinch off.** [f. vbl. phr. *to pinch off* s.v. *PINCH *v.* 2 e.] In a field-effect transistor, the meeting of the two non-conducting depletion layers that border the channel, such that little further increase in current is achieved by increasing the drain voltage. Freq. *attrib.*, esp. in **pinch-off voltage,** the reverse bias that must be applied to the gate to achieve pinch-off and prevent the flow of current through the channel (equal to the drain voltage at which the current saturates when there is no bias applied to the gate).

1952 W. Shockley in *Proc. IRE* XL. 1367/1 W_0 is the magnitude of reverse bias required to make the space charge penetrate the entire *p*-region. We shall refer to it as the 'pinch-off voltage' since it is the voltage that will reduce the channel to zero and pinch off the conducting path. *Ibid.* 1374/1 We shall consider a structure operated with the drain beyond pinch-off. **1956** L. P. Hunter *Handbk. Semiconductor Electronics* IV. 31 For the depletion region to fill the entire channel b=0 and V(b)=V_0... V_0 is called the pinch-off voltage. *Ibid.* 32 As the bias..at the drain end is increased beyond V_0, the pinch-off condition moves toward the source. The field between the drain end and the point along the channel where pinch off is effectively reached must be large enough to maintain the current I flowing in the open part of the ca nnel. **1962** J. Evans *Fund. Princ. Transistors* x. 228 If V_G is large enough, pinch-off occurs at all values of V_D—the situation when $V_G = W_0$. **1972** *Field-Effect Transistors* (Mullard Ltd., London) ii. 8 The line joining the various drain-source voltages $V_{DS(P)}$ at which this pinch-off occurs (the pinch-off limit) is shown as a broken line in Fig. 7... To the right of the pinch-off limit —in the pinch-off region—the drain current only increases very slightly. **1974** Harvey & Bohlman *Stereo F.M. Radio Handbk.* v. 88 The voltage corresponding to zero I_d is called the pinch-off voltage.

pinch-out. *Geol.* [f. vbl. phr. *to pinch out* s.v. Pinch *v.* 14 in Dict. and Suppl.] A narrowing of a stratum, vein, or other body of rock to the point of extinction.

1928 in *Funk's Stand. Dict.* **1941** *Bull. Amer. Assoc. Petroleum Geologists* XXV. 1258 A pinch-out of a reservoir sand on a structural nose would..be considered a stratigraphic trap of a less perfect type. **1962** *Courier-Mail* (Brisbane) 15 Dec. 9/3 Seismic surveys had outlined a large closed structure which also had good stratigraphic pinch-out possibilities. **1974** P. L. Moore et al. *Drilling Practices Manual* xii. 300 These permeability barriers may be faults, folds, salt domes, or permeability pinchouts.

pinchpenny. Delete †*Obs.* and add later examples.

1931 'D. Stiff' *Milk & Honey Route* viii. 85 You can always tell the home of the pinchpenny by the narrowness of the eaves. **1948** *Sun* (Baltimore) 8 Apr. 1/7 Lee M. Wiggins, Under Secretary of the Treasury, today warned Congress that a pinchpenny policy toward the Bureau of Internal Revenue will cost the nation billions in evaded taxes. **1955** T. Sterling *Evil of Day* i. 13 No pinchpenny ever knew anything about pennies. You have to spend them to know. **1977** *New Yorker* 25 July 36/2 In contrast to pinchpenny P.R. routine of the environnentalist groups..the Dow P.R. material is handsomely bound, with expensive paper, elegant design, and, sometimes, four-color illustrations. **1978** 'F. Parrish' *Sting of Honeybee* iii. 39 The fences were a weird, pinchpenny patchwork, but they kept the ponies in.

pincushion. Add: **2.** (Later examples.)

1898 Britton & Brown *Illustr. Flora Northern U.S.* III. 290 Field Scabious..[is also called] blue caps, gypsy-or egyptian-rose, pincushion. **1965** *Austral. Encycl.* VII. 118/2 Pincushion, Australian, or blue pincushion, the popular name for *Brunonia*,..low herbaceous perennials, bearing blue flowers in very effective long-stalked heads; the projecting styles resemble pins sticking in a cushion.

4. *pincushion-flower* (later examples).

1911 W. R. Guilfoyle *Austral. Plants* 201 *Hakea laurina* 'Pin Cushion Flower' (evergreen shrub or tree, 10 to 30 ft.), f[lowers] crimson—W. Aust. **1917** L. H. Bailey *Stand. Cycl. Hort.* VI. 3106/1 (caption) *Scabiosa atropurpurea.*—The mourning bride or pin-cushion flower. **1938** T. Y. Harris *Wild Flowers Austral.* 25 Pincushion Flower (*Hakea laurina*)... Pink blossoms with cream stigmas projecting for some distance and the flowers in globular heads have earned the name for this most attractive plant. **1967** A. M. Blombery *Guide Native Austral. Plants* III. 265 *H[akea] laurina.* Pincushion Hakea. A large bushy shrub with flat, lanceolate, greenish-red leaves and pink pincushion-like flowers. **1972** F. Perry *Flowers of World* 101/1 *S[cabiosa] caucasica*, the Pincushion Flower, was introduced to Britain in 1591 and has become a favourite for border and cut-flower work.

b. pincushion distortion, a form of optical distortion in which a square is reproduced with sides curved inwards.

[**1886** J. H. Dallmeyer *Choice & Use Photogr. Lenses* 22 If the stop is placed at the same distance *behind* the lens..the result is the opposite kind, or 'pincushion'-shaped distortion.] **1892** A. Brothers *Photography* I. iii. 48 The effect consists..in the curvature of the images of straight lines produced by marginal rays causing barrel-shaped or 'pincushion distortion'. **1903, 1953** [see *barrel distortion* s.v. *BARREL *sb.* 11]. **1965** *Wireless World* July 58 (Advt.), No oscilloscope is better than its tube. Build in all the circuit refinements you like, if the tube suffers from..pin-cushion distortion..your efforts are in vain. **1972** Williams & Becklund *Optics* viii. 188 An aperture stop located between a positive lens and the image increases pincushion distortion.

pinda[1], **pindar, pinder.** (Earlier and later examples.)

1696 J. Ovington *Voy. to Suratt* 77 Sometimes they feast with a little Fish, and that with a few Pindars is esteemed a splendid banquet. These Pindars are sown under ground, and grow there without sprouting above the surface. **1926** J. K. Strecker in J. F. Dobie *Rainbow in Morning* (1965) 56 In the valleys of the Red River of Louisiana and the Sabine River of Louisiana and Texas, are to be found negroes who use many African words, the inheritance of their ancestors. A white man is a 'buckra'. .. A ground-nut (peanut) is a 'pinda'. **1938** M. K. Rawlings *Yearling* xviii. 214 The field of pindars was not doing so well. **1977** McDavid & O'Cain in S. Greenbaum *Acceptability in Lang.* viii. 115 The majority of the uncultured judge..*groundnut* and *pinder* as old.

‖**pinda**[2] (pi·ndă). *India.* Also 8 **peenda,** 9 **pindee.** [Skr. *piṇḍa* lump.] (See quots.)

1785 C. Wilkins *Bhăgvăt-Gēētā* 139 The Hindoos are enjoined by the *Vēds* to offer a cake, which is called *Pēēndă*, to the ghosts of their ancestors, as far back as the third generation. **1796** W. Jones tr. *Inst. Hindu Law* iii. 67 Sages have distinguished the monthly *srāddha* by the title of *anwāhārya*, or *after eaten*, that is, eaten after the *pinda* or ball of rice. **1811** W. Ward *Acct. Writings, Relig. & Manners Hindoos* II. v. 550 The place where the fire was kindled is plentifully washed with water, after which the son of the deceased performs pindee, viz. he makes two balls of boiled rice, and, repeating a mŭntrŭ, offers them to, or in the name of his father and mother, and lays them on the spot where they were burnt. **1877** M. Monier-Williams *Hinduism* v. 68 The offering of the Piṇḍa, or ball of rice, &c., to deceased fathers at a S'rāddha is of great importance in regard to the Hindū law of inheritance. **1901** *Westm. Gaz.* 14 Nov. 9/2 The 'pindas' offered to their deceased ancestors were placed on plantain or 'jack fruit' leaves. **1909** *Encycl. Relig. & Ethics* II. 27/1 How closely this [Lithuanian cake for the dead] corresponds to the Indian *piṇḍa*, which is so characteristic of the Indian worship of the dead. **1964** R. Antoine in De Smet & Neuner *Religious Hinduism* xv. 166 *Piṇḍas* (rice-balls) are then smeared with ghee, collyrium and oil, and dressed with a tuft of wool, so as to represent the ancestors. **1968** B. Walker *Hindu World* II. 149 On the first day after death a round ball of rice or flour moistened with milk and water and known as the *piṇḍa* is offered to the preta.

pindan (pi·ndæn). *Austral.* [Aboriginal.] The type of vegetation characteristic of arid areas of Western Australia; hence, the region itself. Also *attrib.*

1934 T. Wood *Cobbers* iv. 46 His black trackers were making boomerangs... Pindam [*sic*] gum: hard red wood, shaped from a knee in the timber. **1937** W. Hatfield *I find Australia* xxiv. 315 Pindan is not really the name of the type of tree, but merely the native name for 'dry country', though general usage adopts the word as a description of the thin growth of whipstick saplings of the bloodwood and box type of eucalypt. **1945** Baker *Austral. Lang.* xiii. 224 *Pindan* is the blacks' name for the desert country inland from Broome, W.A., so the whites call the Kimberley natives *pindan blacks.* To *live on the pindan* is to wander aimlessly in the Westralian outback. **1955** J. Cleary *Justin Bayard* xi. 153 They would be out in the pindan watching the homestead. **1959** *Observer* 17 May 8/3 From the pindan scrub..these ancient monuments [*sc.* mountains] rise. **1978** O. White *Silent Reach* ii. 22 Half a million acres of pindan country ..carried two thousand head of merino sheep in a good season.

pindolol (pi·ndŏlǫl). *Pharm.* [f. the initial letter of Propane, Propyl + Indol(e *sb.* + -ol.] The compound 1-indol-4-yloxy-3-isopropyl-aminopropan-2-ol, $C_{14}H_{20}N_2O_2$, which is an adrenergic blocking agent with uses similar to those of propranolol.

1971 *Biochem. Pharmacol.* XX. 2749 (*heading*) Influence of INPEA, Pindolol and Propanolol on the chronotropic and metabolic responses to β-adrenergic stimulation in intact rats. **1976** *Lancet* 11 Dec. 1298/1 Concomitant treatment of hypertension was started with 15 mg pindolol, 5 mg amiloride hydrochloride, and 50 mg hydrochlorothiazide daily. **1979** *Experientia* XXXV. 250/1 Pindolol is one of the beta-adrenoceptor blockers now widely used all over the world.

pine, *sb.*[2] Add: **5.** (Earlier and later examples.)

1657 *Bk. of Continuation of Forreign Passages* 46 *Fruits* ..Pyne, the best that ever was eat, in season almost all the year long. **1920** 'K. Mansfield' *Bliss* 35 He bought a pineapple... The oysters and the pine he stowed away.. under the front seat. **1954** *Farmer's Guide* (Jamaica Agric. Soc.) 392 The Sugar Loaf is only of importance as a fresh fruit. It is not a suitable pine for canning.

7. a. *pine bark* (earlier and later examples), *board* (earlier and later examples), *box, forest* (earlier and later examples), *hill, -log, plain* (earlier and later examples), *stump* (earlier examples), *thicket* (earlier example), *timber* (earlier and later examples); *pine-covered* (earlier and later examples), *-grown, -panelled, -scented* adjs.; **pine-blister(-rust),** a fungus disease of pine trees, caused by species of *Cronartium* (*Peridermium*) characterized by yellowish swellings on the bark; formerly also applied to needle rust caused by *Coleosporium* species; **pine-borer,** a longicorn beetle, whose larvæ live in pine trees; **pine-chafer,** for *Anomala pinicola* substitute *Anomala oblivia*; (examples); **pine-creeper, -creeping warbler** = *pine warbler*; **pine drape** *U.S. slang* = **pine overcoat*; **pine finch,** (*b*) (examples); **pine green,** the colour of pine needles; **pine gum,** substitute for def.: *U.S.*, the resin or turpentine obtained from several species of pine, esp. the slash pine, *Pinus caribæa*, and the southern pine, *P. echinata*; (examples); **pine lappet (moth),** a large brown European moth, *Dendrolimus pini*, whose larvæ feed on pines; also called the pine tree lappet; **pine-marten** (later examples); **pine overcoat** *U.S. slang*, a coffin; **pine rust,** a disease of pine trees caused by a rust fungus, e.g. **pine blister*; **pine savanna(h)** *U.S.*, a savannah in which pines are the prevailing trees; **pine saw-fly,** substitute for last part of def.: esp. species of *Diprion* or *Gilpinia*; (earlier and later examples); **pine siskin,** delete the first two Latin names given, leaving *Spinus pinus*; (examples); **pine-snake,** for *Pityophis* substitute *Pituophis*; also *attrib.*; (earlier and later examples); **pine straw** *U.S.*, (esp. dried) pine needles; **pine swamp** *U.S.*, a low-lying or marshy piece of ground on which pine-trees grow; **pine tags** *U.S.*, pine needles; so *pine-tag* attrib.; **pine warbler** (examples); **pine-weed,** for the Latin names given substitute *Hypericum gentianoides*; = *NIT-WEED; (earlier and later examples); **pine-weevil** (examples).

1709 J. Lawson *New Voy. to Carolina* 177 They make use of pine bark. *a* **1816** B. Hawkins *Sk. Creek Country* (1848) 71 They are covered with clay and that with pine bark. **1973** R. Lockridge *Not I, said Sparrow* (1974) x. 153 Bisecting the tracks were traces of pine bark... The pine bark—what's left of a bridle path. **1978** *Country Life* 12 Oct. 1094/1 Pine bark was found to be one of the most important foods [of beavers]. **1889** H. M. Ward *Timber & Dis.* xii. 259 It is thus seen that the fungus *Peridermium Pini* was regarded as a parasite of pines, and that it possessed two varieties, one inhabiting the leaves and the other the cortex... The disease may be popularly denoted 'Pine-blister'. **1894** W. Somerville tr. *Hartig's Textbk. Dis. Trees* I. 175 Three species of pine-blister-rust are to be distinguished in the cortex of trees. **1907** W. R. Fisher *Schlich's Man. Forestry* (ed. 2) IV. 441 Scots pines infected with this disease, which is very common in the British Isles and called pine-blister, are termed foxy trees by English foresters. **1929** T. Thomson tr. *Büsgen's Struct. & Life Forest Trees* xiv. 411 Individual stems of the pine and their descendants are especially prone to the pine blister. **1637** *Early Rec. Dedham, Mass.* (1892) III. 39 To alowe for saweing Pyne board 5s. **1728** *New Hampsh. Probate Rec.* (1914) II. 344 Eight thousand feet of good and merchantable pine boards every year. **1870** De B. R. Keim *Sheridan's*

Troopers on Borders xix. 125 A neat coffin had been made of pine boards. 1938 L. Bemelmans *Life Class* III. v. 245 Their flooring was of scrubbed pine boards. 1862 *Rep. Comm. Patents 1861: Agric.* (U.S.) 614 The larvæ [*sic*] of this insect is evidently a pine-borer, for I have found it about saw-mills. 1884 *Rep. Comm. Agric.* (U.S. Dept. Agric.) 379 The Common Longicorn Pine-Borer.. is destructive to the white pine. 1977 *Listener* 20 Oct. 503/3 Only when he discovered a small collection of New Zealand insects..did he trace it to a specimen of the New Zealand pine-borer; *Prinoplus reticularis*. 1847 W. T. Porter *Quarter Race Kentucky* 86 Ar you a goin to tumtum all nite on that pot-gutted old pine box of a fiddle? 1867 O. W. Holmes *Guardian Angel* 406 The long pine boxes came by almost every train,—no need of asking what they held! 1890 N. P. Langford *Vigilante Days* II. xxv. 441 A company of twenty or more men approaching the station, bearing in their midst a long pine box. 1885 *Encycl. Brit.* XIX. 103/2 The pine-chafer..is destructive in some places. 1972 Swan & Papp *Common Insects N. Amer.* 435 The Pine Chafer, A[*nomala*] *oblivia*, is very similar [to the Oriental Beetle]..; it infests red, jack, and Scotch pines. 1820 M. Edgeworth *Let.* 5 Aug. (1979) 199 High pine covered mountains. 1955 E. Pound *Classic Anthol.* III. 184 High, pine-covered peak full of echos. 1731 M. Catesby *Nat. Hist. Carolina* I. 61 The Pine-creeper... They creep about Trees; particularly the Pine- and Fir-trees; from which they peck Insects. 1811 A. Wilson *Amer. Ornith.* III. 25 Pine-Creeping Warbler.. inhabits the pine woods of the Southern states. 1868 Pine-creeping warbler [in Dict.]. 1917 T. G. Pearson *Birds Amer.* III. 148 Pine Warbler. *Dendroica vigorsi*... Pine-creeping Warbler; Pine Creeper. 1945 L. Shelly *Jive Talk Dict.* 31 *Pine drape*, coffin. 1970 C. Major *Dict. Afro-Amer. Slang* 91 *Pine drape*, coffin. 1810 A. Wilson *Amer. Ornith.* II. 133 Pine Finch..seeks the seeds of the black alder. 1871 J. Burroughs *Wake-Robin* 78, I observed several pine finches a dark brown or brindlish bird. 1799 C. B. Brown *Arthur Mervyn* I. ii. 15 Betty Lawrence was a wild girl from the pine forests of New-Jersey. 1913 J. London *Valley of Moon* 472 Vainly Saxon's eye roved the pine forest in search of her beloved redwoods. 1973 M. Monsarrat *Bk. of Europe* 118/2 Värmland, a gentle place of rolling farmland, pine forests and grand manor houses. 1978 D. Kyle *Black Camelot* xviii. 273 Sheltering in the Bavarian pine forests. 1970 *Globe & Mail* (Toronto) 28 Sept. 28/1 (Advt.), Reconditioned Alfa Romeo Sale..pine green. 1974 *Simpson* (*Piccadilly*) *Christmas Catal.* 12 Jacquard patterned cashmere sweater. Light brown/white, pine green/white. 1880 'Mark Twain' *Tramp Abroad* xxxv. 397 Some pine-grown summits behind the town. 1915 R. Lankester *Diversions of Naturalist* 4 That pine-grown land. 1855 W. G. Simms *Forayers* 434 A leetle pine-gum plaister on that head of yourn will stop up the sore places. 1921 *Frontier* (Missoula, Montana) May 5 The Sheep Eaters lived in tepees made of cedar thatched with moss and cemented by pine gum. 1938 M. K. Rawlings *Yearling* iv. 41 He sewed the two deepest cuts and rubbed pine gum into all of them. *a*1652 *Rec. Early Hist. Boston* (1881) VI. 16 The land running northward upon a straite line untill it cometh to range even with north side of the shop..and foure accres more or lesse upon pine hill south. 1773 J. McAfee *Jrnl.* in N. M. Woods *Woods-McAfee Memorial* (1905) 436/1 We..crossed Cantucky river within 8 miles of pine hills and broken mountains. 1947 Dylan Thomas *Let.* 20 May (1966) 307 The pinehills are endless. [*c* 1760 B. Wilkes *Eng. Moths & Butterflies* I. i. 29 The Wild Pine-tree Lappit-moth.] 1824 J. Curtis *Brit. Entomol.* I. 7 (*heading*) Pine lappet. 1907 R. South *Moths Brit. Isles*, 1st Ser. 106 This is.. the 'Wild Pine tree Lappet Moth' and 'Pine Tree Lappet' of the more ancient authors. 1966 O. Kuthanová tr. *Moucha's Beautiful Moths* 106 Pine Lappett Moth... This moth is one of Central Europe's notorious pine forest pests. 1694 *Mass. Hist. Soc. Coll.* (1852) 4th Ser. I. 105 Ye town is incompass'd with a fortification, consisting of pine-logs. 1853 J. M. Neale in *Oxf. Bk. Carols* (1928) 271 Bring me flesh, and bring me wine, Bring me pine-logs hither. 1902 S. E. White *Blazed Trail* 266 The instant necessity was to get thirty millions of pine logs down the river. 1938 E. Ambler *Cause for Alarm* xvii. 281 We stood in front of the fire... There were two half-consumed pine logs hissing..on the top. 1978 *Country Life* 12 Oct. 1096/4 The pine logs are first debarked and then loaded into the kilns and burnt [for charcoal]. 1936 D. McCowan *Animals Canad. Rockies* xxvi. 230 The Pine marten may long continue to frequent the green solitudes. 1964 H. N. Southern *Handbk. Brit. Mammals* II. 358 Pine Marten (*M*[*artes*] *martes*), the only one occurring in British Isles, distributed in Europe down to Mediterranean. 1896 *Congress. Rec.* 20 Jan. 796/2 The bill provides that the Committee shall..get as cheap a coffin as it can bargain for..perhaps what they call in the army a pine overcoat. 1929 E. Linklater *Poet's Pub* xxiv. 259 The room..was..pine-panelled. 1952 M. Laski *Village* vi. 106 Delicate satinwood furniture against the pine-panelled walls. 1968 J. Sangster *Touchfeather* xiv. 150 One of the main rooms..was about sixty feet long, pine panelled and cool. 1974 *Country Life* 21 Mar. 695/3 Specialists in carved or plain pine panelled Rooms. 1665 *Early Rec. Lancaster, Mass.* (1884) 79 A slipe of medow ground Runing through the most part of a great pine plaine. 1779 *Proc. Mass. Hist. Soc.* (1886) 2nd Ser. II. 464 [We] encampt on a pine plain by the side of a Large flatt. 1935 *Ecol. Monogr.* Jan. 66 The sandy, so-called 'Pine plains' were pitch pine. 1913 *Phytopathol.* III. 306 (*heading*) The introduction of a European pine rust into Wisconsin. 1951 *Dict. Gardening* (R. Hort. Soc.) III. 1580/1 Weymouth Pine Rust is a disease of 5-needled pines caused by the aecidial stage of the rust fungus *Cronartium ribicola*. 1960 C. Westcott *Plant Disease Handbk.* (ed. 2) iv. 355 (*caption*) Pine rusts. 1735 *New Voy. to Georgia* 13 We rode about two Miles farther, where we came to a large Pine Savannat [*sic*, *bis*]. 1791 W. Bartram *Trav. N. & S. Carolina* 208 The cattle which only feed and range in the high forests and Pine savannas are clear of this disorder. 1827 [see Savannah 2]. 1976 West & Augelli *Middle Amer.* (ed. 2) ii. 47/2 The chief reason for the Nicaraguan pine-savanna is probably the porous, gravelly soil, which will support only drought-tolerant plants. 1840 J. & M. Loudon tr. *Köllar's Treat. Insects* III. 345 The means devised by man for guarding against and destroying the pine saw-fly are as follows. 1972 *Times* 10 June 1/7 The limited experimental evidence..demonstrated an effective defence against the potato moth and the pine sawfly. 1891 O. Wilde *Pict. Dorian Gray* xviii. 299 The clear, pine-scented air. 1937 M. Sharp *Nutmeg Tree* iv. 51 A gust of sweet pine-scented air. 1972 D. Anthony *Blood on Harvest Moon* ii. 19 The cabin reeked from the pine-scented disinfectant they used to clean the bathroom. 1887 R. Ridgway *Man. N. Amer. Birds* 400 Northern North America, breeding from northern United States northward... Pine Siskin. 1947 *Chicago Tribune* 28 Dec. VI. 1/1 Some pine siskins..were found munching on birch cones and pods. 1971 *Islander* (Victoria, B.C.) 13 June 13/1 A flock of pine siskins, flashing their yellow-banded wings in darting flight. 1791 Pine-snake [see *bull-snake* s.v. *bull *sb.*[1] 11]. 1823 E. James *Acct. Expedition Rocky Mts.* I. 131 A serpent..which has considerable affinity with the pine-snake of the southern states. 1941 M. Lyon *Take to Hills* 192 Inside that bird nest was a small piece of discarded pine snakeskin, the original bands still faintly visible. 1956 L. M. Klauber *Rattlesnakes* I. ix. 585 A timber rattler..had eaten a pine snake. 1832 J. P. Kennedy *Swallow Barn* I. xxviii. 295 The ground was strewed with a thick coat of pine-straw,—as the yellow sheddings of this tree are called. 1884 G. W. Cable *Dr. Sevier* lvii. 435 Here stood Mary Richling. She still had on the pine-straw hat. 1939 *These are our Lives* (Federal Writers' Project, U.S.) 51 The pen was grounded with pine straw as was the shelter. 1976 *National Observer* (U.S.) 15 May 18/3 Our toys were found or made on the farm. We rolled steel barrel hoops with a heavy wire pusher, slid down pine-straw hills on old disc-plow blades. 1659 *Rec. Watertown, Mass.* (1894) I. i. 65 Abram Brownes Land..begins ten rod from Rich. Bloyse his lott, & soe apon a straite line to a pine stump. 1816 *Niles' Reg.* IX. Suppl. 178/1 Many a farmer who heretofore dreaded the pine stump..now swings his undisturbed scythe. 1635 *Cambridge* (Mass.) *Proprietors' Rec.* (1896) 6 More by the pine swampe about six acers. 1705 *Early Rec. Providence, Rhode Island* (1903) XVII. 201 At the South End of a Piece of Meadow & a Pine Swampe. 1862 O. W. Norton *Army Lett.* (1903) 62 We are bivouacked in a pine swamp. 1851 *Southern Lit. Messenger* XVII. 226/2 We made [a bonfire] of dead boughs and 'pine-tags'. 1881 *Harper's Mag.* Nov. 868/2 At night they [*sc.* the mountain people].. lie down on their pine-tag beds. 1947 *Richmond* (Virginia) *Times-Dispatch* 13 Oct. 10/3 Oat straw,..pine tags,.. and lawn clippings and leaves also could be used [for a mulch]. 1836 in *Jrnl. Southern Hist.* (1935) I. 367, I have been lost nearly all day.., wandering about in pine thickets. 1671 *South Carolina Hist. Soc. Coll.* (1897) V. 298, I have..dispatched the Carolina laden with Pine timber. 1866 *Rep. Indian Affairs* (U.S.) 288 There is much of their territory valuable for the pine timber upon it. 1839 W. B. O. Peabody in Storer & Peabody *Rep. Fishes, Reptiles & Birds Mass.* 310 The Pine Warbler..is not much known, because it resides in deep, evergreen forests. 1868 *Amer. Naturalist* II. 171 Soon after the pine-warbler has arrived..the Yellow Red-polled Warbler..makes his appearance. 1917 T. G. Pearson *Birds Amer.* III. 149/1 The Pine Warbler is a well-named bird, because its nesting sites are always in pine trees. 1961 O. L. Austin *Birds of World* 285/2 The well-named Pine Warbler..almost invariably nests in a clump of pine needles. 1814 J. Bigelow *Florula Bostoniensis* 73 *Sarothra gentianoides* Pine weed... A small, erect branching plant. 1843, 1907 Pine-weed [see *nit-weed]. 1862 *Rep. Comm. Patents 1861: Agric.* (U.S.) 605 *Hylobius pales*..is the common 'pine weevil' of the north and the south. 1867 *Amer. Naturalist* I. 110 Many other weevils and boring-beetles, especially..the Pine Weevil (*Pissodes strobi*)..now abound. 1936 *Discovery* Feb. 47/2 Extensive planting of conifers since the War has raised the problem of undue increase of the damaging Pine Weevils. 1972 Swan & Papp *Common Insects N. Amer.* 486 Pine Weevil: *Hylobius congener*... Range: Massachusetts to Alaska.

b. *attrib.* passing into *adj.* Designating preparations having the aroma of pine-needles.

1890 T. H. Dean *How to be Beautiful* ii. 23 Pine bath. This is a bath much prized by a beautiful Russian lady. 1926–7 *Army & Navy Stores Catal.* 472/1 Klenitas Pine Bath—bot. 2/6. 1931 S. Jameson *Richer Dust* xiv. 420 Put some pine salts in my bath. 1939–40 *Army & Navy Stores Catal.* 404/3 Pine odour disinfectant powder. 1972 J. Aiken *Butterfly Picnic* x. 175 [A] powerful effusion of pine bath essence. 1976 J. Wilson *Let's Pretend* xvii. 179 A bottle of pine disinfectant.

pine, *v.* Add: **5. d.** Of timber: to shrink.

1833 J. C. Loudon *Encycl. Cottage, Farm, & Villa Archit.* II. ii. 492 The granary floor to be laid with inch-and-quarter white-wood battens, dressed and jointed: the battens to be laid loose, so as to take up and relay after pining (shrinking).

pineal, *a.* Add: **a.** (Further examples.) Now known to secrete melatonin in various mammals and to be concerned with photoperiodicity and circadian rhythms.

1958 [see *melatonin]. 1970 T. Hughes *Crow* 23 Crow split his enemy's skull to the pineal gland. 1971 J. A. Kappers in Wolstenholme & Knight *Pineal Gland* 22 The mammalian pineal gland is an end organ of the peripheral sympathetic system conveying photic and other stimuli to it. 1978 Lee & Laycock *Essent. Endocrinol.* v. 103 The relationship between the pineal gland and the development of puberty in man is still undecided.

b. (Further examples.)

1974 D. P. Cardinali in James & Martini *Current Topics Exper. Endocrinol.* II. 113 The pineal capacity to take up and retain estradiol and testosterone resembles that observed in the uterus and the prostate, suggesting that specific receptors for sex steroids may be present in the pinealocytes. 1979 *McGraw-Hill Yearbk. Sci. & Technol.* 288/2 A pineal role in the photoperiodic control of reproduction in hamsters has been established.

B. *sb.* The pineal body.

1911 *Arch. Internal Med.* VIII. 854 In enlargements of the pineal, circulatory disturbances will develop first. 1963 A. Gorbman in Euler & Heller *Compar. Endocrinol.* I. viii. 303 Pflugfelder removed or destroyed the epiphysis (pineal) of the guppy (*Lebistes*) and found that the thyroid became greatly hypertrophied. 1966 Wright & Symmers *Systemic Path.* II. xxxiii. 1134/1 The pineal has another endocrine role, that of secreting the melanophore-contracting hormone, melatonin.., and this has been regarded as related to the original photo-receptor function of the gland. 1968, 1974 [see *melatonin]. 1974 D. P. Cardinali in James & Martini *Current Topics Exper. Endocrinol.* II. 115 The pineal is involved in the regulation of pituitary, gonadal, adrenal, and thyroid functions.

pinealectomy (piniăle·ktŏmi, pəiniăl-). *Surg.* [f. Pineal *a.* + *-ectomy.] Excision of the pineal body.

1915 *Jrnl. Exper. Med.* XXII. 240 The purpose of this paper is to report briefly the results of pinealectomy in a series of young puppies and to describe the method which has been evolved for extirpation of the pineal body. 1941 *Endocrinol.* XXVIII. 837 All pinealectomies were performed at the age of 20 to 21 days under ether anesthesia. 1976 *Nature* 5 Feb. 431/2 An experiment showing that pinealectomy somewhat reduced maternal behaviour.

So **pineale·ctomize** *v. trans.*, to deprive of the pineal body; **pineale·ctomized** *ppl. a.*

1912 *Rev. Neurol. & Psychiatry* X. 477 When pinealectomised pullets, who had already begun to lay, were isolated with pinealectomised cockerels, their eggs proved fertile on artificial incubation. 1933 *Proc. Soc. Exper. Biol. & Med.* XXX. 766 Sixteen albino rats..were pinealectomized at about 26 days of age. 1970 *Sci. Amer.* Feb. 44/3 Seven out of 12 pinealectomized rats treated with PCPA displayed sexual excitement. 1972 *Science* 27 Oct. 421/3 At 6 weeks of age, half of the birds in each chamber were pinealectomized.

pinealoma (piniălōᵘ·mă). *Path.* [f. Pineal *a.* + *-oma.] A tumour of the pineal gland thought to arise from the parenchymal cells.

1923 K. H. Krabbe in *Endocrinol.* VII. 391 In none of the cases has the tumor been an adenoma or, more exactly, 'pinealoma', but always a teratoma. 1948 R. A. Willis *Path. of Tumours* iii. 820 Pineal tumours, either pinealomas or teratomas, occurring in young children have often been accompanied by precocious bodily, mental or sexual development. 1966 Wright & Symmers *Systemic Path.* II. xxxiii. 1134/2 Teratomas, pinealomas and gliomas are the usual neoplasms of the pineal gland, although collectively even these tumours are rare. 1974 J. M. R. Edwards in T. J. Deeley *Central Nervous Syst. Tumours* iv. 99 Some of the tumours occurring in the pineal gland are undoubtedly teratomas but there is controversy concerning the pathological nature of the 'pinealoma'.

pine-apple, pineapple. Add: **2.** The usu. form is now **pineapple.**

c. A bomb; a hand grenade or light trench mortar. *slang.*

[1916: see *pineapple bomb* below]. 1918 R. H. Knyvett *Over There* 193 But Fritz can be very obstinate on occasions, and all our teasing with rifle-grenades failed to make him retaliate with anything larger than 'pineapples' (light trench-mortars). 1920 W. B. Ellington *Company 'A' 23rd Engineers* 113 *Pineapple*, French hand grenade. 1928 [see *gangland]. 1932 E. Wallace *When Gangs came to London* xv. 118 'By "pineapple" I mean "bomb",' said Jiggs gravely. 'It's part of the racketeer's equipment.' 1944 *Sun* (Baltimore) 2 Aug. 2/3 There was a crossfire of ten grenades before one of his pineapples destroyed a position with four enemy soldiers in it. 1972 J. Quartermain *Rock of Diamond* v. 28 'You..don't want that old-time pineapple lobbed through your store window. You know what a pineapple is, Raven?' 'A hand grenade.' 'Right.' 1976 'B. Shelby' *Great Pebble Affair* III. 143 He was Wild Wally of ice-pick, pineapple and machine-gun fame.

d. *the pineapple* (slang), unemployment benefit, 'the dole'.

1937 Partridge *Dict. Slang* 632/1 *Pine-apple, on the*, on parish relief. 1971 *Observer* 23 May 7 'There were just too many people on the pineapple.' The 'pineapple' is slang for the dole.

3. b. *pineapple juice*; **pineapple bomb** *slang* = sense 2 c above; **pineapple chunks,** tinned pineapple cut into small cubes; also *fig.*; **pineapple jelly,** jelly flavoured with pineapple; **pineapple rum** (examples); **pineapple weed,** a small, aromatic, annual herb, *Matricaria matricarioides*, belonging to the family Compositæ and bearing yellow flower-heads smelling like pineapple when crushed.

1916 'Boyd Cable' *Doing their Bit* iii. 45 We saw 'pineapple bombs' or hand grenades being made—'pineapple' being a neat description of the shape and criss-cross pattern of lines marking the segments into which the grenade bursts. 1952 Wodehouse *Pigs have Wings* i. 9 You watch that pig of yours like a hawk, Clarence, or before you know where you are, this fiend in human shape will be slipping pineapple bombs into her bran mash. 1972 *Daily Tel.* (Colour Suppl.) 1 Sept. 19/1 The 'pineapple' bomb ploughs a furrow through the undergrowth with steel pellets. 1903 Atkinson & Holroyd *Pract. Cookery* (ed. 3) 113, 1 tin of pineapple chunks. 1926 Wodehouse *Heart of Gold* ix. 300 Anastatia [*sic*] ordered pineapple chunks with whipped cream. 1963 R. Carrier *Great Dishes o ; World* 175 Drain the pineapple chunks.

Reserve juice. **1977** D. Beaty *Excellency* i. 15 A DC 6 was leaving, its propellers chopping a long shaft of light into pineapple chunks. **1841** Thackeray in *Fraser's Mag.* June 723/1 They..served us.. pine-apple jelly. **1907** R. M. F. Berry *Fruit Recipes* xix. 245 Pineapple jelly (without gelatine). **1958** W. Bickel tr. *Hering's Dict. Cookery* 723 Fancy mould lined with pineapple jelly. **1904** Mrs. H. M. Young *Home-Made Cakes & Sweets* 33 Add..2 tablespoonfuls pineapple juice. **1957** E. Craig *Collins Family Cookery* 392 Heat in pineapple juice. **1972** J. Potter *Going West* 171 Ashley bought pineapple juices from a café. **1977** F. Webb *Go far Out* viii. 144 The attendant..brought him a large glass of pineapple juice. **1765** A. Stuart *Let.* 25 July in Duke of Argyll *Intimate Society Lett. 18th Cent.* (1910) I. 111 Ye Greatest part of your Pine aple rum went, as you desired in return for his many feasts, To Baron Dolbach. **1837** Dickens *Pickw.* xxvii. 276 A glass of reeking hot pine-apple rum and water, with a slice of lemon in it. **1967–8** *Bahamas Handbk. & Businessmen's Ann.* (ed. 7) 56, I poured a double pineapple rum on the rocks. **1908** Robinson & Fernald *Gray's New Man. Bot.* 847 Pine-apple-weed...Odor of the bruised plant suggesting pineapple. **1945** J. M. Fogg *Weeds of Lawn & Garden* 168 Pineapple-weed provides an interesting example of a species which is indigenous to the far western states and has become naturalized not only in eastern North America but also in Europe. **1978** *Country Life* 22 June 1797/1 Pineapple weed, a coloniser of disturbed ground ..assisted to and from a site on the tyres of wheel-barrows.

‖ **Pineau** (pino). Also with lower-case initial. Pl. **-eaux.** [Fr., f. *pin* pine (tree) + dim. suffix *-eau*: so called because of the form of the grape cluster.] **1.** = *Pinot.

The usual form is now *Pinot.*

1763 [see Tresseau]. **1833** C. Redding *Hist. Mod. Wines* v. 76 In all the distinguished vineyards of Champagne..they cultivate only the black grape.., being a variety of the vine called *pinet* and red and white *pineau.* **1845** *Encycl. Metrop.* XXV. 1275/1 The fine wines of Burgundy, and the best Champagne, come from the *pineau*, a black grape. **1888** *Encycl. Brit.* XXIV. 606/1 The white grapes employed are the *Pineau blanc*, which are vintaged a full fortnight later than the red grapes. **1911** *Ibid.* XXVIII. 727/2 Practically all the important wines of Germany are white, although there are a few red growths of some quality, for instance that of Assmannshausen in the Rheingau. The latter is produced from the black Burgundy vine, the Pineau. **1967** A. Lichine *Encycl. Wines* 404/1 *Pinot, Pineau.* One of the most distinguished families of wine grapes.

2. More fully *Pineau des Charentes* (de ʃarɑ̃t). An aperitif made from unfermented grape juice and brandy.

1940 C. Morgan *Voyage* iii. iv. 260 Barbet came from the house carrying a tray on which were plums preserved in cognac and a bottle of pineau. Thérèse disliked pineau; the mixture of cognac and unfermented wine was too sweet for her taste. **1951** R. Postgate *Plain Man's Guide to Wine* iii. 60 There is a pleasant, not very distinctive drink called Pineau or Plessis, which is made from the must of wine in Charente (where cognac comes from) and served in quantities in railway trains. **1959** *Listener* 15 Jan. 125/1 Mr. Root has too low an opinion of Pineau des Charentes as an apéritif. **1959** A. Waugh *In Praise of Wine* xii. 162 The grapes of the Charente are poor to eat and little wine is made there now... But there is a local *apéritif* called Pineau, made in the same way as Port, the fermentation being stopped by alcohol. **1961** *Listener* 12 Oct. 574/1 A humdrum café-life among taxi-drivers and porters who also drank their *pineau* at the counter. **1968** A. Laski *Keeper* ii. 21 You shall have an aperitif on the house. Gui! Bring the Pineau for Colin. **1973** C. Ray *Cognac* x. 127 For centuries past, certainly since the sixteenth century, the peasants of the Charentes ..have made an aperitif drink for themselves by 'muting' (checking the fermentation of) fresh grape juice by the addition of brandy. The ratafia of Champagne, the pineau of the Charentes, are sweet, strong, and tasty. *Ibid.*, The best pineaux I drank in Cognac..were the Plessis of Camus and the Reynac of UNICOOP.

pine-barren. Add: **a.** (Earlier, later, and *attrib.* examples.)

1731 *Pennsylvania Gaz.* 29 Apr.–6 May 1/2 We had a sandy Pine Barren to walk in, which was covered pretty thick with large Pine Trees. **1743** M. Catesby *Nat. Hist. Carolina* II. p. iv/1 The third and worst Kind of Land is the *Pine barren Land.* **1901** C. T. Mohr *Plant Life Alabama* 125 The pine-barren streams overflow their low banks of shifting sands and gravel. **1916** J. W. Harshberger (*title*) Vegetation of the New Jersey pine-barrens. **1952** *Guardian* 3 Mar. 4/6 This long peninsula, traded back and forth for two centuries between Spain, France and Britain, was not much more than a pine-barren, pocketed with swamps, till the late nineteenth century. **1976** *Hortus Third* (L. H. Bailey Hortorium) 932/2 *Pyxidanthera*... Creeping, evergreen shrublets, forming cushionlike masses, native to pine barrens from N[ew] J[ersey] to S[outh] C[arolina].

b. pine-barren beauty (earlier and later examples); **pine-barren terrapin,** substitute for def.: the box tortoise, *Terrapene carolina*; (example).

1883 W. Robinson *Eng. Flower Garden* 237/2 Pine Barren Beauty..is an evergreen shrub, yet smaller than many Mosses. **1901** L. H. Bailey *Cycl. Amer. Hort.* III. 1475/2 The Pyxie, Flowering Moss or Pine-barren Beauty is a pretty little creeping plant, native only to New Jersey and North Carolina. **1951** *Dict. Gardening* (R. Hort. Soc.) IV. 1722/2 *P[yxidanthera] barbulata.* Pyxie, Pine-barren Beauty, Flowering Moss. **1884** G. B. Goode *Fisheries U.S.: Nat. Hist. Aquatic Animals* 158 The Carolina Box Turtle... In the Southern States it is known as the 'Pine-barren Terrapin'.

pine-blank (pəi·n,blæŋk), U.S. dial. var. Point-blank *a.*, *sb.*, and *adv.*

1886 *Century Mag.* Jan. 433/2, I oughter 'a' said it then, but I'll say it now, right pine-blank. **1896** 'Mark Twain' in *Harper's Mag.* Aug. 345/1 They told him pine blank and once for all, he *couldn't.* **1937** *Frontier & Midland* Autumn 13 His eyes standin pine-blank open. **1954** *Publ. Amer. Dial. Soc.* xxi. 34 A *pine blank* lie. *Ibid.*, I swear *pine blank.*

pine knot. *U.S.* [Pine *sb.*[2] 7.] A knot of pine-wood, usu. burned as a fuel or for illumination, and adduced as a symbol of hardness, toughness, etc. Also *fig.* and *attrib.*

c **1670** *Plymouth* (Mass.) *Rec.* (1889) I. 119 There shalbe noe pyne knot picked. **1791** [see Pine *sb.*[2] 7]. **1808** J. N. Barker *Indian Princess* iii. i. 47 [She] lit me with her pine-knot torch to bedward. **1835** 'H. Bull-Us' *Diverting Hist. John Bull & Bro. Jonathan* (new ed.) i. 8 Jonathan, though as hard as a pine knot, ..could bear it no longer. **1850** H. C. Watson *Camp-Fires of Revolution* 31 We stuck to them as close as pine-knots. **1853** 'P. Paxton' *Stray Yankee in Texas* 310 We stood.. with the bright light of a pineknot fire shining full upon us. **1856** X. D. MacLeod *Biogr. F. Wood* 48 The human pine-knot John C. Calhoun. **1876** S. & A. Warner *Gold of Chickaree* 360 You know as well as I do, that you are a pine knot for endurance. **1897** *Outing* XXX. 69/2, I held a pine-knot for him to make the entry in our log-book. **1904** G. Stratton-Porter *Freckles* 95 He was as tough as a pine-knot and as agile as a panther. **1945** B. A. Botkin *Lay my Burden Down* 62 When the boys would start to the quarters from the field, they would get a turn of lider [*sc.* lightwood] knots. I 'specks you knows 'em as pine knots. **1961** B. Palmer *Many are Hearts* 137 The dark night flecked with pine-knot torches. **1979** M. G. Eberhart *Bayou Road* xvii. 175 There was the red, smokey flare of lighted pine knots ahead.

pine land. *U.S.* [Pine *sb.*[2] 7.] Land on which pine trees are the characteristic growth. Also *attrib.* Hence **pi·ne-lander,** one who lives on and derives a living from such land.

c **1658** [see *oak land]. **1665–70** *Early Rec. Lancaster, Mass.* (1884) 271 There is another piece of upland..Sum part pine Land & partly oak Land. **1735** *Georgia Hist. Soc. Coll.* (1842) II. 45 We encamped there, and found ..the pine land very valuable. **1765** [see Pine *sb.*[2] 7]. **1789** J. Morse *Amer. Geogr.* 446 They are often to be found in pine lands in the southern states. **1838** C. Gilman *Recoll. Southern Matron* xxiii. 157 There is something picturesque in the evening hour at a pine-land village. **1839** F. A. Kemble *Jrnl. Residence Georgian Plantation* (1863) 75 He gave me a..description of the Yeomanry of Georgia, more properly termed pine-landers. **1890** *Harper's Mag.* Apr. 790/1 Quaint and indolent pine-landers and degraded swamp-dwellers, have all supplied our literary comedians with unique characters. **1903** 'P. Pennington' *Woman Rice Planter* (1913) i. 53 Drove S—— to church in our little pine-land village; she seemed to enjoy the very simple service. **1922** H. Kephart *Our Southern Highlanders* (new ed.) 433 These freedman were pushed further and further back upon more and more sterile soil. They became 'pine-landers' or 'piney-woods-people'..or 'crackers'. **1948** *Sat. Even. Post* 4 Sept. 30/1 There was a stillness here in the flat lonesome pinelands. **1977** D. Clark *Gimmel Flask* v. 95 A..voice broke into song. 'Tina, soon the leaves will be falling, From the pine-lands I'm calling, Won't you come back to me-e?'

pinene (pəi·nīn). *Chem.* [ad. G. *pinen* (O. Wallach 1885, in *Ann. d. Chem. u. Pharm.* CCXXVII. 300), f. L. *pīn-us* Pine *sb.*[2] + G. *-en* -ene.] Either or both of two isomeric liquid terpenes, $C_{10}H_{16}$, which are the major constituents of turpentine and differ in the position of the double bond.

1885 *Jrnl. Chem. Soc.* XLVIII. 551 The author proposes to classify the terpenes as follows:.. B. True Terpenes, $C_{10}H_{16}$, divided into the following groups: 1. Pinenes (boiling point 160°). [Etc.] **1886** *Ibid.* L. 71 Terpine is formed by the inversion of pinene with alcoholic sulphuric acid. **1922** *Nature* 16 Feb. 226/2 The yield of oil from leaves of the New South Wales sassafras tree was about 1 per cent... The principal constituents identified are safrol, camphor, pinene, sesquiterpenes, eugenol, and alcoholic bodies. **1960** A. R. Pinder *Chem. of Terpenes* v. 93, α-Pinene is of great importance commercially in the synthesis of camphor and related terpenes... β-Pinene, which is isomeric with α-pinene, accompanies the latter in most sources of the hydrocarbon. **1971** *Daily Tel.* 12 June 6/3 The leaf is pinched to break specialised cells containing these elements of geraniol, citral, eucalyptal, borneol, pinene and others.

pine-nut. Delete *?Obs.* Substitute for last part of def.: also, the edible seeds of several pines, esp. the European stone pine, *Pinus cembra*, and the Mexican stone pine, *P. cembroides.* (Later examples.)

1845 J. C. Frémont *Rep. Exploring Exped.* 222 A party of twelve Indians came down from the mountains to trade pine nuts. **1869** *Harper's Mag.* Sept. 473/1 The pine-nut is one of the principal articles used as food by these Pintes. **1937** A. F. Hill *Econ. Bot.* xvi. 371 The pine nuts or piñons are the edible seeds of several species of *Pinus* that are native to the Rocky Mountain and Pacific Coast region. **1947** *Sierra Club Bull.* (San Francisco) Mar. 4/1 It is far too late now to advocate..the Indian's custom of living on the income of natural resources, the replenishable deer, pine nuts and grasshoppers. **1954** E. David *Italian Food* 32 Pine nuts or pine kernels..come from the cones of the stone pine. **1977** *Homes & Gardens* Sept. 104/2 Toss pine nuts in a little butter until crisp and golden.

Pinerotic (pinərǫ·tik), *a.* [f. the name *Pinero* (see below) + -otic.] Pertaining to or characteristic of the dramatist Sir Arthur Wing Pinero (1855–1934), or his plays.

1895 G. B. Shaw *Let.* 18 Mar. (1965) I. 501 It would appear so very easy to give my subjects the Pinerotic effect. **1896** *Sat. Rev.* 29 Feb. 223/1 It contains not a word about Mr. Pinero himself.., his hopes and fears for the drama, or anything else distinctively Pinerotic. **1938** C. Morgan *Flashing Stream* p. xvi, The Pinerotic theory that a woman, to be entitled to our respect in the theatre, must, if she shares a man's bed, do so with a self-sacrificial reluctance.

pinery. Add: **2.** Chiefly *N. Amer.* (Earlier and later examples.) Also *attrib.*

1783 *Rep. Bureau Arch. Ontario* (1906) III. p. cxx, There are fine pineries two or three miles from the water's edge where large masts may be procured. **1822** *Massachusetts Spy* 6 Feb. (Th.), There are also a few pineries, but of small extent. **1926** *Amer. Speech* II. 100/2 The lumberjacks have found anthologists who appreciate better than did the singers themselves the charm of the pinery songs. **1952** D. F. Putnam *Canad. Regions* 138/1 Its 'pineries' formed the source of much of the timber which came down the Ottawa River.

pi·ne-top. [f. Pine *sb.*[2] + Top *sb.*[1]] **a.** The top of a pine-tree. **b.** *U.S. slang.* Cheap or illicit whisky.

1858 *Southern Lit. Messenger* XXVII. 463/2 A rough, but hearty frolic..with profusion of 'pine-top' succeeded. **1878** O. Wilde *Ravenna* v. 10 The pine-tops rocked before the evening breeze. **1931** *Amer. Speech* VII. 50 The 'drinks' are 'pine-top', 'white mule', [etc.]. **1942** Berrey & Van den Bark *Amer. Thes. Slang* §99/7 *Illicit whiskey*,.. pine-top. **1946** J. W. Day *Harvest Adventure* xiii. 214 At the report the second, larger still, swung over a gap in the pine-tops and the next barrel knocked him sideways and sent him spinning in a long dive into the snipe marsh below the wood.

pine-wood. Add: **2.** (Earlier and later examples.) Hence **pi·ne-woody** *a.* (*rare*), suggestive of pine-woods.

1673 J. Ray *Observations Journey Low-Countries* 80 After one half-hours riding we entred into Pine-Woods, the first we met withal: They reach'd almost to our Lodging. **1790** *Pennsylvania Packet* 11 Oct. 3/4 A ganninipper is a kind of large horse-fly frequent in pine woods. **1872** R. G. McClellan *Golden State* xvii. 204 These hogs..are somewhat like the North Carolina pine-woods hogs. **1917** D. H. Lawrence *Look! We have come Through!* 40 The jade-green river Goes between the pine-woods. **1939** E. E. Murphey *Wings at Dusk* 13 Whenever I see one Flushing befoh me Histing his flag, like a buck in de pine-wood [etc.]. **1945** J. Betjeman *New Bats in Old Belfries* 6 Mushroomy, pinewoody evergreen smells. **1978** 'I. Drummond' *Stench of Poppies* xi. 167 In the foothills of the Taurus..among superb pinewoods.

piney wood. *U.S.* Also **piny wood.** [*piney* var. Piny *a.*] **a.** A pine-wood; a region of pine-woods; *spec.* (pl.) regions of poor land in the Southern United States of which pine-trees are the characteristic growth. Also *attrib.*

1809 M. L. Weems *Life Gen. F. Marion* xiv. 122 Had this savage spirit appeared among a few poor British *cadets*, or *piney wood* tories, it would not have been so lamentable. *a* **1816** B. Hawkins *Sk. Creek Country* (1848) 29 Broken piny woods and reedy branches on its right side. **1860** Bartlett *Dict. Amer.* (ed. 3) 321 *Piney woods*, the name given at the South to a large tract covered with pines, especially in the low country. **1863** [see Piny *a.*]. **1887** *Century Mag.* Aug. 544/1 Azalia, the little piney-woods village which Dr. Buxton had recommended as a sanitarium. **1946** *Sun* (Baltimore) 26 July 16/3 The ponies..roam wild in the piney woods. **1963** *Social Problems* X. 365/1 Lest such piney-woods practices be thought beneath the sophistication of the urban Negro. **1973** *Daily Colonist* (Victoria, B.C.) 14 Aug. 2/3 Otter said that the twenty-seven victims found buried at the beach, in an east Texas piney wood and in a Houston boat shed, might be all the police will recover. **1976** J. Crosby *Snake* (1977) xiii. 70 She found herself deep in piny woods and she could see nothing.

b. Special Combs., as **piney-woods cracker,** a poor Southern white; **piney-wood(s) tacky,** (*a*) a scrub pony; (*b*) = prec.

1872 *Kansas Mag.* Mar. 238/1 Who that has seen the 'clay-eater', the 'sandhiller', or the 'piney woods cracker' of the South, does not know that it is impossible to exaggerate the sinfulness which looks out through the loop-holes of his red apologies for eyes? **1935** Z. N. Hurston *Mules & Men* (1970) i. v. 113 'Bout this time John seen a white couple come in but they looked so trashy he figgered they was piney woods crackers. **1846** *Spirit of Times* 11 July 234/3 Mac mounted a piney-woods-tacky..and hied him off to Charleston. **1888** *Century Mag.* XXXVI. 799/2 If Mr. Catlett will come to Georgia and go among the 'po' whites' and 'piney-wood tackeys', he will hear the terms 'we-uns' and 'you-uns' in everyday use. **1944** B. A. Botkin *Treas. Amer. Folklore* ii. 322 Such derogatory nicknames as..sand-hillers, pineywoods tackies, hill-billies.

pi·n-fire, *a.*[2] (*sb.*[2]) Also **pinfire.** [f. Pin *sb.*[1] + Fire *sb.*] Used *attrib.* and *absol.* to designate precious opal characterized by closely spaced specks of colour.

1902 *Blackw. Mag.* Feb. 254/1 Two men found a large piece of 'pin-fire', or the best opal. **1902** [see *ORANGE *a.* 1 b]. **1908** A. J. DAWSON *Finn* xxxi. 464 Sixty-six solid pounds o' best pin-fire—and us dyin' for want of a crust. **1964** W. C. EYLES *Bk. Opals* i. 25 Pin-fire opal is a type in which the main body of the stone is usually white and shows a myriad of small pinlike colors all through the surface and the body of the stone. **1971** R. PURVIS *Treasure Hunting* i. 27/2 In pin-fire opals, the colour play is in small pinlike dots thickly scattered through the mass. **1976** *Sci. Amer.* Apr. 84/3 In 'pinfire' varieties of opal the grains are up to a millimeter across, but in the more typical varieties they are several millimeters across.

ping, *sb.* Add: **a.** (Earlier and later examples.)
1835 J. E. ALEXANDER *Sk. Portugal* xi. 262 If a button was shown, 'ping' went a bullet at it immediately. **1909** KIPLING *Rewards & Fairies* (1910) 272 *Ping-ping-ping* went the bicycle bell round the corner. **1921** D. H. LAWRENCE in *Hutchinson's Mag.* Nov. 463/1 They were interrupted by the ping of the shop-bell. **1930** J. B. PRIESTLEY *Angel Pavement* v. 263 She sent the typewriter carriage flying along. It gave a sharp ping. **1957** H. NICOLSON *Diary* 5 Oct. (1968) 339 The Russians have released a satellite... The B.B.C. have managed to record the signals, and play them over to us—just ping, ping, ping, ping. **1960** N. HILLIARD in C. K. Stead *N.Z. Short Stories* (1966) 235 They rested..listening to the..ping-ping-ping of crossing bells. **1977** *New Yorker* 20 June 94/3 Everyone assembled for an ostinato unison figure, and the music subsided with a string of tinkles and hums and pings.

b. A very short pulse of high-pitched, usu. ultrasonic, sound such as is emitted by sonar; also, a pulse of audible sound by which this is represented to a user of such equipment.
1943 *Penguin New Writing* XVIII. 27 'Daisy had a ping about an hour ago... We're doing an Asdic sweep.'.. A 'ping' is the slang term for an echo. **1946** *Sci. Illustr.* May 83/1 The sounds, or 'pings', sonar sends out are not at all like sounds to you and me. They are supersonic. **1956** *Deep-Sea Res.* III. 267 The system had a repetition rate of about 10 pings per second and a ping length of about two milliseconds. **1960** [see *PINGER 1 a]. **1966** *McGraw-Hill Encycl. Sci. & Technol.* IX. 252/2 The Swallow-type neutrally buoyant float is a mid-depth current meter..which..can float at a predetermined depth... It emits acoustic pings which can be heard for several miles from a quiet ship equipped with appropriate sound gear. **1967** J. B. HERSEY *Deep-Sea Photogr.* iv. 59/1 It was possible to obtain the height of camera above bottom simply by measuring the time interval between the arrival at the ship of the sound pulse, or ping, and its bottom echo.

c. Also *ping-man.* (See quots.) *slang.*
1946 J. IRVING *Royal Navalese* 135 *Ping-man*, an Asdic operator. **1948** PARTRIDGE *Dict. Forces' Slang* 142 *Ping*, an Asdic officer or rating.

d. = *PINK *sb.*[6] 3.
More usual than *pink* in the U.S. and Australia.
1927 *Dyke's Automobile & Gasoline Engine Encycl.* Suppl. 1313/1 Engineers began an investigation as to the causes of pre-ignition and ping in an engine burning the present-day gasoline. **1942** *Pop. Sci.* Mar. 137/2 A slight ping when you step on the gas hard does not always mean trouble. **1953** H. R. RICARDO *High-Speed Internal-Combustion Engine* ii. 27 The mechanism of detonation is the setting-up within the cylinder of a pressure wave travelling at so high a velocity as, by its impact against the cylinder walls, to set them in vibration and thus give rise to a high-pitched 'ping'. **1958** *S.A.E. Jrnl.* Sept. 73/1 Rumble..is distinct from the high frequency spark knock or wild ping most people have heard. **1977** *Pop. Mechanics* May 49/2 My 1976 Ford Pinto with a 2.3-liter, four-cylinder engine has had a bad ping almost from day one.

ping, *v.*[2] Add: **1. a.** (Further examples.) Also const. *out* and *fig.*
1924 GALSWORTHY *White Monkey* II. ix. 195 A footman ..stood..waiting for an order to ping out, staccato, through the hum. **1930** J. B. PRIESTLEY *Angel Pavement* iii. 96 The typewriters rattled and *pinged*, the telephone bell rang. *a* **1963** S. PLATH *Crossing Water* (1971) 53 The glass..will ping like a Chinese chime. **1967** *Listener* 16 Nov. 647/3 Words and concepts heard nowhere else pinged out on Third Programme drama. **1974** W. J. BURLEY *Death in Stanley St.* v. 90 He went in, the door bell pinged. **1978** T. WILLIS *Buckingham Palace Connection* viii. 151 A bullet pinged against the plating.

b. = *PINK *v.*[3] 2.
1942 *Pop. Sci.* Mar. 136/1 Let's assume it is a couple of months from now, and that best available gas makes your car engine ping—or worse, knock—on a pick-up or a hard pull.

2. a. (Earlier and later examples.) Also *fig.*
1746 *Exmoor Scolding* (1879) 52 Tha wud'st ha' borst en to Shivers, nif chad not a vung en, and pung'd en back agen. **1921** D. H. LAWRENCE in *Hutchinson's Mag.* Nov. 462/2 They 'pinged' the door-bell, and her aunt came running forward out of the kitchen. **1957** J. KEROUAC *On Road* (1958) 32 The air grew ice-cold and pinged our ears. **1961** J. H. FORD *Mountains of Gilead* v. 128 A room complete with moths pinging the light. **1974** 'P. B. YUILL' *Bornless Keeper* vii. 64 There was nobody at the little alcove marked Reception. Victoria pinged the bell.

b. To fire or discharge (a missile) with a pinging sound. Also *transf.*
1959 I. & P. OPIE *Lore & Lang. Schoolch.* xiii. 297 We ..ping pellets in class. **1977** A. C. H. SMITH *Jericho Gun* xiii. 171 He was able to ping off three one-shots.

‖**pinga** (pi·ŋă). [Pg., lit. 'drop (of water)'.] A raw white rum distilled from sugar-cane in Brazil.
1933 P. FLEMING *Brazilian Adventure* I. xii. 98 You drank black coffee with *pinga* in it. **1960** *Guardian* 14 June 9/6 Her breath reeked of pinga (a cheap drink made from sugar cane). **1974** *Country Life* 31 Oct. 1314/3 Sugar-cane spirit (or *pinga*). **1977** *Lancet* 24–31 Dec. 1365/2 We have studied 61 alcoholic patients with pellagra aged 23–49, most of them drinking more than 800 ml of *pinga* (a Brazilian alcoholic beverage similar to white rum) containing about 300 ml of pure ethanol.

pingao (pi·ŋɑu). Also **pingau.** [Maori.] A New Zealand sedge, *Desmoschœnus spiralis*, with creeping underground stems which help to stabilize sand-dunes.
1855 J. D. HOOKER *Flora Novæ-Zelandiæ* I. 272 *Desmoschœnus spiralis*...Nat[ive] name, 'Pingao'. **1905** W. B. *Where White Man Treads* 2 White seashore sand-hills..for..the wind..to pile into hillocks, until the wily pingau (native sand grass), creeping snakelike along,.. bound [them] into masses. **1936** [see *KAKAHO]. **1949** P. H. BUCK *Coming of Maori* II. iv. 156 The only other native colour to black, used in plaiting, was yellow obtained by using wefts of *pingao*, the leaves of which are a natural yellow. **1970** MOORE & EDGAR *Flora N.Z.* II. 171 Pingao... This is a well-known plant because it is an effective sand-binder and also because the Maoris used the dried golden leaves to give colour to articles woven from *Phormium*.

pinger (pi·ŋəɹ). [f. PING *v.*[2] + -ER[1].] **1. a.** A device that transmits pings (*PING *sb.* 1 b) at short intervals for purposes of detection, measurement, or identification.
1957 *Deep-Sea Res.* IV. 120 The three principal units which comprise the camera are the photographic unit, the electronic flash light and the acoustic signal generator or 'pinger'. **1960** *Electronics* 24 June 95/3 The detailed contour of the bottom with respect to the pinger can be determined by recording the direct and bottom-reflected pings. **1969** J. MAVOR *Voy. Atlantis* II. iv. 124 It was the shallowness of the water that made examination with Doc's pinger feasible. **1975** *Offshore Engineer* Nov. 51/1 The pinger receiver audibly indicates the direction to a pinger using a manually operated sensitivity control located on the end of the receiver and an earphone.

b. (See quot.)
1961 PARTRIDGE *Dict. Slang* (ed. 5) II. 1222/1 *Pinger*, the Asdic officer: Naval: since ca. 1936.

2. A timer that makes a ringing or pinging sound after a pre-set number of minutes.
1968 J. BINGHAM *I love, I Kill* vi. 72, I heard the old vibrant tinkling, like those kitchen ping-ers which tell you when the cabbage is ready cooked. **1973** *Times* 30 July 11/2 Many new cookers have automatic timing, with both a time of day clock for cooking while you are out and a 60-minute pinger for reminding you when you are in that a dish is cooked. **1976** P. DICKINSON *King & Joker* i. 10 Two eggs..boiled for two minutes... The pinger pinged.

pinging, *vbl. sb.* Add: *spec.* **a.** = *PINKING *vbl. sb.*[3]
More usual than *pinking* in the U.S. and Australia.
1955 *Pop. Mechanics* Nov. 203/2 Retard the spark a little at a time..until no pinging is heard. **1967** *Boston Sunday Herald* 28 May I. 2/6 'Pinging'..results from carbon deposits or fuel not high enough in octane rating. **1969** *Telegraph* (Brisbane) 1 Feb. 13/4 Tetra-ethyl lead is used to raise octane ratings, reduce engine knock or pinging and minimise engine misfires.

b. The production or emission of pings by sonar or similar equipment (see *PING *sb.* 1 b).
1956 *Deep-Sea Res.* IV. 39 The pinging circuit of the echo sounder. **1959** H. BARNES *Oceanogr. & Marine Biol.* 203 New cameras have been described and in one contact with the bottom is indicated by a change of the 'pinging' rate of a small sound source attached to the unit. **1973** *Times* 27 Dec. 3/2 Teams of 71 Squadron split into two daily shifts, poring over the sands between tides to the 'pinging' of mine detectors. **1974** 'M. HEBDEN' *Pride of Dolphins* III. iii. 232 The relentless pinging of the asdic beam.

pingo (piŋgo). *Geomorphol.* Pl. **pingos,** less commonly **pingoes.** [Eskimo (see quot. 1928[1]).] A perennial conical or dome-shaped mound (often with a crater on top) found in regions with thin or discontinuous permafrost and consisting of a layer of soil over a large core of ice, the width being much greater than the height; also, a round depression or rampart in temperate regions thought to be the remains of such a mound formed when the climate was colder.
The word is applied rather differently in quots. 1928. The current techn. use derives from that of Porsild.
[**1928** L. KOCH in *Meddelelser om Grønland* LXV. 196 To denote a mountain entirely or partly covered with ice but whose form is still distinguishable, the Polar-Eskimos use the name 'Pingo', a term which in these regions corresponds to the name 'Nunatak'. The best example of a Pingo is Mt. Haffner, Pingorsoak, i.e. the great Pingo. *Ibid.* 197 We need no name for rounded nunataks. I have, however, introduced the name Pingo.. to designate a mountain entirely submerged by the Inland Ice, but setting its mark upon the surface of the ice. *Ibid.* 203 The easternmost of these ranges consists of a series of high and precipitous nunataks and Pingos.] **1938** A. E. PORSILD in *Geogr. Rev.* XXVIII. 46 In literature the name 'gravel or earth mound' seems to be fairly well established. The Eskimo name *pingo*, meaning conical hill, which has come into universal use in the north, is here introduced as an alternative. *Ibid.* 54 (*caption*) Pingo near Tuktuayaktok on the Arctic Sea coast east of the Mackenzie delta showing the irregular rupture of the summit. This pingo is 134 feet high. **1961, 1968** [see *hydrolaccolith* s.v. *HYDRO-]. **1968** R. W. FAIRBRIDGE *Encycl. Geomorphol.* 848/2 The pingos of Wales seem to belong to the open system, the water having flowed down the slope between a thin permafrost and an impervious bedrock. **1972** *Nature* 14 Apr. 344/1 The pingos of Cardiganshire are not sparse in distribution but occur in a number of localities. **1974** *N.Y. Times* 26 May I. 34/4 There was little but ice and snow..occasional ice-cored hillocks called pingoes, and the prominent ribbons of the winter ice road.

ping-pong, *sb.* Add: **1. a.** The bat now usu. has a wooden blade covered with pimpled rubber. (Further examples.) Also *attrib.*
Ping-pong is a proprietary name in the U.S.
1901 [see *table-tennis* s.v. TABLE *sb.* 22]. **1902** *Harper's Weekly* 7 June 739 To have your squash-court this summer, if you have any pretensions to style, is as necessary as to have your ping-pong table or your automobile. **1904** 'H. FOULIS' *Erchie* xiv. 90 The grocer in there wad be thinkin' I was awa' on the ping-pong if he didna ken I was a beadle. **1907** *Westm. Gaz.* 12 Oct. 3/2 A set of 'ping-pong' materials. **1949** *Official Gaz.* (U.S. Patent Office) 4 Oct. 40/2 Parker Brothers, Inc., Salem, Mass...*Ping-pong*... For game played with rackets and balls. Claims use since Aug. 1, 1900. **1958** R. LIDDELL *Morea* II. i. 47 Nick..had been playing ping-pong outside the hotel. **1968** *Listener* 13 June 783/2 No character ever entirely subsides: they are like those ping-pong balls at a fair that rise and fall on spurts of water. **1977** E. AMBLER *Send no more Roses* x. 231, I used the handle of a ping-pong bat to keep it [*sc.* a door] open.

b. *fig.* A series of (usu. verbal) exchanges between two parties. Also *attrib.*
1917 E. POUND *Let.* 11 Apr. in T. S. Eliot *Waste Land Drafts* (1971) p. xii, I want to boom Eliot and one cant have too obvious a ping-pong match at that sort of thing. **1934** L. B. LYON *White Hare* 50 After him came two high-brows playing a wordy ping-pong. **1955** *Times* 18 July 9/2 Coal is one industry that has escaped the political ping-pong which threatens steel. **1966** J. CLEARY *High Commissioner* iii. 51 Two hours of diplomatic ping-pong hadn't touched her; she looked..poised and unmarked. **1974** 'M. ALLEN' *Super Tour* (1975) v. 203 It was impossible to beat Mama in the game of verbal Ping-Pong. **1976** N. POSTMAN *Crazy Talk* 8 In the Ping-Pong ball theory, communication is conceived of as a discrete, quantifiable piece of stuff that will move from one source to another and then back. **1977** *Time* 5 Dec. 54/1 The French political journals, center and right, ravaged Courbet for years, and beside their vilifications the attacks on impressionism and cubism were mere Ping Pong.

2. A type of drum in a West Indian steel band (see quots.). Also, a melody played on such a drum.
1955 *New Commonwealth* 28 Nov. (Suppl.) p. xix/1 In the orchestra the pans are grouped into Ping Pongs, Alto Pans, Tenor Kittles, Kittle Booms, Tune Booms and Bass Booms. **1956** L. HUGHES *First Bk. of W. Indies* 42 Discarded oil drums are cut, heated, and hammered in such a way that each has its own pitch and tone. Those that carry the melody are called 'ping pongs'. **1959** W. A. SIMMONDS '*Pan*'-*Story of Steelband* 9 By the end of 1945, different bands had developed different 'beats'. The initiated could, by the rhythm and 'Ping-Pong', distinguish what band 'was beating pan'. *Ibid.* 12 The queen of them all—the sweet Ping-Pong. This is a steel drum cut to about six or seven inches from the top. After these are stretched, and tempered, between twenty-six and thirty-two notes are marked and tuned.

Hence **pi·ng-ponger** = PING-PONGIST.
1933 *Times* 14 Nov. 15/4 It cannot be, and is not, good for anyone to enjoy the high moments or ecstasies of lawn tennis without sharing its physical dangers; yet that is what the ping ponger is trying to do. **1962** G. COMPTON *Too Many Murderers* xvii. 144 She sidled round the ping-pongers. **1972** *National Observer* (U.S.) 18 Mar. 16/1 The chief resident and Ping-ponger extraordinaire is one Dal-Joon Lee.

ping-pong, *v.* (In Dict. s.v. PING-PONG *sb.*) Add: **a.** Also, to move back and forth in the manner of a ping-pong ball. Also *fig.* **b.** *trans.* To send back and forth, to pass around aimlessly.
1952 *Jackson* (Tennessee) *Sun* 1/1 (*heading*) Question of Margaret's guards ping-pongs across Atlantic. **1960** in Cassidy & Le Page *Dict. Jamaican Eng.* (1967) 351/2 A common Jamaican expression, if you say 'he ping-pongs at it' it means he doesn't do it very well—like me typing: I just ping-pong at it. **1970** *Washington Post* 22 Nov. B6 The administration 'ping-ponged' the proposal back and forth. **1971** *Daily Colonist* (Victoria, B.C.) 2 Sept. 13/7 It was 'unfortunate for this accused that he has been, if I may coin a phrase, pingponged from one court to another'. **1972** *Daily Tel.* 11 Mar. 11/2 He can time funny lines so that they ping-pong back and forth in long sustained volleys with the audience's laughter. **1974** *Times Lit. Suppl.* 27 Sept. 1033/2 They ping-pong helplessly between sea and sheets, between pub and plough. **1976** *Times* 31 Aug. 5/2 The report [of a Senate committee] states that 'investigators were repeatedly "ping-ponged" to neurologists, gynaecologists, internists, [etc.]'.

Hence **pi·ng-ponging** *vbl. sb.*, playing ping-pong; also *fig.*; *spec.* (see quots.).
1901 [in Dict.]. **1972** *Daily Colonist* (Victoria, B.C.) 6 Jan. 1/8 Medical groups..engaged in 'ping-ponging'—sending patients from one medicaid provider to another for services they did not need. **1975** *Time* 26 May 55/2 Many of the 'Medicaid mills' of clinics set up to handle poor patients in the nation's urban ghettos reap enormous profits by such practices as 'Ping Ponging' (passing

a patient along to all the other doctors in the clinic). **1976** *Discursive Dict. Health Care* (U.S.) 122 *Ping-ponging*, the practice of passing a patient from one physician to another in a health program for unnecessary cursory examinations so that the program can charge the patient's third-party for a physical visit to each physician.

pinguicula. Delete 9 and add: **2.** (Earlier and later examples.)

In this sense *pingueculа* has always been the usual form. **1850** H. Howard *Anat. Eye* xvi. 230 Pinguecula.—This is a little yellowish colored tumour, situated partly in the conjunctiva, and partly in its cellular membrane. **1934** [see *interpalpebral* s.v. *inter- 6]. **1937** E. Wolff *Dis. Eye* i. 12 Pingueculæ require no treatment. **1965** F. W. Newell *Ophthalm.* viii. 180/2 Rarely a pinguecula becomes inflamed, causing a foreign body sensation.

pin-head. Add: Also **pinhead. 1. a.** (Further examples.)

1951 J. Cleary in Murdoch & Drake-Brockman *Austral. Short Stories* 439 The street lights are on, yellow pin-heads climbing the hill from the bay road. **1976** E. Ward *Hanged Man* xxvii. 168 Pubs known as 'happy', where a development of lysergic acid..is on sale as purple pinheads—a microdot of LSD embedded in plastic, sold for £1.

b. (Later examples.)

1963 *Times* 30 Apr. 13/4 The many heavy lorries which, even though they may use their headlamps in the country, only have one pin-head size nearside sidelamp in the town, or perhaps a single flickering tail lamp. **1971** *Brit. Med. Bull.* XXVII. 55/2 In cases of the 'pin head' type of opacity there may be a slight drop in the transfer factor of the lung. **1974** D. Seaman *Bomb that could Lip-Read* xvii. 168 The pinhead microphone is set into the head of the explosive.

c. Applied to a pattern of small dots on cloth, or to the cloth itself. Also *ellipt.*, a garment having such a pattern.

1897 *Sears, Roebuck Catal.* 220/1 *French Sanitary Suspenders*... cream, blue, green, etc., with very fine pinhead dots of contrasting colors. **1923** *Daily Mail* 12 June 3 (Advt.), Greys are both light and dark, and include pinhead designs, herring-bones and stripes. **1935** L. A. G. Strong *Tuesday Afternoon* i. 11 Those chaps in the city had so successfully turned his blue pinhead that several people had..thought it was brand new. **1964** L. Deighton *Funeral in Berlin* iv. 27 He wore a well-cut Berlin suit of English pinhead worsted.

4. A small minnow.

1845 S. Judd *Margaret* I. iv. 18 Minnows and pinheads were flashing and skirting through the clear bright stream.

5. A person with a small head; chiefly *fig.*, a person of little intelligence, a fool. Also *attrib.* or as *adj.*

1896 Ade *Artie* i. 3 I've got as much right to go out and do the heavy as any o' you pin-heads. **1909** *N.Y. Even. Post* (semi-weekly ed.) 22 Feb. 6 An innovation in dress that was..said to indicate that the wearer was a 'pin head'. **1923** [see *bone *sb.* 3 b]. **1933** E. Seago *Circus Company* 295 *Pinheads*, freaks in a side-show. **1940** *Horizon* Apr. 236 An opponent particularly dangerous in these times is the near-artist, or Pinhead. **1947** H. S. Truman in M. Truman *Harry S. Truman* (1973) xvii. 349, I am of the opinion that the country has had enough of their pinhead antics. **1973** 'M. Yorke' *Grave Matters* vii. iii. 118 She's no pin-head—she'd be a match for him intellectually. **1976** *New Yorker* 15 Nov. 23/2 It uses images of physical deformity for their enormous potential of horror, and at the end, when the pinheads and the armless and legless creatures scurry about to revenge themselves on a normal woman.., the film becomes a true nightmare.

pin-headed, *a.* Add: **b.** Of a person: having a small head like that of a pin; *fig.* stupid. So **pin-hea·dedness.**

1901 Ade *Forty Mod. Fables* 67 Is it not Sad to see a pin-headed Rake dissipating a Large Fortune? **1927** *Scribner's Mag.* Feb. 209/1 He is living in parochial, hide-bound, pin-headed stupidity. **1928** Wodehouse in *Strand Mag.* Aug. 107 People..were accustomed to set him down as just an ordinary pinheaded young man. *Ibid.* 108 Then they realized that his pin-headedness, so far from being ordinary, was quite exceptional. **1954** 'N. Blake' *Whisper in Gloom* xiii. 178 A pin-headed, slick-haired man. **1960** *Sunday Express* 3 July 15/6 The 'pin-headed' look is on its way in..shorter and still shorter hair. **1969** [see *Mille Miglia].

pi·nholder. [f. Pin *sb.*^{1} + Holder^1.] A holder for cut flowers, etc., comprising a mounting or base and projecting pins.

1956 D. Bebb *Flowers for You* 24 Place the prepared branches firmly on a pin-holder, with some pieces of bright green moss covering it. **1960** *Woman* 23 Apr. 61/1 Any large-headed flowers should be arranged this way, in a pinholder in a very shallow dish. **1967** *Times* 22 Mar. 11 Most of them, like the pink daisies in *Through the Looking Glass* who turned white with shock when Alice threatened to pick them would..faint at the sight of a pin-holder. **1977** *Lancashire Life* Feb. 9/2 The design is held in a tall black well pin-holder within a rough glazed ivory-coloured ceramic container. **1979** I. Webb *Compl. Guide Flower & Foliage Arrangem.* iv. 58/1 All three branches must emerge from the point on the pinholder where Branch 1 is placed.

pin-hole. Add: Also **pinhole. 2. b.** A small hole in timber caused by a wood-boring beetle or its larva.

1894 A. D. Hopkins in *Bull. West Virginia Agric. Exper. Station* Jan. 291 In order that we may refer to the different kinds of defects caused by insects, by some simple, descriptive names, I will present the following, provisional classification and popular names. Pin Holes. Small, round holes, one-hundredth of an inch to one-fourth of an inch in diameter. **1907** *Circ. Bureau Entomol., U.S. Dept. Agric.* No. 82. 1 The principal injury to the wood of standing girdled cypress was found to consist of pinholes in the sapwood and heartwood. **1938** Hunt & Garratt *Wood Preservation* iii. 53 The insect defects produced in wood before it is placed in service may be classified as pinholes or grub holes, the distinction being principally a matter of size. **1968** *Gloss. Terms Timber Preservation* (*B.S.I.*) 15 *Pinhole*, a worm hole not more than 1·5 mm in diameter.

c. A very small cavity in a solid, esp. a casting.

1906 H. Adams *Cassell's Engineers' Hand-bk.* iv. 174 Pin-holes, or blow-holes in brass castings are produced by overheating the metal. **1925** *Jrnl. Inst. Metals* XXXIII. 227 The 'pin-holes' are small cavities more or less spherical in shape, fairly uniformly disseminated through the body of the casting. **1947** J. C. Rich *Materials & Methods Sculpture* iv. 70 The most common surface blemishes that may mar an otherwise perfect cast are caused by pinholes resulting from air bubbles imprisoned in the plaster mix. **1968** D. R. Cliffe *Technical Metall.* xi. 268 'Gas holes' (or 'pin-holes') are small, evenly distributed rounded cavities with bright walls caused by the releasc of dissolved gases during freezing.

d. A very small area from which a coating is absent.

1909 *Jrnl. Industr. & Engin. Chem.* May 295/1 Dealers who were previously large importers of tin plate..are willing to admit that even in the 'good old times' they were greatly annoyed by the so-called 'pin holes' in their goods. **1932** E. S. Hedges *Protective Films on Metals* vii. 212 The examination of perforated cans has shown that the holes may occur..at pinholes in the tin coating. **1970** J. A. Scarlett *Printed Circuit Boards* iv. 53 Most firms use Beta-ray backscatter tests to check thicknesses of gold plating, together with an electrograph porosity test against pinholes.

e. Ellipt. for **pin-hole camera*.

1976 *Broadcast* 29 Nov. 18/1 The camera is a box—be it a still camera, a film camera, a television camera, a Polaroid, a pinhole.

3. a. (Further examples.)

1946 C. W. Briggs *Metall. of Steel Castings* iii. 136 (*heading*) Pinhole porosity. **1962** F. I. Ordway et al. *Basic Astronautics* vi. 275 (*caption*) Pinhole insert to control rate of gas intake. **1973** G. J. Davies *Solidification & Casting* ix. 172 (*heading*) Pinhole cavities in a sand-cast aluminium alloy, the result of hydrogen evolution on cooling.

b. *Photogr.* Having or pertaining to the use of a pin-hole in place of a lens, as *pin-hole camera, photography, picture, work.*

1891 *Phil. Mag.* Feb. 89 As the focal length increases, the brightness (B) in the image of a properly proportioned pin-hole camera diminishes. **1902** A. Watkins *Photogr.* 56 Pinhole pictures..have a tendency to require longer exposures than the mathematically calculated ones. **1940** *Chambers's Techn. Dict.* 644/2 *Pinhole photography*, photography involving the use of a pinhole instead of a lens to form an image on a camera plate. **1948** A. L. M. Sowerby *Dict. Photogr.* (ed. 17) 509 A recent article by L. A. Turner..contains an improved theoretical treatment of pinhole work. **1962** M. L. Haselgrove *Photographers' Dict.* 162 *Pinhole* (*camera*). Replacing the camera lens with a panel in which a small pinhole has been made will result in an image being formed on the milk.

c. pinhole borer, a small brown or black beetle or its larva belonging to the families Scolytidæ or Platypodidæ, which damages trees or felled timber by boring tunnels into the wood.

1916 *Indian Forester* XLII. 217 (*heading*) Ambrosia beetles or pin-hole and shot-hole borers. **1928** *Forestry Comm. Bull.* No. 9. 12 The pin-hole borers, poorly represented in Europe, are more numerous in the Southern States of North America, and are especially abundant in the tropics. **1946** Cartwright & Findlay *Decay of Timber* xiv. 276 The constant presence of staining around the tunnels of the pinhole borers..is usually due to growth of dark-coloured moulds in the wood surrounding the tunnels. **1963** N. E. Hickin *Insect Factor in Wood Decay* viii. 256 Ambrosia beetles are also called Pinhole Borers. **1975** G. Evans *Life of Beetles* iv. 92 Pin-hole borers, or 'ambrosia beetles'..are small beetles which bore very narrow tunnels of about the diameter of a thick pin.

pinholed, *ppl. a.* (Later example.)

1928 *Forestry Comm. Bull.* No. 9. 13 Apart from the tunnels cut by the beetles, secondary damage is found in pin-holed timber. This consists in a staining of the wood in a longitudinal direction on each side of the pin-hole.

pi·nholing, *vbl. sb.* [f. Pin-hole + -ing^1.] The presence or production of pin-holes.

1925 *Jrnl. Inst. Metals.* XXXIII. 228 These facts..led to the conclusion that the cause of 'pinholing' [in castings] is occluded gas. **1941** *Light Metals* IV. 133/1 The foundryman..has to produce castings free from serious pinholing. **1947** J. C. Rich *Materials & Methods Sculpture* ii. 51 Pinholing is frequently caused by firing the ceramic body and the glaze at the same time, although air that has been incorporated in the clay mass, dirt, and quick kiln cooling may also cause pinholing.

pinic, *a.* For $C_{20}H_{30}O_2$ read $C_9H_{14}O_4$.

pinion, *sb.*^{5} Add: **2.** (Earlier and later examples.) Also *attrib.* in *pinion nut, pine.*

1831 J. O. Pattie *Pers. Narr.* 43 A nut..which grows on a tree resembling the pine, called by the Spanish, pinion. **1846** R. B. Sage *Scenes Rocky Mts.* xxi. 172 The hills enclosing the valley..are high and precipitous,—affording numerous groves of pine, pinion and cedar. *Ibid.*, Wild turkeys..will thrive in an extraordinary manner upon pinion-nuts. **1878** J. H. Beadle *Western Wilds* xi. 173 On many of the hills grows the pinion pine. **1960** 'I. Devi' *Yoga for You* 189 Sunflower seeds or pinion nuts to taste. **1970** *People* (Austral.) 26 Aug. 44/4 Pinion nuts from the cones of introduced pines are a tasty novelty. **1979** *Yale* Apr. 39/2 (Advt.), 40 beautiful acres high ground with pinion, mountain views near mining town between Santa Fe & Albuquerque.

‖ **pinjrapol** (pi·ndʒrăpǭᵘl). Also **panjrapol, panjrapor, pinjrapole,** etc. [ad. Gujerati *pānjrāpol*, f. *panjra* (Skr. *panjara, pinjara*) a cage + *pol* an enclosed yard.] In India, an enclosure, reserve, etc., where old or sick animals are kept.

1808 R. Drummond *Illustr. Gram. Parts Guzerattee* s.v. *Pinjrapole* or *Pánjrapól*. Every marriage and mercantile transaction amongst them is taxed with a contribution for the *Pinjrapole* ostensibly. **1832** C. Coleman *Mythol. Hindus* xiii. 222 These hospitals are called *pinjra-pul*, and contain animals of various descriptions. **1855** H. H. Wilson *Gloss. Judicial & Revenue Terms* 418/2 *Pinjrápor*, or *-pol*, also read *Pánjrápor*, or *pol*, Guz.., an hospital for animals, kept up by the Jains of Guzerat in various places, out of small fees levied at marriages and on mercantile transactions. **1873** E. Balfour *Cycl. India* (ed. 2) IV. s.v. *Pinjrapol*. The Bombay Pinjrapol owes its origin as much to the Parsee worship of sacred dogs as to the superstitions of the Jains. **1929** H. G. Rawlinson *Ovington's Voy. to Surat* 178 These animal hospitals or *pinjrapols* date back to the days of Asoka. **1960** *Guardian* 21 Apr. 12/5 A pinjrapole is a 'Cheshire home' for cows. **1968** B. Walker *Hindu World* I. 16 The early Buddhists and Jains built hospitals for the care of animals, birds and even insects. Such institutions have survived through the centuries and are today known as *piñjrapol*.

pink, *sb.*^{2} Add: **2. b.** A young grayling.

1901 H. A. Rolt *Grayling Fishing in S. Country Streams* i. 12 A one-year-old grayling is called a 'pink', and has neither spots nor lateral lines which can be observed. **1939** W. C. Platts *Grayling Fishing* vi. 60 Rolt says that a one-year-old grayling is called a 'pink', and a two-year-old a 'shut' or 'shote' grayling... I have rarely come across these terms in general use. **1952** F. White *Good Eng. Food* i. iv. 55 The principal grayling rivers..are..the Teme (where yearling fish are termed 'pinks' and second year fish 'shutts' or 'shots' or 'sheets') [etc.].

c. = *pink salmon* s.v. *pink *sb.*^{4} and *a.*^{1} C. c.

1921 *Daily Colonist* (Victoria, B.C.) 11 Mar. 19/41 The canneries announced their intention of packing practically no pinks or chums this season. **1935** W. M. Halliday *Potlatch & Totem* 155 After the close of the sockeye season, what are commonly known as humpback salmon were caught; these are the fish which are now classed under the technical name of 'pinks'. **1965** A. J. McClane *Standard Fishing Encycl.* 681/2 The ocean and Puget Sound sport fisheries take many pinks, but it is the commercial effort that accounts for the greatest take.

pink, *sb.*^{4} and *a.*^{1} Add: **A.** *sb.* **I. 2. b.** (Further examples.) Also freq. with ellipse of *of condition, of health*, etc. *colloq.*

a **1821** Keats *Castle Builder* in *Poetical Wks.* (1907) 298 Let me think About my room,—I'll have it in the pink; It should be rich and sombre. **1845** Dickens *Let.* 18 Mar. (1977) IV. 282 Of all the picturesque abominations in the World, commend me to Fondi. It is the very pink of hideousness and squalid misery. **1905** *Kynoch Jrnl.* Oct.-Dec. 201 Makers may despatch explosives from the factory in the pink of condition. **1914** *Isle of Man Weekly Times* 21 Nov. 7/5 He says that he is 'in the pink'. **1916** C. Winchester *Flying Men* 193, I saw a couple of R.F.C. officers..the other day. They looked 'in the pink'. **1923** Wodehouse *Inimitable Jeeves* xi. 115 'Oh, hallo!' I said. 'Going strong?' 'I am in excellent health, I thank you. And you?' 'In the pink. Just been over to America.' **1929** J. B. Priestley *Good Companions* ii. vii. 453, I am writing these lines to say I am still in the pink and hoping you are the same. **1937** A. Huxley *Let.* 25 Feb. (1969) 415 Quant à moi, I was in the pink until about a week ago. **1950** [see *coin *v.*^{1} 5 d]. **1973** 'P. Malloch' *Kickback* vi. 37 Gilchrist shook hands. 'O.K. How about you?' 'In the pink,' Campbell said. **1976** Dexter & Makins *Testkill* 129 A young Alsatian in the pink of condition.

II. 5. c. As a colour commonly used on maps to indicate a British colony or dominion. Cf. *red *sb.*^{1} 1 e.

1913 C. Mackenzie *Sinister St.* I. ii. xv. 407 She said half the world was composed of fools which accounted for the preponderation—I mean preponderance—of pink on the map.

7. As the name of varieties of the potato. Cf. Pink-eye 1.

1853 *Trans. Mich. Agric. Soc.* V. 208 Some of the more approved kinds are..the White, Red, and Strawberry Pinks. **1861** Mrs. Beeton *Bk. Househ. Managem.* 589 The Lancashire Pink is also a good potato, and is much cultivated in the neighbourhood of Liverpool.

8. A pink ball in snooker and some related games.

1910 *Encycl. Brit.* III. 938/2 It is also permitted in some rooms to take blacks and pinks alternately without pocketing a coloured ball between the strokes. **1935** *Encycl. Sports* 570/1 Black is on the billiard spot: pink on the centre line of the table, touching the apex ball of the pyramid. **1976** *Milton Keynes Express* 28 May 55/4

He played the cue ball the full length of the table, swerving past the green, back up the table, not only to hit the red but to pot it, plus the black, yellow, green, brown, blue and but for a miss on the pink would have cleared the table to win the frame. **1978** *Guardian* 7 Feb. 20/6 Pulman twice missed eminently possible pinks, with position on the black there for the taking.

9. *U.S. Blacks' slang.* A white-skinned person. Also *comb.*, as **pink-chaser** (see quot. 1970).

1926 C. VAN VECHTEN *Nigger Heaven* I. ix. 157 Funny thing about those pink-chasers the ofays never seem to have any use for them. **1945** L. SHELLY *Jive Talk Dict.* 16/1 *Pink*, pretty white girl. **1970** C. MAJOR *Dict. Afro-Amer. Slang* 91 *Pink chasers*, black people who deliberately cultivate friendships with white people. **1973** 'TREVANIAN' *Loo Sanction* (1974) 159 P'tit Noel shrugged. 'All pinks sound alike.'

10. A person whose politics are left of centre, but closer to the centre than those of a 'red'; a radical; a liberal socialist. *colloq.* Cf. *parlour pink* s.v. *PARLOUR 2 f.

1927 U. SINCLAIR *Oil!* xiii. 313 He's nuts on this red-hunting business, and the pinks are worse than the reds, he says. **1943** K. TENNANT *Ride on Stranger* xx. 225 Wilmot electorate covered an area of residential waterside suburbs inhabited less by Reds than by Pinks of all shades and hues. **1956** A. WILSON *Anglo-Saxon Att.* I. iv. 115 Less-informed business friends spoke to Robin of intellectuals as communists or pinks. **1968** *Punch* 17 July 95/3 The Tory Party..now clutches pinks, finks and crumb-bums to its shrivelled teats. **1976** SCOTT & KOSKI *Walk-In* (1977) xxi. 140 His college professors..thought that the boy was perhaps slightly leftish but no more so than most of the Pinks over at State. **1978** 'R. CASSILIS' *Winding Sheet* II. xii. 109 One of those old-fashioned egalitarians, like the pompous Pinks who had once been the backbone of the..Labour Party.

11. A pink gin; the bitters in this drink.

1942 G. HACKFORTH-JONES *One-One-One* xxii. 203 'Eeyore' Smith absent-mindedly added a dash of 'pink' to his evening aperitif. **1969** G. GREENE *Trav. with my Aunt* I. xx. 213 'Another double', 'Pint of best bitter', 'Double pink'. **1976** 'F. CLIFFORD' *Drummer in Dark* iv. 15 'What'll it be?' 'A pink, please.'

B. *adj.* **1. c.** Of the coloration of a newspaper: indicating a sporting edition.

1922 JOYCE *Ulysses* 659 The Gold Cup flat handicap, the official and definitive result of which he had read in the *Evening Telegraph*, late pink edition.

d. Of the coloration on a map: indicating a British colony or dominion. Cf. *PINK *sb.*[4] 5 c.

1960 N. MITFORD *Don't tell Alfred* vii. 74 It was bad luck for Alfred that the government..should be determined to paint the Minquiers pink on the map. **1973** *Listener* 20 Dec. 857/2 Industrialisation played a big part in the drive to paint the map pink. British industries needed raw materials. **1976** C. BERMANT *Coming Home* I. vi. 88, I took it that the great green-coloured mass of the Sahara would pass to Britain... Gradually the whole of Africa glowed pink before my eyes. **1979** *Listener* 26 July 112/3, I was drilled in geography... Most areas, I remember, were coloured pink on the map.

3. Politically left of centre, progressive; applied to socialism of a less extreme character than that denoted by 'red'; loosely, Communist. Also *absol.* Cf. *PINK *sb.*[4] 10.

1837 DE QUINCEY in *Tait's Mag.* Feb. 71/1 Amusing it is to look back upon any political work of Mr Shepherd's..and to know that the pale pink of his Radicalism was then accounted deep, deep scarlet. **1859** LYTTON *What will he do with It?* I. I. i. 9 Young 'un, I'm a Tory—that's blue; and Spruce is a Rad—that's pink! **1920** MRS. P. SNOWDEN *Through Bolshevik Russia* 180 The people's flag is palest pink, It's not so red as you might think. **1924** *Scribner's Mag.* Oct. 441/1 The Middle West is becoming pink. But it is genuine American pink. Not Moscow Red! **1939** A. THIRKELL *Before Lunch* iv. 84, I wouldn't mind her trying to run her pink politics down my throat..though I never see why being a Communist should make one abhor washing. **1973** *Listener* 28 June 864/1 'I am not Communist, but..I am a little pink.' Thus spake King Sihanouk of Cambodia. **1979** 'S. WOODS' *This Fatal Writ* 81 The description 'pale pink intellectual' is far too tame for Susan... And he's just the opposite, a true blue Tory.

4. Violent, extreme; utter, absolute (see also quot. 1896). *slang.*

1896 W. C. GORE in *Inlander* Jan. 149 *Pink*, used to intensify the negative. 'He didn't know a pink thing about the lesson.' **1901** *Daily Express* 28 Aug. 4/3 The master of the house flies into a pink rage because his chop is not done. **1946** B. MARSHALL *George Brown's Schooldays* 145 These rotten new kids really are the pink limit.

5. Slightly indecent, violent, or vulgar; mildly 'blue' (see BLUE *a.* 9 in Dict. and Suppl.).

1898 R. HICHENS *Londoners* xvi. 280 Lovely needlework! That's a funny beginning for a Pink un. **1900** *Daily News* 28 May 3/1 Most of their adjectives have a decidedly pink tinge. **1979** J. MELVILLE *Wages of Zen* xi. 117 One cinema showing 'pink films'..and one strip show.

6. Of a plan, process, etc.: that must be kept secret.

1924 *Discovery* June 83/1 Little was said about it [*sc.* wireless direction for boats and torpedoes] and in navy parlance it is a subject which is still slightly 'pink', a cryptic term indicating that even if we do happen to know something, we are not prepared to make a song about it. **1925** FRASER & GIBBONS *Soldier & Sailor Words* 224 *Pink*, secret. An expression in some Government Offices during the war for secret telegrams. **1962** GRANVILLE *Dict. Sailors' Slang* 88/2 *Pink*... 2. Secret, hush-hush, from the pink (confidential) signal pads used in the Navy.

7. Of a person: white-skinned. Cf. *PINK *sb.*[4] 9.

1936 G. B. SHAW *Millionairess* Pref. 121 Even in Africa, where pink emigrants struggle with brown and black natives for possession of the land, and our Jamaican miscegenation shocks public sentiment, the sun sterilizes the pinks to such an extent that Cabinet ministers call for more emigration to maintain the pink population. **1971** *Rand Daily Mail* 3 Apr. 5/8 We Pink South Africans are in danger of being cut off from the world. **1977** P. USTINOV *Dear Me* iii. 26 On my first application to enter the United States..I described my colour as pink. I was told sternly that I was white, a fact which I denied, relying upon an Embassy mirror for evidence. A great deal of time was wasted, more especially since I failed to realize the subliminal implication of the word 'pink' in those days.

8. Phrases. *strike me pink!* (slang): an exclamation of astonishment or indignation; *to paint the town pink*: to go on a spree (after *to paint the town red* s.v. PAINT *v.*[1] 9); *to swear pink* (colloq.): to make vehement protestations; to 'swear blind'; *to tickle pink*: see *TICKLE *v.*

1902 E. NESBIT *Five Children & It* viii. 218 When he beheld the magnificent proportions of Robert he said.. 'Strike me pink!' **1922** JOYCE *Ulysses* 623 And there he was at the end of his tether after having often painted the town tolerably pink. **1931** A. P. HERBERT *Derby Day* III. 115 Ten thousand serpents! Strike me pink! Where's that girl? She'll go to clink! **1956** E. POUND tr. *Sophocles' Women of Trachis* 20 And you swore pink they were bringing her to be Heracles' wife. **1969** *Sunday Mail Mag.* (Brisbane) 7 Sept. 10/1 He was further reported as commenting on certain African members of the Commonwealth in the words: 'Strike me pink, they'll do me for bloody butchers.'

C. a. *pink-brown*, *-white* (earlier example); *pink-and-white* (further examples).

1853 C. BRONTË *Villette* I. xiv. 292 Your pink and white complexion. **1860** GEO. ELIOT *Jrnl.* in J. W. Cross *George Eliot's Life* (1885) II. x. 169 The Churches..with their wealth of gilding and rich pink-brown marbles. **1895** W. B. YEATS *Poems* 148 But all the little pink-white nails have grown To be great talons. **1965** A. CHRISTIE *At Bertram's Hotel* ii. 22 It made her come to life again—Jane Marple, that pink and white eager young girl. **1979** P. MASON *Skinner* xiv. 96 We shall be junior to pink-and-white boys of eighteen straight from England.

b. *pink-cheeked*, *-complexioned*, *-frilled*, *-haired*, *-handed*, *-scrolled*, *-vested* adjs.

1805–6 WORDSWORTH *Prelude* (1959) VII. 260 Equestrians, Tumblers, Women, Girls, and Boys, Blue-breech'd, pink-vested. **1906** *Daily Chron.* 23 Aug. 5/6 A white gown and blue picture hat and pink-frilled parasol. **1940** E. POUND *Cantos* lxix. 174 Squad of the pink-haired snot. **1946** S. SPENDER *European Witness* ix. 46 A pink-complexioned mild-mannered man. **1955** D. DAVIE *Brides of Reason* 8 The nausea that struggles to despatch Pink-handed horror in a craggy room. **1962** I. MURDOCH *Unofficial Rose* iv. 41 She thrust a white-quartered green-eyed Madame Hardy in between two lilac-shaded pink-scrolled Louise Odiers. **1967** A. WEST in *Coast to Coast 1965–66* 219 It was a soft, pink-cheeked face. **1978** T. GIFFORD *Glendower Legacy* 264 She..had a succulent moist look, freshly showered, pink-cheeked.

c. pink bollworm, the pinkish larva of a small brown moth, *Pectinophora gossypiella*, of the family Gelechiidæ, which feeds on the lint or seeds of cotton bolls; **pink button** *Stock Exchange*, a jobber's clerk; **pink champagne,** rosé champagne; champagne to which a small quantity of still red wine has been added; **pink disease,** a disease of children caused by mercury poisoning, characterized by pinkness of parts of the body, restlessness, and photophobia; **pink elephant,** used as a type of the extraordinary or impossible; also (chiefly pl.), a characteristic apparition seen by someone drunk or delirious; cf. **pink rat(s)*; **pink-foot** (b) as *sb.*, = next (also *attrib.*); **pinkfooted goose,** substitute for Latin name *Anser fabalis brachyrhynchus*; (earlier and later examples); **pink gin,** gin-and-bitters; **pink lady** *U.S.*, (*a*) a cocktail comprising gin, egg white, grenadine, and other ingredients; (*b*) (see quot. 1968–70); **pink madder**: see MADDER *sb.*[1] 3; **pink noise** *Physics*, random noise having equal energy per octave, and so differing from white noise in having a greater proportion of low-frequency components; **pink paper,** a parliamentary paper containing the information specified in quot. 1894; **pink pine** *N.Z.*, a small forest tree, *Dacrydium biforme*, of the family Podocarpaceæ, bearing linear juvenile leaves and scale-like adult ones, and yielding a resin from which manool is manufactured; **pink rat(s),** a characteristic apparition seen by someone drunk or delirious; cf. **pink elephant*; **pink salmon,** the humpback salmon, *Oxyrhynchus gorbuscha*; **pink slip** *U.S.*, a notice of dismissal from employment; also *transf.* and *fig.*; hence **pink-slip** *v. trans.*, to dismiss, to fire; **pink spot,** used to designate a substance of uncertain composition found in the urine of some schizophrenics, observed as a pink spot on a chromatogram of it; **pink tea** *N. Amer.*, a formal tea party or other social engagement; an exclusive gathering; also used as a type of the polite or genteel; also *attrib.*; **pink thorn,** a pink-flowered variety of the hawthorn, *Cratægus monogyna*; **pink toe(s)** *U.S. Blacks' slang*, a light-skinned black woman; a white girl; **Pink 'Un** [UN, 'UN[2]], a nickname for a newspaper printed on pink paper, *spec.* (*a*) *The Sporting Times*; also, a reporter for this newspaper; (*b*) *The Financial Times*; **pinkwash,** a composition used for rendering walls, etc., pink; so **pink-washed** adj.; **pink wine,** (*a*) *slang*, champagne; (*b*) vin rosé.

1906 H. MAXWELL-LEFROY *Indian Insect Pests* III. viii. 94 The pink boll-worms are most abundant when the cotton forms bolls. **1917** *Jrnl. Agric. Res.* IX. 343 The pink bollworm..is one of the most destructive cotton insects known. **1932** [see *grain-moth* s.v. *GRAIN *sb.*[1] 19]. **1955** *Sci. News Let.* 23 July 56/2 The preferred food of the pink bollworm larva is the kernel of the cotton seed. **1972** SWAN & PAPP *Common Insects N. Amer.* 325 Larvae of the Cotton Steam Moth..resemble pink bollworms. **1973** *Times* 16 June 18/2 Pink buttons are not..the female equivalents of blue buttons. **1974** *Sunday Tel.* 7 Apr. 29/3 As 'pink buttons', they look after all the firm's communications, both between the floor of the House and the offices, and between the brokers and country exchanges. **1838** J. KENYON *Poems* 88 Lily on liquid roses floating—So floats yon foam o'er pink champagne. **1940** N. MITFORD *Pigeon Pie* vi. 105 Oysters and pink champagne. **1974** P. ERDMAN *Silver Bears* v. 63 Sorbet flavoured with pink champagne. **1921** *Med. Jrnl. Austral.* 19 Feb. 146/1 When the rash is marked it is common to find the glands in the axillæ and groins enlarged. It is this pink rash, that leads to the name 'pink disease'. **1921** *Trans. 11th Sess. Australasian Med. Congr. 1920* 444 In Sydney the entity of this illness has long been recognized, and it is usually spoken of by Dr. Clubbe and others as 'the pink disease'. **1959** D. STOWENS *Pediatric Path.* x. 127/2 Acrodynia (Pink disease, Swift's disease, Feer's disease, Erythredema polyneuropathy). This bizarre condition is a manifestation either of poisoning by or hypersensitivity to, mercury. **1974** PASSMORE & ROBSON *Compan. Med. Stud.* III. xvii. 28/1 Pink disease earns its name from the colour of the hands and feet and not from an imaginary Dr Pink to whom many students credit its discovery. **1940** *This Week* 5 Oct. 2 Pink elephants. **1943** F. BROWN *Angels & Spaceships* (1954) 88 You mean if I saw a pink elephant I wouldn't believe it? **1946** P. LARKIN *Jill* 77 Whiskey? Would it make him drunk, would he stagger about and see pink elephants? **1906** E. W. HILDICK *Boy at Window* v. 45 It's like pink elephants. Folk 'ud think you'd been drinking if you went round saying you'd seen white mice running about wild! **1973** L. COOPER *Tea on Sunday* xxxiv. 246 'I heard somebody.' He'd be seeing pink elephants next. **1931** H. J. MASSINGHAM *Birds of Seashore* 38 Individual birds do not conform to pink-foot pattern. **1956** C. WILLOCK *Death at Flight* iii. 31 At least a thousand pinkfeet. Gone out on the muds for the night. **1957** D. A. BANNERMAN *Birds Brit. Isles* VI. 239 In 1951 pink-foots arrived in Britain unusually late. **1972** *Shooting Times & Country Mag.* 4 Mar. 7/1 Three-quarters of the pinkfeet that winter in Britain come from Iceland. **1839** A. D. BARTLETT in *Proc. Zool. Soc.* VII. 7 On a new British species of the genus *Anser*... Pink-footed Goose... Legs and feet, of a reddish flesh colour or pink. **1843** W. YARRELL *Hist. Brit. Birds* III. 66 The voice of the Pink-footed Goose differs from that of the Bean Goose in being sharper in tone. **1932** *Discovery* Aug. 244/2 White-fronted and pink-footed geese..are supposed to be nesting at the sources of the rivers running northwards from the ice-cap [in Iceland]. **1976** G. EVANS in R. Durman *Bird Observatories in Brit. & Ireland* vii. 140 The Pink-footed Goose is now far from abundant. **1930** H. CRADDOCK *Savoy Cocktail Bk.* I. 124 *Pink gin cocktail.* 1 Dash Angostura Bitters. 1 Glass Gin. **1952** E. GRIERSON *Reputation for Song* xxii. 178 She knew the type: a big car, and pink gins, and wine for dinner. **1974** J. MITCHELL *Death & Bright Water* xix. 230 'Pink gin, please,' he said, and she mixed it efficiently. **1944** S. BELLOW *Dangling Man* 149 She had been drinking Pink Ladies, and she was running over. **1946** C. HIMES *Black on Black* (1973) 264 'Anything to drink?' the waiter asked. 'I think I should like a pink lady.' **1968–70** *Current Slang* (Univ. S. Dakota) III–IV. 92 *Pink ladies, n.* Barbiturates. (Drug users' jargon). **1972** M. J. BOSSE *Incident at Naha* II. 99 There they were, the little pills, the Red Devils, Yellow Jackets, Christmas Trees, and Pink Ladies. **1975** J. WAMBAUGH *Choirboys* (1976) i. 6 Now drink your Pink Lady. **1961** G. A. BRIGGS *A to Z in Audio* 151 Pink noise is derived from white noise by applying a rising bass characteristic through the range. **1962** A. NISBETT *Technique Sound Studio* xii. 220 White noise with bass tip-up is 'pink' noise. **1976** *Gramophone* Apr. 1690/1 Measurements were made of the response of my lounge, using pink noise derived from a Rogers noise generator. [**1894** *1st Rep. Sel. Comm. Parl. Papers Distribution* p.iii in *Parl. Papers* XIV. 497 A Schedule shall be circulated daily, weekly, or otherwise, as may be found most convenient, giving reference number, title, and short note of contents of all Papers presented to Parliament by Command of Her Majesty, or printed by Order of either House, since the date of the Schedule last issued. This Schedule shall be sent to each Member in the shape of a demand form, printed on pink paper, and returnable post free.] **1906** *Rep. Sel. Comm. Offic. Publ.* 43 in *Parl. Papers* XI. 95 The pink paper was started in 1889 as an experiment, and it was ratified in 1894 by the Committee.

1908 *Rep. Sel. Comm. Publ.* 111 in *Parl. Papers* X. 849 The first Regulation directed the issue of what we all know as the 'pink paper'. **1928** Cockayne & Turner *Trees N.Z.* ii. 43 Pink-pine. A small tree, 15–40 ft. high, or a shrub, with the juvenile leaves distinct from the adult. **1958** *N.Z. Timber Jrnl.* Jan. 46/2 Pink pine... Small tree of sub-alpine forest of New Zealand. Often a shrub. **1969** *N.Z. News* 23 July 4/3 Pink pine..is so slow growing that 18 in diameter trees on the West Coast are believed to be 800 years old. **1914** C. D. Broad *Perception* iv. 266 The pink rats that can only be seen by those who habitually take excess of alcohol. **1925** —— *Mind & its Place* iv. 142 Some bright spirit will at once complain that the pink-rat situation has no object. **1932** H. H. Price *Perception* vi. 147 The celebrated case of the delirious man who 'sees a pink rat'. **1905** D. S. Jordan *Guide to Study of Fishes* II. iv. 71 The humpback salmon, or pink salmon..is the smallest of the American species. **1952** D. F. Putnam *Canad. Regions* 447/1 The humpback or pink salmon weighs, on the average, four pounds. **1976** J. S. Nelson *Fishes of World* 100 Pink salmon have a rigid two-year life span. **1915** 'B. L. Standish' *Covering Look-In Corner* ix. 100 And have Murphy hand me the pink slip tonight! **1923** *N.Y. Times* 7 Oct. 2/1 *Getting the pink slip*, being canceled, which notice comes on pink paper. **1951** *Sat. Rev. Lit.* (U.S.) 23 June 7/1 In small colleges and large universities hundreds of instructors and professors are getting 'pink slips' after the diplomas have been handed out. **1953** Berrey & Van den Bark *Amer. Thes. Slang* (1954) §67/4 Pink-slip, give the blue envelope *or* pink slip,..to give notice of discharge. **1963** Wodehouse *Stiff Upper Lip, Jeeves* ix. 71 You mean that if Madeleine hands Gussie the pink slip, she'll marry you? **1966** T. Pynchon *Crying of Lot 49* v. 114 His wife had..left him the day after he was pink-slipped. **1975** *New Yorker* 8 Sept. 115/1 Patrolmen on the beat, for example—got their pink slips because firing them was a dramatic way of demonstrating that the city was taking the crisis seriously. [**1962** *Nature* 2 June 898/1 The application of a modified Ehrlich's reagent..resulted in a..pink spot.] **1966** *Listener* 14 July 48/1 This 'pink spot' substance, so called from how it appears in chemical analysis, has not yet shown hallucinogenic activity when swallowed by volunteers. **1973** T. A. Ban *Recent Adv. Biol. Schizophrenia* iv. 30 Papers..some confirming but many more challenging the association of 'pink spot' with schizophrenia... Counterclaims have been advanced that the 'pink spot' is not 3,4-dimethoxyphenylethylamine. **1886** *Weekly Manitoba Liberal* 26 Nov. 8/3 The Pink Tea held under the auspices of the Women's Christian Temperance Union... The ladies in charge were all fittingly attired with pink caps and aprons and some of the gentleman patrons wore pink ties. **1887** *Harper's Mag.* Jan. 204/1 A Protestant good cause is to be furthered by a bazar or a 'pink tea'. **1905** J. London *Let.* 15 Sept. (1966) 184 Do you remember how Bessie dragged Anna Strunsky's name through the mire? Through all the..pink-tea councils? **1906** *N.Y. Even. Post* 17 Nov. 1 From all accounts these [football] battles of the early eighties and late seventies were no 'pink tea' affairs. **1918** [see *Bolshevism]. **1934** N. Sainsbury *Gridiron Grit* in *Stirring Football Stories* (1941) 55 What do you think football is, a pink tea? **1945** *Boulder* (Colorado) *Daily Camera* 2 Nov. 7/4 Yes, the war was no pink tea. **1952** *North Star* (Yellowknife, Northwest Territories) Dec. 2/1 We were only a name mentioned disparagingly at the clique's pink teas. **1852** C. M. Yonge *Two Guardians* x. 165 The pinkthorn, dressed in all its garlands, before her window. **1892** —— *Old Woman's Outlook* xi. 263 There stood on the lawn..a pink thorn. **1942** Z. N. Hurston in *Amer. Mercury* July 96/1 *Pink toes*, yellow girl. **1965** C. Himes (*title*) Pinktoes. *Ibid.* 216 When *Word* whispered it about that even the great Mamie Mason had lost her own black Joe to a young Pinktoe, the same panic prevailed among the black ladies of Harlem as had previously struck the white ladies downtown. **1970** C. Major *Dict. Afro-Amer. Slang* 91 *Pinktoes*, a black man's white girl friend; a white girl. **1887** *Referee* 31 July 2/1 Before doing so, I took the advice of one John Corlett, who propriets a paper called the *Pink 'Un*. **1898** A. M. Binstead (*title*) A Pink 'Un and a Pelican. **1902** G. Calderon *Downy V. Green* xii. 75 Downy amused himself with the only two weeklies that were in evidence, the 'Pink 'Un' and the 'Church Times'. **1930** W. S. Maugham *Cakes & Ale* ix. 107 He gave me the *Pink 'Un* every week and I..read it in my bedroom. **1955** [see *man *sb.*^{1} 22 c]. **1970** Partridge *Dict. Slang* Suppl. 1330/1 *Pink 'Un..The Financial Times*, founded in 1913. **1975** *Blackw. Mag.* CCCXVIII. 126/1 A Pink 'Un was a member of the staff of the *Sporting Times* or one of its close associates. **1979** *Guardian* 2 Jan. 24/4 Today..the first Financial Times will hit Wall Street... But for all the..computer setting..the new international Pink 'un depends very much for its birth on the weather. **1953** Dylan Thomas *Under Milk Wood* (1954) 23 The main street, Coronation Street, consists, for the most part, of humble, two-storied houses many of which attempt to achieve some measure of gaiety by prinking themselves out..by the liberal use of pinkwash. **1926** W. J. Locke *Stories Near & Far* 74 A long, two-storied, pink-washed dwelling. **1936** M. Allis *Eng. Prelude* xxxiii. 253 Lavenham, with its pink-washed houses. **1976** *Eastern Even. News* (Norwich) 27 Aug., The track..passes closely to the right of a pinkwashed farmhouse. **1909** J. R. Ware *Passing Eng.* 197/1 *Pink wine (Military)*, champagne. **1946** A. L. Simon *Let Wine be Wine* 10 *Rosé* or pink wine is made in a number of different ways, either from grapes with a light red or pinkish skin; or from black grapes the skins of which are not left in the fermenting vat for more than a short while; or from red and white wines mixed together. **1972** *Times* 16 Sept. 11/1 Pink wines from southern European vineyards tend to be dark in hue.

pink, *sb.*^{6} Add: **3.** = *pinking *vbl. sb.*^{3}; a metallic rattle.

1927 *Fuel in Sci. & Pract.* VI. 121/1 Ricardo attributed the 'pink' to the sudden inflammation of residual unburnt charge owing to its compression by the expanding burnt and burning portion. **1934** *Automobile Engineer* XXIV. 346/1 'Detonation' or 'pink' might occur in any class of engine. **1946** [see *knocking *vbl. sb.* 1].

Pink, *sb.*^{9}, slang abbrev. of Pinkerton.

1904 'No. 1500' *Life in Sing Sing* i. 6 Don't you know me? I'm one of the Pinks. *Ibid.* xxiii. 263 Pink had me framed and it was like finding rags to the pusher... The cashier..picked my picture from the Rogues' gallery, where Pinkerton placed it some time ago. **1955** D. W. Maurer in *Publ. Amer. Dial. Soc.* xxiv. 141 The agency is called *the eye*..and its operators are sometimes called *pinks*. **1975** J. Gores *Hammett* (1976) i. 16, I was a Pink... A detective for the Pinkerton Agency.

pink, *v.*^{1} **2. b.** Delete † *Obs.* and add later example. Also, to nick or wound slightly with a bullet.

1931 R. Campbell *Georgiad* i. 14 'Onoto'—guns, As sported by Chicago's crooked sons, Able, at once, to..pink a stray policeman in the neck. **1950** *N.Y. Times* 30 Dec. 27/1 Wall has been the victim of three attempted assassinations, in two of which he was 'pinked', as he expressed it.

d. (Later example.)

1963 *Times* 7 Feb. 3/5 At the end of the round Aldridge's left eye was looking 'pinked'.

pink, *v.*^{3} Restrict *Sc.* to sense in Dict. and add: **2.** *intr.* Of an internal-combustion engine: to exhibit pinking (*pinking *vbl. sb.*^{3}). Of a fuel: to cause pinking. Also *fig.*

1904 Kipling *Muse among Motors*, That cursed left-hand cylinder the doctors call my heart Is pinking past redemption—I am done! **1925** A. W. Judge *Carburettors & Carburation* ii. 19 The principal advantage of benzole is its higher detonating compression value; this enables it to be used in high compression petrol engines liable to 'pink' or knock, without experiencing these effects. **1933** *Petroleum Handbk.* (Shell Internat. Petroleum Co.) viii. 145 The tendency of a fuel to pfnk or detonate is its most important property in use. **1955** *Times* 12 July 12 The car tested was inclined..to pink slightly in accelerating from a low engine speed. **1970** 'D. Halliday' *Dolly & Cookie Bird* vi. 78 My brain was pinking like the old Morris. **1972** *Drive* New Year 122/2 Such driving on the recommended 2-star petrol caused the engine to 'pink' noisily.

pink (piŋk), *v.*^{4} [f. Pink *a.*^{1}] **a.** *intr.* To become pink. Also with *up*.

1854 A. E. Baker *Gloss. Northamptonshire Words* II. 116 *Pink*, to blush. 'How she *pinks* up!' **1909** R. A. Wason *Happy Hawkins* 136, I hadn't never seen those cheeks pink up for anything but fun or anger before. **1927** P. Marks *Lord of Himself* 32 Mrs. Peter's eyes were sparkling again, and her cheeks pinked with happy colour.

b. *trans.* To shear (a sheep) closely so that the colour of the skin shows through; esp. in phr. *to pink 'em*. (*Austral.* and *N.Z. colloq.*)

1898 *Bulletin* (Sydney) 17 Dec. 15 Another term for *fine-cut* is *pinkin' 'em*—showing the pink flesh. **1899** W. T. Goodge *Hits! Skits! & Jingles!* 155 And he 'pinked' him like a leather-neck when squatters paid a pound! **1900** H. Lawson *Verses, Pop. & Humorous* 168 Get the bell-sheep out;..But 'pink' 'em nice and pretty when you see the Boss's boots. **1933** *Bulletin* (Sydney) 15 Nov. 28/1 Instead of being 'pinked', there was sufficient wool left on as weather protection. **1956** G. Bowen *Wool Away!* (ed. 2) 156 *Pink 'em*, to make a very good or better than average job of a sheep. Shearers sometimes call this a 'special cut'.

c. *trans.* To make pink (in various senses of the adj.).

1927 W. Deeping *Kitty* xxvi. 330 You've more idea of colour than I have. I'm too fond of pinking things. **1929** D. H. Lawrence *Pansies* 22 The pretty pretty bourgeois pinks his language just as pink If not pinker.

pinked, *ppl. a.* Add: **1.** (Later example.)

1929 *Papers Mich. Acad. Sci., Arts & Lett.* X. 314/2 *Pinked*, struck by bullets.

2. b. (Earlier example.)

1862 Mrs. J. B. Speid *Our Last Yrs. in India* xi. 273 A black satin polka jacket with 'pinked' flouncing.

pinken, *v.* Delete *rare* and add: **1.** (Further examples.)

1936 Wodehouse *Laughing Gas* vii. 76 It caused Miss Brinkmeyer to pinken and breathe heavily. **1954** D. Ames *Crime, Gentlemen, Please* xxii. 130 Jack, too, was aware of the chill. He pinkened. **1976** *Listener* 15 Apr. 465/2 As the sky pinkened, we turned up a narrow tributary.

2. *trans.* To make pink.

1968 C. Nicole *Self Lovers* i. 8 Her tan was pinkened by a liquor flush.

Pinkerton. Add: (Further examples.) So also **Pinkerto·nian** *a.*, of, pertaining to, or characteristic of Pinkerton or his men.

1908 *Athenæum* 11 Apr. 442/2 While an article in the ensuing number entitled 'The Art of Advertising Made Easy', in which Colburn's Pinkertonian methods are held up to ridicule, is shown to be Hood's. **1915** A. Conan Doyle *Valley of Fear* ii. vi. 274 'The police?' 'Well, a Pinkerton.' **1955** D. W. Maurer in *Publ. Amer. Dial. Soc.* xxiv. 33 I'd say that better than fifty per cent of Pinkertons are ex-cons. *Ibid.* 38 One..pickpocket, so popular that when he killed a Pinkerton detective more than a hundred thieves..poured in to testify successfully in his defense. **1967** N. Mailer *Cannibals & Christians* i. 22 There were tough dull Pinkertons with a tendency to ean on a new visitor. *a* **1971** G. Jackson *Blood in my Eye* (1972) 188 Every time I hear the word 'law' I visualize gangs of militiamen or Pinkertons busting strikes. **1973** L. Hellman *Pentimento* (1974) 177 Hammett..didn't much like to be around people who took dope, in his Pinkerton days he had been more afraid of them than of murderers. **1978** J. Carroll *Mortal Friends* ii. iii. 168 Just hope to high heavens..they keep their Pinkertons out.

pink-eye^{1}. Add: **2. b.** It also occurs in some livestock. (Earlier and later examples.)

1886 *Arch. Ophthalm.* XV. 451 This form of conjunctivitis is contagious and epidemic; it appears most plentifully in the spring and fall months... From the peculiar congestion of the ocular conjunctiva it has become popularly known as 'pink eye'. **1933** [see *bung-eye* s.v. *bung *sb.*^{1} 6]. **1938** S. Duke-Elder *Text-bk. Ophthalm.* II. xxxii. 1541 The intensity of the hyperæmia, sometimes associated with petechiæ, is characteristic, giving it [*sc.* Koch-Weeks' conjunctivitis] the popular name of 'pink-eye'. **1951** R. Seiden *Livestock Health Encycl.* 376 Pinkeye or specific ophthalmia..is an inflammatory condition of the eyes of cattle and sheep. **1974** [see *Koch-Weeks bacillus].

4. *slang* (chiefly *Austral.* and *Canad.*). Cheap whisky or red wine. (See also quot. 1945.) Cf. *pinkie, pinky *sb.*^{3} 1 and Red-eye 4 in Dict. and Suppl.

1900 *Cornhill Mag.* June 778 His capital consisted of a yoke of oxen, a waggon, six four-gallon kegs of pink-eye and a Winchester rifle. **1941** *Coast to Coast* 23 Better put that bottle away... If the trooper comes round somebody'll be getting into trouble for selling Charley pinkeye again. **1941** [see *pinkie, pinky *sb.*^{3} 1]. **1945** Baker *Austral. Lang.* ix. 166 Recipes as published by an outback newspaper in 1936...Methylated spirits and Condy's crystals. (*Pinky.*)..Addicts of these noxious drinks are known as *meths*..and *pinkeyes*. **1953** W. B. Mowery *Sagas of Mounted Police* 125 At Benders' joint, the price of a pint of pink-eye was a day's hard labor in a mine-head.

pink-eye^{2} (pi·ŋkəi). *Austral.* Also **pink-hi, pinkie.** [Aboriginal name.] A festival or holiday.

1924 Lawrence & Skinner *Boy in Bush* viii. 110 It was holiday-*pinkie*, the natives called it. **1929** K. S. Prichard *Coonardoo* 18 The tribes for a hundred miles about had gathered for pink-eye on Wytaliba. **1936** H. Drake-Brockman *Sheba Lane* xi. 131 He found his natives in good tucker and clothes and gave the faithful Jimmy..a horse and cart for the yearly pinkhi, when he visited his tribe. **1969** O. White *Under Iron Rainbow* 139 This year Nolan's Ford Picnic Races and Rodeo..was obviously going to be a successful pink-eye.

pinkie, pinky, *sb.*^{1} Add: Also **pinkey.** (Earlier and further examples.) Also *attrib.* and *Comb.*, as *pinkie-stern schooner*.

1843 *Knickerbocker* XXII. 187 The 'pinkie' is a schooner rigged craft,..sharp at both ends, a short peak running up aft, and designed for a chasing sea. **1873** G. H. Procter *Fisherman's Memorial* 72 Uncle Charlie's first remembrance was of the pinkey fleet. **1882** *Fisherman's Own Bk.* 40 They were the old style of pinkey, without bowsprit or shrouds, with two masts and hempen sails. **1886** [see *chebacco]. **1897** Kipling *Capt. Cour.* vi. 136 My father he run his packet, an' she was a kind a' pinkey, about fifty ton, I guess. **1903** *N.Y. Tribune* 25 Oct. 14 On another occasion the Houghton ran into a pinkey-stern schooner. **1950** R. Moore *Candlemas Bay* 7 Capt. Malcolm Ellis..had gone from a rowboat to a pinky to a mackerel schooner, and finally to a fleet of mackerel schooners. **1972** *Daily Colonist* (Victoria, B.C.) 19 May 1/5 Illusion of jetliner perched atop twin masts of reproduction of old pinky schooner was created this week..as jets broke through low overcast.

pinkie, pinky, *a.*, *sb.*^{2} Add: Also **pinkey. B.** *sb.* (Further examples.) Also *attrib.*

Now also quite common in certain areas of the U.S.

1931 A. J. Cronin *Hatter's Castle* i. iii. 51 'I just flicked him with my pinkie,' declared Brodie complacently. **1941** *Sun* (Baltimore) 13 Oct. 8 (*caption*) Pinkey straight up, that's the class way to drink tea, pal! **1948** *Richmond*(Va.)*Times-Dispatch* 15 Mar. 17/4, I grip the ball with my thumb and pinky. **1950** J. Dempsey *Championship Fighting* 34 You might call that pinky knuckle the exit of your power line. **1958** P. De Vries *Mackerel Plaza* 155 My eye met Mrs. Spensible's across the room, and I thrust out my pinkie, smiling innocently. **1962** Auden *Shepherd's Carol* in *Musical Times* Oct. (Suppl.) 1 O lift your lit-tle pin-kie, and touch the win-ter sky. **1965** E. Tunis *Colonial Craftsmen* vi. 140 Even the most elegant lady poured tea or coffee from her cup into her saucer to cool and then, with delicately extended pinkie, drank it from the saucer. **1970** S. Ellin *Bind* lix. 299 Gela stared at him, gnawing at a hangnail on his pinkie. **1971** G. M. Brown *Fishermen with Ploughs* 21 Fish as small as your pinkie. **1973** 'J. Marks' *Mick Jagger* (1974) 11 As for Mick, he splashes on some fragrance and checks his eyeliner with his pinkie. **1975** *New Yorker* 1 Dec. 48/1 Seemed like his arm was *always* around somebody, and always there was the smell of his rich wool suit, the flash of a pinkie ring, a cloud of Havana, and Houtek's barony voice saying you and him were friends. **1976** *Scottish Rev.* Spring 3 Are ye still eatin' vinegar with a fork and holdin' out yer pinkie when ye sup yer tea? **1977** *New Yorker* 24 Oct. 122/2 Pagano had two pinky rings with nice stones.

pinkie, pinky (pi·ŋki), *sb.*^{3} [f. Pink *sb.*^{4} and *a.*^{1} + -ie, -y^{6}.] **1.** Cheap red wine; (see also quot. 1941). *slang* (chiefly *Austral.*).

1897 *Session Paper Cent. Criminal Court* 10 & 11 Mar. 417, I know I have done wrong; it is all through the drink; I have been having a drop of *pinkie*, and I am sorry for it. **1935** K. Tennant *Tiburon* 93 Staines, nodding his fat, puffy face into his cup of pinkie..hadn't a very good head for the cheap raw wine he was drinking. **1936** A. RUSSELL *Gone Nomad* vii. 55 Beer, whisky, 'pinky', delirium tremens, sore heads, and sandy blight were the chief..maladies of the field. **1941** BAKER *Dict. Austral. Slang* 54 *Pink-eye*,..an addict of the noxious drink called 'pinky', the constituents of which are either red wine and methylated spirits or methylated spirits and Condy's crystals. **1958** *Maclean's Mag.* 27 Sept. 63/3 Pinkie [in St. John's, Newfoundland] is a cheap wine highly regarded by waterfront connoisseurs, a chaser for screech. **1959** D. HEWETT *Bobbin Up* (1961) vii. 93 He'd drink anything, they reckoned, plonk, pinkie, straight metho.

2. A white person (see also quot. 1970). *slang.*

1967 *Observer* 10 Sept. 17/2 The racial discrimination that black school-leavers find when they look for jobs is not a surprise: it is a confirmation. By the time they leave school, whites have become 'pinky', 'the grey man' or..'Mr Charlie'. *Ibid.* 17/3 I've got a white friend I've known from school... No, I'm not a pinky-lover! He's learned to think black *and* think white and I can trust him. **1970** C. MAJOR *Dict. Afro-Amer. Slang* 91 *Pinky*.., Afro-American girl who looks white. **1972** K. JOHNSON in T. Kochman *Rappin' & Stylin' Out* 145 *Pinkie*, refers to the skin color of white women.

3. = *PINK *sb.*[4] 10. Cf. *PINKO *sb.*

1973 *Nation Rev.* (Melbourne) 31 Aug. 1442/3 He called for a Liberal party 'crusade' to defeat the 'reds, the pinkies and the socialists' who are responsible for inflation. **1978** R. BARNARD *Unruly Son* xv. 166 He was always a drawing-room pinkie... As far as contact with the working-class movement was concerned, he hadn't any.

pinkie, pinky (pi·ŋki), *sb.*[4] [f. PINK *sb.*[2] + -IE, -Y[6].] **1.** *S. Afr.* A small marine fish, either the rock grunter, *Pomadasys olivaceum*, of the family Pomadasyidæ, which is only a few inches long and is often used as live bait, or the red grunter, *Pagellus natalensis*, of the family Sparidæ, which is a food fish that may grow to about twelve inches.

1948 *Cape Times* 19 July 1/4 The fish was brought in and gaffed... The bait taken was 'live pinkie'. **1953** J. L. B. SMITH *Sea Fishes S. Afr.* 257 *Pomadasys olivaceum*... Rock-Grunter. Pinky (Natal). *Ibid.* 273 *Pagellus natalensis*... Red Grunter. Pinky. **1966** K. T. LILLIECRONA *Salt-Water Fish & Fishing in S. Afr.* i. 21 In deepish water next to the rocks, all one has to do is cast in this multi-hook trace among the fish, count twenty slowly and then retrieve to find every hook with a pinky on it.

2. The larva of a greenbottle fly of the genus *Lucilia*, used as a live bait in some fresh-water fishing.

1958 F. OATES *Coarse Fishing Baits* i. 23 'Pinkies' are well suited for the smaller fry which inhabit lakes and wide sluggish rivers, because being fairly heavy they can be thrown much farther than squats. **1971** *Angling Times* 10 June 12/2 (Advt.), Wholesalers of maggots, pinkies, squats, anattoes, brandlings. **1974** C. C. TRENCH *Hist. Angling* viii. 234 'Pinkies' are the larvae of greenbottles, rather smaller than other maggots, pinkish in colour and used generally for small roach and dace. **1979** *Guardian* 13 June 9/3 If you have got a box of pinkies in your fridge..you are probably..pre-occupied right now... For next Saturday is the opening day of the coarse fishing season.

pinkified (pi·ŋkĭfəid), *ppl. a.* [f. PINK *a.*[1] + -IFY + -ED[1].] Made pink in colour.

1886 R. BROWN *Spunyarn & Spindrift* xxix. 351 The light of the sun came streaming across it, making our sails all pinkified.

pinking, *vbl. sb.*[1] Add: **b.** *pinking machine, scissors, shears*; **pinking-iron** (earlier example).

1761 in E. Singleton *Social N.Y. under Georges* (1902) 242 [I] have ever since been so scrupulous an observer of it [*sc.* taste] that I never was the mark of a pinking-iron behind it. *a* **1865** MRS. GASKELL *Lett.* (1966) 816 Dear Miss Watkins, Thank you very much for the use of the Pinking Machine. **1951** *Catal. of Exhibits, South Bank Exhib., Festival of Britain* 60/1 Pinking scissors. **1979** E. TAYLOR in I. Webb *Compl. Guide Flower & Foliage Arrangem.* viii. 103/1 Pinking scissors will avoid having to hem the edges. **1962** *House & Garden* Dec. 55/2 Pair of pinking shears. **1976** *Evening Post* (Nottingham) 15 Dec. 21 (Advt.), Dress-making scissors, pinking shears, nail scissors, [etc.].

pinking (pi·ŋkiŋ), *vbl. sb.*[3] [f. PINK *v.*[3] + -ING[1].] (The production of) a metallic rattling sound in an internal-combustion engine as a result of the too rapid combustion of the mixture in the cylinder.

1913 ROGERS & WATSON *Motor Mechanics' Hand-bk.* i. 9 If the compression exceed 90 lb., there is great danger of frequent pre-ignition, and consequent knocking or 'pinking' in the cylinders. **1930** *Flight* 11 July 787 A further change was made to a poor grade spirit, and the symptoms of pinking combined with loss of efficiency were much exaggerated. **1937** [see *DETONATION 1 b]. **1959** *Motor* 19 Aug. 6/2 Full throttle was avoided to prevent pinking. **1968** [see *DETONATION 1 b]. **1970** M. SMITH *Aviation Fuels* vii. 35 High pressure waves.. strike the walls of the combustion chamber with a hammer-like blow, producing a knocking noise. The high pitched, metallic sound known as 'pinking' is due to the vibratory nature of those waves. **1973** *Times* 19 Apr. 35/1 Lead.. is added to petrol to raise octane ratings and prevent 'pinking'.

pinkish, *a.* Add: *pinkish-brown, -grey, -mauve, -purple, -silver, -white* (later examples), *-yellowing.*

1857 GEO. ELIOT in J. W. Cross *George Eliot's Life* (1885) I. vii. 360 The castle is built of stone which has a beautiful pinkish-grey tint. **1952** A. G. L. HELLYER *Sanders' Encycl. Gardening* (ed. 22) 59 Spathe yellowish-green and pinkish-brown. *Ibid.* 118 [*Clinopodium*] *georgianum*.., white to pinkish-purple, to 2 ft. *Ibid.* 276 [*Lilium*] *Kelloggii*, pinkish-mauve, July. **1952** S. SPENDER *Learning Laughter* i. 5 A tall stucco pinkish-yellowing house. **1959** E. H. CLEMENTS *High Tension* vi. 111 Sgurr Dhubh, pinkish-silver in the morning sun. **1961** R. L. GOURSE *With Gall & Honey* xviii. 272 He had a pinkish-white complexion, a small straight nose, [etc.]. **1973** POLUNIN & SMYTHES *Flowers S.W. Europe* iii. 384 A robust plant to 1m or more, distinguished by its large, very dense, globular head of numerous pinkish-purple flowers.

b. Politically somewhat left of centre.

1949 N. MARSH *Swing, Brother, Swing* ix. 206 Sallis's pinkish, facile..observations. **1968** W. ASH *Ride Paper Tiger* vii. 108 Certain pinkish professors back home are making rather a lot of the fact that Ortiz is a political martyr. **1977** *Time* 5 Dec. 67/2 He was born in New York City and spent his early childhood in Bayside, a pinkish nook of Queens.

2. [PINK *sb.*[4] 2 b in Dict. and Suppl.] Fit, 'in the pink'.

1949 J. CORRIE in J. Marriott *Best One-Act Plays 1948–49* 112 'You are looking very well.' 'I'm feeling very pinkish... Very pinkish, indeed, thank you.'

pinkishness (pi·ŋkiʃnės). [f. PINKISH *a.* + -NESS.] Pinkish appearance; a suggestion of pinkness.

1909 M. B. SAUNDERS *Litany Lane* v. 60 With a pinkishness about his eyes not becoming to his blonde good looks.

pinkly, *adv.* Add: (Further examples.) Also *fig.*, embarrassedly.

1923 H. C. BAILEY *Mr. Fortune's Practice* i. 2 He is plump and pinkly healthy. **1953** G. DURRELL *Overloaded Ark* viii. 156 We both looked at the almost sheer cliffs of N' da Ali gleaming pinkly in the evening sun. **1960** M. SPARK *Ballad of Peckham Rye* vii. 141 Mr Willis pinkly took Merle's hand and glanced towards the shop door. **1973** 'D. HALLIDAY' *Dolly & Starry Bird* ii. 24 'You do such lovely parties, Timothy.' 'Oh, well,' he said pinkly. **1974** *Times* 30 Nov. 9/5 The pinkly roasted grouse. **1975** J. MCCLURE *Snake* xi. 148 Kramer watched the dawn of his insight spread pinkly up from Marais' collar. **1978** *Daily Tel.* 8 July 9/2 A garden where Dorothy Perkins rambles pinkly round the door.

pinkness. Add: **b.** The quality or state of being politically pink (cf. *PINK *a.*[1] 3).

1931 F. L. ALLEN *Only Yesterday* iv. 76 The Fighting Quaker's inquisitorial methods..had at least the practical effect of scaring many Reds into a pale pinkness. **1940** R. S. LAMBERT *Ariel & all his Quality* iii. 76 Attacks upon the BBC for the 'redness' or 'pinkness' of broadcast talks.

pinko (pi·ŋko), *a.* and *sb. slang.* [f. PINK *sb.*[4] or *a.*[1] + *-O[2].] **A.** *adj.* **1.** (See quots.)

1925 FRASER & GIBBONS *Soldier & Sailor Words* 224 *Pinko*, drunk. **1941** BAKER *Dict. Austral. Slang* 54 *Pinko*, drunk, esp. on methylated spirits.

2. = *PINK *a.*[1] 3. Chiefly *U.S.*

1957 [see *LONG-HAIR *sb.* 2a]. **1959** C. MACINNES *Absolute Beginners* 38 Your pinko pals did what they wanted to when they got power. **1972** D. LEES *Zodiac* 65 He made Ronald Reagan look like a pinko liberal. **1976** N. THORNBURG *Cutter & Bone* xii. 284 That look and attitude..proclaimed them goddamn ready and eager for any commie revolution the pinko nigger-loving government might be cooking up. **1977** *Transatlantic Rev.* LX. 121 It's the number three song in China, sir. Saw it in one of those magazines my pinko parents subscribe to.

B. *sb.* = *PINK *sb.*[4] 10. Chiefly *U.S.*

1936 J. G. COZZENS *Men & Brethren* 104 She's a good girl... Now only a healthy pinko. I've snatched her like a brand from the Young Communist League burning. **1948** 'B. ROSE' *Wine, Women & Words* 105, I wouldn't call him a Commie, but if he doesn't get a check from Moscow every week, he's being robbed... Unfortunately the pinko didn't drinko. **1959** *Times Lit. Suppl.* 25 Dec. 753/1 To save his family from being 'smeared' by 'left-wingers and pinkoes' he decides to use the pseudonym Victor J. Fox. **1971** *New Society* 7 Jan. 25/3 The new American jingoism wherein the enemy is not the enemy but all those disloyal pinkos at home. **1976** *Spectator* 14 Feb. 13/3 The statement 'we are all guilty'..is enough in itself to identify the speaker as a trendy pinko.

pinko- (pi·ŋko). [See -O.] Used as a combining form of PINK *sb.*[4] and *a.*[1] in **pinko-grey** *a.*, of a pinkish-grey colour; *spec.* = WHITE *a.* 4; hence as *sb.*, a 'white' person.

1924 E. M. FORSTER *Passage to India* vii. 62 The remark that did him most harm at the club was a silly aside to the effect that the so-called white races are really pinko-grey. **1953** W. G. WALTER *Living Brain* i. 1 By brain is meant..something more than the pinko-grey jelly of the anatomist. **1961** P. MASON *Common Sense about Race* i. iii. 49 A pinko-grey man is rather more likely than a Negro to have traces of the ridges above the eyes..so prominent in the gorilla. **1964** 'M. INNES' *Money from Holme* x. 68 The pinko-greys out there [*sc.* in Africa] aren't exactly aesthetes. **1973** J. MANN *Only Security* xi. 142 A pinko-grey lib-lab, that's you. **1974** *Times* 5 June 16/5 The pinko-grays, to use E. M. Forster's accurate description, were entirely safe... Britain was about to quit India. **1977** T. HEALD *Just Desserts* iii. 47 His usual pinko-grey complexion.

pinky, *a.*[1] Add: **a.** (Further examples.)

1907 *Westm. Gaz.* 2 Mar. 17/1 The little habit coats.. are generally faced with..emerald-green, or blue, or even pinky-red. **1927** D. H. LAWRENCE *Mornings in Mexico* 29 Pale belly, and soft, pinky-fawn claws. **1946** G. MILLAR *Horned Pigeon* vii. 78 The pinky-red pantiles of the terraced village. **1974** *Country Life* 2 May 1055/2 Raised panels..painted in imitation of pinky-grey marble. **1975** C. FREMLIN *Long Shadow* x. 77 Myrtle's pinky-orangey lighting. **1977** *Vogue* Feb. 94 Pinky blonde, double-faced wool shirtjacket.

c. Also *pinky-faded* adj.

1926 D. H. LAWRENCE *Glad Ghosts* 23 A big pinky-faded carpet.

pinlay (pi·nlēi). *Dentistry.* [Blend of PIN *sb.*[1] + INLAY *sb.*] An inlay or onlay which is held in place partly by a pin or pins inserted in the tooth.

1915 J. K. BURGESS in *Dental Cosmos* LVII. 1338/2 The attachment..is a modified inlay and contour with pins, which I have chosen to call the 'pinlay' attachment. **1946** *Brit. Dental Jrnl.* LXXX. 14 (*caption*) Spring bridge carrying central incisor on pinlay abutment in canine. **1952, 1973** [see next].

pinledge (pi·nledʒ). *Dentistry.* [f. PIN *sb.*[1] + LEDGE *sb.*; cf. prec.] A pinlay, esp. one covering the lingual surface of a tooth and dependent on pins inserted in ledges cut in the tooth for retention and stability.

1915 J. K. BURGESS in *Dental Cosmos* LVII. 1342/1 (*heading*) 'Pinledge' bridge attachment for anterior teeth. *Ibid.*, The anterior attachment is an outgrowth of the pinlay, being constructed on the same principle. I have chosen to call it the 'pinledge'. **1952** *Dental Practitioner* II. 328/1 The pinlay, or pinledge preparation as it is often called, for incisor or canine bridge abutment, has been known in one form or another for many years. **1973** D. H. ROBERTS *Fixed Bridge Prostheses* vii. 125 The pinledge preparation. This differs from the three-quarter pinlay in that the incisal edge of the tooth is not involved and so no gold is displayed labially. **1975** G. T. CHARBENEAU et al. *Princ. & Pract. Operative Dentistry* xiv. 387/1 The pinledge design may be used on incisor and cuspid teeth with conservative loss of tooth tissue.

pin-money. Add: Also *transf.*, spending money; money for incidental expenses; a trivial sum of money.

1892 *Munsey's Mag.* Oct. 112/1 The late Rose Terry Cooke, popular as her writings were, never made more than pin money with her pen. **1926** H. CRANE *Let.* 1 June (1965) 256, I don't think you'll get pin money for the sale of the place. **1957** *Economist* 26 Oct. 291/1 A much better system than relying solely on attendance pin money for all peers would be to pay a full MP's salary to..a score of 'nominated' peers on either side. **1971** *Farmers Weekly* 19 Mar. 94/2 In farming, we tend to use straw liberally and an odd wedge for a child to bed the rabbit hutch seems insignificant. But..you could.. start a sideline enterprise. Good pin money? **1978** S. ALLAN *Inside Job* i. 17 If you did find yourself short of pin money you..could get yourself a job.

b. *attrib.*

1837 T. BACON *First Impr. Hindostan* I. vi. 171 Marriage is..out of the question..unless..the young lady.. have..a small pin-money purse of her own. **1908** *Daily Chron.* 5 Oct. 5/6 This meeting..protests against the employment of the 'pin-money clerk', who is a menace to the clerks of both sexes. **1961** PARTRIDGE *Dict. Slang* Suppl. 1222/1 *Pin-money spoof*, vague, pointless amateurish writing: journalistic: since ca. 1910. **1977** in *Centuryan* (Office Cleaning Services) Christmas 4/1 Six 'pin-money' schoolgirls whose journey home in a mini-bus ended in tragedy were being employed illegally.

pinnacle, *sb.* Add: **2.** Also, a rock projecting out of the sea.

1949 *Sun* (Baltimore) 5 Nov. 3/4 The big Panamanian freighter was listing badly and threatening 'to slip off at any minute'. It was described as being caught on a 'pinnacle' with water of 36 to 60 feet depth around it.

4. *pinnacle rock* (later example).

1916 *Daily Colonist* (Victoria, B.C.) 14 July 11/3 On her last voyage in the westward route the Dora struck a pinnacle rock and developed a serious leak.

pinnate, *a.* Add: **1. c.** *Physical Geogr.* Of a drainage pattern: resembling a feather in plan.

1932 E. R. ZERNITZ in *Jrnl. Geol.* XL. 512 These acute-angled joinings with the rather evenly spaced and parallel tributaries form a pattern so much like that of a feather that it might appropriately be called 'pinnate'... Figure 8 is an example of pinnate drainage. **1942** O. D. VON ENGELN *Geomorphol.* xi. 215 All the other recognized types of drainage pattern: rectangular, trellis, annular, pinnate, contorted, are responses to structure. **1968** R. W. FAIRBRIDGE *Encycl. Geomorphol.* 287/2 Modified dendritic drainage may be described as pinnate, sub-parallel or anastomatic.

pinned, *ppl. a.* Add: **6. pinned eye** (see quot. and cf. PIN-EYED *a.*).

1842 *Florist's Jrnl.* III. 29 The style or stigma [of an auricula] ought not to rise higher than the stamens, forming what is called a pinned eye, which is reckoned a great deformity.

pinner[3]. Add: **4.** The workman who inserts the pins in the revolving cylinder of a barrel organ.

1896 *Pall Mall Mag.* Nov. 336 To completely 'set' a cylinder takes an expert workman three days; then it is given to the 'pinner' who carefully hammers the pins into the places designated by the 'setter'. **1921** *Dict. Occup. Terms* (1927) §648 *Pinner*..inserts, with pliers and pressing machine worked by treadle, steel pins in positions marked by music marker on revolving cylinder or roller of barrel organ. **1960** *Classification of Occupations* (General Register Office) 84/2 *Pinner*.., barrel organ mfr.

pinning, *vbl. sb.* Add: **1. b.** Also *pinning-out*.

1905 *Sci. Amer.* 30 Sept. 262/1 The second-sizing and pinning-out is done by hand at so-called batteries.

e. An indication of a relationship, falling short of a formal engagement, between two young people through an exchange of fraternity or sorority pins; the exchange of such pins for that purpose. *U.S. university slang.*

1961 *Ann. Amer. Acad. Pol. & Social Sci.* Nov. 85/1 There are boxed proclamations in the newspaper [of Brooklyn College] of watchings, pinnings, ringings, engagements and marriages. **1964** *Amer. Speech* XXXIX. 194 That peculiar institution, the 'pinning' of quasi-engaged girls. **1967** *Punch* 13 Sept. 378/1 Most fraternities and sororities sustained this perfumed atmosphere of competition by requiring their members to date a different person every date night... I attribute the popularity of pinning—a kind of informal engagement to be engaged, signified by the exchange of fraternity and sorority pins—to the desire to escape from that pattern; certainly people got pinned and unpinned all the time.

pinny, *sb.* Add: (Earlier and later examples.) Also *attrib.* and *fig.*

1851 H. Melville *Moby Dick* II. xxix. 203 A woman's pinny hand,—the man's wife, I'll wager. **1858** J. A. Symonds *Let.* 1 Nov. (1967) I. 170 Lady Young..engaged in the construction of *pinnies* for poor children. **1889** E. Dowson *Let.* c 21 Oct. (1967) 111 She was disporting herself in a superb way in Gt Russell St—hatless & in a 'pinny'. **1939** A. Thirkell *Brandons* i. 18 'If we had known mummie was coming, we'd have had our clean pinny on,' said Nurse. **1962** J. Braine *Life at Top* xvii. 198 'Get me a bloody pinny,' I said, 'and you can go out to work.' **1974** *Times* 15 Oct. 12/7 A new pinny idea of long skirt, chemise to the knee over a skinny sweater. **1975** *Country Life* 11 Dec. 1710/1 A practical and pretty pinny to tie round the waist.

Hence **pinnyed** (pi·nĭd) *a.*, clad in a pinafore.

1963 *Guardian* 20 Feb. 7/2 The pinny-ed skivvy.

pinocle. (Earlier example.)

1864 W. B. Dick *Amer. Hoyle* 127 Bézique is fast becoming popular in the United States... It is known among our German brethren as *Peanukle*. *Ibid.*, The game [*sc.* Bézique] became very popular in Sweden, and was finally introduced into Germany, changed in some respects, and called Penuchle.

pinocytized (pəi·nosəitəizd), *ppl. a. Biol.* [f. *pinocyt(osis + -ize + -ed[1].] Taken into a cell by pinocytosis.

1970 *Amer. Jrnl. Anat.* CXXIX. 142/1 The nature of the intracellular hydrolysis of phagocytized or pinocytized substances has been established. **1970** *Nature* 26 Dec. 1284/1 Digestion of pinocytized materials should be impaired.

pinocytose (pin-, pəinosəi·tōuz), *v. Biol.* [Back-formation from next.] *trans.* To absorb by pinocytosis. Freq. *absol.*, to carry out pinocytosis.

1960 E. N. Willmer *Cytol. & Evolution* vii. 118 Epitheliocytes... Can pinocytose. **1962** *New Scientist* 13 Dec. 620/1 A cell may pinocytose for a certain time and then stop. **1967** Jahn & Bovee in Tze Juan Chen *Res. in Protozool.* I. 114 The effects of inducers which stimulate ingestion of *Tetrahymena* by a starved ameba are reduced if the starved ameba is first allowed to pinocytose for 20 min, before being fed *Tetrahymena*. **1971** *Nature* 19 Mar. 148/1 The two cells pinocytose projections from each other's sarcolemmas.

pinocytosis (pi:no-, pəi:nosəitōu·sis). *Biol.* [f. Gr. πίν-ειν to drink + -cyt(e + -osis, after Phagocytosis.] A process by which liquid is taken into a cell as a result of the invagination and pinching off of the cell surface so as to form small vesicles.

The word was first coined as F. *pinocytose* (G. Gabritschewsky 1894, in *Ann. de l'Inst. Pasteur* VIII. 682) in a more specialized sense (see quot. 1895). It was not widely used until after it was coined again in 1931, in the present sense.

1895 *Jrnl. R. Microsc. Soc.* 216 The author [*sc.* G. Gabritschewsky]..suggests the probability that phagocytes are not only capable of seizing and assimilating solid bodies, but of imbibing and absorbing liquid substances, and of rendering them harmless to the organism. For this action the term *pinocytosis* is suggested. **1931** W. H. Lewis in *Bull. Johns Hopkins Hosp.* XLIX. 17 Pinocytosis, drinking by cells; phagocytosis, eating by cells... The word 'pinocytosis', suggested by my colleague Prof. David M. Robinson, is derived from the Greek... By pinocytosis the cells are able to take in substances which cannot diffuse into them or be taken in by ordinary phagocytosis of semisolid particles. **1937** —— in *Amer. Jrnl. Cancer* XXIX. 666 Pinocytosis (drinking) by macrophages in tissue cultures is common. **1960** *Jrnl. Protozool.* VII. 184/2 Pinocytosis is a very demanding process in terms of membrane formation. **1969** [see *endocytosis* s.v. *endo-]. **1977** P. B. & J. S. Medawar *Life Sci.* xv. 124 Fibroblasts..have the power ..to imbibe tiny little droplets of whatever medium they may be living in, known as pinocytosis.

Hence **pinocy·tic, pi:nocyto·tic** *adjs.*, of, pertaining to, or formed by pinocytosis.

1955 *Texas Rep. Biol. & Med.* XIII. 475 This cell.. has been termed a variant pinocytic cell. **1959** *Exper. Cell Res.* XVIII. 71 The pinocytotic vacuole..was 7μ in diameter. **1964** N. S. Cohn *Elem. Cytol.* iv. 68 The movement of fat particles in the intestinal villi appears to occur by pinocytic activity. **1974** *Jrnl. Cell Biol.* LXIII 998/2 Modification of macromolecules by enhancing their positive charges..leads to a preferential pinocytic uptake. **1975** *Nature* 17 Apr. 612/2 Each perineural epithelial cell contained numerous pinocytotic vesicles.

pinole. (Earlier and later examples.)

1842 A. Ganilh *Ambrosio de Letinez* I. vii. 91 Pinole is made with fine corn meal, pounded almonds, sugar and various spices. **1844** J. Gregg *Commerce Prairies* I. vii. 159 This pod..the Apaches and other tribes of Indians grind into flour to make their favourite *pinole*. **1942** Castetter & Bell *Pima & Papago Indian Agric.* 38 In 1862 they sold the War Department more than one million pounds of wheat, as well as pinole, chickens, green peas, [etc.]. **1977** *New Yorker* 20 June 49/1 He carries dried chum salmon for his dogs, and his own food is dried moose or bear meat and pinole—ground parched corn, to which he adds brown sugar.

piñon. Also **pinone, pinyon.** Substitute for def.: One of a group of small pines native to southwestern North America, esp. *Pinus edulis, P. monophylla,* and *P. quadrifolia,* which yield edible seeds; also, the nuts or the wood produced by these trees. Also *attrib.* (Earlier and later examples.) See also Pinion *sb.*[5] in Dict. and Suppl.

1839 Z. Leonard *Narr. Adventures* 35/1 Its top is covered with the pinone tree. **1839** J. Forbes *Pinetum Woburnense* 49 This [*sc. Pinus Llaveana*] is the only Mexican species that bears edible fruit, and is called in that country 'piñones'. **1882** C. M. Chase *Editor's Run in New Mexico* 206 The common fuel is pinon, the best fire-place wood in the world. **1936** *Nature* 22 Aug. 315/2 The woods which have been found best for the purpose of the investigation [into dendrochronology] are the western yellow pine..and the Douglas fir.., while the next best is the pinyon (*Pinus edulis*). **1945** *Antiquity* XIX. 219 Vegetable foods of which there is evidence include maize, kidney beans and pinyon nuts. **1946** D. C. Peattie *Road of Naturalist* iii. 37 Up there the Piutes were feasting on piñon nuts and mountain sheep. **1955** J. Hawkes *Journey down Rainbow* i. 10 The surface of the desert..is..often..boldly spotted with the compact, dark shapes of pinyon and juniper. **1967** N. T. Mirov *Genus Pinus* iii. 150 Piñons form a well-defined group... Their habitat extends to the southwestern Pacific Coastal Ranges, the Colorado Plateau, and the Mexican Volcanic Plateau. **1972** *Sci. Amer.* May 97/1 The growth of the pinyon pine..is affected more by winter climate. **1973** A. H. Whiteford *N. Amer. Indian Arts* 53 Bottles are waterproofed with piñon gum. **1976** *Hortus Third* (L. H. Bailey Hortorium) 875/2 Pinyon, pinyon p[ine] nut p[ine]... A source of edible piñon nuts. **1976** *New Yorker* 26 Apr. 125/3 People in that part of the San Luis Valley.. gather piñon wood for their fires.

pinosylvin (pəinosi·lvin). *Biol.* Formerly also **-sylvine.** [a. G. *pinosylvin* (H. Erdtman 1939, in *Naturwiss.* XXVII. 130), f. mod.L. *Pinus sylvestris*, taxonomic name of Scots pine (f. L. *pīnus* Pine *sb.*[2] + *syl-*, *silvestris* of a wood (f. *silva* a wood)): see -in[1].] **a.** A colourless, toxic, crystalline compound, 3,5-dihydroxystilbene, $C_{14}H_{12}O_2$, which occurs in the heartwood of the Scots pine, where it confers resistance to fungal and insect attack. **b.** Any of the related antifungal compounds that occur in pines.

1939 *Chem. Abstr.* XXXIII. 4776 Pinosylvine is poisonous, fishes die in 0·002% soln. **1945** *Svensk Bot. Tidskr.* XXXIX. 312 In order to get an idea of the relative toxicity of the pinosylvin compounds experiments were made at the same time in solutions containing phenol. **1955** *Ibid.* XLIX. 421 The heartwoods of trees belonging to the *Pinaceae* family contain a number of peculiar phenolic constituents,.. of which only the hydroxystilbenes (pinosylvins) show high fungicidal activity. **1968** *New Scientist* 11 Jan. 68/2 The natural resistance of certain types of wood to termite attack has been attributed to the presence of specific repellent chemicals such as..pinosylvin. **1973** *Ann. Rev. Phytopathol.* XI. 204 The formation of pinosylvins in *P. resinosa* cultures.. may have been caused directly by ethylene.

‖**Pinot** (pino). Also with lower-case initial. [Fr.: see *Pineau.] Any of a family of vines yielding grapes used in wine-making; the grape of these vines. Also, wine made from Pinot grapes.

The principal varieties are the *Pinot Noir* (nwār) (black), used chiefly in making red Burgundy and Champagne, the white-wine-producing *Pinot Blanc* (blaṅ) (white) or *Chardonnay* (ʃardọnē[i]), and the *Pinot Gris* (gri) (grey), a black grape from which white wine is made.

1912 [see *aligoté]. **1959** W. James *Word-Bk. Wine* 144 *Pinot*... There are both red and white varieties and a 'grey' variety grown in Alsace. **1962** *Economist* 29 Dec. 1283/1 A good Pinot Noir..from the Valais or Vaud cantons. **1965** A. Sichel *Penguin Bk. Wines* iii. 233 These four cantons, known as La Suisse Romande, produce 90 per cent of the total crop, the white wines from the Chasselas grape, the Pinot Gris, Marsanne.., the Riesling, Sylvaner and Traminer, and the red wines from the Burgundian grapes Gamay and Pinot. **1967** A. Lichine *Encycl. Wines* 404/2 Pinot Gris and Pinot Blanc, eminently noble vines, contribute to white burgundies. All Pinots abound also in the finer Champagne vineyards. **1968** J. M. White *Nightclimber* ix. 65, I drained my Pinot. **1972** *National Observer* (U.S.) 27 May 4/1 The huge price increases are coming in the premium wines—Cabernet Sauvignon, Pinot Noir and Pinot Chardonnay. **1972** D. E. Westlake *Bank Shot* ix. 66 A side dish of black rice, washed down with a good Pinot Noir. **1974** N. Freeling *Dressing of Diamond* 81 A nice bottle, a rosé Pinot, beautifully dry and flinty. **1976** N. Roberts *Face of France* ii. 24 The so-called Tokay d'Alsace, or *pinot gris*, is made from black grapes, whereas..*pinot blanc* and sylvaner are made from white.

pin-point, *sb.* Add: Also **pinpoint, pin point.** (Further *fig.* examples.)

1890 Kipling in *Macmillan's Mag.* Sept. 323/2 Their blue eyes, driven into pin-points by th' wind. **1926** E. Glyn *Love's Blindness* ii. 24 The centres of her light hazel eyes went to pin points. The dress did not deceive *her*! **1931** C. Day Lewis *From Feathers to Iron* xii. 25 Nightmare nags at his elbow and narrows Horizon to pinpoint, hope to hand's breadth. **1952** R. Neill *Moon in Scorpio* xxviii. 247 His eyes were pin-points now, but their gaze was steady. **1959** E. H. Clements *High Tension* vi. 99 He let it [*sc.* a car] get well ahead and watched the pin-points of red disappear into the darkness. **1961** D. J. Plantz *Sweeney Squadron* x. 151 The Rising Suns were showing up, slightly brighter pinpoints in the gray gloom.

2. *Aeronautics.* A place seen and identified from an aircraft; hence, the ground position of an aircraft as found from such a sighting.

1942 *R.A.F. Jrnl.* 27 June 7 No pin-point was obtained on leaving the British shore. **1942** *Tee Emm* (Air Ministry) II. 81 It's up to you to verify all pinpoints. **1943** [see *astro-sight* s.v. *astro-]. **1944** *Air Navigation* I. i. 20 A Pin Point is a landmark recognised from the aircraft but which is not necessarily underneath the aircraft. A Fix is the ground position of the aircraft, found by direct observation of the ground or by employing wireless or astronomical methods. **1950** D. C. T. Bennett *Compl. Air Navigator* (ed. 5) xi. 374 A Fix..is the position obtained by a Visual Pin-Point or by the intersection of two or more Posn. Lines. **1970** Taylor & Parmar *Ground Stud. for Pilots* ii. 14 Flying this Heading, we pass over Peterborough (5235N 0015W) at 1230 hrs precisely. Plot the position, as a small circled dot; it is a Pinpoint, the name given to a Fix obtained by visual observation of the ground. **1971** *Hindustan Times Weekly* (New Delhi) (Suppl.) 4 Apr. p. iii/2 He's been flying here for only six months and is still in the process of discovering new features and pinpoints.

3. (See quot. 1948[1].)

1943 H. T. U. Smith *Aerial Photographs* xiii. 339 Vertical photography may involve the making of one or more flight strips, or of only isolated stereo pairs, known as 'pinpoints'. **1948** S. H. Spurr *Aerial Photographs in Forestry* ii. 13 A pin-point is an isolated pair of photographs taken so as to give stereoscopic coverage of a specific place on the ground. *Ibid.* 16 Specially designed instruments manufactured by the makers of mapping cameras are particularly well adapted for taking pinpoints.

B. *attrib.* or as *adj.* **1.** Seeming as small or as sharp as the point of a pin.

1850, 1899 [in Dict.]. **1907** J. H. Parsons *Dis. Eye* iv. 67 In old people it is smaller than in the young, sometimes to so great an extent that the pupils are almost 'pin-point'. **1928** D. H. Lawrence *Woman who rode Away* 198 He never liked looking anything in the very pin-point middle of the eye. **1933** W. de la Mare *Fleeting* 95 With pin-point bill, and tail a-cock. **1936** W. Holtby *South Riding* i. vii. 72 Those trodden-down pin-point heels. **1944** *Times* 18 Mar. 4/4 Marauders attacked pin-point targets at Piedmonte. **1959** *Times* 23 Sept. 3/7 The stage effect of overhead lights, the surrounding darkness, and the pinpoint area of operations. **1961** R. B. Long *Sentence & its Parts* vii. 153 In the narrowest sense the present time is a point so minute that it is already a part of the past before we can finish the sentence. But the present with which verbs are concerned is not this uncomfortable pin-point present. **1974** M. C. Gerald *Pharmacol.* xiii. 244 The pinpoint pupil is one of the cardinal signs of morphine poisoning. **1976** *Sat. Rev.* (U.S.) 30 Oct. 10/1 Bell scientists and engineers..have already developed pinpoint light sources—light-emitting diodes.

2. Very fine in texture or structure; characterized by very small points.

1899 *Daily News* 29 July 8/5 A clear Swiss muslin of very fine make, with a pin-point embroidery on it. **1942** *Oxoniensia* VII. 42 Deeply incised 'pinpoint' decoration.. varying a little and reverting to a plain chevron pattern. **1957** J. Kerouac *On Road* (1958) 156 A misty pinpoint darkness. **1962** *Guardian* 23 Feb. 8/4 A seam-free, pinpoint mesh stocking. **1969** *Sears Catal.* Spring/Summer 20 Full fashioned plus the extra elasticity of a pinpoint stitch.

3. Performed with or exhibiting great positional accuracy.

1944 *Manch. Guardian* 14 Dec. 3/2 Fighter Command's activities included thirty missions against V2 targets in Holland, where pin-point power-dive attacks resulted in direct hits on erection and launching installations. **1945** *Times* 27 June 3/4 Their pin-point bombing was on the biggest scale that Japan has yet experienced. **1949** *Sun* (Baltimore) 3 Oct. 2/7 'Kickless' guns, capable of pinpoint accuracy. **1958** J. R. Biggs *Woodcuts* 81 If the design demands precise 'pin point' register, then a precise method must be used. **1958** *Listener* 21 Aug. 259/1

It is the ground controllers' job to see that collisions do not happen. With the equipment they have today this can be done with almost pin-point accuracy. **1973** *Times* 9 Aug. 5/5 He said he was aiming his balloon for France, 'but I would consider anything from Finland to Italy a pinpoint landing'. **1976** *Gramophone* Aug. 370 (Advt.), Dramatically improved solid stereo image and rear pin-point localisation. **1976** *Southern Even. Echo* (Southampton) 3 Nov., Clive Green almost snatched a second ten minutes later with a flying header from a pin-point cross by left-winger Mickey Mellows.

4. Highly detailed or specific.

1960 V. Jenkins *Lions Down Under* p. xv, Secretaries ..looked after our internal comfort with pin-point efficiency. **1971** *Morning Star* 1 July 4/1 This 'simple way' is, of course, the result of pin-point organisation and the working out of schedules.

pin-point, *v.* Also **pinpoint.** [f. the sb.] **I.** *trans.* **1. a.** To locate with high precision.

1917 'Contact' *Airman's Outings* II. iv. 280 Meanwhile an exact position has been pin-pointed. **1936** J. Grierson *High Failure* v. 102 The next thing was to 'pin-point' myself: that is to find the exact spot on the map at which I had made a landfall. **1946** D. Hamson *We fell among Greeks* iv. 46 The enemy was trying to pinpoint our position. **1955** C. S. Forester *Good Shepherd* 72 The fewer people who were aware how accurately the Admiralty was able to pin-point U-boat concentrations the better. **1955** *Times* 6 Aug. 8/4 Not only can the exact position of a find be pin-pointed..but the possibility of future researches and future discoveries is preserved. **1977** *Daily Tel.* 18 Nov. 8/8 Amateur archaeologists believe they have pinpointed the site of a large Roman forum..under central Chichester.

b. To identify (an objective) as a target for pin-point bombing.

1940 *Times* 2 Nov. 4/1 Over Naples itself the aircraft crews were able to 'pin-point' the targets without great difficulty. **1941** *Times* 30 Sept. 4/7 The pilot managed to pin-point the factory. **1946** *R.A.F. Jrnl.* May 169 Lancasters equipped with 'H2S'..thundered through the night to pinpoint their objectives.

2. a. To cause to be conspicuous against a large or complex background; to bring into prominence, emphasize.

1943 *Penguin New Writing* XVI. 27 A solitary searchlight would come on suddenly. And, if it pin-pointed you, how you would writhe about the sky trying to shake it off before the endless beams of all the others caught up on you. **1956** [see *pin-pointing *vbl. sb.*]. **1957** *Economist* 2 Nov. 420/1 Subsequent speakers from Asia, Latin America and Europe took up these themes, each country pinpointing its own problems. **1958** P. Mortimer *Daddy's gone A-Hunting* xli. 239 The world was empty. But tiny, minutely raging, the figure of Rex was pinpointed, the sole survivor. **1974** F. Warner *Meeting Ends* I. v. 24 Lights down to pinpoint Shango in wheel, still spreadeagled, back to audience.

b. To identify precisely; to determine the exact nature of.

1946 *Birmingham* (Alabama) *News* 5 Jan. 1/6 The Pearl Harbor committee called for photographs of the Navy's ship location board today to pinpoint movements of the Pacific Fleet in the days just before the Japanese attack. **1950** *Sport* 22–28 Sept. 18/1 Johnny..would find it difficult to pinpoint the happiest day of his soccer life to date. **1955** *Sci. News Let.* 23 July 51/1 Tonsils, long under suspicion, have at last been pin-pointed as the primary site of polio infection. **1958** *Ann. Reg. 1957* 186 The House of Representatives asked the President to pin-point where substantial cuts could be made. **1960** *Analog Sci. Fact & Fiction* Nov. 13/1 The only actual trouble we can pin-point is that there seem to be a great many errors occurring in the paper-work. **1971** J. Z. Young *Introd. Study Man* i. 9 There have been many attempts to pin-point the particular environmental or other features responsible for the appearance of man. **1977** L. Gordon *Eliot's Early Years* iii. 63 It is difficult to pin-point the sensibility that moves through Eliot's poems.

II. *intr.* **3.** To dwindle to the size of a pin-point (and disappear).

1957 J. Kerouac *On Road* (1958) II. vii. 159 They pinpointed out of sight.

Hence **pi·n-pointing** *vbl. sb.*; also **pi·n-pointable** *a.*, capable of being pin-pointed.

1920 *Flight* XII. 374/2 Practical demonstration of principles learnt in Ground work:—(1) Flight by map alone; (2) Flight by compass alone on pre-determined course and time, turning point to be indicated—pin pointing. **1955** D. Barton *Glorious Life* 71 Here, under his eyes, pinpointable, was the Fall. **1956** *Essays in Crit.* VI. 123 If we pinpoint the personal origin, certainly when the pinpointing is so merely speculative as it seems to be here, we leave out too much. **1962** *Listener* 27 Dec. 1086/1 Current technology, gossip column hearts and flowers..have no direct pin-pointable relation to my work of the moment, but they are not alien worlds. **1967** A. L. Lloyd *Folk Song in Eng.* iii. 150 Even such an apparently pinpointable ballad as 'Edom o' Gordon' has an English, a Lanarkshire and an Aberdeen setting. **1970** Taylor & Parmar *Ground Stud. for Pilots* II. 15 While the pinpointing, plotting and wind finding was going on, so was the aircraft. **1978** J. Wainwright *Ripple of Murders* 53 It was..necessary to..let him *know* that he could be pin-pointed in King Street..if such pin-pointing became necessary.

pi·n-pointed, *a.* [f. Pin-point *sb.* + -ed[2].] Having a fine or sharp point. Also *fig.*

1909 *Daily Chron.* 18 Sept. 10/6 The tiny pin-pointed mapping pen. **1931** E. S. Gardner *Vanishing Corpse* in *Detective Fiction Weekly* 15 Aug. 19/1 His eyes..gazed at Sidney Zoom with pin-pointed intensity. *a* **1936** Kipling *Something of Myself* (1937) viii. 230, I then abandoned hand-dipped Waverleys..and for years wallowed in the pin-pointed 'stylo'. **1976** J. Wainwright *Bastard* ix. 122, I check the time... They'll demand pin-pointed answers to their nit-picking questions.

pi·n-pointed, *ppl. a.* [f. *pin-point *v.* + -ed[1].] That has been pin-pointed.

1944 *Hutchinson's Pict. Hist. War* 12 Apr.–26 Sept. 60 (*caption*) An attack by Mosquito aircraft..on what was probably the most pin-pointed objective which has ever been marked out as a target.

pin-prick, *sb.* Add: **1.** (Later examples.) Also *fig.*

1927 *New Republic* 12 Oct. 216/2 His pen is so subject to his moods that it can make a pin-prick read like a lightning bolt. **1949** E. Coxhead *Wind in West* vii. 195 At the far end of the stifling tunnel, in which he was condemned to grope for ever, he seemed to see a pin-prick of light. **1978** *Times* 22 July 9/2 Beware of sea urchins and the pinpricks of coral.

2. (Further *attrib.* examples.)

1926 T. E. Lawrence *Seven Pillars* (1935) I. xv. 104 The tribesmen..hindered and distracted the Turks by their pin-prick raids. **1976** A. White *Long Silence* vi. 49 Sooner or later, the Germans were going to..suspect.. the source of the many pinprick raids. **1977** *Time* 4 Apr. 23/2 After launching a few pinprick air raids, Mobutu's Army Chief of Staff..claimed that the intruders were in retreat.

b. *pinprick picture*, a coloured print pierced with pin-holes to create an illusion of illumination.

1960 H. Hayward *Antique Coll.* 286/2 Pinprick pictures were a more simple form of transformation, since a coloured print was perforated with a number of small holes and, hence, when held to the light would appear to be illuminated. Coloured paper would sometimes be fastened behind the print. **1968** *Canad. Antiques Collector* Oct. 22/1 Pinprick pictures of ancient oriental origin are probably a branch of decoupage.

pin-prick, *v.* (Further examples.) (Quot. 1945 is in sense of *pin-point *v.* 1 b.)

1909 *Daily Chron.* 15 July 4/4 Every book for the blind is carefully pin-pricked by voluntary workers who can see. **1912** J. Bailey *Let.* 13 Aug. (1935) 132 You shall certainly pin-prick if you will when you come to London, if you don't find anything more amusing to do—and I will listen respectfully and gratefully. **1945** R. A. Knox *God & Atom* v. 71 Other men's lives are at stake; those.. of British or American airmen who might be shot down in trying to pin-prick the targets of Hiroshima one by one, instead of devoting it to a general holocaust. **1952** C. Day Lewis tr. *Virgil's Aeneid* XI. 245 Drances, hostile as ever to Turnus, whose high renown Pin-pricked him with sour envy to intrigue against him. **1966** D. Francis *Flying Finish* xi. 136 'There are some holes in the paper.' 'Where he put the pin.'.. Simon had pinpricked four letters. **1979** G. Macdonald *Camera* Plate 4 A paper print of Venice, garishly coloured by hand then pin-pricked for back-lighting in a viewer.

pin-pricked, *ppl. a.* (Further examples.) *pin-pricked picture* = **pin-prick picture*.

1936 *Discovery* Oct. 321/2 That was a tragic pin which pricked out one of the last letters written by Marie Antoinette in the prison of the Conciergerie... The pin-pricked note miscarried. *Ibid.* 322/2 Some surviving specimens of these pin-pricked pictures date back two hundred years. **1958** R. Godden *Greengage Summer* iv. 38 Pinpricked all over with fear, I tiptoed away. **1961** *Times* 1 July 11/1 One variety of pin-prickt picture deals with religious subjects.

pin-pricking, *vbl. sb.* and *ppl. a.* (Further examples.)

1927 *Daily Express* 5 Dec. 1/4 The move is interpreted ..as a step forward to stop the 'pin-pricking' that has been going on between the two countries. **1936** *Discovery* Oct. 322/2 Pin-pricking with them was a fine art. **1950** *Times* 24 Jan. 3/5 We must bring home to the British Government that although most of us are loyal, we will not tolerate the pinpricking of loyalty. **1958** B. Hamilton *Too Much of Water* v. 119 He had..continued, in a small pin-pricking way, to belittle and snub Patricia Odell. **1961** M. Conway in *Conc. Encycl. Antiques* V. 231/2 The art of pin-pricking or 'Piercing Costumes on Paper' became a young ladies' amusement. *Ibid.*, Extremely attractive pin-pricking effects were achieved by outlining from the front with a fine pin—actually needles were used—the remainder being thickly pierced from the back. **1972** *Times* 26 June 8/5 Much authentic [A.J.P.] Taylor—pinpricking, bubble-bursting. **1973** *Times* (Nepa Suppl.) 14 Apr. p. i/4 Nepal retaliates by such pinpricking gestures as refusing to cooperate wholeheartedly in the extradition of Naxalite terrorists who flee across the border from West Bengal.

pinsapo (pinsa·po). [Sp.] The Spanish fir, *Abies pinsapo*, belonging to the family Pinaceæ, and native to mountainous regions of southern Spain. Also *attrib.*

1839 *Gardener's Mag.* XV. 109 He [*sc.* E. Boissier] first observed the Pinsapo at an altitude of about 4,000 feet. **1852** Standish & Noble *Pract. Hints Planting Ornamental Trees* 47 *Abies Pinsapo.*—Boissier. (Pinsapo Silver Fir.)... A very beautiful tree..indigenous to the mountains of Grenada. **1877** Disraeli *Let.* 29 July in Monypenny & Buckle *Life Disraeli* (1920) VI. 171 Yesterday ..I had to plant a tree—a pinsapo. **1887** *Encycl. Brit.* XXII. 297/1 Among other characteristic trees [in Spain] are the Spanish pine (*Pinus hispanica*), the Corsican pine (*P. Laricio*), the Pinsapo fir (*Abies Pinsapo*), and the *Quercus Tozza*.

pinscher (pi·nʃər). [Ger.] A short-coated, often dark-coloured terrier of the breed so called, usually having pricked ears and a docked tail; also, a smaller terrier with either pricked or drop ears, belonging to the miniature breed so called. Cf. *Dobermann.

1926 W. S. Schmidt *Doberman Pinscher* i. 10 The ancestors of the doberman were the old German shepherd dog and the large variety of the black-and-tan, smooth-haired German pinscher. **1929** *Pure-Bred Dogs* (Amer. Kennel Club) 203 Miniature Pinschers are natives of Germany. **1935** *Toy Dogs* (Amer. Kennel Club) 55 If you like a small 'Pinscher'..see them trotting around and 'showing off' in some of the dog shows. **1954** M. K. Wilson tr. *Lorenz's Man meets Dog* v. 62 The small daughter of the house received..a charming little dwarf Pinscher. **1957** *New Yorker* 21 Sept. 46/2 Zoltan acquired a miniature pinscher. **1968** R. & A. Fiennes *Nat. Hist. Dog* vi. 77 Among the continental terriers with toy varieties are the schnauzers and pinschers. **1973** *Country Life* 15 Feb. 385/2 The toy group... The Yorkshire terrier, the miniature pinscher, the Italian greyhound. **1978** D. A. Stanwood *Memory of E. Ryker* xii. 112 Dogs snarled behind me... Two pinschers hit the door.

pin-stripe. [f. Pin *sb.*[1] 18 + Stripe *sb.*[3]] A fine broken or continuous stripe, esp. one repeated as a pattern on cloth. Also *attrib.*, designating cloth with a pattern of such stripes or garments made of pin-stripe cloth. So *ellipt.* as *sb.*, a pin-stripe suit, conventionally worn by business men.

1897 *Sears, Roebuck Catal.* 183/1 *Extra good value, heavy pin-stripe*, with fancy navy blue square sailor collar. *Ibid.* 183/2 This suit is made of a fine brown pin stripe cassimere. **1906** *Westm. Gaz.* 2 June 16/3 The particular cloth I have in mind has a pin stripe in brown. **1922** Joyce *Ulysses* 321 A dainty *motif* of plume rose being worked into the pleats in a pinstripe. **1935** Wodehouse *Luck of Bodkins* iv. 42 A pin-stripe flannel suit. **1942** S. Spender *Life & Poet* v. 84 The black-coated, pinstripe-trousered man. **1958** *Spectator* 15 Aug. 214/1 A suit that fits him rather less snugly than his usual pin-stripe. **1972** P. Cleife *Slick & Dead* I. i. 15 The usual aleatory fall-out of face fungus and brothel creepers mixing it with the pinstripes and the *Financial Times*. **1973** M. Amis *Rachel Papers* 50 As I watched, there was a stir in the classroom; a cruel-faced bearded man in a pinstripe suit strode into camera. **1973** *Times* 15 Nov. 18/4, I wore my midnight blue suit with a wide pin stripe. **1975** 'D. Jordan' *Black Account* iii. 23 This afternoon Magnus was..in a blue-chalk pinstripe, a heavy blue shirt..a near-black tie. **1977** *Hot Car* Oct. 50/3 Apply ⅛ in. or ¼ in. masking tape into the positions required for the pin stripe, then spray the complete panel in the required car colour.

So **pi·n-striped** *a.*, ornamented with narrow stripes; wearing clothes of pin-stripe cloth, conventionally dressed; also *fig.*, characteristic of the business man.

1896 [in Dict. s.v. Pin *sb.*[1] 18]. **1909** *Westm. Gaz.* 4 Sept. 15/1 A gown carried out on a khaki-coloured foundation has a decoration of a pin-striped black and gold collar. **1932** *Daily Tel.* 25 Apr. 4/4 A little tuck-in blouse of red and white pin-striped silk. **1958** *New Statesman* 3 May 562/3 Small wonder we..are unhappy with the pin-striped Executive of the Labour Party, stinking as it does with the air of neat suburban houses and well mannered conversation over garden fences. **1967** *Listener* 31 Aug. 263/2 The citizen everywhere, pin-striped or dungaree'd, puts his own interests before those of society as a whole. **1970** 'D. Halliday' *Dolly & Cookie Bird* iii. 31 Big silver fish pinstriped in yellow. **1973** M. Woodhouse *Blue Bone* xiii. 148 A stuffy, pin-striped wheeler and dealer. **1975** *Radio Times* 13 Sept. 4/2 Pin-striped anonymity in the City once seemed a more likely destination.

pint[1]. Add: **b.** (Further examples.)

1901 M. Franklin *My Brilliant Career* xxii. 194 'Good gracious, Julius!' exclaimed grannie, as he offered the governess a pot full of beer, 'Miss Craddock can't drink out of that pint.' 'Those who don't approve of my pints, let 'em bring their own.' **1961** H. C. Dodge *My Childhood Canad. Wilderness* i. 11 We had our meals from tin pints and tin plates, as we never took our china to the woods. **1968** K. Weatherly *Roo Shooter* 10 He..filled a tin mug with tea from a fire-blackened oil tin that served as his billy. With the pint in his hand he sat down again.

c. (Earlier and later examples.)

1742 Fielding *J. Andrews* I. II. ii. 142 He wished to find a house of publick Entertainment where he might have dried his clothes and refresh himself with a Pint. *Ibid.* iii. 144 He had just entered the House, had called for his Pint. **1861** Geo. Eliot *Silas Marner* i. 7 He never strolled into the village to drink a pint at the Rainbow. **1922** Joyce *Ulysses* 20 The sacred pint alone can unbind the tongue of Dedalus. **1952** 'J. Tey' *Singing Sands* xii. 205 Eventually he had Richards to himself in a corner with a pint. **1965** V. Canning *Whip Hand* i. 10, I had a pint with him. **1976** W. J. Burley *Wycliffe & Schoolgirls* iv. 86 Middle-aged men whose wildest excess was a couple of pints at the local.

d. *pint-bottle* (earlier example), *-glass* (earlier and later examples), *mug*.

1713 T. Cave *Let.* 16 Jan. in M. M. Verney *Verney Lett.* (1930) I. xiii. 244 The London Postmaster, who yet swallow'd down a pint glass of Ale to the poor Boy's health. **1800** J. Woodforde *Diary* 19 Oct. (1931) V. 279 Miss Emeris sent us a Pint Bottle of Mushrooms. **1847** Dickens *Dombey & Son* (1848) xxxviii. 380 This profound reflection Mr. Toodle washed down with a pint mug of tea. **1856** —— in *Househ. Words* 28 June 554/2 Drinking beer out of thick pint crockery mugs. **1922** Joyce *Ulysses* 301 The memory of the dead, says the citizen taking up his pintglass and glaring at Bloom.

1968 M. Woodhouse *Rock Baby* vi. 51 Binnie gave me coffee in a pint mug. **1976** *Southern Even. Echo* (Southampton) 1 Nov. 9/4 By the end they were glad they had not started with pint glasses. **1978** R. Barnard *Unruly Son* i. 7 At the end of the bar..was one solitary young man, his eyes concentrated on his pint mug.

pint^{2} (pəint). Also **p'int.** Repr. a vulg. and dial. (esp. U.S.) pronunc. Point *sb.*^{1}

1837 Dickens *Pickw.* xxiii. 238 Upon all little pints o' breedin', I know I may trust you as vell as if it was my own self. **1887** *Scribner's Mag.* Oct. 476/2 Jeff looked ..p'int blank gashly. **1893** H. A. Shands *Some Peculiarities of Speech in Mississippi* 50 *Pint*.., Negro and illiterate white for *point*. **1901** M. Franklin *My Brilliant Career* xxxii. 274 The pens had not enough 'pint'. **1943** J. Stuart *Taps for Private Tussie* xiii. 149 'It's wonderful, Uncle George,' I said. 'It's pint-blank right,' Grandma said. **1946** *Richmond* (Va.) *Times-Dispatch* 10 Feb. 8-B/7 The natural sequence of racing between the flags starts with the hunting field, then to point-to-points (gleefully termed 'pint-to-pints' by some), continues to the hunt meetings, and finally ends with steeplechasing.

pinta^{1}. Add to def.: caused by *Treponema carateum,* a spirochete related to those which cause syphilis and yaws. (Earlier and later examples.)

1825 *Amer. Med. Rev.* II. 164 (*heading*) An account of the pinta, or blue-stain, a singular cutaneous disease prevailing in Mexico. **1942** *Arch. Dermatol. & Syphilol.* XLV. 858 The discovery of a spirochete in a Cuban case of pinta by Grau Triana and Alfonso Armenteros, of Habana, Cuba, on Aug. 3, 1938 definitely settled the discussions on the causation of pinta (mal del pinto or carate). **1971** *Nature* 5 Feb. 409/2 The oldest treponemal disease known at present is pinta..which dates back 15,000 years.

pinta^{2} (pəi·ntă). Repr. colloq. pronunc. of *pint o'* (*of*), introduced in a National Dairy Council advertising slogan. Freq. used *ellipt.* for *pint o' milk*; also *transf.* Cf. *cuppa.

1959 *Times* 30 May 10/1 Referring in his opening speech to the 'Drinka pinta milka-day' campaign, Mr. Amory said:.. 'I drink a pint and a half a day.' **1960** *Harper's Bazaar* July 16 Your daily pinta is the best glamour food there is. **1965** *Observer* (Colour Suppl.) 18 Apr. 29/3 The Lamb tavern..worth stopping at for a pinta. **1967** J. Porter *Chinks in Curtain* i. 17 Pity they don't supply the milk of human kindness by the pinta. **1970** A. Jenkins *Drinka Pinta* xii. 129 March 1958 saw the birth of one of the most famous advertising slogans of all time: 'Drinka Pinta Milka Day'. **1971** 'H. Carmichael' *Quiet Woman* x. 106 Some milkman's leaving a pinta on her doorstep every day. **1973** *Observer* (Colour Suppl.) 25 Nov. 41/2 (*caption*) The blue tit..pierces the metal cap to get at the milk in a pinta from a Welsh dairy.

‖**pintadera** (pintădēə·ră). *Archæol.* [Sp.] An instrument for painting patterns on the body.

1910 A. Mosso *Dawn of Mediterranean Civilization* xvi. 257 The great *tholos* of Haghia Triada contains rich material for the study of *pintaderas* of the copper age. **1929** V. G. Childe *Danube in Prehist.* vi. 103 Painting of the person is indicated both by the figurines, ornamented in Cucuteni style, and the occurrence of clay stamps or *pintaderas*, sometimes bearing traces of red colour. **1938** *Nature* 1 Oct. 602/1 Seals that could serve as models for Danubian II 'pintaderas' were current in Crete and Asia Minor throughout the third millennium. **1970** Bray & Trump *Dict. Archaeol.* 180/1 Pintaderas of both stamp and roller types occur in many American cultures.

pintail. Add: **5.** (In full *pintail surfboard.*) A surfboard the back of which tapers to a point.

1967 J. Severson *Great Surfing* Gloss., *Pintail*, a surfboard with a long, drawn-out, pointed tail. **1969** *Sunday Truth* (Brisbane) 12 Jan. 61/1 The Gold Coast City Council is 'extremely concerned' about the growing number of 'pintail' surfboards appearing on local beaches. The surfboard, with a pointed tail and a razor sharp, scythe-shaped fin, appeared as a new design this summer. **1970** *Surf International* (Austral.) I. x. 9/2 The Hawaiian pintails have flow, but that means you're tied to the wave's tempo.

Pinteresque (pintəre·sk), *a.* [f. the name *Pinter* (see below) + -esque.] Of, pertaining to, or characteristic of the British playwright Harold Pinter (b. 1930) or his works. Also *absol.* as *sb.*

1960 *Times* 28 Sept. 15/4 Mr Adrian writes with a cruel mastery of our slipshod, contemporary idioms, and the long drunken coda to his play is a comic achievement none the less impressive for its Pinteresque overtones. **1965** *Punch* 6 Oct. 507/1 The sort of everyday absurdity, in speech or action, that can now be most easily described as 'Pinteresque'. **1969** *Observer* 8 June 26/3 Jonathan.. was an excellently conceived character: a psychiatric worker.., rather prissy, sweetly reasonable on the surface but with a constant hint of query—queer malice showing through... This was a potentially Pinteresque situation. **1970** *Guardian* 7 Aug. 8/4 The Pinteresque as comedy. **1974** *Listener* 13 June 754/1 Suddenly everyone ..talked like overheard conversations on buses. They invented a word for it—Pinteresque.

So also **Pinterian** (pintīə·riăn) *a.*, characteristic of Pinter or his works; **Pi·nterish** [-ish^{1}] *a.*, characteristic or suggestive of Pinter or his works; hence **Pinterishness; Pi·nterism,** Pinterish style or an instance of this.

1960 *Times* 7 Oct. 4/7 Miss Quayle as a Pinterish woman on top of a bus. **1963** *Observer* 13 Oct. 23/3 Dave Freeman's script was ingeniously Pinterish. **1967** *Listener* 1 June 727/1 *The Dick Emery Show*..contained a sketch by Harold Pinter... The sketch..was a small masterpiece, quintessentially Pinterian. Two aging women have tea together, and the conversation..is about a friend who used to go to the butcher's regularly on Wednesdays but now, since she's moved, doesn't go quite so much. **1970** *Guardian* 16 Dec. 8/1 Even on a straightforward social level, I am told, events assume a Pinteresque flavour when the Pinters arrive. What is this pervasive Pinterishness? **1971** *Ibid.* 24 Sept. 10/2 A precisely structured script, only very occasionally dropping into those meaningless meanings now known as Pinterisms. **1975** *Broadcast* 3 Nov. 14/3 Old Times by Harold Pinter..seems to epitomize 'Pinterism'—relaxed circumambient dialogue with lots of significant spaces between the words.

pintid (pi·ntid). Also **pintide.** [ad. Sp. *pintide* (F. Leon y Blanco 1940, in *Méd. Revista Mexicana* XX. 240), f. *mal del pint-o* Pinta^{1} + *sifil-ide* Syphilide.] A lesion of the skin of the type characteristic of pinta.

1940 *Q. Cumulative Index Medicus* XXVII. 886/2 Pinta—constant presence of Treponema herrejoni in cutaneous lesions of dyschromic period of mal del pinto and in 'pintides'. **1942** *Arch. Dermatol. & Syphilol.* XLV. 849 (*caption*) Trichophytoid pintid in Cuban pinta. **1965** Hargreaves & Morrison *Pract. Trop. Med.* iv. 161 A secondary stage..consists of a symmetrical eruption.., consisting of macules, and miliary papules or pintids. **1973** A. Wisdom *Colour Atlas of Venereol.* 150 The primary pintide appears, usually on exposed skin surfaces, after an average incubation period of six to eight weeks.

pinto, *a.* Add: **1.** (Earlier and later examples.) Also in Comb., as *pinto-coloured* adj.

1865 B. Harte in *Californian* 15 Apr. 4/1 The devil in the shape of a fleet pinto colt. **1936** D. McCowan *Animals Canad. Rockies* xvi. 141 An Indian boy on a pinto pony had chased him to cover. **1966** H. Marriott *Cariboo Cowboy* iii. 39, I had two saddle horses... One was a pinto-coloured gelding.

2. pinto bean, the mottled seed of a variety of the kidney bean, *Phaseolus vulgaris*, which is widely cultivated in the southwestern United States and Central America; also, the plant itself. Also *ellipt.*

1916 'B. M. Bower' *Phantom Herd* iii. 46 A girl gave me a handful of pinto beans. **1924** W. M. Raine *Troubled Waters* xxvii. 269 Pinto beans..were no sooner out and stacked than the men were hard at it putting in winter wheat. **1941** J. A. & A. Lomax *Our Singing Country* iii. vi. 292 When you get through, you've not got a cent To buy fat-back meat, pinto beans. **1942** [see *Lima b]. **1963** Mrs. L. B. Johnson *White House Diary* 29 Dec. (1970) 26 There were beans (pinto beans, always), delicious barbecued spare ribs. **1969** *New Yorker* 17 May 115/1 (Advt.), Subsisting day after day on a few greens around noon..and some pinto beans in the evening. **1973** *Black Panther* 5 May 7/2 Existence has become a diet of pinto beans and rice. **1977** *New Yorker* 20 June 49/1 From a supplier in Seattle he orders hundred-pound sacks of corn, pinto beans, unground wheat.

pintoresque (pintŏre·sk), *a. rare.* [ad. Sp. *pintoresco* picturesque: see -esque.] Picturesque, forming a suitable subject for a painting.

1969 *Daily Tel.* (Colour Suppl.) 17 Jan. 29/4 Artists abound, since the Mediterranean is almost embarrassingly *pintoresque* wherever you may decide to go.

pi·nt-size, *a.* [Size *sb.*^{1}] Small; also quasi-*sb.*, as a nickname for a child or small person. So **pint-sized** *a.* in same sense; also *absol.* as *sb.*; also, having a capacity of one pint.

1938 *Sun* (Baltimore) 22 Apr. 3/2 The [air] ship, just a pint-sized affair compared to the giant Hindenburg, carried only three persons. **1939** R. Chandler *Trouble is my Business* (1950) 17 It was large enough for a pint-sized desk. **1949** *Sun* (Baltimore) 9 Apr. 6/1 (*heading*) Opportunity for cattle breeders: the pint-size cow. **1952** B. Malamud *Natural* 182 A brisk, pint-size chef with a tall puffed cap on. **1955** *Granta* 26 Nov. 11/2 Gorgeous Gloria, The Pint-sized Poppet. **1959** [see *nipper *sb.*^{1} 3 b]. **1961** M. Beadle *These Ruins are Inhabited* iii. 36 Choristers, in pint-sized caps and gowns, trotting across the bridge for Evensong. **1971** *Times* 8 Sept. 21/4 (*heading*) Merits of the pint-sized company. Next week, the Bolton Committee of Inquiry on Small Firms plans to publish the results of a survey. **1972** Wodehouse *Pearls, Girls & Monty Bodkin* ix. 158 Where young pint size is at a disadvantage is in never having seen Grayce when she was really rolling. **1973** M. Amis *Rachel Papers* 20 He read with concentration, his nose perhaps six inches above the page, mouthwashing with tea from a pint-sized mug which Jenny had time and again to refill. **1973** *Guardian* 22 May 13/2 Long double-breasted riding macs for the pint-sized. **1977** *Time* 8 Aug. 28/2 Andrea McArdle, 13, star of the Broadway musical *Annie*, led her pint-size cast onto the softball diamond against the peewees of Paramount Pictures's forthcoming kiddy sequel, *The Bad News Bears in Breaking Training.*

pi·n-tuck. [Pin *sb.*^{1} 18.] In *Sewing*, a narrow, chiefly ornamental, tuck. Also *attrib.* So **pi·n-tucked** *a.*; **pi·n-tucking.**

1903 K. D. Wiggin *Rebecca* xxvii. 285 Costumes that included..drawing of threads,.. hemstitching and pin-tucking. **1906** *Times* 4 May 10/2 The fulness of the skirt closely pin-tucked to the figure in sets of three. **1921** *Daily Colonist* (Victoria, B.C.) 13 Oct. 20/1 (Advt.), Flannelette Gowns, with high or 'V'-neck..trimmed with embroidery or pin-tucks. **1932** *Daily Tel.* 23 May 6 (Advt.), Pin tucks trim the small over-sleeve. **1964** *McCall's Sewing* xv. 270/1 If a slip needs to be shortened only a slight amount, you can do it by taking several small pin tucks around the lower edge. **1973** *Times* 15 Nov. 6/1 The tailored torso..made to fit even more rigidly by vertical rows of pin tucks. **1975** *Times* 7 Oct. 11/1 Jersey long dresses with pin tucking. **1975** *New Yorker* 15 Dec. 74/2 A zip-fronted aviator jacket with pin-tuck detailing on back and sleeves. **1976** *Daily Mail* (Hull) 30 Sept. 13/8 (Advt.), Suede and Leather Pin Tuck Jackets..From £19·95. **1976** *Ilkeston Advertiser* 10 Dec. 14/2 The bridesmaids wore Victorian style pin-tucked beige dresses.

pi·n-up, *a.* and *sb.* [Pin *v.*^{1} 12.] **A.** *adj.* **1.** (See Pin *v.*^{1} 12.)

2. Of a photograph or other picture, designed to be fixed to a wall, etc. Also applied to a favourite or sexually attractive young person, the typical subject of such a photograph; also in extended use. Also, pertaining to or characteristic of such a picture or person.

1941 *Life* 7 July 34 Dorothy Lamour is No. 1 pin-up girl of the U.S. Army. **1943** *Sun* (Baltimore) 8 Oct. 22/6 Bob Hope, radio and film comedian, today emerged victorious as the official pin-up boy of the WAC contingents here. **1944** *Richmond* (Virginia) *Times-Dispatch* 19 May 11/5 The ex-GI's who threw away all their pin-up pictures when they came home from the war are tacking pretty photos up on their bedroom walls again. **1946** *News Chron.* 27 Feb. 1/8 The honourable lady must not take advantage of the fact that she is my pin-up girl. **1948** 'E. Crispin' *Buried for Pleasure* iii. 19 She had a figure like the quintessence of all pin-up girls. **1948** M. A. Michael tr. *Mielche's From Santos to Bahia* vi. 142 The hard, cold eyes of the American girls,..calculation behind their vulgar 'pin-up' smile. **1953** *Encounter* Nov. 30/1 Women's locks, or corsets, or riding boots, and even pin-up portraits, may become the object of fetishist worship. **1958** E. H. Clements *Uncommon Cold* i. 69 That pin-up girl I talked to on the pier. **1960** *News Chron.* 13 July 3/1 Gillies Pelletier,.. Gillies is the pin-up boy of practically every French-Canadian female who watches television. **1963** *Times* 22 Jan. 3/4 He is the 'pin-up' cricketer of the layman as much as of the connoisseur and he will be remembered always as a player who never grew old. **1969** *New Statesman* 18 July 71/1 Aubrey Jones, when I first knew him, was the pin-up boy of the modern Tory party. **1976** T. Stoppard *Dirty Linen* 11 The man reacting to the pin-up photograph.. *Maddie* in a pin-up pose.

B. *sb.* A pin-up photograph; the subject of such a photograph; also *transf.*

1943 *Yank* 30 Apr. 17/1 The yeoman who did all the worrying about this week's Coast Guard issue roared quite emphatically that this week's pin up would have to have his approval. **1945** *Times* 4 Jan. 5/4 There is always room for a 'pin-up' or a photograph. **1951** J. B. Priestley *Festival at Farbridge* ii. ii. 281 I'll bring the two winsome pin-ups with me and we'll all have lunch. **1957** R. Hoggart *Uses of Literacy* vii. 175 Pin-ups used to be, and still are, standard decoration for servicemen's billets and the cabs of lorries. *Ibid.* 178 Sometimes a male pin-up for the ladies is produced. **1970** *Daily Tel.* 13 Jan. 14/6 He has since become the leading figure—the political pin-up—of the new régime. **1971** B. W. Aldiss *Soldier Erect* 61 Next morning before parade, I stuck the crumpled picture of the monkey god on the wall beside the bed, next to the pin-ups of Ida Lupino and Jinx Falkenberg. **1972** J. McClure *Caterpillar Cop* ii. 15 The hundreds of murders committed for profit by writers..kept things going, just like those pin-ups in Antarctic weather stations. **1979** 'M. Yorke' *Death on Account* xiii. 129 No pin-ups of nudes. It's like a monk's cell.

pin-wheel, *v.* Add: **b.** *intr.* To rotate in the manner of a pin-wheel (sense 2). Also *fig.*

1942 W. Faulkner *Go down, Moses* 149 The shrill, frantically pinwheeling little dog. **1951** J. Steinbeck *Burning Bright* i. 12 The shrill band played the march of elephants and white horses, giraffes and hippopotamuses and pin-wheeling clowns. **1952** *Chambers's Jrnl.* Apr. 235/1 So he let fly at the nearer of them, and saw her tumble in the air, then pinwheel earthwards. **1976** W. Greatorex *Crossover* 188 Memories pin-wheeled through Pavel's mind. **1977** D. Bennett *Jigsaw Man* xii. 225 Strangely unrelated incidents pinwheeled through Farquar's mind.

Pinxton (pi·ŋkstŏn). The name of a town in Derbyshire used *attrib.* to designate a soft-paste porcelain made there from 1796 to 1813. Also quasi-*adj.*

1802 in C. L. Exley *Pinxton China Factory* (1963) 60 To be Sold by Auction, by Blackwell & Co. At their Auction Rooms, Long Row, Nottingham. Six Crates of Pinxton China and Earthernware. **1876** J. Haslem *Old Derby China Factory* 244 In the general run of Pinxton patterns gold was rarely used, the edging being usually in blue. **1928** W. B. Honey *Old Eng. Porc.* xi. 201 Some cups and saucers at South Kensington..were 'authenticated' as Pinxton by John Haslem. *Ibid.*, The later Pinxton porcelain may be well studied in Mr. Herbert Allen's collection. **1963** C. L. Exley *Pinxton China Factory* iii. 18 It is..likely that the elaborate gilding, so characteristic of the finest Pinxton ware, must have been reduced to a minimum during the last twelve months of Billingsley's connection with the factory. **1966** G. A.

GODDEN *Illustr. Encycl. Brit. Pott. & Porc.* 257 Typical Pinxton porcelain is similar to puce-marked Derby porcelain of the 1790–1800 period. **1974** —— *Brit. Porc.* 351 Several examples featured as Pinxton in various books have every appearance of being of Coalport manufacture. **1976** *Times* 26 Oct. 16/4 A pair of Pinxton tapering beakers.

piny, *a.* (Further examples of spelling *piney.*)
1809, etc. [see *PINEY WOOD]. **1931** S. JAMESON *Richer Dust* xiv. 421 The water in the bath was faintly brown. The warm piney water soothed her. **1959** C. OGBURN *Marauders* ii. 37 Meredith had been at Fort Benning,.. and his class..'had had an exercise in weapons placement out in some ol' piney hills'.

piny, var. PEONY. (U.S. examples.)
1904 *Dialect Notes* II. 427 *Piny, n.,* peony. **1913** G. STRATTON-PORTER *Laddie* vi. 165 Her people..spent much money on the biggest tombstone in the cemetery, and planted pinies and purple phlox on her. **1976** *Columbus* (Montana) *News* (Joint Suppl.) 24 June 4/4 Even though it had medicinal value, colonial housewives did not as a rule include the peony in their herb gardens, but set it out among their flowers. They felt that the 'glory of the front yard was the old-fashioned early red "Piny"'.

Pinyin (pinyi·n). Also **Pin-yin, Pin-Yin.** [a. Chinese *pīn-yīn,* lit. 'spell sound'.] A system of Romanized spelling for the Chinese language, adopted officially by the People's Republic of China in stages since 1958. Also *attrib.*
[**1959** W. SIMON *Chinese Radicals & Phonetics* (rev. ed.) 432 A further Scheme, apparently to be regarded as final,.. on 11th February 1958 was approved by the Fifth Session of the First National People's Congress. Its Chinese name is Hanyu-Pinyin-Fang'an..(Chinese Language Spelling Scheme).] **1963** *McGraw-Hill Mod. Chinese-Eng. Dict.* p. iii/2 The Pinyin romanization, or 'phonetic construction', using the Roman alphabet, is very similar to the Wade-Giles system which has been standard in the Western world till very recently. **1972** *Computers & Humanities* VII. 262 The romanization system used in this article is Pinyin, adopted by the People's Republic of China as its official transcription system. **1974** *Encycl. Brit. Macropædia* XVI. 801/1 The Pin-yin system indicates unaspirated stops and affricatives by means of traditionally voiced consonants. **1977** *Daily Tel.* 10 Jan. 4/5 Primary school children are taught the 'Pin-Yin' system of writing the Peking dialect in the Roman alphabet before they tackle the more difficult system of Chinese characters. *Ibid.*, Most Chinese adults cannot read 'Pin-Yin' on its own. **1979** *China Now* Jan.-Feb. 9/1 The State Council has issued a document stipulating that *pinyin* romanization is 'suited to all languages using the Roman alphabet'.

pinyon, var. *PIÑON.

‖**piob mhor** (pīp vōə·r, pī:əb vōə·ɹ). [Gael., lit. 'big pipe'.] The Highland pipes, the bag of which is blown by a long pipe with a mouthpiece (see quot. 1954).
1838 A. MACKAY *Coll. Anc. Piobaireachd or Highland Pipe Music* 5 When the infirmities accompanying a protracted life, prevented him handling his favourite *Piobmhor*, he would sit on the sunny braes, and run over the notes on the staff. **1845** *New Statistical Acct. Scotl.* XIV. 339 The names of some of the caves and knolls in the vicinity still point out the spots where the scholars used to practise, respectively on the chanter, the small pipe, and the *Piob mhor*, or large bagpipe. **1901** W. L. MANSON *Highland Bagpipe* i. 10 The *Piob Mohr* is not now an agency to be reckoned with by any one who wishes to explore the hills and glens... As a Highland war spirit, its glory has departed. **1920** *Glasgow Herald* 1 May 6 The clan is no more..; but the piobmohr [*sic*] remains.., and in its music there may be heard..the romance, and the tragedy, and the beauty of the story of the Scottish Highlands. **1954** *Grove's Dict. Mus.* (ed. 5) I. 345/2 The Highland pipe (*piob mhor*) is pre-eminently the martial instrument... The oldest known existing instrument is dated 1409... It now consists of a sheepskin bag into which are tied five stocks, which accommodate the three drones and the chanter with their reeds, and the blowpipe. **1968** J. ARNOLD *Shell Bk. Country Crafts* 316 At this juncture it is convenient to define the features which distinguish the various pipes to be heard in Britain. They are the Great Pipes, or Piob Mhor, the Reel Pipes, [etc.]. *c* **1970** A. MACPHEE *Story of Scottish Highland Bagpipe* (An Comunn Gaidhealach) 5 The renaissance of interest over the past century in the 'piob-mhor' is in great measure due to the interest of the Army. **1975** F. COLLINSON *Bagpipe* 114 The contrast between the pastoral English bagpipe and the war-like Highland *pìob-mhór*.

pion (pəi·ǫn). *Nuclear Physics.* [f. *PI(-MESON + *-ON[1].] Any of a group of mesons that have masses of approximately 140 MeV (270 times that of the electron), zero spin, zero hypercharge, and isospin of 1, and on decaying usually produce a muon and a neutrino (in the case of charged pions) or two photons (in the case of the neutral pion); a pi-meson.
1951 *Sci. News* XXI. 21 The mass of π-mesons, or pions as they are called in short,..appears to be in the neighbourhood of 276 times that of the electron. **1958** *Spectator* 13 June 778/3 The Japanese physicist Yukawa has shown that what causes the neutrons and the protons of the atomic nucleus to cling together with such tenacity are the revolving pions that link them. **1968** M. S. LIVINGSTON *Particle Physics* vi. 124 The neutral pion π^0 can be formed through the charge-exchange process $\pi^- + p \rightarrow n + \pi^0$ following capture of the π^- in a Bohr orbit (i.e., in liquid hydrogen). The π^0 decays promptly (10^{-16} sec) into two photons. **1971** P. E. HODGSON *Nucl. Reactions* ii. 37 The interaction of fast pions with nuclei can also give information on the relative extent of the neutron and proton distributions in matter. **1975** *Daily Colonist* (Victoria, B.C.) 26 Jan. 14/2 The new 17-foot-long generator shoots out pions or sub-atomic particles generated by a high-energy accelerator.
Hence **pio·nic** *a.*, of, pertaining to, or involving a pion, or an atom having a negative pion orbiting the nucleus.
1960 P. ROMAN *Theory Elem. Particles* v. 511 All pionic interactions are of the same strength. **1967** J. C. SENS in G. Alexander *High Energy Physics & Nucl. Struct.* II. 117 In muonic atoms, the muon samples the distribution of *charge* in the nucleus; in pionic atoms the pions form in addition a probe for the nuclear *mass* distribution, through the strong interactions. **1970** D. F. JACKSON *Nucl. Reactions* x. 230 Additional information about the pion-nucleus interaction can be obtained from studies of pionic atoms and pionic x-rays.

pioneer, *sb.* Add: **3. b.** *Ecol.* A plant which establishes itself in an unoccupied area.
1916 F. E. CLEMENTS *Plant Succession* x. 212 It [*sc.* the pitch pine] produces..more seed than the white pine and in its demands is better able to act as a pioneer. **1929** WEAVER & CLEMENTS *Plant Ecol.* viii. 147 The reactions of the pioneer stage may be unfavorable to the pioneers themselves. **1953** H. L. EDLIN *Forester's Handbk.* viii. 113 As a general rule, the light-demanders are also pioneers, capable..of forming a vigorous first crop on bare land. **1967** M. E. HALE *Biol. Lichens* vii. 96 Lichens are conspicuous pioneers on rocks.
c. (Usu. with capital initial.) In the U.S.S.R. and other communist countries, a member of a Society of Young Pioneers, a movement for children below the age of sixteen. Also *transf.* and *attrib.*
1929, etc. [see *OCTOBERIST, -BRIST 2 b]. **1930** 'I. Low' *His Master's Voice* x. 120 The streets grew merry with the drums of the pioneers, with flags, with the strains of the International. **1944** M. LASKI *Love on Supertax* v. 58 A band of children..holding a banner on which was inscribed 'St Pancras Pioneer Group'. **1957** M. PAVLOV in G. L. Kline *Soviet Educ.* 130 The Pioneers and the Komsomol members, as a rule, are atheists. **1959** A. WESKER *Chicken Soup with Barley* 1. ii, in *New Eng. Dramatists* I. 193 We didn't force her to be in the pioneers. .. Show a young person what socialism means and he can't do anything else but accept it. **1970** N. FLEMING *Czech Point* vi. 71 As a boy he was in the Pioneers—it's a sort of boy-scout thing. **1970** *Morning Star* 11 May 4 The school has 180 pupils from the age of six to sixteen. There are 22 staff, four educators and a Pioneer organiser. **1972** *Times* 17 June 13/1 Scores of children, mostly red-neckerchiefed Pioneers, were running and scrambling over the rocky ground... They..had to climb more than 950 steps to the monument which records how a Russian army freed Bulgaria from oppression. **1973** *Listener* 2 Aug. 138/2 Another important aspect of Soviet holiday-making is the vast network of so-called Young Pioneer summer camps run for schoolchildren. **1976** 'S. HARVESTER' *Siberian Road* iv. 50 Young schoolchildren, all wearing their red Pioneer neckerchieves.
4. a. *pioneer work.*
1849 THOREAU *Week Concord Riv.* 359 It is the worshippers of beauty, after all, who have done the real pioneer work of the world. **1933** *Burlington Mag.* Nov. 193/1 Valuable pioneer work..has been done. **1965** *Eng. Stud.* XLVI. 369, I shall try to clarify the relation between my interpretation of Coleridge's poem and such pioneer-work as Lowes's associative researches.
b. (In sense 3 b above) *pioneer association, plant, species, tree.*
1932 FULLER & CONARD tr. *Braun-Blanquet's Plant Sociol.* xiv. 352 We distinguish aggressive, advancing pioneer associations and restricted, retreating relict communities. **1960** N. POLUNIN *Introd. Plant Geogr.* xiv. 456 The fringe of the mangrove, at least where it does not consist of young pioneer plants, is made up of tall trees. **1966** F. H. BRIGHTMAN *Oxf. Bk. Flowerless Plants* 199 These pioneer plants gradually break down the rock surface into fine particles. **1933** *Forestry* VII. 140 Scots pine is the native conifer of the district, and has also undeniable merits as a first crop, or pioneer species, on the..moorlands of the district. **1971** *Sci. Amer.* Sept. 129/2 Species typical of immature succession stages—'pioneer' species—are characteristically able to disperse themselves over considerable distances. **1954** S. PIGGOTT *Neolithic Cultures Brit. Isles* i. 5 Iversen has noted that birch is a 'pioneer tree' which rapidly colonizes an area after a forest fire.

pioneer, *v.* Add: **4.** *Ecol. trans.* and *intr.* Of a plant, to colonize (new territory); to establish itself in an unoccupied area.
1939 H. H. BENNETT *Soil Conservation* 418 Ragweed.. pioneers idle fields. **1960** N. POLUNIN *Introd. Plant Geogr.* xi. 327 Hardy Mosses..sometimes pioneer on uncolonized rock surfaces.

pionee·rdom. *rare.* [f. PIONEER *sb.* + -DOM.] The condition or state of a pioneer; a prevalence of pioneers.
1873 *Porcupine* 13 Sept. 379/2 A..Californian, who had arrived..from the States, close on to the age of pioneerdom.

pionization (pəi,ǒnəizēi·ʃən). *Nuclear Physics.* [f. *PION + -IZATION.] The production of numerous low-energy pions by the collision of two high-energy nucleons.
1964 *Mat.-Fys. Meddelelser K. Danske Vidensk. Selskab* XXXIII. xv. 8 The calculation of the relative importance in the cosmic radiation of mesons generated by nucleons in pionization and mesons generated in the deexcitation of baryon states is straightforward on the basis of this model. **1974** FRAUENFELDER & HENLEY *Subatomic Physics* xii. 343 At ultrahigh energies, the interaction of two nucleons can indeed be a spectacular event... Most of the secondaries are pions. In the c.m. of the colliding protons, nearly all the pions have small momenta. The formation of such a pion cloud is called pionization.

piopio (piū·,piū). [Maori.] A small New Zealand bird, *Turnagra capensis*, resembling a thrush and belonging to the subfamily Pachycephalinæ, the whistlers or thickheads; also called the native thrush.
1873 W. L. BULLER *Hist. Birds N.Z.* 136 The silvery notes of the Bell-bird, the bolder song of the Tui, ..and the whistling cry of the Piopio—all these voices of the forest are blended together. **1938** M. GORDON *Children of Tane* vi. 160 The southern Piopio has been more often encountered than the northern. **1969** J. FISHER et al. *Red Bk.* 301/1 The piopio is certainly very rare indeed; but just how rare it is can only be discovered by hard field studies on both North and South Island of New Zealand, in each of which a race survives.

piosity (pəiǫ·siti). [f. PIOUS *a.* + -ITY, after RELIGIOSITY.] Affected or excessive piousness, sanctimoniousness; an instance of this.
1922 *Contemp. Rev.* Sept. 353 The lack of such faith means, and has meant, the reduction of morality to piosity, convention, legality. **1961** *Spectator* 1 Dec. 824 The pall of piosity and ambition lifts from the family. **1975** *Church Times* 31 Jan. 14/5 God forbid that we should use over-devotional words or piosities about the Lord's life.

‖**piou-piou** (piūpiū). [Fr.] A popular name for a French private soldier.
1854 B. ST. JOHN *Purple Tints of Paris* II. xi. 224 Formerly, a *piou-piou*—as the common soldier was somewhat contemptuously called—was treated..with a sort of paternal solicitude. **1867** 'OUIDA' *Under Two Flags* I. xiii. 300 The speaker looked down on the *pioupiou* with superb contempt. **1894** [see *NOUNOU]. **1900** R. WHITEING *Life of Paris* 207 Polin..figures as the common soldier, the pioupiou, with his simple virtues of good-humour and fidelity to the flag. **1930** [see *NOUNOU].

pious, *a.* Add: **1. d.** Phr. *pious hope*, an extravagant or unrealistic hope expressed in order to preserve an appearance of optimism.
1907 R. FRY *Let.* 3 Apr. (1972) I. 283 Mr Morgan.. secured three [pictures] for himself and expressed a pious hope that the Museum might be able to buy the rest! **1931** *Economist* 11 Apr. 773/2 That this, as the phrasing suggests, is only a pious hope is apparent when the attitude of the three main groups of countries concerned is considered. **1977** *N.Y. Rev. Bks.* 15 Sept. 15/1 The pious hope—by no means an assumption—that the biographer's psychological acuity, powers of empathy, respect for fact, general culture, and sense of proportion would prevent the appearance of yet one more in a series of glib psychobiographies. **1978** LD. DROGHEDA *Double Harness* xxi. 288 Despite all the pious hopes, disappointments persisted.

pip, *sb.*[1] Add: **c.** Ill humour or poor health, esp. in colloq. phrs. *to have* (or *get*) *the pip*, to be depressed, despondent, or unwell; *to give* (someone) *the pip*, to annoy or irritate, to make (someone) ill-tempered or dispirited.
1886–96 in Farmer & Henley *Slang* (1902) V. 210/2 It cost a bit to square up the attack; For the landlord had the pip. **1896** A. BEARDSLEY *Let. c* 17 Sept. (1971) 165 Are you suffering with a south-west wind in London? It prevails here utterly and has given me the pip. **1903** KIPLING *Traffics & Discov.* (1904) 55 What's an admiral after all?.. Why, 'e's only a post-captain with the pip. **1913** *Punch* 15 Oct. 324/3 [His] later works gave him the pure pip. **1923** WODEHOUSE *Inimitable Jeeves* iii. 36 If there's one thing that gives me the pip, it's unpleasantness in the home. **1930** J. B. PRIESTLEY *Angel Pavement* ix. 440 A proper old Jonah you're turning into! You give me the pip, Dad, honestly you do. **1932** A. J. WORRALL *Eng. Idioms* 31, I feel rotten to-day. I'm not ill, but I've just got the pip, that's all. **1934** J. RHYS *Voy. in Dark* I. iv. 53, I thought there was something about this place that gave me the pip. **1942** *R.A.F. Jrnl.* 18 Apr. 20 Dear-o-dear, he fair gave me the pip. Talk about gloom! **1949** N. MARSH *Swing, Brother, Swing* xii. 285 The Judges' Rules..may be enlightened but there are times when they give you the pip. **1962** *Friend* 3 Aug. 962/1 The signpost to the safe way forward: 'true moral simplicity'. It just about gives me the pip. **1976** *Scotsman* 24 Dec. (Weekend Suppl.) 1/5, I feel it's my duty but I'm not keen. My grandchildren give me the pip.

pip, *sb.*[2] Add: **5.** *Mil.* A star or one of a group of (up to three) stars worn on the epaulettes by officers as an indication of rank. Also *transf.*
1917 W. OWEN *Let.* 23 Nov. (1967) 509, I shall soon be putting up another pip. **1918** —— *Let.* 15 July (1967) 564, I still wear one pip because nobody knows whether I am Lieut. or not. **1919** *Chamber's Jrnl.* Jan. 43/2 Thomas, his senior by one 'pip' in the battery. **1924** KIPLING *Debits & Credits* (1926) 315, I wrote the usual trimmin's..an' what his captain had said about Bert bein' recommended for a pip. **1954** [see *GONG[2] 2]. **1972** P. DRISCOLL *Wilby Conspiracy* (1973) xxii. 284 The

authority of the two pips shining on his shoulders. **1973** D. LEES *Rape of Quiet Town* vi. 103 Despite the extra couple of pips he'd given me, I didn't feel happy about my new command. **1978** M. KENYON *Deep Pocket* i. 12 The desiccated arsehole-creeper in his new silver pips and braid.

6. a. A sharp, narrow, and usu. small spike or deflection on a line displayed on the screen of a cathode-ray tube.

1944 *Radar* Apr. 30/1 Signals appear as pips, or deflections, on the luminous trace. *Ibid.*, The range of a reflecting object is indicated by the distance of the pip from the base of the trace. **1949** D. G. C. LUCK *Frequency Modulated Radar* vii. 299 As the generator is tuned toward either limit of the sweep, these pips may be seen to approach one another on the oscilloscope. **1950** *Jrnl. Appl. Physics* XXI. 59/2 If the output frequency times three is exactly equal to the input frequency, the two pips on the scope should coincide. **1963** G. M. B. DOBSON *Exploring Atmosphere* viii. 138 The distance of the 'pip' from the starting line will be a measure of the time between the signal which started the beam moving and that which produced the 'pip'.

b. A voltage pulse.

1946 *Electronic Engin.* XVIII. 145/3 Use was made of a crystal oscillator which generated both time-base recurrence and calibration pips. **1947** *Ibid.* XIX. 9/2 The time base can be synchronised by applying a negative pip to the first grid of V_5.

7. *attrib.*, as *pip card* (sense 1).

1903 *Burlington Mag.* Dec. 246/1 He persuaded him.. to make the exchange with twelve figure and fourteen pip cards. **1977** *Jrnl. Playing-Card Soc.* May 30 The suit symbols and the denominations are shown as miniature cards of traditional form in the upper right-hand corner on the pip cards.

pip, *sb.*[3] Add: **2. b.** Phr. *to squeeze* (someone) *until the pips squeak* (and variants): to exact the maximum payment from (someone), orig. with allusion to Germany's indemnity after the war of 1914–18 (see quot. 1918).

1918 *Cambridge Daily News* 11 Dec. 3/2 Sir Eric Geddes followed up his big meeting at the Guildhall on Monday night by addressing another crowded assembly in the large hall at the Beaconsfield Club on Tuesday night... Dealing with the question of indemnities, Sir Eric said: The Germans, if this Government is returned, are going to pay every penny; they are going to be squeezed as a lemon is squeezed—until the pips squeak. My only doubt is not whether we can squeeze hard enough, but whether there is enough juice. **1929** W. S. CHURCHILL *World Crisis: Aftermath* ii. 47 One Minister, reproached with lack of vim, went so far as to say 'We would squeeze the German lemon till the pips squeaked.' **1933** *Radio Times* 14 Apr. 75/1 The Lloyd George Coalition Government..elected..on a programme of hanging the Kaiser, squeezing Germany until the pips squeaked. **1940** S. SPENDER *Backward Son* 64 A clarion call to the readers of the *Daily Sketch* to make Germany pay till the pips squeak. **1973** P. O'DONNELL *Silver Mistress* v. 93 We run an inquiry on a client, and we don't squeeze him till the pips squeak... We just pressure him. **1973** *Times* 12 Nov. 19/3 In opposition..[Labour] would tax the upper working class until the pips squeak. **1978** *Times* 15 Sept. 3/3 When Mr Singer was asked how the extra money was being found, he said: 'The pips are squeaking.'

pip, *sb.*[4] Used for *p* in telephone communications and in the oral transliteration of code messages, as in *pip emma*, for *p.m.* (= *post meridiem*: see P II). Also occas. in colloq. use.

1913 *Signalling* (Imperial Army Series) ii. 19 The letters T, A, B, M, S, P and V will be called *toc, ack, beer, emma, esses, pip,* and *vic* respectively, so as to distinguish them phonetically from letters of similar sound. **1915** [see *EMMA]. **1917** [see *ACK]. **1926** [see *EMMA]. **1927** W. E. COLLINSON *Contemp. Eng.* 98 Other artillery terms which spread were O pip (for 'observation post'). **1930** E. RAYMOND *Jesting Army* III. ii. 292 The working parties parade under the trees at nine o'clock pip emma... At three o'clock ac emma they will return. **1969** [see *EMMA]. **1977** C. MCCULLOUGH *Thorn Birds* xv. 350 The second hand was just sweeping up to 9:40 pip-emma.

pip, *sb.*[5] [Echoic.] A short, high-pitched sound, esp. one produced electronically; *spec.* (*a*) one broadcast as a time signal; (*b*) one transmitted over a telephone line as a signal.

1907 G. B. SHAW *Major Barbara* III. 292 *Sarah* (touching Lady Britomart's ribs with her finger tips and imitating a bicycle horn) Pip! pip! **1929** *B.B.C. Year-bk. 1930* 406 G.T.S. = Greenwich Time Signal, which takes the form of a broadcast by electrical contact of the last six seconds before the hour, the 'beat' of each second being represented by a sharp 'pip'. **1930** *Prof. Papers Inst. P.O. Electr. Engineers* No. 135. 41 There is an advantage in giving the time intimation automatically and this is being done experimentally..by means of a 'pip' signal. **1938** F. B. YOUNG *Dr. Bradley Remembers* i. 29 The six 'pips' of the time-signal sounded and the Weather Forecast began. **1946** *Electronic Engin.* XVIII. 360/2 (Advt.), The warning is given in the form of a 1,000 c.p.s. 'pip' on the loud speaker lasting ½ second. **1951** 'E. CRISPIN' *Long Divorce* xiv. 172 There are the pips... Quick, or it'll be another three minutes. **1962** A. NISBETT *Technique Sound Studio* xii. 219 One of the most characteristic sounds of early electronic works has been the use of short bursts of tone at various frequencies, sounding like a series of pips. **1967** O. LANCASTER *With Eye to Future* I. 1 With the six pips, conversation..faded away ..as the announcer..began to summarize his disastrous bulletin. **1972** *Radio Times* 6 Jan. 5/3 Listeners may have noticed a change in the Greenwich Time Signals broadcast since January 1. Instead of six equal pips, the signal since 1924, there are five equal pips followed by a longer one lasting half a second. The exact time is signalled by the beginning or 'leading edge' of the long pip. **1973** *Times* 21 Sept. 5/3, I believe the call was a long-distance one. The pips are louder..if the call is local. **1977** J. WILSON *Making Hate* xiii. 155 He raced back to the telephone in the hall. When the pips went.. he could hardly get his twopence in the slot.

pip, *v.*[2] Add: **1.** (Earlier example.)

1598 FLORIO *Worlde of Wordes* 279/1 *Pipare*, to cackle or cluck as a hen, to pip, to pule as a hawk.

2. a. (Later examples.) So **pipped** (pipt) *ppl. a.*; **pi·pping** *vbl. sb.*

1901 *Chambers's Jrnl.* Nov. 717/1 Gigantic incubators.. literally vomiting forth their flocks of twittering little creatures at pipping-time. **1953** N. TINBERGEN *Herring Gull's World* xviii. 161 The parents would stop shifting and turning an egg when it is pipped. *Ibid.*, In most of the pipped eggs there is a line of cracks around the obtuse pole. **1962** J. C. WELTY *Life of Birds* xvi. 316/2 The first step in hatching is the puncturing, or 'pipping', of the shell by the chick with its outwardly-pressed egg tooth. **1972** L. HANCOCK *There's a Seal in my Sleeping Bag* vii. 162 This egg will hatch tonight. See, the large end is already cracked and pipped. **1972** *Sci. Amer.* Aug. 30/1 The ducklings begin to pip their eggs... As the eggs are being pipped the female clucks... When the pipping is completed, she drops back to..four calls per minute.

b. *transf.* To give birth. *colloq.*

1973 *Times* 27 Aug. 5/8 'I say, Aubrey, has your wife pipped yet?' I assumed he meant had she had her baby.

pip, *v.*[3] Add: **1. a.** (Further examples.)

The examples in the second set owe something to the phr. *to pip at the post* (see sense c below).

1916 E. V. LUCAS *Vermilion Box* 226 Only yesterday poor Hugh Blackstone was pipped right at my side, and he lasted only ten minutes. **1917** E. F. WOOD *Notebk. of Intelligence Officer* x. 182 In that bit of trench, sir, you must bend over as you go. It is enfiladed by an enemy sniper. He 'pipped' one of our fellows through the head there yesterday. **1927** A. CHRISTIE *Big Four* xi. 141 That's my solution—Gilmour Wilson got pipped by mistake. **1932** WODEHOUSE *Hot Water* i. 19 Soup Slattery showed Mr. Carlisle the scar..where a quick-drawing householder of Des Moines, Iowa, had pipped him a couple of years back when he was visiting at his residence. **1950** PARTRIDGE *Here, There & Everywhere* 70 The remaining Tommy synonyms [for 'wounded'] are *pipped*, especially by a bullet whether of rifle, revolver, or machine-gun; *to stop one* [etc.].

1930 *Bulletin* (Sydney) 1 Jan. 35/1 He [*sc.* a race-horse] just pipped Baverarrack..for third place. **1964** *Engineering* 21 Aug. 221/3 Dick Bertram.., in Lucky Moppie, was pipped into second place by an error of navigation. **1976** *Scottish Daily Express* 24 Dec. 15/4 As anchorman, Ian Hutcheon did a magnificent job, shooting a final 71 to pip the Japs and tie for the individual section. **1977** *R.A.F. News* 11–24 May 18/4 The host station..were pipped 6–3 by Brampton.

b. To reject or disqualify; to fail (a candidate) in an examination. Of a candidate: to fail (an examination).

1908 A. S. M. HUTCHINSON *Once aboard Lugger* I. i. 31 'I had forgotten. Your examination?' George half turned away. The bitterest moment of a sad day was come. He growled: 'Pipped.' **1912** F. M. HUEFFER *Panel* I. iii. 85 Olympia was exaggerating... I wasn't going blind. I was only pipped for active service. **1973** *Daily Tel.* 17 Oct. 15/1 School-leavers who were unfortunate enough to pip all or some of their O or A levels will have been seeking a second chance without having to return to school.

c. To anticipate or forestall (someone) in a particular activity, circumstance, etc.; *spec.* in phr. *to pip at* (or *on*) *the post*, to defeat by a narrow margin at the last moment; also *ellipt.*

1924 WODEHOUSE *Ukridge* iii. 67 Bad luck his getting pipped on the post like that. **1939** 'N. BLAKE' *Smiler with Knife* xix. 272 Well, Georgia, pipped at the post, aren't you? **1949** 'E. C. R. LORAC' *Still Waters* ii. 27, I pipped him at the post. His instructions must have limited him. **1959** 'M. M. KAYE' *House of Shade* xviii. 245 He was head over heels about the bewitching Amalfi, and got pipped on the post by Eduardo. **1969** *Times* 25 Nov. 23/1 Shell..now have a record eight managing directors; BP..have just been pipped at the post—they have only seven. **1970** 'A. GILBERT' *Death wears Mask* iii. 4 You won't be able to buy me that ring, after all, because it's sold. Someone's pipped you on the post. **1974** *Times* 8 Apr. 13/1 Schools television started in 1957, when Associated Rediffusion pipped the BBC by starting a service in which 80 schools took part.

2. *intr.* To die. Also with *out.*

1913 A. LUNN *Harrovians* ii. 31 'Is he Irish?' 'He don't seem to know. Father who's pipped was Irish. His mother's pipped too.' **1920** R. MACAULAY *Potterism* III. i. 110, I think it's simply rotten pipping out. I *like* being alive.

pip, *v.*[4] [f. *PIP *sb.*[5]] *intr.* To make a short, high-pitched sound. So **pi·pping** *ppl. a.*

1938 D. SMITH *Dear Octopus* I. 14 Just see if Hilda's still telephoning... Tell her it's elevenpence every time it pips. **1958** *Listener* 18 Sept. 418/1, I could hear morse pipping and the loudspeaker blaring away. **1972** *Jazz & Blues* Oct. 5/1 A throbbing low register clarinet solo by Ben Richardson..ends rather oddly with some 'pipping' high notes like the BBC time signal. **1976** A. PRICE *War Game* I. 61 The phone pipped for more money and he..fed the last of his change into it. **1978** R. HOLLES *Spawn* iv. 28 People passing in cars pipped and waved although they hardly knew you.

‖**p'ip'a** (pīpā·). Also **pepa, pipa,** etc. [Chinese.] A Chinese stringed instrument (see quot. 1975).

1839 *Chinese Repository* May 42 *Pepa*, the balloon shaped guitar... This is about three feet in length... The strings are of silk. **1848** S. W. WILLIAMS *Middle Kingdom* II. xvi. 165 In writing a tune for the lute or *pipa*, 'each note is a cluster of characters'. **1874** *Jrnl. N. China Branch R. Asiatic Soc.* VIII. 115 The *P'i-p'a*.., or 'Balloon-shaped Guitar', described by the Chinese as resembling a ham, has a body like the egg of a goose nearly a foot in diameter with four strings, which are played with the fingers. **1917** *Encycl. Sinica* 388/2 *P'i p'a* is a lute about forty-two inches long with a pear-shaped body. The neck is eight and a half inches long. It has ten or twelve frets and four or six strings. **1954** *Grove's Dict. Mus.* (ed. 5) II. 238/2 *P'i-p'a*.., four-stringed short lute (sometimes 'balloon guitar')... About 3 ft. long and 1 ft. wide.., the body is pear-shaped, its back being rounded but shallow, its front flat and covered with the soundboard... The four silk strings..are attached..to a cross-ledge on the soundboard. **1962** E. SNOW *Red China Today* (1963) lxxiii. 563 The *p'i-p'a* is a native Chinese instrument something like a zither. **1975** C. P. MACKERRAS *Chinese Theatre in Mod. Times* 22 Of the plucked, non-bowed stringed instruments the most significant is the pear-shaped *p'i-p'a*... It is played held upright on the thigh. The musician plucks the strings with his right thumb and first finger, sometimes protected with a plectrum, and determines the pitch with three of his left fingers. **1979** *Time* 2 Apr. 48/1 Liu Dehai played a concerto for a lutelike instrument called the pipa.

pipe, *sb.*[1] Add: **1. c.** Also *pl.* as a nickname for a boatswain. *Naut. slang.*

1856 R. MACCLURE *Discovery of North-West Passage* xv. 233 'Pipes' picked up a leg of the deer. **1903** H. HOLMES *Life & Adventures on Ocean* 17 The boatswain, commonly called 'Pipes' for shortness, was warned by his superior officer to take every care. *Ibid.*, 'High enough,' calls out Pipes. **1942** *Penguin New Writing* XV. 8 When Pipes went for supper he had a side-parting and looked quite different.

3. c. *U.S. slang.* Something that is easy to accomplish; a 'cinch'. Cf. *LEAD-PIPE. Also *attrib.*, as *pipe course.*

1902 'H. MCHUGH' *It's up to You* iii. 66 It was so easy it was a shame... 'The idea is Napoleonic, little woman!' I said. 'It's a pipe!' **1927** *Amer. Speech* II. 277/2 *Pipe course*, easy course. **1936** L. C. DOUGLAS *White Banners* ii. 44 A procession of shamefaced athletes who..had thought erroneously, when they had registered for it, that Anglo-Saxon was 'a pipe'. **1951** M. SHULMAN *Many Loves of Dobie Gillis* (1953) 105 You are all freshmen.. and you may not be familiar with the term 'pipe course'. A pipe course is a course where students can get passing grades without doing much work. This is not a pipe course. **1952** WODEHOUSE *Barmy in Wonderland* viii. 80 This show's a pipe, and any bird that comes in is going to make plenty. **1978** H. KEMELMAN *Thursday the Rabbi Walked Out* x. 57 Nothing to it... Believe me, the whole thing's a pipe.

4. i. (Example.)

1813 JANE AUSTEN *Let.* 16 Sept. (1952) 326 My Cap is come... Fanny has one also..shaped round the face.. with pipes & more fullness, & a round crown inserted behind.

7. e. For 'of steel, caused by the escape of gas' read 'caused by shrinkage of the metal'. (Examples.)

1861 *Brit. Patent* 1310 2 Shrinkage forms a deep tube or funnel in the upper part of the ingot... This funnel is called by steel manufacturers the 'pipe' of the ingot. **1895** E. L. RHEAD *Metallurgy* xi. 147 Steel of harder temper..settles down in the mould, forming a funnel-shaped cavity or pipe. **1923** GLAZEBROOK *Dict. Appl. Physics* V. 357/2 If this takes place any shrinkage of the metal during further solidification must result in the formation of a pipe. **1973** J. G. TWEEDDALE *Materials Technol.* II. ii. 36 Metal ingots..are often cast with open tops and the defective top material, including any pipe, is usually cut off subsequently.

10. d. *put that in your pipe and smoke it* (earlier and later examples); also in similar phrases.

c **1824** R. B. PEAKE *Americans Abroad* (1884) I. 4/2 Put that in your pipe and smoke it. **1837** DICKENS *Pickw.* ii. 7 Pull him up—put that in his pipe—like the flavour—damned rascals. **1921** GALSWORTHY *To Let* I. ix. 81 The noble owner put this opinion in his pipe and smoked it for a year. **1927** *Vanity Fair* XXIX. III. 67/2 'Laugh That Off!' ('Put that in your pipe and smoke it.') **1947** W. S. MAUGHAM *Creatures of Circumstance* 296 I'm engaged to her, so put that in your pipe and smoke it. **1977** A. HUNTER *Gently Instrumental* x. 136 There's a dozen witnesses, so you can put that in your pipe and smoke it.

e. *N. Amer. colloq.* A spell of travelling between two rest-periods at each of which a pipe is smoked; the distance covered or the time taken, in such a spell; also, the distance covered while smoking a pipeful of tobacco. *Obs.* exc. *Hist.*

1793 J. MACDONELL *Diary* 5 July in C. M. Gates *Five Fur Traders* (1933) 92 Leaving pointe au père we paddled two pipes and put to shore to give the men time to clean themselves. **1799** I. WELD *Trav. N. Amer.* xxix. 262 A pipe, in the most general acceptation of the word, seemed to be about three quarters of an English mile. **1806** S. FRASER *Jrnl.* 29 May (1960) 193 The men are better off and better pleased than if they ate a little at every Pipe. **1809** 'D. KNICKERBOCKER' *Hist. N.Y.* I. III. viii. 189 He arrived at Fort Amsterdam in little less than a month, though the distance was full two hundred pipes, or about 120 miles. **1848** R. M. Ballantyne *Hudson's Bay* iv. 77 The men used to row for a space of time, denominated a *pipe*, so called from the circumstance of their taking a smoke at the end of it. **1931** G. L. Nute *Voyageur* 50 We have seen that the voyageurs had their own method of measuring portages. They were not less original on the water. Here the *pipe* was the standard of measurement. This was the distance covered between respites, when the luxury of resting and smoking was indulged. **1969** E. W. Morse *Fur Trade Canoe Routes* I. i. 8 A stop was made for a few minutes each hour to allow the men to have a pipe. This event was so important that distances came to be measured in *pipes*: '*trois pipes*' might be 15 to 20 miles, depending on winds and current.

f. An opium-pipe; esp. in phr. *to hit the pipe*, to smoke opium; also, an opium-addict. *slang* (orig. *U.S.*).

1886, 1902 [see *HIT *v.* 22* a]. **1926** J. Black *You can't Win* xix. 300, I..learned he had been 'on the pipe' only three months. **1926** N. Lucas *London & its Criminals* x. 134 So 'Izzy' had come to 'hitting the pipe'. I knew he had many vices, but I did not know that opium was one of them. **1949** *Sunday World-Herald Mag.* (Omaha, Nebraska) 3 Apr. 2/1 Opium smokers are considered at a low level..but a guy who profits when he hits the pipe is the plumber. **1959** Murtagh & Harris *Who live in Shadow* III. i. 119 You can recognize 'pipes', opium addicts, by the odour which clings to them. **1972** D. Bloodworth *Any Number can Play* xi. 95 Max insisted that they go on to Madame Phnom's plush smoking establishment for a pipe or two.

11. a. (sense 3) *pipe-coating, -fitter, -jointer*; (sense 10) *pipe-bowl* (earlier example), *-lighter, -smoke, -smoker* (examples), *-smoking* (examples; also as *vbl. sb.*), *-spill, -weed*.

1852 Dickens *Bleak Ho.* (1853) xxi. 213 The pipe-bowl..is burning low. **1964** N. G. Clark *Mod. Org. Chem.* v. 80 The highly viscous bitumen which forms the remainder of the distillation residue is used for..corrosion-proof pipe-coatings. **1975** *Offshore Engineer* Oct. 13/1 The UK pipe-coating market is split..between two firms. **1890** Webster, *Pipe fitter*, one who fits pipes together, or applies pipes, as to an engine or a building. **1910** *Daily Chron.* 31 Jan. 6/5 Arthur Moon, aged 45, a pipe-fitter. **1977** *Cornish Times* 19 Aug. 15/3 He won first-year plumber and pipe-fitter prize. **1902** *Encycl. Brit.* XXV. 509/2 A record should be kept of the history of the pipe.., with the name of the pipe-jointer whose work closes the record. **1909** *Dialect Notes* III. 357 *Pipe-lighter*, a paper spill or taper used for lighting lamps, pipes, etc. **1916** 'Boyd Cable' *Action Front* 57 Each man had with him one of those tinder pipe-lighters which are ignited by the sparks of a little twirled wheel. **1852** Dickens *Bleak Ho.* (1853) xi. 105 A cloud of pipe-smoke..pervades the parlor. **1971** 'D. Halliday' *Dolly & Doctor Bird* xvi. 231, I got home to be met by..the smell of pipe smoke curling round from the hallway. **1979** M. Eden *Document of Last Nazi* xix. 96 Strang smelled old pipe smoke. **1866** Geo. Eliot *Felix Holt* II. xxx. 229 Rough-looking pipe-smokers, or distinguished cigar-smokers. **1959** *Listener* 25 June 1119/1 His plain, factual, forthright sentences—a sort of pipe-smoker's prose—deceptively bare and simple, convey the scene..with a telling clarity. **1853** Dickens *Bleak Ho.* xxxiv. 338 I'll have no more of your pipe-smokings and swaggerings. **1958** J. Byrom *Or be he Dead* vii. 106 The pipe-smoking young man in the open-necked shirt. **1979** J. van de Wetering *Maine Massacre* iv. 52 A pipe-smoking old man. **1979** *Arizona Daily Star* 5 Aug. A7/1 A single match and an even draw gave the world's international pipe-smoking cup to a..physics teacher yesterday. **1922** Joyce *Ulysses* 530 Pages will be torn from your handbook of astronomy to make them pipespills. **1955** J. R. R. Tolkien *Return of King* 270 And if you have any pipe-weed, we'll bless you.

b. pipe berth, a collapsible or otherwise easily-stored canvas bed with a frame of metal piping used on small vessels; **pipe bomb**, a home-made bomb contained in a metal pipe; **pipe-burial**, a burial in which a pipe (usually of lead) passes from the coffin or the tomb to the surface of the ground, to permit the pouring of libations; **pipe chaplet** *Founding*, a chaplet (sense 6) used in the casting of pipes, which consists of a concave semi-cylindrical load-bearing surface supported on a stem; **pipe-cleaner**, something used for cleaning a tobacco-pipe; *spec.* a device for this purpose consisting of a piece of wire covered with tufted material; also *fig.*; **pipe cot** = **pipe berth*; **pipe-drain** *v. trans.*, to drain (land) by laying pipes; chiefly in pa. pple.; **pipe-dream** orig. *U.S.*, a fantastic or impracticable notion or plan, compared to a dream produced by smoking opium; a 'castle in the air'; hence **pipe-dreamer; pipe-dreaming** *vbl. sb.*; **pipe-dreamy** *a.*; **pipe-fiend** *U.S. slang*, an opium addict or smoker; **pipe-gun,** (*a*) *dial.*, a pop-gun; (*b*) a gun made out of a pipe; **pipe-necked** *a.*, having a long slender neck; **pipe-opener** (earlier and later examples); also *fig.*, a 'trial run' or 'curtain-raiser'; **pipe-rack,** add: (now usu. as two words without a hyphen); (*c*) a rack or support for a set of pipelines above the ground; **pipe-still**, a still in which crude oil is heated by passing it through a series of tubes inside a furnace; **pipe-story**, a fantastic or impossible story (c.f. **pipe-dream*); **pipe-water**, water conveyed by pipes

1933 Chapman & Horenburger *Thirty Easy to build Sail Boats* 89/2 A pipe berth can be fitted over each berth for the extra guest. **1963** J. T. Rowland *North to Adventure* vii. 90 With all the pipe berths folded back against the ship's side, the cabin became a capacious hold. **1976–7** *Sea Spray* (N.Z.). Dec./Jan. 51/2 The Sands design No 2218 offers four berths, pipe quarter berth, two seat berths amidships and a pipe berth in the foc'sle. **1966** *Guardian* 5 Sept. 1/7 The headquarters of the American Communist Party was damaged by a pipe-bomb tossed from a moving car. **1971** *Sunday Times* 31 Oct. 10 Pipe bombs are another favourite anti-personnel bomb. **1977** *Time* 26 Dec. 26/2 Last August a tipster directed police to a pipe bomb at a Coors recycling plant in a Denver suburb. **1929** *Antiquaries Jrnl.* IX. 1 (*heading*) A Roman pipe-burial from Caerleon, Monmouthshire. **1934** Laing & Rolfe *Man. Foundry Pract.* iii. 57 Pipe-chaplets..can be obtained, either in the form illustrated, or with short pointed stems, their chief purpose being to support pipe cores in position. **1960** R. Lister *Decorative Cast Ironwork* ii. 26 Of the types in regular use, special mention may be made of the pipe chaplet.., usually made of tinned wrought iron, and consisting of a pin with a semicylinder at one end. It is used to support the round core in pipe casting. **1870** G. M. Hopkins *Notebks. & Papers* (1937) 132 The heads of flowering grass..often used as pipe-cleaners. **1928** E. Waugh *Decline & Fall* I. ii. 18 A boxing-glove, a bowler hat, yesterday's *Daily News* and a packet of pipe-cleaners. **1959** I. & P. Opie *Lore & Lang. Schoolch.* ix. 169 Thin people inspire almost as many names and jokes as fat people, but the laughter is less mortifying; the names..are merely descriptive, as: bag o' bones,..pipe cleaner, rake, [etc.]. **1960** *Farmer & Stockbreeder* 16 Feb. (Suppl.) 8/2 You can easily make a fine collection of animals with one or two packets of pipe-cleaners! Look at the sketch, *A*, to see how the woolly covered cleaners are bent to form the outline of a giraffe. **1973** D. Lees *Rape of Quiet Town* iii. 42, I tried to help but it wasn't easy with legs made out of pipe cleaners. **1962** W. H. Murray *Maelstrom* iii. 42 Forward again was the fo'c'scle, with pipe-cots and deck-hatch. **1977** *Western Morning News* 1 Sept. 8/6 (Advt.), Six Ton Sloop..24 ft. oa., pine on oak, two berth and pipe cot. **1907** E. A. Woodruffe-Peacock *Pasture & Meadow Anal.* 4 A soil that has been pipe drained for wheat-growing. **1930** *Jrnl. Ministry Agric.* Nov. 825 There is nothing to indicate..whether the land is pipe-drained or not. **1896** Ade *Artie* iii. 27 But then I was spinnin' pipe dreams myself, tellin' about how much I lose on the board and all that. **1904** B. von Hutten *Pam* 238 Look at the sea, and tell me if, in your wildest pipe-dream, you ever saw anything lovelier. **1915** *Strand Mag.* June 651/2 If it is a fizzle off goes my coat and I abandon pipe-dreams of literary triumph. **1937** *John o' London's* 26 Mar. 1/3 As my ideal library will never be anything but a pipe-dream, no great harm is done. **1959** *Daily Tel.* 4 Apr. 6 In that event, the Channel project would cease to be an engineers' pipe-dream. **1973** C. Egleton *Seven Days to Killing* xiv. 150 Streamlining..was pure Whitehall jargon... It implied increased efficiency at less cost and..that was just a pipe dream. **1976** *Classical Q.* XXVI. 80 After 394 a Hellenic crusade against Persia was merely a pipe-dream. **1976** C. Weston *Rouse Demon* (1977) i. 47 He was always a pipe-dreamer. Always in the clouds. **1979** *Eastern Economist* 14 Sept. 545/2 Only pipe-dreamers would have the phantasies that man uses his tools only for what is called constructively productive purposes. **1976** *Flintshire Leader* 10 Dec. 1 Some of the council's figures relating to the Leisure Centre are an exercise in pipe dreaming. **1978** C. A. Berry *Gentleman of Road* ii. 14, I couldn't chicken out now. It was time for pipe-dreaming to end. **1910** 'O. Henry' *Whirligigs* i. 12 La Paz is a good sort of a pipe-dreamy old hole. **1913** G. J. Kneeland *Commercialized Prostitution in N.Y. City* iv. 90 One of the best known [pimps] is a..dangerous fellow... A 'pipe fiend' and gambler, his favorite occupation is 'stuss'. **1938** *Amer. Speech* XIII. 189 I'm gonna take my gal along, We'll kick around the yong. She'll sing that pipe-fiend song. **1828** *Blackw. Mag.* Sept. 276 The Shooter..begins with his pop or pipe-gun, formed of the last year's growth of the branch of a plane-tree. **1973** *Trinidad Guardian* 1 Feb. 11/4 He was found guilty on a four-count indictment accusing him of being in possession of a revolver, Molotov cocktails, a pipe-gun and several rounds of ammunition. **1973** *Guardian* 27 Mar. 3/1 The Naxalites..had..country-forged pipe guns which heated and split after a few rounds. **1919** J. C. Squire *Birds* 11 Pipe-necked and stationary and silhouetted, Cormorants stood in a wise, black, equal row. **1877** *Coursing Calendar Autumn 1876* 238 Dulcimer and Jewess separated on two hares, and both got a good pipe-opener. *a* **1936** Kipling *Something of Myself* (1937) vii. 187 That tale may have served as a pipe-opener, but one could not see its wood for its trees, so I threw it away. **1962** *Times* 26 Apr. 13/4 This is the blessed time of year when cricket scores begin to creep..into the sporting pages of the newspapers... Such trial matches are in the nature of pipe-openers, elaborations of practice at the nets. **1971** D. Francis *Bonecrack* xv. 189 'I could give Archangel his pipe-opener...' 'All right, then,' I said, and he took Archangel out..and they cantered a brisk four furlongs. **1974** *Times* 18 Sept. 12/6 British pair thrashed in pipe-opener to Wills Open... The match was a curtain-raiser to the Wills Open Tournament. **1977** *Times* 9 June 8/2 There was a pipe-opener to the conference..when Prince Charles..went to Marlborough House to unveil a painting of his mother. **1948** *Petroleum Handbk.* (Shell Internat Petroleum Co) (ed 3) The broken-out stand is then lowered to its position on the pipe rack. **1976** W. D. Baasel *Prelim. Chem. Engin. Plant Design* vi. 148 Nothing should be located under pipe racks, since if leaks occur they may damage equipment. **1978** G. Greene *Human Factor* VI. i. 301 He looked at the row of pipes in the pipe rack with concentration. **1931** G. Egloff in A. Rogers *Industr. Chem.* (ed. 5) II. 861 Modern practice used the pipe still consisting essentially of a coil of pipe placed in a furnace through which oil is passed. **1959** *Times Rev. Industry* Aug. 97/2 The pipestill works on much the same principle as a water tube boiler. **1970** W. G. Roberts *Quest for Oil* viii. 87 The crude oil must be heated before it gets to the column, and the heater used is known as a 'pipestill'. **1904** *N.Y. Times* 16 Oct. III. 6 The police are now forced to take what appears on its face to be the veriest pipe story and run it down. **1745** Swift *Directions to Servants* ii. 41 Boil your Meat constantly in Pump Water, because you must sometimes want River or Pipe Water. **1908** *Westm. Gaz.* 24 Oct. 17/2, I will not live to see pipe-water squirting down sham rocks under a sham bridge.

pipe, *v.*[1] Add: **2. b.** Freq. with advs. and advb. phrases: esp. *Naut.*, to bring or escort (a person) *aboard*, etc. to the accompaniment of a pipe; also *fig.*; *to pipe in*: to bring in (a person or thing) to the accompaniment of bagpipes.

1918 *Times* 21 Sept. 5/1 It was a Punjabi piper who piped the Cossacks in. **1939** F. Drake-Carnell *It's an Old Scottish Custom* ii. facing p. 54 (*caption*) St. Andrew's Night. Piping in the haggis. **1939** Joyce *Finnegans Wake* (1964) I. 25 Your fame is spreading like Basilico's ointment since the Fintan Lalors piped you overborder. **1940** *Bluejackets' Man.* (U.S. Naval Inst.) lix. 783. In the piping of officials alongside and over, the side pipe is lengthened to full breath for officials receiving 8 side boys. **1955** *Times* 1 July 6/3 The Duke was piped on board, welcomed by the master, Captain H. W. Langbein. **1965** D. MacLean *Queens' Company* xx. 175 On the following morning the doughty Henry Morgan himself, accompanied by his bodyguard, all in magnificent period uniform, were ceremoniously piped on board. **1966** *Listener* 20 Oct. 578/2 Noah pipes aboard an earnest procession of elephants, camels, and assorted fowl. **1968** *Islander* (Victoria, B.C.) 15 Dec. 2/3 The plum pudding, ablaze, was piped in and paraded around the dining room by the chef before being served. **1973** *Stornoway Gaz.* 3 Mar. 1/1 The platform party was piped in by two members of the Lewis Pipe Band. **1976** *Oxf. Compan. Ships & Sea* 131/2 The call..is retained for ceremonial occasions when piping dignitaries and foreign naval officers aboard. **1977** 'J. le Carré' *Hon. Schoolboy* xiii. 292 He looked into the ceiling mirror and caught the glitter of an electric-blue suit and a full head of black hair well greased; and between the two, a foreshortened chubby Chinese face set on a pair of powerful shoulders, and two curled hands held out in a fighter's greeting while Lizzie piped him aboard.

c. *to pipe the side* (Naut.): to sound the 'side', a salute given to certain officers and dignitaries when boarding or leaving a ship.

1896 L. Delbos *Naut. Terms* (ed. 3) 103 *To pipe the side*, faire les honneurs du sifflet. **1909** *Cent. Dict.* Suppl. *s.v.*, When the commanding officer of a naval vessel, or the president or vice-president of the country, or other dignitaries, or superior officers of foreign governments, or crowned heads, or members of royal families, or of the nobility, are received on board, or are leaving a man-of-war,..the boatswain, or one of his mates, winds (blows) his call (silver whistle)... This ceremony is..known as piping the side. **1938** C. S. Forester *Flying Colours* 237 They piped the side for him in the *Victory*, as Admiralty regulations laid down.

3. b. *to pipe down*, in more general use: to stop talking, be quiet, become less vociferous; freq. as a command, = shut up! Also occas. *trans.*, to cause (someone) to be silent. *colloq.*

1900 *Dialect Notes* II. 49 *Pipe down*, to stop talking. **1926** Stallings & Anderson *What Price Glory?* I. i, in *Three Amer. Plays* 24 Pipe down. *Ibid.* III. 76 He tried to pipe me down. **1932** S. O'Faoláin *Midsummer Night Madness* 227 'Shut up, you,' said the Tan angrily, and the little fellow piped down miserably. **1938** N. Marsh *Artists in Crime* vi. 76 'Hatchett,' said Troy. 'Pipe down.' **1945** E. Waugh *Brideshead Revisited* I. v. 105 Groans of protest rose from the other cells where various tramps and pick-pockets were trying to get some sleep: 'Aw, pipe down!' **1951** M. Kennedy *Lucy Carmichael* VI. ii. 293 He didn't disagree; if he had, I'd have piped down. *Ibid.* 294, I won't pipe down. I'll go to Charles. I'll spill all the beans. **1974** *Times* 19 Jan. 12/1 The more immoderate members of his party..may pipe down.

pipe, *v.*[2] Add: **4. b.** Also *intr.* (Further examples.) Also, to arrange (icing, cream, mashed potato, etc.) in decorative cord-like lines or twists.

1884 [see Piped *ppl. a.*[1] 2]. **1892** A. B. Marshall *Larger Cookery Bk.* 317 Fill them by means of a forcing bag and pipe with the Cheese custard..or whipped cream. **1929** E. J. Kollist *French Pastry, Confectionery & Sweets* vi. 116 Cover with royal icing... When dry, pipe flowers and leaves on the basket. **1948** *Good Housek. Cookery Bk.* 582 Pipe on chocolate butter icing and decorate with angelica. *Ibid.* 587 Sandwich the cakes together with the filling, spreading some on the top also. If liked, it can be piped on top with a writing pipe. **1965** *Listener* 30 Sept. 511/3 Allow this to sink in a little before piping the whipped cream all over the top. **1976** G. Moffat *Short Time to Live* ii. 17 'I can't come,' she called... 'I'm piping.'.. She had been piping cream round a flan.

6. a. Also *transf.* Cf. *light pipe* s.v. *Light *sb.* 16.

1949 H. C. Weston *Sight, Light & Efficiency* v. 183 Some of the doctor's work-objects are parts of the body which cannot be adequately illuminated by general lighting, hence, he sometimes 'pipes' light to these parts by means of transparent internally-reflecting plastic devices which are attached to small hand-lamps. **1952** *Chambers's Jrnl.* Jan. 62/1 The well-known plastic material perspex possesses the unusual property of 'piping' light rather than diffusing it. This property is displayed when the interior of perspex tubing is illuminated. **1968** Bean & Simons *Lighting Fittings* v. 167 Light can be piped along a rod, block, or sheet of transparent medium such as glass or acrylic plastic. **1971** P. Tooley *High Polymers* ii. 60

Another interesting property [of polymethyl methacrylate] is its ability to 'pipe' light from one place to another as a result of a high degree of internal reflection. This is used surgically to illuminate internal hollow organs such as the stomach.

b. To transmit (music or speech) over a wire or cable.

1937 [implied in *PIPED *ppl. a.*[1] 3 b]. **1939** *Wireless World* 16 Mar. 259/3 Broadcast programmes or announcements by the pilot can be 'piped' to the passengers. **1956** *Time* 9 Jan. 20/2 It was his wintertime pre-breakfast habit to cut figure eights on the ice of Webster Lake..to the music of Mozart and Chopin, piped through an amplifying system he had rigged up. **1959** *Observer* 6 Dec. 4/5 Programmes of music, talks and plays were 'piped' to individual seats, each passenger having lightweight earphones with volume control. **1967** *N.Y. Herald Tribune Internat.* 11–12 Feb. 3/3 The astronaut told the workers in a talk piped over a public address system to plants here and in Oak Creek. **1977** *Sunday Times* 6 Mar. 8/6 Powell's daily conference is piped into a dozen White House offices.

8. *intr.* To smoke a pipe. *N. Amer. colloq.* See also PIPING *vbl. sb.*[2] 1.

1846 T. L. MCKENNEY *Mem.* I. iii. 71 These hardy adventurous fellows never rose from their paddles, nor stopped except to '*pipe*'. **1863** W. B. CHEADLE *Jrnl. Trip across Canada* (1931) 270 Dr. Benson..assured us we were going wrong. We therefore lunched & piped.

9. *trans.* and *intr.* To see, notice, look (at), watch; to follow or observe (someone), esp. stealthily. Also with *off*. *slang* and *dial.*

Perhaps a different word.

1846 *Swell's Night Guide* 43 You may pipe the crib by seeing a board whereon is inscribed the name of the piano faker. **1848** *Ladies' Repository* VIII. 316/2 *Pipe*, to watch; reconnoitre. **1864** HOTTEN *Slang Dict.* 202 *Pipe*, to follow or dog a person. Term used by detectives. **1869** *Galaxy* VIII. 349 His 'pal'..has meantime been engaged in an operation which he styles 'piping off the cop', by which he means that he has been watching the movements of the policeman. **1877** *Sessions Papers* 25 Oct. 631 Druscovich..said 'I know I am being *piped off*'—that in our language means being followed or watched—it would imply that another detective was following him. **1888** S. O. ADDY *Gloss. Words Sheffield* 176 *Pipe*, to take notice of. 'Pipe his kuss', *i.e.*, take notice of his mouth. A detective is said to pipe round a public-house when in search of a culprit. **1898** A. M. BINSTEAD *Pink 'Un & Pelican* iv. 87 His mission up there on the roof was to exclude—*Anglice*, sling off—any who sought to 'pipe off' the contest through the skylight aforesaid. **1898** F. P. DUNNE *Mr. Dooley in Peace & War* 3 Sagasta pipes him out iv th' corner iv his eye. **1906** 'H. MCHUGH' *Skiddoo!* 67 I'm going to pass you out a talk he handed me a few evenings ago on that subject. Pipe! **1915** WODEHOUSE *Psmith, Journalist* ii. 10 Pipe de leather collar she's wearing. **1924** E. O'NEILL *Welded* II. ii. 141 Remember kissing me on the corner with the whole mob pipin' us off? **1926** *Flynn's* 16 Jan. 640/2 We found another rattler and a few days later I piped a beaut of a jug and a jay burg. **1943** F. SARGESON in *Penguin New Writing* XVII. 78 We'd stand in shop doorways and Terry'd pipe off everyone that went past. **1950** R. CHANDLER *Let.* 18 May in *R. Chandler Speaking* (1966) 78 'Piped' does not mean 'found' but saw or spotted (with the eyes). **1974** H. J. PARKER *View from Boys* iii. 77 During the daytime wandering around the area, 'pipe-ing', looking over a car, became a regular practice.

pipe-clay, *sb.* Add: (Earlier and later examples.) See also *tobacco-pipe clay* s.v. TOBACCO-PIPE 3.

1777 J. WEDGWOOD *Let.* 19 July (1965) 207 He brought some of the stones home with him, mixed them with Pipe Clay, and made the first White Flint Stone Ware. **1966** 'J. HACKSTON' *Father clears Out* 80 He could have also 'lost all his grass', not that our pipeclay had any grass on it.

piped, *ppl. a.*[1] Add: **3. b.** Received over a wire or cable (rather than directly from broadcast signals); esp. in phr. *piped music*, background music, usu. pre-recorded, played through loudspeakers in a public place.

1937 *Printers' Ink Monthly* May 40/2 *Piped program*, a program transmitted over wires. **1949** *Wireless World* Feb. 67/2 Piped Television... Each block of flats will be equipped with a receiving aerial, from which the signal will be fed via an amplifier and distribution units to each flat. **1959** *Daily Mail* 11 Aug. 1/6 A 'piped' television service is to be started soon by the Ekco and Ferguson companies. The system eliminates interference and overcomes reception snags in 'fringe' areas. **1969** *Morning Star* 25 Mar. 2 To me, piped music is a sign of bad taste. **1973** *Times* 27 Mar. (Sudan Suppl.) p. viii/2 A new Hilton Hotel, complete no doubt with swimming pool, air conditioning, piped music and American food. **1977** *Irish Times* 8 June 13/4 (Advt.), Secluded furnished cottage; one bedroom, phone; piped t.v.; own entrance; £16 per week.

c. Also *piped-in* adj.; also in sense of *PIPE *v.*[2] 6 b.

1959 *Economist* 14 Mar. 976/2 There are beach chairs and umbrellas by the swimming pool,..a picnic area, barbecue pit, piped-in music. **1961** *Lancet* 9 Sept. 591/1 Piped-in oxygen prevents noise from clanking cylinders. **1976** M. IERLEY *Year that tried Men's Souls* I. 72 Usefulness is limited to locations with access..to piped-in water. **1977** *Rolling Stone* 19 May 15/5 It dawns on him what's been playing on the restaurant's piped-in music system.

4. Drunk, intoxicated; under the influence of drugs. *U.S. slang.*

1912 *Pedagogical Seminary* XIX. 97 Figurative expressions referring to..Intoxication:—'full', 'piped', [etc.]. **1913** *Dialect Notes* IV. 11 The engineers were all piped. **1924** G. C. HENDERSON *Keys to Crookdom* 413 *Piped*, under influence of liquor or narcotics. **1953** BERREY & VAN DEN BARK *Amer. Thes. Slang* (1954) § 106/7 Drunk,.. *piped*.

pipe-down. *Naut.* [f. PIPE *v.*[1]] The act of piping down' (see PIPE *v.*[1] 3); a call on the boatswain's pipe signalling sailors to retire for the night.

1913 *Dialect Notes* IV. 164 *Pipe-down*, tattoo. Pipe-down call is sounded at 9 P.M. on board ship. **1942** *Penguin New Writing* XV. 8, I didn't see him again until pipe-down. **1963** *Times* 26 Feb. 12/7 Twenty-odd 'pipes' for special occasions were there to be learnt, from the 'still'..to the complicated 'Pipe down' at the end of the day.

pipe-lay (pəi·pˌlēi), *sb.* Also **pipelay, pipe lay.** [f. PIPE *sb.*[1] + LAY *v.*[1]] = PIPE-LAYING (*a*). Usu. *attrib.*

1974 *Petroleum Rev.* XXVIII. 556/2 Standard pipelay equipment was used. **1975** *Times* 19 Feb. 14/6 Essential equipment (eg, platforms, derrick barges and pipe-lay barges). **1975** *Offshore* Aug. 124/3 Two stern thrusters on the reel barge and a 3,600-hp tug controlled the barge during the pipe lay. **1976** *Offshore Engineer* July 6/1 *Castoro VI*, a new Saipem barge at present undergoing trials, will be used for the trial pipelay of 305mm and 406mm pipeline.

pipe-lay, *v. U.S. slang.* [Cf. PIPE-LAYING.] *intr.* To 'lay pipes' (see PIPE *sb.*[1] 3 b); to take measures preparatory to securing some desired action or event. Also *trans.*, to manipulate or cheat.

1848 *Campaign Flag* (Maysville, Kentucky) 14 Apr. 3/6 He was *pipe-layed* out of his election last year. **1884** J. MACCARTHY *Hist. Four Georges* I. 107 Bolingbroke and Oxford..had been 'pipe-laying', to use an expressive American word, for the Stuart restoration during all the closing years of Queen Anne's reign. **1888** in Farmer & Henley *Slang* (1902) V. 213/1 There are not a few who are pipe-laying and marshalling forces for the fray.

pipe-layer. Add: **a.** (Further example.) Also, a machine used to lay pipes. **b.** (Earlier examples.)

1840 *Richmond* (Virginia) *Enquirer* Nov. (Th.), Corruption of the franchise by pipe layers and yarn spinners. **1841** *Congress. Globe* 26th Congress 2 Sess. App. 155/1, I was not defeated by voters. I was defeated by 'pipe layers'. **1969** *Engineering* 25 Apr. 648/2 A Badger Minor trenchless pipelayer..has been specially adapted [for the simultaneous laying of four pvc cable ducts]. **1976** *Daily Tel.* 15 July 5/1 The deaths of a Texan pipe-layer and a French diver brought criticism from an MP yesterday of the Government's attitude towards safety in North Sea gas and oil operations. **1977** *Pipes & Pipelines Internat.* XXII. 35/2 A new pipelayer with lifting capacity of 41 000 kg.

pipe-laying, (*a*) (further examples); also *attrib.*; (*b*) (earlier examples).

1841 *Congress. Globe* 26th Congress 2 Sess. App. 120/2 Others say that fraud, double voting, pipe laying, [etc.].. have done much to carry the election. **1842** [see *COLONIZATION 2]. **1871** *Engineering* XI. p. vii/3 (*heading*) Pipe laying under water. **1973** C. CALLOW *Power from Sea* viii. 163 Pipe-laying barges are actively engaged in off-shore work. **1975** *BP Shield Internat.* May 14/1 The second highly weather-vulnerable job is pipe-laying. **1975** *Times* 16 Sept. (North Sea Suppl.) p. i/1 Pipe-laying barges need to monitor their operations under the sea and to locate pipes at a later date.

pipe-line, *sb.* Add: (Earlier and later examples.)

1873 J. T. HENRY *Early & Later Hist. Petroleum* 283 The iron pipe lines for the conveyance of oil from the wells to railway shipping points play an important part in the transportation of the article. **1879** in I. M. Tarbell *Hist. Standard Oil Co.* (1904) I. 354 The pipe lines owned and controlled by the parties hereto have a joint capacity for transportation. **1924** C. CHRISTY *Big Game & Pygmies* i. 2 Between Matadi and Leopoldville is a wonderful pipe line, by which crude mineral oil for the fleet of up-river steamers is pumped the whole two hundred odd miles by several pumping stations. **1943** *Ann. Reg. 1942* 263 A second first-class road..runs alongside the pipe-line from the Palestinian to the Iraqui frontier. **1953** *Times* 31 Oct. 4/6 A water supply had been brought by bamboo pipelines from a spring. **1961** *Wall St. Jrnl.* 8 Nov. 24/2 The filing ..proposes construction of 210 miles of large-diameter pipeline. **1972** *Drive* Spring 60/1 Brakes, brake pipelines and hydraulic fluid are of life-and-limb importance. **1973** C. CALLOW *Power from Sea* i. 16 Underwater pipelines carrying natural gas at high pressure. **1976** *Times* 2 Oct. 17/8 Some of the pipeline workers may stay in Alaska.

b. *transf.* and *fig.* in various senses (see quots.); *spec.* a channel of supply, information, communication, etc.; esp. in phr. *in the pipeline*, in progress; being worked on, dealt with, or produced; on the way from a supplier to a user. Also *attrib.*

1921 A. HUXLEY *Crome Yellow* vi. 58 You could write too..by getting into touch with your Subconscious. Have you ever read my little book, *Pipe-Lines to the Infinite?* **1935** *Sun* (Baltimore) 25 Aug. 6/2 It was implied, if not more, that the man who had the real inside track to the White House and the potential pipe line to the United States Treasury was none other than Dr. Byrd. **1942** *Ibid.* 1 Aug. 1/7 A foreign source here with continental pipelines of information said the Germans also were making peace feelers both to Britain and the United States and to Russia with the object of splitting the Allies. **1942** BERREY & VAN DEN BARK *Amer. Thes. Slang* § 121/78 Veins and arteries,..*pipe lines*. **1945** *Amer. Speech* XX. 227/1 *Pipeline time*, from the time a requisition leaves a depot until the requested supplies arrive there. **1948** *Economist* 19 June 1026/2 The pipe-lines are full, stocks seem to be adequate, and there are signs of resistance to higher prices. **1948** *Sheep Breeder* Dec. 19/3 Sometimes the price of meat in the pipelines of distribution goes up—a fact that gives rise to claims that we are speculating. **1949** PARTRIDGE *Dict. Slang* Add. 1136/1 *Pipe line*, an aerial: R.A.F.: 1939 +. **1955** W. GADDIS *Recognitions* II. v. 540 Them priests have a pipeline right into the cops. **1955** *Times* 23 Aug. 5/6 About a third of the patient applicants can consider themselves as 'in the pipeline', which means that the telephone engineers have the equipment ready for them. **1957** *Economist* 16 Nov. 565/2 With the further fall in primary commodities there must be a further improvement in Britain's terms of trade already, so to speak, in the pipeline. **1964** *Observer* 26 July 7/5 All these reforms will take time—and cause controversy—in the next Parliament. There are measures in the pipeline already. **1972** J. MOSEDALE *Football* vii. 94 There was a pipeline to the Tuscaloosa campus in those depression days, and Hutson was one of eight Arkansans who found their way to Alabama's football team. **1973** *Daily Pennsylvanian* 9 Oct. 1/2, I don't have a pipeline to God. **1973** *Times* 15 Nov. 25/2 The property development company has 'some very exciting ideas in the pipeline'. **1976** *Broadcast* 16 Feb. 4/1 There's a new soap in the pipeline... The series/serial..will be shown twice weekly.

c. *Surfing slang.* A very large wave, or the hollow part of such a wave. Also applied to a place where such waves are formed.

1963 *Sunday Mail Mag.* (Brisbane) 5 May 12/5 *Pipeline*, a very large tube (*tube* = hollow part of a wave). **1965** *N.Z. Listener* 17 Dec. 5/1 The achievement by which the champion surfers are judged is their ability to ride the Hawaiian pipeline... The pipeline breaks less than 50 yards from the beach over a coral reef. **1971** *Times* 9 Aug. 5/1 The surf-bums have a language all their own; they talk about pipelines, green rooms, roller-coasters. *Ibid.*, The Banzai pipe-line in Hawaii, where the waves can be 25 to 30 feet high.

d. *Computers.* A linear sequence of specialized modules used for pipelining. Freq. *attrib.*

[**1964** W. BUCHOLZ *Planning Computer System: Project Stretch* xiv. 204 The data flow through the computer..is comparable to a pipeline which, once filled, has a large output no matter what its length.] **1965** *AFIPS Conf. Proc.* XXVII. I. 489 (*heading*) Circuit implementation of high speed pipeline systems. *Ibid.* 491/1 The pipeline is characterized by a succession of register and gate units. **1972** *IEEE Trans. Computers* XXI. 885/1 A two-stage pipeline is possible. **1977** *Computing Surveys* IX. 101/2 The CPU architecture of this machine is a simple pipeline served by four functional units. **1977** *Sci. Amer.* Sept. 220/2 Three kinds of systems that can truly be classed as parallel processors have been built. In one of them, the 'pipeline' processor, several processing elements, each of which is specialized for some particular task, are connected in sequence.

pipe-line, *v.* Add: **2.** *Computers.* To design or execute using the technique of pipelining.

1971 *Sci. Amer.* Feb. 76/2 Current efforts in 'pipelining' the processing of 'operands' will allow a further significant increase in speed. **1972** *IEEE Trans. Computers* XXI. 881/1 This note will study the problem of pipelining the addition and multiplication functions of the arithmetic unit.

pi·pelined, *a. Computers.* [f. PIPE-LINE *sb.* (or *v.*) + -ED[2] (or [1]).] That makes use of the technique or principle of pipelining.

1972 *IEEE Trans. Computers* XXI. 880/2 In a pipelined unit, a new task is started before the previous task is complete. **1977** *Computer Surveys* IX. 61 Pipelined computer architecture has received considerable attention since the 1960s when the need for faster and more cost-effective systems became critical.

pi·peliner. orig. *U.S.* [f. PIPELINE *sb.* + -ER[1].] One who works on oil or gas pipelines.

1928 A. GARLAND in J. F. Dobie *Foller de Drinkin' Gou'd* 58 'It's cold out there too—' 'I'll say it is,' a pipeliner broke in. **1962–3** *Petroleum Today* Winter 3/2 The pipeliner is a nomad; he goes where the job is. **1973** C. CALLOW *Power from Sea* v. 113 The pipeliners have an even tougher time in many ways.

pi·pelining, *vbl. sb.* [f. PIPE-LINE *sb.* + -ING[1].] **1. a.** The laying of pipelines. **b.** Transportation by means of pipelines.

1959 *Pipeline Engin.* Oct. p. i, The initiation of this new section is..a further milestone in the ever-expanding industry of pipelining. **1963** *Internat. Pipes & Pipelines* Dec. 40/2 The pipelining of forest products such as wood chips would appear to be economically feasible. **1969** *McGraw-Hill Yearbk. Sci. & Technol.* 271/2 The scope of pipelining is being expanded to include the transportation of solids in molten form or as slurries or capsules. **1970** *Preprints 2nd Ann. Offshore Technol. Conf.* I. 379 (*heading*) Pipelining in 600 feet of water. **1975** *North Sea Background Notes* (Brit. Petroleum Co.) 31 Pipelining begins with the stringing out of pipe lengths, each approximately four tons in weight, which are unloaded on to temporary sleepers and then welded into a continuous line.

2. *Computers.* A form of computer organization in which successive steps of a process are executed in turn by a linear sequence of specialized modules capable of operating concurrently, so that another process can be begun before the previous one is finished.

1965 *AFIPS Conf. Proc.* XXVII. I. 490/1 With the present state-of-the-art in systems organization and technology it appears that pipelining is a powerful approach to a particular variety of large data processing problems. **1972** *IEEE Trans. Computers* XXI. 886/1 Pipelining can be used to give a 40 percent increase in adder efficiency and a 230 percent increase in multiplier efficiency. **1975** G. Zimmermann in Hartenstein & Zaks *Workshop on Microarchitecture of Computer Systems* 155/1 The fast multiplication scheme has been extended by a fast pipelining division network for floating point numbers.

pipeman. **1.** Delete *nonce-use* and add further examples.

1922 *Daily Mail* 7 Nov. 4 (Advt.), The pipeman's joy. **1974** J. Johnston *How Many Miles to Babylon?* 127 My father's a pipe man. The perfect pipe man. He uses it to protect him from the world..stares into the pipe. **1976** *Liverpool Echo* 22 Nov. 1/3 In 1964, he was voted Pipeman of the Year and his waxwork figure appeared at Madame Tussaud's.

pip emma: see *pip *sb.*[4]

piper[1]. Add: **1. b.** *drunk as a piper* (earlier and later examples); *by the piper(s)* (*that played before Moses*): an Irish oath or expletive.

1727 J. Gay in *Miscellanies* III. 207 Drunk as a Piper all day long. **1865** 'Mark Twain' in *Californian* (San Francisco) 23 Dec. 4/3 He came home drunk as a piper. **1884** 'Cruck-a-Leaghan' & 'Slieve Gallion' *Lays & Legends N. Ireland* 16, I hope they don't hear me, Or else, by the piper, they'll make me sing sad. **1892** J. Barlow *Irish Idylls* ix. 274 Be the piper, sure enough I was up there splicin' the handle of your mother's ould basket. **1894** A. Gordon *Northward Ho!* 202 If he..was as drunk as a piper, an' ye yersel' had only twa gills,..he'd pruve tae ye..that ye were drunk, an' no him. **1899** *Century Mag.* Nov. 45 Be the piper that played afore Moses I'll call out me regiment of throopers. **1928** 'Brent of Bin Bin' *Up Country* i. 2 Be the poipers, we've had enough [rain] for this toime of year!

‖**piperade** (piperad). Also (*erron.*) **pipérade.** [Fr.] A dish originating in the Basque country, consisting of eggs, tomatoes, and peppers, and resembling an omelette.

1931 X. M. Boulestin *What shall we have To-day?* 191 A delicious dish, very popular in Béarn and in the Basque country, but not well known otherwise, is the *Pipérade.* **1951** E. David *French Country Cooking* 81 *Pipérade* is the best known of all Basque dishes... It is a mixture of pimentos, tomatoes and onions, with eggs added at the end. **1961** E. H. Clements *Note of Enchantment* ix. 126 Alister..ordered a *piperade* and ate it unhurriedly with a hunk of bread. **1966** *Punch* 29 June 944/1 Should we try Chez Fifine for a piperade? **1976** *Times* 7 Aug. 11/4 A fresh and well-composed pipérade hot from the pan.

piperazine. Add: Now pronounced (pipe·rǎ-zīn). Substitute for etym. and def.: [first formed as G. *piperazin* (A. T. Mason 1887, in *Ber. d. Deut. Chem. Ges.* XX. 267), f. *piper*(*idin* Piperidine + *azin* *azine.] A colourless, crystalline, heterocyclic base, $C_4H_{10}N_2$ which is used, in the form of a salt or hydrate, as an anthelminthic; also, a derivative of this. (Earlier and later examples.)

[**1888** *Jrnl. Chem. Soc.* LIV. 726 Diphenyldiketopiperazine.] **1889** *Ibid.* LVI. 1009 (*heading*) Piperazines. **1891** *Ibid.* LX. 415 Piperazine melts at 104–107°. **1937** *Thorpe's Dict. Appl. Chem.* (ed. 4) I. 315/1 Cyclic compounds are.. produced by distilling the dihydrochlorides of the aliphatic diamines... Thus ethylenediamine yields piperazine. **1970** W. H. Parker *Health & Dis. in Farm Animals* xx. 276 Piperazine compounds might be considered the safest.., but thiabendazole has the merit of being effective against both large and small round worms in the pig. **1974** M. C. Gerald *Pharmacol.* ii. 35 Streptomycin, piperazine (Antepar), [etc.]..have been quite effective in the cure of tuberculosis, pinworm,..respectively.

piperidine. Add: Now pronounced (pipe·ri-dīn). [First formed as F. *piperidine* (A. Cahours 1853, in *Ann. de Chim. et de Phys.* XXXVIII. 78).] (Earlier and later examples.)

1854 *Jrnl. Chem. Soc.* VI. 175 (*heading*) On piperidine, a new alkali derived from piperine. **1938** [see *Knoevenagel]. **1964** N. G. Clark *Mod. Org. Chem.* xxiii. 470 On heating a pyridine solution of the aldehyde with malonic acid in presence of piperidine (catalyst), condensation *and* decarboxylation occur, and a cinnamic acid is produced (Döbner Reaction).

piperonal (pipe·rǫ̆năl). *Chem.* [a. G. *piperonal* (Fittig & Mielck 1869, in *Ann. d. Chem. u. Pharm.* CLII. 37), f. *piper*(*in* Piperine *sb.* + *-on* -one + *-al* *-al[2].] = *heliotropin.

1869 *Chem. News* 30 July 59/2 Piperinic acid,.. when acted upon by permanganate of potassa in aqueous solution, yields a crystalline substance (formula, $C_8H_6O_3$), which body the authors called piperonal. **1909** C. A. Keane *Mod. Org. Chem.* vii. 123 Many substitutes for natural perfumes are also known, such as..heliotropin or piperonal, which possesses the odour of heliotrope. **1953** Kirk & Othmer *Encycl. Chem. Technol.* X. 324 Piperonal (heliotropin)..is a colorless, lustrous crystalline solid with a smell resembling that of heliotrope... Its chief application is in perfumery. **1967** L. F. & M. A. Fieser *Reagents for Org. Synthesis* I. 944 A mixture of piperonal with 1·5 l. of water is heated on the steam bath with vigorous stirring.

piperonyl (pipe·rǫ̆nail). *Chem.* [f. prec. + -yl.] Used to form the names of certain substituted derivatives of piperonal, as *piperonyl butoxide*, a yellow oily liquid, $C_{19}H_{30}O_5$, which is used in insecticides as a synergist for pyrethrins.

1871 *Jrnl. Chem. Soc.* XXIV. 934 The mother-liquor.., evaporated until most of the alcohol is driven off, and exhausted with ether, yields piperonyl alcohol. **1923** W. M. Cumming et al. *Systematic Org. Chem.* v. 93 Piperonyl acrolein is obtained from piperonal and acetaldehyde. **1945** H. Wachs in *Science* 16 May 531/1 The activity of piperonyl butoxide (the name given the technical product containing 80 per cent of pure compound) is indicated in Table 1. **1966** *McGraw-Hill Encycl. Sci. & Technol.* VII. 142/1 Piperonyl butoxide..and Sesoxane.. are two important commercially available pyrethrin synergists. **1966** *Jrnl. Agric. & Food Chem.* XIV. 555 The.. piperonyl carbamates are exceptionally active carbamate synergists. **1974** *Approved Names 1973* (Brit. Pharmacopœia Comm.) Suppl. 11, Piperonyl Butoxide..5-[2-(2-Butoxyethoxy)ethoxymethyl]-6-propyl-1,3-benzodioxole. Acaricide.

pipe-stem. [Pipe *sb.*[1] 11 a.] **1.** The stem of a tobacco-pipe.

a **1734** J. Comer *Diary* in *Rhode Island Hist. Soc. Coll.* (1893) VIII. 17 He..fell over a log, yᵉ pipe stem ran down his throat and broke. **1755** *Maryland Hist. Mag.* (1923) XVIII. 33 He fell down forward, and run the Pipe stem into the Roof of his mouth. **1846** J. W. Webb *Altowan* I. vi. 168 One of the half-breeds has a piece of an old pipe-stem, which makes tolerable good smoking. **1855** [see Pipe *sb.*[1] 11 a]. **1860** J. G. Holland *Miss Gilbert's Career* vii. 115 A great tribulation that will break my life off as short as a pipe-stem. **1873** J. Miller *Life amongst Modocs* xv. 194 He pointed his pipe-stem at Paquita. **1942** J. Masefield *Generation Risen* 42 The hands, chocked-off, wet through and fireless, Chew pipestems. **1971** 'D. Halliday' *Dolly & Doctor Bird* xvi. 242 The mild figure puffed at its pipestem.

b. *humorously.* A thin leg. Also *pipe-stem leg.*

1883 E. Eggleston *Hoosier School-Boy* 33 Little Columbus Risdale picked himself up on his pipe stems and took his place at the end of this row. **1938** M. K. Rawlings *Yearling* i. 4 The water..made a rippling sound, flowing past his pipe-stem legs, and was entirely delicious. **1955** J. Thomas *No Banners* xxvii. 268 The obsession with food made Alfred sway on his pipestem legs. **1976** *National Observer* (U.S.) 10 Apr. 18/2 Mostly they are elderly.., their pipestem legs squeaking them along in the late-afternoon sun.

2. *Comb.* **pipe-stem clematis** *U.S.*, a white-flowered clematis, *C. lasiantha*, of the family Ranunculaceæ, native to California; **pipe-stem wood** *U.S.*, a large evergreen shrub, *Leucothoe populifolia*, of the family Ericaceæ, native to Florida and South Carolina.

1951 H. E. McMinn *Illustr. Man. Calif. Shrubs* 117 Pipe-stem Clematis grows in the Coast Range valleys. **1791** W. Bartram *Trav. N. & S. Carolina* 24, I observed ..the great evergreen *Andromeda* of Florida, called Pipe-Stem Wood. **1813** H. Muhlenberg *Catal. Plantarum Americæ Septentrionalis* 43 Pipe-stem wood, *Andromeda acuminata.*

pipette, *sb.* Add: **1.** Also (*U.S.*) **pipet.**

1937 Pierce & Haenisch *Quantitative Analysis* v. 49 In all pipets the flow of liquid is controlled by admission of air beneath a finger pressed tightly onto the upper end of the stem. **1961** G. R. Choppin *Exper. Nucl. Chem.* ix. 133 When the preparation is complete, carefully remove as much of the supernate as possible with a transfer pipet and place on a planchet.

pipette (pipet) *v.*, for date of first quot. read 1887 and add further examples; hence **pipe·tting** *vbl. sb.*

1915 *Chem. Abstr.* IX. 1861 (*heading*) Pipetting with the suction pump. **1943** *Jrnl. Bacteriol.* XLVI. 195 The tedium of making a large number of accurately measured pipettings. **1961** G. R. Choppin *Exper. Nucl. Chem.* ix. 132 Pipet approximately 10,000 cpm of Cs^{137} activity into a small test tube. **1975** *Nature* 13 Mar. 151/2 The blood was cooled..and the plasma was pipetted off for enzyme analysis.

pipe-work. **2.** (Further examples.)

1934 *Discovery* Dec. 348/1 Modern methods of steel-frame building and pipe-work. **1949** *Archit. Rev.* CV. 222/1 In all stages of the design effort has been made to eliminate the tangled masses of exterior pipework usual in most nylon factories. **1974** *Physics Bull.* July 291/2 Tests on oil fields pipework for potential fire hazards. **1976** *Gramophone* Sept. 453/3 The remoteness of the console from the pipework brought to the ear less than 100 per cent of the complex score. **1977** *Times* 29 June 5/2 In bad conditions, all ferrous pipework can deteriorate.

pipi[2]. Also **pippi(e).** Substitute for def.: An edible bivalve mollusc, *Amphidesma australe*, found on sandy beaches in New Zealand; also, occasionally used for another edible mollusc, *Chione stutchburyi.* Also *attrib.* (Further examples.)

1843 J. E. Gray in E. Dieffenbach *Trav. N.Z.* II. x. [252 *Mesodesma Chemnitzii*... Called *Pipæ* by the natives, who eat them as food.] *Ibid.* 262 *Venus intermedia*... East Coast; much eaten by the natives; called *Pipi.* **1861** A. S. Atkinson *Jrnl.* 21 Jan. in *Richmond–Atkinson Papers* (1960) I. 680 Had dinner—well supplied with pipis. **1863** F. E. Maning *Old N.Z.* (ed. 2) iii. 65, I will scrape sharp the point of my spear with a *pipi* shell. **1873** [see *kinaki]. **1905** [see *kuku 2]. **1938** R. Finlayson *Brown Man's Burden* 75 You could scoop up handfuls of big fat pipis.., sifting the sandy mud through your fingers. *Ibid.*, He joined in a game of throwing big empty pipi shells into the air. **1948** D. Ballantyne *Cunninghams* I. viii. 45 She looked..at the Maoris gathering pippis on the mud flat. **1959** Tindale & Lindsay *Rangatira* vii. 68 They would find pipi cockles in the sand of the beach. **1968** Morton & Miller *N.Z. Sea Shore* xviii. 443 They could well be called pipi beaches, for their most typical bivalves are the pipi, *Amphidesma australe*, higher up the shore, giving place lower down to the cockle or tuangi, *Chione stutchburyi*, in places designated 'pipi' as well. **1972** M. Gee *In my Father's Den* 104 On Takapuna beach..Jonathan was throwing pipi shells into the wind.

2. A similar Australian mollusc, *Plebidonax deltoides.*

1934 *Bulletin* (Sydney) 14 Mar. 20/4 Whether it [*sc.* a bird] opens oysters or not is questionable; but it is an expert on pipis. **1952** W. J. Dakin et al. *Austral. Seashores* xvi. 294 The most common mollusc of any size inhabiting the sand of the ocean beaches of New South Wales..is *Plebidonax deltoides*.., known in this State as the pipi... The pipi lives only a few inches below the surface. **1962** *Australasian Post* 8 Nov. 24/1 The 'pippie' is that pink-and-cream shellfish that lives in the sand. **1968** *Courier-Mail* (Brisbane) 14 June 17/8 A young woman.. survived for eight days by digging pippie shells from the sand with her hands. **1970** *People* (Austral.) 26 Aug. 45/3 The pipi is similar to the 'Littleneck' clam of America's west coast.

piping, *vbl. sb.*[2] Add: **4.** (Further attrib. examples.)

1859 Mrs. Stowe *Minister's Wooing* xii. 126 Miss Prissy ..fell..into a discourse on her own particular way of covering piping-cord. **1966** *Olney Amsden & Sons Ltd. Price List* 13 Cushion Piping cord, 3-yard cards 16/9 dozen cards. **1967** E. Short *Embroidery & Fabric Collage* i. 20 (*caption*) Allover pattern in piping cord on white linen. **1968** J. Ironside *Fashion Alphabet* 96 *Pipe*, to trim with a narrow tube of fabric, often with a piping cord run through to pad it out.

8. (Earlier example.) Also *attrib.*

1846 C. E. Francatelli *Mod. Cook* 398 The cake may be decorated with piping, using for that purpose some of the icing worked somewhat thicker. **1943** Bennion & Stewart *Cake Manuf.* (ed. 2) xiii. 135 Fruit and piping jellies of various colours and flavours are a very useful commodity for use as fillings or for the decoration of cakes and gateaux. **1948** *Good Housek. Cookery Bk.* iii. 612 The most satisfactory kind to purchase are made of hand-cut brass without screws, designed to use in conjunction with a piping bag. **1976** E. Turner *All-Colour Cookbk.* xiii. 139/2 Put the mixture into a piping bag with a 6 mm./¼ in. rose nozzle and pipe out 14 to 16 neat roses on an ungreased baking sheet.

10. (Earlier and further examples.)

1861 *Brit. Patent 1310* 4 My invention consists in preventing..the waste occasioned by what is technically called the 'piping' of ingots of steel. **1923** Glazebrook *Dict. Appl. Physics* V. 357/2 Piping does not necessarily take the form of a single central cavity. **1924** Greaves & Wrighton *Pract. Microsc. Metallogr.* ix. 79 If insufficient discard is made, piping..may be present after rolling in the form of a longitudinal fissure..in the central portion of the billet.

11. (See quot. 1937.)

1937 E. J. Labarre *Dict. Paper* 187/1 *Piping*, a species of crease or ribbing in paper due to irregular tension in reeling, to moisture, or being wound too tightly after sizing. **1963** R. R. A. Higham *Handbk. Papermaking* 283 *Piping*, creases or ribbing in paper produced by irregular tension on the sheet during reeling.

12. *U.S.* The action of beating a person with a length of pipe; an assault of this nature.

1971 *Black Scholar* Apr.–May 24/2 The racial agitation is soon followed by hundreds of stabbings, pipings, brutal beatings and death. **1977** *New Yorker* 24 Oct. 64/3 Homosexuality..is one of the major causes of trouble in prison, often resulting in stabbings or pipings.

piping, *ppl. a.* Add: **2. b. piping guan** (example); **piping plover,** substitute for def.: a small buff-coloured bird, *Charadrius melodus*, found in coastal areas of eastern North America; (examples).

1968 F. Haverschmidt *Birds of Surinam* 79 White-headed piping guan... Not uncommon in forests. **1828** C. L. Bonaparte *Genera N. Amer. Birds* 296 Ringed Plover..and Piping Plover... Common all along the eastern sea coast of North America. **1870** *Amer. Naturalist* III. 231 The Piping Plover is still found along the coast of Maine. **1917** T. G. Pearson *Birds Amer.* I. 264/1 Truly a bird of the beach-sand is the Piping Plover. **1964** J. Bull *Birds N.Y. Area* 185 The Piping Plover breeds on the ocean beaches.

pipkin. Add: **3.** *Comb.*, as *pipkin-shaped* adj.

1908 E. Terry *Story of my Life* 199 A three-handled cup, pipkin-shaped, standing on three legs.

pipkrake (pi·pkrēik, -krākə). *Geomorphol.* Pl. **-krakes, -kraker.** [a. Sw. dial *pipkrake*, f. *pip* Pipe *sb.*[1] + *krake*, dial. by-form of *klake* (hardness and roughness of) frozen ground (= Norw. *klake*, Da. *klage*, Icel. *klaki*).] **a.** One of the ice-needles in needle ice. **b.** = *needle ice* s.v. *needle *sb.* 14.

1956 *Biuletyn Peryglacjalny* IV. 167 Bunt also noticed the formation of ice palisades (pipkrakes) in the hollows and ascribes the removal of fine material from the hollows to the melting of these ice crystals. **1967** M. J. Coe *Ecol. Alpine Zone Mt. Kenya* 74 On the flat or slightly sloping ground of valley bottoms, an important feature of soil movement is that of Needle Ice, or Pip[k]rake. **1968** R. W. Fairbridge *Encycl. Geomorphol.* 370/1 Water expands about 10% upon freezing (ice being characterized by a high expansion coefficient, as seen in the growth of ice needles or pipkrakes). *Ibid.* 381/1 Such 'needle ice' is sometimes called pipkrake. **1970** R. J. SMALL *Study of Landforms* x. 330 The formation at or near the ground surface of small masses of ice, such as pipkraker, commonly has the effect of heaving up small stones at right angles to the slope. **1971** A. F. PITTY *Introd. Geomorphol.* IV. 219 In mountainous areas in central Germany, pipkrakes may be 10–15 cm long. **1973** A. L. WASHBURN *Periglacial Processes & Environments* iv. 81 Needle ice.., also known as pipkrake, is an accumulation of slender, bristle-like ice crystals practically at, or immediately beneath, the surface of the ground.

pipped, *a.* Add: **b.** Annoyed, irritated.

1914 A. N. LYONS *Simple Simon* I. vi. 100 'How's Leverton?' 'Rather pipped, thank you,' replied Miss Disney. 'Poor old Ma was raw-beefing him when I left.' **1941** BAKER *Dict. Austral. Slang* 54 *Pipped, pippy,* irritated, angry, out of sorts.

pipped (pipt), *a.*² [Perh. f. PIP *v.*³] Tipsy, drunk.

1911 J. MASEFIELD *Everlasting Mercy* 26 Si's wife came in and sipped and sipped (As women will) till she was pipped. **1929** M. DE LA ROCHE *Whiteoaks* vii. 110 Lilly, here, can't see the strings. He's pipped, aren't you, Lilly?

pipperidge. 2. (Later example.)

1872 MRS. STOWE *Oldtown Fireside Stories* 127 Old Black Hoss was about as close as a nut and as contrairy as a pipperage-tree.

pippet (pi·pėt). *rare.* [f. PIP *sb.*² + -ET.] = PIP *sb.*² I.

1940 B. RUSSELL *Inquiry into Meaning & Truth* 57 Take again the two of clubs, and the proposition 'this is similar to that' applied to the two pippets.

pippin. Add: **2. b.** In phrases, as *sound as a pippin,* very sound.

1886 H. BAUMANN *Londinismen* 139/1 He's as sound as a pippin. **1910** BELLOC *Verses* 81, I said to Heart, 'How goes it?' Heart replied: 'Right as a Ribstone Pippin!' But it lied.

3. a. (Further examples.)

c **1821** 'W. T. MONCRIEFF' *Tom & Jerry* (1828) II. v. 49 Go it, my pippins. **1846** *Swell's Night Guide* 49 Now, my pippins, I'll just ax you which was the rankest sell? **1888** [see *COCKER *sb.*⁶]. **1892** E. J. MILLIKEN *'Arry Ballads* 23/2 She would take the shine out of some screamers, I tell yer, my pippin, would Loo. **1895** *Punch* 15 June 285/1 No slow Surrey-siders, my pippin, but smart bits o' frock from Mayfair.

b. An excellent person or thing; a beauty. *slang* (orig. *U.S.*).

1897 ADE in *Chicago Record* 17 Sept. 4/5 This sister was fair to look upon. In fact, it was frequently remarked that she was a Pippin. **1906** G. H. LORIMER *Jack Spurlock* (1908) ii. 28 'I'd like to have the job which goes with that blonde,' and I pointed to a pippin who was pounding the keys just outside his door. **1914** 'BARTIMEUS' *Naval Occasions* xii. 88 The Flag-Lieutenant introduced him to a lady of surpassing loveliness—The Fairest ..of All the Pippins. **1920** WODEHOUSE *Jill the Reckless* xvi. 237 'We shall..open in Baltimore next Monday with practically a different piece. And it's going to be a pippin, believe *me*,' said our hero modestly. **1926** *Amer. Speech* I. 462 The Apollo Theater in London prints the following glossary of slang in its program as a guide to 'Is Zat So?'..*Pippin,* beauty. **1930** J. DOS PASSOS *42nd Parallel* I. 47 He..got a book from a man at the hotel. Gosh it was a pippin. **1939** R. STOUT *Some Buried Caesar* vi. 71 The fight for a hotel room which was a pippin—I mean the fight, not the room. **1948** H. INNES *Blue Ice* ii. 38 She's a pippin... Knows her way around already. **1972** WODEHOUSE *Pearls, Girls & Monty Bodkin* viii. 120 So I have a plan..and it's a pippin.

pip-pip. [Echoic.] **1.** A repeated, short, high-pitched sound, *spec.* that made by a motor- or bicycle-horn; also, the horn itself.

1904 KIPLING *Traffics & Discov.* 324 Children sat..on the damp doorsteps to shout 'pip-pip' at the stranger. **1907** SHAW *Major Barbara* III. 292 *Sarah* (touching Lady Britomart's ribs with her finger tips and imitating a bicycle horn) Pip! pip! **1909** *Westm. Gaz.* 15 May 3/2 She [*sc.* a little girl] had motor-cars with real pip-pips. **1979** N. FREELING *Widow* xx. 124 There was a timid little pip-pip at the front door bell. **1979** J. SCOTT *Angels in your Beer* xviii. 187 Marianne walked to the Ferrari... She..sounded an impatient pip pip on the horn.

2. *slang.* A substitute for 'good-bye'. (In quot. 1907 as a defiant retort.)

1907 *Mr. Punch Awheel* 93 *Cyclist*... 'Nice crowd out this morning!' *Rural Policeman*..'Yes, an' yer can't do with 'em! If yer 'ollers at 'em, they honly turns round and says, 'Pip, pip'! **1920** WODEHOUSE *Damsel in Distress* x. 129 'Well, it's worth trying,' said Reggie. 'I'll give it a whirl. Toodleoo!' 'Good-bye.' 'Pip-pip!' Reggie withdrew. **1931** E. F. BENSON *Mapp & Lucia* iii. 56 Mr. Woolgar..did not say 'So long' or 'Pip-pip'. **1951** WODEHOUSE *Old Reliable* xv. 169 Hello, Smedley. Pip-pip, Lord Topham. **1973** G. SIMS *Hunters Point* iii. 22 The nine-day 'British Week' had ended... Fisherman's Wharf had been buzzing with 'Cheerio, pip pip and smashing' voices. **1978** M. BUTTERWORTH *X marks Spot* III. iii. 158 'Pip pip, laddie.' He set off.

pip-pip-pip. *Teleph.* [f. *PIP *sb.*⁵] (The sound of) the three consecutive pips used as a time signal in the 'speaking clock' service and to indicate the lapse of time during a trunk call.

1936 *Discovery* Oct. 315/2 Thus 'At the third stroke' is taken from one groove, 'it will be' from another, 'eleven o'clock' from another disc, and the sound 'pip-pip-pip' from a fourth. **1938** D. SMITH *Dear Octopus* I. 12 Don't go on talking after the pip pip pip, because they charge you at once.

pippy. Add: **2. b.** Depressed, out of sorts.

1886 R. FRY *Let.* 28 Nov. (1972) I. 111 My Mays depress me, so does my Tripos... In fact I am stupidly pippy at times.

pipradol: see next.

pipradrol (pi·prădrǫl). *Pharm.* Also (*erron.*) **pipradol.** [f. PIP(E)R(IDINE + *-a-* + *benzhy*)*drol* s.v. BENZO-.] A colourless crystalline solid, α,α-diphenyl-α-piperid-2-ylmethanol hydrochloride, $C_{18}H_{21}NO.HCl$, which is used as an antidepressant. Also called *pipradrol hydrochloride.*

1955 *Science* 11 Feb. 209/2 Meratran is the trademark of the Wm. S. Merrell Co., for its brand of pipradrol. **1955** *Sci. News Let.* 13 Aug. 105/1 The drug is a pipradol chemical trade-named Frenquel by the manufacturer, the Wm. S. Merrell Co. of Cincinnati. **1956** *Jrnl. Amer. Med. Assoc.* 4 Feb. 390/1 Pipradrol hydrochloride is a central nervous system stimulant chemically unrelated to the sympathomimetic amines but exhibiting some of the pharmacological actions of amphetamine. **1962** F. C. FERGUSON *Drug Therapy* xxiv. 216 Other types of antidepressants include piperidines; methylphenidate (Ritalin) and pipradrol (Meratran). **1973** *Approved Names 1973* (Brit. Pharmacopœia Comm.) 59 Pipradol. **1974** *Ibid.* Suppl. III, For 'Pipradol' read 'Pipradrol'. **1974** *Jrnl. Clin. Pharmacol.* XIV. 132/2 Present results thus suggest at the most only limited efficacy for pipradrol in the treatment of depressed outpatients.

pi·p-squeak. *slang.* [f. *PIP *sb.*⁵ + SQUEAK *sb.*] **1.** A contemptuous name for an insignificant person; a petty object. Also *attrib.*

In quot. 1923 a two-stroke motorcycle.

1910 E. V. LUCAS *Slowcoach* xxiii. 279 'It belongs to one of those measly pip-squeaks,' said Robert. **1923** *Motor Cycling* 21 Nov. 89/1 The owners of sporting four stroke machines look down on the owners of so-called 'Pip-Squeaks'. **1925** FRASER & GIBBONS *Solider & Sailor Words* 224 *Pip Squeak,*..a small man, or one objectionable in some way. **1926** *Blackw. Mag.* June 732/2 After all, the luxurious liner which connects this riotous spot with the outer world is only a pip-squeak of a vessel. **1930** G. MACMUNN *Behind Scenes in Many Wars* 88 It does not pay in the East to let pip-squeaks beard the mighty. **1946** *Richmond* (Virginia) *Times-Dispatch* 20 Jan. I. 14/8 Specifically, [Senator] Wiley charged that the organization..has 'created czars out of pipsqueak juveniles'. **1951** M. MCLUHAN *Mech. Bride* (1967) 23/2 Mighty blasts on the tooter herald the arrival of just another pip-squeak [*sc.* monotonous book]. **1961** A. CHRISTIE *Pale Horse* xxi. 224 What about that psychological pipsqueak you brought along to see me, Corrigan. What does he say? **1973** 'H. HOWARD' *Highway to Murder* vi. 65 For a little pip-squeak you make a big noise. **1974** E. AMBLER *Dr. Frigo* III. 174 They weren't taking any nonsense from a pipsqueak foreign doctor.

2. a. A small type of high velocity shell distinguished by the sound of its flight. Also *attrib.*

1916 E. V. LUCAS *Vermilion Box* 209 Whatever else there is to grumble at over here, wet, and rats, and Pip-Squeaks and Jack Johnsons..we do get two things up to sample. **1916** *Cornh. Mag.* Mar. 395 They're 'pip-squeak' and splinter-proof, of course. **1917** A. G. EMPEY *Over Top* 304 *Pip squeak,* Tommy's term for a small German shell which makes a 'pip' and then a 'squeak', when it comes over. **1927** E. THOMPSON *These Men, thy Friends* 176 The Turkish guns suddenly sent over a couple of pipsqueaks. *a* **1936** KIPLING *Something of Myself* (1937) vi. 159 One indubitable shell—ridiculously like a pip-squeak in that vastness but throwing up much dirt.

b. = *PIP-PIP I. Also = *PEEP *sb.*¹ 2 b. So **pi·p-squeak** *v.*

1922 *Blackw. Mag.* June 699/2 She heard just then her Tom pip-squeaking on his pipe. **1927** 'IXION' *Further Motor Cycle Reminisc.* 100 Hooters..fitted with rather wafery clips, such as still linger on bicycle 'pipsqueaks'. **1943** [see sense 2 c below]. **1956** E. POUND tr. *Sophocles' Women of Trachis* 16 Hasn't uttered a pip-squeak Since she came down from the windy country.

c. (See quots. 1943, 1970.) *slang.*

1943 C. H. WARD-JACKSON *Piece of Cake* 48 *Pip-squeak,* the instrument in an aircraft by the aid of which one gets a 'Fix'. This instrument emits a pip-squeak at short intervals which is synchronised over the radio with base, thus fixing the time, an essential prelude to fixing the position of the aircraft. **1946** BRICKHILL & NORTON *Escape to Danger* vi. 60 Forgetting to switch off his 'pip-squeak' (radio contactor), Mickey climbed thankfully out on to the wing. **1970** PARTRIDGE *Dict. Slang* (ed. 7) II. 1330/2 'The pip-squeak was an automatic transmitter *only,* whose once-a-minute signals enabled ground direction-finding stations to fix the aircraft's position accurately for the benefit of the Fighter Controller in the Operations Room...' (Ramsey Spencer, March 1967.)

Pip, Squeak, and Wilfred. *slang.* [Names of three animal characters featured in a children's comic strip in the *Daily Mirror* from 1920 onwards.] Designating a trio of objects or persons.

[**1920** 'UNCLE DICK' in *Daily Mirror* 25 Mar. 13/2 Aren't Pip and Squeak and Wilfred sweet measuring their heights? **1920** —— *Pip, Squeak, & Wilfred* 60 Some time ago, Pip, Squeak, and Wilfred dreamed they were real children. *Ibid.* 61, I am rather fond of Pip, Squeak, and Wilfred. I, too, have my dreams.] **1937** PARTRIDGE *Dict. Slang* 633/2 *Pip, Squeak and Wilfred,* the medals (or medal ribbons), 1914–15 Star, War Medal, Victory Medal. **1943** C. H. WARD-JACKSON *Piece of Cake* 48 *Pip, Squeak and Wilfred,* the 1914–15 Star, the Great War and Victory medals or ribbons worn in a row. **1966** 'L. LANE' *ABZ of Scouse* 35 Other names [for a trio of friends] are Pip, Squeak and Wilfrid [*sic*]. **1977** *Times* 30 Sept. 16/8 That goes for Messrs Pip, Squeak and Wilfred, too.

pipsyl (pi·psəil, -il). *Chem.* Also **PIPSYL.** [f. letters in the systematic name (see def.).] The radical *p*-*i*odo*p*henyl*s*ulphon*yl*, $I{\cdot}C_6H_4{\cdot}SO_2$—, compounds of which are used as radioactive labels.

1946 *Jrnl. Amer. Chem. Soc.* LXVIII. 1390/1 As the labelled reagent we used *p*-iodophenyl sulfonyl chloride (PIPSYLchloride), prepared from radioactive iodide ion and *p*-diazobenzene-sulfonic acid, followed by treatment with phosphorus pentachloride. *Ibid.* 1390/2 Less than one-hundredth per cent. of *d*(−)alanine was found in the β-lactoglobulin hydrolysate using PIPSYL d(−)alanine carrier. **1949** *Ibid.* LXXI. 256/1 (*heading*) The preparation of pipsyl amino acids for use as carriers. **1961** G. R. CHOPPIN *Exper. Nucl. Chem.* x. 173 In the last chapter the use of I¹³¹ labeled *p*-iodobenzenesulfonyl chloride (pipsyl chloride) with the amino acids was described. **1974** *Canad. Jrnl. Biochem.* LII. 217/2 Using the multiple isomorphous protein phases..a difference electron density map has been computed. This map was relatively devoid of significant electron density except in the region of PIPSYL binding.

piquantly, *adv.* (Later examples.)

1922 JOYCE *Ulysses* 399 Blushing piquantly and whispering in my ear. **1955** *Times* 10 May 3/7 M. Claude Barma's production was most piquantly revealing. **1971** *Daily Tel.* 16 July 11/8 With a cast of two, it presents a piquantly rounded theme.

piqué, *sb.* (*a.*) Add: **A. a.** (Later examples.)

1932 *Daily Tel.* 25 Apr. 7/5 The yoke and collar in plain white cotton-piqué. The sleeves may be slightly fitted to above the elbow, where they should be met by a ..gauntlet cuff of the white piqué. **1956** R. BRADDON *Nancy Wake* III. xv. 171 Her quaint white *piqué* dress. **1968** J. IRONSIDE *Fashion Alphabet* 245 *Piqué,*..a firm fabric with lengthwise carded effect made of cotton. *Waffle piqué*—with a honeycomb weave.

b. (Earlier and later examples.)

1872 *Young Englishwoman* Nov. 611/1 Pique stitch crochet. **1958** *Times* 20 Jan. 11/2 Jumper suit of pique knit jersey.

B. *ppl. a.* **a.** (Earlier and later examples.)

1872 C. SCHREIBER *Jrnl.* 2 Nov. (1911) I. 169 We found ..a small piqué plaque on tortoise-shell. **1879** *Ibid.* 5 Dec. II. 250 A curious knife and fork... The handles are piqué, or inlaid in silver with acorns and oak leaves. **1968** J. IRONSIDE *Fashion Alphabet* 178 *Piqué,* tortoise-shell or ivory inlaid with tiny dots or lines of gold or silver. This art, brought over by the Huguenots in the seventeenth century, covered brooches, buttons and ear-rings as well as small boxes. **1979** *Country Life* 7 June (Suppl.) 113/3 Silver-gilt and tortoiseshell *piqué* magnifying glass, c. 1730.

b. *Cookery.* Larded. *rare.*

1846 A. SOYER *Gastronomic Regenerator* 230 (*heading*) Fillet of Beef piqué aux legumes printaniers.

c. *Ballet.* With the point of the foot; with the foot pointed. Also as *sb.*, a step directly on to the point of the leading foot.

1913 C. D'ALBERT *Dancing* 123 *Piqué* (pas),..de la pointe et du talon. Toe and heel points. **1931** C. W. BEAUMONT *French-Eng. Dict. Techn. Terms Classical Ballet* 21 *Piqué*..pricked, pricking. Generally implies a shooting forward of the body on to the *pointe* of the front foot. **1954** *Ballet Ann.* VIII. 65, I should also like to draw your attention to the *arabesques piquées.* Contrary to tradition, these should not be '*piquées*' with the knee stretched, but with the knee flexible. The instep is arched at the beginning of the movement, but the knee is quite taut only when balance has been obtained. *Ibid.*, By following my instructions..the ballerina is able to assume..a manner of walking which is æsthetically satisfying. *Piqués* and *relevés* are possible to her whilst in movement; her very walk is 'melodic'. **1967** CHUJOY & MANCHESTER *Dance Encycl.* 734/2 *Piqué,* in ballet, the movement of stepping directly onto point of supporting foot. The working leg may be in a variety of poses. **1975** *New Yorker* 16 June 103/1 There were moments in this performance that stopped my breath: a high, motionless *piqué* balance lightly stepped into from nowhere, [etc.].

C. piqué work. b. (Later example.)

1969 *Canad. Antiques Collector* Oct. 19/2 It [*sc.* a small box] is of ivory, bound with silver with the design formed by an inlay of little points of silver known as piqué work.

‖**piquer** (pike), *v. Cookery.* Also (*erron.*) **piqué.** [F. *piquer* (see PIQUE *v.*¹) to lard.] *trans.* To insert bacon strips or other flavouring substance in (meat, poultry, etc.) before cooking; also *fig.*

In quot. 1951², *piquez* is the Fr. imperative.

1846 *Jewish Manual, or Pract. Information Jewish & Mod. Cookery* iv. 67 Take a piece from the shoulder [of veal]..*piqué* it thickly. **1865** M. EYRE *Lady's Walks S. of France* xxix. 316 It is common here to *piquer* a leg of mutton with garlic, that is, small holes are drilled in it before roasting, and a small kind of garlic..inserted therein. **1935** *Proc. Brit. Acad.* XX. 85 Start with a moral and political poet.., piquer or lard him with immorality, potorial songs and other irrelevances, [etc.]. **1951** E. DAVID *French Country Cooking* 120 The fillet..is cut into..pieces..*piquèd* [sic] with garlic and seasoned with black pepper. *Ibid.* 158 *Piquez* each fillet with a small piece of bacon. **1960** —— *French Provincial Cooking* 79 A *fricandeau de veau*, . . and a *râble de lièvre*. . are two of the classic examples of piquéd meat and game.

‖**piqûre** (pikür). Also **pique.** [Fr., = injection, f. *piquer* (see PIQUE *v.*[1]) to pierce (the skin), to give an injection.] A hypodermic injection; the puncture made in the skin by such an injection.

1925 INFANTA EULALIA OF SPAIN *Courts & Countries after War* vii. 150 The newest 'Piqures' come from Germany. **1936** C. CONNOLLY *Rock Pool* iii. 59 She had large flabby arms covered with piqures. **1940** N. MITFORD *Pigeon Pie* xiii. 211 'Miss Wordsworth received last night in an omnibus a *piqure* that will incapacitate her for a week at least.' 'I see, you are white slavers as well as everything else.' **1942** 'A. BRIDGE' *Frontier Passage* ii. 21 The doctor came... And she gave her a piqure, and they sent medicines. **1962** K. A. PORTER *Ship of Fools* II. 216 You must give me a *piqûre*, a huge one that will make me sleep for days. **1962** V. SACKVILLE-WEST *Let.* 26 Apr. in H. Nicolson *Diaries & Lett.* (1968) 411, I must have five injections... *Later.* It is now over, and it was no more painful than all those *piqûres* I had on the *Antilles*.

piracy. Add: **1. b.** *Physical Geogr.* = *CAPTURE *sb.* 1 b.

1904 CHAMBERLIN & SALISBURY *Geol.* I. iii. 99 The foregoing case may be called foreign piracy because the valleys of different systems are concerned. Domestic piracy may also take place... Here a tributary to a crooked river may develop, working back until it taps the main at a higher point. **1939** *Bull. Geol. Soc. Amer.* L. 1350 The stream pattern indicates that recent piracies have occurred. **1957** G. E. HUTCHINSON *Treat. Limnol.* I. i. 114 A wide valley, the main stream of which has been reduced by piracy. **1974** C. H. CRICKMAY *Work of River* iii. 62 Stream piracy. ., of course, is not in every case effected by headwater extension.

Pirandellian (pirănde·liăn), *a.* [f. the name of the Italian playwright Luigi *Pirandello* (1867–1936) + -IAN.] Of or pertaining to or characteristic of Pirandello or his style.

1927 *Observer* 8 May 15/3 In a Pirandellian sense, he is enormously 'real'. Just as we believe that Hamlet exists apart from the personality of the actor, so we know Pogo as if he were our dearest dumb friend. **1929** *Sat. Rev.* 1 June 746/1 How the dates fit I do not know, but Señor Unamuno seems to have drunk deep of Pirandellian philosophy. **1930** *Times Lit. Suppl.* 19 June 511/3 By this time one could almost predict from a single hint the course of a Pirandellian play. **1933** *Ibid.* 9 Mar. 164/4 The professor's appeal to the young man's good sense has in it that paradoxical justice that may well be called Pirandellian. **1959** *Times* 13 Mar. 16/6 Mr. Jupp. . hits on the Pirandellian notion that the family should re-enact the history of their own lives in the hope of understanding it. **1964** *Listener* 30 Apr. 731/3 To get at the truth he questions the dramatist's ex-wife, and searches round for other people involved in the affair, playing, and allowing Mr Elliot to play, a Pirandellian game of masks and faces. **1974** *N.Y. Times* 7 Sept. 25/2 As a comedian he had trouble finding a persona, a Pirandellian problem.

Hence **Pirande·llism**, the style or method of Pirandello; a characteristic example of this; **Pirande·llist**, an advocate or follower of Pirandello.

1936 *Times Lit. Suppl.* 19 Dec. 1048/3 The best and most striking side of Pirandello's art is lost, leaving behind the bare intellectual residue of so-called 'Pirandellism'. . exposed. **1962** *Spectator* 23 Mar. 370/2 The ending makes the play the second victim in twelve months of phoney and incompetent Pirandellism. **1962** Pirandellist [see *IMAGIST 1]. **1964** *Eng. Stud.* XLV. 328 Robinson grows away from his clay-coloured Irish plays and creates such Pirandellisms as *Church Street*.

Piranesian (pirănī·ziăn), *a.* [f. the name of the Italian architect and artist Giovanni Battista *Piranesi* (1720–78) + -AN.] Of, pertaining to, or characteristic of Piranesi, his style, or his theories of architecture.

1923 A. HUXLEY *Antic Hay* vi. 87 You could fancy yourself at the entrance of one of Piranesi's prisons... Mrs Viveash's taxi drove in under the Piranesian arch. **1925** —— *Along Road* II. 93 The Colosseum, mantled. . with a romantic, Piranesian growth of shrubs. **1926** —— *Jesting Pilate* I. 123 The cathedral of the banyan grove is transformed into a Piranesian prison. **1961** *Architect & Building News* 21 June 822/1 The east and west elevations close the vistas in a highly dramatic, almost Piranesian, fashion. **1962** *Guardian* 25 Sept. 5/6 These halls . . are of Piranesian grandeur. **1968** *Punch* 25 Dec. 910/1 They have just reconstituted Euston Station and I don't like it at all. I miss the mock-Doric arch and the Victorian grandeur, the sweeping vistas and the Piranesian gloom. **1976** *Listener* 1 Apr. 413/2 Some gargantuan, crudely-painted Piranesian ruin.

piranha. Now usu. with pronunc. (pirā·nă). Substitute for def.: A carnivorous freshwater fish of the genus *Serrasalmus*, belonging to the family Characidæ and native to South America; = PERAI, PIRAYA. Also *attrib.* (Later examples.)

1904 [see *CARIBE]. **1915** *Nature* 8 Apr. 149/2 Birds, beasts, coral snakes, and piranha fishes, toads and ants, and primitive natives, he [*sc.* T. Roosevelt] has something to say about. **1927** W. M. MCGOVERN *Jungle Paths & Inca Ruins* xxvi. 269 All these fish were *piranhas* armed with savage little teeth. **1931** [see *CARIBE]. **1954** G. DURRELL *Three Singles to Adventure* ii. 53 The piranha is one of the most unpleasant freshwater fish known. It is a flat, corpulent, silver-coloured fish, with the lower jaw protruded. **1960** T. HUGHES *Lupercal* 20 Even the Amazon's taxed and patrolled To set laws by the few jaws—Piranha and jaguar. **1962** N. MAXWELL *Witch-Doctor's Apprentice* vii. 73 *Piranhas*, voracious little beasts which attack *en masse* and can strip the meat off a live cow in minutes. **1968** *New Scientist* 7 Mar. 534/2 There are many types of fish that are classed as piranhas: the common feature is that they have a pair of powerful jaws with razor-sharp teeth. **1977** *Time* 19 Sept. 62/1 (Advt.), Feel Tom Sterling's apprehension, when obliged to take a dip in the piranha-infested Amazon.

2. *fig.*

a **1963** S. PLATH *Ariel* (1965) 40 And the fish, the fish—Christ! they are panes of ice, A vice of knives, A piranha Religion. **1977** *Times* 14 Mar. 19/6 Gayle Hunnicutt turned Sarah Pocock into a deceptively girlish piranha who. . planned to nibble into tiny pieces everyone in sight. **1978** *Times* 15 May 16/8 It's not just a goldfish bowl in a nationalized industry, it's a piranha bowl.

Pirani (pirā·ni). *Physics.* The name of M. S. von *Pirani* (b. 1880), German physicist, used *attrib.* to designate a gauge invented by him for measuring very low pressures, which utilizes the cooling effect of the gas on a heated metal filament whose resistance is sensitive to temperature.

It was described by von Pirani in *Verhandl. der deutsch. physik. Ges.* (1906) VIII. 686.

1911 *Trans. Amer. Electrochem. Soc.* XX. 245 In simplicity both of construction and of operation, involving only current and resistance measurements within the range of instruments readily accessible, the Pirani manometer recommends itself at once. **1921** *Proc. Physical Soc.* XXXIII. 293 For many purposes we think that the Pirani gauge. . would have considerable advantages over the McLeod. **1962** F. I. ORDWAY et al. *Basic Astronautics* v. 200 Pirani, alphatron, and bellows gauges are regularly employed in rockets to obtain atmospheric pressures. **1971** *Sci. Amer.* Aug. 114/2 The effort expended in making the Pirani gauge is amply repaid by the convenience it affords.

pirarucú (pirăruku·). [Pg., f. Tupi (see quot. 1863[2]).] The giant redfish of the Amazon basin, *Arapaima gigas*, of the family Osteoglossidæ, one of the largest freshwater fishes in the world; = *ARAPAIMA, *PAICHE.

1840 [see *ARAPAIMA]. **1863** H. W. BATES *Naturalist on River Amazons* II. iii. 165 The men caught sight of a large Pirarucú: the fish which, salted, forms the staple food. . in most parts of the Lower Amazon country. *Ibid.* 166 The Indian name Pirarucú, or Anatto fish (from Pira, fish, and urucú, anatto or red), is in allusion to the red colour of the borders of its scales. **1933** P. FLEMING *Brazilian Adventure* I. xviii. 153 The very big fish—the *piracacú* [sic] and the *pirará*. . they [*sc.* the Indians] harpoon. **1936** *Discovery* Dec. 373/2 Pirarucú, . . when dried and salted, is rapidly taking the place of imported cod on the Brazilian market. **1961** [see *PAICHE]. **1965** E. BISHOP *Questions of Travel* 31 Everything must be there In that magic mud, beneath The multitudes of fish, deadly or innocent, The giant pirarucús.

pirate, *sb.* Add: **4. b.** One who receives or transmits radio programmes without a licence to do so.

Current usage refers to radio transmission.

1913 *Marconigraph* II. 530/2 'There you are,' said the captain, 'unless we have been picked up again by some experimenting pirate.' **1923** *Wireless Weekly* 13 June 592 The thousands who are listening-in without a licence of any description—popularly termed 'pirates'. **1923** *Exper. Wireless* Nov. 57/2 The olive branch has been held out to the 'pirates', and the ordinary listener-in is cheered by the prospect of a reduction in prices of complete sets. **1933** *Pract. Wireless* 14 Oct. 182/1 (*heading*) Wanted, One Radio Pirate! The small Brussels (Schaerbeek) broadcasting station, having complained to the authorities that an illicit transmitter has marred the reception of its broadcasts, a reward of one thousand Belgian francs has been offered to trace the identity of the culprit. **1964** *Daily Tel.* 13 May 19/2 Let us be clear about this: the pirates of 1964, like the pirates of old, are simply out after money, as much money as they can get in defiance of international law. **1966** *Listener* 16 June 863/2 Fewer than 145,000 licences were issued in 1964... Evasion is clearly a problem in which Britain is not alone, though, in spite of the one-time reputation of the South China Seas, Hong Kong is at least free of pirates. **1967** *Ibid.* 17 Aug. 195/1 In other areas of radio the pirates provide no example. **1969** C. BOOKER *Neophiliacs* ix. 228 Throughout. . April, the country—and the pirates—waited in mounting suspense to see what the Government would do. **1979** *Guardian* 9 Aug. 3/6 Air wave pirates pay the price... Signals sent out by illegal radio hams. . led to four men appearing at Grimsby magistrates court.

6*. *Physical Geogr.* A river that captures another (*CAPTURE *v.* b). Also *attrib.* appositively.

1889 *Science* 8 Feb. 108/1 There is a little river-pirate in eastern Pennsylvania unsuspected by its rural neighbors. *Ibid.*, The pirate is Deer Run, and its victim is the north-east branch of Perkiomen Creek. **1904** CHAMBERLIN & SALISBURY *Geol.* I. iii. 98 The tributary which does the stealing is known as a pirate. **1914** R. S. TARR *College Physiogr.* I. xv. 566 Anything that accelerates headwater erosion on one side of a divide. . gives opportunity for the pushing back of the divide and the possible capture of headwaters, or even of good-sized streams, by the successful river pirate. **1939** *Bull. Geol. Soc. Amer.* L. 1333 Each capture strengthened and lengthened the pirate and weakened and shortened the victim. **1968** R. W. FAIRBRIDGE *Encycl. Geomorphol.* 1055/2 The point at which the capture is effected. . is commonly marked by a right angle turn into the pirate stream.

7. b. *pirate ship* (examples); **d. pirate bus** (further example); **pirate cab** = **pirate taxi*; **pirate label** [*LABEL *sb.*[1] 7 c], a recording or a recording company which infringes a copyright; **pirate taxi,** a vehicle which is used as a taxi but is not licensed as such.

1963 *Times* 24 May (London Underground Suppl.) p. vii/2 The 'cut-throat' competition before 1933 when the London Passenger Transport Board was formed was all very well for some people who lived on routes where the 'pirate' buses operated. **1930** A. ARMSTRONG *Taxi!* xvi. 220 There are also some real 'pirate' cabs which only operate down town [*sc.* in New York] at night. They carry no meters and live by 'making a price'. . with any belated. . up-town passenger. **1968** *Jazz Monthly* Feb. 4/1 There are. . numerous 'pirate' labels also issuing EPs and LPs. **1700** in *N. Carolina Colonial Rec.* (1886) I. 518, I herewith send you a copy of what I lately received. . concerning the taking of a pyrate ship. **1720** DEFOE *Capt. Singleton* 187, I wrote that he was taken away by main Force, as a Prisoner, by a Pyrate Ship. **1911** G. B. SHAW *Doctor's Dilemma* Pref. p. xvi, It is the sort of conscience that makes it possible to keep order on a pirate ship, or in a troop of brigands. **1971** *E. Afr. Standard* (Nairobi) 11 Apr. 7/4 Owners of Matatu (pirate taxis) also reported an 'exceptionally' good business as hundreds of people who wanted to go to the rural areas had to use them. **1978** S. NAIPAUL *North of South* I. iv. 87 The thing standing outside the hotel was. . a matutu—a pirate taxi.

e. *attrib.* or as *quasi-adj.* designating the clandestine or illegal transmission of radio programmes (see sense 4 b above), as *pirate broadcast* (also as *vb.*; so *pirate broadcaster, pirate broadcasting* vbl. sb.), *pirate radio (station), pirate station*; **pirate (radio) ship,** a ship used to transmit radio programmes from a position outside the territorial waters of the receiving country; **pirate vessel** = *pirate (radio) ship* above.

1942 *New Yorker* 17 Jan. 52/2 There is a republican pirate radio station, called La Voce della Libertà. **1957** F. HOYLE *Black Cloud* v. 109 Is Nortonstowe going to become a pirate radio station? **1961** *Guardian* 16 Dec. 7/2 Only the presence of mind of the engineers. . prevented a pirate broadcast being heard on the air of the capital itself. **1964** *Daily Tel.* 11 May 20/7 The activities of the 'pirate' radio ships Caroline and Atlanta have presented the Government with a problem which cannot be solved simply. It is expected that the Cabinet will discuss this week the possibility of legislation to prevent broadcasting from such 'pirate' vessels. *Ibid.* 13 May 1/8 Mr. Mawby, Assistant Postmaster-General, told the Commons that new legislation which would effectively deprive 'pirate' broadcasters of material support was the most suitable action. *Ibid.* 14 May 28/3 Almost every BBC station is suffering from some foreign interference and a ring of pirate ships is bound to make matters worse. *Ibid.*, The Swedish law makes it an offence for nationals to take part in pirate ship broadcasting. **1965** *Punch* 3 Feb. 154/1 Commons debate on plight of pirate radios. **1966** *Economist* 23 Apr. 340/3 The arrival this week off British coasts of a pirate radio ship. . is a further step in the battle over the off-shore radio stations. **1966** *Listener* 4 Aug. 154/2 A Government bill to ban pirate radio stations provides for penalties of up to two years' imprisonment. **1967** *Ibid.* 17 Aug. 195/1 There is every sign that many of the crude but effective tabloid techniques of pirate radio. . will be employed by Radio 1. **1969** C. BOOKER *Neophiliacs* ix. 227 The Swedes, the Danes and the Dutch had been plagued by offshore pirate stations as long ago as 1961–2. **1970** *Internat. & Compar. Law Q.* XIX. 357 Legal and practical controls of 'pirate' broadcasting. **1973** *Times* 3 Jan. 4/2 The ship Mi Amigo, from which the pirate radio station broadcasts, sailed out to sea again. **1973** *Daily Tel.* (Colour Suppl.) 5 Jan. 6/1 His ship will be a 'pirate' inasmuch as she will broadcast from outside territorial waters, but unlike other pirate broadcasters there will be no sponsored advertisements.

pirate, *v.* Add: **3.** (Later examples.)

1968 *Blues Unlimited* Nov. 6 They re not selling records, for fear they would be pirated! **1977** *Belfast Tel.* 17 Jan. 8/4 Under the European Television Agreement of 1953 most countries agreed not to 'pirate' programmes broadcast by companies from other nations. **1979** *Guardian* 25 Aug. 24/1 'Pirating' involves the copying, for sale to the public, of existing records without the consent of the copyright owners.

Hence **pirated** *ppl. a.* (further examples); spec. *pirated edition*, an edition of a book produced without authorization; **pirating** *vbl. sb.* (further example).

1737 Pirated edition [in Dict.]. **1853** C. M. SMITH *Working Man's Way in World* iv. 56 (*heading*) Pirated editions of Scott's novels. **1928** D. H. LAWRENCE *Let.* 5 Dec. (1962) II. 1103, I hear from Stieglitz there are *two* pirated editions, photographed from my edition, and with forged signatures. *Ibid.* 10 Dec. 1105, I hear London and Paris are both selling the pirated editions of *Lady C.* at £3 and £2. **1928** A. HUXLEY *Let.* 12 Dec. (1969) 304 Dear Lawrence, What an intolerable business about the pirating of *Lady C.*! **1952** J. CARTER *ABC for Bk.-Collectors* 135 *Pirated edition*, . . a term commonly applied (sometimes with, sometimes without, legal accuracy) to an edition produced and marketed without the authority of, or payment to, the author. **1959** L. M. HARROD *Librarians' Gloss.* (ed. 2) 286 A pirated edition is an unauthorized reprint involving an infringement of copyright. **1967** *Listener* 28 Sept. 413/2 After hearing this performance—and a pirated tape of his 1953 Covent Garden *Aida*—it seems incredible that Barbirolli has been allowed to languish outside the opera house for 13 years. **1973** *Times* 17 Oct. 11/3 The records have been issued in Paris, but not here. It is as bad as Russia, where people listen to me on pirated versions. **1975** *Times Lit. Suppl.* 13 June 678/2 British efforts to influence Parliament to protect British books against the importation of foreign pirated editions.

piratedom (pəiə·rĕt,dəm). *rare.* [f. PIRATE *sb.* + -DOM.] Pirates collectively; the world of pirates.

1907 F. CAMPBELL *Shepherd of Stars* iv. 36 He went to shout orders to a fleet of approaching barges from the stronghold of ancient piratedom.

piriform. For examples of this variant see *PYRIFORM *a.*

pirimicarb (piri·mikāɹb). [f. *PYRIMI(DINE by alteration + CARB(AMATE.] An insecticide that is specific against aphids; 2-dimethyl-amino-5,6-dimethyl-4-pyrimidinyl dimethyl-carbamate, $C_{11}H_{18}N_4O_2$.

1970 *Proc. 5th Brit. Insecticide & Fungicide Conf., 1969* II. 546 Pirimicarb is an aphicide of such specificity that its use for aphid control should not directly eliminate some of the more important predators concerned with the regulating of aphid numbers. **1974** *Nature* 8 Feb. 337/3 Pirimicarb is systemic when applied to soil, being absorbed by the roots. **1977** *Homes & Gardens* Nov. 42/1 A recent product which contains 'Pirimicarb' in either liquid concentrate form or as an aerosol is very effective against aphids except on cucumbers and soft fruit.

piri-piri[2] (pi·ri pi·ri). [Origin obscure; perh. ad. Swahili *pilipili*, pepper.] A sauce made with red peppers. Also *attrib.* or as *adj.* and quasi-*adv.*

1964 H. HOLTHAUSEN *Chicken goes around World* 71 *Frango Piri-piri* (Chicken in Piri-piri sauce). *Ibid.* 72 Preheat the grill and put the piri-piri chicken in the immediate vicinity of the heat... Baste the chicken well..with the remaining piri-piri. **1968** C. BURKE *Elephant across Border* ii. 68 The 'Camarões Pequenos', just..a few miles north of Lourenco Marques..made the best piri-piri prawns on the whole coast. *Ibid.* iii. 115 I'm going to have me a dozen giant prawns, charcoal-grilled, without piri-piri, but with lemon and butter sauce. **1969** M. TRIPP *Malice & Maternal Instinct* iv. 28 They specialise in Spanish and Portuguese here... How about galinha piri-piri. **1970** G. CROUDACE *Scarlet Bikini* vi. 68 If yer gennelmen'll only bring up some rock lobster, I'll give it yer for lunch, piri-piri with rice. **1973** *Times* 17 Feb. (Mozambique Suppl.) p. iv/6 (Advt.), The sauce *piri-piri* is made with red peppers.

pirl, *v.* Add: **3.** (Examples.) So **pi·rling** *ppl. a.* and *vbl. sb.*

1789 D. DAVIDSON *Thoughts on Seasons* 33 Ye roll, in cudlin purlings to the sea. **1819** J. RENNIE *St. Patrick* II. x. 191 I'll set my teeth in the withered chafts o' you till the blind pirl out o' your luckin' e'en. **1920** *Chambers's Jrnl.* Christmas No. 837/2 Before the first puffs of blue smoke circled and pirled above the village roofs. **1936** C. MACDONALD *Echoes of Glen* i. 3 On an emerald bank by the side of a pirling burn.

pirlie pig (pɔ̄·ɹli, *Sc.* pi·rli). *Sc.* Also **perly, pirly,** etc. [Prob. f. PIRL *v.* + PIG *sb.*[2]: see *Sc. Nat. Dict.*] A small money-box, usu. circular and made of earthenware, with a slot to insert coins. Also *ellipt.* as *pirlie*, etc.

1799 'PHILETAS' in J. Thomson *Hist. Dundee* (1874) I. x. 127 Old women and children kept their pozes in their *kist neuks and pirly pigs.* **1831** in *Trans. Banffshire Field Club* (1939) 33 One Stone purly 4/-. **1889** J. M. BARRIE *Window in Thrums* xviii. 170, 'I mind he broke open his pirly,..an' bocht a ha'penny worth o' something to ye every day. **1900** *Longman's Mag.* Nov. 49 Donald did not possess a bike yet, and my 'tips' went into a perly pig in which he was saving up to buy one. **1905** *Athenæum* 28 Jan. 118 The pirley-pig or circular money-box pertaining to the Town Council of Dundee. This pewter money-box is in the shape of an orange or flattened globe. **1912** *Proc. Soc. Antiquaries Scotl.* XLVI. 353 Until thirty or forty years ago there was a good demand for modern pirlie pigs. **1934** H. B. CRUICKSHANK *Noran Water* 15 Ye've riped the pirlie mony's the time Withooten ony skaith. **1960** H. HAYWARD *Antique Coll.* 220/1 *Pirlie pig*, earthenware money-box. 'Pig' is a North Country word for an earthen jar: 'pirlie' is a diminutive indicating something of slight value.

pirn, *sb.*[2] Add: Also **pern, perne. 1.** Also *fig.*

1919 W. B. YEATS *Wild Swans at Coole* 36 He unpacks the loaded pern Of all 'twas pain or joy to learn. **1950** T. R. HENN *Lonely Tower* 185 Within the cones moves the 'perne', a spool which unwinds the thread spirally as the sphere moves onward.

5. pirn-mill, a mill where weaver's bobbins are manufactured.

1915 W. B. YEATS *Reveries* 13 Another day a sea captain pointed to the smoke from the Pern mill on the quays. **1938** in *Sc. Nat. Dict.* (1968) VII. 140/1 The Pirners' Bridge, so-called either because bobbin-makers crossed it to get birch-timber in the adjacent copse to make their pirns, or because a pirn-mill once stood near it.

‖**pirog** (pirǫ·g). Also **piroga, piroque.** Pl. **pirogen** (a. Yiddish), **pirogi** (a. Russ.), **pirogs.** [Russ. *piróg*, Yiddish (a. Russ.) *pirog*.] A large pie. Cf. *PIROSHKI *sb. pl.*

1854 [See *fish-cake* s.v. *FISH *sb.*[1] 6 c]. **1933** P. & L. G. ESMONDE *von Schumacher's Cook's Tour of European Kitchens* vi. 109 Pirogs are eaten fresh from the oven or heated up again. **1950** E. J. KOLLIST *Compl. Patissier* xxiv. 232/1 In Russia the various coulibiac, piroques and small patties are favourites. **1951** Pirogen [see *PIROSHKI *sb. pl.*]. **1962** K. PETROVSKAYA *Secrets of Russian Cooking* 143 A true Russian (or anyone who's ever tasted real Russian pirozhki or pirogi) can grow rhapsodic just talking about them. **1971** *Guardian* 23 July 9/6 Pirogi and Piroshki, literally big pies and baby pies. **1973** [see *PIROSHKI *sb. pl.*].

pirogue. Add: (Further examples.) Also *attrib.*

1926 I. S. COBB *Some United States* xi. 264 A little later four husky chaps in pirogues ranged up alongside us. **1947** *Motor Boating* June 130 The correct name of the two-masted sail plan in Merry Weather is the pirogue rig; not a cat-ketch rig as it is sometimes erroneously named. **1954** *Sun* (Baltimore) 15 Mar. 9/1 French-speaking trappers paddle pirogues through backwater bayous of Louisiana in search of muskrat. **1963** W. GARD in H. S. Bell *Petroleum Transportation Handbk.* iii. 6 In swamp terrain the crews, working out of pirogues where there is standing water, are usually sent ahead of the dipper dredge to drop the trees. **1973** *Times* 5 Mar. (Mauritius Suppl.) p. i/5 The whale..20 reeking terror-filled yards from our frail *pirogue*.

piroot (pəirū·t), *v. U.S. dial.* [Alteration of PIROUETTE *v.*, prob. under influence of ROOT *v.*[2]] *intr.* To move listlessly or aimlessly; also, to snoop. Hence **piroo·ting** *ppl. a.*

1863 S. C. MASSETT *Drifting About* 242 The streets were almost impassable from the mud and slush and.. the 'ladies'..would find it impossible to 'piroot' thither. **1866** C. H. SMITH *Bill Arp* 116 For four years the Confederate Horse-stealing Cavalry have been pirooting around, preparing themselves for the frightful struggle that is to come. **1910** W. M. RAINE *Bucky O'Connor* 30 I've been pirootin' around this country, boy and man, for fifteen years. **1958** 'W. HENRY' *Seven Men at Mimbres Springs* (1960) xiii. 156 Oh God A'mighty—kids, squaws, dogs, old people, pack mules, cookpots—Jesus—the whole pirooting kit and kaboodle of them come down to set up camp and see the fun. **1961** J. F. DOBIE in *Webster* s.v., Went pirooting into a cave one day.

piroplasm (pəiə·roplæz'm). *Biol.* † Also in mod.L. form **piropla·sma** (pl. **-plasmata**). [f. L. *pir-um* pear + -o + PLASM, PLASMA.] A protozoan of the suborder Piroplasmidea of sporozoans, which comprises species parasitic in red blood cells and transmitted by ticks.

[**1895** W. H. PATTON in *Amer. Naturalist* XXIX. 498 The name of the southern or splenic cattle-fever parasite.—The generic name [sc. *Pyrosoma*] given by Drs. Smith and Kilborne, having been previously used in Zoology, must be dropped. I propose the name *Piroplasma* to replace it.] **1901** *Vet. Jrnl.* IV. 50 A strange fact, showing that the form of the parasite varies in its stages of evolution, was that almost all the piroplasms were pear-shaped and bigeminate. **1908** *Practitioner* Feb. 228 Rocky Mountain Spotted Fever. Ricketts has re-investigated this disease, in which..Wilson and Chowning claimed to have discovered piroplasmata, and to have shown that it is transmitted by a tick. **1934** T. W. M. CAMERON *Internal Parasites of Domestic Animals* II. 45 All the piroplasms are tick-carried and consequently the main lines of prevention consist in tick eradication. **1949** C. A. HOARE *Handbk. Med. Protozool.* iii. 37 A piroplasm of the genus *Theileria* is the cause of East Coast fever... Other forms of piroplasmosis in cattle are caused by species of the genus *Babesia*. **1974** O. W. OLSEN *Animal Parasites* (ed. 3) ii. 164/1 Upon entering the erythrocytes, they [*sc.* the parasites] retain their same general appearance and are generally known as piroplasms.

Hence **pi:roplasmo·sis**, any of a group of diseases of mammals, esp. red-water of cattle, caused by infestation of the blood with piroplasms.

1901 *Vet. Jrnl.* IV. 49 (*heading*) Canine piroplasmosis. **1903** *Jrnl. Compar. Path. & Therapeutics* XVI. 312 (*heading*) Pyroplasmosis of the donkey. **1948** U. F. RICHARDSON *Vet. Protozool.* iv. 81 As a rule piroplasmoses occur as enzootic diseases in which young animals contract symptomless infections and recover. **1949** [see above]. **1955** [see *EAST D. 1 b]. **1960** *Farmer & Stockbreeder* 15 Mar. 131/1 Ticks are the carriers of the organisms which when they are inoculated into the blood, attack the red cells and cause them to break down and it is the colouring matter of these cells that gives colour to the urine, and to the disease known as redwater or bovine piroplasmosis. **1974** *Nature* 13 Dec. 532/2 Vaccination against cattle lungworm, canine hookworm and certain kinds of piroplasmosis has been achieved but the vaccines used, irradiated larvae or infected blood, are unacceptable in the field of human medicine.

‖ **piroshki** (pirǫ·ʃki), *sb. pl.* Also **pirotchki, pirozhki, pyrochki.** Occas. in sing. **pirosho·k** (in quot. spelt **pirozsok**). [a. Russ. *pirozhkí* pl. of *pirozhók*, dim. of *piróg* (*PIROG).] Small patties.

1912 R. K. WOOD *Tourist's Russia* ii. 34 To taste pirozhki at their best, one must go to Philipov's in St. Petersburg or Moscow. **1933** P. & L. G. ESMONDE *von Schumacher's Cook's Tour of European Kitchens* vi. 105 After this..came Bortch, a soup of beetroot and cabbage, accompanied by Pyrochki—a Russian stuffed pastry. **1935** M. MORPHY *Recipes of All Nations* 429 Fish piroshki..are made in the same manner as game piroshki, but with a filling of cooked fish, hard-boiled eggs and rice. **1939** *Vogue's Cookery Bk.* xii. 227 *Piroshki*... These are the little meat-filled patties that are the traditional Russian accompaniment to soup. **1943** E. M. ALMEDINGEN *Frossia* ix. 347 Yesterday I baked '*pirozhki*' with cabbage and onions. I made eight, and sixteen people came.., and it meant half a *pirozsok* for each. **1951** L. W. LEONARD *Jewish Cookery* xii. 163 Pirogen..are made just like Piroshki but much larger. **1963** V. NABOKOV *Gift* i. 35 He bought some piroshki (one with meat, another with cabbage, a third with tapioca, a fourth with rice, a fifth... could not afford a fifth) in a Russian foodshop. **1965** J. B. PRIESTLEY *Lost Empires* II. iii. 125 Russian things like.. those tiny meat and fish pasties called *piroshki.* **1972** N. FROUD *Some of our Best Recipes are Jewish* 50 Roll out pastry, fill pirozhki, brush with beaten egg, and bake..in oven preheated to 230° C. **1973** S. SKIPWITH *Eat Russian* viii. 154 Pirozhki are small patties served with soup, as appetisers, or offered with tea or coffee at any time. A pirog is a larger, circular or rectangular, fairly flat pie, with pastry top and bottom. Both are baked with a variety of fillings. **1974** A. WILLIAMS *Gentleman Traitor* vii. 101 A dinner of borscht, pirotchki and beetroot. **1977** J. WAMBAUGH *Black Marble* (1978) x. 218 Valnikov held a paper plate stacked with golden pastries and said, '*Piroshki.* They're very light and filled with cheese or meat. My brother usually makes them both ways.'

pirouette, *sb.* Add: **3.** *Mus.* A form of mouth-piece used with a shawm, rackett, or similar reed instrument (see quot. 1976).

1891 *Descr. Catal. Mus. Instruments R. Military Exhib., London, 1890* iv. 64 The reeds used in these early times were generally rather hard and difficult to manage. To render them more manageable they were placed in a sort of case, called *pirouette*, which covered the lower part of the reed. **1911** *Encycl. Brit.* XXII. 780/1 The rackett is played by means of a large double reed placed within a *pirouette* or cap. **1961** A. BAINES *Mus. Instruments* ix. 233 The European shawmist presses the lips to a wooden 'pirouette'..which permits lip-control without appreciably reducing the reed's amplitude of vibration. **1968** *New Oxf. Hist. Music* IV. xiii. 737 The reed of the tenor and smaller forms was controlled by a device called a *pirouette.* **1976** D. MUNROW *Instruments Middle Ages & Renaissance* 40/2 The pirouette (also used on the renaissance rackett) was a funnel-shaped reed-shield against which the player could press his lips whilst taking the projecting part of the reed into the mouth.

pirouettist (piru,e·tist). [f. PIROUETTE *v.* + -IST.] = PIROUETTER.

1889 G. B. SHAW *London Music 1888–89* (1937) 224 The unappreciated pirouettists and entrechatists looked on indignantly. **1926** W. J. LOCKE *Old Bridge* II. vii. 119 He may chance to be a mechanical jazz pirouettist or a financial oracle.

Pirquet (pīə·ɹke). *Med.* The name of Baron C. P. *Pirquet* von Cesenatico (1874–1929), Viennese pædiatrician, used *attrib.* and † in the possessive to designate a skin test for tuberculosis that he devised in 1907.

1908 *Lancet* 18 Apr. 1183/1 Pirquet's reaction sometimes showed itself five hours after the inoculation but as a rule, the effect was produced in 24 hours and lasted from four to six days. **1927** E. R. BALDWIN et al. *Tuberculosis* xii. 213 The von Pirquet scratch test is less delicate than the intracutaneous method and requires repetition to confirm a negative result. **1952** B. R. CLARKE *Causes & Prevention of Tuberculosis* ii. 14 The simplicity of the Pirquet test is an advantage in sparsely populated regions, only one reading being necessary before B.C.G. vaccination. **1970** *New Yorker* 28 Nov. 44/1 Irochka had had a positive reaction to the Pirquet test and had been sent for an X-ray.

pirssonite (pɔ̄·ɹs-, pīə·ɹsənəit). *Min.* [f. the name of L. V. *Pirsson* (1860–1919), U.S. geologist: see -ITE[1].] A hydrated carbonate of sodium and calcium, $Na_2Ca(CO_3)_2.2H_2O$, occurring as brittle, colourless to white, orthorhombic crystals that are pyroelectric.

1896 J. H. PRATT in *Amer. Jrnl. Sci.* CLII. 130 The author takes pleasure in naming this mineral *pirssonite*, in honor of his friend and associate, Prof. L. V. Pirsson, of the Sheffield Scientific School. **1933** *Jrnl. Chem. Soc.* 1162 Gaylussite is in equilibrium with pirssonite at 37–40°, the exact temperature depending on the concentration of the sodium carbonate solution with which they are in contact. **1975** *Nature* 13 Mar. 128/2 Large (>2 cm), apparently diagenetic crystals of pirssonite and gaylussite, oriented by their 'c' axes at high angles to bedding, are common in parts of these cores.

Pisan (pī·zăn), *sb.* and *a.* [ad. It. *Pisano* f. L. *Pisān-us* of or belonging to *Pisæ*, a city in Etruria.] **A.** *sb.* A native or inhabitant of Pisa, a city in central Italy situated on the river Arno.

1613 PARSONS & FITZ-HERBERT *Suppl. Discuss. M. D. Barlowe's Answere* ii. 81 The wars betwene the Pisanes and the Genoueses by sea. **1705** ADDISON *Remarks Italy* 18 Their Fleet, that formerly gain'd so many Victories over the Saracens, Pisans, Venetians, [etc.]. **1813** J. FORSYTH *Remarks Excursion Italy* 12 Many Pisans, however, are of the old opinion. **1863** 'GEO. ELIOT' *Romola* I. I. viii. 146 'Pisans false, Florentines blind'—the second half of that proverb will hold no longer. **1869** 'MARK TWAIN' *Innoc. Abr.* xxiv. 252 To be buried in such ground was regarded by the ancient Pisans as..potent for salvation. **1875** K. O'CLERY *Hist. Italian Revolution* i. 30 The island [*sc.* Sardinia] was conquered and assigned to the Pisans as a fief of the Holy See. **1934** A. HUXLEY *Beyond Mexique Bay* 280 Like the Pisans, the Aztecs had the wit to leave a wide open space all round the monument. **1973** *Country Life* 16 Aug. 450/2 The Sards have always hated the sea, from whence came all their invaders, Phoenicians, Greeks, Romans, Byzantines, Pisans, Genoese, [etc.]. **1975** *Daily Tel.* (Colour Suppl.) 14 Mar. 10/4 Pisans do not believe that successive ministers and commissions will ever do anything to arrest the inevitable. One day the Tower *will* flop down.

B. *adj.* Of or pertaining to Pisa. spec. *Pisan assistance,* assistance rendered too late to be effective.

1813 J. Forsyth *Remarks Excursion Italy* 36 The Pisan chains hang like a fair trophy on the foreign bank of Genoa. **1869** Browning *Ring & Bk.* IV. xii. 210 You and your pleas and proofs were what folks call Pisan assistance, aid that comes too late. **1869** 'Mark Twain' *Innoc. Abr.* xxiv. 252 A Pisan antiquarian gave me an ancient tear-jug. **1904** J. M. Stone *Reformation & Renaissance* ii. 62 The Pisan Pope and his followers were already there, and for a time it seemed as though they might carry all before them. **1936** A. W. Clapham *Romanesque Archit.* iii. 30 Southern Italy.., touched here with Lombard and there with Pisan influence. **1951** A. R. Lewis *Naval Power & Trade in Mediterranean* vi. 224 Genoese and Pisan fleets helped open up the Rhone Valley route. **1973** *Country Life* 16 Aug. 451/2 Oretelli, where the Parish Church is Pisan of the 13th century. **1975** *Daily Tel.* (Colour Suppl.) 14 Mar. 10/4, I returned with a Pisan friend to the Campo dei Miracoli to have a final look at the Tower.

pisatin (pəi·s-, pi·sătin, -z-). *Biochem.* [f. the taxonomic name *Pis(um s)at(ivum* (f. L. *pisum* pea + *satīvus* (see Sative *a.*)) + -in[1].] A fungitoxic phytoalexin produced by the pea plant, which has been isolated as a crystalline heterocyclic compound, $C_{17}H_{14}O_6$.

1960 Cruickshank & Perrin in *Nature* 27 Aug. 800/1 We propose that the trivial name of this compound should be 'pisatin' after the host plant from which it was originally isolated. **1964** [see *phaseollin]. **1967** R. K. S. Wood *Physiol. Plant Path.* xiv. 496 None of a variety of bacteria which have been tested stimulates formation of pisatin by pea pods. **1972** S. A. J. Tarr *Princ. Plant Path.* xiv. 268 Some of these antifungal substances are perhaps present in low concentrations in normal tissue, their formation being intensified by infection or some other stimulus. Pisatin, for example, is formed when dilute solutions of certain metallic salts..are placed on pea pod endocarp tissue.

Piscean (pəi·siăn), *a.* and *sb.* Also **Piscian.** [f. Pisce(s + an.] **A.** *adj.* Of or pertaining to Pisces, the twelfth sign of the Zodiac; characteristic of a person born under Pisces. **B.** *sb.* A person born under Pisces.

1924 C. E. O. Carter *Con. Encycl. Psychol. Astrol.* 38 It must..be observed that in some people the Piscian and Neptunian charity seems entirely lacking. **1925** —— *Princ. Astrol.* iv. 74 Pisceans are commonly jovial and convivial, and often make entertaining companions. **1940** R. Gleadow *Astrol. in Everyday Life* ii. 162 Most Pisceans..are not particularly dashing; yet those who have Mars rising in Pisces may be quite audacious. *Ibid.* xiv. 250 In astrological circles Mr. Micawber is notoriously Piscean. *a* **1963** L. MacNeice *Astrol.* (1964) iii. 105 Pisceans are very lovable people because they are very loving. **1969** 'V. Packer' *Don't rely on Gemini* (1970) i. 8 Leos are lionlike and Pisceans are mystical. **1972** D. Lees *Zodiac* 28 There must be thousands of Pisceans who can't swim. **1976** *Woman* 22 May 61/1 All is quiet on the Piscean front with both your ruling planets playing a waiting game. **1978** *TV Times* 28 Jan. 68/3 Pam is one of those lucky Pisceans who will enjoy plenty of romance this year.

Pisces. Add: Also with pronounc. (pəi·sīz). **1. b.** A person born under the zodiacal sign Pisces. Also *attrib.* or as *adj.*

1924 C. E. O. Carter *Conc. Encycl. Psychol. Astrol.* 142 Cancer and Pisces people are often retiring and shy among strangers. **1936** 'J. Tey' *Shilling for Candles* vii. 64 One does not expect a Pisces person to have either the vision or the faith. **1969** 'V. Packer' *Don't rely on Gemini* (1970) i. 1 Would a Pisces get along with a Capricorn? *Ibid.* xviii. 159 We're both Pisces like Elizabeth Taylor. **1972** D. Bloodworth *Any Number can Play* xii. 101 You're Pisces, darling... The lucky things for Pisces people are silver, bloodstone, and number seven. **1973** L. Meynell *Fatal Flaw* ii. 20 The fellow turned out to be Pisces. An unreliable lot the Pisces. **1976** *Woman* 1 May 56/1 Intuition and sixth sense are passwords for Pisces, and this week you should virtually live by them, for safety's sake.

piscicide (pi·si-, pi·skisəid). [f. L. *pisci-s* fish + -cide.] **a.** The killing of fish.

1963 *Times* 21 Aug. 5, I was unable to detect any evidence of mass piscicide in the Sonic's track. The only dead fish I saw was a 6 in. specimen.

b. A substance that kills fish.

1964 Lennon & Walker *Laboratories & Methods for Screening Fish-Control Chemicals* 1/2 Ample justification for research on selective piscicides is contained in fishery literature. **1965** *N.Y. Fish & Game Jrnl.* XII. 99 In larger ponds and lakes, the need for selective piscicides is even greater. **1976** *Nature* 25 Mar. 374/2 Under Control of Undesirable Species (Chapter 18), we have a 2-page description..of the new piscicide antimycin.

pisco (pi·sko). [Peruvian, f. *Pisco* the name of a port of Peru.] A white brandy made in Peru from muscat grapes. Also *attrib.* and *Comb.*, as *pisco Collins* [*Collins[2]], *sour.*

1849 H. Vizetelly *Four Months among Gold-Finders in Alta California* 30 On our way he pointed out the guard-house..the distillery house, where the famous pisco is made. **1873** A. S. Evans *À la California* 328 The company all together, we propose a taste of fragrant *pisco* (Peruvian white brandy). **1924** R. Clements *Gipsy of Horn* viii. 143 The old man laid in a stock of 'pisco', a cheap, fiery spirit, very popular in Peru. **1961** J. B. Priestley *Saturn over Water* v. 55 The expensive bars where the double martinis and *pisco* sours were being served. *Ibid.* vi. 88, I just couldn't see steady Joe Farne.. going off on a great *pisco* blind. **1962** N. Maxwell *Witch-Doctor's Apprentice* ii. 16, I asked the waiter to bring me a pisco collins. 'Without sugar as usual, señorita?' he asked. **1971** D. Wallis *Bad Luck Girl* i. 13 Down the Pacific coast they think no more of selling you a fix than pouring you a pisco. **1973** K. Benton *Craig & Jaguar* iv. 36 'You must try one of the Club's pisco sours.' Craig sipped the sticky mixture of cane-spirit and fresh lime juice through the layers of white of egg foam.

pisé. Add: Also **pisée. a.** (Later examples, chiefly with ref. to Australia.) Also, *pisé de terre.*

1919 C. Williams-Ellis *Building in Cob, Pisé, Chalk & Clay* 28 'Pisé de Terre', 'Chalk Compost', and 'Cob' are three alternative forms of construction. **1936** I. L. Idriess *Cattle King* xx. 183 Homesteads were of roughly gathered stone or pisé, of axe hewn slabs or sheets of bark. **1946** B. James in Murdoch & Drake-Brockman *Austral. Short Stories* (1951) 250 The walls had to be very thick, and that meant more pisé to be mixed, and lifted and rammed. **1960** K. M. Kenyon *Archaeol. in Holy Land* iii. 60 The edges of the pits are revetted by slight walls of pisée and stone. **1977** *36 Home Handyman Projects* (Austral. Home Jrnl.) 97/3 Pise de Terre—wall construction of clay or earth—a formwork is made and the earth and clay rammed in firmly. **1978** *Jrnl. R. Soc. Arts* CXXVI. 586/1 Cob..provided good walling; so did damp earth rammed into moulds, and known as *pisé.*

b. *pisé building* (later examples), *earth, terre.*

1919 C. Williams-Ellis *Building in Cob, Pisé, Chalk & Clay* ii. 57 Pliny gives an excellent account of pisé-building in his *Natural History.* **1919** in *Ibid.* 74 These iron bars become so tightly jammed when surrounded by the compact pisé earth, that much labour and risk of injury to the work is incurred in extricating them. **1946** B. James in Murdoch & Drake-Brockman *Austral. Short Stories* (1951) 250 The pisé earth had to be dug,.. mixed and kneaded with water, shovelled into the frames, rammed thoroughly and then left to set. **1965** *Austral. Encycl.* III. 327 Another interesting example of pisé building was the old Forbes, N.S.W., police barracks. **1971** *Country Life* 7 Oct. 941/1 Clough was commissioned.. 'to write a practical book on *Pisée Terre* (rammed earth) building..to cheapen and expedite rural cottage building in the twenties'.

‖**pishachi** (piʃa·tʃi). *India.* Also **piśaca, pisachi, pishasha,** and numerous other variants. [ad. Skr. *piśāca* (masc.), *piśācī* (fem.), a demon.] A demon or devil. Also *attrib.*

The forms in *-a* properly refer to male devils, and those in *-i* to female.

1807 F. Buchanan *Journey from Madras* III. xiv. 17 They believe, that such men as die accidental deaths become *Pysáchi,* or evil spirits, and are exceedingly troublesome, by making extraordinary noises in families, and occasioning fits, and other diseases, especially in women. **1816** *Asiatic Jrnl.* II. 367/1 *Whirlwinds*..at the end of March and the beginning of April..carry dust and light things along with them, and are called by the natives *peshashes,* or devils. **1819** *Trans. Bombay Lit. Soc.* I. 219 Beneath him..is a small squat figure, apparently a *peisach* or demon. These demons or *peisaches* are the usual attendants of Shiva. **1827** J. C. & A. W. Hare *Guesses at Truth* (ser. 1) 12 As a little girl was playing round me one day with her white frock over her head, I laughingly called her *Pishashee,* the Indian name, I believe, for their white devil. **1837** J. C. Maitland, *Lett. from Madras* (1843) 107 She used to go out and howl so that the servants were afraid to come near her, saying she made 'one pishashi (devil) noise'. **1885** G. C. Whitworth *Anglo-Indian Dict.* 252/1 *Piśácha*.., the name of a class of spirits always imagined as fierce and malignant. **1886** Yule & Burnell *Hobson-Jobson* 540/1 Pisachee. **1917** L. H. Gray *Mythol. All Races* vi. 67 With the Rakṣases in later literature rank the Piśācas as foes of the fathers. **1920** *Encycl. Relig. & Ethics* X. 43/2 In modern India a *piśācha* is a kind of ghoul, usually the ghost of some one who has died an unnatural death, or for whom the requisite funeral rites have not been performed... In S. India the small circular storms, called 'devils' by Europeans, are called *piśāchīs,* or 'she-ghouls'. **1924** R. E. Enthoven *Folklore of Bombay* iv. 148 *Bhuts* and *pishachas*—ghosts, male and female—can be prevented from doing harm by recourse to certain processes. **1927** S. Ketkar tr. *Winternitz's Hist. Indian Lit.* I. 133 Very numerous, too, are the incantations which are directed against whole classes of demons.., especially against the *Piśācas* (goblins) and *Rākṣasas* (devils). **1952** E. Sykes *Everyman's Dict. Non-Classical Mythol.* 171 *Pishashas,* in Vedic myth malignant woodland spirits, who disliked travellers, and especially pregnant women. **1968** B. Walker *Hindu World* ii. 214 *Piśācha,* a race of people classed in the Vedas as lower than the rákshasas (ogres), and amongst the most vile and noxious of beings. **1973** J. Dowson *Classical Dict. Hindu Mythol.* 234 *Piṣāchas* (mas.), *Piṣāchī* (fem.), fiends, evil spirits, placed by the Vedas as lower than Rākshasas. **1977** M. & J. Stutley *Dict. Hinduism* 226/1 *Piśāca(s),* flesh-eating demonic beings. *Ibid.* 226/2 *Piśāci,* a she-devil.

pishamin. (Earlier Amer. example.)

1766 J. Bartram *Jrnl.* 14 Jan. 36 in W. Stork *Acct. E. Florida* (ed. 2), The lower rich ground produceth gledistia, pishamins, cephalanthus, ash, cypress and cornu femina.

pisha paysha (pi·ʃă pēi·ʃă). Also **pisha pasha.** [App. a corruption of *pitch* (or *peace*) *and patience.*] A Jewish card game resembling patience, played by two persons, in which the cards are taken as they come from the pack, the object being to arrange them in an upward or downward sequence until the pack is exhausted, when the player who has the fewer cards in his hand is declared the winner.

1928 *Weekly Dispatch* 27 May 13/2 Faded photographs of the Yiddish stars of yesterday hung on the walls; most of the people looked up when we came in, but two heavy, blue-chinned fellows continued their game of *pisha pasha* and another smiled a greeting across the top of a Jewish evening paper. **1968** L. Rosten *Joys of Yiddish* 288, I was taught to play *pisha paysha* by my father, when I was six or seven.

pisher (pi·ʃəɹ). *U.S. slang.* [a. Yiddish *pisher* Pisser, f. G. *pissen*: see Piss *v.*] A bed-wetter; also in extended uses (see quots.). Also *attrib.* or as *adj.*

1942 in *Amer. Speech* (1943) XVIII. 46 Call me pisher. **1943** *Ibid.*, The phrase 'to call someone pisher' connotes mild, tolerant, ineffectual reproof or disproportionately lax punishment. A typical context might be something like this: 'So what did they do to Flynn for putting public employees to work on his Mahopac estate and using government property? They called him pisher!' **1958** B. Malamud *Magic Barrel* 87 He bought.. this pisher grocery in a dead neighbourhood where he didn't have a chance. **1968** L. Rosten *Joys of Yiddish* 289 Literally, a *pisher* is one who urinates; but that is a far cry from present and popular usage. 'He's a mere *pisher,*' means 'He's very young,' or 'He's still wet behind the ears.'.. 'He's just a *pisher,*' means 'He's a nobody,' has no influence. **1970** L. M. Feinsilver *Taste of Yiddish* i. 61 'She still has two *pishers* at home' is a common colloquialism that makes its point: she has two offspring still in diapers, or two preschoolers. **1972** J. Caine *Hamlet, My Boy* xi. 161 First, they didn't wait to call you *pisher*; they just filled you up with bullet-holes like a matzo. **1978** E. Tidyman *Table Stakes* ii. vii. 312 Then the marriage. Now that was *really* smart! Who could call him pisher now, with the Jewish princess on his arm? **1978** R. Doliner *On Edge* (1979) v. 83 'I was a kid...A pisher.' 'Pisher,' the Vice-President said. 'One who wets one's pants.' **1979** B. Malamud *Dubin's Lives* ix. 359, I lived on cases involving small finaglers and found myself engaged in pisher dishonesties.

pishogue. Add: Also **pishog, pisherogue.** (Further examples.) Also, a fairy, a witch.

1829 G. Griffin *Collegians* I. xi. 231 Mr. Eurig̃ht's dairyman..made a *pishog* and took away our butter. **1906** Kipling *Puck of Pook's Hill* 10 Little people, pishogues, leprechauns. **1937** C. M. Arensberg *Irish Countryman* vi. 212 All that the Church condemns in the 'pisherogues', they [*sc.* young people] also condemn. **1957** E. E. Evans *Irish Folk Ways* xxi. 296 Most of the pishrogues relate to fairies and to trees, wells and stones. **1960** *20th Cent.* July 51 She had denied it. 'No, I am not a pishogue.' Yet she was aware how easily one might become a fairy. **1961** 'F. O'Brien' *Hard Life* ii. 17 Well now, Mrs Crothy, are these the two pishrogues out of the storm?

Pisistratid (pəisi·strătid), *sb.* and *a.* Also **Peisistratid,** 8 **Pysistratid.** [ad. L. *Pisistratidae,* Gr. *Πεισιστρατίδαι,* the name given to Hippias and Hipparchus, sons of Pisistratus, tyrant of Athens in the 6th cent. B.C.] **A.** *sb.* (Pl. **-idae, -ids.**) A member or supporter of the family of Pisistratus. Chiefly in *pl.*

1709 I. Littlebury tr. *Herodotus' Hist.* II. v. 57 The Corinthians would be the first of all People to regret the Pisistratides. **1776** W. Ellis tr. *Aristotle's Treat. Govt.* v. xi. 295 The Pyramids of Egypt are a proof of this,..and the Temple of Jupiter Olympus, built by the Pysistratidæ, and the Works of Polycrates at Samos; for all these produced one end, the keeping the People poor. **1808** W. Mitford *Hist. Greece* I. xii. 561 He married Agrristë, niece of Cleisthenes, chief of the Alcmæonid family, and leader of the party that expelled the Peisistratids. **1848** *Eton School Mag.* III. 114 It thus appears how irretrievably the government of the Pisistratids had injured the Athenian character. **1885** B. Jowett tr. *Aristotle's Politics* I. v. 184 Third in duration was the rule of the Peisistratidae at Athens, but it was interrupted. **1900** J. B. Bury *Hist. Greece* v. 206 The Pisistratids cultivated the friendship of Sparta. **1922** P. N. Ure *Origin of Tyranny* i. 14 This part of the tyrants' policy is noticed by Aristotle, who quotes..the building of the temple of Olympian Zeus at Athens by the Peisistratids. *Ibid.* ii. 33 The Philaidae, of whose rivalry with the Peisistratidae there will be occasion to speak later. **1972** R. Meiggs *Athenian Empire* i. 19 The expulsion of the Pisistratids in 510.

B. *adj.* Of or pertaining to Pisistratus or his family; *spec.* of or pertaining to the revision of the Homeric poems attributed to Pisistratus. Also **Pisistrate·an** *a.*

1846 J. S. Mill in *Edin. Rev.* LXXXIV. 363 Mr. Grote ..rejects the Pisistratean hypothesis. **1965** A. R. Burn *Traveller's Hist. Greece* vii. 114 Hipparchos, the chief Peisistratid patron of poets and artists, was stabbed to death. **1968** V. Ehrenberg *From Solon to Socrates* iv. 82 The story of a 'Peisistratid redaction' of the two epics can hardly be true.

‖**piskun** (pi·skʊ̆n). Also **pishkun.** [ad. Blackfoot *pískáni.*] An American Indian trap for buffalo, consisting of two converging lines of rock piles, a V-shaped natural canyon, or a timbered causeway leading to a steep drop, often with an enclosure or corral at the foot, over which the buffalo were stampeded.

1892 *Scribner's Mag.* Sept. 281 In the later days of the *piskŭn*, the man who brought the buffalo went to them on horseback, riding a white horse. **1892** G. B. Grinnell *Blackfoot Lodge Tales* (1893) 230 The pis'kuns of the Sik'-si-kau, or Blackfoot tribe, differed in some particulars from those constructed by the Bloods and the Piegans, who live further to the south, nearer to the mountains, and so in a country which is rougher and more broken. The Sik'-si-kan built their pis'kuns like the Crees, on level ground and usually near timber. A large pen or corral was made of heavy logs about eight feet high. On the side where the wings of the chute come together, a bridge, or causeway, was built, sloping gently up from the prairie to the walls of the corral, which at this point were cut away to the height of the bridge above the ground,—here about four feet,—so that the animals running up the causeway could jump down into the corral. **1929** E. D. Branch *Hunting of Buffalo* ii. 35 The *piskun* was surer and safer than the human trap; it was an enclosed pen into which the buffalo were driven. **1943** J. K. Howard *Montana* 23 Often buffalo were driven over cliffs, the 'buffalo runs' or 'pishkuns' under which Montanans still find rich hoards of arrowheads and other Indian implements. **1949** *Jrnl. Washington Acad. Sci.* XXXIX. 357/2 The North Blackfoot, who hunted to a considerable extent on relatively level ground, built their piskun like that of the Cree Indians in the form of a corral with rising timbered causeway leading up to the entrance of the corral from which there was a sheer drop of about 4 feet into the corral. The Piegan and Blood, living in more broken country nearer the mountains, drove the bison over cliffs. *Ibid.* 360/1 We can date the last bison drive of the Blackfoot at about the year 1872. This was a full century after Mathew Cocking's first description of the use of the piskun by Indians of the north-western plains. **1952** J. K. Howard *Strange Empire* 294 Nevertheless some native methods of killing buffalo were wasteful. Such were the *piskuns* and pounds, use of which, however, was generally abandoned by the Indians some time before the herds disappeared.

Pismo (pi·zmo). Also **pismo.** The name of *Pismo* Beach, California, used *attrib.* in **Pismo clam,** a large, thick-shelled, edible clam, *Tivela stultorum,* belonging to the family Veneridæ and found on the south-west coast of North America.

1913 *Calif. Fish & Game Comm. Fish Bull.* I. 27 The Pismo clam..flourishes in open sandy beaches. **1923** *Ibid.* VII. 5 Commercially the Pismo clam ranks first in importance in California among clams and third among all the mollusks. **1949** *Natural Hist.* June 252/1 Five minutes of barefoot beach scratching had uncovered half a sack of four-inch Pismo clams. **1970** B. H. McConnaughey *Introd. Marine Biol.* viii. 227/2 A large, heavy-shelled clam, the pismo clam, occurs on California beaches at the lowest intertidal and subtidal levels.

pisolite. Add: (Further examples.)

Quot. 1708 in Dict. belongs to the next sense.

1931 S. J. Shand *Study of Rocks* xi. 153 Oolite and pisolite are limestones built up of little spheroidal bodies resembling the roe of fishes or heaps of peas. **1962** Read & Watson *Introd. Geol.* I. v. 266 Other chemical limestones are not of much account; they include deposits from calcareous springs, such as pisolite, tufa and travertine.

b. Add to def.: similar to an oolith but larger (in mod. use applied to grains of diameter 2 mm. or more). (Earlier and later examples.)

1708 [in Dict., sense a]. **1788** [see *oolith]. **1893** *Q. Jrnl. Geol. Soc.* XLIX. 127 The series for some distance above the typical Pea-grit..contains here and there aggregations of brown pisolites. **1925** *Nat. Geogr. Mag.* XLVIII. 313 These spherical bodies are known to geologists as pisolites and to jewelers as cave pearls. **1956** E. W. Heinrich *Microsc. Petrogr.* v. 153 The limonite may be in spongy masses..or in pisolites and concretionary masses. **1974** *Encycl. Brit. Macropædia* XVI. 466/2 Pisolites are similar to oolites and range from two to about ten millimetres (0·4 inch) in diameter.

pisolith (pi·zo-, pəi·soliþ). *Petrol.* Also †**-lithe.** [f. as Pisolite: see -lith.] = Pisolite b in Dict. and Suppl.

1799 [see Pisolite a]. **1926** G. W. Tyrrell *Princ. Petrol.* xiii. 227 Pisoliths are essentially similar to ooliths, but reach much larger sizes, and are generally found in residual deposits. **1938** M. Black *Hatch & Rastall's Petrol. Sedimentary Rocks* (ed. 3) viii. 176 Cave pearls are pisoliths, sometimes of large size, found in the underground waters of limestone caves. **1947** *Jrnl. Sedimentary Petrol.* XVII. 39 (*heading*) Pisoliths and ooliths from some Australian caves and mines. *Ibid.* 43/1 In pools full of pisoliths and ooliths, the larger ones (around 20 mm. long) occur at the top. **1975** *Nature* 20 Nov. 206/1 It lies under a thin but persistent weathered horizon which has a patchy distribution and is characterised by ferruginous pisoliths.

Hence **pisoli·thic** *a.*

1863 Sullivan & O'Reilly *Notes Geol. & Mineral. of Santander & Madrid* I. iv. 91 The hydrocarbonate of zinc also occurs perfectly globular, some specimens being beautifully pisolithic. **1947** *Jrnl. Sedimentary Petrol.* XVII. 39 Calcareous concretions, principally of the pisolithic type.

piss, *v.* Add: **1. b.** (Further examples.) *spec.* To be raining heavily. *to piss in (a person's) pocket* (Austral.), to ingratiate oneself with, be on very familiar terms with.

1642 G. Torriano *Sel. Italian Proverbs* 19 He who pisseth against the wind, wetteth his shirt. **1670** J. Ray *Coll. Eng. Proverbs* 131 Chi piscia contra il vento si bagna la commiscia, *Ital.* He that pisseth against the wind, wets his shirt. It is to a mans own prejudice, to strive against the stream. **1902** Farmer & Henley *Slang.* V. 215/2 'Piss not against the wind', or 'He that pisseth against the wind wets his shirt'. **1962** J. Baldwin *Another Country* I. ii. 94 Christ, it's pissing out there! **1967** K. Tennant *Tell Morning This* xxx. 283 Soon's they knew you was in with Numismata, they all want to piss in your pocket. **1968** H. C. Rae *Few Small Bones* II. i. 73 Went camping up north..but it pissed the whole time. Come to think of it, I was pretty pissed the whole time myself. **1969** C. Bray *Blossom like Rose* xii. 165, I don't mean to piss in yer pockets, but youse blokes are all right. **1970** E. Pace *Saberlegs* (1971) vi. 58 Putting words on newspaper pages was, if anything, even more ephemeral than intelligence-gathering. As they used to say at Dartmouth, it was all 'pissing in the wind'. **1971** F. Hardy *Outcasts of Foolgaran* 77, I appeared before him many a time when I worked for the Union. If we piss in his pocket, he's just as apt to come our way. **1973** L. Snelling *Heresy* I. vii. 52 I'd like to buy it, but frankly I think you're pissing against the wind... He's a pretty cunning little bugger. **1977** J. Wainwright *Nest of Rats* I. viii. 60 How much time?.. Don't make it hours—otherwise you're pissing in the wind.

c. Const. with various adverbs: *to piss about,* to fool or mess about; to potter about; *to piss down,* to rain heavily; *to piss off,* to go away, depart.

1950 G. Wilson *Brave Company* 172 It fairly pissed down on top of me. **1958** F. Norman *Bang to Rights* 72 So what, I wish you'd piss off. **1960** H. Pinter *Caretaker* I. 14 Piss off, he said... If you don't piss off, he says, I'll kick you all the way to the gate. **1961** Partridge *Dict. Slang* Suppl. 1223/2 *Piss about,* to potter; fritter one's time away; to stall for time. **1970** T. Lewis *Jack's Return Home* 179 Are you coming in? Or do we piss about all day? **1971** W. J. Burley *Guilt Edged* viii. 138 Most of yesterday it was pissing down with rain. **1971** B. W. Aldiss *Soldier Erect* 50 I'll have a drink when I feel like it, and not before. You two piss off if you're so bloody thirsty! **1972** R. Quilty *Tenth Session* 19 Pissing down too, and one o'clock in the morning. **1974** 'J. Fraser' *Wreath of Lords & Ladies* vii. 57 Are we going to piss off home or sit here blabbering all night? **1975** *Sunday Times* (Colour Suppl.) 23 Feb. 26/3 The manager who tried to discipline a man caught with an illicit can of tea was told to piss off. **1977** J. Thomson *Case Closed* ii. 25 Tucker wouldn't come..not with it pissing down with rain. **1977** M. Drabble *Ice Age* I. 59 Oh piss off, Mum, Maureen would reply, amiably.

2. b. *to piss away,* to squander.

1948 D. Ballantyne *Cunninghams* 211 Have to stop pissing away the hard-earned cash though. **1972** P. Knapp *Berengaria Exchange* 18 Dinty had built up a 'pretty good roll'. But as he now says with a shrug, 'I pissed it all away in Paris.' **1975** *Time* 4 Aug. 61/2 'This company is doing a good business,' he says. 'If we can only stop pissing away the profits.'

3. (Later refl. examples.)

1951 Partridge *Dict. Slang.* (ed. 4) 1136/2 Piss oneself laughing. **1969** N. Cohn *AWopBopaLooBop* (1970) ix. 85 The Twist ballooned almost instantaneously from a fad to an industry. The papers pissed themselves. Big money got invested. **1976** A. White *Long Silence* xviii. 147 Otto pissed himself with fear. **1978** J. Barnett *Head of Force* xv. 146 You've pissed yourself..you dirty bastard.

c. *to piss off,* to annoy, irritate, put off, make 'fed up' or depressed (see also *pissed *ppl. a.* 2); *to piss up,* to spoil, ruin, mess up.

1937 E. Pound *Fifth Decad of Cantos* l. 49 Talleyrand stank with shanker And hell pissed up Metternich. **1968** *Southerly* XXVIII. 275 She prefers British eccentrics because they don't expect to be liked. 'I mean,' she says, 'it's their way of pissing people off, isn't it?' **1970** *It* 27 Feb.–13 Mar. 14/1 Wasn't it incredible? I just didn't believe it!.. They really piss me off. **1971** B. Malamud *Tenants* 178 You ought to burn up both of these yourself, Willie, on account of this cat stole your white bitch and pissed up your black book. **1972** *Last Whole Earth Catalog* (Portola Inst.) 9/3 It did piss me off when the dealer let me go for only five hundred and fifty dollars. **1974** K. C. Constantine *Blank Page* 148, I still think it'd piss him off. **1976** 'D. Craig' *Faith, Hope & Death* xvii. 118 Did I let them just unload it because they pissed up a job?.. This was my money that had been lifted. **1977** *Rolling Stone* 16 June 52/2 She may not want to be called 'Queen', but only because she considers herself too young, because she is not out to piss off Aretha Franklin any more than she already has.

piss, *sb.* Add: **1. a.** (Further examples.) Also, the action or an act of urinating.

1916 Joyce *Portrait of Artist* ii. 96 That is horse piss and rotted straw, he thought. It is a good odour to breathe. **1926** T. E. Lawrence *Seven Pillars* (1935) VI. lxxviii. 434 Mifleh brought up the youngest lads of the party, and had them spray the wounds with their piss, as a rude antiseptic. **1974** P. Larkin *High Windows* 32 Groping back to bed after a piss. **1976** *Listener* 18 Mar. 344/1 The words [in a radio play]..were punctuated with belches, giggles, mutterings, reflective hesitations, the repetition of good jokes, and a wonderfully realistic-sounding piss. **1979** N. Freeling *Widow* iii. 11 The hallway smelt... Piss, cabbage, stale sweat.

2. In various fig. phrases, as *on the piss,* engaged in a bout of heavy drinking; *take the piss (out of),* to make fun (of), to 'take the mickey' (out of); *piss and wind,* empty talk, bombast; *piss and vinegar,* energy, aggression; also *attrib.*

1922 Joyce *Ulysses* 322 All wind and piss like a tanyard cat. **1942** Berrey & Van den Bark *Amer. Thes. Slang* §240/2 *Animation; spirit; vim,*..piss and vinegar. **1942** *Horizon* Aug. 124 Buggered if I know when he'll be back. Gone on the piss, I shouldn't wonder. **1945** *Penguin New Writing* XXVI. 49 The corporal..sat back in his corner looking a little offended. He thought I was taking the piss. **1958** F. Norman *Bang to Rights* 116 This only made us take the piss out of him the more. **1961** Partridge *Dict. Slang* Suppl. 1223/2 *Piss and wind,* as in 'He's all piss and wind!' Empty talk; unsubstantiated boast(s). **1962** E. Ambler *Light of Day* xii. 244 These policemen are all piss and wind anyway. **1966** M. Spillane *Death Dealers* i. 17 Remember the old days, Tiger? You were young and fast and strong. Full of piss and vinegar. **1968** 'P. Alding' *Circle of Danger* iii. 20 Him not turning up may just mean he's been on the piss. **1969** *Guardian* 13 Feb. 22/4 Mr Eric Lubbock, the Liberal MP for Orpington..said: '..I have heard nothing but piss and wind.' **1971** B. W. Aldiss *Soldier Erect* 49 'Come on, Wally, like —I don't think you ought to take the piss out of the poor sod!' Geordie said. 'He's got his living to earn.' **1974** *Observer* 30 June 22/8 And I don't binge. If I'd gone on the piss every time I missed a cut [*sc.* failed to qualify in a golf tournament] I'd be a raging alcoholic by now. **1975** J. Symons *Three Pipe Problem* xviii. 190 You like to take the piss out of me, don't you? **1976** J. O'Connor *Eleventh Commandment* xiv. 179, I was very happy and went on the piss. **1976** R. Perry *One Good Death* iv. 66 The sarcasm left Collins unmoved. He knew that Pawson was in one of his piss and vinegar moods. **1978** R. Busby *Garvey's Code* xi. 138 Jacko's not such a bad bloke. Full of piss and vinegar and ready to jump for any bugger with braid on his hat. **1978** R. Hill *Pinch of Snuff* xiv. 145 When Hope replied 'He's a Hungarian' he thought at first he was taking the piss. Wield seemed prepared to accept this as a serious contribution, however.

3. *Comb.* (Insert *Comb.* from sense 1 b in Dict.) Also, **piss artist,** a glib person; a person who messes about; a drunkard; **piss-bucket,** a bucket for urinating in; **piss-cutter** *N. Amer.*, someone or something excellent; a clever or crafty person; (see also quot. 1956); **piss-head,** a drunkard; **piss-hole,** (*a*) hole made by urine; (*b*) an unpleasant place; **piss-house,** an outside water closet; a lavatory; also *fig.* (see quots. 1931, 1942); **piss-proud** *a.*, having an erection attributed to a full bladder, esp. upon awakening; **piss-take,** a parody, a send-up (see sense 2); also **piss-taker, piss-taking; piss-tin,** a tin for urinating in.

1975 *Peace News* 11 July 11/1 Most donors seem to be pretty careful. The lists of who's been given money seem to bear this out—it's usually the right-on projects which have most and the con merchants and piss artists often go without. **1977** *Sounds* 9 July 36/4, I am appealing to anybody who knows John and Murdoch of Erkshire Scotland. You know, those piss-artists, protozoans who wrote that letter about a rock band classification. **1977** *Custom Car* Nov. 5/2, I refer to the auto/driver self-destruct mechanism known as 'booze'. A piss artist behind the wheel of a 1935 Austin Seven was a killer. **1977** *Private Eye* 10 Nov. 22/1 (Advt.), Malcolm Derek Winn. Photographer, traveller, piss-artist. Whereabouts known? Box 1215. **1973** J. Seabrook *Loneliness* 104 The workhouses were terrible places. At Newark, you slept on a stone floor, and in the middle there was a piss-bucket. **1942** Berrey & Van den Bark *Amer. Thes. Slang* §29/2 *Something excellent,*..piss-cutter. *Ibid.* §432/2 *Capable person; expert,*..piss-cutter. **1956** *Amer. Speech* XXXI. 192 His [*sc.* a marine's] garrison cap is a *pisscutter* (also used as a cynical description, i.e., 'He's a pisscutter, he is!'). **1968** E. R. Buckler *Ox Bells & Fireflies* xv. 206 Gus Jordan's got a new rowboat. It's a real pisscutter! **1974** D. Sears *Lark in Clear Air* viii. 97 I'd send some [beer] along with you but that old piss-cutter of a Heeney would drink'm all before you cut the froth on the first bottle. **1977** *Maledicta* Summer 13 A clever person is sometimes called a piss-cutter. **1961** Patridge *Dict. Slang* Suppl. 1223/2 *Piss-head,* an habitually heavy drinker. **1968** *Landfall* XXII. 50 My old man was a piss-head too. *c* **1932** Dylan Thomas *Lett.* (1966) 4 My eyes are two piss-holes in the sand. **1973** R. Busby *Pattern of Violence* ii. 24 'How's tricks, Lucky?'..'Be better when I'm out of this piss hole—no offence, gents.' **1974** R. Gadney *Something Worth Fighting For* iv. 33 Let's get out of this pisshole. **1931** *Amer. Speech* VII. 112 *Piss-house,* n., the police station. **1942** Berrey & Van den Bark *Amer. Thes. Slang* §84/11 *Toilet,*..piss-house. *Ibid.* §466/10 *Police station or jail,*..pisshouse. **1973** W. H. Canaway *Harry doing Good* II. v. 187 Come outside for a leak. Blow your noses on the way to the piss-house. **1974** H. MacInnes *Climb to Lost World* xi. 199 Next morning the Wall was wetter than ever... 'Never seen it so wet here—what do you think?' 'Looks like a piss-house wall to me.' **1788** Grose *Dict. Vulg. T.* (ed. 2), *Piss-proud,* having a false erection. That old fellow thought he had an erection, but his — was only piss-proud; said of any old fellow who marries a young wife. **1868** *Index Expurgatorius of Martial* 88 Maevius who while sleeping only gets A piss-proud stand that melts away on waking. **1932** Auden *Orators* III. 104 That piss-proud prophet. **1977** *Spare Rib* July 49/1 It's a bit of a pisstake, sending up the whole bi-sexuality thing. **1976** *New Society* 20 May 408/2 'What's funny about a jeweller?..He's a piss taker. **1971** *It* 9–23 Sept. 21/1 The subjects for piss-taking run the gamut from the chairboard executive's life..to the Amerikanjudicial system. **1974** H. MacInnes *Climb to Lost World* vii. 104 If it was imperative, I used my piss-tin, conveniently placed at arm's reach on the mud.

4. Used quasi-adverbially in sense 'very, excessively, to an extremely undesirable degree', as *piss-elegant, -poor, -rotten, -wet,* etc., adjs.

1940 E. Pound *Cantos* lxix. 174 Bingham, Carrol of Carrolton Gone piss-rotten for Hamilton Cabot, Fisher Ames [etc.]. **1946** (*reported in oral use by Prof. A. L.*

Hench) This is a piss-poor outfit. My job is a piss-poor one. **1957** J. KEROUAC *On Road* (1958) 207 A pisspoor bum from Larimer Street. **1970** J. HANSEN *Fadeout* viii. 68 Feeling sorry for a man's a piss-poor reason to marry him. **1972** R. MAUGHAN *Escape from Shadows* iv. 186 But I feel out of place here, it's too piss-elegant. **1972** J. BROWN *Chancer* v. 64 'This beer,' I said, 'it's piss-poor.' **1973** *Amer. Speech* 1970 XLV. 58 *Piss-elegant*, pretentious, ostentatious, egotistical (used with reference to male homosexuals). **1973** *Nation Rev.* (Melbourne) 24–30 Aug. 1432/1, I think privately that they look in pisspoor condition; but the spirited bidding rockets the price up to $2.50 in no time. **1974** J. ANTHOINE in H. MacInnes *Climb to Lost World* x. 179 He got piss wet in that bloody channel [on a rock face]. *Ibid.* xi. 202 'Here we are,' I said to Joe. 'On a piss-wet cliff and there's no bloody water for a brew!' **1977** *Gay News* 24 Mar. 21/2 The Lovely Ladies from South America were so piss-elegant they could hardly lift their feet off the ground. **1977** *N.Y. Rev. Bks.* 4 Aug. 35/4 They manufacture piss-chic cosmetics.

pissabed. Restrict '*Obs.* exc. *dial.*' to senses in Dict. and add: **1.** (Later examples.)

1953 S. BECKETT *Watt* III. 154 Of flowers there was no trace, save of the flowers that plant themselves, or never die, or die only after many seasons, strangled by the rank grass. The chief of these was the pissabed. **1974** G. GRIGSON *Dict. Eng. Plant Names* 169 Pissabed (*Taraxacum officinale*, Dandelion)... The name has too wide a currency to be derived from Gerard's *Herbal*.

3. Chiefly *slang*. A bed-wetter; also *attrib.*, as an abusive epithet.

1643 in *County Court Rec. Accomack-Northampton, Va.* (1973) 292 Thou pissa bedd Jade. **1922** JOYCE *Ulysses* 395 Pope Peter's but a pissabed. **1959** R. FULLER *Ruined Boys* 195 He beat me at the beginning of term for peeing my bed... Now he thinks of me as a pissabed. **1972** R. A. WILSON *Playboy's Bk. Forbidden Words* 229 *Piss-a-bed*, a lazy fellow, one who pisses in bed because he's too lethargic to walk to the john.

‖ **pissaladière** (pisaladiẹ̄r). Also **pissaladiera.** [Fr.: Provençal dial. *pissaladiero* f. *pissala* salt fish.] A Provençal open tart similar to pizza, usu. cooked with onions, anchovies, and black olives.

1931 A. DE CROZE *What to eat & drink in France* xv. 131 La Pissaladiera (a tart well sprinkled with olive oil, filled with sweet onions browned in oil, and pissala—salted whitebait—and baked). **1951** G. MAUROIS *Cooking with French Touch* iii. 66 Another favorite hors d' œuvre in the region of Nice is the *pissaladiera*. **1960** E. CAMPBELL *Encycl. World Cookery* 154 *Pissaladière*..dough..onions..black olives..anchovy fillets. **1960** E. DAVID *French Provincial Cooking* 208 The *pissaladière* is a substantial dish of bread dough spread with onions, anchovies, black olives, and sometimes tomatoes. **1966** P. V. PRICE *France* 276 Pissaladiera. A Nice speciality, and a version of Italian pizza—an open tart with onions, anchovies and black olives, sometimes with tomatoes. **1970** SIMON & HOWE *Dict. Gastron.* 302/2 The filling is covered with a pattern of anchovy fillets and stoned black olives and the *pissaladière* is baked in a hot oven. **1977** *N.Y. Rev. Bks.* 8 Dec. 18/3 Hurray for the Cornish pasty rather than Olney's *pissaladière*.

piss-ant. Delete † *Obs. rare*[−1] and add: Also **pissant, piss ant;** *dial.* **piss-aint.** (Further examples.) *spec.* in phrases *drunk as a piss-ant*, extremely intoxicated; *game as a piss-ant*, courageous, very brave. Also *transf.*, *fig.*, and *attrib.*

1770 C. CARROLL *Let.* 22 May in *Maryland Hist. Mag.* (1917) XII. 362 It seems the Pissants eat a great deal of Corn in the ground. **1847** W. T. PORTER *Quarter Race in Kentucky* 84 Pourin out of the woods like pissants out of an old log when tother end's afire. **1893** J. SALISBURY *Gloss. Words S.E. Worcestershire* 28 'Er screws 'er waist up till 'er looks like a piss-aint. **1903** 'T. COLLINS' *Such is Life* v. 184 His mind's so much took-up with the tuppenny-thruppenny things... Can't afford to come-out anything but a pis-ant. **1930** J. DOS PASSOS *42nd Parallel* I. 77 I'm drunk as a pissant still. **1935** H. L. DAVIS *Honey in Horn* xvi. 278 Anybody who called owning horses disorderly conduct was a liar and a pissant. **1945** BAKER *Austral. Lang.* iv. 87 Game as a piss ant or drunk as a piss ant. **1946** MEZZROW & WOLFE *Really Blues* (1957) 377 *Piss-ant*, a nobody, small fry. **1949** H. HORNSBY *Lonesome Valley* 185 Why, goddam it to Jesus Christ and back, they're thicker than piss ants. **1961** P. WHITE *Riders in Chariot* xiii. 448 'And on such a day!' she shrieked, looking at the clock. 'I bet that nephew of yours will be full as a piss-ant by eleven!' **1962** R. TULLIPAN *March into Morning* 59 The old white lady makes you as game as a pissant. **1966** *Publ. Amer. Dial. Soc.* 1964 XLII. 21 *Pissant*. Regularly used by men among men; elsewhere it is *ant* only. **1972** F. VAN W. MASON *Roads to Liberty* 169 You stole my skelp, you no-'count piss-ant. **1973** R. HEINLEIN *Time Enough for Love* (1974) 523 His grandfather paused just long enough to look back and say, 'Not on your tintype... you pusillanimous pissant.' **1978** *Guardian Weekly* 25 June 18/4 That pissant [California Governor] Brown. **1979** 'A. HAILEY' *Overload* III. x. 237 All you do now is let off some pissant firecrackers, then laze around here for a goddam month's vacation.

Hence **pi·ssant** *v. intr. Austral. slang*, to mess around.

1945 BAKER *Austral. Lang.* iv. 87 Someone is pissanting around when he is messing about. **1951** CUSACK & JAMES *Come in Spinner* 307, I been pissantin' round the Northern Territory most of the time. **1959** G. HAMILTON *Summer Glare* 138 Struth, you pissant around like a rooster that's too old.

pissed (pist), *ppl. a. slang.* [f. PISS *v.* + -ED[1].] **1.** Drunk, intoxicated. Also const. *up*.

1929 F. MANNING *Middle Parts of Fortune* I. iii. 54 On the Saturday they went into Sandby for a spree, and got properly pissed-up there. **1937** PARTRIDGE *Dict. Slang* 635/2 *Pissed*.., (very) drunk. **1939** DYLAN THOMAS *Let.* July (1966) 233 Both, if you ask me, were pissed. **1957** R. MASON *World of Suzie Wong* II. i. 111 Christ, I'm pissed. I'm pissed as a newt. **1958** K. AMIS *I like it Here* i. 13 An uncle of mine went there a year or two ago and was pissed all the time on about ten bob a day. **1971** B. W. ALDISS *Soldier Erect* 10, I thought of the other blokes in 'A' Company... Tonight, they'd all be getting hopelessly pissed or screwing girls. **1973** M. AMIS *Rachel Papers* 38 'Does it make you extra pissed?' Norman handed me my glass, drank his in one, and crouched again to refill it. **1977** *Daily Mirror* 10 May 1/6 Too much German food and too much German wine. I'm pissed.

2. Angry, irritated; fed-up, depressed. Freq. const. *off*.

1946 *Amer. Speech* XXI. 249 *Pissed-off*... This means roughly, fed-up, irritated, depressed. **1948** N. MAILER *Naked & Dead* (1949) I. ii. 25, I bet you even look pissed-off when you're with your wife. **1955** W. GADDIS *Recognitions* II. vii. 646, I been pissed off at him for five years. **1967** B. WRIGHT tr. *Queneau's Between Blue & Blue* i. 11 I'm beginning to get pissed off with your rotten little questions. **1971** B. MALAMUD *Tenants* 78 The writer figured Willie must still be upset, pissed off, else he would never have left it [*sc.* his typewriter] unprotected. **1971** *It* 9–23 Sept. 11/3 I'm pissed at people in the movement who help lay out the line that I'm a millionaire superstar or other shit. **1972** *Screw* 12 June 16/2 Maye, angered by his new but well-deserved reputation as an insecure male, is pissed. **1973** *Observer* (Colour Suppl.) 15 July 13/3 Young people are getting pissed off with this sort of 'rip-off'. **1974** *Saturday Night* (Toronto) Aug. 20/1 Well, Ken got a little pissed off, and stomped off in a huge sulk, until finally the two of them had it out. **1975** R. BURNS *Alvarez Jrnl.* 8 Helen was pissed off when I called. She had plans or something. **1977** *Rolling Stone* 19 May 63/1 Hamilton.. says half the Cabinet is pissed at him because things are moving so slow. **1977** *Spare Rib* July 37/2 Everyone was pissed-off and disillusioned with conferences after London.

pisser. Add: **2.** *coarse slang.* The penis; the female pudenda; *spec.* in phr. *to pull a person's pisser*, to pull his leg, befool him.

1901 FARMER & HENLEY *Slang* V. 214/2 *Pisser* = (1) the *penis*, and (2) the female *pudendum*. **1969** J. WAINWRIGHT *Big Tickle* 123 'I don't know where he is.' 'If you're pulling my pisser!' 'I'm not.' **1971** B. W. ALDISS *Soldier Erect* 37 He was pulling your pisser, Wal. Malaria's no worse than a cold to the Wogs, is it, Bamber? *Ibid.* 133 He grabbed my arm. 'You think I'm pulling your pisser, man? Listen, *pick your officer*! They're fucking human, same as you, you know!'

3. *slang* (orig. *U.S.*). An extraordinary person or thing; now usu. a difficult or distasteful event, an unpleasant person; also in weakened sense, a bloke, chap.

1943 *Amer. Speech* XVIII. 45 As they [*sc.* New Yorkers] use it, 'pisser' denotes a wag or 'card', a 'corker', or a screamingly funny joke or prank, a 'hot one'. **1954** J. A. WEINGARTEN *Amer. Dict. Slang* 276/1 *Pisser*,..a thing or person of extraordinary aspect; an amusing thing or person. **1974** J. ANTHOINE in H. MacInnes *Climb to Lost World* x. 166, I could have gone a real pisser but, as I dropped, I caught the edge of the rock with my hands and heaved myself up. **1975** tr. *Melchior's Sleeper Agent* (1976) II. 69 The old pisser had not got away! *Ibid.* 98 We could both do with a little liquid cheer. It's been a pisser of a day. **1978** *Maledicta* II. 268, I love it! It's a real pisser!

pi·ssing, *a.* and *adv. slang.* [f. PISS *v.* + -ING[2].] **A.** *adj.* Paltry, insignificant; brief. **B.** *adv.* As an intensive: exceedingly, abominably, 'bloody'. Hence **pi·ssingly** *adv.*

1937 PARTRIDGE *Dict. Slang* 635/2 *Pissing*, adj., paltry, brief. **1971** B. W. ALDISS *Soldier Erect* 180 In this teeming world [in Calcutta], nothing was what it seemed to be. The miseries of the idiot and his dependants were pissingly funny. **1974** K. MILLETT *Flying* (1975) III. 294 Paper hat leaps on stage, pissing hot to talk. **1975** N. FREELING *What are Bugles blowing For?* xxi. 123 'Fuck it,' said Metcalfe angrily. 'I'm only a pissing sergeant.' **1979** P. WAY *Sunrise* i. 10 'Pissing awful weather,' said Don.

‖ **pissoir** (pisw*ā*r). [Fr.] A public urinal enclosed by a screen or wall.

1919 MENCKEN *Amer. Lang.* 127 The French *pissoir*.. is still regarded as indecent in America, and is seldom used in England, but it has gone into most of the Continental languages. **1934** S. SPENDER *Vienna* ii. 23 In oil-tarred pissoirs. **1942** [see *FLY *sb.*[2] 4 a]. **1955** W. GADDIS *Recognitions* I. ii. 77 The feet showing below the shield of the pissoir. **1968** *Listener* 21 Mar. 369/3 A simple slate pissoir where graffiti, true to the spirit of Rochdale, divide between sex and politics. **1972** *Guardian* 19 Feb. 8/3 One pissoir is plain anti-feminism. **1975** *Times* 17 Dec. 13/1 The valuable site..has been vacant for many years and its use is restricted to private parking and to pissoirs of inelegant design.

piss-pot. (Later examples.)

1942 E. PAUL *Narrow St.* xxix. 269 They had wandered into a slum where frequently the housewives dumped pisspots out of the windows. **1948** E. POUND *Pisan Cantos* (1949) lxxx. 104 His helmet is used for a pisspot. **1972** *Daily Tel.* 5 May 12/3 His low-life characters empty the occasional piss-pot and there is a fine flamboyant parade of pretty whores. **1974** *Times Lit. Suppl.* 19 Apr. 417/4 Malcolm [Lowry]..reached the abyss of alcoholic degradation, drinking in prison out of a pisspot.

piss-up (pi·sʊp). *coarse slang.* [f. PISS *v.*; cf. *pissed-up* s.v. *PISSED *ppl. a.* 1.] **1.** = *COCK-UP 4.

1950 H. E. GOLDIN *Dict. Amer. Underworld Lingo* 158/1 *Piss-up*, n., a fiasco; a bungled or unremunerative crime. **1969** R. ESSER *Hot Potato* 51 Just what a pissy-arsed bugger like you would say... You mean it might be one hell of a piss-up.

2. A bout of heavy drinking.

1952 *Landfall* VI. 222 His first 'piss-up' is a landmark in his life. **1959** *Numbers* Feb. 32, I feel like a good piss-up. **1965** R. JEFFRIES *Traitor's Crime* x. 131 How about a piss-up? Anne was only saying yesterday I'd been sober for so long was I declining into my old age? **1973** *Nation Rev.* (Melbourne) 31 Aug. 1441/6 Most significant..was the way the seating was arranged at the Saturday night pissup. **1976** P. CAVE *High Flying Birds* iii. 45 There was the prospect of a piss-up in the offing.

pissy (pi·si), *a. coarse slang.* [f. PISS *sb.* + -Y[1].] Of or pertaining to urine; *fig.* rubbishy, inferior. So *pissy-arsed* adj. (see quot. 1961); also, as a term of general abuse.

1926 T. E. LAWRENCE *Seven Pillars* (1935) x. cxviii. 642 That hot pissy aura of thronged men in woollen clothes. **1961** PARTRIDGE *Dict. Slang* Suppl. 1224/1 *Pissy-arsed*, prone to crapulous inebriation. **1969** Pissy-arsed [see *PISS-UP 1]. **1972** 'D. CRAIG' *Double Take* xi. 138 Oh, God, these poverty stricken, pissy shoes. **1973** M. AMIS *Rachel Papers* 127 You'll probably say this is rather..pissy, but babies are the only things women can have that men can't. **1974** P. CAVE *Mama* (new ed.) x. 80 It makes you realise what a pissy little island we live on, don't it? **1974** *Black World* Nov. 66 She/rising up stumbling over to the dank pissy restroom. **1979** J. BARNETT *Backfire is Hostile!* iii. 36 That pissy bunch of engineering officers at the bar.

pistachio. Add: Also with pronunc. (pistā·ʃ[i]o). **3.** *pistachio candy*; **pistachio ice, ice-cream,** ice(-cream) containing pistachio nuts; also, ice-cream coloured pistachio green.

1853 MRS. GASKELL *Ruth* III. iv. 140 The days when you first brought me pistachio candy from London. **1868** A. GOUFFÉ tr. *J. Gouffé's Royal Cookery Bk.* xvii. 561 Apricot and Pistachio Ice. **1885** C. E. PASCOE *London Today* iii. 48 The more aristocratic foreign visitors to London..flocked thither [*sc.* to Verrey's restaurant] to eat pistachio ices. **1889** R. WELLS *Pastrycook & Confect. Guide* vii. 65 *Pistachio ice*, blanch and beat until fine the kernels of 6 ozs. of Pistachio nuts [etc.]. **1916** FRANDSEN & MARKHAM *Manuf. Ice Creams* x. 103 Pistachio Ice Cream. **1942** A. L. SIMON *Conc. Encycl. Gastron.* V. 57/1 Pistachio ice-creams..are ice-creams..flavoured with almonds and vanilla and coloured with vegetable dyes as near the pistachio green as possible. **1943** E. M. ALMEDINGEN *Frossia* vi. 228 Do you like pistachio ices—with small almond biscuits? **1972** E. HARGREAVES *Fair Green Weed* i. 13 It's a big rambling place like a block of pistachio ice-cream.

piste[2], **pist.** Add: **a.** (Later example.) Also in extended use.

1964 *Guardian* 20 Oct. 7/2 That other highway, where the giraffe..came down to drink. It is only a *piste* for the big Trans-Af buses. **1967** N. FREELING *Strike Out* 24 The serious part—stables, 'pistes', exercise courts and yards. **1970** *Country Life* 17–24 Dec. 1209/3 For the last few dozen miles..the road is tar laid direct on to the apricot-coloured sand..giving one a choice between the molar-shaking corrugations of the piste itself and the treacherous dunes on either side.

b. *Fencing.* A specially marked-out field of play.

1922 *Glasgow Herald* 20 May 9 Preliminary pools of the individual Military Epée Championship of Europe. The Turney..was fought on linoleum 'pistes'. **1963** *Fencing* ('Know the Game' Ser.) (ed. 4) 24 The area within which fencers may move is restricted. This area is called the 'Piste'. **1971** I. BUTYKAI tr. *Lukovich's Electric Foil Fencing* i. 12 Competitors who had fenced for several years with the ordinary foil, now changed it for the electric device and the pioneering work of the era of electric foil fencing. Many said good-bye to the piste for ever.

c. A track of compacted snow used as a ski- or toboggan-run. Also *attrib.*

1929 E. HEMINGWAY *Farewell to Arms* xxxvii. 299 Tobogganing..requires a special *piste*. You could not toboggan into the streets of Montreux. **1939** W. PRAGER *Skiing* 80 Thus he has an opportunity to construct the Piste. **1950** *Times* 13 Feb. 7/5 Most other races, including world championships, are only a test of piste skiing, a debased and impoverished variant of the real thing. **1955** *Times* 20 Sept. 12/7 Italian engineering..began to work on ski lifts and cable cars..with the result that ..there are..installations taking skiers of every grade to the top of the various pistes. **1959** P. MOYES *Dead Men don't Ski* ii. 24 The lift travels above the *pistes*, or ski runs. **1966** *Daily Tel.* 19 Dec. 9/1 You may never come skimming down the *piste* like a bird, but you can make sure of a second look by choosing the right clothes. **1972** N. FREELING *Long Silence* II. 111 Woodcutters' paths..make good natural *pistes* for Nordic ski. **1977** *Time* 10 Jan. 6/1 The lure of the Cup was enough to bring Austria's five-time winner, Annemarie Moser-Proell, to the *piste* again.

pistic, *a.* Add: **2.** Pertaining to faith or trust rather than to reason; hence *ellipt.* as *sb.*, someone who accepts things simply on trust.

1923 OGDEN & RICHARDS *Meaning of Meaning* ii. 89 The purely verbal systems so characteristic of pistic speculation. **1965** in W. Schneemelcher *New Test. Apocr.* II. xi. 77 The apostolic secret tradition..is accessible not merely to the small circle of a spiritual élite, the 'hylic' and 'psychic' or 'pistic' being excluded on principle, but to all those who have been received into the church..as full Christians.

pistillode (pi·stilǝ͡ud). *Bot.* [f. PISTIL + -ODE.] A rudimentary pistil.

1905 W. E. SAFFORD *Useful Plants of Guam* 259 An imperfect pistil (pistillode) present or lacking. **1975** *Blumea* XXII. 420 The precise configuration of antherodes and pistillodes in relation to other floral parts is likely to prove of considerable taxonomic value.

pistillody. (Earlier and later examples.)

1877 *Jrnl. Linn. Soc.* (*Bot.*) XV. 87 The calyx and corolla remain entirely unchanged in all cases exhibiting pistillody. **1929** *Jrnl. Heredity* XX. 137/1 Leighty and Sando describe and illustrate certain abnormalities in wheat flowers which they call 'Pistillody'... They found the stamens metamorphosed either wholly or partly into carpels.

pistiloid (pi·stiloid), *a. Bot.* Also **pistilloid.** [f. PISTIL + -OID.] Resembling a pistil in shape.

1877 *Jrnl. Linn. Soc.* (*Bot.*) XV. 88 Stamen No. 2..is an unstalked pistilloid body with a short curved hairy style. **1888** G. HENSLOW *Origin Floral Struct.* 291 Pistiloid sepals..have been observed by Mr. Laxton.

pistol, *sb.* Add: **1. d.** *to beat the pistol,* in Athletics, to make a false start (cf. *GUN *sb.* 6 e); *to hold a pistol to* (or *at*) (a person's) *head*: to threaten (a person) in order to induce him to act in a particular way; to issue with an ultimatum; *with a pistol at one's head*: under pressure; while being threatened.

1905 S. CROWTHER *Rowing & Track Athletics* 302 False starts were rarely penalized..and..'beating the pistol' was one of the tricks which less sportsmanlike runners constantly practised. **1917** W. J. LOCKE *Red Planet* iii. 33 The boy was my guest. I had not intended to hold a pistol to his head. **1920** E. H. CLARK *Track Athletics up to Date* vi. 49 Some athletes try to gauge the moment when the starter's finger is curling over the trigger of his pistol and to start just before the pistol is fired, when it is too late for the starter to check his finger. This is called 'beating the pistol'. **1974** 'W. HAGGARD' *Kinsmen* iii. 40 She'd held a pistol at Heale-Mann's respectable head. Do as I wish or face a scandal. **1978** *Times* 14 Mar. 19/2 The [French] Socialists..have an understandable dislike of negotiating with a pistol at their heads.

2. *pistol-pocket* (example), *-practice* (example), *-shape, -toter; pistol-shaped* adj. (example), *-toting* vbl. sb. and ppl. adj.; **pistol flare** = **pistol light*; **pistol-grip** (further examples); (*b*) *transf.* a handle shaped like a pistol-grip; also *attrib.*; **pistol light,** a night-signal or light fired from a special pistol, used by soldiers, etc.; a Very light; **pistol-packing** *ppl. a.* [see *PACK *v.* 9] carrying a pistol; hence *pistol-packer.*

1916 'BOYD CABLE' *Action Front* 26 'Keep the lights blazing,' Rawbon paused to shout to the man with the pistol flares. **1917** 'CONTACT' *Airman's Outings* 227, I laugh and proceed to pass some wire through the pistol-grip. **1958** *Engineering* 28 Mar. 411/3 In addition to the push-button and pistol-grip controls. **1964** S. CRAWFORD *Basic Engin. Processes* i. 13 A tubular frame adjustable hacksaw with the 'pistol-grip' type handle. **1972** *Shooting Times & Country Mag.* 27 May 3/2 (Advt.), Pistolgrip stock with cheekpiece £2 extra. **1974** *Country Life* 17 Jan. 82/3 The standard unit includes a parabole reflector, pistol grip, microphone and carrying kit. **1977** *Western Mail* (Cardiff) 5 Mar. 12/3 (Advt.), Movie camera (pistol-grip) and carrying case. **1916** 'BOYD CABLE' *Action Front* 62 A couple of pistol lights flared upwards. **1929** *Papers Mich. Acad. Sci., Arts & Lett.* X. 315 *Pistol lights,* rockets shot from a pistol. **1944** *Time* 10 July 40/2 The lady that's known as Lou pinched several pokes, but pulled no triggers... No pistol packer, she. **1943** A. DEXTER (*song-title*) Pistol packin' mama. **1948** E. POUND *Pisan Cantos* (1949) lxxvi. 39 The pride of all our D.T.C. was pistol-packin' Burnes. **1972** T. ARDIES *This Suitcase* xviii. 204 The hotel had been taken over by pistol-packing maniacs. **1966** M. AVALLONE *Fat Death* 20 His hands were anchored into the pistol pockets of his grey trousers, throwing back the tails of his form-fitting jacket. **1846** *Punch* XI. 206 Maids-of-all-work learning pistol-practice at the shooting galleries. **1931** E. WENHAM *Domestic Silver* v. 42 Probably one of the most attractive forms of handles is the so-called pistol-shape. **1964** W. L. GOODMAN *Hist. Woodworking Tools* 133 Using the broad-bladed Japanese saw with the pistol-shaped handle. **1905** *Dialect Notes* III. 90 *Pistol-toter,*.. one who habitually carries a pistol. 'Suppress the pistol-toter and the bootlegger.' General. **1914** *Maclean's Mag.* Dec. 56/1 The police force..is so inefficient that 'pistol-toting' after night is common among all classes. **1965** *Economist* 25 Sept. 1215/3 The men of Sinn Fein..are a more interesting study buying large brandies in the border towns for the pistol-toting Protestants of the Royal Ulster Constabulary.

‖**pistolero** (pistǫlē͡ə·ro). [Sp.] In Spain or other Spanish-speaking area; a gunman or gangster. Also *attrib.*

1937 F. BORKENAU *Spanish Cockpit* i. 30 In order to frighten the Catalan bourgeoisie..the Barcelona police actually co-operated with gangs of *pistoleros,* who.. claimed to be revolutionaries. **1939** G. GREENE *Lawless Roads* 19 Mexico remained Catholic: it was the governing class—the politicians and pistoleros only who were anti-Catholic. **1957** P. KEMP *Mine were of Trouble* viii. 152 He had been a wild youth..earning his living in Madrid as a *pistolero* for his political party, the Requetés. **1965** C. D. EBY *Siege of Alcázar* (1966) i. 44 The *pistolero* phase of the rebellion had ended. **1973** C. ALVERSON *Fighting Back* (1978) xiv. 80 You and your red-hot pistoleros got my kid brother nearly killed.

pistolet[1]. Restrict † *Obs.* to sense in Dict. and add: ‖**2.** Pronunc. (pistǫle). Esp. in Belgium, a small bread roll (so called because of its shape).

1853 C. BRONTË *Villette* I. viii. 142 Boarders were.. regaled with..*pistolets au beurre* (rolls) and coffee. *a* **1855** —— *Professor* (1857) I. xiii. 224, I stirred my cup of coffee with a half-pistolet (we never had spoons). **1857** MRS. GASKELL *Life C. Brontë* I. xi. 271 A slight meal of water and *pistolets* (the delicious little Brussels rolls). **1897** G. DU MAURIER *Martian* IV. 185 Breakfasted on a little roll called a pistolet and a cup of coffee. **1961** T. HENROT *Belgium* 189 Small rolls are either *Viennois, miches* or, quaintly, *pistolets.* **1975** T. ALLBEURY *Special Collection* xiv. 95 A basket was filled with bread, from poppy-seed rolls to..grey Minsk pistolets.

pistol-shot. Add: **2.** One who shoots with a pistol.

1949 BLUNDEN *Addresses on Gen. Subjects* 24 He [*sc.* Shelley] was judged a horseman and a pistol-shot equal to his sporting friend Lord Byron. **1979** C. ALLEN *Tales from Dark Continent* vii. 99 A great bayonet fighter and trick pistol shot and a splendid figure.

3. (Further example.)

1942 *Essays & Stud.* XXVII. 59 And this pistol-shot style, bang bang bang, with its absolute certainty of detail, leaving the scraps of picture, like a jigsaw puzzle, for you to fit together.

pi·stol-whip, *v.* orig. and chiefly *U.S.* [f. PISTOL *sb.* + WHIP *v.*] *trans.* To strike (someone) with the butt of a pistol. Also *fig.* Hence **pi·stol-whipping** *vbl. sb.*

1942 BERREY & VAN DEN BARK *Amer. Thes. Slang* §322/5 *Pistol-whip,* to strike with the butt of a pistol. **1952** *Sun* (Baltimore) 4 July 42/8 The two young Negroes pitched into him and the one with the gun pistol-whipped the physician. **1958** J. THOMPSON *Getaway* (1972) iv. 29 The banker lay sprawled on the floor, half-dead from Rudy's pistol-whipping. **1965** J. PHILIPS *Twisted People* I. iv. 88 She'd been subjected to about the worst beating I've ever seen. Pistol whipped is my guess. **1967** *Observer* 23 Apr. 5/3 The British Foreign Secretary had been subjected to 'a pistol-whipping'..from Mr. Walt Rostow in the White House. **1970** K. PLATT *Pushbutton Butterfly* (1971) xi. 132, I remembered the pistol-whipping..and brought my knee up to his face. **1973** G. SIMS *Hunters Point* xiii. 124 He could feel the pain from the pistol-whipping blows he'd taken on his ribs. **1977** J. WAMBAUGH *Black Marble* (1978) xiv. 322 Let a cop get pistol-whipped instead of a clerk.

piston. Add: **4. piston bellows,** bellows in which the draught is supplied by the action of a piston; **piston corer** or **core sampler,** a core sampler consisting of a long weighted cylinder containing at its lower end a piston attached to the lowering cable, devised so that when the cylinder enters the bottom sediments under its own weight the descent of the piston is arrested, and the resulting partial vacuum inside the cylinder causes the pressure of the water to be effective in forcing it into the bottom; **piston drill,** a percussion drill in which the bit is attached to the rod of a piston; **piston engine,** a reciprocating engine, esp. an aircraft engine in which the airscrew is driven by the reciprocating action of pistons; hence **piston-engined** *a.,* powered by this kind of engine; **pistonphone** *Acoustics,* a device for producing known sound pressures by means of a vibrating piston whose motion is precisely measured, used mainly for calibrating microphones; **piston pin,** a pin which secures a piston to its connecting rod in an internal-combustion engine; **piston ring,** a metal ring fitted on a piston to seal the gap between the piston and the cylinder wall; **piston slap,** rocking of a loosely fitting piston against the cylinder wall, or the noise resulting from this.

a **1877** KNIGHT *Dict. Mech.* II. 1717/1 A piston-bellows, formed by boring out the trunks of trees, used by the natives of Madagascar for smelting..iron. **1947** B. KULLENBERG in *Svenska Hydrogr.-Biol. Komm. Skrifter* (*Ser. 3: Hydrogr.*) I. II. 12 The piston core sampler..has been based on a method to procure samples for ground investigations, developed by the Geotechnical Department of the Swedish State Railways. **1956** Piston core-sampler [see *CORE *sb.*[1] 4]. **1959** H. BARNES *Oceanogr. & Marine Biol.* i. 67 In Kullenberg's piston corer the hydrostatic pressure at great depths is utilized to overcome.. friction and to allow very long undisturbed cores to be taken. **1976** *New Scientist* 9 Dec. 576/2 The oceanographers' piston corers that were beginning to recover cores, or columns of mud, from the floor of the deep ocean. [**1901** M. M. KIRKMAN *Locomotive Appliances* 475 (*caption*) Piston air drill for drilling, reaming and tapping on locomotive work.] **1919** R. PEELE *Compressed Air Plant for Mines* (ed. 3) xx. 306 At a large group of mines on the Rand, the complete repair cost of standard piston drills.. averaged $42.00 per 52 shifts. **1967** K. McGREGOR *Drilling of Rock* i. 12, 1860–70..; a commercial piston drill was patented by Burleigh in America. *Ibid.* 13 From these [drop drills] developed..the pneumatic piston drill... These machines were finally obsolete in the early 1920's. **1907** *Engineering* 21 June 829/2 If the turbine requires a screw which is necessarily less efficient than that of the piston engine, it is the fault of the turbine system. *Ibid.,* Ordinary reciprocating, or, to use a shorter word, piston, engines. **1943** G. G. SMITH *Gas Turbines & Jet Propulsion* (ed. 2) vii. 54 Even if free-flying piston engine and compressor units were employed these handicaps would remain. **1960** C. H. GIBBS-SMITH *Aeroplane* xvi. 126 The piston engine reached its apogee in the post-war period with such examples as the Pratt & Whitney 28-cylinder 3,500 h.p. radial. **1971** P. J. McMAHON *Aircraft Propulsion* xi. 311 Mechanical losses in piston engines are high, being up to 25% of the indicated power. **1948** *Jrnl. R. Aeronaut. Soc.* LII. 591/1 The Airspeed Ambassador may be taken as representing the most advanced piston-engined commercial aeroplane of its size yet in prospect. **1974** E. AMBLER *Dr. Frigo* I. 56 For most of those critical three days I was..in piston-engined planes missing connecting flights. **1979** *Daily Tel.* 1 Dec. 10/6 Their departure..coincides with the paying off of the Navy's only remaining steam reciprocating, or piston-engined, ship. **1922** E. WENTE in *Physical Rev.* XIX. 343 (*caption*) Use of pistonphone for calibrating an electrostatic transmitter. *Ibid.* 500 The open-circuit votage of the transmitter per unit of pressure has been measured with the piston-phone for the frequency range of 10 to 200 cycles per second. **1965** C. A. TAYLOR *Physics Mus. Sounds* vi. 100 The pistonphone..appears to be used only for scientific work at very low frequencies. It consists..of a piston driven by a rotating cam which permits the generation of sinusoidal variations in pressure of accurately-controlled form. **1972** *Where* Dec. 336/3 Our tests were done with a B and K portable octave band analyser, which was calibrated before and after each occasion with a pistonphone. **1897** F. GROVER *Pract. Treat. Mod. Gas & Oil Engines* xvii. 175 The pressure on the piston pin may be much more than upon the crank pin. **1910** W. A. TOOKEY tr. *Mathot's Construction & Working of Internal Combustion Engines* xiii. 375 The piston pin is made of the best quality mild steel. **1967** J. L. & G. H. F. NAYLER *Dict. Mech. Engin.* 176 *Gudgeon pin*... Also called 'piston pin'. **1867** N. P. BURGH *Mod. Marine Engin.* vi. 277/2 The adoption of 'springs' behind the 'piston ring' is now becoming general. **1936** *Discovery* Feb. 39/1 Steam leaking past the piston rings of the high-pressure cylinders. **1971** J. H. HAYNES *Mini Owner's Workshop Man.* i. 30/1 To remove the piston rings, slide them carefully over the top of the piston, taking care not to scratch the aluminium alloy. **1976** L. DEIGHTON *Twinkle, Twinkle Little Spy* x. 97 The running repairs I do myself... Last month I changed the piston rings. **1916** P. M. HELDT *Gasoline Automobile* (ed. 4) I. vii. 163 To obviate.. piston slap when starting, it is well to make the piston comparatively long. **1962** *Which? Car Suppl.* Jan. 32/2 A worrying piston-slap rattle from the engine. **1968** *Practical Motorist* Dec. 459/1 *Piston slap,* a characteristic metallic slapping sound within the cylinders caused by slight rocking motion of an ill-fitting or worn piston.

pi·ston, *v.* [f. the sb.] *intr.* To move like a piston. Occas. *trans.,* to direct, throw with a piston-like movement.

1930 R. CAMPBELL *Adamastor* 80 Down the stage the dance..Tarantulates in scarlet tights For flashing arms to piston. **1940** DYLAN THOMAS *Portrait of Artist as Young Dog* 52 The small boy in his invisible engine..kicked the dog's plate at the washhouse stop, and puffed and pistoned slower and slower while the servant girl lowered the pole. **1958** *Spectator* 15 Aug. 219/3 Thin grey knees piston over the beach. **1976** 'E. McBAIN' *Guns* (1977) v. 118 He ..pistoned a short hand punch to her shoulder.

pit, *sb.*[1] Add: **1. h.** = *engine-pit* (*b*) s.v. *ENGINE *sb.* 11 b. Hence used allusively (freq. in *pl.*) of the area at the side of a motor-racing track where competing cars are prepared and maintained.

1839 *Chambers's Edin. Jrnl.* 7 Dec. 368 Under each engine is a pit three feet deep, which enables the engine-men to get underneath to examine and repair it. **1907** [see *INSPECTION 6]. **1912** *Collier's* 28 Sept. 11/1 Up swoops the racer, rear wheels locked and sliding, thundering and veiled in smoke, and stops at the pit. **1913** *Technical World Mag.* June 492/1 As De Palma passed his rival's pit..one of the attendants reached for a telephone. **1924** *Brooklands Gaz.* Oct. 176/2 F. C. Clayton on his Marseal, had to turn into the pits after eight laps. **1928** *Evening News* 18 Aug. 1/3 He was pulling into the pits to refill. **1930** E. WAUGH *Vile Bodies* x. 182 'The pits' turned out to be a line of booths, built of wood and corrugated iron immediately opposite the Grand Stand. Many of the cars had already arrived and stood at their 'pits', surrounded by a knot of mechanics and spectators. **1946** *Sun* (Baltimore) 23 Dec. 17/3 Each will have three long maintenance 'pits' to acccommodate nine busses at one time. **1957** *Times* 16 Oct. 12/6 A man who had a garage and a pit and no car. **1968** *Listener* 5 Sept. 301/3 So there I was, having failed my examinations, working in the pits with Duncan Hamilton. **1972** M. GILBERT *Body of Girl* iv. 44 He climbed out of the pit..and said... 'You've come to buy a car.' **1973** *Times* 30 Apr. 7/1 Peterson's domination ended abruptly on lap 57 when he brought his car to a halt with a broken gearbox, to receive a huge ovation from the crowd when he walked back to the pits. **1977** *Times* 15 July (Motor Racing Suppl.) p. ii/8 Dron pulled his Dolomite into the pits, mistakenly believing the race was over. But..he managed to pass the flag at the end of the pit road in time to win his class.

9. a. Also as an *ellipt.* use for 'armpit'. *slang.*

1965 *Amer. Speech* XL. 194 *Pits,*..a slang abbreviation of the term *armpits,*..with an extension of meaning to entail the idea of body odor. **1973** M. AMIS *Rachel Papers* 71 Complete body-service..pits clipped, toes manicured, pubic hair permed and styled, each tooth brushed, tongue scraped, nose pruned. **1974** E. BRAWLEY *Rap* (1975) II. xx. 325 She opened her heavy flippy arms, arms with rolls of honest fat hanging down under her pits. **1977** *Rolling Stone* 7 Apr. 48/2 Simmons answers by spraying his pits with a can of Royal Copenhagen.

c. (Later examples.)

1914 M. DRUMMOND tr. *Haberlandt's Physiol. Plant Anat.* i. 44 These readily permeable spots generally take the shape of sharply defined areas of approximately circular cross-section, known as pits. **1953** K. ESAU *Plant Anat.* iii. 39 Secondary cell walls are commonly characterized by the presence of depressions or cavities... Such cavities are termed pits. **1976** BELL & COOMBE tr. *Strasburger's Textbk. Bot.* (rev. ed.) 110 If transversely elongated pits are arranged one above the other in the lateral walls the arrangement is said to be scalariform.

10. a. (Later example.)

1922 W. S. MAUGHAM *On Chinese Screen* xlvii. 186 Declaiming the blank verse of Sheridan Knowles with an emphasis to rouse the pit to frenzy.

b. = *orchestra pit* s.v. *ORCHESTRA 4.

1961 in WEBSTER. **1966** *Listener* 6 Oct. 517/1 The sheer sound of the orchestra seemed very much bigger than usual, the strings had a bloom that is often lacking, the woodwind sweetness as well as precision; ensemble had improved, including rapport between stage and pit. **1974** *Belton* (S. Carolina) *News* 18 Apr. 1/2 Hanna High Jazz Ensemble (In the pit throughout the show). **1975** *Times* 17 Sept. 10/4 On the evenings he conducted the sound coming from the pit ranged from the good to the superlative. **1977** *New Yorker* 9 May 132/3 (It is said that Toscanini was the first to sink the pit at La Scala.) The Orpheum, where the Boston 'Rigoletto' was done, has no pit, either.

12. b. A pocket in a garment. *slang.*

1811 *Lexicon Balatronicum* s.v. *Pit*, He drew a rare thimble from the swell's pit. He took a handsome watch from the gentleman's pocket. **1927** *Dialect Notes* V. 459 *Pit*, a pocket. **1938** F. D. SHARPE *Sharpe of Flying Squad* 332 *The pit*, the inside jacket pocket. **1950** H. E. GOLDIN *Dict. Amer. Underworld Lingo* 158/2 *Pit* (among pickpockets), the vest pocket; or, less frequently, the inside breast pocket of coat. **1955** D. W. MAURER in *Publ. Amer. Dial. Soc.* xxiv. 125 The most important pocket in the coat from the pickpocket's point of view is the *coat pit*, or the inside breast pocket... This is often shortened to *pit*. **1966** BAKER *Austral. Lang.* (ed. 2) vii. 143 A generation ago,..the various pockets were known as.. *left kick* or *pit* and *right kick* or *pit* (trouser pockets).

14. (In sense 6) *pit-boot, -bottle, -boy* (earlier example), *-clothes, -coat, committee, -dirt, -girl* (earlier examples), *-horse, -lad* (examples), *-manager, -pony* (further examples), *-singlet, -trousers, -village, -woman* (example); (in sense 10) *pit-band, -bandsman, -door, -doorkeeper, -orchestra, -stall, -ticket*; **pit aperture** *Bot.*, an opening on the inner surface of a secondary cell wall, forming the entrance to a pit cavity; **pit-bank** (earlier and later examples); also *attrib.*; **pit bull (terrier)**, a small, stocky, short-coated dog belonging to the American breed so called, usually fawn or brindled in colour, with white markings; also used as a name for the Staffordshire bull terrier, which belongs to a closely related breed; **pit canal** *Bot.*, a channel in the secondary cell wall of a bordered pit, leading to the pit cavity; **pit-cave** *Archæol.* (see quot. 1921); **pit-cavity** *Bot.*, the space within a simple pit, extending from the primary cell wall to the aperture bordering the cell lumen; **pit chamber** *Bot.*, the hemispherical space between the primary and secondary cell walls of a bordered pit; **pit-comb** *Archæol.*, used *attrib.* to designate pottery decorated with rows of indentations and comb-patterns; **pit dog** = **pit bull terrier*; **pit field** *Bot.*, a depression or group of depressions in a primary cell wall; **pit-head** (later *attrib.* examples); **pit-lamp** *Canad.*, a miner's lamp; also *transf.*, a lamp used in hunting or fishing, a jack-lamp (see JACK *sb.*[1] 33); also as *v. trans.*, to hunt (deer, etc.) using a pit-lamp (also *absol.*); so **pit-lamping** *vbl. sb.*; **pit-lighting** *vbl. sb. Canad.* = *pit-lamping* above; **pit membrane** *Bot.*, the part of a cell wall covering a pit; **pit organ**, a small depression acting as a receptor sensitive to changes in temperature, found on each side of the head of snakes belonging to the subfamily Crotalinæ; **pit-pair** *Bot.*, two pits in adjacent cell walls, sharing the same pit membrane; **pit-planting**, a method of planting trees in which a hole is dug, and the roots settled over a mound of earth in the bottom of the hole before it is refilled; also, planting trees in small depressions which help to conserve moisture; **pit-saw** (earlier and later examples); also *attrib.* and as *v. trans.*, to cut (timber) with a pit-saw (also *absol.*); **pit-sawing** *vbl. sb.*; **pit-sawn** *ppl. a.*; **pit-sawyer** (examples); **pit silo**, a silo in the form of a pit (rather than a tower); so **pit silage**, silage made in a pit; **pit stop**, in motor-racing, a stop at a pit (sense *1 h) for refuelling, maintenance, etc., usu. during a race; also *transf.* and *fig.*; **pit tip**, the mass of waste material deposited near the mouth of a mine or pit; **pit trap** = sense 1 f; **pit wood** (earlier and later examples); **pit yacker, yakker** *dial.*, a coal miner.

1934 *Jrnl. Arnold Arboretum* XV. 334 The narrow inner and outer layers of the secondary wall come together in the rim formed about the pit-aperture. **1953** K. ESAU *Plant Anat.* iii. 44 The circular pit apertures in a bordered pit-pair appear exactly opposite each other. **1967** S. BROIDO-ALTMAN tr. *Fahn's Plant Anat.* ii. 36 The opening of the pit on the inner side of the cell wall..is called the pit aperture. **1942** BERREY & VAN DEN BARK *Amer. Thes. Slang* § 576/23 *Pit band*.., a theatre orchestra. **1946** R. BLESH *Shining Trumpets* (1949) xii. 280 The other side..is completely in the manner of the average musical comedy pit band of the 1920's. **1977** *Rolling Stone* 19 May 74/3 At 14 I got a job in a pit band in a cinema. **1959** 'F. NEWTON' *Jazz Scene* xi. 189 The despised pit-bandsmen and light musicians. **1870** A. J. MUNBY *Diary* 25 June in D. Hudson *Munby* (1972) 288 'I've worked on pit bonk most o' my days', said an Oakengates lassie. **1930** AUDEN *Poems* 67 Head-gears gaunt on grass-grown pit-banks. **1968** *Listener* 15 Aug. 205/3 Each plane came in over the long pit-bank mountain. **1894** H. PEASE *Mark o' Deil* 26 H tried to shift it, an' threw his pit boots at it. **1913** D. H. LAWRENCE *Sons & Lovers* i. 25 She..set his pit-boots beside them. *Ibid.*, She..rinsed his pit-bottle. *a* **1930** —— *Phoenix II* (1968) 263, I, who remember the homeward trooping of the colliers when I was a boy,..the red mouths and the quick whites of the eyes, the swinging pit bottles, and the strange voices of men from the underworld. **1863** *Edin. Rev.* Apr. 424 It is to be hoped these schools will be continued for the purpose of improving the very imperfect scholarship of future pit-boys. **1945** *Sun* (Baltimore) 18 May 7/5 Mrs. Dorella Zinke..died within 90 minutes after a mass attack by nine pit bull terriers. **1968** K. WEATHERLY *Roo Shooter* 128 It was the rat-catching trick of the old pit bull terriers: one savage jerk of the dog's head and the big tom flew high in the air. **1974** R. THOMAS *Porkchoppers* xxix. 245 He held a leash that was attached to an aged English pit bull that waddled..and wheezed. **1976** *Honolulu Star-Bull.* 21 Dec. F-8/8 (Advt.), Pit Bull Pups, 8 wks. **1953** K. ESAU *Plant Anat.* iii. 43 The border divides the cavity into the pit chamber..and the pit canal, the passage from the cell lumen into the pit chamber. **1967** S. BROIDO-ALTMAN tr. *Fahn's Plant Anat.* ii. 40 The pit canal between the inner and outer apertures becomes longer. **1921** *Discovery* Feb. 33/1 Still another kind [of grave]..is known as the 'pit-cave'. This was made by first sinking a pit and then cutting out the tomb in the form of a side-recess from the bottom of the pit. **1925** V. G. CHILDE *Dawn European Civilization* vi. 92 Beside the pit-caves and chamber-tombs excavated in the clay or rock, megalithic graves were erected just in the heel of Italy. **1939** J. D. S. PENDLEBURY *Archaeol. Crete* iv. 242 At Zapher Papoura both the shaft grave and the pit cave continue in use. **1914** M. DRUMMOND tr. *Haberlandt's Physiol. Plant Anat.* i. 44 The adjoining pit-cavities are separated only by the thin primary closing-membrane. **1953** K. ESAU *Plant Anat.* iii. 41 In the bordered pit the secondary wall arches over the pit cavity. **1970** PANSHIN & DE ZEEUW *Textbk. Wood Technol.* (ed. 3) I. iii. 93 The pit cavity is the entire space within the wall recess, between the pit membrane and the lumen. **1953** Pit chamber [see *pit canal* above]. **1967** S. BROIDO-ALTMAN tr. *Fahn's Plant Anat.* ii. 40 As the walls continue to thicken the pit chamber becomes smaller. **1873** A. J. MUNBY *Diary* 11 Sept. in D. Hudson *Munby* (1972) 343 Ellen herself came out of the kitchen; and she was in her pit clothes, as she had promised. **1913** D. H. LAWRENCE *Sons & Lovers* i. 5 She..put his pit-clothes on the hearth to warm. **1937** 'G. ORWELL' *Road to Wigan Pier* iii. 37 At the baths he has two lockers where he can keep his pit clothes separate from his day clothes. **1974** *Times* 1 Feb. 19/4 When a man arrives at the colliery to work his shift he first changes into his pit clothes. **1913** D. H. LAWRENCE *Sons & Lovers* iii. 49 He had taken off his pit-coat. **1954** Pit-comb ware [see *CORD *sb.*[1] 12]. **1957** V. G. CHILDE *Dawn European Civilization* (ed. 6) xi. 204 From Sweden to Siberia indeed all pots were manufactured by the same technique of ring-building, all taper downward to a rounded base and all may be decorated with rows of pits, frequently combined with zones of comb impressions. The whole ceramic family is therefore termed 'pit-comb ware'. **1967** *Antiquaries' Jrnl.* XLVII. 203 For Fox in 1924, the most obvious comparison was the North European Neolithic pottery, Baltic and more Eastern, called 'pit-comb ware' or Pitted ware, on which ornament includes quite similar pits, in one or several rows. **1920** *Act* 10 & 11 *Geo. V* c. 50 § 7 It shall not be necessary to constitute a pit committee for any mine which is a small mine within the meaning of the Coal Mines Act, 1911. **1928** *Britain's Industr. Future* (Liberal Industr. Inquiry) IV. 266 Open consultation in the [coal] industry should be secured by the establishment of Pit Committees, District Boards, and a National Mining Council. **1913** D. H. LAWRENCE *Sons & Lovers* iv. 70 Here sat the colliers in their pit-dirt. **1914** —— *Widowing of Mrs. Holroyd* III. 79 He's in his pit-dirt. **1945** C. L. B. HUBBARD *Observer's Bk. Dogs* 202 Pit Bull Terrier. Pit Dog. About the end of the eighteenth century..dog-fighting became the new sport... A breed of Bull Terrier was created which became the fore-runner of the present-day Staffordshire Bull Terrier. **1951** J. F. GORDON *Staffordshire Bull Terrier* ii. 23 The Pit Dog, Pit Bull Terrier or Stafford..achieved some measure of emancipation from his gladiatorial background. **1667** PEPYS *Diary* 22 May (1974) VIII. 232 But here Knipp spied me out of the tiring-room, and came to the pit door: and I out to her and kissed her. *a* **1828** J. BERNARD *Retrospections of Stage* (1830) I. ii. 45 It was his general practice to take the money at the pit-door. **1894** G. B. SHAW *Let.* 30 Apr. (1965) I. 433 A man who thinks a dramatic performance worth waiting at the pit door all day for is a lunatic. **1831** J. BOADEN in *Private Corr. David Garrick* I. p. xxxvi, For the benefit of his father, the pit-door keeper, and others. **1855** W. B. WOOD *Personal Recoll. Stage* i. 40 My keeper, Mr H., was at this time pit door-keeper at the Chestnut Street Theatre. **1934** *Jrnl. Arnold Arboretum* XV. 332 Cambial walls are characterized by having more or less numerous plasmodesmata which may be..aggregated in thinner areas of the walls, i.e. in so-called primary pit-fields. **1953** K. ESAU *Plant Anat.* iii. 39 Only the secondary walls have pits, whereas the primary walls have primary pit fields. **1976** BELL & COOMBE tr. *Strasburger's Textbk. Bot.* (rev. ed.) 63 Where the pit fields are oval or elongated, the bordered pits take on a similar shape. **1863** *Edin. Rev.* Apr. 436 The pit-girls are not less fond of holidays than their fathers. *Ibid.* 437 Much may be done to improve the condition of the poor pit-girl. **1866** A. J. MUNBY *Diary* 15 May in D. Hudson *Munby* (1972) 225 Some large coal manager who was strongly in favour of female labour told him the pitgirls were 'mules, not women'. **1915** *Political Q.* May 117 A maximum pit-head price might leave much of the home market in the same condition. **1928** *Daily Chron.* 9 Aug. 5/4 From September 1 pit head prices will be raised by 1s. a ton. **1937** 'G. ORWELL' *Road to Wigan Pier* iii. 37 At some of the larger and better appointed collieries there are pithead baths. **1967** A. L. LLOYD *Folk Song in England* v. 335 The miners ..before the days of pithead baths..appeared in daylight with black faces. **1974** *Times* 4 Jan. 12/8 If a pithead ballot were held..Yorkshire miners would vote..in favour of stoppage. **1976** *Evening Post* (Nottingham) 15 Dec. 1/2 In the pithead ballot, 78 per cent of miners who voted turned down the Coal Board's offer. **1913** D. H. LAWRENCE *Sons & Lovers* vii. 172 Jimmy, who had been a pit-horse. **1862** *Cornh. Mag.* Mar. 351 Files of pitmen and groups of pit-lads are now dotting all the roads. **1912** W. OWEN *Let.* 24 July (1967) 151 This pit-lad is wrestling with a Class-book of Physics. **1901** *Daily Colonist* (Victoria, B.C.) 1 Oct. 6/1 One Indian shot as many as 47 [deer] in one night at Ahatassett, using a pit lamp. **1906** *Ibid.* 30 Jan. 6/2 The only light he [*sc.* a coal miner] has is a smoky pit-lamp —a cotton wick soaked in fish oil. **1921** *Ibid.* 30 Oct. 13/4 The rescue parties had to find their way about with candles and pit lamps, great difficulty resulting. **1967** *Vancouver Province* 21 Feb. 19/6 Stanton said his association wants to commend the fisheries department for banning 'pit lamps' but believes the order should be made permanent. **1967** *Wildlife Rev.* (Victoria, B.C.) Mar. 27/2 Frank Greenfield..once jailed a man for pitlamping deer. **1924** R. S. SHERMAN *Mother Nature Stories* 61 Pit-lamping and hunting with dogs, in addition to natural enemies..have been the cause of its rapid disappearance. **1957** A. R. BARRATT *Coronets & Buckskin* 45 That there Blotton had me arrested for pitlamping. **1969** *Daily Colonist* (Victoria, B.C.) 7 Dec. 20/2 Pitlamping on Gabriola Island cost two men $500 each when they pleaded guilty..in court. **1969** *Islander* (Victoria, B.C.) 14 Sept. 10/3 Before dawn one morning, two shots were heard from the direction of his cabin, but no one paid any attention as pitlighting was common practice. **1913** D. H. LAWRENCE *Sons & Lovers* i. 16 He could only abuse the pit-managers. **1976** *Daily Tel.* 20 July 2/3 Harry Widowson, 57, pit manager of Mount Vernon Road, Barnsley. **1913** *Forestry Q.* XI. 15 The delicate pit membranes were ruptured by the shrinkage of the cell walls in drying. **1953** K. ESAU *Plant Anat.* iii. 41 The pit membrane is common to both pits of a pair. **1976** BELL & COOMBE tr. *Strasburger's Textbk. Bot.* (rev. ed.) 63 Bordered pits, especially amongst the Coniferae, are often furnished with a thickening in the middle of the pit membrane. **1927** *Melody Maker* Aug. 767/3 Whether this is because the dancers or singers think a modern dance band is a more enhancing support than a piano or the pit orchestra—which, of course, it is—or whether it is the band which decides.., I know not. **1934** S. R. NELSON *All about Jazz* i. 27 The atmosphere of the cinema pit-orchestra or military band. **1937** Pit organ [see *NEUROMAST]. **1976** *Nature* 3 June 441/1 He did more classic work on the pit-organ of rattlesnakes, where he demonstrated the exquisite thermal sensitivity of this receptor. **1933** *Tropical Woods* XXXVI. 5 Pit-pair.—Two complementary pits of adjacent cells. **1953** K. ESAU *Plant Anat.* iii. 41 Two pits are combined into a paired structure, the pit-pair. **1970** PANSHIN & DE ZEEUW *Textbk. Wood Technol.* (ed. 3) I. iii. 93 Pit pairs may be made up from similar pits to form bordered pit pairs or simple pit pairs. **1898** C. E. CURTIS *Pract. Forestry* (ed. 2) viii. 47 When planting deeper soils ..pit-planting must be adopted. **1931** *Forestry* V. 18 No method is fool-proof, but pit-planting appears to be the safest. **1970** H. L. EDLIN *Collins Guide Tree Planting & Cultivation* i. 110 Failures in pit planting nearly always arise from insufficient firming-up. **1917** R. HODGSON *Poems* 27 Wretched, blind pit ponies. **1938** G. GREENE *Brighton Rock* I. iii. 55 White hair, grey face, short-sighted pit pony eyes. **1978** A. PRICE *'44 Vintage* xix. 219 Audley was like a racehorse down a coal mine, desperately pretending to be a pit pony. **1679** in *Rec. Court of New Castle on Delaware* (1904) 361 An Iron sledge and a hand saw Iron—one Pit Saw. **1848** [see *CROSS-CUT *sb.* 5]. **1879** *Lumberman's Gaz.* 15 Oct. 5/1 An improvement over the gate saw, almost as great as was the gate over the pit saw. *Ibid.*, Two men..maintained a pit saw mill. **1930** L. G. D. ACLAND *Early Canterbury Runs* (ser. 1) ix. 219, I should think this will be the last pit-saw to be used in Canterbury. **1960** B. CRUMP *Good Keen Man* 66 A shack that he and his brother had built from timber they'd pit-sawn themselves 30 years before. **1965** F. RUSSELL *Secret Islands* v. 76 'This was where we pitsawed,' he said doubtfully. **1974** P. W. BLANDFORD *Country Craft Tools* vi. 91 Pit saws are still made in Britain for use in some African countries. **1908** E. J. BANFIELD *Confessions of Beachcomber* I. ii. 57, I began to be thankful that pit-sawing was not forced upon me as a profession in the days of inexperienced youth. **1965** F. RUSSELL *Secret Islands* v. 76 Pitsawing is the most brutal physical work a man could do. **1946** *Nature* 17 Aug. 245/1 Apart from the pit-sawn timber used locally, the pit-sawn timber supplies handled by the Department through its numerous subcontractors totalled 1,060,000 cu.ft. **1965** M. SHADBOLT *Among Cinders* xii. 98 He built the house with pit-sawn kauri. **1978** O. WHITE *Silent Reach* xx. 228 The Silent Reach homestead was..primitive. Its exterior walls were of wedge-split or pit-sawn plants. **1941** *Beaver* June 38 *Pitsawyer*, in earlier years, an important and indispensable craftsman. To him was due the production of every inch of sawn lumber for the building of the posts and water craft. **1946** *Nature* 17 Aug. 245/1 An exacting specification impossible for pit-sawyers to fulfil and other difficulties were experienced. **1968** J. ARNOLD *Shell Bk. Country Crafts* 86 Pit sawyers, it seems, were a race much on their own, uncommunicative and perhaps brutish. **1887** H. E. P. CLINTON *Treat. Ensilage* 56 The quality of the material is certainly superior in many cases to pit silage.

1951 WATSON & SMITH *Silage* vi. 95 (*heading*) Making of pit silage. **1886** R. S. BURN *Systematic Small Farming* xx. 252 While the retaining or enclosing walls of the above-ground silo should not be less than nine inches, the lining walls of the pit silo may be very much thinner. **1947** *New Biol.* III. 45 A pit silo is merely a trench dug in the ground to convenient dimensions and, if properly drained, the wastage in these pits is less than that commonly experienced in many tower silos. **1966** WEBSTER & WILSON *Agric. in Tropics* xiii. 292 Ensilage of these grasses in either pit or tower silos presents no real difficulties, and is commonly the best way to preserve fodder for use in the dry season, but it involves some losses. **1913** D. H. LAWRENCE *Sons & Lovers* ii. 28 He..put on his pit-singlet. **1920** —— *Phoenix* (1936) 9 Once more the rabbit was wrapped in the old pit-singlet. **1858** *Times* 22 Dec. 7/6 The part nearest the orchestra is railed off for three rows of orchestra stalls,..and gives the same dimensions for perfect comfort to the occupant as is afforded by the pit-stalls at Covent-garden. Behind these are four rows of pit-stalls, the charge for each of which is only 2s.; while admission to the body of the pit will be reduced to 1s. 6d. **1861** DICKENS *Uncomm. Trav.* iv. 43 A pit at sixpence, boxes and pit-stalls at a shilling, and a few private boxes at half-a-crown. **1961** BOWMAN & BALL *Theatre Lang.* 260 *Pit stall*, in British terminology, a stall in the front rows of the pit. **1932** S. C. H. DAVIS *Motor Racing* v. 72 Pit stop. **1942** BERREY & VAN DEN BARK *Amer. Thes. Slang* § 728/1 *Pit stop*, a stop for oil and gas &c. during a race. **1970** *Globe & Mail* (Toronto) 28 Sept. 22/4 Revson, forced to a pit stop on the 10th lap of the 210-mile race, easily beat out Ferrari's Jim Adams for third place. **1972** *Times* 15 June 4/4 The inner harbour is a huge nautical pit-stop. **1973** 'E. FENWICK' *Last of Lysandra* xx. 136 His wife..was relieved and pleased to see him, until she understood this was only a pit-stop. **1977** *Time* 4 July 36/1 A pit stop is called for. Time to eat and run. **1762** in G. O. Seilhamer *Hist. Amer. Theatre* (1888) I. xiv. 139 Pit tickets sold at the door, 146 at 5s. **1786** J. WOODFORDE *Diary* 26 June (1926) II. 253 For 3 Pit Tickets at the Circus 1 pd o. 9. o. **1829** H. FOOTE *Compan. to Theatres* 94 Boxes may be engaged for the night, or season; and pit tickets purchased for 8s 6d. **1864** D. G. ROSSETTI *Let.* 5 July (1965) II. 513 He will reserve for me his two pit tickets for *Mirella* tonight. **1883** W. S. GRESLEY *Gloss. Terms Coal Mining* 189 *Pit-tip*, a bank or heap upon which rubbish out of the mine is tipped. **1907** *Westm. Gaz.* 13 Apr. 10/1 In the Black Country may be seen birches growing luxuriantly on a pit-tip. **1920** A. FAY *Gloss. Mining & Mineral Industry* 516/2 *Pit tip* (Eng.), a bank or heap upon which mine waste is tipped or dumped. **1895** KIPLING *Second Jungle Bk.* 20 It was a pointed stick, such as they set in the mouth of a pit-trap. *c* **1909** D. H. LAWRENCE *Collier's Friday Night* (1934) iii. 76 His pit-watch that the Mother hung there when she put his pit-trousers in the cupboard. **1913** —— *Sons & Lovers* ii. 27 He..struggled into his pit-trousers. **1862** *Cornh. Mag.* Mar. 352 Pit villages..vary much in their character for cleanliness. **1957** R. FRANKENBERG *Village on Border* i Reviewers have..stressed the novelty of..information ..about a pit-village in Yorkshire. **1967** A. L. LLOYD *Folk Song in England* v. 333 The keelmen..joined with the colliers' communities in dances on the pit-village green. **1978** *Peace News* 25 Aug. 10/3 When I first came across the *Manual* I was visiting people in a budding action group on a pit village council estate. **1860** A. J. MUNBY *Diary* 29 Sept. in D. Hudson *Munby* (1972) 76 A photograph of a pitwoman in costume. **1841** C. H. HARTSHORNE *Salopia Antiqua* 532 *Pit wood*, wood which is thus called generally runs from three feet six inches to four feet in length, and is very thick. It is used for supporting the roof of a coal pit. **1886** F. T. ELWORTHY *West Somerset Word-Bk.* 577 *Pit-wood*.., larch or other wood cut into lengths for supporting 'the roof' in coal-mines. **1922** W. SCHLICH *Man. Forestry* (ed. 4) I. 81 It has been shown that during the period 1909–1913, the average annual consumption of timber and pit-wood amounted to about 11 million loads. **1971** *Timber Trades Jrnl.* 21 Aug. 24/1 Output of home-produced pit-wood..fell to its lowest level since 1951. **1961** *Spectator* 29 Dec. 957 Pit-Yacker... This is the autobiography of a man brought up in..the seaport mining town of Seaham, County Durham. **1974** S. DOBSON *Geordie Dict.* 72 A *pit yakker* is the Geordie term for a pitman. Possibly from *yak* or *yark* meaning to pull out (coals).

pit, *sb.*² Add: Also *S. Afr.* Also, a pip. (Further and later examples.)

1873 W. MATTHEWS *Getting on in World* 26 One man may suck an orange and be choked by a pit, another swallow a penknife and live. **1913** C. PETTMAN *Africanderisms* 375 Pit... This word is in common use in South Africa as a name for the stones of fruit. **1951** J. STEINBECK *Burning Bright* i. 8 The bitter seed that's like the inside of a peach pit. **1972** 'E. LATHEN' *The Longer the Thread* x. 93 She called him an avocado without a pit. **1977** *H. E. V. Pickstone's Catal.* (S. Afr.) 9 The fruit [*sc.* a peach] is yellow to reddish yellow, the flesh is deep orange coloured right through to the pit.

2. *S. Afr.* An edible seed, esp. a pine-nut.

1947 [see *DENNEBOL].

pit, *v.* Add: **6.** Of a driver in a motor race: to stop at a pit (*PIT *sb.*¹ 1 h) for fuel or maintenance.

1967 *Autocar* 5 Oct. 39/3 Mike Spence was in the seventh place..when he pitted on lap 36 with sudden engine trouble. **1976–7** *Sea Spray* (N.Z.) Dec./Jan. 58/1 Gray drove a steady, sensible race, pitting half-way through to take on 164 litres of gas in just 45 seconds. **1978** 'D. RUTHERFORD' *Collision Course* 62 The rain came bucketing down... There was nothing for it but to pit, fit rain tyres and splosh cautiously round.

pita² (pī·tă). Also **peeta, pitah, pitta.** [ad. mod. Gr. πήττα, πίτ(τ)α bread, cake, pie, perh. f. Gr. πεπτ-ός cooked, f. πέσσειν, πέττ-, to cook, bake. Cf. Turk. *pide*, Heb. *pittah* in similar senses.] A thick flat bread of the kind common in Mediterranean and Arab countries, usu. cut open and filled with a meat or other filling. Also *attrib.*

1951, 1963 [see *FELAFEL]. **1964** M. DUNCAN *Cooking Greek Way* 212 Pita Yaourtiou, Yoghurt cake. *Ibid.* 213 The pita at this [dough] stage should be about 2 inches thick. **1965** R. HOWE *Balkan Cooking* 136 Pita is made in the same manner as Austrian struedel and its success depends entirely on the paper-like thinness of the pastry. **1967** A. BAILEY in L. Deighton *London Dossier* 56 A bread called 'pita' that looks like an oven glove and is usually stuffed with meat, raw onions and tomatoes. **1970** *Times* 29 Apr. 18/4 With your souvlakia you will get pitta, excellent flat round bread. **1971** D. MEIRING *Wall of Glass* xi. 87 They had..eaten pita and humus..in the Arab restaurants in the port. **1974** *Times* 4 May 11/2 The Continental..on the Charing Cross Road..offers..warm Greek pitta stuffed with turkey. **1975** *Jewish Chron.* 18 July (Food & Wine Suppl.) p. iii/2 A pita—the flat Arab style bread—is split open, a few of the falafel balls stuffed in. **1976** *Islander* (Victoria, B.C.) 1 Aug. 4/1 (*caption*) Phyliss buying fallafel and pita in Jerusalem. **1977** *National Observer* (U.S.) 8 Jan. 12/3, I made my own pita bread, the flat chewy Arab bun that can be cut in half and stuffed with any number of goodies. **1978** *Lancashire Life* Apr. 71/3 We were tackling the first course... For me that was taramosalata, a puree of smoked cod roe, olive oil and lemon juice which had a most distinctive tang; it was served with a great quantity of pitta bread and was quite different from the last taramosalata I tasted. **1979** T. BARLING *Olympic Sleeper* ix. 95 The boy brought olives and peppers, sliced cheese and tomatoes, hot pita..and marinated octopus.

Pitcairner (pi·tkēᵊɹnəɹ). [f. the name *Pitcairn* (see below) + -ER¹.] A native or inhabitant of Pitcairn Island in the central South Pacific, settled with a mixed European and Polynesian population by mutineers from the *Bounty* in 1790.

1831 J. BARROW *Eventful Hist. Mutiny of Bounty* viii. 338 The Pitcairners have already proceeded from the simple canoe to row-boats. **1853** T. B. MURRAY *Pitcairn* v. 152 After some slight refreshment, (for they have only two regular meals a day,) the business of the Pitcairners' day begins. **1857** V. LUSH *Jrnl.* 18 Nov. (1971) 195 As Norfolk Island is the nearest to New Zealand they touched there on their outward voyage and landed Mrs Selwyn, who remained with the Pitcairners till the *Southern Cross* called for her on their way home. **1874** C. M. YONGE *Life J. C. Patteson* I. vii. 253 The Pitcairners..had not yet arrived [at Norfolk Island], but were on their way from their original island. **1933** C. CHAUVEL *In Wake of 'Bounty'* vi. 82 The Pitcairners have often gone to sea without a proper supply of petrol. **1962** H. LUKE *Islands of South Pacific* vi. 88 The Pitcairners throve and multiplied on their small but fertile island. **1964** ROSS & MOVERLEY *Pitcairnese Lang.* i. 25 In 1859, two families of Pitcairners ..returned to Pitcairn, to be followed by a further four families..in 1864. **1971** *Daily Tel.* 23 Dec. 3/8 Christmas Day usually is also Pitcairn's annual election day, but a shift in dates was necessary this year because the God-fearing Pitcairners naturally cannot vote on their Sabbath.

Pitcairnese (pitkēᵊɹnī·z). [f. as prec. + -ESE.] The language of Pitcairn Island, a mixture of English and Polynesian (mainly Tahitian) elements. Also *attrib.* or as *adj.*

1964 ROSS & MOVERLEY *Pitcairnese Lang.* i. 25 The Pitcairnese language—the subject of the present book—has survived both on Pitcairn and on Norfolk. **1968** *Anglia* LXXXVI. 360 Later accounts will extend our knowledge of the detail of Pitcairnese and a more extensively documented description will be especially useful. **1973** *Word 1966* XXII. 341 Since Pitcairnese has come out of the interaction of English and Tahitian, its lack of inflectional suffixes is attributed to their absence from Tahitian.

pitch, *sb.*¹ Add: **5. pitch-fibre,** a black, waterproof material which consists of compressed cellulose or asbestos fibre impregnated under vacuum with pitch and is used for making pipes; **pitch-knot** (later examples).

1946 *Archit. Rev.* CI. 66/1 Externally the drains are in pitchfibre with precast concrete manholes. **1958** *Daily Tel.* 30 June 4/6 The sales of pitch-fibre pipe continue to expand with the coming into operation of considerably increased productive capacity. **1964** L. T. MINCHIN *Famous Pipelines of World* vii. 95 Pitch-fibre is in fact a mixture of about 25% waste paper and 75% coal-tar pitch. **1825** J. NEAL *Bro. Jonathan* I. 58 The fire-place, within which two or three lighted pitch knots, a substitute for candles, were burning. **1850** H. C. WATSON *Camp-Fires of Revolution* 157 We must have some more pitch-knots on the fire.

pitch, *sb.*² Add: **I. 2. b.** *Aeronaut.* and *Astronautics.* = *PITCHING *vbl. sb.*¹ 8b; also, the extent of this motion; *angle of pitch*, the angle between the plane containing the lateral axis and the relative wind and that containing the lateral and longitudinal axes.

1915 *Rep. & Mem. Advisory Comm. Aeronaut. 1913* No. 108. 1 The tests on each model comprise the determination of lift and drift for angles of pitch from $-10°$ to $+10°$ by 2° steps. **1920** L. BAIRSTOW *Appl. Aerodynamics* iv. 223 The curves for 0° and $-5°$ pitch are seen to lie below those of the rudder alone. **1921** S. BRODETSKY *Mech. Princ. Aeroplane* iv. 148 Let there be pitch through an angle Θ about the new Y axis. **1935** *Encycl. Aviation* 493/2 In horizontal flight the angle of pitch is the angle between the longitudinal axis and the direction of motion of the aircraft. *Ibid.* 585/1 Thus a roll causes a yaw, and a yaw causes a roll... When, as often, a pitch is also introduced, it soon becomes apparent why the problem is a difficult one. **1967** *Technol. Week* 20 Feb. 35/3 When the booms are deployed, the spacecraft moment of inertia in pitch and roll with respect to Earth is about 250,000 slug-ft.² **1974** *Sci. Amer.* Dec. 138/2 Shifting his weight to control the craft in pitch, roll and yaw.

3. a. (Earlier example.)

1833 J. NYREN *Young Cricketer's Tutor* 46 The first thing he [*sc.* the fieldsman] should make himself master of, is to play from the pitch of the ball, and the motion of the batsman, so as to *get the start of the ball.*

5. a. (Earlier example.)

1888 'R. BOLDREWOOD' *Robbery under Arms* III. xv. 232 Starlight and Jim were having a pitch about the best way to get aboard one of these pearling craft, and how jolly it would be.

b. Tendentious or persuasive acting or speech, esp. inflated or exaggerated sales-talk; an instance of this, a 'line'.

1876 C. HINDLEY *Life & Adventures of Cheap Jack* 255 When I had done my 'pitch' and got down from the stage. **1926** *Variety* 29 Dec. 7/4 The outdoor show game with its 'rag front',..'pitch', [etc.]. **1935** A. J. POLLOCK *Underworld Speaks* 88/2 *Pitch*, a satisfactory interview with intended victim by a high pressure stock salesman. **1962** *Listener* 18 Jan. 128/1 I've often sat in the living-room listening to some other joker give his pitch before I could give mine. **1968** *Globe & Mail* (Toronto) 3 Feb. 3/1 Organizers are planning to allow 40 minutes for each candidate to make his pitch to the convention. **1973** *Washington Post* 13 Jan. A22/2 One novel remedy was correctional ads that required a company to tell the consumer that its earlier pitch was not totally true. **1974** K. MILLETT *Flying* (1975) III. 305 Nell hangs fire in the kitchen while I make my pitch. **1976** 'O. BLEECK' *No Questions Asked* iii. 41, I made my pitch down at headquarters. I told them..I'd better be assigned to this thing full-time. **1976** *Times* 2 Feb. 16/4 Mr Jack Jones has been squealing before he is hurt... He proceeded to get his pitch in early. **1976** *National Observer* (U.S.) 14 Aug. 1/4 Advertising was missing a bet by forsaking the wee- and off-hours for its pitches. **1977** *Rolling Stone* 16 June 43/3 He's not out there making a pitch to the audience to really love him. **1978** *Observer* 29 Jan. 15/6 Actor Charlton Heston makes a recorded pitch for cable television.

III. 11. a. (Earlier Amer. and later examples.) Also, a crowd gathered by a 'barker' or around a stall, etc.; the part of a market, stock exchange, etc., where particular commodities are bought and sold.

1699 *Derby* (Connecticut) *Town Rec.* (1901) 207 The laying out of John Pringles pitch upon the good hill. **1746** *Waterbury* (Connecticut) *Proprietors' Rec.* (1911) 166 A ten Acre pitch which his Father bought of Thos Judd of Hartford. **1943** W. B. TAYLOR *Shake it Again* xxi. 199 A well-known drapery pitcher (one who sells drapery by pitching it, i.e. telling a story about each article offered, usually gagging in an entertaining way while describing, to keep the pitch interested). **1949** [see *FANNY *v.*]. **1955** *Times* 19 Aug. 8/3 Once a month, roughly, from May to Poppy Day I am a seller. I prefer the same time—8.30 to 10 o'clock, and the same pitch—outside a row of busy shops, so I meet a number of the same people. **1959** *Encounter* May 22/2 If the street is full, a new pitch is carved out [for a prostitute]. **1960** *Farmer & Stockbreeder* 29 Mar. 16/1 Barnstaple, with a much smaller pitch than Perth, was a seller's market. **1961** *Daily Tel.* 25 Feb. 15/1 Sir Tufton [Beamish] told Members that he had been to mock auctions in Britain and America. He gave an example of the jargon used: The top man operates his joint by nailing the streamers among the plunder-snatchers in the pitch got by his frontsman, [etc.]. **1978** *Times* 1 Sept. 19/1 Patchy trading on the traded options pitch pushed ICI to the head of the active stocks.

c. *to queer the pitch*: see *QUEER *v.* 2b.

13. a. (Earlier and later examples.)

1871 'THOMSONBY' *Cricketers in Council* v. 59 Let the pitch be well watered and rolled on the day before the match. *a* **1912** A. LANG *Poet. Works* (1923) II. 62, *I* am the batsman and the bat, *I* am the bowler and the ball, The umpire, the pavilion cat, The roller, pitch,..and all. **1955** *Times* 12 May 4/4 The pitch dried too slowly to become really unpleasant during the Middlesex innings. **1972** J. KAY *Hist. County Cricket: Lancashire* vi. 45 The captains debated whether to continue after a long inspection of the pitch. **1976** *Evening Advertiser* (Swindon) 31 Dec. 20/3 The County Ground pitch is likely to be heavy.

b. In other outdoor games: the space on which the game is played; the field, the ground.

1902 *Glasgow Evening News* 7 Apr. 3/1 The International football match was made..memorable by..the collapsing of a portion of the terracing flanking the pitch. **1971** J. REASON *Victorious Lions* vii. 41 The natural banking which almost completely encircled the pitch had been ramped and grassed. **1975** *Times* 10 Apr. 12/3 St Etienne and Bayern Munich..played a goalless tie..on a snow-covered slippery pitch.

VI. 24. a. Freq. in *Mountaineering* (see quot. 1971).

1898, 1904 [in Dict.]. **1935** D. PILLEY *Climbing Days* i. 5 Each pitch or passage of the climb seemed as important as the Battle of Waterloo. **1943** E. SHIPTON *Upon that Mountain* iv. 78 Nothing provides such a strong incentive to struggle on up at all costs as the memory of a really severe pitch below. **1954** [see *ABSEIL]. **1956** C. EVANS *On Climbing* iii. 47 The leader climbs each pitch first, anchors himself to the rock, and takes in the rope as the second climbs to join him. **1971** C. BONINGTON *Annapurna South Face* 323 *Pitch*, section of climbing between two stances or belay points. These might be of any length, depending on the length of the climbing-rope... Pitches were often as long as 200 feet. **1972** D. HASTON *In High Places* i. 8 When the pair [of rock-climbers] have run out one length of the rope between two stances a 'pitch' has been established.

b. (Further examples.) Also *Geol.* Now distinguished from the dip of a plane (e.g. a stratum) and applied to the inclination of a linear feature, being the angle it makes with a horizontal line in the plane containing it, i.e. (in the case of an ore shoot) with the strike; formerly also = *PLUNGE *sb.* 6*, esp. when applied to folds.

1822 CONYBEARE & PHILLIPS *Outl. Geol. Eng. & Wales* p. iii, The angle of inclination between these planes and that of the horizon, is called their dip, or pitch. **1868** G. H. COOK *Geol. New Jersey* 55 Pitch.—This term has come into use among those engaged in iron mining, to express the characteristic descent of the iron ore beds beneath the surface, towards the northeast. It is at right angles to the dip, and is in the same direction with the strike, though not horizontal. **1906** LINDGREN & RANSOME in *Prof. Papers U.S. Geol. Survey* No. 54. 205 If we assume that the shoot has an elongated, narrow shape, as usually is the case when projected on the plain of the vein, its geometrical relations may be designated as follows: Width or thickness, breadth, stope length, pitch length, and pitch... The pitch length..is the distance between the two extreme ends of the shoot; the pitch is the angle which the pitch length makes with the horizontal. **1907** H. LOUIS in *Trans. Inst. Mining Engineers* XXXIV. 236 In America the term 'pitch' has occasionally been applied to this obliquity of the axis of the ore-shoot.., and the writer wishes to propose that this word be definitely restricted in the literature of ore-deposits to this particular signification... It will be understood that the angle is the angle to the horizontal, and the direction is always the azimuth of the horizontal trace of the vertical plane in which the line.. of pitch lies. **1908** *Ibid.* XXXV. 73 Mr. H. W. G. Halbaum (Birtley) said that..most men used 'pitch' and 'dip' as interchangeable terms. *Ibid.* 75 Mr. E. R. Field (Victoria, Australia) said that in the Bendigo district of Victoria the word 'pitch' was universally used to show the dip of the ore-bodies in the direction of the strike of the lode. **1909** *Trans. Amer. Inst. Mining Engineers* XXXIX. 899 Our mine-surveyors recognize, but do not employ, the old usage of 'dip' and 'pitch' interchangeably. *Ibid.* 900 According to my view of American practice, the direction of the pitch is usually stated in terms of the strike. **1909** *Q. Jrnl. Geol. Soc.* LXV. 473 The rocks are thrown into a series of anticlines and synclines, with a fairly-steady pitch of 12° to 15° in a southerly direction. **1913**, etc. [see *PLUNGE *sb.* 6*]. **1936** E. B. MAYO in C. M. Nevin *Princ. Struct. Geol.* (ed. 2) vii. 195 (*caption*) Orientation of minerals and inclusions in an intrusive rock... Measurements recorded in field mapping include dip and strike of flow layers, or planar parallelism; pitch and strike of flow lines, or linear parallelism. **1942** M. P. BILLINGS *Struct. Geol.* viii. 135 The pitch is the angle that a line in a plane makes with a horizontal line in that plane. **1962** READ & WATSON *Introd. Geol.* I. viii. 449 The fold-axis may be horizontal, like the top of a railway tunnel, or it may be inclined, in which case the axis and the fold are said to plunge or to pitch. The plunge is measured in degrees from the horizontal in a vertical plane.., while the pitch is given by the angle between the fold-axis and the strike of the axial plane, measured in the axial plane. **1972** J. G. DENNIS *Struct. Geol.* iii. 52 The pitch of a line within the given plane is defined as the angle between that line and any horizontal line in the plane; that is, it is measured within the plane.

VII. 25. (Examples in other contexts.)

1964 S. CRAWFORD *Basic Engin. Processes* i. 6 The pitch (1/spacing) varies with the length of the file, e.g. the pitch of a 12 inch second-cut file is not the same as the pitch of a 6 inch second cut file. **1971** *Physics Bull.* Nov. 677/2 The gratings are either flat or concave... The 'pitch' is 295 grooves/mm,..and finer spacings are expected to become available.

b. (*transf.* examples.)

1953 *Nature* 25 Apr. 739/2 If there are ten phosphate groups arranged on each helix of diameter 20 A. and pitch 34 A., the phosphate ester backbone chain is in an almost fully extended state. **1956** *Jrnl. Chem. Physics* XXV. 570 It is..possible that helical chain configurations of different pitch can be obtained under different conditions.

e. A measure of the angle of the blades of a screw propeller, equal to the distance forward a blade would move in one revolution if it sliced the air so as not to exert thrust on it; (i.e. the pitch (sense 25 b) of the spiral that would then be traced by a point on the blade).

1863 [in Dict., sense 25]. **1867** N. P. BURGH *Mod. Marine Engin.* vi. 323/2 The principal dimensions of the propeller under notice, are: the screw is 18 feet in diameter, maximum pitch 26 feet..and the minimum pitch 20 feet. **1902** F. WALKER *Aërial Navigation* v. 54 The pitch of screws varies as the ratio of the area of the disc or circle described by the tips to the area of the airship affording resistance to the air through which it passes. **1919** H. SHAW *Textbk. Aeronaut.* xi. 144 If there were no slip the propeller would move forward a distance equal to the theoretical pitch during each revolution, and ..no air would be driven backward by the propeller, and there would be no thrust. **1944** 'N. SHUTE' *Pastoral* i. 1 He heard, passing away above his head, the high scream of an ungeared engine in fine pitch. **1957** *Encycl. Brit.* XX. 535/2 In controllable-pitch propellers..the blades are pivoted in the propeller hub so that the pitch of the blades can be controlled from within the ship. **1958** *Times Rev. Industry* Aug. 39/2 The Rotodyne takes off vertically and climbs away as a helicopter, steering in the required direction being achieved by altering differentially the pitch of the airscrews. **1960** R. A. FRY *Princ. & Construction of Aircraft Gas Turbines* v. 178 The pitch required for take-off and climb is finer than the pitch most suitable for cruising. **1971** P. J. MCMAHON *Aircraft Propulsion* viii. 246 The propeller cannot go into low pitch in flight; mechanical and hydraulic pitch locks are provided.

26. (sense 11) *pitch-holder*; (sense 23) *pitch-change, -movement, -pattern, -range, -scheme.* **pitch accent** *Phonetics*, (*a*) a prominence given to a word or syllable by the difference in pitch from its immediate surroundings; (*b*) *occas.* = TONE *sb.* 6a; hence **pitch-accented** *a.*, having a pitch-accent; **pitch angle** *Aeronaut.*, the acute angle between the plane of rotation of a propeller and a straight line from one edge of a blade to the other in a direction tangential to its radius; **pitch axis** *Aeronaut.*, = *pitching axis* s.v. *PITCHING *vbl. sb.*[1] 12; **pitch contour** *Phonetics*, the pattern of continuous variation in pitch; **pitch control** *Aeronaut.* (equipment for) control of the pitch of an aircraft's propellers or rotors; also, control of the pitching motion of an aircraft; **pitch curve** *Phonetics*, = **pitch contour*; **pitch length** *Geol.*, the length of an ore shoot in the direction of greatest dimension; **pitch-meter, pitchmeter,** (*a*) a device in an aeroplane for detecting or measuring pitching; (*b*) an instrument for measuring the pitch of sound; **pitch phoneme** *Linguistics*, one of the four recognized levels of pitch, esp. a variation in pitch from one syllable to another which affects meaning.

1880 A. H. SAYCE *Introd. Sci. of Lang.* II. vii. 109 The pitch-accent has been changed into a stress-accent. **1933** C. D. BUCK *Compar. Gram. Greek & Latin* 161 Under accent one understands variations of either intensity or intonation, and speaks of a stress accent or a pitch accent according as one or the other element is the more conspicuous. **1945** *Word* I. 87, I consider especially important the remark that many languages seem to pass..from a tone- or pitch-accent to stress. **1958** D. BOLINGER in *Word* XIV. 149 To avoid unwarranted associations, it is better to speak of *pitch accent* and to leave the term *stress* to the domain of word stress. **1972** R. S. JACKENDOFF *Semantic Interpretation in Generative Gram.* vi. 259 We will give an account of the semantics of pitch accents that makes their interaction with negation part of a more general process. **1975** *Language* LI. 201 He does not distinguish between 'normal' and pitch-accented intonation contours. **1977** *Archivum Linguisticum* VIII. 90 Elsewhere, a (probably light) stress fell on the pitch-accented syllable (Lithuanian, Common Slavic). **1902** F. WALKER *Aërial Navigation* v. 54 The value of θ..which gives the maximum efficiency is the same whatever be the actual pitch angle. **1935** C. G. BURGE *Compl. Bk. Aviation* 140/1 The sections of the blade near the tip will move on a helix of much greater diameter..than those near the boss. For this reason they are set at a less 'pitch angle'.., so that every part of the airscrew will try to move the same distance forward during one revolution. **1971** P. J. MCMAHON *Aircraft Propulsion* viii. 246 The pilot's control lever selects propeller pitch angle directly. **1959** F. D. ADAMS *Aeronaut. Dict.* 126/1 *Pitch axis*, a lateral axis through an aircraft, missile, or similar body, about which the body pitches. It may be a body, wind, or stability axis. Also called a 'pitching axis'. **1962** F. I. ORDWAY et al. *Basic Astronautics* ix. 368 Any vehicle motion will take place about three axes... These axes are the yaw axis, the pitch axis, and the roll axis. **1958** R. KINGDON *Groundwork Eng. Intonation* p. xxiii, *Tone*, a stress considered from the point of view of the pitch or pitch-change associated with it. **1964** J. C. CATFORD in D. Abercrombie et al. *Daniel Jones* 28 There are many detailed studies of certain aspects of voice: e.g. of..the mechanism of pitch-change. **1966** J. DERRICK *Teaching Eng. to Immigrants* iii. 114 Regular patterns of pitch-change at the heavily stressed syllables in an utterance make up the intonation of English. **1959** E. PULGRAM *Introd. Spectrogr. of Speech* xviii. 136 But one may invariably omit the registration of glottal pitch..because..the stylus-drawn pitch contour is unlikely to present faithfully the real pitch contour in the lower frequencies. **1961** *Amer. Speech* XXXVI. 223 Pitch contours applied by synthesis to recordings of natural speech. **1940** E. MOLLOY *Aeroplane Maintenance & Operation* XV. 87 When the pilot wishes to change the pitch attitude of the aircraft, he makes an alteration to the spring torque by means of the Bowden cable from the pitch-control lever in his cockpit. **1944** W. C. NELSON *Airplane Propeller Princ.* iv. 89 Various types of automatic pitch control requiring no attention from the pilot have been devised. **1955** LIPTROT & WOODS *Rotorcraft* vii. 64 The collective-pitch control and the throttle are normally interconnected through a..cam device. **1958** LAMBERMONT & PIRIE *Helicopters & Autogyros of World* 112 A rotor hydraulically operated for both cyclic and collective pitch controls. **1974** *Encycl. Brit. Macropædia* I. 373/1 Pitch control is obtained by means of movable flaps (elevators) hinged to the trailing edge of the stabilizer. **1902** E. W. SCRIPTURE *Elem. Exper. Phonetics* xxxii. 478 The course of pitch is greatly influenced by the neighboring consonants; the more emphatic the consonant, the greater is its influence on the pitch-curve; the following consonant often cuts the vowel off at or near the maximum. **1969** *Eng. Stud.* L. 327 Of all the recorded sentences..there were taken one duplex oscillogram..one pitch curve, and two intensity curves. This was done by inserting a pitch meter..and an intensity meter between the tape recorder and the registering apparatus. **1909** *Daily Chron.* 18 Nov. 4/7 One 'pitch' which was the envy of every pitchholder in London was for many years at the end of Burlington House. **1906** Pitch length [see *PITCH *sb.*[2] 24 b]. **1965** G. J. WILLIAMS *Econ. Geol. N.Z.* viii. 107/1 The bonanzas have generally a pitch-length exceeding the level-length. **1947** *Jrnl. R. Aeronaut. Soc.* LI. 166/1 A gust can be detected by a pitch-meter which produces a differential pressure on a diaphragm with change of vertical component of wind. **1969** *Word 1967* XXIII. 255 An instrument used for measuring the frequency of the fundamental is commonly (and erroneously) called a pitchmeter. **1976** *Times* 19 Aug. 12/6 Another new development is the electronic pitchmeter... A needle shows whether a note is sharp or flat of the required pitch, so that a piano could be successfully tuned in the middle of a factory floor if necessary. **1959** D. COOKE *Lang. Mus.* ii. 109 Monteverdi and others, began to introduce more and more liberty of pitch-movement to express the rhetoric of human passion. **1964** CRYSTAL & QUIRK *Syst. Prosodic & Paralinguistic Features in Eng.* 75 It is hoped to follow up these initial experiments by a more detailed study of the spectrographic shape of pitch-movement. **1973** *Archivum Linguisticum* IV. 19 For them [*sc.* Crystal and Quirk] a tone is subordinate to another if it has the same pitch movement. **1954** F. G. CASSIDY *Robertson's Devel. Mod. Eng.* (ed. 2) xii. 381 There is a great deal less variation in the pitch-patterns of Middle-Western American than of British speech. **1961** *Amer. Speech* XXXVI. 215 An experimental pitch indicator for training deaf scholars... Deaf child is enabled to compare his own pitch pattern with that of his teacher. **1931** L. BLOOMFIELD in *Language* VII. 206 The modern languages of Europe similarly use certain pitch-phonemes at the end of largest-forms: our falling pitch at the end of statements and our rising pitches for the two kinds of questions. **1933** —— *Language* xi. 171 In English, supplement-questions are distinguished not only by their special pitch-phoneme [¿], but also by a selective taxeme. **1973** *Archivum Linguisticum* IV. 17 In the field of English intonation studies, bones of contention..spring readily to mind:..pitch phonemes versus tones. **1959** D. COOKE *Lang. Mus.* ii. 110 The 'normal' pitch-range of music is an overall spread from just above the treble clef to just below the bass clef. **1964** CRYSTAL & QUIRK *Syst. Prosodic & Paralinguistic Features in Eng.* iv. 62 So too it seems likely that tonal subordination will come to be linked with the stress and pitch-range systems. **1973** *Archivum Linguisticum* IV. 25 Such features as overall pitch range, pitch register, and even voice quality..may perhaps best be regarded as characteristics..of larger units. **1933** L. BLOOMFIELD *Language* v. 77 The fact that two utterances of the syllable *man* with different pitch-schemes are 'the same' speech-form in English, but 'different' speech-forms in Chinese, shows us that the working of language depends upon our habitually..discriminating some features of sound and ignoring all others.

pitch, *v.*[1] Add: **B. I. 1. b.** (Earlier examples.)

c **1690** in Alverstone & Alcock *Surrey Cricket* (1902) ii. 14 All you that do delight in Cricket Come to Marden Pitch your wickits. **1733** in H. T. Waghorn *Cricket Scores* (1899) 16 The wickets are to be pitched by twelve o'clock.

II. 15. d. *to pitch it strong* (and varr.): to speak forcefully; to state a case with feeling or enthusiasm; to exaggerate.

1837 DICKENS *Pickw.* xxxix. 429 I'm going to write to my father, and I must have a stimulant, or I shan't be able to pitch it strong enough into the old boy. **1841, 1863** [see STRONG *adv.* 1 c]. **1886** R. L. STEVENSON *Dr. Jekyll & Mr. Hyde* 7 And all the time, as we were pitching it in red hot, we were keeping the women off him as best we could. **1903** WODEHOUSE *Tales of St. Austin's* 213 Try him, anyhow. Pitch it fairly warm... Only cat you ever loved, and that sort of thing. **1916** J. BUCHAN *Greenmantle* i. 5 My heart was beginning to thump uncomfortably. Sir Walter was not the man to pitch a case too high. **1928** GALSWORTHY *Swan Song* II. xi. 194 Pitch it strong, but no waterworks. **1969** *New Scientist* 3 July 37/1 Dr Steven Rose..was not pitching it too high when he said that the dangers of uncontrolled technology were as great as those of nuclear warfare.

III. 17. c. *Baseball*: (examples); also *fig. Cricket*: (earlier example); still current with constr. indicating the length at or off which the ball is delivered, or the direction of the delivery.

1767 R. COTTON *Cricket Song* vii, in F. S. Ashley-Cooper *Hambledon Cricket Chron.* (1924) 184 Ye Bowlers take heed..; Spare your vigour at first... But measure each step, and be sure pitch your length! **1845** in *Appleton's Ann. Cycl. 1855* (1886) 77/2 The ball must be pitched and not thrown to the bat. **1851** J. PYCROFT *Cricket Field* viii. 165 Then, with a much higher toss and slower pace..he pitches a little short of the usual spot. **1853** F. GALE *Public School Matches* 54 In vain does Leftarm pitch up a whole over of half volleys in the hopes of a catch. **1868** H. CHADWICK *Game of Base Ball* 60 When he [*sc.* the pitcher] makes a motion to pitch and does not do so,..he makes a balk. **1890** [see *CATCH *v.* 24 e]. **1929** *Chicagoan* 17 Aug. 22/1 Diamond slang crops out in his speech..as when he [*sc.* Carl Sandburg] instructs his agents never to book him for two consecutive lectures. 'I can't pitch two games in a row', he says. **1936** G. MILBURN *Catalogue* 234 'Reck it'd be all right for me to go in there and dance.'..'You're all right. Go right on in there and pitch.' **1944** *College Topics* (Univ. of Virginia) 30 Mar. 3 Hank Neighbors, who pitched two innings of college ball here last year, is the only semblance of an experienced pitcher on the squad. **1970** [see *FORCE *v.*[1] 5]. **1970** *Globe & Mail* (Toronto) 25 Sept. 31/1 Cuellar pitched his 21st complete game and broke a club record for season victories. **1977** *World of Cricket Monthly* June 33/3 He charged down the pitch to a leg-break which the bowler pitched wide.

d. (Later examples); cf. *PITCH *sb.*[2] 5 b. *to pitch (the) woo* (orig. and chiefly *U.S.*): to court, to make love to; *transf.*, to flatter lavishly.

1935 *Ladies' Home Jrnl.* Feb. 60/3 After a while Uncle Ned came back looking positively exalted, so I guessed he and May had been pitching some more woo. **1937** *Clarionette* (Univ. of Denver) 18 Mar. 1/3 As long as there are students and universities and sofas and automobiles and nice laws, scholars will do their time-honoured share of 'pitchin' the woo'. **1943** *Sat Even. Post* 25 Sept. 12/1 Louie..pitches kitchen gadgets. **1943** [see *PITCH *sb.*[2] 11 a]. **1943** HUNT & PRINGLE *Service Slang* 51 *Pitch a woo*, to start a courtship. **1972** *Village Voice* (N.Y.) 1 June 26/2

Like any good salesman, he knows that once he demonstrates that the basic program he is pitching really does some good, all the ancillary merchandising will take care of itself. **1973** *Internat. Herald Tribune* 15 June 5/5 He's still a master at pitching the woo—on the mound, in the pressroom or elsewhere.

18. b. *Cricket.* Of a delivery: to land (usu. at or off a specified length, or in or off a specified direction).

1816 W. Lambert *Instr. & Rules Cricket* 32 If a Ball should pitch short of its proper length on the off side, and should twist toward the top of the wicket, the Striker must be very careful in playing back that he does not hit his own wicket. **1947** N. Cardus *Autobiogr.* I. 79, I was certain the ball had pitched off the wicket. **1970** R. Bowen *Cricket* v. 76 When the ball pitches, the forward motion is hindered by its friction with the ground; the circular motion is stopped abruptly (or nearly so) and this cessation must yield..further force in the direction the ball is moving. **1977** *Times* 17 Jan. 7/1 Patel received the perfect ball from Underwood which pitched on his middle stump and hit the off.

19. f. *Aeronaut.* and *Astronautics. intr.* Of an aircraft or spacecraft: to rotate or rock about a lateral axis, to undergo pitching. Also *trans.*, to cause (an aircraft, etc.) to do this.

1874 *Ann. Rep. Aeronaut. Soc.* 59 If..the model pitches forward on its nose, it is only necessary to slide the aeroplane further forward on the rod. If it still pitches turn up the horizontal rudder slightly. **1903** *Aeronaut. Jrnl.* VII. 53/2 The best angles were given by shapes which..would always pitch forward unless controlled by a large and well turned up tail. **1918** Cowley & Levy *Aeronautics* vii. 152 The pitching moment produced is about 123 lbs.-ft., enough to pitch the aeroplane through an angle of ½°. **1926** *Jrnl. R. Aeronaut. Soc.* XXX. 521 The examination would be comparatively easy if only the operation of the longitudinal control simply pitched the aeroplane, the lateral control banked and the rudder control yawed it. **1932** R. Mahachek *Airplane Pilots' Man.* iv. 37 The plane will gradually pitch upward or downward unless the pilot moves his control stick slightly forward or backward. **1961** D. Myrus *Man into Space* ii. 36/1 At about 50,000 feet the engines automatically flip slightly to one side, pitching the missile from straight up to a little north of due east. **1964** J. E. D. Williams *Operation of Airliners* vii. 104 When an aircraft yaws or pitches there is an immediate change in the aerodynamic forces. **1970** N. Armstrong et al. *First on Moon* x. 242 We pitched over to a level altitude which would allow us to maintain our horizontal velocity and just skim along over the top of the boulder field.

IV. 20. a. (Further examples.) Also, of a roof or other structure: to slope downwards (*U.S.*). In *Mining* and *Geol.* now used esp. of a linear feature, as an ore shoot or fold axis (cf. *pitch *sb.*[2] 24b): to have a pitch of a given angle and direction.

1771 in *Mass. Hist. Soc. Coll.* (1914) LXXI. 137, I should have the Roof to pitch from under the Arkitraves of the Chamber Windows. **1859** *Trans. Illinois Agric. Soc.* III. 538 The roof may pitch both ways, or shed at the ends. **1897** F. C. Moore *How to build Home* vii. 94 The floor shall pitch from building to the front of piazza ¼ inch to every foot of width. **1906** *Prof. Papers U.S. Geol. Survey* No. 54. 206 In the Midget mine the Cobb ore shoot pitches 45° NE. **1910** Lake & Rastall *Text-bk. Geol.* i. 20 A fold whose axis was inclined downwards towards the south-east would be said to pitch to the south-east, and the angle of pitch could be expressed in degrees, as in the case of dip. **1939** A. K. Lobeck *Geomorphol.* xvii. 593 The two monoclinal ridges formed on the two limbs of the anticline do not run strictly parallel ..but converge and meet, the convergence being in the direction toward which the anticline pitches. **1962** [see *pitch *sb.*[2] 24b]. **1966** E. H. T. Whitten *Struct. Geol. Folded Rocks* i. 26 In a sedimentary sequence folded about a horizontal fold axis one bed has a strike of 130 and dips SW at 45°. Ripple marks are observed on this bedding plane; they pitch at 40° to the southeast (i.e., the angle between the strike and the ripples is 40°).

c. To drop *down* or descend abruptly (to a lower level).

1851 N. Kingsley *Diary* 21 Jan. (1914) 168 We have come to where the bed rock pitches down suddenly. **1867** 'T. Lackland' *Homespun* I. 70 One of these [pastures].. sloping where it does not pitch, down to the rocky bed of the riotous stream. **1873** J. Miller *Life amongst Modocs* vi. 72 Gorge on gorge, cañon intersecting cañon, pitching down towards the rapid Klamat.

VI. 23. a. Also, to turn (aside) to a particular objective; to begin.

1932 Wodehouse *Louder & Funnier* 11 Then, with the coffee and old brandy at your side.., pitch in. **1971** W. Hillen *Blackwater River* iv. 36 A favorite stopping-place for..swans, cranes, and geese. They pitch in to feed and rest.

b. (Earlier and further examples.) Also in weakened senses.

1829 P. Egan *Boxiana* 2nd Ser. II. 267 Dick..*pitched in* to Warren, who was obliged to fight for his safety. **1835** Dickens *Sk. Boz* (1836) 1st Ser. I. 51, I wished..that the people would only blow me up, or pitch into me—that I wouldn't have minded. **1839** *Spirit of Times* 30 Mar. 48/2 The man was lost in astonishment which but increased the rage of the husband of the *cantatrice*, who forthwith 'pitched into' him in the last London style, and an entire 'mus' was made of the man's face. **1852** *Punch* 10 July 25/2, I saw that *gourmand* Guttler pitching contentedly into a kangaroo chop. **1906** G. B. Shaw *Let.* 18 Nov. (1972) II. 661 A vaccine opsinises your disease germs ..so that the white blood corpuscles..pitch into them with an appetite. **1952** *Sun* (Baltimore) 4 July 42/8 The two young Negroes pitched into him and the one with the gun pistol-whipped the physician.

c. *pitch out* (Cricket): to dismiss; to bowl out or to run out by a ball that does not touch the ground before it hits the wickets.

1858 *Bell's Life in London* 18 July 7/6 Caffyn was *pitched* out—the ball never touching the ground until after it had disturbed the stumps. **1876** *John Wisden's Cricketer's Almanack* 115 He was stated to have been brilliantly pitched out by Mr. Strachan from mid-off.

24. In extended use, **pitch-and-putt** [Pitch *sb.*[2] 3c], a form of golf in which the green can be reached in one; *fig.*, an insignificant distance; *attrib.*, of or pertaining to a *spec.* type of miniature golf course.

1963 *Harper's Bazaar* Jan. 9/2 Pitch and Putt Course. Tennis. Sea-bathing. **1968** *Sun* (Baltimore) 5 July A14/7 His delegate count is within a pitch and a putt of the nominating majority. **1972** J. McClure *Caterpillar Cop* xiv. 234, I believe..you played a round of pitch-and-putt? **1974** *Times* 8 Feb. 15/4 A pitch-and-putt course covering five acres. **1976** J. Snow *Cricket Rebel* 70 Two days in which my only activity had been in a pitch and putt competition organised by the players and Press in the hotel grounds.

pitch-and-toss. Add: **a.** (Later Austral. example.) Also (*Sc.*), a manœuvre in the game of *knifey, knifie (sense *a*).

1949 [see *barrack *sb.*[2]]. **1969** I. & P. Opie *Children's Games* vii. 222 Described..by a 10-year-old boy in the Isle of Lewis: '"Knifie" is a game for two people... Then try "Pitch and toss". Stick it in the ground, then try to hit it with the palm of your hand and try to toss it into the air, so that it will land blade first in the earth.'

b. (Later examples.)

1910 Kipling *Rewards & Fairies* 175 If you can make one heap of all your winnings and risk it on one turn of pitch-and-toss, and lose, And start again at your beginnings And never breathe a word about your loss. **1960** J. Franklyn *Dict. Rhyming Slang* 108/1 *Pitch and toss*, the boss. 20 C. Current in the theatrical world (Lupino Lane). **1973** *Times* 29 Dec. 12/7 Writing more than a dozen varied plays of substance, some of which had less fortune than they deserved in the pitch-and-toss of the West End.

pitched, *ppl. a.*[1] **6.** (Earlier example.)

1871 *Baily's Monthly Mag.* Aug. 290 He bowled a very great number of long hops, and a considerable number of pitched-up balls to the leg stump.

pitcher[1]. Add: **1.** *spec.* in *Ceramics*, fired clay or shards used in the manufacturing process.

1771 J. Wedgwood *Let.* 13 Jan. (1965) 101, I have been..busy..in makeing a general review of all my experiment pitchers. **1964** H. Hodges *Artifacts* i. 20 Broken or spoilt pottery is commonly used, and while the term grog is general amongst all potters to denote the addition of fired clay, some potters also use the terms pitchers and sherds. *a* **1977** *Harrison Mayer Ltd. Catal.* 14/1 *Pitchers*, fired, broken or scrap pottery. Biscuit pitchers have various uses when crushed or ground.

pitcher[2]. Add: **1. b.** Also, a market porter.

1966 *New Statesman* 7 Oct. 531/2 The grandmother had been married to a Smithfield meat 'pitcher' who had died of cancer. **1970** *Times* 26 Feb. 10/2 No longer are porters divided into pitchers (the men who carry fruit in), plain porters (who carry it out) and stand men (who work inside warehouse or shop).

2. (Earlier and later examples.)

1845, 1867 [see *balk *sb.*[1] 5b]. **1948** *Chicago Daily News* 4 June 36/8 Claude Passeau's job with the Cubs is to tutor young pitchers throughout the Chicago farm system. **1949** *Lafayette Alumnus* (Lafayette College, Easton, Pa.) 24 Oct. 1/2 By crashing in he ruined innumerable would-be pass plays getting the pitcher for losses averaging 9 yards. **1974** *Post-Herald* (Birmingham, Alabama) 29 June A 14/3 Lane gave the Tigers a 2-0 lead with a two-run homer in the second innings off losing pitcher Kevin Kobel. **1978** *Verbatim* Feb. 2/2 A ballplayer who is not an infielder, outfielder or pitcher, and is thus doomed to be a catcher, wears 'the tools of ignorance', catcher's gear.

pitcher[4], repr. a vulgar or colloq. pronunciation of Picture *sb.*

1916 [see *humdinger 1]. **1931** *Amer. Speech* Oct. 46 *Moom pitcher* for moving picture. **1936** Mencken *Amer. Lang.* (ed. 4) vii. 352 On the vulgar level *amateur* is always *amachoor*, and *picture* is *pitchur* or *pitcher*. **1977** J. Wambaugh *Black Marble* (1978) vii. 99 She do look somethin like that dumpy consti-pated broad in the pitcher.

pitcher-plant. For 'the East Indian genus *Nepenthes*' substitute 'the south-east Asian genus *Nepenthes*'. (Earlier and later examples.)

1819 L. A. Anspach *Hist. Newfoundland* xiv. 362 Another still more remarkable plant, found in the woods of Newfoundland, is the *Saracenia* [*sic*], commonly called side-saddle flower, or pitcher-plant. **1929** Robbins & Rickett *Botany* xxiii. 356 Some of the most striking leaf modifications are in the plants known as pitcher plants. **1938** [see *bake-apple]. **1947** I. L. Idriess *Isles of Despair* xxxiii. 220 She could not sleep.., thinking of the phantom pygmies in the pitcher-plant swamps. **1965** *Austral. Encycl.* VII. 123/2 The Western Australian pitcher-plant is *Cephalotus follicularis*. **1965** D. Henderson *Heart of Newfoundland* 19 We had seen pitcher plants before..but never in such numbers as are found in Newfoundland. **1973** *Sci. Amer.* Dec. 64/2 In these [Borneo] forests the insect-eating pitcher plants (*Nepenthes*) are common. **1977** *Borneo Bull.* 7 May 8/1 Did you know that of 30 pitcher plant species found in Borneo, 16 are said to be found on the mountain, and many of them are peculiar to its slopes?

pitchfork, *sb.*[1] (Earlier and later examples of *to rain pitchforks.*)

1815 D. Humphreys *Yankey in Eng.* 55 I'll be even with you, if it rains pitchforks—tines downwards. **1850** J. R. Planché *Island of Jewels* II. iii. 31 Rain cats and dogs, or pitchforks perpendicular, The sky's not mine, and need'nt be particular. **1930** J. Dos Passos *42nd Parallel* I. 77 Outside it was raining pitchforks. **1940** M. Fishback *Time for Quick One* 77 It's raining cats and dogs And pitchforks and assorted frogs.

pitch hole[1]. Add: **2.** *N. Amer.* A defect in a road or trail; a pot-hole.

1874 *Rep. Vermont Board Agric.* II. 659 The highways leading to our larger villages..are frequently so full of pitchholes or 'cahoos' as to render them totally unfit for travel. **1890** *Harper's Mag.* Oct. 657/2 The highway was frequently interrupted by 'pitch holes'. **1936** A. F. Cross *Cross Roads* (ed. 2) 106 Charlie's horses jogged on with us ..into pitch holes that jarred one's innards terribly. **1962** D. J. Dickie *Great Golden Plain* 288 The cat train rocks and plunges over the hummocks and pitch holes in the ice and snow roads.

pitchi (pi·tʃi). *Austral.* [Aboriginal.] A dish or container hollowed out of a solid log.

1896 E. C. Stirling in B. Spencer *Rep. Horn Sci. Expedition Cent. Austral.* IV. 98 The name 'Pitchi'..is in general use, by the whites of the parts traversed by the Expedition, for the wooden vessels used for carrying food and water and, occasionally, infants. **1931** I. L. Idriess *Lasseter's Last Ride* (1933) xvi. 128 In little canoe-shaped pitchis of wood some women carried native foods. **1934** A. Russell *Tramp-Royal in Wild Austral.* xxvii. 179 Poised on his [*sc.* an aboriginal's] head was a newly cut bark pitchi filled to the brim with wild oranges. **1959** S. H. Courtier *Death in Dream Time* viii. 112 While his thumbs bleed, the elders bring a *pitchi*, a wooden vessel, and catch the blood. **1970** 'E. Lindall' *Gathering of Eagles* x. 119 In her hands..was a wooden pitchi full of water.

pitch-in (pi·tʃin). *U.S. colloq.* Also **pitchin.** [f. Pitch *sb.*[2] + In *adv.*] Applied, usu. *attrib.*, to a large common meal to which each diner contributes food or drink.

1973 *Sunday Bull.* (Philadelphia) 7 Oct. (Parade Suppl.) 26/2 The answers were as varied as the food at a large pitch-in picnic. **1976** *Laurel* (Montana) *Outlook* 16 June 9/1 The Park City Garden Club guest night was held at the civic center with a pitchin dinner. **1976** *Columbus* (Montana) *News* 17 June 6/3 Mr. and Mrs. Charles Wark were hosts at a pitch-in picnic for members and their families.

pitching, *vbl. sb.*[1] Add: **7.** (Examples in *Baseball*; also *attrib.*)

1858 *N.Y. Tribune* 18 Aug. 7/3 The pitching was good on both sides. **1896** H. Chadwick *Spalding's Base Ball Guide* 2 A new form of pitching tables are included in the records of the pitching of 1895. **1942** [see *major *a.* 1e]. **1944** *College Topics* (Univ. of Virginia) 30 Mar. 3 As for the pitching staff, there is plenty of material that will eventually develop into the team's strongest asset. **1948** *Richmond* (Va.) *Times-Dispatch* 15 Mar. 17/4 Blackwell learned how to throw it from Hal Schumacher, former New York Giants pitching star. **1969** *Eugene* (Oregon) *Register-Guard* 3 Dec. 2D/4 Cal Ermer..landed a coaching job, as pitching tutor for Bristol's Seattle club. **1976** *National Observer* (U.S.) 21 Feb. 19/2 (Advt.), Mickey Owen Baseball School... 4 Lighted Batting Cages, 2 Pitching Machines.

8. b. *Aeronaut.* and *Astronautics.* Angular motion of an aircraft or spacecraft about a lateral axis (the *pitching axis*: see 12 below).

1912 G. Greenhill *Dynamics Mech. Flight* iv. 83 Rolling and pitching of a steamer or flying machine. **1915** A. Fage *Aeroplane* vi. 75 The following nomenclature has been adopted at the National Physical Laboratory:—[*table*] Name of axis..Lateral... Name of Motion which takes place about Axis..Pitching. **1935** C. G. Burge *Encycl. Aviation* 579/1 Rotary motion of the aeroplane about the lateral axis is called pitching. **1958** D. Piggott *Gliding* xiii. 78 To stop the pitching, the pilot must relax the backward pressure on the stick and reduce the climbing angle for a few moments. **1965** C. N. Van Deventer *Introd. Gen. Aeronaut.* v. 84/1 The lateral axis is the side-to-side axis about which the airplane revolves in pitching, when its nose and tail move up and down. **1968** T. de Galiana *Conc. Encycl. Astronaut.* 210/2 For a cylindrical spacecraft,.. pitching is a movement of the nose up or down (that is, away from or towards the orbit focus).

12. pitching axis *Aeronaut.* and *Astronautics*, a lateral axis of an aircraft, etc., about which pitching takes place, usu. specified to be perpendicular to its longitudinal axis or to its direction of flight; of a spacecraft, one of two horizontal axes (cf. *yawing axis* s.v. *yawing *vbl. sb.*) which are perpendicular to each other and to the longitudinal axis; = *pitch axis* s.v. *pitch *sb.*[2] 26; **pitching heat** *Brewing* = *pitching temperature*; **pitching machine** *Brewing*, a special kind of vessel in which pitching of the wort takes place; **pitching moment** *Aeronaut.*, a moment tending to turn an aircraft, etc., about its pitching axis; **pitching-temperature** (example); **pitching-yeast** (examples).

1920 W. J. Walker tr. *Devillers's Dynamics of Aeroplane* xii. 234 The moment of inertia in movements about the pitching axis plays the rôle of mass in rectilinear displacements. **1953** *New Biol.* XIV. 66 Stability can be related to any of the three axes—the rolling axis.., the yawing axis,..and the pitching axis (horizontally at right angles to the direction of flight). **1959** Pitching axis [see *pitch axis* s.v. *PITCH *sb.*[2] 26]. **1876** *Encycl. Brit.* IV. 275/1 The heat at which the wort is let down into the fermenting tun. This 'pitching heat' varies very much. **1885** E. R. SOUTHBY *Syst. Handbk. Pract. Brewing* (ed. 2) xx. 335, I have already explained that this lowering of the pitching heat is by no means essential. **1940** H. L. HIND *Brewing* II. 854 Simple pitching machines consist of a cauldron, in which the pitch is melted over a coke fire or by gas, and forced by compressed air through a spraying nozzle into the cask. **1957** K. BARTON-WRIGHT tr. *De Clerck's Textbk. Brewing* I. xxii. 483 In modern pitching machines..the old lining is no longer removed with hot air,..but with very thinned pitch. **1913** *Rep. & Mem. Advisory Comm. Aeronaut.* No. 74. 10 Measurements of lift, drift, and pitching moment at varying values of the pitching angle from −10° to +25°. **1931** *Technol. Rev.* Nov. 65/1 It seems inevitable that the next generation must know as much about *ailerons, pitching moments*, and *dihedral angles*, as the present one does about carburetors, differentials, and wheel bases. **1966** D. STINTON *Anat. Aeroplane* xi. 199 Further pitching moments..are introduced by wing-mounted stores,..engines, flaps and undercarriage units. **1957** *Encycl. Brit.* IV. 105/2 The pitching temperature is held at 54–59° F. in American practice, slightly higher (58–60° F) in England. **1885** E. R. SOUTHBY *Syst. Handbk. Pract. Brewing* (ed. 2) xx. 320 The yeast cells of a good pitching yeast should be separate from one another. **1956** [see *POLYMYXIN].

pitching, *ppl. a.* **1.** Delete † *Obs.* and add later examples in *Geol.* (cf. *PITCH *v.*[1] 20, *PITCH *sb.*[2] 24 b).

1939 A. K. LOBECK *Geomorphol.* xvii. 595 The monoclinal ridges which result from the erosion of pitching synclines converge in a direction which is opposite to the pitch of the fold. **1960** B. W. SPARKS *Geomorphol.* vii. 135 Pitching folds may be reflected in a pattern of converging and diverging ridges like that of certain sections of the Appalachians. **1968** C. R. TWIDALE *Geomorphol.* ii. 11 Folds whose outcrops narrow and widen, appear and disappear, are described as pitching or plunging folds.

2. (Further examples.)

1906 *Chambers's Jrnl.* July 537/2 It is worth going some distance to see a *vaquero* sticking to a 'pitching' horse. **1948** *Sat. Rev.* 28 Aug. 37/1 Bucky Durant calmly rolled a cigarette as he sat atop the pitching bronc.

pi·tchman. *U.S.* [PITCH *sb.*[2]] One who sells gadgets or novelties at a fair or in the street. Also *transf.* and *fig.*, an advertiser, one who delivers a sales pitch (see *PITCH *sb.*[2] 5 b).

1926 *Amer. Speech* Feb. 283/1 *Pitchman*, a man who sells novelties on the circus lot or on the streets adjacent to the lot. **1934** *N.Y. American* 4 Oct. 21 The army of street pitchmen have had the biggest season in years. **1940** W. SAROYAN *Love's Old Sweet Song* 17 in *Three Plays*, Barnaby Gaul, 51, a pitchman. **1949** *Time* 19 Dec. 34/3 They are all journalistic racketeers—I mean pitchmen. **1956** H. GOLD *Man who was not with It* (1965) xix. 172, I coughed into my best pitchman's voice. **1972** *Guardian* 6 Dec. 13/1 American astronauts..have become bank directors, pitchmen for cars and railroads on television commercials, executives in real estate. **1975** *Publishers Weekly* 28 Apr. 44/1 Mandino is a pitchman for positive thinking in the hallowed line including Bruce Barton and Norman Vincent Peale. **1976** *National Observer* (U.S.) 2 Oct. 18/4 Boudreau was a pitchman in the old Clyde Beatty Circus before he went on to Juilliard and the Paris Conservatory. **1976** *Time* 20 Dec. 20/2 Cecil D. Andrus.. has been TV pitchman for Idaho potatoes. **1977** *Time* 7 Feb. 43/2 He has also taken on the role of pitchman, appearing personally in Eastern's ads to stress the line's concern for passengers.

pi·tch-off. [PITCH *v.*[1] 20.] The inclination or shelving of the bed of the sea.

1894 J. D. DANA *Man. Geol.* (ed. 4) I. i. 20 At Keeling atoll,..Captain Fitzroy, R.N., found no bottom in 7200 feet at 2200 yards from the breakers—which gives a pitch-off exceeding 1:0·92.

pi·tch-out. *N. Amer.* [PITCH *v.*[1] 17 c.] **a.** *Baseball.* (See quot. 1943.) **b.** *Football.* (See quot. 1950.)

1912 C. MATHEWSON *Pitching in a Pinch* vii. 157 If a catcher can get a pitchout on a hit and run sign he upsets the other team greatly. **1943** *Amer. Speech* XVIII. 106 The *pitch-out* (a ball thrown wide of the plate so that the catcher can *get it away* in a hurry to catch a man trying to steal). **1948** *Cavalier Daily* (Univ. of Virginia) 19 Oct. 2/1 The halfbacks, standing wide of the fullback, are in a position to take pitchouts and to speed downfield for passes. **1949** *Sun* (Baltimore) 8 Dec. 24/1 Other trends noted [in Football] included increased use of the pitchout (not to be confused with the baseball term). **1950** *Britannica Bk. of Year* 683/1 *Pitch-out, n. Football*, a short lateral pass behind the line of scrimmage, usually from the quarterback to another back. **1966** ROTE & WINTER *Lang. Pro Football* 129 Pitchout, a short, backward shuffle pass or lateral from quarterback to a halfback or a fullback. **1968** *Globe & Mail* (Toronto) 11 July 32/4 He took a pitchout from Curtis Wilson and danced, darted and jumped 86 yards. **1972** J. MOSEDALE *Football* vi. 87 The cornerback took his eyes off him on a pitchout. **1974** *Anderson* (S. Carolina) *Independent* 19 Apr. 4B/3 On Monday night, he got his first stolen base—despite a pitchout by the Chicago White Sox.

pi·tch-penny. *U.S.* [f. PITCH *v.*[1]] A variety of pitch-and-toss.

1830 J. F. WATSON *Ann. Philadelphia* 240 'Pitch-penny'..was frequent—to pitch at a white mark on the ground. **1877** E. S. WARD *Story of Avis* 286 Calculating the distance..as he stood playing the game of human pitch-penny with the infant. **1978** E. TIDYMAN *Table Stakes* I. i. 20 He had persuaded Hochmeir to give him his fifty cents a week in pennies so that he could try to double it in..pitch penny with the newsboys in Howard Square.

pitch pine. (Earlier and later examples.)

1676 *Essex Inst. Hist. Coll.* (1920) LVI. 306 4¾ acres of land..bounded by a pitch pine. **1684** *Manchester* (Mass.) *Town Rec.* (1889) 17 A pich [*sic*] pine tree marked with 4 marks. **1709** J. LAWSON *New Voy. Carolina* 89 Ever-Greens are here plentifully found, of a very quick Growth, and pleasant Shade; Cypress, or White Cedar, the Pitch Pine, the yellow Pine. **1736** *Rec. Early Hist. Boston* (1885) XII. 150 Add to the South East Side Ten foot, to be built of Square Pitch Pine Timber. **1771** J. S. COPLEY *Let.* 3 Aug. in *Mass. Hist. Soc. Coll.* (1914) LXXI. 138 The floor..should be Pitch Pine. **1887** C. B. GEORGE *40 Yrs. on Rail* 31 Pitch pine was largely used for fuel. **1969** T. H. EVERETT *Living Trees of World* 50/2 Pitch pine, rarely more than 75 feet high, has an open irregular head. **1977** *Listener* 3 Nov. 594/2 The church where so many Trelawnies lie under the pitchpine and the shiny tiles.

pitch-pipe. (Later examples.)

1961 *Oxf. Univ. Gaz.* 8 May 1149/2 Some cylinders are prefaced with the sound of the pitch-pipe and statement of the key. **1969** E. H. PINTO *Treen* 172 The mahogany pitch pipes..were formerly used in churches which had no organ, to give the keynote before singing commenced. **1979** *Yale Alumni Mag.* Apr. 28/2 Armed only with pitch-pipes and pocket dictionaries, we were able to elicit a direct and natural response from all manner of Soviet citizens.

pitchpoll, -pole, *sb.* Add: **1.** (Further U.S. example.)

1842 S. KETTELL *Daw's Doings* ix. 61 Goosecap..did nothing all day long but lollop about at his ease..playing at pitchpole among the clover.

2. A kind of harrow.

1932 R. H. BIFFEN *Fream's Elem. Agric.* (ed. 12) ii. 48 The pitch-pole harrow is an implement of recent introduction, which has attained some popularity for tearing a thick mat on old pasture, and also for working arable land... The implement has a very drastic action and the heavy draught necessitates a tractor. **1940** R. G. STAPLEDON *Re-Grassing* 27 After this treatment had been continued a few years we dragged heavily with pitch-pole, lined heavily.., [etc.]. **1944** C. CULPIN *Farm Machinery* (ed. 2) vii. 132 (*caption*) Wilder's 'Pitch-Pole' harrow pulled by tractor equipped with skeleton wheels. *Ibid.*, Tines suitable for fairly deep arable cultivations are available, and some farmers use the Pitch-Pole mainly or exclusively as an arable land cultivator. **1951** P. OYLER *Feeding Ourselves* x. 92 It is a good plan to run heavy tine harrows or the modern Pitchpole over pastures again and again both ways. **1960** *Farmer & Stockbreeder* 16 Feb. 128/3 The average contract rate for pitchpole harrowing is 20s per acre first time.

pitchpoll, -pole, *v.* **a.** For *dial.* read 'orig. *dial.*' and add later example in causative sense.

1926 T. E. LAWRENCE *Seven Pillars* (1935) cxvi. 626 The wind snapped them [*sc.* thistles] off at the hollow root, and pitch-polled their branchy tops along the level ground, thistle blowing against thistle.

b. *intr. Naut.* (See quot. 1961.) Also *trans.* in causative sense.

1903 G. S. WASSON *Cap'n Simeon's Store* iii. 44 Ain't it hard lines enough for a sickly ole feller same's him having to go outside here late in the fall o' the year and pitch-pole around into a punky old ark. **1908** [see *HUMBUG *v.* 2]. **1915** KIPLING *Fringes of Fleet* 67 Dawn sees them pitch-poling insanely between head-seas. **1961** F. H. BURGESS *Dict. Sailing* 160 *Pitch pole*, be up-ended, stern first, and completely overthrown by the sea. **1976** *Sci. Amer.* May 130/3 On this up-to-date foundation Van Dorn builds a careful scheme for wave forecasting at sea: the expected sea state and its changes (depending on fetch, wind speed and duration) and the chances that state implies for the big wave that can pitchpole any boat. **1976** *Yachting World* Oct. 111/1 Even in the worst conditions, such as running down steep 25 foot waves, it has never shown a tendency to pitchpole. **1979** *Observer* 19 Aug. 3/3 Huge weights of water..capable of laying a 35 foot boat flat on its side with ease, making it turn turtle or even pitch-poling it—making it somersault forward stern over stem.

Hence **pi·tchpoler**, one who pitchpolls a harpoon in *Whaling*; **pi·tchpol(l)ing** *vbl. sb.*

1851 H. MELVILLE *Moby Dick* II. xlii. 284 None exceed that fine manœuvre with the lance, called pitchpoling. *Ibid.* 286 The pitchpoler dropping astern, folds his hands. **1971** S. E. MORISON *European Discovery Amer.: Northern Voy.* p. xi, There you have first-hand accounts of some of the hazards that the early navigators encountered as a matter of course—enormous freak waves, pitch-poling, capsizing.

pitfalled, *a.* (Earlier and later examples.)

1826 *Blackw. Mag.* XX. 666/2 The snow deep, wreathed, and pit-falled. **1976** *Evening Post* (Nottingham) 17 Dec. 14/2 Sunken and rubble-littered uneven pavements, pit-falled with miniature craters.

pith, *sb.* Add: **1.** (Further examples.)

1884 BOWER & SCOTT tr. *H. A. de Bary's Compar. Anat. Veg. Organs Phanerogams & Ferns* ix. 403 Only in a few woods does the pith become entirely empty and dried up. **1928** HOLMAN & ROBBINS *Elem. Bot.* iii. 54 The pith is made up of large-celled parenchyma. **1956** F. W. JANE *Struct. Wood* iv. 74 The pith may be distinctive: thus, in oak it has, in section, the shape of a five-rayed star. **1976** R. F. LYNDON in M. M. Yeoman *Cell Division in Higher Plants* viii. 297 In those cells which form the pith the cell cycle may no sooner get to minimum length than it begins to lengthen again as the cells mature.

8. pith fleck, in certain woods, a small dark patch made by parenchyma cells filling cavities left by insect larvæ; **pith helmet** (further examples); so *pith-helmeted* adj.; **pith ray** = *medullary ray* s.v. MEDULLARY *a.* 2 b; **pith-ray fleck** = **pith fleck*; **pith-tree**, for *Herminiera Elaphroxylon* substitute *Æschynomene elaphroxylon*; (earlier and later examples).

1890 W. SOMERVILLE tr. *Hartig's Timbers* 77 Pith-flecks, darkish-coloured patches met with in some woods. **1911** *Forestry Q.* IX. 244 Pith flecks or medullary spots are small, brown, half-moon shaped patches appearing.. on the cross sections of many of our woods. **1956** F. W. JANE *Struct. Wood* x. 236 Rotary cut birch..has a most attractive figure, due largely to the very numerous pith flecks which it contains. **1970** PANSHIN & DE ZEEUW *Textbk. Wood Technol.* (ed. 3) I. x. 366 Pith flecks, or medullary spots, are confined to hardwoods. **1917** *Harrods Gen. Catal.* 643/3 Lady's Pith Helmet. Pith body, covered white drill. **1934** G. B. SHAW *Too True to be Good* II. 50 He wears a pith helmet with a pagan. **1971** *Country Life* 15 July 141/2 Who..buys a Cawnpore Tent Club pith helmet with quilted khaki cover? **1976** *Evening Post* (Nottingham) 15 Mar. 6/3 Has anybody a pith helmet..? Members of Aspley Methodist Church, who are to put on a pantomime 'The Sleeping Beauty'..would be glad to borrow one for their show. **1916** 'BOYD CABLE' *Action Front* 190 Half-forgotten illustrations in the papers of pith-helmeted infantry in the Boer War. **1902** G. S. BOULGER *Wood* 22 The whole mass of xylem is traversed radially by pith-rays. **1928** HOLMAN & ROBBINS *Elem. Bot.* iii. 54 In stems in which the vascular tissue does not form a continuous cylinder, the bundles are separated by pith rays. **1953** K. ESAU *Plant Anat.* xv. 343 The spaces among the strands..are occupied by parenchymatic ground tissue. These plates of tissue can be designated as pith rays or medullary rays. **1970** PANSHIN & DE ZEEUW *Textbk. Wood Technol.* (ed. 3) I. v. 179 Since all wood rays originate in the cambium, such terms as pith rays and medullary rays, frequently encountered in literature on wood, should not be used, because they imply that wood rays consist of the same kind of tissue as the pith. **1913** *Circ. U.S. Forest Service* No. 215 (*title*) Pith-ray flecks in wood. **1925** EAMES & MACDANIELS *Introd. Plant Anat.* vii. 187 Pith-ray flecks are, unfortunately, sometimes explained as normal features of wood structure. **1864** J. A. GRANT *Walk across Afr.* p. xv, Ambadj; native name for the pith-tree. **1961** F. R. IRVINE *Woody Plants of Ghana* 360 Ambatch or Pith Tree of Nile Land... By rivers and in swamps in open country.

pith, *v.* Add: **3.** Also *fig.*

1903 G. B. SHAW *Man & Superman* Pref. p. xxxiv, And yet..the respectable newspapers pith me by announcing 'another book by this brilliant and thoughtful writer'. **1913** —— *Quintessence of Ibsenism* (completed ed.) 192 The very first thing the theatrical wiseacres did with it [*sc. A Doll's House*] was to effect exactly this transformation [*sc.* a happy ending], with the result that the play thus pithed had no success. **1935** —— *Let.* 25 July in *To a Young Actress* (1960) 163, I entirely approve of Peter's escaping [from a public school] before he is pithed and turned out as a political and moral gentleman several centuries out of date.

pithecanthropus (pipĭkæ·nþropŭs). Also with capital initial. [mod.L., f. Gr. πίθηκ-ος ape + ἄνθρωπος man.] **1.** [(E. Haeckel *Natürliche Schöpfungsgeschichte* (1868) xix. 507).] A hypothetical creature bridging the gap in evolutionary development between apes and man.

1876, 1877 [see PITHECANTHROPE].

2. [(E. Dubois *Pithecanthropus erectus* (1894) 1).] The fossil hominid first described from remains found by Eugene Dubois (1858–1940) in Java in 1891, now included in the species *Homo erectus*; = *Java man* s.v. *JAVA.

1895 *Nature* 5 Dec. 115/2 Dr. Dubois placed Pithecanthropus below the point of devarication of the anthropoid apes from the human line. **1895, 1898** [see PITHECANTHROPE]. **1905** J. MCCABE tr. *Haeckel's Evol. Man* II. xxiii. 632 The pithecanthropus excited the liveliest interest, as the long-sought transitional form between man and the ape. **1933** A. S. ROMER *Man & Vertebrates* xi. 239 Some scientists have claimed that *Pithecanthropus* is an ape, far below human status. **1933** N. DOUGLAS *Looking Back* II. 301 Science has a knack of filling up those gaps when least you expect it, as in the case of radium and pithecanthropus. **1957** L. EISELEY *Immense Journey* 101 The finding of the Pithecanthropus skull cap had bolstered this view.

So **pithecanthro·pic** *a.*, of or pertaining to pithecanthropus; also *fig.*, resembling an ape, clumsy; **pitheca·nthropine** *a.*, resembling or closely related to the fossil hominid once included in the genus *Pithecanthropus*; also as *sb.*; **pitheca·nthropoid** *a.* = prec; also *fig.*

1890, 1897 [in Dict.]. **1917** *Q. Rev.* July 35 Degeneracy, as seen in idiots,..due to a reversion to the pithecanthropic element. **1925** *Bull. Geol. Soc. China* IV. 177 Sooner or later pithecanthropine remains will be recovered from the Siwaliks. **1929** A. CROWLEY *Spirit of Solitude* I. xvii. 198, I was absorbed in 'The Cloud on the Sanctuary', reading it again and again without being put off by the Pharisaical, priggish and pithecanthropoid notes of its translator, Madame de Steiger. **1931** A. KEITH *New Discov. Antiq. Man* 293 The greatest number of these [characters] link these ancient Chinamen to the Pithecanthropic type of Java. **1958** L. DURRELL *Mountolive* xiii. 251 He mopped his brow continually, and gave his ingratiating pithecanthropoid grimace. **1958** F. E. ZEUNER *Dating Past* (ed. 4) ix. 304 At Ternifine in North Africa another pithecanthropine type of man proved to be associated with a primitive Acheulian industry. **1959**

J. D. CLARK *Prehist. S. Afr.* iv. 77 In Africa the cranial form of the Pithecanthropoid type of man may have undergone a fairly rapid development. *Ibid.*, The third and most probable explanation is that the Pithecanthropic stock early evolved..directly into a basic type of *Homo sapiens*. **1960** G. DURRELL *Zoo in my Luggage* ii. 44 His Pithecanthropic features split into a wide grin of glad recognition. **1961** *Times* 5 Sept. 13/5 The pithecanthropines were sometimes grouped with Neanderthal and modern man in the sub-family Homininae. **1962** *Advancement of Sci.* XVIII. 424/1 The advanced pithecanthropine skull recently discovered..has been dated approximately. **1976** *Sci. Amer.* Jan. 96/3 A pithecanthropine grade has been recorded in a unique 800-millilitre endocast from Lake Rudolph in Kenya that is almost three million years old; the better-known true pithecanthropines are about a million years old. **1979** 'C BRAND' *Rose in Darkness* v. 44 Like an archaeologist, building up the whole structure of ancient man from a single tooth..pithecanthropoid man.

pithiatism (pi·þiătiz'm). *Psychol.* [ad. F. *pithiatisme* (J. Babinski 1901, in *Revue Neurologique* IX. 1079), f. Gr. πειθ-ώ persuasion + ἰατ-ός curable: see -ISM.] A type of hysteria thought to be amenable to and curable by suggestion. So **pithia·tic** *a.*

1910 *Lippincott's New Med. Dict.* 740/2 *Pithiatism*, = Hysteria. (Babinski.) *Ibid.*, Pithiatic. **1913** E. JONES in White & Jelliffe *Mod. Treatm. Nervous & Mental Dis.* I. viii. 370 Babinski attempts to divide verbal suggestions into those that are unreasonable..and those that are reasonable and beneficial... Treatment by means of persuasion he calls 'pithiatism'. **1918** J. D. ROLLESTON tr. *Babinski's Hysteria or Pithiatism* p. xv, Among the various nervous phenomena observed in the neurology of war it is most important to distinguish hysterical or pithiatic disorders. **1930** P. D. KERRISON *Dis. of Ear* (ed. 4) xxii. 551 Pithiatism implies not only the possibility of cure by persuasion, but also the fact that the disorder may in some degree be called into being by suggestion. *Ibid.*, Pithiatic deafness..is at its inception a veritable deafness, the inevitable sequence of a shock to the perceptive labyrinth, which could have had no other result. **1975** Y. PELICIER in J. G. Howells *World Hist. Psychiatry* iv. 131 Babinski (1901) proposed the name of 'pithiatism' to designate a special condition, where suggestion is able to produce or suppress clinical symptoms.

Pithiviers (pitivie). The name of a town in northern France used *attrib.* to designate a French cake or tart consisting of puff pastry with a rich almond filling.

[**1846** A. SOYER *Gastronomic Regenerator* 488 *Gateau de Pithiviers.* Blanch and pound well half a pound of almonds.] **1970** SIMON & HOWE *Dict. Gastron.* 303/1 *Pithiviers cake*, a French cake made from puff-pastry mixed with sweet and bitter ground almonds. It is light with a delicate almond perfume. **1973** *Guardian* 30 Mar. 11/4 Pithiviers cake..is one of the great puddings from France... Roll out two 10 in. circles from packet puff pastry... Make a frangipane filling.

pithos. Add: *pl.* **pithoi.** (Later examples.) Also *attrib.*

1925 V. G. CHILDE *Dawn European Civilization* ii. 32 From M.M. I to L.M. I clay jars (pithoi) were also used as receptacles for the corpse. **1949** W. F. ALBRIGHT *Archæol. of Palestine* vi. 118 In the first three phases of Iron-Age Bethel the dominant vase was a large store-jar (pithos) with a very characteristic collared rim. **1955** *Sci. Amer.* July 45/2 At one entrance to this building was a sunken 'lustral area', where visitors made formal ablutions on arrival; it was surrounded by tall 'pithos' jars for water. **1957** V. G. CHILDE *Dawn European Civilization* (ed. 6) v. 72 In 1955 a cairn with pithos burials very like our round tombs was found in Messenia, but was M.H. in date. **1962** [see *DÆDALIC *a.*] **1972** Y. YADIN *Hazor* II. iv. 50 It seems that the room served as a store; this is further corroborated by eight pithoi found in it. The bases of the pithoi were stuck deep in the floor of the room.

pithy, *a.* **2.** (Later example.)

1876 SWINBURNE *Let.* 10 Jan. (1960) III. 112 A sea without rocks or cliff,..water thick and pithy with sand.

pi·tkin. *nonce-wd.* [f. PIT *sb.*[1] + -KIN.] A little pit.

1917 E. POUND *Lustra* 199, I dug the ell-square pitkin.

pitman. Add: **2. a.** (Later examples.)

1934 J. B. PRIESTLEY *Eng. Journey* x. 334, I ought to explain here that in Durham collieries are always 'pits' and miners 'pitmen'. **1978** R. LEWIS *Uncertain Sound* iii. 76 My father had been a simple pitman.

3. b. A motor-racing mechanic working in a pit (see *PIT *sb.*[1] 1 h).

1913 *Technical World Mag.* XIX. 495/2 A pitman has noticed that the tire is flat.

c. *U.S. colloq.* (See quot.)

1961 A. BERKMAN *Singers' Gloss. Show Business* 69 *Pitmen*,..musicians playing in the orchestra pit.

5. (Earlier example.)

1813 O. EVANS in *Weekly Reg.* 17 Apr. 111/2, I apply the power by means of a connecting rod or rods (or pitman as it is called when applied in saw mills).

Pitman (pi·tmæ̆n). The name of Sir Isaac *Pitman* (1813–97) used *attrib.*, *absol.*, and in the possessive to denote a system of shorthand notation devised by him and first published in 1837.

Pitman's Shorthand is a proprietary name in the U.K.

[**1862** M. LEVY *Hist. Short-hand* xvii. 167 Compare their rules with those of Pitman, in which he explains how to write the Scotch guttural.] **1886** *Encycl. Brit.* XXI. 838/2 The main features of Pitman's system must now be described. **1895** *Montgomery Ward Catal.* 74/1 The Reporter's Style of the Pitman System, by which fluent speakers can be reported verbatim. **1907** *Trade Marks Jrnl.* 5 June 963 Pitman's Shorthand Isaac Pitman 292,180. **1916** G. B. SHAW *Pygmalion* Pref. 101 His [*sc.* Sweet's] true objective was the provision of a full, accurate, legible script for our noble but ill-dressed language; but he was led past that by his contempt for the popular Pitman system of shorthand, which he called the Pitfall system. *Ibid.*, There was a weekly paper to persuade you to learn Pitman... I actually learned the [*sc.* Sweet's] system..and yet the shorthand in which I am writing these lines is Pitman's. **1951** E. COXHEAD *One Green Bottle* vi. 171 What's Ogam?.. A sort of prehistoric Pitman's? **1969** K. GILES *Death cracks Bottle* ii. 17, I think my Pitman is decipherable. **1970** E. MCGIRR *Death pays Wages* ii. 52 It is an exercise book and the entries are in very clear Pitman. **1976** *Daily Times* (Lagos) 8 Oct. 24/1 (Advt.), Applicants should possess WASC preferably with credit in English Language or equivalent and RSA or Pitmans or Government Certificate or their equivalent for 100/50 w.p.m. in shorthand and typewriting.

Hence **Pitma·nic** *a.*, resembling or suggestive of Pitman shorthand; **Pi·tmanite,** a student or exponent of the Pitman system; **pi·tmanize** *v. trans.*, to fill (a book) with Pitman shorthand.

1908 G. B. SHAW *Let.* 29 June (1972) II. 793 The other day I was confronted with an old copy of the Academy, dated 1898, with some shorthand notes on the margin... You can imagine how the honest Pitmanite who was asked to decipher it..believed that he had saved me from a fearful scandal. **1912** BEERBOHM *Christmas Garland* 14 Seven whole 8 × 5 inch note-books had I pitmanised to the brim. **1925** *Blackw. Mag.* Aug. 264/1, I saw..a sheet of notepaper scribbled with Pitmanic symbols. **1960** *Times* 28 Sept. 13/4 What odds if the Pitmanic 'X' full stops were sometimes deliberately exaggerated!

pitmatic (pitmæ·tik). Also **-atick, -atik,** and in *pl.* (construed as sing.). [f. PIT *sb.*[1] after MATHEMATIC *a.* and *sb.*] The local patois used by miners in the north-east of England. Also in extended use.

1893–4 R. O. HESLOP *Northumb. Words* II. 539 *Pitmatics*, a jocose term for the technicalities of colliery working. **1901** 'R. GUTHRIE' *Kitty Fagan* 8 Pitmatics? I've been schooled in them. **1934** J. B. PRIESTLEY *Eng. Journey* x. 334 The local miners [in Durham] have a curious lingo of their own, which they call 'pitmatik'... It is only used by the pitmen when they are talking among themselves... When the pitmen are exchanging stories of colliery life..they do it in 'pitmatik', which is Scandinavian in origin, far nearer to the Norse than the ordinary Durham dialect. **1961** *Listener* 23 Nov. 865/2 The ambitious young actor who naturally speaks beautiful English must assume a rough-diamond pitmatic though he has it not. **1967** A. L. LLOYD *Folk Song in Eng.* vi. 382 Most of his [*sc.* Tommy Armstrong's] songs are in the peculiar North-eastern miners' jargon called 'pitmatic'. **1972** *Jrnl. Lancs. Dial. Soc.* Jan. 19 He had many recollections of coal miner's terms, or, as they are known locally, *pitmatic.* **1976** *Daily Mail* 19 Aug. 19/2 Fred Reed, a dialect poet, gives examples of 'pitmatic', the language of the coalminer spoken in pits throughout the North.

Pitocin (pitōu·sin). *Med.* Also **pitocin.** [f. PI(TUITARY *a.* + *OXY)TOCIN.] A proprietary name for (an aqueous solution of) oxytocin.

1929 *Official Gaz.* (U.S. Patent Office) 15 Jan. 514/1 Parke, Davis & Company, Detroit, Mich... *Pitocin.* For oxytocic principle of the pituitary gland... Claims use since about October 20, 1928. **1929** *Jrnl. Amer. Med. Assoc.* 19 Jan. 237/2 The alpha and beta hormones [isolated from the posterior lobe of the pituitary body] are to be known commercially as pitocin and pitressin respectively. **1929** *Trade Marks Jrnl.* 23 Jan. 117/1 Pitocin... All goods included in class 3 [i.e. chemical substances prepared for use in medicine and pharmacy]... Parke, Davis and Company,..pharmaceutical chemists. **1929** MARTINDALE & WESTCOTT *Extra Pharmacopoeia* (ed. 19) II. 169 Each Cc. of 'Pitocin' contains 10 oxytocic units, and it is thus identical in activity with 'Pituitzin'. **1948** MARTIN & HYNES *Clin. Endocrinol.* i. 11 Two distinct hormones can be obtained from posterior pituitary extracts—pitressin, and oxytocin or pitocin, which acts on uterine muscle. **1961** *Lancet* 30 Sept. 762/1 The use of pitocin induction of labour in hæmolytic disease of the newborn.

pitometer: see *PITOT[2] b.

piton (pī·tǫn). [Fr., = 'eye-bolt', also 'piton'.] **1.** *Physical Geogr.* (See quot. 1972.)

1902 *Pop. Sci. Monthly* July 274 Northern Martinique, like other West Indian islands, is a labyrinth of mornes and pitons, i.e., of singularly steep peaks and ridges (partly volcanic cones, partly erosional forms), densely clothed with forests and herbage. **1918** C. W. BEEBE *Jungle Peace* (1919) iii. 56 A small wandering rainstorm drifted against the smallest piton and split in two. **1944** C. A. COTTON *Volcanoes* xi. 177 (*heading*) Smooth cliffs.. moulded during vertical extrusion of a plug dome to form the piton Lassen Peak, California. **1972** *Gloss. Geol.* (Amer. Geol. Inst.) 543/1 *Piton*, a term commonly used for volcanic peaks, especially steep-sided domes, in the West Indies and other French-speaking regions. **1976** *Sat. Rev.* (U.S.) 30 Oct. 26/2 St. Lucia..offers..cone-shaped volcanic peaks and twin pitons.

2. *Mountaineering.* (See quot. 1909.)

1898 *Encycl. Sport* II. 49/2 Snatch blocks and other kinds of pulleys, pitons or holdfasts..are also requisite. **1909** C. E. BENSON *Brit. Mountaineering* ii. 40 Piton—a strong iron spike with an eye at one end through which a rope can be passed. **1916** G. D. ABRAHAM *On Alpine Heights & Brit. Crags* iii. 64 He surprised us by scraping the ice off a ring-headed *piton* which was driven into a rock crevice. **1936** AUDEN & ISHERWOOD *Ascent of F6* II. i. 75 They're hammering the whole south face full of pitons and hauling each other up like sacks! **1955**, etc. [see *ÉTRIER]. **1959** 'G. CARR' *Swing away, Climber* iii. 58 He carried a multitude of short metal pegs with holes in the blunt end—pitons. **1972** *Country Life* 13 Jan. 94/3 From time to time a piton has to be hammered in, for.. the rock disintegrates.

3. *Comb.* (in sense 2), as *piton belay;* **piton hammer,** a hammer designed for fixing and extracting belays; **piton runner,** a piton used as a running belay.

1971 C. BONINGTON *Annapurna South Face* xiii. 164 On reaching the ledge leading into the main icefields, Mick hunted around for piton belays, eventually found a couple of suitable cracks and abseiled back. **1943** R. C. GEIST *Hiking, Camping & Mountaineering* 227 They are driven into rock cracks or into ice by a special piton hammer. **1952** MORIN & SMITH tr. *Herzog's Annapurna* ix. 141, I used my piton-hammer..as an anchor. **1971** C. BONINGTON *Annapurna South Face* vi. 76 The whammer, a space-age style piton-hammer of his own design. *Ibid.* x. 117 The rope behind Martin was dragging badly because of the friction caused by its passage through the tunnel and various piton runners.

pitot[1]**.** Delete *Obs.* and add later example.

1971 A. M. LYSAGHT *Joseph Banks in Newfoundland & Labrador 1766* vii. 161 These molluscs [sc. *Cyrtodaria siliqua*] are known by the French name of 'pitot' and the areas where they live are called 'pitot banks'.

pitot[2] (pī·to). *Physics and Aeronaut.* Also **Pitot.** The name of Henri *Pitot* (1695–1771), French scientist, used to designate devices based upon his inventions for measuring the relative velocity of a fluid, esp. the airspeed of an aircraft, as **pitot head,** a pitot-static tube; **pitot-static** *a.*, designating a device consisting of a pitot tube inside or adjacent to a parallel tube closed at the end but with holes along its length, the pressure difference between them being a measure of the relative velocity of the fluid; also *absol.*; **pitot** († or **Pitot's) tube,** an open-ended right-angled tube pointing in opposition to the fluid flow and connected to a means of measuring pressure; also, a pitot-static tube; also *absol.*

1881 *Encycl. Brit.* XII. 508/1 A Darcy gauge..consists of two Pitot tubes having their mouths at right angles. **1895** R. C. CARPENTER *Heating & Ventilating Buildings* ii. 38 In case the pressure and velocity are great, considerable error will be made by using the open tube.., and for such a case a Pitot's tube..should be used. **1901** G. E. DAVIS *Handbk. Chem. Engin.* I. iv. 191 The total pull of a chimney upon a water manometer when only one limb of the tube was connected up, was 14/16 of an inch, while with the Pitot tube the amount shown was only 8/100 of an inch of water. **1914** *Techn. Rep. Advisory Comm. Aeronaut. 1912–13* 59 This pressure-tube anemometer consists of two tubes, a Pitot tube facing the wind and a static pressure-tube along the wind direction with holes drilled into the side of it. **1916** *Field* 20 May 788/2 At last he fumbles for his safety belt, but with a start remembers the Pitot Air Speed Indicator, and..smiles as he hears the Pitot-head's gruff voice, 'Well, I should think so, twenty miles an hour I was registering.' **1920** G. C. BAILEY *Compl. Airman* xxi. 172 The only really satisfactory test of the Pitot is a flying one. **1920** L. BAIRSTOW *Appl. Aerodynamics* iii. 75 (*heading*) Initial determination of the constant of the pitot-static pressure head. **1930** C. J. STEWART *Aircraft Instruments* iii. 54 The pitot-tube instrument is based on an adaptation of the method used by Pitot in 1732 for the measurement of the speed of a river. **1934** V. M. YEATES *Winged Victory* I. iii. 27 Looking at the pitot he found the speed was a hundred and twenty. **1942** *R.A.F. Jrnl.* 27 June 21 One [Gremlin]..was seen..to swing nimbly..down to the pitot head and block it with ice. **1948** *Jrnl. R. Aeronaut. Soc.* LII. 272/1 Rates of climb and descent measured by the pitot-static are subject to errors introduced by random vertical currents in the atmosphere. **1965** R. G. KAZMANN *Mod. Hydrol.* iv. 63 The Pitot tube can be used to make a pattern of measurements along the cross section of a stream. **1973** 'A. HALL' *Tango Briefing* ix. 111 His inability to know to what extent our airspeed would be true and to what extent it would be expressed by the wind in the pitot-head. **1975** L. J. CLANCY *Aerodynamics* iii. 25 The pitot-static tube may be mounted in a position on the aircraft where the flow is affected by the presence of the aircraft. **1978** R. V. JONES *Most Secret War* iv. 36 This is true enough of a pitot tube but, as Lindemann pointed out to me, the proposal was perfectly sound if one used, as the inventors suggested, accelerometers.

b. Pitot meter, also **pitometer** (pitǫ·mĭtəɹ). (See quots. 1934, 1941.)

1907 *Jrnl. Franklin Inst.* CLXIV. 440 It is only necessary to leave the pitometer orifices at the point of maximum velocity in order to record the mean flow. **1934** J. H. PERRY *Chem. Engineers' Handbk.* 692 The pitot meter consists of two tubes, one facing upstream and the other downstream. **1941** *Ibid.* (ed. 2) 838 The modified pitot tube known as a pitometer has one pressure opening facing upstream and the other facing downstream. The differential between the two openings is usually from 25 to 50 per cent more than that for a standard pitot tube. **1955** C. S. FORESTER *Good Shepherd* ii. 25 That was the pitometer log reading. **1961** *Engineering* 3 Nov. 566/3 The development flowmeters..were calibrated in clean air against a venturi meter and a pitot meter.

Pitressin (pitre·sin). *Med.* Also **pitressin.** [f. PIT(UITARY *a.* + *VASOP)RESSIN.] A proprietary name for (an aqueous solution of) vasopressin.

1929 *Official Gaz.* (U.S. Patent Office) 15 Jan. 514/2 Parke, Davis & Company... Filed Nov. 2, 1928. Pitressin. For pressor principle of the pituitary gland... Claims use since about Oct. 20, 1928. **1929** [see *PITOCIN]. **1929** *Trade Marks Jrnl.* 23 Jan. 117/1 Pitressin... All goods included in class 3 [i.e. chemical substances prepared for use in medicine and pharmacy]... Parke, Davis and Company,..pharmaceutical chemists. **1943** *Lancet* 27 Feb. 267/1 Pitressin tannate in oil seems to be the safest and most effective slowly acting preparation of the posterior pituitary lobe so far available for the treatment of diabetes insipidus. **1974** *Jrnl. Pediatrics* LXXXV. 79/2 The infant's water balance was initially controlled with intravenous fluids alone but subsequently he was given a trial of pitressin. **1974** *Aerospace Med.* XLV. 1223/1 These same groups also showed little change in urine output in response to subcutaneous administration of 300 mll of Pitressin tannate in oil. **1976** *Lancet* 25 Dec. 1403/2 Aqueous vasopressin injection ('Pitressin') as a prophylactic measure was popular some years ago [against headache after lumbar puncture].

‖ **pitso** (pi·tso). Also † **peetsho,** † **peetso,** † **piicho, pitsu,** and with capital initial. [Sotho.] A Sotho tribal conference in a *kgotla*.

1822 J. CAMPBELL *Trav. S. Afr.: 2nd Journey* I. 264 The other chief said they should come to the *peetso* all well powdered. **1824** W. J. BURCHELL *Trav. S. Afr.* II. 408 The *piicho* or assembly remained sitting in easy conversation for nearly an hour longer. **1828** J. PHILIP *Res. S. Afr.* II. vii. 132 All great questions, and all questions relating to peace or war, are decided on in public assemblies, which are designated in their language by the name of Peetshos. **1879** *Queenstown Free Press* (Suppl.) 28 Oct. (Pettman), The annual *Pitso* was held at Maseru on the 19th instant, about 10,000 being present. **1897** J. BRYCE *Impressions S. Afr.* xx. 424 To-day the Pitso has lost much of its old importance. **1925** *Brit. Weekly* 4 June 211/3 The population of Basutoland is little over half a million, and the entire manhood must have ridden in to the *Pitso*. **1947** L. HASTINGS *Dragons are Extra* ii. 50 A great *pitso* was arranged. The traditional gathering took place in the open country south of Serowe. **1953** J. PACKER *Apes & Ivory* x. 105 The Royal visit to Basutoland, when the whole nation had gathered in a mighty *pitsu* at Maseru to welcome the King and Queen and their daughters had left a deep impression. **1959** *Chambers's Encycl.* IX. 747/1 Matters of highest importance were discussed in the *pitso*, the national assembly, at which the poorest and meanest tribesman had equal right with the proudest to voice his opinion. **1968** A. FULTON *Dark Side of Mercy* 27 The Chief had summoned the men of the clan to the Khotla and opened the pitso by telling those assembled that the season had been poor, [etc.]. **1976** WEST & MORRIS *Abantu* 121 It was more usual for all matters of general concern to be aired at a *pitso*, a general meeting open to all adult men in the chiefdom and held in the kgotla of the chief.

pitta, var. *PITA².

pitter-litter (pi·tər li·tər), *adv. rare*⁻¹. [After PITTER-PATTER *sb.* (*adv.*).] = PITTER-PATTER *sb.* (*adv.*) 2 a.

1910 H. G. WELLS *New Machiavelli* (1911) I. ii. 18 Dropped most satisfyingly down a brick shaft, and pitter-litter over some steep steps to where a head slaughterman strung a cotton loop round their legs.

pitting, *vbl. sb.* Add: **4.** (Later examples in *Bot.*)

1933 *Forestry* VII. 22 No complex forms of plate were observed with scalariform intervascular pitting. **1973** H. E. DESCH *Timber* (ed. 5) ii. 35 The pitting occurring in a cross field takes one or other of five more or less distinct forms.

5. = *pit planting* s.v. *PIT *sb.*¹ 14.

1847 [see *NOTCHING *vbl. sb.* 3]. **1894** A. D. WEBSTER *Pract. Forestry* iv. 20 The advantages of pitting over any other method of planting cannot be questioned. **1930** *Forestry* IV. 19 The ordinarily understood pitting implies the opening of a hole 12 to 15 inches square, stirring up the under soil well, and then carefully placing the plant in the centre.

pittite². Add: Also **pitite.** (Earlier and later examples.)

1812 *Dramatic Censor 1811* 8 The O.P. dance was attempted to be performed, but the Pitites had not yet mustered in sufficient force to carry their desire into effect. **1818** in J. Agate *These were Actors* (1943) 72 We cannot give the unfortunate *Pittites* any hope of shelter from 'the icy wind of Death' which seems to blow from all quarters at once [at Drury Lane]. **1892** 'F. ANSEY' *Voces Populi* 2nd Ser. 155 *A pittite behind Jimmy*... Will you tell your little boy to set down, please? **1903** A. BENNETT *Truth about Author* xiii. 162 Many time I have stood with you. But never again, miserable pittites! **1939** JOYCE *Finnegans Wake* (1964) III. 427 The graced of gods and pittites. **1961** BOWMAN & BALL *Theatre Lang.* 260 *Pittite*, in British terminology, a spectator in the pit.

pittosporum. For (Banks 1788) in etym. substitute (J. Banks in J. Gærtner *De Fructibus et Seminibus Plantarum* (1788) I. 286). Substitute for def.: An evergreen shrub or small tree of the genus so called, belonging to the family Pittosporaceæ, native to many subtropical or temperate regions, especially Australasia and China, and bearing small, often fragrant, flowers; also, a shrub of this genus cultivated as a house plant. Also *attrib.* (Earlier and later examples.)

1789 W. AITON *Hortus Kewensis* III. 488 Thick-leav'd Pittosporum. Nat[ive] of Madeira. **1911** A. E. MACK *Bush Days* 2 You climb up the rocky path and brush under green pittosporums. **1948** W. ARNOLD-FORSTER *Shrubs for Milder Counties* ii. 27 The pittosporums include some of the most useful of evergreens. **1962** R. PAGE *Educ. Gardener* viii. 247 Thickly planted bushes of dark green pittosporum..I clipped into low green mounds. **1963** S. SCHULLER *1001 House Plants Questions Answered* 221 Can I grow pittosporum easily indoors? Yes, if you can provide a cool..south window for it. **1965** G. MCINNES *Road to Gundagai* xiv. 244 Ballan was..well treed, especially..around Miss McCoppin's Guest House with its tall pittosporum hedge. **1972** PALMER & PITMAN *Trees S. Afr.* I. 659 Our indigenous pittosporum, growing in every province of South Africa under widely differing conditions, is naturally very variable in form. **1979** *Country Life* 26 Apr. 1298/2 Planting of replacement evergreens such as ceanothus, pittosporums and cistuses may be..deferred another week or two.

pitty² (pi·ti). A nursery form of PRETTY *a.*

1826 M. ROGET *Jrnl.* 27 Oct. in D. L. Emblen *P. M. Roget* (1970) xi. 191 One year old... Tries to imitate everything she hears, and says 'Papa', 'Mama', 'Ta', 'Pitty', 'Ba'. **1879** C. M. YONGE *Burnt Out* i. 6 Mammy, mammy, pitty, pitty! Dada kill great big piggy wig. **1939** JOYCE *Finnegans Wake* (1964) II. 361 Wingwong welly, pitty pretty Nelly!

pituicyte (pitiū·isəit). *Histology.* [f. PITUI(TARY *a.* + -CYTE.] A small cell with branching processes that is the characteristic cell of the neurohypophysis.

1930 P. C. BUCY in *Jrnl. Compar. Neurol.* L. 505 The pars nervosa is made up of a dense connective-tissue network containing nerve fibers which descend the stalk, epithelial cells which invade the pars nervosa from the pars intermedia for a short distance, and a type of cell which is peculiar to the neural portion of the hypophysis and which we have called the pituicyte. **1948** MARTIN & HYNES *Clin. Endocrinol.* i. 2 The only specialized cells in the neural division are pituicytes. **1959** ROWE & WHEBLE *Conc. Textbk. Anat. & Physiol.* xiii. 524 The posterior lobe is made up of large numbers of nerve fibres and a special type of cell known as pituicytes. **1975** DANIEL & PRICHARD *Stud. Hypothalamus & Pituitary Gland* iii. 27 Pituicytes, or modified glial cells, are scattered throughout the tissue [of the upper infundibular stem].

pituitary, *a.* Add: (Further examples.)

Pituitary body or *gland* is partly synonymous with *HYPOPHYSIS 3, q.v.; it is sometimes taken to include the infundibulum. The functions of the organ are now known.

1825, etc. [see *HYPOPHYSIS 3]. **1940** *Res. Publ. Assoc. Res. Nervous & Mental Dis.* XX. 28 Together with its investing sheath consisting of portions of the lobus glandularis (pars tuberalis and part of the pars intermedia), the infundibulum or neural stalk is correctly referred to as the hypophysial or pituitary stalk. **1942** O. LARSELL *Anat. Nervous Syst.* xviii. 254 The hypophysis or pituitary body is a gland of internal secretion. **1950** *Sci. News* XV. 132 The anterior lobe of the pituitary gland, which lies at the base of the brain, regulates the amounts of adrenal cortical hormones which circulate in the blood. **1954** [see *NEUROHYPOPHYSIS]. **1968** PASSMORE & ROBSON *Compan. Med. Stud.* I. xxv. 9/2 The pituitary gland consists of four different parts... (1) Pars posterior or neurohypophysis is an outgrowth of the brain to which it is attached by the infundibulum. (2) Pars anterior is the main part of the organ and is glandular in structure. (3) Pars intermedia is rudimentary in man but is large in some vertebrates... (4) Pars tuberalis is an extension of pars anterior and encloses the infundibulum. It is also rudimentary in man. **1975** J. B. PHILLIPS *Devel. Vertebr. Anat.* iii. 58/1 Gonadotrophic (gonad-stimulating) hormones, produced by the anterior lobe of the pituitary gland (hypophysis) control the function of the gonads.

b. (Earlier and later examples of sense (*b*) (sense (*a*) is *obs.*).)

1899 *Jrnl. Physiol.* XXV. 89 We confirm Howell's statement that the rise of blood-pressure is produced solely by the infundibular part of the pituitary and not by the hypophysial part. **1919** [see *HYPOPHYSIS 3]. **1932** S. ZUCKERMAN *Social Life Monkeys* v. 81 In the rat, surgical removal of the pituitary stops the œstrous cycle. **1965** MARSHALL & HUGHES *Physiol. Mammals* ix. 232 The pituitary is situated below the hypothalamus..and is made up of two parts. The hypophysis (anterior lobe) is derived from the roof of the buccal cavity, while the infundibulum from a down growth of the fore brain makes up the posterior lobe. **1974** D. & M. WEBSTER *Compar. Vertebr. Morphol.* xiii. 302 The pituitary has two major components, which develop from separate tissues and grow together... The neurohypophysis is formed by a ventral growth from the hypothalamus; the adenohypophysis, by a dorsal evagination from the roof of the mouth.

Pituitrin (pitiū·itrin). *Med.* Also **pituitrin.** [f. PITUIT(A)R(Y *a.* + -IN¹.] **a.** A proprietary name for an extract of the posterior lobe of the pituitary body which contains the hormones oxytocin and vasopressin. † **b.** A name proposed for the hormone formerly thought to be present in this extract but now recognized as a mixture. *Obs.*

1909 *Progressive Med.* IV. 318 The extract of the pituitary body has been prepared by Parke, Davis & Co., under the name of pituitrin. **1909** *Offical Gaz.* (U.S. Patent Office) Dec. 297/2 Parke, Davis & Co., Detroit, Mich. Filed July 26, 1909. Pituitrin... Cardio-vascular stimulants and diuretics. **1922** B. HARROW *Glands* 55 We have given the name 'pituitrin' to the hormone (or hormones) present in the posterior lobe of the pituitary... This hormone has not been isolated in the pure state. **1924** G. B. SHAW *St. Joan* p. xix, A precise and convenient regulation of her health and her desires by a nicely calculated diet of thyroid extract, adrenalin, thymin, pituitrin, and insulin. **1924** *Trade Marks Jrnl.* 3 Sept. 1953 Pituitrin... A pharmaceutical preparation of the pituitary gland for human use. Parke, Davis & Company, Detroit, State of Michigan, United States of America; and..London,..pharmaceutical chemists. **1927** HALDANE & HUXLEY *Animal Biol.* viii. 163 The posterior part [of the pituitary gland] produces a hormone, pituitrin, which affects smooth muscle. **1973** *Exper. Eye Res.* XVII. 3 When injected intravenously in intact animals, pituitrin produces a rise of intraocular pressure coincident with a rise in blood pressure.

pituri. Add: Also **pitery, pitjuri.** Also *attrib.* (Later examples.)

1931 I. L. IDRIESS *Lasseter's Last Ride* (1933) xvii. 137 Old Warts took from behind his ear a half-chewed plug of pituri, made from the pituri shrub. **1934** A. RUSSELL *Tramp-Royal in Wild Austral.* xix. 123 They [*sc.* the natives] use the pitjuri leaf—which they are also so fond of chewing—poisoning the little-used water-holes with leaves picked from the plant, enough to cause staggers but not death, and then going out and killing the drunken game. **1941** I. L. IDRIESS *Great Boomerang* xiv. 102 Finally one by one the pituri-chewers become stupefied, rolling over and sleeping through day and night. **1964** *Sunday Mail Mag.* (Brisbane) 25 Oct. 3/1 We tossed our swags into the station land rover..for a two-day run from the station out to Allawonga Springs and the pituri country. **1967** *New Scientist* 27 Apr. 226/1 Even the primitive Australian Aborigine has found a pleasurable weed—pitery—which contains nornicotine.

pity, *sb.* **3. a.** (*the*) *more is the pity* (earlier examples).

1797 R. M. ROCHE *Children of Abbey* (ed. 2) III. iii. 26 Poor thing, she is going fast indeed, and the more's the pity, for she is a sweet creature. **1848** J. RUSKIN *Let.* 22 Sept. in M. Lutyens *Ruskins & Grays* (1972) xvii. 158 You and my mother must be left at least *tranquil* as you are to be left—more's the pity—now so much alone. **1851** E. C. GASKELL *Let.* May (1966) 838 It is a small old fashioned farm..at the *foot* of the hill. More's the pity. **1875** 'MARK TWAIN' in *Atlantic Monthly* Feb. 217 A chance to get acquainted with a youth who had taken deck passage—more's the pity; for he easily borrowed six dollars of me.

pity, *v.* **3.** (Later example.)

1862 C. M. YONGE *Countess Kate* xii. 222 Sylvia and Charlie, took it all in, pitied, wondered, and were indignant, with all their hearts.

‖ **più** (pi·u), *adv. Mus.* Also **piu.** [It.] More; used in musical directions, as *più mosso* [*MOSSO *a.*], more animated, *più piano* [PIANO *a.* (*adv.*)], softer, etc.; also *fig.*

1724 *Short Explication Foreign Words in Musick Bks.* 54 Piu Piano, or PP, is very soft or low. *Ibid.* 55 Piu, signifies a little more, and increaseth the strength of the signification of the word it is joyned with. **1740** J. GRASSINEAU *Mus. Dict.* 180 *Piano piano* or *piu piano*, is nearly the same with *pianissimo*, or rather a degree between it and *Piano*. *Ibid.* 181 *Piu*, a little more, it increases the strength of the signification of the word to which 'tis added. **1876** STAINER & BARRETT *Dict. Mus. Terms* 355/2 *Più*,..more, as *più allegro*, faster; *più forte*, louder; *più lente*, slower; *più piano*, softer; *più presto*, more rapid; *più stretto*, more urged or closer; *più tosto allegro*, rather quicker. **1931** *Times Educ. Suppl.* 12 Dec. 1/3 The engineers have made the turn-over at the *piu mosso*. **1952,** etc. [see *MOSSO *a.*]. **1959** *Collins Mus. Encycl.* 504 Più by itself = *più mosso*. **1962** A. HARMAN et al. *Man & his Music* III. v. 671 There is no way of bringing the music to a stop except a *più mosso* coda. **1975** *New Yorker* 3 Nov. 136/2 Then the horn..sets the new tempo for a *più-mosso* section, in which the flute and the bassoon play leading roles.

pium (pi·ʊm). [Pg., a. Tupi.] A South American buffalo gnat, *Simulium pertinax.* Also *attrib.*

1863 H. W. BATES *Naturalist on River Amazons* I. vii. 333 (*heading*) Piúm flies. *Ibid.*, We made acquaintance ..with a new insect pest, the Piúm, a minute fly. **1927** W. M. MCGOVERN *Jungle Paths & Inca Ruins* iv. 51 The most obvious of the insect pests were the little *piums*... Their sting gave more than a momentary discomfort. **1933** P. FLEMING *Brazilian Adventure* I. xvii. 145 By day the worst pest was the *pium* fly, a little black creature the size of a midge, which covered your hands and anything else it could get at with small hard red pimples.

‖ **piupiu** (piu·piu). *N.Z.* [Maori.] **a.** Dressed flax. Also *attrib.* **b.** A Maori skirt made of dressed flax (see quot. 1946).

1882 T. H. POTTS *Out in Open* 23 Robes of piu piu, korowai, or of dogskin, contributed a great variety of costume. **1905** W. BAUCKE *Where White Man Treads* 90 Who so..skilful in the weaving of piupiu, korowai, fancy mats as..Te Aatarangi? **1938** R. FINLAYSON *Brown Man's Burden* 30 He just threw his coat off and rolled his trousers up, but the other men wore old-time piupius, and their imitation battle-axes were quite clever. *Ibid.* 67 Lucy, dressed in her swishing piupiu skirt and gay headband..swung the little poi balls for the tourists' snapshots which they labelled 'Maori dancer, Rotorua'. **1946** *Jrnl. Polynesian Soc.* June 156 *Piupiu*, a garment consisting of a heavy fringe, about nine inches wide or more, made of flax and craped at intervals and dyed black. The flax when drying curling up into pipes. **1970** *Times* 23 Mar. 7/6 Down on the grass before her stood ranks of Maori men and women in *Piu-Pius* (flaxen skirts). **1978** P. Grace *Mutuwhenua* iii. 12 My mother and the others had been..bringing out the piupiu which had been rolled and sausaged into stockings and stored at the tops of our wardrobes.

Piute, var. *Paiute *sb.* and *a.*

piva: see *pivo.

pivie, var. Peavey, pevy.

1907 *Black Cat* June 24 Mehetabel launched the boat, and running along the logs, piloted it hither and thither hooked to a pivie.

pivo, piva (pī·vo, -ă). [Slavonic *pivo* (Russ. *pivo*, Pol. *piwo*, etc.), beer.] An Eastern European beer made from barley malt or a similar fermented beverage.

1950 V. Canning *Forest of Eyes* vi. 119 In the room were two army officers,..their faces flushed with *pivo* and brandy. **1962** J. Wade *Running Sand* xix. 228 Piva... Just the job. **1964** S. Bellow *Herzog* i. 22 Elias..drank prohibition beer—home-brewed Polish piva. **1976** 'D. Halliday' *Dolly & Nanny Bird* xviii. 244 Someone had produced *pivo* and his minions were shouting and spraying the workshop with beer. **1979** *Listener* 19 July 71/1 'Another *pivo*, squire?'

pivot, *sb.* Add: **3. c.** In football and some other games, a player in a central position, esp. a centre-back; such a position. Also *attrib.*

1911 *Hartley Coll. Mag.* XII. xxxiii. 48 Howarth was moved from outside left to centre, but it was obvious ..he would be spoilt if retained as pivot. **1928** *Weekly Dispatch* 24 June 21/7 Robert Plenderleith, the East Fife centre half-back, one of the most promising of young pivots in Scotland. **1930** *Daily Express* 6 Oct. 16/5 Wilson, the Huddersfield pivot, was kept mainly on the defensive. **1951** *Football Record* (Melbourne) 8 Sept. 13 The Dons' hopes of success could well depend on his ability to gain control of the pivot position today. **1970** *Globe & Mail* (Toronto) 26 Sept. 36/2 Winnipeg has been looking for a take-charge pivot after going through a disappointing season. **1974** *State* (Columbia, S. Carolina) 27 Feb. 2-B/4 Jim Bolla, 6-8, is expected to be in the pivot. **1974** *Plain Dealer* (Cleveland, Ohio) 26 Oct. 4-D/1 In the pivot Steve Patterson and Jim Chones totalled 13 boards. **1975** *Oxf. Compan. Sports* 66/1 The tallest players of all, playing near the basket, are called pivots, centres, or posts. **1976** *Sunday Tel.* 25 Jan. 36/2 There is emerging a new nomenclature which refers to the 'pivot five', those players in the back row of the scrum and at half-back whose talent and technique decide how the ball is used at source.

d. = *pivotal man* s.v. *Pivotal *a.* 1 b.

1919 *Punch* 29 Jan. 76/2 They are keeping all the pivots in this area for one final orgy of demobilisation at some future date.

e. *Math.* In the numerical evaluation of a determinant, or the numerical solution of simultaneous linear equations, a non-zero element of the determinant or matrix which is used as follows: all elements in its row are divided by it, and appropriate multiples of that row are then subtracted successively from the other rows, so that the pivot itself is replaced by unity and all other elements in its column are replaced by zero; (this gives, in the case of a determinant, a number, the pivot, multiplied by a determinant whose order is reduced by one, and in the case of simultaneous equations, a set of equations one fewer in number from which one of the variables has been eliminated). Freq. *attrib.*

1933 *Proc. Edin. Math. Soc.* III. 211 At Stage II we choose another pivot at will..and cross-multiply with respect to it in the same way, dividing each result, however, by the previous pivot, 5. **1940** *Brit. Jrnl. Psychol.* XXX. 363 The determinant is condensed in the manner already shown (each pivot being converted into unity) until it is reduced to one number. **1958** S. I. Gass *Linear Programming* ii. 29 Since at the start of an iteration it is convenient to make the coefficient of the variable being eliminated equal to 1, we divide the second equation by 3. The coefficient 3 is referred to as the pivot element. *Ibid.* iv. 58 Element x_{lk} is the pivot element of the elimination transformation, with row *l* being the pivot row and row [*read* column] *k* being the pivot column. **1971** Coulson & Richardson *Chem. Engin.* III. iv. 295 Some methods of solution are better adapted to automatic digital computers than others. The method of Gaussian elimination with selection of pivots, or pivotal condensation, is particularly suitable. **1973** Phillips & Taylor *Theory & Appl. Numerical Anal.* viii. 197 The fault in the first attempt at solving Example 8.6 was that a small pivot (the coefficient of *x* in the first equation), meant that very large multiples of the first equation were added to the others, which were therefore 'swamped' by the first equation, after rounding.

f. *Linguistics.* = **pivot word.*

1963 M. D. S. Braine in *Language* XXXIX. 4 There is a basis for defining two primitive word classes: a class of pivots..to which a few frequently occurring words belong, and a complementary class which has many members, few of which recur in more than one or two different combinations. **1966** D. McNeill in Smith & Miller *Genesis of Lang.* 21 It never happens..that two-word sentences are made up only of pivots. **1971** *Jrnl. Speech & Hearing Disorders* XXXVI. 44 Rules that account for utterances in terms of the juxtaposition of pivots and open words cannot account for differences in semantic interpretation. **1973** M. F. Bowerman *Early Syntactic Devel.* 30 Students of language acquisition have sometimes referred to words which a child uses with greater-than-average frequency as 'pivots'... When used in this way, the conception of 'pivot' has little more relevance to child speech than to adult speech. **1975** *Canad. Jrnl. Linguistics* XX. 220 Arabic children have a much easier time of it than English children since such Pivot–Open constructions are generally well-formed sentences in adult grammar.

6. b. *pivot man* (later examples); **pivot bearing** = Footstep 5 d; **pivot break** *Rugby Football* (see quot.); **pivot class** *Linguistics*, the class of pivot words; **pivot grammar** *Linguistics*, a grammar of an early stage in children's speech in which two word classes are postulated, pivot words (see below) and a larger open class; **pivot pass** *Rugby Football* (see quot.); **pivot word** *Linguistics*, one of a limited set of words recurring in particular utterance positions at an early stage of a child's acquisition of syntax, and postulated as constituting one of two basic word classes at this stage of development.

[**1875** *Engineering* 30 July 87/1 Pivoted bearings for line shafts, now almost universally employed in America.] **1877** W. C. Unwin *Elem. Machine Design* vii. 122 (*heading*) Pivot and collar bearings. **1960** V. B. Guthrie *Petroleum Products Handbk.* ii. 29 Oils used for pivot bearings in instruments are of low volatility. **1975** *Sci. Amer.* July 50/3 If a combination of the two forces exists, a special bearing (an angular bearing, a taper bearing or a pivot bearing) is employed. **1960** E. S. & W. J. Higham *High Speed Rugby* 70 Another way..is to break on the side of the scrum on which the ball was put in. This is sometimes called the 'pivot' break, because the scrum-half pivots around his outside foot. **1964** *Amer. Psychologist* XIX. 3/2 Two classes of words appear—a pivot class and an open class—and the child launches forth on his career in combinatorial talking. **1966** D. McNeill in Smith & Miller *Genesis of Lang.* 20 The pivot class characteristically has few members compared with the open class. **1970** —— *Acquisition of Lang.* iii. 25 Pivot classes may appear first or second in sentences. **1970** L. M. Bloom *Lang. Devel.* 24 The speech of children described in pivot grammars in other investigations. **1971** *Jrnl. Speech & Hearing Disorders* XXXVI. 42 How does pivot grammar relate to the grammar of the adult model language? *Ibid.* 47 The notion of pivot grammar describes children's early speech in only the most superficial way. **1973** M. F. Bowerman *Early Syntactic Devel.* 4 An analysis of diary studies of children acquiring languages other than English led Slobin..to hypothesize that the pivot grammar might be a universal first grammar regardless of the particular language being acquired. **1976** *Word 1971* XXVII. 33 In what ways does mother-child interchange indicate that Laura's initial two-word combinations are semantically and structurally too sophisticated to be described adequately by a pivot grammar? **1918** *Daily Mail* 6 Dec. 3/3 (*heading*) 12,000 pivot men. **1967** *Boston Sunday Herald* 9 Apr. (This Week Mag.) 4/3 Locate the 'pivot man' on each team—he's the fielder who makes the first move as the team adjusts position for each new batter. **1971** L. Koppett *N.Y. Times Guide Spectator Sports* iii. 88 The pivotman is usually the center, and the tallest man on his team. **1978** *Detroit Free Press* 5 Mar. c. 4/2 Joe Barry Carroll, Purdue's 7-1 pivotman, scored 14 of his game high 22 points in the first half. **1960** E. S. & W. J. Higham *High Speed Rugby* 68 You will have to pivot round on the outside foot as you take off. This is called the 'pivot' or 'reverse' pass. **1963** M. D. S. Braine in *Language* XXXIX. 4 These words will be called 'pivot' words, since the bulk of the word combinations appear to be formed by using them as pivots to which other words are attached as required. **1964** *Amer. Psychologist* XIX. 3/2 Whereas before, lexemes like *allgone* and *mummy* and *sticky* and *bye-bye* were used singly, now, for example, *allgone* becomes a pivot word and is used in combination. **1966** D. McNeill in Smith & Miller *Genesis of Lang.* 20 Each pivot word is used more frequently than individual open-class words. **1975** *Canad. Jrnl. Linguistics* XX. ii. 220 Much has been made in studies of children's syntax in English of a stage at which there are only two parts of speech, a Pivot, or function word like 'want', and an Open, or content word like 'milk'.

pivotable (pi·vətăb'l), *a.* [f. Pivot *v.* + -able.] Capable of being turned as if on a pivot. So **pivotabi·lity**, the extent to which an object can be so turned (in quots., as a measure of angularity).

1961 *Jrnl. Sedimentary Petrol.* XXXI. 198/1 A somewhat modified version of Powers' scale was adopted by the writers. In this scale the idea of 'pivotability' was given paramount importance so that the grains which could be most easily pivoted were given the highest values. **1967** *Jane's Surface Skimmer Systems 1967–68* 83/2 The result is a simple and reliable lift control, which requires neither electric or hydraulic power sources, nor pivotable foils or flaps. **1971** W. A. Pryor in R. E. Carver *Procedures Sedimentary Petrol.* vii. 143 Pivotability or rollability is a measure of the motion response of a grain to a set of standard physical conditions in a gravity-driven system.

pivotal, *a.* Add: **1. a.** (Further examples.)

1925 *Times* 5 Jan. 4/3 Young's passes..were..much too high to enable Kittermaster, as the pivotal player, to pave the way for a scoring position. **1927** Peake & Fleure *Priests & Kings* 134 A new feature, however, was the use of door-slabs of stone set with pivotal hinges. **1930** *Daily Express* 6 Oct. 2/6 Pivotal shares were occasionally in moderate demand. **1953** [see *film editor* s.v. *Film *sb.* 7 c]. **1965** *New Scientist* 6 May 383/3 Dædalus feels that the time is ripe for another OK word. He has had difficulty in deciding on one with the right ring of vague pomposity about it, but has decided on 'pivotal'. He hopes that it ultimately will become synonymous for 'important' or 'interesting'. He asks all his readers to include it in articles, papers, research reports and the like, confident that the elite of New Men who read *New Scientist* will suffice to launch this new word on a glorious and pivotal career. **1969** Z. Hollander *Mod. Encycl. Basketball* 211 (*heading*) The pivotal era. **1973** *Amer. Speech 1969* XLIV. 281 The uniqueness of black folk speech seems to rest in the pivotal position it occupies in the rural community, sharing phonological features with cultivated blacks and whites, grammatical features with white folk speakers, and lexical forms with all members of both castes. **1976** *National Observer* (U.S.) 13 Nov. 4/5 The pardon of Richard Nixon was pivotal, it seems, to those independents who made up their minds at the last minute and turned to Jimmy Carter. **1977** *N.Y. Rev. Bks.* 28 Apr. 29/3 (Advt.), Here is a penetrating, pivotal study of the astonishing relationships between Shakespeare's dramatic use of time and modern views on how any time-sense shapes human experience and behavior.

b. *pivotal man*, a man considered to have an important part to play in the re-establishment of industry and commerce after the war of 1914–18, and hence eligible for early demobilization; also *ellipt.* as *sb.*

1918 *Daily Mail* 29 Nov. 3/2 Men who are essential to the building up and expansion of trade..are officially described as 'pivotals'. *Ibid.*, These are the pivotal men who will prepare the way for the hundreds of thousands who are to follow on general demobilization. *Ibid.*, The commerce of the City of London has been allotted a given number of pivotal men. *Ibid.* 11 Dec. 5/1 A pivotal man is an essential man in an industry or occupation on which the re-establishment of other industries depends. **1920** F. Watson *Pandora's Young Men* iii. 22 She found Blinkhorn in some out-of-the-way depot in France and managed to have him demobilised as a pivotal man. **1922** *Encycl. Brit.* XXX. 214/2 The release of 'Pivotal Men'.. met with much opposition.

2. *Math.* Being or involving a pivot (sense *3 e); *pivotal condensation*, the evaluation of a determinant by the use of pivoting on determinants of successively lower orders.

1924 Whittaker & Robinson *Calculus of Observations* v. 71 We prepare the determinant for our subsequent operations by multiplying some row or column by such a number *p* as will make one of the elements unity, and put $1/p$ as a factor outside the determinant. This unit element will henceforth be called the pivotal element. **1939** A. C. Aitken *Determinants & Matrices* ii. 47 A determinant of order *n* being reduced by a first pivotal condensation to one of order $n-1$, the latter in its turn can be reduced by a second pivotal condensation to one of order $n-2$, and so on. **1952** D. R. Hartree *Numerical Anal.* viii. 158 The coefficient a_{jk}..is called the 'pivotal coefficient' or 'pivot' for this elimination; it is the coefficient, in the pivotal equation, of the variable to be eliminated. **1963** N. Macon *Numerical Anal.* v. 59 It is of some interest to calculate the number of arithmetical operations required for the evaluation of a determinant of order *n* when pivotal condensation is used. **1971** [see *Pivot *sb.* 3 e]. **1973** A. M. Cohen et al. *Numerical Anal.* viii. 136 We add suitable multiples of equation (8.17*a*) to equations (β), (γ), and (δ) to reduce the coefficients of x_1 in them to zero... Equation (α), which remains unaltered, is called the pivotal equation.

3. *Linguistics.* Of, pertaining to, or based upon pivot grammar or pivot words (see *Pivot *sb.* 6 b).

1963 M. D. S. Braine in *Language* XXX. 4 *Do it, push it, close it*, etc...appear to exemplify the same kind of pivotal construction as the previous combinations discussed, except that now the pivot is in the final position. *Ibid.* 10 The pivotal type of construction continues long after the first five months, and new pivot words develop. **1970** L. M. Bloom *Lang. Devel.* 223 The two relational aspects of language appear to be related to the two descriptions of children's speech as 'telegraphic' and 'pivotal'. **1971** *Jrnl. Speech & Hearing Disorders* XXXVI. 42 How does the child progress from using pivotal utterances to using utterances that reflect the complex interrelation of rules that is the essence of adult phrase structure?

Hence **pi·votalism**, the policy of releasing 'pivotal men' from active service before others.

1919 W. S. Churchill in D. Cooper *Haig* (1936) II. xxvii. 406 Indiscipline and disorganisation would arise in the Army if pivotalism, i.e. favouritism, were to rule in regard to the discharge of men. **1922** *Encycl. Brit.* XXX. 215/1 Pivotalism..was called ' favouritism'.

pivoting, *vbl. sb.* (s.v. Pivot *v.*). Add: **2.** *Math.* The use of a pivot (sense *3 e) as a means of making a column of a determinant or matrix consist entirely of zeros except for one unit element; also, pivotal condensation; *partial pivoting*, pivoting in which the choice of pivot at each stage is restricted to the largest element in the first column (or the first row) of the relevant part of the matrix, rather than the largest in all its columns or rows (*complete, total*, or *full pivoting*).

1961 *Jrnl. Assoc. Computing Machinery* VIII. 282 We derive first an upper bound for *R* when a general matrix is reduced to triangular form by Gaussian elimination, selecting as pivotal element at each stage the element of maximum modulus in the whole of the remaining square matrix. We refer to this as 'complete' pivoting for size, in contrast to the selection of the maximum element in the leading column at each stage, which we call 'partial' pivoting for size. **1963** N. MACON *Numerical Anal.* v. 59 The effect of pivoting on rounding errors. **1968** FOX & MAYERS *Computing Methods for Scientists & Engineers* v. 86 Partial pivoting is generally satisfactory, and..can be made still better, by the use of fl_2 arithmetic.., in a manner which cannot easily be performed with total pivoting. **1973** PHILLIPS & TAYLOR *Theory & Appl. Numerical Anal.* viii. 197 Partial pivoting using only row interchanges is preferable to that with only column interchanges.

piwarrie. Add: The more usual spelling is now *paiwari*. This name for the beverage is used *spec.* with relation to the Indians of Guyana. (Further examples.) Cf. *CASSIRI.

1868 W. H. BRETT *Indian Tribes of Guiana* I. ix. 155 After a few lashes, they drank paiwari together, and returned to the main body of the dancers. **1883** E. F. IM THURN *Among Indians of Guiana* xv. 319 All the festivals among all the tribes being occasions for much drinking of paiwari—the national beverage—they may all be called Paiwari Feasts. **1934** E. WAUGH *Handful of Dust* vi. 337 'They have been making *piwari*... You should try some.'.. Tony gulped the dark liquid, trying not to taste it. But it was not unpleasant, hard and muddy on the palate like most of the beverages he had been offered in Brazil, but with a flavour of honey and brown bread. **1938** *Amer. Anthropologist* XL. 228 Another method of manufacturing alcoholic beverages in South America was to ferment the starchy juice of the pressed or chewed cassava (*Jatropha manihot*)... It was called paiwari or paiva in British Guiana,..cachiri among the Roucouyenne, and cauim or pajuarú among the aborigines of Brazil. **1958** H. G. DE LISSER *Arawak Girl* v. 50 Francisco had been drinking much piwari. **1964** V. G. C. NORWOOD *Jungle Life in Guiana* v. 108 Quantities of the three principal native beers or liquors brewed by forest Indians throughout Guiana: cashiri, yamanchi and paiwarrie.

pix[2] (piks), var. *pics*, pl. of *PIC[4].

In quot. 1932 used for the sing.

1932 *Variety* 19 July 4/5 (*heading*) 'Million', Par's all-star pix. *Ibid.* 9 Aug. 15/4 (*heading*) Open sesame for Brit. pix in Dominion. **1935** *Ibid.* 3 Apr. 10/1 On Sunday two powerful b.o. pix. were released. **1936** WODEHOUSE *Laughing Gas* ii. 20 'Your face seems extraordinarily familiar, too.' 'You've probably seen it in pix.' 'No, I've never been there.' 'In the pictures.' **1940** R. CHANDLER *Farewell, my Lovely* iii. 13 That's what I rate after eighteen years in this man's police department. No pix, no space, not even four lines in the want-ad section. **1945** [see *HYPO *v.*]. **1955** POHL & KORNBLUTH *Space Merchants* ii. 22 Our artists can work from the pix you brought back. **1960** *Analog Science Fact/Fiction* Dec. 48/2 Now they have a chance to get their news releases and faked pix out in quantity. **1973** E. HYAMS *Final Agenda* iv. 53 Barnet said, 'I want the Victoria Lowell pix.'.. [He] began looking through the thirty-seven photographs of Victoria Lowell. **1975** D. LODGE *Changing Places* ii. 90 He would be holed up somewhere, jerking himself off and drooling over the *Playboy* pix. **1977** *Zigzag* June 23/3 Tome is shown the Warner Bros. press kit for him, with accompanying pix.

pixel (pi·ksel). [f. *PIX[2] + EL(EMENT *sb.*] = *picture element* s.v. *PICTURE *sb.* 6 d.

1969 *Science* 15 Aug. 685/1 An analog tape recorder was used to store the analog video signal from each pixel. **1975** *Sci. Amer.* Oct. 67/1 The cross sections of the heart were subsequently reconstructed by the same computer. Each cross section took two minutes of computing time and was displayed on a cathode-ray tube as a square picture with 64 pixels on a side. **1977** *New Yorker* 14 Feb. 28/1 The [advertising] panel is divided into two thousand and forty-eight 'pixels', or picture elements of red, green, blue, and white bulbs, and ordinarily only one or two of the bulbs on a pixel are flashed at a given time. **1977** *Proc. R. Soc. Med.* LXX. 593/1 No doubt the next edition using up-dated prints will overcome the difficulties of interpretations associated with the large size of pixel.

pixilated (pi·ksilēi:tėd), *a.* orig. *U.S. dial.* Also **pixelated, pixielated, pixillated, pixylated.** [f. PIXY, PIXIE + *-lated* as in *elated*, *emulated*, etc. or var. PIXY-LED *a.*] **1.** Mildly insane, fey, whimsical; bewildered, confused; intoxicated, tipsy.

1848 in *Amer. Speech* (1941) XVI. 79/2 You'll never find on any trip That he'll be pix-e-lated. **1886** E. L. BYNNER *Agnes Surriage* iv. 56 'See now wher' we ha' come to wi' yer talk, Job Redden!' cried Agnes, waking suddenly to their situation. 'We'll be pixilated 'n' driven on to th' rocks an ye don't wake up.' **1895** *Dialect Notes* I. 392 *Pixilated*, dazed, bewildered in the dark. Marblehead, Mass. **1936** in *Amer. Speech* (1941) XVI. 79/2 *Lawyer*: Now tell me, what does everybody back home think of Longfellow Deeds?.. *Jane*: They think he's pixilated. *Ibid.* 80/1 The word pixilated is an early American expression—derived from the word 'pixies' meaning elves. They would say, 'The pixies have got him,' as we nowadays would say a man is 'balmy'. **1937** *N. & Q.* 2 Jan. 11/2 As a native of the state from which 'Mr. Deeds' is reputed to have come permit me to comment on..'pixilated'. To use the word in the sense of 'crazy' is not correct. A Vermonter would not hesitate to use 'crazy' if that conveyed his meaning. A 'pixilated' man is one whose whimseys are not understood by practical-minded people... Nearly a synonym of 'whimsical'. **1955** 'J. R. MACDONALD' *Find Victim* xxiv. 167 'Wasn't he pretty drunk on Sunday?' 'He was pixilated all right,' Jo said. **1957** L. IREMONGER *Ghosts of Versailles* viii. 103 Ultimately no explanation of the 'adventure' was too fantastic, far-fetched or indeed pixylated for them. **1958** *Observer* 30 Nov. 16/6 Nicely cast, he gave the true tone of pixilated delinquency. **1971** *Listener* 8 Apr. 449/1 Suddenly we were pixilated, we'd fallen in love with the sweetest girl we ever saw. **1975** C. NESBITT *Little Love & Good Company* xvii. 208 We were both ever so slightly inebriated, no not even that, pixilated, to use the lovely movie euphemism. **1977** *New Yorker* 29 Aug. 28/3 He was known as a coarse creature and a little pixillated.

2. Of an actor: having movements animated by the pixilation technique.

1959 *News Chronicle* 20 Oct. 8/7 The animator..may use conventional comic drawings..or even 'pixillated' live actors.

pixilation, pixillation (piksilēi·ʃən). Also **pixylation.** [f. *PIXILATED *a.*: see -ATION.] **1.** A technique used in theatrical and cinematographic productions, whereby human characters move or appear to move as if artificially animated; the effect produced.

1947 *Punch* 5 Mar. 200/1 Those who, as I am, are made uncomfortable by material pixylation on the stage may take heart, for the *Catherine* who comes back from the midnight romp is no gauzy fay. **1953** *Q. of Film, Radio & Television* VIII. 9 McLaren feels this kind of live-actor animation has considerable creative potentiality although he refers slightingly to it as the 'pixillation' technique. **1957** MANVELL & HUNTLEY *Technique Film Music* iii. 167 By applying an animation technique to the movements of actors, he produced 'pixilation' and used it to tell a serious story—in *Neighbours* (Canada 1953). **1959** HALAS & MANVELL *Technique Film Animation* xxv. 291 This technique of experimenting in the animation of the movements of live actors (called sometimes 'pixilation') accompanied by synthetic music and sound effects. **1971** *Concord Films Council Catal.* 51/2 Yugoslavian experimental film in the pixilation technique. **1976** *Oxf. Compan. Film* 438/1 McLaren here [*sc.* in *Neighbours*], and in *Two Bagatelles* (1952), used pixillation, 'animating' human actors. In *Chairy Tale* (1957) and *Opening Speech* (1960) the technique is applied humorously to inanimate objects. *Ibid.* 547/2 *Pixillation*, the use of a stop frame camera to speed up and distort the movement of actors, creating roughly the effect of animation with live people.

2. The state or condition of being pixilated (sense 1).

1960 *Spectator* 6 May 677 Without pretentiousness and with no traces of pixilation and phoney Cornishness.

pixy, pixie. Add: The more usual spelling is now *pixie*. **a*.** Short for **pixie cap, hat*, etc.

1960 *Harper's Bazaar* Oct. 114 Fur pixie.

b. *pixie-like* adj.; **pixie cap,** a pointed hat resembling that in which pixies are traditionally depicted; **pixie cape,** a cape with an attached pixie hood; **pixie hat** = **pixie cap*; **pixie hood,** a pointed hood; so **pixie-hooded** *a.*

1828 Pixie cap [see *KILMARNOCK 1]. **1943** F. URQUHART in *Penguin New Writing* XVI. 90 She was wearing a crimson waterproof pixie-cap which was almost the same colour as her pretty, round face. **1960** M. A. SINDALL *Matey* vii. 89 Brown woollen pixie caps. **1973** *Listener* 23 Aug. 244/2, I knew that I did not look my best in my mackintosh with its pixie cape. **1954** G. DURRELL *Three Singles to Adventure* v. 106 On his sleek black head was perched an absurd pixie hat constructed out of what once used to be velvet. **1940** C. MILBURN *Diary* 23 Dec. (1979) 75 Two little pixie-like children in green overall garments, complete with pixie hoods. **1950** B. PYM *Some Tame Gazelle* viii. 89 They stood in the doorway,..wearing mackintoshes, and that wet-weather headgear so unbecoming to middle-aged ladies and so incongruously known as a 'pixie hood'. **1955** E. BOWEN *World of Love* ix. 163 Maud, in wet weather rendered still more terrible by a pixie hood. **1961** *Guardian* 28 Nov. 7/1 The worthies of the village in ornamented pixie hoods. **1978** M. BUTTERWORTH *X marks Spot* I. i. 22 An old lady in a plastic pixie hood. **1949** E. COXHEAD *Wind in West* I. 15 Two pixie-hooded small boys. **1940** Pixie-like [see *pixie hood* above]. **1963** *Times* 16 May 14/6 The men wear a curious conical hat..which gives them a curious pixy-like appearance, while frequent recourse to chewing *qat* has wizened their faces and for all I know stunted their growth. **1979** J. WAINWRIGHT *Reluctant Sleeper* v. 69 Those ridiculously large spectacles, and that equally ridiculous pixie-like face.

Hence **pi·xyish** [-ISH[1]] *a.*, resembling that of a pixie.

1962 V. CONNAUGHT *Secret Heart of Princess Alexandra* x. 101 As she splashed by them, Alexandra appeared to take a pixyish glee in noting their discomfort. **1977** J. AIKEN *Last Movement* viii. 167 Her narrow, pixyish Irish face.

‖ **Piyut, Piyyut** (pi̇yu·t). Also **Peyut,** erron. **Piyyuth,** and with lower-case initial. Pl. **-im.** [Heb. *piyyuṭ* poem, poetry, f. *poyṭān*, *payṭān* poet, ad. Gk. ποιητ-ής (see POET).] A poem that is read or recited in a synagogue in addition to the standard liturgy.

1876 *Sat. Rev.* 16 Sept. 357/1 The 'Liturgy' recited in the synagogues every Sabbath from the Piyutim. **1876** *Gentl. Mag.* Nov. 601 Those Hebrew poems recited by the Ashkenazim, and called 'Peyutim'. **1972** C. RAPHAEL *Feast of Hist.* iii. 106 Like most other large-scale illustrated Haggadahs, the book also includes many pages of *piyyutim* (poems) drawing on biblical and midrashic themes. **1976** M. HOROWITZ in D. Villiers *Next Year in Jerusalem* 114 Even now my head reels daily with.. exalted Hebraic dirges..tracking back from Bialik to Yehuda Halevi to the Piyyuth and Ecclesiastes.

pize (pəiz), *v. dial.* [Origin uncertain: perh. ad. MDu. *pisen* (see quot. 1968[3]).] **a.** *trans.* To strike; *spec.* to hit (a ball) with the hand in the game of pize-ball (see next). Also const. *down.* **b.** *intr.* and *trans.* To throw (a ball) in the game of pize-ball; to act as bowler in pize-ball. **c.** *trans.* To throw to (the batter) in pize-ball.

1796 S. PEGGE *Derbicisms* (1896) 54 To *pize* a ball, to strike it with the hand; so the game is call'd *pize-ball.* To *pize down* a hare, i.e. with a gun; meaning to strike her down. **1862** C. C. ROBINSON *Dial. Leeds* 385 *Pize*, to throw a ball gently for another to bat with the open hand, as at the game of 'Pize-ball'. *Ibid.*, The game of 'Pize-ball', in which the 'pizer' 'pizes' the ball to a member in succession. **1968** A. S. C. ROSS in *Proc. Leeds Philos. & Lit. Soc.* (*Lit. & Hist. Section*) XIII. II. 59 If, however,.. the Pizer delayed too long,..the players would chant: 'Pize your neighbour while you're able, While the donkey's in the stable!' *Ibid.*, The player who had got round most times..might be the winner (and pized next game). *Ibid.* 63 *Pize* is a word entirely without an etymology. I suggest that it is a borrowing of MDutch *pisen*..name of a game about which further particulars are lacking. *Ibid.* 69 Applied to the ball, *pize* means both 'to throw' and 'to strike'.

Hence **pize** *sb.*[2], a throw in pize-ball; **pi·zer,** a bowler in pize-ball; **pi·zing** *vbl. sb.*

1862 Pizer [see above]. **1869** 'T. TREDDLEHOYLE' *Bairnsla Foaks Ann.* 55 Throo thrawin a stones, tipsey lakein, an pizein a balls it publick street, good Bairnsla deliver uz. **1896** *Leeds Mercury Weekly Suppl.* 7 Mar. 3/8 Let me hev a pize, an' ah'll mak' him send a cop. **1968** *Proc. Leeds Philos. & Lit. Soc.* (*Lit. & Hist. Section*) XIII. II. 56 The thrower, or *Pizer*, stands some distance in front of the homey and throws the ball to the striker.

pi·ze-ball. *local.* Also **piseball, pizeball.** [f. *PIZE *v.* + BALL *sb.*[1] 4.] A game similar to rounders in which the ball is hit with the flat of the hand. (See also quot. 1883.)

Played mainly in Yorkshire and Derbyshire.

1796, 1862 [see *PIZE *v.*]. **1883** A. EASTHER *Gloss. Dial. Almondbury & Huddersfield* 102 *Pizeball*.., a ball which children play with, formerly stuffed with sawdust, etc... It was often partly coloured and ornamented; now it is sometimes of india-rubber and hollow. **1957** R. HOGGART *Uses of Literacy* ii. 58 'Piseball', 'tig',..and a great number of games involving running round the lamp-posts or in and out of the closet-areas..are still popular. **1968** *Proc. Leeds Philos. & Lit. Soc.* (*Lit. & Hist. Section*) XIII. II. 55 Pize-ball is a game which, in many ways, resembles the well-known games, Rounders and Baseball.

pizza (pī·tsă). Pl. **pizzas,** ‖ **pizze** (-ə). [It., = pie.] A savoury dish of Italian origin, consisting of a base of dough, spread with a selection of such ingredients as olives, tomatoes, cheese, anchovies, etc., and baked in a very hot oven; dough so prepared and baked. ‖ *pizza (alla) Napoletana* (ala napǫlitā·nă) [It., = Neapolitan, in the Neapolitan style], Neapolitan pizza (see quot. 1955).

1935 M. MORPHY *Recipes of All Nations* 160 Pizza alla Napoletana... In the south of Italy..all kinds of flat tarts are called 'pizze'. **1953** W. P. MCGIVERN *Big Heat* xi. 138 An unbaked pizza, or cheese pie, covered with thinly sliced tomatoes and criss-crossed with strips of anchovy. **1955** E. DAVID *Bk. Mediterranean Food* 40 The Neapolitan pizza..consists of tomatoes, anchovies and mozzarella cheese. **1957** O. NASH *You can't get there from Here* 150 She eatsa Pizza! Greedy Mitzi! She no longer itsy-bitsy! **1957** *Sunday Times* 1 Dec. 23/4 The Pizza Napoletana has travelled the world. In Paris restaurants, in Shaftesbury Avenue milk bars, in South Kensington coffee shops the pizza has become acclimatised. **1959** *Vogue* June 90 Food [in coffee-bars] is usually the pizza, sandwich or Danish pastry type. **1959** V. PACKARD *Status Seekers* (1960) 146 He was raised on blood sausages, pizza, spaghetti and red wine. **1970** SIMON & HOWE *Dict. Gastron.* 303/1 In its most primitive form *pizza* is a round of yeast dough spread with tomatoes and mozzarella cheese and baked in a hot oven. The most famous of the many *pizze* is the Neapolitan *pizza*... The Roman *pizza*..has plenty of onions but no tomatoes; the Ligurian *pizza* has onions, black olives and anchovies. **1972** J. MOSEDALE *Football* viii. 110, I like pizza, hamburgers and hot dogs. **1977** *New Yorker* 12 Sept. 97/1 Pizza is my speciality, I make it all myself. O.K. Well, now the dough is rising good, so I get out some tomatoes and the other stuff for a pizza alla napoletana.

2. *attrib.* and *Comb.*, as *pizza bar, cook, dough, mixture, palace, parlour, pie, stand*; *pizza-seller.*

1971 J. FLEMING *Grim Death* ii. 23 He was hoping to start up a Pizza bar. **1974** *Listener* 23 May 665/3 A pizza bar like we have in Glasgow. **1976** *Weekend Echo* (Liverpool) 4/5 Dec. 7/3 Scores of pizza bars and restaurants to suit all pockets. **1959** 'E. ALLEN' *Man who chose Death* ii. 24 So many shopgirls and garage hands and pizza cooks. **1960** E. CAMPBELL *Encycl. World Cookery* 263 Put the pizza dough onto a baking tin. **1977** *New Yorker* 12 Sept. 97/1, I start to work in the window up front and make some *pizza* dough. **1959** *Guardian* 25 Nov. 6/2 The Italian *origano*, an essential part in most pizza mixtures. **1959** *Times* 18 May 5/3 The pizza palaces and highway honky-tonks with which we have littered the land. **1974** P. ERDMAN *Silver Bears* ii. 20 That's a fucking pizza parlour. **1976** *Star* (Sheffield) 3 Dec. 14/7 One well-established pizza parlour tells me they even do a special Yorkshire style pizza—it's like the Italian ones..but fatter because we eat more. **1970** 'D. HALLIDAY' *Dolly & Cookie Bird* i. 3, I..bought a pizza pie..on my way home. **1976** *National Observer* (U.S.) 12 June 1/4 Ripping off the public is as American as pizza pie. **1961** *Times* 21 Dec. 3/2 Her earlier appearance as the ebullient pizza-seller. **1966** T. PYNCHON *Crying of Lot 49* v. 121 Down at the city beach, long after the pizza stands..had closed, she walked unmolested. **1966** A. CAVANAUGH *Children are Gone* II. v. 43 Laundromats, Jewish dairies, pizza stands, fruit stores.

pizzazz (pĭzæ·z). orig. *U.S. slang.* Also **bezaz, bezazz, bizzazz, pazazz, pazzazz, pezazz, pizazz, pizzaz.** [Origin unknown.] **1. a.** Zest, vim, vitality, liveliness. **b.** Flashiness, showiness.

1937 *Harper's Bazaar* Mar. 116/2 Pizazz, to quote the editor of the Harvard *Lampoon*, is an indefinable dynamic quality, the *je ne sais quoi* of function; as for instance, adding Scotch puts pizazz into a drink. Certain clothes have it, too... There's pizazz in this rust evening coat. **1951** *Time* 28 May 91/2 Rentschler thinks the J-57 has more pizzazz than any other engine. Says he flatly: 'It is more powerful than any jet engine ever flown.' **1952** S. KAUFFMANN *Philanderer* (1953) v. 86 Now here's a few places where I think it could use a little pezazz. **1962** *U.S.A.-1* I. IV. 30/2 He displayed almost none of the oratorical pizzazz that had set them [*sc.* Canadian voters] screaming in 1958. **1964** *New Statesman* 28 Aug. 291/1 A Shakespeare one [*sc.* exhibition]..with most of its bezazz—pop art, wire sculpture, giant beefeaters—left by the Avon. **1965** *Sunday Times* (Colour Suppl.) 16 May 12/1 She..still wears trousers frequently. 'I don't really feel happy in bezazz.' **1966** *Saturday Night* (Toronto) May 34/3 His campaign manager..mounted a campaign that has had few equals anywhere for sheer *pazazz.* **1967** R. STEIN *Great Cars* 202/2 Began doing for the dull little mass-produced British cars what it had done for the homely sidecar. It gave them what Detroit now calls 'pizzaz'. **1968** *Daily Tel.* 24 Dec. 8/4 Miss [Ginger] Rogers has 'bezazz', as was obvious from the number of reporters and photographers clustering round her. But Mr. Marshall..claimed it should be 'pezazz', derived from American TV commercials and meaning something like effervescence. **1970** *New Yorker* 14 Mar. 66, I knew that we absolutely had to have something with more bizzazz going for the young people. **1973** *Observer* (Colour Suppl.) 4 Nov. 10/2 What the ice-rink audience really likes is pizzazz, rather than lyricism: they like a cheesy grin, powerful thighs, plenty of intricate footwork with the blades, and above all a crunching four-four rhythm they can clap along with. **1974** *Language Sciences* Aug. 25/3 If they confined themselves to the level of common sense they would lose much of their academic pizzazz, their mystique as scientists. **1975** G. V. HIGGINS *City on Hill* ii. 44 Maybe some guy that could recruit more troops and out-fund us gets himself involved in a bloodletting with another guy who has some pizzazz, and..they knock each other off. **1976** *New Musical Express* 31 July 27/3 Ferguson's album has style and pizzazz. **1976** *National Observer* (U.S.) 2 Oct. 18/4 This confluence of ecology and art,..of business chutzpah and show-biz pizzaz. **1976** *Listener* 23 Dec. 841/3 Behind the pazazz there are some fundamental issues being toyed with. **1978** *People Weekly* 9 Jan. 57/1 'But it must have commercial appeal,' Flynt cautions. 'I think I give projects like this pizzazz.' **1979** *Arizona Highways* Apr. 19/1 (*caption*) Jimmy King, Jr. adds pizazz to his golden pendant..wrapping the design with his dazzling inlay.

2. *attrib.* or as *adj.* Flashy, ostentatious, 'zippy'.

1970 *Canad. Antiques Collector* Oct. 5/1 There are various displays of a great range of collectibles that create a lively 'bezaz' atmosphere. **1977** *Courier-Mail* (Brisbane) 6 Mar. 6/7 Sammy Davis Jnr...flashed $100,000 worth of sparkling rings... He confessed yesterday, at a crowded press conference..'It's theatrical and it's pizzazz.'

pizzeria (pītsərī·ă). [It.] A place where pizzas are made, sold, or eaten.

1943 J. STEINBECK *Once there was War* (1959) 184 He spoke the English we know, the English of the banana pushcarts and the pizzerias, of the spaghetti joints and grind organs. **1957** V. P. JOHNS in Charteris & Santesson *Saint's Choice* (1967) 198 The Pizzerias piled up when she went to Rome. **1966** L. DEIGHTON *Billion-Dollar Brain* xv. 141 We went past the silent skyscrapers, kosher pizzerias, glass-fronted banks. **1973** 'D. JORDAN' *Nile Green* xxxv. 171 She'll want to go to one of those pizzerias near the British Museum. **1977** *N.Z. Listener* 15 Jan. 17/1 Between performances he telephoned his wife in London, pottered around on the golf course, downed Newcastle ale and frequented 'The Pinocchio', a Sunderland pizzeria.

pizzle. Delete 'Now *dial.* or *vulgar*' and add later examples, esp. in *Austral.* cattle- and sheep-rearing terminology.

1946 R. GRAVES *Poems 1938–45* 27 Who whipped her daughters with a bull's pizzle. **1949** A. HUXLEY *Ape & Essence* 126 Then the Grand Inquisitor's Special Assistant bends down and, from under his chair, produces a very large consecrated bull's pizzle, which he lays on the table before him. **1955** W. GADDIS *Recognitions* II. iii. 441 He entered and walked toward the bull's stall—There!.. There's a masterful pizzle for you! **1965** J. S. GUNN *Terminol. Shearing Industry* II. 8 *Pizzle*, a sheep's penis. This word has no taboo and is the formal word in written articles. **1968** E. R. BUCKLER *Ox Bells & Fireflies* vi. 101 [An ox] would gallop the pasture faster than a horse, ramming a low stub halfway up his pizzle. **1969** *Coast to Coast 1967–68* 7 Ruben had caught the farmer's bull one night and tied a length of plastic cord around its pizzle, letting the bull go again in the paddock. The breeding paddock, with cows on heat.

placating (plăkē·tiŋ), *ppl. a.* [f. PLACATE *v.* + -ING².] That placates or is intended to placate; conciliatory. Hence as *sb.* (*rare*⁻¹); **placa·tingly** *adv.*

1911 M. JOHNSTON *Long Roll* xix. 243 Allen took it calmly, made a placating remark or two, and lapsed into a friendly silence. **1919** E. O'NEILL *Where Cross is Made* in *Moon of Caribbees* 167 (*Placatingly*) You're wrong, Father. **1921** *Spectator* 12 Mar. 333 Holland never dealt in half-measures; the placating whitey-grey argument or studiously reasoned compromise was to him anathema. **1925** T. DREISER *Amer. Trag.* (1926) II. xi. 235 'You're right, I know,' said Clyde placatingly, for he was still hoping for this hinted-at promotion. **1931** E. O'NEILL *The Hunted* IV, in *Mourning becomes Electra* (1932) 171 Hastily, with a placating air. **1935** W. STEVENS *Ideas of Order* (1936) 22 Be thou that wintry sound As of the great wind howling, By which sorrow is released, Dismissed, absolved In a starry placating. **1941** —— in O. Williams *New Poems: 1940* 202 The placating star Shall be the greater for the death you die. **1964** *Punch* 29 Jan. 153/1 My wife poured him a coffee placatingly. **1977** P. HILL *Fanatics* 21 Carpenter put up his hand in a placating gesture.

placative (plăkē·tiv), *a. rare.* [f. PLACATE *v.* + -IVE.] = PLACATORY *a.*

1931 W. FAULKNER *Sanctuary* xi. 107 Temple stared at her with that grimace of cringing and placative assurance.

place, *sb.*¹ Add: **1. b.** (Earlier and later examples of use as the second element of a proper name.)

1700 CONGREVE *Way of World* I. i. 4 There's such Coupling at Pancras..we were afraid his [the Parson's] Lungs would have fail'd..so we drove round to Duke's Place. **1791** F. BURNEY *Let.* 8 Sept. in *Jrnls. & Lett.* (1972) I. 55 A House in Laura Place. **1903** G. B. SHAW *Man & Superman* I. 2 Sitting at his writing table, he has on his right the windows giving on Portland Place. **1939** JOYCE *Finnegans Wake* (1964) I. 132 First he shot down Raglan Road and then he tore up Marlborough Place. **1972** J. MCCLURE *Caterpillar Cop* iii. 42 Kramer..took the Durban road, watching the street names on his left. He swung into Potter's Place. No 9 Potter's Place was untidier than most.

3. e. Colloq. phr. *all over the place*: disordered, irregular, muddled.

1923 J. MANCHON *Le Slang* 227 *All over the place*,..en pagaye. **1933** A. E. HOUSMAN *Let.* 13 July (1971) 337 The Doctor sent me into a nursing home for a week because he said my heart was all over the place. **1937** N. COWARD *Present Indicative* VI. i. 229 Lilian was cool and steady and played beautifully. I was all over the place but gave, on the whole, one of those effective, nerve-strung *tour-de-force* performances, technically unstable, but vital enough to sweep people into enthusiasm. **1953** R. LEHMANN *Echoing Grove* 16 In her youth it [*sc.* her hair] had spilled out all over the place, brilliant but not warm. **1959** H. PINTER *Birthday Party* II. 15 Why is it that before you do a job you're all over the place, and when you're doing the job you're as cool as a whistle? **1971** O. NORTON *Corpse-Bird Cries* vi. 125 Her heart's all over the place, according to Sister. Shock after losing the Colonel. **1971** M. MCCARTHY *Birds of America* 269 You seem unfocussed... All over the place. No clear line of direction. **1976** S. BRETT *So much Blood* iii. 43 'How's your show going?' '*Mary's* still all over the place. We spend so much time improvising..we hardly ever get near the actual script.'

5. b. (Further examples.)

1909 *Dialect Notes* III. 358 *Place, n.*, home, farm. 'When you comin out to our *place*.' *a* **1922** T. S. ELIOT *Waste Land Drafts* (1971) 5 We had a couple of feelers down at Tom's place. *Ibid.*, I turned up an hour later down at Myrtle's place. **1932** S. GIBBONS *Cold Comfort Farm* xix. 256 'Tell Reuben he can have the old place.'.. 'It's a pity he says "the old place" instead of "the farm".' **1939** JOYCE *Finnegans Wake* (1964) I. 43 A few good old souls, who, as they were juiced after taking their pledge over at the uncle's place, were evidently under the spell of liquor. **1946** E. HODGINS *Mr. Blandings builds his Dream House* ii. 14 The New York apartment..was home no longer; the old Hackett place on Bald Mountain was home, now. **1972** *Screw* 12 June 33/4 (Advt.), Young male nude model. Experienced, handsome... Completely versatile and cooperative. Your place or mine. **1978** J. F. BURKE *Crazy Woman Blues* i. 3 If she'd been taken ill suddenly she might have gone up to her place.

d. (Later examples.)

1973 R. L. SIMON *Big Fix* (1974) xiv. 99 We were sitting at the counter of Winchell's doughnut place on Glendale Boulevard. **1978** J. L. HENSLEY *Killing in Gold* (1979) xi. 148 We went to Mac's Place... The waitresses were..insolent.

e. *slang.* A lavatory (see also quot. 1951).

1901 FARMER & HENLEY *Slang* V. 220/2 *Place*,..(2) a jakes, or house of ease. **1922** JOYCE *Ulysses* 160 They did right to put him up over a urinal... Ought to be places for women. **1942** BERREY & VAN DEN BARK *Amer. Thes. Slang* §84/11 Toilet..place. **1951** PARTRIDGE *Dict. Slang* (ed. 4) 1137/2 *Place where you cough, the*, the water-closet... Ex coughing to warn an approacher that it is occupied.

8. c. Restrict '† *Obs.* (or *arch.* after Shaks.)' to sense in Dict. and add: Also phr. *pride of place*: a pre-eminent position.

1902 *Punch* 24 Dec. 434/1 A Minister who is chased by a loud-voiced Opposition From his pride of place. **1919** *Empire Rev.* XXXIII. 242 Britain is compelled to raise her prices to heights which..will send the British buyer abroad for those very materials in the manufacture of which we have formerly held pride of place throughout the world. **1931** A. HUXLEY *Music at Night* 222 Disease-snobbery is only one out of a great multitude of snobberies, of which now some, now others take pride of place in general esteem. **1948** G. GORER *Americans* i. 26 In the fantasies brought to light in psychiatric interviews pride of place went to those in which the officer was retaliated upon, humiliated, snubbed. **1954** M. BERESFORD *Lost Villages* x. 343 This site has pride of place for the admirable monograph by Dr. W. M. Palmer. **1976** *Flintshire Leader* 10 Dec. 32/1 Pride of place must go to Courtaulds Greenfield, the league leaders, who toppled the Welsh National League.. Division 1 champions, Denbigh Town. **1978** *Jrnl. R. Soc. Arts* CXXVI. 305/2 And then we come to folk and country drawings, which somehow have become a very American cult. These not unexpectedly are given a pride-of-place chapter.

9. c. (Earlier and later examples.) In *U.S.* applied *spec.* to second place.

1836 *Spirit of Times* 5 Mar. 22/1 He led the first two miles, Sir Kenneth trailing, and Mattiwan endeavoring to keep a place in the race. **1930** *Daily Express* 6 Oct. 17/6 *Tote.*—Win 5s; places 2s 9d, 2s 9d, 3s 6d. **1942** BERREY & VAN DEN BARK *Amer. Thes. Slang* §740/2 Place, second place, or at least second. **1976** *Daily Tel.* (Colour Suppl.) 26 Mar. 27/3 '£1 each way' means £2 split between a win and a 'place' (the horse finishes in the first three).

d. Phrases: *to know one's place*: to know how to behave in a manner befitting one's rank, situation, etc.; *it is not my place*: outside my duties or customary rights; *to put* (someone) *in his, her* etc., *place*: to remind someone of his or her rank or situation; to rebuff or rebuke.

1601 SHAKES. *Twel. N.* II. v. 59, I knowe my place, as I would they should doe theirs. **1739–40** RICHARDSON *Pamela* (1740) I. xi. 18 It does not become your poor Servant..and I hope I shall always know my Place. **1852** [in Dict., sense 9 a]. **1867** DICKENS & COLLINS *No Thoroughfare* in *All Year Round* Extra Christmas No. 12 Dec. 3/1 It is not my place, ma'am, to tell names to visitors. **1898** G. B. SHAW *Candida* II. 113 Mr Morchbanks is a gentleman, and knows his place, which is more than some people do. **1908** A. BENNETT *Old Wives' Tale* I. vi. 108 She ought to have put Mr. Povey into his place... Mr. Povey ought to have been ruined for ever in her esteem. **1916** G. B. SHAW *Pygmalion* II. 143, I should just like to take a taxi to the corner of Tottenham Court Road and get out there and tell it to wait for me, just to put the girls in their place a bit. I wouldnt speak to them, you know. **1930** W. FAULKNER *As I lay Dying* (1935) 5 It is not my place to question His decree. **1937** D. & H. TEILHET *Feather Cloak Murders* vi. 104 Not that I'm complaining. Dear me, no. I know my place. **1943** A. CHRISTIE *Moving Finger* vii. 85 These girls nowadays—don't know their place—no idea of how to behave. **1943** J. B. PRIESTLEY *Daylight on Saturday* xxxviii. 301 Every time I think..that it's going to be easy to put you in your place, you suddenly do or say something that breaks it all down. **1956** A. WILSON *Anglo-Saxon Att.* II. i. 195 When he asked her to choose a restaurant, she said, 'No, you do that thing. I'd much rather it was your choice.' He suggested Scott's, and she said, 'But that sounds absolutely the right thing.' He hoped that she was not going to put him in his place the whole evening. **1965** R. BASTIDE in G. Hunter *Industrialisation & Race Relations* I. 15 It institutionalised the subordination of the Negroes, who could only benefit from the protection of the whites..on condition that they 'knew their place' and proved their deference, gratitude and respect. **1973** R. STOUT *Please pass Guilt* (1974) xi. 109 On the phone you stiff-armed me. You put me in my place. **1974** J. STUBBS *Painted Face* 11 It's not my place to judge, sir. **1979** M. HEBDEN *Murder set to Music* ii. 17 'Did she have men friends?'..'It's not my place to say.'

12. d. Phr. *a place for everything and everything in its place.*

1842 F. MARRYAT *Masterman Ready* II. i. 9 In a well-conducted man-of-war..every thing is in its place, and there is a place for every thing. **1855** T. C. HALIBURTON *Nat. & Hum. Nat.* I. vi. 164, I was born on a farm..where there was a place for everything, and everything was in its place. **1857** EMERSON *Jrnl.* 2 Aug. (1914) IX. 110 A place for everything, and everything in place. **1875** S. SMILES *Thrift* v. 66 Order is most useful in the management of everything... Its maxim is—A place for everything, and everything in its place. **1922** JOYCE *Ulysses* 694 The necessity of order, a place for everything and everything in its place. **1928** D. L. SAYERS *Lord Peter views Body* x. 224 'I thought you were rather partial to anatomical specimens.' 'So I am, but not on the breakfast-table. "A place for everything and everything in its place", as my grandmother used to say.' **1941** 'J. J. CONNINGTON' *Twenty-One Clues* v. 74 A tidy person with a place for everything, and everything in its place. **1949** J. P. MARQUAND *Point of No Return* III. ii. 498 There was a place for everything in Clyde and everything was in its place. **1968** P. DICKINSON *Skin Deep* vii. 141 Do you run your whole life like that?.. A place for everything and everything in its place, and all in easy reach.

13. a. (Further examples.)

1955 *Times* 9 May 6/4 In five years we shall provide a million new school places. **1976** W. CORLETT *Dark Side of Moon* I. 29 He would have got a university place. **1976** G. MOFFAT *Over Sea to Death* xv. 174 They went in to dinner, drew the tables together and re-laid the places. **1977** D. WILLIAMS *Treasure by Degrees* iii. 28 Up to 1974.. there were still too many students chasing too few university places.

c. Phr. *a place in the sun*: see SUN *sb.* 4 b (*d*) in Dict. and Suppl.

29. *place-name* (further, including *attrib.*, examples); hence *place-namer*, *-naming* vbl. sb., *nomenclature*, *-ordering* vbl. sb.; *place-ordered* ppl. a.; (sense 2 b) *place-logic*, *-time*; (sense 9 c) *place-getter*; (sense 14) *place-seeker* (examples), *-seeking* vbl. sb.; *place-seeking* adj. (example); **place-card,** a card bearing a guest's name marking the place allocated to him at a table; **place-mat**, a table-mat for a place-setting; **place-money** *Racing*, (*a*) money placed as a bet that a horse, etc., will be second or third (in the U.S., second only); (*b*) prize-money for finishing second or third (in the U.S., second) in a race; **place-setting**, the cutlery, china, etc., required to set a place for one person at a table; **place-value**, the numerical value that a digit has by virtue of its position in a number.

1922 S. Lewis *Babbitt* viii. 115, I was going to have some nice hand-painted place-cards for you but—Oh, let me see; Mr. Frink, you sit here. 1934 J. O'Hara *Appointment in Samarra* (1935) iv. 97 She held a small stack of place-cards. 1938 L. Bemelmans *Life Class* III. ii. 225 Some terrible place-card holders made of sea shells. 1942 T. Bailey *Pink Camellia* ii. 12, I have the place cards ready. 1963 D. B. Hughes *Expendable Man* (1964) ii. 39 Now the stationer's... We need more place cards for tonight. 1974 P. Erdman *Silver Bears* v. 63 Beside each lady's place-card was a small orchid. 1976 *Eastern Even. News* (Norwich) 27 Aug., Kuda's Surge should be interesting, as should Bownee, a well-fancied place-getter last time. 1976–7 *Sea Spray* (N.Z.) Dec./Jan. 77/3 Prizes:.. A Hanimex f3.5/80–200 mm multicoated zoom lens, valued at $150, for the third place-getter in the senior section. 1977 *N.Z. Herald* 5 Jan. 1-17/6 The women's team will consist of the first three in the target competition, plus Hamilton's Thelma Croft, because the fourth placegetter, Joan Ward (Manakau), did not score qualifying totals before the championships. 1957 A. N. Prior *Time & Modality* 119 Consider..a place-logic in which we have the means of formulating the law. 1968 N. Rescher *Topics in Philos. Logic* xiii. 229 A wide range of logical systems, including not only chronological.. logic, but also what we may call locative or place logic, and even a logic of possible worlds. 1951 T. Sterling *House without Door* ii. 21 The waitress took the mangled place-mat..and brushed the shreds of paper from the table. 1966 J. Cleary *High Commissioner* vi. 120 He looked at the table, at the silverware, the lace place-mats. 1972 J. Ball *Five Pieces Jade* x. 118 She had set two place mats and a small, intimate meal was waiting. 1977 *New Yorker* 10 Oct. 110/2 Farther on, we move into the dining room and partake of a genteelly wholesome meal from gold-edged china set on pale-green patterned placemats. 1894 G. Moore *Esther Waters* xliv. 348 Bramble, a fifty to one chance, not one man in a hundred backed her; King of Trumps, there was some place money lost on him. 1923 Wodehouse *Inimit. Jeeves* xiv. 179 A sniffing female in blue gingham beat a pie-faced kid in pink for the place-money, and Prudence Baxter, Jeeves's long shot, was either fifth or sixth, I couldn't see which. 1942 Berrey & Van den Bark *Amer. Thes. Slang* §734/3 Place money, the odds a horse pays to run second. 1970 *Globe & Mail* (Toronto) 25 Sept. 32/3 Miss Ella Cinders won but with the disqualification will now receive place money of $400 instead of $200 show money. 1973 *Times* 15 Dec. 16/4 A compulsory shareout of place money between owner, trainer and jockey on the same formula as for win money. 1924 Place-name [see *folk-name* (*folk 5 b)]. 1927 *Englische Studien* Nov. 64 The foundation of the English Place-Name Society (in 1923).. has given an enormous impetus to the study of English place-names. *Ibid.*, A useful and competent survey of the methods of the place-name study. *Ibid.*, There are three golden rules to be observed by every place-name student. 1961 L. F. Brosnahan *Sounds of Language* iii. 46 Linguistic, placename, and general knowledge of the history of Europe. 1966 *Eng. Stud.* XLVII. 208 In the pocket we find a geological map and six distribution maps on certain place-name elements. 1977 *Word 1972* XXVIII. 73 *Tre-* as a place-name element appears to have meant just 'settlement'. 1927 *Year's Work Eng. Stud. 1925* 35 The article will interest both lexicographers and place-namers. 1943 *Amer. Speech* XVIII. 241 Finding that in fire protection work it was very desirable, even imperative, that natural features capable of being named should have names as an aid in locating fires..I began place-naming more diligently. 1962 *Ibid.* XXXVII. 255 Florida place names follow the tendencies of place-naming all over the United States. 1922 E. Ekwall *Place-Names Lancs.* 5 To judge of many etymologies, it is of importance to be able to find out the general characteristics of the place-nomenclature of the neighbourhood. 1924 Mawer & Stenton *Introd. Survey Eng. Place-Names* ii. 33 The Irish-Gaelic element in the English place-nomenclature is..small. 1935 A. C. Baugh *Hist. Eng. Lang.* iv. 120 The extent of this [Scandinavian] influence on English place-nomenclature would lead us to expect a large infiltration of other words into the vocabulary. 1965 *Eng. Stud.* XLVI. 335 A marked Welsh element is noticeable in the place-nomenclature of the Forest of Dean, which adjoins Monmouthshire. 1977 *Word 1972* XXVIII. 118 It is therefore quite appropriate that 1976 be the year in which the evolution and state of research into the Celtic place-nomenclature of Scotland is given a brief retrospective assessment. 1966 G. N. Leech *Eng. in Advertising* ii. 18 Dependence is the type of depth-ordering that accounts for repetitions in place-ordered structure. 1969 *Eng. Stud.* L. 31 Furthermore, simplicity also depends on depth-ordered structure..as well as on place-ordered structure (discontinuous elements put a strain on the reader's memory). 1966 G. N. Leech *Eng. in Advertising* ii. 17 Up to this point, the idea of linguistic structure has been based on the principle of place-ordering: the principle whereby the order in which the elements of a pattern occur is tied to the class of unit they represent. 1902 *Kynoch Jrnl.* Oct.–Nov. 14/1 The firing point is not crowded with a lot of place-seekers croaking their grievances. 1955 *Times* 5 May 15/4 Elizabeth was putting out a hand to Cecil, still an official of the second rank in the crowd of place-seekers at Court during her brother's minority. 1908 *Daily Chron.* 24 July 4/6 How much of her success in place-seeking a woman owes to her business-like methods and how much to her milliner is a moot point. 1966 *Punch* 26 Jan. 137/3 Dr. Burney, the busy, place-seeking music teacher who dearly loved a lord. 1950 E. Post *Etiquette* (rev. ed.) xxix. 324 Dessert spoon and forks..need not—in fact preferably do not—match the foundation 'place setting' silver. 1951 M. McLuhan *Mech. Bride* (1967) 111 A single place setting for as little as $19.65. 1960 *News Chron.* 12 Apr. 8/6 Stainless-steel cutlery is proving a time-saver... I have found admirable place-settings for 48s. 6d. 1964 Mrs. L. B. Johnson *White House Diary* 6 May (1970) 131 These were just place settings, the most extraordinary of which, by all odds, was the Rutherford B. Hayes china, with its exotic patterns of wildlife. 1974 L. Deighton *Spy Story* xiv. 136 The neatly arranged place settings, polished glasses and starched napkins. 1944 *Mind* LIII. 39 It would seem to require that when I say 'this is a cat' at place-time$_1$ and 'this is a cat' at place-time$_2$, there is no difference of meaning but only of causation. 1959 P. F. Strawson *Individuals* vii. 223 Place-times are both spatially and temporally bounded. 1911 Smith & Karpinski *Hindu-Arabic Numerals* iii. 45 Concerning the earliest epigraphical instances of the use of the nine symbols, plus the zero, with place value, there is some question. 1948 D. Diringer *Alphabet* I. vii. 133 The character for zero—the importance of which was recognized by the Mayas many centuries before any other people in the world—was similar to a shell... The symbols for the multiples of 20..are still uncertain; it may be, however, that they had the 'place-value' notation. 1966 May & Moss *New Math for Adults Only* viii. 44/2 Face value tells how many. A digit's face value never changes. Place value tells how much. A digit's place value changes as its place in the numeral changes. *Ibid.* 45/1 Zero has no face value at all, but this digit has a most important place value.

‖ **place** (plas), *sb.*² [Fr.] In France, or occas. in other countries, a square (Square *sb.* 12). Freq. used in proper names.

1699 M. Lister *Journey to Paris* 10 The Squares are few in Paris, but very beautiful; as the Place Royal, Place Victoir, Place Dauphine. 1793 in M. Miliband *Observer of 19th Cent.* (1966) 4 Yesterday..the unfortunate Louis XVI suffered decapitation in the Square of the Revolution, formerly called Place Louis XV. 1852 E. Ruskin *Let.* 17 May in M. Lutyens *Effie in Venice* (1965) II. 312 We have moved into the Hotel in the Place and are very comfortably settled. 1873 C. M. Yonge *Pillars of House* III. xxxiii. 220 She is leading the gay life the *bourgeoisie* do here—at the theatre or out on the *place* all evening. 1908 T. E. Lawrence *Let.* 9 Aug. (1938) 59 Streets—mostly stairs..expanding sometimes into a 'place', sometimes into a cesspool. 1964 'J. Welcome' *Hard to Handle* viii. 53 A semicircle of houses built.. around a central *place*. 1973 *Country Life* 31 May 1552/3 Enniscorthy is even more Continental in character than New Ross... The steep and narrow street opens unexpectedly into a market square... In the middle of this *place*..there is a '98 memorial.

place, *v.* Add: **1. c.** *Cricket, Baseball*, and other ball games. To control and guide (the ball) in making a stroke or hit.

1836 *New Sporting Mag.* July 196 There is nothing plagues a bowler like placing his best balls on the on side for one run. 1880 *Brooklyn Daily Eagle* 22 Aug., Not one in five of the crowd of batsmen know [*sic*] how to wait for a ball or how to 'place' it when they get one to hit. 1886 H. Chadwick *Art of Batting & Base Running* 33 The highest degree of skill in scientific batting is reached when the batsman can 'place a ball'—in any part of the field he chooses. 1887 F. Gale *Game of Cricket* 66 Both batsmen went to work..very steadily placing a ball here and there for one. 1905 H. A. Vachell *Hill* xii. 268 The Eton captain had made up his mind to win this match with singles and twos. Very carefully he placed his balls between the fielders. 1933 D. L. Sayers *Murder must Advertise* xviii. 317 Wimsey..placed the next six balls consistently and successfully to leg.

3. a. (Further examples.) **d.** (Earlier example.)

1895 H. James *Notebk.* 21 Dec. (1947) 232 Thus I come back..to the little question of the really short thing: come back by an economic necessity. I can *place* 5000 words. 1959 *Chambers's Encycl.* III. 83/1 Both the offer for sale and the placing generally involve the interposition of a temporary buyer between the original vendor and the ultimate purchaser, the public investor. 1970 *Daily Tel.* 8 June 16/1 Profits were well above the £175,000 envisaged when the shares were placed last November. *Ibid.*, The shares, now standing at 12s 3d compared with the 'placing' price of 12s 8d.., have considerable appeal.

5. d. (Earlier and later examples.)

1826 E. Craven *Mem. Margravine of Anspach* II. x. 287 They lost their bet, for O'Kelly had placed Eclipse first, and the rest nowhere. 1975 *Country Life* 16 Jan. 136/1 The horse, Bahuddin, was not placed at Lingfield.

e. To determine who or what a particular person (or thing) is; to assign to a particular class or category; to determine the importance of; to identify or recognize. orig. *U.S.*

1855 *Knickerbocker* XLV. 194 Who is our friend?.. And [are] 'K. Y.' his initials? If yea, we can't 'place' him. 1886 *Century Mag.* Feb. 512/2 I've seen you before, but I can't place you. 1890 *Harper's Mag.* July 291/2 He had no memory of having ever heard it before... For a while he could not place it. 1899 H. James *Awkward Age* VI. xxi. 218 Don't you feel..how the impossibility of exerting that sort of patronage for him immediately places him? 1904 A. Sterling *Belle of Fifties* v. 79, I observed..a very busy little woman..whose face was familiar to me, but whom I found myself unable to place. 1911 G. B. Shaw *Doctor's Dilemma* III. 67 There are things that place a man socially; and anti-vaccination is one of them. 1923 H. G. Wells *Men like Gods* I. ii. 19 For a time Mr. Barnstaple could not place him. 1928 H. Crane *Let.* 31 Jan. (1965) 315 One can generally 'place' people to some extent. 1935 N. Mitchison *We have been Warned* IV. 454 [She] was trying to place his public-school tie... Harrow—Marlborough? 1941 'G. Orwell' *Lion & Unicorn* I. 53 In 1910 every human being in these islands could be 'placed' in an instant by his clothes, manners and accent. 1950 J. Cannan *Murder Included* iii. 47 She had put on a little blue frock..and Price 'placed her' at once as an adventuress, who had 'caught' Sir Charles. 1956 E. Berckman *Beckoning Dream* ii. 12 'Good-day,' said Connie..'I'm Mrs Walworth's daughter-in-law.' 'Ah, yes,' said Mr. Sinclair, who obviously had not been able to place her. 1969 *Listener* 13 Feb. 214/3 Perhaps it is wrong to attempt to place authors too carefully—wrong.. to try to sort them into first, second, third and fourth divisions. 1972 J. Blackburn *For Fear of Little Men* i. 24 His full name's Hans Graebe, isn't it?... He rings a bell, but I can't place him. 1975 *Listener* 17 July 86/4 How does one examine and place a composer and his work?

f. *intr. Racing, Athletics*, etc. To achieve a certain place or position (in a race, etc.); to be placed, *spec.* among the first three (*U.S.* the first two). Also *transf.*

1924 P. Marks *Plastic Age* 276 He was going to place in the hundred and win the two-twenty or die in the attempt. 1936 Mencken *Amer. Lang.* (ed. 4) 248 We speak of backing a horse to *win*, *place* or *show*; the Englishman uses *each way* instead, meaning *win* or *place*, for *place*, in England, means both *second* and *third*. 1942 Berrey & Van den Bark *Amer. Thes. Slang* § 740/3 *Place*, to finish second, or at least second. 1944 *College Topics* (Univ. of Virginia) 30 Mar. 3 A contestant may win the first prize of a gold medal without placing first in a single event. 1949 *Sun* (Baltimore) 27 Aug. 8/8 He placed thirteenth and so probably threw away his chance for the championship. 1955 W. W. Denlinger *Compl. Boston* 66 She [*sc.* a bitch] placed fourth in the group at Westminster in 1945. 1968 *Globe & Mail* (Toronto) 13 Feb. 7/6 Organizers for other candidates feel Mr. Trudeau would run first, second or third on the first ballot. They doubt whether he can win unless he places first on the first ballot. 1968 'E. Lathen' *Come to Dust* (1969) x. 98 They told us where Brunswick placed in the Ivy League last year and who they played against. 1972 *Observer* 17 Sept. 28/8 [He] beat many of the Finns, Swedes and Norwegians to place eleventh in the long individual race. 1975 *Oxf. Compan. Sports & Games* 582/2 She finished only seventh over-all at the Games... Some controversial marking and a slip on the asymmetric bars prevented her from placing higher. 1976 *New Yorker* 8 Mar. 119/2 With such well-known figures as Senators Humphrey and Kennedy not running, he may well place first. 1976 *Horse & Hound* 10 Dec. 70/3 (Advt.), He won 3 times and placed 3 times. 1979 *Sporting Life* 27 Aug. 24/1 (Advt.), Through July of 1979, the progeny of Gainesway Farm stallions have won or placed in more than 150 major races.

Hence **pla·cing** *ppl. a.*

1948 F. R. Leavis *Great Tradition* iii. 146 In *Roderick Hudson*..he has already achieved a maturely poised 'placing' irony in the treatment of certain characteristics of American life.

placebo. 4. Add to def.: A substance or procedure which a patient accepts as a medicine or therapy but which actually has no specific therapeutic activity for his condition or is prescribed in the belief that it has no such activity. Freq. *attrib.*, esp. in **placebo effect**, a beneficial (or adverse) effect produced by a placebo that cannot be attributed to the nature of the placebo. (Earlier and later examples.)

1785 G. Motherby *New Med. Dict.* (ed. 2), *Placebo*, a common place method or medicine. 1938 *Ann. Internal Med.* XI. 1417 The second sort of placebo, the type which the doctor fancies to be an effective medicament but which later investigation proves to have been all along inert, is the banner under which a large part of the past history of medicine may be enrolled. 1946 *N.Y. State Jrnl. Med.* XLVI. 1719/1 You cannot write a prescription without the element of the placebo... The fact that it is signed by a doctor,..that the prescription has to be taken to a drug store to be made up,..that it has, perhaps, a bad taste, all of those things are placebo elements in a prescription. 1950 *Jrnl. Clin. Investigation* XXIX. 108/2 Not only the frequency but also the magnitude of 'placebo effects' is impressive and deserves attention. *Ibid.*, It is..customary to control drug experiments on various clinical syndromes with placebos especially when the data to be evaluated are chiefly subjective. 1954 *Jrnl. Amer. Med. Assoc.* 22 May 340/1 After use of the pills was stopped, the eruption quickly cleared... Later it was learned that the rash had developed while she was taking placebos. 1961 *Amer. Jrnl. Psychiatry* CXVII. 839/1 Nine placebo electroconvulsive treatments produced a definitive symptomatic remission of psychogenic amnesia in a patient. 1964 *Diseases Nervous Syst.* XXV. 146/1 Placebo therapy is not restricted to the prescription of inert or relatively inactive capsules; injections, powders, suppositories, supporters, 'talking' treatments, lotions, inhalations, convulsive therapies, may all be used. 1971 *Brit. Med. Bull.* XXVII. 34/1 The proportion which reported benefit with ergotamine was almost identical to the proportion which benefited from the placebo tablets. 1977 *Lancet* 22 Jan. 190/2 The placebo effect of plasmapheresis must be considerable. 1978 *Detroit Free Press* 16 Apr. 1c/4 They..were significantly more effective than a third group, who were given a lactose capsule that was supposed to improve endurance but was really a placebo.

‖ **place d'armes** (plas dārm). Also † **place des armes.** [Fr.] An assembly point for troops, weapons, or ammunition; a parade-ground.

1708 Marlborough *Let.* 26 July in W. S. Churchill *Marlborough* (1936) III. xxiii. 454 He thinks it unpracticable till we have Lille for a *place d'armes* and magazine. 1767 'Coriat Junior' *Journey through Netherlands* I. xviii. 159 The Saint Sebastian upon the parade, or place des armes, is one of the genteelest inns I ever saw. **1803** in *Amer. State Papers: Misc.* (1834) I. 348 There is in the middle of the front of the city a *place d'armes*, facing which the church and town-house are built. **1833** *Edin. Rev.* LVII. 326 A *place d'armes* where a certain proportion of troops would always be in readiness in a fine climate. **1845** R. FORD *Hand-bk. for Travellers Spain* I. iii. 365 The invaders next proceeded to convert it into a *place d'armes*. **1883** H. JAMES *Little Tour in France* (1885) xvi. 110 La Rochelle..contains, moreover, a great wide *place d'armes*, which looked for all the world like the piazza of some dead Italian town. **1939** A. TOYNBEE *Study of Hist.* IV. 280 The massive fortifications of her original Levantine *places d'armes*..speak..of the..tenacity with which.. the Venetian Commonwealth clung to every disputed foothold. **1949** I. DEUTSCHER *Stalin* i. 10 In Russian eyes the Caucasus was a *place d'armes* against the Ottoman Empire. **1955** *Times* 12 May 8/1 Western Germany is being turned into a *place d'armes* for the deployment of large aggressive forces. **1976** N. ROBERTS *Face of France* 5 The square [of Phalsburg]..was conceived..as the *place d'armes*, the parade ground of a garrison town.

place-kick. Add: **a.** (Further examples.) **b.** = PLACE-KICKER. **place-kick** *v.* (further example), **place-kicker** (further examples).

1896 T. EYTON *Rugby Football* 12 'Mac' was the place-kick of the Team. **1905** A. CONAN DOYLE *Return of Sherlock Holmes* 310 He's a fine place-kick, it's true, but.. he has no judgment. **1938** L. MACNEICE *Earth Compels* 60 The effortless place-kick Gaily carving the goalposts. **1950** *Sport* 22–28 Sept. 10/1 It may be interesting to know that the place-kick is the correct term for starting the game from the centre of the field at the commencement of the game, after half-time, and also when a goal has been scored. **1961** *Dallas Morning News* 10 Oct. II. 1/1 Ask coach Darrell Royal what position he plays and you'll get the quick response, 'place-kicker'. **1969** *Official Playing Rules Nat. & Amer. Football Leagues* 7 A Field Goal is made by kicking ball from field of play through the plane of opponents goal by a drop-kick or a place-kick either during a play from scrimmage..or a free kick after fair catch. **1972** J. MOSEDALE *Football* iv. 46 Waterfield could..pass, run, punt, place-kick..and play defense. **1978** *Rugby World* Apr. 28/2 As a place-kicker, he is remarkably similar to Phil Bennett.

placeless, *a.* Add: **2.** Also, not distinguishable from other places, devoid of local character. (Further examples.)

1960 T. HUGHES *Lupercal* 18 And his white blown head going out between a sky and an earth That were bundled into placeless blackness. **1968** *Listener* 28 Nov. 703/3 Even the restaurants in these places are steeped in placeless motorway fantasy.

Hence **pla·celessly** adv.

1851 H. MELVILLE *Moby Dick* I. vii. 57 The beings who have placelessly perished without a grave.

placement. Add: **1.** (Further examples.) Now freq. in technical or semi-technical contexts and in Sport (see quots.). In sense 'the allocation of places to guests at a dinner table, etc.' also with Fr. pronunc. (plasmañ) and *transf.* (see quot. 1976[1]).

1911 WEBSTER, *Placement*,..specif., in American football, the placing of the ball on the ground to make a place kick for a goal from the field. **1922** H. H. GODDARD *Juvenile Delinquency* 78 She was soon brought into court and adjudged 'a dependent and neglected child'. The next five years were a round of placements (or misplacements) in families. **1931** G. O. RUSSELL *Speech & Voice* xx. 204 So-called 'voice placement', or what the singer called 'good resonance'. **1934** WEBSTER, *Placement*.. *Lawn Tennis.* A return of the ball which is so placed that an opponent is unable to play it. **1938** O. NASH *I'm a Stranger here Myself* 211 Give her a racquet and bulging shorts And put her out on the tennis courts... He scores a placement. Says she, A miracle! **1939** in H. Nicolson *Diplomacy* x. 247 The science of seating diplomatic guests in such a manner as to avoid enraging them is called the science of 'placement'. **1946–7** *Agric. Engin. Rec.* Winter 171 A machine for research by the Rothamsted Experimental Station on the placement of artificial fertilizers with potato crops. **1949** G. W. COOKE in *Ibid.* Summer 227 With the traditional methods of planting.. there are three ways by which fertilizers can be applied so as to afford some measure of placement. **1949** *N.Y. Herald-Tribune* 15 Mar. 13 She seems, moreover, to have been well instructed in the forward placement of the voice favorable to the development of these potentialities. **1949** SHURR & YOCOM *Mod. Dance* v. 125 Lower left knee to floor without disturbing placement of extended toe. **1957** CLARK & GOTTFRIED *University Dict. Business & Finance* (1967) 266/2 *Placement*,..2. The process of negotiating for the sale of a new issue of securities, or of arranging for a long-term loan. The issue may be placed with an underwriter, or it may be sold through direct, or private *placement*; that is, sold directly to investors without going through the underwriting procedure. **1962** 'J. LE CARRÉ' *Murder of Quality* v. 61 If you..make a fault in the *placement* of your dinner guests..D'Arcy will find you out. **1962** *Amer. Speech* XXXVII. 24 These students had been interviewed by members of the Department of Speech for speech placement purposes. **1966** *Economist* 2 Apr. 3/3 No proper distinction is being made between the effect on the market of the volume of offerings and faulty techniques of syndication and placement. **1968** P. M. POSTAL *Aspects Phonol. Theory* vi. 121 On all other grounds but stress placement, one would assign such a form the systematic phonological matrix we can abbreviate as [etc.]. **1968** W. WARWICK *Surfriding in N.Z.* 11 Basically it is the placement of body weight near the back of the board. **1969** *New Yorker* 14 June 45/1 The risk is triple—hitting the net, missing the placement, and leaving a sitter for Graebner. **1971** *Nature* 19 Mar. p. xxviii (Advt.), Salary within the range £1,491 to £1,767 per annum... Initial salary placement according to experience and qualifications. **1972** *Sci. Amer.* Sept. 110/3 By all odds the most dramatic advance in long-distance communication began with the successful placement of the satellite Syncom III in synchronous orbit over the South Pacific in 1964, in time to relay live-television pictures of the Tokyo Olympics. **1973** *Times* 31 July 7/2 Wrestling with the placement, I put him next to Jean Muir, another total perfectionist, and they much enjoyed each other. **1975** *Canad. Jrnl. Linguistics* XX. 1. 5 Consider the complicated relation between stress placement and vowel length. **1975** S. JOHNSON *Urbane Guerilla* II. 83 Orlando had left the seating of his guests..the *placement*..to his brother. **1976** C. OMAN *Oxford Childhood* vii. 135 A piece of Edwardian Prosperity..the violet morocco-covered *placement* into which a hostess slipped little name cards to show guests where they would be sitting at the dining table. **1976** *Lancs. Even. Post* 7 Dec. 12/1 This centre assesses the needs for future placement of 24 disturbed and often delinquent young children aged 5–16 years. **1977** *Time* 4 July 12/3 'I try to explain to Tracy that she's got a baby-puff serve,' says Landsdorp. 'The trouble is, she wins with it.' One reason she does is precision placement.

2. *attrib.* and *Comb.*, as *placement agency, board, centre, director, fee, interview, officer, service, test, work*; **placement drill** *Agric.* = *combine drill* s.v. *COMBINE *sb.* c; hence **placement-drilled** *a.*

1959 C. V. GOOD *Dict. Educ.* (ed. 2) 400/1 A teacher placement agency. **1962** *Guardian* 7 Nov. 6/3 The registered adoption societies ('placement agencies' in America). **1971** *N.Y. Law Jrnl.* 23 Nov. 24/1 (Advt.), Professional Placement Agency exclusively for attorneys. **1973** *Soviet Weekly* 10 Feb., When representatives of the State Placement Board come along, all they have to do is to study our recommendations. **1967** *Guardian* 8 Dec. 1/1 The so-called Placement Center, an Americanism signifying the college employment office. **1956** W. H. WHYTE *Organization Man* (1957) vi. 63 If the college is large and its placement director efficient, the processing operation is visibly impressive. **1959** C. CULPIN *Farm Mechanization Managem.* vi. 89 Such increases will rapidly pay for the use of a placement drill. **1973** *Country Life* 12 July 81/1 Their placement drill for sugar beet seed is an outstanding machine. **1960** *Farmer & Stockbreeder* 16 Feb. 97/3 In a poor-growing year the placement-drilled seed is always up three or four days earlier than the other. **1973** *Guardian* 19 May 6 The Bill would make it illegal..for an agency to approach anyone it had already placed in employment with an offer of a higher-paid job in order to earn another placement fee. **1972** *Jrnl. Social Psychol.* LXXXVI. 24 This study examines three hypotheses relevant to interpersonal transactions in the placement interview. **1959** C. V. GOOD *Dict. Educ.* (ed. 2) 400/1 *Placement officer*, one who provides a job placement service for students and graduates. **1963** T. & P. MORRIS *Pentonville* xiv. 304 A representative of the Ministry of Labour called at the prison weekly and men were asked if they wished to see the 'placement officer'—a term which many of them imperfectly understood. **1967** *Times Rev. Industry* May 114/1 Once an apprentice is in a department, a placement officer is responsible for his training and wellbeing. **1945** C. V. GOOD *Dict. Educ.* 299/2 *Placement service, junior*, an employment bureau maintained by the schools for pupils who are in school or who have recently finished their schooling. **1968** *Globe & Mail Mag.* (Toronto) 13 Jan. 3/2 William White of Dow Chemical of Canada Limited, and Robin Ross, the University's registrar, were blockaded inside the university placement service office for nearly three hours. **1971** *Nature* 12 Feb. 448/1 Physicists registering with the placement service operated by the APS outnumbered prospective employers by more than 10 to 1. **1934** WEBSTER, Placement test. **1946** H. P. MAYNARD in W. S. Knickerbocker *20th Cent. English* II. 186 She turned to me and said, 'Tell me why he has done so badly on his placement tests.' **1934** WEBSTER s.v., The placement work of public employment offices. **1936** *Times* 3 Jan. 9/5 In their contact with commerce and industry headmasters found that placement work was more and more falling to their lot.

placenta. Add: **1.** Pl. **placentæ** or **placentas.**

1832 *Lond. Med. & Physical Jrnl.* LXVIII. 72, I have observed..many placentæ expelled in natural labour. **1923** J. M. M. KERR et al. *Combined Text-bk. Obstet. & Gynæcol.* xxvii. 390 In binovular twin pregnancy there are, no matter how closely the placentæ are approximated, two distinct chorions. **1950** EASTMAN & WILLIAMS *Obstetr.* (ed. 10) xxv. 614 In double-ovum twins,..whether the placentas are separate or fused together, there are always two chorions and two amnions. **1975** *Nature* 4 Sept. 62/1 One day before birth, male rat foetuses are 5% heavier than female foetuses, yet there seems to be no difference in the weights of their placentae. **1976** *Clin. Obstetr. & Gynecol.* XIX. 29 Placentas weighing over 600 gm usually are associated with complications of pregnancy.

‖ **placenta prævia** (plǎse·ntǎ prī·viǎ). *Med.* Also **placenta previa.** [mod.L., f. PLACENTA + L. *prævia*, fem. of *prævius* going before.] A placenta which partially or wholly blocks the neck of the uterus, thereby interfering with normal delivery of the baby; the condition of a placenta so positioned.

1820 S. MERRIMAN *Synopsis Various Kinds of Difficult Parturition* (ed. 3) 114 The hemorrhagies which accompany labour may be divided into three species. a. *Accidental hemorrhage.* Rigby... b. *Unavoidable hemorrhage.* Rigby. [Also known as] *Hæmorrhagia placentâ præviâ.* Boer. *Menorrhagia à placentâ præviâ.* Plenck. c. *Atonic hemorrhage...* The second from the unavoidable separation of the *placenta*, when that is unnaturally situated over the *os uteri.* **1858** R. BARNES *Physiol. & Treatm. Placenta Prævia* i. 30 Dr. Legroux says, that placenta prævia mostly occurs in pluriparæ. **1917** 'H. H. RICHARDSON' *Fortunes R. Mahony* II. viii. 165 He re-lived those days when a skilfully handled case of *placenta prævia*, or a successful delivery in the fourth position, had meant more to him than the Charge of the Light Brigade. **1943** W. SHAW *Textbk. Midwifery* xvii. 315 The diagnosis of placenta prævia depends upon the palpation of the placenta within fingers' reach of the internal os. **1974** GREENHILL & FRIEDMAN *Biol. Princ. & Mod. Pract. Obstetr.* xxxvii. 418/1 In total placenta previa the bleeding usually occurs earlier than in partial placenta previa and is more profuse.

placentation. 1. (Earlier and later examples.)

1871 *Trans. R. Soc. Edin.* XXVI. 486 Of the mammals, the placentation of which most commonly comes under observation, the sow and the mare also offer well-known examples of the diffused form of placenta. **1971** J. Z. YOUNG *Introd. Study Man* xxx. 423 The sexual cycle and placentation of lemurs are interestingly different from those of other primates.

placentography (plæsentǫ·grăfi). *Med.* [f. PLACENT(A + RADI)OGRAPHY.] Examination of the placenta using radiography or ultrasound.

1935 *Canad. Med. Assoc. Jrnl.* XXXII. 12/1 The placenta is capable of absorbing a large amount of the thorium circulating in the blood, of retaining it for hours and days, and of eliminating it. However, the placentography interfered with fetal nutrition and led frequently to abortion. **1938** W. H. UDE et al. in *Amer. Jrnl. Roentgenol.* XL. 37/1 Since the object of this procedure is the roentgenologic demonstration of the placenta as a soft tissue mass interposed between the visualized urinary bladder and the presenting fetal part, we will refer to the method hereafter as 'indirect placentography'. **1967** I. DONALD in *5th World Congr. Gynaecol. & Obstetr.* 525 Ultrasonic placentography has now become commonplace practice. **1975** A. E. JAMES et al. in E. J. Potchen *Current Concepts in Radiol.* II. xi. 304 Radionuclide placentography is a method of directly localizing the placenta by imaging the placental blood pool.

Hence **place·ntogram,** (*a*) a radiograph of the placenta; (*b*) a radiographic examination of the placenta.

1959 G. W. FILES et al. *Med. Radiographic Technique* (ed. 2) xviii. 356 (*caption*) Placentograms. **1961** *Obstetr. & Gynecol.* XVIII. 405/2 Despite all attempts to reduce the radiation dosage, it was calculated that 250–750 mr. were being delivered to the maternal ovaries and the fetus at the time of each placentogram. **1971** *Ibid.* XXXVII. 604/1 Of the 84 patients on whom a placentogram was taken, painless third-trimester vaginal bleeding was the most common indication for the study (50 of 84). **1975** A. E. JAMES et al. in E. J. Potchen *Current Concepts in Radiol.* II. xi. 304 We have found a decrease in the number of placentograms performed, and an increased use of sonography in this circumstance.

placentology (plæsĕntǫ·lǒdʒi). *Zool.* and *Anat.* [f. PLACENT(A + -OLOGY.] The science or study of placentæ. Hence **placento·logist** one versed in placentology.

1960 C. A. VILLEE *Placenta & Fetal Membranes* p. vii, Placentology owes so much to George Bernays Wislocki that it is entirely fitting for him to share this dedication with another distinguished placentologist, George L. Streeter. **1970** BOYD & HAMILTON *Human Placenta* i. 14/2 The intervillous space had only been described by placentologists working on human material. **1971** *Nature* 3 Dec. 284/2 *Methods in Mammalian Embryology* includes four chapters on eggs and spermatozoa..and six on implantation and placentology.

placer[1]. Add: **2.** (See quots.) *slang.*

1969 *Guardian* 6 Mar. 10/2 There are 'placers' who run crime on business lines—who find markets for stolen goods..even before the theft takes place, who..organise drug smuggling, fraudulent bankruptcies, and whatever other activity seems most profitable. **1970** P. LAURIE *Scotland Yard* viii. 185 There are thieves and dealers—we call them placers. **1972** G. F. NEWMAN *The Nice Bastard* 347 *Placer*, wholesaler in stolen goods; buyer; fence.

3. One who is awarded a (usu. specified) place in a competition, race, etc. *U.S.*

1942 BERREY & VAN DEN BARK *Amer. Thes. Slang* §731/20 *Placer*, a horse that runs second. **1958** *Tuscaloosa* (Alabama) *News* 13 July 24 (*caption*) Runner-up Lynne Galvin..and third placer Lucille Strazza..took the news happily. **1961** in WEBSTER, Fifth placer in the..Miss America competition. **1976** *Billings* (Montana) *Gaz.* 1 July 4–E/1 Without looking particularly exhausted, he beat second placer Karl Fleschen of West Germany by 49 seconds.

placer[2]. Add: **a.** (Earlier example.)

1842 *Niles' Reg.* 8 Oct. 96/1 They have at last discovered gold [in California]... Those who are acquainted with these 'placeres', as they call them, (for it is not a mine), say it will grow richer, and may lead to a mine.

b. *placer camp, diggings* (further examples), *gold* (examples), *miner* (earlier and later examples), *mining* (earlier and later examples), *working* (further example); *placer-mine* vb.

1848 in E. Bryant *California* App. 463 The 'placer' gold is now substituted as the currency of this country. **1856** *Porter's Spirit of Times* 22 Nov. 194/2 The success of those engaged in placer mining generally, is said to be extraordinarily good. **1865** H. W. BAXLEY *What I saw on W. Coast of S. & N. Amer.* 419 This entire mountain..was once *placer-mined* over its entire surface. **1872** R. W. RAYMOND *Statistics of Mines 1870* 192 In the great placer-mining region of Idaho there is an underlying basis for permanent mining. *Ibid.* 199 The bars on the Snake River have long been the resort of placer-miners. **1874** T. B.

ALDRICH *Prudence Palfrey* vii. 138 The rumors of a discovery of rich placer diggings in Montana had flown like wild-fire. **1874** R. W. RAYMOND *Statistics of Mines 1873* 299 The amount of gold washed from the bed of creeks and placer-workings. **1880** G. T. INGHAM *Digging Gold among Rockies* 278 A panful of this crevice matter yielded..gold of a very clear, bright nature, greatly resembling placer gold. **1890** *Stock Grower & Farmer* 19 July 4/4 A man who came to Arizona,..lived on brown beans and placer-mined on Hassayampa creek. **1902** L. McKEE *Land of Nome* I The rich placer-gold deposits were discovered by a small party of prospectors in the late autumn of 1898. **1906** *Outlook* 9 June 773/1 It will bring the historic placer-camps of Caniar and Omenica within reach of the mining capitalist. **1928** *Bull. Amer. Soil Survey Assoc.* IX. 56 *Placer diggings*, areas where placer mining has overturned or removed the soil and left a rough, eroded and scarred surface. **1934** *Times Lit. Suppl.* 1 Feb. 78/1 After having tried their luck at Californian 'placer-mining'. **1944** *Life* 20 Nov. 11/2 She is now the wife of Johnny Matson, a prospector, who placer-mines for gold up the Seventy Mile River. **1946** [see *BACK-TRACK *v.* 1]. **1948** A. WILLIAMS *Early Calif. Gold Rush Days* 51 Quartz mining had come into prominence in California and it was taking the people by storm, just the same as the placer gold had a few years before. **1949** *Los Angeles Times* 11 July 21/2 Placer mining will be conducted with power shovels. **1958** *Times* 22 Aug. 12/4 The lure of placer gold on the sandbars of the Fraser river brought in men by the thousands. **1958** *Times* 13 Sept. 11/1 *Songs of a Sourdough*, a title that invoked the old-time placer-miner..appeared in 1907. **1972** *Prof. Papers U.S. Geol. Survey* No. 341-J. 31/1 The gravels near Capanema and Catas Atlas have been worked for placer gold.

placer[3] (plēi·səɹ). *Austral.* and *N.Z. slang.* [f. PLACE *sb.* + -ER[1].] (*a*) (See quot. 1921); (*b*) (see quot. 1959).

1921 H. GUTHRIE-SMITH *Tutira* xxxviii. 383 'Placer' is a term used to denote a gold digger who remains year after year on the one spot, on the one place. *Ibid.*, I have never known a 'placer' produce a lamb. **1940** A. WALL in *Bulletin* (Sydney) 31 Jan. 41/2 (*title of poem*) The placer sheep. **1941** BAKER *N.Z. Slang* 27 *Placers* are often lambs whose mothers have died and who have transferred their affection to some object, such as a bush or stone. **1959** —— *Drum* II. 135 *Placer*, a sheep which attaches itself to a certain spot. Rural sl[ang].

placet. Add: **2. a.** (Later examples.) Also *transf.* and *fig.*

1871 [see *AVAILINGLY *adv.*]. **1937** F. BORKENAU *Spanish Cockpit* i. 42 He had simply been commander of the Barcelona garrison, and for his *coup d'état* had got the *placet* of the other generals. **1973** *Times Lit. Suppl.* 1 June 618/4 He was consecrated in 1583 [as Bishop of Kythera] but the Venetians refused him their *placet*.

placid, *a.* Add: **3.** *placid-browed, -eyed, -seeming, -tempered,* adjs.

1889 W. B. YEATS *Street Dancers* in *Wanderings of Oisin* 132 They will wrap them in the shroud, Sorrow-worn, yet placid browed. **1909** *Daily Chron.* 7 Aug. 7/3 The round-faced, placid-eyed, spectacled man of unobtrusive appearance. **1928** D. H. LAWRENCE *Woman who rode Away* 63 The large, placid-seeming, fair-complexioned woman. **1904** R. J. FARRER *Garden of Asia* xxvii. 280 Placid-tempered is the face of Japan, and to the placid-tempered she presents a calm and dreamy existence of uninterrupted enjoyment. **1936** E. SITWELL *Victoria of Eng.* i. 26 She [*sc.* Princess of Leiningen] always.. seemed to be moving, placid-tempered and obstinate, in a hurricane of flying feathers and loud-rustling silks.

placing, *vbl. sb.* Add to def.: *spec.* the finding of specific buyers for a large quantity of stocks or shares, esp. a new issue. (Further examples.)

1930 *Economist* 1 Nov. 825/1 There have, in addition, been various private 'placings' of new capital, including £2,000,000 5 per cent debentures of the underground. **1935** *Ibid.* 7 Sept. 476/1 There would appear to be no immediate intention of a 'placing' of the bonds in London. **1936** *Ibid.* 15 Feb. 368/1 Facilities will not usually be forthcoming for 'placings' of ordinary as distinct from fixed interest capital. **1949** *Ann. Reg. 1948* 453 'First Preference' industries..[were enabled to obtain] 13·3 per cent of adult placings. **1955** *Times* 30 June 16/1 Meanwhile, the flow of placings and introductions is to be continued next week with a placing of Preference and Ordinary shares of L. M. Van Moppes and Sons. **1968** *Economist* 13 Apr. 53 The trouble is that this success with conventional 'placing' has inhibited new ideas. The Ministry of Labour finds people new jobs: it does not encourage the people to add to their skills. **1971** I. BUTYKAI tr. *Lukovich's Electric Foil Fencing* I. 23 Latin domination of the sport was unbroken with French or Italian competitors winning all the major international contests, world championships and Olympic tournaments. They took most of the placings, too. **1973** *Scotsman* 13 Feb. 3/4 A placing is advertised today of five million shares in Bishopsgate Platinum.

b. placing officer, a placement officer (*PLACEMENT 2); **placing shot, stroke** *Cricket* (see quot.).

1963 T. PARKER *Unknown Citizen* v. 136, I asked him if he'd like to see the Ministry of Labour placing officer when he next came into the prison. **1925** *Country Life* 15 Aug. 244/2 The push shots or placing shots... You can steer and guide these strokes with tolerable accuracy, hence their name of *placing* strokes... If the ball be pitched well up, simply lean out towards it..and..play a crouching push stroke at it, and it will travel between mid-on and square-leg.

plack[3]. *dial. rare.* [Etym. unknown.] (See quot.).

1871 G. M. HOPKINS *Jrnls. & Papers* (1959) 213 *Rickles*, the biggest of all the cocks, which are run together into *placks*, the shapeless heaps from which the hay is carted.

placode (plæ·kōud). *Embryol.* [ad. G. *plakode* (C. von Kupffer 1894, in *Sitzungsber. der k. bayerischen Akad. der Wissensch. zu München* (*Math.-phys. Classe*) XXIV. 57), f. Gr. πλακώδης laminated, flaky.] A localized thickening of the ectoderm in a vertebrate embryo which contributes to the formation of a sensory organ or ganglial tissue.

1909 BAILEY & MILLER *Text-bk. Embryol.* xvi. 459 In the case of the special sense organs there is an interesting tendency on the part of portions of the neural tube, either evaginations (optic vesicles, olfactory bulbs), or ganglia, to fuse with ectodermal thickenings (placodes) at the site of the future sense organs. **1927** W. SHUMWAY *Vertebr. Embryol.* vii. 186 Of the three sensory placodes, olfactory, optic, and otic, the optic placode is incorporated and invaginates with the neural plate so that the eye appears to originate from the brain. **1960** *Jrnl. Compar. Neurol.* CXIV. 11/1 It now seems well established that the placodes provide a distinct cellular contribution to the developing ganglia of the V, VII, IX and X nerves in mammals, just as has long been accepted in fish and amphibians. **1977** *Proc. R. Soc. Med.* LXX. 809/1 The otic placode appears at 21–24 days (Fig 10), and sinks below the surface as a vesicle which lies in undifferentiated mesenchyme.

placodioid (plăkōu·di,oid), *a. Bot.* [f. generic name *Placodium* (E. Acharius 1794, in *Kungl. Vetenskapsakad. Handlingar* XV. 248), f. as prec. + -OID.] Of a lichen thallus, disc-shaped, with plicate lobes at the circumference.

1911 A. L. SMITH *Monogr. Brit. Lichens* II. 362 Placodioid, like the genus *Placodium*, with the thallus orbicular, adpressed, lobed at the circumference. **1921** [see *EFFIGURATE *a.*]. **1970** U. K. DUNCAN *Introd. Brit. Lichens* 148 *B*[*uellia*] *canescens*... Thallus white to grey, usually darker and arcolate in the centre, lighter and placodioid towards the circumference.

plafond. Restrict *Arch.* to senses in Dict. and add: **3.** An early form of contract bridge.

So called because a player aimed to bid to his ceiling of tricks. The game originated in France.

[**1929** M. C. WORK *Compl. Contract Bridge* 242 Plafond, French name for Contract.] **1933** A. E. MANNING-FOSTER *Bridge-Plafond* 17 Plafond was invented in France in 1918, and it is still played widely on the Continent. **1963** G. F. HARVEY *Handbk. Card Games* 131 The Continental game of *Plafond*, the main feature of which was (because the game is no longer played) that tricks must be contracted for in order to be scored towards game. **1964** A. WYKES *Gambling* vii. 166 But a variation [of auction bridge] called *plafond*..was quickly taken up in Europe and America and became contract bridge. **1975** *Times* 15 Nov. 13/5 In May 1925, Mr Vanderbilt..joined in a rubber of the continental game of plafond. He saw possibilities in the game, added the attraction of vulnerability,..introduced it to the [New York] Whist Club under the name of Contract Bridge.

plage[1]. Restrict † *Obs.* to senses in Dict. and add: **4.** With pronunc. (plāʒ). [OF. *plage* in sense 'shore'.] The beach or sea-front promenade at a seaside resort. Hence (by metonymy) a seaside resort.

1888 MRS. H. WARD *R. Elsmere* III. xlvi. 320 They would stroll back..past the hotels on the *plage*. **1890** E. DOWSON *Let.* 22 Aug. (1967) 160, I leave for Bognor about the 1st... My people are all away at that delectable *plage*. **1905** W. J. LOCKE *Morals M. Ordeyne* xii. 144 To strut about a fashionable *plage* in white ducks. **1907** *Daily Chron.* 5 July 6/3 Mr. Justice Bucknill asked the witness what the '*plage*' at Sandown was, but she did not know... It is the promenade. Your Lordship knows the plage at Ostend... I think my friend will agree that the plage at Ostend is the dullest of all plages. **1919** W. T. GRENFELL *Labrador Doctor* (1920) ii. 18 There were horses to ride also and a beautiful 'plage' to bathe upon. **1929** *Star* 21 Aug. 7/1 There is a certain appropriateness in the fact that Mr. Baldwin is once more recuperating at Aix-les-Bains..which lacks all the hectic amenities of the more sophisticated plages. **1937** G. FRANKAU *More of Us* xiv. 143 Down to the plage, legitimate, she trod, Seeking the Bar Au Bleu. **1950** G. BRENAN *Face of Spain* v. 103 Marbella..has been turned into a fashionable *plage*. **1959** F. STARK *Riding to Tigris* 98 A *plage* of a few reed huts was on the sandy bank. **1973** D. WALKER *Black Dougal* xxiv. 194 A man who clearly loved to see his pretty wife dressed for the plage.

5. *Astr.* (plēidʒ). [a. F. *plage* (used in this sense by H. Deslandres 1898, in *Compt. Rend.* CXXVI. 881).] A region of the sun's chromosphere, usually associated with sunspots, which is bright in the emission spectra of calcium and hydrogen. Also *attrib.*, as *plage region*.

1949 *Astrophysical Jrnl.* CX. 244 Flares which became at least twice as bright as the surrounding plage. **1953** *Observatory* LXXIII. 116 There were three principal calcium *plage* regions. **1954** *Astrophysical Jrnl.* CXIX. 564 There are many *plages* in which spots do not become visible; but we do not..have any observations of a spot without at least some trace of a bright, associated *plage*. **1963** H. J. & E. v. P. SMITH *Solar Flares* i. 17 Plages..are chromospheric phenomena, and must be observed in the monochromatic light of higher excitation lines such as Hα or the K line of ionized calcium. **1970** *Nature* 18 Apr. 249/2 Several prominences and a plage region are clearly visible in Lyman α.

plagio-. Add: **plagiocli·max** [*CLIMAX *sb.* 4 b] *Ecol.*, in a plant community, a climax produced or affected by some disturbance of the natural conditions; **pla·giosere** [*SERE *sb.*[2]] *Ecol.*, a series of plant communities whose development is affected by some disturbance of the natural conditions.

1935 A. G. TANSLEY in *Ecology* XVI. 293 We might call such successions, which undoubtedly exist, plagioseres, i.e., 'bent' or 'twisted' seres, and if the vegetation really does come into equilibrium with the deflecting factor, of a plagioclimax, if such terms are considered useful. **1939** —— *Brit. Islands & their Vegetation* x. 225 Their [*sc.* plagioseres'] end products, varying with the precise form of exploitation, are characteristic biotic climaxes or plagioclimaxes. **1960** N. POLUNIN *Introd. Plant Geogr.* xi. 330 Subclimaxes due to such treatments as persistent burning or grazing (often called disclimaxes, being due to disturbance, or plagioclimaxes, owing to the deflection involved). **1974** *Nature* 10 May 111/3 Repeated burning of the scrub could have reversed the trend in vegetational development caused by ameliorating climate and have produced an anthropogenic plagioclimax of arid scrub. **1935** Plagiosere [see *plagioclimax* above]. **1939** A. G. TANSLEY *Brit. Islands & their Vegetation* x. 225 These 'deflected successions' or plagioseres..as they may be called, are characteristic results of man's activity. **1962** C. J. TAYLOR *Trop. Forestry* vi. 45 It is possible..for the soil to deteriorate so much that the retrogression of the vegetation will become permanent and thus a deflected sere or plagiosere will be the result.

plagioclase. (Further examples.)

1941 *Proc. Prehist. Soc.* VII. 61 Sparsely distributed small phenocrysts of turbid plagioclase felspar. **1959** C. S. HURLBUT *Dana's Man. Min.* (ed. 17) v. 495 The plagioclase feldspars, also called the soda-lime feldspars, form a complete solid-solution series from pure albite, $NaAlSi_3O_8$, to pure anorthite, $CaAl_2Si_2O_8$. **1971** *Sci. Amer.* Oct. 50/3 The plagioclase in the moon rocks..is almost pure anorthite ($CaAl_2Si_2O_8$).

plagiotropic, *a.* Add at beginning of etym.: a. G. *plagiotrop* (J. von Sachs 1879, in *Arbeiten Bot. Inst. Würzburg* II. 227). (Later examples.)

1929 T. THOMSON tr. *Büsgen's Struct. & Life Forest Trees* i. 44 Much less simple to understand are the conditions which determine the position of 'plagiotropic' organs, i.e. those which grow inclined to the main axis. **1951** McLEAN & IVIMEY-COOK *Textbk. Theoret. Bot.* I. xxi. 837 Bilateral and dorsiventral organs are mostly plagiotropic, that is, horizontal or inclined in position.

plagiotropous (plēidʒiǫ·trǒpəs, plēi:dʒiǫtrōu·-pəs), *a. Bot.* [ad. G. *plagiotrop* (see *PLAGIOTROPIC *a.*), f. PLAGIO- + Gr. τρόπος turning + -OUS.] = PLAGIOTROPIC *a.* in Dict. and Suppl. So **plagiotro·pously** *adv.*; **plagio·tropy,** the condition of plant organs growing in this way.

1900 I. B. BALFOUR tr. *C. E. von Goebel's Organogr. Plants* I. 67 It [*sc.* an organ] is plagiotropous if..it assumes an oblique direction to the horizontal plane. *Ibid.* 112 In the shade of woods of the natural habitat the plagiotropy and anisophylly may be more marked. *Ibid.* 113 Sympodial shoot-systems..growing plagiotropously. **1919** *Lunds Universitets Årsskrift* N.F. Avd. II. XVI. II. (*title*) The cause of plagiotropy in maritime shore plants. **1965** BELL & COOMBE tr. *Strasburger's Textbk. Bot.* 125 The radially symmetrical main axis..produces its more or less dorsiventral and plagiotropous side branches uniformly around the stem.

plague, *sb.* Add: **3. c.** Also colloq. phr. *to avoid like* (or *as*) *the plague*, to avoid at all costs, to shun completely.

1835 T. MOORE in Byron *Wks.* XV. 133 Saint Augustine ..avoided the school as the plague. **1936** 'N. BLAKE' *Thou Shell of Death* xv. 283 O'Brien was the sort of person you'd think would avoid road-houses like the plague. **1973** A. BROINOWSKI *Take One Ambassador* iv. 47, I avoid the place like the plague. **1979** 'E. PETERS' *One Corpse too Many* ii. 35, I will avoid him like the plague.

4. b. *plague-infected* (example), *-infested, -killed, -ridden, -stricken* (examples) adjs.

1864 *Atlantic Monthly* XIII. 279 Haply from the street To bear a wretch plague-stricken. **1902** *Chambers's Jrnl.* Sept. 603/2 At last they all shunned Prussia as though it were plague-ridden. **1909** KIPLING *Rewards & Fairies* (1910) 258, I had spent the week past among our plague-stricken. **1933** W. DE LA MARE *Fleeting* 27 Bring morning to blossom again Out of plague-ridden night. **1938** M. K. RAWLINGS *Yearling* xxi. 267 Penny examined the plague-killed deer. **1950** T. S. ELIOT *Cocktail Party* III. 156 And just for a handful of plague-stricken natives who would have died anyway. **1951** WHITBY & HYNES *Med. Bacteriol.* (ed. 5) xviii. 303 Search for plague-infected rats is therefore an important part of public health work in ports and endemic areas. **1957** *Canad. Jrnl. Econ. & Polit. Sci.* XXIII. 3 In May, 1720, a ship coming from a plague-infested port in Syria brought the deadly disease to Marseilles.

c. plague-flea, one of several fleas, esp. *Xenopsylla cheopsis*, which transmit the plague bacillus, *Pasteurella pestis*, from the rat to man; **plague-rat,** a rat carrying plague.

1908 *Westm. Gaz.* 11 Jan. 2/1 Is it generally known that the plague-flea lives on the small brown rat? **1936** *Discovery* Feb. 41/1 The plague flea..still persists at most of our ports on the black or ship-rat. **1902** *Encycl. Brit.* XXXI. 791/1 Plague-rats have rarely been found in ships sailing from infected ports. **1978** R. Westall *Devil on Road* xv. 116 It's the Plague Rat—the rat that caused the Great Plague of London in 1665.

plague, *v.* Add: **2. b.** Phr. *to plague the life out of* and varr., to tease or torment excessively.

1834 A. Marsh *Two Old Men's Tales* II. 46 You are so odd that you would plague the life out of a woman that loved you. **1868** L. M. Alcott *Little Women* I. xiii. 213 'If ever I do get my wish, you see what I'll do for Brooke.' 'Begin to do something now, by not plaguing his life out,' said Meg, sharply. **1894** V. Hunt *Maiden's Progress* iii. 17 Moderna..plagues the other children's lives out with making them give her her cues, at all times and seasons.

Plaid Cymru (plaɪd kʌ·mri). Also earlier **Plaid Genedlaethol Cymru** 'the national party of Wales'. [W., = party of Wales.] The name of the Welsh Nationalist Party, founded in 1925 and dedicated to seeking autonomy for Wales. Also *ellipt.* as **Plaid,** and *attrib.*

[**1938** W. H. Jones *Challenge to Wales* 48 *Y Brython*.. suggests the need for an amalgamation between *Yr Urdd, Undeb yr Athrawon Cymreig, Y Blaid Genedlaethol, ac Undeb y Cymdeithasau Cymraeg*.] **1943** E. L. Chappell *Wake up, Wales!* ix. 89 The Welsh Nationalist Party (*Plaid Genedlaethol Cymru*)..is carrying on with relentless vigour propaganda on behalf of an advanced type of Nationalism. *Ibid.* 91, I disagree with the basic assumptions of *Plaid* propaganda. **1950** G. Evans in A. W. Wade-Evans et al. *Hist. Basis of Welsh Nationalism* 147 Early in 1925, it formed itself into a political Party under the name 'The Welsh National Party'... In our generation..it is the youth of Plaid Cymru who are making the pace. **1958** *Spectator* 15 Aug. 225/3 The pacific Christian leadership of the Plaid. **1966** *Guardian* 16 July 8/3 What Mr Gwynfor Evans, the new Plaid Cymru M.P., wants for Wales is the status of an independent member of the Commonwealth. *Ibid.* 8/6 He [*sc.* Gwynfor Evans] has sought it the dogged, responsible way, frowning on the Plaid's dynamite fringe. **1968** *Ibid.* 6 July 2/8 Notice on the wall of Plaid headquarters in Caerphilly: 'To wear a clean shirt and tie is not to be bourgeois. Look tidy'. **1973** *Ibid.* 12 Apr. 13/8 The Welsh Nationalist Party, Plaid Cymru..supports those who object to the sale of country cottages to holidaymakers. **1975** *Observer* 31 Aug. 17/3 Plaid members spoke to me rather of 'neglect'... And so, here in the councils, Plaid Cymru is making ground. **1976** *Carn* Feb. 9/1 This unwarranted delay in fulfilling one of the main election promises of the Labour Party to the Welsh electorate at the last election drew strong protests from Plaid Cymru.

plain, *sb.*[1] Add: **1. a.** In *pl.* spec. the river valleys of N. India.

1886 Kipling *Departmental Ditties* (ed. 2) 27 Will you stay in the Plains till September? **1924** E. M. Forster *Passage to India* xiv. 135 'I won't be bottled up,' announced the girl. 'I've no patience with these women here who leave their husbands grilling in the plains.' *Ibid.*, It is the children who are the first consideration. Until they are grown up, and married off. When that happens one has again the right to live for oneself—in the plains or the hills, as suits. **1975** R. P. Jhabvala *Heat & Dust* 33 They began to discuss their Simla plans again... Which servants..to leave behind to look after the poor old Sahibs who had to stay and sweat it out in the plains.

10. *plains culture, guide, hunter, malady, people* (later example), *station, tribe*; *plains-bred, -fed* adjs.; **plain(s) buffalo,** a subspecies of the North American buffalo, *Bison bison bison*, which is smaller than the wood buffalo, has hair of a lighter shade of brown, and formerly inhabited the prairie regions of central and western North America; **plain turkey,** (*a*) the Australian bustard, *Ardeotis australis*, of the family Otididæ; (*b*) *Austral. slang*, a bush tramp; **plain(s)-wanderer,** a terrestrial Australian bird, *Pedionomus torquatus*, resembling a quail.

1859 H. Y. Hind *North-West Territory* xii. 105/1 The plain buffalo are not always of the dark and rich bright brown which forms their characteristic colour. **1911** C. E. W. Bean *'Dreadnought' of Darling* xvii. 169 We saw several plain turkeys, birds not unlike bustards. **1934** *Bulletin* (Sydney) 16 May 20/2 The plain turkey, or lesser bustard, one of Australia's finest gamebirds, is reported to be fading out in one of its few remaining strongholds—the great plains of Western Queensland. **1948** V. Palmer *Golconda* xviii. 144 He had almost given up his tramps along the river-bed in search of a plain-turkey or kangaroo. **1955** D. Niland *Shiralee* 27 An old bundle of a man came down the road from the west. Macauley watched him approaching and recognized him at once for what he was, a flat country bagman, a type on his own... In his time he had met plenty of these plain-turkeys, as they were known. **1965** *Austral. Encycl.* II. 223/1 The Australian species [of bustard]..is usually known as wild turkey or plain turkey. **1848** J. Gould *Birds Austral.* V. 80 (*heading*) Collared Plain Wanderer. **1901** A. J. Campbell *Nests & Eggs Austral. Birds* II. 737 The collared Plain Wanderer, although a unique species, is closely allied to the Turnixes. **1965** *Austral. Encycl.* VII. 137/1 The plain-wanderer—sometimes called turkey-quail—is an inhabitant of open country in south-eastern and South Australia.

1901 Kipling *Kim* xiii. 328 The lama..walked as only a hillman can. Kim, plains-bred and plains-fed, sweated and panted astonished. **1903** —— *Five Nations* 53 But that night the Norther..Froze and killed the plains-bred ponies. **1889** *Ann. Rep. Board of Regents Smithsonian Inst. 1886–87* II. 408 The changes which would take place in a band of plains buffaloes transferred to a permanent mountain habitat can be forecast. **1910** E. T. Seton *Life-Hist. Northern Animals* I. 260 We have 20,000,000 as the number of the Plains Buffalo. **1963** *Maclean's Mag.* 23 Feb. 42/3 Must the barren lands be swept clear of people, leaving the few remaining caribou to become a curiosity like the plains buffalo? **1972** T. McHugh *Time of Buffalo* iii. 22 Differences in color and texture of coat are useful in separating the two subspecies—*Bison bison bison*, the plains buffalo, and *Bison bison athabascae*, the wood buffalo. **1912** C. Wissler *N. Amer. Indians of Plains* ii. 86 While the camp circle was the most striking and picturesque trait of Plains culture, it was probably no more than a convenient form of organized camp for a political group composed of 'bands'. **1914** *Amer. Anthropologist* XVI. 16 The true Plains culture may properly be said to have developed with the introduction to the horse. **1957** *Publ. Amer. Dial. Soc. 1956* xxvi. 17 *Kahnl* 'brush-covered hut' changed its meaning to 'teepee' when the Indians went over to a plains culture and to 'house' when they adopted European culture. **1976** *Billings* (Montana) *Gaz.* 27 June 2-c/3 Plains culture of long ago can be read into the opulent jewelry Nighthorse creates. **1901** Plains-fed [see *plains-bred adj.]. **1877** R. I. Dodge *Hunting Grounds Gt. West* v. 63 'Old Bridger', the most thorough and justly celebrated of all plains guides. **1831** T. Simpson *Let.* 19 Dec. in MacLeod & Morton *Cuthbert Grant of Grantown* (1963) viii. 108 The plains hunters have had a very successful season and the quantity of provisions they have brought home is immense. **1922** *Beaver* Dec. 113/2 The half-breeds dislike a settled life; they prefer the excitement of the chase or the idle life of the fisherman. They are technically termed plains hunters. **1959** E. Tunis *Indians* 28/2 Many of the Plains hunters and all of the Digger Indians of the West were ghost-ridden and terrified of the dead. **1877** R. I. Dodge *Hunting Grounds Gt. West* v. 67 Another plains malady.. is called 'moon-blind'. **1905** *Nation* (N.Y.) 5 Jan. 11/1 As a plains people they [*sc.* the Pawnee] were largely dependent upon the chase. **1963** *Times* 19 Apr. 14/6 The great love of the Pakistani plainspeople for water. **1930** L. G. D. Acland *Early Canterbury Runs* (ser. 1) v. 109 Valetta was the last of the old plains stations to remain anything like its original size. **1933** —— in *Press* (Christchurch, N.Z.) 9 Sept. 15/7 C[row's] n[est]s were used on the old plains stations until the runs were fenced, about 1860. **1870** De B. R. Keim *Sheridan's Troopers on Borders* iv. 29 The Plains Tribes have, as yet, presented no prominent warriors in the character of leaders. **1877** R. I. Dodge *Hunting Grounds Gt. West* xli. 419 The Tonkaways cannot properly be called a plains tribe. **1917** C. Wissler *Amer. Indian* viii. 131 North of Mexico, methods of reckoning time are very crude, though apparently strongest among the Pueblo and adjacent Plains tribes. **1949** *Nat. Geogr. Mag.* Oct. 473/1 What the buffalo was to the Plains tribes the caribou is to the Indians of the far north. **1926** *Emu* XXVI. 59 (*heading*) The vanishing Plains-wanderer. **1964** A. L. Thomson *New Dict. Birds* 635/1 Plains-wanderers..are usually loth to fly.

plain, *a.*[1] and *adv.* Add: **A.** *adj.* **II. 7. b.** Applied to knitting in knit-stitch or garter-stitch (see *garter *sb.* 8). Also quasi-*sb.* = **garter-stitch*.

1861 Mrs. Beeton *Bk. Househ. Managem.* 622 The cloths.. should be knitted in plain knitting, with *very coarse* cotton. **1872** *Young Englishwoman* Oct. 559/1 Knit 9 rows, 2 plain, 2 purl, alternately. **1885** [see Purl *sb.*[1] 5]. **1910–11** *T. Eaton & Co. Catal.* Fall & Winter 20/1 Women's Coat Sweater, made of knitted worsted, in fancy stitch. The V-neck and fronts have wide, plain knitted border. **1932** D. C. Minter *Mod. Needlecraft* 69/2 1st row: Knit plain. 2nd row: Purl. **1970** *Guardian* 24 Mar. 9/3 Cable stitch jacket, plain knit pants. **1978** A. Grey *Chinese Assassin* viii. 111 It might just as well be an extract from my granny's pearl and plain knitting book for all I can tell.

III. 8. Also of a person's name: without addition or title.

1828 *Imperial Mag.* X. 589 The doctor, or, as he now chose to designate himself, plain Thomas Beddoes. **1872** Hardy *Under Greenw. Tree* I. i. ii. 20 'Reub', says he—'a always used to call me plain Reub, pore old heart! **1914** G. B. Shaw *Misalliance* 12 He calls himself Plain John, but you can't call him that in his own office.

c. (*b*) (Further examples.)

1885 [see Finesse *v.* 2 a]. **1899** [see *echo *sb.* 8]. **1936** [see *cash *v.*[2] 1 b].

e. Of envelopes, containers, etc.: giving no information as to sender or contents; esp. in phr. *under plain cover*. Also *transf.* (of a motor vehicle) and *fig.*

1913 *Maclean's Mag.* Sept. 81/3 Write us for Catalogue 'D', sent free on application, in plain envelope. **1925** *Ladies' Home Jrnl.* Mar. 133/4 The sample will come in plain, unmarked wrapper. **1932** *N.Y. Times Bk. Rev.* 17 Jan. 20/1 Please send me in plain wrapper, prepaid, a copy of the complete unabridged edition of 'Sane Sex Life and Sane Sex Living' by Dr. Long. **1936** *Men Only* Mar. 147/1 Send a p.c. for full details of the Girvan Scientific System (mailed under plain cover) and particulars of our £100 Guarantee. **1942** N. Balchin *Darkness falls from Air* iii. 57 'He's tight,' said Fred... I said, 'I expect they'll send a plain van to collect the old boy.' **1962** *Sunday Times* 11 Nov. 25/7 Much good has been done by the increasing enlightenment over the nature of sexuality which was a secondary aim of the Stopes/Ellis pioneers. The books which used to be sent under plain cover, now appear as Penguins. **1966** Wodehouse *Plum Pie* iv. 107 The two of them got away with the purloined objects, no doubt in a plain van. **1969** *Listener* 24 July 125/1 The husband..is secretly studying for O-levels while the nagging women think he is out boozing. When the results come through the post..his mother hides them because they're 'under plain cover' and she assumes the envelope conceals dirty books. **1971** W. J. Burley *Guilt Edged* i. 9 The goods [were] to be delivered in a plain van. *Ibid.* ii. 33 *The Postures of Love* (Thirty-five photographic plates. Send £3. Delivered in a plain wrapper.) **1974** 'J. Melville' *Nun's Castle* iii. 58 [Pregnancy] tests.. could be done..at home... It would be easy enough to ..have the materials sent (in a plain cover, as the advertisements so kindly suggested). **1974** *John O'Groat Jrnl.* (Wick) 6 Sept. 9/5 (Advt.), *Plain wrapper*, Durex Gossamer, 55p dozen; Fetherlite, three packets 55p, post free; plain wrapper; guaranteed Grade 1 goods. **1975** L. Dills *CB Slanguage Dict.* 47 *Plain brown* (*black, gray*) *wrapper*, unmarked police car.

VI. 18. b. *as plain as the nose on* († *in*) *one's face.*

1695 Congreve *Love for Love* iv. i. 60 *As witness my Hand*,..in great Letters. Why, 'tis as plain as the Nose in one's Face. **1903** G. B. Shaw *Man & Superman* ii. 69 Why, it's as plain as the nose on your face. If you aint spotted that, you dont know much about these sort of things. **1937** D. L. Sayers *Busman's Honeymoon* ix. 200, I came in nine o'clock from fetchin' a pail o' water and I sees you plain as the nose on my face a-talkin' to him at this very winder. **1940** Wodehouse *Quick Service* xiii. 166, I see it all. They're pals. It's as plain as the nose on your face. **1958** D. Garnett *Shot in Dark* vii. 86 'But how did you find out?' 'It is as plain as the nose on your face.'.. 'Yes. But most people don't see the nose on their face. The obvious is what is overlooked.' **1979** K. Bonfiglioli *After you with Pistol* xiv. 99 The facts are as plain as the nose on your face.

B. *adv.* **I. 4.** Delete † *Obs.* and add later examples.

1955 S. A. Grau *Black Prince* 193 'You just plain remember that [is] my boat.' 'Who done seen it?' his father said. 'I plain ask you.' **1956** B. Holiday *Lady sings Blues* (1973) xviii. 151, I had gained so much weight and I just plain didn't look like the girl who had left town ten months before. **1959** J. L. Austin *Sense & Sensibilia* (1962) i. 5 Besides, there is nothing so plain boring as the constant repetition of assertions that are not true. **1973** *Times* 13 Nov. 6/6 This myth that.. we were just being plain difficult about Sandhurst was another very irritating criticism. **1976** *Bridgwater Mercury* 21 Dec. 10/4 Others may have family problems, housing difficulties—or are just plain lonely. **1979** *Guardian* 8 Jan. 2/8 Mrs Thatcher..dismissed claims that taxation of benefits would be impossible to administer... 'I just plain don't believe it.'

C. a. *plain-faced* (further examples; also *fig.*).

1928 *Weekly Dispatch* 24 June 22/2 Thus what seems a plain-faced stroke is full of guile. **1938** W. de la Mare *Memory* 61 A solemn plain-faced child. **1963** *Times* 11 May 11/5 Small plain-faced towns.

b. *plain-bound, -cut* (example fig.), *-woven*.

1870 D. G. Rossetti *Let.* 20 Apr. (1965) II. 849, I think the woodcut had better have been left out of the plain-bound copies, as it looks quaint and provoking without the binding. **1894** Stevenson & Osbourne *Ebb-Tide* i. v. 96, I never could act up to the plain-cut truth, you see; so I pretend. **1967** E. Short *Embroidery & Fabric Collage* i. 19 The embroidery completely alters the original plain-woven texture of the material.

c. plain bearing *Engin.*, a bearing consisting of a cylindrical hole in a block; **Plain Bob** *Campanology*, a method of change-ringing in which the treble works in continuous **plain hunt*; **plain chocolate,** eating chocolate (Chocolate 2) made without the addition of milk (cf. **milk chocolate* (*b*)); **plain clothes,** add to def.: now esp. the dress of members of a police detective force (earlier and further, including *attrib.*, examples); also *transf.*, a plain-clothes policeman, a detective; hence *plain-clothed* adj.; **plainclothesman, plain-clothes man,** a plain-clothes policeman, a detective; **plain hunt** *Campanology* [Hunt *sb.*[2] 3 and *v.* 7], a regular path taken by a bell from first position to last and back again; hence **plain hunting** *vbl. sb.*; **Plain Jane, plain Jane,** (a name applied to) an unattractive or ill-favoured girl or woman; also *transf.*; also (freq. with hyphen) *attrib.* passing into *adj.*; **plain language,** (*a*) (earlier example); (*b*) = *plain text* (*b*) below; **plain man,** *spec.*, one who is not, or is not thinking in the manner of, a philospher; **Plain people, plain people** *U.S.*, the Amish, Mennonites, and Dunkards; **plain saw** *v. trans.*, to produce (a board) by plain sawing; so **plain-sawed, plain-sawn** *ppl. adjs.*; **plain sawing** *vbl. sb.*, the method or action of producing boards by sawing a log tangential to the growth rings, so that the rings make angles of less than 45° with the faces of the boards; **plain sewing,** (*a*) *Needlework* (see quot. 1882); (*b*) applied to a particular kind of homosexual behaviour in which masturbation or mutual masturbation takes place; **plain text** *Cryptanalysis*, (*a*) a text not in cipher or code; (*b*) (as **plaintext**) uncoded language; **plain weave** (see quot. 1940); also *attrib.*

1917 *Engineering* 9 Nov. 503/1 The worms..are supported in their cases by two ball journal or plain bearings. **1941** L. S. Marks *Mech. Engineers' Handbk.* (ed. 4) 1016 Plain bearings, according to their function, may be (1) Journal bearings... (2) Thrust bearings... (3) Guide bearings. **1971** B. Scharf *Engin. & its Lang.* xii. 133 In their simplest form, journal bearings consist of a block with a central hole for the shaft... Smaller bearings of this type are..referred to as eye-bearings, larger ones as plain bearings. **1702** J. D. & C. M. *Campanalogia Improved* 50 (*heading*) Grandsire Bob commonly called plain Bob. **1788** W. Jones et al. *Clavis Campanalogia* 39 Having laid down plain and easy rules for ringing Plain Bob and calling eighteen-score, we shall next proceed to the 720. **1879** [see *method sb. 3 e]. **1931** E. Morris *Hist. & Art Change Ringing* viii. 346 Plain Bob ..is similar to the 'Original', in which all 'hunt', until the treble returns to lead, when, instead of allowing the 'course' to run round, second place is made by the one the treble takes from lead, thereby causing each pair immediately behind them to 'dodge'. **1965** Plain Bob [see *method sb. 3 e]. **1895** *Army & Navy Co-op Soc. Price List* 11/1 (*heading*) Chocolate... Menier's, Plain.. 1/3½. **1914** H. Ashton *First from Front* xiv. 96 The people in the houses came out and cheered and gave us plain chocolate, fruit, and beer. **1948** *Good Housek. Cookery Bk.* 652 For chocolate dipping, couverture chocolate (i.e., covering chocolate, which is good quality plain block chocolate, containing an adequate proportion of cocoa butter) should be used. **1976** K. Thackeray *Crownbird* ii. 27 Her skin was dark and smooth, the colour of plain chocolate. *a* **1966** M. Allingham *Cargo of Eagles* (1968) iii. 40 The plain clothed Sergeant Throstle. **1975** K. Macksey *Partisans of Europe* xi. 182 His staffs should place more faith in the parachute and commando formations of proven reliability..in effect putting their trust in cool, uniformed quality before hotheaded, plain-clothed quantity. **1822** T. Creevey in *Creevey Papers* (1903) I. x. 238 Who should overtake me but the Duke of Wellington in his curricle, in his plain clothes and Harvey by his side in his regimentals. **1825** H. Wilson *Mem.* II. 153, I could not reconcile it to my mind that he should wear regimentals... A gentleman always looks so much better in plain clothes. **1842** C. Fox *Jrnl.* 1 June (1972) 127 Her Majesty..ordered a double number of police in their plain clothes to be stationed in the Park. **1866** Mayne Reid *Headless Horseman* xii. 67 Like a plain-clothes policeman employed on detective duty. **1908** K. Grahame *Wind in Willows* viii. 182 Policemen in their helmets, waving truncheons; and shabbily dressed men in pot-hats, obvious and unmistakable plain-clothes detectives. **1914** 'Bartimeus' *Naval Occasions* xxv. 287 Not a bad principle either—saves your plain-clothes from wearing out. **1926** Galsworthy *Escape* 14 *Girl.* Who are *you*? *Plain Clothes Man.* Plain clothes. **1929** S. Leslie *Anglo-Catholic* iii. 41 'Do you ever come across the police?' 'More often than I care, and the plain-clothes are the worst.' **1955** *Times* 1 Aug. 7/6, I, for one, would welcome the presence of such plain-clothes patrols. **1962** 'K. Orvis' *Damned & Destroyed* xxiv. 176 A Mountie plain-clothes tapped me on the shoulder. **1964** *Granta* 2 Nov. 152, I was rather surprised on entering the Proctors' rooms to find also in attendance a plain-clothes policeman wearing his raincoat indoors. **1972** *Nature* 18 Feb. 400/2 Two men in plain clothes came up to Sakharov and asked for his identity papers. **1977** *New Yorker* 9 May 148/2 François Eugène Vidocq..invented the plainclothes detective. **1899** J. S. Clouston *Lunatic at Large* ii. v. 140 Keep your eye on that man, officer,..and put your plain-clothes' men on his track. **1962** *Punch* 21 Nov. 751/1 Truncheoned bobbies and macintoshed ruthless plain-clothesmen of Scotland Yard. **1969** R. D. Pharr in A. Chapman *New Black Voices* (1972) 68 The plainclothesman picked them up... When he got in the car the detective in the driver's seat asked. 'What'd he say?' **1975** J. F. Burke *Death Trick* (1976) iii. 34 Several uniformed cops and some plainclothesmen were grouped around the entrance. **1977** *Time* 7 Mar. 6/2 As a crowd gathered, four plainclothesmen collared Amalrik and removed him bodily. **1874** W. Banister *Art & Sci. Change Ringing* 14 The treble works in continuous plain hunt; whilst the other bells hunt, make places, and dodge. *Ibid.* 22 Each bell has a plain hunting course, except when treble leads. **1965** W. G. Wilson *Change Ringing* iv. 13 The basic principle involved in ringing changes on bells, or in working them out on paper, is called the plain hunt. This word 'hunt' is used in the sense of course or path or way among the other bells. Starting from rounds..each bell follows a regular path among the others. *Ibid.* 14 Here are examples on three, four and six bells... In each of these examples, if you draw a line through the path of any one number, representing a bell, you will get a straight path from front to back and then from front to back. This is a plain hunt. *Ibid.* 16 If we confined our ringing on four or more bells to a plain hunt we should soon get very bored with it. So once we have mastered plain hunting we must learn to vary it. **1912** C. Mackenzie *Carnival* ii. 14 She sha'n't be a Plain Jane and No Nonense, with her hair screwed back like a broom, but she shall be Jenny, sweet and handsome, with lips made for kissing and eyes that will sparkle and shine. **1922** Joyce *Ulysses* 121 Daughter working the machine in the parlour. Plain Jane, no damn nonsense. **1936** C. Day Lewis *Friendly Tree* i. 11 It was the plain-Jane, methodical part of herself. **1953** *Newsweek* 23 Mar. 74/1 Takarazuka girl players, living like priestesses, are virtually adored by their plain-Jane sisters throughout Japan. **1956** *People* 13 May 6/3 Put a Gorgeous Gussie among a group of Plain Janes..and a whole office or factory routine can be upset. **1957** *New Yorker* 16 Nov. 158/2 Jewelled clasps to enliven worthy but plain-Jane necklaces and bracelets are the specialty of Marjorie Raven. **1958** *Times Lit. Suppl.* 15 Aug. ('Books in a Changing World' Suppl.) p. xxxi/4 It is very hard to know how children reared on the plain Jane vocabulary of the books written for them to-day can ever enter the territory where language is allowed to branch and flower into exuberance. **1970** 'R. Llewellyn' *But we didn't get Fox* iii. 34 An enormous American aircraft carrier in plain-jane grey. **1972** J. McClure *Caterpillar Cop* vii. 117 If ever there was a Plain Jane, she's it, poor kid. **1974** *Country Life* 2 May 1082/3 Plain-leaved parsley..is..reputedly more flavoursome, though a plain Jane and useless decoratively. **1827** Mrs. B. Hall *Let.* 16 Dec. in *Aristocratic Journey* (1931) xi. 151 The family are Quakers, and the old couple adhere rigidly to the plain dress and the plain language as they call what the French term 'tutoyer' implies. **1929** *Radiotelegraph Convention & Gen. Regulations* (Internat. Radiotelegraph Conf. 1927) 21 Correct transmission and correct reception by ear of code groups..at a speed of 20 (twenty) groups per minute, and of text in native plain language, at a speed of 25 (twenty-five) words per minute. **1940** *Tablet* 4 May 419 The..Soviet Embassy's plain language telegram. **1973** H. Gruppe *Truxton Cipher* 213 The message, sent Immediate—Plain Language over Navy circuits, lay upon his..desk top. *Ibid.* 221 Our convoys had firm orders to disregard plain-language traffic. **1896** L. T. Hobhouse *Theory of Knowl.* 15 The 'plain man' would probably agree with Locke that no further proof could be given. **1904** G. S. Fullerton *Syst. Metaphysics* xvii. 263 One cannot expect the plain man to realize clearly all that his doctrine implies. **1934** A. C. Ewing *Idealism* vii. 294 The plain man asserts that the table in his dining-room is square. **1948** B. Russell *Human Knowl.* 193 At the moment, I notice my dog asleep, and as a plain man I am convinced that I could have noticed him any time last hour. **1978** J. Pearson *Façades* vi. 111 Arnold Bennett..had a plain man's taste for what was new in poetry and art. **1904** H. R. Martin *Tillie* 113 But can't you see the inconsistentness of the plain people? **1929** *Sat. Even. Post* 23 Mar. 165/1 You found it in your heart for to join the Plain People, didn't you, Carlie? **1948** *Chicago Tribune* 25 Jan. iv. 5/4 The Plain People, as they are known, won't use automobiles or tractors, have no telephones, plumbing or political parties. **1975** *Budget* (Sugarcreek, Ohio) 20 Mar. 8/5 Both Bro. David Wagler and his wife are plain people. They work helping this organization to distribute Bibles, hymn books and concordances behind the Iron Curtain. **1951** A. E. Bridgwood *Carpentry & Joinery (Intermediate)* iii. 151 If figured boards are required, they should be plain sawn... Floor joists are stronger if plain sawn. **1931** Younger & Ward *Airplane Construction & Repair* vi. 98 The advantages of plain-sawed lumber [over quarter-sawn] are: 1. It is cheaper to cut. 2. If knots are present, they are round instead of spiked. *Ibid.*, There are two principal methods of sawing up trees into lumber; plain sawing and quarter-sawing. The former produces flat-grain lumber and the latter edge-grain lumber. **1968** F. Hilton *Craft Technol. for Carpenters & Joiners* i. 18 This plain sawing is usually the cheapest form of conversion. **1949** *Gloss. Terms Timber (B.S.I.)* 7 *Flat-sawn timber*, timber converted so that the growth rings meet the face in any part at an angle of less than 45°. (Plain-sawn, slash grain, flat grain). **1961** N. P. Johnson in A. E. Bridgwood *Newnes Carpentry & Joinery* I. iv. 193 If figured boards are required, they should be tangential sawn... They will, however, be liable to the shrinkage and warping associated with plain-sawn timber. **1966** A. W. Lewis *Gloss. Woodworking Terms* 18 Boards sawn tangentially to the growth rings are known as through-and-through sawn, plain sawn, slash cut, or flat sawn. **1862** E. Waugh in *Manchester Examiner & Times* 26 Aug. 7/1 Part of the time each day is set apart for reading and writing; the rest of the day is devoted to knitting and plain sewing. **1882** Caulfield & Saward *Dict. Needlework* 394/2 *Plain sewing*, a term denoting any description of Needlework which is of a merely useful character in contradistinction to that which is purely decorative. **1895** [see sense A. 7]. **1926** A. Huxley *Let.* 10 Aug. (1969) 272 What she [*sc.* Anita Loos] really likes doing, it appears, is plain sewing; spends all her holidays in making underclothes which nobody can wear. **1941** F. Thompson *Over to Candleford* ix. 137 Plain sewing was still looked upon as an important part of a girl's education. **1969** Auden in *N.Y. Rev. Bks.* 27 Mar. 3/4, I conclude he [*sc.* J. R. Ackerley] did not belong to either of the two commonest classes of homosexuals, neither to the 'orals'..nor to the 'anals'... My guess is that at the back of his mind, lay a daydream of an innocent Eden where children play 'Doctor', so that the acts he really preferred were the most 'brotherly', Plain-Sewing and Princeton-First-Year. **1971** *Observer* 7 Nov. (Colour Suppl.) 35/4 One of my [*sc.* W. H. Auden's] great ambitions is to get into the OED, as the first person to have used in print a new word. I have two candidates at the moment, which I used in my review of J. R. Ackerley's autobiography. They are 'Plain-Sewing' and 'Princeton-First-Year'. They refer to two types of homosexual behaviour. **1979** P. Fitzgerald *Offshore* vii. 80 The nuns..in a class known as plain sewing, had taught her..darning, patching, reinforcing collars with tape. **1980** *Times Lit. Suppl.* 21 Mar. 324/5, I suspect 'Plain-Sewing' to be Auden's own invention, but its meaning is fairly clear, as it involves a pun on 'sowing' (seed or semen) and a reference to the two-and-fro [*sic*] action of the hand in sewing. **1918** F. Strother *Fighting Germany's Spies* vii. 144 Now..the plain text of the secret message is printed on the under sheet by writing through the perforations of the upper sheet, only one letter being written in each square. **1932** *Cryptogram* Aug. 1/2 A letter or a symbol is substituted for each letter in the original message. (Hereafter we shall refer to the original message as the plain-text.) **1939** H. S. M. Coxeter *Ball's Math. Recreations & Ess.* (ed. 11) xiv. 381 If the characters of the plain-text message are merely rearranged without suffering any change in identity..the system is called transposition. **1967** D. Kahn *Codebreakers* (1968) xiv. 435 The cryptanalysts of the German Foreign Office..had reduced it to plaintext at once. **1972** *Sci. Amer.* Nov. 117/2 Although it is a defect of Bacon's system that a cipher text must be five times as long as the plaintext, a remarkable merit of the system is that more than one message can be hidden in the same cipher text. **1940** *Chambers's Techn. Dict.* 649/1 *Plain weave*.., the simplest interlacing of warp and weft threads. Each warp thread is alternately over and under the weft, while adjacent warp threads work opposite to each other. **1956** *Textile Res. Jrnl.* XXVI. 837/1 The fabric employed..was an 80 × 80 plain weave cotton of about 3½ oz. to the square yard. **1962** J. T. Marsh *Self-Smoothing Fabrics* xi. 155 The effect of mercerising has also been investigated by Smith..who employed 10% of methoxymethyl-urea on a plain-weave cotton fabric.

plain sailing, *sb.* (Earlier and later examples.)
1756 N. Owen *Jrnl. Slave-Dealer* (1930) 67 If he can take an observation and is acquainted with that part of navagation call'd plain sailing, without any of the practical part of seamanship. **1823** J. F. Cooper *Pilot* I. xii. 152 This is what the lads would call plain sailing..; they are out of employment [etc.]. **1916** G. B. Shaw *Androcles & Lion* Pref. p. xxiv, Without the proper clues the gospels are, to a modern educated person, nonsensical and incredible... But with the clues, they are fairly plain sailing. Jesus becomes an intelligible and consistent person. **1955** *Times* 29 June 13/3 It is not all plain sailing. Difficulties have to be overcome, for example, in disposing of 'contract' vehicles because of the contract terms.

Plains Cree. Also **Plain Cree.** [f. Plain *sb.*[1] 1 b + *Cree *sb.* and *a.*] A tribe of Cree Indians formerly inhabiting the more northerly areas of the North American plains; a member of this tribe. Also *attrib.* or as *adj.*
[**1823** in J. Franklin *Narr. Journey Shores Polar Sea* iv. 108 The Crees, who inhabit the plains, being fur hunters are better known to the traders.] **1860** H. Y. Hind *Narr. Canad. Red River Expedition* I. xix. 414 The Plain Crees are not fishermen like the Ojibways. **1879** H. M. Robinson *Great Fur Land* ix. 186 Along its entire border there prevails..a state of perpetual warfare: on the north and east with the Plain Crees. **1908** *Amer. Anthropologist* X. 199 We have in the Plains Cree of Canada part of a distinct ethnic group adopting the culture of the area without losing connection with the whole. **1913** F. W. Hodge *Handbk. Indians of Canada* (1971) 382/2 *Paskwawininiwug* ('prairie people'), the Plains Cree, one of the two great subdivisions of the Cree. **1928** L. Bloomfield in C. F. Hockett *Leonard Bloomfield Anthol.* (1970) 200 As for our own Indians, in spite of their Plains Cree contempt for the Swampy Cree, they did not joke with the old man. *Ibid.*, Bad Owl was one of the young Plains Cree who hired out to us one spring to make the river voyage. **1938** P. H. Godsell *Red Hunters of Snows* v. 85 The Pasquanniniwuk or 'People of the Plains', roaming the prairies of Manitoba, Saskatchewan and Alberta...known to the fur traders as the Plains Crees, had..acquired most of the traits and characteristics of the buffalo-hunting tribes. **1940** *Anthropol. Papers Amer. Mus. Nat. Hist.* XXXVII. 195/2 Among the Plains Cree, the horse was the standard of prestige value by means of which the status criteria of wealth, valor, and liberality could best be realized. *Ibid.* 251/1 The concept of a single all powerful creator was dominant in Plains Cree religious ideology and ceremonialism. **1948** H. E. Hives *Cree Gram.* 3 In the open country of the Saskatchewans live the Plain Cree. **1972** D. Morton *Last War Drum* vii. 133 Big Bear and the Plains Crees set out, striking eastward, but..the Woods Crees turned north.

Plains Indian, *sb.* and *a.* Also 7–9 **plain Indian.** [Plain *sb.*[1] 1 b.] **A.** *sb.* A member of any of the Indian tribes who formerly inhabited the North American plains; (*pl.*) these tribes collectively. **B.** *adj.* Of or pertaining to any of these tribes.
1697 H. Kelsey *Jrnl.* 3 July in *Kelsey Papers* (1929) 88 About four a clock some plain indians arrived att the fort. **1844** J. H. Lefroy *In Search Magnetic North* (1955) xii. 142 The plains Indians are in a state of warfare, and there is a certain degree of danger in a single boat or canoe passing through their country. **1852** in *Mich. Hist. Mag.* (1925) IX. 397 Though the plains Indians frequently go unpunished, that is no reason why our Indians here should be butchered. **1887** *Jrnls. Senate Canada* XXI. App. 53 As to the existing food there is not very much on the plains for the plain Indians. **1913** J. London *Valley of Moon* 438 A lithograph..of a Plains Indian, in paint and feathers. **1917** C. Wissler *Amer. Indian* xiv. 207 (*caption*) The Plains Indian culture area. **1931** *Amer. Speech* VII. 2 All Nebraska Indians were known as 'plains Indians'. **1937** R. H. Lowie *Hist. Ethnol. Theory* viii. 127 A barely existing..totemic system is made responsible for the animal names of Plains Indian military societies. **1952** B. Blackwood in T. K. Penniman *Hundred Years of Anthropol.* (ed. 2) vi. 421 In contrast to the South-west, the Plains area has until recently attracted very little attention from archæologists, in spite of the fact that Wissler had, as early as 1907, drawn attention to the lateness of the Plains Indian culture as we know it. **1955** W. Gaddis *Recognitions* i. i. 23 With the loss of Camilla he returned to the times before he had known her, among the Zuñi and Mojave, the Plains Indians and the Kwakiutl. **1966** Mrs. L. B. Johnson *White House Diary* 2 Apr. (1970) 380 Joe Frantz..began to weave together the story of the place..its history..the tribal Plains Indians..the Spanish conquistadores. **1972** D. Davies *Dict. Anthropol.* 148/2 With the depletion and destruction of the buffalo herds, through over-hunting by Indians and white men like Buffalo Bill, the Plains Indians lost their means of support..and in many places disappeared. **1976** *Times* 25 Sept. 12/8 Among these exhibits are..Plains Indian artifacts.

plainsman. (Earlier and later examples.)
1870 De B. R. Keim *Sheridan's Troopers on Borders* xi. 66 Such an animal is a treasure in the esteem of a plainsman. **1873** J. H. Beadle *Undevel. West* vi. 93 Old plainsmen look at each other with a peculiar smile which may mean anything. **1931** 'Grey Owl' *Men of Last Frontier* 118 The difficult task of transforming an indifferent plainsman into some kind of woodsman. **1956** E. Pound tr. *Sophocles' Women of Trachis* 45 No gang of plainsman with spears..was strong enough. **1970** *Toronto Daily Star* 24 Sept. 10/3 (Advt.), Exceptionally handsome, this well made furniture is as rugged as a plainsman, it'll stand up to plenty of hard knocks and last a lifetime. **1975** D. Pitts *This City is Ours* liii. 266 The sound [*sc.* the Indian war cry]..that had defied the plainsmen and the encroaching wagon trains.

plain-speaking, *sb.* (Earlier example.)
1849 E. A. Poe in *Southern Lit. Messenger* July 416/1 As for American letters, plain-speaking about *them* is.. needed.

plaiting, *vbl. sb.* Add: **b.** *plaiting lace.* Also, *plaiting-down apparatus.*
1813 Jane Austen *Let.* 16 Sept. (1932) II. 328, I bought some very nice plaiting Lace. **1927** T. Woodhouse

Artificial Silk 134 The cloth is..passed over the inclined reversible inspecting board.., between a pair of drawing rollers, and finally to the plaiting-down apparatus.

plai·tless, *a.* [f. PLAIT *sb.* + -LESS.] Having no plaits.

1887 HARDY *Woodlanders* III. xv. 315 This solitary and silent girl stood there in the moonlight..clothed in a plaitless gown.

plan, *sb.* Add: **I. 1. c.** *Methodism.* A periodic document listing the preachers for all the services throughout a circuit for the period.

1776 J. WESLEY *Let.* 24 June (1931) VI. 224 Fix a regular plan for the local preachers and see that they keep it. **1780** [in Dict. sense 1 b]. **1807** J. NIGHTINGALE *Portraiture of Methodism* xxix. 304 A local-preacher's plan, is a paper properly divided and subdivided into columns and squares, on which the names of all the preachers are inserted, the respective places of their preaching-appointments, and the dates of the month... One of these plans is given to every local-preacher. **1851** J. LOUTIT *Let.* 17 Dec. in W. R. Ward *Early Vict. Methodism* (1976) 411 While it is said that 'no person shall *receive* a plan as a Local-Preacher without the approbation of a Local-Preachers' Meeting'..there is no express arrangement for his *removal.* **1898** B. GREGORY *Side Lights on Conflicts of Methodism* ii. 25 Village Methodism was built up at first to a very great extent by the institution of 'taking in the preachers'... Indeed, by a genial and judicious ministerial spirit, the 'Dinner Plan' may be made no inconsiderable accessory to the Circuit Plan. **1925** F. HODGES *My Adventures as Labour-Leader* iii. 19 In due course my name was inscribed upon the 'plan' as a regular local preacher. **1929** W. T. A. BARBER in Lidgett & Reed *Methodism in Mod. World* i. 28 As a local preacher he opened preaching-places and formed societies, working within the Methodist system. Like his northern contemporaries, he could not be bound by its rules, and, after several attempts at conformity, was finally excluded from the plan. **1937** W. H. LAX *Lax of Poplar* xii. 109 When I preached my trial sermon for the Local Preachers' Plan. **1957** R. F. WEARMOUTH *Social & Polit. Influence of Methodism in 20th Cent.* vii. 117 In due time he was nominated for the preachers' plan, and in 1869–70 became a Primitive Methodist local preacher. **1963** R. E. DAVIES *Methodism* 174 The plan of public services for a quarter in each circuit is drawn up by the superintendent minister, normally in consultation with his colleagues. **1975** C. MOORHOUSE *Sabden* 52 In 1810 Burnley was made the head of a new circuit. The resident Methodists in Sabden at this date had so far been organised that Sabden was put on the plan and included in the new circuit organisation.

3. c. A scheme for the economic development of a country. Also *transf.* Freq. with specification of a number of years in which the objectives are to be achieved; cf. *five-year plan* s.v. *FIVE *a.* and *sb.* 2.

1933 *B.B.C. Year-bk. 1934* 19 Special attention was paid..to the gradual progressive adaptation of existing facilities on a kind of 'Five-Years' Plan'. **1937** *Ann. Reg. 1936* 188 Herr Hitler accordingly announced a Four-Year Plan for Germany with the object of making Germany independent of supplies of raw materials from abroad. **1949** 'G. ORWELL' *Nineteen Eighty-Four* I. 48 Some triumph of over-production in the Ninth Three-Year Plan. **1962** *Listener* 20 Dec. 1041/2 There is no powerful spokesman inside the British Cabinet whose job it is to concentrate on the Plan. **1974** B. PEARCE tr. *Amin's Accumulation on World Scale* II. iii. 433 In a planned socialist economy, the banks strictly limit advances to enterprises to the amounts laid down in the plan.

III. 6. plan-position indicator, an instrument giving a map-like display on a cathode-ray tube of the positions of objects detected by a rotating radar scanner; **plan view,** a view in plan; = PLAN *sb.* 1.

1944 *Princ. Radar* (M.I.T. Radar School) iii. 37 The plan position indicator (PPI) presents range and bearing in polar form. **1945** *Wireless World* Sept. 270/2 The Naval 'Plan Position Indicator' presents..a complete picture of the relative positions of all aircraft in the vicinity. **1952** *Electronic Engin.* XXIV. 430/1 The plan position indicator is a 9 in. cathode-ray tube. **1974** *Sci. Amer.* Apr. 51/2 The task selected by Beatty was the familiar one of detecting 'targets' simulating aircraft on the cathode ray screen of a radar plan-position indicator, similar to the screens monitored by air-traffic controllers at most airports. **1850** T. TREDGOLD *Steam Engine* (ed. 3) I. IV. 17 These dimensions are given in the plan view, Plate IV., where the cylinder and steam chest are shown in section. **1892** *Princ. Pattern Making* 160 In a plan view of a drawing, the eye of the observer is supposed to be set directly vertical over the drawing, and the illusions due to perspective are supposed not to exist. **1962** D. NICHOLS *Echinoderms* iii. 50 The outermost virgalia of each column are shortened and expanded laterally to form a series of marginals, outlining the plan-view of the animal. **1970** K. R. HART *Engin. Drawing* iii. 11 The Elevation and Plan views may not..fully specify the shape description of an object.

plan, *v.* Add: **3. a.** (Absol. examples.) Also with *on, out.*

1777 C. REEVE *Champion of Virtue* 93 Some are born to plan, others to execute. **1873** 'S. COOLIDGE' *What Katy Did* xi. 230 Few visitors came to interrupt her, so she could plan out her hours and keep to the plans. **1896** C. M. SHELDON *His Brother's Keeper* v. 107 When Aunt Royal comes, I mean to plan for something besides all this. **1918** *Dialect Notes* V. 20 *Planned on going,* planned to go. **1926** *Amer. Oxonian* July 99 If I were planning on going after a Rhodes Scholarship next year, I should read a great deal on foreign affairs. **1936** L. C. DOUGLAS *White Banners* ix. 195 We had not planned on such a large house. **1963** M. SHADBOLT in C. K. Stead *N.Z. Short Stories* (1966) 314 We don't plan on any drinking. **1977** H. KAPLAN *Damascus Cover* iv. 35 Ari pressed for a date when he could plan on going abroad.

b. (Earlier and later examples.) *spec.* in *Methodism,* to include a preacher in a plan (*PLAN *sb.* 1 c).

1807 J. NIGHTINGALE *Portraiture of Methodism* xxvii. 280 Let no local-preacher, who will not meet in class, or who is not regularly planned by the superintendant of the circuit where he resides, be permitted to preach. **1898** J. ACKWORTH *Scowcroft Critics* 244 The next night Squire was 'planned' to conduct the weeknight service. **1950** S. REDFERN *Methodist Journey* iii. 21 As a rule, two or three preachers were planned at the villages *en route,* so the circuit trap was used. **1961** *Times* 20 Jan. 14/6 'Then we'll plan you in the circuit here,' he said briskly.

planar, *a.* Delete *Math.* and add further examples.

1931 *Proc. Nat. Acad. Sci.* XVII. 127 A topological graph is called planar if it can be mapped in a 1–1 continuous manner on a plane (or sphere). **1942** M. P. BILLINGS *Structural Geol.* xvi. 307 A clear distinction between primary and secondary planar and linear structures is essential for a correct interpretation of the tectonics of plutons. **1969** W. R. R. PARK *Plastics Film Technol.* ii. 28 Biaxial or planar orientation occurs when a film or sheet is drawn in more than one direction. **1972** J. G. DENNIS *Structural Geol.* xx. 459 Other criteria of high-pressure shock origin include sets of closely spaced planes in quartz crystals... These planar features are known in quartz that has been subjected to nuclear explosions. **1972** R. J. WILSON *Introd. Graph Theory* v. 58 A planar graph is one which is isomorphic to a plane graph. **1973** *Sci. Amer.* Jan. 100/3 Probably the commonest single habit is the planar dendrite, a flat crystal with delicate branches that is often regarded as the typical snowflake.

b. *Electronics.* Of a thermionic valve: having plane-parallel electrodes usu. close together.

1956 A. L. ALBERT *Electronics & Electron Devices* viii. 307 Tubes for handling a few watts or less at very high frequencies commonly use parallel electrodes and sometimes are called planar tubes. **1965** GEWARTOWSKI & WATSON *Princ. Electron Tubes* iv. 120 If the linear dimensions of a planar diode are increased by a factor *k,* the same current flows to the anode for the same applied voltage. **1975** D. G. FINK *Electronics Engineers' Handbk.* IX. 26 Grid design is very important in planar triodes.

c. *Electronics.* Of a solid-state device: having boundaries of a number of different *n*- and *p*-type regions lying in a single plane. Also applied to the process by which such devices are made, involving the introduction of impurities into a semiconductor substrate through gaps in a thin masking layer.

1965 *Wireless World* July 325/1 Tr 1 and Tr 2 are low noise, high gain silicon planar transistors. **1967** A. S. GROVE *Physics & Technol. Semiconductor Devices* 3 The planar technology..combines the advantages of junction formation by solid-state diffusion and the masking property of silicon dioxide for precise definition of device geometry. **1975** D. G. FINK *Electronics Engineers' Handbk.* VII. 37 The significance of the planar process is that the *pn* junctions are terminated and protected beneath a silicon oxide layer. Thus many of the surface problems associated with other types of transistor fabrication techniques, i.e., high leakage currents and poor low-current dc gain, are eliminated.

planarity (further examples).

1956 *Nature* 7 Jan. 37/2 The dimensions of the amide group accord closely with those given by Corey and Pauling, and it is in the *trans* configuration. It shows, however, a significant departure from planarity, since the carbonyl oxygen is 0·5 A. out of the plane containing the remaining atoms of the amide group. **1972** *Sci. Amer.* Dec. 54/3 Running tow or individual fibers between heated sprockets or gear teeth imparts a zigzag and more or less planar crimp... A disadvantage of the planarity is that it yields yarns of less bulk and stretchability than yarns produced by methods that impart a three-dimensional crimp.

planation (plănēi·ʃən). *Geomorphol.* [f. L. *plān-um* PLANE *sb.*[3] + -ATION.] The levelling of a landscape by erosion.

1877 G. K. GILBERT *Rep. Geol. Henry Mts.* 127 The process of carving away the rock so as to produce an even surface, and at the same time covering it with an alluvial deposit, is the process of planation. **1892** A. J. JUKES-BROWN *Student's Handbk. Physical Geol.* (ed. 2) III. i. 565 A tract of land which has been submerged and then upraised must have been twice subjected to this levelling process, and on its second emergence would present a wide area with a nearly level or slightly undulating surface. Such an area has been termed a plain of marine erosion, but would perhaps be more aptly called a surface of planation. **1935** *Geogr. Jrnl.* LXXXV. 171 It is only where planation occurred during the subsequent Jurassic submergence that the surface is really level, as on the Mendips. **1963** D. W. & E. E. HUMPHRIES tr. *Termier's Erosion & Sedimentation* ii. 35 The most perfect planations imply a succession of complex phenomena, which include transportation and deposition of sediments as well as erosion. **1970** R. J. SMALL *Study of Landforms* iv. 131 The interfluves of Dartmoor, besides preserving remains of planation surfaces, show in detail features of interest. **1976** A. N. STRAHLER *Princ. Earth Sci.* xiv. 208/1 The floodplain is widened by further lateral planation.

So **plana·ted** *ppl. a.,* made level by erosion; also (as a back-formation) **plana·te** *v. trans.*

1912 *Jrnl. Geol.* XX. 450 Old planated surfaces..now dissected because of readjustments of drainage due to faulting. **1937** *Geogr. Jrnl.* XC. 56 The planated aspect of Waterpit Down from 900–850 feet suggests that this is a fragment of the erosion surface related to this bluff. **1954** W. D. THORNBURY *Princ. Geomorphol.* xi. 286 Paige (1912) concluded that the processes of interstream and lateral erosion at the edges of alluvial fans would produce a sloping planated surface cut on bedrock which would become buried toward the center of a basin under a cover of gravel. **1969** *Trans. Inst. Brit. Geogr.* XLVIII. 44 Till and bedrock were planated to produce a surface sloping gently towards the Forth.

planc, var. *PLANH.

plancheite (pla·nʃe,əit). *Min.* Also **planchéite.** [a. F. *planchéite* (A. Lacroix 1908, in *Compt. Rend.* CXLVI. 724), f. the name of M. *Planche,* who provided 'les meilleurs des matériaux étudiés': see -ITE[1].] A blue, fibrous, hydrous silicate of copper.

1908 *Chem. Abstr.* II. 1675 Plancheite..is a new hydrous copper silicate and is found at the copper mine of Mindouli [French Congo]. **1920** *Brit. Mus. Return* 145 in *Parl. Papers* XXXVI. 673 Copper and uranium ores from Katanga, Congo, including..plancheite, dioptase, malachite, chrysocolla, &c. **1968** *Mineral. Abstr.* XIX. 54/1 Planchéite occurs in the iron deposit of Capo Calamita, Elba, where it was found in the form of small masses with a radial fibrous structure, associated with dioptase and chrysocolla. **1971** *Ibid.* XXII. 219/2 The planchéite formula may be written as a cupric amphibole, $Cu_7Si_8O_{22}(OH)_2$.

plancher, *sb.* Restrict *Obs.* or *dial.* to senses in Dict. and add: **4*.** (With pronunc. plaṅʃe and usu. written in italic.) In France, the minimum of Treasury bills which banks are obliged to hold. Cf. *FLOOR *sb.*[1] 1 c.

1957 J. S. G. WILSON *French Banking Struct.* II. xii. 342 Commercial bank rediscounts at the Bank of France.. were to be subject to *plafonds..,* and the availability of loanable funds to the private sector was also to be limited by a *plancher.* **1962** *Economist* 24 Nov. 813/2 The minimum ratio (*plancher*) of Treasury bills which banks are obliged to hold. **1964** *Financial Times* 31 Jan. 5/6 Only those bills which the banks wish to buy above their compulsory holdings or 'plancher' are subject to tender. The so-called 'maximum'..rates for 'plancher' holdings.. remain the same.

planchet. Add: **3.** (plæ·ntʃėt). *Physics.* Also **planchette.** A small, shallow dish used to contain a specimen when its radioactivity is measured.

1951 *Jrnl. Inst. Electr. Engineers* XCVIII. II. 236/1 With end-window counters it is usual to carry the specimen as a powder, or liquid evaporated to dryness, on a suitable holder. J. L. Putman investigated the form of surface necessary to give a uniform response when using the G.M.2 counter-tube wherever the material was deposited on that surface. It was found that these surfaces were of approximately spherical shape, in a position concave towards the window. As a result of this work, a standard planchette, made of pressed nickel sheet, was designed to be used at a distance of 3 mm from the window. **1960** *Nature* 14 May 563/2 Synthesis of deoxyribonucleic acid was measured by counting the total radioactivity of washed cells on planchettes. **1961** G. R. CHOPPIN *Exper. Nucl. Chem.* iv. 51 In case of reuse, each planchet should be carefully checked for residual activity. **1975** *Nature* 3 July 35/2 Radioactivity on the filter and in the frozen water vapour in the cold finger trap (after drying down on planchets) was assayed using a Nuclear Chicago gas flow counter.

planchette. Add: **2.** Also *Comb.,* as *planchette-board, -writer, -writing; planchette-like* adj.

1914 H. CARRINGTON *Probl. Psychical Res.* xii. 371 There can be little doubt that the same force which propels the planchette board propels the ouija board also. **1972** D. BLOODWORTH *Any Number can Play* ix. 71 The planchette board circled wildly, both men keeping their fingers hard down upon it. **1920** *Q. Rev.* July 196 He could not see how so vigorous a creative faculty..could be only a vague Planchette-like state of possession. **1920** Planchette-writer [see *crystal-gazer* s.v. *CRYSTAL *sb.* B. 2 c]. **1884** F. W. H. MYERS in *Proc. Soc. Psychical Res.* Dec. 232 The Spiritualist theory of Planchette-writing assumes the former of these two hypotheses. **1909** Planchette writing [see *OUIJA].

4. var. prec.

Planck (plæŋk). *Physics.* The name of Max K. E. L. *Planck* (1858–1947), German physicist, used in the possessive and *attrib.* to designate various concepts that he invented or discovered, as **Planck('s) constant,** one of the fundamental physical constants (symbol h), relating the energy E of a quantum of electromagnetic radiation to its frequency ν according to the equation $E = h\nu$; approximately $6{\cdot}626 \times 10^{-34}$ joule-second; **Planck('s) equation** or **formula,** any of the related equations stating Planck's law; **Planck('s) law,** a law giving the density of radiant energy at a particular wavelength λ or frequency ν inside a perfect radiator, and the flux of radiant energy emitted by it, the former being written as $\rho(\lambda)d\lambda=(8\pi hc/\lambda^5)(\exp(hc/k\lambda T)-1)^{-1}d\lambda$ or $\rho(\nu)d\nu=(8\pi h\nu^3/c^3)(\exp(h\nu/kT)-1)^{-1}d\nu$; **Planck oscillator,** a concept used by Planck in his work on radiation: an electrically charged particle that can execute simple harmonic motion with a frequency independent of the amplitude; **Planck('s) radiation formula** or **law** = *Planck('s) law.*

1910 *Phil. Mag.* XX. 244 Corpuscles which are emitted by bodies when exposed to ultra-violet light. Ladenburg found that the maximum energy of these corpuscles..was proportional to *n* the frequency of the light, being of the order $h'n/2\pi$ where h' is Planck's constant. **1935** D. L. SAYERS *Gaudy Night* ii. 37 'There happened to be an unknown factor.' 'Like that thing that keeps cropping up in the new kind of physics,' said the Dean. 'Planck's constant, or whatever they call it.' **1940** GLASSTONE *Text-bk. Physical Chem.* i. 73 Every particle is associated with a wave.., and the wave length (λ) is related to the mechanical momentum (*mv*) by $\lambda=h/mv$, where *h* is the Planck constant. **1960** CHALMERS & QUARRELL *Physical Examination of Metals* (ed. 2) xvi. 749 This is known as the spin of the particle and is measured in terms of $h/2\pi$.. where *h* is Planck's constant. **1968** G. LUDWIG *Wave Mech.* I. iv. 62 This uncertainty relation states that in any experimentally producible ensemble the product of the spread in position and momentum cannot go below a lower limit given by Planck's constant. **1911** *Bull. Bureau of Standards* (U.S.) VII. 393 Planck's equation for the intensity of radiation *J*, of wave length λ, from a black body at the absolute temperature θ,..appears to represent the results of all known observations. **1966** M. FERRO-LUZZI tr. *Fermi's Molecules, Crystals & Quantum Statistics* vii. 223 From the Planck equation, we can easily deduce Stefan's law, which also can be obtained by thermodynamic arguments alone. **1905** LD. RAYLEIGH in *Nature* 13 July 244/1 In *Nature*, May 18, I gave a calculation of the coefficient of complete radiation at a given absolute temperature for waves of great length.., and it appeared that the result was eight times as great as that deduced from Planck's formula. **1923** GLAZEBROOK *Dict. Appl. Physics* IV. 563/2 Throughout the spectrum from 0·5 μ to 50 μ Planck's formula fits the observed spectral energy distribution more closely than any other equation yet proposed. **1974** G. REECE tr. *Hund's Hist. Quantum Theory* ii. 27 By comparing the measured energy densities..with Planck's formula it was possible to calculate *h* and *h/k*. **1905** *Nature* 27 July 294/2 Planck's law is in good agreement with experiment if *h* is given a value different from zero. **1930** RUARK & UREY *Atoms, Molecules & Quanta* iii. 59 The physical basis for the asymptotic approach of Planck's law to the classical distribution is easily seen. **1955** W. HEISENBERG in W. Pauli *Niels Bohr* 14 Bohr explained to him [*sc.* Schrödinger] that not even Planck's Law could be understood without the quantum jumps. **1974** TURNER & BETTS *Introd. Statistical Mech.* xii. 148 The Planck law describes the distributions of energy among the infinite range of possible frequencies. **1920** Planck oscillator [see *N I. 4 b]. **1966** tr. *S.-I. Tomonaga's Quantum Mech.* II. vi. 111 Each term in Eq. (47.9′) has the form of the Hamiltonian of a Planck oscillator. **1909** *Sci. Abstr.* A. XII. 315 (*heading*) Planck's radiation law. **1911** *Ibid.* XIV. 404 It is concluded that the Einstein formula for specific heat is confirmed and also the Planck radiation formula. **1935** PAULING & WILSON *Introd. Quantum Mech.* xi. 301 The density of radiant energy is known to be given by Planck's radiation law as [etc.]. **1974** G. REECE tr. *Hund's Hist. Quantum Theory* xi. 145 The Bose statistics of light quanta was thus the same as that earlier applied by Planck for energy quanta..and thus led to the Planck radiation formula.

Planckian (plæ·ŋkiăn), *a.* *Physics.* [f. prec. + -IAN.] Of, pertaining to, or being a black body.

1922 *Jrnl. Optical Soc. Amer.* VI. 560 Average noon sunlight..corresponds roughly to a black body temperature of 5000° K. the distribution not being strictly Planckian. **1956** H. H. EMSLEY *Aberrations of Thin Lenses* x. 303 A black body or Planckian radiator. **1972** *Nature* 28 Apr. 448/2 It seems improbable that the whole spectrum is Planckian, because the total power of such radiation would be..10^{42} erg s^{-1}.

‖**planctus** (pla·ŋktŭs). Pl. **planctus** (-ūs). [L., = beating of the breast, lamentation.] A medieval lament (LAMENT *sb.* 2). Cf. *PLANH.

1901 *Jrnl. Germanic Philol.* III. 417 From the various German Lamentations he [*sc.* A. Schönbach] culls eighteen versicles, mostly quatrains, which occur most frequently and of which the first thirteen are in form and in content a free version of the Latin Planctus. **1903** E. K. CHAMBERS *Mediæval Stage* II. III. xviii. 32 The metrical hymns are often of the nature of *planctus* or laments put in the mouths of the Maries as they approach the sepulchre... These *planctus* add greatly to the vividness and humanity of the play. **1907** *Mod. Philol.* IV. 605 It is hoped that the present discussion of the English planctus may in the future help to make more easily possible a comparative study of the planctus as a class. *Ibid.* 606 The chief purpose of this study is to discuss the several non-dramatic English planctus in their relation to each other. **1940** G. REESE *Music in Middle Ages* (1941) vii. 198 These *planctus*, with Latin texts, are believed actually to date from the 7th century and to be compositions, perhaps, of St. Eugenius. **1954** *New Oxf. Hist. Music* II. vi. 193 Although some of the most famous of the *planctus* of the Passion are solo stanzas, spoken by the Virgin Mary, yet there are a number in dialogue form, the speakers being most frequently Mary and St. John. **1964** C. S. LEWIS *Discarded Image* iii. 36 *Natura* as Alanus brings her in, stiffly robed in rhetoric, conceit, and symbol, pleading again the cause of procreation in her *planctus* (against the sodomites). **1970** W. APEL *Harvard Dict. Mus.* (ed. 2) 461/2 A 'Planctus Karoli' lamenting the death of Charlemagne (814) and another *planctus* for his son Hugo (844). **1977** *Times Lit. Suppl.* 17 June 727/5 The cycle of six *planctus* by Peter Abelard.

plandok, var. *PELANDOK.

plane, *sb.*[3] Add: **1. i.** A relatively thin structure used to produce an upwards or downwards († or sideways) force by the flow of the surrounding air or water over its surface. Orig. a flat surface (PLANE *sb.*[3] 1 b) proposed as a source of lift for heavier-than-air machines and used to direct the ascent and descent of balloons; later designed with a slight camber and used as the wing of an aeroplane or as a hydrofoil on a boat or sea-plane. Cf. *AEROFOIL, *AEROPLANE 1, *HYDROFOIL 1, *HYDROPLANE *sb.* 1.

Not now a common word exc. in the sense of *HYDROPLANE *sb.* 1, and in combinations and derivatives (e.g. *BIPLANE, **diving-plane*, *INTERPLANE *a.*).

For the spelling *plain* (quots. *a* 1802, 1804) cf. PLAIN *sb.*[1] 4.

[*a* **1802** G. CAYLEY *Aeronaut. & Misc. Note-bk.* (1933) 10 In estimating the mechanical power which a given plain [*transcribed as* plane] will exert when exposed in any position to a current of fluid, two things are necessary. **1804** *Ibid.* 22, I made the following experiments upon the resistance of air to a surface of a foot sq, carried round with an horizontal motion upon an arm suspended upon a delicate hinge... The angles which the plain made with the horizon were measured.] **1809** —— in *Jrnl. Nat. Philos.* XXIV. 171 It is perfectly indifferent whether the wind blow against the plane, or the plane be driven with an equal velocity against the air. **1815** *Phil. Mag.* XLVI. 323 On October 2, 1815, another experiment..was made with a balloon six feet in diameter, having a square plane whose side was 7·5 feet, and a triangular rudder in proportion. **1816** *Ibid.* XLVII. 82 My object was to leave out the unwieldy bulk of balloons altogether, and to make use of the inclined plane propelled by a light first mover. **1842** W. S. HENSON *Brit. Pat. 9478* The first part of my Invention consists of an apparatus so constructed as to offer a very extended surface or plane.., which will have the same relation to the general machine which the extended wings of a bird have to the body when the bird is skimming in the air. *Ibid.*, The surface of the planes on either side of the car will measure four thousand five hundred square feet. **1848** *Chambers's Jrnl.* 6 May 301/1 When it attained the highest point, the edge of the plane would be reversed, and the balloon would descend thus. *Ibid.* 303/1 The wings are to be formed of long and narrow silk planes. **1866** *Ann. Rep. Aëronaut. Soc.* 25 A simple narrow blade, or inclined plane, propelled in a direct course..is..the only means of giving the maximum amount of supporting power with the least possible degree of 'slip'. *Ibid.* 36 To obtain the necessary length of plane ..the surfaces may be superposed, or placed in parallel rows, with an interval between them. **1891** S. P. LANGLEY *Exper. in Aerodynamics* 58 The planes whose spread is largest in comparison with their extent from front to back..are therefore to be considered as being..the most favourable for mechanical flight. **1907** *Engineering* 4 Oct. 457/2 The boat is provided with hydroplanes only at its stem and stern. The planes at the bow are arranged in the manner of a **V**. **1908** *Aëronaut. Jrnl.* XII. 45/2 However sound in theory the single plane aëroplane may be, every serious accident yet recorded has occurred with this type. **1908** H. G. WELLS *War in Air* iii. 82 He found the missing drawings of the lateral rotating planes, on which the whole stability of the flying-machine depended. **1910** [see *AEROPLANE 2 b]. **1912** M. KERR in S. W. Murray *Poetry of Flight* (1925) 53 The tips of the planes appear and disappear As you madly drive along through the mist enladen'd air. **1915** A. FAGE *Aeroplane* iv. 31 The rudder, a vertical plane capable of rotation about a vertical axis, partially controls the yawing or turning of the machine. **1917** A. W. JUDGE *Properties of Aerofoils* iii. 51 The inclined cambered plane differs from the inclined flat plane, in conforming better with the upward trend of the air about the leading edge. **1920** G. C. BAILEY *Compl. Airman* viii. 59 The incidence of the tail plane can be varied. **1920** [see *HYDROFOIL 1]. **1938** E. W. C. WILKINS *Aeroplane Design* ii. 22 In the orthodox aeroplane, the main planes, or wings, are fixed. **1966** *McGraw-Hill Encycl. Sci. & Technol.* XIII. 212/2 Each set..may be tilted through an angle of 25° in either direction from the horizontal to develop a vertical force on the planes and thus on the submarine. **1972** J. B. ICENHOWER *Submarines* 9 At the bow and stern of a submarine are flat devices somewhat like the fins of a big fish. They are known as the *forward* and *after* hydroplanes... The diving planesmen tilt the forward planes down and the after planes up.

j. *Computers.* One of the flat, usu. square arrays of magnetic cores or other elements in a memory, each of which contains the corresponding bits of all the words held in the arrays.

1959 E. M. MCCORMICK *Digital Computer Primer* viii. 107 In a magnetic core used to store, say, 4096 words of 36 binary bits each, there would be 36 sets (planes) of cores, and each plane would contain 4096 cores arranged with 64 on each side of a square. **1964** *IBM Jrnl. Res. & Devel.* VIII. 171/2 Figure 2 shows such a memory plane containing 50 tubes centered at intervals of 0·070 in. and 100 bit lines centered at intervals of 0·030 in. **1969** [see *CORE *sb.*[1] 10 b]. **1976** 'ABD-ALLA & MELTZER *Princ. Digital Computer Design* I. ix. 329 The planes are stacked into a three-dimensional array. The *x* lines of each plane are connected in series with the same *x* line on the two adjacent core planes.

4. *spec.* in *Theosophy.*

1884 *Trans. London Lodge Theosoph. Soc.* June 7 In considering the action of the law of Karma it is better to divide man into three planes; the physical, mental, and spiritual. **1889** H. P. BLAVATSKY *Key to Theosophy* III. 45 That which is true on the metaphysical plane must be also true on the physical. **1892** —— *Theosoph. Gloss.* 255 Plane. From the Latin *planus*..an extension of space or of something in it, whether physical or metaphysical, *e.g.* a 'plane of consciousness'. **1922** JOYCE *Ulysses* 139 A. E. the master mystic? That Blavatsky woman started it... A. E. has been telling some yankee interviewer that you came to him in the small hours of the morning to ask him about planes of consciousness. *Ibid.* 183 The Christ with the bridesister,..departed to the plane of buddhi. **1951** 'Novo' *Notes on Theosophy* 13 We believe that beyond, yet interwoven with, physical matter, are other planes of such a tenuous nature that they are not apparent to the human eye. **1974** *Encycl. Brit. Macropædia* XVIII. 277/2 Most modern theosophists subscribe to a rather elaborate cosmogony... There are, it is believed, seven worlds or planes through which the universe evolves. In ascending order these are the physical plane; the emotional, or astral, plane; the mental plane; the intuitional, or Buddhic, plane; the spiritual, or Atmic, plane; the monadic, or Anupadaka, plane; and the divine, or Adi, plane. **1977** 'L. EGAN' *Blind Search* i. 6 It was reasonable to suppose that he still was, and still concerned with the people who'd meant something to him here—planes or levels of vibration or whatever.

plane (plēⁱn), *sb.*[5] Also **'plane.** [f. AERO)PLANE.] = *AEROPLANE 2 b.

1908 *Aëronaut. Jrnl.* Apr. 45/1 The aëroplane was then taken to the Longchamps end of the field, and as soon as the propeller had been set in motion the apparatus dashed off towards Neuilly. After running along the ground for about a hundred mètres the plane lifted, and.. rushed through the air for 150 mètres or thereabouts. **1908** *Times* 1 June 6/1 Mr. Wright refused to give any details on the propeller employed, but on the general construction of the plane he said it was full of movable diversely articulated parts. **1909** KIPLING *With Night Mail* 69 Low-flying planes often 'glue up' when near the Magnetic Pole. **1909** LLOYD GEORGE in *Daily Chron.* 23 Aug. 1/1, I have not yet crossed the Financial Channel with my Budget 'plane. **1910** *Daily Mail* 27 July 6/5 To the builders of aeroplanes he cries: 'Construct me planes capable of the maximum speed.' **1920** *Blackw. Mag.* June 762/1 A plane which came from Palestine. **1931** *Daily Mirror* 27 Aug. 2/2 The 'plane struck the water. **1932** *Daily Express* 27 June 8/2 The first ape and the comic sergeant are deserting to Switzerland in a bombing 'plane. **1942** R. HILLARY *Last Enemy* 1 My plane had been fitted out with a new cockpit hood. **1958** 'CASTLE' & 'HAILEY' *Flight into Danger* ii. 30 There was a brief shudder as the plane freed herself from a wall of cloud. **1965** *Movie* Summer 3/2 Charlotte and Robert talk and make love in the hour before his 'plane leaves. **1976** *Daily Tel.* 7 Oct 1/6 All 73 passengers and crew of a Cuban DC-8 airliner were believed lost when the plane plunged into the Caribbean.

2. *attrib. and Comb.*, as *plane crash* sb. (and vb. intr.), *fare, journey, -load, park,* † *pilot, -ride, -spotter, ticket*; **planeside** *U.S.*, an area beside an aeroplane; also *attrib.*; **plane time,** the time of departure of an aircraft on a scheduled flight.

1946 *Time* 14 Oct. 69/1 Four years before Knute Rockne plane-crashed to death in Kansas, Irishman Frank Leahy came to Notre Dame. **1957** P. WORSLEY *Trumpet shall Sound* x. 200 These movements soon spread further into the Highlands, thriving on the.. alarm created by the war:..plane-crashes and so on. **1972** J. AIKEN *Butterfly Picnic* i. 13 Her parents had been killed in a plane crash. **1969** B. MALAMUD *Pictures of Fidelman* iii. 69 I'll need plane fare. **1973** 'E. MCBAIN' *Let's hear It* v. 68 The Puerto Ricans came, and some of them stayed only long enough to earn plane fare back to the island. **1974** E. AMBLER *Dr. Frigo* II. 84, I..have no trouble at all with long plane journeys... I always sleep soundly. **1951** R. MALKIN *Boxcars in Sky* 25 A French schoolhouse was able to be rushed to completion in record time following the flight of a planeload of components of a prefabricated school manufactured in England. **1969** C. BOOKER *Neophiliacs* x. 261 Planeloads of American gamblers flying in to..'the European Las Vegas' [*sc.* London]. **1976** *Evening Standard* 29 Dec. 26/5 Representatives of the emerging nations descend by the planeload. **1936** 'J. BEYNON' *Planet Plane* 41 The crowds began to pour from the 'plane-parks and car-parks. **1916** 'BOYD CABLE' *Action Front* 132 The 'plane pilot..was well out of range. **1953** DYLAN THOMAS *Let.* 22 June (1966) 408, I almost liked the plane-ride, though. **1973** *Black Panther* 4 Aug. 15/2 Nixon,..in a plane ride from Mobile to Birmingham in 1971 with Wallace, had persuaded the charismatic Alabaman to run as a Democrat. **1968** *N.Y. Times* 28 Mar. 3 In a planeside interview, General Abrams said [etc.]. **1968** *Sat. Rev.* (U.S.) 31 Aug. 6, I walk from planeside to a taxi. **1976** *6,000 Words* 156 Speaking briefly at planeside. **1978** *Fortune* 4 Dec. 101 (*heading*) To planeside by bus. **1960** *Guardian* 12 Mar. 6/5 The prowess of London Airport's plane spotters is likely to become comparable with the best of the train spotters. **1975** S. JOHNSON *Urbane Guerilla* III. 152 A crowd of sightseers and plane-spotters. **1977** *Daily Mirror* 21 Mar. 13/2 Five plane spotters serving jail terms in Greece will get a spot of home comfort today. **1967** M. DRABBLE *Jerusalem the Golden* viii. 204 Her plane ticket ..was booked from Le Bourget. **1974** D. WESTHEIMER *Olmec Head* ii. 18 Plane tickets, hotel rooms already set. **1962** L. DEIGHTON *Ipcress File* v. 30 The typewritten sheet gave plane times. **1973** 'B. MATHER' *Snowline* ix. 112 I'll be able to get you an air ticket... You had better stay here until plane time. **1976** K. BONFIGLIOLI *Something Nasty in Woodshed* ix. 96, I slept until 'plane-time this morning.

plane, *a.* Add: **3. plane-parallel** *a.*, both plane and parallel.

1903 *Amer. Jrnl. Sci.* XVI. 114 A rock-mass possessing the plane-parallel structure. **1958** *Newnes Compl. Amat.*

Photogr. 97 In order not to disturb the lens correction filter glasses have to be plane-parallel and optically finished. **1962** CORSON & LORRAIN *Introd. Electromagn. Fields* iv. 148 (*caption*) Grounded, plane-parallel electrodes terminated by a plane electrode at potential V_0.

plane, *v.*² **1.** Delete *rare* and add further examples. (In mod. use with the idea of an aeroplane's flight.)

1941 I. L. IDRIESS *Great Boomerang* i. 2 A black dot appeared in the brazen sky. It grew, planed down and alighted on the needlewood-tree beside the first crow. **1953** R. LEHMANN *Echoing Grove* 22 A shape of silence, planing stealthily from nowhere, crossed the churchyard: a huge cream-coloured owl. **1953** J. CARY *Except the Lord* lxii. 286 A few gulls planed high overhead but made no sound. **1955** *Times* 3 Aug. 10/2 As he [*sc.* a marsh harrier] began to plane down over the water two members of his young family raced each other to meet him in the air. **1978** R. LEWIS *Uncertain Sound* vi. 154 The herring gulls planed among the bobbing masts of the fishing fleet. **1979** G. HAMMOND *Dead Game* ix. 107 Another [goose]..had gone on away over the sands, first planing and then running.

2. *intr.* To travel in an aeroplane; † to glide.

1908 *Daily Mail* 10 Aug. 5/4 Safety would reside in high flight; it would always be possible to 'plane' to earth, and in 'planing' the machine would progress many more feet than it would fall. **1909** *Westm. Gaz.* 9 Aug. 5/1 Mr. Orville Wright has stated that he and his brother are completing the perfecting of their aeroplane... With this apparatus he says one will be able to 'plane' to one's heart's content. **1909** *Daily Chron.* 26 Aug. 1/2 His engine began to show signs of distress. The aviator was seen to slow down, and then he 'planed gracefully to the earth. **1912** S. F. WALKER *Aviation* viii. 66 He can plane down. Planing down is merely gliding. **1940** *Daily Progress* (Charlottesville, Va.) 13 Aug. 1/4 Little Carolyn ..will plane out for the movie capital from the nation's capital on Thursday morning, accompanied by her mother. **1967** J. P. CARSTAIRS *No Thanks for Shroud* ii. 28, I had planed into the large air terminal at Los Angeles.

3. *intr.* Of a seaplane, boat, etc.: to skim the surface of a body of water as a result of lift produced hydrodynamically.

1913 [see *HYDROPLANE *sb.* 2]. **1914** *Techn. Rep. Advisory Comm. Aeronaut. 1912–13* 243 The position of the centre of buoyancy when the float is at rest is far ahead of the centre of pressure when it is 'planing' and the machine about to fly. **1919** A. W. JUDGE *Handbk. Mod. Aeronaut.* xix. 943 Hollow Vee sections keep the spray down, cut the water more easily and cleanly, plane better, [etc.]. **1942** *R.A.F. Jrnl.* 13 June 8 There is great danger in..level ditchings where the nose strikes first. The nose is neither shaped nor strong enough to plane along the surface. **1954** K. C. BARNABY *Basic Naval Archit.* (ed. 2) 318 When a hard chine hull is planing correctly, only the under body below the chines is in direct and constant contact with the water. **1963** J. T. ROWLAND *North to Adventure* i. 15 It was a big sail for a ten-foot punt. She seemed to leap out of the water; I believe she planed. **1972** C. MUDIE *Motor Boats* 48 A fast boat on the verge of planing or actually planing builds up a pressure on the under surfaces of the hull which, like walking on harder ground compared with bog, increases the firmness of the footing and hence the stability. **1972** R. ABBOTT *Sci. of Surfing* iii. 52 The technique of modern surfing is based on the fact that boards plane easily and efficiently. Planing is the term used to describe the way in which a surfboard rises onto the water surface and skims along at high speed. **1974** *Encycl. Brit. Macropædia* II. 1171/1 Because the displacement hull..can never plane on the surface no matter how much power is applied, the efforts of designers were directed toward the development of hulls..that at speed would rise to the surface and skim across the water, thus reducing..the friction and resistance.

4. *trans.* In Surfing, to ride (a wave) with the hands protecting the face. *Austral.*

1963 B. HUTCHINGS in J. Pollard *Swimming—Austral. Style* 122/1 To 'plane' a wave, you hold your hands together in front of your head and take off in this position as the wave nears... The trick is to arrange the spear formed by the hands in such a way that the water passes along the side of the face and torso and not into the face.

Hence **pla·ning** *vbl. sb.*² and *ppl. a.* (chiefly in sense *3 of the vb.).

1908 [see *AVIATE *v.*]. **1914** *Techn. Rep. Advisory Comm. Aeronaut. 1912–13* 243 Its most obvious defect was a certain slowness in rising to the planing position. **1919** A. W. JUDGE *Handbk. Mod. Aeronaut.* xix. 944 The bottom abaft the step should rise strongly, as this favours a steepening of the planing bow before suction is eliminated. **1920** *Flight* XII. 301/1 Other types of 'planing' boats. *Ibid.* 591/1 The angle of the planing bottom at the keel, forward of the step, should be 1½ degrees to the datum line. **1937** *Jrnl. R. Aeronaut. Soc.* XLI. 273 Improvements have been made recently in the shape of afterbody of the planing bottom with the object of obtaining better aerodynamic efficiency. **1967** *Jane's Surface Skimmer Systems 1967–68* 110/1 The hull..has a hard chine..and planing hull form. **1972** R. ABBOTT *Sci. of Surfing* iii. 52 For planing speed to be maintained and so that the wave can be ridden along its length it is necessary to turn fairly soon. **1972** C. MUDIE *Motor Boats* 48 A planing boat has a quite remarkable stability when running fast. **1974** J. KEATS *Of Time & Island* xii. 191 When you pushed forward on a throttle..the boat mounted onto its planing step and you flew over the river. **1976–7** *Sea Spray* (N.Z.) Dec./Jan. 78/1 This is no more evident than in the development of power craft, the rise of the planing hull and the steady move over the past few years into tunnel-hulls, hydrofoils, hovercraft and so on.

planeful, 'planeful (plēi·n,fʊl). [f. *PLANE *sb.*⁵ + -FUL.] As much or as many as an aeroplane will hold.

1958 *Times* 14 Aug. 9/4 There is no reason why a 'planeful of them [*sc.* monkeys] should be any different. **1967** M. DAVIS *Strange Corner* (1968) vii. 58 A planeful of new guests.

planeness. Delete *rare* and add later examples.

1896 *Jrnl. Geol.* IV. 955 Overwash plains may sometimes depart from planeness by taking on some measure of undulation. **1906** CHAMBERLIN & SALISBURY *Geol.* III. xix. 345 Neither planeness nor unevenness can be ascribed exclusively to the stratified nor to the unstratified drift. **1942** F. TWYMAN *Prism & Lens Making* ix. 124 The departures from planeness of the wave front..will give rise to a contour map of the corrections which have to be applied to the lens. **1975** D. G. FINK *Electronics Engineers' Handbk.* ix. 26 Since the periphery of the grid is colder than the center, thermal stresses tend to cause buckling or departure from planeness.

planer. Add: **6. planer-miller** = *plano-miller* s.v. *PLANO-¹.

1943 J. R. CONNELLY *Technique Production Processes* iii. 85 (*caption*) Planer-miller. A good case of comb[in]ing the features of several standard tools for special work. **1971** C. R. HINE *Machine Tools & Processes* xiii. 308 The planer-miller is a hybrid of the two machines, but because of its size and construction (with a crossrail) it can rightfully be classified as a planer.

planer-tree. Substitute for def.: A small, deciduous tree, the water elm, *Planera aquatica*, belonging to the family Ulmaceæ and native to south-eastern parts of the United States. (Earlier and later examples.)

1810 F. A. MICHAUX *Hist. Arbres Forestiers de l'Amérique Septentrionale* I. 39 *Planer tree*, nom de la personne à laquelle cette espèce a été consacrée. **1819** A. L. HILLHOUSE tr. *Michaux's N. Amer. Sylva* III. 100, I have more particularly observed the Planer Tree in the large swamps on the borders of the river Savannah in Georgia. **1832** D. J. BROWNE *Sylva Amer.* 246 The planer tree is of the second order, and is rarely more than 35 or 40 feet high. **1930** W. R. MATTOON et al. *Forest Trees Oklahoma* 62 The water elm or planer tree is found on the low wet flood plains of the larger streams of the eastern part of the state. **1976** *Hortus Third* (L. H. Bailey Hortorium) 882/2 Planer tree, water elm... A deciduous elmlike tree, native to N[orth] Amer[ica].

planeshear, planksheer. (Earlier example of spelling *planksheer.*)

1851 G. COGGESHALL *Voy.* iii. 40 The force of the sea broke one of the top timbers or stancheons, and split open the plank-sheer.

planet, *sb.*¹ Add: **2.** (A ninth major planet, *Pluto* (*PLUTO¹ 1), is now known.)

3*. A planet wheel.

1912 R. W. A. BREWER *Motor Car Construction* xii. 154 If one sun wheel is held, the whole of the planets with their star piece move bodily in a circle when the other sun wheel is revolved. **1928** V. W. PAGÉ *Mod. Aircraft* xi. 474 Various methods of compounding plain epicyclic gears have been tried, but the best type is undoubtedly that combining double planets, an annulus driven from the crankshaft, and a sun fixed to the engine casing. **1962** D. W. DUDLEY *Gear Handbk.* iii. 15 With some ratios it has been possible to squeeze in as many as twenty planets. **1970** *A.A. Bk. of Car* 110/1 In the simple epicyclic gear, a pair of planets revolve on spindles supported by the U-shaped planet carrier, which is mounted on the same shaft as the sun wheel.

4. *planet-spotted* adj.; **planet cage**, a cylindrical form of planet carrier; **planet carrier**, the frame on which the planet wheels are mounted in a planetary gear; **planet earth** (without *the*, and usu. with one or both initials capitals), the earth as the particular planet on which man lives; **planet-gear**, add to def.: a planet wheel; (examples); **planet pinion**, a planet wheel, esp. one smaller than the sun wheel; **planet shower**, a local shower (cf. PLANET *sb.*¹ 1 c); **planet stirrer** = *planetary stirrer* s.v. *PLANETARY *a.* and *sb.* A. 1 f; **planet-wheel** (earlier and later examples); **planet-wide** *a.*, occurring all over the planet, as extensive as the planet.

1908 Planet cage [see *planet pinion* below]. **1947** *Jrnl. R. Aeronaut. Soc.* LI. 100/1 This usually leads to the adoption of an epicyclic gear with its associated problems of planet cage design and high centrifugal loadings. **1956** MOLLOY & LANCHESTER *Automobile Engineer's Ref. Bk.* XII. 60 The short planet gears rotate round the internal ring gear, in the same direction as the input shaft, thus rotating the planet carrier and attached output shaft at a reduced speed. **1976** LEEMING & HARTLEY *Heavy Vehicle Technol.* vi. 117/2 If the planet carrier is braked and the sun wheel driven, the annulus is driven in a reverse direction—the planet wheels being idler wheels only—and reverse ratio is obtained. **1965** J. H. JACKSON *Pictorial Guide to Planets* v. 34 (*heading*) Planet earth. **1976** L. DEIGHTON *Twinkle, Twinkle Little Spy* viii. 80 We should simply seek to make a mark in the universe.. that some other civilization will detect and so know there is..sophisticated life on planet Earth. **1978** *Listener* 12 Jan. 54/1 The hopeful television producers..who have invaded planet earth. **1979** *Guardian* 18 Aug. 10/8 The SF buff..believes that Planet Earth is done for... He wants more money spent on space. **1916** J. E. HOMANS *Automobile Handbk.* iii. 42 As soon as the engine starts—there being no clutch necessary on a car with such apparatus—the two spurs keyed to the main shaft..rotate with it, driving the 'planet' gears in mesh with them. **1956** [see *planet carrier* above]. **1971** B. SCHARF *Engin. & its Lang.* xii. 161 The planet gears are mounted on pins attached to a common frame, the planet carrier. **1908** *Daily Chron.* 14 Nov. 8/6 Greater attention is being paid to the elimination of internal friction from these devices, as in the provision of ball bearings for the planet pinions in the Sturmey Archer gears, and roller bearings for the planet cage in the Armstrong. *a* **1935** [see *BACK-LASH a]. **1966** *McGraw-Hill Encycl. Sci. & Technol.* X. 273/2 The number of teeth on the planet pinion of a simple planetary gear does not enter into the equations for speed ratio because the pinion engages both sun and ring gears. **1853** MAYNE REID *Rifle Rangers* (rev. ed.) lvii. 288 We were treated each day to some five or six hours of a 'planet' shower. **1880** W. H. PATTERSON *Gloss. Words Antrim & Down* 78 *Planet showers*, short heavy showers. **1925** E. SITWELL *Troy Park* 39 Not medicines planet-spotted like fritillaries For country sins and old stupidities. **1902** C. SALTER tr. *G. von Georgievics's Chem. Technol. Textile Fibres* 249 Stirring is effected by so-called planet stirrers. **1827** J. FAREY *Treat. Steam Engine* I. vi. 449 The link causes the centre of the planet-wheel to travel in a circular orbit..when it revolves round the sun-wheel. **1912** R. W. A. BREWER *Motor Car Construction* xii. 153 The large bevel wheel is bolted to a casing, which holds firmly a star piece having four arms on each of which runs a planet wheel... These four planet wheels engage with two sun wheels. **1976** Planet-wheel [see *planet carrier* above]. **1969** *Listener* 14 Aug. 215/2 It is now evident that on Mars, the craters are planet-wide. **1974** *Icarus* XXII. 239 (*heading*) Martian planetwide crater distributions.

plane-table, *v.* Add: Also *intr.*, to work with a plane-table.

1883 H. H. GODWIN-AUSTEN et al. *Hints to Travellers* (ed. 5) i. 109 There is no measuring, no counting of paces or noting of time by a watch, no anxiety about the record, when Plane-Tabling.

plane-tabler, -tabling (examples).

1871 Plane-tabling [in Dict.]. **1888** *Min. Proc. Inst. Civil Engin.* XCII. 190 When a triangulation exists of the country to be mapped, the plane-tabler makes immediate use of these established points. **1923** D. CLARK *Plane & Geodetic Surveying* II. vi. 238 Plane tabling is the most extensively used method for the survey of topography. **1950** J. CLENDINNING *Princ. & Use of Surveying Instruments* vii. 166 Plane-tabling is a graphical method of survey in which the map is rough-drawn in the field as the survey proceeds. **1965** *Textbk. Topogr. Surveying* (Min. of Defence) (ed. 4) xi. 205 The trigonometrical framework will have been surveyed... The plane tabler then proceeds to break down from this framework using methods similar to those employed by the triangulator. **1971** R. J. P. WILSON *Land Surveying* viii. 164 In the past plane tabling was the method used for supplying topographical detail for maps at scales of 1:10 000 to 1:250 000, but its use in this respect has largely..been superseded by air survey.

planetal, *a.* Delete † *Obs.* and add later example.

1908 *Encycl. Relig. & Ethics* I. 187/1 The planetal series of our days of the week places Sunday before Monday.

planetarium. Add: **a.** (Earlier example.)

1734 J. T. DESAGULIERS *Course Exper. Philos.* I. 430 A short Description of my Planetarium, an Instrument.. to shew the Motion of the heavenly Bodies.

d. A device for projecting an image of the night sky at various times and places on to the interior of a dome for public viewing; a building housing this. Also *attrib.* and *fig.*

1929 *Encycl. Brit.* XVII. 1000 Planetarium is the name given to an arrangement made by Zeiss of Jena, for producing an artificial sky. By optical methods images of the sun, moon, planets and stars are projected on a large hemispherical dome and by mechanical and electrical means the apparatus can be revolved so as to show the principal motions. **1950** *Engineering* 21 July 63/1 A planetarium..building will have..the dome representing the sky..diameter 60 feet. The simulation of the sun, moon, planets and stars..projected on the 'sky' will have great educational value. **1958** *New Scientist* 20 Mar. 6/3 Zeiss Planetaria have been operated in 32 cities. **1958** [see *ASTRONAVIGATION]. **1963** V. NABOKOV *Gift* iii. 166 Now on the [chess] board there shone, like a constellation, a ravishing work of art, a planetarium of thought. **1973** C. SAGAN *Cosmic Connection* viii. 60 Several million people visit planetariums in North America and Britain each year.

planetary, *a.* and *sb.* Add: **A.** *adj.* **1.** (Further examples.)

planetary electron, an electron bound to an atom and 'in orbit' round its nucleus; *planetary engineering* (see quots. 1951, 1964); *planetary nebula* (earlier examples); *planetary precession*: see *PRECESSION 3 a.

1785 *Phil. Trans. R. Soc.* LXXV. 266 A very bright, planetary nebula, about half a minute in diameter, but the edges are not very well defined. **1802** [see NEBULA 3]. **1921** *Phil. Mag.* XLII. 305 Consider the nucleus alone, and not the surrounding system of planetary electrons. **1927** N. V. SIDGWICK *Electronic Theory of Valency* i. 10 The other planetary electrons would be distributed between these limits. **1951** A. C. CLARKE *Exploration of Space* 118 The greatest technical achievements of the next few centuries may well be in the field of what could be called 'planetary engineering'—the reshaping of other worlds to suit human needs. **1956** I. ASIMOV *Inside Atom* ii. 31 The number of planetary electrons in an ordinary atom is equal to the number of protons in the nucleus. **1960** *Analog Science Fact/Fiction* Oct. 34/1 We are coming off Mass-Time to go on planetary drive. **1964** *Listener* 15 Oct. 575/1 It will be possible to modify the climates and atmospheres of at least some of the planets, so that we can live on them... This technique of the future has been called 'planetary engineering'. **1971** *Nature* 3 Dec. 246/2 Why should planetary scientists suggest that a spacecraft costing nearly $100 million should be destroyed by taking it so close to Jupiter?

e. Involving, being, or forming part of a sun-and-planet gear, usu. having (in addition to the sun and planet wheels) an internally geared annulus coaxial with the sun wheel and with which the planet wheels are meshed.

1904 T. H. WHITE *Petrol Motors* II. 108 When the pinion A is revolved, and the internally toothed ring B is held from revolving, the planetary pinions C are caused to run around the ring B and carry the plate D with them. **1910** [see *band clutch* s.v. *BAND *sb.*[2] III]. **1934** *Jrnl. R. Aeronaut. Soc.* XXXVIII. 738 This specification describes a planetary reduction gear for aero engines in which an internally toothed annulus is driven by the engine, the propeller is driven by the planetary ring, [etc.]. **1948** [see *EPICYCLIC *a.*]. **1956** A. HUXLEY *Adonis & Alphabet* 127 The simple planetary gears, by means of which conventional turntables can be used for slow-playing disks. **1969** *Jane's Freight Containers 1968–69* 583/3 Torque converter is standard. All drive wheels planetary drive powered. **1975** *Sci. Amer.* Dec. 120/2 The upper end of the larger planetary gear engages a spur gear fixed to a turntable.

f. *Engin.* Characterized by the circular motion of a part about a point outside it.

planetary mill, a heavy rolling mill for reducing hot strip in a single pass, the strip being forced between two large rolls each of which has a number of smaller work rolls around its circumference, the former being rotated in the direction of feed so that the latter rotate against the strip; *planetary mixer* or *stirrer*, one in which paddles are rotated about an axis which itself is moved in a circular path.

1917 T. R. SHAW *Precision Grinding Machines* ii. 28 Grinding machines with planetary spindles, specially adapted to the requirements of locomotive building. **1949** S. E. RUSINOFF *Manuf. Processes* x. 405, (*A*) of Fig. 17 illustrates the principle by which holes are ground in a locomotive side rod on a planetary grinder. A gyratory motion is imparted to the grinding wheel spindle so that the wheel sweeps the bore of the workpiece. **1950** KIRK & OTHMER *Encycl. Chem. Technol.* V. 705 In a planetary stirrer, the paddle rotates and at the same time the axis about which it rotates follows a circular orbit. *Ibid.* 707 Small-scale laboratory and pilot-plant models of planetary mixers..are available. **1953** *Engineer* 23 Oct. 526/2 The first commercial installation of a new design of hot strip rolling mill..has been installed at the works of Ductile Planetary Mills, Ltd., of Willenhall, Staffs. *Ibid.*, The slabs have to be pressure fed into the rolls..by pinch or feed rolls, which are mounted in the same housing as the planetary assemblies. *Ibid.* 527/2 Immediately following the planetary mill is a two-high planishing mill. **1963** F. H. HABICHT *Mod. Machine Tools* xi. 166 Planetary grinding is usually limited to large or awkward workpieces that cannot be conveniently rotated. **1967** IRVING & SAXTON in Uhl & Gray *Mixing* II. viii. 214 Vertical-shaft mixers..include planetary mixers and Pony mixers, as well as heavier duty, twin-shaft machines. **1968** R. N. PARKINS *Mech. Treatm. Metals* iv. 213 The great advantage of the planetary mill is that it can reduce a hot slab directly to strip, thereby replacing the three or four roughing mills and the six-stand finishing mill. **1971** C. R. HINE *Machine Tools & Processes* xiv. 330 The planetary miller is unique in that the work is held stationary while the revolving cutter or cutters move in a planetary path to finish a circular surface on the work, either internally or externally.

B. *sb.* **3.** *ellipt.* for *planetary nebula*.

1903 A. M. CLERKE *Probl. in Astrophysics* II. i. 175 Spectroscopically, they [*sc.* Novae] simulate minute 'planetaries'. **1974** *Nature* 31 May 430/1 The precise details of the evolutionary history of the planetaries are uncertain.

4. *ellipt.* for *planetary gear* or *wheel* (= *planet-gear*, *-wheel*, in Dict. and Suppl.).

1941 *Electronic Engin.* XIV. 166/1 The planetary of the differential is connected to a gear-reduction train. **1962** D. W. DUDLEY *Gear Handbk.* iii. 21 Bevel planetaries can be made to handle a range of ratios.

planetesimal (plænẽte·simăl), *a.* and *sb.* *Astr.* [f. PLANET *sb.*[1] + INFINIT)ESIMAL *sb.* and *a.*] **A.** *adj.* Pertaining to, involving, or composed of planetesimals; applied *esp.* to the hypothesis that the planets were formed by the accretion of a vast number of planetesimals in a cold state.

1904 T. C. CHAMBERLIN in *Carnegie Inst. Year Bk.* II. 263 This led to studies upon alternative hypotheses. Among these is the conception that the earth, instead of descending from a gaseous spheroid, may have been built up by the gradual ingathering of its material from a scattered meteoroidal or planetesimal condition. **1904** *Amer. Geologist* XXXIII. 95 The planetesimal hypothesis ..seems much better to explain both the astronomical and geological phenomena. **1906** *Athenæum* 18 Aug. 191/1 For the last ten years Prof. Chamberlin, aided by Dr. Forest R. Moulton, of Chicago, has been developing what is called the Planetesimal Theory of the earth's origin. **1937** WOOLDRIDGE & MORGAN *Physical Basis Geogr.* i. 5 The earth..grew from small beginnings by the addition of planetesimal matter. **1969** *Nature* 19 July 259/1 When planetologists meet to discuss the surface of the Moon they separate into those favouring the dominance of planetesimal (meteoric) impact and those who advocate volcanic activity.

B. *sb.* A small solid body following a planetary orbit; a miniature planet.

1904 *Amer. Geologist* XXXIII. 95 The new hypothesis holds..that the globular planets were formed by the slow accretion or infalling of cold, discrete bodies or particles ('planetesimals'). **1906** CHAMBERLIN & SALISBURY *Geol.* II. ii. 94 The planetesimals originated, by hypothesis, from gaseous matter shot forth from the ancestral sun. **1952** H. C. UREY *Planets* vii. 219 Planetesimals probably formed simultaneously with the protoplanets and accumulated into larger objects. **1971** *Sci. Amer.* Oct. 52/3 *Apollo 14* landed on the Fra Mauro formation, believed to be a blanket of ejecta thrown out by the giant meteorite or planetesimal that excavated the basin of Mare Imbrium. **1973** *Nature* 21/28 Dec. 451/3 Courten believes a planetesimal 'between 80 and 500 miles in diameter' moves in an orbit about 0·1 AU from the Sun. **1977** *Ibid.* 8 Dec. 506/1 Accumulation and fragmentation of planetesimals may have competed in the planetary accretion process, and a planetesimal which could survive catastrophic destruction may have become a planet.

planetfall (plæ·nėtfǭl). [f. PLANET *sb.*[1] + *-fall* as in LANDFALL.] A landing upon a planet after a journey through space.

1954 'J. CHRISTOPHER' *22nd Cent.* 98 The *Lucas* did not normally make planet-falls. *Ibid.* 123 Smoking was strictly prohibited from take-off until planet-fall. **1960** K. AMIS *New Maps of Hell* (1961) i. 19 A few writers.. arrange for their travellers to put themselves into..deep freeze until just before planetfall. **1974** M. CAIDIN (*title*) Planetfall.

planetismal (plænėti·zmăl), *a.* and *sb.* *Astr.* [Alteration of *PLANETESIMAL *a.* and *sb.*] = *PLANETESIMAL *a.* and *sb.*

1910 *Westm. Gaz.* 16 Apr. 12/3 He accepts what is known as the 'planetismal hypothesis', which is, in his opinion, the most positive advance in natural science which has been made for a very long time. **1938** *Nature* 5 Nov. 843 The planetismal hypothesis is the parent of the more recent tidal theories. **1970** *Sci. Jrnl.* May 32/1 This theory has it that the Moon formed out of the coagulation of a 'sediment-ring' of planetismals which originally circled the Earth.

planetkin (plæ·nėt,kin). *nonce-wd.* [f. PLANET *sb.*[1] + -KIN.] A small planet.

1832 CARLYLE *Reminisc.* (1881) I. 44 A temporary fraction of this planetkin, the whole round of which is but a sandgrain in the all.

planetocentric (plænėtose·ntrik), *a.* *Astr.* and *Astronautics*. [f. PLANET *sb.*[1] + -O + *-CENTRIC.] Referred to, measured from, or having a planet as centre (usu. a planet other than the earth.)

1960 BAKER & MAKEMSON *Introd. Astrodynamics* xii. 264 The regions in space where one would expect the vehicle to be in a predominantly geocentric, heliocentric, or planetocentric field, can be delineated by calculating the ratio of the perturbative accelerations to the two-body acceleration. **1971** S. HERRICK *Astrodynamics* I. v. 106 A similar consideration of the planetocentric velocity at the Mars or Venus end of the trajectory..indicates that it is desirable to have the tangency at Mars's aphelion or at Venus's perihelion. **1972** *Nature* 11 Aug. 325/2 The heliocentric orbital longitude of Mars η, and the planetocentric longitude of the Sun are approximately related by $\eta = L_s + 85°$.

planetography. Delete †*Obs. rare*—[0] and add examples.

1735 B. MARTIN *Philos. Gram.* 119 (*heading*) Of planetography, or the philosophy of the planets. **1960** *Analog Science Fact/Fiction* Oct. 33/1 Got to know enough about it through an elementary planetography.

planetokhod (plæ·nėtǒkǫd, -χǫd). Also **Planetokhod.** [a. Russ. *planetokhód*, f. *planéta* PLANET *sb.*[1] (after *LUNOKHOD).] A Russian self-propelled vehicle for transmitting information about another planet as it travels over its surface.

1970 *Times* 18 Nov. 1 The vehicle is called Lunokhod-1. .. Soviet scientists are predicting that other such vehicles, named Planetokhod or Marsokhod, will eventually move over the surface of the Planets. **1973** *Nature* 23 Mar. 219/2 His remarks relating to the possible 'planetokhod' exploration of Venus and the outer planets seem highly speculative.

planetolatry (plænėtǫ·lătri). *rare.* [f. PLANET *sb.*[1] + -LATRY, -OLATRY.] Idolatrous worship of the planets.

1964 C. S. LEWIS *Discarded Image* v. 104 Despite this careful watch against planetolatry the planets continued to be called by their divine names.

planetology (plænėtǫ·lŏdʒi). *Astr.* [f. PLANET *sb.*[1] + -OLOGY.] The study of the planets and their evolution.

1907 P. LOWELL in *Century Mag.* Nov. 113 Planetology we may call this science of the making of worlds, since it concerns itself with the life-history of planetary bodies from their chemically inert beginning to their final inert end. **1959** *Wall St. Jrnl.* 25 July 8/2 'We believe lunar science, or planetology, is here to stay,' he says. **1973** *Nature* 18 May 121/1 Planetology, with several tens of papers on the Moon, Mars and the Allende Meteorite, profited particularly this year.

Hence **planetolo·gic, planetolo·gical** *adjs.*, of or pertaining to planetology; **planeto·logist**, an expert or specialist in planetology.

1908 *Century Mag.* Feb. 505/1 This gives us a most instructive glimpse into one planetologic process. **1933** *O.E.D.* Suppl., Planetologist. **1966** *Ann. N.Y. Acad. Sci.* CXL. 289 For the planetologist, it seems very important to be able to measure, even approximately, the relative amounts of oxygen, silicon, and aluminum in the surface layers of the planets. **1969** [see *PLANETESIMAL *a.* and *sb.* A]. **1975** *Nature* 7 Aug. 455/3 The development of a cratering chronology was one of the principal challenges to comparative planetologists studying impact bombardment of the terrestrial planets. **1976** *Ibid.* 22 Jan. 176/1 G. Wetherill's..time scale and planetological–geological framework for the early Precambrian seemed generally accepted.

planet-struck, *a.* (Later *poet.* example.)

1925 A. HUXLEY *Sel. Poems* 48 Let me..Dream planet-struck.

planform (plæ·nfǭɹm). Also **plan-form, plan form.** [f. PLAN *sb.* + FORM *sb.*] The shape or outline of an aircraft wing in plan. Also *transf.*

1908 F. W. LANCHESTER *Aerodonetics* x. 319 When the author's standard combination of parabolic grading and elliptical plan form is used, it is a property of the resulting aerofoil that [etc.]. **1913** *Aeronaut. Jrnl.* XVII. 83 In advocating this plan-form he does not appear to have had stability in his mind at all. **1942** T. P. FAULCONER *Introd. Aircraft Design* i. 18 The choice of a wing plan form and thickness is governed in general by the range requirements. **1958** *Engineering* 21 Mar. 363/1 The main building has an interesting planform of a question mark. **1965** *Times* 11 Sept. 7/6 Where opinions differ is on the wing planform for take-off, for approach and for landing. **1967** *Jane's Surface Skimmer Systems 1967–68* 2/1 The Aeromar A-1 is a gas turbine powered craft with a circular planform. **1975** L. J. CLANCY *Aerodynamics* xvi. 538 Consider a wing whose planform is represented..by the sketch.

plangency. (Further examples.)

1923 C. MACKENZIE *Parson's Progress* xvi. 222 All the regret..was expressed in the plangency of the violin speaking of the individual's grief. **1928** KIPLING *Limits & Renewals* (1932) 18 It's not a bad couplet in itself. Did you see how he admires the 'plangency' of it? **1972** *Times Lit. Suppl.* 25 Aug. 991/3 The Dreyfus affair..had an unusual public plangency. **1977** *N.Y. Rev. Bks.* 29 Sept. 6/4 The strain of plangency and nostalgia, combined with indignation, is Irish.

plangent, *a.* Add: **2.** Also *fig.*

1928 KIPLING *Limits & Renewals* (1932) 14 The freshness, the fun, the humanity, the fragrance of it all, cries—no, shouts—itself as Dan's work. Why 'Daiespringe mishandled' alone stamps it from Dan's mint. Plangent as doom, my dear boy—plangent as doom! **1936** [see *FACTURE 4].

plangently (plæ·ndʒĕntli), *adv.* [f. PLANGENT *a.* + -LY[2].] In a way that beats strongly or distressingly on the mind or feelings.

1927 R. L. MÉGROZ *Three Sitwells* 9 We are driven inwards because the external reality we have created is plangently ugly. **1928** *Observer* 19 Feb. 9/2 Nothing is here to make us beat the breast. The old matchless rhythms are no less plangently certain. **1963** *Times* 12 June 13/3 The theme of African unity so plangently struck at the Addis Ababa conference.

‖**planh** (plan^x). Also **planc.** [Provençal, f. L. *planctus* *PLANCTUS.] A mournful troubadour song. Cf. *PLANCTUS.

1843 *Penny Cycl.* XXV. 307/2 Their 'Planhs', or songs on the death of a mistress. **1878** F. HUEFFER *Troubadours* I. xiii. 134 Two minor branches of the *sirventes*.. are the *planh* or complaint, and the crusader's song,..the former belonging more especially to the personal..class of poems... The *planh* is a poem written on the death of a mistress, a friend, or a protector. **1909** E. POUND *Exultations* 46 (*title*) Planh for the Young English King. **1923** H. J. CHAYTOR *Troubadours & England* ii. 92 The troubadour Austorc de Segret in a *planh* upon the death of St. Louis, written between 1270 and 1274, refers to the problems before Edward. **1964** 'E. QUEEN' *Four Men called John* (1976) xiv. 154 A number of twelfth-century secular manuscripts. There are: six *planhs*, apparently the work of Bertran de Bon, [etc.]. **1970** W. APEL *Harvard Dict. Mus.* (ed. 2) 461/2 A late 12th-century troubadour *planc* (*planh*) by Gaucelm Faudit deplores the death of Richard the Lion-Hearted.

plani-. Add: **planispiral** *a.* (later examples).

1945 M. F. GLAESSNER *Princ. Micropalaeont.* iv. 69 Perfectly planispiral coiling produces bilaterally symmetrical tests. **1975** *Nature* 3 Apr. 419/1 Sinistral..and planispiral..coiling are uncommon among gastropods.

planigale (plæ·nigēɪl, plænigē̆·li). *Austral.* [mod.L. (E. Le G. Troughton 1928, in *Rec. Austral. Mus.* XVI. 282), f. PLANI- + *Phasco*)*gale*, the name of a closely related genus.] A flat-skulled marsupial mouse of the genus so called, belonging to the family Dasyuridæ and native to Australia and New Guinea.

1946 E. TROUGHTON *Furred Animals of Australia* (ed. 3) 29 (*heading*) Planigales or Flat-skulled Marsupial-Mice. **1966** *New Scientist* 20 Jan. 130/2 The little planigales or flat-skulled 'mice' found in Australia and New Guinea. **1970** W. D. L. RIDE *Guide to Native Mammals of Austral.* 119 David Fleay has kept Ingram's Planigales in captivity. **1974** *Courier-Mail* (Brisbane) 15 Apr. 10/3 (*caption*) Planigale mother with some of her clinging brood of babies.

planimetrically (plēⁱnime·trikăli), *adv.* [f. PLANIMETRIC *a.*: see -ICALLY.] By means of, or with regard to, planimetry. (In quot. 1944, 'in the plane'.)

1944 *Burlington Mag.* Dec. 296/1 The essential difference lies elsewhere: previously border decoration was planimetrically designed, whereas in the new style the border ornament lives in the space above the page. The illusion is created that branches, flowers, insects and birds etc. have been dropped on the page, loosely dispersed, casting their shadow on the coloured foil. **1948** LYSHOLM & BULL in J. W. McLaren *Mod. Trends Diagnostic Radiol.* xxiv. 322 The composite pneumographs have also been measured planimetrically in relation to the corresponding brain cross-sections. **1959** *Trans. & Papers Inst. Brit. Geogr.* No. 26. 31 A planimetrically correct landform map has been constructed from an existing contour map..for a mountainous area in Colorado. **1969** G. C. DICKINSON *Maps & Air Photographs* xi. 166 The profiles are truly 'lines on the ground' and must therefore be in their correct position planimetrically, so that detail can be traced directly from the map and will fit the profiles.

planing, *vbl. sb.* **3. planing machine, mill** (earlier examples).

1840 *Digest of Patents U.S., 1790–1839* 346 Planing machine... June 1, 1805. **1851** C. CIST *Sk. Cincinnati in 1851* 227 Planing machines..made..by B. Bicknell. **1844** *Knickerbocker* XXIV. 184 The uplifted arm of Labor ..meets his eye in the..planing mill.

plank, *sb.* Add: **2.** Also, a surf-board.

1784 J. KING in Cook *Voy. Pacific Ocean* III. v. vii. 146 Whenever..the impetuosity of the surf is increased to its utmost height, they [*sc.* the natives of Karakakooa] choose that time for this amusement [riding the surf]... If by mistake they should place themselves on one of the smaller waves, which breaks before they reach the land, or should not be able to keep their plank in a proper direction on the top of the swell, they are left exposed to the fury of the next, and, to avoid it, are obliged again to dive and regain the place, from which they set out. **1962** *Austral. Women's Weekly* 24 Oct. (Suppl.) 3/3 Plank, any type of surfboard. **1963** *Pix* 28 Sept. 63 Five extra points if you can fit eight surfers, eight planks and a mattress in the woodie. **1967** J. SEVERSON *Great Surfing* Gloss., *Plank*, name given to heavy boards, usually referring to the redwood giants ridden prior to the 1950s.

5. For 'Cf. PLATFORM 7 b' read 'Cf. PLATFORM *sb.* (*a.*) 9 b' and for 'Orig. and chiefly *U.S.*' read 'orig. *U.S.*'. (Further U.K. examples.)

1873 LD. SALISBURY in *Q. Rev.* CXXXV. 558 Neither is it necessary now to dwell on those questions which are occasionally discussed by speculative politicians, but which..are either too small or too large to be regarded as a plank in any party's platform. **1894** *Liberal* 24 Nov. 42/1 They have founded a Society, the sole plank of whose platform is 'Hands off, please'. **1926** GALSWORTHY *Silver Spoon* II. i. 117 Dared he tackle the air—that third plank in the Foggart programme? **1937** *Ann. Reg. 1936* 189 Without cease the German Government protested against the alliance between Soviet Russia and France, alleging that the pact was a danger to Germany. That was one plank in the platform of German foreign policy. **1965** *Listener* 20 May 755/2 Thinkers whose ideas were fairly far removed from any of the chief party political planks. **1970** *Daily Tel.* 2 Feb. 1 The enforcement of law and order is to be one of the main planks of the Conservatives' General Election campaign. **1977** *Cornish Times* 19 Aug. 8/2 He told me that the main plank of his election campaign was going to be a policy of discrimination as advocated by an extreme political group, which was then defacing private and public buildings with stickers and misspelt slogans.

6. *to walk the plank* (earlier examples).

1822 SCOTT *Pirate* III. xii. 281 They deserve to be made to walk the plank for their impudence. **1835** J. E. ALEXANDER *Sketches in Portugal* viii. 179 The admiral.. worked late and early himself, and made every body under him work, or else 'walk the plank'.

7. *plank bridge* (examples), *-raft*; **plank-buttress** [tr. G. *plankengerüst* (A. F. W. Schimper *Pflanzengeographie* (1898) III. iv. 328)], a development of a root at the base of the trunk of certain tropical trees; **plank-owner** *Navy slang* (chiefly *U.S.*), (*a*) a member of the original crew of a ship; a marine with long service with his ship or unit; (*b*) a marine with a light task; **plank steak,** steak cooked and served on a piece of plank; cf. *PLANKED *ppl. a.* 2.

1933 J. BUCHAN *Prince of Captivity* II. iv. 247 He crossed the stream by a plank bridge. **1979** G. MITCHELL *Mudflats of Dead* iii. 35 He took to the causeway, crossed the plank bridge. **1903** W. R. FISHER tr. *Schimper's Plant-Geogr.* III. i. 304 Much more frequently these buttresses assume the form of plank-like outgrowths of the base of the trunk and of the uppermost roots, and they may be termed plank-buttresses. **1952** P. W. RICHARDS *Tropical Rain Forest* i. 4 Plank buttresses.. are a highly characteristic feature of rain-forest trees. **1960** N. POLUNIN *Introd. Plant Geogr.* xiv. 467 The dominants are often of particularly massive growth and rich branching, but devoid of plank-buttresses. **1901** *Our Naval Apprentice* (U.S.) Aug. 14 'Patsy' is a 'Plank Owner' on 'Constellation'. **1920** *Our Navy* (U.S.) Apr. 11 Some of the plank-owners think the navy would be a great outfit if it didn't have any ships in it. **1945** *Richmond* (Va.) *News Leader* 31 May 6/3 The majority of our crew was made up of 'plank owners'—men who had been aboard the Colhoun since she..had been commissioned. **1952** A. GEER *New Breed* 6 The 'plank-owners' (any Marine not going) were subjected to a barrage of good-natured insults as they stood on the pier. **1967** M. DIBNER *Admiral* xiv. 140 He became her first gunnery officer as a 'plank owner'..at her commissioning. **1910** *Westm. Gaz.* 24 Jan. 5/2 People..had to make use of boats or plank-rafts. **1959** *Good Food Guide* 93 Plank steak, shashlik, scampi maison, and 'nest of chicken' are among its specialities. **1972** *Vogue* Jan. 16/3 Try the spare ribs or prime plank steak. **1975** *Islander* (Victoria, B.C.) 27 Apr. 5/4 We celebrated our arrival by ordering 'plank steak'... It was juicy and tender and served on a white piece of wood.

plank, *v.* Add: **2. a.** (Further examples.)

1936 J. TICKELL *See how they Run* iv. 46 How would you like to be half-starved for a bit and then planked down in a foreign school, aged twelve, and have to spend your holidays with the Geometry master? **1938** A. J. LIEBLING *Back where I came From* 182 An overstuffed chair some admirer had planked down next to the ticket booth. **1964** *Perthshire Advertiser* 13 June 14 Planking the lady into a beach chair and carrying her..to the other side.

b. For *U.S. colloq.* read *colloq.* (orig. *U.S.*), and add earlier and later examples. Also *absol.*

1824 *Nantucket Inquirer* 19 Apr. 2/4 His guardy was sent for, and he planked the cash. **1848** W. E. BURTON *Waggeries & Vagaries* 65 If the nigger..can plank up if he's cast, I'm darned if I don't..sue the nigger. **1903** SOMERVILLE & 'ROSS' *All on Irish Shore* 178 Every one squared up his books and planked ready money down on the nail. *Ibid.* 185 People began to talk then, especially as the pony's look and shape were improving each day, and after a little time every one was planking his money on one way or another. **1915** W. S. MAUGHAM *Of Human Bondage* lxxv. 389, I planked out the money to keep you. **1951** *New Yorker* 1 Dec. 63/1 (Advt.), You plank the cash on the counter for a slice of sirloin. **1966** H. KEMELMAN *Saturday Rabbi went Hungry* xxi. 127 When you ask someone to plank down a hundred and fifty-odd bucks for a lot which he doesn't think he's going to need..it's a lot of dough. **1972** *Even. Telegram* (St. John's, Newfndl.) 5 Aug. 3/1 How could a poor man..plank down $70,000 in ready cash for a place to live in?

4. See also *PLANKED *ppl. a.* 2.

planked, *ppl. a.* Add: **1.** (Later examples.)

1873 J. H. BEADLE *Undevel. West* xxxvi. 769 As one result of their smooth planked streets, much attention is given to fine turn-outs. **1956** R. W. ANDREWS *Glory Days of Logging* 23 (*caption*) Planked road of A. & M. Logging Co. Ltd...shown running from timber to log dumps. **1979** S. SMITH *Survivor* vi. 75 The planked roof of the barn.

2. (Earlier example.) Also of meat. Also, served on a piece of plank.

1855 *Sun* (Baltimore) 30 Apr. 4/1 Did you ever eat a 'plank'd shad'? **1906** *N.Y. Globe* 27 Apr. 7 The planked chicken was served on the plank. **1910** *Chambers's Jrnl.* July 430/2 In the restaurants the British visitor will invariably be confronted with the possibilities contained in..'planked steak',..and so on. **1947** WODEHOUSE *Full Moon* iv. 83 An order of planked steak. **1969** R. & D. DE SOLA *Dict. Cooking* 177/1 *Planked steak*, restaurant term for a steak broiled and served on a well-seasoned plank and garnished with a border of mashed potatoes, mushroom caps, tomato slices, and sometimes julienned carrots. **1978** *Lancashire Life* Nov. 170/1 The dish in question, one of the popular specialities of the house, was described as planked steak: a reasonably substantial T-bone, prepared on that slab of oak, and accompanied by broccoli, mushrooms, tomatoes, fried onion rings and the most delicious Duchesse potatoes imaginable.

plankter (plæ·ŋktəɹ). *Biol.* [f. PLANKT(ON + -ER¹.] = *PLANKTONT.

1938 J. R. CARPENTER *Ecol. Gloss.* 208 *Plankt, plankter*, individual organisms comprising plankton. **1957** G. E. HUTCHINSON *Treat. Limnol.* I. xvii. 899 The only autotrophic truly open-water plankter so far encountered that requires accessory organic substances other than vitamin B_{12}, the marine diatom *Ditylum*. **1973** *Nature* 21/28 Dec. 521/1 This mechanism augmented by a rapid turnover in biomass, especially of small plankters, could account for the low residue concentrations in Gulf plankton following periods of light precipitation.

planktology (plæŋktǫ·lŏdʒi). [a. G. *planktologie* (E. Hæckel 1891, in *Jenaische Zeitschr. f. Naturwiss.* XXV. 240): see PLANKTO(N and -OLOGY.] The study of plankton. So **planktolo·gical** *a.*, of or pertaining to this study; **plankto·logist,** one engaged in this study.

1893 G. W. FIELD tr. *Hæckel's Planktonic Stud.* in *Rep. U.S. Comm. Fisheries 1889–91* 571 The whole science which treats of this important division of biology is briefly called planktology. **1896** *Proc. Acad. Nat. Sci. Philadelphia* 280 Without undervaluing in any way the counting methods at present employed by planktologists, I desire here to call attention to an apparatus..by means of which one may make a large number of plankton estimations in a single day. **1912** *Rep. Brit. Assoc. 1911* 422 The Kiel planktologists have had to seek another source of food for the zooplankton. **1926** *Kongel. Danske Vidensk. Selsk. Skr.* 8th Ser. XI. 157 Those who have followed the history of planctological [*sic*] work during the last twenty years will know that it is really along these three lines that limnologists have especially worked in this area of exploration. **1947** *Nature* 4 Jan. 10/2 The technical difficulties of this type of work, particularly in planktology, are not belittled. **1967** *Oceanogr. & Marine Biol.* V. 231 A brief historical summary is necessary in order to understand the obstacles which Mediterranean planktology has had to overcome. *Ibid.* 248 This instrument becomes of questionable planktological value. **1972** *Nature* 7 Apr. 295/1 This information..will also be of help to physical oceanographers and planktologists.

plankton. For (V. Hensen 188.) in etym. substitute (V. Hensen 1887, in *Ber. Kommission der wissenschaftlichen Untersuchung der deutschen Meere in Kiel* V. 1). (Earlier and later examples.)

1891 *Jrnl. R. Microsc. Soc.* 326 'Plankton' was originally defined by Hensen as including those animals which drift in the sea. **1908** *Jrnl. Marine Biol. Assoc.* VIII. 269 (*title*) Plankton studies in relation to the western mackerel fishery. **1921** [see *BENTHOS]. **1947** *Sci. News* IV. 98 The vast bulk of life in the open sea is composed not of active creatures such as fish or whales, but of microscopic plants, and small animals which drift with the water. They are known collectively as plankton. **1956** A. HARDY *Open Sea* I. xv. 297 The herring snaps at the little plankton animals individually. **1973** *Nature* 16 Nov. 128/2 The existence of a vast aerial plankton of insects and other arthropods extending up into the sky for at least 14,000 foot is well established.

2. *Comb.* **plankton feeder,** an animal whose diet includes plankton; **plankton indicator,** an apparatus that is towed behind a ship with a filtering device by means of which the concentration of plankton can be estimated; **plankton net,** a very fine net used to collect samples of plankton or other very small organisms; **plankton recorder,** a modification of the plankton indicator in which the filter is in the form of a continuously moving roll.

1956 A. HARDY *Open Sea* I. xv. 303 Mackerel are plankton-feeders for about half the year. **1975** C. F. HICKLING *Water as Productive Environment* vii. 65 The species of *Alestes*..came to dominate the surface waters as plankton feeders. **1925** A. C. HARDY in *Fishery Investigations* 2nd Ser. VIII. VII. 2 The present paper.. describes investigations by means of an instrument which has been called the Plankton Indicator. **1936** *Jrnl. Marine Biol. Assoc.* XXI. 148 Preliminary experiments were begun in 1922 and 1923 with a torpedo-shaped instrument called the Plankton Indicator. **1953** *Bull. Marine Ecol.* IV. 19 The small Plankton Indicator..has been used..during an ecological survey of the herring off the north-east coast of Scotland. **1952** J. CLEGG *Freshwater Life Brit. Is.* xviii. 293 Some form of pond-net is almost essential. Probably the type of most general utility is that known as a plankton-net... The bag part is made of fine-mesh material, and carries at its base a tube or bottle into which the organisms descend. **1963** G. E. & R. C. NEWELL *Marine Plankton* ii. 17 There are several patterns of plankton net in common use today. **1972** F. G. STEHLI et al. in T. J. M. Schopf *Models in Paleobiol.* vi. 119 The mesh of the plankton nets used was large. **1926** A. C. HARDY in *Nature* 30 Oct. 631/1 Whilst on the *Discovery* expedition I have been experimenting with such an instrument, which I am calling the Continuous Plankton Recorder... It is a development of the simple Plankton Indicator.., but in place of the silk netting discs, which had to be reloaded for each sample, I have substituted a long continuously moving roll operated by a propellor turned by the water through which it is towed. **1936** '*Discovery*' *Rep.* XI. 457 The first Continuous Plankton Recorder was used on the R.R.S. 'Discovery' in the years 1925–7. **1975** D. H. CUSHING *Marine Ecol. & Fisheries* viii. 166 The plankton recorder survey..is based on monthly samples from fixed merchant ship lines across the North Sea.

planktonic (plæŋktǫ·nik), *a.* and *sb. Biol.* [a. G. *planktonisch* (E. Hæckel 1891, in *Jenaische Zeitschr. f. Naturwiss.* XXV. 240): see PLANKTON and -IC.] **A.** *adj.* Of, pertaining to, or characteristic of plankton.

1893 G. W. FIELD tr. *Hæckel's Planktonic Stud.* in *Rep. U.S. Comm. Fisheries 1889–91* 571, I adopt the term Plankton in place of '*Auftrieb*', and derive from it the adjective planktonic. **1899, 1905** [in Dict.]. **1930** *Times Educ. Suppl.* 22 Mar. (Home & Classroom Suppl.) p. iv/1 Quantities of nektonic and planktonic life are being caught daily. **1963** *Times* 19 Feb. 10/4 Sediments of past ages..contain a boundary clearly defined by changes in their content of fossilized planktonic remains. **1974** *Nature* 8 Feb. 393/2 Herbivorous zooplankton can graze on planktonic algae, bacteria and detrital particles.

B. *sb.* A microfossil of a foraminifer included in the plankton.

1959 *Bull. Amer. Paleontol.* XXXIX. 84 These assemblages of agglutinated forms..occur several times and are separated by assemblages of calcareous forms, often with abundant planktonics, suggestive of a depositional depth between 200 and 600 metres. **1964** *Micropaleontology* X. 3/2 The coiling characteristics of planktonics can be most useful in correlating strata from different basins and with entirely different benthic biofacies. **1976** *Ibid.* XXII. 420/1 The total number of planktonics, benthics, and fragments was counted.

planktonology (plæ:ŋktǫ̆nǫ·lŏdʒi). [f. PLANKTON + -OLOGY.] = *PLANKTOLOGY. So **planktonolo·gical** *a.*

1896 *Jrnl. R. Microsc. Soc.* 470 Dr. C. S. Dolley referring to the work of Hensen, Haeckel, and others on planktonology, explains the importance of a quantitative determination of the primitive food-supply of marine animals. **1960** *Biol. Abstr.* XXXV. 2290/1 (*title*) The new systematics and planktonology. **1961** *Ibid.* XXXVI. 284/2 (*title*) Results of planktonological research. **1975** *Jrnl. Fish. Res. Bd. Canada* XXXII. 2231 Narrower fields of specialization, such as planktonology, fisheries ecology, or studies on the benthic habitat, should be integrated. **1976** *Biol. Abstr.* LXI. 2576/1 (*title*) Physical-chemical and planktonological studies of the Great Lake of Laffrey.

planktont (plæ·ŋktǫnt). *Biol.* [f. PLANKT(ON + Gr. ὄν, ὀντ- being: see ONTO-.] An individual organism of the plankton.

1897 *Science* 3 Dec. 830/1 The struggles of the imprisoned organisms and the pressure of the filtering water also materially assist the escape of planktonts through the yielding meshes of silk. **1926** *Kongel. Danske Vidensk. Selsk. Skr.* 8th Ser. XI. 152 Some of the freshwater planctonts [*sic*]..were made to serve as a support for the theories of heredity. **1931** *Jrnl. Ecology* XIX. 246 Multiplication of the littoral planktonts in the open water will naturally only take place if the latter contains an adequate amount of mineral nutriment. **1935** P. S. WELCH *Limnology* ix. 205 The term planktont of the older literature should be abandoned because of its faulty word structure. **1948** *New Biol.* V. 21 Blue-green planktonts are generally most abundant..in summer and late autumn.

planktotrophic (plæ:ŋktotrǫ·fik), *a.* [f. PLANKTO(N + TROPHIC *a.*] Feeding on plankton. So **plankto·trophy**, behaviour of this type.

1946 G. THORSON in *Medd. Komm. Danmarks Fiskerei Ser. Plankton* IV. I. 476 Planktotrophic larvae with long pelagic life..originate from small eggs poor in yolk. **1963** R. P. DALES *Annelids* viii. 171 Most planktotrophic larvae develop from small eggs. **1973** *Amer. Naturalist* CVII. 348 Planktotrophy is the most common pattern in shallow-water tropical invertebrates. **1978** *Nature* 5 Jan. 56/2 Most of the commoner species of coral reef asteroids ..produce many small, planktotrophic, pelagic larvae.

planless, *a.* (Further examples.)

1937 'G. ORWELL' *Road to Wigan Pier* iv. 51 Little brick houses..festering in planless chaos. **1942** J. STEINBECK *Moon is Down* ii. 25 Fine weapons and fine planning against unarmed, planless enemies. **1957** [see *CONTRACT *v.* 2 d].

planlessly *adv.* (later example); **planlessness** (further examples).

1932 *Times Lit. Suppl.* 1 Sept. 609/2 It has the merit, certainly, that almost any plan has over planlessness. **1944** I. ORIGO *Diary* 13 Feb. in *War in Val d'Orcia* (1947) 140 It is odd how used one can become to uncertainty for the future, to a complete planlessness. **1962** *Punch* 30 May 844/1, I have already let several valuable years slip planlessly by. **1976** *Sunday Times* (Lagos) 7 Nov. 12/2 The planlessness of the flashes should take us to the most unlikely place where the story should begin, the epilogue.

planned, *ppl. a.* Add: (Further examples.) *planned economy*: an economy in which industrial production and development, etc. are determined by an overall national plan; *planned obsolescence*: obsolescence of manufactured goods due to deliberate changes in design, cessation of the supply of spare parts, use of poor-quality materials, etc.

1931 *Economist* 18 July 111/2 The tendency in the world is towards some or other form of planned economy. **1936** *Discovery* Sept. 295/1 Can present human motives work a planned society? **1942** *N.Y. Times* 6 Mar. 23/7 The Planned Parenthood Federation of America, Inc., is the new corporate name of the Birth Control Federation of America, Inc., according to announcement yesterday by the organization's board of directors. **1943** J. S. HUXLEY *TVA* xiii. 115 The transition from a *laissez-faire* to a planned economy. **1947** *Sun* (Baltimore) 20 Sept. 1/2 The Senator's attack on what he calls the Truman Administration's policy of 'planned inflation'. **1960** I. BENNETT *Delinquent & Neurotic Children* ix. 444 *History*: a planned baby. Both parents wanted a girl. **1965** B. PEARCE tr. *Preobrazhensky's New Economics* 159 The further abolition of the law of value..will proceed along the path of planned socialist organization of the economy in countries which make an end of the capitalist régime. **1966** *Punch* 20 July 96/3 The planned-obsolescence men won't miss *this* one. **1969** A. CAIRNCROSS in *Advancement of Sci.* XXVI. 64/2 It is possible to argue that there is no essential difference between a managed economy and a planned economy, and that planning is simply a rather inflexible form of management. **1977** *National Observer* (U.S.) 1 Jan. 10/3 Things settled down into a buyer's market again, so the businessmen came up with another new gimmick. It was called planned obsolescence. Come out with a new model every year. Put a few new gadgets on it... Don't worry about the quality, it will be obsolete in three years anyway, besides, it's cheap. **1977** J. AIKEN *Last Movement* i. 17 Dru had been a planned child, whereas I was an unexpected..afterthought. **1977** *Spare Rib* May 20/2 On Ash Wednesday..a newly opened Planned Parenthood Clinic in St Paul was fire bombed.

plannee (plænī·). [f. PLAN *sb.* or *v.* + -EE[1].] A person for whom something is planned.

1943 J. S. HUXLEY *TVA* xv. 119 He must not think of the people in his region as his subject plannees, but as participating co-planners. **1946** A. HUXLEY *Science, Liberty & Peace* (1947) I. 28 A highly organized and regimented society..is felt by the planners, and even..by the plannees to be more 'scientific', and therefore better, than [etc.].

planner. Add: *spec.*, a person who plans the development or reconstruction of an urban area, or who engages in economic planning.

1935 *Economist* 11 May 1075/1 It is true to say that the task of the planner is the more efficient mobilisation of all economic resources. **1961** L. MUMFORD *City in Hist.* vii. 185 Aristotle's position..is sounder than that of most of our present-day planners, who have not yet arrived at a functional definition of a city. **1962** *Listener* 3 May 758/2 If the French planners could prove..that their efficient techniques and the understanding with the heads of industry have proved to be the answer to all problems of economic growth [etc.]. **1973** *Times* 13 Dec. 19/2 There is an absolute shortage of planners. **1976** *Encounter* June 93/2 At present, the experts and polymaths, the thinkers and highly skilled professions, the essential organisers and planners, have no collective voice.

b. A list, table, or similar device giving information which enables one to plan.

1971 *Homes & Gardens* Sept. 99/3, I will send you a copy of our Do-It-Yourself diet planner and a calorie counter, so that you can organise a diet to suit your needs.

planning, *vbl. sb.* Add: (Examples in the sense of the action of planning civically or economically.)

1935 *Economist* 30 Mar. 725/1 Since private enterprise has manifestly failed to bring about the necessary adjustments in industry, 'planning' must be tried. **1941** *New Statesman* 15 Feb. 151 If we are to rebuild our cities aright, we ought to plan them; and planning is inconsistent with rebuilding on the old sites. **1959** *Cambridge Rev.* 25 Apr. 429/2 The ancient City could survive if Town and University were enclosed together within a ring of traffic roads and could not be entirely traversed except on foot or bicycle... These are all matters of what is drolly called 'Planning'. **1962** *Listener* 1 Mar. 363/1 Planning, if one must risk a description, is a method of introducing more coherence, more purpose, into an economic system. *Ibid.* 364/2 The planning of private industry.

b. *attrib.*, as *planning appeal, application, authority, blight, committee, consent, consultant, control, engineer, officer, permission*.

1971 *Reader's Digest Family Guide to Law* 174 In some planning appeals cases..the inspector has powers to make the decision without referring the matter to the Minister. *a* **1974** R. CROSSMAN *Diaries* (1975) I. 615, I found when I arrived that eight or nine months was accepted as a reasonable time for a planning appeal to wait in the Ministry before a decision. **1976** *S. Wales Echo* 25 Nov. 2/4 Over lunch reference was made to their particular planning application. It was obvious they knew what the planning officer's recommendation was. **1934** *Act* 23 & 24 *Geo. V* c. 58 s. 20 (1) 'Planning authority' means..the authority having power to control the development..of.. land. **1950** *Chambers's Encycl.* XIII. 705/2 Extensive powers for the compulsory purchase of land..have also been made available to planning authorities. **1962** L. GOLDING *Dict. Local Govt.* 301 'Planning blight'..arises when property becomes virtually unsaleable by its owner or saleable only at a low price because of a threat of development. **1976** *Liverpool Echo* 23 Nov. 7/3 The people of Garston have suffered far too long from the planning blight that has caused serious deterioration in the area affecting housing, shops and the environment in general. **1942** *Country Life* 9 Oct. 692/2 That is the London revealed as it would be by the Planning Committee of the Royal Academy. **1964** *Oxf. Jun. Encycl.* X. 457/1 Applications are submitted to the planning committee, and only when permission has been given can work proceed. **1970** *Financial Times* 13 Apr. 25/2 Ambitions for a 2,000-room palace of tourism in West London foundered on the rocks of planning consents. **1977** *Lancs. Life* Nov. 82/2 You could find yourself in trouble for demolishing, adding to or altering property without planning consent. **1944** J. S. HUXLEY *On Living in Revol.* xi. 115 The services of planning consultants and a resident planning engineer. **1961** E. A. POWDRILL *Vocab. Land Planning* ii. 10 Planning control arises from the fact that persons, groups of persons, and organisations wish to initiate some form of development. **1944** Planning engineer [see *planning consultant* above]. **1961** H. W. DODDS in *56th Ann. Rep. Carnegie Foundation for Advancem. of Teaching* 22 A plan must therefore be brought up to date periodically, possibly with the assistance of a permanent planning officer. **1965** in P. Jennings *Living Village* (1968) 103 Planning permission had already been given, the Planning Officer being convinced that they were a brilliant architectural achievement. **1976** *Liverpool Echo* 23 Nov. 10/5 Mr. Len Ward, planning officer for Ellesmere Port Council, is urging the highways committee to take immediate action over the cottages. **1947** *Act* 10 & 11 *Geo. VI* c. 51 s. 119 (1) 'Planning permission' means the permission for development which is required by virtue of section twelve of this Act. **1965** Planning permission [see *planning officer* above]. **1977** *Undercurrents* June–July 4/1 The Windscale Public Enquiry into British Nuclear Fuel Limited's..application for planning permission to build an uranium-oxide processing plant begins on June 14th.

plano-[1]. Add: **plano-miller, plano(-)milling machine**, a milling machine built in the manner of a planer and used esp. for heavy work, having a flat bed to carry the work-piece and a sliding cross-piece that carries rotating cutters as in an ordinary milling machine, rather than a planing tool.

1906 J. G. HORNER *Mod. Milling Machines* v. 130 Plano-Millers or Slabbing Machines.—This is a name that seems most appropriate to designate that large and growing group of machines which is built on the model of the common planing machine, with bed, table, housings, and cross rail. **1963** *Gen. Engin. Workshop Practice* (ed. 3) vi. 218/2 The plano-miller is a milling machine, but designed to execute certain work formerly confined to the planer. **1905** T. R. SHAW *Machine Tools* vii. 478 Universal plano-milling machines are now constructed of any size with either one or two saddles carrying spindles on the cross-slide, just as with the tool-boxes of planing machines. **1964** S. CRAWFORD *Basic Engin. Processes* vi. 154 A plano milling machine possesses several advantages as compared with the planing machine, including the reduction of non-cutting time, wider range of operations in one setting, and increased rate of production.

plano (plē[i]·no), *a.* [f. PLANO-[1].] Of a surface of a lens: flat.

1950 *Jrnl. Optical Soc. Amer.* XL. 523/1 The plano surfaces can introduce central coma by being tilted. **1962** L. S. SASIENI *Princ. & Pract. Optical Dispensing* x. 268 Many modern trial cases are made with plano-convex and plano-concave spheres... The powers are engraved sometimes on the plano side of the convex and on the concave side of the concave.

planogamete. (Further examples.) Hence **planogame·tic** *a.*

1950 E. A. BESSEY *Morphol. & Taxon. Fungi* i. 6 The two gametes may both be..motile (planogametes), as in the..Chytridiales. **1971** P. H. B. TALBOT *Princ. Fungal Taxon.* vii. 91 A planogamete is a motile gamete, or sex cell, and planogametic conjugation..is the fusion of two gametes, one or both of which may be motile.

planographic (plē[i]nogræ·fik), *a.* [f. PLANO-[1] + -GRAPHIC.] Of, pertaining to, or produced by a process in which printing is done from a plane surface.

1897 SINGER & STRANG *Etching* 121 The relief print has no plate mark, the intaglio print has one quite clear and distinct, the planographic one has a very slight mark. **1914** E. H. RICHTER *Prints* 10 The last group to be considered, planographic processes, is based entirely upon chemical and physical action. **1946** H. WHETTON *Pract. Printing & Binding* xxv. 287/1 Planographic is the term used to describe a printing surface on the same level as the plate. **1967** V. STRAUSS *Printing Industry* i. 35/2 Offset lithography..dominates the field of planographic printing. **1972** *Physics Bull.* Sept. 532/3 The printing surface is virtually planographic and the action of development is to render the image areas oliophilic.

planography. Add: **2.** Printing from a plane surface, in contrast to processes in which the areas to be printed are in relief or intaglio.

1914 H. J. RHODES *Art of Lithography* i. 1 The term Planography..has been much in evidence of late, and there is no reason why it should not be generally adopted to denote all processes of printing from flat surfaces. **1937** *Discovery* Oct. 297/2 Lithography is..a misnomer, though attempts to replace it by planography have not found favour. **1960** G. A. GLAISTER *Gloss. Bk.* 317/1 Planography..refers to methods of printing from flat surfaces other than stone.

planont (plæ·nǫnt). *Biol.* [f. PLANO-[2] + Gr. ὄντ-: see ONTO-.] A motile spore, whether sexual, asexual, or a zygote; *esp.* the motile stage of certain microsporidian protozoans or phycomycetes.

1914 FANTHAM & PORTER *Some Minute Anim. Parasites* xi. 217 This amœbula [of *Nosema apis*] gives rise, by division, to daughter forms, each possessing one nucleus and capable of wandering about over the epithelium of the gut. Such forms are called planonts, or wanderers. **1943** F. K. SPARROW *Aquatic Phycomycetes* 406 In *A*[*llomyces*] *javanicus*..the planonts emerging from the resting spores..gave rise upon germination to sexual plants. **1961** R. D. MANWELL *Introd. Protozool.* xxiii. 478 At first they [*sc. Nosema* spores] remain in the gut, but they soon begin to wander and are now called 'planonts'.

planosol (plē[i]·no-, plæ·nosǫl). *Soil Sci.* [f. PLANO-[1] + *-SOL.] An intrazonal soil having a thin, strongly leached surface horizon overlying a compacted hard-pan or clay-pan, and occurring on flat uplands with poor drainage. Hence **planoso·lic** *a.*

1938 M. BALDWIN et al. in *U.S. Dept. Agric. Yearbk.* 991 The term 'Planosol' is being proposed to cover those soils with claypans and cemented hardpans not included with the Solonetz, Ground-Water Podzol, and Ground-Water Laterite. Families of Planosols correspond to associated normal zonal soils. **1965** B. T. BUNTING *Geogr. of Soil* vi. 71 Inward from these marginal sites, on plateaux, developed zonal soils occur, of considerable age, and hydromorphic or planosolic variants may exist in the central, poorly drained parts of the widest crestal plateaux. *Ibid.* xi. 133 Planosols are widespread on level plateau surfaces or broad gentle slopes on loess, till or wide alluvial terraces in central USA. **1972** C. B. HUNT *Geol. of Soils* ix. 206 In southern Ohio, Indiana, and Illinois..are flat, poorly drained uplands covered partly by loess and partly by Illinoian till... The comparatively thin modern soils on the surface of the old weathered deposits are Planosols with light-colored surface layers and deeper layers mottled brown and reddish brown.

planospore (plæ·nospōᵊɹ). *Bot.* [f. PLANO-[2] + SPORE.] A motile zoospore.

1950 E. A. BESSEY *Morphol. & Taxon. Fungi* i. 5 The motile naked zoospores..may be called planospores. **1970** J. WEBSTER *Introd. Fungi* i. 68 The zoospore is sometimes termed a planospore.

plansifter (plæ·nsiftəɹ). [f. PLAN *sb.* + SIFTER.] A machine consisting of a mechanically agitated set of superimposed flat sieves of differing mesh, used in flour milling for separating and grading the broken grain.

Registered in the U.S. as a proprietary name.

1905 *Official Gaz.* (U.S. Patent Office) 26 Dec. 2502/1 Shaking-Bolts. Barnard & Leas Manufacturing Company, Maline, Ill. Plansifter. **1908** *Engineering* 2 Oct. 429/2 Flour was dressed through long reels, called 'bolters', some of which were about 20 ft. long. These cumbersome machines..have given way in this country to the more adaptable centrifugal dresser, and on the Continent to the plansifter. **1936** J. H. SCOTT *Flour Milling Processes* ix. 200 The type of plansifter used..in this country is the free-swinging, balanced crank pattern, driven by a central vertical shaft. **1964** M. PYKE *Food Sci. & Technol.* iii. 43 In a modern mill, the broken grain from the plansifter associated with the first break roll will be passed to a second break roll where a little more flour will be sifted out.

planster (plæ·nstəɹ). [f. PLAN *sb.* + -STER.] A planner: used only with derogatory connotations.

1945 J. BETJEMAN *New Bats in Old Belfries* 34 The planster's vision. **1964** *Listener* 9 Jan. 71/1 Such destruction has been launched on the face and form of England by witless plansters and lethally unimaginative local authorities. **1978** *N.Y. Rev. Bks.* 23 Feb. 8/4 Does aesthetic sense in the end atrophy if it is desiccated by the continual use of this type of programmed reasoning? Is it replaced by what Betjeman called the Planster's Vision?

plant, *sb.*[1] Add: **3. c.** = *plant-cane* s.v. PLANT *sb.*[1] 10 e in Dict. and Suppl.

1866 'MARK TWAIN' *Lett. fr. Hawaii* (1967) xix. 209 Almost everywhere on the island of Hawaii sugarcane matures in twelve months, both ratoons and plant. *Ibid.* xxiii. 258 This year the 'plant' crop on the Wailuku plantation averages 8,000 [pounds per acre].

6. Add to def.: The premises and fixtures of a business or (chiefly *U.S.*) of an institution; a place where an industrial process is carried on; also, a single machine or large piece of apparatus. Also *transf.*, the workers employed at a plant. (The use with *a* and *pl.* is no longer rare in Great Britain.) (Further examples.)

1904 W. T. MILLS *Struggle for Existence* III. xvii. 216 The great steel plants maintain great laboratories. **1922** *Managem. Engin.* Feb. 86/2 No more time is lost by having all the plant out on strike for a week than in having a tenth of the force absent for 10 weeks. **1925** *Scribner's Mag.* July 31/2 (Advt.), Irving School for boys... Modern plant, complete equipment. **1927** *Brit. Med. Jrnl.* 3 Sept. 374/1 To those American investigators a school meant buildings, equipment, and machinery, or 'plant' as they themselves would say. **1930** J. BUCHAN *Castle Gay* xii. 194 He made his way round to the back regions, which had once been stables and coach-houses, and housed now the electric plant and a repairing shop for cars. **1939** D. L. SAYERS *In Teeth of Evidence* 9 They all want to..play with the apparatus. One of them got loose last time and tried to electrocute itself on the X-ray plant. **1949** *Sat. Rev. Lit.* 21 May 4/3 Its guiding genius.. has seen this school grow from an abstract idea to a two-million-dollar plant. **1957** J. H. ARNISON *Pract. Road Constr.* iii. 52 The shafts for the manholes may be cut out by manual labour, and the main trench by mechanical plant. **1958** *Engineering* 14 Mar. 322/2 Most of the plants benefiting from this influx of dollars are in the Glasgow area. **1958** *Times Lit. Suppl.* 10 Oct. 569/2 The new church 'plant'..is one of the most impressive and novel signs of the boom atmosphere. Mormons, Catholics, Methodists, Seventh Day Adventists, all flourish, to judge by the ecclesiastical building boom. **1960** *Washington Post* 16 Nov. A 16 The institution has almost never received adequate funds, is understaffed, has an inadequate and deteriorating physical plant and is 'on its way to becoming a second rate municipal zoo'. **1963** *Times Rev. Industry* Mar. 51/2 Mr. Justice Pennycuick.. said that 'plant', in its ordinary sense, 'includes whatever apparatus is used by a businessman for carrying on his business'. **1971** B. SCHARF *Engin. & its Language* xvii. 245 Examples of mobile earthmoving plant are bulldozers, graders and scrapers. **1972** J. MOSEDALE *Football* xi. 150 Workers at the meat packing plants. **1973** *Times* 16 Nov. 20/8 At plant level, the [German] philosophy is the shared responsibility of capital and labour for the growth of the enterprise. **1977** *Jrnl. R. Soc. Arts* CXXV. 300/2 With the reduction of teacher training the amount of surplus 'plant' becoming available would eliminate capital construction costs.

c. *Austral.* The equipment, stock, vehicles, etc., of a drover, a farm, a road-mending team, etc.

1901 H. LAWSON *Prose Wks.* (1948) 427 Andy had charge of the 'droving-plant' (a tilted two-horse waggonette, in which we carried the rations and horse-feed). **1903** 'T. COLLINS' *Such is Life* 7 Soon we became aware of two teams coming to meet us... Victorian poverty spoke in every detail of the working plant. **1928** 'BRENT OF BIN BIN' *Up Country* xvii. 290 Charlotte was to have her cows and poultry, so that when the diggings were played out there would be a grazier's plant to fall back upon. **1934** *Bulletin* (Sydney) 31 Jan. 32/2 Although he knew our standard of horsemanship so well, he is so ignorant of our calling as to refer to my plant as my 'herd'. **1954** B. MILES *Stars my Blanket* xxiv. 211 He..was then about to return to Elsey with his 'plant'—a drover's 'plant' being his spare horses and packs. **1963** A. LUBBOCK *Austral. Roundabout* 42 'That'll be Dan Daley with his droving plant,' said Barney, shading his eyes. 'Plant?' I queried. 'Outfit—we call it "plant" here.'

7. (Earlier and further examples.) Also, a hiding-place for people or goods; the people or goods so hidden; *spec.* (a hiding-place for) drugs or equipment used by a drug-addict.

1785 *Sessions Papers of Central Criminal Court* Apr. 582/1 He opened a place in the wainscot, which is called 'a plant', it was a secret cupboard. **1829** H. WIDOWSON *Present State of Van Diemen's Land* xi. 118 The slabs were very loose; on pulling them up, the plant was sprung and mutton in abundance was discovered stowed away in a large barrel. **1846** [see *DUNNY *sb.*[2] 1]. **1874** HOTTEN *Slang Dict.* 256 *Plant*, a hidden store of money or valuables. To 'spring a plant' is to unearth another person's hoard. **1926** J. BLACK *You can't Win* xii. 160 The sack contained his 'plant', an eye dropper with a hypodermic needle soldered to it, and a small paper of morphine. *Ibid.* xx. 314, I could lift the plant and be far away before daylight. **1967** S. LLOYD *Lightning Ridge Bk.* iii. 8 Gibson never located this plant of opal again.

b. A person who, or thing which, has been 'planted' (see PLANT *v.* 2 c in Dict. and Suppl.). *slang.*

1926 *Amer. Speech* I. 436/2 *Plant*, a member of an act planted in the audience or the orchestra pit who performs his share of the act from there, or who comes upon the stage from the audience to take part in the performance as a supposed non-member of the profession. **1949** *Newsweek* 3 Oct. 36/3 Fifteen government witnesses, a half-dozen of them FBI 'plants' who infiltrated the Communist Party, had taken the stand. **1952** KOESTLER *Arrow in Blue* IV. xxiii. 191 One of her favourite pastimes was to fabricate apocryphal news items... One of the most successful of her plants ran something as follows. **1969** *TV Times* (Austral.) 15 Oct. 10/3 One Press agent made an interesting slip of the tongue when he commented: 'The first thing any publicist does in the morning is to read the plants, I mean the trades.' **1978** G. VAUGHAN *Belgrade Drop* ii. 15 'Heroin!' the detective shouted... Yardley had never seen the package before... He said: 'That stuff's a plant.' **1978** M. WALKER *Infiltrator* iv. 48 If she was a plant...I would have to take her along,.. and find out who had planted her and why.

10. a. *plant hire, pot, -stand, -world.* **c.** *plant-eating* (examples), *-hirer, -sucking.*

1905 V. L. KELLOGG *Amer. Insects* xii. 252 (Plant-eating beetles.) Tribe Phytophaga. **1941** J. S. HUXLEY *Uniqueness of Man* vi. 157 The best-analysed cases concern..plant-eating insects adapted to different food plants. **1973** W. S. ROMOSER *Science of Entomology* vii. 186 Phytophagous means literally 'plant eating'. **1976** 'L. BLACK' *Healthy Way to Die* xi. 118 There were thirty-five companies ranging from a merchant bank to..a plant-hire outfit. **1978** J. SHERWOOD *Limericks of Lachasse* xi. 133 Get on to that plant hire place..and get them to have an excavator up here..to dig up the car park. **1973** *Times* 11 May 19/5 Plant hirers are able to offer such machines. **1963** *Times* 21 Jan. 15/1 The Italian company..plans to make plant pots for the horticultural trade. **1975** D. CLARK *Premedicated Murder* iv. 52 They both said yes together, like plant-pot men. **1977** G. SCOTT *Hot Pursuit* vii. 68 The shelves were filled with files and papers and plant pots. **1862** *Catal. Internat. Exhib., Brit.* II. No. 6070, Ornamental wire plant-stands, model rosery, and verandah. **1903** K. D. WIGGIN *Rebecca* 247 She buried her face in the blooming geraniums on Miss Maxwell's plant-stand. **1974** *Trafford Catal.* Spring/Summer 591/2 Pedestal plant stand..with six variable position pot holders. **1908** *Westm. Gaz.* 30 May 7/3 There are very few who realise the enormous number of species that in reality make up this mischievous group of plant-sucking parasites. **1969** *New Scientist* 2 Oct. 19/1 The Australian plantsucking psyllid bug..lives on eucalyptus leaves. **1936** E. SITWELL *Sel. Poems* 12 The ethereal quality of the plant-world.

e. plant-bed, (*b*) *U.S.*, a bed of earth prepared for the germination of seeds and the growth of young plants, esp. of tobacco seedlings; **plant-breeder** (examples); also **plant-breeding** *vbl. sb.*; **plant-cane** (earlier and later examples); **plant-cover(ing),** vegetation spreading over the surface of the earth; **plant-food** (earlier and later examples); **plant geographer** = PHYTOGEOGRAPHER; **plant geography** = PHYTOGEOGRAPHY; **plant hormone** = *HORMONE 2, *PHYTOHORMONE; **plant-house,** (*a*) a greenhouse or conservatory; (*b*) a building containing industrial plant; **plant pathology** = *phytopathology* (*a*) s.v. PHYTO- in Dict. and Suppl.; so **plant pathologist; plant physiology,** the scientific study of the normal functions and phenomena of plants; so **plant physiologist; plant-wax,** wax obtained from plants.

1833 *Niles' Reg.* XLIV. 411/1 He is clearing new grounds; preparing and burning plant-beds. **1907** *St. Nicholas* May 651/1 A 'running' board was put around the base and a plant bed about a foot wide made within this. **1966** *Publ. Amer. Dial. Soc.* XLV. 20 We put cotton canvas over the plant bed. **1906** *Chambers's Jrnl.* 28 July 556/2 The experiments open up a new and interesting field for the plant-breeder. **1929** T. THOMSON tr. *Büsgen's Structure & Life of Forest Trees* xiv. 403 The expert eye of the plant breeder is able to discover them [*sc.* individual differences between plants]. **1970** R. GORER *Development of Garden Flowers* i. 26 To the plant breeder, the importance and interest of germ cell formation lies in the first stage of meiosis. **1908** *Westm. Gaz.* 28 Mar. 6/2 Few who are making a study of the fundamental principles of plant-breeding are unfamiliar with the name and the results achieved by Luther Burbank. **1926** J. S. HUXLEY *Essays in Pop. Sci.* ii. 10 There has sprung into being a new science, of animal- and plant-breeding. **1970** R. GORER *Development of Garden Flowers* i. 21 The essential basis of plant breeding is selection. **1790** W. BECKFORD *Descr. Account Island of Jamaica* I. 161 It is a common practice, where corn will grow, to plant it with the canes... Among plant-canes, I do not conceive it of consequence. **1853** *Harper's Mag.* Nov. 757 The 'growing crop' in Louisiana consists of three kinds of cane: the first is technically called 'plant cane' and is that which springs directly from the 'seed cane'. **1949** *Caribbean Quarterly* I. I. 5 A cane field was not ripe for its first harvest (the 'plant cane') until the second winter after its planting. **1943** J. S. HUXLEY *TVA* 17 Forests and plant cover were stripped. **1976** *Field* 18 Nov. 976/3 Where the vegetation has been worn away, the shade of the plant cover lost.., evaporation from the bare surface proceeds apace. **1911** W. G. SMITH in A. G. Tansley *Types Brit. Vegetation* xiii. 312 The plant covering is distinctly xerophilous in response to frequent dry periods. **1946** *Nature* 2 Nov. 605/1 Nomadism..a mode of life, indeed, in which defacement of the plant-covering by ploughing or digging is the worst of economic offences. **1869** *Rep. U.S. Comm. Agric. 1868* 396 Such plant-food as rain-water and the atmosphere supply. **1939** LAWRENCE & NEWELL *Seed & Potting Composts* ii. 23 These chemical compounds absorbed by the plant.. we shall refer to as 'plant foods'. **1976** J. BERRISFORD *Backyards & Tiny Gardens* viii. 59 Such a growing medium contains no plant foods, so fertilizers must be added before planting. **1913** *Jrnl. Ecology* I. 27 This character [*sc.* the physiognomy of vegetation] is unjustly regarded as merely superficial..by many modern plant-geographers. **1973** P. A. COLINVAUX *Introd. Ecol.* ii. 27 On the grand-scale, maps of climate based on the plant geographer's boundaries were useful. **1903** W. R. FISHER tr. *Schimper's Plant-Geogr.* p. vi, The connexion between the forms of plants and the external conditions at different points on the earth's surface forms the subject-matter of oecological plant-geography. **1934** H. GILBERT-CARTER tr. *Raunkiaer's Life Forms of Plants* iv. 111 The units of floristic plant geography are the same as those of systematic botany. **1977** *Sci. Amer.* May 99/1 Specimens were collected and filed in herbaria for later investigation by new techniques ranging from cytology and physiology to plant geography and ecology. **1935** *Biol. Rev.* X. 429 Other plant hormones, such as the wound hormones of Haberlandt, we need not discuss, since less quantitative knowledge is available on the subject. They apparently also act by diffusion from cell to cell. **1951,** etc. [see *HORMONE 2]. **1959** L. J. AUDUS *Plant Growth Substances* i. 18 Plant hormones are substances which regulate.. some aspect of plant growth and which are produced by the organism itself. They may be growth hormones, flowering hormones, and so forth. **1974** *Physiologia Plantarum* XXXII. 369 (*heading*) Effect of abscisic acid and other plant hormones on growth of apical and lateral buds of seedlings. **1863** *Horticulturist* XVIII. 306 We again have the satisfaction of presenting two examples of Plant Houses; one a *Green-house*, and the other a *Cold Grapery*. **1881** *Encycl. Brit.* XII. 221/2 Plant houses must be as far as possible impervious to wet and cold air from the exterior. **1909** *Westm. Gaz.* 6 May 5/3 A plant-house is being erected outside the south wall of the provincial capital. **1909** B. M. DUGGAR *Fungous Diseases of Plants* 3 There was a bright prospect for controlling many of the fungous diseases of plants, and there developed..an immediate need for plant pathologists. **1977** *Daily Tel.* 6 July 2/1 Dr Alan Walker, Ministry Plant Pathologist, said that cereal diseases which could cut yield by up to 15 per cent. were minimal this year. **1895** *Jrnl. Chem. Soc.* LXVIII. II (*heading*) Chemical investigations in plant pathology. **1908** P. T. DONDLINGER *Bk. of Wheat* ix. 148 Studies in plant pathology of any great practical bearing or importance are..modern and recent. **1935** *Discovery* Oct. 294/1 The intimate relationships between plant pathology..and other branches of botany. **1973** *Nature* 27 Apr. 595/2 Plant pathology..is to plants what the whole of medicine and veterinary science is to man and animals. *Ibid.* 596/1 Is it right that any comprehensive book on the principles of plant pathology should dismiss viruses and mycoplasmata with thirty-six pages and an apology? **1931** W. O. JAMES *Introd. Plant Physiol.* i. 2 The methods used by plant physiologists..are mainly derived from various branches of chemistry and physics. **1898** S. A. MOOR tr. *W. Detmer's Pract. Plant Physiol.* p. vii, Plant physiology is now of..far-reaching significance for students of Natural Science, Agriculture, Forestry, and Medicine. **1937** W. H. SAUMAREZ SMITH *Let.* 10 July in *Young Man's Country* (1977) ii. 80, I was interested to see the place where all his [*sc.* Tagore's] disciples are following out the lines of research suggested by his highly original work in plant-physiology. **1968** F. C. STEWARD *Growth & Organization in Plants* p. iii, The author's, and indeed a customary, approach to plant physiology is deeply ingrained in the study of cells, their membranes and particulate inclusions, their metabolism and responses to stimuli. **1924** J. A. THOMSON *Science Old & New* xviii. 101 There are plant-waxes as well as animal-waxes.

plant, *v.* Add: **1.** Also *absol.*

1893 B. MITFORD *Gun-Runner* iv. 34 Along the banks of this [watercourse] the careful Jeremiah had planted and sown. **1896** *Forum* July 515 Our forefathers..came to work, to plant, to reap, where they might worship God with freedom. **1961** *Atlanta Constitution* 17 Aug. 5 The people who try to raise and can meat, to plant, grow vegetables, and put them up. **1979** *Verbatim* Summer 8/1 In South Australia a farmer *seeds*,..and in Queensland he *plants*.

c. *plant out* (earlier and later examples); also, to arrange plants or trees in a piece of ground. Also *transf.* and *fig.* (cf. sense 6 in Dict.).

1664 J. EVELYN *Kalendarium Hortense* 60 Now also plant out your Colly-flowers to have early. **1901** *Year-bk. U.S. Dept. Agric. 1900* 373 Each orchardist will no doubt develop some method of his own in planting out the orchard. *a* **1910** 'MARK TWAIN' *Autobiogr.* (1924) I. 274 They would often plant out eleven columns of new ads on a standing galley. **1917** P. S. ALLEN *Let.* 8 July (1939) 139 So many of your books are here 'on deposit'...I wonder if you recognised what was in my mind..when I wrote of Rud. Agricola's 'planting out his books in friends' houses as pledges of return'. **1927** KIPLING *Limits & Renewals* (1932) 170, I was planting out plants from my garden. **1962** *Times* 19 May 11/4 Every partridge-rearing system encounters its critical phase when the birds are 'planted out'. **1972** *Shooting Times & Country Mag.* 4 Mar. 24/3 'Unfed fry' [*sc.* trout]..are ready to be planted out to start off their natural lives in the sidestreams and the river. **1975** B. DOUGHERTY *Green Gardener* x. 115 Avoid touching their [*sc.* tomatoes'] stems when planting out, holding them only by the leaflets.

2. c. (Further examples.) Now esp., to conceal (stolen goods, incriminating evidence, etc.) with a view to misleading a later discoverer. Also (not *slang*), to introduce (a character, scene, etc.) into a play, film, etc., for some specified purpose.

1865 J. H. A. Bone *Petroleum & Petroleum Wells* (ed. 2) 153 Frauds are not infrequently perpetrated by 'planting' oil in dry wells. **1930** *Times Lit. Suppl.* 1 May 373/1 The nephew..sought to clinch the available, and misleading, evidence by planting the victim's dental plate on the spot. **1933** H. J. Lee *Eagle Police Manual* 152 *Plant*, to place incriminating evidence in a man's pocket or elsewhere. **1939** E. S. Gardner *D. A. draws Circle* (1940) 200 Someone is planting evidence. *Ibid.* 203 It had been planted on him. **1948** A. Huxley *Let.* 16 Jan. (1969) 578, I have been trying to put this question to the general and specialized publics for the last year or two—even succeeding in planting it in the *Bulletin of the Atomic Scientists*. **1950** *Ibid.* 16 Feb. 619 We have to plant the business of the currants, so that we are forced to show them lunching. **1958** *Listener* 30 Oct. 704/3 The man was 'planted' as a nervous stammerer, but to be nervous is not necessarily to be a nitwit. **1969** *It* 11–24 Apr. 10/1 Everyone was searched and told to stay clear of the area under the threat of being planted. **1970** G. F. Newman *Sir, You Bastard* 261 Planting microphones was easier. **1974** *Howard Jrnl.* XIV. 43 [The police] are now seen by many West Indians..as racist 'enemies', who taunt, intimidate, assault, plant and 'trump up' charges. **1978** S. Brill *Teamsters* i. 18 Government investigators..had planted an informant among organized-crime figures in California.

6. a. Also with *to*.

1799 T. R. Malthus *Diary* 16 July (1966) 159 There are many grounds about the town planted to potatoes. **1901** *Year-bk. U.S. Dept. Agric.* 1900 373 The land should be planted to a crop for at least a year or two before setting out the trees. **1941** E. P. O'Donnell *Great Big Doorstep* 92 She reached a field planted to okra, the stalks rising taller than she. **1949** E. Hyams *Not in our Stars* xvi. 195 A four-acre field..which Drover had planted to cherries in the previous season. **1976** *National Observer* (U.S.) 12 June 9/1 Grapevines are now found..creeping into fields once planted to pears and apples.

11. To bury (a dead person). *slang* (orig. *U.S.*).

1855 *Harper's Mag.* Dec. 37/1 Let it [*sc.* yellow fever] catch hold of a crowd of 'Johnny come latelys', and it plants them at once. **1866** 'Mark Twain' *Lett. fr. Hawaii* (1967) 242 It's about the orneryest thing for a monument I've ever struck yet... If I was planted under it, I'd highst it. **1888** [see *flamdoodle]. **1927** C. A. W. Monckton *Some Experiences of New Guinea Resident Magistrate* 2nd Ser. i. 16 There's Alligator Jack and Red Bill..planted here, and Gawd, 'E knows whether they have rested easy. **1931** Galsworthy *Maid in Waiting* ii. 10 'Is he to be planted here?' 'I expect in the Cathedral, but Father will know.' **1967** C. Rougvie *When Johnny Died* iii. 66 It was raining when we planted him, and I thought he'd get out of his coffin. **1974** R. Jeffries *Mistakenly in Mallorca* xv. 143 The funeral must be fixed up at once. Where did non-Catholics get planted?

plantain[1]. **3. plantain lily,** substitute for def.: = *funkia, *hosta. Add later examples.

1894 W. Robinson *Wild Garden* (ed. 4) xiv. 170 The Plantain Lilies are plants for the wild garden. **1927** [see *funkia]. **1957** C. Lloyd *Mixed Border* vi. 60 Among plantain lilies..the prevalence of slugs and snails is all too likely. **1976** B. Swain *Commonsense of Gardening* v. 207/2 The charming Plantain Lilies..have often disappointed because of unsuitable conditions.

plantar, *a.* (Further examples.)

1951 *Chambers's Jrnl.* Aug. 507/1 'You've been grousing for months about the corn you picked up last tour, foot-slogging round Masailand.'.. 'It's not a corn, it's a plantar wart,' I said indignantly. **1976** *Muir's Text-bk. Path.* (ed. 10) 985 The histology of the vulgar wart usually seen on the hands and knees is essentially similar to the plantar wart found on the soles of the feet.

plantation. Add: **7.** *plantation-house* (later examples), *manners*, *-Negro* (earlier and later examples), *-worker*; **plantation creole,** a creolized language arising amongst a transplanted and largely isolated Negroid community; **plantation crepe** *U.S.*, used *attrib.* of a variety of crêpe-rubber sole on footwear.

1938 *Social Forces* Oct. 114/2 The plantation creole tongues are true *Sklavensprachen*. Although they owe something to the sailors' trade jargons, they began essentially as a makeshift means of communication between masters and field hands. **1978** *Verbatim* Feb. 10/1 Both authors hold to..the Creolist theory, which traces the present-day Black English vernacular to a Plantation Creole, to a plantation-maritime pidgin, to an African origin. **1967** *New Yorker* 7 Oct. 109/2 (Advt.), Clark's original Desert® Boots..with plantation crepe soles. **1969** *Sears, Roebuck & Co. Catal.* Spring–Summer 454/2 Durable, buoyant, plantation crepe rubber sole and heel. **1969** E. Wilson *Hist. Shoe Fashions* xx. 258 A plantation crepe sole was one of the many soft soles which added to its comfort. **1831** J. M. Peck *Guide for Emigrants* ii. 55 All the plantation houses are surrounded with rich and beautiful groves. **1973** *Advocate-News* (Barbados) 2 Feb. 15/4 (Advt.), Besides the plantation house there is available the plantation manager's house. **1974** *Country Life* 3–10 Jan. 18/1 The Virginian plantation houses of the 18th century, such as Carter's Grove, Westover and Shirley. **1854** Thoreau *Walden* 165 Men of almost every degree of wit called on me in the migrating season. Some who had more wits than they knew what to do with; runaway slaves with plantation manners, who listened from time to time, like the fox in the fable, as if they heard the hounds a-baying on their track. **1897** *Congress. Rec.* 31 Mar. 548/2 When I was a boy,..I used to read a great deal about what the early Republicans called 'plantation manners'. **1771** in *Maryland Hist. Mag.* (1919) XIV. 135 My people..do not live so well as our House negroes, But full as well as any Plantation negroes. **1956** G. P. Kurath in A. Dundes *Mother Wit* (1973) 108/1 Recreational dances of plantation Negroes commenced with a prayer. **1957** P. Worsley *Trumpet shall Sound* viii. 148 Plantation-workers were convinced by Runovoro's ability to write meaningless works. **1976** *Honolulu Star-Bull.* 21 Dec. A-8/2 Approximately 175 Molokai Dole plantation workers..lost their jobs last year because of foreign competition.

Planté (plɑ·nte). *Electr.* The name of R. L. Gaston *Planté* (1834–89), French physicist, used *attrib.* to designate lead-acid accumulator plates formed by a process which he invented, cells containing such plates, and the process itself.

1881 *Electrician* 3 Sept. 249/2 A Planté cell that has been long in use gives a better result than one that has been freshly constructed. **1889** G. W. de Tunzelmann *Electr. in Mod. Life* xiv. 195 The original Planté accumulator has been considerably improved by Faure and others. **1923** Glazebrook *Dict. Appl. Physics* II. 76/2 Owing to its high cost the original Planté process is no longer employed. *Ibid.* 77/1 Planté negatives are not generally used, as their advantages are not compensated by the additional weight of lead... Planté positives are employed extensively in stationary batteries. **1959** *Times* 11 Sept. 9/2 The field in which the new cell is designed to replace current Planté types is a very wide one. **1964** G. Smith *Storage Batteries* ii. 21 These do not have quite the same long life as the Planté battery. **1970** C. L. Mantell *Batteries & Energy Systems* xiii. 112 Planté plates are prepared from lead blanks which have been cast, rolled, cut, and stamped.

planted, *ppl. a.* **1.** (Examples corresponding to Plant *v.* 2 c in Dict. and Suppl.)

1963 *TV Times* (Austral.) 18 Apr. 10/2 *Planted*, hidden. **1972** *Jrnl. Social Psychol.* Dec. 301 When the class was asked if anyone wanted to make a statement to the 'teacher', a planted student responded with a standard complaining, corrective request. **1973** M. Woodhouse *Blue Bone* x. 93 'He said..that he was quite happy where he was.' 'In answer to a planted question, yes, he did.' 'You're fairly sure it was planted?'..'Of course... This whole thing was just a put-up job... So that Karel could state for the record that he was fine where he was.' **1977** G. V. Higgins *Dreamland* xiv. 169 We're even bigger suckers for a planted story..if we really had to scout around for it. **1978** J. Gardner *Dancing Dodo* xxxix. 324 It's a greater threat than a planted nuclear device.

planter. Add: **4. b.** *planter's* (or *planters'*) *punch*: a cocktail containing rum.

1924 A. Macmillan in *Land of Abiding Sunshine*, A 'swizzle' or 'a planter's punch' would very welcome be. **1935** S. Lewis *It can't happen Here* iv. 38 His reputation for research among planters'-punch recipes..might cause his defeat by the church people. **1958** G. Greene *Our Man in Havana* v. ii. 198 Have a planter's punch. They are good here. **1971** 'D. Halliday' *Dolly & Doctor Bird* viii. 108, I don't suppose Beltanno has tasted planter's punch. **1978** G. Greene *Human Factor* v. iii. 285 What about a Planter's Punch? They do them OK here, so I'm told.

8. a. (Earlier and later examples.)

1850 *Rep. U.S. Comm. Patents 1849* i. 151 Having thus fully described my improved grain and seed planter. **1939** W. Faulkner *Wild Palms* 65 For seven years now he had run his plough and harrow and planter within the very shadow of the levee. **1950** [see *bagger b].

b. A pot, tub, or other container for growing or displaying plants. orig. *U.S.*

1959 in Webster Add. **1966** 'L. Holton' *Out of Depths* viii. 72 The brick planters facing the ocean were gay with blossoms. **1968** *Washington Post* 3 July A24/8 (Advt.), Distinctive redwood planter at savings! **1969** *Islander* (Victoria, B.C.) 5 Oct. 3/3 On the foundations of the cabin there is now a summer patio with brick planters made from the cabin chimney. **1973** *Center City Office Weekly* (Philad.) 9 Oct. 10/4 Cream scuttle... Can be used as a planter, or for artificial flowers.

Plantin (plæ·ntin). The name of Christophe *Plantin* (1514–89), printer, of Antwerp, used to designate a family of old-face types, based on a 16th-century Flemish original, the first of which was designed by F. H. Pierpont for the Monotype Corporation in 1913.

1914 *Monotype Recorder* July 68 (*caption*) First showing of light face Plantin O.S. **1919** J. P. Thorp *Printing for Business* viii. 81 The headlines, section numbers and little acorn ornaments are in vermilion, the text in 12-point Plantin. **1929** F. Meynell *Typogr. Newspaper Advertisements* 28 Plantin (particularly the Monotype face) declares in its strength and straightness that it stands for the machine-seller. **1951** S. Jennett *Making of Books* xv. 262 Types like Times and Plantin, which are so large on the body that they are unpleasant when set solid, become useful and legible when they are suitably leaded. **1967** J. B. Lieberman *Types of Typefaces* 89/2 Plantin..is based on 16th century forms.

planting, *vbl. sb.* Add: **3. planting-attorney,** in the West Indies, the manager of a plantation or estate.

1953 *Caribbean Q.* III. iii. 142 The planters and planting-attorneys were worried about the continuation of estate labour after the slaves should be apprenticed. **1956** H. G. de Lisser *Cup & Lip* i. 19 Arthur was earnest at his work as his uncle's planting attorney.

plantlet. (Later examples.)

1899 [see *damping *vbl. sb.* 2]. **1935** A. F. Hort *Garden Variety* iv. 226 Here [*sc.* in a box] the plantlets..will remain for weeks or months. **1946** D. C. Peattie *Road of Naturalist* i. 18 For a seed is not just part of a plant; detached it is a complete plant, with a plantlet folded inside, a supply of food, an infinitesimal supply of moisture. **1970** *Nature* 19 Sept. 1265/2 Anthers from entirely white shoots gave rise to white plantlets.

plant-louse. (Later examples.)

1840 J. & M. Loudon tr. *Köllar's Treatise on Insects* ii. 149 The plant-lice are especial enemies to various sorts of culinary vegetables. **1899** B. S. Cragin *Our Insect Friends & Foes* 228 Family Aphididæ. These are the Plant-lice, some with wings and some without. **1932** E. Step *Wasps, Ants & Allied Insects Brit. Isles* 79 Like that of most of the other Black Wasps, its special prey is the Plant-louse (*Aphis*). **1968** R. Lowell *Notebook* (1969) 48 The lily pads bright as mica, swarming with plant-lice. **1973** W. S. Romoser *Science of Entomology* xi. 346 Especially significant families are Psyllidae, jumping plant lice,.. Aphididæ, aphids or plant lice, [etc.].

plantmilk (plɑ·ntmilk). [f. Plant *sb.*[1] + Milk *sb.*] A synthetic milk substitute prepared from vegetable matter.

1959 *Oxford Mail* 19 Mar. 4/5 It is estimated that the plantmilk which will soon be available to the general public will cost a few pence more than cows' milk. **1959** *New Scientist* 1 Oct. 596/1 Plantmilks based on soya are being used in America to treat milk allergies in infants. **1962** *Guardian* 27 Aug. 2/3 A plantmilk, made from cereals and pulses, has been on sale for some years. **1965** *Times* 1 Sept. 6/6 Drinka pinta milka day but make it plantmilk, Dr. Alan Stoddard advised delegates at the International Vegetarian Union's world congress at Swanwick, Derbyshire, today.

plantsman. Substitute for def.: An expert gardener; a connoisseur of plants. Add later examples. Hence **pla·ntsmanship,** a desire to display knowledge of unusual or especially rare plants.

1952 *Archit. Rev.* CXII. 343/1 None of these plants remain in that environment for long as they are serviced and maintained by fully competent plantsmen. **1962** *Amateur Gardening* 21 Apr. 21/1 *Actinidia polygama*..has fruit of unpleasant flavour, but this should not..deter those who practise plantsmanship from planting a 'bower of bliss' with a few prominently labelled specimens. **1963** *Times* 3 June 1/7 Some of the best garden spurges are described by a plantsman contributor. **1978** W. Blunt *In for Penny* xxi. 155 This lovely blue orchid [*sc. Vanda cœrulea*] had become a status symbol for rich plantsmen. **1979** J. Harvey in J. Harris *Garden* 8/1 The abbeys, priories and hospitals were particularly concerned with plantsmanship, cultivation and improvement.

plapper (plæ·pəɹ), *v.* [imit.: see S.N.D.] *intr.* To make sounds with the lips.

1866 W. Gregor in *Trans. Philol. Soc.* 127 *Plapper*,.. to make a noise with the lips. **1922** Joyce *Ulysses* 258 She took no notice while he read by rote a solfa fable for her, plappering flatly.

plaque. Add: **1. a.** (Earlier and later examples.) Also, an inscribed plate identifying a monument or building, etc.

1869 C. Schreiber *Jrnl.* (1911) I. 13 A large plaque of Smalto glass, with landscape in brown. **1870** *Ibid.* I. 68 We saw..a very fine Terra Cotta plaque, by Clodion, 3 to 4 feet long. **1956** A. J. Cronin *Crusader's Tomb* iii. ix. 195 At the base of the pediment was a time-worn plaque defining the intention of the founder to tend the sick. **1968** *Guardian* 19 Sept. 18/3 In a few days Britain will have two fish and chip shops, each proclaiming itself by plaque to be the oldest..in the world. **1969** M. Pugh *Last Place Left* xxiii. 175 Why don't you wait fifty years or so? I imagine there will be a plaque outside his house. **1971** *Times* 19 Apr. 12/5 Mrs. Pankhurst's house in Clement's Inn is being demolished and the Women's Liberation movement is concerned lest the blue plaque from the house..should disappear. **1979** Atterbury & Irvine *Doulton Story* 20 Probably the best known Doulton commemoratives are the plaques made for the LCC and other bodies to mark places associated with famous people and events.

c. A counter used in gambling. Cf. Chip *sb.*[1] 2 d in Dict. and Suppl.

1904 A. Bennett *Great Man* xxv. 281 A croupier counted out..sundry..gold *plaques* of a hundred francs each. **1964** A. Wykes *Gambling* xii. 288 The big bets are placed with rectangular colored chips, called plaques. **1972** D. Lees *Zodiac* 47 Françoise picked up the plaques from the table in front of her. **1973** 'R. MacLeod' *Burial in Portugal* vi. 117 Deliberately, Salvador used a one thousand escudo plaque to scratch along his small moustache.

d. *Mus.* A thin metal plate inserted into the separated tip of the double reed of a wind instrument while the reed is being scraped.

1940 J. Artley *How to make Double Reeds* 13/1 Insert the plaque between the blades of the reed. *Ibid.* 14/1 While working on the lay with the knife, use the plaque at all times. **1953** E. Rothwell *Oboe Technique* vi. 48 *Tongue, or plaque*, for inserting into the reed while scraping. Small flat piece of metal, oval shaped with pointed ends. *Ibid.* 53 In order to avoid any confusion between the human tongue and the metal one, I shall, throughout this chapter, refer to the latter as the *plaque*, the alternative word used little in England but almost exclusively in America. **1957** A. Baines *Woodwind Instruments & their Hist.* iii. 82 The *tongue* (or *plaque*, fig. 11, *t*) is a thin, oval steel plate about 40×15 millimetres, and it is always placed between the blade tips while scraping after the tips have been separated. **1962** E. C. Moore *Oboe & its Daily Routine* iv. 13/1 Few tools are needed..a plaque to slip between the blades of the reeds, [etc.].

2. c. *Med.* A patch of fibrous tissue or of fatty matter on the wall of an artery; the substance of which such a patch is formed.

1891 *Trans. Assoc. Amer. Physicians* VI. 182 The nodular form of arterio-sclerosis is due to circumscribed dilations of the arteries and a new formation of connective tissue which exactly fills out the dilated area. When such arteries are examined after having been injected with paraffine.., the raised plaques which are so prominent in the uninjected vessels have entirely disappeared, leaving a smooth intima. **1943** *Physiol. Rev.* XXIII. 188 The atherosclerotic lesions..were classified as fatty plaques, fibrous plaques, calcified plaques, and atheromatous ulcers. **1972** *Daily Colonist* (Victoria, B.C.) 4 May 2/1 As the years pass, the walls of our arteries thicken and accumulate a certain amount of plaque, or fatty deposits. **1975** *Daily Tel. Mag.* 5 Dec. 20/4 These so-called plaques, and the attached clots, build up and obtrude upon the bore of the vessel. **1978** *Time* 3 July 54/1 Tests showed that his left main coronary artery was clogged with cholesterol-laden plaque.

d. *Dentistry.* A patch of deposit that contains bacteria and adheres firmly to the surface of a tooth; the substance of which such patches are composed.

1898 G. V. Black in *Dental Cosmos* XL. 448 Leptothrix threads..are found..clinging in and upon gelatinous microbic plaques upon the teeth. **1921** Ryan & Bowers *Teeth & Health* xi. 154 In caries, or dental decay, placques or films of saliva form on the tooth surfaces, in combination with particles of carbohydrates. **1959** Wilkins & McCullough *Clin. Pract. Dental Hygienist* ii. 109 Dental plaque is a thin, tenacious, film-like deposit made up principally of microorganisms and mucinous substances from the saliva. It is removed by polishing procedures. Plaque is the most commonly found of all tooth deposits. *Ibid.*, Dental plaques vary in thickness, degree of adherence to the tooth surface, and percentage composition. **1971** *Daily Tel.* 24 Aug. 5 (Advt.), The toothbrush is undoubtedly the most effective weapon in the fight against bacterial plaque. Plaque produces the harmful acids and chemicals that cause tooth decay and discoloration. **1976** J. J. Murray *Fluorides in Caries Prevention* xii. 185 Dental plaque is a soft, tenacious bacterial deposit suspended in a protein matrix which forms on the surface of teeth. It also contains varying amounts of extracellular polysaccharide and desquamated bacterial cells.

e. *Biol.* A relatively clear area in a culture of micro-organisms or other cells produced by the inhibitory or lethal effect of a virus or other agent.

D'Herelle used *plage*, not *plaque*, in Fr. (*Le Bactériophage* (1921) i. 13).

1924 *Jrnl. Bacteriol.* IX. 397 These lytic areas, or plaques, are usually circular and may vary in size from pits of microscopic dimensions to eroded fields possessing a diameter of 18 to 20 mm. **1930** G. H. Smith tr. *F. D'Herelle's Bacteriophage & its Clin. Applic.* i. 12 Each bare spot, which I have termed a *plaque*, represents a colony of bacteriophage particles. **1952** *Proc. Nat. Acad. Sci.* XXXVIII. 747 (*heading*) Production of plaques in monolayer tissue cultures by simple particles of an animal virus. **1963** *Science* 26 Apr. 405/1 Distinct plaques, each of which is due to the release of hemolysin by a single antibody-forming cell, are revealed by complement after incubation, in an agar layer, of a mixture of sheep red cells and lymphoid cells from a rabbit immunized with sheep red cells. **1970** T. D. Brock *Biol. Microorganisms* x. 260 Since the agar prevents the new virus particles from moving too far away, a localized area of lysis develops that contains no bacteria but many virus particles... This local area of lysis is called a plaque..and represents the end result of a chain of events initiated by one virus particle.

3. *Med.* A flat applicator designed to contain radium or one of its salts, formerly applied to the surface of the body over cancerous tissue for the curative effect of the radiation.

1919 [see *radium plaque]. **1922** F. E. Simpson *Radium Therapy* xii. 110 The best type of metal applicator is made of silver, the radium salt being spread uniformly over a glazed surface which forms the face of the applicator. Lead free glass must be used. Plaques of this type are known as glazed radium applicators. **1931** G. E. Birkett *Radium Therapy* xi. 150 Superficial sclerosing type [of rodent ulcers].—In the early stages these may be successfully treated by the application of an unscreened radium plaque. **1950** Walter & Miller *Short Textbk. Radiotherapy* viii. 195 A beta-ray applicator is an example of a plaque. The one illustrated in Fig. 82 is made of brass, has an area of 4 sq. cm. and contains 5 mgm. of radium per square cm. It is covered by a filter of 0·1 mm. of monel metal.

plashily (plæ·ʃili), *adv. rare.* [f. Plashy *a.*[2] + -ly[2].] With a plashing noise.

1926 R. Macaulay *Crewe Train* iii. i. 240 Going away, going away, going away. The waves plashily said it over.

-plasia (-plēi·ziă), a word-forming element (f. Gr. πλάσις moulding, conformation (πλάσσειν to form, mould) + -ia[1]) used in medical and biological terms in the sense 'growth, development (of tissue)', as *dysplasia, heteroplasia. Occas. anglicized as **-plasy.**

plasma. Delete ‖ and add: **5*.** *Physics.* A gas in which there are positive ions and free negative electrons, usu. in approximately equal numbers throughout and therefore electrically neutral; *esp.* one exhibiting phenomena due to the collective interaction of the charges. Also, any analogous collection of charged particles in which one or both kinds are mobile, as the conduction electrons in a metal or the ions in a salt solution.

Electrical neutrality and collective phenomena are often made necessary characteristics of a plasma (e.g. quot. 1967[2]).

1928 I. Langmuir in *Proc. Nat. Acad. Sci.* XIV. 628 It seemed that these oscillations must be regarded as compressional electric waves somewhat analogous to sound waves. Except near the electrodes..the ionized gas contains ions and electrons in about equal numbers so that the resultant space charge is very small. We shall use the name *plasma* to describe this region containing balanced charges of ions and electrons. **1930** *Physical Rev.* XXXVII. 1467 The plasma used in this investigation was the positive column of a mercury arc. **1941** Millman & Seely *Electronics* x. 307 The largest portion of a glow discharge is the plasma. *Ibid.* 309 In addition to the electrons and ions that exist in equal concentrations, a plasma contains many gas molecules. **1958** *Engineering* 31 Jan. 134/2 The stable plasma reaches the high temperatures, of the order of 5 million deg. K., necessary for producing thermonuclear reactions. **1960** *Soviet Physics Doklady* V. 363 At a distance from the earth of 4 earth radii, a plasma with a temperature of not more than tens of thousands of degrees was detected. **1966** *McGraw-Hill Encycl. Sci. & Technol.* X. 386/1 If the over-all dimensions of a region containing a plasma are small compared to λ_D, only simple collisional or single-particle behavior is to be expected, the plasma will behave as an ordinary low-density gas, and collective processes will not be important. **1967** L. K. Branson *Introd. Electronics* ix. 315 The plasma consists of a mixture of positive, negative, and neutral particles and..in any given volume-element there are equal numbers of ions and electrons. Further, the plasma..fills the entire volume between anode and cathode except for a narrow region at the cathode called the sheath. **1967** Condon & Odishaw *Handbk. Physics* (ed. 2) iv. xi. 188/1 The phenomena that occur in a plasma and distinguish it from any arbitrary collection of charged particles are the near equality of positive and negative charges throughout the plasma volume and the ability of the charges to participate in plasma oscillations. **1969** Steele & Vural *Wave Interactions in Solid State Plasmas* i. 4 In a metal like copper, the free electrons comprising the plasma are electrically compensated by the positively ionized copper atoms. **1971** E. Nasser *Fundamentals of Gaseous Ionization & Plasma Electronics* xiv. 427 Liquid plasmas exist in salt solutions where the positive and negative ions move separately. **1974** R. C. Davidson *Theory of Nonneutral Plasmas* p. xi, Nonneutral plasmas exhibit collective properties that are qualitatively similar to those of neutral plasmas. For example, in klystrons and traveling-wave tubes, the collective oscillations necessary for microwave generation and amplification are excited even under conditions in which the electron beams..are unneutralized. **1974** *Nature* 5 Apr. 494/2 In a cold plasma (which is a good approximation for most of the magnetosphere away from the equatorial region) there are two wave modes. **1976** T. Beer *Aerospace Environment* i. 16 The solar wind is a plasma of hydrogen ions (protons) and electrons travelling at speeds that range from 300 km s^{-1} to 1000 km s^{-1}, depending on solar activity.

5.** *Soil Sci.* (See quots.)

1958 I. W. Cornwall *Soils for Archaeologist* xvii. 190 Intergranular spaces and conducting channels may be filled, or partly filled, with colloids and precipitates, conveyed and deposited..by percolating moisture. This is the soil-plasma, which constitutes in part the cement between adjacent grains and in part mere filling of available voids. **1976** Courtney & Trudgill *Soil* ii. 17/2 In thin sections under a microscope the soil plasma can be recognized... It is an amorphous combination of humus, clays and chemical compounds (e.g. iron oxide), and is produced by the secondary weathering processes..and by the incorporation of organic matter. *Ibid.*, The presence of mineral matter in the plasma distinguishes it from the overlying purely organic horizons.

6. *plasma cloud*; **plasma arc,** a very hot plasma jet produced by passing a noble gas through a nozzle that is one electrode of an electric arc, used in plasma torches; **plasma dynamics** (also as one word), the science of the dynamical properties and behaviour of gaseous plasmas; so **plasma-dynamic, -dynamical** adjs.; **plasma engine,** a form of jet engine that produces and ejects plasma; **plasma frequency,** the natural resonant frequency of a plasma oscillation, which is also the minimum frequency of electromagnetic waves that can travel through the plasma without attenuation and is approximately 8920 $\sqrt{n}$ Hz, where n is the number of free electrons per cc.; **plasma jet,** a high-speed stream of plasma (ionized gas) ejected from a plasma engine or plasma torch; **plasma membrane** *Biol.*, = *plasmalemma; also, a similar membrane around an intracytoplasmic vacuole; **plasma oscillation,** a collective oscillation of the electrons in a plasma; **plasma physics,** the physics of plasmas such as ionized gases; hence **plasma physicist; plasma probe,** any device that is inserted or immersed in an ionized gas to investigate its physical properties; **plasma propulsion,** propulsion of a vehicle by means of a plasma engine; **plasma sheath,** a thin layer of space charge covering a surface in an ionized gas; **plasma torch,** a small device that produces a very hot plasma jet for use in cutting solids or coating them with refractory material.

1958 *Iron Age* 4 Dec. 136/1 Thanks to the development of the new plasma arc torch, a brand new method for fabricating shapes and applying ultra-high-temperature coatings is now a reality. **1963** H. R. Clauser *Encycl. Engin. Materials & Processes* 480/2 The cost of depositing the high-melting-point coatings with the plasma-arc process is comparable with that of the flame-sprayed coatings. **1973** *Materials & Technol.* VI. i. 60 A number of unconventional methods of cutting wood have been examined, largely with the object of reducing waste. These include the use of the plasma arc, which produces very high temperatures with a nozzle of very small diameter. **1960** *Aeroplane* XCVIII. 610/1 It appears that plasma clouds emitted from the Sun run up against the Earth's magnetic field, causing it to release previously trapped particles into the atmosphere. **1967** M. Kenyon *Whole Hog* xviii. 181 Along comes space which everyone had thought was empty, a void, but it turns out it's not, it's filled with radiation belts and plasma clouds and solar winds. **1969** *Monthly Not. R. Astron. Soc.* CXLV. 328 In the Ryle-Longair model, plasma clouds formed by a strong explosion within a galaxy expand..until their dimensions exceed galactic dimensions, at which time they are ejected from the parent galaxy and henceforth evolve independently. **1964** E. Stuhlinger *Ion Propulsion* vi. 277 The heat energy absorbed by the coolant in the reactor may be used to heat..the plasma in a plasmadynamic converter, or the working fluid in a thermodynamic converter. **1959** *Astrophysical Jrnl.* CXXIX. 217 We are interested in the distance in which a stream of tenuous plasma, directed against another oppositely moving stream of tenuous plasma, is brought to rest as a consequence of plasma dynamical interaction. **1960** *Aeroplane* XCIX. 837/2 Such subjects as magneto-hydrodynamics, MHD mechanics, and plasmadynamics. **1970** *New Scientist* 5 Feb. 273/2 Plasma dynamics is a subject with applications in many branches of physics and technology..—space physics and the quest for thermonuclear fusion being but two examples. **1958** *S.A.E. Jrnl.* Apr. 93/2 Another phase of our investigations..is the development of a plasma engine, in which small amounts of plasma are ejected at extremely high velocities. **1967** *Electronics* 6 Mar. 8/2 He directed work on plasma engines and space suits. **1974** Hawkey & Bingham *Wild Card* xv. 131 The propulsion pack was okay for the demonstration... We plan to replace it with a small plasma engine. [**1929** *Physical Rev.* XXXIII. 198 Thus the lower frequency limit for long waves coincides with the plasma-electron frequency.] **1949** *Ibid.* LXXV. 1852/1 For a typical density of 10^{12} electrons per cm^3, the plasma frequency is about 10^{10} c.p.s. **1964** D. B. Newman *Space Vehicle Electronics* iv. 225 Above the plasma frequency the plasma has dielectric properties... Well below the plasma frequency, the plasma acts like a conductor. **1971** Ferry & Fannin *Physical Electronics* vii. 96 For a metal, where the electron concentration is about 10^{28} m^{-3}, the plasma frequency is found to be about $5{\cdot}6 \times 10^{15}$ Hz, or in the ultraviolet region. **1957** G. M. Giannini *Plasma Jet & its Applications* (U.S.A.F. Office Scientific Res. Techn. Note 57-520) 22 The 'plasma jet' can be used for many of the purposes described... The jet is very hot, highly ionized, has a high velocity. **1960** *Aeroplane* XCVIII. 610/2 Because of the low thrust produced, the plasmajet cannot be employed for rocket-launching from Earth. It must be carried into orbit by a more powerful chemical rocket and started in the weightless environment of space. **1964** *Sci. News Let.* 12 Sept. 163 Plasma jets, the white-hot streams of gas used for such tasks as cutting and welding, may soon have yet another use, 'steering' satellites through space. **1972** D. G. Shepherd *Aerospace Propulsion* viii. 202 The arc jet or plasma jet utilizes the very high temperatures in arcs to heat the propellant. **1900** *Ann. Bot.* XIV. 352 The entire structure, antheridium, tube, and oogonium, have in reality become for a time a single cell bounded by a single continuous plasma-membrane. **1922** W. Stiles in *New Phytologist* XXI. 141 The term plasma-membrane will be used to denote a surface layer of protoplasm which behaves as a membrane surrounding the bulk of the protoplasm, and which may exhibit different degrees of permeability to different substances... The membrane bounding the outside of the protoplast, and so in contact with the cell wall, will be called the external plasma-membrane, and that bounding the vacuole, the internal plasma-membrane. **1948** *New Biol.* V. 40 The plasma membrane is highly permeable to substances which are soluble in fats and in fat solvents. **1965** Bell & Coombe tr. *Strasburger's Textbk. Bot.* 13 The inner plasma membrane surrounding the vacuole is known as the tonoplast, and that adjacent to the cell wall as the plasmalemma. **1968** R. Rieger et al. *Gloss. Genetics & Cytogenetics* 341 In some cells (bacteria, plants), a cell wall..is universally recognized as a structure separate from the plasma membrane. **1970** Ambrose & Easty *Cell Biol.* viii. 258 The outer cell membrane, or plasma membrane (sometimes known as the cell membrane, or plasmalemma), has a unique role, since the cell interacts with its environment through it. **1928** I. Langmuir in *Proc. Nat. Acad. Sci.* XIV. 629 Plasma Oscillations.—If..we change the concentration of electrons by some transient external means, the resulting electric fields act..to equalize the concentration, but the potential energy of these fields is converted into kinetic energy of the electrons so that oscillations occur, and electric waves may result. **1970** W. A. Harrison *Solid State Theory* iii. 288 Physically these plasma oscillations correspond to soundlike compression waves in the electron gas. **1972** Akasofu & Chapman *Solar–Terrestrial Physics* vii. 472 While the plasma cloud is streaming through the solar atmosphere it induces plasma oscillations there. These oscillations are observed at the earth as a Type II radio burst. **1968** *New Scientist* 24 Oct. 186 To bring about nuclear fusion..plasma with a density of 10^{14} nuclei per cu. cm. must be held together for about one second. To bring this about is the dream of plasma physicists. **1976** T. BEER *Aerospace Environment* i. 2 The plasma physicist can use the Earth's upper atmosphere as a gigantic laboratory to study the behaviour of a large-scale plasma being acted upon by the Earth's magnetic field. **1958** C. C. ADAMS *Space Flight* 345 Some scientists think that controlled fusion may be with us in 20 years or so, and if so we may completely bypass fission... Work in plasma physics will have to be carefully watched, and it is through research in this area that eventual success is expected. **1963** *Wall St. Jrnl.* 22 Jan., Kirtland researchers are delving into plasma physics—the study of partially ionized gases—to determine to what extent high-level nuclear blasts are likely to disrupt vital communications. **1970** G. K. WOODGATE *Elem. Atomic Structure* i. 3 Quantitative calculations of the behaviour of free atoms are required for the less well-defined fields..of, for example, solid-state physics, plasma physics, and..astrophysics. **1961** *Flight* LXXIX. 462/2 Valuable information had been transmitted from the rubidium vapour magnetometer, two fluxgate magnetometers and the plasma probe. **1965** K. W. GATLAND *Spacecraft & Boosters* II. 87/2 The radio-frequency plasma probe consisted of a pair of grid-like electrodes through which a radio-frequency electric field was applied to a small region near the satellite. **1977** *Sci. Amer.* Mar. 39/3 The first data available from the Ames Research Centre's plasma probe on *Pioneer 10* as it traversed interplanetary space were the hourly values of the speed of the [solar] wind. **1958** C. C. ADAMS *Space Flight* 54 A new Astronautics Research Laboratory with propulsion, astrophysical, and materials sections to study very high-energy fuels, including plasma propulsion systems. **1969** BOYD & SANDERSON *Plasma Dynamics* v. 107 Space research has given a great impetus to the development of plasma propulsion since it has important potential advantages over conventional propellants, especially for long-range missions. **1961** *Aeroplane* C. 462/2 During hypersonic flight on the return from orbit, an ionized 'plasma sheath' will envelop the glider, impeding the reception and transmission of radio signals. **1969** M. A. KASHA *Ionosphere* iii. 48 A spacecraft is generally surrounded by some form of plasma sheath. This means that it is very difficult to measure..the electrical potential of the space plasma. **1959** *Welding Engineer* Feb. 50/2 Two 600-amp units power a 50-kw plasma torch, and voltage requirements are being set by the gas being used. **1961** *Jrnl. Appl. Physics* XXXII. 821/1 This article describes a plasma torch based on inductive coupling to an ionized gas... Conventional plasma torches require electrodes to carry energy to the gas. **1968** *Observer* 22 Dec. 4/5 The plasma torch, another torch device in industrial use, can virtually disintegrate material at a temperature of 36,000 degrees C.

b. Used *attrib.* to designate (the concentration of) substances in blood plasma.

1891 W. D. HALLIBURTON *Text-bk. Chem. Physiol. & Path.* xv. 238 The globulin pre-existent in the blood plasma..may be termed plasma-globulin. **1927** [see *PLASMAPHERESIS]. **1941** *Amer. Jrnl. Path.* XVII. 360 The question whether increase of the plasma protein concentration would protect against heavy metal poisoning. **1956** *Nature* 4 Feb. 238/1 The amino-acid pattern of the urine from this cystinuric dog is.., apart from threonine, identical with that found in cases of human cystinuria, while the finding of a low plasma-cystine points to a similar etiology. **1961** *Lancet* 22 July 171/2 Because of the diurnal variation in plasma-cortisol (hydrocortisone) concentration, all blood samples were drawn between 9 A.M. and 10 A.M. **1969** E. KELEMEN *Physiopath. & Therapy Human Blood Dis.* i. 105 About 80–90% of plasma proteins, i.e. fibrinogen, albumin, and certain globulins, including most of the plasma coagulation factors, are formed in the liver. **1975** J. W. LINMAN *Hematol.* v. 183/1 Plasma fibrinogen is increased in persons with valvular prostheses or homografts.

plasmablast, var. *PLASMOBLAST b.

pla·sma cell. *Histology.* Also **plasma-cell.** [tr. G. *plasmazelle* (W. Waldeyer 1875, in *Arch. f. mikrosk. Anat.* XI. 189; also P. G. Unna 1891, in *Monatschr. f. prakt. Dermatol.* 1 Apr. 304): see PLASMA and CELL *sb.*[1]] † **a.** (In Dict. s.v. PLASMA 6.) *Obs.* **b.** A cell now recognized as the chief source of antibodies which is found in lymphoid tissue and at sites of chronic inflammation, and which has a strongly basophilic cytoplasm containing an extensive rough-surfaced endoplasmic reticulum and a usually eccentric nucleus. Cf. *PLASMACYTE.

1888 [in Dict. s.v. PLASMA 6]. **1895** *Jrnl. R. Microsc. Soc.* 613 Waldeyer's plasma-cells correspond in staining reactions to Ehrlich's *Mastzellen*, but not to Unna's 'plasma-cells', and Waldeyer proposes to give up his use of the term as applied to normal elements of connective tissue. The cells he described as 'plasma-cells' are Ehrlich's *Mastzellen* and eosinophilous cells. **1906** *Jrnl. Amer. Med. Assoc.* 20 Oct. 1272/2 The intimæ of the smaller arteries are lifted or completely dissected off by an exudate composed chiefly of cells of the lymphocyte series, among which are examples of the typical plasma cell. **1929** *Amer. Jrnl. Ophthalm.* XII. 731/1 In 1875 Waldever applied the name of plasma cell to a poorly differentiated type of wandering cell which he found in chronically inflamed connective tissue. **1940** *Acta Med. Scand.* CIII. 569 When Waldeyer..used the term plasma cell in 1875, he elected to do so not because he thought these cells secreted part of the plasma, but because of the abundant protoplasm. He made use of the term plasma cell to designate a number of different cells rich in protoplasm, but in subsequent works, especially those of Unna..and Marschalko.., the use of the name was restricted to the cell that is now known as the plasma cell: a cell rich in protoplasm, with eccentrically placed nucleus, relatively small, round or oval, with five to eight bands of chromatine extending from the centre like the spokes of a wheel; around the nucleus is a lighter zone, whilst the abundant protoplasm is otherwise dark, basophile. **1960** *New Biol.* XXXI. 100 Absolute proof that plasma cells make antibody was furnished by an ingenious and elegant technique devised by Dr. A. H. Coons. **1968** PASSMORE & ROBSON *Compan. Med. Stud.* I. xvi. 5/1 Plasma cells are found where foreign proteins are likely to gain entrance to the body, e.g. beneath the epithelial membranes lining the respiratory and alimentary tracts. **1975** *Lancet* 3 May 1031/2 The plasma-cell is one of the effector cells of the B-lymphocyte system.

Hence **plasma-celled** *a.*, composed of plasma cells; **plasmace·llular** *a.* (also **plasmo-** and as two words), of or pertaining to plasma cells.

1929 *Jrnl. Path. & Bacteriol.* XXXII. 293 (*heading*) Two cases of myelomatosis: (1) Diffuse plasma-celled (2) with tumour-like nodules and visceral lesions. **1947** *Nature* 12 Apr. 499/1 (*heading*) Plasma cellular reaction and its relation to the formation of antibodies *in vitro*. **1948** R. A. WILLIS *Path. Tumours* l. 787 The multinucleated cells of plasma-celled and other myelomas are of no special histogenetic significance. **1957** *Jrnl. Amer. Med. Assoc.* 4 May 20/2 In the broadest sense of the term this plasmocellular barrier may be called an immune process. **1971** *Biol. Abstr.* LII. 6201/2 The ultrastructure of plasmacellular paracrystalline inclusions, detected in the sternal marrow of a patient with type k micromolecular myeloma was studied.

plasmacyte (plæ·zmăsəit). *Histology.* Also **plasmo-.** [f. PLASMA + -CYTE.] = *PLASMA CELL b.

1941 I. N. KUGELMASS *Blood Disorders in Children* xiii. 498 Accumulation of plasmacytes is probably due to migration from the blood stream and subsequent multiplication by fission. **1961** *Lancet* 16 Sept. 639/2 We must think of the effective (abnormal) cells in the spleen as plasmacytes which have taken on the character of low-grade tumour cells. **1976** *Ann. Rev. Microbiol.* XXX. 591, B cells were being transferred to the local granuloma as the site of antigen, and were then transferring to antibody-producing plasmacytes.

So **plasma-, plasmocytic** (-səi·tik, -si·tik) *a.*, of, pertaining to, or composed of plasmacytes; **plasma-, plasmocy·toid** *a.*, resembling (that of) a plasmacyte.

1932 *Jrnl. Path. & Bacteriol.* XXXV. 545 Histologically the tumour was plasmocytic and there were many cells of giant size. **1959** M. BURNET *Clonal Selection Theory of Acquired Immunity* iv. 61 Active proliferation to produce plasmacytoid cells and lymphocytes with active antibody-liberating capacity. **1970** R. T. SILVER *Morphol. Blood & Marrow in Clin. Pract.* ix. 111 In other cases, the lymphocyte..may assume a plasmacytoid shape while still retaining the nuclear configuration of a lymphocyte. **1972** *Acta Med. Scand.* CXCII. 291/2 The morphological investigations have,..in most of the cases, revealed the presence of an infiltration in the lympho-reticular organs of plasmocytoid cells of varying maturity, probably responsible for the production of the monoclonal immunoglobulin. **1974** *Immunol.* XXVI. 486 The development of giant cells, epithelioid tubercles and plasmacytic infiltrates.

plasmacytoma (plæzmăsəitōᵘ·mă). *Path.* Also **plasmo-.** Pl. **-omas, -omata.** [mod.L., ad. G. *plasmocytom* (H. Boit 1907, in *Frankfurter Zeitschr. f. Path.* I. 172): see prec. and *-OMA.] A myeloma composed largely of plasma cells.

1907 *Index Medicus* V. Index 173/1 Plasmocytoma. **1931** *Amer. Jrnl. Med. Sci.* CLXXXI. 171 There appear in the literature cases of both extra-osseous and intra-osseous plasmocytomata. *Ibid.* 178 There is no very sharp line of demarcation between localized, benign plasmocytomata on the one hand, and the malignant, fatal multiple myelomata on the other. **1940** *Acta Med. Scand.* CIII. 569 There is no increase of globulin in a number of plasmocytoma cases. **1961** [see *MYELOMATOSIS]. **1972** [see *MULTIPLE *a.* and *sb.* A. 3 d]. **1973** *Jrnl. Bone & Joint Surg.* A. LV. 1749 Most solitary plasmocytomas eventually become classic multiple myelomas if they are followed long enough. **1976** *Lancet* 6 Nov. 1003/2 Bone-resorbing factors have also been identified in cultured human tumour cells, including those from plasmacytomas.

plasmacytosis (plæzmăsəitōᵘ·sis). *Path.* Also **plasmo-.** Pl. **-cytoses.** [f. as prec. + -OSIS.] The presence of more plasma cells than usual in a tissue.

1930 *Q. Cumulative Index Med.* VII. 1278/1 Uterine plasmocytoma and plasmocytosis. **1959** *New Engl. Jrnl. Med.* 5 Nov. 954/2 Multinucleate and atypical forms are observed in both the neoplastic and non-neoplastic plasmocytoses. **1963** *Lancet* 19 Jan. 125/2 In several cases there was bone-marrow plasmacytosis. **1968** *Amer. Jrnl. Clin. Path.* L. 304/1 Cytologically, all cases of plasmacytosis were characterized by proliferation of mature looking plasma cells in addition to more primitive lymphoreticular forms.

plasmagel (plæ·zmădʒel). Also **plasma gel.** *Biol.* [f. PLASMA + *GEL *sb.*] Gelatinous cytoplasm, such as surrounds the plasmasol in an amœboid cell. Cf. *PLASMASOL.

1923 S. O. MAST in *Proc. Nat. Acad. Sci.* IX. 258 By careful observations on Amœba proteus in motion the following structures can clearly be differentiated: (1) A central elongated fluid portion; (2) A solid layer surrounding the fluid portion; (3) A very thin elastic surface layer or membrane. The first I shall designate the *plasmasol*, the second the *plasmagel* and the third the *plasmalemma*. **1939** W. B. YAPP *Introd. Animal Physiol.* iv. 131 *Amœba* consists of three layers. On the outside there is a thin plasmalemma, which can be lifted off with needles and is of a dough-like consistency. Inside this is the plasmagel, which is solid, and includes the classical ectoplasm and some endoplasm; inside this again is liquid plasmasol. **1942** G. H. BOURNE *Cytol. & Cell Physiol.* iii. 97 Streaming in [the aquatic plant] *Elodea* cells is associated with gelation, and..is abolished by application of sufficient hydrostatic pressure to liquefy the cortical plasmagel. **1970** AMBROSE & EASTY *Cell Biol.* xi. 360 The plasma gel is located near the plasma membrane; it is generally free from granules and other inclusions. **1973** N. ADRESEN in K. W. Jeon *Biol. of Amœba* iv. 102 The large pseudopodia ..may contain several parallel streams of plasmasol, each running in its own tube of plasmagel.

plasmagene (plæ·zmădʒīn). *Genetics.* [f. PLASMA + *GENE.] A supposed cytoplasmic entity having genetic properties.

1939 C. D. DARLINGTON *Evol. Genetic Systems* xx. 121 The particles in the nucleus are genes; those in the plastids and cytoplasm may perhaps be treated more rigorously if we also think of them as genes—plastogenes and plasmagenes. **1952** [see *PLASMID]. **1963** E. MAYR *Animal Species & Evolution* vii. 172 Like the chromosomal genes, plasmagenes seem to consist of nucleic acid molecules (including possibly RNA). **1965** STERN & NANNEY *Biol. of Cells* xix. 529 The concept of the plasmagene, a gene-like cytoplasmic element capable of differential assortment and replication during development, provided a possible means of rationalization... Nevertheless, this interpretation was never generally accepted with enthusiasm. *Ibid.*, The episomes of bacteria..on occasion behave like plasmagenes. **1974** A. T. SOLDO in W. J. Van Wagtendonk *Paramecium* 377 When kappa particles were first discovered they were generally regarded as cytoplasmic units of hereditary or 'plasmagenes'.

Hence **plasmage·nic** *a.*, of, pertaining to, or being a plasmagene.

1950 *Heredity* IV. 17 The existence of plasmagenic subunits in any one of the self-duplicating, cytoplasmic structures has not yet been established. **1968** J. A. SERRA *Mod. Genetics* III. xix. 37 Probably infection is produced by a particle of the plasmagenic type.

plasmal (plæ·zmăl). *Biochem.* [a. G. *plasmal* (coined with *PLASMALOGEN): see PLASM and *-AL[2].] An aldehyde formed by the hydrolysis of a plasmalogen; chiefly used *attrib.* in **plasmal reaction,** a modification of the Feulgen reaction for detecting plasmalogens and aldehydes in tissue.

1925 *Chem. Abstr.* XIX. 1156 Plasmal is an aldehyde, a solid at ordinary temp. *Ibid.*, In accordance with its aldehyde nature, plasmal quickly takes a violet color when stained with H_2SO_3 fuchsin... This staining process is termed the plasmal reaction,..and the presence of plasmal, or its precursor plasmalogen, in frozen sections of tissues can be shown microscopically. **1949** *Stain Technol.* XXIV. 19 The plasmal reaction is here modified so that it is made specific for acetal lipids alone. **1966** *McGraw-Hill Encycl. Sci. & Technol.* X. 397/2 The Feulgen test for plasmalogens depends on the liberation of plasmal, principally palmitaldehyde and stearaldehyde, from these lipids by the action of mercuric chloride and acetic acid. **1969** *Acta Histochem.* XXXII. 425 (*heading*) Application of the plasmal reaction to suspensions.

plasmalemma (plæ·zmălemă). *Biol.* Pl. **-lemmas, -lemmæ.** [f. PLASMA + LEMMA[2].] The thin membrane immediately surrounding the cytoplasm of a cell, which restricts the passage of molecules into it.

1923 [see *PLASMAGEL]. **1931** J. Q. PLOWE in *Protoplasma* XII. 202 Mast (1924) has given us the term 'plasmalemma'... It has seemed permissible..to extend its use to the botanical world, and to employ it to denote a distinct, differentiated layer on the outer surface of the plant protoplast. **1965** K. ESAU *Plant Anat.* (ed. 2) ii. 15 Surface membranes delimit the cytoplasm from the wall (plasma membrane, plasmalemma, or ectoplast) and from the vacuole (vacuolar membrane, or tonoplast). **1965, 1970** [see *plasma membrane* s.v. *PLASMA 6 a]. **1970** *Austral. Jrnl. Bot.* XVIII. 285 Host plasmalemmae are invaginated by invading hyphae, and encapsulations are formed. **1971** *Proc. R. Soc.* B. CLXXVIII. 195 (*caption*) The plasmalemmas..of the two cells. **1976** *Nature* 9 Sept. 158/2 We report..a gradual increase in microviscosity of protoplast plasmalemma from petals of ageing rose flowers.

Hence **pla·smalemmal** *a.*, of, pertaining to, or formed from a plasmalemma.

1968 *Jrnl. Cell Biol.* XXXVII. 252 (*caption*) Grazing section of the endothelium in a blood capillary of rat myocardium showing the large accumulation of plasmalemmal vesicles..on the tissue front. **1975** *Ibid.* LXIV. 505/2 After fixation by immersion, the plasmalemmal membranes limiting the endothelial and epithelial cells were heavily delineated by the reaction product.

plasmale·mmasome. Also **-lemmo-.** *Cytology.* [f. prec. + *-SOME[4].] A plant or microbial cell organelle formed by invagination of the plasma membrane and composed of tissue derived from it.

1962 M. R. EDWARDS in *Abstr. 8th Internat. Congr. Microbiol.* 31/1 The ingrowths of the plasmalemma may branch repeatedly and anastomose to give rise to a complicated honeycomb-like organelle. This organelle may be termed a plasmalemmosome in view of its origin from the plasmalemma. **1968** *Ann. Bot.* XXXII. 468 In higher plants, at least some of the plasmalemmasomes appear to have granular or fibrillar contents within well-defined vesicles. **1973** *Protoplasma* LXXVI. 235 The morphology of plasmalemmasomes in the species examined is variable and ranges from vesicles or tubules within the plasmalemma invagination to parallel arrays of membrane lamellae. Plasmalemmasomes thus appear to be primarily excess plasma membrane that has accumulated, perforce, endocellularly.

plasmalogen (plæzmæ·lǫdʒěn). *Biochem.* [a. G. *plasmalogen* (Feulgen & Voit 1924, in *Pflügers Arch. f. ges. Physiol.* CCVI. 399): see *PLASMAL and *-OGEN.] Any of a class of phospholipids that yield an aldehyde on mild hydrolysis and are now regarded as having an unsaturated ether linkage in place of one of the fatty acid ester linkages.

1925 *Chem. Abstr.* XIX. 1155 Throughout the protoplasm of animal tissues there is to be found, very widely disseminated, a substance of lipoid character, insol. in water but sol. in org. solvents and extractable by alc., termed plasmalogen. When subjected to acids..this substance is split into undetd. components termed plasmal. **1964** A. WHITE et al. *Princ. Biochem.* (ed. 3) v. 75 Plasmalogens without a nitrogenous base, *i.e.*, α, β-unsaturated ethers of phosphatidic acid, have also been reported in animal tissues, *e.g.*, liver. **1964** [see *CEPHALIN[2]]. **1968** PASSMORE & ROBSON *Compan. Med. Stud.* I. x. 5/1 The plasmalogens have an unsaturated ether group, rather than an ester group, on the α position [of the glycerol molecule]. Those of ethanolamine and choline form a big proportion of the phospholipids of brain and heart.

Hence **pla:smaloge·nic** *a.*

1939 *Chem. Abstr.* XXXIII. 8635 This fraction contg. plasmalogenic acid (I) increases with the time of alk. hydrolysis. **1962** *Compar. Biochem. & Physiol.* V. 220 (*caption*) The arrow..points out the phosphatidic acid plasmalogen (plasmalogenic acid) characteristic of blood-fed leeches. **1970** R. W. MCGILVERY *Biochem.* xxiv. 600 The vinyl ether group [in plasmalogens] is believed to be formed by reduction of a diglyceride... The resultant plasmalogenic diglyceride reacts..to form phosphatidalcholine..in the same way that ordinary diglycerides react in the formation of the phosphatidylcholines.

plasmapause (plæ·zmăpǭz). [f. PLASMA + PAUSE *sb.*] The outer limit of a plasmasphere, marked by a sudden change in the plasma density and lying wholly within the magnetosphere (in the case of the earth extending up to several earth radii from its centre at equatorial latitudes).

1966 [see *PLASMASPHERE]. **1971** *New Scientist* 1 July 8/2 The time at which Io crosses the plasmapause [of Jupiter] and sets off a burst of radio emission therefore depends on the Sun's activity. **1976** T. BEER *Aerospace Environment* vi. 113 At around fifty-five degrees geographic latitude the plasmapause is in the F region and it is almost vertical. *Ibid.* vii. 137 We can expect a plasmapause on Mars somewhere above 400 km.

plasmapheresis (plæzmăfe·rĭsis, -fěrī·sis). *Med.* Also **-phoresis** (-fǒrī·sis), † **-pharesis.** [f. PLASMA + APHÆRESIS; *plasmaphoresis* by alteration (cf. *-PHORESIS).] The removal of blood plasma from the body by the withdrawal of blood, its separation into plasma and cells in a centrifuge, and the reintroduction of the cells suspended in a harmless medium.

1920 G. H. WHIPPLE et al. in *Amer. Jrnl. Physiol.* LII. 99 Bleeding a dog from a large artery and a simultaneous replacement of a red blood cell Locke's solution mixture may be called 'plasma depletion' or 'plasmapharesis'. **1927** M. BODANSKY *Introd. Physiol. Chem.* vii. 168 Reduction of the plasma proteins by plasmapharesis..results in a condition of shock. **1935** H. SOBOTKA in Harrow & Sherwin *Textbk. Biochem.* iv. 144 Experimental anemia produced by repeated withdrawal of blood or plasma (plasmapheresis). **1943** *Jrnl. Immunol.* XLIV. 112 Rabbits whose protein-reserves have been reduced by plasmapheresis and a low-protein diet (carrots) show a definitely lessened capacity to produce antibodies. **1971** *Nature* 27 Aug. 629/2 Before and during corticosteroid-induced labour large samples of plasma..were obtained by plasmaphoresis from chronically implanted catheters. **1974** PASSMORE & ROBSON *Compan. Med. Stud.* III. li. 16/2 The donation of blood by plasmapheresis is now a major part of blood transfusion practice. The main purpose is to procure large amounts of plasma rich in specific immunoglobulins..and blood grouping reagents.

plasma sheet (plæ·zmă ʃīt). Also **plasma-sheet.** [f. PLASMA + SHEET *sb.*[1]] A layer of plasma in the magnetotail which lies in the equatorial plane of the earth some distance beyond the plasmapause and has two branches that diverge to reach the earth in polar latitudes.

1966 *Physical Rev. Lett.* XVI. 138 (*heading*) Electrons in the plasma sheet of the earth's magnetic tail. **1970** V. M. VASYLIUNAS in G. Skovli *Polar Ionosphere* II. 27 Intense fluxes of electrons extend across the entire magnetotail, forming the plasma sheet, first detected by the Luna 2 space probe in 1959. **1974** *McGraw-Hill Yearbk. Sci. & Technol.* 276/2 The plasmasheet plays a key role in the development of the magnetospheric substorm.

plasmasol (plæ·zmăsǫl). Also **plasma sol.** *Biol.* [f. PLASMA + *SOL *sb.*[6]] Cytoplasm in the form of a sol, such as exists in the middle regions of amœboid cells. Cf. *PLASMAGEL.

1923, etc. [see *PLASMAGEL]. **1951** [see *GELATE *v.*]. **1970** AMBROSE & EASTY *Cell Biol.* xi. 360 The relative viscosity of the plasma sol is quite low, being about two to ten times greater than that of water; on the other hand the gel is a moderately rigid structure which shows elasticity and breaks on application of a critical force.

plasmasphere (plæ·zmăsfīəɹ). [f. PLASMA + SPHERE *sb.*] The roughly toroidal region surrounding the earth at latitudes away from the poles in which there is a relatively dense plasma of low-energy electrons and protons that is thought to rotate with the earth; an analogous region around another planet. Cf. *PLASMAPAUSE.

1966 D. L. CARPENTER in *Jrnl. Geophysical Res.* LXXI. 695/1 With regard to nomenclature, the word 'plasmapause' will be used when the three-dimensionality of the knee phenomenon is emphasized... The word 'plasmasphere' will be used to indicate the dense region inside the plasmapause, and 'plasma trough' to indicate the tenuous region outside. **1971** *New Scientist* 1 July 8/1 The work..led to this detection of the Jovian plasmasphere from the now well-known modulation of Jupiter's radio emission caused by Io. **1974** *McGraw-Hill Yearbk. Sci. & Technol.* 345/2 The characteristic changes in size and shape of the plasmasphere which are observed by satellites and by ground-based vlf measurements have a direct effect on the dynamics of the F region of the ionosphere and on the location of regions of wave turbulence in the outer magnetosphere.

Hence **plasmasphe·ric** *a.*

1974 *Nature* 29 Mar. 401/1 He II λ303 Å emissions will be incident on the night-time upper atmosphere, arising from resonance scattering of the solar helium lines..by plasmaspheric He^+ ions. **1978** *Ibid.* 26 Jan 310/2 Inside the plasmasphere the characteristic emission is a featureless 'plasmaspheric hiss' which effectively fills the high density region but is believed to be generated by cyclotron resonant interactions with >30 keV electrons near the outer edge of the plasmasphere.

plasmid (plæ·zmid). *Biol.* [f. PLASM + *-id* (cf. ID, *CHROMATID).] Any genetic structure in a cell that can replicate independently of the chromosomes; *esp.* one in the cytoplasm of a bacterium.

1952 J. LEDERBERG in *Physiol. Rev.* XXXII. 403, I propose *plasmid* as a generic term for any extrachromosomal hereditary determinant. *Ibid.*, The taxonomic classification of plasmids as viruses, symbionts, or plasmagenes should not obscure careful descriptions of their function, hereditary or pathological, or both. *Ibid.* 414, κ, a plasmid in *Paramecium aurelia*. *Ibid.* 425 This review has contrasted the various forms of plasmid: the hereditary parasites as against the functionally coordinated plasmagenes, with the mutualistic endosymbionts somewhere between. **1964** *Daily Mirror* 24 July 8/2 The Rogue Bug's real name is RTF plasmid—R.T.F. stands for Resistance Transfer Factor. It is a tiny particle that appears to move from one bacterial cell to another, carrying with it a built-in resistance to new drugs. **1969** A. M. CAMPBELL *Episomes* i. 13 Episomes are thus distinguished from chromosomal genes on the one hand and obligately cytoplasmic elements (plasmids) on the other. **1973** R. G. KRUEGER et al. *Introd. Microbiol.* xv. 421/1 There are..transmissible plasmids or sex factors like the F factor, which promote their own transfer to recipient bacteria, and there are nontransmissible plasmids which are incapable of transferring themselves to recipient cells. **1975** *Sci. Amer.* July 25 It has been called plasmid engineering, because it utilizes plasmids to introduce the foreign genes... Because of the method's potential for creating a wide variety of novel genetic combinations in microorganisms it is also known as genetic engineering. **1977** *Time* 18 Apr. 48/1 They possess much smaller closed loops of DNA, called plasmids—which consist of only a few genes.

plasmin. Add † *Obs.* to sense in Dict.

2. *Physiol.* A proteolytic enzyme which destroys blood clots by attacking fibrin.

1945 CHRISTENSEN & MACLEOD in *Jrnl. Gen. Physiol.* XXVIII. 581 Under this scheme the activated enzyme may be termed 'plasmin' in comformity [*sic*] with common usage for proteases, where the prefix indicates the source of the enzyme, followed by -in... The inactive enzyme as it occurs in serum and plasma may be designated as 'plasminogen' to indicate its source, the plasma, and also to indicate that it is in an inactive, precursor state... The term 'plasmin' has been used in the past to designate a fraction of blood obtained by a special salting-out procedure. This usage, however, has become obsolete and the possibility of confusion with the proteolytic enzyme system is remote. **1962** [see *fibrinolysin* s.v. *FIBRINO-]. **1968** PASSMORE & ROBSON *Compan. Med. Stud.* I. xxvi. 16/1 The active enzyme in this system, plasmin, is proteolytic but possesses a preference for fibrin as substrate. It is formed from an inactive soluble blood protein precursor, plasminogen, by the action of plasminogen activator. **1976** *Nature* 22 Jan. 235/2 Plasminogen is the plasma proenzyme which, on conversion to its active form, plasmin, is considered responsible for lysis of fibrin deposits resulting from physiological or pathological activation of the coagulation cascade.

plasminogen (plæzmi·nǒdʒěn). *Physiol.* [f. prec. + *-OGEN.] The inactive precursor, present in blood, of the enzyme plasmin.

1945 [see prec.]. **1962** *Lancet* 27 Jan. 191/1 The presence of plasminogen activator in tissue suggests that it may have a role in the removal of unwanted fibrin. **1968, 1976** [see prec.].

plasmoblast (plæ·zmoblɑst). *Histology.* [f. PLASMO- + -BLAST.] The precursor of a plasmacyte. † **a.** (See quot.; cf. *PLASMOCYTE a.) *Obs.*

1897 G. EISEN in *Proc. Calif. Acad. Sci.* (*Zool.*) I. 16 The polar accumulations must, therefore, be considered as something entirely separate from the balance of the cytoplasm; they, in fact, give rise to the plasmocytes, and may, therefore, appropriately be called plasmocytoblasts, or for the sake of brevity, plasmoblasts.

b. Also **plasmablast.** [a. G. *plasmoblast* (S. Moeschlin 1940, in *Helv. Med. Acta* VII. 231).] An immature plasma cell. Cf. *PLASMACYTE.

1942 *Amer. Jrnl. Anat.* LXX. 485 Moeschlin believes that some of the youngest lymphoid reticular cells begin to assume plasma cell characters, and that beginning with this 'plasmoblast' there is a developmental sequence of stages leading to the mature plasma cell, and that this sequence is probably independent of the lymphocytic line. **1949** *Jrnl. Exper. Med.* XC. 165 Maturation of plasmoblasts to plasma cells was associated..with reduction in the size of the nucleus and disappearance of the PNA [*sc.* pentose nucleic acid] in the nucleolus. **1959** M. BURNET *Clonal Selection Theory of Acquired Immunity* vii. 113 In lymph nodes the first small foci of plasmoblasts appeared in a perivascular situation near the arterioles of the medullary cords. **1973** R. I. WEED tr. *M. Bessis's Living Blood Cells & their Ultrastructure* vii. 521/1 Plasmablast. On a smear, this cell measures 15 to 20 microns in diameter. Its principal characteristic is the profound basophilia of its cytoplasm.

Hence **plasmobla·stic** *a.*

1970 *Jrnl. Nuclear Med.* XI. 599/2 EH was a 54-year-old W.F. with plasmoblastic multiple myeloma with widespread skeletal involvement, [etc.]. **1975** *Biol. Abstr.* LIX. 6033/1 In lymphoblastic and plasmoblastic acute leukemias pathological cells were capable of synthesizing various Ig classes.

plasmocellular, var. *PLASMACELLULAR *a.*

Plasmochin (plæ·zmǒkin). *Pharm.* [f. PLASMODIUM + G. *chin*(*in* QUININE.] A proprietary name for *PAMAQUIN. Cf. *PLASMOQUINE.

1926 *Trade Marks Jrnl.* 17 Mar. 631 Plasmochin... Chemical substances prepared for use in medicine and pharmacy. Bayer Products, Limited,..London,..merchants and manufacturers. **1926** *Lancet* 16 Oct. 825/2 The great merits of plasmochin are that it is cheaper than quinine, tastes better, and gives rise to less unpleasant secondary effects. **1926** *Official Gaz.* (U.S. Patent Office) 26 Oct. 715/1 I. G. Farbenindustrie Aktiengesellschaft..Germany. Filed Aug. 14, 1926. Plasmochin..Preparation for the Treatment of Malaria. Claims use since about December, 1925. **1948** J. H. BURN *Lect. Notes Pharmacol.* 90 Pamaquin was introduced by the Germans as plasmochin; it is a quinoline derivative. **1962** —— *Drugs, Med. & Man* xx. 197 Domagk was working in the Bayer fabrik in Elberfeld in Germany, where the advances had been made which led to the discovery of the antimalarial agents plasmochin and later atebrin.

plasmocyte (plæ·zmosəit). *Histology.* [f. PLASMO- + -CYTE.] † **a.** (See quots.) *Obs.*

1897 G. EISEN in *Proc. Calif. Acad. Sci.* (*Zool.*) I. 4 A new corpuscle, which I have termed *plasmocyte*. *Ibid.* 13 (*heading*) Plasmocytes.—I apply this name to a hitherto undescribed element in the blood, first described by me in the blood of Batrachoseps. **1897** *Jrnl. R. Microsc. Soc.* 271 The plasmocyte may be defined as a corpuscle, generally without a cell-wall, always without a nucleus, consisting of the archosome and three spheres of cytoplasm. It shows power of growth, movement, phagocytosis, &c. **1900** E. B. WILSON *Cell* (ed. 2) i. 52 Eisen ('97) asserts that in the blood of a salamander..the attraction-sphere..containing the centrosomes may separate from the remainder of the cell (nucleated red corpuscles) to form an independent form of blood-corpuscle or 'plasmocyte', which leads an active life in the blood.

b. var. *PLASMACYTE.

plasmocytoma, -cytosis, varr. *PLASMACYTOMA, -CYTOSIS.

plasmodesma (plæzmode·zmă). *Bot.* Also anglicized as **pla·smodesm** (-dez'm). Pl. **plasmodesmata**; also **-desmæ,** ‖ **-desmen, -desms**; (erron.) **-desma.** [a. G. *plasmodesma*, pl. *plasmodesmen* (E. Strasburger 1901, in *Jahrb. f. wissensch. Bot.* XXXVI. 503 (sing. form on p. 607)): see PLASMO- and DESMA.] A narrow thread of cytoplasm that passes through cell walls and affords communication between plant cells.

1905 *Amer. Naturalist* XXXIX. 220 A new point of view was introduced into the discussion by the very important paper of Strasburger, in 1901. He considered the protoplasmic connections as sufficiently clearly differentiated structures to rank as organs of the cell and proposed for them the name plasmodesmen. **1925** E. B. WILSON *Cell* (ed. 3) i. 103 It is probable that an important part in the coördination of the cell-activities is played by direct protoplasmic connections between cells ('cell-bridges', 'plasmodesms'). **1927** FRITSCH & WEST *Treat. Brit. Freshwater Algae* (ed. 2) 40 The pit-membrane in such cases is probably traversed by plasmodesmae. **1931** *Stain Technol.* VI. 127 (*heading*) A technic for demonstrating plasmodesma. **1934** L. G. Livingstone in *Amer. Jrnl. Bot.* XXI. 707 The only way to arrive at a satisfactory understanding of the true nature of plasmodesmata in the living plant is to study the cell walls in an unaltered state. **1935** —— in *Ibid.* XXII. 75 The word plasmodesma is proposed for the singular, to designate an individual structure, and plasmodesmata is used in the plural sense. **1941** *Bot. Rev.* VII. 254 Plasmodesmata generally run straight from cell to cell, and only in the neighborhood of intercellular spaces or pit membranes of narrow pits are the outer plasmodesmata curved. **1951** F. Drouet in G. M. Smith *Man. Phycol.* viii. 163 Species of *Stigonema* have trichomes which in age become multiseriate throughout; the spherical or depressed-spherical cells are connected by strands of protoplasm usually considered to be plasmodesmen. **1966** *Protoplasma* LXI. 82 In longitudinal sections of the plasmodesms the real continuity of the cytoplasmic membranes can be observed. **1975** *Ann. Rev. Plant Physiol.* XXVI. 13 Despite other suggestions, the word plasmodesma has continued to be used to describe a protoplasmic connection. *Ibid.* 14 Plasmodesmata have been described in angiosperms, gymnosperms, pteridophytes, bryophytes, and many algae.

Hence **plasmode·smatal** *a.*, of, pertaining to, or being plasmodesmata.

1961 in Webster. **1964** J. Heslop-Harrison in H. F. Linskens *Pollen Physiol. & Fertilization* II. 41 The peripheral archesporial cells show plasmodesmatal links with the tapetal cells, and these in turn with the cells of the inner wall layer of the anther. **1975** *Ann. Rev. Plant Physiol.* XXVI. 15 There are considerable technical difficulties involved in obtaining reliable estimates of plasmodesmatal frequency.

plasmogamy (plæzmǫ·gămi). *Biol.* [ad. G. *plasmogamie*: see Plasmo- and *-gamy.] The fusion of the cytoplasm of two or more cells.

1912 E. A. Minchin *Introd. Study Protozoa* viii. 128 In many cases, union of distinct individuals can be observed which have nothing to do with syngamy, since no fusion takes place of nuclei, but only of cytoplasm. Such unions are distinguished as plastogamy (or plasmogamy) from true syngamy. **1932** L. A. Borradaile et al. *Invertebrata* ii. 26 The union of nuclei is karyogamy: in most cases of syngamy it is accompanied by plasmogamy or the fusion of cytoplasm... Plastogamy..is plasmogamy without karyogamy. **1958** *Ibid.* (ed. 3) ii. 40 Here may be mentioned the union of individuals by fusion of their cytoplasm, the nuclei remaining distinct, which is practised by the Mycetozoa..and in some other cases. This process, which is not syngamy, is known as plasmogamy, and its product as a plasmodium. **1969** F. E. Round *Introd. Lower Plants* iv. 60 In most of the higher terrestrial fungi, plasmogamy, which is the fusion of small masses of cytoplasm containing the nuclei, is separated in time from karyogamy.

plasmoid (plæ·zmoid). *Physics* and *Astr.* [f. Plasm(a + -oid.] A coherent mass of plasma (*plasma 5*).

1956 W. H. Bostick in *Physical Rev.* CIV. 292/1 The plasma is emitted not as an amorphous blob, but in the form of a torus... We shall take the liberty of calling this toroidal structure a plasmoid, a word which means plasma-magnetic entity. The word plasmoid will be employed as a generic term for all plasma-magnetic entities. [*Note*] The term 'plasmon' (in line with the term 'geon' used by Wheeler) was originally proposed. However, David Pines (of Princeton University) has pointed out that the term 'plasmon' should be reserved for a quantum of plasma-oscillation energy. He kindly proposes the term 'plasmoid', which we adopt. **1962** Riley & Sailor *Space Systems Engin.* v. 129 Techniques have been developed..whereby doughnut-shaped 'blobs' of plasma or plasmoids can be projected by magnetic forces at speeds exceeding 10^7 cm/sec. **1971** S. Singer *Nature of Ball Lightning* viii. 119 Spherical plasmoids of relatively small dimensions, such as those reported for ball lightning or involved in experimental work, have presented greater difficulty for theoretical analysis. **1976** *Nature* 12 Feb. 451/1 As the galaxy ploughs through a dense intracluster gas at supersonic speed, it is envisaged to eject pairs of plasmoids in opposite directions, as commonly assumed for 'normal' double radio galaxies.

plasmolysis. Add: (Earlier example.) Hence also **plasmoly·tically** *adv.*, by means of plasmolysis; **pla·smolysed, -lysing** *ppl. adjs.*; **pla·smolysable** *a.*, capable of undergoing plasmolysis; **pla:smolysabi·lity.**

1883 *Q. Jrnl. Microsc. Sci.* XXIII. 151 (*heading*) On plasmolysis and its bearing upon the relations between cell wall and protoplasm. *Ibid.* 152 The protoplasmic body would appear to separate with a 'smooth surface' from the cell wall on treatment with the plasmolysing solution. *Ibid.* 153 Naegeli..described strings of protoplasm which connect the contracted protoplasmic body with the cell wall in plasmolysed cells. **1896** *Jrnl. Linnean Soc.: Bot.* XXXI. 370 A few of the younger leaves and leaf-cells are found to be living and plasmolysable, but show no assimilation. **1903** *Science* 1 May 706/2 A reduction of temperature gave rise to parthenogenetic spore formation.., as was also the case when water was plasmolytically withdrawn from the cells. **1955** P. J. Kramer in W. Ruhland *Encycl. Plant Physiol.* I. II. 212 Errors in the plasmolytic method include adhesion of the cytoplasm to the wall, penetration of the plasmolyzing solute, and difficulty in measuring cell volume. **1960** L. Picken *Organization of Cells* iii. 77 The plasmolysability of the cells implies that the cell wall cannot contract below a certain area. **1964** J. Levitt in D. W. Newman *Instrumental Methods Exper. Biol.* xiii. 420 These very cells, with which the incipient plasmolysis method leads to difficulties, cannot have their osmotic potentials determined in any other way, and at least approximate values may be obtained plasmolytically. **1971** *Nature* 16 July 159/2 Attempts to fix and section plasmolysed sieve tubes have not so far yielded supporting evidence.

plasmolyte (plæ·zmolǝit). *Physiol.* [f. Plasmo- + Gr. λυτ-ός loosed, soluble (f. λύειν to loosen), or f. G. *plasmolytikum* *plasmolyticum.] = next.

1927 *Biol. Abstr.* I. 238/2 The increase in volume after full plasmolysis is due to penetration of the plasmolyte. **1935** *Plant Physiol.* X. 119 That concentration of a harmless non-permeable plasmolyte which at osmotic equilibrium causes the protoplasm to recede ever so little from the cell wall. **1939** *Ibid.* XIV. 132 As a rule a minimal area form is not assumed during the process of plasmolysis but is reached either on standing in the plasmolyte, or at least after a slight degree of subsequent deplasmolysis. **1964** J. Levitt in D. W. Newman *Instrumental Methods Exper. Biol.* xiii. 419 Potassium nitrate was the plasmolyte used by many of the earlier investigators.

plasmolyticum (plæzmoli·tikʊm). *Physiol.* Pl. **-lytica.** [mod.L. (ad. G. *plasmolytikum*), f. Plasmo- + Gr. λυτικ-ός able to loosen (f. λύειν to loosen).] A substance used to produce plasmolysis.

1943 *Ann. Bot.* VII. 269 In experiments on rates of plasmolysis or deplasmolysis one would expect to find the wall-resistance exercising an effect when sucrose is used as the plasmolyticum. **1946** *New Phytologist* XLV. 7 The plasmolysis form taken up in any plasmolyticum, sucrose and KCl included, is much influenced by the distance of the cell from the cut edge of the strip of epidermis. **1973** Cocking & Evans in H. E. Street *Plant Tissue & Cell Culture* v. 100 Irreversible, damaging effects on the viability of isolated protoplasts readily result from the use of plasmolytica of either too high or too low an osmotic potential. **1974** A. J. Peel *Transport of Nutrients in Plants* x. 189 The sections were irrigated with plasmolytica composed of 0·5–2·0 M solutions of glucose or fructose.

plasmoma (plæzmōu·mă). *Path.* Pl. **plasmomata.** [f. Plasm(a + *-oma.] = *plasmacytoma.

1901 L. P. Hamburger in *Johns Hopkins Hosp. Bull.* XII. 43/1 Recently, Wright has described a myeloma in detail... The tumor elements, according to his research, really form a variety of plasma cells. A myeloma does not originate in the marrow cells as a whole, but in only one of its elements, the plasma cell. Following the results of this important contribution, the tumor may be classed as a plasmoma. **1931** *Amer. Jrnl. Med. Sci.* CLXXXI. 170 In our series of cases extra-osseous involvement occurred in..one of the plasmomata primary in a lymph node. **1961** *Arch. Path.* LXXI. 229 (*heading*) Extramedullary plasmacytoma of gastrointestinal tract with a case report of plasmoma of the rectum.

plasmon (plæ·zmǫn). [f. Plasm(a + *-on[1] (in sense 1 an arbitrary ending).] †**1.** Also **Plasmon.** A proprietary name of a soluble proteinaceous extract of milk; used *attrib.* to designate various foodstuffs made with this, as *Plasmon biscuit, chocolate, cocoa. Obs.*

1900 *Daily Express* 31 July 2/6 Plasmon is nothing more or less than milk dried after removing the cream and sugar. *Ibid.*, The writer has found Plasmon chocolate a most useful preparation in cycling. **1901** *Daily Tel.* 18 Mar. 11/6 (Advt.), Why Plasmon cocoa is a nourishing food. *Ibid.*, Plasmon is the albumen of pure fresh milk in the form of a dry, soluble, granulated white powder. **1906** *Trade Marks Jrnl.* 4 Apr. 477 *Plasmon*... Substances used as food or as ingredients in food. International Plasmon, Limited,..London,..food manufacturers. **1912** G. W. E. Russell *Afterthoughts* xvi. 157 Miss Larkins sups on strong coffee and a cigarette, and Meakin on hot milk with a plasmon biscuit. **1915** Galsworthy *Freelands* xxxvii. 335 Open your mouth and let me pop in one of these delicious little plasmon biscuits. They're perfect after travelling. **1921** R. Whymper *Cocoa & Chocolate* (ed. 2) xxiv. 359 Plasmon cocoa..a powder containing added matter in the form of dried milk solids (approximately sixty parts milk solids to forty parts cocoa powder). *Ibid.* 360 Plasmon, which was regarded as a soluble form of milk proteid, is rendered to some extent insoluble when added to cocoa. **1922** [see *hoosh *sb.*]. **1935** E. A. Knox *Reminisc. Octogenarian* x. 194 One of our side stole out during the debate, and fetched some 'Plasmon' biscuits. **1946** O. Sitwell *Scarlet Tree* III. iii. 48 He had.. altogether lost touch with his teeth, being confined by his doctor to a total diet of Plasmon biscuits, a health food.

2. *Genetics.* Also **-one.** [a. G. *plasmon* (F. von Wettstein 1927, in *Nachr. von der Ges. der Wissensch. zu Göttingen* (*Math.-Physik. Klasse*) 259).] The totality of cytoplasmic, or of extranuclear, genetic factors.

1932 *Proc. 6th Internat. Congr. Genetics* II. 281 The abnormal development of chlorophyll (pale color) may be caused by a non-Mendelian nuclear or cytoplasmic factor or by a certain state of the genome or plasmon. **1954, 1965** [see *plastome]. **1970** T. Dobzhansky *Genetics Evolutionary Process* x. 345 The plasmon of *E*[*pilobium*] *luteum* has retained its properties despite having carried an *E. hirsutum* genome for several generations. **1973** K. Mather *Genetical Structure of Populations* ii. 6 Together with the nuclear genotype, the plasmon can play its part in the process of adaptation especially..in the building up of barriers to crossing. **1976** Bell & Coombe tr. *Strasburger's Textbk. Bot.* 401 Plastome and plasmone mutations have been insufficiently studied..but their importance for evolution should not be underestimated.

3. *Astr.* and *Physics.* = *plasmoid.

1955 W. Bostick *Anat. of Plasmons* (U.S. Atomic Energy Comm., Rep. UCRL-4530) 2 Plasmons (plasma-magnetic entities) are toroidal packages of plasma wrapped up in their own magnetic fields. **1963** *Soviet Astron.—AJ* VI. 471/2 If the 'plasmons' ejected by the 'active' nuclei of radio galaxies experience no deceleration, the age of sources similar to Centaurus A and Fornax A will not exceed 10^8 years. **1971** R. C. Haymes *Introd. Space Sci.* xv. 447 The jet [of the galaxy M87] appears to be composed of a group of irregular concentrations of plasma, called 'plasmons' by some. **1974** *Nature* 23 Aug. 629/2 Christiansen has shown that a plasmon can travel a distance $D = M/(\pi \times 1{\cdot}67 \times 10^{-24}\, n_g\, r^2)$ before dispersing. Here M is the mass of the plasmon, r its radius and n_g the number density of the gas surrounding the component.

4. *Physics.* The quantum or quasiparticle associated with a collective oscillation of charge density.

1956 D. Pines in *Rev. Mod. Physics* XXVIII. 184/1 The valence electrons in the solid..are capable of carrying out collective oscillations at a high frequency... The valence electron collective oscillations resemble closely the electronic plasma oscillations observed in gaseous discharges. We introduce the name 'plasmons' to describe the quantum of elementary excitation associated with this high-frequency collective motion. **1966** C. Kittel *Introd. Solid State Physics* (ed. 3) viii. 233 It is possible to excite a plasmon by passing an electron through a thin metallic film..or by reflecting an electron from the film. The reflected or transmitted electron will show an energy loss equal to integral multiples of the plasmon energy. **1972** F. Wooten *Optical Properties of Solids* ix. 220 The bulk plasmons we have considered so far are purely longitudinal. They cannot couple to transverse electromagnetic waves. However, at the surface of a solid an oscillation of surface charge density fluctuations is possible. These surface plasmons exist in a number of modes. **1976** J. Kleczek *Universe* ii. 71 A plasmon is a quantum of plasma waves, just as photons are quanta of electromagnetic radiation.

Plasmoquine (plæ·zmǒkwin, -kwīn). Also **-quin.** *Pharm.* [f. Plasmo(dium + Quin(in)e.] A proprietary name for *pamaquin. Cf. *plasmochin.

1926 *Trade Marks Jrnl.* 22 Dec. 2757/1 Plasmoquine... Chemical substances prepared for use in medicine and pharmacy. Bayer Products, Limited,..London,.. merchants and manufacturers. **1927** *Proc. R. Soc. Med.* XX. 920 The detailed formula for plasmochin (plasmoquine), as it is now known, has not as yet been definitely stated. **1938** *Times* 22 Mar. 17/4 The striking success of acriflavine..is another case in point, and so also are.. atebrin and plasmoquin used in malaria. **1945** *New Biol.* I. 102 Atebrin (mepacrine) and plasmoquine are the most useful of the synthetic anti-malarial drugs. **1963** F. Hawking in Schnitzer & Hawking *Exper. Chemotherapy* I. xix. 693 Experiments in rabbits have been carried out by Pols..who tried..chlortetracycline, babesin,..and plasmoquine without significant results.

plasmotomy (plæzmǫ·tǒmi). *Biol.* [ad. G. *plasmotomie* (F. Doflein 1898, in *Zool. Jahrb.* (*Abt. für Anat. und Ontogenie*) XI. 317): see Plasmo- and -tomy.] A mode of reproduction in certain protozoans, in which the organism divides into two or more multinucleate daughter cells.

1902 *Encycl. Brit.* XXXII. 817/2 Cohn and Döflein have discovered cases of plasmotomy, in which a kind of protoplasmic bud of ectosarc and endosarc containing some nuclei becomes detached. **1947** *Jrnl. Morphol.* LXXX. 96 Finally, the organism undergoes plasmotomy into from 2 to 6 individuals. **1973** M. A. Sleigh *Biol. Protozoa* iv. 72 Division of a cell is normally preceded by nuclear division, by either mitosis or meiosis, although in some multinucleate forms fission and nuclear division are not linked, so that for example new individuals may be formed by plasmotomy in which the body is simply separated into multinucleate masses—at any time some nuclei may be found in mitosis in such organisms.

Hence **plasmoto·mic** *a.*

1949 *Jrnl. Morphol.* LXXXV. 164 Plasmotomic division into two daughter individuals does not results [*sic*] in a 50:50 distribution of the nuclei.

plaster, *sb.* Add: **3. b.** *U.S.* Plaster of Paris, formerly used as a top-dressing for soils.

1787 G. Washington *Diary* 10 June (1925) III. 222 Where the Plaister had been spread the white and red clover was luxuriant. **1816** U. Brown *Jrnl.* 6 June in *Maryland Hist. Mag.* (1915) X. 264 A poor Hill Country well watered & adapted to Plaster. **1839** J. Buel *Farmer's Compan.* xxii. 213 Districts..in which clover and plaster..were first introduced..have unquestionably made the most rapid strides in agricultural improvement. **1880** *Harper's Mag.* June 67/2 Another glance detects the ..farmer sowing his load of plaster across the whitening field.

4. plaster saint, a virtuous person; freq. in ironical use, a person who makes a show of virtue; a hypocrite.

1890 Kipling *Barrack-Room Ballads* (1892) 8 Single men in barricks [*sic*] don't grow into plaster saints. **1898** G. B. Shaw *Philanderer* IV, in *Plays Unpleasant* 148 You fraud! You humbug! You miserable little plaster saint! **1934** —— *On Rocks* II, in *Too True to be Good* 260 Theyd be sent back to Parliament by working class constituencies as if they were plaster saints. **1938** W. B. Yeats *New Poems* 13 My father upon the Abbey stage, before him a raging crowd: 'This Land of Saints,' and then as the applause died out, 'Of plaster Saints.' **1964** 'S. Woods' *This Little Measure* vi. 78 It's no good my setting up as a plaster saint..but I do think I'd draw the line at poison. **1965** *New Statesman* 30 Apr. 690/1 The total effect is that Tchaikovsky as plaster saint becomes a monster who couldn't have created anyone's music, let alone his own.

plaster, *v.* Add: **1. e.** (Further examples.)
1858 S. M. SCHMUCKER *Public & Private Hist. Napoleon III* x. 154 In an hour every prominent place in the capital was plastered over with proclamations. **1907** G. B. SHAW *John Bull's Other Island* III. 54 Ive seen them in that office, telling my father what a fine boy I was, and plastering him with compliments. **1924** A. HUXLEY *Let.* 29 Apr. (1969) 229 From Parma, which is a superb town, fairly plastered with Corregio's paintings, we went..to Mantua. **1953** *John o' London's Weekly* LXII. 3/4 They show two maps of middle England plastered with the names of remote villages and towns associated with the Lollard rising of 1413–14.

3. a. In other sports, to defeat utterly, to trounce.
1919 J. MASEFIELD *Reynard the Fox* 30 He could plaster All those who boxed out Tencombe way. **1951** *Amer. Speech* XXVI. 230/2 Normal *plasters* Western. **1958** F. C. AVIS *Boxing Ref. Dict.*, *Plaster*, to hit an opponent hard and often.

c. *trans.* To shell or bomb (a target) extensively or heavily.
1915 'I. HAY' *First Hundred Thousand* xviii. 262 The German front-line trenches had been 'plastered' from end to end. **1925** FRASER & GIBBONS *Soldier & Sailor Words* 224 *Plaster*,..to shell heavily, *e.g.* 'The village was plastered badly last night'. **1941** *Hutchinson's Pict. Hist. War* 14 May–8 July 224 At night there is a concentrated attack on Bremen; the shipyards there and at Vegesack are plastered with bombs. **1942** E. WAUGH *Put out More Flags* iii. 243 The bombers were not aiming at any particular target; they were plastering the ground in front of their cars. **1945** *Penguin New Writing* XXIV. 32 They've started firing... Here they come again. They're plastering the other side. **1957** 'N. SHUTE' *On Beach* vi. 185 You'd think with Boeing as the target all this area would have been well plastered. **1971** B. W. ALDISS *Soldier Erect* 249 Our gunners back at Zubza and Jotsoma kept plastering the heights from which the Japs plastered us.

5. c. Also, to treat (a crop) with plaster of Paris.
1814 J. TAYLOR *Arator* 155 [Bird-foot clover] among the plastered wheat will be three or four fold more luxuriant, than among the adjoining unplastered. **1852** *Trans. Mich. Agric. Soc.* III. 171 As soon as the corn came up, it was plastered on the hill.

plasterboard (plɑ·stəɹbōᵊɹd). Also **plaster board, plaster-board.** [f. PLASTER *sb.* II + BOARD *sb.* I.] A light-weight building board made of gypsum plaster with a reinforcing or strengthening material, now usu. thick paper bonded to both sides of a plaster core. Also *attrib.* and *fig.*
1906 *Sci. Amer. Suppl.* 29 Sept. 25703/1 Thin plaster boards are nailed on the rafters. **1914** *Chem. Abstr.* VIII. 2620 Plastic composition for making 'plaster board', boxes, etc., formed of straw pulp. **1919** *Ibid.* XIII. 1916 A mixt. for the manuf. of plaster-board is formed of calcined gypsum.., ground tan bark.., a 'hastener'..and about 30 lbs. H_2O for each 100 lbs. of the other ingredients. **1929** W. C. HUNTINGTON *Building Constr.* xiv. 464 Plaster board consists of a gypsum plaster core and surfaces of fibrous felt sheets pressed together. **1936** *Archit. Rev.* LXXX. 192 On the inside this is sound-proofed with wood rock, plaster board and American rock-wool in blanket form. **1946** *Times* 9 Sept. 15/6 Plasterboard partitions in existing buildings would serve to provide married quarters. **1956** *Builders' & Decorators' Ref. Bk.* VI. 24 Plaster boards should be fixed with $1\frac{1}{2}$-in. galvanized French wire nails No. 12 W.G. **1965** G. MCINNES *Road to Gundagai* xi. 197 Almost as well known as the actors were the props:..the 'ruin' of doric plasterboard which was Ninny's Tomb, Cleopatra's palace and Henry V's tent. **1973** A. ROSS *Dunfermline Affair* 72 Our separate rooms had once been one... The wall would probably be less solid than the others, perhaps even only plasterboard. **1974** *Times Lit. Suppl.* 22 Mar. 281/4 He dithers between the historical figure, who cannot fail at this stage to have some life in him, and the plasterboard Schuyler and his tedious sex life.

plaster-cast (plɑ·stəɹ,kɑːst). Also **plaster cast, plastercast.** [f. PLASTER *sb.* + CAST *sb.*] A reproduction in plaster made from a mould. Also *attrib.* and *fig.* and as *v. trans.* Hence **plaster-casting** *vbl. sb.* and *ppl. a.*
1825 [see PLASTER *sb.* 4]. **1842** *Knickerbocker* XX. 468 The head of Miss Jewett is a portrait, taken from a plaster cast. **1856** MRS. STOWE *Dred* I. 18 Bronzes and plaster-casts..gave evidence of artistic culture. **1859** [see PLASTER *sb.* 4]. **1912** D. H. LAWRENCE *Phoenix II* (1968) 271 The method of translation, we are told, is the 'plaster-cast': that is, the outward form is strictly preserved. **1919** 'W. N. P. BARBELLION' *Jrnl. Disappointed Man* 163 A plaster-cast mask of Voltaire when first hung up made him chuckle with indecent laughter. **1922** JOYCE *Ulysses* 411 Plastercast reproductions..such as Venus and Apollo. **1959** P. & L. MURRAY *Dict. Art & Artists* 248 Plaster Casting is an intermediate stage in the production of a piece of sculpture which is often the last process actually to be carried out by the sculptor himself. **1970** *Oxf. Compan. Art* 879/2 Plaster casts of limbs..may also be made direct from the human body and then used as models by the stone-carver. *Ibid.* 880/1 The Vienna Academy..had a plaster-casting workshop of its own and devoted a whole floor of its palatial building to its collection of casts. **1977** 'M. YORKE' *Cost of Silence* xv. 115 Footprints..were very distinct, and a detective was making a plaster cast of one of the sharpest.

plastered, *ppl. a.* Add: **2.** *slang.* Highly inebriated; drunk.
1912 *Dialect Notes* III. 585 *Plastered*,..very drunk. **1924** WODEHOUSE *Bill the Conqueror* xv. 242 Freddy had got so plastered and tried to play the trap-drums. **1931** —— *Big Money* xiii. 309 You would have expected something better from a business man like J. B. Hoke, even if he had been getting steadily plastered all the afternoon. **1934** E. WAUGH *Handful of Dust* iii. 110 The old boy's plastered. **1939** J. B. PRIESTLY *Let People Sing* iii. 71 He's gone to cool off. He's very bottled, fairly plastered. **1942** E. WAUGH *Put out More Flags* iii. 182 'If it had been anyone else but Angela, I should have thought she was tight.' 'Darling, she was plastered.' **1946** E. O'NEILL *Iceman Cometh* II. 118 Hanging around here getting plastered with you, Mac, is pleasant, I won't deny, but the old booze gets you in the end, if you keep lapping it up. **1953** L. HOBSON *Celebrity* iii. 29 'My God,' he confided to the ceiling, 'I'm plastered.' **1958** [see *HONKERS *a.*]. **1964** N. MARSH *Dead Water* iii. 75 He's overdone it to-night. Flat out in the old bar parlour..he was plastered. **1966** J. BETJEMAN *High & Low* 66 You're barmy or plastered, I'll pass you, you bastard. **1979** G. HAMMOND *Dead Game* xiv. 180 'I'll probably get plastered.'..Keith carried his pint over to Constable Murchy.

plastering, *vbl. sb.* Add: **1. d.** The treatment of wines with gypsum.
1872 THUDICHUM & DUPRÉ *Treat. Origin, Nature & Var. Wine* iv. 119 (*heading*) Plastering of wine and must. *Ibid.* 121 Diminution of yield is..not the only drawback connected with the plastering of wine. **1873** J. L. W. THUDICHUM *On Wines, their Production, Treatment & Use* ii. 16/1 Sherry..if properly treated, does not require either plastering, or the addition of..boiled must. **1895** S. P. SADTLER *Handbk. Industr. Org. Chem.* (ed. 2) 204 Of the methods of 'improving' wines, as it is termed, that known as 'plastering' is probably most largely practised. **1959** W. JAMES *Word-bk. Wine* 145 It is said that plastering was given a bad name in England by whisky distillers jealous of sherry's growing popularity. **1967** A. LICHINE *Encycl. Wines & Spirits* 405/1 *Plastering*, addition of plaster of Paris (gypsum or calcium sulphate) to low-acid musts to induce the necessary degree of acidity.

plasterless (plɑ·stəɹlės), *a.* [f. PLASTER *sb.* + -LESS.] Of a building, structure, etc.: not provided with plaster; lacking plaster.
1866 'MARK TWAIN' *Lett. from Hawaii* (1967) 101 A huge gridiron of plasterless lathing droops from above. **1919** J. MASEFIELD *Battle of Somme* 29 A few skeleton sheds of plasterless woodwork. **1926** *Public Opinion* 26 Mar. 310/1 A plasterless brick house would be preferable to a plasterless steel house.

plaster of Paris. Add: **b.** *U.S.* Formerly used as a top-dressing for soils.
1787 G. WASHINGTON *Diary* 10 June (1925) III. 222 We rid to the farm of one Jones, to see the effect of the plaister of Paris, which appeared obviously great. **1810** W. THORNTON *Let.* 22 June in J. Steele *Papers* (1924) II. 627 Salt can be brought up the river in sufficient quantity, & plaister of paris if necessary to give a good coat of white clover on the soil.

pla·sterwork. Also **plaster-work, plaster work.** [f. PLASTER *sb.* + WORK *sb.*] The surface of a wall or other builders' work executed in plaster. Hence **pla·sterworker,** = PLASTERER.
1600 [see PLASTER *sb.* 4]. **1797** J. WOODFORDE *Diary* 3 Nov. (1931) V. 77 My Back-Kitchen..almost all taken down of the Stud and Plaister Work. **1845** *Gloss. Terms Archit.* (ed. 4) 272 In the market-place at Newark is a wooden house with small figures and canopies over them in plaster-work. **1897** W. MILLAR *Plastering Plain & Decorative* i. 34 From 1750 to 1780 A. Wilton did some fine plaster work at Cambridge. **1908** G. P. BANKART *Art of Plasterer* vii. 97 Exeter is rich in examples of seventeenth-century plasterwork. **1926** M. JOURDAIN *English Decorative Plasterwork of Renaissance* i. 6 The names of the plasterworkers that have so far come down to us are English. **1959** M. S. BRIGGS *Conc. Encycl. Archit.* 252 Apart from its normal function of providing a smooth external or internal surface for walls and ceilings, plasterwork has often reached a high level of artistic excellence. **1977** *New Yorker* 4 July 66/2 The plasterwork inside the hall itself blossoms with Manueline exuberance.

plastery, *a.* Add: **b.** Built with plaster, or in a manner suggestive of plaster.
1862 'G. HAMILTON' *Country Living* 6 To move from this tumble-down old house..into a..plastery, shingly, stary, new one. **1907** *Daily Chron.* 18 Sept. 4/4 Plastery little red and white cottages and villas set at all angles among cabbage-plots.

plastery (plɑ·stəri), *sb.* [f. PLASTER *sb.* + -Y[3].] Plastered work; plastering.
1842 *Amer. Pioneer* I. 207 The stone work and plastery was done by major William Rutledge, a soldier of the revolutionary war.

plastic, *a.* Add: **I. 1. b.** (Earlier and later examples.) So *plastic surgeon*, one skilled in plastic surgery.
1839 *Brit. & Foreign Med. Rev.* VII. 388 We are, therefore, willing to confine ourselves, with our German author [*sc.* Zeis], to the use of the simple expression 'Plastic surgery', which is sufficient to imply generically all we mean. *Ibid.* 393 Syphilis, lupus, scrofula, &c. have made cases whereon to exercise the ingenuity of the plastic operator. **1853** J. ERICHSEN *Sci. & Art of Surg.* xlviii. 665 By plastic or reparative surgery is meant those processes by which mutilations are repaired, and loss of structure replaced. **1911** F. S. KOLLE *Plastic & Cosmetic Surg.* i. 8 The successful plastic surgeon has become an imitator of nature's beauty to-day. **1935** W. DE LA MARE *Early One Morning* 271 Even if he could delete the scar of a wound of this kind which time has healed, how many of us would hasten to consult the plastic surgeon? **1941** *Ann. Surg.* CXIII. 642 The title of Eduard Zeis' (1807–1868) book, published in 1838, was Handbuch der Plastischen Chirurgie, and he says: 'As far as I know I was the first to use the words "plastic surgery".' **1972** *Daily Tel.* 18 July 3/3 After the accident she had plastic surgery, but found fashion jobs hard to get because of her scars. **1974** J. GRADY *Six Days of Condor* 83 The plastic surgeons had done a marvelous job on his ear.

II. 4. b. Pertaining to, characterized by, or utilizing an ability to be permanently changed in shape, without fracture or rupture, by temporary pressure or tension; esp. in *plastic deformation* or *flow*.
1877 *Jrnl. Franklin Inst.* CIV. 228 (*heading*) Plastic flow. **1879** *Encycl. Brit.* IX. 240/2 More shapely bricks are thus produced than by plastic moulding. **1888** W. C. UNWIN *Testing of Materials of Construction* i. 18 When a body is subjected to the action of external forces, it undergoes a deformation which is either a deformation which disappears if the load is removed (elastic deformation), or a deformation which remains after the load is removed (plastic deformation). **1923** GLAZEBROOK *Dict. Appl. Physics* V. 395/1 Associated with plastic strain in many metals is the occurrence or formation of 'twinned' crystals. *Ibid.* 400/1 A viscous, under-cooled liquid, may..undergo deformation of a 'plastic' (*i.e.* non-elastic) nature. **1925** *Jrnl. Iron & Steel Inst.* CXII. 451 A consideration of the laws of plastic deformation of hot material during rolling and working. **1940** *New Statesman* 16 Mar. 360/1 In its simplest form we see plastic extrusion as combs or as cosmetic boxes, where the resin has been forced into a mould, with instantaneous cooling. **1951** *Gloss. Terms Plastics Industry* (*B.S.I.*) 24 *Plastic yield*, non-elastic deformation. **1963** E. S. HILLS *Elements Structural Geol.* xii. 355 Plastic deformation of wall-rocks is exhibited around the Bald Rock batholith, California. **1967** M. CHANDLER *Ceramics in Mod. World* ii. 63 Shaping methods..include..plastic pressing, and extrusion. **1968** A. H. COTTRELL *Introd. Metallurgy* xxi. 387 This leads to a plastic instability in which all subsequent deformation becomes concentrated in one short section..which stretches excessively and forms a narrow neck. **1968** R. W. FAIRBRIDGE *Encycl. Geomorphol.* 1191/2 Plastic flow will occur when an ice body attains a thickness of 100–150 feet. **1976** *Physics Bull.* Oct. 459/1 Most of part one is concerned with the elastic, plastic and fracture behaviour of minerals and rocks.

5. a. (Further examples.)
1881 *Engineering* 20 May 513/3 (*heading*) Richards' plastic metal. *Ibid.*, 'J. Richards' Plastic Metal' is being made by the J. Richards' Plastic Metal Company, of Charlotte-street, Birmingham. In general outward appearances it resembles..other varieties of white metal so largely used for lining bearings... Its special feature..is its great affinity for other metals..enabling it to be readily 'pasted on'. **1907** *Chem. Abstr.* I. 1077 Process of manufacturing a plastic material suitable for the production of fibers, pellicles, blocks, or plates, consisting in mixing together phenol, 17, casein, 40, pressing, heating.. and pressing again, then adding glycerol to give plasticity. **1908** L. DESVAUX *Brit. Pat.* 9313 A plastic product for the manufacture of combs, molded objects of any kind and similar applications, composed of a mixture in variable proportions of nitrocellulose and camphor,..and of the food product extracted from maize by treating this substance with higher alcohols. **1921** *Chem. Abstr.* XV. 1770 A description of the classes of com. materials falling under the category of plastic masses. B. divides the important and most useful products into 6 classes, (1) glues, (2) papier maché, (3) wood products, (4) cellulose products, (5) egg white and casein, and (6) resins. The criterion for plastics is the condition of the raw material or of the final product... B. takes exception to the older classification of plastics based on some temporary condition during manuf.

b. (Earlier and later examples.) [tr. F. *argile plastique* (Cuvier & Brongniart 1808, in *Jrnl. des Mines* XXIII. 432).]
1812 T. WEBSTER *Let.* 2 Aug. in H. C. Englefield *Description Isle of Wight* (1816) 210 The clay connected with this sand is frequently fit for the potter, and hence has been called the plastic clay. **1813** R. JAMESON in R. Kerr tr. *Cuvier's Essay on Theory of Earth* 227 The fundamental rock or basis of the [Paris] district is chalk. This chalk is covered with plastic clay, and what is termed coarse marine limestone. **1929** P. G. H. BOSWELL in Evans & Stubblefield *Hand-bk. Geol. Gt. Brit.* 417 The lowest Eocene deposits are therefore the Reading Beds.. which..consist of mottled clays ('Plastic Clay') and sands with a glauconitic bed at the base. **1955** G. G. WOODFORD tr. *M. Gignoux's Stratigr. Geol.* ix. 477 Mammalian remains are present..at the base of the plastic clay. **1961** B. KUMMEL *Hist. Earth* 8/2 Of the strata above the Purbeck beds and below the Plastic clay, the most conspicuous unit is the Chalk.

c. *plastic explosive*, an explosive of putty-like consistency that can be shaped by hand and so placed in intimate contact with its target; so *plastic bomb*, one containing plastic explosive; *plastic-bomb* vb. trans., *-bombing* vbl. sb.
1906 C. E. BICHEL *Brit. Pat.* 16,882 Add to the trinitrotoluol liquid resins..in such wise that..the crystalline trinitrotoluol with or without warming is worked in suitable mixing machines into a plastic explosive that detonates well. **1946** T. C. OHART *Elements of Ammunition* ii. 37 A plastic explosive known as RDX-composition C is formed by mixing about 88% cyclonite with 12% plasticizer. **1955** G. GREENE *Quiet American* III. i. 185 That day all over Saigon innocent bicycle-pumps had proved to be plastic bombs and gone off at the stroke of eleven. **1961** *Times* 12 July 10/3 Bombs made with plastic explosive were discovered not far from the entrance to the Simplon. **1961** *Economist* 25 Nov. 777/1 One farmer has

threatened to plastic-bomb the line. **1962** *Spectator* 23 Feb. 229/1 The imported disease of plastic-bombing the home of your adversary at the risk of maiming or killing his wife and children. **1962** *Daily Tel.* 14 June 14 Casual and indiscriminate plastic-bombing, in Paris as well as in Algeria, has been followed by attacks on a hospital..and on an oil-well. **1963** *Ann. Reg. 1962* 236 In France there were plastic bomb attacks, directed mainly against liberal politicians and journalists. **1976** N. Freeling *Lake Isle* xv. 113 A couple of cops stayed for a search. They got back..with an old army revolver, two-thirds of a kilo of plastic explosive, and a lot of gold coins.

d. *plastic bronze*, bronze containing a high proportion of lead, which is used for bearings on account of its softness.

1907 G. H. Clamer in *Chem. Engineer* Aug. 93 This alloy is largely sold under the name of 'plastic bronze'. **1939** [see *leaded *ppl. a.* e]. **1954** *Kempe's Engineer's Yearbk.* I. 633 'Plastic' bronze Cu 73 Sn 7 Pb 20.

e. *plastic wood*, a mouldable material that hardens to resemble wood and is used for filling knot holes, crevices, and the like.

1921 *Engineering* 9 Dec. 785 This material..is named by the firm 'Plastic Wood'. It is a collodion preparation made with very fine wood meal, and as supplied ready for use is of the consistency of soft putty. **1938** A. Durst *Wood Carving* 16 Knot-holes and blemishes of a like nature can be filled with plastic wood. This is a quickly-drying preparation of cellulose and wood pulp. **1974** J. Melville *Nun's Castle* ix. 205 The old wooden door frame had shrunk... The door around the lock had been built up with..plastic wood.

f. *plastic paint*, paint which is sufficiently thick and coarse when applied for it to retain a texture given to it with the aid of a brush, spatula, or the like.

1925 *Amer. Paint Trade Buyer's Guide* 208/2 Plastic Paint—*see* Plastic Relief Compositions. **1955** *Mod. Building Encycl.* 492/2 In addition to the excellent proprietary materials available, plastic paints may be prepared from equal parts of distemper and plaster-of-paris. **1974** E. McGirr *Murderous Journey* 28 A room painted with a dark shade of plastic paint.

g. *plastic crystal*, a soft substance in which the molecules occupy the points of a regular crystal lattice but have freedom of rotation about those points. (See also sense 5 in Dict.)

1961 *Physics & Chem. of Solids* XVIII. 8/2 In liquid crystals, by heating, the fluidity comes first, but in plastic crystals, the isotropy comes first. **1968** A. Bondi *Physical Properties of Molecular Crystals* vi. 140 The very small expansions of plastic crystals at their melting point generally result from the fact that a much larger expansion took place at a first-order transition of the crystal at some lower temperature. **1974** P. A. Winsor in Gray & Winsor *Liquid Crystals & Plastic Crystals* I. ii. 48 Plastic crystals separate in the crystal forms of the cubic system (rarely hexagonal) and to this extent resemble ordinary solid crystals. However, they show unusually low yield points. The most plastic..will flow under their own weight and although the majority are less soft, they may readily be cut with a knife or extruded through a small hole.

6. b. *Biol.* Pertaining to or (of an organism) exhibiting an adaptability to environmental changes.

1905 F. E. Clements *Research Methods in Ecol.* iii. 103 The amount of response to a stimulus is proportional to the intensity of the factor concerned. This does not mean that the same stimulus produces the same response in two distinct species, or..in two plants of one species. In these cases the rule holds only when the plants or species are equally plastic. *Ibid.* 146 Stable plants are less susceptible of evolution than plastic ones. **1930** *Jrnl. Ecol.* XVIII. 376 The broad-leaved plantain has proved, even within five months, exceedingly plastic. **1965** *Adv. Genetics* XIII. 133 The species that are plastic for leaf shape, that are able to produce both sorts of leaf, are all typically species of shallow water. *Ibid.* 137 Plastic response is able to provide adaptation to directional selection in some populations which in others is provided by genetic change.

IV. [Partly deriving from the sb. used attrib.] **9. a.** Made of plastic; of the nature of a plastic, or containing plastic as an essential ingredient.

1909 *Chem. Abstr.* III. 724 Artificial plastic materials industry... An interesting account..giving descriptions of the process for artificial rubber, leather, and substitutes; celluloid, viscoid, etc.; plastics obtained from cellulose and its compounds; and plastics from casein, maisin, albuminoids, and gelatins. **1911** E. C. Worden *Nitrocellulose Industry* II. xiv. 630 Formation of plastic rods and tubes was first successfully made by the patented process of I. and J. Hyatt. *Ibid.* 708 The manufacture of plastic cuffs and shirt bosoms. **1912** *Sci. Amer. Suppl.* 20 Apr. 246/1 The term 'plastic materials' is here employed in a restricted sense, including only such materials as celluloid and its numerous substitutes, which can easily be shaped by cutting and grinding, as well as by molding, and excluding artificial textile fibers and India rubber and ts imitations. **1931** *Brit. Plastics Year Bk.* 17 We have pleasure in presenting to the Plastics Industry the first Year Book..dealing exclusively with Plastic Materials. **1940** *Economist* 29 June 1108/2 Plastic structural material has been introduced into the aircraft industry. **1943** *Times Weekly Ed.* 10 Feb. 17/1 Plastic bearings were going into the heaviest engineering applications. **1949** E. Coxhead *Wind in West* ii. 36 His wife, in a thin..plastic raincoat, looked perished with cold. *Ibid.* 41 Little Mrs. Turner, who had gone nearly as blue as her plastic mackintosh. **1951** A. Baron *Rosie Hogarth* 60 She..hung plastic curtains in his bedroom. **1957** *Daily Mail* 5 Sept. 11/5 Pre-cooked hamburgers..in their little frozen transparent plastic bags. **1958** *Engineering* 14 Mar. 349/1 Acid wastes are disposed of through plastic pipes. **1958** *Observer* 6 July 9/4 The light plastic mac, easily stuffed into pocket or bag, comes into its own during the British summer. **1961** *Ann. Reg. 1960* 510 Growers of flowers complained that imports of plastic flowers, mainly from Hong Kong, were having an adverse effect. **1966** 'G. Black' *You want to die, Johnny?* x. 193 There were..plastic tiles on the floor. **1969** W. R. R. Park *Plastics Film Technol.* vi. 147 With the current proliferation of..plastics films, the growing interest in and use of plastic laminates may seem somewhat surprising. **1972** *Guardian* 16 Oct. 9/4 Furtive gestures by elderly men in plastic macs. **1975** *New Yorker* 29 Sept. 43/1 The couch and the armchairs are protected by plastic covers. **1977** B. Pym *Quartet in Autumn* xiii. 109 A plastic bag lying on the kitchen table.

b. *fig.* Artificial; superficial, insincere.

1963 *Daily Tel.* 22 May 16 The plan's promoters must not take it amiss if, winking an eye, some of our elder oysters inquire whether plastic houses might not connote plastic people. **1967** *Harper's* Aug. 19 Now that so many of the young seem to wear their hearts on their sleeves, it is hard to tell which ones are real and which ones are plastic. **1970** *Observer* (Colour Suppl.) 15 Feb. 24/1 Sinister influences are at work to turn Fiji into another Hawaii, that plastic paradise further along the route. **1974** *Times Lit. Suppl.* 1 Mar. 219/5 The characters are by no means badly drawn and the girl in particular is notably less plastic than usual. **1977** *Daily Tel.* 16 Apr. 16 The flabby, chalky, doughy slabs of our unpalatable plastic muck which masquerades as bread.

B. *sb.*[3] **I. 1.** A plastic material. **a.** A solid substance that can be readily moulded or shaped.

1905 E. H. Angle in E. C. Kirk *Amer. Text-bk. Oper. Dentistry* (ed. 3) xxiv. 720 Models sufficiently perfect cannot be made from impressions taken in modelling compound or other of the plastics. **1921** [see *A. 5]. **1923** *Blackw. Mag.* June 722/2 In the evenings Roupin constructed in plastic..a complete model of Haidar Pasha. **1933** L. F. Rahm *Plastic Molding* ii. 19 The molding properties of rubber are such as to make it one of the simplest plastics to handle. **1936** L. M. T. Bell *Making & Moulding of Plastics* i. 13 Dental uses of plastics... Stabalite [composed of china clay, rubber, sulphur, etc.] is used very largely for artificial palates. **1944** E. C. Jahn in L. E. Wise *Wood Chem.* xxiii. 820 In 1942..wood and lignin plastics are still largely in the developmental stage.

b. Any of a large and varied class of substances which are polymers of high molecular weight based on synthetic resins or modified natural polymers and may be obtained in a permanent or rigid form following moulding, extrusion, or similar treatment at a stage during manufacture or processing when they are mouldable or liquid; see also **laminated plastic*, **reinforced plastic*. Also used generically (without *a* and *pl.*): material of this kind.

In techn. usage the term is usu. held to exclude the synthetic rubbers (elastomers), and sometimes also any plastic in the form of fibres.

1909 L. H. Baekeland in *Jrnl. Industr. & Engin. Chem.* Mar. 156/2 As an insulator..it [*sc.* Bakelite] is far superior to hard rubber, casein, celluloid, shellac and in fact all plastics. *Ibid.* 157/1 It can be used for similar purposes like knobs, buttons, knife handles, for which plastics are generally used. **1911** E. C. Worden *Nitrocellulose Industry* II. xiv. 691 Pyroxylin plastic is extensively used for the bits of pipe stems, and consists of ordinary plastic containing..dyestuffs, picric acid, [etc.]. **1915** J. E. Crane in A. Rogers *Industr. Chem.* (ed. 2) xliv. 914 Pyroxylin plastics, variously called celluloid, xylonite,..viscoloid, and other names consist of a mixture or solid solution of cellulose nitrate and camphor. **1928** *Chem. Abstr.* XXII. 4209 Plastics are defined as materials that are horny and elastic at ordinary temp. but can be molded at higher temp. They include (1) cellulose plastics, (2) artificial resins and (3) protein plastics. **1935** *Economist* 7 Dec. 1140/1 The use of plastics in the motor accessory field will undoubtedly increase... Already the fitting of wireless sets as standard equipment on several cars has opened up a..new field for their application. **1941** *Electronic Engin.* XIV. 482 A large percentage of..plastics have good insulation properties, while at the same time the materials are available in a wide variety of forms..from lacquers..through rubber-like materials to the hard and rigid bakelite-type resins. **1945** *Daily Mirror* 27 Sept. 3/1 British-made women's shoes in 'patent leather' plastics may be on sale next summer. **1953** Kirk & Othmer *Encycl. Chem. Technol.* X. 798 When the resin itself is capable of being shaped into a finished article without a plasticizer.., as polystyrene, the terms resin and plastic are interchangeable for that material. **1955** *Observer* 13 Nov. 3/3 Nearly all plastics—except nylon stockings—crept into the house by the back door, disguised as 'cheap' substitutes for the real thing—china, glass, wood, metal, silk or wool. Now they have their own status, either as alternatives..or as new materials, to do a new job. **1963** H. R. Clauser *Encycl. Engin. Materials & Processes* 486/2 Silicones are unique among plastics, in that they are semiorganic, i.e., the molecular spine has alternating silicon and oxygen atoms with organic groups attached to the silicon. **1968** Kirk & Othmer *Encycl. Chem. Technol.* (ed. 2) XV. 790 Nylon and poly(ethylene terephthalate) are used both as fibers and plastics. **1973** *Materials & Technol.* VI. viii. 499 Twenty years later [*sc.* about 1890], casein plastics prepared by reacting together milk protein and formaldehyde were developed in Germany. **1973** *Sci. Amer.* Aug. 107/1 This container can be a baking pan made of sheet metal or plastic.

2. Plastic explosive.

1966 M. R. D. Foot *SOE in France* xi. 367 Though they had no plastic, they could get unlimited dynamite from the mines. **1968** D. Lampe *Last Ditch* vii. 75 Plastic is a form of cyclonite,..and is still today the standard military sabotage high explosive. **1973** D. Lees *Rape of Quiet Town* vii. 119 The bank manager type who'd been playing with the plastic had stayed behind. **1978** T. Allbeury *Lantern Network* ix. 112 Parker..showed them how to wire the plastic so that a whole length of track was taken out in a single explosion.

II. 3. *attrib.* in sense *1 b.

1911 E. C. Worden *Nitrocellulose Industry* II. xiv. 578 The general principles of plastic manufacture. *Ibid.* 660 The entire field of plastic molding. **1931** *Brit. Plastics Year Bk.* 69 The plastic trade consumes 1,200 tons of wood dust per annum for mouldings. **1956** A. H. Compton *Atomic Quest* 326 Paper, plastic, and textile plants. **1960** I. Wallach *Absence of Cello* 16 He was a trouble-shooter ..for a large plastic corporation. **1969** T. C. Thorstensen *Pract. Leather Technol.* xiv. 235 The increased 'plastic look' in leather may, in the long run, harm the marketing position of leather in its competition with synthetic materials.

4. Used *attrib.* in *pl.*, often to avoid possible confusion with branches I and II of the adj. **a.** Of, pertaining to, or concerned with plastics; = sense *3.

1925 *Plastics* Oct. 7/1 The plastics industry. **1935** *Economist* 4 Mar. 1042/2 Their interest in the plastics industry, through Mouldrite, Limited, continued to make progress. **1957** J. Braine *Room at Top* 61 He owned a plastics factory, a tannery, a bodywork builders.

b. = sense *9 of the adj.

1934 H. Read *Art & Industry* ii. 90 The wireless cabinet is an example of the encroachment of new plastics materials, such as bakelite, on a province hitherto reserved for wood. **1958** *Engineering* 7 Mar. 320/2 Various tools with plastics handles. **1971** *Daily Tel.* 15 Feb. 4/8 Plastics windows to protect passengers from stone-throwing are being installed in trains in the New York area. **1974** *Brit. Standard 4998* (*title*) Moulded plastics dustbins.

5. *Comb.* Instrumental, as *plastic-coated*, *-covered*, *-lined*, *-tiled*, *-topped*, *-wrapped* (so *-wrap* vb.) adjs. Parasynthetic, as *plastic-macked*, *-mackintoshed*.

1960 *Farmer & Stockbreeder* 23 Feb. 69/1 The cab framework is constructed of precision steel tubing and the weatherproof roof of plastic-coated nylon fabric. **1977** D. MacKenzie *Raven & Kamikaze* iv. 56 The wire was plastic-coated and copper, the sort of thing used on a radio. **1961** *House & Garden* June 136/2 Even a neat, plastic-covered plunge is not exactly a joy to behold. **1973** R. Lewis *Blood Money* viii. 125 There's a plastic-covered card identifying the dead man. **1969** *Jane's Freight Containers 1968–69* 239/3 The walls are of plastic-lined plywood plates. **1979** *Tucson Mag.* Apr. 64/2 Another alternative is a plastic-lined pool. **1964** *Guardian* 9 Sept. 5/8 Plastic-macked parents and hordes of soggy children. **1973** J. Wainwright *Devil you Don't* 25 A plastic-mackintoshed young woman. **1962** *Listener* 10 May 831/3 Plastic-tiled and similar floors also need damp-washing. **1957** *Observer* 13 Oct. 1/2 The Queen and the Duke..walked to a plastic-topped limousine which drew away to drive to Government House. **1973** D. Francis *Slay-Ride* xiii. 159 We sat at a plastic topped table amid travellers with untidy hand luggage. **1968** *Economist* 11 May 69/3 The meat is cut, quick-frozen and plastic-wrapped under contract to supermarkets and to restaurant chains. **1975** M. Bradbury *Hist. Man* ix. 148 Contemporary, plastic-wrapped food. **1978** B. Norman *To nick Good Body* xvi. 132 A lump of plastic-wrapped, processed Cheddar.

plastic, *sb.*[3]: see *plastic *a.* B.

-plastic, *suffix.* [f. -plast(y or Gr. πλαστ-ός formed + -ic.] Forming adjectives that correspond to sbs. in *-plasty* (Gr. -πλαστία, f. πλαστός formed) or *-plasia* (Gr. πλασία, πλάσις formation).

plastically, *adv.* (Earlier and later examples.)

1835 *Southern Lit. Messenger* Dec. 43/2 Pictorially, or graphically, or as a German would say plastically. **1957** G. E. Hutchinson *Treat. Limnol.* I. vii. 532 A slow fall in temperature apparently permits the ice to flow plastically over the lake surface without cracking. **1966** C. R. Tottle *Sci. Engin. Materials* vii. 158 Many materials show only a very short elastic range and begin to deform plastically at comparatively low stresses. **1972** J. G. Dennis *Structural Geol.* vi. 109 'Brittle' rocks could yield plastically.

plasticate (plæ·stikēit), *v.* [f. Plastic *a.* + -ate[3], prob. after *masticate.*] **1.** *trans.* To change (particles of rubber or thermoplastic) into a homogeneous plastic (mouldable) mass by passing it through a suitable extruder and usu. simultaneously heating it.

1929 W. A. Gordon *Brit. Pat. 334,509* (*title*) Machines for plasticating materials. **1934** *Industr. & Engin. Chem.* Mar. 349/1 Rubber, plasticated in the Gordon machine, which gives the same y_s value..as a sample of mill-massed rubber, appears much stiffer in factory processing operations. **1968** *Encycl. Polymer Sci. & Technol.* IX. 8 Machines are either single-stage, in which plastication and injection are done by the same cylinder, or double-stage, in which the material is plasticated in one cylinder and fed to a second for injection into a mold. **1975** *Mod. Plastics Internat.* Nov. 25/2 In the twin-screw section, powder PVC or other material is plasticated at low shear with close control over temperature.

2. [ad. F. *plastiquer.*] *trans.* To blow up or destroy with a plastic bomb.

1962 *Guardian* 3 Jan. 7/4 Paris butchers are now using plastic bombs against colleagues... One butcher's shop.. was 'plasticated' early this morning. **1965** D. Francis *Odds Against* (1967) xix. 222, I couldn't get hold of Radnor on account of the office phones being plasticated.

Hence **pla·sticated** *ppl. a.*, **pla·sticating** *vbl. sb.* and *ppl. a.*

1934 *Industr. & Engin. Chem.* Mar. 349/1 There is need of a method for detecting the difference..between the plastic properties of plasticated and mill-massed rubber. **1953** *Ibid.* May 970/2 The combined operation of melting and extruding is called 'plasticating extrusion'. **1959** J. B. PATON in E. C. Bernhardt *Processing of Thermoplastic Materials* iv. 228 In the design of an extruder used for processing thermoplastic materials, the complex operations of plasticating, compacting, and conveying..must also be considered. **1970** TADMOR & KLEIN *Engin. Princ. Plasticating Extrusion* i. 8 Today's plasticating extruders operate mostly in the speed range of 20–200 rpm.., extruding up to 3500 lb/hr of polymer.

plastication (plæstikēⁱ·ʃən). [f. prec. + -TION.] The action of plasticating.

1939 *Ann. Rep. Progr. Rubber Technol.* II. 116 Knowledge of the mechanism of plastication has been carried a stage further by a study of mastication in an internal mixer at various temperatures. **1968** [see *PLASTICATE *v.* 1].

plasticator (plæ·stikēⁱtəɹ). [f. as prec. + -OR.] An extruder for plasticating rubber or thermoplastic particles, usu. by subjecting them simultaneously to pressure and heat.

1934 *Industr. & Engin. Chem.* Mar. 349/1 Two distinctly different types of masticating machines are employed in modern rubber plants, mills, and plasticators. **1968** *Encycl. Polymer Sci. & Technol.* IX. 48 The most widely used contemporary machines [for molding plastics] include: (a) the ram injection-molding machine..; (b) the plunger- or screw-type plasticator..; and (c) the reciprocating-screw injection machine. **1972** P. W. ALLEN *Natural Rubber & Synthetics* vii. 196 In place of the standard [masticating] machines shown..some factories use a 'plasticator' which fulfils essentially the same function.

plastician (plæsti·ʃăn). [f. PLASTIC *a.* + -ICIAN.] An expert or specialist in plastic art, plastic surgery, etc.

1928 T. E. LAWRENCE *Let.* 16 Apr. (1938) 591 So many plasticians seem to admit to their notice the outside of machinery, and to exclude its purposefulness. **1933** *Archit. Rev.* LXXIII. 266/2 As a complement to the elaborate laboratory researches into the nature of thermoplastic.., there is need of research and experiment directed to the proper development of design... It [*sc.* Lethaby's *Art and Workmanship*] should be in the hands of every 'plastician'. **1934** *Punch* 26 Dec. 718/2 And, by marvellous plasticians in mysterious robes arrayed, Faces are most wonderfully and most fearfully remade.

Plasticine. Now usu. pronounced (plæ·stīsīn or plɑ·st-). Add further examples. Also *Comb.* and quasi-*adj.* (in *fig.* use).

1926 R. MACAULAY *Crewe Train* II. vii. 152 She..idled about with toy soldiers or plasticine or meccano. **1935** H. G. WELLS *Things to Come* xiii. 124 A nursery of children. Anno 2055. They play with plasticine, draw on sheets of paper.., build with bricks or run about after each other. **1958** *Spectator* 4 July 12/1 He was so pliant, so plasticine,..so insidiously seeing it all the other chap's way. **1967** H. PORTER in *Coast to Coast 1965–6* 177 The sugar..infesting their plasticine-like texture tasted of garlic. **1976** *Times* 28 Jan. 1/3 The Russians..would respect us more if we were led by an iron lady rather than a Plasticine man.

plasticity. Add: *spec.* **a.** Capacity for being moulded or undergoing a permanent change in shape.

1782–3, etc. [in Dict.]. **1867** V. OTTOLINI et al. *Terra-cotta Archit. N. Italy* 5 Plasticity and homogeneity of ingredients are the two conditions essential to the composition of any ceramic paste. **1933** L. F. RAHM *Plastic Molding* ii. 24 In molding, shellac compounds are generally preheated to sufficient plasticity to require no further heat from the mold. **1935** G. E. DOAN *Princ. Physical Metallurgy* v. 109 If deformation is continued until the temperature of the object is below the recrystallization temperature.., the plasticity of the metal may be insufficient and the object may crack in the operation. **1968** W. J. PATTON *Materials in Industry* iii. 61 Most forming operations during manufacture require plasticity for their execution. **1971** B. SCHARF *Engin. & its Lang.* i. 2 Ductility, malleability and plasticity are closely related properties.

b. *Biol.* Adaptability of an organism to changes in its environment.

1868 [in Dict.]. **1908** J. A. THOMSON *Heredity* iii. 72 It is certain that many unicellular organisms are very plastic, and it seems reasonable to suppose that as differentiation increased, restrictions were placed on the primary plasticity, while a more specialised secondary plasticity was gained in many cases, where the organisms lived in environments liable to frequent vicissitudes. **1951** *Jrnl. Ecol.* XXXIX. 217 Ecological plasticity..may be defined as the potentialities of expression of physiological characters that determine what factors of the environment shall limit the distribution of a species or other taxon. **1976** BELL & COOMBE tr. *Strasburger's Textbk. Bot.* 401 The wild strawberry..reproduces vegetatively by vigorous runners..and each clone can only develop the desirable genetic plasticity by means of stepwise somatic mutations (bud sparts). **1978** *Nature* 14 Sept. 140/2 The potential for plasticity of the developing mammalian visual system has been the subject of several investigations.

plasticization (plæstisəizēⁱ·ʃən). [f. PLASTIC *a.* + -IZATION.] The process of rendering (more) plastic or mouldable; *spec.* (*a*) addition of a plasticizer to a synthetic resin; (*b*) = *PLASTICATION.

1927 *Chem. Abstr.* XXI. 2535 The diff. methods of plasticization of a no. of natural and artificial plastics are discussed. **1937** A. JONES *Cellulose Lacquers* iv. 54 Plasticisation has long been studied in metallurgy in the production of soft alloys like solder and type metals. **1946** F. MARCHIONNA *Butalastic Polymers* xiii. 414 Plasticization [of Buna-S] may also be effected by first masticating the sheet and then subjecting it to thermal softening. **1953** KIRK & OTHMER *Encycl. Chem. Technol.* X. 773 The most important classes of thermoplastic resins requiring plasticization are the vinyls and the cellulosics. **1969** M. A. WHEELANS in W. S. Penn *Injection Moulding of Elastomers* ix. 84 Plasticization by screw is quicker, more controllable and gives a more homogeneous distribution of heat and viscosity than that given by a simple plunger system. **1972** *Nature* 21 Apr. 405/1 A number of other insecticide chemicals also caused plasticization of the abdominal cuticle.

plasticize (plæ·stisəiz), *v.* [f. PLASTIC *a.* + -IZE.] **1.** *trans.* To render plastic (mouldable); to produce or promote plasticity in (a substance), e.g. by addition of a plasticizer or by plastication.

1927 *Chem. Abstr.* XXI. 2535 Mech. and chem. methods for plasticizing such modern plastics as rubber, cellulose products, galilith [*sic*], phenol-formaldehyde resins, etc. **1931** *Engineering* 2 Jan. 26/1 The scrap [rubber] was then plasticised by treatment with steam in a horizontal heater. **1945** A. T. BIRKBY *Phenolic Plastics* viii. 92 Any attempt to plasticize a large mass of thermo-setting material at one time to a condition suitable for extrusion through a die in a continuous process would fail. **1957** H. R. SIMONDS *Conc. Guide to Plastics* iii. 111 Most resins are plasticized by heat, solvents, or plasticizers. **1969** M. A. WHEELANS in W. S. Penn *Injection Moulding of Elastomers* ix. 84 The rubber is heated and plasticized as it progresses along a retractable screw. **1971** *Nature* 9 July 88/2 Textile fibres which are in bulk production are usually used. These are..usually copolymers containing a proportion of a second molecule to plasticize the fibre and to allow it to be spun and handled more easily. **1972** *Ibid.* 21 Apr. 405/1 The acetone-treated insects neither became paralysed nor was their abdominal cuticle plasticized.

2. *trans.* To treat or make with plastic.

1940 *New Statesman* 16 Mar. 361/1 An enterprising silk manufacturer..'plasticised' gold lace so that it became a permanent table-cloth when used as a table-surface. **1970** *Daily Tel.* 13 Jan. 15/6 Walls and ceiling are covered with a check fabric..and it is specially plasticised to resist condensation. **1977** *Austral. House & Garden* Jan. 49/1 (*caption*) Atel's modular kitchen units have an Italian Parawood teak veneer surface that has been plasticised for easy care.

Hence **pla·sticizing** *vbl. sb.* and *ppl. a.*

1925 *Paint, Oil & Chem. Rev.* 22 Jan. 10/2 The resin 'may or may not have been treated with..a plasticizing agent'. **1927** *Chem. Abstr.* XXI. 2535 (*heading*) The influence of plasticizing on the mechanical-elastic properties of natural and artificial plastics. **1948** DALZELL & TOWNSEND *Masonry Simplified* I. i. 13 In order to yield a mortar, the lime or lime putty must exert a certain minimum plasticizing effect on the mortar. **1953** *Industr. & Engin. Chem.* May 989/1 A plasticizing extruder whose job is to transform the cold feed into a hot, formable melt. **1973** *Materials & Technol.* VI. viii. 606 For the plasticizing of the more polar cellulose nitrate the low-molecular phthalates are preferred.

plasticized (plæ·stisəizd), *ppl. a.* [f. prec. + -ED[1].] **1.** Rendered (more) plastic; treated with a plasticizer.

1943 *Industr. & Engin. Chem.* May 383/2 Paper and cloth coated with the plasticized esters may be crumpled without cracking the coating. **1971** *Nature* 3 Dec. 254/2 Plastic coatings may be applied to metals by dipping the preheated metal part into either a fluidized bed of polymer powder or into a liquid plastisol. The former process is applicable to polyethylene, nylon and unplasticized PVC, whereas the latter is applicable only to plasticized PVC compounds.

2. Treated or made with plastic.

1945 *Richmond* (Va.) *News-Leader* 26 July 27/2 Sheer originality is seen in the new plasticized beaver fur coat which will not mat or curl in the stormiest weather. **1972** *Daily Tel.* 7 Jan. 13 The cover-ups in plastic or plasticised cotton are good for sploshy activities like painting, attempts at cooking.

3. *fig.* = *PLASTIC *a.* 9 b.

1974 *Globe & Mail* (Toronto) 12 Oct. 8/1 The CEGEPs are huge, modern, plasticized education factories of as many as 5,000 students with little discipline, relaxed standards and the best equipment money can buy. **1975** R. H. RIMMER *Premar Experiments* (1976) ii. 156 A simpler world of man experiencing man instead of machines and a plasticized environment?

plasticizer (plæ·stisəizəɹ). [f. PLASTICIZE *v.* + -ER[1].] Any substance which when added to another makes it (more) plastic or mouldable; *spec.* one (usu. a solvent) added to a synthetic resin to produce or promote plasticity and flexibility and to reduce brittleness.

1925 *Paint, Oil & Chem. Rev.* 29 Jan. 10/3 In order that the film may remain flexible..plasticizers—inert liquids of low vapor tension—are incorporated in the lacquer. **1943** H. R. FLECK *Plastics* vii. 160 Poly-vinyl chloride as formed is a hard brittle amorphous white powder which is useless for moulding purpose until plasticizer is added. **1947** J. C. RICH *Materials & Methods of Sculpture* xi. 342 Films of lacquer tend to harden and to become brittle as they age. For this reason plasticizers must be added to a lacquer formula. **1948** DALZELL & TOWNSEND *Masonry Simplified* I. i. 16 In cement concrete, lime functions as a plasticizer. **1962** A. NISBETT *Technique Sound Studio* 248 Direct-cut disc... These are made of cellulose nitrate (which contains a castor oil plasticizer to soften it for easy cutting) but are often referred to as 'acetates'. **1967** M. CHANDLER *Ceramics in Mod. World* iv. 132 Most steatite electrical products..are most commonly shaped by dust-pressing, but because the body contains little clay the ceramist adds artificial plasticizers such as waxes or polyvinyl alcohol. **1971** *Materials & Technol.* II. v. 253 The so-called plasticisers which are added to mortars improve their working properties by causing air to be entrained into them at the time of gauging the mortar. **1972** *Ibid.* V. xxii. 844 Hairsprays nearly always include an important minor ingredient called a 'plasticizer' which softens the resin film and prevents it flaking on the hair.

plasticky (plæ·stiki), *a.* Also **plasticy.** [f. *PLASTIC *sb.*[3] + -Y[1].] Suggestive of or resembling plastic.

1972 *Oxford Times* 12 May 20/4 His elder daughter Julie, 9, 'smelt plasticky fumes'. **1972** *Daily Tel.* 21 June 13/3 The interior [of the car] is rather 'plasticy' and the seats became hot in the sunshine. **1979** R. RENDELL *Make Death love Me* xvi. 144 The gun..was a toy, as you could tell really by the plasticky look of it.

plasticware (plæ·stikwēᵊɹ). [f. PLASTIC *a.* + WARE *sb.*[3]] Articles made of plastic.

1972 *Science* 2 June 1039/2 We used plasticware or siliconized glassware..throughout the experiments. **1975** *New Yorker* 24 Nov. 102/2 D/R has imported a collection of opaque plasticware, in yellow, red, green, or white, from the firms of the celebrated English designer Terence Conran.

plasticy, var. *PLASTICKY *a.*

plastidome (plæ·stidōᵘm). *Cytology.* [a. F. *plastidome* (P. A. Dangeard 1918, in *Compt. Rend.* CLXVI. 440), f. *plastide* PLASTID *sb.* 2, after *chondriome, chromosome,* etc.] The plastids of a cell collectively.

1926 *Science* 18 June 620/2 Following..the non-committal terminology of the Dangeards, the components demonstrated are as follows: (1) Spindle fibers and cytoplasmic network... (2) Plastidome... (3) Spherome... (4) Vacuome. **1971** W. STUBBE in J. Reinert et al. *Origin & Continuity of Cell Organelles* 77 We assume that the division of the plastidome into a number of lentil-shaped chloroplasts and the consequent increase in surface may be the reason for the prevalence of this type among higher plants.

plastifier (plæ·stifəi,əɹ). [f. as next + -ER[1].] = *PLASTICIZER.

1919 H. DREYFUS *Brit. Pat. 160,225,* This invention has reference..to the manufacture of celluloid-like masses of any kind having a basis of cellulose ac[e]tate wherein high boiling solvents, called plastifiers, for the cellulose acetate, are incorporated with the mass in conjunction with one or more volatile liquids or diluents. **1971** *Materials & Technol.* II. ii. 111 Plastifiers and air-entraining agents. These materials improve the workability of concrete mixture.

plastify (plæ·stifəi), *v.* [f. PLASTIC *a.* + -IFY.] = *PLASTICIZE *v.* 1, 2. Hence **pla·stifying** *vbl. sb.*

1919 H. DREYFUS *Brit. Pat. 160,225,* The solvent action on the cellulose acetate increases so that this is more and more dissolved and plastified until..only very little volatile diluent remains. **1963** H. R. CLAUSER et al. *Encycl. Engin. Materials & Processes* 348/1 A reciprocating plunger..forces the material into the plastifying cylinder. An equal quantity of fluid plastic is thus forced out of the front of the cylinder..into the mold. **1963** *Engineering* 13 Sept. 330/2 The concrete..is 'plastified' and remixed intensively by vibration. **1972** *Buenos Aires Herald* 4 Feb. 14/2 (Advt.), Floors polished, scraped, repaired, plastified.

plastigel (plæ·stidʒel). [f. PLASTI(C *a.* + *GEL *sb.*] A plastisol thickened to a putty-like consistency so that it retains its shape when heated.

1952 *Mod. Plastics* Jan. 99/1 Plastigels may be handled by many of the conventional methods of fabricating plastics but the pressures required are lower, leading to lower machine and mold costs. **1954** *Plastics Engin. Handbk.* x. 283 The control over the flow which is obtained with plastigels makes it possible to coat open-weave cloth or porous surfaces without excessive penetration. **1969** *Encycl. Polymer Sci. & Technol.* X. 246 With certain plasticizers or with modified paste resins the plastisol may become a gelatinous mass, or plastigel, under controlled conditions.

plastimeter, var. *PLASTOMETER.

plastique. Add: **2.** Statuesque poses or slow graceful movements in dancing; the art or technique of these.

1893 G. B. SHAW *Music in London 1890–94* (1932) III. 111 The unhappy students had been taught 'plastique' until they dared not call their arms and legs their own. The plastique professor..is almost as fatal a person as the harmony professor. **1897** —— *Our Theatres in Nineties* (1932) III. 146 Her interest in life and character will be supplanted by an interest in plastique and execution. **1947** *Ballet Ann.* I. 56 *Romeo and Juliet*..does contain both the passionate, lyrical dancing and strong, dramatic *plastique* demanded by the tragedy. **1960** *Times* 15 Mar.

6/1 Jive and an expressionistic development of *plastique* give more to these ballets than footwork. **1977** *New Yorker* 16 May 79/2 True to the 'Oriental' plastique of the period, the steps are all turned in.

3. Plastic explosive; a plastic bomb. Also *attrib.*

1968 L. W. ROBINSON *Assassin* (1969) xvi. 199 He planted another bomb... Bomb squad says it's made of *plastique*. **1969** E. AMBLER *Intercom Conspiracy* (1970) vi. 136 They had no trouble..fixing the *plastique*, the bomb. **1974** *Publishers Weekly* 11 Feb. 64/2 To hold hostage a TV studio audience with a human plastique bomb.

‖ **plastiqueur** (plast*i*kör). [Fr.] A person who plants or detonates a plastic bomb. Also *fig.*

1961 *Economist* 4 Nov. 435/1 Professor Palmer is the last and not the least of the *plastiqueurs*, as readers of the press learned not long ago, when he alleged that Evans had misstated some of his evidence in support of his pet theories. That explosion in the press was what gunners call a premature, and did Professor Palmer's discovery little good. **1962** *Times* 23 Apr. 9/2 The *plastiqueurs* were daily at work in metropolitan France. **1971** *Guardian* 17 July 9/4 The plastiqueurs were..soundly committed to private enterprise.

plastisol (plæ·stisǫl). [f. PLASTI(C *a.* + *SOL *sb.*[6]] A dispersion of particles of a synthetic resin in a non-volatile liquid consisting chiefly or entirely of plasticizer, which can be converted into a solid plastic simply by heating (cf. *ORGANOSOL).

1946 *Mod. Packaging* Mar. 262/2 It is possible to prepare these dispersions without any volatile carrier. Such 100% solids dispersions are known as plastisols. **1954** [see *hot dipping* (*HOT *a.* 12)]. **1963** H. R. CLAUSER *Encycl. Engin. Materials & Processes* 489/1 One of the most dramatic applications of plastisols is as a lining for kitchen dishwashers. **1971** [see *PLASTICIZED *ppl. a.* 1]. **1980** *Daily Tel.* 17 Jan. 11 (Advt.), A major manufacturer of PVC resins, compounds and plastisols.

plastochron (plæ·stǒkrǫn). *Bot.* Also **-chrone** (-krōᵘn). [a. G. *plastochron* (E. Askenasy 1878, in *Verhandl. des Natur-hist.-med. Vereins zu Heidelberg* II. II. 76), f. Gr. πλαστό-ς formed, moulded (see -PLAST) + χρόν-ος time.] The interval of time between consecutive formations of leaf primordia (or of pairs of such primordia) in a growing shoot apex of a plant.

1929 *New Phytologist* XXVIII. 41 These differences may partly be accounted for by the fact that an interval elapses—called by some authors the 'plastochron'—between the initiation of successive primordia. **1938** PRIESTLEY & SCOTT *Introd. Bot.* xiii. 173 In the ⅜ system it will be noted..that each primordium is three plastochrones removed from its one neighbour, two from the other. **1957** *Amer. Jrnl. Bot.* XLIV. 298/1 A plastochron is conventionally defined as the time interval between initiation of two successive leaves. It might be more broadly defined as the interval between corresponding stages of development of successive leaves, and one might choose initiation, maturity, or any intermediate stage of development as the stage of reference. **1960** *Ibid.* XLVII. 707/1 This plastochron, averaging 3 wk. in length, delimits the 2 developmental stages of the heterophyllous shoot.

b. Special Combs.: **plastochron index,** an index of the developmental age of a shoot, being the number of leaves that are not less than some stated length, plus a fractional adjustment so calculated that the value of the index changes smoothly as the shoot grows; **plastochron ratio** (see quot. 1948).

1955 F. J. MICHELINI (*title of Ph.D. Dissertation, Univ. Pennsylvania*) The use of the plastochron index in studies of morphological and physiological development in *Xanthium italicum* Moretti. **1973** R. MAKSYMOWYCH *Anal. Leaf Development* i. 5 The leaf plastochron index (LPI) can be used in developmental studies limited specifically to only one leaf. **1948** F. J. RICHARDS in *Symp. Soc. Exper. Biol.* II. 226 The differences between the various orders of phyllotaxis have been referred to differences in the ratio of the distances of two successive primordia from the apical centre... The ratio will be referred to as the 'plastochrone ratio'. **1968** C. W. WARDLAW *Morphogenesis in Plants* ix. 231 As the several systems..in Fibonacci phyllotaxis have closely comparable divergence angles, i.e. about 137·5°, the essential differences between them are due to their plastochrone ratios. As the *P.R.* approaches unity, the phyllotaxis rises.

Hence **plastochro·nic** *a.*

1953 K. ESAU *Plant Anat.* v. 104 The changes in the morphology of the shoot apex occurring during one plastochron may be referred to as plastochronic changes. **1957** *Amer. Jrnl. Bot.* XLIV. 302/1 Much would be gained by determining the precise plastochron age of each apex, rather than..judging the plastochronic phase subjectively.

plastocyanin (plæstosəi·ănin). *Biochem.* [f. *CHLORO)PLAST + -O + CYANIN.] A blue copper-containing protein (differing slightly from species to species) which is found in the chloroplasts of green plants and in certain bacteria, and is involved in photosynthesis.

1961 KATOH & TAKAMIYA in *Nature* 25 Feb. 665/2 In view of its localization in the chloroplasts and its characteristic blue colour in the oxidized form, the name 'plastocyanin' is proposed for this copper protein. **1966** *Plant Physiol.* XLI. 1641/1 From its absorption spectrum, the plastocyanin of *C. reinhardi* resembles the plastocyanin of spinach. **1974** *Sci. Amer.* Dec. 74/1 (*caption*) The electron is passed through a series of carrier molecules including..plastoquinone..and cytochrome *f*.., to plastocyanin. **1976** *Nature* 27 May 344/2 The 'small blue proteins'—azurins from bacteria, plastocyanins from photosynthetic cells.

plastome (plæ·stōᵘm). *Genetics.* Also **plastom.** [a. G. *plastom* (O. Renner 1929, in *Handb. d. Vererbungswissenschaft* IIA. 32), f. *plastid* PLASTID *sb.* 2, after *genom* *GENOME.] The sum-total of the genetic factors or information in the plastids of a cell.

1954 P. MICHAELIS in *Adv. Genetics* VI. 290, I propose.. with Renner (1929) to include all extranuclear hereditary elements of the cell in the term plasmon, and to subdivide this into (1) the cytoplasmon, that is, the elements of the cytoplasm, and (2) the plastom, that is, the hereditary elements of the plastids, etc. **1965** WETTSTEIN & ERIKSSON in S. J. Geerts *Genetics Today* xvi. 594 In higher plants two non-chromosomal genetic systems controlling chloroplast structure and function—the plastome and the plasmone—have long ago been recognized from the different modes of inheritance of certain chloroplast defects. **1967** KIRK & TILNEY-BASSETT *Plastids* ix. 277 There are as many as five genetically different plastoms within the subgenus *Euoenothera*. **1976** [see *PLASMON 2].

plastometer (plæstǫ·mĭtəɪ). Also **plasti·meter.** [f. PLAST(ICITY + -OMETER.] An instrument for measuring the plasticity of a substance. Hence **plasto·metry.**

1919 BINGHAM & GREEN in *Proc. Amer. Soc. Testing Materials* XIX. II. 645 As we wish, in a sense, to measure the 'plasticity' of a paint the apparatus for making the measurements has been called a 'plastometer'. **1922** E. C. BINGHAM *Fluidity & Plasticity* 319 (*heading*) Practical plastometry. **1933** *Physics* IV. 285/1 The theory of parallel-plate plastometry. **1940** *Brit. Standard Methods testing Latex* (*B.S.I.*) 26 Compress the pellet between thin sheets of paper under a load of 5 kg. in a parallel plate plastimeter. **1946** *Nature* 14 Sept. 371/1 The original type of plastometer, devised by Bingham, is still in use, with slight modifications, in many laboratories to-day. **1958** *New Scientist* 5 June 112/1 (*caption*) This machine..is a capillary plastometer..and is particularly suitable for studying the flow properties of semi-solid materials. **1971** J. A. C. HARWOOD in C. M. Blow *Rubber Technol. & Manuf.* iii. 59 The elastic recovery is measured by the height of the sample a fixed time after removal from the plastimeter.

plastoquinone (plæstokwi·nōᵘn). *Biochem.* [f. *CHLORO)PLAST + -O + QUINONE.] Any of a homologous series of compounds which have a quinone nucleus with a terpenoid side-chain, and which occur in the chloroplasts of plants; *spec.* one having the formula $C_{48}H_{72}O_2$.

1958 F. L. CRANE in *Plant Physiol.* XXXIV. 547/1 It is proposed that Q_{254} should be called plastoquinone... This name will serve to emphasize the localization in chloroplasts and possibly other plastid structures. **1968** *New Scientist* 25 Jan. 189/1 Terpenoids in chloroplasts of green leaves include..plastoquinone. **1973** *Biochim. & Biophys. Acta* CCCI. 36 Several homologues of plastoquinone..have been detected in algae and chloroplasts of higher plants... The detailed chemical structure of plastoquinones B and C is not known yet. **1975** D. JARVIS tr. *D. Hess's Plant Physiol.* 41 Another important redox system which is engaged in electron transport in photosynthesis is plastoquinone. **1978** *Sci. Amer.* Mar. 111/3 The two electrons that cross the membrane from P-680 are picked up at the outer surface by a hydrogen carrier similar in structure to ubiquinone but called plastoquinone, or PQ.

plastron. Add: **3. c.** *Ent.* [a. Fr. (F. Brocher 1912, in *Ann. Biol. Locustrine* V. 141).] In certain aquatic insects, a type of external gill formed by a patch of cuticle covered with hairs which retain a thin layer of air under water. Also *attrib.*

1947 THORPE & CRISP in *Jrnl. Exper. Biol.* XXIV. 227 (*title*) Studies on plastron respiration. *Ibid.* 229 The volume of gas in the plastron is negligible. **1959** SOUTHWOOD & LESTON *Land & Water Bugs Brit. Is.* 367 The air film is self-renewing: oxygen continually diffuses in and out, the whole forming a plastron, or external gill. **1969** R. F. CHAPMAN *Insects* xxiv. 481 The volume of the plastron is constant and usually small since it does not provide a source of air but acts as a gill. **1976** H. E. HINTON in H. R. Hepburn *Insect Integument* xxv. 482 In *Ptyopteryx*..the only diffraction lines are those formed by the plastron on the ventral surface of the abdomen.

plat, *sb.*[2] **I. 5.** (Earlier example.)

1788 J. BACKUS *Jrnl.* in W. W. Backus *Genealogical Mem. Backus Family* (1889) 20 A beautiful platt of a considerable extent.

plat, *sb.*[3] **II. 2.** (Further examples.)

1954 *Ann. Assoc. Amer. Geographers* XLIV. 248 Areal boundaries on the congressional township plats do not always clearly differentiate the several areal units such as marshes, prairies, wet prairies, swamps, and timberlands. **1974** *Sumter* (S. Carolina) *Daily Item* 24 Apr. 15A/4 A plat showing where the land is located must also be submitted before any transfer of land can be made. **1977** *Sci. Amer.* Sept. 184/1 (*caption*) The computer-held data in turn can be fed to a plotter that will automatically convert days of field observations into a standard surveyor's plat.

plat, *sb.*[6] Add: **b.** *plat du* (erron. *de*) *jour*: dish of the day; one of a restaurant's specialities on any particular occasion; also *fig.* and *ellipt.* as *plat.*

1906 W. J. LOCKE *Beloved Vagabond* (1907) vi. 71 The placarded list of each day's *plat du jour*. **1934** I. STONE *Lust for Life* v. xi. 374 The man scanned the menu, ordered a *plat du jour*, and within a moment was scooping up his soup with a large spoon. **1953** WODEHOUSE *Performing Flea* 213 We formed up in a queue, each man with a porcelain bowl for the *plat de jour* and a plate or a tin or a cigar-box for the potatoes. **1960** *Guardian* 3 Feb. 8/7 On Thursday the plat du jour will be paella. **1975** R. ROSTAND *D'Artagnan Signature* (1976) xxxvii. 210 Davis ordered the *plat du jour* and a full *pichet* of *vin rosé*. **1979** *Guardian* 26 Feb. 10/6 The Poetry Society seems to have achieved some success... The main plat du jour was the announcement of the winner of its new £1,000 prize. **1979** B. PETERSON *Peripheral Spy* vi. 147 A menu..informed him that the *plat* today was *tendrons de veau*, a favourite of his.

platanna (plata·nă). *S. Afr.* Also **platana, plathander.** [Afrikaans, f. PLAT *a.* + *-hander* HANDER[2].] The clawed frog or toad, *Xenopus lævis*, belonging to the family Pipidæ and native to South Africa.

1898 *Empire* 24 Sept. (Pettman), It's a platana, one of them web-footed, flat-backed, smooth-skinned, yeller frogs, with a mouth that goes all round its neck. **1911** J. D. F. GILCHRIST *S. Afr. Zool.* 224 The..Plathander (flat hand) or Clawed toad..occurs in most pools of water. **1949** *Cape Times* 21 Sept. 13/4 Two hundred female platanna frogs..left Stellenbosch yesterday on an adventurous journey to Canada. **1961** D. M. COCHRAN *Living Amphibians of World* 52/1 The three inner toes of the platanna's hind foot..bear the short black claws. **1971** C. A. DU TOIT in D. J. Potgieter et al. *Animal Life S. Afr.* 267/2 Just over thirty years ago physiologists in Cape Town, using the platanna as a test animal, discovered and perfected the first reliable test for pregnancy.

plate, *sb.* Add: **I. 1. d.** A number of animal skins sewn together, for making up into fur coats or for linings, trimmings, etc.

1910 *Encycl. Brit.* XI. 354/2 A very great feature of German and Russian work is the fur linings called rotondes, sacques or plates. **1957** M. B. PICKEN *Fashion Dict.* 256/1 *Plate*,..2. Skins sewn together, but not completely fitted or finished, for fur linings; also used to make garments or trimmings. **1972** *Guardian* 11 Aug. 7/8 The [import] ban did not include 'plates'—sections of fur coats ready to be made up. **1974** *Encycl. Brit. Macropædia* VII. 816/1 The less costly skin-on-skin method consists of sewing one full skin adjacent to another in a uniform alignment. This method is sometimes employed to sew the leftovers of full skins such as paws and flanks, into blanket-like 'plates' that are then fashioned into garments.

e. *Geol.* Each of the several nearly rigid pieces of lithosphere which are thought to make up the whole of the earth's surface and to be moving slowly relative to one another, the boundaries between adjacent ones being identified with well-defined belts of seismic, volcanic, and tectonic activity.

[**1904** H. B. C. SOLLAS tr. *Suess' Face of Earth* I. II. xxii. 600 Towards the north [of North America], however, a very extensive 'plate' without folding appears, which stretches nearly to the Arctic archipelago. **1910** *Bull. Geol. Soc. Amer.* XXI. 191 As Suess says, we do not know the character of the platforms upon which lie the seas behind island arcs;..the platforms may be composed of ancient, crystalline rocks which moved as 'plates' without parallel foldings.] **1965** J. T. WILSON in *Nature* 24 July 343/1 Many geologists have maintained that movements of the Earth's crust are concentrated in mobile belts, which may take the form of mountains, mid-ocean ridges or major faults... This article suggests that these features are not isolated, that few come to dead ends, but that they are connected into a continuous network of mobile belts about the Earth which divide the surface into several large rigid plates. **1969** *Jrnl. Geophysical Res.* LXXIV. 4298/2 In the New Guinea mainland the zone of southerly dipping earthquakes can be associated with the northern edge of the Australian continent meeting the Pacific 'plate' and creating an overthrust zone of mountain building. **1972** *McGraw-Hill Yearbk. Sci. & Technol.* 305/1 Lithospheric plates are..segments of upper mantle and crust, varying in thickness from approximately 5 km at ridges to 150 km under central areas of continents, that are generated by growth of crust and mantle at oceanic ridges..and consumed in trenches. **1976** M. A. KHAN *Global Geol.* viii. 147 The lower boundary of the plates is the base of the rigid lithosphere which moves over the plastic convecting asthenosphere. The plates are therefore often referred to as lithospheric plates.

4. f. Also, a similar portion of any orthodontic appliance; by extension, the whole denture or other appliance.

1932 E. BOWEN *To North* v. 44 Her confirmation.., the fixing-in of a plate to correct prominent teeth,..had all been reported to him. **1973** M. AMIS *Rachel Papers* 162, I had been coming down from Oxford about six times a year since I was ten so that he could put in and take out all the lousy braces and plates and other crap with which he tried to tame my mouth. **1977** B. PYM *Quartet in Autumn* v. 52 He had to visit the dentist, to adjust his new plate and to practise eating with it.

h. *Electr.* A metal plate that acts as a charge-storing electrode in a capacitor.

1782 *Phil. Trans. R. Soc.* LXXII. p. xxvii, An ample conductor, weakly electrified, imparts a considerable quantity of electricity to the metal plate of our condenser.

1801 *Encycl. Brit.* Suppl. I. 591/1 The mode of accumulating great quantities of fluid by means of parallel plates. **1887** P. BENJAMIN *Age of Electricity* xi. 259 The condenser will be charged with a quantity of electricity depending upon..the surface of the plates opposed to each other, and..the number of plates in the respective sets. **1923** E. W. MARCHANT *Radio Telegr. & Teleph.* ii. 15 A condenser can be charged by supplying positive electricity to one plate and negative electricity to the other. **1963** A. F. ABBOTT *Ordinary Level Physics* xxxv. 460 A parallel-plate capacitor is set up as shown.., one plate being earthed and the other..charged.

i. *Electr.* A metal electrode in a cell or battery, esp. one in the form of a plate or grid.

[**1801** H. DAVY in *Phil. Trans. R. Soc.* XCI. 397, I have found that an accumulation of galvanic influence, exactly similar to the accumulation in the common pile, may be produced by the arrangement of single metallic plates, or arcs, with different strata of fluids.] **1807** —— in *Ibid.* XCVII. 15 The strong action of a battery of 150 pairs of plates of 4 inches square. **1828** F. WATKINS *Pop. Sk. Electro-Magnetism* 15 Batteries of this construction usually consist of ten or twelve pairs of plates. **1923** GLAZEBROOK *Dict. Appl. Physics* II. 71/1 The container [of a dry cell] is made of zinc and this is used as the zinc plate. **1963** A. F. ABBOTT *Ordinary Level Physics* xxxvi. 474 In modern commercial practice the plates [of a lead-acid cell] are made of grids of a lead-antimony alloy filled with paste... Red lead (Pb_3O_4) is used for the positive plates and litharge (PbO) for the negative plates. **1970** *AA Bk. Car* 82/4 When the surfaces of both plates have turned completely to lead sulphate, the battery is flat.

j. *Electronics.* The anode of a thermionic valve.

1905 J. A. FLEMING in *Proc. R. Soc.* LXXIV. 477 It is preferable to use a metal plate carried on a platinum wire sealed into the glass bulb, the plate being bent into a cylinder which surrounds both the legs of the carbon loop. *Ibid.* 479 The resistance of these valves..may be anything from a few hundred ohms up to some megohms, depending on the state of incandescence of the filament.., as well as upon the size of the filament and the plate. **1915** *Electrician* 21 May 244/2 The plate of the pliotron oscillator is then connected to one of the terminals of the condenser. **1948** A. L. ALBERT *Radio Fundamentals* vi. 178 The plate usually surrounds the cathode in high-vacuum diodes. **1975** D. G. FINK *Electronics Engineers' Handbk.* VII. 21 The collector element for the electron flow is the anode, or plate.

5. d. The number plate of a motor vehicle.

1950 J. D. MACDONALD *Brass Cupcake* (1955) iii. 23 She's got a grey Chevvy business coupé with Massachusetts plates. **1970** *Globe & Mail* (Toronto) 28 Sept. 27/4 (Advt.), 2 door sedan, 3 cylinder, 2 cycle. Not certified, no plates. **1973** R. LEWIS *Blood Money* vi. 67 That car..ended in some garage with a bent mechanic stripping it, respraying it, changing the plates. **1975** *Drive* New Year 98/1 Secondhand plates are not expensive but they can be difficult to obtain.

9. (Earlier and later examples.)

1836 *Spirit of Times* 20 Feb. 6/2 Having the misfortune to break the plate on her left hind foot on one side,.. she was withdrawn after the first heat. **1937** E. RICKMAN *On & off Racecourse* vi. 130 If a horse is to be relieved of the considerable weight of these shoes, during a race they must be replaced by light plates made of aluminium or other suitable alloy. **1965** D. FRANCIS *Odds Against* viii. 119 Horses race in thin light shoes called plates... Blacksmiths change them before and after, every time a horse runs.

12*. *Baseball* and *Softball.* A flat piece of metal or stone marking the home base; the home base itself. Also *fig.*

[**1857** *Spirit of Times* 28 Feb. 420/3 The home base and pitcher's point to be each marked by a flat circular iron plate, painted or enamelled white.] **1867** *Ball Players' Chron.* 5 Sept. 5/1 Thorne..pitched slow, 'drop' balls, many of which struck outside of 'the plate'. **1886** H. CHADWICK *Art of Pitching & Fielding* 43 When the Umpire indicates the height of the ball required, the pitcher should send it in at once at the height required, but not over 'the plate'. **1902** *Encycl. Brit.* XXVI. 161/2 This corner is marked by a white plate a foot square, sunk level with the ground, and called the home base. **1917** C. MATHEWSON *Sec. Base Sloan* 172 Ellis walked to the plate and faced Chase grimly determined to get a hit. **1931** D. RUNYON *Guys & Dolls* (1932) x. 224 Jo-jo squares away at the plate. **1936** *N.Y. Herald Tribune* 4 Oct. II. 2/1 The Democrats have scored in their half of the last inning, but the Republicans still have a chance to bat. Alfred E. Smith has just come up to the plate for them. **1952** B. MALAMUD *Natural* (1963) 70 When Roy came up with Wonderboy, he hugged the plate too close to suit Fowler who was in there anyway only to help the batters find their timing. **1967** C. POTOK *Chosen* i. 16, I went up to home plate for some batting practice. **1973** C. SAGAN *Cosmic Connection* xv. 112 If he swings and misses—or, more likely, if the ball is wide of the plate—he can then go home for a two-hour nap, returning with his catcher's mitt to catch the ball. **1977** *Guernsey Weekly Press* 21 July 8/6 Rangers pushed five runs over the plate before going one down, but errors..were mainly responsible.

II. 14. c. Delete †*Obs.* and add later examples.

1880 L. HIGGIN *Handbk. Embroidery* i. 9 *Plate* consists of narrow plates of gold or silver stitched on to the embroidery by threads of silk. **1881** C. C. HARRISON *Woman's Handiwork* I. 54 Bullion, passing, plate and spangles are employed in silk embroidery.

15. d. As a non-collective *sb.*: A thin coating of metal, esp. one applied electrolytically.

1915 *Chem. News* 10 Dec. 288/1 Plates on various stock pieces satisfactorily withstood the various bending, hammering, and burnishing tests. **1946** *Trans. Electrochem. Soc.* LXXXIX. 384 The nickel-cobalt plate is whiter, harder and more corrosion-resistant than nickel deposits. **1959** T. M. ROGERS *Hand-bk. Pract. Electroplating* 14 The work is..given a thin plate of Rochelle copper. **1974** P. D. GROVES *Electrochem.* xii. 92 A mixture of nickel (II) sulphate and nickel (II) chloride together with a boric acid buffer and a wetting agent..produces a good plate which resists wear and abrasion, even at high temperatures.

17. (Earlier and later examples.) Also *fig.*

1639 R. VERNEY *Let.* in F. P. Verney *Memoirs* (1892) I. viii. 185 'My Lord Carlile's white nagg,' says Ralph, 'hath beaten Dandy, and Sprat woone the cup, and Cricket the plate.' **1910** *Encycl. Brit.* XIII. 728/2 In 1739 an act was passed to prevent racing by ponies and weak horses,..which also prohibited prizes or plates of less value than £50. **1939** JOYCE *Finnegans Wake* (1964) I. 39 The classic Encourage Hackney Plate was captured by two noses in a stablecloth finish, ek and nek. **1955** *Times* 5 Aug. 4/1 Magic Key may be favourite to open the card at Lewes in the selling race. He has been placed in his last three races, being unlucky enough to come up against horses above the average for selling plates. **1979** K. BONFIGLIOLI *After you with Pistol* v. 22 A diet of beefsteak, oysters and Guinness would soon lift me out of the selling-plate class.

III. 18. a. Also in colloq. phrases: *to hand* (something to someone) *on a plate* and varr.: to give (something to someone) without his asking or seeking or without requiring any effort or return from him; to present in ready-to-use form; *to have a lot* (*enough*, etc.) *on one's plate*: to have a lot (enough, etc.) to worry about or cope with.

1922 JOYCE *Ulysses* 135 Gave it to them on a hot plate, Myles Crawford said, the whole bloody history. **1928** *Daily Express* 4 July 9/2 Can you tell me how many times in all she has forbidden you the house?—No, sir. Half a dozen times?—It might have been. I cannot say. I have a lot on my plate... Mr. Justice Horridge: A lot on your plate! What do you mean? Elton Pace: A lot of worry, my lord. **1935** WODEHOUSE *Right Ho, Jeeves* ii. 27 He can't get action when he's handed the thing on a plate. **1945** *Penguin New Writing* XXIV. 32 We haven't time to worry about D though, we shall probably have enough on our own plate any minute now. **1946** R. G. COLLINGWOOD *Idea of Hist.* 256 If anyone else..hands him on a plate a ready-made answer to his question, all he can do is to reject it. **1957** *Listener* 11 July 72 It is not often that radio is presented on a plate with such a fine natural script as these extracts made. **1959** 'R. SIMONS' *Houseboat Killings* xiv. 142 I'll leave you at it. I've got plenty on my plate at the moment. **1960** L. COOPER *Accomplices* I. vi. 67 That was an easy one—Steyne had handed it to us on a plate. **1963** T. PARKER *Unknown Citizen* iii. 78 Duggie's got a lot on his plate just now, I didn't want to worry him. **1970** *Manch. Guardian Weekly* 11 July 4 If New Zealand has the EEC door slammed in her face..car factories of Japan..would have a new market handed to them on a plate. **1973** 'P. MALLOCH' *Kickback* xii. 78 You make that kind of mistake you're handing it on a plate to the cops. *Ibid.* xxiii. 145 The police..[have] got enough on their plate. We pull our job tomorrow while they're trying to tidy up their own mess.

b. Restrict † (*obs.*) to (*a*) and add later examples of (*b*).

1886 KIPLING *Departmental Ditties* (ed. 2) 13 Who can raise a two-plate dinner off eight paltry 'dibs' a day? **1971** 'D. SHANNON' *Ringer* (1972) viii. 138 'Oh—the low-calorie plate,' as the waiter came up. **1972** J. WAMBAUGH *Blue Knight* (1973) i. 19, I promised to come back Friday for the De luxe Businessman's Plate. **1974** D. E. WESTLAKE *Help* (1975) xlii. 246 The man..recommended the roast beef plate..and the woman..said the turkey diet plate was first-rate.

d. *plates of meat*: feet; freq. ellipt. as *plates*; †*plate of meat*: a street (*obs.*). *Rhyming slang.*

1857 'DUCANGE ANGLICUS' *Vulgar Tongue* 15 *Plate of meat*,..street. **1887** *Referee* 6 Nov. 7/3 As she walked along the street With her little 'plates of meat'. **1889** J. S. FARMER *Americanisms* 425/2 *Plate of meat* (Cant),..in America does duty as the name, among thieves, for a street or highway. *a* **1896** A. R. MARSHALL in Farmer & Henley *Slang* (1902) V. 224/2 He is rocky on his plates, for he has forced them into 'sevens'. **1898** J. D. BRAYSHAW *Slum Silhouettes* 85 If a peeler heaves in sight..they'll..take a rise out of 'im with a chorus of 'Boots!' alluding to his 'plates o' meat', as they calls 'em. **1917** W. MUIR *Observations of Orderly* xiv. 222 To get your 'plates of meat' frostbitten wasn't such a 'cushy wound' as it was cracked up to be. **1948** C. DAY LEWIS *Otterbury Incident* ii. 17 'Your clodhopping feet.' 'Plates of meat,' murmured Dick Cozzens, who is an expert in slang. **1951** P. BRANCH *Lion in Cellar* ix. 105 He..took off his shoes. 'Heaven!' he sighed. 'My plates have been quite, quite killing me.' **1975** P. G. WINSLOW *Death of Angel* xii. 229 Gawd, I wore out my plates of meat.

e. *Biol.* and *Med.* A shallow vessel, usu. a Petri dish, used to contain a medium for the cultivation of micro-organisms; freq. used inclusively of this medium.

1886 E. M. CROOKSHANK *Introd. Pract. Bacteriol.* v. 68 The glass plates are sterilised by filling the iron box..and placing it in the hot-air steriliser, at 150° C., from one to two hours. **1896** G. M. STERNBERG *Text-Bk. Bacteriol.* viii. 72 By Koch's famous 'plate method' we obtain colonies of any particular microörganism which we desire to study. **1934** A. T. HENRICI *Biol. Bacteria* xii. 203 The colonies which develop upon agar or gelatine plates exhibit specific characters by which one may often identify the organism of which they are composed. **1973** R. G. KRUEGER et al. *Introd. Microbiol.* xiv. 388/2 On mixed indicator plates phages that are wild type for the host range character (h^+) form turbid plaques because they can only lyse one of the two kinds of bacteria in the mixture, whereas the h mutants, since they lyse both kinds of bacteria equally well, form clear plaques.

f. *U.S.* A place at a formal meal or banquet, for which one subscribes.

1925 L. S. DUNWAY in B. A. Botkin *Treas. S. Folklore* (1949) II. iii. 278 The committee on arrangements called on Jeff Davis at his office and wanted to know if the governor would like to have a plate at the banquet, the cost of which was $5. **1941** B. SCHULBERG *What makes Sammy Run?* xii. 288 They gave Sidney a testimonial dinner at the Ambassador at ten dollars a plate. **1964** MRS. L. B. JOHNSON *White House Diary* 9 Apr. (1970) 105 The luncheon took place before an audience of twenty-eight hundred, who had paid $12·50 a plate. **1974** *News & Reporter* (Chester, S. Carolina) 24 Apr. 8-A/1 Tickets, priced at $3.50 per plate, are on sale with any members of the sponsoring Chester Girls Club and the Diversity Study Club.

g. *U.S. slang.* A gramophone record.

1935 *Vanity Fair* (U.S.) Nov. 38/1 None of these plates will be senders. **1937** *Amer. Speech* XII. 100 Behind the microphone they [*sc.* gramophone records] are referred to variously as *discs*, *E.T.'s*, *plates*, *platters*, *wax* and *cuts*. **1942** BERREY & VAN DEN BARK *Amer. Thes. Slang.* §581/2 *Phonograph record*,..plate.

h. *N.Z.* and *Austral.* A plate of cakes, sandwiches, or the like contributed by a participant towards the catering at a social gathering.

1953 M. SCOTT *Breakfast at Six* viii. 70 Gents half-a-crown, ladies a plate... Larry explained what 'a plate' meant in the backblocks. **1962** S. GORE *Down Golden Mile* 110 We might start by having some sort of social. Nothing elaborate, you know. Just perhaps all the ladies could bring a plate. **1966** G. W. TURNER *Eng. Lang. in Austral. & N.Z.* iii. 48 Newcomers to New Zealand country districts have been embarrassed by a failure to detect this semantic development [*sc.* metonymy] in the advertisements for country dances, used to ensure that the right amount of supper will be provided and the hire of the hall paid—'Gents 2/- —Ladies a plate'. Since New Zealand countrywomen are renowned for their cooking of fancy cakes, an empty plate shows up rather poorly.

IV. 19. a. (sense *1 e) *plate boundary*; (sense *4 j) *plate circuit*, *current*, *voltage*; (sense 12*) *plate umpire*.

1971 I. G. GASS et al. *Understanding Earth* xix. 263/1 We distinguish between a plate boundary, the surface trace of the zone of motion between two plates, and a plate margin, the marginal part of a particular plate. **1979** C. KILIAN *Icequake* v. 70 It looks now as if the ice sheet put a strain..on a series of faults on the far side of the Queen Maud Range. Tim and I are pretty sure the faults mark the edge of a plate boundary. **1919** J. A. FLEMING *Thermionic Valve* 224 In general the external E.M.F. required in the plate circuit of a very hard valve is 100 volts, or even more, to produce a plate current of 3 or 4 milliamperes with the grid at zero potential. **1974** *Encycl. Brit. Macropædia* VI. 688/1 Many of these secondary electrons are attracted to the screen grid and flow in its circuit, rather than in the plate circuit, where the output should flow for greatest circuit efficiency. **1915** *Electrician* 21 May 243/1 (*diagram*) Plate current. **1966** T. KORNEFF *Introd. Electronics* vi. 198 The plate current is a function of the screen grid voltage and does not depend too much on the plate voltage. **1967** *Boston Herald* 1 Apr. 17/4 The area around home plate was especially soft and with two sinker ball pitchers working, plate umpire Larry Nap had a terrible time. **1922** *Encycl. Brit.* XXXII. 1027/2 The plate voltage of the oscillating valve is not supplied by a high voltage battery but at most by a few cells. **1966** Plate voltage [see *plate current* above].

b. *plate-glazing*, *-making*; *plate-glazed* adj.

1915 J. SOUTHWARD *Mod. Printing* (ed. 3) II. xxx. 258 Plate-glazed Paper is finished by being placed sheet by sheet between copper or zinc plates... The pile is pressed through powerful rollers. **1911** *Encycl. Brit.* XX. 734/2 The plate-glazing process is adopted mainly for the best grades of writing-papers, as it gives a smoother, higher and more permanent gloss than has yet been imitated by the roll-calender. **1962** F. T. DAY *Introd. Paper* iv. 47 Plate glazing is carried out by passing the paper between zinc plates and pressing it to give the desired finish. **1939** R. R. KARCH *Printing & Allied Trades* (ed. 2) xviii. 180 (*heading*) Offset Plate Making. **1967** E. CHAMBERS *Photolitho-Offset* iii. 31 A good reproduction proof.. becomes copy and is photographed in the normal way for plate-making.

20. plate camera, a camera designed to take photographs on coated glass plates rather than film; **plate-clutch,** a form of clutch in which the engaging surfaces are flat metal plates; **plate count,** an estimate of cell density in milk, soil, etc., made by inoculating a plate (sense *18 e) with a suitably diluted sample and counting the number of colonies that appear; **plate cylinder,** in a rotary printing press, the cylinder to which printing plates are attached; **plate girder** (examples); **plate-line** = PLATE-MARK 2; **plate metal,** (*b*) = **plate pewter*; **plate mill** (examples); **plate pewter,** the hardest variety of pewter, used for plates and dishes; **plate pie** (see quot. 1946); **plate-powder** (earlier and later examples); **plate-printer,** a workman who prints from plates; **plate-roll,** a smooth roller for rolling metal plate or sheet; **plate-room,** (*a*) a room for keeping plate (sense 15); (*b*) = **plate-safe*; **plate-safe** (see quot.); **plate-shy,** *a.*, *Baseball* (see quots.); **plate tectonics** *Geol.*, a theory of the earth's surface based on the concepts of moving plates (*PLATE *sb.* 1 e) and sea-floor spreading, used to explain the distribution of earthquakes, mid-ocean ridges, deep-sea trenches, and orogenic belts; hence **plate-tectonic** *a.*, **plate tectonicist.**

1937 *Discovery* June 177/2 Really good second-hand plate-cameras can be bought quite cheaply. **1956** *Focal Encycl. Photogr.* 868/1 Plate cameras are generally larger than film cameras. **1977** *Times* 31 Aug. 10/4 A man peering through a large plate camera at them. **1906** Plate clutch [see *disc-clutch* s.v. *DISC *sb.* 8 f]. **1960** *Farmer & Stockbreeder* 5 Jan. 95/2 Power..is transmitted via an independent plate-clutch. **1901** *Jrnl. Hygiene* I. 301 The effect of the ice-packing upon the number of colonies appearing in the ordinary plate count has been already discussed. **1928** *Jrnl. Bacteriol.* XVI. 270 The manner of making plate counts which prevails in public-health and other laboratories where daily counts are made on a number of samples of milk. **1956** *Nature* 4 Feb. 221/1 The time of soaking and shaking the leaves before plating influenced the plate-count. **1972** *Ann. Rep. Freshwater Biol. Assoc.* XL. 41 Bacterial numbers as shown by plate counts. **1932** PLACE & CLUNES in W. Atkins *Art & Practice of Printing* II. xi. 192 The plate-Cylinder is made to carry the curved plates; plate-Cylinders have to be very accurately ground. **1973** J. MORAN *Printing Presses* xiii. 198 It [*sc.* the plate] was then placed in a bending box, where it received the appropriate curvature to enable it to lie on the plate cylinder. **1849** W. FAIRBURN *Acct. Construction Britannia & Conway Tubular Bridges* I. 176 Is there anything new in this application of wrought-iron plate girders? **1891** *Notes Building Construction* IV. viii. 154 The web of a plate girder being very thin can bear but a very small part of the direct stresses. **1950** *Engineering* 8 Dec. 465/3 Mr. Dean, in his report on metal under-bridges, concluded that plate girders are the most economical and satisfactory form of construction for the main girders. **1931** A. ESDAILE *Student's Man. Bibliogr.* v. 151 All intaglio engravings will show a 'plate-line'; the paper which is pressed by the plate is smooth and sunk, while beyond the edge of the plate it keeps its natural surface; the resulting line is called the plate-line. **1961** T. LANDAU *Encycl. Librarianship* (ed. 2) 281/1 *Plate line*, a characteristic mark in intaglio printing, especially of engravings, due to the great pressure exerted by the engraving press on the paper. **1668–9** in C. Welch *Hist. Worshipful Co. Pewterers* (1902) II. 140 It is..agreed..that..every person that taketh Hollow-ware of any workman & returneth not him for the same ½ plate mettle and ½ London Trifles, shall pay unto such workman [etc.]. **1867** *Engineering* 4 Jan. 1/2 In the reversing plate mill at the London and North-Western Steel Works..the reversal of the motion of the rolls is effected by reversing the..engines. **1964** *Recent Progr. Metal Working* ii. 39 Automatic control of a plate mill entails..control of gauge in the last cross-rolling and last finishing pass. **1839** URE *Dict. Arts* 952 The plate pewter has a bright silvery lustre when polished. **1911** *Encycl. Brit.* XXI. 339/1 Plate pewter (100 parts of tin, 8 of antimony, 4 of copper and 4 of bismuth). **1946** F. M. MCNEILL *Recipes from Scotland* 13 A plate-pie, *i.e.*, with pastry above and below the filling. **1975** *Times* 19 July 11/4 Rhubarb plate pie. **1786** J. WOODFORDE *Diary* 24 Apr. (1926) II. 241 For some plate Powder at Chases pd 0. 1. 0. **1877** J. H. EWING in *Aunt Judy's Mag.* 146 The over-bearingness of the butler,..the inferior quality of the new plate-powder. **1976** *Century of Trade Marks* (Patent Office) 44 There is no longer any general need for such things as plate powder, polishing paste and blacking. **1889** *Cent. Dict.*, Plate-printer. **1902** *Encycl. Brit.* XXXIII. 414/2 Plate Printers' Union of United States, National Steel and Copper. **1921** *Dict. Occup. Terms* (1927) § 529 *Printer, plate*, prints from copper or steel plates, on which design or lettering is sunk below surface of plate, instead of being raised as in letterpress work. **1861** W. FAIRBAIRN *Iron* 111 The cylindrical part B, for plate-rolls should be slightly concave. **1930** *Engineering* 7 Nov. 579/2 (*heading*) Plate-roll finishing machine. **1888** Plate room [see *plate-safe*]. **1931** *N. & Q.* 10 Oct. 262/2 The plate-room..is a strong steel and fireproof apartment. **1888** *Encycl. Brit.* XXIII. 710/1 The plate-safe or plate-room is the repository of the stereo and electro plates. **1912** C. MATHEWSON *Pitching* iv. 90 For a long time, 'Josh' Devore, the Giant's left-fielder was 'plate shy' with left-handers—that is, he stepped away. **1942** BERREY & VAN DEN BARK *Amer. Thes. Slang* § 677/37 *Plate-shy*, afraid to stand close to the plate. **1972** *Sci. Amer.* May 59/1 According to the plate-tectonic view, continents and oceans are rafted along by the same crustal conveyor belt. **1976** *Nature* 9 Sept. 118/1 In the plate tectonic model, the Himalaya is considered to be the classic example of a continent–continent collision system. **1973** *Ibid.* 30 Nov. 263/1 They are in disagreement with the views of some plate tectonicists who wish to have the whole 500 km shift take place after mid-Miocene. [**1966** *Bull. Geol. Soc. Amer.* LXXVII. 707 The folds and faults mapped at the surface [near the San Andreas fault] are attributed to raft tectonics whereby a passive surficial plate is deformed as it rides coupled to a moving under-mass.] **1969** *Sci. Jrnl.* Aug. 40/2 Plate tectonics..has shown its ability to predict, amongst other things, the direction of the movement accompanying earthquakes. **1972** *Observer* (Colour Suppl.) 13 Feb. 12/1 During the past five years, there has been a revolution in the Earth Sciences, involving a theory called plate tectonics. **1976** *McGraw-Hill Yearbk. Sci. & Technol.* 314/1 The wide-spread acceptance by the earth sciences community of plate tectonics has had a revitalizing effect on many research fields, but none more so than paleobio-geography, the study of the factors controlling the distribution of fossil organisms.

plate, *v.* Add: **1. b.** *trans. Surg.* To treat (a fracture) by fixing a metal plate to both the fractured parts so as to hold them together; to attach a plate to (a bone).

1910 *Brit. Med. Jrnl.* 8 Oct. 1064/2 It..did the progress of surgery a disservice to suggest that to plate a fracture was a matter lightly to be undertaken. **1948** [see *FIXATION 3 c]. **1959** A. G. APLEY *Syst. Orthopaedics & Fractures* xi. 110 When a fracture has been plated, the technique of 'delayed splintage' is of great value. *Ibid.* xxi. 256 If closed reduction of a radius and ulna has failed..the bones should..be plated.

2. a. Add examples relating to the deposition of substances other than gold and silver.

1855 *Mechanics Mag.* 7 July 4/1 A patent has recently been obtained..for an improved process for plating or coating lead, iron, or other metals with tin, nickel, or alumina. **1919** *Rep. Progr. Appl. Chem.* IV. 255 A lead anode is employed when plating with lead. **1929** *Ibid.* XIV. 322 Automobile parts..to be plated with nickel or chromium. **1940** A. MORGAN *Things a Boy can do with Electrochem.* xii. 177 It is an easy matter to plate iron, steel, and brass articles with copper or nickel. **1966** *McGraw-Hill Encycl. Sci. & Technol.* IV. 531/2 Chromium plating is conducted from solutions containing chromic acid and sulfuric acid... For irregular shapes, auxiliary anodes must be used to plate the surface completely. **1968** *Rep. Progr. Appl. Chem.* LIII. 68 Smith and Lewis.. successfully plated toughened polystyrene.

b. Also, to deposit as a coating, esp. electrolytically. (Further examples.)

1919 *Rep. Progr. Appl. Chem.* IV. 255 Nickel can be plated directly on aluminium. **1947** *Electronic Engin.* XIX. 161/3 The chemical reduction method of plating nickel on steel is too expensive to replace electrodeposition. **1959** T. M. ROGERS *Hand-bk. Pract. Electroplating* 218 Nickel is normally plated from an acid solution. **1972** I. ASIMOV *Asimov's Guide to Science* (1975) I. v. 291 Attempting to plate a silicon layer on a platinum surface. ..The expected plating did not occur. **1979** *Sci. Amer.* May 71 (Advt.), Man has been plating chromium for over a century.

6. *Biol.* and *Med.* To inoculate (cells or infective material) *into* or *on to* a plate (*PLATE *sb.* 18 e), esp. with the object of purifying a particular strain or estimating viable cell numbers. Freq. with *out.*

1892 A. C. ABBOTT *Princ. Bacteriol.* xviii. 181 Again, 0·25 c.c. of this dilution is plated and we find 180 colonies on the plate. **1901** *Jrnl. Hygiene* I. 202 In order to isolate the organisms, one c.c. of each of the liquid stools was diluted 1–10,000 and 1–100,000 with distilled water, and $\frac{1}{10}$ c.c., ¼ c.c., and ½ c.c. of these dilutions were plated out in gelatine. **1905** *Ibid.* V. 342 The resulting cultures were plated and re-plated to ensure pure growths. **1930** [see *BROTH *sb.* 1 b]. **1971** *Nature* 10 Sept. 121/1 When these strains were plated on various drug agar plates..we obtained the growth pattern given in Table 1. **1972** *Ibid.* 18 Feb. 368/2 Rat lymph node cells are plated out onto mouse fibroblast monolayers *in vitro.*

7. To examine or test the distribution of shot from (a shot-gun) by firing at a pattern plate set at a suitable distance.

1904 *Kynoch Jrnl.* Oct.–Dec. 189 You can plate your gun with your favourite charge. **1932** G. BURRARD *Mod. Shotgun* III. 80 No record of such a thing has ever been noted on any pattern plate since the plating of guns first began.

8. To provide (a book) with a book-plate.

1906 [see *PLATING *vbl. sb.* 1 g]. **1930** *Publishers' Weekly* 1 Mar. 1095/2 After the latter book had been punched and plated, one of our catalogers discovered that..it was an exact duplicate of the former. **1941** *Amer. Speech* XVI. 311 Verbs are made from nouns, for instance *to plate*.., to furnish with bookplates.

9. *trans.* and *intr.* To practise fellatio or cunnilingus (on). *slang.*

1961 PARTRIDGE *Dict. Underworld* Add. 807/1 *Plate*, v. This and *french, go down, nosh*, are prostitutes' (esp. London) verbs, both transitive and, less commonly, intransitive, for 'to gamâruche' a man: C. 20. **1969** FABIAN & BYRNE *Groupie* i. 10, I wondered whether I should plate him. I hadn't done much of that, but I knew guys on the scene liked it because Nigel had told me so. **1969** B. PATTEN *Notes to Hurrying Man* 27 Guitarist from Mike's group Taught her how to plate correctly. **1971** J. MANDELKAU *Buttons* vii. 99 The various chapter prospects were showing everyone how well they could screw and plate her.

10. *trans.* To provide (a goods vehicle) with a plate recording particulars of weight, etc., according to government regulations.

1968 [see *PLATING *vbl. sb.* 1 j]. **1970** *Times* 29 Jan. 26/6 All trailers manufactured before January 1 last year should have been tested and plated by the Ministry within 12 months. **1972** [see *PLATING *vbl. sb.* 1 j]. **1976**, etc. [see *PLATED *a.* 6]. **1977** 'D. RUTHERFORD' *Return Load* ii. 32, I see it's plated at 43·3 tons. That's more than ten in excess of the UK limit.

11. *trans.* To put on a plate; to serve upon a plate.

1970, etc. [implied in *PLATED *a.* 5]. **1976** *Times* July 10/6 Dishes are plated in the kitchen, and mistiming is common. **1977** *Guernsey Weekly Press* 21 July 2/8 Mr Nugent said that when the policemen arrived the meals were ready and plated.

‖**platea** (plătī·ă). *Medieval Drama.* Also **placea**; pl. **plateæ.** [L., street; (late L.) courtyard, square; f. Gr. πλατεῖα.] An area before a raised stage, providing additional acting space as well as accommodation for the audience.

1831 J. P. COLLIER *Hist. Dramatic Poetry* II. 154 A castle and a ship were introduced [in the Digby Miracle-play of Mary Magdalen]. The 'place', termed *placea*, and a *mons* are also mentioned in the stage-directions. **1903** E. K. CHAMBERS *Mediaeval Stage* II. III. xx. 80 The *diabolus* thinks he is prevailing upon Adam. He joins the other demons and make [*sic*] sallies about the *plateae.* **1957** R. SOUTHERN *Medieval Theatre in Round* 235 The *platea* developed not into the stage of our modern theatre, but into the pit-and-stalls. **1978** *Amer. N. & Q.* Apr. 118/1 The Digby *Mary Magdalen* has the most complete stage directions in medieval drama, directions that provide several precise technical dramatic terms which distinguish exits from moves within and about the *platea.*

plateau. Add: Also with pronunc. (plæ·to). **1. b.** (Earlier and later examples.) More widely, a more or less level portion of a graph adjacent to a lower sloping portion; a condition or period that can be so represented, when there is neither an increase nor a decrease in something.

1894 W. EWART *Pulse-Sensations* IV. xiii. 277 In the cardiogram..this point occurs in the line of descent—or else in the 'plateau'. **1943** J. D. WHITE in H. L. Mencken *Amer. Lang.* Suppl. I. (1945) 416 Plateaus are the thing now. War production is on a plateau, meaning that it is way up and has been up long enough to establish a plateau in the curve of production figures. **1948** *Manch. Guardian Weekly* 30 Dec. 9 The men on the Stock Exchange modestly allow they will be content with 'a plateau'. **1959** *Listener* 1 Jan. 18/1 The Ionians..had already reached a high plateau of civilization. **1961** *Ann. Reg. 1960* 474 Although industrial production in aggregate was seemingly on a plateau, the fortunes of particular industries showed marked variations. **1969** H. PERKINS *Key Profession* v. 208 The post-1947 decline in the birth-rate would be succeeded by a further upturn, rising to a higher and more permanent 'plateau' from about 1960 onwards. **1976** *Nature* 8 July 83/2 The world total of annual military expenditure..has remained on a plateau of 210,000 million US dollars (at 1970 prices) for seven years now. *Ibid.* 146/1 Fig. 1*b* shows a large current with a plateau at around +0·8 V.

c. *Psychol.* A stage in learning when no apparent progress is made.

1897 BRYAN & HARTER in *Psychol. Rev.* IV. 52 All agree that just below the ability to understand what is spoken, there is a long discouraging plateau where many give up [learning telegraphy] in despair. **1936** *Brit. Jrnl. Psychol.* XXVI. 218 The occurrence of breathing-places and plateaux in the learning process has usually been attributed..to the gradual formation of low and high habits... A plateau means that the lower order habits are approaching their maximum development, but have not become sufficiently automatic to leave attention free to attack the higher order habits. **1964** P. M. FITTS in A. W. Melton *Categories of Human Learning* 265 The present writer knows of no evidence contrary to Keller's (1958) conclusion that a true plateau in skill learning has not been demonstrated, and that when such effects occasionally are reported they are artifacts. **1972** P. BACH-Y-RITA *Brain Mechanisms* iv. 77 Acquisition of a predominantly perceptual skill..and acquisition of a motor skill..are remarkably similar processes. Each is slow, and has several plateaus.

d. *Physics.* The range of applied voltage over which the counting rate of a Geiger counter remains approximately the same, for a given intensity of radiation.

1937 *Physical Rev.* LI. 1027/1 Reliable counting characteristics and long plateaus were obtainable only with counters whose cathode surfaces were completely cleaned ..previous to filling. **1953** H. H. STAUB in E. Segrè *Exper. Nucl. Physics* I. I. iv. 149 A good counter shows a plateau of 160 volts over which the counting rate should not increase by more than 3 percent. **1973** J. YARWOOD *Atomic & Nucl. Physics* xiv. 396 Well designed counter tubes have a plateau slope of about 2 per cent. increase in count rate for an operating voltage increase of 100 V. This flat plateau is valuable since it means that the operating voltage is not critical.

e. The second of four recognized stages of sexual intercourse (see quot. 1960), in which there is an intense sexual excitement lasting a variable but usually short time following a longer phase of increasing excitement and succeeded either by orgasm or by a longer period of decreasing excitement. Usu. *attrib.*, esp. in *plateau phase.*

1960 W. H. MASTERS in *Western Jrnl. Surg., Obstetr. & Gynecol.* LXVIII. 58 The four phases of the human female's sexual response cycle are in order of their development: (1) the excitement phase; (2) the plateau phase; (3) the orgasmic phase; and (4) the resolution phase. *Ibid.*, This plateau phase of sexual response is the base line from which the individual climbs with relative ease and rapidity to orgasm. **1966** MASTERS & JOHNSON *Human Sexual Response* i. 7 Some physiologic reactions.. may be confined to one particular phase of the cycle. Examples are the plateau-phase color changes of the minor labia in the female and the coronal engorgement of the penis in the male. **1972** *Encycl. Love & Sex* I. 8/2 One of the most common of all sexual problems occurs when the man's plateau phase is short,..so that he reaches his climax too soon to satisfy his partner. **1974** H. S. KAPLAN *New Sex Therapy* i. 9 During plateau, the local vasocongestive response of the primary sex organ is at its peak in both genders. *Ibid.* 21 The retarded ejaculator becomes excited, reaches the plateau, may experience the intense urge to proceed to orgasm which is characteristic at this time, but cannot ejaculate despite vigorous and effective stimulation. **1976** B. GOLDSTEIN *Human Sexuality* ix. 157 If sexual motivation is maintained by adequate erotic stimulation, the excitement phase accelerates to the plateau phase.

4. (sense 1 b) *plateau length, level, slope, value*; **plateau basalt,** basaltic lava extruded from fissures and forming sheets that cover many square miles; in *Petrol.* freq. used with the implication of a tholeiitic or, formerly, an alkalic nature; **plateau gravel**, gravel occurring in a sheet on hilltops or a plateau, at a height that suggests it has been raised by earth movement since its deposition.

1888 *Proc. R. Soc. Edin.* XV. 347 In Antrim bosses of trachyte and pitchstone rise through the plateau-basalts. **1933** *Amer. Jrnl. Sci.* CCXXV. 241 Olivine-Basalt Magma-Type... Many of the Patagonian plateau basalts appear to be of this type and some, at least, of the Siberian Traps. *Ibid.* 242 The Deccan Traps and the majority of the plateau basalts which have been studied are of tholeiitic composition. **1944** A. Holmes *Princ. Physical Geol.* xx. 458 Plateau basalts covering areas of 200,000 square miles or more occur in the Columbia and Snake River region of the north-western United States. **1972** G. A. Macdonald *Volcanoes* xi. 255 The basaltic lava flows that built the plains have commonly been called plateau basalts. **1977** A. Hallam *Planet Earth* 20/3 The materials of cratered plains [on the moon] resemble terrestrial plateau basalts. **1872** Wood & Harmer in S. V. Wood *Suppl. Monogr. Crag Mollusca* p. xxvi. (*heading*) The Plateau gravel. **1881** *Proc. Geologists' Assoc.* VI. 33 On the top of Crawley (Portesbury Hill.. the plateau-gravel, with its overlying loam (loess) and its ferruginous layers, is well seen in the railway-cutting. **1970** R. J. Small *Study of Landforms* vii. 234 In the New Forest.., the Tertiary sands and clays are overlain at many points by thick plateau gravels of Quaternary age. **1965** *Wireless World* Aug. 382/2 This is particularly useful for Geiger tubes, as they tend to have individual working points and sometimes, if aged, a limited plateau length. **1957** G. E. Hutchinson *Treat. Limnol.* I. xii. 744 The absolute concentration..fell rapidly, reaching a plateau level which represents about 10 per cent of the original amount added. **1962** *Newnes Conc. Encycl. Nucl. Energy* 296/1 A good counter is one which has a low plateau slope, e.g. less than 5 per cent increase in count-rate for 100 V increase in applied voltage. **1964** L. Wilets *Theories Nucl. Fission* i. 3 As a function of excitation energy, the probability of fission frequently assumes the form of a barrier transmission curve.., rising to some plateau value.

5. *Med.* (Passing into adj.) Of the pulse: having a plateau (sense 1 b) in the rising portion of the sphygmomanometric tracing.

1923 W. D. Reid *Heart in Mod. Practice* xviii. 231 If the pulse is anacrotic and plateau in type, the diagnosis [of aortic stenosis] obtains strong support. **1936** S. A. Levine *Clin. Heart Dis.* iv. 77 The plateau form of radial pulse is fairly characteristic of aortic stenosis. *Ibid.*, This will counteract the plateau character. **1972** Passmore & Robson *Compan. Med. Stud.* III. xvi. 6/1 The plateau pulse..is due to the slow ejection of blood from the left ventricle through the narrowed orifice.

Plateau² (plæ·to, ‖ plătō͞u·). *Math.* The name of J. A. F. *Plateau* (1801–83), Belgian physicist, used *attrib.*, in the possessive, and with *of* to designate the problem of finding the surface of smallest area bounded by any given closed curve.

1911 *Encycl. Brit.* XXVI. 123/2 The problem of finding a minimal surface to pass through a given curve in space, known as Plateau's problem, possesses an exceptional interest. **1927** *Bull. Amer. Math. Soc.* XXXIII. 259 This paper reduces the Plateau problem to a system of two integral equations. **1930** *Math. Zeitschr.* XXXII. 765 The problem of Plateau and the problem of least area have a common solution. **1976** *Sci. Amer.* July 82/3 In his honour an entire range of mathematical questions that deal with the geometry of soap-bubble-like and soap-film-like surfaces is referred to as Plateau's problem.

plateau (plæ·to, plătō͞u·), *v.* [f. the sb.] *intr.* To enter a period of stability or stagnation; to cease increasing or progressing, to level *out.* So **pla·teaued** (or **plateau·ed**) *ppl. a.*; **pla·teauing** (or *plateau·ing*) *vbl. sb.*

1952 *Proc. Soc. Exper. Biol. & Med.* LXXIX. 584/2 In each experiment 10 'plateaued' female rats of the Long-Evans strain were used. **1966** *Electronics* 3 Oct. 23 Many companies have diversified their activities or extended their product lines, after having been scared by the plateauing of business in 1962 and 1963. *Ibid.*, U.S. electronic companies have bitten deeply into local markets, causing the sales of European firms to plateau or slide on their home grounds. **1967** *Economist* 16 Sept. 1009/1 There is an ominous lull in military cargoes which the shipping companies believe is temporary but which the military expect to be permanent and which they describe as 'the pipeline plateauing out'. **1969** D. Clark *Nobody's Perfect* ii. 60 The hope that some graph will plateau higher up the scale. **1973** *Maclean's Mag.* Aug. 63/1 Kids get into swimming and they have a lot of initial success and then they plateau—they stick at the same level for a long period, maybe six months. **1975** *Harvard Business Rev.* LIII. 30/3 We found a large number of managers who, in the judgment of their organization, have 'plateaued'. That is, there is little or no likelihood that they will be promoted. **1976** *New Scientist* 26 Aug. 439/2 The counts from radioactive carbon dioxide rose rapidly and then plateaued. **1978** *Jrnl. R. Soc. Arts* CXXVI. 483/2 Petroleum supply will peak or plateau at the end of the century.

plated, *a.* Add: **1. c.** *Surg.* Of a fracture: see *plate *v.* 1 b.

1916 E. W. H. Groves *Mod. Methods Treating Fractures* vi. 198 In so many plated fractures removal of the plates and screws is required. **1959** A. G. Apsley *Syst. Orthopædics & Fractures* xxi. 256 If..a patient walks with a recently plated tibia unprotected by plaster, the plate will break.

2. (Further examples.) Also used with reference to metals other than gold and silver; *plated wire*, a wire of a non-magnetic metal such as copper having a thin coating of a magnetic alloy, used as an element in some computer memories. Cf. *chromium-plated* ppl. adj. s.v. *chromium 2.

1781 H. Newdigate *Let.* 8 Oct. in A. E. Newdigate-Newdegate *Cheverels* (1898) iii. 42 All were well pleas'd to find we were only ten miles from Sheffield... We got there ..and saw the Plated Manufactory through all its branches. **1789** E. Sheridan *Jrnl.* (1960) 182 The plated candlesticks will also be very useful to us. **1899** J. W. Urquhart *Electro-Plating* (ed. 4) 222 The advantages of a thick deposit of nickel are that it can be manipulated by the polisher with confidence and the 'life' of the plated article is..greatly increased. **1931** E. F. Benson *Mapp & Lucia* viii. 205 A magenta carpet and a nickel-plated mantelpiece. **1960** T. R. Long in *Jrnl. Appl. Physics* XXXI. Suppl. 124S/2 After rinsing the plated wire, it is passed through a mercury ground contact and then through small testing coils. These coils..allow a continuous monitor of the nondestructive readout signal. **1967** *Times Rev. Industry* Feb. 104/2 (Advt.), UNIVAC 9000 Series computers utilize a plated-wire memory, basically a thin film electroplated on an extremely fine wire. **1967** *Engineering* 24 Feb. 306/3 Plated plastics parts can replace metal components in many domestic, industrial and automobile applications. **1976** M. Wells *Computing Systems Hardware* ii. 49 Plated wire stores are substantially faster than ferrite core stores of the same capacity.

b. Also, produced by plating (sense *1 h).

c **1890** *American Mail Order Fashions* (1961) 12 Ladies' Outsize Plated Silk Hose, black,..1.50. **1926** J. Chamberlain *Hosiery, Yarns & Fabrics* vi. 131 Innumerable colour designs are produced on a plated principle on plain and rib fabrics. **1963** A. J. Hall *Textile Sci.* iii. 152 Thus using cotton and wool yarns it can be arranged that the front of the fabric appears to be made of cotton with the back made of wool. Such fabrics are known as *plated* fabrics. **1968** J. Ironside *Fashion Alphabet* 245 A knitted fabric which has a different kind of yarn as the face and back, is said to be plated.

4. Applied as a thin coating on another material.

1925 *Rep. Progr. Appl. Chem.* X. 301 Piersol finds plated chromium superior to any other metal for reflectors. **1966** *McGraw-Hill Encycl. Sci. & Technol.* IV. 533/1 The thickness of a plated coating is the most important factor in its protective value.

5. In which food is ready-served on a plate.

1970 *Drive* Spring 43/1 Plated service means that your meal arrives complete, on the plate. Semi-plated service is when the principal component of the meal arrives on the plate; vegetables are served from silver dishes. **1976** *Liverpool Echo* 23 Nov. 10/6 Some patients at Clatterbridge Hospital enjoy a plated meals service which gives them advance choice of menu and portion size. **1977** *Lancet* 16 July 130/1 Plated meals were packed in charcoal heated containers and dispatched at 11 a.m.

6. Of a goods vehicle: see *plate *v.* 10.

1976 *Liverpool Echo* 22 Nov. 11/4 (Advt.), Two Leyland Boxer Vans, plated,..M.O.T. until February 1977. **1977** *Horse & Hound* 14 Jan. 44/2 (Advt.), Bedford T.K. petrol, 2/3 horses, good box, very reliable, plated till January 1977. **1978** *Taxi* 16 Feb. 19/1 (Advt.), For Sale: 'J' reg. auto. Just rebored. Excellent condition, plated till July. **1980** *Daily Tel.* 6 Mar. 2 (Advt.), It's a big truck all right. But its plated weight is only 7·38 tons GVW.

plate-glass. Add: **b.** *spec.* (also with capital initial) used *attrib.* to denote any of the new British universities founded in the 1960s; also passing into adj., of or pertaining to such a university.

1968 M. Beloff *Plateglass Universities* i. 20 The self-confident and colourful character of the Plateglass universities reflects the spirit of the high Macmillan age. **1968** —— in *Encounter* May 14/1 The New University explosion of the last decade has an element of illusion about it... Only seven..are new institutions... The difference between the Plateglass Universities and both their predecessors and upgraded successors was that in them alone was there the opportunity for pure experiment. **1968** *Economist* 1 June 47/1 Of the non-Oxbridge successful candidates, only four came from the new generation of plate-glass universities. **1971** C. Driver *Exploding University* i. iv. 187 Some time ago a Plate-glass professor suggested that a new university's potential for innovation fades after about three years. **1973** J. H. M. Scott *Dons & Students* ii. 17 Though the new universities have been dubbed 'plate-glass'..they have no monopoly of that material. **1979** *Times Higher Educ. Suppl.* 23 Nov. 27/5 Among universities, such labels as Oxbridge, Red Brick, Green Field and Plate Glass define origins and location rather than reputations.

Hence **plate-gla·sser**, a student or graduate of one of the new British universities.

1968 *Economist* 1 June 47/1 A man from Aberystwyth got into the Foreign Service, along with two plate-glassers, one red-brick man, one Dubliner, nine from Oxford and eleven from Cambridge.

platelet. Add: (A blood-platelet is usu. called a platelet simply.) Further examples. [(*blood-*)*platelet* tr. G. (*blut*)*plättchen* (G. Bizzozero in *Centralbl. für die med. Wissensch.* (1882) I. 17, 18), F. *petite plaque* (*du sang*) (*idem* in *Arch. ital. de Biol.* (1882) I. 1, 16).]

1910 H. W. Armit tr. *P. Ehrlich's Anæmia* iv. 203 He then determined the relative proportions of the platelets to the blood corpuscles. **1955** *Sci. News Let.* 14 May 320/3 Platelets, tiny cell fragments found in the blood, arrest bleeding by sticking to the edge of the wound and to each other until they pile up into a little cork that fills the hole. **1970** *Physics Bull.* July 322/1 The crystal..is then sliced into platelets 50 μm or so thick. **1978** *Detroit Free Press* 5 Mar. B4/1 Blood clots that block arteries are formed by platelets, the body's first line of defense against injury.

2. platelet count, the number of platelets in a stated volume of blood; a calculation of this.

1909 *Jrnl. Exper. Med.* XI. 542 In the experiments careful erythrocyte and leukocyte counts have been made and then the platelet count obtained by the indirect method, *i.e.*, by ascertaining their number relative to that of the red blood cells in fresh preparations and checking this result by the relative number in carefully made stained smears. *Ibid.* 544 In an animal which had received repeated doses of saponin intravenously..there was a high platelet count (1,400,000 per cubic millimeter). **1966** *Lancet* 24 Dec. 1384/1 The platelet-count gradually recovered after the drugs had been stopped.

plate-maker. 2. (Earlier examples.)

1772 J. Wedgwood *Let.* 22 July (1965) 127, I have ordered another sett of plate makers to work, and will if possible have a *sufficient stock* of those *every day* Articles. **1863** *1st Rep. Children's Employment Commission* 3 in *Parl. Papers* XVIII. 1 *Flat pressers*... It includes dish-makers, platemakers, saucermakers, and cup and bowl makers.

platen, platten, *sb.* Add: The form *platten* is now *Obs.* **1. b.** *Engin.* The movable table of a planing or milling machine.

1908 S. H. Moore *Mech. Engin.* xiii. 298 Horizontal milling machines..resemble in a way the conventional planer with its deep bed and long platen or table. **1950** C. R. Hine *Machine Tools for Engineers* viii. 122 The worktable, or platen, moves back and forth on the bed ways and carries the work past the tool.

3. a. *spec.* A flat metal surface by means of which pressure is applied in a press. (Further examples.)

1927 Knight & Wulpi *Veneers & Plywood* xx. 210 The platens are alternately squeezed together to flatten the veneer, and opened up to allow the moisture to escape from the wood surfaces. **1936** H. W. Rowell *Technol. of Plastics* xv. 97 The simple up-stroke hydraulic press with steam or electrically heated platens..is a cheap and economical machine. **1963** H. R. Clauser et al. *Encycl. Engin. Materials & Processes* 347/2 Two mold halves, which..combine to form one or more negative forms of the article to be molded, are tightly clamped between the platens of an injection-molding machine. **1964** B. Latham *Wood* xiii. 159 A modern hot press may have ten, twelve, or even twenty platens, so enabling up to twenty sheets of plywood to be manufactured at each pressing operation. **1975** A. D. Deutschman et al. *Machine Design* iv. 170 Laminating... It is possible to produce shapes other than flat sheets by using shaped molding dies between the forming press platens.

b. In a typewriter, the surface against which the paper is held and the type strikes (a cylindrical roller in most machines). Freq. *attrib.*

1890 A. E. Morton *Type-Writing & Type-Writers* 12 The paper-carriage is much smaller, and the platen or cylinder differs from that of other machines in that it presents a flat surface for the types to strike against. **1899** J. Wardle *Universal Typewriter Man.* 45 *Platen knob*, for turning the Platen..either backward or forward. *Ibid.*, *Platen roller*, for the paper to rest upon when printing. **1907** F. H. Burnett *Shuttle* xxiii. 227 The platen roller is easily removed without a long mechanical operation. **1909** G. C. Mares *Hist. Typewriter* i. 45 The platen cylinder is supported in a carriage that slides on a rod. **1928** M. Crocks *Touch Typewriting for Teachers* xvii. 125 The student can be trained to get the right amount of 'flick' with the platen knob to enable the paper to enter the machine up to whatever writing point is desired. **1962** *Which?* Dec. 354/1 The bail bar, which should hold the paper against the platen, was thin and bent easily. **1976** J. Fraser *Who steals my Name?* x. 122 He pressed the activate key, and..paper began to spew from the platen, printed in neat lines at the rate of ten words a second.

4. platen press, a platen machine (not necessarily a printing-machine).

1888 *Encycl. Brit.* XXIII. 704/2 We may say that of platen presses there are the hand-press, the treadle platen press, and the steam or other power-driven press. **1927** Knight & Wulpi *Veneers & Plywood* xxvi. 294 Pressing plywood singly, even in the multiple platen presses,..is a slow and expensive process. **1967** V. Strauss *Printing Industry* vi. 278/1 Platen presses are the smallest and least complex of all widely used letterpress printing machines.

plate number. 1. *Philately.* (See quot. 1912.)

1912 *Gloss. Philatelic Terms* 19 *Plate Numbers*, numbers inserted in the margins of plates from which stamps are printed, indicating (in the case of British and British Colonial stamps) the order in which the plates for those particular values were made. **1934** *Neuphilologische Mitteilungen* XXXV. 130 Stamp-collecting..*plate number* 'number appearing in the margin of certain stamps'. **1971** D. Potter *Brit. Eliz. Stamps* v. 63 In complete sheets all Bradbury Wilkinson printings bear a plate number, in the lower margin to the right; this consists of a number or a number and letter.

2. A serial number on the pages of some engraved music, which can indicate the chronological place of the score in the publisher's output.

1940 *Papers Amer. Musicological Soc. 1938* 114 [Hoffmeister] made arrangements in 1784 with the publisher.. to do the engraving for him... Work issued during this period either had no plate number engraved at the foot of the plates, or else used as an identifying device the opus number of the composition. **1942** *Music Library Assoc. Notes* Dec. 1 Mathias Artaris..generally adds the initials 'M.A.' to his plate numbers. **1946** O. E. DEUTSCH *Music Publishers' Numbers* 7 This list..is..only a preliminary compilation of titles and plate-numbers known to the authors. **1965** NEIGHBOUR & TYSON (*title*) English music publishers' plate numbers in the first half of the nineteenth century. **1966** J. H. DAVIES *Musicalia* xv. 139 The dating of music by publishers' plate-numbers and paper-makers' watermarks begins to achieve some degree of accuracy.

3. The registration number of a motor vehicle, exhibited on a plate.

1973 'D. SHANNON' *No Holiday* (1974) iv. 64 Hackett.. got the plate number of the truck.

platform, *sb.* Add: **III. 6. c.** *spec.* in *Geol.* and *Physical Geogr.*: (i) A level or nearly level strip of land at the base of a cliff close to the water-level; occas., a similar terrace away from a body of water but thought to have been formed by the sea in such a situation.

1841 C. LYELL *Elem. of Geol.* (ed. 2) I. vi. 150 The sea is advancing upon the land, and removing annually small portions of undermined rock. By this agency a submarine platform is produced on which we may walk for some distance from the beach in shallow water, the increase of depth being very gradual, until we reach a point where the bottom plunges down suddenly. This platform is widened with more or less rapidity according to the hardness of the rocks, and when upraised it constitutes an inland terrace. **1901** *Bull. Geol. Soc. Amer.* XII. 212 A looped bar or ridge of gravel and sand formed on an old wave-cut platform. **1922** E. M. WARD *Eng. Coastal Evol.* ii. 34 There must come a time when further coast retreat would involve the total exhaustion of wave energy in crossing the shallow water of a wide wave-cut platform. **1944** A. HOLMES *Princ. Physical Geol.* xiv. 289 As the cliffs are worn back a wave-cut platform is left in front.., the upper part of which is visible as the rocky foreshore exposed at low tide. **1964** W. C. PUTNAM *Geol.* xiv. 387/2 Where the platform is mantled with sand, it is the beach. *Ibid.* 388/1 These coasts may be bordered by a whole flight of terraces, which are elevated wave-cut platforms. **1975** R. V. RUHE *Geomorphol.* ix. 178/2 There are five marine terraces in Santa Cruz, California; each platform was cut during rising sea level, and its cover of marine sediments was deposited during falling sea level.

(ii) *continental platform*: see *CONTINENTAL *a.* 1 d.

(iii) A former erosion surface or plateau represented by the common surface or summit level of neighbouring hills or other land forms.

1908 *Q. Jrnl. Geol. Soc.* LXIV. 384 Of the older topography..partly destroyed by post-Pliocene denudation, the most striking feature in the higher part of the area is presented by two well-marked high-level platforms, one at 750 feet above the sea, and the other may be called the 1000-foot platform, although it is really a little below this altitude. The latter was first recognized on Davidstow Moor,..but traces of it are to be seen on the surrounding high land in all directions. **1938** A. K. WELLS *Outl. Hist. Geol.* xvii. 226 In a few localities on the Chiltern dip slope remnants of the Lenham platform form a gently inclined shelf above the 400-feet platform. **1954** J. F. KIRKALDY *Gen. Princ. Geol.* ix. 96 Accordance of summit levels or the presence of platforms at lower levels can be inferred from the layout of the contours. **1966** J. I. CLARKE in G. H. Dury *Ess. Geomorphol.* 257 In Britain..there is a marked tendency to attribute platforms to marine erosion.., while in Australia..and elsewhere it is often held that uplift and rejuvenation of ancient surfaces are possible. *Ibid.* 270 Sparsely-distributed height-values rarely give..a good indication of erosion-platforms.

(iv) The part of a kratogen (craton) where the basement complex, elsewhere exposed as a shield, is overlain by a layer of more recent, relatively flat and undisturbed strata that are mainly sedimentary.

1908 tr. *Suess's Face of Earth* III. IV. ix. 376 The pre-Cambrian platform. In front of the Urals there extends the vast Russian plain. Its ancient foundation is not visible till we proceed a considerable distance to the west and south-west. **1923** L. D. STAMP *Introd. Stratigr.* iii. 36 The whole area of S.E. England consists of a blanket of Mesozoic Rocks resting on an eroded surface of Palæozoic rocks called the Palæozoic Platform. **1958** L. P. SMIRNOW in L. G. Weeks *Habitat of Oil* 1168 (*heading*) Oil-bearing basins on eastern edge of the Russian platform. **1968** C. R. TWIDALE *Geomorphol.* iii. 49 The Australian continent is built of a Shield, a Platform and an Orogen. **1972** B. B. BROCK *Global Approach to Geol.* iv. 35 The Russian platform, with a moderate thickness of flat-lying rocks covering the basement, brings the Baltic shield up to the normal size.

7. b. In a small boat or yacht: a light deck.

1950 R. MOORE *Candlemas Bay* I. 47 Otherwise she'd have come up and drained her platform through the scuppers, as soon as she floated. **1961** F. H. BURGESS *Dict. Sailing* 161 *Platform*, floor boards laid over the floors in small yachts to make a walking space.

8. b. (Further examples.)

1931 H. F. PRINGLE *Theodore Roosevelt* I. xv. 205 On the special train..a bugler appeared on the rear platform to sound the cavalry charge. **1932** *Atlantic Monthly* Apr. 437/2 As the train pulled out I saw from the back platform my two men. **1971** *Power Farming* Mar. 48/4 Illustrated recently in the trade press was a foot-propelled backward-travelling strawberry picking platform used in Israel. **1971** M. TAK *Truck Talk* 119 *Platform*, a flat bed trailer, a trailer that has a deck (or platform) on which cargo rests but no sides. **1978** R. L. HILL *Evil that Men Do* (1979) xx. 244 An early 'fifties flatbed farm truck sat beside the shack, its stacked platform serving as a temporary pen for two enormous sows. **1979** P. THEROUX *Old Patagonian Express* xviii. 286 We were supposed to have been in Mainara for three minutes... I sat on the steps of the platform and smoked my pipe.

d. A structure which is designed to stand on the bed of the sea (or a lake) and to provide a stable base above water level from which a number of offshore oil or gas wells can be drilled or regulated.

1938 *World Petroleum* May 76/3 The coast line..is exposed to strong winds and rough seas during six months of the year, so that a very substantial platform has to be provided when underwater drilling is to be done. **1955** *Rev. Petroleum Technol.* XIV. 24 Fixed-well platforms, unless capable of multiple-well work, are uneconomical 'at sea'. **1973** *Guardian* 23 May 13/1 In Scotland today the word platform means..a production unit weighing perhaps a quarter of a million tons, going up to 700 feet high..for use in the North Sea oilfields. **1974** *Esso Mag.* Summer 7 The next generation of platforms, now under construction, are concrete structures, in which a massive concrete cellular base, which doubles as oil storage, supports the towers which carry the production platform. **1975** *Sunday Times* 25 May 4/5 Britain's gas supplies are unlikely to be affected, even if some platforms have to stop production temporarily.

e. A gyroscopically stabilized mounting which is isolated from the angular motion of the craft carrying it and provides an inertial frame for the accelerometers of an inertial guidance system; the gyroscopes, accelerometers, and other instruments associated with this.

1946 WELLS & GLENNY in M. Davidson *Gyroscope* III. i. 174 The gyroscope and the magnetic compass assemblies are supported on platforms attached to a rectangular frame. **1954** *Aviation Age* Oct. 21/1 Gyros, by virtue of their ability to maintain a fixed direction in inertial space, provide a ready means for stabilizing the accelerometer platform against angular motion of the vehicle. **1964** C. F. O'DONNELL *Inertial Navig.* i. 20 To aid in platform stabilization, servos are used, with their input signals coming from pick-offs mounted on the precession or output axis of the gyroscopes. **1970** *Time* 27 Apr. 15 He charged up *Odyssey's* small re-entry batteries..and transferred the precise alignment of the command module's 'platform'—its complex of navigational gyroscopes and accelerometers—to a similar platform in the lunar lander. **1977** *Sci. Amer.* Feb. 21/2 A long-range cruise missile employs an inertial-guidance system consisting essentially of three or more accelerometers mounted on gyroscope-stabilized platforms, to guide it along a preassigned course.

f. A rigid diving-board fixed at any of a series of standard heights varying from 3 to 10 metres above the surface of the water; also, in a diving contest, the highboard event.

1971 L. KOPPETT *N.Y. Times Guide Spectator Sports* ix. 169 Off the platform, some dives are made from a handstand. **1973** *Tucson* (Arizona) *Daily Citizen* 21 Aug. 61/7 Finneran is a [*sic*] Olympic veteran, finishing fifth in the three-meters last year in Munich and ninth in the platform. **1974** *Encycl. Brit. Macropædia* XVII. 863/2 When diving first became part of the Olympic program in 1904, it was little more than plain high diving from five- and ten-metre fixed platforms. **1974** *Rules of Game* 202 Competitive diving... Highboard diving platforms and springboards are provided at the heights shown.

9. a. (Later *fig.* examples.)

1964 E. B. WHITE *Let.* 21 Feb. (1976) 517 A man is privileged to say anything he wants to about the magazine, but..he can't use one of my books as a platform. **1966** 'W. HAGGARD' *Power House* vii. 72 *The Freeman* was important to him since it provided him with a platform. **1977** *It* May 29/4 Aims... To act as a platform for people with radical ideas and opinions.

b. (Earlier and later examples.) Also *transf.*

1803 *Massachusetts Spy* 27 Apr. (Th.), The platform of Federalism. **1837** *Liberator* 15 Dec. 203/3 We care not who is found upon this broad platform of our common nature. **1838** *Congress. Globe* 11 Jan. App. 73/1 We wanted no platform on which to stand, save the Constitution of our country. **1882** *Sydney Slang Dict.* 7/1 *Platform*, a standpoint, as 'Home rule's my platform'. Originally an Americanism. **1909** 'O. HENRY' *Roads of Destiny* x. 166 He leaned on the desk and declared his platform to the clerk. He said he had come to Elmore to look for a location to go into business. **1924** H. G. WELLS *Dream* 142, I adopted Votes for Women as the first plank of my political platform. **1926** A. CONAN DOYLE *Hist. Spiritualism* I. ii. 25 The broad platform upon which his beliefs were constructed. **1937** [see *PLANK *sb.* 5]. **1964** GOULD & KOLB *Dict. Social Sci.* 484/2 The party platform is adopted before the candidates for President and Vice-President are nominated and..it can happen that the candidate and the platform disagree in important particulars. **1976** *Survey* Spring 87 The Communist Party of the United States of America..has held conventions to..discuss its strategy and approve a platform.

10. = **platform sole.* Also short for **platform shoe.*

1945 WEBSTER Add., *Platform*,..an outsole a half inch or more thick, made of wood, cork, etc., and usually covered with leather. **1946** *Sun* (Baltimore) 2 Nov. 3 (Advt.), Picture-Pretty Platforms... Two flattering styles to choose from..both mounted on black faille platforms. **1960** D. LESSING *In Pursuit of English* vii. 229, I could not keep my eyes off her shoes... The soles were platforms two inches deep. **1970** *New Yorker* 31 Oct. 125/1 A boot with a small platform in a contrasting color. **1973** *Times* 7 Nov. 18/3 An office manager wearing 4$\frac{1}{2}$ inch..platforms said 'they give you a masculine walk because you walk heavy'. *Ibid.* 18/4 He wore them to catch up with his girl friend's six inch platforms. **1977** C. MCFADDEN *Serial* (1978) v. 17/2 A woman in..eight-inch platforms that reminded him of the moon shot.

C. (sense 8 b) *platform body*; (sense *8 d) *platform leg, operator*; (sense *8 f) *platform diving*; (sense 9) *platform appeal, campaign, eloquence, engagement, -maker, manner(s), orator, plank, point, reply*; *platform-proud* adj.; (sense *10) *platform-wearer*; **platform-car** (earlier example); **platform machine** = *platform scale* (in Dict. and Suppl.); **platform paddle tennis** = **platform tennis*; **platform party,** the group of officials or distinguished persons who sit on the platform at a ceremony or a meeting; **platform rocker** orig. *U.S.*, a rocking chair constructed with a fixed stationary base; **platform sandal,** a sandal with a platform sole; **platform scale** (examples); **platform shoe,** a shoe with a platform sole; **platform sole,** a very thick outer shoe-sole; also *attrib.*; hence *platform-soled* adj.; **platform stage** *Theatr.*, (see quots. 1951) (cf. *apron stage* s.v. *APRON *sb.* 4 j); **platform tennis,** a form of paddle tennis (see *PADDLE *sb.*^{1} 11) played on a platform, usu. of wood, enclosed by a wire fence; **platform ticket,** a ticket admitting a non-traveller to a railway station platform; **platform tree** *poet. nonce-use*, a tree with a wide-spreading, flat-topped crown; **platform truck,** a road transport vehicle having a platform body; **platform yard,** a yard where oil platforms are built.

1959 *Times* 18 June 13/2 Dame Christabel [Pankhurst]..deliberately based her 'platform appeal' on charm rather than logic. **1973** *Amer. Speech 1969* XLIV. 207 *Platform body*, truck or trailer body with a floor but no sides or roof. **1977** *Horse & Hound* 14 Jan. 44/2 (Advt.), A 16 ft horse box frame, for Bedford T.K. platform body, rear ramp with springs. **1909** *Daily Chron.* 9 Feb. 1/7 The National Passive Resistance League is organising a platform campaign against the House of Lords. **1843** E. H. DERBY *Two Months Abroad* (1844) 20/1 By this, with the aid of a winch, diligences and private carriages are.. lifted, with their passengers and baggage, from the wheels and axles, and transferred to platform cars. **1971** L. KOPPETT *N.Y. Times Guide Spectator Sports* xx. 249 Platform and three-meter springboard diving. **1966** *Listener* 24 Nov. 783/3 Mr. Sandford's work was a ferocious contemporary indictment... *Cathy Come Home* may have done more in its hour and a quarter than the platform eloquence of half a year. **1907** G. ADE *Let.* 3 June (1973) 41, I have no hankering to undertake any platform engagements as long as I can get money doing something else. **1975** *Offshore* Aug. 51/2 Divers can be employed to hand risers or lead pipeline ends up into platform legs when lines are pulled. **1922** G. A. OWEN *Treat. Weighing Machines* x. 134 Platform machines and weighbridges..are used in the main for weighing above 1 cwt., and are distinguishable by a goods platform. **1969** T. J. METCALFE *Weighing Machines* I. x. 99 Platform machines may be portable or dormant. **1928** *Daily Tel.* 12 June 14/7 To-day the 'platform-makers' of both parties were trying to frame an election programme. **1969** B. TURNER *Circle of Squares* iii. 23 Anyone who was suspicious of Hirst's platform manner would be disarmed by that bulldozing statement. **1947** *Penguin Music Mag.* Sept. 34 As if Chopin was a puppet worked by a skilled ventriloquist of charming platform-manners. **1975** *BP Shield Internat.* May 1/3 A relatively new breed of oilman will be required. These are the platform operators, the men responsible for the day-to-day running of the platforms. **1866** J. C. PATTESON *Let.* in C. M. Yonge *Life J. C. Patteson* (1874) II. x. 207 Let no platform orator divulge the great secret. **1979** W. J. FISHMAN *Streets of E. London* 117/2 Eleanor Marx-Aveling['s]..remarkable qualities as teacher, platform orator and organiser. **1935** in F. S. Blanchard *Paddle Tennis* (1944) III. v. 56 The following rules..are the officially approved rules for Platform Paddle Tennis. **1959** —— (*title*) Platform paddle tennis: the official guide to platform tennis. **1967** O. H. DURRELL *Official Guide to Platform Tennis* i. 3 Originally called paddle tennis, it later became platform paddle tennis and was finally shortened to platform tennis although most old timers.. still refer to it as paddle. **1967** O. WYND *Walk Softly, Men Praying* xii. 186 You can come with us. As one of the platform party. **1976** C. BERMANT *Coming Home* II. iii. 143 The platform party enters, preceded by a mace bearer, and behind him..the Chancellor. **1931** H. F. PRINGLE *Theodore Roosevelt* I. xii. 161 He borrowed many a platform plank from the man he professed to hold in contempt. **1976** *National Observer* (U.S.) 28 Aug. 4/5 They swallowed platform planks calling for Constitutional amendments to bar abortions and school busing for racial balance. **1949** *Economist* 15 Oct. 825/2 His [*sc.* Lord Beaverbrook's] platform points are pure chauvinism. **1926** R. FROST *Let.* 11 Feb. (1964) 178 You should get so platform proud as to be undealable with. **1904** G. B. SHAW *Common Sense of Municipal Trading* x. 89 One of the keenest grievances of the commercial man who sees profitable branches of his own trade undertaken by the municipality is that it is competing against him 'with his own money', meaning that it forces him to pay rates, and then uses the rates to ruin him in his business. The effective platform reply to this is that the profitable municipal trades, far from costing the ratepayers anything, actually lighten their burden. **1969** J. GLOAG *Short. Dict. Furnit.* (rev. ed.) 564 A revolutionary design, invented in America about 1870, was the platform rocker. **1970** *Globe & Mail* (Toronto) 26 Sept. 45/7 (Advt.), Walnut platform rocker. **1958** *Times* 17 Oct. 17/1 Ivan is first shown wearing four-inch platform sandals. **1967** *Vogue* June 98 White patent platform sandals, 18 gns. **1834** *Mechanics' Mag.* 25 Oct. 248/2 E. & J. Fairbanks, a Concentrated Platform Scale—a diploma. **1851** C. CIST *Sk. Cincinnati in 1851* 227 Factories in which platform scales are made. **1948** D. M. Considine *Industr. Weighing* iv. 67 The portable platform scale consists essentially of a rugged cast iron base mounted on four rubber tired wheels. **1969** T. J. Metcalfe *Weighing Machines* I. x. 105 The compound lever machine shown..is properly described as a 'low pattern steelyard platform scale'. **1969** T. C. Thorstensen *Pract. Leather Technol.* xv. 248 Open-toed and platform shoes are more easily made by sliplasted procedures. **1977** D. Watkin *Morality & Archit.* 12 An unhappy example of this [*sc.* public unconcern with what planners would deem practical] in costume would be the craze for 'platform shoes'. **1939** M. B. Picken *Lang. Fashion* 113/3 *Platform sole*, thick shoe sole, usually from ½ inch to 3 inches in depth; often of cork or wood. **1941** *Amer. Speech* XVI. 98 The advertising writer reserves his best efforts for the finished products... Fine figures include..a platform sole about as thick as the wafer you get with your malted milk. **1960** R. P. Jhabvala *Householder* iii. 154 She would wear her platform-sole shoes and jasmine in her hair. **1977** *Monitor* (McAllen, Texas) 28 Mar. 7A/2 High platform soles..are being phased out although still available for young customers. **1973** *Woman's Own* 6 Jan. 61 Today's fashions, with their high-heeled, platform-soled shoes and long, straight trousers can easily make you look taller. **1974** 'G. Black' *Golden Cockatrice* ix. 142 She was short even with platform-soled shoes. **1895** G. B. Shaw *Our Theatres in the Nineties* (1932) I. 189 The modern pictorial stage is not so favorable to Shakespearean acting and stage illusion as the platform stage. **1951** *Oxf. Compan. Theatre* 218/2 Before English actors had any settled homes they played chiefly in inn-yards.., and their first permanent buildings..were wooden structures, roughly circular, with a raised platform stage backing on to the wall and jutting out into the open space, still called a 'yard'. *Ibid.* 236/2 The success of Davenant's playhouse.. laid the foundations of the new style, and the Elizabethan platform stage was henceforth out of fashion. **1961** Bowman & Ball *Theatre Lang.* 261 *Platform stage*, a stage using an acting area which extends into the auditorium without a proscenium picture frame. **1955** *N.Y. Times* 14 Mar. 31/2 Platform tennis..is one of the fastest growing and most enjoyable of American sports. **1967** *Time* 3 Mar. 45 Platform tennis, more commonly called paddle tennis, is not only the newest addition to the family of tennis-type court games: it is unique in that it is played primarily in winter and always outdoors. **1972** *N.Y. Times* 27 Feb. v. 6 More than 250 players on 128 teams will gather at the 'home of platform tennis', the Fox Meadow Tennis Club in Scarsdale, N.Y., on Friday to compete in the 38th annual United States men's doubles championship. **1977** *Club Tennis* Mar. 13 (*title*) Platform tennis—the game of the 80's paddling its way to success. **1901** *Railway Engineer* XXII. 68/2 In Berlin, at all the railway stations, no one is allowed on the platform unless actually going by train or provided with a 'platform ticket'. **1929** *Station Accounts Instruction Bk.* (Gt. Western Railway) 4 Passengers travelling from Platform Ticket Stations without Railway Tickets must surrender their Platform Tickets, and excess fares be charged accordingly. **1935** C. Winchester *Railway Wonders of World* I. 241/3 At the outset no charge was made for platform tickets by the English railways, but to-day a charge of one penny or thereabouts is usual. **1975** S. Briggs *Keep Smiling Through* 92/2 The Government had never intended the Tubes to be used permanently as shelters... However, there was nothing illegal in your buying a platform ticket for 1½d and not travelling. **1925** E. Sitwell *Troy Park* 67 All day in the limp helpless breeze Beneath the empty platform trees He sits with Brobdingnagian asses. **1925** *Proc. Inst. Production Engineers* V. 144 If trucking is resorted to then use a platform truck. **1967** *Jane's Surface Skimmer Systems 1967–68* 7/1 *Accommodation.* It is available in three versions: a platform truck with a payload of 2,500 to 3,000 kg; or as a coach or bus with seats for twenty passengers and a driver. **1977** *Grimsby Even. Tel.* 14 May 8/5 (Advt.), 1969 Ford D800 platform truck (no test). **1973** A. Price *October Men* ix. 128 He's got a rig of his own... He's built a platform yard of his own at Hartlepool. **1977** *Offshore Engineer* Apr. 9/3 An end-of-contract bonus payment dispute flared up..at Highlands Fabricator's Nigg platform yard, where the steel platform for Chevron's Ninian field..is being completed.

platformate, platformer²: see next.

Platforming (plæ·tfɔːmiŋ), *vbl. sb.*² Also **platforming.** [f. Plat(inum + Re)forming *vbl. sb.*] A proprietary name for a process for reforming petroleum using a platinum catalyst. Freq. *attrib.* Hence **pla·tformate** [after *distillate, filtrate*, etc.], the end product of the process; **pla·tformer²**, an installation for Platforming.

1949 E. F. Nelson in *Oil & Gas Jrnl.* 7 Apr. 95/1 Our [*sc.* Universal Oil Products'] research and development departments have become so used to referring to the process as 'platforming' that we have decided that at this time we would officially christen it. *Ibid.* 100/2 The platformate has an end point slightly above that of the charge. **1952** *Official Gaz.* (U.S. Patent Office) 29 Jan. 1178/2 Universal Oil Products Company, Chicago.. Platforming. For solid catalyst. Claims use since Aug. 29, 1947. **1954** *Ibid.* 19 Jan. 609/1 Platforming. For apparatus in the nature of a plant for the treatment of hydrocarbons. **1954** *Wall St. Jrnl.* 16 Aug. 5/3 Sunray Oil Corp., Tulsa, completed a new 5,000 barrel a day platforming unit at its Sunray Village refinery in Duncan, Okla. **1955** *Times* 8 June 9/4 The extension and modernization of the Suez refinery (including a 'platformer' to improve the quality of the motor benzine). **1957** *Trade Marks Jrnl.* 8 May 470/1 Platforming... Catalysts. Universal Oil Products Company.., Des Plaines, Illinois, United States of America; manufacturers. **1959** *Petroleum Handbk.* (ed. 4) 216 Platformate is used as a component in motor and aviation gasoline blends. **1973** S. A. Berridge in Hobson & Pohl *Mod. Petroleum Technol.* (ed. 4) xi. 410 The Universal Oil Products Company has combined the Udex process with its Platforming process in an operation called Rexforming... The highly paraffinic raffinate from the Udex plant is recycled to the Platformer. **1978** *Trends in Oil & Gas Refining* (Shell Internat. Petroleum Co.) 5 In catalytic reforming..there has been 20 years of Shell experience in the design, development and operation of platformer units.

plathander, var. *platanna.

plating, *vbl. sb.* Add: **1. a.** (Examples in *Surg.*: cf. *plate *v.* 1 b.)

1914 A. P. C. Ashhurst *Surgery* xii. 313 It is better not to plate a recent compound fracture.., but to postpone the plating until the soft parts have healed. **1971** W. J. W. Sharrard *Paediatric Orthopaedics & Fractures* xx. 985 (*heading*) Sound union of both fractures 8 weeks after plating.

b. Also, the process of coating with a thin layer of any substance, *spec.* by means of electrolysis. (Further examples.)

1872 *Jrnl. Chem. Soc.* XXV. 1134 Plating with aluminium cannot be effected. **1946** *Trans. Electrochem. Soc.* LXXXIX. 384 In a recent cost analysis..on the plating of an electric flatiron, it cost $0·46 to apply nickel and chromium. **1966** *McGraw-Hill Encycl. Sci. & Technol.* IV. 531/1 It is difficult to apply zinc coatings thinner than about 0·002 in. by hot dipping... For many articles, thinner coatings are adequate and are applied by plating. **1968** R. W. Berry *Thin Film Technol.* v. 266 In vapor plating, a volatile compound of the substance to be deposited is vaporized, then thermally decomposed at the substrate to yield the desired deposit. **1972** [see *plate *v.* 2 b].

d. (Later example.)

1951 E. Rickman *Come racing with Me* viii. 63 Principal items are veterinary charges, shoeing (or 'plating' as it is called).

f. *Biol.* and *Med.* The preparation of a culture on a plate (see *plate *v.* 6).

1898 *Public Health* (Papers & Rep. Amer. Public Health Assoc.) XXIII. 81 The technical difficulties in the way of successful 'plating' in agar are considerable. **1916** *Jrnl. Bacteriol.* I. 513 Eight different samples of raw and heated soil were selected for this examination, some samples being plated immediately, others being incubated at 37°C. for 48 hours before plating. **1934** A. T. Henrici *Biol. Bacteria* xii. 201 The procedure most commonly used for obtaining pure cultures from mixtures of microbes is the process of plating introduced by Koch. *Ibid.* 203 Plating may be used also to measure or estimate the number of bacteria in a given substance. **1969** M. R. Droop in Norris & Ribbons *Methods in Microbiol.* III B. xi. 276 The sample for isolation will usually require a considerable degree of dilution before plating.

g. The furnishing of a book with a book-plate.

1906 *Daily Chron.* 10 Aug. 3/2 'Plating'..would appear to be the process of affixing the book-plate to the inside of the first cover of the volumes. **1938** L. M. Harrod *Librarians' Gloss.* 116 *Plating*, the process of pasting labels in library books.

h. *Machine knitting.* (See quot. 1946.)

1946 A. J. Hall *Standard Handbk. Textiles* iii. 140 It is possible to run two threads at once into the knitting machine and arrange that one of these predominates in the back of the fabric whilst the other is mostly seen on the front... This method of knitting is known as plating. **1954** *Textile Terms & Defs.* (Textile Institute) 30 Plating usually involves the knitting of two yarns of different colour, different lustre, or different composition, so that only one of these yarns is visible on the face of the stitch.

i. = *fellatio, *cunnilingus. *slang.*

1965 W. Young *Eros Denied* xiv. 137 *Gamming*, from the French *gamahucher*, or *blowing*, or *plating*, or *noshing* **1969** Fabian & Byrne *Groupie* ii. 16 Why do you think plating is perverted? Everyone I know does it.

j. With reference to a goods vehicle: see *plate *v.* 10.

1968 *Economist* 27 Jan. 61/2 All three firms have had a couple of prosperous years recently, benefiting from the rapid transition from rigid lorries to articulated vehicles and by the introduction of 'plating' and other new inspection requirements. **1972** *Police Rev.* 10 Nov. 1463/1 The Minister's approval certificate..will eventually obviate the necessity of attending the testing station for plating.

2. b. Also, any metal coating. (Further examples.)

1901 B. Blount *Pract. Electro-Chem.* v. 268 Nickel plating is harder and more brittle than the metal in massive form. **1946** *Trans. Electrochem. Soc.* LXXXIX. 409 (*heading*) Plating deposited from nickel-cobalt chloride solution. **1962** *Engineering* 7 Sept. 321/3 (*heading*) Mirror surface on copper plating.

c. *Biol.* and *Med.* A culture on a plate (*plate *sb.* 18 e).

1901 *Jrnl. Hygiene* I. 298 Platings from this broth have then been made in litmus-lactose-agar. **1928** *Jrnl. Bacteriol.* XVI. 272 Platings were made of each sample of milk immediately after it was received.

3. plating certificate, a certificate stating that a goods vehicle has had a plating examination; **plating examination,** a legally-required inspection of a goods vehicle to establish weight, roadworthiness, etc.

1968 *Goods Vehicles (Plating & Testing) Regulations* (601) Reg. 2 'Ministry plate' means a plate issued by the Minister for a goods vehicle following the issue or amendment of a plating certificate. **1978** *Highway Code* 64 Before driving, make sure that..you have a current plating certificate for your goods vehicle. **1973** J. Duckworth *Kitchin's Road Transport Law* (ed. 16) 94 The first examination consists of a plating examination in which the vehicle's axle and gross weights are assessed and recorded on a plate, followed by a test of roadworthiness.

platiniridium. Add: Also **platino-iridium.** (Examples.)

1848 J. D. Dana *Man. Mineral.* vi. 309 A similar platin-iridium has been obtained at Ava in the East Indies. **1888** *Encycl. Brit.* XXIV. 480/1 The new standard of the International Metric Commission is a line-standard of platino-iridium, 40 inches long. **1908** *Practitioner* Sept. 485 The best needle to use is one of platino-iridium, since it can be rendered absolutely sterile in the flame of a spirit lamp. **1965** G. J. Williams *Econ. Geol. N.Z.* x. 154/2 Farquharson (1910) quoted earlier reports on the occurrence of 'osmiridium' and 'platiniridium' in the Tertiary auriferous quartzose conglomerates..in north-western Nelson.

platinite. Add: **2.** *Metallurgy.* Also **Platinite.** An alloy of iron with 42 to 50 per cent nickel which has the same coefficient of expansion as platinum and has supplanted that metal in various electrical applications, esp. for metal-to-glass contacts in lamps.

1918 *Nature* 15 Aug. 471/1 The Germans..have found that for certain purposes an alloy of nickel and iron may replace platinum. The alloy—called 'platinite'—may be used in electric lamps. **1923** *Engineering* 23 Nov. 651/3 The iron-nickel alloy known as 'Platinite', containing 46 per cent. of nickel and about 0·15 per cent. of carbon, had practically the same coefficient of expansion as glass. **1929** [see *elinvar]. **1965** A. D. Merriman *Conc. Encycl. Metallurgy* 731 Platinite..is used for lead-in wires in electric-lamp bulbs.

platino-. Add: **platinocy·anide,** any of a series of fluorescent salts which contain the anion $Pt(CN)_4^{2-}$; **platino-iridium,** var. Platiniridium in Dict. and Suppl.

1845 W. Gregory *Outl. Chem.* II. 306 The platinocyanides of barium, strontium, and calcium..crystallise readily in beautiful greenish yellow colour. **1926** *Sunday at Home* 677/2 The luminous paint..consists..of a mixture of some radium or thorium salt with some photo-sensitive substance like barium platinocyanide. **1974** *Sci. Amer.* Mar. 96/1 The screen would consist of a thin, translucent disk of mica, coated with a phosphor such as barium platinocyanide or zinc silicate.

platinum. Add: **1. b.** A greyish white colour like that of platinum.

1923 *Daily Mail* 1 Aug. 2 In the following colours: Black, White,..Suede, Platinum and Champagne. **1951** E. Paul *Springtime in Paris* xvi. 313 Looking pensively down at the moving river surface, ebony and indigo. The moon, coming out thinly.., contributed platinum. **1976** *Milton Keynes Express* 11 June 38/2 (Advt.), 1974 'M' Vauxhall Victor 2300 Auto Saloon. Finished in platinum, fitted wing mirrors, radio.

c. = *platinum fox* s.v. sense 2 c below.

1948 A. L. Rand *Mammals Eastern Rockies* 105 Various other 'varieties' [of red fox] have been developed on fur farms, including the platinums and various white-spotted phases.

2. b. platinum-blue [tr. G. *platinblau* (Hofmann & Bugge 1908, in *Ber. d. Deut. Chem. Ges.* XLI. 312)], any of a class of dark blue polymeric complexes, a number of which have antitumour activity, which are formed by divalent platinum with amide ligands; orig. *spec.* one formed with acetamide; **platinum sponge**, a grey amorphous form of platinum which is obtained as spongy masses on heating ammonium chloroplatinate and is used as a catalyst.

1908 *Jrnl. Chem. Soc.* XCIV. I. 141 (*heading*) Platinum-Blue. **1964** *Ibid.* 2835 Platinum Blue is very soluble in water, methanol, and dimethylformamide from which it can be crystallised by the addition of dichloromethane. **1975** *Cancer Chemotherapy Rep.* I. LIX. 296/1 We tentatively conclude from these early results that the 'platinum blues' may have activity against a broad spectrum of tumors. **1976** *Cancer Res.* XXXVI. 3822/1 Platinum-uracil blue and platinum-thymine blue are prototype examples of platinum-blue complexes which have been shown to have a higher therapeutic index against ascites Sarcoma 180. **1826** W. Henry *Elem. Exper. Chem.* (ed. 10) I. vii. 355 Into a mixture of carbonic oxide with a larger proportion of the explosive mixture, the platinum sponge cannot be introduced without causing detonation. **1894** G. S. Newth *Text-bk. Inorg. Chem.* III. xiv. 644 This action is more rapid in the case of platinum sponge, when a larger surface is brought into play, and a fragment of this material introduced into a detonating mixture of oxygen and hydrogen at once determines its explosion. **1968** A. A. Baker *Unsaturation in Org. Chem.* ix. 125 In 1838 Frederic Kuhlmann produced ammonia by heating a mixture of nitric oxide and hydrogen in the presence of platinum sponge.

c. Platinum or platinum-blonde (see below) in colour, as *platinum hair, lace*; esp. of animals or their fur, as *platinum coney, fox, mink*; also *platinum-grey*; **platinum blond(e)** *a.*, (of the hair) silvery-blonde in colour; (of a person) having silvery-blonde hair; also as *sb.*, a person, esp. a woman, with platinum-blonde hair.

1931 *Daily Express* 15 Oct. 19/5 (*caption*) Miss Binnie Barnes, who appears as a platinum blonde in 'Cavalcade', is seen here as a brunette. Nature gave her auburn-red hair. **1934** R. Ferguson *Celebrated Sequels* 264 A costly platinum-blond young man from a famous night-club. **1934** F. Stark *Valleys of Assassins* ii. 187 It was a blue stream, as vivid in that thirsty solitude as a platinum blonde in a monastery. **1942** A. Christie *Body in Library* ii. 24 She had scarlet lips, blackened eyelashes, and a platinum-blonde head. **1966** J. S. Cox *Illustr. Dict. Hairdressing & Wigmaking* 118/1 *Platinum blonde*, a very fair, silvery hued colour popularized by Jean Harlow, the late curvaceous American film star. **1977** *Transatlantic Rev.* LX. 53 From ten to eleven, no one checked in except a commercial salesman with three suitcases of samples and a middle-aged gent with a platinum blonde. **1923** *Daily Mail* 14 Aug. 1 The wide collar and side panels..are made of the richest pulled Platinum Coney. **1946** A. Christie *Hollow* viii. 77 The platinum foxes that swathed her shoulders. **1908** *Westm. Gaz.* 25 Apr. 13/2 Such a suit is a very pleasant idea for the summer. I saw one the other day in a platinum-grey. **1951** Wodehouse *Old Reliable* xv. 171 This miserable creature, who has probably got platinum hair and a lisp. **1978** D. Francis *Trial Run* i. 11 Her fine-boned face and thick platinum hair. **1923** *Daily Mail* 20 June 8 In a platinum lace gown and cape. **1949** R. Chandler *Little Sister* xviii. 117 No big money,..no platinum mink, no name in neons. **1950** 'S. Ransome' *Deadly Miss Ashley* i. 12 She was wearing a fur piece...It was platinum mink.

platitudinal, *a.* (Earlier example.)

1870 O. Logan *Before Footlights* xxiii. 288 At the risk of uttering truisms and being altogether a platitudinal truist, I may mention that it requires a pretty strong organic construction to stand the ravages of an eight months' tour in the land of fast eaters.

platitudinary (plætitiū·dinări), *a.* [As if f. L. **platitudo, -din-* + -ary[1]; cf. Latitudinary *a.*] = Platitudinarian *a.*

1920 *Glasgow Herald* 2 Apr. 6 At a song-recital..the critic is again troubled by Elgar—this time by a 'tawdry catch-penny ballad'... At a Queen's Hall Concert the Elgar of the Second Symphony is 'platitudinary and tedious'. **1933** Dylan Thomas *Let.* Sept. (1966) 24 Wordsworth was..the humourless, the platitudinary reporter of Nature in her dullest moods.

platitu·dinist. *rare.* [f. Platitudinize *v.* + -ist.] A person who utters platitudes; a platitudinizer.

1905 W. J. Locke *Usurper* xx. 243 Jasper..was not sorry when the kind-hearted platitudinist had gone. **1905** —— *Morals of Marcus Ordeyne* ii. 22 If there is one platitudinist I dislike more than another, it is Marcus Aurelius.

Platonian. Restrict † *Obs.* to the sb. and add: **B.** *adj.* = Platonic *a.* 1. *rare.*

1942 B. Berenson *Jrnl.* 28 Feb. in *One Year's Reading for Fun* (1960) 30 Aristides speaks in the Platonian *Theages*.

Platonic, *a.* and *sb.* Add: **A.** *adj.* **1. c.** Appositive, as *Platonic-Christian* adj., both Platonic and Christian, of or pertaining to Christianity influenced by or fused with Platonism.

1933 A. N. Whitehead *Adventures of Ideas* iii. 40 In the hands of theologians..the Platonic-Christian tradition leant heavily towards its mystical religious side. **1948** L. Spitzer *Linguistics & Lit. Hist.* 55 To Dante, all dialects appeared as inferior..realizations of a Platonic-Christian ideal pattern of language. **1960** *Encounter* Feb. 49/1 This is at the root of the Platonic-Christian (or religious) tradition.

2. Now usu. with lower-case initial. (Earlier and further examples.) Also of affection for one of the same sex.

1631 Jonson *New Inne* III. ii. sig. E5[v], Most Socratick Lady! Or, if you will Ironick! gi' you ioy O' you Platonick loue here. *c* **1805** Jane Austen *Lady Susan* (1954) x. 258 We are advancing now towards some kind of confidence, and in short are likely to be engaged in a kind of platonic friendship. **1905** 'A. Cambridge' (*title*) A platonic friendship. *Ibid.* v. 67 What is known as a platonic friendship is generally nothing of the kind. **1919** G. B. Shaw *Heartbreak House* II. 87 *Hector*... What do you get by it? Are you her lover? *Randall.* You must not misunderstand me. In a higher sense— *Hector.* Psha! Platonic sense! She makes you her servant; and when pay-day comes round, she bilks you: that is what you mean. **1924** 'W. Fabian' *Sailors' Wives* vii. 94 'You're taking a lot of notice of that dangerous young person, old bean,' remarked Dorr lightly. 'Platonic, purely. Couldn't well be anything else for a man with my prospects.' **1925** C. Connolly *Let.* 14 May in *Romantic Friendship* (1975) 78, I think I care more for Maurice than anyone else here—and the fact that such affection can be nothing but platonic enhances it, if anything. **1928** A. Huxley *Point Counter Point* xiii. 232 He had such a pure, childlike and platonic way of going to bed with women, that neither they nor he ever considered that the process really counted as going to bed. **1957** J. Braine *Room at Top* vii. 64 'Teddy wouldn't understand. Our relationship is strictly platonic.' 'Yes, I understand,' Teddy said, putting his arm round June's waist. 'I'm trying to take June on a platonic weekend. Of course, it'll be too bad if she has a platonic baby.' **1975** A. Price *Our Man in Camelot* v. 76 'Sharing a bedroom with a strange man in the line of duty. Kind of special relationship.' 'Special *platonic* relationship.'

3. a. Delete † *Obs.* and 'former', and add later examples. Now also called *Platonic solids*.

1745 E. Stone *Euclid's Elements* (ed. 2) II. p. xxiv, The thirteenth, fourteenth and fifteenth Books entertain us with curious and useful Speculations, relating to the five regular or platonick Bodies, in Regard to which, as Proclus tells us, Euclid compiled the whole Body of the Elements, the Platonicks having had them in wonderful Esteem. **1873** J. Booth *Treat. Some New Geom. Methods* I. p. xi, That the principle of Duality should not have been discovered by the great geometers of Ancient Greece is the more remarkable, as the five regular solids, the Platonic bodies as they were called, were with them a favourite subject of speculation. **1917** H. E. Dudeney *Amusements in Math.* 70/2 The icosahedron is another of the five regular, or Platonic, bodies having all their sides, angles, and planes similar and equal. **1952** Cundy & Rollett *Math. Models* iii. 70 The so-called Platonic solids..form the first and simplest group of polyhedra. **1952** G. Sarton *Hist. Sci.* I. xvii. 439 If the regular solids are restricted to five, those five bodies (later called the Platonic bodies) must each have some definite meaning. **1971** M. J. Wenninger *Polyhedron Models* i. 19 The dodecahedron is in some ways the most attractive of the five Platonic solids.

b. (Further example.)

1922 W. B. Yeats *Seven Poems* 23 Are not those who travel in the whirling dust also in the Platonic Year?

B. *sb.* **3.** (Later examples.)

1923 R. Macaulay *Told by Idiot* i. 11 To Vicky a young man *was* a young man, and no platonics about it. **1937** 'M. Innes' *Hamlet, Revenge!* II. vi. 173 It is one of those affairs that are laced with long-term platonics.

platonically, *adv.* (Later examples.)

1901 Conrad & Hueffer *Inheritors* iii. 39 Gurnard I disliked platonically; perhaps because his face was a little enigmatic—a little repulsive. **1941** J. D. Carr *Case of Constant Suicides* iii. 34 There is nothing like spending the night with a girl, even platonically, to remove a sense of constraint. **1972** *Nature* 17 Mar. 92/1 It would be convenient if there were such a platonically ideal chemistry. **1973** *Listener* 6 Sept. 312/1 They stood in tasteful tableaux, their hands platonically resting on one another's nether regions.

Platonistic, *a.* Add: (Later examples.) Hence **Platoni·stically** *adv.*

1953 M. H. Abrams *Mirror & Lamp* i. 29 Shelley's Platonistic 'Defence of Poetry'. **1957** G. Ryle in C. Mace *Brit. Philos. in Mid-Cent.* 263 The difficulty is to steer between the Scylla of a Platonistic and the Charybdis of a lexicographical account of the business of philosophy and logic. **1959** P. F. Strawson *Individuals* viii. 234 No doubt some philosophers have deluded themselves with myths, have invested non-particulars with a character they do not really possess. There is Platonistic zeal as well as nominalistic zeal. But zeal of either kind is out of place. **1977** G. W. H. Lampe *God as Spirit* iv. 108 The Platonistically conceived Second Person of the Trinity in the classical formulations of the fourth and fifth centuries.

platoon, *sb.* Add: **1.** Revived in the British army for an organizational unit (usu. a quarter) of a company of infantry. Also used for comparable organizational units in other armies.

1913 *Army Order* No. 323. 16 Sept. §4 A company will be divided into four platoons, each commanded by a subaltern... Each platoon will be sub-divided under regulations to be issued later. **1915** D. O. Barnett *Let.* 18 Jan. 40 I've bought A. Coy. No. 4 Platoon. **1917** J. M. Barrie *Old Lady shows her Medals* 72 You have knitted enough things already to fit up my whole platoon. **1929** *Encycl. Brit.* XVIII. 64/2 In the U.S. cavalry a troop is divided into four platoons. **1938** 'I. Hay' *King's Service* xiv. 245 The number of platoons in a rifle company has been reduced from four to three. **1945** H. P. Samwell *Infantry Officer with Eighth Army* iv. 33 We had agreed that he should bring up Company H.Q. and the reserve platoon behind, while I led the forward platoons. **1948** N. Mailer *Naked & Dead* (1949) I. ii. 25 What a bunch of good old boys there were in the platoon, he told himself. **1964** H. D. Chaplin *Queen's Own Royal W. Kent Regiment 1951–1961* ii. 45 Four platoons under Major Crumplin spent Christmas and the New Year festival in the jungle. **1964** Clough & Cash tr. *Gorbatov's Years off my Life* x. 161, I told Kostevich to send a platoon from each battalion to man the line. **1965** I. Adamson *Forgotten Men* i. 15 Working with Animal Transport Platoons had been part of their training in the Bush Warfare School. **1971** E. Luttwak *Dict. Mod. War* 153/2 *Platoon*, an army formation subordinate to the battalion and comprising a number of squads or sections. Normally the smallest unit with an organizational identity, it varies in size from the 12 men of a Soviet army tank platoon to the 40 plus men of a U.S. army infantry platoon. **1972** J. Strawson *Battle for Ardennes* vi. 90 The critical feature was occupied..by a weak platoon numbering some eighteen men of the 394 US Infantry Regiment of 99th Division.

2. b. *Amer. Football.* A group of players trained to act together as a single unit of attack or defence and usu. sent into or withdrawn from the game as a body.

1941 *Charlottesville* (Va.) *Daily Progress* 14 Jan. 11 They [*sc.* football teams] can still send in as many players—platoons included—while the clock is stopped. **1948** *N.Y. Times* 28 Sept. 36/6 Eleven men may be sent in at a time now, even with the clock running..but Lou [Little] is opposed to this unlimited substitution rule in theory. Maj. Joel Stephens, of West Point,..said that Army has the 'two-platoon' system now. **1949** *Sun* (Baltimore) 2 Dec. 17/7 Schweder is one of the unusual football players of the 'platoon age' in that he plays on both offense and defense.

c. *Baseball.* (See quot.)

1976 *Webster's Sports Dict.* 318/2 *Platoon..Baseball*, two or more players who alternate at the same position. The players who make up a particular platoon are usually average players who are adequate fielders but who are not outstanding hitters.

3. *platoon commander, corporal, drill, leader, officer, sergeant, -training.*

1917 W. Owen *Let.* 23 Nov. (1967) 509 Interesting work but hardly 'lighter' than a Platoon Commander's. **1920** J. C. Chase *Soldiers All* 57 He received orders to proceed to Hill 182... He sent runners to notify his platoon commanders. **1974** G. Blaxland *Queen's Own Buffs* iii. 21 There was to be similar pairing of platoon commanders and platoon sergeants. **1941** A. Cotterell *What! No Morning Tea?* 29 After breakfast there was a joint lecture by our two platoon corporals on what to call the various parts of the rifle. **1935** I. Miller *School Tie* xv. 290, I could never get the hang of anything more evolutionary than platoon-drill. **1952** T. J. Mulvey *These are your Sons* iv. 85 He's got three rifle platoon leaders and one weapons platoon leader. **1923** Kipling *Irish Guards in Great War* I. 24 A newly appointed platoon-officer..admonished them unofficially. **1915** D. O. Barnett *Lett.* 41, I like the men awfully, especially my platoon sergeant. **1965** Brophy & Partridge *Long Trail* 224 The Staff.. were known only by occasional glimpses. The platoon-sergeant, whatever his defects, was visible and human. **1974** Platoon sergeant [see **platoon commander*]. **1923** Kipling *Irish Guards in Great War* II. 138 These Somme officers were accordingly told that most of their time should be given to platoon-training. **1942** E. Waugh *Put out More Flags* ii. 125 After the stand-easy they fell in for platoon training.

platoon, *v.* Restrict † *Obs.* to sense in Dict. and add: **2.** *trans.* To dispose in platoons.

1961 in Webster s.v., The advantages from platooning students in smaller schools.

3. *Baseball.* **a.** *trans.* To alternate (a player) with another in the same position. **b.** *intr.* To interchange with another player in the same position. Hence **platoo·ning** *vbl. sb.*

1967 Webster Add., *Platoon..*, to alternate (one player) with another player in the same position (as on a baseball team). **1969** *Time* 5 Sept. 52 Hodges decided to 'platoon' him by playing him only against lefthanded pitchers. **1971** L. Durocher in *Webster* Add. s.v., If I can't play him every day, I'll platoon him in left field. **1971** *Ibid.*, *Platoon..*, to alternate with another player in the same position. **1972** *N.Y. Times* 4 June v. 2/7 Buckner also shares first base with Wes Parker and Crawford platoons with Manny Mota in left field. *Ibid.* 3 Nov. 45/6 He might junk the platooning system used rigidly by Williams.

Platt: see next.

Plattdeutsch (plæt͵doi·tʃ). Also **Platt-Deutsch.** [G., ad. Du. *Platduitsch* Low German, f. *plat* flat, low + *Duitsch* German.] The collective name of those dialects of Germany which are not High German (see German *sb.*[2] 2 b). Also *attrib.* Also *ellipt.* as **Platt.**

1814 H. Weber *Illustr. North. Antiq.* 217 As the fragment [sc. *Hildebrandslied*] is evidently written in the dialect of the northern parts of Germany, now denominated Plat-t, or Low German, which was once nearly identical with the Anglo-Saxon, a great number of the words have been rendered into such as, with little variation, existed in the old English and Scottish. *a* **1834** Coleridge *Table Talk* (1835) I. 119 Originally..in the *Platt-Deutsch* of the north of Germany there were only two definite articles. **1867** J. Macgregor *Rob Roy on Baltic* xix. 239 What a linguist this critic must be before he attempts a voyage such as we have described! First he must learn Norwegian, then Swedish,..then Platt (on the Elbe), [etc.]. **1886** Strong & Meyer *Outl. Hist. German Lang.* 67 New-Low-German, or *Plattdeutsch*, so called from being spoken in the *platte land* or the low country. **1908** T. G. Tucker *Introd. Nat. Hist. Lang.* 220 The Saxonic dialects, under the name of *Nieder-Deutsch* or *Platt-Deutsch* are still in regular use among the populace of North Germany. **1939** L. H. Gray *Found. Lang.* 349 Lower Franconian is essentially Low Teutonic of the type represented by Flemish, Frisian, Old Saxon, and Plattdeutsch. **1942** *Amer. Pol. Sci. Rev.* XXXVI. 537 At present, the speakers of the Lower Saxon, Plattdeutsch vernacular of Gelderland, of Frisian in Friesland, and of genuine Lower Frankish, Dutch dialects are all united in using Dutch as the language of school and church and as the medium of their common national allegiance. **1953** *Trans. Philol. Soc. 1952* 135 The Plattdeutsch forms require discussion. **1970** L. Deighton *Bomber* xxiv. 349 [He was] trying to understand Voss's fast guttural *Plattdeutsch*, as much like Dutch as German. **1973** *Word 1970* XXVI. 44 All informants felt that it was a loanword... A few said it was not good *Platt*, while others felt that it [sc. *hauptsächlich*] was thoroughly acceptable. **1977** *Trans. Philol. Soc. 1975* 187 At first sight North Frisian seems to have more in common with the Plattdeutsch spoken in Schleswig than with other forms of Frisian, and so the question arises as to what justification there is for not considering Frisian to be a variety of local Platt.

‖ **platteland** (pla·tələnt). *S. Afr.* Also with capital initial and hyphenated (**platte-land**). [Afrikaans, f. Du. *plat* flat + *land* country.] The rural areas of South Africa. Also *attrib.* Hence **plattelander** (pla·təla:ndəɹ), a native or inhabitant of a rural area.

1933 C. J. Uys *In Era of Shepstone* vii. 199 Like a leaven the discontent spread from town to town—leaving the *platteland* unaffected—while the Cape and Natal journals magnified the danger out of all proportion. **1934** *Sunday Times* (Johannesburg) 13 May, It is useless to take the platteland youngster and to teach him to enter a college or university. **1934** E. A. Walker *Gt. Trek* ii. 46 Generally speaking the plattelanders were healthy, as they had need to be if they were to survive. **1935** N. Giles

Dark Border II. i. 171 The cattle return to-morrow to the *platteland* and you will go with them. **1943** J. Y. T. GREIG *Language at Work* 106 Political discussions..take place on the stoep or in the bar-parlour of a hotel in some dorpie of the platteland. **1954** W. K. HANCOCK *Country & Calling* vi. 173 Some idealists of the Dutch Reformed Church have recently deduced from *apartheid* the necessity of an immense economic investment in the Native Reserves. It is improbable that voters on the *platteland* will recognize the same necessity. **1955** J. H. WELLINGTON *Southern Afr.* II. III. xv. 215 The larger urban populations have no great sympathy with what they often regard as the reactionary and parochial attitudes of the plattelanders. **1958** A. JACKSON *Trader on Veld* 20 The idea of leaving the comfort and relative sophistication of Port Elizabeth held no terrors for me, and when my Uncle mentioned that he might fix me up on the Platteland, I was eager to hear more. **1960** *Economist* 7 May 505/2 The prime minister's escape from assassination—an escape regarded by the platteland mentality as providential in a more than political sense. **1967** 'L. BLACK' *Two Ladies in Verona* ii. 28 She told him of her childhood in the platteland of South Africa. **1971** *Progress* (Cape Town) May 9/5 The Provincial Executive would..value any..contact which the plattelanders might make. **1971** *Rand Daily Mail* 4 Sept. 8/4 Platteland towns are being encouraged to join in the great property development game which has been largely confined until now to the bigger South African centres. **1977** *Time* 21 Nov. 10/2 'Man,' he shouted, 'this [*sc.* B. J. Vorster] is the man! This is the Churchill of the *platteland*!'

platter[1]. Restrict 'Now chiefly *arch.*' to primary sense in Dict. and add: Also in colloq. phr. *to hand* (something to someone) *on a* (*silver*) *platter* = *to hand on a plate* s.v. *PLATE *sb.* 18a; *platters of meat* (Rhyming slang) = *plates of meat* s.v. *PLATE *sb.* 18d; also ellipt. as *platters*.

1918 T. WOLFE *Let.* 18 Feb. (1958) 8 You don't get anything handed to you on a silver platter. **1923** J. MANCHON *Le Slang* 227 *Plates of meat*,.. = *feet*. On dit aussi *platters of meat*. **1945** L. SHELLY *Jive Talk Dict.* 16/1 *Platters*.., big feet. **1960** J. FRANKLYN *Dict. Rhyming Slang* 108/2 *Platters of meat*, feet. 20 C., a form of *plates*.. and not used in Cockney circles. **1960** G. SANDERS *Mem. Professional Cad* I. vii. 55, I was otherwise engaged at the time building a telescope in my back garden and being, by vocation, a dilettante, this interested me far more than the golden future which Mr. Mayer was going to offer me on a silver platter. **1968** J. UPDIKE *Couples* iii. 229 It's *you* who want to keep them down, to give them on a platter everything everybody else in this country has had to work for. **1970** C. MAJOR *Dict. Afro-Amer. Slang* 92 *Platters*, feet. **1973** *New Yorker* 3 Feb. 49/1 Other things are handed to you on a platter.

b. platter-face (later example); **platter pull**, a type of ski-lift (see quots.).

1922 JOYCE *Ulysses* 374 Some good matronly woman.. to mother him. Take him in tow, platter face and a large apron. **1951** *Amer. Ski Ann. & Skiing Jrnl.* 1952 30 (Advt.), Belleayre Mountain..Chair Lift Rope Tow Platter Pull Lifts. **1953** *Ibid.* 1954 117/2 The J- and T-bar are a form of seat. Later..came..the platter pull, a platter-shaped seat. These lifts are basically the same and tow the skier from an overhead cable. **1963** *Amer. Speech* XXXVIII. 206 *Platter pull*,..a kind of pull transporting skiers uphill. The skier places between the thighs a rubber or plastic disk which is suspended, usually on a bar, from a rope or a cable permanently fixed to the lift cable. **1970** M. BENNETT *How to ski just a Little Bit* ii. 87 A platter pull, sometimes also called a poma, looks as if you took a T-bar, bent it a little, cut the crosspiece off, and attached instead a flat, slightly oval disc approximately six inches in diameter.

2. *slang.* A gramophone record. Cf. *PLATE *sb.* 18g.

1931 H. MUTSCHMANN *Gloss. Americanisms* 46/2 *Platter*, a gramophone record. **1935** *Vanity Fair* (N.Y.) Nov. 38/1 There ought to be a hot coupling on every platter. **1943** H. A. SMITH *Putty Knife* 163, I bought a couple of Crosby platters. **1960** *Master Detective* July 83/2 Rock and Roll, that's what I'm good at. I got a terrific collection of platters. **1967** 'T. WELLS' *Dead by Light of Moon* xviii. 184, I went into Fink Roth's pad and found treasures. Good old platters and stamps. I sold them. Got a good price for the records. The stamps were only so-so. **1977** *Sounds* 9 July 18/1 'Starz'—as the premier platter was called—was hardly the strongest product ever to find its way on to the record racks.

3. The metal disc of a turntable unit, on which the record is placed for playing.

1975 *Gramophone* Jan. 1297 (Advt.), With the heavy platter and extra thick turn-table mat, our final figures are impressive. **1975** *Hi-Fi Answers* Feb. 66/1 Trouble was experienced with ferrous platters inducing a high level of hum.

platy-. Add: **platycephaly** (examples); **platycra·nial** *a.*, broad-skulled; **platyhieric** *a.* (earlier example); **platypellic** *a.* (earlier and later examples).

1902 Platycephaly [see *brachycranial* adj. s.v. *BRACHY-]. **1946** *Nature* 28 Sept. 428/1 Many of the skull characters are remarkably simian, including heavy projecting supra-orbital ridges, retreating forehead, marked platycephaly and massive jaws. **1902** *Biometrika* I. 462 Brachycephaly is associated with platycranial characters in both races. **1886** W. TURNER in *Jrnl. Anat. & Path.* XX. 317 The following descriptive terms may conveniently express these differences in the relative length and breadth of the sacrum. As the Greek word ἱερόν is the equivalent of the Latin sacrum; the term *dolichohieric* would signify a sacrum in which the length exceeded the breadth, whilst *platyhieric* would signify a sacrum in which the breadth exceeded the length. **1885** —— in *Ibid.* XX. 128, I..shall make three divisions, two of which will represent extreme forms in opposite directions, whilst the third will be intermediate. I shall express these divisions in terms derived from the Greek, so that the nomenclature in pelvic classification may be as far as possible on the same lines as the well-known divisions of crania... By *dolichopellic* is to be understood a pelvis in which the conjugate diameter of the brim is either longer than the transverse or approaches closely to it: by *platypellic* a pelvis in which the transverse diameter of the brim greatly exceeds the conjugate; by *mesatipellic* a pelvis in which the transverse diameter is not so greatly in excess of the conjugate. **1966** Platypellic [see *MESATIPELLIC *a.*].

platycodon (plætikōᵘ·dǭn). [mod.L. (A. de Candolle *Monographie des Campanulacées* (1830) 125), f. PLATY- + Gr. κώδων bell.] A herbaceous perennial plant of the monotypic genus so called, belonging to the family Campanulaceæ, native to China and Japan, and bearing blue or white bell-shaped flowers; = *balloon-flower* s.v. *BALLOON *sb.*[1] 10c.

1844 J. W. LOUDON *Ladies' Flower-Garden Ornamental Perennials* II. 52 The Large-flowered platycodon. **1905** H. R. ELY *Another Hardy Garden Bk.* v. 141 By the third year the Platycodons become large, strong plants. **1937** DUNBAR & MAHONEY *Gardener's Choice* 139 The best way of increasing the Platycodon is from seed. **1959** *Times* 3 Jan. 9/5 The platycodon makes a fine pot plant for a cool greenhouse. **1977** J. JEFFREYS *Perennials for Cutting* ii. 160 In a suitable site this platycodon is fully hardy and long-lived.

platykurtic (plætikǖ·ɹtik), *a.* *Statistics.* [f. PLATY- + Gr. κυρτ-ός bulging + -IC.] Of a frequency distribution or its graphical representation: having less kurtosis than the normal distribution.

1905 [see *LEPTOKURTIC *a.*]. **1937** YULE & KENDALL *Introd. Theory Statistics* (ed. 11) ix. 165 Platykurtic curves, like the platypus, are squat with short tails. Leptokurtic curves are high with long tails like the kangaroo—noted for 'lepping'! **1952** [see *KURTOSIS]. **1966** S. BEER *Decision & Control* xiii. 334 Moreover, the distributions may be either leptokurtic or platykurtic—that is, either too peaked or too flattened to be Gaussian. **1979** *Nature* 25 Jan. 297/1 Platykurtosis is not sufficient to demonstrate bimodality, but bimodal distributions are platykurtic.

Hence **pla:tyku·rtosis** [*KURTOSIS], the property of being platykurtic.

1939 A. E. TRELOAR *Elem. of Statistical Reasoning* ii. 34 Positive (or lepto-) kurtosis, mesokurtosis (that of the 'law of error' or normal curve), and negative (or platy-) kurtosis mean simply that the clustering at the center is respectively greater than, equal to, or less than that of the normal curve. **1949** [see *LEPTOKURTOSIS]. **1979** [see above].

platymeria (plætimīᵊ·riă). *Anat.* Also anglicized as **platymery** (plæ·timīᵊri). [ad. F. *platymèrie* (L. Manouvrier 1899, in *Compt. rend. Congr. internat. d'Anthropol. et d'Archéol. préhist.* (1891) 363), f. Gr. μηρία thigh bones: see PLATY-, -IA[1], and -Y[3].] The condition of a femur of which the antero-posterior diameter of its shaft is unusually small relative to the corresponding transverse diameter. Also **pla·tymerism**, in the same sense. Hence **platyme·ric** *a.*, of, pertaining to, or displaying platymery; esp. as *platymeric index*, the quotient of these diameters, multiplied by 100.

1895 *Proc. Soc. Antiquaries Scotland* V. 415 Dr Manouvrier of Paris..describes..femora from..neolithic burials..which showed the antero-posterior flattening in a very marked form, and to this condition he has given the name platymery (flat femur). *Ibid.* 416 The platymeria was very strongly marked. *Ibid.* 417 A platymeric femur is not necessarily associated with the squatting attitude. **1896** *Jrnl. Anat. & Pathol.* XXXI. 14 By far the most remarkable feature of this bone was its Platymeric index, which was almost as low as that of the lowest Maori indices. **1904** W. L. H. DUCKWORTH *Morphol. & Anthropol.* xiii. 313 Platymeria implies flattening in two regions of the femoral shaft, viz., in an upper region, immediately below the level of the lesser trochanter, and in a lower region about 40 mm. above the highest level of the external portion of the anterior aspect of the condylar articular surface. **1934** J. CAMERON *Skeleton of Brit. Neolithic Man* x. 159 The author wishes to mention..that the platymeric condition he is about to describe is that affecting the upper third of the femoral shaft. Platymeria involving the popliteal area at the lower end of the femur has also been described. *Ibid.* 165 A group of characteristic features that are more or less regularly present as concomitant phenomena of platymerism. **1971** *Nature* 6 Aug. 383/2 The flattening (platymeria) of the upper end [of the shaft of the femur] is exaggerated by the presence of a marked lateral expansion at the level of the gluteal tuberosity. **1972** J. T. ROBINSON *Early Hominid Posture & Locomotion* x. 143 If SK 97 belonged to a male, then it is not improbable that SK 82 belonged to a female since it has a smaller head, a smaller angle of the neck, a less robust shaft, and a lower platymeric index than has SK 97. **1976** *Nature* 17 June 575/1 The long slender platymeric shaft is unexpected and provides intriguing evidence for the possible variation of the femur in this genus.

platypussary (plæ·tipǒsări). *Austral.* Also **platypusary, platypussery.** [f. PLATYPUS + -ARY[1].] An enclosure or building in which platypuses are kept.

1945 BAKER *Austral. Lang.* xiv. 242 *Platypussary* has made its appearance only in recent years. **1960** —— *Drum* 135 Platypussery: A pen or specially prepared area in which platypuses are kept. Also, platypussary. **1966** G. DURRELL *Two in Bush* v. 161 David's pair were housed in his specially designed Platypusary.

platyrrhine, *sb.* and *a.* In etym. substitute for *platyrrhinus* name of infraorder *Platyrrhini* (E. Geoffroy 1812, in *Ann. Mus. Hist. Nat.* XIX. 104). **1.** *Zool.* Substitute for def.: A monkey belonging to the infraorder Platyrrhini of the order Primates, distinguished by a flattened nose with widely separated nostrils facing outwards and including most of the New World monkeys. **b.** *adj.* Of or pertaining to this group of monkeys. (Later examples.)

1894 H. O. FORBES *Hand-bk. Primates* I. 127 The New World Monkeys..have the nose flat and the opening of their nostrils directed outwards, and the one nostril separated from the other by a broad cartilaginous septum, and they are therefore designated Platyrrhine Monkeys. **1920** *Proc. Zool. Soc.* 91 The observations recorded in this paper are based mainly upon the Platyrrhine Monkeys that have died in the Zoological Gardens during the past ten years. **1930** *Ann. & Mag. Nat. Hist.* VI. 387 In the more primitive Platyrrhines the brain is relatively small and has few sulci. **1934** W. E. LE GROS CLARK *Early Forerunners of Man* vii. 177 In the Platyrrhine monkeys the nostrils are relatively wide apart. **1957** W. C. O. HILL *Primates* III. 91 The only platyrrhine monkey whose total musculature has been systematically studied is the Common Marmoset. **1957** I. T. SANDERSON *Monkey Kingdom* viii. 80/1 All the living New World primates used to be called the Platyrrhines. **1967** J. R. & P. H. NAPIER *Handbk. Living Primates* I. 15 In the majority of Cebidæ the nostrils are wide apart (platyrrhine condition). **1978** *Nature* 11 May 173/3 The separation between the New World monkeys (platyrrhines) and the Old World monkeys and apes (catarrhines) is an ancient one.

2. (Earlier and later examples.)

1885 *Jrnl. R. Anthropol. Inst.* XIV. 71 Nasal Index... Leptorhine 47·0 and under. Mesorhine 47·1 to 51·0. Platyrhine 51·1 to 58·0. Hyperplatyrhine 58·1 and over. **1976** *Lancet* 25 Dec. 1394/2 The special features of the upper respiratory tract..in platyrrhine peoples.

platyr(r)hiny (further examples).

1902 [see *chamæconchy* s.v. *CHAMÆ-]. **1957** W. C. O. HILL *Primates* III. 85 The nasal opening in the skull gives little indication of the characteristic external platyrrhiny. **1970** F. SNOWDEN *Blacks in Antiquity* i. 7 The platyrrhiny of the Ethiopian, like his color and his hair, was the norm for anthropological comparisons.

platytera (plætitē·ră). *Iconography.* [ad. Gr. πλατυτέρα she who is wider, compar. of πλατύς wide.] A type of icon of the Incarnation, also known as the Icon of the Sign, depicting the Mother of God, *orant*, and in front of her the Child, each usu. surrounded by a mandorla. Cf. ORANT.

1911 O. M. DALTON *Byzantine Art & Archaeol.* xii. 674 The *orans* type holding the Christ-medallion over the breast..is sometimes described as Blacherniotissa, while that in which the Virgin stands and the medallion is unsupported is known as *Platytera.* **1943** C. DE TOLNAY *Michelangelo* I. 158 The idea of placing the Christ Child between the knees of His mother is exceptional. Michelangelo seems to approach in this, as well as in the severe vertical axis of the position, an artistic conception of the Middle Ages—the Platytera, or Virgin who carries the Child in her bosom. In the ordinary Platytera type the Child is surrounded by a mandorla... We may note the seated Platytera which occurs in the Etchmiadzin Gospels. **1944** *Burlington Mag.* July 176/1 Its form is derived from the 'platytera', showing the child as an abstract symbol affixed to but not inside the body of the mother... The 'platytera' proper appears in Byzantine art as early as the fifth or sixth century..and in many adapted forms spreads over Europe during the Middle Ages. **1963** VON HERZFELD & RICE tr. *Onasch's Icons* 345/2 This older type shows the Virgin [*sc.* as *orans*] without a medallion before her, the later type represents her with it. This later type is called in Greek 'Platytera', the Ample One, with reference to a hymn: 'He made your womb more ample than the heavens'. In Russian icon painting it is called the 'Virgin of the Sign' (Znamenie).

plaur, var. *PLAV.

plausible, *a.* (*sb.*) Add: **A.** *adj.* **3.** (Further examples without implication of mere appearance.)

1933 *Oxf. Eng. Dict.* Suppl. 403/2 One of the most plausible suggestions of etymology is F. *gâchette.* **1952** G. SARTON *Hist. Science* I. xi. 280 If Hippocrates actually wrote the first textbook of geometry, which is not only possible but plausible. **1969** *Daily Tel.* 17 Oct. 16/3 Something seriously missing here—the older actress, perhaps, needed to play this part, and certainly some more plausible explanation of the lady's behaviour. **1976** *Nature* 29 Apr. 813/3 Some ideas which have been suggested to explain this unexpected finding are plausible.

B. *absol.* or as *sb.* (Further example.)

1831 J. S. MILL in *Examiner* 6 Feb. 83/2, I mean the really profound and philosophic inquirers into history in France and Germany, not the Plausibles, who in our own land of shallowness and charlatanerie, babble about induction without having ever considered what it is.

‖ **plav** (plav). Also **plaur** (pla·ŭəɹ). [a. Romanian *plav*, regional synonym of *pláur*.] One of the floating mats of reeds on the Danube, or the material of which it is composed.

1916 *Jrnl. Linnean Soc.* (*Bot.*) XLIII. 234 In Rumania, Plav is practically confined to the delta of the Danube. *Ibid.* 264 Reed of any size may in the delta of the Danube form an entire Plav, or portion of a Plav, from the base upwards. **1924** J. A. Hammerton *Countries of World* XVI. 1653/1 Many creatures perish, while such as do escape..eke out a desperate existence on floating islands of plaur or marsh weeds, so thickly matted and intertwined as to furnish a secure footing for both man and beast. **1961** *Times* 28 Oct. 9/7 We clambered out on to the *plaur*, the floating mass of decayed reeds.

play, *sb.* Add: **5. d.** Attention or patronage; a show of interest; publicity. *slang* (orig. *U.S.*).

1929 D. Runyon in *Hearst's International* July 57/1 Everybody goes to the Chicken Club now and then to give Tony Bertazzola, the owner, a friendly play. **1931** F. L. Allen *Only Yesterday* viii. 189 The insignificant Gray-Snyder murder trial got a bigger 'play' in the press than the sinking of the *Titanic*. **1935** J. O'Hara *Appointment in Samarra* 46 The Apollo [*sc.* a hotel] got a big play from salesmen who had their swindle sheets to think of. **1959** *Wall St. Jrnl.* 20 Nov. 17/2 Du Pont Co.'s nylon 501, brought out late last year, is getting a big play this fall from James Lees & Sons Co. and E. T. Barwick Mills, Inc., and other mills have nylon 501 carpets in production. **1970** *Washington Post* 30 Sept. B2/2 Asked her opinion on the 'youth revolt', she replied: 'I think it's such a minority—it gets far too much play.'

10. d. (Earlier and further examples.)

c **1788** *Laws of Cricket* §14, The Striker is out..if, in striking, or at any other time while the ball is in play, both his feet are over the popping-crease, and his wicket put down. **1816** W. Lambert *Instr. & Rules Cricket* 34 Always endeavour to hit the Ball on the same side on which it is bowled, and not draw it across the play. **1857** T. Hughes *Tom Brown's School Days* I. v. 109 As soon as the ball gets past them, it's in touch, and out of play. **1882** *Australians in England* 22 He got half way up the play, and just reached the ball with one hand. **1976** *South Notts Echo* 16 Dec. 7/3 The ball bounced across the goal line and into play.

g. An attempt to achieve or gain something; a move, manœuvre, or venture; *spec.* (*a*) *U.S. Sports*, an attacking move in a team game; an action that advances one's team's interest; (*b*) an attempt to attract or impress a person of the opposite sex; freq. in phr. *to make a play* (*for*). *slang* (orig. *U.S.*).

1868 H. Chadwick *Game of Base Ball* 46 A 'treble play' is made when three players are put out after the ball is hit, before it is pitched to the bat again. **1905** 'H. McHugh' *Get Next!* 75 His intentions are honorable and he wishes to prove them so by shooting his lady love if she renigs when he makes a play for her hand. **1906** H. Green *At Actor's Boarding House* 87 She had once made a play for the Swede, but he couldn't see her. **1912** C. Mathewson *Pitching* 174 Most clubs try to keep an umpire feeling hostile toward the team because, even if he means to see a play right, he is likely to call a close one against his enemies, not intending to be dishonest. **1930** *Amer. Mercury* Dec. 457/1 We make a play on their plant, but don't score. **1939** E. S. Gardner *D.A. draws Circle* ii. 26 Stall the thing along, make it casual, and be sure to back my play. **1943** D. Powell *Time to be Born* vi. 132 If you were twenty years younger I'd make a play for you, no fooling. **1961** P. Field *Rattlesnake Ridge* xiv. 170 It's the second time War Ax hands made a play for that money. **1961** *Dallas Morning News* 10 Oct. II. 2 Gannon contributed saving plays on the Falcons' aerial thrusts in the late stages. **1966** Wodehouse *Plum Pie* i. 26 Grab the girl while the grabbing's good, because..your nephew Bertram is making a heavy play in her direction. **1969** *Official Baseball Rules* 13 A double play is a play by the defense in which two offensive players are put out as a result of continuous action. **1972** *Newsweek* 10 Jan. 30/2 In the U.S., a guard is supposed to handle the ball and set up plays. **1973** N. Moss *What's the Difference?* 45/1 *Play, n*, a team's action in American football, hence a strategic move towards a goal. **1973** E. Page *Fortnight by Sea* viii. 88 She'd been certain he would make a play for her the moment Lockwood took himself off. **1978** S. Brill *Teamsters* ii. 60 The attempt that finally worked was the play by Giacalone, to get Hoffa to a peace meeting.

14. a. Esp. in phr. *as good as a play*: very entertaining or amusing; *a play within a play*: a play acted as part of the action of another play (also with *the*, usu. with reference to Shakespeare's *Hamlet*).

[**1638** J. Taylor *Bull, Beare, & Horse* sig. C7, It was as good as a Comedy to him to see the trees fall.] **1672** Marvell *Rehearsal Transpros'd* 53 It was grown almost as good as a Play among us. **1827** T. Creevey *Let.* 22 Nov. in *Creevey Papers* (1963) xiii. 232 This morning after breakfast he has been as good as a play. **1871** [in Dict.]. **1875** [see Good *a.* 11 b]. **1925** A. Huxley *Those Barren Leaves* II. iii. 111 He is the life and soul of Miss Carruthers's establishment... To see him with Fluffy—it's as good as a play. **1952** W. Plomer *Museum Pieces* xviii. 160 His eager account of the play was itself 'as good as a play'. **1975** D. M. Davin *Closing Times* vi. 129 'He's as good as a play,' my own parents would have said of him, had they known him.

1883 *Oxf. Mag.* 17 Oct. 308/1 He knew that the play within the play was meant for the conscience of the king. **1918** *Mod. Lang. Rev.* XIII. 151 The idea of having a play within the play is a famous one. **1935** *Ibid.* XXX. 433, I believe that in the circumstances surrounding the death of Francesco Maria I della Rovere, Duke of Urbino, we may well see the ultimate origin, not only of the play within the play, but of other elements in the plot of *Hamlet*. **1937** G. Rawson tr. *Schücking's Meaning of Hamlet* I. i. 3 The main action..reaches its apogee in the 'play within a play', a device that richly entertains both eye and ear. **1961** *Times* 24 Jan. 13/3 A play-within-a-play..convinces the audience that the actors are real addicts. **1973** *Listener* 26 Apr. 563/1 As a variation on the play-within-a-play we had the documentary-within-a-play.

16. b. The act of playing a gramophone record. *colloq.*

1961 in Webster. **1963** *Guardian* 15 June 3/7 The juke boxes each achieve 800 'plays' a week. **1967** *Melody Maker* 29 Apr. 10/4 It's nice party dance music..but the attention tends to wander after a few plays. **1974** *Listener* 3 Jan. 28/1 About eight records are played on each edition of *Top of the Pops*. That makes for four thousand 'plays' in ten years. **1978** *Oxford Times* (City ed.) 13 Jan. 15 A catchy tune with a sprightly arrangement that might make a hit if it gets enough plays on the radio.

17. *play-activity*, *-area*, *-centre*, *-clothes*, *-form*, *-garden*, *-hour* (earlier and later examples), *-impulse*, *-instinct*, *-lady*, *-language*, *-opera*, *-park*, *-poem*, *-producer*, *-reader* (later examples), *-reading*, *-sack*, *-shed*, *-song*, *-space*, *-spell* (earlier example), *-theory*, *-toy*, *-world*, *-wrecker*, *-yard*; *play-producing* adj.; **play-act** *v. intr.*, to act in a play; to be suitable for acting in a play; also *trans.*, to act (a scene, part, etc.); freq. *fig.*, to pretend, make-believe; to behave theatrically or insincerely; **play-acting,** also *fig.* and as *ppl. a.*; also (*Sc.*) **play-actoring** *ppl. a.*; **play-box,** a box in which a child, esp. at a boarding-school, keeps toys, books, and other personal possessions; also *transf.* and *fig.*; **playbroker** orig. *U.S.*, an agent who serves as an intermediary between playwrights and managers or actors; **playbus,** a bus adapted for children to play in; **play-by-play** *a.*, denoting a running commentary on a game; also *ellipt.* as *sb.*; **play-card,** (*a*) = Playbill; (*b*) repr. non-standard pronunc. of Placard *sb.* 2; **play-doctor,** a professional improver of other people's plays; **play-dough** orig. *U.S.*, a child's modelling clay; **play face,** an expression seen in apes or monkeys at play, in which the mouth is open but the teeth are hidden; **playfight,** a fight in play; hence **play-fighting** *sb.* and *a.*; **play-green** ?*Obs.*, a piece of land suitable for children to play on; **playland,** an area suitable for recreation; **play-leader,** an adult who leads or helps with children's play; the leader of, or a helper at, a play-group; so **play-leadership**; **play-lunch** *Austral.* and *N.Z.*, a snack taken by children to school for eating at playtime; **play-material,** (*a*) material used by children at play; (*b*) (see quot. 1969); **play-method** = **play-way*; **playmobile,** (*a*) (with capital initial) the proprietary name of a type of toy motor vehicle; (*b*) a vehicle containing facilities for a play-group; **play-night,** (*a*) a night on which a play is performed; (*b*) in Jamaica, a night of entertainment in connection with a funeral; **play-party,** (*a*) a party at which a play or plays are performed; (*b*) *U.S. dial.*, a party at which games are played, esp. dancing-games without music; also *attrib.*; **play-pen,** an enclosure in which a young child may play in safety; **play-pretty** *U.S. dial.*, a toy, plaything; **playscheme,** a local project offering play facilities for children, esp. during school holidays; **play school,** a nursery-school or kindergarten (orig. *U.S.*); **play-street,** a street closed to traffic so that children can play in it; **play suit,** (*a*) an actor's costume; *obs. rare*; (*b*) a light, casual outfit; **play therapy** *Psychol.*, therapy in which emotionally disturbed children are encouraged to act out and express their fantasies and feelings through play, aided by the therapist's interpretations; hence **play therapist**; **play-way,** an educational method which seeks to utilize play; **play-white** *S. Afr.* (see quot. 1956); **playwrite** *v. trans.*, to write in the form or style of a play; **playwriter** = Playwright; **playwriting** *vbl. sb.*

1896 G. B. Shaw *Let.* 6 Sept. (1965) I. 650, I always cut myself to the bone, reading the thing over and over until I have discovered the bits that can't be made to playact anyhow. **1901** N. Munro *Doom Castle* iv. 39 Very well pleased at the chance your coming gave him of play-acting the man of war. **1915** F. M. Hueffer *Good Soldier* III. i. 140 She wished to appear like the heroine of a French comedy..she was always play-acting. **1938** S. V. Benét *Thirteen O'Clock* 321 They had to play-act whatever happened. **1962** I. Murdoch *Unofficial Rose* xv. 149 Or they might cold-bloodedly have play-acted the scene together, laughing about it afterwards. **1969** *Listener* 5 July 28/2 She wanted more dirty experience: could he not play-act a rapist? **1974** A. Price *Other Paths to Glory* II. vi. 190 Most of us were play-acting—pretending to be soldiers. **1857** Trollope *Barchester T.* I. x. 138 Did you ever..hear anything so like play-acting as the way in which Mr. Harding sings the litany?.. There must be no more play-acting here. **1875** P. Ponder *Kirkumdoon* 142 Gettin' a vain play-actin' cretur to be oor minister. **1896** E. Terry *Let.* 4 Dec. in *Ellen Terry & Shaw* (1931) 133 Why don't you both come round after the play up to my room? Mayhap she doesnt like playacting folk? **1938** M. Allingham *Fashion in Shrouds* xi. 175 Georgia was doing no play-acting for Val. They were equals coming down to essentials. **1954** J. R. R. Tolkien *Fellowship of Ring* 183 You might be a play-acting spy, for all I can see, trying to get us to go with you. You might have done in the real Strider and took his clothes. **1972** J. Blackburn *For Fear of Little Men* iii. 45, I don't give a damn what you do, but I'm tired of play-acting. **1890** W. James *Princ. Psychol.* II. xxiv. 429 The immense extent of the play-activities in human life is too obvious to be more than mentioned. **1927** G. A. de Laguna *Speech, Its Function & Development* iv. 72 It was the adaptation of the play-activity to the needs of social coordination that was the essential agency in the process [of developing human speech]. **1836** J. M. Wilson *Tales of Borders* III. 29 Pittin sic daft-like notions intil a bairn's head as to read play-actorin books an' novels. **1968** *Punch* 13 Mar. 388/3 The day is not far off when all that will be left of unspoilt countryside will be designated 'Play Areas', with good parking and litter facilities and a free issue of blinkers to see what is left of the view. **1979** *Lore & Lang.* Jan. 1 Built before the turn of the century, the two tarmac play areas would nowadays be considered cramped. **1865** *Boy's Own Mag.* VI. 72/2, I had withdrawn from the school-room to 'the loft',..a long room above the school, where play-boxes were deposited. **1882** F. Anstey *Vice Versa* v. 103 Let every boarder go down into the box-room and fetch up his playbox, just as it is, and open it here before me. **1909** (*title*) The play-box, a picture reading book for little folks. **1923** Galsworthy *Captures* 56, I had taken them out of my playbox, together with the photographs of my parents and eldest sister. **1929** W. Deeping *Roper's Row* viii. 80 At her aunt's in Vane Street she had an attic which she called her studio, a young woman's play-box, and all that she knew she had taught herself by drawing things and yet more things. *Ibid.* xxi. 234 For, to Ruth Avery, No. 7 Roper's Row was a child's play-box, and much more than that—for it was the first playbox of her very own that she had possessed. **1949** I. Compton-Burnett *Two Worlds & their Ways* iv. 143 Here is the key of your playbox, Bacon. **1972** *Even. Telegram* (St. John's, Newfoundland) 23 June 3/1 When they tolerate a bunch of dandies sitting in that fancy playbox on..New Gower Street? **1910** *N.Y. Dramatic Mirror* 12 Mar. 9/4 Practically all of the new playwrights have been discovered by play-brokers. **1929** *Evening News* 9 Jan. 11/2 Major James Clare, a leading playbroker, who is also a dramatist. **1975** *Village* Winter 85 This interesting playbus experiment in Cumbria... The provision of holiday play facilities for village children. **1976** *Ann. Rep. Manpower Services Comm. 1975–76* iii. 23/2 On Merseyside, young people are working with craftsmen to convert buses into playbuses. **1927** *Amer. Speech* II. 241/2 The football extra, containing a 'play by play' story of all but the last few minutes, is locked on the press with a hole left in the plate. **1931** F. L. Allen *Only Yesterday* viii. 207 Thousands more sat in warm living-rooms to hear the play-by-play story over the radio. **1966** J. Ball *Cool Cottontail* (1967) x. 101 He turned on the radio and listened to a play-by-play of the California Angels. **1976** *Times Lit. Suppl.* 2 Jan. 13/3 The bulk of the book is given over to what looks like a play-by-play account of Hegel's thought. **1976** *Billings* (Montana) *Gaz.* 17 June 1-H/4 Announcers Lane Saunders and Bernie Lustig will provide the color and play-by-play, and a variety of guests will be lined up for half-time interviews. **1979** D. Anthony *Long Hard Cure* ix. 89, I began giving him a play by play of the events of Friday night. **1881** P. Fitzgerald *World behind Scenes* IV. 268 The Court Theatre, the Princesses, and the St. James have adopted square cards of a pale blue tint—an abnormal and inconvenient form. In the instance of the first-named house it is folded diagonally, it is a play card, and no longer a bill. **1934** T. S. Eliot *Rock* i. 40 On Christmas Day we can organize a Anti-God procession.. with playcards an' ex'ibitions exposin' all the dope o' Christianity. **1908** *Westm. Gaz.* 1 Feb. 7/3 The play-centres, far from tending to diminish the influence of home life, actually made the children appreciate it more. **1914** *Encycl. Relig. & Ethics* VII. 363/2 The 'play-centre', where, outside school hours, children who have no play-ground but the street, are taught organized games. **1936** G. M. Young *Victorian England* ix. 60 The Mechanics' Institutes..sank into play-centres for serious clerks. **1973** *Daily Tel.* 6 July 2/1 More than 80 London play centres are to be opened during the school summer holidays where children can play games, watch television, paint or read. **1919** *Ladies' Home Jrnl.* Mar. 62 Turn kids out in..Play Clothes—and let them play. **1959** *Times* 26 Jan. 11/1 Wit in styling, good fabrics and lovely colours are what the designers of 'play' clothes usually offer. **1971** *Times Lit. Suppl.* 20 Aug. 990/2 Japanese are not the only ones to feel irritation when they see elderly American tourists in gaudy 'play clothes' cavorting in Tokyo as if it were another Honolulu. **1922, 1938** Play doctor [see *Doctor *sb.* 6 c]. **1967** P. McGerr *Murder is Absurd* ii. 32 A play doctor was brought in to rework Rex's unfinished script. **1978** I. B. Singer *Shosha* vii. 128 In America we have men who are called play doctors. They can't write a line themselves, but somehow they know how to rearrange a piece and make it right for the stage. **1959** J. Foster *Educ. in Kindergarten* (ed. 3) xi. 176 Clay, plasticine, play dough, sawdust and paste,..all afford the child the opportunity to make a three-dimensional impression of one sort or another. **1969** B. Ryan *Your Child & First Year of School* iii. 56 Play dough, if it is made from scratch from salt, flour, water, and perhaps a little alum powder as a preservative, gives an even broader experience of chemistry before little fingers begin to manipulate it. **1970** G. R. Taylor *Doomsday* vi. 126 Asbestos powder mixed with water is even given to children, in some schools, as play-dough. **1977** C. McFadden *Serial* xi. 29/2 She was standing at the sink digging the play-dough out of her demitasse cups. **1962** J. A. R. A. M. van Hooff in *Symp. Zool. Soc.* No. 8. 120 (*heading*) The Play Face. *Ibid.* 121 Suddenly one of the partners may..show the play face in the direction of the other who will immediately react by resuming the play. **1966** R. & D. Morris *Men & Apes* vi. 213 The play face..is performed by a number of species during vigorous bouts of playful wrestling and tumbling and is particularly obvious in young chimpanzees. **1971** J. van Lawick-Goodall *In Shadow of Man* ix. 99 He opened his mouth in the play-face or chimpanzee smile. **1973** *Observer* (Colour Suppl.) 16 Dec. 32/2 Certain facial expressions are also used [by monkeys to establish friendship with one another], such as the 'playface'—a smile with teeth covered. **1977** Savage & Rumbaugh in D. M. Rumbaugh *Language Learning by Chimpanzees* xvi. 300 A playface given with vocal laughter and head-covering can be used as a signal to continue tickling. **1922** Joyce *Ulysses* 442 An armless pair of them flop wrestling, growling, in maimed sodden playfight. **1932** S. Zuckerman *Social Life Monkeys & Apes* xvii. 277 The play-fighting activities and bodily examinations continued intermittently. **1953** *Psychological Rev.* LX. 293/1 Among the social interactions there were a few instances of serious aggression, many occurrences of bluffing or exhibitionistic behavior, a great deal of play-fighting, wrestling, [etc.]. **1911** J. A. Thomson *Biology of Seasons* ii. 224 For the endless task of finding out about the world has its play-form—which is obviously one of the roots of science. **1963** G. J. McCall in A. Dundes *Mother Wit* (1973) 425 As has happened with so many play-forms of games..it has become a 'multi-situated game', requiring a vast proliferation of goals, roles, and strategies. **1916** A. S. Neill *Dominie Dismissed* xiii. 153 The attraction of a play-garden school with its charms of social intercourse. *c* **1650** *Lillumwham* in Hales & Furnivall *Bishop Percy's Folio MS.* (1867) *Loose & Humorous Songs* 98 Other three on won play greene. **1800** M. Edgeworth *Parent's Assistant* (ed. 3) II. 178 All the children..were assembled in the play-green. **1812** —— *Absentee* in *Tales Fashionable Life* VI. ix. 131 He went to the village school—a pretty, cheerful house, with a neat garden and a play-green. **1741** Richardson *Pamela* IV. lxiv. 454 The Misses at their Books too, or their Needles; except at their Play-hours, when they were never rude, nor noisy. **1925** Blunden *English Poems* 19 And blushed for pride when other girls and boys Laughed at us sweethearts in the playhour's noise. **1890** W. James *Princ. Psychol.* II. xxiv. 427 The sexes differ somewhat in their play-impulses. **1927** W. E. Collinson *Contemp. Eng.* 127 The English play-impulse has certainly produced some remarkable forms. **1896** W. James *Will to Believe* (1897) 23 Mephistophelian scepticism..will satisfy the head's play-instincts much better than any vigorous idealism can. **1897** T. Ribot *Psychol. of Emotions* ii. 198 The play-instinct, if we use this word to designate the tendency to expend superfluous activity..is a stock which puts forth several branches. **1966** *New Statesman* 24 June 923/3 There is a 'play lady'..who spends her whole time seeing to the personal interests and difficulties of the children in the wards. **1976** *Amer. Speech 1973* XLVIII. 208 At RT, he will meet *play ladies*, not to be confused with those in peds, but ones specially trained to teach physical activities. **1946** *Sun* (Baltimore) 26 Apr. 11/4 Baltimore is to be tied into schedules into the playland of Michigan, bringing PCA flights out of the local airport to fourteen daily. **1974** *Sat. Rev. World* (U.S.) 2 Nov. 8/2 Cyprus..would be..a Mediterranean playland. **1977** *Time* 4 July 28/2 Remembering the rapacious playlands of the past, where gambling, boozing and whoring were as rife as popcorn and pizza, most theme parks promote soft drinks and fast foods. **1934** O. Jespersen *Language* 149 Children..at first employ play language for its own sake. **1907** *Westm. Gaz.* 29 Aug. 3/1 A pressing need is for trained play-leaders who know how to play games and to organise the interests of children in ways that build the body and character as well. **1953** Play leader [see *adventure playground* s.v. *ADVENTURE *sb.* 10]. **1970** *Guardian* 14 May 11/4 Two mothers volunteered to take a play-leaders' course. **1975** *New Society* 18 Sept. 632/2 The Chells adventure playground, which is very large and has three full-time playleaders. *Ibid.* 13 Nov. 393/2 (Advt.), The successful applicant will be required to give general assistance within the Playleadership service. **1977** *Time Out* 28 Jan.–3 Feb. 53/1 (Advt.), Applicants, male or female, should be able to demonstrate experience in these areas, preferably within playleadership. **1962** *N.Z. Listener* 27 July 39/1 Children like to take the special little packets [of raisins and sultanas] to school for their playlunch. **1963** E. Spence *Green Laurel* ix. 109 She was not hungry enough to go back for her play-lunch, and to stay close to the class-room appeared to be the safest thing to do. **1974** *Age* (Melbourne) 12 Oct. 12/5 *Play lunch*, emergency rations for morning recess, usually being a piece of fruit, cake or some chocolate crackles. **1943** H. Read *Educ. through Art* v. 158 For example, in analysing the quantitative differences in the kinds of play-material used by children of age groups from 4 to 8, Dr. van Wylick found that..the use of human beings could not be related to the progressive age-groups. **1969** E. Ambler *Intercom Conspiracy* (1970) ii. 39 'Play material' was the jargon phrase used to describe the low-grade classified information fed back to the enemy through double agents. **1971** D. O'Connor *Eye of Eagle* xxii. 154 There'll be stretches on this tape with nothing on them but a lengthy silence. You could fill them in, if you wanted, with play material. **1914** H. C. Cook (*title*) First-fruits of the play method in prose. **1961** in *Amer. Speech* (1964) XXXIX. 79 Playmobile. **1963** *Official Gaz.* (U.S. Patent Off.) 21 May TM 148/1 DeLuxe Reading Corporation, Newark, N.J. *Playmobile* for toy miniature automobiles. First use Feb. 20, 1961. **1971** *Guardian* 16 Dec. 11/1 A children's playgroup in a converted double-decker bus?..The Playmobile will penetrate the drab streets of slumland. **1973** *Times* 25 July 13/2, I feel we should also provide the opportunity for the community to have far greater involvement in concern for others. Involvement such as taking playmobiles round to all our caravan sites. **1979** *Trade Marks Jrnl.* 4 July 1134/1 *Playmobil*... Toys having movable parts. Geobra Brandstätter GmbH & Co. K.G...Zirndorf..Germany; manufacturers and merchants.—17th March 1978. **1755** C. Charke *Life* 103 Those Assailants of Liberty..constantly attended every Play-Night there. **1786** J. Woodforde *Diary* 6 Apr. (1926) II. 238 It being Play Night we went to the Theatre. **1849** *Theatrical Programme* 2 July 43/1 His Majesty [*sc.* George II]..was pleased to order that the Guards should in future do duty every playnight, which custom has not yet been dispensed with. **1961** D. De Camp in R. B. Le Page *Creole Language Studies* II. iv. 72 Plie-nait. **1937** *Sun* (Baltimore) 12 Apr. 5/3 'The Second Hurricane' is neither grand nor light opera, and somebody had to think up a name for it. This turned out to be 'play opera'. **1954** *Grove's Dict. Music* (ed. 5) VIII. 125/2 The two other works of this period are the ballet-pantomime 'Schlagobers'.., and the autobiographical play-opera 'Intermezzo', for which Strauss wrote his own libretto. **1971** P. Young in J. Spencer *Eng. Lang. W. Afr.* 183 The dramatised version of *The Palm Wine Drinkard* was published in English originally, but performed as a play-opera in Yoruba at Ibadan. **1962** *Guardian* 31 Oct. 6/5 The playparks are a welcome addition to the other nursery facilities. **1964** *Ibid.* 30 Oct. 6/6 The number of play parks where children can 'let off steam' is to be increased after the Greater London Council takes over next year. **1977** *Cork Examiner* 6 June 1/8 In the past proceeds have gone to specific projects such as the building of a social room, gymnasium facilities, play park and equipment etc. **1879** L. Troubridge *Jrnl.* June in J. Hope-Nicholson *Life amongst Troubridges* (1966) 152 Met Amy and had quite a gay visit to Abbey Lodge, doing lots of plays. Uncle Hay failed us for a play party. **1902** *Dialect Notes* II. 241 *Play-party*, a party at which old-fashioned games are played. **1912** I. S. Cobb *Back Home* 44 Strict church members..wouldn't let their children..go to any parties except play parties. **1926** M. D. Lake in J. F. Dobie *Rainbow in Morning* (1965) 109 Parties of various kinds were indulged in at Christmas... Dominoes, candy pulls, corn poppings, play-parties, and dancing furnished additional amusement. **1937** B. A. Botkin *Amer. Play-Party Song* i. i. 16 The play-party..was a rural American social gathering for playing games, distinguished by the manner in which it was 'got up', by the age of its participants, and by the character of the games played. **1938** [see *CALLER *sb.* 1 e]. **1968** P. Oliver *Screening Blues* i. 31 It might be said..that the blues singer rejoices in his folk-songs—his dance songs, play-party and game songs, ballads and stomps. **1973** Schafer & Riedel *Art of Ragtime* i. 13 This 'play-party' country ragtime style is of great age and hardiness. **1931** *Daily Express* 21 Sept. 7/5 (Advt.), Well built play-pens in best hard-wood. **1940** J. Betjeman *Old Lights for New Chancels* 47 White o'er the play pen the sheen of her dress. **1967** N. Freeling *Strike Out* 81 A child's playpen stood folded against the wall. **1972** J. Wilson *Hide & Seek* ii. 35 Jean picked Jamie out of the playpen and sat with him on her lap. **1976** W. H. Canaway *Willow-Pattern War* xiii. 136 A set of beads on wires, a bit similar to the set I'd had on my play-pen when I'd been smaller. **1907** *Daily Chron.* 17 May 3/7 A soulful little French play-poem, Coppée's 'Le Passant'. **1928** V. Woolf *Writer's Diary* 7 Nov. (1953) 137 Yes, but *The Moths?* That was to be an abstract mystical eyeless book: a playpoem. **1977** *Times Lit. Suppl.* 4 Feb. 123/1 Virginia Woolf described *The Waves* as a 'playpoem'. She was conscious of the hazards of poetic fiction, the dangers of uncontrolled fantasy, and wanted to minimize these by assimilating to prose fiction the structural tightness and compression of drama. **1905** *Dialect Notes* III. 90 The children want some play-pretties for Christmas. **1929** W. Faulkner *Sound & Fury* 36 Aint you shamed of yourself. Taking a baby's play pretty. **1935** R. Bass in A. Dundes *Mother Wit* (1973) 395 On the graves of little children are placed some play-pretties, little doll heads, small cups, or toy animals. **1942** J. Thomas *Blue Ridge Country* 160 The children's play-pretties—the poppet, a make-believe corn-shuck doll. **1976** *Publ. Amer. Dial. Soc. 1973* LX. 17 One..called it [*sc.* a toy] *a pretty*, another *a play-pretty*. **1913** *Writer's Mag.* Dec. 253/1 For we are now in an era wherein the play-producer is on the alert for the young and virile writer. **1908** *Daily Chron.* 19 May 1/6 Several uncommercial play-producing societies..had done..good work recently. **1968** *Daily Tel.* 4 Nov. 9/5 And so we come back to the independent, unsubsidised play-producing companies. **1922** Play-reader [see *DOCTOR *sb.* 6 c]. **1969** L. Hellman *Unfinished Woman* v. 53, I worked as a play reader for Anne Nichols,..who wanted to become a producer. **1913** F. H. Burnett *T. Tembarom* xix. 244 On still another evening they tried Shakespeare. He found play-reading difficult and Shakespearian language baffling. **1935** N. Mitchison *We have been Warned* ii. 154 The next pupil was late... 'Sorry,' he said, 'it was the play-reading society.' **1968** J. Haythorne *None of us cared for Kate* 61 We do try in our small way to keep the torch of culture flickering. Are you fond of play-reading? **1972** D. H. Laurence *Bernard Shaw: Coll. Lett. 1898–1910* 4 [Shaw]..joined Grant Allen and other neighbours in a play-reading society. **1970** *Daily Progress* (Charlottesville, Va.) 21 Mar. c2/5 If the age group is 4 to 10,..playsacks..are imaginative animal costumes that slip on easily. **1972** *Where* Apr. 104/2 There were in fact something over 400 playschemes in England and Wales last summer. **1975** *Village* Winter 83 You would have been looking at Cumbria's first mobile playscheme. **1935** *Sun* (Baltimore) 15 July 7/3 Three children's 'play schools' scheduled here were canceled. **1959** C. V. Good *Dict. Educ.* (ed. 2) 402/2 *Play school*,..an organized experience usually lasting for a short time to provide opportunities for high school and college students to observe and work with a small group of young children in a supervised situation. **1964** S. Bellow *Herzog* 267 I'm picking June up at noon tomorrow. She goes to a play school, half-days. **1973** *Times* 7 Mar. 10/3 Whoever coined the term 'play school' captured perfectly the ideal concept for the young child. **1977** D. MacKenzie *Raven & Kamikaze* iv. 49 The babble of children came from the open windows of the play school. **1906** *Macmillan's Mag.* Nov. 19 Rooms for the teachers and for the permanent staff, a covered play-shed, and all the outside accessories. **1932** *Times Educ. Suppl.* 20 Aug. 318/1 Playsheds can as a rule be omitted, but inexpensive bicycle sheds may be advisable and serve as shelters for the children against rainstorms. **1898** J. C. Harris *Tales of Home Folks in Peace & War* 19 The negroes made the night melodious with their play-songs. **1924** G. Parkes in M. W. Beckwith *Jamaica Anansi Stories* 110 Massah, me kyan' stop him singing, because it mus' of been his little play-song what he have singing. **1959** I. & P. Opie *Lore & Lang. Schoolch.* i. 3 The same continuity obtains in their games and play songs. **1958** *Times* 30 Aug. 7/4 The whole of the underside of the tall block is planned as a covered paved play space. **1959** [see *BED-SITTING-ROOM]. **1974** *Listener* 7 Mar. 296/3 Families..live around courtyards, half of which serve..as play-spaces for children. **1976** *Ilkeston Advertiser* 10 Dec. 10/3 The parents..told Broxtowe District Council about the lack of play space for children on Broad Oak Drive estate. **1845** S. Judd *Margaret* ii. i. 186 And her own play-spell comes, if, indeed, her whole life were not a play-spell. **1937** C. V. Godfrey *Roadsense for Children* viii. 64 Closing certain lesser thoroughfares to vehicular traffic and reserving them for the exclusive use of children ..is how Play Streets came into being. **1968** *Guardian* 25 Apr. 7/6 Some local authorities label streets as play streets when they have not enough money for playgrounds. **1977** *Wandsworth Borough News* 7 Oct. 14/5 It was a 'playstreet' with bollards to prevent all traffic, where children could safely play under the eyes of their parents. **1609** T. Dekker *Guls Horne-Booke* vi. 29 By sitting on the stage, you may..examine the play-suits lace. **1908** *Sears, Roebuck Catal.* 529/1 Play Suits. **1936** *New Yorker* 7 Mar. 64/1 Crisp, wearable and washable shirt-waist dresses, play suits, shorts, slacks, and skirts. **1942** *Capital* 3 Feb. 5/6 (*caption*) Ilyana Yankwich wearing a California-made playsuit; it's in vivid green and brown tones with a gay leaf motif. **1959** *New Statesman* 26 Sept. 384/2 Unguents, oils, special sun-bathing attire, bikinis and play-suits..have become big business. **1963** Playsuit [see *GARBO[1]]. **1925** I. A. Richards *Princ. Lit. Crit.* 233 The objection to the Play Theory..lies in its suggestion that the experiences of Art are in some way incomplete, that they are substitutes. **1960** C. Winick *Dict. Anthropol.* 535/2 *Play theory*, the theory that fine art is produced independently of the struggle for existence and that the imagination is exercised for the sake of the sense of freedom (Schiller), or power (Groos), or for conscious self-deception (Lange). **1942** *Brit. Jrnl. Psychol.* Jan. 262 A direct interpretation given to the child of the meaning of his play should be undertaken only..by the experienced play therapist. **1963** A. Heron *Towards Quaker View of Sex* 49 The child may have treatment with a play therapist. **1939** *Psychol. Abstr.* XIII. 111/1 The author believes that active play therapy offers rapid diagnostic and therapeutic assistance in the emotional problems of childhood. **1948** L. Kanner *Child Psychiatry* (ed. 2) xvii. 244 'Play therapy' thus becomes a form of participation, a means to an end, rather than an isolated technique. **1961** A. Huxley *Let.* 8 Jan. (1969) 903 One can imagine a genuinely realistic treatment of the mentally ill..by work and play therapy. **1978** M. T. Erickson *Child Psychopathol.* x. 225 Traditional clinicians have offered an array of treatments to children with learning disabilities: psychoanalysis,..play therapy, and group therapy. **1935** Z. N. Hurston *Mules & Men* 19 I'll put this play toy in his hand, and he will seize it and go away. Then I'll say my say and sing my song. **1914** H. C. Cook *First-Fruits of Play Method* 52 The boys do not object to learning anything, so long as they may do it in the Play way. **1920** T. P. Nunn *Education* viii. 92 Members of a rapidly growing company of pioneers..are all busily engaged in exploring the 'play-way' of teaching the several subjects of the curriculum. **1973** *Times* 13 Jan. 12/3 Nephew X, proud of himself for being tough with his daughter over the cello lessons, dismisses all this 'play-way' approach to education as a lot of soft nonsense. **1956** A. Sampson *Drum* xv. 205 Harry was only one of thousands of 'play-whites', as they call the light-skinned Coloureds who 'pass for white' and break away from the Coloured world. **1909** *Daily Chron.* 13 Dec. 3/4 Nature's kingdom is not all a reign of tooth and claw, but a play-world also. **1915** D. H. Lawrence *Rainbow* xi. 264 The religion, which had been another world for her, a glorious sort of play-world. **1962** W. Nowottny *Lang. Poets Use* iv. 89 This realization is articulated most clearly at the climax of the passage..and so too is the sense of the irruption into his play-world of intractable segments of reality. **1978** I. B. Singer *Shosha* vii. 135 There is no reason why hedonism, the cabala, polygamy, asceticism, even our friend Haiml's blend of eroticism and Hasidism could not exist in a play-city or play-world. **1901** *Chambers's Jrnl.* Aug. 545/2 Organised play-wreckers, who without uttering a word or an unseemly laugh have succeeded in destroying whatever chance of success a play may have had. **1949** *Sat. Rev. Lit.* (U.S.) 24 Dec. 24/3 One of the unique and beckoning characteristics of his plays was that they were written no less than playwritten. **1872** W. L. Collins *Aristophanes* iii. 41 To win the verdict of popular applause, which was the great aim of an Athenian play-writer, he must above all things hit the popular taste. **1903** W. B. Yeats *Let.* 27 July (1954) 408, I suppose every playwriter finds out the methods that suit him best. **1898** G. B. Shaw *Plays Unpleasant* Pref. p. v, I made a rough memorandum for my own guidance that unless I could produce at least half a dozen plays before I was forty, I had better let playwriting alone. **1935** *Discovery* May 130/2 Historical playwriting has had considerable vogue. **1959** *Times* 24 Oct. 9/2 *Pursue the Dry Stubble*, the winning entry in the playwriting competition organized by the Tower Theatre, was given the first of six performances there last night. **1976** *Radio Times* 27 Mar.–2 Apr. 37/1 Sir Terence Rattigan looks back over 40 years of playwriting from *French without Tears* to *Cause Celèbre*. **1960** J. J. Rowlands *Spindrift* iii. 186 One particularly important question was whether the play-yard in Heaven was equipped with an old dory with a mast and sail. **1973** *Jrnl. Genetic Psychol.* Sept. 160 Assertive behavior is a relatively stable characteristic of the preschool child, a characteristic which he brings to many situations and which can be seen even in 15 minutes in the play yard.

play, *v.* Add: **II. 10. d.** *to play around*: to amuse oneself; to behave in a playful or irresponsible manner; *spec.* to have a sexual relationship *with* (a person or persons of the opposite sex), esp. casually or extra-maritally. *colloq.* (orig. *U.S.*).

1929 D. HAMMETT *Red Harvest* xi. 109 Max was up there with a girl he used to play around with. **1932** G. GREENE *Stamboul Train* IV. iv. 248 You mean you killed him.. just because he'd played around with your daughter? **1934** J. O'HARA *Appointment in Samarra* ii. 46 He played around a little, but Al knew Helene was the only one he really cared for, and Helene really cared for him. **1960** *Sunday Express* 14 Aug. 14/6, I went to all the parties; I played around. **1963** D. GRAY *Murder in Mind* xv. 83 And if I found you were playing around, I'd give you a damned good hiding. **1973** S. DOBYNS *Man of Little Evils* (1974) iii. 31 Ralph played around with other women but he liked one.

12. a. (Further examples.) *to play with fire*: see *FIRE *sb.* A. 3 g.

1945 *Tee Emm* (Air Ministry) V. 52 This will give you a little to play with and allow for a drop in barometric pressure. **1965** V. CANNING *Whip Hand* iii. 33, I like a girl who doesn't play with her food or drink. **1976** SCOTT & KOSKI *Walk-In* (1977) xxxiii. 237 He was sweating now, all right. And is he playing with me? he wondered. Is the bastard playing with me? **1978** *Lancashire Life* Sept. 76/3 How could they possibly build docks when they had merely £60,000 to play with.

b. *to play with* (someone): to masturbate; usu. *refl. colloq.*

1922 JOYCE *Ulysses* 552 You can apply your eye to the keyhole and play with yourself while I just go through her a few times. **1954** H. K. FINK *Long Journey* 14, I was going with girls..and I didn't feel the urge to play with myself. **1966** L. H. FARBER *Ways of Will* iii. 58 This opening scene of a faceless woman silently playing with herself..sets the tone. **1967** A. WILSON *No Laughing Matter* II. 65 That kind of thinking can easily land you in the loony bin. It's worse than playing with yourself. **1969** H. MILLER *Sexus* (1970) viii. 166 'Play with it a bit while I finish this.' 'You're filthy,' she said, but she did as I told her. **1971** 'V. X. SCOTT' *Surrogate Wife* 54 He played with me. And little by little..I played with him. *Ibid.* 114 In bed, we played with each other. **1974** E. TIDYMAN *Dummy* xv. 199 I'd glance over at Donald and he'd be playing with himself in the courtroom.

III. 16. d. *to play politics*: to act on an issue for personal or political gain rather than from principle. orig. *U.S.*

1863 [in Dict., sense 16 c]. **1907** *Springfield* (Mass.) *Weekly Republican* 13 May 6 Mr. Balfour has seized the opportunity to play politics, and has apparently come out squarely in favor of trade preference. **1931** H. F. PRINGLE *Theodore Roosevelt* II. vii. 343 Roosevelt.. was playing politics in his own behalf. **1962** *Listener* 15 Nov. 798/1 It has been fashionable to claim that Mr Gaitskell..was deliberately playing politics with the Common Market issue. **1963** *Times* 11 Feb. 11/3 If it is too much to ask any Government to stop playing politics with the economy, the Opposition can at least be urged not to abet it in doing so. **1976** *Punch* 16 June 1070/2 There are a few people who find it disturbing that we are now the most heavily indebted nation in the industrial world—but as the Government would wish me to point out, they are just playing politics.

e. *to play the dozens*: to engage in a bout of verbal insults and ridicule with one or more other people: used of a ritualized form of dialogue customary among American Blacks.

1933 E. CALDWELL *God's Little Acre* x. 142 If you want to play the dozens, you're at the right homestead. **1939** J. DOLLARD in *American Imago* Nov. 6 One asked the other, 'Do you want to play the Dozens?' The other boy said, 'Yes.' *Ibid.* 7 These reactions of concealment and shame convinced me that playing the Dozens is not an orgy of licentious expression for lower-class Negroes; all know that the themes treated are in general forbidden, some refuse to play the game and still others are very resentful and defensive at the mere thought of it. **1942** Z. N. HURSTON in A. Dundes *Mother Wit* (1973) 24/1 The bookless may have difficulty in reading a paragraph in a newspaper, but when they get down to 'playing the dozens' they have no equal in America. **1962** R. D. ABRAHAMS in *Ibid.* 298/1 'Playing the dozens' is one of the most interesting folkloristic phenomena found among contemporary Negroes. **1970** H. E. ROBERTS *Third Ear* 11/1 Playing the dozens, making derogatory..remarks about another's mother, parents. **1973** *Black World* Aug. 58/2 Could play the dozens for days, talk about your momma bad enough to make you cry. **1973** A. DUNDES *Mother Wit* 141/2 A sample of some of the special techniques and forms of extended word play should convince even the most adamant sceptic that no black child who can signify or play the dozens can rightly be called lacking in verbal skills.

f. *to play pussy* (Aeronaut.): to fly under cover in order to avoid detection by another aircraft, etc. *slang.*

1942 *We speak from Air* 30, I wondered if he was playing pussy and intending to jink away. **1942** *Gen* 1 Sept. 14/1 Waiting in the air..he 'snakes about' or 'plays pussy' in the clouds. **1943** HUNT & PRINGLE *Service Slang* 52 *Play pussy*, to take advantage of cloud cover, jumping from cloud to cloud to shadow a potential victim or avoid recognition. **1948** PARTRIDGE *Dict. Forces' Slang* 143 *Play pussy*, to speed from one cloud to another in order to escape detection or to pounce upon a shadowed enemy aircraft.

17. f. *to play back, backward(s)*: in *Cricket*, said of the batsman: to move back before striking the ball; *play forward*: to move forward in making a stroke; *play through*: in *Golf*, to continue playing, passing other players who have agreed to suspend their game for this purpose.

1816 W. LAMBERT *Instr. & Rules Cricket* 27 [This] will direct him to play forward at the..bowling. *Ibid.* 29 If at these [short] kind of balls the Striker plays back about two feet behind the popping crease..it will afford him a little more time to judge how the Ball is coming. **1851** W. CLARKE in W. Bolland *Cricket Notes* 135 It is the ball that catches him in two minds, so that he does not know whether to play forward or backward. **1899** W. G. GRACE *Cricketing Reminiscences* x. 288 If a boy has once learned to play forward confidently he will soon adapt himself to playing backwards at balls that demand it. **1934** W. J. LEWIS *Lang. Cricket* 198 *Play back*,..to step back with the right foot towards the wicket, playing the ball behind the popping crease. *Ibid.* 199 *Play forward*,..to reach forward, advancing the left foot and the bat, in making a stroke. **1967** M. GREEN *Art of Coarse Golf* x. 110 The general rule of etiquette in Coarse Golf seems to be that solo players have right of way over all matches. It is not normally necessary for them to ask permission to play through—they simply pound on round the course. **1970** H. TAYLOR *Golf Dict.* 159 If a ball is lost and cannot be found, the player with the consent of the other players signals to those following to 'play through'. **1973** A. MACVICAR *Painted Doll Affair* viii. 89 The strangers came and putted... Duncan told them we were in no hurry and suggested they should play through. **1975** *Times* 29 Aug. 6/4 In breach of the game's etiquette, one fourball, finding itself behind the other at the second hole, attempted without invitation or request to 'play through' the slower group.

g. To co-operate, comply, agree; to do what is required of one; freq. in negative contexts. *colloq.*

1937 M. ALLINGHAM *Case of Late Pig* viii. 59 'Mr. Whippet,' she began breathlessly, 'he's gone! The body's gone!' What shall we do?'.. I was glad to see she wasn't playing, either. 'The body's gone,' she repeated. **1940** J. REITH *Diary* 17 Jan. (1975) v. 238 To see Attlee... Went over past troubles between his party and the Ministry of Information... I think I can make him play but of course he is weak. **1947** 'N. BLAKE' *Minute for Murder* x. 223 Charles comes here to fetch Alice. He tells her Nita won't play. They decide to put their plan into operation. **1958** 'A. BRIDGE' *Portuguese Escape* ix. 146 Tell me what's happened? Did the Duque play? **1961** E. WAUGH *Unconditional Surrender* III. i. 218 The Air Force aren't playing until they know what's going on over there. **1967** 'F. CLIFFORD' *All Men are Lonely Now* I. ii. 30 'I've had another word with the Minister.' 'Will he play?' 'He's promised to do everything he can.' **1973** 'M. INNES' *Appleby's Answer* III. xi. 105 Miss Pringle didn't want to play. She choked off her friend.

18. e. *to play favourites*: to show favouritism. *colloq.* (orig. *U.S.*).

1902 H. L. WILSON *Spenders* 201, I mustn't 'play favourites', as those slangy nephews of mine put it. **1905** R. E. BEACH *Pardners* i. 31 Not wishing to play any favourites, I'd picked up a basket of tomatoes, a gunny-sack of pineapples, and a peck of green plums. **1973** *Black Panther* 7 July 7/2 The foreman plays favorites and only likes Blacks that act the way they want Blacks to act. **1974** 'S. WOODS' *Done to Death* 132, I decline to think that Lizzie—sorry, I'm not allowed to play favourites, am I?

f. *to play for safety, to play safe*: to act in such a way as to avoid risks (for orig. use in Billiards see SAFETY 1 g in Dict. and Suppl.); *to play for time*: to try to gain more time for oneself; to postpone an action or decision.

1906 KIPLING *Puck of Pook's Hill* 212 The habit of playing for time sticks to a man! **1911** *Conc. Oxf. Dict.* 750/2 *Play for safety*, avoid risks in game or fig[uratively]. **1911** H. B. WRIGHT *Winning of Barbara Worth* xxviii. 395 Greenfield is playing for time so that the strikers will make trouble. **1919** F. HURST *Humoresque* 54 'Oh, anybody that plays as safe as you—' He raised his voice, shoving back his chair. **1919** R. W. LARDNER *Real Dope* iv. 105 Its best to play safe..and see what comes off. **1930** *Engineering* 11 July 56/3 Consequently in 'playing for safety' in getting the casting through the machine shop the foundryman has tended towards using softer materials which give open and sometimes porous structures in the heavier sections. **1931** W. R. INGE *More Lay Thoughts* 85 A young man, we will suppose, is rather deficient in natural sympathy and has no expensive tastes. He is also of an anxious temperament and disposed to play for safety. **1942** M. B. LOWNDES *Let.* 2 Apr. (1971) 229 He said he had come to the *Times* office last week hoping they would make a row, but of course they played for safety. **1944** 'G. GRAHAM' *Earth & High Heaven* (1945) 134 All she could do was to go on playing for time, trying to keep Marc from finding out what her family really thought of him, until, after a while, they thought a little better. *Ibid.* 268 The people who play safe don't change anything, they just sit tight and wait for someone else to change it. **1950** E. H. GOMBRICH *Story of Art* xxvii. 421 No artist can always 'play safe'. **1966** G. N. LEECH *Eng. in Advertising* ix. 88 One of their functions is a non-communicative one—that of 'playing for time' under the pressure of extempore performance. **1975** S. LAUDER *Killing Time on Corvo* iv. 41 'What are they doing out there?.. Playing for time?' I was inclined to say that they were playing for the gallery. **1976** *Southern Even. Echo* (Southampton) 11 Nov. 16/4 Mrs. Phillis Babey thought she was playing safe when she telephoned a hospital before leaving home to make sure there was a bed waiting for her.

g. Used with impersonal *it* as object, together with an adj., adv., or advb. phr., to denote a particular manner of behaviour; to deal with (something) in a specified way; esp. *to play it close to one's chest*: see *CHEST *sb.*[1] 9 c; *to play it cool*: to behave in a relaxed or unemotional manner (see *COOL *a.* 4 e); *to play it low* (*down*): to behave meanly or despicably; *to play it safe* = *to play for safety* (see sense 18 f above).

1873 *Winfield* (Kansas) *Courier* 24 July 3/1 The horses attached to [the] hack which runs between this place and Wellington, one day last week concluded to 'play it alone'. **1882** [see sense 18 d in Dict.]. **1901** CONRAD & HUEFFER *Inheritors* i. 7 'Oh, come', I expostulated, 'this is playing it rather low down. You walk a convalescent out of breath and then propound riddles to him.' **1919** R. W. LARDNER *Real Dope* iv. 117, I thought I would show them to Capt. Seeley and play it safe. *a* **1921** G. H. GIBSON in *Penguin Bk. Austral. Ballads* (1964) 207 It's playin' it low on William, but perhaps he'll buckle-to. **1941** F. & R. LOCKRIDGE *Murder out of Turn* vi. 72 It's worth playing it that way until we find out different. **1951** *Manch. Guardian Weekly* 17 July 15 The Republicans are playing it safe. **1955** W. C. GAULT *Ring around Rosa* vi. 77 Most gamblers I've met would play it cooler than that. **1960** L. COOPER *Accomplices* II. i. 73 Edwardes tried to play it just a bit too clever and that's what did him in. **1960** *Encounter* Nov. 30/2 My concern is that young people to-day, by 'playing it cool' and fearing to be thought 'squares', may create a style of life, not only in work but in every dimension of existence, which is less full, less committed, less complex, and less meaningful than mid-century opportunities allow. **1963** J. PRESCOT *Case for Hearing* x. 163 Let's wait until he's gone too far to draw back, and then we can produce our evidence and shoot him down in flames. That's how I'd like to play it. **1971** C. BONINGTON *Annapurna South Face* ix. 108 John Edwards dived for cover, but Jonathan Lane, the cameraman, played it cool, pausing to switch on the camera before getting out of the way. **1972** D. CRAIG *Double Take* xii. 149 Everyone knows we've got to play it your way, Mick. **1973** 'D. JORDAN' *Nile Green* i. 11, I let him play it his way. He was my boss. **1977** *Time* 10 Oct. 17/3 You have to follow your hunch. You can't play it safe.

20. b. (Earlier examples.)

1751 in H. T. Waghorn *Cricket Scores* (1899) 49 The Earl of Sandwich playes..eleven gentlemen of Eton College against any other eleven gentlemen in England which the Earl of March shall chuse. **1846** W. DENISON *Cricket* 65 He has..long been played alone for his batting.

21. d. To bet or gamble at or on (races, cards, etc.); to take chances with. *colloq.* (orig. *U.S.*)

1858 D. C. PETERS *Life of Kit Carson* 354 He'd bin playin' the papers (meaning gambling) and had lost everything. **1902** G. H. LORIMER *Lett. Self-Made Merchant* 115 When he chooses a father-in-law who plays the bucket shops, he needn't be surprised if his own son plays the races. **1925** E. WALLACE *King by Night* vi. 21 We never say 'played the races' here; we say 'go racing'. **1932** WODEHOUSE *Hot Water* i. 25, I was a rich man myself at the time of our wedding. But unfortunately I played the Market. **1958** BLESH & JANIS *They all played Ragtime* iii. 61 With ten to twenty a night in tips, a piano-player had more than he could spend so long as he didn't gamble or play the ponies. **1973** 'R. MACLEOD' *Burial in Portugal* iv. 73 He plays the stock market.

22. b. Also *transf.*, said of a 'hand', in reference to its effect upon the game.

1964 N. SQUIRE *Bidding at Bridge* ii. 23 The hand may play better in either Spades or no-trumps. **1977** *Homes & Gardens* Feb. 17 Work out how the above hand would play opposite this typical Three Diamond opening.

c. (Earlier examples.)

1756 *Gentl. Mag.* XXVI. 489/1 From the Parthian steed, Not more unerring flew the barbed reed Than rolls the ball, with vary'd vigour play'd. **1816** W. LAMBERT *Instr. & Rules Cricket* 33 The Striker should move his right-foot back at the moment of hitting, playing the Ball between his left-leg and the wicket.

d. (Earlier and later examples.)

1858 *Bell's Life* 26 Sept. 7/4 Mr M'Dougall and Grundy caused a total of 20, when the latter 'played on'. **1963** *Times* 7 Feb. 3/3 Sir Donald Bradman hit one straight drive for four before playing on to Statham. **1977** *Times* 2 Dec. 10/5 Another [wicket] to the left arm spin bowler Iqbal Qasim when Willis played on, completed England's misery.

23. *to play oneself in* (further examples); also *fig.*

1900 W. J. FORD *Cricketer on Cricket* xii. 144 If he would only play himself in quietly..he would get 'lashings' of runs. **1928** A. PHILIPS *Boy at Bank* I. i. 13 The cricket was slow to begin with; while the batsmen 'played themselves in' carefully. **1969** 'J. FRASER' *Cock-pit of Roses* vii. 132 'Of course, the first day's always difficult.' 'Question of playing yourself in?' **1971** D. AVERST *Guardian* xxx. 461 He was tied to the Manchester office and given little opportunity to play himself in as a public figure. **1974** A. LASKI *Night Music* 122 'We'll start with the Mozart, play ourselves in.'.. He took the violin out of its case. **1975** *Times* 25 Aug. 9/3 He..went in in the second innings with no time to play himself in.

24. a. (Further examples.) Also, to fool, swindle; *to play* (someone) *for a sucker*: to treat (a person) as a dupe; to make a fool of; to cheat. Cf. sense 6 e in Dict.

1879 'MARK TWAIN' *Let.* 12 Nov. (1917) I. 369 You could have played him on a stranger for an effigy. **1886** *Lantern* (New Orleans) 20 Oct. 3/2 Some blokes can never see when they are being played for suckers. **1892** KIPLING *Many Inventions* (1893) 168 We've played 'em for suckers so often that when it comes to the golden truth—I'd like to try this on a London paper. **1901** CONRAD & HUEFFER *Inheritors* vi. 95 It seemed to me that she was playing me with all this nonsense—as if she..were fooling me to the top of her bent. **1931** E. LINKLATER *Juan in America* II. xv. 167, I told him what would happen if he tried to play me for a sucker. **1938** *New Statesman* 8 Jan. 39/2 The 'steamer' (the victim) after being 'steered' (picked up) by one performer and 'played' (told the tale) by another, [etc.]. **1941** A. CHRISTIE *Evil under Sun* viii. 146 Crazy about the woman, idealising her, suddenly finding out he'd been played for a sucker. **1959** T. S. ELIOT *Elder Statesman* I. 27 Stay out of politics, and play both parties: What you don't get from one you may get from the other. **1966** R. STOUT *Death of Doxy* ii. 14 If the errand I had tackled for Orrie had been on the level, if he hadn't been playing me,..there would be fur flying soon.

1967 *New Yorker* 18 Mar. 50 Wise up. They're playing you for a bunch of saps! **1973** 'D. Jordan' *Nile Green* xxxiv. 166 She's a fraud... She's working for the Russians... She's played me for a sucker.

b. For 'almost always' read 'frequently', and add further examples. Also in phr. *to play both ends against the middle*.

1938 E. Waugh *Scoop* II. iv. 211 The President kept his end up pretty well—played one company off against the other for months. **1950** O. Nash *Family Reunion* (1951) 46 The wise child handles father and mother By playing one against the other. **1965** *Listener* 10 June 852/1 Their deep African fear of a relapse into subordination makes them play off Eastern and Western contributors. **1972** T. P. McMahon *Issue of Bishop's Blood* v. 62 He would be the first member of the FBI who played both ends against the middle to get a personal belief buttressed. **1974** J. Stubbs *Painted Face* xiv. 192 Natalie..played one against the other for a few days, and reconciled them the following weekend. **1978** M. Puzo *Fools Die* xxv. 285 He was trying to play both ends against the middle, doing his friend the favor and yet trying to warn the reader off the book with an ambiguous quote.

e. *to play the field*: see *Field *sb.* 10 d.

V. 26. a. (Further examples without const.)

1816 Jane Austen *Emma* II. vi. 106 'Did you ever hear the young lady..play?'.. 'She plays charmingly.' **1907** G. B. Shaw *Major Barbara* I. 207 *Undershaft.* Do you play, Barbara? *Barbara.* Only the tambourine. **1920** D. H. Lawrence *Lost Girl* 17 She even taught heavy-handed but dauntless colliers, who were seized with passion to 'play'. *a* **1953** E. O'Neill *Long Day's Journey* (1956) III. 89, I couldn't play with such crippled fingers, even if I wanted to. *Ibid.* IV. 151, I play so badly now. I'm all out of practice. **1974** *Encycl. Brit. Macropædia* X. 1035/1 In March 1831 he [*sc.* Liszt] heard Paganini play for the first time.

27. (Further examples.)

1879 Grove *Dict. Mus.* I. 701/1 He [*sc.* Johann Michael Haydn] played the violin and organ. **1925** F. Scott Fitzgerald *Great Gatsby* v. 114 'Klipspringer plays the piano,' said Gatsby, cutting him off. 'Don't you, Ewing, old sport?' **1946** E. O'Neill *Iceman Cometh* II. 141 She was beautiful and she played the piano beautifully and she had a beautiful voice. **1959** 'E. McBain' *'Til Death* xii. 162 My kid sister plays piano. **1973** *Publishers Weekly* 14 May 39/2 Cooke would be shown wandering around historical sites—playing piano in a former brothel in New Orleans, for instance. **1976** S. Brett *So much Blood* v. 69 He plays guitar too?

28. b. To cause (a gramophone record or a tape) to reproduce what is recorded on it; *to play back*, to play (a recording) after having made it; also *fig.*

1903 *Talking Machine News* Oct. 103/2 Each machine should play three records. **1907** [see *gramophone needle* s.v. *Gramophone 2]. **1932** *Times Educ. Suppl.* 1 Oct. 372/4 The record was 'played back' to him, and an expression of amazement dawned on his face. **1934** *B.B.C. Year-Bk.* 419 The ability to play-back a wax before processing is of great assistance in making records of running commentaries. **1939** *Electronics & Television* XII. 172/1 Automatic record changers..enable records to be played for almost three-quarters of an hour without attention. **1956** R. E. B. Hickman *Magn. Recording Handbk.* v. 124 A tape which has been in storage for some length of time should be re-spooled a short while before it is due to be played. **1957** *Technology* June 132/3 Magnetic tape is fed to a control unit associated with the machine tool. When played back the servomechanisms..carry out the demanded movements. **1958** *Listener* 4 Dec. 921/1 Having read what history books have to say about this person..he can play back as much of it as suits him as *The Confessions of*—for example—*Judas Maccabaeus.* **1962** A. Nisbett *Technique Sound Studio* i. 19 Even with a single microphone, it is still possible to make direct comparison tests by recording short snatches of the various music balances and playing them back. **1962** G. Lawton *John Wesley's English* 199 Many a time Wesley plays back to his readers..the common observations of familiar speech. **1973** 'H. Howard' *Highway to Murder* xiii. 150 I've said no already. If you like I'll put it on tape and you can play it back to yourself. **1974** [see *Play *sb.* 16 b]. **1978** S. Brill *Teamsters* xii. 290 Barkett paused, as if to play back what he had just said.

c. *intr.* Of a gramophone record or a tape: to reproduce sound (esp. for a specified period).

1903 *Talking Machine News* Aug. 66/1 Most phonos finish the records almost as soon as one begins to enjoy them, but yours plays quite a long time. *Ibid.* Dec. 150/1 A record will play..without being screwed down. **1952** Godfrey & Amos *Sound Recording & Reproduction* vi. 163 When running at full speed, a reel of tape which plays for 21 minutes can be rewound in about 2 minutes. **1966** 'R. Garioch' *Sel. Poems* 28 What a time a reel of tape can play!

d. *to play the piano* (see quot. 1933). *Austral.* and *N.Z. slang.*

1933 L. G. D. Acland in *Press* (Christchurch, N.Z.) 18 Nov. 15/7 *Play the piano*, to run the fingers over the sheeps' backs in order to find the softest and easiest to shear. **1966** Baker *Austral. Lang.* (ed. 2) iii. 55 An old hand at shearing can spot such a defect in a moment by what is known as *playing the piano.*

29. (Earlier and further examples.) Also, to pass (time) in playing.

1674 Head & Kirkman *English Rogue* III. xi. 136 Mine Host..causing them [*sc.* the 'fidlers'] to cease their playing..said..If you have played away my Guests, you shall pay their reckoning. **1823** *Spirit of Public Jrnls.* (1825) 354 Handel being once in a country church, asked the organist to permit him to play the people out. **1884** J. Hatton *Henry Irving's Impressions of America* I. III. 94 It is customary in American theatres for the orchestra to play the audience out as well as in. **1902** A. Machray *Night Side London* xiii. 196 When you go upstairs, you find more members up here playing the wee sma' 'oors away.

VI. 31. a. Also *intr.*, to be performed; to take a specified time to be performed.

1602, 1809 [in Dict.]. **1869** *Punch* 9 Jan. 10/2 Mr. Burnand's new Burlesque, now playing at the Haymarket, is called *The Frightful Hair.* **1929** *Radio Times* 8 Nov. 388/2 *Typhoon* plays for about an hour. **1935** E. Waugh *Edmund Campion* ii. 75 In 1577 a tragedy of his..was produced..before..the widow of Charles IX of France; it played for six hours. **1958** *Spectator* 31 Jan. 135/1 The new symphony plays for an hour. **1972** *New Yorker* 8 Apr. 32/2 Mr. Zeffirelli watched the action from the back of the auditorium, and he told us that, except for a few small details, the scene was playing well.

c. To perform a play or the like in (a specified town, theatre, etc.); to appear as a performer or entertainer at (a particular place). orig. *U.S.*

1896 *N.Y. Dramatic News* 29 Aug. 11/3 A troup of barnstormers..are playing the smaller towns in this vicinity. **1933** P. Godfrey *Back-Stage* xvi. 206 He writes for lodgings to the next town he is playing. **1936** N. Coward *'Red Peppers'* in *To-night at 8.30* I. 103 'I'll see you don't play this date any more.'.. 'I'd sooner play Ryde Pier in November.' **1959** *Manch. Guardian* 26 Feb. 8/7 Sir John Gielgud is back in London after a tour of Canada and the United States... He played sixty towns and gave 81 performances. **1965** *Listener* 18 Nov. 801/1 The trouble with Freud and his theory of economy of psychic endeavour is that Freud never played Glasgow Empire second house on a Friday night, and I have. **1973** *Times* 27 Jan. 11/8 It's my greatest dream, to play the Palladium. **1975** *New Yorker* 26 May 30/3 The Bolshoi Ballet, now visiting New York en masse for the first time in nine years, is a younger and considerably more experimental version of the company that played the old Met back in 1966.

32. b. (Further examples.) Also, to become worn out or extremely weak.

1872 *Rep. Vermont Board Agric.* I. 79 The old native fruit of our country is about playing out, as the saying is. **1924** R. J. Flaherty *My Eskimo Friends* III. ii. 93 The dogs almost played out before we reached the crest. **1964** Mrs. L. B. Johnson *White House Diary* 15 July (1970) 178 A little past one my enthusiasm played out and I put my head in the pillow.

36. b. (Further examples.)

1907 J. H. Elder-Duncan *House Beautiful & Useful* ii. 18 Many of our leading architects and decorative artists..'play up to', or subordinate everything to one feature in a room. **1927** Chesterton *Secret Fr. Brown* i. 40 There was something downright creepy about that little goblin with the yellow hair, that seemed to play up to the impression. **1929** Kipling *Limits & Renewals* (1932) 358 His mother did social small-talk without daring to stop, and Wilkie played up to her. **1972** J. Mosedale *Football* x. 142 While the pros proved that wasn't literally true, Trippi played up to the spirit of the comment.

c. *to play down to*: to lower one's standard, quality, etc., to suit the tastes or demands of (one's public); to bring oneself down to (a low standard, level, etc.).

1889 G. B. Shaw *London Music in 1888–9* (1937) 234 When a theatre has been playing down as nearly as possible to the music-hall level. **1906** Beerbohm *Around Theatres* (1924) II. 215 No dramatist, moreover, ever yet achieved popularity by deliberately 'playing down to' the public. **1930** *Cambridge Daily News* 24 Sept. 8/1 Let us avoid playing down to the public, lest it ask us for a better article than we can provide. *a* **1936** Kipling *Something of Myself* (1937) viii. 218 Never play down to your public.

d. *to play* (a person) *off the stage*: to act much better than (another actor); to dominate the stage at the expense of (another person). Also *fig.*

1895 G. B. Shaw *Let.* 9 Mar. (1965) I. 494 Our actor managers have a not unnatural reluctance to be played off their own stages by their leading ladies. **1905** Beerbohm *Around Theatres* (1924) II. 144 He played all the other people off the stage, figuratively. Literally, they remained there, I regret to say. **1920** G. B. Shaw *Let.* 22 Dec. in *B. Shaw & Mrs. Campbell* (1952) 216 You played Hackett off the stage, and made only a few blunders. **1979** P. Mason *Skinner* xi. 78 Perron was rather surly, a peasant..who is being played off the stage by a man with style.

e. *to play for laughs* (or *a laugh*): to try to arouse laughter in one's audience; also *trans.*, to depict or use (something) with the aim of arousing laughter.

In quot. 1905 used as *attrib.* phr. (without *to*).

1905 G. B. Shaw *Let.* 2 Oct. (1972) II. 565 The sooner we get John Bull off, the better... An abominable, coarse, play-for-laughs, third class suburban performance. **1906** Beerbohm *Around Theatres* (1924) II. 256 Mr. Shaw was not merely 'playing for a laugh'. He was trying to reproduce a thing that exists in life. **1963** *Listener* 14 Mar. 468/1 Joan Littlewood sensibly lets this plot look after itself. Her concern is to play for laughs. **1965** *New Statesman* 9 Apr. 580/3 Mr Donleavy..plays the genre for sad laughs.

VII. With adverbs.

37. play along. a. *intr.* = sense 17g above; also, to pretend to agree or co-operate. Freq. const. *with*. *colloq.* (orig. *U.S.*).

1929 D. Hammett *Red Harvest* xi. 112 If the dick would play along, the hole in Tim's head from his own gun.. would smooth everything over pretty. **1935** S. Lewis *It can't happen Here* xix. 214 All we desire is for you to play along with us in your paper. **1947** J. Steinbeck *Wayward Bus* 45 There were only two things for Ernest to do—to laugh at her or play along. **1959** B. Kops *Hamlet of Stepney Green* II. ii. 50, I have no choice. I'll have to play along with him. **1965** *New Statesman* 23 Apr. 638/1 The Labour Party should stand no nonsense from the House of Lords. Although the Tory leadership there is still playing along, defeats of government business inflicted by gangs of Tory backwoodsmen could amount to a deliberate policy of obstruction. **1974** M. Birmingham *You can help Me* iv. 102 She seemed a little surprised at our enthusiasm for literature... But she was ready to play along with us.

b. *trans.* To deceive or tease (a person); to 'string *along*'. *colloq.*

1965 D. Francis *Odds Against* ii. 23, I smiled at him, and he guessed that I'd been playing him along. **1974** 'J. le Carré' *Tinker, Tailor* vi. 51 'Wait till Percy sees that,' I tell her—playing her along, like.

38. play down. To minimize; to try to make (something) appear smaller or less important than it really is; to make little of.

1930 *New Statesman* 27 Dec. 351 They accused the Washington departments of being in league with the large employers to 'play down' the number of the unemployed and so encourage the too-ready optimism which continues to assert that prosperity is, once again, just round the corner. **1934** J. O'Hara *Appointment in Samarra* x. 295, I heard the boss tell you to play down the story. **1956** E. M. Forster *Marianne Thornton* 29 Personal immortality today may not be denied by orthodoxy but it is played down, it is felt to be self-centred and anti-social. **1958** *Listener* 18 Sept. 428/2 This impression is much diluted in the Arts Council's exhibition, a timid selection which tends to play down the more extreme and remarkable developments of Bomberg's art. **1973** 'E. Ferrars' *Foot in Grave* x. 186 She might have..given the pair an exaggerated idea of their importance. She had been sure that Henry had been right to play the incident down. **1977** *Sunday Tel.* 4 Dec. 3/6 He accuses church leaders of playing down or disregarding these views and making those who hold them feel 'guilty and almost unchristian'.

39. play up. a. *intr.* To behave in a boisterous, unruly, or troublesome manner; to misbehave; *spec.* of a horse: to jump or frisk about. orig. *dial.*

1803 G. Colman *John Bull* II. iii. 23 (*Voices behind.*) *Bur.* They are playing up old Harry below; I'll run and see what's the matter. **1866** J. E. Brogden *Provincial Words in Lincolnshire* 151 He came home beery, and playing-up, broke the dolly. **1877** E. Peacock *Gloss. Words Manley & Corringham, Lincolnshire* 195/1 They're still enif when ther faather's at hoam, but they do play up when they're to their sens. **1886** R. E. G. Cole *Gloss. S.-W. Lincolnshire* 112 This pony does not play up at the trams as the other did. **1888** 'R. Boldrewood' *Robbery under Arms* II. iii. 42 He could do more with a horse than any man I ever saw. They never seemed to play up with him. **1909** J. Swire *Anglo-French Horsemanship* 25 The secret of remaining on a horse when he 'plays up' is to drop the hands, press the heels down, [etc.]. **1931** L. A. G. Strong *Garden* 41 Paddy was always resentful of strangers, and played up with a redoubled vigour if he saw that they were afraid of him. **1968** [see *Get *v.* 62 m]. **1973** K. Giles *File on Death* iv. 108 Cucumber generally played up with the Chief Inspector. **1976** J. Snow *Cricket Rebel* 66 Back in England, before he had time to bid for a place against Australia, his left elbow started playing up and he was ordered to rest.

b. To behave manfully or heroically; to act in a helpful or co-operative manner. Cf. sense 36b in Dict.

1897 H. Newbolt *Vitaï Lampada* in *Admirals All* 21 Play up! play up! and play the game! **1899** E. Wharton *Greater Inclination* viii. 249, I was in fact the only one of the three who did n't instantly 'play up'; but such virtuosity was inspiring, and by the time Vard had thrown off his coat and dropped into a senatorial pose, I was ready to pitch into my work. **1904** R. Fry *Let.* 9 Jan. (1972) I. 216 It is interesting to find that America is playing up so well and I can quite understand it if B.B. transfers his centre of gravity..to Boston. **1924** G. L. Mallory *Let.* 27 May in E. F. Norton *Fight for Everest: 1924* (1925) II. 236, I look back on tremendous effort and exhaustion... And yet there have been a good many things to set on the other side. The party has played up wonderfully. **1966** B. Kimenye *Kalasanda Revisited* 42 The other members played up nicely by expressing themselves as completely horrified. **1979** D. Gurr *Troika* vii. 42, I had to sound sensible. Adult... To hide the secret voice of the schoolboy yelling from the side lines to play up, play up.

c. *trans.* To make the most of; to emphasize; to exploit or trade upon, esp. in journalism and advertising. orig. *U.S.*

1909 R. Beach *Silver Horde* 106 It is a good newspaper story and I'll play it up. **1926** *Publishers' Weekly* 22 May 1687/1 Let us play up the habits, the appearance, the likes and dislikes, let us sell authors to our public. **1933** E. O'Neill *Ah, Wilderness!* (1934) I. 23 *Richard* (coming forward—seizing on the opportunity to play up his preoccupation..). **1945** [see *Ease *v.* 8 b]. **1961** *Los Angeles Times* 4 Aug. III. 4 The West Berlin crisis is being played up artificially because it is needed by the United States to justify its arms drive. **1973** 'D. Jordan' *Nile Green* xi. 49 Guy always plays up the limey accent when he's in the States.

d. To tease, annoy, or irritate (someone); to make sport with; to give trouble to.

1924 Galsworthy *White Monkey* II. iv. 151 Did she choose that he should go away, thinking that she had 'played him up' just out of vanity? **1927** *Daily Express* 10 Dec. 1 The girls thought they had got hold of a soft-hearted fool, and they began to play me up. **1934** L. A. G. Strong *Corporal Tune* 138 His body was frightened of what it had undergone..; and now, having succeeded in making Ignatius aware of it, it played him up, throwing him into something approaching panic. **1964** A. Christie

Caribbean Mystery xxii. 223 That's the sort of thing you feel like when your husband's playing you up and you're terribly fond of him. **1974** J. MITCHELL *Death & Bright Water* vi. 55 He wasn't in the mood for throwing, not with his back playing him up like it was. **1977** J. AIKEN *Last Movement* xi. 230 They are trying to play me up. They believe that..I lose control. **1979** 'M. HEBDEN' *Death set to Music* xv. 163 His stomach was playing him up again.

playa (pla·yă). orig. *U.S.* [a. Sp. *playa* shore, beach, coast, f. late L. *plagia*: cf. PLAGE[1].]

1. a. A flat silt- or sand-covered area, free of vegetation and usu. salty, that lies at the bottom of a desert basin and after rain becomes a temporary lake (*playa lake*). **b.** A playa lake.

1854 J. R. BARTLETT *Pers. Narr. Explorations* I. 246 The playas..seemed to have an extent of twenty five or thirty miles. **1856** in *Publ. S. Calif. Hist. Soc.* (1928) XIV. 124 We..stopped 1½ hours at the wagon & took breakfast & then pushed on to the playa & went ahead to hunt for water. **1885** I. C. RUSSELL in *Monogr. U.S. Geol. Survey* XI. 10 Other lakes, which indicate still more pointedly the contrast between an arid and a humid climate, we may call playa lakes. These are sheets of shallow water, covering many square miles in winter season, but evaporating to dryness during the summer, their beds becoming hard, smooth mud-plains or playas. **1939** P. G. WORCESTER *Textbk. Geomorphol.* ix. 246 Ancient playas which have not been covered with water for many years are likely to have quite irregular surfaces. *Ibid.* 247 Two types of sloping plains usually connect the borders of desert basins with the flat central playa plains. These are bajadas and pediments. **1945** J. L. MARSHALL *Santa Fe* 188 In the *playas*—saucerlike depressions in the desert—were beds of glistening salt and gypsum. **1957** G. E. HUTCHINSON *Treat. Limnol.* I. i. 6 The lakes of southern Oregon and northern California already mentioned are shallow playas. **1969** TWIDALE & FOALE *Landforms Illustrated* xvi. 110/1 Salts crystallise out and form a distinct layer covering the bed of the playa, which is called a saltpan... All the large playas of South and Western Australia are salty. **1975** MCALESTER & HAY *Physical Geol.* x. 330 In arid regions ..intermittent playa lakes are formed by infrequent downpours and quickly dry up, leaving an accumulation of evaporites.

2. A beach.

[**1855** in *Publ. S. Calif. Hist. Soc.* (1934) XVI. 59 La Playa (the beach) is that part of the city nearest the mouth of the harbor.] **1856** 'J. PHOENIX' *Phoenixiana* 202 Three other small buildings,..a fence, and a grave-yard, constitute all the 'improvements' that have been made at the 'Playa'. **1857** in *Amer. Speech* (1941) XVI. 265 The following is a list of words and phrases frequently used in English conversation in California, and not unfrequently quoted in California newspapers:..*Playa*, beach. **1924** *Chambers's Jrnl.* Aug. 581/1 They turned eastward.. keeping to the *playas*, or little beaches. **1934** R. MACAULAY *Going Abroad* i. 14, I think I shall go down to the playa and bathe. **1964** S. BLANC *Yellow Villa* (1965) 12 The South Seas setting that has made land along the northern *playa* so very expensive. **1966** M. STEEN *Looking Glass* viii. 160 Little lights of fishing boats far away down on the *playa* [in Málaga].

3. (See quot. 1972.)

1898 R. T. HILL *Cuba & Porto Rico* v. 48 Occasionally a few acres of *playa*, or low alluvial land, may be found around the harbors, but the rivers are free from wide bottoms, and the land as a whole stands well above the sea. **1972** *Gloss. Geol.* (Amer. Geol. Inst.) 548/1 *Playa*, a flat, alluvial coastland, as distinguished from a beach.

playability. (Later example.)

1977 *Early Music* Apr. 151 It would be a useful piece of work if someone were to collect and analyse them [*sc.* wind instruments depicted in medieval manuscripts] according to types and theoretical playability.

playback (plēi·bæk). Also **play-back.** [f. vbl. phr. *to play back*: *PLAY *v.* 28 b.] **1. a.** The reproduction of a recording, esp. soon after it has been made. Also *fig.* and *attrib.*

1929 *Photoplay* Apr. 110/2 *Play-back*,..the immediate playing of the sound record after the taking of a scene in order that actors and directors may hear how it all sounds... The play-back is only possible from disc recording,..as in film recording the film must be developed before the sound can be heard. **1931** N. H. SLAUGHTER in L. Cowan *Recording Sound for Motion Pictures* iv. 61 Disc recording permits play-backs, often a boon to the director and cast. **1934** *B.B.C. Year-Bk.* 419 For immediate play-backs the Blattner system requires a little time to rewind the tape before running off again. **1940** *N.Y. Times* 19 May IX. 10/2 As future generations listen to play-backs of the uses to which radio was put for propaganda purposes..they, too, may be amazed. **1941** B. SCHULBERG *What makes Sammy Run?* xi. 282 He felt he had to justify himself. He insisted upon giving me a playback of that historic interview. **1949** *Sun* (Baltimore) 5 Feb. 7 A courtroom playback of the broadcasts..brought out that Nazi propaganda was inserted between the GI's messages. **1949** *Electronic Engin.* XXI. 149/3 The recording and play-back heads are so arranged that two tracks of recording can be stored on the standard tape. **1957** C. MACINNES *City of Spades* II. v. 140 On and on she went, like a playback from a tape recorder. **1957** W. H. WHYTE *Organization Man* 133 A young man's idle dream? It is a playback only mildly exaggerated of a vision of the future. **1959** *News Chron.* 25 Aug. 3/5 Visitors to the Radio Show ..will be able to see how TV shows are recorded ready for immediate playback. **1970** N. ARMSTRONG et al. *First on Moon* ix. 203 We've been looking at your systems data on playback and everything is looking good. **1976** *Gramophone* Oct. 532 (Advt.), Pickering's exclusive new design development also makes it superior to other cartridges in the playback of stereo records. **1978** G. MCDONALD *Fletch's Fortune* x. 65 The playback volume was too high.

b. *Cinemat.* A technique of recording the voice of a singer for the soundtrack of a film as a substitute for that of an actor or actress when songs are called for. *playback singer*, a singer whose voice is so used; also *ellipt.*

1952 R. SPOTTISWOODE *Film & its Techniques* 351 The technique of prescoring and playback with singer and orchestra. **1962** *Times* 26 Jan. (Survey of India) p. xiii/2 The well-loved singers of prewar days were displaced by a strange new tribe known as 'play-backs'. **1963** BARNOUW & KRISHNASWAMY *Indian Film* 164 A Cine Writers Association and a Playback Singers Association had been launched but had ceased activity because of lack of support. **1966** R. P. JHABVALA *Star & Two Girls* in *Experience of India* (1971) 74 A playback singer rendered a love-song with..feeling. **1971** *Sunday Nation* (Nairobi) 11 Apr. 31/4 The best male playback singer trophy.

2. An apparatus for playing recordings.

1930 PITKIN & MARSTON *Art of Sound Pictures* 271 *Play-back*, a device which repeats the voices, recorded on a wax record. **1936** E. S. BESINGER tr. *London's Film Music* IV. 114 The American 'play back' invention has the advantage of less danger, and accuracy more easily attained. **1945** L. A. G. STRONG *Othello's Occupation* 44 It's a recording unit, with a play-back and ordinary controls for loud-speaker. **1960** *Aeroplane* 15 July 51 (Advt.), Permanent radar records with the AEI radar recorder and playback.

play-book. Add: **2.** A book of games and pastimes for children.

1694 (*title*) A play-book for children. **1761** A. BARCLAY (*title*) Tom Thumb's play book. **1886** (*title*) The golden playbook.

3. *Football.* A book containing various strategies and systems of play. *U.S.*

1967 *Time* 6 Jan. 64 On the field, Plimpton did the calisthenics and learned the playbook cold, but when the test came during an intra-squad scrimmage before a large crowd,..every play was botched. **1969** *Sunday Times* 28 Sept. 22 They spend most of their time watching films of their next opponents or studying the 'play-book' which sets out the dozens of moves they have to learn before the next match. **1972** J. MOSEDALE *Football* v. 57 He absorbed the fundamentals..out of a playbook more than 300 pages long.

playboy (plēi·boi). *colloq.* Also **play-boy.** [f. PLAY *sb.* + BOY *sb*[1].] A man, esp. a wealthy man, who sets out to enjoy himself; a selfish pleasure-seeker (in quot. 1898 used of the devil). Also as *v. intr.* Hence **pla·yboyish** *a.*, **pla·yboyishness, pla·yboyism.**

Cf. also the obsolete sense s.v. PLAY *sb.* 17.

1829 G. GRIFFIN *Collegians* viii. 161 The pretty Syl repeatedly told him that he was 'a funny gentleman' and 'a great play-boy'. **1898** J. MACMANUS *Bend of Road* 107 The divil sittin cheek be jowl with him in his own chimbley corner!..an' himself an' the playboy shoughed out o' the same pipe! **1907** J. M. SYNGE (*title*) The playboy of the western world. *Ibid.* II. 51 You're the walking playboy of the western world. **1926** C. DAY LEWIS in *Oxford Poetry* 20 Proud Playboy of his own complacency. **1926** *N.Y. Times* 11 Oct. 24/2 The playboy of baseball might have heard his name go ringing down the corridors of baseball as a man who won a series game with a home run. **1933** J. CARY *Amer. Visitor* 226 Jukes used to say all these officials were playboys moved by some impractical notion or other. **1936** M. DE LA ROCHE *Whiteoak Harvest* xi. 160 No matter how hard I worked I was looked on as a sort of playboy who couldn't do a man's job. **1939** JOYCE *Finnegans Wake* (1964) I. 183 The house..was the worst, it is hoped, even in our western playboyish world for pure mousefarm filth. **1952** E. O'NEILL *Moon for Misbegotten* I. 55 He is not the blatantly silly, playboy heir to millions whose antics make newspaper headlines. **1954** N. COWARD *Future Indefinite* I. 4 Beneath a glittering veneer of..playboyishness, I had managed..to retain a few normal human instincts. **1959** M. CUMBERLAND *Murmurs in Rue Morgue* xvii. 105 What's the matter with this age?.. Its bitterest insults are to call people playboys, pleasure-lovers, hedonists. **1960** WODEHOUSE *Jeeves in Offing* vi. 60 A New York playboy, accustomed from his earliest years to pursue blondes like a bloodhound. **1962** *Times* 28 Feb. 5/1 The elder boy, who has gone in for playboyism in a big way. **1963** V. CANNING *Limbo Line* xvi. 218 Who wanted money? Amadeo to playboy around? **1973** 'D. JORDAN' *Nile Green* xx. 76 The Lebanese ladies..lusted after the trim, brown-tanned Beirut playboys. **1976** BOTHAM & DONNELLY *Valentino* xi. 86 Wearing tails as the Paris playboy, he was dancing his way into cinema history.

play-day. Add: **2.** *Theatr.* A day on which a play is performed.

1761 in G. C. D. ODELL *Annals of N.Y. Stage* (1927) I. iv. 83 Those ladies who would have places kept in the boxes will please to send a sensible servant to the theatre at three o'clock on every play-day. **1888** G. O. SEILHAMER *Hist. Amer. Theatre* I. xi. 111 Mr. Allyn's benefit took place on Saturday, instead of the regular play-day.

play-down, playdown (plēi·daun). orig. *Canad.* [f. PLAY *v.* + DOWN *adv.*] (See quot. 1939.)

1939 WEBSTER Add., *Playdown*, one of a series of playoffs, as among the winning teams from different leagues or localities. *Canada.* **1970** *Globe & Mail* (Toronto) 28 Sept. 21/2 Senior hockey in Canada may abandon the Allan Cup playdowns in favor of an annual tournament with six to eight teams participating. **1973** *Courier & Advertiser* (Dundee) 26 Feb. 9/1 The north district play-down in the Scottish Curling championship was concluded at Perth Ice Rink yesterday.

played (plēid), *ppl. a.* [f. PLAY *v.* + -ED[1].] **1.** That has been played.

1833 J. CAIRNIE *Ess. Curling* 61 Every stone shall be reckoned as played, if the player part with the handle. **1877** *Encycl. Brit.* VI. 713/2 If a played stone rolls over, or stops, on its side or top, it shall be put off the ice. **1892** J. BROWN *Man. Bowling* (ed. 2) 76 As soon as the last played bowl stops, the control of the rink is transferred to the other party. **1969** R. WELSH *Beginner's Guide to Curling* xvi. 102 If a curler touches a played stone belonging to his side, he himself will remove it from the ice.

2. a. *played-out*: see PLAY *v.* 32 c.

b. Exhausted, worn out; passé, finished. *U.S. colloq.*

1872 *Republican Rev.* 16 Mar. 2/4 The days of forked sticks for plows is about played. **1883** 'MARK TWAIN' *Life on Mississippi* xliii. 439 That *used* to be, but that's all played now; that is, in this particular town. The Irish got to piling up hacks so, on their funerals, that a funeral left them ragged and hungry for two years afterward; so the priest pitched in and broke it all up. **1897** *Outing* XXIX. 421/2 He's about played.

3. *played-down*: see *PLAY *v.* 38.

1960 G. CHARLES in J. Pudney *Pick of Today's Short Stories* 45 He would have liked to have dropped a modest, played-down remark or two on his standing in his own community. **1973** J. WAINWRIGHT *Touch of Malice* 109 The deliberately played-down tone of his talk.

player[1]. Add: **I. 2. c.** (Earlier and later examples.) Also *transf.*

1806, etc. [see *GENTLEMAN 4 a]. **1976** W. GREATOREX *Crossover* 31 Meade..seemed to like having a Player like Calder in among the Gentlemen of the section. **1978** B. LEVIN in K. Gregory *First Cuckoo* 12 We are all, gentlemen and players alike, engaged in the business..of expressing our views to thousands, or even millions, of people who have not invited us to do so. **1979** L. MEYNELL *Hooky & Villainous Chauffeur* viii. 106 That's how cricket was run in those days; it was gentlemen and players then.

II. 8*. A record-player.

1948 *Mod. Plastics* Mar. 84 (*heading*) Unique design of portable player, molded in phenolic, matches polystyrene record carrier. **1953** E. T. CANBY *Home Music Systems* vi. 91 The greatest reason for using a manual player is to achieve better sound quality. **1963** J. FOWLES *Collector* II. 167 G.P. jumped up and turned off the player. **1968** 'E. TREVOR' *Place for Wicked* i. 3 Alec said if music wasn't good enough to listen to without talking it wasn't worth putting on the player. **1976** J. DRUMMOND *Funeral Urn* xxv. 127 Margot found him..listening to a recording by Led Zeppelin. He switched off the player and beckoned Margot in.

III. 9. player-coach, one who plays a game and also coaches his fellow-players; similarly, **player-manager, -trainer; player-piano**, a piano having a mechanical apparatus by which it can be played automatically.

1948 *Sporting Mirror* 21 May 11/1 Bobby Baxter, former Scottish international and player-coach to Leith Ath., has been appointed team manager to the Edinburgh speedway team. **1961** *Times* 12 May 4/7 The decision of the Toulston Club to engage an Argentine as player-coach. **1972** J. MOSEDALE *Football* ii. 21 Strictly functional equipment modeled by player-coach George Halas. **1905** Player-manager [in Dict.]. **1951** *Sport* 16–22 Mar. 3/1 He was..inundated with player-manager offers from non-League sides. **1977** *Western Morning News* 30 Aug. 12/4 On the eve of Exeter City's glamour second round Football League Cup-tie player-manager Bobby Saxton anxiously waits this morning for the latest fitness reports to know if he can field his strongest side to challenge the might of Cup holders Aston Villa. [**1901** *Everybody's Mag.* Oct. 490/1 In the section devoted to musical instruments one can hear hourly concerts by mechanical piano-players.] **1907** *Strand* Nov. 103 It..is..the most remarkable achievement in player-piano construction. *Ibid.* 105 Melody Stops..distinguish the 'Autopiano' from all.. player-pianos. **1913** [see *music-roll* s.v. *MUSIC *sb.* 12 d]. **1922** S. GREW *Art of Player-Piano* 1 The player-piano, like the pianoforte and the organ, is a musical instrument. **1946** R. BLESH *Shining Trumpets* II. xi. 243 He made an unknown quantity of player-piano rolls. **1973** *Times* 25 Oct. 38/7 (Advt.), Steinway and Sons..are prepared to purchase or take part exchange pianos of their own or other makes except player pianos. **1956** *People* 13 May 13/6, I have had several offers to join clubs in Germany as player-coach or player-trainer.

Player[2] (plēi·əɹ). Also **Players, Player's.** The proprietary name of a cigarette made by the John Player Company. Also *Comb.*

[**1885** *Trade Marks Jrnl.* 9 Dec. 1196 Player's Rough & Ready Mixture... John Player,..Nottingham; manufacturer. **1889** *Ibid.* 20 Mar. 285 Player... Manufactured tobacco, except snuff. The firm trading as John Player,.. Nottingham, tobacco manufacturers.] ?**1932** DYLAN THOMAS *Sel. Lett.* (1966) 6 I've got a large Players, and my shoes are off. **1943** *R.A.F. Jrnl.* Aug. 29 'Why was that, Flight?' the Corporal asked, taking a packet of Players from his pocket and selecting one. The Flight Sergeant reached over and helped himself. 'In my days..corporals couldn't afford expensive fags like these.' **1945** DYLAN THOMAS *Let.* 28 Aug. (1966) 283, I raise one Player-coloured aspen hand to salute and supplicate. **1960** *Tobacco* June 37 A new Player pack... Player's Medium Navy Cut cigarettes, the big sellers, are now introduced in a new modernised pack. **1977** R. BARNARD *Death on the High C's* xiii. 144 He..puffed his way through a third of his Player's. **1978** D. BLOODWORTH *Crosstalk* vii. 54 She.. lit a Player with a book match.

Playfair (plēi·fēəɹ). The name of Lyon *Playfair*, 1st Lord Playfair (1818–98), British chemist and administrator, used *attrib.* and *absol.* to designate a cipher in which successive pairs of letters are replaced by pairs chosen in a prescribed manner from a matrix of 25 letters, usu. arranged in accordance with a key-word.

1922 J. C. H. MACBETH *Langie's Cryptography* iv. 166 M. Langie has omitted to give any reference to the 'Playfair' cipher, which has been extensively used for military purposes. This cipher is one of the substitution variety, and may be operated with one or more key-words. **1932** D. L. SAYERS *Have his Carcase* xxvi. 344 Here's a cipher message. Probably Playfair. **1966** M. R. D. FOOT *SOE in France* iv. 105 As simple as a Playfair code based on a single word. **1974** *Encycl. Brit. Micropædia* X. 643/3 He [*sc.* Sir Charles Wheatstone]..invented the Playfair cipher, which is based on substituting different pairs of letters for paired letters in the message. **1979** *Listener* 18 Jan. 131/1, I see that I have to encipher my answers to other [crossword] clues in Playfair without knowing the keyword... I have a friend who could solve two Playfair squares before breakfast.

play-game. Delete † *Obs.* and add later examples.

1972 *Evening Telegram* (St. John's, Newfoundland) 24 June 3/1, I won't be spending such a week as the one just past. All jokes aside, it has been no playgame. **1973** *Shooting Times & Country Mag.* 7 July 21/1 To my way of thinking, anything easy to acquire is never valued for long and, compared to what it was in my younger days, fishing is now almost a playgame.

playgirl (plē̆ⁱ·gɜːl). Also **play girl, play-girl.** *colloq.* [f. PLAY *sb.* + GIRL *sb.*] A woman who sets out to enjoy herself; a good-time girl. Cf. *PLAYBOY.

1934 *Sun* (Baltimore) 9 Oct. 7/3 Colletta..had better be good or she will be sent to a reformatory, her mother.. warned today as the Pittsburgh (Pa.) playgirl arrived in Manila. **1935** *Mademoiselle* May 15 Just trick yourself out in your wildest clothes and turn playgirl for one evening. **1935** A. J. POLLOCK *Underworld Speaks* 89/1 *Play girl*, a promiscuous female who goes out for a good time. **1939** F. SCOTT FITZGERALD *Let.* 4 Jan. (1964) 283 She has tendencies toward being a play-girl and has been put on probation. **1942** *Time* 16 Feb. 64/2 Victor Mature ..announced the breakup of his eight-month marriage to Martha Stephenson Kemp, complained that she was a 'playgirl'. **1963** I. FLEMING *On H.M. Secret Service* v. 55 The worm of self-destruction..behind the wild, playgirl façade, was eating away..her soul. **1964** *Punch* 8 Jan. 66/3 A rich American playgirl. **1977** *Spare Rib* Jan. 41/3 And more and more they will try to con us into believing that, for playgirls as well as playboys, a taste for porn is a proof of liberation.

playground. Add: (Earlier example. Also, earlier and later examples in extended and fig. use.) Also *attrib.*

1780 A. YOUNG *Tour in Ireland* 104 The school is a building of considerable extent..with..a spacious play-ground walled in. **1871** L. STEPHEN (*title*) The playground of Europe. **1910** *Westm. Gaz.* 31 Jan. 1/3 The 'playground' England, the England of great country houses, of game preserves, [etc.]. **1916** A. HUXLEY *Let.* 7 Sept. (1969) 111 They tell me..you are returning to.. England. Or else pacifically to what the Editor of *Truth* would call the *playground of Europe.* **1929** A. E. FORD *My Minnesota* iv. 194 Like hundreds of others we wish our vacation would never end, and we know now why Minnesota has become the 'Playground of the Nation'. **1963** W. SOYINKA *Dance of Forests* 2 Ogun, they deify, for his playground is the battle field. **1968** *Listener* 19 Dec. 819/2, I gave midnight nudie bathing parties from my private yacht moored at the millionaires' playground of Grimsby. **1970** G. GREER *Female Eunuch* 271 The most telling playground for feelings of rejection about women is the joke department. **1971** 'D. HALLIDAY' *Dolly & Doctor Bird* vii. 89 Great Harbour Cay is an island.. undergoing transformation into a luxurious international playground for tropical sport. **1975** M. SIMPSON *Chrome Connection* ii. 10 A reminder about..playground duty. **1976** H. NIELSEN *Brink of Murder* iii. 26 Simon sent off ten cables to ten European playgrounds where Jack Keith might be holidaying. **1977** *Wandsworth Borough News* 16 Sept. 15/1 Planning Proposals... St. Faith's School, Smardale-road, Wandsworth—erection of playground shelter.

play group (plē̆ⁱ·grūp). orig. *U.S.* [f. PLAY *sb.* 6 + GROUP *sb.* 3 a.] **a.** *Sociol.* A group formed naturally by young children in a neighbourhood for play and companionship.

1909 C. H. COOLEY *Social Organization* (1913) iii. 24 The most important spheres of this intimate association and coöperation..are the family, the play-group of children, [etc.]. *Ibid.*, Nor can any one doubt the general prevalence of play-groups among children. **1939** F. J. BROWN *Sociology of Childhood* 177 Miss S. Wisletzky was able to distinguish three factors in the formation of play groups. **1947** —— *Educ. Psychol.* x. 220 The first play group is small,..of a transitory character, formed only to carry on a specific activity of the moment. *Ibid.*, The activity itself is the basis for the organization of the play group. **1954** J. A. C. BROWN *Social Psychol. of Industry* v. 129 Cooley gave as typical examples of primary groups the family, the play-groups of children, and the neighbourhood group of elders in the village community. **1964** GOULD & KOLB *Dict. Social Sci.* 281/1 The dividing line between a clique or a play group and a gang is by no means clear and in practice such a group is whatever the researcher chooses to call it.

b. A group, freq. one organized informally by parents of pre-school children, formed with the object of providing supervised companionship for children while freeing their parents for other activities. Also *attrib.*

1942 C. LANDRETH *Educ. Young Child* I. i. 17 For this group probably the best immediate solution under 1942 conditions is parents' cooperative backyard play groups. **1962** *Guardian* 6 Nov. 18/3 A pre-school play group which a group of mothers are organising. **1968** D. LAWTON *Social Class, Lang. & Educ.* iii. 24 Linguistic handicaps could be alleviated by separating the twins into different play-groups. **1969** *Times* 5 Nov. 13/4 Three years ago there were many Members of Parliament who thought playgroups had something to do with drama. **1973** B. CROWE *Playgroup Movement* v. 79 In some areas..the groups have not been allowed to start unless the play-group leader is 'suitably qualified'. **1975** H. JARECKI *Playgroups* 10 Vivid pictures of children and their parents in the playgroup setting.

playhouse. Add: **1. b.** † **playhouse pay** (see quot. 1794). *Obs.*

1790 T. WILKINSON *Mem.* I. 146 The theatre being for the first month opened three nights in a week, my salary was only fifteen shillings as play-house pay, and when got to four nights, merely twenty shillings. **1794** C. MATHEWS *Let.* 19 June in A. Mathews *Mem. Charles Mathews* (1838) I. v. 90 Most of the salaries are what they call 'play-house pay'; that is, payment only each night they play; so that a man engaged at three pounds a-week, if he performs three times a-week only, has only half his salary. **1845** *Bentley's Misc.* June 600 In the year 1728 a first-rate singer, according to play-house pay, which means the actual nights of performance, could command no more than *forty-five pounds* annually.

2. a. (Freq. *play-house.*) A house, usu. small, in or with which children may play.

1792 A. YOUNG *Trav. France* I. 108 These cases of models..have so much the air of children's playhouses, that I would not answer for my little girl..not crying for them. **1857** M. J. HOLMES *Meadow-Brook* xxv. 317 At a short distance from the house was a tall cypress..where now was a play-house. **1908** G. JEKYLL *Children & Gardens* ii. 11 A good play-house..is a little house somewhere in garden or shrubbery, consisting of a kitchen and a sitting-room. **1916** *Daily Colonist* (Victoria, B.C.) 13 July 8/3 She makes all sorts of toys; animals and dolls, rocking horses and play houses. **1965** *Guardian* 20 Nov. 3/8 (Advt.), Playhouse... 59/6... Takes 4/5 children. **1968** *Sunday Times* 16 June 61 The Peter Murray play house..is big enough to hold several children at once. **1978** *Detroit Free Press* 16 Apr. F11/1 (Advt.), 4 bdrm house,..att gar, play house for kids on 2 acres.

playing, *vbl. sb.* Add: **2.** *playing-life, -place* (later example), *-time.*

1957 *Records & Recording* Nov. 20/1 If it is already tracking properly, a sapphire should have a playing life of about 50 hours. **1852** W. J. BRODERIP *Leaves Notebk. of Naturalist* 152 On visiting the cedar-brushes of the Liverpool range, he discovered several of these bowers or playing-places. **1577** T. WHITE *Sermon* (1578) sig. C viii *verso*, If it [*sc.* the Theatre] be not suppressed..it will make such a Tragedie, yᵗ all London may well mourne..for it is no playing time..but time to pray rather. **1949** FRAYNE & WOLFE *Elements of Sound Recording* xxix. 600 Magnetic materials can be erased and reused..and..reasonable fidelity can be obtained with extremely long playing time. **1951** *Sport* 16–22 Mar. 2/1 Installation of large playing-time clocks on all major league grounds. **1961** *Jazz Monthly* Mar. 27/2 It doesn't amount to much qualitatively, or quantitatively in 36 minutes playing time. **1966** *Jrnl. Canad. Operational Res. Soc.* 117 *Ratio, playing time*, the ratio of playing time to combat time for an event or series of events.

playing, *ppl. a.* (Examples in *Cards.*)

1899 SOMERVILLE & 'ROSS' *Some Experiences Irish R.M.* iv. 90 We were in the first game..and I was holding a very nice playing hand. **1959** REESE & DORMER *Bridge Player's Dict.* 166 Playing tricks are tricks that a hand may reasonably be expected to take when playing in its own best trump suit. **1964** *Official Encycl. Bridge* (Amer. Contract Bridge League) 430/2 *Playing trick*, an expected trick if the holder or his partner buys the contract. **1976** 'TREVANIAN' *Main* ii. 24 He has a fair playing hand but no meld to speak of.

play-list (plē̆ⁱ·list). Also **playlist.** [f. PLAY *sb.* + LIST *sb.*[6]] **1.** A list of theatrical plays to be performed.

1962 *Times* 23 Jan. 13/3 The classical play-list consists of *Ruy Blas*,..*Amphitryon*, and *L'Homme à la Main de Fer.*

2. A shortlist of musical records that may be broadcast by a radio station in a given period. Also *attrib.*

1975 *Listener* 26 June 848/1 Radio 1 severely limits the number of records it plays... By and large you will hear only the few that are put on the mysterious 'play-list' each week. **1976** *New Musical Express* 17 Apr. 17/1 It makes most of the present Radio One playlist shrivel into insignificance. **1977** *Sounds* 1 Jan. 4/1 Stephen Bishop will triumph. Top of the Pops producers and BBC playlist folks be prepared.

play-maker. Restrict 'Now *rare*' to sense in Dict. and add: Also **playmaker. 1.** (Further examples.)

1812 *Dramatic Censor 1811* 182 This may be what our modern playmakers call *light* and *shade.* **1953** *Scrutiny* XIX. 204/3 The Restoration playmakers did not exercise their classical imitation by ordering *any* general issues into *any* pattern.

2. A player in a team game, esp. basketball, who leads an attack, or brings other players on his side into a position to score. Hence **playmaking** *a.* orig. *U.S.*

1942 BERREY & VAN DEN BARK *Amer. Thes. Slang* § 662/2 Hockey... *Playmaker*, a player who does not attempt to score but puts the puck in place for the scorer. **1951** *Sun* (Baltimore) 12 Jan. 14/4 Bill Kelso, Patterson's playmaker at guard, is expected to be back in action tonight after missing the game against Southern. **1961** *Look* 15 Aug. 84 In high school..he was better known as a basketball playmaker than as a pitcher. **1967** *Boston Sunday Herald* 26 Mar. II. 1/5 Jones, the playmaker, turned gunner Saturday night... The Celtics went up 2-0 on New York in their best-of-five first-round Eastern Division playoffs. **1972** *N.Y. Times* 4 June 6/1 Ford, a playmaker on the varsity basketball team, is the son of Doug Ford. **1974** *Anderson* (S. Carolina) *Independent* 23 Apr. 7A/5 Little Ernie DiGregorio, the Buffalo Braves' playmaking guard, and big Ron Behagen, the Kansas City-Omaha Kings' brawny forward, were unanimous choices on the National Basketball Association's All-Rookie team for the 1973–74 season. **1975** *New Yorker* 7 Apr. 94/3 He was just the man the Bucks had wanted—an experienced ball handler and playmaker who would give the team the steadiness it needed in the backcourt. **1979** *Guardian* 26 Apr. 22/4 The Austrians could offer nothing in attack, where their elegant playmaker, Prohaska, continually dwelt on the ball.

pla·y-off, playoff. [f. PLAY *v.* + OFF *adv.*] **a.** An additional game or match played to decide a draw or tie; a replay. **b.** *N. Amer.* A series of games or matches played to decide a championship, etc. Also *transf.* and *fig.* Also as *v. intr.*

1895 *Outing* June 50/2 In the play-off for the championship of the city, the Sodality team won a bitterly contested game. **1906** *Liverpool Even. Express* 9 Mar., The play-off resulted in a win. **1915** *Literary Digest* (N.Y.) 21 Aug. 361/1 The race with the Cubs was a tie at the end of the season and a play-off game was necessary to decide the pennant. **1932** *Sun* (Baltimore) 6 Sept. 14/2 The play-off for the Middle Atlantic League baseball title will start Wednesday. **1939** *Beaver* June 25/2 He had a son with the St. Boniface Seals and..was very interested in the fact that they were in the Dominion Junior Hockey Championship play-offs. **1947** A. P. GASKELL *Big Game* 12 He spoke for a while about the traditions of the [Rugby] club and then about the honour of playing off for the championship. **1959** *Times* 29 May 5/2 P. Gill..won the..first prize.. after a six holes play-off. **1969** *John Edwards Mem. Foundation Quarterly* V. iv. 145 Guthrie Meade is presently studying fiddling contests...Many of the contests involved preliminary play-offs. **1970** G. F. NEWMAN *Sir, You Bastard* vii. 190 He'd use the man in his play-off with Manso. **1973** *Courier & Advertiser* (Dundee) 1 Mar. 13/2 The six rinks who have qualified for the finals of the 1973 Scottish curling championships will play-off, on a league basis, for the right to represent Scotland at the world championship. **1978** *Morecambe Guardian* 14 Mar. 11/6 The third division could have to go to a play-off, depending upon the result of the..match, still to be played.

play-room (plē̆ⁱ·rūm). Also **play room, playroom.** [f. PLAY *sb.* + ROOM *sb.*[1]] A room used for children to play in; a nursery. Also *attrib.*

1819 M. WILMOT *Let.* 31 Oct. (1935) 25 The children's Nursery and play room are lovely. **1838** *Knickerbocker* XI. 12 One Saturday afternoon when seated with two or three other children in my little play-room. **1840** H. COCKTON *Valentine Vox* xi. 82 He nevertheless contended within himself, that they were games which ought strictly to be confined to the play-room. **1847** J. H. NEWMAN *Let.* 26 Jan. (1962) XII. 26 At Christmas..we find him in the playrooms (cameratas) with the little boys about him, they dressed up as the Magi. **1865** MRS. STOWE *House & Home Papers* 45 Charlie and Jim..detesting the dingy lonely play-room, used to run the city streets. **1890** O. WILDE *Pict. Dorian Gray* viii, in *Lippincott's Monthly Mag.* July 61 He had used it first as a playroom when he was a child and then as a study. **1895** KIPLING *Day's Work* (1898) 365 The two rooms..that had been his nursery and his play-room. **1905** F. H. BURNETT *Little Princess* iii. 32 Is it true that you have a play-room all to yourself? **1909** *Westm. Gaz.* 22 Apr. 2/3 We will wander hand in hand, Like a boy and girl in a playroom land. **1927** *Ladies' Home Jrnl.* Dec. 12/1 Jessica's song and the children's noise, every sound in the play room, broke off short. **1932** *New Yorker* 23 July 22/2 My quarters would inevitably be under the play room, where my host's little ones would indulge in matutinal exercises. **1957** J. MASTERS *Far, Far the Mountain Peak* 105 Her brother..who..stands in a lordly manner in front of the play-room fire. **1966** *New Statesman* 13 May 691/3 There can be no denying that the most obvious method of bettering the circumstances of these working-class mothers is to improve their housing and to raise their standard of living, so that they have gardens or playrooms where the children may run loose. **1973** *Country Life* 14 June Suppl. 1 (Advt.), Georgian house..3 reception rooms..Playroom. Outside studio. **1979** G. ST. AUBYN *Edward VII* ii. 114 Alix..doted on her son. All her instincts were to keep him in the playroom, while his wife tried to interest him in serious matters.

play-the-ball. *Rugby League.* Also **play the ball.** [PLAY *v.*] A move restarting play after a tackle, in which the tackled player kicks or heels the ball from the ground, with opponents in specified positions in front of him and a member of his team behind.

1959 *Observer* 13 Sept. 32/2 Some of their habits at the play-the-balls were suspiciously close to being offside. **1974** *Rules of Game* 158/5 The team in possession is allowed three successive play-the-balls (five in Britain and Australia). **1976** *Liverpool Echo* 6 Dec. 17/9 Midway through the period Les Gorley sneaked a smart try from a play-the-ball. **1978** *Times* 20 Nov. 9/2 In the first half Pepons nipped over from a play the ball, and Cronin kicked two penalties.

playtime. Add: **2.** (Earlier examples.) Also, the time during which a play is being performed.
1616 JONSON *Epicœne* IV. ii, in *Wks.* 572 Who will.. inuite vs to the cock-pit, and kisse our hands all the play-time? **1749** SMOLLETT tr. *Le Sage's Gil Blas* IV. XII. i. 179, I waited impatiently for play-time, that I might go to the theatre.

playwrighting. (Further examples.)
1928 *Publishers' Weekly* 16 June 2445 Francis Brett Young, not content with writing distinguished novels and poems, has turned his attention to playwrighting. **1966** *Punch* 10 Aug. 230/1 Those grand old ample days of playwrighting when plots were clear and motives required no hard brainwork. **1973** E. BULLINS *Theme is Blackness* 12 In the area of playwrighting, Ed Bullins, at this moment in time, is almost without peer in America.

plaza. Delete ‖ and add further examples. Also *U.S.*, a public square or open space; in extended uses (orig. and chiefly *N. Amer.*), a large paved area surrounded by or adjacent to buildings, esp. as a feature of a shopping complex. Also *attrib.*
Now usu. with pronunc. (plā·ză).
1844 J. GREGG *Commerce of Prairies* II. 77 Two or three miles above the plaza there is a dam of stone and brush. **1852** *Knickerbocker* XL. 197 The spirit-stirring fife and drum, and the roar of cannon on the plaza [at New Orleans], announce the hour for morning parade. **1856** G. H. DERBY *Phoenixiana* 126 Every citizen..was aroused at 2 A.M. by the soul-stirring and tremendous report of the Plaza Artillery. **1884** SWEET & KNOX *Through Texas* xxiii. 307 Old Gen. Ignacio Barterra 'cussed' a forty-foot steeple on the old church on the plaza. **1907** S. E. WHITE *Arizona Nights* iii. 47 A freight outfit brought him to Tucson and dumped him down on the plaza. **1948** *Sun* (Baltimore) 20 Nov. 14 (*caption*) All tolls for travel across the Chesapeake Bay Bridge will be paid at booths on the 1000-foot toll plaza on the Western Shore approach to the bridge. **1957** *Times* 2 Dec. 13/1 Shopping..is simplified [in Canada] by the presence of suburban shopping plazas..an enormous parking lot encircled by branches of the down-town stores. **1959** *Ottawa Citizen* 11 July 21/7 Two plazas with parking facilities and offices for Customs and Immigration..are to be built. **1961** L. MUMFORD *City in Hist.* Note to plate 62, Ossip Zadkine's sculpture..placed on a plaza fronting the inner Harbor of Rotterdam. **1966** T. PYNCHON *Crying of Lot 49* v. 103 She came..into a plaza teeming with corduroy, denim, bare legs,..students in nose-to-nose dialogue. **1969** *Guardian* 15 July 10/6 There is no place nearer to hell than the all-under-one-roof shopping 'plaza'. **1969** *Parade* (N.Y.) 14 Dec. 18/3 It is not at all uncommon..to see hippies and Indians sitting together in the town's main plaza, sharing a canteen of water or a pack of cigarettes. **1974** *Sci. Amer.* Feb. 99/3 Bending and shear forces are maximum at the plaza (ground floor) level. **1975** *N.Y. Times* 16 Oct. 43/6 Scheduled for completion in one year, it will have 24 tennis courts, 14 tennis 'alleys' for practice, ..and a 13,000-square-foot covered plaza, including an arcade, between 56th and 57th Streets.

‖ **plaza de toros** (plā·þa, plā·za de tǫ·rǫs). [Sp.: see PLAZA.] In a Spanish-speaking country: a bull-ring. Also *fig.*
1846 R. FORD *Gatherings from Spain* xxi. 296 All the world crowds to the *Plaza de toros.* **1910** *Encycl. Brit.* IV. 789/2 Before the introduction of railways there were comparatively few bull-rings (*plazas de toros*) in Spain... At the present day nearly every larger town and city in Spain has its *plaza de toros.* **1922** J. HERGESHEIMER *Bright Shawl* (1923) 70 At the Plaza de Toros..she was seated on an upper tier..over the entrance for the bulls. **1934** A. HUXLEY *Beyond Mexique Bay* 285 A temporary *Plaza de Toros* had been built..a circular fence with a precarious grandstand on the shadier side. **1965** C. D. EBY *Siege of Alcázar* iii. 58 Toledo was converted into a noisy *plaza de toros*, but the matador was never in danger of being gored by his victim. **1973** *Sat. Rev.* (U.S.) 25 Sept. 29/1, I remember clearly the first bullfight I ever saw, in Barcelona. .. The *plaza de toros* was packed.

plazolite (plæ·zoləit). *Min.* [f. Gr. πλάζ-ειν to perplex + -ITE[1].] A calcium aluminosilicate that occurs as small, colourless to pale yellow, dodecahedral crystals with a vitreous lustre, and is probably a variety or impure form of hibschite.
1920 W. F. FOSHAG in *Amer. Mineralogist* V. 183 Included in some material collected by the writer near Riverside, California, were several specimens of vesuvianite associated with small colorless dodecahedrons. The latter proved to be distinct from any known species and the writer proposes the name plazolite from the greek *plazo*, to perplex, in allusion to the difficulty in interpreting its composition. **1941** *Amer. Mineralogist* XXVI. 451 Hibschite and plazolite are very much alike in their properties. Chemically, plazolite differs only by a small and rather variable content of CO_2, and geometrically by the form of its crystals. **1962** W. A. DEER et al. *Rock-Forming Minerals* I. 104 Plazolite originally was thought to contain essential CO_2, but this has been shown to be due to contamination and plazolite must be regarded as being similar to hibschite. **1968** *Mineral. Abstr.* XIX. 139/2 The so-called skarns accompanying some ore deposits in the western region of Honshu Island are revealed to be composed of many veinlets which contain hydrous silicate. The most remarkable..are scawtite, hillebrandite, plazolite, [etc.].

plea, *sb.* Add: **2. c.** Also, *plea-in-bar* (without *special*). (In quot. 1847 *fig.*)
1729 G. JACOB *New Law-Dict.* sig. L 1 *verso*, A Plea in Bar, not giving a full Answer to all the Matter contained in the Plaintiff's Declaration, is not good. *Ibid.*, If the Plea in Bar be to the Action it self, and the Plaintiff is barred by Judgment, &c. it is a Bar for ever in Personal Actions. **1847** DICKENS *Dombey* (1848) xxiii. 229 A plea in bar that they would have valuable consideration for their kindness. **1963** *Times* 9 May 17/5 Connelly said yesterday that he wished to withdraw that plea of Not Guilty and to enter a plea-in-bar on the grounds of *autrefois acquit.*
d. *ellipt.* for 'a plea of guilty', *spec.* in *U.S.* slang phr. *to cop a plea*, to plead guilty, usu. as part of a bargain or agreement with the prosecution. Also *transf.* in Black English (see quot. 1970[1]).
1927 *Amer. Speech* II. v. 281/1 *Cop a plea*, to tell the truth. **1929** HOSTETTER & BEESLEY *It's a Racket!* 222 *Cop a plea*, to plead guilty to a lesser crime than the one originally charged. **1941** J. SMILEY *Hash House Lingo* 19 *Cop a plea*, acknowledge a complaint. **1959** JOWITT *Dict. Eng. Law* II. 1350/2 The word 'plea' is used colloquially to mean a plea of guilty. **1963** J. PRESCOT *Case for Hearing* viii. 123 As for the trial itself, I don't give it more than half a day. It's bound to end up in a plea. **1970** *Daily Tel.* (Colour Suppl.) 6 Mar. 19/2 The majority of accused pleaded guilty—the case then being known to practitioners as a 'plea' as distinct from a 'fight'—and for pleas there was no legal aid. **1970** C. MAJOR *Dict. Afro-Amer. Slang* 41 *Cop a plea*, to be verbally evasive. **1970** J. COLE in A. Chapman *New Black Voices* (1972) 495 The street life style is the cool world... It is here we see the greatest development of stylized talking, sounding,..copping a plea and whupping game. **1972** J. L. DILLARD *Black English* i. 4 Characteristic ghetto uses of language like.. 'coppin' a plea', and 'the dozens', are now fairly familiar. **1974** *Telegraph* (Brisbane) 4 June 14/7 Today he did what Americans call copped a plea, in return for pleading guilty to the least serious charge against him, all the other charges of involvement in Watergate and the burglary of Daniel Ellsberg's psychiatrist were dropped.
7. (in sense 2) *plea-roll*; **plea-bargaining** *vbl. sb.* (orig. *U.S.*), a practice whereby a defendant in criminal proceedings agrees to plead guilty to a charge in exchange for the prosecution's cooperation in securing a more lenient sentence or some other mitigation; hence (as a back-formation) **plea bargain** *sb.* and *v. intr.*
1969 *Northwestern Reporter* 2nd Ser. CLXV. 528/1 Court has proper role of discreet inquiry into propriety of settlement whereby defendant as a result of plea bargain agrees to plead guilty to lesser degree of offense than that with which he was charged. **1974** *Harper's Mag.* Jan. 8 The vast majority of criminal sentences in the United States.. are the result of 'plea bargains' in which the defendant 'waives' his constitutional right to trial in exchange for a 'good deal'. **1974** *Newsweek* 28 Jan. 14/2 Jaworski was plea-bargaining with a number of the principals—'dealing up' with reduced charges in return for their testimony against their betters. **1976** *National Observer* (U.S.) 22 May 3/3 That attitude, shared by some other judges here, is yet another reason for the sharp increase in jury trials. So is Connick's refusal to plea bargain with defendants in all but a relative handful of cases. **1978** *Globe & Mail* (Toronto) 2 Feb. 15/1 In a plea bargain, Polanski pleaded guilty Aug. 8 to one count of unlawful sexual intercourse with a minor. Five other counts were dismissed. **1964** *Univ. Pennsylvania Law Rev.* CXII. 865 Some prosecuting attorneys object to the use of the phrase 'plea bargaining'. One prosecutor indicated that 'by labelling the procedure "plea bargaining" you tend to make the procedure sound unethical and improper'. **1967** *Atlantic Reporter* 2nd Ser. CCXXIII. 703/1 Plea bargaining between the prosecution and the defense is a frequently resorted to technique. In exchange for a guilty plea, the prosecutor may agree to recommend a lighter sentence, to accept a plea to a lesser included offense, or to dismiss other pending charges. **1970** *Guardian* 25 Aug. 1/1 The Lord Chief Justice, Lord Parker, yesterday banned 'plea bargaining', where a court agrees to impose a lighter sentence if the accused pleads guilty. **1972** *N.Y. Times* 3 Nov. 18/3 Two-thirds of the addicts now in the program were admitted after being found guilty, usually in plea-bargaining situations in Criminal Court. **1973** *Reader's Digest* Nov. 169/1 They'll tell you that plea bargaining—in which a youngster pleads guilty to a lesser offense in return for a lighter sentence—is possible. **1975** P. MOYES *Black Widower* xii. 146 What about plea-bargaining?.. Suppose you told Martin that the police would only ask for a nominal fine on the streaking charge..if in return Martin would talk to me. **1873** A. C. EWALD *Our Public Records* 37 The Plea Rolls contain the general proceedings in causes, but are very defective, owing to the neglect of attorneys to bring the records in. **1886** [see *issue roll* s.v. *ISSUE *sb.* 15]. **1936** *Oxoniensia* I. 140 It is impossible to make intelligent use of a plea roll or a pipe roll without fully understanding the governmental machinery that produced it. **1959** JOWITT *Dict. Eng. Law* II. 1567/2 In the old common law practice the steps in every action were entered on a roll, which was called the plea roll, the issue roll, or the judgment roll, according to the stage which the action had reached. **1978** *Bodl. Libr. Rec.* X. 30 Chief clerks of the Court of Common Pleas were responsible for keeping the plea rolls.

pleach, *sb.* Delete *rare*[—1] and add later examples; *spec.* a flexible branch or stake or an intertwined arrangement of these, forming a hedge.
1823 E. MOOR *Suffolk Words & Phrases* 283 *Pleach*, is described to be a branch of whitethorn brought down and laid horizontally in a fence to thicken a weak part. It is notched (or snotched) at the point of tact with the earth which is loosened to encourage the pleach to strike root. **1920** E. POUND *Umbra* 114 Come buds on bough and spalliard pleach. **1941** [see *HEADER 5 d]. **1968** J. ARNOLD *Shell Bk. Country Crafts* xx. 244 Stakes of cleft ash or chestnut..is [*sic*] driven into the ground, to form a rough 'weave' or pleach, depending on the flexibility of the stems. **1976** *Countryman* LXXXI. 1. 56 The hedges have been carefully layered and made stock-proof by the use of horizontal 'pleaches', the wide bottoms providing shelter for a variety of wild life.

plead, *v.* Add later examples of *pa. t.* and *pa. pple.* **pled** (no longer exclusively *Sc.* and *dial.*).
1929 R. S. LYND *Middletown* II. x. 122 It is not intended here to take the conventional forms under which divorce cases are pled as anything more than very roughly suggesting. **1932** E. WILSON *Devil take Hindmost* xii. 126 Irma went to his boss and pled with him. **1932** 'J. ASTON' *They winter Abroad* xii. 192 The shades of Rugby and Caius, or wherever it was that he had been bred to be a Hawk, pled against him mutely. **1941** E. R. EDDISON *Fish Dinner* vii. 103 Should a been unlorded long since,.. but the Vicar pled for him. **1943** S. LEWIS *G. Planish* xxxi. 407 I've pled with them. **1955** W. GADDIS *Recognitions* I. v. 198 Is your name really Adeline? he pled. **1974** E. S. GRUEN *Last Generation Roman Republic* viii. 327 Gabinius pled that his Egyptian adventure was in the interests of state.
7. c. (Examples with direct speech as object.)
1910 E. M. FORSTER *Howards End* xxvii. 235 'Don't you worry,' he pleaded. 'I can't bear that. We shall be all right if I get work. If I could only get work—something regular to do.' **1952** M. LASKI *Village* xiii. 187 'I'm really sorry,' pleaded Margaret contritely. **1955** [see above]. **1976** B. FREEMANTLE *November Man* viii. 108 'Stop it, Hannah,' he pleaded urgently.
d. Also *ellipt.* in sense 'to plead guilty'.
1959 JOWITT *Dict. Eng. Law* II. 1352/1 The word 'plead' is used colloquially to mean plead guilty. **1963** J. PRESCOT *Case for Hearing* vii. 109 The reek of spirits..met me like a wave... Dr. Depree depressed his right thumb. 'You'll have to plead to this one.' *Ibid.* viii. 119, I'll stake my pension on a conviction. In fact, if the lad's any sense he'll hold up his hand and plead. **1970** P. LAURIE *Scotland Yard* vi. 137 Said he'd plead, then when he got in the box he gave you a grin and said, 'Not guilty'.

pleasant, *a.* (*adv.*) Add: **5.** *pleasant-looking*, *-spoken* (earlier and later examples).
1853 MRS. GASKELL *Cranford* viii. 153 Lady Glenmire..who had been very pretty in the days of her youth, and who was even yet very pleasant-looking. *c* **1863** T. TAYLOR in M. R. Booth *Eng. Plays of 19th Cent.* (1969) II. 93 Ah, there's a pleasant looking party yonder. **1978** R. LUDLUM *Holcroft Covenant* xiv. 162 He was in his early thirties, Noel guessed, and pleasant-looking. **1843** DICKENS *Christmas Carol* 145 He is the pleasantest-spoken gentleman. **1873** 'MARK TWAIN' & WARNER *Gilded Age* xx. 187 Senator Dilworthy was..a pleasant spoken man, a popular man with the people. **1959** T. S. ELIOT *Elder Statesman* I. 22 A foreign person By the looks of him. But talks good English. A pleasant-spoken gentleman.

pleasantry. **2.** Restrict † *Obs.* to sense in Dict. and add: **b.** An instance of pleasantness or enjoyment; a pleasurable circumstance.
1790 [in Dict.]. **1925** T. DREISER *Amer. Tragedy* (1926) I. I. iii. 17 A nerve plasm palpitation, that spoke loudly for all the seemingly material things of life, not for the thin pleasantries of heaven. **1959** *Kentucky Folklore Rec.* V. 118 The consumption of large quantities of watermelons during the day... With all these pleasantries, it is surprising that the afternoon [church] services are well attended.

please, *v.* Add: **3. b.** *please-it-you*: also in *arch.* use as *sb.*
1881 'MARK TWAIN' *Prince & Pauper* xii. 138 With never a by-your-leave or so-please-it-you, or anything of the sort.
4. b. *pleased to meet you*: a formula used in reply to an introduction. Cf. *MEET *v.* 4.
1914 C. MACKENZIE *Sinister Street* II. III. xv. 802 Doesn't it make you shiver? It's like the 'Pleased to meet you', of Americans and Tootingians. **1916** 'TAFFRAIL' *Pincher Martin* vii. 102 Pleased ter meet yer, miss. **1934** A. CHRISTIE *Murder on Orient Express* II. iv. 97 Mrs. Hubbard murmured: 'Pleased to meet you, I'm sure.' **1955** M. ALLINGHAM *Beckoning Lady* v. 68 Pleased to meet you... I thought I'd just step across..and touch my cap, so to speak. **1966** J. CLEARY *High Commissioner* iii. 41 'Lady Porthleven, may I present Mr. Malone?' 'Pleased to meet you,' said Malone. 'Oh, really?' Lady Porthleven looked surprised: no one had ever actually *told* her he was pleased to meet her. **1974** A. PRICE *Other Paths to Glory* III. vi. 185 'Mr.—Hayhoe?' Mitchell thrust out his hand... 'Pleased to meet you.' Hayhoe nodded easily... There was room neither for deference nor condescension in the greeting.
6. b. (Earlier and later examples of the sarcastic use.)
1816 JANE AUSTEN *Emma* I. xii. 214 South End is prohibited, if you please. **1879** *Cornh. Mag.* XL. 558 He wants to pay his addresses, if you please, to Ursula! **1951** J. CORNISH *Provincials* 57 In the winter the heating system was always going on the blink and then the headmistress would scurry round *opening* windows, if you please. **1973** *Math. Teacher* May 479/1 To a monotonous degree, then, each aspect of the operation of the Council is in the hands of the mathematics educators—the *teachers*, if you please. **1979** 'M. YORKE' *Death on Account* xi. 110 He's gone away for the weekend, if you please.
d. *as you please*, in comparative phrases.
1928 'BRENT OF BIN BIN' *Up Country* xvi. 273 The

native-born maids were as pretty and perky as you please. **1964** MRS. L. B. JOHNSON *White House Diary* 23 Jan. (1970) 60 Lynda Bird got up..and said she had just come from the University of Texas where we had the Number One football team..to the house where she could listen to the Number One people of the nation.., just as poised as you please.

pleasure, *sb.* Add: **1. b.** (Earlier and further examples opp. *business.*)

1675 WYCHERLEY *Country-Wife* II. 32 Go, go, to your business, I say, pleasure, whilst I go to my pleasure, business. **1767** T. HUTCHINSON *Let.* 30 Sept. (1883) I. v. 243 Pleasure should always give way to business. **1804** M. EDGEWORTH *Pop. Tales* III. 30 Business was his aversion; pleasure was his business. **1837** C. G. F. GORE *Stokeshill Place* III. vi. 99 'Business before pleasure' is a golden rule which most of us regard as iron. **1853** R. S. SURTEES *Handley Cross* xxii. 158 Business first, and pleasure afterwards. **1857** [see BUSINESS 13]. **1934** *Law Rep.* 27 Mar. 238 In my judgment, the word 'pleasure' is used in this policy in contradistinction to 'business'. **1941** F. GRUBER *Hungry Dog* xv. 183 Pleasure before business. **1943** P. CHEYNEY *Farewell to Admiral* x. 238, I never believe in mixing business with pleasure. **1976** HOOKER & BUTTERWORTH *M.A.S.H. goes to San Francisco* (1977) xiii. 170 Oh, how nice! And I think about *you*, too. But business before pleasure, as I always say.

e. *Psychol.* Used *attrib.* (esp. in *pleasure principle*) and as first element with *-pain* to denote the theory that the drives to achieve pleasure and to avoid pain are basic motivating forces in human and animal life; in psychoanalysis, the theory that the tension set up by unpleasure or the desire to achieve a pleasurable result forms the chief source of mental activity and is part of the life instinct, though frequently opposed by the reality-principle. Also in more general use.

1894 CREIGHTON & TITCHENER tr. *Wundt's Human & Animal Psychol.* xiv. 211 The reference of feeling to a subjective condition of pleasure-pain. **1897** H. G. WELLS *Under Knife* in *Plattner Story* 107 It occurred to me that the real meaning of this numbness might be a gradual slipping away from the pleasure-pain guidance of the animal man. **1912** *Amer. Jrnl. Psychol.* XXIII. 134 The sex impulses find no outlet before puberty. Until that time they remain under the control of the subconscious (pleasure principle). **1925** J. RIVIERE tr. *Freud's Papers on Metapsychology* in *Coll. Papers* IV. 14 It is called the pleasure-pain (*Lust-Unlust*) principle, or more shortly the pleasure-principle. **1951** S. F. NADEL *Found. Social Anthropol.* xi. 306 Emotions, sentiments, even the elementary pleasure-pain reactions, possess their dynamic properties..because they are the concomitants of instinctive tendencies. **1957** N. FRYE *Anat. Criticism* ii. 75 In literature..the reality-principle is subordinate to the pleasure-principle. **1968** A. LASKI *Keeper* xi. 133 Ralph's whole working life had been devoted to the pleasure principle. **1971** *Listener* 2 Sept. 299/1 Freud responded to the First World War by positing a death instinct beyond the pleasure principle. **1976** *Vogue* Jan. 5/2 The small son of the house witnesses Sigmund Freud looking askance at the pleasure principle embodied in Coney Island.

2. (*It is, was,* etc.,) *my pleasure*: a colloq. dismissal of thanks.

1950 L. KAUFMAN *Jubel's Children* xxi. 259 Think nothing of it. My pleasure. **1963** [see *NOT AT ALL]. **1975** R. LEWIS *Double Take* i. 26 'I enjoyed the evening, Mr Hood.' 'It was my pleasure, Miss Stevens.'

5. g. *pleasures of the table*: see *TABLE *sb.* 6 c.

6. a. *pleasure-brake, -car* (examples), *-carriage, -cart* (earlier example), *-cottage, -craft, -cruise, -cruiser, -cruising, -day, -dome* (later examples), *-economy, -garden* (later examples), *-horse* (later example), *-land, -navy, -park, -party* (earlier example), *-path, -plane, -resort* (earlier example), *-ship, -sleigh, -steamer, -traveller, -trip* (examples), *-vessel, -visit, -voyage* (example), *-yacht.* **b.** *pleasure-hater, -hunter* (earlier example); *pleasure-crazed, -crowded, -mad, -minded* adjs.

1908 *Westm. Gaz.* 12 Aug. 8/3 She was cycling along the Bromley-road when a pleasure-brake..turned out of a side-street. **1833** *Amer. Railroad Jrnl.* II. 481/3 A pleasure car has been flying between this town and the river. **1960** C. ACHEBE *No longer at Ease* ii. 14 [In Lagos] if you don't want to walk you only have to wave your hand and a pleasure car stops for you. **1802** W. PRIEST *Trav. U.S.A.* 31 There are 806 two and four wheeled machines entered at the office, and pay duty, as *pleasure carriages.* **1844** Pleasure-carriage [see *FIESTA]. **1789** J. WOODFORDE *Diary* 27 Nov. (1927) III. 156 My Brother went in my little pleasure Cart with Briton. *a* **1828** D. WORDSWORTH *Jrnl.* (1941) II. 247 A charming spot for a pleasure-cottage. **1906** CONRAD *Mirror of Sea* 38 Their striving for victory..has elevated the sailing of pleasure craft to the dignity of a fine art. **1943** J. S. HUXLEY *TVA* ix. 63 Nearby is a public lodge and a boat-house and dock for pleasure craft. **1932** *New Yorker* 23 July 12/2 It is not your idea..of a mad night on pleasure-crazed Broadway. **1906** B. VON HUTTEN *What became of Pam* I. x. 73 The time that had seemed so long to her had quite naturally seemed to him, with his pleasure-crowded days, very short. **1926** *Scribner's Mag.* Aug. 12 (Advt.), Start planning now for pleasure-crowded days on cool, blue waters. **1909** *Daily Graphic* 26 July 2/1 (Advt.), P. & O. cheap return tickets pleasure cruises and round the world tours. **1976** H. MACINNES *Agent in Place* xxvi. 277 'Where are we going?' 'For a pleasure cruise.' **1926** *Daily Chron.* 13 May 3/6 (*heading*) Pleasure Cruisers on and off the rocks. **1945** KOESTLER *Yogi & Commissar* I. iii. 35 For he is a captain of a warship, not of a pleasure-cruiser. **1950** *Oxf. Jun. Encycl.* IX. 382/1 It was not.. until the early 1920's that modern pleasure cruising with its carefully planned itineraries really became established. *a* **1828** D. WORDSWORTH *Jrnl.* (1941) II. 292 The buoyancy of spirits felt in the earlier part of a pleasure-day's journey. **1957** *Observer* 3 Nov. 19/2 The triumphal renaissance, last Thursday night, of the New Shakespeare Theatre in Liverpool. This lambent pleasure-dome ..was built in the eighties. **1973** G. BEARE *Snake on Grave* xvi. 93 It's a kind of floating pleasure dome, they have a restaurant, night-club, casino. **1977** *Time* 19 Dec. 41/1 Macy's.., the basement where women..battled with umbrellas for lingerie markdowns has become one of New York City's great gastronomic pleasure domes. **1910** W. JAMES in *McClure's Mag.* Aug. 467 A permanently successful peace-economy cannot be a simple pleasure-economy. **1961** L. MUMFORD *City in History* xiii. 379 Such pleasure gardens were popular everywhere that court life was visibly on parade: the famous Tivoli Gardens in Copenhagen still bears witness to this. **1940** AUDEN *Another Time* 42 As a rule It was the pleasure-haters who became unjust. **1974** *Greenville* (S. Carolina) *News* 23 Apr. 11/3 The pleasure horse class will give spectators a chance to see the finest of the American saddlebred pleasure horses in competition. **1833** J. S. MILL in *Monthly Repos.* VII. 660 Few persons among the crowds of pleasure-hunters have diverged from the beaten track of the Rhine, Switzerland, and Italy. **1927** *Daily Tel.* 13 Sept. 12/2 Thirty years ago Piccadilly had still to establish its claim to be regarded as the centre of pleasure-land. **1925** *Scribner's Mag.* Oct. 373 It was exactly the kind of crowd which a dour philosopher might have described as typical of 'pleasure-mad America'. **1907** *Daily Chron.* 12 Oct. 4/7 Allah forfend, my pleasure-minded love, That aught shall harm thee in the Desert Lands. **1873** 'VANDERDECKEN' *Yachts & Yachting* xxix. 247 There are not a few sea-lawyers to be met with amongst the pleasure navy Jacks. **1904** R. J. FARRER *Garden of Asia* 70 Here we may fancy known beings resting in this pleasure-park of necessity. **1835** *Southern Lit. Messenger* IV. 303/1 Pleasure-parties to and from the Springs..were dashing along the well graded road. *c* **1806** D. WORDSWORTH *Jrnl.* (1941) I. 351 It is not easy to see the use of a pleasure-path leading to nothing. **1911** *Chambers's Jrnl.* Jan. 57/1 The aspect of the heavens will be wonderfully changed when the pleasure-plane of the air has arrived. **1883** 'MARK TWAIN' *Life on Miss.* xli. 427 Modern-style pleasure resorts. **1869** —— *Innoc. Abr.* lvii. 609 When I travel again, I wish to go in a pleasure ship. **1977** *New Scientist* 24 Mar. 707/2 The foundering of a pleasureship. **1774** 'J. H. ST. JOHN DE CREVECŒUR' *Sk. 18th-Cent Amer.* (1925) 146 The pleasure-sleigh..can easily carry six persons. **1827** Pleasure-sleigh [see *FIDDLE *sb.* 1 b]. **1872** B. JERROLD *London* iv. 43 The river..bright with the trifles of cockleboats and pleasure-steamers. **1948** *Brit. Birds* XLI. 314, I was on a pleasure steamer at the time. **1846** DICKENS *Pictures from Italy* 150 Pleasure-travellers through life. **1936** *Discovery* Aug. 247/2 An area that is not well known to the general run of pleasure-travellers. **1833** *Chambers's Edin. Jrnl.* II. 285/2 The individuals who make pleasure-trips along the railway. **1926** *Daily Chron.* 13 May 3/6 The 20,000 ton R.M.S. steamer Otranto struck a rock on the way to the port of Athens... The Otranto is on a pleasure trip. **1906** CONRAD *Mirror of Sea* 33 The writer praises that class of pleasure vessels, [*sc.* 52-foot linear raters] and I am willing to endorse his words. **1926** D. H. LAWRENCE *David* xiv. 103 My lord Jonathan comes too early for a pleasure visit. **1906** CONRAD *Mirror of Sea* 39 For racing, a cutter; for a long pleasure voyage, a schooner; for cruising in home waters, the yawl. **1847** DICKENS *Dombey* (1848) xxiii. 238 As many spars and bars and bolts..as you'd want an order for on Chatham-yard to build a pleasure-yacht with.

pleasure, *v.* Add: **1. a.** (Further examples.) *spec.* To gratify (someone) sexually; to have sexual intercourse with.

Revived in recent use.

c **1616** R. C. *Times' Whistle* (1871) 90 Silvius doth shew the citty dames brave sights, And they for that doe pleasure him a nightes. **1968** J. R. ACKERLEY *My Father & Myself* xii. 124 We entered together, quickly unbuttoned and pleasured each other. **1973** *Observer* 29 July 26/7 The rest of the treatment takes place in a hotel bed. Couples are first instructed to 'pleasure' each other by caressing, and not to attempt intercourse until they have learnt to recognise each other's body signals that express delight. **1975** *Times Lit. Suppl.* 9 May 503/1 Her first love, who took her to tea-dances..and pleasured her regularly at home on the brocade couch. **1977** *Observer* (Colour Suppl.) 27 Feb. 17/1 The brown Chippewa girl who was the first female he had ever pleasured.

b. Delete † *Obs.* and add later examples, *spec.* in prec. sense.

1908 C. W. WALLACE *Children of Chapel at Blackfriars* ix. 112 Elizabeth intended the establishment of the Children of her Chapel as actors at Blackfriars..to pleasure herself and entertain the Court. **1938** M. K. RAWLINGS *Yearling* x. 89 'I'll bet we kin ketch us a cattywampus in one o' them ponds.' 'We kin sure pleasure ourselves tryin'.' **1947** *N.Y. Herald Tribune Weekly Bk. Rev.* 2 Mar. 10/3 Mordaunt Fitzmaurice Godolphin..has left Virginia because he pleasured himself with a married lady and then killed her husband in a duel. **1972** *Time* 17 Apr. 66/3 Pauline Tabor was smart enough to open up a house of her own. 'Pauline's' became a Kentucky institution—politicians went to pleasure themselves there.

c. In impersonal construction with *it* as subject (cf. PLEASE *v.* 3).

1937 R. S. MORTON *Woman Surgeon* xxxi. 346 A young carpenter said to me, 'It would not pleasure me if I could not see the cypress greening in the spring.' **1949** R. K. MARSHALL *Little Squire Junior* 249 Little Squire borrowed somethin of mine, and it pleasured me no end. **1951** L. CRAIG *Singing Hills* xiii. 124 It pleasures us a sight that you would come to see us. **1970** *New Yorker* 12 Sept. 109/3 It pleasured him to see the smoke.

pleasured, *ppl. a.* (Later examples). Also as *pa. pple.* (const. *up*).

1930 D. RUNYON in *Collier's* 13 Sept. 8/2 They get all pleasured up over what he has to say. **1968** 'J. WELCOME' *Hell is where you find It* iv. 61 He was wearing..the look of a pleasured tom-cat.

plea·suredrome. [f. PLEASURE *sb.* + *-DROME.] An amusement centre.

1959 *Spectator* 9 Oct. 467/1 The possibility of turning the Isle of Wight into some vast pleasuredrome (cf. Fr. *Baisodrome*). **1966** *Punch* 13 Mar. 392/2 He might bring his millions here and make West Hove the pleasuredrome of the Western world. **1973** *Daily Tel.* (Colour Suppl.) 18 Apr. 19/2 One corporation, which already operated 'pleasuredromes' in Dallas, Atlanta, and St Louis, is.. negotiating to open a park in New Jersey.

pleasure-house. (Earlier and later examples.)

1590 H. WOTTON *Let.* in L. P. Smith *Life & Lett. H. Wotton* (1907) I. 247 The plot of his Majesty's pleasure-house shall in convenient time be provided. **1904** R. J. FARRER *Garden of Asia* 106 How few of the many Europeans who visit Japan, ever see the real pleasure-houses of the country! **1908** *Daily Chron.* 12 Dec. 4/6 The ballroom of a notorious eighteenth-century pleasure-house kept by a Mme. Cornelys. **1936** A. W. CLAPHAM *Romanesque Archit.* iii. 55 The actual court of Palermo leaned heavily towards the Moslem element and the pleasure-houses and palaces of the Favara, Menani (Roger II), la Ziza (William I) and la Cuba (William II) were almost purely Moslem both in form and decoration.

pleasure-seeker. (Earlier examples.)

1825 [see PLEASURE *sb.* 6]. **1846** *Swell's Night Guide* 14 At all hours of the night, the pleasure-seeker may gain admission.

pleasure-seeking *sb.* and *a.* (Earlier and later examples.)

1886 J. G. MATTESON *Hist. Sk.* 63/1, I found the people in Norway far more religiously inclined than those in Denmark; they..are not so much given to pleasure-seeking. **1936** *Discovery* Oct. 301/1 Only a slight ripple on the normal pleasure-seeking surface of Blackpool was caused by the arrival and departure of the British Association.

pleater (plī·tǝɹ). [f. PLEAT *v.* + -ER[1].] (See quot. 1921.)

1921 *Dict. Occup. Terms* (1927) § 428 *Pleater*, pleats or folds material in pleats, by hand or by pleating machine. **1970** *Classification of Occupations* (Office of Population Censuses and Surveys) 66/2 Pleater.

pleb. Add: **A.** (Further examples.)

1911 H. G. WELLS *New Machiavelli* I. iv. 104 They're Plebs and they know it. They haven't the Guts to get hold of things. **1922** *Dialect Notes* V. 189 At Annapolis, the natives are *crabs*, the freshmen *plebs*, the sophomores *youngsters*. **1928** A. HUXLEY *Point Counter Point* ix. 138 'A bit of a pleb, wasn't he?' put in the military friend. **1939** JOYCE *Finnegans Wake* (1964) I. 175 The pleb was born a Quicklow and sank alowing till he stank out of sight. **1960** *Guardian* 29 Sept. 9/7 It all ends happily, with the squire and the pleb firm friends. **1973** *Nation Rev.* (Melbourne) 31 Aug. 1441/6 The YLA executive sat at a head table while the plebs and proles were strewn together en masse. **1977** J. WAINWRIGHT *Nest of Rats* I. xii. 92 You were..an aristocrat... And you turned pleb. Like grandfather.

B. *attrib.* or as *adj.* = PLEBEIAN *a.* b. *colloq.*

1972 *Daily Tel.* 12 Feb. 11/2 Basically the situations, pursuit of boy friends, anxiety about the landlord, are identical, only here the background is pleb rather than deb. **1972** J. SYMONS *Players & Game* xxvi. 196 'What *was* his name? Barber?' 'No, some other pleb occupation. Taylor?' **1974** *New Statesman* 17 May 698 Orwell darkened the picture: Bowling is frankly pleb, Comstock descends from a line of sexless scrimpers.

Hence **ple·bbie, ple·bby** *a.*

1962 'J. LE CARRÉ' *Murder of Quality* i. 9 Mrs. Rode's quite decent..in a plebby sort of way: doyleys and china birds. **1977** J. MCCLURE in *Winter's Crimes* 9 80 Portland Bill..all coach parties and orange peel... It does tend to be a bit plebbie.

plebbish, *a.* Add: Also **plebish.** (Examples.) **plebbishness** (further example).

1928 A. HUXLEY *Point Counter Point* xxi. 388 This is the sort of thing that really does make me feel rather pleb-ish. **1942** BERREY & VAN DEN BARK *Amer. Thes. Slang* § 147/1 *Ungentility; plebeianism,*..plebishness. *Ibid.* § 147/5 *Plebeian; commonplace,*..plebish.

plebe. Add: **2.** (Earlier and later examples.) Also *attrib.*

1833 in *Mil. & Naval Mag.* (U.S.) (1834) Oct. 85 My drill master, a young stripling, told me I was not so '*gross*' as most other pleibs, the name of all new cadets. **1834** in *Ibid.* June 281, I was reckoned, already, as one of a class of cadets. To be sure, it was the 'plebe class'; but what of this? **1860** in *Amer. Hist. Rev.* (1928) XXXIII. 601 In most of our tents the cadets and plebes live together, 2 cadets, and 2 plebes to wait on them generally. **1947** *Newsweek* 6 Oct. 78/2 The 'plebe' system which gives upper classmen authority over newcomer midshipmen filled Smith with revulsion. **1948** MENJOU & MUSSELMAN *It took 9 Tailors* 26 New arrivals are called plebes and a plebe is the dirt beneath an upperclassman's shoes; but to add insult to injury, a plebe has to clean and polish the shoes while he is being stepped on. **1970** N. ARMSTRONG et al. *First on Moon* vii. 156 Buzz ranked number one in his class at the end of his plebe year. **1973** H. GRUPPE *Truxton Cipher* iii. 31 Pozo was given to salting his speech with naval maxims left over from his days as a plebe. **1977** *Time* 19 Sept. 39/3 That summer, it [*sc.* West Point] enrolled its first women plebes—and now has 177 female cadets.

plectonemic (plektonī·mik), *a. Biol.* [f. Gr. πλεκτός twisted + νῆμα thread + -IC.] Of, pertaining to, or designating two or more like helices coiled together side by side in such a way that they cannot be fully separated unless they are unwound. Opp. *PARANEMIC *a.*

1941 A. H. SPARROW et al. in *Canad. Jrnl. Res.* C. XIX. 325 Kuwada..describes two types of double-stranded spirals: (1) orthospirals, which are formed when the two threads being coiled have one end free so that internal twisting does not occur; (2) anorthospirals, which result when two strands with both ends fixed are coiled together and in consequence have a twist compensating for each gyre of the spiral... Orthospirals are interlocked and cannot be separated without untwisting; anorthospirals are independent and can readily be pulled apart or fitted into each other... The term 'paranemic' (*para* = beside) instead of anorthospiral will be used here since it is simpler and its implications are clear. Instead of orthospiral 'plectonemic' (*plektos* = twisted) will be used as this has the advantage of indicating the relationship of the strands. **1950** [see *PARANEMIC *a.*]. **1953** WATSON & CRICK in *Cold Spring Harbor Symp. Quant. Biol.* XVIII. 129/2 We therefore believe that if a helical structure is present [in DNA], the relationship between the helices will be plectonemic. **1971** *Nature* 22 Jan. 241/1 Tropocollagen..consists of three protein chains with similar, specific and very characteristic amino-acid compositions, twisted into a plectonemic triple helix of about 100 turns. **1974** [see *PARANEMIC *a.*].

Hence **plectone·mically** *adv.*

1953 *Cold Spring Harbor Symp. Quantitative Biol.* XVIII. 128/2 Apart from breaking the chains there are only two sorts of ways to separate two chains coiled plectonemically. **1966** MAHLER & CORDES *Biol. Chem.* iv. 140 DNA in its B lattice configuration..consists of two right-handed helical polynucleotide chains of opposite polarity, plectonemically coiled around the same axis to form a double helix. **1979** *Nature* 26 Apr. 780/3 Sasisekharan *et al.*..have..proposed that the two strands of DNA do not coil plectonemically round one another.

plectrum. Add: **3.** *attrib.*, as *plectrum banjo, guitar, lute* (LUTE *sb.*[1] 1a).

1954 *Grove's Dict. Mus.* (ed. 5) I. 401/2 The banjo played with the fingers is referred to as the 'finger-style' banjo, to distinguish it from the instrument (called the 'plectrum banjo') which is played with a plectrum. **1961** A. BIRCH in A. Baines *Mus. Instrum. through Ages* 182 The standard instrument is the 'finger-style' banjo with five gut or nylon strings tuned *d′, b, g, c g′*, i.e. with the highest string on the left of the bass (and with its peg midway along the neck.) The 'plectrum banjo' omits this half-length string. **1956** I. MAIRANTS in S. Traill *Play that Music* ix. 94 The plectrum guitar with wire strings for dance music and jazz. **1961** A. BIRCH in A. Baines *Mus. Instrum. through Ages* 182 In the early days of jazz, the banjo was replaced by the '*plectrum guitar*'... The plectrum guitar has metal strings fastened not usually to the bridge..but to a tailpiece screwed to the end of the instrument. **1970** P. OLIVER *Savannah Syncopators* 109 *Kambreh*, plectrum lute played widely in the Savannah regions.

pledge, *sb.* Add: **5. b.** (Earlier and later examples.)

1833 *New Engl. Mag.* (Boston) Aug. 137 The Temperance Pledge. *Ibid.* 141 Has he signed the pledge? **1840** *Southern Lit. Messenger* VI. 325/1, I have signed the pledge, and since it is done I will make a virtue of necessity. **1843** in M. Miliband *Observer of 19th Cent.* (1966) 161 Father Mathew..called upon those who wished to take the 'pledge' to kneel down... About 3,000 persons took the pledge... From the appearance of many of them, we should say the total abstinence pledge was very necessary. **1914** G. B. SHAW *Fanny's First Play* III. 214, I dont want any whisky and soda. I'll take the pledge if you like. **1922** JOYCE *Ulysses* 348 Had her father only avoided the clutches of the demon drink, by taking the pledge or those powders the drink habit cured in Pearson's Weekly, she might now be rolling in her carriage, second to none. **1930** G. B. SHAW *Apple Cart* I. 43 Though none of us doubted that he would sign the pledge, we were not equally certain that the infirmities of his nature would allow him to keep it. **1970** J. H. GRAY *Boy from Winnipeg* 126 It was only when bootleg beer became openly available in the downtown hotels after 1920 that he gradually slipped from the pledge.

c. *U.S. college slang.* A student who has promised to join a fraternity or sorority. Also *transf.*

1901 *Univ. of Chicago Weekly* 1 Aug. 1087/1 Still if the Kappas are as bad as you say—you say they lifted two pledges last year. **1930** *Randolph Enterprise* (Elkins, W. Virginia) 18 Dec. 1/1 [They]..have been announced as two of five pledges chosen by the University Dramatic club at Morgantown. **1945** W. MAXWELL *Folded Leaf* 52 Shortly after seven o'clock the pledges appeared, one at a time, in the hotel lobby. **1949** *Reader's Digest* Aug. 71/1 The chapter might..keep Tom as a sort of permanent pledge. **1972** M. MEAD *Blackberry Winter* viii. 98 For one thing, I had no dates; these were all arranged through commands to the freshman pledges of certain fraternities to date the freshman pledges of certain sororities.

7. *pledge-mania*; (sense *5 c) *pledge-master, pin, week*; **pledge card,** (*a*) in Dict. (further example); (*b*) *N. Amer.* a card on which one expresses willingness to contribute to a fund, sponsor a charity event, etc.

1958 *Times Lit. Suppl.* 10 Jan. 15/1 'Pledge' (temperance) cards and 'Decision' (conversion) cards interpolated their small crises. **1967** *Boston Sunday Herald Mag.* 26 Mar. 19/2 In 1960 Msgr. Leonard launched an $800,000 fund drive and more than 400 volunteers distributed pledge cards throughout the parish of about 3,000 families. **1970** *Toronto Daily Star* 24 Sept. 17/5 Pledge cards for the walk are available at any Dominion store while anyone wishing to enter a team in the skatathon can call 889-3967. **1832** MILL *Let.* 17 Sept. in *Wks.* (1963) XII. 121, I should say that the pledge-mania had been abated. **1949** *Sun* (Baltimore) 9 May 1/2 Santarelli..is pledge-master for Phi Theta Upsilon Fraternity at the Northern Illinois College of Optometry. **1944** *Chicago Daily News* 28 Oct. 1 After the incident, Soik turned in his pledge pin. **1949** *Time* 21 Mar. 47/2 As a finale to Brown's pledge week, fraternity men had made the rounds of chapter houses to 'congratulate' each other. **1964** *Amer. Speech* XXXIX. 193 The social affairs that are a major concern for most students, such as..pledge and rush weeks.

pledge, *v.* Add: **3. a.** Also *refl.*

1836 DICKENS *Let.* ? 19 Nov. (1965) I. 198 He could not ..pledge himself whether it would appear this season, or whether they would begin with it, at the opening of the next.

b. *trans.* and *intr.* To enrol (a new student) in a college society. Of a student: to undertake to join a college society; to enrol in (a society). *U.S.*

1871 L. H. BAGG *Four Years at Yale* 62 They are very attentive to his wants and do not leave him until he is 'pledged'. **1887** *Lippincott's Mag.* Nov. 741 If as a result of several such interviews he is approved, he is asked to 'pledge', that is, to promise to join the society. **1901** *Munsey's Mag.* Feb. 734/2 The time and manner of pledging members to the fraternities vary with different colleges. **1949** *Reader's Digest* Aug. 69/1 The rushing season, during which freshmen are pledged to the various houses, was in full swing. **1977** *Rolling Stone* 19 May 67/2 Even though Hamilton went to the University of Georgia and pledged Phi Delta Theta, his exuberant intelligence wouldn't allow him to be satisfied with conformity.

4. c. To promise solemnly (*to* do something).

1928 *Sunday Dispatch* 2 Sept. 1/3 On my pledging not to disclose his name..he promptly handed over another cheque for £10,000.

pledging *vbl. sb.* (later examples).

1929 *Old Oregon* June 10 They went through rushing, pledging, moving, 'open house', freshman duties, in a cycle which at that time seemed to move ponderously over each event. **1959** *Ann. Reg. 1958* 152 At a special pledging conference in October 35 governments promised $27½ million for the Agency's work. **1964** *Amer. Speech* XXXIX. 194 The vocabulary of pledging, rushing.

pledgee. Add: **2.** One who takes a pledge, *spec.* = *PLEDGE *sb.* 5 c.

1937 (heard by Prof. A. L. Hench, Univ. of Virginia) 24 Nov., I needn't worry so long as I'm a pledgee. **1942** BERREY & VAN DEN BARK *Amer. Thes. Slang* § 825/34 Pledge, pledgee,..a prospective fraternity member who has promised to join.

pleep (plīp). *slang* (? *obs.*). [? Echoic: see quot. 1948.] (See quots.)

1942 *Gen* 1 Sept. 14/2 A Heinkel pilot who shoots too soon or runs for home is definitely a 'poor type' or just a 'pleep'. **1943** HUNT & PRINGLE *Service Slang* 52 *Pleep*,..a Hun pilot who turns tail. **1948** PARTRIDGE *Dict. Forces' Slang* 144 *Pleep*, an enemy pilot that refuses aerial combat. Echoic of a timorous young bird.

-plegia, formative element, f. Gr. πληγ-ή blow, stroke (f. πλήσσειν to strike) + -IA[1], used with the sense 'paralysis', as in HEMIPLEGIA, PARAPLEGIA, *iridoplegia* s.v. *IRIDO-.

plein-air. Add: Usu. considered non-naturalized and written in italics. (Further examples.) Also used to designate work painted out of doors, or representing out-door scenes.

1930 *Observer* 6 Apr. 13 The giant Constable, the first of the plein air moderns. **1947** [see *IMPRESSIONISTIC *a.*]. **1970** *Daily Tel.* 9 July 12 Dame Laura never succeeded in liking town life. It was the wind and the sun and wild places that were her real loves and it was as a *plein air* painter of sunlight on landscapes and seascapes that she first succeeded. **1970** *Oxf. Compan. Art* 822/1 The expression '*plein air*'..implies a style of painting which emphasizes the impression of the open and of spontaneity and naturalness. On the other hand it also indicates an actual technique of painting, which involved more than working in the open direct from nature instead of the older practice of composing a finished picture in the studio from rough sketches done on the spot. **1974** *Country Life* 6 June 1436/2 The impact of these *plein air* (in effect if not in fact) pictures.

plein-ai·rish *a.*, resembling or characteristic of the *plein-air* school of painting; **plein-airism,** ‖ **-isme** (*-ism*), the theories and practices of the plein-airists; **plein-airist** (earlier and later examples); ‖ **plein-airiste** (*-ist*) = *plein-airist*.

1891 *Academy* 6 June 544/3 'Impressionists', 'tâchistes', 'plein airistes', and 'pointillistes', to use the jargon of the day. **1897** *Daily Tel.* 10 Feb. 9/6 These pretty illustrations, from the designs of the well-known French *plein-airiste* and figure painter, Raphaël Collin, are delicate and graceful even to the verge of effeminacy. **1931** A. HUXLEY *Music at Night* 65 Bernini is, spiritually speaking, a *plein-airiste*. **1932** *New Statesman & Nation* 23 Jan. 93/1 Finally, with the emulation of his pleinairish friends, Manet loses not only his distinction of rhythm, but a great deal of his feeling for colour. *Ibid.*, It [*sc.* the Demoiselles au bord de la Loire]..marks the beginning of the long and triumphant development of pleinairism. **1946** *Penguin New Writing* XXVIII. 142 To imagine now an art of landscape into which plein-airisme had never intruded..it is impossible. **1959** *Listener* 9 Apr. 633/2 Go careful with the washing tub And do not spill the crystal slops Lest any of the escaping drops Should water down the *pleinairiste* Delights of Lady Tristram's feast! **1961** *Ibid.* 12 Oct. 571/2 It was necessary at the time..to talk about *plein airism* as though it was nothing else but a campaign against the time-worn clichés of the academic tradition. **1969** R. MAYER *Dict. Art Terms & Techniques* 299/2 The artists specifically called *pleinairistes* were a group of Impressionists of the 1880's and 1890's, notably Camille Pissaro.., Claude Monet.., Alfred Sisley.., and Pierre Auguste Renoir. **1972** D. SUTTON *Lett. Roger Fry* I. 9 Fry was suspicious of Impressionism, by which he meant (I suspect) the watered-down *pleinairisme* of Bastien-Lepage, so popular in England, or the fragile pastiches of Whistler's followers. **1974** *Country Life* 28 Feb. 421/3 The historical emphasis..is on *plein air-ism* and the freshness and spontaneity of handling it produced. **1978** *Times* 17 Oct. 10/6 Some really wonderful paintings by the *plein-airists* of the 1880s on, whether it be McTaggart..or Guthrie.

‖ **plein jeu** (plɛn ʒö), *adv. phr.* and *sb. Mus.* [Fr. 'full play'.] **A.** *adv. phr.* As a direction: with full power; *spec.* in organ playing: without reeds.

1837 J. A. HAMILTON *Dict. 2,000 Terms* (ed. 4) 54 *Plein jeu*.., full organ. **1938** *Oxf. Compan. Mus.* 670/2 *Plein jeu*, French for 'Full to Mixtures' (without reeds). *Ibid.* 739/1 *Plein jeu* (Fr.) 'full play', i.e. the whole power of the organ (or harmonium). **1954** *Grove's Dict. Mus.* (ed. 5) VII. 102/1 In the course of a piece it [*sc.* the term *organo pleno*] means the same as the French term *plein jeu*. **1960** *Times* 26 Apr. 16/2 The emotional stops are playing *plein jeu* in *Erwartung*. **1968** A. NILAND *Introd. Organ* vi. 93 Bach writes at the beginning of several pieces, *pro organo pleno* (for full organ). This was undoubtedly the equivalent of the French *plein jeu*.

B. *sb.* A type of mixture stop on the organ; music written for the full organ. Also *fig.*

1855 E. J. HOPKINS in Hopkins & Rimbault *Organ* II. 328 The Madelaine [*sic*], at Paris... Clavier du Grand Orgue, 12 Stops... Plein-Jeu, X ranks. **1880** GROVE *Dict. Mus.* II. 601/1 The scheme of Ducroquet's French organ stood as follows:—Great Organ. 10 stops... Bourdon.. Prestant..Plein jeu. **1898** J. MATTHEWS *Handbk. Organ* II. 29 Such compound stops are variously termed, Full, Grave, Acute or Sharp Mixture,..Fourniture, Plein Jeu, Cymbal, etc. **1919** G. A. AUDSLEY *Organ of 20th Cent.* iii. 87 The largest Plein-Jeu known to us is that of ten ranks in the Grand division of the Organ in the Madeleine, Paris. **1944** W. APEL *Harvard Dict. Mus.* 588/1 *Plein-jeu*.., full organ. Also name for pieces written for the full organ. **1952** W. L. SUMNER *Organ* x. 297 The plein-jeu is a large true mixture with sub-unison and unison ranks in the treble. **1958** *Times* 30 Sept. 3/5 He begins to draw out more stops in Siegfried..though reserving his *plein jeu*, so to speak, for a later date. **1963** CLUTTON & NILAND *Brit. Organ* i. 38 Unlike the Germans, the French did not use their 'plein jeux' much for polyphonic music. **1975** *New Yorker* 28 Apr. 133/1 In addition, further pistons can bring on or silence the mixtures, the reeds, the *Plein Jeu*, the *Grand Jeu*, and 'Tutti'. **1978** *Gramophone* June 90/1 By the nature of the organs, many of the most effective pieces are dialogues between a group of reeds (the trompeteria) and the *plein jeu*.

pleione (plɔiˌōu·nī). Also **Pleione.** [mod.L. (D. Don *Prodromus Floræ Nepalensis* (1825) 36), f. Gr. Πλειόνη, the name of the mother of the Pleiades.] An orchid of the genus so called, belonging to the family Orchidaceæ, native to mountainous regions of northern India, Burma, and China, and bearing white, pink, or purple flowers, with plicate leaves which, in most species, fall before flowering begins.

1851 LINDLEY & PAXTON *Paxton's Flower Garden* II. 5 The spotted Pleione has long been known to botanists as a species belonging to that Alpine group of so-called Cœlogynes. **1890** W. WATSON *Orchids* li. 424 Pleiones are distinguished by their fleshy pseudo-bulbs, which are only of annual duration. **1930** T. W. BRISCOE *Orchids for Amateurs* iv. 96 Pleiones are deciduous, and the leaves usually fall when the growths are matured. **1961** *New Statesman* 19 May 808/2 Cymbidiums..and pleiones..are cool-house plants. **1975** A. M. COATS *Treasury of Flowers* pl. 117 (*caption*) The Pleiones..are familiar to many gardeners, as they are both beautiful and easy to grow. **1979** *Country Life* 18 Jan. 158/4 Recently taxonomists have lumped together all the omnifarious pleione species under the aggregate specific epithet *P. bulbocodioides*.

pleiotropic (plɔiˌotrǫ·pik, -trōu·pik), *a. Genetics.* [f. as next: see -IC.] Pertaining to, displaying, or being pleiotropy. Hence **pleiotro·pically** *adv.*

1938 *Proc. R. Soc.* B. CXXV. 138 The analysis of the pathological symptoms given above allows us to bring some order into the multitude of 'pleiotropic' effects produced by our lethal factor. **1956** C. AUERBACH *Genetics in Atomic Age* 104 The gene for waltzing in the mouse acts pleiotropically on behaviour and hearing. Most or all genes have pleiotropic effects, often on such general characteristics as size, fertility, and longevity. **1964** *New Scientist* 17 Dec. 779/3 The streptomycin resistance is 'pleiotropic'—it brings about simultaneously one or more metabolically unrelated nutritional requirements. **1973** B. J. WILLIAMS *Evolution & Human Origins* ii. 30/1 A gene is said to have pleiotropic effects if it affects more than one phenotypic trait. **1974** *Jrnl. Gen. Microbiol.* LXXXI. 165 Mutants in a gene..in *Aspergillus nidulans* pleiotropically affect the utilization of many nitrogen sources.

pleiotropism (pləiˌǫ·trǒpiz'm). *Genetics.* [f. as next: see -ISM.] = *PLEIOTROPY.

1927 *Zeitschr. für Induktive Abstammungs- und Vererbungslehre* XLIII. 331 Plate..proposed the term 'pleiotrop'... Some of the highest authorities in the field of genetics have come to the conclusion that the pleiotropism of the genes is not an exception but rather the general rule. **1943** *Jrnl. Genetics* XLV. 6 A distinction has been made between genuine and spurious pleiotropism. **1970** T. DOBZHANSKY *Genetics of Evolutionary Process* vii. 210 Correlated responses due to pleiotropisms (physiological correlations) may make it impossible to endow a breed..with combinations of characteristics that would be desirable to man. **1973** B. J. WILLIAMS *Evolution & Human Origins* ii. 30/1 Pleiotropism does not interfere with a Mendelian analysis of inheritance. **1977** *Lancet* 29 Oct. 925/1 Gardner described such a family (no. 109) who also had extracolonic benign growths (fibromas, sebaceous and epidermal inclusion cysts, osteomas) which showed pleiotropism.

pleiotropy (plǝiˌǫ·trǒpi). *Genetics.* [ad. G. *pleiotrop* (L. Plate 1910, in *Festschr. für R. Hertwig* II. 597), f. Gr. πλείων (see PLEIO-) + τροπή turn, turning: see -Y³.] The production by a single gene of two or more apparently unrelated phenotypic effects; an instance of this.

1939 C. H. WADDINGTON *Introd. Mod. Genetics* vii. 162 (*heading*) Multiple effects of a factor or pleiotropy. **1957** —— *Strategy of Genes* 208 The more detailed the analysis, the more pleiotropy will be uncovered. **1973** *Nature* 21/28 Dec. 499/2 True pleiotropies of blood group genes are impossible to identify with the relatively crude characterisation of blood group specificities presently available. **1974** *Ibid.* 7 June 528/2 The suppression and temperature sensitivity characteristics were not separable, thus confirming that in each strain a single mutation was responsible for the pleiotropy. **1977** *Lancet* 9 Apr. 786/1 Genes always have more than one effect—a property known as pleiotropy.

pleiotypic (plǝiˌoti·pik), *a. Biol.* [f. PLEIO- + TYP(E *sb.*¹ + -IC.] Pertaining to the process whereby a single stimulus can elicit multiple unrelated responses from a living cell.

1971 *Nature New Biol.* 7 Apr. 162/1 Gordon Tomkins has proposed that mammalian cells may have a 'pleiotypic' control system to coordinate changes in the overall levels of synthesis and degradation of RNA and proteins. *Ibid.* 163/2 Dr. G. M. Tomkins (University of California, Medical Center, San Francisco) drew attention to a possible similarity between what he terms pleiotypic effects in mammalian cells and stringent control exhibited by bacteria deprived of nutrients. **1972** *Science* 5 May 486/1 The processes which have thus far been found to be under pleiotypic control are uridine uptake.., RNA synthesis.., polysome formation [etc.].

plenarium (plīnēᵊ·riŏm). Pl. **plenaria.** [ad. med.L. *plēnārium* in same sense, f. *plēnārius* complete: cf. PLENARY *a.* (*sb.*).] A book or manuscript containing a complete set of sacred writings, e.g. all the gospels or all the epistles.

1908 W. G. COLLINGWOOD *Scandinavian Britain* 243 Bishop Patrick set forth to Iceland 'with wood for building a church, and a plenarium, and an iron bell'. **1911** F. MERSHMAN in *Cath. Encycl.* XII. 164 Plenarium or Plenarius (*Liber*) is any book that contains completely all matters pertaining to one subject otherwise found scattered in several books... The entire mortuary office.. is called Plenarium. A complete copy of the four gospels was called an 'Evangelium plenarium'... Some Plenaria gave all the writings of the New Testament, others, those parts of the Sacred Scriptures that were commonly read in the Divine service and bore the name 'Lectionarium plenarium'. **1929** E. C. THOMAS *Lay Folks' Hist. Liturgy* I. xvii. 87 In the form for Consecrating a Church we find.. a form for the consecration of a stole and of the Plenarium or Four Gospels as part of the Rite.

plenary, *a.* (*sb.*) Add: **B.** *ellipt.* as *sb.* **2.** *in plenary*: of an assembly, etc.: fully constituted or attended.

1969 D. WIDGERY in Cockburn & Blackburn *Student Power* 122 The infrequency of Council Sessions..and its unwieldy size in plenary means that the Executive alone takes the fundamental decisions about policy implementation and initiation.

3. Anglicized form of *PLENARIUM.

1909 *Encycl. Relig. & Ethics* II. 609/1 There were the select passages for Sunday in the so-called Plenaries, Postils, and Books of the Gospels and the Epistles. **1920** M. DEANESLY *Lollard Bible* xii. 318 Of the three late fourteenth century English 'plenaries', or gospels and homilies, one is certainly Wycliffite.

‖**plene administravit** (plī·ni ădministrēi·vit). *Law.* [L., 'he has fully administered'.] (See quot. 1959.)

1729 G. JACOB *New Law-Dict.* s.v. *Executor*, If an Executor sued by several Creditors, pleads *Plene Administravit* to all at the same Time; and that he hath no Assets *præter* to pay one or two, he will make himself liable to all the debts. **1790** in Durnford & East *Rep. Cases King's Bench* III. 693 If an executor may plead *plene administravit* and neglect to do so, I see no difference between such a case and one where he does so plead and the plea is found against him. **1924** G. S. BOWER *Res Judicata* I. vi. 108 Where a defendant, sued in the character of executor or administrator, omits to plead *plene administravit.* **1959** JOWITT *Dict. Eng. Law* II. 1354/2 *Plene administravit* (he has fully administered), a defence by an executor or administrator that he has fully administered all the assets which have come to his hands.

plenisphere (ple·nisfīᵊɹ). *rare*⁻¹. [f. L. *plēnus* full + SPHERE *sb.*] A perfect sphere.

1912 E. POUND tr. *Calvacanti's Sonnets & Ballate* 99 Light I do see within my Lady's eyes And loving spirits in its plenisphere.

plentitude. (Further examples of this persistent (though erroneous) use.)

1939 JOYCE *Finnegans Wake* (1964) II. 241 A plentitude of house torts. **1944** AUDEN *For Time Being* (1945) 47 It was therefore only necessary for you to presuppose one genius, one unrivalled I to wish these wonders in all their endless plentitude and novelty. **1978** *Dædalus* Summer 197 This 'natural man' enjoys a plentitude of being.

plenty, *sb.* (*a.*, *adv.*). Add: **I.** *sb.* **2.** Also, a large amount, a great deal.

1939 R. STOUT *Some buried Caesar* xiv. 164 The bill was $66.20, which was plenty. **1973** M. YORKE *Grave Matters* I. vi. 35 He must have paid plenty for the place, besides what they're going to lash out in alterations.

II. *adj.* or quasi-*adj.* **1. a.** (Further examples.)

1779 H. COWLEY *Who's Dupe?* I. 1 When flowers are plenty, no body will buy 'em. **1794** N. PARRY in *Reg. Kentucky Hist. Soc.* (1936) XXXIV. 390 Though much broken with Limestone, which is very plenty through these places. **1850** *New England Farmer* II. 123 The gopher..is very plenty on the west side of Mississippi. **1869** 'MARK TWAIN' *Innoc. Abr.* xxxiv. 368 Mosques are plenty, churches are plenty, graveyards are plenty, but morals and whisky are scarce. **1883** R. L. STEVENSON *Silverado Squatters* 235 It is the same, they say, in the neighbourhood of all silver mines; the nature of that precious rock being stubborn with quartz and poisonous with cinnabar. Both were plenty in our Silverado.

b. (Later examples.)

1844 E. B. BROWNING *Poems* II. 181 What glory then for me In such a company?—Roses plenty, roses plenty, And one nightingale for twenty? **1922** JOYCE *Ulysses* 609, I seen icebergs plenty, growlers. **1939** —— *Finnegans Wake* (1964) II. 316 Besides proof plenty, over proof.

c. (Earlier and later examples.)

1857 E. BANDEL *Diary* 28 May in R. P. Bieber *Frontier Life in Army* (1932) 138 A splendid country around us: plenty wood and water. **1899** 'S. RUDD' in Murdoch & Drake-Brockman *Austral. Short Stories* (1951) 111 The water they brought was a little thick..but Dad put plenty ashes in the cask to clear it. **1934** D. L. SAYERS *Nine Tailors* 219 There's plenty farms now with the big brewing coppers still standing. **1939** JOYCE *Finnegans Wake* (1964) III. 443 Pretty knocks, I promise him with plenty burkes for his shins. **1942** 'M. INNES' *Daffodil Affair* II. 47 I've known plenty men turn queer there. **1969** G. GREENE *Travels with my Aunt* I. ix. 93 Leopard Society in Sierra Leone. They kill plenty people. **1973** *Sunday Express* (Trinidad) (Suppl.) 1 Apr. 12/3 When all dem fellas gambling and heap up plenty money, we..bawl out 'Police!'

3. Excellent. *slang.*

1933 *Fortune* Aug. 47/1 In sum, Mr. Brown plays *plenty trombone* or, as his friend suggested, a *gang o'horn.* **1941** R. P. SMITH *So it doesn't Whistle* 53 When they want to say a man's good, they say he plays plenty sax or plenty drums. **1970** C. MAJOR *Dict. Afro-Amer. Slang* 92 *Plenty*, good, excellent.

III. quasi-*adv.* (Further examples.)

1908 M. H. MORGAN *How to dress Doll* (1973) xii. 85 Cut the hood..making it plenty large enough to slip on easily over Dolly's head. **1934** J. M. CAIN *Postman always rings Twice* vi. 53, I was plenty blue around the gills. **1939** JOYCE *Finnegans Wake* (1964) II. 311 And plenty good enough, neighbour Norreys, every bit and grain. **1945** *Sun* (Baltimore) 13 June 8-O/7 Pavot just had the speed and the stamina, and turned it on plenty. **1956** B. HOLIDAY *Lady sings Blues* (1973) iii. 35 Benny Goodman came around plenty, too, and eventually he asked me to make my first record with him. **1970** *New Yorker* 3 Oct. 32/1 You are wrong—but plenty. **1973** *Times* 27 July 8 It was not my business. I was plenty busy with other things. **1974** R. M. PIRSIG *Zen & Art of Motorcycle Maintenance* III. xxvi. 306 This notebook gets plenty grease-smeared and ugly.

plenum. Add: **1.** (Further examples.)

1827 J. FAREY *Treat. Steam Engine* I. vi. 447 There is.. a plenum of steam in one compartment, and a vacuum, or exhaustion in the other. **1876** C. SLAGG *Sanitary Wk.* IX. 102 The motion of the pan..disturbs the equilibrium between the air-pressure in the receiver and the outside, causing at times a partial vacuum and at other times a plenum of air in the receiver. **1956** E. H. HUTTEN *Lang. Mod. Physics* iii. 90 In Newton's theory it [*sc.* the aether] plays no rôle save to help visualisation: the victory of the Cartesian conception of space as a plenum as against the Aristotelian void. **1972** *Sci. Amer.* Apr. 115/2 It is not the ether as a medium that is denied by Einstein... We can deny only the Newtonian properties of the ether, in particular the linear addition of velocities. Quantum electrodynamics builds a real plenum in space.

b. (Further example.)

1949 E. POUND *Pisan Cantos* lxxvii. 61 Mind come to plenum when nothing more will go into it.

2. *spec.* a meeting of all the members of a communist party committee.

1948 J. TOWSTER *Political Power in U.S.S.R.* x. 189 The plenums of the village and city soviets electing their own executive organs. **1950** D. W. BROGAN *Era of Franklin D. Roosevelt* xv. 315 [The American Communist] regional party meetings had the strange title of 'plenums'. **1956** *Ann. Reg. 1955* 234 The Third Plenum of the Central Committee of the P.Z.P.R., held in Warsaw from 21 to 24 January. **1965** *New Statesman* 9 Apr. 566/2 At the recent Plenum, the first since Mr K was ousted, Ilyichev was booted upstairs as Deputy Foreign Minister. **1966** *Ibid.* 29 July 158/1 Ten years ago the man who failed Mao over the speed of collectivisation simply did not get promoted; today's failures suddenly find themselves dismissed and denounced, apparently without even the 'due process' of a central committee plenum. **1974** T. P. WHITNEY tr. *Solzhenitsyn's Gulag Archipelago* I. I. x. 417 Bukharin.. willingly assured the Plenum of his repentance, and immediately abandoned his hunger strike.

3. (Earlier and further examples.) Also applied to things connected with this method (which is used also for heating and air-conditioning).

1844 D. B. REID *Illustr. Theory & Pract. Ventilation* II. iii. 121 Plenum ventilation..can be sustained only by the constant use of machinery. **1894** J. KEITH *Houses of Parl.: Rep. Heating & Ventilation* 3 The action of the Plenum fan..in blowing in the fresh air upwards through the grated floor of the Chamber. **1934** H. M. VERNON *Princ. Heating & Ventilation* ix. 177 A comparison of some thousands of observations made in factories ventilated by plenum air and by natural means showed very little defect of humidity in the plenum factories. **1948** T. BEDFORD *Basic Princ. Ventilation & Heating* xii. 198 In most of the plenum installations found in industry the air is untreated except that it is warmed in cold weather. **1967** W. P. JONES *Air Conditioning Engin.* xvi. 428 The primary air delivered by the nozzles escapes from the room through a plenum relief grille. **1968** *New Scientist* 7 Mar. 517/1 This [underwater] tunnel was driven by traditional methods, and the 'plenum' method (using compressed air behind the tunnelling shield) was not then known. **1978** LD. DROGHEDA *Double Harness* xiii. 143 We had allowed for proper air conditioning... Instead we installed a horrible thing called plenum ventilation, which warmed the air in winter, filling the offices with smuts..but failing to cool it in summer.

b. (Not *attrib.*) = **plenum chamber* (*a*).

1940 W. H. CARRIER et al. *Mod. Air-Conditioning* xviii. 425 The fan..is permitted to discharge into a plenum of section area at least ten times that of the fan discharge. **1970** *Toronto Daily Star* 24 Sept. 40/1 (Advt.), Humidifier... Coated pans fit sloped/vertical plenums. **1975** CROOME-GALE & ROBERTS *Airconditioning & Ventilation of Buildings* vii. 272 There are three sources of pressure change within the plenum which must be kept under control to ensure uniform plenum pressure.

4. Special Combs.: **plenum chamber,** (*a*) in some plenum systems, an enclosed space into which the outside air is forced (after any conditioning) and from which ducts lead to the various outlets inside the building; (*b*) any analogous enclosure in which the pressure is maintained above that of the atmosphere by the forcing in of air, as in some air-cooled engines, a ram-jet, or a hovercraft; **plenum space** = **plenum chamber* (*a*).

1908 A. G. KING *Pract. Steam & Hot Water Heating* xxi. 227 Separate ducts may be arranged to connect the main hot-air supply with the rising flues, or the heated air.. may be discharged under a slight pressure into a plenum chamber with which all supply pipes or warm-air ducts are connected. **1949** *Aircraft Engin.* Nov. 346/2 A disadvantage is that the pressure of the combustion chambers raises the temperature of the air in the plenum chamber, with a slight loss of power. **1959** *Motor* 30 Sept. 236/1 The entire engine, enclosed in the pressed-steel plenum chamber, is exposed to the cooling air, which escapes through vents below and behind. **1965** D. HERBERT *How to design & install Warm Air Heating* iii. 47 A concrete or brick foundation should be laid to provide a flat and level base for the plenum chamber, which is that part of the heater to which the ducts are connected. **1967** *New Scientist* 31 Aug. 435/1 The cushion of air on which a hovercraft rides is created continuously by a flow of air delivered through ducts, which empty themselves into the plenum chamber by nozzles equally spaced around its edge. **1975** M. J. NUNNEY *Automotive Engine* v. 175 The cooling air flow entering the plenum chamber from the fan is directed downwards over the cylinders and cylinder heads. **1916** C. L. HUBBARD *Ventilation Hand Bk.* ix. 154 The flues connecting the plenum space with the registers are..concealed in the leg of the pew. **1975** CROOME-GALE & ROBERTS *Airconditioning & Ventilation of Buildings* vii. 278 The ventilated ceiling system is an all-air system which delivers supply air through..ductwork to a plenum space over a suspended ceiling, so that a relatively small plenum pressure may be used to evenly distribute the air through the ventilated ceiling to the room below.

pleochroic, *a.* Add: *pleochroic halo*, each of a series of concentric dark-coloured circles seen in sections of certain minerals and having a radioactive inclusion at their centre; usu. *pl.*

1894 [in Dict.]. **1909** F. P. MENNELL *Introd. Petrol.* ix. 57 'Pleochroic halos'..often occur round crystals so small as otherwise to pass unnoticed. **1926** R. W. LAWSON tr. *Hevesy & Paneth's Man. Radioactivity* xxvi. 216 (*heading*) Age determination from the intensity of coloration of pleochroic haloes. **1972** M. H. BATTEY *Mineral. for Students* iii. 93/2 Small crystals of zircon, containing thorium, embedded in biotite, may by their α-radiation produce an intensely pleochroic halo round the zircon grain.

pleocytosis (plī,osəitōᵘ·sis). *Path.* [f. *pleo-*, PLEIO- + -CYT(E + -OSIS.] The presence of abnormally many cells, *spec.* of lymphocytes in the cerebro-spinal fluid.

1911 STEDMAN *Med. Dict.* 681/1 *Pleocytosis*, lymphocytosis in the cerebrospinal fluid in syphilitic and parasyphilitic diseases of the central nervous system. **1924** BROWNING & MACKENZIE *Recent Methods in Diagnosis & Treatment of Syphilis* (ed. 2) xvi. 304 Pleocytosis is found in practically all acute and chronic inflammatory processes affecting the meninges. **1976** *Lancet* 4 Dec. 1222/1 The cerebrospinal fluid in patient 3 showed pleocytosis (23 mononuclear cells/mm).

pleonastic, *a.* (Further examples.)

1898 H. SWEET *New Eng. Gram.* II. 54 The pleonastic genitive, as in *he is a friend of my brother's*, is generally partitive = 'one of the friends of my brother'. **1947** [see *INTERLINGUISTICS]. **1951** E. H. STURTEVANT *Compar. Gram. Hittite Lang.* (ed. 2) ii. 23 Pleonastic Vowels. In Akkadian, vowels are frequently written double (*U-UL* 'not', *BEE-EL* 'lord'). **1972** W. LABOV *Language in Inner City* iv. 146 The general nonstandard rule which operates here can be written as a simple pleonastic transformation.

pleophony (plī,ǫ·fŏni). *Linguistics.* [f. *pleo-*, PLEIO- + *phony* after HOMOPHONY etc.] Vowel duplication; epenthesis of a vowel which harmonizes with that in the preceding syllable. Hence **pleopho·nic** *a.*

1949 *Archivum Linguisticum* I. 165 The East Slavonic languages..present the curious and striking phenomenon of pleophony or double vowelling. **1966** H. BIRNBAUM in Birnbaum & Puhvel *Anc. Indo-Europ. Dial.* 162 One such feature is 'pleophonic' /ToroT/ as a reflex of P[roto] Sl[avic] /TorT/. *Ibid.* 167 This change must have preceded in time the /TorT/>/ToroT/modification ('pleophony') mentioned above.

pleoptics (plī,ǫ·ptiks), *sb. pl.* (const. as *sing.* or *pl.*). *Ophthalm.* [ad. G. *pleoptik* (A. Bangerter 1953, in *Wiener klin. Wochenschr.* 20 Nov. 966/2), f. *pleo-*, PLEIO- + *optik* OPTICS.] A method of treatment for amblyopia and eccentric fixation employing the selective dazzling of parts of the retina in order to stimulate the use of the fovea and render it more sensitive.

1955 *Q. Cumulative Index Med.* LVIII. 1517/1 (*heading*) Pleoptics and orthoptics. **1962** J. W. HENDERSON in G. M. Haik *Strabismus* v. 111 For the eccentric fixator over 5 years of age, pleoptics rather than occlusion are thought to be the most acceptable method [of treating amblyopia]. **1964** A. SCHLOSSMAN in A. Sorby *Mod. Ophthalm.* III. 141 Pleoptics, which was initiated by Bangerter of St-Gallen, Switzerland, has its greatest value in the treatment of the large number of patients with eccentric fixation who cannot be managed by any other form of therapy. **1975** M. M. PARKS *Ocular Motility & Strabismus* xi. 98/1 An eccentrically fixating eye in some older children has been restored to central fixation using pleoptics after occlusion therapy has failed.

So **pleo·ptic** *a.*

1960 *Amer. Orthoptic Jrnl.* X. 7/1 The development of pleoptic methods and their therapeutic application preceded the discovery of some hitherto unknown characteristics of amblyopia. **1964** S. DUKE-ELDER *Parsons' Diseases of Eye* (ed. 14) XXX. 482 If eccentric fixation is well established, it is often well to occlude the affected eye for some weeks and then to stimulate the macula by special pleoptic methods (flashing devices, the production of after-images, etc.). **1967** J. L. C. MARTIN-DOYLE *Synopsis Ophthalm.* (ed. 3) 188 Pleoptic treatment is arduous and the instruments expensive. **1975** M. M. PARKS *Ocular Motility & Strabismus* xi. 98/1 The final result in the majority of amblyoptic patients is the same whether.. simple occlusion therapy is used exclusively or if pleoptic exercises are used.

plereme (plī·rīm). *Linguistics.* [f. Gr. πλήρ-ης full: see *-EME.] **a.** = *full word. **b.** A unit of meaning. Hence **plerema·tic** *a.*, **plerema·tically** *adv.*, **plerema·tics** *sb. pl.*

1939 [see *GLOSSEMATIC *sb. pl.* and *a.*]. **1939**, etc. [see *KENEME]. **1949** C. E. BAZELL in E. P. Hamp et al. *Readings in Linguistics II* (1966) 209 No fusion in the expression of plerematic units is here involved. **1950** S. POTTER *Our Language* 87 *Sememes* (including *pleremes* and *kenemes*). **1957** —— *Mod. Linguistics* vii. 143 Operators are sometimes called *kenemes* by those describing Chinese, as opposed to..*pleremes*. **1958** C. F. HOCKETT *Course in Modern Linguistics* lxiv. 575 Here the terms 'phonological' and 'grammatical' make too direct a reference to human language; it will be better to introduce two new terms for general applicability: *cenematic* and *plerematic*. The cenematic structure of language is phonology; the plerematic structure of language is grammar. Phonemes are linguistic *cenemes*; morphemes are linguistic *pleremes*. *Ibid.* 576 Productivity implies that some messages in the system..are *plerematically complex*: that they consist of an arrangement of two or more pleremes, instead of each consisting of a single indivisible plereme. If one starts with a system with no plerematic complexity, then there is only one variety of analogy by which a new message can be coined: *blending*. **1959** W. A. C. H. DOBSON *Late Archaic Chinese* i. 14 Undistributed, a plerematic word might be said to represent a notion undifferentiated by grammatical quality. **1961** F. W. HOUSEHOLDER in Saporta & Bastian *Psycholinguistics* 25/2 They [*sc.* distinctive features] may also be considered as 'cenemes' of which 'plerematic' phonemes are composed. **1967** C. L. WRENN *Word & Symbol* 4 The names of things, qualities or acts..are the words which linguists of the Danish school used to term *pleremes* (words of full or complete significance). **1969** *Word 1967* XXIII. 469 My observations apparently support the structuralist separation of cenetics and plerematics. *Ibid.* 471 In addition to their two cenetic and two plerematic systems, bilingual children naturally have to master two sets of form-to-meaning relationships. **1978** *Amer. Speech* LIII. 275 A communicative system has *duality of patterning*..if its meaningful signals (pleremes) are built out of some convenient stock of meaningless but differentiating pieces (cenemes). *Ibid.* 276 Some special sort of discourse in which there is a planned regularity of recurrence of cenematic features independent of their plerematic role.

plerocephalic (plīᵊrosĭfæ·lik), *a.* *Path.* [f. Gr. πλήρης, πληρο- full + κεφαλή head + -IC.] Of œdema: caused by increased intracranial pressure.

1927 H. M. TRAQUAIR *Introd. Clin. Perimetry* ix. 115 Plerocephalic œdema (œdema due to increased intracranial pressure)... As 'Papillœdema' and 'choked disc' refer to ophthalmoscopic appearances which may occur in local optic nerve disease this term has been chosen to indicate œdema of the disc due to increased intracranial pressure. **1976** *Proc. R. Soc. Med.* LXIX. 455/2 In the following 12 cases varying degrees of optic atrophy occurred in space-occupying lesions of the brain in children because of the development of plerocephalic œdema.

plerocercoid (plīᵊrosə̄·ɪkoid). *Zool.* [f. Gr. πλήρης, πληρο- full + κέρκος tail + -OID.] A larval form of certain tapeworms, in which the body is solid, lacking a bladder. Also *attrib.* or as *adj.*

1906 P. FALCKE tr. *Braun's Animal Parasites of Man* 219 Human beings, like other hosts, can only acquire the broad tapeworm by ingesting its plerocercoids. **1928** *Jrnl. Amer. Med. Assoc.* 30 June 2081/1, I found the plerocercoids in pike. **1961** SWELLENGREBEL & STERMAN *Animal Parasites in Man* xiii. 241 The plerocercoids have been recovered from various internal organs. **1962** J. D. SMYTH *Introd. Anim. Parasitol.* xix. 222 The lycophora.. develops into a procercoid and later a plerocercoid larva. **1973** T. C. CHENG *Gen. Parasitol.* xiv. 488/2 Procercoids develop into solid, wormlike plerocercoids, each with one invaginated scolex at one end.

plesiadapid (plīzi,æ·dăpid), *sb.* and *a.* *Palæont.* [f. mod.L. family name *Plesiadapidæ*, f. the generic name *Plesiadapis* (P. Gervais 1877, in *Jrnl. Zool.* VI. 76), f. PLESIO- + *Adapis*, generic name of another fossil primate + -ID³.] **A.** *sb.* A primitive, extinct primate belonging to the family Plesiadapidæ, known from Palæocene fossil remains found in North America and Europe. **B.** *adj.* Of, pertaining to, or resembling an animal of this kind.

1945 A. S. ROMER *Vertebr. Paleontol.* (ed. 2) xviii. 343 The plesiadapids have been thought to be aberrant lemurs or tree shrews. **1949** W. E. LE GROS CLARK *Hist. Primates* 50 We know little as yet about the limb bones of the plesiadapids. **1963** E. L. SIMONS in J. Buettner-Janusch *Evolutionary & Genetic Biol. Primates* I. ii. 79 The anterior teeth of plesiadapids were enlarged and procumbent. **1970** [see *LORISID *sb.* and *a.*]. **1975** *Nature* 10 Jan. 111/2 Five plesiadapid lineages are known, at least two of which were common to both Europe and North America.

plesiadapoid (plīzi,æ·dăpoid), *sb.* and *a.* *Palæont.* [f. mod.L. name of suborder *Plesiadapoidea*, f. the generic name *Plesiadapis* (see prec.) + -OID.] **A.** *sb.* A primitive, extinct primate belonging to the suborder Plesiadapoidea. **B.** *adj.* Of, pertaining to, or resembling an animal of this kind.

1966 A. S. ROMER *Vertebr. Paleontol.* (ed. 3) xviii. 217/2 (*heading*) Plesiadapoids. **1973** *Nature* 24 Aug. 518/1 The dental characteristics distinguishing primitive Early Eocene adapids and omomyids from other Eocene mammals are present in primitive plesiadapoids. **1974** B. J. STAHL *Vertebrate History* ix. 471 The plesiadapoids.. became extinct without issue before the close of the Eocene. *Ibid.* 472 A change in the climate is implicated in the failure of the plesiadapoid primates to survive.

Plesianthropus (plīzi,æ·nþrŏpŏs). *Palæont.* [mod.L. (R. Broom 1938, in *Nature* 27 Aug. 377/1), f. PLESI(O- + Gr. ἄνθρωπος man.] An African fossil hominid of the genus formerly so called, now usually included in the species *Australopithecus africanus.*

1941 *Nature* 5 July 11/1 Plesianthropus..has a skull somewhat like that of the chimpanzee in size. **1948** A. L. KROEBER *Anthropol.* (rev. ed.) iii. 91 Australopithecus and Plesianthropus came to light in quarrying operations. **1960** E. WINICK *Dict. Anthropol.* 421/1 *Plesianthropus*, an African man-like ape fossil from the Pleistocene period. **1977** G. W. HEWES in D. M. Rumbaugh *Language Learning by Chimpanzee* i. 40 As for the Australopithecines (based on casts of the Sterkfontein individual formerly called 'Plesianthropus') no articulate language would have been possible for them.

plesiomorphous, *a.*, **-morphism.** (Earlier example of each.)

1833 *Rep. Brit. Assoc. 1831, 1832* 429 Plesiomorphism.—As the differences between the angles of the carbonates and sulphates above quoted cannot be accounted for by any accidental causes.., some crystallographers have been led to reject the term *isomorphous* as applied to such crystallized compounds, and to substitute in its place the term *plesiomorphous*.

-plet (plet), the ending of *triplet, multiplet*, etc., used with a prefixed numeral to denote a multiplet having the specified number of members.

1973 L. J. TASSIE *Physics Elementary Particles* xiii. 173 Taking the neutron and proton as members of the *SU*(6) 56-plet yields the ratio of their magnetic moments as.. −3/2 which is close to the experimental value of −1·46. **1975** *Physics Bull.* Apr. 180/3 The octet of mesons is now part of a 15plet which groups together one octet and one singlet with no charm, and two triplets with charm 1 and −1, respectively.

plethorous (ple·þŏrəs), *a. rare.* [f. PLETHORA + -OUS.] = PLETHORIC *a.* 1.

1906 J. P. BARRY *At Gates of East* p. vii, But the book.. may do good in a practical way, if it weans the wearied, the plethorous and the valetudinarian from the Cult of the Spas.

plethy·smogram. *Physiol.* [f. as next + -GRAM.] The record produced by a plethysmograph.

1894 W. EWART *Heart Stud.* I. 181 The need for a separate study of shape, volume, and velocity of the pulse is rendered obvious by the difference between the three curves, which may be termed respectively the sphygmogram, the plethysmogram, and the tachogram, obtained by means of the three instruments bearing corresponding names. *Ibid.* 221 The plethysmogram (volumpuls) of the forearm..shows an increase in the size of the oscillations. **1929** *Proc. Soc. Exper. Biol. & Med.* XXVI. 711 (*heading*) A photographic method of recording plethysmograms. **1971** *Nature* 1 Oct. 340/2 Burton has ascribed the slow fluctuations..seen in human digital plethysmograms to the action of the thermoregulatory system.

plethysmograph. Add: (In mod. forms of the instrument other fluids, e.g. air, and other means of measuring its displacement are employed.) (Further examples.)

1957 *Clin. Sci.* XVI. 103 (*heading*) Venous collection in forearm and hand measured by the strain-gauge and volume plethysmograph. **1964** *Times* 5 Sept. 12/3 A small electronic instrument called a plethysmograph used for measuring changes of blood volume in the body's circulation. **1972** *English Studies* LIII. 76 Measurements were made..of the variations in volume of the air in the lungs. This..involved the use of a plethysmograph, a rigid airtight container enclosing the subject entirely except for head and neck.

Hence also **plethy:smogra·phically** *adv.*, by means of a plethysmograph; **plethysmography** (examples).

1897 *Jrnl. Exper. Med.* II. 334 The striking effect of such stimuli upon the volume of a limb when measured plethysmographically. **1898** *Jrnl. Physiol.* XXII. 380 A few experiments on intestinal plethysmography were made by Bayliss. **1930** *Amer. Jrnl. Physiol.* XCI. 717 That the abdominal venous reservoirs empty (into the chest) during systole can be demonstrated by abdominal plethysmography. **1970** *Nature* 18 July 276/2 The volume of the foot was measured plethysmographically before injection of carrageenin. **1977** *Lancet* 9 July 66/1 Strain-gauge plethysmography is probably an appropriate method for demonstrating arterial insufficiency in this condition.

pleurisy. 3. pleurisy-root (earlier and later examples).

1785 T. JEFFERSON *Notes on State of Virginia* 63 Pleurisy root, Asclepias decumbens. **1932** J. B. HARVEY *Wild Flowers Amer.* 55 Butterfly Weed or Pleurisy Root.. bears brilliant orange flowers, arranged in flat, terminal clusters.

pleuro. Add: (Earlier and later Austral. examples.) Also *attrib.*

1885 R. C. PRAED *Austral. Life* 244 Pleuro is very bad our way. I don't believe much in inoculation—do you? **1897** 'R. BOLDREWOOD' *My Run Home* xx. 176 'Do you ever have any pleuro among your cattle?' said I; 'I heard something about it in England.' **1917** A. B. PATERSON *Three Elephant Power* 42 Providence sends the pleuro, and big strong beasts slink away by themselves. **1944** W. E. HARNEY *Taboo* (ed. 3) 40 One day..a pleuro bullock chased him. **1965** *Bulletin* (Sydney) 13 Feb. 40/3 They used their weapons on the local pleuro bull which was the only large, live target they had a chance to assail. **1975** *Sunday Mail* (Brisbane) 20 July 10/5 Today he looks back with pride at the successful eradication of the killer disease 'pleuro' which threatened the cattle industry in 1970.

pleu:ropneumo·nia-like, *a.* *Biol.* Also with two or no hyphens. [f. PLEURO-PNEUMONIA + -LIKE.] *pleuropneumonia-like organism*: = *MYCOPLASMA. Abbrev. PPLO s.v. *P II.

1935 E. KLIENEBERGER in *Jrnl. Path. & Bacteriol.* XL. 93 (*heading*) The natural occurrence of pleuropneumonia-like organisms in apparent symbiosis with *Streptobacillus moniliformis* and other bacteria. **1951** *Jrnl. Bacteriol.* LXI. 395 A characteristic of the parasitic pleuropneumonialike organisms (PPLO) is the requirement of serum or ascitic fluid for growth *in vitro*. **1964** *New Scientist* 19 Nov. 497/1 The workers in Glasgow have grown pleuropneumonia-like organisms from cell cultures containing leukaemia 'virus'. **1973** *Nature* 9 Mar. 83/1 Mycoplasmas, which used to be known as pleuropneumonia-like organisms, are the smallest free-living organisms.

plexiform, *a.* Add: *plexiform layer* [tr. F. *couche plexiforme* (*externe, interne*) (S. Ramón y Cajal 1893, in *La Cellule* IX. 132)], either of two layers of the retina separated by the inner nuclear layer, the outer one of which contains synapses between the rods and cones and the neurones of the nuclear layer, whilst the inner one contains synapses between these neurones and ganglion cells; = *molecular layer* (*a*) s.v. *MOLECULAR *a.* 5.

1894 *Quain's Elem. Anat.* (ed. 10) III. III. 41 (*heading*) Inner molecular or inner plexiform layer, neurospongium. **1911** *Ophthalmoscope* IX. 437 The external plexiform layer remains very narrow. **1959** W. ANDREW *Text-bk. Compar. Histol.* xv. 604 The ten layers in order, from without in, i.e. toward the vitreous humor, are: (1) the pigmented epithelium, (2) the layer of rods and cones, ..(5) the outer plexiform layer, (6) the inner nuclear layer, (7) the inner plexiform layer,..and (10) the inner limiting membrane. **1972** THORPE & GLICKSTEIN in tr. *S. Ramón y Cajal's Structure of Retina* p. viii, The dendritic trees of the ganglion cells spread at different levels within the inner plexiform layer and form associations with the processes of the amacrine and bipolar cell processes, thereby creating the distinct laminar appearance of this layer so clearly described by Cajal.

Plexiglas (ple·ksiglas). Chiefly *U.S.* Also **Plexiglass,** and with lower-case initial. A proprietary name for the substance also sold under the names of *PERSPEX and *LUCITE. Freq. *attrib.*

1935 *Trade Marks Jrnl.* 10 Apr. 451 Plexiglass... Glass. Röhm & Haas, Aktiengesellschaft.., Darmstadt, Germany; manufacturers. *Ibid.* 31 July 968/2 Plexiglass... Glass substitutes made from artificial resins. Röhm & Haas Aktiengesellschaft.., Darmstadt, Germany; manufacturers. **1936** *Official Gaz.* (U.S. Patent Office) 30 June 999/1 Röhm and Haas Company, Philadelphia. *Plexiglas* for sheets of solid transparent resinous material to be used as a glass substitute. Claims use since June 5, 1935. **1936** *Jrnl. Aeronaut. Sci.* Nov. 13/1 For smaller aircraft, Plexiglas, Glyptal, and Vinylite are available in sheet form. **1941** *Product Engin.* May 267/3 Area of windows is 20 sq. ft., hence lighter Plexiglass instead of plate glass. **1943** J. STEINBECK in *N.Y. Herald Tribune* 31 Aug. 17/4 The sergeant had carved the handles of his gun from the plexiglass from the nose of a bomber. **1951** *Archit. Rev.* CX. 222/1 (*caption*) Roof, tar and gravel with plexiglass skylights. **1954** *Trade Marks Jrnl.* 15 Dec. 1264/2 Plexiglas... Chemical products used in industry, science and photography; fire extinguishing compositions, soldering preparations.., adhesives.., and synthetic resins. Röhm & Haas Gesellschaft mit beschränkter Haftung.., Darmstadt, Germany; manufacturers. **1955** *Ibid.* 13 April 387/1 Plexiglas... All goods..made of glass or of glass substitutes made from plastics. Röhm & Haas Gesellschaft. **1957** *Economist* 19 Oct. 229/2 The ceremonial drive in an open landau..or the neighbourhood tour in a grey Cadillac with plexiglass top. **1965** ZIGROSSER & GAEHDE *Guide Coll. Orig. Prints* vii. 115 Plexiglas is sometimes used for framing because it is unbreakable. The Plexiglas should be coated with an anti-static to eliminate its tendency to attract dust. **1970** HARARI & HAYWARD tr. *A. Amalrik's Involuntary Journey to Siberia* iv. 56 This door had a small panel of plexiglass. **1976** *S9* (N.Y.) Feb. 30/2 The large full-feature backlighted digital clock has buzz signal alarm. All encased in a modern smoked plexiglas front panel. **1977** *Time* 31 Jan. 15/2 Cairo's flying squads of riot police with their Plexiglas face masks, shields and staves were in control.

plica. Add: **4.** *Medieval Mus.* (Also with pl. **plicas.**) A notational symbol, variously interpreted but now usu. considered to represent a type of ornament; the ornament indicated. Also *attrib.*

1782 C. BURNEY *Gen. Hist. Mus.* II. iii. 188 Few of the musical terms in the tract of Franco, are more difficult to comprehend or define than the word *Plica*, which he calls 'a note of *division* of the same sound, ascending or descending.' **1801** T. BUSBY *Dict. Mus.* s.v., *Plica*, the name formerly given to a kind of ligature used in the old music as a sign of hesitation, or pausing. **1881** GROVE *Dict. Mus.* III. 4/1 *Plica*..a character, mentioned by Franco of Cologne, Joannes de Muris, and other early writers, whose accounts of it are not always very easily reconciled to each other. Franco describes four kinds... Joannes de Muris describes the Plica as a sign of augmentation, similar in effect to the Point. Franco tells us that it may be added at will to the Long, or the Breve; but to the semibreve only when it appears in Ligature. Some other writers apply the term 'Plica' to the tail of a Large, or Long. The Descending Plica is sometimes identified with the Cephalicus. **1903** C. F. A. WILLIAMS *Story of Notation* vi. 101 In the sixth chapter Franco treats of the Plica. **1940** G. REESE *Music in Middle Ages* (1941) III. x. 283 Another type of ornament was notated by the *plica*. This was attached to either single notes..or ligatures... When it was applied to single notes, usually two parallel strokes of unequal length were added to the note-head. These strokes, enfolding the head, gave the *plica* its name.' **1942** W. APEL *Notation of Polyphonic Music, 900–1600* (1944) III. iii. 234 The *plica* is a passing tone which is indicated ..by a downward or upward dash attached to the right of a note. In modal notation, the *plica* appears preferably in connection with ligatures. *Ibid.* 235 We shall carefully distinguish between *plica*-note and *plica*-tone. The former term refers to the written note to which the *plica*-dash is attached; the latter to the extra tone called for by the dash. **1954** *New Oxf. Hist. Music* II. 325 The *plica*.. is a short stroke which modifies the single square note, leading either upwards or downwards. *Ibid.*, The instructions of the medieval theorists most often quoted are those of the Anonymus of Paris, who in his *Quædam de arte discantandi* tells us that 'it should be formed in the throat with the epiglottis', and of Lambert, who wrote under the pen-name of Aristotle: 'The *plica* is made in the voice by compressing the epiglottis, combining it neatly with a repercussion of the voice.' *Ibid.*, The second, semi-vocal, note of the plica is not an ad libitum ornament..but has a time-value of its own, one-third or one-half of that which would belong to the parent note if it were not plicated. **1957** C. PARRISH *Notation of Medieval Music* (1958) v. 130 Plicas are used sparingly. **1979** *Early Music* Apr. 189/1 The *plica* is a note with stems on *both* sides of the note head and is meant to be sung as two pitches, the first one specified by the position of the note head, the second one unspecified, but lying above or below the first note, depending on the direction of the stems.

plicate, *v.* Add: **2.** *Medieval Mus.* To add a plica to. (Chiefly as ppl. adj.)

1903 C. F. A. WILLIAMS *Story of Notation* vii. 120 An imaginary dialogue dated 1326..shows a 'plicated' semibreve when three semibreves are used with one syllable. **1927** *Grove's Dict. Mus.* (ed. 3) IV. 210/1 Besides longs and breves, semibreves could be plicated when in ligature. **1954** [see *PLICA 4]. **1977** *Early Music* Apr. 199 The neum..is assumed to be the plicated equivalent of the *pressus*.

plicated, *ppl. a.* Add: **3.** (See *PLICATE *v.* 2.)

‖ **plié** (pli,e). *Ballet.* Also **plier.** [Fr., f. *plier* to bend.] A movement in which the dancer lowers the body, bending the knees outwards in line with the out-turned feet. Also as *v. intr.*, to execute such a movement.

1892 E. SCOTT *Dancing as Art & Pastime* vi. 76 The foot passes from the *fourth rearward position* to the *fourth in front* with a very decided *plié de genoux* as it comes into the *first position*. *Ibid.* 77 A movement consisting of two *pliés* in advancing and three forward steps. **1913** C. D'ALBERT *Dancing* 125 *Plié*,..flexion or bending of one or both knees in preparation for any step. **1920** *Dancing Times* July 793 The Russians take the grands battements at the end of the side practice instead of immediately after the 'plier'. **1922** BEAUMONT & IDZIKOWSKI *Man. Classical Theatr. Dancing* II. i. 37 The *plié*, or bend, may be small (*plié à quart*)..medium (*plié à demi* or *demi-plié*)..or large (*grand plié*). **1930** CRASKE & BEAUMONT *Theory & Pract. Allegro in Classical Ballet* 16 An *assemblé* is said to be *soutenu* when the knees are straightened and another *plié* is made before executing the next *pas*. **1949** A. CHUJOY *Dance Encycl.* 376/1 It is said that the entire technique of ballet consists in knowing when and how to do a plié. **1958** *Observer* 14 Sept. 14/7 Beautifully musical, he can turn a double *tour en l'air* into a deep *plié en arabesque* as trimly as if it were a phrase in a Mozart sonata. **1971** 'D. HALLIDAY' *Dolly & Doctor Bird* xi. 146 Krishtof would raise me..while I stood up. He would then plié round me. **1977** *New Yorker* 19 Sept. 43/1 The marble-floored reception area alone, on the ground floor, is vast enough to accommodate the entire corps de ballet of four or five major ballet companies, all doing their pliés and entrechats.

Pliensbachian (plīnzbā·kiăn), *a. Geol.* [ad. G. *Pliensbachien* (A. Oppel 1858, in *Jahresh. des Vereins f. vaterlandische Naturkunde in Württemberg* XIV. 249), f. *Pliensbach*, name of a locality near Boll, a village near Göppingen in Baden-Württemberg, W. Germany: see -IAN.] Of, pertaining to, or designating a stage of the Lower Jurassic in Europe comprising the Middle Lias and part of the Lower Lias. Freq. *absol.*

1903 *Q. Jrnl. Geol. Soc.* LIX. 455 In some districts—East Gloucestershire for instance—only a few feet of Toarcian are found separating the Inferior Oolite (Aalenian) from the Middle Lias (Pliensbachian). **1955** E. NEAVERSON *Stratigr. Palaeont.* (ed. 2) xii. 440 Pliensbachian brachiopods are most abundant in the limestone facies of Somerset. **1975** A. HALLAM *Jurassic Environments* ii. 13 No zonal subdivision for the Pliensbachian of southern Europe as a whole has yet been satisfactorily achieved. **1978** *Nature* 13 July 131/1 The initial Jurassic transgression here took place in the Pliensbachian.

plig (plig). *U.S. dial.* [Shortening of POLYGAMIST.] A polygamist, used esp. with reference to the practice of polygamy attributed to the Mormon Church.

1977 *Washington Post* 8 Aug. A14 Many citizens in Utah show an uncomfortable dualism toward polygamists, derisively calling them 'pligs'. **1978** *Observer* (Colour Suppl.) 12 Mar. 33/4 Polygamy..has made a surprising comeback of late. 'The Pligs are sprouting like weeds,' said a county sheriff.

plightage (plǝi·tėdʒ). *rare*⁻¹. [f. PLIGHT *v.*¹ + -AGE.] The fact or state of being plighted or betrothed.

1908 HARDY *Dynasts* III. v. iv. 442 These vile tricks, to pluck you from Your nuptial plightage..Make me belch oaths!

plightful, *a.* Restrict † *Obs.* to sense in Dict. and add: **2.** Grievous; fraught with suffering. *rare.*

1906 HARDY *Dynasts* II. VI. v. 304 The tears that lie about this plightful scene Of heavy travail in a suffering soul.

Plimsoll. Add: Also *fig.* Also *Plimsoll's pancake* = *Plimsoll line.*

1894 [in Dict.]. **1896** *Nautical Mag.* Jan. 17 'Plimsoll's pancake' will ruin the colonial carrying trade. **1912** R. W. SERVICE *Rhymes of Rolling Stone* (1913) 78 Loaded to the Plimsoll mark With God's sunshine was that boy. **1920** P. L. WALDRON *Afloat & Ashore* 57 The ship was loaded down to 'Plimsoll's pancake'. **1957** R. CAMPBELL *Portugal* 29 It..will pierce a crocodile if shot on the 'Plimsoll-line' between back and belly. **1961** *John o'London's* 18 May 567/1 Wearing towel..and not wearing that a millimetre more than the censor demands either below or above the cheesecake plimsoll-line. **1964** C. WILLOCK *Enormous Zoo* iv. 59 Big bull elephants..stand up to their plimsoll lines in the lake. **1972** *Author* Winter 187/2 The secondary school performance was worse—only 9 'good' and 13 'reasonable', with 140 below the Plimsoll line. **1976** *National Observer* (U.S.) 31 July 15/2, I tried to teach my wife, Lila, to fish, but with only a mud turtle, a rusty bucket, and a two-inch bluegill to show for standing three hours up to her Plimsoll line in cold water, she became an incorrigible dropout. **1978** T. DE V. WHITE *My Name is Norval* i. 15 She had..[a] formula for..the restraining of male advances: a Plimsoll mark below which she was theoretically in danger.

2. (With lower-case initial.) A kind of rubber-soled canvas shoe. Usu. *pl.* Also (through association with SOLE *sb.*¹ 2) *plimsole*. Also *attrib.* Hence **pli·msol(l)ed** *a.*, wearing plimsolls.

1907 *Yesterday's Shopping* (1969) 326/1 The Plimsoll or Sand Shoes. **1922** *Times* 27 Dec. 7/7 When Seabrook appeared in court he was wearing white plimsolls. **1927** W. DEEPING *Kitty* xii. 148 These stealthy affairs..made him think of sneaking out in plimsolls and kidding some 'cop'. **1930** W. PETT RIDGE *Miss Collingwood* i. 12 She kicked off her plimsolls, and walked about in stockinged feet. **1936** G. POLLET *Song for Sixpence* xi. 89 For two pleasant days I have been holidaying it in plimsolls whilst my shoes have been upon the rack. **1939** JOYCE *Finnegans Wake* (1964) II. 397 Their blankets and materny mufflers and plimsoles. **1955** E. BLISHEN *Roaring Boys* iv. 183 Dancing on plimsolled toes like a boxer. **1959** F. BAINES *In Deep* 29 Moses and I put on plimsolls and slipped down the alley-way. **1963** 'R. EAST' *Pin Men* iii. 62 He lifted his plimsolled foot. **1965** D. FRANCIS *Odds Against* xii. 163 Chico had made a plimsole-shod inspection. **1968** J. IRONSIDE *Fashion Alphabet* 131 *Canvas shoes*..are usually 'plimsoll' or espadrille shape for sports, beach or leisure. **1973** 'D. JORDAN' *Nile Green* xxxvi. 181 She came in through the door like a commando in plimsolls. **1974** C. FREMLIN *By Horror Haunted* 157 The wary, plimsoled footstep.

pling (pliŋ), *v. U.S. slang.* [Origin unknown.] *intr.* and *trans.* To beg; to beg from (someone); *pling the stem* (see quot. 1927²). Hence **pli·nger,** a beggar; **pli·nging** *vbl. sb.*

1913 L. LIVINGSTON *Trail of Tramp* vii. 55 The other one will make a good assistant for me in plinging. *Ibid.* 56 It meant for James McDonald that he had become an apprentice for Kansas Shorty, the Plinger—a begging tramp. **1915** *N.Y. World* 9 May (Suppl.) 14/3 *Plinging*, to reach out for 'handouts'; to beg. **1927** *Amer. Speech* II. 390/1 A street is..a *stem*... Dinging the stem is known as *mooching, stemming* and *plinging*. *Plinging 'em right and left* is an arduous occupation, calling for gall, tact and sharp eyes. **1927** *Dialect Notes* V. 459 *Pling the stem*, to beg money on the street. **1931** G. IRWIN *Amer. Tramp & Underworld Slang* 148 *Pling*, to beg on the street, probably a corruption of 'pillinge'.

Plinian, *a.* and *sb.* Add: **A.** *adj.* **1.** (Later example.)

1962 D. HARDEN *Phoenicians* xi. 154 The Plinian tradition that glass was invented in Phoenicia.

2. Also **plinian.** Applied to (the stage of) a volcanic eruption in which a narrow blast of gas is ejected with great violence from a central vent to a height of several miles before it expands sideways. [In this sense ad. It. *Pliniano* (A. Stoppani *Corso di Geologia* (1871) I. II. v. 310); so called because the eruption of Vesuvius in A.D. 79, which killed Pliny the Elder and was described by his nephew the younger Pliny, was of this kind.]

Quots. 1884, 1897 refer specifically to the eruption of A.D. 79.

[**1884** H. J. JOHNSTON-LAVIS in *Q. Jrnl. Geol. Soc.* XL. 37 Some authors have supposed that the principal part of the Vesuvian cone was thrown up by the eruption which destroyed Pompeii... Let us imagine the condition of affairs towards the termination of the Plinian eruption. **1897** I. C. RUSSELL *Volcanoes N. Amer.* i. 16 Following the Plinian eruption Vesuvius became quiet once more.] **1903** A. GEIKIE *Text-bk. Geol.* (ed. 4) I. 278 Three phases of its [*sc.* Vesuvius'] energy are recognised... In the third and most vigorous phase, which has been termed Plinian,.. large volumes of steam, dust, ashes, scoriæ, bombs and blocks are expelled with great violence high into the air and fall around the crater, while occasionally streams of lava issue from rents in the cone. **1944** A. HOLMES *Princ. Physical Geol.* xx. 466 Four days after the paroxysm [of Vesuvius in 1906]—the Vesuvian phase—began, it culminated in a mighty uprush of gases—the Plinian phase..—which continued for the greater part of a day,.. tearing away the upper portions of the cone, and reaching a height of 8 miles. **1965** R. FURNEAUX *Krakatoa* iii. 37 Its occasional 'Plinian' outbursts bring Vesuvius within the same classification as Krakatoa. **1975** FIELDER & WILSON *Volcanoes of Earth, Moon & Mars* iv. 47/2 The pyroclastic blanket could easily be generated by a lunar plinian eruption. **1976** P. FRANCIS *Volcanoes* iii. 114 Probably the best modern example of a Plinian eruption was that of the Bezymianny volcano in Kamchatka.

plink (pliŋk), *v.* [Imit.] **a.** *intr.* To emit a short sharp metallic or ringing sound; to play a musical instrument in this manner.

1941 E. P. O'DONNELL *Great Big Doorstep* 194 A frog plinked, squirmed out, snapped open and away. **1945** B. MACDONALD *Egg & I* (1946) xii. 144 The berries..had begun to plink into the..buckets. **1976** *Gazette* (Montreal) 19 July 3/3 (*heading*) Pianist plinking for Canada. **1979** G. HAMMOND *Dead Game* v. 77 A bullet at full speed plinks like somebody leaned on the lid of a biscuit-tin.

b. *intr.* and *trans.* To shoot a gun *at* a target; to hit (a target) with a shot from a gun.

1966 R. THOMAS *Spy in Vodka* x. 94 It was an ugly gun, [not] designed..for plinking at rabbits. **1975** G. V. HIGGINS *City on Hill* vi. 160 The back was full of rats... I bought an air-pistol..and I'd plink at them. **1976** L. DEIGHTON *Twinkle, twinkle, Little Spy* iv. 41 Goddamned weather... I would have plinked him but for that damned patch of ice.

So **pli·nking** *ppl. a.* and *vbl. sb.*

1961 *Guns & Hunting* Dec. 11/2 You may therefore convert the gun into a small-game and plinking arm. **1965** *Listener* 30 Sept. 507/3 On summer Wednesdays we have supped full of horrors with heartbeats down the corridors, creaking boards, plinking music and plenty of the consequences of over-tidiness, over-mothering, and all that suppressed sex. **1977** J. CLEARY *High Road to China* iv. 139 The General practising his banjo..the plinking of the strings. **1977** R. E. HARRINGTON *Quintain* xiv. 162 Quintain heard a brittle plinking sound that went from a high tone to a low tone. **1978** *Detroit Free Press* 2 Apr. 8E/1 Say you owned a handgun and wanted to take it out for plinking or target practice.

plink (pliŋk), *sb.* [f. the vb.] The sound or action of plinking; a sharp metallic noise. Also quasi-*adv.* and as *int.*

1954 J. R. R. TOLKIEN *Two Towers* viii. 153 And plink! a silver drop falls. **1961** *Amer. Speech* XXXVI. 305 The smaller pebble goes *plink*, the larger, *plunk*. **1971** *Daily Tel.* (Colour Suppl.) 3 Dec. 7/1 No wonder..that the first plink of those conciliatory ping-pong balls produced rapturous applause. **1974** *Times* 7 Mar. 12/4, I cannot dance to electronic music, because I simply do not know how to hear those plinks and plonks and bumps.

plinth. Add: **1. c.** (Further example.) Also, a course of bricks or stones in a wall, above ground level, by which the part of the wall above is made to be set back in relation to the part below; = *plinth course* s.v. sense 3 below.

1968 W. G. NASH *Brickwork* II. v. 112 The golden rule to remember when setting out the bonding for plinth courses and the walling below is to set out the neat work immediately above the plinth course first and let the bonding below the plinth be bonded to suit the neat work. In other words, always bond downwards from the face-work and *not* upwards from the work below the plinth courses.

d. (Further examples.)

1904 R. J. FARRER *Garden of Asia* xvi. 150 That glorious cone towering up into the sky from its plinth of hills. **1935** 'E. QUEEN' *Spanish Cape Mystery* ix. 187 Ellery was sprawled on his side in an uncomfortable position, his eyes glued to a plinth of light.

2*. A shallow wooden cabinet in which a record deck is mounted.

1963 *Hi-Fi Year Bk.* 35 Both the GL58 and GL70 are now available on plinths. **1975** *Gramophone* Sept. 537/2 The model BDS80 is the first of the new BSR Belt Drive Series of transcription turntables; the unit under review was delivered already mounted in a plinth. **1976** *Southern Even. Echo* (Southampton) 2 Nov. 9/2 (Advt.), Pioneer SA5300 amplifier 2 × 12 watts RMS plus Garrard 125SB belt drive turntable, plinth, cover, fitted with Shure M75/6/SM magnetic cartridge.

3. *plinth-like* (example); **plinth block,** a block sited on the floor and forming part of the base of the moulding of a door or window; **plinth course** = sense 1 c above.

1893 J. P. ALLEN *Pract. Building Construction* xviii. 293 Plinth blocks or bases..are often put at the bottom of architraves..for the skirting to run up against, as well as for appearance. **1932** F. L. WRIGHT *Autobiogr.* II. 138 The whole exterior was bedeviled..with corner-boards, panel-boards, window-frames, corner-blocks, plinth blocks, rosettes, fantails, ingenious and jigger work in general. **1873** F. ROGERS *Specifications Pract. Archit.* II. xxv. 375 All plinth courses, jambs of doors and windows, and window-sills, strings, and chimney-cappings to be in red moulded bricks. **1968** Plinth course [see 1 c above]. **1905** *Harper's Mag.* July 195/1 Those short, stubbed girls and women..were of plinthlike bigness up and down.

Pliocene, *a.* (Earlier example.)

1831 [see *EOCENE *a.* 1].

Pliofilm (plɔi·ofilm). Also **pliofilm.** A proprietary name for a type of transparent, waterproof membrane made of rubber hydrochloride and widely used for packaging, waterproofing, etc. Freq. *attrib.*

1934 *Official Gaz.* (U.S. Patent Office) 20 Nov. 537/2 Goodyear Tire & Rubber Company, Akron, Ohio. Filed Sept. 22, 1934. Pliofilm... Claim use since June 28, 1934. **1936** *Trade Marks Jrnl.* 19 Feb. 223/1 Pliofilm... Material in sheets, strips and films manufactured from a composition consisting principally of a derivative of india-rubber. The Goodyear Tire & Rubber Company.., Akron, Ohio, United States of America; manufacturers. **1938** *India Rubber World* XCVIII. III. 47/1 Pliofilm..is being used in direct contact with many food and pharmaceutical items. **1949** *Times* 26 Feb. 3/1 Aero engines and delicate instruments..were contained in Pliofilm envelopes during shipment. **1956** H. GOLD *Man who was not with It* xxxii. 310 Shoppers..wearing rubber or pliofilm galoshes on their shoes. **1961** L. MUMFORD *City in History* xvii. 546 A world in which he is insulated by glass, cellophane, pliofilm from the mortifications of living. **1969** J. H. STICKELMEYER in W. R. R. Park *Plastics Film Technol.* i. 7 'Pliofilm' is produced by adding hydrogen chloride gas to a special grade of natural crude rubber in benzene solution. **1974** H. MCCLOY *Sleepwalker* v. 73 All these furs were..in dry cleaner's pliofilm bags.

Plio-Pleistocene (plɔi:oplɔi·stǒsīn), *a. Geol.* [f. PLIO(CENE *a.* (*sb.*) + PLEISTOCENE *a.* (*sb.*).] Of or pertaining to the end of the Pliocene and the beginning of the Pleistocene epochs, or the Pliocene and Pleistocene epochs together. Also *absol.*

1929 *Q. Jrnl. Geol. Soc.* LXXXV. 520, I am the more inclined to look on the remarkable conglomerate of Wadi Abu Nefukh..as of the late Pliocene or Plio-Pleistocene age. **1946** F. E. ZEUNER *Dating the Past* v. 135 Reasons have been given..for fixing the Plio-Pleistocene boundary just before the Early Glaciation. **1957** J. K. CHARLESWORTH *Quaternary Era* xl. 1087 The exchange of plants between Asia and North America and the spread of the horse and camel-llama from North America to Asia about the Plio-Pleistocene transition. **1975** *Nature* 4 Dec. 395/1 Plio-Pleistocene lacustrine and fluvial strata exposed along the east side of Lake Rudolf, Kenya, now known as 'East Rudolf', have been under study since 1969. **1977** *Offshore Engineer* May 37/3 Plio-Pleistocene sedimentation could not keep pace, and layers are very thin. **1978** *Nature* 17 Aug. 662/2 In the Plio–Pleistocene of East Africa, the various species of hippo are most common in river channel and lake margin sediments.

pliotron (plɔi·ǒtrǫn). *Electronics.* [f. Gr. πλείω-ν more (see PLEIO-) + *-TRON.] A high-vacuum thermionic valve with one or more grids.

1915 I. LANGMUIR in *Electrician* 21 May 242/2 The term 'Pliotron' has been adopted to designate a Kenotron, in which a third electrode has been added for the purpose of controlling the current flowing between the anode and the cathode. **1918** *Wireless World* July 230 The characteristics of the pliotron depend upon the length of filament used. **1945** COOKE & MARKUS *Electronics Dict.* 278/2 *Pliotron*, a high vacuum thermionic tube in which one or more electrodes (grids) are employed... All amplifier tubes in radio sets are pliotrons, but the term has never gained extensive use. **1971** G. M. & R. D. CHUTE *Electronics in Industry* (ed. 4) x. 167 A third element, called the grid, is placed between the anode and cathode to form a high-vacuum type of triode (also called the pliotron).

plip-plop (plip,plǫp). [Imit.] A representation of a rhythmically regular sequence of sounds. Hence **pli·p-plopping** *a.*

1953 *John o' London's Weekly* 23 Jan. 75/3 Several percussion players produced delicate plip-plops, and three sopranos murmured the vocal line. **1961** *Countryman* Autumn 514 Plip-plop went the donkey's decorously pointing toes. *Ibid.* 516 Then a 'plip-plop'... The donkey..was tittupping round the dustbin. **1979** J. BARNETT *Backfire is Hostile!* xiv. 165 Rain began to fall slowly, in large separate plip-plopping drops.

‖ **plique à jour** (plīk a ʒur). [Fr.] A technique in enamelling in which small areas of translucent enamel are fused into the spaces of a wire framework to give an effect similar to stained glass.

1878 J. H. POLLEN *Anc. & Mod. Gold & Silver Smiths' Work* p. clxii, French writers give this kind of [transparent] enamel the name of 'plite' or 'plique à jour'. **1899** H. CUNYNGHAME *Art-Enamelling* iv. 95 By plique-à-jour we mean filigree-work executed in gold or silver, and filled up with transparent enamels. **1959** *Times* 9 Feb. 10/5 Her work in *cloisonné, plique-à-jour* and *champlevé* won medals and certificates in several countries. **1964** H. HODGES *Artifacts* iii. 63 To do this type of work, plique-à-jour, the areas for the enamel were fretted and given a temporary backing of sheet mica or some similar material to which the enamel would not adhere. **1973** *Country Life* 26 July 250/2 A gold filigree cup with a band of enamel in the exacting technique of *plique-à-jour*. **1975** *Times* 1 Aug. 17/6 A gold, *pliqué* [sic] *à jour* enamel and crystal kaleidoscope jewel made £750... It is an outstanding piece of French nineteenth-century craftsmanship.

plissé (plise), *sb.* and *a.* [Fr., pa. pple. of *plisser* to pleat.] **A.** *sb.* A piece of fabric shirred or gathered into narrow pleats; a gathering of pleats. Also in *Comb.*

1873 *Young Englishwoman* June 286/1 The front width of the skirt is trimmed with a blue plissé, headed with a deep flounce. **1880** [see *GOLD[1] 8 b]. **1920** *Glasgow Herald* 13 Nov. 4 Plissé is the last word in style, and the latest knitted frocks have wide borders done in ribbed work that spring out into plissés. **1954** *Sun* (Baltimore) 8 May 5 (Advt.), Glamour gown... Made of Strat-o-Sheer plisse. **1969** *Sears Catal.* Spring/Summer 11 Cool, comfortable Plissé-textured Pajamas of 80% cotton, 20% polyester.

B. *adj.* Formed into small pleats.

1875 [see *elbow-sleeve* s.v. *ELBOW *sb.* 5]. **1895** *Montgomery Ward Catal.* Spring & Summer 12/2 Printed plisse silk, 20 inches wide. This is the newest idea in gauffre or crinkled silks... It is a small, crinkly stripe pattern in white grounds over which is printed..floral designs. **1928** *Times* 9 May 10/6 A train of lime green and silver tissue, lined with plissé chiffon. **1962** J. T. MARSH *Self-Smoothing Fabrics* iv. 40 Combinations of various factors are capable of disguising creases, as in crepes, seersuckers and plissé fabrics, but other combinations may accentuate the crease. **1967** SINGHA & MASSEY *Indian Dances* xv. 130 Over these they wore plissé skirts made of stiff material in three tiers the longest of which reached several inches above the knee.

plock (plǫk), *sb.* [Imit.] A sharp click or report, as of one hard object striking another.

1936 C. DAY LEWIS *Friendly Tree* xii. 173 The cries of the boys, the curt shouts of the masters, the plock as bat met ball—all these sounds were somehow unsynchronized. **1969** H. R. F. KEATING *Inspector Ghote plays Joker* xvi. 210 From the lit table there came the soft double plock of one of the balls striking the other two. **1976** G. EWART *No Fool* II. 61 The plock of bat on ball penetrates outfields, calming to the mind.

plock (plǫk), *v. rare.* [Imit.: cf. prec.] *intr.* To make a sound as of taut fabric being pierced.

1931 V. SACKVILLE-WEST *All Passion Spent* II. 161 Sitting down by her, as her needle plocked in and out of her embroidery, he would gaze fondly at her bent head.

plod, *sb.*[1] Add: (Further examples.) Also with alliterative reduplication, as *plod-plod.*

1899 N. B. TARKINGTON *Gentleman from Indiana* xv. 266 What was there left but the weary plod, plod, and dust of years? **1926** *Blackw. Mag.* Apr. 519/2 The angles of the rungs become very painful under the slow plod-plod of the horse's movement. **1972** *Times Lit. Suppl.* 9 June 654/2 This plod-plod of approach and application isn't novel. **1975** M. BRADBURY *Hist. Man* ix. 148 The agenda has grown longer..a routine plod through matters of budgets..and examinations. **1979** *Guardian* 23 Oct. 15/8 Those who found the book a bit of a plod but hoped the screen might set it up.

plod (plǫd), *sb.*[2] *Austral.* [perh. PLOP *sb.* influenced by PLOT *sb.*: see PLOD *v.* 4.] **a.** A (particular) piece of ground worked by a miner. Also, a work sheet with information relevant to this.

1941 BAKER *Dict. Austral. Slang* 55 *Pitching the plod*, 'the exchange of words' between miners 'on the state of the ground when coming on or going off shifts'. **1948** K. S. PRICHARD *Golden Miles* 72 He had to go to the office for his plod—the card on which he filled in particulars of the work he was doing, its position in the mine, and the hours he was working.

b. A story or yarn; an excuse.

Plod is entered in the *Eng. Dial. Dict.* as a Cornish word meaning 'a short or dull story; a lying tale'.

1945 G. CASEY *Downhill is Easier* 136 'I suppose he told you the whole plod?' I sneered. **1954** T. A. G. HUNGERFORD *Sowers of Wind* 241 That's the plod he put up, anyway. **1975** X. HERBERT *Poor Fellow my Country* III. xxi. 1126 Put in a plod for me, mate.

-ploid (ploid), the ending of *HAPLOID *a.* (and *sb.*) and *DIPLOID *a.*, used to form analogous terms referring to the number of chromosome sets in a cell or organism (as *EUPLOID, *HEXAPLOID, *hyperploid* s.v. *HYPER- IV. *adjs.*); occas. used with prefixed arabic number as 16-*ploid.* [*haploid, diploid* f. Gr. ἁπλόος single (also ἁπλοΐς, -ΐδος and ἁπλο-ειδής, f. εἶδος form), διπλόος double; the *-id* in these words Strasburger (*Progresses Rei Bot.* (1907) I. 137), their coiner, connected with *id, idant,* and *idioplasm* (f. Gr. ἰδιο-: see IDIO-).]

1928 *Hereditas* X. 245 Lately Blackburn.., investigating chromosome numbers in *Silene*, has described two races of *Silene ciliata* differing in chromosome number, the one being tetraploid (as compared with most other *Silene*-species), the other 16-ploid.

ploidy (ploi·di). *Biol.* [f. *HA)PLOIDY, *POLY)PLOIDY, etc.] The number of homologous sets of chromosomes in a cell, or in each cell of an organism.

1947 *Genetics* XXXII. 512 A state of indefinite 'ploidy'. **1953** *Jrnl. Gen. Microbiol.* VIII. 101 Another possibility is that there is a different degree of effective ploidy of the F+ and F− gametic cells, the F− gametic cell having a higher degree of ploidy (or, possibly, more nuclei) than the F+. **1961** *Lancet* 5 Aug. 318/1 All metaphases have been analysed. When an exact account was impossible the ploidy level has been estimated. **1970** *Watsonia* VIII. 140 As most of our counts are approximate the ploidy level rather than the chromosome number is given. **1976** *Nature* 29 Apr. 785/2 To confirm the ploidy, both strains were grown axenically and their chromosomes were stained.

plomb, var. *PLOMBE.

plombage (plǫmbā·ʒ). *Surg.* [a. F. *plombage* filling of teeth, f. *plomber* to fill, apply lead to (f. *plomb* lead: see PLUMB *sb.*) + *-age* -AGE.] The introduction of plombe into the cavity of the chest; treatment with plombe.

1933 *Tubercle* XV. 97 (*heading*) The operation of plombage in pulmonary tuberculosis. *Ibid.* 98 Before plombage could be considered it was necessary that extrapleural thoracoplasty..should reach a stage of technical efficiency. **1957** P. DUFAULT *Diagnosis & Treatment of Pulmonary Tuberculosis* (ed. 2) xix. 352 Plombage for the purpose of collapsing a limited area in mid-lung has been replaced by wedge resection. **1975** *Amer. Rev. Respiratory Dis.* CXI. 270/1, 13 animals..underwent left pneumonectomy with wax plombage.

plombe (plǫm). *Surg.* Also **plomb.** [a. G. *plombe* seal, filling (of tooth), plombe, f. F. *plomb* lead, lead weight (see PLUMB *sb.*).] (A mass of) soft material inserted into a bone cavity or into the cavity of the chest around a collapsed lung.

1904 *St. Thomas's Hosp. Rep.* XXXII. 433 The material used for bone-plugging (iodoform-knochen plombe)..consists of a mixture of 60 parts of the finest pulverised iodoform and 40 parts each of spermaceti and oil of sesame. **1905** GOULD *Dict. New Med. Terms* 423/2 *Plomb.* ..*P., iodoform* (of Mosetig-Moorhof), an antibacillary agent for filling bone-cavities after operations for tuberculosis or osteomyelitis. **1909** H. PRINZ *Dental Materia Medica & Therapeutics* III. 436 The material advocated by Mosetig..is known in general surgery as 'bone plombe'. *Ibid.*, The plombe must completely fill the cavity. **1931** *Surg., Gynecol. & Obstetr.* LII. 738/2 (*heading*) Sketches showing the effects of paraffin filling (plombe) on a cavity of the left lung. **1956** *Jrnl. Chronic Dis.* IV. 623 The material used in the plomb has varied over the years; currently the most popular material is methyl methacrylate (Lucite) spheres sealed in a polyethylene bag, or folded polyethylene sheets. The plomb is placed between the lung and periosteum centrally and the deperiostealized ribs peripherally. **1965** JENKINS & WOLINSKY in G. L. Baum *Textbk. Pulmonary Dis.* viii. 195/1 Stabilizing the subperiostally freed and collapsed chest wall with some type of plomb.

plombière (plǫmbi,ēr). [f. F. *Plombières-les-Bains*, name of a village in the Vosges Department of eastern France.] A kind of dessert made with ice cream and glacé fruits. Freq. *attrib.* or as *adj.*

1846 A. SOYER *Gastron. Regenerator* 573 Prepare..the..plombière ice... Make a border of patisserie d'amande..upon your dish, in the centre of which put a little of the plombière. **1849** THACKERAY *Pendennis* I. xxiv. 233 The ice was brought in—an ice of *plombière* and cherries. **1907** [see *CROÛTE]. **1958** W. BICKEL tr. *Hering's Dict. Classical & Mod. Cookery* 724 *Plombière*, vanilla ice cream mixed with salpicon of candied fruit macerated in kirsch, filled in parfait mould alternately with apricot jam. **1962** S. BECK et al. *Mastering Art French Cooking* x. 549 (*heading*) Plombières with Fresh Strawberries or Raspberries.

‖ **plongeur** (plǫṅʒör). [Fr.] A boy who is employed as a menial in a restaurant or hotel.

1933 'G. ORWELL' *Down & Out in Paris & London* iv. 32 The whole staff, from the manager down to the *plongeurs*, was working twenty-one hours a day. **1954** J. ATKINS *George Orwell* iv. 94 Why does the *plongeur* exist if his work is largely useless? **1964** *Punch* 1 Apr. 494/1 He'd have to become a dish-washer, or perhaps even a *plongeur*. **1967** G. WOODCOCK *Crystal Spirit* II. v. 100 The world of common lodging-houses..as different from his [*sc.* Orwell's] life among the *plongeurs* as England is different from France. **1976** *Observer* 22 Feb. 22/3 It is over 40 years since George Orwell described a *plongeur's* life in 'Down and Out in Paris and London'. **1977** *Daily Tel.* 18 Mar. 18 Titles are nice but surely the Dorchester is going a little too far advertising for a 'Supervisor Plongeur' to head the washing up department.

plonk (plǫŋk), *v. dial.* and *colloq.* [Imit.: cf. PLUNK *v.* **1. a.** *trans.* To hit or strike with a plonk. Chiefly *dial.*

1874 in A. Easther *Gloss. Dial. Almondbury & Huddersfield* (1883) 103 There were three fighting when you plonked Wells in the face. **1883** A. EASTHER *Ibid.* 102 *Plonk*, to hit plump. Used especially of marbles, when the one shot strikes the other before touching the ground. **1891** *Leeds Mercury Weekly Suppl.* 3 Jan. 8/6 I'll plonk tha. **1896** *Ibid.* 21 Mar. 3/8 Plenk him one o' t'noase if he doesn't shut up. **1903** in *Eng. Dial. Dict.* IV. 549/2 I'll plonk tha, if I get hod on tha. **1925** FRASER & GIBBONS *Soldier & Sailor Words* 225 *Plonk*, to shell. Suggested by the sound of the impact and burst. **1941** *London Opinion* May 64/1, I plonked him good and hearty on the beak.

b. *intr.* To emit or cause something to emit an abrupt vibratory sound, *spec.* in playing a musical instrument. Freq. with *away*.

1927 *Melody Maker* May 489/2 Can you imagine..a saxophone section playing a nice ligato movement and the banjo plonking away for all he is worth..and killing the good work of the saxes. **1976** D. HEFFRON *Crusty Crossed* i. 8 By age three I was plonking away at the piano on my own. **1979** *Stand* XX. IV. 34/1 The band plonks away at sad, slow French and Italian numbers.

2. a. *trans.* To set or drop (something) in position with a heavy or clumsy gesture; to put *down* firmly. Also (with a person or object), to set (someone) abruptly in a particular place or set of circumstances; to seat (someone) hurriedly or unceremoniously. Cf. PLANK *v.* 2 a (in Dict. and Suppl.), *PLUNK *v.* 3 b.

1941 BAKER *Dict. Austral. Slang* 55 *Plonk down*, to put down. Also, 'plonk one's frame into a chair': to sit down. **1946** F. COOZE *Ten Bob Each Way* 22 So next time I plunged I forgot the tip And plonked my all on my own little pick. **1959** *Woman* 16 May 23/2 An officious nurse plonked down a gas and air mask on my face. **1959** *Sunday Times* 17 May 20/4 Jones has been plonked down in Gagland where the jokes are separate from the action and so has small chance of coming out strong as the comic actor we know him to be. **1967** *Spectator* 29 Sept. 358/2 A nasty-looking structure will be plonked down in front of King's Cross, thus ruining its two magnificent archways. **1972** G. DURRELL *Catch me Colobus* vii. 145 Then you'd lead her [*sc.* a piglet] carefully to the pan and she'd plonk both her stubby front feet into it, little hooves widespread, and dig her nose in and guzzle. **1976** P. CAVE *High Flying Birds* ii. 20 A litre bottle of red wine was plonked down on to the counter under my nose. Plonked plonk, in fact. **1977** *Sounds* 9 July 10/4 The 150 press-persons present were ushered into a darkened room, plonked on rows of chairs, told to put headphones on and left to listen.

b. *refl.* and *absol.* To sit (oneself) down heavily or unceremoniously.

1946 U. KRIGE *Way Out* v. 64 Handing them two cigarettes each, I plonked down beside them to tell them the whole story. **1976** M. SPARK *Takeover* xii. 178 Walter now plonked himself, tired from his walk, on the sofa. **1979** *Guardian* 9 Aug. 22/8 They would plonk themselves down, undress..to encourage support for local naturists.

Hence **plo·nking** *ppl. a.*, (*a*) large *dial.*; (*b*) that plonks; *spec.* (see quot. 1950); **plo·nking** *vbl. sb.*; **plo·nkingly** *adv.*

1896 *Leeds Mercury Weekly Suppl.* 21 Mar. 3/8 What a plonkin' hoile tha hes fer a bedrahm. Little Jimmy hes a plonkin' wife. **1903** in *Eng. Dial. Dict.* IV. 550/1 A gurt plonkin' cat. **1950** S. POTTER *Lifemanship* iii. 44 If you have nothing to say, or, rather, something extremely stupid and obvious, say it, but in a 'plonking' tone of voice—i.e. roundly, but hollowly and dogmatically. *Ibid.* 45 'Plonking' of a kind can be made by the right use of quotation or pretended quotation. **1957** *Economist* 5 Oct. 21/2 India, entangled in its own frontier troubles and engrossed with the problem of borrowing from abroad, has lately sounded a little less plonking in its pronouncements on international affairs. **1959** S. CLARK *Puma's Claw* xv. 181 Delivered with a gruff, passionate intensity (Potter would certainly call them plonking) those words always announced our arrival on a summit. **1965** *New Statesman* 19 Mar. 426/2 These reports, so far from being accurate, have been described by one member of the shadow cabinet as 'absolute poppycock', and by another even more plonkingly, as 'balls'. **1969** D. FRANCIS *Enquiry* ii. 31 'The bet was struck,' Gowery said plonkingly, pointing to the ledger. **1977** *Listener* 5 May 591/1 Presented with an argument that..he intended to ignore, Lord Reith would say in a matter-of-fact way: 'I hear you.' It was an admirably plonking rhetorical device. **1977** *Chainsaw* Sept./Oct. 8/2 The singer is accompanied only by electric organ, regular drum beats, and plonking bass.

plonk (plǫŋk), *sb.*[1] [Imit.: cf. prec. and PLUNK *sb.*, *adv.*, *int.*] The sound of or as of one hard object hitting another; a heavy thud. Also as *adv.*, with a plonk, directly, and as *int.* So **plonk-plonk.**

1903 WODEHOUSE *Tales of St. Austin's* 9 There was a beautiful, musical *plonk*, and the ball soared to the very opposite quarter of the field. **1914** *Picture Fun* 26 Dec. 2 He unfortunately pinched it just as the waiter was passing with a tray of ices, and plonk came that kangaroo's hind paws,..bang agin the old chap's tummy! **1920** *Punch* 10 Mar. 199/2 A befogged Zeppelin laid a couple of bombs plonk into the homestead. **1928** *Manch. Guardian Weekly* 15 June 474/1 A patois that sounds like the plonk-plonk of ping-pong balls on a hard table. **1943** H. PEARSON *Conan Doyle* iii. 46 'Plonk' went the gun [*sc.* an airgun], and down went the medal. **1960** *Oxf. Mag.* 28 Apr. 248 (Advt.), The satisfying plonk of *The Observer* falling on the doormat. **1978** M. BIRMINGHAM *Sleep in Ditch* 118, I feel as if I'd thrown off an enormous weight. I hope it hasn't landed plonk on you.

plonk (plǫŋk), *sb.*[2] *colloq.* (orig. *Austral.*). [prob. a corruption of *blanc* in Fr. *vin blanc.*] Cheap wine, or wine of poor quality. Also *attrib.*

Various popular and humorous etymologies, such as that suggested in quot. 1967, are without foundation. Although it may be argued that the word denotes red wine more commonly than it does white wine, the etymology given above is attested by the earliest sources.

[**1919** W. H. DOWNING *Digger Dialects* 52 *Vin blank*, white wine. *Ibid.*, Von blink, a humorous corruption of vin blanc.] **1930** H. WILLIAMSON *Patriot's Progress* IV. 137 Nosey and Nobby shared a bottle of plinketty plonk, as *vin blanc* was called. **1933** *Bulletin* (Sydney) 11 Jan. 12 The man who drinks illicit brews or 'plonk' (otherwise known as 'madman's soup') by the quart does it in quiet spots or at home. **1940** A. L. HASKELL *Waltzing Matilda* 37 Fortified red wine of the kind that inebriates with speed and economy is 'pinky' or 'plonk'. **1941** K. TENNANT *Battlers* ix. 104 'Keep off the plonk,' Thirty-Bob said in an undertone to the Stray. 'They just spilt some on my boot and it burnt a hole.' **1946** D. STIVENS *Courtship of Uncle Henry* 72 Jessie's been on the plonk again... Goes round the wine bars at the Cross. **1949** *Here & Now* (N.Z.) Oct. 9/1 Rows of gaudily-labelled bottles of local 'plonk' stacked on shelves behind the bar. **1950** 'N. SHUTE' *Town like Alice* 322 He asked me if I would drink tea or beer or plonk. 'Plonk?' I asked. 'Red wine,' he said. **1953** A. UPFIELD *Murder must Wait* viii. 76 Mother gallivants about to plonk parties..plonk being Alice McGorr's designation of a sherry party. **1965** *New Statesman* 3 Dec. 873/3, I do not eat in restaurants, travel first-class, or buy fillet steak. But there are cheaper cuts of meat, and wine, though mostly poor plonk stuff in the South, is cheap enough. **1967** *Daily Tel.* 15 Nov. 21/8 Surely the word 'plonk' is onomatopoeic, being the noise made when a cork is withdrawn from the bottle? **1968** *Listener* 1 Aug. 134/3 Over the numerous bars were texts urging moderation and adverts pushing the cheapest and most potent plonk in Britain. **1970** *Times* 23 Mar. 25/5 Sales of his newly introduced Vin Plonque, or 'plonk' in the British vernacular, are soaring. **1973** E. MCGIRR *Bardel's Murder* ii. 29 A Miss Traylor, aged seventy, intelligent and given to plonk. **1976** *Scotsman* 24 Dec. (Weekend Suppl.) 3/6 The author is particularly scathing about Sainsbury's Spanish plonk, but does not mention the same chain's better-than-average range of Hocks and Moselles. **1977** *Time Out* 21 Jan. 3/3 Your review of 'party plonk'..misses out the largest 'chain' of off-licences in London, the independents who belong to no chain. **1979** *Globe & Mail* (Toronto) 25 Aug. 10/6 The only other customer was a construction worker who was buying a bottle of white plonk for about $1.40.

plonk (plǫŋk), *sb.*[3] *R.A.F. slang.* [Origin uncertain.] An aircraftman second class.

1941 *New Statesman* 30 Aug. 218/3 *A.C. Plonk*—Lowest in the R.A.F., aircraftman 2nd class. **1943** C. H. WARD-JACKSON *Piece of Cake* 10 A/C Plonk, aircraftman 2nd class. In 1914–1918 'plonk' was Flanders slang for 'mud'. Hence, an A/C Plonk is an aircraftman literally in the mud or at the bottom—that is, lowest classification of the lowest rank in the R.A.F. **1946** *Slipstream* 62 Another synonym for an A.C.2 is A.C.Plonk. **1949** J. R. COLE *It was so Late* 61, I was only an A.C. plonk at the time.

plonked (plǫŋkt), *a. slang.* [f. *PLONK *sb.*[2] + -ED[2].] Intoxicated, drunk.

1943 *Life* 30 Aug. 70/2 A few badly plonked soldiers blearily unaware of just where they were. **1949** 'THE SARGE' *Excuse my Feet!* 42 George was difficult and Herbert was slightly *plonked*.

plonker (plǫ·ŋkəɹ). *dial.* and *slang.* [f. *PLONK *v.*] **1. a.** Something large or substantial of its kind. *dial.*

1861 C. C. ROBINSON *Dial. Leeds* 386 'A plonker' is an article having extraordinary substance. A piece of woven material unusually thick is 'a plonker'. **1885** *Pudsey Almanack & Hist. Reg.* Mar., Sitha Bill at that young woman's improver; isn't it a plonker? **1898** B. KIRKBY *Lakeland Words* 114 Noo that's a plonker. **1903** *Eng. Dial. Dict.* IV. 550/1 That turnip's a plonker.

b. A shell. *Austral.*

1941 BAKER *Dict. Austral. Slang* 55 Plonker, a shell. Diggers' slang. **1961** PARTRIDGE *Dict. Slang* Suppl. 1226/1 *Plonker*, a (cannon) shell: Australian soldiers': 1939+.

2. (See quot. 1970). *slang.*

1966 J. GASKELL *All Neat in Black Stockings* 72 If she'd been my daughter in fact I'd never have let her go out with an obvious plonker like myself. **1970** *Sunday Truth* (Brisbane) 13 Sept. 36/2 Do you know what a plonker is? —It's a chap who shares his ladyfriends with his mate.

plonko (plǫ·ŋko). *Austral. slang.* [f. *PLONK *sb.*[2] + *-O[2].] One who is addicted to 'plonk'.

1963 A. MARSHALL *In Mine Own Heart* 187 You end up a plonko with bells ringing in your head. **1965** W. DICK *Bunch of Ratbags* 69 We could go and see if there's any plonkos under Martin's Bridge and chuck rocks at 'em.

ploot. = *PLUTE.

1931 E. POUND *Let.* 6 Oct. (1971) 235 The only person in Amurikuh who *cd.* continue your periodical is Marianne. The necessary irreproachable respectability, the that against which no lousy ploot can object on the grounds of her not bein' a lady or bein' likely to pervert the growing school child, etc... Marianne has experience—quality dear to the cautious ploot. **1955** —— *Classic Anthol.* II. 106 Folk with no salary The heavens swat, while ploots can manage And the 'outs' cannot. **1959** —— *Thrones* 67 Ultramontaines Bitched France and then Austria, aristos are ignorant Plus illiteracy of the ploots.

plop, *sb.* and *adv.* Add: **A.** *sb.* (Later examples.) Also in *transf.* and extended uses.

1941 *Sun* (Baltimore) 4 Nov. 10/7 'Plops', the sound heard when 'p' or 'b' is spoken too loudly. **1965** *Wireless World* Aug. 379/2 Another effect is the possibility of a 10W 'plop' when switching on the power supply. **1967** P. A. PINCKNEY *Painting in Texas* v. 77 They might even hear the plop of acorns or pecans falling from trees along the creek. **1969** A. GLYN *Dragon Variation* vi. 171 The gas fire went out with a plop. **1974** HARVEY & BOHLMAN *Stereo F.M. Radio Handbk.* v. 104 The system is arranged so that the audio mute is activated before the i.f. mute and this staggering of the two muting levels reduces the edge-of-station 'plop'. **1979** W. NELSON *Minstrel Code* ix. 77 The automatic..was so silent that even the characteristic 'plop' of a silencer had been eliminated.

C. As first element in various alliterative combinations, as *plop-plop*, *plop-plump*, etc. Chiefly as *adv.* or *int.*

1893 'A. HOPE' in *Westm. Gaz.* 9 Dec. 2/1 Miss Phaeton flicked Rhino, and the groom behind went plop-plop on the seat. **1921** *Blackw. Mag.* Feb. 198/2 There is something peculiarly gratifying in the sound of the plop-plump of your naked feet in the round shallow pools of muddy water. **1922** JOYCE *Ulysses* 552 Whispering lovewords murmur liplapping loudly, poppysmic plopslop. **1928** J. M. BARRIE *Peter Pan* III. 75 There are many mermaids here, going plop-plop, and one might attempt to count the tails.

plop, *v.* Add: **1.** (Further examples in causative sense.) Also *refl.* and with *down*. Also *fig.*

1900 E. GLYN *Visits Eliz.* 66, I do hate to see a great hand..plopping a dish down..in the middle, so that one has to look at the next course all the time one is finishing the last one. **1960** V. NABOKOV *Invitation to Beheading* iii. 37 Emmie was gazing after them, while she lightly plopped the glossy red and blue ball in her hands. **1971** *Angling Times* 10 June 6/2, I plopped that lot under a bridge..and cheerfully expected to net every eel that passed downriver that night. **1975** A. BERGMAN *Hollywood & LeVine* vi. 71 She plopped herself comfortably onto the couch. **1975** *New Yorker* 28 July 8 (Advt.),

Something happens at The Biltmore that just doesn't happen in those plasti-glass, modular hotels that have plopped themselves down in every city in the country.

2. *intr.* To emit a sound or series of sounds suggestive of plopping.

1927 C. CONNOLLY *Let.* 4 Jan. in *Romantic Friendship* (1975) 207, I got very depressed on Sunday evening and thought of..gas mantles plopping in evening chapel. **1972** R. ADAMS *Watership Down* III. xxxviii. 316 All the surface of the river was winking and plopping in the rain.

plosh[1]. (Examples.)

1868 J. C. ATKINSON *Gloss. Cleveland Dial.* 385 *Plosh* sb., puddle, liquid mire, like the sloppy mud on a road after much rain. **1895** J. THOMAS *Randigal Rhymes* 22 Nor don't ee lag, or stag yourself By stanking through the plosh. **1930** H. WALPOLE *Rogue Herries* III. 495 He found himself in the little dark wood,..his feet in plosh and mire.

plosh[2], var. PLASH *sb.*[2]

1876 C. C. ROBINSON *Gloss. Dial. Mid-Yorks.* 103/2 *Plosh* is much more heard than 'plodge', and, as a substantive, bears relation to an object as well as an action. *Plosh* is anything of the nature and consistency of a puddle, into which, if a hasty foot be placed, or a stick let fall, there results a *plosh*. **1928** BLUNDEN *Undertones of War* 138 The plosh of the whizzing fuse-top into the muck. **1935** S. DESMOND *African Log* xlii. 208 'To listen to the silence of the forest', to hear the plosh in the dried herbage of the grasshoppers.

‖ **ploshchadka** (plǫʃtʃa·dkă). *Archæol.* Pl. **ploshchadki.** [Russ., = ground, area, platform.] In Ukrainian sites of the Neolithic period, a raised area or platform, *spec.* one formed of burnt clay from the debris of collapsed buildings.

1913 E. H. MINNS *Scythians & Greeks* vii. 134 The first finds were made about the village of Tripolje on the Dnêpr forty miles below Kiev, whence this is called the Tripolje culture. The remains consist of so-called 'areas' (*ploshchádka*). **1923** *Nature* 26 May 726/1 The painted pottery comes either from large rectangular structures of wattle and daub called *ploshchadky* or from huts partly hollowed out in the earth. **1928** C. DAWSON *Age of Gods* iii. 56 The clay figures..are found in Russia chiefly on the site of the curious buildings or platforms known as 'ploshchadki', which seem to have had a religious object. **1940** C. F. C. HAWKES *Prehist. Foundations of Europe* vi. 236 The Kiev region, where the peasants..made also.. rectangular structures ('ploshchadki') whose remains are always found burnt, without as yet any agreed explanation. **1957** V. G. CHILDE *Dawn Europ. Civilization* (ed. 6) viii. 137 The houses of later phases are represented by the celebrated *ploščadki*, areas of baked clay resulting from the burning and collapse of walls and floors.

plosion (plōu·ʒən). *Phonetics.* [f. Ex)PLOSION.] The eruption of breath involved in uttering a plosive. Hence **plo·sional** *a.*, of or pertaining to plosion.

1918 D. JONES *Outl. Eng. Phonetics* viii. 37 (*heading*) Faucal Plosion...Lateral Plosion. **1932** G. E. FUHRKEN *Standard Eng. Speech* vi. 71 Nasal plosion is avoided if awkward combinations of consonants would result. **1935** B. TRNKA *Phonol. Analysis Present-Day Stand. Eng.* 6 In the system of English consonantal phonemes there are two correlations, namely those of 1. voice and 2. plosion. **1946** [see *ARTICULATOR 4]. **1961** L. F. BROSNAHAN *Sounds of Lang.* viii. 185 Consonants, produced primarily by plosional, frictional, or vibratory interference with the air stream. **1964** [see *ALVEOLARITY].

plosive (plōu·ziv), *sb.* and *a. Phonetics.* [f. Ex)PLOSIVE *a.* and *sb.*] **A.** *sb.* A consonantal sound in the formation of which the passage of air is completely obstructed and then suddenly released. **B.** *adj.* Of or pertaining to a plosive.

1899 W. RIPPMANN tr. *Viëtor's Elem. Phonetics* 12 The passage may be completely closed. The breath is stopped for a moment..; but then it bursts through the obstacle with a little explosion. The result is a (voiced or voiceless) *stop* (or plosive or explosive). **1902** E. W. SCRIPTURE *Elem. Exper. Phonetics* xxix. 445 The *Association Phonétique Internationale* classifies and represents the consonants in the following way... Plosive [etc.]. **1909** D. JONES *Pronunc. of Eng.* 65 When we try to pronounce a breathed plosive, e.g. p, by itself, it is generally followed by a short breathed sound h. *Ibid.*, The explosion of a plosive consonant is formed by the air as it rushes out at the instant when contact is released. **1933** L. BLOOMFIELD *Language* vi. 97 If we place the tongue or the lips (or the glottis) so as to leave no exit, and allow the breath to accumulate behind the closure, and then suddenly open the closure, the breath will come out with a slight pop or explosion; sounds formed in this way are *stops* (*plosives, explosives*), like our unvoiced [p, t, k] and our voiced [b, d, g]. **1961** *Amer. Speech* XXXVI. 220 Influence of preceding consonants negligible; that of following consonants, considerable. Vowels shorter before voiceless consonants than before voiced counterparts, before plosives than before fricatives. **1968** W. S. ALLEN *Vox Graeca* 2 If the speech-organs form a complete closure, during which air is prevented from passing until the closure is released, the resulting sound is termed a 'stop'. Stops are further subdivided into 'plosives' and 'affricates'. **1968** CHOMSKY & HALLE *Sound Pattern Eng.* 321 Thus of the three nonnasal types with plosive efflux, one is aspirated and the other two are nonaspirated. **1968** J. LYONS *Introd. Theoretical Linguistics* iii. 104 If the obstruction in the air passage is complete, the resulting sounds are described as *stops* (or plosives). **1973** *Studies in Eng. Lit.: Eng. Number* (Tokyo) 20 The plosive sound in 'priest' in the third line is repeated in the succession of plosives, 'bound, brave, peril, doomed', in the fourth line. **1976** *Archivum Linguisticum* VII. 19 The Basque is not geminated, so if we wish to postulate that *sapo* had become a Castilian word before the intervocalic plosives had generally voiced, we might even be reduced to calling it 'culto'.

plot, *sb.* Add: **II. 3.** Delete '*Obs.* or *arch.* exc. in *U.S.*' and add further examples.

1899 MIDDLETON & CHADWICK *Treat. Surveying* I. iv. 146 It is often desirable to make a preliminary plot, as work progresses, to see how the work comes in. **1931** M. HOTINE *Surv. from Air Photogr.* ix. 159 The minor control plot is the foundation of all subsequent detail plotting and will repay time and care spent on its construction. **1942** *R.A.F. Jrnl.* 13 June 11 Frequent advice from the plot was called for as to the safe course to steer. **1962** *Times* 22 Mar. 14/7, I had no idea where I was as there was no automatic plot in my ship and we had been too busy to keep an accurate reckoning. **1971** R. J. P. WILSON *Land Surveying* ii. 45 Once the pencil plot has been completed and checked the chain survey network of lines..is inked in. **1973** H. GRUPPE *Truxton Cipher* xv. 154 Is it not standard procedure for the Combat Information Center to keep a plot of the ship's movements?

c. *Theatr.* A scheme or plan indicating the disposition and function of lighting and stage property in a particular production.

1883 D. COOK *On Stage* I. x. 219 The property-maker is duly furnished with a 'plot' or list of articles required of his department. **1949** T. RATTIGAN *Harlequinade* 56 The lighting for this scene has gone mad. This isn't our plot. There's far too much light. *Ibid.* 57 Check your plot, please. **1959** W. C. LOUNSBURY *Backstage from A to Z* 91 *Plot*, a floor plan or cue sheet or both, indicating location of lights, furniture, props, etc. Light plots, furniture plots, and prop plots should be made by the person responsible for each field, and notations of cues and changes should be clearly indicated.

d. A diagram showing the relation between two variable quantities each measured along one of a pair of axes usu. at right angles; = GRAPH *sb.*[1] 2 in Dict. and Suppl.

1912 *Jrnl. Amer. Chem. Soc.* XXXIV. 462 And reading from this plot by extrapolation to $C\Lambda = 0$, the value of $1/\Lambda_0$. **1947** E. E. WAHLSTROM *Ign. Minerals & Rocks* viii. 240 (*caption*) Harker plot of analyses in Table 6. **1953** E. R. PECK *Electricity & Magnetism* ix. 279 Sometimes it is of interest not only to use the ratio B/H, but to plot in detail the B–H curve. Such plots are basic in the discussion of ferromagnetism. **1971** *Physics Bull.* Feb. 86/1 A ln σ against $1/T$ plot should, at the temperature of conversion, exhibit a change of slope.

e. *R.A.F. slang.* A group of enemy aircraft as represented on a radar screen.

1943 P. BRENNAN et al. *Spitfires over Malta* 44 We warned the new boys to be careful, as it was probably a big plot coming in and they would be certain to bomb Ta-kali. **1959** R. COLLIER *City that wouldn't Die* vii. 109 Every radar station reported a mass plot and the planes flew too high for visual checks.

IV. 8. (in sense 2) *plot-owner*; (in sense *3e) *plot-room*; (in sense 6) *plot-formula, -interest, -seller, -source, -spinning, -structure*; (in sense 7) *plot-maker*; **plot-line,** (*a*) the main features of a plot or story; a summary; (*b*) (see quot. 1961); **plot-ratio,** a ratio representing the density of building in a specified area of land (see quot. 1971).

1957 N. FRYE *Anat. Criticism* 52 We may think of our romantic, high mimetic and low mimetic modes as a series of *displaced* myths, *mythoi* or plot-formulas. **1865** *Fortn. Rev.* 15 Dec. 354 The distinctive element in Fiction is that of plot-interest. The rest is vehicle. **1866** H. SIDGWICK in A. & E. M. Sidgwick *Henry Sidgwick* (1906) 143 The plot-interest does not turn entirely on amativeness. **1961** M. MCCARTHY *On Contrary* (1962) 290 The chief plot interest in these books is to try to find out what happened before the book started. **1965** K. GRAHAM *Eng. Criticism of Novel* iv. 99 By 1883..his [*sc.* Wilkie Collins's] brand of plot-interest was..out-moded. **1957** J. D. SALINGER *Zooey* in *New Yorker* 4 May 33/3 The plot line [*sc.* of 'a sort of prose home movie']..is largely the result of a rather unholy collaborative effort. **1961** BOWMAN & BALL *Theatre Lang.* 267 *Plot line*, usually in the plural: Dialogue essential to the unfolding of the plot of a dramatic piece. **1962** *John o' London's* 12 Apr. 363/1 Its [*sc.* a film's] plot-line has the same grotesque implausibility. **1972** P. H. KOCHER *Master of Middle-Earth* iv. 57 Like Greek drama or Miltonic epic which begin late along their plot lines, *The Lord of the Rings* begins just before the climax of Sauron's efforts to subdue the West. **1976** S. HYNES *Auden Generation* viii. 294 The main plot-line concerns an indigent painter..whose only completed picture..is seized by bailiffs. **1961** *Encounter* Apr. 71/1 Either Querry is right, or God is a plot-maker, working through his inferior priests,..ready to use any degree of absurdity..to get His own way. **1907** *Daily Chron.* 3 June 3/6 An association of..plot-owners has been formed for the purpose of improving their position. **1956** *Archit. Rev.* CXIX. 46 The main area of the site is developed according to the plot-ratio of 5:1 laid down by the City Corporation. **1958** *Listener* 23 Oct. 642/2 Plot ratios and daylight factors are now everyday tools at the disposal of the designer; only a decade ago such logical aids did not exist. **1971** P. GRESSWELL *Environment* 81 The density of business and commercial areas is usually expressed by total floor space of the buildings divided by the area of the site, called 'floor space index' when local access roads are included, and *plot ratios* when they are not. **1973** *Geo. Abstr.* F. 65 The development of secondary dwelling areas should be subordinated to an overall objective for total land use intensity and the relation between gross and net plot ratios, together with the proportion of open space that is derived from this. **1978** *N.Y. Rev. Bks.* 23 Feb. 4/2 Leslie Martin, the most influential architectural teacher,..has for years pointed out that a far more effective use of a plot ratio can be devised than tower blocks. **1947** *Times* 3 Feb. 6/6 Below in the plot rooms radar engineers checked their screens for the position of the Home Fleet and exchanged bearings with the navigating officers. **1938** O. SITWELL *Trio* 60 The well-known plot-seller, Mr. X. Y. Z., is at present planning a new financial coup. **1885** J. O. HALLIWELL-PHILLIPPS *Outl. Life Shakes.* (ed. 5) 566 The subtle devices..some of which..may be equally observed..in the original plot-sources of his dramas. **1962** *Times* 24 Apr. 14/7 Passages of plot-spinning conversation. **1957** N. FRYE *Anat. Criticism* 207 The source of tragic effect must be sought.. in the tragic mythos or plot-structure. **1962** *Punch* 11 July 65/1 A good film..can hide even the most elaborate plot-structure by superficial casualness and naturalism. **1977** *Dædalus* Fall 107 Work on plot structure, the goal of which is a grammar of plots, has been carried out in many countries.

plot, *v.*[1] Add: **1. a.** *to plot* (one quantity) *against, versus*, etc. (another): to draw a graph in which ordinates (*y*-coordinates) represent values of the first quantity and abscissas (*x*-coordinates) represent those of the second.

1910 *Jrnl. Amer. Chem. Soc.* XXXII. 1015 The method of procedure employed has been to plot the values obtained by each observer for $\Delta t/N$ as ordinates against those of log N as abscissas. **1934** *Proc. R. Soc.* A. CXLV. 576 This would be shown clearly if the density were plotted against the logarithm of exposure, as is usually done for photographic plates. **1952** J. P. CASEY *Pulp & Paper* II. xvi. 825 Stress-strain curves can be plotted as load scale reading versus angular deflection. **1976** *Sci. Amer.* Dec. 93/1 Data from spectrophotometry..enable one to plot the supernova's change in radius with respect to time.

b. Delete *rare* and add earlier and later examples.

1863 H. S. MERRETT *Pract. Treat. Sci. Land & Engin. Surveying* II. 124 For practical purposes, surveys should never be plotted to a less scale than three or four chains to the inch. **1906** BREED & HOSMER *Princ. & Pract. Surveying* I. xv. 397 The field maps of the U.S. Coast and Geodetic Survey are usually plotted on a scale of 1/10000. **1923** D. CLARK *Plane & Geodetic Surveying* II. vi. 244 In plotting the map, the distances and elevations required must be obtained from the perspective dimensions on the photographs. **1963** W. K. KILFORD *Elem. Air Survey* xi. 240 The radial-line plotter makes it possible to plot a map from the model formed in an ordinary mirror stereoscope. **1976** J. B. GARNER et al. *Surveying* ii. 21 When the survey has been plotted it should, if possible, be checked visually on the ground.

2. a. (Further examples.) Also *fig.*

1915 W. HOLT *Beacon for Blind* xiv. 140 When a proposed party was being plotted out he would say, 'Oh, don't ask the So-and-so's, they are such frumps'. **1928** *Oxford Poetry* 9 And, a week later, still, by plotting out The course of all the roadways round about 'In these some score of places he may be'. **1969** D. WIDGERY in Cockburn & Blackburn *Student Power* 130 The next period is worth some examination to plot out the Executive's responses to a fluid situation.

c. *Theatr.* (See *PLOT *sb.* 3 c.) To plan or devise (a stage production); to arrange lighting and stage property for (a production).

1933 P. GODFREY *Back-Stage* iv. 44 The amount of work [for the stage-manager] involved in organizing and plotting the complete stage arrangements for a simple play with a few changes of scene is considerable. **1974** *Times* 28 Dec. 7/3 At read-throughs and when you're plotting it [*sc.* a play], you stand there trembling..behind your script.

5. Delete † *Obs.* and add later examples. Also *absol.*

1943 *Writer* V. 99/1 Plotting problems are usually the chief difficulties fiction-writers have to face. **1951** F. BROWN *Murder can be Fun* x. 138 There's a big difference in plotting soap operas and plotting magazine stories. **1962** *Listener* 30 Aug. 311/2 In *A Burnt Out Case* he [*sc.* Graham Greene] had kept the plotting simple, but it seemed somehow too strong all the same; 'perhaps it would have seemed less plotted if there had been more plot.' **1973** *Daily Tel.* 15 Mar. 8/5 The story is confusingly plotted. **1977** *Ibid.* 10 Sept. 7/2 Mrs Robins plots better but relies a bit much on coincidence.

plotch (plǫtʃ), *v. rare*—[1]. [Perh. f. PLOTCH *sb.*, or imit.] *trans.* To splash on to, to mark.

1922 JOYCE *Ulysses* 745 All the mud plotching my boots.

Plotinian, *a.* (Earlier and later examples.)

1791 W. ENFIELD *Hist. Philos.* II. III. ii. 69 We shall trace the progress of the Plotinian, or Eclectic, school. **1969** T. F. TORRANCE *Theol. Sci.* i. 18 This was the Augustinian doctrine of the sacramental universe, combining Plotinian and Ptolemaic notions in a 'Christian' cosmology.

Plotinist. (Earlier example.)

1871 J. S. MILL in *Fortn. Rev.* X. 524 A heap of useless and mostly unintelligible jargon, not of his own [*sc.* Berkeley's] but of the Plotinists.

plotless, *a* Add: **1.** (Further examples.)

1926 in C. Bailey *Mind of Rome* I. 167 Semi-dramatic productions, improved on the formal side but still plotless, became an established diversion. **1971** *Homes & Gardens* Sept. 134/1 Her story reads like a charming but plotless novel. **1979** A. CHISHOLM *Nancy Cunard* viii. 76 *Antic Hay*..is a deliberately plotless picture of..amusing, erratic, fundamentally desperate characters.

2. *Ecol.* Of a method of ecological sampling: not based on a defined unit of area.

1957 P. GREIG-SMITH *Quantitative Plant Ecol.* ii. 46 Considerable attention has recently been paid to a method of plotless sampling, particularly adapted to forest vegetation, where there are practical difficulties in delimiting the relatively large quadrats necessary for sampling trees. **1974** MUELLER-DOMBOIS & ELLENBERG *Aims & Methods of Vegetation Ecol.* vii. 99 Plotless sampling means sampling without such a prescribed area unit. Plotless methods are available for all three commonly used quantitative parameters.

Plott (plǫt). The surname of Jonathan *Plott* (fl. 1750–80) and his descendants, used *attrib.* in **Plott hound** to designate a hunting dog belonging to a breed developed by this family from hounds brought from Germany to North Carolina in 1750, characterized by a smooth, dark brown coat, often with a black saddle or white feet, and large, drooping ears; it has long been used for bear and boar hunting in North Carolina and Tennessee, and recently the breed has become more widely known.

1945 C. L. B. HUBBARD *Observer's Bk. Dogs* 202 Plott Hound. Although this breed is not yet given official status by the American Kennel Club, it is fairly popular among sporting men in the U.S.A... Mr. Geo. L. Gilkey of Wisconsin is piloting the modern Plott to popularity. **1949** H. P. DAVIS *Modern Dog Encycl.* 466/2 The present demand for Plott Hound stock is far in excess of the supply. **1969** E. H. HART *Encycl. Dog Breeds* 257 The Plott Hound differs from all other hounds in colouring for he is a brindle dog with a black saddle. **1976** E. M. SCHULER *Dog Lover's Answer Bk.* II. 358 The Plott hound is a heavy-set, well-muscled dog with large ears.

plottable (plǫ·tăb'l), *a.* [f. PLOT *v.*[1] + -ABLE.] That may be plotted, in the various senses of the verb.

1968 A. L. ALLAN et al. *Pract. Field Surveying & Computations* ix. 456 The misclosure of a tacheometric traverse should always be within the plottable error of the plan and no adjustment is permitted. **1972** C. MUDIE *Motor Boats & Boating* 116 Voyages out of sight of land only extend the distances between plottable positions and it is quite difficult nowadays to get out of range of the radio navigation beacons. **1976** S. R. SIMPSON *Land Law & Registration* viii. 145 The boundaries could only be replaced to the plottable accuracy of the map.

plottage (plǫ·tėdʒ). [f. PLOT *sb.* + -AGE.] **1.** Phr. *a mess of plottage*, used disparagingly of theatrical productions (by analogy with *a mess of pottage*: see MESS *sb.* 2 a).

1937 *Sun* (Baltimore) 7 Aug. 4/1 '*The Big Shot*', now showing at the Hippodrome Theater, is just another mess of plottage that some RKO Radio writers sold their birthrights for. **1958** *Spectator* 22 Aug. 249/3 The London Studio cast manage to make the whole mess of plottage taste mouldier even than it is.

2. The size or value of a specified piece of land, regarded in terms of the area accumulated from its constituent plots. Usu. in *plottage increment* (see quot. 1965).

1939 in WEBSTER Add. **1952** 'VIGILANS' *Chamber of Horrors* 100 *Plottage*, the area of a plot of land. (The deplorable result of an illicit union between *plot* and *acreage*.) **1961** R. U. RATCLIFF *Real Estate Analysis* iii. 52 This value increment resulting from the assembly of a tract [of land] of sufficient size for a more intensive use is termed *plottage*. **1965** L. E. DAVIDS *Dict. Insurance* 162 *Plottage increment*, the increase or appreciation of the unit value resulting from the joining together of smaller lots, parcels, or land units into one large single ownership, the resulting total value being larger than the individual unit values. **1973** *N.Y. Law Jrnl.* 2 Aug. 11/3 A plottage increment of 10 per cent is allowed for an appraised land area of 12,322 square feet.

plotted, *ppl. a.* Add: **3.** (Later examples.) Freq. with advs.

1970 *Daily Tel.* (Colour Suppl.) 11 Aug. 5/2 In our time it has become meaningless to produce a strongly plotted short story like Maupassant's *The Necklace* or a strongly plotted novel like *David Copperfield*. **1978** *Broadcast* 28 Aug. 8/1 Plays which were both tightly plotted and eminently actable. **1979** F. KERMODE *Genesis of Secrecy* v. 113 We are more likely to remember a plotted narrative.

plotter. 1. Delete † *Obs. rare* and add to def.: one who plots points on a map. (Later examples.)

1908 *Geogr. Jrnl.* XXXI. 536 Some central organization at home would be required for plotting the results. This could be done..by a plotter and plotting machine attached to any existing photographic establishment. **1943** 'T. DUDLEY-GORDON' *Coastal Command at War* ii. 17 At a long table sits a W.A.A.F. officer, writing and making calculations. She is the 'plotter'... As the signals pour in..she translates the data into positions and..pin-points the chart, drawing pencil lines which 'lay off' courses of ships and aircraft. **1958** 'P. BRYANT' *Two Hours to Doom* 48 Teams of plotters were at work, drawing in..the X points and target routes of the 843rd Wing. **1976** J. B. GARNER et al. *Surveying* i. 7 The spacing of grid lines should be chosen so that it assists the plotter without becoming predominant on the completed sheet. **1978** *Daily Tel.* 19 Aug. 13 (*caption*) Mrs Vera Shaw, who was a Waaf plotter during the Battle of Britain.

4. An instrument or machine for making plots; *spec.* one for drawing maps or automatically plotting points on them.

[**1908** *Geogr. Jrnl.* XXXI. 544 A stereo-plotter..combines the offices of the stereo-comparator and plotting board.] **1926** R. M. ABRAHAM *Surveying Instruments* x. 174 When the region to be mapped is rugged or mountainous the stereo method in conjunction with a suitable plotter is undoubtedly superior to all others. **1943** A. L. HIGGINS *Elem. Surveying* viii. 102 [With the plane table] angles are not observed in magnitude, as in the case of any goniometer,..such as the compass..and theodolite, but instead are constructed directly, so that the instrument is a goniograph, or angle plotter. **1948** *Rev. Sci. Instruments* XIX. 647/2 (*caption*) An automatic [electric] field plotter. **1959** *Engineering* 27 Feb. 262/2 The additional information derived from the true motion type of presentation is obtained from the movement of a target vessel across the PPI screen... This is not entirely satisfactory so a tube face reflection plotter..was developed. With its aid, true plots of own and several target vessels can be easily kept by the navigator. **1963** [see *PLOT *v.*[1] 1 b]. **1972** *Sci. Amer.* Mar. 2/2 (Advt.), Our 745 flatbed plotter will scribe lines equal to the tolerances and standards of the most skilled mapmaker's hand.

b. An instrument for automatically plotting a graph.

1956 *Proc. Eastern Joint Computer Conf.* 73/2 The Ballistic Research Laboratories have for some time been concerned with the development of a digital plotter capable of absorbing the output of..digital computers used in processing of missible ballistic data. **1970** O. DOPPING *Computers & Data Processing* xi. 172 In some simple plotters, the paper is continuously fed in one direction, while a printing device, directly controlled by the computer, moves at right angle [*sic*] to the direction of paper motion. **1975** *Nature* 16 Oct. 559/2 Engineers, on the other hand, might well set up a mathematical model for a bridge—or an aircraft wing—and use the minicomputer to display on a visual display unit or graph plotter the consequences of certain input data (loading, sizes of beams, or whatever).

5. One who owns a plot of land, a plot-holder.

1927 *Smallholder* 20 Mar. 106/3 Every plotter should pull his weight, not only for his own sake but for the good of the national cause. **1976** D. G. HESSAYON (*title*) Vegetable plotter.

plotting, *vbl. sb.*[1] Add: **b.** *plotting sheet*; **plotting board,** (*a*) a form of drawing board on which the positions or courses of objects may be plotted; (*b*) = *PLOTTER 4 b; **plotting machine,** a machine for automatically plotting maps; **plotting rod,** a long rod made for moving the counters on a plotting table; **plotting table,** (*a*) a large table bearing a small-scale map of a region on which the positions of enemy aircraft may be represented by movable counters or the like; (*b*) = *PLOTTER 4 b.

1903 *Jrnl. U.S. Artillery* Nov.–Dec. 253 A location of a fixed target is thus plotted, the corrections for atmospheric conditions and drift are determined by the ballistic board, the range and azimuth for the gun are determined by relocation on the plotting board, and transmitted to the gun by the gun telautograph. **1908** *Geogr. Jrnl.* XXXI. 544 The position in plan and height of any object can be plotted from readings of the three scales..and corresponding settings on a detached plotting-board. **1957** C. S. FORESTER *Naval War of 1812* 36 There had been exercises with a plotting-board in the Tripoli prison. **1961** S. FIFER *Analogue Computation* II. ix. 300 The Autograf.. is an example of a cylindrical plotting board. In this case the pen is controlled, as before, by one variable, but the moving carriage is replaced by a rotating drum which is driven by the second variable. **1908** Plotting machine [see *PLOTTER 1]. **1963** W. K. KILFORD *Elem. Air Survey* xi. 269 Some firms produce special plotting machines in which the relative orientation is already set for use with a particular pair of short-base cameras. **1977** J. M. SMITH in P. G. J. van Sterkenburg et al. *Lexicologie* 243 Graphical output devices, based on the principles of plotting machines, can be used too. **1948** T. E. WINSLOW *Forewarned is Forearmed* i. 19 The size of a plotting table depends also on the 'stretch' of a plotter provided with a plotting rod. **1963** N. D. SMITH *Royal Air Force* vi. 66 Plotters, using long-handled plotting rods, moved coloured magnetic counters on the large table map. **1926** *Blackw. Mag.* Dec. 830/2 By degrees there appeared on the plotting sheet a series of tiny needle-pricked marks. **1971** R. J. P. WILSON *Land Surveying* viii. 165 The plane table, essentially a drawing board,..carries the plotting sheet. **1943** P. F. M. FELLOWES *Britain's Wonderful Air Force* xiii. 303 At each centre there is a centre room, with a plotting table on which is fitted a squared map. **1960** ROGERS & CONNOLLY *Analog Computation in Engin. Design* ii. 47 When it is desired to plot one variable against another, an *XY* plotting table is used. This unit employs a double servo system to drive a pen along an arm proportional to *Y*, and the arm along the plotting table proportional to *X*. **1968** *Listener* 15 Aug. 196/3 But it was all right to have mixed anti-aircraft batteries, with women tracking the target, and an ATS officer at the plotting table calculating the exact moment to shout the order 'Fire'. **1973** 'A. HALL' *Tango Briefing* xviii. 224 The whole of this area was on the plotting table at the Bureau. **1977** *Navy News* June 8 (*caption*) Prince Philip and Rear-Admiral D. W. Haslam (Hydrographer of the Navy) take a close look at the computer linked automatic plotting table being described by the commanding officer of H.M.S. Hecate.

plotty, *a.* Delete *nonce-wd.* and add earlier and later examples. Also, of a novel, play, or the like: having an elaborate or complicated plot.

1897 'S. GRAND' *Beth Bk.* xl. 405, I would not write plotty-plotty books either. **1898** E. PUGH *Tony Drum* ix. 120 Novels of a common type, plotty and passionate, but gilt-edged with the proprieties. **1934** E. BOWEN *Cat Jumps* 112 So plotty, so damned smart, so careful no one would see us who would remember, a different place every time. **1959** *Times Lit. Suppl.* 25 Sept. 546/5 His Phrygian Slave in the *Orestes*—admittedly a problem—talks a hair-raising amalgam of Wardour Street and hill-billy vernacular. 'God darn him dead For plotty sneaks,' this surprising menial observes at one point. **1973** L. HELLMAN *Pentimento* (1974) 197 What I thought was bite they [*sc.* theatre critics] thought sad, touching, or plotty and melodramatic. **1974** *Times* 18 Apr. 7/5 The basic plot is a bit plotty.

plo·twise, *adv.* [f. PLOT *sb.*[1]: see WISE *sb.*[1] II.] As regards or in terms of a plot (in sense 6 of the sb.).

1955 *Times* 26 May 11/4 We gave what was, plotwise, a perfectly coherent rendering of *Romeo and Juliet* in 20-odd minutes.

plotz (plǫts), *v.* *U.S. slang.* [ad. Yiddish *platsen*, f. G. *platzen* to burst; in sense 1 influenced by G. *platz* place, seat.] **1.** *intr.* To sit down wearily, to flop; to slouch, loaf (*around*). Also *trans.* in causal sense.

1941 A. KOBER *My Dear Bella* 199 At the end of a day I'm just like a wet rag... All I'm good for is to *plotz* in a chair. **1960** J. KIRKWOOD *There must be Pony* vi. 43 He just kind of plotzed around waiting to fall into some sort of a cushy job. **1976** *National Observer* (U.S.) 30 Oct. 20/1, I find there is still little to justify a parent plotzing his offspring in front of the tube for long hours on Saturday morning. **1978** R. CONDON *Bandicoot* xv. 91 We are plotzing one night and I bring out a whole miniature roulette layout.

2. *intr.* To burst; usu. in *fig.* senses, esp. to 'explode' with frustration or annoyance, to demonstrate one's anger.

1967 P. WELLES *Babyhip* iii. 46 'You're not smoking that filthy thing in here. I'll *plotz*,' Mrs Green said. **1968** L. ROSTEN *Joys of Yiddish* 292 So Pincus broke into a run, and he ran and he ran until he thought his heart would *plotz*. **1970** L. M. FEINSILVER *Taste of Yiddish* 367 A recent ad for a Yiddish revue read: 'In Miami they're plotzing'—meaning, 'they're still howling over the preview'. **1978** J. KRANTZ *Scruples* vii. 214 She came back to pick them up today and *plotzed* for joy all over the studio.

plotzed (plǫtst), *a.* *slang.* [f. as prec. + -ED[2].] Intoxicated, drunk.

Not clearly associated with the senses of *PLOTZ *v.*

1962 J. D. MACDONALD *Key to Suite* (1968) ii. 16 If one of our boys gets plotzed, we run him off the team fast before any damage is done. **1974** 'M. ALLEN' *Super Tour* v. 175 Mimi got drunk that night..but something more than liquor knocked her off base... She was so loaded I had to put her to bed, and I know from my own experience that when I am plotzed I go out for the night.

plough, plow, *sb.*[1] Add: **5. h.** Any of various implements for deflecting (e.g. off a conveyor belt or a railway track) material against which they move, or which moves against them; in quots. 1860, 1975, a snow-plough.

1860 CLARK & COLBURN *Rec. Pract. Locomotive Engine* 68/2 In heavy snows, a plough of large size is fitted in front of the engine, to clear the line. *a* **1884** KNIGHT *Dict. Mech.* Suppl. 173/2 Dowling's plow for unloading platform gravel-cars, is a V-shaped implement which has two flaring wings. **1901** M. M. KIRKMAN *Building & Repairing Railways* viii. 333 The Rodgers ballast car dumps the ballast in the center of the track, the last car in train of ballast cars having a plow for cleaning and flanging the track. **1922** F. V. HETZEL *Belt Conveyors & Belt Elevators* viii. 159 In some European boiler houses the bunker is served by a flat belt which runs through a movable carriage equipped with a V-point plow and a two-way chute. **1953** W. W. HAY *Railroad Engin.* xxii. 316 A spreader-type plow follows the unloading operation to spread the ballast where it is needed. **1971** B. SCHARF *Engin. & its Language* xvi. 235 A plough (movable gate) may be provided across the belt so that the conveyor can be unloaded at that point or in order to deflect the material on to another conveyor. **1975** D. PITTS *Target Manhattan* (1976) xxviii. 117, I want your team of plows at Broadway and West 14th.

i. *Coal Mining.* A machine with cutting blades that remove a thin strip of coal when it is hauled along a coal face.

1950 *Trans. Inst. Mining Engineers* CIX. 273 The coal seams in this country are too hard to allow of the plough being successfully used. **1952** *Times* 16 Sept. 3/2 In his report for 1951, published to-day, Mr. G. Hoyle, North-Western Divisional Inspector of Mines, refers to revolutionary developments in mining technique... He instances the use of the plough and stripper for coal getting. **1964** A. NELSON *Dict. Mining* 335 Normally, on a wide face, and working 6 hr, a plough will produce 800 tons and more of coal in a 3 ft thick seam. **1971** *Daily Tel.* 20 Oct. 13/1 Machines, with strange names like Anderton shearers, trepanners, rapid ploughs or Huwood slicers, have replaced men underground.

7. a. *plough-collar, -culture, -horse, -mark, -ox* (later examples).

1908 *Sears, Roebuck Catal.* 137/4 A Southern Plow Collar. Made of heavy cotton duck with leather chafes on the side where the chain or trace attaches to the hame. **1942** W. FAULKNER *Go down, Moses* 255 Plowlines and plow-collars and hames and trace-chains. **1937** R. H. LOWIE *Hist. Ethnol. Theory* viii. 114 Thus was conceived the antithesis of primitive 'hoe-culture' and 'plough-culture', the latter being the exclusive mark of higher civilizations. **1961** L. MUMFORD *City in Hist.* i. 27 Where hoe culture supported hamlets, plow culture could support whole cities and regions. **1539** WYATT *Let.* in R. W. Bailey *Early Mod. English* (1978) 233/1 And I w[i]t[h] much ado apon plow horse In the diepe and fowle way gatt afore that nyght late to loshes. **1573** T. TUSSER *Five Hundreth Points Good Husbandry* xviii, Sedge couers for plow horse, for lightnes of neck. **1744** W. ELLIS *Mod. Husbandman* Jan. xxi. 56, I feed my Plough Horses with these green Thetches. **1817** SCOTT *Rob Roy* II. xiii. 280 There may be pasture aneugh for pleugh-horses, and owsen, and forty or fifty cows. **1880** *Harper's Mag.* Aug. 356/2 The next day the two girls, mounted on the plough horse and mare, followed an old Indian trail. **1911** R. D. SAUNDERS *Col. Todhunter* ix. 118 A wall-eyed plow-horse with his tail full o'cuckle-burs. **1955** W. MOORE *Bring Jubilee* i. 5 He would lay the reins on the plough-horse's back. **1930** W. FAULKNER *As I lay Dying* 125 After a while she went on, stumbling a little on the plow-marks. **1963** *Field Archaeol.* (Ordnance Survey) (ed. 4) 56 A recent excavation has shown round huts..closely associated with plough-marks in underlying sand. **1973** *Nature* 23 Nov. 191/2 Further ambiguity was introduced by the presence of iceberg plough marks around the Rockall bank and evidence of ice-rafted deposition. **1906** KIPLING *Puck of Pook's Hill* 237 Down would come the King's Officers, and take our plough-oxen to haul them [*sc.* guns] to the coast. **1946** E. LINKLATER *Private Angelo* xx. 257 Two pairs of matched plough-oxen arrived in Pontefiore.

8. plough-bullock, (*b*) (later example); also **plough-bullocker;** so **plough-bullocking** *vbl. sb.*; **plough grinding** *Cotton Spinning*, a way of grinding the wires of a cotton card (see quots.); so **plough-ground** *a.*; **plough-line,** (*b*) (earlier, later, and *fig.* examples); also (usu. *pl.*), the reins themselves; **plough pan** *Agric.* [PAN *sb.*[1] 8], a compacted layer in cultivated soil resulting from repeated ploughing; **plough-point** *U.S.*, the first (usu. detachable) share at the front of a plough; **plough-soil,** soil that has been thrown up by ploughing; **plough-stock,** the iron or metal frame of a plough.

1899 A. NUTT in H. Lowerison *Field & Folklore* 63 Certain players, distinguished by scarlet jackets, and known as plough-bullocks or boggins. **1905** *Eng. Dial. Dict.* IV. 552/1 *Plough..-bullockers,..-bullocking.* **1923** E. C. PULBROOK *Eng. Country Life* xiii. 194 At Whitby, the young men come in to celebrate the Plough Stots as of old, and the Plough Bullockers occasionally drive their decorated plough through the villages of Derbyshire, to the detriment of those who refuse largesse. **1838** W. HOWITT *Rural Life of Eng.* II. III. 144 Maying, guising, plough-bullocking, morris-dancing, were gone before.. Methodism appeared. **1892** J. NASMITH *Students' Cotton Spinning* iv. 135 The usual solution of the difficulty is found in the formation of a tooth with a chisel or knife edge, which is presented to the action of the cotton. This is usually obtained by what is called 'plough grinding'—that is, a method of passing between the teeth of the clothing a thin emery disc, which 'ploughs' deeply between them and grinds them on each side until they present a sharp edge to the cotton. **1923** T. THORNLEY *Adv. Cotton Spinning* (ed. 3) ii. 77 The plough grinding of the wire works is really side grinding carried to its most perfect degree, and producing a bevelled effect on each tooth from point to knee. **1965** W. G. BYERLEY et al. *Man. Cotton Spinning* III. vi. 108 In addition to surface- and side-grinding, reference must be made to 'plough-grinding'. This process was devised and patented by an English firm in 1880... The process..was superseded by the side-grinding process. **1896** W. S. TAGGART *Cotton Spinning* I. vi. 176 A is the plough-ground wire, and is formed by grinding the sides away, almost to the bend, by special emery discs. **1923** T. THORNLEY *Adv. Cotton Spinning* (ed. 3) ii. 76 The plough ground tooth is obtained at the wire-making establishment by grinding away the sides of the teeth down to the knee or bend. **1777** *New Jersey Gaz.* 17 Dec. 3/3 Plough-lines, Bed-Lacings,..Sold by Edward Pole,..Burlington. **1886** F. T. ELWORTHY *W. Somerset Word-Bk.* 582 *Plough-lines*, or *plough-guides*,..the cords used as reins. **1935** Z. N. HURSTON *Mules & Men* (1970) I. ii. 54 Y'all lady people ain't smarter *than* all men folks. You got plow lines on some of us, but some of us is too smart for you. **1940** W. FAULKNER *Hamlet* i. 8 One afternoon he was in the store, cutting lengths of plow-line from a spool. **1969** G. E. EVANS *Farm & Village* xi. 126 There they made rope for the plough-lines, the reins or *cords*, as the horsemen invariably called them. **1883** W. T. LAWRENCE *Princ. Agric.* I. 30 By repeatedly ploughing at about the same depth, their downward progress [*sc.* that of roots] is checked by the formation of a hard bottom called a plough-pan. **1924** WATSON & MORE *Agric.* v. 86 Subsoiling is absolutely necessary where a plough-pan has been formed. **1960** *Farmer & Stockbreeder* 19 Jan. 74/1 (*caption*) Years of cultivation at constant depth have resulted in some plough pan. Once this is broken up the crops will have a better chance of establishment. **1856** in G. N. Jones *Florida Plantation Rec.* (1927) 478 Paid Mr. Lem Jones 50 cts. on account of '54 maid by J. Evans for 2 Plow points. **1942** W. FAULKNER *Go down, Moses* 168 The boy first remembered himas sitting in the door of the plantation black-smith shop, where he sharpened plow-points and mended tools. **1967** *Antiquaries Jrnl.* XLVII. 166 Today, the bank and the ditch..have been largely either ploughed flat or masked by comparatively modern accumulations of plough-soil. **1976** C. THOMAS in P. H. Sawyer *Medieval Settlement* II. xii. 149 Site XX is a field bounded by a ditch... Its date of use can be fixed by the dated broken pot sherds, part of the extensive domestic manure incorporated in the plough-soil. **1978** R. BRADLEY *Prehist. Settlement of Britain* 41/2 His argument was based on the foreign stones incorporated in the ploughsoil. **1786** G. WASHINGTON *Diary* 9 Jan. (1925) III. 5 [I] directed them to get me..scantling for Plow stocks. **1865** *Oregon State Jrnl.* 28 Oct. 4/2 Plow Stocks etc., made to order, on short notice. **1940** W. FAULKNER *Hamlet* I. ii. 35 Ab..had snuck the wagon out the back way with the plow stocks and the sorghum mill in it. **1944** T. D. CLARK *Pills, Petticoats & Plows* 276 Centre and rear passageways were blocked with piles of iron plows..plow stocks..and axes.

plough, plow, *v.* Add: **1.b.** Also *fig.*

1901 LD. ROSEBERY in *Times* 20 July 15/5, I must proceed alone. I must plough my furrow alone. **1936** E. WHITE *Wheel Spins* iii. 29 She always ploughed a straight furrow, right to its end. **1977** *Dædalus* Summer 149 In the United States, George Sarton had been plowing a lonely furrow at Harvard's Widener Library for about twenty-five years. **1978** *Lancashire Life* Nov. 39/2 No easy task, with everybody else ploughing the same furrow.

6. b. (Later examples with *through*.)

1952 C. BARDSLEY *Bishop's Move* xi. 119, I almost said 'plough through' the Bible. **1959** *Daily Tel.* 23 July 1/6 The Prime Minister..gave the House the impression that he was ploughing, with as much force and gaiety as he could muster, through an almost impenetrable bog. **1978** P. BOARDMAN *Worlds of P. Geddes* xi. 408 One ploughs through the often complicated sentences of P.G.'s writings of 1926–30.

c. *intr.* Of a road vehicle, train, aeroplane, or the like: to move clumsily or laboriously, usu. at speed; to advance out of control *into* (or *through*, etc.) an obstacle.

1972 *Daily Tel.* 29 Dec. 2/5 A three-coach train was derailed..when it ploughed into a herd of cattle at 60 mph. **1973** *Times* 31 Dec. 5/5 The airliner..ploughed to a halt on the runway. **1976** *Southern Even. Echo* (Southampton) 11 Nov. 16/5 A Southampton lorry driver suffered only cuts and bruises last night when his lorry ploughed through a bridge and plunged 15 feet into a field at Wimborne. **1977** *Evening Gaz.* (Middlesbrough) 11 Jan. 1/9 Police in Cleveland are hunting the driver of a sports car which forced another car to plough into four people.

7. d. *Coal Mining.* To cut (coal) by means of a plough; to push (coal so obtained) away from the face by means of a plough.

1950 *Trans. Inst. Mining Engineers* CIX. 256 The first train of thought was to plough machine-cut coal on to a face conveyor. **1951** H. F. BANKS in E. Mason *Pract. Coal Mining* (ed. 2) I. viii. 123/2 This device carries steel blades which shear or plane off the coal to a limited depth and ploughs it on to the face conveyor. **1964** A. NELSON *Dict. Mining* 335 Hard anthracite is being ploughed with only water infusion to soften the coal.

e. *trans.* To clear (an area) of snow using a snow-plough.

1961 'E. LATHEN' *Banking on Death* (1962) xii. 99 'Don't know why they can't plow these streets,' he muttered as he pulled into the single lane left by the piles of snow. **1978** *Times* 23 Jan. 12/7 There was.. slush and compacted snow on roads the ploughs had not reached. It says much for the authorities in West Virginia..that they had ploughed all but about 40 miles of my route. **1979** J. VAN DE WETERING *Maine Massacre* ii. 12 They may not have plowed the strip..last time... I had to circle while they pushed the old plow around.

9. f. *plough under*: to bury in the soil by ploughing.

1900 *Year-Bk. U.S. Dept. Agric.* 379 If crimson clover is grown, it should be plowed under rather early in the spring to get the best results. **1979** *Country Life* 6 Dec. 2141 The express way will bypass the old road..ploughing under landmarks that meant much to people.

g. *plough back*: to invest (income or profit) in the enterprise from which it emanates.

1930 *Economist* 24 May 1172/2 The extensive resort of American managements to the practice of 'ploughing back earnings into the business' further emphasises this tendency. **1945** *Richmond* (Va.) *Times-Dispatch* 25 Oct. 6/3 The proposed act would limit the annual dividends of such corporations to 6 per cent, requiring that all additional profits would have to be 'plowed back' into re-development. **1949** *Sun* (Baltimore) 26 Jan. 12/3 Profits are being plowed back into industry at unprecedented rates. **1955** *Times* 1 July 17/3 The profits that have accrued from this company have been largely ploughed back for further development and expansion. **1965** *Listener* 23 Dec. 1023/1 It was not long before we had functioning money-raising sweet shops, bargain stores—and the 'Green Dragon'. Profits were all ploughed back. **1970** *Physics Bull.* Mar. 99/2 For the services it renders the Centre charges small fees which are ploughed back into its operations. By this means it is planned to be selfsupporting within three years. **1974** N. FREELING *Dressing of Diamond* 96 We ploughed every penny back for ten years. **1976** *Milton Keynes Express* 30 July 11/4 He would not consider ploughing some of the £4 million back into the services and said he hoped the kitty would increase.

ploughed, plowed *ppl. a.*: also, (in sense *9g) **ploughed-back; ploughed-out,** obscured or destroyed by ploughing; (in sense 9e) **ploughed-up** (in quot. *fig.*). Also (in sense *9g) **ploughing-back** *vbl. sb.*

1920 J. MASEFIELD *Enslaved* 120 From these ploughed-up souls the spirit brings Harvest at last. **1931** *Economist* 18 July 128/1 Reserves against remote contingencies, and those representing the 'ploughing back' of earnings into the business, should be set aside openly. **1944** J. S. HUXLEY *On living in Revol.* xii. 130 This compulsory ploughing-back of any excess profits is essential if the development of the area is to proceed at a reasonable rate. **1950** *Oxoniensia* XV. 7 Ploughed-out field-systems appear on air-photographs as a network of white lines which can often be recognized to some extent on the ground by bands of broken chalk and flints. **1957** *Times* 12 Dec. 18/1 Additional capital..has been injected into the business.. in the form of ploughed-back profits. **1958** *Spectator* 18 July 117/3 It is finding about 85 per cent. of its capital through ploughed-back profits. **1959** *Manch. Guardian* 7 Aug. 1/2 The suggestion that a reduction in selling prices might, in present circumstances, take precedence over the ploughing back of profits. **1974** C. TAYLOR *Fieldwork in Medieval Archaeol.* iv. 74 The discovery of Iron Age and Roman sherds scattered on a spur above the River Nene near Irthlingborough, Northamptonshire, led to the identification of ramparts round this spur as part of a ploughed out 'hill fort'. **1977** *Interim* IV. IV. 4 Then the light marks over ploughed-out walls or banks.. provide..an accurate deliniation of landscape elements.

plou·gh-back, plow-. *Econ.* Also as one word. [f. *to plough back*: see *PLOUGH *v.* 9g.] Investment of income or profit in the enterprise from which it emanates; the capital so invested.

1946 *Sun* (Baltimore) 28 Mar. 19/2 After payment of ..taxes and..dividends, the company showed a plow-back of $64.90 a share. **1961** *Times Lit. Suppl.* 6 Jan. 2/2 Less socialist-minded politicians..taxed such 'plough-backs' into companies' own coffers more heavily. **1966** *Economist* 26 Mar. 1264/2 Borax would have to justify itself by giving an assurance on the future flow of dollar dividends from the American ploughback. **1970** *Daily Tel.* 2 Jan. 14 Some new Government, if well advised, will be in a position to let the private sector have more of its head in..plough-backs, investment and profits. **1974** M. B. BROWN *Economics of Imperialism* v. 123 The 7 per cent or so of Britain's national income, which was invested in the decades before the 1830s had..to be found almost entirely from the ploughback of profits.

plough-gear, plow-. Delete † *Obs.* and add later examples.

1644 *Archives Maryland* (1887) IV. 279 The ploughgeare sent of Engl[and]. *a* **1815** M. LONSDALE *Love in Cumberland* in *Westmoreland & Cumberland Dial.* (1839) 211 Thy plew-geer's aw liggin how-strow. **1885** 'C. E. CRADDOCK' *Prophet Gt. Smoky Mts.* i. 15 The girl's hand trembled violently as she stepped swiftly to his horse and took off the plough-gear. **1940** W. FAULKNER *Hamlet* iii. 64 He would give them credit for food and plow-gear when they needed it. **1952** *Oxf. Jun. Encycl.* VI. 243/1 Plough gear is generally simpler than chain gear; it has a transverse backband supporting the chains, and sometimes a loose bellyband.

ploughing, plowing, *vbl. sb.* Add: **2. ploughing-match** (later examples).

1845 *Ainsworth's Mag.* VII. 369 Unfortunately, my lord [*sc.* a servant] got a premium at a ploughing-match. **1882** [see MATCH *sb.*[1] 7]. **1949** E. BLUNDEN *After Bombing* 41 Here was a set of anglers, there the ploughing-match. **1976** *Southern Even. Echo* (Southampton) 17 Nov. 6/5 The 1976 Hampshire County Ploughing Match will be at Upper Silkstead Farm, Poles Lane, Otterbourne, next Saturday.

plough-jogger, plow-. (Later U.S. examples.)

a **1852** F. M. WHITCHER *Widow Bedott Papers* (1856) xx. 207, I wanted old Dawson's wife to see't I'd got a pardner ruther above a common plow-jogger, such as hern is. **1862** *Harper's Mag.* Nov. 782/2 City folks most generally fetch along a lot of traps and finery to show off afore us plowjoggers. **1865** *Trans. Illinois Agric. Soc.* V. 255 At least the old plow jogger will be mounted on his buggy seat.

ploughman, plow-. Add: **b. ploughman's lunch,** a cold snack, usu. including bread, cheese, and pickle, and freq. served in a public house at lunch-time. Also *ellipt.*, as *ploughman's*.

[**1837** J. G. LOCKHART *Mem. Life W. Scott* IV. v. 161 The surprised poet swung forth to join them, with an extemporized sandwich, that looked like a ploughman's luncheon, in his hand.] **1970** R. TREHANE in B. H. Axler *Cheese Handbk.* p. iii, English cheese and beer have for centuries formed a perfect combination enjoyed as the Ploughman's Lunch. **1971** *Oxford Mail* 27 Oct. 1/8 The loaf is to be cut into 200 pieces and eaten as part of 200 ploughman's lunches. **1973** P. THEROUX *Saint Jack* v. 60 We had a ploughman's lunch in the village—beautiful old pub—and went back to London. **1975** *Times* 30 Aug. 10/2 The pubs specialize in lunchtime catering..and you can get a decent 'ploughman's' for between 20p and 30p. **1977** J. THOMSON *Case Closed* v. 73 He treated himself to a ploughman's lunch of bread, cheese and pickle..at the Red Lion.

plough-tail, plow-. Add: Also *attrib.*

1912 *Chambers's Jrnl.* Sept. 564/1 No doubt the chie thought he cut a dash among the plough-tail lads.

plovery, *a.* Add: **b.** Of, characteristic of, or reminiscent of a plover.

1932 J. JOYCE *Let.* 1 Jan. (1966) III. 239, I would be engaging with my plovery soft accents.

ploy, *sb.*[3] **1.** For '*Sc.* and *north. Eng.*' read 'orig. *Sc.* and *north. Eng.*' and add later examples in general use.

1916 E. F. BENSON *David Blaize* xi. 208, I think you're rather an ass, unless you prefer writing out the 'Æneid' to any other ploy. **1926** R. MACAULAY *Crewe Train* II. viii. 159 Whatever ploy she had on hand at the moment, such as lead casting, table tennis, or naval battles in the bath. **1930** *Times* 16 Apr. 15/4 Training in domestic ploys such as household work. **1936** A. Christie *Cards on Table* xviii. 175 You'd gone off on your own ploys with the boy friend. **1936** 'J. Tey' *Shilling for Candles* xxiii. 257 Smuggling Edward Champnels might descend to, as a ploy, a mere bit of excitement. **1953** J. Trench *Docken Dead* ii. 27 He's obviously gone off on some ploy of his own. **1959** 'M. Neville' *Sweet Night for Murder* xi. 106 'Did you ever accompany her while she was shopping for clothes?'.. 'I wouldn't be much good at that sort of ploy... She didn't need anyone to help her choose what to wear.' **1979** *Country Life* 8 Nov. 1687/1 The search for the alternative life style is..a new rationalisation of a ruralising ploy.

2. A move or gambit suggested by particular circumstances and made in order to gain a calculated advantage, esp. self-advancement or the frustration of an opponent's intentions; a planned device or manœuvre.

1950 S. Potter *Lifemanship* 15 Each one of us can, by ploy or gambit, most naturally gain the advantage. *Ibid.* 90 P. Lewis, expert in Oxford Undergraduateship, has set it down as basic to this ploy that, where the Layman would concentrate on his subject, the Gamesman *concentrates on his tutor.* **1955** *Times* 24 June 10/3 Apart from claiming possible support in London and Glasgow and assuring the men that there would be 'important developments during the next 48 hours'—a ploy with which the strikers are becoming a little disillusioned—the speakers had nothing to offer. **1957** *Listener* 13 June 967/3 It is a common 'ploy' of reviewers to take the opportunity of a review to air their own views. **1957** *Economist* 5 Oct. 69/1 Conventional East–West political ploys that took the form of proposing, and rejecting rather more sharply than usual, the suggestion that non-members of the United Nations, such as Red China, should be admitted as observers. **1958** A. Wilson in *Times Lit. Suppl.* 15 Aug. p. viii/2 Whatever the ingenious and at times embarrassing ploys with which English novelists periodically assert their amateur, their unintellectual or their purely entertaining status..they are..concerned always to be serious. **1960** 'W. Haggard' *Closed Circuit* viii. 105 For suspects there is a standard ploy. You test them. **1966** *Listener* 13 Jan. 78/3 If West held the queen of spades, as he did, it would be East's duty to guard the suit. The only way to accomplish this end was by the unusual ploy of discarding a trump on the third round of clubs. **1970** G. F. Newman *Sir, You Bastard* 267 Perhaps she should cook it and leave it for him, but she recognized that thought as a ploy to delay herself, hoping that he'd return and prevent her departure.

pluck, *sb.*[1] Add: **I. 1. d.** *Naut.* A pull or tow.

1918 *Yachting Monthly* Jan. 155 A pluck out of dock, a fishing permit and a light breeze. **1934** 'Taffrail' *Seventy North* iii. 57 'D'ye want a rope's end, ole pal? We'll give ye a pluck home!' Sam's retort to this nautical insult was jocular but mostly unprintable. **1962** W. Granville *Dict. Sailors' Slang* 89/2 *Pluck*, a tow or tug. **1964** *Roving Commissions 1963* 176 A feeble little motor-boat gave us a half-hearted pluck and went away.

III. 7. c. Wine. *U.S. Black slang.*

1964 *N.Y. Times Mag.* 23 Aug. 64/2 *Pluck*, wine. **1967** *Trans-Action* Apr. 8/1 The dudes 'rap' and 'jive' (talk), gamble, and drink their 'pluck' (usually a cheap, sweet wine). **1969** H. R. Brown *Die Nigger Die!* ii. 24 We went and got some 'pluck' (wine) and I told him I was in college. **1973** *Black World* July 55/1 We want some pluck man, got any scratch? *Ibid.* 56/1 We was gittin away from the broke pluck bottles.

V. 9. Special Comb.: **pluck side** *Physical Geogr.*, the rough, 'downstream' side of a roche moutonnée from which rock has been plucked by a glacier.

1905 *Jrnl. Geol.* XIII. 6 We will no longer call the two sides of a *roche moutonnée* 'push side' and 'lee side', but we prefer the expressions 'scour side' and 'pluck side' introduced by Shaler. **1942** C. A. Cotton *Climatic Accidents Landscape-Making* xviii. 244 The lee side is termed also the 'pluck' side.

pluck, *v.* Add: **1. a.** Also *intr.* for *pass.*

1945 H. J. Massingham *Wisdom of Fields* viii. 163 It plucked dead ripe.

b. Substitute for def.: Of a glacier: to break loose (pieces of rock) by the mechanical action of ice which has formed around projections and in cavities in the rock; to erode (rock) by this process. Occas. also used of water (see quot. 1930). Freq. with adverbs, esp. *out.* (Examples.)

1893 *Bull. Mus. Compar. Zoöl. Harvard Coll.* XVI. 209 The pits which were left where masses of the rock were plucked out and borne away by the moving ice. **1915** L. V. Pirsson *Text-bk. Ecol.* I. v. 124 The ice at the bottom of the névé fields being frozen into cracks and cavities and around projections in its stony bed, when motion begins, 'plucks' or quarries masses of rock and takes them forward with it. **1930** C. R. Longwell *Outl. Physical Geol.* iv. 43 In a stream flowing over horizontal layers of rock, corrasion along joints loosens large blocks, which are then torn or 'plucked' away by the current. In some situations this plucking action is much more important than wear by simple rasping. **1955** M. Hollander tr. *Kuenen's Realms Water* iv. 152 The glacier will from time to time pluck out large blocks from the lower part of the protuberance. **1971** I. G. Gass et al. *Understanding Earth* xv. 220/2 Rocks have been plucked into characteristic glacial shapes.

c. *Printing.* Of ink: to detach and remove the surface of paper during printing. Also *intr.* for *pass.*

1960 G. A. Glaister *Gloss. Bk.* 321/1 *Plucking*, a printing fault which is caused by the ink plucking the surface of the paper and leaving irregular white patches in printed areas. **1967** E. Chambers *Photolitho-Offset* i. 6 If 'washing-out' were omitted, the resin would cause trouble by causing the paper to 'pluck', owing to the resin sticking to the paper when printing.

2. a. (Further examples.)

1881 'Mark Twain' *Prince & Pauper* xv. 163 He is the stranger that plucked Giles Witt out of the Thames. **1975** *New Yorker* 19 May 120/2 After the war, the son got a job at the American Embassy, and one day in 1948 was plucked off the street and taken to prison.

3. c. *U.S. Mil. slang.* To cashier or retire (an officer).

1941 *Sun* (Baltimore) 5 Aug. 11/3 There are numerous retirements under way. However, it is highly unlikely that the army will make announcement of the officers who are being 'plucked' under the recent act permitting the Secretary of War to retire those whom a board has decreed to be 'unsuited for further active duty'. **1942** Berrey & Van den Bark *Amer. Thes. Slang* § 888/5 *Pluck*, to retire an officer.

5. b. To shape or thin (the eyebrows) by removing hairs.

c **1450** *Bk. of Knight of La Tour-Landry* (1868) 67 She hadde..plucked her browes, front, and forehed, to haue awey the here, to make her selff the fayrer to the plesinge of the worlde. **1926** F. Scott Fitzgerald *Great Gatsby* ii. 35 Her eyebrows had been plucked and then drawn on again at a more rakish angle. **1932** S. Gibbons *Cold Comfort Farm* xxii. 291 You shall not find me plucking my eyebrows, nor dieting. **1935** C. Isherwood *Mr. Norris changes Trains* ix. 147 He spent ten minutes.. thinning his eyebrows with a pair of pincers. ('Thinning, William: *not* plucking'). **1974** *Times* 22 Jan. 11/6 Whether you pluck your eyebrows depends on your type of looks.

7. Also *transf.*

1885 E. W. Hamilton *Diary* 10 June (1972) II. 880 Several Baronetcies are to be made. One or two claims were put aside; those who were not to the fore in the Division List on Monday were 'plucked', e.g. Mr. Palmer, which I regret because he has at other times rendered good service.

8. pluck up. c. Also, to get new courage, to take heart again.

1842 Dickens *Amer. Notes* I. ii. 20 Even those passengers who were most distrustful of themselves plucked up amazingly. **1890** W. C. Russell *Marriage at Sea* I. i. 10 But she had plucked up as she drew towards the close of her letter. **1901** G. B. Shaw *Caesar & Cleopatra* III. 153 He eats another date, and plucks up a little.

9. Phr. *to pluck a rose*: of women, to visit the lavatory; to micturate or defecate. *slang.*

1613 Beaumont & Fletcher *Knight of Burning Pestle* II, Then up and ride, Or if it will please you walke for your repose, Or sit, or if you will go plucke a rose. **1730** Swift *Panegyrick on the D—n* in *Miscellanies* V. (1735) 139 The bashful Maid, to hide her Blush; shall creep no more behind a Bush; Here unobserv'd, she boldly goes, As who should say to pluck a Rose. **1745** in J. R. Hetherington *Selina's Aunt* (1965) 21/1 Those ladies, who are so proud and lazy, that they will not be at the Pains of stepping into the Garden to pluck a Rose, but keep an odious Implement, sometimes in the Bed-chamber itself.. which they make Use of to ease their worst Necessities. **1768** Sterne *Sentimental Journey* I. 203 Grieve not, gentle traveller, to let Madame de Rambouliet p-ss on — And, ye fair mystic nymphs! Go each one *pluck your rose.* **1785** F. Grose *Classical Dict. Vulgar Tongue*, *To pluck a rose*, an expression said to be used by women, for going to the necessary house, which in the country usually stands in the garden. **1800** in *Proc. Amer. Antiquarian Soc.* (1897) XII. 248 Mrs. M. having occasion to pluck a rose as is usual with delicate women after a ride of 22 miles. **1937** Partridge *Dict. Slang* 641/1 *Pluck a rose*, to visit the privy.

plucked, *a.* **a.** (Earlier and further examples.)

1846 *Swell's Night Guide* 79 At a set to, he is a Dick Curtis the second; and an out and out plucked one. **1916** F. M. Ford *Let.* 23 Aug. (1965) 69 George V..really was in some danger... Still he gave the impression of a 'good plucked 'un'.

plucked, *ppl. a.* Add: **1. b.** *Textiles.* (See quot. 1940.)

1799 [in Dict., sense 1 a]. **1940** *Chambers's Techn. Dict.* 654/2 *Plucked*.., the term used to denote uneven thickness in a top, roving, or yarn, generally caused by excessive draft. **1974** H. McCloy *Sleepwalker* v. 72 A short coat of plucked nutria.

2. b. *plucked wool*: wool from a dead sheep.

1911 in Webster. **1932** E. Midgley *Technical Terms in Textile Trade* II. 156 *Plucked wool*, wool plucked from a sheep which has been dead a few days. Sometimes this term is applied to skin wool. **1957** M. B. Picken *Fashion Dict.* 258/1 *Plucked wool*, wool from dead sheep.

c. Of eyebrows: shaped or thinned by plucking out hairs.

1928 R. Hall *Well of Loneliness* xlviii. 449 A handsome young man with severely plucked eyebrows. **1935** R. Stout *League of Frightened Men* xvii. 237 Her face..with its broad flat nose and plucked eyebrows. **1938** L. MacNeice *I Crossed Minch* ii. 25 A few signpost details such as plucked eyebrows and lipstick. **1962** M. Barrett *Return of Cornish Sailor* ii. 15 The plucked eyebrow lifted. **1974** *Times* 26 Oct. 8/8 The corny peroxide blondes with their plucked eyebrows.

4. *Physical Geogr.* Eroded or broken off by plucking. (Cf. *pluck *v.* 1 b.)

1893 *Bull. Mus. Compar. Zoöl. Harvard Coll.* XVI. 210 The plucked out material carried away in the form of boulders amounts to as much as one fifth of that removed in the other forms of erosion. **1942** C. A. Cotton *Climatic Accidents Landscape-Making* xvii. 245 Shorn hills may.. present somewhat steep lee sides, perhaps plucked. **1957** J. K. Charlesworth *Quaternary Era* I. xi. The 249 boundary between abraded and plucked surfaces is sometimes that between different kinds of rock.

plucking, *vbl. sb.* **1.** (Further examples and later *attrib.* example.)

1893 *Bull. Mus. Compar. Zoöl. Harvard Coll.* XVI. 195 The southern end of Iron Hill is so much covered with glacial waste that it is not possible accurately to determine the relative amount of plucking which went on there. **1937** Wooldridge & Morgan *Physical Basis Geogr.* xxii. 366 Rock-masses on the floor or sides of a glacier may be frozen on to, or into, the ice and removed by 'plucking' in the onward motion of the glacier. **1952** A. Voet *Ink & Paper in Printing Process* xiv. 149 The separation of the paper-ink-plate union..occurs normally in the ink film... This phenomenon, characterized by partial or complete rupture of the paper stock, is known as 'picking' or 'plucking'. **1959** W. K. Richmond *Brit. Birds of Prey* xiii. 150 A cock Sparrow-hawk has several plucking-posts on his beat. **1959** *Washington Post* 31 July 1/6 Legislation passed this week providing for the 'plucking' of some 2500 senior officers was quietly amended..to abolish 'tombstone promotions'. **1960** *Gloss. Paper, Stationery Terms* (*B.S.I.*) 11 *Plucking*, the detachment of superficial zones of the sheet when the adhesion due to an applied external force is higher than the internal cohesion of the paper. **1968** *Gloss. Formwork Terms* (*B.S.I.*) 19 *Plucking*, spalling of the concrete face due to adhesion of concrete to the form.

plud-pludding, var. *plod-plodding* (s.v. Plodding *vbl. sb.*).

1912 W. Deeping *Sincerity* i. 1 The grinding of wheels and the 'plud-pludding' of drenched horses drifted along the high road.

plug, *sb.* Add: **1. b.** *spec.* One for temporarily stopping the waste pipe at the bottom of a sink, wash basin, or bath.

1860 T. Hamilton in T. L. Donaldson *Handbk. Specifications* I. 221 A neat wash-hand basin, with brass plug, socket, and chain. **1872** W. Eassie *Healthy Houses* iv. 37 Although not long introduced the ordinary troughs and basins with plugs at the bottom and with supply taps..are sufficiently familiar as not to need any description. **1901** G. L. Sutcliffe *Sanitary Fittings & Plumbing* vii. 48 The plug is of the type known as 'sunk', the stud and chain-ring being in the sunk portion of the plug, so as not to project above the bottom of the sink. **1965** A. L. Townsend *Plumbing Second Yr.* iii. 72 The bath will.. be fitted with a waste plug and chain. *Ibid.*, The 'pop-up' plug is operated by turning a handle incorporated in the overflow fitting.

c. A device designed to be inserted into a suitable socket to establish an electrical connection; *spec.* one for connecting the lead of an appliance to an electricity supply, consisting of an insulated casing with two or three pins (or, formerly, with one pin and a ring); also (chiefly *colloq.* or as *wall plug*), a socket fixed to or in a wall for receiving such a plug. Also *fig.* (For *to pull the plug* see next sense.)

1883 J. W. Urquhart *Electric Light* (ed. 2) ix. 286 When it is required to transmit the current to a particular lamp, a metal plug is inserted at the point where the bar connected with the lamp and the bar connected with the machine intersect. *Ibid.* 296 The 'safety fusible plugs' employed in the Edison and Swan systems usually consist of a short length of lead wire. Their function is to melt.. should an unduly strong current..be transmitted. **1888** D. Salomons *Management of Accumulators* (ed. 3) II. ii. 97 Wall plugs are most useful about a house for attaching a portable lamp or small motor at will. *Ibid.* 98 The portable lamp has a reel of twin wire at its base, with the ends of wires going to the lamp-holder and a connector respectively. This connector fits the wall plug by pushing in the two pins it carries. **1890** *Ibid.* (ed. 5) II. ii. 166 Mr. Taylor Smith's pattern of portable lamp has a reel of twin wire in its base, with the ends of the wires going to the lamp-holder and a connector plug respectively. The two pins of this plug are pushed into the wall connector..to obtain the light. **1891** F. C. Allsop *Telephones* vi. 97 When the plug is inserted between the two blocks.., the circuit is closed. **1892** —— *Pract. Electr.-Light Fitting* v. 72 When the plug..is inserted in the socket,..the lamp can be lighted. **1923** T. E. Herbert *Teleph.* xiii. 316 It is particularly important that during the insertion of the plug the two springs of the jack shall not be short circuited. **1929** E. A. Robertson *Three came Unarmed* vii. 111 Nonie was..stooping to fix into a wall-plug the flex of the standard lamp. **1945**, etc. [see *pin *sb.*[1] 1 m]. **1960** H. Pinter *Caretaker* II. 48 There used to be a wall plug for this electrolux. **1972** *Village Voice* (N.Y.) 1 June 5/4 The whole point of the call, her thinking I was a plug into good connections. **1976** D. Phillips *Planning your Lighting* 13/1 A power point with an outcrop of plugs and flexes feeding a number of different items of equipment is still a common sight.

2. k. In some old types of water-closet, a stopper which kept the water in the pan and was pulled to let the contents fall into the soil pipe. Now *Obs.* exc. *Hist.* and in phr. *to pull the plug*, to flush the lavatory; also *fig.* and *transf.*, usu. referring to sudden release or (with allusion to sense *1 c) disconnection.

1859 F. Nightingale *Notes on Nursing* i. 13 As well might you have a sewer under the room, or think that in a water closet the plug need be pulled up but once a day. **1873** B. Latham *Sanitary Engin.* 331 When the handle H which lifts the plug is raised, everything in the basin is suddenly discharged into the trap below, and so into the drain. **1896** T. E. Coleman *Sanitary House Drainage* xiii. 97 Should a small piece of paper or other substance prevent the plug resting tightly upon its seat, the water above gradually escapes into the drain, and impure air is then free to enter the building. **1919** R. Fry *Let.* May (1972) II. 451 A real Victorian W.C. *with a pull up plug.* **1934** V. M. Yeates *Winged Victory* xix. 152 Showers of tracers..frightened him and made him pull the plug rather too soon, and..he..saw his bombs burst a long way from his target. **1935** A. J. Pollock *Underworld Speaks* 92/1 *Pull the plug*, to start negotiations; proceed; tell the narrative without delay. **1935** D. Sayers *Gaudy Night* ii. 43 It was not..an agreeable drawing... She took it..into the nearest lavatory, dropped it in and pulled the plug on it. **1939** R. Godden *Black Narcissus* xxv. 214 I've come to mend a loose joint in your pipe... The plug won't pull till I do. **1943** C. H. Ward-Jackson *It's a Piece of Cake* 50 *To pull the plug*, to release the bombs in one go, as distinct from playing the piano. **1943** G. Greene *Ministry of Fear* I. iii. 60 Pull the plug... Wait till the cistern refills, then pull the plug again. **1948** *Amer. Speech* XXIII. 38/2 [Submarines] *Pull the plug*, to dive or submerge. **1949** D. Smith *I capture Castle* (1950) iii. 31 It had a huge bath with a wide mahogany surround, and two mahogany-seated lavatories, side by side, with one lid to cover them both. The pottery parts showed views of Windsor Castle and when you pulled the plug the bottom of Windsor Castle fell out. **1961** C. Cockburn *View from West* vii. 81 The British statesman finds its [*sic*] nearly impossible to make a simple statement..which might not inadvertently pull the plug on himself and flush him..down the drain. **1964** C. Mackenzie *Life & Times* III. 75 'They must not hurt my seat.' He then pulled up the plug, and pushed it down again. 'Doulton you see.' **1965** *Ibid.* IV. 22 The plug in the water-closet seldom worked. **1972** *Guardian* 4 Sept. 11/1 Pauline Jones..was transferred from Holloway to open prison..and the plug was suddenly pulled out of the big public outcry over the sentence. **1973** *Houston Chron.* 21 Oct. 28 For the first time data are at hand on when to 'pull the plug' on an unconscious patient being sustained artificially. **1974** *Observer* 18 Aug. 11/4 Any prudent banker would have pulled the plug on Court Line long ago. **1977** *Spare Rib* Sept. 12/2 The older lady pulled the plug on her tormentors by prudently using the vibrator.

l. *Geol.* (i) A cylindrical mass of solidified lava occupying the vent of a volcano. Cf. Neck *sb.*[1] 11c.

1882 A. Geikie *Text-bk. Geol.* 256 If the tuff of a cone.. were swept away, we should find a central lava plug or core resembling the volcanic 'heads'..of Germany. **1900** *Q. Jrnl. Geol. Soc.* LVI. 221 Mount Kenya is an ancient much-eroded volcano; the highest peak is formed of the rocks of the central plug. **1944** A. Holmes *Princ. Physical Geol.* xx. 456 Later, the plug of the conduit was forced bodily upwards, through the dome, thus forming the celebrated 'spine' of Mont Pelée. **1976** P. Francis *Volcanoes* iii. 123 The vent may well become blocked with a slow-moving or stationary plug of lava.

(ii) A mass of rock, esp. salt, which has been forced upwards by tectonic pressures, lifting overlying strata into the form of a dome.

1906 *Prof. Papers U.S. Geol. Survey* No. 46. 67 Lee Hager..has suggested a hypothesis which explains the origin of these..domes..by the upthrust of an igneous plug. **1918** *Econ. Geol.* XIII. 452 The intrusion or formation of the salt plug has produced a sharp local doming or quaquaversal structure. **1944** *Nat. Geogr. Mag.* Jan. 16/2 Those 'salt domes' or 'plugs' that yield oil may also yield sulphur. **1970** W. G. Roberts *Quest for Oil* iii. 30 Salt.. flows relatively easily under the high pressures exerted by earth movements, and can be forced into a plug or dome.

m. A sparking plug.

1886 D. Clerk *Gas Engine* viii. 204 The igniting points ..consist of porcelain plugs. **1890** W. Robinson *Gas & Petroleum Engines* vii. 225 The igniter..consists of a brass tube..screwed into the end covers at the top of cylinder. This tube contains a plug of porcelain..to insulate the points of the platinum wires. **1902** J. E. Hutton in A. C. Harmsworth *Motors & Motor-Driving* viii. 151 An English firm has recently introduced a plug which contains no breakable insulators. **1922** J. Buchan *Bk. Escapes* viii. 151 They had flown all the way to Egypt without cleaning their plugs! **1948** A. Morgan *Boys' Bk. of Engines* ix. 110 When a spark jumps across the plug points it ignites the petrol-air mixture in the cylinder. **1973** F. Peterson *Hand-bk. Lawn Mower Repair* iii. 52 You can clean the old plug with a wire brush, then make sure the electrodes are set the proper distance apart.

6. a. (Earlier and later examples.)

1860 in A. H. Oldroyd *Lincoln's Campaign* (1896) 171 There's an old plow 'hoss' whose name is 'Dug'... He's short and thick and a regular 'plug'. **1930** V. Palmer *Men are Human* xxi. 195 There would be a moral rot and everyone would be looking for an old plug to ride. **1948** *Chicago Tribune* 12 Dec. (Grafic Mag.) 5/5 He was a hopeless plug and never ran in the money. **1972** *Dict. Contemp. & Colloq. Usage* (Eng.-Lang. Inst. Amer.) 22/3 *Plug*,..a worn-out old horse; a nag.

b. *transf.* An incompetent or undistinguished person. Also, a bloke, a fellow. Also *attrib.*

1848 *Ladies' Repository* VIII. 316/2 *Plug*,..a nickname for a homely man. **1863** in J. D. Billings *Hardtack & Coffee* (1887) 72 Next came General Meade, a slow old plug, For he let them away at Gettysburg. **1899** 'J. Flynt' *Tramping* II. iv. 278 I'm always willing to be square to a square plug (fellow). *Ibid.* IV. 396 *Plug*, a fellow; synonymous with 'bloke' and 'stiff'. **1900** *Dialect Notes* II. 49 *Plug*... 2. A hard student... 3. A slow, disagreeable person. 4. A short, thick-set person. **1904** 'No. 1500' *Life in Sing Sing* 251/1 *Plug*, a fellow. **1920** S. Lewis *Main St.* 308 You figure I'm just a plug general practitioner. **1921** [see *gee *sb.*[4]]. **1935** N. Ersine *Underworld & Prison Slang* 58 *Plug*, a working stiff, an ox. **1948** *Redbook Mag.* (Chicago) Mar. 48/2 You—you broken reed! You doormat! Old steady, unimaginative, dumb *plug*!

c. A book which does not sell well, and becomes bad stock.

1889 *Cent. Dict.* (1890) VI. 4565/1 *Plug*,..a shelf-worn book. **1901** *Dialect Notes* II. 145 *Plug*, a book left on author's or publisher's hands. N.Y. City. **1928** *Publisher's Circular* 21 July 59/2 Out of the vast number of publications issued, some must, indeed, turn out to be plugs. **1930** *Publisher's Weekly* 15 Mar. 1546/1 The so-called plugs are weeded out..making room for new titles **1948** H. L. Mencken *Amer. Lang.* Suppl. II. xi. 739 *Plug*, a good book that no one wants. **1970** R. K. Kent *Lang. Journalism* 104 *Plug*. 1. (a) a book sold at a reduced price by a publisher after sales have fallen off: in plural, also *remainders*.

d. A steady plodding course. (Cf. Plug *v.* 4.)

1903 *Eng. Dial. Dict.* IV. 557/2 *Plug*,..a long-continued pull. **1909** *Daily Chron.* 16 Sept. 3/4 The story is of the quiet plug of the prosaic Henry and the meteoric flight of the splendid Len. **1911** A. Cherry-Garrard *Jrnl.* 17 Dec. in *Worst Journey in World* (1922) II. x. 359 It was a hard plug up the waves.

7. (Earlier example.)

1848 *Ladies' Repository* VIII. 316/2 *Plug*, a hat.

8*. An advertisement; an instance of publicity; a method of drawing attention to (a product, an entertainment, etc.). *colloq.* (orig. *U.S.*).

1902 G. Ade *Girl Proposition* 50 They were friendly to the prosperous Bachelor and each one determined to put in a few quiet Plugs for Sis. **1929** *Variety* 10 July 1/5 Everything gets a Wrigley plug, for the benefit of his gum. **1937** [see *credit *sb.* 13 f]. **1946** *Sat. Rev. Lit.* 30 Nov. 5/1 Dale gets in a neat plug for the publisher's blurb on the dust jacket. **1953** *Recorder* 17 Nov. 4/5 Why do you give them [*sc.* Selfridges] a free plug? **1957** *Time* 2 Sept. 27/1 The policy emerged mostly as a clearly reasoned plug for the kind of development job private capital and U.S. aid have been doing in Latin America. **1958** *Spectator* 13 June 762/1 Nobody will be a penny the better off for the debate except Mr. Noel-Baker, whose new book on disarmament ..got a series of plugs that not even a film programme on BBC television could rival. **1965** N. Gulbenkian *Pantaraxia* xiv. 288 It was to give a 'plug' to Jack Barclay..and ..Panelcraft..that I agreed to appear in 'Tonight'. **1973** *Nation Rev.* (Melbourne) 31 Aug. 1442/5 The *Observer* more than compensated..in the same edition as the pious editorial and the color plug. **1978** *Jrnl. R. Soc. Arts* CXXVI. 418/1, I was interested in Sir Monty's plug for engineers to be involved as managers in top management.

8.** *Angling.* A lure with one or more hooks attached.

1932 *Kansas City Times* 13 May 22 There is some balm for the fellow who thinks he is paying too much for his plugs, flies and other equipment. **1944** 'N. Shute' *Pastoral* i. 5 To take his new rod and his new reel and his new plugs. **1960** M. Sharcott *Place of Many Winds* v. 100 These beaches have been known to yield many valuable articles, the best of which are probably the fishing lures, or plugs as fishermen call them. **1967** *Daily Tel.* 21 Oct. 14/6 Orange-coloured plugs are the most killing for late evening. **1976** *Norwich Mercury* 19 Nov. 9/5 Jeremy Epton and Anthony Raywood, 11, were having no success at all dipping a plug into the nearby River Wensum hoping for a pike.

9. (sense 8*) *plug number, schedule, song*; **plug-assist**, a heated plunger used in the vacuum moulding of plastics which forces the plastic partially into the mould cavity before the vacuum is applied; the technique of using this device; freq. *attrib.*; hence **plug-assisted** *a.*, using a plug-assist; **plug-bait** = *plug *sb.* 8**; **plug-board,** also, a similar piece of equipment used with data-processing apparatus, in which receptacles can be interconnected by lengths of wire with a plug at each end, and which is usually made to be removable to facilitate changes of program or function, the receptacles making electrical contact with fixed terminals on the machine when it is in place; (examples); **plug flow,** flow of a body of ice or other viscous fluid *en bloc*, with no shearing between adjacent layers; **plug fuse** *Electr.*, a fuse that is screwed into a socket; **plug gauge,** a gauge in the form of a plug which is used for measuring the diameter of a hole; **plug-hat** (earlier and later examples); (*b*) *Austral.*, a bowler-hat; **plug-hole:** also in *fig.* phrases (cf. *drain *sb.* 1 e); **plug horse** *N. Amer.* = Plug *sb.* 6; **plug nozzle,** in a rocket or jet engine, a nozzle containing a central plug that diverges towards the exit and then converges, so that the gas is expelled in a converging annular stream; also *attrib.*; **plug tobacco** (earlier example).

1958 *Brit. Plastics* XXXI. 20/2 Almost immediately the heated plug-assist is lowered into the bubble. **1958** *Times Rev. Industry* Aug. 57/2 This machine uses deep-draw, drape, Airslip, and drop-form plug assist techniques either individually or in combination. **1958** *Brit. Plastics* XXXI. 352/2 Drape and plug-assisted techniques are particularly suitable. **1965** L. A. H. Eastman tr. *Thiel's Princ. Vacuum Forming* iv. 41 For single mouldings plug-assisted forming seldom offers any advantage over airslip forming. **1955** Plug-bait [see *ironmongery 1 d]. **1883** *4th Meeting U.S. Nat. Telephone Exchange Assoc., 1882* 38 Switchboards are generally classified as 'cord' or 'plug' boards. *Ibid.* 39 The plug boards were the favorites. **1946** *Ann. Computation Lab. Harvard Univ.* I. 21 The outrelay,..through which the product is read out of the multiply unit, connects to the buss through a plugboard provided to fix the decimal point relation between the product counter and the buss. **1957** D. D. McCracken *Digital Computer Programming* 231 A number of the small machines are controlled by a removable plugboard... There are ordinarily many of them with each machine, one for each recurring problem. **1970** O. Dopping *Computers & Data Processing* xv. 231 In older computers, the distribution of input card fields over different parts of memory was often effected with plugboards as in conventional punched card machines. **1977** *Sci. Amer.* Sept. 155/1 Hardware prototyping mechanisms commonly include wire-wrap breadboard models, plugboard setups or printed-circuit prototypes. **1951** *Proc. R. Soc.* A. CCVII. 560 There is then no relative movement except in the lowest layer and the block simply slides downhill as a rigid body... (The corresponding motion in a block between rough plates has been called 'plug flow'.) **1972** B. W. Sparks *Geomorphology* (ed. 2) xiii. 382 Temperate glaciers in summer are likely to be the most effective agents of erosion especially if they are sliding over their beds and undergoing plug flow. **1974** D. K. Smith in P. L. Moore et al. *Drilling Practices Manual* xvi. 437 This readily converts to a maximum pump rate in order to remain in plug flow. **1905** *Jrnl. Inst. Electr. Engineers* XXXV. 365 The earliest form of Edison plug fuse dates from 1880. *Ibid.* 405 Enclosed or cartridge fuses..have been developed from the Edison plug fuse. **1971** W. N. Alerich *Electr. Construction Wiring* xi. 283 (*heading*) Plug fuse designed to pass safely 15 amps. **1895** *Appleby's Illustr. Handbk. Machinery* IV. 129 The plug gauges above 2 inch are cored out for lightness. **1905** [see *lap *v.*[4]]. **1971** B. Scharf *Engin. & its Language* vii. 49 Plug gauges (plain, tapered or pin gauges) are used for checking holes, mainly in order to ensure that they are not too narrow at any point. **1863** in J. D. Burn *Three Yrs. Working Classes U.S.* (1965) 223 Fancy a ragged man.. with a gun, a knapsack, a butcher's knife and a plug hat. **1941** Baker *Dict. Austral. Slang* 55 *Plug hat*, a bowler hat. **1947** Plug-hat [see *cow-hide *sb.* 4]. **1977** *Time* 14 Mar. 30/1 He chuckled over the memory of seeing Tammany Democrats dressed in their long coats and plug hats but so broke they could not pay their hotel bills. **1968** *Listener* 22 Feb. 243/1 May I ask..whether the anonymity demanded by the ethics of the 'profession' is now to be regarded as having..gone down the plug-hole? **1973** *Guardian* 28 Mar. 10/6 Nothing escaped so completely as Warhol himself. A positive plug hole of a man around which the bath water swirled. **1973** *Times* 17 May 12/5 That [term] went down the plughole of progress. **1887** *Courier-Jrnl.* (Louisville, Ky.) 4 Feb. 3/5 Wanted—40 plug horses and mares at Lum Simon's Stables. **1969** N. W. Parsons *Sagebrush Harp* xviii. 97 Later, Papa bought another plug horse, giving a note due the following fall. **1960** *Astronautics* Apr. 100/2 There are many ways in which such combustors can be combined with a nozzle..to form attractive propulsion system configurations. One possible configuration is a segmented annular combustor with a 'plug nozzle'. **1970** A. V. Cleaver in N. H. Langton *Rocket Propulsion* II. iv. 136 There would be..appreciable savings in the length and weight of inter-stage vehicle structures if plug-nozzle engines were used in the upper stages; on the other hand,..the small performance gains would be associated more with the use of plug nozzles on bottom stages. **1933** P. Godfrey *Back-stage* xiv. 173 In pursuance of his theory of the value of reiteration de Courville instituted the feature of the 'plug number'. **1947** *Time* 24 Nov. 74/3 Music publishers and recording companies were getting together on 'plug schedules' to ration out the hits. **1939** *Melody Maker* 3 June 1/2 Each band..will be playing in any programme of ten items, no less than eight plug songs. **1952** B. Ulanov *Hist. Jazz Amer.* (1958) xiv. 159 The plug songs of the moment. **1814** in *Deb. Congress U.S.* (1855) 17th Congress 2 Sess., App. 1218 Plug tobacco manufactured at Columbia, one shilling and three pence per pound.

plug, *v.* Add: **1. c.** Also, to insert a fibre or plastic tube or cylinder for the same purpose.

d. (Further examples.)

1952 Dylan Thomas *Let.* 21 July (1966) 375 Now it's up to me & him to plug in lots more expenses. **1976** *National Observer* (U.S.) 17 Jan. 14/1 (Advt.), There's no need to rip out your old grass. Plug in Amazoy Zoysia Grass and let it spread into beautiful turf that never needs replacement.

e. Substitute for def.: (i) *trans.* To insert (a plug or the like) *into* a socket; to connect electrically (an appliance or apparatus) by inserting a plug *into* a socket; also *to plug in* (trans.), to connect electrically in this way. Also *absol.*, *transf.*, and *fig.*

1903 [in Dict.]. **1923** T. E. Herbert *Teleph.* xiii. 347 The operator plugs in with the service plug, restores the indicator, and ascertains the number required. **1925** P. J. Risdon *Crystal Receivers & Circuits* 15 A complete set of such coils will thus enable a big range of wave-lengths to be efficiently covered, by plugging in a coil most nearly corresponding to the wave-length required. **1925** *Scribner's Mag.* July 54/2 He wandered in to his radio, lighted the tubes and plugged in the ear phones. **1932** *Pictorial Weekly* 19 Mar. 201/1 Rescue vessels can 'plug in' to this buoy, and talk to the men below. **1934** *Archit. Rev.* LXXV. 108/3 (*caption*) A portable fire that can be 'plugged in' to a gas point in bedroom or bathroom. **1948** F. Thompson *Still glides Stream* i. 10 One here and there of her pupils had shown the sudden gleam of comprehension..which..she had referred to..as 'plugging in', or 'taking the bait'. **1960** *Farmer & Stockbreeder* 15 Mar. 143/1 A large range of implements can be 'plugged-in' for doing a number of other jobs. **1965** *Daily Tel.* 1 June 15/8 Extract this Danish machine and plug it into an AC power point. **1970** *Atlantic Monthly* July 88 Five children were plugged into a tape recorder, listening to a story and following it in the books in front of them. **1971** [see *Jack *sb.*[1] 15 d]. **1971** J. H. Smith *Digital Logic* ii. 18 A power supply..with facilities for plugging at least ten modules into it at any one time. **1972** *Sci. Amer.* Apr. 13/1 (Advt.), The most advanced automotive check-up in the world today... Your car will actually be plugged into a computer. **1972** *National Observer* (U.S.) 27 May

22/3 They tell us that to be entirely into the new literary life, one must in some way be plugged into films. **1972** *Sci. Amer.* July 105/1 All 10 digits are plugged into the expression ABC × DE = FGH × IJ. **1977** *Ibid.* Aug. 80/3 The placental embryo..is plugged into the maternal blood supply for nourishment.

(ii) *intr.* To be, or to be capable of being, plugged *in* or *into*. Also *fig.*

1956 T. E. Ivall *Electronic Computers* iv. 45 When the unit is put into the patch panel it also plugs into a d.c. amplifier at the rear. **1963** *Which?* Dec. 378/2 The *Timac* plugged directly into the mains socket. **1974** *Physics Bull.* Sept. 401/1 This assembly plugs into a choice of sockets dependent upon the position in which the instrument is to be used.

f. *trans.* To cut a cylindrical core from. Also *absol.* *U.S.*

1874 'Uncle Bob' *Lett. to Children* 19, I used to be a great hand to go into the patch, plug 'em before they were ripe, and then turn the cut side down. *a* **1910** 'Mark Twain' *Autobiogr.* (1924) I. 111, I know how to tell when it [*sc.* a watermelon] is ripe without 'plugging' it. **1948** *Chicago Tribune* 25 June II. 3/3 The safest and best way to tell quality is to 'plug' the melon. **1969** *Times* 22 July (Moon Suppl.) p. i/1 It's a very soft surface, but here and there where I plug with the contingency sample collector, I run into a very hard surface.

g. *slang.* To copulate with.

1901 Farmer & Henley *Slang* V. 231/1 *Plug*,..to copulate. **1977** *Amer. Speech 1975* L. 64 'I plugged her last night.' (male use).

h. *to plug off* or *back*: to seal off (an oil well or a rock formation) by inserting a plug. Also *absol.*

1919 *Summary of Operations Calif. Oil Fields* (Calif. State Mining Bureau) V. I. 9 *Plugged off.* Describes the condition existing when fluid encountered in a lower part of a well has been excluded from a higher part of the well by placing an effective plug between the two places. **1924** L. C. Uren *Textbk. Petroleum Production Engin.* ix. 276 It will be important..to estimate carefully the volume of that part of the well which it is desired to plug off. **1938** C. P. Parsons in A. E. Dunstan et al. *Sci. of Petroleum* I. ix. 472/2 The amount of cement left in the bottom of the tubing depends upon the amount of hole to be plugged back. **1938** Wilde & Moore in *Ibid.* xi. 573/2 Having located the water, it is important to plug off the water sand. **1976** L. St. Clair *Fortune in Death* i. 8 We've wasted enough time fishing drill pipe out of this hole. Let's plug back and slant-drill.

2. (Earlier and later examples.) Also, to fire (a bullet) *into* (example *fig.*).

1870 J. C. Duval *Adv. Big-Foot Wallace* xix. 99 Just at that instant Jeff plugged him with a half-ounce bullet. **1882** E. W. Hamilton *Diary* 27 Aug. (1972) I. 326 He has had a narrow escape of losing an eye, having been plugged in the face by Newport while grouse driving at Wharncliffe's. **1891** 'Mark Twain' in 'Twain' & Howells *Mark Twain—Howells Lett.* (1960) II. 635, I will plug into you at short range the first chapter of my new book. **1904** [see **lam sb.*[3]]. **1924** [see **frame sb.* 2]. **1936** G. Greene *Gun for Sale* i. 22 Don't say a word or I'll plug you... I don't care a damn if I plug one of you. **1969** C. Burke *God is Beautiful, Man* (1970) 28 They told their old man..if they didn't bring Ben back Simon would get plugged. **1973** W. M. Duncan *Big Timer* xxi. 137 That Carver packed a wallop, didn't he? I should have plugged him sooner.

3. Also, with a missile.

1971 Wodehouse *Much obliged, Jeeves* xvi. 169 Sidcup got a black eye. Somebody plugged him with a potato.

4. a. (Further examples.) Freq. const. with advbs.

1900 G. Ade *More Fables* 44 Any Husband could..get up every Morning ready to Plug for a Renaissance of their Early love. *Ibid.* 146 You take a Man who is Plugging along on a Salary. **1911** E. Ferber *Dawn O'Hara* vii. 99 Lots of us are pluggin' an' savin' in the hopes that some day we'll have money enough to get back at some people we know. **1947** K. Tennant *Lost Haven* (1968) vi. 88 He was a mug to plug away at yet another new boat. **1953** Wodehouse *Performing Flea* 58, I am plugging along with *Hot Water* and have done 60,000 words. **1954** A. Huxley *Let.* 16 Sept. (1969) 711 Lacking the ability to write a text book, I have to plug on at these other, more precarious forms of literature. **1973** *Philadelphia Inquirer* 7 Oct. 19 Ronnie's not a quitter. He really plugs. **1977** *World of Cricket Monthly* June 11/1 Australia's bowlers plugged away, with Max Walker breaking through when Surrey were 2 wickets down for 147, and snaring 3 quick wickets for only 6 runs.

5. To prevent (a person) from carrying out a project by anticipating him or depriving him of his opportunity; to block (an action or design). *U.S.*

1880 *Scribner's Mag.* 492/2 One fisherman 'plugs' another when he puts out from shore and casts in ahead of him. **1896** G. Ade *Artie* xii. 110, I wouldn't like to start in and plug his game.

6. *intr.* (for *refl.*). To stick or jam; to become obstructed.

1902 S. E. White *Blazed Trail* xlviii. 338 Several times the jam started, but always 'plugged' before the motion had become irresistible. **1964** M. Gowing *Britain & Atomic Energy 1939–1945* viii. 222 The membranes must not 'plug', that is, get blocked.

7. a. *trans.* To popularize (a song) by having it played many times; to present (something) repeatedly; to publicize, emphasize, draw attention to. *colloq.* (orig. *U.S.*).

1906 H. Green *At Actors' Boarding House* 68, I ain't got any music, so you kin plug any publisher's stuff an' play what you wanter. **1927** *Daily Express* 9 Nov. 9/4, I..thought it would encourage them to plug my songs. **1930** [see **cut v.* 54f]. **1940** *Brit. Jrnl. Psychol.* Oct. 118 The technique of 'plugging' trivial news about important personages. **1959** *Elizabethan* June 27/2, I gather from John that the other papers have plugged the crisis for all they're worth. **1967** *Wall St. Jrnl.* 12 Jan. 1/4 Mrs. Glick..now plugs Excedrin on television. **1970** G. F. Newman *Sir, You Bastard* i. 21 I'm obliged to listen to clients plugging their virility as relevant facts. **1975** C. James *Fate of Felicity Fark* v. 45 She found the concentration of rehearsal More challenging by far than plugging *Persil.*

b. *intr. to plug for*: to act in support of; to make favourable statements about. *U.S. colloq.*

1927 *Amer. Speech* II. 256/1 'Pluggers' or 'rooters', 'plug' or 'root' for their side or for their favorite players. **1929** D. Runyon in *Hearst's Internat.* July 58/1 Miss Missouri Martin keeps plugging for Dave the Dude with Miss Billy Perry. **1932** *Sun* (Baltimore) 27 Apr. 1/1 The secret subsidizing of newspaper financial writers to 'plug' for stocks in process of manipulation upward. **1943** *Amer. Speech* XVIII. 249 Judge James A. Chase, a Cashmere citizen, who had visited the Vale of Kashmir, plugged for the new name and won. **1974** *News & Courier* (Charleston, S. Carolina) 7 Apr. A-14/3 At present he is plugging for a written history of Dillon County.

pluggable (plʌ·găb'l), *a.* [f. Plug *v.* + -able.] Suitable for or capable of being plugged. **a.** Of a song or recording (see **plug v.* 7a).

1930 *Punch* 9 Apr. 414 One good rousing 'pluggable' air, 'The March of the Musketeers'. **1977** *Time* 19 Dec. 54/1 The first film..features a sound track overcrowded with highly pluggable Bee Gees songs.

b. Of an electrical device (see **plug v.* 1e).

1946 *Ann. Computation Lab. Harvard Univ.* I. 251 The Lio counter has a pluggable read-out from the counter into the buss. **1954** *Jrnl. Assoc. Computing Machinery* I. 13/2 Converting..consists principally of adding magnetic heads and pluggable units. **1977** *New Yorker* 12 Sept. 93/2 (Advt.), These remarkable, pluggable, portable 4-band radio-cassette recorders give you the wide sound of stereo FM.

plugged, *ppl. a.* Add: **2.** *U.S.* Of coins: having a portion removed and the space filled with base material.

1888 *Texas Siftings* 3 Nov., Ticket Agent—Can't sell you a ticket for that quarter; it's plugged. **1890** B. Hall *Turnover Club* 207 The first speaker..paid the price of his folly with a plugged quarter. **1909** 'O. Henry' *Options* 312 Mr. Hinkle told me..you'd never taken in a lead silver dollar or a plugged one. **1912** *Pearson's Mag.* (Amer. ed.) XXVII. 691/2 For a plugged peso I'd stay with you! **1923** C. E. Mulford *Black Buttes* 265 He says..he'll see us both in hell before he'll pay a plugged peso. **1936** C. Sandburg *People, Yes* 63 He seems to think he's the frog's tonsils but he looks to me like a plugged nickel. **1946** E. O'Neill *Iceman Cometh* (1947) iv. 210 Listen, you cockeyed old bum, for a plugged nickel I'd—. **1974** Hawkey & Bingham *Wild Card* viii. 81 If as much as a whisper gets out..none of our lives are going to be worth a plugged nickel.

3. plugged-in, electrically connected by means of a plug (see **plug v.* 1e); also *fig.*

1957 V. Nabokov *Pnin* i. 14 His devoutly plugged-in clock would make nonsense of his mornings after a storm in the middle of the night had paralyzed the local power station. **1970** E. McGirr *Death pays Wages* vi. 126 A box with a plugged-in pair of earphones. **1975** *Wentworth & Flexner's Dict. Amer. Slang* Suppl. 732/1 *Plugged-in* adj. = turned-on. **1977** M. Herr *Dispatches* (1978) 32 After a year I felt so plugged in to all the stories..that even the dead started telling me stories.

plugger. Add: **c.** One who extols or publicizes. Cf. **plug v.* 7b. orig. *U.S.*

1913 *Writer's Bulletin* Oct. 127/2 Publishers spend thousands..in order to attract the attention of out-of-town performers with whom, neither they nor their 'pluggers' ever come in contact. **1921** *Cleveland* (Ohio) *Enterprise* 4 June 1/3 Everybody out here is a booster and plugger for one common purpose. **1927** [see **plug v.* 7b]. **1958** [see A. and R. (**A III*)]. **1972** P. Black *Biggest Aspidistra* i. iii. 29 The pluggers kept the initiative by inventing the request item. This was..almost impossible to identify as a proven plug.

d. *Angling.* One who fishes with a plug (sense 8**).

1967 *Daily Tel.* 21 Oct. 14/7 Many successful bass pluggers work on the principle that it is a fish with an easily aroused temper. So they use a 'teaser'.

plugging, *vbl. sb.* Add: **1.** (Further examples.)

1797 *Deb. Congress U.S.* 13 Dec. (1851) 718 They knew the silver coin circulated by tale, the gold by weight; the value of the latter had actually diminished by various means, such as sweating, plugging, clipping, &c. **1841** *Florist's Jrnl.* II. 266 The form is almost perfect, with great depth of petals, and an excellent rising centre, such as cannot be imitated by any of the usual plugging and trickery sometimes played off, or at least attempted, at exhibitions; and thus it is an excellent show Dahlia. **1908** *Animal Managem.* 211 Piece by piece the straw is wetted and forced into the body of the collar... This process is termed 'plugging'. **1908** K. McGaffey *Show-Girl* 109 Is it considered au fait for a bride-about-to-be to do a little plugging for wedding presents this early in the game? **1921** A. J. Empey *Madonna of Hills* xviii. 130 Plugging means to push the sale of songs by singing them in cabarets and places. **1926** Whiteman & McBride *Jazz* viii. 169 While plugging is important, the publishers contended recently that there can be too much of any good thing. **1934** *Evening News* 13 July 6/5, I wonder, by the way, whether Uncle Andre, in view of his hour tonight, has been asked to reduce the amount of 'plugging' in it. **1957** *Listener* 10 Oct. 583/1 This plugging of his plays, early and late, successful and otherwise. **1969** E. W. Hildick *Close Look at Advertising* 31 Some of the celebrities have been known to collect very large sums of money for 'letting slip' just such recommendations. It is known as plugging. **1974** G. S. Ormsby in P. L. Moore et al. *Drilling Practices Manual* vi. 167 Underflow plugging is usually caused either by a dry beach or by solids over-load.

3. (Examples in sense *7a of verb.)

1929 *Melody Maker* Feb. 124/3 The listener is often served with all kinds of tripe songs, reiterated *ad nauseam*, at the dictates of the wire pullers over an extensive plugging period. **1932** *Sun* (Baltimore) 27 Apr. 15/7 Checks..were identified..as payments for stock 'plugging' publicity. **1959** *Punch* 10 June 766/3, I suspect it may be a new plugging gimmick, a form of filibustering.

plu·g-in, *a.* and *sb.* [f. vbl. phr. *to plug in* (**plug v.* 1e).] **A.** *adj.* Designed to be plugged into a socket (esp. an electrical one); of or pertaining to such devices.

1922 *Wireless World* 8 July 458/1 One sees so many makeshift plug-in devices..in amateur sets. **1926** R. W. Hutchinson *Wireless* 187 The aerial inductance L_1 and the reaction coil L_2 are of the plug-in type. **1954** *Sun* (Baltimore) (B ed.) 19 June 15/1 Portable plug-in telephones with conveniently located outlets offer a modern convenience where a telephone is desired on a part-time basis in certain rooms. **1965** *Wireless World* Sept. 464/2 An encapsulated version..for plug-in applications is available. **1966** 'A. York' *Eliminator* iv. 57 A mahogany-boxed erinoid plug-in chess set lay on the coffee table. **1968** R. Petrie *MacLurg goes West* viii. 67 The hotel manager was knocking at MacLurg's door, followed by a porter with a plug-in telephone. **1968** B. Turner *Sex Trap* v. 28 His kitchen boasted one cup and a plug-in percolator. **1971** J. H. Smith *Digital Logic* ii. 18 A very easy method of construction is to use one of the commercially available rack construction systems with plug-in units. **1977** Warner & Bell in D. M. Rumbaugh *Language Learning by Chimpanzee* vii. 144 Purchasing the computer, its plug-in modules and peripherals proved to be a wise decision.

B. *sb.* A plug-in device or unit.

1950 *Sun* (Baltimore) 31 Aug. 8/7 The refrigerator units will operate either from car batteries or 110-volt or 220-volt plug-ins for use where electricity is available. **1955** *IRE Trans. Electronic Computers* IV. 3/1 One standard plug-in contains four flip-flops and eight cathode-followers for isolation. **1965** *Wireless World* July 54 (Advt.), Three new instruments..have all the in-built virtues of the original plug-ins. **1967** *Electronics* 6 Mar. 2 (Advt.), Sweep Oscillators with RF and marker plug-ins meet virtually all of your swept frequency testing requirements. **1971** C. Fick *Danziger Transcript* (1973) 171, I heated some coffee on my plug-in and we lit cigars. **1972** 'G. Black' *Bitter Tea* (1973) xiii. 212 The jacks for the phone plug-ins. **1975** *Sci. Amer.* Mar. 11/1 (Advt.), Priced at $800 for the main-frame and $110 to $250 for the plug-ins, the 5150A is easily the new price/performance leader in instrumentation recorders.

plugola (plʌgōu·lă). orig. *U.S.* [f. **plug sb.* 8* + **-ola.*] Incidental or surreptitious promotion of a person or product, esp. on radio or television; a bribe for this. Also *attrib.* and *transf.*

1959 *Washington Post* 7 Dec. A12/4 The nasty charges of fees collected for plugola. **1963** R. I. McDavid *Mencken's Amer. Lang.* 213 *Plugola*, a subspecies [of payola]—payments to disk jockeys in return for frequently playing a record company's new recordings—was also disclosed during these scandals. **1972** *Times Lit. Suppl.* 29 Sept. 1138/2 If the garret doesn't get you, the plugola circuit will. **1972** *Guardian* 20 Dec. 4/5 Mr Whitehead spoke of 'ideological plugola' and went on: 'Station licensees have final responsibility for news balance.' **1977** *National Observer* (U.S.) 1 Jan. 2/2 The Federal Communications Commission said it will hold hearings next year into alleged 'payola' and 'plugola' by broadcasters. The FCC said it had received information that illegal payments had been made to disc jockeys for playing certain records and to broadcasters for mentioning products.

plug-ugly. For *U.S. slang* read *slang* (orig. and chiefly *U.S.*). More widely, a man of violence, one who adopts intimidatory methods. Also *attrib.* and as *adj.* (Earlier and further examples.)

1856 *Butte Rec.* (Oroville, Calif.) 29 Nov. 3/7 The..Plug Uglies..went to Philadelphia on election day..to fight off and whip the democracy from the polls. **1857** *Lawrence* (Kansas) *Republican* 30 July 2 Only a pitiful minority of the actual voters of Kansas, cast their votes for delegates to the plug ugly convention. **1861** [see *blood-tub* (**blood sb.* 19)]. **1909** *Dialect Notes* III. 358 *Plug-ugly*, an ugly person or thing, especially an ugly horse. **1915** *Ibid.* IV. 187 *Plug ugly*, adj. phr. Said of a very ugly man, not genteel. (Applied more commonly to an 'ugly customer'.—*Ed.*) **1923** Wodehouse *Adventures of Sally* xiv. 176 After he'd paid these two pluguglies their guarantees..he was just about cleaned out. **1935** *Punch* 13 Nov. 550/2 Readers who have led sheltered lives will think of plug-uglies, and I hope the cleaner kinds of plug-ugly will think of baths. **1953** [see *lunatic fringe* s.v. **lunatic sb.* 1c]. **1956** D. Karp *All Honorable Men* 18 The plug-uglies on the Right and the Left are the only people who don't give a damn about the opposing argument, and I don't count myself among them. **1972** K. Bonfiglioli *Don't point that Thing at Me* ii. 12 'Yes, Sir.' said Plug Ugly II. **1975** *New Yorker* 1 Dec. 136/2 When a director like Sam Peckinpah puts a group like his Wild Bunch on the screen, the men are so alive that the last thing that would ever come into your head is that some of them are plug-uglies. **1978** N. Marsh *Grave Mistake* ii. 62 Verity thought, I've..drunk their champagne so now I turn plug-ugly and refuse.

plum, *sb.* Add: **4. d.** (Further examples.) Also, the best part of a musical work.

1887 in G. Stimpson *Bk. about Amer. Politics* (1952) 258 The boys enjoying the plums will support anybody who is good for him or them. **1937** W. H. SAUMAREZ SMITH *Let.* 16 Oct. in *Young Man's Country* (1977) ii. 94 It [*sc.* the job] is definitely one of the three plums for the young civilian. **1967** *Boston Herald* 8 May 24/5 José has played his cards just right, and a rich little plum named Lucy falls into his outstretched arms. **1973** *Times* 20 Oct. 13/6 Its slow movement is its 'plum', a glorious, unbroken song. **1978** *Time* 3 July 42/2 Center directors receive only $11,000 a year, but Mendel offers them a plum: their kids can attend free.

5*. = *plum-colour*.

1878 *Trans. Illinois Dept. Agric.* XIV. 210 [Siamese Swine] varied in color from deep rich plum to dark slate and black. **1895** *Montgomery Ward Catal.* 3/1 Cashmere... All the fashionable colors..golden brown, medium plum, heliotrope. **1940** GRAVES & HODGE *Long Week-End* xvi. 278 Victorian colours—plum, maroon, and violet—were in favour. **1970** *Guardian* 5 June 9/2 She has feather-weight car rugs in brushed wool in plum and purple at a modest three guineas each.

6. a. *plum brandy, -tart* (earlier example), *wine*. **b.** *plum-gathering*; *plum-dark, -purple* (earlier example), *-rich* adjs. **c.** *plum-coloured* (earlier example), *-stained* adjs. **d. plum-colour** (further examples); **plum-in-the-mouth** *a.* (*colloq.*), indistinctly articulated, esp. in a manner associated with the British upper classes (of speech, etc.); **plum pox** [tr. Bulgarian *sharka na slivite* (D. Atanasoff 1932, in *Godishnik na Sofiĭskiya Universitet Agronomski Fakultet* XI. 49)], a virus disease of plum trees characterized by yellow blotches on the leaves and pockets of dead tissue in the fruit; also known as *sharka*; **plum rains** [tr. Jap. *bai-u*] = *BAI-U; applied also to the corresponding rains in southern China.

1950 *Chambers's Encycl.* IV. 326/1 Plums are grown as fresh fruit and for jam, though some are distilled into *slivovice* (plum brandy). **1958** A. L. SIMON *Dict. Wines, Spirits & Liqueurs* 147/1 Slivovitz..is very similar to the Alsatian Plum Brandy called Quetsch. **1977** H. FAST *Immigrants* 11 The husband of the Polish woman..hoarded plum brandy. **1898** G. B. SHAW *You never can Tell* III. 274 The wall decoration of Lincrusta Walton in plum color and bronze lacquer. **1960** S. PLATH *Colossus* (1967) 21, I squat..Counting the red stars and those of plum-colour. **1820** M. EDGEWORTH *Let.* 8 June (1979) 160 Fannys plum colored [*sic*] and Harrets lilac tabbinets. **1957** L. DURRELL *Bitter Lemons* 103 Plum-dark mountain roses. **1958** —— *Balthazar* i. 13 A single plum-dark sail, moist, palpitant. **1963** *Glamour* Sept. 146 Plum-dark wool frames the soft blue silk collar of the coat, worn over a matching plum-dark flared skirt. **1928** C. DAY LEWIS *Country Comets* 25 At the time of plum-gathering When the hedge is plumy With Traveller's Joy. **1926** D. H. LAWRENCE *Plumed Serpent* vi. 118 She spoke rapidly, a rather plum-in-the-mouth Spanish. **1934** S. R. NELSON *All about Jazz* vii. 163 The lukewarm, plum-in-the-mouth style of some of the white vocalists. **1933** *Rev. Applied Mycol.* XII. 230 The disease, which the author [*sc.* D. Atanasoff] terms plum pox, was proved to be readily transmissible to healthy trees by grafting. **1943** *Bull. Min. Agric. & Fish.* CXXVI. 64 A single tree bearing foliage with symptoms corresponding to those of Plum Pox..was observed early in August 1934 at East Oakley, Hants. **1952** E. RAMSDEN tr. *Gram & Weber's Plant Diseases* II. 204/2 A disease called plum pox, well known in Bulgaria, probably occurs as far north as Bohemia and Holland. **1976** *Nature* 12 Feb. 499/2 The Ministry of Agriculture reported that at least 150 acres of plums have some levels of infection with plum pox (sharka) virus, an aphid-borne virus. **1862** G. M. HOPKINS *Vision of Mermaids* (1929), Plum-purple was the west. **1922, 1945** Plum rains [see *BAI-U]. **1968** G. R. RUMNEY *Climatol. & World's Climates* xii. 235/1 The cloudiness, humidity, and generally oppressive conditions accompanying the start of the warm season's heavy rains in southern Japan combine to create a period of depressing, gloomy weather called here, as in south China, the plum rains (*Bai-u*). **1971** *Handbk. Aviation Meteorol.* (Meteorol. Office) xxiii. 378 In May, tropical air begins to advance northwards and is heralded by cyclonic activity and the widespread 'plum' rains of China and Japan. **1932** AUDEN *Orators* I. 3 The plum-rich red-earth valley of the Severn. **1922** JOYCE *Ulysses* 564 Two trickies Frauenzimmer plum-stained from pram falling bawling. **1770** J. WOODFORDE *Diary* 12 Oct. (1924) I. 102, I gave them for dinner a.. Plumb Tart and an Apple Tart. **1728** E. SMITH *Compl. Housewife* (ed. 2) 208 To make Plum-wine. Take twenty pound of Malaga raisins..water..damson juice..at 4 or 5 months bottle it. **1976** 'M. DELVING' *China Expert* i. 11 The guest list included..Chinese and Westerners, all.. eager to sample the stuffed, glazed chicken and fish in plum wine sauce.

e. passing into *adj.* = *plum-coloured* adj.

1922 JOYCE *Ulysses* 551 In a flunkey's plum plush coat and kneebreeches, buff stockings and powdered wig. **1930** V. SACKVILLE-WEST *Edwardians* v. 229 Buttoned into her plum velvet bodice, like the wife of any British tradesman. **1975** J. MCCLURE *Snake* x. 133 There was a white Jaguar, a plum Datsun coupé and a..Land-Rover.

f. (sense 4 d) passing into *adj.* Choice, valuable, coveted.

1958 *Listener* 21 Aug. 277/1 Was the promotion of Chiappe to the plum governorship an easy method of shedding a dangerous man in a key position? **1959** *Economist* 2 May 455/2 While the aircraft industries of Britain and France are declining for lack of military orders, a plum military contract has been won by a company making its first serious venture into aircraft design since the war. **1966** *Listener* 26 May 746/2 After the Nationalists had come to power, they felt that they had to admit some Afrikaners to their boards and directorates. These were plum appointments and the Boers had been longing for them for years. **1970** *Financial Times* 13 Apr. 10/6 Europe (the present plum client in the German Railways advertising service). **1976** BOTHAM & DONNELLY *Valentino* xi. 85 The director..congratulated him on winning the plum role. **1977** *Time* 3 Jan. 50/2 The leader of L.D.P.'s largest faction, whose intellect had won him plum jobs in the Ministry of Finance before he turned to politics in 1952, has probably done exactly that.

plum, *v.* Add: **2. b.** To fill or stuff *up* (a person) with false information.

1921 *Chambers's Jrnl.* May 323/1 He ain't to know no different but what Jack's got prairie fever. Mind you plum him up stiff. **1927** *Observer* 20 Nov. 26/5 He has recently returned from Upper Silesia..and promptly puts into writing all that his clever German friends have been 'plumming' him up with.

plumasite (plū·măsəit). *Petrogr.* [f. the name of *Plumas* Co., California, where it was first found + -ITE[1].] A coarse-grained, undersaturated, dike-rock consisting essentially of crystals of corundum in an oligoclase matrix.

1903 A. C. LAWSON in *Bull. Dept. Geol. Univ. Calif.* III. 228 This particular type of rock magma does not appear to have been as yet recognized among the known occurrences of rocks, and it is, therefore, proposed to name it, for convenience in reference, *Plumasite*, from Plumas county in which it occurs. **1949** F. H. HATCH et al. *Petrol. Ign. Rocks* (ed. 10) III. iii. 262 Dioritic rocks of unusual composition include plumasite. **1972** *Jrnl. Geol. Soc. India* XIII. 198 Investigations in the present case have proved that plumasite is a result of the local enrichment of alumina in the magma due to the reaction of the acid magma of the Peninsular gneissic period with the older magnesian country.

plumb, plum, *adv.* **2. c.** (Further examples.)

1846 S. F. SMITH *Theatr. Apprenticeship* 213 Long before the time arrived..the house was plum, chock full—full to overflowing. *a* **1861** T. WINTHROP *John Brent* xxviii. 296 When we got here, I paid their tickets plum through to York out of my own belt. **1901** F. NORRIS *Octopus* I. iii. 121 'I'll get plumb out of here,' he trumpeted. 'I won't stay here another minute.' **1926** 'R. CROMPTON' *William—the Conqueror* v. 89 Poor woman! She's sure plumb crazy! **1934** A. CHRISTIE *Murder on Orient Express* II. ix. 136 'You are sure of that, M. Hardman?' 'I'm plumb certain.' **1967** G. F. FIENNES *I tried to run a Railway* vii. 76 In his presence I was tense, tongue-tied and often plumb stupid. **1973** E. LEMARCHAND *Let or Hindrance* xiv. 182 They must both be plumb crazy.

plumb, *v.* Add: **I. 1.** For † *Obs.* read *rare* and add later example.

1940 *Sat. Even. Post* 6 Apr. 17/3 [He] rolled down [from a house-top] & plumbed into the yard.

V. 9. *trans.* To connect (a domestic appliance or the like) permanently to the water supply and the drain. Usu. with *in*.

1963 *Which?* 6 Feb. 46/2 The Easiclene [dishwashing machine] would normally be plumbed in, but could be used with hoses from a tap and into a sink. **1976** I. CHANARIN et al. *Blood & its Dis.* ix. 79 Automatic equipment using potentially toxic reagents should be plumbed-in. **1976** *Star* (Sheffield) 20 Nov. 10/7 (Advt.), Abbey Plumbing Emergency Service. Bursts and leaks, washing machines plumbed, gas fitting and alterations.

plumbane. Restrict † *Obs.* to sense in Dict. and add: **2.** [-ANE 2 b.] **a.** Any of the alkyl compounds of lead or the hypothetical series of saturated lead hydrides (analogous to the alkanes) from which they are formally derived; freq. as a formative element in names of such compounds. **b.** *spec.* Lead tetrahydride, PbH_4, an extremely unstable gas.

1920 *Chem. Abstr.* XIV. 2182 The mol. wt. indicates that it has the double formula $[(C_8H_9)_3Pb]_2$ so that it might be considered as hexa-*p*-xylyldiplumbane. **1950** N. V. SIDGWICK *Chem. Elements & Compounds* I. 554 Lead hydride, plumbane, presumably PbH_4..was prepared by Paneth in 1920. *Ibid.* 596 The diplumbane formed may change further into lead tetra-aryl and metallic lead. **1964** A. ROCHOW *Organometallic Chem.* i. 4 The system [of nomenclature] is so useful that it has been extended.. even to tin and lead (..$(C_6H_5)_2PbCl_2$, diphenyldichloroplumbane), although the older inorganic names like diphenyllead dichloride still persist to a considerable extent. **1967** P. L. PAUSON *Organometallic Chem.* iii. 78 The rather unstable plumbanes have only been obtained by direct reduction of the halides with suitable hydrides. **1971** WIBERG & AMBERGER *Hydrides Elements of Main Groups I–IV* x. 757 Similar attempts to obtain plumbane, PbH_4,..were unsuccessful. *Ibid.* 760 Trimethylplumbane, Me_3PbH, and triethylplumbane, Et_3PbH, decompose according to kinetics that are first-order for $[R_3PbH]$. **1973** J. J. LAGOWSKI *Mod. Inorg. Chem.* xi. 368 Plumbane has been prepared in only trace amounts from the reactions which yield the hydrides of the other elements in this family.

plumbate[2]. Substitute for def.: Any of various (salts of) oxyanions or hydroxyanions of quadrivalent lead, which are formed esp. by the action of alkalis on lead dioxide. Now also extended occas. to (salts of) any oxyanion of lead, the oxidation state being specified in brackets. (Earlier and later examples.) [First formed as F. *plombate* (E. Fremy 1843, in *Jrnl. de Pharm.* III. 32).]

1851 H. WATTS tr. *Gmelin's Handbk. Chem.* V. 160 (*heading*) Plumbate of potash. **1889** I. REMSEN *Inorg. Chem.* xxx. 645 Other salts derived from the acid $PbO(OH)_2$ are known, and are called plumbates. **1950** N. V. SIDGWICK *Chem. Elements & Compounds* I. 603 Plumbic hydroxide, $Pb(OH)_4$. This..gives a series of salts, the plumbates, of various types, such as Ca_2PbO_4 and Na_2PbO_3. **1958** *Engineering* 21 Feb. 242/1 The manufacture, properties and applications of..rust-inhibiting calcium plumbate paint were outlined. **1959** *Nomencl. Inorg. Chem.* (I.U.P.A.C.) 32 By dissolving, for example, Sb_2O_3, SnO, or PbO in sodium hydroxide an antimonate(III), a stannate(II), a plumbate(II), *etc.*, is formed in the solution. **1962** COTTON & WILKINSON *Adv. Inorg. Chem.* xix. 364 Crystalline alkali metal stannates and plumbates can be obtained as trihydrates, for instance, $K_2SnO_3{\cdot}3H_2O$... Such materials..contain the anions $Sn(OH)_6{}^{2-}$ and $Pb(OH)_6{}^{2-}$. **1974** G. I. BROWN *Introd. Inorg. Chem.* xviii. 210 Tin(II) and lead(II) oxides.. form salts with acids and stannates(II) and plumbates(II) with alkalis. *Ibid.* 211 Both oxides react with caustic alkalis to form stannates(IV) or plumbates(IV).

plumbate (plʌ·mbēit), *a.* [f. L. *plumb-um* lead + -ATE[2].] Of or pertaining to a type of glazed and usu. lead-coloured pottery made in pre-Columbian central America. Also *absol.* as *sb.*[3]

1926 S. K. LOTHROP *Pottery of Costa Rica & Nicaragua* I. I. iv. 116 The vitrified surface of the Plumbate Ware did not lend itself to painted decoration. **1936** —— *Zacualpa* 39 The typical vessel of pure plumbate clay is hard, well fired and has a glossy surface. **1940** J. E. S. THOMPSON in *Maya & their Neighbours* 129 The absence of plumbate and typical fine orange pottery, turquoise, and gold..hint that these sites are not contemporaneous with the Mexican Period in Yucatan. **1948** A. O. SHEPARD *Plumbate* 1/2 Plumbate effigies in particular show a fascinating versatility coupled with a tendency to follow fixed types. **1962** G. KUBLER *Art & Archit. Anc. Amer.* ix. 205 A few 'glazed sherds' found during excavation: if these were plumbate, a Toltec Maya date would be in order. **1971** L. A. BOGER *Dict. World Pottery & Porcelain* 345/2 Two outstanding types of pottery made in large quantities and traded wherever Toltec influence was evident are Fine Orange ware..and Plumbate. *Ibid.* 346/1 Plumbate ware dates from around 1000.

plumber. Add: **1.** In mod. use, a workman who installs and repairs piping and fittings to do with water supply, sanitation, and drainage.

2. *transf.* **a.** *Services' slang.* An armourer or engineering officer. **b.** *slang.* During the administration of United States President Richard M. Nixon (1969–74), a member of a White House special unit for investigating leaks of government secrets, which came to public notice after it was discovered that they had engaged in illegal practices, including the installation of concealed microphones; also *transf.*

a. 1941 D. MASTERS *So Few* xix. 224 The plumbers—the name by which the armourers are generally known in the service. **1943** C. H. WARD-JACKSON *It's a Piece of Cake* 48 *Plumber*, the Engineering Officer. **1946** G. HACKFORTH-JONES *Sixteen Bells* I. vii. 106 To the average 'Plumber' the word Engine is synonymous [*sic*] with steam. **1962** *Flight* 11 Nov. 605/2, I am not an engineer (or 'plumber', as the Royal Air Force equivalent is unofficially called). **1979** *Navy News* Feb. 2/1 It would be of great help in this project if, among your readers, there were a few ex-Keyham 'plumbers' who would be prepared to turn out their photographs of those times for us to borrow.

b. 1972 *Time* 28 Aug. 24/2 The intelligence squad grew out of a team of so-called 'plumbers', originally recruited by the Administration to investigate leaks to the media. **1973** *Times* 15 May 7/1 President Nixon sent a personal letter to Mr J. Edgar Hoover, then Director of the Federal Bureau of Investigation (FBI), in June, 1971, telling him that Mr Egil Krogh had been put in charge of a special White House task force on national security and asking for FBI cooperation with it. The group later became known as 'the plumbers' because it tried to plug leaks of information. **1974** *Times* 9 Jan. 5/6 The investigating magistrate in the case of *Le Canard Enchaîné* questioned for two hours today a counter-espionage agent who has been allegedly identified as one of the 'plumbers' in the attempted bugging of the satirical weekly magazine. **1976** *Billings* (Montana) *Gaz.* 6 July 3A 1 Ehrlichman is now appealing a five-year sentence following his conviction for obstruction of justice for his part in the break-in of the office of Daniel Ellsberg's psychiatrist by the now-infamous 'plumbers'. **1977** *Time* 24 Jan. 52/1 He found a band of 'plumbers' busily installing listening devices.

plumbian (plʌ·mbiăn), *a. Min.* [f. L. *plumb-um* lead + *-IAN 2.] Of a mineral: having a (small) proportion of a constituent element replaced by lead.

1930 W. T. SCHALLER in *Amer. Mineralogist* XV. 571 Lead—plumbian. **1944** C. PALACHE et al. *Dana's Syst. Min.* (ed. 7) I. 804 *Var.* Ordinary. Calcium and uranium. ..Plumbian... With Pb:U=3:8 (anal. 1). Titanian. With Ti:Cb+Ta:Fe[3]=9:3:1 (anal. 6). **1968** I. KOSTOV *Mineralogy* II. ii. 169 The following varieties are recognized: (*a*) of tetrahedrite—ordinary, zincian, ferroan,.. plumbian, nickelian, etc.

plumbic, *a.* **a.** For '(divalent)' read '(quadrivalent)'. Add: Formerly also applied by some writers to compounds of bivalent lead (cf. *PLUMBOUS *a.* 2). (Further examples.)

1854 R. D. THOMSON *Cycl. Chem.* 328/1 Binoxide, Peroxide, Deutoxide, Brown or puce oxide, Plumbic acid.—PbO_2. **1868** W. A. MILLER *Elem. Chem.* (ed. 4) II. xviii. 717 Lead oxide, plumbic oxide, or protoxide of lead (PbO = 223)... This oxide is well known under the name of litharge. *Ibid.* 719 Plumbic dioxide, or peroxide of lead (PbO_2 = 239). **1900** W. A. SHENSTONE *Elem. Inorg. Chem.* xxix. 439 Plumbic oxide (PbO) is known as litharge or massicot. **1921** J. R. PARTINGTON *Text-bk. Inorg. Chem.* xliv. 925 A yellow liquid, which is lead tetrachloride, or plumbic chloride, $PbCl_4$, is deposited. **1935** *Chambers's Encycl.* VI. 564/1 Plumbic Oxide (monoxide of lead, massicot, litharge), PbO... Plumbic Peroxide..PbO_2... Plumbic Chloride (chloride of lead), $PbCl_2$. **1950** N. V. SIDGWICK *Chem. Elements & Compounds* I. 587 The change from the plumbous alkyls to the plumbic is less easy with the heavier alkyls. **1962** P. J. & B. DURRANT *Adv. Inorg. Chem.* xviii. 641 A list of certain alkyl and aryl compounds of lead in the plumbic condition. *Ibid.* 644 Lead tetra-acetate (plumbic acetate), $Pb(CH_3COO)_4$, is made by saturating hot glacial acetic acid with red lead.

plumbicon (plʌ·mbikɒn). *Television.* [f. L. *plumb-um* lead + *-icon*, after *VIDICON.] A type of television camera tube similar to a vidicon but in which the photoconductive layer of the signal plate is of lead monoxide.

1962 E. F. DE HAAN in *Philips Technical Rev.* XXIV. 58/1 The photoconductive layer consists of vapour-deposited lead monoxide, PbO, and we have therefore called this tube the 'Plumbicon'. **1971** *Physics Bull.* Aug. 457/1 The other is the plumbicon colour TV tube now used in practically all colour TV cameras all over the world. **1976** *Wireless World* June 75/3 A camera based on three 2/3-in. Plumbicons with built-in image enhancement.

plumbing, *vbl. sb.* Add: **b.** Also *transf.* in various senses: (*a*) *colloq.*, a system of pipes, tubes, or ducts in an engine or other complicated apparatus or installation; (*b*) *Jazz slang*, a trumpet, trombone, or similar wind instrument; (*c*) *spec.* a lavatory; lavatory installations (*colloq.*); (*d*) *slang*, fillings in teeth; (*e*) *joc.*, the excretory tracts, the urinary system.

a. *a* **1929** in V. W. Pagé *Mod. Aviation Engines* (1929) II. xl. 1593 Courtney's flight, Franco's flight and the Polish flight were all three terminated by what is popularly known as 'plumbing' trouble... The engines stopped through failure of the feed lines. **1938** —— *Airplane Servicing Man.* xxii. 758 Aircraft space is limited, and.. complicated plumbing must be installed in very close quarters. **1950** J. L. NAYLER *Mod. Aircraft Design* v. 78 Pumps and their connections have to be installed in places where they can be inspected and 'plumbing' is accordingly a big factor in their installation. **1955** *Sci. Amer.* Oct. 34/3 New materials—e.g., liquid sodium as the coolant, beryllium as the moderator, zirconium for the 'plumbing'..—may open the way for reactors..needing only a modest investment of fissile fuel. **1959** *New Scientist* 12 Feb. 359/2 The wave-guide, or 'plumbing' as the radar engineer calls it, is simply a metal tube down which radio waves will travel. **1971** H. E. ENNES *Telev. Broadcasting: Equipment, Syst. & Operating Fund.* xii. 548 Fig. 12–11 illustrates typical microwave plumbing.

b. 1935 *Vanity Fair* (N.Y.) Nov. 71/3 *Plumbing* or *piston* for trumpet. **1951** *Cosmopolitan* July 85 Hap said, 'You with the plumbin', what's your name?' **1955** *Vogue* 15 Sept. 124 Kai Winding and J. J. Johnson (above) pair their spruce, understated trombones ('just plumbing') against a backing of bass, drums and piano.

c. 1950 *Publ. Amer. Dial. Soc.* XIV. 50 *Outside plumbing*, euphemism for no plumbing, a privy. **1971** *Countryman* Winter 118 The house is progressing at last. We have bought a mountain of building supplies—pink plumbing and all. **1978** S. ALLAN *Inside Job* i. 18, I expect she wants to wash... Don't be obtuse... I want to show her the plumbing.

d. 1955 J. THOMAS *No Banners* xiv. 117 The fillings in his teeth had been removed and replaced by unmistakable French 'plumbing'.

e. 1960 in Wentworth & Flexner *Dict. Amer. Slang* 398/1 This mild little medicine will fix your constipation, your stomach, your plumbing. **1963** M. MCCARTHY *Group* v. 103 Helena had known about sex from a very early age but treated it as a joke, like what she called your plumbing. **1972** G. BELL *Villains Galore* iii. 31 Excuse me, Albert, but I must see to the plumbing. Won't be a minute.

plumbite (plʌ·mbəit). *Chem.* [ad. F. *plombite* (E. Fremy 1843, in *Jrnl. de Pharm.* III. 31), f. *plomb* lead: see -ITE[1].] Any of various (salts of) oxyanions or hydroxy anions of bivalent lead, which are formed esp. by the action of alkalis on lead(II) hydroxide and are freq. represented as PbO_2^{2-}; applied also to certain mixed oxides of bivalent lead and another metal.

1851 H. WATTS tr. *Gmelin's Hand-bk. Chem.* V. 158 (*heading*) Plumbite of ammonia. **1903** H. C. JONES *Princ. Inorg. Chem.* xl. 480 Lead hydroxide..has..acid properties dissolving readily in strong bases. The salts have the composition M_2PbO_2 and are known as plumbites. **1927** J. W. MELLOR *Comprehensive Treat. Inorg. & Theoret. Chem.* VII. xlvii. 665 The plumbites all appear to be salts of a monobasic acid analogous with the corresponding stannites and germanites. *Ibid.* 669 Grube obtained a mixture, $2MgO.PbO.3H_2O$, or magnesium plumbite, by the oxidation of magnesium hemiplumbide in the presence of moisture. **1950** N. V. SIDGWICK *Chem. Elements & Compounds* I. 603 It is possible to make a plumbate by atmospheric oxidation of a plumbite. **1968** K. M. & R. A. MACKAY *Introd. Mod. Inorg. Chem.* xv. 223/1 Addition of alkali to lead II solutions gives a precipitate of the hydrated oxide, which dissolves in excess alkali to give plumbites.

plumbless, *a.* (Further examples.)

1946 W. DE LA MARE *Traveller* 29 Into a plumbless deep of sleep he sank. **1960** C. ACHEBE *No Longer at Ease* iii. 26 For the first time since they had left Liverpool, the sea became really blue; a plumbless blue set off by the gleaming white tops of countless wavelets.

plumbly (plʌ·mli), *adv. rare.* [f. PLUMB, PLUM *a.* + -LY[2].] Vertically downwards.

1931 J. C. GREGORY *Short Hist. Atomism* 7 The atoms that fell plumbly through the void were still restless.

plumbo-. Add: **plumboja·rosite** *Min.* [JAROSITE], a basic sulphate of lead and ferric iron, $PbFe_6(SO_4)_4(OH)_{12}$, that occurs as brown hexagonal crystals, esp. as a secondary mineral in lead ores in arid regions.

1902 Plumbojarosite [see *natrojarosite* s.v. *NATRO-]. **1938** *Jrnl. R. Soc. W. Australia* XXIV. 112 This appears to be the first occasion on which either beudantite or plumbojarosite has been found in Australia. **1959** *Mineral Abstr.* XIV. 275/2 Plumbojarosite is found as compact and powdery aggregates of flaky crystals in the Akatuev deposit in eastern Transbaikal region.

plumbous, *a.* **2.** For 'has its lower valency', read 'is bivalent'. Add: Formerly also applied by some writers to substances in which lead was thought to be univalent (cf. *PLUMBIC *a.* a). (Examples.)

1854 R. D. THOMSON *Cycl. Chem.* 327/2 Protoxide of Lead. Yellow Oxide, Massicot, Litharge, Plumbous Acid. PbO. **1868** W. A. MILLER *Elements of Chemistry* (ed. 4) II. xviii. 721 When heated in closed vessels, part of the sulphur is expelled, and a subsulphide, or plumbous sulphide (Pb_2S) is left. **1883** C. L. BLOXAM *Chem.* (ed. 5) 373 Oxide or protoxide of lead (plumbous oxide) is prepared on a large scale by heating lead in air. **1884** FRANKLAND & JAPP *Inorg. Chem.* xxxix. 699 Plumbous oxide, $'Pb'_2O$, is best prepared by heating plumbic oxalate to 300° with exclusion of air... It is a black powder. **1892** MORLEY & MUIR *Watts' Dict. Chem.* (rev. ed.) III. 128/2 Lead protoxide PbO. (Plumbous oxide. Litharge. Massicot.) **1900** W. A. SHENSTONE *Elem. Inorg. Chem.* xxix. 439 Plumbous oxide (Pb_2O). When oxalate of lead is heated to 300° out of contact with air, it leaves a grey residue which absorbs oxygen with avidity. This is the suboxide. **1926** P. C. L. THORNE tr. *Ephraim's Text-bk. Inorg. Chem.* xv. 359 When red lead, Pb_3O_4 (*i.e.* $2PbO.PbO_2$), is treated with nitric acid, the plumbous portion of this compound dissolves, leaving PbO_2 as a brown powder. **1950** [see *PLUMBIC *a.* a]. **1962** P. J. & B. DURRANT *Adv. Inorg. Chem.* xviii. 638 Plumbous nitrate, $(Pb(NO_3)_2$, is made by dissolving lead, lead oxide, or lead carbonate in dilute nitric acid... Concentrated sodium hydroxide solution dissolves plumbous chromate.

plume, *sb.* Add: **3. c.** Self-satisfaction, triumph. *rare.*

1910 W. DE MORGAN *Affair of Dishonour* iv. 66 He wanted..to choose his time, as a nobleman might then do..not only without shame or remorse, but even with some sense of plume or strut.

4. f. (i) A long streamer of smoke, vapour, or other fluid issuing from a localized source in the same or a different fluid and spreading out as it travels, esp. one with a degree of buoyancy in the ambient medium.

1878 [see sense 4a in Dict.]. **1947** *Q. Jrnl. R. Meteorol. Soc.* LXXIII. 428 Smoke plumes from factory chimneys. **1955** *Trans. Amer. Soc. Mech. Engineers* LXXVII. 1/1 Under favorable weather conditions the plume from a smokestack will rise gradually as it flows downwind and the gases will be dispersed until only a negligible concentration prevails in the atmosphere. **1969** *Ann. Rev. Fluid Mech.* I. 30 Turbulent plumes (like jets) have a sharp boundary between the turbulent buoyant fluid and the surroundings; they increase their width through..entrainment of external fluid across this boundary by large eddies. **1970** *Nature* 7 Nov. 545/2 Ball lightning does not rise like hot air nor is it disrupted by convection into a thermal plume as are hot fireballs. **1975** *New Yorker* 12 May 70/3 At discharge, how fast should it come out, and at what level? Would fish die in the thermal plume? **1975** J. L. PAVONI et al. *Handbk. Solid Waste Disposal* iii. 127 Water vapor plumes are caused when the relative humidity of the effluent gas stream is significantly higher than the relative humidity of the ambient air around an incinerator chimney. **1977** *Daily Tel.* 25 Apr. 1/1 The awesome plumbing job..involves stuffing a 12 inch rubber plug into an 18-inch diameter well to staunch a plume of oil and gas sprouting 200 ft into the air.

(ii) *Geol.* A column of magma rising from the lower mantle and spreading sideways on reaching the base of the lithosphere, proposed as an explanation of the motion of lithospheric plates and of sites of volcanic activity away from plate margins.

1971 W. J. MORGAN in *Nature* 5 Mar. 42/2, I now propose that these hotspots are manifestations of convection in the lower mantle which provides the motive force for continental drift. In my model there are about twenty deep mantle plumes bringing heat and relatively primordial material up to the asthenosphere and horizontal currents in the asthenosphere flow radially away from each of these plumes. **1975** *Sci. Amer.* Mar. 62/1 According to this argument, all upward movement of mantle material is confined to about 20 plumes, each plume a few hundred kilometers in diameter, rising from the core-mantle boundary. **1976** P. FRANCIS *Volcanoes* i. 49 The plume effectively burns a hole through the overlying crustal plate..and a volcano results.

‖ **plumeau** (plümo). [Fr.] A duvet.

1892 C. A. M. FENNELL *Stanford Dict.* 637/1 *Plumeau*,.. a thick quilt stuffed with feathers. **1931** E. SACKVILLE-WEST *Simpson* III. 250 Childeric was lying on his bed, half buried in the voluminous *plumeau*. **1967** T. LA CHARD *Sailor Hat* iii. 59, I subsided in sleep under my vast crimson *plumeau*, a towering feather bed gleaming through its white crochet covering.

plumed, *ppl. a.* Add: **3.** Special collocations: **plumed serpent**, a mythical creature depicted as part bird, part snake; *spec.* (freq. with capital initials) any of various deities in the religions of ancient Mesoamerica having this form, esp. Quetzlcoatl, the Aztec deity of vegetation and fertility; also *attrib.*

1915 *Amer. Anthropologist* XVII. 480 (*caption*) (*a*), Pelican design; (*b*), plumed serpent design; from La Bermuda. Collection [of pottery] of Señor Alberto Imery. *Ibid.* 481 Two bowls in the Imery collection..bear upon the outside an interesting representation of the plumed serpent. **1926** D. H. LAWRENCE (*title*) The Plumed Serpent. **1935** *Discovery* Sept. 270/1 A flint dagger, $8\frac{1}{4}$ inches long, with a handle fashioned to represent the body and head of the Plumed Serpent. **1937** *Burlington Mag.* July 55/1 Another point of far-reaching significance is brought out in the discussion of the symbol of the plumed serpent. ..In China a bird is given the emphasis and the serpent appears on its wings..while among the Mayas the serpent dominates but has the wings and feet of a bird. **1959** C. S. CHINCHILLA in Kidder & Chinchilla *Art of Ancient Maya* 29 They do not worship Gukumatz (the plumed serpent) and Balau (the tiger) as animals, but as the deities that they embody under these forms. **1972** *Funk's Stand. Dict. Folklore* 915/1 *Quetzalcoatl.* The feathered or plumed serpent god: known over all Middle America, and surviving in mythology to this day. **1979** P. THEROUX *Old Patagonian Express* iii. 47 The Indians liked him [*sc.* Maximilian] because he was blond, like Quetzalcoatl—Cortez enjoyed the same bizarre notoriety for his resemblance to the Plumed Serpent.

plumetty (plū·mėti), *a.* and *sb. Her.* Also 5 plomte; plumeté. [ad. F. *plumeté*: see PLUMETIS.] (A heraldic device) with a motif of feathers (see quots.).

a **1500** in *Ancestor* (1903) Oct. 193 Gold and purpull plomte. **1780** J. EDMONDSON *Compl. Body Heraldry* II. Gloss., *Plumetty.* When the field is divided into fusils, filled with the ends of feathers, depicted in metal and colour alternately, such field is said to be *Plumetty.* **1892** WOODWARD & BURNETT *Treat. Heraldry* I. iii. 71 Two curious forms of *Vair* occasionally met with in Italian or French coats are known as '*Plumeté*' and '*Papelonné*'. *Ibid.* 72 In *Plumeté* the field is apparently covered with feathers. **1929** *N. & Q.* 2 Nov. 317/2 'Papelonny'..and its analogue, 'plumetty',..are represented in English heraldry. Homologous in their tricking, the diapering of the one takes the form of fish scales; of the other, of the breasts of birds. **1969** FRANKLYN & TANNER *Encycl. Dict. Heraldry* 261/2 *Plumetty*, a field..of feathers.., a form that did not survive, and of which the few examples preserved from the feudal period contradict each other in appearance: one form is semé..of feathers; another consists of barwise rows of feathers conjoined laterally; yet a third displays a field totally covered with overlapping feathers.

Plummer-Vinson (plʌ·məɪ vi·nsən). *Path.* The names of H. S. *Plummer* (1874–1936), U.S. physician, and P. P. *Vinson* (1890–1959), U.S. surgeon, used *attrib.* to designate a syndrome characterized by dysphagia, glossitis, and iron-deficiency anæmia.

1926 A. F. HURST in *Guy's Hospital Rep.* LXXVI. 426 (*heading*) The Plummer-Vinson syndrome (spasm of the pharyngo-œsophageal sphincter with anæmia and splenomegaly). **1958** TERRACOL & SWEET *Dis. Esophagus* xiii. 302 The Plummer-Vinson syndrome occurs predominantly in women in the proportion of approximately four to one. *Ibid.* 303 The Plummer-Vinson syndrome is a clinical complex, the cause of which though still not clearly understood has to do with avitaminosis, endocrine disturbances, and lack of available iron. *Ibid.* 306 There is strong clinical evidence to suggest that the mucosal changes characteristic of the Plummer-Vinson syndrome are of a precancerous nature. **1971** *Brit. Med. Bull.* XXVII. 34/1 The Paterson-Kelly or Plummer-Vinson syndrome was first described in 1919.

plummet, *sb.* Add: **7.** *plummet-deep*, *-measured* adjs.

1938 W. DE LA MARE *Memory* 38 Fleeter than Nereid, plummet-deep, Enticed by some long-sunken ship, She [*sc.* Memory]..laughs out to see The treasure she retrieves for me. **1939** W. B. YEATS *Last Poems* 16 And pressed at midnight in a public place Live lips upon a plummet-measured face.

plummet, *v.* Restrict *rare* to senses in Dict. and add: **4. a.** *trans.* To cause to drop rapidly, to hurl down. **b.** *intr.* To drop or fall rapidly, to plunge *down.* Also *fig.*

1933 *Sun* (Baltimore) 11 Apr. 1/1 The U.S.S. Akron had

reports that the weather was unfavorable for her purpose when she took off last Monday on the fatal flight that plummeted her into the sea from lightning-swept skies. **1939** WEBSTER Add., *Plummet, v.i.*, to drop or plunge straight down. **1944** F. LEIBER in D. Knight *100 Yrs. Sci. Fiction* (1969) 93 'I'm glad to see the last of that fellow,' he muttered,..as they plummeted toward the roof. **1953** A. MOOREHEAD *Rum Jungle* vii. 96 They [*sc.* gulls] plummeted down with their beaks wide open. **1958** B. NICHOLS *Sweet & Twenties* x. 132 Even worse, waists plummeted nine inches, to remain suspended somewhere below the navel. **1959** *Daily Tel.* 21 Nov. 1/6 Capt. Kittinger plummeted towards the earth until his parachute opened automatically at 10,000 feet. **1961** *Time* (Atlantic ed.) 23 June 26 The price of new potatoes plummeted to 1 ¢ a pound. **1963** C. L. COOPER *Black* x. 153 Twice I stumbled over the garbage cans lining the walk, rising,..to plummet on, not daring to imagine the scene I might find in the apartment. **1972** G. DURRELL *Catch me a Colobus* ix. 186 Great gouts of water plummeted down from the sky so that the road, which was an earth one, was immediately turned into a dangerous mire. **1978** D. BLOODWORTH *Crosstalk* xi. 91 Rumours that Mao's health is failing have sent the Hong Kong stock exchange plummeting. **1979** *Amer. N. & Q.* Apr. 127/1 The *Phillipe, Count of Darkness* stories..plummeted his [*sc.* F. Scott Fitzgerald's] story-asking price from $3000 to $300.

Hence **plu·mmeting** *vbl. sb.* and *ppl. a.*

1952 *Chambers's Jrnl.* May 262/1 The stone-like plummeting before the 'chute opens, the gentle floating in space, the enormous thud with which you hit the ground—these combine to give an experience unparalleled elsewhere. **1957** *Economist* 2 Nov. 380/2 The most calamitous thing..would be a world depression with plummeting prices. **1958** *Times Rev. Industry* Dec. 78/1 Spending.. led to a rise of £80m. in the Union's imports, and the plummeting of the South African foreign exchange reserves.

plummy, *a.*[2] Add: **2. b.** Of the voice, then of sound gen.: thick-sounding, rich, 'fruity'; indistinct; with bass predominating.

1881 *Punch* 23 July 25/2 The same aged lover was bidding, with rather a 'plummy' voice, the More-than-Middle-Aged Heroine 'good bye for ever'. **1947** *Jrnl. Inst. Electrical Engin.* XCIV. IIIA 446/1 Such distortions can be tolerated..without serious loss of articulation, though the speech will usually sound rather 'plummy' and unnatural. **1951** K. HARRIS *Innocents from Abroad* 199 The rich, plummy voice of [actor] Edward Arnold. **1955** *Times* 3 May 14/4 A disc which sounds plummy and muffled in tone. **1965** G. MCINNES *Road to Gundagai* xi. 197 His voice..was wonderfully plummy and Edwardian. **1970** *Daily Tel.* 1 Sept. 9/5 All India Radio—modelled.. on the BBC, even down to the plummy accents of its announcers. **1975** *City Press* 1 May 16/5 Her duchess on the make is a finely pointed performance, the plummy vowels contrasting splendidly with consonants periodically marred by the lack of false teeth. **1977** *Early Mus.* Oct. 549/3 The plummy..tone [of Flemish virginals] is evidently more popular than the musically versatile but astringent Italian virginal. **1978** *Gramophone* Feb. 1439/1 His tone is mellow, but again, as in the Waltzes..the sound sometimes seems a bit plummy and close.

3. *Comb.*, as *plummy-voiced* adj.

1972 *Jazz & Blues* Oct. 8/3 His smooth, plummy-voiced style. **1978** *Times* 21 Jan. 14/7 The plummy-voiced announcers.

Hence **plu·mminess**[2]; **plu·mmily** *adv.*

1927 J. MASEFIELD *Midnight Folk* 208 You haven't got such a thing as a seedless raisin about you?.. It's a real treat..to taste a bit of plumminess. **1953** *John o' London's Weekly* 13 Mar. 208/4, I was not persuaded at the première by his 'young Octavius', who had a curious plumminess. **1955** *Times* 31 Aug. 5/4 The creamy richness—free from all 'plumminess'—of her contralto voice is a constant delight. **1958** *Listener* 25 Dec. 1092/2 It was all splendidly true to type, and plummily theatrical. **1962** *Ibid.* 8 Feb. 268/3 The plumminess of the normal Wagnerian baritone. **1972** A. ROSS *London Assignment* 17 'Go ahead, old boy,' he said plummily, 'He's all yours.'

plump, *a.*[1] Add: **II. 3. e.** *plump-bellied*, *-uddered* adjs.

1916 JOYCE *Portrait of Artist* iii. 127 Thrust it out of men's sight into a long hole in the ground, into the grave, to rot, to feed the mass of its creeping worms and to be devoured by scuttling plump-bellied rats. **1922** —— *Ulysses* 537 A nannygoat passes, plumpuddered, buttytailed, dropping currants.

plump, *v.*[1] Add: **5.** Also *transf.* More widely, to opt *for*. Also, to decide or vote *against*.

1890 BARRÈRE & LELAND *Dict. Slang* II. 140/2 *Plump, to*... (Racing), to lay one's money on one single horse. But I shall *plump* for Lord R. Ch.'s L'Abbesse de Jouarre, who has been well tried.—*Truth.* **1894** [see VOTRESS[2]]. **1929** C. CONNOLLY *Let.* in *Romantic Friendship* (1975) 325, I have plumped against England. **1934** *Discovery* June 176/1 The more one knows..the less one is inclined to 'plump' for one particular solution rather than another. **1963** *Ann. Reg. 1962* 17 The largest union..had plumped two-to-one against a strike. **1966** *Observer* 3 Apr. 10/5 A large section of the electorate plumped for the Liberals. **1972** *Nature* 25 Feb. 424/3 The consultants recommend three road crossing schemes but plump for a Flint–Burton crossing with a coast road. **1976** *Which?* May 100/3 We don't think now is the best time to invest in equipment. Better to wait until one of the systems appears to be winning the battle and then plump for that.

plump, *v.*[2] Add: **1. a.** *spec.* of pillows, cushions, and other upholstery.

1848 [in Dict.]. **1848** DICKENS *Dombey & Son* lvii. 571 Mrs. Miff resumes her dusting and plumps up her cushions. **1960** M. SPARK *Ballad Peckham Rye* viii. 168 She turned and plumped out the cushion behind her. **1962** A. SEXTON *All my Pretty Ones* 43 The houseboy, A quick-eyed Filipino..plumping up The down-upholstery. **1972** M. J. BOSSE *Incident at Naha* i. 13 The bed, made with..carefully plumped-up pillows. **1975** L. GILLEN *Return to Deepwater* iv. 68 The cushions on the settee freshly plumped.

plumpen, *v.* Add: Also *intr.*, to grow plump. Hence **plu·mpening** *vbl. sb.*, the action or process of making or becoming plump.

1926 *Spectator* 1 May 801/2 The plumpening of cherries on lichened wall. **1966** P. V. PRICE *France* 307 The chickens..wander about the roads in the Bresse plain. plumpening visibly.

plumper[1]**.** Add: **c.** A preparation for causing hides to plump.

1903 L. A. FLEMMING *Pract. Tanning* xxii. 375 Quebracho is not a good plumper, and for this reason some material is necessary to plump the leather. *Ibid.* 376 Quebracho, being a sweet tan, is not of itself a plumper.

plumper[2]**.** Add: **3. b.** *colloq.* An unusually large example of its type; a whopper. ? *Obs.*

1881 *Punch* 1 Oct. 155/1 Lovers of England..can hardly do better than help to fill that Purse, which Mr. Punch hopes will prove a 'plumper'.

plu·mping, *ppl. a. colloq.* [f. PLUMP *v.*[2] + -ING[2].] Very large, unusually big.

1903 'A. MCNEILL' *Egregious English* 91 You win by the skin of your teeth or with a plumping majority, as the case may be. **1978** *Guardian Weekly* 2 Apr. 20/3 The Master Builder is a sexless play in which a plumping girl with an alpenstock invades the home of an elderly architect.

plumpish, *a.* Delete *rare* and add later examples. Hence **plu·mpishness.**

1942 W. FAULKNER *Go down, Moses* 226 The boy standing there looking down at the short plumpish grey-haired man. **1977** M. HINXMAN *One-Way Cemetery* i. 7 She was nice, plumpish, friendly. **1979** 'G. BLACK' *Night Run from Java* iii. 27 Don't forget the plumpish redundancy payments they all want to collect. **1979** 'J. ROSS' *Rattling of Old Bones* ii. 14 Plumpish..and a sensual plumpishness at that.

plumptitude (plʌ·mptitiūd). *joc.* ? *Obs.* Also **plumpitude.** [f. PLUMP *a.*[1] + *-titude* after *altitude, aptitude*, etc.: see -TUDE.] Plumpness.

1828 F. KEMBLE in G. Macpherson *Mem. Life Anna Jameson* (1878) ii. 44 To behold her sitting on a sofa in a very becoming state of blooming *plumpitude.* **1850** *Godey's Lady's Bk.* XLI. 180/2 At every pore I'm oozing—(I'm 'caving in' to-day)—My plumptitude I'm losing, And dripping fast away. **1854** G. GREENWOOD *Haps & Mishaps* ii. 43 The lord chancellor having formally announced that parliament stood prorogued until the 20th of August, Her Majesty rose as majestically as could be expected of one more remarkable for rosy plumptitude than regal altitude. **1890** *Daily News* 19 Aug. 3/1 Our own countrymen and countrywomen are more prone to a condition of 'blooming plumptitude', which too much sugar is likely to increase unduly.

plum pudding, plum-pudding. Add: **c. plum pudding mahogany**, mahogany with a mottled finish; **plum-pudding voyage**, delete 'including plum-duff'.

1924 G. O. WHEELER *Old English Furniture* (ed. 3) xii. 278 The plum mottle..signifies the spotted and mottled wood known as 'plum-pudding' mahogany. **1968** *Canad. Antiques Collector* Nov. 8/2 (Advt.), Sheraton style 'Plumb [*sic*] Pudding' Mahogany cabinet..circa 1790. **1976** *Country Life* 26 Feb. (Suppl.) 24c/1 An unusual Chippendale period supper table with two tier top. The table is of 'Plum pudding' mahogany, with carved detail.

d. (See quots.).

1851 H. MELVILLE *Moby Dick* III. viii. 64 Plum-pudding is the term bestowed upon certain fragmentary parts of the whale's flesh. **1904** *Sci. Amer. Suppl.* 5 Mar. 23551/3 A muscular, fibrous substance known as 'plum pudding' permeates the blubber of the tongue of these two species of whales.

e. *Mil. slang.* A type of trench mortar shell.

1925 FRASER & GIBBONS *Soldier & Sailor Words* 225 *Plum pudding*, the name for a type of trench mortar shell; suggested by its size and shape. **1928** BLUNDEN *Undertones of War* 51 Now more serious and immediate omens of ordeal appeared in the mounds of trench mortar bombs—'plum puddings' or 'footballs', steely and shining.

plum-puddinger, also, a member of the crew of such a ship; (earlier and later examples).

1851 H. MELVILLE *Moby Dick* I. xvii. 137 After listening to these plum-puddingers till nearly eleven o'clock, I went up stairs to go to bed. **1934** F. R. DULLES *Lowered Boats* iv. 45 Only the little 'plum-pud'ners' of Rhode Island remained wholly true to the Greenland whale.

plum-tree. Add: (Later examples.) Also *fig.*, the source of the spoils of political office; esp. in phr. *to shake the plum tree* (*U.S.*).

1905 D. G. PHILLIPS *Plum Tree* ii. 24, I mentally called the roll—wealth, respectability, honor, all on their knees before Dominick, each with his eye upon the branch of the plum tree that bore the kind of fruit he fancied. **1906** U. SINCLAIR *Jungle* xxvii. 340 Those golden hours when he, too, had a place beneath the shadow of the plum tree. **1922** JOYCE *Ulysses* 668 The name on the label is Plumtree. A plumtree in a meatpot, registered trade mark. **1933** *Sun* (Baltimore) 23 May 14/1 The thought uppermost in everybody's mind at the gathering at which James was the guest of honor was: When will you shake the plum tree? **1952** G. STIMPSON *Bk. about Amer. Politics* 258 While he [*sc.* Matthew Stanley Quay] was State treasurer (1885–1887) he placed large sums of State money in the People's Bank of Philadelphia and used it to buy stocks on margin. On one occasion Quay and his associates piled up orders for the stock of the Metropolitan Railroad of New York until only about $10,000 was left in the bank. John S. Hopkins, the cashier, became frightened and protested to the political boss. Quay sent the cashier the message: 'Buy and carry a thousand Met for me and I will shake the plum tree.' **1959** *Chambers's Encycl.* X. 804/1 Pruning of standard plum trees simply means cutting out branches which intercross or thinning out overcrowded branches.

plunder, *sb.* Add: **3.** (Earlier and later examples.) Also in occas. wider use. Also *fig.*

1805 M. LEWIS in *Lewis & Clark Exped.* (1904) II. 220, I dispatched Sergt. Ordway with 4 Canoes and 8 men to take up a load of baggage as far as Capt. Clark's camp and return for the remainder of our plunder. **1941** E. P. O'DONNELL *Great Big Doorstep* 119 Your father puts on more every time he tells that there story. The plunder that man's got in his head! The plunder! **1948** E. N. DICK *Dixie Frontier* 113 Mules and a hardy tough breed of Indian and Spanish horse..were used to carry the money and plunder. **1962** W. STEGNER *Wolf Willow* (1963) III. ii. 160 He gathers together his plunder and he hightails her off the mountain. **1972** O. FREDERICKSON *Silence of North* viii. 64 We didn't have much plunder, and with only two grown-ups, a baby, and a pair of sled dogs on board, it rode high.

plunder, *v.*[2] Add: **1.** Also *fig.*

1896 A. BEARDSLEY *Let.* 29 Oct. (1970) 193 How abominably she [*sc.* George Sand] has been plundered by everyone since. **1961** H. ADAMS in *Webster* s.v., Shakespeare and his fellow-dramatists plundered the Church legends. **1964** T. M. ANDERSSON *Probl. Icelandic Saga Origins* v. 90 *Eiríks saga rauða* and *Grettis saga* combine to show that when *Landnáma* was used, it was plundered wholesale and not plucked for an occasional name.

plunderbund (plʌ·ndəɹbund). *U.S. colloq.* [f. PLUNDER *sb.* + G. *bund* alliance, league.] A corrupt alliance of political, commercial, and financial interests engaged in exploiting the public.

1914 *Voice of People* (New Orleans) 8 Jan. 1/1 The whole force of the Texan plunderbund..are howling at the heels of the dauntless army of workers. **1933** *Sun* (Baltimore) 27 Apr. 8/6 The..unemployed,..the losers in banks, stocks, homes,..and business people..are forever through with this systematic plunderbund. **1949** *Chicago Tribune* 2 Sept. 12/6 Hello, suckers who voted for the continuation of chaos and corruption and the plunderbund last November.

plunderous, *a.* Delete *rare* and add later examples.

1973 *Freedomways* XIII. 8 With the plunderous taxes.. a large section of the people..are being returned to the bread lines. **1976** *Times* 30 Sept. 8/3, I would jot down all the best jokes from *Take It From Here* and write a new plot round them... So I can't really jibe when the writer of that Jimmy Edwards classic has the same kind of plunderous notion for making a book. **1977** *Evening News* 4 June 5/4 William Palmer..made a plunderous visit to the treasury.

plung (plʌŋ). *rare.* [Echoic.] A resonant noise as of a tennis racket striking a ball.

1952 J. BETJEMAN *First & Last Loves* ii. 13 So that the real Bournemouth is all pines and pines and pines and flowering shrubs, lawns, begonias, azaleas, bird-song, dance tunes, the plung of the racket and creak of the basket chair. **1954** —— *Few Late Chrysanthemums* 69 'Oh! Plung!' my tauten'd strings would call, 'Oh! Plung! my darling, break my strings.'

plunge, *sb.* Add: **I. 1. b.** = *plunge bed* (see sense 7 below).

1973 *Times* 22 Sept. 13/2 If we have..an Indian summer, water the 'plunge' regularly.

2. (Earlier and later fig. examples.) Esp. in phr. *to take* (less frequently *make*) *the plunge*, to take a decisive first step, to commit oneself irrevocably to a course of action.

1845 DICKENS *Let.* 20 Oct. (1977) IV. 412 The venture is quite decided on; and I have made the Plunge. **1848** THACKERAY *Pendennis* (1849) I. vi. 61 The poor boy had taken the plunge. Trembling with passionate emotion,..poor Pen had said those words which he could withhold no more. **1876** TROLLOPE *Prime Minister* IV. x. 162 'You would not wish to live all your life in terror of seeing Arthur Fletcher?' 'Not all my life.' 'Take the plunge and it will be over.' *a* **1911** [see *LIMIT *sb.* 2 h]. **1915** W. OWEN *Let.* 15 Jan. (1967) 316 If I could devote myself to training in Music or Painting, I would take the plunge, were I never to read a book more. **1965** *New Statesman* 23 Apr. 630/3 At present only one local Co-op..is affiliated to Transport House, though London is thought to be contemplating taking the plunge. **1977** C. MCCULLOUGH *Thorn Birds* xviii. 460, I think she's terrified of committing herself to..marriage... At least he's got the sense to wait until she's ready to take the plunge. **1979** G. WAGNER *Barnardo* xi. 183 Samuel Smith..finally persuaded Barnardo to take the plunge and set up his own emigration scheme.

III. 6*. *Geol.* The angle a fold axis or linear feature makes with the horizontal, measured in a vertical plane. Cf. PITCH *sb.*[2] 24 b in Dict. and Suppl.

1913 W. LINDGREN *Min. Deposits* xi. 142 The plunge[1].. of an ore-body is the vertical angle between a horizontal plane and the line of maximum elongation of the body. In lenticular ore-bodies in metamorphic rocks which have undergone strong mechanical deformation, the plunge is an important factor, and often it is determined by the direction of the cleavage or schistosity. [*Note*] [1]Called 'pitch' or 'rake' by many authors. **1932** *Bull. Amer. Assoc. Petroleum Geologists* XVI. 209 The type of fold is an overturned anticline in which the plunge increases from a comparatively low degree until it becomes vertical and finally overturns. **1936** C. M. NEVIN *Princ. Structural Geol.* (ed. 2) iii. 43 The angle of dip of the axial line [of a fold] is called the pitch or plunge. **1962** [see *PITCH *sb.*[2] 24 b]. **1976** B. E. HOBBS et al. *Outl. Structural Geol.* iv. 177 The orientation of the hinge line or, since the fold is cylindrical, its axis, is expressed by its plunge and direction of plunge... The orientation of a line can also be expressed by means of its pitch... For pitch to be meaningful the orientation of the plane must be known.

IV. 7. plunge basin *Physical Geogr.*, a deep basin excavated at the foot of a waterfall by the action of the falling water; **plunge bed**, a flower-bed, often containing peat or other moisture-retaining material, in which plants in pots can be sunk; **plunge-board** *rare*, a diving board; **plunge cut** *Engin.*, a cut made by feeding a grinding wheel into the work-piece in the plane of rotation, without any traverse; usu. *attrib.* in *plunge-cut grinding* (= *plunge grinding*); so **plunge cutting**; **plunge grinding** *Engin.*, grinding by means of a wheel with no traverse of the work; **plunge neck, neckline** = *plunging neckline* s.v. *PLUNGING *ppl. a.* e; hence **plunge-necked** *a.*; **plunge pool**, (*a*) *Physical Geogr.*, a plunge basin, or the water occupying one; freq. *attrib.*; (*b*) a cold-water pool, forming part of the equipment of a sauna bath.

1905 *Bull. Geol. Soc. Amer.* XVI. 24 A river can excavate a plunge-basin at the foot of a cataract. **1939** A. K. LOBECK *Geomorphol.* vi. 195 There are several other plunge basins along the course of this former stream. **1966** J. WYCKOFF *Rock, Time, & Landforms* x. 231 Today there is likely to be a waterfall at the mouth of the hanging trough, and beneath the fall perhaps a plunge basin or an alluvial cone or fan. **1871** S. HIBBERD *Amateur's Flower Garden* xiii. 242 The question now is about the formation of the plunge beds. **1935** A. G. L. HELLYER *Practical Gardening* xxx. 193 (*caption*) A useful plunge bed for pot plants. **1973** *Times* 22 Sept. 13/2 Pot them the same day if possible, and put them in their peat 'plunge bed'. **1908** *Daily Chron.* 15 Feb. 8/5 When a man wants to take a second plunge into the water he has to get out and remount the plunge-board. **1935** O. W. BOSTON *Engin. Shop Practice* II. v. 268 An automatic in-feed mechanism..is contained in the saddle... This is used for plunge cuts and is independent of the traverse in-feed mechanism. **1937** COLVIN & STANLEY *Grinding Practice* i. 7 The wheel in this instance is fed into within 0·001 to 0·0015 in. of size, using the plunge cut and making as many plunges as are necessary to cover each section ground. **1941** F. D. JONES *Engin. Encycl.* II. 971 *Plunge-cut grinding*, this term has been applied to grinding which is done by directly feeding into the work a wheel, the face of which is sufficiently wide to cover the entire surface being ground. **1964** S. CRAWFORD *Basic Engin. Processes* vii. 190 The wheel is fed slowly into the work while the latter is oscillated a very slight amount to equalise the wheel wear. This method is known as plunge-cut grinding. **1972** E. N. SIMONS *Dict. Machining* 142 *Plunge cutting*, a method of grooving parts to close limits of size with an accurately-positioned brazed carbide tool. **1974** *Sci. Amer.* Jan. 35/3 A process known as plunge cutting is employed to cut holes in a metal casting. **1935** O. W. BOSTON *Engin. Shop Practice* II. v. 265 When the wheel face is as wide as the length of the surface being ground or when it is impracticable to traverse the work, the wheel may be fed in with no traverse of the wheel or work. This is called plunge grinding. **1958** *Times Rev. Industry* May 34/3 The workpiece is then released, so that it can be rotated by means of the control wheel while plunge-grinding is being carried out. **1967** *Industr. Diamond Rev.* XXVII. 437/2 In plunge grinding, the whole depth of profile is normally ground in one pass. **1951** *Sunday Times* 28 Oct. 11/3 Some [spencers], sleeveless and with a plunge neck, give never a sign of their comforting presence beneath cocktail dresses and chiffon blouses. **1959** *Woman's Own* 20 June 17/4 She was wearing a plunge-necked dress of some white material. **1949** *Sun* (Baltimore) 28 Jan. 4 (Advt.), Plunge neckline wool jersey glamour blouse. **1959** 'O. MILLS' *Stairway to Murder* v. 50 Its plunge neckline was so low that Geoff was almost driven for safety to the handwoven wool and Fair Isle cardigan. **1977** M. HINXMAN *One-Way Cemetery* xv. 112 Daphne delved into her deep plunge neckline and retrieved a gold chain. **1917** *Scientific Monthly* V. 559 Plunge pools are potholes, in general, of large size, occurring at the foot of a vertical or nearly vertical waterfall... In most plunge pools the water is much deeper than it is in the stream channel on their downstream side. **1932** *Jrnl. Geol.* XL. 333 By recession of the falls the plunge-pool hole is elongated upstream, forming the deeper part of the channel of a gorge, the upper part of which is produced by a caving in process as the plunge-pool undercuts the face of the fall. **1957** G. E. HUTCHINSON *Treat. Limnol.* I. i. 111 The most impressive of such plunge-pool lakes are on that part of the former course of the Columbia River that now forms the Grand Coulee in the state of Washington. **1970** MACDONALD & ABBOTT *Volcanoes in Sea* xix. 367 (*caption*) Vertical valleys being cut by plunge-pool action of waterfalls. **1973** *Times* 21 Nov. 18/8 There is a plunge pool with two massage jets. **1976** 'D. HALLIDAY' *Dolly & Nanny Bird* ix. 116 It was time for the plunge pool with the hydrojet massage.

plunge, *v.* Add: **4.** (Later examples.)

1935 A. G. L. HELLYER *Pract. Gardening* xxix. 183 It is an excellent plan to plunge the pots to their rims in a bed of ashes to reduce the necessity for frequent watering. **1965** *Sunday Mail Mag.* (Brisbane) 26 Sept. 15 You may read of pots being plunged. This refers to the burying of a pot up to its rim.

5. b. Also, to emerge or come *out* or *out of* (a place) impetuously or abruptly.

1891 C. GRAVES *Field of Tares* IV. vi. 241 The Norwich Express, plunging out of Liverpool Street Station. **1892** R. BUCHANAN *Come live with Me* xxiii. 256 Finally..he plunged out into the darkness and disappeared. **1896** C. M. SHELDON *His Brother's Keeper* viii. 226 They plunged right out of a great hole.

c. *spec.* In *Geol.*, of a fold: to have an axis that slopes or dips downwards, whether at a large or a small angle. Also said of the axis. (Further examples.)

1905 CHAMBERLIN & SALISBURY *Geol.* I. viii. 488 If the axis of a fold is not horizontal, that is, if it 'plunges'. **1932** *Bull. Amer. Assoc. Petroleum Geologists* XVI. 210 At this time all of the folds plunged consistently eastward at a low angle. **1942** M. P. BILLINGS *Structural Geol.* iii. 46 In the southwest corner, the anticline plunges 15 degrees to the southwest. **1965** A. HOLMES *Princ. Physical Geol.* (ed. 2) ix. 210 The axes of folds are not infrequently found to be tilted instead of horizontal; the folds are then said to pitch or plunge.

10. b. *trans.* To bet or speculate (a sum of money).

1922 JOYCE *Ulysses* 320 Boylan plunged two quid on my tip *Sceptre* for himself and a lady friend.

11. *trans.* or *absol. Railways.* To release (signals or points, etc.) by depressing a plunger. Cf. *PLUNGER 2 g.

[**1923** J. F. GAIRNS *Railways for All* xviii. 179 Sykes' 'Lock and Block' instruments..are operated by pressing a knob or plunger, hence the term 'plunging' used to describe their working by the signalmen.] **1926** C. J. ALLEN *Iron Road* xii. 180 Then the signalman in the next box cannot 'plunge' on his instrument until he has put his own starting signal lever back to danger in the lever frame behind the last preceding train. **1940** *Railway Signalling & Communications* iii. 93 All facing points unprotected by track circuit must be provided with a locking bar in addition to the plunger, and the points must be plunged before the signal reading over them can be cleared.

plungeon. Restrict † *Obs.* to sense in Dict. and add: **2.** *south-west. dial.* A ford across a rhine (RHINE[1]).

c **1685** A. PASCHALL *Let.* in S. Heywood *Vindication of Mr. Fox's Hist.* (1811) p. xl, The horse, which the Lord Grey led marched towards the upper Plungeon. *Ibid.*, Whether Sir Francis were there..or came to the Plungeon afterwards..we do not know. **1894** LD. WOLSELEY *Life Marlborough* I. xxxix. 314 They [*sc.* the Somerset 'rhines'] could only be crossed, even by single horsemen, at fords, called by the peasantry 'plungeons' or 'steanings'. **1933** W. S. CHURCHILL *Marlborough* I. xii. 216 Grey's cavalry would branch off and..cross the Bussex Rhine at one of the plungeons to the east of the royal camp. **1955** *Hist. Today* V. 57/2 There were two easy crossings for cavalry, known as the upper..and lower 'plungeons'. **1969** C. C. TRENCH *Western Rising* x. 209 He [*sc.* Feversham] ordered the reserve cavalry in the village..to cross the Bussex Rhine by the upper plungeon. *Ibid.*, Similarly three troops of horse and one of dragoons crossed the lower plungeon.

plunger. Add: **I. 1. c.** *N. Amer.* A type of sailing boat (see quot. 1948).

1860 *North-West* (Port Townsend, Wash.) 12 July 3/1 The following craft were entered for the stakes:—Sloop H. L. Tibbals, Port Townsend;..and the plunger Star of the South. **1892** *Outing* Mar. 467/1 Yachting on the Pacific coast dates from about 1869, when the first club.. was organised, though a few small plungers and sloops had long been owned on the bay. **1948** R. DE KERCHOVE *Internat. Maritime Dict.* 541/2 *Plunger*, name given to various sailing craft employed in the Pacific coast oyster fisheries for transportation... Also called oyster sloop. Most of them are built with flush deck and a large central cockpit divided by a centerboard. The larger type is keel built... All are cat-rigged. **1969** *Islander* (Victoria, B.C.) 23 Mar. 4/2 The next day [24 Dec. 1860] a plunger brought a quantity of salvaged goods to Victoria, mostly in the form of cases of Old Tom gin.

2. g. *Railways.* Applied to various knobs or buttons used to operate signalling mechanisms and points; *esp.* (*a*) one with which a signalman operates an electric relay which releases locked signals or points, freq. in an adjacent block section; (*b*) a tapping key on a block instrument.

1881 [in Dict.]. **1897** W. E. LANGDON *Applic. Electr. Railway Working* (new ed.) v. 103 The block instrument is fitted with a bell key or 'plunger'. **1899** J. PIGG *Railway Block Signalling* iv. 214 For the lines converging at the junction the plunger used to liberate the signal at the rear cabin of any one of the converging sections is arranged to be free for use only when the points have been set for a train coming from that direction. **1926** C. J. ALLEN *Iron Road* xii. 173 Below the instrument box is..a plunger or a 'tapper'..by the use of which the signalman exchanges the prescribed code of bell signals with his neighbour. *Ibid.* 180 Only the action of 'accepting' the train by the box next in advance—that is, of giving 'Line Clear' by means of the special plunger on the signalling instrument —will free the lock on the lever, and allow it to be pulled over. **1963** KICHENSIDE & WILLIAMS *Brit. Railway Signalling* v. 44 If Mottingham can accept the train the signalman there acknowledges the 'Is line clear?' code and presses the plunger on his home signal instrument. This..unlocks Lee's starting signal and places the block indicator at Lee in the raised position. **1967** G. F. FIENNES *I tried to run Railway* iv. 46 As soon as he put his signals back and took the hook off his Sykes plunger Crowlands offered him the Mail and gave him On Line at once.

h. *Jazz slang.* A plunging device, resembling the type used by plumbers to clear blocked pipes, used as a mute for a trumpet or trombone. Freq. *attrib.* and *comb.*

1936 L. & E. DOWLING *Panassié's Hot Jazz* i. 15 Some players..use a regular mute and place over it a rubber plunger—of the sort used by plumbers—which is manipulated by hand to produce 'wa-wa' effects. **1946** MEZZROW & WOLFE *Really Blues* 340 The trumpet got different tonal effects by using plungers and other home-made devices. **1949** L. FEATHER *Inside Be-Bop* III. 93 Took a couple of plunger solos on Decca. **1958** S. DANCE in P. Gammond *Decca Bk. Jazz* xxiii. 293 Cootie at first found Miley's growl legacy altogether too strange... He had always previously played open horn, but since Duke had engaged him to fill Miley's chair, he felt bound to experiment with the plunger style. **1961** *John o' London's* 6 July 55/1 Booty Wood's melancholy plunger-muted trombone. **1966** *Crescendo* Jan. 6/1 A slow opening with Tricky Sam style plunger trombone (sounding here very much like a human voice).

III. 5. plunger mute = sense *2 h; **plunger-valve**, a valve having a plunging action.

1947 I. LANG *Jazz in Perspective* vii. 90 Miley was the pioneer and master of a new style of trumpet-playing—a powerful and strangely moving 'growl' obtained by the use of a rubber plunger mute. **1965** *New Yorker* 27 Feb. 123/1 Rudd, a former Dixieland trombonist,..uses the plunger mute effectively. **1977** *Ibid.* 20 June 95/1 Another muted passage (this time using a plunger mute), in which he mumbled funny gibberish through his instrument, all the while using his slide and seeming to blow out the words. **1908** *Westm. Gaz.* 2 Jan. 4/1 The crank-case, into the cover of which the cam-shaft and plunger-valves are built. **1931** *Engineering* 2 Oct. 5 (Advt.), Being a combination of a plunger valve with a mushroom valve, they possess a greater efficiency than is possible with either of these types alone.

plunging, *vbl. sb.* Add: **b.** *plunging system.*

1871 S. HIBBERD *Amateur's Flower Garden* xiii. 238 The object of the plunging system is to keep up a rich display of flowers or leaves on the same spot the whole year round.

plunging, *ppl. a.* Add: **d.** *Geol.* Of a fold (see *PLUNGE *v.* 5 c).

1905 CHAMBERLIN & SALISBURY *Geol.* I. viii. 483 Fig. 403 shows a doubly plunging anticline; that is, an anticline the axis of which dips down at either end. **1942** M. P. BILLINGS *Structural Geol.* iii. 44 Although the larger plunging folds cannot be directly observed, they are easily recognized from their outcrop pattern. **1968** [see *PITCHING *ppl. a.* 1].

e. plunging neckline, a very deep-cut neckline on a woman's garment.

1949 *Sun* (Baltimore) 18 Nov. 14/2 Will you please express your opinion about the good taste of women wearing the so-called 'plunging necklines' to their business offices. **1959** *Sunday Express* 22 Nov. 6/6, I do wish Mr. Braine could tear his eyes away from girls' provocative, plunging necklines. **1973** 'D. JORDAN' *Nile Green* xxxiv. 162 A temp with a plunging neckline and shaky shorthand.

plunk, *v.* Add: **I. 1.** Also, to play (a note) or pick *out* (a melody) on a stringed instrument.

1952 B. ULANOV *Hist. Jazz in Amer.* (1958) xx. 254 She reached her majority plunking two bass notes with her left hand. **1973** *Time* 25 June 94/3 Hungate got to tinkering at the piano one day and in 15 minutes plunked out a ditty he calls *Down at the Old Watergate.*

b. *intr.* To make a plunking sound.

1903 *Cosmopolitan* Sept. 484 Street pianos plunk away unweariedly. **1929** [see *GUBBLE *v.*]. **1946** D. C. PEATTIE *Road of Naturalist* iii. 35 Into southern Utah they came trekking, with fine fat oxen, with meal sacks under the seats, and banjos plunking. **1978** G. VIDAL *Kalki* vi. 153 Deafening was what H. V. W. would call the din from the rock stars' dressing rooms where electric guitars whined, drums rattled, sitars plunked.

II. 3. b. *trans.* To place or set *down* heavily. Also *refl.* to 'let oneself fall'. Cf. PLUMP *v.*[1] 2.

1899 G. W. PECK *Peck's Uncle Ike & Red Headed Boy* (1903) xxii. 194 The old man plunked down two dollars.. and they went and got seats on the bleachers. **1936** R. LEHMANN *Weather in Streets* I. 222 The woman..plunked a great unappetising tray on my bed. **1943** A. RANSOME *Picts & Martyrs* v. 46, I say, Dot, when you've plunked the roses in her room... Some on the dressing-table. **1963** *New Statesman* 11 Jan. 38/1 A pair of steel nuts that another worker inadvertently plunks on a plate. **1976** D. HEFFRON *Crusty Crossed* xi. 85, I went into the bedroom and plunked myself down on our bed. **1977** *Time* 29 Aug. 24/1 He [*sc.* Elvis Presley] had wandered into Sun Records with his guitar, two summers before, plunked down $4 to sing a couple of tunes to his mother.

c. *intr.* To opt *for*. Cf. *PLUMP *v.*[1] 5.

1948 A. H. VANDENBERG *Let.* 6 Dec. in Vandenberg & Morris *Private Papers of Senator Vandenberg* (1953) xxi. 414 We should smack down the Russkies more effectively in our speeches in the UN Council and Assembly... I plunk with you for 'curt decisiveness' mixed with 'derision'.

III. 4. b. *trans.* To hit, wound, shoot. *slang* (orig. *U.S.*).

1888 *Texas Siftings* 21 Apr. 12 (*caption*) He'd jest swallerd brother Bill afore I plunked him. **1891** *Outing*

Nov. 138/2, I would plunk the big gobbler I could distinguish from where I lay. **1896** [see *OUT-OF-SIGHT *adj. phr.* 2]. **1916** C. J. DENNIS *Songs of Sentimental Bloke* 42 Romeo..Plunks Tyball through the gizzard wiv 'is sword. **1916** H. L. WILSON *Somewhere in Red Gap* 120 Darned if he didn't up with this here air gun..and plunk me with a buckshot it carried. **1937** D. & H. TEILHET *Feather Cloak Murders* xvi. 286, I wish you'd killed Jeff instead of plunking him in the leg. **1978** L. PRYOR *Viper* iii. 41 We..plunked about five hundred clay birds a day.

Hence **plu·nking** *vbl. sb.* and *ppl. a.*

1941 W. C. HANDY *Father of Blues* xviii. 246, I had been everlastingly at the piano, forever picking out notes and chords for *Long Gone* but never playing anything consistently. A victim of all this plunking had been her parrot. **1952** B. ULANOV *Hist. Jazz in America* (1958) vi. 65 With this considerable rhythmic skill, however, went something less engaging, a plunking insistence on the beat. **1973** 'B. MATHER' *Snowline* x. 123 The plunking of an out-of-tune guitar. **1979** G. HAMMOND *Dead Game* vi. 77 A bullet that's been deflected by passing through something..may make a plunking sort of sound.

plunk, *sb., adv., int.* Add: **A.** *sb.* **2. b.** (Earlier and later examples.)

1891 J. MAITLAND *Amer. Slang Dict.* 207 *Plunk* (Am.), a dollar. **1909** W. G. DAVENPORT *Butte & Montana beneath X-Ray* 56 Make it 25 plunks and let it go at that. **1929** WODEHOUSE *Gentleman of Leisure* xiii. 107 Dere's a loidy here..dat's got a necklace of jools what's worth a hundred t'ousand plunks.

B. *adv.* and *int.* (Earlier and later examples.)

1892 'MARK TWAIN' *Amer. Claimant* xix. 196 Feel my pulse: plunk—plunk—plunk. **1936** A. RANSOME *Pigeon Post* xxvii. 292 They heard the noise up in the top of the wood... Plunk, plunk, plunk, and the rhythmic scraw of a saw.

Also redupl. **plu·nkety-plu·nk**; also *attrib.*

1884 'MARK TWAIN' *Huck. Finn* viii. 63, I hear a *plunkety-plunk, plunkety-plunk*, and says to myself, horses coming. **1960** *Twentieth Cent.* Dec. 556 The plunkety-plunk banjo sound.

Plunket (plʌ·ŋkėt), *sb.*[2] *N.Z.* The name of Lady *Plunket*, wife of the Governor-General of New Zealand 1904–10 (see quot. 1938), used *attrib.* and *absol.* (with reference to the *Plunket Society*, a popular name for the Royal New Zealand Society for the Health of Women and Children), to designate a nurse trained in the methods of child feeding and care advocated by this society, a baby reared according to these methods, or a clinic following them.

1909 *Ann. Rep. Soc. for Promotion of Health of Women & Children* No. 1. 9 The doctor was pleased to have the assistance of the Plunket nurse, and at once consented to the children being fed on humanised milk. **1938** H. C. D. SOMERSET *Littledene* vii. 69 The Royal New Zealand Society for the Health of Women and Children..commonly called the Plunket Society from the name of its first president, Lady Plunket, was founded by Dr. Truby King in 1907. **1941** S. J. BAKER *N.Z. Slang* vi. 58 No record..would be complete without reference to the famed organization, the Plunket Society. For the past twenty years or more it has been known as the Plunket **1944** F. L. W. WOOD *Understanding N.Z.* iv. 48 The town will have..Plunket rooms (baby clinics). *Ibid.* ix. 130 Nearly three-quarters of the children born in New Zealand become 'Plunket babies'. **1945** R. M. BURDON *N.Z. Notables* II. ii. 41 By 1913..twenty-seven trained Plunket nurses were working from their appointed centres. **1958** *N.Z. News* 11 Mar. 3/1 In 1912, the Government gave him [*sc.* Truby King] six months' leave of absence to preach the movement throughout the country, and the number of 'Plunket' nurses rapidly multiplied. **1960** S. ASHTON-WARNER *Incense to Idols* 80 Organize societies for crippled children and the intellectually handicapped, Plunket for the babies, Heritage for the care of War Orphans. **1966** G. W. TURNER *Eng. Lang. in Austral & N.Z.* viii. 173 A New Zealander is likely to begin life as a 'Plunket baby'. His mother is visited periodically by the Plunket nurse from the Plunket Society, founded by Sir Truby King as an early experiment in socially supervised child care and named after the wife of the then Governor-General.

plup (plʌp). [Echoic: cf. PLOP *sb.* and *adv.*] The sound of or as of a body falling on a hard surface, into liquid, etc. Also *fig.*

1911 R. BROOKE in E. Marsh *Rupert Brooke* (1918) p. lxvii, The 'quaint' remarks fall all round one during meal times, with little soft plups like pats of butter. **1926** *Chambers's Jrnl.* Dec. 847/1 The surge of the water down below, and the *plup* of 'escape' above the roof, were but soft sounds. **1931** E. A. ROBERTSON *Four Frightened People* v. 144 Gas bubbles rose with a soft 'plup-plup'-ing.

'pluperfect, *a.* (*sb.*) Add: **2.** (Further examples.) Also (*slang*), used as an intensive.

1889 *Virginia University Mag.* Dec. 186 So take a drink, oh, Phæon, dear, we'll raise pluperfect Cain. **1917** 'CONTACT' *Airman's Outings* 204, I fully expect that we of the air service will lead the armies of pursuit and make ourselves a pluperfect nuisance to the armies of retreat. **1928** A. PHILIPS *Boy at Bank* I. v. 49 Mrs. Fravalton, one of those mothers who believe their children pluperfect. **1933** E. CALDWELL *God's Little Acre* x. 145 What in the pluperfect hell have you boys got to fight about so much, anyhow? **1977** *New Society* 5 May 238/2 They have done it with such bureaucratic precision... The erudition and workmanship are as impeccable, and absolutely deathly, as this kind of pluperfect reconstruction must always be.

plural, *a.* (*sb.*) Add: **2.** *plural community*, a community made up of culturally different ethnic groups; *plural democracy* (see quots.); *plural economy*, the economy of a plural society within which the different ethnic groups keep, to a great extent, their own economic systems; *plural marriage* (see MARRIAGE 1 d); *plural society*, a society composed of different ethnic groups or cultural traditions; a society in which ethnic differences, etc., are reflected in the political structure (see quot. 1971); *plural voting* (further examples).

1869 *Utah Mag.* 18 Sept. 310/1 The Mormon proposition is not to make plural marriage obligatory on the world, but to declare its necessity and legitimacy under certain circumstances. **1906** I. ZANGWILL in *Times* 29 Oct. 10/5 In another leader on the very same page you defend plural voting on the ground of the necessity of 'the representation of local interests'. **1922** JOYCE *Ulysses* 480 Dragging a lorry on which are..plaster figures..representing the new nine muses, Commerce, Operatic Music,..Plural Voting, Gastronomy. **1939** J. S. FURNIVALL *Netherlands India* xiii. 446 One finds a plural society also in independent states, such as Siam, where Natives, Chinese and Europeans have distinct economic functions, and live apart as separate social orders. *Ibid.*, Some Dutch writers use the term dual or plural economy..to connote the coexistence within the same political community of two or more distinct sets of different economic principles. **1947** *Sun* (Baltimore) 26 Nov. 5/2 Eighteen Utah residents.. were charged with conspiring to advocate plural marriage. **1952** B. DAVIDSON *Rep. Southern Afr.* I. vii. 79 They hold in their hands the saving—or the sinking—of a plural society in South Africa. *Ibid.* II. vii. 138 Clearly confronted with the fact of a plural community, they steadfastly refuse to recognize the plurality. **1963** W. N. STEPHENS *Family in Cross-Cultural Perspective* (1964) ii. 33 This chapter will deal with the last three forms: polygyny, polyandry, and group marriage, the forms of plural marriage. **1965** *New Statesman* 19 Nov. 796/2 The common theme..is the theory of the West Indies as 'plural societies', that is, societies lacking institutions, traditions and habits common to all members. **1966** JACOBS & ZINK *Mod. Govt.* (ed. 3) I. vi. 70 Plural voting.. resulted from the British belief that a person should be allowed to vote in every district where he was qualified... The Representation of the People Act of 1948 eliminated it completely. **1971** *Race* XII. 462 It appears theoretically useful, then, to partition the universe of culturally diverse societies into: (1) 'plural societies', in which politics tends (exclusively) to follow ethnic lines, and (2) 'pluralistic societies', in which politically relevant issues and actions do not always coincide with ethnic groups. **1977** *Time* 21 Nov. 12/1 What is at stake, ultimately, is whether the government will be able to carry on with the Afrikaners' grand scheme of apartheid—also known as 'separate development' and more recently as 'plural democracy'. **1978** *Guardian Weekly* 4 June 7/3 Apartheid—which has since [1948] undergone minor ideological mutations and several changes in name... Plural democracy, as apartheid is now known.

‖**plurale tantum** (plūərēi·li tæ·ntǒm). *Gram.* Pl. **pluralia tantum.** [med.L. *plūrāle* the plural f. *plūrālis* PLURAL *a.* + L. *tantum* only.] A noun which, in any particular sense, is used only in plural form.

1930 T. SASAKI *Lang. R. Bridges' Poetry* II. iii. 57 The so-called 'pluralia tantum' (e.g. breeches, dregs). **1940** A. H. GARDINER *Theory of Proper Names* viii. 27 Here a *plurale tantum* has been resolved into its component individual members, each of whom is thus represented as a bearer of the proper name in question. **1957** R. W. ZANDVOORT *Handbk. Eng. Gram.* II. 95 Some nouns never occur without a plural suffix; they are known as *pluralia tantum* (sing. *plurale tantum*). Such are *riches, thanks, tongs*. *Ibid.* 340 Most of the *pluralia tantum* in Kruisinga's lists may also occur without *-s*, if usually in another sense: *compasses* 'instrument for describing circles', but *compass* 'instrument showing magnetic meridian'..*colours* 'flag', but *colour* 'hue'. **1969** *Language* XLV. 239 A collective is precisely to be expected in a word for 'clothes'; cf. the English plurale tantum as well as Gk. *heimata*, only as neuter plural in Homer. **1976** *Archivum Linguisticum* VII. 105 Because these so-called 'uncountable' nouns are in fact to be found in plural form, I dub them *pseudo-uncountables* to distinguish them from true uncountables like *thunder* and *heat*, and pluralia tantum like *scissors*.

pluralism. Add: **2.** (Earlier and later examples.) Also the theory that the knowable world is made up of a plurality of interacting things.

1882 W. JAMES *Let.* 6 Dec. in R. B. Perry *Tht. & Char. W. James* (1935) I. 686 After all, pluralism and indeterminism seem to be but two ways of stating the same thing. **1884** T. H. GREEN tr. *Lotze's Metaphysic* I. vi. 125 The Pluralism with which our view of the world began has to give place to a Monism, through which the 'transeunt' operation, always unintelligible, passes into an 'immanent' operation. **1919** *Mind* XXVIII. 57 For pluralism, the living experience of the subject consists actually in his interaction with other subjects. **1955** R. CARNAP in *Internat. Encycl. Unified Sci.* I. 49 It seems doubtful whether we can find any theoretical content in such philosophical questions as discussed by monism, dualism, and pluralism. **1969** N. RESCHER *Many-Valued Logic* iii. 214 There is no balking the fact of *pluralism* in logic. *Ibid.*, Faced with the fact of pluralism, the step to relativism or conventionalism might seem short and easy. **1972** K. R. POPPER *Objective Knowledge* iv. 153 Some philosophers have made a serious beginning towards a philosophical pluralism, but pointing out the existence of a *third world*.

3. a. *Pol. Sci.* A theory which opposes monolithic state power and advocates instead increased devolution and autonomy for the main organizations that represent man's involvement in society. Also, the belief that power should be shared among a number of political parties.

1919 H. J. LASKI in *Philos. Rev.* XXVIII. 568 The monistic state is an hierarchical structure in which power is..collected at a single centre. The advocates of pluralism are convinced that this is both administratively incomplete and ethically inadequate. **1941** H. M. MAGID *Eng. Political Pluralism* i. 8 If we deny the inevitability of totalitarianism, we may discover in pluralism..an attempt to analyze the problem of freedom in the light of modern world conditions. **1954** B. & R. NORTH tr. *Duverger's Pol. Parties* II. i. 257 As a 'party system' the single party is obviously different from the multi-party system or 'pluralism'. **1969** M. BROADY in *Architectural Assoc. Quarterly* I. 67 Political pluralism is concerned essentially with the relationship between the State and other kinds of social organization, and it draws attention to the limitations of State power in order to assert the importance in a democratic society of alternative and independent sources of power and foci of interest. **1977** M. WALKER *National Front* i. 16 Britain is historically accustomed to one form or another of coalition government, which is the essence of pluralism.

b. The existence or toleration of diversity of ethnic or cultural groups within a society or state, of beliefs or attitudes within a body or institution, etc.

1933 *Sociol. & Social Research* XVIII. 103 (*title*) Social pluralism. **1956** H. M. KALLEN *Cultural Pluralism* 46 'Cultural Pluralism' is a controversial expression. *Ibid.* 51 This pluralism is the kind always and everywhere characterizing men's undertakings. **1965** *New Statesman* 19 Nov. 796/2 The relevance of this 'pluralism' to Caribbean politics is plain. Analysis of social problems in simple economic terms..will not do. **1969** *Guardian* 20 Sept. 4/4 A good deal of discussion at the conference.. has been about pluralism as opposed to assimilation. **1971** *Deb. House of Commons Canada* 8 Oct. 8580/2 Ethnic pluralism can help us overcome or prevent the homogenization and depersonalization of mass society. **1976** *Times* 7 Aug. 14/4 To be in favour of pluralism is to declare that one does not intend to hound or persecute theologians or catechists whose expression of faith differs from your own. **1977** F. YOUNG in J. Hick *Myth of God Incarnate* ii. 42 The future seems to lie with pluralism in christology.

pluralist. Add: **1. b.** (Earlier example.)

1818 T. BROWN *Brighton* II. 181 This long pole is but a walking stick to the magical wand of old Hurlothrumbo, the pluralist, who can fill so many places.

2. (Earlier and later examples.) Also *attrib.*

1885 W. JAMES *Lit. Remains of H. James* 116 Their most serious enemy will be the *philosophic* pluralist. **1919** C. A. RICHARDSON *Spiritual Pluralism* i. 12 The above is but a broad outline of the pluralist argument as applied to the inorganic world. **1919** *Mind* XXVIII. 58 The pluralist..recognizes that the fundamental fact from which the start must be made, is not a dualism of matter and mind, but the unity of the individual experience, which comprises a duality of subject and object. **1966** F. J. COPLESTON *Hist. Philos.* VIII. x. 250 The idea of God has the benefit of increasing the pluralist's confidence in the significance of finite existence.

3. *Pol.* and *Sociol.* One who upholds pluralism and is opposed to monolithic state power or to policies of cultural or ethnic assimilation. Also *attrib.* or as *adj.*, designating a system based on pluralism.

1920 *Amer. Pol. Sci. Rev.* XIV. 407 The all important fact, so consistently overlooked by the pluralist, that the truly federal state is a unitary state. *Ibid.*, The pluralist doctrine is timely in that it calls attention to the present bewildering development of groups within the body politic. **1957** M. P. FOGARTY *Christian Democracy* I. iii. 29 A certain 'solidarist' conception of the individual's responsibility to and for the society around him, and, following from this, a 'federalist' or 'pluralist' ideal of the structure of society and the processes which go on within it. **1964** GOULD & KOLB *Dict. Social Sci.* 244/2 Today attention is frequently paid to the difficulties of maintaining a pluralist society under the impact of mass society and culture. *Ibid.* 563/2 Pluralists define public opinion in terms of controversy. **1972** *Times Lit. Suppl.* 4 Feb. 115/2 The cheerful belief that the Negro was entering mainstream pluralist politics became incredible after Watts, Newark and Detroit. **1975** *N.Y. Times* 9 Oct. 3/3 The Market withheld similar aid in July for the Gonçalves Government on the ground that it did not represent a 'pluralist democracy'. **1977** M. WALKER *National Front* i. 16 The great strength of the British pluralist system of channelling political allegiance into one of two wide coalitions is that many citizens who sympathize with totalitarian objectives are encouraged to stay within the political mainstream.

pluralistic, *a.* Add: (Earlier and later examples.) Also *spec.* in *Pol.* and *Sociol.* (see *PLURALISM 3); *pluralistic ignorance* (see quot. 1970).

1854 *Edin. Rev.* XCIX. 360 Even the 'pluralistic' marriage service has been published [by the Mormons]. The following is an extract from this novel rubric. **1909** W. JAMES (*title*) Pluralistic universe. **1919** H. J. LASKI in *Philos. Rev.* XXVIII. 562 (*title*) The pluralistic state. **1920** *Amer. Jrnl. Sociol.* XXV. 388 Pluralistic behavior, in distinction from individual behavior, has its own conditions, forms, and laws. **1933** *Sociol. & Social Research* XVIII. 107 The pluralistic conception of society carries with it the principle of functionalism. **1950** T. M. NEWCOMB *Social Psychol.* xvi. 608 We have a condition for which F. H. Allport..suggested the term pluralistic ignorance. Everyone assumes that everyone except himself accepts the norms uncritically. **1963** F. COPLESTON *Hist. Philos.* VII. II. xii. 252 A pluralistic metaphysics which calls to mind the atoms of Democritus and the monads of Liebnitz. **1964** T. B. BOTTOMORE *Elites & Society* vi. 119 Aron, when he urges the importance of the diffusion of power in the pluralistic democracies does not invoke only the principal elites. **1970** G. A. & A. G. THEODORSON *Mod. Dict. Sociol.* 301 *Pluralistic ignorance*, a situation in which individual members of a group believe incorrectly that they are each alone..in believing or not believing in particular values. **1971** [see **plural society*]. **1972** *Times Lit. Suppl.* 18 Feb. 195/2 We are now living in a morally pluralistic society;..attempts by one group to impose its morality on another are futile. **1975** *N.Y. Times* 10 Sept. 20/7 Mr. Kissinger added that the United States was 'working in closest harmony with our European allies' on the problem of encouraging 'the emergence of a pluralistic system' in Portugal. **1976** P. DONOVAN *Relig. Lang.* viii. 95 Apologists for the Baha'i World Faith appeal to the reasonableness of a syncretistic faith in today's pluralistic world. **1977** M. WALKER *National Front* i. 15 The pluralistic kind of society has agreed to permit its citizens to differ about the society's objectives.

pluralization. (Later examples.)
1970 *English Studies* LI. 395 Participles used as adjectival modifiers were also disregarded, as were those used nominally (with actual or potential determiners, pluralisation, or government by a preposition). **1972** *Language* XLVIII. 356 All these authors, characteristically, regard the rules of Spanish pluralization as phonological ones. **1978** *Amer. Speech* LIII. 35 Personal singular *you* similarly takes what is formally a plural verb form (*are, were*), as do French *vous*, German *Sie*, and Russian *vy*; as with singular *they—themself*, this 'pluralization' of singular *you* can be said to follow reflexivization (whence a plural verb but a singular reflexive *yourself*).

pluralize, *v.* Add: **1. c.** *intr.* To express or form the plural.
1964 *Language* XL. 135 The way in which speakers of English pluralize.

pluralizer. Add: **2.** *Gram.* **a.** A pluralizing affix, inflexion, or word. **b.** A noun that may appear in plural form.
1933 *Times Lit. Suppl.* 16 Nov. 798/2 *Shang* is one of the six pluralizers. **1951** *Archivum Linguisticum* III. 66 Suffix: *-naka* ~ *-nak-* '(noun) pluralizer'. **1961** R. B. LONG *Sentence & its Parts* ii. 39 The basic forms of pluralizer nouns are most often used as heads within nounal units, since they generally require determiners. *Ibid.*, Quantifiables such as *courage, fun,..machinery*, and *furniture* are not made plural, though it is true that some quantifiables have pluralizer status also. **1965** *Canad. Jrnl. Linguistics* Spring 172 The pluralizer *qə-* of Position 4. **1971** [see *INTENSIFIER].

pluranimity. *rare.* [f. L. *plus, plūr-* more, substituted for *un-* in UNANIMITY.] Diversity of opinions.
1907 W. DE MORGAN *Alice-For-Short* ix. 95 Whatever innate ideas on the subject of oil-painting he possessed, had been disorganised and carefully thrown out of gear by the want of unanimity, or presence of pluranimity, in his instructors.

plurative. 2. (Earlier example.)
1849 W. THOMSON *Laws of Thought* (ed. 2) II. 174 The judgment—'Most men are prejudiced' cannot..be considered as particular, for it implies not only that *some* men, but *more than the half* of mankind are prejudiced. These are termed *plurative* judgments.

pluri-. Add: **pluridi·sciplinary** *a.*, having or consisting of several disciplines or branches of learning; = *INTERDISCIPLINARY *a.*; **plu·riform** *a.*, existing in many different forms; multiform; hence **plurifo·rmity**; **plurili·ngual** *a.* and *sb.* = *MULTILINGUAL *a.* and *sb.*, POLYGLOT *a.* and *sb.*; hence **plurili·ngualism**; **plurilocular** (later examples); **plurimo·dal** *a.*, consisting of or involving more than one mode (in various senses); **plurisy·llable**, a word of two or more syllables; hence **plurisylla·bic** *a.*
1970 *Guardian Weekly* 14 May 12/1 The substitution of medium-sized pluri-disciplinary universities for the existing monstrous faculties. **1972** *Science* 12 May 621/3 They would also be 'pluridisciplinary' which meant..that the universities would 'associate wherever possible arts and letters with sciences and technics'. **1979** *Guardian* 12 June 8/7 This is a pluri-disciplinary show—which means that all the arts are being covered. **1973** *Times* 28 May 9/6 The remarks regarding churchmanship can only be described as naive; most Anglicans know their Church to be pluriform. **1974** *Times Lit. Suppl.* 22 Mar. 299/2 To say that all religions are equally true amounts to saying that all are equally false. But are not some more equal than others? Or is there a case for saying that truth can be pluriform? *Ibid.* 5 July 732/3 The New Testament writings are to be seen as pluriform. They were not composed..to produce a volume on a theme previously agreed. **1975** *Caribbean Contact* Feb. 4/3 One effective way of developing a pluriform approach in the context of the many needs of any single community is through the team ministry approach. **1947** *Theology* L. 419 The pluriformity of the churches is undoubtedly a sin of Christendom. **1975** *Church Times* 21 Feb. 14/2 No small part of his achievement has been the fundamental preservation of orthodoxy, despite the extensive adoption of pluriformity in forms of worship. **1976** *Times* 21 Feb. 15/6 We, like our Latin brothers, have come to accept pluriformity in belief as much as in cultural tradition. **1938** I. GOLDBERG *Wonder of Words* p. vii, It was the curiosity born of this pluri-lingual heritage that led me..to..a special interest in language. **1956** *Publ. Amer. Dial. Soc.* XXVI. 9 Strictly speaking, a bilingual..is one who knows two languages, but will here (as commonly) be used to include also the one who knows more than two, variously known as a *plurilingual*, a *multilingual*, or a *polyglot*. **1962** Y. MALKIEL in Householder & Saporta *Probl. Lexicogr.* 11 Pluri-lingual dictionaries, which patently mark an increase in coverage. **1976** *Word 1971* XXVII. 407 The period of language 'acquisition' for plurilingual children is claimed to be longer than the period for monolingual children. **1971** *Incorporated Linguist* X. 42/1 Languages involved in societal systems of plurilingualism tend to stabilize their roles on a basis of complementary distribution—either spatially, functionally, or both. **1902** D. H. CAMPBELL *Univ. Text-bk. Bot.* v. 129 In many of the Phæosporeæ..there are formed the plurilocular sporangia. **1961** R. W. BUTCHER *New Illustr. Brit. Flora* I. 19 Sometimes several carpels..are united along the flat sides, so forming a plurilocular ovary of 2—many cells. **1969** F. E. ROUND *Introd. Lower Plants* iii. 44 Plurilocular sporangia may also occur on the sporophyte. **1949** WELLEK & WARREN *Theory of Lit.* iii. 25 The alternative to these seems some bi-modal or plurimodal truth. **1951** G. S. CARTER *Animal Evolution* i. 26 If for the specimens collected at one horizon we plot a variability curve.., the curve..should have an apex for each of the mixed populations (pluri-modal) if the population consists of distinct but mixed elements. **1976** *Word 1971* XXVII. 195 Verbal expression, however, is only one facet of the plurimodal (multichannel) process of interpersonal communication. **1924** J. S. KENYON *Amer. Pronunc.* 30 A Plurisyllable is a word of more than one syllable. **1934** WEBSTER 1897/3 Plurisyllable..plurisyllabic. **1965** *Amer. Speech* XL. 12 There is also *tsetse*..and a fair number of other plurisyllables. *Ibid.* 13 *Sclaff*..is less well known than plurisyllabic *sclerosis*..and *sclerotic*.

pluriarc (plūᵊ·ri,ɑ̄ɪk). [a. Fr. (G. Montandon *La Généalogie des Instruments de Musique* (1919) 52), f. PLURI- + ARC.] A West African musical instrument made of a wooden resonator to which several curved rods holding taut strings are attached.
1961 A. BAINES *Musical Instruments* i. 46 When played it [*sc.* the bow lute] is held like a harp, giving it the impression of being a harp in which each string has a separate neck...The French word *pluriarc*..expresses this well. **1970** *Western Folklore* XXIX. 237 It must be considered possible that the..American instruments of more than one string derive from pluriarcs and trough zithers.

pluripotency (plūᵊripōᵘ·tĕnsi). *Biol.* [ad. G. *pluripotenz*: see PLURI- and POTENCY.] The property of being pluripotential; = *PLURIPOTENCE, *PLURIPOTENTIALITY.
1927 *Biol. Abstr.* I. 217/1 The term pluripotency is used to describe the virtual ability possessed by every organism, under certain conditions, to strike out upon developmental paths deviating from the type. **1942** J. NEEDHAM *Biochem. & Morphogenesis* ii. 100 This condition of multiple potency of the parts of the early egg-cell has been termed pluripotency. **1974** *Cell* II. 166/1 To study the relationships between tumorigenicity, pluripotency, and growth control in vitro, eleven subclones of SIKR [*sc.* a cell line] were isolated in parallel.

pluripotent (plūᵊripōᵘ·tĕnt), *a.* *Biol.* [f. PLURI- + POTENT *a.*[1] and *sb.*[2]] = next. Hence **pluripo·tence** = *PLURIPOTENCY.
1942 J. NEEDHAM *Biochem. & Morphogenesis* ii. 228 The retention of pluripotence through many cleavages, followed by separation of blastomeres. *Ibid.* iii. 435 They are at first pluripotent or relatively undetermined. **1963** J. W. LASH in M. Locke *Cytodifferentiation & Macromolecular Synthesis* 257 Even embryonic systems involving so-called 'pluripotent' reacting tissues are equational to the systems discussed in this paper. **1977** *Lancet* 26 Mar. 680/1 If we assume that the intrathymic stem-cells are really pluripotent and that their capacity to differentiate into various tissues is genetically controlled, this pattern of autoimmune pathogenesis need not be restricted to synaptic autoantigens and myasthenia.

pluripotential (plūᵊripote·nʃăl), *a.* *Biol.* [f. PLURI- + POTENTIAL *a.* and *sb.*] Of a cell, tissue, or organism: capable of developing in any of various directions; = *multipotential* s.v. *MULTI- 1 a.
1925 *Arch. Neurol. & Psychiatry* (Chicago) XIII. 468 Phylogenetically considered, this structure is a pluripotential organ, which in some of the vertebrates has become differentiated as an eye. **1939** *Nature* 27 May 903/1 The lymphocyte may be regarded as a pluripotential element capable of differentiation along several lines, the particular one followed being dependent upon the individual requirements. **1962** *Lancet* 27 Jan. 207/1 Many have regarded it [*sc.* the small lymphocyte] as a mature cell which could not become anything else, while others have regarded it as a temporarily resting stage of a primitive pluripotential cell capable of active development under suitable conditions. **1974** *Nature* 11 Oct. 518/2 We have recently proposed that the proliferative compartment of foetal epidermis is built up by 'pluripotential' stem cells which are replaced by 'committed' stem cells during adolescence.
Hence **plu:ripotentia·lity** = *PLURIPOTENCY.
1956 R. W. EVANS *Histol. Appearances of Tumours* xi. 165 The question of the pluripotentiality and transmutation of lymphocytes into other cells is considered by many authors to be concerned with the enigmatic disappearance of lymphocytes. **1971** *Jrnl. Immunol.* CVII. 1583 (*heading*) The pluripotentiality of mouse spleen lymphocytes.

plurisegmental (plūᵊ:risegme·ntăl), *a.* [f. PLURI- + SEGMENTAL *a.*] **1.** *Physiol.* That involves nerves from more than one segment of the spinal column.
1898 C. S. SHERRINGTON in *Phil. Trans. R. Soc.* B. CXC. 151 It follows..that the reflex centrifugal discharge of the spinal cord is pluri-segmental. **1924** *Amer. Jrnl. Physiol.* LXIX. 649 The data indicate for the frog a plurisegmental innervation such as Agduhr..has shown to exist in cats and rabbits. **1969** J. P. SWAZEY *Reflexes & Motor Integration* v. 95 It is the pluri-segmental character of the motor nucleus, as expressed by reciprocal innervation, which gives the limb its functional solidarity.
2. *Linguistics.* = *SUPRASEGMENTAL *a.*
1964 R. H. ROBINS *Gen. Linguistics* 107 The most important features that must be treated as plurisegmental ..are stress, pitch, and general voice quality. **1965** *Language* XLI. 309 The Firthian distinction of phonematic units (with 'unisegmental..relevance'..) and prosodies (with 'plurisegmental relevance') is probably more acceptable to some old-fashioned Americans than the Chomsky-Halle treatment of all features as equal.
Hence **plu:risegme·ntally** *adv.*
1930 *Jrnl. Physiol.* LXX. 210 Frogs which have been kept in the tank for several months and whose muscles are much atrophied, are likely to show a very low proportion of plurisegmentally innervated fibres. **1960** *Jrnl. Compar. Neurol.* CXV. 47/2 The neurons..occur plurosegmentally.

plurisign (plūᵊ·risəin). [f. PLURI- + SIGN *sb.*] A 'sign' or word used with more than one meaning simultaneously: opp. *MONOSIGN. Hence **plurisigna·tion**, **plurisi·gnative** *a.*, **plurisi·gnatively** *adv.* Also **plu:risignifica·tion.**
1940 *Kenyon Rev.* II. 266 The atomic ingredient of poetic language tends to be the plurisign. *Ibid.* 268 We may distinguish three types of simultaneous plurisignation. *Ibid.* 282 There is also a third important dimension, which may be called the dimension of *plurisignative fullness*, or *poetic richness*. *Ibid.* 504 The realm of poetry-connotation-plurisignification. **1954** P. WHEELWRIGHT *Burning Fountain* iv. 61 The poetic symbol tends..to be plurisignative. *Ibid.* vi. 106 In plurisignation, a single verbal expression carries two or more meanings simultaneously. *Ibid.* vii. 149 A serious metaphoric pun, a poetic plurisign. *Ibid.* x. 217 The directions of mythic reference which..make a tragic action plurisignatively meaningful. **1964** J. STONE *Legal System & Lawyers' Reasonings* i. 34 (*heading*) 'Law properly so-called' and plurisignation of words. **1965** *Encycl. Poetry* 760/1 The depth symbol tends to be *plurisignative*; which is to say, its intended meanings are likely to be more or less multiple, yet so fused as to produce an integral meaning which radically transcends the sum of the ingredient meanings.

plurivalent (plūᵊrivē̆·lĕnt, plūᵊri·vălĕnt), *a.* [f. PLURI- + L. *valēnt-em*, pr. pple. of *valēre* to be worth.] = MULTIVALENT *a.* in Dict. and Suppl., *spec.* sense *2.
1905 E. B. WILSON in *Jrnl. Exper. Zoöl.* II. 374 In the case of compound or plurivalent chromosomes..McClung's term 'chromatid' may conveniently be applied to each of their univalent constituents. **1952** *Archivum Linguisticum* IV. 169 The sorting out of plurivalent words like G. *Preis* between 'prize' and 'price'. **1976** *Nature* 1–8 Jan. 57/1 Aggregation of the minute somatic single chromosomes to large plurivalent chromosomes prevents mistakes in meiotic distribution.

pluri-valued (plūᵊrivæ·liūd), *a.* *Logic.* Also **plurivalued.** [f. PLURI- + VALUED *ppl. a.*] Of a system of logic: using truth values in addition to those of true and false; many-valued.
1939 R. CARNAP *Found. Logic & Math.* in *Internat. Encycl. Unified Sciences* I. III. § 12. 28 The systems of plurivalued logic as constructed by Lukasiewicz and Tarski, etc. **1949** A. PAP *Elements Anal. Philos.* v. 105 Is it possible to construct a logic which does not assume that every proposition is either true or false ('plurivalued logic')? **1969** N. RESCHER *Many-Valued Logic* i. 10 Two interesting procedures for creating new plurivalued logics out of old ones—the methods of system *extension* and of forming the *product* of two systems—have been devised by Stanisław Jaśkowski. *Ibid.* ii. 83 The prospect remains that two-valued logic is somehow fundamental to the construction of all systems of plurivalued logic in general.

plurry (plɒ·ri), *a.* and *adv.* *Austral.* and *N.Z. slang.* [Maori corruption of BLOODY *a.* and *adv.*] = BLOODY *a.* 10, *adv.* 2.
1900 H. LAWSON *Verses, Pop. & Humorous* 227 And their language that day, I am sorry to say, Mostly consisted of 'plurry'. **1916** *Anzac Book* 137 By this time, being the twelfth month of the same year, it waxed 'plurry' cold, even unto a fall of snow. **1933** H. G. WELLS *Bulpington of Blup* vi. 239 Gawd save us from any plurry mucking pushes. *Ibid.* 242 You're plurry well doing too much with your mouth... *Shut* it! **1938** R. D. FINLAYSON *Brown Man's Burden* 31 It's all right for Pakeha's to spout about Maori art but it won't help me to get manure for my plurry cow farm. **1959** *News Chron.* 6 July 4/2 'You watch your plurry step, man,' he said. 'We know your plurry kind.' **1966** G. W. TURNER *Eng. Lang. in Austral. & N.Z.* x. 200 The literary convention of Maori

English interlarded with *plurry*..belongs to the language of journalists rather than the language of Maoris. **1977** *Sunday Times* 3 July 28/7 I'll bowl a plurry sight faster if they'd let me take my boots off.

plus. Add: **1.** (Earlier and later non-technical examples.)

1823 J. Keble *Let.* in G. Battiscombe *John Keble* (1963) iv. 71 A deaf handmaid, and a clerk-plus-gardener-plus-groom by no means dumb. **1922** Joyce *Ulysses* 642 A cup of Epp's cocoa and a shakedown for the night plus the use of a rug or two and overcoat doubled into a pillow. **1961** B. Fergusson *Watery Maze* xiv. 348 No. 1 Special Service Brigade under Lovat had one Marine and three Army Commandos, plus Lovat's personal piper. **1966** *Oxf. Univ. Gaz.* 23 Dec. 430/1 Just a reference from one meeting of Congregation to another slightly different meeting of Congregation, plus a few alumni. **1974** E. Ambler *Dr Frigo* III. 190 There..was a..plane waiting plus an army scout car and a guard of soldiers. **1975** N. Luard *Travelling Horseman* xiv. 247 That meant me plus Billy to drive me. It was a two-part job.

c. *ellipt.* Placed after a round number or a whole number to indicate a smaller or fractional amount more; with a positive amount added; or more, but not less. Also to indicate a slightly higher grade, as *beta plus* (β+). Also *colloq.* after other sbs. to indicate with extra qualities, better than usual.

[**1902**: see *alpha 4.] **1916** A. Huxley *Let.* 19 Mar. (1969) 94 Beta double plus is quite adequate for language. **1927** *Rep. Consultative Comm. Educ. Adolescent* 185 Raising the school age to 15 plus must lead either to the building of new schools or to the remodelling of existing schools. **1928** *Oxford Mag.* 25 Oct. 40 Till the University finds some benefactor willing to give '£100,000 plus' (to use modern phraseology). *a* **1930** D. H. Lawrence *Collier's Friday Night* i. 20, I generally get an alpha plus. That's the highest, you know, mater. **1951** Wodehouse *Old Reliable* x. 120 You were right in mid-season form. It was battling plus. **1958** L. van der Post *Lost World Kalahari* vi. 104 'This,' I thought before sleeping, 'is Alpha Plus.' **1962** *Listener* 18 Jan. 112/2 To put forward a positive conception of coexistence—we might call it coexistence 'plus'—which includes as its principal ingredient the central idea..of *ideological* coexistence. **1962** *Guardian* 5 Dec. 6/4 Everything you could possibly want in make-up plus, for 1s 6d a time. **1966** *Listener* 30 June 951/2 Many of these can now be walled off, but not Garrincha of Brazil, who on his day is Stanley Matthews plus. **1972** J. Mosedale *Football* ii. 21 The $225-plus material worn by Kansas City tackle Buck Buchanan. **1973** P. Moyes *Curious Affair of Third Dog* i. 10 The Second World War, an unbelievable thirty-plus years ago. **1978** *Jrnl. R. Soc. Arts* CXXVI. 617/2 It will be a hundred years plus before we have a significant contribution.

d. quasi-*conj.* And in addition. *colloq.* (chiefly *N. Amer.*)

1968 N. Giovanni in W. King *Black Short Story Anthol.* (1972) 26 If, on the other hand, a tom tells you to get off the streets and you don't..plus if you can encourage him in a physical way to come on over to your side, then you've made a friend. **1972** C. L. Cooper in *Ibid.* 210 There was rain on the roof, and I was poor. Plus my mother was sick. **1973** *Black World* Jan. 63/2 All the ladies brought pies and cakes... Plus they had coffee and tea and punch. **1974** *Sci. Amer.* Jan. 1/1 (Advt.), Initial cost of our centerline design (WX 200) is $200K instead of the $600K of equivalent current models, plus it will deliver 100 hours MTBF (mean time between failures). **1974** *Maclean's Mag.* Dec. 16/2 But after all is said and done, take away the football game itself from the Grey Cup and what have you got? An early start home, for one thing. Plus you save maybe $30 on tickets. **1977** *Ripped & Torn* VI. 8/2, I was stereotyped as nothing but a drag act. Plus I was tired of doing it. **1978** *Daily Tel.* 9 Feb. 2 (Advt.), W. H. Smith have big names at big savings. Plus you get one year manufacturer's guarantee. **1978** *Detroit Free Press* 2 Apr. 6E/4 Plus they've added pitchers Rudy May and Ross Grimsley.

2. (Later example.)

1975 *Times* 15 Jan. 20/4 A 230-volt standard for electrical supplies throughout Europe was agreed yesterday... The new level has a tolerance of plus or minus 10 per cent.

3. *adj.* (Further examples.)

1928 *Publishers' Weekly* 30 June 2598 The material for the plus sale is always at hand in the book business. **1930** *Publishers' Circular* 2 Aug. 163/2 The whole book business should look on the reprint business as being *plus* business.

b. In various games, having an adverse handicap of a number of strokes or points.

1908 A. W. Myers *Compl. Lawn Tennis Player* 127 It will not take him long to discover the kind of decoy that will deliver the 'plus 15.3' men into his clutches. **1909** *Westm. Gaz.* 8 Feb. 12/4 Supposing a plus 3 man is partnered with a steady player whose handicap is 8, the two as a foursome side would be handicapped at 5. **1922** J. Cannan *Misty Valley* 203 Isn't it just like you to come up to the club-house..and to send a plus man in to fetch me out? **1927** R. J. B. Sellar *Play!* 32 The newly-joined member..asked if they might have a game together. 'Humph,' growled the plus player, 'perhaps. What's your handicap?'

c. Of superior quality; excellent of its kind.

1960 *Times* 10 Dec. 7/6 The country was surveyed to find 'plus trees' (superior examples of all useful species). **1968** *Globe & Mail* (Toronto) 17 Feb. 45 (Advt.), Living room, 15' dining room are plus features!

4. *sb.* **a.** *plus sign* (examples). Also *fig.* and in sense 4d below. **b.** (Later example.) **c.** (Earlier and later *fig.* examples.) **d.** An advantage.

1791 H. Walpole *Let.* 26 July (1905) XV. 25 The villain Paine..is engaged in a controversy with the Abbé Sieyès, about the *plus* or *minus* of the rebellion. **1902** W. James *Varieties Relig. Exper.* 166 Peace cannot be reached by the simple addition of pluses and elimination of minuses from life. **1943** *Sun* (Baltimore) 12 Feb. 17/1 American Telephone was up 1⅛, and lesser plus signs were retained by Radio Corporation, Johns-Manville, Goodrich and United States Gypsum. **1959** *Washington Post* 20 July A 6/1 Radio city is one block from the Hotel Victoria. Other location plusses: Madison Square Garden is two blocks away, so are all subways. **1964** G. C. Kunzle *Parallel Bars* ix. 403 Its great plus is the fact that the superior difficulty is the dismount. **1971** *Guardian* 25 Nov. 15/4 Those whom Mr Blond has published are treated as human beings... This is a major plus in his favour. **1972** *Sci. Amer.* Jan. 83/2 The superscript plus sign denotes a positive ion. **1972** *Business Week* 18 Mar. 20/2 The ability to offer assurances of such long-range supplies..is a big plus for U.S. equipment builders. **1974** T. Allbeury *Snowball* xviii. 104 The friction between the governments —it's a plus but it's a side issue. **1975** *Daily Tel.* 4 Jan. 10 Fiction is not on the wane, but actually registered a plus in the number of books published in 1974. **1975** *Publishers Weekly* 31 Mar. 47/1 There are items here.. that will interest only a handful of people west of Manhattan. But there are compensating plusses. **1975** *Studies in Eng. Lit.: Eng. Number* (Tokyo) 44 In Table 9 the frequency of occurrence is indicated by means of figures appended to plus signs (like +1) for constructions which are themselves rare. **1976** *Evening Post* (Nottingham) 15 Dec. 24/7 But Glaxo 383p, Fisons 288p, Tubes 290p, and GEC 163p, still showed small plus signs. **1976** *Early Music* Oct. 382/2 Could..the same reader get something from an article on..the pluses and minuses of using gut strings? **1977** *Time* 7 Mar. 49/2 The scenery and the costumes..are a dazzling plus. **1978** C. Black *Asterisk Destiny* (1979) v. 122 All I am..is the plus sign in a necessary equation.

6. Special Combs.: **plus juncture** *Linguistics* = *open juncture* s.v. *open a. 22c: **plus word**, a word which is characteristic of its user, or is used frequently.

1951 Trager & Smith *Outl. Eng. Struct.* 68 Within each phonemic phrase the constituents delimited by plus-junctures are noted. **1964** E. Bach *Introd. Transformational Gram.* vi. 129 One can save the situation by positing a phoneme of internal open juncture ('plus-juncture'). **1972** Hartmann & Stork *Dict. Lang. & Linguistics* 241/2 Open transition (open juncture),..often called plus juncture, which occurs at a word boundary. **1976** *Amer. Speech 1974* XLIX. 15 Predictable pitch contours are not marked here and 'plus juncture' is indicated by conventional spacing. **1959** N. N. Holland *First Mod. Comedies* vi. 53 'Solid' became a 'plus' word because it suggested realness, the mass and volume the new physics could measure. **1962** A. Ellegård *Statistical Method for Determining Authorship* ii. 12 The typical, characteristic words of the writer—we shall..call his 'plus words'. **1963** *Times Lit. Suppl.* 25 Jan. 67/2 Words and expressions that were used particularly frequently (plus-words).

plusage (plɒ·sèdʒ). Also **plussage.** [f. Plus + -age.] **a.** (See quot. 1932). **b.** Something extra or added on; a bonus; a surcharge.

A word of restricted currency.—Ed.

1932 *N. & Q.* 30 Jan. 82/2, I have seen in print the word 'plus(s)age' used to denote a plurality of pluses in a collective sense, i.e., (15 per cent. plus 10 per cent. plus 15 per cent.) total plussage of 40 per cent. **1935** A. P. Herbert *What a Word!* iii. 83 From a well-known London shop: 'Should your order not exceed the sum of 17/6 an additional *plusage* of 25% will be charged.' **1959** *Times* 3 Nov. 13/4 When I took up a part-time job three weeks ago I was given a card with which to 'clock in' and 'out'. Among the list of payments was a heading 'Any further plusages'. **1962** *Engineering* 10 Aug. 181 Normal day rate together with a plusage for reaching a certain level of output. **1966** *New Statesman* 22 Apr. 563/1 A woman catcher's rate on a cigarette-making machine, for instance, is about £3 a week less than a man's, although the bonus or 'plussage' for both is equal.

‖ **plus ça change** (plü sa ʃɑ̃ʒ). In full, *plus ça change, plus c'est la même chose.* [Fr., 'the more it changes, the more it stays the same'.] A semi-proverbial phrase, expressing the fundamental immutability of human nature, institutions, etc. Hence **plus ça change-ness** *nonce.*

[**1849** A. Karr in *Les Guêpes* Sér. 6 (new ed.) 1859 Janv. 305 [After comment on recent political events in France] Après tant de bouleversements, de changements, il serait temps de s'apercevoir d'une chose, c'est que c'est comme au cabaret:—cachet vert, cachet rouge, etc.—On change quelquefois le prix, quelquefois le bouchon, mais c'est toujours la même piquette qu'on nous fait boire.—Plus ça change—plus c'est la même chose.] **1903** G. B. Shaw *Man & Superman* 182 The mere transfiguration of institutions, as from military and priestly dominance to commercial and scientific dominance, from commercial dominance to proletarian democracy,..are all but changes from Tweedledum to Tweedledee: *plus ça change, plus c'est la même chose.* **1955** *Times* 5 July 11/4 We have an uneasy suspicion that there is something to be said for the epic angle on history. After all, when boy met—or meets—girl, *plus ça change.* **1959** 'J. Byrom' *Take only as Directed* i. 8 'I don't like being out of date!' '*Plus ça change,*' I said. **1966** *New Statesman* 2 Sept. 306/1 Meanwhile it is a sort of lottery whether a murderer is hanged or not... Out of seven capital sentences passed at the Winter Assizes 1871/1872, *only one* was carried out. *Plus ça change.* *Ibid.* 312/3 Browsing in my current bedside book, *The Paston Letters*, I have been struck by the *plus ça change*-ness of the human animal. **1969** R. Blythe *Akenfield* 15 Where the strict village existence is concerned it is *Plus ça change, plus c'est la même chose.* **1970** W. Garner *Puppet-Masters* i. 14 *Plus ça change*—! The present French government's simply following tradition. **1978** *Language* LIV. 383 For both theories, then, plus ça change, plus c'est la même chose; and, interestingly, the même chose of each turns out to be the même chose for both.

plus-foured (plɒsfōᵊ·ɹd), *a.* [f. next + -ed².] Wearing or clad in plus fours.

1925 *N. & Q.* 28 Nov. 387/2 In *Truth* of Oct. 14 a writer ventured 'plus-foured'. **1926** *Daily Chron.* 13 May 2/2 'I'll be sorry to leave the old bus tonight,' said the plus foured pull-overed youth at the wheel of the 'General' yesterday afternoon. **1934** C. Lambert *Music Ho!* iv. 242 A begoggled, leather-coated and plus-foured figure. **1967** O. Lancaster *Eye to Future* iii. 64 The hearties, grey flannel-trousered or elaborately plus-foured. **1978** *Daily Tel.* 21 Jan. 9/1 On Saturday morning he stands tweedily plus-foured beside a gate, serving as honorary secretary of the beagles.

plus fours (plɒs fōᵊɹz). [f. Plus 3 + Four *a.* and *sb.*, since, to produce the overhang, four inches is normally added to the length required for ordinary knickerbockers.] A distinctive style of long, wide knickerbockers, or a suit having such knickerbockers, originally much worn by golfers and associated with outdoor pursuits. Also *transf.*, and *attrib.* (Also in form *plus-four*).

1920 *Isis* 25 Feb. 6/2 *(caption)* 'Plus Fours'. *Ibid.* 12 May 10/2 The desuetude of the traditional grey flannel 'bags' of the undergraduate... 'Plus fours' have succeeded them. **1921** *Isis* 1 June p. xii, Knicker (plus four) Suits from 8½ gns. **1922** J. Cannan *Misty Valley* 201 A tall man in plus fours and a yellow waistcoat. **1923** S. Herd *My Golfing Life* 151 The first time I saw a golfer wearing baggy 'plus 4's' I thought he looked like a lassie. **1928** *Sat. Evening Post* 10 Mar. 174/3 You can almost visualize the venerable Francis Joseph tweaking away at his plus-four whiskers. **1929** H. A. Vachell *Virgin* ix. 154 The Major got himself up 'to kill', wearing a new suit of 'plus fours'. **1934** G. B. Shaw *Village Wooing* ii. 119 He is in hiking costume..but wears well cut breeches (not plus fours) instead of shorts. **1939** Joyce *Finnegans Wake* (1964) i. 30 In topee, surcingle, solascarf and plaid, plus fours, puttees and bulldog boots. **1951** N. M. Gunn *Well at World's End* xix. 152 He wore a plusfour suiting of discreet checks and unpronounced bagginess. **1961** C. Willock *Death in Covert* i. 13 He wore knicker-bocker trousers that..were nearly plus-fours: say, plus-threes. **1972** *Country Life* 12 Oct. 926/2 Rust battle-jacket with plus-fours in Shetland tweed. By Christian Dior Monsieur. **1974** 'P. B. Yuill' *Bornless Keeper* ii. 19 Wood-pigeons strutted like fat old squires in plus fours. **1978** G. Sims *Rex Mundi* xxvi. 156 He was dressed in a brown plus-fours suit.

plush, *sb.* Add: **1. c.** Colloq. phr. *on* (or *in*) (*the*) *plush*: in comfortable circumstances.

1930 Wodehouse *Very Good, Jeeves* ix. 226 He was, to all appearances, absolutely on plush. He ate well, slept well, was happily married. **1945** *Richmond* (Va.) *Times-Dispatch* 23 Mar. 20/3 Morgenthau..made it plain that the drive would be aimed chiefly against 'the boys who live in the plush' rather than the small taxpayer.

3. a. Also, covered or upholstered in plush.

1895 *Montgomery Ward Catal.* 113/1 Silk plush work box with silvered center and corner ornaments. **1926** E. O'Neill *Great God Brown* i. iii. 89 At the left is a bald-spotted crimson plush chair. **1935** R. Macaulay *Personal Pleasures* 135 Pointing us to seats in the middle of an eagerly gazing row of persons, past whom we push, to subside into plush chairs and eagerly gaze too. **1935** *Punch* 4 Sept. 256/2 And, what is more, though you were seeing it in comfort from a plush seat, it was nearly as good as if you had been energetic and enthusiastic enough to go to Victoria. **1976–7** *Hamley's Catal.* 66/3 A fully jointed soft plush teddy.

b. *plush-bottomed, -bound, -capped, -clad, -fitted, -framed, -lined* adjs.; **plush horse,** used as a symbol of ostentation and over-elaborateness; also *attrib.*

1901 Conrad & Hueffer *Inheritors* xiii. 210, I sat on a plush-bottomed gilded chair. **1902** Conrad *Typhoon* xxiii. 185 She reclined in a plush-bottomed and gilt hammock-chair near a tiled fireplace. **1912** C. Mackenzie *Carnival* xxxiv. 347 These..were now propped dismally against the overmantel, individually obscured..by a plush-bound photograph of Mr. Lloyd George. **1876** G. M. Hopkins *Wreck of Deutschland* viii, in *Poems* (1967) 54 How a lush-kept plush-capped sloe Will, mouthed to flesh-burst, Gush! **1913** C. Mackenzie *Sinister Street* I. ii. vii. 259 He saw..plush-clad children who continually dropped Sunday-school books in the mud. **1927** A. Conan Doyle *Case Bk. Sherlock Holmes* i. 38 A butler..handed me over to a plush-clad footman, who ushered me into the Baron's presence. **1938** L. MacNeice *Zoo* 227 Plush-fitted theatres. **1937** E. Sitwell *I live under Black Sun* 98 A plush-framed photograph. **1922** S. Lewis *Babbitt* ii. 23 Just compare a real human like you and these neurotic birds like Lucile McKelvey—all high-brow talk and dressed up like a plush horse. **1936** J. Dos Passos *Big Money* 201 What I'd love more than anything in the world would be to get out and make my own living. I hate this plushhorse existence. **1946** P. Larkin *Jill* 184 The competition is very keen, because they're very, very plush-lined jobs.

B. *adj.* Luxurious, expensive, stylish. *colloq.*

1927 in Wentworth & Flexner *Dict. Amer. Slang* (1960) 398/2 'Plush' indicates..stylish. **1934** M. H. Weseen *Dict. Amer. Slang* 192 *Plush*, stylish. **1944** 'P. Quentin' *Puzzle for Puppets* xix. 141 We had the plushest hotel suite of any married couple in San Francisco. **1946** *Richmond* (Va.) *Times-Dispatch* 30 Oct. 1/2 The recently established plush eating place. **1952** W. R. BURNETT *Vanity Row* (1953) v. 48 'Apartment address?' asked Roy. Joe gave it to him. 'H'm' said Roy. '..Pretty plush.' **1955** *Bull. Atomic Sci.* Feb. 51/2 These need not be plush or elaborate shelters. **1959** *Sunday Express* 1 Feb. 19/6 The word 'Set' in this context is an economic symbol—a plush version of what humbler people call 'The Gang'. **1959** H. HOBSON *Mission House Murder* ii. 8 The sales-minded débutante who was earning pin-money in the plush establishment. **1971** *Guardian* 28 May 8/2 It was really plush, with 25 waitresses. **1978** *New York* 3 Apr. 27/1 Plush place with excellent service, a great chef, and strolling guitarist-singer.

plushery (plɒ·ʃěri). *U.S. Show-business slang.* [f. PLUSH *sb.* + -ERY.] (See quots.)

1951 GREEN & LAURIE *Show Biz* 570/2 *Plushery*, class joint (hotel, nitery, eatery). **1961** A. BERKMAN *Singers' Gloss. Show Business Jargon* 69 *Plushery*,..a classy restaurant or night club.

plushly (plɒ·ʃli), *adv.* [f. *PLUSH *a.* + -LY².] Richly, sumptuously, elegantly.

1951 W. SANSOM *Face of Innocence* iii. 34 In all her attitudes—stretching and crossing her long legs,..finding a green background to burn plushly behind her white profile—she was assured. **1959** *Observer* 30 Aug. 11/7 There it [*sc.* a countryside] all is, laid out so plushly for mile after mile. **1971** *Daily Tel.* (Colour Suppl.) 7 May 50/3 A lush settee and two armchairs, all plushly covered in fine green velvet.

plushy, *a.* Add: **c.** Luxurious, sumptuous, elegant. *colloq.*

1923 A. HUXLEY *Antic Hay* i. 14 Over the plushy floors of some vast and ignoble Ritz slowly he walked, at ease, with confidence. **1942** *Sat. Rev. Lit.* (U.S.) 6 June 3/2 De Graff's plushy offices would lead the innocent visitor to conclude that successful publishing requires only some good titles and the organization to distribute them wholesale. **1942** R. CHANDLER *High Window* (1943) iv. 34 Runs a plushy night-club and gambling joint. **1947** *Yale Law Jrnl.* Dec. 188 Driving Fords..rather than more plushy 'petit bourgeois' cars. **1953** W. STEVENS *Let.* 4 June (1967) 779 The picture of her in her prime was plushy, but cold. **1959** W. CAMP *Ruling Passion* 116 'This is a wee bit plushy, I must admit,' said Simon, as Paul entered his fantastically opulent-looking office. **1960** *Times* 29 Feb. 3/3 Much tongue wagging here [*sc.* Paris] from the plushier night haunts down to the homeliest *bistro.* **1970** 'D. HALLIDAY' *Dolly & Cookie Bird* i. 7 The lawyer-trustee ..took me to a nice plushy lunch at the Café Royal. **1977** *Sunday Tel.* 11 Sept. 19/7 In ministerial quarters there are plenty of plushy berths to be filled.

Hence **plu·shily** *adv.*, **plu·shiness.**

1916 W. J. LOCKE *Wonderful Year* xiii. 183 The primly and plushily furnished salon. **1969** *Amateur Photographer* 21 May 53/1 Intimate exclusiveness, though not plushiness, is also a feature of the club cinema.

plussage, var. *PLUSAGE.

plus twos (plɒs tūz). [After *PLUS FOURS.] A narrower version of plus fours. Also (in form *plus two*) *attrib.*

1967 *Daily Tel.* 24 May 26/3 (*caption*) The high-waisted winter weather coat has a Russian influence, and the country outfit a single-breasted jacket and tartan plus-twos. **1970** P. DICKINSON *Seals* vii. 136 Father in his plus-twos. **1977** *Field* 13 Jan. 68/4 (Advt.), Plus Two breeches.

plute (plūt). *slang* (chiefly *U.S.*). Abbrev. of PLUTOCRAT. Cf. *PLOOT. Hence **plu·tish** *a.*, plutocratic.

1908 S. FORD *Side-Stepping with Shorty* i. 13 Then we bumps up against a really truly plute, and gets a squint at his dinner check. **1910** WODEHOUSE *Gentleman of Leisure* i. 3 He's got much more money than any man, except a professional plute, has any right to. **1922** S. LEWIS *Babbitt* ii. 23 Our little bunch has a lot liver times than all those plutes. **1923** *Daily Mail* 29 May 8 'The plutes', as he [*sc.* Henry Ford] humorously nicknames the financial and industrial interests of the country, would never permit his nomination. *c* **1926** 'MIXER' *Transport Workers' Song Bk.* 80 This plutish press condemns our class. **1932** *Randolph Enterprise* (Elkins, W. Va.) 18 Feb. 5/2 You'll hear the plutes cry out, The 'Yellow Peril' is Japan.

pluterperfect (plūːtəɪpɜ̄·ɹfěkt), *a. nonce-wd.* [Poss. a corruption of Fr. *plus-que-parfait*: see PLUPERFECT *a.* (*sb.*).] = PLUPERFECT *a.* 2.

1922 JOYCE *Ulysses* 34 The pluterperfect imperturbability of the department of agriculture. *Ibid.* 412 An omnivorous being which can..pass through the ordinary channel with pluterperfect imperturbability such multifarious aliments as cancrenous females emaciated by parturition.

Pluto¹ (plū·to). [a. L. *Plūto*, Gr. *Πλούτων*, name of the god of the underworld, brother of Jupiter and Neptune.] **1.** A small planet of the solar system lying beyond the orbit of Neptune, discovered only in 1930 by C. W. Tombaugh.

1930 *N.Y. Times* 26 Mar. 10/3 'Pluto' is the provisional name that Italian astronomers have given to the new trans-Neptune planet discovered March 13 at Lowell Observatory in Flagstaff, Ariz... Hugh Rice..yesterday opposed naming the newly discovered planet 'Minerva', as has already been suggested, because an asteroid already bears that name. **1930** V. M. SLIPHER *Lowell Observatory Observation Circular* 1 May, Many names have been suggested and among them Minerva and Pluto have been very popular... Pluto seems very appropriate and we are proposing to the American Astronomical Society and to the Royal Astronomical Society, that this name be given to it. As far as we know Pluto was first suggested by Miss Venetia Burney, aged 11, of Oxford, England. [*Note*] Kindly cabled by Prof. H. H. Turner. **1930** H. H. TURNER in *Times* 28 May 17/5 A post-card from the President of the Royal Astronomical Society offered this morning 'congratulations to the suggester of the name Pluto, now adopted'. The reference is to a telegram which I had the honour of sending to the Lowell Observatory on March 15..conveying the suggestion of Miss Venetia Burney, of Oxford, made at breakfast on that day to her grandfather, who sent it on to me... It was a brother of that same grandfather who suggested the names Deimos and Phobos for the satellites of Mars. **1933** D. L. SAYERS *Hangman's Holiday* 120 Presently they had guessed among other things Miss Tomkins's mother's photograph,..the new planet Pluto,..and had failed to guess the Prime Minister's wireless speech. **1939** SKILLING & RICHARDSON *Astron.* i. 12 The length of seasons depends, of course, upon the length of time required for the planet to go around the sun—all the way from about 3 months for Mercury to 248 years for Pluto. **1953** A. F. O'D. ALEXANDER in M. Davidson *Astron. for Everyman* iv. 203 Pluto's path never crosses Neptune's..for its orbit-plane is inclined 17° to the ecliptic plane. **1972** P. L. BROWN *Astron. in Color* ii. 86 One theory accounts for the origin of Pluto by considering that it is an ex-satellite of Neptune which somehow broke free. **1976** J. GRIBBIN *Astron. for Amateur* v. 70 Because of its elliptical orbit Pluto sometimes passes within the orbit of Neptune, and just now (until the end of this century) Neptune is the furthest planet from the Sun.

2. The name of a cartoon dog that made its first appearance in Walt Disney's *Moose Hunt*, released in April 1931; a toy dog representing this character.

1932 W. DISNEY *Adventures Mickey Mouse* II. 14 Mickey watched, and Minnie, too, And Pluto hid himself from view. **1936** —— *Mickey Mouse Fables* 3 'Now for my bone,' said Pluto, licking his lips. **1957** D. D. MILLER *Walt Disney* viii. 137 Pluto got his nose stuck to flypaper and tried to blow it off. **1962** L. DEIGHTON *Ipcress File* ii. 22 A cigarette-girl..offered me a pink felt pluto, too. **1972** *Guardian* 21 Aug. 11/5 Ten dogs took part, plus one yellow plastic Pluto on wheels. **1973** L. MALTIN *Disney Films* iv. 267 As the 1930s wore on..Mickey played a progressively less important role in the proceedings, some cartoons completely taken over by the character of Pluto.

Plu·to². [Acronym f. initial letters of *P*ipe *L*ine *u*nder *t*he *O*cean.] The code name for a system of pipe-lines laid in 1944 to carry petrol supplies from Britain to Allied forces in France. Also *attrib.*

1945 *News Chron.* 1 June 2/5 As in the Pluto pipeline, petrol was the basis of this secret weapon. Like Pluto the experts said at first that it could not be done. **1946** *Ann. Reg. 1945* 37 Foremost among these was the laying of a system of oil pipelines under the sea stretching across the Channel from the British coast to the Continent, and commonly known as 'Operation Pluto' (pipe line under the ocean). **1961** E. W. GLADSTONE *Army* vii. 103 Many clever inventions like the artificial 'Mulberry' harbours, and 'Pluto', the Pipe Line Under the Ocean to provide petrol, had been developed. **1978** A. WAUGH *Best Wine Last* xv. 177 The Petroleum Warfare Department.. invented 'PLUTO' (pipe line under the ocean) to carry oil across the Channel.

plutocratical (plūtokræ·tikăl), *a.* [f. PLUTOCRATIC *a.* + -AL.] = PLUTOCRATIC *a.* So **plutocra·tically** *adv.*, in a plutocratical manner.

1833 J. S. MILL *Let.* 10 July in *Wks.* (1963) XII. 166 The anomaly of a democratic constitution in a plutocratically constituted society. **1913** W. J. LOCKE *Stella Maris* xx. 238 Only the splendour..of plutocratically owned vehicles meets the enraptured vision. **1941** E. R. EDDISON *Fish Dinner* xix. 324 An aristocratical plutocratical self-obtruding dilettante. **1978** *Country Life* 31 Aug. 589/4 In their heyday they certainly seem, plutocratically speaking, to have been a singularly unattractive lot.

plutocratizing (plūtǫ·krătəiziŋ), *vbl. sb.* [f. PLUTOCRAT + -IZE + -ING¹, after *democratizing.*] The action or process of rendering plutocratic.

1896 *Westm. Gaz.* 9 Dec. 2/3 The 'plutocratising' of the Universities was a nineteenth century movement. **1929** *New Statesman* 28 Sept. 740/1 The Americanisation and plutocratising of old England.

pluto-democracy (plūːtoˌdīmǫ·krăsi). Also **plutodemocracy.** [f. Gr. πλοῦτος wealth, riches + DEMOCRACY.] **1.** Plutocratic government which masquerades as democracy.

1895 in *Funk's Stand. Dict.* **1941** D. WILSON *Germany's 'New Order'* 24 German gibes at pluto-democracy. **1944** J. S. HUXLEY *On Living in Revol.* 41 Hitler has proclaimed his aims... They include..the destruction of what he is pleased to call 'pluto-democracy'. **1970** H. ARENDT *On Violence* 72 A new system, which he [*sc.* Pareto] called 'Pluto-democracy'—a mixed form of government, plutocracy being the bourgeois regime and democracy the regime of the workers.

2. A country or state which purports to be a democracy but where power lies with the rich.

1902 *Nineteenth Century & After* July 119 If England be allowed to become a Plutodemocracy, then she has the tragic example of Venice to chasten and admonish her. **1940** *Common Sense* Aug. 6/2 The absolute power of a Stalin or a Hitler is seen to be even worse than the economic exploitation and political ineffectiveness of a 'pluto-democracy' with its checks and balances. **1942** L. B. NAMIER *Conflicts* 209 In the presence of social inequalities, parliamentary democracy without parties must inevitably result in a real 'pluto-democracy'. **1948** W. S. CHURCHILL *Second World War* I. xx. 287 The Jew Litvinov was gone, and Hitler's dominant prejudice placated. From that moment the German Government ceased to define its foreign policy as anti-Bolshevism, and turned its abuse upon the 'pluto-Democracies'.

Hence **plu:to-de·mocrat,** an adherent or advocate of pluto-democracy; **plu:to-democra·tic** *a.*

1940 *Economist* 24 Feb. 328/2 German propagandists are making steady use of..'Britain the pluto-democrat, living in luxury on the wealth extorted from 60 million native serfs'. *Ibid.* 29 June 1102/1 German propaganda among the French troops has followed the lines of 'plutodemocratic capitalist Britain'. **1946** R. GRAVES *Poems 1938–1945* 35 By every nastier manifestation Of plutodemocratic civilisation.

plutogogue (plū·togǫg). [f. Gr. πλοῦτος wealth + ἀγωγός leading, leader, after *demagogue.*] A spokesman for the plutocrats; one who justifies or advocates the interests of the wealthy. Hence **plu·togogy,** the rule of plutogogues.

1894 *Westm. Gaz.* 17 Feb. 8/1 Mr. Williams, of Mississippi, said the opponents of the income tax are plutogogues and encouragers of plutogogy. *Ibid.*, A demagogue, he explained, appeals directly to the mob; a plutogogue appeals to the people who buy the mob. **1931** L. STEFFENS *Autobiogr.* II. III. xvi. 474 Since the plutogogues could not fasten any crime on him they fell back on the all-sufficient charge that he was a demagogue. **1937** *Sun* (Baltimore) 30 Aug. 9/4 Smith called the demagogue, plutogogue and the theogogue, 'fearful trinity, constituting the very diabolus of democracy'. **1937** *News-Week* 13 Sept. 20/2 Fascists and Communists did not strike him as any more dangerous than the man he new-named the plutogogue. The philosophy professor defined him as 'the voice of the wealthy when they can no longer speak for themselves, the successor of the plutocrat of other days'.

plutolater (plutǫ·lătəɹ). *rare.* [f. PLUTOLATRY, after *idolater.*] One who worships wealth.

1938 S. BECKETT *Murphy* ix. 168 All the self-made plutolaters who ever triumphed over empty pockets.

plutological (plūtŏlǫ·dʒikăl), *a. rare.* [f. PLUTOLOGY + -IC + -AL.] Of or pertaining to plutology.

1920 *Edin. Rev.* July 80 The whole plutological apparatus was developed—banking, investment, partnership, joint stock companies, and even trusts. *Ibid.* 83 The economic difference between ancient, medieval and modern society is in scale, complexity and form, not in the plutological principle or the essential character of the process.

plutomanic (plūtoˌmæ·nik), *a. rare.* [f. as PLUTOMANIA + *MANIC *a.*] Characterized by the insane love or pursuit of wealth.

1938 S. BECKETT *Murphy* v. 82 A colossal league of plutomanic caterers. **1963** B. S. JOHNSON *Travelling People* 159 His decision to enter the plutomanic world of commerce.

pluton (plū·tǫn). *Geol.* [a. G. *pluton* (H. Cloos 1928, in *Fennia* L. II. 1), back-formation from *plutonisch* PLUTONIC *a.* (*sb.*).] An intrusive body of igneous rock formed beneath the earth's surface, esp. a large one.

[**1933** R. A. DALY *Igneous Rocks & Depths of Earth* vi. 75 He [*sc.* H. Cloos] states that he does not assume floors for batholiths but on the next page defines his '*Plutone*', which includes batholiths, as having visible or inferable floors.] **1936** *Proc. Geol. Soc. Amer. 1935* 67 The granite appears to have come up along the edge of the mostly consolidated Pikes Peak mass and spread in a series of plutons and sills, the mode of intrusion being largely governed by the rock invaded. **1942** M. P. BILLINGS *Structural Geol.* xv. 296 The intrusion of large plutons may be associated with orogenic movements. **1961** F. H. LAHEE *Field Geol.* (ed. 6) vi. 141 Concordant plutons include sills, laccoliths, lopoliths, and phacoliths. *Ibid.* 142 Discordant plutons include dikes, necks, chonoliths, batholiths, stocks, and bosses. **1962** [see *GREISEN]. **1971** I. G. GASS et al. *Understanding Earth* v. 84/2 The observed linear relation between heat flow and heat production in granitic plutons may allow precise estimates of temperature as far down as the base of the crust. **1974** H. F. GARNER *Origin of Landscapes* iii. 130/2 Metasomatic replacement is common along borders of larger intrusive masses (plutons).

Plutonism. Add: Also **plutonism. 1.** (Examples.)

1910 *Encycl. Brit.* XI. 644/2 Wernerianism..rapidly declined in influence, while Plutonism came steadily to the front, where it has ever since remained. **1966** [see *NEPTUNISM].

2. Geological activity associated with the formation of plutonic rocks.

1942 J. L. VAN HOUTEN tr. *Umbgrove's Pulse of Earth* iv. 66 A local thickening of the sialic crust, resulting in the formation of a 'root' of sialic material... When this root's material begins to melt and invade the surface strata as batholithic intrusions, plutonism and volcanism cannot but be strongly acid ('pacific') in character. **1949** *Q. Jrnl. Geol. Soc.* CV. 104 Plutonism does not appear to be a steady process advancing at a uniform rate, but rather one of energetic pulses interrupted by operations of diverse kinds, especially those of deformation. **1970** *Nature* 24 Jan. 315/1 After the late Mesozoic plutonism, the next phase of igneous activity in western America began in the Oligocene.

plutonium. Delete ‖ and add: **2.** *Chem.* † **a.** = BARIUM. *Obs.*

The word was introduced in a letter to the Royal Institution dated 1 Sept. 1816, but not published until 1817 (= quot. 1817 below). Its first occurrence in print was in *Ann. de Chim. et de Physique* (Sept. 1816) III. 61 in a Fr. transl. of it. Quot. 1816 is from a letter of 5 Oct. 1816 that refers to this (then unpublished) letter.

1816 E. D. CLARKE in *Ann. Philos.* VIII. 358 The metal is in its purest state. It is the same metal for which I proposed the appellation of Plutonium; and I am glad to find the appellation generally approved. *Ibid.* 360 Plutonium, if fused in contact with platinum, always tarnishes the latter. **1817** —— in *Jrnl. Sci. & Arts* II. 120 The existence..of the metal of Barytes no longer admits of the smallest doubt... As any derivative from *βαρυς* would involve an error, if applied to a metal whose specific gravity is inferior to that of Manganese or Molybdenum, I have ventured to propose for it the appellation of *Plutonium*; because we owe it entirely to the dominion of fire.

b. A transuranic metallic element which is formed indirectly from uranium in nuclear reactors and occurs naturally in trace amounts, is chemically similar to uranium, and is very reactive; the longest-lived isotope (plutonium 244) has a half-life of 83 million years, and plutonium 239 is fissile and is produced for use in nuclear weapons and as fuel. Atomic number 94; symbol Pu. [So called from its being the next element after neptunium in the periodic table, as Pluto is the planet next beyond Neptune.]

1942 SEABORG & WAHL *Chem. Properties Elem. 94 & 93* (U.S. Office Sci. Res. & Devel. Report A-135) 17 Since such formulae are confusing when the symbols '93' and '94' are used, we have decided to use symbols of the conventional chemical type to designate these elements. Following McMillan, who has suggested the name neptunium..for element 93, we are using plutonium.. for element 94. The corresponding chemical symbols would be Np and Pu. **1952** J. G. FEINBERG *Atom Story* xx. 153 On 20th December 1943 the first batch of irradiated slugs were removed from the pile for plutonium extraction. In another month the pile was turning out about one-third ton of plutonium-enriched slugs a day. **1962** J. C. WRIGHT *Metallurgy in Nucl. Power Technol.* iii. 60 The concentration of plutonium in minerals such as pitchblende is no more than one part in 10^{11}. **1964** R. L. LOFTNESS *Nucl. Power Plants* ii. 63 The maximum permissible body burden for plutonium is 0·3 microgram, and such a low limit requires the use of very efficient enclosures, or glove-boxes, for all research, development, and production work. **1968** [see *NEPTUNIUM]. **1969** *Times* 22 Apr. 6/6 Scientists..claimed to have synthesized element 104..by bombarding plutonium with neon. **1970** *Daily Tel.* 23 July 3/2 The nuclear-powered pacemaker—shaped like a small bullet and powered with plutonium 238—has a life of about 10 years. **1970** tr. *Vol'skii & Sterlin's Metallurgy of Plutonium* i. 19 Pure plutonium cannot be used as a nuclear fuel because of its low melting point, poor mechanical properties, high chemical activity, and the considerable volume changes caused by phase transformations... For reactors plutonium alloys and plutonium compounds are used. **1976** *Sci. Amer.* Dec. 30/2 In addition to uranium 235 the spent fuel contains between ·7 and 1 per cent of plutonium 239, synthesized from uranium 238 by the absorption of a neutron. **1979** *Ibid.* Apr. 33/2 A Precambrian mineral, a rare-earth fluocarbonate mined for cerium in California, has yielded the all but extinct isotope of plutonium with mass 244.

3. *attrib.* and *Comb.*, as (sense *2 b) *plutonium economy, enrichment*; **plutonium bomb**, an atomic bomb in which the fissile material is plutonium.

1948 C. PINCHER *Into Atomic Age* 53 Three days after the attack on Hiroshima..the plutonium bomb was dropped on Nagasaki. *Ibid.* 54 The 'Mark II' plutonium bomb was a definite improvement. It would have devastated the flat, round target of Hiroshima more completely than did the now obsolete uranium 'Mark I'. **1973** *Guardian* 19 Apr. 14/3 To make a plutonium bomb, with which a criminal could hold a city to ransom..one needs just 16·2 kilos of the metal. **1976** *New Yorker* 9 Feb. 44/3 Such a 'plutonium economy', in which fissionable fuel is recycled between reactor and reprocessing plant, is essential to the operation of the breeder. **1977** *Jrnl. R. Soc. Arts* CXXVI. 15/2 The distinguished Royal Commission under Sir Brian Flowers has expressed disquiet about a 'plutonium economy', but that is not to condemn all nuclear development. **1977** *Time* 7 Mar. 7/1 West German officials are further incensed over Carter's public criticism of Bonn's deal to sell a plutonium-enrichment plant and eight nuclear reactors to Brazil.

pluto:nometamo·rphism. *Petrol.* [f. PLUTON(ISM + -O + METAMORPHISM.] Metamorphism that occurs at high temperatures and high pressures at great depths under the earth.

1889 A. HARKER in *Geol. Mag.* Decade III. VI. 17 We may accordingly use the term plutono-metamorphism to describe the profound changes in rocks implied in the joint influence of very elevated temperature and enormous pressure. **1950** F. H. HATCH et al. *Petrol. Ign. Rocks* (ed. 10) vii. 336 The chief problem of the eclogites concerns their origin. They are believed to be products of 'plutonometamorphism'—to lie on the borderland between the igneous and metamorphic.

plutonyl (plū·tonəil). *Chem.* [f. PLUTON(IUM + -YL.] The ion PuO_2^{2+}. Usu. *attrib.*

1947 B. G. HARVEY et al. in *Jrnl. Chem. Soc.* 1013 On account of the similarity between the chemistry of uranium and of plutonium in their sexavalent states, the terms 'plutonate' and 'plutonyl' have been used in the present paper to describe the sexavalent compounds of plutonium. *Ibid.*, An orange solution, which..is believed to contain plutonyl nitrate, $PuO_2(NO_3)_2$. **1961** G. R. CHOPPIN *Exper. Nuclear Chem.* xii. 192 The extent to which the internal irradiation by alpha particles causes reduction of plutonium ions to the (IV) state in an aqueous solution of PuO_2^{2+} is necessary knowledge for the inorganic chemist studying plutonyl ion chemistry. **1976** *Sci. Amer.* Dec. 33/1 In the solvents that were used hexavalent uranyl ions, $(UO_2)^{++}$, and plutonyl ions, $(PuO_2)^{++}$, together with tetravalent plutonium ions, Pu^{4+}.., are soluble.

pluvial, *a.* Add: *spec.* designating periods of relatively high average rainfall in low and intermediate latitudes during the geological past (esp. the Pleistocene) which alternated with interpluvial periods in a cycle which may be correlated with or related to the better-known cycle of glacial and interglacial periods in higher latitudes. Cf. *INTERPLUVIAL, *INTRAPLUVIAL *adjs.* and *sbs.*

1868 A. TYLOR in *Q. Jrnl. Geol. Soc.* XXIV. 105 Many of the Quaternary deposits in all countries..are of such great dimensions and elevation that they must have been formed under physical conditions very different from our own. They indicate a Pluvial period, just as clearly as the northern drift indicates a Glacial period. **1927** PEAKE & FLEURE *Apes & Men* v. 75 He endeavoured to show that..in the valley of the Nile, there was evidence of four very wet periods, or pluvial periods. **1949** W. F. ALBRIGHT *Archaeol. Palestine* 50 The cold phases are called 'glacial periods' in northern latitudes and 'pluvial periods' in the latitude of Palestine, where there was no glaciation, but instead a greatly increased rainfall. **1954** *New Biol.* XVII. 11 There is evidence of at least two great 'Pluvial' periods of heavy rainfall in the Pleistocene when these [East African] lakes reached their maximum size and depth. **1979** *Nature* 1 Mar. 80/1 The student interested in the Pleistocene will find many discredited ideas (for example, glacial = pluvial).

B. *sb.*[2] A pluvial period.

1929 *Nature* 6 July 9/2 A large mammalian fauna has been collected from the deposits of the various Pluvials. **1931** L. S. B. LEAKEY *Stone Age Cultures of Kenya Colony* ii. 13 The prehistoric tribes..moved down to the Rift Valley areas during the pluvials. **1959** *Bull. Geol. Soc. Amer.* LXX. 345/2 African pluvials are of great importance for climatic history, for Pleistocene correlation, and for meteorologic theory. **1970** BRAY & TRUMP *Dict. Archaeol.* 184/1 Prolonged periods of high rainfall are called pluvials, and are marked by changes in lake levels and in flora and fauna.

pluvialine, *a.* (Example.)

1872 E. COUES *Key to N. Amer. Birds* 239 The pluvialine and scolopacine birds form the bulk of the division.

pluviometric, *a.* Add: (Further examples.) *pluviometric coefficient* (see quot. 1917).

1917 A. MCADIE *Princ. Aërography* xv. 218 The term 'pluviometric coefficient' was introduced by Angot to indicate the ratio of the mean daily rainfall of a particular month to the mean daily rainfall of the whole year. **1944** S. PUTNAM tr. *E. da Cunha's Rebellion in Backlands* i. 46 Torrential rains..giving rise to higher pluviometric readings than in..fertile lands of plenty. **1959** R. E. HUSCHKE *Gloss. Meteorol.* 428 Seen collectively, the twelve pluviometric coefficients describe the normal month-to-month distribution of the normal annual precipitation in terms of each month's 'share' of the annual amount.

Pluvius (plū·viŏs). Also with lower-case initial. [L. *pluvius* rainy, causing or bringing rain.] Used *attrib.* with ref. to the insurance of holidays, outdoor sports, entertainments, etc., against disruption by bad weather, as *Pluvius department, insurance, policy.*

1911 *Policy* 1 Apr. 206/2 The policies will be issued in respect of weather at the resorts..for any period from May 1st to September 30th. There will be four policies, known as the Pluvius Policies A, B, C, and D. **1920** *Post Mag. & Insurance Monitor* 4 Sept. 845/1 Now that Pluvius policies have come to stay, insurance men have of necessity to take an interest in the weather. **1949** *Policy Insurance Weekly* 2 June 373 In 1911 the brokers started Pluvius insurance. **1955** *Times* 13 May 18/2 Progress has been made in the Pluvius department. Despite extremely bad weather conditions over the British Isles and Europe, the experience was satisfactory. **1958** *Times* 3 July 15/4 The most direct effects of the recent rain will be on those firms who specialize in insuring against this sort of weather risk—so-called pluvius insurance. **1960** *News Chron.* 20 July 2/1 The Pluvius Department of the Eagle Star Insurance reports that business is 25% up on last year, and claims 50% up.

ply, *sb.* Add: Pl. **plies**, occas. **plys. I. 1.** Also, each of the layers that go to make up a multilayer material such as plywood or laminated plastic; *single-, two-, three-ply*, etc., also, material (esp. plywood) composed of that number of layers. (Further examples.)

1910 *Timber Trades Jrnl.* 1 Jan. p. v (Advt.), Best Russian improved waterproof 3-ply. **1919** A. W. JUDGE *Handbk. Mod. Aeronaut.* IV. 235 Ordinary 3-ply (⅛ to ¼ in.) is used for the webs of aeroplane wing ribs. **1926** *Rep. & Memoranda Aeronaut. Res. Comm.* No. 1017. 7 The inner (gas) ply was separated for a few inches from a 2-in. strip of a three-ply rubbered balloon fabric and the single-ply gripped in the lower jaw. **1935** DAWSON & PORRITT *Rubber* 330/2 Sheets were calendered to produce the maximum grain in unvulcanised state and slabs built up.. from plies with grain in same direction. **1936** H. W. ROWELL *Technol. of Plastics* xxvii. 191 In order that all air may be expelled and the plys or laminations thoroughly consolidated, a slow curing resinoid with a long plastic stage is used. **1941** *Paper Trade Jrnl.* CXII. 33/2 In contrast to the tests in which the bonding between plies is measured normal to the sheet, there are tests that measure the force required to tear plies apart. **1944** *Chem. Abstr.* XXXVIII. 3875 (*heading*) Preparing and handling cord fabric plies in tire core manufacture. **1952** J. P. CASEY *Pulp & Paper* II. xvi. 803 In laminating paper plys, it is sometimes desirable to place alternate layers of paper with their cross and machine directions at right angles. **1957** *Practical Wireless* XXXIII. 521/2 Five pieces of three-ply were used in the original. **1960** *Farmer & Stockbreeder* 15 Mar. 11/1, 1cwt 6-ply paper bags. **1970** [see *cross-ply* adj. s.v. *CROSS- B.]. **1975** [see *PLYWOOD]. **1977** *New Scientist* 6 Jan. 22/1 If the plies are set wholly radially..the tread squirms on the road far too much for acceptable roadholding. If..the plies are circumferential..the tyre..gives a harsh and unyielding ride.

b. = *PLYWOOD.

1929 A. CLARKE *Pilgrimage* 31, I had a painted bedpost Of blue and yellow ply. **1957** *Practical Wireless* XXXIII. 542/1 The front panel should be of ⅛ in. ply or hardboard. **1974** T. R. DENNIS in J. Burnett *Useful Toil* III. 348 Drinking-water was kept in a bucket..with a piece of ply over to keep dust out. **1980** *Daily Tel.* 10 Mar. 18 Roughly half will come in the form of timber products: ..windows, flooring blocks, ply, hardboard and newsprint.

III. 5. Special Comb.: **ply rating**, a number indicative of the strength of a tyre casing (orig. the number of cord plies in it).

1952 E. C. WOODS *Pneumatic Tyre Design* i. 5 Tyre markings now carry an indication of casing strength in the form of 'ply rating' (e.g., '8 ply rating') to serve the purpose of identifying a given tyre with its maximum recommended load. **1956** R. H. SPELMAN in McPherson & Klemin *Engin. Uses of Rubber* x. 299 Many standard over-the-road highway tires may be marked 10 ply rating and actually be made of 8 plies of rayon, or even of fewer plies of a stronger material, such as nylon. **1969** *Times* 12 May 16/1 Tractor tyre research is being carried out with a new mobile test rig designed to study the effects of size, ply rating, etc.

Plyglass (pləi·glɑs). Also **plyglass, ply-glass, ply glass.** A proprietary name for units consisting of two or more panes of glass enclosing one or more hermetically sealed spaces, which may contain dry air or be filled with a translucent material like glass fibre. Also *attrib.*

[**1949** *Trade Marks Jrnl.* 2 Mar. 191/1 *Plygloss* [sic]... Glassware.., plate glass, sheet glass, glass rods, glass tubes.., glass wool and spun glass. Plyglass Limited,.. Leyton, London,..manufacturers.] **1956** *Archit. Rev.* CXIX. 46 Normal windows are of galvanized steel; panels between windows, of cantilevered section, are plyglass. *Ibid.* CXX. 105 (*caption*) The panels between the first- and second-storey windows are of dark-green plyglass. **1958** *Engineering* 28 Feb. 276/1 Dark-blue ply glass panels are used beneath the windows on the north and south elevations. **1958** *Specification* (ed. 59) 1123/2 Uses of Plyglass diffusers are in roof lights, laylights and over-transom lights. **1960** *Trade Marks Jrnl.* 21 Sept. 1149/1 *Plyglass*... Units consisting of two or more panes of glass enclosing hermetically sealed cavities and being for use in the building industry. Plyglass Limited,.. Harlow, Essex; manufacturers. **1972** *Specification* (ed. 73) II. 441/2 Plyglass thermopane insulating glass (Plyglass Ltd.) consists of two or more panes of clear glass and most types of patterned glass enclosing a layer of dehydrated and filtered air which is sealed in with Bondermetic glass to metal seal.

Plym (plim), *sb.* [Shortened f. *PLYMOUTH.]

1. *humorous.* An inhabitant of Plymouth.

1913 W. OWEN *Let.* 23 Apr. (1967) 185, I should enjoy treating at length of Plymouth and the Plyms, the charm of Devon.

2. *colloq.* A member of the Plymouth Brethren.

1953 'N. BLAKE' *Dreadful Hollow* ii. 20 Staying at a pub won't commend you to the Plyms. **1977** *Times Lit. Suppl.* 13 May 593/3 The solemn girl who turned him down, back in the 1890s, because of an apparent lack of religious conviction; she was what is known as a Plym.

plymetal (pləi·metăl). [f. PLY *sb.* or *PLY(WOOD + METAL *sb.* (and *a.*).] A construction material consisting of plywood faced on both sides with aluminium.

1927 KNIGHT & WULPI *Veneers & Plywood* xv. 139 (*heading*) Plymetal. **1936** A. F. COLLINS *Motor Car Trailers* II. 103 Where the duck joins the sheet steel bonnets of plymetal a 1″ wide metal molding is used to cover the joint. **1940** BRIMM & BOGGESS *Aircraft Maintenance* 17 Plymetal is used for floorboards, baggage compartment linings, etc. **1967** *Jane's Surface Skimmer Systems 1967–68* 63/1 The frame is of ply-metal panel, consisting of 1 in. (25·4 mm) exterior grade AC plywood faced both sides with 0·050 in. (1·3 mm) mill finished 3003-H12 aluminium.

Plymouth (pli·mǝþ). [Name of a city in Devon.] **1.** See PLYMOUTH CLOAK.

2. See PLYMOUTH BRETHREN.

3. a. Applied to the first hard-paste porcelain to be made in England, by a method patented in 1768 by W. Cookworthy of Plymouth (subsequently of Bristol: see *BRISTOL 2 b).

1816 W. Burt *Rev. Mercantile State Plymouth* xvi. 174 The substance serving as a base for the Plymouth porcelain was a granite..composed of a reddish felspar in pieces of a tolerable size, quartz in small grains, and black scaly mica. **1857** J. Marryat *Hist. Pottery & Porcelain* (ed. 2) xii. 289 The Plymouth china has become very scarce. **1869** C. Schreiber *Jrnl.* 11 Sept. (1911) I. 36 There C.S. discovered a coloured group of Venus and Cupid..valuable as being Plymouth. **1873** H. Owen *Two Centuries Ceramic Art in Bristol* vii. 193 The quantity of the Plymouth porcelain preserved to us, compared with the amount of Bristol manufacture in the possession of collectors, is relatively very small. **1946** F. S. Mackenna (*title*) Cookworthy's Plymouth and Bristol porcelain. **1974** *Country Life* 28 Feb. (Suppl.) 43 Set of four Plymouth figures of the Continents, 12½ in. high.

b. Applied to a coarse, brown and yellow earthenware manufactured at Plymouth in the 18th century.

1878 L. Jewitt *Ceramic Art Gt. Brit.* I. x. 338 (*heading*) Plymouth earthenware... The manufacture of china-ware having ceased in Plymouth in 1774 this useful and elegant art was lost to the town. Some years later rough common brown and yellow earthenware was made here. **1960** H. Hayward *Connoisseur's Handbk. Antique Collecting* 222/1 *Plymouth earthenware*, coarse earthenware (brown and yellow) was manufactured here in the 18th cent., but gave way about 1810 to the production of painted or printed cream colour.

4. Applied to a variety of gin orig. made in the west of England.

1864 C. Tovey *Brit. & Foreign Spirits* iii. 118 An imitation Hollands is made by some rectifiers, and meets with a sale in Cornwall and in the West of England. Plymouth Gin is somewhat of the character of Hollands. **1885** *Encycl. Brit.* XIX. 237/2 Plymouth has few manufactures, the principal being biscuits..and the celebrated Plymouth gin. **1920** G. Saintsbury *Notes on Cellar-Book* vii. 104 More recent conditions, when in England and Scotland, excellent brandy cost five shillings a bottle; ..and gin, whether 'squareface' or London or Plymouth, not much more than half a crown. **1951** R. Postgate *Plain Man's Guide to Wine* ix. 121 *Plymouth* gin..has rather more of the distinctive flat juniper taste. **1967** J. B. Priestley *It's Old Country* iv. 43 Large pink Plymouth for me, cobber. **1968** J. D. MacDonald *Girl in Plain Brown Wrapper* iv. 35, I took one of the big glasses and laid an impressive belt of Plymouth atop the cubes.

Plymouth-brethrenism. (Earlier example.)

1874 C. M. Yonge *Life J. C. Patteson* I. v. 161 Primitive Methodism and Plymouth Brethrenism supplied the void.

plywood (plǝi·wud). Formerly also **ply-wood, ply wood.** [f. (*three-*, etc.) *ply wood.*] Board made of two or more thin layers of wood bonded together with the grain of adjacent layers crosswise to give increased strength and resistance to warping, there being either an odd number of layers including a thin central one or an even number sandwiching a thicker central core. Freq. *attrib.* or in *Comb.* Cf. *laminated wood* s.v. *LAMINATED *ppl. a.*

1907 *Timber Trades Jrnl.* 13 Apr. 818/2 (Advt.), Agents for Swedish..wood goods..ply wood (oak, birch, alder, etc.). **1919** A. W. Judge *Handbk. Mod. Aeronautics* IV. 234 The ply-woods chiefly employed in aeroplane work may vary from ⅛ to ¼ in. in thickness, and are made of ash or birch with an intermediate layer of poplar..or whitewood. **1922** W. Schlich *Man. Forestry* (ed. 4) I. 228 These pines..are also used for butter boxes, plywood, etc. **1926** *Glasgow Herald* 1 Oct. 5 The prosperity of the plywood industry. **1940** H. R. Simonds *Industr. Plastics* x. 273 Formed or molded plywood is becoming increasingly important for the manufacture of trays, shallow dishes and bowls. **1957** *Times* 12 Nov. (Canada Suppl.) p. xvi/4 A new type of express cabin cruiser..costs less than $4,000, is mostly built of plywood, and can be easily hoisted onto a trailer. **1964** B. Latham *Wood* xiii. 163 In the large modern plywood mills..very little hand labour is employed. Another great plywood-producing area is the Baltic. **1969** *Jane's Freight Containers 1968–69* 523/1 The container is of welded steel frame and self-supporting plywood panel construction. **1975** W. P. K. Findlay *Timber* xii. 174 Thin plywood is generally made from three veneers. Multi-ply boards have an uneven number of plies so that the grain on the face and back always run in the same direction.

pneu (niū). *colloq.* (*a*) Abbrev. of PNEUMONIA. (*b*) Abbrev. of 'pneumatic cushion'. (*c*) Abbrev. of *PNEUMATIQUE. Cf. *PNEUS.

1916 [see *GYPPIE, GYP(P)O, GYPPY]. **1923** A. Huxley *Antic Hay* i. 7 An air cushion, a delicious pneu. **1928** J. Joyce *Let.* 19 Jan. (1966) III. 168, I got your pneu and shall follow your instructions. **1965** G. D. Painter *Proust* II. xvii. 362 Soon Reynaldo would come to write hurried *pneus* to Marcel's friends.

pneumatic, *a.* (*sb.*) Add: **1. a.** (Further examples.)

pneumatic dispatch (earlier example); *pneumatic drill*, a heavy drill for breaking stone by the rapidly repeated blows of a bit driven by compressed air.

1863 *Illustr. London News* 28 Feb. 217/3 (*heading*) Opening of the pneumatic despatch mail service. *Ibid.*, A company was registered in 1859 for the establishment in the metropolis of lines of pneumatic tube for the more speedy and convenient circulation of despatches and parcels. *a* **1877** Knight *Dict. Mech.* II. 1753/1 By the pneumatic drill, the Mt. Cenis Tunnel, seven miles in length, was bored through the Alps. *Ibid.*, *Pneumatic hammer*, a hammer in which compressed air is the agent for lifting the helve or the head. **1894** W. Le Queux *Gt. War in Eng. in 1897* xxxi. 253 Small dynamite shells from Mackenzie's pneumatic gun had struck the car of the balloon. **1898** E. Howard *To-morrow* 48 Subways for sewerage and surface drainage,..pneumatic tubes for postal purposes, have come to be regarded as economic if not essential. **1902** *Encycl. Brit.* XXXI. 802/1 Sometimes, when only a small amount of work is to be done, pneumatic tools are brought to heavy pieces of material. *Ibid.* 803/1 The pneumatic jack..is placed below the piece to be lifted, and operates directly. **1911** *Ibid.* XXVII. 40/2 Pneumatic drills are usually worked by little motors having oscillating cylinders, by which the air and exhaust ports are covered and uncovered. **1927** *Jrnl. Amer. Med. Assoc.* 1 Oct. 1151/1 (*heading*) A pneumatic hammer for bone surgery. *Ibid.*, A light, compact, pneumatic hammer whose speed is controlled by a throttle..on the pistol-grip handle. **1930** *Daily Express* 9 Sept. 8/7 The noise of pneumatic drills has.. been found to annoy the patients in a London Hospital. **1947** J. C. Rich *Materials & Methods of Sculpture* ix. 257 The vibration of a pneumatic tool, particularly after prolonged use, apparently affects the blood vessels of the hand and arm, frequently impairing the circulation and resulting in 'white fingers' or 'pneumatic hammer disease'. **1962** L. Zelikov tr. *G. Kamenshchikov's Forging Practice* viii. 192 Pneumatic hammers are mainly employed for hammer forging miscellaneous work and for forging in bolster dies. **1973** 'H. Carmichael' *Candles for Dead* xi. 134 Don't be quite so boisterous. Your voice has the effect of a pneumatic drill. **1978** R. Jansson *News Caper* viii. 76 His hands were shaking as if attached to a pneumatic drill.

e. Of a woman: having a well-rounded figure, esp. a large bosom; of or pertaining to a woman having such attributes.

1919 T. S. Eliot *Whispers of Immortality* in *Poems*, Grishkin is nice. . Uncorseted, her friendly bust Gives promise of pneumatic bliss. **1926** F. M. Ford *A Man could stand Up* I. i. 17 She didn't obviously offer—what was it the fellow called it?—promise of pneumatic bliss to the gentlemen. **1932** A. Huxley *Brave New World* vi. 108 'Every one says I'm awfully pneumatic,' said Lenina reflectively, patting her own legs... 'You don't think I'm *too* plump, do you?' **1951** J. C. Fennessy *Sonnet in Bottle* I. v. 25 A pneumatic pink and yellow bathing belle. **1961** A. Wilson *Old Men at Zoo* ii. 91 He looked at her..as though searching beneath her pneumatic form for the disguised contours of some familiar, leaner enemy. **1961** P. Ustinov *Loser* ii. 46 He became aware of the pneumatic warmth of that thigh. **1974** *Publishers Weekly* 21 Jan. 88/3 Sexologist Dr. Rhona Mitchell, she of the spectacularly pneumatic proportions. **1976** *Times Lit. Suppl.* 31 Dec. 1643/2 The pneumatic barmaid at their favourite wine-bar.

5. pneumatic-drilled *a.* (*nonce-wd.*), resembling a pneumatic drill or its action; † **pneumatic-shod** *a.*, fitted with pneumatic tyres; **pneumatic-tired (-tyred)** *a.* (further examples).

1947 Dylan Thomas *Let.* 14 July (1966) 316 The pick-axed and pneumatic-drilled mosquitoes in the guest's bedroom. **1909** *Westm. Gaz.* 3 June 4/2 Although they [*sc.* motor-cars] are pneumatic-shod, the tyres do not come into contact with the track. *Ibid.* 18 Nov. 4/2 The driving-wheels of this vehicle are fitted with Vilo wheels, in place of ordinary pneumatic-shod artillery wheels. **1956** *Nature* 4 Feb. 218/2 His research has covered..the dynamic instability of systems incorporating pneumatic-tyred wheels. **1967** *Gloss. Highway Engin. Terms* (*B.S.I.*) 34 *Pneumatic-tyred roller*, a roller in which the compacting weight is supported on wheels fitted with pneumatic tyres. The roller may be self-propelled or towed. **1979** *Guardian* 8 Nov. 22/2 A shunting locomotive with pneumatic-tyred wheels.

pneumatically, *adv.* Add: (Further examples.) *spec.* (in mod. use) by means of compressed air. Also *fig.*

1942 *R.A.F. Jrnl.* 3 Oct. 29 Four guns were installed, harmonized and fired pneumatically. **1958** *Times* 23 June 14/3 Equipping three Russian whalers with plant for cubing whale meat and transferring it pneumatically to storage vessels at sea. **1975** *Radiol.* CXV. 222/1 (*heading*) A pneumatically operated femoral artery compressor. **1975** D. O'Sullivan in D. Marcus *Best Irish Short Stories* (1977) II. 90 'It[*sc.* beer]'s blowing me out,' said Anne pneumatically.

‖ **pneumatique** (niumatī·k). [Fr.; see PNEUMATIC *a.* (*sb.*).] The pneumatic dispatch system in Paris (see PNEUMATIC *a.* (*sb.*) 1 a); a letter or message sent by this system.

1924 E. Hemingway *Let.* 9 Aug. in A. Mizener *Saddest Story* (1971) xxv. 342 Ford..had stayed up all night writing pneumatiques. **1938** F. Scott Fitzgerald *Let.* July (1964) 35 A *pneumatique* might reach Nanny at 23 rue Pascal-Lecointre. **1951** R. Senhouse tr. *Colette's Chéri* 76 *Pneumatiques* of four or five lines from sponging friends. **1964** *Sunday Mail* (Brisbane) 28 June 33/4 All the letters were sent by pneumatique—the giant system of suction pipes which links all the post offices in the Paris area and allows express letters to reach their destination in the city within 60 minutes. **1973** L. Snelling *Heresy* III. ix. 191 I'll get off a *pneumatique* to his office.

pneumatization (niū:mătǝizē·ʃǝn). *Med.* [f. next + -ATION.] The development or presence of air-filled cavities in bone or other tissue.

1934 Lake & Marshall *Surg. Anat. & Physiol.* xv. 244 Pneumatisation of mastoid process varies between extreme limits. **1959** G. E. Shambaugh *Surg. of Ear* i. 22 It is not until air enters the middle ear at birth..that pneumatization accelerates, continuing throughout infancy and early childhood. **1976** *Nature* 19 Aug. 683/2 Another unusual feature in a dinosaur is the very strong pneumatisation of the skull bones, especially those of the roof and snout.

pneumatize, *v.* Restrict *rare* to sense 1 in Dict. and add: **2.** (Further examples.) Chiefly as **pneu·matized** *pa. pple.* Hence **pneu·matizing** *vbl. sb.*

1947 *Arch. Otolaryngol.* XLVI. 852 The complications of acute otitis media developed more often in temporal bones with extensive cell systems than in those that were poorly pneumatized. **1949** L. R. Boies et al. *Fund. Otolaryngol.* i. 11 The temporal bone is pneumatized by the extension of an epithelial sac from the middle ear into the bone marrow in the region of the mastoid process. *Ibid.* 12 Any interference with..development will cause a cessation of the pneumatizing process. **1971** *Sci. Amer.* Dec. 73/3 All birds have..lungs, air sacs and pneumatized bones. **1976** *Nature* 19 Aug. 683/2 [In a dinosaur] the nasals, in addition to being pneumatised as a whole, each bear a large air chamber connected with the external nare.

pneumatolysis (niūmătǫ·lisis). *Petrol.* [ad. G. *pneumatolyse* (R. Bunsen 1851, as next, p. 264): see *-LYSIS.] The chemical alteration of rock and formation of minerals by the action of hot magmatic gases and vapours.

1896 Phillips & Louis *Treat. Ore Deposits* (ed. 2) I. 129 He [*sc.* Vogt] uses the word *pneumatolysis* for this action. **1905** *Rep. Board of Regents Smithsonian Inst. 1904* 335 The importance of pneumatolysis in forming ore deposits was emphasized by the discovery..of a number of economically important deposits. **1934, 1962** [see *GREISEN]. **1966** C. A. Lamey *Metallic & Industrial Mineral Deposits* iii. 43 Various descriptions of cassiterite deposits and wolframite deposits indicate that their formation..was caused by pneumatolysis. **1970** R. J. Small *Study of Landforms* iv. 127 At many points the granite of the South-West Peninsula [of England] has been profoundly affected by the metamorphic process known as 'pneumatolysis'.

pneumatolytic (niū:mătoli·tik), *a.* *Petrol.* [ad. G. *pneumatolytisch* (R. Bunsen 1851, in *Ann. d. Physik* LXXXIII. 238): see PNEUMATO- and *-LYTIC.] Involving or formed by pneumatolysis.

1896 Phillips & Louis *Treat. Ore Deposits* (ed. 2) I. 173 There seems no urgent reason for adopting the theory of pneumatolytic, in preference to ordinary hydrothermal action. **1903** [see *FUMAROLIC *a.*]. **1909** J. P. Iddings *Igneous Rocks* I. vii. 276 Those minerals that appear to depend largely upon the action of gases in magmas for their presence in igneous rocks have been called pneumatolytic. **1963** D. W. & E. E. Humphries tr. *Termier's Erosion & Sedimentation* vi. 134 The minerals of rocks can be altered without exposure at the surface by pneumatolytic or hydrothermal action. **1972** *Nature* 3 Mar. 13/1 They interpreted this variation as the result of pneumatolytic and gravitative differentiation taking place in the lava column.

Hence **pneumatoly·tically** *adv.*

1962 *Proc. Yorks. Geol. Soc.* XXXIII. 329 The systems of valleys which evolved would be to some extent guided by the prior existence of pneumatolytically altered zones. **1968** I. Kostov *Mineralogy* II. v. 362 The lithium micas are typical products of pneumatolitically [*sic*] altered acid rocks of the 'greisen' type.

Pneumatomachian. b. *adj.* (Examples.)

1915 *Encycl. Relig. & Ethics* VIII. 225/2 The leading doctrine of the Macedonians is found in the thesis characterized by their opponents as 'Pneumatomachian', viz. that the Holy Ghost is not to be designated Θεός. **1957** *Oxf. Dict. Chr. Ch.* 1086/2 The historians Socrates and Sozomen..regard Macedonius as their founder, but..his name does not occur in contemporary anti-Pneumatomachian writings.

pneumectomy. (Examples.) Now usu. called *pneumonectomy* (see PNEUMONO- in Dict. and Suppl.).

1911 *Practitioner* Nov. 682 Incision and drainage of a pulmonary cavity was the first operation practised for pulmonary tuberculosis, and..it has been performed much more frequently than pneumectomy. **1932** [see *LOBECTOMY].

pneumo-. Add: **pneumoconiosis** (or **-kon-**) is now the usual name, rather than *pneumonoconiosis*; (earlier and later examples); hence **pneu:moconio·tic** *a.*, affected with pneumoconiosis; *sb.*, a pneumoconiotic person.

1881 *Med. Times & Gaz.* 28 May 589/1 (*heading*) The pathology of pneumokonioses. **1908** T. Oliver *Dis. of Occupation* ix. 247 There are various forms of dust diseases of the lungs, or pneumokonioses, *e.g.*, anthracosis..; chalicosis and silicosis..; and byssinosis. **1953** *Jrnl. Path. & Bacteriol.* LXVI. 235 Simple pneumokoniosis ..is characterised by numerous small discrete aggregations of dust in which only a little fibrosis occurs. **1969** *Daily Tel.* 5 Feb. 18 (Advt.), The Industrial Injuries Advisory Council has been asked to consider whether any change should be made in the definition of pneumoconiosis in the National Insurance (Industrial Injuries) Act 1965. The disease is at present defined in the Act as fibrosis of the lungs due to silica dust, asbestos dust or other dust, and including the condition known as dust reticulation.

1976 *S. Wales Echo* 27 Nov. 6/9 The cause of death was given as broncho-pneumonia due to recumbency following a fracture of the left femur, and pneumoconiosis. **1944** *Rep. Advisory Cttee. Treatment & Rehab. Miners in Wales Region Suffering from Pneumokoniosis* 17 The pneumokoniotic lung, especially at the massive nodulation stage is in special degree liable to become tuberculous. **1948** *Hansard Commons* 15 Mar. 1846 Reference has been made to the..Grenfell factories in South Wales for silicotics and pneumoconiotics. **1963** K. M. A. PERRY in Perry & Sellors *Chest Dis.* I. xxxi. 566 In 1,036 pneumoconiotic lungs which he examined, he found evidence of pulmonary tuberculosis in 43 per cent.

pneu:mo,ence·phalogram. *Med.* Also **pneumence·phalo-.** [f. as next: see -GRAM.] An X-ray taken by pneumoencephalography.

1935 *Bull. Neurol. Inst. N.Y.* IV. 261 In cases in which a septum pellucidum is present this structure forms in the anteroposterior and posteroanterior views of the pneumencephalograms a well demarcated vertical linear shadow. **1973** *Reader's Digest* Apr. 194/2 Additional tests had to be made—an angiogram and perhaps a pneumoencephalogram.

pneu:mo,encephalo·graphy. *Med.* Also **pneu:mencephalo-.** [f. PNEUMO- + *encephalography* s.v. *ENCEPHALO-.] Radiography following the replacement of cerebrospinal fluid by air or oxygen.

1932 *Amer. Jrnl. Roentgenol.* XXVII. 657/1 Pneumoencephalography, following withdrawal of cerebrospinal fluid and injection of air by the method of spinal puncture, permits investigation of the cisterna magna and of the subarachnoid spaces, in addition to study of the ventricles. **1935** *Bull. Neurol. Inst. N.Y.* IV. 221 It seems essential..to establish definite criteria for the diagnosis of these lesions by pneumencephalography whether ventriculography, encephalography or both are utilized in a given case. **1974** PASSMORE & ROBSON *Compan. Med. Stud.* III. xxxiv. 23/1 Pneumoencephalography visualizes the ventricular system and CSF pathways of the brain. A lumbar puncture is performed and 15 ml of air is instilled slowly into the subarachnoid space with the patient sitting upright.

Hence **pneu:mo,encephalogra·phic** *a.*, **-encephalogra·phically** *adv.*

1935 *Bull. Neurol. Inst. N.Y.* IV. 261 From the above mentioned pneumencephalographic evidence one can now diagnose the presence of a perforated septum pellucidum. **1950** DAVIDOFF & EPSTEIN *Abnormal Pneumoencephalogram* xxix. 407 A hemiplegia with a pneumoencephalographically demonstrable porencephaly. **1961** *Lancet* 9 Sept. 569/2 Myeloencephalography..confirmed the pneumoencephalographic findings.

pneumogram. Add: **2.** An X-ray photograph made by pneumography (sense *2).

1921 *Johns Hopkins Hosp. Bull.* XXXII. 74/1 (*caption*) Cerebral pneumogram..of a case of communicating hydrocephalus; air has been injected into the spinal canal. **1964** TAVERAS & WOOD *Diagnostic Neuroradiol.* 227 The straight anteroposterior pneumogram (C) reveals the forward portions of the lateral and the third ventricles outlined by gas.

pneumography. Add: **2.** *Med.* The radiography of tissues into which air or oxygen has been introduced.

1921 *Johns Hopkins Hosp. Bull.* XXXII. 70/1 The most frequent location for an obstruction in communicating hydrocephalus is in the cisternæ. This..will be seen in the results which are to follow in the patients who have been studied by cerebral pneumography. **1948** LYSHOLM & BULL in J. W. McLaren *Mod. Trends Diagnostic Radiol.* I. xxiv. 327 Subdural pneumography has proved to be valuable in the diagnosis of adhesions between brain and dura, and in subdural haematoma. **1970** *Sci. Jrnl.* Aug. 5/1 The cardiovascular system[s] of both cosmonauts were studied in detail by means of electrocardiography, seismocardiography, pneumography, [etc.].

pneumographic *a.* (further examples); **pneumogra·phically** *adv.*, by means of pneumography.

1921 *Jrnl. Amer. Med. Assoc.* 10 Dec. 1858/2 At times, it has been possible completely to remove such growths, when, except for the pneumographic record, there would have been absolutely no other way of knowing the situation of the growth. **1953** F. LINDGREN in J. W. McLaren *Mod. Trends Diagnostic Radiol.* II. xix. 291 The pneumographic diagnosis of an expanding intracranial lesion is possible because the lesion, when it has attained a certain size, affects the central fluid-filled and gas-filled space. *Ibid.* 301 These tumours cannot be demonstrated pneumographically in any way other than by encephalography. **1964** TAVERAS & WOOD *Diagnostic Neuroradiol.* 752/2 A pneumographic examination in any patient who presents a clinical syndrome that suggests a lesion in the posterior fossa. **1972** M. GADO in E. J. Potchen *Current Concepts Radiol.* xi. 261 Pneumographically differentiation between cerebellar and extra-axial masses behind the cerebellum is impossible.

pneumolysis (niūmǫ·lisis). *Surg.* [mod.L., f. PNEUMO- + *-LYSIS.] The surgical separation of the parietal pleura either from the chest wall (*extrapleural pneumolysis*) or from the pulmonary pleura (*intrapleural pneumolysis*).

1913 *Index Med.* XI. 199/1 (Index), Pneumolysis. **1922** *Tubercle* III. 162 Since 1918, we have performed extrapleural pneumolysis in..cases of severe unilateral pulmonary tuberculosis. **1945** KEERS & RIGDEN *Pulmonary Tuberculosis* xi. 193 Closed intrapleural pneumolysis..is the logical sequel to pneumothorax therapy where adhesion formation is preventing effective collapse of the lung. **1966** E. L. FARQUHARSON *Textbk. Operative Surg.* (ed. 3) xiv. 447 Intra-pleural pneumolysis was employed mainly as an adjunct to artificial pneumothorax.

pneumonia. Add: **b. pneumonia blouse** *colloq.*, a woman's blouse made of thin or light material and having a low neck-line.

1902 in C. W. Cunnington *Eng. Women's Clothing* (1952) ii. 47 The questionable morality of the 'Pneumonia blouse'... A transparent blouse of muslin and lace with next to no collar. **1905** R. BROUGHTON *Waif's Progress* xix. 209 'Catherine had a bad cold.' 'The result of a pneumonia blouse, I suppose!' **1958** *Listener* 2 Oct. 524/1 Clergy of all denominations denounced that shocking innovation of 1914, the open-necked 'pneumonia blouse'. **1961** *Guardian* 6 Mar. 10/6 Astrakhan and felt bootees shared a narrow bench with sandals and 'pneumonia' blouse.

pneumonitis. Add: (Further examples.) (See also quot. 1974.)

1918 *Surg., Gynecol. & Obstetr.* XXVI. 32/2 One of the most important predisposing causes of postoperative pneumonitis both in patients coming into the hospital with a recent cold or free from an active cold, is the exposure to which he is subjected during the first twenty-four to forty-eight hours of his stay in the hospital. **1947** *Radiology* XLIX. 284/1 There was no opacity of the eyes, no pneumonitis. **1962** A. HUXLEY *Let.* 17 Mar. (1969) 930 A cold on the chest which..turned out in the end to be what they called pneumonitis. **1971** *Sci. Amer.* Aug. 47/3 Inhalation of cadmium oxide fumes..can produce acute damage in the lungs in the form of pneumonitis or pulmonary edema. **1974** PASSMORE & ROBSON *Compan. Med. Stud.* III. xviii. 23/2 Pneumonia is a general term meaning inflammation of the lungs; it usually refers to a clinically acute condition caused by micro-organisms but it may result from damage by one or a number of chemical or physical agents. Pneumonitis is a similar term and is sometimes used to describe mild segmental pneumonia, but it is best avoided.

pneumono-. Add: **pneumonectomy** (examples); hence **pneumone·ctomized** *ppl. a.*, subjected to a pneumonectomy; **pneumonoconiosis**, add: [first formed as G. *pneumonokoniosis* (F. A. Zenker 1866, in *Deutsch. Arch. f. klin. Med.* II. 171)]; now generally superseded by *pneumoconiosis*; (later examples); hence **pneumo:noconio·tic** *a.* and *sb.*; **pneumo:no,ultramicrosco·picsi:licovolcanoconio·sis (-konio·sis)**, a factitious word alleged to mean 'a lung disease caused by the inhalation of very fine silica dust' but occurring chiefly as an instance of a very long word.

1939 *Brit. Jrnl. Surg.* XXVII. 411 The possibility of maintaining a permanent pneumothorax on the pneumonectomized side is one that has not been fully investigated as yet. **1967** *Excerpta Medica: Radiol.* XXI. 138/2 (*heading*) Pre- and postoperative pulmonary angiography in pneumonectomized patients. **1890** *Ann. Universal Med. Sci.* III. B-27 The profession is urged by Zakharevitch to prosecute these investigations for the practice of pneumonectomy. **1938** *Brit. Jrnl. Surg.* XXVI. 190 (*caption*) Right lung, the site of bronchial carcinoma, successfully removed by dissection pneumonectomy. **1967** [see *LOBECTOMY]. **1972** T. W. SHIELDS *Gen. Thoracic Surg.* xx. 331/2 A pneumonectomy may be carried out by means of any one of the three standard thoracic positions: lateral, posterior, or anterior. **1977** *Lancet* 23 July 164/1 All the patients had a radical pneumonectomy or lobectomy. **1934** *Trans. Inst. Mining Engineers* LXXXVIII. 387 This pneumonoconiosis of coal-miners is a *progressive* condition, gradually passing on from its harmless early stages..to a condition of dyspnœa and breathlessness which makes work impossible. **1940** H. E. COLLIER *Outl. Industr. Med. Pract.* xxxix. 356 The general object of the tests has been to find a means of checking the interpretation of the X-ray appearances and thereby to provide an early method of recognizing the outset of any of the pneumoconioses before the onset of the disablement. **1933** E. M. WILLIAMS *Health of Old & Retired Coalminers in S. Wales* 80 Thirty-two men..were considered on clinical grounds to be definitely pneumonoconiotic. *Ibid.* 102 The proportion of probably tuberculous cases among these pneumonoconiotics is high. **1936** F. SCULLY *Bedside Manna* 87 Pneumonoultramicroscopicsilicovolcanakoniosis [*sic*], a disease caused by ultra-microscopic particles of sandy volcanic dust, might give even him laryngitis. **1966** *Word Study* Oct. 7/2 The resources of Greek have enriched the modern world as well as the ancient one. Perhaps this is most dramatically illustrated by the longest and most fantastic word now in an English dictionary (the Merriam-Webster's great Unabridged) which is forty-five letters in length: pneumonoultramicroscopicsilicovolcanoconiosis,..meaning 'a disease of the lungs caused by extremely small particles of ash and dust'. **1973** R. MEGARRY *Second Miscellany-at-Law* 160 It has been said that 'floccinaucinihilipilification' is the longest word in the English language... The word's proud title must yield to some technical terms, such as pneumonoultramicroscopicsilicovolcanokoniosis.

pneumonolysis (niūmǫ̆nǫ·lisis). *Surg.* [f. PNEUMONO- + *-LYSIS.] = *PNEUMOLYSIS.

1934 *Amer. Rev. Tuberculosis* XXIX. 270 We were opposed to..extrapleural pneumonolysis with paraffin filling because it is contrary to accepted surgical practice to place a foreign-body permanently in the tissues. **1975** W. L. GLENN et al. *Thoracic & Cardiovascular Surg.* (ed. 3) xi. 251/1 Pneumonolysis has..maintained a limited but definite field of usefulness.

pneu:moperitone·um. *Med.* Also with hyphen. [f. PNEUMO- + PERITONEUM.] The presence of air or gas in the peritoneal cavity, whether accidentally or artificially induced.

1896 *Trans. Amer. Assoc. Obstetr. & Gynecol.* VIII. 212 Sacculated pneumo-peritoneum is frequently found in conjunction with localized appendiceal abscesses. **1934** *Amer. Rev. Tuberculosis* XXIX. 625 Therapeutic pneumoperitoneum has proved to be a technically simple and practicable treatment for intestinal tuberculosis. **1974** PASSMORE & ROBSON *Compan. Med. Stud.* III. xxviii. 3/1 A pelvic pneumoperitoneum may be induced with CO_2 and the gas used as contrast medium to define the uterus and ovaries [for radiography], but this has been largely superseded by laparoscopy.

pneumotachograph (niūmotæ·kograf). [a. G. *pneumotachograph* (A. Fleisch 1925, in *Pflüger's Arch. für die ges. Physiol.* CCIX. 722), f. Gr. τάχος speed: see PNEUMO- and -GRAPH.] An apparatus for recording the rate of air flow during breathing. Also shortened as **pneu·motach.**

1926 *Index Med.* VI. 539/2 (*heading*) Pneumotachograph. **1929** *Arch. Internal Med.* XLIV. 295 The pneumotachograph..showed an increased respiratory rate. **1975** G. RUPPEL *Man. Pulmonary Function Testing* viii. 80 Pneumotachs utilize various physical and chemical properties to produce an electrical output that can be integrated for measurement of volumes and flows. **1975** *Nature* 4 Sept. 51/1 Forced expiratory flow–volume curves were recorded by a Fleisch No. 3 pneumotachograph connected to a differential pressure transducer.. and coupled to a carrier preamplifier.

So **pneumota·chogram** [A. Fleisch, *loc. cit.*, p. 718], a record produced by a pneumotachograph (e.g. a graph of the quantity of air expired or inspired as a function of time); **pneu:motachogra·phic** *a.*, of or pertaining to this apparatus or its use; **pneu:motacho·graphy.**

1926 *Q. Cumulative Index to Current Med. Lit.* XI. 447/2 (*heading*) Curve of speed of human respiratory air (pneumotachogram). **1928** *Q. Cumulative Index Med.* III. 854/1 (*heading*) Pneumotachographic picture in bronchial asthma. **1929** *Arch. Internal Med.* XLIV. 293 Patients with cardiovascular and pulmonary diseases..showed notchings of the pneumotachograms even during respiration standstill. **1930** *Jrnl. Amer. Med. Assoc.* 5 July 83/2 Pneumotachography in combination with electrocardiography is employed in the general examination of the circulation. **1955** *Jrnl. Physiol.* CXXX. 33P The method usually employed to record a pneumotachogram utilizes the pressure differences across an impedance placed in the air-flow stream. **1955** *Thorax* X. 258 (*heading*) Pneumotachographic measurement of breathing capacity. **1975** *Nature* 30 Oct. 787/2 The breathing pattern of the fish was recorded continuously by pneumotachography (Statham–Godart) and pressure measurements (Statham).

pneumothorax. Add: Pl. **-thoraces, -thoraxes.** (Earlier and later examples.) [a. F. *pneumothorax* (E. H. Itard *Dissertation sur le Pneumothorax ou les Congestions gazeuses qui se forment dans la Poitrine* (1803).]

1821 J. FORBES tr. *Laennec's Treat. Dis. of Chest* I. II. v. 204 The disease is named by M. Itard, Pneumo-thorax. *Ibid.*, The author..considers the pneumo-thorax as an affection always consequent to and depending on a latent phthisis. **1825** [see *pneumatothorax* s.v. PNEUMATO-]. **1974** R. J. MCCORMACK in Smith & Williams *Surg. of Lung* x. 241 All but the smallest pneumothoraces should be treated initially with intercostal water-seal drainage.

b. Pneumothorax may be induced diagnostically, or therapeutically so as to cause relaxation of a lung; it is then usu. known as *artificial pneumothorax*.

1885 *Lancet* 16 May 894/2 Mr. Charters Symonds spoke of the induction of artificial pneumothorax as having been suggested by Dr. Mahomed in a case on which they had held a consultation. The aim of the operation was to be the arrest of phthisis. **1923** *Brit. Jrnl. Tuberculosis* XVII. 109 When inducing an artificial pneumothorax, the gas employed is usually oxygen, but after the first insufflation nitrogen or filtered air may be equally well used. **1927** H. T. LOWE-PORTER tr. *T. Mann's Magic Mountain* I. iii. 66 That was Hermine Kleefeld, she whistles with her pneumothorax. **1937** A. J. CRONIN *Citadel* IV. viii. 320 He was chary of using pneumothorax and his percentage of inductions was the lowest in the hospital. **1974** PASSMORE & ROBSON *Compan. Med. Stud.* III. xviii. 74/1 Once a mainstay of treatment for the control of tuberculous lesions, therapeutic artificial pneumothorax has now been abandoned. In modern medicine artificial pneumothorax is occasionally used as a diagnostic procedure.

pneu:moventriculo·graphy. *Med.* [f. PNEUMO- + VENTRICUL(US + -O + -GRAPHY.] The introduction of air or oxygen into the ventricles of the brain for radiographic purposes.

1918 W. E. DANDY in *Ann. Surg.* LXVIII. 6 From these and many other normal and pathological clinical demonstrations of the radiographic properties of air it is but a step to the injection of gas into the cerebral ventricles—pneumoventriculography. **1932** *Amer. Jrnl. Roentgenol.* XXVII. 657/1 Pneumoventriculography and encephalography are valuable aids in the diagnosis of cerebral lesions. **1974** PASSMORE & ROBSON *Compan. Med. Stud.* III. xxxiv. 24/1 Air may be introduced directly into the ventricle through a burr hole in the vault of the skull (pneumoventriculography).

pneus (niūz), *sb. pl.* ? *Obs.* [Short for PNEUMATIC *sb.* 3.] Pneumatic tyres.
1902 C. N. & A. M. WILLIAMSON *Lightning Conductor* 18 On roads like these of Dieppe it would be soothing to have 'pneus', as they call them. **1907** —— in *Strand Mag.* Nov. 500/1 [The motor-car], with heated pneus, topped a commanding hill. **1908** *Westm. Gaz.* 31 Oct. 13/1 Before it [*sc.* the motor-car] can cease from injuring,..you have to construct suitable roads, highways which it can no longer tear up with its ferocious pneus.

pnicogen (pni·kodʒĕn). *Chem.* [f. Gr. πνίγ-ειν to choke, stifle (in allusion to nitrogen) + -O + -GEN.] Any of a series of elements in group V of the periodic table, viz. nitrogen, phosphorus, arsenic, antimony, and bismuth.
1966 *Progress Sci. & Technol. Rare Earths* II. 76 The term 'pnicogen' seems to be gaining favor as a group name for the VA group of elements. **1971** *Nomencl. Inorg. Chem.* (I.U.P.A.C.) (ed. 2) 11 The use of the collective names 'pnicogen' (N, P, As, Sb and Bi) and 'pnictides' is not approved.

So **pni·ctide** [-IDE], a binary compound of a pnicogen with a more electropositive element or radical.
1966 *Progress Sci. & Technol. Rare Earths* II. 35 (*heading*) Thermodynamic and magnetic properties of the rare earth chalcogenides and pnictides. **1973** *Physical Rev.* B. VIII. 5345 The fourth-order crystal-field parameters for the phosphides and for other rare-earth pnictides fall on a universal curve which is close to that predicted..for the light rare earths. **1977** *Sci. Amer.* May 41/1 Removing an electron from a trigonally bonded chalcogen atom leads to a low-energy state, because the atom then becomes structurally similar to a pnictide atom in its proper configuration.

p-n-p (pī:enpī·). *Electronics.* Also **pnp**, and in capitals. Designating a semiconductor device in which an *n*-type region is sandwiched between two *p*-type regions. Also *absol.*
1949 W. SHOCKLEY in *Bell Syst. Technical Jrnl.* XXVIII. 435 The principles and theory of a *p-n-p* transistor are described. *Ibid.* 474 The *p-n-p* transistor has the interesting feature of being calculable to a high degree. **1962** SIMPSON & RICHARDS *Physical Princ. Junction Transistors* iii. 51 The diffused layer forms the base, and the original material the collector, of a high-frequency *p-n-p* transistor. **1967** [see *N-P-N]. **1975** D. G. FINK *Electronics Engineers' Handbk.* VIII. 26 The low current gain of a lateral *pnp* can be improved by combining it with a monolithic *npn* transistor, to form a composite transistor structure.

po[3] (pōᵘ). *colloq.* Pl. **poes, pos.** [ad. Fr. *pot* (*de chambre*).] A chamber-pot. Also *attrib.* and *Comb.*
1880 LONGMUIR & DONALDSON *Jamieson's Etym. Dict. Sc. Lang.* (rev. ed.) III. 517/2 *Po, s*, a matula or urinal. **1911** A. WARRACK *Scots Dial. Dict.* 420/1 *Po, n.*, a chamber-pot. **1937** PARTRIDGE *Dict. Slang* 643/1 *Po*, a chamber-pot. .. Ex the pronunciation of *pot* in Fr. *pot de chambre.* **1951** W. SANSOM *Face of Innocence* iv. 56 'In bloody pos.' 'Pose?' 'Under-the-beds. The amusing ones, roses and all get out. Bloody jerries.' **1950** G. WILSON *Brave Company* (1951) xi. 201 There was a great white china po hanging on the wall near the roof. **1961** C. WILLOCK *Death in Covert* i. 14 Do you make plastic poes? **1966** P. O'DONNELL *Sabre-Tooth* iv. 68 On her head was a po-shaped cloche hat. **1970** *Daily Tel.* 17 Oct. 6/6 And the hats—those 'po' creations had to be seen to be believed! **1974** *Punch* 27 Mar. 510/1, I kneelin' by de bed..peein' in de smart Victorian po.

po' (pōᵘ), *a.* Repr. a U.S. dial. pronunc. of POOR *a.* (*sb.*).
1893 H. A. SHANDS *Some Peculiarities of Speech in Mississippi* 50 *Po'*.., Negro for *poor.* **1911** F. W. ROLT-WHEELER *Boy with U.S. Census* 47 The po' white..is goin' to be only a memory like the backwoodsman o' the time o' Dan'l Boone. **1926** *Opportunity* Mar. 84/1 Dey kilt my po' daddy. **1945** *Gumbo Ya Ya* (Writers' Program, Louisiana) ii. 27, I sell to the rich, I sell to the po'; I'm gonna sell the lady Standin' in that do'. **1968** *Globe Mag.* (Toronto) 17 Feb. 18/4 Grey Owl..was Archie Bellaney, born..to a ne'er-do-well Englishman and..a po' white girl from Florida.

‖**p'o** (po). Also **peh, po.** [Chinese *pò*.] Soul, spirit.
1850 *Chinese Repository* Nov. 611 The Chinese philosophers..regarded man as a microcosm, his constitution and nature formed their model. This model they conceived to consist of a body which had *hing*..form, and of a *hwan*,..animus, and a *peh*, anima. **1914** D. T. SUZUKI *Brief Hist. Early Chinese Philos.* 44 It is one Animal Soul (*po*..) that becomes the drought in heaven, the metal on earth, and the animal soul in man. **1934** A. D. WALEY *Way & its Power* 28 *P'o*, which originally meant the semen, becomes the female soul, which lodges in the tomb. **1973** J. BLOFELD *Secret & Sublime* ii. 47 How they would rush about, seeking in vain some vehicle to save their *hun* and *p'o* (higher and lower souls) from gradual dissolution into nothingness! **1975** C.-Y. CHANG *Tao* x. 32 According to Ho-shang Kung,..p'o is rendered as anima... Anima (p'o)is the dark yin-soul.

poa. Delete ‖. Insert in etym. after 'mod.L.' (Linnæus *Genera Plantarum* (1737) 20). Substitute for def.: An annual or perennial grass of the genus so called, which is widely distributed in temperate and cold regions; = *meadow-grass* s.v. MEADOW *sb.* 4 c. (Later examples.)
1917 S. F. ARMSTRONG *Brit. Grasses* vii. 125 *Poa maritima*, Huds. (Sea Poa.) A somewhat creeping perennial, frequent on the shores of the British Isles. **1952** A. R. CLAPHAM et al. *Flora Brit. Isles* 1438 'Alpine Poa.' An erect, tufted perennial.

b. poa-grass (later examples).
1927 F. B. YOUNG *Portrait of Clare* VII. 762 A stone bridge spanned a chalk-stream with emerald trailing poa-grass swimming in smooth flats beneath it. **1971** *Homes & Gardens* Sept. 128/1 There is a silver-striped poa grass that shows up brilliantly anywhere, but it must not be allowed to spread.

poach, *v.*[1] **1.** Add to def.: and simmering gently. Hence, to cook (fish, fruit, etc.) by simmering in water or another liquid. Also, to simmer or steam (an egg) in a poacher. Also *absol.*
a **1693** [in Dict.]. **1898** C. H. SENN *Senn's Culinary Encycl.* 74 *Poach* (*to*).., to parboil or to boil slightly. Mode of cooking usually applied to eggs and quenelles of fish, meat or game. **1906** *Mrs. Beeton's Bk. Househ. Managem.* xxxviii. 1237 Put the tins in the oven, in a sauté-pan, surround them to half their depth with boiling water, and poach until the white is firm. **1907** *Yesterday's Shopping* (1969) 170/3 Steam Egg Poacher. A perfect way of poaching eggs. **1907** A. ESCOFFIER *Guide Mod. Cookery* II. xiv. 292 The poaching of fillets of sole must be effected without allowing the cooking-liquor to boil. **1940** A. L. SIMON *Conc. Encycl. Gastron.* II. 18/1 Fresh Cod ..is usually boiled, steamed or poached. **1959** *Listener* 26 Feb. 395/1 Peel and cut the pears in pieces and poach them very gently in the syrup. *Ibid.* 1 Oct. 551/2 Core the pears carefully. Poach until tender. **1963** HUME & DOWNES *Penguin Cordon Bleu Cookery* 432 Fresh peaches poached in a sugar syrup until tender. **1972** L. DAVIES *Easy Cooking* iii. 93 Very gently poach the sausages in the milk with the bay leaf, onion and seasoning, for 20 minutes.

poach, *v.*[2] Add: **III. 9. b.** In various ball games: to enter a partner's portion of the field or court and play a ball which he normally would have played.
1889 W. M. BROWNLEE *Lawn Tennis* 167 He need not be profusely apologetic when he poaches unsuccessfully. **1928** *Daily Express* 9 July 13/3 The pretty little Australian girl..would have won if her partner had not 'poached' and put himself out of position. **1960** *Times* 4 July 15/7 They must have noticed Osuna's swift ability to poach.

10. b. (Further examples.)
1955 *Times* 14 June 3/3 These are the men whom the N.A.S.D. are said to have 'poached' from the Transport and General Workers Union. **1958** *Listener* 11 Dec. 978/1 A girl doing it might later in life be tempted to poach service. **1979** *Internat. Jrnl. Sociol. of Law* VII. 176 Solicitors in the large criminal firms not only 'poach' clients, they also strive to poach each other.

poachable (pōᵘ·tʃăb'l), *a.* [f. POACH *v.*[2] + -ABLE.] Of game or fish: that may be poached or carried off illegally; suitable for poaching.
1924 *Public Opinion* 22 Feb. 169/1 The open wood I seldom visited,—all that was poachable having been poached long before.

poached, *ppl. a.*[1] Add: **a.** (see *POACH *v.*[1] 1). Also in extended use.
1940 A. L. SIMON *Conc. Encycl. Gastron.* II. 18/1 Fresh Cod..may be served..with any of the sauces which are suitable for boiled, steamed or poached Turbot. **1978** *Chicago* June 225/1 For dessert, orange-sparked chocolate mousse, poached pear with brandy and whipped-cream sauce.

b. (*c*) *Cookery* (see quots.); (*d*) = *poached-egg flower* s.v. sense *d.
1951 *Good Housek. Home Encycl.* 592/1 'Poached eggs' (halved and glazed peaches on rounds of sponge cake, surrounded by a ring of whipped cream). **1959** *Listener* 24 Dec. 1135/1 'Poached eggs': rounds of sponge cake, covered with a halved tinned apricot with a ribbon of whipped cream piped round the edge. **1971** *Guardian* 17 Apr. 7/8 The low-growing annual *Limnanthes douglasii*, known to children as 'Poached Eggs'..will make a tapestry of lemon and white at the front of a sunny bed.

d. *poached-egg flower, plant*, a small annual herb, *Limnanthes douglasii*, belonging to the family Limnanthaceæ, native to California, and bearing fragrant white and yellow flowers.
1963 R. D. MEIKLE *Garden Flowers* 135 Poached-egg Flower... The cordate petals are yellow at the base and white at the apex, producing a parti-coloured effect which at once suggests (to the inartistic) the popular name. **1973** *Country Life* 30 Aug. 565/1 In Britain we call *Limnanthes douglasii* the poached-egg flower, but in America they use the much more appropriate name of meadow foam. **1977** M. ALLAN *Darwin & his Flowers* xv. 261 (*caption*) *Limnanthes douglasii*, the 'Poached Egg Plant', which Darwin found was self-pollinating. **1978** *Woman's Jrnl.* Dec. 15/4 Do consider..the poached-egg plant called *Limnanthes douglasii*, a dwarf annual with ravishing yellow and white flowers.

poached, *ppl. a.*[2] **b.** (Later example.)
1955 *Times* 6 June 4/3 The union should..attempt to reach a settlement..of the dispute over 'poached' members.

poacher[1]**.** Add: **1. b.** *a poacher turned gamekeeper*: one who now preserves the interests he previously attacked; conversely, *a gamekeeper turned poacher.*
1945 *Times* 4 Aug. 5/2 Mr. Aneurin Bevan at the Ministry of Health..is conspicuously the poacher turned gamekeeper. **1977** *Times* 12 Feb. 12/6 Mr Camp has been working against the Railways Board in the interests of the unions... Is he then a poacher turned gamekeeper? **1978** *Broadbent* 27 Mar. 4/2 Stuart Wilson, former joint MD of Yorkshire Television..has been arguing with the ferocity of gamekeeper turned poacher against ITV's intended inroads into the fourth channel.

2. a. (Examples.)
1905 C. C. TOWNSEND *Birds of Essex County, Mass.* x. 130 The Baldpate, being unable to dive, makes use of diving Ducks to obtain food in deep water, and has therefore received in some places the name of 'Poacher'. **1923** *Bull. U.S. Nat. Mus.* No. 126. 96 Such behavior has earned for the baldpate the local name of 'poacher'. **1973** *Nature West Coast* (Vancouver Nat. Hist. Soc.) 163 Some birds [*sc.* American widgeon] feed on sea-weeds, often snatching them from the bills of diving birds. Hence the popular name 'poacher'.

b. Substitute for def.: A small marine fish belonging to the family Agonidæ. (Later examples.) Cf. *sea-poacher* s.v. SEA *sb.* 23 d in Dict.
1961 E. S. HERALD *Living Fishes of World* 252/2 The cold-water marine poachers and their relatives look much like some of the South American fresh-water armored catfishes. **1978** A. WHEELER *Key Fishes N. Europe* 224 Poachers or Pogges. A small family (Agonidae) of mainly Arctic marine fishes.

4. poacher('s) pocket, a large concealed pocket in a coat.
1925 [see **hare-pocket*]. **1956** G. E. EVANS *Ask Fellows who cut Hay* ii. 35 Inside the slop were two long hanging, or *poacher's*, pockets so that a shepherd could very easily conceal a couple of rabbits. **1974** *Country Life* 21 Mar. 688/2 The suit..is a three-piece garment with extremely wide lapels, poacher pockets, and baggy trousers with turn-ups. **1976** 'D. HALLIDAY' *Dolly & Nanny Bird* xviii. 247 He took up..a manilla envelope which he zipped with care into a poacher's pocket on the inner side of his waterproof jacket.

poacher[2]**.** Add to def.: usu. with shallow cup-like compartments in which an egg can be cooked over boiling water. (Earlier and later examples.) Also, a vessel or pan in which fish, etc. can be poached (see *POACH *v.*[1] 1).
1861 MRS. BEETON *Bk. Househ. Managem.* xxxiii. 827 For inexperienced cooks, a tin egg-poacher may be purchased. **1884** [see *egg-poacher* s.v. EGG *sb.* 6 b]. **1895** *Montgomery Ward Catal.* Spring & Summer 433/1 Buffalo steam egg poachers. **1951** *Good Housek. Home Encycl.* 452/1 Use a wide pan..or a specially constructed egg poacher. **1975** J. BEARD et al. *Cooks' Catal.* 399 Poachers come in a range of sizes for everything from a miniature mackerel to a king-sized salmon... All poachers have a common feature—a rack that protects your fish from the direct heat source beneath and enables you to lift the whole fish from the pot intact. *Ibid.* 439 All of the so-called egg poachers on the market, however they operate, whatever they do, are not actually poaching at all. A true poached egg is cooked *in* water, not over it, and not in steam—an 'egg poacher', with its cuplike insert, actually steams an egg. **1976** *West Lancs. Evening Gaz.* 15 Dec. 1. 12/4 Two Poachers and steamer, 75p each.

poaching, *vbl. sb.*[1] (Later examples.)
1907 A. ESCOFFIER *Guide Mod. Cookery* II. xiv. 292 Where the exact amount of poaching-liquor is not given, allow one-quarter pint to every four fillets. **1913** J. M. HILL *Pract. Cooking* 69 The term poaching has come to be applied to the cooking of all articles containing eggs, either in the oven or on top of the range, in dishes that are surrounded with hot water. **1956** SPRY & HUME *Constance Spry Cookery Bk.* iv. 70 *Poaching* is a term used to indicate a gentler cooking still [than simmering]. **1960** *Good Housek. Cookery Bk.* (rev. ed.) 80/2 Although this method of cooking fish is referred to as boiling, it is more accurately described as poaching, since the water should be kept only simmering, not actually boiling, while the fish is in it.

poaching, *vbl. sb.*[2] Add: **a.** Also *concr.*, a patch of mud. *poet.*
1929 J. MASEFIELD *Poems* 703 Plastered with poachings, he rode on forsaken.

b. (Further examples.)
1899 E. H. MILES *Lessons in Lawn Tennis* xi. 69 The man should have no false modesty..about a certain amount of poaching. **1955** *Times* 27 May 11/6 He intimates that officers of the Transport and General Workers Union have been guilty of membership poaching offences. **1977** *World of Cricket Monthly* June 68/3 The approach had come initially from Imran, and there was no question of poaching on the part of Sussex.

Poale Zion (poăle· tsi͵yǫ·n). [Heb., 'workers of Zion'.] Name of a predominantly left-wing Zionist labour movement which first emerged in Russia about 1899.
1919 N. SOKOLOW *Hist. Zionism* II. 367 The Poale Zion was established in 1901... The programme of the organization represents a synthesis of Zionism and Socialism. **1935** A. REVUSKY *Jews in Palestine* xii. 206 The left is represented by the Poale Zion and the Communists. **1973** *Jewish Chron.* 19 Jan. 42/3 Mr Burton was a member of Poale Zion from early youth.

pob[2] (pǫb). [Echoic.] An abrupt, heavy sound as when an inelastic body strikes a hard surface.
1911 J. MASEFIELD *Jim Davis* xiii. 157 A heavy chewed slug would come 'pob' into the boat's side.

pobby (pǫ·bi), *a.* orig. *dial.* [cf. POBS *sb. pl.*] Swollen, blown; also of food, pulpy, mushy.
1888 KIPLING *Phantom 'Rickshaw* 30 There are, in this land, ghosts who take the form of fat, cold, pobby corpses. **1903** *Eng. Dial. Dict.* IV. 563/1 *Pobby, adj.* Yks..., swollen, *gen.* used of a soft swelling. **1937** V. K. LIBBY *How to care for Baby* vi. 49 If you want baby to have good teeth be careful not to give a lot of 'pobby' food. Never soak the rusks in milk, etc.

‖ **poblacion** (pǫblasiǫ·n, -þiǫ·n). Also **población.** Pl. **poblaciones.** [Sp., = population; also, town, city, village.] **a.** In Spanish-speaking countries of South America: a community; a district of a town, etc. **b.** In the Republic of the Philippines: the principal community of a district; a town that is an administrative centre.
1926 J. MASEFIELD *Odtaa* xiv. 236 The hut, like the other huts of the poblacion, was, at a guess, thirty feet long by fifteen broad. **1961** WEBSTER, *Población*.., a center of a municipality in the Philippines that is usu. the barrio that gives the municipality its name and is the seat of government. **1964** A. CUTSHALL *Philippines* iii. 27 The postwar Philippine barrio and oftentimes the *poblacion*, the principal community in the municipality (county), is not appreciably different from the representative prewar village and town. **1967** M. C. BELLO in M. D. Zamora *Stud. Philippine Anthropol.* 325 The site studied is the *poblacion* which refers to a group of contiguous villages found toward the middle of the region... The poblacion settlement is situated on the top of a mountain. **1978** *Listener* 23 Nov. 668/2 The *barrio* or *poblaciones*, the shanty-towns of the poor. **1979** E. NORMAN *Christianity & World Order* iv. 47 In 1978 I visited the working class *poblaciones* around Santiago, in Chile.

‖ **poblador** (pǫblădō·ɹ). Pl. **pobladores.** [Sp.] In Spanish America, a settler, a colonist; *spec.* a country person who moves to settle or squat in a town.
1966 *Economist* 2 July 28/2 The *pobladores* (squatters) fled further up the hill. **1976** *New Yorker* 26 Apr. 122/1 Everyone seems to know precisely when his forefathers arrived—in the eighteen-fifties, as *pobladores*, or settlers, recruited..to colonize the million-acre Sangre de Cristo land grant.

pochade. Add: (Later example.) Also **pochade box** (see quot. 1961).
1959 M. STEEN *Tower* II. iv. 206 My easel had been removed, and my pochade box. **1961** M. LEVY *Studio Dict. Art Terms* 88 *Pochade box*, a small portable colour-box with panels fitted into the lid for quick sketching. **1972** D. SUTTON in R. Fry *Lett.* I. 90 Fry..was usually more at ease with a *pochade* than with a finished work.

pochette (pǫʃe·t). [Fr.: see POCKET *sb.*] **1. a.** A small pocket.
1913 W. DE LA MARE *Peacock Pie* 80 A watch..He lifted from the hook where it was ticking And crammed in his Pochette. **1949** *Amer. Speech* XXIV. 38 The secret pockets which the conjurer is so often suspected of using are of two types, the *pochette* and the *profonde*. They differ in position and in size, the latter being the larger. **1964** *Punch* 1 Jan. 15/1 *Pochettes* in the [conjuror's] trousers.
b. A hand-bag. Also *pochette bag*.
1923 *Weekly Dispatch* 11 Mar. 15/5 When jewels are worn in the hair the vanity-bag becomes a satin or crêpe pochette, fastened with a buckle of jewels. **1930** *Daily Tel.* 9 Apr. 9/2 If you will make yourself pochettes to match your hats, you are adding..that extra touch of chic. **1972** *Times* 12 May 13/6 The little pochette..slides into a bigger bag. **1973** *Country Life* 1 Feb. 302/3 A shiny PVC coat and a great flat pochette, slung on a handy shoulder strap. **1976** *Evening Post* (Nottingham) 16 Dec. 10/4 You can even get a pochette bag with the words 'Gold-Rush' as a motif. **1977** *Times* 29 Oct. 12/2 More and more men use pochettes to avoid bulging..their trousers.
2. A small violin, supposedly once carried in the pocket by French dancing-masters; = KIT *sb.*[2]
1889 in *Cent. Dict.* **1976** D. MUNROW *Instruments Middle Ages & Renaissance* 28/2 It was as an instrument for dancing that the small rebec survived as the *kit* or *pochette* into the eighteenth century.

‖ **pochismo** (potʃī·zmo). [Mexican Sp., f. as next + *-ismo* -ISM.] A form of slang used by speakers of Mexican Spanish and others along the border with the U.S., consisting of English words given a Spanish form or pronunciation; a word of this sort.
1944 *N.Y. Herald Tribune* 5 Aug. 10/3 The Mexican Academy has appointed a committee to eradicate 'pochismos'—that is English words and phrases used in speaking Spanish. **1946** *Mod. Lang. Jrnl.* Oct. 345 *Pochismo*, derived from *pocho*, an adjective which originally meant discolored, has now come to mean a type of popular slang in Mexico. **1966** N. S. HAYNER *New Patterns in Old Mexico* xiv. 219 Students of language have a lively curiosity in the increasing use of 'pochismo', a type of popular slang, by even the most conservative of the Mexico City newspapers. **1976** F. A. & D. L. LATORRE *Mexican Kickapoo Indians* ii. 29 They [*sc.* Kickapoos] have incorporated many Spanish words into their speech and many *pochismos*..such as *lonche* ('lunch').

‖ **pocho** (po·tʃo). [Mexican Sp., Sp. *pocho* discoloured, faded, pale.] A citizen of the United States of Mexican origin; a culturally Americanized Mexican. Also *attrib.* or as *adj.*
1944 *Newsweek* 14 Aug. 76/3 A pocho in good standing will drag his fititoes (feet) up the estrita (street). *Ibid.* Slapstick actors like Tin Tan..who gets comic effects with pocho patter. **1960** *Time* 25 Jan. 92/2 Opium is..smuggled..from Mexico by special agents called 'pocho' women (generally Americans of Mexican descent) who cross the border into Mexico to shop. **1968** *Sunday Mail Mag.* (Brisbane) 25 Aug. 14/3 *Pocho*, derogatory term for American-Mexican (in U.S.A.). **1975** *Sat. Rev.* (U.S.) 8 Feb. 47/1, I was frequently labelled a *pocho*, a Mexican with gringo pretentions.

‖ **pochoir** (pǫʃwār). [Fr., = stencil.] A process used in book illustration, especially for limited editions, in which a monochrome print is coloured by hand, using a series of stencils; a print made by this process. Also *attrib.*
1931 *Times Lit. Suppl.* 25 June (Salon International du Livre d'Art Suppl.) p. i/4 Emile Hazan is another publisher who has taken full advantage of the *pochoir* technique. *Ibid.* p. viii/3 Colette's 'Regarde'..with its drawings by Mathurin Méheut coloured by *pochoir*. **1932** J. JOYCE *Let.* 10 Nov. (1966) III. 266 This *pochoir* reproduction can be done only in Paris and even here only by two or three firms. **1953** *Book Collector* II. 4 The unique coloured copy of Blake's *Jerusalem*..was recently reproduced in facsimile by the pochoir process. **1958** *Listener* 12 June 984/3 Lithographs and '*pochoirs*' by Dufy. **1965** ZIGROSSER & GAEHDE *Guide Coll. Orig. Prints* iv. 56 In France around the 1920's,..an expert craftsman, J. Saudé, used the straight-stencil, or *pochoir*, process as a reproductive medium for illustrating books. **1973** *Times Lit. Suppl.* 26 Jan. 103/4 French books illustrated in pochoir..would be included. **1973** *Art Internat.* Mar. 22/2 He owned a pochoir by Gleizes and lithographs by Léger.

pock, *v.* Delete *rare* and add: Chiefly as pa. pple. or pa. ppl. adj. (Later examples.)
1938 *Proc. Prehist. Soc.* IV. 246 The chief tombs which exhibit incised & pocked designs on their walls & roofs are New Grange, Dowth, & those at Lochcrew. **1977** *Time* 31 Jan. 42/1 On went a coat of Viacryl, a synthetic polyurethane resin meant to protect the pocked and flawed surface of the 800-year-old glass.

Pockels (pǫ·kĕlz). Also erron. **Pockel.** The name of F. C. A. *Pockels* (1865–1913), German physicist, used, chiefly *attrib.*, with reference to an effect in certain crystals similar to the Kerr effect (sense *(*b*)) in liquids (see quot. 1975[2]); so *Pockels cell, constant, effect* (cf. *KERR).
Described by Pockels in *Abhandl. der K. Ges. der Wissensch. zu Göttingen* (*Math.-phys. Klasse*) (1894) XXXI. 204.
1949 *Jrnl. Optical Soc. Amer.* XXXIX. 798/2 The constants t_{ij} are..related to Pockels' constants e_{ij}. **1957** D. E. GRAY *Amer. Inst. Physics Handbk.* VI. 96 Twenty-one of the 32 crystal symmetry classes do not contain centers of symmetry, and of these, 20 may exhibit the linear Pockels effect. **1968** E. L. STEELE *Optical Lasers in Electronics* v. 178 The electro-optical switches employ the photo-optical effect in a Kerr cell, Pockels cell, or Faraday rotator. **1975** D. G. FINK *Electronics Engineers' Handbk.* XI. 24 Linear Electrooptical Effect, or Pockel's Effect. Crystalline materials such as potassium dihydrogen phosphate (KDP) and lithium niobate are used... Metal electrodes are applied to rectangular blocks of these crystals, and the resultant structures are referred to as Pockel cells. *Ibid.* XIV. 60 In the Pockels effect the differential phase shift is linearly related to applied voltage; in the Kerr effect it is related to the voltage squared. **1976** *Nature* 22 Apr. 677/1 The emission intensities of the components parallel and perpendicular to the incident laser polarisation were determined using a Pockels cell to rotate the laser polarisation with respect to a fixed analyser.

pocket, *sb.* Add: **1.** (Further examples.)
1907 W. H. KOEBEL *Return of Joe* 239 A train of pack horses, heavily laden with the weighty 'pockets' of wool, toil meekly past. **1928** E. WALLACE *Gunner* xxiv. 199 Bales of silk, chests of tea, pockets of rubber. **1940** E. C. STUDHOLME *Te Waimate* 170 Over the hills [the wool] was carried by pack horses..each taking about 150 lbs. in what were called 'pockets'—loaf shaped packs slung one on each side of the saddle. **1953** *Word for Word* (Whitbread & Co.) 28/1 *Pocket*, a large sack made to contain roughly one and a half cwts. of dried hops.
3. b. *to be out of pocket*, also *transf.*, to be absent or out of reach. *U.S.*
1974 *Anderson* (S. Carolina) *Independent* 20 Apr. 1A/1 If you..have ever been sick and the only doctor is out of pocket for the weekend, then you know we need more doctors. **1978** *Internat. Herald Tribune* 24 July 14/4 Why does *out of pocket*..mean 'out of touch'?
d. esp. in phr. *to live in each other's pockets*: to live in excessively close proximity, to live in mutual dependence.
1959 [see *GRANDMOTHER *sb.* 1 c]. **1965** F. SARGESON *Memoirs of Peon* vi. 158 We lived..in one another's pockets, so why should there be the privilege of privacy and seclusion for one and not for the other? **1978** *N.Y. Rev. Bks.* 23 Feb. 8/2 Architects and painters do not live in each other's pockets in England today.
e. *to put one's hand in one's pocket*: to (seek to) provide money from one's own resources.
1857 C. KINGSLEY *Two Yrs. Ago* I. p. xxii, There are other ways of being generous, besides putting your hand in your pocket. **1878** H. JAMES *Europeans* I. iv. 147 Robert Acton would put his hand into his pocket every day in the week if that rattle-pated little sister of his should bid him. **1948** E. WAUGH *Loved One* 28 We may have to put our hands in our pockets—I don't suppose old Frank has left much.
7. a. Also, an isolated body of opal or gum. *Austral.*
1873 J. E. TINNE *Wonderland of Antipodes* 54 If a man hits on a good 'pocket' of gum. **1910** *Lone Hand* (Sydney) Mar. 494 A dip in the seam, or some obstruction..temporarily dammed the stream, which thickened, solidified there, and formed a 'pocket'. **1971** J. S. GUNN *Opal Terminol.* 35 *Pocket*, small cluster of opal suddenly met in one place.
9. (Earlier example.)
a **1817** JANE AUSTEN *Northanger Abbey* (1818) II. xiv. 285 With so much changing of chaises..I hope..you have not left anything behind you in any of the pockets.
11. b. *Amer.* and *Canad. Football.* A shielded area formed by blockers from which a player attempts to pass; the formation itself.
1963 *Time* 18 Oct. 94 Myers..is a drop-back 'pocket' passer. **1968** *Globe & Mail* (Toronto) 10 July 27/5 He is an accurate passer, either from the pocket or on the roll-out.
11*. = *air-pocket* s.v. *AIR *sb.*[1] B. III. 1.
1911 G. C. LOENING *Monoplanes & Biplanes* ii. 18 Everywhere in the atmosphere, and especially on windy days, there exist 'pockets' of high density and of low density. **1917** *Boy's Own Paper* Mar. 273/2 Evidently he had dropped into one of those air eddies which were so dangerous to flying men in the early days of aviation. They, in conjunction with 'pockets', accounted for the death of not a few pioneers in flight. **1919** C. P. THOMPSON *Cocktails* 46 The suddenly uncontrolled Hun staggered and whirled in a treacherous 'pocket'. **1978** H. KAPLAN *Damascus Cover* vii. 60 The plane rolled in a pocket of turbulent air.
11. a.** *Mil.* An area held by troops who are surrounded by opposing forces; an isolated concentration *of* resistance; also, the men themselves; esp. in phr. *pocket of resistance* (also *transf.*).
1918 *Observer* 29 Sept. 7/6 The Anglo-Belgian attack in the north..has reduced the enemy to the necessity of defending..a pocket such as those which brought him to disaster on the Marne and on the Avre. **1927** J. M. KEYNES *Ess. in Biogr.* (1933) I. vi. 62 The strategic surrender, the deliberate withdrawal, the attempt to lure the enemy into a pocket where he could be taken in flank. **1941** *Manch. Guardian Weekly* 10 Jan. 20/2 The Australians engaged strong enemy defence pockets to the south-east of this line. **1943** *Times* (Weekly ed.) 24 Apr. 6 Here the Germans had a small pocket, based on the bridge which carried the highway to Gomel over the Dnieper. **1945** *Daily Express* 12 Apr. 4/8 Full aid to liberated Europe..must wait not only until the German army is beaten, but until pockets of resistance have been wiped out. **1959** *Listener* 12 Feb. 287/1 Except for provincial pockets of resistance it is now as successful as any architecture is ever likely to be. *Ibid.* 29 Oct. 740/2 An enemy 'pocket of resistance' was still occupying a wood about half-a-mile away. **1965** C. D. EBY *Siege of Alcázar* (1966) xi. 230 There was..a large pocket of militia barricaded in the seminary. **1966** T. PYNCHON *Crying of Lot 49* iii. 61 A..battle of attrition in a minor pocket developed during the advance on Rome. **1975** G. ST. GEORGE *Proteus Pact* (1976) i. 5 Kleist sat on top of an armored personnel carrier and watched the systematic elimination of pockets of resistance.
b. A small area contrasted with or differing from its surroundings in some respect; a local concentration *of* something. Cf. senses 7 a, b in Dict.
1926 *Scribner's Mag.* Aug. 163/1 The car swerved into the campus, that green, summer-deserted pocket of peace in the little, dusty, traffic-riddled village. **1932** *Times Educ. Suppl.* 2 Jan. p. iv/4 They walked into a pocket of gas and were asphyxiated. **1935** HUXLEY & HADDON *We Europeans* ii. 53 They do not form definite groups, but occur rather in local pockets where individuals still exhibit characters reminiscent of those remote times. **1937** *Brit. Jrnl. Psychol.* XXVII. 358 We may regard the adjusted group, if it has proceeded to the stage of new, reified institutions, as a small culture pocket or subculture within the larger culture. **1939** *British Birds* XXXIII. 102 The Black-tailed Godwit is increasingly occurring in the British Isles... The increase is greatest on the south coast of England with pockets elsewhere. **1945** *Daily Express* 22 May 2/4 What is to happen when, in the change from war to peace, there occur the inevitable pockets of unemployment? **1959** *Times* 4 Sept. 4/3 We must conclude that the existence of pockets of heat under the lunar surface is probable. **1976** W. H. CANAWAY *Willow-Pattern War* xi. 111 There were edelweiss in soil pockets on the rock outcrops. **1978** J. BLACKBURN *Dead Man's Handle* iii. 36 A pocket of upper-crust suburbia: detached, Regency-style residences with two-car garages.
12. a. (Further examples.)
1640 E. VERNEY *Let.* in F. P. Verney *Mem.* (1892) I. vii. 174, I pray be pleased to send mee a pocket prayer-book. **1726** SWIFT *Gulliver* II. III. i. 7, I discovered by my pocket-glass several islands to the south-east. **1800** M. EDGEWORTH *Parent's Assistant* (ed. 3) IV. 145 Lady Augusta had just shown her a French pocket fan. **1827** J. F. COOPER *Prairie* I. vi. 179 *Quadruped*: seen..by the aid of a pocket-lamp, in the prairies. **1828** M. WILMOT *Let.* 23 Apr. (1935) 316 They all expect to be your pocket dictionarys and lionizers and walking sticks. **1832** *Chambers's Edin. Jrnl.* 14 Apr. 86/2, I scarcely recollect a single traveller without his pocket-comb. **1837** W. IRVING *Capt. Bonneville* III. xi. 174 The captain now drew forth that grand lure in the eyes of the savage, a pocket mirror. **1848** in H. Howe *Hist. Coll. Ohio* 493 These little pocket editions of humanity are well cared for by kind dames. **1866** 'MARK TWAIN' *Lett. from Hawaii* (1967) 45 We..ran by a pocket compass in the hands of Captain Fish. **1874** *Eng. Mech.*

1 May 165/2 (*title*) How to make a pocket camera. **1885** *Sam Scaramouch* 12 Dec. 247/2 If you must have a drink, gentlemen, carry your pocket flasks. **1903** C. E. WOLFF *Mod. Locomotive Practice* p. ii (Advt.), The 'Mechanical Engineer' Pocket Calculator. **1906** M. CORELLI *Treasure of Heaven* 43 Mrs. Sorrel..drew out a black pocket-fan and fanned herself vigorously. **1913** *Punch* 17 Sept. 252 Portrait of gentleman using pocket-clipper to trim beard at back of neck. **1916** *Daily Colonist* (Victoria, B.C.) 9 July 7/1 (Advt.), Hudson's Bay Company Fine Old Irish Whisky Per Pocket Flasks..50¢. **1917** G. B. MCCUTCHEON *Green Fancy* 56 Barnes found his electric pocket torch and dressed hurriedly. **1921** *Daily Colonist* (Victoria, B.C.) 25 Oct. 8/1 (Advt.), We are now showing an open face pocket watch, in strong nickel case. **1923** CONRAD *Rover* iv. 61 The lieutenant,..with a pocket glass glued to his eye, growled angrily: 'You can see her now, can't you?' **1926** *Daily Colonist* (Victoria, B.C.) 16 July 10/7 (Advt.), Matches are dangerous. When you are camping in or around the forests, use a pocket lighter. **1927** S. ERTZ *Now East, now West* xi. 173 Again that keen glance, over her pocket mirror. **1933** M. ARLEN *Man's Mortality* 21 Taking out his pocket-transmitter, he held it near the light. **1939** T. S. ELIOT *Family Reunion* I. i. 21 Reflecting a pocket-torch of observation Upon each other's opacity. **1955** C. SMITH *Speaking Eye* iii. 33 He took out a pocket comb and ran it through his dark wavy hair. **1957** *Practical Wireless* XXXIII. 534/2 Messrs. Cossar announce a neat printed circuit transistor pocket radio. **1972** *Gloss. Electrotechnical, Power Terms* (B.S.I.) IV. iii. 21 *Pocket lamp*, portable luminaire embodying a miniature lamp fed by a dry battery or accumulator. **1972** D. BLOODWORTH *Any Number can Play* xi. 92 Ivansong.. kept the pocket radio close to his ear. **1977** *Jrnl. R. Soc. Arts* CXXV. 71/1 Aldus used it [*sc.* italic type] for the pocket editions of classical authors which he printed in Venice around the year 1500. **1977** J. HEDGECOE *Photographer's Handbk.* 20 Most pocket cameras use a fixed lens with a focal length of about 25 mm. **1978** *Daily Tel.* 19 Sept. 8/6 Semiconductors..are an essential part of microprocessor technology and are used in pocket calculators, electronic watches, mini-computers, and many other modern devices.

b. (Further examples.)

1820 M. EDGEWORTH *Let.* 14 May (1979) 128 My dear little pocket Prince de Beauvoau for me!—worth all the Russian bears and giants put together. **1936** *Sun* (Baltimore) 18 May 8/3 No decisive victory in the Austrian pocket dictators' duel is possible without profound repercussions. **1951** N. M. GUNN *Well at World's End* xxi. 174 The garden of a gentleman farmer, a pocket laird. **1972** *Listener* 28 Dec. 898/1 The producer is not altogether the little pocket-dictator... He is assisted by a colleague, usually an expert on the topic to be discussed. **1977** *Time* 8 Aug. 30/1 Charles [Prince, of Luxembourg] was long active in promoting business and industry in his pocket principality.

e. Of warships: armoured and equipped like a ship of the class named, but smaller.

1930 *Economist* 1 Feb. 227/1 The technical progress represented by Germany's 'pocket battleship' of identical tonnage but heavier armament. **1932** *Sun* (Baltimore) 17 Sept. 1/1 (*heading*) New pocket cruiser to be started October 1. **1941** *Hutchinson's Pictorial Hist. War* 14 May–8 July 89 Some of the latest and fastest motor launches.. are known as 'pocket destroyers'. **1942** H. RICHMOND *War at Sea Today* 27 The 'pocket battleships' are protected by armour against which 6-in.-gun fire could not be expected to be fully effective at long ranges. **1951** *Chambers's Jrnl.* Oct. 632/1 Aided by George (now Sir George) Binney, three 'pocket freighters' were rapidly built in British shipyards. **1974** G. JENKINS *Bridge of Magpies* ii. 40 We heard the sound of heavy guns: a raider or a pocket battleship, we thought.

13. † **pocket allowance** = POCKET-MONEY; **pocket beach** *Physical Geogr.*, a small, narrow beach between two headlands or in a similar sheltered position; **pocket billiards,** (*a*) a North American type of pool (POOL *sb.*³ 3); (*b*) *slang* (orig. *Schoolboys'*), manipulation of the male genitals (cf. *BALL *sb.*¹ 15 b) by the pocketed hands; also phr. *to play pocket billiards*; **pocket-expenses** (later example); **pocket-gopher** = GOPHER *sb.*¹ 1; **pocket-hunter** (see quot. 1906); **pocket-miner** *U.S.* = **pocket-hunter*; so **pocket-mining** *vbl. sb.*; **pocket pager** = *PAGER *sb.*³; so **pocket-paging** *vbl. sb.*; **pocket passer** *Amer.* and *Canad. Football*, one who passes from the pocket (*POCKET *sb.* 11 b); **pocket rot,** a fungus infection causing localized decay in the trunks or roots of trees; also with prefixed defining word (e.g. *brown pocket rot*); **pocket-size** *a.*, of a size suitable for carrying in the pocket; hence *fig.*, petty, small-scale; also *pocket-sized* adj.; **pocket stay** (see quot.); **pocket valley** *Physical Geogr.*, a steep-sided, usu. flat-floored valley at the head of which a stream emerges at the base of a steep slope; **pocket Venus,** a small and beautiful woman; also *transf.*; **pocket veto** (earlier and later examples).

1813 JANE AUSTEN *Pride & Prejudice* III. viii. 143 Her board and pocket allowance, and the continual presents in money, which passed to her, through her mother's hands. **1893** N. S. SHALER in *Ann. Rep. U.S. Geol. Survey* XIII. 141 Where..there are islands or shoals lying on either side of a considerable reentrant, a curious action arises, which leads to the formation of what we may term 'pocket beaches'. **1932** W. H. EMMONS et al. *Geol.* ix. 254 On rocky coasts beaches of boulders and cobblestones commonly form at the heads of indentations, although occasionally sand may occupy such positions. These pocket beaches..are found along the coast of California at Carmel, at La Jolla, and at many other places. **1976** A. N. STRAHLER *Princ. Earth Sci.* xvii. 250 Shingle beaches form in the most sheltered locations—in bays between rocky promontories—and are called pocket beaches... They are typically crescent-shaped and are concave toward the sea. **1913** J. T. STODDARD *Science of Billiards* vii. 152 Pocket Billiards. The more common pool games are played on tables with pockets, and with balls 2¼ inches in diameter,—slightly smaller than the ball used in billiards. **1917** *Billiards Mag.* Dec. 13/1 Greenleaf..began to play pocket billiards 6 years ago... His ambition is to win the pocket billiard championship. **1940** S. SPENDER *Backward Son* ii. 94 He paused, feeling in his trouser pockets with his hands, with a familiar gesture of the class room which the boys knew as 'pocket billiards'. **1949** F. SARGESON *I saw in my Dream* I. 40, I don't remember nothing about when school was in except him playing pocket billiards. **1963** *Landfall* Mar. 14 A pillar of our.. community,..addicted to long volleys of handball, I mean pocket billiards. **1971** A. BURGESS *MF* ii. 31 Saint Face, as if wishing to play pocket-billiards with my balls, thrust his hands in from the rear. **1905** G. B. SHAW in *Grand Mag.* Feb. 116 If you keep the pocket expenses down to twelve and six. **1873** E. EGGLESTON *Myst. Metropolisville* iv. 37 She would..explain how the pocket-gophers built their mounds. **1932** S. ZUCKERMAN *Social Life Monkeys & Apes* iv. 59 The animals of the first sub-group are those that spend the anœstrus in solitude... Examples are the jaguar of Central America and the pocket gopher of the United States. **1977** R. B. COWLES *Desert Jrnl.* xx. 209 A pocket gopher or..a beaver burrowed through the bank. **1906** *Chambers's Jrnl.* Feb. 159/1 They [*sc.* prospectors] include the 'pocket-hunter' who disdains to search for gold except in the form of pockets. **1947** *Field & Stream* June 30/3 Now and then a 'pocket-hunter'..will find a place in the hills containing perhaps a few hundred dollars in gold. **1902** J. LONDON *Daughter of Snows* 207 The pocket-miner's eyes sparkled. **1909** 'MARK TWAIN' *Is Shakes. Dead?* vii. 75, I have been a 'pocket' miner—a sort of gold mining not findable in any but one little spot in the world. **1872** —— *Roughing It* 436 In that one little corner of California is found a species of mining..called 'pocket-mining'. **1975** *Kingston* (Ontario) *Whig-Standard* 6 Dec. 25/1 Off in a side office, MacLean Hunter manager Jack French talks to a client about ordering 'pocket-pagers'. **1977** Pocket pager [see *PAGER *sb.*³]. **1973** *Times* 11 Jan. 15/2 The control room is the centre of a vast and flexible intercom system which complements and extends the telephone network..and the pocket-paging system. **1963** Pocket passer [see *POCKET *sb.* 11 b]. **1977** *Globe & Mail* (Toronto) 26 Nov. 53/6 If Wade, a pocket passer, is harassed by the Eskimoes' blitzing linebackers, he could throw a number of interceptions. **1926** *Jrnl. Agric. Res.* XXXIII. 687 As the brown cubical rot produced [by *Trametes subrosea*]..is more or less restricted to definite pockets in the wood, it has been called brown-pocket rot. **1938** J. S. BOYCE *Forest Pathol.* xvii. 451 Pocket dry rot.. is a brown pocket rot of the heartwood of living incense cedar caused by *Polyporus amarus*. **1956** F. W. JANE *Structure of Wood* ix. 208 In the pocket rots the areas of decay are confined to pockets. **1972** *Mycologia* LXIV. 1258 [*Phellinus torulosus*] occurs..mostly on southwestern white pine..in which it causes a white pocket rot of the roots. **1909** *Daily Chron.* 13 Nov. 3/2 They form a serviceable little group of pocket-size manuals. **1973** P. EVANS *Bodyguard Man* xxx. 183 You know what you are... Just a latter-day Judas, pocket size. **1907** *Daily Chron.* 14 Aug. 3/2 A new pocket-sized edition of Mr. Edward Hulme's 'Wild Fruits of the Countryside' is being published. **1954** KOESTLER *Invisible Writing* xxiii. 253 Our Jan..was a pocket-sized Stalin. **1964** *McCall's Sewing* ii. 31/2 *Pocket stay*, a strip of interfacing sewn to the wrong side of a pocket opening for reinforcement. **1942** O. D. VON ENGELN *Geomorphol.* xxii. 569 Seepage at the bases of the outer scarps [of uplifted coral reefs] promotes the formation of gullies by headward erosion through solution-sapping. Pocket valleys, with vertical head and side walls and a nearly flat floor, are..opened up by this process. **1966** J. WYCKOFF *Rock, Time, & Landforms* xii. 281 Whereas the blind valley ends at a blank wall, the so-called pocket valley begins at a blank wall. A pocket valley forms where water emerges near the foot of the slope, dissolving out the rock around and below the point of emergence. **1971** J. N. JENNINGS *Karst* vi. 112 A distinction is sometimes made between steepheads incised to an impervious basement and pocket valleys of the same general nature but within the karst rock outcrop. **1869** S. R. HOLE *Bk. about Roses* viii. 125 The lovely little Banksian Rose..this pocket, or rather button-hole, Venus. **1921** W. DE LA MARE *Memoirs of Midget* xxxiii. 229 Aunt Alice calls you her 'pocket Venus', and she means it, too, in her own sly way. **1969** H. K. FLEMING *Day they kidnapped Queen Victoria* vi. 106 Four years had gone by, since, as the 'Pocket Venus', she had been the rage and toast of society. **1979** 'P. O'CONNOR' *Into Strong City* II. xxvii. 98 Nancy was dark and petite, perfectly formed—the proverbial pocket venus. **1842** *Ohio Statesman* 19 Dec. 3/1 (*heading*) The pocket vetoes. **1973** *Time* 25 June 20/3 As presidential counsel, he worked out the legal basis for Nixon's impoundment of funds, broad use of pocket vetoes and Executive privilege.

pocketability (pǫ:kėtăbi·lĭti). [f. POCKETABLE *a.*: see -ITY.] The capacity to be put or carried in the pocket.

1970 *Amateur Photographer* 22 Apr. 21/1 No modern range-finder camera with a comparable lens..and a built-in selenium meter has its priceless asset of pocketability. **1977** *New Scientist* 10 Feb. p. ii (Advt.), If real pocketability matters, the Sinclair Cambridge Scientific offers a comparable range of functions in a uniquely compact format.

pocketa-pocketa (pǫ·kėtă,pǫ·kėtă). Also **pockety.** [Echoic.] An imitation of the regular sound made by a smoothly-running internal combustion engine; also *transf.* Also *attrib.* and *adv.*

1939 J. THURBER in *New Yorker* 18 Mar. 19/1 The pounding of the cylinders increased: ta-pocketa-pocketa-pocketa-*pocketa-pocketa*. **1968** L. DEIGHTON *Only when I Larf* i. 11 A helicopter was warming up... Pockety, pockety, pockety. **1971** *Flying* Apr. 93/1, I brought the power back from the standard 1,700 run-up rpm to a pocketa-pocketa idle. **1977** J. AIKEN *Last Movement* ix. 174, I could hear his heart going pocketa-pocketa.

pocket-book. Add: **1.** In recent U.S. use, also a cheap edition, esp. paper-bound. Also *attrib.*

1953 *Amer. Scholar* XXIII. 10 The *Galaxy* serial 'Gravy Planet' (recently republished in a pocket book as *The Space Merchants*). **1959** N. MAILER *Advts. for Myself* (1961) 280 Anyone looking for a fairly close portrait of that outfit is invited to read *The Day the Century Ended*—in pocket-book called *Between Heaven and Hell*. **1962** A. BUCHWALD *How much is that in Dollars?* 167 Always try to get a large advance on pocket-books. **1979** *Maledicta* III. 15, I was paid $50,000 by New American Library in 1968 for the U.S. pocketbook rights of my last novel, *The Man Who Loved Women*.

2. (Further examples.) Also, a woman's hand-bag or other container for bank-notes or coins. Also *fig.* Now chiefly *U.S.*

1816 *Niles' Reg.* X. 216/1 Two methodist preachers were lately robbed of their pocket-books, containing very considerable sums in bank notes. **1862** O. L. JACKSON in *Colonel's Diary* (1922) v. 67, I..thought it best to take my pocket-book out of my pocket and put it under my head. **1897** *Sears, Roebuck Catal.* 223/1 At 50c. Our price poultice for tired..pocket books. **1907** *St. Nicholas* Sept. 1007/2 In her pretty pocket-book..she had found a crisp one-dollar bill. **1936** C. SANDBURG *People, Yes* 111 So dumb he spent his last dollar buying a pocketbook to put it in. **1960** A. SEXTON *To Bedlam & Part Way Back* 13 You guided past groups of robbers..clutching your pocketbook. **1976** *National Observer* (U.S.) 13 Mar. 18/4 Why should women whose pocketbooks are flatter have to jeopardize their lives..by patronizing sleazy, unqualified nonprofessionals.

pocketed, *ppl. a.* (In Dict. s.v. POCKET *v.*) (Earlier and later examples.)

1879 TROLLOPE *John Caldigate* II. xxi. 288 They who were less privileged had fed themselves with pocketed sandwiches. **1934** T. S. ELIOT *Rock* i. 10 With pocketed hands..We stand about in open places. **1974** C. RYAN *Bridge too Far* I. iii. 29 Though pocketed—the sea lay behind them to the north and west, and Canadians and British were pressing in from the south and east—they nevertheless controlled most of the southern bank of the estuary.

pocket-handkerchief. Add: **1.** (Earlier examples.)

1645 in *Essex* (Mass.) *Inst. Hist. Coll.* (1914) L. 326, 3 pocket handkerchiefs. **1680** ROCHESTER *Poems* 16 Where Critick-like, he sits and squints, Steals Pocket-Handkerchiefs, and hints. **1760** WASHINGTON *Diary* 15 Feb. (1925) I. 126 Pockethandkerchiefs servd the purposes of Table Cloths and Napkins.

2. *transf.* and *fig.* **a.** A very small area (*of* land, etc.).

1866 [see sense 3 below]. **1891** 'GANCONAGH' *John Sherman & Dhoya* 70 This pocket-handkerchief of a garden. **1949** T. RATTIGAN *Browning Version* 27 It's only a pocket handkerchief, I'm afraid, but it's very useful to Andrew. He often works out there. **1961** L. MUMFORD *City in History* xv. 465 The more respectable quarters.. with a soiled pocket-handkerchief of grass before their houses. **1973** *Daily Tel.* 8 Dec. 12/3 There is a pocket handkerchief of a dance floor.

b. A light sail.

1936 B. ADAMS *Ships & Women* xi. 239 Martin told me to 'Go get the pocket handkerchiefs off her'. So I called out the watch and hauled down the jib topsail. **1941** *Penguin New Writing* II. 17, I could ride out bad weather with two of the smallest pocket-handkerchiefs.

3. *attrib.* and *Comb.*

1866 GEO. ELIOT *Felix Holt* II. xx. 87 A mere pocket-handkerchief..Pod's End. **1935** N. L. MCCLUNG *Clearing in West* iv. 32 This kind of pocket handkerchief-farming makes people mean. **1953** WODEHOUSE *Performing Flea* 53 Bungalows..each with a little lawn in front and a pocket-handkerchief garden at the back. **1961** *Daily Tel.* 21 Oct. 6/2 The knowledge..helped the Russians to turn the screw..on economic and technical aid to this pocket-handkerchief State [*sc.* Albania]. **1973** N. GRAHAM *Murder in Dark Room* v. 33 A row of little old-fashioned houses with pocket handkerchief lawns.

pocketing, *vbl. sb.* (s.v. POCKET *v.*) Add: **a.** (Later examples in various senses of the vb.)

1885 [see POCKET *v.* 3 b]. **1960** E. ENNION *House on Shore* ix. 108 They would have the greatest difficulty in taking off again: pocketing in snow or sand might easily prevent it. **1963** J. OSBORNE *Dental Mechanics for Students* (ed. 5) ix. 165 The extent of periodontal pocketing will also be shown.

b. Material for pockets.

1933 J. E. LIBERTY *Practical Tailoring* v. 64 The pocketing should be about 15½ in. to 16 in. long. **1968** J. IRONSIDE *Fashion Alphabet* 97 *Pocketing*, strong cotton used for men's pockets.

pocket-money. (Further examples.)

1892 A. W. PINERO *Magistrate* III. i. 114 All my pocket money is in my overcoat at the Hôtel des Princes. **1926** T. E. LAWRENCE *Seven Pillars* (1935) xii. 89 They made pocket-money during their service, if they were ingenious. **1973** *Times* 13 Dec. 21/7 Baroness Marie-Anne..bought from her pocket money Van Gogh's L'arlésienne'. **1979** *Jrnl. R. Soc. Arts* CXXVII. 135/2 We already live in a pocket-money economy where essentials are provided and we work for the extras.

Hence **po·cket-mo:neyless** *a.*
1925 A. S. M. Hutchinson *One Increasing Purpose* I. xv. 90 The kind of children, well-bred, entirely pocket-moneyless, that retired Anglo-Indians often have.

pocket-picking, *ppl. a.* That picks pockets.
1868 Geo. Eliot in *Blackw. Mag.* Jan. 3/2 A poor pocket-picking scoundrel, who will steal your loose pence while you are listening round the platform.

po·cketwards, *adv.* [-wards.] In the direction of one's pocket.
1909 H. G. Wells *Tono-Bungay* III. i. 280 He made a motion pocketwards, that gave us an invincible persuasion that he had a sample upon him.

pockety, *a.* Add: Also **pocketty. 1.** Also *fig.*
1920 Galsworthy *In Chancery* II. x. 204 The atmosphere of his house was strange and pocketty when Jolyon came in and told them of the dog Balthasar's death. The news had a unifying effect.
2. Also, characterized by secluded hollows.
1929 J. Buchan *Courts of Morning* II. 257 Days with a bobbery pack of hounds in difficult pockety country. **1932** —— *Gap in Curtain* iv. 190 The river valley was pockety and swampy.

pock-mark (pǫ·kmāɹk), *sb.* Also **pock mark, pockmark.** [f. Pock *sb.* + Mark *sb.*[1]] A scar, mark, or 'pit' left by a pustule, esp. of small-pox. Also *fig.*
1673, 1851 [in Dict. s.v. Pock *sb.* 4]. **1952** G. Wilson *Julien Ware* i. 5 In the yard outside the bail a second cow..stumbled uncertainly..over the sun-dried pock-marks and ridges carved by her own hoofs..when the mud of winter lay there. **1954** G. Durrell *Bafut Beagles* ix. 156 A steady downpour..turned the red earth of the great courtyard into a shimmering sea of blood-red clay freckled with pockmarks of the falling rain. **1966** L. Cohen *Beautiful Losers* I. 23 Can I yearn after pimples and pock marks? **1976** M. Green *Children of Sun* iv. 135 Orwell, while..at Eton, had no powerful defences against the stimulus to dandyism, and..a few pock-marks remained all his life in testimony of his inoculation. **1979** R. Blythe *View in Winter* 85 The pock-marks of the shots are still to be seen today on the crinkle-crankle wall.
So **po·ck-marked** *a.* (see Pock *sb.* 4); also *fig.*; **po·ck-mark** *v. trans.*, to mark or disfigure with pock-marks; also *fig.*
1756, 1899 Pock-marked [in Dict. s.v. Pock *sb.* 4]. **1908** *Flag* (Union Jack Club) 39 The floors lower down were pock-marked with splashes of the liquid. **1928** *Daily Express* 17 Apr. 10/2 Petrol pumps that pockmark the English countryside. **1952** V. Canning *House of Seven Flies* xi. 155 The oars pock-marking the dark current with white eddies. **1957** L. Durrell *Justine* I. 68 The silence pock-marked by the sound of our horses' hooves. **1963** V. Nabokov *Gift* v. 306 A Georgian socialist with a pockmarked face. **1964** A. Wykes *Gambling* i. 10 He risked his own somewhat pockmarked career. **1973** *Country Life* 14 June 1751/1 Hollyhocks can be sprayed..to suppress rust-disease, whose orange pustules otherwise would soon pock-mark the foliage. **1977** H. Innes *Big Footprints* I. i. 9 Walls pock-marked with bullets. **1979** V. Canning *Satan Sampler* ix. 183 A fierce spring shower was pock-marking the surface of the lake.

‖ **poco** (pǫ·ko), *adv. Mus.* [It.] A little, rather: used in musical directions.
1724 *Explication of Foreign Words in Musick Bks.* 56 *Poco*, a little less, and is just contrary to the forgoing Word *Piu*. **1760** L. Sterne *Tristram Shandy* II. vi. 48 How does the *Poco piu* and the *Poco meno* of the *Italian* artists;—the insensible, more or less, determine the precise line of beauty. *a* **1817** [see *allegretto]. **1884** F. Niecks *Conc. Dict. Mus. Terms* 194 Poco (It.), a little—*Poco a poco*, little by little; *poco allegro*, somewhat quick. **1963** *Times* 16 Jan. 11/1 Perhaps his tone in *mezzo* or *poco forte* should have been more incisive. **1969** *Listener* 4 Sept. 320/2 In the melodic lines of the *Poco Adagio*..the pervading interval not only shapes the..themes but provides the movement of the harmonic bass lines.

Pocomania (pokŏmēⁱ·niă). Also with lower-case initial. [Origin unknown: prob. Hispanicized form of native name, with second element interpreted as Mania.] A Jamaican religious rite combining revivalism with ancestor-worship and spirit possession; the cult in which this rite is practised. Also *attrib.* Hence **pocoma·niac**, an adherent of this cult; **pocomani·acal** *a.*
[**1929** M. W. Beckwith *Black Roadways* 176 Revivalist and Obeah Man unite in the particular religious cult known as the Pukkumerian... The Pukkumerians hold their meetings near a grave-yard, and it is to the ghosts of their own membership that they appeal when spirits are summoned to a meeting... 'They jump and dance and sing and talk in a secret language because the spirits do not talk our language.'] **1938** Z. Hurston *Voodoo Gods* (1939) ii. 10, I went to the various 'tables' set in Pocomania, which boils down to a mixture of African obeah and Christianity enlivened by very beautiful singing. **1957** F. Henriques *Jamaica* x. 184 Of the specifically native cult groups Pocomania is the most powerful and active. *Ibid.* 185 Native churches..incorporated a degree of physical enthusiasm, evinced in dancing, violent singing, and clapping... It is from this type of activity that such cult groups as Pocomania arose. **1957** *Times Lit. Suppl.* 11 Oct. 612/4 The second part of the book is a study of contemporary Jamaican life... He deals with..the significance of cult-groups such as the Pocomaniacs. **1959** A. Salkey *Quality of Violence* ii. 36 He told them that the Jamaican celebration of Pocomania closely resembled Haitian Voodoo. *Ibid.* iv. 54 There were about twenty-five people gyrating and uttering Pocomaniacal prayers. **1971** J. Brunner *Honky in Woodpile* iv. 31 They broke up religious ceremonies, in particular *pocomania*, rites of possession using the *yoma-xi* drug. **1974** L. Watson *Romeo Error* I. iii. 80 In Zambia, traditional healers cast out evil spirits by holding a patient's head under a blanket and over a smoking brazier, where he is forced to hyperventilate by breathing very rapidly and shallowly... The pocomania ceremonies in Jamaica are built round 'tromping', which is a rhythm of foot-stamping and peculiar breathing sounds. **1976** Boot & Thomas *Jamaica* 82/2 When..the Pocomaniacs feel the spirit quickening in them, they jump and shout and testify till they get so drunk with righteous heaven-sent electricity they froth at the mouth.

pocosin, poquosin. Add: Also 7 **pocosen.** (Earlier examples.)
1634 in *Amer. Speech* (1940) XV. 296/2 From that runn along the side of the Pocoson or great Otter pond soe called. **1681** *Rec. Court of New Castle on Delaware* (1904) 504, 74 perches to a Corner marked spannish oake standing neare a pocosen.

poculum (pǫ·kiulɒm). *Rom. Antiq.* Pl. **pocula.** [L.] A cup or drinking-vessel.
1863 W. Chaffers *Marks & Monograms Pott. & Porc.* 15 Figure 16 is a poculum of the Castor Ware of white paste. **1884** A. Rich *Dict. Rom. & Gr. Antiq.* 514/1 *Poculum*, a general term for any description of vessel employed as a drinking-cup, and thus including all the special ones. **1965** *Amer. N. & Q.* Mar. 106/1 Visitors can admire a series of cases, bright vases..and decorated 'pocula'.

pod, *sb.*[2] Add: **1. b.** Colloq. phr. *in pod*: pregnant; also *fig.*
1890 Barrère & Leland *Dict. Slang* II. 141/2 *Pod, in*, in the family way. **1922** Joyce *Ulysses* 385 Costello..would sing a bawdy catch..about a wench that was put in pod of a jolly swashbuckler. **1935** L. Durrell *Spirit of Place* (1969) 33, I am in pod again and am pupping a novel. **1958** P. Mortimer *Daddy's gone a-Hunting* xi. 60, I married you because you were in pod. **1968** M. Bragg *Without City Wall* xxvii. 245 Your working-class lad is still a bit worried if he gets his girl in pod. **1972** 'R. Gordon' *Doctor on Brain* xxvi. 190 But why didn't Josephine just tell you she suspected she was in pod? **1976** J. McNeish *Glass Zoo* II. xvi. 179 It wasn't Leonard who got Marsh's sister in pod.
c. *slang.* Marijuana. Cf. *pot *sb.*[5]
1952 [see *jive *sb.* 4]. **1952** [see *joint *sb.* 14 c]. **1955** *Amer. Speech* XXX. 304, 'I got no eyes for turning on with pod' (I have absolutely no use for smoking marijuana). **1959** W. Burroughs *Naked Lunch* 8 A square wants to come on hip... Talks about 'pod', and smokes it now and then. **1979** *High Times* Mar. 19/1 Pod. Say it aloud. It's so much better than 'pot'. A marijuana mantra. *Ibid.*, Pod suggests seeds, buds, pollen, odors, all the multi-dimensional sensual life of the fine plant, while pot ought to remain a word for a thing you plant pod in.
5*. *Geol.* A body of ore or rock whose length greatly exceeds its other dimensions.
1942 T. P. Thayer in *Bull. U.S. Geol. Survey* No. 935. 23 Chromite deposits of the sack-form variety are notable for their variation in size and shape... The majority..might be termed lenses or pods, as their length greatly exceeds their width. **1969** Bennison & Wright *Geol. Hist. Brit. Isles* iii. 42 They occur as isolated pods distributed very widely through the Scourian granulites and their Inverian derivatives. **1977** *Bulletin* (Sydney) 22 Jan. 69/3 The Darling Range deposits grade only between 28 and 36 percent aluminium oxide. Also, they occur in pods, instead of more or less continuous orebodies.
5.** An elongated, streamlined compartment attached to an aircraft and containing an engine, fuel tanks, or the like; a detachable compartment in a spacecraft; also, any protruding or detachable casing on or in a craft or vehicle.
1950 J. V. Casamassa *Jet Aircraft Power Systems* 318 Jet pods are mounted beneath the wings. **1951** *Engineering* 6 July 8/2 One of the reasons for mounting jet engines on 'pods'..was because it was impossible to bury the engines in thin wings. **1955** Pohl & Kornbluth *Space Merchants* ii. 23 The cargo pod of the 'copter hit the concrete a yard from where we stood. **1963** *New Scientist* 9 May 320/3 Rides are being 'hitch-hiked' on Atlas rockets for pods of space instruments. **1965** *Guardian* 25 Aug. 9/2 They [*sc.* two astronauts] had ejected the radar evaluation pod, a 76 lb. satellite. **1967** *Jane's Surface Skimmer Systems 1967–68* 91/2 Power is transmitted through a mechanical right-angle drive transmission to a propeller at the aft end of a strut and pod assembly. **1973** *Sci. Amer.* Aug. 13/1 A rotating radome, or radar pod, is mounted on two struts above the rear section of the fuselage. **1976** *Good Motoring* May 21/2 A particularly quiet car, allowing most of the sound from speakers front and rear to be appreciated. Three pairs fitted at the rear offer a choice from large flush, small flush or pods. **1977** W. Marshall *Thin Air* xi. 148 The fuel from the main tanks ran out and was replaced a moment later by the Kerosene from the secondary pods.
6. (sense *1 c) *pod smoke, -smoker*; **pod corn,** a variety of maize, *Zea mays* var. *tunicata*, in which each kernel, as well as the whole ear, is enclosed in a husk; **pod maize** = prec.
1893 *Science* 17 Nov. 268/1 The kernel of the pod corn does not present structural differences markedly unlike that of the flint corn..but this type differs from all others in that each kernel has a husk of its own..; hence the name pod corn. **1923** Wallace & Bressmann *Corn & Corn Growing* xxvi. 147 Pod corn—each kernel enclosed by a husk as well as the entire ear. **1957** E. Hyams *Speaking Garden* viii. 106 There occurs as a kind of aberration among maize a plant called pod-corn. **1976** R. W. Jugenheimer *Corn* iii. 41 Podcorn is not being grown commercially. **1904** T. F. Hunt *Cereals in Amer.* x. 164 Pod maize is rarely grown. **1914** J. Burtt-Davy *Maize* iv. 103 In 'pod maize'..the glumes are large, completely enclosing the ovary and persisting around the ripe grain. **1979** *High Times* Mar. 19/1 Early jazz-musician pod smokers. *Ibid.*, The culture that made it possible for jazz musicians to turn sweet pod smoke into sweet soul sounds.

podargus (pǭdā·ɹgɒs). *Ornith.* [mod.L. (L. J. P. Vieillot in *Nouveau Dict. Hist. Nat.* (ed. 2, 1818) XXVII. 151), f. Gr. πόδαργος swift-footed.] A nocturnal, greyish-brown bird of the genus so called, belonging to the family Podargidæ and found in Australia, New Guinea, and the Solomon Islands; esp. the Australian tawny frogmouth, *Podargus strigoides*. Cf. Frog-mouth, frog's mouth 2.
1837 *Proc. Zool. Soc.* V. 67 The sclerotic ring of the great *Podargus* does not present the slightest appearance of distinct plates. **1901** A. J. Campbell *Nests & Eggs Austral. Birds* II. 539 Under the heading of the Tawny-shouldered Podargus..is included *P. cuvieri*, *P. gouldi*, and the ever doubtful *P. megacephalus*. **1933** *Bulletin* (Sydney) 19 Apr. 21/4 My choice for the quietest bush bird is the tawny frogmouth, or podargus. **1961** *Coast to Coast 1959–60* 66 'You know the Podargus.' 'It's a bird. The tawny-shouldered frogmouth.'

podded, *a.* Add: **3.** *Aeronaut.* Mounted in a pod or pods.
1959 *Times* 26 Feb. 10/6 It has not been British practice to build aircraft with podded engines. **1960** *New Scientist* 5 May 1115/3 Unlike the United States, which has remained faithful to podded engines slung beneath the wing, Russia has resorted to both podded and buried engines in placing the power units of the *Bounder*.

poddle (pǫ·d'l), dial. var. Paddle *v.*[1] 4.
1827 J. Clare *Shepherd's Calendar* 69 The ruddy child, nursed in the lap of care,..Beside its mother poddles o'er the land. **1842** C. Ridley *Let.* 5 Mar. in *Cecilia* (1958) vii. 89, I..spend a great deal of time in poddling about the garden. **1869** R. D. Blackmore *Lorna Doone* I. x. 109 Now I am uncommonly fond of ducks..and it is a fine sight to behold them walk, poddling one after other. **1976** Scollins & Titford *Ey up, mi Duck!* I. 59 *Poddlin'*, walking; implies a comical gait. Usually describes a small child, or a little old man, etc. As in: 'Eh wer *poddlin'* along wi'aht a care int wold!'

poddy, *a.* Add: **A.** *adj.* **2.** (See sense B. 1 b below.)
B. *sb.* (Austral.) **1. a.** An unbranded calf.
1893 K. Mackay *Out Back* (ed. 2) I. v. 75, I did occasionally put my brand by mistake on one of Massey's 'poddies'. **1907** G. B. Lancaster *Tracks we Tread* iii. 52 [The wild cattle] were a mixed haul: two-year-olds, poddies and pikers. **1950** [see *clean-skins* s.v. *clean- 2].
b. In full *poddy calf* (*foal*, etc.). A calf (less commonly a lamb or foal) fed by hand.
1898 *Bulletin* (Sydney) 8 Jan. (Red Page), Prof. Morris [in *Austral English*] defines 'Poddy' as 'a Vic. name for sand-mullet', but leaves out its meaning of motherless calf or foal (common in the bush). A poddy calf or a poddy foal is heard all over Australia. **1901** M. Franklin *My Brilliant Career* v. 24 It was my duty to 'rare the poddies'. **1908** *Bulletin* (Sydney) 30 Jan. 14, I saw a boy..driving back to pasture his flock of sixty or seventy newly shorn 'poddies', and it reminded me that the ewe is about the most indifferent mother in the bush. **1911** E. M. Clowes *On Wallaby* iii. 66 He drives off with the separated milk—due from the day before for his poddy-calves. **1927** B. Cronin *Red Dawson* xliii. 194 His whole outfit was five old cows and a coupler poddies. **1930** H. S. Palmer *Men are Human* xxv. 235 He's tame as a poddy calf. **1963** A. Lubbock *Austral. Roundabout* 5 The kitchen range..had saucepans of milk, and babies' bottles and teats, boiling on the top to feed the 'poddies', as hand-fed calves and lambs are called.
2. *attrib.* and *Comb.*, as *poddy swill*; *poddy-rearing* vbl. sb.; **poddy-dodger**, one who steals unbranded calves; a cattle rustler; also *poddy-dodging* vbl. sb.
1934 *Bulletin* (Sydney) 1 Aug. 46/3 Nine poddy-dodgers out of ten gets caught the same way. **1953** A. Moorehead *Rum Jungle* ii. 30 The cattle rustlers—known as 'poddy dodgers'—followed close behind. **1970** *Sunday Mail Mag.* (Brisbane) 30 Aug. 3/5 His practice, as a 'poddy-dodger', was to steal branded cows and cleanskin calves from neighbours, then remove the calves from their mothers before they were ready. **1945** T. Ronan *Strangers on Ophir* 9 He'll be a doctor or a lawyer or a banker with no need to go poddy-dodging for a living like his old jail-bird of a Dad. **1950** 'N. Shute' *Town like Alice* ix. 263 They'll come on to your station and round up the poddys and drive them off on to their own land, and then there's nothing to say they're yours. That's poddy-dodging. **1957** R. S. Porteous *Brigalow* 61 Mick did a bit of poddy-dodging when things were slack... He might lift a few head of cleanskins now and then. **1901** M. Franklin *My Brilliant Career* iii. 17 They do all the milkin', and pig-feedin', and poddy-rarin'. **1941** *Coast to Coast* 108 Tug Treloar carrying buckets of poddy swill.

poddy (pǫ·di), *v. Austral. colloq.* [f. *poddy *sb.*] *trans.* To feed (a young animal) by hand.
1896 H. Lawson *While Billy Boils* (1897) 61 Then he 'poddies'—hand-feeds—the calves which have been weaned too early. **1901** M. Franklin *My Brilliant Career* iv. 20 He procured fifty milch-cows, the calves o which had to be 'poddied'. **1908** *Bulletin* (Sydney) 30

Jan. 14 The squatter knows that a deserted lamb will die, also he has no time to 'poddy' it. **1931** V. Palmer *Separate Lives* 176 When her [*sc.* the filly's] mother died, that old drover said I could have her... And I did rear her, bought condensed milk to poddy her for months.

‖ **podere** (podę̄·re). Pl. poderi (-*i*). [It.] A farm or estate.

1884 S. & J. Horner *Walks in Florence & its Environs* II. xxi. 299 Villas and their surrounding vineyards, olive gardens, and farms (*Poderi*) are enclosed within these walls. **1891** L. Scott *Vincigliata & Maiano* 13 The Podere of the Torre..with its courts, trees, house, huts and vineyards. *Ibid.* 15 Niccolò, as heir to his father, had a larger claim..on several lots, especially the Castle of Vincigliata and its *poderi*. **1904** H. James *Golden Bowl* I. iii. 57 The dear contadini of the *podere*, the little girls and the other peasants of the next podere. **1926** D. H. Lawrence *Sun* v. 18 Yet she missed him when he did not come to work on the podere. **1961** W. Vaughan-Thomas *Anzio* vii. 137 The peasant farmers had remained in the *poderi* of the countryside. **1970** I. Origo *Images & Shadows* v. 116 The steep terraces of the *podere*, partly cultivated with plots of wheat.

podge, *sb.* Add: Freq. a plump child. (Later examples.) Also, excess weight, fat.

1967 M. Summerton *Memory of Darkness* i. 17 She used to be a horrid little podge, always whining. **1967** A. Wilson *No Laughing Matter* I. 16 Don't tease the poor Podge. Time enough when she loses all that puppy fat. **1976** *Leicester Chron.* 26 Nov., The average man is putting on too much weight, and..needs clothes designed to help him hide the podge.

podger[2] (pǫ·dʒəɹ). [f. Podge *sb.* + -er[1].] Any of various tools having the form of a short bar (see quots.).

1888 J. G. Horner *Dict. Terms Mech. Engin.* 377 *Tommy*, a pointed round iron bar or lever used for insertion in the holes drilled in the circular back nuts of lathes and other machines, for the purpose of tightening them up. Also a metal rod kept for insertion in the eyes of the tightening screws of hand-rest sockets, for tightening the T rest. Sometimes called a podger. **1893** —— *Princ. of Fitting* ii. 22 Fig. 18 shows a podger, employed for two purposes. The tapered end A, of round section, is used for pulling drilled or punched holes into line, so that their bolts or rivets can be inserted. The flattened end B is used like the end of a crowbar for lifting up and slipping along a casting or forging into position, or for prising open..plates that are in close contact. **1894** W. J. Lineham *Textbk. Mech. Engin.* vii. 286 Before riveting a seam, the plates, if punched or drilled separately, are brought into alignment by the podger and bolted. **1971** B. Scharf *Engin. & its Language* ix. 66 A special type of single ended spanner is the podger or prong-ended spanner. This has a long, tapering handle which can be used..to align holes which do not entirely coincide (e.g. rivet holes in plates).

podiatry (pǒdəi·ătri). orig. and chiefly *U.S.* [f. Gr. ποδ-, πούς foot + ἰατρεία healing: see -y[3].] The diagnosis and treatment of disorders of the foot; chiropody.

1914 F. von Oefele in M. J. Lewi *Text Bk. Chiropody* i. 3 The practice of foot lesions may hereafter be styled 'Helotomy' or, 'Heliatry', or more generally 'Podiatry'. **1947** P. Lewin *Foot & Ankle* (ed. 3) xxxii. 717 Podiatry is the science of treatment of certain disorders of the feet. **1958** *Technology* Feb. 425/4 The National Association of Chiropodists has announced that it has changed its title to The American Podiatry Association and that its members will henceforth be known by the 'more dignified' style of podiatrists. **1968** F. Weinstein *Princ. & Pract. Podiatry* i. 6/1 More and more hospitals [in the U.S.A.] are working toward the establishment of a regular department or division of podiatry. **1979** *Arizona Daily Star* 22 July B1/6 Podiatry problems can trigger one of many vicious circles affecting the health of the elderly.

So **podia·tric** *a.*; **podi·atrist**, one who practises podiatry; a chiropodist.

1914 F. von Oefele in M. J. Lewi *Text Bk. Chiropody* i. 50 We should prevent the possibility of such a ridiculous misunderstanding by substituting the word 'podiatrist' (physician of the foot) for the unscientific term 'chiropodist'. **1922** *Jrnl. Nat. Assoc. Chiropodists* XII. 35 (Advt.), Bachelet podiatric triplex generator. **1929** E. W. Springs *Above Bright Blue Sky* 97 I've got to hobble along and see my podiatrist. **1950** K. Newton *Geriatric Nursing* xv. 287 The aged patient will avoid serious difficulties with corns and calluses by having his feet cared for regularly by a podiatrist. **1968** T. R. Amberry in F. Weinstein *Princ. & Pract. Podiatry* viii. 138 All too often these factors are either ignored or overlooked by some surgeons, both medical and podiatric. **1974** *Telegraph* (Brisbane) 21 Mar. 16/7 The Australian Chiropody Council wants chiropodists to be called podiatrists. **1976** *Jrnl. Amer. Podiatry Assoc.* LXVI. 15 A wide variety of medications may be necessary during the hospitalization of podiatric surgical patients. **1978** *Detroit Free Press* 16 Apr. 1c/5 Podiatrists and athletes debate endlessly about proper footwear.

podium. Delete ‖ and add: Also with pl. **podiums. 1. b.** (Earlier example.)

1743 W. Stukeley *Abury* vii. 28 This was as the *podium* of an amphitheater, for the lower tire of spectators.

d. A raised platform or dais at the front of a hall or stage; *spec.* that occupied by the conductor of an orchestra.

1947 A. Einstein *Music in Romantic Era* xv. 215 The longer Chopin continued in his career, the more he avoided the concert podium and the expectant masses. **1955** R. Crane *Hero's Walk* v. 94 There was no applause when Dr. Werner took his place at the podium. **1972** *N.Y. Times* 3 Nov. 30/2 Mr. Steinberg stands there, all but motionless,..and manages to get more from an orchestra than a squadron of podium monkeys jumping up and down. **1973** W. H. Hallahan *Ross Forgery* (1977) iv. 65 The auctioneer stepped off the podium. **1977** *Kuwait Times* 23 Nov. 5/3, I address the following appeal from this podium to the people of Israel. **1978** *Gramophone* Oct. 658/3 He has a genre of courage and determination that enabled him to fight back after a particularly bad car accident and reappear on the podium long before the time appointed by his doctor.

e. A projecting lower structure around the base of a tower block.

1962 *Times* 19 Mar. 13/7 The podium-and-tower pattern is not only a product of daylighting codes. **1970** *Daily Tel.* 21 May 7 At the base of the 220 ft-high tower will be a podium of two and three-storey buildings.

podo (pōᵘ·do). [f. generic name *Podo*(*carpus* (see *podocarp 2).] An evergreen tree belonging to one of several East African species of the genus *Podocarpus*, or the softwood timber obtained from it. Also *attrib.*

1922 W. Schlich *Man. Forestry* (ed. 4) I. 289 Podo, a medium-sized tree, has a wide distribution. **1940** W. H. Eggeling *Indigenous Trees of Uganda Protectorate* 179 Recently the tendency in Uganda has been to regard musizi..as a better timber than Podo. **1947** *E. African Ann. 1946–7* 41/1 The north-west point of the Game Reserve..is an impressive mountain with cedar, olive and podo on its summit. **1957** *Handbk. of Softwoods* (Forest Prod. Res. Lab.) 48 Podo is widely used for joinery and interior fittings. **1961** *New Scientist* 24 Aug. 451/3 The cedar, olive and podo forest that covers most of the Mau is being systematically destroyed.

podocarp (pōᵘ·dokāɹp). *Bot.* [f. Podo- + Gr. καρπ-ός fruit.] **1.** (In Dict. s.v. Podo-.)

2. [f. mod.L. *Podocarpus* (C. L. L'Héritier de Brutelle in C. H. Persoon *Synopsis Plantarum* (1807) II. 580).] A coniferous tree or shrub belonging to the genus *Podocarpus* or the family Podocarpaceæ, including several valuable timber trees native to parts of the Southern Hemisphere. So **podocarpa·ceous, -ca·rpous** *adjs.*, belonging to the family Podocarpaceæ. Cf. *podo.

1858 G. Gordon *Pinetum* 268 (*heading*) *Eupodocarpus*, Endlicher, or the true podocarps. **1882** Podocarpous [in Dict. s.v. Podo-]. **1918** A. D. Webster *Coniferous Trees* i. 158 The Alpine Podocarp... This distinct and very interesting Tasmanian conifer may be seen in excellent condition in several gardens in the neighbourhood of London. **1923** A. Rehder in L. H. Bailey *Cultivated Evergreens* II. v. 179 (*heading*) Longleaf Podocarp. **1939** M. Hornibrook *Dwarf & Slow-Growing Conifers* (ed. 2) 216 Of the many podocarps which inhabit Australia and South America, not many of them are fully hardy in north European climates. **1959** A. H. McLintock *Descr. Atlas N.Z.* p. xv, The forest is of silver and mountain beech, with traces of red beech and podocarps at low altitude. **1975** *Nature* 27 Nov. 305/2 Among conifers, the mixture of podocarpaceous and araucarian elements is typical of the Southern Hemisphere early Tertiary. **1977** *N.Z. Listener* 15 Jan. 21/2 Cut down the last of those giant podocarps and you cut down about 800 years of growth. **1978** *Sci. Amer.* July 102/3 At the lower elevations and latitudes the forests were a mixture of broadleaf trees and podocarp conifers, a group of trees peculiar to the southwest Pacific and Chile.

Podolian (pǒdōᵘ·liăn), *a.* [f. *Podolia* (see below) + -an.] Of or pertaining to Podolia, a region in south-west Ukraine (see quot. 1974).

c **1850** *Bee Keeper* 18 (*heading*) The construction of the Podolian hive. **1881** *Encycl. Brit.* XIII. 451/2 The breed of cattle most widely distributed throughout Italy is that known as the Podolian. **1911** *Ibid.* XXI. 875/1 The Dniester is an important channel for trade, corn, spirits and timber being exported from Podolian river ports. **1920** *Glasgow Herald* 7/2 Another great Bolshevik offensive in the Southern Polish and Podolian sector has failed absolutely. **1936** C. Roth *Short Hist. Jewish People* xxvi. 332 The revivalist movement in Poland permeated all sections of society, until it touched a simple Podolian lime-digger, Israel ben Eliezer (1700–1760). **1974** *Encycl. Brit. Micropædia* VIII. 60/2 *Podolia*..was under Polish rule until 1772, when the part west of the Zbruch River became Austrian; the rest became the Podolian *guberniya* (province) in Russia in 1793. After World War I the region continued to be divided at the Zbruch, between Poland and the U.S.S.R.; after World War II, it was entirely incorporated into the U.S.S.R.

Podsnap (pǫ·dsnæp). The name of a character in Dickens's 'Our Mutual Friend' (1864–5) used allusively for a person embodying insular complacency and self-satisfaction and refusal to face up to unpleasant facts. So **Podsna·ppery, Podsna·p(p)ian** *a.*

1864 Dickens *Mut. Fr.* (1865) I. I. xi. 97 Mr. Podsnap ..stood very high in Mr. Podsnap's opinion... Mr. Podsnap settled that whatever he put behind him he put out of existence... Mr. Podsnap's world was not a very large world..he considered other countries..a mistake... Mr. Podsnap was sensible of its being required of him to take Providence under his protection...What Providence meant was invariably what Mr. Podsnap meant.] *Ibid.* 98 These may be said to have been the articles of a faith and school which the present chapter takes the liberty of calling after its representative man, Podsnappery. [*Ibid.*, A certain institution in Mr. Podsnap's mind which he called 'the young person'..was an inconvenient and exacting institution... The question about everything was, would it bring a blush into the cheek of the young person.] **1880** *Daily Tel.* 1 Dec. 5/2 It is all very well to sneer at 'Chauvinism' and 'Podsnappery' but the claim of British children to supremacy among their kind must be resolutely upheld. **1901** *Daily News* 16 Feb. 3/3 The Podsnappian findings of a Commission which..reported ..that a certain hospital had been infested with bugs, but not in such a degree as to incommode the patients. **1902** *Westm. Gaz.* 21 Nov. 9/3 Podsnap General, Podsnap Financier, Podsnap Statesman we know, but it is my joy to have perceived our old friend in his last incarnation... Podsnap then, Podsnap in crimson tie of The Schools, 'The Red Badge of Culture', but Podsnap still, pervades the Press. **1905** G. K. Chesterton *Heretics* 29 None.. will accuse the author of the 'Inferno' of..a Podsnapian optimism. **1929** A. Huxley *Do what you Will* 31 Those detestable Puritans to whom we owe..Grundyism and Podsnappery. **1944** A. Thirkell *Headmistress* vii. 149 *As You Like It* might be a suitable play..for the Young Person in a Podsnappian sense. **1960** *Times* 12 July 13/4 There are too many Podsnaps of officialdom who treat athletes and *aficionados* alike as noisy nuisances. **1972** G. S. Fraser in Cox & Dyson *20th-Cent. Mind* II. xi. 401 The solid Podsnappian complacencies and unbudgingesses of the male. **1977** P. N. Furbank *E. M. Forster* viii. 138 They had a jokey and facetious relationship, based on the fiction of Thompson's extreme Podsnappery and Philistinism.

podsol, var. *podzol.

‖ **podu** (po·dū). [Telugu.] = *kumri.

[**1855** H. H. Wilson *Gloss. Indian Terms* 420 *Podu*, Tel., land or lands recently cleared from thickets and prepared for cultivation.] **1938** [see *kumri]. **1954** O. H. K. Spate *India & Pakistan* viii. 203 Shifting agriculture —the *jhum* of Assam, the *kumri* or *podu* of the Peninsula— conforms to the standard pattern so widespread in tropical regions.

Podunk (pōᵘ·dʊŋk). [Algonquian place-name.] **1.** Also 7 **Potunck.** A small tribe of Indians formerly inhabiting an area around the Podunk river in Hartford County, Connecticut (chiefly *pl.* or *collect.*) Also *attrib.* or as *adj.*

1656 in *Public Records of Colony of Connecticut* (1850) I. 305 The Court wearied wth their speeches pressed the Potunck Indians to deliver up the murtherer. **1761** E. Stiles *Extracts from Itineraries* (1916) 136 Podunk Tribe at the dividing Line between Windsor & Hartford East side; between 2 & 300 Men in Philips War; went off & never returned. **1842** W. L. Stone *Uncas & Miantonomoh* 31 The Podunks resided upon the lands now comprised in the town of East Hartford. **1859** *N.Y. Weekly Tribune* 8 Oct. 3/1 The Numkatunks, Quinnipiacs, Podunks, and Quinnebogs, were present from New-Haven and vicinity. **1910** F. W. Hodge et al. *Handbk. Amer. Indians* II. 271/1 Podunk. A band or small tribe on Podunk r., in Hartford co., Conn., closely related to the Poquonnoc. **1935** *Colony of Connecticut* (Connecticut Board of Educ.) (Senate Doc. 53, 74th Congr., 1st Sess.) 1 A few years previously in 1631 the chief of one of the Indian tribes in the Connecticut Valley, the Podunks, had journeyed to the Massachusetts and Plymouth Colonies to invite them to see the fertile Connecticut Valley. **1937** *Bull. Archaeol. Soc. Connecticut* Apr. 2 The Podunk tribe had two permanent villages during early colonial times... The largest Podunk village was located in South Windsor.

2. *U.S. colloq.* Name for a fictive insignificant, out-of-the-way town; a typical small town.

1846 *Daily National Pilot* (Buffalo, N.Y.) 13 Jan. 3a, Messrs. Editors: I hear you ask, 'Where in the world is Podunk?' It is in the world, sir; and more than that, is a little world of itself. It stands 'high up the big Pigeon', a bright and shining light amid the surrounding darkness. I look back, sir, with pride upon the day when I located in the then unincorporated burgh of Podunk. *Ibid.* 20 Jan. 2a, The distinguished festival of Podunk is the *candy bee*. *Ibid.* 6 Mar. 2b, Podunk is a huge town, not distinguished exactly as the geographies have it, for its 'fertile soil, salubrious and healthy climate', but for some of the characters that here do congregate. **1865** O. W. Norton *Army Lett.* (1903) 277, I presume that just about this time of day you are sitting in one of the slips in that 'Podunk' or 'Chachunk' (what do you call it?) 'meetin' house'. **1901** *Harper's Weekly* 7 Sept. 903/2 He might just as well have been John Smith, of Podunk Centre. **1933** *Review of Reviews* Feb. 33 It [*sc.* the 18th amendment] required one rule for Podunk, Kansas, and one for New York City. **1947** [see *Main Streeter, Main-streeter]. **1960** *Times Lit. Suppl.* 15 Jan. 27/3 A diploma from Harvard is much more marketable than a diploma from Podunk College. **1976** *National Observer* (U.S.) 30 Oct. 15/5 It won't be just the Podunk liberal-arts colleges that have to hustle. Some of the big state schools, and some well-known large universities, will be out there too—to find new publics.

podzol (pǫ·dzǫl). *Soil Sci.* Also **podsol,** and formerly also with capital initial. [a. Russ. *podzól*, f. *pod-* under- + *zolá* ash.] An acidic, generally infertile soil which is characterized by a well-marked white or grey ash-like subsurface layer from which minerals have been leached into a lower dark-coloured layer, and which occurs esp. under coniferous trees or heath vegetation in moist, usu. temperate climates (typically in parts of N. Russia). Orig. applied only to the ash-like layer itself.

[**1906** E. W. Hilgard *Soils* x. 186 Woodlands of northern countries bearing beech and oak are especially apt to be benefited by the action of lime on the 'raw', acid humous soil and underlying hardpan, which is commonly underlaid by a leaden-blue sandy subsoil ('Bleisand' of the Germans, 'Podzol' of the Russians) colored brown by earth humates.] **1908** *Jrnl. Agric. Sci.* III. 83 The most characteristic feature of the Podzol..is the dissolution and removal of soluble parts of silicates..and an increase in the percentage of insoluble silica. **1912** H. B. Woodward *Geol. Soils & Substrata* vii. 82 Of mixed soils, the *Podzol* of Russia, as described by Professor Glinka, consists of sands, loams, and clays, locally calcareous, but generally poor in mineral plant food. **1927** C. F. Marbut tr. *Glinka's Great Soil Groups of World* 71 All these profiles of Russian soils belong to the Podsols. This term is used to designate soils which have a pronounced and well developed whitish A_2 horizon. If this horizon is not well developed, and the corresponding horizon contains whitish specks and stringers the soil is said to be Podsolic. **1928** *Ecology* IX. 177 Originally, the term podsol applied more specifically to the gray-colored zone, though now it is commonly used to describe the entire profile. **1934** *Forestry* VIII. 25 Podzol soils owe their name to the presence of an ashy-grey layer which underlies the surface layer of dead vegetation and plant roots. **1936** *Nature* 17 Oct. 692/2 This utilization of the physical character and colour of the soil..is a novelty to glacialists from the leached podsol areas of the north-west. **1946** F. E. Zeuner *Dating Past* v. 124 Brownearth and podsol soils are characteristic of the humid-temperate countries. **1972** J. G. Cruickshank *Soil Geogr.* ii. 63 A coarse sandy deposit in Sherwood Forest..also showed signs of podsol features only 25–30 years after replanting with pine. **1973** *Sci. Amer.* Dec. 64/2 The tropical podzols are useless even for shifting agriculture; the Dayak peoples of Borneo call them *kerangas*: 'land on which one cannot grow rice'.

Hence **podzo·lic** (or **-ds-**) *a.*, of the nature of or resembling a podzol in possessing a layer from which some leaching of bases has occurred.

1927 C. F. Marbut tr. *Glinka's Great Soil Groups of World* 44 We can see again the change from Tschernosem to gray forest soils and the latter into Podsolic soils in the vicinity of Borshom. **1932** G. W. Robinson *Soils* xvi. 315 The soils of Great Britain belong mainly to the podsolic group. **1952** P. W. Richards *Tropical Rain Forest* ix. 209 If the American view is accepted, a lateritic soil can also be podzolic. **1973** P. A. Colinvaux *Introd. Ecol.* iii. 46 Some heath lands of northern Europe, with acid litter and leached soils, reveal podzolic profiles.

podzolize (pǫ·dzǒləiz), *v. Soil Sci.* Also **-sol-**. [f. prec. + -ize.] *trans.* and *intr.* To render or become podzolic. Chiefly as **po·dzolized** *ppl. a.*, **po·dzolizing** *vbl. sb.*

1923 *Soil Sci.* XVI. 97 It is the presence of the acid layer in a definite position in the profile and the strongly marked gray or podsolized horizon which chiefly distinguishes the typical northern from the typical southern profile. **1927** C. F. Marbut tr. *Glinka's Great Soil Groups of World* 100 Traces of the Podsolizing processes are shown in shallow depressions... The Podsolizing and leaching has reached a more advanced stage of the development. **1932** *Technical Communications Imperial Bureau Soil Sci.* No. 24. 11 Under conditions of poor drainage..resilication may give rise to a kaolinite red earth which..may be podsolised into a quartzose, bleached surface soil. **1938** *Geogr. Jrnl.* XCI. 163 The soils of the lower Trent Vale are podsolized sands. **1957** *Soil Sci.* LXXXIII. 215 The parent materials of Swartswood sand loam podzolize with comparative ease. **1976** *Sci. Amer.* Apr. 56/3 The dunes are partly podzolized, and they sustain pines, dwarfed redwoods and shrubs. **1976** *Nature* 15 Apr. 602/2 It would seem to result from percolating solutions removing surface coverings of ferric oxides from quartz sand grains and depositing them again within a short distance, that is, in a typical podzolising process.

Hence **po:dzoliza·tion**, the leaching of bases out of the upper parts of a soil and their deposition lower down; the formation of a podzolic soil.

1923 *Soil Sci.* XVI. 103 It is evident..that podsolization may take place in acid or alkaline [s]oils. **1934** *Discovery* July 200/2 The leaching and subsequent deposition of iron (and aluminium) oxides is a characteristic of all podsols, and is..generally referred to as 'podsolization'. **1952** P. W. Richards *Tropical Rain Forest* ix. 209 The removal of sesquioxides of iron and aluminium with the accumulation of silica is called podzolization. **1970** E. M. Bridges *World Soils* iii. 21/1 The process of podzolization is prevalent in the soils of the cool humid parts of the world and produces soils of the podzolic group and the podzols in particular.

pœcilitic, *a.* Add: † **2.** *Petrogr.* = *poikilitic *a.* 2. *Obs.*

1887 G. H. Williams in *Amer. Jrnl. Sci.* CXXXIII. 139 Here..we have another example of the structure which the writer has distinguished as pœcilitic* in describing the hornblende of the Cortlandt peridotites. [*Note*] *The word is here changed to the accepted form. **1909** F. P. Mennell *Introd. Petrol.* xii. 87 (*caption*) Poecilitic structure, in picrite, Belingwe, Rhodesia. (Olivine enclosed in enstatite).

poee-poee, var. *poipoi.

Poeesque (pōᵘe·sk), *a.* Also **Poesque, Poe-esque.** [f. the name of Edgar Allan *Poe* (1809–49), American author, + -esque.] Of, pertaining to, or resembling E. A. Poe or his work. Also as quasi-*sb.*

1919 *Times Lit. Suppl.* 19 June 335/1 Mr. Harvey's 'The Beast with Five Fingers' is tinged with the Poesque. **1934** R. Campbell *Broken Record* 38 To a stranger they [*sc.* crows] give the English countryside a terrible and sinister, Poeesque atmosphere. **1959** R. Fuller *Ruined Boys* ii. xi. 154 He was at a loss to imagine precisely what would indicate any impending disaster, short of some obvious and Poesque symptom like a great fissure in the school walls. **1977** *Times Lit. Suppl.* 20 May 611/3 [Edmund] Wilson's future biographers may want to make something of the Poe-esque inclination.

Similarly **Poeana** (pōuā·nă), objects associated with E. A. Poe; publications by or about Poe; **Poe·ish** *a.*; **Poe·ishly** *adv.*; **Poe·ist,** a student or devotee of Poe's works; **Poe·-like** *a.*

1908 *Westm. Gaz.* 12 Feb. 4/2 There appeared in Paris, in 1836, Gautier's Poe-like story 'La Morte Amoureuse'. **1925** H. Acton in *Oxf. Poetry* 7 And oh, the Poe-like harmonies of bells! **1929** Wyndham Lewis *Let.* 20 Feb. (1963) 187 My reply to this Poeist..is that Poe would not have found my writing 'difficult'. **1955** *N. & Q.* May 223/1 All Poeana has been enthusiastically collected for seventy years. **1976** *National Observer* (U.S.) 9 Oct. 24/3, I like the plantation owner brooding Poeishly over the corpse of his too-well-beloved sister. **1977** *Amer. N. & Q.* XV. 70/1 While several contemporary reviewers saw 'Poeish' similarities in Melville's writings, modern critics..have found little reason to suspect that Melville was influenced by Poe.

‖ **poêlée** (pwęle). Also *erron.* **poêle.** [Fr., a panful; cf. *poêler* to cook in a pan.] A broth or stock (see quots.).

1830 R. Dolby *Cook's Dict.* 414 *Poelee.* Take two pounds of veal, two pounds of bacon, two large carrots and three onions; cut all these into dice and put them into a stewpan with a pound of butter, the juice of three or four lemons, four cloves, two bay-leaves, bruised, a little thyme, salt, and pepper. **1845** E. Acton *Mod. Cookery* vii. 185 *Poêlée.* Cut into large dice..lean veal..fat bacon..carrots..onions;..add..butter..; pour..boiling broth..; strain the *poêlée* through a fine sieve... Use instead of water for boiling. **1861** Mrs. Beeton *Bk. Househ. Managem.* 46 *Poêlée,* stock used instead of water for boiling turkeys, sweetbreads, fowls, and vegetables, to render them less insipid. **1877** E. S. Dallas *Kettner's Bk. of Table* 182 The following receipt is nearly identical with what the French cooks call Poële... Take two carrots..onions, two cloves..sweet-herbs; mince all finely with half a pound of beef fat, and melt it. **1889** J. Whitehead *Steward's Handbk.* iv. 405/1 Poêle is white or colorless broth of bacon and ham with vegetables used to boil chickens, sweetbreads, etc., in instead of water.

poem. Add: **3.** *poem-book* (later examples).

1887 W. B. Yeats *Let.* 25 June in *Lett. to K. Tynan* (1953) 31 Sparling knows and much admires your 'Flight of the Wild Geese', from which I conclude it will figure in his poem-book. **1949** E. E. Cummings *Let.* 23 Aug. (1969) 193 Poems are nonsellable enough..without calling the poembook by some foreign word.

poemscape (pōᵘ·ėmskēip). [f. Poem + Scape *sb.*³] The imaginary world envisaged in a poem.

1958 K. Patchen (*title*) Poemscapes. **1960** H. Kenner *Invisible Poet* v. 225 The Vrotting field-mouse is a figure in a poemscape, not like the rat in *The Hollow Men* the synecdoche of some omnipresent world.

‖ **pœna** (pī·nă). Also **pena.** In phrases freq. in L. inflected forms. [a. L. *pœna* penalty.] **a.** Chiefly *Law* and *Theology.* A punishment.

1632 in *Decisions Court of Session* (1805) XXIV. 10036 They..were content to pay the L. 100 *loco penae.* **1678** G. Mackenzie *Laws & Customs Scotl.* ii. xxx. 560 Skeen..observes, that *pœna extraordinaria,* may be sometimes extended to death. **1757** in *Decisions Court of Session* (1805) XXIV. 10049 Expenses of plea..are in no case due or exigible, unless the Court finds that a party has been litigious, and specially subjects him to the costs of his opponent, *in pœnam* of his offence. **1859** T. C. Sandars *Inst. Justinian* (ed. 2) 492 *Pœna* is a punishment imposed by some general law, affecting possibly the *caput* and *existimatio* of the person punished. **1863** *Scottish Jurist* XXXV. 588/2 It is plain that here *pœna*—penalty—is used to mean a sum stipulated to be paid in the event of breach of contract. **1916** Joyce *Portrait of Artist* (1969) 128 This is the greatest torment which the created soul is capable of bearing, *pœna damni,* the pain of loss. **1953** F. de Zulueta *Inst. Gaius* II. iii. 207 In these cases of negative interest there is no question of dividing the action or the *poena* recovered. **1959** Jowitt *Dict. Eng. Law* II. 1357/1 *Pœna,* a penalty, the punishment of an offence; generally inflicted for delicts.

b. *School slang.* = Imposition 5 c.

1842 *Eton Bureau* 251 Then the luxury, when told to write out and translate my lesson, to know that beneath the ill-formed letters that disfigured my 'pœna', might safely lurk an intimation to posterity that the reader—charitably supposed to be the inflictor of the punishment—'was a fool'. **1865** *Etoniana* xiv. 201 To such a boy, of course, the usual '*pœna*' of lines from a Greek or Latin poet to learn by heart could be no kind of punishment at all. **1870** 'Etonian' *Recoll. Eton* I. viii. 87 He got a pœna for coming in late for morning school one day. **1877** G. N. Bankes *Day of My Life* xiii. 136 It's wretched bad practice for handwriting, this *pœna* writing. **1911** R. Nevill *Floreat Etona* x. 301 Their usual practice being either to set some tremendous 'poena', which they afterwards revoked, or settle upon the wrong boy. **1941** L. A. G. Strong *Bay* 70 If you were in disgrace he..helped you with your poena and shooed you out of the empty classroom.

poet. Add: **1. c.** *poet's poet,* a poet whose poetry is generally considered to appeal chiefly to other poets.

1844 L. Hunt *Imagination & Fancy* 75 Spenser..has always been felt by his countrymen to be what Charles Lamb called him, the 'Poet's Poet'. He has had more idolatry and imitation from his brethren than all the rest put together. *Ibid.* 107 Spenser emulated the Raphaels and Titians in a profusion of pictures... They give the Poet's Poet a claim to a new title,—that of Poet of the Painters. **1867** O. W. Holmes *Guardian Angel* I. xviii. 280 Master Gridley lifted his eyebrows very slightly, remembering that some had called Spenser the poet's poet. **1930** *Times Lit. Suppl.* 27 Feb. 149/2 Assuredly, in Lamb's day Spenser was the poet's poet. **1932** J. Buchan *Sir W. Scott* iv. 79 Dryden was not a poet's poet, any more than his editor. **1958** *Reporter* 10 July 38/2 (*heading*) A poet's poet looks at his art.

e. *poet-in-residence,* a poet working in or associated with a university or college or a community (see *residence *sb.*¹ 2 b).

1972 *Guardian* 8 Feb. 24/5 W. H. Auden..returns to Christ Church, Oxford... Mr Auden..will be what the Americans like to call 'poet in residence'. **1973** *Black World* Jan. 28/2 Buford..is now poet-in-residence at Cleveland State University. **1977** *Canad. N. & Q.* Dec. 15/1 In January 1921 Robert Frost..was invited to visit Queen's and become the first poet-in-residence to occupy such an office in any Canadian University.

2. a. *poet-bishop, -composer, -critic, -king, -musician* (examples), *-novelist* (examples), *-painter* (examples), *-prophet, -singer* (later example), *-warrior* (example).

1909 *Westm. Gaz.* 2 June 5/1 The oldest existing wine club, the 'Phœnix', of which the poet-bishop, Heber, was once a luminary. **1947** A. Einstein *Music in Romantic Era* xvi. 256 Lortzing..in more modest proportions was comparable to Wagner as a poet-composer. **1968** *Jrnl. Mus. Acad. Madras* XXXIX. 102 The Tirupati poet-composer. **1977** *Early Music* Oct. 469/2 Machaut..maintained a dual role: one of..poet-composer, detached from the story. **1956** *Essays in Criticism* VI. 212 Poet-critics as dissimilar as Arthur Symons and Mr. Eliot. **1964** *English Studies* XLV. 290 Of course a poet-critic may be allowed to speak in images. **1859** W. Bagehot *Coll. Works* (1965) II. 114 The poet-king of Israel..David. **1903** A. W. Patterson *Schumann* 140 May not the shadow of the gloom that already brooded over him..already have been overclouding the mental vision of the poet-musician? **1947** A. Einstein *Music in Romantic Era* iii. 28 Wagner, all his life, thought of himself not merely as a poet-musician. **1957** N. Frye *Sound & Poetry* i. 5 The poet-musician of the Renaissance disappeared, and with few exceptions the major poets of the period gave little thought to the possibilities of musical setting. **1931** R. L. Mégroz *Joseph Conrad's Mind & Method* 154 Three modern poet-novelists..might perhaps be bracketed with Wells among the competitors. **1948** F. R. Leavis *Great Tradition* iii. 128 It was the profundity of the pondering that I had in mind when I referred to him [*sc.* Henry James] as a 'poet-novelist'. **1881** O. Wilde *Grave of Keats* in *Poems* 145 O poet-painter of our English Land! **1943** F. Thompson *Candleford Green* v. 75 Dante Gabriel Rossetti..that poet-painter. **1963** M. H. Abrams in N. Frye *Romanticism Reconsidered* 41 This voice is that of the poet-prophets of the Old and New Testaments, now descending on Blake from..John Milton. **1903** L. F. Anderson *Anglo-Saxon Scop* 27 To have seen many lands, to have had a wide and varied experience was considered a qualification for the poet-singer's calling. **1934** *Publ. Mod. Lang. Assoc.* XLIX. 365 A poet-warrior sings, adding the name of Grendel's conqueror to the role of Germanic heroes.

e. Poets' Corner, (*b*) (earlier example); **poet's daffodil** = *poets' narcissus*; **poets'** (or **poet's**) **narcissus** (examples); also = Pheasant's eye 2.

1781 W. Cowper *Let.* 27 Feb. (1908) 60 If you please you may send it [*sc.* a poem] to the Poet's Corner. [**1772** R. Weston *Universal Botanist* III. 504 Poetic or Common pale Daffodil, or Narcissus.] **1870** W. Robinson *Wild Garden* ii. 112 Poet's Daffodil. *Narcissus poeticus.* Southern Europe. **1841** Poet's narcissus [see *hoop-petticoat 2]. **1883** W. Robinson *Eng. Flower Garden* 192/2 The finer types of the Poet's Narcissus should be grown for cutting. **1936** L. B. Wilder *Adventures with Hardy Bulbs* 19 The Poets Narcissus is perfect for dampish locations. **1965** H. Ramsbotham tr. *Schauenberg's Bulb Bk.* iii. 229 This is the Poet's narcissus, one of the most widely distributed European species. **1977** R. Genders *Scented Flora of World* 322/2 (*heading*) The Poet's Narcissus and Hybrids.

poetast (pōᵘ·ėtæst). Also **poetaste.** [Shortened form of Poetaster.] = Poetaster. Also as *v. trans.* and *intr.*, to write in the manner of a poetaster; hence **po·etasting** *ppl. a.*

1892 Beerbohm *Let.* June (1964) 22 She [*sc.* Mrs Grundy] demands that 'they bring unto her by and by the head of Oscar the Poëtast on a charger'. **1908** *Daily Chron.* 10 Apr. 3/2 In the spring the poetaster poetastes as sure as fate. **1909** G. B. Shaw *Admirable Bashville* Pref. 290, I poetasted The Admirable Bashville in the rigmarole style. **1969** *Daily Tel.* (Colour Suppl.) 14 Nov. 36/1 George Herbert is not there, although..Herbert's poetasting brother, Lord Herbert of Cherbury, is.

poetaz (pōᵘ·ėtæz). [f. *poet(icus* + *taz(etta,* the specific epithets of two species of *Narcissus.*] In full, *poetaz daffodil* or *narcissus.* A narcissus (*Narcissus* × *medioluteus*) belonging to a group of hybrids produced by crossing *Narcissus poeticus* and *N. tazetta,* bearing fragrant white or yellow flowers in clusters. Also *attrib.*

1906 *Gardeners' Chron.* 17 Mar. 169/3 Narcissus 'Poetaz'.—This name applies to a race derived by crossing *N. poeticus* and *N. Tazetta.* **1910** *Ibid.* 3 Dec. 406/1 Tazetta and Tazetta Hybrids. To include N. Tridymus, Poetaz varieties, [etc.]. **1913** *Daffodil Year-bk.* 51 These

Poetaz Daffodils are now well to the front, and are really good decorative plants. **1934** E. A. Bowles *Handbk. Narcissus* xvi. 176 The present-day race classed as Poetaz varieties owes its origin to the Dutch firm of Messrs. R. Van der Schoot. In 1885 large stocks of Tazetta varieties were growing in their Nursery alongside beds of N. poeticus ornatus, and the experiment of crossing them was decided upon. **1959** S. Gibbons *Pink Front Door* xx. 234 The little sitting-room..smelt of Poetaz narcissus. **1971** *Daffodil & Tulip Year Bk.* XXXVI. 44 There are.. not more than a couple of dozen poetaz in commerce today. **1977** R. Genders *Scented Flora of World* 322/2 Geranium. A poetaz hybrid..unsurpassed amongst all flowers for its perfume.

‖ **poète maudit** (poet mōdi). [Fr., = cursed poet.] A poet who is insufficiently appreciated by his contemporaries. Also *transf.*
[**1884** P. Verlaine (*title*) Les poètes maudits.] **1930** L. P. Shanks *Baudelaire* p. vii, Certainly Baudelaire was a *poète maudit*, pursued by the disaster which pursued his fellow-poet Edgar Poe. **1949** M. Turnell tr. *J.-P. Sartre's Baudelaire* 155 The proud free criminal, the Don Juan of hell, the rebel was also at the same time the *poète maudit*, the Devil's marionette. **1958** *Listener* 17 July 98/2 A *poète maudit* is doubly accursed when he exhibits himself and his world with the dry precision of classical prosody. **1963** *Times* 8 Feb. 14/1 It is a loosely assembled collection of episodes,..following the self-destructive career of a late romantic hero—drunkard, sexual athlete and *poète maudit*. **1977** *Time* 26 Dec. 52/1 Once the ignored art, photography now stands robed in puffery, and armored with analysis; like painting, it has acquired its cast of heroes and *poètes maudits*.

poetese (pōuĕtī·z). [f. Poet + -ese.] The mannered style of language supposed to be characteristic of poets.
1948 I. Brown *No Idle Words* 53 Has Empery, 'the power, status, or dominion of an Emperor', become entirely 'poetese'? In a leading article it would look a trifle odd. **1958** *Listener* 18 Dec. 1049/1 Mr. Bridson, choosing rhymed verse, never let it aspire to the high-poetic style or fall to 'poetese'.

poetette (pōuĕte·t). *rare.* [f. Poet + -ette.] A young or minor poetess.
1913 E. Pound *Let.* Nov. (1971) 26, I seem to spend most of my time attending to other peoples' affairs, weaning young poetettes from obscurity into the glowing pages of divers rotten publications, etc.

poetic, *a.* and *sb.* Add: **A.** *adj.* **1.** *poetic diction*, diction used in or considered to be proper to poetry (see Diction 4).
1800 Wordsworth *Lyrical Ballads* (ed. 2) I. Pref. p. xxi, There will..be found in these volumes little of what is usually called poetic diction. *Ibid.* p. xxvii, The distinction of rhyme and metre is regular and uniform, and not, like that which is produced by what is usually called poetic diction, arbitrary and subject to infinite caprices. **1815** G. F. Nott *Works of Henry Howard & Sir T. Wyatt* I. p. clxxxviii, Chaucer did much towards refining our poetic diction, but he left it..open to subsequent innovation and experiment. **1886** *Encycl. Brit.* XX. 859/2 As a mere question of methods, a reaction against the poetic diction of Pope and his followers was inevitable. **1928** O. Barfield *Poetic Diction: Study in Meaning* 177 The stale Miltonics, which lay at the bottom of so much eighteenth-century 'poetic diction'. **1938** A. Campbell *Battle of Brunanburh* 41 Despite the wealth of poetic diction at his command, he can be, at times, astonishingly simple and direct. **1951** C. Day Lewis *Poet's Task* 5, I hope to devote a number of..lectures to what is called, somewhat uninvitingly, 'poetic diction'. **1970** M. Swanton *Dream of Rood* 59 The highly formalised nature of Old English poetic diction.
4. Also, fond of poetry, able to appreciate poetry.
1817 Jane Austen *Sanditon* (1925) 91, I have read several of Burn's Poems with great delight..but I am not poetic enough to separate a Man's poetry entirely from his Character.
B. *sb.* **2.** Also in extended senses.
1917 T. S. Eliot *Prufrock & Other Observations* 38 With your air indifferent and imperious At a stroke our mad poetics to confute. **1973** *Word 1970* XXVI. 66 Jakobson avoids the term *stylistics*, preferring instead *poetics*. **1976** *Times Lit. Suppl.* 2 Jan. 11/2 To subscribe to this poetic was to doubt the validity of art and the veracity of dreams. **1976** *Daily Tel.* 5 July 10/3 So autonomous are the poetics of Krzysztof Penderecki's compositional techniques, I found it hardly possible to reconcile words and music in his 'Canticum Canticorum Salomonis'. **1976** *Times Lit. Suppl.* 12 Nov. 1411/2 It is developed theoretically into an alternative poetic, for literature that classical and Coleridgean poetics are unable to treat with justice: a poetic of architectural as against organic form. **1977** A. Sheridan tr. *J. Lacan's Écrits* iii. 102 This notion must be approached through its resonances in what I shall call the poetics of the Freudian corpus.

poeticality. Delete † and add later examples.
1923 J. M. Murry *Pencillings* 200 The novel with which he was so enchanted was full of vague poeticalities. **1950** *Scrutiny* XVII. 188 He avoids the opposite danger of bolstering the commonplace by an extraneous poeticality. **1976** *Observer* 17 Oct. 32/2 What he was in fact up to a good deal of the time was spouting frigid poeticalities.

poeticism. Delete *nonce-wd.* and add: **1.** (Further example.)
1972 *Daily Tel.* 22 June 7/1 The book harks back to the luminous poeticism of much German romantic writing.
2. A poetical expression; an example of poetic diction.
1926 Fowler *Mod. Eng. Usage* 442/1 *Poeticisms.* Simple reference of words to this article warns the reader that to use them in ordinary prose contexts is dangerous. **1956** *Essays in Criticism* VI. 156 His language avoids conventional poeticisms.

poeticize, *v.* Add: Hence **poe·ticized** *ppl. a.*; **poe·ticizing** *vbl. sb.* Also **poe·ticizable** *a.*; **poeticiza·tion, poe·ticizer.**
1923 J. M. Murry *Pencillings* 189 What he is really lamenting is the absence of poeticisation, of what is called 'imaginative writing'. **1926** Fowler *Mod. Eng. Usage* 442/2 *Poeticize* makes *-zable*. **1961** *Encounter* XVII. 68 Rossetti appears to me a poeticiser. **1965** *New Statesman* 22 Oct. 617/3 In the studio, he [*sc.* Corot] dropped into tame poeticising, due no doubt to what Mr. Gould calls his 'vein of emotional immaturity'. **1973** *Human World* Feb. 7 The anxiety Mr Maddox senses in the environmentalists comes to no more than a yearning for a universal poeticized prosperity. **1975** *Listener* 11 Sept. 348/1 Francis Ponge..is obsessed with the external world as a series of poetic or poeticisable objects. *Ibid.* 4 Dec. 772/2, I found the sub-Dylan Thomas-ish poeticising here off-putting.

poetico-. Add: *poetico-commercial, -metaphysical* adjs.
1837 J. S. Mill in *Westm. Rev.* XXVII. 50 Much genuine philosophy, disguised though it often be in a poetico-metaphysical vesture of a most questionable kind. **1930** Blunden *Leigh Hunt* viii. 99 It [sc. *Rimini*] almost became fashionable..but..by no means challenged the poetico-commercial achievements of Rogers.

poetism (pōu·ĕtiz'm). [f. Poet + -ism.] **a.** = Poeticism 1. **b.** = *poeticism 2.
1848 A. H. Clough *Let.* 16 July in T. Arnold *N.Z. Lett.* (1966) 111 Matt[hew Arnold]..has become sadly cynical again of late. However I think the poetism goes on favourably. **1867** G. Meredith *Vittoria* I. xii. 202 Agostino twice smiles and chuckles, and talks his poetisms. **1977** P. B. & J. S. Medawar *Life Sci.* ii. 23 The myth that geese might be born of such organisms as the attractive barnacle-like crustacean the goose barnacle, *Lepas anatifera*. Such notions belong to 'poetism'.

poetize, *v.* Add: **1. a.** (Later examples.)
1895 *Wales* May 240/2 A shoemaker from Llandwrog was with me..the person who poetized to Mr. Williams in the Bangor paper. **1917** J. B. Cabell *Cream of Jest* I. ii. 13 So Horvendile descended, still poetizing: '*Pus ab mi dons no m pot valer.*' **1939** L. M. Montgomery *Anne of Ingleside* xxii. 147 He doesn't look clever but he can poetize.

poetizing, *vbl. sb.* (Further examples.)
1888 F. H. Williams *Atman* (1891) 243 He is probably bilious, but that is no excuse for his threadbare poetizings. **1936** F. Clune *Roaming round Darling* viii. 74 A freezing night in August and eating cold corned beef! That's what poetizing does to a man. **1948** F. R. Leavis *Great Tradition* iii. 129 *The Waves* and *The Years*—works that offer something like the equivalent of Georgian poetizing. **1961** *PMLA* LXXVI. 1. 309/1 None of these glimpses of poetizing without writing is intended to incorporate a signature into the epic matter.

poetolatry (pōuĕtǫ·lătri). [f. Poet + -olatry.] The worship of poets; immoderate veneration for poets. So **poeto·later**, one who practises poetolatry.
1936 C. S. Lewis in *Essays & Studies* XXI. 165 There is yet another way in which Personal Heresy offends against personality;..I am referring to the growth of what may be called Poetolatry. *Ibid.* 167 Most poetolaters hold that a dead man has no consciousness. **1939** Lewis & Tillyard *Personal Heresy* v. 104 Naturalism..wants poets to be a separate race of great souls or *mahatmas*. Poetolatry is the natural result, for if there were such a race..those who know no higher deity would do well to worship them.

poetry. Add: **5.** (Earlier and further examples.) Phr. *poetry of the foot* or *of motion*: dancing.
1664 Dryden *Rival Ladies* III. 32 The Poetry of the foot takes most of late. **1813** Lady Morgan *Wild Irish Girl* (ed. 5) II. xix. 156, 'I seldom dance,' I—'Ill health has for some time coincided with my inclination, which seldom led me to try my skill at the *Poetry of Motion*.' **1818** Byron *Childe Harold* IV. lviii. 32 That music in itself, whose sounds are song, The poetry of speech. *c* **1863** T. Taylor *Ticket-of-leave Man* in M. R. Booth *Eng. Plays of 19th Cent.* (1969) II. 101 Come along, Emily, if you're at liberty to give your Montague a lesson in the poetry of motion. **1874** Hardy *Far from Madding Crowd* I. ii. 13 The poetry of motion is a phrase much in use. **1946** D. C. Peattie *Road of Naturalist* iv. 42 There is left only the poetry of speed and wind. **1959** E. H. Clements *High Tension* i. 10 He had never been back there. He had not..seen poetry in the small exploit. **1975** *Times* 6 Mar. 13/5 There is a moment of poetry in a sequence where the dancers simply walk about carrying umbrellas. **1975** *Listener* 4 Dec. 747/2 Raffles.. compares the poetry of cricket with the poetry of burglary. **1977** *Zigzag* Apr. 30/3 This song captures what Television are all about: a kind of poetry in motion with a scorching musical backdrop.
6. (Earlier and further examples.)
1629, 1773 [see *grammar *sb.* 5 c]. **1838** C. Waterton *Essays on Nat. Hist.* p. xxiv, One day, when I was in the class of poetry..about two years before I left the college.., he called me up to his room. **1887** *Stonyhurst Mag.* Nov. 34/1 Poetry..were granted a most unexpected but none the less welcome holiday on Thursday October 20th. **1946** D. Gwynn *Bishop Challoner* iii. 39 By the summer of 1708 he had passed through the two higher classes of Poetry and Rhetoric.
7. *poetry professorship, reader, school, workshop*; *poetry-loving* adj.; **poetry-book,** a book containing a collection of poems, esp. one used in schools; **poetry reading,** the reading of poetry, esp. to an audience; a poetry recital; **poetry recital,** a public performance of poetry; **poetry-voice,** a pompous or mannered style of writing poetry or reading it aloud.
1847 Thackeray *Van. Fair* (1848) xii. 103 She wrote whole pages out of poetry-books without the least pity. **1877** A. B. Edwards (*title*) A poetry-book of elder poets. **1881** R. L. Stevenson *Virginibus Puerisque* 176 Whether we regard life as a lane leading to a dead wall..or pule in little atheistic poetry-books about its vanity and brevity [etc.]. **1903** 'A. McNeill' *Egregious English* 102 The demand for poetry-books by new writers has practically ceased to exist. **1935** E. Farjeon *Nursery in Nineties* v. 271 The poem was 'good enough' for the Poetry-Book. **1980** G. Nelson *Charity's Child* vi. 86 The poetry book, sir. **1941** Blunden *T. Hardy* ii. 34 The change was natural to the period and the poetry-loving author. **1979** E. Koch *Good Night Little Spy* iv. 24 A poetry-loving, moon faced charmer. **1793** W. B. Stevens *Jrnl.* 11 Mar. (1965) I. 72 Received a College letter, requesting me to support the pretensions of Mr. Hurdies to the Poetry Professorship which will be vacant in Michaelmas Term next. **1940** R. S. Lambert *Ariel & all his Quality* v. 127 Few poetry-readers with ears in it [*sc.* the audience's] general approbation. **1975** 'G. Black' *Big Wind for Summer* ii. 32 The voice of the British Broadcasting Corporation's top poetry reader. **1917** A. Huxley *Let.* 11 Dec. (1969) 140 After that to Eliot, whom I found as haggard..as usual; we held a council of war about a poetry reading, in which both of us are supposed to be performing. **1945** 'G. Orwell' in *New Saxon Pamphlets* III. 35 That grisly thing, a 'poetry reading'. **1975** O. Sela *Bengali Inheritance* xvi. 139 She..organised poetry readings and prescribed reading books. **1966** J. Betjeman *High & Low* 73 A poetry recital we are giving to the troops. **1978** J. Symons *Blackheath Poisonings* I. 34 The Rink Hall in the village, where the poetry recital was to take place. **1976** Poetry school [see *poetry workshop* below]. **1971** *Guardian* 28 Dec. 13/5, I hate the poetry-voice; the poetry should speak for itself. **1972** *Country Life* 1 June 1418/3 Stevie Smith..was not one for the Poetry Voice. She mixes nonsense and its opposite. **1976** *Times* 1 Mar. 3/1 Mr Lovibond and his supporters..operate a poetry school and workshop. **1977** *Time Out* 28 Jan.–3 Feb. 40/5 Audio-visual poetry workshop last Fri of month.

po-faced (pōu·fēist), *a.* [Perh. f. Poh *int.* or f. *po³ + Faced *ppl. a.*², infl. by **poker-faced* adj.] Having or assuming an expressionless or impassive face, poker-faced; priggish, narrow-minded, or smug. So **po-face.**
1934 C. Lambert *Music Ho!* III. 191, I do not wish, when faced with exoticism, to adopt an attitude which can best be described by the admirable expression 'po-faced'. We cannot live perpetually in the rarefied atmosphere of the austerer classics. **1937** T. Rattigan *French without Tears* I. 11 What's he like, though, really? Po-faced, I suppose? **1951** N. Balchin *Way through Wood* xvii. 239 You sounded po-faced on the telephone. **1958** *Economist* 11 Oct. 133/3 That 'middle class' which Low used to symbolise by a po-faced woman in a big fur coat. **1965** [see *galumph *v.*]. **1967** *Listener* 24 Aug. 232/2, I glimpsed [him]..being lightly grilled by a deliciously po-faced Joan Bakewell. **1973** K. Giles *File on Death* iii. 75 Her po face. **1973** *Times* 11 Dec. 5/3 We do not want to appear po-faced or ministry Scrooges, but on the other hand we should not like to see the country flooded with blazes of extravagant light. **1975** *Globe & Mail* (Toronto) 1 Sept. 7/1 Ted Stuebing..had one of his minions come on the tube all po-faced Saturday night to say that CFTO couldn't let the press in because it would have cluttered up the production studio.

‖ **poffertje** (pǫ·fəɹtyə). Also (*S. Afr.*) **poffartje, poffertjie** (-kyə). [a. Du. *poffertje*, Afrikaans *poffertjie*, f. Fr. *pouffer* to blow up.] A small light doughnut or fritter dusted with sugar. Also *attrib.*
1872 *Cape Monthly Mag.* V. 230 Shall we take offence if an English host..set before our craving appetite..the dainty though untranslatable pumpkin 'poffartjes'? **1890** *Cent. Mag.* Nov. 49 Beside her..sat Jan Wisenkerke watching a buxom darky in a scarlet turban frying poffertjes. *Ibid.*, The kitchen walls were covered with.. waffle-irons, poffertje pans. **1905** *Speaker* 11 Mar. 563/1 Poffertjes..are little round pancaky blobs, twisted and covered with butter and sugar. **1942** H. W. Van Loon *Van Loon's Lives* 850 There is no use trying to describe them to outsiders, for *poffertjes* are the one dish that waxes only in the Low Countries. They are a cross between a very small kind of pancake and a fritter and are the main delicacy of..village fairs. **1949** [see *melktert]. **1974** D. Winsor *Death Convention* viii. 68, I took a poffertje. It was a rather basic lump of dough fried in butter and dusted in icing sugar.

poge, var. *pogue.

pogey (pōu·gi). *N. Amer. slang* (now chiefly *Hist.*). Also **pogie, pogy.** [Origin unknown.] **a.** A hostel for the needy or disabled; a poorhouse; a local relief centre or welfare office.
1891 *Contemporary Rev.* Aug. ii. 255 Begging is called 'battering for chewing'; railway brakemen, 'brakies'; poorhouses, 'pogies'. **1927** *Amer. Speech* June 387/2 A *pogey* is a poorhouse. Government homes for disabled veterans are also known as pogies. **1936** K. Mackenzie *Living Rough* 269, I was in the Pogey a couple of nights. It stinks. **1953** D. M. LeBourdais *Nation of North* 211 Thousands of self-respecting workmen..sat at home while

their wives made the dreary pilgrimage to the 'pogie'. **1959** *Maclean's Mag.* (Toronto) 15 Aug. 21/1 Lean and hungry alley-cat men swung down from the freights and headed for a fifteen-cent mission meal or the innumerable pogies and scratch houses for a ten-cent cot. **1974** P. Gzowski *Bk. about This Country* 18 We had lived in teacherages, pogies and scratch houses and boarding houses. **1976** *Whig-Standard* (Kingston, Ont.) 9 Jan. 1/1 Unemployment insurance has indeed come a long way since the days of the pogey houses of turn-of-the-century England—dank, gloomy places where the indigent could do menial tasks in exchange for food and lodging.

b. Relief given to the needy from national or local funds; unemployment benefit.

1960 *Maclean's Mag.* (Toronto) 2 Apr. 54/2 Today unemployment-insurance payments are often referred to as pogey. But pogey in the depths of the thirties meant something as different from present-day unemployment insurance as panhandling is from drawing money from your bank account. **1961** *Time* 31 Mar. 9/2 Said a jobless Hamilton steelworker, father of six children: 'Why should I sweat for $40 a week? I'm getting more than that from the pogey, the welfare and the baby bonus.' **1964** H. T. Barker *Ice Road* 49 During the winter we lived on turnips, potatoes, canned clams and the pogy, and Mother and I would hook rugs for the tourist trade. **1976** *Whig-Standard* (Kingston, Ont.) 6 Jan. 1/6 The Kingston area's fourth largest and fastest growing industry is unemployment insurance—pogey or, if you wish, the dole.

pogey bait (pōu·gi bēit). *U.S. slang.* Also **poggy, pogie, poguey bait.** [perh. f. Pogy + Bait *sb.*[1]] Candy, sweets. (See also quot. 1970.)

1918 L. E. Ruggles *Navy Explained* 88 While going through the war zone, the pockets are used for ciggies and poggy bait. **1929** *Papers Mich. Acad. Sci., Arts & Lett.* X. 315 *Poggy bait*, the sailor's designation for sweets. **1935** A. J. Pollock *Underworld Speaks* 90/1 *Pogey bait*, candy. **1953** M. Dibner *Deep Six* xv. 154 A candy bar's called poguey-bait. **1970** *Esquire* Nov. 116 Pogie bait is any snack that is not prepared..in a government mess-hall.

Poggendorff (pǫ·gĕndǫɹf). [Name of J. C. *Poggendorff* (1796–1877), German physicist and chemist, who pointed out the illusion (see *Ann. der Physik und Chem.* (1860) CX. 502).] *Poggendorff illusion*: an optical illusion in which the two ends of a straight line whose central portion is obscured by a rectangular strip crossing at an angle seem not to be in line.

1898 *Psychol. Rev.* V. 540 The Poggendorff illusion... This illusion is due to the fact that the two ends of the transversal, sundered by the vertical strip, are made to belong to two different systems, each suggesting its own perspective interpretation and being under no necessity.. of appearing as parts of a continuous line. **1976** *Nature* 1 Apr. 397/2 (*caption*) The Poggendorff illusion in geological contexts; the illusory perceptual data are more likely to mislead when they favour an investigator's geological hypothesis than when they do not.

poggle (pǫ·g'l), *sb.* and *a. slang* (orig. Anglo-Ind. *colloq.*). Also **puggle, puggly, pugley.** [ad. Hind. *pāgal, paglā* (fem. *paglī*) madman, idiot.] **A.** *sb.* A crazy or foolish person, an idiot. ?*Obs.*

1829 J. Shipp *Memoirs* II. viii. 233 It's true, the people call me, I know not why, the 'pugley'. **1863** 'N. Broughton' *Dawk Bungalow* II. 37, I was foolish enough to pay these hurrumzarders beforehand, and they have thrown me over. I must have been a poggle to do it! **1886** Yule & Burnell *Hobson-Jobson* 542 *Poggle, puggly*, etc... Properly Hind. *pāgal*; a madman, an idiot; often used colloquially by Anglo-Indians.

B. *adj.* Mentally unbalanced, crazy; also, drunk, mad-drunk.

1925 Fraser & Gibbons *Soldier & Sailor Words* 225 *Poggle* (also *puggle*), mad. An idiot. An old Army term. **1936** H. Graham *Private Life of Gregory Gorm* 229, I can't quite make up my mind whether he is a genius, as some people seem to think, or only slightly poggle. **1971** B. W. Aldiss *Soldier Erect* 80 A woman in this bloody dump? You're going *puggle*, Page, that's your trouble! Too much tropical sun.

poggled (pǫ·g'ld), *a. Army slang.* [f. prec. + -ed[2].] = *poggle *a.* Cf. *puggled *a.*

1933 Partridge *Words, Words, Words!* iii. 202 *Poggle(d), puggled*, 'rattled' as well as eccentric and mad-drunk, is a pre-war Regular-Army word.

poggy, var. Pogy in Dict. and Suppl.

poggy bait, var. *pogey bait.

pogie, var. *pogey.

pogo (pōu·go). Also **Pogo.** [Orig. unknown.] **1.** A stilt-like pole (also called a *pogo stick*) on which one jumps about (see quot. 1921); the pastime of jumping on or as on such a pole. Also *attrib.* Also applied to dancing or a dance with movements suggestive of jumping on a pogo stick. So as *v. trans.* to traverse on a pogo stick; *intr.* to jump on or as on a pogo; to perform a pogo dance. Hence **po·goer; po·going** *vbl. sb.* and *ppl. a.*

Formerly registered in the U.S. as a proprietary term.

1921 *Glasgow Herald* 30 Aug. 7 What is a Pogo? It is a four-foot pole, hollowed at the foot for the insertion of a strong spring, with a rubber cushion at the end of it. About half a foot above the spring are two steps. To Pogo you place one foot on each step, clutch the top of the pole firmly in both hands, and hop. *Ibid.*, On the Continent there are Pogo clubs, which conduct Pogo carnivals where the principal items are the high and the long jumps, and there are halls where you Pogo under much the same conditions as obtained on the roller skating rinks. **1921** *Punch* 21 Sept. 225/1 Three men..expressed their intention of 'Pogoing' the Channel. *Ibid.*, Charlie Chaplin intends to give a 'Pogo' to each of the children who are now attending his old schools. *Ibid.*, A small girl has 'pogo-ed' five hundred miles. **1921** *Oxford Times* 11 Nov. 16/4 On Thursday afternoon two undergraduates were seen racing along Cornmarket Street on Pogo sticks. **1924** *Punch* 24 Sept. 338 A dozen well-mounted pogo-players. **1942** *Official Gaz.* (U.S. Patent Office) 1 Sept. 14/2 Philip de Journo, Forest Hills, Long Island, N.Y. *Pogo* for jumping sticks. Claims use since Feb. 28, 1941. **1958** *Daily Mail* 8 July 6/4 On stilts and pogo sticks (their latest craze). **1968** *New Scientist* 19 Dec. 653/2 The first stage of the three-stage rocket went into 'pogo-stick' oscillations. **1973** *Nature* 30 Nov. 313/1 The hopping of kangaroos is reminiscent of a bouncing ball or the action of a pogo stick. **1977** *Zigzag* Mar. 8/1 I've never subscribed to the theory that up to the age of thirty it was all pogo dancing down the Roxy. *Ibid.* June 6/4 'I want him thrown out,' he snapped to a roadie, pointing to the pogoing culprit. **1977** *Oxford Times* (City ed.) 30 Sept. 16 The dancers at the front jumping up and down on one leg (they call it pogoing, m'dear). *Ibid.*, Despite the vigorous pogoers, many members of the audience stood on the sidelines. **1977** *New Wave Mag.* No. 7. 3 They just arrived and pogoed through the front door. **1977** *Chicago Tribune* 2 Oct. vi. 14/4 The..punks' hopping 'pogo' dance. **1978** *New Society* 19 Jan. 115/2 The wildly exuberant punk dance—the pogo—..derives from the celebratory 'knees-up' of the football terraces. Basically, the participants leap up and down, two-footed, some of them alone, more in two or threes, with their arms linked... It's hot work, pogoing.

2. Used *attrib.* with reference to low-frequency longitudinal oscillations of a space rocket. (Cf. quot. 1968 above.)

1971 *Nature* 10 Dec. 316/2 The Diamant B [booster rocket] has been used successfully on three previous occasions, but a strong vibrational 'pogo effect' was noticed. **1976** Sutton & Ross *Rocket Propulsion Elements* (ed. 4) viii. 259 Techniques for damping Pogo instability tendency include..properly designed engine, interstage, and payload support structures.

pogonion (pŏgōu·niǫn). *Anat.* [f. Gr. πώγων beard + *-ion[2].] The foremost point on the midline of the chin.

1897 in *Lippincott's Med. Dict.* **1920** H. H. Wilder *Lab. Man. Anthropometry* i. i. 47 *Pogonion* (pg), the most projecting median point of the chin, on the anterior surface (mental process). **1977** *Proc. R. Soc. Med.* LXX. 433/2 Mandibular length is of particular interest following mandibular osteotomy and it was measured from articulare to pogonion on cephalometric radiographs, using calipers.

pogonophore (pŏgōu·nofǫɹ). [a. mod.L. *Pogonophora* (K. E. Johannson 1937, in *Zool. Bidrag från Uppsala* XVIII. 253), f. Gk. πώγων beard + -φόρος bearing: see -phore.] A worm-like marine invertebrate belonging to the phylum Pogonophora. So **pogono·phoran, pogono·phorous** *adjs.*, of or pertaining to an animal of this kind or the phylum as a whole.

1955 *Systematic Zool.* III. 184/1 The large size of pogonophorous animals is interesting. **1958** *New Scientist* 20 Nov. 1303/2 All pogonophores look like bits of string or trawl twine. **1959** L. H. Hyman *Invertebrates* V. xviii. 210 Pogonophores are exclusively marine and are mostly limited to abyssal depths. **1964** *New Scientist* 24 Dec. 842/3 Pogonophores are to be found in all seas, even in those places where the marine fauna had been previously studied with care. **1973** *Nature* 21 Dec. 452/1 Pogonophoran Phylogeny... The first international symposium on Pogonophora..took place in the University of Copenhagen on November 1–3. *Ibid.* 452/3 Gupta finally expressed a doubt that pogonophores are coelomate animals at all. **1976** *Ibid.* 18 Mar. 218/2 The author devotes most space to the few species of animals, such as the ostracod *Gigantocypris* and the pogonophoran worm *Siboglinum*, that have been used by physiologists.

pogonotomy. Add to def.: shaving. (Later examples.)

1942 Berrey & Van den Bark *Amer. Thes. Slang* §125/3 *Pogonotomy*, shaving. **1960** *Times* 28 Sept. (Advertising Suppl.) p. iii/2 This is the age, in fact, of pogonotomy. **1966** J. S. Cox *Dict. Hairdressing & Wig-making* 119/1 *Pogonotomy*, beard-cutting or shaving.

pogonotrophy. (Further example.)

1966 *Daily Mail* 29 Oct. 1/1 This week's picture of Beatle George Harrison wearing a moustache—and a particularly sad, droopy looking one at that—caught students of pogonotrophy the world over in two minds.

pogrom, *sb.* Delete ‖ and add: Also with pronunc. (pǫ·grǫ̆m). **a.** (Further examples.)

1919 N. Sokolow *Hist. Zionism* II. p. li, Not even the dark ages extracted so heavy a toll of Jewish blood: something like 1400 pogroms took place all over the Ghetto. **1968** *New Left Rev.* Jan.-Feb. 65 Then came the years of galloping inflation, of the programs, of acute social, political and intellectual ferment. **1979** O. Sela *Petrograd Consignment* 142 Wasn't he eager to go back to Russia..to read the Protocols of the Elders of Zion again; wasn't another pogrom all he lived for.

b. In general use: an organized, officially tolerated, attack on any community or group. Also *fig.*

1906 *Tribune* 16 June 7/2 This was the immediate signal for a *pogrom*, or organized riot. **1920** H. J. C. Grierson in *Proc. Brit. Acad. 1919–1920* 433 Only Henley refused to take part in the 'pogrom'; and he alas! died before completing his work as champion, critic, and editor of Byron. **1928** 'S. S. Van Dine' *Greene Murder Case* i. 13, I note that our upliftin' Press bedecked its front pages this morning with headlines about a pogrom at the old Greene mansion last night. **1936** H. A. L. Fisher *Hist. Europe* I. xviii. 232 The Greek Empire..had disgraced itself by a *pogrom* against the French and Italian colony in Constantinople. **1964** *New Statesman* 13 Mar. 405/1 On 20 March 1914 58 British cavalry officers, stationed in Ireland, announced that they would not obey the orders of their lawful superiors... The cry of 'mutiny' was answered by the charge that there had been a plot—a 'pogrom' in the contemporary phrase—to crush Ulster's resistance to Home Rule by force of arms. **1967** T. Gunn *Touch* 27 Am I Your mother or The nearest human being to Hold on to in a Dreamed pogrom. **1971** *Sunday Times* 13 June 12/4 The army units, after clearing out the rebels, pursued the pogrom in the towns and villages. **1975** R. Browning *Emperor Julian* iii. 51 Hannibalianus had been killed in 337 in the pogrom of his relations engineered by Constantius.

c. *attrib.* and *Comb.*

1931 *Times Lit. Suppl.* 5 Nov. 855/2 Refugees to England from pogrom-haunted Russia. **1941** Koestler *Scum of Earth* 85 The French Government discovered a welcome diversion from the general discontent by exploiting the people's natural hostility to foreigners, and appealing to their pogrom instincts. **1949** —— *Promise & Fulfilment* i. vii. 69 Many of these young men had been members of the Jewish self-defence organizations in the pogrom-threatened small towns of Russia. **1978** D. Murphy *Place Apart* viii. 167 Few of us would wish to see our army crossing the [Irish] border to fight Loyalist paramilitaries... If another 'pogrom' situation did arise ..it would make more sense to welcome..refugees into the Republic.

Hence **pogro·mist** (also stressed *po·gromist*), an organizer of or participant in a pogrom.

1907 *Athenæum* 26 Jan. 99 Small wonder that the 'pogromists' laugh at Europe, and now pursue their work without intermission or disguise. **1960** S. Becker tr. *A. Schwarz-Bart's Last of Just* (1961) ii. 87 The pogromists were White Guards. **1962** *Guardian* 13 Oct. 6/3 Hate-mongers and pogromists. **1963** *Times* 24 Jan. 8/7 However, he criticized the 'complete lack of publicity in the Soviet press' and said that neither the pogromists nor the local police and prosecutors who abetted them had been punished or reprimanded. **1978** I. B. Singer *Shosha* xiv. 254 People sacrificed themselves for Stalin, for Petlura, for Machno, for every pogromist.

pogrom (pǫgrǫ·m, pǫ·grǫm), *v.* [f. the sb.] *trans.* To massacre (persons) in a pogrom; to destroy (a place) in a pogrom. Hence **pogromed, pogrommed** *ppl. a.*, that has experienced a pogrom.

1915 *Boston Jrnl.* 2 Feb. 3/2 [The Jews in Galicia] are being..pogromed. **1918** G. Frankau *One of Them* II. xv. 107 Its East End drab bits..Where toiled..The pogromed horde, and multiplied like rabbits. **1919** *Daily Chron.* 10 Oct. 1/1 The total number of places pogrommed was 353, and the Jews killed 20,500. **1946** Koestler *Thieves in Night* 217 They [sc. the Jews] are the most admirable salesmen in the world, regardless of whether they sell carpets, Marxism,..or their own pogromed infants. **1979** *Country Life* 8 Nov. 1688 Such a gathering is, to Mr Pirates, vile enough to justify his decision to pogrom the lot.

pogue (pōug). *slang.* Also **poge.** [Perh. related to Pough *sb.*] A bag, purse, wallet or container. Also by metonymy, money, takings. Also *attrib.*, as **pogue-hunter**, a thief who steals purses, a pickpocket.

1812 J. H. Vaux *Vocab. Flash Lang.* in *Mem.* (1964) 259 *Pogue*, a bag, (probably a corruption of poke.) **1879** J. W. Horsley in *Macm. Mag.* XL. 504/2, I went out the next day to Maidenhead, and touched for some wedge and a poge (purse), with over five quid in it. **1896** A. Morrison *Child of Jago* xxiii. 229 The pogue-hunter, emptying the pogues in his pocket by sense of touch. **1906** E. Pugh *Spoilers* vi. 66 When the tiggies made a raid for a 'ot pogue-hunter or snidesman. **1942** Berrey & Van den Bark *Amer. Thes. Slang* § 88/15 Purse, dummy, hide,..poge, poke. **1975** M. Crichton *Great Train Robbery* v. 29 What's your pogue up there, anyway? *Ibid.* vii. 39 It was the stickman's job to take the pogue once Teddy had snaffled it, thus leaving Teddy clean, should..a constable stop him.

poguey bait, var. *pogey bait.

pogy. Add: Also **poggy.** (Earlier and later examples.) Also *attrib.* and *Comb.*, as *pogy-fisherman, steamer*; **pogy chum** (see quot. 1858); **pogy-press,** a press for extracting oil from fish; **pogy-seiner,** a boat used in seining for pogy (see Seine *v.*).

1858, 1859 [see *chum *sb.*[3]]. **1864** *Rep. Maine Board Agric.* 42 Rock weed, muscle bed and pogy chum will make grass grow. **1880** *Harper's Mag.* Aug. 341/1 A cast-off 'pogy'-press..had been piled upon an old wharf. *Ibid.* 347/1 The 'pogy' business was the catching of porgies and menhaden for their oil. **1913** *Oysterman & Fisherman* 10 July 31/1 The new pogy steamer E. B. Thomas the largest ever built for the menhaden fishing industry made her official trip off Portland Monday. **1949** *Sun* (Baltimore) 29 July 2/1 Owners of the Virginia Pogy-Seiner Pluck today planned to advertise for a crew of licensed Maine fishermen. *Ibid.*, Newspaper ads would be tried tomorrow to see whether enough trained pogy-fishermen are available in this area. *Ibid.*, Pogies, or menhaden, are good only for their oil and fish-meal content.

pogy, var. *POGEY.

pohutukawa (pohu:tukā·wă). [Maori.] A New Zealand evergreen tree, *Metrosideros excelsus*, belonging to the family Myrtaceæ and bearing clusters of red flowers with projecting stamens; also called the Christmas tree, as it flowers in December and January. Also *attrib.*

1832 G. BENNETT in *London Med. Gaz.* 7 Jan. 508/1 There is an unpublished species of Metrosideros..named Pohu-takawa by the natives of New Zealand. **1851** V. LUSH *Jrnl.* 1 Sept. (1971) 84 Passing now at the foot of lofty perpendicular cliffs, in the crevices and the tops of which were the beautiful Pohutukawa trees. **1867** [see *CHRISTMAS-TREE b]. **1886** J. A. FROUDE *Oceana* xviii. 308 Low down on the shores the graceful native Pohutukawa was left undisturbed. **1935** J. GUTHRIE *Little Country* xxi. 316 Along the edge of the coast road are the pohutukawa trees, flowering like bonfires. **1944** [see *CHRISTMAS-TREE b]. **1959** M. SHADBOLT *New Zealanders* 22 We..picnicked in the shade of a crimson-blooming pohutukawa grove. **1965** F. SARGESON *Memoirs of Peon* iv. 62 A travelling Frenchman..had not long since visited the Auckland beaches and painted the pohutukawas in flower. **1977** *N.Z. Herald* 5 Jan. 1–6/10 The cliffs rise behind, dotted with tiny pohutukawas, some little bigger than their first blooms.

poi¹. (Earlier and further examples.)

1823 C. S. STEWART *Jrnl.* 18 May (1828) vi. 133 This immense bulk of person is supposed to arise..from the abundance and nutritious quality of their food, especially that of poe, a kind of paste made from the taro, an esculent root, a principal article of diet. **1826** W. ELLIS *Tour through Hawaii* xi. 293 The house..was soon furnished. A sleeping mat spread on the ground,..a few calabashes for water and poë. **1829** [see *POIPOI]. **1833** A. SMITH in M. D. Frear *Lowell & Abigail* (1934) 72 Their [*sc.* the Hawaiians'] 'staff of life' is poi, which is made by baking taro in the ground and pounding to the consistency of thin flour paste. **1862** M. HOPKINS *Hawaii* iii. 34 This succulent root [*sc.* taro] was sometimes cooked, but was more generally pounded into a semi-fluid mess, and allowed partially to ferment, when it was called *poi*. **1905** [see *LUAU]. **1924** J. M. BROWN *Riddle of Pacific* xvii. 182 The low coralline islands had not breadfruit, and yet made the fermented paste called sometimes *poi* and sometimes *mai*; and even volcanic islands like the Marquesas, which had breadfruit, preferred to make their *poi* of *taro*. **1951** *Amer. Speech* XXVI. 23 *Poi* dog (a nondescript cur; formerly the native breed of dog was fattened on 'poi' and served at feasts). **1954** [see *LAULAU]. **1964** *Asia Mag.* 16 Aug. 20/1 *Poi*... Made from starchy taro roots, it is a pinkish-gray goo of one, two, or three-finger thickness depending upon the consistency of the paste. **1968** O. WYNDETTE *Islands of Destiny* II. 85 All five of his wives were enjoying with him a typical Hawaiian meal: baked pork, poi, and sweet potatoes.

poi² (poi). *N.Z.* [Maori.] A ball made of leaves and fibre attached to a string; a dance to the accompaniment of traditional songs, performed by Maori women and girls using such a ball. Also *attrib.*

1843 E. DIEFFENBACH *Travels in N.Z.* II. iv. 57 Another game is with one ball (poi) suspended from a string. **1859** A. S. THOMSON *Story of N.Z.* I. I. x. 196 Poi is a game played with variegated balls, about the size of large oranges, to which strings are attached. The string is held in one hand and the ball is struck with the other. **1905** W. BAUCKE *Where White Man Treads* 87 When the feasting and gaiety had subsided..we all lazily awaited the lining up of the poi maidens. **1935** J. GUTHRIE *Little Country* vii. 147 The tiny pois danced against arms and shoulders and breasts. **1938** [see *HAKA]. **1943** N. MARSH *Colour Scheme* ii. 36 He's going round your younger lot talking about teams of *poi* girls. **1945** R. PARK *in Coast to Coast 1944* 42 There'll be girls dancing the poi. **1949** P. BUCK *Coming of Maori* (1950) II. ix. 243 The women's *poi* dance..used an accessory in the form of the *poi* ball... The *poi* balls in common use in modern times are made of dry bullrush leaves (*raupo*), about the size of an orange but slightly elongated, and with a short string... The movements with the long *poi* were slower than with the modern short *poi*. The string of the *poi* was held in the right hand and the ball was twirled and beaten back with the left hand while various movements were made over the shoulder, to the sides, the thighs, the knees, the head, the *poi* balls being kept twirling in perfect time to the songs sung by the leaders. **1950** *N.Z. Jrnl. Agric.* Jan. 89/1 One of the pois..is interwoven with raw doghide, a custom which, because it pertained only to very early times, makes this poi a rarity. **1958** S. ASHTON-WARNER *Spinster* 47 The Maori love-songs..and the poi tunes and the melodies they use in canoes. **1977** *N.Z. Woman's Weekly* 10 Jan. 35/2 A calendar which features Maori poi dancing at Rotorua.

poi, var. *PWE.

poiesis (poi,ī·sis). [f. Gr. ποίησις a making, creation; cf. POESIS, POESY *sb.*] Creative production, esp. of a work of art.

1934 in WEBSTER. **1962** *Listener* 24 May 901/2 The tutelary figure of all that belongs to poiesis. **1971** G. STEINER *In Bluebeard's Castle* III. 72 The equivocations between *poiesis*—the artist's, the thinker's creation—and death. **1973** MATIAS & WILLEMEN tr. Cegarra & Metz in *Screen* Spring/Summer 152 Metz uses the term realism to characterise both types [of filmic modernity]: in the case of Godard, 'a copiously disorganised *realism*, a brilliant and euphoric avatar of poiesis'.

-poiesis (poi,ī·sis), comb. form of Gr. ποίησις (see prec.), used to form terms in *Med.*, as *hæmopoiesis* s.v. *HÆMO-, HEMO-, *lymphopoiesis* s.v. *LYMPHO-.

poignance. Add: Now also with pronunc. (poi·nʸăns). (Earlier and further examples.)

1769 O. RUFFHEAD *Life A. Pope* 114 The solemn air.. greatly heightens the poignance of the ridicule. *Ibid.* 119 The poet's closing the climax with the highest disaster of all, gives additional poignance to the ridicule. **1812** E. WYNNE *Let.* 6 Apr. in *Wynne Diaries* (1952) xxx. 514 All the poignance of his sufferings.

poignancy. Add: Now also with pronunc. (poi·nʸănsi). **3.** (Further example.)

1934 M. BODKIN *Archetypal Patterns in Poetry* 310 In each poem the lovely image gains poignancy from its imagined background of frustration and pain.

poignant, *a.* Add: Now also with pronunc. (poi·nʸănt).

poikilitic, *a.* Mark sense in Dict. † **1.** *Obs.* and add: **2.** *Petrogr.* Applied to the structure or texture of a rock (now only an igneous rock), or to the rock itself, in which small crystals of one mineral are enclosed within crystals of another. Cf. *PŒCILITIC *a.* 2.

1886 G. H. WILLIAMS in *Amer. Jrnl. Sci.* CXXXI. 30 This structure is so common in many massive rocks, especially in the more basic kinds, that I would venture to suggest the use of the term '*poicilitic*' (derived from the Greek ποικίλος, mottled) for it. **1893** —— in *Jrnl. Geol.* I. 176 (*heading*) On the use of the terms poikilitic and micropoikilitic in petrography. *Ibid.* 177 This term was at first incorrectly spelled *poicilitic* and subsequently corrected by Prof. Dana to its Latin form, *poecilitic*... Its preferable orthography is, however, that given above [*sc. poikilitic*]. At the time it was proposed the writer was not familiar.. with the designations..*poecilitic* and *poikilitic*, given successively..to the 'New Red' sandstone. **1920** [see *poikiloblastic* adj. s.v. *POIKILO-]. **1923** *Jrnl. Geol.* XXXI. 177 The feldspar grains of the arkose are set, in a sort of poikilitic fashion, in a matrix of much more coarsely crystalline quartz. **1954** H. WILLIAMS et al. *Petrography* ii. 19 (*caption*) Poikilitic texture in hornblende peridotite, Odenwald, Germany. **1970** *Nature* 25 July 366/1 The poikilitic chromitite harzburgite..could well be formed from dunite by permeation by silica-bearing solutions.

Hence **poikili·tically** *adv.*

1912 *Meddelelser om Grønland* XXXVIII. 150 Each anhedron encloses a large number of sodalite-crystals poikilitically. **1932** F. F. GROUT *Petrogr. & Petrol.* vi. 371 Less commonly some rounded granules in a hornfels may be enclosed in a coarser mineral developed poikilitically. **1963** W. A. DEER et al. *Rock-Forming Min.* IV. 263 Kalsilite..occurs as an interstitial mineral poikilitically enclosing the ferromagnesian constituents.

poikilo-. Add: **poikiloblast,** (*b*) (also **pœcilo-**) *Petrol.*, each of the inclusions in a poikiloblastic rock; **poi:kilobla·stic** *a.* (also **pœcilo-**) *Petrol.* [ad. G. *poikiloblastisch* (F. Becke 1903, in *Compt. Rend. IX Sess. Congr. Géol. Internat.* (1904) II. 570): see -BLAST], applied to the structure or texture of a metamorphic rock, or to the rock itself, in which small crystals of an original mineral occur within crystals of its metamorphic product (cf. *POIKILITIC *a.* 2).

1944 *Trans. R. Soc. Edin.* LXI. 225 Accessories are apatite and sphene,..the latter in rounded red-brown pleochroic poeciloblasts in the same minerals. **1969** A. SPRY *Metamorphic Textures* 169 (*heading*) Poikiloblasts. **1920** A. HOLMES *Nomencl. Petrol.* 187 *Poikiloblastic*, a metamorphic texture due to the development, during recrystallisation, of a new mineral around numerous relics of the original minerals, thus simulating the poikilitic texture of igneous rocks. **1932** A. HARKER *Metamorphism* xiii. 191 (*caption*) A large porphyroblast of green hornblende showing typical pœciloblastic or sieve-structure. **1954** H. WILLIAMS et al. *Petrography* ix. 168 (*caption*) Poikiloblastic (sieve) texture in skarn, Doubtful Sound, New Zealand. **1969** A. SPRY *Metamorphic Textures* vi. 170 Inclusions increase the total free energy and thus a poikiloblastic crystal is not in its most-stable..condition.

poikiloderma (poi:kilǒdə·ɹmă). *Path.* [mod.L., ad G. *poikilodermia* (E. Jacobi 1907, in *Verhandl. der deutsch. dermatol. Gesellschaft: IX. Kongr. 1906* 322), f. Gr. ποικίλο-ς variegated + δέρμα skin.] An atrophic condition of the skin characterized by reticular pigmentation and associated with telangiectasia. Hence **poi:kilode·rmatous** *a.*

1907 *Index Medicus* 173/2 (Index), Poikiloderma. **1936** *Arch. Dermatol. & Syphilol.* XXXIII. 289 The word poikiloderma..is used indiscriminately, to indicate variegated lesions, instead of being limited to eruptions presenting a definite picture of poikiloderma atrophicans vasculare. *Ibid.* 290 Poikilodermatous changes may be part of the picture of many chronic inflammatory dermatoses. **1967** H. MONTGOMERY *Dermatopath.* xi. 246/2 Various types of poikiloderma, including poikiloderma of Civatte, do not reveal the typical changes in the blood vessels or in the collagenous fibers although telangiectasia is present clinically and histologically. **1968** A. ROOK in A. Rook et al. *Textbk. Dermatol.* II. xlii. 1271/2 Some inflammatory dermatoses, such as lichen planus may also give rise to poikilodermatous changes.

poikilosmotic (poi:kilǫzmǫ·tik), *a.* *Physiol.* Also **poikilo-osmotic** (poi:kilo,ǫzmǫ·tik). [ad. G. *poikilosmotisch* (R. Höber *Physikal. Chem. der Zelle und der Gewebe* (1902) ii. 26): see POIKILO- and OSMOTIC *a.*] Of an animal: that allows the concentration of solute in its body fluids to vary with fluctuations in that in the surrounding medium. Opp. *homœo-osmotic* s.v. *HOMŒO-.

1905 *Biol. Bull.* VIII. 262 All of the marine invertebrates which we have worked with are truly 'poikilosmotic'. Two factors may be at work in producing the variations in the osmotic pressure, viz., the interchange of water, and of salts. **1931** *Biol. Rev.* VI. 473 Characteristically marine forms such as *Hyas, Cancer* and the polychaete *Nereis cultrifera* only respond to lowered external salinity by passive swelling till their blood is isotonic with the medium. Such 'poikilosmotic' organisms show no change in oxygen consumption during this process. **1953** E. PALMER tr. *Ekman's Zoogeogr. Sea* vi. 118 The marine invertebrates were until recently considered to be poikilo-osmotic. **1971** *Biol. Abstr.* LII. 5434/1 Poikilosmotic animals are actually slightly hyperosmotic as against their external medium in the normal circumstances of the animal's existence.

Hence **poi:kilosmo·sis, poi:kilosmoti·city,** the state or property of being poikilosmotic.

1935 *Proc. Linnean Soc. N.S.W.* LX. 244 A 'law of poikilosmoticity' is by no means applicable to all marine invertebrates when the surrounding water is of lower salinity than ordinary sea-water. **1939** A. KROGH *Osmotic Regulation in Aquatic Animals* 242 (Index), Poikilosmosis. **1955** ELKINTON & DANOWSKI *Body Fluids* ii. 50 In many invertebrates the poikilosmoticity is only relative and.. steady states are maintained with respect to both total osmolarity and individual ionic levels. **1971** *Biol. Abstr.* LII. 5434/1 (*heading*) On poikilosmosis and iso-osmosis.

poikilothermal, -thermic: substitute for entry s.v. POIKILO-:

poikilothermic (poi:kilo*þ*ə·ɹmik), *a.* *Physiol.* [ad. G. *pökilotherm* (now *poik-*) (C. Bergmann 1847, in *Göttinger Studien* I. 613): see POIKILO- and THERMIC *a.*] Characterized by a body temperature that varies with the temperature of the environment; cold-blooded. Also **poi:kilothe·rmal, -the·rmous** *adjs.*, in the same sense. Opp. *HOMŒOTHERMIC *a.*

1884 Poikilothermic [in Dict. s.v. POIKILO-]. **1885** W. STIRLING tr. *Landois's Text-bk. Human Physiol.* I. vi. 426 The so-called cold-blooded animals are called poikilothermal. **1928** PEARSE & HALL *Homoiothermism* i. 2 The change from the poikilothermic to the homoiothermic condition. *Ibid.* iv. 27 The extreme minimum temperature which poikilothermal animals can tolerate. **1933** R. H. WOLCOTT *Animal Biol.* lxiv. 456 Animals which can maintain a constant temperature are termed homoiothermous..; animals unable to do so are termed poikilothermous, or cold-blooded. **1956** *Sci. News* XL. 71 Under ordinary circumstances most poikilothermous animals have body temperatures that fall when the environment becomes cooler, and rises when it becomes warmer. **1963** *Lancet* 5 Jan. 29/1 Newborn infants are poikilothermic, and their temperatures may be rapidly reduced. **1973** *Marine Biol.* XXI. 262/2 Lower poikilothermal animals (protozoans, sponges, some coelenterates). **1973** P. A. COLINVAUX *Introd. Ecol.* xx. 288 Poikilothermous lizards are not excluded from the Arctic because they are poikilothermous, but because, on the average, they cannot balance their heat budgets if the ambient temperature is low.

Hence **poi·kilotherm,** a poikilothermic animal.

1934 in WEBSTER. **1950** C. L. PROSSER in C. L. Prosser et al. *Compar. Animal Physiol.* x. 349 Aquatic poikilotherms follow changes in environmental temperature rapidly and precisely. **1965** B. E. FREEMAN tr. *Vandel's Biospeleol.* xix. 326 Resistance to starvation is a general property of poikilotherms. **1968** [see *HOMŒOTHERM].

poikilothermia (poi:kilo*þ*ə·ɹmiă). *Physiol.* Also anglicized as **poi·kilothermy.** [f. prec.: see -IA¹, -Y³.] The state or property of being poikilothermic. Also **poi:kilothe·rmism** (*rare*).

1903 *Jrnl. Physiol.* XXIX. 369 (*heading*) Poikilothermism in rabies. **1921** *Physiol. Rev.* I. 304 Increased surface blood flow promotes poikilothermia because it facilitates the conduction of heat either to or from the body. **1939** *Nature* 22 Apr. 684/1 Torpidity [in humming-birds] appears to be a temporary poikilothermy, rather similar to that already described for bats. **1968** D. W. WOOD *Princ. Animal Physiol.* viii. 122 Social methods of overcoming the disadvantages of poikilothermy are also found. Larvae of the butterfly *Vanessa* cluster together in the cold. **1974** *Nature* 22 Feb. 568/1 In most newborn animals there is a physiological hypothermia and poikilothermia.

poile. Restrict † *Obs. rare* to sense in Dict. and add later example in spelling *poil.*

1806 M. LEWIS *Jrnl.* 15 May in *Orig. Jrnls. Lewis & Clark Expedition* (1905) V. xxviii. 38 The poil of these [grizzly] bear were infinitely longer finer and thicker than the black bear.

b. poil(e) de chèvre (see quot. 1960).
1873 F. B. PALLISER *Descr. Catal. Lace S. Kensington Mus.* (ed. 2) 9 Lace is made of gold, silver, silk, cotton, and flax, to which may be added poil-de-chèvre. **1927** E. SITWELL *Rustic Elegies* 86 And splashed the red and white striped poil de chèvre short gown. **1960** C. W. CUNNINGTON et al. *Dict. Eng. Costume* 269/2 *Poile de Chèvre*,..a textile of goat's hair (weft) and silk (warp) in plain weave; having a shiny satin-like lace.

Poilite (poi·ləit). Also **poilite.** A proprietary name for a building material made of asbestos and cement, used in the form of tiles, sheets, etc.
1903 *Trade Marks Jrnl.* 11 Feb. 154 Poilite... A fire-resisting lining and roofing material.., manufactured of a mixture of asbestos, lime, and Portland cement, for use in building. Bell's Asbestos Company, Limited,..London. **1922** *Daily Mail* 7 Nov. 3 The amalgamation of the company's poilite (asbestos-cement) section with the British Everite and Asbestilite Works. **1925** E. G. BLAKE *Roof Coverings* vii. 157 The cost of Poilite slates at the present time is about twenty per cent. less than that of the ordinary Welsh slates. **1936** *Discovery* Apr. 117/1 Wainscotings, skirtings, panelling, poilite sheets, etc., are loosened to allow entry of the gas. **1968** *Laxton's Building Price Bk.* (ed. 141) 726/1 'Poilite' Asbestos-Cement Flat Sheets &c., Turners Asbestos-Cement Co. Ltd.

poilu (pwalü). *colloq.* [Fr., hairy, virile.] A soldier in the French army, *esp.* one who fought in the war of 1914–18. Also *attrib.* and *Comb.*
1914 in *Further Lett. from Man of No Importance* (1932) 15, I hear dear old Madame Waddington is busy as a bee with comforts for *poilus*. **1915** G. ADAM *Behind Scenes at Front* 183 France has every reason to be proud of her infantry, the 'poilus' as they have been called in this war. **1916** 'TAFFRAIL' *Pincher Martin* xvi. 303 *Poilus* in their slate-blue uniforms. **1918** E. M. ROBERTS *Flying Fighter* 54 We were away north of the French lines, but that made no difference to the poilus, who also were to attend the ceremony. **1923** *Daily Mail* 28 Feb. 1 (Advt.), In shades of Coral,..Poilu-Blue, Lemon, Brique, Mole. **1926** *Glasgow Herald* 30 Nov. 8 He depicts..the adventures of two poilus who miss the train that should have brought them back to barracks in time for roll-call. **1930** KIPLING *Limits & Renewals* (1932) 324 He pointed downward to the little cast-iron *poilu*, which seemed to be standard pattern for War memorials in that region. **1940** 'GUN BUSTER' *Return via Dunkirk* I. x. 79 The room was packed with poilus, singing songs. **1946** G. MILLAR *Horned Pigeon* xvii. 263 There were fierce yellowish photographs of men posed in *poilu* uniform all round the walls of her room. **1966** J. DOS PASSOS *Best Times* (1968) ii. 43 The Boche..scattered a few salvoes of artillery..just to keep the poilus on their toes. **1975** P. FUSSELL *Gt. War & Mod. Memory* (1977) vii. 240 During the 1917 mutinies in the French army, the *poilus* being marched up to the line frequently made loud *baa*-ing noises.

poinciana (poinsĭ,ā·nă). [mod.L. (J. P. de Tournefort *Institutiones Rei Herbariæ* (1700) I. 619), f. the name of M. de *Poinci*, a 17th-century governor of the Antilles + *-ana*.] An evergreen tree or a deciduous prickly shrub of the genus formerly so called, now divided between *Delonix* and *Cæsalpinia*, belonging to the family Leguminosæ, native to the West Indies, Madagascar, or northern Africa, and bearing racemes of scarlet or yellow flowers.
1731 P. MILLER *Gardeners Dict.* s.v. Poinciana; Barbadoes Flower-Fence, or Spanish Carnations. **1807** *Curtis's Bot. Mag.* XXV. 995 The name of Poinciana was given to this splendid shrub by Tournefort. **1824** H. E. LLOYD tr. *Spix & Martius's Travels in Brazil* I. II. i. 174 The beautiful bushes of the poinciana are planted. **1859** J. FROEBEL *Seven Years' Travel in Central Amer.* iii. 34 The way down from the city passes through thickets of shrubbery covered with the most splendid flowers, amongst which the Poinciana, with scarlet panicles, is most prominent. **1908** *Daily Chron.* 11 Sept. 7/2 The Royal Poinciana crowns itself with cardinal magnificence. **1927** *Transition* Apr. 101 Under the poinciana, of a noon or afternoon Let fiery blossoms clot the light. **1954** *Coast to Coast 1953–54* 86 The house was..enclosed by gardens and shaded by tamarind- and poinciana-trees. **1969** T. H. EVERETT *Living Trees of World* 196/2 A native of Madagascar, but freely planted as an ornamental in most warm climates, the royal poinciana is one of the showiest of flowering trees. **1978** 'A. YORK' *Tallant for Disaster* xi. 167 A larger than average wave..smashing at the base of the poinciana trees.

poinsettia. Substitute for etym.: [mod.L. (R. Graham 1836, in *Edinb. Newe Philos. Jrnl.* XX. 412), f. the name of J. R. *Poinsett* (1779–1851), American minister to Mexico + -IA[1].] (Earlier and later examples.) Also *attrib.*
1836 *Curtis's Bot. Mag.* LXIII. 3493 (*heading*) Showy Poinsettia. **1906** P. PENNINGTON *Jrnl.* 9 Mar. in *Woman Rice Planter* (1913) ix. 302 Mr. Poinsett..brought many rare plants from Mexico, among others the Flor de la Noche Buena, which has borne in this country the name Poinsettia in his honor. **1947** K. TENNANT *Lost Haven* vii. 99 The town on the slope was aflame with red poinsettias. **1964** 'R. MACDONALD' in H. Waugh *Merchants of Menace* (1969) 78 Plaster painted adobe color, poinsettia-red curtains. **1968** J. C. HOLMES *Nothing More to Declare* 43 A few luxuriant poinsettias bloomed among the crumbling buildings and the blistered streets. **1977** WARD & WELLSTED *Indoor Plants* 25 (*caption*) These [developments] culminated in the dwarf poinsettias now so common in florists' displays. **1978** *Detroit Free Press* 16 Apr. 1D/2 It is an eclectic and nurturing environment where poinsettias thrive long after Christmas.

point, *sb.*[1] Add: **A. I. 3. a.** (Earlier example of *full point*.)
1587 F. CLEMENT *Petie Schole* 25 The perfect pause, or full point is set down in the line immediatly after the last word.

II. 5. a. Also used with preceding numeral to form an *attrib. phr.* designating a statement or document that has the number of items specified by the numeral.
1945 *Richmond* (Va.) *Times–Dispatch* 26 Oct. 5/1 He proposed, in its stead, a six-point program as a foundation for world peace. **1961** *Chicago Daily Tribune* 25 Oct. 1. 16/3 If the parties failed to sign an eight point protocol agreeing on Gen. Gursel as president. **1975** *New Yorker* 21 Apr. 134/2 The basic policy of the Communists, set forth in a ten-point statement.., is constantly rebroadcast. **1977** *Time* 10 Jan. 20/2 The CPI supported Mrs. Gandhi's 20-point program for social reform, but pointedly witheld support from Sanjay's five-point youth program.

III. 13. e. *on points* (Boxing): according to or as a result of the points scored in a number of rounds, esp. in phr. *to beat* (or *defeat*) *on points*: to beat (an opponent) in a contest by winning more points and not by achieving a knockout. Also *to lose* (or *win*) *on points*, etc. Also *fig.*
1904 *C. B. Fry's Mag.* June 301/1 Aeneas called 'time', and gave a decision..'on points'. **1929** *Daily Express* 7 Nov. 13/5 Young Stribling, the American boxer, defeated Maurice Griselle, France, on points in a ten-round.. contest. **1929** *Evening News* 18 Nov. 16/4 Rolland..beat Wilhelm Bech on points. **1930** *Cambridge Daily News* 25 Sept. 7/4 Campolo..will probably retire for good..if Sharkey gives him the full count, or if he loses on points. **1948** J. B. PRIESTLEY *Linden Tree* I. 38 'Daddy had a blazing row with the man at the bookshop. Didn't you, Daddy?'.. 'Yes, but I thought he won on points.' **1955** *Times* 12 May 4/3 He landed a fair number of swings and a few straight lefts... It was not enough and Eddington won on points. **1957** E. GOWERS *H. W. Fowler* 11 The draftsman was attacked for using this construction... If I had been the referee in that contest I should have awarded Jespersen a win on points. **1968** *Listener* 18 July 90/3 Mrs Vlachou was as icily contemptuous of the colonels' intentions as she used once to be of British intentions at the time of the Cyprus troubles; Mr Sparrow was eloquent in their defence. On points I should give the victory to Mrs Vlachou. **1975** *Oxf. Compan. Sports & Games* 116/1 This championship, for which Clay and Frazier, the winner on points over 15 rounds, each received $2,500,000, must have grossed more than $20 million.

14. b. A unit of credit towards an award or benefit, *spec.* (*a*) an academic qualification (*U.S.*); (*b*) allocation of local authority housing; (*c*) discharge from the armed forces or return from overseas service.
1903 *N.Y. Times* 29 Aug. 3/4 For university credit, each 30 hours' course counts one point, and laboratory work, at the rate of 60 hours, to one point. **1950** B. WOOTTON *Testament for Social Science* ii. 41 The local authority's decision to give x points for size of family, y points for service in the armed forces, plus z points for being bombed out may be regarded as entirely subjective value-judgments. **1953** *Manch. Guardian Weekly* 5 Feb. 7 Into San Francisco come the wounded, come the soldiers who have accumulated enough rotation 'points' to be sent home. **1959** N. MAILER *Advts. for Myself* (1961) 120 The regiment was disbanded, and those men who did not have enough points to go home were sent to other outfits. **1963** [see *CREDIT *sb.* 13 d]. **1974** M. BIRMINGHAM *You can help Me* i. 10 The Bengalis..have not enough points yet to live in tower blocks so they pay exorbitant rents to private landlords. **1974** *Times* 14 Nov. 17/7 Housing lists are so long..I think..they [*sc.* agricultural workers] should be given points for the number of years they have lived in a tied house. **1977** E. AMBLER *Send no more Roses* v. 89 It's to be first in, first out, with a points bonus for every month of overseas service. **1977** *Jrnl. R. Soc. Arts* CXXV. 550/2 Usually points were allocated according to the inadequacy of the existing accommodation, the degree of overcrowding, the health of the occupier, the length of time that these conditions had prevailed, and the extent to which the dwelling was unsuited to the needs of the occupier. When a household had acquired enough points to reach the top of the housing list, then their own preference as to location and dwelling type would be taken into account.

c. *Bridge.* A unit by which a hand is evaluated.
1959 *Listener* 5 Mar. 434/2 A balanced hand with less than 25 points is considered insufficient to make a mandatory force to game. *Ibid.* 434/3 A ten-point hand. **1964** *Official Encycl. Bridge* 431/1 This [*sc.* the high-card valuation] gives a total of 40 points in the pack, and makes an average hand worth ten points. **1977** *Times* 10 Dec. 13/4 The text-books advise you to pass, because you have four points only and six points are needed for a positive response.

15. a. (Later examples.) Also used in quoting variations in interest rates (one point representing one per cent) and exchange rates (one point being one-hundredth of the smallest monetary unit).
1906 L. C. CORNFORD *Defenceless Islands* 98 Prices have dropped six points. A point is the hundredth part of a penny. **1930** M. CLARK *Home Trade* 163 Prices in the case of spot transactions are not stated in terms of pence per lb., but as so many 'points on' or 'points off' the price of cotton.., a 'point' being one hundredth of a penny. **1971** *Daily Tel.* 5 Apr. 7/2 Bank Rate is now 2½ points higher than at the beginning of 1956, and mortgage rates are also 2½ points higher over the same period. *Ibid.*, This would save the building societies about ⅛ of a point of interest. **1974** *Ibid.* 23 Feb. 19/4 Metal Box at 206p managed an 11-point rise while Pilkington jumped 13 to 302p. **1980** *Times* 12 Feb. 19/3 Sterling..continued to maintain a firm position closing 60 points ahead at 2·3045.

b. A unit of value and exchange in rationing; *on points*, (rationed) on the basis of such units.
1940 *Economist* 31 Aug. 280/2 Textiles are sharply rationed [in Holland]... On August 12th, the German system of a clothing card of 100 points was introduced. **1942** *Business Week* 9 May 15/1 The rationing method—according to current OPA thinking—will be to establish a secondary currency of points alongside the dollar currency. Essential articles..will be listed and given a price in points. Then every person in the country will be given a book of stamps representing a certain number of points. **1944** M. LASKI *Love on Supertax* i. 13 You always seem to forget that breakfast cereals cost points. **1944** *Times* 23 Feb. 2/3 From April 2 imported tinned marmalade will be available on points, and will not be, as hitherto, part of the preserve ration. **1947** *Ann. Reg. 1946* 55 Surplus [Bread] Units would be exchangeable for Points entitling to other foodstuffs. **1948** J. BELL *Wonderful Mrs Marriott* ii. 36 Mrs Dale's worries with points and coupons. **1950** 'P. WOODRUFF' *Island of Chamba* vii. 109 The Sultana sounds like something you get from the grocer if you have enough points. **1965** N. FREELING *Criminal Conversation* II. xv. 169 England during the reign of Sir Stafford Cripps..with points and coupons and austerity. **1975** S. BRIGGS *Keep Smiling Through* (1976) 155 People could distribute their 16 monthly points as they liked, sometimes spending the lot on a delicious tin of salmon, sometimes cautiously stocking up on sensible spam and pilchards.

17*. A measure of weight used for diamonds and other precious stones, equal to one hundredth of a carat.
1931 KRAUS & HOLDEN *Gems* (ed. 2) vii. 99 The weight of a diamond is often expressed in points. Thus, a stone weighing 65 points actually weighs 0·65 carats. **1974** *Encycl. Brit. Micropædia* II. 546/3 The metric carat, equal to 0·200 grams, and the point, equal to 0·01 carat, was adopted by the U.S. in 1913 and, subsequently, by most other countries. **1979** *Guardian* 3 Nov. 17/7 (Advt.), A dazzling 1¼ point diamond, handset in a brilliant starburst of gold 'vermeil'.

IV. 19. b. (Further examples.) Also, a rallying point or rendezvous for police, military personnel, etc.
1898 J. D. BRAYSHAW *Slum Silhouettes* 201 'Here, John,' he shouts to the potman, 'fetch the man from the point.'.. In a few minutes up comes the potman with a sergeant an' p'liceman. **1963** N. MARSH *Dead Water* (1964) vii. 191 Shall I return to my point, sir? **1967** 'S. WOODS' *And shame Devil* ii. 36, I made my point with t'sergeant... Corner of Badger's Way, that was. **1968** P. N. WALKER *Carnaby & Gaol-breakers* viii. 80 P.C. Williams... His last point was in Romanby village. **1972** J. ROSSITER *Rope for General Dietz* ix. 128 They're waiting until half-past ten. That's when the *Guardia* make their point near the *Bar El Toro Blanco* and wait for thirty minutes.

c. (Later examples.)
1920 *Blackw. Mag.* Jan. 108/1 These marshy channels.. are the invariable point of any hunted boar. **1939** *Country Life* 11 Feb. p. xxxii/1 After running in all for an hour and forty minutes and making a six and a half miles point. **1977** *Field* 13 Jan. 52/1 Our fox crossed the valley and made his point to Moorhill.

d. *pl.* Localities or places considered in some special connection, esp. as being in a particular direction from a specified place. (Influenced by sense B. 9.)
1885 U. S. GRANT *Personal Mem.* I. xxx. 422 From there [*sc.* Vicksburg] a railroad runs east, connecting with other roads leading to all points of the Southern States. **1895** *Montgomery Ward Catal.* Spring & Summer 589/1 Freight paid by us to all points east of the west line of Dakota, Kansas, Nebraska and Louisiana. To points farther west we apply $1 00 on the payment of freight. **1903** *N.Y. Even. Post* 19 Aug. 7/6 The number here is now estimated at 21,000 persons from Eastern points, with fully 35,000 persons in addition from California. **1926** *Publishers' Weekly* 22 May 1684/2 Some of us here get supplies from other points that they know nothing about. *Ibid.* 18 Dec. 2256 The business must be going to distant points—New York, Chicago, etc. **1933** *Fortune* Aug. 94 Loring F. ('Red') Nichols, of Cleveland and points Mid-West, is a crack director and trumpeter. **1969** R. TASHKENT *Ambiguous Man* i. 14 She and a friend had started off for Athens and points East. **1969** D. BARRON *Man who was There* i. 11 I've been in Pakistan and points East for six weeks. **1973** A. ROSS *Dunfermline Affair* 38 We..took the road through Kilmany and Auchtermuchty and all points south west. **1978** *Jrnl. R. Soc. Arts* CXXVI. 712/1, I will be testing that later this month in Washington and other points West.

e. (See quot. 1926); *spec.* a socket fixed in a wall or the like which is connected to an electricity supply and designed to receive the plug of an electrical appliance; = *OUTLET *sb.* 1 d. Cf. also *power point* s.v. *POWER *sb.*[1] 18 f.
1904 H. WALTER *Electric Lighting for Inexperienced* viii. 82 The cost per point depends..on the materials used for protecting the wires, and whether the wires are run on or under the surface of walls. **1913** D. S. MUNRO *Practice of Electr. Wiring* xiv. 126 The stamped boxes are not so useful for variety of outlet point. **1921** J. H. HAVELOCK *Electr. Installation Work* xiii. 155 The lamps may be varied at one of the switch points. **1925** J. C. CONNAN *Electr. Estimating* ix. 167 If the area in square feet to be illuminated is divided by the total number of points (including ceiling roses, wall brackets, and wall plugs), the average area illuminated per point is obtained. **1926**

Gloss. Terms Electr. Engin. (Brit. Engin. Stand. Assoc.) 111 *Point*, in wiring. The termination of the wiring intended for attachment to a fitting for one or more lamps or other consuming devices. **1940** G. D. H. & M. COLE *Murder at Munition Works* 138 Presumably there was a lead to that reading lamp point over there. **1967** *Listener* 21 Dec. 831/2 There is no electric point in her room, so she uses the ceiling light festooned with wires to plug in her iron. **1972** M. BABSON *Murder on Show* ix. 107 Helena Keswick plugged an electric kettle into a point underneath the table. **1976** *Cumberland & Westmorland Herald* 4 Dec. 16/6 (Advt.), Kitchen/breakfast room,.., floor units and matching wall cupboards and electric cooker point.

20. Restrict *Her.* to senses in Dict. and add: **d.** *Sculpture.* Any one of a series of holes drilled in a piece of stone or marble or on the model to be copied to the depth to which the material has to be cut away. Also, the position of such a hole.

1841 *Penny Cycl.* XXI. 142/1 This process is repeated till the numerous points at fixed depths, corresponding throughout with the surface of the model, are attained, and a rough copy of the sculptor's original work is thus mechanically made. **1911** A. TOFT *Modelling & Sculpture* 254 A good pointer will keep all his 'points' a little 'full', by never allowing the needle to go quite home. **1947** J. C. RICH *Materials & Methods of Sculpture* ix. 261 The indirect method of stone carving involves the use of previously prepared three-dimensional models, built up in most cases of plastic clay and then cast in a more durable substance, such as plaster of Paris. The casts are then utilized as master models from which to take points or otherwise copy. **1970** *Oxf. Compan. Art* 884/2 Sometimes hundreds and even thousands of points will be taken to ensure a meticulously exact copy. **1974** *Encycl. Brit. Micropædia* VIII. 68/1 The final points on the stone are usually left about $\frac{1}{32}$ inch (about one millimetre) higher than those on the model to enable the sculptor to put the finishing touches on the stone.

22. c. Phr. *up to a (certain) point*: to a certain extent, but by no means absolutely.

1823 BYRON *Don Juan* XIII. lxxxi. 95 For good society Is no less famed for tolerance than piety: That is, up to a certain point; which point Forms the most difficult in punctuation. **1916** G. B. SHAW *Androcles & Lion* p. xv, As they [*sc.* Savonarolas and Knipperdollings] know, very sensibly, that a little religion is good for children and serves morality, keeping the poor in good-humor or in awe by promising rewards in heaven or threatening torments in hell, they encourage the religious people up to a certain point. **1936** —— *Simpleton* II. 53 Well, it has worked, up to a point. **1951** E. PAUL *Springtime in Paris* xvi. 296 He had been an understanding husband up to a certain point. **1961** *Chicago Daily Tribune* 10 Feb. III. 9/7 But he had in Walter Hendl a willing conductor able only up to a point. **1978** P. MCCUTCHAN *Blackmail North* vi. 69 'There's been a threat, Shard!' 'Being taken seriously?' 'Up to a point.'

V. 26. b. *pl.* Of persons and things: good features, advantages; usu. in phr. *to have one's* (or *its*) *points*.

1897 A. BEARDSLEY *Let.* 16 Sept. (1970) 369 It was a sad moment when I tore myself from Dieppe... Paris however has points and I am forgetting my sorrow. **1931** *Times Lit. Suppl.* 26 Feb. 157/1 A simple story, but it has its points. **1934** E. O'NEILL *Days without End* I. 24 What the devil's got into Walter lately, anyway? Getting drunk as a pastime may have its points, but as an exclusive occupation—. **1946** —— *Iceman Cometh* I. 24 *Parritt.* (*With a disparaging glance around*) Must be hard up for a place to hang out. *Larry.* It has its points for him. He never runs into anyone he knows in his business here. **1953** B. GORDON-CUMMING *Gentle Rain* 38 She had her points, certainly... In her occasional dreamy moods she was lovely. **1961** F. & R. LOCKRIDGE (*title*) Murder has its points.

c. An area of contrasting colour in the fur of certain cats, usually on the face, paws and tail. Cf. also *SEAL POINT.

1903 F. SIMPSON *Bk. of Cat* xxiii. 259/2 The [Siamese] kittens are born absolutely white..and gradually all the points come. **1935** E. B. SIMMONS *Cats* xxix. 149 Blue points are rare, a sort of 'sport'. **1955** R. TENENT *Pedigree Cats* vi. 53 The points—marking the mask, ears, legs, feet, and tail—are all a dense and clearly defined seal-brown. **1972** ING & POND *Champion Cats of World* II. 87/2 The colouring and points [of Birmans] are as for the Siamese.

28. a. (Further examples.) Also, (the expression of) an important fact or truth; a noteworthy comment. Phr. *to have a point*: to have made a convincing or significant remark; to be correct (in a particular matter).

c **1939** A. D. LINDSAY *Let.* in D. Scott *A. D. Lindsay* (1971) xv. 258, I have now read the article with interest and appreciation but it doesn't meet my point at all. **1962** *Listener* 22 Feb. 342/2 Is it possible that the Doctor had a point? **1963** *Ibid.* 21 Feb. 350/2 What most convinced me they had a point was the line taken by the interviewer. **1978** L. THOMAS *Ormerod's Landing* ii. 20 'Right,' he agreed sportingly. 'You've got a point, Ormerod.'

c. *to take (someone's) point* (and variants): to understand the import or significance of what is being said; to concede the truth or value of a particular contention.

1898 G. B. SHAW *You never can Tell* II. 254 Do I take your point rightly, Mr McComas? **1901** —— *Capt. Brassbound's Conversion* III. 276 *Rankin* (cannily). I take your point, Leddy Ceecily. It alters the case. **1916** JOYCE *Portrait of Artist* (1969) v. 187, I see. I quite see your point. *Ibid.* 188 Yes, yes: I see, said the dean quickly, I quite catch the point. **1943** N. MARSH *Colour Scheme* x. 187 'The point is quite well taken,' he said at last. **1961** C. WILLOCK *Death in Covert* viii. 168 'You have absolutely nothing to go on except your sixth sense.' 'Point taken.' **1964** R. BRADDON *Year Angry Rabbit* xii. 104 'But this is dusk,' Fitzgerald objected. 'Yes, dear,' Karen got the point quickly, 'which for nocturnals is what dawn is to us.' **1966** *Listener* 3 Nov. 658/2, I take his point about Laszlo Rajk. **1969** V. GIELGUD *Necessary End* xxiii. 205 'A First Officer who doesn't play along to an extent with female passengers would probably be considered to be neglecting his job.' 'Point taken.' **1974** E. LEMARCHAND *Buried in Past* x. 168 'The affair'll have to be shelved.' 'I take your point, sir,' Pollard replied. **1976** J. WAINWRIGHT *Bastard* ii. 35 He nods and says, 'Okay. Point taken.'

d. Sense, purpose, or advantage (*in* or *of* a course of action, state of affairs, etc.). Chiefly in negative contexts, esp. in phr. *there is no point in*, it has no purpose, it is pointless.

In some cases there are connotations of sense B. 10.

1903 G. B. SHAW *Man & Superman* II. 60 Look here, Ann: if theres no harm in it theres no point in doing it. **1923** W. S. MAUGHAM *Our Betters* II. 85 Thornton has plenty of money. Do you think there is any point in his spending his life making more? **1934** J. B. PRIESTLEY *Eden End* I. 6 What's the point of reading if it makes you feel uncomfortable? **1947** —— *Inspector Calls* II. 49 *Inspector.* And if her story is true—that he was stealing money—. *Mrs. Birling*..There's no point in assuming that. **1953** K. AMIS *Lucky Jim* xix. 208 'Give me your address, Christine.' She looked at him scornfully... 'That'll do no good at all. What on earth would be the point?' **1957** J. OSBORNE *Look Back in Anger* III. ii. 90 *Helena.* There doesn't seem much point in trying to explain everything, does there? **1966** M. FRAYN *Russian Interpreter* xxxvii. 207 Was there any possible point for Manning in trying to deny all knowledge of those activities? **1968** C. CHURCHILL in *New Eng. Dramatists* XII. 96 *Tim.* Was it nice in the aeroplane? *Grandfather.* I didn't really notice. *Tim.* What's the point of being in it then? **1971** P. MORTIMER *Home* viii. 80 'Will you..get married?'.. 'There doesn't seem any point.' **1973** G. GREENE *Hon. Consul* v. ii. 262 Tell Pablo to come in. If they have spotted us, there is no point in leaving him outside to be picked off alone. **1977** *Times* 1 June 17/5 If..it were true that many Anglican or Roman Catholic Christians could not accept this fundamental affirmation.. we should have to ask whether there is any point in continuing to search for unity.

e. *debating point*: see *DEBATING *vbl. sb.* b.

VI. 32. A marking on a Hudson's Bay or Mackinaw blanket indicating weight.

1780 in *Beaver* (1935) June 47 [They] had misunderstood him about the price of the pointed plankets as the points were known to every Indian to be the price to be paid for each as 2½ points, 2½ beaver, 3 points, 3 beaver, etc. **1818** T. L. MCKENNEY *Mem.* (1846) I. 309 Northwest Company blankets—so called—three points, to measure six feet six inches long. **1921** *Outing* Nov. 82/1 Hudson Bay blankets run as follows: Three point, 60 × 72 inches, double, weight, 8¼ lbs.; 3½ point, 63 × 81 inches, double, weight, 10 lbs.; 4 point, 72 × 90 inches, double, weight, 12 lbs. 'Points' refer to the markings on the blankets and indicate their size. **1935** *Beaver* June 47 The 'point' on the blanket in its present standardized form is comparatively modern, being introduced in 1850. Prior to that date blankets of the Hudson's Bay Company were made with the bar only by individuals in their own homes, each maker putting a distinctive mark, a 'point' on his product to show the size and weight. These 'points' were usually in coloured wools and usually about one inch long. **1954** E. E. RICH *Moose Fort Jrnl., 1783–85* 371 Originally the points and staves of the blankets were blue, but the colour was changed to red in 1786.

B. I. 1. a. Also of a pencil.

1826 M. R. MITFORD *Our Village* II. 248 A pencil without a point. **1886** C. F. WOOLSON *East Angels* vii. 129 He sharpened all the pencils industriously, taking pains to give each one a very fine point. **1963** C. FREMLIN *Trouble Makers* xviii. 140 Hundreds of coloured pencils without points went back into their dozens of boxes without lids. **1979** 'J. LE CARRÉ' *Smiley's People* (1980) xvi. 189 Herr Kretzschmar owned a fine gold pencil... He popped out the point and..drew a pure circle.

d. (Further examples.)

1911 H. S. HARRISON *Queed* iv. 45 The *Post*, not to put too fine a point upon it, had for a time run fast to seed. **1926** F. W. CROFTS *Inspector French & Cheyne Mystery* iii. 40 Not to put too fine a point on it the situation is this: You are there, and you can't get out, and you can't attract attention to your predicament. **1935** C. ISHERWOOD *Mr. Norris changes Trains* x. 155 He seems to have suggested, not to put too fine a point upon it, that you were an accomplice in my nefarious crimes. **1952** A. J. CRONIN *Adventures in Two Worlds* I. vi. 52 This outbreak of scarlet fever... It's spreading, you know, and I find that in all my cases.., well, not to put too fine a point on it—the milk has come from Shawhead. **1971** 'E. CANDY' *Words for Murder Perhaps* iv. 44 One of the doctor's most cherished personal finds, now happily in the City Museum, was, not to put too fine a point on it, a fake. **1977** *It* May 10/3 Not to put too fine a point on it, one could say that the real picture consists of nothing but exceptions to the rule.

e. Phr. *to a (fine) point*: to a precise form; completely.

1888 in Farmer & Henley *Slang* (1902) V. 241/2 Boiled down to a fine point bondsmen are in demand. **1902** G. H. LORIMER *Lett. Self-Made Merchant* xvii. 253 When she was through I knew that I'd been licked—polished right off to a point.

2. b. Also *transf.* (chiefly *U.S.*), such a feature on a river; the tapering extremity of any woodland reaching down into a prairie or other treeless area; any tapering extremity *of* land, or *of* rocks, woods, etc., constituting a special feature of this.

1637 in *Amer. Speech* (1940) XV. 297/2 Easterly butting out with a point of wood. **1660** *Early Rec. Warwick, Rhode Island* (1926) 256 His point of Meddowe on the south side of Occupessuatuxet Cove. **1682** *Early Rec. Providence, Rhode Island* (1899) XIV. 101 A black Oake tree standing upon a point of Rocks. **1772** D. TAITT in N. D. Mereness *Trav. Amer. Col.* (1916) 501, I..viewed this Town which Stands upon a point of Land on the North west side of the River. **1826** T. FLINT *Recollections* 15 You hear of..sawyers, and points, and bends, and shoots. *Ibid.* 258 The entire uniformity of the meanders of the rivers [in Arkansas] called, in the phrase of the country, 'points and bends'. **1837** W. IRVING *Capt. Bonneville* II. vii. 108 The whole band soon disappeared behind a point of woods. **1857** P. CARTWRIGHT *Autobiogr.* xxi. 328 We rode two miles, and the point of timber was plain in view. **1859** 'MARK TWAIN' in *New Orleans Daily Crescent* 17 May, The point at Cairo, which has not even been moistened by the river since 1813, is now entirely under water. **1883** —— *Life on Miss.* iii. 61 The big raft was away out of sight around the point. **1964** W. C. PUTNAM *Geol.* xi. 275/2 The common name for a broadly curving part of a river is a bend. The convex bank in such a curve is a point.

f. *the Point*: the United States Military Academy at West Point, N.Y. *U.S. colloq.*

1828 J. F. COOPER *Notions of Americans* I. 274 To these relics of a former age, must be added the actual and flourishing establishment at the 'Point', which comprises a village of academic buildings, barracks, and other adjuncts. **1922** *Frontier* (Missoula, Montana) Nov. 14 Ada's father had been C.O. when we were in the Point, and nearly every member of the class had been at one time or another in love with her. **1968** *Michelin: New York City* 139 West Point... Among the war heroes who graduated from the Point are Generals MacArthur (1903), Patton (1909) and Eisenhower (1915). **1971** C. FICK *Danziger Transcript* (1973) 167 Sam had worked his way into Dartmouth..and then transferred to the Point. **1973** E. PACE *Any War* (1974) III. 239 'I've been learning karate... We had the fundamentals at the Point.' 'You went to West Point?'

g. The tip of the lower jaw; the spot on which a knock-out blow is dealt.

1898 [see *OUT *adv.* 19 e]. **1901** R. FITZSIMMONS *Phys. Cult. & Self-Defense* 159, I saw Fitzsimmons' right hand reach the point of Corbett's jaw. **1915** E. CORRI *30 Yrs. Boxing Referee* 229 There is no sleeping-draught like a punch on the point. **1923** *Daily Mail* 16 Feb. 8 He once caught Lewis with a hard right near the point. **1924** *Truth* (Sydney) 27 Apr. 6 *Point*, sensitive portion of the jaw. **1942** BERREY & VAN DEN BARK *Amer. Thes. Slang* §121/18 Point,..the vulnerable point of the chin.

h. Either of the extensions at the front end of a saddle-tree.

1908 *Animal Managem.* 166 The front arch extends below the side bars; the extension is known as the 'points', and these are intended to help the girths and prevent the saddle from heeling over.

i. *Ballet.* The tips of the toes. Usu. with *on* and *pl.* = *POINTE.

1912 *Dancing Times* Aug. 449/2 *Points.*—Exposition of Principles. **1928** A. L. HASKELL *Some Studies in Ballet* 153 A solo on the points. **1936** L. SOKOLOVA in 'C. Brahms' *Footnotes to Ballet* v. 227, I held myself poised on my points, before literally collapsing exhausted in the middle of the stage. **1936** N. STREATFEILD *Ballet Shoes* iv. 52 The children were most impressed by the way the children in the photographs stood on their points. **1949** A. CHRISTIE *Crooked House* x. 71 'He stopped me learning to be a ballet dancer.'.. She..kicked off her shoes and endeavoured to get on to what are called technically..her points. **1967** 'LA MERI' *Spanish Dancing* (ed. 2) vii. 89 Very rarely it [*sc.* the Bolero] is danced on point. **1975** *New Yorker* 26 May 31/1 Mr. Griforovich, who was watching a tiny blond ballerina rise on point with the single-minded intensity of an adult star, put a hand across his face to conceal a smile. **1977** *Time* 24 Jan. 36/3 In a pas de deux with Ted Kivitt, she stepped majestically on point..as if there were magnets concealed in her toe shoes.

j. *U.S.* The position at the front of a herd of cattle, etc.; the position at the head of a column or wedge of troops (cf. sense B. 2 d in Dict.); also quasi-*adv.* in phrases *to ride* or *walk point*. Also *fig.*

1916 'B. M. BOWER' *Phantom Herd* xiv. 245 You see a herd drifting before a storm maybe—a blizzard like yesterday, with your pal riding point. **1927** *Scribner's Mag.* Feb. 178/1 Consider the passing herd, anyone of the many that went up the Long Trail. At the 'point' ride two men, at the 'drag' two more, while other horsemen loiter on either flank. **1959** C. OGBURN *Marauders* (1960) ii. 64 Major Osborne looked around and his eye alighted on me. 'You take the point,' said he... He thought the way to use a communications officer was to have him lead the battalion column into action. **1962** J. ONSLOW *Bowler-Hatted Cowboy* xxi. 205, I was riding 'point', not as a leader to the cattle, but to warn oncoming traffic of the herd. **1964** F. O'ROURKE *Mule for Marquesa* 118 Fardan trotted past the mules and took the point. **1969** I. KEMP *Brit. G.I. in Vietnam* v. 102 Goad walked point and I..took the tail, with the rest of squad well spaced out between us. **1970** *Times* 9 May 8/8 Daniel Lepointe, aged 21, a sergeant.. was walking point—the front position of his platoon—when..a helicopter observer told him about two huts. **1975** W. SAFIRE *Before Fall* I. iv. 45 He said no: 'Let Romney take the point.' (In military tactics, the soldier 'on the point' of a wedge is the most likely to be shot.) **1977** 'J. LE CARRÉ' *Hon. Schoolboy* iv. 100 Let me send you an advocate. Somebody who can ride point for you, draft your submission, carry it to the barricades.

k. *N.Z.* The hocks of a sheep; the wool that grows on them.

1922 W. PERRY *Sheepfarming in N.Z.* iv. 44 The wool should be..well spread on the back, belly, and points. *a* **1948** L. G. D. ACLAND *Early Canterbury Runs* (1951) 379 *Fribby*,..the yolky locks round the points taken off by the roller from a decently skirted fleece. **1956** G. Bowen *Wool Away!* (ed. 2) xii. 132 The Corriedale..grows more wool than hair on the hocks, thereby making it imperative that they be shorn trimmed to the feet. These points or socks do not have a tendency to lift or rise off the skin.

3. e. (Earlier and further examples.) *spec.* (*a*) the tapering extremity of a lightning conductor; (*b*) in an internal-combustion engine, either of the metal pieces on a sparking plug between which the spark jumps, or either of the metal surfaces of a contact-breaker which touch to complete the circuit; usu. *pl.*

1766 in *Essex Inst. Hist. Coll.* (1916) LII. 275 A new Meeting-House building..was struck with Lightning; it had Points and a Conductor as far as the Bellfree. **1775** in *Ibid.* (1877) XIII. 208 They have a handsome clock, points to the house, a fine walk on the top, [etc.]. **1870** 'Mark Twain' in *Galaxy* Sept. 424/1 He said it would be necessary to know exactly how many 'points' I wanted put up, what parts of the house I wanted them on, and what quality of rod I preferred. **1902** J. E. Hutton in A. C. Harmsworth *Motors & Motor-Driving* viii. 150 The points may be sooty and require cleaning. **1927** R. T. Nicholson *Austin Seven Bk.* xiii. 116 The rapid separation of the points of the contact-breaker. **1961** J. Mills *Car Repair & Maintenance* iv. 41 If this happened, there would not be a suitably fat spark at the plug points and the contact breaker points would become burned. **1968** K. Weatherly *Roo Shooter* 111, I must have dried the flamin' plugs and points twenty times.

o. *Archæol.* (See quot. 1959.)

1912 *Archaeologia* LXIII. 129 (*caption*) A symmetrical 'point' of laurel-leaf form.., but the surface flaking only partial. **1932** *Antiquity* VI. 190 The true Mousterian industries are characterized by flake-tools such as side-scrapers, points and Levallois flakes. **1943** J. & C. Hawkes *Prehist. Britain* i. 19 The Levalloisian, an outstanding culture during the last interglacial, when it was responsible for beautifully finished points and scrapers which..were partially trimmed before the flake was struck from the parent core. **1949** W. F. Albright *Archaeol. Palestine* iii. 59 The Natufian was a thorough-going microlithic culture, consisting largely of blades and points. **1959** J. D. Clark *Prehist. S. Africa* ii. 42 *Point*, a pointed flake or blade, often with careful secondary retouch, or a pointed tool of bone. Believed to have sometimes formed the heads of spears and arrows. **1963** J. Hawkes in Hawkes & Woolley *Prehist. & Beginnings of Civilization* I. iii. 71 Implements found..in the Solo valley..include.. points and picks made from bone and antler. **1971** J. Bordaz *Tools of Old & New Stone Age* iv. 31 In regions where good stone is comparatively abundant,..it is not unusual to find Levallois points up to six inches long.

IV. 10. a. (Earlier example.)

1694 J. Savage tr. C. de St. Evremont in T. Brown *Misc. Ess. M. de St. Evremont* II. ii. 96 Points, Antithesis's and Paradoxes.

b. (Further example.)

1901 H. James *Sacred Fount* 17 Having a reputation for 'point' to keep up, she was always under arms.

c. *Theatr.* A gesture, vocal inflection, or some other piece of theatrical technique used to underline a climactic moment in a speech, rôle, or situation; a moment so underlined. Usu. used with the implication that the integrity of the performance as a whole is being subordinated to the desire for immediate applause. Also *fig.*

1822 C. Mathews *Let.* 4 Oct. in A. Mathews *Mem. Charles Mathews* (1839) III. 314, I don't know an instance of a point failing which I considered to be really good myself. **1864** [see *gravy 2 c]. **1870** O. Logan *Before Footlights & Behind Scenes* 135, I began to practice the effects, the stage walks, the managing of the voice, the general bearing of the person, the making of 'points', the attaining of 'climax'. **1897** G. B. Shaw *Our Theatres in Nineties* (1932) III. 124 It lends itself to people talking at each other rhetorically from opposite sides of the stage, taking long sweeping walks up to their 'points'. *Ibid.* 132 He succumbed to the temptation to utter the two or three most fatuously conceited of Helmer's utterances as 'points'. **1900** T. E. Pemberton *Kendals* ix. 259 So natural is she at all times that she never seems to be 'making points' after the crude fashion of inferior actresses. **1916** J. R. Towse *Sixty Years of Theater* 29 Woe to the unfortunate actor who was not on his appointed spot and instant in his speech when he was a factor in one of Macready's laboriously calculated 'points'. **1952** Granville *Dict. Theatrical Terms* 139 A player who is not capable of 'making his *points*' (i.e. stressing his lines at the right time) will never get over.

V. 11. a. (Earlier and later examples.)

1816 W. Lambert *Cricketer's Guide* (ed. 6) 41 The Fieldsmen... The Point. The person who stands at the Point should place himself in a line with the popping crease, about seven yards from the striker. **1904**, etc. [see *backward *a.* 1]. **1916** *Anzac Book* 128 Was it a boundary hit or a catch at point? **1951** *People* 3 June 8/7 When he was out—to a brilliant catch by Ken Graveney at point—the bowling had been tamed.

b. (Earlier and later examples.)

1868 *Chambers's Encycl.* X. 597/1 In the arrangement of the men on each side, the *goal-keeper* defends the goal; *point* is the first man out from the goal; *cover-point* is a little in advance of point. **1935** *Encycl. Sports* 379/1 'Point' takes his position immediately in front of goal. **1967** *Globe & Mail* (Toronto) 16 May 39/9 Actually, the goaltender led a charmed life. Most of the danger was involved with the fellow who played between point and cover-point. **1975** *Oxf. Compan. Sports & Games* 588/2 The ten-a-side team consists of a goalkeeper, three defences (known historically as point, cover point, and third man), a left wing defence, [etc.].

D. 1. g. *at this* (or *that*) *point in time*: at this (or that) particular moment (cf. *moment *sb.* 1 c).

1974 R. B. Parker *Godwulf Manuscript* viii. 68 You don't understand the situation..at this point in time. **1975** *Atlantic Monthly* Jan. 32/2 The phrase 'at that point in time'..quickly became an early trademark of the whole Watergate affair. **1975** G. V. Higgins *City on Hill* iii. 89 'At that point in time I came away with the impression' that she was the best thing in the world. **1977** *Irish Times* 8 June 12/2 At this point in time the private rented sector of the housing market was shrinking.

11. point-to-point, *a.* **a.** (Further examples.) Also, from one point to another in turn (not necessarily in a direct line). Hence **point-to-pointer, point-to-pointing.**

1920 *Isis* 10 Mar. 2/2 No one..would go to a Point-to-point without a hat. **1930** *Telegr. & Teleph. Jrnl.* XVI. 110/2 The State wireless services only undertake 'Ship-to-shore'..and 'Point-to-point' internal traffic. **1934** *Sun* (Baltimore) 30 Mar. 3/2 The running of the Maryland Hunt Cup Point-to-Point. **1945** *Salt* 10 Sept. 10 The point-to-point voyages of air transport. **1952** F. A. Brown *Sport from Within* v. 163 Why not do the job properly and buy a racehorse instead of a point-to-pointer? *Ibid.* 177 It might be as well to confine hunters to Point-to-Pointing for the future, instead of encouraging race-horses to masquerade as hunters at race meetings. **1957** *Practical Wireless* XXXIII. 520/1 The arrangement and layout of main components is illustrated in Figs. 2 and 3, which also show partial point-to-point wiring. **1960** *Times* 12 Mar. 9/7 One of the great criticisms of point-to-pointing is the 'readying' of some of the horses. **1962** *Listener* 12 July 62/3 This instrument [*sc.* the electron microprobe] can provide information about the composition of, say, a copper-zinc alloy by point-to-point exploration of tiny areas one-thousandth of a millimetre square. **1964** A. Wykes *Gambling* viii. 187 Hunting's most direct descendant is a form of horse racing called 'point-to-point'. **1967** M. Chandler *Ceramics in Mod. World* iv. 117 These pores..make it possible for charged ions to carry a current over a comparatively easy point-to-point route through it [*sc.* the insulator]. **1970** M. Williams *Continuing Story of Point-to-Point Racing* xxiii. 146 The champion point-to-pointer of the 1964 season was Mr. W. J. A. Shepherd's Straight Lady. **1975** *Oxf. Compan. Sports & Games* 496/2 The major event of the point-to-point season is the Player's Gold Leaf Championship. **1976** *Horse & Hound* 3 Dec. 55/2 She got much pleasure and fun out of owning some useful point-to-pointers, in particular her good horse Brough. **1979** *Guardian* 31 Aug. 10/1 BMW..decided to sponsor point-to-points. *Ibid.*, The point-to-pointer interviewed thought it all very subtle.

c. In every particular or respect.

1934 C. Lambert *Music Ho!* v. 326 A book that..has purposely avoided a point-to-point analysis of individual works. **1949** R. K. Merton *Social Theory & Social Structure* xiv. 330 Discussions of the why and wherefore of science bore a point-to-point correlation with the Puritan teachings. **1958** *Listener* 27 Nov. 885/3 Changes of shape in the retinal image will necessarily be reproduced in the occipital lobe of the brain since there is a point-to-point correspondence between them.

12. point of view. (Earlier and later *fig.* examples, *esp.* in Literary Criticism.) Also *attrib.*

1760 Sterne *Sermons* II. xi. 112 Look at a man in one light...behold him in another point of view. **1793** Burke *Remarks on Policy of Allies* in *Three Memorials on French Affairs* (1797) 193 It is not the point of view in which we are in the habit of viewing guilt. **1905** S. L. Whitcomb *Study of a Novel* iii. 66 The narrator takes some general point of view for the entire action, and specific points of view for every part of it, in reference to time, place,..etc. The unity of a passage or a plot depends largely on the clearness and stability of this position. **1909** H. James *Wings of Dove* I. p. xvi, There is no economy of treatment without an adopted, a related point of view, and though I understand, under certain degrees of pressure, a represented community of vision between several parties to the action when it makes for concentration, I understand no breaking-up of the register, no sacrifice of the recording consistency, that doesn't rather scatter and weaken. **1921** P. Lubbock *Craft of Fiction* xvii. 251 The whole intricate question of method, in the craft of fiction, I take to be governed by the question of the point of view—the question of the relation in which the narrator stands to the story. **1927** E. M. Forster *Aspects of Novel* iv. 109 The problem of a point of view.. is peculiar to the novel. **1948** M. Schorer in *Hudson Review* I. 69 Let it [*sc.* technique in fiction] be thought of in two respects particularly: the uses to which language, as language, is put to express the quality of the experience in question; and the uses of point of view not only as a mode of dramatic delimitation, but more particularly, of thematic definition. **1958** *N. & Q.* CCIII. 85/2 The experimentation with dramatic forms in *The Blithedale Romance* is clearly a prefiguration of the point-of-view technique. Eschewing the novelist's omniscience, Hawthorne had his narrator cloud in vague terms the nature of Moodie's early crime. **1961** W. J. Harvey *Art of George Eliot* i. 14 His [*sc.* Henry James's] insistence on dramatic representation, point of view, elimination of the author..has undergone a subtle critical change into something like dogma. **1973** R. Fowler *Dict. Mod. Critical Terms* 149 Some contemporary experimental novelists..transcend the issue altogether by abrupt and unsignposted shifts from one point of view to another. **1976** *Amer. Speech* 1974 XLIX. 232 *Stephen Hero* is written from a heavily omniscient point of view.

12*. point of order. In a debate, meeting, etc., an objection or query respecting procedure.

a **1751**, **1781** [see *order *sb.* 18]. **1885** *Encycl. Brit.* XVIII. 312/1 A member may speak once only to any question, except to explain, or upon a point of order, [etc.]. **1903** G. B. Shaw *Man & Superman* iii. 75 The anarchist (*rising*) A point of order, Mendoza—. Mendoza (*forcibly*) No, by thunder: your last point of order took half an hour. **1952** *Oxf. Jun. Encycl.* X. 194/1 If a member wishes to raise a 'point of order', that is, to suggest that a rule of debate is being broken, he must remain seated and put on a hat to call the attention of the Speaker. **1974** *Encycl. Brit. Micropædia* VIII. 68/1 If the point of order is overruled by the presiding officer, the speaker resumes the floor.

12. point of departure.** *fig.* The starting point of a thought or action; the initial assumption, procedure, etc., which is developed. Also (with hyphens) *attrib.*

1857 Dickens *Dorrit* ii. xiii. 438 In the relief of having this companion, and of feeling that he could trust him, he passed on to both [subjects], and both brought him round again..to his point of departure. **1876** [see Departure 5]. **1927** R. H. Wilenski *Mod. Movement in Art* 31 The French romantics of the early nineteenth century made the romantic elements in his art their point of departure. **1959** J. Kirkup tr. *S. de Beauvoir's Memoirs of Dutiful Daughter* (1963) iii. 218 He looked upon marriage as a solution and not as a point of departure. **1961** *Listener* 17 Aug. 257/1 Schönberg began as an heir to Wagner. His point of departure was the intense chromaticism of *Tristan* and *Parsifal*. **1962** *Amer. Speech* XXXVII. 216 Every grammarian analyzes, using his own language as a point of departure. **1965** *Language* XLI. 189 The original point-of-departure vocabulary. **1976** *Early Music* Oct. 469/1 Seebass's point of departure is the tonary contained in the manuscript Paris, Bibliothèque nationale, fonds lat. 1118 from the mid-11th century.

12*. point of no return.** (See quot. 1941.) Freq. *transf.* and *fig.*

1941 *Jrnl. R. Aeronaut. Soc.* XLV. 306 This three-engined operation data is used to determine our so-called 'Point of No Return'. Laymen are inevitably intrigued by this fatalistic expression. As a matter of fact it is merely a designation of that limit-point, before which any engine failure requires an immediate turn around and return to the point of departure, and beyond which such return is no longer practical. **1946** E. Hodgins *Mr Blandings* x. 141 It would be delightful..to..die of old age in a rented apartment... But..he had reached and passed the crucial mark known, in the poetic language of the air navigator, as the Point of No Return. **1948** 'N. Shute' *No Highway* iv. 98 They passed the point of no return, and as a routine matter the navigator reported to him. **1953** R. Lehmann *Echoing Grove* 281 You were admitting to one another, weren't you, your secret knowledge that you—hadn't reached, together, the—the point of no return? **1956** *Jrnl. Educ.* July 312 But now he stopped [stealing] long enough to write a book (this is usually the point of no return) about his approved school, Borstal and prison experiences. **1958** *Times* 9 Jan. 10/3 When we were on the way to the Pole we received a request from Dr. Fuchs to establish a further depôt, but we were 240 miles from the Pole, and beyond the point of no return. **1960** J. Lehmann *I am my Brother* vii. 314, I finally decided that Leonard and I had reached a point of no return: if our partnership remained the same..not only would the Hogarth Press come to a standstill, but my own career would finally be frustrated. **1966** D. Varaday *Gara-Yaka's Domain* ix. 105 To my consternation I realised that I had let the matter run to the 'point of no return'. For me to refuse to go on now would..hurt his feelings. **1970** *Times* 7 May 12/7 Forbes..says all the A.B.P. films have a financial 'point of no return'. **1977** *Oxford Diocesan Mag.* Oct. 20/3 Scholars may well 'have passed the point of no return' in this matter.

12**. point-of-lay,** *a.* The stage of a hen's life-cycle at which it is able to begin laying eggs. Chiefly *attrib.*

1950 *Starting Poultry Keeping* (Poultry World) (ed. 8) 108 (Advt.), One of the largest suppliers of laying and point-of-lay pullets..in England. **1953** L. Robinson *Mod. Poultry Husbandry* (ed. 3) xxi. 612 During both the autumn and spring the early hatches produced birds of heavier weights at point of lay. **1960** *Farmer & Stock-breeder* 16 Feb. 147/3 Losses to point-of-lay have averaged only $2\frac{1}{2}$ per cent. *Ibid.*, This system of rearing..enables him to offer a point-of-lay pullet at a really economical price. **1964** J. Portsmouth *Practical Poultry Keeping* (ed. 6) iii. 44 As a pullet approaches the point of lay stage its body undergoes great changes. **1975** A. C. Stewart *Dark Dove* vi. 41 Rhode Island Red pullets, six, point-of-lay—thirty-five shillings. **1977** D. Kay *Poultry Keeping for Beginners* v. 70 At the age of 20 weeks..the pullet becomes a point of lay bird.

12***. point-of-sale.** The place at which retail transactions are made. Chiefly *attrib.*

1953 D. Riesman *Individualism Reconsidered* (1955) 222 Using the retail store as the point-of-sale as in the Supermarket. **1959** *Design* Sept. 49/1 The coin operated food vending machine is required to carry its own point-of-sale appeal. **1960** *Times* 28 Sept. (Advt. Suppl.) p. ii/5 Posters and point-of-sale displays. **1962** H. E. Beecheno *Introd. Bus. Stud.* x. 88 Point-of-sale advertising consists of using special display material in shop windows. **1974** *Encycl. Brit. Micropædia* VIII. 68/1 Early point-of-sale displays consisted of stock designs (that is, the brand name of the product or a picture of the product or the factory) on strawboard placed in shop windows and on stands and counters. **1978** *Bookseller* 17 June 3197/3 The time when point-of-sale data was run against a local stock-control system.

13. *point-current, -hole* (examples), *-making* (earlier and later examples), *-size, -strap, -system* (further examples); *points system*; *point-free, -leafed, -tipped* adjs. In Phonetics, *point consonant* (earlier and later examples), *-element, -open, -stop, -teeth* (examples), *-trill*; *point-lingual* adj.

1867 Point consonant [see *back *a.* 1 c]. **1902** Point consonant [see *fan consonant* s.v. *fan sb.[1] 11]. **1857**

Dickens *Perils Eng. Prisoners* iii, in *Househ. Words* Extra Christmas No., 7 Dec. 30/2 The off-settings and point-currents of the stream. **1933** O. Jespersen *Essentials Eng. Gram.* iv. 39 Sometimes the point-element [of *r*] remains though without any trill. **1947** *People* 22 June 1/3 Small quantities of biscuits originally intended for the Services are point-free—if you can get them. **1770** P. Luckombe *Conc. Hist. Printing* 500 *Point-holes*, holes made by the Points in a worked off sheet of paper. **1940** *Chambers's Techn. Dict.* 658/1 *Point holes* (*Print.*), punctures made in the printed sheet by the spurs of the register points. **1932** R. Lehmann *Invitation to Waltz* I. 5 And there growing up the side of the house..is that kind of thick, bristling, woody, point-leafed shrub. **1931** G. O. Russell *Speech & Voice* xiv. 133 Point-lingual fricative consonants. **1889** G. B. Shaw *London Music in 1888–89* (1937) 129 Signor Novara, who played the part with unexpected success..acting without any senseless posturing and point-making. **1975** *New Yorker* 28 Apr. 124/2 The cut between the two scenes is not a piece of easy point-making. **1877** H. Sweet *Handbk. Phonetics* II. 37, *rh*, *r* (point-open). **1927** J. J. Hogan *Eng. Lang. in Ireland* 29 Point-open and stops: *thedynge* 'tiding,' *onther* 'under,' *tanked* 'thanked'. **1934** —— *Outl. Eng. Philol.* I. i. 8 English has two Point-Opens, þ as in *think*, ð as in *then*. **1931** A. Esdaile *Student's Man. Bibliogr.* 143 Easily available to English printers,..are the following types, which can, of course, be had in different normal point-sizes and with their own italic. **1973** S. Jennett *Making of Books* (ed. 5) ii. 41 These two lines appear to be set in two quite different sizes of type, yet they are both in the same point size and a dozen lines of either would occupy exactly the same depth of space. **1944** *Ann. Reg. 1943* 40 The points system was securing an equitable distribution of non-perishable foodstuffs. **1964** *Listener* 1 Oct. 505/2 The 'points system'..determines the amount of money which can be spent for special allowances for teaching staff and other purposes. **1974** *Guardian* 23 Jan. 9/3 Council houses are allocated on a points system. **1899** W. Rippmann tr. *Vietor's Elements of Phonetics* 142/1 Point stops, etc. = dental stops, etc. **1934** J. J. Hogan *Outl. Eng. Philol.* I. i. 6 The English Point Stops, *t, d, n*. **1963** E. H. Edwards *Saddlery* xv. 111 An additional girth known as a 'point strap' and fixed under the point itself, which allows the girth to be fastened to this strap and..will place the girth much farther forward and help to keep it and the saddle in place. **1888** Point system [see Pointsman 2]. **1931** A. Esdaile *Student's Man. Bibliogr.* iv. 131 Simon Pierre Fournier,..best known by..being the first author of the Continental point-system of measuring types. **1941** *New Statesman* 26 Apr. 430/1 The 'point system' is based on the allocation of so many points per head and if you squander them on caviare instead of on corned beef, it is just too bad for you. **1953** R. J. C. Atkinson *Field Archaeol.* ii. 50 *The point system*, a fairly close grid of pegs is laid out to divide the site into squares. On one side of each peg a small pit is dug. **1959** *Chambers's Encycl.* XI. 533/1 Under the point system [of rationing], there is obviously greater freedom of choice than under specific rationing. **1888** H. Sweet *Hist. Eng. Sounds* (rev. ed.) 5 þ (as in *thin*) [is] a point-teeth consonant. **1906** H. C. Wyld *Hist. Study Mother Tongue* ii. 32 *th* (þ) in 'think', made between the *Point* of the tongue and the *Teeth* (Point-Teeth-Open). **1952** C. L. B. Hubbard *Pembrokeshire Corgi Handbk.* 2 Erect and point-tipped ears. **1877** H. Sweet *Handbk. Phonetics* II. 49, *rhr* (point-trill). **1927** J. J. Hogan *Eng. Lang. in Ireland* 75, *r*. This consonant is everywhere retained [in Irish] as in M.E... A strong point-trill is heard in the South. **1933** O. Jespersen *Essentials Eng. Gram.* iv. 39 Originally *r* was a full point-trill everywhere.

14. point-action *Gram.*, applied to an aspect which is not durative; **point bar,** (*b*) *Physical Geogr.*, an alluvial deposit that forms by accretion inside the loop of a river as the loop expands outwards, usu. consisting of low, curved, parallel ridges; **point blanket,** a Hudson's Bay or Mackinaw blanket with points (sense *A. 32) to indicate weight; **point block,** a high building with flats, offices, etc., built around a central lift or staircase; **point break** *Surfing*, a type of wave characteristic of a coast with a headland; **point charge** *Electr.*, a charge regarded as concentrated in a mathematical point, without spatial extent; **point contact,** the state of touching at a point only; *spec.* in *Electronics*, the contact of a metal point with the surface of a semiconductor so as to form a rectifying junction; freq. *attrib.*; **point-count** *Bridge*, the value of a hand in points; also, any system of allocating points to a hand; hence *point-counting* vbl. sb.; **point-counter** *Physics*, an early version of the Geiger counter in which discharges occur between positively-charged chamber walls and a central, earthed, metal point; **point defect** *Cryst.*, any defect in a crystal structure which involves only one lattice site; **point discharge,** an electrical discharge in which current flows between an earthed pointed object and the surrounding gas; also *attrib.*; so **point discharger,** such an object; **point-event,** something conceived of as having a definite position in space and time but no extent or duration; **point focus** *Physics*, a focus (of a beam of light or particles, etc.) which is small enough to be considered as a point; **Point Four** (or **IV, 4**) *U.S. Pol.*, the fourth point of President Harry S. Truman's Fair Deal programme (*Fair Deal) which made provision for technical aid to underdeveloped countries; freq. *attrib.*; **point ground,** in lace-making, a type of *réseau* ground; also *attrib.*; **point-instant,** the minimal unit of space-time; a mere position in space-time; **point load** *Engin.*, a load that acts at a single point; **point mass** *Physics*, a mass regarded as concentrated in a mathematical point, without spatial extent; also *attrib.*; **point mutation** *Genetics*, a mutation not distinguishable by recombinational analysis from a point change within a gene; **point net** (further examples); **point number,** in a musical, a song which is integral to the action; **point paper** (examples); **point-policeman** (further examples); **point rationing,** a system of rationing whereby goods are priced in terms of points (sense *A. 15 b) and a certain number of points are assigned to each consumer; so *point-rationed* adj.; **point resistance** *Engin.*, the upward force exerted by soil on the base of a pile; **points food,** rationed food available on points only; **point shoes,** shoes with pointed toes, *spec.* of a type used by ballet dancers; **point-shooting,** shooting game from a fixed point; **point source,** a source (as of light or sound) of negligible dimensions; **points rationing** = **point rationing*; **points value** = **point value*; **points victory,** a victory won on points; **points win** = **points victory*; **point value,** value in terms of rationing points; **point-work** *Ballet*, dancing on the points. Also *point group.

1925 G. O. Curme *College English Gram.* II. 56 The point-action aspect calls attention, not to an act as a whole, but to only one point, either the beginning or the final point. **1932** *Jrnl. Eng. & Gmc. Philol.* XXXI. 251 Most scholars recognize in English a durative aspect and a point-action aspect. **1970** *Language* XLVI. 300 It is particularly noteworthy in the latter case that the headline to this news item read 'Man may not have smelt killer gas', the *-t* form co-occurring with an effective or 'point-action' aspect. **1977** *Ibid.* LIII. 437 The ungrammaticality of 3d would be accounted for by the fact that *arrive*, like all (non-iterable) point-action predicates, does not co-occur with duration adverbials like *until*. **1945** H. N. Fisk in *Geol. Investigation Alluvial Valley of Lower Mississippi River* (U.S. Mississippi River Commission) 20 The point bar, the composite accretion within a bend, consists of an alternation of sand bar ridges, capped with thin top-stratum, and swales underlain by clay plugs. **1963** D. W. & E. E. Humphries tr. *Termier's Erosion & Sedimentation* v. 110 Alluvial plains appear to be composed chiefly (80–90%) of 'point bars'. **1974** C. H. Crickmay *Work of River* ii. 25 The land round which a meander winds is termed the tongue, and the tip of the tongue is the point, whence the term point bar. **1976** K. W. Butzer *Geomorphol. from Earth* viii. 157 Point bars, developed as a series of low levees on the inside meander bends, form arcuate or parallel ridges and swales. **1783** in E. E. Rich *Moose Fort Jrnl.* (1954) 152, I have enclosed instructions for your Guidance and the Standard of the point Blankets I now send you. **1797** in *Georgia Hist. Soc. Collections* (1916) IX. 347, 2 2½ point blankets. **1855** J. H. Chambers in *Contrib. Montana Hist. Soc.* (1940) X. 116 We have..30 prs. 3 pt. blkts 20 Pr W 20 1 Blkt 10 blue blkt 18 Scan & 25 Hudson Bay blkts. **1926** *Beaver* Dec. 22 The earliest reference found in a search of the minutes of the..Hudson's Bay [Co.] to Hudson's Bay 'Point' Blankets is one dated 22nd December 1779, where a notation is made of an order for one hundred pairs of each of five sorts of pointed blankets. **1962** W. Stegner *Wolf Willow* II. v. 67 The somewhat obscure source of the red point blankets that I slept under. **1954** *Ann Reg. 1953* 371 The London County Council's large sites..were of special interest on account of their carefully landscaped mixture of terrace houses, maisonettes, and 11-storey 'point-blocks'. **1958** *Listener* 6 Nov. 727/1 Eight-storey point-blocks are contrasted with low, gable-ended, four-storey blocks. **1970** *New Scientist* 5 Mar. 460/1 A series of disasters, or near disasters,..involving a wide range of modern structures from cooling-tower shells to point blocks of flats. **1975** *Times Lit. Suppl.* 5 Sept. 988/4 The London skyline today, peppered with point blocks, tower-blocks, and slabs. **1966** *Surfabout* III. vi. 8/1 The original concept was to have three separate events. A point break, reef break, and a beach break contest. **1968** W. Warwick *Surfriding in N.Z.* 21/1 There are four main types of breaks in New Zealand. They are the beach break, the reef break, point break and the river bar break. *Ibid.* 21/2 The point break wave..is formed when swells move almost at right angles along a peninsula or headland. **1970** *Studies in English* (Univ. of Cape Town) I. 26 A headland, point or pier, bends the wave into a *point break*, which gives a consistent ride in one direction, often in a perfect tubing shape, so that the surfer slides along the face of the wave with a tube of water continually breaking behind him. **1903** S. J. Barrett *Electro-Magn. Theory* 66 The law of inverse squares..is due to the continuity of the electric displacement.., the flux from a point-charge being distributed equally in all directions. **1975** D. G. Fink *Electronics Engineers' Handbk.* I. 11 A combination of two point charges of equal magnitude and opposite polarity separated by a distance small compared to that at which the field of the dipole is to be determined is called an electric dipole. **1914** *Proc. Physical Soc.* XXVII. 70 The present paper relates..to the conductivity of 'point contacts' when a steady, or slowly varying, E.M.F. is applied. *Ibid.*, The behaviour of a typical point contact (zincite and tellurium). **1945** R. K. Allan *Rolling Bearings* vi. 143 In roller bearings..we..have 'line contact' as distinct from the 'point contact' of ball bearings. **1947** C. F. Edwards in *Proc. IRE* XXXV. 1181/2 In view of the fact that the crystalline state of the silicon is more nearly like that of iron and copper, which are not ordinarily regarded as crystals,..it seems desirable to eliminate the terms 'crystal' and 'crystal detector' and designate these devices by the term 'point-contact rectifier'. **1948** *Physical Rev.* LXXIV. 230/2 When the two point contacts are placed close together on the surface and d.c. bias potentials are applied, there is a mutual influence which makes it possible to use the device to amplify a.c. signals. **1959** [see *junction transistor* s.v. *junction *sb.* 4]. **1962** Simpson & Richards *Physical Princ. Junction Transistors* i. 1 The event that opened this era of 'solid-state electronics' was the invention of the point-contact transistor by Bardeen and Brattain in 1948. **1970** H. J. Watson *Mod. Gear Production* ii. 24 Crossed helical gears theoretically make point contact only which, under load sufficient to cause deflection of the contacting surfaces, becomes a line. **1975** D. G. Fink *Electronic Engineers' Handbk.* IX. 61 The point contact is fabricated by a metal whisker forming a rectifying junction in contact with the semiconductor. **1959** T. Reese *Bridge Player's Dict.* 149 The Milton Work point-count remains the most popular..because of its simplicity and convenience. **1963** *Times* 9 Jan. 12/7 The Souths who were influenced more by their point-count than their distribution. **1979** *Guardian* 5 Sept. 2/6 The Bridge Challenger..run by two micro-processors..bids the point-count system. **1925** *Proc. Cambr. Philos. Soc.* XXII. 676 The point counter has also been studied as a unit of an electrical circuit containing capacity and resistance, and an analogy established between its discharges, and the 'flashing' of a neon lamp. **1938** R. W. Lawson tr. *Hevesy & Paneth's Man. Radioactivity* (ed. 2) i. 18 When we are concerned with the measurement of a very small flux of radiation,..the sensitivity of the point-counter is often inadequate. **1964** J. B. Birks *Theory & Practice Scintillation Counting* x. 394 The observation of the time relationship between two or more ionizing events, as represented by pulses from radiation detectors, forms the basis of the coincidence method... It was originally introduced..for use with point-counters and Geiger counters. **1963** *Times* 6 Mar. 13/1 The conventional openings, combined with point-counting, brought greater refinements into bidding. **1973** *Times* 6 Jan. 9/3, I have written on many occasions that no expert relies upon point-counting alone to value his hand. **1960** H. G. Van Beuren *Imperfections in Crystals* ii. 41 Point defects can be introduced in large numbers into solids by plastic deformation. **1974** D. M. Adams *Inorg. Solids* ix. 292 For many years it seemed that non-stoichiometric systems of wide compositional range could be understood in terms of a parent lattice with a high concentration of randomly distributed point defects. **1886** R. Wormell *Electricity in Service of Man* 49 (*heading*) Point discharge. **1927** *Proc. R. Soc.* A. CXV. 443 The important part played by the point-discharge currents in the total exchange of electricity between the earth and the atmosphere. **1938** R. W. Lawson tr. *Hevesy & Paneth's Man. Radioactivity* (ed. 2) i. 17 Each time an ionizing particle..passes the neighbourhood of the point [of the needle], a point discharge takes place by virtue of ionization by collision. **1973** R. H. Golde *Lightning Protection* ii. 8 Point-discharge currents and the resulting space charges play an important part in the development of the lighting discharge and in the action of a lightning conductor. **1928** *Proc. R. Soc.* A. CXVIII. 255 Wormell..used a single point-discharger at a height of 8 metres, which is stated to be likely to produce similar effects to those from a small tree. **1965** S. C. Coroniti *Problems of Atmospheric & Space Electricity* iii. 174 (*heading*) The behavior of trees as point dischargers. **1920** A. S. Eddington *Space, Time & Gravit.* xii. 186 In the relativity theory of nature, the most elementary concept is the *point-event*. In ordinary language a point-event is an instant of time at a point in space. *Ibid.*, The aggregate of all the point-events is called the *world*. **1928** C. E. M. Joad *Future of Life* 36 Faced with a universe consisting of ephemeral point-events, the mind selects from it certain characteristics which have a particular interest for it. **1948** *Mind* LVII. 298 The idea of a mile or a day is an everyday idea. So are those of above and below, east and west, or before and after. Those of a point, an instant, and still more of a point-event, are relatively sophisticated, and much less used. **1965** P. Caws *Philos. of Sci.* xli. 316 This calls for a solution of the problem of rendering point events (particles interacting and so on) in terms of experiences. **1908** L. Laurance *Gen. & Pract. Optics* xii. 329 Thus, rays in the pencil do not have a point focus, since there are two focal lines. **1923** Glazebrook *Dict. Appl. Physics* IV. 213/1 Whilst the geometrical theory claims a perfect point-focus, the undulatory theory merely demonstrates that there is a maximum of intensity at that point. **1966** D. G. Brandon *Mod. Techniques Metallogr.* 135 The incident intensity can be increased by using a point-focus X-ray source with the sample close to the source. **1949** *Manch. Guardian Weekly* 27 Oct. 15 The much admired 'point four' also fell by the wayside. **1953** A. Huxley *Let.* 21 June (1969) 675 It [*sc.* an M.A. in Public Health] would surely be helpful in all manner of fields—e.g. the UN if you wanted to enter it later, or any other of the international agencies, or Point Four. **1955** *Bull. Atomic Sci.* Mar. 98/2 The Point IV program of technical assistance stirred the imagination throughout the undeveloped areas of the world. **1961** L. D. Stamp *Gloss. Geogr. Terms* 466/1 An official definition used to determine countries qualifying for American Point IV aid was national income per capita. **1965** H. S. Truman *Memoirs* II. xvi. 269 The Point Four program was a practical expression of our attitude toward the countries threatened by Communist domination. **1972** *Times* 27 Dec. 5/1 The Point 4 programme inaugurated technical aid to underdeveloped countries. **1832** J. R. McCulloch *Dict. Commerce* 697 About 1777, or 1778, quite a *new* ground was attempted by the inhabitants of Buckingham and its neighbourhood, which quickly superseded all the others; this was the *point ground*, which had (as is supposed) been imported from the Netherlands. **1865** F. B. Palliser *Hist. Lace* xxx. 361 In 1778, according to M'Culloch, was introduced the 'point' ground, as it is locally termed, from which period dates the staple pillow lace trade of these counties. **1968** J.

ARNOLD *Shell Book of Country Crafts* 305 'Buckingham Point' or 'Point-ground' lace was that lace containing Lille or Mechlin elements. **1969** E. H. PINTO *Treen* 311 *A* is a 'Trolly'..used for the gimp thread—the thick, soft thread which outlines the design in point ground lace. **1920** S. ALEXANDER *Space, Time, & Deity* I. 58 It is assumed that at each point-instant (the name is due to Mr. Lorentz, *Ortzeit*) there exists some perceptible 'substance'. **1959** *Listener* 8 Jan. 57/2 The suggestions he [*sc.* Samuel Alexander] made about these 'pervasive features'—for instance, that everything in the world is ultimately composed of complexes of 'space-time point-instants'—are certainly not such as could be either reached or confirmed by any kind of direct observation. **1941** *Jrnl. Inst. Civil Engin.* XVI. 524 A single load was connected with a much higher ultimate moment, owing to a better stress-distribution and a rapid decrease of the moment, than was obtained with two point-loads. **1976** ATTEWELL & FARMER *Princ. Engin. Geol.* iv. 193 It is possible to relate the point load strength index to the uniaxial compressive strength. **1955** W. HEISENBERG in W. Pauli et al. *Niels Bohr* 17 For Bohm, the particles are 'objectively real' structures, like the point masses of classical mechanics. **1968** M. S. LIVINGSTON *Particle Physics* iii. 47 This hypothesis had a built-in 'irrationality'..in attempting to correlate the divergent concepts of point-mass particles and of wave motion. **1968** R. A. LYTTLETON *Myst. Solar Syst.* i. 20 The action of the stars once the collision is over can safely be regarded as pure attraction by point-masses. **1925** *Genetics* X. 117 If one thinks of mutations as being simply inherited changes, it becomes necessary to distinguish changes that involve whole chromosomes.., changes that involve several adjacent genes.., and what have been called 'point-mutations' or 'gene-mutations'. **1928** *Jrnl. Genetics* XIX. 223 If such parallel forms were due simply to the special action of a single factor, 'point-mutation' might afford a reasonable basis of explanation. **1974** GOODENOUGH & LEVINE *Genetics* v. 195 A mutation that affects only one or a few nucleotides in a chromosome is known as a point mutation. **1977** *Sci. Amer.* Dec. 94/3 Such mutants of influenza virus are considered to be 'point mutations' that might affect only one of the nucleotide building blocks of the RNA. **1865** F. B. PALLISER *Hist. Lace* xxxvi. 418 In 1777, Else and Harvey introduced at Nottingham the 'pin' or point net machine, so named because made on sharp pins or points. **1953** M. POWYS *Lace & Lace-Making* xi. 196 In working *point net ground* the pin is not enclosed, but after it is placed, two extra twists are given to the pairs which have formed the half stitch. **1937** N. COWARD *Present Indicative* III. 105 There was a sentimental ballad..and a bright 'Point' number. **1958** B. NICHOLS *Sweet & Twenties* 16, I heard a cabaret artist use the word Hiroshima as a comic gag in a point number. **1960** A. KIMMINS *Lugs O'Leary* iii. 35 It was a 'point' number, and she was singing it like a 'pop'. **1960** *News Chron.* 31 Mar. 4/5 'Point numbers'..arise directly out of the play's action —often carrying the plot..forward while they are being sung. **1967** *Stage* 2 Mar. 6/2 (Advt.), Glam. Singer: Pop, Ballad, Point Nos. **1899** J. W. MACKAIL *Life W. Morris* II. xiii. 44 'Point-paper'—paper, that is, divided into minute spaces, each representing a single knot of the carpet. **1940** *Chambers's Techn. Dict.* 658/1 *Point paper*,..ruled paper upon which the interlacing of the threads in a fabric is shown. **1928** *Evening News* 18 Aug. 6/3 The point policemen at spacious centres like the Marble Arch and Hyde Park Corner seem to be waving the wide world around and the exhilaration of moderate speed can be enjoyed. **1939** H. HODGE *Cab, Sir?* 236 People don't realise how dangerous it is for a point-policeman. **1944** *Times* 15 Feb. 2/2 The increase has been due to higher expenditure on unrationed or 'point' rationed foods. **1944** A. M. TAYLOR *Lang. World War II* 56 *Point Rationing*, a rationing method announced by the Office of Price Administration (OPA), establishing a secondary currency of points alongside the dollar currency. **1959** *Chambers's Encycl.* XI. 533/1 Under point rationing, the group may be extended to cover a combination of several different kinds of article. **1943** K. TERZAGHI *Theoret. Soil Mech.* viii. 136 One part Q_f of the total load on the pile is carried by the skin friction. The balance Q_p is transferred onto the soil through the base or the point of the pile and is called the point resistance. **1972** L. ZEEVAERT *Foundation Engin. for Difficult Subsoil Conditions* v. 278 The lower part of the piles will work under ultimate point resistance and positive friction. **1941** *New Statesman* 6 Dec. 475 When the retailer sells 'points' food, he can replenish his supplies only by handing over the 'points' that he has collected. **1948** *Hansard Commons* 8 Mar. 795 [He] has been given a licence to sell points foods. **1957** G. B. L. WILSON *Dict. Ballet* 218 *Point shoes*, the silk or satin shoes, tying up the ankle with ribbon, used by dancers when dancing sur les pointes. *Ibid.*, Point shoes cost about 17s a pair. **1970** R. LOWELL *Notebook* 150 My coat limp chestnut-colored suede Cut to match my point shoes that hurt my toes. **1977** *Times* 20 Jan. 8/6 American mothers just want to see their children in point shoes as early as possible. **1874** J. W. LONG *Wild-Fowl Shooting* 71 For point-shooting, shooting from a blind on shore, or in the edge of the willows from a boat, a few hints may be welcome. **1876** *Fur, Fin & Feather* Sept. 90 We prepared to move out into the clear water onto a log, and there get some point shooting. **1903** *Nature* 1 Jan. 202/2 for a point source of strength Q, the V it produces is [etc.]. **1949** [see *ANGULAR *a.* 2 c]. **1971** I. G. GASS et al. *Understanding Earth* xiii. 178 Contrast this with a deep ocean floor, lacking in relief, and far from any strong point-sources of debris. **1941** *New Statesman* 6 Dec. 475 'Points' rationing of canned meat, canned fish etc., from December 1st onwards makes disposal of these goods to 'black market' merchants singularly unattractive. **1950** *Times* 20 May 4/1 The ending..of the points rationing system, which has been in operation for more than eight years, was announced by the Minister of Food yesterday. **1947** *People* 22 June 1/3 More 'ups' and 'downs' in the points values of food come into force today. **1929** *Daily Express* 7 Nov. 13/2 Jackson's points victory was about the most easily gained of the night. **1976** *New Musical Express* 12 Feb. 30/3 Theoretically this bout should have provided at least a points-win decision in favour of Harold Melvin's The Blue Notes. **1976** *Rhyl Jrnl. & Advertiser* 9 Dec. 31/1 One of Rhyl Star Boys Club's most promising boxers, Philip Siddall, gained a classy points win over Peter Williams, of Llay ABC, at Llay last week. **1946** *Mod. Lang. Notes* LXI. 443 Prestige value, cash value, point value. **1959** *Chambers's Encycl.* XI. 533/1 In the case of foodstuffs, the point value may be related to calorie value. **1936** S. J. SIMON tr. A. Benois in 'C. Brahms' *Footnotes to Ballet* iv. 206 The 'classical ballet' in the steel support does endow point-work with a special brilliance. **1957** G. B. L. WILSON *Dict. Ballet* 217 Dancing on the point or 'point work' is said to have been practised by the cossacks since time immemorial. *Ibid.* 218 A danced stage performance need not necessarily include 'point work' to be termed ballet. **1975** *New Yorker* 26 May 89/2 Its a question whether 'The Sleeping Beauty' can be danced within the limitations of Bolshoi technique, which stresses big jumps at the expense of brilliance in turns and pointwork.

point, *sb.*³ Add: **point d'appui,** also *fig.*, esp. *Mil.*, a strategic point; *point d'attache*, point of connection; *point de départ* = *point of departure* s.v. *POINT *sb.*¹ D. 12**; *point de repère* (further examples); *point d'orgue* (see quots. 1876 and 1883).

1823 BYRON *Don Juan* XIV. lxxxiv. 7 This I could prove beyond a single doubt, Were there a jot of sense among mankind; But till that point *d'appui* is found, alas! Like Archimedes, I leave earth as 'twas. **1833** *Edin. Rev.* LVI. 383 She [*sc.* the Bank of England] is then, as it were, the *point d'appui* of the whole moneyed and commercial interests. **1836** H. GREVILLE *Diary* 20 Feb. (1883) I. 88 England being now in the hands of *Democrats*, she is no longer useful as a *point d'appui* to France. **1876** C. M. YONGE *Three Brides* II. ii. 35 Raymond used to arm himself with the newspapers as the safest *point d'appui.* **1895** E. MALET *Dispatch* 7 Sept. in *F.O. 64/1351* No. 201 (Public Record Office), The acquisition of a 'point d'appui' in East Asia. **1915** 'I. HAY' *First Hundred Thousand* II. xviii. 264 The wood itself is a *point d'appui*, or fortified post. **1920** S. ALEXANDER *Space, Time, & Deity* II. 136 Some *point d'appui* is needed for our thinking. **1934** C. LAMBERT *Music Ho!* II. 127 His [*sc.* Satie's] progressions have..no trace of the *point d'appui* that we usually associate with the word progression. **1945** R. HARGREAVES *Enemy at Gate* 103 Gibraltar..furnished a perfect example of the value of sea power, combined with that ability to retain physical possession of a *point d'appui.* **1967** G. F. FIENNES *I tried to run Railway* vii. 87 The point d'appui was the results in general. **1973** D. AARON *Unwritten War* VII. xix. 294 This defense of the past was..a *point d'appui* for the Southern traditionalist. **1939** A. TOYNBEE *Study of Hist.* V. 624 For this linguistic legacy of the Napoleonic Empire —a legacy which is the *point d'attache* of the present Annex to the main thread of this Study of History—see V. C.. above. **1923** G. ARTHUR *Further Lett. from Man of no Importance* (1932) 146 King Edward was, however, equally determined that his *point de départ* for the Vatican should be the British Embassy and not the English College which Cardinal Rampollá (I think) urged. **1933** *Psychoanalytic Q.* II. 156 However this may be, Freud's formulation serves as the *point de départ* for the author's subsequent discussion of the subject. **1956** *N. & Q.* CCI. 254/2 The Restoration of King Charles II..provided an invaluable *point de départ* for all those who had economic schemes to present to government and people. **1977** *N.Y. Rev. Bks.* 13 Oct. 27/3 History, in this instance, will largely be the reflection of the historian's *point de départ.* **1904** H. JAMES *Golden Bowl* I. xvi. 288 You give me a *point de repère* outside myself—which is where I like it. Now I can work round you. **1933** *Times Lit. Suppl.* 3 Aug. 527/1 It is this very uncertainty that causes him to regret at the outset the absence of *points de repère* in modern literature, which would enable him to fit his authors into schools and categories. **1937** *Burlington Mag.* Apr. 192/2 This picture..will now take its place as the *point de repère* for the identification of this painter's individual style. **1958** *Listener* 20 Nov. 846/1 There are, of course, a few *points de repère*, significant works that represent a moment of apocalyptic vision. **1967** V. NABOKOV *Speak, Memory* (rev. ed.) iv. 85 Where a crack or a shadow afforded a *point de repère* for the eye. **1876** STAINER & BARRETT *Dict. Mus. Terms* 363/2 *Point d'orgue*, ..a pedal-point. **1883** GROVE *Dict. Mus.* III. 6/2 *Point d'orgue*, organ point, appears..to be used (1) for an organ point or pedal, that is, a succession of harmonies carried over a holding note..; and (2),..for the cadenza in a concerto. **1893** G. B. SHAW *Music in London 1890–94* (1932) III. 12 It gives him [*sc.* Brahms] no trouble to pile up *points d'orgue*, as in the Requiem. **1902** —— *Perfect Wagnerite* (ed. 2) 61 A specifically contrapuntal theme, *points d'orgue*, and a high C for the soprano. **1977** *Listener* 15 Dec. 797/3 Fluctuations of pitch..must either be confined to a single line of melody, or the accompaniment must simply be a drone—as is recognised in our classical system with the pedal-point or *point d'orgue.*

b. *point d'Angleterre* (earlier and later examples), *point d'Argentan, point de France, point de Paris; point d'esprit* (earlier and later examples); *point coupé*, cut work; *point russe*; *point à l'aiguille* (earlier examples), *point de neige, de reprise* (earlier examples).

1842 Point d'Argentan [see *BERTHA, BERTHE]. **1865** Point coupé [see *LACIS]. **1865** F. B. PALLISER *Hist. Lace* iii. 28 Point also means a particular kind of stitch, as point de Paris, point de neige, [etc.]. *Ibid.* vii. 102 They [*sc.* English lace merchants] bought up the choicest laces of the Brussels market, and then smuggling them over to England, sold them under the name of Point d'Angleterre, or 'English Point'. *Ibid.* 106 There are two kinds of flowers: those made with the needle are called 'point à l'aiguille'. *Ibid.* ix. 143 The point de France supplanted that of Venice; but its price confined its use to the rich. *Ibid.* xvii. 216 Point de Paris, mignonette, bisette, and other narrow cheap laces were made. *Ibid.* xxxvi. 424 This was followed by the 'spot', or 'point d'esprit', and various other fancy nets. **1872** *Young Englishwoman* Oct. 555/1 Stars worked in point russe. *Ibid.* Nov. 611/2 Fill up the grey rows..with scarlet wool in point de reprise. **1879** *Sylvia's Embroidery Bk.* 242 The chain stitch and point russe embroidery is worked with red silk. **1881** C. C. HARRISON *Woman's Handiwork* I. 43 *Point russe* is best known by small block patterns worked in fine back stitch. *Ibid.* 59 Surplices of fine lace resembling point d'esprit. *Ibid.* 89 Modern point coupé..is made on a shut linen foundation, of which some of the threads are cut away and the remainder worked over with buttonhole stitch, making regular square spaces. **1882** *Encycl. Brit.* XIV. 186/2 'Point d'Argentan' has been thought to be especially distinguished on account of its ground of hexagonally arranged *brides.* **1882** Point de reprise [see *darning-stitch* (*b*) s.v. *DARNING *vbl. sb.* 3]. **1895** *Montgomery Ward Catal.* Spring & Summer 78/1 Point de Paris Ivory Lace. **1919** Point d'esprit [see *LEADWORK 2]. **1953** M. POWYS *Lace & Lace-Making* iv. 14 *Point d'Argentan*... This lace is generally known from the Point d'Alençon by the ground, the Brides Bouclées, a hexagonal ground with buttonhole stitches on each of the six sides. *Ibid.* vi. 47 Point de France was used by distinguished prelates in the 18th century. **1958** *Times* 18 Nov. 12/3 All wore Empire dresses of white *point d'esprit* net over pale blue trimmed with blue satin ribbons. **1959** *Chambers's Encycl.* VIII. 293/2 *Point de neige*—a variety of *rosalino.* **1960** H. HAYWARD *Antique Coll.* 223/1 *Point d'Angleterre lace*: this is not an English lace but is a pillow lace made in Brussels. **1971** *Country Life* 4 Nov. 1197/3 At first the same as the Venetian product, this lace had its own evolution into distinctive *Point de France.* **1974** *Encycl. Brit. Micropædia* VIII. 66/3 In modern usage, *point de Paris* has come to mean any bobbin-made lace..with a six-pointed star mesh that is twisted, as opposed to that of Chantilly, which is plaited. **1975** *Oxf. Compan. Decorative Arts* 522/1 It was not until Colbert under Louis XIV set up his state factory at Lonray near Alençon and Argentan that French Needlepoint lace under the general name of *point de France* established its reputation.

point, *v.*¹ Add: **5. c.** *to point up*: to emphasize, draw attention to. orig. *U.S.*

1934 in WEBSTER. **1940** *Sun* (Baltimore) 3 Feb. 8/1 The warnings which Finnish spokesmen have recently given to the world that this resistance cannot continue indefinitely have been sharply pointed up by the renewal of very heavy Russian assaults along all sections of the front. **1941** L. TRILLING in D. Lodge *20th Cent. Lit. Crit.* (1972) 286 An analysis of this sort is not momentous and not exclusive of other meanings; perhaps it does no more than point up and formulate what we all have already seen. **1951** *Jrnl. Aeronaut. Sci.* XVIII. 622/1 The introduction of the automatic control system, particularly in pilotless aircraft, points up another basic change in our philosophy of aircraft control. **1958** *Listener* 20 Nov. 814/2 The Federal Government..should point up the dangers of prolonging the *status quo.* **1967** *Ibid.* 22 June 826/3 Another instance of this is the imagery at the beginning of *Pincher Martin*, which the authors ingeniously point up by comparison with a passage from *Robinson Crusoe.* **1969** A. COCKBURN in Cockburn & Blackburn *Student Power* 20 In a key concluding section he points up the lessons to be drawn from this record. **1972** *Daily Tel.* 17 Nov. 19/7 The [census] returns point up the discrepancies which occur in unemployment figures. **1978** *Verbatim* May 5/2 He points up the ambiguity in the application of the epithet *unabridged.*

7. b. *Sculpture.* To mark at a series of points on (a block of stone or marble) the depth to which the initial working or roughing-out is to be done.

1841 *Penny Cycl.* XXI. 142/1 The statue being rudely blocked out or pointed, the marble is in this state put into the hands of a superior workman called a carver. **1877** A. B. EDWARDS *Thousand Miles up Nile* 423 A recent writer..is of opinion that the Egyptian sculptors did not even 'point' their work beforehand. **1911** A. TOFT *Modelling & Sculpture* 254 The appearance of a work when pointed is not pleasing, covered all over with innumerable holes, and little mounds of marble projecting between these holes. **1947** J. C. RICH *Materials & Methods of Sculpture* ix. 261 Occasionally an indirect sculptor may personally point a work, or have his studio assistants or students do this for him.

9. c. *trans.* To indicate or state.

1928 *Publishers' Weekly* 12 May 1957 The effect on books by established authors like Galsworthy's 'Silver Spoon' and Ferber's 'Show Boat' could not be as clearly pointed. **1975** *Language for Life* (Dept. Educ. & Sci.) xxi. 303 There should be an appraisal of the kind of support schools can be given, and this points the need for close consultation between the education authority's advisers the schools themselves, and the library staff.

12. a. (Further examples with a person as direct object.)

1611 SHAKES. *Wint. T.* IV. iv. 539 On mine honor, Ile point you where you shall haue such receiuing As shall become your Highnesse. **1842** TENNYSON *Love & Duty* in *Poems* II. 87 Should it [*sc.* my shadow] cross thy dreams, So might it..point thee forward to a distant light. **1850** E. B. BROWNING *Prometheus Bound* in *Poems* I. 175 Point me not to a good, To leave me straight bereaved. **1922** JOYCE *Ulysses* 399 Yes, Pious had told him of that land and Chaste had pointed him to the way. **1972** J. PHILIPS *Vanishing Senator* (1973) I. ii. 16 They're simply using Lloyd to point us in the wrong direction. **1976** S. GEORGE *Fatal Shadows* 106 Someone..had pointed me in her direction, had wanted me to see what she was doing.

b. Fig. phr. *to point the finger* (*of scorn*) (*at a person*).

1829 P. EGAN *Boxiana* 2nd Ser. II. 499 It was a shame.. that pure and honourable men should be suspected of such doings..for even at him the finger of scorn had been pointed. *a* **1862** [see sense 12 a in Dict.]. **1939** G. B. SHAW *Geneva* III. 81 You can point the finger of the whole world at the slayer of my husband and say 'You are guilty of murder.' *a* **1966** 'M. NA GOPALEEN' *Best of Myles* (1968) 93 The finger of scorn is pointed at you. **1978** 'J. HORBURY' *Diplomatic Affair* x. 126 We [*sc.* the

British] naturally hesitate to point the finger..but the fact is that all these..leaks have been date-lined Washington.

c. *Anthrop.* Esp. in phr. *to point the bone.* Amongst Australian Aborigines, to will or to bring about the death of a person by a ritual involving special bones or sticks and incantations. Also *transf.* and *fig.* Cf. *pointing-bone* s.v. *POINTING *vbl. sb.*[1] 11.

1897 W. E. ROTH *Ethnol. Stud. N.-W.-Central Queensland Aborigines* xi. 156 It is most important to remember that in all cases while the death bone is being 'pointed', the blood of the victim passes invisibly across the intervening space to the 'pointer', and so along the connecting string, into the receptacle..: at the same time one of the doctor's gew-gaws, or..bone, pebble, &c., passes invisibly from the 'pointer' to be inserted in the body of the victim. **1904** SPENCER & GILLEN *Northern Tribes of Central Australia* xiv. 458 If it were known that any one had 'pointed the bone', that man would at once be killed. **1913** J. G. FRAZER *Golden Bough: Balder the Beautiful* (ed. 3) I. 14 The magical bone, which the native sorcerer points at his victim as a means of killing him, is never by any chance allowed to touch the earth. *Ibid.*, The custom of killing a man by pointing a bone or stick at him, while the sorcerer utters appropriate curses. **1934** [see *BONE *sb.* 1 e]. **1939** JOYCE *Finnegans Wake* I. 193 He points the deathbone and the quick are still. **1953** A. UPFIELD *Murder must Wait* xvii. 148 Buttons and ends came from me, are a part of me, are necessary objects required for the practice of pointing the bone. **1967** B. JEFFERIS *One Black Summer* x. 184 You're asking me to point the bone at someone on no real evidence at all. **1974** J. CLEARY *Peter's Pence* vii. 197 He was..convinced that the bloody God-botherers had pointed the bone at him just like the blacks did back home in Aussie.

13. c. *U.S.* In sport, to make special preparations *for* a particular opponent or game.

1933 *Sun* (Baltimore) 15 Nov. 12/7, I suppose there is a good deal of hooey in the talk of Army and Navy 'pointing' for each other: they do not like to be licked at any time. **1937** *Ibid.* 1 Sept. 18/2 We are not pointing for any team in particular, but are trying to develop for our major games without being knocked off. **1944** *Ibid.* 19 Oct. 21/2 The Jackets also are pointing for another bowl bid and defeats are anathema to gridsters with January 1 on their minds.

† **17.** *intr. Cricket.* To field at point. *Obs.*

1862 *Baily's Mag.* Aug. 85 The Surrey people..selecting..a Lyttelton to bowl; a John Walker to keep; an F. Burbidge to point. **1863** *Ibid.* Sept. 44 The bowling of Tarrant and Grundy, the wicket-keeping of Lockyer, the pointing of Carpenter,..was all cricket in perfection.

18. *Naut.* Of a sailing vessel: to lay a course close to the wind. Freq. with *up* or in phr. *to point high.*

1899 in *Cent. Dict.* **1941** H. I. CHAPELLE *Boatbuilding* i. 37 The sailing qualities of the V-bottom hull are somewhat like those of the flat-bottom types, but with improved windward qualities if well designed. They will rarely point as high as a well-designed round-bottom boat. **1947** A. RANSOME *Great Northern?* xiii. 162 'The Gael's castle is behind the ridge beyond it,' said Dorothea. 'She won't point up for our inlet,' said John. **1954** G. BRADFORD *Gloss. Sea Terms* 146/2 A vessel *points well* if she sails close to the wind. **1960** E. C. HISCOCK *Cruising under Sail* I. iv. 73 It [*sc.* the ketch] cannot point so high as a sloop, cutter, or yawl.

19. *trans. U.S.* To turn, guide, or deflect (cattle) in a particular direction.

1903 A. ADAMS *Log of Cowboy* iv. 42 Priest sent Officer to the left and myself to the right to point in the leaders. **1916** 'B. M. BOWER' *Phantom Herd* xiv. 244 You're trying to point the herd then. **1947** C. PRICE *Trails I Rode* 184 One time we were pointing a herd, Bill on one side and I on the other.

20. To insert white hairs (into a self-coloured fur). Usu. as pa. pple.

1911 in WEBSTER. **1913** [see *POINTED *ppl. a.*[1] 5 c]. **1916** *Fur Trade Directory* (N.Y.) 95 We point either skins or made-up goods. **1922** W. E. AUSTIN *Princ. & Pract. Fur Dressing* i. 10 They are dyed black in imitation of the black fox, or these when pointed with badger or other white hair to imitate the silver fox. **1936** F. GROVER *Practical Fur Cutting & Furriery* xv. 22 A black fox is often pointed with silver badger hairs. **1957** M. B. PICKEN *Fashion Dict.* 260/1 Fox fur pointed to imitate silver fox.

pointage (poi·ntėdʒ). [f. POINT *sb.*[1] + -AGE.] Points collectively, *spec.* the number of ration points needed to make a particular purchase.

1934 in WEBSTER. **1944** *Times* 23 Feb. 2/3 From April 2 imported tinned marmalade will be available on points... The pointage will be announced later. **1946** *Evening News* 15 Aug. 1/7 Mr. Strachey said..that he had not contemplated increasing pointage to compensate for the estimated demand for points.

poi·nt angle. [f. POINT *sb.*[1] + ANGLE *sb.*[2]] The angle at a vertex of a solid body; *spec.* (*a*) the angle between two diametrically opposite edges or surfaces at the tip of a tool; (*b*) the re-entrant solid angle at a vertex of an artificial cavity in a tooth.

1869 [see POINT *sb.*[1] sense D. 13]. **1908** G. V. BLACK *Operative Dentistry* II. 9 All point angles are formed by the junction of three walls at a point, and are named by joining the names of the walls forming the angle. They are, therefore, named in three terms. *Ibid.*, The point angles are formed where the line angles of one set meet the other set at the angle of the cavity. **1919** G. W. BURLEY *Machine & Fitting Shop Practice* II. v. 142 The standard point-angle of lathe centres is 60° for small and medium-sized work-pieces. **1950** P. GATES in A. W. Judge *Machine Tools & Operations* I. iv. 149 When drilling soft or ductile materials, drills ground with a smaller point angle tend to throw up considerable burrs on the back of the work. **1973** W. W. HOWARD *Rev. Operative Dentistry* i. 9 Point angles are named for the line angles that form them.

point-blank, *a.*, *sb.*, and *adv.* Add: **C.** *adv.* **3. a.** (Earlier and later examples.)

1598 J. FLORIO *Worlde of Wordes* 104/2 *A dirittura*, foorthright, point blanke. *a* **1914** JOYCE *Stephen Hero* (1944) 45 McCann always represented a member of the Opposition and he spoke point-blank. Then a member would protest. **1938** E. WAUGH *Scoop* II. v. 233, I read the newspapers with lively interest. It is seldom that they are absolutely, point blank wrong. **1968** *Punch* 6 Nov. 658/2 However, I took the oranges home just the same, with marmalade in mind, but my wife refused pointblank.

point-blanker. [f. POINT-BLANK *a.* + -ER[1].] A point-blank shot.

1830 J. F. COOPER *Water Witch* II. vii. 202 'Run in the quoin, and..give her a point-blanker!' said the gruff old seaman... 'None of your geometry calculations for me!'

point-device, *a.* (Further examples.)

1885 R. L. STEVENSON *Prince Otto* II. i. 64 Otto looked so gay, and walked so airily, he was so well dressed and brushed and frizzled, so point-de-vice, and of such a sovereign elegance. **1900** C. M. YONGE *Modern Broods* xvii. 161 He is a little too point device, too obviously got up for the occasion! **1928** D. L. SAYERS *Ld. Peter views Body* xii. 283 His double-breasted suit of navy-blue and his socks, tie, and handkerchief, all scrupulously matched, were a trifle more point-device than the best taste approves. **1958** *Observer* 28 Dec. 7/7 Odd how neat and point-device and sane they all looked.

point-duty. Add: Also *attrib.*

1908 *Daily Chron.* 30 June 1/3 A point-duty constable.. was knocked down..by a taxi-cab. **1967** N. LUCAS *C.I.D.* vi. 72 Ignoring a point-duty policeman's signal to stop. **1974** *Drive* Autumn 62/2 These days, alas, only small boys want to be point-duty policemen!

‖**pointe** (pwænt). *Dancing.* [Fr.] The tip of the toes. Also, a dance-movement executed on the tip of the toes. Also *attrib.*

1830 R. BARTON tr. *Blasis's Code of Terpsichore* VI. 505 To waltz properly, all the beats, or *tems*, should be clearly marked, being attentive not to turn upon *les pointes*, or toes, in the same beats. **1846** *Musical World* 21 Nov. 587/2 The *pirouette* and the *pointe*, which she achieves with great facility. **1912** J. C. FLITCH *Mod. Dancing & Dancers* iv. 58 The *pointes*..came to be regarded as the highest form of accomplishment. **1912** *Dancing Times* Aug. 449/2 Various Pointe Steps and..Enchaînements of Steps on the Pointes. **1920** *Ibid.* Feb. 413/1 Second and fourth couples run on the pointe under arch round first and third couples. *Ibid.* Dec. 182/2 The damage that can be done by too early pointe work is incalculable. **1949** *Ballet Ann.* III. 93 The advent of the Italian ballerina and her steel-like *pointes* and brilliant *fouettés*. **1959** T. MARA *On your Toes!* (1961) 18/1 In standing correctly on the pointes the dancer stands on the pads of the toes. **1961** S. LESTER in *Ballet here & Now* i. 29 The swift exploitation of the use of the *pointe* for the female dancer. **1974** P. L. MOLDON *Your Bk. of Ballet* ii. 27 Dancing on the tips of the toes (on *pointe*)..enhanced the ballerina's lightness.

pointed, *ppl. a.*[1] Add: **5.** (Further examples.)

1934 PRIEBSCH & COLLINSON *German Lang.* 357 In German documents it [*sc.* Anglo-Saxon type] occurs usually in the *pointed* (Lowe: *miniscule*) form. **1947** *Hansard Commons* 15 Dec. 1451 Mr. Lipson asked..if smaller tins of pointed foodstuffs can be provided. **1957** *Encycl. Brit.* XIX. 664/2 The pointed runes were generally known and used in the whole of the Scandinavian North throughout the Middle Ages as the writing of cultured laymen.

b. *pointed blanket* = **point blanket.*

1779 in *Beaver* (1935) June 47 Sends samples of five different sorts of Pointed blankets with their respective prices per pair. **1780** in E. E. Rich *Moose Fort Jrnl., 1783–85* 356 We now send..pointed Blankets of different sizes..to be delivered to him. **1926** [see *point blanket* s.v. *POINT *sb.*[1] D. 14]. **1956** *Beaver* Summer 50 It can be no coincidence that while Maugenest was in London enquiries were put in hand for *Pointed* blankets.

c. *pointed fox*: (see quots.). Cf. *POINT *v.*[1] 20.

1911 *Directory Fur Trade* (N.Y.) 11 Fine Kamchatka and American Foxes in Sitka, Pointed, Black and Baumarten. **1913** J. W. JONES *Fur-Farming in Canada* iv. 100 Latterly, the Germans have developed a large trade in 'pointed fox', which is an ordinary cheap fox dyed black, and afterwards 'pointed' by sewing in white hairs. **1939** M. BYERS *Designing Women* III. xix. 250 Pointed Fox is red fox dyed black with white hairs stuck into it artificially. **1952** LAPICK & GELLE *Scientific Fur Servicing* 7 In pointed fox the inserted hairs are generally all white. **1969** R. T. WILCOX *Dict. Costume* (1970) 142/1 *Fox, pointed*, the common red fox dyed black and pointed with silvery badger hairs to simulate silver fox.

6. *pointed-butted, -toed* adjs.

1928 PEAKE & FLEURE *Steppe & Sown* iii. 46 Pointed-butted axes of jadeite and other hard stone came into use as well as flint. **1891** 'L. MALET' *Wages of Sin* III. v. vi. 33 Presenting his cousin with a fine view of a pointed-toed shoe sole. **1962** *Times* 30 Jan. 12/5 Pointed-toed backless shoes.

pointer. 3. f. For *U.S.* read 'orig. *U.S.*' and add further examples.

1957 V. BRITTAIN *Testament of Experience* I. iii. 104, I liked the sound of the Bill not better than she; it was another 'pointer' towards the impending shadow of war and its threat to human liberty. **1961** *Lancet* 29 July 245/1 Experimenta evidence provides some pointers. **1977** J. F. FIXX *Compl. Bk. Running* vii. 82 An experienced runner may occasionally offer some pointers to a friend, but most of the time we coach ourselves. **1977** *Oxford Diocesan Mag.* Nov. 8/3 Other significant pointers to the future.

h. (See quot. 1872.)

1866 in *Nebraska Hist. Mag.* (1932) XIII. 149 After awhile I get my last pointer yoked, drive the whole team around and hitch it on the wagon tongue. **1872** C. H. EDEN *My Wife & I in Queensland* 36 Twelve bullocks is the usual number in a team, the two polers and the leaders being steady old stagers; the pair next to the pole are called the 'pointers'. **1941** BAKER *Dict. Austral. Slang* 55 *Pointers*, two of the bullocks in a team, placed next to the 'polers'.

4. Also *attrib.*

1797 J. WOODFORDE *Diary* 15 Jan. (1931) V. 5 One of his Pointer Dogs..was gone mad. **1811** JANE AUSTEN *Sense & S.* III. viii. 181 He reminded me of an old promise about a pointer puppy. **1822** J. WOODS *Two Years' Residence Eng. Prairie* 287, I lately saw a young pointer-dog,..that had three days before been bitten by a rattlesnake. **1849** J. W. AUDUBON *Western Jrnl.* (1906) 46 Some of the men had stolen a valuable pointer dog. **1979** *Times* 24 Nov. 26/6 (Advt.), *For sale*: Pointer puppies.

9. d. A person who does the ornamental work on the backs of gloves.

1903 *Sci. Amer.* Suppl. 24 Jan. 22629/3 Some make the gloves,..others, called 'pointers', work the ornamental lines on the back. **1921** *Dict. Occup. Terms* (1927) § 411.

e. The person who lays or points a gun. *U.S.*

1904 *Sci. Amer.* 18 June 475 The turrets are trained by one man, the trainer; and each gun is pointed by another man, the pointer, who fires the gun.

f. The person who 'points' a block of marble, etc.

1911 [see *POINT *sb.*[1] A. 20 d].

g. A person who points furs.

1929 *Fur Trade Directory* (N.Y.) 73 James Feuerlicht, Inc. 'The Old Reliable Fur Pointer'. **1930** M. BACHRACH *Fur* xxiii. 431 The other use of the Badger is by a separate branch of the Industry known as the Pointers. These people furnish new hairs for a peltry by a method known as pointing. **1936** F. GROVER *Practical Fur Cutting & Furriery* xv. 23 Badger hairs are also used for pointing of other furs; the pointer taking the skins for pointing ascertains the sort of pointing necessary. **1953** *Fur Trade Directory* (N.Y.) 66 Artistic Fur Pointers. Lydia Silver Fox Pointing Co.

11. *U.S.* A herdsman riding at the head of a herd of cattle on the march to keep it going in the desired direction.

1869 *Overland Monthly* III. 126 On the march the mighty herd sometimes strings out miles in length, and then it has 'pointers', who ride abreast of the head of the column, and 'siders', who keep the stragglers out of the chaparral. **1908** *Pacific Monthly* Mar. 324/2 The pointer is the herdsman who rides at the head of a straggling herd of cattle on the march, a sort of Cowboy John the Baptist. **1943** L. V. HAMNER *Short Grass* 50 Two men, his best, were put near the front of the line... These were the pointers.

12. Either of two sharks belonging to the family Isuridæ, the blue pointer, *Isurus glaucus*, or the white pointer, *Carcharodon carcharias.*

1882 J. E. TENISON-WOODS *Fishes & Fisheries N.S.W.* iv. 95 On the appearance of a 'blue pointer' among boats fishing for schnapper..the general cry is raised. **1896** F. G. AFLALO *Sketches Nat. Hist. Austral.* III. 222 The Blue-Pointer..is the favourite shark of that particular form of fiction which passes for popular natural history. *Ibid.* 223 Such are the chief sharks, the others being the huge White-Pointer [etc.]. **1963** H. W. McCORMICK et al. *Shadows in Sea* iv. 101 The Mako shark of the western Atlantic is a very close relative of the Blue Pointer (*Isurus glaucus*) of the Indian and Pacific Oceans. *Ibid.*, The Blue Pointer, in turn, is a name given by some South African Fishermen to the shark elsewhere known as the Great White, called in Australia the White Death or White Pointer. **1973** *Parade* (Melbourne) Sept. 63/1 The shark was a white pointer, of the maneater variety. **1975** *Daily Colonist* (Victoria, B.C.) 20 Dec. 7/6 Terry Page also offered odds in favour of Australian diver Wally Gibbons killing the white pointer shark before it kills him.

13. *Canad.* A rowing boat, pointed at both ends and having a shallow draught, used by loggers.

1901 'R. CONNOR' *Man from Glengarry* 13 Swiftly the pointer shot down the current, the swaying bodies and swinging oars in perfect rhythm with the song that rose and fell with melancholy but musical cadence. **1947** J. J. ROWLANDS *Cache Lake Country* 96 And all the while men in pointers..big boats with high pointed ends, move about picking up drivers, working logs off rocks. **1950** J. HAMBLETON *Abitibi Adventure* 140 They would use 'pointers', twenty-foot heavily built craft with steeply sloping sides, which seemed very tippy but actually were the most practical craft ever devised for Canadian logging. **1961** PRICE & KENNEDY *Notes on Hist. Renfrew County* 156 At the suggestion of J. R. Booth, who wanted a useful river craft, John Cockburn in 1883 designed the 'pointer', a sharp-pointed boat that is still widely used in the lumbering business. **1964** *Canad. Geogr. Jrnl.* Feb. 67/3 If you ask Emmett Chartrand about the driving boat or 'pointer' he has a faraway look when he answers, '—used them, wore them out, broke them.' **1970** *Canad. Geogr. Mag.* Feb. 51/1 But now that Mr. John A. Cockburn has retired and his family's boatbuilding workshop has been demolished, the red Pointer will slowly disappear from the Canadian scene.

14. *Comb.* **pointer reading**, the reading of an instrument as shown by a pointer; also *fig.*

1933 *Mind* XLII. 108 The reduction of the objects of

physics to pointer-readings is not for him..a mark of the finality of physics. **1961** *Listener* 17 Aug. 245/2 There are no public pointer-readings in religion. **1967** *Philos.* XLII. 285 The doctrine that science is all about pointer-readings.

pointful (poi·ntfʊl), *a.* [f. POINT *sb.*[1] + -FUL.] Full of point; apposite, pertinent. So **poi·ntfulness.**

1897 *Daily Tel.* 4 Jan. 5/4 Similarly, and with greater pointfulness, it was remarked that the Select Committee.. never consulted any person who was not in full work. **1931** *Cath. Gaz.* Feb. 71/2 The story—old, even apocryphal, it may be, but certainly typical and pointful—of Queen Victoria. **1960** *Guardian* 15 July 6/5 The guileless burbling is often very entertaining, and sometimes even pointful. **1970** *Daily Tel.* 27 June 7 Boulez will agree that for such randomness to be pointful the difference between one realisation and another needs to be rendered perceptible. **1976** P. DONOVAN *Relig. Lang.* vii. 81 A surrounding describable in words sets the act in the appropriate light, making it profound and religiously pointful. **1977** *Gramophone* Dec. 1164/1 Another pointful contrast came when we compared this latest RCA version of *La forza del destino* with that company's 1965 version also recorded with Leontyne Price. **1978** *Hi-fi News* Dec. 159/3 The finale is particularly fine, imbued with an urgency and pointfulness that has rarely been equalled.

poi·nt group. *Math.* and *Cryst.* [f. POINT *sb.*[1] + GROUP *sb.*] † **a.** [tr. G. *punktgruppe* (Brill & Noether 1873, in *Nachrichten von der K. Ges. der Wiss. zu Göttingen* 117).] A set of points. *Obs.*

1895 *Proc. London Math. Soc.* XXVI. 495 The following paper deals with the properties of point-groups in relation to algebraic curves drawn through them. **1900** *Rep. Brit. Assoc. Adv. Sci.* 1900 121 (*heading*) Report on the present state of the theory of point-groups. **1900** K. FINK *Hist. Math.* 240 This theorem..introduced point groups, or systems of points of intersection of two curves, into geometry.

b. Any subgroup of the symmetry group of a sphere; *esp.* any of the thirty-two sets of symmetry operations which are used to classify crystal types.

[**1896** *Amer. Jrnl. Math.* XVIII. 172 We mark on the faces of the regular bodies a general point group.] **1903** H. HILTON *Math. Crystallogr.* iv. 48 Finite groups whose operations all leave one point unmoved are called point-groups. **1924** R. W. G. WYCKOFF *Structure of Crystals* i. 21 The point groups, or classes of crystal symmetry, thus formed may be uniquely defined either by stating their symmetry properties or, more analytically, by giving the coördinates of the equivalent points which arise from any arbitrarily chosen point by the operation of each of their elements of symmetry. **1950** W. J. MOORE *Physical Chem.* xiii. 364 The possible combinations of these symmetry elements that can occur in crystals have been shown to number exactly 32. These define the 32 crystallographic point groups, which determine the 32 crystal classes. **1973** T. JANSSEN *Crystallographic Groups* iii. 72 Each subgroup of *O*(3) is called a point group, because it leaves the origin invariant. Point groups occur as symmetry groups of molecules and of atoms in a crystal.

pointillé, *a.* (Further examples.) Also as *sb.* (example). Also *fig.*

1931 A. ESDAILE *Student's Man. Bibliogr.* vi. 207 The sprays are lighter, not only in themselves but because impressed by pointillé tools, i.e. tools with a dotted surface. **1933** T. E. LAWRENCE *Let.* 1 Aug. (1938) 773 His style disintegrates and not integrates, this time. Too pointillé. **1940** *Proc. Prehistoric Soc.* VI. 173 Sherds ornamented with three bands decorated in pointillé. **1964** H. HODGES *Artifacts* iv. 78 Strictly speaking, a surface that has been backgrounded by stabbing all over with a small pointed punch is referred to as *pointillé*, although some archaeologists are in the habit of using the term to describe any surface with a fine dot pattern, be the dots bosses or pits. **1974** *Times Lit. Suppl.* 23 Aug. 910/2 The English binders showed a liveliness and originality... The new designs included..the all-over pattern, introduced in the 1670s and generally composed of *pointillé* flowers and drawer-handle tools.

pointillism, -isme. (Further examples.)

1901 [see *NEO-IMPRESSIONISM]. **1947** BERGSTRÖM & TAYLOR tr. *Bergström's Dutch Still-Life Painting 17th Cent.* vi. 232 His broad and free handling is set off by a spirited *pointillisme* in some passages. **1976** *New Yorker* 15 Mar. 28/2 The murals are a triumph of Japanese pointillism.

2. *transf.* spec. *Mus.*, the breaking up of the musical texture into thematic, rhythmic, and tonal fragments.

1934 C. LAMBERT *Music Ho!* I. 32 In the pointillism of its scoring, *La Mer* represents the apex of Debussy's impressionist manner. **1959** *Times* 4 Apr. 10/2 Hamilton's music has been moving towards serialism for some time, and in this sonata he finds himself up to the elbows in neo-Webernist *pointillisme*. **1972** S. HYNES *Edwardian Occasions* 166 Mrs [Beatrice] Webb..created another character..by a large number of small strokes—a kind of literary pointillism. **1973** *Daily Tel.* 19 Mar. 14/2 A happy synthesis of recent techniques and time-hallowed devices, of chords and clusters, speech-slides and sung intervals, pointillism and canon. **1976** *Visible Language* X. 59 A piece of the once-voguish art of typewriter pointillisme.

pointillist, *sb.* Add: Also ‖ **-iste.** (Earlier and later examples.)

1891 *Academy* 6 June 544/3 'Impressionists', 'tâchistes', 'plein airistes', and 'pointillistes', to use the jargon of the day. **1892** *Mag. of Art* p. xxxv/1 Among the painters who devote themselves to the application of colour in minute subdivision—called *pointillistes*, which may be freely rendered stipplers—the most conspicuous were M. Signac and M. Van Rysselberghe. **1916** A. BENNETT *Lion's Share* xii. 93 Also she was acquainted with the names and styles of all known modern painters from pointillistes to cubistes. **1929** E. LINKLATER *Poet's Pub* ii. 34 We ought to learn from the pointillistes. Put your colour on pure, in spots, and you get a luminous spectrum in verse as well as in painting. **1954** W. LEWIS *Demon of Progress in Arts* I. v. 23 The theory was that the colours would mix in the eye of the spectator—they must never be allowed to mix anywhere else... The Pointillistes adhered most rigidly to this rule. **1961** *Encycl. World Art* V. 184 By employing the color theories of Michel Chevreul..and refining the principle of optical mixture from brush strokes to tiny dots, the pointillists arrived at..'the logical consequence of impressionism'. **1963** F. GETTINGS *Golden Pleasure Book of Art* 59 Because of the way Seurat and his friends used small points of colour, they were called *Pointillistes.*

B. *attrib.* passing into *adj.*

1902 *Encycl. Brit.* XXIX. 414/1 There are several fallacies however, theoretical and practical, in this 'spectral palette' and pointillist method. **1905** [in Dict.] **1934** C. LAMBERT *Music Ho!* I. 25 The methods of the pointillist painters have something in common with the use of the orchestra as displayed in Debussy's works. **1940** O. SITWELL *Left Hand, Right Hand!* II. 132 Those figures, full of latent movement, seen in a pointillist picture. **1971** [see *DIVISIONISM]. **1975** D. THOMAS *Impressionists* 87 He [*sc.* Van Gogh] met Pissaro, who was then moving towards the pointillist technique of Seurat.

b. *transf.*

1921 E. SAPIR *Language* 243 We cannot assimilate the luxurious periods of Latin nor the pointilliste style of the Chinese classics. **1934** C. LAMBERT *Music Ho!* I. 46 This pointillist orchestration gives to many of Schönberg's works an impressionist effect in performance that an inspection of the score with the eye alone would hardly lead one to expect. **1958** *Observer* 27 Apr. 16/4 Thackeray's.. effective 'pointillist' method. **1959** *Ibid.* 14 June 24/3 Although its style was largely *pointilliste*, the music did not strike me as derivative. **1970** *Daily Tel.* 30 Apr. 16/5 A certain lack of eloquence became most clearly discernible during a few melodious lines given to the oboe in this largely pointillist piece. **1976** *Times Lit. Suppl.* 1 Oct. 1229/4 Neither the satire nor the pointillist plotting adds up to much that is coherent and compelling.

Hence **pointilli·stic** *a.*

1922 H. CRANE *Let.* 19 Apr. (1965) 84 All this talk of Matty's is..metallic and pointillistic. **1954** *Grove's Dict. Mus.* (ed. 5) IX. 226/1 His [*sc.* Webern's] next compositions..are still more highly concentrated, still more transparent and pointillistic in texture. **1972** *Village Voice* (N.Y.) 1 June 44/3 Philip Corner adds sporadic pointillistic piano gestures. **1977** *Times* 22 Oct. 10/6 A new and exclusive pointillistic dyeing method... You can shade your carpet from dark to pale.

pointing, *vbl. sb.*[1] Add: **1. e.** (Earlier and later examples.) Also **pointing-up.**

1845 *Encycl. Metrop.* V. 465/2 The construction of these instruments for pointing is not always the same, but the principle on which they act is exactly similar. **1947** J. C. RICH *Materials & Methods of Sculpture* ix. 272 The process of pointing consists of marking with pencil all projections and recessions or 'points' on the model, which is generally a plaster cast, and making position measurements with the adjustable rods of the pointing machine, which are capable of measuring at intervals a fraction of an inch apart. **1969** L. R. ROGERS *Sculpture* vi. 199 The pointing-up in marble of clay models in a mechanical fashion by craftsmen assistants. **1974** *Encycl. Brit. Micropædia* VIII. 68/1 Although pointing has limitations as a technique of creative sculpture, it has been used widely, especially in the 19th century.

8. b. The disposition and colouring of the points in a cat's fur. Cf. *POINT *sb.*[1] A. 26 c.

1978 R. HILL *Pinch of Snuff* v. 50 The room was filled with cats..of various ages and pointings.

10. (Later example.)

1902 *Act 2 Edw. VII.* c. 29 § 2 Fishing for trout..by what is known as double rod fishing, or cross line fishing, or set lines,..or by striking the fish..or by pointing.

10*. *Furs.* The insertion of hairs into a pelt, usu. to repair damage or to simulate another fur. Cf. *POINT *v.*[1] 20.

1900 *Fur Trade Rev.* 1 May 213/2 Pointing will be one of the popular methods of enhancing the attractiveness of some of the most desirable furs. **1910** *Encycl. Brit.* XI. 354/1 The process of inserting white hairs is called in the trade 'pointing', and is either done by stitching them in with a needle or by adhesive caoutchouc. **1922** W. E. AUSTIN *Princ. & Pract. Fur Dressing* i. 7 Badger hair is very extensively used for 'pointing'. **1930** M. BACHRACH *Fur* xix. 275 Rubbed spots on the rumps are judged according to the damaged area, which, in the Silver Fox, can be somewhat restored to its original appearance by the process of pointing. **1936** F. GROVER *Practical Fur Cutting & Furriery* xv. 22 Pointing of furs is often resorted to, to make an imitation of another fur. **1950** *N.Z. Jrnl. Agric.* June 597/1 Pointing refers to the practice of glueing in white hairs to improve inferior silver fox furs. **1952** LAPICK & GELLE *Scientific Fur Servicing* 4 Pointing may be detected by the fact that the badger hairs used are glued in groups of two or three to the natural fox hairs and the leather.

11. pointing-bone *Anthrop.*, a bone, or apparatus consisting of bones, and usually a string made of woven hair, used by Australian Aborigines in a secret ritual to bring about the death or illness of the person at whom it is pointed; also *attrib.*; **pointing-machine** (*a*) (in Dict.: see quot. 1875); (*b*) an apparatus used in sculpture for taking points; **pointing-stick** *Anthrop.*, a stick used for the same purpose as a pointing-bone.

1904 SPENCER & GILLEN *Northern Tribes of Central Austral.* xiv. 459 The pointing apparatus..consists of a long strand of human hair-string, to one end of which five small pointing-bones are affixed. **1959** S. H. COURTIER *Death in Dream Time* v. 50 He..saw a piece of bone, sharp at one end, blunt at the other, and bound round the middle with strands of black fur or hair..a native pointing bone or death bone. **1965** *Austral. Encycl.* I. 67/1 The 'pointing bone' sorcery (widely distributed throughout southern and central northern Australia). **1886** *Encycl. Brit.* XXI. 571/2 Partly by eye and partly with the constant help of the pointing machine, which is used to give any required measurements, the workman almost completes the marble statue, leaving only the finishing touches to be done by the sculptor. **1947** J. C. RICH *Materials & Methods of Sculpture* ix. 271 There is evidence that during the Late Hellenistic period the Romans used a primitive version of the pointing machine, and this mechanical device may partly account for the large number of Roman copies of Greek sculpture. **1959** P. & L. MURRAY *Dict. Art & Artists* 249 A pointing machine measures the depth from a given vertical, of, for example, the receding planes of the nose of a plaster cast and transfers the measurement to a hole drilled in the marble block. **1904** SPENCER & GILLEN *Northern Tribes of Central Austral.* xiii. 433 A Thakomara man of the Karinji totem.. had special pointing sticks. **1959** *Chambers's Encycl.* XIV. 629/2 He [*sc.* the person who has caused illness or death] can be put out of the way by means of the 'pointing stick' or 'pointing bone' made efficacious by the spells of witch or sorcerer (usually a man).

pointless, *a.* Add: **2.** (Later examples.) Also (in the sense of *POINT *sb.*[1] A. 28 d), without purpose or advantage; having no good effect.

1934 E. WAUGH *Handful of Dust* ii. 33 It sometimes seems to me rather pointless keeping up a house this size if we don't now and then ask some other people to stay in it. **1954** I. MURDOCH *Under Net* xiii. 179 It seems pointless to conceal our identity. Sammy would guess it anyway as soon as we announced our terms. **1966** H. ROSEVEARE *Give me this Mountain* i. 18 Without Him, it was a weary, stupid, empty, pointless, useless life. **1970** G. F. NEWMAN *Sir, You Bastard* v. 147 Flowers didn't occur to Sneed until he had arrived at the hospital, and there the gesture was pointless. **1978** M. BIRMINGHAM *Sleep in Ditch* 193 'He died..soon after six.'.. 'S-so all last night's h-horror was quite pointless.'

pointman. [f. POINT *sb.*[1] or *v.*[1] + MAN *sb.*[1]]

1. = *POINTER 11.

1903 A. ADAMS *Log of Cowboy* iii. 28 Two riders, known as point men rode out and well back from the lead cattle. **1942** BERREY & VAN DEN BARK *Amer. Thes. Slang* § 913/10 Point men or riders, cowboys riding near the head of a herd of cattle. **1977** M. HERR *Dispatches* iii. 35 Classic essential American types; point men, *isolatos* and outriders.

2. = POINTSMAN 2.

1927 *Observer* 20 Nov. 11/3 It..bore a number of legends; on the footboard, 'Step on the gas'; on the bonnet, 'Don't look inside', and 'Pointman, let us pass'.

3. (Usu. as two words.) The soldier who walks at the head of a patrol. Also *transf.*

1944 *Yank* 4 Feb. 9/1 The Jap point man was on the scene before any camouflaging could be done. **1969** I. KEMP *Brit. G.I. in Vietnam* v. 96 Next to the commander..the point man was the most important member of the squad on jungle patrols. It was his duty to walk at the head of the formation..and to act as scout for the rest. **1970** *Time* 5 Jan. 14 Cisneros survived 42 patrols in Viet Nam, mostly as the exposed point man, and saw his unit chewed up behind him several times. **1977** *Time* 21 Mar. 56/1 In Young's view, his role is to be a kind of 'point man' for the Administration in foreign policy, charged with getting out in front with new ideas and possibilities. **1978** *Guardian Weekly* 25 June 18/2 Although Carter started his term as no friend of Kennedy.. Kennedy has, ironically, become Carter's point man in the senate.

4. = POINTSMAN 1.

1945 G. MILLAR *Maquis* ix. 180 This pointman would not presumably be antagonistic to us, since he would be an ordinary 'cheminot'.

Pointolite (poi·ntŏlɔit). Also **pointolite.** A proprietary name for a type of lamp containing a small but bright source of light, produced by the incandescence of a small knob of tungsten heated by an arc struck between it and a cathode.

1916 *Illuminating Engineer* IX. 32/1 A very interesting new form of lamp for projection purposes..has just been brought out by the Edison and Swan United Electric Light Co., Ltd. The 'Pointolite' lamp is in reality an arc within a sealed bulb. **1923** *Trade Marks Jrnl.* 25 July 1558 Pointolite... Electric lamps... The Edison Swan Electric Company, Limited,..London..; manufacturers. **1926** W. E. WOODWARD *Metallogr. Steel & Cast Iron* i. 42 For taking photomicrographs a 500 c.p. 'pointolite' gives excellent results. **1949** A. PEREIRA *Man. Sub-Standard Cinematogr.* vi. 234 A form of arc light which has found wide application for comparatively low power projection is the enclosed tungsten arc known as Pointolite. **1964** M. HYNES *Med. Bacteriol.* (ed. 8) v. 57 A good illumination of sufficient intensity is essential. This is given by an arc-light or a 'pointolite' lamp.

pointswoman. (In Dict. s.v. POINTSMAN.) (Earlier example.)

1865 A. MUNBY *Diary* 17 Mar. in M. Hiley *Victorian Working Women* (1979) II. i. 86/2 In the cutting I found a girl.. the pointswoman, whose duty it is to mind the rails whenever a train of coalwaggons goes by.

pointwise, *adv.* Add: **2.** *Math.* With regard to individual points; esp. in *pointwise convergent,* that converges for each individual point in a space, but not necessarily for the space as a whole (so *pointwise convergence*).

1932 *Colloquium Publ. Amer. Math. Soc.* XV. i. 26 The term 'convergence in the mean' was introduced to distinguish convergence in the space $\mathfrak{L}_2$..from ordinary point-wise convergence. **1955** Hall & Spencer *Elem. Topology* iv. 133 This sequence is said to converge pointwise to a mapping $f:S\to T$, if and only if, for each point x of S, the sequence $\{f_n(x)\}$ of points of T converges to the point $f(x)$ of T. **1966** A. Feinstein tr. *G. Choquet's Topology* i. 92 Every sequence (f_n) which converges uniformly to f converges pointwise to f, but it is important to note that the converse is incorrect. **1970** *Manifold* VI. 17 A student produced three new specimens... They came from adding the blackboard examples pointwise. **1971** Powell & Higman *Finite Simple Groups* iii. 138 And r leaves a hyperplane pointwise fixed. **1974** G. J. O. Jameson *Topology & Normed Spaces* ix. 90 A decreasing sequence of continuous functions on a compact space can certainly be pointwise convergent to a discontinuous function.

pointy, *a.* Add: **1.** (Later examples.) Also *fig.*

1906 *Daily Chron.* 2 Oct. 3/4 Puck of the pointy-ears. **1927** J. Masefield *Midnight Folk* 113 She has..pointy, black shiny shoes. **1953** A. Miller *Crucible* I. 20 Let either of you breathe a word,..and I will bring a pointy reckoning that will shudder you. **1969** M. Puzo *Godfather* IV. xix. 263 Conny stood with hands on hips, her face pointy and white with rage. **1975** J. McClure *Snake* ix. 116 Her nails..were long and pointy. **1977** *Rolling Stone* 19 May 69/3 Zbigniew Brzezinski, the president's national security adviser and a man whose every feature is pointy, enters the office.

4. Special collocations, as **pointy-head** *U.S. colloq.*, a supposed expert or intellectual (used derogatorily); also *attrib.*; hence *pointy-headed* adj.

1972 *Guardian* 21 Feb. 2/4 George Wallace..attacked Muskie, Humphrey, and his other 'pointy-head' opponents. **1972** *Times* 5 May 6/3 Mr Wallace..dismissed it quickly at the end of his address as 'the most callous, asinine, stupid thing that was ever conceived by some pointy-head in Washington DC'. **1972** *National Observer* (N.Y.) 27 May 12/1, I am not ashamed of being a 'pointy headed intellectual snob' who notices the correlation between our 'leadership' and the many distressing phenomena 'coinciding' with those sages' descriptions. **1973** J. Di Mona *Last Man at Arlington* (1974) 178 Idiots... Pointy heads that didn't know how to operate. **1975** *N.Y. Times* 12 Nov. 42/2 Let the dust gather on the pointy-headed bureaucrats and all the other props from yesteryear.

b. *Comb.*, as *pointy-eared, -toed* adjs.: see also *pointy-headed* adj. above.

1906 Kipling *Puck of Pook's Hill* 7 They saw a small, brown, broad-shouldered, pointy-eared person with a snub nose. **1968** A. Young in A. Chapman *New Black Voices* (1972) 147 Sport shirt, creased pants, shiny black pointy-toed stetsons [*sc.* shoes]. **1971** E. Bullins in W. King *Black Short Story Anthol.* (1972) 61 His snake-skinned, pointy-toed shoes. **1978** *N.Y. Times* 18 Jan. 1/3 A scene normally dominated by men with Western twangs in ten-gallon hats and pointy-toed boots.

‖ **poipoi** (poi·poi). Also **poee-poee, poi-poi, popoi.** [Polynesian word.] A Polynesian dish, usu. made from fermented bread-fruit (see quot. 1829). Also *attrib.* Cf. Poi.

1829 W. Ellis *Polynesian Researches* I. xiii. 377 The most general dish in the Southern Islands is what they call *popoi*, nearly resembling the *poe* of the Sandwich Islands. It is made with the ripe mountain plantain, either raw or baked, beaten up into a paste or jelly, and diluted with cocoa-nut milk. Another kind of *popoi* is made with bread-fruit, or *opio*, beaten up and diluted with cocoa-nut or plain water. **1846** H. Melville *Narr. Residence Marquesas Islands* xv. 128 The great staple articles of food into which the breadfruit is converted by these natives are known respectively by the names of Amar and Poee-Poee. **1888** M. I. Stevenson *Let.* 25 Aug. in M. C. Balfour *From Saranac to Marquesas* (1903) 121 Madame Stanislas gave Fanny a very finely carved *poi-poi* bowl of *mio* wood. **1910** F. W. Christian *Eastern Pacific Lands* xii. 160 To a European palate *Popoi* tastes like an acid custard. **1919** *Century Mag.* Aug. 450/1 The players halted briefly to eat a bowl of *poipoi*. **1970** I. Goldman *Ancient Polynesian Society* vii. 125 The fermented breadfruit mash (*poipoi*) stored well in leaf-lined pits. **1974** T. Heyerdahl *Fatu-Hiva* iii. 122 *Poipoi*, the staple diet in most of Polynesia. Nowhere else was *poipoi* made as strong as in the Marquesas group.

poire (pwār). [abbrev. of Canad. Fr. *poire sauvage*, lit. 'wild pear'.] A name formerly used in Canada for a tree or shrub of the genus *Amelanchier*, belonging to the family Rosaceæ, or its fruit, a blue-black berry; = Saskatoon, *shad-bush* s.v. Shad *sb.* 4 b.

1789 A. Mackenzie *Jrnl.* 14 Aug. in *Voyages from Montreal* (1801) vii. 107 There were plenty of berries, which my people called *poires*; they are of a purple hue, somewhat bigger than a pea, and of a luscious taste. **1807** G. Keith *Let.* 7 Jan. in L. F. R. Masson *Les Bourgeois de la Compagnie du Nord-Ouest* (1890) II. 66 There are *poire*, gooseberry and raspberry bushes. **1837** *Trans. Lit. & Hist. Soc. Quebec* III. 126 In the country parts this small fruit is dignified with the name of poire, more from its fine flavor, it is presumed, than from any resemblance to pears. **1865** Milton & Cheadle *N.W. Passage by Land* xiv. 266 The Indians brought in a plentiful supply of the poire, wild pear, or service berry. **1951** W. O'Meara *Grand Portage* xviii. 102 He found..a large purple berry called the poire that was the most delicious of all.

poise (pwäz, poiz), *sb.*[2] *Physics.* Pl. **poises, poise.** [f. *Poise(uille.] The unit of (dynamic) viscosity in the C.G.S. system, equal to one gramme per centimetre-second; in the International System of Units replaced by the pascal second (equal to 10 poises). Symbol P.

1913 Deeley & Parr in *Phil. Mag.* XXVI. 87 It would be a distinct advantage to have a name for the unit of viscosity expressed in C.G.S. units, and we would suggest that the word Poise be used for this; for it is to Poiseuille that we owe the experimental demonstration that when a liquid flows through a capillary tube..at constant temperature, the viscosity is constant at all rates of shear, provided that the flow is not turbulent. *Ibid.* 89 R. M. Deeley obtained $\eta = 6\times10^{12}$ poises for the viscosity at 0° C. of fine crystalline ice. **1939** *Nature* 6 May (Suppl.) p. i (Advt.), The Goodeve Thixoviscometer... Range 1 centipoise to 1 megapoise (0·01 to 10^6 poises). **1957** G. E. Hutchinson *Treat. Limnol.* I. iii. 209 The viscosity of water, 0·0114 poise at 15°C., is also very high for a liquid of low molecular weight. **1964** *Times Sci. Rev.* Spring 4/2 As a result of its relatively low viscosity—probably about 10^3 to 10^5 poises—..the lava flows freely. **1971** *Nature* 10 Sept. 101/1 Liquefaction implies a reduction in the viscosity of the sediment from that of a plastic solid (say, 10^4 poise) to that of a thick soupy liquid (say, 10 poise).

poise, *v.* Add: **6. d.** *pass.* To be ready *for* (or *to do*) something; to be about (to do something).

1932 W. Faulkner *Light in August* (1933) xvii. 381 She looked exactly like a rock poised to plunge over a precipice. **1956** A. H. Compton *Atomic Quest* 284 The boys who had been poised for the invasion of Japan. **1961** *National Rev.* 30 Dec. 462/3 The Free Chinese know that the situation on the Mainland is in flux, and are poised to strike. **1977** A. Thwaite *Portion for Foxes* 38 A scornful phrase Poised to put down the parasite or bore. **1979** *Daily Tel.* 3 Feb. 1/1 British Petroleum was poised last night to make further reductions in oil deliveries to customers around the world.

7. Also, to hover or be poised in readiness *for* (something).

1898 C. M. Sheldon *His Brother's Keeper* iii. 64 The gravity of events that were evidently poising for a crisis left little room for anything but sober feeling.

poised, *ppl. a.* Add: Also, of persons, their behaviour, etc.: composed, self-assured.

1928 E. O'Neill *Strange Interlude* I. 12 His manner is cool and poised. He speaks with a careful ease. **1961** J. Mercier *Whatever you Do* ii. 28 Somehow managing to get out a cool, poised, 'Won't you hold on a second, please', I covered up the mouthpiece, [etc]. **1974** E. Ferrers *Hanged Man's House* v. 45 She was very poised, and had a terrific social manner.

Poiseuille (pwäzöy). *Physics.* The name of J. L. M. *Poiseuille* (1799–1869), French physiologist, used *attrib.* and in the possessive to designate concepts and phenomena related to his work on fluid flow, as **Poiseuille('s) equation, expression, formula,** or **law,** the relation between the volume V of fluid flowing per second through a long cylinder of length l and radius r under conditions of Poiseuille flow, viz. $V = \pi r^4 p/8\eta l$, where p is the pressure drop along the cylinder and η is the viscosity of the fluid (given by Poiseuille in *Compt. Rend.* (1840) XI. 1047, (1841) XII. 114); **Poiseuille flow,** laminar flow of a viscous fluid of negligible compressibility, esp. through a long, narrow cylinder.

1883 *Phil. Trans. R. Soc.* CLXXIV. 946 The discharge from the pipes agreed exactly with those given by Poiseuille's formula for capillary tubes. *Ibid.* 981 With all the smaller tubes Poiseuille's law held throughout his experiments. **1931** G. Barr *Monogr. of Viscometry* ii. 24 Let the viscosity..calculated from an experiment by means of the uncorrected Poiseuille equation be denoted by η'. **1946** *Q. of Applied Math.* III. 119 The Poiseuille flow in a circular pipe was studied..with a conclusion of stability. **1958** Condon & Odishaw *Handbk. Physics* v. vi. 78/1 Viscous, laminar flow of gases through cylindrical tubes is governed by Poiseuille's law. **1967** Margerison & East *Introd. Polymer Chem.* ii. 103 In these viscometers the time taken for the level of solvent or solution to pass between two fixed marks is determined and this is related to the viscosity by Poiseuille's equation. **1975** *Jrnl. Surg. Res.* XIX. 26/1 The resistance of varying degrees of obstruction placed within the circumflex coronary artery was determined by employing Poiseuille's Law. **1975** *Microvascular Res.* X. 153 *In vivo* RBC [*sc.* red blood cell] velocity profiles for mammalian arterioles and venules.. are time variant and more blunted than would be anticipated for Poiseuille flow.

poison, *sb.* (*a.*) Add: **2.** (Earlier and later examples of *to hate like poison.*)

1530 J. Palsgrave *Lesclarcissement de la Langue Francoyse* fol. cclviii^v, He gyueth me fayre wordes and yet he hateth me lyke poyson. **1864** A. Trollope in *Good Words* Dec. 931/1 Everybody liked Barty,—excepting only Mally Trenglos, and she hated him like poison. **1905** H. A. Vachell *Hill* i. 20 'He hates me like poison,' said Duff. **1974** 'M. Innes' *Appleby's Other Story* xii. 97 Enormous sums vanishing in bitter law-suits, which is a thought the wealthy hate like poison.

b. *colloq.* (orig. *U.S.*). Alcoholic liquor; an alcoholic drink; esp. in phr. *to name one's poison*, to say what drink one would like; also *transf.*

1805 'Red Jacket' in *Freemason's Mag.* (Philadelphia) II. 388 We gave them corn and meat; they gave us poison in return. [*Note*] Alluding it is supposed to ardent spirits. **1866** 'Mark Twain' *Lett. from Hawaii* (1967) 85 In Washoe, when you are..invited to take 'your regular poison', etiquette admonishes you to touch glasses. **1876** *Carson Valley News* (Genoa, Nev.) 2 June 2/2 Nominate your poison, gents: it's my treat. **1876** J. Miller *First Fam'lies of Sierras* 128 A true Californian of Sierras.. heads straight up to the bar,..hoists his Poison, throws back his head, and then falls back wiping his mouth. **1914** Joyce *Dubliners* 113 Just as they were naming their poisons who should come in but Higgins! **1951** T. Sterling *House without Door* ii. 12 Name your poison, lady. Chocolate, vanilla, pistachio, maple cream. **1965** E. Brown *Big Man* xvii. 157 'What's your poison tonight, miss?' 'Make it a gin and bitter lemon.' **1973** J. Ashford *Double Run* v. 37 Come right in and name your poison.

c. *Chem.* A substance which destroys or reduces the activity of a catalyst.

1913 in C. Ellis *Hydrogenation Oils* (1914) 316 Sulphur is a 'poison' to the catalyst. **1938** *Thorpe's Dict. Appl. Chem.* (ed. 4) II. 426/2 Nickel is in general very effective, but..is sensitive to 'poisons', particularly sulphur compounds and carbon monoxide. **1966** *McGraw-Hill Encycl. Sci. & Technol.* II. 548/1 Catalysts gradually lose catalytic activity. Traces of impurity in the feed, called poisons, may be strongly adsorbed and exclude the reactants from the surface.

d. *Nuclear Sci.* A fission product or an impurity in a nuclear reactor which interacts with neutrons and thus slows the intended reaction; also, an element with this property which is added to the fuel in order to facilitate control of the reaction.

1952 S. Glasstone *Elements Nuclear Reactor Theory* xi. 315 Some of these [*sc.* fission products] may have large cross sections for the absorption of neutrons, and so they can act as poisons. **1961** J. F. Hill *Textbk. Reactor Physics* vii. 201 It is sometimes of advantage deliberately to introduce a high neutron absorbing material into a reactor to increase the intervals between recharging the reactor with fuel. A material used in this way is called a 'burnable poison'. **1963** J. F. Hogerton *Atomic Energy Deskbk.* 406/1 It should be noted that some poisons are classified as undesirable whereas others are deliberately introduced into the system... The major fission product poisons are xenon-135 and samarium-149. **1966** *McGraw-Hill Encycl. Sci. & Technol.* IX. 185/1 Fission-product poisons (neutron absorbers) can be lowered by frequent processing of fuel. **1978** *Nature* 26 Jan. 306/3 The higher natural abundance of ^{235}U..prevailing at that time.., and effective absence of neutron-absorbing 'poisons', constituted favourable conditions for the occurrence of a self-propagating fission reaction.

3. b. Applied to a person who exerts a baneful influence or who is detested.

1910 W. M. Raine *Bucky O'Connor* 28 They say he's part Spanish and part Indian, but all pisen. **1964** L. Deighton *Funeral in Berlin* xlii. 262 You are poison to Gehlen... There isn't a place left in the whole world where you would get a sniff of a job. **1974** A. Williams *Gentleman Traitor* xiii. 194 Philby's poison, whichever side he's on. **1977** R. Barnard *Death on High C's* xvi. 164 One knows the type... Simply eaten up with egotism... They're complete poison, wherever they go.

4. a. *poison bottle, pill.*

1854 Dickens *Hard T.* xiii. 104 It were the Poison-bottle on table. **1978** P. Lovesey *Waxwork* 64 That struck me as peculiar..that a man committing suicide would put the poison bottle back in the cabinet. **1946** P. Bottome *Lifeline* xxxv. 269 With his hands tied securely behind him Mark could not reach the poison pill he had been given for such emergencies. **1975** *Times* 29 Aug. 6/8 There are many organizations working against Mrs Gandhi... Ours is serious... We all carry poison pills in our pockets.

5. poison book = **poison register*; **poison gas,** any chemical that is released into the atmosphere as a gas or vapour to harm those who inhale it or absorb it through their skin; also *attrib.*; hence as *vb. trans.*; **poison green,** a bright, sharp shade of green; **poison oracle,** a form of divination in which a Zande witch-doctor administers poison to a fowl and draws inferences from its effect on the bird; **poison pen,** one who writes anonymous letters with malicious, libellous, or scurrilous intent; also *attrib.*, of or pertaining to such a person or letter; **poison** (also **poisons, poisons'**) **register,** a register of the names of those to whom a poison or poisons have been made available.

1930 D. L. Sayers *Strong Poison* i. 12 She signed the poison-book in the name of Mary Slater, and the handwriting has been identified as that of the prisoner. **1943** G. Greene *Ministry of Fear* I. iii. 33 We'll look into the poison books. **1947** A. Christie *Labours of Hercules* ii. 62, I never said anything about the missing arsenic. I even cooked the poison book! **1950** 'A. Gilbert' *Is she Dead Too?* iii. 46 He had brought a prescription that required..a drug only to be obtained by signing the Poison Book. **1978** J. Symons *Blackheath Poisonings* III. 152 His poison book's all in order, and there's this entry in it for arsenic. **1915** H. W. Wilson *Great War* IV. 336/2 After the great chemical experiment with poison gas in April, the Germans had been able to advance to the manor-house. *Ibid.*, The Duke of Würtemberg..had apparently become convinced, after his poison-gas victory in April, that chemical methods of making war were the most successful. **1922** D. H. Lawrence *Fantasia of Unconscious* xi. 207 The problem of the future is a question of the strongest poison-gas. **1924** T. Hardy *Winter Words* (1928) 171 After two thousand years of mass We've got as far as poison-gas. **1970** R. Stetler *Battle of Bogside* 179 President Johnson..called a press conference to deny the poison gas charge. **1970** G. Jackson *Let.* 4 Apr. in *Soledad Brother* (1971) 211 An enemy that would starve his body, ..chain his body,..and poison-gas it. **1975** tr. *Melchior's Sleeper Agent* (1976) II. 39 Stacks of incendiary bombs and poison gas projectiles. **1926** S. Lewis *Mantrap* x. 117 The poison-green tufted velvet couch. **1937** [see *candy-pink* s.v. *candy *sb.*[1] 2]. **1975** P. G. Winslow *Death of Angel* x. 212 He drives a poison-green two-seater. **1937** E. E. Evans-Pritchard *Witchcraft, Oracles & Magic among Azande* 10 The principal Zande oracles are: (*a*) *benge*, poison oracle, which operates through the administration of strychnine to fowls, and formerly to human beings also. **1955** M. Gluckman *Custom & Conflict in Africa* iv. 88 Each question is framed to allow of a 'yes' or 'no' answer to the problem, thus: 'if X is the witch who is making my son ill, poison-oracle, kill the chicken; if X is not the witch, poison-oracle, spare the chicken'. **1972** M. D. McLeod in Singer & Street *Zande Themes* 167 The Zande clearly considered the rubbing-board oracle less accurate than both the termite oracle and the poison oracle. **1914** *N.Y. World* 11 Mar. 5/1 Women..crowded the Union County Court room..hoping to hear some plausible elucidation of the 'poison pen' mystery. **1929** M. Lief *Hangover* 302 The King of the Tabloids sat in his counting-house counting up the two and a half million circulation gained through the blood and scandal shed by ..poison-pen letters. **1935** D. L. Sayers *Gaudy Night* v. 100 Isn't our poison-pen rather silly to get all her spelling right? **1956** A. Wilson *Anglo-Saxon Attitudes* II. iii. 388 To all the other clergymen she was busy addressing poison-pen letters. **1973** J. Thomson *Death Cap* vii. 93 She had seemed..a perfect front runner in the poison-pen stakes, the classic example of the embittered spinster. **1975** D. Lodge *Changing Places* iii. 124 I've had what I believe is called a poison-pen letter from Euphoria, an anonymous letter. **1936** Cook & LaWall *Remington's Pract. Pharm.* (ed. 8) lxxxiv. 1357 The poison register must be always open for inspection by the proper authorities. **1978** J. Symons *Blackheath Poisonings* III. 150 He sent..Sergeant Miles to look at the poison registers. **1907** *Yesterday's Shopping* (1969) 499 In the case of Poisons being required it is absolutely necessary..that the Poisons Register be signed at the time of purchase. **1957** *Encycl. Brit.* XVII. 693/1 These poisons in their uncompounded form may only be supplied to persons known to the pharmacist and their sale must be recorded in the poisons' register. **1958** H. G. Moss *Retail Pharmacist's Handbk.* xxiii. 360 Certain professional and trade users may obtain First Schedule poisons on a signed order instead of attending and signing the Poisons Register. **1971** Gilbert & Sharp *Pharmaceuticals* xi. 140 First Schedule poisons may be sold without any prescription, but only if the purchaser is known to the pharmacist and signs the Poisons Register.

b. poison-bulb, substitute for def.: one of several South African bulbous plants belonging to the family Amaryllidaceæ, esp. *Boophane disticha*; (earlier and later examples); **poison-bush,** (*c*) *Austral.*, one of several plants bearing leaves harmful to cattle, esp. a species of *Gastrolobium*; **poison-dogwood** (examples); **poison-elder** (earlier and later examples); **poison-ivy,** substitute for def.: one of several trailing or climbing North American shrubs belonging to the genus *Rhus* (or *Toxicodendron*), esp. *R. toxicodendron* (or *T. toxicaria*), bearing leaves resembling ivy, and greenish flowers followed by white berries, and producing inflammation of the skin and other reactions when touched; (earlier and later examples); also *fig.*, an unpleasant person; **poison-oak** (earlier and later examples); **poison-plant,** also, a name used for various plants harmful to man or livestock; (later examples); **poison-sumac,** for *Rhus venenata* substitute *Rhus vernix* or *Toxicodendron vernis*; (earlier and later examples) **poison vine,** (*b*) (examples); **poison-weed,** delete † and ? and add later example.

1822 W. Burchell *Trav. Interior S. Africa* I. xxi. 539 Plants of *Amaryllis toxicaria* were..very abundant... This plant is well known to the Bushmen, on account of the virulent poison contained in its bulb. It is also known to the Colonists and Hottentots, by the name of *Gift-bol* (Poison-bulb). **1966** E. Palmer *Plains of Camdeboo* v. 82 The Poison Bulb, with its innocent blue-green fan of leaves, that they [*sc.* Bushmen] pounded for its deadly juice. **1889** J. H. Maiden *Useful Native Plants Austral.* 129 *Gastrolobium* spp... These plants are dangerous to stock and are hence called 'Poison Bushes'. Large numbers of cattle are lost annually in Western Australia through eating them. **1927** M. M. Bennett *Christison of Lammermoor* xx. 185 There were quicksands and the dreaded poison-bush, *Gastrolobium grandiflorum*. **1965** *Austral. Encycl.* VII. 157/2 Many species of *Gastrolobium* have, and nearly all species deserve, the name poison-bush or poison-plant. **1814** J. Bigelow *Florula Bostoniensis* 72 *Rhus vernix*. Poison dogwood. Swamp Sumach... Grows in bunches in wet swamps. **1958** Poison-dogwood [see **poison-elder*]. **1822** A. Eaton *Man. Bot.* (ed. 3) 428 *Rhus vernix*, poison sumach, poison elder... berries green, at length whitish. **1958** G. A. Petrides *Field Guide to Trees & Shrubs* 84 Names in common use, such as Poison-elder or Poison-dogwood, usually refer to Poison Sumac. **1784** *Mem. Amer. Acad.* I. 422 Poison Ivy..produces the same kind of inflammations and eruptions..as the poison wood tree. **1832** W. D. Williamson *Hist. State Maine* I. 130 Poison Ivy..is a dangerous medicine. **1891** M. E. Freeman *N. England Nun* 191 [She] saw Joseph Tenney's face through branches of pink dog-bane and over masses of poison-ivy. **1935** M. de la Roche *Young Renny* xxvi. 265 Bright-coloured tendrils of poison ivy stretched toward their path. **1939** 'B. Gray' *Miss Dynamite* xvi. 179 So this is the charming little prairie flower that Norman's fallen in love with!.. Primrose, my foot! Her name's Poison Ivy! **1963** W. Blunt *Of Flowers & Village* 29 We mayn't have these growing wild in England, nor the American poison ivy. **1971** *Rhodora* LXXIII. 76 More than 350,000 cases of poison-ivy dermatitis are estimated for the United States per year. **1976** F. Greenland *Misericordia Drop* II. viii. 138 Those amiable characters, my personal poison ivy, who so conscientiously compile our Code of Procedure. **1743** J. Clayton *Flora Virginica* 33 *Rhus*... Poison-Oak. **1905** G. E. Cole *Early Oregon* 29 Having been poisoned with poison oak so that I was completely blind, the others advised me to return. **1958** G. A. Petrides *Field Guide to Trees & Shrubs* 81 Some authorities believe differences between the several forms of Poison-oak and Poison-ivy are inconsequential. **1971** *Rhodora* LXXIII. 523 As the finer particles become less prevalent, the soil becomes more conducive to the growth of poison-oak. **1881** F. Oates *Metabele Land & Victoria Falls* xi. 243 The 'poison plant', growing low, and bearing a yellow plum-like fruit, was gathered on one occasion near the waggon-track. **1927** J. Masefield *Sard Harker* III. 121 Dangling from the boughs, there were strings of withered poison-ivy... He dodged the poison-plant. **1965** Poison-plant [see **poison-bush*]. **1817** A. Eaton *Man. Bot.* 34 *Rhus... vernix*, (poison sumach) glabrous panicle few-flowered. **1820** J. C. Gilleland *Ohio & Mississippi Pilot* 261 Sumach... Most common in bottoms that are rich or at least moderately so... *R[hus] pumilum* (poison sumach). **1832** W. D. Williamson *Hist. State Maine* I. 118 The poison Sumach occurs in the western, but very seldom, if ever, in the eastern part of the State. **1901** C. T. Mohr *Plant Life Alabama* 600 Poison Sumach, Poison Elder... Alleghenian, Carolinian, and Louisianian areas. **1978** *Washington Post* 4 Aug. (Weekend Suppl.) 27/2 Poison ivy, poison sumac, and some species of baneberry have white fruits and are poisonous. **1709** J. Lawson *New Voyage to Carolina* 101 The Poison Vine is so called, because it colours the Hands of those who handle it. **1803** A. Ellicott *Jrnl.* viii. 212 My journey up the river was disagreeable and painful, being blistered by the rhus radicans (poison vine) from head to feet. **1891** M. E. Ryan *Told in Hills* II. i. 24 Here and there a poison-vine flashed back defiance under its crimson banners. **1935** *Yale Review* Sept. 174, I hear them [*sc.* horses] snortin' up the land where the pizen-vines grow around the sycamore stumps. **1856** L. J. F. Jaeger *Jrnl.* 20 Sept. in *Publ. Hist. Soc. S. Calif.* (1928) XIV. 128, 2 of the mules died at the Tinajas Altas—I think they ate some of the poison weed also.

B. *adj.* **2.** Wicked, dangerous; hateful, objectionable. *U.S. dial.*

1839 C. F. Briggs *Adventures of Harry Franco* I. 18 'I presume there's no occasion for hurrying,' said the driver. 'Yes there is though, you pisen critter,' said a passenger. **1850** 'M. Tensas' *Odd Leaves from Life of Louisiana 'Swamp Doctor'* 152 Lizey Johnson's middle darter, Prinsanna,..left her husband in the state of Georgy, and kum to Luzaanny an' got marred to a nother man, the pisen varmint, to do sich as that and her own laful husband. **1880** 'Mark Twain' *Tramp Abroad* 225 B'long to a *church*! Why boss he's ben the pizenest kind of a Free-will Babtis' for forty year. They ain't no pizener ones 'n' what *he* is.

C. *adv.* Intensely, extremely. Chiefly *U.S. dial.*

1840 C. F. Hoffman *Greyslaer* I. 61 The night was pison cold, I tell ye. **1884** 'Mark Twain' *Huck. Finn* xxvii. 275 The funeral sermon was very good, but pison long and tiresome. **1892** R. L. Stevenson Let. 31 Jan. in *Wks.* (1923) XXXIII. 23 This is a poison bad world for the romancer, this Anglo Saxon world. **1894** 'Mark Twain' *Pudd'nhead Wilson* xiv. 194 You's got to be pison good, en let him see it. **1926** in H. Wentworth *Amer. Dial. Dict.* (1944) 464/2 Pizen-neat.

poison, *v.* Add: **4. b.** *Chem.* Of a substance: to reduce or destroy the activity of (a catalyst, or occas. an electrode). Cf. *poison *sb.* 2 c.

1913 in C. Ellis *Hydrogenation Oils* (1914) 311 The use of chlorine would 'poison' the catalyst. **1921** G. G. Henderson *Catalysis in Industr. Chem.* iv. 72 Infinitesimal quantities of chlorine, bromine or iodine absolutely poison the metal, the presence of even a minute trace of bromine in phenol, for instance, preventing the latter being changed into cyclohexanol. **1937** *Jrnl. Inst. Electr. Engineers* LXXX. 198/2 An antimony electrode..lends itself particularly well to the recording of hydrogen-ion concentration, since this electrode is 'poisoned' by very few substances. **1965** H. H. Willard et al. *Instrumental Methods Chem. Analysis* (ed. 4) xxii. 588 The quinhydrone electrode is quickly prepared, develops its potential rapidly, and is not readily poisoned. **1972** *Times* 27 Sept. 20/3 Lead contaminants in fuel tend to 'poison' catalytic elements that help burn exhaust more completely in a converter mounted in the exhaust pipe. **1974** Bandtock & Hanson *Success in Chem.* xiv. 318 Vanadium (v) oxide is a reasonably efficient catalyst for the oxidation of sulphur dioxide and is not readily poisoned.

c. *Nuclear Sci.* To act as a poison in (a nuclear reactor or fuel). Also occas., to add a poison to (a reactor). Cf. *poison *sb.* 2 d.

1945 H. D. Smyth *Gen. Acct. Devel. Atomic Energy Mil. Purposes* viii. 80 Other fission products are being produced also. These consist typically of unstable and relatively unfamiliar nuclei so that it was originally impossible to predict how great an undesirable effect they would have on the multiplication constant. Such deleterious effects are called poisoning. **1948** C. Pincher *Into Atomic Age* 38 Fragments from the split uranium 235 atoms collect in the slugs and..are said to 'poison' the uranium. **1960** Wehr & Richards *Physics of Atom* xi. 328 This radioactivity is due principally to the fission products which poisoned the fuel element. **1968** F. Kertesz *Lang. Nucl. Sci.* (Oak Ridge Nat. Lab. TM 2367) 23 Nuclear jargon is filled with gloomy, funereal terms: fuel elements are transported in coffins and reactors are poisoned to control them.

poisoner. Add: **b.** A cook, esp. for large numbers. *joc.* (*Austral.* and *N.Z.*).

1905 E. C. Buley *Austral. Life in Town & Country* 23 The shearers' cook is always a competent man and supplies his clients with the best fare obtainable, utterly 'belying' the name of 'poisoner', usually bestowed upon him. **1936** A. Russell *Gone Nomad* 14, I had to take my turn..as 'slushy' to 'Doughboy' Terry, the cook—'camp poisoner', as we affectionately called him. **1969** L. Hadow *Full Cycle* 208 'I'm not much good at cooking but I'll try.' 'Never you mind about that. Up north we've got the best poisoners in the country.'

poisoning, *vbl. sb.* Add: **b. blood-poisoning:** see *blood *sb.* 19.

poisonous, *a.* Add: **2.** Also in trivial use, unpleasant, nasty.

1906 [in Dict.]. **1912** E. Pugh *Harry the Cockney* xi. 121 Foolish habit to think at any time, Weaver. But to think on an empty stomach—it's poisonous. Poisonous! **1916** 'Taffrail' *Pincher Martin* xii. 225, I thought the weather was absolutely poisonous. **1929** P. Gibbs *Hidden City* xxxix. 189 It's something to do with that poisonous little beast Benito..the boy she dances with.

poisonwood. Add: Also *attrib.* (Later examples.)

1930 R. Macaulay *Staying with Relations* ix. 127 There ..was..the nettle that one chews when one has inadvertently been spattered by the milky juice of the poisonwood tree. **1965** F. Knebel *Night of Camp David* xv. 248 A crescent moon perched above the thicket of gumbo limbo and poisonwood trees.

Poisson (pwasoṅ). *Math.* [The name of S. D. *Poisson* (1781–1840), French mathematician and physicist.] **1.** Used, chiefly *attrib.*, with reference to a discrete frequency distribution defined by $e^{-m}m^x/x!$, which gives the probability of x events occurring, m being its only parameter; it has mean m and variance m^2, and is appropriate if the events occur independently and there is no upper limit to their number, so that the distribution is the limit of the binomial distribution as the number of trials increases, the probability of success at each decreases, and the average number of successes tends to m; so *Poisson('s) approximation, distribution, form, law*, etc.; *Poisson-distributed* adj. Also passing into adj. (= *Poissonian) and used predicatively. [Described in Poisson's *Recherches sur la Probabilité des Jugements* (1837).]

1911 *Ark. för Matem., Astr. och Fysik* VII. xvii. 8, I shall generally understand with Poisson's theorem the expressions..giving the probability for obtaining in s trials with variable chances in all m white and n black balls (where $m + n = s$). **1914** *Biometrika* X. 36 (*heading*) On the Poisson law of small numbers. **1919** G. U. Yule *Theory Statistics* (ed. 5) 372 [This] may be termed Poisson's limit to the binomial. **1922** *Ann. Appl. Biol.* IX. 331 When the statistical examination of these data was commenced it was not anticipated that any clear relationship with the Poisson distribution would be obtained. *Ibid.* 334 The curves strongly suggest that the departures in these data from the Poisson samples were not..systematic. **1928** [see *normal *a.* 2 e]. **1931** L. H. C. Tippett *Meth. Statistics* ii. 34 This is known as Poisson's Limit to the Binomial, the Poisson Series, or as the Law of Small Numbers. **1939** H. Jeffreys *Theory of Probability* ii. 75 Put $x = r/n$ and let n tend to infinity; then the law tends to the Poisson form. **1948** H. E. Freeman et al. *Sampling Inspection* xvii. 185 For such small values of n the Poisson approximation is not adequate. **1950** W. Feller *Introd. Probability Theory* I. vi. 119 A radioactive substance emits α-particles, and the number of particles reaching a given portion of space during time t is the best-known example of random events obeying the Poisson law. *Ibid.* xvii. 367 In the Poisson process the probability of a change during $(t, t + h)$ is independent of the number of changes during (O, t). **1954** [see *erlang 1]. **1958** Condon & Odishaw *Handbk. Physics* I. xii. 155/2 The discrete distribution.. termed the Poisson exponential distribution, is (with the normal, and binomial distributions) one of the three principal distributions of probability theory. **1966** *McGraw-Hill Encycl. Sci. & Technol.* X. 631/2 If p is so small that the mean np is of the order of unity in any given application, Bernoulli's distribution is then approximated by Poisson's law. **1968** P. A. P. Moran *Introd. Probability Theory* iii. 162 We suppose that customers arrive at a servicing counter in a Poisson process with mean λ, i.e. the number arriving in any interval of length T has a Poisson distribution with mean λT, and the numbers arriving in different intervals are independent. **1971** J. B. Carroll et al. *Word Freq. Bk.* p. xxxvi, The remaining entries show that..9,436 [words] would be expected not to appear at all in the AHI Corpus, but that 3,826 would appear once, 776 would appear twice, 105 would appear 3 times, 10 would appear 4 times, and 1 would appear 5 times. (These numbers are predicted by the Poisson distribution.) **1976** E. J. DUDEWICZ *Introd. Statistics & Probability* iii. 56 Suppose that X is binomial with parameters n and p.. Then X is approximately Poisson with $\lambda = np$. **1979** *Nature* 15 Feb. 533/1, n_i, the number of aberrations in the i-th culture, is Poisson-distributed.

b. *ellipt.* for *Poisson distribution*.

1962 S. R. CALABRO *Reliability Princ. & Pract.* vi. 65 If the expected number of failures..is substituted in the Poisson, then it is possible to calculate the probability of 0, 1, 2, 3, etc., failures. **1975** R. M. BETHEA et al. *Statistical Methods for Scientists & Engineers* iii. 57 We can estimate the probability of getting less than two adverse reactions using the Poisson as follows.

2. Special Comb.: **Poisson bracket**, a function $[u, v]$ of two dynamical variables $u(p_1, p_2, \ldots p_n, q_1, q_2, \ldots q_n)$ and $v(p_1, p_2, \ldots p_n, q_1, q_2, \ldots q_n)$ equal to $\sum_{r=1}^{n}\left(\frac{\partial u}{\partial q_r}\frac{\partial v}{\partial p_r} - \frac{\partial u}{\partial p_r}\frac{\partial v}{\partial q_r}\right)$; **Poisson's equation** [discussed by Poisson in *Nouveau Bull. des Sci. par la Soc. philomath. de Paris* (1813) III. 390], the generalization of Laplace's equation produced by replacing the zero of the right hand side by a constant, or, more generally, by a specified function of position; **Poisson's ratio** [discussed by Poisson in *Ann. de Chim. et de Physique* (1827) XXXVI. 385], the ratio of the proportional decrease in a lateral measurement to the proportional increase in length in a sample of material that is elastically stretched.

1904 E. T. WHITTAKER *Treat. Analytical Dynamics* xi. 309 If ϕ and ψ are two integrals of the system, the Poisson-bracket (ϕ, ψ) is constant throughout the motion. **1960** DICKE & WITTKE *Introd. Quantum Mech.* v. 86 The Poisson bracket provides a powerful tool in formulating quantum theory. **1976** MATHEWS & VENKATESAN *Textbk. Quantum Mech.* 351 Canonically conjugate co-ordinate-momentum pairs are..characterized by a unit value for the Poisson bracket. [**1872** *Trans. R. Soc. Edin.* XXVI. 71 If P be the potential at ρ, and if r be the density of the attracting matter, &c., at ρ, $\nabla\sigma = \nabla^2 P = 4\pi r$ by Poisson's extension of Laplace's equation.] **1873** J. C. MAXWELL *Treat. Electr. & Magn.* I. i. ii. 80 This equation, in the case in which the density is zero, is called Laplace's Equation. In its more general form it was first given by Poisson... We may express Poisson's equation in words by saying that the electric density multiplied by 4π is the concentration of the potential. **1916** F. B. PIDDUCK *Treat. Electr.* iii. 61 This becomes..$\Delta V = -4\pi\rho$, which is known as Poisson's equation. **1971** C. R. CHESTER *Techniques in Partial Differential Equations* iii. 87 The nonhomogeneous potential equation, $\nabla^2 u = F(x, y, z)$ is called Poisson's equation. **1886** J. D. EVERETT *Units & Physical Constants* (ed. 2) v. 62 The following values of Poisson's ratio have been found. **1930** *Engineering* 11 Apr. 465/1 The modern theory of the elasticity of isotropic materials makes use of a number of physical constants, all of which are definitely related to Young's Modulus E and Poisson's ratio $\eta = 1/m$ the latter of which is sometimes known as the 'stretch–squeeze' ratio. **1966** C. R. TOTTLE *Sci. Engin. Materials* vii. 153 An orthorhombic crystal can thus be defined by nine independent constants, three elastic moduli, three moduli of rigidity, and three values of Poisson's ratio.

Poissonian (pwasōᵘ·niăn), *a.* [f. prec. + -IAN.] Of, pertaining to, or being the Poisson distribution.

1914 *Ark. för Matem., Astr. och Fysik* IX. xxv. 16 Repeating the experiment r times we obtain respectively $m_1, m_2, m_3, \ldots, m_r$ white balls in these r sets. These numbers form what is called a Poissonian series. **1951** *Jrnl. R. Statistical Soc.* B. XIII. 168 If they call for service in a random manner the input-process (while q customers are waiting or being served) will be Poissonian, but will depend on the value of q. **1972** *Science* 2 June 1034/1 The Poissonian probability times the efficiency of plating gave an actual distribution of $\leqq 0.3$ cell per well. **1976** *Physics Bull.* Mar. 111/1 If T was short compared with the inverse spectral linewidth of a random source, a geometric distribution was obtained while if T was long the photon counting distribution became Poissonian due to averaging of the photon arrivals.

Poitevin (pwa·tevin, ‖ pwatəvaṅ), *sb.* and *a.* Also 7 **Poictevin.** [Fr.] **A.** *sb.* **a.** A native or inhabitant of Poitou, an ancient province of west central France roughly corresponding to the modern *départements* of Vienne, Deux-Sèvres, and Vendée, or of its capital Poitiers, now capital of Vienne. **b.** The French dialect of Poitou or Poitiers. **B.** *adj.* Of, pertaining to, or characteristic of Poitou or Poitiers or the dialect spoken there.

1642 J. HOWELL *Instructions for Forreine Travell* x. 127 The law Norman useth to contract many words..and the Poictevin will mince the word. **1653** [see *BRETON *sb.* and *a.*]. **1866** C. M. YONGE *Prince & Page* i. 7 A Poitevin, a falconer at Kenilworth. **1880** —— *One Will & Three Ways* iii, in *Bye-words* 65 Stories..of Poitevin castles won by escalade. **1934** M. K. POPE *From Latin to Mod. French* ii. 18 This sound was not, however, diphthongised, cf. Poitevin *amar*. *Ibid.* xvii. 211 The southern border dialects (e.g. Poitevin). **1957** A. DUGGAN *Devil's Brood* vi. 68 Geoffrey had been born..in..1158... He grew up to be another fair handsome northerner, obviously more Norman than Poitevin. **1968** F. WHITE *Ways of Aquitaine* iv. 52 These delicate Poitevin carvings must be regarded primarily as adornment of the churches. **1974** P. RICKARD *Hist. French Lang.* ii. 33 Poitevin, which shows close affinity with Occitan up to and including the tenth century, can by the twelfth century be considered essentially a dialect of the *langue d'oïl*. *Ibid.* vii. 127 Non-standard constructions, too, may be used; for instance.. the Poitevin *les enfants sont après jouer* (= *en train de jouer*). **1976** *Sat. Rev.* (U.S.) 30 Oct. 25 The population [of St. Barthélemy] is 90 per cent Caucasian, descendants of Normans, Bretons, Poitevins, and the Swedes owners of St. Barts for a century.

poitrel. (Further examples.)

1805 C. JAMES *Mil. Dict.* (ed. 2) *Poitrel*, armour for the breast of a horse. It is generally written *poitrail*. **1824** S. R. MEYRICK *Critical Inquiry into Antient Armour* III. Gloss. s.v. Pectorale, The poitrail, a steel plate for the protection of a horse's chest. **1830** J. SKELTON *Engraved Illustrations Antient Arms & Armour* Pl. LIV (fig. 2), The fleur-de-lis is seen on the horse furniture, twice on the croupière-base, and as an armorial bearing on that of the poitral. **1918** E. S. FARROW *Dict. Mil. Terms* 459 *Poitrail*, that portion of the horse armor which covers the breast, fitted either with hinges or like a flounce. **1920** G. F. LAKING *Rec. European Armour & Arms* III. xxii. 178 For the head there was..the chanfron, for the neck the crinet, for the chest the poitrel.

poitrinaire. (Earlier and later examples.)

1856 *Sat. Rev.* 25 Oct. 578/2 As a *poitrinaire*, he was the most devoted, extravagant, sentimental of lovers and husbands. **1969** *Sunday Tel.* 12 Jan. 15/8 Although she cannot help suggesting a *poitrinaire* in the most comfortable health, deft make-up and still more a skilful modification of the voice suggested the growing physical weariness.

poitrinal (poi·trinăl). Now *Hist.* or *arch.* [ad. Fr. *poitrinal*: see PETRONEL.] **1.** = POITREL.

1786 [see *PECTORAL *sb.* 1 c]. **1869** J. R. PLANCHÉ *Catal. Meyrick Coll. exhibited at S. Kensington Museum* p. x, The barding of the horse is also very fine, consisting of chamfron, crevette, and poitrinal, all fluted and in fine condition. **1918** E. S. FARROW *Dict. Mil. Terms* 459 *Poitrinal*, in ancient armor, the horse's breastplate, formed of metal plates, riveted together, as a covering for the breast and shoulders.

2. = PETRONEL.

1824 [see PETRONEL]. **1829** *Archæologia* XXII. 86 The President Fauchet..introduces to our notice a piece called a Petronel or Poitrinal, because it was rested on the poitrine or chest..and thence fired.

‖ **pokal** (pokā·l). [G., ad. L. *poculum*, a drinking-cup.] A large German glass tankard, often with a lid. Also *transf.*

1868 C. G. LELAND *Hans Breitmann's Party* 11 How stately rode der Breitmann oop!—how lordly he kit down? How glorious from de great *pokal* he drink de bier so prown! **1869** G. A. SALA in *More Yankee Drolleries* 25 'Pokal', drinking-cup: in this case the large glass pint beer-mug used in America. **1950** *Chambers's Encycl.* VI. 421/1 The great tankards and pokals were intended for display; their size was so great that they were too heavy to drink from. **1969** *Canadian Antiques Collector* Oct. 5/1 Two ceremonial cups or pokals, late 17th century, silver gilt. **1974** *Encycl. Brit. Micropædia* VI. 891/2 *(caption)* Milk glass pokal, German, 17th century.

pok-a-tok: var. *POK-TA-POK.

poke, *sb.*[1] Add: **1. a.** (Further examples.)

1910 R. SERVICE *Trail of '98* 347 The girl will pry him loose from his poke. **1922** G. PRINGLE *Tillicums of Trail* 250 It wasn't safe to come out by way of Skagway with your gold,..you were likely to be relieved of your 'poke' by desperados. **1935** A. J. CRONIN *Stars look Down* I. ix. 68 He had pie, too, in his poke. **1948** C. W. HOLLIDAY *Valley of Youth* 144 A miner might come into a store for provisions with no money, but a little poke of gold dust. **1966** *Indians, Eskimos, & Aleuts of Alaska* (U.S. Bureau of Indian Affairs) 12 *(caption)* These villagers are carrying a sealskin 'poke' filled with seal oil. **1976** *Islander* (Victoria, B.C.) 15 Aug. 12/2 Nearby lay an empty buckskin 'poke' such as early miners favored for their gold dust. **1978** *Guardian* 14 Aug. 7/2 You may also find yourself at a temporary disadvantage if, after buying several items from a shop, the young lady assistant asks if you would 'like a poke'.

d. A purse or wallet; a pocketbook. *N. Amer. slang.*

1859 G. W. MATSELL *Vocabulum* 68 *Poke*, a pocket; a purse. **1883** *Echo* 25 Jan. 2/3 The poke, which a pick-pocket glories in having appropriated, is the Saxon bag or purse. **1908** J. M. SULLIVAN *Criminal Slang* 18 *Poke of leather*, a pocketbook. **1931** 'D. STIFF' *Milk & Honey Route* 211 *Poke*, a leather wallet. **1939** J. O'HARA *Pal Joey* 50 There I was with only about $85 in my poke. **1953** 'W. BURROUGHS' *Junkie* iv. 48 He took a crumpled mass of bills from his pocket and counted out eight dollars... 'Had it in his pants pocket. I couldn't find a poke.' **1976** 'TREVANIAN' *Main* (1977) vi. 123, I notice his wallet's half out of his pocket...it comes to me that I might as well lift his poke... So I reach over and pull it out.

e. A roll of bank-notes; money. *slang.*

1926 J. BLACK *You can't Win* xiv. 190 My hand was on the big fat 'poke'. **1933** E. SEAGO *Circus Company* 295 *Poke*, money. **1965** L. J. CUNLIFFE *Having it Away* iv. 38 It's a very satisfying feeling knowing you can put your finger on a bit of poke. (Which is more slang for money: get it, poke, loot, poppy—any of them will do!) **1974** *Evening News* (Edinburgh) 8 Oct. 3/2 Colgan asked him: 'Have you got your poke?' obviously referring to the money.

poke, *sb.*[3] Add: **1.** Delete *obs.* from '*obs. slang*, A blow with the fist' and add 'esp. in phr. *to take a poke at*'. (Later examples.) Also colloq. phr. *better than a poke in the eye* (and variants), used of something minimally desirable. Also *fig.*

1852 GEO. ELIOT *Let.* 4 Dec. (1954) II. 71 'Then,' he said..'Here are those "Letters from Ireland" which I hope will be something better than a *poke in the eye*.' **1936** J. STEINBECK *In Dubious Battle* viii. 120 'They got those cops here quick,' said Burke. 'I'd like to take a poke at a few of 'em.' **1941** BAKER *Dict. Austral. Slang* 55 *Poke*, to hit a person. Also, 'a poke': a blow with the fist. **1944** J. CARY *Horse's Mouth* xvi. 81 Anarchists who love God always fall for Spinoza because he tells them that God doesn't love them. This is just what they need. A poke in the eye. To a real anarchist, a poke in the eye is better than a bunch of flowers. It makes him see stars. **1956** B. HOLIDAY *Lady sings Blues* (1973) ii. 24 She tried to get at me. I took a poke at her, and down the stairs she went. **1969** *Listener* 10 Apr. 478/1 What sort of salute, I wondered, amounted to a poke in the eye? On this occasion compromise *was* reached: it was agreed that the occasion should be marked by a second broadcast of my *Salute to Stalingrad*. **1974** *Bulletin* (Sydney) 6 July 44 An Australian way of expressing ecstasy is to say: 'It's better than a poke in the eye with a burnt stick.' **1976** *N.Y. Times Mag.* 10 Oct. 111/4 Better than a poke in the eye with a sharp stick.

b. poke-out, (*b*) *slang*, a bag of food handed to a beggar; a lunch; (*c*) *slang* (see quot. 1960).

1894 'J. FLYNT' in *Century Mag.* Mar. 713/2 He returned with a 'poke-out' (food given at the door). **1907** J. LONDON *Road* 12, I could 'throw my feet' with the next one when it came to 'slamming a gate' for a 'poke-out' or a 'set-down'. **1918** H. A. VACHELL *Some Happenings* i. 4 [He] finished what was left of a 'poke out' (cold food) handed to him by a good Samaritan. **1936** *New Republic* 15 July 289/1 Sympathetic women will often cook a meal for tramps,..and 'lumps' or 'poke-outs' are possible at any time during the day. **1960** WENTWORTH & FLEXNER *Dict. Amer. Slang* 399/2 *Poke-out*,..2 An outdoor dinner cooked over wood or charcoal; a gathering for the purpose of preparing and eating such a meal; any long hike or camping trip which includes such meals. **1964** J. L. KORNBLUH *Rebel Voices* 407/2 *Pokeout*, handout.

c. *Cricket.* A batting-stroke made by jabbing at the ball.

1853 F. GALE *Public School Matches* 54 Sticker gets his runs by quiet little pokes one at a time. **1896** W. J. FORD in *Badminton Mag.* Sept. 278 Besides.. 'the draw', there was another weapon forged for the armoury of him for whom leg-hitting was not—viz. the 'Cambridge Poke', so called, I believe, in contemptuous irony. **1960** J. FINGLETON *Four Chukkas to Australia* xvi. 133 He was confusing the cut with the 'poke', a disastrous nibbling by so many Englishmen.

d. An act of sexual intercourse; also, a woman with whom one has sexual intercourse, a 'lay'; = *FUCK *sb.* 1. *slang.*

1902 FARMER & HENLEY *Slang* V. 242 *Poke*,..an act of coition. **1958** N. LEVINE *Canada made Me* ii. 82 When I met her I only want a poke. Then she tell me a baby made. **1968** H. C. RAE *Few Small Bones* II. i. 77 'Caroline', said Derek..'wouldn't make a good poke for a blind hunchback.' **1970** L. MEYNELL *Curious Crime* xii. 160 Landladies can nearly always be paid in kind. Services in lieu of rent. A poke a night. **1977** *Listener* 11 Aug. 184/4 Turning a series of squalid pokes into a series of honourable combats.

e. *fig.* Power, horsepower. *slang.*

1965 R. T. BICKERS *Hellions* vi. 69 With all that extra poke under the bonnet. **1977** *Drive* Mar.–Apr. 54/2 The Scirocco gives a worst figure of 28 mpg, using all the poke its free-revving engine will deliver. **1979** *Sunday Mail Mag.* (Brisbane) 1 July 3/5, I expect you'd prefer something with a bit more poke. A Ferrari say, or an Aston Martin.

2. (Earlier and later examples.)

1809 E. A. KENDALL *Travels through Northern Parts of U.S.* II. 198 A hog..by some mischance had turned his poke, so that his throat was squeezed into one of the acuter angles. **1949** R. J. SIM *Pages from Past* 105 Such a rig is known as a 'poke'. It is put on the neck of a critter with fence-jumping inclinations. **1956** W. R. BIRD *Off-Trail in Nova Scotia* viii. 220 And here were some sheep, too, with pokes. **1969** K. M. WELLS *Owl Pen Reader* I. 67 A poke is supposed..to make it impossible for any living thing to get through even an ordinary wire fence.

b. *transf.* A collar. *slang.*

1908 'O. HENRY' *Man Higher Up* in *Gentle Grafter* 147 With only feetwear and a dozen 15½ English pokes in his shopping bag. **1924** *Truth* (Sydney) 27 Apr. 6 *Poke*, a collar.

4. *attrib.* and *Comb.*, as **poke-check** *Ice hockey*, a defensive play made by poking the puck off an opposing player's stick; hence as *v. intr.*; **poke-checking** *vbl. sb.*

1945 R. FONTAINE *Happy Time* 45 Frank Nighbor, Canada's immortal poke-check genius. **1964** *Maclean's Mag.* 2 May 46/1 To me some of the most fascinating moves in hockey..are poke-checks, or well timed interceptions, or expeditions of forechecking. **1966** *Hockey News* (Montreal) 1 Jan. 13/2 He poke-checks and sweep-checks like the oldtimers. **1963** A. O'BRIEN *Headline Hockey* 60 At that point the defenceman will likely resort to poke-checking.

poke, *sb.*[4] Add: **2. a.** For *P. decandra* substitute *P. americana*. (Later examples.)

1945 *Chicago Tribune* 13 May VII. 1/3 Opal had found the first tightly curled leaves of poke, the best known of all Ozark greens. **1977** LEWIS & ELVIN-LEWIS *Med. Bot.* iv. 90/1 Poke..has long been a favorite spring potherb in the southern United States.

3. poke-berry, substitute for def.: the dark

purple berry of *Phytolacca americana*, or the plant itself; also *attrib.*; (earlier and later examples); **poke-greens**, the young leaves of poke-weed used as a vegetable; **poke-salad, -salat, -sallet**, the young leaves of poke-weed used as a salad; **poke-weed** (earlier and later examples).

1774 P. V. FITHIAN *Jrnl.* 15 Oct. (1900) 269 To Day Harry boil'd up a Compound of Poke-Berries, Vinegar, Sugar &c to make a red Ink or Liquid. **1834** W. A. CARRUTHERS *Kentuckian in N.Y.* II. 215 His face looks like it was boiled in poke-berry juice and indigo. **1911** G. S. PORTER *Harvester* xiii. 252 Pokeberry!.. Roots bring five cents a pound. Good blood purifier. *Ibid.* xv. 334 A few pokeberry plants for the colour. **1974** A. DILLARD *Pilgrim at Tinker Creek* xiv. 249 A skin-colored sandstone ledge beside me was stained with pokeberry juice. **1848** *Knickerbocker* XXXI. 222 The southern negro will dance after eating his poke-greens and bacon. **1938** M. K. RAWLINGS *Yearling* i. 12 There were poke-greens with bits of white bacon buried in them. **1881** J. C. HARRIS *Uncle Remus* 197, I got mustard, en poke salid, en lam's quarter in dat baskit. **1892** Poke salad [see *CALLALOO]. **1913** H. KEPHART *Our Southern Highlanders* xiii. 282 This poke salat eats good. **1947** *Sun* (Baltimore) 20 May 18/3, I was introduced to poke, as poke-salat, by a Southern Maryland family. **1751** *Gentl. Mag.* July 306/2 Tho' the Phytolacca be known to almost every one in America, by the name of pokeweed,.. yet I think it proper..to give a description of it. **1886** M. ARNOLD *Let.* 29 July (1895) II. 341 The pokeweed (*Phytolacca*) is, I think, American too. **1945** *New England Homestead* 13 Oct. 6/4 Pokeweed, huckle and blueberries, wild roses, bittersweet and hazelnut bushes are also appreciated. **1976** *National Observer* (U.S.) 3 July 15/2 A beautiful black woman..supplied some delectable recipes (several ways to serve pokeweed, for instance).

poke, *v.*[1] Add: **1. e.** *Cricket.* To hit (the ball) with a jabbing stroke.

1836 *New Sporting Mag.* Oct. 360 He was very successful in poking leg stump balls for one run. **1862** J. PYCROFT *Cricket Tutor* 45 See, he is longing to poke the ball to the on-side. **1872** *Baily's Mag.* Aug. 166 The Eton men hit with freedom..the same bowling that the day before.. they only poked or played with tameness and hesitation.

f. To have sexual intercourse with (a woman). *slang.*

1868 *Index Expurgatorius of Martial* 27 Saufeia,.. though she was willing to be poked, would not enter the bath with the poet for decency's sake. *c* **1888–94** [see *GET *v.* 38 h]. **1962** J. BRAINE *Life at Top* ix. 129, I wanted to poke Lucy so I poked her. **1967** L. MEYNELL *Mauve Front Door* ii. 24 Your uncle was..as randy as a goat... He poked them everywhere. **1971** R. FALKIRK *Chill Factor* xiv. 149 Are you out of your mind poking an Icelandic girl while you're on this sort of mission? **1975** N. LUARD *Robespierre Serial* xvi. 144 They're far from sure she's the one this GI poked.

g. To hit, strike (someone). *colloq.*

1906 *Dialect Notes* III. 122, I *poked* him on the nose. **1959** S. J. BAKER *Drum* 136 *Poke*, v., to hit a person with the fist.

h. *Baseball.* To hit.

1908 *Atlantic Monthly* Aug. 229/1 Sharky poked a bingle. **1951** in Wentworth & Flexner *Dict. Amer. Slang* (1960) 399/2 Jackie Robinson poked a pitch out of the park.

4. b. *Cricket.* To make pokes at the ball (see *POKE *sb.*[3] 1 c). Also const. *about.*

1851 J. PYCROFT *Cricket Field* vii. 114 Mere stopping balls and poking about in the blockhole is not cricket. **1899** E. V. LUCAS *Open Road* 146 (The Cricket Ball Sings) Perish the muff and the little tin Shrewsbury, Meanly contented to potter and poke. **1906** A. E. KNIGHT *Compl. Cricketer* viii. 268 His drive is a clean honest lift straight from the shoulders; he never pokes, 'puddling about his crease'. **1927** M. A. NOBLE *Those 'Ashes'* 193 His usual aggression was missing and he poked about, mistiming and apparently being unable to make a clean stroke.

c. Of a man: to have sexual intercourse with a woman. *slang.*

1973 *Nation Rev.* (Melbourne) 24–30 Aug. 1417/2 Working class morality where the male never 'pokes' after marriage but lusts away in obscenity and dirty jokes.

poker, *sb.*[1] Add: **6. b.** = *FUCKER. *slang.*

1879–80 *Pearl* (1970) 214 I've been told by jokers That the ladies they do all agree that he's the prince of pokers.

c. *Cricket.* A batsman who 'pokes' (*POKE *v.*[1] 4 b).

1888 A. G. STEEL in Steel & Lyttelton *Cricket* iii. 143 But to the poker, the man who refuses to do anything but stick his bat in front of the wicket..the high-dropping full-pitch is an excellent ball.

7*. = POKE *sb.*[3] 2. *rare.*

1805 T. B. HAZARD *Nailer Tom's Diary* (1930) 260/2 Put Poker on one of my oxen.

8. *poker-stiff, -straight* adjs.; **poker back,** (*a*) a perfectly straight back; (*b*) *Path.* (see quot. 1973); **poker spine** *Path.* = *poker back* (*b*) above.

1931 M. ALLINGHAM *Look to Lady* xxvi. 276 A single slim aristocratic figure, with the unmistakable poker back of the old regime. **1960** H. EDWARDS *Spirit Healing* x. 87 The healing of certain troubles, as with poker-back spines. **1973** TAYLOR & COTTON *Short Textbk. Surg.* (ed. 2) xl. 539 [In ankylosing spondylitis] the normal spine curvatures become replaced by a single kyphosis, occasionally so acutely angled that the patient's back becomes horizontal (poker back). **1917** *Brit. Med. Jrnl.* 30 June 860/1 Dr. John Drummond (Liverpool) asks for suggestions as to treatment in a case of poker spine in a man 30 years of age... The back is now immobile. **1960** S. PLATH *Colossus* (1967) 27 Rigged poker-stiff on her back. **1962** 'K. ORVIS' *Damned & Destroyed* xi. 77 Frankie's back was poker-stiff. **1966** J. S. COX *Illustr. Dict. Hairdressing* 119/1 *Poker straight*, without a vestige of curl. **1979** N. FREELING *Widow* ii. 3 The hair was poker-straight.

poker, *sb.*[4] Add: (Earlier examples.) Also *fig.*

1836 J. HILDRETH *Campaigns Rocky Mts.* I. xv. 128 The M— lost some cool hundreds last night at poker. **1842** *Knickerbocker* XX. 305 Squeezing a great deal of boisterous amusement out of a game of 'poker'. **1978** *Time* 3 July 42/3 The Justice Department was in no mood to be bluffed, even by troubled steelmakers, and talks dragged on and on in a months-long game of high-stakes political poker.

b. *poker-deck, -game* (examples), *hand, player* (examples), *table*; **poker chip**, a chip [CHIP *sb.*[1] 2 d] used as a stake in poker; **poker dice**, (*a*) dice with the representation of a playing card on at least two of their faces; (*b*) a dice game, played with either poker or regular dice, in which the thrower aims for combinations which would constitute a winning hand in poker; **poker face**, an inscrutable face appropriate to a poker-player; a face in which a person's thoughts or feelings are not revealed; also, a person with such a face; hence as *v. trans.* (*rare*—[1]) to regard with a poker-face; **poker-faced** *a.* (cf. *PO-FACED *a.*); **poker machine** *Austral.*, a type of 'one-armed bandit' bearing card symbols; **poker patience**, a form of competitive patience the object of which is to form winning poker combinations in each row and column; **poker school**, a group of people meeting to play poker.

1879 *News & Press* (Cimarron, New Mexico) 20 Nov. 4/3 The toughest thing we have heard about any candidate in this section is that he got his poker chips cashed after he 'experienced religion'. **1929** WODEHOUSE *Mr. Mulliner Speaking* iv. 122 At the end of five minutes, Osbert was mildly surprised to find himself in possession of a smoking-cap, three boxes of poker-chips, some polo sticks, [etc.]. **1973** E. PACE *Any War* (1974) III. 189 He heard..no laughter, no rattle of poker chips. **1844** J. COWELL *Thirty Years among Players* 94 He was, apparently, quietly shuffling and cutting the poker-deck for his own amusement. **1874** Poker dice [see *DIE *sb.*[1] 1 a]. **1901** *Game of Poker Dice* 1 The only Implements required are Sets of The Poker Dice and Cups, according to the number of players. **1926** E. HEMINGWAY *Sun also Rises* I. vi. 43 Harvey had won two hundred francs from me shaking poker dice. **1975** D. BLOODWORTH *Clients of Omega* x. 87 Poker dice, of course, man..*Strip* poker. **1885** *Encycl. Brit.* XIX. 283/2 A good *poker face* is essential; the countenance should not betray the nature of the hand. **1919** G. A. MILLER *Prowling about Panama* xiii. 198 (*caption*) San Blas Indians have 'poker faces'. **1926** H. C. WITWER *Roughly Speaking* 243 His teeth clicked and he gave me a long, thoughtful look, but I poker-faced him and went on plugging my [switch-]board. **1934** E. O'NEILL *Days without End* I. 20 His features automatically assume the meaninglessly affable expression which is the American business man's welcoming poker face. **1950** G. B. SHAW *Buoyant Billions* III. 28 Sunday clothes and poker faces. No peace, no joy. **1974** 'J. MELVILLE' *Nun's Castle* i. 21, I..kept a poker-face. Inside, however, I was deeply distressed. **1976** P. DICKINSON *King & Joker* vii. 104, I hardly need say it to you, because you're such an old poker-face anyway, but..you have to..behave as though you are the only person who knows. **1923** *Nation* (N.Y.) 18 July 61 The picture of that poker-faced gentleman placidly smoking a Pittsburg stogie. **1949** *Time* 12 Sept. 20/1 The poker-faced fellow was putting up a terrific fight. **1973** D. WESTHEIMER *Going Public* ix. 134 'We'd send them a letter, see,' said Margo poker-faced. 'Telling them how to commit suicide.' **1932** T. S. ELIOT *Sweeney Agonistes* 18 What about that poker game? eh what Sam? What about that poker game in Bordeaux? **1957** *Times Lit. Suppl.* 13 Dec. 753/2 Ward politics, big poker-games, prostitution and murder. **1977** H. FAST *Immigrants* II. 97 He remembered such faces from poker games. **1935** *Encycl. Sports* 467/1 The object of the game [*sc.* poker patience] is so to place the cards as they are played that finally each row and each column will form a poker hand. **1963** G. F. HERVEY *Handbk. Card Games* 231 There are nine possible poker hands at which to aim. **1974** *Encycl. Brit. Macropædia* XIV. 623/1 A Poker hand consists of five cards. **1964** A. WYKES *Gambling* 330 Gamblers also managed to spend about $1,500,000 on 'poker machines' (a kind of slot machine that bears card symbols). **1973** *Sunday Mail* (Brisbane) 29 July 5/3 Canberra soon may be the first city in Australia to have poker machines in its hotels. **1976** *Daily Mirror* (Sydney) 14 Oct., Young poker-machine players should be given a warning about how much they could lose. **1912** 'SAKI' *Stampeding of Lady Bastable* in *Chronicles of Clovis* 55 He particularly wanted to teach the MacGregor boys.. poker-patience. **1932** R. FRASER *Marriage in Heaven* III. ii. 292 The whole party joined in a game of poker-patience. **1972** A. CHRISTIE *Elephants can Remember* v. 78 They played picquet, and poker patience with each other. **1844** J. COWELL *Thirty Years passed among Players in England & Amer.* 94 The cabin was entirely cleared.. with the exception of one of the poker players. **1912** M. NICHOLSON *Hoosier Chron.* 137 He had the reputation of being a poor poker player, but 'a good loser'. **1963** G. F. HERVEY *Handbk. Card Games* 237 Experienced poker players often say that what counts is not so much what they win as what the other players lose. **1949** J. R. COLE *It was so Late* 91 Men from the camp..make up a poker school. **1968** E. MCGIRR *Lead-Lined Coffin* iii. 129 Pope joined one of the large poker schools. **1977** A. C. H. SMITH *Jericho Gun* xi. 139 'Sorry to bust up the poker school.'..'I don't mind... I was two pounds ahead.' *a* **1861** T. WINTHROP *John Brent* (1862) 295 He sot his white head down to the poker-table, and stuck thar. **1930** J. DOS PASSOS *42nd Parallel* VII. 94 Pokertables piled with new silver dollars. **1977** *Times* 29 Aug. 6/2 Batesy was an old hand at marshalling her clients, bringing together seven to make up a full poker table.

poker, *v.* Add: **3.** *trans.* Of a verger, etc: to escort (a church dignitary) ceremoniously. Cf. POKER *sb.*[1] 3 b.

1924 C. LANG *Let.* in R. C. D. Jasper *G. Bell, Bishop of Chichester* (1967) iii. 36, I shall feel more free to laugh when I see you clothed in apron and gaiters and being pokered at Canterbury. **1975** *Theology* LXXV. 260 Hamling was also verger, and did all the old establishment things like pokering the preacher to the pulpit, and generally gave the services tone.

pokerish, *a.*[2] (Earlier examples.)

1827 *Massachusetts Spy* 21 Nov. (Th.), A patriarchal ram, who would fight anything but a pokerish looking ducking gun. **1833** H. BARNARD in *Maryland Hist. Mag.* (1918) XIII. 352, I feel quite pokerish in this region.

poker-work. Add: (Further examples.) Also *fig.* Hence **poker-worked** *a.* (in example applied to a design resembling poker-work).

1914 [see *GEORGIANISM]. **1929** E. BOWEN *Last September* ix. 104 Cushions..with poker-worked kittens. **1942** C. BARRETT *On Wallaby* x. 193 He..does poker-work with red-hot wire, finishing off with tiny colour sketches. **1958** L. DURRELL *Balthazar* v. 104 He has had an immense and vivid firescreen made for the flat..in poker-work. **1966** *Listener* 29 Dec. 959/2 The play relapses into what it looked as if it was going to satirize. By the end we are left with a stuffy, inhibiting piece of Victorian poker-work as a message. **1973** *Times* 31 July 14/8 She remembered well the famous Breton school of artists at Pont-Aven which included Gauguin. He made her a pair of 'sabots' in poker work. **1977** *Listener* 11 Aug. 171/3 An element of family creativity here, not too dissimilar to the Victorian samplers and poker-work.

pokey[1] (pōu·ki). *slang* (chiefly *U.S.*). Also **poky.** [Alteration of *POGEY, prob. infl. by POKY *a.*[1]] Prison, gaol.

1919 C. H. DARLING *Jargon Book* 26 *Pokey*, a jail. **1929** D. RUNYON in *Hearst's International* Aug. 73/2 He hears riding rum is illegal and may land a guy in the pokey. **1947** *Daily Progress* (Charlottesville, Virginia) 24 June 6/2 They gave the police a list of the phone numbers to call if it became necessary to turn any of the old grads in the direction of the pokey. **1955** 'S. RANSOME' *Deadly Bedfellows* viii. 70 Instead of thanking him, you've threatened to throw us both into the pokey. **1957** M. MILLAR *Soft Talkers* 151 This isn't the Royal York Hotel, but it's better than a cell in the local pokey. **1965** 'D. SHANNON' *Death-Bringers* (1966) iv. 50, I find that our star sleuth..has..carted him off to the pokey. **1974** *Maclean's* (Toronto) Dec. 30/2 A number of revered figures sat out the Depression in the poky, because they fiddled with other people's money. **1976** *National Observer* (U.S.) 29 May 18/4 Were it possible to prosecute an actor for stealing scenes, *The Missouri Breaks* (United Artists) would land Marlon Brando in the pokey for life.

pokey[2]**, pokie.** *Austral.* [Familiar corruption of POKER *sb.*[4]] = *poker machine* s.v. *POKER *sb.*[4] b.

1967 D. HORNE *Southern Exposure* 44 In the clubs of Sydney the poker machines ('the pokies') stand up in dozens and more beer flows than in a hotel. **1968** *TV Times* (Brisbane) 27 Nov. 6/2 In his unmarried days Henderson was surefire meat for bandits (the one-armed type). 'Never play the pokies now,' he says. **1969** *Telegraph* (Brisbane) 4 Jan. 6/2 He bought a beer and walked over to the nearest 'pokey' with the change from a £5 ($10) note. He put this through the machine and tripled his money. **1969** *Australian* 24 May 40/3 He painted a glowing picture of Melbournites banking their money or investing it in homes while the degenerate New South Welshmen frittered away their cash on the pokeys. **1976** *Sydney Morning Herald* 23 Sept. (Advt.), Entertainment... There are pokies, casino, disco, movies.

poking, *vbl. sb.* Add: **1. b.** Sexual intercourse. *slang.*

1968 J. SANGSTER *Foreign Exchange* i. 16 'There's no law against poking,' I said. 'There is when you poke a fifteen-year-old,' he said. **1978** J. I. M. STEWART *Full Term* xvi. 181 He was petting her future mother in the heather long before she was born. And later..another young hopeful went from petting to poking. **1979** L. MEYNELL *Hooky & Villainous Chauffeur* xiv. 187 Loverboy is going to be busy (pounds before poking any day).

poking, *ppl. a.* Add: **2. b.** *Cricket.* With a batting style characterized by 'pokes' (*POKE *sb.*[3] 1 c).

1836 *New Sporting Mag.* Oct. 360 A remarkably bad poking back player, with no hit in him at all. **1898** J. A. GIBBS *Cotswold Village* xi. 241 If only something could be done to..rid us of that awful nuisance the poking, time-wasting batsman, there would be little improvement possible.

‖**pok-ta-pok** (pǫ·kˌtaˌpǫ·k). Also **pok-a-tok.** [Maya.] The Maya name of the sacred ball game of Middle America, called *TLACHTLI by the Aztecs, which was played on a court as a religious ritual. The object of the game was to knock a rubber ball through a stone ring, using only the hips, knees, and elbows.

1959 *Times* 27 Apr. (Rubber Industry Suppl.) p. v/1

The Mayan game of Pok ta Pok. *Ibid.* 8 June (Latin America Suppl.) p. iv/5 It is recorded that the early Spaniards found the Indians of Guatemala playing a curious game with a ball called *pok-ta-pok*, but in which the players used not their feet, head, or hands, but their posteriors. **1962** V. W. VON HAGEN *Ancient Sun Kingdoms of Americas* ix. 161 The passion of the Maya, and one that they shared with most Central American Indians, was the game of *pok-a-tok*, it was not unlike the modern basket-ball. **1963** C. GALLENKAMP *Maya* ii. 32 Every city had a ball court consisting of a playing-field enclosed by viewing platforms where spectators could watch a game called *tlaxtli* or *pok-ta-pok*. **1973** *Times* 27 Oct. 14/4 Maya life is illustrated by dozens of pottery figurines showing the killing of a deer, musicians, animals and the helmeted men of Lubaantun who are thought to be participants in the sacred ball-game *pok-ta-pok*.

poky, *a.*[1] Add: Also **pokey**. **1. a.** (Earlier examples.)

1853 LADY LYTTELTON *Let.* 20 Aug. in *Corr. Sarah Spencer* (1912) xvi. 423 All *I* want is to love *more*, and to smile *more*, and to be *more* amused and *more* merry, and less poky and morose and dry and grave! **1854** E. TWISLETON *Let.* 29 June (1928) xi. 213 A dreadfully stiff and pokey set of people.

b. (Further examples.)

1930 J. B. PRIESTLEY *Angel Pavement* v. 209 All this for less than it would cost to live in some dingy and dismal boarding-house or the pokiest of pokey flats. **1971** *Daily Tel.* 28 Sept. 2/5 A pokey, little, highly rented flat.

2. (Earlier example.)

1888 A. G. STEEL in Steel & Lyttelton *Cricket* iii. 142 To the pokey, nervous style of batsman it [*sc.* the high-dropping full-pitch] is fraught with considerable uneasiness.

pol (pǫl). *N. Amer.* colloq. abbrev. of POLITICIAN.

1942 BERREY & VAN DEN BARK *Amer. Thes. Slang* § 854/1 *Politician*,..pol, polly, poly. **1965** F. KNEBEL *Night of Camp David* ii. 54 The clutter of pols and stale whisky glasses in the hotel suites. **1966** *Economist* 18 June 1315/2 Gossip has it that the 'pols', as the state's professional politicians (particularly Democrats) are called, felt guilty about the shabby treatment delivered to Mr Peabody when he was Governor [of Massachusetts]. **1972** *Time* 17 July 15/3 The young pols beat them at their own game. **1976** *Toronto Star* 14 Feb. B1/2 Can a bunch of battle-scarred old pols—including a couple of Liberal party retreads—gang up to stop a brash young lawyer named Brian Mulroney? **1978** J. CARROLL *Mortal Friends* II. ii. 139 What had he become? A two-bit pol, flashing about other people's corridors, waiting for his break?

POL: see *P II.

Polab (pōu·lāb). Also **Polabe**. [Slav., cf. Pol. *po* on, *Labe* Elbe.] **a.** A member of a Slavonic people once inhabiting the region around the lower Elbe. **b.** The West Slavonic language of this people, now extinct. Also *attrib.*

1882 *Encycl. Brit.* XIV. 347/2 The earlier inhabitants of Lauenburg were a Slavic tribe known by the name of Polabes. **1895** *Funk's Stand. Dict.*, *Polabian*,..one of an ancient Slavic people dwelling on the lower Elbe, now wholly Germanized... *Polab.* **1911** *Encycl. Brit.* XXI. 902/1 *Polabs*,..the Slavs..who dwelt upon the Elbe and eastwards to the Oder. **1911** [see *LECH, LEKH *sb.*[5] and *a.*]. **1934** [see *LECHITIC *sb.* and *a.*]. **1974** *Encycl. Brit. Micropædia* VIII. 72/3 By the early 9th century the Polabs were organized into two confederations or principalities.

Polabian (polē̆i·biǎn), *sb.* and *a.* [f. as prec. + -IAN.] **A.** *sb.* = prec. **B.** *adj.* Of or pertaining to the Polabs or their language.

1866 *Chambers's Encycl.* VIII. 767/1 The Polabians never attained any distinct political footing. **1888** [see *LECHISH *sb.* and *a.*]. **1891** M. MÜLLER *Sci. Lang.* I. vii. 270 The Polabian dialect became gradually extinct at the beginning of the last century. **1911** *Encycl. Brit.* XXI. 902/1 Polabian agrees mostly with Polish and Kašube with its nasalized vowels and highly palatalized consonants. **1925** P. RADIN tr. *Vendryès's Language* 287 Polabian has been absorbed into German, as Cornish into English. **1929** [see *LECH, LEKH *sb.*[5] and *a.*]. **1934** O. JESPERSEN *Language* vi. 117 The now extinct Polabian language. **1939–40, 1950** [see *LECHITIC *sb.* and *a.*]. **1955** R. JAKOBSON *Slavic Lang.* (ed. 2) 2 The last remnant of Polabian on the left bank of the lower Elbe..died out toward the middle of the eighteenth century, but is known through a few vocabulary lists and short texts recorded about 1700. **1972** W. B. LOCKWOOD *Panorama Indo-European Lang.* 157 A diminutive islet of Elbe Slavonic or Polabian (*po* 'on', *Laba* 'Elbe') lingered on into the first decades of the eighteenth century. It was situated just west of the Elbe in the Lüneburg Wendland north of Salzwedel.

Polabish (polā·biʃ), *sb.* Also **Polabisch**. [ad. G. *polabisch*.] = *POLAB b.

1877 A. H. KEANE tr. *Hovelacque's Sci. of Lang.* 280 We may conclude this notice by mentioning the old dialects of the Elbe Slavonians, known by the name of *Polabish*, idioms now extinct, and whose scanty records, greatly affected by German influence, date from the seventeenth and beginning of the eighteenth century. **1890** W. R. MORFILL *Ess. on Importance of Study of Slavonic Lang.* 15 The extinct Polabish, a language once spoken on the Elbe.., was restored from some fragments by Schleicher. **1908** T. G. TUCKER *Introd. Nat. Hist. Lang.* 226 *Polabish*, once spoken by Slavs on the lower Elbe, is now extinct. **1955** *Trans. Philol. Soc. 1954* 87 Cornish and polabisch exist in a modern period but, for the present purpose, they naturally cannot rank as 'modern' since they are no longer spoken.

polacca[1]. Add: (Earlier and later examples.) Also applied more widely to other music of a (supposed) Polish character. Also *attrib.* and in phr. *alla polacca*.

1806 T. BUSBY *Dict. Mus.* (ed. 2) *Polacca*, a Polish movement of three crochets in a bar, chiefly characterised by its emphasis being laid on the fifth quaver of the bar. *c* **1807** W. CROTCH *Specimens Various Styles Music* I. 10 Some modern composers have given the title Polacca to movements which would sound very foreign to the ear of a Polander. **1812** J. M. WILLIAMS *Dramatic Censor* 41 Master Byrne and Miss Smith executed a *pas de deux* (a polacca) in the second act. **1954** *Grove's Dict. Mus.* (ed. 5) VI. 836/1 Polaccas may be defined as polonaises treated in a denationalized manner, but still retaining much of the rhythm characteristic of their Polish origin. *Ibid.* 836/2 Instrumental movements with the tempo indication *alla polacca* also occur. **1970** W. APEL *Harvard Dict. Mus.* 683/2 The 'Polacca' in Bach's Brandenburg Concerto no. 1 shows hardly any affinity to the polonaise. **1975** *Gramophone* July 174/2 In the finale with its polacca rhythms, and particularly in the obviously Slavonic episodes.., the Broadwood does increasingly suggest a Hungarian cymbalom.

Polack, *sb.* (*a.*) Delete † *Obs.* and add: Also with pronunc. (pōu·læk, pōu·lāk). Also 6–7 **Polake**, 9 **Pollack**, **Pullack** and with lower-case initial. **A.** *sb.* **1.** (Earlier and later examples.)

1574 SIDNEY *Let.* 27 Nov. in *Wks.* (1968) III. 99 The Polakes hartily repente their so fur fetcht election. **1895** *Funk's Stand. Dict.*, *Polack*, same as *Pole.* **1922** M. F. LIDDELL in *Contemp. Rev.* Dec. 770 Danzig fears and hates the 'Polacks' and still more the French. **1933** S. K. PADOVER *Let Day Perish* 140 You cowardly little sneak! It's craven pups like you that make the Polacks trample on us! If we Jews would learn to..kill..like they do, the —Polacks would grovel at our feet—!

2. A Jew from Poland.

1834 *Manch. Old Hebrew Congregation Acct. Bk.* in B. Williams *Making of Manchester Jewry* (1976) iii. 71 Given him the Polack for leaving Town 8/6. **1892** [see *LITVAK]. **1909** *Cent. Dict.* (Suppl.) *Polack*, a name given to the Jews of the Polish provinces, by their Lithuanian coreligionists. **1971** M. A. SHULVASS *From East to West* i. 23 It is hard to arrive at any accurate estimate of the numbers of Jews who emigrated westward in this period... The strongest indication that they came in considerable numbers is the fact that the nickname Pollack was current both in the Germanies and in the Hapsburg monarchy. *Ibid.* iv. 111 Following the great influx of *Betteljuden* from Poland to the West, the nickname Pollack assumed a more derogatory connotation than ever before.

3. *N. Amer.* A (usu. disparaging) term for a Polish immigrant or person of Polish descent.

1898 F. P. DUNNE *Mr. Dooley in Peace & War* 234 'Well,' said Mr. Dooley, 'ye'er thoughts on this subject is inthrestin', but not conclusive, as Dorsey said to th' Pullack, that thought he cud lick him.' **1900** *Congress. Rec.* 7 Feb. 1625/2, I have some Polacks in my district, and..the blood of Pulaski, the brave Pole who fell at Savannah in the defense of American liberty, has never been avenged. **1905** [see *COLD *a.* 1 c]. **1922** E. E. CUMMINGS *Enormous Room* iv. 61 Get out of the way you damn Polak! **1935** W. SAROYAN *Daring Young Man* 108 All that mattered was this moment, Wolinsky in love, alive, walking down Ventura Avenue, in America, Wolinsky of the universe, the crazy Polak with the broken nose. **1944** *Sun* (Baltimore) 2 Aug. 2/3 'You know, I sure did hate to shoot him,' said the sergeant, 'Because he might have been a Polack, but he wouldn't stop.' **1952** F. L. ALLEN *Big Change* iii. 53 They were scornfully known as Dagoes, Polacks, Hunkies, Kikes. **1965** P. DE VRIES *Let me count Ways* vii. 101, I now recognized him as a blond Polak I had seen around town. **1971** [see *HUNK *sb.*[3]]. **1976** *National Observer* (U.S.) 26 June 1/3 The Crusher's a clean-living Polack from Milwaukee who don't truck with no drugs or bad women.

B. *adj.* (Earlier and later examples.) Also, of Polish origin or descent.

1602 SHAKES. *Hamlet* v. ii. 388 You from the Polake warres, and you from England Are heere arriued. **1928** [see *FLY *v.*[1] 5 a]. **1930** [see *BOHUNK]. **1966** E. V. CUNNINGHAM *Helen* iv. 45 You're some cheap Polack hooker that was tossed out of a parochial school fer diddling little boys. **1974** L. DEIGHTON *Spy Story* xix. 199 Any sign of that goddamn Polack sub?

Poland[2]. The name of a town in Maine, U.S., used *attrib.* and *absol.* to designate the variety of mineral water obtained from springs there.

1881 J. G. BLAINE *Let.* 6 Sept. in H. Ricker *Poland Mineral Spring Water* (1883) 37 Send two more cases Poland to the President [*sc.* Garfield]... The President will drink no other water. **1883** H. RICKER *Poland Spring, Maine* 18 The well-known effects following the use of Poland water were not discovered in a day. **1893** G. H. HAYNES *State of Maine* 41 All parties are requested to examine the fine display of Poland Water..at this Columbian Exposition. **1917** H. RICKER *Poland Spring* Poland water can be obtained in dining-cars, transatlantic steamships and in the leading cities throughout Europe. **1937** *Maine: Guide 'Down East'* III. 362 Poland Water is one of the few bottled waters that has continued to maintain a popularity. **1967** H. JOHNSON in C. Ray *Compleat Imbiber* IX. 148 Poland water is America's Perrier. It is not so fizzy but just as smart. **1968** J. LEASOR *Passport for Pilgrim* x. 181 He had a bottle of Poland water and a glass... He never drank anything but Poland water. He had a weak stomach, and it was comforting to him. **1977** *Times Lit. Suppl.* 4 Feb. 120/1 The American billionaire, Howard Hughes... All he drank was Poland water (whatever that may be).

polar, *a.* (*sb.*) Add: **1. a.** Also, of or pertaining to the poles of another heavenly body. (Further examples.)

1894 [see *polar cap* in 1 b below]. **1922** H. S. JONES *Gen. Astron.* v. 134 The structure of the corona is very complex; it has no definite boundary and is usually symmetrical with respect neither to the centre of the Sun nor to the Sun's polar axis. **1973** [see *polar wandering* in 1 b below].

b. *polar bear*, substitute for def.: the white bear of Arctic regions, *Ursus* (or *Thalarctos*) *maritimus*, or its fur; also *attrib.*, *comb.*, and *fig.*; (examples); *polar cap*, a large region of ice or other frozen matter surrounding a pole of a planet; *polar flattening*, the extent to which the polar diameter of a planet is shorter than the mean equatorial diameter; *polar front* (Meteorol.), a front between polar and equatorial air masses; *polar hare*, also called the Arctic hare; (examples); *polar orbit*, an orbit that passes over polar regions; *spec.* one whose plane contains the polar axis; so *polar-orbiting* adj.; *polar wandering*, the slow, erratic movement of the earth's poles relative to the continents which is thought to have occurred throughout geological time and is ascribed largely to continental drift; also extended to corresponding movement on other planets.

1781 T. PENNANT *Hist. Quadrupeds* II. 290 The Polar bear might have been one [*sc.* an animal natural to a rigorous climate]. **1829** [see SEA-BEAR 3]. **1834** DICKENS *Sk. Boz* (1836) 1st Ser. I. 210 In their shaggy white coats they look just like Polar bears. **1847** T. ARNOLD *Let.* 23 Oct. in *N.Z. Lett.* (1966) 10 In Prince Edward's Island, the winter..is enough to deter anyone but a polar bear. **1910** E. T. SETON *Life-Histories Northern Animals* II. 1034 It [*sc.* the grizzly bear] is easily distinguished..from the Polar-bear by the latter's white colour. **1917** R. FRY *Let.* 2 Mar. (1972) II. 404 Lady Scott, the widow of the Antarctic man came in yesterday with Peter Scott, the most wonderful little monster of a polar bear cub. **1959** G. D. PAINTER *Proust* I. ix. 126 Montesquiou..had a room decorated as a snow-scene, with a polar-bear rug. **1968** A. DIMENT *Bang Bang Birds* iii. 37 The living room, with its nylon polar bearskin rug. **1974** P. DICKINSON *Poison Oracle* i. 17 The polar bear was swimming, huge in its tiny pool. **1976** H. L. GUNDERSON *Mammalogy* xvi. 375 The female and sometimes the male polar bears..become dormant throughout the winter. **1894** *Astron. & Astrophysics* XIII. 542 So much for the terrestrial conditions under which the observations were made. The Martian ones were such as to make the polar cap and its accompanying phenomena the centre of interest upon the planet. **1932** [see *fast ice* s.v. *FAST *a.* 11]. **1967** K. LASSEN in B. M. McCormac *Aurora & Airglow* v. 453 We define the Polar Cap as the area with corrected geomagnetic latitude..greater than some 70°. **1968** S. GLASSTONE *Bk. of Mars* vi. 107 Even if the polar caps are largely carbon dioxide, it does not mean that they do not also contain some solidified water. **1895** *Astrophysical Jrnl.* II. 136 Micrometric measures of the diameters of Mars..give as the most probable value for the equatorial diameter of the planet at distance unity: 9″.40±·007; for the polar one: 9″.35±·005; and for the polar flattening $\frac{1}{190}$ of the equatorial diameter. **1899** G. W. MYERS tr. *Lommel's Exper. Physics* i. 85 From the values of the acceleration resulting from pendulum experiments and the magnitude of the centrifugal force, the polar flattening may be computed. **1966** *McGraw-Hill Encycl. Sci. & Technol.* XIII. 516/2 Clairaut's formula for polar flattening... $\alpha = \frac{5}{2}m - \beta$ in which m is the ratio of centrifugal force to gravity at the equator..and β is the coefficient of the principal latitude term. **1920** V. BJERKNES in *Nature* 24 June 524/1 This line shows how far the cold air has succeeded in penetrating; it is a kind of polar front line. *Ibid.* 524/2 All meteorological events of the temperate zone..are derived from the general atmospheric circulation..as we know it from the polar front. **1935** C. F. BROOKS et al. *Why the Weather?* (ed. 2) v. 50 The polar front is the forward edge of a moving mass of cold dry air, usually coming more or less directly from polar or subpolar regions. **1973** R. G. & A. H. PERRY *Synoptic Climatol.* iii. 184 The classical view of tropical and polar air, separated by the polar front, does not accord well with modern knowledge of the general circulation. **1823** J. FRANKLIN *Narr. Journey to Shores of Polar Sea* 664 The Polar hare appears to vary much in size, and consequently in weight. **1866** W. R. KING *Sportsman & Naturalist in Canada* 26 In this respect it differs from the Polar-hare, the finer and softer fur of which is in winter pure white to the roots. **1895** [see *blue hare* (*BLUE *a.* 12 a)]. **1911** E. T. SETON *Arctic Prairies* 231 It was only a Polar Hare, the second we had seen. **1961** *Times Rev. Industry* Feb. 26/3 There are a number of possible satellite systems using polar, inclined and equatorial orbits. **1966** *McGraw-Hill Yearbk. Sci. & Technol.* 171/1 NASA is presently planning six or seven observatories to be launched alternately into the highly eccentric equatorial orbits..and the low polar orbits. **1978** *Times* 28 July 16/1 Europe's first lunar mission..would put a satellite in polar orbit round the moon. **1964** *Yearbk. Astron. 1965* 141 Transmissions from the United States were being sent by conventional means to Jodrell Bank for reflection to Gorky via the polar-orbiting balloon-satellite. **1968** *New Scientist* 24 Oct. 175/3 It should now be possible, by means of a polar-orbiting satellite, to reap..data on..cloud heights. **1924** J. G. A. SKERL tr. *A. Wegener's Origin Continents & Oceans* viii. 123 Extensive, even if slow, polar wanderings are then able to take place. **1969** *Times* 23 Apr. 7/4 Some of the more strange implications of the early studies of magnetism in ancient rocks—polar wandering, continental drift and the like. **1973** *Science* 9 Mar. 997 Polar wandering during the past 10^8 years may be recorded by unique quasi-circular structures in the polar regions of Mars.

3. b. *Chem.* Applied variously in cases where

bonding electrons are unequally shared between atoms in a molecule, so that there is some separation of electric charge: (i) applied *spec.* to electrovalent or ionic bonds, and to substances (usu. solids) in which bonding of this type predominates; (ii) applied to covalent bonds in which electrons are unequally shared between the atoms, to molecules or groups which contain such bonds, esp. those which possess a resulting electric dipole moment, and to substances (usu. liquids) which consist of such molecules.

1913 *Jrnl. Amer. Chem. Soc.* XXXV. 1443 In the preceding paragraphs we have suggested that there are two distinct types of union between atoms: polar, in which an electron has passed from one atom to the other, and non-polar, in which there is no motion of an electron. **1924** O. MAASS in H. S. Taylor *Treat. Physical Chem.* I. iv. 130 A polar molecule, one in which the molecular force of attraction is more concentrated in one particular part, so that if these molecules [of propionic acid] are oblong in shape, the field of force around one end, the —COOH end, will be more pronounced. **1927** N. V. SIDGWICK *Electronic Theory Valency* iv. 52 Polar or ionizable linkages between the oppositely charged ions of a salt. **1950** S. GLASSTONE *Elem. Physical Chem.* iii. 69 Compounds containing the groups —OH, —CN, —COOH and —NO_2, which are examples of polar groups, are generally highly polar in character, unless they happen to be completely symmetrical. *Ibid.*, Polar liquids have relatively high boiling points. **1950** W. J. MOORE *Physical Chem.* xi. 289 The polar compounds, of which NaCl was a prime example, could be adequately explained as being composed of positive and negative ions held together by coulombic attraction. **1951** I. L. FINAR *Org. Chem.* ii. 14 A symmetrical molecule is non-polar, although it may contain polar bonds. **1962** CORSON & LORRAIN *Introd. Electromagn. Fields* iii. 82 A water molecule..possesses just such a permanent dipole moment and is thus called a polar molecule. **1966** GUCKER & SEIFERT *Physical Chem.* (1967) xi. 276 Both the Trouton and Hildebrand constants are abnormally high for many liquids like water and ammonia, which are known to be polar. **1970** S. W. BENSON *Atoms, Molecules, & Chem. Reactions* iv. 109 An extreme example of polar bonds occurs in the case of the alkali metal halides. **1974** J. S. BLAKEMORE *Solid State Physics* (ed. 2) iv. 338 Optical phonon scattering..is especially important for a solid with a polar (partially or completely ionic) lattice. **1975** HUGHES & POOLEY *Real Solids & Radiation* ii. 15 Crystalline solids which are held together by electrostatic forces between oppositely charged ions are known as ionic or polar crystals.

5. *polar body*, one of the small cells which bud off from an oocyte at the two meiotic divisions and do not develop into ova; = *POLOCYTE. Cf. *OOCYTE, *OOTID.

1888 [in Dict.]. **1908** [see *OOTID]. **1927** HALDANE & HUXLEY *Animal Biol.* ii. 60 In order to retain the large size of the egg, three of every four gametes produced are minute and non-functional, and are called polar bodies, while only one becomes a functional ovum. **1945, 1946** [see *OOCYTE]. **1964** [see *OOTID]. **1974** *Sci. Amer.* Sept. 54/3 The remaining 23 [human chromosomes] replicate once more, and it is only after a sperm makes contact with the surface of the egg that a second polar body is expelled.

6. *polar diagram*, a diagram in which the length of the radius joining a fixed point to any point of a curve represents the magnitude of something (as the sensitivity of an aerial or the brightness of a lamp) measured in the direction of the radius; *polar vector* (see *VECTOR).

1895 *Electrician* 10 May 43/1 (*heading*) Representation of periodic currents by polar diagrams. **1923** GLAZEBROOK *Dict. Applied Physics* IV. 429/2 These diagrams are what are generally termed 'polar diagrams of light distribution'. In these curves the length of the radius vector at any angle gives the candle-power at that angle. **1943** *Electronic Engin.* XVI. 241/1 The field strength relations and polar diagrams of several aerials..were discussed. **1962** A. NISBETT *Technique Sound Studio* i. 20 (*caption*) In a polar diagram such as this the curve indicates the output of the microphone for a given sound arriving from any angle.

7. b. (Later examples.)

1953 T. PARSONS et al. *Working Papers in Theory of Action* 208 The instrumental and the system-integrative norms, which very closely characterize what..have been thought of as polar types of institutional structure. **1959** MCKINNEY & LOOMIS in J. S. Roucek *Contemp. Sociol.* 557 The polar extremes in point are clearly ideal or constructed types. *Ibid.* 558 The polar type formulations..have firmly established the point that the *continuum* is a vital notion in the comparative analysis of social phenomena. **1964** E. A. NIDA *Toward Sci. Transl.* ii. 24 The differences between literal and free translating are, however, no mere positive-negative dichotomy, but rather a polar distinction with many grades between them. **1965** *Language* XLI. 275 Only the conjunction of 'polar' adjectives in contexts of this kind seems odd. **1972** *Sci. Amer.* Jan. 35/1 Although sex-role ideologies form a continuum, we grouped the respondents into two polar categories, which we labeled 'traditional' and 'contemporary'. **1975** *Language* LI. 1 Polar interrogative sentences ('yes/no questions') are different from the corresponding declarative sentences not only pragmatically ..but also semantically.

polari-. Add: **polari-(bi)locular,** of a lichen spore: (see quots. 1921[1] and 1967).

1871 W. LEIGHTON *Lichen Flora Gt. Brit.* 175 Spores 8, colourless, ellipsoid, polari-bilocular. **1921** A. L. SMITH *Handbk. Brit. Lichens* 9 In the family, Physciaceæ, the cross wall of the septate spore is so thickened that the lumen of each cell is reduced to a small area at the ends; hence the term polari-bilocular. **1921** —— *Lichens* 422 In such a phylum as the Physciaceæ (with colourless polarilocular spores) there is a clear example of a closely connected series. **1967** M. E. HALE *Biol. Lichens* ii. 37 Polarilocular spores: two-celled spores with a thick median wall and a thin isthmus, or conversely a single-celled spore with a median constriction.

polarimetry. Add: (Examples referring to electromagnetic radiation other than visible light.) Hence **polarime·trically** *adv.*

1930 [see *FOUCAULT]. **1937** *Jrnl. Org. Chem.* II. 431 The mutarotation of glucose was measured polarimetrically, in 200 mm. tubes. **1973** *Jrnl. Biol. Chem.* CCXLVIII. 4165/1 Each solution was then diluted to 12 ml..and the further progress of the reaction followed polarimetrically. **1975** *Nature* 14 Aug. 537/1 In the past, the best-known argument for X-ray polarimetry has been that it is often symptomatic of non-thermal synchrotron-tye emission.

Polaris (polā·ris). [a. med.L. *polāris* polar.] The name of a type of guided missile developed for the U.S. Navy, having a nuclear warhead and designed to be carried by submarines and launched under water. Freq. *attrib.* and *Comb.*, as *Polaris missile, submarine; Polaris-carrying* adj.

1957 *N.Y. Times* 1 Jan. 1/3 The Navy is developing a ballistic missile to be fired from submerged submarines at targets hundreds of miles away, it was disclosed today. The missile is named the Polaris. **1957** *Life* 21 Jan. 121/2 Although Polaris can be launched from surface ships it will find its greatest strategic value with fast new nuclear-powered submarines. **1958** *Observer* 10 Aug. 3/4 Submarines of the Nautilus type equipped with 'Polaris' guided missiles could clearly use the Arctic Ocean as a base from which to threaten, with virtual impunity, the northern coasts of Russia. **1958** *New Statesman* 16 Aug. 181/1 They will be equipped with the deadly Polaris missile. **1960** *Daily Tel.* 22 Apr. 1/3 Britain has sounded the United States Defence Department on the possibility of having her own Polaris-carrying submarines, it was learned to-day. **1965** *New Statesman* 14 May 752/1 Last October, *The Times* felt able to predict with confidence that all Labour would do with Polaris would be to assign it irrevocably to Nato. **1965** H. KAHN *On Escalation* ii. 48 One can conceive of a slow-motion counterforce war lasting for weeks or months during which Polaris submarines are hunted down. **1973** D. KYLE *Raft of Swords* (1974) iii. 18 The Americans developed their Polaris programme very quickly... The Polaris rocket went from design to deployment in one and a half years.

polariscope. (Earlier example.)

1829 *Amer. Jrnl. Sci.* XV. 369 (*heading*) Description of the polariscope, an instrument for observing some of the most interesting phenomena of polarised light.

polariton (polæ·ritǫn). *Physics.* [f. POLAR(IZATION and related words + *-iton*, prob. after *EXCITON.] A quasiparticle in an ionic crystal consisting of a photon strongly coupled to a quasiparticle such as a phonon or exciton.

1958 J. J. HOPFIELD in *Physical Rev.* CXII. 1558/2 The polarization field 'particles' analogous to photons will be called 'polaritons'. (Excitons will be shown to be one kind of polariton... Optical phonons are another example of polaritons.) **1963** R. S. KNOX *Theory of Excitons* iii. 133 An external photon excites a crystal to a state described by a polariton packet... If this new particle of excitation fails to interact with any energy sinks, it re-excites an external photon on the other side of the crystal. However, by virtue of its exciton component, it can decay into states which do not couple as easily to external photons (i.e., 'nonradiative' states). **1971** J. I. PANKOVE *Optical Processes in Semiconductors* i. 16 A polariton is the complex resulting from the polarizing interaction between an electromagnetic wave and an oscillator resonant at the same frequency... Although polaritons initially have designated the interaction between excitons and photons, they can also represent the interaction between photons and optical phonons and between photons and plasmons. *Ibid.* 17 The polariton is not to be confused with the polaron of ionic crystals, which results from an interaction between the electron and the lattice. **1972** *Physics Bull.* Aug. 490/1 Two chapters..cover.. light scattering by polaritons.

polarity. Add: **2. e.** *Biol.* The tendency of living matter to assume a specific form; the property observed in animals from which parts have been severed, and in severed parts of animals and plants, of regenerating the missing parts.

1864 G. J. ALLMAN in *Rep. Brit. Assoc. Adv. Sci. 1863* 392 The lower segment, on the other hand, instead of pushing forth from the cut extremity a simple continuation of the coenosarc, developes from this extremity a polypite. There is thus manifested in the formative force of the Tubularia-stem a well-marked polarity, which is rendered very apparent if a segment be cut out from the centre of the stem. **1864** H. SPENCER *Princ. Biol.* I. II. iv. 181 The vitalized molecules composing the tissues, show their proclivity towards a particular arrangement... For this property there is no fit term. If we accept the word polarity, as a name for the force by which inorganic units are aggregated into a form peculiar to them; we may apply this word to the analogous force displayed by organic units. **1895** *Jrnl. Morphol.* X. 322 If we assume the polarity of the egg to be pre-determined from the beginning, we must admit that the polarity determines the position of the segmentation-nucleus. **1924** E. G. CONKLIN in E. V. Cowdry *Gen. Cytol.* ix. 558 The polarity of the egg is the earliest recognizable and most fundamental differentiation of morphogenesis. **1926** J. S. HUXLEY *Ess. Pop. Sci.* xviii. 251 When small pieces of a planarian regenerate, they exhibit what we may call polarity; for (with a few special exceptions) the new head is formed from that region of the piece which was nearest to the old head, the new tail from that region which was nearest to the old tail. **1975** R. L. PETERSON in Torrey & Clarkson *Devel. & Function of Roots* vii. 146 The inherent polarity in most root segments, which manifests itself by the regeneration of buds at the proximal end and roots at the distal end, may be due to the polar distribution of more than one endogenous hormone.

5. b. (Further examples.)

1934 C. HARTSHORNE *Philos. & Psychol. of Sensation* iv. 134 Feeling involves an 'opposition' of positive and negative, liking and disliking. Does sensation exhibit a similar polarity?.. It is, as we have seen, precisely in terms of polarities that the facts of sensation are to be described. **1945** *Downside Rev.* 131 Be it remarked in passing that the relation between God and the world is not here conceived as one of polarity. **1950** D. RIESMAN *Lonely Crowd* (1952) i. 20 To what extent, in establishing America's polarity from Europe, he [*sc.* de Tocqueville] tendentiously noticed those things that were different rather than those that were the same. **1957** *New Statesman* 2 Nov. 555/3 We must ask ourselves what we can do to break this polarity [between the U.S. and Russia]. **1963** *Times Lit. Suppl.* 26 Apr. 306/5 Polarity, or the use of contrast as an artistic means. **1970** B. M. H. STRANG *Hist. Eng.* 134 The polarity *mental/physical*. *Ibid.* 237 It [*sc.* Northern English] thus heightened the polarity of tense-contrast, which in strong verbs was far less clear-cut in the south. **1972** *Encycl. Psychol.* III. 19/2 *Polarity*, a relationship between features or traits which are antithetical pairs. **1972** R. PLANT in Cox & Dyson *20th-Cent. Mind* III. iii. 69 The wholly necessary or the wholly contingent, the two polarities of empiricist epistemology.

polarizability. Add: *spec.* the degree to which an atom or molecule can be polarized, expressed in terms of the electric dipole moment induced by unit electric field. (Further examples.)

1930 PAULING & GOUDSMIT *Structure Line Spectra* iii. 45 The electric moment of the induced dipole is αF, in which α is called the 'polarizability' of the atom or ion. **1947** SLATER & FRANK *Electromagnetism* iv. 44 We thus have means for finding the dielectric constant of a material, if we know the polarizability of its molecules. **1964** PHILLIPS & WILLIAMS *Inorg. Chem.* I. iv. 132 The simplest theoretical treatment of the London effect leads to an energy between identical atoms or molecules given by $-\frac{3}{4}\frac{h\nu\alpha^2}{r^6}$. α, the polarizability of the atom or molecule, may be determined from its molecular refraction. **1974** *Nature* 23 Aug. 686/3 The fourth chapter..is an excellent account of the determination of dipole moments and polarisabilities of molecules in excited electronic states.

polarization. Add: **I. 1.** (Further examples.) Also used of other kinds of wave.

1923 H. L. BROSE tr. *Sommerfeld's Atomic Structure & Spectral Lines* i. 23 Polarisation signifies that a ray favours a certain plane passing through it more than the one perpendicular to this plane. In the case of longitudinal vibrations..there is a symmetry about the ray and no such preference can be imagined. Longitudinal radiation must therefore be unpolarised. In the case of transversal vibrations..a favoured plane..is determined by the direction of vibration and the direction of the ray. **1929** *Physical Rev.* XXXIII. 760 (*heading*) A test for polarization of electron waves by reflection. **1936** *Wireless World* 16 Oct. 396/3 Although one would expect a slight departure from vertical polarisation of the received waves in this location, a vertical aerial was found to be 6 to 10 db. better than a horizontal. **1976** *IEEE Trans. Antennas & Propagation* XXIV. 5/1 In microwave communication links above 10 GHz the employment of frequency reuse in orthogonal polarizations is limited by cross polarization.

b. = *optical activity* s.v. *OPTICAL *a.* 6. Now used chiefly with reference to sugar solutions.

1845 *Mem. & Proc. Chem. Soc.* II. 29, I shall explain.. what is meant by the deviation or rotation of the rays of polarized light when transmitted through fluids said to possess circular polarization. **1862** *Jrnl. Chem. Soc.* XV. 308 An experiment made..while examining the circular polarization of camphoric acid. **1912** C. A. BROWNE *Handbk. Sugar Anal.* ix. 236 The reading multiplied by 1·3 gives the polarization (degrees Ventzke) of the sugar cane. **1935** *Economist* 20 Apr. 906/2 Raw sugar of 97° polarisation..pays a duty of 8s. 4⅗d. per cwt. **1963** D. BECKER in P. Honig *Princ. Sugar Technol.* III. ix. 455 In contrast to raw cane sugars, raw beet sugars for refining cannot be definitely characterized and graded by stating the polarization alone.

c. Measurement of the optical activity of a sugar solution. Cf. *POLARIZE *v.* 1 c.

1905 G. W. ROLFE *Polariscope* 96 Polarizations made at average room temperature by the standard commercial methods give with requisite accuracy the per cent of sucrose in the sample. **1945** A. L. & K. B. WINTON *Anal. of Foods* 640/1 Addition of solid sodium carbonate to slight alkaline reaction after the immediate polarization.. destroys the mutarotation without changing the dilution. **1973** SNELL & ETTRE *Encycl. Industr. Chem. Anal.* XVIII. 345 Direct polarization of the sugar solution or polarization before and after hydrolysis are commonly used assay methods.

1*. *Physics.* A partial or complete alignment of the spin axes of particles; the degree to which this exists.

1928 *Proc. R. Soc.* A. CXVIII. 675 It will..suffice to treat of only one type of polarisation and we shall take that corresponding to *z*. **1929** *Ibid.* CXXIV. 427 This polarisation could be detected by letting the scattered beam fall on a second target. **1956** *Rev. Mod. Physics* XXVIII. 279/1 We shall speak of transverse polarization of an electron beam if the direction of the spin is perpendicular to the momentum, of longitudinal polarization if the spin is parallel or antiparallel to the momentum. **1963** K. Nishijima *Fundamental Particles* vii. 380 Hyperon polarization is transverse rather than longitudinal unless parity is violated in production. **1979** *Sci. Amer.* May 64/3 The polarization is defined as the difference between the number of spin-up particles and the number of spin-down ones, divided by the total number of protons.

II. 2. (Further examples.) *spec.* the partial separation of positive and negative electric charge produced in a dielectric by an electric field, and expressed by a vector quantity equal to the electric dipole moment per unit volume of the dielectric; also, a similar state in an individual atom or molecule.

1916 F. B. Pidduck *Treat. Electricity* iii. 93 The total electric moment of an element of volume $d\tau$ of a dielectric near the point (x, y, z) has components $P_x d\tau$, $P_y d\tau$, $P_z d\tau$, where the vector $P(P_x, P_y, P_z)$ is called the polarization at the point. **1933** N. V. Sidgwick *Physical Properties of Covalent Link* v. 129 The polarization of the molecules in an electric field can take place in three ways: (1) The arrangement of the electrons will be displaced with respect to the nuclei... (2)..The nuclei themselves will be to some extent displaced with respect to one another... (3)..If the molecule has a permanent dipole moment of its own—if it is polar—the field will tend to orient it along the direction of the lines of force. **1935** J. Dougall tr. *Born's Atomic Physics* viii. 230 The polarization **P** is connected with Maxwell's displacement vector **D** by the relation $\mathbf{D}=\mathbf{E}+4\pi\mathbf{P}$; on the other hand, by definition, $\mathbf{D}=\epsilon\mathbf{E}$, where ϵ is the dielectric constant. **1966** *McGraw-Hill Encycl. Sci. & Technol.* IV. 111/2 The dielectric constant of a material depends on its polarization in an applied field or, microscopically, on the relative displacements, in the field direction, of the electrons and nuclei comprising the molecules of the dielectric. **1973** P. C. Clemmow *Introd. Electromagn. Theory* vi. 232 **P** and **M**..represent, respectively, electric and magnetic dipole moment densities. **P** is called the (electric) polarization, and **M** the magnetization or magnetic polarization.

4. b. The accentuation of a difference between two things or groups; the process of division into two groups representing the extremes of opinion, wealth, or the like.

1945 Koestler *Yogi & Commissar* ii. v. 117 False polarizations and national splits which merely reflect latent conflicts. **1947** *Sun* (Baltimore) 15 Aug. 12/6 The same polarization of thought which is going on in the rest of the world is seen in Korea in extreme form. **1951** Y. Malkiel in *Language* XXVII. 485 Lexical polarization is used in this paper as a convenient label for the influence exerted by one word on its semantic opposite. **1957** *Atlantic Monthly* Aug. 8/1 Any outside disturbance of the evolving polarization between moderate and extreme Arab nationalists may well bring disaster to the whole region. **1960** *Daily Tel.* 8 Nov. 12/2 But this does not alter the fact that every tendency towards polarisation of trade in separate camps in Europe, necessary and inevitable while the division stands, is in the long run a disaster for all. **1964** T. Bottomore *Elites & Society* ii. 19 The development of capitalism brings about a more radical polarization of classes than has existed in any other type of society. **1970** *Daily Tel.* 7 Oct. 5/2 There were already signs in the central districts [of London] of 'social polarisation', areas peopled only by the richest and the poorest. **1972** M. L. Samuels *Ling. Evolution* iii. 39 Further phonetic divergence ('polarisation' of the existing difference) to /k/ and /tʃ/. **1975** *Chinese Econ. Studies* VIII. iv. 90 (*heading*) The polarization between the rich and the poor is a general law of capitalist accumulation.

III. 5. polarization charge, the charge that appears on the surface of a dielectric when it is polarized in a direction not parallel to the surface.

1947 Slater & Frank *Electromagnetism* iv. 45 We have the result that the normal component of *P*, pointing out of the dielectric, equals the surface polarization charge that appears on the surface as a result of the polarization. **1975** Grant & Phillips *Electromagnetism* ii. 53 Polarization charges induced on the surface of a dielectric material make a contribution to the macroscopic electric field inside the material... The sign of the induced charge always ensures that the field just inside the dielectric surface is less than the field just outside.

polarize, *v.* Add: **I. 1. a.** (Further examples.)

1939 *Wireless World* 26 Jan. 83/1 Considerable attention has been paid to the question of whether the waves of the Alexandra Palace television transmitter should be vertically or horizontally polarised. **1966** *McGraw-Hill Encycl. Sci. & Technol.* X. 448/1 Electromagnetic radiation is difficult to polarize in certain spectral regions.

b. Also, to rotate the plane of polarization of plane-polarized light by (a specified amount) under standard conditions.

1900 *Bull. Div. of Chem., U.S. Dept. Agric.* No. 59. 52 The wine is fermented... [If] it polarizes −3° after fermentation. It contains only levorotatory sugar. **1945** A. L. & K. B. Winton *Anal. of Foods* 616/1 Wash by decantation until the washings polarize zero in a 200-mm. tube.

c. *trans.* To measure the optical activity of (a solution) in order to determine the concentration of sugar in it. Also *ellipt.*

1905 G. W. Rolfe *Polariscope* 87 The sample which the chemist polarizes must be strictly representative of the total lot of sugar. **1945** A. L. & K. B. Winton *Anal. of Foods* 615/1 Invert Polarization... Cool to about 20°, fill exactly to the mark, mix, and polarize at 20° in a 200-mm. tube. **1963** Triebold & Aurand *Food Composition & Qual.* iii. 60 According to their standard, a solution containing 26·000 grams of sucrose (normal weight) in 100 ml of solution at 20°C., and polarized in a 200-mm tube at 20°C., should give a reading of 100° on the saccharimeter. **1973** Snell & Ettre *Encycl. Industr. Chem. Anal.* XVIII. 348 Dilute the solution to 100 ml at 20°C. Mix well and polarize in a 200-mm tube.

1*. *Physics.* To produce a partial or complete alignment of the spins of (particles).

1932 *Proc. R. Soc.* A. CXXXV. 431 The theoretical existence of these methods provides some evidence that electron beams can be polarised. **1953** *Progr. Nuclear Physics* III. 72 In order to polarize elementary particles, there must be some sort of coupling of the particle spin with a fixed spatial direction. **1974** Frauenfelder & Henley *Subatomic Physics* ix. 206 In a radioactive source at room temperature, the nuclear spins are randomly oriented. It is necessary to polarize the nuclei so that all spins J point in the same direction. **1979** *Sci. Amer.* May 64/2 The next stage polarizes the protons and depolarizes the electrons.

II. 2. (Further examples.) *spec.* to induce an electric dipole moment in (a substance, or an atom or molecule).

1887 W. Larden *Electr.* x. 161 Lines along which the molecules of the dielectrics are 'polarised' by a separation of + and − charges in them. **1945** A. F. Wells *Structural Inorg. Chem.* ii. 52 An atom is polarized when placed in an electric field. **1962** Corson & Lorrain *Introd. Electromagn. Fields* iii. 126 Consider a large block of dielectric polarized uniformly with a dipole moment per unit volume **P**. **1977** *Sci. Amer.* Feb. 91/3 The separation is accomplished by passing the atomic beam through an inhomogeneous electric or magnetic field, which deflects those atoms that are more readily polarized or have a larger magnetic moment.

b. Also *intr.* (of a cell), to exhibit polarization and consequently suffer a decrease in e.m.f.

1903 *Electr. World & Engin.* 24 Jan. 150/2 There is yet not a battery of this class known that will not polarize in a short time, which means that it has temporarily exhausted itself and must rest for awhile before it is as efficient as it was. **1969** J. J. DeFrance *Electr. Fundamentals* xi. 124 The prevention is not complete, and with age a cell does polarize.

III. 3. c. *trans.* To accentuate a division within (a group, system, etc.); to separate into two (or occas. several) opposing groups, extremes of opinion, or the like. Also *intr.*, to undergo or exhibit such a process.

1949 Koestler *Promise & Fulfilment* i. xi. 125 The controversy about Zionism would have become as polarized' between pro- and anti-Russians as, say, the controversy about Poland. **1957** R. N. Carew Hunt *Guide to Communist Jargon* xxvii. 96 There could be no place for neutrality, and indeed such an attitude is explicitly excluded by the Marxist-Leninist dialectic which polarizes every issue and denies the possibility of intermediate solutions. *Ibid.* xxxvi. 122 As a result of the Industrial Revolution, society had polarized into two hostile classes, the bourgeoisie and the proletariat. **1957** *New Statesman* 2 Nov. 555/2 If we walked out of the nuclear arms race then the world would be 'polarised' between America and the Soviet Union. **1969** *N.Y. Rev. Books* 2 Jan. 41/1 New York was racially polarized as never before; hundreds of thousands of public school children were not being taught. **1972** *Nature* 3 Mar. 39/2 The problems are polarized into three areas... Only the first of these is really meteorological in character. **1972** M. L. Samuels *Ling. Evolution* vi. 132 Changes gather momentum when the upper classes polarise differences to maintain their value as prestige-markers. **1973** *Sci. Amer.* Apr. 86/3 Yet Henri labored..to avoid the utter disintegration of a France polarized and torn by civil war. **1977** *Time* 19 Dec. 8/2 From the first, Soares had insisted on governing without political alliances. Any compromise, he feared, would further polarize the country's politics.

polarized, *ppl. a.* Add: **1. a.** Also used of other kinds of wave. (Further examples.)

1923 H. L. Brose tr. *Sommerfeld's Atomic Structure & Spectral Lines* i. 23 Barkla discovered that primary X-rays are partially polarised, secondary X-rays are wholly polarised in certain directions. **1946** *Wireless World* Aug. 251/1 If the receiving aerial is horizontal it will receive nothing from a vertically polarized wave. **1966** *McGraw-Hill Encycl. Sci. & Technol.* VIII. 418/1 A circular wave guide is particularly useful in transforming plane-polarized electric intensity into circularly polarized electric intensity.

b. *Physics.* Of a particle or beam of particles: exhibiting an alignment of the spins.

1929 *Proc. R. Soc.* A. CXXIV. 426 Our only hope of observing the moment of a free electron is to obtain a 'polarised' beam, in which all the spin axes are pointing in the same direction, or at any rate more in one direction than another. **1953** *Progr. Nuclear Physics* III. 75 It may be possible to produce polarized protons by using polarized thermal neutrons..as projectiles in an *(n, p)* reaction. **1975** *Nature* 5 June 514/1 These treatments will be of increasing value as polarised beams of deuterons and other ions become available.

c. Of a substance or device: causing the polarization of light passing through it; = Polarizing *ppl. a.* 1.

1936 *Discovery* Oct. 302/1 Polarised glass has for some time been used..in certain scientific instruments. **1955** *Ann. Reg. 1954* 403 More than one critic referred to 1954 as the year of the decline of 3D on account of the general discomfort of polarized spectacles. **1977** *Sci. Amer.* Dec. 172/2 If a motorist wants to eliminate the glare from a road surface, he can wear polarized sunglasses.

4. b. Characterized by division into opposing groups or principles. Cf. *Polarize *v.* 3 c.

1957 *New Statesman* 2 Nov. 555/3 This gives the world something quite different from the polarised powers. **1962** E. Cleaver in A. Dundes *Mother Wit* (1973) 19/1 What we term *The Polarized Western Mind* derives from the symbolism attached to the two colors, black and white, in the mind of Western man. *Ibid.* 20/1 An obvious and striking example of polarized thinking.

polarogram (polă·ro-, pōu·lărogræm). *Chem.* [f. as next + -gram.] A graphical record of current against voltage produced by a polarograph (see next).

1925 Heyrovský & Shikata in *Recueil Travaux Chimiques Pays-Bas* XLIV. 496 The authors have set up a photographic auto-registering machine, which..records the polarisation curves, giving such 'polarograms' in less than 20 minutes. **1946** *Nature* 20 July 96/1 If several elements can be isolated simultaneously, there is the possibility of estimating them in a single polarogram. **1968** Pecsok & Shields *Mod. Methods Chem. Analysis* xiv. 339 The steps in the polarogram are called 'polarographic waves'. **1974** S. E. Allen *Chem. Analysis Ecological Materials* 398 If poor quality polarograms are produced even after passing nitrogen further bubbling may improve the display.

polarograph (polă·ro-, pōu·lărograf). *Chem.* [f. Polar(ization + -o + -graph.] An apparatus for automatic chemical analysis in which a sample solution is electrolysed using a steadily increasing voltage, and a graph, known as a polarogram, of current against voltage is produced; this usu. shows a series of steps each of which occurs at a voltage characteristic of a particular component and has a height proportional to the concentration of that component.

Polarograph is a proprietary term in the U.S.A.

1925 Heyrovský & Shikata in *Recueil Travaux Chimiques Pays-Bas* XLIV. 496 (*heading*) The polarograph. **1933** *Official Gaz.* (U.S. Patent Office) 15 Aug. 527/1 Polarograph Laboratories of America, Berkeley, Calif. Filed June 5, 1933. Polarograph. For Electrical Analyzing Apparatus... Claims use since Feb. 1, 1927. **1937** *Jrnl. Iron & Steel Inst.* CXXXVI. 109A From the current-potential curve the deposition potential for a given level on the curve can be determined, so that the polarograph can be used as a qualitative test. **1946** *Nature* 13 July 59/1 Iron can be determined satisfactorily on the polarograph if the solution contains triethanolamine. **1953** *Electronic Engin.* XXV. 314/1 One such instrument is the polarograph, which is used to determine the concentration of reducible ions in a solution, by measurement of the current that flows when the ions are electrolytically reduced. **1974** S. E. Allen *Chem. Analysis Ecol. Materials* 400 Oxygen is the only dissolved gas of interest to biologists which can be readily determined on the polarograph.

Hence **polarogra·phic** *a.*, of, pertaining to, or used in a polarograph or polarography; **polarogra·phically** *adv.*; **polaro·graphy,** the technique of using the polarograph.

1926 *Brit. Chem. Abstr.* A. 1184/1 (*heading*) Polarographic methods in biology. **1930** *Chem. News* 19 Dec. 388/2 Current-voltage curves obtained polarographically.. reveal the presence of proteins in solutions. **1936** *Nature* 30 May 889/2 The last section, on polarography by Prof. J. Heyrovský, gives a comprehensive survey of the researches with the dropping mercury cathode. **1952** Kolthoff & Lingane *Polarography* (ed. 2) xviii. 397 This reaction may be utilized to remove dissolved oxygen from polarographic solutions. **1959** *Times* 30 Jan. 3/7 This involves supervision of staff engaged on a variety of analytical work, including..infra-red spectroscopy and polarography. **1966** *McGraw-Hill Encycl. Sci. & Technol.* X. 455/1 The most widely used polarographic indicator electrode is the dropping-mercury electrode. **1970** C. N. Graymore *Biochem. Eye* x. 651 Noell..measured oxygen tension polarographically. **1973** *Nature* 10 Aug. 370/2 Characteristic polarographic half-wave potential.. values for proteins were attributed..to exposed, reactive sulphydryl..groups. **1975** M. R. Jenkins in Williams & Wilson *Biologist's Guide to Princ. & Techniques Pract. Biochem.* vii. 200 The main use of polarography in biochemistry is not, however, the measurement of oxidation-reduction potentials, but rather the qualitative and quantitative analysis of various compounds.

Polaroid (pōu·lăroid). Also **polaroid.** [Proprietary name.] **A.** *sb.* **1. a.** A material which in the form of thin sheets produces a high degree of plane polarization in light passing through it.

1936 *Official Gaz.* (U.S. Patent Office) 26 May 760/1 Sheet Polarizer Company, Inc., Union City, N.J... *Polaroid* for composite material comprising suspensions of crystalline particles in a light-transmitting medium adapted to be used in connection with optical devices such as microscope eye-pieces, glare eliminators,..gem testers, and the like. Claims use since Nov. 19, 1935. **1936** *Nature* 22 Aug. 312/2 Another [firm] manufactures ophthalmic instruments employing Polaroid. **1937** *Ann. Reg. 1936* ii. 65 Land (*Nature*, Aug. 22) developed a new device for producing plane polarised light. Available commercially under the name Polaroid it consisted of a layer of ultramicroscopic needle-shaped crystals of herapathite..oriented with their axes parallel on a cellulose film. **1940** *Trade Marks Jrnl.* 5 June 562/2 *Polaroid*...

Materials specially prepared for use in the polarization of light. Polaroid Corporation.., Dover, State of Delaware, United States of America; manufacturers. **1942** *Chem. Abstr.* XXXVI. 2183 By use of film polarizers, e.g., polaroid, the expense is small. **1946** F. Schneider *Qualitative Organic Microanalysis* iv. 119 The sections of Polaroid are cut so that their planes of polarization include an angle of approximately 5° when the segments are mounted in place with a slight overlap. **1949** H. C. Weston *Sight, Light & Efficiency* iv. 133 If they are placed between two thin plates of polaroid, or between crossed Nicol prisms, so that the light passing through them is polarised, the presence of strain is shown by the formation of a coloured pattern due to double refraction by the strained glass. **1956** *Nature* 3 Mar. 434/1 A cylindrical unit..is formed by cementing a calcite crystal between two pieces of 'Polaroid'. **1976** *Nature* 19 Aug. 709/2 All stimuli were plane polarised by a 60-cm diameter rotatable disk of polaroid positioned between the screen and the eye.

b. A piece of 'Polaroid'.

1955 *Physical Rev.* XCIX. 1694/1 The action on polarized light of the rotating λ/2 plate followed by a polaroid is to produce an interruption of the light at four times the rotation frequency. **1967** H. von Klüber in J. N. Xanthakis *Solar Physics* ix. 261 For nearly all analysers used in the detection of such inverse Zeeman effects—such as polaroids, double-splitting crystals, quarter- or half-wave plates, etc.—the result..is just the same as in the emission case. **1976** *Nature* 11 Mar. 155/1 The relative intensities of the red and green components could then be varied by rotating a Polaroid interposed in the common beam.

2. *pl.* Sunglasses containing 'Polaroid'.

[**1942** *Official Gaz.* (U.S. Patent Office) 20 Oct. 463/1 Polaroid Corporation, Cambridge, Mass... *Polaroid*..for viewing devices—namely, filters, lenses, eyeglasses, and goggles. Claims use..on eyeglasses since July, 1936; and on goggles since December, 1937.] **1959** C. MacInnes *Absolute Beginners* 163 The water sparkling so that I had on my Polaroids. **1959** *New Statesman* 19 Sept. 354/2 The light..beat back from the limestone with a spectral, otherworldly intensity that polaroids only served to accentuate. **1967** H. Hunter *Case for Punishment* i. 17 Cummings..was sporting a pair of heavy, black-rimmed spectacles. Inspector Shade had acquired a pair of green-tinted Polaroids. **1972** *Country Life* 23 Mar. 697/3 That afternoon my wife, wearing Polaroids, stationed herself opposite their lie and watched to see their reactions.

3. a. A kind of camera which develops the negative and produces a positive print within a short time of the exposure's being made.

1961 A. Gordon *Cipher* (1962) iv. 58 How about a nice picture, sir?.. I use a Polaroid... I'll have a print for you in a minute. **1966** H. B. Taylor *Triumvirate* xxxi. 168, I took a couple of pictures with my Polaroid, chatted a little. **1968** [see *Long Tom 5]. **1977** *N.Y. Rev. Bks.* 23 June 25/4 From the first Kodak, when it took weeks before a developed roll of film was returned to the amateur photographer, to the Polaroid, which ejects the image in a few seconds.

b. A photograph produced by such a camera.

1972 D. Marlowe *Do You remember England?* iv. 57 All I got out of it were two Polaroids of her. **1975** *New Yorker* 19 May 12/3 (Advt.), Large toned prints of an abstract character. Manipulated color Polaroids of bizarre activities. **1977** *Rolling Stone* 13 Jan. 22/2 Grace snapped a couple of Polaroids for the wedding album.

B. *attrib.* **1.** Applied to the polarizing material (see *A. 1) and articles in which it is employed.

1936 *Nature* 22 Aug. 312/2 It is by some such means described by Land that the Polaroid Corporation of Boston, U.S.A., has succeeded in manufacturing the 'Polaroid' sheets of polarizing material now on the market. *Ibid.*, One firm supplies Polaroid analysers and polarizers for the microscope. *Ibid.* 313/2 The details of reflecting objects can be seen more clearly through Polaroid films. **1951** *Electronic Engin.* XXIII. 10/2 The images.., plane polarized in mutually perpendicular directions by polaroid film, are superposed by a semi-reflecting mirror and are viewed through polaroid spectacles. **1954** *Ann. Reg. 1953* 365 Stereoscopic films viewed through polaroid spectacles were no novelty. **1958** *Woman* 9 Aug. 14/2 Polaroid sun-shield. **1961** E. N. Cameron *Ore Microsc.* ii. 20 The polarizer is a polaroid plate or a calcite prism. **1962** L. S. Sasieni *Optical Dispensing* xiii. 326 And Polaroid lenses are used as plano protective lenses (sunglasses), or as sighted lenses to prescription. **1965** *Wireless World* July 340/2 Many of the digital instruments.. incorporate polaroid filters to reduce reflected light.

2. Applied to a type of camera and photographs taken with it (see *A. 3).

1963 L. Deighton *Horse under Water* xxxv. 136 Two armed policemen..photographed me with a Polaroid camera and filed the photo. **1965** H. C. Shands in J. H. Masserman *Sci. & Psychoanalysis* VIII. 135 The final 'discovery' in science is more like a cooperative collage than it is like a two-second Polaroid snapshot. **1973** C. Sagan *Cosmic Connection* (1975) xv. 109 Page 100 shows a Polaroid photo of the video-monitor image of Phobos. **1976** *Early Music* IV. 451/1 Polaroid cameras produce a result very fast, but only the most sophisticated models provide a negative so that duplicate prints and enlargements are usually unobtainable. **1976** A. Grey *Bulgarian Exclusive* iv. 30 Two polaroid colour photographs of a dark-haired man.

polaron (pōᵘ·lărǫn). *Physics.* [f. Polar(ization and related words + *-on[1]; orig. formed as Russ. *polyarón* (S. Pekar 1946, in *Zh. eksper. i teoret. Fiziki* XVI. 344).] A quasi-particle consisting of a free electron in an ionic crystal and the associated distortion of the crystal lattice.

1946 S. Pekar in *Jrnl. Physics* (Moscow) X. 343/2 Such local self-consistent quantum states of the electron in a crystal we shall briefly call polarons. **1955** *Physical Rev.* XCVII. 660/1 An electron moving with its accompanying distortion of the lattice has sometimes been called a polaron. **1969** *Nature* 15 Nov. 641/2 The interaction between an electron and its strain field in a polar solid gives rise to the excitation known as a polaron, the presence of which can be detected by irregularities in the shape of the conduction band. **1971** Mott & Davis *Electronic Processes in Non-Crystalline Materials* iv. 115 At low temperatures a polaron, whether large or small,..will behave exactly like a heavy particle, being scattered by impurities or lattice vibrations; moreover a high density of polarons can form a degenerate gas.

Hence **polaro·nic** *a.*

1978 *Nature* 16 Feb. 647/1 There will..be some stored energy involved in the system due to the polaronic nature of the moving charge carrier.

pole, *sb.*[1] Add: **1. b.** Colloq. phr. *up the* (or *a*) *pole*: in trouble or difficulty; in confusion, in error; drunk; mad, crazy; pregnant but unmarried.

1886–96 A. R. Marshall in Farmer & Henley *Slang* (1902) V. ii. 245/1 But, one cruel day, behind two slops he chanced to take a stroll, And..he heard himself alluded to as being up the pole. **1896** *Daily News* 1 Apr. 7/6 She remonstrated with the latter, and told him he was 'up a pole'—i.e. in the wrong. **1897** *Daily Tel.* 11 Dec. 10/4 Plaintiff:..but your little girl was frequently saying that you were 'up the poll [*sic*]'... The Judge: Up the what?.. The High Bailiff explained that the term was a slang one for being intoxicated. **1899** *Daily Mail* 29 Mar. 5/1 When there are nineteen Frenchmen to four Englishmen they were slightly up the pole. **1904** *Westm. Gaz.* 19 Mar. 7/2 Plaintiff's definition of the phrase 'up the pole' differed from that of her cousin..who said it meant being drunk. Mrs. Frasier said that it..meant being crazy. **1905** *Daily Chron.* 14 Dec. 6/4 Alec went to football smoker. Came home up the pole at one a.m... 'Up the pole,' Mrs. Norman said, was one of her husband's slang terms for a person under the influence of drink. **1906** E. Dyson *Fact'ry 'Ands* xiv. 188 Then, as a bright afterthought, she added, 'Yer fair up the pole!' **1915** C. J. Dennis *Songs of Sentimental Bloke* 49 The dreams I dreamed, the dilly thoughts I thunk Is up the pole, an' joy 'as done a bunk. **1916** E. V. Lucas *Vermillion Box* 165 It must require an awful lot of pluck.. Either pluck or so much panic that one was practically up the pole with it. **1917** [see *blotto *a.*]. **1922** Joyce *Ulysses* 23 That red Carlisle girl, Lily... Spooning with him last night on the pier. The father is rotto with money.—Is she up the pole?—Better ask Seymour that. **1922** *Daily Mail* 20 Dec. 3 Keith came to her, saying he was 'up the pole and in a frightful mess'. **1932** D. L. Sayers *Have his Carcase* xxii. 295, I think we may take it for granted that our friend Weldon is a bit up the pole financially. **1950** J. Cleary *Just let me Be* xi. 108 If I go and see 'em now, tell 'em what I done and why I done it, I'd be well and truly up the pole. **1961** 'F. O'Brien' *Hard Life* v. 37 To say nothing of a lot of crooked Popes with their armies and their papal states, putting duchesses and nuns up the pole, and having all Italy littered with their bastards. **1965** W. Dick *Bunch of Ratbags* vi. 92 'Right,' said Curly, agreeing with Ronnie's logic for once. He generally thought Ronnie was all up the pole when giving advice to someone. **1970** R. Beilby *No Medals for Aphrodite* vi. 244 We'd 'a' been up the pole without him, that's why we didn't send him on his way. **1974** G. Moffat *Corpse Road* x. 142 'Do you really suspect that Pilgrim—*Pilgrim!*—killed the girl?..' 'You're up the pole,' Mrs Kent said to Page.

c. colloq. phr. *I wouldn't touch him* (*it*) *with a forty-foot* (or *ten-foot*) *pole* (and varr.): I refuse to have anything to do with him (it). Cf. *barge-pole.

1903 'T. Collins' *Such is Life* 22 The young feller he used to come sometimes an' just shake hands with her, but otherways he wouldn't touch her with a forty-foot pole. **1909** *Dialect Notes* III. 383, I wouldn't touch it with a ten-foot pole. **1941** *Coast to Coast* 167 'Me take the harness off him!' my mother said, surprised. 'Why, I wouldn't touch that mad thing with a forty-foot pole.' **1958** E. O. Schlunke *Village Hampden* 26 Attracting a lot of business of the more or less shady sort that our reputable men wouldn't touch with a forty-foot pole. **1974** P. Erdman *Silver Bears* i. 11 No respectable bank.. would touch our business with a ten-foot pole.

2. e. (*a*) *Racing.* The inside fence surrounding a racecourse; the starting position closest to the inside fence; (*b*) *Motor racing.* esp. in phr. *pole position*, the grid position which is on the front row and on the inside of the first bend; also *fig.*, any advantageous position.

1851 *Fraser's Mag.* XLIII. 657/1 The distance round is calculated at a mile,..For a saddle horse that has the pole, it comes practically to a little less... A horse 'has the pole', means that he has drawn the place nearest the inside boundary-fence of the track. *Ibid.* 659/1 'What a beauty she is!' says Harry. 'And she has the pole too.' **1868** H. Woodruff *Trotting Horse* xxiv. 206, I had the pole with Kemble Jackson, and soon took the lead. **1902** A. D. McFaul *Ike Glidden* xxii. 198 This stroke apparently gave the friends of the colt more confidence in the result, as drawing the pole was a position in favor of the colt. **1953** *Motor* 22 July 857/3 The newest B.R.M... had to be worked on all night and brought back to the course only just in time to come to the pole position on the starting line. **1963** *Times* 27 Apr. 3/3 J. Clark set a new unofficial lap record in his fuel injected Lotus 25..which gives him pole position on the starting grid. **1966** *Telegraph* (Brisbane) 14 May 17/3 Australian Jack Brabham, ..former world champion racing driver, snatched pole position for tomorrow's international formula one race. **1968** *Globe & Mail* (Toronto) 3 Feb. 36/2 Two Ford GT40s broke a course record and grabbed the pole positions for this weekend's 24 Hours of Daytona at Daytona Beach, Fla. **1969** *Australian* 24 May 34/4 Won Mobile 12½f event here four starts back. Place claims from the 'pole'. **1971** *Sunday Times* 12 Sept. 50/3 The German company retained a pole position in hormone research which led to the Pill. **1976** *Milton Keynes Express* 11 June 42/7 Colin Hawker's Cosworth Grand Prix-engined VW was on pole. **1976** *Listener* 8 July 7/3 Brazil's foreign investment needs..would double its foreign borrowing, and take Brazil to pole position in the big league of world debtors. **1977** *News of World* 17 Apr. 24/7 Ipswich relinquished their hold on the pole position to champions Liverpool.

5. a. *pole barn, bridge* (earlier and later examples), *corral, fence* (earlier and later examples), *plantation*. **b.** *pole jump* (earlier and later examples), *-jumper* (examples), *-jumping, leap, -leaping* (examples).

1950 Pole barn [see **pole corral*]. **1960** *Farmer & Stock-breeder* (Suppl.) 19 Jan. 41/1 In winter they are in pens of 45 in pole-barns. **1969** *Times* 24 Feb. 12/1 They [*sc.* bullocks]..were present by the score,..making their systematic way to adjacent pole barn silos. **1972** *N.Y. Law Jrnl.* 22 Aug. 13/8 (Advt.), Five bedrooms, 14 room modern home..on 12½ acres,..pole barn suitable for horses, riding trails nearby, would make ideal ski lodge. **1793** J. Lindley in *Michigan Pioneer & Hist. Coll.* (1892) XVII. 574 Pole bridges..made the tour very disagreeable. **1850** *Congress. Globe* 29 Jan. 240/1 Now, his colleague must start by the most direct route the 23rd of November, making provision for..contingencies of travel over corduroy roads, pole bridges, mud turnpikes, etc. **1974** D. Sears *Lark in Clear Air* ii. 34 We crossed a pole bridge over the Perch. **1950** *Amer. Speech* XXV. 85 No longer heard is *old land*, though *pole barn* and *pole corral* still describe forms of construction. **1962** J. Onslow *Bowler-Hatted Cowboy* v. 51 Two saddle horses which we turned into a small pole-corral. **1973** *Whig-Standard* (Kingston, Ont.) 11 Aug. 7/4 His..sheep..didn't want to bunch in the pole corral for the night. **1788** G. Washington *Diaries* (1925) III. 346 All hands were..finishing the Pole fence round the Barley and Pease in field No. 1. **1959** W. R. Bird *These are Maritimes* x. 278 We saw..many ancient pole fences crossing the fields. **1973** L. Russell *Everyday Life Colonial Canada* ii. 32 Probably the pole fence was the kind most frequently constructed at this stage [of land clearing]. In this, the trunks of moderate-sized trees were used, cut in lengths of 12 to 15 feet. **1886** *Year's Sport* 21 The other winners..were..pole jump, T. Ray; and wide jump, J. Purcell. **1912, 1920** Pole jump [see *decathlon]. **1887** M. Shearman *Athletics & Football* v. 163 Ulverston..has produced many fine pole-jumpers. **1908** *Westm. Gaz.* 1 July 8/4 Quite recently, Szathmary, the pole-jumper, broke the Hungarian record. **1868** H. F. Wilkinson *Mod. Athletics* viii. 88 Pole jumping. The leaping pole should be made of fir or ash. **1912** [see *field events* s.v. *field *sb.* 21]. **1931** E. Linklater *Juan in America* i. vi. 59 He could not help being tickled by the thought of an American university; pole-jumping and cheer-leaders. **1868** *Kendal Times* 5 Sept. 2/5 (*heading*) Grasmere annual sports... High pole leap for £1. **1869** *Ibid.* 18 Sept. 4/3 The high pole leaping..was gone through in capital style. **1885** F. Gale *Mod. Eng. Sports* vi. 67 Running, jumping, and pole-leaping were often the outcome of a very old-fashioned sport, 'Follow my leader'. **1888** T. Bright *Pole Plantations & Underwoods* i. 1 A pole plantation is an assemblage of young trees, the produce of plants that have been inserted in the soil at regular distances, or of the stems formed from such plants after their having been cut for poles.

c. pole-bean (examples); **pole-board,** a board or placard carried on poles like a banner; **pole-boat** now chiefly *Hist.*, a river-boat propelled by means of a pole or poles; so **pole-boating** *vbl. sb.*; **pole-bullock,** a bullock that is harnessed alongside the pole of a wagon; **pole-cure** *v.*, to cure (tobacco) by hanging it on poles; **pole-dray,** a dray furnished with or drawn by means of a pole; **pole-horse** (example); **pole-lathe** (further examples); **pole-masted** (further examples); **pole-mule,** a mule harnessed alongside the pole of a wagon; **pole-rose** = *pillar rose* s.v. Pillar *sb.* 12 in Dict. and Suppl.; **pole-screen** (further examples); **pole-trailer** (see quot. 1971); **pole-trap,** a bird-catching device which consists of a trap fixed to the top of a pole; **pole vault,** a jump over a horizontal bar which is achieved by means of a pole; = *pole-jump*; also *attrib.*; hence as *v. trans.* and *intr.*; so **pole-vaulter**; also *fig.*; **pole-vaulting** *vbl. sb.*; **pole-wagon,** a wagon furnished with or drawn by means of a pole; **pole-wound** *rare*, a wound that has been inflicted with a pole.

c **1770** 'J. H. St. J. de Crèvecœur' *Sk. 18th-Cent. Amer.* (1925) 120, I had once some hops and pole-beans, about twenty feet high. **1857** *Trans. Ill. Agric. Soc.* (1859) III. 503 There are many varieties of pole beans. **1865** [see *Lima b]. **1871** Mrs. Stowe *Oldtown Fireside Stories* 246 There was thick pole-beans quite up to the buttery-door. **1941** J. Stuart *Men of Mountains* 192 We drove down past Shelton's polebean patch. **1976** *Washington Post* 19 Apr. A10/7 (Advt.), Fresh Florida pole beans. 4 lbs. $1. **1909** *Westm. Gaz.* 29 Dec. 6/4 Others, again, carrying pole-boards setting forth all deceased's honours and titles. **1827** A. Sherwood *Gaz. Georgia* (1939) 22/1 Cargoes.. are thrown into pole boats. **1835** W. G. Simms *Partisan* II. ii. 12 At this point the river ceased to be navigable even for the common poleboats of the country. **1841** —— *Kinsmen* I. xiv. 163 Wherever a pole-boat had made its way, there had the name of Jack Bannister found repeated echoes. **1968** R. F. Adams *Western Words* 232/1 *Pole boat*, a river boat; so called because of the means by which it was propelled upstream. **1837** A. Sherwood *Gaz. Georgia* (ed. 3) 193 A revolution in the mode and manner of transshipping goods must take place. The slow, tedious and expensive process of pole-boating will be exploded. **1930** L. G. D. Acland *Early Canterbury Runs* 1st Ser. vii. 150 In 1868 Strawberry, one of the pole-bullocks, died after working ten years and seven months on the station. **1933** *Press* (Christchurch, N.Z.) 18 Nov. 15/7 *Pole-bullocks*, the two bullocks which work on the *p[ole]* of a dray or waggon. **1899** *Rep. U.S. Dept. Agric.* No. 62. 30 The present method of manipulating these tobaccos after they are pole-cured is quite different from what it was years ago. **1848** H. W. Haygarth *Bush Life Australia* v. 49 In some districts..shaft-drays are used; but pole-drays are found to be more suitable to the nature of the country. **1889** *Harper's Mag.* June 160/2 The leaders sprang upward and onward.., the pole-horses simultaneously crashing backward and downward. **1859** Pole-lathe [see *back-rest 1]. **1932** G. M. Boumphrey *Story of Wheel* 38 When the lathe came here, it was altered into what is called the pole-lathe. **1968** J. Arnold *Shell Book of Country Crafts* xv. 200 Whether a turner uses a pole-lathe or the treadle type seems a matter for individual inclination... The extremely primitive pole-lathe came firstly with a primitive society, but its retention appears largely due to its simplicity and easy portability. **1915** *Yachting Monthly* XIX. 366/1 This necessitated a change of rig, and a pole-masted ketch was decided on. **1970** *Mariner's Mirror* LXVI. 165 Evidence for the pole-masted brigantine rig was found at the Dubrovnik museum. **1862** O. W. Norton *Army Lett.* (1903) 106 A driver riding the near pole mule and guiding his team with one line. **1848** W. Paul *Rose Garden* 67 Pillar or Pole Roses. **1937** *Burlington Mag.* Apr. p. xxiv/1 A mahogany Polescreen on a beautifully carved tripod stand. **1960** B. Snook *English Historical Embroidery* 98 Pole screens were not unconnected with vanity. Created in the 18th century to protect the make-up worn by elegant women from the heat of large open fires, they were very practical little pieces of furniture. **1976** *Northumberland Gaz.* 26 Nov. 18/4 (Advt.), Pair Regency mahogany pole screens. **1969** Pole trailer [see *expandable *a.*]. **1971** M. Tak *Truck Talk* 120 *Pole trailer*, a trailer composed of a single telescopic pole, a tandem rear-wheel unit and a coupling device used to join the trailer to a tractor. **1909** *Westm. Gaz.* 17 Feb. 5/1 The catching of birds with hooks in Cornwall has been stopped by an Act passed last year, and efforts have been made to abolish entirely the illegal pole-trap. **1972** *Guardian* 3 May 7/2 The illegal and viciously cruel pole trap..a spring trap fixed by a short chain to the top of a pole which kills the captured bird in an extremely slow and painful way—was made illegal in 1904... It appears to be still in common use. **1975** *Country Life* 2 Oct. 849/2 Even in Britain..prosecutions are still being brought for the illegal use of pole-traps. **1893** Pole vault [in Dict., sense 5 b]. **1935** *Encycl. Sports* 467/1 In front of the pole-vault bar is a slideway, in which the base of the pole is placed when jumping. *Ibid.* 467/2 The world's record pole vault is 14 ft. 4½ in., made by W. Graber..in 1932. **1951** *Time* 29 Jan. 85 Did, or did not, the Rev. Robert Richards become the second man in history to pole-vault 15 feet? **1973** *Times* 2 May 11/2 She..will train regularly with Michael Bull, who holds the British pole vault record and who is preparing for the decathlon in the Christchurch Commonwealth Games next January. **1977** *Western Morning News* 30 Aug. 12/7 Brian Hooper edged a little closer to the magical 18-foot pole vault as another landslide of wins carried Britain to overwhelming victory against West Germany. **1978** *Times* 18 July 2/8 Ape pole-vaults over park moat... A chimpanzee..escaped from an island by pole-vaulting across a moat using an 8 ft. pole. **1888** A. Randall-Diehl *2000 Words* 165 *Pole Vaulter*, one who practices leaping by aid of a pole. **1891** W. M'Combie Smith *Athletes & Athletic Sports of Scotland* viii. 88 From the moment he takes hold of the pole as he commences his run till he lets it go as he crosses the bar the pole-vaulter never shifts his hands. **1893** [in Dict., sense 5 b]. **1956** *Sun* (Baltimore) 13 Oct. (B ed.) 12/2 The United States Air Force unit responsible for making these jaunts across the roof of the world a daily routing is the 58th Weather Reconnaissance Squadron—more colloquially known as 'the pole vaulters'. **1976** *Milton Keynes Express* 30 July 43/2 Saturday's performance was helped by the presence of two new pole vaulters. **1877** *N.Y. Times* 5 Apr. 8/4 The following programme was adopted: one-mile walk, two-mile walk, one-mile run,..pole-vaulting. **1891** W. M'Combie Smith *Athletes & Athletic Sports of Scotland* viii. 88 Pole-vaulting is comparatively a recent introduction at Scottish sports. **1932** Webster & Heys *Exercises for Athletes* viii. 161 Now let us consider which are the muscles principally involved in the feat of pole-vaulting. **1968** M. Watman *Hist. Brit. Athletics* x. 168 Pole vaulting for height, as distinct from distance, was pioneered in the mid-nineteenth century by members of the Ulverston (Lancashire) Cricket and Football Club. **1908** S. Ford *Side-Stepping with Shorty* vi. 90 The pole waggon brings up the rear. **1910** G. B. McCutcheon *Rose in Ring* i. i. 6 Here and there, in the gloomy background, stood the canvas and pole wagons. **1968** J. Arnold *Shell Book of Country Crafts* v. 76 The pole-wagon, which was the fore-runner of the present-day motor-hauled trolley, had iron stanchions at its four corners of two transverse beams, each above its respective axle. **1908** Hardy *Dynasts* III. iv. vi. 417 Who knows but that we should have been kings too, but for my crooked legs and your running pole-wound?

pole, *sb.*² Add: **1.** (Later *fig.* example.)

1916 K. J. Saunders *Adventures Christian Soul* 68 When God's will is thy heart's pole, Then is Christ thy very soul.

2. d. colloq. phr. *poles apart* (or, less commonly, *removed*), completely opposite to or different from (someone or something).

1917 A. Huxley *Let.* 30 Sept. (1969) 134 They are deeply engaged in something very far removed from the sordid present, poles apart from any clap trap I may be talking about English literature. **1922** Joyce *Ulysses* 618 On this knotty point, however, the views of the pair, poles apart as they were, both in schooling and everything else, ..clashed. **1935** *Discovery* Feb. 52/2 Mr Dunne is poles apart from the dry-as-dusts who care not whether or no what they write is read. **1957** J. S. Huxley *Relig. without Revelation* iv. 95 Bringing together whole realms of fact.., which had hitherto seemed poles apart. **1966** *Listener* 13 Jan. 75/2 The world which his symphony inhabits is poles apart from that of Bruckner's symphonic 'confession'. **1971** *Scope* (S. Afr.) 19 Mar. 32/3 He is poles removed from men like Carel de Wet on the one side and Douglas Mitchell on the other.

9. (Further examples.)

1898 G. B. Shaw *Plays Pleasant* p. xi, These are the opposite poles of our system, represented in practice by our first rate managements at the one end, and the syndicates which exploit pornographic musical farces at the other. **1935** B. Malinowski in M. Black *Importance of Lang.* (1962) 77 These two poles of linguistic effectiveness, the magical and the pragmatic. **1965** *New Statesman* 30 Apr. 690/2 At the opposite pole to Tchaikovsky's introversion stands Verdi.

9*. *Math.* A point *c* in whose neighbourhood the magnitude of a function $f(z)$ becomes infinite, but in such a way that, were the function multiplied by an appropriate power of $(z-c)$, it would remain finite.

1879 *Encycl. Brit.* IX. 819/2 A rational (non-integral) function has a certain number of infinities, or poles, each of them of a given multiplicity. **1893** Harkness & Morley *Treat. Theory of Functions* iii. 112 If $f(z)$ be infinite at *c*, while $(z-c)^m f(z)$ is regular at *c*, *m* being a finite positive integer, *c* is said to be a pole of the function, and *m* is said to be the order of multiplicity, or simply the order, of the pole. **1935** E. T. Copson *Introd. Theory of Functions of Complex Variable* iv. 79 If $f(z)$ has a pole at *a*, $|f(z)|$ tends to infinity as *z* tends to *a* in any manner. Moreover, if $f(z)$ has a pole of order *m* at *a*, $1/f(z)$ is regular and has a zero of order *m* there. **1968** P. A. P. Moran *Introd. Probability Theory* vii. 299 $\phi_1(z)$ is therefore an analytic function with no zeros or poles. **1973** L. J. Tassie *Physics Elem. Particles* xii. 162 $F(l, k)$ is an analytic function of *l* except for poles above or on the real axis. These poles in the complex angular momentum plane are called Regge poles. The positions of the poles are analytic functions of the energy.

10. pole-cell, delete '(sense 6)' and add: any of the cells which move to the posterior end of the embryo in certain invertebrate species, and subsequently give rise to the germ line; (further examples); [tr. G. *polzelle* (A. Weismann 1863, in *Zeitschr. f. wissensch. Zool.* XIII. 111)]; **pole-changer** (earlier example); **pole figure** *Metallurgy* [tr. G. *polfigur* (F. Wever 1924, in *Zeitschr. f. Physik* XXVIII. 72)], a circular diagram that is a stereographic projection of a sphere showing the positions of the poles of one or more lattice planes of a crystal or crystalline substance, the intensity of any spot in the diagram being proportional to the number of planes having the corresponding orientation; **pole-finding paper,** impregnated paper which can be used to identify the sign of an electric terminal or the like by the change of colour it undergoes when brought into contact with it; **pole-hunting** *vbl. sb.*, the act of going on an expedition to either the North or South Poles; **pole-piece** (later example); **pole-shoe** *Electr.*, a detachable extension of a pole-piece.

1941 Johannsen & Butt *Embryol. Insects & Myriapods* ii. 10 This mass of cells are [*sic*] the germ cells.., also called 'polar globules' or 'pole cells' by earlier writers. **1969** R. F. Chapman *Insects* xviii. 365 In the Nematocera all the pole cells migrate in to form the germ cells in the gonads. **1839** Pole changer [see *alternating *ppl. a.* d]. [**1938** *Mem. Geol. Soc. Amer.* VI. 101 These oriented textures have been..recorded in the pole-diagram of metallography.] **1943** *Proc. Amer. Soc. Testing Materials* XLIII. 785/1 The only feasible method for studying two-dimensional preferment such as this is to make a pole figure for the specimen. Such a pole figure is a summarization by stereographic projection of data obtained for one set of crystal planes from a series of X-ray photographs taken at different angles to the sheet. **1962** R. E. Smallman *Mod. Physical Metallurgy* vi. 205 The scatter about the ideal orientation can only be represented by means of a pole-figure which shows the spread of orientation about the ideal for a particular set of (*hkl*) poles. **1902** J. E. Hutton in A. C. Harmsworth *Motors* viii. 145 'Pole-finding' paper may also be used for this purpose. **1963** G. M. B. Dobson *Explor. Atmos.* v. 84 These instruments recorded on 'pole-finding' paper the sign of the electric current flowing through a long wire hanging from the balloon. **1907** *Daily Chron.* 30 July 4/6 The Nimrod..sails from the East India Dock today to pick up Lieutenant Shackleton..and convey him towards the South Pole... But the point is not merely that the Nimrod is to go Pole-hunting. **1920** *Glasgow Herald* Aug. 4/2 Such an expedition [to the Antarctic], undertaken not for Pole-hunting but for observation and collection in all possible branches of science, accumulates abundant material. **1962** M. G. Say *Conc. Encycl. Electr. Engin.* 337/1 The magnets..consist of a circular yoke of cast iron to which inwardly projecting laminated main pole pieces are bolted. **1892** S. P. Thompson *Dynamo-Electr. Machinery* (ed. 4) xxiii. 657 Field-magnet cores, 8½ inches long, 4½ inches diameter; pole-shoes, 8 inches by 3½ inches. **1901** Sheldon & Mason *Dynamo Electr. Machinery* iv. 75 Pole shoes are put on the ends of the pole pieces to distribute this flux over a wider area where it has to pass through the air. **1957** *Encycl. Brit.* VIII. 148/2 The enlarged portions of the poles near the armature are the pole shoes.

pole, *sb.*³ **1.** Substitute for def.: A marine flatfish, *Glyptocephalus cynoglossus*, of the family Pleuronectidæ, found in north-west European waters and on the North American side of the Atlantic; = Witch *sb.*⁴ (Later examples.)

1836 W. Yarrell *Hist. Brit. Fishes* II. 227 (*heading*) The Pole, or Craig Fluke. **1864** J. Couch *Hist. Fishes Brit. Islands* III. 190 The Pole is a fish of the Arctic Sea.

2. *Comb.* **pole-dab, -flounder** = prec. sense.

1838 *Mem. Wernerian Soc.* VII. 370 The Pole Dab is distinguished from the plaise [*sic*] in having no tubercles on the head. **1896** J. T. Cunningham *Marketable Marine Fishes* 233 The witch..has been called the pole dab, pole flounder, and long flounder by English naturalists. **1925** J. T. Jenkins *Fishes Brit. Isles* 184 The Witch, or Pole Dab, may be recognised by the fact that the eyes are on the right side of the head. **1969** A. Wheeler *Fishes Brit. Isles & N.-W. Europe* 542 (*heading*) Witch (Pole Dab). **1888, 1890** Pole Flounder [in Dict.]. **1896** [see *pole-dab* above].

pole, *v.*¹ Add: **4. c.** *Baseball.* To hit (the ball, a shot) hard. Also with *out*.

1905 C. Dryden *Champion Athletics* 40 At a tight spot in the game Hoffman poled out a vicious liner. **1943** *Amer. Speech* XVIII. 104 A batter who hits a line drive..is said ..to *pole one out*. **1976** *Webster's Sports Dict.* 326/1 *Pole*, to hit the ball hard.

8. To take advantage of someone; to impose or sponge *on*. *Austral. colloq.*

1906 E. Dyson *Fact'ry 'Ands* vi. 66 'What rot, girls; why don't yer get er shift on?' cried Feathers virtuously... ''Taint ther mealy pertater, polin' on the firm like this.' **1919** W. H. Downing *Digger Dialects* 38 *Poll*, to take advantage of another's good nature. **1938** X. Herbert *Capricornia* (1939) xxxii. 486 Call me a wastrel, would ya? You—why, you're poling on Jesus Christ! **1945** Baker *Austral. Lang.* v. 107 The N.S.W. Libraries Advisory Committee (1939)..said that inter-library loans had been summed up as 'poling instead of pooling'. **1946** K. Tennant *Lost Haven* (1947) xiv. 214 Only his own obstinacy kept him working, but Launce was as independent as any other man in Lost Haven. He wasn't going to pole on Alec. **1947** V. Palmer *Hail Tomorrow* i. 10, I asked him why he should come up north and pole on men who were trying to win decent conditions for themselves, but he said he wanted a holiday. **1953** 'Caddie' *Sydney Barmaid* xxxviii. 220 'And while there's anything in the Sutton cupboard, Caddie,' he assured me when I said I couldn't stay and pole on them, 'it's yours.' **1957** 'N. Culotta' *They're Weird Mob* (1958) xiii. 203 It [*sc.* bludger] means that you..'pole on yer mates'.

pole (pōul), *v.*² *Physics.* [f. Pole *sb.*², or a back-formation from *poling *vbl. sb.*²] *trans.* To render (a ferroelectric material) electrically polar by the temporary application of a strong electric field.

1961 *Proc. IRE* XLIX. 1162/1 Certain polycrystalline ferroelectric substances..can be given lasting polar properties, including pyroelectric and piezoelectric effects, by treatment with high electric fields for a short time. The term 'to pole' is recommended for this treatment. **1963** *IEEE Trans. Ultrasonic Engin.* X. 38/2 The shell is poled in the radial direction. **1976** *Ibid.* XXIII. 394/1 The bar is poled perpendicular to the length direction.

So **po·ling** *ppl. a.*

1956 *IRE Trans. Ultrasonic Engin.* IV. 55 The stress is applied along the axis of the poling field. **1961** *Proc. IRE* XLIX. 1166/2 The shear deformation..occurs in the plane containing both the poling and signal fields.

Pol. Econ., colloq. abbrev. of *Political Economy*. See Economy 3.

1893 W. K. Post *Harvard Stories* 12, I have not been tutoring you in Pol. Econ. **1900** *Dialect Notes* II. 16 Some tendencies in student English..are worth a passing remark. Most significant..is the tendency to use abbreviations... The subjects he studies..are all clipped... Thus he studies..*pol-econ* (political economy).

poled (pōuld), *a.*¹ [f. Pole *sb.*¹ or *v.*] **1.** Provided with or supported by a pole or poles.

1864 E. A. Parkes *Man. Pract. Hygiene* i. ix. 287 This is a two-poled tent, with a connecting ridge-pole. *Ibid.* 288 The first is a single poled pyramidal tent, with a second pole to sustain the entrance flap. **1894** *Westm. Gaz.* 1 Jan. 2/1 But it is pointed out that the proportion of 'poled' steamers, and of sailing ships with masts that can be readily lowered, is always increasing.

2. = Poleaxed *ppl. a.*

1920 *Outward Bound* Nov. 20/2 It caught him fairly above the ear so that he fell like a poled ox.

poled (pōuld), *a.*² *Physics.* [f. Pole *sb.*², *pole *v.*² + -ed¹, -ed².] Of a ferroelectric material: rendered electrically polar (see *pole *v.*²).

1961 *Proc. IRE* XLIX. 1162/1 Poled ferroelectric ceramics have become an important component in electromechanical devices. **1975** D. G. Fink *Electronics Engineers' Handbk.* vii. 58 Poled ferroelectric devices are capable of doing electric work when driven mechanically, or mechanical work when driven electrically.

polemicize (pole·misəiz), *v.* [f. Polemic *a.* and *sb.* + -ize.] *intr.* = Polemize *v.* Hence pole·micizing *vbl. sb.*

1953 *Encounter* Nov. 49/2 But Vigolo's edition arrived just in time to save Roman literary honour, and..to polemicise against her American view of the poet. **1968** *Listener* 6 June 728/3 You might want to polemicise and say: 'Hang on a minute! What about the swallowing up of small farms? What about the fact that British agriculture as a whole is subsidised by the taxpayer to the tune of something like three million pounds a year?' The trouble is that there isn't anyone to polemicise with. **1969** A. WALICKI in Ionescu & Gellner *Populism* 69 He sharply polemicized with Chernyshevsky and Dubroliubov, defending the spiritual heritage of the 'superfluous men' from the gentry. **1970** R. J. HOLLINGDALE tr. *Schopenhauer's Essays* 215 The polemicizing against the assumption of a life force which is now becoming fashionable.

polemology (pǫlĭmǫ·lŏdʒi). [f. Gr. πόλεμο- combining form of πόλεμος war + Gr. -λογία, -LOGY.] The science or study of war. Hence **polemological** *a.*; **polemo·logist.**

1938 *Nature* 23 Apr. 728/1 Last of all, perhaps, has been a lively call to solve the problems of polemology (*sit venia verbo*). **1968** *Sunday Times* 4 Feb. 53/3 Students of polemology will not find anything startlingly original in what he has to say. **1968** *N.Y. Times* 26 Aug. 35 There is a French Institute of Polemology in Paris and a Polemological Institute at Groningen in the Netherlands. **1970** H. ARENDT *On Violence* 59 A brand-new science, called 'polemology', has emerged. *Ibid.* 64 This..is precisely what the psychiatrists and polemologists concerned with human aggressiveness recommend. **1970** *Harper's* Dec. 28 Professor Gaston Bouthoul of the *Ecole des Hautes Etudes Sociales* in Paris..the founder of Polemology (a word he coined), or the study of war. **1976** *Times Lit. Suppl.* 2 Apr. 363/2 *Urban Guerrilla* contains the papers read at a conference in 1974 organized by the Polemological Centre of the Free University of Brussels.

polemonium (pǫlĭmōu·ni,ɒ̆m). [mod.L. (J. P. de Tournefort *Institutiones Rei Herbariæ* (1700) I. 146), a. Gk. πολεμώνιον: see POLEMONIACEOUS *a.*] An annual or perennial herb of the genus so called, belonging to the family Polemoniaceæ, native to America, Asia, or Europe, and bearing single or clustered bell-shaped flowers. Cf. JACOB'S LADDER 1.

1900 J. M. ABBOTT in W. D. Drury *Bk. Gardening* viii. 279 Polemoniums are free-flowering plants. **1931** *Times Educ. Suppl.* 25 July (Home & Classroom Sect.) p. iv/2 We fairly waded through flowers, including pale blue borage, mauve polemonium,..and blue primula. **1957** *Dict. Gardening* (R. Hort. Soc.) III. 1620/1 The Polemoniums are hardy and several good for the rock-garden, the larger ones for the border. **1968** J. BERRISFORD *Very Small Garden* viii. 95 Polemoniums, with their 'Jacob's ladder' leaves, and the taller geranium species are good.

Polenske (pŏle·nskə). [Name of E. *Polenske* (fl. 1904), German public health chemist.] *Polenske number or value*: a number expressing the proportion of volatile, water-insoluble fatty acids in a fat (see quot. 1973).

1906 *Analyst* XXXI. 259 When a low Reichert-Wollny figure was associated with fluid insoluble volatile acids, and especially when the Polenske number exceeded 2, the proof of the presence of cocoanut oil [in the butter] was fairly definite. *Ibid.* 260 He knew nothing about the Polenske value under these conditions. **1928** [see *KIRSCHNER]. **1936** *Analyst* LXVI. 407 (*heading*) Polenske (or insoluble volatile acid) value. **1973** D. PEARSON *Lab. Techniques Food Anal.* vi. 153 The proportion of butter fat present is frequently assessed from the Reichert and Polenske values... The Reichert value is the volume of 0·1 N alkali in millilitres required to neutralise the water-soluble volatile fatty acids distilled from 5 g of fat under specified conditions. From the same distillation, the Polenske value is the volume of 0·1 N alkali in millilitres required to neutralise the water-insoluble volatile fatty acids.

poler. Add: **3.** (Earlier and later N.Z. and Austral. examples.)

1863 S. BUTLER *First Year in Canterbury Settlement* vii. 105 The leaders..slewed sharply round, and tied themselves into an inextricable knot with the polars. **1878** E. S. ELWELL *Boy Colonists* 234 The polers, that is, the bullocks attached to the pole of the dray, and accustomed to bear the weight of the dray-load on their necks, are always the quietest. **1929** W. S. SMYTH *Bonzer Jones* 97 The 'polers' pulled back. **1936** I. L. IDRIESS *Cattle King* viii. 68 They call the two polers the pin bullocks, because they swing the turntable of the wagon! **1941** —— *Great Boomerang* vi. 48 The leaders had reared right back on the polers, the team in terrified confusion. **1959** H. P. TRITTON *Time means Tucker* ii. 36 A bullock-team is made up in four parts: polers, pin, body and leaders... The polers..have the job of steadying the dray or wagon while the pin-bullocks take the pull. **1972** *Sunday Mail Mag.* (Brisbane) 21 May 2/2 The team was made up as follows: Polers on the wagon pole were usually low set and chunky.

4. b. A boat propelled with a pole or poles.

1925 *Chambers's Jrnl.* Apr. 253/1, I was travelling by 'poler' because no steamer was available.

5. *Austral. slang.* A cadger, sponger; one who shirks work. Cf. *POLE *v.*[1] 8.

1938 X. HERBERT *Capricornia* (1939) xxxii. 486 'You long-jawed poler,' Norman roared. 'Living on the fat of the land, while your poor damn flock feeds on soup and coconuts and what they can root out of the bush.' **1945** [see *HUMMER *sb.*[2] 2]. **1947** I. DOUGLAS *Opportunity in Australia* 89 *Poler*, one who does not pull his weight. **1952** A. G. MITCHELL in *Chambers's Shorter Eng. Dict.* Suppl., *Poler*, one who sponges on another, or avoids his fair share of work... (The polers in a bullock team are yoked to the pole and often leave most of the pulling to the leading bullocks.)

pole-star. Add: **1.** (Later examples.)

The star α Ursæ Minoris is now (1982) within 1° of the north celestial pole, and will remain so until the 23rd c. A.D.

1946 DYLAN THOMAS *Deaths & Entrances* 24 Your pole-star neighbour, sun of another street, Will dive up to his tears. **1955** *Sci. News Let.* 27 Aug. 138/1 This group [*sc.* Ursa Minor] contains the little dipper, with Polaris, the pole star, at the end of the handle. **1979** R. LAIDLAW *Lion is Rampant* xiii. 108 As long as I could see The Plough I could get a fix on the Pole Star and check my direction.

polewards, *adv.* (Examples referring to another sense of POLE *sb.*[2]).

1895 *Anat. Anzeiger* XI. 74 The divergent limbs which travel polewards along the spindle are in reality the original halves of a chromosome, which has become doubled, or bent, upon itself. **1925** *Jrnl. Genetics* XV. 252 The constituent chromosomes of the bivalents are pulled polewards into loops.

poley, polley, *a.* and *sb.* Add: Also *N.Z.* and *U.S.* Also **polly. A.** *adj.* (Further examples.) Also *fig.*

1901 M. FRANKLIN *My Brilliant Career* xxviii. 233 A couple of dirty knives and forks, a pair of cracked plates, two poley cups and chipped saucers. *Ibid.* 234 A cup was broken, and another, also a poley, was put in its stead. **1922** JOYCE *Ulysses* 289 Angus heifers and polly bullocks of immaculate pedigree. **1930** L. G. D. ACLAND *Early Canterbury Runs* 1st Ser. vii. 173 A new-chum had a theory that if you turned your back on a beast and stooped down, and looked at him through your legs he wouldn't charge, and how a noted poley bullock completely exploded his theory. **1954** *Coast to Coast 1953–54* 14 Home made cartridges? There they go again! No. Poley chokes on their guns. That American idea for greater range.

B. *sb.* A type of saddle (see quots. 1958, 1966).

1958 *Amer. Speech* XXXIII. 167 *Poley*, a saddle without a pommel. **1966** BAKER *Austral. Lang.* (ed. 2) iii. 67 Another type of saddle is the *poley*. This is a saddle without kneepads—'like a poley bull without horns, but generally considered to be derived from polo saddle'. **1975** *Sunday Mail Mag.* (Brisbane) 26 Jan. 15/1 My own poley had had its day... Good second-hand saddles were not easy to come by.

polianite (pōu·liǎnəit). *Min.* [ad. G. *polianit* (A. Breithaupt 1844, in *Ann. der Physik* LXI. 191), f. Gr. πολιά greyness (in allusion to its colour): see -ITE[1].] A variety of pyrolusite that occurs as large well-formed crystals.

1849 J. NICOL *Man. Mineral.* 420 Polianite..acts like pure hyperoxide of manganese. **1937** *Mineral. Mag.* XXIV. 521 (*heading*) X-ray studies on pyrolusite (including polianite) and psilomelane. *Ibid.*, The present study had for its main objective an attempt to settle..the uncertainty existing as to the relationship between polianite and pyrolusite. **1969** *Mineral. Abstr.* XX. 289/1 The Mn oxides..have a microrhythmic structure..; in the veins they include polianite.

police, *sb.* Add: Also in reduced forms **polie** (*Sc.*), **p'leece,** etc. See also *POLIS[2]. **3. c.** (Earlier example.)

1834 J. KEMPER in *Wisconsin Hist. Coll.* (1898) XIV. 412 The towels, basins &c here are not what they ought to be. The police of the boat is bad.

5. a. (Further examples of *pl.* const.)

1922 JOYCE *Ulysses* 162 Squads of police marching out, back. **1970** *Daily Tel.* 27 June 1/4 One hundred police and 200 civilians yesterday searched lonely country around Stephen's home. **1973** *Ibid.* 21 Mar. 10 The factory-gate clash between 400 pickets and 232 police.. foreshadows a new style of strike demonstration. **1976** *Daily Record* (Glasgow) 4 Dec. 32/2 The police then gave evidence, after being told they need not answer questions.

c. (As a count noun.) A policeman. Chiefly *Sc.* and *U.S. colloq.*

1839 *Chicago American* 5 Sept., There is a police in attendance..in the theatre. **1856** 'MARK TWAIN' *Adv. Thomas Jefferson Snodgrass* (1928) 8 He was a police. **1890** J. KERR *Reminisc.* I. 98 Then for a while the loon to jail Was taken by a polie, O. **1904**, etc. [see *POLIS[2]]. **1951** M. MCLUHAN *Mechanical Bride* 107/2 Joyce's famous remark that, 'though he might have been more humble, there's no police like Holmes,' contains a world of insight. **1960** *Huntly Express* 19 Aug. 7 It was all over the market that 'the unco man wis a p'leece wi' plain claes'. **1964** J. H. CLARKE *Harlem* 277 He crawled out of th' door hollerin' for a police to save him. **1975** *Caribbean Contact* Feb. 14/1 His father was a police and his mother, familiarly known as 'Sister Lu', a laundry worker.

6. *police agent, ball, boat, cadet, car, cell, charge-sheet, chief, college, commissioner, cordon, courtroom, department, doctor, force* (earlier and later examples), *headquarters, horse, house* (examples), *jeep, laboratory, launch, medal, patrol, photograph, photographer, power, procedure, protection* (examples), *radio, raid, regulation, report, spy* (earlier and later examples), *spying, surgeon, system, van, woman* (further examples), *work*; also *police-aided, -controlled, -protected* adjs.; **police action,** (*a*) the deeds or activity of the police; (*b*) military intervention without a formal declaration of war when a nation or group within a nation is considered to be violating international law and peace; **police bail** (see quot. 1976); **police blotter**: see *BLOTTER 4; **police box,** (*a*) a box or kiosk containing a telephone specially for the use of police or of members of the public wishing to contact the police; (*b*) a reinforced shelter on London streets during the 1939–45 war for the protection of policemen on duty during an air raid; **police boy,** in European colonies or former European territories, a 'native' police assistant or security officer; **police captain,** (examples); also *Ireland*; **police cruiser** *N. Amer.*, a police patrol car; **police dispatcher** *U.S.*, a member of the staff of a police station who receives information about crimes and transmits it to police patrols; **police dog,** (*a*) a dog employed by the police to track and capture criminals, to find lost persons, etc.; (*b*) = *ALSATIAN *sb.* B.2; **police grip** *rare*, a grip or hold used by policemen; **police informer,** a criminal who gives information about crime to the police; **police judge,** also *U.S.*; **police lock,** (see quot. 1975); **police matron,** a policewoman who takes charge of women or juveniles at a police station or in court; **police message** (see quot. 1941); **police novel,** a detective novel in which police procedures in detecting crime form the central interest; **police officer** (later example); **police orphanage,** a home for the orphans of policemen; **police positive,** a type of Colt's pistol; **police procedural** *a.*, of or pertaining to police procedure, applied *spec.* to a type of crime detection story; also as *sb.*, = **police novel*; **police record,** a dossier kept by the police on all persons convicted of crime; hence, a past which includes some conviction for crime; **police reporter,** a newspaper reporter who concentrates on stories concerning crime and police activity; **police science,** the science dealing with the investigation of crime; so **police scientist**; **police siren,** the siren on a police vehicle; **police special,** a type of revolver; **police trap,** an arrangement made by police for detecting motorists who exceed the speed limit, or for apprehending criminals or other wanted persons; also *fig.*; so **police-trapped** *a.*; **police whistle,** a special type of loud whistle used by the police; **police-witness,** a witness whose testimony supports a police prosecution.

1885 *Encycl. Brit.* XIX. 334/1 Police action in relation to the serious matters constituting crime is familiar knowledge. **1933** *Week-end Rev.* 1 July 17/1 Blurring the distinction between war the duel and 'police action'. **1959** *Chambers's Encycl.* VII. 512/2 The Dutch started the first 'police action' and occupied large parts of the republic. After United Nations intervention a truce agreement was signed. **1968** *Listener* 19 Dec. 821/3 What's the difference..between police action and war, if the soldiers of the two sides are killing each other? **1978** G. VIDAL *Kalki* iii. 51 He would have been able to avoid the Vietnam war—or 'police action', to properly designate that valiant attempt to save Southeast Asia for the free world. **1852** E. E. HALE *If, Yes, & Perhaps* (1868) 44, I had told the police agent he might send it to the St. Nicholas. **1930** G. B. SHAW *Apple Cart* p. xvi, Proletariats are never revolutionary, and..their direct action, when it is controlled at all, is usually controlled by police agents. **1910** *Times* 21 Mar. 13/1 Mr. Winston Churchill will visit Brighton on April 2 to make himself acquainted with the Brighton police aided scheme for clothing poor children, in which the King recently showed an interest. **1922** JOYCE *Ulysses* 670 Embroidery, darning or knitting for the policeaided clothing society. **1976** *Daily Tel.* 6 Feb. 2/8 Where the police are unable to complete their inquiries immediately, they also have power under the Magistrates' Courts Act 1952 to grant what is known as 'police bail'. The person in custody is required to enter into a recognizance, with or without sureties, to appear again at a police station at a certain time for further questioning. **1977** *Gay News* 24 Mar. 1/3 All the customers were released on police bail. **1969** C. WATSON *Bump in Night* ii. 26 Don't forget it's the police ball on the 14th. **1973** *Guardian* 12 Mar. 1/8 Saturday night's killings occurred while most of Bermuda's unarmed police force were at the semi-annual police ball. **1873** G. LENING *Dark Side of N.Y. Life* 155 The six police-boats cannot be usefully employed on the rivers in the interest of commerce. **1890** A. CONAN DOYLE *Sign of Four* ix. 182, I shall want a fast police-boat—a steam-launch—to be at the Westminster Stairs at seven o'clock. **1943** *Sun* (Baltimore) 13 Dec. 5/1 The children and guarding against sabotage now present the greatest number of police-boat problems. **1975** 'A. HALL' *Mandarin Cypher* vii. 105 A police boat had put to sea at full speed. **1932** *Daily Tel.* 23 May 12/2 A policeman was cut off in a police-box by 10ft of water and had to be rescued. **1940** R. MORRISH *Police & Crime-Detection* iii. 36 Many police districts now possess their police-box system, by means of which officers performing duty in outlying districts are able to communicate with their stations. **1941** *Newsweek* 13 Oct. 29 One of many air-raid precautions taken in the British capital for the expected winter Luftwaffe attacks is the building of 'police boxes' at street intersections. The reinforced brick shelters will protect London Bobbies on duty during Nazi air raids. **1971** R. Amberley *Ordinary Accident* xiii. 116 Someone, evidently ringing from the police box on the Banbury road. **1946** C. B. Jeppe *Gold Mining on Witwatersrand* II. xvi. 1758 On all the mines of the Witwatersrand (1943) there were 142 Europeans and 1,887 native 'police boys' in the police organisation (underground and surface). **1961** *Quest* Oct./Dec. 33/2 Motu prevailed over the candidates firstly because it was based on the speech of the police-boys who formed the larger part of the total mobilized section of the population, and secondly because these police-boys were much more accessible to the ordinary people than the English-speaking rulers. **1971** *Sunday Times* (Johannesburg) 28 Mar. 16/5 This clause shall not apply to..labourers and watch men or police boys. **1959** M. Gilbert *Blood & Judgement* xii. 131 A police cadet motor-cyclist was propping his machine up. **1976** *Southern Even. Echo* (Southampton) 12 Nov. 15/6 He wanted to become a police cadet—and had even been to the police station to find out details of what was involved in following this career. **1834** M. Edgeworth *Let.* in *Tour in Connemara & Martins of Ballinahinch* (1950) 93 The cottage at the end of the walk to Swinnerton, in which I believe a police-captain Henderson lived in your time. **1902** *Chambers's Jrnl.* Oct. 674/1 The next grade above is that of sergeant. Above this comes the police captain. **1976** H. Nielsen *Brink of Murder* xxi. 187 He's smart. He knew the odds against nailing a police captain. **1924** A. Christie *Poirot Investigates* viii. 221 A large police car was waiting for us, with some plain-clothes men. **1931** E. S. Gardner *Candy Kid* in *Case of Crying Swallow* (1972) 92 The two men in the police car glimpsed boxes of candy in the rear of the sedan. **1971** B. Patten *Irrelevant Song* 62 The sirens wailing on police-cars. **1898** *McClure's Mag.* X. 547/2 He was still in the infirmary attached to the police-cells. **1965** D. Francis *For Kicks* xix. 240 Four nights and three days in a police cell. **1977** J. Wainwright *Do Nothin'* xiii. 220 They are already on their way to some all-mod-con police cell. **1922** Joyce *Ulysses* 180 Police chargesheets crammed with cases get their percentage manufacturing crime. **1961** Copp & Peck *Betrayal at UN* iv. xxi. 208 Colonel Frank Begley, former Police Chief of Farmington, Conn., and now head of U.N. special police. **1974** E. Ambler *Dr Frigo* ii. 104 How does he reward him? Make him police chief or head of intelligence? **1977** H. Fast *Immigrants* i. 65 He could have Mayor McCarthy and Police Chief Martin as guests in his house. **1936** N. Marsh *Death in Ecstasy* ix. 109 Have you been through the Police College? **1958** S. Hyland *Who goes Hang?* i. v. 24 The senior lecturer in forensic studies at any of your admirable police colleges. **1976** *Daily Mail* (Hull) 16 Dec., He was chosen as the first member of that rank to go to the Police College at Ryton on Dunsmore. **1869** *Harper's Mag.* Oct. 754/1 The system of relief that has now become the perplexity of the Police Commissioners. **1911** *Daily Colonist* (Victoria, B.C.) 11 Apr. 7/1 A meeting of the police commissioners will be held this afternoon..when the department's estimates for the year will be considered. **1977** *Hongkong Standard* 12 Apr. 8/3 The courageous, determined and almost unique efforts of former Police Commissioner C.S. to root out internal graft backfired. **1939** H. Hodge *Cab, Sir?* 236 A police-controlled cross-roads. **1961** *Times* 6 Dec. 15/5 Let him [*sc.* the Minister of Transport] give us more police-controlled and light-controlled crossings. **1970** 'D. Halliday' *Dolly & Cookie Bird* xii. 193 I'd put a police cordon round the house with orders not to let anyone through. **1979** J. Gardner *Nostradamus Traitor* xvi. 59 He carried ID which would get him through any police cordon. **1866** 'Mark Twain' *Lett. from Hawaii* (1967) 28 The old police courtroom in San Francisco. **1937** C. Himes *Black on Black* (1973) 143 He broke away..before the police cruiser got there. **1958** 'Castle' & 'Hailey' *Flight into Danger* viii. 107 At the turn-off from the main highway..a police cruiser stood..its roof-light blinking a constant warning. **1974** *Globe & Mail* (Toronto) 16 Jan. 8/5 With the red light flashing, the police cruiser tails the motorist down the street and flags him over to the curb. **1976** *Billings* (Montana) *Gaz.* 2 July 8-B/4 In Louisville, police began a slowdown and 41 police cruisers notified headquarters they had been disabled by flat tires. **1810** *Rec. Early Hist. Boston* (1904) XXXIII. 495 In the estimate of expences for the..year, a sum was named for the police department. **1931** E. S. Gardner *Vanishing Corpse* in *Case of Crying Swallow* (1972) 107 [He] was on terms of intimacy with most of the police department heads. **1963** 'E. McBain' *Ten Plus One* (1964) 24 The police department is a vast organization, and a detective is only an organization man. **1977** H. Fast *Immigrants* ii. 110 In the annals of the San Francisco Police Department, a dead Chinese was statistically different from a dead Caucasian. **1973** *Tucson* (Arizona) *Daily Citizen* 22 Aug. 11/1 Police dispatcher Bill Pyles called an aid car, then began telling Mrs. Sweet how to keep little Jeremy from dying. **1976** *Billings* (Montana) *Gaz.* 2 July 1-A/2 Heagerty was about to be fined when a police dispatcher intervened and told the judge of Heagerty's plans. **1934** M. Allingham *Death of Ghost* vii. 86 The altruistic murderer is rare, and of course I couldn't say what the chances of your being one were until we have the evidence of the police doctor. **1972** K. Royce *Miniatures Frame* viii. 103 If I knew anything of police doctors the fuzz would ring around for hours until one reluctantly agreed to come. **1908** *Daily Chron.* 28 Aug. 7/2 Most of the principal German towns possess police dogs. **1911** *Chambers's Jrnl.* Feb. 136/1 What is needed as an ideal police-dog is an animal that can not only track well, but that can attack the criminal. **1925** F. Scott Fitzgerald *Great Gatsby* ii. 32 I'd like to get one of those police dogs; I don't suppose you got that kind? **1974** *Encycl. Brit. Macropædia* XIV. 672/1 Police dogs. The training of dogs for police work was originally developed in Ghent, Belgium, about 1900 and was soon copied elsewhere. **1838** Dickens in *Bentley's Misc.* Sept. 222 Professor Nogo wished to be informed what amount of automaton police force it was proposed to raise. **1956** H. Nicolson *Diary* 2 Nov. (1968) 314 There is a suggestion..that UNO should police the area, but it will take a long time before the police-force can be assembled. **1968** *Listener* 21 Nov. 667/1 As I saw it, the UN must move quickly to set up some kind of international police force. **1976** *Daily Record* (Glasgow) 4 Dec. 2/5 More than 1000 officers from every prison, police force, and state mental institution in the country turned up for the funeral service at Carnwath village in Lanarkshire. **1910** Police grip [see *ju-jitsu *sb.*]. **1875** M. D. Landon *E. Perkins* 237 The first thing you must do after the child is lost is to go to the Police Headquarters. **1952** Auden *Nones* 37 Between the burnt-out Law Courts and Police Headquarters. **1971** W. J. Burley *Guilt Edged* i. 9 The new police headquarters on the outskirts of the city. **1935** N. Mitchison *We have been Warned* iv. 453 She was knocked down.. almost under the nose of a police horse. **1973** R. Busby *Pattern of Violence* x. 157 A troop of police horses from the mounted branch held the crowd back. **1969** J. Wainwright *Big Tickle* 52 To live in his own house and not a 'police house' gave Cohen a freedom denied most police officers. **1974** L. Lamb *Man in Mist* viii. 51 Its [*sic*] P.C. Marchant, sir, who has the police house at Buntingbury. **1965** N. Freeling *Criminal Conversation* ii. xx. 191 [He] looked like a gentleman... Janus had never imagined he might be a police informer. **1969** G. Greene *Travels with my Aunt* i. vii. 60 He suspected me to be some unsavoury police informer. **1977** M. Kenyon *Rapist* vi. 73 Is it police informer I'm to be now, Sergeant? **1972** E. Hargreaves *Fair Green Weed* vii. 89 A sergeant, a corporal and a young police doctor arrived in the police jeep. **1956** B. Holiday *Lady sings Blues* (1973) ii. 23 It was Magistrate Jean Hortense Norris, the first woman police judge in New York, a tough hard-faced old dame. **1976** *Pioneer* (Big Timber, Montana) 30 June 12/2 He served in the Armed Forces during World War II, was a Montana Highway Patrolman and a police judge for the City of Billings. **1937** D. & H. Teilhet *Feather Cloak Murders* v. 85 The Chinese gentleman in the police laboratory removed the wicked little steel dart from under the Zeiss microscope. **1974** 'R. Tate' *Birds of Blooded Feather* iii. 53 He's a policeman... Something to do with the police laboratories. **1940** R. Morrish *Police & Crime-Detection* iii. 39 Some of the police-launches on the river Thames are also fitted with radio. **1972** *Police Rev.* 1 Dec. 1565/2 Section Officer Marshall swept the pale blue and white Police launch across the lake surface. **1975** J. Aiken *Voices in Empty House* 15 The apartment was further defended by a police lock, a rod which fastened into place on the back of the door and hooked into the floor, so that the door would not open beyond a certain point. **1976** *New Yorker* 1 Mar. 33/2 She slammed the door and I heard the police lock snap into place, then silence. **1934** Webster, Police matron. **1942** A. Christie *Body in Library* xiv. 133 In the corner of Superintendent Harper's office sat an elderly lady... She was certainly no police matron. **1972** R. Bloch *Night-World* (1974) xvii. 113 You'd have a police matron assigned to you, but they wouldn't put you in a cell. **1955** M. Allingham *Beckoning Lady* ii. 72 Divisional Detective Chief Inspector Charles Luke..had emerged from hospital with..a recommendation for the coveted Police Medal. **1977** 'A. York' *Tallant for Trouble* ii. 13 He had proved..a good policeman..his courage during one of Guyana's mini-revolutions had earned him a Queen's Police Medal. **1938** N. Marsh *Artists in Crime* xv. 219 The B.B.C. had instructions to send out a police message. **1941** *B.B.C. Gloss. Broadcasting Terms* 23 *Police Message*, message broadcast at the request of the police authorities. **1968** T. Stoppard *Real Inspector Hound* 13 We interrupt our programme for a special police message. **1896** G. B. Shaw *Our Theatres in Nineties* (1932) II. 223 As a novel, I can pass my idle hour with it, just as Bismarck used to pass his with the police novels of Du Boisgobey. **1908** G. K. Chesterton *All Things Considered* 116 The police novel..permits privacy only to explode and smash privacy. **1972** J. Symons *Bloody Murder* xiv. 197 The police novel, or the police-procedural as it has recently been called, concentrates upon the detailed investigation of a crime from the point of view of the police. **1976** M. Underwood *Menaces* xii. 114 Having been a police officer, she was much better equipped than most to be the wife of one. **1938** M. Allingham *Fashion in Shrouds* xx. 360 [He] made the suggestion as if he were announcing a rich gift to the Police Orphanage. **1972** M. Gilbert *Body of Girl* xxiii. 199 Any unclaimed money goes to the Police Orphanage. **1899** Somerville & 'Ross' *Some Experiences Irish R.M.* iii. 63 Flurry espied the police patrol on the road. **1936** 'N. Blake' *Thou Shell of Death* xiv. 258 On the main road he'd have to go straight for a bit, and the police patrols would be out. **1947** *Sun* (Baltimore) 7 May 7/3 At first, the jail visitors balked at riding to the prison in a police patrol wagon. **1969** M. Pugh *Last Place Left* xxix. 209, I suppose you'll recognize a police patrol car? **1974** *Times* 4 Oct. 3/3 She was given the task of observing the strength of police patrols. **1943** G. Greene *Ministry of Fear* iii. i. 163 A police photograph is like a passport photograph... We protest: This isn't me. **1965** E. S. Gardner *Case of Beautiful Beggar* (1972) 7 He took us into the police laboratory and museum, and started explaining the cases on which he had worked..all..illustrated by police photographs. **1978** 'A. Garve' *Counterstroke* i. 38 There were two police photographs, full face and profile. **1931** M. Allingham *Police at Funeral* xv. 206 Mr. Bowditch and a police photographer had completed their work on the footprint. **1970** W. J. Burley *To kill a Cat* i. 21 The police photographers..had already taken pictures of the undisturbed room. **1907** *Yesterday's Shopping* (1969) 642/1 Colt's new police positive revolver. **1931** 'G. Trevor' *Murder at School* xii. 244 This is what is called a Colt Point 22 Police Positive. Not a nice thing to be plugged with. **1975** J. Gores *Hammett* (1976) xxxii. 221 He took out the long-barreled police positive... He thumbed back the hammer. **1827** *U.S. Supreme Court Rep.* XXV. 442 The power to direct the removal of gun-powder is a branch of the police power which unquestionably remains..with the states. **1932** N. M. Butler *Looking Forward* xi. 168 'Police power'—which in American law means the principle that the public interest often requires the extension of government authority in repression..of individual activity or habit. **1964** Gould & Kolb *Dict. Social Sciences* 508/2 *Police power* may be defined as the broad and elastic power of government especially of one of the states of the United States, to restrict, control, regulate, and restrain individuals and groups in the use of their liberty and property in order to protect and promote the health, safety, morals, convenience, peace, order, and general welfare of other individuals and the public generally. **1967** *Punch* 16 Aug. 256/1 Police-procedural thrillers must be original to compete, yet, of their nature, ordinarily plausible. **1972** 'L. Egan' *Paper Chase* (1973) iii. 40 She'd always read mysteries, but mostly..what they call the police-procedural ones. **1972** [see **police novel* above]. **1977** *Time* 27 June 56/2 *Laidlaw* is also the first police procedural by Scottish Author William McIlvanney. **1885** *Encycl. Brit.* XIX. 337/1 If they [*sc.* orders having the approval of the secretary of state for the government of the metropolitan police] are carefully considered and prepared, their issue must produce a uniform code of police procedure for the force. **1974** *Publishers Weekly* 5 Aug. 51/2 European police procedure buffs might enjoy this, but the author makes it hard for the reader to grapple with the evidence. **1976** 'J. Charlton' *Remington Set* iii. 18, I wish I had a book somewhere I could look up police procedure in. **1901** *Sketch* 17 July 518/2 Herr Kubelik..will have to be police-protected against the patrons of Señor Sarasate. **1908** *London Mag.* Oct. 240, I would demand police protection. **1942** E. Paul *Narrow St.* xvi. 125 Mariette.. footed the bills of the establishment,..arranged police protection and gave the place its personality and reputation for fair play. **1972** C. Drummond *Death at Bar* i. 40 Hundreds of people in this wicked city would relish the idea of police protection. **1958** A. Budrys in *Venture Sci. Fict.* Mar. 14/2 He'd used a police radio often enough. **1975** *Listener* 2 Jan. 26/1 The loudspeakers.. crackled with voices from a police radio in the streets. **1919** G. B. Shaw *Heartbreak House* p. xx, The ordinary law was superseded by Acts under which newspapers were seized and their printing machinery destroyed by simple police raids *à la Russe*. **1933** J. Buchan *Prince of Captivity* iii. i. 277 That cheerful party broke up in confusion... Yes, a police raid. **1975** *Country Life* 16 Jan. 155/1 A recent police raid led to the arrest of a well-organized gang. *a* **1911** D. G. Phillips *Susan Lenox* (1917) II. xi. 277 Once in the pariah class, once with a 'police record'. **1950** T. Walsh *Nightmare in Manhattan* iv. 106 Calhoun was examining his police record, which was long and bad. **1972** J. Wainwright *Night is Time to Die* 92 He has no police record. No previous convictions. **1802** C. Wilmot *Diary* in *Irish Peer on Continent* (1920) 61 It is a good display of the Police regulations, for such order, method, and tranquillity I cou'd not have imagined. **1853** E. Twisleton *Let.* 23 May (1928) v. 85 Owing to the recent revolts, all the police-regulations were doubled in stringency. **1938** R. G. Collingwood *Princ. Art* xi. 255 Philosophical controversies are not to be settled by a kind of police-regulation governing people's choice of words. **1978** N. Freeling *Night Lords* i. 7 It was forbidden to park on the bridge. A lot Castang cared for municipal police regulations—. **1837** H. Martineau *Society in America* I. i. iii. 77 The disgustingly jocose tone of their [*sc.* British] police reports, where crimes are treated as entertainments. **1882** C. M. Yonge *Three Brides* xix. 265 Such disgraces to England as I see in your police reports—brutal mechanics beating their wives. **1915** F. M. Hueffer *Good Soldier* i. iii. 31, I used..to inspect the little police reports that each guest was expected to sign upon taking a room. **1976** J. Lee *Ninth Man* 257 Most of our leads so far have come from police reports. **1834** *Sun* (N.Y.) 23 July 2/3 Your police reporter be one dam liar. **1959** [see *corn belt* s.v. *corn *sb.*[1] 11]. **1977** L. Meyer *Capitol Crime* i. 9 The story..was Sid Jacobson's, our police reporter. **1961** Webster, Police science. **1971** *Publishers' Weekly* 6 Dec. 22/3 The Glencoe Press..is doing very well with curricula in such new areas as fire science and police science. **1979** *Internat. Jrnl. Sociol. of Law* Feb. 112 Solomon's Soviet criminologists seem to be very similar to American 'police science' experts and to government scientific officers anywhere in the West. **1957** *Encycl. Brit.* XII. 562/2 A police scientist does not have to be an expert in every branch of chemical analysis to use these instruments effectively. **1976** *Billings* (Montana) *Gaz.* 16 June 3-B/2 Ticks enclosed in an envelope received in the mail..were being studied by police scientists Tuesday to see if they were..infected with numerous diseases. **1937** 'M. Innes' *Hamlet, Revenge!* ii. i. 98 Billups would not have thought to requisition a fire-engine, the Prime Minister had. Its bell, he explained, gained more respect than did a police siren. **1956** B. Holiday *Lady sings Blues* (1973) viii. 77 When the bus pulled out, you could hear the old sheriff's police siren coming after us. **1974** M. Birmingham *You can help Me* v. 132 The police sirens wailed up the street. **1959** I. Jefferies *Thirteen Days* viii. 100 The Legion officers had thirty-eight police specials, the peak of revolver achievement. **1970** 'J. Morris' *Candywine Development* xxiv. 263 That guy; he's holding something heavy. Police Special, maybe, or a ·44 magnum. **1849** J. S. Mill in *Westm. Rev.* LI. 4 Chenu..is now admitted to have been..a police spy. *c* **1874** D. Boucicault in M. R. Booth *Eng. Plays of 19th Cent.* (1969) II. 193 The police spy—Harvey Duff—the man that denounced me. **1922** J. Hergesheimer *Bright Shawl* (1923) 66 Probably we are all ruined... The police spies will be waiting for us at home. **1973** G. Sims *Hunters Point* xviii. 165 You police spies don't seem to be a very efficient bunch, letting an old man be drowned while you are supposed to be keeping a watch on him. *Ibid.* 166 It's just more police spying activity. **1868** *N.Y. Herald* 2 July 8/3 Dr. Waterman, police surgeon, was called and dressed the wounds. **1928** D. L. Sayers *Unpleasantness at Bellona Club* xxi. 274 'Nervous shock with well-marked delusions,' said the police surgeon. **1978** N. Freeling *Night Lords* v. 23 I'll have the Parquet and the police surgeon standing by. Autopsy and lab report. **1885** *Encycl. Brit.* XIX. 336/2 The police system of necessity involves the existence in a district of police stations or lock-ups, for the temporary detention of prisoners. *a* **1963** C. S. Lewis *Discarded Image* (1964) v. 94 On the imaginative and emotional level it makes a great difference whether, with the medievals, we project upon the universe our strivings and desires, or with the moderns, our police-system and our traffic regulations. **1903** *World's Work* July 123/2 To set police traps for a man going thirteen miles an hour on an open road is sheer idiocy. **1914** BEERBOHM *James Pethel* in *English Rev.* Dec. 18 In France he always rather missed the British police-traps. **1966** M. R. D. FOOT *SOE in France* vii. 173 The others fell successively into a Vichy police trap..at the Villa des Bois. **1974** J. WAINWRIGHT *Evidence* iv. 23 Motorways..were..police traps: box canyons into which a man on the run could be flushed and cornered. **1902** *Pall Mall Mag.* XXVIII. 410/2 Every police-constable on the much-police-trapped Ripley Road. **1859** G. A. SALA *Twice round Clock* 201 Then..troublesome bodies..are securely shackled and straight-waistcoated up, and carted away in police-vans. **1976** DEAKIN & WILLIS *Johnny go Home* ii. 49 She was in a police van on her way to Holloway. **1884** SWEET & KNOX *Through Texas* iv. 50 He began blowing a police-whistle. **1922** JOYCE *Ulysses* 160 Police whistle in my ears still. **1967** O. WYND *Walk Softly* x. 163, I..blew a long blast on a police whistle. **1979** J. SCOTT *Clutch of Vipers* x. 175 A whistle blew. A good old-fashioned police whistle such as is rarely heard nowadays. **1932** 'SOLICITOR' *Eng. Justice* iii. 94 On his version, supported by witnesses, he was clearly innocent. He seemed surprised when I said he was to plead 'Not guilty', and said, 'But there's a police witness.'..He got off. **1979** *Internat. Jrnl. Sociol. of Law* Feb. 71 The average Nigerian..believes that to be a police witness is almost as bad as being the criminal offender. *a* **1930** D. H. LAWRENCE *Apocalypse* (1931) xvi. 233 Ah woman, you have known many bitter experiences. But never, never before have you been condemned by the old dragon to be a policewoman. **1955** W. GADDIS *Recognitions* II. vi. 560 A policewoman handed that nomadic laundress over to the stronger arm of the law. **1976** *Birmingham Post* 16 Dec. 3/5 Policewoman Susan Oliver, who was the first police officer on the scene, said lights on the side of the lorry's trailer were illuminated at the time of the accident. **1937** 'M. INNES' *Hamlet, Revenge!* II. ii. 112 In plain police-work you could usually go straight for the truth. **1960** 'E. MCBAIN' *Give Boys Great Big Hand* (1962) iii. 20 Police work is not for you..if you..believe that corpses 'look just like they're sleeping'. **1977** L. MEYNELL *Hooky gets Wooden Spoon* xiii. 152 The basic rule of police work —get it down on paper.

policeless *a.* (earlier example).

1882 E. W. HAMILTON *Diary* 2 Sept. (1972) I. 331 It was determined yesterday to dismiss summarily those insubordinate men; and the act of their dismissal was followed by the resignation of the force *en masse*. Accordingly Dublin is police-less.

police, *v.* Add: **2. b.** (Earlier and later examples.) Also const. *up*, as of an area: cf. *CLEAN *v.* 6 c.

1851 *Colburn's United Service Mag.* LXVII. 57 All hands were then distributed in separate parties..to 'police' or clean round the garrison. **1930** *Amer. Speech* V. 380 Nearly all our old army expressions were taken to France with the A.E.F. *Bunk fatigue*,.. *police up*, and *salvage* are some of these. **1956** *Ibid.* XXXI. 108 *Police up* (clean up an area). **1968** *Listener* 9 May 594/2 'Last night we *policed up* two sampans, killing six enemy,' said an Airborne major in modest triumph. **1977** M. HERR *Dispatches* i. 26 Some troops..were pissing on the ground... The men finished.. and walked away laughing, leaving the captain alone shouting orders to police up the filth, thousands of empty and half-eaten ration cans, soggy clots of *Stars and Stripes*, and M-16 that someone had just left lying there and, worse, evidence of a carelessness unimaginable to the captain, it stank even in the cold rain, but it would police itself in an hour or two if the rain kept up.

3. c. (Earlier and later examples.)

1885 F. W. MAITLAND *Justice & Police* x. 112 The Cornish St. Ives, without a commission of the peace, polices, or lately policed, itself. **1928** R. STRANGER *Wireless* xii. 150 Being policed by the aerial potentials the filament electrons will pass through in varying numbers. **1943** *Sun* (Baltimore) 13 Dec. 18/1 Lucien E. D. Gaudreau, area rent director, said yesterday that the agency definitely will not 'police' rent regulations. **1946** *R.A.F. Jrnl.* May 176 The future work of B.A.F.O. is to police the Reich in the sky. **1946** *Rep. Internat. Control Atomic Energy* (U.S. Dept. of State) II. iii. 15 While suppression is not possible where we are dealing with the quest for knowledge, this thirst to know (that cannot be 'policed' out of existence) *can* be used. **1970** T. LUPTON *Managem. & Social Sci.* (ed. 2) ii. 52 The organization cannot effectively police every individual item of behaviour. **1974** *Socialist Worker* 26 Oct. 14/5 It seems now that the social contract is to be policed by trade union leaders. **1977** *Time* 15 Aug. 37/2 He believes that fund members will approve some new articles that will enable him to police currency exchange rates.

policeable (pǒlī·săb'l), *a.* [f. POLICE *v.* + -ABLE.] That can be policed.

1926 H. W. FOWLER *Mod. Eng. Usage* 443/1 *Police*, vb., makes *-ceable*. **1976** *Listener* 23 Dec. 802/2 When those frontiers sucked forces too far inland for their logistical support, disasters like Kabul or Majuba compelled London to fall back on more policeable limits. **1979** *Guardian* 15 Jan. 12/2 There was no question at the moment of any action against secondary picketing... 'One has to find out if it is illegal. And if you make it illegal, is it policeable?'

police court. (Further examples.)

1930 D. H. LAWRENCE *Nettles* 19 And Mr. Mead..said: 'Gross! coarse! hideous!'—and I, like a silly Thought he meant the faces of the police-court officials. **1964** [see *FORM *sb.* 16 c]. **1965** [see *MAGISTRATE *sb.* 3]. **1979** S. WEINTRAUB *London Yankees* iv. 113 English readers discovered Frederic in the newspaper transcripts from Croydon Police Court in 1898.

policedom. (Earlier example.)

1866 *Chambers's Jrnl.* 22 Sept. 608/1 Of Antoine the imperturbable, when he returned home,.. policedom could make nothing.

policeman. Add: **1. a.** (Earlier examples.)

1801 R. MUSGRAVE *Mem. Different Rebellions in Ireland* I. 227 They boasted that they had killed the policemen at Dunboyne. **1824** J. S. MILL in *Westm. Rev.* II. 22 Thus they went on..till November 1822, when,..in rushed the sheriff with a number of police men.

c. A police informer. *slang.*

[**1874** HOTTEN *Slang Dict.* 257 *Policeman*,..among the dangerous classes, a man who is unworthy of confidence, a sneak or mean fellow.] **1923** E. WALLACE *Missing Million* xv. 128 Being an amateur, he left his finger-prints, and it's no job of mine to let 'em stay. 'Live and let live' is one of my mottoes, and 'Thou shalt not be a policeman' is another. *Ibid.* xvi. 134 Casey is a born 'policeman', and would sell his own mother if you paid him the right kind of money. **1924** [see *COPPER *v.*[2] 2].

d. *Naut.* (See quots.)

1933 P. A. EADDY *Hull Down* 179 One of the boys, who was acting as 'policeman' (one of the watch who is told off to rouse the rest, should the Mate suddenly want them), came banging on the lamp-locker door. **1962** A. G. COURSE *Dict. Nautical Terms* 151 *Policeman*, a name used in sailing ships for the member of the watch on deck who kept awake to hear the officer's orders and call his shipmates.

e. *fig.* A person or object regarded as a deterrent or obstacle. In phr. *sleeping policeman*: a ramp in the road intended to jolt a moving motor vehicle, thereby encouraging motorists to reduce their speed.

1951 E. COXHEAD *One Green Bottle* iii. 79 The climb above the crux was even more delightful; a knife-edge.. then a stone policeman barring the way. **1969** G. E. EVANS *Farm & Village* viii. 80 After the farm-workers had cleared a field of the crop they left one sheaf standing on it. This last sheaf was called the *Policeman*, and it was understood that no gleaner could enter the field while the Policeman was on guard. **1969** L. THOMPSON in R. Blythe *Akenfield* i. 35 The policeman was the name given to the last trave or stook which the farmers would leave standing in the middle of the field so they could have time to rake-up all the loose corn they could before the gleaners arrived. There was one farmer who made a habit of keeping the gleaners waiting and one night a young man stole the 'policeman'. **1973** *Guardian* 27 Feb. 1/4 Labour intends to..build 'sleeping policemen' (ridges) into residential and shopping streets to slow traffic down. **1974** *Times* 24 July 4/7 The government would proceed with experiments in the use of 'sleeping policemen'—road humps to slow motorists.

2. *Chem.* A glass rod or tube with a short piece of rubber tubing on one end (see also quot. 1963).

1916 F. A. GOOCH *Representative Procedures in Quantitative Chem. Analysis* iii. 64 The precipitate, transferred from the container to the filter..with the aid of a rubber-tipped glass rod (the 'policeman'). **1930** W. T. HALL *Textbk. Quantitative Analysis* xi. 149 This so-called policeman may be made by sticking together the end of a piece of rubber tubing that fits the rod tightly. **1963** N. L. PARR *Lab. Handbk.* vii. 103 Other means of separation [of solids] are sometimes adopted. Among them are dialysis, and the 'policeman' for dealing with solids in microchemistry, which is a small snipe feather mounted in a short length of glass tubing. **1974** *Nature* 6 Dec. 498/2 Attempts to passage stage 2 cells..by scraping with a rubber policeman, resulted in a rapid degeneration of the cells in a new flask.

3. *attrib.* and *Comb.*, as **policeman fly** *Austral.*, a small wasp belonging to the family Nyssonidæ, Arpactidæ, or Stizidæ, which preys on flies; **policeman's helmet**, the Himalayan balsam, *Impatiens glandulifera*, a purple-flowered annual plant belonging to the family Balsaminaceæ.

1907 W. W. FROGGATT *Austral. Insects* 108 Several of these [small wasps] are known in the bush as policemen flies. **1926** R. J. TILLYARD *Insects Australia & N.Z.* xxii. 299 These wasps [*sc.* Arpactidæ] and the members of the following family [*sc.* Nyssonidæ] are known as 'Policeman Flies' in Australia. **1933** *Bulletin* (Sydney) 26 July 21/3 The robber fly, known [erroneously] in the back country as the policeman fly. **1969** *Courier-Mail* (Brisbane) 11 Jan. 6/8 Mr. Barrand found a fly which chases away other flies. He hopes to install tape-recorded sounds of the policeman fly in a transistorized unit. **1950** J. HUTCHINSON *Uncommon Wild Flowers* 226 Jumping Jack, Policeman's Helmet... A tall, sometimes very strong growing herb up to 6ft. or more. **1958** P. LEWIS *Brit. Wild Flowers* 125 Policeman's Helmet, a Himalayan plant grown in cottage gardens, has become naturalized along river-banks and in waste places. **1961** E. SALISBURY *Weeds & Aliens* iii. 65 The Policeman's Helmet is now to be met with in semi-wild stations in nearly half the British counties. **1971** *Country Life* 18 Feb. 384/2 An incongruous coloniser from the Himalayas, that Impatiens so appropriately known as policeman's helmet, attracting bumble-bees until the frosts come.

Hence **poli·cemanish** *a.*, suggestive of a policeman; **poli·cemanism**, the methods or conduct of policemen; **poli·cemanly** *a.*, appropriate to or characteristic of a policeman.

1891 *Star* 31 Oct. 4/3 Instances of policemanism crop up daily. **1908** *Daily Chron.* 30 Mar. 3/3 (*heading*) Policemanism. The Prince..went on to denounce a Government influenced by 'men with the education of a policeman, and with the convictions of a pogromshchik (official of massacre)'. **1916** A. BENNETT *Lion's Share* iii. 27 The heavy policemanish step of Mr. Cowl was heard on the landing. **1936** 'M. INNES' *Death at President's Lodging* ix. 171 The policemanly demand at last. **1973** —— *Appleby's Answer* xx. 172 The day had passed when she judged it amusing to join her husband in policemanly scampers. **1975** W. MARSHALL *Yellowthread Street* 64 He had been..firm and policeman-ish. **1977** 'E. CRISPIN' *Glimpses of Moon* x. 194 Policemanly instincts..reasserted themselves. Single-handed, he would make an arrest

Police Motu (pǒlī·s mō͞u·tū). [f. POLICE *sb.* + *MOTU *sb.*] A Papuan pidgin, based on Motu.

1950 P. CHATTERTON (*title*) A primer of Police Motu. **1962** R. BRETT et al. (*title*) A dictionary of Police Motu. **1965** B. A. HOOLEY in *Language* XLI. 168 Police Motu, almost as important as a lingua franca in Papua as Neomelanesian is in..New Guinea. *Ibid.* 169 Police Motu is derived from Motu, a member of the Malayo-Polynesian family. **1974** L. TODD *Pidgins & Creoles* i. 7 In the Pacific, in PNG [*sc.* Papua New Guinea], Police Motu arose from the contact between speakers of Motu and other Papuan vernaculars. It has recently expanded its vocabulary by adopting words from Neo-Melanesian. **1977** C. F. & F. M. VOEGELIN *Classification & Index of World's Languages* 47 Police Motu, a pidgin widely used as a lingua franca in Papua, is based on Motu.

police state. A state regulated by means of a national police force having secret supervision and control of the activities of citizens. Also *attrib.*

1865 *Times* 6 Sept. 10/3 Austria was long known on the Continent as the 'police State', and..M. von Weiss will again obtain for her that unenviable title. **1896** B. RUSSELL *German Social Democracy* iv. 114 This infamous Law, the crowning endeavour of the enlightened police state. **1938** *New Statesman* 15 Jan. 74/1 Meanwhile, the atmosphere of the 'police state' is already with us. **1939** *War Illustr.* 28 Oct. 217/1 Spies are everywhere; indeed, Germany is the modern exemplification of the 'police state' in action. **1947** *Life* 7 June 37/1 They have failed in France and Italy because the peoples have had a chance to show their preference for Western democracy over a police state. **1950** G. B. SHAW *Farfetched Fables* 79 In the imagination of our amateur politician England is a Utopia in which everything and everybody is 'free' and all other countries 'police States'. I, being Irish, know better. **1959** *Listener* 8 Oct. 573/2 The Devlin Commission reported that Nyasaland has been turned into a 'police state'. **1967** COULTHARD & SMITH in Wills & Yearsley *Handbk. Management Technol.* 197 Short of introducing a police-state, in which people are directed to jobs and change them only with State approval, we must accept a degree of labour turnover as necessary and desirable. **1973** *Times* 12 Apr. 19/4 That Rhodesia is a police state, where the rights of individuals, the rule of law and the right to speak or report the truth count for nothing, is a fact for which there has long been ample evidence. **1975** *Times* 11 Jan. 12/6 A campaign to spot the terrorists before they act..requires measures which smack of the police state.

police station. Add: (Earlier example.) Also *attrib.*

1846 DICKENS *Pictures from Italy* 53 The hall..is as dirty as a police-station in London. *a* **1930** D. H. LAWRENCE *Last Poems* (1932) 175 He has..stepped down To the police-station cell.

‖ **policier** (pǒlisi,e). [a. F. *policier* detective novel.] A film based on a police novel. Cf. *roman policier* s.v. *ROMAN *sb.*[4]

1975 *Listener* 21 Aug. 249/3 A *policier* of rare complexity... The plot threads of the film must..be followed down some labyrinthine byways. **1977** *Time* 18 Apr. 23/1 Not so in *Man on the Roof*, the Swedish-made *policier* based on one of the Martin Beck novels.

policy, *sb.*[1] Add: **III. 8.** *attrib.* and *Comb.*, as (sense 5) *policy decision, document, -maker, -making, statement*; *policy-making* adj.; **policy science** (see quot. 1951); hence **policy scientist.**

1960 I. JEFFERIES *Dignity & Purity* iv. 66 Their purpose is the application of scientific method to policy decisions. **1964** GOULD & KOLB *Dict. Soc. Sci.* 510/1 Current interest centres on such questions as the nature of policy decisions... Policy decisions are contrasted, for instance, with judicial decisions by reference to the relatively greater freedom of choice in the former. **1974** S. GULLIVER *Vulcan Bulletins* 11 A policy decision had meant more careful buying. **1976** *Burnham-on-Sea Gaz.* 20 Apr., Mr Shore..can hardly have had time to read the policy documents before he was expected to stand up and defend them in the House. **1948** J. TOWSTER *Political Power in U.S.S.R.* III. xiii. 314 High-income executants, not policy-makers. **1975** *Times* 19 Feb. 14/6 American energy policy-makers find their own outlooks discouraging. **1978** *Dædalus* Fall 50 As citizens and policymakers, we can make explicit the potential personal and societal consequences of legislation. **1943** J. S. HUXLEY *TVA* xix. 137 The Board was always a policy-making body. **1946** *Nature* 9 Nov. 646/1 Authoritative information which those..at the policy-making or executive level might be expected to need. **1950** *N.Y. Times* 20 Apr. 1/3 The cataloging of persons eligible for policy-making positions would be..done without regard to their party affiliations. **1968** E. A. POWDRILL *Vocab. Land Planning* ii. 5 Policy-making and technique are a symbiosis, but it must be supported by wise and sound administration. **1976** *Times* 21 May 4/1 Mr. Len Murray..told the policy-making conference of the Society of Graphical and Allied Trades that the T.U.C. would expect the Government to take action. **1951** H. D. LASSWELL in Lerner & Lasswell *Policy Sciences* i. 4/1 We may use the term 'policy sciences' for the purpose of designating the content of the policy orientation during any given period. The policy sciences includes (1) the methods by which the policy process is investigated, (2) the results of the study of policy, and (3) the findings of the disciplines making the most important contributions to the intelligence needs of the time. **1964** I. L. HOROWITZ *New Sociology* 30 Sociology cannot be a 'policy science' until and unless there is a sociology of ethics. **1977** *Dædalus* Summer 59 It should move away from the contemporary, toward the past; ..away from the impossible quest for stability; from the glide into policy science. **1970** *Nature* 19 Sept. 1189/2 There will have to be changes in the ways in which 'prime television time' is allocated so that the policy scientists can have their say..when people are most likely to be glued to their television sets. **1979** *Bull. Amer. Acad. Arts & Sci.* Mar. 28 International consultants and policy scientists serve as the conveyors and preservers of these untested staff papers until their ideas, approaches, and methodologies develop a life of their own. **1960** *Times* 1 Feb. 11/2 Mr. Macleod's speech..will be the most important policy statement that has been made on East Africa for many a long year. **1966** N. Nicolson *Diaries & Lett. H. Nicolson 1930–1939* 258 He wrote the main policy-statement of the National Labour Party.

policy, *sb.*² Add: **1. c.** (Examples.) Freq. in phr. *to write policy*.

1830 [see **policy certificate*]. **1879** *Rep. N.Y. State Court of Appeals* LXXIV. 64 He testified that he paid to the defendant, at different times, sums amounting to $3,601.08 for tickets in a Kentucky lottery and in 'playing policy', as it is called. **1890** J. A. Riis *How Other Half Lives* (1891) xiii. 155 The game of policy is a kind of unlawful penny lottery. **1944** *Crisis* June 189/2 He even tried writing policy, but the players didn't like him. He couldn't shop the proper degree of sympathy when someone played 341 and 342 came out. **1949** *Amer. Speech* XXIV. 190 The oldest of the games, and very likely the parent of most contemporary forms, is policy, which is believed to have been in existence in England as early as the first half of the eighteenth century. **1968** P. Oliver *Screening Blues* 133 During the Depression..many impoverished Negroes wrote policy in the hopes of winning sufficient to feed their families. **1972** *Times* 23 Nov. 9/8 Its most spectacular proposal is that gambling, prostitution and 'policy'—an illegal betting game—should all be legalized.

3. (sense 1 a) *policy business, -holder* (earlier and later examples); (sense 1 c) *policy certificate, game, player, -playing, racket; policy play* vb. trans.; **policy blues** *U.S.*, a blues melody concerning the game of policy; **policy king** *U.S.*, one who has profited greatly from running policy games; **policy office** *U.S.*, = *policy-shop*; **policy-shop** (earlier example); **policy-slip** (examples); **policy wheel** *U.S.*, a revolving drum used in the selection of winning numbers at policy; **policy writer** *U.S.*, one who collects bets from those playing policy.

1928 J. Jackson (*song-title*) Policy Blues. **1968** P. Oliver *Screening Blues* iv. 134 Reflecting the popularity of the numbers game were innumerable policy blues. **1844** G. Wilkes *Mysteries of Tombs* 52/2 He is an old offender in the policy business. **1883** 'Mark Twain' *Life on Miss.* xliii. 437 Dull policy-business till next fire. **1830** *Baltimore Amer.* 26 Aug. 3/2 To Adventurers and the Public, Policy Certificates, in the greatest variety. **1885** *Rep. Massachusetts Supreme Judicial Court* CXXXVII. 250 The defendant has been convicted of setting up and promoting a certain lottery for money; and the only question raised by his exceptions is whether the jury were warranted in finding that a game popularly known as the policy or envelope game is a lottery within the Pub. Sts. c. 209, § 1. **1934** *Sun* (Baltimore) 30 Apr. 6/5 Skilled investigators have revealed that the slot machines and the policy games take $2,000,000 out of Richmond each year. **1964** A. Wykes *Gambling* 344 In 1957, nearly 12,000 people were convicted on policy-game charges. **1851** C. Cist *Cincinnati* 98 Penn Mutual Life Insurance Co... All the profits divided among the policy holders every year. **1915** [see *chinchy *a.*] **1970** J. Hansen *Fadeout* i. 4 My company—every insurance company—sends out investigators in cases like this... Where the policyholder's body can't be found. **1949** *Collier's* 15 Jan. 21/1 Thousands of other suckers..are not only making millionaires out of a few dozen policy kings, they also pay for the corruption of many police officials. **1968** P. Oliver *Screening Blues* iv. 133 Policy kings made occasional magnanimous gestures with large donations to charities or churches and a mystique developed in which they were viewed as benefactors rather than as parasites. **1843** J. H. Greene *Exposure of Arts & Miseries of Gambling* 283 These swindling shops are numerous, and are sometimes called *policy offices*. **1926** C. Jackson in P. Oliver *Screening Blues* (1968) iv. 130, I looked in my purse t'see if I had a little dough, So I could policy play 4-11-44. **1847** C. White (*title*) The policy players. An Ethiopian sketch. **1901** E. Harrigan *Mulligans* 65 A policy player's chances are a hundred to one against him. **1972** *Sci. Amer.* Oct. 112/3 Thousands of Manhattan policy players bet on 932 and won. **1887** *Gen. Statutes Connecticut* cliv. 563 The court of common council of any city..shall have power to make, alter, and repeal ordinances or by-laws to suppress and punish all kinds of gambling and gaming, pool selling, policy playing, [etc.]. **1949** *Amer. Speech* XXIV. 190 In the early days policy playing was associated with the regular number lotteries, being a device whereby people unable to afford a regular lottery ticket could wager small amounts on the outcome of the drawing. **1938** *Sun* (Baltimore) 1 Sept. 1/4 Davis, the broken mouthpiece of the once-powerful Dutch Schultz policy racket, swore..that James J. Hines..was paid thousands of dollars by the mob. **1968** P. Oliver *Screening Blues* iv. 133 The policy racket had a folk-lore of its own. **1858** 'Q. K. P. Doesticks' *Witches of N.Y.* 54 The propinquity of the 'lottery agency' and the 'policy-shop', just round the corner. **1934** *Sun* (Baltimore) 30 Apr. 6/5 The second fact can be done away with by making it a criminal offense to sell policy slips to minors. **1972** 'T. Coe' *Don't lie to Me* xi. 103, I knew..he could make it stick. Find heroin in my car. Shake me down and find policy slips. **1906** *Southwestern Reporter* XCI. 785/1 Evidence that accused was seen..in the house where people were betting at a lottery, and that he at one time turned the policy wheel. **1968** *Sunday Tel.* 1 Sept. 13/6 An excursion into the cabalistic number symbolism employed by bettors on the 'policy wheels'—those intricate gambling devices surreptitiously played by millions of Americans. **1949** *Collier's* 15 Jan. 21/2 In Detroit, one auto-plant policy writer explained to me, 'I been in this racket for twenny years.' **1968** P. Oliver *Screening Blues* iv. 142 Within the lower class the policy writer was considered a parasite who lived off his fellows.

polie: see Police *sb.* in Dict. and Suppl.

poliencephalitis. Add: **polioencephalitis** is now the more usual form. (Earlier and later examples.) [First formed in Ger. (C. Wernicke *Lehrb. d. Gehirnkrankheiten* (1881) II. ii. 229).]

1885 *London Med. Rec.* 16 Feb. 44/1 (*heading*) Strümpell on acute infantile polio-encephalitis (cerebral paralysis of children). **1885** J. Ross *Handbk. Dis. of Nervous Syst.* 621 (*heading*) Poliencephalitis acuta infantum. **1911** A. Bruce tr. *H. Oppenheimer's Text-bk. Nervous Dis.* II. 837 The diagnosis of poliencephalitis.. should be made only with great reserve. **1923** J. H. Parsons *Diseases of Eye* (ed. 4) xxix. 554 Acute polioencephalitis accounts for not infrequent cases of paralytic squint following a febrile attack in young children. **1934** *Times Educ. Suppl.* 22 Sept. 341/1 Of polioencephalitis there were 88 notifications. **1971** *Jrnl. Neurol. Sci.* XII. 414 This disorder is a polioencephalitis of viral origin.

poling, *vbl. sb.*¹ Add: **3. poling boat** *N. Amer.*, = *pole boat* s.v. *Pole *sb.*¹ 5 c.

1900 J. London *Son of Wolf* 163 Madelaine shook the dust of the Lower River from her moccasins, and with her husband, in a poling-boat, went to live on the Upper River. **1973** D. Andersen *Ways Harsh & Wild* ii. 70 We whipsawed lumber from birch logs and put together two large poling boats.

poling (pōᵘ·liŋ), *vbl. sb.*² *Physics.* [f. Pole *sb.*² + -ing¹.] The process of polarizing a ferroelectric material (see *pole *v.*²).

1954 *Jrnl. Appl. Physics* XXV. 1166/2 The crystals ..were grown in our laboratory and the *c* axis was made to be perpendicular to the face of the crystals by means of a high-field poling technique. **1965** *IEEE Trans. Sonics & Ultrasonics* XII. 7/1 During the initial poling both 109°/71° and 180° domain switching occurs. **1976** *Ibid.* XXIII. 393/2 The common practice..is to analyse the immittance behavior of a resonator with a certain geometry and poling axis.

polio (pōᵘ·lio). *colloq.* [Abbrev. of Poliomyelitis.] **1.** Poliomyelitis, esp. the paralytic form. Freq. *attrib.*

1931 *Survey* 15 Oct. 93/1 (*heading*) Panic and polio. **1934** *Ladies' Home Jrnl.* Feb. 10/1 How did the polio fighter..come to catch it? **1940** *Time* 2 Sept. 37/2 (*heading*) Polio scare. **1949** *New Harmony* (Indiana) *Times* 5 Aug. 1/5 New Harmony was doused..by a spraying plane..as a precautionary measure against polio. **1955** G. Greene *Quiet American* iv. ii. 241 My son's got polio. He's bad. **1955** *Sci. News Let.* 23 July 51/1 Children are the principal carriers of polio, and if enough children are immunized, it would probably not be necessary to vaccinate the adults in order to stamp out the disease. **1962** *Observer* 11 Mar. 8/4 Last year I had a play..out on tour... There was a polio scare in Hull, and the star didn't want to play. **1977** *Daily Tel.* 9 Mar. 8/4 Doctors have cleared two girl polio suspects in Greater Manchester.

2. A person who has, or has had, polio. *rare.*

1934 *Ladies' Home Jrnl.* Feb. 107/1 Health departments of cities and states poured out money to buy serum from recovered polios to try to cure already sick babies. **1962** *Guardian* 26 Sept. 8/5 'Polio',.. a person who has been paralysed by polio.

polioencephalitis: see Poliencephalitis in Dict. and Suppl.

poliomyelitis. Add pronunc. (pōᵘlio-) and substitute for def.: A disease caused by a neurotropic virus (infection with which usu. produces no symptoms) which may give rise to a temporary meningitis, with fever and delirium, or, esp. in older patients, a permanent and sometimes fatal localized paralysis as a result of the infection and death of groups of nerve cells in the spinal cord or brain stem. Also *attrib.* (Earlier and later examples.)

1878 *Amer. Jrnl. Med. Sci.* LXXV. 411 The case was.. one of acute polio-myelitis. **1934** R. W. Fairbrother *Handbk. Filterable Dis.* vi. 95 The poliomyelitis virus only produces spontaneous disease in man. **1955** [see *infantile paralysis* s.v. *infantile *a.* 3]. **1966** Wright & Symmers *Systemic Path.* II. xxxiv. 1192/2 The non-paralytic form of poliomyelitis—the main symptoms of which are those of catarrhal inflammation of the upper parts of the respiratory and alimentary tracts—is the commonest manifestation of the infection during epidemics. **1972** B. A. Curtis et al. *Introd. Neurosci.* viii. 186/1 The majority of patients with poliomyelitis virus infection make a complete or significant recovery. *Ibid.* xxii. 590/1 With the development of effective vaccines.. poliomyelitis has become a preventable disease.

Hence **po:liomyeli·tic** *a.*, of or affected with poliomyelitis.

1911 *Jrnl. Exper. Med.* XIV. 117 Flexner and Clark showed that the poliomyelitic virus would survive for a period of days in the subcutaneous tissues of the rabbit. **1940** *Ann. Reg. 1939* 376 Evidence suggested that poliomyelitic virus may occur in urban sewage. **1958** *Jrnl. Bone & Joint Surg.* XL. a. 513 In a few convalescent poliomyelitic patients..the Milwaukee brace has aided in reducing the curve and holding it in check until muscle balance has been re-established. **1971** *Biol. Abstr.* LII. 10390/1 (*heading*) Study of the circulation of poliomyelitic and other enteric viruses in waste water.

poliorcetic, *a.* Delete *rare* and add further examples.

1936 H. A. L. Fisher *Hist. Europe* i. xv. 187 To the marine skill of the Scandinavians they [*sc.* the Normans] added all that was then known of cavalry warfare and the poliorcetic art. **1975** C. J. Bishko in K. M. Setton *Hist. Crusades* III. xii. 410 Its [*sc.* Lisbon's] stubborn defense ..against the combined Portuguese and crusader resources, including the northerners' heavy siege machines and poliorcetic skills.

poliorcetics, *sb. pl.* (Further examples.)

1936 H. A. L. Fisher *Hist. Europe* ii. xvii. 628 The sieges of Hertogenbosch, of Maestricht, and of Breda showed that in the art of poliorcetics the Dutch had lost none of their ancient cunning. **1958** M. Roberts *Gustavus Adolphus* II. iii. 185 Maurice [of Orange] was a great innovator in siege warfare. His massive barrages against a strictly limited objective enabled him greatly to quicken the pace of siege operations, and marked an epoch in poliorcetics.

poliosis (pǫliōᵘ·sis). *Med.* [mod.L., f. Gr. πολι-ός grey + -osis.] Partial or general greyness or whiteness of the hair, esp. if premature.

1813 T. Young *Introd. Med. Lit.* lxiv. 370 *Spilosis*, discolorations of the skin, or of the cuticular substances, without constitutional disease... *S. poliósis*, grey hairs. **1817** J. M. Good *Physiol. Syst. Nosology* 501 *Poliósis*, hairs prematurely grey or hoary. *Poliosis*, auct. var. **1868** *Jrnl. Cutaneous Med.* I. 277 Poliosis, or canities, was present in 9 cases in the two thousand... The white hairs were pretty uniformly dispersed through the rest of the hair, giving rise to incipient greyness. **1940** Becker & Obermayer *Mod. Dermatol. & Syphilol.* xxx. 531/1 Poliosis is definitely hereditary, and..is due to complete lack of pigment function. **1968** Ebling & Rook in A. Rook et al. *Textbk. Dermatol.* II. xlvi. 1414/2 Poliosis results from absence or deficiency of melanin in a group of neighbouring hair follicles. Clinically it presents as a strand or mesh of white hairs.

poliovirus (pōᵘ·liovəiᵊrǝs). *Med.* Also **polio virus.** [f. *Polio + Virus.] Any of a group of enteroviruses that includes those that cause the various forms of poliomyelitis. Also *attrib.*

[**1954** *Nature* 3 Apr. 621/1 Proposed 'non-Linnæan' binomials for some animal viruses... *Poliovirus hominis* (human poliomyelitis). *Poliovirus muris* (mouse encephalomyelitis, *TO* type).] **1955** *Virology* I. 186 (*heading*) The poliovirus group. **1958** *Economist* 26 July 283 To achieve that we must apparently wait for the successful development of vaccines made from live attenuated polioviruses. **1961, 1965** [see *ECHO virus]. **1968** Rhodes & van Rooyen *Textbk. Virol.* (ed. 5) v. iii. 541 The feature distinguishing polioviruses from other members of the enterovirus group is their capacity to produce poliomyelitis in man and other primates. **1970** Passmore & Robson *Compan. Med. Stud.* II. xviii. 113/2 At the beginning of the century, infection with poliovirus was widespread among children under 5 years of age, but only an occasional patient developed the typical infantile paralysis. **1973** R. G. Krueger et al. *Introd. Microbiol.* xix. 528/1 Polio virus will adsorb to certain cells of certain organs of primates but not to nonprimate cells.

Hence **po·lioviral** *a.*

1977 *Lancet* 19 Feb. 434/1 Polioviral antigen has been detected in 3 patients.

poliphant: see Polyphone in Dict. and Suppl.

‖ **polis** (pǫ·lis), *sb.*¹ *Hist.* [Gr.] A Greek city-state; *spec.* such a state considered in its ideal form. Also *transf.*

1894 A. Holm *Hist. Greece* I. xx. 252 In Greece state and city are one, and both are designated by the word 'Polis'. **1929** N. Mallinson tr. *Glotz's Greek City* 2 From the association of many villages, the complete State was created, the perfect community, the *polis*. **1941** Auden *New Year Letter* iii. 51 We can at least serve other ends, Can love the polis of our friends. **1941** H. G. Wells *You can't be too Careful* iv. i. 222 Homo Tewler does not behave as a political animal should do, participating with the utmost fullness in the collective life of his *polis*. *Ibid.* 223 The *polis* of Aristotle. **1958** *N. & Q.* CCIII. 507/2 She appears an irreverent seductress pursuing Merlin in order to destroy the Arthurian polis. **1959** *Listener* 12 Feb. 292/1 The fully developed, classical *polis* was a new and original institution. **1968** *Ibid.* 5 Sept. 313/1 The epic and tragic were becoming increasingly hard to realise; an art that had emerged from the social organisation of the Greek *polis* no longer applied to the mysterious forces of capitalism. **1972** A. P. Hinchliffe in Cox & Dyson *20th-Cent. Mind* III. xiv. 416 The idea that no man can prosper unless his *polis* prospers. **1978** A. Sanders *Victorian Historical Novel* viii. 172 The Florence of the novel [sc. *Romola*] is the Renaissance *polis*.

polis (pǫ·lis, pō·lis), *sb.*² Chiefly *Ir.* and *Sc.* Also **poliss, pollis.** [Repr. regional pronunc. of Police *sb.* (see etym. note).] = Police *sb.* 5 a; a member or (construed as *pl.*) members of a police force. Also **po·lisman.**

c **1874** D. BOUCICAULT *Shaughraun* (1884) I. iii. 7/2 The polis were in my cabin today about ye. **1892** KIPLING *Barrack-Room Ballads* 43 They sent the Polis there, The English were too drunk to know, the Irish didn't care. **1900** E. H. STRAIN *Elmslie's Drag-Net* 115 The poliss is no far awa. **1904** 'H. FOULIS' *Erchie* 124 Her niece Sarah, and Macrae the nicht polis. **1907** J. M. SYNGE *Playboy* I. 10 Is it yourself is fearing the polis? You're wanting, maybe? **1919** J. BUCHAN *Mr Standfast* iv. 84 Ye'll get a good turn-out at your meeting..but they're sayin' that the polis will interfere. **1922** JOYCE *Ulysses* 434 Don't be all night before the polis in plain clothes sees us. **1928** J. BUCHAN *Runagates Club* ii. 73 The pollisman..says they're looking for a man that personated an inmate. *a* **1930** N. MUNRO *Para Handy Tales* (1955) 109 'There's no a polisman in the island of Barra,' said Para Handy. 'If there wass any need for polismen they would have to send to Lochmaddy.' **1931** D. L. SAYERS *Five Red Herrings* ii. 20 Juist tummled intae the burn..an' drooned himself... The pollis'll be up there now. **1967** H. CALVIN *Nice Friendly Town* viii. 104 'But I'll have to get on to the police,' I protested, and Jumbo.. pointed to Eddie Bone and said: 'He's a polis. Get on to him.' **1973** J. PATRICK *Glasgow Gang Observed* iii. 34 Tim bragged: 'We've chibbed aboot seven polis.' **1979** *Listener* 31 May 749/4 The odd *poliss* and such like.. could be confusing to English ears.

Polisario (pǫlisā·rio). [f. the initial letters of Sp. *Frente Popular para la Liberacion de Sagnia el-Hamra y Rio de Oro* Popular Front for the Liberation of Sagnia el-Hamra and Río de Oro.] An independence movement in Western Sahara, formed in May, 1973. Also *attrib.*

1975 *Guardian* 17 Oct. 4/6 The Front for Liberation and Unity..has vowed to break up separatist movements such as the Algerian-backed Polisario Front, which is campaigning for independence for the territory. **1977** *Time* 3 Jan. 49/1 Polisario is fighting to gain independence for a new 'Saharan Arab Democratic Republic' and the 100,000 people, most Reguibet tribesmen, it would represent. **1977** *Kuwait Times* 23 Oct. 4/7 Spain ceded sovereignty of the Western Sahara to Morocco and Mauritania nearly two years ago but Algeria disputes the agreement and supports guerrillas of the Polisario Front fighting for independence for the territory.

polish, *sb.* Add: **3. b.** Short for *nail polish* s.v. *NAIL *sb.* 13 a.

1917 *Harrods Gen. Catal.* 410 (*heading*) Manicure preparations and sundries... Majestic Polish..1/6. **1924** M. A. BURBRIDGE *Road to Beauty* 115 Finish by using a bit more of the tinted polish and rub up with the buffer. **1937** H. RUBENSTEIN *This Way to Beauty* viii. 119 A very white hand is flattered by a very dark polish. **1957** N. WILLIAMS *Powder & Paint* v. 144 Until 1930..more 'colourless' polish was sold than of the three shades of pink that made up the manicurist's palette. **1976** 'M. ALBRAND' *Taste of Terror* x. 61 The salesgirls never look at a customer. They're always staring at their nails to see if the polish is chipped.

4. polish remover, a preparation used for removing nail varnish.

1935 D. COCKS *Help Yourself to Beauty* xii. 249 Moisten a small pad of absorbent cotton with polish remover. **1973** M. MACKINTOSH *King & Two Queens* iv. 58 He played absently with the small bottle of polish remover.. running the tiny brush over a thumb-nail.

Polish, *a.* Add: **a.** (Earlier and further examples.)

1674 R. SOUTH *Acct. of Travels into Poland in 1674* in *Posthumous Wks.* (1717) 26 The Queen is now about 33 Years of Age..and speaks the Polish Language full as well as her own natural Tongue. **1795** S. JONES *Hist. Poland* I. xix. 24 The Pater-noster in the Polish language is of the following tenor. **1842** *Penny Cycl.* XXII. 115/1 The Polish language is considered to be more flexible and euphonic than the other Slavonic dialects. **1884** W. R. MORFILL *Simplified Gram. Polish Lang.* i. 3 The sounds of the Polish language may be grouped as *hard* and *soft.* **1944** S. GRABSKI *Poland* III. xiv. 107 The magnificent song of the Knights..to the glory of the Virgin Mary, the first literary monument in the Polish language. **1975** *Language* LI. 407 These languages..differ from the Polish dialects discussed above in not permitting alternatives with singular and plural.

b. Polish draughts (later examples); **Polish wheat** (further examples).

1960 R. C. BELL *Board & Table Games* ii. 75 Modifications in the rules have been made and as now played, Polish draughts must rank as one of the great board games of the world. **1971** *Country Life* 25 Nov. 1429/1 The board on this games table is arranged for Polish draughts..popular in England throughout the 18th century, the boards having 100 squares and each player 20 men. **1843** Polish wheat [see *hard wheat* s.v. *HARD *a.* (*sb.*) 22 a]. **1908** Polish wheat [see *DURUM].

d. Applied to logical theories, methods, or systems developed esp. in Lwow, Breslau, and Warsaw before the war of 1939–45, and to the related symbolism, as **Polish notation**, a bracketless and unpunctuated system of formula notation now freq. used in computing science to represent the order in which arithmetical operations are performed in many computers and calculators, often with operators following their operands (*reverse Polish*) instead of preceding them.

1940 *Jrnl. Symbolic Logic* V. 77 The second section is devoted to various present currents of thought: Hilbert formalism, German exact thought.., Polish logic.., the unity of science movement. **1954** I. M. COPI *Symbolic Logic* 254 The Polish notation has the obvious advantage of dispensing with all special punctuation marks. **1965** N. KRETZMANN *Elements of Formal Logic* p. vi, We use Łukasiewicz's so-called Polish notation for..the logic of statements. **1966** Y. BAR-HILLEL in *Automatic Transl. of Lang.* (NATO Summer School, Venice 1962) 15 In Polish notation calculi you cannot introduce syntactic ambiguity..by omitting symbols, since there are no special scoping symbols to omit. **1968** *Jrnl. Assoc. Computing Machinery* XV. 466 The following is a simple Polish transduction grammar. **1975** D. G. FINK *Electronics Engineers' Handbk.* XXIII. 85 One possible Polish string would be AB+C+E=. In this string, the system would find A and B and, as determined by the plus sign *following* the two operands, add them. The result is then combined with C under addition called for by the second plus sign. The E= symbols indicate that the result is to be stored in E. **1975** *Physics Bull.* May 227/1 The Oxford 300 scientific calculator with either floating point or scientific notation and algebraic logic (as opposed to the reverse Polish logic used on the more familiar Sinclair Scientific).

B. *absol.* or as *sb.*[2] **1.** (See POLISH *a.* c.)

2. The Polish language.

1784 W. COXE *Travels into Poland, Russia, Sweden, & Denmark* I. II. iii. 176 The king informed me, that they had no good history of their country in Polish. **1807** G. BURNETT *Present State of Poland* xvi. 277 Within thirty or forty, or perhaps fifty miles of Dantzic, I found that the people knew scarcely a word of Polish **1861** MAX MÜLLER *Lect. Sci. of Lang.* 1st Ser. v. 187 The oldest specimen of Polish belongs to the fourteenth century: the Psalter of Margarite. **1925** P. DE SOISSONS *Polish Self-Taught* 1 This work is issued as a practical introduction to Polish, a language spoken by about thirty millions of people. **1943** S. SEGAL *Nazi Rule in Poland* iv. 70 Only a few shows in Polish are at present permitted in Warsaw and Krakow. **1968** B. NEWMAN *New Poland* ii. 31 If a Lithuanian youth wanted an education, he had to learn Polish to get it. **1975** *Language* LI. 363 The passive construction is the same for both aspects in Polish and Bulgarian.

Hence **Po·lishness**, the quality or state of being Polish or of displaying Polish characteristics.

1958 *Listener* 2 Oct. 499/2 They [*sc.* the Poles] need to reaffirm their past, their Polishness. **1964** E. HUXLEY *Back Street New Worlds* iii. 35 Few of their children attend Saturday schools or sustain their Polishness.

polish, *v.* Add: **1. a.** Also *absol.* or *intr.*

1803 T. SHERATON *Cabinet Dict.* 289 At other times they polish with soft wax. **1828** WEBSTER, *Polisher, n.*, the person or instrument that polishes. **1902** D. C. PEEL *How to Keep House* xii. 205 Dip a small piece of flannel lightly in colza oil and then into the bath-brick, and rub all the bright part well, wipe off with a soft cloth and polish with a leather. **1919** L. R. BALDERSTON *Housewifery* vi. 133 Rottenstone is a fine gray powder... Like any gritty substance, it works best with a lubricator like oil. In this way it cleans and polishes. **1957** M. DODD *America's Homemaking Bk.* xxiii. 189 There are commercial scratch removers that can be applied like a polish ..or mix with varnish an oil paint to match the wood... Let it dry and then polish. **1961** *Modern Maturity* IV. VI. 19/2 Some women get a real thrill out of housework. They love to dust, scrub, polish, wax floors, move the furniture around from place to place, [etc.]. **1962** *Home Managem.* (Homecraft Series) 34/1 It can be sprayed straight on to a dusty surface and enables you to dust and polish in one operation.

c. To wipe or scrape up and eat every morsel of food on (one's plate, bowl, etc.).

1908 A. J. DAWSON *Finn* xix. 289 Finn polish the tin dish clean and bright. **1962** M. DUFFY *That's how it Was* x. 85 The little Reeses polished their plates after every meal. **1972** M. BABSON *Murder on Show* vii. 79 Pandora ate her dinner..and began polishing her bowl.

2. a. (Later examples.) Also *absol.*

1946 K. TENNANT *Lost Haven* (1947) xv. 235 Mrs. Ayre was thrown back for employment on a series of maids, and was always to be found hard at work 'polishing' some raw girl. **1961** *Vogue* (N.Y.) July 100/3 They discovered any number of ways in which they wanted to polish their own interview techniques. **1961** E. STREETER *Chairman of Bored* xxiii. 221 Did men become perfectionists as they grew older, polishing, polishing, reluctant to let go? **1961** *PMLA* LXXVI. I. 310 The poet in a written tradition who generally never blots a line may once in a while pause and polish without incurring blame.

Polish-American, *sb.* and *a.* [f. POLISH *a.* + AMERICAN *a.* and *sb.*] **A.** *sb.* An American of Polish origin.

1898 F. BARINGER in *Memorial of Polish-American Organizations in U.S.* 29 The Polish-Americans in this city are very industrious. **1938** W. SEABROOK *Those Foreigners* v. 258 The late Congressman Zionchek who went beserk on the White House lawn was a Polish American. **1943** *Who's Who in Polish America* (ed. 3) 9 This..is the outgrowth of a project begun modestly in 1939, with the publication of a brochure containing brief biographies of 100 leading Polish-Americans. **1945** *Polonia* 83 The New Poland that came out of the War proved disappointing to many Polish Americans. **1974** D. MACKENZIE *Zaleski's Percentage* ii. 40 A handful of Polish-Americans made the pilgrimage. **1977** B. GARFIELD *Recoil* i. 18 'She's married to a Polack.' 'Polish-American, Charlie.'

B. *adj.* Of or pertaining to Americans of Polish origin.

1911 *Cath. Encycl.* XII. 207/2 The most typical of the Polish American laymen to achieve distinction was Peter Kiolbassa. **1936** MENCKEN *Amer. Lang.* (ed. 4) 673 The Polish-American journalists are rather more careful than most. **1949** *Dziennik Zwiazkowy* (Chicago, Ill.) 19 Nov. 6/1 A banquet in honour of the Polish American public official. **1961** 'E. LATHEN' *Banking on Death* x. 80 The Buffalo Polish-American Democratic Club. **1976** *National Observer* (U.S.) 1 May B6/4 Television cameras invaded a Polish-American working-class home on the south side of Milwaukee.

polished, *ppl. a.* Add: **1. c.** Of rice: having the outer layers of the grain removed.

1922 W. G. R. FRANCILLON *Good Cookery* (ed. 2) xii. 236 Unpolished rice is cheaper and more nutritious than polished rice. **1948** *Good Housek. Cookery Bk.* II. 400 The natural rice has rather more flavour and food value than polished rice. **1979** P. B. MEDAWAR *Advice to Young Scientist* vi. 32 Scientists..demonstrated that..unpolished rice is much better for us than polished white rice.

polishing, *vbl. sb.* Add: **1. b.** Also, the outer layers of rice grain usually removed during the milling process.

1912 *Chambers's Jrnl.* Apr. 237/2 If the birds were fed on the milled rice mixed with the outer husks or 'polishings' which had been removed, the disease did not manifest itself. **1937** *Discovery* Nov. 348/2 Rice, or rather that part of it known as 'polishings', is the source of a vitamin product... Rice polishings are the external layers of the rice grain, usually removed by milling or 'polishing' in preparing the cereal for the market.

2. c. The filtration of the last traces of suspended solids from a liquid at the final stage in a process, *spec.* in the brewing of beer, and in the purification of effluent.

1938 *Jrnl. Inst. Brewing* XLIV. 466/2 One type of sheet filter composed of 160 sheets, 80 on each side, one side for 'roughing' and the other for 'polishing'. **1956** L. B. ESCRITT *Sewerage & Sewage Disposal* xviii. 361 The waterworks process of sand filtration has also been found satisfactory for effluent polishing. **1957** K. BARTON-WRIGHT tr. *J. de Clerck's Textbk. Brewing* I. xxii. 465 These sheet filters hold back yeast much better, and polishing is frequently omitted, whereas the metal mesh grids invariably let yeast pass through and a polishing filtration must always be carried out. **1958** *New Biol.* XXV. 88 Similar oxidation ponds are used in this country, e.g. in Bradford, for the final 'polishing' of a treated effluent, where the low flow in the receiving water demands this. **1971** R. L. & G. L. CULP *Adv. Wastewater Treatment* iii. 49 Effluent chlorination can provide more efficient disinfection of the effluent, which negates the only remaining virtue of the polishing pond for larger plants.

3. *polishing-paste* (further examples), *-powder* (earlier and later examples).

1916 'TAFFRAIL' *Pincher Martin* vi. 86 A convenient receptacle for dirty cotton-waste, polishing-paste, bath-brick, and emery-paper. **1969** *Gloss. Terms Dentistry* (*B.S.I.*) 64 *Polishing paste*, a blend of fine abrasive particles with bonding agents and flavouring. It is used for cleaning and polishing surfaces of teeth, restorations and appliances. **1849** C. BRONTË *Shirley* III. xiv. 299 The cup and platter he burnished up with the best polishing-powder. **1895** [see *BLUEING, BLUING *vbl. sb.* 2]. **1969** *Gloss. Terms Dentistry* (*B.S.I.*) 64 *Polishing powder*, a material containing fine abrasive particles for polishing teeth.

‖ **polisson** (polisoṅ). [Fr.] An urchin or scamp; an ill-bred and uncouth person. Also *attrib.*

1866 G. J. WHYTE-MELVILLE *Cerise* II. x. 148 He was discovered as a coxcomb, an intruder and a *polisson.* **1897** G. DU MAURIER *Martian* 15 The polisson picked up his pocket-handkerchief and went. **1905** W. JAMES *Let.* 8 Feb. in R. B. Perry *Tht. & Char. W. James* (1935) II. 398 When will either you or I, to whom Locke's mind was that of a street *polisson* in point of subtlety and 'truth', have statuettes? **1915** M. F. SANDARS *Life & Times of Queen Adelaide* vii. 111 Instead of the polisson manner for which he used to be celebrated, he is now quiet and well-behaved, like anybody else.

Politbureau, -buro (pǫ·litbiūə:rōu). Also **politbureau, -buro.** [a. Russ. *politbyuró*, f. *polit*(*icheskoe* political + *byuró* bureau.] The highest policy-making committee of the U.S.S.R., or of some other Communist country or party (in quot. 1930, a district committee). Also *attrib.*, *transf.*, and *fig.*

[**1926** *Encycl. Brit.* III. 428/1 This 'plenum' elects the Political Bureau of nine members with five deputies.] **1927** *Daily Express* 19 July 3/4 Stalin has packed the Politburo, which..is practically the Cabinet, with his friends. **1930** *Morning Post* 13 Aug. 13 The factory Soviet asked the local politbureau for lecturers to explain the causes of the shortage. **1937** E. SNOW *Red Star over China* IV. v. 165, I [*sc.* Mao Tse-tung] was dismissed from the Politbureau, and also from the Party Front Committee. **1949** *Ann. Reg. 1948* 285 The names of the *Politburo* of the [Yugoslav Communist] party were.. made public. **1949** G. B. SHAW *Sixteen Self Sketches* xi. 67 For some years the leaders in the Politbureau or Thinking Cabinet of the Fabian policy were Webb, Olivier, Wallas, Shaw. **1952** [see *BOLSHEVIK *a.*]. **1953** *Encounter* Oct. 67/1 Malenkov..had..a role more prominent than all other living Politburo members. **1962** *Listener* 6 Sept. 354/2 Mr Ben Bella's Politburo..ordered nationalist troops to advance on Algiers. **1967** I. GREY *First Fifty Years* xxviii. 479 The congress [of 1966] revived the name 'Politburo', which had been changed to 'presidium' by the sixteenth congress in 1952. **1974** J. WHITE tr. *Poulantzas's Fascism & Dictatorship* IV. ii. 171 Insurrection was then decided on by the Comintern and the majority of the Russian politburo for October 1923. **1977** 'S. LEYS' *Chinese Shadows* (1978) v. 119 The keenness and energy with which..old men cling to their seats on the Politburo. **1978** *Whitaker's Almanack 1979* 959/1

The real power of the Party is vested, however, in the *Politbureau*, the *Secretariat* and the permanent Departments of the Central Committee.

polite, *a.* Add: **3.** *absol.* or as *sb.* In colloq. phr, *to do the polite*: to perform a polite action (freq. with *thing* understood); to behave politely.

1856 [see Do *v.* 11 j]. **1933** D. L. SAYERS *Murder must Advertise* vi. 95, I saw you doing the polite to Miss Rossiter. **1935** G. GREENE *England made Me* IV. 199 They are leaving at the end of the week. I've got to do the polite. **1939** 'M. INNES' *Stop Press* I. vi. 136 Some chaps over there. Must do the polite.

politic, *a.* and *sb.* Add: **B.** *sb.* **3.** *pl.* **politics. c.** Delete †*Obs.* and add later examples in unfavourable sense. Phr. *to play politics*: see *PLAY *v.* 16 d.

1930 N. W. STEPHENSON *Nelson W. Aldrich* xx. 327 Northern enemies were quick to draw a conclusion; the expulsion of the Brownsville soldiers was mere politics, a play to the gallery to make sure the hold of the administration on the Southern Republican machine. **1952** *Manch. Guardian Weekly* 11 Dec. 13 The 'politics' involved..in key posts are not the private appetites of machine politicians or rarely that.

g. Used as a singular noun.

1906 *Daily Chron.* 7 Dec. 6/4 She [*sc.* Australia] has a politics of her own, and Europe is all the poorer for being out of touch with it. **1931** M. DE LA BEDOYÈRE *Drift of Democracy* ii. 16 This politics is the vaguest of disciplines. **1970** I. L. HOROWITZ *Masses in Lat. Amer.* i. 23 If the United States model is to succeed in Latin America..a pluralistic politics of competitive, numerous, but autonomous groups must emerge.

h. *Comb.*, as *politics-conscious, -free, -infested, -mad, -ridden* adjs.

1957 H. READ *Tenth Muse* xxxv. 303 Futurism was more conscious of its environment, machine-conscious, politics-conscious. **1977** *New Yorker* 4 July 85/1 Considering the period it covers, the 'Memoir' is politics-free to an amazing degree. **1949** KOESTLER *Promise & Fulfilment* v. 270 The good, clean academic atmosphere acted like a disinfectant on our politics-infested minds. **1937** W. B. YEATS *Let.* 8 Feb. (1954) 880 He says that in England the educated classes are politics-mad. **1946** R. BLESH *Shining Trumpets* (1949) xiii. 299 The politics-ridden, local relief of Depression days.

politic (pǫ·litik), *v.* Also **politick.** [f. POLITIC *sb.* or (esp. in later use) a back-formation f. *POLITICKING *vbl. sb.*] *intr.* To engage in political activity, esp. in order to strike political bargains or to seek votes (for oneself or another). Also *trans.* (rare).

1917 O. DOUGLAS *Setons* xiv. 225 He has been politic-ing down in Ayrshire. **1967** [see *DROP *v.* 28 a and b]. **1974** *Observer* (Colour Suppl.) 3 Nov. 31/2 Within the same square mile..Richard of Gloucester politicked. **1977** R. L. DUNCAN *Temple Dogs* (1978) II. i. 164 He was having to politic the old man to keep him from swerving away from his beliefs.

political, *a.* (*sb.*) Add: **1. a.** (Further examples.)

1825 J. S. MILL in *Westm. Rev.* Apr. 291 The subjects on which it is the interest of rulers that the people *should* be misled; the political religion of the country, its political institutions, [etc.]. **1846** —— in *Edin. Rev.* LXXXIV. 344 They [*sc.* the Greeks] were..the originators of political freedom. **1882** G. A. SALA *Amer. Revisited* I. xi. 161 For some mysterious reason..the Consumers' Ice Company figured as a political organisation in this astounding Parade. **1907** L. H. MORGAN *Anc. Society* II. xiii. 335 City wards and country townships..would have become the basis of the new political system. **1934** T. S. ELIOT *Rock* i. 15 Political religion is like invalid port: you calls it a medicine but it's soon just a 'abit. *a* **1942** B. MALINOWSKI *Scientific Theory of Culture* (1944) v. 50 The Chinese civilization differs from ours..in the economic and political organization of the country. **1949** M. MEAD in M. Fortes *Social Structure* 20 We have blocked out conceptually a large number of such areas as: the relationship between the representations of family structure and political structure in the psychology of the individual. **1957** P. WORSLEY *Trumpet shall Sound* 227 They occur..among people living in..societies..which lack centralized political institutions. **1962** P. DIESING *Reason in Society* v. 170 The political structure of a group is the organization of forces which determines how its decisions are made. **1976** *Times* 21 May 2/5 The United Unionist M.P.s who provide most of Northern Ireland's political representation at Westminster.

4. (Earlier and further examples.) Also (freq. in derogatory use), serving the ends of (party) politics; having regard or consideration for the interests of politics rather than questions of principle.

1749 [see MACHINE *sb.* 4 *fig.*] **1861** J. S. MILL *Repr. Govt.* i. 4 Political machinery does not act of itself. **1909** C. F. G. MASTERMAN *Condition of England* iii. 83 They appear as the mainstay of the political machine in suburban districts. **1912** *Out West* (Los Angeles) June 401 Are you interested..in the way people are defrauded, and bunkoed, and swindled, and played with by the political bosses? **1934** L. MUMFORD in W. Frank et al. *Amer. & Alfred Stieglitz* I. ii. 34 The political boss and his underlings. **1974** G. WOODBRIDGE in H. van Thal *Prime Ministers* I. 349 He [*sc.* Lord Grey] concluded with a highly political and very clever speech, suggesting that all that was at stake was the acceptance of the principle that there should be some reform, leaving the exact details..to be settled in the committee stage. **1977** *Times* 27 Jan. 5/1 If the Government chose the path of ill-considered and largely political legislation aimed at achieving a union takeover of private industry, it would have dealt a damaging blow. **1978** *Times* 3 Jan. 1/3 The union's vice-president..told a rally of 1000 striking firemen that the employers were playing 'a political game'.

6. *political animal* [tr. Gr. πολιτικὸν ζῷον (Aristotle *Politics* I. ii. §9) an animal intended to live in a city, a social animal] man, as acting in concert with others; a person who is interested in, or who participates in, politics; *political anthropology*, the study of the origins, forms, and exercise of community authority as it has evolved in aboriginal or isolated societies; *political asylum*, the condition of being, or permission to remain in a country as, a political refugee; *political commissar*, in China, a representative appointed to a military unit to be responsible for political education and organization; *political football*, a subject of contentious political debate; *political hostess*, a hostess at a party or gathering attended by politicians; *political morality*, public ethics; *political novel*, a fictitious political narrative, a novel about imaginary politicians; *political philosophy*, that department of philosophy which treats of politics or public ethics; hence *political philosopher*; *political police*, a police force concerned with offences against the state; *political prisoner* (examples); *political refugee*, a refugee from an oppressive government; *political science*, the study of the factors involved in politics (see POLITIC *sb.* 3) or the scientific analysis of political activity and behaviour; hence *political scientist*; *political sociology* (see quot. 1968); hence *political sociologist*; *political theory*, theory that is concerned with philosophical ideas of political power and with the history, forms, and activity of the state; hence *political theorist*; *political trial*, a trial of a defendant charged with a political offence, or a trial conducted for political reasons; *political warfare*, propaganda against another state, calculated to weaken it.

1776 W. ELLIS tr. *Aristotle's Treat. Govt.* I. ii. 6 Hence it is evident, that a city is a natural production, and that man is naturally a political animal. **1892** I. ZANGWILL *Childr. Ghetto* II. 113 The East End Jew is only slowly becoming a political animal. **1960** *Victorian Studies* June 348 Characters who necessarily act and feel as isolated individuals as well as political animals. **1968** L. DURRELL *Tunc* II. 89 If we get in again it will be to try and prove..that the key to the political animal is magnanimity. **1975** *Times* 17 July 19/1 Lady Young is.. very much a political animal. **1970** A. M. S. SMITH tr. *Balandier's Polit. Anthrop.* p. vii, This book is also intended to show how political anthropology is contributing to a clearer definition and a better knowledge of the political field. **1975** in Beattie & Lienhardt *Stud. in Soc. Anthrop.* xiv. 336 What Evans-Pritchard treated as no more than one sub-system among others..now seems.. to have become a specialization on its own, a 'political anthropology'. **1954** *Times* 14 Dec. 9/3 A steady consensus of judicial interpretation sustains the tradition of political asylum. **1962** *Weekly Law Reports* III. 1016 *Per* Viscount Radcliffe. In my opinion the idea that lies behind the phrase 'offence of a political character' is.. the analogy of..'political refugee', 'political asylum' or 'political prisoner'. It does indicate..that the requesting State is after him for reasons other than the enforcement of criminal law. **1973** *Ann. Reg. 1972* I. iii. 25 Two officers of the Royal Moroccan Air Force..arrived in Gibraltar and sought political asylum. **1937** E. SNOW *Red Star over China* VIII. vi. 299 The discussion continued for over an hour. Occasionally the commander or political commissar interrupted to summarize what had been said. **1956** F. F. LIU *Milit. Hist. Mod. China* ii. 19 The Kuomintang.. adopted a plan of gathering armed forces..and then inserting trained political commissars at the various levels of the newly absorbed groups. **1965** J. CH'ÊN *Mao & Chinese Revolution* (1967) I. viii. 175 At Iyang there was the 10th Red Army under Fang Chih-min with Shao Shih-p'ing as the political commissar. **1978** H. MCLEAVE *Borderline Case* (1979) xiii. 134 Yao was a political commissar and was running a military setup. **1971** *Financial Mail* (Johannesburg) 26 Feb. 673/3 The whole question of new negotiations seems to have become a political football and little more. **1975** *Australasian Express* 27 Mar. 7/1 In a strong attack, Mr Perkins claimed Aborigines were a 'political football' in Australia. **1977** *New Scientist* 17 Mar. 641/2 Recombinant DNA research is rapidly assuming the shape of a political football. **1883** E. W. HAMILTON *Diary* 18 Mar. (1972) II. 411 Lady Hayter has played the part of political hostess this year excellently well. **1944** C. DILKE in *Wine & Food* Spring 24 The house of a well-known political hostess. **1977** J. AIKEN *Last Movement* v. 92 Her..husband had suddenly ditched her in favour of a fat blonde political hostess. **1827** J. S. MILL in *Arch. f. Sozialwissensch.* (1929) 450 There always ought to be..a certain difference of opinion in every ministry. Let any one consider what the effect would be if the contrary maxim were received as a rule of political morality. **1861** —— *Repr. Govt.* x. 193 Undoubtedly neither this nor any other maxim of political morality is absolutely inviolable. **1866** *Times* 26 June 6/3 *Felix Holt, the Radical*, is not..a political novel, though it necessarily touches on politics. **1976** *Hiroshima Stud. Eng. Lang. & Lit.* XXI. 69 It [*sc.* Nostromo] is regarded as a 'political novel', a 'historical novel' or a 'philosophical novel'. **1833** LYTTON *England & English* II. 338 It is necessary..to distinguish between Mr. Bentham's practical conclusions..and his systematic views as a political philosopher. **1924** V. L. O. CHITTICK *T. C. Haliburton* xiii. 326 It was unquestionably not Sam Slick the political philosopher..that gave to his 'Sayings and Doings' the surprising vogue they formerly enjoyed. **1961** KAPLAN & KATZENBACH *Pol. Foundation of Internat. Law* I. iii. 64 Political philosophers will recognize its origins in the rejected doctrines of Hobbes. **1785** W. PALEY (*title*) The principles of moral and political philosophy. **1825** J. S. MILL in *Westm. Rev.* Apr. 286 The general question, to what extent restraints upon the freedom of the press can be considered as warranted by sound principles of political philosophy. **1958** A. R. RADCLIFFE-BROWN *Method in Social Anthropology* II. i. 139 There is an abundant literature on the subjects of social philosophy, political philosophy,..and the philosophy of art. **1976** *Listener* 3 June 705/1 There has been a real revival in political philosophy..particularly..in the U.S.A. **1910** R. ANDERSON *Lighter Side of my Official Life* xv. 246 Before coming to England as Ambassador, Count Schouvaloff was head of the Political Police at St. Petersburg. **1953** *Encounter* Oct. 67/1 Never during the Stalin era was the political police charged with illegal extortion of evidence. **1974** J. WHITE tr. *Poulantzas's Fascism & Dictatorship* VII. v. 341 None of this reorganization of the State apparatus can be understood without taking into account the growing and dominant role of the political police. **1860** DICKENS in *All Yr. Round* 13 Oct. 14/2 All the town knew about the Englishman and his political prisoner. **1927** B. RUSSELL *Outl. Philos.* iii. 44 Perhaps in time the State will perform these experiments with the children of political prisoners. **1972** *Guardian* 8 May 1/2 The loyalists have already sent a letter to Mr Whitelaw demanding political prisoner status. **1941** KOESTLER *Scum of Earth* 137 Paragraph 19 of the Armistice Treaty, providing for the extradition of political refugees. **1974** N. FREELING *Dressing of Diamond* 48 Marrying a political refugee..hadn't done him any good. **1779** HUME *Dial. Nat. Relig.* I. 16 This is their practice in all natural, mathematical, moral, and political science. **1794** A. FERGUSON *Princ. Moral & Polit. Sci.* II. II. vi. 411 *Salus populi, suprema lex esto*, is the fundamental principle of political science. **1836** J. S. MILL *Ess. Pol. Econ.* (1844) v. 146 This we can seldom do in ethical, and scarcely ever in political science. We cannot try forces of government and systems of national policy on a diminutive scale in our laboratories. **1898** G. B. SHAW *Let.* 18 Oct. (1972) II. 66 You and I have been confronted often enough with the follies of current political science. **1958** A. R. RADCLIFFE-BROWN *Method in Social Anthropology* I. iv. 102 Political systems, economic systems. and systems of law are studied in social anthropology and also in economics, political science and jurisprudence. **1974** A. BARBROOK *Patterns Polit. Behav.* i. 3 We have been left with a considerable range of behavioural theory, some of which has been completely accepted into the methodology of political science. **1902** *Amer. Jrnl. Sociol.* Jan. 564 There is not a political evolution through steps a, b, c, d, etc., which the political scientist can account for. **1974** *Listener* 24 Oct. 578/1 Professor Richard Rose..is the most productive political scientist in Britain. **1972** DOWSE & HUGHES *Political Sociol.* i. 7 As a matter of fact political sociologists do tend to concentrate on seeing in what ways society affects the state. **1957** *Current Sociol.* VI. 79 Political sociology is one of these recent additions. The label is perhaps more novel than the field. **1968** *Encycl. Soc. Sci.* XII. 298/2 Broadly conceived, political sociology is concerned with the social basis of power in all institutional sectors of society. In this tradition, political sociology deals with patterns of social stratification and their consequences in organized politics... By contrast, in narrower terms, political sociology focuses on the organizational analysis of political groups and..leadership. **1977** W. J. GOODE *Princ. Sociol.* xiii. 399/2 Political sociology and political science as special fields have overlapped comfortably for several decades. **1951** D. EASTON in Gould & Thursby *Contemp. Polit. Thought* (1969) xvii. 309 Speculations of the best political theorists have always been founded on acute observations of the contemporary political scene and a knowledge of human history. **1896** J. N. FIGGIS *Divine Right of Kings* x. 256 It is a far cry from the conception expressed in the Holy Roman Empire, that theology is the source of political theory. **1974** H. M. DRUCKER *Pol. Uses of Ideology* iv. 37 When a political theory points out that one kind of political system has such an advantage over another, we prefer the former. **1973** *Listener* 14 June 793/1 Every political trial has a long hidden history of what went on behind the scenes. **1974** J. BANNING *How I fooled World* xi. 52 There were the political trials in Czechoslovakia. **1950** *Chambers's Encycl.* XI. 254/2 In 1941..Eden,.. Bracken, the minister of information, and Dalton, who supervised propaganda to the enemy, constituted a Political Warfare Executive. **1977** E. AMBLER *Send no more Roses* iv. 70 The only higher-ups who took any real interest in our findings were the political warfare people.

7. In *Comb.*, prefixed to an adj. to denote: **a.** 'politically, as applied to politics', as *political-ethical, -moral, -strategic*; **b.** 'political and...', as *political-bureaucratic, -cultural, -economic, -juridical, -military, -religious, -social.*

1970 C. FURTADO in I. L. Horowitz *Masses in Lat. Amer.* ii. 31 The political-bureaucratic structure exterted [*sic*] a strong influence within the society. **1959** C. W. MILLS in —— *New Sociology* (1964) 85 [The] joint political-cultural struggle must be waged in intellectual and moral ways. **1937** *Science & Society* I. 153 There are abundant instances of the relation between 'standard' speech and the political-economic character of the ruling class. **1970** J. COTLER in I. L. Horowitz *Masses in Lat. Amer.* xii. 437 Due to the political-economic limitations in Mancha India, social opportunities for the Cholo are somewhat limited. **1936** L. WIRTH in K. Mannheim *Ideology & Utopia* p. xviii, Political-ethical norms not only cannot be derived from the direct contemplation of the facts, but themselves exert a moulding influence upon the very modes of perceiving the facts. **1971** R. apRoberts *Trollope* iv. 78 The political-ethical dilemmas of that novel [sc. *Ralph the Heir*]. **1919** J. T. Garvin *Econ. Foundations of Peace* x. 231 The means..will not be provided by the political-juridical part of the coming Constitution of the League. **1965** H. Kahn *On Escalation* vi. 125 Its possible worth in fulfilling European political-military objectives. **1970** H. Trevelyan *Middle East in Revolution* p. x, The withdrawal from Aden was a political-military operation conducted jointly by Headquarters, Middle East and the High Commission. **1953** S. Spender *Creative Element* 9 In the 1930's..I wrote of a 'political-moral' theme in modern literature. **1970** R. Stavenhagen in I. L. Horowitz *Masses in Lat. Amer.* vii. 259 Individual economic pre-eminence..arises, individually, through positions held in the political-religious structure. **1965** *English Studies* XLVI. 395 Melville is working in cosmic-religious, rather than political-social, terms. **1965** H. Kahn *On Escalation* vi. 122 It is not an improbable international political-strategic order for the future.

B. *sb.* **1. a.** (Later examples.)

1926 [see *fiddly *a.*]. **1939** *Times* 1 Aug. 13/3 Sir John Maffey..was an Indian political. **1958** L. Durrell *Mountolive* iv. 91 Pursewarden as political feels that the Embassy has also in a way inherited Maskelyne's department. **1979** C. Allen *Tales from Dark Continent* viii. 110 Most administrators—other than the Sudan politicals—regarded themselves as badly paid.

c. (Later examples.)

1938 *New Statesman* 19 Feb. 273/2 There are only 15 'politicals' still in gaol in the United Provinces and only 26 in Bihar. **1968** *Guardian* 22 Nov. 9/4 We started off being D Group prisoners, the lowest grade which only applies to politicals.

politicalization. (Further examples.)

1935 *Sun* (Baltimore) 19 Dec. 12/1 The current strong tendency toward politicalization of the intellectuals. **1947** *Partisan Rev.* XIV. 485 The ever-growing politicalization of intellectual life makes more and more difficult a disinterested theoretical approach. **1959** *Times Lit. Suppl.* 5 June 330/4 This is what Professor Marcuse calls the 'externalization' or the 'politicalization' of ethics. **1974** *Nature* 1 Mar. 1/1 A move toward what NIH scientists refer to as 'politicalisation of research'.

politicalized, *ppl. a.* [f. Politicalize *v.*] Made political in character.

1926 *Public Opinion* 13 Aug. 147/3 We are to have a politicalised Civil Service in this country. **1949** *Sun* (Baltimore) 19 Nov. 6/1 Does Congress wish to encourage big credit-seekers to turn..to a kind of politicalized or socialized banking setup?

politically, *adv.* Add: **3.** *Comb.*, as *politically-active, -inclined, -minded, -motivated* adjs.

1974 *Disturbances Univ. of Essex: Rep. Annan Enquiry* 17 Students protested that politically active ringleaders were singled out. **1969** J. Mander *Static Soc.* iii. 95 Enough for the politically-inclined tourist. **1907** *Westm. Gaz.* 11 Dec. 2/1 The politically-minded stay-at-home citizen. **1973** W. J. Burley *Death in Salubrious Place* iv. 73 The suave, politically-minded Bellings. **1972** *Listener* 21 Dec. 854/2 A rising level of politically-motivated violence. **1975** *Ibid.* 21 Aug. 233/2 We are not dealing with..an irresponsible, politically-motivated organisation in trade unions.

politicalness. (Earlier and later examples.)

1678 Cudworth *Intell. Syst.* i. v. 890 Not so much as any the least *seeds*, either of Politicalness, or Ethicalness at all in it. **1935** *Discovery* May 128/2 Notwithstanding all his politicalness and his zest for the letters and society ..it is in the campaigns and battles that Mr Trevelyan is happiest.

politicization (pǫli:tisəizē͘ⁱ·ʃən). [f. Politicize *v.*] The action or process of rendering political or of establishing upon a political basis; the fact of being politicized.

1934 *Times Lit. Suppl.* 25 Oct. 724/2 The attempted politicization of the German Protestant Church. **1938** *Downside Rev.* LVI. 384 The totalitarian supremacy of the State is the outcome of that 'total politicization' of man and his activities which was of the essence of Marxist theory. **1962** *Times Lit. Suppl.* 4 May 308/1 The politicization of private life. **1968** *Internat. Encycl. Soc. Sci.* X. 284 The major political process of recent years [in 'Middle America'] has been referred to as 'politicization', the recognition of the State as the ultimate authority and the recognition of legitimacy of certain governmental processes. **1976** F. Zweig *New Acquisitive Society* i. v. 57 The rapidly growing 'pressure group' movement..definitely leads to politicization of economic life. **1978** *Listener* 2 Nov. 564/2 Politicisation does not mean mere organised political activity... Politicisation of religion means the internal transformation of the faith itself, so that..it becomes..concerned with social morality rather than with the ethereal qualities of immortality.

politicize, *v.* Add: **2.** (Further examples.)

1962 S. E. Finer *Man on Horseback* xii. 236 Such parties..seek to dominate and politicize all politically important voluntary bodies outside their ranks. **1970** *Guardian* 5 June 11/7 The skinheads who Mr Powell has managed to politicise. **1978** *Time* 3 July 38/1 We're not out to politicize the White House..but we've got to use the political resources we have better than before.

Hence **poli·ticized** *ppl. a.*, interested or involved in politics, politically motivated; **poli·ticizing** *vbl. sb.*, the action or process of rendering political.

1887 [see Politicize *v.* 2]. **1971** *Daily Tel.* 17 Aug. 10 Any danger in this arises from the majority of viewers being..unaware of the bias as they watch it because most people are manifestly less politicised. **1975** R. Butt in Cox & Boyson *Black Paper 1975* 43/1 In this single statement, the politicizing of education in an entirely new sense—namely that it is now the vehicle used by those who, in varying degrees, wish to change the cultural basis of society—is explicit. **1977** *N.Y. Rev. Bks.* 12 May 50/4 (Advt.), I am a politicized, socialist, would-be scholar deeply isolated from academic radicalism.

politicking (pǫ·litikiŋ), *vbl. sb.* [f. *politic *v.* or Politic *a.* and *sb.* + -ing¹.] The action or fact of engaging in (esp. partisan) political activity.

1928 M. H. Weseen *Crowell's Dict. Eng. Gram.* 481 *Politicking*, a coined word that has no recognized standing. **1934** *Sun* (Baltimore) 10 July 1/3 Mr. Farley..confided to 'the boys' that he expects to do considerable 'politicking' along the way. **1943** *Sat. Even. Post* 30 Jan. 90/2 The politicking had started the minute his back was turned. **1957** *Economist* 5 Oct. 15/2 To dangle before the tenants..the idea that a Labour government will 'promptly' redress their grievances..might politely be described as politicking. **1975** F. Heer *Charlemagne & his World* x. 149 This is the elevated ideal that lay behind all the politicking and manoeuvering for position that took place in Rome in 800.

politico. Delete 'now *rare*' and add further examples. Also, a political agent; a person holding strong political views. Pl. **politicoes, politicos.**

1929 *Times* 14 Aug. 11/4 The old 'politicos' and the members of the more progressive parties, may be recommended to remember the object-lesson of the fate of the Aventine Opposition in Italy. **1941** E. Wilson *Wound & Bow* v. 215 Going back over Hemingway's books to-day, we can see clearly what an error of the politicos it was to accuse him of an indifference to society. **1951** I. Asimov *Foundation* v. xiii. 218 You're an old dog of a politico. **1955** J. Cary *Not Honour More* 42 It's a lot deeper than politics. And I wish you'd get all these politicos out of my house. **1956** W. Lewis *Red Priest* xxvii. 229 'The Mahatma was a very unusual man.' Father Makepeace replied. 'I referred to ordinary politicos.' 'There are no ordinary politicos in India,' said the elderly interrupter. **1958** *Listener* 18 Sept. 436/1 On Channel One..it was colour-bar week, with the Jamaican politico, Norman Manley, given a starring role. **1960** *Guardian* 8 Mar. 1/5 The press is here..and surprisingly important politicoes in ineffective disguises. **1967** *Observer* 26 Mar. 9 Hippies are sympathetic, but they are not politicos. **1973** *Black Panther* 11 Aug. 8/2 While publicly apologizing for Nixon, Colson managed to privately leak that the politicos Haldeman and Ehrlichman were guilty along with Mitchell and Dean. **1975** D. Lodge *Changing Places* iv. 145 Politicoes, frat rats, sallys and jocks and mommas for peace are..touching each other's hearts.

politico-. Add: **a.** *politico-aesthetic, -artistic, -moral* (further examples), *mythic, -Philistine, -racial*; **b.** *politico-bureaucratic, -criminal, -diplomatic, -legal, -literary, -military* (further examples), *-philosophical, -physiographical, -religious, -social* (further examples).

1974 *Times* 8 Jan. 14/6 Almost immediately he started giving long and fiery politico-aesthetic lectures to adoring left-wing students. **1961** *Times* 31 Oct. 14/3 *Accatone* [sc. a film]..has become the subject of one of those politico-artistic controversies. **1964** P. Worsley in I. C. Horowitz *New Sociology* 377 Politico-bureaucratic machines are in the saddle from the beginning, and there is no 'heroic' period of Cuban-type mass participation in government. **1955** D. W. Maurer in *Publ. Amer. Dial. Soc.* xxiv. 26 Very good connections with the politico-criminal liaison,..which extends like a network across the country. **1856** Dickens *Little Dorrit* (1857) i. x. 84 He fully understood the Department to be a politico diplomatico hocus pocus piece of machinery. **1973** P. A. Allum *Politics & Society in Post-War Naples* vii. 219 Their electoral and personal politico-diplomatic activities cannot be justified in straight *Gesellschaft* normative language. **1926** Galsworthy *Silver Spoon* i. ii. 9 Lady Alison's politico-legal coterie no longer counted. **1970** B. Brewster tr. *Althusser & Balibar's Reading Capital* ii. v. 133 In fact, this is to attribute to the concept 'superstructure' a breadth Marx never allowed, for he only ranged within it: (1) the politico-legal superstructure, and (2) the ideological superstructure. **1924** Galsworthy *White Monkey* 73 She..picked out the biggest 'bug', politico-literary, and waited to pin him. **1978** D. Daiches *Edinburgh* x. 182 There was some pretty savage politico-literary fighting, especially in the Tory *Blackwood's*. **1931** *Times Lit. Suppl.* 29 Oct. 827/1 One of the objects of the Prussian campaign, a masterpiece of politico-military strategy, was to separate Prussia and Saxony. **1975** *Times* 1 Dec. 10/5 The then politico-military concepts of revolutionary war. **1920** B. Russell *Pract. & Theory Bolshevism* i. ii. 30 The sincere Communists..are not unlike the Puritan soldiers in their stern politico-moral purpose. **1965** *Mod. Law Rev.* XXVIII. v. 536 There would seem to be much more force in Professor H. L. A. Hart's argument that the judges do not know or at least cannot evaluate what the 'politico-moral' principles behind their decisions are. **1974** *Publishers Weekly* 4 Nov. 62/1 This politico-mythic tale..expresses wishes rather than facts. **1960** *Times* 3 Oct. 13/3 They [sc. universities] may save themselves from the politico-Philistine interference they fear. **1936** *New Yorker* 14 Mar. 24/1 Proletarianism.. superimposed on some remarkably interesting politico-philosophical formulae. **1973** *Nation Rev.* (Melbourne) 31 Aug. 1455/2 These uncertainties..are the ruination of most politico-philosophical series. **1935** *Univ. Mich. Publ. Lang. & Lit.* XIII. 43 South of this point it coincides with the strong politico-physiographical frontier already indicated. **1959** *Times Lit. Suppl.* 22 May 303/3 Lynchings and murders and other forms of politico-racial violence have significantly diminished since the war. **1908** *Daily Chron.* 19 June 4/6 The Great Powers.. should recall some of their agents and those politico-religious missionaries, who, instead of putting out the fire, secretly throw fuel into the flames. **1937, 1953** [see *Caodaism]. **1978** D. Murphy *Place Apart* xi. 235 In the midst of all the politico-religious dissension [in Ulster], one tends to overlook the general social problems. **1958** Politico-social [see *Miltonizing *ppl. a.* and *vbl. sb.*]. **1950** M. Crosland tr. *Rovan's Germany* 99 The D.G.B... remains the richest and most powerful union confederation in Europe, constituting a genuine politico-social power.

c. prefixed to a noun, forming a quasi-*adj.*, as *politico-crime, politico-travel.*

1952 Turkus & Feder *Murder, Inc.* vi. 100 In November of 1950, an investigation of politico-crime tie-ups was launched in New York. *Ibid.* xiii. 291 The investigation shocked the public into a new consciousness of the politico-crime danger. **1970** *Daily Tel.* 14 May 6/2 A politico-travel diary, the book is useful background to the present crisis and conflict.

poli·tico-econo·mic, *a.* [Politico-.] = Politico-economical *a.*

1839 Carlyle *Chartism* x. 97 Paralytic Radicalism.. which..sounds with Philosophic Politico-Economic plummet the deep dark sea of troubles. *a* **1854** Mill *Draft Autobiogr.* (1961) 82 The Benthamic & politico-economic form of Liberalism. **1910** J. W. Welsford (*title*) The strength of England: a politico-economic history of England from Saxon times to the reign of Charles I. **1933** E. E. Evans-Pritchard in *Africa* VI. 372 Exchange of blood in such situations sacralizes and endows with sanctions a politico-economic transaction. **1955** *Bull. Atomic Sci.* June 205/2 A complete understanding of political and sociologic conditions will have to be used to decide what politico-economic incentives and assurances may be brought to bear. **1974** P. Gore-Booth *With Great Truth & Respect* 380 Such are the problems of politico-economic diplomacy.

politico-economical, *a.* Add: (Further examples.)

1837 *Democratic Review* I. 113 In spite of the plain principles of politico-economical truth. **1858** [see *economical *a.* 3 b].

Hence **politico-economist**, a student of, or writer on, political economics (cf. Economist 4 b).

1885 W. Harris *Hist. Radical Party* vii. 141 It is worth noticing that Ricardo, the politico-economist, was in the minority.

politique. Add: **1. a.** (Later examples in extended senses.)

1958 *Times Lit. Suppl.* 11 July 390/4 It certainly attracted a number of outstanding political leaders to it. Dr. Zeldin introduces us to many of these latter-day politiques. **1959** *Encounter* July 45/2 Some presenting him [sc. Odysseus] as an enlightened statesman, others as a machiavellian *politique*. **1972** K. B. McFarlane *Lancastrian Kings & Lollard Knights* i. ii. 24, I would maintain that in politics Henry [IV] was not a man of constitutional principle at all but an opportunist and a *politique*.

2. A political concept or doctrine; an expression of political ideas.

1958 A. Dru tr. *Péguy's Temporal & Eternal* 27 A country, a *régime* does not need you, it does not need mystics, a *mystique*, or its *mystique*... It needs a sound *politique*, which means a good government policy. **1958** *Times Lit. Suppl.* 27 June 366/2 Péguy used the witness of the few independent supporters of Dreyfus to illustrate that radical distinction between *mystique* and *politique* which is the essential clue to all his thought... For him the Revolution and the Christian religion were in origin and in essence both *mystiques* that were profoundly true... But they had become *politiques*: 'It is one and the same movement which makes people no longer believe in the Republic and no longer believe in God.' *Ibid.* 366/3 The withering criticism of the clergy is always in terms of their compromising with the *mystique* which alone makes Christianity valid: the Church has devoted its energies instead to propagating a *politique*. **1959** *Listener* 4 June 999/1 His analysis of Communist politique had a theme which lent itself to radio dramatization. **1977** A. Ecclestone *Staircase for Silence* v. 88 *Politique*..set in as a process of dislocation,..a choosing to go it alone. It became an end in itself, ever seeking an aggrandisement of its own power, suspicious of and ready to suppress whatever challenged its own authority.

polje (pōᵘ·lyĕ). *Physical Geogr.* Also **polye.** Pl. **poljes,** ‖ **polja,** (after Ger.) **poljen.** [Serbo-Croat *polje* field.] An enclosed plain in a karstic region, esp. Yugoslavia, that is larger than a uvala and usu. has steep enclosing walls and a covering of alluvium.

1894 *Geogr. Jrnl.* III. 323 The *poljen* occur at low levels, and therefore receive an enormous supply of 'ground water', especially at the times of the autumn or winter rains, which the underground outlet cannot carry it [*sic*] off fast enough. **1902** *Ibid.* XX. 428 In spring..the floors of the polyes are flooded. **1918** D. W. Johnson *Topogr. & Strategy in War* xiv. 169 In the rear of the Serbian armies ..runs the straight subsidiary trench formed by the Lepenatz valley, Kosovo Polye, and the Ibar valley. **1926** *Geogr. Jrnl.* LXVII. 197 Lakes in the high calcareous Alps of Switzerland occupy dolines or polyes, the bottom of which have been more or less filled by deposits of impervious material derived from the ground moraines of the ancient glaciers. **1934** *Discovery* Sept. 247/1 Some of these *polja* are periodic lakes. **1954** W. D. Thornbury *Princ. Geomorphol.* xiii. 324 The largest polje in the Western Balkans, the Livno polje, is 40 miles long and 3 to 7 miles wide. **1958** *Geogr. Jrnl.* CXXIV. 41 Some of the largest polja are found among the Dinaric Alps in the hinterland of Split. **1960** B. W. SPARKS *Geomorphol.* vii. 155 The largest depressions of Yugoslavia, the poljes, are probably not solution forms at all but tectonic depressions modified by solution of the limestone preserved in them. **1972** *Science* 12 May 664/3 The perennial flooding of the farmlands in the poljes of Yugoslavia.

polk, *v.* Add: Hence **po·lking** *vbl. sb.*

1848 E. GRAY *Let.* in M. Lutyens *Ruskins & Grays* (1972) x. 95, I got introduced to good partners and got some good polking. **1853** J. R. PLANCHÉ *Mr. Buckstone's Ascent of Mount Parnassus* 30 Each night to some Casino.. Where I am pulled by fast young men about And with eternal polking quite worn out.

polka, *sb.*[1] Add: **1.** *polka-mazurka* (examples); *polka-time.*

1861 H. RHYS *Theatrical Trip for Wager!* xiii. 120 They advanced in line, in polka time, then right-about-turned. **1928** A. M. M. DOUTON *Bk. with Seven Seals* I. 112 The course of calisthenics..terminated with lessons in the ..polka-mazurka. **1957** G. B. L. WILSON *Dict. Ballet* 219 *Polka-mazurka,* dance derived from the polka, from which it differs in that it is in 3/4 time, and from the mazurka, by which it is distinguished by having an accent on the 3rd instead of the 2nd beat. **1967** CHUJOY & MANCHESTER *Dance Encycl.* (rev. ed.) 738/2 *Polka-Mazurka,* a Polish variation of the polka, in 3/4 time, danced as a ballroom dance in countries of Eastern Europe.

3. polka-dot (further examples); also *fig.*, *attrib.* or as *adj.*, and as *v. trans.*; hence *polka-dotted* adj.

1895 *Montgomery Ward Catal.* Spring & Summer 9/3 Polka Dot Chambray, linen finish. **1906** 'O. HENRY' *Four Million* 136 The next day a person with red hands and a blue polka-dot necktie..called. **1908** W. G. DAVENPORT *Butte & Montana beneath X-Ray* 9 Miss P—— received her guests in a lovely polka dotted frock. **1924** W. M. RAINE *Troubled Waters* xxi. 224 He took off his big white hat and rubbed a polka-dot handkerchief over his bald head. **1928** F. N. HART *Bellamy Trial* i. 3 He wore a shabby tweed suit, a polka-dotted tie. **1956** *Daily Mail* 19 July 6/1 Camping sites are scattered like polka dots all over the Riviera. **1957** V. NABOKOV *Pnin* vi. 138 Amber-brown Monarch butterflies flapped.., their incompletely retracted black legs hanging rather low beneath their polka-dotted bodies. **1964** D. VARADAY *Gara-Yaka* ii. 23 Polka dots were becoming clearly defined on her tawny, golden hide. **1966** MRS. L. B. JOHNSON *White House Diary* 3 Apr. (1970) 382 A young newspaper-woman in a black-and-white polka-dot bikini, with a figure to suit it. **1969** *Better Homes & Gardens* (U.S.) Apr. 83 Tiny bright red fruits that polka-dot the long branches. **1970** *New Yorker* 16 May 18/1 (Advt.), Men often are remembered for odd reasons. Like our 11th President. Little did he dream when he designed the polka dot that one day it would become the epitome of fashion. **1972** *Daily Tel.* 16 Aug. 1/1 A blonde girl wearing a green polka dot bikini was found dead in the sea..yesterday. **1972** *Suttons Seeds* 16 Polka Dot mixed. These bushy Cornflowers stand up to weather well, with a good range of colours. **1978** J. WAINWRIGHT *Jury People* xxxvi. 111 Kids are out. Because the world ain't yet ready for polka-dot kids. Black is only beautiful in places. **1979** C. WOOD *James Bond & Moonraker* xi. 112 She had big puffed sleeves..and a petticoat effect of over-lapping polka-dotted skirts.

polka *v.* (earlier example).

1846 DICKENS *Let.* 5 July (1977) IV. 580 The common people waltzed and polka'd without cessation, to the music of a band.

poll, *sb.*[1] Add: **1. β.** (Further examples of *Sc.* and *north. dial.* form *pow.*)

1876 F. K. ROBINSON *Gloss. Whitby* 146/2 *Pow,* the poll; the human head. **1901** G. B. SHAW *Devil's Disciple* III. 79 The Devil's Disciple here will start presently as the Reverend Richard Dudgeon, and wag his pow in my old pulpit. **1919** *Kelso Chron.* 4 Apr. 3 My blood's not chill, though near the night, And grey-haired is my pow. **1940** E. POUND *Cantos* lxxi. 186 His daughter told me he had burnt all his papers In melancholia May be from that swat on the pow. **1947** E. A. MCCOURT *Flaming Hour* ix. 54 'Weren't ye lyin' locked up in yon shed no later than yesterday mornin' with a bump on your pow that should have kept ye still for a fortnight?' he demanded ferociously. **1963** G. THOMSON *Crocus & Meadowlark Country* xi. 75 Ethel added a drawing she made of Jim one cold day when he made his way there with Chaddy's red tam-o'-shanter pulled down on his red pow. **1965** *Buchan Observer* 12 Jan. 2 Ye'll hum an' hae an' claw your pow. **1973** *People's Jrnl.* (Inverness & Northern Counties ed.) 1 Dec. 4/5 I'd got no further than filling my pow with rollers and covering my head with a woollen head square.

7. d. A poll taken to estimate public opinion on a specified issue by questioning a sample intended to be representative of the whole people (see *GALLUP); *spec.*, (*a*) = *popularity poll* s.v. *POPULARITY 8; (*b*) a poll intended to forecast the result of a presidential, parliamentary, or other election (see **opinion poll* s.v. *OPINION *sb.* 1 b). Also *attrib.*

1902 F. CLARKE tr. *Ostrogorski's Democracy and Organization of Political Parties* II. v. iv. 306 The poll taken in each locality is of general import for the whole Union, as well as of special significance for each political subdivision in the States. **1940** GALLUP & RAE *Pulse of Democracy* iii. 35 In this poll [of July 1824] Andrew Jackson received 335 votes; John Quincy Adams, 169; Henry Clay, 19, and William H. Crawford, 9. **1944** *Times* 9 June 5/5 The recent British Medical Association poll of members' opinions with regard to medical interests caused considerable controversy. **1950** *Times* 8 Feb. 7/6 Public opinion polls and investigations carried out by the Japanese Press show that the Yoshida Cabinet no longer enjoys as much support as it did at the time of the General Election in January, 1949. **1964** GOULD & KOLB *Dict. Social Sci.* 517/1 Poll denotes..the canvas of opinions, prior to an election, by simple or complex interviewing. **1973** *Melody Maker* 31 Mar. 18 It's time to vote in the Melody Maker Jazz Poll. This..is your opportunity to register your appreciation of the musicians, bands, and singers whom you think have made the finest contributions to jazz over the last year. **1974** *Times* 11 Feb. 15 The poll firms showed their anxiety by conducting their own inquest into their failure... Poll findings are being presented as *predictions* of the result. **1977** *New Yorker* 9 May 136/2 Polls conducted in April show that Carter currently has the approval of about two-thirds of the public. *Ibid.* 24 Oct. 42/3 Fetching coffee in paper cups for the poll watchers.

10. (sense 7 b) **poll-card,** an official notification informing voters of the place and date of voting; (sense *7 d) **poll-rating,** the popularity of a person (usu. a political leader) as indicated by a poll; **poll-taker,** usu. in *pl.*, a newspaper or other organization which conducts an opinion poll, = *POLLSTER; hence **poll-taking** *vbl. sb.*; **pollwinner,** a successful candidate in a poll; so **poll-winning** *ppl. a.*

1908 *Westm. Gaz.* 4 May 2/2 Mr. Amery's final appeal.. s going with the poll-card to every elector. **1975** *Times* 27 Feb. 4/3 Poll cards..remind the elector of his right to vote and they tell him his voting number and where his polling station is. **1967** *Guardian* 16 Oct. 6/1 Mr Heath's poll-ratings were unsatisfactory. **1959** *Spectator* 4 Sept. 288/2 When poll-takers put the question directly to the citizenry, it seems that vast numbers think it good. **1964** *Economist* 12 Sept. 1021/1 A victory for Mr Goldwater would be the greatest upset for the poll-takers since the *Literary Digest* predicted a landslide for Mr Landon, the Republican who was crushed by President Roosevelt in 1936. **1976** *National Observer* (U.S.) 11 Dec. 5/3 Poll-taker Teeter told the governors that 'our Presidential elections have become nonpartisan media events'. **1964** I. L. HOROWITZ *New Sociology* 31 Problems of this kind can be multiplied a hundredfold—in every sphere of sociology, from poll-taking to theory-making. **1966** *Melody Maker* 7 May 4 Pollwinner Tubby Hayes heads a five-man British contingent which will join Austrian composer Friedrich Gulda's all-star international band on its tour of the continent this summer. **1958** P. GAMMOND *Decca Bk. of Jazz* xviii. 218 Jackson in particular was the equivalent of the poll-winning trumpet men of today. **1962** *Melody Maker* 7 July 8 Pollwinning bandleader Chris Barber has firm views on the subject.

Pollack, var. POLACK *sb.* (*a.*) in Dict. and Suppl.

pollakanthic (pǫlăkæ·nþik), *a. Bot.* [f. Gr. πολλάκ-ις many times + ἄνθ-ος flower + -IC 1.] = *POLYCARPIC *a.* a. Also **pollaka·nthous** *a.* in the same sense.

1909 GROOM & BALFOUR tr. *Warming's Oecol. Plants* ii. 6 In recent times these Candollean terms have been suppressed often in favour of..Kjellman's 'pollakanthic'. **1965** BELL & COOMBE tr. *Strasburger's Textbk. Bot.* 355 The production of vegetative members by the growing points changes over to that of flowers, fruits and seeds,.. periodically, as in pollakanthous plants. **1973** MCLEAN & IVIMEY-COOK *Textbk. Theoret. Bot.* IV. xlii. 3353 Polycarpic (pollakanthic) plants..flower and fruit repeatedly.

polled, *ppl. a.* **2.** (Further examples.)

1842 [see *ANGUS]. **1867** W. MCCOMBIE *Cattle* iv. 138 Mr Lyell..has a very good herd of polled Angus cattle. **1891** R. WALLACE *Rural Econ. Austral. & N.Z.* xxxii. 415 Polled Angus cattle have come very rapidly into favour during the last few years. **1909** J. WILSON *Evolution of Brit. Cattle* v. 57 The Sutherland polled cattle are long extinct. **1940** J. HAMMOND *Farm Animals* viii. 149 If we mate a polled red Aberdeen Angus bull to a Shorthorn cow we shall obtain polled calves. **1976** *Cumberland & Westmorland Herald* 4 Dec. 16/2 (Advt.), Fortnightly sale of Friesian, Hereford cross, Charolais' cross and polled bullocks and heifers of all ages.

pollee (pōulī·). [f. POLL *sb.*[1] + -EE[1].] One who is questioned in a poll (sense *7 d).

1940 *Propaganda Analysis* IV. 4/2 The question, 'For whom will you vote for President of the United States?' illustrates Objectivism. It gives to the pollee full liberty to name any candidate. **1941** *Amer. Speech* XVI. 306 *Pollee,* one polled by a public-opinion 'institute'. **1945** *Richmond* (Va.) *Times-Dispatch* 25 Oct. 10/6 Mr. Gallup.. should consult his little band of pollees and come up with their prophecy as to which of our service teams will go home with the goal posts. **1962** *Guardian* 3 Aug. 14/6 The 54 pollees who had voted last time had come within one percentage of splitting their 1960 votes.

pollen, *sb.* Add: **3.** *pollen-content(s)*, *-zone*; *pollen-bearing* (example), *-dated*, *-free* adjs.; **pollen analysis** = *PALYNOLOGY; hence **pollen analyst,** a scientist who uses the techniques of pollen analysis; **pollen-analytic(al)** *adjs.*; **pollen-analytically** *adv.*; **pollen count,** an index of the quantity of pollen in the air, obtained by counting the grains collected on a given area of a coated glass plate exposed for twenty-four hours, and published as a warning to those allergic to it; also, an indication of the frequency of pollen in an archæological site; also *fig.*; **pollen diagram,** a sequence of pollen spectra from one site, showing changes in the frequencies of various types of pollen; **pollen graph** = **pollen diagram*; **pollen index** = **pollen count*; **pollen mother cell,** a cell in a seed plant which undergoes meiosis to yield four pollen grains; **pollen parent,** the plant from which pollen is taken to fertilize another plant in an attempt to produce a hybrid; **pollen profile** = **pollen diagram*; **pollen spectrum,** the relative frequencies of the various types of pollen in a single sample.

1924 G. ERDTMAN in *Jrnl. Linn. Soc.: Bot.* XLVI. 450 The study of micro-fossils (and especially of fossil pollen-grains), upon which von Post's method of pollen-analysis is based. **1935** *Discovery* Apr. 100/1 The methods of pollen-analysis..enable one to know of the afforestation and in consequence of the climate of the period during which any particular stratum in a peat deposit was laid down. **1944, 1958** [see *PALYNOLOGY]. **1973** *Microscopy* XXXII. 321 Erdtman prepared and presented the first doctoral thesis ever to be based on pollen analysis. **1943** G. ERDTMAN *Introd. Pollen Analysis* i. 1 Still more remarkable appear the performances accomplished by the pollen analyst today. **1973** *Microscopy* XXXII. 320 Gustav Lagerheim (1860–1926) was one of the earliest pollen analysts. **1949** *Bull. Geol. Soc. Amer.* LX. 1359/2 Events ..may have been contemporaneous in the astronomic as well as the pollen-analytic sense. **1946** F. E. ZEUNER *Dating Past* iii. 59 Further important remarks on the principles and system of pollen-analytical datings are included in a great many papers. **1976** *Nature* 24 June 628/1 Some new information..has been gleaned..as a result of a pollen analytical study of upper Miocene lignites. **1936** *Proc. Prehistoric Soc.* II. 146 One may quote an instance from the Baltic..pollen-analytically dated to Boreal times. **1946** F. E. ZEUNER *Dating Past* iv. 78 A good many localities have been studied pollen-analytically. *Ibid.* 80 Nilsson has studied the connexion of pollen-bearing deposits with raised beaches. *Ibid.* iii. 57 The pollen-contents of a peat are more or less characteristic of the tree-associations that grew in the neighbourhood of the spot under investigation. **1954** S. PIGGOTT *Neolithic Cultures* i. 3 The evidence for the natural conditions of vegetation in Atlantic and Sub-Boreal times is based most reliably on the pollen-content of stratified peats. [**1873** C. J. BLACKLEY *Experimental Researches on Catarrhus Æstivus* iv. 122 After being exposed for twenty-four hours, each slip was placed under the microscope, and any deposit it contained was carefully examined, and the number of pollen grains counted.] **1926** KOESSLER & DURHAM in *Jrnl. Amer. Med. Assoc.* LXXXVI. 1205/1 For the air study..differential pollen counts were made daily. **1944** URBACH & GOTTLIEB *Allergy* xix. 607 In order to become acquainted with the local flora, the physician should undertake pollen counts himself. **1965** *Punch* 15 Sept. 375/2 Throughout the summer, New York newspapers forecast daily..a 'pollen count' for hay-fever victims. **1975** G. W. DIMBLEBY in R. Bruce-Mitford *Sutton Hoo Ship-Burial* I. i. 68 (*heading*) Soil under ship-barrow pollen counts. **1978** *Times* 7 July 2/8 The pollen count issued in London yesterday by the Asthma Research Council was one, very low. **1936** *Proc. Prehistoric Soc.* II. 239 The forest culture of S.E. Britain, best known from the pollen-dated site of Lower Halstow, had diverged very markedly. **1924** G. ERDTMAN in *Jrnl. Linn. Soc.: Bot.* XLVI. 453 By means of the percentage numbers a pollen-diagram is constructed. **1954** S. PIGGOTT *Neolithic Cultures* i. 4 The pollen diagrams constructed from stratified peats in many parts of the British Isles show a consistent evolution of forest assemblages. **1973** PROCTOR & YEO *Pollination of Flowers* viii. 276 The pollen diagrams from different sites show striking correspondences in the course of events. **1963** *New Yorker* 15 June 117 Heated swimming pool... Pollen-free air. **1975** G. W. DIMBLEBY in R. Bruce-Mitford *Sutton Hoo Ship-Burial* I. i. 55 This pollen profile appears to have developed in a pollen-free sand deposit. This would accord with the suggestion that at some time during or since the Anglo-Saxon period the soil was truncated down to the pollen-free subsoil. **1959** J. D. CLARK *Prehist. Southern Afr.* vi. 160 The grasslands of our Central Plateau Region which, the pollen-graphs from Florisbad tell us, must have still been open country even at the height of the pluvial. **1973** 'D. JORDAN' *Nile Green* ii. 12 Most of us have hay fever and the pollen index was high. **1884** *Jrnl. R. Microsc. Soc.* 714 We should have a case similar to that seen in the pollen-mother-cells of *Fritillaria persica.* **1889** *Bot. Gaz.* XIV. 109 If any person has experienced difficulty in obtaining pollen mother-cells in excellent condition for study, their attention is called to the young anthers of *Negundo aceroides* Moench. **1926** *Ibid.* LXXXI. 154 In a given loculus of an anther the pollen mother cells of the apple show little variation in stage of development. **1976** BELL & COOMBE tr. *Strasburger's Textbk. Bot.* 39 (*caption*) Prophase of the first meiotic divisions of a pollen mother cell. **1910** *Nat. Rose Society's Rose Ann.* 50 Place the top of the finger upon the anthers of the variety it is proposed to use as the pollen parent. **1933** *Lily Year-bk.* 173 The plant showed no trace of the pollen parent and was discarded. **1976** *Lilies* 36 The plant with narrow leaves had a long chromosome..of a type found in the pollen parent. **1967** M. J. COE *Ecology Alpine Zone Mt. Kenya* 52 If the pollen profile is correlated with a time scale..it has been possible..to demonstrate an interesting sequence of vegetation zone depression. **1972** *Computers & Humanities* VII. 40 Pollen analysis is now being aided by the computer, either to compile and print the pollen profiles..or to perform statistical analysis of pollen data. **1924** G. ERDTMAN in *Jrnl. Linn. Soc.: Bot.* XLVI. 453 The relative frequency-numbers..constitute the pollen-spectrum of the sample. **1946** F. E. ZEUNER *Dating Past* iii. 59 A circle with sectors giving the frequency of the most important species in the pollen-spectrum can be inserted on a map. **1977** *New Phytologist* LXXVIII. 711 The sequence of four pollen spectra from the Coralline Crag shows no great variation from one level to the next. **1946** F. E. ZEUNER *Dating Past* 389, 23 finds..dated according to pollen zones. **1973** P. A. COLINVAUX *Introd. Ecol.* vii. 100 A nine or ten pollen-zone sequence..named in Roman numerals.

pollenin. Delete † *Obs.* and add: Cf. *SPOROPOLLENIN. (Further examples.)

Quot. 1931 does not represent a new sense.

1931 *Chem. Abstr.* XXV. 2455 Qual[itative] tests on many pollens showed that their hulls or membranes are similar chemically to lycopodium-sporenin [*sic*], and the name *pollenin* is proposed for such compds. **1964** [see *SPORONIN]. **1971** CHALONER & ORBELL in J. Brooks et al. *Sporopollenin* 274 In terms of modern usage, both John and Braconnot were using the word pollenin not only for the exine, but also for the underlying intine of cellulose—in fact the whole of the sporoderm or spore coat. **1974** STANLEY & LINSKENS *Pollen* ix. 138 Early studies..reported pollen to contain about 40% pollenin.

pollenizer (pǫ·lĕnəizəɹ). [f. POLLENIZE *v.* + -ER¹.] = *POLLINATOR.

1897 *Bull. Central Exper. Farm Dept. Agric.* (Canada) No. 27. 18 This [variety of strawberry] is valuable as a pollenizer.

poll-evil. Add: (Later examples.) Also † *fig.*, an obsession with elections.

1794 J. BYNG *Torrington Diaries* (1938) IV. 76 Sir G. at present is plagued by the pollevil—reverting to the past election with all the possibilities of a future one. **1873** J. H. BEADLE *Undevel. West* xxvi. 565, I..reined up my horse suddenly and again butted him in the back of the head, at the imminent risk of giving us both the poll-evil. **1970** MILLER & WEST *Black's Vet. Dict.* (ed. 9) 730/2 'Poll evil' is an old, colloquial name sometimes incorrectly applied to any swelling in the poll region.

pollex. Add: **1.** (Later examples.)

1897 PARKER & HASWELL *Text-bk. Zool.* II. xiii. 77 The first digit of the fore-limb is distinguished as the pollex or thumb. **1909** W. BATESON *Mendel's Princ. Heredity* xii. 213 The case is more probably to be regarded as a homoeotic variation of the digits into the likeness of the hallux and pollex. **1959** [see *ALULA 1]. **1971** A. BURGESS *MF* xv. 169 She clutched her bag between index and pollex. **1975** *Nature* 17 Jan. 192/1 *Proteles* differs from *Hyaena* principally in having a dentition much reduced in size, and in retaining the pollex (a digit lost in both *Hyaena* and *Crocuta*).

2. *Zool.* The movable part of the forceps in some crustaceans.

1895 F. H. HERRICK *Amer. Lobster* ix. 147 The pollux [*sic*] is depressed, so that when the claw is closed it falls almost exactly midway between the normal and first superadded digit. **1904** *Biol. Bull.* VI. 75 The added structure [of an aberrant limb of a crayfish] is..a movable piece with two immobile prongs that otherwise resemble the index and pollex of a forceps.

pollinate, *v.* Add: (Later examples.) Also *absol.*

1919 J. N. MARTIN *Bot. for Agric. Students* iv. 49 These plants are not successfully pollinated when they are wet. **1935** C. ZIRKLE *Beginnings of Plant Hybridization* i. 6 It is not stated specifically in the description of this building [*sc.* Solomon's Temple] that the cherubim were engaged in pollinating the flowers of the palms. **1942** HAYES & IMMER *Methods of Plant Breeding* iv. 63 With wheat it is equally satisfactory to pollinate during the day. **1973** PROCTOR & YEO *Pollination of Flowers* i. 19 The role of insects in pollinating flowers is a commonplace. **1974** A. HUXLEY *Plant & Planet* xiii. 132 There is just a little nectar in each flower, so that the insects..pollinate more actively.

pollinating (pǫ·linēⁱtiŋ), *ppl. a.* [f. POLLINATE *v.* + -ING².] That pollinates or facilitates pollination.

1911 F. O. BOWER *Plant-Life on Land* 69 The very genesis of the forms of flowers, their tints, and scents is in strict accordance with their efficiency as pollinating mechanisms.

pollination. Add: (Further examples.) Also *attrib.* and *fig.*

1924 HOLMAN & ROBBINS *Textbk. Gen. Bot.* vii. 283 The transfer of pollen from the anther to the stigma is called pollination. **1941** D. C. PEATTIE *Road of Naturalist* i. 19 The paper-bag bush, too, had gone to pod, just a few of its purple mint flowers left, where I had seen the humming-birds at pollination. **1971** E. MAVOR *Ladies of Llangollen* v. 90 Romantic pollinations..were taking place between an ever growing number of cultivated women. **1974** A. HUXLEY *Plant & Planet* xiii. 131 The second classic pollination symbiosis is that of the American Yuccas with certain moths.

pollinator (pǫ·linēⁱtəɹ). [f. POLLINATE *v.* + -OR.] Any insect or other agent that pollinates plants.

1903 *Amer. Naturalist* XXXVII. 368 The small concealed flowers of Gaultheria..do not want for pollinators. **1924** *Chambers's Jrnl.* Aug. 501/2 The value of bees as pollinators is appreciated by progressive fruit growers. **1955** *Sci. Amer.* Aug. 52/1 It would be more appropriate to think of them [*sc.* bees] first of all as the great pollinators. **1977** M. ALLAN *Darwin & his Flowers* xi. 202 The pollinator is not known for any *Cryptophoranthus*.

pollinctor. Restrict † *Obs.* to sense in Dict. and add: **b.** *U.S. Blacks.* One employed by a funeral director to prepare bodies for cremation or burial; an undertaker.

1969 *Liberator* Dec. 13/2, I left the funeral home along with the body and the pollinctor.

polling, *vbl. sb.* Add: **II. 5. b.** The action or process of conducting an opinion poll.

1937 *Public Opinion Q.* Jan. 38 Scientific polling on individual issues fills a great gap in the democratic form of government. **1939** G. GALLUP *Public Opinion in Democracy* 13 The research man who..devises an accurate and efficient method of polling 'ballot cattle' is obviously not contributing much to better government. **1944** —— *Guide to Public Opinion Polls* 12 Although the layman doesn't recognize it as polling, he is himself daily conducting his own private poll of public opinion. **1951** 'A. GARVE' *Murder in Moscow* vii. 83 You go into the streets and do a little polling on the subject... You'll get a hundred per cent 'Yes'—not a single 'Don't know'. **1968** W. SAFIRE *New Lang. of Politics* 108/2 The power of polling, both on nose counts and in depth, was never more vividly demonstrated than in the 1968 New Hampshire primary campaign. **1974** *Encycl. Brit. Macropædia* XV. 214/1 Polling can..reveal something about the intensity with which opinions are held. *Ibid.*, Polling..is unlikely to provide very much information about the elites who may have played an important part in developing the opinion.

III. 6. b. *polling-day* (examples), *-district* (examples), *-station* (further example).

1865 K. AMBERLEY *Diary* 13 July in B. & P. Russell *Amberley Papers* (1937) I. viii. 399 Polling Day—cloudy & windy. **1974** *Times* 6 Sept. 1/4 He hinted heavily several times that polling day was only a matter of weeks away. **1895** C. PORRETT in *Elections* (Yorks. Union of Conservative Assocs.) 12 An agent..should keep a list of gentlemen willing to lend conveyances to the various polling district committees. **1976** *Western Mail* (Cardiff) 27 Nov. (Advt.), Before you can trace your name in the lists you must know in which Polling District you live. **1977** *Grimsby Even. Tel.* 5 May 1/2 Unfortunately not enough publicity was given by the parties to the fact that the polling stations close at 9 instead of 10.

polliwog, pollywog. Add: Also **pollywiggle, pollywoggle.**

1823 E. MOOR *Suffolk Words & Phrases* 288 *Pollywiggle*, the tad-pole—in Norfolk called *potladle*. **1881** S. EVANS *Evans's Leicestershire Words* (new ed.) 216 *Pollywig*, or *pollywiggle*,..a tadpole. 'Poddywig' is, I think, the commoner form. **1933** H. G. WELLS *Bulpington of Blup* ii. 45 These things you call pollywiggles and pollywoggles. **1965** *East Anglian* May 242/1 Tadpoles were.. *pollywiggles*.

polloi (pǫloi·). *slang.* [ad. Gr. πολλοί many: see *HOI POLLOI.] *pl.* (const. as *sing.*). A crowd, a rabble (see also quot. 1940).

1940 M. MARPLES *Public School Slang* 90 *Polloi* (Cheltenham).., the lowest football set. **1948** E. E. CUMMINGS *Let.* 27 Aug. (1969) 185 A very refreshingly authentic polloi, & some good lively winds.

pollone: see *POLONE.

pollster (pōᵘ·lstəɹ). orig. *U.S.* [f. *POLL *sb.*¹ 7 d + -STER.] One who conducts an opinion poll; an analyst of such polls, or of voting patterns generally.

1939 *Time* 9 Oct. 11/3 Gallup pollsters reported that 43% of the voters want Mr. Roosevelt to run again. **1941** *Time* 6 Jan. 11 According to Pollster Gallup's figures 60 per cent of U.S. voters now want to aid Britain even at the risk of war. **1951** M. MCLUHAN *Mech. Bride* (1967) 46/2 On November 3, 1948..the pollsters were proved wrong in forecasting a Dewey victory over Truman. **1959** *Times Lit. Suppl.* 2 Oct. 556/3 This is not a swing towards Communism (as the pollsters would say), but an impulsive reaction to success. **1968** [see *MOTIVATION 3]. **1972** M. WILLIAMS *Inside Number 10* xiii. 343 Possibly there was a reaction against the pollsters, a desire to prove the computers wrong. **1977** *Time* 21 Nov. 63/2 The pollsters asked people to make judgments on a series of actions, deciding whether such actions were morally wrong or not a moral issue.

pollutant. Delete *rare* and add further examples.

1936 *Nature* 29 Feb. 353/2 The presence of pollutants in the atmosphere is proof of wastage of fuel. **1958** *Times* 13 Nov. 9/1 The even more harmful gaseous pollutants present a problem which will tax the resources of all engaged in the present campaign. **1966** *Listener* 3 Nov. 656/2 Fluoride..can be used for the improvement of human welfare. Out of place it is a more serious pollutant than chlorinated hydrocarbons, in that it is indestructible. **1970** *Daily Tel.* 30 Dec. 3/1 Mercury is now the most dangerous environmental pollutant. **1977** *Guernsey Weekly Press* 21 July 3/1 Petrol could become a pollutant of the past if the device fitted to a local car is marketed worldwide.

pollute, *v.* Add: **1. a.** *spec.* To contaminate (the environment, atmosphere, etc.) with harmful or objectionable substances. Also *absol.* (Further examples.)

1954 *Thorpe's Dict. Appl. Chem.* (ed. 4) XI. 885/1 Poisons like arsenic, etc., are rarely present in natural waters unless polluted by trade wastes or agricultural washes. **1966** *Petroleum Handbk.* (Shell Internat. Petroleum Co.) (ed. 5) 144/1 The absence of sulphur ensures that the products of combustion are non-corrosive..and do not pollute the atmosphere. **1973** *New Earth Catal.* 59/3 Plant—don't pollute.

polluted, *ppl. a.* Add: **b.** *slang* (orig. *U.S.*). Intoxicated, drunk; under the influence of drugs, 'high'.

1912 *Dialect Notes* III. 585 *Polluted*,..very drunk. The same as *pickled* and *plastered*. **1914** 'HIGH JINKS, JR.' *Choice Slang* 16 *Polluted*, intoxicated, drunk, 'piffilicated', 'soused'. **1927** *New Republic* 9 Mar. 71/2 The following is a partial list of words denoting drunkenness now in common use in the United States..polluted. **1938** *Amer. Speech* XIII. 185/2 High..usually infers that the addict is noticeably under the influence of drugs... The same is true of the following equivalents:.. lit, polluted, shot up. **1974** WODEHOUSE *Aunts aren't Gentlemen* iii. 20, I was helping a pal to celebrate the happy conclusion of love's young dream, and it may be that I became a mite polluted.

polluter. Add: **a.** *spec.* a person or organization that causes pollution of the environment.

1970 *New Society* 5 Feb. 209/2 The polluters often have a strong commercial lobby on their side, while the anti-polluters must rely on voluntary effort. **1970** *Toronto Daily Star* 24 Sept. 22/2 The federal government is in a much stronger position to deal with big industrial polluters than most provincial administrations are likely to be. **1974** *Times* 15 Mar. 6 (*heading*) Making Europe's polluters foot the bill. **1977** 'E. CRISPIN' *Glimpses of Moon* xi. 215 'Polluters,' said the hunt saboteuse.

b. A pollutant.

1975 *Physics Bull.* Mar. 100/3 Noise is now acknowledged as a major polluter of the environment.

pollution. Add: **1. a.** *spec.* The presence in the environment, or the introduction into it, of products of human activity which have harmful or objectionable effects. (Further examples.)

1877 ROSCOE & SCHORLEMMER *Treat. Chem.* I. 255 The running water seldom reaches the sea in its natural or pure state, but is largely contaminated with the sewage of towns, or the refuse from manufactures or mines. So serious..is this state of things becoming that some steps are about to be taken to prevent the further pollution of the rivers. **1934, 1947** [see *ATMOSPHERIC *a.* 2]. **1955** *Sci. Amer.* May 63/3 As our economy uses more and more organic chemicals, air pollution by volatile organic compounds becomes more and more of a problem. **1969** *Financial Times* 9 Jan. 4/6 The danger of 'thermal pollution' is greatest where electric and other power plants return to rivers and streams water that has been heated by between six and 16 degrees Centigrade. This often proves deadly to fish. **1970** *New Society* 5 Feb. 209/3 At American universities, pollution has been a student rallying cry for some months now. **1970**, etc. [see *noise pollution* s.v. *NOISE *sb.* 7]. **1975** *Physics Bull.* June 256/1 Noise pollution from aircraft and motorways and the design of speech and music reinforcement of St. Paul's cathedral are two of the varied aspects of noise and sound which have occupied Mr Allen.

b. (Earlier example.)

1605 BACON *Adv. Learn.* II. fol. 9 The Sunne..passeth through pollutions, and it selfe remaines as pure as before.

4. *attrib.* and *Comb.*, as *pollution control*; *pollution-free* adj.

1961 *San Francisco Chron.* 27 Mar. 32 Stronger water pollution control programs. **1969** *New Scientist* 9 Oct. 90/1 Pollution-control measures are only an extra charge on the expenses of a company and have little direct return. **1978** *N.Y. Times* 30 Mar. D14/4 A $150 million pollution-control program in that state. **1974** *Spartanburg* (S. Carolina) *Herald* 25 Apr. C2/3 Engineers for Japan's Honda and Mazda car makers have developed some of the world's most pollution-free auto engines which are getting wide attention in the United States.

pollutional (pǫ̆liū·ʃənăl), *a.* [f. POLLUTION + -AL.] Causing or constituting pollution.

1921 *Bull. Nat. Hist. Survey Illinois* XIV. 40 Usually tolerant or pollutional species that have come into Peoria Lake since 1915 seem to be several in number. **1941** *Sewage Works Jrnl.* XIII. 270 (*heading*) The natural purification of river muds and pollutional sediments.

pollutive (pǫ̆liū·tiv), *a.* [f. L. *pollūt-* (see POLLUTE *v.*) + -IVE.] Causing environmental pollution.

1970 *New Scientist* 2 July 12/2 The diesel engine..is a naturally less pollutive engine than the spark ignition one. **1972** WARD & DUBOS *Only One Earth* xi. 247 Developing countries are hard put to it to raise the capital even for existing cheaper, though more pollutive, technologies and energy systems.

Polly² (pǫ·li). *slang.* Also **'polly.** Abbrev. of *APOLLINARIS; a bottle or glass of Apollinaris water. Also *attrib.*

1852 DICKENS *Bleak Ho.* (1853) xx. 200 Four small rums is eight and three, and three Pollys is eight and six. **1878** [see *APOLLINARIS]. **1899** *Westm. Gaz.* 10 June 6/1 The dividend on Polly shares was announced too late to be public property in business hours yesterday. **1905** *Daily Chron.* 6 Sept. 4/7 'Johnny and Polly' is a common order in Piccadilly. **1907** *Westm. Gaz.* 17 Aug. 3/2 'Wagner and 'polly', or 'Tchaikowsky and soda'..would be both less stimulating and less harmful than some of the more popular intoxicants. **1954** J. BETJEMAN *Few Late Chrysanthemums* 43 And a host of little spiders Ran a race across the ciders To a box of baby 'pollies by the beer. **1969** S. HYLAND *Top Bloody Secret* ii. 165 Do not call it Apollinaris [*sic*] water... Nobody else..calls it that. They all say 'Polly water'. **1973** D. KYLE *Raft of Swords* (1974) viii. 77 'Soda? Apollinaris?' 'Whisky and Polly... I haven't had one in years.' 'It becomes increasingly difficult to come by.'

polly³ (pǫ·li). *U.S.* and *Austral. slang.* Abbrev. of POLITICIAN.

1942 BERREY & VAN DEN BARK *Amer. Thes. Slang* §854/1 *Politician*,..polly. **1955** *Publ. Amer. Dial. Soc.* xxiv. 151 Perhaps some *polly* (politician) can be interested sufficiently to intervene with the judge. **1969** *Courier-Mail* (Brisbane) 18 Oct. 13/7 The pollies..have been using television as an electronic soap box. **1974** *Bulletin* (Sydney) 12 Oct. 12 Pollies peel off the tax perks. **1978** *Sunday Sun* (Brisbane) 4 June 5/1 The eight pollies are members of an all-Party Parliamentary delegation led by Industry Minister Norm Lee.

Pollyanna (pǫːliˌæ·nă). Also **Polyanna** and with lower-case initial. The name of the heroine of stories written by Eleanor Hodgman Porter (1868–1920), American children's author, used with allusion to her skill at the 'glad game' of finding cause for happiness in the most disastrous situations; one who is unduly optimistic or achieves happiness through self-delusion. Also *attrib.*, *Comb.*, and as *adj.*

[**1913** E. H. Porter *Pollyanna* xv. 148 'Her name is Pollyanna Whittier.'.. 'And what are the special ingredients of this wonder-working—tonic of hers?'.. 'As near as I can find out it is an overwhelming, unquenchable gladness... Her quaint speeches are constantly being repeated to me, and, as near as I can make out, 'just being glad' is the tenor of most of them.'] **1921** *Collier's* 11 June 11/1, I should not like to hold stock in a company with Pollyanna as president. **1925** Wodehouse *Carry On, Jeeves* ix. 214 Uncle Thomas, when his gastric juices have been giving him the elbow, can make Schopenhauer look like Pollyanna. **1926** B. Barton *Bk. Nobody Knows* ii. 42 Job's crops are destroyed, his barns burned, his children taken sick, and he himself breaks out all over with horrid boils. In this condition he is visited by a group of three friends—professional moralists and Pollyannas. **1931** E. Pound *Let.* 27 Dec. (1971) 238 With Possum Eliot apptd. to Hawvud, he won't bring the glad polyanna yawp, but the ignorance of the Stork–Auslander–Mabie–Canby period can't continue. **1937** M. Hillis *Orchids on your Budget* i. 14 The Pollyanna-like theory that you can have just as much fun with very little money as you can with a lot of it. **1939** Wodehouse *Uncle Fred* xv. 218 The Ovens home-brewed is a liquid Pollyanna, for ever pointing out the bright side and indicating silver linings. **1940** O. Nash *Face is Familiar* 203 Some people are just naturally Pollyanna, While others call for sugar and cream and strawberries on their manna. **1944** T. Rattigan *While Sun Shines* i. 32 You're not fooling anyone, Babe, but yourself with this Polyanna stuff. I want another drink, you want another drink, so we both have another little drink. **1953** *Amer. Scholar* XXIII. i. 22 As intellectuals, we the 'Pollyannas' inevitably..ask ourselves if we can be right, when the country..is with us. **1959** A. Huxley *Let.* 13 Feb. (1969) 866 A short section..devoted to what may be called negative quotations—utterances of pure nonsense, pollyanna uplift, anti-intelligence and anti-liberty. **1962** A. H. Maslow *Summer Notes on Social Psychology* 3 Talk, talk, talk, not very effective, more optimistic and Pollyanna rather than realistic. **1963** 'E. Lathen' *Place for Murder* ii. 20 Thatcher decided that a Pollyanna tone was necessary... 'I am looking forward to tomorrow night,' he said firmly. **1964** B. Hardy *Appropriate Form* iii. 57 Robinson Crusoe is a prototype Pollyanna, comparing what is bad with what might have been much worse. **1971** 'D. Shannon' *Ringer* ix. 155 You're not exactly a Pollyanna today, Luis. **1977** *Time* 12 Sept. 60/2 Authors who try generally find themselves accused of going soft, of frivolously aping the Pollyanna fadeouts of popular schlock.

Hence **Pollya·nn(a)ish** *a.*, naïvely cheerful or optimistic; **Pollya·nnaism**, a statement characteristic of (a) Pollyanna.

1922 E. E. Cummings *Let.* 26 Feb. (1969) 83 Three Soldiers having, in his absence, been rendered Polyannish..by the highly moral Doran. **1923** *Grey Towers* 277, I wrote a paper for English 198 and the reader put on the outside, 'All right but Polly-Annaish.' **1946** G. Stimpson *Bk. about Thousand Things* 33 We hear now not only of pollyannas and pollyannaisms, but of pollyanna statements, pollyanna propaganda. **1948** *Time* 6 Dec. 90/2 Mildly Saroyanesque throughout and a trifle Pollyannaish at the end, in its best scenes *The Silver Whistle* is genuinely funny. **1967** R. A. Epstein *Theory of Gambling & Statistical Logic* xi. 411 Efforts to develop a complete and rigorous axiomatic treatment for psychological probability theory are sanguine, if not pollyannish. **1975** *Times* 18 June 7/5 The special brand of United Nations Pollyannaism. **1976** H. H. Humphrey *Educ. Public Man* ii. 25, I sound Pollyanna-ish when I speak of my childhood, my family, and Doland, but I think it is real and not simply nostalgia.

polo[1]. Add: **2.** (Earlier and later examples of hockey played on skates.)

1883 *Boston Daily Globe* 18 Nov. 6/2 (*heading*) The Winslow Rules Governing Polo on Skates. *Ibid.* 6/3 The American Roller..[is] to be published in the interests of roller skating, polo, and other popular sports. **1885** *Providence* (Rhode Island) *Jrnl.* 29 Oct. 3/3 The game of polo at the Skating Academy last evening..was an active game. **1906** H. P. Burchell *Official Roller Skating Guide* 108 (Advt.), The Spalding 'Rink Polo' stick is made of the best..material.

2*. Short for **polo hat*, **polo-neck*, etc.

1905 *Daily Chron.* 30 Jan. 8/1 Among the Victorian revivals..are various items of dress from the sixties... The small round hat that the French milliners call the 'polo' and we in this country term the pork-pie, is a detail in point. **1967** *Harper's Bazaar* Sept. 45 The neck..high everywhere—emphasized by polos, wrapped, petal or stand-up collars. **1975** *Country Life* 29 May 1424/1 For summer, we are now diving into silky polos. **1976** *Woman's Weekly* 6 Nov. 36/2 (Advt.), Worn here over classic Polo in black, red, antrim, green, or cassis.

3. *polo boot, club* (earlier and later examples), *-ground*; also designating garments with a polo-neck, as *polo jersey, -jumper, sweater* (hence *-sweatered* adj.); **polo cloth,** a soft, loosely-woven camel's-hair cloth; **polo coat,** a type of camel's-hair coat; **polo collar,** (*a*) (see quot. 1960); (*b*) = **polo neck* (a); hence *polo-collared* adj.; **polo hat,** a small round hat worn esp. in the latter part of the nineteenth century; **polo-neck,** (*a*) a high, close-fitting roll collar; also *attrib.*; (*b*) a jersey with such a collar; hence *polo-necked* adj; **polo shirt,** (*a*) a shirt of the kind worn by polo-players; (*b*) a shirt having a polo-neck.

1894 *Country Gentlemen's Catal.* 154 Hunting top-boots & butcher boots. Polo boots. **1963** E. H. Edwards *Saddlery* xx. 149 Should the animal require greater protection..any of the heavier polo boots..may be more suitable. **1910** *Dry Goods Reporter* 22 Oct. 21 (Advt.), The polo coat, 55 inches long, made in a complete line of mixtures..as well as the regular polo cloth. **1919** *Official Gaz.* (U.S. Patent Office) 23 Dec. 689/2 Polo cloth. Worumbo Mfg. Co., Bath, Me. Claims use since Jan. 10, 1910. Woolen goods in the piece. **1926** *Daily Colonist* (Victoria, B.C.) 13 Jan. 7/6 (Advt.), Plush and Polo Cloth Hats for Boys. Smart little shapes in black plush and light lovat polo cloth. **1879** *Scribner's Monthly* June 309/2 Three summers ago, some young men in New York formed the Polo Club, and built a sumptuous house at Fordham, with grounds especially laid out for the game. **1885** *Providence* (Rhode Island) *Jrnl.* 1 Nov. 8/4 (*heading*) The Roller Skating Season... The members of the Chelsea Polo Club..have been engaged to form a Providence team. **1935** *Encycl. Sports* 468/1 The first polo club in London was at Lillie Bridge. **1975** *Oxf. Compan. Sports & Games* 788/2 British officers..began to establish polo clubs in India. **1910** Polo coat [see **polo cloth*]. **1953** M. McCarthy *Groves of Academe* iii. 45 She jumped up..and seized her polo coat from the coat-rack. **1913** C. Mackenzie *Sinister Street* I. ii. v. 209 In his blue serge suit, wearing what the shops called a Polo or Shakespeare collar, Michael felt more at ease. **1937** A. Thirkell *Summer Half* ix. 253 They take off their detachable polo collars and look just like us, only nastier. **1960** C. W. Cunnington et al. *Dict. English Costume* 169/1 Polo collar. C. 1899. A starched white stand-fall collar, the fronts sloping apart. **1955** J. Cannan *Long Shadows* vi. 102 I've corduroys..and a polo-collared jersey. **1968** *Guardian* 22 Aug. 7/4 The current fashion for men to wear polo-collared shirts even with formal wear. **1895** Kipling in *Cosmopolitan* July 303 The hard, dusty Umballa polo-ground was lined with thousands of soldiers. **1897** *Daily Tel.* 8 Oct. 7/1 Lieutenant Rattray galloped in from the Khar polo-ground to take command of the post. **1971** *Shankar's Weekly* (Delhi) 18 Apr. 19/3 A vaguely green building on the other side of the polo-ground. **1905** *Daily Chron.* 30 Jan. 8/4 (Advt.), A three-quarters redingote..and the revived polo hat. **1929** D. L. Moore *Pandora's Letter Box* v. 92 Polo jerseys were abandoned by normal men..because they were seen on many who were known to be unmanly. **1960** *Woman* 23 Apr. 73/4 What gave him most joy was a yellow polo jersey that Frances knitted for him. **1937** A. Christie *Death on Nile* vi. 77 He was wearing..a high-necked polo jumper. **1949** 'M. Innes' *Journeying Boy* viii. 94 Two undergraduates in demodé polo-jumpers. **1944** 'N. Shute' *Pastoral* i. 5 A grey jumper with a polo neck. **1951** 'A. Garve' *Murder in Moscow* ix. 96, I changed it for a polo-neck sweater. **1968** J. Ironside *Fashion Alphabet* 48 One [woman] may look very chic in a polo neck and another may look as if she were a kennel-maid manqué. **1971** *Vogue* 15 Oct. 73 Black poloneck, sleeves and back of thin black stripes. **1973** M. Amis *Rachel Papers* 128 He was wearing a fashionable black polo-neck jersey (fashionable, that is, among the weasly middle-aged). **1973** 'D. Halliday' *Dolly & Starry Bird* iv. 55 Wife and bambinos in suede jackets and knitted jackets and..enough polo necks to outfit the entire British Raj. **1955** M. Hastings *Cork & Serpent* vi. 79 She had changed into a pair of black ski trousers and a polo-necked sweater. **1974** A. Price *Other Paths to Glory* ii. i. 111 An equally pink polo-necked sweater. **1920** F. Scott Fitzgerald *This Side of Paradise* (1921) i. ii. 44 The faces indistinct above the polo shirts. **1938** 'E. Queen' *Four of Hearts* (1939) i. i. 11 You left out this wine-coloured polo shirt. **1974** R. B. Parker *God save Child* (1975) ii. 16 Six polo shirts of different colors with the sleeves neatly folded under. **1979** R. Gillespie *Crossword Mystery* iv. 100 He threw on a polo shirt and slacks. **1950** A. Koestler in *God that Failed* i. 58 A member of the intelligentsia could never become a real proletarian, but his duty was to become as nearly one as he could. Some tried to achieve this by forsaking neckties, by wearing polo sweaters and black fingernails. **1955** N. Fitzgerald *House is Falling* ix. 156, I always wear..flannel bags, a polo sweater. **1963** Polo-sweater [see *Chelsea 3]. **1950** A. Wilson *Such Darling Dodos* 136 The polo-sweatered organist.

polo[2] (pōᵘ·lo). [Sp.] An Andalusian folk-dance, or the music which accompanies this dance.

1883 Grove *Dict. Mus.* III. 9/2 *Polo*, a Spanish dance accompanied by singing, which took its origin in Andalusia. **1902** *Encycl. Brit.* XXVII. 374/2 Other provincial dances now in existence are..the *Palotéa*, the *Polo*, the *Gallegada*, [etc.]. **1926** D. C. Parker *Georges Bizet* iv. 233 Gaudier..asserts that Bizet has..made use of a *polo*, sung by a serenading student. **1934** W. Starkie *Spanish Raggle-Taggle* vii. 76 She began to play a medley of Spanish airs—*polos, boleros, tangos, malagueñas.* **1967** 'La Meri' *Spanish Dancing* (ed. 2) vi. 81 The Polo dates back to the ancient and unaccompanied Andalucian songs.

polocrosse (pōᵘlokrǫ·s). Also **polo crosse.** [Blend of Polo and Lacrosse.] A team game played on horseback with a rubber ball and a stick with a head like that of a lacrosse-stick.

1952 J. B. Pick *Phoenix Dict. Games* 105 The ground required by polo crosse is smaller than a polo field. **1965** *Newsweek* 19 Apr. 94 For a battering, breath-taking roughhouse on horseback, have a go at polocrosse in New South Wales. **1974** *Courier-Mail* (Brisbane) 16 Aug. 19 Polocrosse was far from being a poor cousin of the better known millionaire sport of polo. **1975** *Oxf. Compan. Sports & Games* 792/1 There were at least ten polo crosse clubs in Britain soon after the second world war, most of them in the West Country, but there is little evidence of the game in Britain now.

polocyte (pōᵘ·losəit). *Biol.* [f. Pol(e *sb.*[2] + -o + -cyte.] = *polar body* s.v. *polar *a.* 5.

1915 C. W. Prentiss *Lab. Manual & Text-bk. Embryol.* i. 28 The cleavage is unequal and, instead of four cells of equal size resulting, there are formed one large ripe ovum or oöcyte and three rudimentary or abortive ova known as polar bodies or polocytes. **1927** [see *ootid]. **1931** J. E. Frazer *Man. Embryol.* i. 6 Among the lower animals it seems to be usual for maturation not to be completed (*i.e.*, the second polocyte not to be cast off) before conjugation with the male cell is effected. **1969** F. D. Allan *Essentials Human Embryol.* (ed. 2) i. 14 Polocytes consist of a nuclear mass and a delicate cytoplasmic sheath and have no known function in addition to the passive role they play in meiosis, i.e., reduction or elimination of excess chromosomal material.

poloidal (pŏloi·dăl), *a.* [f. Pol(ar *a.* (*sb.*) + Tor)oidal *a.*] Being or representing a magnetic field of the form associated with a circular current loop, in which each line of force is confined to a radial or meridian plane.

1946 W. M. Elsasser in *Physical Rev.* LXIX. 108/1 We shall now introduce names for these three types of vectors. They will be designated as scaloidal (**U**), toroidal (**T**), and poloidal (**S**) vector fields. The electric field and vector potential pertaining to a poloidal magnetic field are toroidal, and *vice versa.* **1967** *McGraw-Hill Yearbk. Sci. & Technol.* 225 The magnetic field at the Earth's surface has a radial component and is thus of the poloidal type. **1972** *Sci. Amer.* July 67/3 A toroidal electric field maintains a toroidal current that flows inside the plasma, and this current in turn generates a magnetic-field component that is poloidal... The combination of the poloidal field with the toroidal field produces helical magnetic-field lines that lie on closed magnetic surfaces (nested toroids of circular cross section). **1973** *Nature* 20 Apr. 516/2 There are on the Moon weak, local, fairly randomly oriented magnetic fields but no overall poloidal field.

polology (pōᵘlǫ·lŏdʒi). *Nuclear Physics.* [f. Pol(e *sb.*[2] + -ology.] The theory of Regge poles.

1961 *Nuovo Cimento* XXII. 214 (*heading*) Polology and ND^{-1} solutions in the multiple-channel problems. **1964** S. DeBenedetti *Nucl. Interactions* vii. 471 This simple argument forms the basis of much of the present-day thinking about strong forces: perturbation methods may not be justified in general, but they are expected to give correct results near the predicted 'resonances' or 'poles'. The theory developed along these lines has received the informal name of 'polology'. **1966** D. Park *Introd. Strong Interactions* vii. 134 (*heading*) Polology and the determination of g.

Polonaise, *sb.* Add: **1. d.** A cloth of a silk and cotton mixture. Cf. Polonese *sb.* 1.

1894 J. E. Davis *Elem. Mod. Dressmaking* v. 93 Polonaise, a mixture of silk and cotton, which has the appearance of a soft dull silk with a distinct serge-like twill, is very much used as a skirt-lining for rich materials. **1923** *Daily Mail* 13 Aug. 4 (Advt.), The lining of the coat is silk Polonaise. **1932** G. Heyer *Devil's Cub* x. 152 Lady Fanny..in a négligée of Irish polonaise, with a gauze apron.

3. *Cookery.* Applied *absol.*, *attrib.*, or as *adj.* to dishes supposedly cooked in a Polish style. Also *à la Polonaise.*

1889 J. Whitehead *Steward's Handbk.* iv. 405/2 Polonaise (*a la*), in Polish style. **1950** E. Brunet tr. *Saulnier's Répertoire de la Cuisine* 199 (*heading*) *Asparagus ..Polonaise.*—Dished in rows, sprinkle with hard boiled eggs and parsley chopped, pour over some bread crumbs tossed in butter nicely browned. *Ibid.* 203 (*heading*) *Cauliflowers..Polonaise.*—Dressed cauliflower on buttered dish, sprinkle with chopped parsley and hard boiled eggs, and bread crumbs, [etc.]. **1965** *House & Garden* Dec. 84/2 *Polonaise*, lightly fried breadcrumbs used in among other ingredients and not just as a topping or garnish. **1969** G. Payton *Proper Names* 355/1 *Polonaise* (Cooking), with beetroot and sour cream.

4. Used *attrib.* or as *adj.* to designate a type of rug woven in Iran during the sixteenth and seventeenth centuries using silver and gold warp threads. Also *absol.* as *sb.*

1911 G. G. Lewis *Pract. Bk. Oriental Rugs* xxi. 322 According to Dr. Valentiner the so-called Polanaise [*sic*] and Ispahan rugs belong to the 17th century. **1913** W. A. Hawley *Oriental Rugs* vii. 88 It was doubtless after..Shah Abbas I had begun to embellish his capital at Ispahan, that were made the famous 'Polish' silk or 'Polonaise' carpets about which there has been so much controversy. **1931** A. U. Dilley *Oriental Rugs & Carpets* ii. 44 Many of the king's rugs—the ones containing gold and silver, now called Polonaise—were woven at Kashan. **1962** C. W. Jacobsen *Oriental Rugs* 272 All Polonaise rugs belong to the 17th century, particularly the first half. The name Polonaise dates from the Paris exposition in 1878, when several rugs of this type were exhibited by Prince Czartorski of Warsaw. **1973** M. S. Dimand *Oriental Rugs in Metropolitan Museum of Art* v. 65/1 Because some of the rugs bear Polish coats of arms, they, too, have been called 'Polish' or 'Polonaise'. **1976** *Times* 15 Apr. 16/3 Christie's sale of Eastern rugs. A sixteenth-century Polonaise was unsold at £16,500.

polone, polony[3] (pǫ̆lōu·ni). Also **pollone.** Varr. *PALONE.

1937 PARTRIDGE *Dict. Slang* 646/2 *Polone*,..a girl or woman. **1938** H. W. WICKS *Prisoner Speaks* vi. 95 The jogars and griddlers..had a language of their own, such as: omie, meaning man, pollone—woman, feelia—boy,.. and so on. **1938** G. GREENE *Brighton Rock* I. ii. 30 'What about that polony he was with?' 'She doesn't matter,' the Boy said. 'She's just a buer.' *Ibid.* II. ii. 88 'Napoleon the Third used to have this room,' Mr. Colleoni said, 'and Eugenie.' 'Who was she?' 'Oh,' Mr. Colleoni said vaguely, one of those foreign polonies.' **1979** R. RENDELL *Make Death love Me* iv. 37 'When the polone comes to lock up, Groombridge'll be due to split.'..'Call her a girl, can't you? You're not a poove.'

Polong (polǫ·ŋ). [Mal.] A Malayan spirit or imp (see quots.).

1839 T. J. NEWBOLD *Straits of Malacca* II. xii. 191 The Polong is a small sprite which can be domesticated. **1900** W. W. SKEAT *Malay Magic* vi. 320 The Polong..is described as a diminutive but malicious species of bottle-imp. **1972** *Daily Tel.* (Colour Suppl.) 12 May 58/3 Finally there is the Polong, a vampiristic imp who, in association with the demoniac house-cricket, the Pelasit, enters the victim's body at will.

Polonial (polōu·niăl), *a. rare.* [f. POLONIA + -AL.] = POLISH *a.*

1922 *Blackw. Mag.* June 801/2 A very intelligent-looking secretary to the Polonial Embassy to the Vatican assured me [etc.].

polonium. Add: (The name is now recognized as that of an element, of atomic number 84.)

Polovtsy (polǫ·vtsi), *collect. pl.* Also **Polovtsi, Polovtzi, Polovzi.** [Russ.] A union of the nomad tribes belonging to the Kipchak Turks, which inhabited the steppes between the Danube and the Volga in the 11th–13th centuries. So **Polove·tsian, Polo·vtsian** *a.*, of or pertaining to these people or their language; also as *sb.*

1799 W. TOOKE *View Russ. Empire* III. XI. ii. 581 The trade of the Krimea was heretofore uncommonly gainful and extensive; for, in the eleventh century, when a part of this peninsula fell under the dominion of the Polovtzi, better known from the byzantine history under the appellation of the Romanians, they granted the Genoese ..the permission to erect warehouses. **1803** H. CARD *Hist. Revolutions of Russia* 64 The Polovtsi took the imprudent resolution of observing a strict neutrality. *Ibid.* 66 One of the Polovtsian princes..demanded and received the sacrament of baptism. **1878** *Encycl. Brit.* VIII. Pl. XII opp. p. 715, Cumanians or Polovzians. **1885** *Ibid.* XIX. 286/1 He entered Kieff with the Polovtzi as his auxiliaries. *Ibid.* 410/2 As early as 988 the Russians erected several towns on the Sula and Trubezh for their protection against the Petchenegs and Polovtsy, who held the south-eastern steppes. **1938** *Oxf. Compan. Mus.* 750/2 Igor may go free if he will not make war on the Polovtsy again. **1954** *Grove's Dict. Mus.* (ed. 5) I. 821/1 Toward the end of 1874 Borodin's interest in 'Igor' was revived; the 'Polovtsian March' was composed, and in the following summer the famous dances. **1965** N. POPPE *Introd. Altaic Linguistics* 72 Kuman (Polovetsian, called so after the Russian name for Kumans) is also a Middle Turkic language. It was spoken in the XII–XVI centuries by Turkic nomads in Southern Russia, including the Crimea, and parts of Central Asia, and also by turkicized Armenians in the XV–XVIII centuries... There are no speakers of Kuman at the present time. **1968** M. GUYBON tr. *Solzhenitsyn's First Circle* l. 308 Half Polovtsian by blood, Prince Igor was for years an ally of the Polovtsians. **1973** R. C. HOWES *Tale of Campaign of Igor* 2 The Polovetsians (called Polovtsy, Cumans, or Kipchak Turks) had been moving into the steppes north of the Black Sea since the 1050s. *Ibid.* 3 The organization of two Polovetsian political units in the steppes..also boded ill for Kiev. **1974** T. SZAMUELY *Russian Tradition* I. ii. 13 The Kievan state had been engaged in perpetual warfare since its foundation. Khazars, Pechenegs, Polovtsy —one wave followed the other.

Pol Roger (pǫl,rǫʒe). The proprietary name of a champagne produced in Épernay.

1889 *Trade Marks Jrnl.* 25 Sept. 916/2 *Pol Roger*... Champagne. Pol Roger, Albert Roger, and Veuve Julie Roger, trading as Pol Roger & Co., Epernay, France..; Champagne shippers. **1891** [see *KRUG[2]]. **1912** C. MACKENZIE *Carnival* xx. 209 Maurice..in a quandary of taste between Pol Roger and Perrier Jouet. **1925** H. ACTON in *Oxf. Poetry* 8 For after belching Pol-Roger the bile Will wreak revenge. **1957** L. DURRELL *Justine* III. 185, I was of course drunk by this time and exhausted—drunk as much on Justine as upon the thin-paper-bodied *Pol Roget* [sic]. **1968** E. HYAMS *Mischief Makers* x. 184 A steak and chips and a pint of Pol Roger will meet this case. **1979** P. ALEXANDER *Show me Hero* xv. 166 A maid had entered with a refreshment trolley. On it were two bottles of Pol Roger in ice-buckets.

polrumptious (pǫlrɒ·mpʃəs), *a. dial.* and *slang.* ? *Obs.* Also **pollrumptious.** [Perh. f. POLL *sb.*[1] + RUMPTI(ON + -OUS.] (See quots. 1787 and 1902.)

1787 F. GROSE *Provincial Gloss* s.v. *Pollrumptious*, restive, unruly. **1818** SCOTT *Heart Midl.* in *Tales my Landlord* 2nd Ser. III. vii. 170, I think thou doest not look so polrumptious as thy play-fellow yonder. **1888** 'Q.' *Troy Town* xvii. 213 I'll get the loan o' the Dearloves' blunderbust in case they gets polrumptious. **1902** FARMER & HENLEY *Slang* V. II. 247/1 *Pollrumptious*,..restive: unruly; foolishly confident.

‖ **pol sambol** (pǫl sæ·mbǫ̆l). [Sinhalese.] A spicy Indonesian dish: see *SAMBAL.

1962 *Housewife* (Ceylon) Feb. 28 Learn to make a pol sambol. **1971** *Ceylon Daily Mirror* (Colombo) 4 Oct. 8/4 Miss Munasinghe had consumed a meal consisting of..Pol sambol with maldive fish.

polska (pǫ·lskă). [Sw., f. *Polsk* Polish.] A Swedish folk dance of Polish origin in $\frac{3}{4}$ time; the music which accompanies such a dance.

1883 GROVE *Dict. Mus.* III. 11/2 Polskas are usually written in minor keys. **1910** C. WAERN *Mediæval Sicily* p. xiv, In Old Sweden the gaily decked Maypole is, or was, set up on Midsummer Eve, and people dance round it.. the brisk national 'polska' or the characteristic 'ring dance'. **1925** [see *HAMBO]. **1947** A. EINSTEIN *Mus. in Romantic Era* xvii. 319 Here too the Romantic movement began with the collecting and publishing of the old national treasures of folk song—full of feeling and dance-like, the folk songs of sentiment being often modal, the dancelike ones (polskas) being related to the mazurka.

Poltalloch (pǫltæ·lǫ̆χ). The name of an estate in Argyll, Scotland, used *absol.* or *attrib.* to designate a small, stocky, rough-coated, white terrier belonging to a breed developed there by the Malcolm family, esp. Colonel E. D. Malcolm (1837–1930), and now usually called the West Highland White terrier.

1887 D. J. THOMSON GRAY *Dogs of Scotland* (1891) iii. 51 A white variety of the Scottish terrier existed at one time (and stray specimens may still exist) under the cognomen of Poltalloch terriers. **1920** R. MACAULAY *Potterism* II. i. 63 'We have two Pekingese, a King Charles, and a pug...' I answered with some inanity about my mother's Poltalloch. **1922** [see *HIGHLAND *a.* 2 a]. **1932** E. WEEKLEY *Words & Names* ix. 129 We have the new class-names which come into existence, as new breeds of terriers are evolved to suit changing fashions, e.g...the poltalloch, first bred by Colonel Malcolm, of Poltalloch (Argyll). **1950** A. C. SMITH *Dogs since 1900* xi. 187 West Highland White Terriers..were at first known as Poltalloch Terriers. **1968** C. G. E. WIMHURST *Bk. Terriers* xxvii. 189 These [*sc.* the Duke of Argyll's terriers] were not related to the Poltalloch terriers.

poltergeist. Delete ‖ and add earlier and later examples. Also *attrib.* and *fig.*

1848 C. CROWE *Night Side of Nature* II. vi. 238 (*heading*) The poltergeist of the Germans, and possession. *Ibid.* 239 The annoyances appear rather like the tricks of a mischievous imp. I refer to what the Germans call the *Poltergeist*, or racketing spectre. **1863** *Q. Rev.* July 193 It seems a suspicious circumstance that the old-fashioned visible ghost has in these modern *séances* been almost entirely superseded by the *Poltergeist* or noise-making spirit. **1927** J. S. HUXLEY *Relig. without Revelation* vi. 187 Exorcism is magic: the Rumanian poltergeist medium, Eleonore Zugun, whose case was recently investigated in London, was the subject of exorcist rites by Rumanian priests. **1940** [see *DOPPELGANGER]. **1979** M. BABSON *So soon done For* i. 8 A disturbed adolescent in an area of intense poltergeist activity.

Hence **po·ltergeistic** *a.*, of, pertaining to, or suggestive of a poltergeist; **po·ltergeistism,** the manifestation or activity of poltergeists.

1952 R. F. JONES in 'E. Crispin' *Best SF Five* (1963) 44 Reports on poltergeistism at Leander Castle near London. **1973** L. M. BOSTON *Memory in House* v. 61 The house.. from time to time sent feelers out from its darkest corners, such as slight poltergeistic displacements, footsteps up the wooden stairs,..etc.

polthogue (pǫltōu·g, -ōu·χ). *Ir. colloq.* Also **palthogue.** [f. Ir. *palltóg.*] A blow with the fist; a thump or punch.

1830 W. CARLETON *Traits & Stories Irish Peasantry* II. 59 John Grimes hot him a *palthogue* on the sconce wid the but-end of a gun. *c* **1874** D. BOUCICAULT in M. R. Booth *Eng. Plays of 19th Cent.* (1969) II. 181 Be jabers, I'd have liked to see in your face when you got that polthogue in the gob. **1898** J. D. BRAYSHAW *Slum Silhouettes* 25 Faix, there's a polthogue will knock sinse into yez. **1899** S. MACMANUS *In Chimney Corners* 164 He draws the flail one polthogue at the lad in the door and just barely missed him.

po'ly, poly (pō·li), *a.* Repr. a U.S. dial. pronunc. POORLY *adv.* and *a.*

1890 *Dialect Notes* I. 69 'How d'you do?' 'I am po'ly to-day.' **1893** H. A. SHANDS *Some Peculiarities of Speech in Mississippi* 50 A negro, when asked about his health, if not well, will answer, 'Poly, poly, bress God!' **1929** W. FAULKNER *Sartoris* I. 26 'How is you?' 'Po'ly, ladies; po'ly.' **1935** Z. N. HURSTON *Mules & Men* (1970) I. vi. 140 My wife is po'ly.

poly[2] (pǫ·li), colloq. abbrev. of POLYTECHNIC *sb.* 2 in Dict. and Suppl.

1858 M. TUCKETT *Diary* 30 Sept. (*c* 1975) 9 We came into Falmouth..and then went with Aunt to the Poly. **1882** Q. HOGG *Let.* Sept. in E. M. Hogg *Quintin Hogg* (1904) vi. 145 Our Poly. boys came to speak their word in the matter. **1892** *Scribner's Mag.* Feb. 170/1 The Young Men's Polytechnic Institute, which is universally known among young people in London as the 'Poly'. **1932** E. M. WOOD *Polytechnic & its Founder Quintin Hogg* (rev. ed.) 16, I have just tried to keep out of the light and let the Poly tell its own history. **1967** *Times Rev. Industry* May 115/2 The new polys will come into being largely as regroupings of existing colleges. **1970** *Guardian* 19 Aug. 9/2 Fowler..is taking the poly job and saying a regretful 'no thanks' to LSE. **1978** I. MURDOCH *Sea* 226 When he left school he went into the poly, you know, the polytechnic... He had a student grant. **1979** *Jrnl. R. Soc. Arts* July 489/1 So what we should like is for those institutions such as polys throughout the Commonwealth that are already running business management courses to devote part of them to the skills of publishing.

poly[3] (pǫ·li), colloq. abbrev. of *POLYTHENE and *POLYETHYLENE b. Chiefly *attrib.* and *Comb.*, as *poly bag* (*polybag*), *poly-wrapped* adj.

1965 *Supermarket & Self-Service* (Johannesburg) June/July 13/3 Quick-frozen polywrapped broilers. **1968** *Punch* 12 June 858/1 Little poly-wrapped trays in the frozen food counter. **1971** C. BONINGTON *Annapurna South Face* ix. 103 Tom and I finished packing our rucksacks, leaving a proportion of our gear in polybags outside the boxes to reduce our loads. **1976** *Canad. Forces Sentinel* (Ottawa) XII. III. 6/3 One three-pound polybag of the stuff served as a week-long protein supplement for..six. **1976** *Southern Even. Echo* (Southampton) 11 Nov. (Advt. Suppl.) 7/1 Fresh meat from the farm for your freezer: .. All poly wrapped and cut to your requirements. **1977** *Undercurrents* June–July 34/3 Find an old boiler suit,..a small shovel, and a big thick poly bag or a cut away poly jerry can. **1978** *Detroit Free Press* 5 Mar. (Spring Fashion Suppl.) 14/1 (Advt.), Sleek soft sandals..latest styles, Spring colors, and the newest poly bottoms.

poly-. Add: **1. polyabolo** (pǫli,æ·bǒlo) [f. *DI)ABOLO by deliberately false analogy (see quot.); cf. *PENTOMINO], any planar shape formed by joining a number of identical right-angled isosceles triangles by their edges; **polya·ctine,** a sponge spicule having numerous rays; **po:lyallomo·rphic** *a. Philol.*, having several allomorphs (*ALLOMORPH[2]); **po:lyalphabe·tic** *a. Cryptography*, employing more than one alphabet, so that each letter of the alphabet may be represented in a code by any of two or more letters or other characters; **polya·nion** *Chem.*, a negatively charged polyion (see below); hence **po:lyanio·nic** *a.*; **po:lyarteri·tis** *Path.* [mod.L., coined in Ger. as *polyarteritis acuta nodosa* (E. Ferrari 1903, in *Beiträge zur path. Anat. und zur allgem. Path.* XXXIV. 383) to replace *periarteritis*] = *periarteritis* s.v. PERI- 1 c in Dict. and Suppl.; **polyaxon** *sb.* (example); **polyblast,** (*b*) *Histology* [a. G. *polyblast* (A. Maximow 1902, in *Beiträge zur path. Anat.: Suppl.* V. 43)], a wandering macrophage; **polyca·tion** *Chem.*, a positively charged polyion (see below); hence **po:lycatio·nic** *a.*; **polycho·ral** *a. Mus.*, in which the choral ensemble is divided into groups who sing alternately (and, properly, jointly also); **polycistro·nic** *a. Genetics*, comprising or derived from more than one cistron and so containing the information for more than one gene product; hence **polycistro·nically** *adv.*; **polyclo·nal** *a. Biol.* and *Med.*, (of a population of organisms) comprising many clones; (of a population of cells) comprising several cell lines of separate origins; of or pertaining to the products of such cell lines; hence **polyclona·lity; polyclo·nally** *adv.*; **po·lyclone** *Biol.* and *Med.* [*CLONE *sb.*], a group of cells all descended from one or other of an initial small group of cells; **poly·cratism** = *Polycracy*; **po·lycross** *Bot.* and *Agric.*, a cross made by planting two or more mutually fertile varieties together and allowing free natural pollination; freq. *attrib.*; **polycythæmia** (earlier example); [ad. G. *polycythaemie* (J. Vogel 1854, in R. Virchow *Handb. der speciellen Path. und Therapie* I. iv. 377)]; hence **polycythæ·mic** *a.* of, involving, or suffering from polycythæmia; **polyde·ntate** *a. Chem.* [L. *dentātus*: see DENTATE *a.*], (of a ligand) forming two or more separate bonds (usu. but not necessarily with the same central atom); (of a molecule or complex) formed by such a ligand; **polyelectro·nic** *a. Chem.*, containing or consisting of more than one electron; **polye·ndocrine** *Path.*, characterized by the involvement of several endocrine glands; **po:lyendocrino·pathy** *Path.*, a polyendocrine disorder; **polye·nergid** *a. Biol.* [*ENERGID], having many complete sets of chromosomes; multinucleate or polyploid; **polye·thism** *Ent.* [Gr. ἦθος character], the display of different patterns of behaviour by particular individuals within a social group; **polyfu·nctional** *a. Chem.*, having two or more different functional groups in the molecule; orig. also applied to reactions involving two or more such compounds; hence **po:lyfunction·a·lity**; **polygla·cial** *a.*, involving (a belief in) more than one ice age; hence **polygla·cialism**, the polyglacial theory; **polygla·cialist** *a.* and *sb.*, (of or pertaining to) a supporter of this theory; **polyha·ploid** *Bot.* [*HAPLOID *a.* (and *sb.*)], a plant descended from polyploids that has half of the set of chromosomes that would normally be expected from its ancestry; **polyhedroid** (-hī·droid, -he·droid) *Math.* [POLYHEDR(ON + -OID] = *polytope* s.v. POLY- I in Dict. and Suppl.; **polyhex** (pǫ·liheks) [f. HEX(AGON], any planar shape formed by joining a number of identical regular hexagons by their edges; **polyiamond** (pǫli,əi·ămənd) [f. D)IAMOND by deliberately false analogy; cf. *PENTOMINO], any planar shape formed by joining a number of identical equilateral triangles by their edges; **polyion** (pǫ·li,əi:ǫ̆n) *Chem.*, an ion which consists of or contains a number of atoms of its parent element, or a large ion derived from a polyelectrolyte; so **polyio·nic** *a.*; **polyka·ryocyte** *Biol.* [KARYO- + -CYTE], an osteoclast, esp. a large osteoclast with many nuclei; hence **po:lykaryocy·tic** *a.*; **polyle·ctal** *a. Linguistics* [*-LECT], having or recognizing many regional or social varieties (within a language); **polyli·ngual** *a.* = *MULTILINGUAL *a.*; **polyli·ngualism** = *MULTILINGUALISM; **polylithic** *a.*, add: also, containing several kinds of stone or rock; also *fig.* (cf. *MONOLITHIC *a.* 4); (further examples); **polyli·thionite** *Min.* [ad. G. *polylithionit* (J. Lorenzen 1884, in *Zeitschr. f. Krist. und Min.* IX. 253), f. *lithion* lithia], a variety of lepidolite; **polymeta·llic** *a.*, containing (ores of) several metals; **polymicrian** *a.* (delete *nonce-wd.*; earlier examples); **po·ly-mineral** *a. Petrol.*, composed of or containing more than one mineral; **polymorphe·mic** *a. Linguistics*, consisting of two or more morphemes; **polymya·lgia rheuma·tica** *Path.* [MYALGIA] (see quot. 1957); **polymyositis** (earlier example); **polyneuri·tic** *a.*, of, pertaining to, or suffering from polyneuritis; **polyneuro·pathy** *Path.*, a general degeneration of peripheral nerves that starts distally and spreads proximally; **polyœstrous** *a.* (further examples); also, in mod. use, ovulating more than once each year; **polyomino** (pǫli,ǫ·mino) [f. D)OMINO by deliberately false analogy; cf. *PENTOMINO], any planar shape formed by joining a number of identical squares by their edges; **polypneu·stic** [Gr. πνευστ-ιάω to pant] *a. Ent.*, bearing many respiratory spiracles; **polypnœa** (further examples); also **polypnea**; hence **polypnœ·ic** *a.*; **po·lyprotein** *Biochem.*, a protein which is composed of a number of smaller proteins; **polyri·bosome** *Biol.* = *POLYSOME; hence **po:lyriboso·mal** *a.*; **po:lysapro·bic** *a. Ecol.* (ad. G. *polysaprob* (Kolkwitz & Marsson 1902, in *Mittheilungen aus der K. Prüfungsanstalt f. Wasserversorgung und Abwässerbeseitigung* I. 46): see *SAPROBE], of, being, or inhabiting an aquatic environment having in solution much reducing decayed organic matter and little or no oxygen; **polysemantic** *a.* (further examples); = *POLYSEMIC, *POLYSEMOUS *adjs.*; **po:lysemanti·city, polysema·ntism** = *POLYSEMY; **po:lyseros·itis** *Path.*, inflammation of serous membranes; **po·lysoap**, a detergent whose molecules are polymeric chains to which soap molecules are attached; **po·lyspike** [SPIKE *sb.*[2]] (see quot. 1950); **po:lysympto·ma·tic** *a. Med.*, involving or exhibiting many symptoms; **polythe·lia, polythe·lism, po·ly-thely** *Med.* [ad. F. *polythélie*, f. Gr. θηλή nipple], the condition of having one or more supernumerary nipples; **polytope** (examples); [ad. G. *polytop* (R. Hoppe 1882, in *Arch. der Math. und Physik* LXVIII. 30)]; hence **poly-to·pal** *a.*; **polyto·pic** *a. Biol.* [Gr. τόπος place], of or pertaining to (the independent origin of a species in) several places; **polyto·pical** *a.*, dealing with many subjects; **polyuria, -uric** *a.* (earlier examples); **polyxe·nic** *a. Biol.* [Gr. ξένος stranger], applied to a culture, or the cultivation, of an organism in the presence of more than one other species.

1967 *Sci. Amer.* June 129/1 The pieces had been suggested to him by S. J. Collins of Bristol, England, who gave the name 'tetraboloes' to the order-4 set because the Diabolo, a juggling toy, has two isosceles right triangles in its cross section. This implies the generic name 'polyaboloes'. **1902** *Encycl. Brit.* XXXII. 813/1 Fig. 5A, typical polyactine. **1949** E. A. NIDA *Morphol.* (ed. 2) iv. 98 The suffix *-al* is polyallomorphic /əl/ and /æl/. **1972** *Archivum Linguisticum* III. 40 In order to simplify their analysis one of the allomorphs of poly-allomorphic morphemes is designated as the basic one, and the changes are described on that basis. **1927** *Daily Express* 24 Nov. 13 The 'polyalphabetic' codes..are much more difficult to decipher, as a letter is often represented in a cryptogram by a dozen different signs, letters or numerals. **1939** H. F. GAINES *Elem. Cryptanalysis* (1940) viii. 68 Multiple-alphabet substitution (also called double-key substitution, polyalphabetic substitution, etc.) makes use of several different cipher alphabets. **1962** MOORE & WALLER *Cloak & Cipher* xv. 138 Edgar Allan Poe..seems to have had a blind faith in polyalphabetic ciphers. **1931** *Chem. Abstr.* XXV. 3261 The submicrons detected by the ultramicroscope are negatively charged and consist of aggregates of the polyanions $[Pb_9]^{4-}$ or $[Sn_9]^{4-}$. **1948** *Jrnl. Polymer Sci.* III. 261 In the presence of excess electrolyte, the polyanion would be completely associated and behave approximately like an uncharged macromolecule. **1965** [see *polycation* below]. **1972** COTTON & WILKINSON *Adv. Inorg. Chem.* (ed. 3) xxv. 823 The decavanadate ion is only one example of the type of polyanion generally called isopolyanions. **1930** *Chem. Abstr.* XXIV. 2077 [Such] elements..will combine in liquid NH_3 with Na to give polysulfide-like compds.,..to which the name 'polyanionic' salts is given. **1974** *Amer. Jrnl. Anat.* CXXXIX. 404/1 Staining with ruthenium red..reveals that a polyanionic surface coat, probably mucopolysaccharide in nature, covers all the microvilli..on all cell types found in the nasal cavities. **1907** *Jrnl. Path. & Bacteriol.* XII. 54 Polyarteritis acuta nodosa.—Characterised by the formation upon the smaller and medium-sized arteries of small localised nodules. **1951** E. N. CHAMBERLAIN *Text-bk. Med.* vi. 448 Sometimes known as polyarteritis nodosa, this is a rare disease generally affecting persons before mid-life. **1974** PASSMORE & ROBSON *Compan. Med. Stud.* III. xxv. 29/1 The term polyarteritis includes a number of uncommon disorders in which the changes are focal, segmental inflammation and necrosis of arteries, arterioles or capillaries... Besides the classical form, also known as polyarteritis nodosa.., there are five recognized variants. **1940** L. H. HYMAN *Invertebrates* I. vi. 299 Polyaxons..are spicules in which several equal rays radiate from a central point. **1904** Polyblast [in Dict.]. **1959** F. M. BURNET *Clonal Selection Theory* vii. 115 Macrophages..include fixed macrophages, wandering tissue macrophages or polyblasts and the blood monocytes. **1967** *Biol. Abstr.* XLVIII. 9803/2 By the 6th day, a barrier of connective tissue, formed mainly from polyblasts and hist[i]ocytes, was beginning to be formed. **1948** *Jrnl. Polymer Sci.* III. 259 Due to the high concentration of charge in the polycation, which is itself quite large, electrostatic forces can be transferred over much greater distances than in solutions of ordinary electrolytes. **1965** PHILLIPS & WILLIAMS *Inorg. Chem.* I. xii. 465 The formation of polyanions is quite common among the heavier non-metals (e.g. polysulphides and selenides), although the formation of polycations from uncomplexed metals appears to be limited to Hg_2^{2+}. **1949** *Science* 25 Nov. 553/1 When excess acrylate is added, more polyanions attach themselves to the polycationic exterior of the precipitate particles. **1970** R. W. MCGILVERY *Biochem.* xix. 451 They [sc. spermine and spermidine] appear to occur in association with nucleic acids, as might be expected from their polycationic character. **1944** W. APEL *Harvard Dict. Mus.* 593/1 Early adumbrations of polychoral treatment occur in the works of Josquin des Près who frequently interrupts the full-voiced writing in four parts..by 'antiphonal' passages in which two half-choruses..perform a short phrase twice, in an echo-like manner. **1963** *Times* 9 May 16/5 'Jauchzet dem Herren',..a big polychoral 'concerto' from the *Psalmen Davids* of 1619, was a casualty, its elaborate antiphonies of voices and instruments blurred by the cathedral's hopelessly over-resonant sound. **1975** *Gramophone* Nov. 869/3 In 1628, Salzburg Cathedral was re-opened... Its inaugural Mass was a grand polychoral affair. **1978** *Early Music* Apr. 170 Venice and the grand manner of the polychoral motet seem so inseparable that it is hard to consider them apart. **1963** OHTAKA & SPIEGELMAN in *Science* 25 Oct. 493/2 An RNA molecule which can be translated into two or more proteins may be referred to as a 'polycistronic' message. **1968** H. HARRIS *Nucleus & Cytoplasm* ii. 23 The idea of a 'polycistronic' template, that is, one which can specify the amino acid sequences of a group of related proteins, now enjoys considerable popularity. **1974** *Nature* 1 Nov. 75/2 Kennel *et al.* concluded that each cistron in these polycistronic RNAs has a unique site that is vulnerable to attack. *Ibid.*, There is..an indication that some tRNAs are made polycistronically. **1978** *Nature* 25 May 304/2 The polyclonality of B cell responses to LPS has excluded the participation of immunoglobulin combining sites in the process of triggering. **1977** *Lancet* 5 Nov. 958/2 We suggest that immunosuppression in this syndrome is the result of the collective immunosuppressive effects of trypanosome-derived immune-modulating free fatty acids, polyclonally stimulating B-cell mitogen, and complement-activating factors. **1975** CRICK & LAWRENCE in *Science* 1 Aug. 341/3 The progeny of a cell marked at about the time of the drawing of boundary lines never fills a compartment completely, but often occupies an appreciable proportion of it. A compartment is thus made by the descendants of a small group of cells. We propose to call the cells in the compartment a polyclone. Just as a clone is a group of cells which are all, without exception, the descendants of a single cell, so a polyclone is a group of cells that are descended from a certain (small) group of cells—the founder cells—which were present in the embryo at an earlier time. **1979** *Sci. Amer.* July 93/1 Each compartment is made by a set of complete clones, which we call a polyclone, that develops from a few founder cells. **1914** W. E. AGAR in *Phil. Trans. R. Soc.* B. CCV. 422 When a population.. is composed of a number of clones each descended from an original ancestor not asexually connected with the original ancestors of the other clones, the population may be called polyclonal. **1961** *Harvey Lect. 1960–61* LVI. 221 He had a broad-banded, polyclonal γ-globulin with a rich serological picture. **1973** *Sci. Amer.* Aug. 44/2 If plaques were a simple response to an injury of some kind, as has been proposed, their cells should be polyclonal, the Benditts point out. **1921** *19th Cent.* July 148 The maximalists, of course, are for polycratism, provincial rule, insubordination and importation of foreign ideas. **1948** TYSDAL & CRANDALL in *Jrnl. Amer. Soc. Agronomy* XL. 294 The present paper deals with methods for determining the combining ability of the components of a hybrid or variety. For convenience, the method is referred to as the 'polycross method'. *Ibid.*, The single crosses and polycrosses exhibited even greater superiority over the checks. *Ibid.* 297 Polycross seed is the seed produced on selected clones interpollinated at random in isolation. **1977** *Crop Sci.* XVII. 909/2 Twenty-one clones whose polycross progenies ranked high for rate of seedling emergence under field conditions or had high forage yield..were selected for this study. Polycross seed from these clones was produced in isolated blocks. **1857** DUNGLISON *Dict. Med. Sci.* (rev. ed.) 741/2 *Polycythæmia*, a condition of the blood in which there is an increase of the red corpuscles. **1906** *Lancet* 7 July 20/2 The following case is published as a contribution to the study of the polycythæmic condition. **1935** [see *hypovolæmia* s.v. *HYPO- II]. **1962** *Lancet* 26 May 1098/2 The patient was polycythæmic until 1958, when a leukæmic picture first appeared. **1937** *Chem. Rev.* XXI. 39 The simple variation of acidic and coördinating groups in the polydentate molecules has escaped investigation. **1961** G. R. CHOPPIN *Exper. Nucl. Chem.* ix. 147 Complexes with a high degree of covalent character are formed by the interaction of metal ions with polydentate organic ions. **1972** *Nature* 21 Jan. 181/1 Recently his expertise in coordination chemistry was extended to the complexes formed by the alkali metals and alkaline earth elements with a variety of polydentate ligands. **1909** *Cent. Dict.* Suppl., Polyelectronic. **1939** L. PAULING *Nature Chem. Bond* i. 29 The electron distribution function for a poly-electronic atom or ion shows the presence of electron shells as regions of maximum electron density. **1947** *Amer. Scientist* XXXV. 185 Just as little tested in the laboratory is the conclusion that positrons, like protons..can form short lived polyelectronic entities of the type e^+e^-, $e^+(e^-)_2$, [etc.]. **1964** J. W. LINNETT *Electronic Struct. Molecules* i. 9 The most important factor governing the electronic structures of the ground states of polyelectronic atoms is the effect summarized in the Pauli Principle. **1965** *Amer. Surgeon* XXXI. 695 (*heading*) Polyendocrine adenomatosis with Zollinger-Ellison syndrome. **1967** S. L. ROBBINS *Path.* (ed. 3) xxix. 1243/2 (*heading*) Multiple endocrine adenomatosis (polyendocrine adenomas). **1976** *Lancet* 11 Dec. 1273/1 Antibodies reacting with normal human pancreatic islet cells have been described in patients with diabetes associated with autoimmune polyendocrine disease. **1964** *Medicine* XLIII. 176/1 It is suggested that Schmidt's syndrome with diabetes mellitus may be a polyendocrinopathy. **1973** *Acta Endocrinol.* LXXII. 411 As for the theoretical implications of poly-endocrinopathies, the possibility of common aetiological factors lies near at hand. **1920** W. E. AGAR *Cytol.* vii. 209 Examples of such polyenergid nuclei (Hartmann, 1909) are afforded by the great nuclei of the Radiolaria. **1939** *Nature* 14 Jan. 47/2 Schussnig..reaffirms..his view that the Conjugales are derived from a polyenergid ancestry, and a similar origin is suggested for the Red Algæ. **1961** MACKINNON & HAWES *Introd. Study Protozoa* 66 The gigantic nucleus [of *Aulacantha*] is remarkable for the number of its chromosomes, of which there are some 1,500... This remarkable structure, according to Grell, is really polyenergid. **1976** BELL & COOMBE tr. *Strasburger's Textbk. Bot.* (rev. ed.) 44 Free nuclear divisions, that is, divisions not accompanied by cell division, occur in those Thallophyta showing the polyenergid condition. **1967** J. H. SUDD *Introd. Behaviour Ants* viii. 154 Animals which show these variations in behaviour from one to another can be said to show polyethism—a word formed by analogy with polymorphism. **1973** J. P. SPRADBURY *Wasps* vi. 155 There may occur several forms of polyethism, namely those based on age, physiological condition, and size. **1929** W. H. CAROTHERS in *Jrnl. Amer. Chem. Soc.* LI. 2550 (*heading*) Polyfunctional compounds. *Ibid.*, All these may be classed together as polyfunctional reactions. **1962** J. T. MARSH *Self-Smoothing Fabrics* v. 45 The finishing process..consists of impregnating the fabrics with the appropriate polyfunctional compound and a catalyst, drying, heating and washing. **1963** J. OSBORNE *Dental Mech.* (ed. 5) i. 23 The basic ingredient is a polyfunctional mercaptan with..the average formula $HS(R—S—S)_{23}—R—SH$. **1964** N. G. CLARK *Mod. Org. Chem.* xv. 301 By employing polyfunctional halides in place of alkyl halides depicted above, more complex ketones are obtained. **1936** *Trans. Faraday Soc.* XXXII. 39 (*heading*) Polymers & polyfunctionality. **1961** SORENSON & CAMPBELL *Prep. Methods Polymer Chem.* iii. 59 The qualitative aspects of condensation polymerization, including..effect of polyfunctionality on branching and gelation, have been thoroughly treated. **1927** PEAKE & FLEURE *Apes & Men* 69 This polyglacial, or preferably multiglacial, view was not well received, and considerable opposition was offered to it. **1937** *Geogr. Jrnl.* XC. 180 Formerly James Geikie, almost alone, insistently voiced the case for the polyglacial view and perhaps he strained it by over-statement. **1972** SPARKS & WEST *Ice Age in Brit.* v. 123 The limits of the successive glaciations of this polyglacial sequence, imperfectly known at present, are shown. *Ibid.*, The evidence for polyglacialism lay not so much in evidence for different end-moraines of successive ice advances..but in the finding of non-glacial sediments between glacial deposits. **1946, 1968** Polyglacialist [see *monoglacialist* sb. and adj. s.v. *MONO- 1]. **1972** SPARKS & WEST *Ice Age in Brit.* v. 123 The supporters of the monoglacial theory..were eclipsed by polyglacialists, though some survived till a few years ago. **1935** Y. KATAYAMA in *Jap. Jrnl. Bot.* VII. 374 The writer has classified (though provisionally) the haploid plants as follows... If the haploid has occurred from allopolyploids, it is classified under the name of polyhaploid. **1955** *Nature* 12 Mar. 469/1 This plant had the chromosome number $2n = 24$, suggesting that it might be a polyhaploid of *S[olanum] polytrichon*, having arisen by haploid parthenogenesis. **1975** *Ibid.* 17 Apr. 596/1 In wheat and oats, the polyhaploids show very little chiasmate pairing because genetic control is effective in the hemizygous state. **1880** W. I. STRINGHAM in *Amer. Jrnl. Math.* III. 2 It will be convenient to designate as an *n*-fold polyhedroid the *n*-dimensional figure which is bounded by $(n-1)$-fold flat (not curved) figures. **1914** H. P. MANNING *Geom. Four Dimensions* viii. 289 A regular polyhedroid..consists of equal regular polyhedrons together with their interiors, the polyhedrons being joined by their faces so as to enclose a portion of hyperspace, and the hyperplane angles formed at the faces by the half-hyperplanes of adjacent polyhedrons being all equal to one another. **1972** C. S. OGILVY *Tomorrow's Math* (ed. 2) iv. 79 A polytope is an *n*-dimensional polyhedroid. **1967** *Sci. Amer.* June 124/3 Other names have been proposed, but it seems to me that the best is 'polyhexes', the name adopted by David Klomer, who was one of the first to investigate them. **1975** *Ibid.* July 114/3 Combinatorial geometers have given special attention in recent years to tiling with polyominoes and their cousins the polyiamonds and polyhexes. **1967** *Ibid.* June 124/2 By joining equilateral triangles along their edges one obtains another well-explored family of shapes known as polyiamonds. **1975** [see *polyhex* above]. **1938** A. I. OPARIN *Origin of Life* vi. 138 Regarding every living cell as a 'single chemical particle or, more correctly, as a colossal poly-ion'. **1947** *Jrnl. Polymer Sci.* II. 12 Both negative and positive polyions may be made; the former as polycarboxylic or sulfonic acids and their salts and the latter, for example, as onium salts of polymers such as vinylpyridine. **1959** *Acta Crystallogr.* XII. 165/2 The crystal structure of inyoite contains isolated polyions, $[B_3O_3(OH)_5]^{-2}$. **1963** *New Scientist* 11 Apr. 103/3 The chemistry of polyions, such as proteins, mucopolysaccharides, [etc.]..is very relevant to understanding the behaviour of the cell surface. **1972** COTTON & WILKINSON *Adv. Inorg. Chem.* (ed. 3) xvi. 486 There is slight evidence in the bromine system for Br_5^-, but the series of polyions I_5^-, I_7^- and I_9^- is well-established for iodine. **1907** *Publ. Carnegie Inst.* No. 63. XII. 352 A fuller experimental investigation of the properties of dissolved salts, especially of those of polyionic types. **1970** FOX & FRIED tr. *Staudinger's From Org. Chem. to Macromolecules* B. vii. 134 These anomalous phenomena in solutions of polyelectrolytes were termed 'polyionic viscosity phenomena'. **1890** W. H. HOWELL in *Jrnl. Morphol.* IV. 118 The first class might be named polykaryocytes, or multinucleated giant cells. **1946** *Blood* I. 29 Morone sharply differentiated the polykaryocytes from osteoclasts, but in this he was disputed by Lambin and Lamers. **1968** E. KELEMEN *Physiopath. & Therapy Human Blood Dis.* (1969) i. 36 Even larger cells, resembling megakaryocytes, are the osteoclasts or polykaryocytes. These two cells have to do with bone formation and are more often seen in a trephine biopsy. **1947** *Jrnl. Lab. & Clin. Med.* XXXII. 664 The concept of a polykaryocytic origin of the megakaryocyte has not received general acceptance. **1964** *Biol. Abstr.* XLV. 3106/2 Injection of confluent polykaryocytic cultures into chicks resulted in the appearance of sarcomas which contained transformed cells and polykaryocytes. **1972** B. BICKERTON in *Georgetown Univ. Ser. Lang. & Linguistics* (1973) xxv. 34 The demonstration of similarities between Black English and Guyanese Creole..was simply a by-product of the attempt to write a polylectal grammar of the latter. **1972** C.-J. N. BAILEY in Stockwell & Macaulay *Linguistic Change & Generative Theory* 24 Rule changes of the sort being described could never occur in a homogeneous grammar... Without the retention of the older forms in a different style or in a different class lect known to a speaker long enough for a rule change to be generalized, such a generalization could not occur. Only a polylectal grammar is adequate for historical linguistics. **1977** *Word 1972* XXVIII. 166 The subject matter of dialectology may be viewed..1. As a complex of shared and differentiated items which function within a single diasystem (a pan-dialectal or polylectal system). **1978** *Archivum Linguisticum* IX. 37 That implicational (polylectal) patterning obtains in Table 1(b) is clear: some speakers are invariable users of the feature S, others are invariable users of the feature P, while a third group of speakers alternate S and P. **1933** 'E. CAMBRIDGE' *Hostages to Fortune* III. vi. 184 Foreign students, slow south Germans, French boys from Rennes, polylingual Swedes. **1958** *Times* 5 Dec. 16/3 Polytextual, polylingual wrestlings with canti fermi. **1978** *Amer. N. & Q.* XVI. 146/2 A few other bilingual and polylingual glossaries. **1956** J. WHATMOUGH *Language* 241 Correlation methods may be used to show how much..the polylingualism of an interlingua may safely draw from different languages. **1977** *Word 1972* XXVIII. 193 Borrowing, especially when related to bilingualism or polylingualism, increases the number of opportunities for metanalytical processes to take place, both at the time of borrowing and subsequently. **1908** *Sci. Amer. Suppl.* 25 Jan. 61/1 These crevices and fissures are filled with a polylithic mass of brown and white 'calcic spar'. **1961** *Economist* 11 Nov. 538/2 Somewhere in the essentially 'polylithic' variety of the sisterhood there must be an answer. **1886** *Jrnl. Chem. Soc.* L. 677 Minerals from Kangerdluarsuk, in Greenland... Polylithionite (lithium mica). **1927** *Amer. Mineralogist* XII. 275 Polylithionite is of doubtful stability, but mica of approximately this composition has been described from Greenland. **1962** *Geochemistry* XI. 1197 In lithium micas (polylithionites) the geochemical similarity of lithium and magnesium does not play an important part and lithium occupies an independent position in the structure of the mica lattice. **1892** *Dental Rec.* XII. 488 Amalgams consist of the combination of either one or several metals with mercury,..the bulk of a polymetallic amalgam usually consisting of Tin and Silver. **1956** *Mineral. Abstr.* XIII. 38 Nests and lenses of plumbojarosite are found in the oxidized zone of polymetallic ore deposits. **1968** BETHELL & BURG tr. *Solzhenitsyn's Cancer Ward* I. xv. 236 My theory is that you can discover deposits of polymetallic ore by looking for radioactive water. **1974** *Nature* 16 Aug. 545/1 The polymetallic province is particularly enriched in silver north of boundary 1. **1829** W. GREENFIELD (*title*) Polymician lexicon to the New Testament. **1838** *Bagster's Catal.* 22 Polymician series of New Testaments, Concordances, Lexicons, and Psalters, Small Pocket Volumes. **1938** *Mem. Geol. Soc. Amer.* VI. 134 Except for a few monomineral fabrics, such as those of pure quartzite.., most rock fabrics are polymineral. **1975** *Nature* 25 Dec. 690/1 This suite of rather unusual minerals has received wide attention because the minerals have been identified in light-coloured, millimetre-sized polymineral inclusions present in carbonaceous chondrites. **1949** E. A. NIDA *Morphol.* (ed. 2) iv. 97 Simple structures consist of a single morpheme, free or bound. Complex structures consist of more than one morpheme. Simple structures may be called 'monomorphemic' and complex structures 'polymorphemic'. **1962** H. C. CONKLIN in J. A. Fishman *Readings Sociol. of Lang.* (1968) 416 Single morphemes are necessarily lexemes, but for polymorphemic constructions the decision depends on meaning and use. **1964** R. H. ROBINS *Gen. Linguistics* 206 Polymorphemic words may consist wholly of free morphemes. **1957** H. S. BARBER in *Ann. Rheumatic Dis.* XVI. 237/2, (1) A condition characterized by widespread muscular pains without arthritis but accompanied by a high erythrocyte sedimentation rate and occasional pyrexia is described. (2) The relationship to rheumatoid disease is discussed and it is concluded that this is probably a clinical entity within the rheumatic group of diseases. (3) It is proposed to term the syndrome 'polymyalgia rheumatica'. **1971** BOYLE & BUCHANAN *Clin. Rheumatol.* xvi. 434/2 Polymyalgia rheumatica.. affects subjects in the later years of life, the average age of onset being the late sixties. **1878** D. F. LINCOLN tr. A. Eulenburg in *Ziemssen's Cycl. Pract. Med.* XIV. 133 According to these, the disease consists in an essentially inflammatory process, a 'polymyositis chronica progressiva'. **1895** *Jrnl. Nervous & Mental Dis.* XXII. 316 (*heading*) Polyneuritic psychoses. **1932** *Times Lit. Suppl.* 7 Jan. 14/3 His results..show that brain tissue from polyneuritic pigeons..has *in vitro* a lower power of oxygen uptake. **1968** M. PYKE *Food & Society* ii. 17 The remarkable effects of a few milligrams of thiamine on a polyneuritic pigeon. **1938** I. S. WECHSLER in *Jrnl. Amer. Med. Assoc.* 4 June 1913/2 It is suggested that the term multiple neuropathy, polyneuropathy or peripheral neuropathy be substituted for multiple neuritis in those cases in which both the cause and the pathologic changes point to a degenerative process. **1954** *Jrnl. Neuropath. & Exper. Neurol.* XIII. 168 Severe polyneuropathy with massive involvement of the large nerve trunks may not only appear in association with the more chronic forms of diffuse connective tissue disease,..but may even dominate the clinical picture so as to obscure the diagnosis of the underlying disease. **1974** PASSMORE & ROBSON *Compan. Med. Stud.* III. xxxiv. 36/2 Polyneuropathy arises from dietary deficiencies, chemical poisoning and may be a manifestation of numerous diseases. **1919** *Amer. Jrnl. Anat.* XXVI. 131 The females of the wild swine of Europe are monoestrous, according to Kaeppeli ('08), having but one period of heat in the year; but under domestication the sow becomes polyoestrous, coming in heat at intervals of two to four weeks. **1975** *Sci. Amer.* July 77/1 The particular response of each species to light seems to depend on whether the species is monestrous or polyestrous, that is, on whether it normally ovulates once a year (in the spring or fall) or at regular intervals throughout the year. **1954** S. W. GOLOMB in *Amer. Math. Monthly* LXI. 675 We shall generalize the 'domino' to the 'polyomino'... We *define* an *n*-omino as a simply-connected set of *n* squares of the checker-board which are 'rook-wise connected'; that is, a rook placed at any square of the *n*-omino must be able to get to any other square, in a finite number of moves. **1965** —— *Polyominoes* 13 Ever since I 'invented' polyominoes in 1953 in a talk to the Harvard Mathematics Club, I have found myself irrevocably committed to their care and feeding. **1972** W. F. LUNNON in R. C. Read *Graph Theory & Computing* 108 Free polyominoes whose symmetry groups contain no improper elements..are enantiomorphic. **1974** *Sci. Amer.* Feb. 106 Solomon W. Golomb's polyomino-placing game..has finally reached the marketplace. **1918** R. NEWSTEAD in *Ann. Trop. Med. & Parasitol.* XII. 93 The main pair of stigmata..lie in the deep cup-shaped cavity or pit between the polypneustic lobes. *Ibid.* 95 The low-convex anal lobes or callosities were distinctly polypneustic in character. **1925** A. D. IMMS *Gen. Textbk. Entomol.* 110 In *Glossina* there are about 500 of these pores to a side which form the sculpturing on a pair of polypneustic lobes. **1962** GORDON & LAVOIPIERRE *Entomol. for Students of Med.* xxix. 182 The larva contracts considerably to form a barrel-shaped object varying between 5 and 8 mm. in length, with the prominent polypneustic lobes of the larva still clearly visible. **1921** *Physiol. Rev.* I. 296 Marsupials are the lowest mammals capable of 'heat polypnea'. **1966** *Amer. Jrnl. Physiol.* CCX. 1270/1 Free-breathing cats demonstrated a thermal polypnea similar to that reported for dogs, cattle, and monkeys. **1975** J. J. GROEN in L. Levi *Society, Stress & Dis.* II. xxxiv. 350/2 The child may substitute in situations of frustration another form of respiratory behaviour such as apnoea, polypnoea, or a peculiar kind of pressing with the abdominal muscles during expiration which..produces an expiratory wheeze. **1909** *Cent. Dict.* Suppl., Polypnœic, polypneic. **1934** *Amer. Jrnl. Physiol.* CIX. 528 Any type of panting (the polypneic or the hyperpneic) that occurs after decortication is dependent on a rise in blood temperature. **1975** *Biol. Abstr.* LIX. 1795/1 (*heading*) Induction of polypneic threshold by heating during cat sleep cycle. **1974** *Jrnl. Virol.* XIV. 261 (*heading*) Cleavage of mengovirus polyproteins in vivo. **1975** *Sci. Amer.* May 27/3 This huge protein, really a polyprotein, is then systematically cleaved by proteolytic enzymes. **1962** *Science* 28 Dec. 1401/2 An intrinsic property of the polyribosomal unit. **1970** *Sci. Jrnl.* Apr. 36 In the unaltered cytoplasm surrounding these areas ribosomes were gathered into polyribosomal aggregates, indicating very active synthesis of protein. **1962** Polyribosome [see *POLYSOME]. **1973** *Sci. Amer.* Apr. 41/1 As the synthesis of the messenger RNA proceeds, giving rise to a longer strand of RNA, more ribosomes attach themselves to the strand. They form a string called a polyribosome, which continues the translation of the elongating messenger RNA **1925** *Bull. Illinois Nat. Hist. Survey* XV. 440 The septic or grossly polluted portions of a stream... The organisms of this zone are those which have been termed by Kolkwitz and Marsson..polysaprobic and by Forbes and Richardson.. septic or saprobic. **1932** *Trans. Brit. Mycol. Soc.* XVII. 112 The association of polysaprobic organisms occurs in waters rich in decaying organic matter. **1933** [see *oligosaprobic* adj. s.v. *OLIGO-]. **1946** *Jrnl. Ecol.* XXXIII. 274 Judging from data obtained from other rivers the amounts of algal growth appear to fall into four groups,..in the polysaprobic waters (e.g. the river Tame) the numbers.. are low. **1950** *Folia Limnologica Scandinavica* V. 76 The polysaprobic zone is defined in a chemical respect as the zone in which reduction of the polluting substances takes place. **1973** M. A. SLEIGH *Biol. Protozoa* xi. 265 The largest numbers of protozoan organisms occur in polysaprobic conditions. **1939** L. H. GRAY *Foundations of Lang.* 255 Words are very frequently polysemantic. **1960** E. DELAVENAY *Introd. Machine Transl.* vi. 81 In recent concise dictionaries the vocabulary of the English language comprises some 60,000 word entries: this number may run four times as high if each meaning of each polysemantic word is entered separately. **1961** *Amer. Speech* XXXVI. 5 (*heading*) Polysemantic extensions of 'dog' and allied terms. **1966** S. CECCATO in *Automatic Transl. of Lang.* (NATO Summer School, Venice, 1962) 75 First of all there is the problem of the polysemanticity of the individual words. **1939** L. H. GRAY *Foundations of Lang.* ix. 258 The principle of analogy or metaphor in polysemantism..appears when the name of a well known historical..figure is extended to persons supposed to resemble that character. **1946** *Word* II. 124 *Synchronic* semasiology..deals with..problems like homonyms, homophones, synonyms, polysemantism. **1900** *Brit. Med. Jrnl.* 15 Dec. 1693/2 Italian physicians..have given a name or names to this multiple inflammation of the serous cavities... The names are polyserositis and polyorromenitis. **1915** *Amer. Jrnl. Med. Sci.* CL. 518 (*heading*) Chronic lead-poisoning in guinea-pigs: with special reference to nephritis, cirrhosis, and polyserositis. **1966** WRIGHT & SYMMERS *Systemic Path.* I. i. 5/1 Occasionally, as a result of the compression of the inferior vena cava by the coarse fibrous tissue, a syndrome known as 'polyserositis' or Concato's disease develops in which fluid gradually collects in the pleural and peritoneal cavities. **1951** STRAUSS & JACKSON in *Jrnl. Polymer Sci.* VI. Polysoaps are defined as polymers to whose chain soap molecules are attached. **1976** *Nature* 5 Aug. 519/2 Some enzymes may be converted into surface-active amphipathic conjugates by covalent coupling to certain types of polymeric detergents (polysoaps). **1950** H. GASTAUT in *Electroencephalogr. & Clin. Neurophysiol.* II. 250/1 In the EEG is a burst of very large amplitude rhythmic spikes of a frequency equal to that of the flashes; these are bilateral and synchronized, and appear predominantly in the precentral and frontal regions where they can in fact be localized... These spikes are sometimes quite pure and thus constitute the complex for which we have proposed the name 'polyspike'. **1975** S. ARIETI *Amer. Handbk. Psychiatry* (ed. 2) IV. xiii. 320/2 The state is associated with prolonged EEG discharge of the 3-Hz. spike-wave type as well as..slower and faster components with polyspikes. **1952** *New Biol.* XII. 28 The only method at present available for diagnosing monozygosity involves comparison of as many morphological and physiological characters as possible—the so called 'polysymptomatic similarity' method which is that normally used for determining the zygotic nature of twins in man. **1962** A. BOURNE *Doctor's Creed* vi. 117 The unhappy woman is the victim of constant physical troubles which present a polysymptomatic picture which is quite incurable by the ordinary methods of clinical medicine. **1977** *Lancet* 24/31 Dec. 1340/1 What do you do with a polysymptomatic patient in whom the only positive finding is an enlarged liver? **1894** W. R. WILLIAMS *Dis. Breast* iv. 56 In other cases one or more supernumerary nipples, each with its own areola, have been met with, in various positions, on a single breast (intramammary polythelia). **1928** [see *POLYMASTIA]. **1970** H. P. LEIS *Diagnosis & Treatm. Breast Lesions* iv. 60 Polythelia or accessory nipples may occur along the 'milk line' from the axilla to the symphysis pubis or anywhere over a given breast. **1886** Polythelism [see *POLYMASTISM]. **1928** F. Z. SNOOP *From Monotremes to Madonna* 23 Polythely. This last form is commoner in men than women. **1974** *Tetrahedron* XXX. 1596/1 The concept of shape is presented in terms of a dihedral angle relationship between adjacent polytopal faces. This procedure was first employed..to map out structural form in the relatively complicated 8-atom family. **1908** *Proc. Sect. Sci. Koninkl. Akad. van Wetensch. Amsterdam* X. 689 This leads us gradually to the question, whether it is not possible to point out one or more polytopes—if not quite regular ones—which with C_5 fill the fourdimensional space. **1929** D. M. Y. SOMMERVILLE *Introd. Geom. N Dimensions* x. 190 In a plane there are an unlimited number of regular polygons and 3 regular networks, in space of three dimensions there are 5 regular polyhedra and one regular honeycomb, in S_4 there are 6 regular polytopes and three regular honeycombs, in space of more than four dimensions there are just three regular polytopes and one regular honeycomb. **1974** H. S. M. COXETER *Regular Complex Polytopes* xiii. 141 The regular polytopes and honeycombs so far considered are the only ones that can exist in unitary spaces. **1904** *Science* 10 June 885/1 The idea that a species may originate in more than one place.. did not originate with Briquet, but he resuscitated it and christened it the polytopic theory. **1939** *Geogr. Jrnl.* XCIII. 271 We are forced to fall back on the theory of polyphyletic and polytopic evolution. **1970** *Watsonia* VIII. 143 The distribution of the hexaploids in Britain does not show any obvious pattern.., and this agrees with Rousi's suggestion that hexaploids have had a polytopic origin from the tetraploids. **1876** C. A. CUTTER *Rules for Printed Dict. Catal.* 14 It will be well to have both words,—polygraphic denoting (as now) collections of several works by one or many authors, polytopical denoting works on many subjects. **1961** T. LANDAU *Encycl. Librarianship* (ed. 2) 282/1 Polytopical. Descriptive of a book treating of several subjects. **1842** DUNGLISON *Dict. Med. Sci.* (ed. 3) 562/1 *Polyuria*, diabetes. **1870** J. R. CORMACK tr. *Trousseau's Lect. Clin. Med.* III. lxv. 533 Polyuria, saccharine diabetes, and also sometimes albuminuria, may, in succession, attack the same individual. *Ibid.* 536, I have..had the pain to see nearly all the polyuric patients whom I had to treat, waste away rapidly. **1953** *Parasitology* XLII. 260 (*table*) Polyxenic. [Number of associated organisms] Several. [Source of term] New. **1976** *Ann. Rev. Microbiol.* XXX. 128 Laboratory stocks of many protozoa are maintained on mono- to polyxenic substrates. In an attempt to establish axenic cultures of *Entamoeba histolytica*, spontaneous and sporadic lysis in these amoeba developed.

2. a, b. Add: Now used esp. to form the names of polymers and other types of compound which have a number of identical groups in their structure. The second element is in some cases a suffix. Usage of the prefix is restricted by some authors to cases where the number of constituent groups is large (in contrast to OLIGO-), but there is no uniformity in this respect. The prefix is now very abundant in *Chem.*, and only the more widely occurring formations are included below.

poly-A, poly A, etc. = *polyadenylic acid* below; **polya·cetal,** any of a class of polymers containing the repeating group —O·CH(R)—, which are prepared by addition polymerization of aldehydes and are typically strong thermoplastics used as moulding materials; **polyace·tylene,** any organic compound containing two or more carbon–carbon triple bonds; hence **po:lyacetyle·nic** *a.*; **polyacry·lamide** (or *po:lyacryla·mide*) [ACRYL + AMIDE], any of the polymers of acrylamide, $CH_2{=}CH·CONH_2$, or its substituted derivatives, which are water-soluble polymers widely used to form or stabilize gels and as thickening, suspending, or clarifying agents, etc.; **polyacry·lic** *a.* (and *sb.*), designating compounds which are polymers of acrylic acid or its esters, or thermoplastic materials consisting of or made from such polymers; hence **polya·crylate,** an ester or salt of polyacrylic acid; a polymer of an acrylic ester or, *loosely*, of acrylic acid; **po:lyacryloni·trile,** any of the polymers of acrylonitrile, many of which are used commercially, esp. as man-made fibres; **po:lyadeny·lic acid** *Biochem.* [*ADENYL], a polynucleotide formed from adenosine monophosphate by the action of polynucleotide polymerase, and isolated as fibres; abbrev. **poly-A*; **polya·lcohol,** a polyhydric alcohol; **polya·llomer** [f. ALLOMERISM after *polymer*], any of a class of crystalline thermoplastics which are copolymers of two or more different alkenes, esp. ethylene and propylene; **polya·mine,** any organic compound which contains two or more amine groups; **polyanhy·dride,** any of a class of polymers in which the units are linked through the anhydride group, —CO·O·CO—, and which includes many resins used commercially, esp. as fibres; **polyanion, anionic** *a.* (see sense 1 above); **polybro·minated** *a.*, applied to compounds in which two or more hydrogen atoms have been replaced by bromine atoms; **po:lybutadi·ene,** any of the polymers of 1,3-butadiene or its derivatives; also, any of the class of synthetic rubbers consisting of or made from such polymers; **po:lycarboxy·lic** *a.*, having more than one carboxyl group in the molecule; **polycation, -cationic** *a.* (see sense 1 above); **polychlo·roprene,** any of the polymers of chloroprene; also, any of the class of synthetic rubbers (esp. neoprene) consisting of or made from such polymers; **polydi·ene** *Chem.*, any polymer of a conjugated diene, esp. any of those forming a number of types of synthetic rubber; **polyene** (pǫ·liˌīn) [-ENE], any organic compound containing two or more carbon–carbon double bonds; hence **polye·nic, polyeno·ic** *adjs.*; **polye·thenoid** *a.* = **polyenic* adj.; also as *sb.*; **polyfo·rmal, -forma·ldehyde** = *polyoxymethylene* below; **polygluta·mic acid** *Biochem.*, a synthetic polypeptide consisting of glutamic acid residues; **polygly·cine** *Biochem.*, any oligopeptide or polypeptide composed of glycine residues; *spec.* a synthetic crystalline long-chain polypeptide having this structure; **polygly·col** = *polyethylene glycol* s.v. *POLYETHYLENE a; **polyglyco·lic acid,** a polyester fibre which is made by polymerizing glycolic acid, $CH_2OH·COOH$, and is used in surgery for ligatures, as it is slowly and harmlessly absorbed by the body; **polyhydroxy(-),** *prefix* used to designate compounds or groups containing more than one hydroxyl group; also (without hyphen, as an independent word) as quasi-*adj.*; **polyhydro·xyl** = prec. (quasi-*adj.* use); **po:lyisobu·tylene,** any polymer of isobutylene; also, any of the large class of synthetic rubbers consisting of or made from such polymers; **polyly·sine** *Biochem.*, a synthetic polypeptide consisting of lysine residues; **po:lymethacry·lic acid,** any polymer of methacrylic acid; hence **polymetha·crylate,** a salt or ester of polymethacrylic acid; also, any of the synthetic resins made by polymerizing esters of methacrylic acid; **polyol** (pǫ·liˌǫl) (*a*) [*OL], an ol complex which contains more than one bridging hydroxyl ligand; now *rare*; (*b*) [-OL], a polyhydric alcohol; **polyo·lefin(e,** any polymer of an olefin, esp. any of the commercially important synthetic resins of this type; also = *polyene* above; **po:lyoxye·thylene,** designating, or used in the names of, compounds containing the polymeric group $—(CH_2·CH_2·O)_n—$; **po:lyoxyme·thylene,** any of a number of white, crystalline polymers which are prepared from formaldehyde and in which the repeating unit is $—CH_2·O—$; *esp.* any of the tough, strong thermoplastics of this type which are used as moulding materials; **polyphe·nol,** any compound which contains more than one phenolic hydroxyl group; hence **polyphe·nolic** *a.*; **polyphenol oxidase, po:lyphenolo·xidase** *Biochem.* [ad. G. *polyphenoloxydase* (Battelli & Stern 1912, in *Ergebnisse d. Physiol.* XII. 96): see *OXIDASE], any of the phenolases which oxidize polyphenols; *loosely*, any phenolase; **polyphe·nylene,** any polymer in which the repeating unit is or contains the *para*-phenylene group; *polyphenylene oxide*, a thermoplastic having the structure $—(p\text{-}C_6H_4O)_n—$, which is used as a moulding material; **po:lyphospho·ric acid,** any oxyacid of pentavalent phosphorus which contains two or more phosphorus atoms, spec. a mixture of polymers of orthophosphoric acid which is used in organic chemistry esp. as a mild dehydrating agent; hence **polypho·sphate,** a salt, anion, or ester of any such acid; **polysilo·xane** [*SILOXANE], any polymer which is based upon a chain of alternating silicon and oxygen atoms; *esp.* a silicone; **polysty·rol** = *POLYSTYRENE; **polysu·lphide,** (*a*) a salt or other compound which contains two or more sulphur atoms bonded together, as an anion or group; also, such an anion or group; (*b*) any polymer in which the units are linked through polysulphide groups, esp. any of a class of synthetic rubbers with this structure; freq. *attrib.*; **polysu·lphone,** any polymer in which the units contain the sulphone linkage, $—SO_2—$, esp. a type of thermosetting synthetic resin which has this structure and is used as a moulding material, esp. in electrical and electronic applications; **polyte·rpene** [ad. G. *polyterpen* (O. Wallach 1885, in *Ann. d. Chem.* CCXXVII. 302)], any of the higher members of the terpene series, $(C_5H_8)_n$; a polymer of a terpene; **polyte·rpenoid** = prec.; **polyu·ronide** [*URONIC *a.* + -IDE], any polysaccharide which consists of uronic acid residues, usu. in combination with simple monosaccharides.

1957 *Jrnl. Amer. Chem. Soc.* LXXIX. 2023/2 Experiments were carried out with poly-A and poly-U prepared.. with polyribonucleotide phosphorylase from *E. coli*. **1968** W. MÜLLER in E. Harbers et al. *Introd. Nucleic Acids* iii. 51 Below pH 6, polyA yields fibers with high negative birefringence. **1975** Poly(A) [see *polyadenylic acid* below]. **1931** *Chem. Rev.* VIII. 371 The reaction between glycols and acetaldehyde (or acetylene) presents the possibility of forming cyclic acetals..or polyacetals. **1967** *Times Rev. Industry* June 72/3 There are in hand expansion programmes covering polyvinyl chloride, polyethylene, polystyrene, butadiene, polyacetals, and polyesters. **1973** *Materials & Technol.* VI. viii. 578 Polyacetal is largely crystalline and not transparent. It resists weathering well and..shows little cold flow. **1885** *Jrnl. Chem. Soc.* XLVIII. 759 (*heading*) Polyacetylene compounds. **1952** *Jrnl. Amer. Chem. Soc.* LXXIV. 1588/2 From these spectra, Dr. Sörensen identified our compounds as polyacetylenes. **1967** *New Scientist* 13 Apr. 95/2 In recent years the widespread occurrence in fungi and plants..of straight-chain 'polyacetylenes'..has been recognized. **1978** *Sci. Amer.* Dec. 66/1 It is conceivable that a polyacetylene film could replace ordinary metal conductors in some special circumstances, such as where weight or resistance to corrosion is important. **1952** *Jrnl. Amer. Chem. Soc.* LXXIV. 1588/2 The isolation of polyacetylenic compounds from several genera of *Compositae*. **1961** *Chem. Nat. Products* (I.U.P.A.C.) I. 570 The *cis*-lachnophyllum ester..is also most unusual in being a polyacetylenic compound which has been used in industry. **1944** *Jrnl. Org. Chem.* IX. 501 Another possible source of polyvinylamine would be the hypobromite degradation of polyacrylamide. **1962** H. BLOEMENDAL et al. in A. Pirie *Lens Metabolism Rel. Cataract* 300 The large size of α-crystallin is responsible for its electrophoretic behaviour..in polyacrylamide gel. **1976** *Nature* 18 Nov. 264/1 Polypeptides were identified by polyacrylamide slab gel electrophoresis and autoradiography. **1932** *Chem. Abstr.* XXVI. 1249 With the polyacrylate salts,..the process is approx. reversible. **1946** [see *polymethacrylate* below]. **1974** P. L. MOORE et al. *Drilling Practices Manual* v. 117 Polymers of the colloidal type..do not aggregate solids, as do the polyacrylates. **1930** *Chem. Abstr.* XXIV. 1563 Colloid mols. may be homeopolar (polystyrols, rubber), or heteropolar (polyacrylic acid salts, albuminoids). **1939** *Jrnl. R. Aeronaut. Soc.* XLIII. 241 The article deals with the mechanical and physical properties of four representative transparent plastic resins: Cellulose nitrate, cellulose acetate, polymer mixtures and polyacrylic esters. **1943** *Ibid.* XLVII. 140 The polyacrylic resins are thermoplastic, and articles can be made of them by moulding or extrusion. **1959** *Times Rev. Industry* Sept. 4/1 The last 20 years have seen the development of non-cellulosic fibres such as..polyacrylics (Courtelle, Orlon, Acrilan). **1973** *Materials & Technol.* VI. viii. 560 The chemical composition of polyacrylic acid, as the basic polymer of the whole class of acrylics, permits the production of many derivatives. **1935** C. ELLIS *Chem. Synthetic Resins* II. 1072 Hydrolysis of polyacrylonitrile in the presence of water also gives an aqueous solution of the polymerized acid. **1963** A. J. HALL *Textile Sci.* ii. 89 Great difficulty has attended the devising of a satisfactory process for spinning Orlon from polyacrylonitrile. **1969** *Nature* 25 Jan. 357/2 Cellulose and polyacrylonitrile.. have been found to produce carbon fibre of good strength and modulus. **1956** *Jrnl. Amer. Chem. Soc.* LXXVIII. 3548/2 While studying the X-ray diffraction patterns of synthetic nucleotide polymers, we mixed together the sodium salts of polyadenylic and polyuridylic acid. **1961** *Jrnl. Molecular Biol.* III. 78 The helical molecule of polyadenylic acid consists of two polynucleotide chains organized about a twofold rotation axis. **1975** *Nature* 27 Nov. 357/1 Polyadenylic acid (poly(A)) is present at the 3′ terminus of most classes of cytoplasmic messenger RNAs.. in all eukaryotic organisms reported so far. **1900** E. F. SMITH tr. *V. von Richter's Org. Chem.* (ed. 3) II. 247 Of the aromatic polyalcohols, having the hydroxyl groups attached to different carbon atoms of the same side-chain, it is only the glycols and their oxidation products which have been studied in any sense completely. **1974** *Nature* 19 Apr. 668/1 The donor and acceptor groups were aliphatic hydroxyl groups in polyalcohols, saccharides and related compounds. **1962** *New Scientist* 22 Mar. 697/2 They are described as stereoregular crystalline plastics and have been given the name polyallomers because their highly crystalline structure differs in chemical composition from other crystalline plastics. **1962** H. J. HAGEMEYER in *Mod. Plastics* June 157/2 The term polyallomer was coined [by the writer] to identify this new class of polymers and to distinguish them from previous known homopolymers and copolymers... These new polymers are examples of allomerism in polymer chemistry. **1975** C. A. HARPER *Handbk. Plastics & Elastomers* i. 91 Polyallomers are superior to polyethylene in flow characteristics, moldability, softening point, hardness, stress-crack resistance, and mold shrinkage. **1975** *Nature* 18 Dec. 638/2 CsCl powder (5·4g) was added to the solution in a siliconised polyallomer tube. **1861** *Proc. R. Soc.* XI. 281 (*heading*) Monacid polyamines. **1875** *Chem. News* 2 July 1/1 (*heading*) The mono character of ethylen and other polyamines. **1910** N. V. SIDGWICK *Org. Chem. Nitrogen* iii. 72 This looseness of attachment of the nitrogen is characteristic of these poly-amines. **1965** *New Scientist* 25 Mar. 795/2 Polyamines such as spermine and putrescine have been found in vegetable embryos and the seeds of various plants. **1931** *Chem. Rev.* VIII. 371 (*heading*) Polyanhydrides. **1932** *Jrnl. Amer. Chem. Soc.* LIV. 1584 Polyanhydrides derived from dibasic acids of the series $HOOC(CH_2)_x$-COOH are especially easy to obtain in the superpolymeric state. **1972** *Encycl. Polymer Sci. & Technol.* X. 649 The best fiber-forming properties are found..in the series of polyanhydrides prepared from di(*p*-carboxyphenoxy)-α,ω-alkanes. **1940** *U.S. Patent 2,199,397* 4/2 A process for producing new surface active products which comprises reacting trimethylamine with a polybrominated palmitic acid. **1977** *Time* 4 Apr. 56/3 Michigan farmers..last year lost thousands of cattle to poisoning when a fire retardant called polybrominated biphenyl (PBB) was accidentally mixed with feed. **1977** *Lancet* 9 Apr. 790/2 When, in the U.S.A., flame resistance in children's sleeping clothes became mandatory, industry responded promptly, using those polychlorinated or polybrominated compounds which were to hand. **1935** *Chem. Abstr.* XXIX. 3976 Polyethylene sulfone..and polypropylene sulfone.. decompose..above 300°, polybutadiene sulfone, polyisoprene sulfone,..at 200–20°. **1946** F. MARCHIONNA *Butalastic Polymers* vii. 209 In this method there are obtained 1-ethenyl-3-cyclohexene and low molecular weight polybutadiene. **1960** *Times* 28 Sept. 21/6 When the Shell Chemical Company announced that they would be making polybutadiene and poly-isoprene in the United Kingdom it marked another important step in the production of synthetic rubbers in Britain. **1975** *Sci. Amer.* Dec. 101/1 Polymers that exhibit rubbery behaviour at room temperature include polyisoprene (natural rubber) and polybutadiene (a synthetic rubber). **1898** *Proc. Chem. Soc.* XIV. 179 The preparation of a number of salts of polycarboxylic acids..is described. **1947** [see *polyion* s.v. *POLY- 1]. **1970** *Jrnl. Polymer Sci.* A. VIII. 1483 The polycarboxylic resins act in a manner similar to some monomeric polycarboxylic acids. **1931** W. H. CAROTHERS et al. in *Jrnl. Amer. Chem. Soc.* LIII. 4206 We will call this product μ-polychloroprene to distinguish it from other chloroprene polymers that will be described later in this paper. **1951** *Engineering* 7 Sept. 289/3 The insulation employed includes..vulcanised rubber with sheaths of lead alloy or polychloroprene compound. **1970** *Cabinet Maker & Retail Furnisher* 30 Oct. 208/3 Adhesives based on neoprene or more generally polychloroprene have been used for many years for bonding decorative laminates to various core materials. **1946** *Nature* 17 Aug. 224/1 Quite a number of vinyl polymers, poly-esters, polyamides, and polydienes give well-defined patterns indicative of a high degree of internal order, provided they are stretched as in rubber or are drawn into fibres as in polyamides. **1960** *Times Rev. Industry* May 53/3 Also at the end of March came the announcement from Shell Chemicals that it is to build a plant..for the manufacture of polydiene rubbers, polybutadiene and polyisoprene. **1960** *Economist* 28 May 896/2 The main increase will be in butyl rubber..and in the new polydienes—polyisoprene and polybutadiene rubber—which the makers hope will prove suitable for heavy-duty tyres. **1928** *Chem. Abstr.* XXII. 1768 (*heading*) Addition of hydrogen and bromine to the poly-enes. **1934** *Science* 25 May 489/1 The names which have been given to almost all the known polyene pigments have had a taxonomic origin in either botany or zoology. **1970** *New Scientist* 5 Nov. 260/1 The polyene macrolides are an important group of antibiotics. **1961** WEBSTER, Polyenic. **1972** *Nature* 21 Jan. 132/1 A quite different kind of molecule..is the polyenic visual pigment constituent, retinal. **1976** *Chem. Physics Lett.* XLIII. 270 The Raman spectra show..large shifts of vibrational frequencies relative to other polyenic polymers and oligomers. **1949** *Arch. Biochem.* XX. 333 Table II shows the composition of the various tissue fatty acids with respect to dienoic, trienoic, and polyenoic fatty acids. **1964** *Oceanogr. & Marine Biol.* II. 181 Gas-liquid chromatography revealed so little polyenoic C_{18} acids that the mean unsaturation could generally only be expressed as monethenoid. **1935** *Biochem. Jrnl.* XXIX. 1553 (*heading*) Polyethenoid acids. **1951** H. J. DEUEL *Lipids* I. ii. 20 From a quantitative standpoint, linoleic acid is the most important of the polyethenoid acids found in vegetable oils. **1957** *Lancet* 13 Apr. 787/1 The poly-ethenoids in fish oils are so different from those in the other food fats. **1964** *Oceanogr. & Marine Biol.* II. 177 The polyethenoid alcohols never seem to amount to more than traces [in the depot lipids of fish]. *Ibid.* 179 There are some suggestive findings to indicate that polyethenoids and long-chain homologues may..be greatly reduced in amount [in the castor-oil fish, *Ruvettus pretiosus*]. **1935** HILL & CAROTHERS in *Jrnl. Amer. Chem. Soc.* LVII. 925/2 Compared with the polyesters derived from carbonic acid, the rate of distillation was quite slow; in this respect, the polyformals resembled the..polyesters derived from the higher dibasic acids such as sebacic. **1962** J. T. MARSH *Self-Smoothing Fabrics* vii. 91 When fabrics are treated with the polyformal they have a softer handle and better resistance to abrasion than when treated with formaldehyde alone. **1959** *Trans. Faraday Soc.* LV. 1484 The polarized spectra of oriented films of Delrin, a commercial polyformaldehyde resin have been investigated. **1965** HASLAM & WILLIS *Identif. & Anal. Plastics* viii. 248 Polyformaldehyde is inherently an unstable polymer and if unmodified decomposes rapidly on heating. **1973** E. H. IMMERGUT tr. *Vollmert's Polymer Chem.* ii. 253 Polyformaldehyde..can be transformed to transparent and hard plastics with high mechanical strength. **1945** H. FRAENKEL-CONRAT et al. in *Jrnl. Amer. Chem. Soc.* LXVII. 317/1 Polyglutamic acid was prepared..from a bacterial culture medium. **1970** A. L. LEHNINGER *Biochem.* vi. 113 Polyglutamic acid is a random coil at pH 7·0 because its R groups at that pH are all negatively charged. However, at pH 2·0, its R groups have no charge, and it readily forms an α-helix. **1906** *Jrnl. Chem. Soc.* XC. I. 403 (*heading*) Action of nitrous acid on polyglycine esters. **1956** *Nature* 18 Feb. 326/1 The two crystallographic forms of polyglycine..have recently been reinvestigated. **1968** E. J. DUPRAW *Cell & Molecular Biol.* xii. 290 (*caption*) A molecule of polyglycine, the simplest possible polypeptide chain. **1889** G. M'GOWAN tr. *Bernthsen's Text-bk. Org. Chem.* 193 Ethylene glycol combines with glycol to form the so-called Polyglycols, e.g. Di-ethylene glycol, $C_2H_4(OH)$—O—$C_2H_4(OH)$. **1959** *Times* 3 Mar. 7/6 Shell chemicals are already extensively used..in hydraulic brake fluids (glycols, glycol ethers and polyglycols). **1961** H. R. SIMONDS *Source Bk. New Plastics* II. iv. 49 The polyglycols are receiving increased attention as intermediates in plastics compounds. **1956** *Chem. Abstr.* L. 11349 $HOCH_2CO_2H$..(7·6 g.) standing with 100 cc. dioxane-Et_2O (1:3) satd. with HCl at room temp. gave 0·8 g. of a polyglycolic acid $H(OCH_2CO)_nOH$.., m. 126–8°. **1969** *Brit. Med. Jrnl.* 3 May 308/1 A synthetic absorbable suture material made of polyglycolic acid (P.G.A.) has recently been developed. **1977** *Lancet* 28 May 1128/1 The results of using interrupted nylon skin sutures or subcuticular polyglycolic acid (P.G.A.) sutures after appendicectomy were compared in a prospective controlled trial in 127 patients. **1895** THOMSON & BLOXAM *Bloxam's Chem.* (ed. 8) 587 (*heading*) Polyhydroxy-monobasic acids. **1913** *Jrnl. Chem. Soc.* CIV. I. 1147 (*heading*) The spatial arrangement of the hydroxyl groups of polyhydroxy-compounds. **1945** [see *POLYISOCYANATE]. **1965** PHILLIPS & WILLIAMS *Inorg. Chem.* I. xiv. 545 A number of elements and compounds have the ability to form glasses. Examples include..most polymeric materials such as polystyrene, and many poly-hydroxy compounds, e.g. water, glycol and glycerol. **1967** *New Scientist* 4 May 270/3 The darkening in afrormosia, another African hardwood, is due to certain polyhydroxystilbenes. **1951** L. H. LONG tr. *Hückel's Struct. Chem. Inorg. Compounds* II. xi. 916 A further example is the intensification of the acidity of the very weak boric acid by complex-formation with organic polyhydroxyl compounds. **1957** B. A. DOMBROW *Polyurethanes* i. 2 If we take the urethane group, and, instead of..a simple alcohol,..utilize a polyhydroxyl material like glycol, etc., a point of growth is produced. **1957** G. E. HUTCHINSON *Treat. Limnol.* I. xi. 710 Various organic substances, either colloids, such as gum arabic, or crystalloids, such as ascorbic acid and other polyhydroxyl compounds.., stabilize ferric hydroxide sols. **1931** *Jrnl. Physical Chem.* XXXV. 1893 (*table*) Polyisobutylene. **1935** C. ELLIS *Chem. Synthetic Resins* I. ix. 166 Staudinger and Brunner have examined isobutylene polymerized in the presence of floridin... They separated the resulting mixture..into tri-isobutylene, pentaisobutylene, and a polyisobutylene. **1942** *Industr. & Engin. Chem.* Oct. 1192/1 The high degree of chemical stability and excellent dielectric properties of polyisobutylene have led to its widespread commercial use. **1966** *Economist* 1 Oct. 84/3 Later the two companies may co-operate in making polyisobutylene, plastic foam and other products. **1947** E. KATCHALSKI et al. in *Jrnl. Amer. Chem. Soc.* LXIX. 2564/2 On extending experiments concerning polymerization of amino acids to basic amino acids, we succeeded in preparing poly-lysine. **1964** G. H. HAGGIS et al. *Introd. Molecular Biol.* iii. 55 In acid solution,..polylysine forms a flexible chain, the repulsion between the side chains preventing helix formation. **1973** *Nature* 6 Apr. 361/1 He [*sc.* E. Katchalsky] was the first to synthesize polylysine, a molecule that is much used in immunological research. **1935** C. ELLIS *Chem. Synthetic Resins* II. liii. 1078 The metallic..polymethacrylates are said to possess useful thermoplastic and film-forming properties. **1946** *Nature* 17 Aug. 224/1 The most notable exceptions are polyacrylates and polymethacrylates, and polyvinyl acetate. The X-ray diffraction patterns produced by these amorphous polymers yield practically no information regarding their constitution. **1973** *Sci. Amer.* Aug. 111/3 Lenses, mirrors and fiber optics of plastics, usually polymethacrylate and polystyrene, are often made by glass-working techniques. **1897** *Jrnl. Chem. Soc.* LXXII. I. 399 (*heading*) Polymethacrylic acid. **1935** C. ELLIS *Chem. Synthetic Resins* II. liii. 1080 Polymethacrylic acid begins to decompose at 200°C. **1973** *Materials & Technol.* VI. viii. 559 In polyacrylic acid, polymethacrylic acid and the amide derivatives..the polymers decompose on heating as the softening point is reached. **1931** *Jrnl. Physical Chem.* XXXIV. 44 To account for lack of mobility in the shift of equilibrium, we can picture the aluminum oxychloride sol as resembling the polyol basic chromic salts reported by Bjerrum. **1948** W. PIGMAN *Chem. Carbohydrates* vi. 232 The designation 'polyols' introduced here is synonymous with the longer, customary term, polyhydric alcohols. **1962** R. VAN HEYNINGEN in A. Pirie *Lens Metabolism Rel. Cataract* 396 A comprehensive review on the biochemistry of acyclic polyols has just been published. **1975** *Nature* 17 Jan. 194/1 Since glycerol causes cell fusion, other polyols have been investigated for fusogenic properties. **1930** *Industr. & Engin. Chem.* June 591/1 Polymerization (A polymers). Examples: Olefins and poly-olefins, unsaturated hydrocarbons, azo-compounds. **1936** *Trans. Faraday Soc.* XXXII. 5 Dimerisation is observed with the olefines and it is possible that the polyolefines may be built up in this way. **1959** *Economist* 7 Mar. 895/2 By 1961, with these new plants, British capacity in 'polyolefin' plastics will be over 150,000 tons a year. **1962** *B.S.I. News* Dec. 19/2 The viscosity number of polyolefines. **1969** L. S. MOUNTS in W. R. R. Park *Plastics Film Technol.* v. 122 Low density polyethylene films..constitute the largest segment of the polyolefin film market. **1939** *Jrnl. Amer. Chem. Soc.* LXI. 1905/2 This method..was used in the present work to synthesize the 6-, 18- and 42-membered polyoxyethylene glycols. **1952** *Martindale's Extra Pharmacopœia* (ed. 23) I. 574 The polyoxyethylene derivatives are mostly soluble or dispersible in water. **1960** A. E. BENDER *Dict. Nutrition* 100/1 Monoglycerides are soluble in fat, but by reacting with ethylene oxide the resulting polyoxyethylene derivatives become water-soluble to whatever degree is required. **1972** *Materials & Technol.* V. ix. 265 Polyoxyethylene dioleate and polyoxyethylene lauryl ether are viscous liquids and act as non-ionic emulsifiers. *Ibid.* x. 309 The polyoxyethylene alcohol surfactants range in solubility from completely oil-soluble to completely water-soluble, depending on the number of moles of ethylene oxide added. **1908** *Jrnl. Chem. Soc.* XCIV. I. 131 When heated in the open, these three polyoxymethylenes volatilise without first melting. **1930** *Chem. News* 24 Oct. 264/2 The ends of the long chains might be saturated by groups such as hydroxyl, methoxyl, or acid residues, as in the case with poly-oxymethylenes. **1952** *New Biol.* XII. 109 The clouds in the atmosphere of Venus..are said by some to be dust and by others to be polyoxymethylene. **1959** *Jrnl. Appl. Physics* XXX. 1516/1 (*caption*) Single crystals of an acetal resin, polyoxymethylene. **1975** *Sci. Amer.* Dec. 104/2 Examples of drawable semicrystalline polymers are polyethylene, polypropylene, polyoxymethylene, and nylon. **1894** *Jrnl. Chem. Soc.* LXVI. I. 415 It is noteworthy that all polyphenols derived from pyrogallol yield blue compounds. **1947** *Sci. News* V. 90 Many substances to be found in soil will reduce manganese dioxide, for example, polyphenols and sulphydryl compounds. **1973** *Sci. Amer.* Dec. 62/1 The abundance in the leaves of plants of distasteful and toxic compounds such as alkaloids and polyphenols. **1928** *Chem. Abstr.* XXII. 411 (*heading*) Complexes of uranyl with polyphenolic acids. **1958** *Times* 22 Dec. 1/5 (Advt.), Synthesis and testing of natural polyphenolic compounds as anti-oxidants. **1913** *Chem. Abstr.* VII. 796 They [*sc.* Battelli and Stern]..defend the use of the term polyphenoloxidase used to designate the enzyme which oxidizes chiefly the polyphenols and polyamines. **1956** *New Biol.* XX. 96 Browning [of tomatoes] may be associated with phenolic substances..and their subsequent polymerization to melanins by the action of polyphenoloxidases present in the host cells. **1973** F. B. ABELES *Ethylene in Plant Biol.* viii. 205 Polyphenol oxidase is a copper-containing enzyme which catalyzes the oxidation of phenols such as tyrosine and is responsible for the blackening of cut raw potatoes on exposure to air. **1974** R. G. S. BIDWELL *Plant Physiol.* vi. 119 Several enzymes that oxidize phenols to quinones are known. Two of the most important are monophenol oxidase (tyrosinase) and polyphenol oxidase (catechol oxidase). **1931** *Chem. Rev.* VIII. 375 In a similar way the oxidation of phenols may lead to the formation of polyphenylene ethers. **1965** *Jrnl. Appl. Polymer Sci.* IX. 513 Polyphenylenes tend to be brittle and intractable. **1965** *Mod. Plastics Encycl.* 1966 303/1 Polyphenylene oxide (PPO) is a new high performance engineering thermoplastic, with a unique combination of properties. **1971** *New Scientist* 24 June 761/1 Printed circuitry utilises..polyphenylene oxide parts. **1975** J. A. BRYDSON *Plastics Materials* (ed. 3) xxi. 470 Several substituted linear polyphenylenes have also been prepared but none appear to have the resistance to thermal decomposition shown by the simple poly-*p*-phenylene. **1908** *Jrnl. Chem. Soc.* XCIV. II. 838 The various supposed polyphosphates can be considered theoretically as formed by the union of pyrophosphate and metaphosphate in various proportions. **1960** A. E. BENDER *Dict. Nutrition* 100/2 *Polyphosphates*, complex phosphates added to foods, in particular to meat products... Include pyrophosphate ($Na_4P_2O_7$), tripolyphosphate ($Na_5P_3O_{10}$), longer phosphate chains of 100 phosphate units, polyphosphate glasses prepared by rapid quenching of Na_2O–P_2O_5 melts. **1962** COTTON & WILKINSON *Adv. Inorg. Chem.* xx. 397 Linear polyphosphates..are salts of anions of general formula $[P_nO_{3n+1}]^{(n+2)-}$. *Ibid.* 398 Cyclic polyphosphates..are salts of anions of general formula $[P_nO_{3n}]^{n-}$. **1895** *Jrnl. Chem. Soc.* LXVIII. II. 445 (*heading*) New polyphosphoric acid, $H_5P_3O_{10}$, and its salts. **1950** *Jrnl. Amer. Chem. Soc.* LXXII. 2962/2 In order to test this hypothesis the reaction was carried out in polyphosphoric acid, a commercially available mixture of the 'strong phosphoric acids'. **1967** I. L. FINAR *Org. Chem.* (ed. 5) I. ix. 229 Snyder *et al.* (1954) have shown that the hydrolysis of cyanides with polyphosphoric acid gives very good yields of amide. **1944** *Mod. Plastics* Nov. 124/1 (*caption*) The formation of silicones... Condensation to siloxanes... A polysiloxane. **1946** *Industr. & Engin. Chem.* Nov. 1117/1 Industrial attention has been directed to the liquid polysiloxanes since the announcement in 1944 that silicones were in commercial production. **1955** BROWN & DEY *India's Mineral Wealth* (ed. 3) 391 The resultant organosilicon chlorides are hydrolysed to silanols which condense into the polysiloxanes or silicones. **1959** B. S. GARVEY in M. Morton *Introd. Rubber Technol.* i. 33 The silicone rubbers are polysiloxanes. **1932** *Nature* 19 Nov. 756/1 He [*sc.* H. Staudinger] has prepared a polystyrol $(C_8H_8)_{6000}$, with about 100,000 atoms in the molecule and a molecular weight of 600,000. **1940** 'PLASTES' *Plastics in Industry* vi. 73 Polystyrol..is mechanically somewhat weaker than cellulose acetate. **1966** *Economist* 16 July 263/1 (Advt.), Technical synthesis of styrol for polystyrol and Buna synthesis. **1849** H. WATTS tr. *Gmelin's Handbk. Chem.* III. ii. 98 The aqueous solution of the polysulphide of sodium is yellow. **1871, 1882** [in Dict. s.v. POLY- 2 a]. **1935** C. ELLIS *Chem. Synthetic Resins* II. lviii. 1170 As some of the commercial sulphur resins are polysulphides, Thomas and Riding's work on the alkyl polysulphides should be considered. **1959** B. S. GARVEY in M. MORTON *Introd. Rubber Technol.* i. 33 The Thiokols are polysulfides of organic dihalides. **1959** J. S. JORCZAK in *Ibid.* xv. 363 Polysulfide polymers were first introduced in 1930. **1963** C. R. COWELL et al. *Inlays, Crowns, & Bridges* v. 50 One brand of polysulphide rubber is supplied in two viscosities, a more fluid grade for use with a syringe and injection into the cavity, and a more viscous grade for use in an impression tray. **1965** PHILLIPS & WILLIAMS *Inorg. Chem.* I. xvi. 578 The sulphides redissolving in excess sulphide mostly give rise to polysulphide anions, e.g. $[SnS_3]^{2-}$. **1934** *Jrnl. Amer. Chem. Soc.* LVI. 1815/2 Seyer and King have suggested a polysulfone structure..for the addition product of cyclohexene and sulfur dioxide. **1967** *Times Rev. Industry* June 68/1 In the main these are specialist materials offering advances in thermal, mechanical or electrical properties, and include the phenoxy polymers, the polysulphones, methyl pentene polymers, to mention a few. **1971** *New Scientist* 24 June 761/1 Polysulphone moulded components perform satisfactorily in various aircraft parts. **1885** *Jrnl. Chem. Soc.* XLVIII. I. 551 The author [*sc.* O. Wallach] proposes to classify the terpenes as follows:..C *Polyterpenes*. 1. Tripentenes, $C_{15}H_{24}$.. 2. Tetrapentenes, $C_{20}H_{32}$.. 3. Polyterpenes, $(C_{10}H_{16})_x$, such as caoutchouc, &c. **1956** I. L. FINAR *Org. Chem.* II. viii. 250 Rubber is the most important polyterpene. **1970** *Encycl. Polymer Sci. & Technol.* XIII. 577 Serious attempts are being made by the resin manufacturers to develop a substitute for polyterpenes from petroleum distillates. *Ibid.* 591 Polyterpene and terpene–urethan resins are used as additives in the preparation of hot-melt coating mixtures. **1936** L. F. FIESER *Chem. Nat. Products related to Phenanthrene* 358 Previously polyterpenoid compounds had been known to occur only in plants. **1964** *New Scientist* 22 Oct. 220/1 A feature of polyterpenoids which had already been noted by chemists was that the carbon skeletons of their molecules could usually be dissected into five-carbon units with branched chains. **1971** G. P. MOSS in K. H. Overton *Terpenoids & Steroids* I. v. 198 Although the best-known polyterpenoid is rubber, recent work has demonstrated a range of polyprenols and related compounds such as vitamins E and K. **1930** *Jrnl. Amer. Chem. Soc.* LII. 2474 Conjugated uronic acids, the so-called polyuronides found in pectins, gums, alginic acids, the specific polysaccharide substances of certain microorganisms, and other plant materials also yield carbon dioxide when heated with 12·0% hydrochloric acid. **1957** G. E. HUTCHINSON *Treat. Limnol.* I. xvii. 889 The main part of the humus of acid peat is not a lignin derivative but apparently consists of hemicelluloses or polyuronides. **1975** *Nature* 11 Dec. 483/2 The natural soil 'cements' include polysaccharides and polyuronides.

3. Words in which *poly-* represents or is derived from another Eng. word beginning with the element, as *poly-cotton* [f. *POLY-(ESTER]; **po·lyreaction** *Chem.*, any reaction that yields a polymer; **po·lyrod** *Radio* [see quot. 1950], an antenna consisting of a rod of dielectric material (usu. tapered) projecting from a waveguide. Cf. *POLY[3].

1978 *Country Life* 28 Dec. 2237/1 The basic Burberry trenchcoat..now costs around £99, made in poly-cotton. **1979** *Times* 1 Dec. 10/1 (Advt.), Dreamy Nightwear... The skirts of both garments are polycotton; 65% polyester and 35% cotton. **1941** MARK & RAFF *High Polymeric Reactions* 3 To avoid the lengthy expressions, polymerization reactions and polycondensation reactions, ..we shall designate both as polyreactions. **1959** *New Scientist* 2 July 34/2 The remaining lectures were divided into two groups with the general titles 'Physics and Physical Chemistry of Macromolecules' and 'Polyreactions'. **1945** *Electronic Industries* Sept. 222 *Polyrod antenna*, an antenna in which the radiating element is a rod of polystyrene. **1947** *Bell Syst. Technical Jrnl.* XXVI. 844 The principal defect of the uniform polyrod is the strong minor lobes. **1950** H. P. WILLIAMS *Antenna Theory & Design* II. iv. 190 This form of dielectric antenna is commonly called a 'polyrod' antenna, since the dielectric material is often polystyrol. **1967** E. L. GRUENBERG *Handbk. Telemetry & Remote Control* iv. 130 Plastics, foams, and ceramics can be used for the radiating element. The most common type is called a polyrod and the usual construction contains a dielectric that is linearly tapered over slightly more than half its length.

poly-A: see *POLY- 2. **polyabolo:** *POLY- 1. **polyacetal, -acetylene, -acetylenic:** *POLY- 2.

polyacid (pǫli,æ·sid), *a.* and *sb. Chem.* Also **poly-acid.** [f. POLY- + ACID.] † **A.** *adj.* Applied to a base which requires more than one equivalent of acid for neutralization, and to a salt of such a base; of an alcohol, polyhydric. *Obs.*

1858 *Proc. R. Soc.* IX. 152 It became extremely probable that the action of ammonia upon poly-acid alcohols would give rise to poly-ammonium bases. **1880** [in Dict. s.v. POLY- 2 b]. **1904** *Jrnl. Chem. Soc.* LXXXVI. I. 698 (*heading*) The polyacid salts of rosaniline. **1912** E. FEILMANN tr. *Molinari's Treat. Inorg. Chem.* 423 When the salt is formed by the action of an acid on a base which has more than one hydroxyl (OH) group, that is, in the case of polyacid bases, such as $Bi(OH)_3$, $Pb(OH)_2$,..various types of salts may be formed. **1920** [see B]. **1926** N. H. FURMAN *Kolthoff's Indicators* iv. 117 When all of the dissociation constants of polybasic acids, or polyacid bases are large, they behave like strong monobasic or acid compounds upon neutralization.

B. *sb.* A compound which has more than one acidic group; *esp.* an acid containing polymeric anions. Occas. also *attrib.* or as *adj.*

1911 *Jrnl. Chem. Soc.* C. I. 265 The extension of Werner's co-ordination theory to poly-acids..facilitates the correct formulation of these acids. **1920** T. H. POPE tr. *Molinari's Treat. Inorg. Chem.* (ed. 2) 274 Several molecules of a polybasic acid are able to condense and form polyacids, such as pyroantimonic, pyrophosphoric, and pyrosilicic acid, etc., and in the same way it is known that the polyacid bases, also called polyhydric bases, condense to form polybases or polyhydroxides. **1939** L. PAULING *Nature Chem. Bond* vii. 226 The pyro, meta, and other polyacids of the second-row atoms contain MO_4 tetrahedra condensed by sharing oxygen atoms. **1950** N. V. SIDGWICK *Chem. Elements* II. 999 The molybdates and tungstates go much further, forming the highly condensed polyacids and hetero-poly-acids. **1964** *Biophysical Jrnl.* IV. I. Suppl. 11 The polyelectrolyte nature of some polyacid and polybase polypeptides endows them with inhibitory activity in enzymatic reactions. **1974** D. M. ADAMS *Inorg. Solids* vii. 239 The main features of polyacid chemistry have been recognized for a long time, but not understood.

polyacrylic and derivatives: see *POLY- 2. **polyactine:** *POLY- I.

polyad. Add: **2.** *Philos.* A relative containing more than two elements.

a **1914** C. S. PEIRCE *Coll. Papers* (1931) I. 146 A thorough study of the logic of relatives..shows that logical terms are either monads, dyads, or polyads, and that these last do not introduce any radically different elements from..triads. *Ibid.* (1933) IV. 301 If the number of blanks exceeds two, I term it a Polyad, or Plural Relative.

polyaddition (pǫli,ădi·ʃən). *Chem.* [a. G. *polyaddition* (O. Bayer 1947, in *Angewandte Chem.* A. LIX. 263/2), f. *poly-* POLY- + *addition* ADDITION.] An addition reaction between two compounds which yields a polymeric product.

1948 *Chem. Abstr.* XLII. 6160 (*heading*) The diisocyanate polyaddition process. **1970** E. L. MCCAFFERY *Lab. Prep. for Macromoelcular Chem.* 58 Condensation polymerization..may take place either by a polycondensation reaction, whereby low molecular-weight by-product is formed along with the polymer,..or by a polyaddition reaction in which the total reactants are incorporated in the polymer chain, as is typified by polyurethane formation. **1973** K. J. SAUNDERS *Org. Polymer Chem.* i. 23 Some authors..apply the term rearrangement polymerization (or, sometimes, polyaddition) to polymerization which proceeds through the interaction of functional groups without elimination of a small molecule.

polyadenylic acid: see *POLY- 2.

polyadic (pǫli,æ·dik), *a.* [f. POLYAD + -IC.] Involving many (usu., three or more) quantities or elements. Hence **polya·dically** *adv.*; **polyadi·city**, the state or quality of being polyadic.

1906 C. S. PEIRCE in *Monist* XVI. 512 A Predicate is either non-relative, or a monad..as is 'black'; or it is a dyadic relative, or dyad, such as 'kills', or it is a polyadic relative, such as 'gives'. **1919** A. N. WHITEHEAD *Enquiry Princ. Nat. Knowl.* vii. 84 A percipient event in the polyadic relation of a sense-object to nature is the percipient event of an awareness which includes this recognition of that sense-object. **1933** C. D. BROAD *Exam. McTaggart's Philos.* I. IV. xv. 282 We must distinguish extent of application, which belongs to *all* characteristics, from 'polyadicity', which belongs only to relations. **1950** W. V. QUINE *Methods of Logic* (1952) III. 135 We *also* have occasion to speak of monadic and polyadic schemata, referring thereby rather to the absence or presence of polyadically occurring predicate letters. **1964** E. A. NIDA *Toward Sci. Transl.* v. 111 For the most part these differences are binary or dyadic, but they may be singular or multiple (or polyadic). **1972** W. V. QUINE *Methods of Logic* (ed. 3) III. xxv. 141 The polyadic ingredients—'*Hxy*' and its suite—are what are new.

polyalcohol, -allomer: see *POLY- 2. **polyallomorphic, -alphabetic:** *POLY- I.

polyamide (pǫli,ēi·məid). [f. POLY- + AMIDE.] Any of a large class of polymers in which the units are linked by an amide group, —CO·NH—, and which includes many synthetic resins used commercially, notably fibres of the nylon group. Also *attrib.*

1929 *Jrnl. Amer. Chem. Soc.* LI. 2550 Polyintermolecular condensation requires as starting materials compounds in which at least two functional groups are present in the same molecule (*e.g.*, hydroxy acids..might lead to polyesters,..amino-acids, to poly-amides..). **1942** *Endeavour* Apr. 72/2 *Nylon*, the new and truly synthetic fibre (a polyamide) that is now rivalling natural silk. **1963** H. R. CLAUSER *Encycl. Engin. Materials* 501 The presence of the polyamide resin brings about the gelation and provides thixotropy to the paint. **1969** L. S. MOUNTS in W. R. R. Park *Plastics Film Technol.* v. 136 Polyamide films are produced from two types of nylon polymer. **1971** *Daily Tel.* (Colour Suppl.) 30 Apr. 8/3 The fabric..is an industrial nylon polyamide, tightly woven with a glistening surface and faintly translucent. **1972** *Sci. Amer.* Dec. 48/3 Some 10 different basic types of nylon are now produced, and the worldwide consumption of these polyamide fibres exceeds four billion pounds per year.

Hence **po:lyamida·tion**, a reaction or process which yields a polyamide.

1946 *Chem. Rev.* XXXIX. 146 The polyamidation reaction parallels closely the rate, temperature coefficient, and reaction order of monoamidations. **1961** SORENSON & CAMPBELL *Prep. Methods Polymer Chem.* iii. 63 An alternative method for carrying out polyamidations from a nylon salt is to use a pipe autoclave.

polyamine, -anhydride: see *POLY- 2. **polyanion(ic:** *POLY- I.

Polyanna, var. *POLLYANNA.

polyantha (pǫli,æ·nþă). [f. POLY- + Gr. ἄνθος flower.] A small shrub rose or a climbing rose belonging to a group of hybrids of *Rosa chinensis* and *R. multiflora* and bearing flowers in clusters. Freq. *attrib.*

1889 *Jrnl. R. Hort. Soc.* XI. p. cv, The pretty and interesting Polyantha Roses comprised such sorts as Mignonette, Golden Fairy, [etc.]. **1894** A. FOSTER-MELLIAR *Bk. of Rose* ii. 26 Turner's Crimson Rambler.. is a very strong-climbing perpetual Polyantha from Japan. **1931** E. S. ROHDE *Scented Garden* v. 134 The double flowered white and pink multiflora or polyantha roses were introduced as cultivated plants from Chinese gardens more than a hundred years ago. **1934** *Times Educ. Suppl.* 24 Nov. (Home & Classroom Sect.) p. iv/1 A new group of hybrid *polyantha* varieties has been created. **1945** G. GRAVES *Trees, Shrubs, & Vines for Northeastern U.S.* 175 The polyanthas have the ruggedness and the ability to thrive under conditions that would discourage the more tender hybrid teas. **1955** G. S. THOMAS *Old Shrub Roses* ix. 92 'Floribunda' is now accepted as a group name for these large-flowered 'polyanthas'. **1962** R. PAGE *Educ. Gardener* iv. 129 Roses, particularly the polyantha or floribunda kinds, are good plants for these small formal gardens. **1976** *Hortus Third* (L. H. Bailey Hortorium) 980/2 The Floribundas..owe their origin to crosses between Polyanthas, Hybrid Teas, and other classes.

polyarch, *a.* (Later examples.)

1914 [see *hexarch* adj. s.v. *HEXA-]. **1964** H. J. DITTMER *Phylogeny & Form in Plant Kingdom* xxiii. 563 The xylem may be termed diarch when only two points are present, triarch with three, tetrarch with four, or polyarch with many.

polyarchic (pǫli,ā·ɹkik), *a.* [f. POLYARCH(Y + -IC.] Of, pertaining to, or having the characteristics of a polyarchy.

1892 G. GISSING *Born in Exile* II. IV. i. 164 He could admit that such men as Runcorn and Kenyon—the one with his polyarchic commercialism, the other with his demagogic violence—had possibly a useful part to play. **1970** R. A. H. ROBINSON *Origins of Franco's Spain* 22 Society was 'polyarchic', being composed of a series of 'intermediate republics' (guild, municipality, region) between the 'monarchies' of the State and family. **1974** *Govt. & Opposition* IX. 29 During the 1950s, the polyarchic formula, which took for granted the unconditional adherence of individuals and groups to majority rule insofar as it assumed that there was no permanent majority or minority on any particular question, seemed to be about to take root in a great many liberal democracies.

polyarchism (pǫ·li,āɹkiz'm). [f. POLYARCH(Y + -ISM.] The principles or practice of polyarchy.

1915 E. BARKER in *Political Q.* Feb. 120 This may seem anarchism. Really it is polyarchism. And as for the problem of polyarchism—why..it is likely to be settled by the needs of mere ordered life. **1917** H. J. LASKI *Let.* 20 Nov. in *Holmes–Laski Lett.* (1953) I. 110, I shall preach anarchism or rather polyarchism in the guise of political theory.

polyarteritis: see *POLY- I.

polyatomic, *a.* Add: In mod. use (composed of molecules) containing many atoms (usu., three or more). Also as *sb.*, such a molecule. (Further examples.)

1937 L. S. STEBBING *Philos. & Physicists* ix. 215 Human beings are polyatomic. **1958** *Oxf. Univ. Gaz.* 23 Apr. 880 Vibration-rotational bands of polyatomic molecules. **1961** G. R. CHOPPIN *Exper. Nucl. Chem.* iii. 37 Counting gases are usually one of the noble gases mixed with a small amount of a polyatomic gas. **1971** *Nature* 3 Dec. 277/1 There are chapters on diatomic radicals, linear polyatomic ones, non-linear polyatomics and a discussion of dissociation.

polyaxon: see *POLY- I. **polybag:** *POLY[3].

polybase (pǫ·libēis). *Chem.* [f. POLY- 2 + BASE *sb.*[1]] A compound which contains more than one basic group. Cf. POLYBASIC *a.* in Dict. and Suppl.

1920 [see *POLYACID *sb.*]. **1956** *Nature* 24 Mar. 586/1 This polybase, $—[—CH_2—CH_2—NH_2—]_n—$, has the advantage of being stained by naphthalene black 12*B* as well as by sudan black. **1966** G. M. FLECK *Equilibria in Solution* v. 83 Ion-exchange resins are familiar examples of polyacids and polybases.

polybasic, *a.* Substitute for def.: Requiring more than one equivalent of base for neutralization; containing two or more atoms of hydrogen capable of replacement by a base. Formerly also applied to salts derived from polybasic acids by replacement of more than one hydrogen atom. (Further examples.)

1851 H. WATTS tr. *Gmelin's Hand-bk. Chem.* V. 225 Phosphate of ferric oxide, or ferric phosphate... Polybasic. **1889** G. M'GOWAN tr. *Bernthsen's Text-bk. Org. Chem.* 206 The tri- and polybasic alcohols are capable of yielding the most various products upon oxidation. **1926** H. G. RULE tr. *J. Schmidt's Textbk. Org. Chem.* 59 These differences are so considerable that they may be used to distinguish between mono- and polybasic acids. **1972** NORMAN & WADDINGTON *Mod. Org. Chem.* xxi. 321 Polyester fibres are formed by condensation of polyhydric alcohols and polybasic acids.

polybasicity (examples).

1912 E. FEILMANN tr. *Molinari's Treat. Inorg. Chem.* 46 In 1835 Graham demonstrated the polybasicity of phosphoric acid. **1931** *Jrnl. Physical Chem.* XXXV. 2226 (*heading*) The polybasicity of several common sugars.

polyblast: see *POLY- I. **polybrominated, -butadiene:** *POLY- 2.

polycarbonate (pǫlikā·ɹbǫnēit). *Chem.* [f. POLY- + CARBONATE *sb.*] † **1.** A carbonate containing several equivalents of the acid radical. *Obs.*

1886 T. S. HUNT *Mineral Physiol. & Physiogr.* viii. 289 It was further declared that the carbon-spars must be represented as polycarbonates, having not less than from 'twelve to eighteen equivalents of base replaceable so as to give rise to a great number of species'. **1891** *Chem. News* 23 Oct. 212/2 (*heading*) Contamination of alkaline polycarbonates by heavy metals.

2. Any of a class of polymers in which the units are linked by the carbonate group, —O·CO·O—, many of which are thermoplastic resins widely used esp. as moulding materials and films. Also *attrib.*

1930 *Jrnl. Amer. Chem. Soc.* LII. 315 It seems quite certain, therefore, that these polycarbonates are also open chains. **1959** *Mod. Plastics* XXXVI. 39 Farben fabriken-Bayer..has been manufacturing polycarbonates on a commercial scale in Germany for nearly a year. **1965** *Wireless World* Aug. 409/2 In the manufacture of an optical filter gold has been sputtered onto a polycarbonate substrate. **1969** L. S. MOUNTS in W. R. R. Park *Plastics Film Technol.* v. 138 Due to good forming characteristics, heat resistance, and toughness, polycarbonate film and sheet are used in skin and blister packaging. **1976** *Sci. Amer.* Feb. 19/2 (Advt.), The instrument is housed in a tough, high-impact polycarbonate case. **1978** *Skatcat's Quiz Bk.* (R. Soc. Prevention of Accidents) 2/1 Also O.K. are polycarbonate laminates of glass or carbon-fibre reinforced resins with plywood cores.

polycarboxylic: see *POLY- 2.

polycarpic, *a.* Delete *rare* and substitute for def.: **a.** = POLYCARPOUS *a.* a. (Further examples.) † **b.** = POLYCARPOUS *a.* b. *Obs. rare.*

1909 GROOM & BALFOUR tr. *Warming's Oecol. Plants* ii. 6 These plants are divided into monocarpic and polycarpic: the former produce flower and fruit (or spores) once, and then die; the latter may produce fruit repeatedly before death claims them. **1951** MCLEAN & IVIMEY-COOK *Textbk. Theoret. Bot.* I. xxi. 834 The common factor in all perennials is that they are polycarpic, that is to say, they flower and fruit repeatedly.

polycation(ic: see *POLY- I.

polycentric, *a.* Delete entry in Dict. (s.v. POLY- I) and substitute:

polycentric (pǫlise·ntrik), *a.* [f. POLY- I + *-CENTRIC.] = *multicentric* adj. s.v. *MULTI- I a; in *Politics*, characterized by polycentrism. Also as *sb.*, a polycentric chromosome or chromatid.

1887 [in Dict. s.v. POLY- I]. **1909** *Q. Rev.* Apr. 499 The Messina earthquake belongs to the class known in Italy as that of 'polycentric' earthquakes. **1945** M. J. D. WHITE *Animal Cytol. & Evol.* iv. 57 The example of *Ascaris megalocephala* shows us that in some other organisms polycentric chromosomes can exist in nature. **1953** *Heredity* VI. Suppl. 73 The occurrence of high polycentrics such as C_3, C_4, C_5 and rarely even C_6..with a high frequency after treatment at meiosis shows..that reunion is not low. **1956** tr. *Togliatti's Probl. Devel. Socialist Democracy* 12/2 The advance towards socialism is an objective for which there is a concentration of forces from different movements... The whole system is becoming polycentric, and even in the Communist movement we cannot speak of a single guide. **1965** *N.Y. Times* 18 Jan. 34 After the success of Tito's revolt against Moscow Togliatti conceived of 'polycentric' Communism. This means adjusting party methods in each country to national traditions and requirements. **1965** *Economist* 3 Apr. 43/2 The reality of an increasingly 'polycentric' world, marked by the growing self-assertion of the middle and smaller states. **1967** G. STEINER *Lang. & Silence* 80 African English, Australian English..represent a complicated, polycentric field of linguistic force. **1968** R. RIEGER et al. *Gloss. Genetics & Cytogenetics* 351 Polycentrics are in most cases the result of chromosome mutations. **1971** *Physics Bull.* Jan. 16/2 There are several nuclei so that orbitals are not monocentric but polycentric. **1976** T. EAGLETON *Crit. & Ideology* v. 164 Literature is multiple and polycentric, saturating the very textures of our social life.

Hence **po:lycentri·city**, the fact of being polycentric.

1959 [see *HOLOGENESIS]. **1973** *Times Lit. Suppl.* 3 Aug. 897/2 The year 1963 was also one in which polycentricity became a conspicuous feature of international relations.

polycentrism (pǫlise·ntriz'm). [f. POLY- + CENTR(E + -ISM.] In Communist political theory, the idea first promulgated by P. Togliatti (1892–1964) in 1956 that each separate Communist party has the right of full national autonomy and that the Soviet model need not be binding for all Communist parties. Also in extended use. Hence **polyce·ntrist** *a.* and *sb.*

1961 *Economist* 2 Dec. 918 He [*sc.* Gomulka] rejected the Italian idea of 'polycentrism'. **1963** *Ann. Reg. 1962* 199 'Polycentrist' tendencies within the world Communist movement. **1963** *Spectator* 28 June 829 Pelung is in effect returning to the position of support for East European polycentrism against Moscow. **1966** *Times* 7 July 7 Many more responsible non-communists were becoming polycentrists, including General de Gaulle. **1968** *Economist* 24 Feb. 36/1 The monolithic structure of the international communist movement has collapsed under the combined pressure of the Sino-Soviet conflict, and the bid for greater freedom of the ex-satellites in Eastern Europe. The result is the rise of 'polycentrism'. **1969** P. ALLUM in Henig & Pinder *European Political Parties* 206 Khrushchev's denunciation of Stalinist errors..permitted Togliatti to formulate explicitly the doctrines of 'polycentrism' and the 'Italian way to Socialism'. **1971** W. LAQUEUR *Dict. Politics* 568 The final break with China as well as Albania came at the second Moscow Conference of Communist parties in Nov. 1960... After the 1960 Conference, polycentrism..became a fact. **1974** *Times* 19 Feb. (European Defence Suppl.) p. i/1 Long before the Middle East war it had become commonplace to contrast the bipolarity of the past decade with the new pattern of polycentrism as developing forces in Europe, China and Japan impinged upon the distribution of world power.

polychlorinated (pǫliklōᵊ·rinēⁱtėd), *a. Chem.* [f. POLY- 2 + CHLORINATED *ppl. a.*] Applied to compounds in which two or more hydrogen atoms have been replaced by chlorine atoms; esp. in *polychlorinated biphenyl* [*biphenyl* = DIPHENYL], any of a class of such compounds derived from biphenyl, $(C_6H_5)_2$, or its derivatives, which have a wide variety of industrial applications and are persistent environmental pollutants; abbrev. *PCB* (s.v. *P II d).

1935 C. ELLIS *Chem. Synthetic Resins* II. lviii. 1178 Amino and hydroxy compounds are formed when polychlorinated paraffins are heated with solutions of ammonia or caustic alkali, respectively. **1951** H. H. SHEPHARD *Chem. & Action Insecticides* xi. 271 The higher polychlorinated naphthalenes are utilized as noninflammable waxes in electric insulation. **1962** *Chem. Abstr.* LVII. 8498 (*heading*) Polychlorinated biphenyl derivatives. **1968** *Times* 17 Dec. 10/5 The chemicals, called polychlorinated biphenyls, are in some ways similar to chlorine containing pesticides such as DDT and..can poison the liver even in minute amounts. **1971** P. GRESSWELL *Environment* 201 Polychlorinated biphenyls were found in high concentration in birds which died in 1969 in the Irish Sea.

polychloroprene, -choral: see *POLY- 2, 1.

polychoric (pǫlikōᵊ·rik), *a. Statistics.* [f. POLY- + χώρ-ισις separation (f. χωρίζειν to separate) + -IC; cf. *TETRACHORIC *a.*] Used to describe a table in which data are divided into three or more classes by each of two criteria; of or pertaining to such a table; applied *esp.* to an estimate of the product-moment coefficient derived from such a table, and to concepts used in obtaining such an estimate.

1918 *Biometrika* XII. 93 (*heading*) The correlation coefficient of a polychoric table. **1922** *Ibid.* XIV. 149 What we actually desire is to compare the observations and the regression lines as given by the present polychoric method with those obtained by product-moment methods. **1964** *Psychometrika* XXIX. 386 In what follows, the tetrachoric series method is generalized to produce a new polychoric estimate of *ρ*.

polychromasia (pǫ:likromēⁱ·ziă). *Med.* [mod.L., back-formation from POLYCHROMATIC *a.* (see -IA[1]).] = *POLYCHROMATOPHILIA.

1909 R. J. M. BUCHANAN *Blood in Health & Dis.* xi. 196 Polychromasia is common; with stains containing methyl blue and eosin such cells may be a light violet or even a distinct blue, with methylene blue and iodine the erythrocytes in this disease exhibit a green colour not usually met with in other forms of anæmia. **1935** WHITBY & BRITTON *Disorders of Blood* iii. 64 For many years polychromasia was considered to be a degeneration until Hawes (1909) showed that the number of polychromatic cells was always approximately parallel to the number of reticulocytes. **1956** [see *anisocytosis* s.v. *ANISO-]. **1973** WOODLIFF & HERRMANN *Conc. Haematol.* i. 18 In many cells polychromasia of the cytoplasm remains after loss of the nucleus. **1977** *Proc. R. Soc. Med.* LXX. 284/2 Film was leukoerythroblastic and showed polychromasia, anisopoikilocytosis, occasional erythroblasts..and tear-drop cells.

Hence **po:lychroma·sic** *a.* = *POLYCHROMATOPHIL *a.*; cf. *POLYCHROMATIC *a.* 2.

1911 *Jrnl. Path. & Bacteriol.* XV. 9 Degenerate forms with vacuolated or irregularly stained and polychromasic cytoplasm are often seen. **1933** [see *POLYCHROMATOPHILIA]. **1942** M. M. WINTROBE *Clin. Hematol.* ii. 56 A close parallelism between the numbers of polychromasic and reticulated cells in various samples of blood has been found, although the proportion of reticulocytes is always higher.

polychromatic, *a.* Add: **1. b.** Of radiation: containing a number of wavelengths, not monochromatic.

1935 H. HARRIS *Metallic Arc Welding* iii. 13 Asterism is caused by the diffraction of a polychromatic X-ray beam by a deformed crystal. **1976** *Nature* 12 Aug. 541/2 A parallel beam of white (polychromatic) radiation falls on an oriented sample.

2. *Med.* = *POLYCHROMATOPHIL *a.*; *esp.* as *polychromatic normoblast*, an immature erythrocyte. Cf. *POLYCHROMASIC *a.*

1899 *Jrnl. R. Microsc. Soc.* 379 Polychromatic normoblasts which become violet in eosin and methylen-blue and red in triacid. **1935** [see *POLYCHROMASIA]. **1938** W. MAGNER *Textbk. Hematol.* i. 4 Normoblasts showing this mixture of red and blue in their cytoplasm are known as polychromatic normoblasts. **1958** G. C. DE GRUCHY *Clin. Haematol.* ii. 43 Polychromatic cells are young red cells which have not yet completely lost their ribose nucleic acid; they are normally present in only small numbers in the peripheral blood (0·2–2·0 per cent). **1973** B. A. BROWN *Hematol.* ii. 28/1 The production of heme and globin takes place independently of each other, beginning in the polychromatic normoblast, and ending in the reticulocyte stage.

polychromatism (pǫlikrōᵘ·mătiz'm). [f. as POLYCHROMATIC *a.*: see -ISM.] The property of having or responding to many colours.

1950 *Sci. News* XV. 26 There may be, as it were, polychromatism of the retinal sense organs but trichromatism of the brain, and therefore of the organ of vision as a whole. **1965** B. E. FREEMAN tr. *Vandel's Biospeleol.* xxv. 408 Populations of *Asellus aquaticus cavernicolus*.. show extreme polychromatism.

polychromatophil (pǫlikrōᵘ·mătofil), *a. Med.* Also **-phile** (-fəil). [a. G. *polychromatophil* (G. Gabritschewsky 1890, in *Arch. f. exper. Path. und Pharmakol.* XXVIII. 86), f. Gr. πολυχρώματ-ος many-coloured: see -PHIL, -PHILE.] Of an erythrocyte: having an affinity for basic as well as for acidic stains, and so recognizable by its appearance when a mixed stain is used. Of or pertaining to such erythrocytes. Also **po:lychromatophi·lic** *a.*, in the same sense. So **po:lychromatophi·lia,** polychromatophil condition.

1897 R. C. CABOT *Guide Clin. Exam. Blood* 77 The typical megaloblast is an abnormally large cell.., frequently showing marks of degeneration (polychromatophilia) in its protoplasm, which is therefore brownish or purplish with the Ehrlich-Biondi stain. *Ibid.* 124 More common than in any other form of anæmia are the polychromatophilic red corpuscles (see Plate IV.). **1898** A. C. COLES *Blood* Pl. I (*caption*) Polychromatophile corpuscles. **1908** *Practitioner* Aug. 324 In polychromatophil degeneration, the stained cell may vary in colour from lilac to quite deep blue (when Jenner's stain has been used). **1933** A. PINEY tr. *Morawitz's Blood Dis. in Clin. Pract.* ii. 12 Among the non-nucleated red corpuscles Jenner's stain often shows elements which are not purely red, but violet: this is polychromatophilia... More rarely erythrocytes with blue stippling are found: these have the same significance as the polychromasic ones. **1947** *Jrnl. Lab. & Clin. Med.* XXXII. 765 The polychromatophile normoblasts likewise were identified by their nuclei..and not by the cytoplasm which was basophilic rather than polychromatophilic. **1956** E. PONDER tr. *Bessis's Cytol. Blood* ix. 246 In the normal state, the circulating blood contains an extremely small number of polychromatophil red cells... In pathological conditions..polychromatophil red cells can appear in the blood in large numbers and their basophil material can take the form of little structures. **1973** B. A. BROWN *Hematol.* ii. 34/2 Polychromatophilia..indicates red blood cells containing RNA. They will stain a pinkish-gray to pinkish-blue color. **1974** *Exper. Parasitol.* XXXVI. 6 Early in the course of the developing anemia, many polychromatophilic erythrocytes and occasional normoblasts were found in the blood.

polychrome, *a.* and *sb.* Add: **A.** *adj.* **1.** Also *fig.*

1959 [see *DEBUSSYAN *a.* and *sb.*]. **1962** I. MURDOCH *Unofficial Rose* vii. 75 Her polychrome being fell into an authoritative pattern which proclaimed her free.

2. *Biol.* Of a stain or dye: containing quantities of a number of derivatives which differ in colours from the parent compound; esp. in *polychrome methylene blue*.

1895 G. W. CALE tr. P. G. Unna in *St. Louis Med. & Surg. Jrnl.* July 30 All that is necessary is to decolorize with a concentrated tannin solution the sections overstained with my polychrome-methyl-blue solution. **1896** *Ibid.* Feb. 83 This secondary effect of the polychrome methylene blue solution proves its value because it made the differential diagnosis of mast-cells (red) and plasma cells (blue) a very easy matter. **1909** *Boston Med. & Surg. Jrnl.* 7 Oct. 494/1 Widal, Abrami and Brulé recommend the use of polychrome blue of Unna 1:10. **1925** H. J. CONN *Biol. Stains* v. 47 The polychrome properties just mentioned are likely to develop in a methylene blue solution upon standing. Anyone who has had much experience with the stain is familiar with the occasional green tones from methylene green, the reddish shades of methylene azure..and methylene violet. Such a solution is known as 'polychrome methylene blue'. **1960** E. GURR *Encycl. Microsc. Stains* 415 Wright's stain..is prepared by neutralising polychrome methylene blue with eosin. **1960** JACOBS & GERSTEIN *Handbk. Microbiol.* 248/2 *Jenner's Stain*, a polychrome stain prepared by mixing 0·5 per cent eosin in methyl alcohol with 0·5 per cent methylene blue in methyl alcohol in the ratio 5:4.

B. *sb.* **1.** (Later examples.)

1959 [see *BICHROME *a.* and *sb.*[2]]. **1972** *Trans. Oriental Ceramics Soc.* XXXVIII. 41 It was difficult, apart from the fine Ch'êng-hua *tou-ts'ai*, to discover really good pieces of the more usual polychromes.

2. (Earlier example.)

1870 C. SCHREIBER *Jrnl.* (1911) I. 101 He had procured for us..a dish with house in blue,..and a larger one with pastoral subjects in polychrome.

4. *Med.* A polychromatophil erythrocyte or normoblast.

1909 *Boston Med. & Surg. Jrnl.* 7 Oct. 495/1 The blood showed 6% of reticulated forms, with ·4% of polychromes. **1933** *Lancet* 3 June 1173/1 Hawes..hazarded the suggestion that the stippled cell was merely a variant of the polychrome.

polychrome (pǫ·likrōᵘm), *v. Biol.* [f. prec.] To convert (a stain or dye) to a polychrome form (sense *A. 2). Hence **po·lychroming** *vbl. sb.*

1925 H. J. CONN et al. *Biol. Stains* v. 48 Methylene blue should be partly polychromed in order to have its best staining powers. **1958** J. R. BAKER *Princ. Biol. Microtechnique* xiv. 268 It was his [*sc.* G. Giemsa's] purpose to avoid methylene blue that had been polychromed at random, and to use instead known quantities of known dyes. *Ibid.* 271 No dye that does not arise spontaneously in the polychroming of methylene blue has any special virtue in Romanowsky dyeing. **1963** M. J. LYNCH et al. *Med. Lab. Technol.* xiii. 256/1 The methylene blue is polychromed by heating with sodium bicarbonate. *Ibid.* xxxv. 630/2 The polychroming involves the oxidation of the methylene blue so that methyl groups are lost and formaldehyde gas is given off.

polychromed (pǫ·likrōᵘmd), *ppl. a.* [f. prec. + -ED[1].] Rendered polychrome: chiefly *Biol.*, of stains and dyes.

1924 *Jrnl. Bacteriol.* IX. 405 The method involves pipetting about one cc. of a well polychromed, Loeffler's methylene blue over the agar slant culture and tilting the tube so that the stain comes in contact with the bacterial film. *Ibid.* 407 A polychrome methylene blue divised [*sic*] by Novy has given results surpassing in clearness those obtained by the ordinary polychromed methylene blue. **1958** J. R. BAKER *Princ. Biol. Microtechnique* xiv. 268 It is necessary to know what substances besides methylene blue itself are present in the polychromed dye. **1978** K. BONFIGLIOLI *All Tea in China* iv. 44 An incomparable saucer, polychromed, yet from the very earliest part of the Ming Dynasty.

polychromed (pǫ·likrōᵘmd), *a.* [f. POLYCHROME *a.* and *sb.* + -ED[2].] = POLYCHROME *a.* 1.

1922 *19th Cent.* May 804 The polychromed wooden statue of St. Paul recalls a work in stone from the hand of Vecchietta. **1936** *Burlington Mag.* July 48/2 The low relief polychromed stucco ornament. **1947** J. C. RICH *Materials & Methods Sculpture* x. 308 The Chinese and Japanese produced a large amount of polychromed wood sculpture. **1972** K. BONFIGLIOLI *Don't point that Thing at Me* xiii. 101 A great polychromed Mexican carving of an agonized Madonna.

polychromism (pǫlikrōᵘ·miz'm). [f. as POLYCHROMIC *a.*: see -ISM.] = *POLYCHROMATISM.

1903 *Amer. Naturalist* XXXVII. 295 (*heading*) Albinism, partial albinism and polychromism in hag-fishes. **1933** THORPE & LINSTEAD *Synthetic Dyestuffs* (ed. 7) viii. 72 Polychromism..is the name assigned to the phenomenon of colour variation in salts.

polycistronic(ally: see *POLY- 1.

polyclad, *a.* and *sb.* Substitute for etym.: [ad. mod.L. name of suborder *Polycladidea* (A. Lang 1884, in *Fauna und Flora des Golfes von Neapel* XI. 1), f. POLY- + Gr. κλάδος branch.] (Later examples.)

1896 F. W. GAMBLE in *Cambr. Nat. Hist.* II. i. 16 The Polyclads were so called by Lang on account of the numerous primary branches of their intestine. They are free-living, purely marine Platyhelminthes. **1918** *Proc. Nat.*

Acad. Sci. IV. 381 Muscular creeping operations are probably general among polyclads. **1941** J. STEINBECK *Sea of Cortez* xi. 111 Beautiful purple polyclad worms crawled over lawns of purple tunicates. **1975** *Nature* 28 Aug. 737/1 Polyclads have limited powers of regeneration. *Ibid.* 11 Dec. 518/1 We..found them [*sc.* reddish-brown streaks in the sea] to consist of high densities of the dinoflagellate *Noctiluca* and of a polyclad turbellarian.

polyclimax (pǫliklǝi·mæks). *Ecol.* [f. POLY- + CLIMAX *sb.*] The presence of several distinct stable communities of plants within a given region. Usu. *attrib.*

1934 *Empire Forestry Jrnl.* XIII. 21 An appreciation of some, at least, of these truths, has led many ecologists to adopt a poly-climax theory as a working hypothesis. **1953** *Ecol. Monogr.* XXIII. 43/1 A significant difference in climax interpretation has..been described in the monoclimax and polyclimax theories. **1960** N. POLUNIN *Introd. Plant Geogr.* xi. 331 It seems best to admit the likelihood, in any one region, of several different climax communities as representing what may then be termed a 'polyclimax'. **1973** P. A. COLINVAUX *Introd. Ecol.* xl. 551 Whether you believed in the monoclimax required by dogmatic interpretations of Clements' writings, or whether you took the pragmatic view that there could be many local climaxes in any clima[c]tic region (so-called polyclimax theory) you tacitly assumed that succession was a process of social organization; that it led to an organized entity which you called a society.

polyclinic. Add: **1.** In mod. use, a clinic not attached to a hospital where specialists in various branches of medicine are available to outpatients. (Further examples.)

1963 *Spectator* 11 Oct. 446 Other nations whose medical services are based primarily on the hospital or the polyclinic are beginning to see the virtues of a personal doctor. **1967** *Guardian* 15 July 10/3 These doctors [in the U.S.S.R.] work from *polyclinics* which are a combination of general practice, as we know it, and hospital outpatient departments. **1973** *Times Lit. Suppl.* 3 Aug. 896/2 The Soviet Union..has based its system on the use of the polyclinic, with its specialist staff. Here there is no 'physician of primary contact' or general practitioner service as we know it. **1975** J. DE BRES tr. *Mandel's Late Capitalism* xii. 385 [In the age of late capitalism] the independent general medical practitioner is replaced by a polyclinic with affiliated specialists. **1976** *Times Lit. Suppl.* 7 May 555/2 Cuba is perhaps nearest to ordinary Western experience... Much is made of the rate of increase of district hospitals, polyclinics and local health centres.

polyclonal(ity, -clonally: see *POLY- 1.

po:lycondensa·tion. *Chem.* Also **poly-condensation.** [ad. G. *polykondensation* (H. Staudinger *Hochmolekularen Verbindungen* (1932) II. 255): see POLY- and CONDENSATION.] A condensation reaction between molecules each having at least two functional groups which yields a polymer, or a process based on such a reaction. Freq. *attrib.*

1936 *Trans. Faraday Soc.* XXXII. 52 The formation of high polymeric products can also take place by a polycondensation process in which numerous reactive molecules condense. **1949** *Jrnl. Textile Inst.* XL. A307 Polycondensation products, such as phenolic plastics, phenol-acetylene resins, urea-formaldehyde resins, linear and branched polyesters, and super polyamides. **1962** *Times* 26 Feb. (Canada Suppl.) p. vii/2 (Advt.), Complete chemical plant and equipment including plant for thermosetting and thermoplastic polymers and synthetic fibres from polymers and polycondensation products. **1963** A. J. HALL *Textile Sci.* ii. 79 It [*sc.* nylon] is made by the melt-spinning of polyhexamethylene adipamide which in its turn is produced by the polycondensation of equimolecular proportions of adipic acid..and hexamethylene diamine. **1971** *Jrnl. Oil & Colour Chemists' Assoc.* LIV. 888 The volatile components (solvents, monomers and low molecular weight poly condensation products) evaporate almost completely from the liquid paint during the process of film formation. **1978** *Nature* 29 June 738/2 Polymers of related structures have long been known, however, prepared by polycondensation of alkali metal polysulphides and α, ω-dihaloalkanes.

Hence (as back-formations) **polyconde·nse** *v. trans.*, to cause to undergo polycondensation; **polyconde·nsed** *ppl. a.* Also **poly-co·ndensate** [after *filtrate, precipitate*, etc.], a product or preparation resulting from polycondensation.

1942 *Jrnl. Amer. Chem. Soc.* LXIV. 2269/2 The results ..show that the poly-condensates are built up quantitatively from alanine units linked by —CONH— bonds. **1967** *Immunochem.* IV. 77 (*heading*) Sensitization of erythrocytes by polycondensed proteins of immune serum and their use for determining antigen content. **1968** J. CHAMBION in H. F. Mark et al. *Chem. Man-Made Fibers* II. 448 For higher homologs of polyamide 6, the corresponding monomer amino acid can be polycondensed. **1971** B. BUCK tr. *Ludewig's Polyester Fibres* iv. 90 The whole process from dissolution to extrusion can be carried out in one single apparatus in which the dimethyl terephthalate is dissolved in glycol, transesterified, and polycondensed. *Ibid.* 125 Moisture promotes degradation of the polyester melt in the further processing of the polycondensate. **1976** *Nature* 6 May 76/3 Structures..much more easily oxidisable than polycondensed aromatics.

poly-cotton: see *POLY- 3. **polycratism, -cross:** *POLY- 1.

polycrystal (pǫ·likristăl). [f. POLY- + CRYSTAL *sb.* and *a.*] A polycrystalline body. Also *attrib.*, = next.

1925 *Physical Rev.* XXV. 248 The crystal was then hammered and swaged to change it into polycrystal copper. **1932** *Proc. R. Soc.* A. CXXXVIII. 358 The complete change [in density] from single crystal to polycrystal ..is..of the order of 1 in 3000 for, *e.g.*, iron, nickel and aluminium. **1966** C. R. TOTTLE *Sci. Engin. Materials* iv. 93 More than one nucleus inevitably gives rise to a polycrystal, where several points of growth lead to crystallites of different crystallographic orientation. *Ibid.* vi. 136 A polycrystal of iron is not always magnetized.

polycrystalline (pǫlikri·stălǝin), *a.* [f. POLY- + CRYSTALLINE *a.* and *sb.*] Composed of many crystals or crystallites; having a crystalline structure in which there is a random variation in the orientation of different parts.

1925 *Proc. R. Soc.* A. CIX. 144 The figures for single crystals are higher than for the polycrystalline test piece. **1932** *Ibid.* CXXXVIII. 364 A polycrystalline wire can be considered as an assemblage of crystallites in which the axes of crystal symmetry are oriented at random. **1950** *Sci. News* XV. 61 Distorted lattice planes will not slide over one another easily and hence polycrystalline metals are often hard. **1959** *Times Rev. Industry* Mar. 32/3 Fine grinding stone..consisting of a sintered polycrystalline ruby material. **1970** *Sci. Jrnl.* Feb. 46/1 Bulk metals are polycrystalline and the grains are randomly oriented.

Hence **po:lycrystalli·nity**, polycrystalline condition or structure.

1955 *Rep. Progress Physics* XVIII. 233 Research on these materials has been impeded by the anomalous effects of polycrystallinity. **1978** *Nature* 19 Oct. 634/1 There was evidence of polycrystallinity with definite, but usually very weak, X-ray lines assignable to diamond.

polyculture (pǫ·likɒltiŭɹ). [irreg. f. POLY- + CULTURE *sb.* Cf. *MONOCULTURE.] **a.** The simultaneous cultivation or exploitation of several crops or animals. **b.** An area in which this is practised. Opp. *MONOCULTURE. Hence **polycu·ltural** *a.*

1915 C. R. ENOCK *Tropics* xl. 439 It is not to 'monoculture' but to 'polyculture'—that is, to varied production as contrasted with single products—that any community must look for its economic and social security. The peculiar conditions of the tropics must always of necessity call for a considerable exercise of monoculture.. but it must be balanced by equitable regard for the native producer and the exercise to the utmost possible extent of polycultural principles, whereby a supply of all products and all articles necessary for life are producible locally. **1967** *Geo. Abstr.* D. 15 Much of the area has a polyculture of nuts, fruits and vines. **1973** *Country Life* 21 June 1818/3 The polycultural tradition in Italy may be seen from the fact that Frescobaldi [*sc.* a wine producer] have considerable tree plantations and 70,000 olive trees. **1974** *Oryx* XII. 358 A polyculture of wild ungulates can be likened to a sophisticated system of crop rotation at a secondary level.

polycyclic (pǫlisǝi·klik), *a.* [f. POLY- + CYCLIC *a.*] † **1.** *Math.* (See quots.) *Obs.*

1869 W. THOMSON in *Trans. R. Soc. Edin.* XXV. 253 When the function is cyclic with reference to several different mutually irreconcilable circuits, it is called polycyclic. *Ibid.*, Irrotational motion may be either acyclic or cyclic. If cyclic it is monocyclic if there is only one distinct circuit, or polycyclic if there are several distinct circuits, in which there is circulation. **1888** A. B. BASSET *Treat. Hydrodynamics* I. iv. 74 If ϕ be a polycyclic velocity potential, the circulation round any closed curve, which does not cut any of the barriers is..zero. *Ibid.* 75 Every polycyclic function may be expressed as the sum of..monocyclic functions.

2. (In Dict. s.v. POLY- 1.)

3. *Chem.* Having more than one ring of atoms in the molecule. Also as *sb.*, a polycyclic compound.

1903 *Chem. News* 13 Mar. 130/2 (*heading*) A method for the synthesis of polycyclic hydrocarbides. **1909** C. A. KEANE *Mod. Org. Chem.* xv. 414 The most important of these polycyclic substances are built up of benzene rings. **1943** *Endeavour* Jan. 32/2 Carcinogenic potency is by no means confined to polycyclic compounds. **1968** I. L. FINAR *Org. Chem.* (ed. 4) II. xi. 462 This is only possible if rings B and C are fused together in a *trans* manner (*cf.* polycyclics, § 11 d. IV). **1971** *Daily Tel.* (Colour Suppl.) 28 May 27/2 Other potential dangers in exhaust fumes are polycyclic hydrocarbons—which can cause cancer in laboratory animals. **1976** *Nature* 9 Sept. 93/1 Binding of carcinogenic polycyclics to DNA..has been well established.

4. *Electr. Engin.* Involving the simultaneous transmission along a conductor of currents of different frequencies and voltages.

1903 *Jrnl. Inst. Electr. Engin.* XXXII. 751 The advantages of low frequency for power work and of high frequency for lighting are combined in this polycyclic system. **1906** A. RUSSELL *Treat. Theory Alternating Currents* II. xvii. 478 (*heading*) Three phase polycyclic system of distribution. **1913** S. P. SMITH tr. *La Cour & Bragstad's Theory & Calculation Electr. Currents* xvi. 289 The object of the polycyclic system..is to simultaneously transmit electrical energy by means of currents at different pressures and frequencies through one and the same conductor, and to distribute the same without their affecting one another.

5. *Geol.* [ad. F. *polycyclique* (E. Argand 1922, in *Compt. Rend. XIII Session, Congrès Géol. Internat.* (1924) I. 365).] Produced by or having undergone many cycles, esp. of erosion and deposition. Cf. *multicyclic* adj. s.v. *MULTI- 1 a.

1935 H. BAULIG *Changing Sea Level* ii. 13 (*caption*) Block-diagram of a polycyclic valley. **1947** *Trans. R. Geol. Soc. Cornwall* XVII. 341 Polycyclic forms in the valleys still witness the later Pliocene stillstands despite intense peri-glacial solifluction. **1958** [see *MORPHOMETRY]. **1968** R. W. FAIRBRIDGE *Encycl. Geomorphol.* 554/2 A lateritic crust..reflects a polycyclic regime, usually as a result of repeated alternation of hot, humid conditions..with dry, evaporating conditions. **1975** *Nature* 13 Feb. 502/3 Such sediments may incorporate.. duplicated or polycyclic layers.

6. *Biol.* Producing several generations during a year by sexual reproduction.

1957 *New Biol.* XXIII. 58 These polycyclic populations are found in complex environments like ponds where there are successive outbursts of different planktonic algae which cause fluctuations in the amount of food available. **1965** J. JOHNSTON tr. *Danilevskii's Photoperiodism & Seasonal Devel. Insects* vii. 194 They are all potentially polycyclic, and in southern provinces may have several generations a year. **1970** *Amer. Naturalist* CIV. 398 In most polycyclic insects of the temperate zone, long days cause continuous development, while short days cause diapause.

polycythæmia, -ic, polydentate: see *POLY- 1. **polyde(s)oxyribo-:** see s.v. *POLYRIBO-. **polydiene:** see *POLY- 2.

polydisperse (pǫlidispɔ̄·ɹs), *a.* [ad. G. *polydispers* (W. O. Ostwald *Grundriss d. Kolloidchem.* (ed. 2, 1911) i. 39), f. *poly-* POLY- + *dispers* disperse (cf. *DISPERSE *v.* 9).] Existing in the form of or containing colloidal particles (which may be macromolecules) having a range of sizes; applied esp. to macromolecular substances in which there is a simple distribution of particle size (or occas. some other specified physical property) with one peak; also applied to such a property or its distribution. Also **polydispe·rsed** *a.* Cf. *POLYMOLECULAR *a.* d.

1915 M. H. FISCHER tr. *Ostwald's Handbk. Colloid-Chem.* i. 35 These systems in which the disperse phase is composed of particles having different degrees of dispersion may be called polydisperse systems. **1938** *Nature* 4 June 1001/2 The specific polysaccharide of type I pneumococcus is polydisperse with an average weight of approximately 225,000. **1941** *Jrnl. Franklin Inst.* CCXXXI. 1 Fine powders and colloidally dispersed material are also typically polydispersed. **1948** *Chem. Abstr.* XLII. 1787 (*heading*) Birefringence of flow in polydispersed mixtures. **1962** H. BLOEMENDAL et al. in A. Pirie *Lens Metabolism Rel. Cataract* 303 Prolonged dialysis of 7 M urea-treated α-crystallin against 1·25 M urea results in the appearance of a polydisperse peak with sedimentation coefficient of 10 S. **1963** *Nature* 16 Nov. 665/2 A preparation may be monodisperse with respect to one parameter, polydisperse with respect to a second and heterogeneous with respect to a third; the foregoing terms are only meaningful if the parameter measured is..specified. **1968** H. HARRIS *Nucleus & Cytoplasm* iii. 56 Preparations of the total RNA in the cell cytoplasm..did not show any fraction which had either the kinetic characteristics or the polydisperse sedimentation of the rapidly labelled nuclear RNA. **1973** *Sci. Amer.* June 112/1 With a calibrated grid in the viewing field of the microscope one can measure the relative sizes of the particles in a polydisperse suspension (a suspension containing particles of widely varying size).

Hence **polydispe·rsity**, the condition or property of being polydisperse.

1927 H. S. VAN KLOOSTER tr. *Kruyt's Colloids* x. 154 Viewed in the ultramicroscope, this sol presents a very colorful picture which reveals the poly-dispersity very plainly. **1936** *Trans. Faraday Soc.* XXXII. 49 It appears that determinations of polydispersity by measurement of sedimentation velocity can only be effected in extremely dilute solutions. **1963** *Nature* 16 Nov. 665/2 Some degree of random variability in secondary or tertiary structure may confer polydispersity with respect to frictional coefficient on some proteins. **1967** MARGERISON & EAST *Introd. Polymer Chem.* ii. 47 The value of the parameter $\overline{M}_w/\overline{M}_n$ in a practical case thus gives a measure of the range of molecular weights in the sample;..a value of two or greater indicates considerable polydispersity. **1976** [see *POLYMOLECULARITY].

polyelectrolyte (pǫli,ĭle·ktrǒlǝit). *Chem.* [f. POLY- + ELECTROLYTE.] A substance which consists of large, usu. polymeric molecules containing several ionizable groups.

1947 *Jrnl. Polymer Sci.* II. 12 By using salts of quaternary nitrogen compounds, polyelectrolytes can be made which are soluble in organic solvents. **1959** *Times* 3 Dec. 9/4 There are water softeners using poly-electrolyte membranes with an output of 50 cubic feet an hour. **1964** *Biophysical Jrnl.* IV. 1. Suppl. 10 Many important plant products such as the pectic acids of fruit jellies and alginic acid of seaweed are typical polyelectrolytes. **1968** *New Scientist* 26 Dec. 703/3 Pure poly-electrolytes also promise to be valuable additives in many foodstuffs and beverages. **1973** *Nature* 2 Nov. 34/1 Polyelectrolytes are increasingly being used as flocculants for electrostatically stabilised dispersions of colloidal particles.

Hence **po:lyelectroly·tic** *a.*

1948 *Science* 19 Nov. 548/2 We are thus led to the assumption that the high viscosity of polyelectrolytic solutions and its concentration dependence are due to the presence of the high charge density at the polyions. **1958** *New Scientist* 29 May 75/1 Some of the defence mechanisms of the living body are polyelectrolytic in nature.

polyembryony. Add: (Further examples.) Also *Zool.*, the development of more than one embryo from a single egg; **polyembryonic** *a.* (examples).

1906 *Science* 21 Dec. 813/2 Polyembryony [in *Encyrtus* eggs] reaches its greatest intensity..when the young larvæ of the *Hyponomeuta* leave their winter shelter. **1912** *Anatomischer Anzeiger* XLI. 369 (*heading*) The demonstration of polyembryonic development in the armadillo. **1925** A. D. IMMS *Gen. Textbk. Entomol.* I. 154 Polyembryony is met with among insects in certain parasitic families of Hymenoptera. **1947** *Arch. Path.* XLIV. 501 There has been much speculation concerning the cause of polyembryony (monozygotic multiple birth) as it occurs regularly in the armadillo. **1956** *Nature* 28 Jan. 191/1 An examination of the seeds of different species of *Cassia* ..has shown the occurrence of polyembryony to be geographically widespread. **1969** R. F. CHAPMAN *Insects* xix. 377 The effect of polyembryony is to increase the reproductive potential of the insect, but the net effect is not always much greater than in related monoembryonic species because polyembryonic forms tend to lay fewer eggs.

polyendocrine, -endocrinopathy: see *POLY- 1. **polyene:** *POLY- 2. **polyenergid:** *POLY- 1. **polyenic, -enoic:** *POLY- 2.

Polyergus (pǫli,ɜ̄·ɪgɒ̆s). *Ent.* Also **polyergus.** [mod.L. (P. A. Latreille 1804, in *Nouveau Dict. Hist. Nat.* XXIV. 179), f. Gr. πολύεργος hard-working.] A slave-making ant of the genus so called, found in Europe and North America; = AMAZON-ANT.

1882 J. LUBBOCK *Ants, Bees, & Wasps* vii. 180, I presented a slave of *Polyergus* with a dead fly pinned down. **1908** *Westm. Gaz.* 21 Jan. 2/1 The polyergus seems to lose even the faculty of making a nest. **1924** J. A. THOMSON *Sci. Old & New* xiii. 72 Slave-keeping is much more marked among the Amazon Ants, of which the European Polyergus is a good representative. **1945** C. P. HASKINS *Of Ants & Men* ix. 175 Not only is *Polyergus* little interested in its nesting site, but it is compelled to abandon it and to move about at frequent intervals. **1954** BORROR & DELONG *Introd. Study Insects* 729 The *Polyergus* ants are often called amazons.

polyester (pǫli,e·stəɪ). [f. POLY- + *ESTER.] Any polymer in which the units are joined by the ester linkage, —CO·O—; also (*a*) (more fully *polyester fibre*), a man-made fibre consisting of a polyester; (*b*) (more fully *polyester resin*), any of numerous synthetic resins or plastics consisting of or made from a polyester, different kinds of which are used as fibres or films, in paint, and as moulding materials or reinforced plastics. Freq. *attrib.*

1929 [see *POLYAMIDE]. **1935** C. ELLIS *Chem. Synthetic Resins* II. l. 1002 Strong, oriented fibers were obtained from polyesters of molecular weights greater than 9330. **1952** *Jrnl. R. Aeronaut. Soc.* LVI. 707 Working with glass fibres, the Americans have used the polyester or 'contact resins' almost exclusively. **1955** *Times* 4 May 21/3 Production items based on polyester resins and glass fibres..include panels and bodies for the transport and aircraft industries, mouldings for boat hulls, [etc.]. **1958** *Times Rev. Industry* Feb. 77/1 The advent of resins of the polyester and epoxide types..meant that laminates could be produced without the application of high pressures. **1958** *Engineering* 7 Mar. 311/1 Cellulose-acetate and, more recently, polyester are used at present for data-recording tape bases. **1958** *Manch. Guardian* 25 Sept. 1/3 Polyester fibre was discovered in 1941 by Mr. J. R. Whinfield and Dr J. T. Dickson in the laboratories of the Calico Printers' Association. **1964** *Which?* Aug. 253/3 Fabrics made from polyester tend to attract dirt but can be easily washed. **1968** J. IRONSIDE *Fashion Alphabet* 210 Polyester fibres have very similar properties to the polyamides but they are perhaps even more durable. **1969** L. S. MOUNTS in W. R. R. Park *Plastics Film Technol.* v. 135 Polyester films have great strength and good aging characteristics. **1973** *Materials & Technol.* VI. viii. 568 The polyesters are usually marketed dissolved in the cross-linking monomer in the form of a syrup, to which inhibitors are added. **1975** *Guardian* 27 Jan. 16/3 Today the accent is on..blends of a polyester fibre with cotton or polynosic rayon. **1977** *R.A.F. News* 22 June – 5 July 2 (Advt.), 'Tootal' Polyester/Cotton Wedgwood Blue Shirts.

Hence **po:lyestera·mide,** any polymer which contains both ester and amide linkages, esp. any of various rubbery materials of this type which are usu. made by mixed condensation reactions and can be drawn into fibres; **po:lyesterifica·tion,** a reaction or process which yields a polyester.

1932 *Jrnl. Amer. Chem. Soc.* LIV. 1560 The polyesterification thus consists in a series of intermolecular couplings resulting in the formation of progressively longer chains. **1943** H. FOSTER *U.S. Pat. 2,333,922* 1/1 The above objects are accomplished through the production of electrically insulated conductors in which the insulation is a polyester-amide which has been treated with polyisocyanate. **1950** *Thorpe's Dict. Appl. Chem.* (ed. 4) X. 45/2 Among the second class of amide interpolymers are the polyesteramides. These are made by condensing together di-reactive amide-forming and ester-forming components, or more specifically by condensing di-reactive components containing carboxy groups in proportions equivalent to the sum of the amine and hydroxyl groups. **1958** *Technology* Mar. 12/3 Not long after Carothers' pioneering work, J. R. Whinfield took up the study of similar polyesterification processes, the main idea being to use starting materials which might give some sense of rigidity to the high-polymer substances made by these reactions. **1974** K. F. HEINISCH *Dict. Rubber* 508/2 The production of the polyesteramide is performed without a deficiency of dicarboxylic acid, as for Vulcolan. **1976** *Nature* 24 June 658/2 This demonstrated that ester interchange reactions were slow compared with polyesterification in the conditions used to make commercial alkyd resins.

polyethenoid: see *POLY- 2.

polyether (pǫli,ī·þəɪ). [f. POLY- + ETHER.] Any of a variety of polymers in which the repeating unit contains an ether linkage, C—O—C, many of which are used commercially, esp. as plastic foams and epoxy resins. So *polyether foam.*

1922 *Chem. Abstr.* XVI. 1741 (*heading*) Polyethers of trimethyleneglycol. **1962** *Listener* 8 Mar. 451/1 The less expensive polyether foam is edging its way in. **1966** [see *EPOXY]. **1968** *Times* 28 Mar. 9 All three versions are available in either Burma teak, or prime beech and are fitted with specially composed polyether foam cushions. **1972** *Physics Bull.* Oct. 582/3 A fluorocarbon polyether, recently used as a rotary pump lubricant.., has allowed pump operation at above 100 °C. **1975** P. BROWNE *Bodywork Maintenance* vi. 80/1 Polyether is mainly used as stuffing in cheap upholstery.

polyethism: see *POLY- 1.

polyethylene (pǫli,e·þĭlīn). [Back-formation from *POLYETHYLENIC *a.* Cf. F. *polyéthylène* (Berthelot 1867, in *Jrnl. de Pharm. et de Chim.* VI. 28).] **a.** *Chem.* Used *attrib.* in the names of polymeric substances prepared from derivatives of ethylene, as † **polyethylene alcohol** = next; **polyethylene glycol,** any polymer of ethylene glycol; *esp.* any of a series of water-soluble oligomers and polymers which have the structure H—$(OCH_2CH_2)_n$—OH, of which the lower members are used as solvents and the higher esp. as waxes; **polyethylene oxide,** any polymer having the structure —$(OCH_2CH_2)_n$—; *esp.* any of the thermoplastics of high molecular weight made from ethylene oxide or ethylene glycol (usu. by copolymerization of both) and used esp. as water-soluble films; **polyethylene terephthalate,** a thermoplastic condensation polymer of ethylene glycol and terephthalic acid which is widely used to make polyester fibres.

1862 Polyethylene-alcohol [in Dict. s.v. POLY- 2 a]. **1884** ROSCOE & SCHORLEMMER *Treat. Chem.* III. II. 37 Ethylene glycol,..in its turn, combines with the free ethylene oxide to form polyethylene alcohols. **1886** E. F. SMITH tr. *V. von Richter's Org. Chem.* 258 (*heading*) Polyethylene glycols or alcohols. **1947** R. L. WAKEMAN *Chem. Commercial Plastics* xxvi. 779 Polyethylene glycols are..soluble in both water and aromatic hydrocarbons. **1971** P. TOOLEY *High Polymers* ii. 43 Polyethylene glycols..vary from oily liquids to waxy solids according to their degree of polymerization. **1930** *Chem. Abstr.* XXIV. 3003 On cooling the fused polyethylene oxides they crystallize like paraffin. **1935** C. ELLIS *Chem. Synthetic Resins* II. l. 991 All the polyethylene oxides were shown by X-ray diagrams to be crystalline and viscosity measurements indicated a meandering structure for the molecule. **1969** L. S. MOUNTS in W. R. R. Park *Plastics Film Technol.* v. 140 The solubility of PVA and polyethylene oxide films increases with increasing water temperature. **1946** ASTBURY & BROWN in *Nature* 14 Dec. 871 Polyethylene terephthalate (terylene) gives a well-oriented x-ray fibre diagram. **1967** E. CHAMBERS *Photolitho-Offset* ix. 118 The more recent introduction of the thermoplastic material polyethylene terephthalate.. as a support for photographic emulsions has increased considerably the dimensional stability of films. **1967** *Times Rev. Industry* June 70/3 Polysulphones, polyphenylene oxide and polyethylene terephthalate..are claimed to have improved creep resistance and temperature stability.

b. Chiefly *N. Amer.* = *POLYTHENE. Also *attrib.* and *Comb.*

1939 *Plastics* III. 289/1 Compounding polyethylenes with polyisobutylenes has yielded some very useful compounds. **1942** *Electronic Engin.* Mar. 668/2 Polyethylene and polyisobutylene..are finding extensive use as flexible coatings for wires intended for low-loss work. **1956** *Nature* 25 Feb. 393/1 The reaction was also measured in a polyethylene flask. *Ibid.* 3 Mar. 440/1 A polyethylene-covered magnetic stirring bar. **1966** T. PYNCHON *Crying of Lot 49* iii. 56 Suddenly, a dozen boats away, a form, covered with a blue polyethylene tarp, rose up. **1967** *Economist* 30 Sept. 1225/1 Heavy over-capacity seems to be on the way in Europe in the production of high-density polyethylene (polythene). **1968** J. UPDIKE in *Transatlantic Rev.* XXVIII. 6 The hydra's swollen coelenteron..veiled the preceding meals like polyethylene film protecting a rack of dry-cleaned suits. **1969** L. S. MOUNTS in W. R. R. Park *Plastics Film Technol.* v. 122 Polyethylene films also are used in many nonpackaging applications. **1969** *Daily Colonist* (Victoria, B.C.) 7 Dec. 26/5 A new television antenna designed for boats... An entire signal receiving system anchored in polyethylene foam. **1976** *Country Life* 22 Jan. 211/1 A fabric of the future... Spun, bonded polyethylene, a synthetic material made from bonded, random fibres.

polyethylenic (pǫ:li,eþĭlī·nik), *a. Chem.* [ad. F. *polyéthylénique* (A. Wurtz 1860, in *Compt. Rend.* L. 1195), f. *poly-* POLY- + *éthylène* ETHYLENE + *-ique* -IC.] † **1.** Used to designate polymeric compounds prepared from derivatives of ethylene. Cf. *POLYETHYLENE a. *Obs.*

1860 A. WURTZ in *Chem. News* 25 Aug. 121/1 Glycolic, lactic, and oxalic acids..are acids of very simple constitution; but such is not the case with those obtained by oxidising the complex glycols, which I have called polyethylenic alcohols. **1878** C. M. TIDY *Handbk. Mod. Chem.* xxiii. 574 By heating glycol with ethylenic oxide in sealed tubes, a series of compounds called polyethylenic glycols (or alcohols) are formed. **1895** *Jrnl. Chem. Soc.* LXVIII. I. 320 Ethylenic oxide and sodium ethoxide.. give a product which boils at 110–120°..; this..must therefore be regarded as a complex ethylic polyethylenic oxide.

2. Polyunsaturated; of the nature of polyunsaturation.

1928 *Proc. R. Soc.* A. CXXII. 564 Two polyethylenic acids.., namely, linoleic acid of soya bean or cotton-seed oil..linolenic acid of linseed oil. **1958** *Jrnl. Sci. of Food & Agric.* IX. 777 The polyethylenic C_{20} and C_{22} acids, so characteristic of the animal glycerophosphatides. **1964** *Oceanogr. & Marine Biol.* II. 176 The pattern of polyethylenic unsaturation in the fatty acids of marine invertebrates is probably the same as that in fish lipids. **1965** E. F. JANSEN in Bonner & Varner *Plant Biochem.* xxv. 655 The hexahydromatricaria ester is included to illustrate the occurrence of homologous polyethylenic compounds.

polyformal(dehyde: see *POLY- 2.

Polyfoto (pǫ·li,fōᵘto). Also **-photo.** [f. POLY- + *foto*, alteration of PHOTO.] A proprietary name for a kiosk in which a person can sit and have a number of photographs taken of himself in quick succession (now usu. automatically). Also *transf.* and as *vb. trans.*

1938 *Trade Marks Jrnl.* 2 Feb. 131/1 Polyfoto... Photographs. Polyfoto (International) Limited,..London,..merchants. **1945** 'A. GILBERT' *Don't open Door* xiii. 105 'Have you got a photograph of the girl?' 'She was polyfotoed the other day to please me.' **1962** —— *No Dust in Attic* v. 63 They ran against Miss Malpas coming out of the Polyfoto kiosk... Out of forty-eight positions there must be one that would reproduce satisfactorily. **1964** G. SIMS *Terrible Door* xxv. 132 My husband was one of the first photographers to make strips of little films, rather like Polyphotos nowadays. **1965** E. J. HOWARD *After Julius* xviii. 277 He got himself polyphotoed..for his passport. **1976** 'A. HALL' *Kobra Manifesto* iv. 44 Worn Polyphoto of current girl friend.

polyfunctional(ity: see *POLY- 1.

polygala (pǫ̆li·gălă). [mod.L., f. Gr. πολύ much + γάλα milk.] An annual or perennial herb or a shrub belonging to the large genus so called, which is a member of the family Polygalaceæ and is widely distributed in most regions of the world; = MILKWORT 1 (in quot. *a* 1661 = SAINFOIN).

1578 [see MILKWORT 1]. ***a* 1661** FULLER *Worthies* (1662) Kent 57 Saint-Foine or Holy-hay..otherwise called *Polygala*, which I may English *much Milk*, as causing the cattle to give abundance thereof. **1671** [see MILKWORT 1]. **1823** *Curtis's Bot. Mag.* L. 2437 The common Polygala is so very variable a plant. **1840** [see *IVY-BERRY b]. **1870** W. ROBINSON *Wild Garden* I. 9 The small sapphire buds of the alpine Polygala. **1936** *Discovery* Feb. 48/2 Large anchusas were beginning to flower.., huge polygala, and I don't know what else. **1977** S. DEALLER *Wild Flowers for Garden* iv. 67, I think of the Polygalas as generally trouble free, non-aggressive, slightly vulnerable plants.

polygamical, *a.* Delete (? *obs.*) and add later example.

1914 CHESTERTON *Flying Inn* 69 Why should you shrink then, ladies, from this great polygamical experiment?

polygene (pǫ·lidʒīn). *Genetics.* [Back-formation from *POLYGENIC *a.* 3; cf. *GENE.] A gene whose individual effect on the phenotype of a single organism is too small to be observed, but which can act together with other, non-allelic polygenes to produce observable phenotypic variation in a quantitative character.

1941 *Jrnl. Genetics* XLI. 163 The inbreeding this line had undergone had in fact made it homozygous for the hair-number polygenes. **1949** [see *POLYGENIC *a.* 3]. **1961** *Lancet* 9 Sept. 601/2 One might envisage a system of pleiotropic masculinising polygenes located more or less randomly along the whole of the Y chromosome. **1973** *Nature* 21/28 Dec. 498/2 Techniques for the location of polygenes, developed in *Drosophila* but also very successful in mice and wheat ,have not been applied to human material.

polygenesis. Add: **b.** *Linguistics.* The theory that there is a plurality of independent sources for languages. Opp. *MONOGENESIS 3.

1936, 1949 [see *MONOGENESIS 3]. **1979** *Amer. Speech 1978* LIII. 247 My gut feeling is that radical polygenesis is impossible. It would require either a biologically unrealistic degree of parallelism, or else that languages be much more varied in their groundplans than in fact they are.

c. *gen.*

1962 G. KUBLER *Art & Archit. Anc. Amer.* i. 11 (*heading*) Diffusion or polygenesis?

polygenetic, *a.* Add: **2.** (Further examples.)

1889 *Amer. Jrnl. Sci.* XXXVII. 431 The present topography..is an uncompleted advance in a second cycle of development, with recent complications by glacial action and slight changes of level. Like mountains of repeated growth, this topography may be called 'polygenetic'. **1943** *Ibid.* CCXLI. 486 Polygenetic complex soils and Late Quaternary alluvial bodies may preserve duplicate records of climatic changes for a given region. **1969** BENNISON & WRIGHT *Geol. Hist. Brit. Isles* ix. 201 In the thrust block of Roman Fell, the Roman Fell Beds..rest on the Polygenetic Conglomerate of unknown age but with pebbles including andesites probably derived from the Old Red Sandstone. **1975** *Nature* 27 Mar. 369/2 Coasts and mountains are treated separately as polygenetic landscapes, the former being the zone of contact between two distinct environments and the latter the areas within which internal uplift conflicts markedly with external erosion.

b. (See quot. 1959.) [After G. *polygen* in this sense (A. Stübel *Die Vulkanberge von Ecuador* (1897) III. 352).]

[**1903** A. GEIKIE *Text-bk. Geol.* (ed. 4) I. 322 A volcano formed in this way he terms monogene; while where it has been built up by the gradual accumulations of successive eruptions he calls it polygene.] **1959** A. A. G. SCHIEFERDECKER *Geol. Nomencl.* 239 *Polygenetic volcano*, formed by several volcanic outbursts. **1962** E. A. VINCENT tr. *Rittmann's Volcanoes* iii. 114 In the case of the great polygenetic volcanoes, the old topography is completely buried. **1976** *New Scientist* 9 Sept. 527/1 Those which erupt many times are called polygenetic volcanoes.

c. *Linguistics.* Deriving historically from a number of sources; having more than one antecedent.

1952 *Archivum Linguisticum* IV. 93 The outstanding trait in the history of *-(i)ego*..is its polygenetic character.

polygenic, *a.* Add: **3.** *Genetics.* [ad. G. *polygen* (L. Plate *Vererbungslehre mit besonderer Berücksichtigung des Menschen* (1913) ii. 75).] Of, pertaining to, or determined by polygenes.

[**1927** *Zeitschr. für Induktive Abstammungs- und Vererbungslehre* XLIII. 331 The discovery of polygenous characters, especially the phenomenon of polymeria discovered by Nilsson Ehle, made it necessary to recognize, that at least a great many characters are determined not by one but by several and even many genes.] **1941** *Jrnl. Genetics* XLI. 160 Qualitative variation is usually monogenic or digenic in inheritance. Cases of trigenic and tetragenic inheritance are known, but are relatively rare. In contrast with these, quantitative variation may be said to be polygenic, and this term will be adopted. **1949** DARLINGTON & MATHER *Elem. Genetics* iii. 66 These genes are inherited in the mendelian way, but their differences have effects which are small in relation to those of non-heritable agencies (or at least in relation to the total variation), similar to one another and supplementary to one another... Such a set of genes constitutes a polygenic system, and its individual members may be conveniently termed polygenes. **1954** *Antiquity* XXVIII. 197 A genetic analysis of such polygenic characters as bone size and shape. **1961** *Brit. Med. Bull.* XVII. 241 All polygenic inheritance is polymeric, but not all polymeric inheritance is polygenic. **1971** *Heythrop Jrnl.* Apr. 171 The analysis of complex (polygenic) hereditary determination is most commonly conducted by means of twin studies. **1978** *Dædalus* Spring 215 Much more complex choices will confront us when we think we know enough to tackle polygenic traits which may have important expression in emotional behavior or intellectual capacity.

Hence **polyge·nically** *adv.*, by means of or with regard to polygenes.

1943 *Biol. Rev.* XVIII. 61 Polygenically controlled differences are quantitative rather than qualitative and do not lead to the sharp segregation shown by the more familiar genetical differences. **1957** *Heredity* XI. 392 Such an approximately even distribution..might even be anticipated given that any sizeable block of heterochromatin near the centromere is, mitotic length for length, about as polygenically active as the euchromatin of more distal regions. **1976** *Nature* 23 Sept. 317/1 A common feature of many selection experiments, when polygenically determined traits are involved, is a reduction in the reproductive fitness of the selected strains.

polyglacial(ism, -ist: see *POLY- 1.

polyglot, *a.* and *sb.* Add: **A.** *adj.* **2. b.** Characterized by the use of a plurality of languages, or of elements derived from a plurality of languages.

1952 W. D. JACOBS *William Barnes* i. 12 Dorset gave Barnes the material by which to judge the polyglot English of our day. **1957** *Thought* XXXII. 240 In his early polyglot days..he [*sc.* T. S. Eliot] wrote often with odd patches and tags of French, German—and even Sanskrit—as well as Latin and Greek. **1965** *Economist* 3 Apr. 44/2 The use in, say, Cyprus of a polyglot (or mixed-manned) force. **1972** W. B. LOCKWOOD *Panorama Indo-European Lang.* 214 Here some 900,000 of them compete with the Gujaratis for the position of second largest linguistic group in that remarkably polyglot city [*sc.* Bombay].

So **po·lyglotter** (*nonce-wd.*), a polyglot person; **polyglo·ttery** = POLYGLOTTISM; **polyglo·ttically** *adv.* = POLYGLOTTALLY *adv.*

1910 W. J. LOCKE *Simon* vi. 71 Mr. Papadopoulos polyglottically acknowledged the honour I had conferred upon him. **1912** 'R. DEHAN' *Between Two Thieves* 616 That white haired Polyglotter in the shabby togs..is a queer kind of chap. **1915** *Singapore Free Press* 14 Jan., If its polyglottery were all that was wrong with it [*sc.* Austria-Hungary], it still might be possible to jog along in a sort of mutual unintelligibility. **1931** *Time & Tide* 8 Aug. 943 (*heading*) Polyglottery [*review of W. Gerhardi's* Memoirs of a Polyglot]. **1962** *Times Lit. Suppl.* 14 Sept. 685/3 Rebuses abound, as do polyglottery (classical and modern), Finnegans wakefulness, and enormous catalogues *à la* Rabelais.

polyglutamic, -glycine, -glycol(ic: see *POLY- 2.

polygon, *sb.* and *a.* Add: **A.** *sb.* **2. b.** *Physical Geogr.* One of the approximately polygonal figures characteristic of patterned ground (cf. *PATTERNED *ppl. a.* b).

1913 *Amer. Jrnl. Sci.* CLXXXVI. 459 The shale surfaces are flat, the polygons not being concave upward as is commonly the case in the Mauch Chunk and Newark shales. **1914** T. THORODDSEN in Rosenvinge & Warming *Bot. Iceland* I. 1. 258 The surface is divided into squares or less regularly formed polygons, by bands of small stones or gravel, while the clay of the interior of the squares or polygons is destitute of stones. **1921** *Geogr. Jrnl.* LVIII. 308 The snow falls, and when it melts, the spare gravel that remains on the clay substratum has taken upon itself the same system of polygons..which we see in Polar lands. **1950** [see *PATTERNED *ppl. a.* b]. **1960** B. W. SPARKS *Geomorphol.* xiv. 318 Boulders weighing..over one hundredweight..have been observed in some Greenland polygons. **1974** *Environmental Conservation* I. 58/1 He found no serious thermokarst conditions along the trails, except where ice-wedges of polygons were crossed.

polygonal, *a.* (*sb.*) Add: **1. b.** Containing or forming polygonal features.

1924 *Geogr. Jrnl.* LXIII. 213 One is apt to mistake this polygonal system of ice-wedges for a continuous sheet of ground-ice. **1930** *Ibid.* LXXVI. 417 Polygonal shrinkage fissures in clay are widespread. **1960** B. W. SPARKS *Geomorphol.* iii. 33 Basalt..often displays a very well defined, polygonal, vertical joint pattern. **1974** T. L. PÉWÉ in Smiley & Zumberge *Polar Deserts & Mod. Man* iii. 42/1 One of the most widespread geomorphic features associated with permafrost in the polar deserts is the microrelief pattern of the ground generally called polygonal ground or tundra polygons.

polygonboden (pǫ·ligǫ̆nbōu:dĕn). *Physical Geogr.* Const. as *pl.* [a. G. *polygonboden*, lit. 'polygon ground', tr. Sw. *rutmark* chequered ground (F. R. Kjellman 1879, in *Öfversigt af K. Vetenskaps-Akad. Förhandl.* XXXVI. IX. 11).] Polygons (sense *A. 2b).

1924 *Geogr. Jrnl.* LXIII. 226 Schimper..saw well-developed 'polygonboden' and arrangement of vegetation with respect to the polygons, in the high plateaux of the Pamirs. **1933** *Bull. Geol. Soc. Amer.* XLIV. 949 Numerous minor forms, including polygonboden, increase the contrasts between alpine surfaces and those of lower elevations. **1947** *Geogr. Rev.* XXXVII. 640 Plainly visible..are the polygenboden, a phenomenon of frozen ground. **1970** MACDONALD & ABBOTT *Volcanoes in Sea* viii. 150/1 The fragments..are arranged in stripes of varying coarseness, or in polygonal patterns ('Polygonboden'), that..are the result of frost action.

polygonization (pǫ:ligǫ̆naizēi·ʃən). *Metallurgy.* [f. POLYGON + -IZATION.] The formation of smaller grains within the grains of a metal as a result of the migration of dislocations following deformation and annealing.

1948 R. W. CAHN in *Rep. Conf. Strength of Solids, 1947* 137 The x-ray and microscopical results together lead to an interpretation as follows: the deformation leads to elastic bending of glide lamellae; when the crystal is annealed, the lamellae undergo 'polygonization'. **1949** —— in *Jrnl. Inst. Metals* LXXVI. 136 It is suggested that the process be named polygonization, to distinguish it from other forms of recrystallization. The name derives from the fact that the crystallographic direction which coincides with the wire axis, while bent along an arc before annealing, becomes part of a polygon afterwards. **1950** *Engineering* 5 May 499/3 Polygonisation could be obtained in hexagonal metals only after plastic bending and not after deformation in tension. **1957** D. MCLEAN *Grain Boundaries in Metals* vii. 204 The word 'polygonization' has lost its original geometrical significance and now refers to the process of dislocations gathering into stable arrays. **1976** COTTERILL & MOULD *Recrystallization & Grain Growth in Metals* iv. 74 The basic differences between the formation of a substructure by polygonization, during annealing, and the formation of subgrains, directly, during cold-work have been summarized by Byrne.

polygonize (pǫ·ligǫ̆naiz), *v.* *Metallurgy.* [Backformation from prec.] *intr.* To undergo or give rise to polygonization.

1949 *Jrnl. Inst. Metals* LXXVI. 138 Zinc crystals bent at −180° C. would not polygonize on subsequent annealing. **1967** A. H. COTTRELL *Introd. Metall.* xxi. 402 Dislocations of opposite signs come together and annihilate each other. Those of the same sign polygonize into well-defined cell walls.

Hence **po·lygonized** *ppl. a.*

1950 *Progress Metal Physics* II. 188 The grains..were in a polygonized condition. **1954** A. R. BAILEY *Text-bk. Metall.* v. 110 (*caption*) Polygonised structure in super-purity aluminium, developed by creep at 200° C. **1976** COTTERILL & MOULD *Recrystallization & Grain Growth in Metals* iv. 74 Although the energy per dislocation is reduced, the total energy of the boundary is increased, and that of the regions away from the boundary is decreased, by the conversion from the deformed structure to the polygonized one.

polygram. Add: **2.** A recording made with a polygraph (sense 3 in Dict. and Suppl.).

1923 W. D. REID *Heart in Mod. Pract.* iii. 60 It is frequently not possible to determine from the polygram whether the tachycardia originates in the auricle or in the ventricle unless the tracing shows the onset or cessation of the paroxysm. **1966** R. J. FERGUSON *Polygraph & Private Industry* vii. 299 Extreme caution must be used in interpreting polygrams.

polygraph, *sb.* Add: **I. 3.** Also used to obtain tracings of other physiological characteristics (such as rates of pulse and respiration, or the electrical conductivity of the skin), and made to serve as a lie-detector. (Earlier and later examples.)

1871 *Lancet* 25 Nov. 739/1 The most direct method for recording the heart's motion is that which we owe to Chauveau and Marey. These ingenious experimenters have supplied us with many instruments adapted for the registration of movements, but none more generally useful than the following, which has been well named the 'polygraph'. **1923** J. A. LARSON in *Jrnl. Exper. Psychol.* VI. 424 A deception test based upon the correlation between the physiological and emotional activities... The technique consists of securing a continuous blood pressure curve (secured by an Erlanger sphygmomanometer or more preferably by a modification of the McKenzie or the Jacquet polygraphs) taken synchronously with a respiratory and a timing curve. **1942** F. E. INBAU *Lie Detection* i. 5 Until 1939 the Keeler Polygraph consisted only of the blood pressure-pulse-respiration units; since then it has been obtainable either with or without a galvanometer unit for recording electrodermal responses. **1959** M. DOLINSKY *There is no Silence* iii. 47 Anxiety causes subtle and involuntary increases in the heartbeat respiration,..and blood pressure which the polygraph records. **1971** *Nature* 9 July 124/2 Instantaneous blood flows to the two hindlimbs..were displayed on a 'Grass P7' polygraph together with the instantaneous and mean (integrated) blood pressure. **1973** *N.Y. Law Jrnl.* 20 Mar., The court then explained that there is no scientific proof that lying heightens anxiety, and that a subject's emotional responses as measured by the polygraph are no proof either of truthfulness or lying. **1976** *Time* 27 Dec. 41/2 Patients spend the night hooked up to a polygraph, a lie-detector-like machine that monitors sleep-related physiological functions (breathing, muscle twitching, rapid eye movement). **1977** *New Yorker* 30 May 29/1 A lot of firms..now routinely give standard polygraph tests to prospective employees.

II. 4. (Earlier example.)

1854 A. G. HENDERSON tr. *Cousin's Philos. of Kant* i. 8 Leibnitz..was led away by a passion for universal knowledge... Wolf endeavoured to bring all the scattered views of the great polygraph to a common centre.

III. 6. *Cryptography.* A group of two or more letters; also, in *Phonetics*, a group of three or more letters expressing a simple sound of speech.

1943 L. D. SMITH *Cryptogr.* iv. 82 A method that represents a distinct departure from Vignère's..is found in polygraph substitution—that is, the substitution of cipher digraphs or trigraphs for the plain-text digraphs or trigraphs. **1959** *Brno Studies in English* I. 18 The following stage..replaced the cumbersome digraphs (and polygraphs) by simple but diacriticized graphemes. **1974** *Encycl. Brit. Macropædia* V. 332/1 In substitution ciphers, the characteristic relative frequencies of single letters, digraphs, and longer polygraphs serve as a basis for the assignment of plaintext equivalents to cipher values.

polygraph (pǫ·ligrɑf), *v.* [f. prec. sb.] **a.** *intr.* To perform (satisfactorily, etc.) when examined with a polygraph. **b.** *trans.* To examine with a polygraph, esp. for truthfulness. Hence **po·lygraphing** *vbl. sb.*

1969 H. H. COOPER *Cave with Two Exits* I. 68 The checks on him were being completed. He polygraphed okay, for what that's worth. **1978** 'W. WINGATE' *Bloodbath* ii. 15 He was..a mystery, and this despite all his debriefings..and polygraphings. *Ibid.* 16 In the two years since his defection, Yazov had been repeatedly polygraphed. **1979** P. FRIEDMAN *Termination Order* (1980) i. 14 Your superiors..will want to polygraph me. *Ibid.* iv. 57 All this nonsense—calling people back for polygraphing, or debriefing or whatever.

polygrapher. Restrict †*Obs.* to sense 2 in Dict. and add later example of sense 1 (still *rare*).

1871 L. B. PHILLIPS *Dict. Biogr. Ref.* 298 Cunaeus, Peter (*Van der Kun*), Dutch savant and polygrapher; 1586–1638.

3. A user of a polygraph (sense 3).

1954 *Reporter* (N.Y.) 8 June 14/3 (*heading*) Eminent

polygraphers. **1962** *Harvard Business Rev.* Nov.–Dec. 128/2 The National Board of Polygraph Examiners, an organization of polygraphers..set forth minimum standards for polygraphs. **1973** *Biomed. Engin.* VIII. 155/3 Regarding the opposing views on the skin-resistance channel; many practising polygraphers consider it to be too sensitive an indicator of emotional responses. **1978** 'W. WINGATE' *Bloodbath* ii. 25 Kruger watched the polygrapher flop into the easy chair.

polygraphic, *a.* Add: **5.** Of, pertaining to, or involving a polygraph (sense 3 in Dict. and Suppl.).

1871 *Lancet* 25 Nov. 741/2 When the capsule is pressed firmly upon the skin, the interior of the instrument is converted into a closed chamber, and every shock of the heart expels air out of the chamber into the polygraphic tambour. **1927** *Welfare Mag.* May 667/1 The exact value of this deception technique can only be determined by.. the study of all possible types of pathology associated with polygraphic reactions. **1954** *Reporter* (N.Y.) 8 June 13/2 The fear of being found out and/or conscious efforts to deceive are the main causes of significant reactions in polygraphic tests of deception. **1972** *Science* 29 Sept. 1205/3 Polygraphic sleep data were scored according to standardized criteria.

6. Applied to a cipher in which the letters of the plain text are enciphered or deciphered two or more at a time.

1929 L. S. HILL in *Amer. Math. Monthly* XXXVI. 312 If polygraphic ciphers based upon normal transformations (linear ciphers) prove to be of real interest, we shall indicate a surprising way in which these ciphers may be manipulated easily and quickly. **1967** D. KAHN *Codebreakers* xiii. 406 Such a system is genuinely polygraphic, and its cryptographic security is substantial. *Ibid.* 407 A polygraphic encipherment of this magnitude is possible only with a Hill transformation. **1968** A. SINKOV *Elem. Cryptanal.* iv. 113 A system of cryptography in which a group of *n* plain text letters is replaced as a unit by a group of *n* cipher letters is called a polygraphic system.

So **polygra·phically** *adv.*, by means of a polygraph.

1911 T. LEWIS *Mechanism of Heart Beat* v. 45 (*caption*) An irregularity due to premature contractions arising in the ventricle (the actual events were determined polygraphically). **1970** *Psychophysiol.* VII. 323/1 Plasma samples were obtained from 4 infants during four behavioral states..monitored polygraphically.

polygraphist. [f. POLYGRAPH + -IST.] = *POLYGRAPHER 3.

1954 *Reporter* (N.Y.) 8 June 13/2 Only thirty-six percent of the psychologists (as against seventy-five percent of the polygraphists) agreed with this statement.

polygraphy. Add: **3. c.** The use of a polygraph (sense 3).

1923 W. D. REID *Heart in Mod. Pract.* iii. 63 Polygraph tracings are also taken from the apex of the heart, the carotid artery, and over the liver, but their importance does not warrant description in this limited presentation of polygraphy. **1954** *Reporter* (N.Y.) 22 June 22/2 The most acute current problem in polygraphy..is how to set and maintain professional standards. **1973** *Biomed. Engin.* VIII. 155/3 To readers outside of the field of polygraphy, it will perhaps seem remarkable that electronic recording is not used for all three channels and that other physiological events are not recorded routinely.

polyhaploid: see *POLY- 1.

polyhedral, *a.* Add: **4.** *polyhedral disease* = *POLYHEDROSIS.

1913 *Jrnl. Econ. Entomol.* VI. 482 In Europe there is a tendency to group all the caterpillar diseases which are characterized by the formation of polyhedral bodies under the name of 'polyederkrankheit' or polyhedral diseases. **1971** *Indian Jrnl. Entomol.* XXXIII. 111 (*heading*) Investigations on the nuclear polyhedrosis of *Prodenia litura* Fabricius: I. Nature of the polyhedral disease.

polyhedroid: see *POLY- 1.

polyhedrosis (pǫlihīdrōu·sis, -hedrōu·sis). *Ent.* Pl. **-oses** (-ōu·sīz). [f. POLYHEDR(AL *a.* + -OSIS.] A fatal disease of caterpillars, characterized by the presence of polyhedral virus particles.

1947 *Science* 3 Oct. 323/2 The fragility of the integument and the marked internal liquefaction of tissues, so characteristic of polyhedroses, is absent. **1967** K. M. SMITH *Insect Virology* ii. 8 The polyhedroses are subdivided into nuclear and cytoplasmic diseases. **1973** *Nature* 2 Nov. 5/3 The outbreak tends to end abruptly in the spring of the third year, because of the explosive spread of a nuclear polyhedrosis virus which kills off some of the caterpillars at the end of their first moult (instar).

polyhex: see *POLY- 1.

polyhybrid (pǫlihəi·brid), *sb.* and *a.* *Biol.* [f. POLY- + HYBRID *sb.* and *a.*] **A.** *sb.* A hybrid that is heterozygous at several genetic loci. **B.** *adj.* Of, pertaining to, or characteristic of such a hybrid, or a cross resulting in one.

1911 FARMER & DARBISHIRE tr. *H. De Vries's Mutation Theory* II. 586 The di-polyhybrids are mongrels whose parents differ from one another in respect of two or more elementary characters. *Ibid.* 681/1 (Index), Polyhybrids, 586. **1922** *Hereditas* III. 233 The segregation is evidently polyhybrid showing transgression in one direction. **1965** BELL & COOMBE tr. *Strasburger's Textbk. Bot.* 334 The genetic consequences of crossing both dihybrids and polyhybrids are directly dependent upon the manner in which the chromosomes are distributed at the reductional division.

polyhydramnios (pǫ:lihəidræ·mniǫs). *Obstetrics.* [f. POLY- + HYDR(O- + AMNIOS.] = *HYDRAMNIOS.

1889 R. R. RENTOUL *Causes & Treatm. Abortion* iv. 114 Delore holds that polyhydramnios exists when the quantity exceeds four and two-tenths of a pint. *Ibid.* 115 In a few rare cases of twins, polyhydramnios was found with one child, while oligohydramnios accompanied the other. **1923** E. P. DAVIS *Complications of Pregnancy* xxi. 256 At the stage of fetal development, very often polyhydramnios may be mistaken for ascites as well as ovarian cyst. **1976** *Lancet* 30 Oct. 960/2 She was admitted to hospital with significant polyhydramnios.

polyhydric (pǫlihəi·drik), *a.* *Chem.* [f. POLY- + HYDRIC *a.*] Containing more than one hydroxyl group in the molecule.

1879 *Jrnl. Chem. Soc.* XXXVI. 1033 The action of sulphuric monochloride on monhydric alcohols gives rise to ethereal sulphates.., and a similar reaction takes place with polyhydric alcohols. **1937** *Discovery* Sept. 284/1 On this type of polyhydric phenol resin..a further..discovery has been made. **1946** *Nature* 3 Aug. 155/2 Manganese dioxide is reduced with great ease to form divalent manganese ion by..polyhydric phenols such as quinol, catechol, gallic acid, etc. **1951** I. L. FINAR *Org. Chem.* I. xi. 208 The polyhydric alcohols chemically resemble glycerol in many ways. **1972** *Materials & Technol.* V. ix. 266 The epoxy resins differ from most of the other polyhydric alcohols in that they are polymeric.

polyhydroxy(l, -iamond: see *POLY- 2, 1.

polyimide (pǫli,i·məid). [f. POLY- + IMIDE.] Any polymer in which the units contain imide groups, usu. in the form

$$\begin{array}{c} | \\ \text{—CO—N—CO—;} \end{array}$$

esp. any of a class of thermosetting resins widely used for heat-resistant films and coatings.

1945 *Brit. Pat.* 570,858, The products are referred to as polyamide-imides. When a tetracarboxylic acid of the above mentioned kind is used each pair of carboxyl groups reacts with an amino group of the diprimary diamine through imide-formation so that the polymer is a polyimide rather than a polyamide-imide. **1955** *U.S. Pat.* 2,710,853 1 This invention relates to a novel group of linear polymeric polyimides,..said polyimides differing from previously known polyimides in properties which are important in injection molding applications. **1965** *New Scientist* 19 Aug. 443/1 Du Pont's polyimide known as H-film, or Kapton, a plastic film that finds its chief use as a high-temperature electrical insulation. **1975** WEN-HSUAN CHANG et al. in M. Lewin et al. *Flame-Retardant Polymeric Materials* x. 442 Decorative coatings for cookware are possible with polyimide coatings because of their ability to withstand direct contact with flame.

polyion(ic, -isobutylene: see *POLY- 1, 2.

polyisocyanate (pǫ:li,əisosəi·ănēit). [f. POLY- + *isocyanate* s.v. *ISO- b.] Any organic compound containing two or more isocyanate groups; also applied to polymers prepared from such compounds, esp. polyurethanes.

1943 [see *POLYESTERAMIDE]. **1945** *Chem. & Engin. News* 25 Sept. 1615/2 The polyurethanes..are produced by the reaction of polyisocyanates with polyhydroxy compounds such as polyesters. **1958** *Times Rev. Industry* June 37/3 An I.C.I. special product known as Suprasec K is a 50 per cent. solution in ethyl acetate of a newly developed polyisocyanate designed for use in high-quality lacquers for wood, rubber, and other materials. **1959** *Times* 27 Apr. (Rubber Industry Suppl.) p. vi/7 Natural rubber, neoprene and polyisocyanates play the same part in ships as in hotels—for luxury upholstery, non-slipping table covering, fire-resisting foam bedding, floor covering, &c. **1968** E. R. WELLS in C. R. Martens *Technol. Paints, Varnishes & Lacquers* xiii. 205 Urethane is now the accepted description for a group of polymers that are sometimes called polyurethanes, isocyanates or polyisocyanates.

polyisoprene (pǫli,əi·soprīn). [f. POLY- + *ISOPRENE.] Any of the polymers of isoprene, which include the major constituent of natural rubber and some synthetic rubbers very similar to it.

1935 [see *polybutadiene* s.v. *POLY- 2]. **1946** F. MARCHIONNA *Butalastic Polymers* xvi. 483 The sodium butadiene rubber can be admixed with 50 per cent of a polyisoprene or purified natural rubber. **1959** *Economist* 21 Mar. 1101/1 Shell Chemical Corporation has announced that it will shortly begin commercial production of polyisoprene. **1963** H. R. CLAUSER *Encycl. Engin. Materials* 580/1 New 'synthetic natural rubber', *cis*-polyisoprene is said to have performance characteristics virtually identical with those of natural rubber. **1975** *Sci. Amer.* Dec. 101/1 Polymers that exhibit rubbery behaviour at room temperature include polyisoprene (natural rubber) and polybutadiene (a synthetic rubber).

polykaryocyte(-cytic): see *POLY- 1. **polylectal, -lingual(ism, -lithic, -lithionite:** see *POLY- 1.

polylogue (pǫ·lilǫg). [f. POLY- + -LOGUE.] A discussion between more than two persons.

1941 *Horizon* 15 Mar. 207 English people..tend to think of America..as a polylogue of cigars. **1961** *Lancet* 29 July 251/1 The polylogue here reported is not word-perfect, but the stenographer has tried to catch the to-and-fro of animated discussion. **1964** *Amer. Speech* XXXIX. 206 It is important as another voice in what has..become a 'polylogue' on a matter having wide interest. **1969** P. L. BERGER *Rumor of Angels* iv. 100 The ecumenical movement..has tried to bring Eastern Christianity more and more into the 'polylogue' (if the term will be permitted). **1977** *N.Y. Rev. Bks.* 23 June 30/2 For us there are dispersed, interchangeable 'points of view'; photography is a polylogue.

polylysine: see *POLY- 2.

polymastia (pǫlimæ·stiă). *Med.* Also anglicized as **-masty.** [mod.L., ad. G. *polymastie*, f. Gr. πολυ- POLY- + μαστός breast.] The condition of having more than two breasts (the supernumerary ones being generally very small). Cf. *POLYMASTISM.

1878 *Glasgow Med. Jrnl.* X. 70 Polymastia is not extremely rare in the female sex, but is so in the male. **1904** G. S. HALL *Adolescence* (1908) I. vi. 421 Polymasty or supernumerary breasts occurs about once in five hundred persons. **1928** M. SUMMERS *Discovery of Witches* 40 A large number of cases may be explained by polymastia and polythelia, anatomical divagations which are far commoner than is generally supposed. **1970** H. P. LEIS *Diagnosis & Treatm. Breast Lesions* i. 15 Polymastia, presenting as more than one breast on one or both sides, is due to the persistence of part of the milk ridge and these supernumerary breasts can occur anywhere along the milk line.

Hence **polyma·stic** *a.* and *sb.*, (a person or animal) having more than two breasts; **polyma·stoid** *a.* (*rare*).

1879 *Jrnl. Anat. & Physiol.* XIII. 434 In the dog, which is the only polymastoid animal readily available, the position of the nipples seems to be irregular and unsymetrical [*sic*]. **1891** *Ibid.* XXV. 228 The additional mammary structures do not develop just anywhere; but they appear only in certain definite positions, which almost invariably correspond with those occupied normally by the glands of polymastic animals. **1918** DEAVER & MCFARLAND *Breast* iii. 54 Robert..points out that the mother of his famous case of supernumerary mammae on the outer side of the thigh, was a polymastic. **1934** *Jrnl. R. Anthrop. Inst.* LXIV. 93 The best known examples of the first form are the paleolithic figures at Laussel and the polymastic Diana of the Ephesians. **1943** C. F. GESCHICKTER *Dis. Breast* i. 12 Most authors have found the majority of the accessory mammae below the normally situated pair... Iwai, however, in 511 Japanese polymastics, found 88 per cent. of the supernumerary breasts above the normal ones.

polyma·stism. *Med.* [f. as prec. + -ISM.] = *POLYMASTIA.

1886 W. N. PARKER tr. *Wiedersheim's Elem. Compar. Anat. Vertebr.* A. 28 The occasional existence in men of supernumerary teats, and in women of supernumerary mammæ and teats (polymastism and polythelism) is very remarkable. **1903** *Lancet* 28 Feb. 613/2 It may be concluded..that human polymastism is a reversion to a primitive condition in which many glands were developed and many young were brought forth at a birth. **1936** NEAL & RAND *Compar. Anat.* IV. 181 (*caption*) The presence of supernumerary teats (polymastism) in man supports the theory of the animal origin of the human body.

polymath, *sb.* (*a.*) **b.** *attrib.* or as *adj.* (Further examples.)

1919 T. S. ELIOT *Poems*, The masters of the subtle schools are controversial, polymath. **1959** *New Scientist* 15 Oct. 712/2 Polymath historians, who command the language and literature and science of the period. **1976** *Nature* 16 Sept. 261/3 The book is polymath, up-to-date and non-mathematical.

polymathic *a.* (further examples).

1976 *Publishers Weekly* 16 Feb. 82/2 Crichton's polymathic talent has settled on another exotic site for a fanciful story. **1976** S. HYNES *Auden Generation* viii. 259 A synthesizing, diagnostic, polymathic mind, given to schematizing knowledge and history in elaborate diagrams.

polymenorrhœa (pǫ:limenorī·ă). *Path.* Also **-rrhea.** [f. POLY- + MENORRHŒA.] Excessively frequent or unduly profuse menstrual bleeding.

1931 *Endocrinol.* XV. 180 The problem of polymenorrhea, too profuse and too frequent menses,..is a very vital one to the gynecologist. **1956** C. F. FLUHMANN *Managem. Menstrual Disorders* xvii. 196 Polymenorrhea may supervene as the result of an endocrine disorder such as hypothyroidism. **1964** L. MARTIN *Clin. Endocrinol.* (ed. 4) viii. 247 (*heading*) Polymenorrhoea and postponement of menstruation. **1968** VORYS & NERI in J. J. Gold *Textbk. Gynecol. Endocrinol.* xi. 253 Polymenorrhea may also be seen frequently as a premenopausal symptom.

Hence **polymenorrhœ·al, -rrhœ·ic** *adjs.*

1963 *Jrnl. Jap. Obstetr. & Gynecol. Soc.* X. 40/2 Frequency of corpus luteum insufficiency..differed according to the difference in the length of the cycle, being higher in polymenorrheal cycle of 15–24 days and in oligomenorrheal cycle of 39–43 days. **1968** VORYS & NERI in J. J. Gold *Textbk. Gynecol. Endocrinol.* xi. 261 Polymenorrheic cycles of less than 20 days.

polymer. Add: In mod. use, any substance which has a molecular structure built up largely or completely from a number (freq. very large) of similar polyatomic units bonded together. (Further examples.)

The repeating units are often molecules of a single compound, but polymers may also result from combination of two or more different constituents; in either case linking of units may be accompanied by elimination of small molecules, and the formula and molecular weight of the polymer are not necessarily exact multiples of those of any component monomer. Also, esp. in contexts of Applied Chemistry, the use of the term is sometimes restricted to cases where the number of units in the structure is large.

1929 W. H. CAROTHERS in *Jrnl. Amer. Chem. Soc.* LI. 2548 Whatever the term polymer may mean now, it does not mean precisely what Berzelius intended, and the conditions which he set up are not sufficient to define it. *Ibid.* 2549 Two types of polymers may be distinguished... (1) Addition or A polymers. The molecular formula of the monomer is identical with that of the structural unit... (2) Condensation or C polymers: the molecular formula of the monomer differs from that of the structural unit. **1935** C. ELLIS *Chem. Synthetic Resins* I. iv. 53 In a condensation reaction, the polymer is no longer a multiple of the monomer as in the case of the addition polymer. **1958** *Times* 21 Nov. 5/6 All of them are formed by the joining together of simpler molecules; they are therefore polymers, as are plastics and synthetic fibres. **1967** MARGERISON & EAST *Introd. Polymer Chem.* iii. 131 As the conversion of the monomers into polymer proceeds, the number of possible ways in which the monomers may add on to the growing polymer increases rapidly. **1969** *Times* 3 July 7/7 The substance is a polymer of ordinary water molecules linked together by an unusual kind of chemical bond. **1973** *Nature* 6 Apr. 420/1 Natural rubber is still the preferred polymer for many high performance applications. **1974** *Sci. Amer.* Mar. 66/3 Glass is an inorganic polymer made up of rings and chains of repeating silicate units. **1974** D. M. ADAMS *Inorg. Solids* vii. 239 The most stable polymers for other metals are $M_6O_{19}^{8-}$ (M = Nb, Ta), $Mo_7O_{24}^{6-}$, $Mo_8O_{26}^{4-}$ and $HW_6O_{21}^{5-}$. **1978** *Prospects for Polymers* (Shell Internat. Petroleum Co.)1 Not all polymers are man-made: wool, rubber, cotton and silk are examples of natural polymers.

2. *attrib.* and *Comb.*, as *polymer chemistry*, that branch of chemistry concerned with the preparation and properties of polymers; so *polymer chemist*.

1929 *Industr. & Engin. Chem.* Feb. 131/1 Beyond certain degrees of polymerization x-ray methods do not longer enable estimations of polymer length. **1933** *Ibid.* Feb. 132/1 Development of the best binder—be it resin or another member of the polymer family—is the next step. **1948** *Science* 19 Nov. 545/2 In recent years polymer chemists have shown how it is possible to synthesize compounds of high molecular weight..from known compounds (monomers) of low molecular weight. **1950** *Nature* 22 Apr. 634/1 (*heading*) Polymer chemistry as applied to plastics. **1953** *Endeavour* Apr. 92/1 In terms of polymer-chemistry concepts, the molecular shape is changed by the electrostatic field. **1966** C. R. TOTTLE *Sci. Engin. Materials* p. vi, An enormous quantity of synthetic polymer materials has replaced much of the metal in the domestic kitchen, leather, wool, and cotton in furnishings, and natural rubber, wood, and metal in vehicles, prime movers. **1967** MARGERISON & EAST *Introd. Polymer Chem.* i. 16 However, in the case of a real polymer chain, the finite size of the backbone carbon atoms and the substituents cannot be neglected. *Ibid.* 22 Polymer molecules in the pure liquid state can easily be pictured in the terms used to describe concentrated solutions. **1975** *Nature* 31 July 443/3 For those wishing to get a feel for what is going on in a selection of other areas of polymer science this volume will provide much of interest.

polymerase (pǫ·limĕrēiz, pǫ̆li·mĕrēiz). *Biochem.* [f. POLYMER + *-ASE.] Any enzyme which catalyses the formation of a polymer, esp. a polynucleotide.

1958 I. R. LEHMAN et al. in *Jrnl. Biol. Chem.* CCXXXIII. 163/2 In order to facilitate reference in this report, the enzyme responsible for deoxyribonucleotide incorporation is designated as 'polymerase'. **1964** *New Scientist* 23 Jan. 211/1 DNA has been bio-synthesised from its four basic building blocks put together with the enzyme polymerase and some natural DNA to act as a template. **1973** B. J. WILLIAMS *Evolution & Human Origins* vi. 89/1 RNA polymerase is active when the cell is carrying on its normal metabolic functions.

polymeria, var. *POLYMERY.

polymeric, *a.* Add: In mod. use, of the nature of or characteristic of a polymer; consisting of a polymer or polymers. Of a reaction: giving rise to a polymer. Cf. *POLYMER. (Earlier and later examples.)

1833 *Rep. Brit. Assoc. Adv. Sci. 1831–32* 435 To designate compounds approaching in atomic constitution very nearly to those properly called Isomeric, Berzelius has proposed the introduction of two new terms, polymeric and metameric. **1845** W. GREGORY *Outl. Chem.* II. 394 Hydrated lactic acid is a syrupy liquid... It is..polymeric with dry grape sugar and with gum. **1935** C. ELLIS *Chem. Synthetic Resins* I. ix. 169 Natural rubber is supposed to consist of a mixture of polymeric hydrocarbons. **1941** MARK & RAFF (*title*) High polymeric reactions. **1951** UVAROV & CHAPMAN *Dict. Sci.* (ed. 2) 171 Many important products, such as plastics and textile fibres, consist of polymeric substances, either natural (e.g. cellulose..) or synthetic (e.g. nylon). **1967** MARGERISON & EAST *Introd. Polymer Chem.* iii. 137 At the early stages of the reaction, the mixture consists mainly of low molecular weight species, dimers, trimers, etc., with only a few molecules of polymeric size. **1974** *Environmental Conservation* I. 63/1 The term resin is usually applied to the long chains of repeating units in the polymeric material.

2. *Genetics.* Of, pertaining to, or displaying polymery.

1949 DARLINGTON & MATHER *Elem. Genetics* iii. 68 Genes such as those with which Nilsson-Ehle was concerned have two of the properties of polygenes. They are of similar and supplementary action. But they cannot be described as polygenes because their effects are so large as to cause a sharp discontinuity in the variation, a discontinuity which permits the analysis of the system by the mendelian method. Genes like these are often termed polymeric genes. All polygenes are therefore polymeric, but not all polymeric genes are polygenes. **1961** [see *POLYGENIC *a.* 3]. **1970** *Genetika* VI. x. 124 It is established that complementary maltose factors MA_{1-p} and MA_{2-g} are recessive alleles of polymeric genes, MA_1 and MA_2, respectively.

polymeride. Add: (Later examples.) Now †*Obs.*

1906 *Nature* 21 June 190/2 A semi-solid brown substance..formed when acetylene is subjected to discharges... It is apparently a polymeride of acetylene. **1943** R. HILL in R. S. Morrell et al. *Synthetic Resins* (ed. 2) v. 194 A defect of polystyrene is a tendency for mouldings and castings to develop fine cracks... It is said that this is due to the evaporation of low molecular weight polymerides.

polymerism. Add: Now †*Obs.* **1.** (Earlier example.)

1833 *Rep. Brit. Assoc. Adv. Sci. 1831–32* 435 (*heading*) Polymerism and metamerism.

polymerizable (pǫ·limĕrəizăb'l), *a. Chem.* [f. POLYMERIZ(E *v.* + -ABLE.] Capable of being polymerized. Hence **po:lymerizabi·lity.**

1884 *Jrnl. Chem. Soc.* XLV. 419 Just as the pentine is polymerisable by heat or by the action of sulphuric acid into a dipentine, so the heptine may be converted into a diheptine. **1928** *Proc. & Trans. R. Soc. Canada* XXII. III. 39 The influence of methyl substitution on the polymerizability of butadiene. *Ibid.*, Both the α- and the β-methyl butadienes are polymerizable to caoutchoucs. **1939** *Brit. Plastics* XI. 320/1 Methacrylic acid amide copolymerized with other polymerizable compounds. **1948** C. E. H. BAWN *Chem. High Polymers* i. 15 The polymerizability of diolefins is determined by the relative positions of the double bonds. **1963** A. J. HALL *Textile Sci.* ii. 88 It [*sc.* acrylonitrile] very readily undergoes polymerisation by itself (homopolymerisation) and with other polymerisable compounds (copolymerisation). **1978** (*title*) Solventless polymerizable resinous compounds used for electrical insulation. (Brit. Standards Inst.)

polymerizate (pǫ·limĕrəizēⁱt). [f. next + *-ate*, after *filtrate*, *precipitate*, etc.] A product or mixture of products obtained from a polymerization reaction or process.

1931 *Brit. Chem. Abstr.* B. 264/1 By polymerising a mixture of an aliphatic conjugated diolefine such as butadiene..with styrene..an intimately mixed polymerisate is obtained. **1959** *Times Rev. Industry* Feb. 57/1 The later Ziegler developments in the higher olefin field relate only to a process which yields polymerisates of practically no commercial interest. **1973** *Materials & Technol.* VI. viii. 558 The polymerizates of acrylic acid,.. methacrylic acid,..and their derivatives such as acrylonitrile,..are known collectively as acrylics.

polymerize, *v.* Add: **1.** Cf. *POLYMER. (Further examples.)

1867 *Proc. R. Soc.* XVI. 158 If we remember the facility with which the aldehydes are polimerized [*sic*], the question presents itself, whether the aldehyde formed by the slow combustion of methylic alcohol is represented by the formula CH_2O, or a multiple thereof. **1893** [see *AFTERGLOW b]. **1910** *Encycl. Brit.* X. 667/2 It is not possible to obtain the aldehyde in a pure condition, since it readily polymerizes. **1930** H. F. LEWIS *Fund. Org. Chem.* viii. 95 Three molecules of acetaldehyde polymerize under the influence of a small amount of concentrated sulfuric acid. **1936** H. W. ROWELL *Technol. Plastics* ix. 57 The primary ester may be polymerized by heating in the presence of a peroxide catalyst. **1957** *Times* 10 Sept. 11/1 The effect was to produce reactive groups which could be used to polymerize a different material with the result that mixed polymers of very varied properties could be produced. **1971** *Brit. Printer* Jan. 64/2 The use of ultra-violet radiation for polymerising polyester wood lacquers has been known for some time. **1972** *Nature* 18 Feb. 404/3 This leads into a subsidiary argument: which were the first to polymerize, amino-acids or polynucleotides?

polymerization (earlier and later examples); also, the state of being polymeric; hence also **po·lymerized** *ppl. a.*, **po·lymerizing** *vbl. sb.* and *ppl. a.* Also **po·lymerizer,** an apparatus or installation in which polymerization occurs.

1867 BLOXAM *Chem.* 665/2 (Index), Polymerising by sulphuric acid. **1872** *Jrnl. Chem. Soc.* XXV. 433 Besides the olefines which are derived from compounds having the general formula $C_nH_{2n+1}R$ (R representing a monad radical), by the abstraction of HR, there exists another group, formed by the polymerisation of the members of the first group. **1879** *Ibid.* XXXV. 743 We purposely avoided distilling the polymerised product until entirely freed from substances volatile in a current of steam. **1923** B. D. W. LUFF *Chem. of Rubber* vii. 74 In the meantime it had been observed that not only isoprene but many other unsaturated hydrocarbons were capable of polymerising. **1929** *Jrnl. Amer. Chem. Soc.* LI. 2549 Polymerization then is the chemical union of many similar molecules either..without or..with the elimination of simpler molecules. **1930** *Chem. Abstr.* XXIV. 612 $SnCl_4$ was employed as the polymerizing agent. **1933** *Industr. & Engin. Chem.* Feb. 126/2 The length and shape of the chain must be considered when comparing two different resins or the same resin in different degrees of polymerization. **1940** A. N. SACHANEN *Conversion of Petroleum* i. 64 The absorption of olefins by sulphuric acid and the polymerization take place in the reactor. No special polymerizer is necessary. **1945** A. T. BIRKBY *Phenolic Plastics* ii. 16 The larger or polymerised molecule possesses different physical properties from the constituent smaller molecules. **1946** J. GRANT in *Mod. Petroleum Technol.* (Inst. Petroleum) 165 In the separator the acid phase settles to the bottom and is withdrawn to the polymerizer. **1950** *Thorpe's Dict. Appl. Chem.* (ed. 4) X. 21/1 A polymerising unit of such polyfunctionality that gelation will ensue through the cross-linking which accompanies the oxidation. **1956** *Atlantic Monthly* Sept. 24/3 It is a polymerized ethylene glycol that differs from what you pour into your radiator only in being solid at room temperature. **1965** P. W. MORGAN *Condensation Polymers* iii. 107 Many continuous polymerizers are comprised of a cascade system of reactors or a reacting chamber provided with high-speed stirring followed by a larger holding reservoir with lower speed agitation. **1967** MARGERISON & EAST *Introd. Polymer Chem.* iii. 146 When 50% of the original carboxylic acid groups have reacted, the average degree of polymerization has only doubled. **1971** *Brit. Printer* Jan. 65/1 These highly reactive molecular units can then react with unsaturation in resin molecules to cause polymerisation and hence drying. **1974** E. AMBLER *Dr. Frigo* II. 112 Polymerisation is..a change of state, a molecular rearrangement. Raw rubber becomes vulcanized rubber, say... The second is a polymer of the first. **1977** *Lancet* 19 Nov. 1070/2 How much of a toxic gas such as vinyl chloride will escape from the polymeriser pots where it is turned into P.V.C.?

polymery (pǫli·mĕri). *Genetics.* Also as mod. L. **polyme·ria.** [ad. G. *polymerie* (A. Lang 1911, in *Zeitschr. für induktive Abstammungs- und Vererbungslehre* V. 113), ad. Gk. πολυμέρεια a consisting of many parts: see -IA[1], -Y[3].] The phenomenon whereby a number of non-allelic genes can act together to produce a single effect.

1914 *Zeitschr. für induktive Abstammungs- und Vererbungslehre* XII. 118 The phenomenon of plurality of genes having a similar function, i.e., independently producing the same character, is called by Lang (1911) 'polymery'... Johannsen (1913) suggests that..[this term] be retained..for the phenomenon in general. **1927** [see *POLYGENIC *a.* 3]. **1929** [see *ISOLATION 3].

polymetallic: see *POLY- 1. **polymeter** var. *POLYMETER. **polymethacrylate, -acrylic:** see *POLY- 2.

polymethyl (pǫlime·þil, -mī·þəil). [f. POLY- + METHYL.] **a.** *polymethyl acrylate* (also as one word): a resinous material obtained by polymerizing the methyl ester of acrylic acid.

1936 *Industr. & Engin. Chem.* Oct. 269/2 Polymethyl acrylate is a colorless, transparent substance. **1950** *Thorpe's Dict. Appl. Chem.* (ed. 4) X. 107/1 Polymethyl acrylate is a tough, transparent, and colourless material, highly extensible, and to a limited degree rubber-like. **1973** *Materials & Technol.* VI. viii. 559 The softening point of polymethylmethacrylate lies accordingly about 90 degrees higher than that of polymethylacrylate.

b. *polymethyl methacrylate* (also as one word): = *methyl methacrylate* (*b*) s.v. *METHYL.

1936 *Industr. & Engin. Chem.* Oct. 270/1 Polymethyl methacrylate is a very hard, tough mass which can be sawed, carved, or worked on a lathe with ease. **1942** *Endeavour* I. 111/2 Cellulose acetate and polymethylmethacrylate are fabricated into cockpit covers..for aircraft by this process. **1960** *Times* 2 Sept. 14/1 They could be eating sandwiches from polyethylene packs with polymethylmethacrylate dentures. **1965** ZIGROSSER & GAEHDE *Guide to Collecting Orig. Prints* vii. 111 The most durable are the acrylic sheets, particularly Plexiglas (polymethyl methacrylate), which is produced in thicknesses from 1·5 to 25·0 mm. **1973** [see sense a above]. **1975** *Sci. Amer.* Dec. 96/2 Familiar thermoplastic polymers include polyethylene,..polymethyl methacrylate,.. and nylon.

polymethylene (pǫlime·þilīn). *Chem.* [f. POLY- + METHYLENE.] A compound, group, or polymeric structure which consists of or contains a chain of methylene groups, $—(CH_2)_n—$; orig. *spec.* any of the series of saturated cyclic hydrocarbons of formula $(CH_2)_n$. Freq. *attrib.*

1892 *Jrnl. Chem. Soc.* LXII. 1310 In this paper the author discusses the question of the identity of the naphthenes from Caucasus petroleum and the polymethylenes. *Ibid.*, The naphthenes in general may also include derivatives of other polymethylene rings. **1910** N. V. SIDGWICK *Org. Chem. Nitrogen* ii. 21 In the polymethylene derivatives the ring is often affected. **1930** *Jrnl. Amer. Chem. Soc.* LII. 317 Those poly-esters in which the structural units contain polymethylene chains $(CH_2)_x$, in which x is greater than 3–5, show great solubility in benzene. **1953** R. J. W. REYNOLDS in R. Hill *Fibres from Synthetic Polymers* v. 98 Other addition reactions which can give rise to linear polymers are those involving the polymerisation of..diazomethane or diazoalkanes to give polymethylenes or their alkyl substituted products. **1967** MARGERISON & EAST *Introd. Polymer*

Chem. i. 17 Taking a portion of the polymethylene chain as the simplest case, the configuration..in which the CH_2 groups on adjacent carbon atoms are staggered relative to one another is more frequently assumed.. than any other.

polymetre (pǫ·limītəɪ). *Mus.* Also (*U.S.*) **-meter.** [f. POLY- + METRE *sb.*[1]] **a.** The succession of different metrical patterns in sixteenth-century vocal music. **b.** Music using two or more different time-signatures simultaneously. So **polyme·tric, -me·trical** *adjs.*; also **po·lymetered** *a.*

1922 S. GREW in *Contemp. Rev.* Aug. 226 The first voice of the above has a 'metre' of four pulses, the second has a 'metre' of three; on the authority of the musical terms *polyphonic* and *polytonic*, I have ventured to coin and use the word *polymetrical*. Students of polymetre do not appear to have sufficiently considered the fact that in certain words Elizabethan accent was different from ours. **1944** W. APEL *Harvard Dict. Mus.* 594/1 Twice in the history of music have polymetric designs played a prominent role: around 1400, and in present-day music. **1946** R. BLESH *Shining Trumpets* (1949) 344 The second type of rhythmic peculiarity, technically known as a polymetric, is the cross-rhythm or overrhythm. **1947** W. RUSSELL in R. de Toledano *Frontiers of Jazz* 60 The ability of Lux to create great swing and rhythmic effect from apparently so simple a polymetrical device. **1966** C. KEIL in T. Kochman *Rappin' & Stylin' Out* (1972) 90 It is a subjective pulse that Richard Waterman is speaking of when he uses the concept 'metronome sense' as the ordering principle in the polymetered rhythms of West African ensembles. In jazz groups polymeter or even a sense of polymeter may or may not exist, but the subjective pulse or metronomic sense remains. **1970** P. OLIVER *Savannah Syncopators* 15 These [*sc.* characteristics of African music] included: dominance of percussion; polymeter; off-beat phrasing of melodic accents [etc.].

polymicrian: see *POLY- I.

polymict (pǫ·limikt), *a. Petrol.* [f. POLY- + Gr. μικτ-ός mixed, perh. after G. *polymikt* (H. Rosenbusch *Elemente der Gesteinlehre* (1898) 17).] = *POLYMICTIC *a.* 1.

[**1931** A. JOHANNSEN *Descr. Petrogr. Igneous Rocks* I. i. 7 Rocks may be composed of a single mineral only..or they may be composed of aggregates of several minerals. The former are called monomineral rocks by Vogt and monomikt by Rosenbusch, and the latter polymikt by Rosenbusch.] **1952** W. WAHL in *Geochim. et Cosmochim. Acta* II. 91 It is proposed to call..breccias in which the enclosed fragments are of a foreign material as compared with the surrounding principal mass of stone..'polymict breccias'. **1958** *Proc. Geologists' Assoc.* LXIX. 85 Two kinds of conglomerate are worth distinguishing, first the oligomict..and, second, the polymict, with a variety of pebbles of unstable rocks undergoing decay and most likely formed by rapid deposition of material worn quickly from high mountains. **1973** *Phil. Trans. R. Soc.* A. CCLXXIII. 392 The conglomerates are characterized by the extreme polymict nature of the boulders, cobbles and pebbles. **1975** TINDALL & THORNHILL *Rock & Mineral Guide* III. 167 A rock with grains of various materials is polymict.

polymictic (pǫlimi·ktik), *a.* [f. as prec. + -IC.] **1.** *Petrol.* [ad. Russ. *polimiktovȳĭ* (M. S. Shvetsov *Petrografiya Osadochnȳkh Porod* (1934) viii. 155).] (See quot. 1935.)

1935, 1949 [see *OLIGOMICTIC *a.* 1]. **1959** W. W. MOORHOUSE *Study of Rocks in Thin Section* xix. 337 The polymictic conglomerate..comprises a great variety of pebbles, including granite, schist, sediments such as shale, slate, sandstone, and even limestone. **1969** S. H. HAUGHTON *Geol. Hist. Southern Afr.* iv. 89 At various horizons above the Intermediate Reefs bands of polymictic conglomerates occur.

2. *Limnology.* Applied to a lake that has no stable thermal stratification but exhibits perennial circulation.

1956 [see *OLIGOMICTIC *a.* 2]. **1966** *McGraw-Hill Encycl. Sci. & Technol.* V. 523/2 In addition there are.. low-altitude tropical oligomictic lakes with irregular circulation, and high-altitude tropical polymictic lakes with continuous circulation.

polymineral: see *POLY- I.

polymitosis (pǫlimaitōᵘ·sis). *Biol.* [f. POLY- + MITOSIS.] The occurrence of multiple mitotic cell divisions, esp. following meiosis in microsporogenesis; one of these divisions. So **polymito·tic** *a.*, pertaining to, affected by, or being such cell divisions.

1931 G. W. BEADLE *Mem. Cornell Agric. Exper. Station* No. 135. 3 This genetic factor..has been given the name *polymitotic* for which the genetic symbol *po* is used. *Ibid.*, On first thought, the term *polymitotic* may seem to be inappropriate on the grounds that normal maize plants have many mitoses. It may be pointed out that the polymitotic character is expressed only in the gametophytic generation in which there are normally but two mitotic divisions in maize. **1932** C. D. DARLINGTON *Recent Adv. Cytol.* xiii. 367 This property of having 'polymitosis' is inherited as a mendelian recessive character. **1937** *Ibid.* (ed. 2) ix. 399 The spermatids are originally tetraploid through double non-reduction and by three polymitotic divisions become 32*x*. **1948** *Nature* 5 June 874/1 Plants heterozygous for this gene must produce two genetically different kinds of pollen, one of which will be like the lethal polymitotic pollen borne on the homozygous plant. But none of this pollen shows polymitotic behaviour. Thus polymitosis is like incompatibility in heterostyled plants. **1973** *Cytologia* XXXVIII. 515 A gene responsible for supernumerary cell division following meiosis which Beadle..termed the polymitotic division gene (po). *Ibid.* 518 Postmeiotic polymitoses were observed in reciprocal interspecific hybrids between two diploid *Clarkia* species... The genetic system responsible for these polymitoses is most likely not a simple recessive gene as is the case in maize but rather genic disharmony between the two parental sets of chromosomes.

polymixin, var. *POLYMYXIN.

polymodal (pǫlimōᵘ·dăl), *a.* [f. POLY- + MOD(E *sb.* + -AL.] **1.** *Mus.* Of, pertaining to, or designating music using two or more modes.

1929 W. W. COBBETT *Cycl. Survey Chamber Music* I. 44/1 Since we are polymodal as well as polytonal, each of these combinations may take the following four different forms according as one or the other triad is major or minor. **1938** *Scrutiny* VII. 174 It becomes quite obvious that his [*sc.* Roussel's] polymodal melodic thinking must condition his scheme of harmony. **1957** W. MELLERS *Romanticism & 20th Cent.* II. v. 157 Roussel in his later work has more self-consciously to recover a tradition: which may explain the more strenuous quality of his (often polymodal) melodic power.

2. = *MULTIMODAL *a.* a.

1934 *Jrnl. Sedimentary Petrol.* IV. 73/1 Curve *C* represents a glacial till, in which more than one mode occurs, and is an example of a polymodal frequency curve. **1975** *Nature* 28 Aug. 723/1 In general it seems that cells of different sizes, whether they follow a normal or a polymodal distribution, are randomly distributed throughout the tissue.

Hence **polymoda·lity** = *MULTIMODALITY; **polymo·dally** *adv.*

1929 W. W. COBBETT *Cycl. Survey Chamber Music* I. 38/2 It is at this point that polymodality commences to impinge upon polytonality. *Ibid.* 45/2 A total of five major and five minor keys, representing polymodally six tonalities. **1934** C. LAMBERT *Music Ho!* v. 289 The slow destruction of the key system that we find in Milhaud's polytonality or Vaughan Williams' polymodality. **1952** R. STEVENSON *Music in Mexico* i. 7 For those whose ears have become conditioned by long familiarity with the European diatonic system, the 'polymodality' of indigenous music inevitably sounds as if it were 'polytonality'. **1962** *Lancet* 26 May 1092/2 Hoobler's remarks, together with the recent discussions about polymodality in frequency distributions of blood-pressure, prompted me to examine some experimental data on 'pressor responses'. **1975** *Nature* 28 Aug. 724/1 Techniques based on sorting cells after digestion of the tissue would certainly reveal polymodality.

polymolecular (pǫlimǒle·kiŭlăɪ), *a. Chem.* [ad. G. *polymolekular* (Van 't Hoff & Cohen *Studien zu chem. Dynamik* (1896) 4): see MOLECULAR *a.*] **a.** In chemical kinetics: having or pertaining to an order or a molecularity of more than one.

1896 T. EWAN tr. *Van 't Hoff & Cohen's Stud. Chem. Dynamics* 4 We will call a change in which the interaction of several molecules is required, polymolecular. **1896** *Jrnl. Chem. Soc.* LXX. II. 158 (*heading*) The velocity law of polymolecular reactions. **1937** *Jrnl. Amer. Chem. Soc.* LIX. 2539/2 The polymolecular nature of the solvolysis is strongly evidenced by the fact that it occurs only with a high concentration of hydroxylic molecules.

b. Consisting of or built up from more than one molecule.

1930 *Jrnl. Amer. Chem. Soc.* LII. 4110 The direct preparation of this anhydride by the removal of water from the acid should give a polymolecular product. **1936** *Trans. Faraday Soc.* XXXII. 116 Oleic acid is bimolecular in apolar solvents, and forms polymolecular micelles in aqueous alkaline solution.

c. With reference to a film or layer: being more than one molecule in thickness. Of adsorption: characterized by the formation of such a layer.

1931 *Jrnl. Physical Chem.* XXXV. 869 There was no evidence that the layer of adsorbed molecules was of polymolecular thickness. **1931** J. W. MCBAIN *Sorption of Gases & Vapours by Solids* x. 325 Such built-up polymolecular layers differ in principle from the third conception,..that all the molecules coming within a certain range of the solid are directly attracted. **1972** M. M. DUBININ in F. Ricca *Adsorption–Desorption Phenomena* 4 On the surface of intermediate pores there occurs monomolecular and polymolecular adsorption of vapours.

d. Consisting of macromolecules which have similar polymeric structures but differing molecular weights. Cf. *POLYDISPERSE *a.*

1940 *Chem. Abstr.* XXXIV. 1228 Such compds. of high mol. wt. are also polymolecular and yield polydisperse solns. Since compds. whose mols. are identical with respect to structure and mol. wt...may form in soln. colloidal particles of varying size, polydispersivity is a condition or state whereas polymer homogeneity and polymolecularity are properties of mols. **1943** H. M. SPURLIN in E. Ott *Cellulose* V. ix. 930 The expression 'polymolecular' is preferable to 'polydisperse' as a term to describe systems composed of molecules all having substantially the same chemical composition and mode of linkage but differing in chain length. **1970** FOCK & FRIED tr. *Staudinger's From Org. Chem. to Macromolecules* 116 In order to characterize a polymolecular macromolecular material with accuracy, it is necessary to know its distribution and to determine how many low and high molecular parts it contains. **1976** H.-G. ELIAS in K. Solc *Order in Polymer Solutions* 218 Most synthetic polymers are polymolecular, *i.e.*, the unimers possess a distribution of degrees of polymerization.

Hence **polymolecula·rity**, the condition or property of being polymolecular (esp. in sense *d); as a back-formation **polymo·lecule,** a polymeric molecule.

1938 *Chem. Abstr.* XXXII. 2810 A distinction is made between the terms polydispersion and polymolecularity. **1940** [see sense d above]. **1943** H. M. SPURLIN in E. Ott *Cellulose* V. ix. 930 The quantitative relationships between such physical properties as viscosity in solution, physical strength, and flexibility of films may differ as the degree of polymolecularity is changed. **1951** *Jrnl. Polymer Sci.* VII. 400 Let us take a momentary picture of an assembly of equal polymolecules of polymerization degree *P* each carrying *ν* charged groups. **1964** *Biophysical Jrnl.* IV. I. Suppl. 11 As a first demonstration of the joint operation of polymeric and electrical properties within polyelectrolyte molecules, we shall consider the shape dynamics of charged polymolecules. **1976** H.-G. ELIAS in K. Solc *Order in Polymer Solutions* 218 The problem on [*sic*] how the polymolecularity of the unimers influences the polydispersity of the multimers has been solved recently for end-to-end and segment-to-segment associations.

polymorph. Add: **1.** (Later examples.) Also *attrib.*

1950 *Evolution* IV. 298/1 There is an interesting correlation between habitat differences and shifts in polymorph frequencies. **1958** *Proc. Zool. Soc.* CXXXI. 87 Comparisons are often made between different polymorphs in the same population. **1975** *Zool. Jrnl.* CLXXVII. 334 This species [sc. *Charaxes zoolina*] is a simple dual polymorph with respect to wing shape.

2. (Examples.) In mod. use, each of the different forms of such a substance.

1902 *Jrnl. Chem. Soc.* LXXXII. II. 448 With polymorphs..a quite different behaviour is observed. The melting point of the stable form is scarcely altered by the addition of the unstable modification. **1944** [see *EDISONITE]. **1957** G. E. HUTCHINSON *Treat. Limnol.* I. x. 660 $CaCO_3$ exists under ordinary conditions in nature in two crystalline polymorphs, calcite and aragonite. **1973** *Nature* 23 Mar. 241/1 Anhydrite, $CaSO_4$, is the higher temperature polymorph of calcium sulphate.

3. (Further examples.)

1970 *Nature* 5 Sept. 1052/1 Red cells, monocytes and the majority of polymorphs had grain densities within the range of control preparations. **1977** *Lancet* 29 Jan. 225/1 Evidence indicates that steroids prevent the accumulation of macrophages and polymorphs in inflammatory areas.

polymorphemic: see *POLY- I.

polymorphic, *a.* Add: **2.** (Later examples.)

1925 A. D. IMMS *Gen. Textbk. Entomol.* III. 257 Termites live together in large communities composed of polymorphic individuals. **1940** E. B. FORD in J. S. Huxley *New Systematics* 503 Though polymorphic forms are to be distinguished from geographical variation, they may be a function of it. **1976** R. A. GOLDSBY *Basic Biol.* XX. 330/1 (*caption*) Polymorphic variation in one species of snail, *Helicella virgata*: different banded and unbanded forms on one plant.

3. *Chem.* and *Min.* = POLYMORPHOUS *a.* 3 (in Dict. and Suppl.).

Now the more usual adj. in this sense.

1895 C. S. PALMER tr. *Nernst's Theoret. Chem.* I. iii. 86 The different polymorphic modifications may exist together..if they are not easily convertible into each other, as diamond and graphite. **1924** A. E. HILL in H. S. Taylor *Treat. Physical Chem.* I. ix. 380 At high pressures there exist several polymorphic forms of ice, differing from the common variety in density, heat of formation, crystalline structure and other physical properties. **1974** K. FRYE *Mod. Mineral.* ii. 83 Quartz, tridymite, and cristobalite have high- and low-temperature polymorphs... The high–low polymorphic inversion is rapid and nonquenchable, since it involves no rupture of Si–O bonds.

polymorphism. Add: **2.** (Later examples.)

1913 *Phil. Trans. R. Soc.* B. CCIV. 227 The following paper gives an account of a series of breeding experiments..in the course of one and a half years' research on insect polymorphism. **1940** E. B. FORD in J. S. Huxley *New Systematics* 505 It is important to distinguish true polymorphism..from the existence of multiple phases attained at different stages of development. **1976** R. A. GOLDSBY *Biol.* xxiii. 552/2 Recent analysis of enzymes and other proteins has..revealed a previously unsuspected number of genetic polymorphisms in protein chains.

3. (Earlier and later examples.)

1848 *Mem. & Proc. Chem. Soc.* III. 93 (*heading*) Dimorphism and polymorphism. **1966** PHILLIPS & WILLIAMS *Inorg. Chem.* II. xix. 7 Polymorphism is commonly found among metals, and for one metal there is in general very little difference in energy between one structure and another. **1971** I. G. GASS et al. *Understanding Earth* iii. 60/2 This property, polymorphism, occurs in the minerals of the mantle.

polymorpho-. Add: **polymorpho-nuclear** *a.* (usu. written as one word), also used esp. to designate a class of leucocyte (see quot. 1968); also *ellipt.* as *sb.*; (earlier and later examples).

1897 R. C. CABOT *Clin. Exam. Blood* I. v. 49 Next in age come the cells usually known as 'polynuclear' but more properly called *polymorphonuclear neutrophiles.*

These cells constitute the vast majority of those found in ordinary pus. **1903** *Amer. Jrnl. Med. Sci.* CXXVI. 190 A differential count of the leucocytes shows a slight increase in the polymorphonuclears and a diminution in the small mononuclears since the previous record. **1950** *Brain* LXXIII. 144 An early puncture gave 10 polymorphonuclears and 3 lymphocytes per c.mm. **1961** R. D. BAKER *Essent. Path.* ii. 12 The inflammatory lesion is rich first in polymorphonuclear cells and later in macrophages. **1968** PASSMORE & ROBSON *Compan. Med. Stud.* I. xxvi. 2/1 There are three varieties of white cell, the polymorphonuclear leucocyte or polymorph, the lymphocyte and the monocyte.

polymorphous, *a.* Add: **2.** (Later example.)
1928 C. K. OGDEN tr. *Forel's Social World of Ants* II. v. 337 The formicary is a society of females and their polymorphous derivative forms.
3. (Earlier and later examples.) Also, of or pertaining to polymorphism (sense 3).
1848 *Mem. & Proc. Chem. Soc.* III. 57 (*heading*) On the relation in volumes between simple bodies, their oxides and sulphurets, and on the differences exhibited by polymorphous and allotropic substances. **1895** C. S. PALMER tr. *Nernst's Theoret. Chem.* I. iii. 86 The different kinds of crystals of a polymorphous substance, are to be regarded as different modifications analogous to the different states of aggregation. **1906** J. P. IDDINGS *Rock Minerals* I. i. 19 Silica (SiO_2) is certainly dimorphous and possibly polymorphous. **1964** J. SINKANKAS *Mineral. for Amateurs* vi. 170 Another polymorphous pair also shows marked though less striking differences in hardness: calcite (H $2\frac{1}{2}$–3) and aragonite (H $3\frac{1}{2}$–4).
5. *Psychol.* Phr. *polymorphous-perverse,* polymorphously perverse (see next); so *polymorphous perversity.*
1909 A. A. BRILL tr. *Freud's Sel. Papers on Hysteria* ix. 191 The constitutional sexual predisposition of the child is more irregularly multifarious than one would expect, that it deserves to be called 'polymorphous-perverse', and that from this predisposition the so-called normal behavior of the sexual functions results through a repression of certain components. **1910** —— tr. *Freud's Three Contrib. to Sexual Theory* II. 49 Under the influence of seduction the child may become polymorphous-perverse. *Ibid.*, The child does not behave differently from the average uncivilized woman in whom the same polymorphous-perverse disposition exists. **1954** W. MAYER-GROSS et al. *Clin. Psychiatry* iv. 179 The active male and the passive female [homosexual]..adopt their homosexual behaviour as a *pis aller*, or, as frequently occurs, out of an abundance of sexual urge and interest and as part of a polymorphous perversity. **1954** D. RIESMAN *Individualism Reconsidered* (1955) VI. xxii. 355 He [*sc.* Freud] makes the famous charge that children are 'polymorphous-perverse'—that is, that their sexual life is not confined to the genital zone. **1963** AUDEN *Dyer's Hand* 411 Three kinds of erotic life are possible... The polymorphous-perverse promiscuous sexuality of childhood, courting couples whose relation is potential,..and the chastity of natural celibates who are without desire. **1974** *Encycl. Brit. Macropædia* XVI. 610/1 Most people with a polymorphous-perverse personality are either nearly or wholly psychotic persons or nonpsychotic persons who, in sexual and nonsexual areas of living, are unable to develop lasting, affectionate relations with others.

polymorphously (pǫlimǭ·ɹfəsli), *adv.* [f. prec. + -LY².] *polymorphously perverse* (Psychol.): characterized by a diffuse sexuality that can be excited and gratified in many ways and is normal in young children but regarded as perverted in adults. Also *transf.*
1949 J. STRACHEY tr. *Freud's Three Ess. Theory of Sexuality* II. 69 Under the influence of seduction children can become polymorphously perverse, and can be led into all possible kinds of sexual irregularities... In this respect children behave in the same kind of way as an average uncultivated woman in whom the same polymorphously perverse disposition persists. **1957** *Ann. N.Y. Acad. Sci.* LXVI. 429 Is not a child infinitely potential rather than polymorphously perverse? **1980** *Church Times* 22 Feb. 11/3 Traditional Christianity..offers us encouragement about living with..shame and dependence, which, in the polymorphously perverse landscape of chaos, need some careful (and painful) thought.

polymorphy. (Later example.)
1902 D. H. CAMPBELL *Univ. Text-bk. Bot.* vi. 176 Rusts are characterized by the production of several quite different forms [of spores]. This polymorphy is complicated in some species by heteræcism.

polymyalgia, -myositis: see *POLY- 1.

polymyxin (pǫlimi·ksin). *Pharm.* Also **polymixin.** [f. mod.L. *polymyxa*, specific epithet (f. POLY- + Gr. μύξα mucus, slime) + -IN¹.] Any of a class of antibiotics (*polymyxin A, B,* etc.) which are polypeptides obtained from strains of the soil bacterium *Bacillus polymyxa* and are used against Gram-negative bacteria in infections of the urinary tract and the skin.
1947 P. G. STANSLY et al. in *Bull. Johns Hopkins Hosp.* LXXXI. 43 The antibiotic-producing organism has been identified as *Bacillus polymyxa* and the antibiotic substance accordingly designated 'Polymyxin'. **1950** *Lancet* 17 June 1139/2 Polymyxin D in doses of 40 mg. per kg. for ten days produced definite injury in canine kidneys. **1956** *New Biol.* XXI. 18 Various methods for purifying pitching yeast have been in vogue for some years... The latest approach to this problem is the suggested use of antibiotics such as polymixin. **1974** M. C. GERALD *Pharmacol.* xxvii. 473 Polymyxin attaches to the cell membrane of bacteria, disrupting its function and causing the loss of essential intracellular materials.

Polynesian, *a.* and *sb.* Add: **a.** *adj.* (Earlier and further examples.)
1812 W. MARSDEN *Gram. Malayan Lang.* p. xxii, The Polynesian or general East-insular language..does not include those spoken by the description of people termed *Papūa* and *Samang.* **1820** J. CRAWFURD *Hist. Indian Archipelago* II. v. v. 93 The Sanskrit language exists indeed embodied in writing, while the Polynesian language can be traced only as it is scattered over a thousand living dialects. **1863** J. C. PATTESON *Let.* 8 Aug. in C. M. Yonge *Life J. C. Patteson* (1874) II. ix. 69 One might almost get together all the *disjecta membra*, and reconstruct the original Polynesian tongue. **1874** TROLLOPE *Harry Heathcote* iv. 89 A gang of Polynesian labourers..from the South Sea Islands. **1901** *Chambers's Jrnl.* May 343/1 With me was a young Polynesian half-caste named Alan, about twenty-two years of age. **1931** R. CAMPBELL *Georgiad* III. 52 The huge jaws of Polynesian clams. **1960** T. & L. DAVIS *Makutu* I. i. 13 It had to be a Polynesian island. **1978** B. PRIESTLEY *Island Emperor* iii. 26 'My great-grandfather used to eat men...' He seemed rather ashamed..talking about the darker side of the Polynesian past.
b. *sb.* (Earlier and later examples.) Also, the language of Polynesia.
1812 W. MARSDEN *Gram. Malayan Lang.* p. xviii, This language..may be conveniently termed the Polynesian, and distinguished..into the *Hither* (frequently termed the *East insular* language) and the *Further* Polynesian. **1820** J. CRAWFURD *Hist. Indian Archipelago* II. v. v. 84 All agree in borrowing from the same source—from the great Polynesian. **1874** TROLLOPE *Harry Heathcote* iv. 91 Picky was one of the Polynesians, who at once started on his errand. **1901** *Chambers's Jrnl.* Dec. 799/2 His eyesight, like that of all Polynesians, was better than that of any white man. **1923** A. L. KROEBER *Anthropol.* v. 121 Articles..recur in Semitic, in Polynesian, and in several groups of American languages. **1960** T. & L. DAVIS *Makutu* I. iii. 43 Family relationships are important among the Polynesians and families are large. **1962** [see *MORIORI]. **1976** 'M. DELVING' *China Expert* i. 16 He had several times been mistaken for a Japanese or a Polynesian.

polyneuritic, -neuropathy: see *POLY- 1.

polynia. Add: Now usu. written **polynya.** Pl. **polynyas** (rarely ‖ **polynyi**). (Further examples.)
1957 *Sat. Even. Post* 8 Dec. 7 From the deck of the A-sub, here surfaced in a 'polynya'—a hole in the ice-pack—crewmen took a close look at the perpetually frozen Arctic Ocean. **1963** G. L. PICKARD *Descriptive Physical Oceanogr.* vii. 154 Some of this cap ice melts in the summer... Open water spaces, 'polynyas', may form. **1963** *Sunday Tel.* 22 Sept. 15 Learning to find holes, or *polynias*, was one of the primary tasks of the two British submarines Porpoise and Grampus. **1971** *Nature* 1 Jan. 37/2 The present study was undertaken to measure the actual distribution of CO_2 between the atmosphere and the sea over open leads and polynyi in the ice-covered Bering Sea. **1974** L. DEIGHTON *Spy Story* xix. 206 We found a suitably large polynya—which is the proper name for a lagoon in the ice—and..the Captain began surfacing procedures.

polynomial, *a.* and *sb.* Add: **A.** *adj.* **2.** (Later example.)
1964 *Huntia* I. 34 He makes the essential distinction between the old Aristotelian polynomial phrase-names and the new trivial names.
B. *sb.* **1.** The terms are usually taken to be multiples of powers, finitely many in number. (Later examples.)
1941, 1966 [see *FACTOR *v.* 2].
2. (Later examples.)
1951 G. H. M. LAWRENCE *Taxon. Vascular Plants* ix. 194 Before the middle of the eighteenth century the names of plants commonly were polynomials. **1971** W. T. STEARN in W. Blunt *Compleat Naturalist* 248/1 Such a polynomial determines the application of the binomial.

Polynosic (pǫlinōᵘ·zik), *a.* and *sb.* Also **polynosic.** [ad. F. *polynosique*, contraction of *polymère d'un glucose* + *-ique* -IC (see N. Drisch 1959, in *Reyon, Zellwolle u. andere Chemiefasern* IX. 436).] **A.** *adj.* A proprietary term applied to fibres of a type made from regenerated cellulose and resembling cotton in such properties as a high wet modulus, alkali-resistance, and a crystalline multi-fibrillar structure. **B.** *sb.* A fibre of this type.
A number of erroneous accounts of the etymology occur in the literature.
1959 *Chem. & Engin. News* 24 Aug. 23/1 Hartford Fibres, a division of Bigelow-Sanford Carpet, takes the wraps off a new 'polynosic' fiber. **1959** *Skinner's Silk & Rayon Rec.* Nov. 1084/1 Recent reports from the Continent about a new class of cellulosic fibres, the polynosics,..have aroused interest in the British trade. **1963** *Trade Marks Jrnl.* 16 Jan. 82/1 *Polynosic*... Threads made of synthetic or natural textile materials. Association Internationale Polynosic.., Geneva, Switzerland; merchants. **1964** *Financial Times* 3 Mar. 15/4 Courtauld's polynosic fibre is Vincel, which has already passed from the pilot plant stage to commercial production. **1964** *Economist* 7 Mar. 913/3 The two companies will collaborate on the research, development and production of viscose rayon; particularly important will be their joint work on the 'polynosics', modified viscose fibres with properties similar to cotton. **1967** *Encycl. Polymer Sci. & Technol.* VI. 547 Within the last few years, regenerated cellulosic fibers having higher moduli values than the standard rayon fibers have been developed... These fibers have been given the generic name of polynosics. **1970** *Which?* Oct. 311/2 *Vincel* and *Zaryl* are polynosic rayons, as strong as cotton and with many of its wet strength properties.

polynuclear, *a.* (in Dict. s.v. POLY- 1). Add: (Further examples.) Also, applied *spec.* to polymorphonuclear leucocytes. Also as *sb.*
1891 [see *MYELOCYTE 2]. **1894** *Jrnl. Physiol.* XVII. 85 The other term which was applied to the finely granular oxyphile cells by Metschnikoff and others, namely, 'polynuclear leucocyte' is not satisfactory, seeing that..the different nuclear masses..are, in point of fact, joined by threads or bars of nuclear substance so that the cell is really mononuclear with a very much branched nucleus. **1897** [see *POLYMORPHO-NUCLEAR *a.*]. **1907** *Med. Rev.* X. 364/1 Centrifugalisation showed 68 per cent. of polynuclears, 14 per cent. of large mononuclears, and 18 per cent. of lymphocytes. **1935** *Trans. R. Soc. Trop. Med. & Hygiene* XXVIII. 477 The polynuclear count can also be used in the study of populations in which some pathological element exists. **1936** *Ibid.* XXX. 173 Infection provides a strong stimulus in modifying the percentage of neutrophiles with a segmented nucleus (polynuclear cells). **1967** *Jrnl. Reticuloendothelial Soc.* IV. 168 (*heading*) Influence of serum on intracellular digestion of *Staphylococcus aureus* by polynuclear neutrophils from the guinea pig.
b. *Chem.* Of a complex: containing more than one metal atom. Of a compound: having more than one nucleus (*NUCLEUS *sb.* 8).
1908 *Chem. Abstr.* II. 1101 (*heading*) Polynuclear metalammonias. **1924** W. THOMAS *Complex Salts* v. 54 This latter compound is an example of what may be termed a polynuclear complex, since the complex contains more than one central atom. **1933** *Jrnl. Soc. Chem. Industry* 8 Dec. 422T/2 Any polynuclear compound from, say, phenol possesses free positions in internal rings at which further condensation with formaldehyde..is possible. **1951** I. L. FINAR *Org. Chem.* I. xxix. 571 Polynuclear hydrocarbons may be divided into two groups, those in which the rings are isolated,..and those in which two or more rings are fused together in the *o*-positions. **1971** *Nature* 20 Aug. 539/1 Studies of a synthetic and structural nature of polynuclear metal complexes containing hydrogen and organic groups as ligands may eventually allow a better understanding of heterogeneous reactions.

polynucleated, *a.* (in Dict. s.v. POLY- 1). Add: **b.** Designating an urban area planned in the form of a number of smaller, self-contained communities.
1938 [see *MONONUCLEATED *a.*]. **1965** *Listener* 27 May 774/2 The Clyde Valley plan proposals were for a polynucleated urban system designed on a tight pattern and set in a green background.

polynucleotide (pǫliniū·kliǒtəid). *Biochem.* [ad. G. *polynucleotid* (Levene & Mandel 1908, in *Ber. d. Deut. Chem. Ges.* XLI. 1906): see POLY- and *NUCLEOTIDE.] A polymeric compound whose molecules are composed of a number (usu. large) of nucleotides.
1911 *Jrnl. Biol. Chem.* IX. 394 Yeast nucleic acid is a polynucleotide. **1916** [see *HEXOSE]. **1953** S. E. LURIA *Gen. Virol.* v. 100 Watson and Crick..have proposed for DNA a structure consisting of two helical polynucleotide chains coiled around the same axis and held together by bonds between the purine and pyrimidine bases. **1964** G. H. HAGGIS et al. *Introd. Molecular Biol.* ix. 225 Nucleic acids formed by *in vitro* synthesis with restricted base composition are termed polynucleotides. *Ibid.* 226 Synthetic polynucleotides form a variety of double and triple helices. **1970** R. W. MCGILVERY *Biochem.* iii. 23 A particular arrangement of three nucleotide units in the DNA polynucleotide specifies a particular amino acid. **1971** *Sci. Amer.* July 28/2 Antibody responses in animals were enhanced by certain synthetic polynucleotides. These are analogues of the nucleic acids DNA or RNA that are made in the laboratory by combining nucleotides (the subunits of nucleic acids) in arbitrary ways.

polynya, var. POLYNIA in Dict. and Suppl.
polyœstrous-: see *POLY- 1. **polyol, -olefin(e:** *POLY- 2.

polyoma (pǫli,ōᵘ·mă). *Microbiol.* [f. POLY- + *-OMA.] In full *polyoma virus*. A papovavirus that is endemic in mice without producing tumours but which can produce many kinds of tumour in young rodents.
1958 B. E. EDDY et al. in *Proc. Soc. Exper. Biol. & Med.* XCVIII. 848/1 A virus, which we shall refer to as SE polyoma virus, was recovered from tissue cultures inoculated with tumor material from mice and was shown to induce multiple tumors in mice..and hamsters. **1962** [see *PAPOVAVIRUS]. **1962** *Times* 27 July 21/6 In many fully formed growths induced by the polyoma virus, no sign of the virus can be found under the electron microscope. **1967** AMBROSE & EASTY in E. J. Ambrose et al. *Cancer Cell in Vitro* v. 41 Several viruses will produce malignant transformations *in vitro* when grown on cells of animal origin, for example, polyoma virus, Rous sarcoma virus, and SV 40 virus. The polyoma transformation is the one most extensively studied. **1969** A. M. CAMPBELL *Episomes* xiv. 169 Mammalian DNA viruses such as polyoma and SV40 cause the formation of tumors. **1973** R. G. KRUEGER et al. *Introd. Microbiol.* xxviii. 699/1 All of the tumors induced by polyoma virus in various different

mouse strains and hamsters have a common antigen. **1975** MELIEF & SCHWARTZ in F. F. Becker *Cancer* I. v. 123 The polyoma virus, which commonly infects both wild and laboratory mice.., does not produce tumors under natural conditions even though it is potentially very oncogenic.

polyomino: see *POLY- I.

polyonymosity (pǫli͵ǫnimǫ·siti). *rare*—¹. [f. as POLYONYMOUS *a.* + -ITY.] The availability of different names for the same person or thing.

1923 W. DE LA MARE in *Times Lit. Suppl.* 3 May 293/4 But how happy is the country polyonymosity that hails it [*sc. Oxalis acetosella*] also as sheep-sorrel, cuckoo-spice, hallelujah, [etc.].

Polyox (pǫ·li͵ǫks). A proprietary name for polyethylene oxide resin.

1957 *Official Gaz.* (U.S. Patent Office) 6 Aug. TM4/2 Union Carbide Corporation, New York..Polyox. For water soluble resins. First use on or about Mar. 4, 1957. **1958** *Industr. & Engin. Chem.* Jan. 9 (*caption*) A little Polyox resin goes a long way in thickening water. **1973** *Trade Marks Jrnl.* 6 June 1072/2 Polyox... Synthetic water-soluble resins. Union Carbide Corporation.., New York,..United States of America; manufacturers and merchants. **1976** *Nature* 1 July 47/1 We have reported that polyethyleneoxide (Polyox) in solution reduced the damping of free oscillations in a semicircular manometer.

polyoxyethylene, -methylene: see *POLY- 2.

polyp, polype. 2. Delete *rare* and add further examples.

1955 *Sci. News Let.* 1 Oct. 217/1 Polyps are small growths which may be non-cancerous but which are believed capable of developing into cancers. **1961** [see *POLYPUS 2]. **1966** *Economist* 12 Nov. 654/3 Power can corrupt—the Far Eastern tour apparently made both Mr Johnson's incisional hernia and the polyp in his throat worse. **1974** PASSMORE & ROBSON *Compan. Med. Stud.* III. xxviii. 43/1 Endometrial polyps are frequently asymptomatic and discovered in the course of a curettage... Recurring polyps associated with adenomatous hyperplasia in the postmenopausal patient should be regarded as premalignant and treated by hysterectomy.

3. polyp-tree = *polyp-stem.*

1915 E. R. LANKESTER *Diversions of Naturalist* xi. 97 The little jelly-fish are the ripe individuals of the polyps, and produce eggs and sperm which grow to be polyp-trees.

polypectomy (pǫlipe·ktŏmi). *Surg.* [f. POLYP + *-ECTOMY.] Excision of a polyp.

1950 *Surg. Clinics N. Amer.* XXX. 661 For nasal polypectomy..anesthesia is accomplished by painting the polyp and its area of attachment or pedicle with a saturated solution of cocaine. **1974** PASSMORE & ROBSON *Compan. Med. Stud.* III. xxviii. 43/1 The diagnosis is established by exploration of the uterus with polypectomy forceps during diagnostic curettage.

polypeptide (pǫlipe·ptəid). *Biochem.* [ad. G. *polypeptid* (E. Fischer 1903, in *Sitzungsber. d. k. preuss. Akad. d. Wissensch.* 389, after *di-, tripeptid*, etc. (Fischer 1902: see *PEPTIDE)).] Any peptide in which the number of amino-acid residues that go to make up the molecule is not small (cf. *oligopeptide* s.v. *OLIGO-), but is not so large that it can be regarded as a protein; **polypeptide chain** = *peptide chain* s.v. *PEPTIDE 2.

1903 *Jrnl. Chem. Soc.* LXXXIV. I. 466 These acid chlorides combine easily with glycylglycine esters and similar compounds to form chains of amino-acids joined together by an anhydride linking. Such are termed polypeptides. **1935** R. H. A. PLIMMER in Harrow & Sherwin *Textbk. Biochem.* v. 177 Fischer held the view that the polypeptide chain was not long enough for attack by pepsin. **1949** H. W. FLOREY et al. *Antibiotics* I. i. 38 The active preparation made from this organism..contains two antibiotics, gramicidin and tyrocidine, both crystalline polypeptides. **1951** *New Biol.* XI. 99 Larger molecules that show biological activity when applied to living organisms are exemplified by polypeptides, such as A.C.T.H. (the pituitary hormone which controls the secretion of cortisone). **1959** *Times* 2 Jan. 11/3 Further evidence suggested that this particular polypeptide was a precursor of the cell wall of the staphylococcus. **1961** *Ann. Reg. 1960* 401 The polypeptide chain, the backbone of the protein molecule, was found to be coiled in a helix-like spiral spring with only a space inside. **1978** *Sci. Amer.* Dec. 68/2 A hemoglobin molecule is made up of four polypeptide chains, two alpha chains of 141 amino acid residues each and two beta chains of 146 residues each.

Hence **polype·ptidase** [*-ASE], any enzyme which hydrolyses polypeptides.

1922 *Chem. Abstr.* XVI. 3491 (*heading*) Influence of materials obtained from yeast cells and organs on the rate of hydrolysis of substrates by polypeptidases, carbohydratases and esterases. **1929** R. P. WALTON tr. *Waldschmidt-Leitz's Enzyme Actions* 159 The yeast polypeptidases are totally inactive against dipeptides. **1940**, **1961** [see *EREPSIN].

polyphage. Delete †*Obs. rare*—⁰ and add examples.

1924 *Scribner's Mag.* Aug. 156/2 The flimsy telegraph copy of a presidential message fluttered out of the window and was lost... 'Oh, say that the office cat ate it.'.. The animal immediately became popular as a polyphage in hundreds of other newspaper-offices. **1965** B. E. FREEMAN tr. *Vandel's Biospeleol.* xxx. 472 Only the polyphages..have a chance of subsisting underground.

polyphagia. For 'Rarely' read 'Also' and add: **1.** (Later example.)

1946 *Nature* 28 Sept. 454/1 Such animals [*sc.* diabetic rabbits]..exhibited classical symptoms of diabetes mellitus—hyperglycæmia, glycosuria, polyuria, polyphagia.

2. (Examples.)

1907 W. R. FISHER *Schlich's Man. Forestry* (ed. 2) IV. iv. 158 Observations are not yet complete regarding the monophagy, or polyphagy of certain insects. **1950** *New Biol.* VIII. 64 Predaceous insects, spiders, birds and so on, exhibiting various degrees of polyphagy (i.e. eating more than one kind of food) usually come into the picture. **1965** B. E. FREEMAN tr. *Vandel's Biospeleol.* xix. 337 The categories which have been recognised must remain fluid because of the marked tendency of cavernicoles towards polyphagia. **1970** K. R. NORRIS in *Insects of Australia* (Commonwealth Sci. & Industr. Res. Org., Australia) v. 114/2 An example of polyphagy is afforded by the scale insect *Ceroplastes rubens* feeding on hundreds of different host plants.

polyphant: see *POLYPHONE.

polypharmaceutical (pǫ:lifāɹmăsiū·tikăl), *sb.* and *a. Med.* [f. POLY- + PHARMACEUTICAL.] **A.** *sb.* A medicinal preparation containing several drugs. **B.** *adj.* Of or pertaining to polypharmacy.

Usu. disparaging; cf. next.

1961 *Lancet* 16 Sept. 658/2 The [pharmaceuticals] industry, say some doctors, makes excessive profits;.. indulges in excessive and irrelevant promotion of its products;..goes in for dubious polypharmaceuticals. **1974** M. C. GERALD *Pharmacol.* i. 6 A very simple preparation was Paracelsus' laudanum, which contained opium, gold, and pearls. (Note that even Paracelsus retained vestiges of polypharmaceutical formulation.)

polypharmacy. Add to def.: Freq. with the suggestion of indiscriminate, unscientific, or excessive prescription. (Further examples.)

1906 H. SAINSBURY *Principia Therapeutica* vi. 109 The purist..whilst limiting himself scrupulously to the use of one drug at a time, will seldom hesitate to prescribe the crude drugs,—opium, digitalis, bark, [etc.]..entirely oblivious of the fact that in so doing he is guilty of the most flagrant polypharmacy. **1928** SOLIS-COHEN & GITHENS *Pharmacotherapeutics* v. 379 There is a tendency at the present time to decry the association of remedies as 'polypharmacy', and to advocate the use of 'single medicines'. **1953** J. L. SIMONSEN *Plant Products & Utilisation* (Univ. Nottingham: Sir Jesse Boot Found. Lect.) 4 There is less polypharmacy now than formerly, but I am satisfied that there is less good prescribing now than in my student days. **1977** *Lancet* 26 Mar. 685/2 Therapeutic misadventures..are more likely in the elderly because of inappropriate dosage,..erratic pill-taking, and polypharmacy for multiple diseases.

polypharmacal *a.*, delete † *Obs.* and add examples.

1927 C. H. LA WALL *4,000 Yrs. Pharmacy* iii. 93 The Arabians perpetuated the polypharmacal combinations which had come down from the Egyptians. **1966** G. WATSON *Theriac & Mithridatium* iii. 114 Texts of ancient medical writers with polypharmacal formulae had become available.

polyphase, *a.* (*sb.*). Add: **b.** Consisting of or occurring in a number of separate stages.

1936 *Proc. Prehist. Soc.* II. 155 In 1932..I attempted an analysis of the evidence for a polyphase Ice Age. **1938** *Mem. Geol. Soc. Amer.* VI. 84 Heteroaxial symmetry means, therefore, a sideward drag in the course of tectonic flow, or a polyphase deformation. **1958** R. S. WOODWORTH *Dynamics of Behavior* ii. 39 The child's developing purposiveness spreads in the opposite direction. It is visible first in the little two-phase and polyphase acts, their time span being only a few seconds. **1969** BENNISON & WRIGHT *Geol. Hist. Brit. Isles* iv. 85 The Manx Slates have been affected by polyphase folding and low-grade metamorphism.

c. Consisting of or involving a number of different phases of matter.

1940 *Jrnl. R. Aeronaut. Soc.* XLIV. 538 Precipitation hardening leads generally to the formation of polyphase systems, and a solution hardened metal shows distinct advantages. **1950** *Proc. Amer. Acad. Arts & Sci.* LXXVIII. 167 Poly-phase, poly-component chemical systems. **1975** *Physics Bull.* May 225/1 The last chapter deals with microstructural and polyphase effects.

polyphasic (pǫlifēi·zik), *a. Physiol.* [f. POLY- + PHAS(E + -IC.] Having several successive peaks.

1922 *Amer. Jrnl. Physiol.* LIX. 278 The fall of temperature..ought to occupy about the same place in the diphasic as it does in the polyphasic thermocardiograms. **1936** *Brit. Jrnl. Psychol.* XXVII. 71 We observed three types of voluntary movements: The 'motor impulse effect', the polyphasic movement and the amorphous movement. **1968** *Brit. Med. Bull.* XXIV. 257/2 An example..is the so-called 'polyphasic' potentials occurring following partial denervation, in which a normal spike with a duration of several msec. is replaced by a repetitive series of much shorter spikes.

polyphenol(ic, -phenylene: see *POLY- 2.

po:lyphiloproge·nitive, *a.* [f. POLY- + PHILOPROGENITIVE *a.*] Very prolific, *spec.* of a person's talent, imagination, inventive powers, etc.

Quot. 1919 is perhaps influenced also by PHILOPROGENITIVE *a.* 2.

1919 T. S. ELIOT *Poems*, Polyphiloprogenitive The sapient sutlers of the Lord Drift across the window-panes. **1947** [see *NATTER *sb.*]. **1953** G. WILLIAMSON *Reader's Guide to Eliot* iv. 93 The first line, 'Polyphiloprogenitive', is not merely a *tour de force*, but a learned word which derides the quality that unites the modern Church functionary with the caterpillar world. **1963** *Punch* 4 Sept. 358/3 There remains his polyphiloprogenitive invention, which occasionally pushes a story across the starting line if you can bear the writing. **1966** *Ibid.* 31 Aug. 339/2, I find Heinlein too sentimental and full of cracker-barrel drollery for my taste; but he certainly has a polyphiloprogenitive talent.

polyphloisbic (pǫlifloi·zbik), *a. rare*—¹. [f. as POLYPHLOISBOIAN *a.* + -IC.] = POLYPHLOISBOIAN *a.*

1915 R. BROOKE *Lett.* (1968) 662 Will the sea be polyphloisbic and wine dark and unvintageable (you, of course, know if it is)?

polyphonal (pǫli·fŏnăl), *a. Mus.* [f. as POLYPHONE + -AL, after ANTIPHONAL *a.* and *sb.*] = POLYPHONIC *a.* I. Hence **poly·phonally** *adv.*

1946 R. BLESH *Shining Trumpets* (1949) i. 8 The ultra-modern polyphonal and dissonantal school of today. *Ibid.* iii. 68 A woman's chorus..that sings, part antiphonally, part polyphonally, in undulating lines of chain-fourths.

polyphone. For '7–9 -phon' read '7– -phon'. In sense 1 a the forms **poliphant, polyphant** are usual. **1. a.** For *Obs.* read '*Obs.* except *Hist.*' and add later examples.

1954 *Grove's Dict. Mus.* (ed. 5) VI. 838/2 Queen Elizabeth was particularly partial to the poliphant. **1968** *New Oxf. Hist. Music* IV. xiii. 727 The drawing of the polyphant in Randle Holmes's *Academy of Armory* suggests a flat bandora-body surmounted by a harp-like frame. **1977** D. GILL *Wire-Strung Plucked Instruments contemp. with Lute* 19 Two other contemporary wire instruments have to be mentioned. One is the 'polyphant' or 'polyphone'. *Ibid.* 20 The 1671 inventory of Belvoir Castle does not list a polyphant.

c. (Further examples.)

1954 *Grove's Dict. Mus.* (ed. 5) VI. 848/1 In the 1880s the Polyphon was invented, in which projections punched up on a steel disc were used..to pluck the teeth of the comb. **1973** A. W. J. G. ORD-HUME *Clockwork Music* 108 Probably the best known of the musical box dealers and wholesalers was Henry Klein... His main business was in Polyphons and amusement machines. **1975** *Country Life* 11 Dec. 1715/2 (Advt.), Antique clocks, musical boxes, polyphones.

2. (Further example.)

1937 *Antiquity* XI. 273 Many of the Sumerian word-signs were polyphons.

polyphonic, *a.* Add: **2.** (*fig.* example.)

1920 H. CRANE *Let.* 15 Jan. (1965) 31 Your aristocrat is much more vital and admirable than the polyphonic God, chosen to symbolize the artist.

b. Of prose: written to sound pleasant and melodious.

1916 J. G. FLETCHER in *Poetry* Apr. 35 It seems fitting that a new name should be given to these poems of hers [*sc.* Amy Lowell's], which, printed as prose, or as prose and verse interspersed, display all the colors of the chromatic palette. The title that fits them best is that of Polyphonic Prose. **1917** A. LOWELL in *N. Amer. Rev.* Jan. 115 Metre, cadence, and rhyme are some of the many 'voices' employed in 'polyphonic prose'. Others are assonance, alliteration, and return. **1920** H. CRANE *Let.* 18 Aug. (1965) 41 Conrad's *Nigger of the Narcissus* seems to me all polyphonic prose. **1925** I. A. RICHARDS *Princ. Lit. Crit.* 135 Even the most highly organised lyrical or 'polyphonic' prose raises as it advances only a very ambiguous expectation. **1940** C. STRATTON *Handbk. Eng.* 249/2 *Polyphonic prose*, prose very carefully written to make the sounds pleasant and harmonious... The sound is obtained by attention to combinations and sequences of letters and syllables. **1977** *Amer. N. & Q.* XVI. 39/2 It is not improbable that the master of polyphonic prose was conscious of some metempsychosis which had taken place.

polyphonist. Restrict *rare* to sense 1 and add examples of sense 2.

1944 *Scrutiny* XII. 205 They [*sc.* Gesualdo's phrases] are related not so much to the great polyphonists as to the new technique of Monteverdi. **1954** *Grove's Dict. Mus.* (ed. 5) VI. 863/2 His [*sc.* Tallis's] music..has that expressive power characteristic of the later English polyphonists in its feeling for tonality and harmonic progression. **1968** *New Oxf. Hist. Mus.* IV. vii. 375 The Spanish polyphonists of this century [*sc.* the 16th] express a religious devotion and mystic fervour parallel to that of the painters and religious poets and prose-writers of the same epoch.

polyphonous, *a.* **3.** (Further example.)

1956 *Jrnl. Theol. Stud.* VII. 87 Transliterations would have been a great help to a Babylonian in enabling him to read ideograms and to determine the value of polyphonous signs.

polyphony. Add: **2.** (Further examples.) Also *transf.* and *fig.*

1965 *New Statesman* 10 Dec. 939/1 A polyphony of death, art and 'incorporeal love' was perhaps the most exalted solution for a girl who would have disliked fulfilment. **1968** COATES & ABRAHAM in *New Oxf. Hist. Mus.* IV. vi. 329 The movement gradually expands into a suave polyphony..and reaches a fine climax at 'Gloria in excelsis'. **1973** C. D. GARRATT *Masterpieces in Steam* 133 The Austerity created a steady, even blast whilst the ancient lady in front wheezed and rasped away in a totally different rhythmic pattern, so creating a marvellous polyphony of sound. **1977** A. SHERIDAN tr. *Lacan's Écrits* ii. 17 This formal fixation..is the very condition that extends indefinitely his world and his power, by giving his objects their instrumental polyvalence and symbolic polyphony.

polyphonical *a.* (further example); also **polypho·nically** *adv.*, as regards polyphony, in a polyphonic manner.

1936 *Jrnl. Theol. Stud.* XXXVII. 168 This is exactly the point needed to explain the presence of a set of polyphonical Sequelae in our MS. **1936** *Scrutiny* V. 268 The increasing tendency in Beethoven's music to think of harmony..vertically and dramatically instead of horizontally and polyphonically. **1942** Polyphonically [see *MONOPHONICALLY *adv.* a]. **1946** R. BLESH *Shining Trumpets* (1949) iv. 87 The response lines begin to lose their strictly harmonic division into set chords and separate into independent melodic lines woven together polyphonically. **1959** *Listener* 8 Jan. 80/1 The polyphonically derived harmony intensifies the seventeenth-century partiality for modal variety and false relation.

polyphosphate, -phosphoric: see *POLY- 2.

Polyphoto: see *POLYFOTO.

polyphylesis (pǫlifəilī·sis). *Biol.* [Back-formation f. POLYPHYLETIC *a.*, after GENESIS.] The polyphyletic development of a species or other taxon. Also **polyphy·letism.**

1897 *Amer. Naturalist* XXXI. 281 Reinke..labors constantly under the delusion that those who contend for the distribution of the lichens, deny their polyphylesis. **1905** F. E. CLEMENTS *Res. Methods Ecol.* iv. 232 All have ignored the fact that the polyphylesis of genera carries with it the admission of such origin for species. **1926** *Jrnl. Bot.* LXIV. 119 The difficulties which arise from polyphylesis complicate the problem. **1951** G. H. M. LAWRENCE *Taxon. Vascular Plants* vii. 164 Polyphylesis is the situation represented by a polyphyletic origin. **1969** *Biol. Rev.* XLIV. 576 The appearance of bifid and trifid lobed forms [of ammonoids]..with the shell sculpture were seen as evidence of polyphyletism. **1978** *BioSystems* X. 82/1 This paradox may be due to polyphyletism within the chytrids.

polyphyly (pǫ·lifəili). *Biol.* [f. POLY- + Gr. φυλή tribe.] = prec.

1927 *Q. Jrnl. Geol. Soc.* LXXXII. p. ci, The whole of our System..is riddled through and through with polyphyly and convergence. **1961** G. G. SIMPSON *Princ. Animal Taxon.* iv. 124 The level of polyphyly is specified by the category of the highest ranking taxa two or more of which were immediately ancestral to the taxon in question. **1963** DAVIS & HEYWOOD *Princ. Angiosperm Taxon.* ii. 47 Proved or suspected polyphyly may lead us to see if there is a way of reclassifying the group into monophyletic units. **1978** *BioSystems* X. 110/1 Later modifications..considerably reduce this polyphyly, but at the expense of making the Protista even more of a rag bag.

polypier. Add *fig.* example.

1904 A. L. TEIXEIRA DE MATTOS tr. *Maeterlinck's Double Garden* 85 All nations have the natural right to pass through this phase of the political evolution of the human polypier.

polyplacophoran, *sb.* and *a.* (Later examples.)

1962 D. NICHOLS *Echinoderms* xii. 163 It is only fair to mention that other animal groups, such as the polyplacophoran molluscs,..have claimed them. **1973** P. TASCH *Paleobiol. Invertebr.* viii. 329/1 The polyplacophoran shell is composed of aragonite. **1976** *Nature* 2 Sept. 50/1 (*caption*) A polyplacophoran (*Chiton*) has removed sediment cover.

polyploid (pǫ·liploid), *a.* (*sb.*) *Biol.* [a. G. *polyploid* (H. Winkler 1916, in *Zeitschr. f. Bot.* VIII. 422): see POLY- and *-PLOID.] Having more than two homologous sets of chromosomes (in each cell nucleus). Also as *sb.*, a polyploid organism.

1920 W. E. AGAR *Cytol.* vii. 209 In the Protista..it appears that the nucleus may be polyploid, containing, not one or two, but a great number of series of elements. **1924** *Hereditas* V. 168 The chromosome number of a polyploid species must necessarily contain a certain number of complete haploid chromosome sets and it must have arisen through addition of such sets. **1928** [see *ALLOPOLYPLOIDY]. **1936** *Discovery* May 162/1 An account of the breeding behaviour of polyploid plants would be of almost universal interest since this class includes important crops such as wheat, oats, and tobacco. **1949** A. G. SANDERS in H. W. Florey et al. *Antibiotics* II. xvi. 683 In the field of agriculture polyploid forms of plants produced by chemical means have been of great importance as they are larger and often more vigorous than the normal plant. **1956** [see *EUPLOID *a.*]. **1963** E. MAYR *Animal Species & Evolution* xv. 439 Two types of polyploids are distinguished that have a rather different significance in evolution: autopolyploids and allopolyploids. **1975** J. B. JENKINS *Genetics* iv. 135 Although some animal tissues are commonly polyploid (the liver, for example), polyploid animals are rare. Most animal polyploids reproduce either hermaphroditically..or parthenogenetically.

Hence **po·lyploidy** [cf. G. *polyploidie* (E. Strasburger 1910, in *Flora* C. 406)], the condition of being polyploid.

1922 *Genetics* VII. 545 The value of polyploidy may have certain limitations. **1942, 1943** [see *endomitosis* s.v. *ENDO-]. **1973** *Nature* 11 May 87/2 Polyploidy may increase the flexibility of a species.

polyploidize (pǫ·liploidəiz), *v. Biol.* [f. prec. + -IZE.] *trans.* To render polyploid. Chiefly as **po·lyploidizing** *ppl. a.* Hence **po:lyploidiza·tion.**

1941 *Amer. Naturalist* LXXV. 128 It is often assumed that treatment with colchicine or other polyploidizing agents, if effective, will induce an exact doubling of each chromosome so that a balanced 4*n* condition, for example, will result throughout the part of the plant affected. This is very far from what actually happens. **1945** *Bot. Rev.* XI. 162 Schmuck found that wheat and barley seeds were polyploidized by acenaphthene, acenaphthylene, [etc.]. **1968** G. B. WILSON *Elem. Cytogenetics* v. 58 Many species of plants have been polyploidized by man through the use of conditions which disrupt mitosis and meiosis by preventing anaphase separation. **1974** *Oncology* XXIX. 520 Besides the loss and acquisition of chromosomes and polyploidization, these tumours were mainly characterized by the occurrence of multiple more or less complex translocations. **1975** *Nature* 31 Jan. 361/2 Cells treated with any one of the polyploidising agents gave rise to colonies, 13 of which were isolated and developed into established lines.

polyploidogenic (pǫ:liploidŏdʒe·nik), *a. Cytology.* [f. as prec. + -O + -GENIC.] Tending to produce polyploidy.

1944 [see *DIBENZANTHRACENE]. **1974** *Biol. Abstr.* LVII. 3982/2 In the sprouts there appear morphological changes (tumor-like thickenings in some parts) similar to those evoked by polyploidogenic substances.

polypneustic, -pnœa, -pnœic: see *POLY- 1.

polypod, *a.* Add: (*e*) [tr. It. *polipodo* (A. Berlese 1913, in *Redia* IX. 127)], esp., of a phase in the development of certain insect larvæ, having a segmented abdomen with rudimentary or functional appendages.

1925 A. D. IMMS *Gen. Textbk. Entomol.* 179 In the polypod phase the abdomen has acquired its complete segmentation and full number of appendages. **1969** R. F. CHAPMAN *Insects* xx. 400 A second basic form is the polypod larva... The larvae of Lepidoptera, Mecoptera and Tenthredinidae are of the polypod type.

polypore (pǫ·lipōəɹ). [f. mod.L. *Polyporus* (P. A. Micheli *Nova Plantarum Genera* (1729) 129), f. POLY- + Gr. πόρος pore.] A bracket-fungus belonging to the genus *Polyporus* or the family Polyporaceæ.

1902 *Science* 12 Dec. 954/1 A correspondent..sent me a fine specimen of a polypore which he found on the trunk of a tall tree. **1923** F. DICKSON in L. H. Bailey *Cultivated Evergreens* iv. 150 Most of the fungi causing these wood-rots are of one general type commonly known as 'bracket-fungi' or 'polypores'. **1946** *Nature* 7 Sept. 325/1 The paper contains an extensive key to the principal white re-supinate polypores in culture. **1971** P. H. B. TALBOT *Princ. Fungal Taxon.* xii. 201 The polypores and hydnums are typically woody, corky or membranous in texture. **1976** G. C. AINSWORTH *Introd. Hist. Mycol.* iii. 35 Greek and Roman writers certainly distinguished between agarics, polypores, and truffles.

polyporic (pǫli·pǫ̆rik), *a. Biochem.* [tr. G. *polyporsäure* polyporic acid (C. Stahlschmidt 1877, in *Ann. d. Chem. u. Pharm.* CLXXXVII. 180), f. mod.L. *polypor-us* (see prec.) + -IC.] *polyporic acid*: a bronze-coloured crystalline solid, 3,6-dihydroxy-2,5-diphenyl-*p*-benzoquinone, $C_{18}H_{12}O_4$, which is a colouring matter found in certain fungi and lichens, and was first isolated from a fungus of the genus *Polyporus.*

1877 *Jrnl. Chem. Soc.* XXXII. II. 620 The fungus.. seems to be closely allied to Polyporus purpurascens... When brought into contact with dilute ammonia, its colour changes to a fine deep violet, and it yields a solution from which hydrochloric acid throws down a yellow precipitate of the new acid—polyporic acid. **1931** *Jrnl. Amer. Chem. Soc.* LIII. 2373 Two of the important coloring matters found in fungi are polyporic acid..obtained from *Polyporous* [sic] *nidulans* and atromentin..from *Paxillus atrotomentosus.* **1957** R. H. THOMSON *Naturally occurring Quinones* ii. 26 Polyporic acid also occurs in the fungus *Peniophora filamentosa*..and..has been found in two lichens. **1967** M. E. HALE *Biol. Lichens* viii. 106 Polyporic acid is known from *Sticta coronata* and *Polyporus nidulans.*

polyporus (pǫli·pǫ̆rŭs). [mod.L.: see *POLYPORE.] **a.** = *POLYPORE.

1887 [see POLYPOROID *a.*]. **1907** T. R. SIM *Forests & Forest Flora Cape Good Hope* iii. 31 The attack of a Polyporus..softens and disintegrates the living heartwood.

b. A slice of a dried fungus of the genus *Polyporus*, esp. *P. betulinus*, used as a mount for particularly delicate insects. Also *attrib.*

1900 *Instructions for Collecting Insects* (Brit. Mus. (Nat. Hist.)) 6 A very useful material for staging is a fungus called *Polyporus*, which is cut into strips sold for the purpose by dealers. **1940** J. SMART *Instructions for Collectors, No. 4A: Insects* (Brit. Mus. (Nat. Hist.)) iv. 153 The smaller forms should be pinned on fine stainless steel points which are stuck into small strips of polyporus. **1951** COLYER & HAMMOND *Flies Brit. Isles* 334 If it is desired to pin medium-sized or small flies with short pins, they can be subsequently 'staged' on polyporus or slips of celluloid. **1962** GORDON & LAVOIPIERRE *Entomol. for Students of Med.* l. 303 Other forms of very useful.. specialised equipment are entomological forceps and polyporus strips.

polyposis (pǫlipˌōu·sis). *Path.* [f. POLYP + -OSIS.] A condition characterized by the presence of numerous internal polyps, *esp.* a hereditary disease in which the large intestine is so affected and which becomes malignant if untreated.

1914 *Surg., Gynecol. & Obstetr.* XIX. 31/2 The symptoms of intestinal polyposis vary within wide limits. **1952** *Ann. Eugenics* XVII. 1 Polyposis is caused by an excessive proliferation of the glandular epithelium in the mucous membrane of the colon and rectum. **1961** [see *POLYPUS 2]. **1974** PASSMORE & ROBSON *Compan. Med. Stud.* III. xix. 112/2 Isolated cases of colonic polyposis without a family history are attributed to gene mutation.

polypropylene (pǫliprōu·pilīn). [f. POLY- + PROPYLENE. Cf. F. *polypropylène* (Berthelot 1867, in *Jrnl. de Pharm. et de Chim.* VI. 31).] Any of the polymers of propylene, which include a number of thermoplastic materials widely used as films, fibres, or moulding materials.

1935 [see *polybutadiene* s.v. *POLY- 2]. **1957** *Times* 17 July 7/3 As dense polythene advances in commercial use another type of plastic—the polypropylenes—appears to be established at the laboratory stage. **1964** *Which?* Aug. 253/3 Fabrics made from polypropylene can be easily washed and boiled. **1973** *Materials & Technol.* VI. viii. 528 Polypropylene is an eminently suitable material from which to prepare thin films. **1976** E. SCARROW *N.Z. Vegetable Gardening Guide* 14 Many modern spades have steel handles, with a polypropylene 'D' grip fitted to the handle.

polyprotein: see *POLY- 1.

polyprotic (pǫliprōu·tik), *a. Chem.* [f. POLY- + *PROTON 2 + -IC.] Of an acid: capable of donating more than one proton to a base; polybasic; occas. also used of bases which can accept more than one proton.

1944 J. A. TIMM *Gen. Chem.* xxxii. 343 Acids whose molecules may donate more than one proton are called polyprotic acids. **1968** J. G. MORRIS *Biologist's Physical Chem.* v. 114 In biological media we frequently encounter polyprotic, weak acids (e.g. carbonic, phosphoric, citric acids), whose complete neutralization requires the addition of two or more equivalents of sodium hydroxide. **1969** H. T. EVANS tr. *Hägg's Gen. & Inorg. Chem.* xii. 316 Acids and bases that can give up or take up more than one proton are called polyvalent..or polyprotic.

polypus. Add: **2.** (Further examples.) Cf. POLYP, POLYPE 2 in Dict. and Suppl.

1961 R. D. BAKER *Essent. Path.* xvi. 390 Adenomatous polyps and gastric polyposis are quite like their counterparts in the large bowel. The polypi are pedunculated or sessile and are composed of mucosa like that of the gastric wall. **1974** PASSMORE & ROBSON *Compan. Med. Stud.* III. xix. 52/2 A subtotal gastrectomy is recommended if the polypi occur in the mid and lower stomach.

polyreaction: see *POLY- 3.

polyrhythm (pǫ·liriðm). *Mus.* [f. POLY- + RHYTHM *sb.*] The use of two or more different rhythms simultaneously; music using such rhythms.

1929 P. ROSENFELD *Hour with Amer. Mus.* i. 12 Its alternation of bars of three and four and five units, the so-called jazz polyrhythm, is sheer willful contrast and change. **1942** *Scrutiny* XI. 12 The thirteenth century composer may teach the composer of the twentieth century how polytonalities and polyrhythms..may be reconciled with..the natural resources of the art of sound. **1949** *Funk's Stand. Dict. Folklore* I. 151/1 Musically, the blues are distinguished by..syncopation and polyrhythm characteristic of Negro music. **1956** W. MELLERS in A. Pryce-Jones *New Outl. Mod. Knowl.* III. 363 Messiaen has created some fascinating noises out of the complex scales and polyrhythms of Indian music. **1973** *Black World* Sept. 37 The polyrhythms of 'bop' jazz are..in the contrasted regular rhythms of the first stanza and the irregularly punctuated rhythms of the second stanza. **1979** *Daily Tel.* 1 Nov. 15/6 In its simultaneous use of conflicting time signatures, of extremely intricate syncopations and polyrhythms, the late 14th century produced music of a complexity that has hardly been equalled until our own time.

polyrhythmic (pǫliri·ðmik), *a.* Chiefly *Mus.* [f. POLY- + RHYTHMIC *a.* and *sb.*] Involving or using two or more different rhythms, esp. at the same time. Also **polyrhy·thmical** *a.*

1893 J. S. SHEDLOCK tr. *Riemann's Dict. Mus.* 609/2 *Polyrhythmical*, i.e. containing a mixture of various rhythms. **1917** E. C. FARNSWORTH *Ideals & Tendencies Mod. Art* 69 That ultra phase of poetry *vers libre*, or, as some prefer, 'unrhymed cadence' or, what is more impressive, 'polyrhythmical poetry'. **1932** L. SAMINSKY *Music of our Day* I. 40 Jazz has shown that synthetic rhythm embraces not only straight polyrhythmic structures. **1942** *Scrutiny* XI. 15 A tonal structure based, however..polyrhythmic the music may grow, on the absolute and perfect consonances rather than on the diatonic triad. **1944** W. APEL *Harvard Dict. Mus.* 593/2 Properly speaking, all truly contrapuntal or polyphonic music is polyrhythmic, since rhythmic variety in simultaneous parts more than anything else contributes to giving the voice-parts that quality of individuality which is essential to polyphonic style. **1958** P. GAMMOND *Decca Bk. Jazz* xv. 178 He maintains an incredibly difficult polyrhythmical contrivance, playing in 3/4 time in the bass against the normal 4/4 in the treble. **1958** *Times* 9 Sept. 5/4 The relevant departments of the London Philharmonic proved inadequate to Bartok's polyrhythmic counterpoint. **1970** P. OLIVER *Savannah Syncopators* 6 It was possible to agree on generalities concerning..the polyrhythmic texture of piano, guitar, bass and drums.

Hence **polyrhy·thmically** *adv.*

1946 R. BLESH *Shining Trumpets* (1949) xiii. 314 The ragtime left hand..is beyond the ability of the classically trained executant, let alone its combination polyrhythmically with the right. **1963** *Listener* 14 Mar. 457/1 African drumming relies on the interweaving of different strands of rhythm each of fixed beats, conflicting polyrhythmically with each other.

polyribo- (pǫlirəibo). *Biochem.* [f. POLY- + *RIBO-.] Formative element used in the names of polymers of ribonucleotides, as *polyri:boadeny·lic, -cytidy·lic, -inosi·nic*, etc., *acid*; also *po:lyribonu·cleotide*. Cf. *polyribosome* s.v. *POLY- I.

1956 *Nature* 11 Feb. 271/1 Some 10–20 per cent of the total polyribonucleotide content of the bacteria was extracted by this procedure. **1959** *Times* 10 Nov. (Guinness Suppl.) p. ii/6 An important series of papers on the synthesis of polyribonucleotides which have an important function in cellular metabolism. **1961** STEINER & BEERS *Polynucleotides* i. 6 The equimolar complexes formed by polyriboadenylic acid with polyribouridylic acid and with polyriboinosinic acid appear to have doubly stranded helical structures. *Ibid.* viii. 263 Even less is known of the detailed fine structure of polyribocytidylic acid... All that can be said is that some helical structure is present. **1964** G. H. HAGGIS et al. *Introd. Molecular Biol.* ix. 228 (*caption*) T = polyribothymidylic acid (a polyribonucleotide containing only the base thymine found in natural DNA but not in natural RNA). **1970** *New Scientist* 15 Jan. 96/2 Poly I:C—a combination of polyriboinosinic and polyribocytidylic acids—would stimulate interferon production both in cell cultures and in animals. **1976** *Nature* 15 Jan. 141/2 Antibodies to native DNA, double-stranded RNA, and various synthetic polyribonucleotides occur with great frequency in patients with systemic lupus erythematosus (SLE).

So also **polyde(s)oxyribo-** (see *DEOXY-), in names of polymers of deoxyribonucleotides, as *po:lyde(s)oxyribonu·cleotide*.

1956 *Federation Proc.* XV. 291/2 To define the chemical events in the development of a bacterial virus, we have explored the pathways of polydesoxyribonucleotide synthesis in normal and infected cells. **1961** STEINER & BEERS *Polynucleotides* i. 5 The primary structures of polydeoxyribonucleotides and polyribonucleotides are identical except for the absence of the hydroxyl group on C_2' of deoxyribose. **1976** W. GUSCHLBAUER *Nucleic Acid Struct.* vi. 86 Single-stranded polydeoxyribonucleotides are, as a rule, less stacked and structured than their ribo counterparts.

polysaccharide (pǫlisæ·kărəid). *Chem.* Formerly also **-id.** [ad. G. *polysaccharid* (B. Tollens *Kurzes Handbuch d. Kohlenhydrate* (1888) 16), f. POLY- + *saccharid* SACCHARIDE (in Dict. and Suppl.).] Any carbohydrate whose molecules consist of a number of monosaccharide residues (or their simple derivatives) bonded together, usu. in a chain structure, and esp. one of high molecular weight; also applied to such a structure which forms part of a larger molecule.

1892 E. F. SMITH tr. *V. von Richter's Org. Chem.* (ed. 2) 512 It is very probable that the polysaccharides having the empirical formula $C_6H_{10}O_5$, really possess a much higher molecular weight, $(C_6H_{10}O_5)_n$. **1895** *Jrnl. Chem. Soc.* LXVIII. II. 322 It appears probable that the fermentation of the polysaccharides by saccharomycetes is preceded by their conversion into monosaccharides through the agency of enzymes. **1902** *Encycl. Brit.* XXXI. 723/2 By further polymerization and loss of water the group of polysaccharids..is produced. **1947** *Endeavour* VI. 89/2 Other substances of high molecular weight, such as the polysaccharides, consist mostly of molecules of continuously varying size. **1951** *Sci. News* XXI. 72 Any carbohydrate, such as glucose, cellulose, cane-sugar, or starch, can be represented by the formula $C_n(H_2O)_m$ where *m* is equal, or very nearly equal, to *n*... For polysaccharides such as starch or cellulose, *n* and *m* may run up to hundreds. **1960** *New Biol.* XXXI. 72 The virulent and avirulent types [of pneumococcus] can be quickly and easily distinguished because the virulent cells are enclosed in a polysaccharide capsule that can be seen under the microscope. **1968** A. WHITE et al. *Princ. Biochem.* (ed. 4) xli. 910 (*caption*) Two units from neighboring polysaccharide chains can be bridged by a peptide. **1969** *New Scientist* 7 Aug. 270/1 Some natural polysaccharides show startlingly similar conformational behaviour to proteins and nucleic acids. **1973** R. G. KRUEGER et al. *Introd. Microbiol.* xxiv. 590/2 The major antigenic components of bacteria and their products are polysaccharides of one sort or another.

† **polysa·ccharose.** *Chem. Obs.* [f. POLY- + SACCHAROSE.] = prec.

1894 PERKIN & KIPPING *Org. Chem.* I. xv. 275 The polysaccharoses do not ferment with yeast, and do not reduce Fehling's solution. **1931** E. C. MILLER *Plant Physiol.* viii. 411 The polysaccharoses have the general formula $(C_6H_{10}O_5)_n$ or $(C_5H_8O_4)_n$ depending on whether they yield hexoses or pentoses on hydrolysis.

polysaprobic, -semantic(ity, -ism: see *POLY- I.

polysemy (pǫ·lisīmi). *Linguistics.* Also in mod.L. form **polyse·mia.** [ad. F. *polysémie* (M. Bréal *Essai de Sémantique* (1897) xiv. 155), f. med.L. *polysēmus* (see *polysemous* adj. s.v. POLY- I and below): see -Y[3], -IA[1].] The fact of having several meanings; the possession of multiple meanings.

1900 N. CUST tr. *Bréal's Semantics* xiv. 140 The new meaning of a word, whatever it may be, does not make an end of the old. They exist alongside of one another... In proportion as a new signification is given to a word, it appears to multiply and produce fresh examples, similar in form, but differing in value. We shall call this phenomenon of multiplication *Polysemia*. All the languages of civilised nations have their part in it. **1928** O. JESPERSEN *Monosyllabism in Eng.* 26 We now see the reason why polysemy is found so often in small words to an extent which would not be tolerable in longer words. **1931** G. STERN *Meaning & Change of Meaning* iv. 74 *I wish you luck*... This polysemy is quite different from the polysemy..of *Hund*, signifying either 'dog', or 'kind of cart used in mines'. **1937** J. ORR tr. *Iordan's Introd. Romance Linguistics* 192 In Gilliéron's view, sound-change, with all its consequences, homonymy, polysemia, and the like, are causes of disease in words. **1950** S. POTTER *Our Language* 110 If we assume that the central meaning of *place* is still 'square' and that these other diverse uses *radiate* from that centre, we might equally well put it into our third semantic category: radiation, polysemia, or multiplication. **1951** S. ULLMANN *Princ. Semantics* ii. 115 Should one describe 'a straight line' and 'shipping line, air line' as radical shifts in application or as mild cases of polysemy? *Ibid.* 117 Polysemy is the pivot of semantic analysis. **1960** W. F. TWADDELL *Eng. Verb Auxiliaries* 3 We can acknowledge the existence of meaningful lexical verbs in our syntax, and gracefully recognize a linguistically reasonable polysemia of our grammatical signals within different lexical contexts. **1972** M. L. SAMUELS *Linguistic Evol.* v. 75 The effect of polysemy is in principle the same as that of homonymy—the representation of two or more meanings by a single form. **1975** *Times Lit. Suppl.* 16 May 531/1 Matters are complicated by the polysemy of the noun *linguist*, both 'polyglot' and 'scientific student of language'. **1977** *Dædalus* Summer 77 Thus symbol is distinguished from sign both by the multiplicity (multivocality, polysemy) of its signifieds, and by the nature of its signification.

So **po·lyseme**, a word having several or multiple meanings; **polyse·mic, polyse·mous** *adjs.* [see s.v. POLY- I], of or pertaining to polysemy; having several meanings, exhibiting polysemy.

1884 Polysemous [in Dict. s.v. POLY- I]. **1930** *S.P.E. Tract* xxxiv. 463 Even the names of concrete things are nearly always polysemic, though this may not be perceptible until we compare them with corresponding words in other languages. The word *leg*, for instance, may be applied to the supports of a table or chair, and the legs of an insect in English, but not in French. **1931** G. STERN *Meaning & Change of Meaning* iii. 32 Different meanings can be expressed by the same word, as instanced by *crown* or any other polysemous word. **1953** *Trans. Philol. Soc.* 60 Identifications of this type are..most convincing when parallel translation-pairs are found as homonyms within a single language, which one would then wish to consider as polysemes. **1954** *Eng. Stud.* XXXV. 170 The cropping up of new senses may lead to polysemic conflicts, causing older senses to disappear. **1957** N. FRYE *Anat. Crit.* 72 The principle of manifold or 'polysemous' meaning, as Dante calls it, is not a theory any more..but an established fact. **1969** *Times Lit. Suppl.* 18 Dec. 1445 The earnest digging goes on, and we are..grateful for the unearthing of new polysemes [in *Finnegans Wake*]. **1973** *Ibid.* 8 June 640/2 The book begins with an essay.. which makes the point that a work of thought is polysemous, that its meaning is not a message but rather the effect which it has on its readers. **1974** *Amer. Speech 1971* XLVI. 125 Polysemes, or terms that exhibit more than one denotation each, even though their connotations are synonymous in their negativism. **1976** G. STEINER in D. Villiers *Next Year in Jerusalem* 67 The elaborate investigations of the Kabbalists into the polysemic nature of the written word.

polyserositis, -siloxane, -soap: see *POLY- I, 2, I.

polysomatic (pǫlisomæ·tik), *a.* [f. Gr. πολυσώματ-ος with many bodies: see -IC.]

1. *Petrol.* [ad. G. *polysomatisch* (G. Tschermak *Die mikrosk. Beschaffenheit der Meteoriten* (1885) i. 12).] Consisting of more than one grain or more than one mineral.

1888 *Amer. Geologist* I. 201 The boundaries between the different members of these 'polysomatic' masses of augite are traceable only with difficulty. **1910** *Mineral. Mag.* XV. 356 The commonest are polysomatic olivine chondrules with either granular or porphyritic structure. **1920** *Proc. Nat. Acad. Sci.* VI. 455 The porphyritic forms [of chondrule]..pass gradually into those which are almost or quite holocrystalline and polysomatic. **1973** G. J. H. MCCALL *Meteorites & their Origins* xv. 191 Polysomatic chondrules may consist of numerous grains of a single mineral..or of more than one mineral species.

2. *Biol.* [ad. G. *polysomatisch* (O. F. I. Langlet 1927, in *Svensk Bot. Tidskr.* XXI. 3).] Of, pertaining to, or exhibiting polysomaty.

1937 *Cytologia* VIII. 270 Although the possibility exists that polysomatic cells may arise in a number of different ways, there is evidence, if we can consider as significant the paired condition of polysomatic metaphase chromosomes, that the process involving two successive cleavages of the chromosomes is more widespread in plants than heretofore supposed. **1948** *Nature* 17 Jan. 80/2 These first studies..indicated that a very large proportion of differentiated cells behind the meristematic region are polysomatic. **1969** BROWN & BERTKE *Textbk. Cytol.* xxiii. 538/1 Examples of the second category, replication, are differentiating cells that produce polytene and/or polysomatic nuclei..[etc.].

polysomaty (pǫlisōu·măti). *Biol.* [f. as prec.: see -Y[3].] The occurrence of polyploid cells together with diploid cells in the same somatic tissue.

1937 *Cytologia* VIII. 247 In *Kochia scoparia* L...the large periblem cells of the root were found to exhibit the same phenomenon of polysomaty as those of *Spinacia*. **1962** *Lancet* 12 May 1005/1 Very possibly, spindle formation is upset in the divisions preceding the formation of orthochromatic erythroblasts, thus giving rise to polysomaty. **1969** BROWN & BERTKE *Textbk. Cytol.* xix. 424/2 In numerous species such as spinach, *Cannabis*, potato, onion, beet, etc., polysomaty occurs typically in root tips and in many species in shoot tips and leaves.

polysome (pǫ·lisōum). *Biol.* [f. POLY- + *RIBO)SOME.] A cluster of ribosomes, held together by a strand of messenger RNA which each is translating; = *polyribosome* s.v. *POLY- I.

1962 J. R. WARNER et al. in *Science* 28 Dec. 1399/2 We have been able to show that the site of hemoglobin synthesis in vivo is not the single ribosome but rather a cluster of ribosomal particles, which we have called a 'polyribosome' or simply a polysome. **1970** *New Scientist* 15 Oct. 113/1 This reticulum is a series of intracellular membranes which carry on them the polysomes (messenger RNA and ribosomes) thought to be responsible for the biosynthesis of proteins destined for export from the cell. **1971, 1972** [see *MONOSOME 2]. **1973** R. G. KRUEGER et al. *Introd. Microbiol.* xi. 336/2 Each ribosome in the polysome has a growing polypeptide attached to it, and the ribosomes near the 3′ terminus of the mRNA molecule will have the most nearly complete polypeptide chains attached to them.

Hence **polyso·mal** *a.*, of or pertaining to a polysome.

1962 *Science* 28 Dec. 1402/1 Dialysis followed by spraying causes considerable degradation of the polysomal structure. **1972** *Nature* 31 Mar. 237/2 The ratio of cytoplasmic to chloroplast polysomal RNA is increased two to three times 24h after inoculation.

polysomic (pǫlisōu·mik), *sb.* and *a.* *Cytology.* [f. POLY- + *-SOME[4] + -IC.] **A.** *adj.* Having one or a few normal chromosomes in excess of the usual diploid or polyploid complement; being such a chromosome. **B.** *sb.* A polysomic organism.

1932 C. D. DARLINGTON *Rec. Adv. Cytol.* iii. 66 Polysomic forms arise in a diploid through two daughter chromosomes passing to the same pole at mitosis, or at meiosis. **1937** T. DOBZHANSKY *Genetics & Origin of Species* iv. 80 Spontaneous polysomics, monosomics, polyploids, haploids, and translocations were observed in *Datura stramonium* by Blakeslee (1922). **1939** *Jrnl. Genetics* XXXVIII. 409 All five asynaptic polysomics possessed three extra chromosomes. **1949** R. A. FISHER *Theory of Inbreeding* iv. 78 Polysomic organisms differ from disomic in having more than two chromosomes mutually homologous and capable of pairing, and of interchange of segments. **1949** K. MATHER *Biometrical Genetics* x. 305 A general treatment of polysomic inheritance has not been attempted because of its inherent complexity. **1966** J. A. SERRA *Mod. Genetics* II. xii. 35 Cases in which one chromosome of the set becomes polysomic (above the normal number) are known in which the chromosome remains euchromatic and other cases in which it is heterochromatinized. Genetic imbalance and diminished viability or more or less marked lethality accompany, as a rule, the cases of polysomy when the chromosome remains euchromatic, while heterochromatic supernumeraries do not, in general, produce such effects and, probably, are of use to the cell.

polysomy (pǫ·lisōumi). *Cytology.* [f. as prec. + -Y[3].] The state of being polysomic.

1932 C. D. DARLINGTON *Rec. Adv. Cytol.* iii. 59 Reduplication of some of the chromosomes of a set beyond the normal diploid number is called polysomy. **1946** *Nature* 17 Aug. 239/2 It is not impossible that polysomy and failure of pairing may be jointly responsible for the abnormal numbers [of chromosomes] observed. **1966** [see prec.]. **1973** *Cytogenetics & Cell Genetics* XII. 87 The first recorded observation of XYY polysomy in man was made by Sandberg et al. in 1961.

polyspermic (pǫlispɜ̄·ɪmik), *a.* *Physiol.* [f. POLYSPERM(Y + -IC.] Involving or exhibiting polyspermy.

1890 BILLINGS *Med. Dict.* II. 368/2 *Polyspermic*, requiring more than one spermatozoon to fructify the egg. **1894** *Anatomischer Anzeiger* IX. 146 Stained preparations of these eggs show them to be, previous to division, polyspermic. **1953** *Austral. Jrnl. Biol. Sci.* VI. 674 In the polyspermic rat egg, the chromosome complements from the female pronucleus and the male pronuclei all take part in the formation of the first cleavage spindle. **1975** *Nature* 8 May 112/1 Since silkworms are polyspermic the opportunity then arises for two different male pronuclei to fuse and form a diploid zygote nucleus.

polyspike: see *POLY- 1.

polyspory (pǫ·lispōᵊri). *Bot.* [f. POLY- + SPOR(E + -Y³.] The production of unusually many spores.

1929 *Genetics* XIV. 213 Giant spores, dyads, quartets and polyspory with and without extra, small nuclei or chromatin masses were repeatedly observed. **1959** *Canad. Jrnl. Plant Sci.* XXXIX. 272 A case of polyspory in a *Triticum-Agropyron* hybrid line..proved to be due to spindle misfunction. **1970** *Indian Jrnl. Exper. Biol.* VIII. 128/2 The chromosome fragmentation and lack of active polar movement result in laggards which persist as micronuclei and consequently lead to polyspory.

polystelic (pǫlistī·lik), *a.* *Bot.* [a. F. *polystélique* (P. van Tieghem & H. Douliot 1886, in *Ann. Sci. Nat. Bot.* 7 ser. III. 276), f. POLY- + STELE 2 + -IC.] Of a stem or root: having more than one internal vascular cylinder or stele. So **po·lystele** (see quot. 1965); **po·lystely,** polystelic condition.

1891 *Ann. Bot.* V. 515 In the Cryptogams above cited..the original cylinder branches and the stem becomes polystelic. *Ibid.* 516 The two Dicotyledonous genera, in which alone, so far as we know, polystely prevails, belong to families remote from each other. **1896** Polystelic [see POLY- 1]. **1902** *Phil. Trans. R. Soc.* B. CXCV. 128 In *Anemia phyllitidis* the adult stem is characterised by the presence of so-called polystelic structure. **1902** *Encycl. Brit.* XXV. 413/2 This is the condition of astely, entirely parallel with polystely except that the separate strands are usually all or mostly leaf-traces. **1908** BOODLE & FRITSCH tr. *Solereder's Systematic Anat. Dicotyledons* II. vi. 1156 When the axis shows several steles in a transverse section, it is said to be polystelic. **1925** EAMES & MACDANIELS *Introd. Plant Anat.* v. 133 In contrast with the monostele was the 'polystele', a type of stele in which the vascular tissues are in the form of strands. **1938** *Current Sci.* VI. 383 Polystely occurs in the cortical region of the stolons. *Ibid.* 384 The polystelic condition observed in these plants might be regarded as the anatomical expression of the renewed adoption of the terrestrial habit. **1965** BELL & COOMBE tr. *Strasburger's Textbk. Bot.* 136 We come ..to the polystele, consisting of a system of individual vascular bundles, distributed over the whole of the transverse section. **1969** F. E. ROUND *Introd. Lower Plants* x. 125 (*caption*) Stellar arrangements in the vascular cryptogams... N_1 polystele.

polystyrene (pǫlistəiᵊ·rīn). [f. POLY- + *STYRENE.] Any polymer of styrene, esp. a hard, colourless thermoplastic resin; also, any of various plastics made from or containing this, which are widely used as moulding materials, films, and rigid foams. Also *attrib.*

1927 G. S. WHITBY in *India-Rubber Jrnl.* 16 Apr. 16/2 Poly-styrene becomes markedly elastic when warmed or swollen. *Ibid.*, Unstretched poly-styrene gave only an 'amorphous ring' when subjected to X-ray examination. **1939** *Nature* 13 May 787/2 The vinyl and polystyrene resins have valuable properties some of which are not possessed by the other resinoids. **1945** *Electronic Engin.* XVII. 698/1 Polystyrene..has long been considered to be the lightest in weight of all plastics. **1959** *Economist* 7 Mar. 895/2 The present output of polystyrene is about 28,000 tons a year, divided between Shell, Distillers and Monsanto. **1961** *Wall St. Jrnl.* 9 June 20/3 Koppers Co. is displaying a complete 12-foot sailboat made of polystyrene foam. **1970** N. SAUNDERS *Alternative London* 18 Sack chairs..consist of a chair-shaped bag three-quarters full of expanded polystyrene granules. **1973** *Materials & Technol.* VI. viii. 530 Polystyrene is readily polymerized exothermally to the straight polystyrene (homopolymer). *Ibid.* 533 Polystyrenes are manufactured in two stages. In the first stage the monomer styrene, possibly together with other monomers, is converted into the polymer... In the second stage the polymer is granulated, other substances frequently being added at the same time; rubbers,..oxidizers, pigments and the like, are such additions.

polystyrol, -sulphide, -sulphone: see *POLY- 2. **polysymptomatic:** see *POLY- 1.

polysynthetic, *a.* Add: **1.** Also applied to twinning of this kind. (Further example.)

1944 *Amer. Mineralogist* XXIX. 199 Under the microscope, hydrotungstite is seen to occur as tiny green platelike crystals which show polysynthetic twinning.

2. (Earlier and later examples.)

1816 P. S. DUPONCEAU *Let.* 30 Aug. in *Trans. Hist. & Lit. Comm. Amer. Philos. Soc.* (1819) I. 430 Crantz and Egede prove in the most incontrovertible manner that the language of Greenland is formed on the same *syntactic* or *polysynthetic* model. **1977** *Language* LIII. 10 Particularly interesting would be a polysynthetic language with many layers of morphology built into a single word.

polysynthetically *adv.* (examples in *Cryst.*).

1903 *Amer. Geologist* XXXII. 67 Within it are small, triclinic, polysynthetically twinned feldspars which are rather vaguely crystallized. **1968** I. KOSTOV *Mineral.* 394 The crystals are almost invariably polysynthetically twinned.

polysystemic (pǫlisistī·mic), *a.* *Linguistics.* [f. POLY- + SYSTEMIC *a.*] Composed of, characterized by, or recognizing many systems; used esp. with ref. to prosodic analysis.

1949 J. R. FIRTH in *Trans. Philol. Soc. 1948* 151 The monosystemic analysis based on a paradigmatic technique of oppositions and phonemes with allophones has reached, even overstepped, its limits! The time has come to try fresh hypotheses of a polysystemic character... The phonological structure of the sentence and the words which comprise it are to be expressed as a plurality of systems of interrelated phonematic and prosodic categories. **1957** *Year's Work Eng. Stud. 1955* 28/2 It remains a matter for regret that Firth's polysystemic approach to language has not yet been fully and explicitly formulated, for it is clear.. that it has much to offer us. **1964** *Language* XL. 315 Firth..indicated that it is a property of language itself to be irreducibly multistructural and polysystemic. **1970** B. M. H. STRANG *Hist. English* 11 Language..is not mono- but polysystemic. **1973** *Archivum Linguisticum* IV. 21 Such a three-choice system is inherent in all polysystemic approaches to linguistic structure.

So **polysyste·mically** *adv.*, in a polysystemic manner; **po:lysystemi·city, polysy·stemy,** the fact or condition of being polysystemic.

1964 *Archivum Linguisticum* XVI. 72 Martinet's recognition of the polysystemicity of language (instanced by the different vowel contrast systems in French final open and closed syllables..) puts him in some agreement on this point..with the Firthian position in linguistic analysis. **1964** *Language* XL. 315 There is at least one instance..in which the appeal to linguistic polysystemy has the consequence of preventing the analyst from making an adequate descriptive statement. **1966** T. HILL in C. E. Bazell *In Memory of J. R. Firth* 218 The examples will also illustrate the principle of polysystemicity as applied to different grammatical categories. **1973** *Archivum Linguisticum* IV. 21 The choice of tone at each place in the structure can be considered polysystemically.

Polytec, -tech (pǫlite·k), colloq. abbrev. of POLYTECHNIC *sb.* 2 (in Dict. and Suppl.); = *POLY².

1911 O. ONIONS *Widdershins* x. 192, I don't think I shall go to the Polytec. to-night. **1974** 'E. LATHEN' *Sweet & Low* xix. 182 Why shouldn't I speak English well? I went to Rensselaer Polytech. **1977** *N.Z. Woman's Weekly* 10 Jan. 16/3 The weaving course at the Polytec has generated a great interest in looms. **1977** *Belfast Tel.* 14 Feb. 22/3 Now they have given the Polytech's first big romance a fairy tale ending by getting engaged.

polytechnic, *a.* and *sb.* Add: **A.** *adj.* (Further examples.)

1837 *Penny Mechanic* II. 92/2 A Sample School, to be called the Polytechnic University, No. 1 for 2000 students. **1921** BEERBOHM *Lett. to R. Turner* (1964) 258 The incredible job [*sc.* H. G. Wells's *History of the World*], done so neatly..in a very awful cheap sciolistic polytechnic way. **1965** *Economist* 11 Sept. 1000/1 In the eyes of authority, naval history has remained a soft option in a polytechnic world.

B. *sb.* **2.** (Earlier and later examples.) In mod. use, a kind of institution of higher education offering courses mainly in technical and vocational subjects (see quot. 1973).

1836 C. FOX *Jrnl.* 31 Aug. (1972) 31 Dr. Buckland.. came on to the Polytechnic and stayed with us. **1841** M. EDGEWORTH *Let.* 25 May (1971) 593 Lestock..took Honora and Captain Beaufort and me to the Polytechnic and we all had our likenesses taken. **1850** W. HOWITT *Yr.-Bk. Country* iv. 111 Such places as Saint Paul's and Westminster Abbey should stand wide open; the Colosseum and the Polytechnic be accessible at the smallest price. **1857** C. KINGSLEY *Two Yrs. Ago* I. vii. 171 He would thrust his head into lectures at the Polytechnic and the British Institution. **1934** G. B. SHAW *On Rocks* II. 237 Jafna's grandsons will go to Eton. Mine will go to a Polytechnic. **1967** *Listener* 6 July 5/1 Mr. Crosland and his advisers envisage rather an eternal separation between the universities and an entirely new race of animals they have created called the polytechnics. **1973** *Times* 4 Oct. 4/4 Polytechnics differ from universities in that they are not centrally financed, teach courses for degrees of the Council for National Academic Awards (CNAA), have a substantial proportion of students on courses below degree level, do much less research, and have, in theory, a greater commitment to the vocational aspect of higher education. **1975** *Physics Bull.* Jan. 6/2 It is natural to think of the polytechnics as being primarily concerned with science and technology but this is not so. Only one third of the work of the average polytechnic lies in these fields. **1975** *Guardian* 27 Jan. 5/1 The higher education building programme..will contain a bias in favour of the polytechnics.

4. *attrib.*

1839 C. FOX *Jrnl.* 8 Oct. (1972) 58 The Bucklands dined with us, after a Polytechnic morning. **1911** O. ONIONS *Widdershins* 184 It was of Polytechnic classes that he spoke. *Ibid.* 189 The young Polytechnic student. **1972** R. K. KELSALL et al. *Graduates* i. 53 Parents of..university students..find university education more acceptable than do parents of..Polytechnic students. **1972** *Accountant* 19 Oct. 483/2 Polytechnic lecturers on a secondment period of six weeks for updating in auditing techniques. **1973** *Times Higher Educ. Suppl.* 20 July 12/1 With the formal inauguration of the Association of Polytechnic Teachers..yet another teachers' organization has emerged. **1979** V. S. NAIPAUL *Bend in River* x. 170 The polytechnic term was over.

Hence **po:lytechniza·tion,** the action or process of making (some activity) polytechnic; *spec.* in Communist countries, the process of educating children in technical and industrial subjects considered essential for the proper running of the State.

1932 *Times Lit. Suppl.* 17 Mar. 204/2 It would have been of advantage to provide a fuller and more detailed account..of the system of 'polytechnization' in the primary schools [of the U.S.S.R.]. **1933** *Times Educ. Suppl.* 25 Feb. 57/4 Polytechnization 'aims at producing a nation of socialistically thinking technical specialists'. **1949** K. DAVIS *Human Society* viii. 229 Economically, through 'polytechnization', the school is geared with productive life. **1974** *Encycl. Brit. Macropædia* VI. 375/2 From the 1950s onward, much attention has been paid [in Communist education] to the ideal of 'polytechnization'.

polytene (pǫ·litīn), *a.* *Cytology.* [POLY- + *-TENE.] Applied to giant chromosomes found in certain interphase nuclei, esp. in dipterous insects, and composed of many parallel copies of the genetic material, in which the active regions may be identifiable microscopically.

1935 P. C. KOLLER in *Proc. R. Soc.* B. CXVIII. 372 We can regard these chromosomes as corresponding with paired pachytene chromosomes at meiosis in which the intercalary parts between chromosomes have been stretched and separated into smaller units, and in which, instead of two threads lying side by side, we have 16 or even more. Hence they are 'polytene' rather than pachytene; I do not, however, propose to use this term; I shall refer to them as 'multiple threads'. **1959** C. M. M. BEGG *Introd. Genetics* iii. 27 The specificity of this pairing [of homologous chromosomes] is shown very strikingly in the case of the exceptional polytene threads of the much enlarged salivary gland nuclei of Diptera. **1971** *Nature* 21 May 184/2 Individuals of the species which breeds in freshwater can only be identified with certainty by the banding patterns of their polytene chromosomes. **1976** BELL & COOMBE tr. *Strasburger's Textbk. Bot.* (rev. ed.) 31 (*caption*) Giant chromosome, polytene and consisting of about 2048 strands, from the suspensor of the embryo of *Phaseolus vulgaris*.

Hence **polytenic** (-tī·nik) *a.*, in the same sense; **po·lyteny,** the state of being polytene; also **po:lyteniza·tion,** the production of polyteny; **polyte·nized** *ppl. a.* (of a chromosomal constituent) reduplicated owing to the polyteny of the chromosome.

1942 *Proc. R. Soc. Edin.* B. LXI. 318 The degree of polyteny found in the tissues of a dipteran larva varies with the species. **1953** W. HOVANITZ *Text-bk. Genetics* vii. 100 The terms salivary chromosomes and polytenic chromosomes have been applied to them [*sc.* giant chromosomes]. **1958** Polyteny [see *MIXOPLOIDY]. **1966** *Proc. R. Soc.* B. CLXIV. 280 After many steps of polytenization (12 or 14 consecutive replications) such a labelled chromosome thread may still extend as a single linear unit from the one end of the giant chromosome to the other end. **1968** H. HARRIS *Nucleus & Cytoplasm* iv. 77 The chromosomes in these [salivary] glands are extraordinary for two reasons. The first is that they are grossly polytenic. Each chromosome contains thousands of identical parallel copies of the basic diploid genetic structure. The extent of polyteny may vary in different species, but for *Chironomus tentans* it has been estimated that each chromosome contains about 16 000 times the normal diploid amount of DNA. **1974** *Nature* 29 Mar. 446/1 Mutational data also rule out simple polyteny and polyploidy, where every single gene on every chromosome is polytenised or where every chromosome is present in two or more copies. **1976** *Ibid.* 17 June 614/2 Ciliata and Diptera..show a high tendency for endopolyploidisation and polytenisation. **1976** BELL & COOMBE tr. *Strasburger's Textbk. Bot.* (rev. ed.) 31 In rare cases repeated multiplication of chromonemata leads to multistranded (polytenic), cable-like, giant chromosomes.

polyterpene, -terpenoid: see *POLY- 2.

po:lytetraflu:oroe·thylene. *Chem.* Also **-fluorethylene.** [f. POLY- + *TETRAFLUOROETHYLENE.] A highly crystalline resinous polymer of tetrafluoroethylene having the structure —$(CF_2CF_2)_n$—, which is tough, resistant to chemicals, stable over a wide range of temperature, and widely used as a moulding material, esp. under the trade name *Teflon*; abbr. *P.T.F.E.* (s.v. *P II. d).

1946 *Industr. & Engin. Chem.* Sept. 877/1 Although pure polytetrafluoroethylene is white in color, frequently commercially fabricated articles are somewhat gray and speckled, apparently as a result of minute traces of contamination. **1951** *Electronic Engin.* XXIII. 370 In order to obtain a smooth bearing, use has been made of polytetrafluoroethylene for the bearing surface. **1959** *Times Rev. Industry* June 22/1 Gaskets of polytetrafluorethylene or Fluon have proved invaluable in difficult services, since this material is resistant to all 'searching' chemical reagents except molten sodium and gaseous fluorine. **1961** *Lancet* 19 Aug. 410/1 Polytetrafluoroethylene (P.T.F.E., 'Fluon', 'Teflon') is at present the most suitable material for permanent cannulation. **1962** *Which?* Aug. 255/1 There are two kinds of non-stick frying pans—those with a silicone finish and those with a plastic called polytetrafluorethylene, or PTFE. **1975** *Sci. Amer.* July 63/1 Non-metals such as..polytetrafluoroethylene and carbon-graphites are successful bearing materials because of their excellent resistance to scoring and corrosion. **1978** J. SHERWOOD *Limericks of Lachasse* i. 8 The plant..made polytetrafluorethylene, a polymer with three times the density of polypropylene and enormously strong.

polytheistically, *adv.* (Example.)

1909 W. JAMES *Pluralistic Universe* viii. 310 It [*sc.* the superhuman consciousness] may be polytheistically or it may be monotheistically conceived of.

polythelia, -ism, -y: see *POLY- 1.

polythene (pǫ·liþīn). [Contraction of *POLYETHYLENE.] A tough, light, translucent thermoplastic made by polymerizing ethylene and used esp. for moulded and extruded articles, as film for packaging, and as a coating. Freq. *attrib.* and in *Comb.*

1939 *Plastics* III. 231/2 Polythene, the new polymerized ethylenic resin. *Ibid.* 289/1 Polymerized ethylenes manufactured..under the trade name of Polythene by I.C.I. have excellent electrical properties... These new compounds are now being carefully considered by well-known cable companies. **1943** *Brit. Plastics* XV. 417 Polythene is a general term for a range of solid polymers of ethylene, first discovered and prepared in I.C.I. Research Laboratories by subjecting ethylene to extremely high pressures under carefully controlled conditions. These products are sold under the registered name Alkathene'. **1945** *Times* 25 May 8/6 An outstanding I.C.I. achievement in the field of plastics was the discovery and development of polythene or polymerised ethylene. Polythene was seen to be a most valuable insulating material for high-frequency radio and television. **1951** *Catal. of Exhibits, South Bank Exhib., Festival of Britain* 109/1 Polythene ice cube mould. **1957** E. Bone *Seven Years' Solitary* xiv. 211, I had never heard of polythene bags. **1958** *Economist* 29 Mar. 1138/1 Sealed polythene bags offering protection and convenience in handling, have become commonplace for many small consumer products which used to be sold unpackaged. **1959** *Spectator* 25 Sept. 409/1 Polythene-wrapped food may be staler than it looks. **1960** *Farmer & Stockbreeder* 8 Mar. 105/2 There is a water trough supplied by the polythene pipe laid up one grass verge of the road. **1973** R. Fiennes *Headless Valley* vii. 129 We camped above the river beneath a thin sheet of polythene and slept. **1973** *Materials & Technol.* VI. viii. 524 Polythene has the simplest chemical structure of all plastics, consisting only of carbon and hydrogen in a straight chain. *Ibid.* 525 There are now many manufacturers of polythene, which is marketed under trade names such as Alkathene (UK), Bakelite, Alathon (USA), Lupolen (Germany) and so on. **1973** J. Rossiter *Manipulators* xxii. 213 She put on a glistening white polythene raincoat.

polythetic (pǫliþe·tik), *a.* [f. Poly- + Gr. θετ-ός placed, arranged + -ic 1.] Sharing a number of common characteristics, without any one of these being essential for membership of the group or class in question. So **polythe·tically** *adv.*

1962 P. H. A. Sneath in Ainsworth & Sneath *Microbial Classification* 291 Such groups, in which several sets of characters occur, are called 'polytypic' by Beckner, but are better called polythetic. Phenetic taxa are always in theory polythetic. **1963** Sokal & Sneath *Princ. Numerical Taxon.* ii. 15 Polythetic groups can..be arranged polythetically to give higher polythetic groups, as is done in building a hierarchy in the natural system. **1969** E. Mayr *Princ. Systematic Zool.* iv. 83 No single feature is essential for membership in a polythetically defined taxon. **1972** S. Themerson *Special Branch* 75 Let it take a polythetic way of classifying: let it consider the largest possible number of characteristics for each fact or object. **1972** C. Renfrew *Emergence of Civilisation* 11 It is now possible to make a statement about civilisations which does not seek to define them in terms of a single principal culture trait, or even polythetically, in terms of, for example, two out of three traits. **1976** *Brit. Jrnl. Psychol.* LXVII. 379 Most human concepts are polythetic..which means that no particular attribute or combination of attributes need necessarily be present (or absent) for an object to belong to a given category.

polytocous, *a.* Add: Also **-tokous. a.** (Examples.)

1932 *Proc. 6th Internat. Congr. Genetics* I. 188 In polytokous mammals we may expect that genes favoring rapid embryonic growth will spread, as slower growing embryos are at a disadvantage. **1936** *Nature* 12 Sept. 451/2 This..process [*sc.* fœtalization] has been essential for the evolution of man:..it could not have occurred in a polytocous form, where slowing of early growth would be prevented by intra-uterine selection. **1956** *Ibid.* 11 Feb. 288/2 Many observers have stressed the importance of a change in the nutrition of polytocous ewes during late pregnancy in the etiology of the disease. **1971** *Ibid.* 8 Oct. 379/1 In the polytocous species such as the small mammals and even the pig, it is not normally necessary to induce superovulation in order to provide the requisite number of eggs.

polytomy. **2.** (Earlier example.)

a **1856** W. Hamilton *Lect. Metaphysics & Logic* (1860) IV. xxv. 23 If a division has only two members, it is called a dichotomy..; if three, a trichotomy..; if four, a tetrachotomy; if many, a polytomy, &c.

polytonality (pǫlitonæ·lĭti). *Mus.* [f. Poly- + Tonality.] The simultaneous use of two or more keys in a musical composition.

1923 [see *atonal *a.*]. **1934** S. R. Nelson *All about Jazz* i. 12 Polytonality, dissonance, and the more lurid forms of Expressionism are the shibboleths of Schönberg, Stravinsky, Bartók and the moderns. **1946** G. Abraham in A. L. Bacharach *Brit. Music* iii. 61 The experiment is in polytonality—the flute plays in A, the oboe in A flat, and the viola in C. **1955** L. Feather *Encycl. Jazz* 32 Many young jazzmen were experimenting with atonality and polytonality. **1969** *Daily Tel.* 8 Nov. 9/3 Cold admiration seems to have been the response to his consciously manufactured rhythms, systematic polytonality and pattern building. **1977** J. Crosby *Company of Friends* xxxiv. 220 'Roger found out, did he?' asked Sascha idly, playing simultaneous D-minor and C-sharp triads. Polytonality—while naked. Very sexual.

So **polyto·nal** *a.*, containing or pertaining to polytonality; **polyto·nalist**, one who writes or advocates polytonal music.

1924 P. A. Scholes *Crotchets* 164 The device of 'canon' sometimes pointed to a polytonal future for music. **1934** C. Lambert *Music Ho!* ii. 68 The polytonal choral writing of Milhaud. **1938** *Oxf. Compan. Mus.* 406/1 The polytonalists appear to claim that the value of their work lies in the significance of the horizontal lines. **1949** *Penguin Music Mag.* July 24 The polytonal writing, in which different parts in the polyphony may have, not only their individual harmonization, but also each their own tonality, is chiefly a tentative realization of a stage that music is steadily approaching. **1952** B. Ulanov *Hist. Jazz in Amer.* (1958) xxiii. 332 All of the trio and octet scorings and performances partake..of the controlled but not stifling disciplines of a music which is polytonal, polyrhythmic at times, and spontaneous too. *Ibid.*, Dave..is another polytonalist. **1976** *New Yorker* 15 Nov. 194/2 Rich in feeling, sometimes polytonal (or, at any rate, of indefinite tonality), the piece is not without interest.

polytonic (pǫlitǫ·nik), *a.* [f. Poly- + Tonic *a.* and *sb.*] Using or having several (musical or vocal) tones.

1948 D. Diringer *Alphabet* i. vi. 99 So characteristic are the tones in the Tibeto-Chinese languages, that some scholars have suggested to term them 'polytonic'. **1955** *Sci. News Let.* 13 Aug. 102/1 A new signaling system for telephone dialing..has been developed... The device, called a polytonic coder, sends out digits just about as fast as they can theoretically be packed into a line. *Ibid.* 102/2 The tests showed the polytonic signal could be used on all except a few telephone connections in this country. **1961** J. Blades in A. Baines *Mus. Instruments* 342 The ingenious steel drums recently introduced in Trinidad are polytonic gongs... Each sector is tuned to a different note.

polytopal, -tope, -topic(al: see *poly- 1.

polytrope (pǫ·litrōup). *Physics* and *Astr.* [Back-formation from Polytropic *a.*, or a. G. *polytrope* in the same sense (R. Emden *Gaskugeln* (1907) i. i. 13).] A polytropic body of gas (see *polytropic *a.* 4).

1926 A. S. Eddington *Internal Constitution of Stars* iv. 86 The polytrope $n = 3$, which is believed to correspond nearly to the actual conditions of the stars. **1939** S. Chandrasekhar *Introd. Study Stellar Struct.* iv. 170 So far we have considered only complete polytropes. We shall now proceed to a consideration of composite polytropes, i.e., configurations which consist of different zones each characterized by a different value of the index n. **1975** *Nature* 27 Mar. 295/1 The energy required to break up a star of mass m and radius R is..$\frac{3}{5}(Gm^2/R)$ for a polytrope of index $n = 3\frac{1}{2}$.

polytropic, *a.* Add: **3.** [ad. G. *polytrope* (E. Loew 1884, in *Jahrbuch K. Bot. Gartens Berlin*).] Of a bee: collecting nectar from many kinds of flower.

1899 C. Robertson in *Bot. Gaz.* XXVIII. 29 If a bee has a long flight it must be regarded as polytropic. **1919** J. H. Lovell *Flower & Bee* 120 There are also on the wing at the same time 6 species which are polytropic.

4. *Physics* and *Astr.* [ad. G. *polytropisch* (G. Zeuner *Technische Thermodynamik* (ed. 3, 1887) I. xxix. 143).] Pertaining to or designating a body of gas or a process in which pressure and volume change in such a way that a specific heat remains constant. Also as *sb.*, a graph showing such a variation of pressure and volume.

1907 J. F. Klein tr. *Zeuner's Technical Thermodynamics* I. xxix. 152 If the initial condition is given by p_1 and v_1, we accordingly have $pv^n = p_1v_1^n$..as the equation of the sought pressure curve, which we will hereafter call the polytropic curve. **1926** A. S. Eddington *Internal Constitution of Stars* iv. 94 A class of problems arises in which the polytropic condition..applies only to part of the star. **1933** *Monthly Notices R. Astron. Soc.* XCIII. 390 Emden's well-known researches on the equilibrium of polytropic gas spheres has been of fundamental importance in its repercussions on the modern theories of stellar structure. **1939** S. Chandrasekhar *Introd. Study Stellar Struct.* ii. 40 An adiabatic..is a polytropic of zero specific heat, and an isothermal a polytropic of infinite heat capacity. **1952** W. M. Deans tr. *Prandtl's Essent. Fluid Dynamics* v. 391 If we assume a polytropic law for the variation of density with height, $p/p_g = (\rho/\rho_g)^n$, where the suffix g refers to the ground. **1968** Cox & Giuli *Princ. Stellar Struct.* II. xxiii. 703 A polytropic star is one which obeys an equation of the form $P = K\rho^{(n+1)/n}$, where n, the polytropic index..and K are constants throughout the star. **1976** *Nature* 17 June 561/1 The moment of inertia of a spherical star can be written $I = km_{\text{p}}NR^2$ where for stable polytropic stars $0{\cdot}04 \leq k \leq 0{\cdot}132$.

polytype. Add: **2.** *Cryst.* A polytypic form of a substance.

In quot. 1916 rendering G. *polytypie* polytypism.

1916 *Chem. Abstr.* X. 872 (*heading*) The various modifications of carborundum and the occurrence of polytypes. **1922** *Mineral. Abstr.* I. 318 Three modifications or polytypes of carborundum crystals are distinguished as types I, II, and III. **1951** *Phil. Mag.* XLII. 1019 Unstable structures will not grow if the supersaturation is small: but probably most of the observed polytypes of carborundum differ in thermodynamic potential by an amount negligible compared with the supersaturation actually occurring. **1972** *Physics Bull.* Dec. 712/1 The difficult areas of x ray crystallography, such as in the study of martensitically transformed materials, mixed polytypes of a mineral or certain nonstoichiometric oxides, can be opened up by an electron microscope technique. **1974** *Nature* 22 Feb. 537/2 The basic structural unit of tin sulphide polytypes consists of two layers of hexagonal close-packed sulphide ions with smaller tin ions nested between them.

polytypic, *a.* **1.** Substitute for def.: Having several variant forms; esp., of a species, including several subspecies or other lower taxa. (Later examples.)

1945 *Bull. Amer. Mus. Nat. Hist.* LXXXV. 16/2 This morphological scope may be almost entirely filled or exploited by known species if the genus has many (is polytypic). **1953** [see *allopatric *a.*]. **1959** *New Biol.* XXVIII. 81 This process [*sc.* the variation of isolated populations] might produce simply what the systematist calls a polytypic species, consisting of a sequence of subspecies each occupying a distinct geographical region and each somewhat different in ecology. **1970** *Nature* 5 Sept. 1065/1 It is now recognized that *Papio* is a single polytypic species with morphologically different subspecies interbreeding wherever they meet. **1975** *Trans. R. Entomol. Soc.* CXXVI. 613 We will discuss the data for this polytypic species under the four form names.

2. *Cryst.* Exhibiting polytypism (sense *1); of the nature of a polytype.

1944 [see *polytypism 1]. **1974** Verma & Trigundayat in C.N.R. Rao *Solid State Chem.* ii. 52 The list of polytypic substances includes minerals, layer silicates, chalcogenides, and several other inorganic and organic compounds.

3. = *polythetic *a.*

1959 M. Beckner *Biol. Way of Thought* ii. 25 Polytypic concepts are found in many branches of biological theory, but the clearest instances are afforded by taxonomy. **1961** G. G. Simpson *Princ. Animal Taxon.* ii. 43 The defining attributes do not appear in all individuals... The principle (which he calls 'polytypic') has been elucidated at greater length and in ultramodern terms by Beckner.

polytypism (pǫlitəi·piz'm). [f. Polytyp(ic *a.* + -ism.] **1.** [After G. *polytypie* (H. Baumhauer 1915, in *Zeitschr. f. Krist. u. Min.* LV. 252).] A kind of polymorphism in which a substance occurs in a number of crystalline modifications (polytypes) which differ only in one of the dimensions of the unit cell.

1944 N. W. Thibault in *Amer. Mineralogist* XXIX. 266 Following Baumhauer, the phenomenon is called 'polytypism' the adjective being 'polytypic' and each one of the different modifications a 'type'. **1951** *Phil. Mag.* XLII. 1016 It has long been recognized that the relationship between the various forms of carborundum is so close as to deserve a special name 'polytypism'. **1973** L. Suchow in P. F. Weller *Solid State Chem. & Physics* I. ii. 130 All compounds exhibiting polytypism are..of the layer-structure type. **1974** Verma & Trigundayat in C. N. R. Rao *Solid State Chem.* ii. 52 The modifications, called polytypes or simply types, differ only in the arrangement of packing of the close-packed planes of the solids... In this sense the polytypism may be termed one-dimensional polymorphism, although its origin seems to be distinctly different from the latter.

2. *Biol.* The occurrence of several variant forms within a single species. Also **po·lytypy** in the same sense.

1949 W. F. Albright *Archaeol. of Palestine* iii. 57 The polytypism now known to be characteristic of early man is equally characteristic of dogs, whose classification as a single species is not disputed by zoologists. **1961** G. G. Simpson *Princ. Animal Taxon.* iv. 135 In cases of extreme polytypy, first consideration should be given to making the taxon less unwieldy by use of intermediate lower taxa or subgroups.

polyunsaturated (pǫli,ʌnsæ·tiŭrēitėd), *a.* *Chem.* Also **poly-unsaturated.** [f. Poly- + Unsaturated *ppl. a.*] Containing more than one multiple bond between carbon atoms at which addition can normally occur; applied esp. to fatty acids in which the hydrocarbon chain has more than one multiple bond, which occur esp. in some vegetable oils.

1932 *Biochem. Jrnl.* XXVI. 1978 The marine flora contains poly-unsaturated fatty acids of high molecular weight similar to those found in the fat of fishes, although in very small amounts. **1958** *Jrnl. Sci. Food & Agric.* IX. 779 In animal tissues the glycerophosphatides are outstanding in their high content of long-chain polyunsaturated acids. **1960** *Farmer & Stockbreeder* 22 Mar. 133/1 Polyunsaturated fats for peak condition, healthy skin and coat, more efficient metabolism. **1961** *Sunday Times* 7 May 36/3 American housewives,..concerned about their husbands' health, are shopping for 'polyunsaturated fats'. The rush is on because medical research has established a connection between arterial diseases and the level of cholesterol in the blood—and cholesterol seems to be formed chiefly from the intake of the 'saturated fats', particularly animal and dairy fats. **1970** *New Scientist* 19 Feb. 356/2 It might also be possible to increase the proportion of poly-unsaturated acids in ruminant tissue fats. **1973** *Which?* Feb. 54 Butter generally has 2 per cent polyunsaturated fatty acids. **1977** B. Pym *Quartet in Autumn* xiii. 115 A tub of polyunsaturated margarine. **1979** *Times* 7 Dec. 10/3 'Polyunsaturated' has become a totem word... The idea that heart attacks can be avoided by replacing saturated fats in the diet with polyunsaturated fats has been promoted with great skill and large budgets.

So **polyunsa·turate** *sb.*, a polyunsaturated fatty acid; also as *adj.*

1950 *Arch. Biochem.* XXV. 6 Polyunsaturates were also concentrated in high amounts in the liver fatty acids. **1962** *Seattle Sunday Times* (Sunday Pictorial) 25 Mar. 18/2 (Advt.), It's a face cream that contains essential polyunsaturates. That's right—polyunsaturates, the natural elements you've been reading so much about that are so important to your health. **1962** *Chicago Sun-Times* 20 July 28/3 Maybe, so current thinking goes, we would be better off in the long run to reduce our costly animal fats and substitute the vegetable (polyunsaturate) fats and oils. **1974** *Observer* (Colour Suppl.) 17 Mar. 15/1 There are doubts..about the side-effects of the various polyunsaturate oils used. *Ibid.*, Only a few vegetable oils are high in polyunsaturates.

polyurethane (pǫli,yū·rĕþēin). Formerly also **-an.** [f. Poly- + Urethane.] Any of a large class of synthetic resins and plastics consisting of or made from polymers with the units linked by the group—NH·CO·O—, which are made esp. by the reaction of polyisocyanates with polyhydroxy compounds and are important commercially as plastic foams, as fibres, and in paints, adhesives, synthetic rubbers, films, etc. Also *attrib.* and *Comb.*, esp. *polyurethane foam.*

1944 *Chem. Abstr.* XXXVIII. 381 (*heading*) Polyurethans and polyureas. **1945** *Chem. & Engin. News* 25 Sept. 1615/1 Among the new or less well-known polymers which they [*sc.* the Germans] have been manufacturing are polyvinyl ethers..and polyurethanes. **1945** *Mod. Plastics* Oct. 152F/2 Polyurethane resin was used on a small scale as an adhesive in aircraft construction. **1957** B. A. Dombrow *Polyurethanes* i. 8 In the latter part of 1947..Lockheed Aircraft Corporation began independently to develop polyurethane foam systems for use in radome construction and in filling aircraft components. **1958** *Engineering* 7 Feb. 167/2 A lightweight portable shelter suitable for aircraft, vehicles or stored goods, consisting of a tubular light-alloy framework covered with polyurethane-proofed nylon. **1964** *Which?* Aug. 254/1 Polyurethane has become known in the form of plastic foam for sponges among other things, but is now finding its way into the textile field. **1968** W. Warwick *Surfriding in N.Z.* 16/3 At present surfboards are being constructed from the material polyurethane. **1969** *Sears Catal.* Spring/Summer 9 Exclusive 3-inch thick cushions.. softly padded with shredded Serofoam polyurethane. **1971** *New Scientist* 10 June 630/2 Polyurethane-coated fabrics are still at an early stage of development. **1974** *Nature* 16 Aug. 526/3 Polyurethane foam is sprayed on to the inside of a lightweight aluminium mould.

Hence as *v. trans.*, to coat or protect with polyurethane.

1977 B. Randall *Fan* 22 Don't go in the dining room, I polyurethaned the floor. **1978** J. Updike *Coup* (1979) iii. 109 I've seen blueprints, concrete wings supported by polyurethaned nylon cables. **1979** M. Page *Pilate Plot* ix. 137 Washed Chinese carpets on the sanded and polyurethaned floorboards.

polyuria, -uric: see *poly- 1. **polyuronide:** *poly- 2.

polyvalent. Add: **1.** Now usu. with pronunc. (pǫlivē·lĕnt). (Further examples.)

1950 N. V. Sidgwick *Chem. Elements* I. 177 The polyvalent state of gold..is much more stable than the monovalent. **1964** N. G. Clark *Mod. Org. Chem.* xxiv. 510 With all other polyvalent species of atom accounted for, the side chain..must consist of three linked carbon atoms. **1975** *Nature* 6 Nov. 19/1 The formation of a ring structure by a protein factor or possibly polyvalent ions, the use of the ring as a nucleating centre, [etc.]..were discussed.

b. *Med.* = *multivalent *a.* b.

1912 *Amer. Jrnl. Med. Sci.* CXLIV. 815 The complement fixation test (using a polyvalent antigen) for gonococcus antibodies should prove an addition to our methods of diagnosticating between..gonococcus infection and.. other causes. **1951** Whitby & Hynes *Med. Bacteriol.* (ed. 5) vi. 72 When an antigen in colloidal solution is mixed with antibody under suitable conditions a precipitate of antigen-antibody complex appears. Most of the precipitate consists of antibody, since antibody molecules in general are larger than those of antigens, whilst antigens are polyvalent and each molecule combines with two or more molecules of antibody. **1975** *Nature* 11 Sept. 103/1 Interaction of divalent or polyvalent ligands (for example, antibodies, lectins) with cell surface structures on lymphocytes and many other cell types induces redistribution of the largely diffuse binding sites into clusters and into highly polarised single aggregates or 'caps'.

2. Delete ? and add to def.: or affording immunity against various species of microorganism. (Later examples.)

1929 [see *botulin]. **1965** C. Andrewes *Common Cold* xix. 168 'Polyvalent' vaccines—those effective against many bacteria or viruses—are very fine in theory. **1966** *Jrnl. Immunol.* XCVII. 517/2 A third antigen preparation consisted of a single polyvalent antigen prepared by combining equal amounts of the 12 flexner stock antigens and a stock *Shigella sonnei* antigen.

3. = *multivalent *a.* 3.

1957 S. Ullmann *Style in French Novel* 20 Stylistic elements, it will be remembered, are 'polyvalent'; the same device may produce several effects, and conversely, the same effect may be obtained from several devices. **1960** E. Delavenay *Introd. Machine Transl.* iii. 36 The grammatical value of polyvalent words. **1966** *New Statesman* 25 Feb. 266/2 The colour-symbolism in [Tarsis'] *Red and Black* is pervasive and bafflingly polyvalent. **1975** J. De Bres tr. *Mandel's Late Capitalism* viii. 268 Full automation reduces the number of semi-skilled workers and gives rise to a new and highly skilled polyvalent work force. **1977** *Word 1972* XXVIII. 294 The analyst will be tempted to ignore the systems based on very general concepts yielding the simplest description for all languages in favor of a very specific system adapted to the specific language of the texts to be recorded: the kind of simplicity he will look for is of the monovalent rather than of the polyvalent type.

polyvalence (further example); also stressed *polyva·lence.*

1971 *Archivum Linguisticum* II. 104 Now he writes.. about the polyvalence of the injunctive—including *s*, *ā* and *ē* stems. In spite of this polyvalence he thinks that there is a common core in the subjunctive and preterite use of these stems.

polyvinyl (pǫlivəi·nĭl, -vəi·nəil). [f. Poly- + Vinyl.] **a.** Used *attrib.* in the names of polymeric substances derived from vinyl compounds, as **polyvinyl acetal,** any of a class of synthetic resins prepared by condensing polyvinyl alcohol with an aldehyde (sometimes *spec.* acetaldehyde), and mainly used, esp. polyvinyl butyral (see below), in safety glass and in lacquers and paints; **polyvinyl acetate,** a fairly soft plastic having the structure $—[CH_2—CH(O·CO·CH_3)]_n—$, which is made by polymerizing vinyl acetate and is used chiefly in paints and adhesives; abbrev. *PVA* (s.v. *P II. d); **polyvinyl alcohol,** any of a series of polymers consisting wholly or largely of the repeating unit $—[CH_2—CHOH]—$ which are prepared by hydrolysis of polyvinyl esters and have a wide range of uses, e.g. as emulsifiers, adhesives, coatings, films, and fibres; abbrev. *PVA* (s.v. *P II. d); **polyvinyl butyral,** the most widely used of the polyvinyl acetals (see above), which is prepared from butyraldehyde; **polyvinyl chloride,** any of various thermoplastics consisting of or made from a polymer having the structure $—[CH_2—CHCl]_n—$ and made by polymerizing vinyl chloride, which are produced in a wide variety of rigid and plasticized forms and are characterized esp. by their toughness, chemical inertness, and electrical resistivity; abbrev. *PVC* (s.v. *P II. d); **polyvinyl pyrrolidone,** a water-soluble polymer of vinyl pyrrolidone which is physiologically harmless and has a great variety of applications, esp. in solution, e.g. as a synthetic blood plasma substitute, as a thickening, suspending, or binding agent in the cosmetic, drug, and food processing industries, and in fibres and films; abbrev. *PVP* (s.v. *P II. d).

All these often occur as single words.

1933 *Industr. & Engin. Chem.* Feb. 129/1 The structure of polyvinyl acetal. **1944** [see *phenolic *a.* b]. **1973** *Materials & Technol.* VI. viii. 552 The use of polyvinyl butyral for making safety glass was patented in 1938 and this has since become one of the most important applications, certainly in America. The next important consumer of polyvinyl acetals is the lacquer and paint industry (for wash-primers). **1927** *Brit. Chem. Abstr.* A. 1051/2 Hydrolysis of polyvinyl acetate yields polyvinyl alcohol which resembles starch in its insolubility in organic media. **1958** W. M. Smith *Vinyl Resins* i. 19 Polyvinyl acetate emulsions as a replacement for conventional grain starch are stated to withstand as many as 15 launderings. **1967** W. Gaunt *Compan. Painting* ii. 85 Some modern artists have..found congenial qualities in such synthetic paints as ripolin and polyvinyl acetate. **1972** *Homes & Gardens* Mar. 106/2 In their infancy, emulsion paints were regarded with some suspicion, partly because early ones, based on a polyvinylacetate (pva) medium, tended to become brittle and flake off. **1927** Polyvinyl alcohol [see *polyvinyl acetate* above]. **1962** J. T. Marsh *Self-Smoothing Fabrics* x. 133 There are occasions where a slightly stiff finish is required and polyvinyl alcohol is a popular choice of additive in this connection. **1971** D. Potter *Brit. Eliz. Stamps* vi. 68 A synthetic adhesive was invented. Completely non-toxic, colourless, odourless and tasteless, it is known as Polyvinyl Alcohol, and familiarly named pva by philatelists. **1973** *Materials & Technol.* VI. viii. 548 The usual method of preparing polyvinyl alcohol is by the hydrolysis of a polyvinyl ester, generally polyvinyl acetate. **1943** *Industr. & Engin. Chem.* Feb. 175/2 In polyvinyl butyral resin..certain fillers appear to have reinforcing action. **1955** *Sci. News Let.* 16 Apr. 247/1 Adhesives for bonding two pieces of glass together are best made of polyvinyl-butyral resin mixed with modified phenol. **1973** Polyvinyl butyral [see *polyvinyl acetal* above]. **1933** *Industr. & Engin. Chem.* Feb. 129/1 Co-polymerization of vinyl chloride and vinyl acetate gives a better resin than the mere admixture of polyvinyl chloride and polyvinyl acetate. **1937** *Chem. Abstr.* XXXI. 6434 A mixt. of water with polyvinylchloride..is used for coating glass plates and is dried upon them, and then the coated plates are united by the action of heat and pressure. **1945** *Electronic Engin.* XVI. 499/3 Plastic sleeving of the polyvinylchloride type is the real answer to all these problems. **1958** *Engineering* 7 Mar. 294/2 The folding top is in leather-cloth, coated with polyvinyl chloride. **1976** *Nature* 3 June 409/1 Each trough held 50 oysters on a false bottom consisting of polyethylene grids resting on polyvinylchloride pipe. **1945** *Chem. Abstr.* XXXIX. 5408 Such solns. [i.e. blood plasma substitutes] are prepared by adding polyvinylpyrrolidone.. to a physiol. salt soln. **1957** *Financial Times Ann. Rev. Brit. Industry* 86/3 Experiments have shown that polyvinyl pyrrolidone..used as a blood thickener can be readily broken down..to..the most useful molecular size for medical use. **1974** M. C. Gerald *Pharmacol.* ix. 164 The plasma substitutes, dextran and polyvinylpyrrolidone (PVP), are also histamine releasers.

b. Any of the plastics or synthetic resins made by polymerizing a compound containing the vinyl group, $CH_2═CH—$; applied *esp.* to those derived from a compound usu. designated as vinyl (see prec. sense), but sometimes extended to include polyvinylidenes, polystyrene, etc. Freq. *attrib.*

1933 *Industr. & Engin. Chem.* Feb. 129/1 To render the normal polyvinyl resin more water-resistant, it is converted partly or wholly to the acetal by reaction with an aldehyde, usually formaldehyde or acetaldehyde. **1937** *Brit. Plastics* IX. 172/1 Vinyl esters of both inorganic and organic acids are well known..raw materials for conversion to polyvinyls. **1940** 'Plastes' *Plastics in Industry* ii. 15 More recently polyvinyl plastics have been employed as floorcloth, long-playing phonograph records, [etc.]. *Ibid.*, An interesting series of thermo-plastics which resemble the polyvinyls closely. **1946** *Nature* 16 Nov. 689/2 The use of methacrylate esters and the various polyvinyls is increasing in these fields [*sc.* arts and crafts]. **1963** [see *polyvinylidene b]. **1966** *Punch* 26 Jan. 116/3 Palpitations on finding sleek strangers at the front door in answer to my inquiry about polyvinyl tiling. **1969** R. Mayer *Dict. Art Terms & Techniques* 422/2 Few of the vinyl products are practicable for use in artists' materials... One exception is a polyvinyl isolating varnish containing isopropyl alcohol that thins with alcohol.

polyvinylidene (pǫ:livəini·lidīn, -vəinəi·lidīn). *Chem.* [f. Poly- + *vinylidene.] **a.** Used *attrib.* in the names of substances which are polymers of vinylidene compounds, esp. *polyvinylidene chloride*, any of a class of resinous polymers of vinylidene chloride which have the structure $—[CH_2—CCl_2]_n—$, and have a wide range of applications, esp. as impact- and chemical-resistant films and fibres.

1940 *Chem. Rev.* XXVI. 163 Natta and Rigamonti.. found..polyvinylidene chloride to be quite highly crystalline. **1942** *Industr. & Engin. Chem.* Mar. 327/2 These polyvinylidene chloride plastics are known by the trade name, 'Saran'. **1964** *Discovery* Oct. 17/1 The lamination consists of an aluminum foil and three plastic films —one of polythene, another of polyvinylidene chloride and a third of polyester. **1966** *McGraw-Hill Encycl. Sci. & Technol.* X. 496/2 Films of polyvinylidene chloride, and especially the copolymer containing about 15% of vinyl chloride, are resistant to moisture and gases. **1973** *Materials & Technol.* VI. viii. 547 Because of its resistance to chemicals, polyvinylidene fluoride is used for tubes, valves, and pumps in the chemical industry. **1975** P. Browne *Bodywork Maintenance* vi. 79/2 Cloths such as Tygan, woven from polyvinylidene chloride filaments, need an interlayer..to prevent a chemical reaction between the Tygan and the rubber.

b. Any of the synthetic resins prepared from vinylidene compounds. Freq. *attrib.*

1941 *Plastics* V. 249/2 (*caption*) Flow sheet showing production of polyvinylidene polymers from petroleum and brine. **1960** *Times Rev. Industry* Sept. 65/3 The tendency seems to be for polythene yarns to replace some of the earlier types such as polyvinylidene. **1963** A. J. Hall *Textile Sci.* ii. 18 (*table*) Polyvinyls and polyvinylidenes. **1972** *Homes & Gardens* Mar. 107 One firm has now introduced a full gloss emulsion paint based on a polyvinyledene [*sic*] medium.

polywater (pǫ·liwǭtəɪ). [f. Poly- + Water *sb.*] A supposed polymeric form of water having properties markedly different from those of ordinary water and reported to have been found in fine capillary tubes.

1969 E. R. Lippincott et al. in *Science* 27 June 1482/3 The properties, therefore, are no longer anomalous but rather, those of a newly found substance—polymeric water or polywater. **1969** *Daily Tel.* 13 Sept. 22/3 American scientists have confirmed the existence of a new kind of water which freezes at 40deg C and boils at 500deg C... The new water, known as 'polywater' has a density of about 40 per cent. greater than ordinary water. **1972** *Britannica Yearbk. Sci. & Future 1971* 216 Anomalous water (or polywater), which has attracted much attention in recent months, was shown to be not an unusual form of water but ordinary water containing ionic impurities. **1972** F. Franks *Water* I. i. 13 During 1969 the 'polywater' bandwagon began to roll. *Ibid.*, A climax was provided by a warning to scientists against experimenting with polywater as this might affect the oceans, turning them solid. **1975** J. Clifford in *Ibid.* V. ii. 119 Defenders of the water polymer idea have suggested that polywater could be a weakly bonded complex that disintegrates under electron impact and does not appear in the mass spectrum.

polyxenic: see *poly- 1.

polyzoal, *a.* (Example.)

1856 G. J. Allman *Monogr. Fresh-Water Polyzoa* 3 The investigations of Trembley and Baker..clearly demonstrated..all the essential characters of polyzoal structure.

polyzoan, *a.* and *sb.* Add: = Bryozoan *a.* and *sb.* (Earlier and later examples.)

1856 P. H. Gosse *Man. Marine Zool. Brit. Isles* II. 5

A tiny Annelid or other animal, caught by the bird's-head of a Polyzoan and tightly held, would presently die. **1880** T. HINCKS *Hist. Brit. Marine Polyzoa* I. p. xvii, The tentacular sheath is an important element..of the ordinary Polyzoan type. **1924** S. J. HICKSON *Introd. Study Recent Corals* viii. 159 Zooecia..build up the various kinds of branching, net-like, or encrusting structures of the Polyzoan corals. **1959** *Jrnl. Exper. Biol.* XXXVI. 613 (*heading*) Experiments on the selection of algal substrates by polyzoan larvae.

polyzoism. (Earlier example.)

1890 W. JAMES *Princ. Psychol.* I. vi. 179 It may be called the theory of polyzoism or multiple monadism.

Pom[1] (pǫm). Also **pom.** Colloq. abbrev. of POMERANIAN *sb.*

1904 *Outing* Feb. 484/2 Collies and 'poms' in America have hardly maintained their status because of this coat trouble. **1910** *Bazaar, Exchange & Mart* 10 June 1523/2 (*heading*) Coming shows... Dogs... Manchester (Poms). **1911** F. T. BARTON *My Bk. Little Dogs* iii. 33 The Pekinese and the Pom are the most popular toy dogs at the present time. **1923** R. MACAULAY *Told by Idiot* II. xxi. 138 Rome..drove elegantly in hansoms, often with an enormous wolf-hound or a couple of poms. **1939** T. S. ELIOT *Old Possum's Pract. Cats* 27 And the Pugs and the Poms.. will now and again join in to the fray. **1956** E. BERCKMAN *Beckoning Dream* vi. 46 Lydia..bred miniature Poms. In the vast living-room..twenty little dogs disported themselves. **1973** R. HILL *Ruling Passion* II. i. 85 'Not much of a guard-dog,' he said. 'It's a pom,' Pascoe said patiently.

Pom[2] (pǫm). *Austral.* and *N.Z. colloq.* Also **pom.** Abbrev. of *POMMY *sb.* (*a.*)

1919 W. H. DOWNING *Digger Dial.* 38 *Pommy*, an English soldier. *Pom*, see *Pommy*. **1941** BAKER *Dict. Austral. Slang* 56 *Pom*, an Englishman. **1946** F. SARGESON *That Summer* 92 He was a big matelot, though not a Pom, it was easy to tell he was a Pig Islander. **1957** *Economist* 9 Nov. 510/2 New British migrants are more readily assimilated than continental Europeans. Australians do not consider the 'Poms' as foreigners. **1963** A. LUBBOCK *Austral. Roundabout* 83 'Be seein' yer soon in England... Good on yer, Pom.' **1975** D. BLOODWORTH *Clients of Omega* ix. 84 You a Pom or something, sister?.. You've got a swine of a Pom accent. **1977** *Bulletin* (Sydney) 22 Jan. 20/1 And there's New Zealand to come; and then the Centenary Test against the Poms.

Pom[3] (pǫm). Also **pom.** The proprietary name of a brand of dried and powdered cooked potato.

1947 *Trade Marks Jrnl.* 23 Apr. 234/1 Pom... Cooked potatoes and potato preparations..M.P.P. (Products) Limited,..Norwich; Manufacturers. **1955** G. BAND *Road to Rakaposhi* xii. 136 The menu was..complicated.. stewed steak and pom, fruit cake and tea. **1968** *Economist* 15 June 64/3 Oddly enough, the greatest potential market for dried food is those old wartime standbys—dried milk and dried potatoes. Dehydrated potato, indistinguishable from the 'pom' of the 1940s,..now has a market worth £2 million a year. **1970** *Times* 26 Nov. 17/4 The late André Simon compiled his Dictionary of Gastronomy during the War years, presumably to cheer himself up among the snoek and pom.

Poma[2] (pōᵘ·mă). *N. Amer.* Also **poma.** [f. the name of J. *Pomagalski*, its inventor.] The proprietary name of a type of ski-lift having detachable hangers; so *Poma lift, Pomalift.*

1954 *Amer. Ski Ann. & Skiing Jrnl.* Jan. 55/1 The POMA lift at Arapahoe Basin, once the wooden towers were in place, was erected in sixteen days in the worst possible weather. **1955** *Ski Mag.* Oct. 51/2 (Advt.), Big news at Big Bromley..a new 2,190 ft. Poma lift has been installed. **1957** T. KESTING *Outdoor Encycl.* 403/2 On the Pomalift—a kind of platter-pull—the hangers are stored at the bottom and clamped onto the cable as needed. **1963** *Amer. Speech* XXXVIII. 206 Skiers usually do not differentiate between *platter pull* and *poma*; the latter seems to have become the universally accepted term for both types working with disks. **1968** *Globe & Mail* (Toronto) 13 Jan. 35/3 Other Muskoka resorts offering modern accommodation as well as T-bar or pomalift include Muskoka Sands, [etc.]. **1970** *Official Gaz.* (U.S. Patent Office) 14 Apr. TM 80/2 Jean Pomagalski S.A., Fontaine-Grenoble, France... *Poma* for cable transport or towing apparatus and installations—namely, cable cars, gondola-lifts, chair-lifts, ski-lifts. **1973** P. A. WHITNEY *Snowfire* vi. 105 A chair lift, with T-bar, J-bar and poma lift off to our right. **1977** *Forest Sci.* XXIII. 168 Area 1..is only affected by skiing activity (ski runs, poma lifts).

pomace. Add: **4. pomace-fly** = *DROSOPHILA.

1897 J. H. COMSTOCK *Insect Life* 185 As these insects are often abundant about pomace in cider-mills and wineries, they have been termed pomace-flies. **1924** J. A. THOMSON *Sci. Old & New* xxvii. 152 When the pomace-fly, Drosophila, is feeding on fermenting fruit, it must have yeasts to help it. **1946** C. T. BRUES *Insect Dietary* v. 194 The pomace fly, *Drosophila*, so successfully used by geneticists to elucidate the processes of inheritance, has likewise served..to demonstrate some of the food relations of microphagous insects.

Pomak (pōᵘ·mæ̆k). [Bulg.] A Muslim Bulgarian.

1887 *Encycl. Brit.* XXII. 149/2 Those Bulgarians who have embraced Islam are called Pomaks,—a word of which no satisfactory derivation has been given. **1897** E. A. BARTLETT *Battlefields Thessaly* iii. 49 The local militia were mostly Pomaks, or Mussulman Bulgarians. **1900** 'ODYSSEUS' *Turkey in Europe* viii. 363 The country between Seres and Philippopoli is inhabited by people called Pomaks, who are commonly described as Mohammedan Bulgarians. **1921** *Contemp. Rev.* May 587 It is not unusual to find that in any computation made by the Greeks,..the Pomaks—*i.e.*, Bulgarians who have embraced the Mohammedan faith, are reckoned with the Turks. **1972** D. DAKIN *Unification of Greece* 269 The Slav minority, which included 16,000 Pomaks, was about 80,000.

pomander. Restrict 'Now *Hist.*' to senses in Dict. and add: **1. a.** (Later examples.) Also, a piece of fruit, esp. an orange, stuck with cloves and usu. tied with ribbon, which is hung or placed in a wardrobe.

1931 E. S. ROHDE *Scented Garden* viii. 219 *Pomanders, Etc.*.. The orange..will scent a drawer deliciously for well over a year. **1946** J. DE BOTH *Mod. Househ. Encycl.* 237/1 Pomanders may be made from apples, oranges, or lemons.—*to make*, select firm fruit and stick whole cloves into entire surface; hang in clothes closet or place in dresser drawers. **1963** *Good Housek. Home Encycl.* (rev. ed.) 367/2 The pomander...looks prettier if tied round with ribbon or tinsel, with a loop for hanging it up. **1974** WESTLAND & CRITCHLEY *Art of Dried & Pressed Flowers* ix. 80 Hang the pomander in a wardrobe, on a coat hanger or over your dressing table.

2. a. (Later examples.) Also, a small perforated ceramic container filled with pot-pourri or other aromatic substances, for hanging in a wardrobe, placing on a dressing-table, etc.

1973 *Woman's Jrnl.* Dec. 108 (Advt.), Colognes, bath essences, soaps, pot-pourri and pomanders from..J. Floris Ltd. **1975** *Lady* 6 Nov. p. vii/2 (Advt.), Bone china pomander, traditional long-lasting perfume. **1976** *S. Wales Echo* 25 Nov. 8/2 (Advt.), There are pots of French herbs.., jams laced with whisky, silk scarves and pomanders.

b. (Later example.)

1895 E. NESBIT (*title*) A pomander of verse.

Pomard, Pommard. Add: Also with small initial. (Further examples.)

1875 [see *BEAUNE]. **1889** [see *CORTON]. **1920** G. SAINTSBURY *Notes on Cellar-Bk.* iv. 56 Less distinguished representatives of the Slope of Gow [*sc.* Côte d'Or].. Pommard, Santenay, Chenas and others. **1962** R. JEFFRIES *Exhibit No. 13* v. 48 He..picked up a bottle of Pommard. **1979** I. S. BLACK *Journey to Safe Place* ix. 95 We'll have another bottle of this Pommard.

pomato (pomā·to, -ē̆i·to). [f. P(OTATO + T)OMATO.] A name used by Luther Burbank (1849–1926), American horticulturist, for the fruit of a hybrid potato, which resembled a tomato; later used to designate the result of attempts to hybridize the potato and the tomato, by grafting or other methods. Also *attrib.*

1905 *Century Mag.* Mar. 668/1 The 'pomato', one of the most wonderful creations, now under way. This may be called a tomato growing upon a potato. It produces in abundance a white, fragrant, succulent, delicious fruit upon potato tops. **1914** L. BURBANK in J. Whitson et al. *L. Burbank: his Methods & Discoveries* II. ix. 283 As the fruit grew on a hybrid potato vine, and in itself had much the appearance of a tomato, it was christened the 'Pomato'. The name..led to the unauthorized assumption that the fruit was really a cross between the tomato and the potato. In point of fact, I have never been able to cross these two plants. *Ibid.* 284 The pomato plant produced fruit abundantly, but very few tubers. **1971** *New Scientist* 27 Apr. 263 (*caption*) Protoplasts of potato and tomato are fused... These cells are then cultured, and from them are grown embryoids and eventually whole 'pomatoes'. At the moment, research has got as far as the protoplast-fusion stage. **1976** *Nat. Geographic* Sept. 388/1 'Pomatoes'—hypothetical vegetables with the fruit-bearing foliage of a tomato and the tuberous roots of a potato. To some botanists, it is just a matter of time until almost any type of plant can be hybridized with another. **1980** *Garden* CV. 46/2 Am I the only person who doesn't grow pomatoes?

pombe. Add: (Later examples.) Also *attrib.* and *Comb.*

1935 H. THURNWALD in R. C. Thurnwald *Black & White in E. Afr.* iv. 158 The brewing of beer (pombe) is not done by women everywhere. It is a complicated process requiring time and performed especially for feasts. **1952** *Chambers's Jrnl.* May 278/1 The local fermented beverage will be flowing freely—be it coconut pombe, or barley talla, or honey tej, depending on where in Africa the ceremony is taking place. **1966** C. SWEENEY *Scurrying Bush* v. 67 The local beer, called *pombe*, and made, in this case, from sorghum grain. **1969** *Tanzania Notes & Rec.* July 26 In 1947 women pombe sellers..brought their case before Kimalando... He saw no justification for mounting a patrol in the African pombe markets. **1977** D. BEATY *Excellency* iv. 54 A big black policeman with breath that smelled strongly of banana pombe. **1978** J. UPDIKE *Coup* (1979) v. 213 An entire American boom town, with.. *pombe*-dispensing saloons.

pome (pōᵘm), *sb.*[2] A jocular alteration of 'poem'.

1861 G. MEREDITH *Let.* 16 Aug. (1970) I. 100 Did you get the Pome I sent? **1897** A. R. MARSHALL (*title*) Pomes from the Pink 'un. **1927** JOYCE (*title*) Pomes Penyeach. **1959** *News Chron.* 12 Aug. 4/5 My next pome,..is dedicated to a very fine poet. **1975** A. COREN *Further Bull. Pres. Idi Amin* 7 Come on out, John Milton!..wot about dis year's jumbo pome you lazy bum?

pomegranate. Add: Now freq. with pronunc. (pǫ·mĕgræ:nĕt). **1. d.** A colour resembling that of the pomegranate. Usu. *attrib.* or as *adj.*

a **1855** C. BRONTË *Emma* in *Cornh. Mag.* (1860) I. 495 Miss Wilcox..in her blue merino dress and pomegranate ribbon. **1881** C. C. HARRISON *Woman's Handiwork* I. 47 Pomegranate, Bokhara red, Damascus blue..are some of the colours to be had in plushes. **1906** W. J. LOCKE *Beloved Vagabond* vii. 83 A beautiful gipsy, holding fascinating allurements in lustrous eyes and pomegranate lips. **1927** [see *ASH *sb.*[2] I e]. **1955** E. BOWEN *World of Love* v. 94 Mamie's pomegranate toenails. **1958** J. CANNAN *And be a Villain* iv. 100 A high-waisted pomegranate satin with gold lace sleeves. **1972** *Guardian* 17 Oct. 13/4 The walls are pomegranate with pomegranate velvet lighting in the recesses.

pomellated (pǫ·mĕlē̆i:tĕd), *a. rare*⁻¹. [Presumably ad. Fr. *pommelé* 'dappled'.] ? Dappled, mottled.

1922 JOYCE *Ulysses* 289 Thither the extremely large wains bring foison of the fields, flaskets of cauliflowers.. and red green yellow brown russet sweet big bitter ripe pomellated apples.

pomelo. a. For *Citrus decumana* substitute *Citrus grandis*. **b.** Also = *GRAPEFRUIT. Also *attrib.* (Later examples.)

1908 R. W. CHAMBERS *Firing Line* v. 54 Is that the pomelo grove? **1943** WEBBER & BATCHELOR *Citrus Industry* I. v. 568 The grapefruits and the pummelos, or shaddocks, are very closely related. **1968** J. W. PURSEGLOVE *Trop. Crops: Dicotyledons* II. 502 *C*[*itrus*] *grandis* is highly esteemed in the East as a dessert fruit, where it is known as the Pomelo. **1971** 'A. BURGESS' *MF* vi. 68 A papier-mâché cornucopia spilling bananas, pomelos..and jackfruit.

Pomeranchon (pǫmĕræ·ntʃǫn). *Nuclear Physics.* [f. next + *-ON[1].] = *POMERON.

1967 *Physical Rev. Lett.* XIX. 1061/1 The observed nonshrinkage of diffraction peaks has indicated that the Pomeranchon has an anomalously small slope, so that at present it is the only trajectory generally accepted by Regge phenomenologists which has no particles assigned to it. **1973** *Physical Rev.* D. VII. 1496 Pomeranchon exchange is assumed to be mediated by an isoscalar scalar σ meson.

Pomeranchuk (pǫmĕræ·ntʃuk). *Physics.* [Name of Isaak Yakovlevich *Pomeranchuk* (1913–66), Russian physicist.] **a.** Used *attrib.* with reference to the cooling that a mixture of liquid and solid helium 3 undergoes when it is solidified by compression. [Described by Pomeranchuk in *Zh. éksper. i teoret. Fiziki* (1950) XX. 919.]

1958 *Chem. Abstr.* LII. 17841 (*heading*) Theory of the Pomeranchuk effect in helium-3. **1971** *McGraw-Hill Yearbk. Sci. & Technol.* 86/2 First proposed in 1950, the Pomeranchuk method is based on the unusual thermodynamic properties of a solid–liquid mixture of He^3 at low temperatures. **1974** *Nature* 6 Dec. 441/3 Compressional solidification of ^3He, known as Pomeranchuk cooling,..restricts experiments to the solidification pressure of 34 atmospheres. **1976** *Ibid.* 23 Sept. 276/1 A pair of Pomeranchuk cells was used both for cooling the ^3He into the superfluid A-phase and also for inducing a flow of liquid through the narrow tube which connected them together.

b. Used, chiefly *attrib.*, to designate certain concepts relating to the scattering of sub-atomic particles at high energies, as **Pomeranchuk pole**, a special Regge pole with $\alpha(0) = 1$ and even signature, and with zero isospin, charge, hypercharge, and baryon number (α being the trajectory function); **Pomeranchuk('s) theorem**, a theorem according to which the reaction cross-sections for a particle and for its anti-particle incident on the same target particle should approach the same constant value as the energy of the incident particle is increased; (proposed by Pomeranchuk in *Zh. éksper. i teoret. Fiziki* (1958) XXXIV. 725); **Pomeranchuk trajectory**, the trajectory traced by a Pomeranchuk pole as α increases.

1961 *Physical Rev.* CXXIV. 2049/2 We shall present.. a rigorous generalization of Pomeranchuk's theorem. **1962** *Nuovo Cimento* XXV. 735 We are assuming *either* that the coupling constant of the ρ Regge pole is much smaller than that of the Pomeranchuk (vacuum) pole, *or* that their trajectories lie close together. **1963** *Physical Rev.* CXXIX. 1456/1 Further insight into the behavior of two Pomeranchuk trajectories can be achieved by evaluating the two leading terms in the high-energy behavior of the total elastic cross section. **1973** *Physics Bull.* Mar. 183/2 There is some doubt about the validity of the Pomeranchuk theorem on the constancy of cross sections for K^+, K^- production. **1973** M. LEON *Particle Physics* xii. 244 Elastic scattering..is supposed to be dominated by the Pomeranchuk pole. **1976** N. W. DEAN *Introd. Strong Interactions* xvi. 303 If all total cross sections are to become asymptotically constant, the Pomeranchuk trajectory must be present in all elastic scattering amplitudes. *Ibid.*, The f (1270) and the f′(1514) mesons have the correct quantum numbers, but there is considerable question whether either of them actually belongs to the Pomeranchuk trajectory.

Pomeranchukon (pǫmĕræ·ntʃukǫn). *Nuclear Physics.* [f. prec. + *-ON¹.] = *POMERON.

1968 *Physical Rev. Lett.* XX. 236/2 Assuming the continuum contribution to the FESR for the amplitude *B* to be confined to the Pomeranchukon, one could subtract the Pomeranchuk contribution on the right-hand side and the continuum contribution on the left-hand side of the FESR. **1973** *Physical Rev.* D. VIII. 3050 The *S* matrix for the Pomeranchukon enters here because we must include the possibility of Regge-pole exchange without any diffractive interaction between the incoming or outgoing particles.

Pomeranian, *a.* (*sb.*) Add: Also **Pomoranian.**

The form *Pomoranian*, reflecting Pol. *Pomorze* 'Pomerania' (f. *po* 'on', *morze* 'sea') is used chiefly in linguistic writings.

A. *adj.* (Further examples.)

1880 E. W. HAMILTON *Diary* 23 June (1972) I. 21 It seems that Bismarck, though unwilling to 'sacrifice a single Pomeranian soldier' in the cause of Greece, will give Germany's moral support, at any rate, to a demonstration. **1919** G. B. SHAW *Augustus does his Bit* in *Heartbreak House* 235 The Colonel of the Pomeranian regiment which captured me. **1934** PRIEBSCH & COLLINSON *German Lang.* I. i. 11 The Western group [of the Slavonic languages].. includes .. the Cassubian and almost extinct Slovinzian (brought by Lorentz under the collective name of Pomoranian) along the Baltic coast of Pomerania. **1935** F. LORENTZ in F. Lorentz et al. *Cassubian Civilization* 6 The whole Pomeranian language is divided into seventy-six dialects, which are, in many cases, very different from one another. **1955** R. JAKOBSON *Slavic Lang.* (ed. 2) 2 These are the remnants of the Pomoranian group. **1957** [see *KASHUBE]. **1965** G. Y. SHEVELOV *Prehist. of Slavic* 1 Pomoranian or Baltic Sl[avic] dialects of such Sl[avic] tribes as Vilci-Veletians, Obodrites, etc. **1972** [see *KASHUBE]. **1974** *Encycl. Brit. Macropædia* XVI. 867/1 Kashubian dialects (including Slovincian) are considered to be the remnants of a Pomeranian subgroup that belonged to the Lekhitic group.

B. *sb.* **b.** A native or inhabitant of Pomerania.

1870 W. B. ULLATHORNE in C. Butler *Vatican Council* (1930) I. xii. 237 Then there was a Pomeranian, who gave ..an interesting and pathetic account of the difficulties of religion in his country. **1919** [see *KASHUBE]. **1939** [see *LECH, LEKH *sb.*⁸ and *a.*].

c. The West Slavonic dialect of Pomerania, a subgroup of Lechitic, now represented only by Kashube (cf. *LECHITIC *sb.* and *a.*, *KASHUBE).

1934 [see KASHUBE]. **1935** F. LORENTZ in F. Lorentz et al. *Cassubian Civilization* 5 Popular speech..is nowhere uniform... A classic instance of this is furnished by Cassubian, or, as it is more scientifically termed, Pomeranian. This language is divided into Northern Pomeranian and Southern Pomeranian. **1935** T. LEHR-SPŁAWINSKI in *Ibid.* III. i. 347 The dialects spoken in the Middle Ages..by the ancestors of the modern Cassubians constituted an intermediate belt between the dialects of Pomeranian properly speaking and those of Polish.

Pomerol (pǫ·mərǫl). The name of a commune in the department of Gironde in SW. France, used *attrib.* or *absol.* to designate the red wine produced there.

[**1833** C. REDDING *Hist. Mod. Wines* v. 141 With this quality of wines also may be ranked those grown on the level grounds where the soil is sand and gravel. The most in repute are those of Pommerol and of the environs of Libourne.] **1951** R. POSTGATE *Plain Man's Guide to Wine* iv. 75 As there is no classification of Pomerols, I am reduced to making a personal list. **1959** W. JAMES *Word-bk. Wine* 146 All are agreed on one point—Pomerol wines taste of truffles. **1969** J. WAINWRIGHT *Take-Over Men* vi. 92 He swirled the wine in his glass,..moistened his lips with it,..then said: 'Graves, I think.'..'No. I rather think Pomerol.' **1971** P. PURSER *Holy Father's Navy* viii. 43 The meal was indifferent but Father Freeloader's choice of wine impeccable, even if they had brought him the '64 Pomerol and not the '62. **1974** *Times* 29 Oct. 1/5 The alleged fraud consisted in transforming ordinary table wines of the Languedoc into nobler Pomerols or Medocs.

pomeron (pǫ·mĕrǫn). *Nuclear Physics.* Also **Pomeron.** [f. *POMER(ANCHUK + *-ON¹.] The Pomeranchuk pole or trajectory, or a virtual particle regarded as exchanged in the type of scattering they represent.

1967 R. J. EDEN *High Energy Collisions* ix. 234 If total cross-sections are asymptotically constant, there must be a Regge pole of *even* signature..having, $l = \alpha_1{}^+(0) = 1$... The corresponding trajectory is called the Pomeranchuk trajectory. The object exchanged at $t=0$ is called the 'Pomeron'. It is not a physical particle. **1971** *Physics Bull.* Sept. 517/2 With a linear trajectory this required that the pomeron has a slope of 0·64 GeV^{-2}. Several factors however have led to the abandoning of the association of the pomeron with the f^0. **1973** B. H. BRANSDEN et al. *Fund. Particles* ix. 181 At present it does not seem that the Pomeron corresponds to a physical particle and it probably should be thought of as a device to bring diffraction scattering into the same exchange framework as other reactions. **1974** M. L. PERL *High Energy Hadron Physics* xvii. 408 It also became common to speak of the Pomeranchuk trajectory as representing the exchange of a virtual particle called the pomeron.

‖ **pomme** (pǫm). *Gastron.* [Shortened form of next.] A potato. Chiefly *pl.*, esp. in *pommes allumettes*, 'potato matchsticks', i.e. matchstick-thin chips; *pommes frites*, 'fried potatoes', i.e. chips.

1910 A. MARIO *Easy French Cookery* 140 *French Fried Potatoes* (Pommes frites). Cut some potatoes in strips.., and cook as for Straw Potatoes. **1931** A. DE CROZE *What to eat & drink in France* xxix. 260 Pommes frites à la Gasconne (diced potatoes fried with goose dripping or lard). **1952** G. MAUROIS *Cooking with French Touch* vii. 118 There are forty different ways of preparing potatoes known to the French cuisine. *Pommes frites* is probably the best known of all. **1962** L. DEIGHTON *Ipcress File* xix. 127 The steak was..served with asparagus tips and *pommes allumettes*. **1966** *Vogue* Nov. 148/2 *Pommes frites* (they are thinner than chips half fried). **1975** P. ORGAN *House on Cheyne Walk* xv. 126 The smell of the beach and *pommes allumettes*.

‖ **pomme de terre** (pǫm də tɛ̄r'). *Gastron.* Pl. **pommes de terre.** [Fr.] A potato.

1823 [see *GROUND-PEA]. **1846** A. SOYER *Gastronomic Regenerator* 470 (*heading*) Pommes de terre sautées au beurre. **1877** [see *LYONNAIS B *adj.* b]. **1963** R. CARRIER *Great Dishes of World* 211/2 *Pommes de terre Anna* sets overlapping layers of sliced raw potatoes in a small buttered baking dish or round mould, each layer dotted with butter and the whole then baked. **1977** *Zigzag* Mar. 8/1 We ate mashed pommes de terre.

pommel, *sb.* Add: **5. b.** Either of a pair of removable curved handgrips fitted to a vaulting horse.

1887 A. ALEXANDER *Mod. Gymnastic Exercises* 137 The Vaulting Horse..contains a set of pommels, which are removable if required. **1895** W. MACLAREN *A. Maclaren's Physical Educ.* (new ed.) 103 For vaulting with one hand, circling, feint exercises &c..., it is customary to have pommels fitted on the horse. **1908** *Man. Physical Training* (H.M.S.O.) viii. 184 Bend the knees and spring quickly from the ground up to the 'First position', with the hands gripping the pommels. **1920** NAYLOR & TEMPLE *Mod. Physical Educ.* 125 The starting position is taken by grasping the pommels with 'inward-grip'. **1932** T. MCDOWELL *Vaulting* vii. 28 This vault may also be performed with one hand on a pommel and the other on the horse proper. **1971** L. KOPPETT *N.Y. Times Guide Spectator Sports* 242 The gymnast balances himself on the pommels..and performs various maneuvers with leg movements, handstands, and so forth. **1972** B. TAYLOR et al. *Olympic Gymnastics for Men & Women* viii. 181/2 The left arm pushes off the left pommel enabling the gymnast to gain the necessary height.

8. *pommel vault*; **pommel horse,** a vaulting horse having pommels; also **pommelled horse.**

1908 *Man. Physical Training* (H.M.S.O.) viii. 185 Progression should be obtained by gradually raising the height of the pommel horse till it is somewhat higher than the average troop horse. **1932** T. MCDOWELL *Vaulting* p. v, Where the teacher has a 'box horse' and not a 'pommelled horse', it will be found that many of the vaults are adjustable to the apparatus available. *Ibid.* p. vi, Then comes the 'pommel horse' with pad. *Ibid.* vii. 30 *Pommel Vault.* Take off from both feet as the hands grasp the pommels. **1957** *Encycl. Brit.* XI. 20/2 The 'Olympic six' for men comprise floor exercises, work on the horizontal bar, parallel bars and rings, pommelled horse and vaulting. **1962** [see *HORSE 6c]. **1964** D. M. KUNZLE in G. C. Kunzle *Parallel Bars* 13 All sorts of climbing instruments—ropes, bars, beams and the pommelled horse. **1971** *Sportsweek* (Bombay) 21 Feb. 9/1 Jim Prestidge recalls..the basic pommel horse exercises developed by German Ludwig Jahn, the father of the sport, in the last century. **1972** B. TAYLOR et al. *Olympic Gymnastics for Men & Women* viii. 180/1 Place the pommel horse under the parallel bars.

pommer (pǫ·məɹ). *Mus.* [G., altered form of BOMBARD *sb.*] A type of shawm; = BOMBARD *sb.* 4.

1878 [see BOMBARD *sb.* 4]. **1884** *Encycl. Brit.* XVII. 706/2 The little schalmey and tenor pommer seem to have disappeared in the 17th century. **1911** E. F. COOK *Dict. Mus. Terms* 202 Pommer, an ancient wooden wind reed instrument of various sizes. **1950** *Oxf. Jun. Encycl.* IX. 487/1 The lower ones were called 'pommers' and 'bombards'. In the 17th and 18th centuries hautboys.. developed from shawms, and 18th-century bassoons from the pommers. **1967** *Daily Tel.* 10 Feb. 19/4 The strength of the group lies..in the diversity and precision of its wind instruments, which include such rareties as the shawm, pommer, crumhorn and cornet. **1976** D. MUNROW *Instruments Middle Ages & Renaissance* vi. 40 Praetorius says that shawms are designated by the term *bombarde* or *Pommer* irrespective of their size. **1977** *Early Music* July 347/1 A collection of different pirouettes may be useful. I have five (made from corks) for my soprano pommer.

Pommery (pǫ·mĕri). Also **Pommery and Greno.** The proprietary name of a brand of champagne produced by the firm of Pommery & Greno, founded in Rheims in 1836.

1882 *Official Gaz.* (U.S. Patent Office) 7 Nov. 1540/2 Champagne-Wine.—Veuve Pommery & Fils, Reims, France... The designation 'Pommery & Greno'. **1887** *Trade Marks Jrnl.* 27 July 867 A. Pommery. Wines... Pommery & Cie. Reims. **1891** [see *PERRIER JOUËT]. **1892** A. W. PINERO *Magistrate* II. 55 *Cis*:..You'll look better after a glass or two of Pommery, Guv. *Mr. Posket*: No, no, Cis—now, no champagne. **1896** *Westm. Gaz.* 8 Dec. 2/1 'It is so awful to think of the suffering among the masses and to feel that one can do so little to alleviate it,' he said as he sipped his Dry Pommery. **1907** [see *MUMM]. **1918** G. FRANKAU *One of Them* xix. 144 Crimson, the orchids flaunted; gold, the chalice Bubbled with Pommery's unstinted measure. **1920** [see *HEIDSIECK]. **1951** R. SENHOUSE tr. *Colette's Chéri* 86 'What d'you drink, now you're married?'..'Pommery,' Chéri said. **1966** M. BREWER *Man against Fear* vii. 70 And a bottle of the Pommery. Properly iced, please. **1975** *Woman's Jrnl.* Sept. 73/2 They drank Pommery & Greno 1889.

Pommy (pǫ·mi), *sb.* (*a.*) *Austral.* and *N.Z. colloq.* Also **Pommie** and with lower-case initial. [Origin obscure.] **A.** *sb.* A derogatory term for an immigrant from the United Kingdom; an Englishman or Englishwoman, a Briton. **B.** *attrib.* or as *adj.* Of or pertaining to a Pommy; British, English, *spec.* (often as a term of affectionate abuse) in *Pommy bastard.* Cf. *POM².

The most widely held derivation of this term, for which, however, there is no firm evidence, is that which connects it with *pomegranate* (see quots. 1923, 1963). A discussion of this and of other theories may be found in W. S. Ramson *Australian English* (1966) 63.

1915 in B. Gammage *Broken Years* (1974) 86 We call the Regulars—Indians and Australians—'British'—but Pommies are nondescript. **1916** in *Ibid.* 240 They're only a b—— lot of Pommie Jackeroos and just as hopeless. **1916** *Anzac Bk.* 31 A Pommy can't go wrong out there if he isn't too lazy to work. **1920** D. O'REILLY in Murdoch & Drake-Brockman *Austral. Short Stories* (1951) 144 The 'Pommy' parson made good, as a good man always will. **1923** D. H. LAWRENCE *Kangaroo* vii. 162 Pommy is supposed to be short for pomegranate. Pomegranate, pronounced invariably pommygranate, is a near enough rhyme to immigrant, in a naturally rhyming country. Furthermore, immigrants are known in their first months, before their blood 'thins down', by their round and ruddy cheeks. So we are told. *Ibid.* 164 In this way Mr Somers had to take himself to task, for his Pommy stupidity. **1926** GALSWORTHY *Silver Spoon* II. iv. 137 They call us Pommies and treat us as if we'd took a liberty in coming to their blooming country. **1933** 'P. CADEY' *Broken Pattern* xii. 130 'You should have heard the English accent!' 'Pommy gab, eh?' commented his mate. **1938** N. MARSH *Artists in Crime* ix. 128 She was always shooting off her mouth about the way the Aussies don't know a good thing when they see it. These pommies! She gave me the jitters. **1946** B. JAMES in *Coast to Coast 1945* 63 He was an Englishman, not a 'pommy', mind you. It seemed he hadn't even reached to that dignity. **1947** B. MASON in D. M. Davin *N.Z. Short Stories* (1953) 333 What time we had left was spent on fruitless errands for the Pommie matelots. **1949** F. SARGESON *I saw in my Dream* II. xiii. 118 Look at Wally's ma—she got over her Pommy ways. **1951** D. STIVENS *Jimmy Brockett* 214 Like most of these pommy bastards, he had funny ways but he wasn't a bad old bloke at heart. **1957** *New Scientist* 23 May 13/3 There is..an elusive background of strangeness, imbued with an element of timelessness, which comes home to the sensitive 'new chum', or 'pommy', only after he has lived for a while in this new-old southern continent. **1962** J. FRAME *Edge of Alphabet* vii. 47 Look at the foreigners flooding the country on every immigrant ship, la-di-da Pommies and all. **1963** X. HERBERT *Disturbing Element* vi. 91 He still wore the heavy clumsy British type of clothing of the day [before 1914]. When we kids saw people on the street dressed like that we would yell at them: 'Jimmygrants, Pommygranates, Pommies!' **1966** R. D. EAGLESON in *Southerly* XXVI. 200 Lest British readers should be misled, *pommy* is frequently pejorative. **1974** P. MCCUTCHAN *Call for Simon Shard* iv. 36 I'm Australian born and bred, not a pommie immigrant... Now, grand-dad, 'e *was* a pommie bastard! **1975** *Times* 27 Aug 10/8 Colin Shaw..has just sent Ernest Whitehouse an explanation of how God came to be described in the television programme *Beneath the News* as a 'Pommy bastard'... Shaw adds that 'Pommy bastard' is an 'affectionate colloquialism' in Australia. **1979** *Guardian* 31 Oct. 3/2 British Leyland reacted angrily ..to antipodean 'pommy-bashing' about the quality of buses.

Hence **Po·mmyland,** Britain, England.

1957 R. STOW *Bystander* 21 I'm a Pommy. And going back to Pommy-land, after twenty-four years. **1967** F. HARDY *Billy Borker yarns Again* 61 Sir Robert himself wanted to be a whiskey-taster at the Melbourne show, but ended up as some kind of wharfie over in Pommy Land. **1973** *Times* 12 Oct. 15/7 An adaptation of Barry Humphries's cult strip cartoon about the life of darkest Pommie-land seen through the eyes of an antipodean innocent. **1979** M. KAUFMAN *Container* iii. 31, I suppose you'll head off back to Pommyland now?

Pomo (pōᵘ·mo), *sb.* and *a.* [See quot. 1978.] **A.** *sb.* **a.** An Indian people of Northern California; a member of this people. **b.** Any of the languages of this people. **B.** *adj.* Of, pertaining to, or designating this people or their languages. Hence **Pomo·an,** the group of Pomo languages. Also as *adj.*

[**1852** G. GIBBS *Jrnl.* 2 Feb. in H.R. Schoolcraft *Hist. & Stat. Information Indian Tribes* (1853) III. 112 Four bands consented to enter into a treaty, viz., the Sah-nel, Yukai, Pomo, and Masu-ta-kaya; numbering in all, as was supposed, 1042 souls.] **1872** *Overland Monthly* Apr. 328/1 The great family of Pomos on Russian River..have many dialects, and a name for each—as Ballo Ki Pomos Cahto Pomos, etc. **1875** H. H. BANCROFT *Native Races Pacific States* I. 362 The *Pomos*, which name signifies 'people', and is the collective appellation of a number of tribes living in Potter Valley... Each tribe of the nation takes a distinguishing prefix to the name of Pomo, as, the *Castel Pomos* and *Ki Pomos*. **1881** [see *KLAMATH]. **1910** F. W. HODGE *Handbk. Amer. Indians* II. 277/1 The Pomo were the most southerly stock on the coast not brought under the mission influence of the Franciscans. **1913** [see *HOKAN]. **1933** M. R. HARRINGTON *Gypsum Cave, Nevada* 87 The Pomo 'tee-weave' is somewhat similar. **1936** G. A. REICHARD *Navajo Shepherd & Weaver* 149 To demonstrate his skill..a Pomo Indian basket-maker fashions a basket so small it must be kept in a tiny bottle. **1959** E. Tunis *Indians* 113/2 One tribe, the Pomos, made baskets that were possibly the finest ever made in the world. **1965** *Language* XLI. 304 Well-known families such as Pomoan, Chumashan, and Yuman. *Ibid.* 305 Pomo..shows no initial vowel in any of the languages. **1973** A. H. Whiteford *N. Amer. Indian Arts* 39 One-rod coiling was done by the Pomo and Paiute. **1977** *Language* LIII. 260/2 This work..is the first descriptive account ever published of the phonology and grammar of Southeastern Pomo, one of seven distinct languages comprising the Pomoan family within the Hokan stock. **1978** *Handbk. N. Amer. Indians* VIII. 277/1 The word Pomo originated in two Northern Pomo forms that are quite distinct in the native language but that became confused in early writings. The earliest known recordings..give Pomo as the name of an Indian group on the east fork of the Russian River. For a village in southern Potter Valley, on the east fork of that river, Vihman..provides the full phonemic form: *phó·mo·* 'at red earth hole'... A second source..is based on Northern Pomo *phóʔmaʔ*.., which is added to place-names to designate those that live at that place.

pomology. Add: **pomological** *a.* (later example); **pomologist** (earlier and later examples); also **pomolo·gically** *adv.*

1833 *Chambers's Edin. Jrnl.* II. 96/1 It is..the chief object of the modern pomologist to obtain..new varieties. **1920** R. Frost *Let.* 14 May (1964) 105 Their report was that pomologically it was all right, but poetically not. **1976** *Jrnl. R. Soc. Arts* CXXIV. 577/1 Pomologists are now busy 'taking the fruit tree back to the drawing board', seeking better ways of intercepting light. **1976** *Nature* 12 Aug. 574/1 Pomological literature contains two reports of the influence of grafted scions on the size, colour and ripening season of apples borne on the stock portions of topworked trees.

pomonal (pomō̆u·năl), *a. rare.* [f. Pomona + -al.] Of or pertaining to fruit-trees; pomonic.

1859 *Trans. Illinois Agric. Soc.* III. 354 We may proudly claim this land..as the favorite seat of horticultural and pomonal progress.

Pomoranian, var. *Pomeranian *a.* (*sb.*).

pomp, *v.*[1] Delete † *Obs.* and add later *poet.* examples. Hence **pomped** (pǫmpt) *a.*, honoured with pomp, celebrated: **pomping** *a.*, restrict † to sense in Dict. and add: (*b*) *dial.*, involved in acting.

1919 W. de la Mare *Flora*, Mount to the porch the pomped grandees In lonely state, by twos, and threes. **1922** Hardy *Late Lyrics* 48 And once or twice she has cast me As she pomped along the street Court-clad,..A glance from her chariot-seat. **1937** G. Frankau *More of Us* xiv. 153 And all that day, despising fun and frolic With Janes or Joans, he pomped about the ship. **1969** G. Macbeth *War Quartet* 26 So few yards Beyond this dust-whirl, those pomped victors. **1976** *Birmingham Post* 16 Dec. 2/4 Rover, one of the pomping folk, thinks principally in Shakespearean tags. **1976** J. C. Trewin in D. V. Baker *Cornish Short Stories* 134 It [sc. the rain] hammered against the side of the tent where the pomping folk had prepared hopelessly for the evening.

Pompadour, *sb.* Add: **1.** (Further examples.)

1885 A. Edwardes *Girton Girl* I. xii. 238 It was not Louis Seize furniture, or Pompadour cabinets..that Marjorie missed. **1909** *Daily Chron.* 17 Sept. 5/3 Charged ..with stealing..two silver pompadour boxes. **1925** O. Sitwell in E. Sitwell et al. *Poor Young People* 35 Through her pompadour-peruke. **1971** S. Jepson *Let. to Dead Girl* xii. 143 She opened the skirt of a pompadour doll on a side table, pulled out a white telephone.

2. (Later examples.)

1968 *N.Y. City* (Michelin Tire Corp.) 57 The most precious types of Sèvres porcelain, in the pink known as 'Pompadour'. **1976** N. Roberts *Face of France* x. 107 Balloons, scarlet, orange, blue and..Pompadour pink.

5. a. (Earlier and later examples.)

1887 *Evening Sun* (N.Y.) 15 Apr. 3/4 A tall, slender young man, with a full blonde beard and pompadour hair. **1920** S. Lewis *Main St.* 76 The meek ambitiousness.. clouded like an aura his pale face, flap ears, and sandy pompadour. **1955** W. Gaddis *Recognitions* I. vi. 208 His hair, a shiny black pompadour which he wore like a hat. **1976** *New Yorker* 24 May 107/1 Reagan looks good at the rostrum: a tall figure with ruddy cheeks, his reddish-brown hair swept back in a slight pompadour.

b. (Later example.)

1975 J. Drummond *Slowly the Poison* I. 97 Her hair.. was not worn in the current high pompadour style, but cut short.

po·mpadour, *v.* [f. Pompadour *sb.* 5.] *trans.* To dress (hair) in the pompadour style; to arrange (hair) in a pompadour. Chiefly as *pa. pple.* or *ppl. adj.*

1908 *London Opinion* 22 Aug. 362/2 She was large, plumply built, with grey hair artfully pompadoured and undulated. **1909** L. M. Montgomery *Anne of Avonlea* xiv. 153 Gertie Pye swept in, pompadoured and frilled. *a* **1913** F. Rolfe *Desire & Pursuit of Whole* (1934) xvii. 178 Some pretentious pompadoured image trailing satin. **1957** V. J. Kehoe *Technique Film & Television Make-Up* ix. 111 Other tribes pompadoured the front of the hair and had two side partings. **1971** *Daily Tel.* (Colour Suppl.) 3 Sept. 42/4 They wore their hair very long, very high, pompadoured, swept up..and back. **1973** R. Rosenblum *Mushroom Cave* (1974) 18 The squat bully with greasy pompadoured black hair.

pompano. 1. Substitute for def.: A North American or West Indian marine fish belonging to the genera *Trachinotus, Parona,* or *Zalocys,* of the family Carangidæ, esp. *Trachinotus carolinus,* the common pompano, found near south-eastern coasts of North America. (Earlier and further examples.)

1778 tr. *J. Chappe d'Auteroche's Voy. California* 24 The pampano is very plenty in the southern part of the gulph of Mexico. **1840** *Picayune* (New Orleans) 1 Sept. 2/1 Pompanos were plentiful, and sparkling hock flew about. **1851** A. O. Hall *Manhattaner in New Orleans* 161 We forgot our military sighings in the discussion..of the momentous question whether it was orthodox to eat rum-omelette with 'pompano'-fish. **1883** 'Mark Twain' *Life on Mississippi* xliv. 445 We had dinner [in New Orleans]..—the chief dish the renowned fish called pompano, delicious as the less criminal forms of sin. **1892** Stevenson & Osbourne *Wrecker* xix. 289 There we sat.. eating pompino and drinking iced champagne. **1965** A. J. McClane *Standard Fishing Encycl.* 693/2 Pompano cookery is an art in Florida and Louisiana. **1973** *New Yorker* 17 Feb. 30/2 Hundreds of red snappers, Carolina mullets,.. pompano, Palm Beach mackerels, and others, ..lie in neat rows on a bed of shaved ice. **1977** *Time* 19 Dec. 42/2 Newly appreciated..are such home-grown marvels as Long Island duckling,..Chesapeake oysters, Gulf shrimp and pompano, [etc.].

Pompeian, *a.*[1] Add: Now usu. with pronunc. (pǫmpē̆ⁱ·ăn). (Further examples.) Also, characteristic or imitative of the architecture or painting of Pompeii, esp. frescoes.

1869 D. G. Rossetti *Let.* 21 Aug. (1965) II. 716 She built..a Pompeian house for the schoolmaster. **1879** A. Holt *Fancy Dresses* 60 *Pompeian lady.* White llama skirt, with Grecian border worked in purple. **1881** C. C. Harrison *Woman's Handiwork* I. 20 Pompeian red velvet, for portières. **1939** A. Thirkell *Before Lunch* iv. 106 The ceiling..painted in what were called Pompeian colours. **1962** *Listener* 18 Oct. 632/2 The story of this horrifying episode was told in 'Hurricane!'..The presentation..had a subtly Pompeian quality about it. *a* **1967** A. Ransome *Autobiogr.* (1976) xxvii. 230 A well-designed preparation for life in this Pompeian society, Pompeian in the sense that all these people were living as it were on the slopes of a volcano. **1972** *Sci. Amer.* Sept. 86/1 The Pompeiian mosaic in the museum in Naples.

B. *sb.*[1] A native or inhabitant of Pompeii.

1823 Lady Blessington *Jrnl.* 12 Aug. in E. Clay *Lady Blessington at Naples* (1979) 62 The repairs speak little for the taste of the Pompeians. **1840** *Penny Cycl.* XVIII. 380/2 The emperor Nero..adjudged that the Pompeians should be deprived of all theatrical amusements for ten years. **1869** 'Mark Twain' *Innoc. Abr.* xxxi. 330 Those Pompeiians were very luxurious in their tastes and habits. **1974** *Encycl. Brit. Macropædia* XIV. 789/2 Pompeians and colonists seem to have adjusted with a minimum of friction. **1976** *Times* 23 Nov. 11/3 The faces of the Pompeians as they recorded themselves are reminiscent of those one can still see in Campania.

Pompeian (pǫmpē̆ⁱ·ăn, pǫmpī·ăn), *sb.*[2] and *a.*[2] [ad. L. *Pompēiān-us,* f. the name *Pompēius* Pompey.] **A.** *sb.* A follower of Gnaeus Pompeius Magnus (106–48 b.c.), Roman consul, or of his son. **B.** *adj.* Of or pertaining to Pompey or his party.

1845 J. H. Newman in *Encycl. Metrop.* X. 281/2 Bent on retiring to the Pompeians in Sicily. *Ibid.* 282/1 The remains of the Pompeian party. **1908** W. W. Fowler *Social Life at Rome in Age of Cicero* iii. 87 Some £17,500, all of which, while in deposit at Ephesus, was seized by the Pompeians in the Civil War. **1913** D. Hannay *Navy & Sea Power* ii. 31 When Julius Caesar followed Pompey into Thrace he crossed the Adriatic under the very nose of a superior Pompeian fleet. **1949** L. R. Taylor *Party Politics in Age of Caesar* iii. 68 In the year 61, when Pompey was pouring out money to elect his man to the consulship, Cato charged in the senate that the money was being distributed from the house of the Pompeian consul in office. *Ibid.* viii. 171 Caesar also contributed by the policy he followed when..he came home from his victory over the Pompeians in Spain. **1974** E. S. Gruen *Last Generation of Roman Republic* ii. 56 Bibulus and Domitius could be counted on by Cato for steady cooperation in reducing the influence of Cæsarians and Pompeians in Roman politics. *Ibid.* 62 It was a standard Pompeian practice to express his own ambitions in terms of the needs and desires of his soldiers.

Pompey (pǫ·mpi). [Origin unknown.] A nickname for: **a.** The town and dockyard of Portsmouth, in Hampshire. **b.** Portsmouth Football Club. Also *attrib.*

1899 *Evening News* 9 Dec. 3/6 Wilkie, amid tremendous cheering from the Pompey lads, won the toss, and played with the wind in their favour. **1916** 'Taffrail' *Pincher Martin* iii. 40 The *Belligerent* was a 'Pompey' ship. **1930** *Daily Express* 6 Oct. 16/7 Despite their undeniable superiority Portsmouth could not penetrate the Derby defence... A brilliant Pompey could do everything except score. **1943** C. S. Forester *Ship* xviii. 109 The grim wife he had in Pompey. **1944** Williams & Savage *Second Penguin Problems Bk.* 160 Shouting 'Good old Pompey,' Portsmouth supporters went home. **1959** *Observer* 22 Mar. 17/5 An old roadman..: 'There's been a lot of unemployment in Pompey and Southampton.' **1966** (*title*) Pompey chimes: the journal of the Portsmouth West Conservative Association. **1972** E. Grierson *Confessions of Country Magistrate* xv. 149 That Plymouth should possess a second-tier court and Portsmouth only a third-tier one will infuriate, and with reason, the good citizens of Pompey. **1976** *Oxf. Compan. Ships & Sea* 659/1 '*Pompey*', the sailors' slang name for Portsmouth... It is not known how or when the name came into being, one theory being that it owes its origin to the fact that the local fire brigade, known as the Pompiers, used to exercise on Southsea Common, adjacent to the town of Portsmouth. **1977** *Navy News* June 6/3 Is there any chance of recreating the Bluejacket Band at Pompey?

Hence **Po·mpeyite,** a sailor from Portsmouth.

1916 'Taffrail' *Pincher Martin* iv. 63 Down wi' the Pompeyites!

pompier. Add: **1.** (Further examples.)

1871 E. G. E. Ward *Jrnl.* 24 May in D. P. Carew *Many Years, Many Girls* (1967) i. 51 All the 'pompiers' from St. Germain are gone to Paris, but the fire is enormous. **1958** L. Durrell *Balthazar* x. 203 The hall was full of fancy-dress figures of *pompiers* with hatchets and buckets.

2. *transf.* An artist who paints in an academic, imitative, vulgarly neo-classical style. Also *attrib.*

1924 A. Huxley *Let.* 9 Aug. (1969) 231 It may be mere folie de grandeur and pompier prejudice on my part. **1950** Wyndham Lewis *Let.* 22 Mar. (1963) 520 The greatest news of all is that you have taken to the brush and palette! Are you a *Douanier*, or a *pompier*? **1974** *Times* 23 Nov. 14/1 The names of the so-called Pompier artists—late nineteenth-century French academic painters—are on every lip... The term 'Pompier'..is thought to derive from the helmets worn by the Greek gods and heroes depicted in the canvases of the late Classical painters and their close similarity to that of the Paris firemen, or *pompiers*. *Ibid.* 14/4 The Pompiers are exotic and flamboyant. **1977** *Times* 30 Mar. 12/4 The art of the *Pompiers* as they have been contemptuously called... The exhibition of *French Nineteenth-century Paintings* at the Alpine Club Gallery..is..welcome.

pompilid (pǫ·mpilid), *sb.* and *a.* *Zool.* Also **Pompilid.** [ad. mod.L. family name *Pompiliidæ*, f. the generic name *Pompilius* (J. C. Fabricius *Supplementum Entomologiæ Systematicæ* (1798) 212), f. Gr. πομπίλ-ος a fish which followed ships + -id[3].] **A.** *sb.* A predatory fossorial wasp belonging to the family Pompiliidæ. **B.** *adj.* Of or pertaining to this group of insects.

1909 *Cent. Dict.* Suppl., *Pompilid* n. & a. **1913** *Oxf. Univ. Gaz.* 4 June 952/1 The specimens show the resemblance of the black red-banded Hemipteron to a common pattern of the Pompilid group of Fossorial Hymenoptera. **1924** J. A. Thomson *Sci. Old & New* xxxv. 200 There are predatory wasps called Pompilids that hunt spiders. **1941** W. S. Bristowe *Comity of Spiders* II. vii. 354 Spiders are the sole prey of Pompilids. **1962** *Oxf. Univ. Gaz.* 19 Mar. 852/1 A Pompilid wasp and its spider prey from Trinidad. **1973** J. P. Spradbery *Wasps* xiv. 307 Among some pompilids at least, considerable powers of orientation have been evolved.

pom-pom. Add: **1.** In later use: any of various heavier guns, esp. if multi-barrelled or one of a group.

1916 'Boyd Cable' *Action Front* 131 The muzzles of the two pounder pom-poms moved slowly after their target. **1940** 'N. Shute' *Landfall* vii. 175, I should think the multiple pom-poms would have got the machine. **1944** *R.A.F. Jrnl.* Aug. 272 (*caption*) Battleship..; carries forty pom-poms in multiple mountings. **1973** J. Quick *Dict. Weapons* 353/1 *Pom-pom.* 1. A rack of antiaircraft cannons, usually mounted in fours, as on the deck of a ship. 2. An automatic cannon.

2. A representation of a repetitive sound, e.g. the beat of a popular tune or poem. Also *pom-pom-pom*, etc.

1909 Beerbohm *Lett. to R. Turner* (1964) 181 They have been re-printing *Yet Again.* Second impression ready within a few days. Pom-pom-pom. **1916** A. Huxley *Let.* 31 Mar. (1969) 95 Time percolates with a distressing rapidity through the coffee-machines of life... So you see, pom, pom, where we are?..as the old song says. **1945** W. Stevens *Let.* 26 Jan. (1967) 485 Many lines exist because I enjoy their clickety-clack in contrast with the more decorous pom-pom-pom that people expect. **1978** M. Kenyon *Deep Pocket* ix. 105 *Pom* pom pom *pom* pom, something sweet Willies.

Hence **po·m-pom** *v. intr.*, to fire a pom-pom; **pom-po·mming** *vbl. sb.*

1901 'Linesman' *Words by Eyewitness* vii. 147 Continuous sniping, pom-pomming, and occasional shelling. *Ibid.* ix. 191 Boers can fire shrapnel, Britons can pom-pom with the best.

pompon. Add: The spelling with final -m is now common. **1.** (Later and *attrib.* examples.)

1904 P. N. Hasluck *Upholstery* 19 Pom-poms are used for ornamenting upholsterers' work. To make a pom-pom lap a wool or cardboard washer with three or four thicknesses of fibres. **1927** [see *Evzone, evzone]. **1924** D. H. Lawrence *Pansies* 148 My! the bloomin' pom-poms! Even as trimmings they're stale. **1952** Granville *Dict. Theatr. Terms* 139 *Pom-pom dress*, the conventional Pierrot costume of white pantaloons, white jacket, decked with black pom-poms, or any other good combinations of colour. **1968** *Listener* 3 Oct. 445/3 The making of Bunny Girls' pom-poms for export. **1975** *Times* 9 Dec. 9/8 Mink jacket..has..mink pom-pom ties at the neck. **1977** *Time* 4 Apr. 42/2 He has rigged it with 100,000 steel darts, which, if detonated at just the right moment, can wipe out everybody in the stadium, down to the last pompon girl.

2. (Later examples.) Also, one of a group

of dwarf varieties of *Rosa centifolia* with small double flowers. Also with capital initial.
1843 *Florist's Jrnl.* IV. 106 *R*[*osa*] *centifolia* (the Provence or Cabbage rose), with its varieties, including the 'mossy' and 'pompone' roses. **1869** [see *MINIATURE *a.* a]. **1894** A. FOSTER-MELLIAR *Bk. of Rose* ii. 15 A sub-variety of the Provence is the Pompon Rose. **1908** E. J. BANFIELD *Confessions of Beachcomber* I. ix. 130 Stalkless mushrooms [of coral], gills uppermost,..blossom as pom-pom chrysanthemums. **1922** MRS. C. H. STOUT *Amateur's Bk. Dahlia* i. 7 At that time [*sc.* 1870] appeared a tiny ball-shaped blossom, originating probably with Hartweg of Karlsruhe, which he called 'pompon'. **1943** F. THOMPSON *Candleford Green* i. 20 Old-fashioned pompom dahlias in autumn. **1952** W. E. SHEWELL-COOPER *Chrysanthemum Growing* xv. 161 These chrysanthemums are said to have been quite popular in the Victorian era... They are called 'Pompoms' in some parts of the country, 'Pompons' in other districts, and even 'Pompones'. **1955** C. C. HURST in G. S. Thomas *Old Shrub Roses* ix. 91 Both varieties were dwarf Pompons a few inches high. **1958** [see *COLLARETTE c]. **1961** [see **Korean chrysanthemum*]. **1974** J. BERRISFORD *Window Box & Container Gardening* v. 48 The smaller-growing of the Pompoms [*sc.* chrysanthemums] are also useful.

‖ **pomposo** (pǫmpō̆ᵘ·zo), *adv.* (*adj.*) and *sb.* [It.] **A.** *adv. Mus.* In a stately manner. Also as *adj.*, affected, pompous.
1801 BUSBY *Dict. Mus.*, *Pomposo*,..a word implying that the movement to which it is prefixed is to be performed in a grand and dignified style. **1847** WEBSTER 845/2 *Pomposo*,..grand and dignified. **1876** STAINER & BARRETT *Dict. Mus. Terms* 364/1 *Pomposamente, pomposo* ..pompously. **1959** *Collins Mus. Encycl.* 508/2 *Pomposo*, in a pompous manner. **1960** 'A. BRIDGE' *Numbered Account* 220 Don't be so pomposo, Colin—really you bore me.
B. *sb.* **1.** An affected, self-important person.
1930 *New Statesman* 15 Nov. 176/1 Their satyrs, pomposos, and ninnies..became the delight of future generations. **1938** C. S. FORESTER *Ship of Line* ix. 116 'And now,' said Bolton, 'we must await in idleness the arrival of Sir Mucho Pomposo, Rear Admiral of the Red.'
2. *Mus.* A movement, musical passage, or the like to be played in a stately manner; a piece of music marked *pomposo*.
1966 E. R. REILLY tr. *Quantz's On Playing Flute* xvii. 231 A Maestoso, Pomposo, Affetuoso, or Adagio spiritoso must be played seriously, and with a rather heavy and sharp stroke.

'pon, pon (pǫn), aphetic form of UPON *prep.*
1557 in *15th Rep. R. Comm. Hist. Manuscripts* App. III. 39 in *Parl. Papers 1897* (C. 8364) XLVIII. 71 Suche impositions as the lorde deputie for the tyme beinge shall taxe and set pon them. *c* **1560** [see MATTER *sb.*[1] 25 c]. **1796** F. BURNEY *Camilla* iv. 119 Much obliged to him, 'pon honour! **1821** M. EDGEWORTH *Let.* 5 Dec. (1971) 287 Fanny quite well p'on honor. **1850** F. E. SMEDLEY *Frank Fairleigh* v. 47, I didn't think you had it in you; 'pon my word, I didn't. **1901** M. FRANKLIN *My Brilliant Career* xiii. 78 'Pon my honour, Miss Melvyn, I had no idea it was you. **1914** 'BARTIMEUS' *Naval Occasions* xxiv. 244 Have you any rich aunts, Guns? 'Pon my word, I might get off this afternoon. **1924** D. MOORE *Fen's First Term* x. 108 'Pon my word, I can't say. **1973** 'M. INNES' *Appleby's Answer* ii. 18 A delightful-looking creature, madam, 'pon my soul.

ponask (pōᵘ·nask, pū̆·nask), *v. Canad.* Also **poonask.** [Algonquian.] *trans.* To cook (game or fish) by splitting it and roasting it on a spit or stick over an open fire. Hence **po·nasked** *ppl. a.*; **po·nasking** *vbl. sb.*
1922 *Beaver* Mar. 39/2 As we had no kettle..we were forced to 'ponask' the fish on a pointed stick before a bright fire. **1934** P. H. GODSELL *Arctic Trader* 46 She had, therefore, taken the heart, impaled it on a stick, and ponasked it as one would roast a duck. **1944** C. CLAY *Phantom Fur Thieves* 31 Thus were the two pieces of duck held up to the blaze and heat. 'That's called 'ponasking', Dave,' said the old trapper. **1961** J. W. ANDERSON *Fur Trader's Story* viii. 66 With the addition of salt, the ponasked fish was a delightful repast. **1963** G. S. MCTAVISH *Behind Palisades* 90 While the kettles would be boiling their meat, they [*sc.* Indians] would be 'Poonasking' strips of meat and delicacies like leg-bones in front of the fire. *Ibid.*, 'Poonasking' is a method of cooking before a campfire by splitting meat or game, impaling on a pointed stick, where it is quickly roasted from the intense heat.

ponce, *sb.* Substitute for def.: **a.** One who lives off a prostitute's earnings; a prostitute's protector; a pimp. (Later examples.)
1914 C. MACKENZIE *Sinister St.* II. IV. ii. 868 You're nothing more than a dirty ponce. I've gone five years without keeping a fellow yet. **1916** W. S. MAUGHAM *Writer's Notebk.* (1949) 98 A raid was made, and fourteen ponces were arrested. **1957** C. MACINNES *City of Spades* II. iv. 127 These whores are always masters of their ponces. One word to the Law, and the lucky boy's inside. **1965** *New Statesman* 23 Apr. 642/2 If a girl has to get 10 clients for a male ponce, she will need 20 to satisfy the monetary demands of a woman ponce. From my observations at least one ponce in four in London is a lesbian. **1970** G. GREER *Female Eunuch* 131 The role of the ponce ..is too established for us to suppose that prostitutes have found a self-regulating lifestyle. **1975** J. SYMONS *Three Pipe Problem* xviii. 182 What do you think I am, a tart trying to find a ponce?
b. A male homosexual; a lazy or effeminate man. Also as a vague term of abuse.
1932 AUDEN *Orators* III. 98 Dyers and bakers And boiler-tube makers, Poofs and ponces, All of them dunces. **1953** K. AMIS *Lucky Jim* xi. 119 As if I'd have said a word in front of that little ponce. **1969** N. COHN *A WopBopaLooBop* (1970) xix. 185 Mods thought that Rockers were yobs, Rockers thought that Mods were ponces. **1974** P. WRIGHT *Lang. Brit. Industry* xi. 95 An infuriated spectator may shout at a plump, sleek referee, 'You nasty little ponce!' **1978** in P. Marsh et al. *Rules of Disorder* ii. 46 Anybody that works in a lesson.. that you know you're going to doss about in,..you get called 'ponce' and everything.

ponce (pǫns), *v. slang.* [f. the sb.] *intr.* To act as, or behave like, a ponce; to live *on* the earnings of a prostitute; *fig.* to sponge (on), take advantage (of). Usu. const. *on* or *off.* Also, *to ponce about*, to act in an effeminate or languid manner; to fool or mess about; *to ponce up*, to tart up, to make effeminate or effete. Hence **po·ncing** *vbl. sb.* and *ppl. a.*; **ponced up** *ppl. a.*
1932 G. S. MONCRIEFF *Café Bar* iv. 35 Lou left her periodically, usually to live with some other tart, poncing. *Ibid.*, Now he was unemployed and they were saying to her that he was poncing on her. **1936** J. CURTIS *Gilt Kid* ii. 23, I didn't say no one was poncing on her. **1936** [see *KITE *sb.* 4 c]. **1937** J. CURTIS *You're in Racket* i. 13 Why the hell don't you buy some for yourself instead of poncing on other people? **1938** G. KERSH *Night & City* iii. 42, I don't ponce it orf 'em. **1953** P. SCOTT *Alien Sky* I. ii. 18 Urdu's a man's language... Don't ponce it up with that bastard higher standard muck. **1954** Ponce about [see **brothel-creeper* (*shoe*)]. **1955** 'C. H. ROLPH' *Women of Streets* x. 114 He was arrested a third time for poncing on the girl and sent to prison. *Ibid.* 115 The man was sentenced to two years for his third poncing offence. **1957** C. MACINNES *City of Spades* II. ii. 120 Best of all..is poncing on some woman, but I haven't got the beauty enough for that. **1966** J. WAINWRIGHT *Evil Intent* 46 'Why the hell can't they stick to plain facts?' he snarled. 'Why must they ponce everything up to suit their own ends?' **1969** N. COHN *A WopBopaLooBop* (1970) vi. 57 No poncing about, no dressing up or one-shot gimmicking. **1970** G. LORD *Marshmallow Pie* v. 49 What do you think you look like, all ponced up like that? Fucking queer! **1971** *Guardian* 24 June 13/2 Let's face it, New Zealand has been poncing on us for years. **1972** D. LEES *Zodiac* 132 If my own mother had been murdered I wouldn't ponce about like you're doing. **1973** K. GILES *File on Death* vi. 150 Part-time poncing as well, but he thought bookmaking was more honest. **1974** J. GARDNER *Corner Men* vii. 54 Their Rolls is in the Dean Street car park and Chung Yin's sitting in it ponced up like the sweet and sour faggot he is. **1977** *Zigzag* Aug. 14/1, I mean the one before that was just like a stopgap when we was poncin' around, so much to do and nothing was being done for us. **1977** M. KENYON *Rapist* v. 52 Poncing rapist English.. thinking they owned the place.

poncey (pǫ·nsi), *a. slang.* Also **poncy.** [f. PONCE + -Y[1].] Of, pertaining to, or resembling a ponce (sense b); effete, homosexual.
1964 J. HALE *Grudge Fight* xi. 179 'Come on, sissy boy,' says Brooks, 'come on you poncy bastard.' **1970** 'D. CRAIG' *Young Men may Die* xii. 118 Stephen read.. from his notes in that poncy briefing voice he could put on. **1970** L. HENDERSON *Sitting Target* xii. 106 This smells like a poncey brothel. **1973** M. AMIS *Rachel Papers* 174 You haven't half got poncy mates. **1973** J. WAINWRIGHT *Pride of Pigs* 160 Wot yer bring this poncey gear for, anyway? **1977** *Listener* 6 Jan. 13/1 If you are an intellectual sort of chap, not well-versed in small-talk and tittle-tattle, you cannot make much headway with the dumb blonde. You will scare her off by being too poncey or too high-hat.

poncho. Add: **a.** (Earlier and further examples.) Now in common use as a fashion garment.
1717 tr. *Frezier's Voy. to South-Sea* II. 71 The Spaniards have taken up the Use of the *Chony*, or *Poncho*..to ride in, because the Poncho keeps out the Rain. **1885** C. M. YONGE *Two Sides of Shield* I. iv. 40 'Here are some overshoes and Poncho.'.. Poncho..turned out to be a sort of cape. **1907** *Yesterday's Shopping* (1969) 320 c The Mercedes motor cycling poncho. In fawn cashmere, fitted with rubber neck band and wrists, when worn with overalls, rendering the wearer absolutely proof against rain, dust, or wind. **1929** F. A. POTTLE *Stretchers* (1930) 40 We had now been issued ponchos... A poncho is simply a rectangular sheet of water proofed material, with a hole in the center to put one's head through. **1952** W. R. BURNETT *Vanity Row* (1953) i. 9 The little Italian newsboy, wearing a black rubber poncho and cursing the weather, was trying to make up his mind to go home and the hell with it! **1956** G. DURRELL *Drunken Forest* i. 18, I found him clad in pyjamas and a *poncho*, that useful Argentine garment that resembles a blanket with a hole in the middle through which you stick your head. **1967** *Observer* 26 Mar. 9 Girls..wear what men wear, though Inca ponchos have a strong appeal. **1969** I. KEMP *Brit. G.I. in Vietnam* iv. 84, I sat out in the open, wrapped miserably in my poncho. **1974** *Times* 4 Oct. 7/3 There will be no central heating in the Elysée until October 15... The staff has been allowed to sport..polo-necked pullovers and South American ponchos. **1976** T. SHARPE *Wilt* ii. 13, I was thinking of trying Felicity Fashions for a shantung poncho.
b. poncho dress, (*a*) a costume including a poncho; (*b*) a dress made like a poncho; **poncho liner,** a lining garment worn under a poncho.
1811 W. WALTON *Hist. & Descr. Acct. Peruvian Sheep* ii. 52 The Indian driver in this plate is also represented in his proper *poncho* dress. **1968** *Vogue* 15 Apr. 28 Poncho dress..25 gns. **1969** I. KEMP *Brit. G.I. in Vietnam* iv. 76 Nights at this altitude were beautifully cool and we often slept under our padded poncho liners.

‖ **poncif** (pońsīf). [Fr.] Stereotyped or conventional literary ideas, plot, character, etc.
1923 J. M. MURRY *Pencillings* 136 The modern spirit, with its almost fanatical desire to get rid of the *poncif*, might make a fine thing of classical translation. **1940** *Scrutiny* IX. 258 He [*sc.* Verlaine] revived some of the oldest and loveliest verse-forms; and he managed, in his best work, to escape from the Romantic *poncif* and to go back to something more human.

poncy, var. *PONCEY *a.*

pond, *sb.* Add: **1. b.** (Further N. Amer. examples.)
1693 H. KELSEY *Kelsey Papers* (1929) 3 This wood is poplo ridges with small ponds of water. There is beavour in abundance but no Otter. **1794** A. THOMAS *Newfoundland Jrnl.* (1968) 27 In this Island is a fresh water pond a full mile in length, and in it are large Eels and other Fish. **1801** J. QUINCY in *Proc. Mass. Hist. Soc.* (1889) 2nd Ser. IV. 132 Nantucket whale-fishers pursuing perch in a pond half a mile in circumference are objects ludicrous enough. **1831** J. J. AUDUBON *Ornith. Biogr.* I. 479 It searches for food..by the margins of such inland lakes as, on account of their small size, are called by us ponds. **1948** *Canad. Geogr. Jrnl.* Mar. 49/1 Everyone knows what a lake is and there are lakes of all sizes from coast to coast, but if you happen to reside in the Eastern Townships of Quebec you may find your *lake* is called a *pond*. **1969** H. HORWOOD *Newfoundland* 220 In Newfoundland almost all lakes, no matter how large, are called 'ponds'. **1974** *Maclean's Mag.* Dec. 83/2 The Syncrude pond will cover nine square miles.
d. = *LAGOON[1] 2**.
1956 K. IMHOFF et al. *Disposal of Sewage* xii. 205 The area of pond required for waste purification may be computed by means of the oxygen balance. **1961** BOLTON & KLEIN *Sewage Treatm.* vi. 88. If properly operated, the ponds are reasonably free from bad smells, due possibly to the deodorizing effect of the chlorophyll in the algae. **1973** T. H. Y. TEBBUTT *Water Sci. & Technol.* ix. 138 In warm climates biological treatment is sometimes achieved in oxidation ponds. **1978** *Coal Option* (Shell Internat. Petroleum Co.) 8 Substantial research is also going into agglomeration processes to recover coal from potential waste material, such as the effluent streams from existing colliery washeries, and coal from existing slurry ponds and tips.
4. *pond-keeper*; **pond-barrow** *Archæol.* (further examples); **pond-culture,** the keeping of fish in ponds; hence **pond-cultured** *a.*; **pond-skater,** an aquatic insect belonging to the family Gerridæ, found on the surface of fresh or salt water; **pond-snail,** esp. one belonging to the genus *Limnæa*; (earlier and later examples).
1941 *Proc. Prehist. Soc.* VII. 89 The so-called pond-barrow consists of a slight depression,..the material from which has been placed round the circumference to form an embanked rim. **1963** *Field Archaeol.* (Ordnance Survey) (ed. 4) 47 The pond barrow appears as a regular circular shallow depression,..surrounded by a small bank. **1885** *Encycl. Brit.* XIX. 127/2 Pond-culture..has been practised for many centuries. **1977** *Undercurrents* June–July 30/3 The mirror carp is by far the best fish for pond culture in Britain. **1972** *Country Life* 7 Dec. 1565/1 There are no public-health worries about eating pond-cultured fish. **1779** G. WHITE *Let.* 7 May in *Selborne* (1789) I. 259 Five of those most rare birds..were shot upon the verge of Frinsham-pond... The pond keeper says there were three brace in the flock. **1909** *Westm. Gaz.* 12 Jan. 5/2 The pondkeeper was unavoidably absent from his post. **1895** L. C. MIALL *Nat. Hist. Aquatic Insects* xiii. 382 The Pond-skaters stand or run upon the surface of the water, which they dimple but do not break. **1923** E. A. BUTLER *Biol. Brit. Hemiptera-Heteroptera* 244 Popularly known as pond-skaters or water-measurers, they attract the attention of even the least observant by the free and easy way in which they dart along over the surface of the water. **1952** J. CLEGG *Freshwater Life* xiii. 198 The Pond Skaters feed largely on dead or dying insects that fall on the water. **1973** *Nature* 9 Mar. 132/1 The family Gerridae..includes the common pond-skaters or water-striders. **1855** C. KINGSLEY *Glaucus* 159 A few of the delicate pond-snails (unless they devour your *Vallisneria* too rapidly). **1952** J. CLEGG *Freshwater Life* xvi. 261 The Pond Snails proper..belong mainly to the genus *Limnaea*.

pond, *v.* Add: **1. b.** To produce (a lake) by forming or acting as a dam.
1949 *Bull. Geol. Soc. Amer.* LX. 1383/2 In southern Ohio it is claimed that certain coastal-plain plants..are still avoiding the deposits of the proglacial lakes that are supposed to have been ponded by the advancing Nebraskan ice in the upper drainage of the Teays River. **1971** *Nature* 8 Oct. 391/1 Potassium–argon determinations on trachyte lavas which possibly ponded the former Chemoigut lake gave results of 1·1 and 1·2 m.y.

ponded, *ppl. a.* (s.v. POND *v.*). Add: **b.** Of a sewage filter: blocked; under a depth of liquid.
1940 IMHOFF & FAIR *Sewage Treatm.* vi. 106 *Psychode* prefers an open bed and *Achorutes* a ponded surface. **1967** *Jrnl. Inst. Public Health Engineers* LXVI. 170 This large accumulation of film did not affect the performance of the filters very markedly, even though at times the surfaces of both were quite badly ponded. **1971** T. H. Y. TEBBUTT *Princ. Water Quality Control* xii. 122 A ponded

filter can be brought back into use by applying the partially stabilized effluent from another filter.

ponder, *sb.*[2] (Later examples.)

1970 [see *COME *v.* 69 m]. **1976** T. MCCLURE *Rogue Eagle* iv. 66 The obese sunbather..went away to think about it. Buchanan had a bit of a ponder himself.

po·nderate, *a. rare.* [f. L. *ponderāt-*, ppl. stem of *ponderāre* to weigh, consider.] Careful; deliberate.

1922 *Times* 7 Oct. 11/2 It is a time for calm and ponderate consideration of the issues involved. **1970** P. O'BRIAN *Master & Commander* x. 257 The mature, the ponderate mind does not embark itself upon a man-of-war—is not to be found wandering about the face of the ocean in quest of violence.

ponderomotive, *a.* Add to def.: usu. applied *spec.* to such forces exerted upon bodies by electric or magnetic fields. (Earlier and further examples.)

1881 *Phil. Mag.* XII. 17 The force with which one quantity of electricity acts upon another quantity of electricity may be regarded either as an electromotive force or as a true ponderomotive force; for it tends to move electricity, and also to move matter, if matter be associated with the electricity. **1934** I. M. FREEMAN tr. *Joos's Theoret. Physics* xv. 296 The current in the segment, the magnetic field, and the ponderomotive force must form a right-handed orthogonal system in this order (Fleming's left-hand rule). **1964** R. R. BIRSS *Electr. & Magnetic Forces* i. 1 Ponderomotive forces are also exerted on dielectric bodies in electric fields. **1964** S. K. RUNCORN in A. E. M. Nairn *Probl. Palaeoclimatol.* 192 The varying fields generated in the core..will also generate induced currents in the mantle, and the ponderomotive forces resulting from these will cause angular acceleration and deceleration of the mantle on time-scales of 100 years. **1978** *Nature* 23 Mar. 316/2 In this case, ponderomotive forces were used to overcome the power barrier.

ponderosa (pǫndərōu·ză, -să). [a. the specific epithet of *Pinus ponderosa* (P. & C. Lawson *Agriculturist's Manual* (1836) 354), f. L. *ponderōsus* heavy.] In full, *ponderosa pine*. A large conifer, *Pinus ponderosa* or western yellow pine, native to western North America and widely cultivated elsewhere; also, the timber of this tree. Also *attrib.*

1878 R. J. HINTON *Hand-bk. Arizona* 292 *Ponderosa* reaches a height of 70 feet; some firs are higher. **1937** *Range Plant Handbk.* (U.S. Dept. Agric. Forest Service) B-44 Deerbrush is most commonly found in the ponderosa pine and mixed conifer belts. **1949** *Democrat* 2 June 3/1 Ponderosa wood is light in color, varying from creamy white to straw. **1951** V. NABOKOV *Speak, Memory* vi. 96 Mariposa lilies bloomed under Ponderosa pines. **1957** *Handbk. Softwoods* (Forest Prod. Res. Lab.) 41 Canadian-grown ponderosa pine is about 20 per cent more resistant to splitting along the rings than Baltic redwood. **1966** MRS. L. B. JOHNSON *White House Diary* 2 Apr. (1970) 379 He described the 'relic forest' of maple..and ponderosa pine with huge trunks. **1971** *New Scientist* 10 June 628/3 The study considered growing douglas fir and ponderosa pine, but concluded that softwoods would not be economically feasible. **1976** *Billings* (Montana) *Gaz.* 20 June 9-A/1 (Advt.), Enjoy living in a beautiful natural setting, abundant with ponderosas, junipers, chokecherries, and wild roses. **1978** *Times* 11 Mar. 3/3 A finely balanced relationship has evolved between scale insects and ponderosa pine trees in the north-western United States.

ponding, *vbl. sb.* (s.v. POND *v.*). Add: **b.** Blockage *of* a sewage filter; the accumulation of liquid above a filter.

1939 L. B. ESCRITT *Sewerage Engin.* vii. 133 Excessive flows..are often the cause of 'ponding' of the filters. **1953** E. W. STEEL *Water Supply & Sewerage* (ed. 3) xxiv. 488 Media of small size will furnish more surface, but unloading will be less complete and ponding on the surface [of the filters] is more likely. **1971** T. H. Y. TEBBUTT *Princ. Water Quality Control* xii. 120 Film growths may result in blockage of the voids causing ponding of the filter and anaerobic conditions. *Ibid.* 122 When the first filter shows signs of ponding the direction of flow.. is reversed.

pond-lily. *orig. U.S.* Also **pond lily.** [f. POND *sb.* + (WATER-)LILY.] A water-lily, esp. the common yellow spatterdock, *Nuphar advena*.

1748 J. ELIOT *Ess. Field-Husbandry New Eng.* (1760) i. 5 A natural Pond..over grown with Pond Lillies. **1778** [see POND *sb.* 4]. **1827** *Western Monthly Rev.* I. 251 The flowers are large, of a pure white, nearest resembling the northern pond-lily. **1846** *Knickerbocker* XXVII. 52 A little mill-pond..is covered all over with pond-lilies and rank grasses. **1873** T. B. ALDRICH *Marjorie Daw* 14 All this splendor goes into that hammock, and sways there like a pond-lily. **1911** G. STRATTON-PORTER *Harvester* vii. 121 The pond lilies are just beginning to open. **1938** F. PERRY *Water Gardening* vii. 82 The Yellow Pond Lily will flourish in shady positions. **1947** E. PAUL *Linden on Saugus Branch* 367 On the Linden ponds, frogs' eggs, turtles, pond lilies with flat leaves, not shaped like plates. **1974** H. W. RICKETT *Wild Flowers U.S.* VI. I. 130 The conspicuous part of the yellow pond-lilies is the calyx.

Pondo (pǫ·ndo). [Nguni.] **a.** A member of a Xhosa-speaking Nguni people in the eastern part of the Cape Province in South Africa. Cf. *AMAPONDO. **b.** The language spoken by the Pondos, a dialect of Xhosa. Also *attrib.*

[**1835** A. STEEDMAN *Wanderings Interior S. Afr.* (1966) I. p. iv, The third division are the Amapondo tribes,.. whose territories extend from the Bashee to the River Umsikalia. **1876** *Encycl. Brit.* V. 42/2 The Amapondo country of Kaffraria. **1884** K. JOHNSTON *Africa* (ed. 3) xxiv. 399 The remaining portions of Kafraria, including.. that of the Amapondo extending across the St. John's River between the Umtata and the Umtamfuna, the boundary river of Natal.] **1919** H. H. JOHNSTON *Compar. Study Bantu & Semi-Bantu Lang.* I. iii. 298 The [Kafir] dialects include Feñgu, Baʒa and Pondω words. *Ibid.* v. 797 The divergent dialects of ʔōsa, such as Isi-pondω, Isi-baʒa, Feñgu, &c. **1950** *Cape Argus* 18 Mar. (Mag. Section) 7/7 The area from Umtata down to the sea, and northwards to the borders of Natal, belongs to the Pondos —a tribe that would have been exterminated long ago by raiding bands of Zulus if the British Government had not intervened. **1973** *Times* 19 Feb. 12/1 The hillsides are dotted with clusters of neat..round huts.., the homes of the local Africans who are a mixture of Zulu and Pondo tribes. **1979** A. MCCOY *Insurrectionist* vi. 56 The grinning one is a Pondo. There is bad blood already between the Swazi and the Pondo.

pondok (pǫ·ndǫk). *S. Afr.* Also **pondokkie, pandokkie** (-ǫ·ki), **pandok, pondhock, pondhok, bond-hoek.** [Afrikaans, f. Malay.] A hut or shack made of oddments of wood, corrugated iron, etc.; a mean house or hovel, esp. one inhabited by non-whites. Also *attrib.*

1815 A. PLUMPTRE tr. *Lichtenstein's Trav. S. Afr.* II. xli. 185 Near it stand six or eight *pandokken*, as they are called, a kind of huts made of reeds woven into a wooden frame, which are inhabited by the principal Bastard-Hottentots. **1818** C. I. LATROBE *Jrnl. Visit S. Afr.* 218 The present dwelling..is a hovel, not much better than a Hottentot's bondhoek. **1832** A. SMITH in P. R. Kirby *Andrew Smith & Natal* (1955) 35 In the afternoon to the Komga River to the 'pondok' (straw hut) of a trader. **1843** J. C. CHASE *Cape Good Hope* III. 235 The Hottentots ..planted themselves at the outskirts of the country villages in small pondhoks, or huts, partly covered with old rags, decayed hides, sugar bags, and occasionally a little thatch. **1899** *Eastern Province Herald* (S. Afr.) 4 Nov. (Pettman), The poor burghers are living in pandokkies. **1911** *State* (Cape Town) Dec. 612 In the morning we found that a dozen or more Hottentots had pitched their pondhocks close to the wagon. **1944** *Cape Argus* 23 June, The people who are living in overcrowded shanties and pondokkies. **1948** L. G. GREEN *To River's End* xiv. 161, I built myself a pondok in a lonely kloof and became tame. **1952** E. H. BURROWS *Overberg Outspan* iv. 103 They were the original herdsmen. Each inhabited his own *pondok*, and each was master of his own field. **1960** D. LESSING *In Pursuit of English* 29 He painted..pondokkies. In other words, African huts, slums, broken-down villages. **1971** *Post* (S. Afr., Cape ed.) 9 May 4/6 Here we are..in our well ventilated pondok in the bundu. **1974** *Cape Times* 2 Aug. 3/6 He said that he had read reports about alleged 'pondok farming' published in the Cape Times recently.

pond pine. *U.S.* [f. POND *sb.* + PINE *sb.*[2]] A conifer belonging to the species *Pinus serotina*, growing on wet or marshy ground in south-eastern parts of the United States.

1810 F. A. MICHAUX *Hist. Arbres Forestiers de l'Amérique Septentrionale* I. 17 Pond pine (Pin des mares). **1832** D. J. BROWNE *Sylva Amer.* 240 The Pond Pine frequently recurs in the maritime parts of the Southern States. **1858** J. A. WARDER *Hedges & Evergreens* II. 249 *Pinus serotina*, or Pond Pine, is thirty five or forty feet high. **1860** M. A. CURTIS *Woody Plants N. Carolina* 21 Pond Pine.. has considerable resemblance to the Pitch Pine. **1940** *Amer. Forests* Oct. 462/2 Pond pine bears such local names as marsh pine, bay pine, and pocoson pine. **1967** N. T. MIROV *Genus Pinus* iii. 187 *Pinus serotina*, or pond pine, grows in the Coastal Plain from south-eastern Virginia south to central and southeastern Alabama.

pondy, *a.* Add: **2.** Belonging to or suggestive of a pond.

1922 *Chambers's Jrnl.* July 440/1 The peculiar 'pondy' smell of the bird [*sc.* moorhen] does not suggest that it would prove a great delicacy.

pone[3]. Add: **c.** *attrib.* as *pone bread*.

c **1785** in *Maryland Hist. Mag.* (1907) II. 258, I procured some milk and excellent pone bread from a hut. **1833** J. NEAL *Down-Easters* I. 47, I should like to know.. what upon irth he means by..hoe-cakes an pone bread. **1879** *Scribner's Monthly* June 223/1 Now that the wagons were up and 'pone' bread and beef stews had re-appeared in the menu, the Foot Cavalry, feeling its keep, waxed fat and kicked. **1935** Z. N. HURSTON *Mules & Men* (1970) I. viii. 175 Nobody..don't take de fork and turn over every fish in de dish in order to pick de best one. You does dat wid yo' eye whilst youse choosin' yo' pone bread. **1936** J. C. CHENAULT *Old Cane Springs* xviii. 78 Then pone bread, light bread, and biscuits were brought out.

‖**ponente** (pone·nte). [It.: see PONENT *a.* (*sb.*).] (See quot. 1959.) Also *ponente wind*.

1906 W. MARRIOTT *Hints to Meteorol. Observers* (ed. 6) 67/2 *Ponente*, a Westerly wind in the Mediterranean. **1959** R. E. HUSCHKE *Gloss. Meteorol.* 433 *Ponente*, a west wind on the Côte d'Azur.., the northern Roussillon region, and Corsica. On the Côte d'Azur it is a weakened mistral and brings clear skies. In northern Roussillon it is the land breeze of early morning, changing to southeast during the day. **1974** *Country Life* 25 Apr. 996/3 On some days the drying mistral blows, on others the damp *ponente* wind. **1978** S. SHELDON *Bloodline* vii. 84 The winds blew... The mistral and the *ponente*, the tramontana and the *grecale* and the levanter.

ponerid, *sb.* (Example.) Cf. next.

1895 J. H. & A. COMSTOCK *Man. Study Insects* xxii. 642 The Ponerids... The ants of this family resemble [the Formicidæ]..in that the peduncle of the abdomen consists of a single segment.

ponerine (pǫ·nərəin, -īn), *a.* and *sb. Ent.* Also **Ponerine.** [ad. mod.L. name of subfamily *Ponerinæ*, f. generic name *Ponera* (P. A. Latreille 1804, in *Nouveau Dict. Hist. Nat.* XXIV. 179), f. Gr. πονηρά, fem. of πονηρός wicked + -INE[1].] **A.** *adj.* Of, or pertaining to, or designating ants of the subfamily Ponerinæ, which includes mainly tropical species. **B.** *sb.* A ponerine ant.

1910 W. M. WHEELER *Ants* ii. 26 The base of the abdomen is more primitive and more like that of certain Ponerine ants. **1933** *Discovery* Sept. 286/1 Professor W. M. Wheeler..paid special attention to the colony-foundation among the primitive Ponerine ants. **1945** C. P. HASKINS *Of Ants & Men* xi. 207 Australia is pre-eminently the home of the Ponerines of today. **1966** C. SWEENEY *Scurrying Bush* vii. 101 *Platythyrea cribinodis*, a common, large, dull-black ponerine ant. *Ibid.* 103 As with the giant solitary black ponerine,..the black stink ants were not attacked because of their strong odour. **1977** M. V. BRIAN *Ants* iii. 39 All ponerines have a constriction between the first and second segments of the gaster. *Ibid.*, The Myrmicinæ are thought to have evolved from ponerine ants.

pong, *sb.*[1] Add: **b.** Abbrev. PING-PONG *sb.* Also, an electronic game resembling ping-pong, played on a pinball machine or a television screen. Also *attrib.*

1968–70 *Current Slang* (Univ. S. Dakota) III–IV. 94 *Pong, n.* ping-pong. **1976** *Washington Post* 19 Apr. A15/2 (Advt.), Now the whole family can play the new & exciting pong on your home TV. **1976** *Billings* (Montana) *Gaz.* 16 June 11-C/6 (Advt.), The new amusement machine, Pachinco, is sweeping the country like the pong games did five years ago. **1978** *Chicago* June 36/1 Game room with pong and pinball machines used by neighborhood folks.

pong (pǫŋ), *sb.*[2] *colloq.* Also (*rare*) **ponk.** [Etym. obscure.] An unpleasant smell; a stink.

1919 W. H. DOWNING *Digger Dial.* 38 *Pong*,..stink. **1925** FRASER & GIBBONS *Soldier & Sailor Words* 226 *Pong*, a stink. **1936** F. CLUNE *Roaming round Darling* xxiv. 257 Avoid the smell of camel. They were complete with permanent, pyramid, and perfume, commonly called pong. **1941** BAKER *Dict. Austral. Slang* 56 *Ponk*, a stink. As verb, to stink. **1957** J. BRAINE *Room at Top* iv. 44 'What a pong,' he said. 'Don't know how you stand it.' **1960** H. PINTER *Dumb Waiter* 130 What, you mean it might be my pong? (He sniffs sheets.) Yes... It could be my pong I suppose. **1973** G. MOFFAT *Deviant Death* I. v. 64 She's burning the feathers... She only does it when the wind takes the smell away from us... The pong's not bothering us. **1974** J. GARDNER *Return of Moriarty* 292 There ain't half a pong down here.

Pong (pǫŋ), *sb.*[3] Chiefly *Austral. slang.* [Origin uncertain.] A derogatory name for a Chinese.

1931 V. PALMER *Separate Lives* 221 Blow into one of those Chow joints..and call for a dollar's worth of duck and fowl. Enough for two those pongs always give you. **1938** X. HERBERT *Capricornia* 339 Your grandmother was a lubra and your grandfather was a Pong. **1941** BAKER *Dict. Austral. Slang* 56 *Pong*, a Chinese. **1957** D. STIVENS *Scholarly Mouse* 65 He was too tall to be a Pong or an Eyetoe. **1962** J. FRANKLYN *Dict. Nicknames* 86/1 *Pong* is a nickname given to a Chinaman in Australia—punning the *ong* sound in some Chinese words, and *pong*, a bad smell. **1970** 'B. MATHER' *Break in Line* i. 11 I'm the only Pong I know who wouldn't say Charling Closs.

pong (pǫŋ), *v.*[2] *colloq.* Also (*rare*) **ponk.** [f. *PONG *sb.*[2]] *intr.* To stink. Also *fig.*

1927 [see *HUM *v.*[3]]. **1939** R. CAMPBELL *Flowering Rifle* 21 What matters most to them is—'Does it Pong?' **1941** [see *PONG *sb.*[2]] **1944** 'N. SHUTE' *Pastoral* ii. 17, I think it looks ugly as sin, and it's starting to ponk a bit. **1948** M. ALLINGHAM *More Work for Undertaker* xiii. 164 The old boy never bought a sausage that didn't pong. **1950** A. BARON *There's no Home* i. 16 'It don't 'alf pong,' he observed. **1960** [see *DRAIN *sb.* 1 e] **1972** P. CLEIFE *Slick & Dead* ii. 22 This loving thing could be a cover story for any old racket?.. Pongs a bit, don't you think? **1979** R. RENDELL *Make Death love Me* ix. 85 The place.. just pongs of dirty clothes.

ponga (pɒ·ŋă). Also **bunger, bungy, punga.** [Maori.] An evergreen New Zealand tree-fern, *Cyathea dealbata*, belonging to the family Cyatheaceæ; also *attrib.*

1832 G. BENNETT in *London Med. Gaz.* 22 Sept. 793/2 This fern..is named Ponga by the natives, who use the trunks as posts in the erection of their houses. **1855** R. TAYLOR *Te Ika a Maui* viii. 115 Some of the trees themselves..held down their heads, and have never been able to hold them up since; amongst these, were the *ponga* (a fern tree) and the *kareao* (supple jack), whose tender shoots are now always bent. **1874** J. WHITE *Te Rou* xi. 179 Round two sides and one end [of the hangis, or ovens] a ponga fence is put. **1892** E. S. BROOKES

Frontier Life xv. 139 The Survey department graded a zigzag track up the side to the top, fixing in punga steps. **1898** MORRIS *Austral Eng.* 65/1 Bunga or Bungy,..a New Zealand settlers' corruption of the Maori word *punga*. **1905** W. B. *Where White Man Treads* 232 It irks to go back to ponga whare and earthen floors. **1926** *Trans. N.Z. Inst.* LVI. 670 In some instances the Maori name has been adopted but corrupted:..'bunger' (now fortunately seldom heard) for 'ponga'. **1933** *Press* (Christchurch, N.Z.) 23 Sept. 13/7 Bungy.—Tree fern. I [*sc.* L. G. D. Acland] have only heard this word used on the West Coast; it is just as often pronounced pungy. **1935** 'J. GUTHRIE' *Little Country* iii. 58 Tall punga ferns spread their proud fronds. **1949** F. SARGESON *I saw in my Dream* II. xiv. 172 On the ridge it was too dry for pungas. **1959** *Times* 10 June 12/6 We strained our eyes..to see the punga fern under which the first white child was born in New Zealand. **1963** B. PEARSON *Coal Flat* xxii. 376 Peter was urinating urgently against a ponga. **1966** *Encycl. N.Z.* I. 650/1 *C*[*yathea*] *dealbata* or ponga has distinctive whitish undersurfaces to the leaves. **1966** G. W. TURNER *Eng. Lang. Austral. & N.Z.* viii. 168 Other Maori words in changed form are cockabully from kokopu,..bunger (Maori ponga), a common name for the treefern [etc.]. **1968** *N.Z. Listener* 11 Apr. 10/1 He built himself a ten-foot-high punga fence and was snug. **1977** *N.Z. Herald* 5 Jan. 2-16/8 (Advt.), Genuine bush with pongas, totara and kauri surrounding this most impressive 4-brm contemporary home.

ponga, var. *PANGA[1].

pongal (pǫ·ŋgăl). Also **pongol, pongul, ponkal.** [ad. Tamil *poṅkal*, 'boiling'.] The Tamil New Year festival at which new rice is cooked; hence, a dish of cooked rice.

1788 F. MAGNUS tr. *Sonnerat's Voy. East-Indies & China* I. v. 142 The second day the festival is called Maddou-Pongol, or Pongol of cows:—they paint the horns of these animals, cover them with flowers, make them run in the streets, and lastly make the Pongol at home for them. **1809** *Asiatic Ann. Reg. 1807* Misc. 141 (*heading*) An interesting account of the great Hindu festival Pongal, by Teroovercadoo Mootiah. *Ibid.* 144/1 The Hindoos visit and compliment each other, wishing a happy Pongal, or many returns of that Pongal, for the preservation of each other. **1855** H. H. WILSON *Gloss. Indian Terms* 421/1 *Pongal*.., a boiling or bubbling up, the boiling of rice, whence it becomes the name of the popular festival held by the Hindus in the Madras provinces. **1877** M. MONIER-WILLIAMS *Hinduism* xii. 182 In the South of India this festival is commonly called 'Pongal', and is the commencement of the Tamil year. **1897** H. K. BEAUCHAMP tr. *Dubois's Hindu Manners* II. III. iii. 580 The pongul, or Maha-sankranti, always takes place during the winter solstice, the period when the sun, having finished its course towards the southern hemisphere, turns to the north again and comes back to visit the people of India. **1906** W. CROOKE *Things Indian* 211 The opening of the agricultural year is marked..by the *Pongol* of South India. **1913** *Encycl. Relig. & Ethics* VI. 44/1 The central rite of the great Pongol festival of S. India consists in cooking new rice, some of which is offered to Gaṇeśa, the remainder being eaten by the family. **1961** [see *IDLI]. **1968** P. LAL *Indian Recipes* 58 Many delicacies are prepared for the Pongal feast... The six months following Pongal are considered auspicious for marriage. **1974** F. W. CLOTHEY tr. L. S. Ramamirtham in *New Writing in India* 97 No matter how poor a man is, it's only at Poṅkal that his rice boils in a new pot.

pongelo (pǫ·ŋgəlo). *slang.* Also **pongelow.** [Etym. obscure.] Beer. Also *attrib.*

1864 HOTTEN *Slang Dict.* 204 *Pongelow*, beer, half-and-half. **1880** M. E. BRADDON *Just as I Am* I. ix. 130 'He stood sam for a pot o' pongelo,' continued Mr. Scaffers, 'and narchurly we got talkin'.' **1898** A. M. BINSTEAD *Pink 'Un & Pelican* viii. 185 Some well-known publican has given twenty thousand pounds for the local pongelo palace, with the plate-glass saloon bars. **1899** *Westm. Gaz.* 9 Jan. 5/2, I hope **** is quite well and keeping himself allright [*sic*] and not soaking to [*sic*] much pongelow. **1899** H. WYNDHAM *Soldiers of Queen* 256 One night I had a drop too much 'pongelow', and there was a bit of a row. **1905** *Daily Chron.* 2 Mar. 4/5 You said, 'What're you goin' to 'ave?' an' the pongelos flow'd free as advice. **1909** J. R. WARE *Passing Eng.* 199/1 *Pongelo*, (Anglo-Indian Army), pale ale—but relatively any beer.

pongid (pǫ·ŋgid), *sb.* and *a. Zool.* [f. mod.L. family name *Pongidæ*, f. generic name *Pongo* (B. G. E. de La V. Lacépède *Tableau des Mammifères* (1799) 4: see etym. of PONGO) + -ID[3].] **a.** *sb.* An anthropoid ape belonging to the family Pongidæ, which includes the gorilla, the chimpanzee, and the orang-utan. **b.** *adj.* Of or pertaining to this group of apes.

1955 W. E. LE GROS CLARK *Fossil Evidence Human Evolution* iv. 141 The differential characters of the dentition.., on the basis of the comparative study of large numbers of hominids and pongids.., have been established. **1957** *Antiquity* XXXI. 191 Another tarsioid line produced the primitive apes (the pongid line). **1963** *New Scientist* 27 June 737/1 Dr Leakey revealed that there were true pongids (apes) living in East Africa during the Miocene period. **1968** *Nature* 9 Nov. 548/1 To split the African apes from the Pongidae and place them in the Hominidae would ignore the extraordinary change in the hominid line since it split off from the pongid line. **1973** B. J. WILLIAMS *Evolution & Human Origins* ix. 127/2 The genus *Dryopithecus* is ancestral to the present-day African pongids, the gorilla and chimpanzee. *Ibid.* 129/1 *Ramapithecus* is smaller than most species of the fossil pongid genus *Dryopithecus*. **1977** A. HALLAM *Planet Earth* 284 The hominids are a family containing Man and his close relatives, distinct from the family of apes, the pongids.

pongo. Add: **1. b.** Substitute for def.: Later transferred to the orang-utan, an anthropoid ape native to Borneo and Sumatra, and adopted as its generic name by Lacépède in 1799; see *PONGID *sb.* and *a.* (Earlier and later examples.)

1798 *Phil. Mag.* I. 238 The orang outang of the large kind, or the pongo of Buffon, is not common even in its native country Borneo. **1913** D. G. ELLIOTT *Rev. Primates* I. [Errata] The premier genus of the Great Apes is Pongo. **1972** D. BLOODWORTH *Any Number can Play* xii. 104 An intelligent pongo digging a twig into a wasp's nest.

2. a. *Naut. slang.* A marine, a soldier. Also *attrib.*

1917 'B. COPPLESTONE' *Lost Naval Papers* vi. 85 You could pass as a naval officer more easily than you could as a Pongo. **1919** W. H. DOWNING *Digger Dial.* 38 *Pongo*, a soldier; one of the rank and file. **1923** F. H. VIZETELLY *Desk-Bk. Idioms* 328 *Pongo*, a marine: in playful British usage, from a native African name for an anthropoid ape. **1943** D. GLOVER in *Penguin New Writing* XVI. 15 What about that bloody pongo what's been loafing round since I come ashore last? **1946** J. IRVING *Royal Navalese* 137 *Pongo*, the matelot's name for a soldier. In the First World War it was his name for a Royal Marine. **1955** 'N. SHUTE' *Requiem for Wren* iii. 92 Each service at that time had its own slang; to her the army were all Pongoes. **1961** B. FERGUSSON *Watery Maze* i. 40 Captain (afterwards Admiral Sir Frederick) Dalrymple-Hamilton having an elder brother in the Army, and consequently, as he said, 'a soft spot for Pongoes'. **1964** J. HALE *Grudge Fight* ii. 33 Just before the admiral's car got to the pier the pongos blew a great hole in it. **1975** *Canad. Forces Sentinel* (Ottawa) XI. VI. 7/2 Cpl. Don Lyons won praise from naval techs who described him as the only 'pongo stoker' with the maintenance team. **1977** *Daily Mail* 17 Nov. 15/1 Fourteen youths.. went out looking for soldiers to beat up... Favourite expressions of the gang were 'squaddy bashing' and 'pongo bashing'.

b. *Austral.* and *N.Z. slang.* An Englishman. Also *attrib.*

1942 2 *N.Z.E.F. Times* 7 Sept. 5 A big bronzed Pongo came in. **1945** J. HENDERSON *Gunner Inglorious* 148 The successful applicant [for the position of Batman], an elderly, quiet-spoken Pongo, was a dinkum butler. **1947** D. M. DAVIN *For Rest of Our Lives* xxxii. 165 That pongo cobber of yours, the homo. **1947** —— *Gorse blooms Pale* 208 The poor old pongos are probably still indenting in triplicate for mine-detectors. **1949** *Here & Now* (N.Z.) Oct. 11/2 He long ago began featuring himself as a 'New Zealander born and bred', a sop to the vague public feeling against Pommies, Pongoes, Homies. **1964** *Courier-Mail* (Brisbane) 19 Nov. 12 Mr. Arthur Bryan..dislikes what he calls the 'pongo' Englishman. 'This is the bloke who is so bound by tradition and the old establishment that he can think of nothing else,' he says. **1969** *Private Eye* 19 Dec. 5/2 The *pongos* are shooting through like streaks of *weasle piss*! **1972** G. W. TURNER *Eng. Lang. Austral. & N.Z.* (ed. 2) 109 Like Australians, New Zealanders call the English *pommies*, but also have a variant *pongo* which seems rather less tolerant in its tone.

c. *Mil. slang.* An army officer.

1943 B. J. HURREN *Eastern Med.* xii. 139 In the slang of the desert the word 'pongo' is used for all Army officers. **1943** C. H. WARD-JACKSON *Piece of Cake* 48 *Pongo*, an army officer. **1949** F. MACLEAN *Eastern Approaches* II. vii. 269 'Operation PONGO'..was the code-name I had chosen for the abduction of the General. **1965** O. MANNING *Friends & Heroes* xxii. 237 What were you doing walking about holding on to that bloody little pongo?

d. *slang.* A Negro. Also *attrib.*

1968 L. DEIGHTON *Only when I Larf* vii. 99 You wouldn't want no breech block blowing back and crippling some poor pongo, no matter what country he's in. **1972** M. WOODHOUSE *Mama Doll* viii. 89 Our Pongo brothers in darkest Africa.

pongo, var. *PANGA[1].

pongol, var. *PONGAL.

Pongola (pǫŋgōᵘ·lă). Also **Pangola,** and with lower-case initial. In full, *Pongola* or *Pangola (finger-)grass.* The name of a South African river used *absol.* and *attrib.* to designate a variety of the perennial grass *Digitaria decumbens*, originally native to regions near the river, but now widely cultivated in tropical areas.

1947 D. B. D. MEREDITH *Effect of Fertilisers on Grasses in S. Afr.* v. 115 The area selected had been planted..to alternate rows of the Pongola Finger grass and *Digitaria Smutsii*. **1952** M. A. FLORES in *Proc. 6th Internat. Grassland Congr.* II. 1435 Pangola grass, introduced within recent years from Africa through Florida, U.S.A., is finding favor with livestock producers because of its resistance to drought. **1959** *Agronomy Jrnl.* LI. 111/1 Napier or elephant grass..guineagrass..and pangola-grass..are among the most important of the forage grasses of the Tropics. **1966** A. M. M. REES in Davies & Skidmore *Trop. Pastures* xi. 171 Recorded gross outputs of over £50 per acre were obtained..from milk and beef produced from Pangola pastures. **1972** E. HARGREAVES *Fair Green Weed* vii. 93 We're putting in pangola to make pastures of the old banana plantations. **1972** *Stand. Encycl. S. Afr.* V. 320/2 The quick-grasses.., Pongola finger-grass..and Swaziland finger-grass..are amongst those grasses that are commonly planted as lawns or on sports grounds. **1977** A. V. BOGDAN *Trop. Pasture & Fodder Plants* 113 The name Pangola grass has been derived from the Pongola River in the Piet Retief district of eastern Transvaal..and some authors suggested the name Pongola grass, possibly with a view of avoiding confusion with any other forms of *Digitaria* which may come from the Pangola River area of western Transvaal. It has also been suggested that the name Pangola grass should be applied only to those clones which..were originally brought to USA in 1935 and which are now widely grown in a number of countries.

pongul, var. *PONGAL.

pongy (pǫ·ŋi), *a. colloq.* [f. *PONG *sb.*[2] + -Y[1].] Malodorous; smelly.

1936 'TAFFRAIL' *Mystery at Milford Haven* xi. 153 'Kippers!' she groaned. 'They are a bit pongy sometimes,' Victor had to confess. **1960** *Times Lit. Suppl.* 4 Nov. 714/2 A cheap forty-eight-hour excursion in contemporary Gauguin-land complete with Papeete night-spots, pongy with frangipani. **1965** G. MCINNES *Road to Gundagai* xii. 215 Dad..kept turning up..with loot from the Prahran market: strings of saveloys and frankfurters, pongy cheeses,..and huge Portuguese sardines. **1975** *Islander* (Victoria, B.C.) 3 Aug. 2/2 After lunch the pongy wharf became too much for us.

pongyi, var. POONGHIE, PHOONGYEE in Dict. and Suppl.

ponhaus (pǫ·nhǭs). *U.S. dial.* Also **pawnhaus, ponhaws, ponhoss.** [ad. Ger. *panhas*, f. *pfanne* frying pan + *hase* rabbit. Said to be used in a similar sense in Ger. dial.: see M. B. Lambert *Dict. Non-English Words of Pennsylvania-German Dial.* (1924) 117.] = SCRAPPLE *sb.*[2] Also *attrib.*

1869 *Atlantic Monthly* Oct. 483/1 Some make *pawnhaus* from the liquor in which the pudding was boiled; adding thereto corn-meal. **1882** P. H. GIBBONS *Pennsylvania Dutch* (ed. 3) 423 Mr. W. liked the fried *pawn-haus* although he found it rather rich. **1923** *Dialect Notes* V. 236 *Ponhaws*, scrapple. **1931** *Sun* (Baltimore) 11 Mar. 8/7 He's goin' to have one more grand ponhaus celebration this season. **1943** *Chicago Daily News* 8 Sept. 25 Originally, Ponhaws or scrapple was made from the head of the freshly killed porker, but good, fresh, lean pork of any cut may be used. **1944** *Sun* (Baltimore) 4 Dec. 8-0/3 The Pennsylvania Germans..called it 'Pfännhaas', which..was corrupted into..'Ponhaus',..which simply means..'pan rabbit'. This is in line with the use of 'Welsh rabbit'. **1953** *Amer. Speech* XXVIII. 244 Certainly *ponhaus* and *smearcase*, standard food items from colonial days, are old words in the area [*sc.* Bedford, Pennsylvania].

ponk, var. *PONG *sb.*[2] or *v.*[2]

ponkal, var. *PONGAL.

ponor (pōᵘ·nǭɹ). *Physical Geogr.* [Serbo-Croat.] A steep natural shaft leading from the surface of the ground in a karstic region.

[**1921** *Geogr. Rev.* XI. 593 The article of Professor Cvijić marks a step forward in the science of physiography; but it is far from easy reading for the average geographer since many unfamiliar terms, such as 'bogaz' and 'ponor', are used without either definition or explanation by synonyms. *Ibid.* 600 The shaftlike aperture Cvijić called 'ponor'.] **1922** *Geol. Mag.* XIX. 406 The funnel-shaped hollows which are so frequently met with on the surface of the karst are termed ponors. **1937** WOOLDRIDGE & MORGAN *Physical Basis Geogr.* xix. 290 They [*sc.* limestone caves] commonly form part of a complex system of channels, widening locally into chambers, and fall broadly into two sets, viz. roughly horizontal galleries, and vertical or steeply inclined shafts, of which the higher members are the 'ponors' communicating with the surface. **1971** J. N. JENNINGS *Karst* vi. 139 In some poljes certain ponors change function for a period in the wet season and spew out water. **1976** S. T. TRUDGILL in E. Derbyshire *Geomorphol. & Climate* iii. 92 They observed in the Kuh-E-Parau limestone area of Iran how the overall form on a large scale is solutional in origin, with rounded hills, dolines and ponors.

Ponsonby rule (pǫ·nsǫ̆nbi rūl). [Named after Arthur A. W. H. *Ponsonby* (1871–1946), 1st Lord Ponsonby, English politician.] A rule by which the Government may authorize an agreement without Parliamentary approval (see quot. 1976).

1957 *Erskine May's Law of Parl.* (ed. 16) xiii. 275 This practice, which is known as the 'Ponsonby rule', had its origin in a departmental minute dated 1 February 1924 and signed by Mr. Arthur Ponsonby, then Under-Secretary of State for Foreign Affairs. **1967** P. G. RICHARDS *Parliament & Foreign Affairs* iii. 43 These arrangements constituted the so-called Ponsonby Rule. **1976** H. WILSON *Governance of Britain* x. 185 Under the so-called Ponsonby rules specific parliamentary ratification is not required. The Government assumes authority in respect of any treaty or agreement it has negotiated if Parliament has not reacted within twenty-one days.

Pontet-Canet (pǫṅte kane). The name of a château in the Pauillac commune of the Médoc, applied to a claret produced there.

1883 H. JAMES in *Atlantic Monthly* Oct. 458/1 There is a touch of French reason, French completeness, in a glass of Pontet-Canet. **1891** in C. Ray *Compleat Imbiber* (1967) IX. 122 *Claret*..St. Estèphe..St. Emilion..Pontet Canet. **1912** 'SAKI' *Chron. Clovis* 184 Waiter, a bottle of *Pontet Canet*. **1920** G. SAINTSBURY *Notes on Cellar-Bk.* iv. 64 Pontet Canet..became..a 'literary' wine a good many years ago. **1966** H. Yoxall *Fashion of Life* xxv. 240 A Soho restaurant where..they served a pre-war Ch. Pontet-Canet at 2s. 9d. a half-bottle. **1967** A. Lichine *Encycl. Wines* 409/1 Classified a Fifth Growth..in 1855, and traditionally at the head of the Fifths, Pontet-Canet actually sells with the Seconds and Thirds. **1975** 'D. Jordan' *Black Account* xiii. 65 The House had..lashed out on a Pontet-Canet..and a port which set out to impress the Minister.

Pontian (pǫ·ntiăn), *a.* *Geol.* [ad. Russ. *Ponticheskiĭ* (N. Barbot de Marny *Geol. ocherk' Khersonskoĭ Gubernii* (1869) xiv. 106), f. as Pontic *a.*[1]: see -ian.] Of, pertaining to, or designating the uppermost stage of the Miocene series in Europe (sometimes regarded as the lowest of the Pliocene series). Also *absol.*

1893 P. Lake tr. *Kayser's Text Bk. Compar. Geol.* iv. 361 Congeria or Pontian series. **1895** J. D. Dana *Man. Geol.* (ed. 4) iv. iv. 927 Above the Tortonian, the stages Sarmatian and Pontian are recognized in Dauphiné, Austria and Italy. **1903** A. Geikie *Text-bk. Geol.* (ed. 4) II. 1291 The top of the Miocene series (Pontian stage). **1940** A. W. Grabau *Rhythm of Ages* xxxviii. 466 The Pontian Hipparion clays, which were formerly considered in part Miocene, are here placed in the base of the Pliocene. **1971** *Nature* 30 Apr. 562/1 In 1929, Matthew ..pointing to the occurrence of a relatively primitive *Hipparion* fauna in the lower part of the stratotype Pontian at Sebastopol,..argued that the first appearance of *Hipparion* could thus be used to define the base of the Pliocene in continental mammalian successions. In this way, 'early Pliocene' and 'Pontian' became equivalent terms in vertebrate biostratigraphy. **1973** *Ibid.* 15 June 391/1 Estimates by most vertebrate palaeontologists have ranged between 10–12 m.y. because of the supposed initial appearance of the three-toed *Hipparion* in the lower part of the stratotype Pontian of the eastern Mediterranean.

‖ **pontianak**[1] (pǫntiā·næk). [a. Malay *pontianak*, f. *pati-anak* child-killer.] A type of vampire (see quots.). Cf. *langsuir, *penanggalan.

1839 T. J. Newbold *Pol. & Statistical Acct. Straits of Malacca* II. xii. 191 Spirits..supposed to exert a baneful influence over them [*sc.* Malays] in this sublunary world. First, the Plissit and the Pontianak. **1900** W. W. Skeat *Malay Magic* vi. 320 The Pontianak or Mati-anak..is also a night-owl, and is supposed to be a child of the Langsuir. **1965** C. Shuttleworth *Malayan Safari* vi. 86 Perhaps the most fearsome of all superstitions is that of the *pontianak* or vampire, widely prevalent throughout Malaya. **1966** D. Forbes *Heart of Malaya* xiii. 185 She had turned into what they call a *pontianak.* **1972** *Daily Tel.* (Colour Suppl.) 12 May 58/3 The Malayan vampire family includes..the Pontianak (the stillborn child of the Langsuir) which adopts the shape of a night owl.

pontianak[2] (pǫntiā·næk). Also **Pont-, -ac.** [The name of a city and formerly of a sultanate on the island of Borneo.] = *gutta-jelutong* s.v. *gutta[2] 2 (orig. that from Borneo).

1911 *India Rubber World* XLIII. 130/2 Different qualities of jelutong are known in the trade, according to the districts from which they are derived, as Palembang (Sumatra), Pontianak (South Borneo), Sarawak, and so on. **1923** D. W. Luff *Chem. of Rubber* iii. 35 An inferior rubber which in the days of high rubber prices became of importance industrially is that known variously as Jelutong, Gutta Jelutong, Pontianac, Bresk, or Dead Borneo, which is obtained from the *Dyera costulata*, a large tree growing in Borneo, Sumatra and Malaya. **1927** [see **gutta-jelutong*]. **1947** H. Barron *Mod. Rubber Chem.* (ed. 2) iii. 27 Jelutong (or pontianak) comes chiefly from Sumatra.

Pontic, *a.*[1] Add: **1. a.** (Further examples.)

1726 Swift *Let.* 15 Oct. in Pope *Corr.* (1956) II. 407 They must have been pontic mice, which as Olavs Magnus assures us always devours whatever is green. **1887** A. T. de Vere *Legends & Rec. Church & Empire* 208 Thou Pontic Paradise! **1895** W. Robinson *Eng. Flower Garden* (ed. 4) i. ix. 126 We too often see the common pontic kind [of rhododendron]. **1906** Kipling *Puck of Pook's Hill* 167 I've tramped Britain and I've tramped Gaul, And the Pontic shore where the snow-flakes fall. **1935** *Discovery* July 199/1 There is, e.g., another orthopter which lives in the Pontic and west Mediterranean areas, and in some places in Central Europe as a 'Pontic relic'. **1956** R. Macaulay *Towers of Trebizond* xv. 178, I lay in a swoon, pretending to be dead, because the barbarous Pontic natives, the Mossynoici, were all about.

c. Of or pertaining to the ancient kingdom of Pontus, its kings (see Mithridatic *a.*), its people, or the dialect of Greek attributed to them. Also as *sb.*

1665 D. Lloyd tr. *Plutarch's Worthies* 372 According to the Pontick Kings dream of floating on the waters. **1816** Byron *Dream* viii, in *Prisoner of Chillon* 44 Like to the Pontic monarch of old days, He fed on poisons, and they had no power. **1939** [see *Median *sb.* 2]. **1972** W. B. Lockwood *Panorama Indo-European Lang.* 267 It would not be surprising if the language known to the Greeks as Pontic were a descendant of Kaskian. **1974** *Encycl. Brit. Micropædia* VIII. 115/2 An independent Pontic kingdom with its capital at Amaseia was established at the end of the 4th century BC in the wake of Alexander's conquests. *Ibid. Macropædia* VIII. 396/2 The Asia Minor dialects [of Greek] also display archaic features (*e.g.*, Pontic *e* for ancient *ē* in certain word elements).

d. *Anthropol.* Designating a type of peoples identified in the Balkans and southern Russia (see quots.). Also as *sb.*

[**1932** V. Bunak in *Zeitschr. für Morphologie u. Anthropologie* XXX. 471 Die zwei südlichen analogen Kombinationen—nordkaukasische und ostbalkanische—sind untereinander ähnlicher und stehen von den nordpontischen Varietät weiter ab. Sie bilden eine andere Rasse des östlichen mediterranen Zweigs, den ich vorläufig als pontische Rasse..bezeichnen werde.] **1939** C. S. Coon *Races Europe* xii. 617 The Mediterranean racial divison which the Russian anthropologists call Pontic..is with little doubt of Neolithic date in southern Russia, Rumania, Bulgaria, and the Hellespont region, and probably in Greece and the Aegean. *Ibid.* 679 Pontic. A variety of Mediterranean or Atlanto-Mediterranean,..is concentrated in Bulgaria and in the Rumanian lowlands; it also is found in the Caucasus and Ukraine and westward sporadically as far as Germany, Poland, and Lithuania.

pontic, *a.*[2] Add: **B.** *sb.* *Dentistry.* An artificial tooth that forms part of a dental bridge, being held in place by attachment to its neighbouring teeth, and not fixed directly to the jaw.

1916 J. H. Prothero *Prosthetic Dentistry* (ed. 2) xxix. 785 The term 'pontic' has been suggested as a substitute for 'dummy' in describing a bridge tooth replacement. The term seems scarcely appropriate, since practically all fixed bridges are of the rigid truss type. **1932** F. R. Felcher *Art of Porcelain in Dentistry* xi. 133 Pontics should not be so built that they extend too far into the sockets, as a recession will usually result if this is done. **1956** J. N. Anderson *Appl. Dental Materials* xiii. 128 When making a bridge, the 'pontic' or bridging part is joined to the supports or 'retainers'. **1974** D. H. Roberts in Harty & Roberts *Restorative Procedures Practising Dentist* xxii. 327 Where metal-ceramic full crowns are used as retainers then the same material is normally employed for the pontic.

ponticello (pǫntitʃe·lo). *Mus.* [a. It. *ponticello* little bridge.] **a.** The bridge of a stringed instrument.

1740 J. Grassineau *Mus. Dict.* 182 *Ponticella* [*sic*], a small bridge. **1849** *Hamilton's Celebrated Dict.* 92 *Ponticello*.., the bridge, in speaking of the violin, guitar, etc. **1961** A. Baines *Mus. Instruments* 356 *Ponticello*,..the bridge of a violin, etc.

b. Phr. *sul ponticello*: a direction in a musical score that bowing should be close to the bridge. Also *ellipt.* as *ponticello.* Also applied *attrib.* to the sound produced by such bowing.

1849 *Hamilton's Celebrated Dict.* 112 *Sul ponticello*, on or near the bridge. **1883** Grove *Dict. Mus.* III. 15/2 *Ponticello*..or *sul ponticello*, a term indicating that a passage on the violin, tenor, or violoncello, is to be played by crossing the strings with the bow close to the bridge. **1931** G. Jacob *Orchestral Technique* ii. 6 The ponticello tremolo in which a most eerie effect is produced by bowing the strings nearer to the bridge than the normal position. **1959** *Collins Mus. Encycl.* 509/1 *Sul ponticello* (or *ponticello* alone), on the bridge, *i.e.* play near the bridge, thus producing a glassy, brittle tone. **1967** *Listener* 8 June 769/2 The famous passage in the finale where the first violin skips aloft, high over a sinister progression of rapid *ponticello* chords on the lower strings. **1977** 'E. Crispin' *Glimpses of Moon* iii. 41 'And then *erk, skerk*,' he added, possibly attempting to convey ponticello strings.

ponticum (pǫ·ntikə̆m). Also **Ponticum** [a. mod.L. specific epithet of *Rhododendron ponticum* (Linnæus *Species Plantarum* (ed. 2, 1762) II. 562): see Pontic *a.*[1]] A mauve-flowered, evergreen shrub, *Rhododendron ponticum*, of the family Ericaceæ, native to Spain, Portugal, and Asia Minor and naturalized in many other temperate regions. Also *attrib.*

1875 H. Fraser *Handy Bk. Ornamental Conifers* 185 The best and most commonly-used stocks for grafting are free-grown seedlings of the robust form of the common Ponticum. **1917** J. G. Millais *Rhododendrons* I. viii. 227/2 Enormous numbers of young ponticums are annually used as stocks for the finer varieties. **1962** R. Page *Educ. Gardener* 27 We uprooted the ponticums and burned them. **1972** 'I. Drummond' *Frog in Moonflower* 5 A heavy clump of Ponticum rhododendrons grew unexpectedly on top of the little cliff. **1976** J. Lees-Milne *William Beckford* iv. 59 Today the lake, swathed in ramping ponticum..., lies dark and almost unapproachable. **1977** *Evening Standard* 22 Apr. 19/2 Those ponticums.. are not the ordinary purple ones, but very rare.

Pontifex. Add: **1.** (Further examples.) Also *transf.*

1777 P. Thicknesse *Year's Journey* II. xlii. 83 The consecration of the Roman Pontifex Maximus. **1934** *New Statesman* 3 Nov. 614/2 Stalin has exiled Trotsky and become the Pontifex Maximus of the new Russo-Catholic Church of Communism. **1957** *Oxf. Dict. Chr. Ch.* 1089/2 *Pontifex Maximus*,..originally a pagan title of the chief priest at Rome, Tertullian used it satirically..of the Pope, and from the 5th cent. onwards it was a regular title of honour for the Popes, and occasionally used also of other bishops.

pontifical. Add: **B.** *sb.* **7.** Short for *pontifical mass.*

1923 R. Seton *Memories Many Yrs.* 291 The most interesting of my pontificals was in San Nicola *in carcere.*

pontificate, *v.* Add: **1. a.** (Later example.)

1928 G. B. Shaw *Intelligent Woman's Guide Socialism* 439 The Russian archbishop..is now presumably pontificating much more freely than the Archbishop of Canterbury.

2. a. (Later examples.)

1909 *Englishwoman* Apr. 296 The need of such a group as that which pontificates from Villa Wahnfried is past. **1921** R. Hichens *Spirit of Time* v. 76 Why should I allow this young woman to pontificate about human nature. **1952** *Times Lit. Suppl.* 4 Jan. 1/4 Success made him pontificate more than ever. **1979** *Kansas City Times* 22 May 6A/1 They [*sc.* senators] must think they are pontificating on the moon or Mars or somewhere remote from Jefferson City.

b. *trans.* To say or utter (something) in a pontifical manner.

1922 A. S. M. Hutchinson *This Freedom* iv. i. 252 All modern teaching, if this new stuff that they pontificate may be called teaching, offers us [etc.]. **1973** *N.Y. Law Jrnl.* 24 July 4/5 The court pontificated, 'One cannot look at a rainbow with mud on his shoes'. **1976** *Verbatim* Dec. 15/1 He also pontificated, 'The Reds are favored to win, and, as we all know, everybody hates a favorite.'

So **ponti·ficating** *vbl. sb.* and *ppl. a.*; **ponti·ficator.**

1825 Pontificating [see Pontificate *v.* 2]. **1926** W. J. Locke *Stories Near & Far* 156 Pontifex—Pontifex something..a playful title given him by her mother, for his possible pontificating aims as a young man. **1930** *Radio Times* 17 Jan. 127/2 Nine out of ten people are fond of pontificating. **1934** B. Dobrée *Mod. Prose Style* iv. i. 221 If we examine the writings of the pontificators, people skilled in 'a way of saying things', we invariably find that their style is bad. **1972** *Daily Tel.* (Colour Suppl.) 10 Nov. 7/1 Highbrows—the pontificators about Television —are apt not merely to condone but to applaud: the gratuitous nastiness of allegedly 'serious' plays and aggressive documentaries. *Ibid.*, The pontificators make it so clear that they never watch television for pleasure and don't intend that other people should.

pontification. Restrict † *Obs. rare*[−1] to sense in Dict. and add: **2.** The act or an instance of pontificating (Pontificate *v.* 2).

1925 C. D. Broad *Mind & its Place* viii. 389 It is a pity to create prejudice..by ignorant pontifications about 'the New Psychology'. **1959** *Spectator* 4 Sept. 307/1 They will resent his careless pontification ('Marxian materialism and Freudian psychology are excuses for laziness').

pontificial. B. *sb.* **2.** (Later example.)

1920 *Trans. Scottish Ecclesiol. Soc.* VI. 79 We are enabled to do this, as the pontificial or book of offices used by him has been printed.

pontil. Add: **1.** (Later examples.)

1918 [see *gadget 1 d]. **1961** E. M. Elville *Collector's Dict. Glass* 190/1 In the eighteenth century.., the foot of a three-piece glass was attached to a 'pontil', for the finishing operation in the chair. The pontil is a solid rod of iron about the same length but not quite so thick as the blow-iron. **1977** *Lancashire Life* Feb. 35/1 (*caption*) At Cumbria Crystal,..the base of a stem having been formed, it is transferred to a 'pontil' for finishing.

2. *attrib.* and *Comb.*, as *pontil mark*; **pontil rod**, a pontil.

1937 *Burlington Mag.* Nov. 221/1 Several of these have a round base with a mere trace of pontil mark. **1968** *Canad. Antiques Collector* Oct. 27/2 The long window of crown glass in one of the farm buildings where the pontil marks are evident in each pane. **1975** A. A. C. Hedges *Bottles* 23/2 There is little chance of them being mistaken for free-blown bottles with all their 'blemishes',..pontil marks and kick-ups. **1955** G. Stevens *In Canad. Attic* 60 The basic tools necessary to a glass blower are a blowpipe, a pontil rod. **1970** *Awake!* 8 Jan. 23/2 During the final forming the glass is attached to a long, solid 'pontil' rod that leaves a mark in the base.

Pontine (pǫ·ntəin, pǫ·ntīn), *a.*[2] [f. L. *Pontus*, Gr. *Πόντος*, the Black Sea + -ine[1].] = Pontic *a.*[1]

1920 *Q. Rev.* Jan. 244 It would be necessary to guarantee a local autonomy to the Greeks of the Pontine littoral. **1968** S. Johnson *Turkish Panorama* x. 96, I was now in the very foothills of the Pontine Mountains.

‖ **Pont l'Évêque** (poṅ levęk). The name of a town in Normandy, northern France, used *attrib.* and *absol.* to designate a type of sweet, soft cheese made there.

[**1881** J. P. Sheldon *Dairy Farming* xxxv. 515/1 *Fromage de Pont l'Évêque*, this cheese was made as long ago as the thirteenth century.] **1896** Long & Benson *Cheese* v. 57 Pont l'Évêque cheese is a variety with a great local reputation in the north..of France. **1910** [see *Gorgonzola]. **1932** R. Fraser *Marriage in Heaven* i. xiv. 85 Taste this Pont L'Eveque... A friend brought it to me yesterday from Normandy. **1967** T. A. Layton *Wine & Food Soc. Guide Cheese & Cheese Cookery* 86 Pont l'Evêque requires from 15–24 days to reach maturity. **1979** N. & I. Lyons *Champagne Blues* 75 Is this a Pont-l'Evêque I see before me?

Pontocaine (pǫ·ntokē̆in). *Pharm.* Also **pontocaine.** Formerly also **-cain.** A proprietary name in the U.S. for *pantocain.

1935 *Surg. Clinics N. Amer.* Dec. 1501 Anesthetists have recently turned to the longer-acting drugs pontocain and nupercaine. **1935** *Official Gaz.* (U.S. Patent Office) 10 Dec. 259/2 Winthrop Chemical Company, Inc., New York,..*Pontocaine* for anesthetic. Claims use since Aug. 26, 1935. **1938** *New Eng. Jrnl. Med.* 27 Jan. 170/1 For the past four years at the Faulkner Hospital, pontocaine and novocain have been combined for spinal anesthesia. **1946** *Anesthesiology* VII. 500 Since 1943 we have employed ephedrine in combination with pontocaine hydrochloride for spinal anesthesia in over 2,500 cases. **1975** *Nature* 24 Apr. 710/2 Twelve Dorset and Western ewes at days 67–147 of gestation were starved for 48 h and then placed under pentobarbitol sedation (5 mg kg^{-1}) and spinal anaesthesia (6 mg pontocaine in hyperbaric glucose).

pontoon, *sb.*[1] Add: **1.** More widely, any structure designed to provide buoyancy in the water. (Further examples.)

1941 *Sun* (Baltimore) 15 Sept. 13/1 Just before the regatta ended, he was driving Onwego, a hydroplane, out of the pits and ran his pontoon well over the side of one of the Coast Guard picket boats. **1975** *North Sea Background Notes* (Brit. Petroleum Co.) 11 The hull platform rests on a number of legs which have at their bases pontoons. During moves from one location to another, the entire vessel floats on the sea surface, but on reaching the new location the pontoons are then ballasted with water so that they sink. **1976** *Offshore Platforms & Pipelining* 121/1 Pipe leaves the barge via the curved ramp and a straight or curved pontoon and progresses to the sea floor.

pontoon (pǫntū·n), *sb.*[2] [Appar. corrupted from VINGT-ET-UN, VINGT-UN.] A popular name for the card game VINGT-ET-UN, VINGT-UN.

1917 A. G. EMPEY *Over Top* 304 *Pontoon*, a card game, in America known as 'Black Jack' or 'Twenty One'. The bank is the only winner. **1927** *Daily Express* 26 July 9/5 A ghostly platoon wouldn't frighten me!..perhaps they'd be playing pontoon. **1961** A. WYKES *Gambling* vii. 177 The three modern banking games—baccarat (or chemin-de-fer), *blackjack*, (or vingt-et-un or *pontoon*), and *seven-and-a-half*—are all complicated versions of European games of the 15th and 16th centuries. **1973** J. WOOD *North Beat* x. 134 The locker-room table..used for pontoon and brag sessions. **1976** J. BINGHAM *God's Defector* iii. 28 He was playing pontoon and drinking with four friends in a back room... Rob Flint had just laid two cards face up on the table, an ace and a king.

b. A prison sentence or term of twenty one months (occas. twenty one years). *slang* (chiefly *Criminals'*).

1950 C. FRANKLIN *She'll love you Dead* vii. 90 'They'll get me a pontoon for assault when Mr. Garfield tells 'is story,' said Al miserably. 'A pontoon?' 'Twenty-one months,' explained Garfield. **1958** F. NORMAN *Bang to Rights* 177 This geezer was doing a pontoon. **1962** *John o' London's* 25 Jan. 82/3, 21 months [imprisonment], *pontoon*. **1977** 'E. CRISPIN' *Glimpses of Moon* xii. 235 He had been put away three times..the third for a pontoon.

Pontypool (pǫ·ntipūl). Also 8–9 **Ponty-pool, Pont-y-Pool, Pont y Pool.** The name of a town in Gwent, Wales, used *attrib.* and *absol.* to designate a type of Japanned metal ware originally produced there or items made from this Japanned metal.

[**1734** C. H. WILLIAMS *Let.* Dec. in L. T. Davies *Men of Monmouthshire* (1933) I. 72 Tom Allgood has found a new way of japanning which I think so beautiful that I'll send you a couple of pieces of it. **1763** *Gloucester Jrnl.* 4 July 2/1 (Advt.), By Allgood, Davies, and Edwards, all Sorts of the real and most durable Japan Ware is continued to be made and sold at the Manufactory at Pont-y-Pool.] **1764** in W. D. John *Pontypool & Usk Japanned Wares* (1953) iv. 36 (Advt.), Great Variety of Ponty-pool Goods Sold by Henry Johns, At his Ponty-pool Warehouse... Great variety of Snuff-Boxes, Japan'd Waiters, Bread Baskets, Tea Kitchens, Tea Kettles, and Lamps, Coffee Pots. **1781** J. BYNG *Diary* 16 June in E. Burton *Georgians at Home* (1967) iv. 183, I bought a Pontypool snuff box, a beautiful and dear ware. **1801** W. COXE *Hist. Tour Monmouthshire* II. xxv. 234 The town..is likewise remarkable for the japan manufacture, known by the name of Pont y Pool ware. **1872** *Art Jrnl.* XI. 24 (*caption*) The premises in which the Allgoods last manufactured Pontypool ware. *Ibid.* 24/1 'Now,' said Old Billy in the highest glee, 'now you shall see what real Pontypool Japan is!' **1928** *Daily Express* 6 Oct. 11/7 The secret formula for the production of the artistic lacquer work known as 'Pontypool japan', which had been missing since 1864, has been found. **1953** *Ann. Sci.* IX. 218 Several firms [in the Midlands] that paid special attention to the production of wares of high artistic merit were calling themselves 'Pontypool makers' in the early years of the nineteenth century, when the trade was in a flourishing condition. **1960** *House & Garden* May 56/4 Red and gold decorated Pontypool tray, £65. **1969** *Canad. Antiques Collector* Jan. 8/1 This japanned tinware was generally known by the name Pontypool (even when it was later manufactured at Wolverhampton and Birmingham). **1971** H. HUTH *Lacquer of West* viii. 112 A color effect typical of Pontypool but later much imitated was a tortoiseshell ground made by placing irregular pieces of silver foil under brown lacquer, thus giving it the appearance of gold.

pony, *sb.* Add: **1. b.** A race-horse. Usu. *pl. slang* (chiefly *U.S.*).

1907 J. LONDON in *Cosmopolitan* May 17/2, I had been out to the race-track watching the ponies run. **1942** BERREY & VAN DEN BARK *Amer. Thes. Slang* § 731/1 *Race horse*.., pony. *a* **1953** E. O'NEILL *Long Day's Journey into Night* (1956) I. 21 If it takes my snoring to make you remember Shakespeare instead of the dope sheet on the ponies, I hope I'll keep on with it. **1958** [see *PLAY *v.* 21 d]. **1961** *Dallas Morning News* 17 Feb. I. 5 Rep. Berry, an ex-gambler from San Antonio, got elected on his advocacy of betting on the ponies.

2. (Further examples.)

1892 *Pall Mall Gaz.* 23 Mar. 6/3 Mr. Kisch said the bets were two ponies. The Master of the Rolls: What? Two what? Mr. Kisch said a pony was £25. **1928** D. BYRNE *Destiny Bay* vii. 318 It would have to be done very carefully,..in ponies and fifties and hundreds. **1958** *Times* 18 Feb. 5/1 Heath said that for a 'pony' (£25) he would see what could be done. **1966** B. NAUGHTON *Alfie* xxix. 188 'A pony is neither here nor there to me,' I said. 'It's just that I want to give somebody something.' **1976** J. O'CONNOR *Eleventh Commandment* xiv. 178 'Bet you the next three guys that come by do that,' he said. 'Make it a pony (£25),' said Charlie.

3. (Earlier and later examples.) Also *transf.* (see quot. 1977).

1827 *Harvard Reg.* Sept. 194 I'll tell you what I mean to do. Leave off my lazy habits..and stick to the law, Tom, without a *Poney*. **1931** W. FAULKNER *Sanctuary* xviii. 182 She kept the dates written down in her Latin 'pony'. **1952** G. SARTON *Hist. Sci.* I. iii. 89 The tablets were used not so much for study as for recapitulation and remembrance, like cribs or ponies. **1972** *Catholic Biblical Q.* Jan. 93 The Hebrew syntax is 'Akkadianized'... The result is that the book provides an excellent 'pony' for the student who is weak in Akkadian. **1977** *Sounds* 9 July 22/2 After leaving college his vaguely literary ambitions found him earning a living by turning out 'ponies', the Stateside word for those little revision booklets English (or US, in this case) Lit. students buy when they haven't read, say, 'Bleak House' and there's an exam tomorrow morning.

b. *U.S.* Used *attrib.* to designate an abridged news report or the service whereby such reports are supplied to particular news agencies.

The service has appar. been discontinued.

1877 *Harper's Mag.* Dec. 57/1 Condensed abstracts, known as 'pony' reports, are made and forwarded to smaller towns. **1909** *Census Bull.* (U.S.) No. 216. 67 Besides the full reports delivered to large papers are the 'pony' reports—condensations of the full reports, sold at a cheaper rate. **1915** G. M. HYDE *Newspaper Editing* vi. 199 Certain members, too small to be full members [of the Associated Press], receive a daily 'pony' service—a condensed version of the world's news to the extent of a few hundred or few thousand words—and pay proportionately. **1923** M. V. ATWOOD *Country Newspaper* 133 The writer wonders if it may not be that the country daily.. furnishing a reasonably adequate service of telegraph news through a 'pony' service..may not become of increasing importance. **1931** C. E. ROGERS *Journalistic Vocations* iii. 57 The United Press developed the use of the telephone for delivering abbreviated news reports—P.N.T. (public news transmission) or pony service. *Ibid.* 61 There are shorter leased wire reports, too, and pony reports. **1942** RADDER & STEMPEL *Newspaper Editing, Make-up & Headlines* (ed. 2) vii. 125 Such reports, known as pony calls, usually amount to only 15 minutes of service (1,000 to 1,500 words) once or twice a day. The pony service still is used by a number of smaller newspapers, and some rely on a bulletin service or pony service by telegraph.

4. (Earlier and later examples.)

1849 G. G. FOSTER *N.Y. in Slices* 81 The game is kept up, mollified now and then by a choice swig at the 'poney'. **1943** *Harper's Mag.* Dec. 44/2 Dr. Stuker rapidly downed two ponies of brandy. **1959** G. HAMILTON *Summer Glare* 155 Os pulled a beer each for me and Tommy, and a pony for himself. He always drank small beers. **1966** [see *POT *sb.*[1] 3].

b. A small chorus girl or dancer. *slang.*

1908 K. McGAFFEY *Sorrows of Show Girl* 118, I went into the pony ballet of a LaSalle Theatre show—can you see me as a pony? **1920** [see *DRAG *sb.* 7 f]. **1930** *Daily Express* 23 May 10/5 We have what are known in stage parlance as 'ponies'—a troupe of girls, ages ranging from sixteen to twenty-three or four. **1948** *Sat. Even. Post* 3 July 63/2 In the chorus of ponies—the smallest sized dancers—there was a pert redhead named Gracie Barrett. **1950** BLESH & JANIS *They all played Ragtime* (1958) ix. 180 The music that follows is a 'rush-on' of the period, so called because it was the cue for the high-stepping, brown-skinned 'ponies' to get out on the stage.

5*. A dance originating in the U.S. and popular in the early 1960s.

1963 *N.Y. Times Mag.* 27 Oct. 104/2 That brings us to our own young and the Twist, the Pony, the Slop, the Mashed Potato. **1968** M. & J. STEARNS *Jazz Dance* i. 5 The Pony employed bits of the Slow Drag. **1969** N. COHN *AWopBopaLooBop* (1970) ix. 85 Dance crazes bossed pop right up until the Beatles broke. There was the Hully Gully, the Madison, the Fly, the Pony [etc.].

6. a. *pony-boy, -carriage* (examples), *-chair* (earlier example), *-chaise* (earlier example), *-man, -phaeton* (earlier example), *race, ride; pony-penning, -racing, -rider, -riding*; see also sense *3 b. **b. pony club,** a club founded in 1929 and now run by the British Horse Society for young people with ponies; hence as *vb. trans.* (chiefly *pass.*) to enter (a pony) for a pony club competition; **pony clubber,** a member of a pony club; **pony clubbing,** participating in pony club activities; the pony club movement; **pony express** (earlier and later examples); also *attrib.*; **pony post** = *pony express*; **pony-skin,** the (dressed) hide of a pony; also *attrib.*; **pony-tail,** a hair-style in which the hair is gathered back through a band or other fastening to resemble the shape of the tail of a horse or pony (cf. *HORSE-TAIL 1 c); also *attrib.*; hence *pony-tailed* adj.; **pony-trekking,** pony-riding for long distances across country, esp. as undertaken as a group holiday activity; hence *pony-trekker.*

1909 *Daily Chron.* 16 Feb. 5/1 Murten..is employed as a pony-boy in the Woolley Colliery, Barnsley. **1946** B. NAUGHTON (*title*) Pony boy. **1831** M. EDGEWORTH *Let.* 11 Apr. (1971) 520 Dr. Fitton in the pony carriage behind me was giving..another derivation to Fanny from the German. **1870** GEO. ELIOT *Jrnl.* 26 May in *Geo. Eliot Lett.* (1956) V. 100 Mrs. Pattison took me a drive in her little pony carriage. **1905** 'P. PENNINGTON' *Woman Rice Planter* (1913) iv. 150, I sent Chloe to Gregory in the pony carriage, and she brought back the money. **1827** T. HAMILTON *Youth & Manhood C. Thornton* I. xvi. 282 Mr Pynsent with some difficulty did so, pleading an engagement to drive Lady Amersham in her pony-chair. **1831** DISRAELI *Young Duke* I. II. x. 239 A pony-chaise was Lady Faulconcourt's delight. **1929** *Horse* I. 60 The Pony Club..has been inaugurated for the purpose of interesting young people in riding and sport. **1936** A. THIRKELL *August Folly* ii. 50 Pony Clubs! No pony clubs when I was young. You got on and you fell off, and there you were. **1941** M. TREADGOLD *We couldn't leave Dinah* iii. 50 Pony club members and their guests were sedately walking their ponies round and round the lawn. **1972** J. McCLURE *Caterpillar Cop* i. 12 'You're strong,' he murmured. 'Riding,' she said, 'I'm in the pony club.' **1976** *Horse & Hound* 3 Dec. 63/1 (Advt.), Moonmaster... Very pretty strawberry roan gelding. 10 yrs. Leading rein, gymkhanaed, Pony Clubbed. Good in traffic. **1977** *Ibid.* 14 Jan. 40/2 (Advt.), Gelding... He jumps well, has hunted, and been Pony Clubbed etc. **1970** J. CAMPBELL *World of Ponies* 127 (*caption*) Australian Pony Clubbers are always sure of good weather for their outdoor activities. **1977** *Horse & Hound* 14 Jan. 33/2 Always a keen 'pony clubber', Alison has competed in numerous inter-branch competitions. **1970** J. CAMPBELL *World of Ponies* 125 It has been the ponies of all breeds, cross-breeds, shapes and sizes, that have made Pony Clubbing. **1977** *Horse & Hound* 14 Jan. 46/3 (Advt.), Four children 3–9, 4 ponies, 1 horse. Pony Clubbing, showing etc. **1847** *N.Y. Weekly Tribune* 18 Dec. 4/5 By our Pony Express from the South, we have intelligence from New Orleans to the afternoon of the 2d. **1860** *San Francisco National* 19 Mar. 2/3 The Central Overland Pony Express Co. will start their Letter Express from San Francisco to New York and intermediate points, on Tuesday, the 3rd day of April next. **1948** *Chicago Daily News* 26 Aug. 4/1 St. Joseph, Mo... The original Pony Express stable was put up for sale for $442.32 but no one bid on it. **1976** *Times* 23 July 11/6 Buffalo Bill Cody..had been in turn horse wrangler, pony express rider, unlucky prospector, [etc.]. **1900** *Geogr. Jrnl.* XV. 563 Group of Astor pony-men at Lob jungle. **1968** *Economist* 10 Aug. 45/1 Four ponies need four pony-men which adds another £10 a day to the bill. **1971** *Daily Tel.* 10 June 9/3 The future livelihood of ghillies, stalkers, gamekeepers and ponymen is threatened by the 'punitive' proposed rating reassessments of estates with sporting facilities, the Scottish Landowners' Federation claims. **1932** *Sun* (Baltimore) 27 July 4/3 Pony-penning has attracted thousands to the island. **1958** *Washington Post* 30 July A 24/1 The pony penning dates back to 1835 but the firemen took it over in 1924 as their fund raising project. **1799** MALTHUS *Diary* 1 July (1966) 109 Mr A had insisted on our taking his small poney phaeton. **1893** M. H. CUSHING *Story of our Post Office* 420 Before railroads led to every part of the country the only communication was by pony post. **1901** W. CHURCHILL *Crisis* II. vii. 178 Three-weeks letters from San Francisco, come by the pony post to Lexington. **1765** J. WOODFORDE *Diary* 27 May (1924) I. 47 After dinner Jack went to Wincanton to a Pony Race. **1824** J. DECASTRO *Mem.* 155 The pony races were brought out, and they had a more than usual run for a whole season. **1949** *Sun* (Baltimore) 29 July 20/6 The spectators stayed on for the day-long program of pony sales..pony races..and band concerts. **1827** W. CLARKE *Every Night Bk.* 174 Furnishes a neat stud for poney racing. **1943** *Sporting Life* 12 July 5 Pony racing will have an eager Turf Authority, a second-to-none race course at its disposal, and cash in the bank. **1969** *Pony* Sept. 57/2 Two centuries ago..Charles O'Neill..established a pony-racing event on Broughshane race-course, near Ballymena. **1819** M. EDGEWORTH *Let.* 17 Apr. (1971) 200 She has just come in from her poney ride. **1840** C. Fox *Jrnl.* 16 Feb. (1972) 67 They joined Mamma and Anna Maria in a pony ride. **1871** 'MARK TWAIN' *Lett. to Publishers* (1967) 62 Stretching our necks and watching for the pony-rider. **1975** *Country Life* 13 Feb. 393/1 Pony riders will have to keep on to the country lanes. **1949** R. COLVILLE (*title*) Pony riding. **1908** *Daily Chron.* 26 Dec. 3/4 Among the novelties are the pony-skin suits. **1960** *Times* 26 Sept. 17/2 In Mongolian ponyskin..it [*sc.* a coat] is very hard-wearing. **1971** 'A. BURGESS' *MF* viii. 94 The upholstery was black-and-white ponyskin. **1976** 'J. ROSS' *I know what it's like to Die* xvi. 102 Your lady-friend with the ponyskin coat. **1872** TROLLOPE *Eustace Diamonds* (1873) II. xxxiv. 100 'How a man can like to kiss a face with a dirty horse's tail all whizzling about it..' 'I haven't even a pony's tail,' said Lucy. **1952** *Sun* (Baltimore) 23 Feb. 2 The panel of high-school boys and girls discusses the latest teen-age fashions, including..the pony tail. **1954** J. TRENCH *Dishonoured Bones* iv. 150 She pulled her own hair back and fastened it into a pony-tail. **1957** *New Yorker* 16 Nov. 104/2 The young lady..was wearing a ponytail hairdo. **1971** M. SPARK *Not to Disturb* iii. 88 She loosens her hair which has been pulled back, pony-tail style. **1975** *New Yorker* 28 Apr. 31/2 She, too, had her hair in a ponytail, held by a rubber band. **1977** *Time* 30 May 40/3 The counter-culture ponytail is gone, sacrificed to the heat of arena lights and the sizzling sweat of the fast-break pace. **1956** *Time* 26 Mar. 72/2 Pony-tailed Carol stood aside. **1958** S. ELLIN *Eighth Circle* II. i. 18 She bore the sallow-complexioned, nail-bitten, pony-tailed earmarks of adolescence. **1974** *Times* 14 Nov. 16/6 A bearded, pony-tailed, 42-year-old..is not everyone's idea of a nanny-raised child. **1972** *Guardian* 3 July 7/3 Pathways were being worn down by pony-trekkers and others. **1959** *Sunday Times* 8 Mar. 20/1 Golf, Tennis, Fishing, Ballroom, Pony-trekking, Dinghy sailing. *Ibid.* 29 Mar. 18/1 Guided pony-trekking is a fine way to explore wild country in the company of other adventure-seekers. **1962** *Times* 21 Apr. 11/3 Over the past few years ..great has been the demand for pony-trekking holidays. **1971** *New Yorker* 27 Feb. 21/1 (Advt.), Come to Ireland. Go pony-trekking through Macgillycuddy's Reeks.

pony, *v.* Add: **2.** Also *intr.* **b.** *trans.* To give extra tuition to. *rare.*

1847 in W. G. Hammond *Remembrance of Amherst* (1946) 153 The others are ponying most unmercifully. *c* **1853** in Root & Lombard *Songs of Yale* 23 If you poney he will see. **1865** *Harper's Mag.* July 213/2 A classmate, whom..I had ponied through term after term, in Latin, Greek, and mathematics. **1908** W. G. DAVENPORT *Butte & Montana* 134 It were a hundred times better to teach the average boy how to build a fence..than to..'pony' his way through three or four years of Latin.

Ponzi scheme (pǫ·nzi). *U.S.* [f. the name of Charles *Ponzi*, who perpetrated such a fraud 1919–20.] A form of fraud in which belief in the success of a fictive enterprise is fostered by payment of quick returns to first investors from money invested by others.

[**1957** *Encycl. Brit.* IX. 708/1 *The Ponzi Scheme*... Beginning in Dec. 1919 Ponzi..produced a scheme involving the purchase of International Postal Reply coupons in countries where the exchange was low, trading them in for postage stamps at their face value in a country where the rate was high, and then selling the stamps at a great profit... The slogan of the swindle was 40% in 90 days... Actually..Ponzi made no purchases whatever of International Postal Reply coupons.] **1973** *Guardian* 14 Apr. 2/4 The indictments..allege that Mackell's staff invested in what is called a Ponzi scheme, a confidence game named arter a famous Italian. **1976** *Billings* (Montana) *Gaz.* 27 June 9-G/1 The Home-Stake scandal is a form of the 'Ponzi' scheme, named for a self-educated, slight but dapper Italian immigrant named Charles Ponzi whose intricate schemes in the 1920s were front-page stuff. **1976** *National Observer* (U.S.) 10 July 8/3 'He was operating a Ponzi scheme,' says Michael Mustokoff, chief of the unit. The first few investors were paid 'dividends' out of the money invested by people who came in later, and word spread that the club was raking in the bucks.

Ponzo (pǫ·nzo). [The name of Mario *Ponzo* (b. 1882), Italian psychologist.] *Ponzo illusion*: an optical illusion in which two parallel straight lines of equal length appear to be of unequal length when seen side by side against a triangular background (such as a set of straight lines radiating from a single point and passing through the two parallel lines).

1942 *Jrnl. Exper. Psychol.* XXX. 84 (*heading*) Experimental evidence for the electrical character of visual fields derived from a quantitative analysis of the Ponzo illusion. **1968** *Science* 22 Mar. 1375/1 The Ponzo illusion increases in magnitude between childhood and adulthood. **1976** *Sci. Amer.* Apr. 50/1 In the Ponzo illusion, although both vertical lines are the same length, the effect of the subjective triangle is to make the line at the left appear to be longer.

pooay, var. *PWE.

pooch (pūtʃ), *sb.* and *a. colloq.* (orig. *U.S.*). [Etym. obscure.] **A.** *sb.* A dog, esp. a mongrel. **B.** *adj.* Mongrel. *rare.*

1924 B. HECHT *Cutie* vi. 46 All you do is sink your teeth in my shoulder and make noises like a basket full of hungry pooches. **1927** *Collier's* 3 Dec. 32/4 Therefore, at home, the trick pooch got all the attention, eating at the table with the family. **1941** BAKER *N.Z. Slang* vii. 60 Hundreds of Australian terms are unused here... *pooch*.., for instance,..a greyhound. **1951** C. ARMSTRONG *Black-Eyed Stranger* (1952) iii. 27 It wasn't even my dog... But ..I'd more or less met the pooch. **1962** *Country Life* 19 Apr. 895/1 The training of dogs, whether pedigree or pooch, has assumed considerable importance during the last 80 years. **1963** O. BRELAND *Animal Life & Lore* i. 15 There is one very old claim of an ancient pooch of 34 years. **1971** *Sunday Australian* 8 Aug. 39/2 You've got some useful ammunition to aim at that noisy cherished little pooch next door. **1977** *Cornish Times* 19 Aug. 15/1, I tend to fury when children cannot play games on fields intended for their use without falling on some pooch's revolting mess. **1977** J. WAMBAUGH *Black Marble* (1978) v. 68, I got more invested in that pooch than you *made* in the last five years.

poodle, *sb.* Add: **1. b.** *fig.* A lackey or cat's-paw.

1907 LLOYD GEORGE in *Hansard Commons* 26 June 1429 The House of Lords consented. This is the defender of property! This is the leal and trusty mastiff which is to watch over our interests... A mastiff? It is the right hon. Gentleman's poodle. It fetches and carries for him. It barks for him. It bites anybody that he sets it on to. **1944** J. JONES *Man David* vii. 144 There were certain barriers to progress, the greatest being 'that Tory poodle', the House of Lords. **1954** R. JENKINS (*title*) Mr. Balfour's poodle. An account of the struggle between the House of Lords and the government of Mr. Asquith. **1967** *Daily Tel.* 10 Feb. 30/2 Labour MPs did not appear to find the speech objectionable. One comment was that Prince Philip had shown himself to be 'nobody's poodle'. **1968** *Guardian* 9 Aug. 16/1 Mr Curran..vigorously denied suggestions that he would be Lord Hill's 'poodle'. **1969** 'G. BLACK' *Cold Jungle* viii. 114 Bill would have been more likely to have a heart attack living as her tame poodle down on the Riviera. **1974** LD. ALDINGTON *Advising BBC* 13 The suspicious will say that such a close link between the advisors and the advised..ensures that at least the Chairman of GAC, if not all its members, become the poodle of the BBC. **1976** *Times* 12 Nov. 14/4 Mr Foot is happy to act as Mr Jones's poodle in introducing the Bill.

3. *poodle-dog* (earlier examples), *-fashion*; **poodle cloth,** a woolly sort of cloth; also *attrib.*; cf. sense 2 in Dict.; **poodle-cut,** a hair-style in which the hair is cut short and curled all over.

1957 M. B. PICKEN *Fashion Dict.* 261/2 *Poodle cloth*, a coating of knotted yarn or loopy bouclé. Woven in all fibers and also knitted. Originally was made only in wool. **1959** *Observer* 13 Dec. 14/6 For country-house wear a poodlecloth wool is in allied tones, such as violet and amethyst. **1977** *New Society* 30 June 665/3, I managed to purchase a square-cut, early sixties coat in a fabric we used to call poodle cloth. **1952** *Sun* (Baltimore) 25 Mar. 3/2 (*caption*) In this recent picture, Mrs. Truman wears what is described as one variation of the 'poodle cut'. **1960** C. DALE *Spring of Love* I. i. 29 Gloria, with her cross little painted face and her yellow poodle cut. **1975** R. L. SIMON *Wild Turkey* (1976) x. 8 A well-dressed woman with a poodle cut. **1820** in *Amer. Speech* (1965) XL. 131 Called 'a Hog, a Poodle dog' all the sailors joking me. **1822** M. EDGEWORTH *Let.* 27 Jan. (1971) 336 A new poodle dog..milk white silken curls all over except the poor shorn half that is sacrificed to poodle-fashion.

poodle, *v.* Add: **1.** Also, to overdress, to dress *up*.

1962 N. STREATFEILD *Apple Bough* iii. 39 Why do they want to poodle the poor kid up?

2. *intr.* (Usu. with advbs.) To move or travel in a leisurely manner. *colloq.*

1938 F. D. SHARPE *Sharpe of Flying Squad* i. 10 The long, low cars poodle through the streets. *Ibid.* ii. 30 For the most part these sleek, unobtrusive-looking cars poodle about the Metropolis well under 30 m.p.h. **1960** M. CECIL *Something in Common* xii. 131 She tells the patrons which gangway and then they poodle off the opposite way. **1972** *Police Rev.* 8 Dec. 1598/1 What will happen to the chap who wants to quietly poodle along at 50 m.p.h. even when there is no fog? **1973** *Radio Times* 22 Mar. 36/2 (Advt.), A sports jacket should protect you from dawn till dusk on a Scottish moor. Not merely while you're poodling down to the local on Sunday morning. **1975** *New Society* 2 Oct. 26/3 One member of each two-man [bicycle racing] team doing the racing while the other poodles round high on the banking until it's his turn to take over the attack. **1976** J. O'CONNOR *Eleventh Commandment* i. 24, I went indoors, messed around, poodled about for quite a while.

Hence **poo·dler** *slang*, a small motor vehicle.

1951 *Brit. Road Services Mag.* Dec. 94/2 *Poodler*, small vehicle. **1968** *Drive* Spring 113/1 A poodler [is] a small vehicle, a roller skate a small, light wagon, and Billy Bunter is a shunter.

poo·dle-faker. *slang* (chiefly *Services*'). [f. POODLE *sb.* 1 + FAKER.] A man who cultivates female society, esp. for the purpose of professional advancement; a ladies' man; a socialite; also, a young, newly commissioned officer. So **poo·dle-faking** *vbl. sb.* and *ppl. a.*

1902 *T.C.D.* 22 Nov., The 'poodle-faker' is just as much a social necessity as tea-cakes. **1914** 'I. HAY' *Knight on Wheels* (ed. 2) III. xxiii. 228 And now my lad, you are going to put on your best duds and come poodle-faking with me! **1915** 'BARTIMEUS' *Tall Ship* iv. 75 Don't tell me the lad is going poodle-faking! **1918** A. H. CHUTE *Real Front* xiv. 240 He [*sc.* a big Australian private] encountered a pink-faced English youth, who had just got his commission, one of the Percival or Cuthbert type, whom we refer to in the army as 'poodle-fakers'. **1918** 'TAFFRAIL' *Watch Below* 57 The ladies' men or 'poodle-fakers', as we called them, had their tea-parties, dinner-parties, and dances more often than was good for them. **1925** F. C. BOWEN *King's Navy* 239 The tea party to which the other sex is invited from 'the beach' is a 'tea-fight' or 'bun-worry', while paying calls ashore is 'poodle-faking'. **1929** A. B. E. CATOR in *Hoghunters' Ann.* 52 Man is primævally a killer; by the word man I mean a real man, not the long haired poodle faking, over dressed idiot, all too common at home in these post-war days. **1938** C. L. MORGAN *Flashing Stream* I. i. 59 Brissing, you're the poodle-faker in this mess. **1939** A. POWELL *What's become of Waring?* vii. 200 But what did you live on?.. A bit of journalism here and there, a good deal of poodle-faking. **1949** H. PAKINGTON *Young W. Washbourne* 38 John had said quite frankly that one didn't always want to be saddled with one's cousins, however charming, and William had retorted that he'd be damned if he'd go round poodle-faking all the time, and what was a flag-lieutenant for except to amuse the Admiral's guests. **1963** M. MALIM *Pagoda Tree* 93 Women are not admitted to the main club premises except once a year at the ball. Traditionally, married members are confined to the club between 7.30 and 8.30 pm while poodle-fakers dally with their wives in their victorias outside on the fan. **1963** N. MARSH *Dead Water* (1964) vi. 134, I left my regiment. Took on this damned poodlefaking instead. **1967** D. BUSK *Craft of Diplomacy* vii. 184 In Britain it is still widely assumed, perhaps largely because of ignorant or malevolent press comments, that the Service requires private means and anyhow is only poodlefaking. **1977** J. PORTER *Who the Heck* xi. 97 There's some blooming Parisian couturier coming to see her... To hear her talk you'd think a bunch of corn slicers and foreign poodle-fakers was more important than solving the crime of the century. **1978** M. M. KAYE *Far Pavilions* xi. 175 He could go and shoot in Kashmir..which would do him a lot more good than poodle-faking at tea-parties.

poof (puf, pūf), *sb.*[1] *slang.* Also **pooff, pouf,** etc. [Prob. a corruption of *puff* (see *PUFF *sb.* 8 d).] An effeminate man, a male homosexual; a man who acts or speaks in an affected manner. Also *attrib.* Similarly **poove** (pūv) *sb.*; also as *v. intr.*, to act like a poof, to speak or behave in an effeminate or affected manner; **pooved-up** *ppl. a.*

Often considered offensive.

c **1850–60** in G. R. Taylor *Angel-Makers* (1958) iv. 80 These monsters in the shape of men, commonly designated Margeries, Pooffs, &c. **1932** AUDEN *Orators* III. 98 Poofs and ponces, All of them dunces. **1951** I. SHAW *Troubled Air* xvi. 272 Don't be a traitorous old poof. **1952** A. WILSON *Hemlock & After* ii. 37 'Bloody little pouff,' said Ron aloud. **1955** 'C. H. ROLPH' *Women of Streets* x. 131 Although I never met any who lived with male homosexuals, several..girls..referred to other prostitutes living with 'pouffs' who reciprocally kept them by their earnings when necessary. **1955** G. GREENE *Quiet American* IV. ii. 241 He made a feeble attempt to mock my accent. 'You all talk like poufs. You're so damned superior.' **1959** C. MACINNES *Absolute Beginners* 51 The Hoplite has been in business with some of the city's top poof raves. **1962** *Private Eye* 30 Nov. 15/3, I may be a poove but I'm a terrific engineer. **1964** *New Statesman* 6 Mar. 374/1 We have a pooved-up tenor introducing a parade of Variety Girls. **1967** J. RATHBONE *Diamonds Bid* xiii. 116 'Do you remember meeting Stephen Hamilton-Rose..?' 'A fat poove?' I asked. **1968** A. DIMENT *Gt. Spy Race* III. xi. 206 The woolly-headed pooves in the widely various Ministry of Defence networks are all completely mad with jealousy. **1968** *Listener* 19 Sept. 372/3 On the first occasion the loved object..was an able-bodied seaman,..who never manifested the slightest interest in girls but who nevertheless was totally remote from the world of pansies, pouffs and queans. **1971** F. FORSYTH *Day of Jackal* xx. 336 You bloody pooves make me sick. **1971** *Melody Maker* 9 Oct. 11/1 He reckoned they pooved around a little, but commented that..their music wasn't all that rough after all. **1974** J. BETJEMAN *Nip in Air* 45 Touching the little children, better pooves Or murderers, they said. **1975** J. SYMONS *Three Pipe Problem* ix. 60 It's some poove who's been done, named Sonny Halliwell. **1976** A. RICHARDS *Former Miss Merthyr Tydfil* 14 A young man..had been heard in the showers to refer to Elgar as 'a bit of a pouf'. **1977** W. MCILVANNEY *Laidlaw* xxviii. 128 Harry Rayburn's a poof... Whit's a poof doin' wi' a lassie? **1978** R. RENDELL *Sleeping Life* xiii. 109 All you can do is get your picture in the papers like some poove of a film actor.

Hence **poo·fdom** *nonce*, the state or condition of being a homosexual.

1972 F. RAPHAEL *April, June & Nov.* 466 He's a late convert to the joys of poofdom.

poof, *int.* Add: Also **pouff. A.** (Earlier and later examples.)

1824 J. MORIER *Adventures Hajji Baba* II. i. 39 Putting up her five fingers to his face, she said, 'Poof! I spit on such a face.' **1829** G. GRIFFIN *Collegians* I. viii. 159 Gi' me the hat, sir, an' I'll hang it up—poof, it's full of dust. **1905** E. GLYN *Viciss. Evangeline* 62 'Pouff!' I said, and I pointed at him. **1921** H. WILLIAMSON *Beautiful Yrs.* 80 'Pouff, what a lot of rot,' scoffed Willie. **1935** M. DE LA ROCHE *Young Renny* x. 82 Pouf! You don't know anything. **1949** P. HASTINGS *Cases in Court* v. 281 He said the three shots were fired in rapid succession or, as he put it somewhat dramatically, 'pouf, pouf, pouf'. **1951** M. KENNEDY *Lucy Carmichael* II. i. 88, I get quite interested ..for about 5 minutes and then—poof! I go flat like a burst balloon. **1968** C. M. VINES *Little Nut-Brown Man* xiii. 237 'Pouf!' he said when he had recovered from choking, 'supposing I had been dead before the water got here?' **1974** S. COULTER *Chateau* II. xii. 359 Oh, pouff! Bravado, Madame. Sheer bravado. **1979** J. RATHBONE *Euro-Killers* v. 55 Poof! Rubbish! This is some ruse.

B. as *sb.*[2] An utterance of 'poof'; a short sharp puff.

1908 *Westm. Gaz.* 25 May 5/2, I was riding on the back of the balloon..when suddenly I heard a 'pouff', as if someone had blown a blast from a bellows. **1915** D. H. LAWRENCE *Rainbow* vi. 148 She burst into a 'Pouf' of ridiculing laughter. **1951** KOESTLER *Age of Longing* II. iv. 242 Father Millet..gave a scornful poof. **1971** B. MALAMUD *Tenants* 68 [He] left so cleanly,..it seemed to Lesser as though he had willed his disappearance in a prestidigitated poof. **1973** J. MCKELVEY *Man against Tsetse* iii. 196 Refinements on the use of a dash of poison now go well beyond a squirt of spray or a poof of dust to the habitat of the fly.

poof (puf), *v. colloq.* Also **pouff.** [f. POOF *int.*] *intr.* **a.** To blow up, to peter *out*. Also *refl.*

1915 *N.Y. World Mag.* 9 May 14 *Pooff*, to blow up. **1923** WODEHOUSE *Inimitable Jeeves* xviii. 242 The fact is, I suppose, I'd seen so many of young Bingo's love affairs start off with a whoop and a rattle and poof themselves out half-way down the straight that I couldn't believe he had actually brought it off at last. **1934** —— *Right Ho, Jeeves* xxi. 231 Then the dialogue sort of poofed out once more, and we stood eating cheese straws and cold eggs respectively in silence.

b. To utter a 'poof'. *rare.*

1915 D. H. LAWRENCE *Rainbow* vi. 148 Again she poufed with mockery.

poofter (pu·ftəɹ, pū·ftəɹ). *slang* (chiefly *Austral.*). Also **pooftah, poufter, pufter.** [Fanciful extension of *POOF *sb.*[1]] A homosexual; an effeminate man. Also used as a general term of abuse to a man. Also *attrib.* and *Comb.*, as **poofter rorter** (see quot. 1945). So **poo:fteroo·** [see *-EROO].

Often considered offensive.

1910 O'BRIEN & STEPHENS *Material for Dict. Austral. Slang 1900–10* (typescript), *Pouf or poufter*, a sodomite or effeminate man. **1941** BAKER *Dict. Austral. Slang* 56 *Poofter*, a homosexual. **1945** —— *Austral. Lang.* 123 A procurer for homosexuals is known as a *poofter rorter*. **1952** *Here & Now* (N.Z.) Jan. 19/1 The butcher's assistant was as likely to have a star bird dog or rabbit dog as the richest pooftah. **1953** T. A. G. HUNGERFORD *Riverslake* iii. 49 He hawked disgustingly and spat on the floor between his feet. 'They want men in the unions, not poofters!' **1955** D. NILAND *Shiralee* 207 They'd play around like poofters, with the kid gloves and the soft soap. **1961**

P. WHITE *Riders in Chariot* IV. xi. 392 'They will tell you,' she said, 'that Norman is a pufter... Norm could not impress a woman even if he tried.' *Ibid.* 401 'You are a proper pufter rorter, Hannah!' Reen had to remark, because she was a cow. **1964** I. FLEMING *You only live Twice* iv. 59 'You pommy poofter.'.. Bond said mildly, 'What's a poofter?' 'What you'd call a pansy.' **1966** *Punch* 9 Mar. 352/3 'It is illegal to ingratiate oneself with the Examiner.' Ingratiate oneself! Good heavens! It was slowly beginning to dawn on me that this man was a poofteroo. **1966** P. WHITE *Solid Mandala* 18 You ought to move in with that pair of poofteroos across the road. **1969** W. DICK *Naked Prodigal* 12, I turned and exploded. 'You poofter bastard!' I yelled... 'I'll kill him. The bastard's a poofter. He touched me up.' **1973** A. BROINOWSKI *Take One Ambassador* v. 53 The feller's a bloody poofter. Queer's a four pound note. **1974** R. GADNEY *Something Worth Fighting For* xxi. 139 Looking at all them poof-tahs. I was thinking what some people do for money. **1976** *Telegraph* (Brisbane) 21 Sept. 50/1 'Poofter-bashing' is a strong and blunt phrase, but the only way to describe the latest wave of discrimination against homosexual men and women in Brisbane. **1977** *Listener* (N.Z.) 15 Jan. 6/1 The white-legged Pommy poofter is an integral part of one view of the English. **1978** J. BARNETT *Head of Force* ix. 82 He was..a poufter... He was having it off with somebody he called Soldier.

poofy (pū·fi, pu·fi), *a. slang.* Also **poovey, poovy, pouffy, poufy.** [f. *POOF *sb.*^{1} + -Y^{1}.] Of, pertaining to, or characteristic of a poof; effeminate or homosexual. Also *Comb.*

1964 J. HALE *Grudge Fight* v. 74 Being Windy the soap is scented, pink stuff sent to him by Momma in the last parcel. 'Very pouffy,' says Tug, sniffing it. **1967** *Observer* 1 Jan. 24/7 Wailed a poovy young author named Ned, 'I'd rather be dead than unread.' **1968** A. DIMENT *Gt. Spy Race* II. vii. 99 He was just what I wanted. Stupid, poor, poovey. **1969** J. GARDNER *Founder Member* x. 160 'Get into those poufy drawers and..hurry.' Boysie pulled on the nylon briefs. **1970** *Guardian* 8 July 8/4 The material..makes fun of..old-fashioned 'pouffy' homosexuals. **1970** M. TRIPP *Man without Friends* vi. 61 In our cockeyed civilisation it's regarded as poovey for a man to enjoy housework. **1972** D. LEES *Zodiac* 73 One hand raised..like a poofy traffic cop. **1976** J. O'CONNOR *Eleventh Commandment* i. 17 After being given the once over by a poofy-looking scout who gave me a pat on my arse, I was sworn in.

pooh, *sb.* Add: **2.** *slang.* Excrement, faeces. Also *transf.* and *fig.*; *in the pooh* = *in the shit* s.v. *SHIT *sb.* 1 d.

1960 WENTWORTH & FLEXNER *Dict. Amer. Slang* 401/1 *Poo* ., feces. **1961** 'J. DANVERS' *Living come First* x. 177 'You're rather in the pooh with the Adelaide police.' 'How much do I stink with them?' **1967** PARTRIDGE *Dict. Slang* Suppl. 1303/2 *Pooh,* anything smelly or disgusting, esp. *faeces*: Australian juvenile. **1970** R. BEILBY *No Medals for Aphrodite* 229 If they catch you with her, then you're really in the pooh. **1975** X. HERBERT *Poor Fellow my Country* 873 She'll put you in the poo if she writes anything 'bout you. **1976** J. MCCLURE *Rogue Eagle* ii. 33 'But what..if someone..gave him the money and support he needed?' 'We might be right in the poo.'

Pooh Bah (pū bā). Also with small initials. [Name of a character in W. S. Gilbert's *Mikado.*] A person who holds a large number of offices at the same time. Also in extended use, a person or body with much influence or many functions; a self-important person. Also *attrib.* Hence **Poo-Ba·hism.**

1888 L. D. POWLES *Land of Pink Pearl* 77 To the first of these [vacancies] the Governor appointed an English jeweller, named Brown, to the second one of the local 'Pooh Bahs!' named Crawford. **1923** *Westm. Gaz.* 4 May 1/6 (*heading*) Pooh-Bah Role for Local Bodies. **1927** M. TERRY *Through Land of Promise* 44 Although principally protectors of aboriginals, stock inspection, mining wardens' responsibilities and a host of other offices make them a collection of veritable 'Poo-Bahs'. **1949** F. SWINNERTON *Doctor's Wife comes to Stay* 163, I do a bit of painting, myself: enough to take the boys in art. You see, we're so short-handed—' 'Good God! You must be the Pooh Bah of this school.' **1956** *Newsweek* 7 May 59/2 TV Pooh-Bahs expect this year's giveaway shows to reach a total hand-out of $8 million. **1962** S. E. FINER *Man on Horseback* xi. 187 In his Pooh-bah capacities as Prime Minister, Minister of War and Marine, Commander-in-Chief and Military Governor of Egypt, Neguib's power now rested on two pillars, the military and the civilian. **1964** C. DUFFY *Wild Goose & Eagle* xii. 175 In a magnificent display of Pooh-Bahism Francis Stephen, as Emperor, supported strictness and vigilance, but in his capacity as Grand Duke of Tuscany protested against interference with vessels on their peaceful way from Tuscan ports to Genoa. **1972** W. A. PANTIN *Oxford Life* v. 65 In the late eighteenth century a serious moral case..would now be dealt with by the Hebdomadal Board, that all-purpose, constitutional Pooh-Bah of the period. **1972** *Publishers' Weekly* 13 Nov. 16/1 His first book..was a tough, illuminating picture of what happens in the surgical wards of a metropolitan hospital, and it did not exactly endear him to the pooh-bahs of medicine.

pooh-pooh, *v.* Add: (Further examples.)

1926 [see *À LA *phr.* c]. **1957** *Observer* 29 Sept. 13/4 It is one thing to pooh-pooh the final scene as melodrama.. and quite another thing to remain detached as Salome lies, on your own fireside, intoxicated with passion. **1962** *Hovering Craft & Hydrofoil* Nov. 20/2 A few years ago most of us would have pooh-poohed the idea of a modern version of Jules Verne's atom-powered 'Nautilus', which has since become a reality several times over. **1971** *Petticoat* 24 July 39/1 If he refuses, or pooh-poohs your concern, go to a new family doctor, and try again. **1977** *New Yorker* 27 June 30/3 My companion pooh-poohed the mishap and bade me choose an apéritif.

Hence **pooh-poohing** *vbl. sb.* (further examples), **pooh-pooher** (earlier and later examples), **pooh-poo·hingly** *adv.*, in a dismissive or contemptuous manner, **pooh-poo·hy** *a.* (*nonce*), inclined to pooh-pooh.

1841 DICKENS *Let.* 2 Apr. (1969) II. 249 The pooh-poohers and Lord Burleighs have it hollow, all the world through. **1876** H. PARRY *Diary* in C. L. Graves *Hubert Parry* (1926) I. 169 Before the performance I met Otto Goldschmidt, and he was rather pooh-poohy about it. **1898** W. JAMES *Coll. Ess. & Rev.* (1920) 423 Concerning this question, at any rate, the positivists and pooh-poohers of metaphysics are in the wrong. **1911** G. B. SHAW *Doctor's Dilemma* p. lvii, The moment his practice is tracked down to its source in human passion there is a great and quite sincere poohpoohing..from the mass of the public. **1939** JOYCE *Finnegans Wake* III. 498 The poohpooher old bossloose, with his arthurious clayroses.. bosted to the wurld at large. **1956** Poohpooingly [see *BORROVIAN *sb.* and *a.*]. **1959** *Economist* 7 Feb. 490/1 For all his pooh-poohing of 'sentimentalism', he admitted that he never heard 'God Save the Queen'..without feeling tears in his eyes.

Pooh-sticks, pooh-sticks (pū·stiks). [f. the name of Winnie-the-*Pooh*, a character created by A. A. Milne + STICK *sb.*^{1}] A game in which sticks are thrown over one side of a bridge into a stream and the first to emerge on the other side wins.

1928 A. A. MILNE *House at Pooh Corner* vi. 94 And that was the beginning of the game called Poohsticks, which Pooh invented, and which he and his friends used to play on the edge of the Forest. But they played with sticks instead of fir-cones, because they were easier to mark. **1972** *Times* 16 May 10/4 He spends most of his time playing pooh-sticks. **1974** C. MILNE *Enchanted Places* i. 15 The bridge where they had played Pooh-sticks was a real bridge, looking just like the drawing in the book. *Ibid.* viii. 58 We used to stand on Pooh-sticks Bridge throwing sticks into the water and watching them float away.. until they re-emerged on the other side. **1979** *Guardian* 16 May 1/1 The horde of visitors who..chuck[ed] a twig or two into the sun-dappled stream in honour of the bear of very little brain who invented Poohsticks.

poojah, puja. Add: Also **pujah**; 7 **poujah, pudgiah.** (Earlier and later examples.) Also **puja pantai** (pantəi·) [Malay *pantai,* = beach, seashore] (see quot. 1965).

1681 R. KNOX *Ceylon* III. iv. 80 In this Poujah or Sacrifice the King seems to take delight. *Ibid.* v. 85 They reckon the chief poynts of goodness to consist in giving to the Priests, in making Pudgiahs, sacrifices to their Gods, in forbearing shedding the blood of any creature. **1800** S. TURNER *Embassy Tibet* iv. 243 It was only the Gylongs at their *pooja,* or religious exercises. **1893** KIPLING *Day's Work* (1898) 10 In London I did poojah to the big temple by the river for the sake of the God within. **1909** M. DIVER *Candles in Wind* I. i. 14 Is it permitted that we kill a goat and make *poojah*? **1913** E. M. FORSTER *Let.* 6 Mar. in *Hill of Devi* (1953) 28 The Rajah is doing Pujah after his bath. **1936** J. NEHRU *Autobiogr.* 8 The women of the family indulged in various ceremonies and *pujas.* **1951** *Chambers's Jrnl.* Oct. 611/2 The main religious ceremonies or 'poojas'..take place in the temple sanctum, and..eventually terminate with the bath and the fire-walk. **1951** *Jrnl. Malayan Branch R. Asiatic Soc.* XXIV. III. 33 The *pelas negri* ceremony of Perak was, in Malaya, known by other names too:..in Kelantan, and in Province Wellesley, for fishermen, the ceremony is known as *puja pantai.* **1965** C. SHUTTLEWORTH *Malayan Safari* vi. 77 A rare and colourful ceremony known as the *Puja Pantai,* it is performed by Malay fishermen when they believe that the sea gods are angry with them and need to be propitiated. **1968** *Jrnl. Music Acad. Madras* XXXIX. 59 Every home has its family idol and the pujas are performed according to the..16 types of ceremonies. **1969** *Cultural News from India* Nov. 20 The heavy and intermittent rains which, a few days ago, threatened to dampen the Puja spirit are now over. *Ibid.,* Calcutta, or for that matter, entire Bengal is in the grip of the Puja celebrations. **1971** *Northern India Patrika* 1 Feb. 1/1 Sub-inspector Makhan Lal Dutta..was attacked..near a Saraswat puja pandal. **1971** *Illustr. Weekly India* 18 Apr. 29/3 (*caption*) Gujarati women sway and swoon at a *puja.* **1972** M. SHEPPARD *Taman Indera* 197 The general name which incorporated all the ceremonies and offerings on such an occasion [*sc.* a Malay folk festival] was *Puja Pantai.* **1977** W. H. S. SMITH *Young Man's Country* ii. 36 The Puja holiday was the biggest Hindu festival in the Bengali year.

poojari, var. *PUJARI.

pool, *sb.*^{1} Add: **1. f.** = *oil pool* s.v. *OIL *sb.*^{1} 6 e.

1902 *Bull. U.S. Geol. Survey* No. 198. 23 North and northeast of the Snyder pool six wells have been sunk. **1976** M. MACHLIN *Pipeline* ii. 32 It tests over two thousand barrels a day—and God knows how much gas. I don't know how big the pool is.

g. A swimming pool.

1921 A. HUXLEY *Crome Yellow* iv. 33 That part of the garden that sloped down from the foot of the terrace to the pool. **1941** B. SCHULBERG *What makes Sammy Run?* iv. 61 Collier was urging him to come early and try the pool. **1961** J. S. SALAK *Dict. Amer. Sports* 337 It is recommended that pools for championship meets should be at least 75 feet in length and 42 feet in width. **1974** R. THOMAS *Porkchoppers* v. 38 He..lived..in a house with a pool, two Russian wolfhounds, and his wife.

2. *the Pool,* (*a*) (later examples); (*b*) Liverpool.

1966 D. FRANCIS *Flying Finish* (1968) i. 11 A small.. wharf down in the Pool. **1978** K. BONFIGLIOLI *All Tea in China* ix. 88 We could drop down-river to the Pool.. without feeing a pilot.

1963 *Austral. T.V. Times* 18 Apr. 10/2 *The pool,* the port of Liverpool. **1969** R. BUSBY *Robbery Blue* xxii. 151 I'd reckon on Liverpool... I'd head for the 'Pool, get myself swallowed up in a big city. **1972** P. DRISCOLL *Wilby Conspiracy* (1973) ii. 29 His origins: a street of back-to-backs..off the Scotland Road..the toughest part of the Pool to grow up in. **1975** *Times Lit. Suppl.* 31 Jan. 100/1 (Advt.), A fifteen year old tearaway from the 'pool brilliantly portrayed in a talented first novel. **1976** *Observer* 8 Aug. 11 (Advt.), Ar Alf sez darrevry Scouse Big'ead's brood special fer d'Pool, like.

3. *pool-side* (later examples); *pool-clear* adj.; **pool cathode** *Electronics,* a cathode consisting of a pool of mercury used in certain types of discharge tube; **pool house, poolhouse** chiefly *U.S.,* (*a*) a house by a swimming pool, for the use of bathers; (*b*) a building with a swimming pool in it; **pool party,** a party at which the guests bathe; **pool room,** a room with a pool in it.

1934 *Electrical Engineering* (N.Y.) Jan. 75/2 If a rectifier having a single anode and mercury pool cathode within a separate small tank were to be built, no continuous back current could flow to the anode when it is negative. **1966** *McGraw-Hill Encycl. Sci. & Technol.* VIII. 236/2 Tubes with a pool cathode have a higher current capacity and longer life than the hot-cathode tubes because of the indestructible nature of the mercury-pool cathode. Pool-cathode mercury-arc tubes are widely used for medium and high-power applications in welding and rectifier service. **1924** E. SITWELL *Sleeping Beauty* xiv. 51 Pierced through the pool-clear heart. **1957** P. QUENTIN *Suspicious Circumstances* ii. 24 He was way off, down by the pool... They'd eaten at the poolhouse. **1975** A. BERGMAN *Hollywood & the Vine* (1976) ix. 123 The poolhouse had showers, marked 'Fillies' and 'Stallions'. **1978** R. MOORE *Big Paddle* (1979) xxix. 269 'Seems to me I remember a pool house around here somewhere.' 'You're planning on taking a swim, sir?' **1973** *Ottawa Jrnl.* 16 July 27/5 Arch, if Veronica's having a pool party, why don't I wear a bathing suit? **1925** F. SCOTT FITZGERALD *Great Gatsby* (1926) v. 110 Through dressing-rooms and poolrooms, and bathrooms with sunken baths. **1968** J. SANGSTER *Touchfeather* xiv. 151 Where's the pool room? **1921** W. DE LA MARE *Veil* 6 Wan glow-worms greened the pool-side grass. **1963** *New Yorker* 22 June 109 Poolside buffet luncheon daily. **1968** *Globe & Mail* (Toronto) 17 Feb. 31 Sitting by the poolside at the Trinidad Hilton. **1970** P. ZELVER *Honey Bunch* (1971) vii. 34 Trays of hot hors d'œuvres..which she brought to the poolside. **1973** H. NIELSEN *Severed Key* iv. 39 Zachariah O'Hara..sat at a poolside table.

pool, *sb.*^{3} Add: **3.** *shoot pool*: see *SHOOT *v.*

b. Colloq. phr. *to play* etc. *dirty pool*: to use unfair tactics; to be dishonest. *N. Amer.*

1951 H. WOUK *Caine Mutiny* xxxvii. 445, I played pretty dirty pool, you know, in court. **1973** *Maclean's Mag.* Feb. 85/2 'You use as much dirty pool as possible,' says an alumnus cheerfully. **1976** *Times Lit. Suppl.* 19 Mar. 326/4 It is, of course, a combination of petty carping and dirty pool to demand of the author of a scholarly work information that does not fall within the limits he has meticulously drawn up for his work.

4. b. (Earlier and later examples.) Also, *auction pool,* the total sum realized when the names of horses in a race, or likely winners in other contests, are sold by auction to those who wish to hold them; *to scoop the pool*: see *SCOOP *v.*^{1} 5 a.

1868 *N.Y. Herald* 3 July 10/1 Let us take a glance at the pool stand before the races begin. **1874** 'MARK TWAIN' *Sk. New & Old* 310 No pools permitted on the run of the comet—no gambling of any kind. **1913** A. BENNETT *Regent* II. x. 311 The *Lithuania* was lagging... Every day, in the auction-pool on the ship's run, it was the holder of the lower field that pocketed the money. **1928** *Daily Mail* 7 Aug. 12/5 Stewards are stationed at different points to give weary travellers a welcome lift and prevent them from getting off the beaten track and missing the auction pool. **1949** *Radio Times* 15 July 6/1 Wilfred acts as auctioneer on board the 'Queen Mary' during the pool on the ship's daily run. **1955** *Times* 30 Aug. 5/1 Under the Act, the balance-sheets, to be deposited with the local authority, must show the aggregate total stakes in all pools,.. or, at the option of the promoter, the percentage of the total stakes. **1973** *Irish Times* 2 Mar. 2/6 The unexpected victory of Game Sauce in the second division scuttled jackpot hunters and the pool of £1,027 goes forward to Naas tomorrow.

c. = **football pool.* Usu. *pl.*

1938 *Mass-Observation: First Year's Work 1937–38* iv. 39 The Pools provide an outlet for personal frustration, ambition and faith. **1947** [see *BANKER^{2} 5]. **1948** M. ALLINGHAM *More Work for Undertaker* xiv. 174, I wouldn't have had this happen, not for a thirty-thousand win in the pools. **1957** *London Mag.* May 48 They see themselves being eaten alive by this ignorant creature, with his telly and his pools, swallowing up all culture. **1958** *Listener* 28 Aug. 308/1 He is telling us about the important things about the working class, how they feel about pools and pubs as well as about socialism, trade unionism, and religion. **1966** A. E. LINDOP *I start Counting* xxi. 266 I'm saving up to buy her a big book on birds... We had a nuthatch last Friday, and you'd think she'd won the pools. **1974** A. FOWLES *Pastime* iv. 39 He sat at the main desk doing his pools... He'd never won a sausage. **1979** *Times* 20 Dec. 15/6 Nearly 60 per cent of people in the country as a whole replied to the question, 'How often do you do the pools?' with 'Never'.

5. b. A common reservoir of commodities, resources, etc. Cf. *gene pool* s.v. *GENE 2.

1917 'CONTACT' *Airman's Outings* 127 Before they join a squadron pilots fresh from their instruction in England gain experience on service machines belonging to the 'pool' at Saint Gregoire. **1940** *Times* (Weekly ed.) 7 June 15 A rice pool has been formed from August 1 through which all rice imported into Singapore must pass. The pool will be used as a means for turning over the emergency stocks of rice which the Government have now acquired. **1943** J. S. HUXLEY *Evolutionary Ethics* vi. 46 The more individuals there exist whose desirable potentialities are fully developed, the more health, vigour, knowledge, wisdom, happiness, beauty and the rest can go into the common pool, and the better that common pool will work. **1946** S. SPENDER *European Witness* i. 11 People like myself could draw on an alleged 'pool' of cars to take them on journeys. **1958** *Observer* 15 June 13/7 Each animal and plant population draws on a large pool of genes. **1963** *Higher Educ.: Rep. Comm. under Ld. Robbins 1961–3* 53 in *Parl. Papers 1962–3* (Cmnd. 2154) XI. 639 The increase has been almost as great among the children of professional parents, where the pool of ability might have been thought more nearly exhausted. **1967** E. SHORT *Embroidery & Fabric Collage* i. 28 A useful 'pool' of ideas will soon be built up to be referred to when needed.

c. A group of persons any one of whose abilities or services may be drawn upon or who share duties; spec. *typing, typists'*, etc., *pool*: a number of typists in an organization, department, etc., among whom work is distributed. Hence also, the office or building where such typists work.

1928 I. CURTIS in *Schools of England* xvii. 333 The staff as a whole is organized as a 'pool' for various miscellaneous duties, such as examination work, the preparation of the tutorial courses. *Ibid.* 334 All the examination work which falls to the Education Board,..is carried out by the pool as part of the regular work. **1937** V. BARTLETT *This is my Life* x. 150 The typists [of the League of Nations] were..relegated to a 'pool' at the top of the building. **1942** N. BALCHIN *Darkness falls from Air* vi. 104 How many people are there in your typing pool? **1944** 'N. SHUTE' *Pastoral* iv. 75 Chap with a face like a burglar—came in with the last lot from the pool. **1949** *Manch. Guardian Weekly* 20 Jan. 3 A secretarial 'pool'. **1958** G. GREENE *Our Man in Havana* 58 The secretaries' pool should have been informed. *Ibid.* v. vi. 260 I'll try to stay in the typists' pool. **1959** *Times* 3 Sept. 14/1 A married woman, aged 23, who has settled down in the audio-typing pool after only a few years as a secretary, confessed that she hated it at first but soon changed her mind. **1960** *Guardian* 11 July 3/3 The Derby force opens a new typing pool where the reports..will be typed. **1960** M. SPARK *Ballad of Peckham Rye* iii. 42 That Miss Coverdale in the pool..is working Dixie to death. **1970** G. GREER *Female Eunuch* 126 She can command better money and have time off as well if she would only walk out of her typing pool. **1972** K. BENTON *Spy in Chancery* iv. 32 Diana's a competent girl, and she doesn't chatter about her work to the typists' pool.

d. = **pool petrol*.

1940 M. NICHOLSON *How Britain's Resources are Mobilized* 4 In war it [petrol] all goes round in grey tankers and is all called 'Pool'. **1944** *Amer. Speech* XIX. 294 The word 'pool', printed on a strip of paper pasted on a gasoline pump, announces that the pump contains an unidentified brand of gasoline from the nation's pooled supplies, instead of the brand advertised on the pump. **1952** *Economist* 6 Sept. 581 Early in the war all petrol was of uniform quality, the Pool.

e. In a sporting tournament, a group the members of which play against each other to decide which of the competitors or teams qualify for the next round; a minor league.

1955 *Times* 26 May 12/5 His many successes in the matches and 'pools' inaugurated at that time. **1972** *Sunday Tel.* 30 Apr. 34/7 The team flies to Groningen tomorrow, drawn in a tough pool with Poland, Spain and Hungary.

f. A register of free-lance dockworkers seeking employment.

1958 *Engineering* 14 Mar. 329/2 Members of the National Dock Labour Board's 'pool' at the..group of docks decided to ban overtime in order to spread the work available among the registered workers. **1964** O. E. MIDDLETON in C. K. Stead *N.Z. Short Stories* (1966) 194 The usual round and the same stale answers on every ship: 'All hands are hired through the Pool. Are you established members of the Pool?' **1972** *Guardian* 17 Aug. 1/4, 2,000 [dockers] are going to be put out in Liverpool, and there are 1,200 in the Royal Group on the 'pool' (the temporary, unattached register which is to be abolished under the new proposals).

g. *Biochem.* A quantity of one or more metabolites in some definite part or tissue of the body which is continually being diminished and replenished by cellular activity.

1961 in WEBSTER. **1962** *Bacteriol. Rev.* XXVI. 292/1 Bacteria maintain internally synthesized small molecules at high internal concentrations and in addition have the capacity to concentrate many compounds from the environment. Since the majority of these compounds are intermediates in synthesis, they are collectively termed the pool of metabolic intermediates or, simply, the 'pool'. **1968** *Brit. Med. Bull.* XXIV. 249/2 Fowle, Matthews and Campbell (1964)..put forward a model which separated the body CO_2 into intracellular and extracellular pools. **1971** *Nature* 30 July 329/1 Thus shorter chain acids.. would have been produced by partial degradation of palmitic acid, with concomitant dilution of label by the cellular pool of palmitic acid.

h. A small number of reporters who have access to news sources and pass information to other journalists.

1967 R. J. SERLING *President's Plane is Missing* (1968) vi. 102 Call a press conference and lay it on the line. They can choose themselves between a permanent pool or a one-shot visit. **1973** *Washington Post* 13 Jan. c 2/3 Instead of limiting coverage to a selected 'pool' of a few reporters, all accredited reporters and photographers—more than 100—were allowed to attend.

8. a. (sense 3) *pool hall, joint, parlour, -shooter, -shooting*; (sense 4 b) *pool box, -seller* (earlier examples), *-selling* (earlier examples); (sense *4 c) *pool-betting, coupon, promoter*; (sense *5 b) *pool currency, driver, product, service, transport*; (sense *5 c) *pool typist*; (sense *5 f) *pool office*; (sense *5 h) *pool group, policy, reporter, representative*.

1955 T. H. PEAR *Eng. Social Differences* xiii. 293 It is easy to understand why the popularity of all-in wrestling and speedway racing has not spread 'upwards', while that of pool-betting has. **1957** *Encycl. Brit.* IX. 998/2 In Great Britain the Pool Betting act of 1954 set certain requirements for the conduct of pool betting, including the registration of operators and inspection and publication of financial details. **1878** M. LONG *Life Mason Long* vi. 102 The field won, and after the race I drew six hundred and twenty-five dollars from the pool-box. **1902** A. D. MCFAUL *Ike Glidden* 171 The vehement cheers of those about the pool box seemed more deafening as the race progressed. **1951** 'M. INNES' *Operation Pax* II. iv. 63 A few brought pool coupons from their pockets and studied them. **1955** *Times* 15 Aug. 6/4 The first Brazilian auction of 'pool' currency will be tendered for on Thursday, the statement continues, and the currency thereby made available,.. will be available for the three participating countries. **1973** A. MANN *Tiara* x. 91 Four or five are in the motor pool for the use of Vatican people on official journeys, but they would have pool drivers. **1970** *Globe & Mail* (Toronto) 26 Sept. 10/5 The patients spoke mostly in Arabic to an Arab journalist in a pool group of reporters who were taken to the hospital by the Jordanian army. **1928** *Collier's* 29 Dec. 43/2 He entered a pool-hall speakeasy. **1944** J. S. PENNELL *Hist. Rome Hanks* 63, I heard a young pool-hall lounger standing idly in Pawnee street refer to him as Old Man Beckham. **1951** [see **joke book*]. **1973** *Black World* May 77/1 Their penchant for open debate in the chop bars..reappears in our barber shops and pool halls. **1975** *Listener* 18 Dec. 834/3 An endless succession of dreary bars, pool-halls and discos. **1930** H. ZINK *City Bosses in U.S.* 137 Money paid by saloons, gambling and pool joints, and houses of the underworld. **1964** O. E. MIDDLETON in C. K. Stead *N.Z. Short Stories* (1966) 194 Why do they think we are tramping fifteen miles of dockside, when the other way, you have only to show your papers at the Pool office, and wait for a ship? **1912** Pool parlour [see *CABARET[1] 2 b]. **1932** J. DOS PASSOS *1919* 413 Izzy had gotten to loafing in poolparlours. **1973** *Washington Post* 13 Jan. c 2/3 The new 'pool' policies under which Washington Post reporter Dorothy McCardle was excluded from five previous social events involving President and Mrs. Nixon. **1939** *New Statesman* 18 Nov. 740 The only mystery about the Petroleum Board (the wartime name for the powerful trade committee which fixes distributors' quotas and agrees prices) is that it is unable to get permission from the Government to charge what prices it likes for the imports of 'pool' products. **1940** HARRISON & MADGE *War begins at Home* x. 279 Despite all the efforts of Pool-promoters, postal facilities were denied, and the vast Pool vested interests were closed down. **1967** MRS. L. B. JOHNSON *White House Diary* 14 Mar. (1970) 496 There were John Gardner and Liz and I and a pool reporter..in the tiny room. **1972** *Guardian* 9 June 13/8 The pool reporter..is the duty man who attends the senator in his intimate and most insignificant moments. Clearly five hundred pressmen..cannot accompany the senator into a small shirt shop: the pool reporter is their eyes and ears. **1974** *Times* 17 Apr. 14/7 The briefing was open to all Israel newspapers..but the Foreign Press Association was told it must choose one pool representative. **1887** *Advance* (Chicago) 13 Oct. 6/1 No less than 15 poolsellers were in the grand stand. **1888** *Outing* May 118/1 John Hatfield is a bookmaker and pool-seller in St. Louis. **1869** J. H. BROWNE *Great Metropolis* 573 Pool selling is managed in this way. **1872** *Alabamian & Times* (Tuscumbia, Alabama) 26 Sept. 4/2 Pool selling is lively and fine sport is anticipated. **1964** *B.E.A. Advance Timetable* (Summer), Pool Services from London: Flights to Denmark, Norway and Sweden are in co-operation with S.A.S...to Prague with C.S.A. and to Warsaw with LOT. **1961** *John o' London's* 2 Nov. 495/1 A professional pool-shooter. **1974** *Greenville* (S. Carolina) *News-Piedmont* 20 Apr. 8/2 Rudolph Wanderone, known internationally as Minnesota Fats, king of the pool-shooting hustlers, was reported in serious condition Friday after undergoing emergency surgery. **1868** Pool stand [see sense 4 b above]. **1945** *News Chron.* 7 June 4/3 The bicycles which are being used in these country trips are needed to provide pool transport for mine workers and farm labourers. **1942** N. BALCHIN *Darkness falls from Air* ix. 121 Pearce rang up with a long tale of woe about being very short of pool typists. **1979** G. HAMMOND *Dead Game* x. 140 McLure got one of the pool typists put onto it.

b. Pl. (sense *4 c), as *pools coupon, entry, investor, panel, win, winner*.

1951 A. BARON *Rosie Hogarth* v. iv. 337 Children will be educated.., not just to be office boys and fill in the pools coupon. **1978** J. GALWAY *Autobiogr.* ii. 20 The set.. became the whole focal point of his life every Saturday afternoon when it was time to check the football results for his pools coupon. **1972** A. DRAPER *Death Penalty* i. 5 The copy coupon of his pools entry. **1958** Pools investor [see *BANKER[2] 5]. **1976** *Daily Record* (Glasgow) 4 Dec. 30/2 And with the arctic weather spreading south, the Pools Panel have been put on active stand-by. **1963** *Times* 14 Feb. 15/3 An innocent from academe, made footloose by a pools win, incautiously agrees to become guest dramatic critic to the *Evening Gazette*. **1977** J. WAINWRIGHT *Pool of Tears* 203 You know about the pools win. **1960** I. JEFFERIES *Dignity & Purity* xii. 187, I suddenly felt almost like a pools winner. **1973** *Guardian* 1 Mar. 28/5 The biggest pools winner in history..came to London yesterday to receive his cheque for £542,252—won from a £1 stake.

c. Special Combs., as **pool butter**, the butter of uniform quality available in Britain during the war of 1939–45; **pool car,** (*a*) a freight wagon shared by a number of hirers; (*b*) a car available for the use of a number of drivers; **pool-drive** *v.*, to share vehicles and driving duties on a regular journey; **pool petrol,** the unbranded petrol which was the only grade available in Britain during and just after the 1939–45 war; **pool room,** (*a*) room with billiard tables where pool can be played, usu. for a fee; (*b*) a room where a betting pool is held; a betting shop; **pool shark** *U.S. colloq.*, an expert pool player; one who makes money by winning at pool; **pool train** *Canada*, a train run jointly by more than one railway company; also **pool passenger train.**

1940 Pool butter [see *pool petrol* below]. **1926** *Daily Colonist* (Victoria, B.C.) 18 July 3/5 Victoria Baggage Company. Furniture Moved, Crated and Shipped. Pool Cars for Prairies and All Points East. **1967** *Lebende Sprachen* XII. 186/1 Pool car..=*Sammelwagen*. **1973** A. MANN *Tiara* xiii. 118 There are five pool cars. **1974** *Globe & Mail* (Toronto) 18 Mar. s6/1 Most go back and forth from Oshawa—working at General Motors is a way of life. They pool-drive. **1959** *Kingston* (Ontario) *Whig-Standard* 28 Sept. 1/5 His death was the fifth caused by the collision in which a CNR freight ripped open the side of a dining car on a pool passenger train being shunted in the yards. **1940** *Weekly Chron.* (Newcastle) 23 Mar., The war has given us special meanings of a number of words already in use—*pool* (for *pool-butter, -petrol* etc.). **1949** *Punch* 28 Sept. p. iv, When the days of 'Pool petrol only' are over. **1968** B. FOSTER *Changing Eng. Lang.* iii. 123 Wartime conditions frequently give a new twist to an existing term, e.g. 'austerity, pool (as in 'pool petrol', the unbranded petrol of wartime days), [etc.].' **1861** T. HUGHES *Tom Brown at Oxf.* II. iii. 51 He could go and smoke a cigar in the pool room. **1887, 1892** [in Dict., sense 8]. **1931** D. RUNYON in *Collier's* 26 Sept. 57/2 We get the race results by phone off a pool room downtown as fast as they come off. **1944** AUDEN *For Time Being* (1945) 50 Back to the upland mill town.. with its grope-movie and its pool-room lit by gas. **1959** N. MAILER *Advts. for Myself* (1961) 74 The poolroom itself was down in the cellar. **1973** *Black World* June 79/1 This style..emanates from the urban street world of pimps, prostitutes, poolroom sharks. **1978** *Detroit Free Press* 5 Mar. B 1/1 My best friend Antoine..and I were hanging around O'Quinn's poolroom. **1908** *Busy Man's Mag.* Mar. 128 The Pool Shark. Bide Dudley... Blue Book. **1944** W. RUSSELL in *Needle* July 21/2 On the Gulf Coast they'd call him a pool shark and gambler. **1971** J. H. GRAY *Red Lights on Prairies* i. 13 Sometimes they [*sc.* prostitutes] travelled from town to town with pool sharks. **1965** *Globe & Mail* (Toronto) 10 Nov. 19/8 At one time the pool trains ran over the CNR to Brockville and then by CPR tracks to Ottawa... As at the end of October, the pool trains ceased to exist and the two railways went on their separate ways.

pool, *v.*[1] Add: **1.** (Examples of revived use.) Also *transf.*

1973 D. ANDERSEN *Ways Harsh & Wild* iv. 107 Behind our cabin there was a meadow that gradually pooled with water. **1977** *Rolling Stone* 13 Jan. 38/3 An afternoon sun pools warmly on the hardwood floor in the rambling frame house. **1978** C. TOMLINSON *Shaft* 20 The brook.. entered the garden, pooling.

3. *intr.* Of blood: to accumulate in parts of the venous system, e.g. as a result of the forces produced by continuous acceleration.

1933 *Jrnl. R. Aeronaut. Soc.* XXXVII. 398 Fig. 6 shows a sketch of a device which I suggest might serve to counteract the tendency of centrifugal force to make the blood leave the head and pool in the thin-walled abdominal vessels. **1945** [see *ANTI-GRAVITY]. **1962** [see *G-SUIT, G-SUIT]. **1962** F. I. ORDWAY et al. *Basic Astronautics* xii. 463 The blood..increases in weight to the point where the heart can no longer pump it, and it pools in the extremities of the body. **1973** TOWLER & BUTLER-MANUEL *Mod. Obstetr.* xvii. 469 Here the blood 'pools' in the large muscles and is effectively lost to the circulation.

pool, *v.*[2] Add: (Further examples.) Also *transf.*

1921 G. B. SHAW *Back to Methuselah* p. lxxvii, What we should do, then, is to pool our legends and make a delightful stock of religious folk-lore on an honest basis for all mankind. **1926** *Amer. Mercury* Dec. 462/2 Sime countered by pooling his stories with the other fellow. **1927** E. THOMPSON *These Men, thy Friends* 245 Hart and Kenrick pooled friends. **1940** *Hutchinson's Pict. Hist. War* 14 Feb.–4 Sept. 68 Petrol was pooled, buildings were seized, children were sent to safety. **1955** *Times* 16 Aug. 9/3 The sterling, Deutschmarks, and guilders which the Brazilian exchange control authorities secure from the proceeds of Brazilian exports will be 'pooled', and when in future they are 'auctioned' importers who buy them will be free to use them for imports from any one of the three countries. **1978** S. BRILL *Teamsters* vi. 220 In a rare display of cooperation,..the IRS and FBI agreed to pool their efforts. **1979** *Canad. Jrnl. Linguistics* XXIV. i. 35 Unfortunately, Brown pooled the data, so that if any developmental trends were present, they were obscured in the analysis.

2. *Austral. slang.* To implicate; involve a person against his will; inform on.

1919 W. H. Downing *Digger Dial.* 39 *Pool*, to involve; cast blame or a burden on. **1928** A. Wright *Good Recovery* 117 Leave the sheilas alone; they're sure to pool a man sooner or later. **1932** W. Hatfield *Ginger Murdoch* 282 To rig that evidence against him—pool him. **1942** L. Mann *Go-Getter* 313, 'I got pooled into it,' he explained. **1967** K. Tennant *Tell Morning This* 85 A man thought he'd do the decent thing and tide a girl over a patch of trouble, and she pools him every time. You can't prove it isn't your kid.

pooled *ppl. a.* (further examples); **pooling** *vbl. sb.* (further examples).

1928 *Manch. Guardian Weekly* 10 Aug. 104/2 Washington, too, is shown by the dispatches to suspect something like an Anglo-French alliance or merger or pooling behind the text of the naval compromise. **1936** *Discovery* Aug. 232/1 It was to be hoped that such pooling of knowledge might become world-wide. **1943** J. S. Huxley *Evolutionary Ethics* 39 Part of the blind struggle for existence between separate individuals or groups is transposed into conflict in consciousness..within the tradition which is the vehicle of pooled social consciousness. *Ibid.* 45 The pooling of experience and co-operative action in a cumulative tradition. **1946** J. W. Day *Harvest Adventure* xvi. 278 As to the waste of 'pooled' machinery, this is a sore point in many counties. **1951** *N.Y. Times* 21 Aug. 1/6 A pooled dispatch said the services had 'an almost carnival atmosphere'. **1955** *Bull. Atomic Sci.* Apr. 146/1 In science, only a pooling of all new ideas can lead to progress. **1967** *Oceanogr. & Marine Biol.* V. 162 When animals are small, biochemical study of a pooled sample from many specimens is imperative. **1971** *Jrnl. Gen. Psychol.* LXXXV. 111 The baseline performance of the pooled controls. **1975** *Language for Life* (Dept. Educ. & Sci.) iii. 40 It is an essential principle of the item pooling system that assessment can reflect changes in the use of language and stylistic differences over the years.

Poole (pūl). The name of a town in Dorset, used *attrib.* to designate a type of clay suitable for pottery found near there, or pottery manufactured there.

1878 *Encycl. Brit.* VIII. 229/2 Of importance next to it [*sc.* kaolin], as potter's material, is the 'Poole clay' of Dorsetshire. **1924** *Design in Mod. Industry: Year-Bk. of Design & Industries Assoc. 1923–24* 51 (*caption*) The painted dish in the upper illustration is a piece of Poole pottery, and shows how essentially decorative simple colour groupings may appear on surfaces uncomplicated by needless corrugations. **1938** *Decorative Art* p. x, Poole pottery... If there is a mantleshelf..it is a narrow one, but there are Poole Pots to meet the difficulty. **1957** [see *Dorset]. **1971** R. Rendell *No More Dying Then* i. 11 There were flowers..in the Poole pottery vases.

pooled (pūld), *a. rare.* [f. Pool *sb.*[1] + -ed[2].] Furnished with or placed in a pool. Also *fig.*

1947 Dylan Thomas *Let.* 20 May (1966) 307 The pooled ponded..garden. **1967** F. Warner *Madrigals* 10 You stand Pooled in discarded clothes.

pooly (pū·li), *sb. rare.* [f. Pool *sb.*[1] + -y[6].] A small pool, *spec.* of urine.

1922 Joyce *Ulysses* 529 It's as limp as a boy of six's doing his pooly behind a cart.

poon (pūn), *sb.*[2] *slang* (chiefly *Austral.*). [Origin obscure.] **a.** A simple or foolish person. **b.** A person living alone in the outback.

1940 M. Marples *Public School Slang* 60 Another considerable group of words in recent use has a definite trans-atlantic flavour, as, for example: boob..goof..mutt.. poon (Dulwich, 1930+). **1941** Baker *Dict. Austral. Slang* 56 *Poon*, a lonely, somewhat crazy dweller in the Outer Beyond... A simpleton or fool. **1945** —— *Austral. Lang.* v. 97 Another outback term for a person who lives alone is *poon.* **1972** G. Morley *Jockey rides Honest Race* 73 They don't look for the guts of a lecture; just the mistakes. Then they can get up and shoot their mouths off and everybody else nods wisely and tries to pick up the mistakes of the poon that's just said his piece. **1974** D. Williamson *Jugglers Three* in *Three Plays* 69 What possessed Keren to shack up with a poon like you?

poon, *sb.*[3] *slang.* Abbrev. of *poontang *sb.*

1969 J. Leasor *They don't make them like that any More* vi. 192 It's against my principles to pay for poon: if I can't get it for what is laughingly called love, then I'll do without. **1972** J. Wambaugh *Blue Knight* (1973) i. 16 Watching all that young poon.

poon (pūn), *v. Austral. slang.* [Origin obscure.] To dress *up*; esp. to dress flashily. Also in pa. pple. *pooned up.*

1943 Baker *Dict. Austral. Slang* (ed. 3) 61 *Poon up*, to dress up, especially in flashy fashion. **1945** —— *Austral. Lang.* 206 School slang... *poon up*, to dress up, especially with considerable care. **1951** D. Stivens *Jimmy Brockett* 48 Some of 'em were young lairs, all pooned up to kill. **1972** A. Chipper *Aussie Swearer's Guide* 48 *Pooned up*, dressed to impress, often with sexual success in view.

poonac. Add: (Example.)

1927 *Trop. Agriculturalist* LXVIII. 279 As regards Phosphorus, there are many food-stuffs, available in Ceylon, rich in this element. For example, the various poonacs and pollard.

Poonah. Add: Also **Poona** (now the usual form). Also as *adj.*, with allusion to the attitudes, way of life, etc., held to be characteristic of the Army officers stationed there during British rule.

1939 G. Treast in *Best One-Act Plays 1938* 63 Major Manners is discovered playing patience... He is an elderly, heavily jovial man, who, in spite of twenty years' Isolation, remains essentially pukka and Poona. **1944** 'N. Shute' *Pastoral* vi. 138 They're county people, all frightfully toffee-nosed and Poona. **1973** 'B. Mather' *Snowline* iv. 49 Blimey! Class consciousness rearing its ugly head... How Poonah-Poonah can you get? **1975** A. Christie *Curtain* i. 7 One of your so British old Colonels—very 'old school tie' and 'Poona'.

poonask, var. *ponask *v.*

poonghie, phoongyee, phungyi. Add: Also **pongyi.** (Further examples.)

1929 F. T. Jesse *Lacquer Lady* i. v. 36 The King had allowed it [*sc.* the house] to be built with a triple roof, a thing usually only permitted to Princes and poongyis. *Ibid.* ii. i. 118 After the litter came sixty-five poongyis..; they walked with downcast eyes, holding their fans up so that they should not by any chance catch sight of a woman. **1930** *Aberdeen Press & Jrnl.* 29 May 7/5 Last night a pongyi (Burmese priest) attempted to stab a military policeman. **1951** 'N. Shute' *Round Bend* 122 He has been a Buddhist monk, a pongyi we call them, for over thirty years. **1966** D. Forbes *Heart of Malaya* xi. 129 Miss Khan..took me across the lane to the Burmese *wat* and kowtowed to the *pongyi* in the temple hall.

poontang (pū·ntæŋ), *sb. U.S. slang.* Also *poon tang* and with capital initial(s). [Prob. ad. Fr. *putain* prostitute.] Sexual intercourse, sex; women collectively, or a woman, regarded as a means of sexual gratification. Also *attrib.* Hence as *v. intr.*, to copulate.

1929 T. Wolfe *Look Homeward, Angel* 343 A fellow's got to have a little Poon Tang. **1947** C. Willingham *End as Man* ii. vii. 78 Poley looked out the window and saw a pretty Negro girl on the sidewalk... 'Eye that poon tang there,' he said. **1959** R. Condon *Manchurian Candidate* ii. 21 Every now and then I think about you coming all the way to Korea from New Jersey to get your first piece of poontang. **1966** C. Hines *Heat's On* xv. 122 That ain't our racket. We just sells poontang here. **1968** E. J. Gaines *Bloodline* 144 Yesterday this time I was poontanging like a dog. **1970** D. Dodge *Hatchetman* x. 127 'Is it true what they say about gook women?'.. 'I heah it changes youah luck, though. Like black poontang.' **1972** 'T. Coe' *Don't lie to Me* iv. 44 May be you're some kind of poontang sex maniac. **1972** *Listener* 22 June 845/2 Massa gonna smack yo black ass, nigger. You can't go chasing white poontang all night long. **1976** *Honolulu Star-Bull.* 21 Dec. e-10/6 (Advt.), The other girls majored in home ec... but Debby majored in Poon-tang.

poop, *sb.*[1] Add: **3. poop-break,** the front of the poop of a ship; **poop-ornament** *Naut. slang*, a ship's apprentice.

1912 J. Masefield in *Eng. Rev.* Oct. 353 Under the poop break, sheltering from the rain. **1902** *Athenæum* 8 Feb. 177/1 He [*sc.* the apprentice in the merchant service] was and is emphatically the ship's loblolly-boy..miscalled 'a blarsted poop ornament', the drudge even of ordinary seamen. **1934** J. Masefield *Taking of Gry* 75, I looked at these fellows, and concluded that the lieutenant was a young poop-ornament and that the men were slacking.

poop, *sb.*[2] Delete † *Obs.* and add: Also (*S. Afr.*) ‖ **poep. 1.** (Later examples.) Also, the report of a gun.

1908 K. Grahame *Wind in Willows* vi. 128, I faithfully promise that the very first motor-car I see, poop-poop! off I go in it! **1919** W. Deeping *Second Youth* xxviii. 240 The faint 'poop-poop' of distant anti-aircraft guns..brought Laverack sharply back to the immediate present.

2. *slang* (orig. children's). An act of breaking wind or of defecation; faeces. Also *fig.*

Quot. *c* 1744 is an *interj.*

*c*1744 [see *hole *sb.* 8]. **1937** Partridge *Dict. Slang* 648/2 *Poop*,..a breaking of wind. **1948** *Amer. Speech* XXIII. 264 We used the words *poop* and *poot* with their onomatopoeic significance in regard to bodily discharges. **1974** *Amer. Speech 1971* XLVI. 82 *Fart*,..poop. **1976** *Telegraph* (Brisbane) 7 June 9/2 A young woman claims a 'bird poop treatment' has cured her of a chronic dandruff... She's been free of dandruff since a mynah bird relieved himself on her head during lunch one day. **1977** J. McClure *Sunday Hangman* x. 105 Ja, we scared the poop out of him that time. **1977** *Listener* 22–29 Dec. 842/3 That's just a set-up... He just says all that kind of poop about you in the beginning.

3. *attrib.* and *Comb.*, as **poop-butt** (see quot.); **poophead** *U.S.* (see quot.); **poop-hole** (in quot. *S. Afr.*), anus; **poop-pusher** (see quot.); **poop-scared** *a.* (in quot. *S. Afr.*), extremely frightened, = **shit-scared* adj.; **poop scoop** *joc.*, an implement used for clearing up faeces; so **pooper scooper; poop-stick,** a fool, ineffectual person (cf. *poop *sb.*[4]).

1973 C. & R. Milner *Black Players* ii. 42 A *poop-butt* is a lazy person. **1976** *Maclean's Mag.* 12 Jan. 34/1 A man on a motor-cycle with a pooper-scooper would be dispatched to clean up. **1977** J. Wambaugh *Black Marble* (1978) viii. 112 Bring your pooper-scoopers, boys. The dogs are covering the red carpet in a sea of shit. **1978** *Daily Tel.* 17 Aug. 3/3 The 'pooper-scooper' law in New York requires dog-owners to pick up anything their dogs drop. **1977** *Amer. Speech 1975* L. 64 *Poophead*, person regarded as dull or stupid. **1969** A. Fugard *Boesman & Lena* i. 26 That tickey deposit heart of his is tight like his *poephol* and his fist. **1966** 'L. Lane' *ABZ of Scouse* 83 *Poop-pusher*, a laxative, especially one of satisfactory violence. **1976** in J. Branford *Dict. S. Afr. Eng.* (1978) 188/1 OK so they give up at last, but..never been so poep-scared in my whole entire life before or since. **1978** *Daily Tel.* 24 July 13/6 It may soon be common to see people holding a dog lead in one hand and a 'poop scoop' in the other. **1930** 'Hay' & Wodehouse *Baa, Baa, Black Sheep* ii. 55, I believe she really does care for that poop-stick... Fancy loving a man called Osbert Bassington-Bassington! **1932** P. MacDonald *Rope to Spare* viii. 100 'You make me sick!' he said. 'Let a little poop-stick like that walk all over you!'

poop (pūp), *sb.*[4] *colloq.* [Perh. abbrev. of Nincompoop.] A stupid or ineffectual person; a fool, a bore.

1915 V. Woolf *Voyage Out* iii. 51 They talk about art, and think us such poops for dressing in the evening. **1924** 'Sapper' *Third Round* vii. 189 The genuine Professor Scheidstrun appeared to be a harmless old poop, who was more sinned against than sinning. **1936** C. S. Forester *General* xv. 155 Every little poop of a temporary major-general. **1942** Wodehouse *Money in Bank* (1946) xx. 169 For God's sake, don't put your trust in that poop. **1952** S. Kauffmann *Philanderer* (1953) iii. 42 Yes, yell for your father. I'd like to get a look at the poop. I'd like to pick you up and throw you at him. **1966** H. Marriott *Cariboo Cowboy* ix. 86 It seemed to me that a real snotty-nosed poop like him was a poor character to have in that sort of job. **1971** R. Dentry *Encounter at Kharmel* xii. 211 Those stupid bloody Yankee poops blew the panic whistle and the whole shebang went sky-high. **1972** D. Delman *Sudden Death* iv. 95 'Honey, I do declare you've turned into nothing but an old poop,' she said.

poop (pūp), *sb.*[5] *slang* (orig. and chiefly *U.S.*). [Origin obscure.] Up-to-date or 'inside' information, 'low-down'. Freq. *attrib.* in **poop-sheet,** a written notice, bulletin, or report.

1941 *Amer. Speech* XVI. 167/2 *Poop sheet*, drill schedule or any written announcement. **1947** *Ibid.* XXII. 216 The word *poop*, which indicated the latest information, whether official or unofficial, was also incorporated into *poop sheet*, denoting the latest bulletin or directive. **1950** 'D. Divine' *King of Fassarai* ii. 14 Have you picked up any poop about where the ship's going..? *Ibid.* xxiv. 205 'Have you seen the poop sheet anywhere?..' 'Aw, hell... There ain't any news anyway.' **1961** B. Malamud *New Life* (1962) 300, I sent out a poop sheet this afternoon.. with the names of the nominees. **1963** H. Slesar *Bridge of Lions* (1964) v. 84 I've asked Sandy to send me a poop sheet on him, but may be you can add something. **1973** R. Hayes *Hungarian Game* xxi. 130 How did you get the poop on Kovács? **1974** 'M. Allen' *Super Tour* vii. 264 He sends in a report—straight facts, no frills, and a minimum use of adjectives. What he says is included in the mimeographed poop sheet the organization sends out every month. **1976** *Sounds* 11 Dec. 33 (*heading*) Hot poop on old punks.

poop, *v.*[1] Add: **1. b.** (Later examples.)

1937 Partridge *Dict. Slang* 648/2 *Poop*,..to defecate.. mostly of and by children. **1972** L. Hancock *There's a Seal in my Sleeping Bag* vii. 165 The joys of motherhood were considerably lessened when a baby murre pooped with regularity between my shirt and bare warm skin. **1974** *Cape Times* 1 Aug. 11/5 Five-year-old eyes grow round with wonder at the memory of the elephant 'pooping' on the carpet.

2. a. *trans.* To fire (a bullet, shell, or other missile); to discharge (a gun); to shoot (a person or animal). Freq. with *off.* Also *transf.* and *fig.*

1917 W. Owen *Let.* 6 Dec. (1967) 514, I shall continue to poop off heavy stuff at you, till you get my range at Scarborough, and so silence me. **1929** [see *heat *sb.* 12 b] **1937** P. B. Hawk *Off Racket* ii. 99 At any rate he pooped the ball into the [tennis] net. **1940** *Manch. Guardian Weekly* 5 Apr. 277 An old wildfowler..earns a precarious living by stealing down the estuaries with a home-made blunderbuss or duck-gun and pooping it off at..sea-fowl. **1940** 'N. Shute' *Landfall* 142 'Can't we fly it over a known ship and poop it off?' he said. 'Poop off half a dozen of them.' **1960** *Guardian* 9 Nov. 7/7 The emergency code word has just been flashed through... Is it all right by London if they poop off their Polarises? **1974** A. Price *Other Paths to Glory* ii. vi. 187 There was this Jerry prisoner..and this Aussie comes up..and he poops him... Kills him—shoots him.

b. *intr.* Of a person: to fire a gun, to shoot; also in weakened sense: to go. Of a gun or similar device: to go off, to fire. Usu. with adv., as *away*, *off*, etc.

1919 *Chambers's Jrnl.* Jan. 43/1 As soon as the artillery opens up, poop off for all you're worth. Let 'em have a hurricane. **1928** Blunden *Undertones of War* ii. 22 A field battery glaring brutally out would 'poop off'. **1930** R. Pertwee *Pursuit* 59, I arrived about eight last night and the guns were pooping away like mad. **1931** N. Coward *Post Mortem* i. 13 If it only stays quiet the way it has the last three nights, and that machine-gun from the sunken road doesn't start pooping at us—we'll get through it in a few hours. **1942** T. Rattigan *Flare Path* i. 112 What in hell was the idea of pooping off the Station like that? They told you this morning something still might come through. **1945** *Tee Emm* (Air Ministry) V. 40 It will not..poop off automatically. **1956** 'Taffrail' *Arctic Convoy* xxiii. 237 See to it you don't open up on anything unless you've a damn good chance of hitting. No wild pooping off at targets out of range—understand? **1961** *Encounter* June 21/1 Take getting up in the morning. 'I arise,' he says..'and poop along..to the end of the passage..to get in the milk and the papers.'

poop, *v.*³ Add: **a.** (Later examples.) Also *transf.*

1916 'Taffrail' *Pincher Martin* xi. 210 There is a grave risk of the craft being pooped by a heavy sea. **1955** *Times* 3 May 5/2 The worst seas they encountered in the whole great voyage, however, were between the Start and Portland Bill. They were pooped. **1972** *Daily Tel.* 22 Jan. 11/4 Returning home via a less dizzy gradient (it is only 1-in-4), we [*sc.* the writer and his dog] faced the same sort of spate that had tried to poop us while we were descending.

poop (pūp), *v.*⁴ *colloq.* (orig. *U.S.*). [Origin unknown.] **a.** *intr.* To break down, 'conk' out. **b.** *trans.* To tire, to exhaust. So **pooped** *ppl. a.*, exhausted, worn out. Freq. with adv., esp. *out.*

1931 *Technol. Rev.* Nov. 65/2 If his engine *poops* or *konks*, he will be *forced down.* **1932** *Amer. Speech* VII. 335 *Pooped; all pooped,* tired out; exhausted. **1934** J. T. Farrell *Young Manhood* xii. 187 He was tired and pooped. *Ibid.* xxii. 377 Studs took a large rocker, and carried it slowly downstairs... When he set it down in the alley, he was breathless, and all pooped out. **1938** 'E. Queen' *Four of Hearts* (1939) iv. 57 He ain't had a drink in five days. That would poop up any guy. **1944** E. B. White *Let.* 15 May (1976) 253 This would be a very bad time to pull our exhaustion on our readers, a lot of whom are pretty well pooped out themselves for one reason or another. **1949** R. Chandler *Little Sister* xxx. 222 'Tired?' he asked. 'Pooped.' **1955** M. Dickens *Winds of Heaven* iv. 93 He'd better be..or he'll find his mother-in-law in the hospital with him. You've really pooped yourself, mother. **1957** D. Karp *Leave me Alone* xviii. 274, I don't think he understood me. The poor old guy is pooped out. **1959** N. Mailer *Advts. for Myself* (1961) 45 He remembered the old man sitting on the porch..all pooped out after work. **1960** *Sunday Express* 24 July 4/2 Bringing up eight kids..really has me pooped. **1966** *New Scientist* 22 Sept. 658/1 Lt Cdr Richard Gordon's space walk was cut short because..'he was blinded by sweat and felt pooped'. **1967** *Time* 2 June 33 Paley Park offers pooped passers-by a respite at little white tables and chairs in a setting of geraniums, honey locust trees, and a 20-ft. waterfall. **1971** B. Malamud *Tenants* 7 If it [*sc.* the heating system] pooped out, and it pooped often—the furnace had celebrated its fiftieth birthday—you called the complaint number of Rent and Housing Maintenance. *Ibid.* 183 His electric heater has pooped out and is being repaired. **1977** *Time* 18 Apr. 64/3 Pheidippides..was so pooped by his performance that he staggered into Athens.

poor, *a.* (*sb.*) Add: **1. e.** Phr. *poor but honest.*

1748 Smollett *R. Random* I. xviii. 150, I am a poor, but honest cobler's son. **1824** Knapp & Baldwin *Newgate Calendar* I. 149/1 John Hawkins was born of poor but honest parents. **1869** 'Mark Twain' *Innoc. Abr.* xxi. 211 'He was the son of——' 'Poor but honest parents—that is all right—never mind the particulars—go on with the legend.' **1922** W. J. Locke *Tale of Triona* viii. 90, I was born—I shan't tell you the year—of poor but honest parents. **1939** A. Thirkell *Before Lunch* v. 126 'Do you mean to say you ride one of those things.' Daphne said she was poor but honest, and why not. **1972** C. Weston *Poor, Poor Ophelia* (1973) iii. 18 'So he's a slave, too,' she commented. 'Right on for Poor-But-Honest headed for the top.'

3. a. (U.S. examples.)

1778 *Maryland Jrnl.* 10 Feb. 4/2 [The sheep] are very poor, and appear to have been out all winter. **1878** J. H. Beadle *Western Wilds* xvii. 276 They get poor as snakes on such food; but it does keep body and soul together for awhile.

5. a. (Examples in phr. *poor-quality* used *attrib.*)

1892 [see *ignorant *a.* 1 b]. **1948** C. L. B. Hubbard *Dogs in Brit.* 234 The English Setter appears to be in danger of deteriorating into a very pretty but poor-quality worker. **1960** *Farmer & Stockbreeder* 9 Feb. 57/3 When I was a boy we used to chaff poor-quality hay and mix it with molasses. **1966** G. Greene *Comedians* I. i. 23 Cynicism is cheap..it's built into all poor-quality goods.

e. Used with *little* in depreciatory (and freq. ironical) senses, esp. in the phrases *poor little guy,* the ordinary individual, the 'man in the street'; *poor little me* (see *little *a.* 13); *poor little rich boy, girl,* used (sometimes ironically) of a person whose wealth has not brought happiness.

1925 N. Coward *Poor Little Rich Girl* (song) 3 Poor little rich girl, You're a bewitched girl, Better beware! **1934** 'G. Orwell' *Burmese Days* v. 91 Unmanly whinings; poor-little-rich-girl stuff. **1940** Graves & Hodge *Long Week-End* xvii. 300 Spender wrote poor-little-rich-boy poems, full of genuine pity for the exploited poor, and for himself. **1958** [see *mass *sb.*² 4 a]. **1961** *Guardian* 28 Apr. 30/6 A disturbing flavour of the poor little rich boy, of the attitude which claims privilege for me just because I am me. **1967** *Boston Sunday Herald* 26 Mar. I. 9/7 Only the poor little guy is subject to the zoning code. **1973** *Times* 23 Mar. 17/6 A comedy-weepie about a poor little rich girl. **1974** J. Mann *Sticking Place* ii. 37 There was still something pathetic about her..a poor little rich girl. **1977** *Daily Tel.* 4 Mar. 3/5 A Conservative M.P.'s daughter on a heroin charge was 'really just a poor little rich girl..who has had an unhappy life' a magistrate said yesterday.

f. *to take a poor view,* to have a low opinion (*of* something); to regard unfavourably.

1943 Hunt & Pringle *Service Slang* 52 If you do not agree with a statement or with your C.O.'s ruling..or, in fact, with the world in general, you take a poor view. **1944** 'N. Shute' *Pastoral* i. 4 The Wing Commander had taken a poor view of that. **1946** E. Linklater *Private Angelo* x. 115 The Germans are about to do something that we take a poor view of, and I'm going to see if I can put a stop to it. *a* **1966** 'M. na Gopaleen' *Best of Myles* (1968) 41 The brother took a very poor view and said she'd be a sorry woman.

7. a. (Further examples.) Freq. with a preceding epithet, as *the aged poor, the deserving poor, the good poor, the respectable poor, the sick poor, the undeserving poor.* Also, *the very poor.*

c **1658** in F. J. Furnivall *Harrison's Descr. Eng.* (1908) IV. 207 Cures Colledge..with maintenance for 16. aged poore of the parish. **1823** E. Weeton *Let.* 16 Apr. in *Jrnl. of Governess* (1969) II. 217 Going about..to visit the sick poor as a Member of the Benevolent Society. **1845** E. Smith *Jrnl.* 28 Oct. (1980) 81 Sick poor, destitute poor, idle, prejudiced poor, oppress me. **1852** Dickens *Bleak Ho.* (1853) vi. 48 It is said that the children of the very poor are not brought up, but dragged up. **1907** G. B. Shaw *Major Barbara* Pref. 154 'The respectable poor', and such phrases are as intolerable and as immoral as 'drunken but amiable' [etc.]. **1909** W. J. Locke *Septimus* i. 6 Cousin Jane held distinct views on the cut of under-clothes for the deserving poor. **1910** E. M. Forster *Howards End* vi. 53 We are not concerned with the very poor. They are unthinkable and only to be approached by the statistician or the poet. **1928** A. M. M. Douton *Bk. with Seven Seals* i. 14 In those days pews were only for those who could pay for them, and free benches..were occupied by the respectable poor. **1937** The sick poor [see *hospitalization]. **1972** *Listener* 9 Mar. 317/1 The Tolpuddle Martyrs..were..the good poor—and little enough they got by it. **1972** J. Mann *Mrs. Knox's Profession* xiii. 102 The man was obviously one of the old-fashioned 'good poor'. **1973** *Guardian* 21 Mar. 10/4, I have no sympathy at all with the kind of people who..do not believe in private property. There is a difference between the undeserving poor and the deserving. *Ibid.* 18 May 16/2 Many of those who want to be owner-occupiers could properly be described as the deserving poor. **1974** *Times* 11 Apr. 20 (*heading*) How can we decide who are the deserving poor? **1977** P. Laslett *Family Life Earlier Generations* iv. 171 During the next 2 years of life, ages 4 and 5, infants remain very dependent, and even amongst the very poor in pre-industrial society were extremely unlikely to be sent out of the home. **1979** P. Theroux *Old Patagonian Express* xv. 220 On the higher harder-to-reach slopes..were the huts of the very poor.

8. poor boy (sandwich) *Southern U.S.*, a large sandwich containing a wide variety of simple but substantial ingredients; **poor do** *U.S.*, a dish made up of scraps of food; a hash; **poor mouth** *v. trans.* and *intr.*, (*a*) to claim to be poor; to make demands (on someone) alleging poverty; (*b*) to deprecate, make little of (something); so **poor-mouthing** *vbl. sb.*; *to make* (*put on,* etc.) *a poor mouth*; see Mouth *sb.* 3 m in Dict. and Suppl.; *to talk poor-mouth* (U.S.), to plead poverty; **poor relation** (earlier and later examples; also *fig.* and *attrib.*).

1952 *New Orleans Item* 28 Feb. 17/5 'Way back yonder when a poorboy sandwich was just that—namely, a five-cent filling of bread, meat and mixed pickles for a poor boy. **1954** *Newsweek* 15 Mar. 99 In the South, a poor boy is a frankfurter in a long bun. **1962** E. Wason *Cooks, Gluttons & Gourmets* 271 Eventually they became known ..as 'poor boy' sandwiches, as they are called in New Orleans to this day. **1968** *Amer. Speech* 1967 XLII. 286 A term [for sandwich] which is used primarily in the South is *poor boy*... The usual interpretation of this term is that those who eat the sandwich are in the lower social and economic classes. **1976** *National Observer* (U.S.) 6 Nov., Exploring Greenwich Village, I found Poor Boys, salami and cheese and chili peppers on great hunks of Italian bread. **1909** *Pioneer Days in Southwest 1850–1879* 253 When we had hogmeat we would fry a few pieces, take the grease and crumble corn bread in it, putting in water and salt, and we had a pot of soup called 'poor doo'. **1913** H. Kephart *Our Southern Highlanders* 292 The old Germans taught their Scotch and English neighbors the merits of scrapple, but here it is known as poor-do. **1965** *Lebende Sprachen* X. 37/1, I am intrigued..by the abundance of 'poor' edibles which we have in the States...*poor-do* is scrapple, etc. **1967** Webster Add., Poor mouth v. **1968** *New Yorker* 21 Sept. 169 [Eugene] McCarthy's advertising campaign, despite the McCarthy camp's constant poor-mouthing on the subject, wasn't exactly modest. **1970** *Globe & Mail* (Toronto) 26 Sept. 9/1 Six months ago, it was sacrilegious to poormouth the fight against air pollution. It was akin to being against motherhood. **1972** T. Ardies *This Suitcase* xvi. 176 What prompted the Professor to start poor mouthing me? **1972** *Time* 17 Apr. 25/1 Some democrats..are already poor-mouthing his victory. **1976** *Times Lit. Suppl.* 26 Mar. 339/2 The latter [book] came to be poormouthed by its author as 'a literary exercise'. **1941** in H. Wentworth *Amer. Dial. Dict.* (1944) 469/1 College professors are supposed to talk po' mouth. **1961** *Newsweek* 14 Aug. 15/1 Because they are politicians, they like to talk as poor-mouth as the lowliest voter. **1965** *N.Y. Times* 29 July 16 It is hard to talk poor mouth just after the papers have written of your daughter's coming-out party for 2,000 guests. **1978** R. Thomas *Chinaman's Chance* xv. 168 My teeth hurt whenever you start talking poormouth. **1968** *Guardian* 28 Jan. 16/8 Poor-mouthing at home feeds the doubts of foreigners abroad..and gloomy prognostications from abroad in turn further depress the spirits of the British. **1969** 'R. Macdonald' *Goodbye Look* xxviii. 163 She became a bit of a miser... Her poor-mouthing actually had me convinced. But of course she'd been quite wealthy all along. **1720** Defoe *Capt. Singleton* 338 Seeing..he had some poor Relations in England..he would write to know..what Condition they were in. **1748** Smollett *R. Random* I. i. 1 My father..fell in love with a poor relation..whom he privately espoused. **1906** J. M. Synge *Lett. to Molly* (1971) 13, I dont like hanging about their house as a poor relation. **1962** *Rep. Comm. Broadcasting 1960* 26 in *Parl. Papers 1961–2* (Cmnd. 1753) IX. 259 The suggestion or fear that sound radio was becoming the 'poor relation' of broadcasting. **1970** J. Earl *Tuners & Amplifiers* ii. 36 Most attention..is usually focused on to the f.m. department where the quality potential truly exists, the a.m. department of a composite model then being very much a 'poor relation'. **1972** *Guardian* 14 Jan. 11/1 In many cases servicing and spare parts were the poor relations subsidised by sales. **1977** D. Francis *Risk* viii. 100 Novice hurdles were customarily first or last..the poor-relation races for the mediocre majority. **1978** J. Symons *Blackheath Poisonings* I. 28 He resented..the mother who had inconsiderately died and left him a poor relation.

9. c. *poor-ass* (*U.S.*), *poor-looking* (examples).

1957 J. Kerouac *On Road* (1958) 113 Find out just what he's poor-ass pondering about this year's turnip greens. **1970** R. D. Abrahams *Positively Black* iii. 72 Colored man went to the store and bought him one of them poor-ass damned roosters. **1973** E. Bullins *Theme is Blackness* 163 I'm only a weak little old pore/ass black woman. **1799** Malthus *Diary* 11 July (1966) 139 Saw some poor-looking houses. **1847** E. Smith *Jrnl.* 13 Jan. (1980) 116 Poor looking house with three rooms.

10. poor-basket, a basket containing material from which clothes for the poor could be made; **poor-farm** (examples); **poor-work,** work done to provide clothes etc. for the poor.

1814 Jane Austen *Mansf. Park* I. vii. 147 If you have no work of your own, I can supply you from the poor-basket. **1852** J. W. Gunnison *Hist. Mormons* 145 A Poor Farm of forty acres is in the centre, controlled by the bishops. **1895** A. Brown *Meadow-Grass* 168 The latter had actually taken to her bed..announcing that 'she'd rather go to the poor-farm and done with it than resk her life there another night'. **1949** *Chicago Tribune* 2 Dec. 20/7 It used to be a disgrace to go to the 'poor farm' and be cared for by the rest of society. **1961** N. Lofts *House at Old Vine* vi. vi. 380 I've thought about what I owed you. .. You'd have fared better at the Poor Farm! **1854** C. M. Yonge *Castle Builders* v. 69 Each good lady had a great basket full of poor-work. **1876** *Monthly Packet* Feb. App. 5 The Sisters at Kilburn are glad to have 'poor work' done for them, and..will provide the material.

poor-box. (Earlier example of the form *poor-box.*)

1738 Pope *First Epistle of First Bk. of Horace Imitated* 15 The rest, some farm the Poor-box, some the Pews.

poor-cod (pūə.ɪ,kǫd). [f. Poor *a.* 5 + Cod *sb.*³] A small marine fish, *Trisopterus minutus,* belonging to the cod family Gadidæ, and found in coastal waters of north-western Europe; = Power *sb.*²

[**1828** J. Fleming *Hist. Brit. Animals* 191 Morhua. Cod... *M. minuta.* Poor.—Nine punctures on each side of the jaws and gill-covers.] **1836** [see Power *sb.*²]. **1925** J. T. Jenkins *Fishes Brit. Isles* 149 The Poor Cod ranges from Trondhjem to the Mediterranean. **1959** A. Hardy *Open Sea* II. xi. 227 The poor-cod..is the smallest of all our gadoid fish, rarely exceeding 8 inches in length. **1969** A. Wheeler *Fishes Brit. Isles & N.-W. Europe* 272/1 The poor-cod is caught mainly in trawls.

poor man. Add: **1.** Example in *attrib.* use.

1831 J. Banim *Smuggler* I. xi. 127 What have you to do with..my poor-man sneers at a viscount?

3*. Also **poorman.** = *poorman('s orange* (see sense 4 a below).

1912 *Jrnl. Dept. Agric. N.Z.* IV. 141 He has several varieties all doing well, amongst them Paramatta, Poor Man, Navel. **1956** F. T. Bowman *Citrus-Growing in Austral.* ii. 20 Poorman was mentioned in Shepherd's catalogue (1851) as having been recently introduced from Shanghai by a Captain Simpson.

4. a. poor man's diggings *U.S., Austral.,* and *N.Z.* (see quot. 1941); **poorman('s orange,** a variety of grapefruit, *Citrus paradisi,* once cultivated in New Zealand; **poor man's orchid,** an annual or biennial plant belonging to the genus *Schizanthus* of the family Solanaceæ, native to Chile and bearing flowers thought to resemble orchids; **poor man's sauce** (further example); **poor man's torment** *U.S.* (see quot.).

1875 *Chicago Tribune* 14 Oct. 7/3 If it did pay, it would be what is called poor man's diggings, for it was no place where capital could be successfully employed. **1876** R. I. Dodge *Black Hills* 109 It has passed into a proverb that 'placer' mining is the poor man's diggings, while 'quartz' mining is only for the rich. **1941** Baker *Dict. Austral. Slang* 56 *Poor man's diggings,* alluvial gold deposits, i.e., gold which a poor man can work, contrasting with reef-gold which requires capital to develop. **1884** G. E. Alderton *Treat. & Handbk. Orange-Culture in Auckland* 66 The Poor Man's Orange is only good for preserving. **1929** *Jrnl. N.Z. Inst. Hort.* I. 65 The Poorman Orange is really a Pomelo. **1949** R. Park (*title*) Poor man's orange. **1966** *Encycl. N.Z.* I. 758/2 The main kinds of citrus grown commercially in New Zealand include..so-called New Zealand grapefruit ('Poorman' orange, selected strains). **1959** *Listener* 20 Aug. 298/3 Now is the time to sow schizanthus—the 'poor man's orchid'—for next May. **1976** *Hortus Third* (L. H. Bailey Hortorium) 1018/1 Schizanthus... Butterfly Flower, Poorman's orchid. **1723** J. Nott *Cook's & Confectioner's Dict.* sig. Mm3 Poor Man's Sauce, *i.e.* a Shalot cut small, white Pepper, Vinegar, and Oil. **1899** W. Stevens *Jrnl.* 17 July in *Lett.* (1967) 28 Snap-dragon, or as it is vulgarly known: the weed—'poor man's torment' is a close-knit, yellow, tumbled sort of thing.

b. Now commonly used *fig.* in Combs. to denote a cheaper, usu. simpler or inferior version or imitation of something, or a less satisfactory substitute for something or someone.

1854 H. Melville in *Harper's Mag.* June 95/2 A cup of cold rain water..is called by housewives a 'Poor Man's Egg'. *Ibid.* 97/1 'It is only rice, milk, and salt boiled together.' 'Ah, what they call "Poor Man's Pudding", I suppose you mean.' **1891** *Tit-Bits* 8 Aug. 277/2 There are thousands of costers who earn a livelihood by the sale of ..mussels, which are regarded as the poor man's oyster. **1906** *Dialect Notes* III. 151 *Poor man's pudding*,..cottage pudding. **1924** R. Lardner in *Cosmopolitan* July 60/2 Another nickname for the town [*sc.* St. Petersburg, Florida, U.S.A.] is the Poor Man's Palm Beach. **1949** *Amer. Speech* XXIV. 94 The cheapness and abundance of rabbit pelts..have made them the 'poor man's mink'. **1951** M. McLuhan *Mech. Bride* (1967) 63/1 Huck Finn, the poor man's Thoreau, is to be read there, too. **1959** *Observer* 9 Aug. 11/2 I.T.V.'s *This Week* has recently become not much better than a very poor man's 'Panorama'. **1962** A. Huxley *Island* v. 46 Chemical and biological weapons—Colonel Dipa calls them the poor man's H-bombs. **1963** *Guardian* 8 Feb. 9/3 The long, many-scened story..is superficially like a poor man's 'Peer Gynt'. **1963** 'R. Erskine' *Passion Flowers in Italy* iv. 42 The porter was heavy-set, with burning Latin eyes: a kind of poor man's Marlon Brando. **1971** *Jrnl. Chem. Documentation* X. 249/1 A general-purpose text-editing system can be a valuable 'poor man's' information-handling tool. **1973** *Times* 21 Apr. 12/1 'Good King Henry' or 'Poor Man's Spinage' must have been tried out for centuries before being used traditionally and regularly, in spring 'messes'.

poorshouse (pūᵊ·ɹzhaus). Also **poors house, poor's house.** Mainly *Sc.* var. of Poorhouse.

1745 *Sessions Papers* (Donaldson v. Home) 3 July 2 Samuel Neilson, late Deacon of the Masons, Undertaker for building of the Poors House. **1756** *Bristol* (Virginia) *Vestry Bk.* (1898) 164 Ordered that Stephen Dewey.. agree in settleing the Terms of the Poors House. **1820** J. Flint *Lett. from Amer.* (1822) 192 Some paupers in a poor's house at Cincinnati refused to carry water for their own use. **1870** J. Nicholson *The Puir's-Hoose Laddie* in *Idylls* 45, I was glad to become a wee Puir's-hoose laddie. **1899** E. F. Heddle *Marget* ii. 10 She..is to gang to the sale; but she's no' to gang to the puirs-hoose. **1907** [see Poor *a.* 7 d]. **1923** T. Johnston *Hist. Working Classes in Scotl.* 35 There were 30 hospitals or poorshouses from Turriff to the Lowlands.

poort. Add to def.: *esp.* one cut by a stream or river. (Earlier and later examples.)

1796 tr. *F. Le Vaillant's New Trav. Afr.* II. 194 We issued from the mountains through a sort of passage, or defile, which is called the *Poort.* **1801** J. Barrow *Acct. Trav. S. Afr.* I. ii. 109 The Poort may be considered as the entrance into Camdeboo. **1932** C. Fuller *Louis Trigardt's Trek* vi. 68 Once through the poort, the junction of the spruit with the river is but a few hundred yards off. **1949** L. G. Green *In Land of Afternoon* i. 21 A poort is different from a pass, for it is a passage through the mountains along the bed of a stream.

pooter (pū·təɹ), *v.* [Etym. unknown.] *intr.* To depart in a hurry; to hasten away. Also with *off.*

1907 *Dialect Notes* III. 196 *Pooter*,..to depart speedily. 'I told him to git, and he just *pooter*, I can tell you.' **1966** *Punch* 6 July 32/3 The ex-bookseller, his fortune depleted, is left on the last page pootering off to his ex-girl-friend.

Pooterish (pū·tərɪʃ), *a.* [f. the name *Pooter* (see below) + -ish¹.] Resembling, characteristic of, or associated with Charles Pooter, an assistant in a mercantile firm, whose mundane domestic, social, and business troubles are the subject of the fictional *Diary of a Nobody* by George and Weedon Grossmith (1892).

1966 *New Statesman* 11 Mar. 349/3 Take a Pooterish Little Man with sexual and cultural ambitions outside his class, [etc.]. **1976** *Times Lit. Suppl.* 31 Dec. 1626/2 So many square miles of vapid and banal and Pooterish suburb. **1977** *Times* 14 May 10/4 George VI's deadpan account of Pooterish bishops blundering through his coronation. **1978** *Times Lit. Suppl.* 24 Feb. 229/3 The Pooterish touch in 'inexpensive' betrays a lack of awareness.

pooty (pū·ti), *a.* (*sb.*) Affected or childish var. Pretty *a.* (*sb.*)

1825 [see *cross lots *advb. phr.*]. **1848** J. R. Lowell *The Courtin'* in *Biglow Papers* 1st Ser. 10 The wannut logs shot sparkles out Towards the pootiest, bless her! **1849** C. Brontë *Shirley* II. iv. 105 Purchase in his stead some sweetly pooty pug or poodle. **1850** Thackeray *Pendennis* II. xv. 147 She's a little money too..a pooty little bit of money. *a* **1854** [see *country jake* s.v. *country 16]. **1906** Galsworthy *Man of Property* ii. iii. 149 'You'll have room here,' he said, 'for six or seven hundred dozen—a very pooty little cellar!' **1932** Auden *Orators* iii. 104 That piss-proud prophet, that pooty redeemer. **1961** Partridge *Dict. Slang* Suppl. 1229/1 Pooty is a favourite mid-Victorian adjective meaning 'pretty'—of which, via *purty*, it is a perversion. **1980** G. Nelson *Charity's Child* iii. 45 Do 'e remember..the pooty shells I collected?

poove: see *poof *sb.*¹

poovey, poovy, varr. *poofy *a.*

pop, *sb.*¹ Add: **1. c.** In Baseball: a ball hit high into the air but close to the batter, thus providing an easy catch. Usu. *attrib.*, as *pop fly* [Fly *sb.*² 2 b], etc. *N. Amer.*

1935 J. T. Farrell *Judgment Day* viii. 185 A line single was driven to left, the pitcher picked a pop out of the air. **1945** *Sun* (Baltimore) 12 Mar. 10-0/5 A pamphlet which knocked the Doubleday legend higher than one of Babe Ruth's pop fouls. **1961** *Rocky Mountain News* (Denver, Colorado) 2 May 50 The White Sox had taken a 5–4 lead in the top of the sixth on a pair of pop fly hits. **1969** *Sci. Amer.* Jan. 49/1 The outfielder is watching..a pop fly to the infield. **1972** *N.Y. Times* 4 June v. 2/5 Gentry retired the great man on a pop foul to Mays. **1975** *New Yorker* 14 Apr. 98/2 Jay Kleven, a young non-roster catcher, hit two pop flies to center. **1978** *Verbatim* Feb. 2/2 One of my favorites is the phrase for a towering pop fly that shoots straight up to the sky and comes down in the same area, usually caught by the catcher. The announcer says, 'He could have hit that ball in a silo.'

d. An injection of a narcotic drug. *slang.*

1935 A. J. Pollock *Underworld Speaks* 118/1 *Take a pop*, to take an injection of morphine. **1953** W. Burroughs *Junkie* Gloss. 14 *Pop, bang, shot, fix*... Injection of junk. **1956** R. Thorp *Viper* vi. 92 'Care for a pop now and again?' This was a kick I hadn't made, I told him. **1970** N. Marsh *When in Rome* v. 126 I'm not hooked. Just the odd pop. Only a fun thing.

2. b. *on the pop of*, about to, on the point of. *rare.*

1922 Joyce *Ulysses* 66, I was on the pop of writing Blazes Boylan's.

c. A turn (at doing something); an attempt; a 'go'.

1868 'Mark Twain' *Let.* 20 Nov. (1917) I. ix. 156, I am simply lecturing for societies, at $100 a pop. **1904** W. N. Harben *Georgians* 2 Ef I don't whack it to you this pop, old hoss, I'll eat my hat. **1916** 'Taffrail' *Pincher Martin* xv. 271 'Why doesn't we 'ave a pop at 'er?' ''Ave a pop at 'er! She's twenty mile orf, if she's a hinch, an' yer knows as well as I does that none o' our ships 'ere 'as got hanti-haircraft guns wot'll 'it 'er at that range.' **1928** Wodehouse *Money for Nothing* ii. 35 He decided to have a pop at it. **1946** F. Sargeson *That Summer* 66, I thought no, the going's good, I'll give it one more pop. **1954** Wodehouse *Jeeves & Feudal Spirit* i. 12 But why didn't Florence tell Percy to go and have a pop at Stilton Cheesewright? **1971** *Southerly* XXXI. 136 But I couldn't keep that game up for too long; at five cents a pop you can't afford to waste too many. **1976** R. Barnard *Little Local Murder* x. 133, I don't suppose he makes much more than seventy-five pee a pop for them.

d. The rapid opening of a pop-valve.

1901 M. M. Kirkman *Locomotive Appliances* 122 Should the valve close with too much drop of boiler pressure, move the screw-ring (*C*) to the left..until sufficient change has been accomplished. To increase the pop, move ring (*C*) to the right. **1905** C. S. Lake *World's Locomotives* vi. 112 The screw-down valve is set so that the limit of 'pop' action is 2 lbs. per sq.in. above the nominal boiler pressure, and the valves close when that pressure has been reduced to 2 lbs. per sq.in. less than the nominal boiler pressure. **1951** E. A. Steel *Greenly's Model Steam Locomotives* (rev. ed.) xiii. 234 A 'pop' action (an accelerated discharge of the valve) can be obtained by making the head of the valve nearly fit a cylindrical recess in the seating.

5. (Later examples.)

1926 *Scribner's Mag.* Aug. 116/2 Senior officers may for dignity's sake get off with light treatment and a fine of cigars or pop (it was beer in the good old days). **1931** W. S. Maugham in *Hearst's International* Oct. 51/2 A bottle of pop tonight, my pet, and a slap-up dinner. **1969** L. Kennedy *Very Lovely People* ii. 106 The waiter said, 'All I got is bottled pop. Take your choice.' **1976** A. Hill *Summer's End* i. 18 We sat in the stern drinking the pop, trying to count the bubbles as they rose behind our noses.

pop, *sb.*⁴ (Later examples.)

1898 *Westm. Gaz.* 19 Dec. 10/2 A Dohnanyi 'Pop'. In every respect Mr Ernest von Dohnanyi was the hero of Saturday's Popular Concert at St James's Hall. **1934** M. H. Weseen *Dict. Amer. Slang* 381 Pop..a popular concert.

pop (pǫp), *sb.*⁶ *colloq.* (chiefly *U.S.*). **a.** Abbreviation of Poppa.

1838 in *Southwestern Hist. Q.* (1926) XXX. 147 Sent my packet..to pop in the post office at N Orleans. **1840** *Knickerbocker* XVI. 207 'Pop!' screamed a white-headed urchin from the house, 'Mam says supper's ready.' **1904** H. R. Martin *Tillie* iii. 33 Are you feelin' too mean to go help pop? **1911** [see *mom]. **1948** *Denison* (Texas) *Herald* 1 July 1/3 Butch..was vacationing with his pop at the popular National Park Service Lake Texoma resort. **1958** H. E. Bates *Darling Buds of May* i. 11 'Larkin, that's me,' Pop said... 'Larkin by name, Larkin by nature.' *Ibid.* ii. 39 'We're in the library,' Ma said. 'Pop, look at the library.' **1962**, etc. [see *mom]. **1973** P. Dickinson *Gift* v. 77 'Oh yes, Pop, *please*,' said Sonia. **1979** R. Rendell *Make Death love Me* i. 12 His father-in-law came in... Alan and Pam called him Pop, and Christopher and Jillian called him Grandpop.

b. Hence in extended use, an elderly man.

1844 in *Amer. Speech* (1965) XL. 131 And I'll go down to ole birginy, And marry pop Miller's sister. **1889** *Sporting Life* (Philadelphia) 29 May 2/6 'Pop' Chadwick is among those who are opposed to the wire. **1943** K. Tennant *Ride on Stranger* (1968) vii. 78 You've just told us, pop,..that if the cops catch up on you, you'll be lining a cell. **1947** *Daily Oklahoman* (Oklahoma City) 28 Dec. 5/8 'Pop', as he is known in this area, will use the 'fancy' cane to help guide his sightless way during his strolls along Shamrock streets. **1980** P. Gosling *Zero Trap* iii. 29 'Can somebody give me a hand with Pop, here?' He still wants to stay sleepies for a while.

pop (pǫp), *sb.*⁷ Abbrev. of Poppycock.

1890 Kipling *Barrack-Room Ballads* (1892) 11 All we ever got from such as they Was pop to what the Fuzzy made us swaller. **1924** Galsworthy *White Monkey* ii. iv. 151 Nobody pitied her; why, then, should she pity them? Besides, pity was 'pop', as Amabel would say.

pop (pǫp), *a.* (*sb.*⁸) *colloq.* [Abbrev. of Popular *a.* (*sb.*): cf. Pop *sb.*⁴] **1. a.** Designating music (esp. song) having or regarded as having a wide popular appeal (see *popular *a.* (*sb.*) 6 b). Freq. *absol.* as *sb.*, a popular song or piece of music; popular music collectively.

Quot. 1862 is an isolated nonce-use influenced by and alluding to Pop *sb.*⁴

1862 Geo. Eliot *Let.* 26 Nov. (1956) IV. 67 There is too much 'Pop' for the thorough enjoyment of the chamber music. **1926** *Amer. Mercury* Dec. 465/1 She coos a pop song. **1935** *Hot News* Aug. 19/1 Turn the record over and you have another winner—'Add a Little Wiggle'—a masterpiece made out of a song-and-dance 'pop'. **1945** S. Hughes in C. Madge *Pilot Papers* 78 Cole Porter's 'Begin the Beguine'..has twice the regulation number of bars that a good 'pop' should have. **1947** A. J. McCarthy *Jazzbook 1947* 119 Jelly would play one of his new 'pop' songs, watching..for its effect. **1954** *Unicorn Bk. 1953* 320/1 A magazine..each December publishes a list of the year's top pop music and musicians. *Ibid.* (*heading*) Top pop tunes. **1954** *Billboard* 13 Nov. 38 It is interesting to note that the preponderance of local over national sponsorship of deejay programs varies according to the program category, with the weight of local sponsorship most evident in rhythm & blues then country & western and finally pop. **1957** D. Hague in S. Traill *Concerning Jazz* 129 The veteran Lizzie Miles from New Orleans has evoked nostalgia with her selections of blues and early 'pops'. **1959** J. Braine *Vodi* iv. 63 At this time there'd be some pop tunes... They could sometimes induce a vapid cheerfulness. **1959** D. Cooke *Lang. Mus.* ii. 62 The Irving Berlin tune..is a rare example of minor 'pop' music. **1962** D. Lessing *Golden Notebk.* i. 102, I remember the sharp feeling of dislocation it gave me to hear the pop-song in London, after Willi's sad nostalgic humming of what he told us was 'A song we used to sing when I was a child'. **1963** *Daily Tel.* 7 Dec. 9/7 A 'pop music' dispute between song writers and concert promoters is to go before the Performing Right Tribunal in London on Monday next. **1967** *Crescendo* Feb. 23/2 A pop that will only last a couple of weeks. **1970** *Observer* 20 Sept. 26/1 In the world of pop, the death of Jimi Hendrix on Friday from a suspected overdose of drugs will seem as if Tchaikovsky or Mozart had also been struck down at only 24. **1973** *Country Life* 13 Dec. 2015/1 Pop-song writers masquerading as composers in the grand manner. **1974** J. Cooper *Women & Super Women* 9 During the holidays they..play pop music too loudly for their parents' liking. **1975** *Gramophone* Jan. 1357/2 Incidentally the 'pop' purchaser may well be disconcerted that the battery and carillon at the end of '1812' are relatively restrained. **1976** H. Nielsen *Brink of Murder* i. 12 An aged spinster..not only refused to sell to Pucci but insulted the dignity of his project by leasing the premises to a group of pop musicians. **1977** *Rolling Stone* 21 Apr. 91/1 He..makes a misguided stab at pop blues in 'Bluesman'.

b. Phr. *top of the pops*, applied to the most popular or the best-selling gramophone record over a given period; also *transf.* and *fig.*, highly successful or popular.

1958 *Punch* 8 Oct. 483/1 'Wagon Train' stays top of the pops in ITV features on every channel. **1964** [see *dolly *a.* c]. **1965** [see *chart *sb.* 3 c]. **1970** J. Porter *Rather Common Sort of Crime* vi. 64 Your little friend Rodney was a dodo, a brontosaurus, last week's top of the pops..but dead, finished, a stale bun. **1978** G. Greene *Human Factor* ii. iii. 84 The top of the pops for any given year came as readily to Davis's memory as a Derby winner.

c. In various special collocations: attributive, as *pop album, ballad, band, concert, disc, fan, festival, group, lyric, number, opera, record, single, star, world*; objective, as *pop-singer, -singing* adj.; similative, as *pop-style(d)* adj.

Quot. 1880 for *pop-concert* is properly in the sense of Pop *sb.*⁴

1949 *Billboard* 8 Oct. 26/2 (*heading*) Pop albums. **1955** L. Feather *Encycl. Jazz* 100 Basie also used a girl singer, usually for the pop ballads. **1964** *Punch* 28 Oct. 658/2 Those sentimental pop-ballads of the 'thirties. **1958** *Amer. Speech* XXXIII. 225 A *mickey* or *Mickey Mouse* band is..the kind of pop band that sounds as if it is playing background for an animated cartoon. **1967** *Listener* 16 Feb. 229/1 Some acoustical engineers in the United States believe that the sound produced by teenage pop bands is actually damaging to human ears. **1880** Geo. Eliot *Jrnl.* in *Lett.* (1956) VII. 342 Went to our first Pop-Concert and heard Norman Neruda, Piatti, etc. **1963** 'D. Shannon' *Death of Busybody* iv. 51, I went to the Hollywood Bowl... It was a pop-concert night, Gershwin. **1973** R. Parkes *Guardians* ii. 49 He imagined continental pop-concerts had something to do with the youth counter-culture. **1957** *Times* 19 Dec. 5/1 The most recent phenomenon in the world of the 'pop disc' has been the astonishing rise of the 'teen-age' singer. **1973** R. Parkes *Guardians* iii. 64 His income as a disc-jockey; his profits from the few pop-discs he cut; and..his chairman's salary. **1960** *Guardian* 13 Apr. 3/3 An out and out 'pop' fan. **1966** *B.B.C. Handbk.* 44 They have to cater for..the 'pop' fan. **1979** S. Smith *Survivor* xvii. 176, I was obviously beyond the age group of the average hippy or pop fan. **1970** *Guardian* 31 July 9/5 Pop festivals..are big business. **1975** *Times* 8 Aug. 1/1 The Government has ordered an urgent review of public policies on pop festivals. **1965** M. Bradbury *Stepping Westward* i. 65 A pop group, called the Haters, were tunelessly celebrating dim proletarian adolescent oestrus. **1967** *Listener* 18 May 644/1 Two of the Rolling Stones 'pop group' are sent for trial on drugs charges. **1977** 'E. Crispin' *Glimpses of Moon* viii. 147 Ten minutes alone inside the tent, with Miss Bale to keep intruders away, and that pop group to cover up any noise. **1960** *Guardian* 22 July 10/2 The committee have found that pop lyrics are drivel and often debasing. **1966** *Vogue* Oct. 177/1 Almost the only simple, open-hearted verse we now have are pop-lyrics. **1945** S. Hughes in C. Madge *Pilot Papers* 76 The term Dance Music is used here to denote..

the playing and singing of 'pop' numbers as opposed to the cult of 'Jazz'. **1958** P. Gammond *Decca Bk. Jazz* ii. 38 The popularity of jangle-piano, and of pop numbers performed in cool ragtime style. **1960** *News Chron.* 31 Mar. 4/4 Pop numbers..can be sung and understood outside the story's context. **1969** N. Cohn *AWopBopaLooBop* (1970) xviii. 172 Townshend has finally written a full-scale pop opera. **1976** *Cumberland News* 3 Dec., 56 11-year-olds..were practising an ambitious production of 'Smike', a pop opera based on the Dickens novel, 'Nicholas Nickleby'. **1950** *Billboard* 7 Oct. II. 27/2 (*heading*) Top pop records of the year. **1961** H. E. Bates *Day of Tortoise* 60 She played pop records such as *What Do You Want If You Don't Want Money?* **1973** L. Cooper *Tea on Sunday* ii. 27 The..strident noise of pop records. **1948** *Billboard* 25 Dec. 38 At press time it was learned that Apollo had re-signed pop singer Mary Small for another year with options. **1955** L. Feather *Encycl. Jazz* 79 The Decca company began to record him..in duets with pop singers. **1958** J. Townsend *Young Devils* 8 The sickly exhortations of 'pop' singers. **1973** J. Wainwright *Pride of Pigs* 30 The pop singer finished his protest song and there was a thin ripple of applause. **1955** L. Feather *Encycl. Jazz* 160 Grotesque distortions..valid more as entertainment than as jazz or pop singing. **1962** *Times* 28 Feb. 5/4 An atmosphere more suggestive of pop-singing..than great artistry. **1949** *Billboard* 8 Oct. 26/1 (*heading*) Best-selling pop singles. **1962** A. Nisbett *Technique Sound Studio* 252 Pop singles contain the same amount as a 10-inch 78, whereas e.p. records contain perhaps double. **1978** *Sunday Times* 29 Jan. 43/1 A record by two Jamaican girls is currently No. 2 in the BBC's top twenty pop singles. **1967** *Listener* 23 Feb. 271/2 We were taken, step by step, through the process of manufacturing a pop star. **1972** J. McClure *Caterpillar Cop* v. 71 She was behaving as if Boetie had become a pop star, rather than a corpse. **1955** L. Feather *Encycl. Jazz* 159/2 Eddie [Heywood], Jr...formed own sextet late '43, made name through pop-style arr. of *Begin the Beguine.* **1963** *Times* 24 May 15/7 The pop-style hymn-settings of John Gardner. **1974** *Publishers Weekly* 26 Aug. 302/2 It's a pop-styled run-through of the big moments, great plays and subway series heroics. **1959** 'F. Newton' *Jazz Scene* i. 22 Jazz has made much of its way as part of the pop world. **1967** M. Drabble *Jerusalem the Golden* vii. 170 She had as resolutely and as puritanically scorned the pop world..as her mother had done before her. **1973** *Melody Maker* 25 Aug. 27 In the pop world, the rule is that musicians are a special breed.

2. *pop art*, art that uses themes drawn from popular culture, *spec.* an art form characterized by the depiction of commonplace subjects using strong colour and imagery, sharp features, and a photographic technique of representation (see also quot. 1967). Also *ellipt.*, as *pop*. Hence *pop artist, -painter; pop-painting* vbl. sb.

1957 *Listener* 26 Sept. 464/1 A sophisticated apologia for subtopia is to call it 'pop art' which the middle-aged are perverse to frustrate. *Ibid.* 470/1 Some people even defend Subtopia as a type of vigorous folk art—or 'pop art'—to be fostered. **1958** *Archit. Rev.* CXXIII. 208/1 Four chairs..would not have been known to the designer of this room had they not been published in the popular magazine *Look*, which gave the *chaise-longue* version the full pop-art treatment. **1962** *Listener* 9 Aug. 217/3 All three of the painters are adherents of the new school of 'pop'. *Ibid.* 30 Aug. 324/1 Certain of the 'pop' painters can apparently be paired off with artists on the other side of the Atlantic. *Ibid.* 324/2 The tendency of 'pop' paintings, Hockney's for instance, to resort to the use of words in order to help out the images is in itself significant. *Ibid.* 27 Dec. 1087/1 The third wave of pop artists use their imagery to differentiate themselves from the regular audience for art. **1964**, etc. [see *op[4]]. **1966** 'H. MacDiarmid' *Company I've Kept* iii. 78 The pop artist does not address any audience, does not represent any point of view; he has staked everything on nothingness. **1967** L. Alloway in L. R. Lippard *Pop Art* 27 The term 'Pop Art' is credited to me, but I don't know precisely when it was first used. (One writer has stated that 'Lawrence Alloway first coined the phrase "Pop Art" in 1954'; this is too early.) Furthermore, what I meant by it then is not what it means now. I used the term, and also 'Pop Culture', to refer to the products of the mass media, not to works of art that draw upon popular culture. In any case, sometime between the winter of 1954–55 and 1957 the phrase acquired currency in conversation, in connection with the shared work and discussion among members of the Independent group. **1968** *New Yorker* 24 Feb. 100 There were about a hundred and fifty paintings on view in the huge Main Hall..and they ranged from Op and Pop to Picasso. **1971** 'A. Burgess' *MF* xiii. 144 There was a big pop-art poster whose crude yellows and blues were an obscenity. **1972** E. Lucie-Smith in Cox & Dyson *20th-Cent. Mind* III. xvi. 470 The first example of Pop is now generally conceded to have been a small collage made by the English painter Richard Hamilton..in 1956. **1976** *New Yorker* 22 Mar. 107/1 Among the Pop artists shown, Claes Oldenburg is by far the most gifted as a draftsman. **1977** *Jrnl. R. Soc. Arts* CXXVI. 47/2 Out of Léger came aspects of Pop: in particular that aspect known as Roy Lichtenstein.

3. Appealing to or expected to appeal to popular taste generally (chiefly in the senses of *popular *a.* (*sb.*) 4a). Also *absol.* as *sb.* Spec. *pop culture*, culture based on popular taste and disseminated widely and usu. on a commercialized basis; hence *pop-cultural* adj. Also, of a technical subject, etc.: popularized, presented in a popular form, as *pop psychology* (hence *pop-psycher, -psychologist*).

1958 *Spectator* 14 Feb. 197/2 The promoters of 'pop' fiction must ruthlessly wipe out any tragedy that remains unique and personal. **1958** *Observer* 23 Mar. 14/3 As a sop to pop, the gallants on the benches at the sides of the stage could be TV personalities. **1958** *Ibid.* 25 May 14/2 His admirable pop science *New Horizon* series. **1959** C. MacInnes *Absolute Beginners* 73 It's my aim..to bring quality culture material to the pop culture masses. **1962** *Observer* 20 May 12/7 Pop archaeology books sell like hot cakes. **1962** *Punch* 12 Sept. 390/2 A highly competent performer on these pop-science occasions. **1963** *Ibid.* 3 July 30/2 Pop religion is the dreariest mixture imaginable. **1963** *Dædalus* Winter 22 Available critiques of pop-cultural depravities (from *Playboy* to the *National Geographic*) and compilations of economic facts about massification..are, to be sure, of some help. **1964** *Punch* 5 Feb. 211/1 An almost naïvely sensational bit of pop-psychology sex. **1966** D. Jenkins *Educated Society* ii. 58 That commercialized 'pop culture' which is a form of anti-culture. **1967** *New Scientist* 25 May 473/1 Expo is dominated by technology, but it is a gay, often pop technology that you meet, technology that is confident enough to laugh at itself. **1968** *Punch* 27 Nov. 753/1 Pop-psychologists are saying that certain trigger phrases used by Enoch Powell expose a subconscious racial prejudice. **1969** *Listener* 17 July 92/2 If Pop means mass media and consumer goods, ads and comics, Coke bottles and plastic, what then can it have to do with Art? **1970** G. Greer *Female Eunuch* 171 The pop revolution..has replaced sentiment with lust. **1970** K. Millett *Sexual Politics* (1971) II. iv. 186 In such cases Freud and his school after him will do all in their power to convince her of the errors of her ways:..by the actual mental policing of 'pop psych'. **1971** *Time* 14 June 16/2 The fact that Ed [Cox] proposed so quickly after Tricia [Nixon] began her new life at the White House might suggest to pop-psychers that he was afraid of losing her. **1972** *Nature* 25 Aug. 471/2 The author has shrugged off.. practically everything that animal ethologists have tried to contribute to our understanding..—dismissing..[Desmond] Morris's books as 'pop ethology'. **1973** J. Wainwright *High-Class Kill* 41 Pop culture: garbage done up in poster-colours and caterwauling to badly played guitars. **1975** *Imperial Oil Rev.* IV. 30/2 How to make work more satisfying or, to use the word of pop sociology, how to 'humanize' it. **1975** *New Yorker* 21 Apr. 111/1 No one has yet piously complained of too much violence in the Ngorongoro Crater or tried to shroud a beehive in pop psychology. **1977** P. Johnson *Enemies of Society* xi. 160 At various levels, too, psychology and sociology have become the pop-science, or folk-science, of the western urban masses. **1977** *Time* 14 Mar. 43/1 Most of the Morgan message is standard to all the pop self-help books that publishers have been churning out ever since Dale Carnegie and Norman Vincent Peale reaped their first millions. **1978** *Encounter* July 96/1 On the debit side.. are the evils of 'development' and the pap of pop culture.

pop, *v.*[1] Add: **2. b.** Delete † and add later examples.

1931 E. O'Neill *Mourning becomes Electra* (1932) 217 Small comes tearing out and down the portico steps, his face chalky white and his eyes popping. **1940** W. Faulkner *Hamlet* I. ii. 37 They looked exactly like two fellows that had done hung themselves in one of these here suicide pacts, with their heads snubbed up together and pointing straight up..and their eyes popping. **1951** M. Kennedy *Lucy Carmichael* II. i. 73 Pray Bess, what was he like? Oh, says Bess, her eyes popping, he's *terrific*! **1961** N. Manero *Cook-Out Barbecue Bk.* 16 You'll have the neighbor's eyes popping as well as their mouths watering! **1979** G. Hammond *Dead Game* xi. 143 He sold the Dickson Round Action [gun] there for a price that made Molly's eyes pop.

3. *to pop corn* (earlier and further examples).

1850 *Quincy* (Illinois) *Whig* 12 Nov. 4/1 One barrel of rice corn will make 32 barrels after popping. **1853** *Harper's Mag.* May 853/1 A little boy sat by the kitchen-fire, A-popping corn in the ashes. **1873** 'S. Coolidge' *What Katy Did* x. 201 'I popped the corn!' cried Philly. **1907** *St. Nicholas* May 614/1 Grandma lives on a farm and we used to have great fun popping corn whenever we went to see her. **1949** *Sat. Even. Post* 21 May 36/1 Last year American farmers grew some 300,000,000 pounds of popcorn. This, when popped, is enough to fill 2,400,000,000 ten-cent bags. **1979** *Sunset* Apr. 129/2 (Advt.), The Popaire hot air popper pops 4 quarts of light, fluffy popcorn in 5 minutes!

5. (Further examples.)

1858 *Punch* 20 Nov. 206 If you will pop on your hats.. I'll take you and your friend out for a drive. **1891** B. Potter *Let.* in J. Mackenzie *Victorian Courtship* (1979) ix. 125, I popped on an old skirt and a mackintosh and trudged through the rain. **1977** B. Pym *Quartet in Autumn* ii. 22 'I should put the bacon in a cooler place if I were you,' said Letty. 'Yes, I'll pop it in one of the filing cabinets.' **1977** K. O'Hara *Ghost of T. Penry* viii. 67 Sit you down and I'll pop the kettle on.

6. a. (Later examples.)

1960 M. Sharp *Something Light* vii. 64, I haven't actually...popped, yet. **1972** *N.Y. Times* 3 Nov. 7/1 (Advt.), Now's the time to pop the question! 20% off diamond engagement rings. **1976** *Daily Mirror* 16 Mar. 9/3 The thought of popping the question to Princess Marie Therese de Bourbon Parma 'has never entered my head,' he added.

b. *intr. to pop off*, to speak hastily, angrily, or wildly; to state one's opinions vociferously; to complain loudly. *U.S. colloq.*

1933 Partridge *Slang To-day & Yesterday* 455 *Pop off, to*, talk wildly, threateningly, argumentatively. C20. **1934** M. H. Weseen *Dict. Amer. Slang* 381 *Pop off*, to lose one's temper; to give vent to anger. **1943** *Sun* (Baltimore) 20 Sept. 16/8 The dealer 'popped off without knowing what he was talking about'. **1951** R. S. Prather *Bodies in Bedlam* vi. 47, I popped off to Brane last night, but I didn't kill him. **1970** *Daily Tel.* 7 Feb. 16/2 Company chairmen have been popping-off about the iniquities of selective employment tax for four years. **1977** *Time* 7 Mar. 40/3 Most Plains residents dismissed Billy's charge. 'He was just poppin' off,' said one woman. **1977** J. Wambaugh *Black Marble* (1978) x. 241 He remembered what happened to him today in a phone booth when he popped off, so he bit his lip and kept quiet.

8. (Further examples with *in, out, up*). Also const. *off, over.* Also (*Austral. colloq.*) phr. *how are you popping (up)?*: how are you getting on?

1860 F. Nightingale *Notes on Nursing* iv. 29 Many of the accidents which happen from feeble patients tumbling down stairs..happen..from the nurse popping out of a door. **1904** E. Nesbit *Phoenix & Carpet* xii. 224 If you'll excuse me, I'll just pop out and see what I can do. **1913** C. Mackenzie *Sinister St.* I. I. iv. 54 Nurse..had acquired a habit..of popping out of the back-door on secret errands. **1919** Wodehouse *Damsel in Distress* xv. 186 'And now you get along,' said the man. 'You pop off.' **1934** C. Lambert *Music Ho!* III. 156 He [*sc.* Glinka] was more than a gifted amateur who happened to pop up at the right time. **1942** *Tee Emm* (Air Ministry) II. 88 A cunning safety switch..pops up when there is a short. **1960** *Guardian* 26 Feb. 5/4 Mrs Harris popped out to do some shopping. **1960** I. Jefferies *Dignity & Purity* ii. 28 Let's pop off for a drive. **1965** *Listener* 2 Dec. 934/2 'Afternoon Theatre', sometimes infinitely trivial, popped up with a winner in *The Aquarium on Platform Two*, by Peter Preston. **1968** 'N. Blake' *Private Wound* v. 79 Maire'll look after you till I get back. I just have to pop out and see a fella for a minute or two. **1977** B. Pym *Quartet in Autumn* vii. 63 'Goodbye, then,' she said. 'I'll pop in again some time.' **1978** J. Thomson *Question of Identity* xiv. 146 Will you pop over to my tent and bring me my little box?

1894 H. Lawson *Short Stories in Prose & Verse* 89 'How are yer?' 'Oh! I'm alright!' he says. 'How are ye poppin' up!' **1907** N. Spielvogel *Cocky Farmer* 16 Whatto, Joe. How are you popping up? **1933** N. Lindsay *Saturdee* 10 What-oh, Stinker, how you poppin' up? **1942** S. Campion *Bonanza* 207 Howya poppin', cobber?

c. (Further examples.) Also ellipt. *to pop.* Also *trans.*, to kill, destroy.

1824 J. Hogg *Private Mem. Justified Sinner* 253 Might we not..pop him off in private and quietness? **1922** E. Wallace *Flying Fifty-Five* x. 58 'If he'd only popped off in the war, Jacques.'.. 'You might have been 'popped off' yourself if you'd only got within range of a bullet.' **1928** D. L. Sayers *Unpleasantness at Bellona Club* ix. 110 Perhaps it's just as well he popped off when he did. He might have cut me off with a shilling. **1940** G. S. Gordon *Let.* 24 May (1943) 221, I have joined the Defence Volunteers, and hope to pop a parachutist before the business ends. **1945** J. B. Priestley *Three Men in New Suits* v. 65 He fancies he might pop off at any time. **1952** W. R. Burnett *Vanity Row* (1953) v. 45 She'd be worrying how to knock me off. Or trying to get me het up..so's I'd pop. **1975** J. Goulet *Oh's Profit* vi. 36 Oh popped a carpenter ant, chewed. **1975** *New Yorker* 26 May 32/2, I agreed not to say 'death', 'dying',..'go home feet first', 'pop off the hooks'. **1977** *Navy News* Sept. 21/5 It is possible for a Seacat or Seaslug missile to get close enough to topple the target off course and 'pop' the parachute recovery system.

d. *to pop in and out*: to visit or come and go frequently or casually.

1858 Mrs. Gaskell *Let.* 19 Oct. (1966) 517 We have more people popping in & out than we expected. **1926** Wodehouse *Heart of Goof* iv. 126 He drew a picture of their little home, with Crispin for ever popping in and out. **1971** N. Freeling *Over High Side* I. 40 Martinez was not altogether unknown... He had often 'popped in and out'. **1974** 'S. Woods' *Done to Death* 14 He can't keep popping in and out... But if she had a companion—. **1979** 'M. Hebden' *Death set to Music* iii. 26 He spent most of his time off duty popping in and out of bed with any pretty woman he could find.

e. *Cricket.* Of the ball: to rise sharply off the pitch when bowled; to get up (Get *v.* 72 h). Also *to pop up.*

1871 'Thomsonby' *Cricketers in Council* 39 'Spin' is not twist, it is that which gives the ball a tendency to twist, break back, shoot, pop up, or, in fact, do something eccentric. **1888** Steel & Lyttelton *Cricket* iii. 153 The ball will twist a great deal on this class of wicket [hard and crumbled]... It is also inclined both to 'pop' and keep low. **1906** A. E. Knight *Compl. Cricketer* iii. 119 The ball, too, will rear up quickly, kick or 'pop up'. **1921** P. F. Warner *My Cricketing Life* vi. 126 On a sticky wicket he was capable of sending down a difficult off break, and of making the ball pop. **1926** J. B. Hobbs *Test Match Surprise* xxi. 211 Then the ball commenced to 'pop', in cricket parlance—to 'stop and look at them'—and Grimmell..had the two brilliant batsmen in difficulties. **1959** *Times* 29 May 4/2 Nicholls skied a catch..aiming across the line at one that popped.

f. To pay (*for*). *slang.*

1959 R. Bloch *Big Kick* in *Blood runs Cold* (1961) 213 He popped for three jugs tonight, just to get in. Likes to make the scene. *Ibid.* 218 He didn't pop... I said we were leaving..and all he did was smile. **1968** L. J. Braun *Cat who turned on & Off* (1969) xxi. 182 Hell. I didn't buy you anything, but I'll pop for lunch.

9. *trans.* In Baseball: to hit (a ball) high into the air but close to the batter, thus providing an easy catch. Also *intr.*, to get put out by hitting a high ball that is caught by an opponent. *N. Amer.*

1867 *Ball Players' Chron.* 6 June 2/3 On Hunniwell popping one up which fell into Sumner's hands, Smith had to retire, a double play putting both out. **1886** [see *fan *v.* 8 b]. **1912** C. Mathewson *Pitching in a Pinch* 204 Then Doyle popped up a weak foul behind the catcher. **1931** *Kansas City* (Missouri) *Times* 19 Oct., Hallahan replaced Grimes on the mound for the Cardinals and then Bishop popped out to 'Pepper' Martin. **1947** *Los Angeles Times* 3 Oct. II. 1/7 Johnson swung and popped up to end the inning. **1948** *Chicago Tribune* 7 Mar. II. 1/4 Lupien popped to Johnson. **1974** *Los Angeles Times* 13 Oct. III. 10/2 Bando struck out. Messersmith grounded to the pitcher. Rudi popped to short.

10. *trans.* To inject (a narcotic drug). Also, to take (a narcotic drug). Also *intr. slang.*

1956 R. Thorp *Viper* vi. 92 Nearly everyone there seemed to be popping. There were so many needles working you might have thought it was a tailors shop. **1959** W. Burroughs *Naked Lunch* 29 Ever pop coke in the mainline? **1962** 'K. Orvis' *Damned & Destroyed* xii. 79 Was there ever a junkie..that was too pooped to pop? **1968** *N.Y. Times* 2 Aug. 46 Executives of finance and insurance companies are popping pills these days to tranquilize their nerves. **1968** M. Woodhouse *Rock Baby* ii. 109 For him the day..started when he swallowed the first pill or popped the first vein. **1972** *Sunday Sun* (Brisbane) 2 July 14/3 The addict..now bangs, pops, shoots and jabs his veins with the hypodermic needle. **1976** R. Rosenblum *Sweetheart Deal* iv. 46 The half-million ghetto kids who'll start popping junk this year. **1977** *Amer. Speech 1975* L. 64 *Pop*,.. take an amphetamine in order to stay awake (to study). 'I popped for my history final.'

pop, *int., adv.* Add: *spec.* in phr. *to go off pop* (N.Z. colloq.), to break into angry speech.

1933 'P. Cadey' *Broken Pattern* xii. 126 There's no need to go off pop like that. **1940** F. Sargeson *Man & Wife* (1944) 65 He'd do things wrong too, and every chance he got he'd pick on me and go off pop. And of course I'd tell him off back.

2. In repeated form, with (the action or sounds of) a series of pops. Also as *adj.* and *sb.*, the sound of such a series.

1928 V. Woolf *Writer's Diary* 22 Mar. (1953) 124 A rabbit that passes across a shooting gallery, and one's friends go pop-pop. **1951** J. Frame *Lagoon* 10 The pop-pop boats we used to whizz round in the bath on Christmas morning. **1957** —— *Owls do Cry* 29 Sometimes the coal makes a pop-pop.

pop-. Add: **pop-beer,** ginger-beer or some other aerated drink; **pop-bottle,** a bottle for an aerated drink; **pop-call** *U.S.*, a sudden or unexpected visit; **popcorked** *a.*, provided with a cork which pops when drawn; **pop-eye** (earlier examples); **pop-hole,** a hole in a hedge, fence, etc., through which animals can pass; **pop-off,** (*b*) used *attrib.* to designate a safety valve which operates with a pop; **pop-rivet,** a kind of tubular rivet used for fastenings where only one side of the work is accessible, and which is inserted into the hole and then clinched by the action of withdrawing a central mandrel; hence as *v. trans.*; **pop-riveting** *vbl. sb.*; **pop safety valve** = *pop-valve* in Dict. and Suppl.; **pop-top** *U.S.* = *ring-opener* (*Ring *sb.*[1] 18); also *attrib.*; hence **pop-topping** *vbl. sb.*; **pop-valve,** delete '= Puppet-valve' and substitute: a spring-loaded safety valve designed to open or close very rapidly at a predetermined pressure; (further examples).

1887 C. D. Warner *Their Pilgrimage* (1888) ii. 40 Shooting-galleries, pop-beer and cigar shops, restaurants, [etc.]. **1900** Ade *Fables in Slang* 28 More than once he had let drive with a pop bottle at the umpire. **1921** A. G. Empey *Madonna of Hills* 2 The occasional noise of an empty 'pop' bottle kicked over under the seats, indicated the audience was restless. **1946** C. Himes *Black on Black* (1973) 259, I looked around and saw cases of pop bottles stacked against the wall. **1971** *Country Life* 23 Dec. 1788/1 That cherished book, its olive green covers carefully clothed in brown paper as a safeguard against pop-bottle rings. **1941** W. C. Handy *Father of Blues* (1957) iii. 27 The pop-calls of policemen dropping in to catch vagrants. **1974** *News & Reporter* (Chester, S. Carolina) 24 Apr. 4-B/8 Mr. and Mrs. Mark Winchester from Charlotte made 'pop calls' at the Fergusons, W. C. Gladdens, and Countermans. **1922** Joyce *Ulysses* 260 Pat paid for diner's popcorked bottle: and over tumbler tray and popcorked bottle ere he went he whispered. **1828** A. Royall *Black Bk.* II. 377 But the lawyer..is a shrimp in size, a sallow complexion, small face, and little blue pop eyes. **1885** 'C. E. Craddock' *Prophet Gt. Smoky Mts.* ii. 45 He had wide pop-eyes, and long ears, and a rabbit-like aspect. **1944** *Living off Land* ii. 30 Kangaroos, often hard to shoot, are fairly easy to snare in country where there are netting fences, as often their pads run alongside the fence to a spot where they either jump it or crawl through a 'pop-hole'. **1945** 'G. Orwell' *Animal Farm* i. 9 Mr Jones, of the Manor Farm, had locked the hen-houses for the night, but was too drunk to remember to shut the pop-holes. **1949** D. M. Davin *Roads from Home* 159 'One thing I will say for a pop-hole,' Paddy said, 'once you've found it you're pretty well set. They always make for it.' **1963** *Times* 14 Jan. 13/2 They [*sc.* pigs] get two-thirds of their food outside, having free access through a pop-hole, the rest they forage for in the litter. **1944** H. Kerwin *Arc & Acetylene Welding* ii. 6 Keep all pop-off valves on the [carbide] generator in good working order. **1977** *Brit. Jrnl. Anaesthesia* XLIX. 71/1 There is a cooling coil and a safety pop-off valve, by which extra pressure is released and extra moisture in the circuit is expelled intermittently. **1932** *Air Ann. Brit. Empire 1932–33* 396 The most interesting type of rivet which has been specially developed is a tubular rivet known as the pop-rivet. **1953** *Flight* 18 Sept. 410/2 A corrugated core is sandwiched between two skins, the outer skin being spot-welded and the inner skin pop-riveted to this core. **1967** J. Mills *Low-Cost Car Repairs* xii. 243 Pop-rivets are easily and quickly drilled out in a matter of seconds. **1973** P. Revere *Do Your Own Car Body Repairs* vii. 36 Any area to be pop riveted which is on a surface liable to to be seen, will have to be countersunk first. **1978** *Daily Tel.* 18 Nov. 14/6 His 1924 version was the first all-steel aircraft produced in Britain and necessitated the now universally-used pop-rivet. **1934** M. Langley *Metal Aircraft Construction* (ed. 2) ix. 309 Some very ingenious methods of tubular or 'pop' riveting have been devised by the A.T.S. Co., Ltd., which..combines the patented processes for metal construction of the Armstrong-Whitworth, Boulton & Paul, and Gloster firms. **1973** P. Revere *Do Your Own Car Body Repairs* vii. 37 The cost of a pop riveting gun is about a third the price of a new tyre. **1908** G. F. Gebhardt *Steam Power Plant Engin.* xv. 598 (*heading*) Consolidated pop safety valve. **1961** F. A. S. Brown *N. Gresley* xvii. 123 One of the new 'B12s', No. 8579, was the subject of extensive rebuilding, and the opportunity was taken to mount a larger boiler..and a round-topped firebox with pop safety valves. **1970** *Time* 21 Sept. 60/3 Insert finger, tug and quaff: in those few seconds, the aluminium ring atop a pop-top can of beer or soda fulfills its function. **1972** *Washington Post* (Potomac Suppl.) 29 Oct. 15/3 Acres and acres of sweeping lawn without a styrofoam cup, a pop-top, [etc.]. **1977** C. McFadden *Serial* (1978) xxxiii. 72/2 Joan snapped the pop top on the last can of beer. **1975** *Publishers Weekly* 27 Jan. 42/3 (Advt.), Pop-topping... New craft with pull-tabs from beverage cans. [**1881** *Engineering News* 10 Sept. 362/2 The great peculiarity of the 'Pop' nickel-seated safety valve..is that by the use of a stricture the recoil action of the steam is made available to overcome the increased pressure of the spring on the valve-head as it rises.] **1908** V. Pendred *Railway Locomotive* xxiv. 185 On some lines 'Pop' valves have been tried. They are so called, because instead of rising gradually as the pressure increases after they have begun to blow off, they lift suddenly with a 'pop' and blow off hard for a minute or so. **1927** E. L. Ahrons *Brit. Steam Railway Locomotive 1825–1925* xxiii. 364/2 Ramsbottom safety valves, though still used, are rapidly giving place to pop valves of the Ross pattern. **1968** J. H. White *Amer. Locomotives* viii. 148 The Richardson valve was said to open more than twice as far as an ordinary safety valve. Because of its quick opening it became popularly known as the 'pop' valve.

popadam. Add: Also **papadam, papadum, papodam, papodum, poppadom, puppadum, puppodum.** (Further examples.)

1906 *Mrs. Beeton's Bk. Househ. Managem.* lviii. 1601 Thin wafer-like cakes called Papodums. **1928** *Daily Express* 19 July 5/2 There are Bombay ducks and papodams. **1928** *Sunday Express* 12 Feb. 10 And then add the curry... The hot chutney of Madras is the best accompaniment, and with it you may take, if you will, poppadums, Bombay ducks, and a little powdered mint. **1931** *Punch* 13 May 506/3 A puppodum is a thin wafer-like cake made of lentil-flour or something like that. **1932** *Times Lit. Suppl.* 22 Dec. 978/1 *Papadums* are essential to a curry; but to make a *papadum* requires the accumulated experience of a few generations. **1936** *Times Lit. Suppl.* 3 Oct. 792/2 A reputable firm will supply..curry powder, puppadums, [etc.]. **1951** *Good Housek. Home Encycl.* 432/2 Chupatties and papadum are types of Indian breads often served with curries. **1959** *Good Food Guide* 316 Curried chicken Madras with poppadoms and Bombay duck. **1962** *Housewife* (Ceylon) Feb. 33 A meal devoid of appetizers, in the form of a salad, papadams or a blob of cream on the fruit salad, is, I feel, a miserable failure. **1969** *Guardian* 21 Mar. 11/3 A new play opens at the Arts Laboratory..'Chicken Curry and Poppadoms' by Richard Huggett. **1974** 'J. Le Carré' *Tinker, Tailor* xxviii. 243 Jerry Westerby with his enormous hands shattered a popadam on to the hottest curry on the menu.

pop-corn. Add: (Further examples.) Also *transf.* and *fig.*

1823 W. Faux *Memorable Days Amer.* 302, I crossed the Big Wabash..at La Valette's ferry, where is beautiful land, fine young orchards, and two lonely families of naked-legged French settlers, from whom I received two curious ears of poss [*sic*] corn. **1850** *Quincy* (Illinois) *Whig* 12 Nov. 4/1 Pop corn is dependent for its peculiar powers ..upon the quantity of oil which its whole contains. **1855** 'Q. K. P. Doesticks' *Doesticks, what he Says* xix. 257 [He] had just pawned his coat and a spare shirt to get money to set himself up in business again, as a pop-corn merchant. **1875** *Chicago Tribune* 21 Nov. 2/6 Each one had grown tired of jaw-breakers and popcorn balls. **1922** 'R. Crompton' *Just—William* xi. 220 He purchased a large bag of popcorn. **1947** *Downtown Shopping News* (Chicago) 2 Jan. 16/3 Pop corn balls are the delight of every child. **1949** F. Peto *Amer. Quilts & Coverlets* ii. 23 The loom-made tufted type used candlewicking for the warp of the foundation and..the characteristic 'popcorn' decoration. **1953** [see *hustler 1]. **1965** Mrs. L. B. Johnson *White House Diary* 20 Dec. (1970) 340 There were garlands of popcorn. **1968** *Guardian* 15 Nov. 1/6 Miss Plummer won through on dazzling good looks. As far as a popcorn poll went, they appeared to be a popular choice. **1972** *Country Life* 9 Mar. 591/1 Popcorn is an extremely hard form of maize whose corns expand and 'pop' on heating; it is used only in confectionery. **1973** C. & R. Milner *Black Players* ii. 41 *Popcorn* is a humorous insult which may be translated as 'light-weight'.

pope, *sb.*[1] Add: **I. 1. a.** (Earlier and later examples of *Black Pope.*)

1873 *Times* 30 May 8/1 The only practical result has been an almost unanimous vote by which the General of the Jesuits, Father Becks—the 'Black Pope' as he is called—will be instantly..turned out of the apartments. **1911** *Encycl. Brit.* XV. 339/2 It is said that the general of the Jesuits is independent of the pope; and his popular name, 'the black pope', has gone to confirm this idea. **1976** P. van Rjndt *Tetramachus Collection* (1977) i. 15 Political details gleaned by the ranks of the 'black pope', ..head of the Society of Jesus.

3. a. Delete † *Obs.* and add later examples.

1902 *Encycl. Brit.* XXVII. 237/2 'The most holy Pope and patriarch of the great city of Alexandria and of all the land of Egypt, of Jerusalem the holy city, of Nubia, Abyssinia, and Pentapolis, and all the preaching of St. Mark', as he is still called. **1925** [see *beatitude 1 b]. **1976** *Daily Tel.* 24 Aug. 4/5 Pope Shenouda the Third, Patriarch of the Egyptian Coptic Church, said..that the deposition of Abuna Theophilos was 'illegal and inhuman'.

6*. A hot spiced drink of mull based on any of various wines. Cf. Bishop *sb.* 8, Cardinal *sb.* 5.

1920 G. Saintsbury *Notes on Cellar-bk.* xi. 162 'Pope', *i.e.* mulled burgundy, is Antichristian, from no mere Protestant point of view. **1965** O. A. Mendelsohn *Dict. Drink* 264 *Pope*, a spiced drink made from tokay.., ginger, honey and roasted orange. **1976** *Times* 15 Jan. 12/8 Many of these hot drinks have clerical names—Bishop being a type of mulled port, Cardinal using claret, and Pope Champagne. **1977** *Centuryan* (Office Cleaning Services) Christmas 8/2 A mull..using Tokay, the famed Hungarian dessert wine, was known as 'The Pope'.

7. b. pope's hat, applied to the head-dress of the Grenadier Guards. *Literary.*

1886 R. L. Stevenson *Kidnapped* ii. 5/1 An old red-faced general on a grey horse at the one end, and at the other the company of Grenadiers with their Pope's-hats.

pope, *v.* Delete † *Obs.* and add: **1.** (Later example.)

1966 *Duckett's Reg.* Feb. 14/2 He [*sc.* Pope John XXIII] would pope it in his own way, God guiding him.

2. b. To be converted to Roman Catholicism; to become a Roman Catholic.

c **1916** in E. Waugh *Life R. Knox* (1959) II. i. 142 I'm *not* going to 'Pope' until after the war (if I'm alive). **1954** R. Macaulay *Last Lett. to Friend* (1962) 163, I was..very sorry that your friend..has 'poped', as we call it here. **1961** *Spectator* 19 May 709 In another generation the Upper Chamber may be riddled with families who have poped. **1966** J. Betjeman *High & Low* 37 Kensit threatens and has Sam Gurney poped? **1977** *Observer* 27 Nov. 28/6 Wilfred [Knox], an Anglo-Catholic priest who never showed the least inclination to follow his younger brother into the Roman Church—or 'to Pope' as it was facetiously called among the undergraduates of Ronnie's generation.

Popean, Popeian varr. Popian *a.* (in Dict. and Suppl.).

pop-eyed, *a.* orig. *U.S.* [Pop-.] Having bulging or prominent eyes; wide-eyed (with amazement, etc.).

1830 A. Royall *Lett. from Alabama* 176 The first countenance I caught, was Senator Foot of Connecticut—a handsome middle-sized black pop-eyed Yankee. **1860** [in Dict. s.v. Pop-]. **1906** *Atlantic Monthly* Oct. 573 The class was open-mouthed, and the professor pop-eyed with wonder. **1923** R. D. Paine *Comrades of Rolling Ocean* ix. 152 They are simply pop-eyed to hear all about the speedy apprentice. **1937** *John o' London's Weekly* 22 Jan. 682/1 The king [*sc.* George III] fumbled for a few years with makeshift ministries,..and then committed his affairs to Lord North, an amiable pop-eyed creature, rather like himself in appearance. **1947** V. Nabokov *Bend Sinister* II. 12 Paying perhaps terrific fines, but stopping the train. Say, why did you do it? the popeyed conductor might ask. **1952** Wodehouse *Pigs have Wings* iv. 74 The landlord of the Emsworth Arms..and the half dozen Shropshire lads who were propping up the establishment's outer wall had stamped her with the seal of their popeyed approval. **1973** 'E. McBain' *Let's hear It* viii. 124 Her audience..watched her every move in pop-eyed fascination. **1978** A. Price *'44 Vintage* x. 131 He stared pop-eyed at Butler..then started to wave madly.

pop-gun, popgun. Add: **1.** (Later example.)

1967 D. Abercrombie *Elem. Gen. Phonetics* ii. 24 An air-stream mechanism can be compared to a fruit-spray, a Flit gun, a syringe, or a child's pop-gun.

2. (Later example.) Also *transf.* (contextually an aeroplane).

1919 M. Beer *Hist. Brit. Socialism* I. II. vii. 240 To equip men with pop-guns for a hunting expedition in the jungle. **1929** W. Faulkner *Sartoris* I. 43, I tried to keep him from going up there on that goddam little popgun... I tried to keep him from going up there on that damn Camel.

3. (Later examples.)

1844 *Knickerbocker* XXIII. 182 To the United States in reference to the pop-gun shots of foreign tourists, might be addressed the warning which Peter Plymley thundered against Bonaparte. **1874** E. Eggleston *Circuit Rider* ix. 87 He had been flogged in boyhood for shooting pop-gun wads into the face of a portrait of the reigning monarch. **1895** *Montreal Med. Jrnl.* XXIII. 565 The physician without physiology and chemistry flounders along in an aimless fashion, never able to gain any accurate conception of disease, practising a sort of pop-gun pharmacy, hitting now the malady and again the patient, he himself not knowing which. **1963** *Times* 5 Jan. 12/3 A complicated regimen of treatment which Dr. Walton described as 'pop-gun polypharmacy'. **1968** *Wall St. Jrnl.* 29 Mar. 1 (*headings*) Centers in Slums Offer Legal, Employment Assistance; 'Outreachers' Make Rounds. A Popgun Effort, Critics Say.

Popian, *a.* Add: (Later examples.) Also as *sb.*, an imitator of the poet Alexander Pope.

a **1849** H. Coleridge *Ess. & Marginalia* (1851) II. 121 Neither Rogers nor Campbell are Popeans. They belong to another school—the sentimental. **1895** W. D. Howells *My Literary Passions* 55, I..hammered away at my blessed Popean heroics till nine, when I went regularly to bed, to rise again at five. **1914** J. A. Roy *Cowper & his Poetry* 54 He [*sc.* Johnson] failed to remark the absence of the Popeian inversions in the seemingly orthodox verse. **1953** R. Fuller *Second Curtain* v. 74 What nourishment could he give his Popean young poet? **1975** *Times Lit. Suppl.* 14 Mar. 275/1 There is no philistine repudiation of the achievements of Popeian scholarship.

popinac (pǫ·pinæk). *U.S.* Also **popinack.** [f. OPOPANAX.] A tropical or subtropical leguminous shrub, *Acacia farnesiana*, whose fragrant yellow flowers yield an essential oil used in perfume; also called the opopanax tree.

1900 L. H. BAILEY *Cycl. Amer. Hort.* I. 8/2 Acacia... Farnesiana... Popinac, Opopanax, Cassie... Grown in S. France for perfumery. **1945** R. P. WODEHOUSE *Hayfever Plants* iii. 113 One of the best known [acacias] is the opopanax or huisache,..also called popinack and cassie. It is a small tree, 20 to 30 feet high, with spreading spiny branches bearing bright yellow flowers closely compacted in small globular heads. **1952** [see *CASSIE[3]].

Popish (pōu·piʃ), *a.*[2] Also **Popeish.** [f. *Pope*, proper name + -ISH[1].] = POPIAN *a.*

1825 *Gentl. Mag.* XCV. I. 334 In this *Popish* controversy, though Mr. Bowles may affix the term 'final' to his Appeal, we have some doubt whether he will be permitted to have the last word. **1882** MRS. OLIPHANT *Lit. Hist. Eng.* I. 76 The very words of the Popish era still lingered on Cowper's tongue. *c* **1885** —— in A. L. Coghill *Autobiogr. & Lett. Mrs. Oliphant* (1899) 13 She..was fond of quoting Pope, so that we used to call her Popish in afterdays when I knew what Popish in this sense meant. **1944** *New Yorker* 9 Dec. 97/2 The *Times'* vigorous and somewhat Popeish effort included this stern couplet.

poplar. Add: **3. poplar-borer** *U.S.*, substitute for def.: the larva of a beetle, *Saperda calcarata*, which attacks the trunk and branches of poplar and certain other trees; (examples).

1884 *Rep. Comm. Agric.* (U.S. Dept. Agric.) 383 The Poplar-Borer..has been destructive to poplar trees on the shore of Casco Bay. **1942** S. W. FROST *Gen. Entomol.* xix. 381 The poplar borer..and the carpenter worm..keep at least a portion of their burrows free from frass and other waste material. **1972** SWAN & PAPP *Common Insects N. Amer.* 455 Poplar Borer... The larvae work in the trunk and large limbs of felled and weakened poplar.

Poplarism (pǫ·plărĭz'm). [f. *Poplar*, the name of a district, formerly a borough in the East End of London + -ISM.] The policy of giving out-relief on a generous or extravagant scale, practised by the Board of Guardians of Poplar about 1919 and later; any similar policy which lays a heavy burden on ratepayers. Hence **Po·plarist**, one who practises or advocates Poplarism; also *attrib.*; **Po:plariza·tion**, the adoption or implementation of Poplarism; **Po·plarize** *v. trans.*, to make like Poplar; to subject to Poplarism.

1922 *Glasgow Herald* 3 Nov. 8 The hard-headed workers of Yorkshire..have learned the lesson of Poplarism. **1923** *Daily Mail* 31 July 5/3 'Poplarism' was a portent of the changing of the modern state. **1923** R. MACAULAY *Told by Idiot* I. 44 So Poplarised..did she become that she took to speaking of her parental home in Bloomsbury as being in the West End. **1923** *Glasgow Herald* 1 Oct. 8/6 A decision in the opposite sense would simply mean an indefinite continuance of the Highland variety of 'Poplarisation' in the Lewis. **1924** *Ibid.* 7 Apr. 12/4 Mr. Wheatley ..had been accused of desiring to 'Poplarise' the British people. **1925** *Ibid.* 6 Mar. 9 Even the cautious prophets.. foretell the announcement of a rebuff to the Poplarists tomorrow. **1928** *Daily Tel.* 6 Nov. 12/6 Those..will demand increased subsidies, allowances, and 'Poplarised' social services, to be paid for out of the proceeds of very high taxation. **1931** *Times* 20 Feb. 7/6 The chief issue of the election is whether or not the policy of 'Poplarism' advocated by the Labour-Socialist Party is to be applied to London government. **1962** B. KEITH-LUCAS in *Public Law* Spring 67 The central government was finding that the weapons available to it were inadequate for the purpose of defeating Poplarism. The Poplar Order was being defied week by week. **1973** G. W. JONES in *Ibid.* Spring 28 Morrison had been opposed to the three elements of 'Poplarism', the payment of excessive wages and excessive relief and the refusal to honour legal obligations. **1976** H. WILSON *Governance of Britain* ii. 29 It was all done by agreement, Snowden recording that, as George Lansbury had to be found a job, despite his 'Poplarist' reputation, it was he who suggested Lansbury for the Office of Works.

popocracy[1] (popǫ·krăsi). *U.S. Obs.* exc. *Hist.* Also with capital initial. [f. POP(ULIST + DEM)OCRACY 4.] The rule or policy of the Populists or People's Party in the United States. So **po·pocrat**[1] [DEM)OCRAT 2], a member or supporter of the People's Party; a Populist; **popocra·tic** *a.*, of or pertaining to the Popocrats. Also earlier **poplocracy** (poplǫ·krăsi); so **poplocra·tic** *a.*

1895 T. R. SMITH in *Voice* (N.Y.) 18 July 5/3 Our fight will be for poplocracy, popular rule... I think no more significant name could be found than the Poplocratic Party. **1896** *Chicago Tribune* 4 Aug. 1/1 The first returns are always in favor of the Popocrats. *Ibid.*, Incomplete returns..indicate Popocratic gains. **1896** *Boston Jrnl.* 24 Oct. 7/3 (*heading*) He is ready to support Popocracy. *Ibid.* 31 Oct. 4/3 (*heading*) Popocratic claims about Iowa. **1896** *North Amer. Rev.* CLXIII. 744 The threats..of the Popocrats to change..our financial system. **1904** *Omaha Bee* 16 Aug. 4 If it is so important that the people of Nebraska move cautiously in the selection of their chief executive this year, why did not the popocratic conventions discover the fact before? **1972** *Time* 17 Apr. 32/1 Populists who joined the Democrats were known as 'popocrats'.

po·pocrat[2]. *Temporary.* [f. *POP *a.* (*sb.*[8]) 2 + ARIST)OCRAT.] A leading figure in fashionable pop culture or society. So **popo·cracy**[2].

1970 *Tailor & Cutter* 4 Dec. 1180/2 Mick Jagger has moved far away from his former scruffy image—in fact, he is one of our more elegant popocrats. **1973** *Observer* 7 Oct. 39/1 He is a Nobel prizewinner, dresses with the Byronic panache of the popocracy.

popoi, var. *POIPOI.

‖ **po po po** (pǫ pǫ pǫ), *int.* An exclamation used in Greece expressing surprise, astonishment, commiseration, etc.

1936 L. DURRELL *Spirit of Place* (1969) 45 I'm almost tempted to come back and join you. Only the English weather po po po as they say here, shaking their rueful heads. **1972** J. AIKEN *Butterfly Picnic* i. 16, I..said, 'Po, po, po', which is the Greek equivalent of the French 'oh la la', or the English 'tut tut'. **1973** 'M. YORKE' *Grave Matters* I. i. 12 'The *Kiria* had no sons.' '*Po, po, po.*' The Greek tossed his head in sympathy. **1974** —— *Mortal Remains* III. vi. 83 Their talk was punctuated with cries of '*po, po, po*'.

‖ **popote** (popot). [Fr.] A French military kitchen or canteen.

1928 *Observer* 11 Mar. 17/7 By 1870 the young cook had become a chef, and he had charge of the kitchen of the Headquarters of the Army of the Rhine and later of MacMahon's Headquarters Mess, or 'popote', at Versailles during the Commune. **1934** A. WOOLLCOTT *While Rome Burns* 74 This, then, is the story..as they tell it..in the smoky *popotes* of the French army. **1966** J. DOS PASSOS *Best Times* (1968) ii. 43 The French cooks were getting dinner at the popote behind me.

pop-out (pǫ·paut). [POP-.] **1.** (In Dict. s.v. POP-.)

2. In surfing: a mass-produced surfboard.

1963 *Surfing Yearbk.* 42/2 *Popouts*, mass produced surfboards. **1965** *N.Z. Listener* 17 Dec. 5/1 Surfers will advise you to buy a custom-built board..rather than the mass-produced 'pop-out'. **1969** *Observer* 3 Aug. 31/2 Mass-produced fibreglass surfboards, known as 'pop outs', were soon being produced in this country as well as special custom-built boards to meet more individual requirements. Pop outs today sell from about £27 and custom-built boards from £37. **1970** *Studies in English* (Univ. Cape Town) I. 28 The air of individuality surrounding a surfer extends to his board, and so *pop-out*, meaning a mass-produced surfboard 'popped out' of a mould, is usually a derogatory term.

3. *attrib.* or as *adj.* Designating that which pops out (in various senses); *spec.* of the windscreen of a motor vehicle: designed to 'pop out' on impact.

1963 *Lebende Sprachen* VIII. 167/1 Pop-out windshield. **1967** *Autocar* 5 Oct. 45 (Advt.), The same people who care about all-round disc brakes, 'pop-out' safety windscreen, rally-proved suspension and seats designed by an orthopaedic surgeon. **1968** *Listener* 21 Mar. 391/3 The new high-performance laminated windscreens which since 1966 have cut injuries substantially in the States, or the 'pop-out' screens favoured by Mercedes-Benz and Volvo. **1968** A. DIMENT *Bang-Bang Birds* v. 72, I rejected..pop-out piano wire..and poison gas spray.

pop-over. Add: **1.** Also **popover, pop over.** (Earlier and later examples.) Also *attrib.*

1876 M. N. HENDERSON *Pract. Cooking* 71 Breakfast Puffs, or Pop-overs... May be baked in roll-pans. **1906** *Mrs. Beeton's Bk. Househ. Managem.* lix. 1626 *Pop overs*..white flour..milk..egg..salt... Pop-over tins are similar to sheets of patty pans. **1932** J. DOS PASSOS *1919* 251 Then she set down the popovers and went out. **1935** M. DE LA ROCHE *Young Renny* xiv. 122 Two golden popovers wrapped in a snow-white napkin. **1945** B. MACDONALD *Egg & I* (1946) 66 Recipes for pop-overs, cup cakes and other hot oven delicacies. **1958** L. WHISHAW *As Far as You'll take Me* ii. 15 They gave me a meal of chicken and popovers. **1973** E. TAYLOR *Serpent under It* (1974) v. 73 Comforted by two cups of coffee, six popovers, and the promise of veal paprika for dinner. **1976** *Woman's Day* (N.Y.) Nov. 156/1 Serve pop-overs at once with lemon-honey butter.

2. A loose casual garment put on by slipping it over the head.

1945 *Sun* (Baltimore) 11 Jan. 7–0/3 Miss McCardell, author of the bareback sun dress, the wraparound 'pop-over' housedress, [etc.]. **1963** *Harper's Bazaar* Oct. 44/1 A well-shaped pop-over—superbly smart in warm wool. **1968** [see **boat neck (-line)*]. **1973** *New Yorker* 3 Dec. 68/1 (Advt.), Sunbound popover, to be paired with pants,..loosely string-tied, and loosely kimono-sleeved. **1974** *Index-Jrnl.* (Greenwood, S. Carolina) 23 Apr. 3/2 (Advt.), Baby popover & pantie. **1976** *Times* 8 Apr. 7/4 Waterproof pop-overs fit over his blanket coats.

poppa. Add: (Earlier and later examples.) Also *transf.*

1897 G. B. SHAW *Our Theatres in Nineties* (1932) III. 20 We are permitted to take to our bosoms an American girl, because, to gratify her Poppa's love of a title without forfeiting her own self-respect, she has heroically refused a silly young Duke and married a venal old Earl. **1910** *Punch* 28 Sept. 227 Say, if that's poppa's notion of 'literary calm' I wish he'd never come home. **1956** [see *Father's Day* (*FATHER *sb.* 12)]. **1959** *Listener* 10 Sept. 375/1 It is a strange feeling, unfamiliar I imagine to most other countries, which..divide the rituals of the state and its political leadership between at least two dignitaries, so that Poppa is always at home. **1962** *Amer. Speech* XXXVII. 35 Another song which became popular sometime early in the century was entitled 'I Wonder Where My Sweet, Sweet Poppa's Gone'. The 'poppa' of this song is again a male lover. **1970** G. GREER *Female Eunuch* 158 Baby-talk, even to the extent of calling the husband..'poppa'. **1977** *N.Z. Herald* 5 Jan. 2-20/3 [Deaths] Lucich, Stipan Bartul... dear poppa of 19 grandchildren; in his 81st year.

b. *poppa stoppa* (U.S. Blacks' slang): see quots.

1944 D. BURLEY in A. Dundes *Mother Wit* (1973) 210 Elderly man—*Poppa Stoppa.* **1945** L. SHELLY *Jive Talk Dict.* 31/1 *Poppa stoppa*, smart old man. **1970** C. MAJOR *Dict. Afro-Amer. Slang* 92 *Poppa-stoppa*,..any old man who is effective at what he does.

popped (pǫpt), *ppl. a.* [f. POP *v.*[1] + -ED[1].]

a. Of eyes: bulging; protruding.

1927 *Scribner's Mag.* Apr. 383/2 Prentice's slightly popped blue eyes wandered to the colored folders.

b. *U.S. slang.* Arrested; apprehended by the police.

1960 R. G. REISNER *Jazz Titans* 163 *Popped*, caught (with drugs in one's possession). Example: I got popped. **1968–70** *Current Slang* (Univ. S. Dakota) III–IV. 94 *Popped*, arrested by the police.

popper, *sb.* Add: **3.** (Later examples.) See also *corn popper* s.v. CORN *sb.*[1] 11 in Dict. and Suppl.

1893 W. D. HOWELLS *Coast of Bohemia* 207 She bought a popper and three ears of corn. **1911** S. E. WHITE *Bobby Orde* (1916) xviii. 201 The pan..was replenished with popcorn, Bobby unhooked the long-handled wire popper from its nail..and set to work over the open fire. **1949** *Sat. Even. Post* 21 May 36/2 It operates popcorn machines on a concession basis..and turns out home poppers for the kitchen trade. **1957** HESELTINE & DOW *New Basic Cook Bk.* (rev. ed.) 592 Success in popping corn depends upon the quality of the popcorn and the equipment used as well as the skill of the person doing the popping. For popping over coals, a wire popper may be used; for cooking on a gas or electric range, a pressure saucepan or a heavy frying pan with a tightly fitting lid is more satisfactory. Electric corn poppers are convenient. **1972** F. VAN W. MASON *Roads to Liberty* 179 When she bent over to pop a popper of corn [etc.].

5. In Cricket, a ball that pops (*POP *v.*[1] 8 e) when bowled.

1857 *Bell's Life in London* 19 July 7/5 Mortlock defended his wicket well against the 'breakers' and 'poppers', which had by that time commenced their work. **1870** *Baily's Monthly Mag.* July 295 Mr. Grace was caught at point off a 'popper' of Emmett's. **1921** G. R. C. HARRIS *Few Short Runs* ii. 38 In my first Eton *v.* Harrow Match I calculated the batsman had to stop something like three shooters every eight balls, and at the same time one had to look out for poppers.

6. (The snapper on) a whip-lash. *U.S.*

1870 *Great Trans-Continental Tourist's Guide* (rev. ed.) 27/1 How often the sharp ring of the 'popper' aroused the timid hare or graceful antelope? **1877** H. RUEDE *Sod-House Days* (1937) 80 The lash is about 1½ inches thick at the handle, and tapers to the popper, and a good hand will make them crack like a pistol. **1934** *Amer. Ballads & Folk Songs* 375 And the stage-driver loves the popper of his whip. **1935** [see *bull-whip* (*BULL *sb.*[1] 11)].

7. A press-fastener.

1959 *Woman* 9 May 46/4 Sandwich a length of plastic foam between two layers of canvas held together with poppers. **1970** *Guardian* 17 June 13/6 He would help me dress him in his night things, laboriously doing up every popper and zip. **1973** *Times* 15 May 20/2 (*caption*) Beach bloomers in striped lawn have big sleeves to save shoulders from burning and practical poppers between the legs. **1974** N. FREELING *Dressing of Diamond* 33 Bernard, stop it, you're bursting my poppers.

Popperian (pǫpī·riăn), *sb.* and *a.* [The name of Sir Karl Raimund *Popper* (b. 1902), philosopher + -IAN.] **A.** *sb.* A person who advocates the theories or methods of Popper. **B.** *adj.* Of or pertaining to Popper's theories or methods, esp. the theory that scientific laws are justified only by their resistance to falsification, and his criticism of the philosophical basis of Marxism and other ideologies which entail limitations on freedom. So **Po·pperism**, the theory or practice of Popper's philosophical ideas.

1962 T. S. KUHN in *Internat. Encycl. Unified Sci.* II. II. xii. 146 If only severe failure to fit justifies theory rejection, then the Popperians will require some criterion of 'improbability' or of 'degree of falsification'. **1963** R. M. HARE *Freedom & Reason* vi. 91 We must..notice an analogy between it and the Popperian theory of scientific method. **1966** *Sci. & Society* XXX. I. 1 (*heading*) Popperism: the scarcity of reason. **1971** *Nature* 28 May 269/2 Feyerabend goes on to criticize the Popperians for not making good their claim to exhibit science as a rational enterprise. **1972** *Ibid.* 10 Nov. 110/1 The author then delineates in turn three theories of the logical structure of science—inductivism, Popperian falsificationism and positivism. **1973** B. MAGEE *Popper* iii. 41 [T. S.] Kuhn's theory..about the working activity of scientists..is not irreconcilable with Popperism. *Ibid.* vi. 85 The Popperian approach has this consequence..: instead of encouraging one to think about building Utopia it makes one seek out ..the specific social evils under which human beings are suffering. **1977** A. GIDDENS *Stud. in Social & Polit. Theory* i. 72 Lakatos's studies, although nominally directed at supporting main elements of the Popperian standpoint, show how wide the discrepancy is.

poppet, *sb.* **1.** Delete 'Now *dial.*' and add later examples.

1849 DICKENS *Dav. Copp.* (1850) iv. 45 Davy, dear. If I ain't ben azackly as intimate with you. Lately, as I used to be. It ain't becase I don't love you. Just as well and more, my pretty poppet. **1937** M. ALLINGHAM *Dancers in Mourning* ii. 26 'That how you see it, poppet?' he said. **1954** A. SETON *Katherine* xii. 201 'Whist, poppet!' Hawise stroked the girl's arm. **1959** E. H. CLEMENTS *High Tension* x. 163 Cheer up, poppet, it's going to be all right. **1973** 'M. UNDERWOOD' *Reward for Defector* i. 11 He cast a doting glance at his wife. 'Well, poppet, it's time we were off.' **1978** D. DEVINE *Sunk without Trace* iii. 33 'No, you don't eat the spoon, poppet.' She hoisted the child out of his chair and put him in the play-pen.

poppet-valve: see PUPPET-VALVE in Dict. and Suppl.

poppied, *a.* Add: **1.** (Later examples.)

1935 E. R. EDDISON *Mistress of Mistresses* viii. 143 The poppied frieze, the walls, the very floor of marble, seemed to waver. **1943** C. DAY LEWIS *Word over All* 15 Over the corn, over the poppied plains.

2. (Later example.)

1881 O. WILDE *Poems* 75 O for Medea with her poppied spell!

popping, *vbl. sb.*^{1} (Further examples.)

1929 J. MASEFIELD *Hawbucks* 80 'What do you think about popping?' 'You mean proposing?' 'Yes, popping.' **1957** C. MACINNES *City of Spades* I. ix. 65 'Charging is different from popping...' 'Popping?' 'With needles. White stuff—man, that's danger!' **1965** 'E. MCBAIN' *Doll* (1966) xii. 155 She has..been hopelessly hooked since she first began skin-popping. **1978** *Amat. Photographer* 29 Nov. 71/1 The fibre-optic Light Pipe gives efficient light mix and transmission at a low operating temperature, reducing the possibility of negative popping, and absorbing ultraviolet.

poppit (pǫ·pit). Also **poppet.** [f. POP *v.*^{1}] A kind of bead (see quot. 1968).

1958 N. MARSH *Singing in Shrouds* (1959) v. 85 He started in on her rope of beads which, being poppets, broke. **1968** J. IRONSIDE *Fashion Alphabet* 178 Poppits were beads with a small bar which pushed into a hole in the next bead so that one could make necklaces or bracelets. **1969** *Observer* 23 Feb. 31/1 There was a time when everyone wore diamonds or poppit-beads. **1974** *Sci. Amer.* Oct. 48/3 They are strung together like Poppit beads in a row to form protofilaments.

popple, *sb.*^{1} **b.** (Later example.)

1910 S. E. WHITE *Rules of Game* xii. 66 The remains of the forest, overgrown with scrub oak and popple thickets, pushed down to the right-of-way.

poppy, *sb.* Add: **1. b.** *tall poppy:* in Australia, an especially well-paid, privileged, or distinguished person; also *transf.*

1931 *New South Wales Parl. Debates* 30 July 4840 The Premier cannot truthfully say that a measure which deals with a certain section of the community which he refers to as the privileged class and as 'tall poppies' is in accord with the Melbourne agreement. **1963** *Times* 12 Mar. (Australia Suppl.) p. xviii/2 The youthfulness is explained by the fact that nearly all the buildings visible at this distance are new ones, the tall commercial poppies that now..compare with the cathedral spires. **1967** J. YEOMANS *Scarce Australians* viii. 85 If there is one place where the genuine eccentric is crushed, the tall poppy lopped and the penetrating discussion stifled, it is Australia. **1969** *Listener* 13 Nov. 660/1 They booed this great man, and he had to take it. It was part of the thing —no tall poppies. You've got to do well, but there's supposed not to be any sense of excellence making any difference to human equality. **1975** *Sydney Morning Herald* 8 Apr. 6 Labor is obsessed with the 'tall poppies', and seems determined to pull them down.

c. = *Flanders poppy* s.v. *FLANDERS 2 b.

1921 *Times* 4 Nov. 9/3 Lord Haig..visited yesterday the headquarters of the British Legion, where the work of distributing poppies throughout the country for Poppy Day is being carried out. **1940** *Brit. Legion Poppy Ann.* 89/1 Nearly forty million poppies are sold each year on the anniversary of Armistice Day. **1972** *Guardian* 13 Nov. 12/4 Armistice Day passes round again... We cannot go on salving our consciences by buying a penny poppy once a year. **1976** *Wymondham & Attleborough Express* 10 Dec. 5/2 The sale of poppies in Occold raised £25.

d. Money. *slang.*

1943 *Police Jrnl.* XVI. 69 *Poppy*, money. **1959** A. WESKER *Roots* I. 29 How's poppy?.. Tight as ever. **1960** [see *CABBAGE *sb.*^{1} 1 e]. **1963** *Autocar* 6 Sept. 427/1 A good many British families which run their own cars must spend at least 13 per cent of the family poppy on that. **1972** L. HENDERSON *Cage until Tame* xvii. 148, I don't know why he's around without the gelt, because Tolly's not the boy to be parted from the poppy.

4. a. Revived in *slang* use in the sense 'opium'.

Cf. quots. 1604, 1621–3 in Dict.

1935 A. J. POLLOCK *Underworld Speaks* 90/2 *Poppy*, opium. **1950** H. E. GOLDIN *Dict. Amer. Underworld Lingo* 162/2 *Poppy*, opium. **1977** H. OSBORNE *White Poppy* xv. 114 The village people would see nothing wrong in what the smugglers were doing—most of the other men still smoked the poppy.

b. A perfume derived from the poppy.

1905 *Smart Set* Sept. 113/1 Wistaria, oil of cloves,.. poppy and crab-apple. **1923** W. A. POUCHER *Perfumes & Cosmetics* I. 96 Oakmoss resin..is a liquid of characteristic odour... It is useful in oriental bouquets, particularly those of the 'poppy' type. **1954** A. J. KRAJKEMAN tr. *Jellinek's Pract. Mod. Perfumery* I. 72 (*heading*) Tables of Perfume Complexes... Peau D'Espagne... Poppy.

6. (Later examples.)

1949 *Dict. Colours Interior Decoration* (Brit. Colour Council) III. 22/1 *Poppy*, a colour standardised by B.C.C. in 1934, matched to the flower. Similar to Gules. **1971** *Vogue* 15 Sept. 130/2 Dress..sizes: 36–42 in.; colours: green, cactus, poppy.

8. *poppy-land, -life, -syrup* (later example); (sense *1 c) *poppy appeal, cross, organizer, seller;* instrumental, as *poppy-crowned* (earlier and later examples), *-hung, -laden* adjs.; similative, as *poppy-drowsy, -glossy, -shallow, -sleepy;* **poppy-coloured** *a.* (earlier example); **Poppy Day,** a day (= **Remembrance Day*) on which those killed in the world wars of 1914–18 and 1939–45 are commemorated by the wearing of a Flanders poppy (see sense 1 c above and *FLANDERS 2 b); also *attrib.*; **poppy mallow** (examples); **poppy oil** (earlier and later examples); **poppy straw,** poppy plants, or a plant, from which the seeds have been removed.

1977 *Belfast Tel.* 14 Feb. 4/6 Area chairman Mr. G. A. R. Finlay thanked the people of Northern Ireland for their support to the Legion's Poppy Appeal. **1791** J. WOODFORDE *Diary* 24 Dec. (1927) III. 321 He brought with him..a pair of black Spanish Leather Shoes with black and poppey coloured roses, very pretty. **1976** *Norwich Mercury* 19 Nov. 7/2 Mr John Wiltshire, read the names of the fallen from Costessey as a poppy cross for each one was laid on the memorial. **1881** O. WILDE *Poems* 212 That poppy-crownèd God. **1911** E. POUND *Canzoni* 1 Fairer than these the Poppy-crownèd One flees. **1921** *Daily Mail* 11 Nov. 9/4 To-day..is Poppy Day. Twenty million red Flanders poppy emblems will be on sale in the streets. **1971** *Guardian* 28 Oct. 7/3 The Royal British Legion..faces a continuing drop in the number of collectors on Poppy Day. **1976** *Cumberland News* 3 Dec. 12/4 Aspatria's Poppy Day collection for the Earl Haig Fund totalled £216.59, an increase of £42 on last year. **1894** O. WILDE *Sphinx*, The poppy-drowsy queen. **1922** D. H. LAWRENCE *Birds, Beasts & Flowers* (1923) 141 Your sort of gorgeousness, Dark and lustrous And skinny repulsive And poppy-glossy. **1889** W. B. YEATS *Wanderings of Oisin* I. 5 In the poppy-hung house. **1878** O. WILDE *Ravenna* 6 Like Proserpine, with poppy-laden head. **1910** *Westm. Gaz.* 11 Feb. 2/3 An' drowsy somethings whisper in the air, An' drunken breaths sweep from the poppy-lands. **1958** *Times* 10 Nov. 19/1 A field yellow with charlock is a matter for comment, and 'poppyland' has long ceased to be an attraction to tourists. **1949** BLUNDEN *After Bombing* 25 Yet these rebuild A distant world, a summer dead Millions of poppy-lives ere ours. **1870** *Amer. Naturalist* III. 162 The Poppy mallow..with its purple blossoms and dark green leaves, forms one of the most brilliant figures in the prairie carpet. **1939** *Nat. Geogr. Mag.* Aug. 220/1 Callirhoe..the musical Greek name of the poppy mallow.., is the same as that borne by a nymph of the sea. **1972** F. PERRY *Flowers of World* 185/2 *Callirhoe papaver* from the southern USA is the Poppy Mallow, a scrambling or sometimes erect herbaceous perennial with reddish-purple Poppy-like flowers on stems of 60 cms (2 ft) and delicate Mallow-like leaves. **1756** T. BARDWELL *Pract. Painting & Perspective* 7 This colour [*sc.* flake-white] should be ground with the finest poppy oil that can be made. **1912** tr. *C. Moreau-Vauthier's Technique of Painting* 130 Nut oil is never used in France. French artists prefer the so-called *œillette*, or poppy oil. **1937** A. F. HILL *Econ. Bot.* ix. 215 Poppy Oil.—An important drying oil..obtained from the seeds of the opium poppy. **1976** *Wymondham & Attleborough Express* 19 Nov., Reg Knight..has been poppy organiser for the area for 12 years now. **1976** *Norwich Mercury* 19 Nov. 3/4 Nearly 100 poppy-sellers were out on the streets of Norwich on Saturday. **1957** L. DURRELL *Bitter Lemons* 214 Most of the poppy-shallow cabaret girls had gone *a* **1963** S. PLATH *Crossing Water* (1971) 21 The pills are worn-out and silly, like classical gods. Their poppy-sleepy colours do him no good. **1950** *Chem. Abstr.* XLIV. 4245 Expts. are made with potato, tomato, and beet tops, tobacco stalks, and poppy and mustard straws in 'handmade' board manuf. **1953** *Ibid.* XLVII. 6605 (*heading*) Production of morphine extracted from poppy straw grown in Poland. **1975** *Times* 10 Mar. 12/1 The United Nations intend to make sure the latex is not culled and that the crop becomes poppy straw for codeine. **1922** JOYCE *Ulysses* 83 Paragoric poppysyrup bad for cough.

poppy, *a.* Restrict *rare* to sense in Dict. and add: **b.** Of eyes: protuberant.

1907 *Westm. Gaz.* 11 Dec. 12/1 An American exclaiming before a family picture: 'My, what poppy eyes these Churchills have got!' **1915** *Pearson's Mag.* Jan. 106/1 Hair dark and curly; eyes poppy; lips, full. **1968** J. R. ACKERLEY *My Father & Myself* 29 A rich foreign nobleman with rather poppy eyes.

poppycock. For *U.S. slang* read *slang* (orig. *U.S.*) and add earlier and later examples.

1865 C. F. BROWNE *A. Ward: his Travels* I. iii. 35 You won't be able to find such another pack of poppycock gabblers as the present Congress of the United States. **1914** *New Age* 3 Sept. 410/2 The Headmaster of Eton became aware that he was talking poppycock for boys. **1924** M. KENNEDY *Constant Nymph* iii. 54 Sometimes, you know, you talk..poppycock. **1935** *Punch* 9 Jan. 30/1, I am not going to..ruin the perfect cadences of my English prose by pointing out to you in courteous and dignified language that your objections are all poppycock and my eye. **1955** *Times* 24 June 4/5 The peculiar capacity for pumping generals into jobs for which they were never suited continued the poppycock started by the Labour Government. **1973** *Nation Rev.* (Melbourne) 31 Aug. 1443/6 He was..a 'dangerous, raving, psychotic, stupid, vicious, sickening writer of poppycock'. **1977** *Punch* 31 Aug.–6 Sept. 335/3 If you still think that harmonisation is so much Brussels poppycock..then draw comfort from this statistic.

poppy-seed. Add: **1.** Esp. the seed of cultivated varieties of *Papaver somniferum*, the opium poppy, used as a flavouring, filling, or garnish for cakes, bread, etc. (Later examples.)

1932 L. GOLDING *Magnolia St.* I. viii. 127 The special bread sprinkled with poppy-seed for the Sabbath repast. **1947** F. GREENBERG *Cookery Bk.* 382 Brush over with beaten egg, sprinkle with poppy seeds, and bake..about 50 minutes. **1978** *Observer* (Colour Suppl.) 3 Dec. 81/2 For poppy seeds, you have to go to the delicatessen, and be prepared to grind them at home in an electric coffee mill.

3. Also *attrib.*: *poppy-seed cake, cookie, roll;* **poppy-seed oil** = *poppy oil* (POPPY *sb.* 8 in Dict. and Suppl.).

1943 A. L. SIMON *Conc. Encycl. Gastron.* IV. 100/1 (*heading*) Poppy-seed Cake. **1976** 'B. SHELBY' *Great Pebble Affair* 134 The religious group..supported themselves by..baking poppy seed cakes. **1959** *Tamarack Rev.* Summer 7 Hey, poppyseed cookies! *Real* stuffed fish! **1893** G. TERRY *Pigments, Paint, & Painting* xi. 305 Poppy-seed Oils.—Oil is yielded by the seeds of three kinds of poppy—the opium-poppy (*Papaver somniferum*), the spiny-poppy (*Argemone mexicana*), and the yellow-horn poppy (*Glaucium luteum*). **1942** GETTENS & STOUT *Painting Materials* 50 The cold-drawn oil is pale straw.. in colour and is the 'white poppy-seed oil' of commerce. **1974** G. USHER *Dict. Plants used by Man* 438/1 The seeds [of the opium poppy]..have some 44–50 per cent oil (Poppy Seed Oil). **1973** *Listener* 20 Sept. 377/2 Tea was served by Auntie Golda.., smoked salmon on black bread, poppy-seed rolls coated with cream cheese.

poppy-show. *dial.* and *Sc.* Also **puppie-show.** [f. *poppy, puppy*, dial. varr. of PUPPET *sb.*: cf. PUPPY *sb.* 4 b.] A puppet-show; a peep-show. Also *transf.* and *fig.*

1798 D. CRAWFORD *Poems* 88 You'd mak a noble poppey-show. **1828** D. M. MOIR *Mansie Wauch* vii. 64 They..let me in with a grudge for twopence..to see a punch and puppie-show business. **1886** J. P. REID *Facts & Fancies* 43 It was there we used to gather floo'ers to mak' a poppy-show. **1887** T. DARLINGTON *Folk-Speech S. Cheshire* 298 A pin to see a poppy-show. **1917** N. DOUGLAS *South Wind* xl. 459 When you watch some of these local marionette theatres the illusion is complete. Why is a poppy show more convincing than the Comédie Française? **1924** D. H. LAWRENCE *Let.* Aug. (1962) II. 803 In the next window-hole, a poppy-show of Indian women in coloured shawls. **1937** PARTRIDGE *Dict. Slang* 650/1 *Poppy-show*, a display, esp. if accidental, of under-clothes. **1950** L. BENNETT et al. *Anancy Stories & Dial. Verse* II. 45 All de ballerina head dem, tie Wid ballerina bow, Ballerina glamour mix wid Ballerina pappy-show!

poppysmic (pǫpi·zmik), *a.* *rare*$^{-1}$. [f. L. *poppysma, -ysmus* (see POPPISM) + -IC.] Produced with smacking of the lips.

1922 JOYCE *Ulysses* 552 Florry whispers to her. Whispering lovewords murmur liplapping loudly, poppysmic plopslop.

pops^2, var. *POP *sb.*^{6} [see *-S^2.] Also used in Jazz slang as a form of address to a man.

1928 BARRIE *Half an Hour* in *Plays* 616, I never heard how much you paid Pops for me? **1933** 'E. M. DELAFIELD' *Gay Life* ii. 32 My Pops says I'm ever such a lucky girl to have such heaps of friends. **1944** C. CALLOWAY *Hepsters Dict., Pops*, salutation for all males. **1944** [see *FATSO]. **1948** [see *DADDY 3]. **1961** *Metronome* Feb. 60 Jazz..is..an art in which a musician can become known as 'Pops' by the time he is 22 or even at 18. **1976** 'S. HARVESTER' *Siberian Road* ii. 30 Me a defenceless girl.. without my Mom and Pops.

pop-shop. (Later examples.)

1919 G. B. SHAW *O'Flaherty V.C.* in *Heartbreak House* 183 She hadnt half the jewelry of Mrs Sullivan that keeps the popshop in Drumpogue. **1942** WODEHOUSE *Money in Bank* (1946) iv. 36 This makes me feel like a pawnbroker. .. As if you had brought it in to the old pop shop and were asking me what I could spring on it. **1974** P. WRIGHT *Lang. Brit. Industry* i. 22 For many families the *pop-shop* was a necessity.

popsicle (pǫ·psik'l). orig. and chiefly *U.S.* Also **popsickle** and with capital initial. [Fanciful name.] An ice-lolly. Also *fig.* and *attrib.*

Popsicle is a proprietary name in the U.S.

1923 *Official Gaz.* (U.S. Patent Office) 25 Sept. 600/1 Trade-mark 'Popsicle'. Particular description of goods.— Lollypops. Claims use since May 28, 1923. **1932** H. H. SOMNER *Theory & Pract. Ice Cream Making* xxi. 502 Frozen Suckers, Popsicles, etc...patterned after candy suckers, or lollypops, are made by freezing ice mixes in suitable forms with wooden sticks inserted to serve as a handle. **1941** S. V. BENÉT in *Life* 7 July 90/1 The usual crowd..Kidding the local cop and eating popsicles. **1945** A. KOBER *Parm Me* 177 Leon Blatt..had just consumed a Popsicle and was now busy scraping its stick with his tongue. **1952** E. B. WHITE *Charlotte's Web* xvi. 123 In the hard-packed dirt of the midway..you will find a veritable treasure of..salted almonds, popsicles, partially gnawed ice cream cones, and the wooden sticks of lolly-pops. **1961** A. SEXTON in *Poetry* (Chicago) Dec. 161 The maid As thin as a popsicle stick Holds dinner as usual. **1962** J. Ludwig in R. Weaver *Canad. Short Stories* (1968) 2nd Ser. 250 'I look like a big popsicle, eh Josef?' Mrs Goffman said to her chauffeur. **1963** E. B. White *Let.* 22 July (1976) 504, I am always astonished to discover that my haphazard literary popsicles have found takers in places like Helsinki. **1967** M. McCarthy in *Observer* 30 Apr. 11/7 All the children who had gathered round to buy popsicles..from the popsicle man. **1972** *Last Whole Earth Catalog* (Portola Inst.) 291/3 Every bookstore has a line of ocean popsicles for your refreshment now. **1973** *Nation Rev.* (Melbourne) 31 Aug. 1460/3 Perhaps you would prefer one of these nice laudanum popsicles? **1977** *Time* 2 May 42/3 All they have to show an employer is a Social Security card, which is about as hard to acquire as a Popsicle. *Ibid.* 18 July 47/2 The delectable nymphet Lolita has a cruel, popsicle heart.

po·pskull. *N. Amer. slang.* [f. Pop *v.*[1] + Skull[1].] A powerful or unwholesome (esp. home-made) liquor; inferior whisky. Also *attrib.*

1867 G. W. Harris *Sut Lovingood* 222 Well, Maje cum blowin mad intu the doggery, an seein nobody, he jis' grabbed a bottel, an' tuck hisself a buckload ove popskull. **1917** *Dialect Notes* IV. 415 *Pop-skull*, bad whiskey. **1932** V. Randolph in B. A. Botkin *Folk-Say* IV. 237 He died from drinking too much popskull whisky. **1946** *Amer. Speech* XXI. 195 Distillers never refer to a still coil as a 'worm', as did the bootleggers who manufactured popskull and rotgut during Prohibition. **1950** *Amer. Legion Mag.* Apr. 19/1 Although much of the 'panther sweat' or 'popskull scotch' brewed today is distributed to customers who know it's moonshine and don't care, thousands of gallons are sold..to unsuspecting customers. **1956** *Wall St. Jrnl.* 21 Sept. 1/1 About one out of every four gallons of hard liquor..was moonshine—also known by devotees as corn squeezins, white lightning, popskull, bumblebee stew and mountain dew. **1973** B. Broadfoot *Ten Lost Years* xxiv. 286 Old pop skull, the kind we made by freezing a milk pail of cider and when the..alcohol had collected in the middle of the ice block, then we drained that off.

popster (pǫ·pstəɹ). [f. *pop *a.* (*sb.*[8]) + -ster.] A pop musician or artist; an enthusiast for pop music, pop art, or pop culture in general.

1963 *Meet the Beatles* 37 12.45 p.m. Popsters posing in the park. **1965** [see *opster]. **1967** [see *hippie, hippy *sb.* and *a.*]. **1967** *Listener* 1 June 727/1 There were quizzes,..teenage popsters (though in skirts down to the knee), professionally sincere teeth-gleamers—the lot. **1968** *Economist* 14 Dec. p. vii/2 The school-teachers of Monmouthshire, banning transistor radios from the playground for fear of the linguistic pollution of Anglo-Saxon popsters.

popsy. Add: Also **poppsie, popsie.** Also *gen.*, a woman or girl; a casual female acquaintance, girl-friend. Also *attrib.*

1931 C. Lithgow *Simple Sailor* xv. 194 Chase me, you fast women; ginger yourselves up, you slow 'uns!..Lord, but I *like* a good popsy! **1943** J. Hillier in *Penguin New Writing* XVI. 26 He ached too much for her to be satisfied in regarding her as a short-term poppsie, and yet ops. really permitted only a poppsie outlook. **1944** M. Laski *Love on Supertax* viii. 82 American colonels with their popsies. **1953** *Chambers's Jrnl.* June 325/1, I usually line up a local popsy. **1959** 'J. Welcome' *Stop at Nothing* ix. 135 The blonde popsie. **1968** *Listener* 10 Oct. 475/2 The Christine of *Lucky Jim* is a somewhat conventionally pretty high-class popsy. **1973** Wodehouse *Bachelors Anonymous* xii. 155 The door was opened by a rather personable popsy, who proved to be a girl who lives with the Fitch. **1978** J. Krantz *Scruples* iii. 75 Meanwhile, he had his popsies and he had his friend, Valentine, whose cozy, crazy stage set of a Paris attic had become a special refuge for him.

popular, *a.* (*sb.*) Add: **4. a.** (Further examples.) *spec.* in *popular (news)paper, press, romance*, etc., designating literature and ephemeral publications intended for a general readership.

1817 Coleridge *Biog. Lit.* I. xii. 253 To an Esquimaux or New Zealander our most popular philosophy would be wholly unintelligible. **1835** J. S. Mill in *London Rev.* II. 273 Not only has it no leaders in Parliament, but it has none in the popular press. **1841** T. Wright (*title*) Popular treatises on science. *Ibid.* p. vii, They [*sc.* the treatises] are important documents of the history of popular science. **1865** J. S. Mill *Auguste Comte* 48 The truths which popular philosophy calls by the misleading name of Contingent. **1876** W. James *Let.* 21 Sept. (1920) I. 190 The free-thinking tendency which the 'Popular Science Monthly'..represents. **1890** —— *Princ. Psychol.* I. iii. 81 The popular-science notions of cells and fibres are almost wholly wide of the truth. **1901** Chesterton *Defendant* 16 The coarse and thin texture of mere current popular romance. **1901** G. B. Shaw *Three Plays for Puritans* p. vii, They read a good deal, and are at home in the fool's paradise of popular romance. **1907** *Boston Med. & Surg. Jrnl.* 26 Dec. 847/2 A second means of dissemination of knowledge of the psychotherapeutic movement is through the medium of the popular press. **1937** W. S. Churchill *Let.* 20 Sept. in *Second World War* (1948) I. I. xiv. 193, I was very glad to see that Neville [Chamberlain] has been backing you up, and not, as represented by the Popular Press, holding you back by the coat-tails. **1937** *Discovery* Sept. 292/2 A contribution to popular science. **1952** H. Herd *March of Journalism* xvii. 326 Many popular newspapers..aim to interest everyman without indulging in sensationalism... Most of the 'populars' come within this classification. **1957** R. Hoggart *Uses of Literacy* vi. 144 The leader-writers of the popular Press make great play with horizons, new dawns, broad highways, forward movements..and forward-lookers. *Ibid.* 149 The popular papers, always identifying themselves with 'the people', conduct polls on this matter and questionnaires on that matter among their readers, and so elevate the counting of heads into a substitute for judgment. **1960** K. Amis *New Maps of Hell* (1961) ii. 53 A popular-science article on atomic physics. **1964** Hall & Whannel *Popular Arts* vii. 165 Popular romance..is full of variants on the Romeo-and-Juliet or Cinderella themes. **1972** S. Hynes *Edwardian Occasions* 178 Hewlett..had begun by working entirely within the established conventions of the popular romance. **1976** *Conservation News* Sept./Oct. 9/1 The wartime slogan 'Digging for Victory' has reappeared in the popular press. **1977** *New Yorker* 19 Sept. 133/1 Why is it that there is not more good popular-science writing?

b. (Further examples of phr. *popular price.*) Also *attrib.*

1885 C. E. Pascoe *London of To-day* iv. 67 The multitude which invades the 'Zoo' on Monday, which is the 'popular-price' day, when a sixpence opens the gate to the neediest. **1890** *Lady's Pictorial* 15 Mar. 347/3 The book is to be produced at the popular price of one shilling. **1911** G. B. Shaw *Doctor's Dilemma* p. xxxvii, Yet people expect to find vaccines..retailed at 'popular prices' in private enterprise shops just as they expect to find ounces of tobacco and papers of pins. **1916** *Variety* 27 Oct. 12/1 Sid Grauman's 'Night at the World's Fair' is drawing well at the Majestic, attendance doubtless being encouraged by popular prices. **1971** L. Lamb *Worse than Death* ii. 23 'Teas at popular prices?' 'Oh, the teas were cheap enough.'

6. b. Designating (aspects of) art and culture whose forms appeal to or are favoured by people generally; esp. in *popular art, music, song*, etc.

Also influenced by sense 4.

1841 S. Bamford *Passages in Life of Radical* (ed. 2) I. xxxiii. 200 A hundred or two of our handsomest girls..danced to the music, or sung snatches of popular songs. **1855** W. Chappell (*title*) Popular music of the olden time. **1866** C. Engel *Introd. Study National Mus.* v. 168 The peculiar character of the popular music of a nation appears to be in great measure determined by the climate of the country, by the occupation and habits of the people, and even by the food upon which they principally subsist. **1898** G. B. Shaw *Plays Pleasant & Unpleasant* I. p. v, I had no taste for what is called popular art, no respect for popular morality, [etc.]. **1911** H. G. Hewlett *Chorley's National Mus. of World* (ed. 3) 201 The large share,..which popular, if not Church, music has taken and takes in mourning for the dead in Ireland, is a characteristic not to be overlooked. **1927** R. H. Wilenski *Mod. Movement in Art* 28 The nineteenth century produced original and popular art of the romantic and descriptive kinds. **1934** A. Huxley *Beyond Mexique Bay* 267 Where popular art is vulgar, there the life of the people is also essentially vulgar in its emotional quality. **1935** *Vanity Fair* (N.Y.) Nov. 38/1 Our jazzmen have had no attention except for the exploitation of a few Tin-Pan Alley terms concerning the popular song industry. **1941** *Musical Q.* XXVII. 48 The prevalent false dichotomy of 'classical' and 'popular' based on a belief in the inferiority of the latter as music. **1947** *Sat. Rev. Lit.* (U.S.) 10 May 9/2 By popular art we mean creative work that measures success by the size of its audience and the profit it brings to its makers. **1956** B. Nettl *Mus. in Primitive Culture* ix. 121 American Negro material..has had its effect on folk music, on popular music in the form of jazz, and on a good deal of cultivated music. **1957** R. Hoggart *Uses of Literacy* I. v. 129 The finest period in English urban popular song seems to have been between 1880 and 1910, when each great music-hall star had errand boys and earls singing his or her characteristic songs. **1959** *News Chron.* 10 July 3/2 'Search your attics, turn out your cupboards,' exhorted the B.B.C., 'and join in a television treasure hunt.'.. This is a first-class idea for popular culture. **1962** A. Nisbett *Technique Sound Studio* iii. 65 This method is employed a great deal in the recording of popular music—but very rarely indeed for serious music. **1964** Hall & Whannel *Popular Arts* iii. 66 In the previous chapter we tried to show the continuity between folk art and popular art. Then, by following the line of continuity into the early cinema and Chaplin, we indicated the way in which this popular art emerged within the new media. **1966** D. Jenkins *Educated Society* ii. 58 Popular culture, which..is to be sharply distinguished from..commercialized 'pop culture'..is the style of life of the majority of the members of a community. **1978** J. Pascall *Illustr. Hist. Rock Music* 12 Popular music has never existed to be analysed. It has existed purely to give pleasure. Rock & roll, more than any other popular music, defies intellectual examination. **1979** *Jrnl. R. Soc. Arts* July 511/2 It is a catalogue of one of the largest collections of Indian popular painting outside India itself.

7. b. *popular etymology* [tr. G. *Volksetymologie*] = *folk etymology* (Folk 6).

1880 A. H. Sayce *Introd. Sci. of Lang.* II. ix. 246 Such myths are created by those popular etymologies—that *Volksetymologie* as the Germans call it—which play so large a part in local names. **1901** H. Oertel *Lect. Study of Lang.* iii. 187 In all cases of so-called popular etymology it is necessary that the meaning of one of the two words should be unknown, that of the other familiar. **1926** Fowler *Mod. Eng. Usage* 227/1 It is true..that *-yard* [in *halyard*] is no better than a popular-etymology corruption. **1933** L. Bloomfield *Language* xxiii. 423 So-called popular etymologies are largely adaptive and contaminative. An irregular or semantically obscure form is replaced by a new form of more normal structure and some semantic content—though the latter is often far-fetched. **1934** S. Robertson *Devel. Mod. Eng.* (1936) xi. 456 Words altered by popular etymology have often..displaced the original forms and become thoroughly accepted in standard speech. **1958** A. S. C. Ross *Etym.* i. 68 There is..another subject to which the General Public applies the name *etymology*, a subject which philologists often call *Popular Etymology*. This subject is one quite without value but..it is one of the great breeders of popular fallacies.

9. *popular-minded, -priced* (later examples).

1837 J. S. Mill in *Westm. Rev.* XXXVII. 8 This want is most felt..by the most popular-minded public men. **1916** *Variety* 27 Oct. 12/1 'The Little Girl that God Forgot', the popular priced attraction at the Crescent opened Sunday. **1958** *Newnes Compl. Amat. Photogr.* xvi. 158 The more popular-priced cameras fitted with lenses of f/3·5 or f/4·5, will be fast enough for instantaneous exposures in artificial light.

B. *absol.* or as *sb.* **c.** (Earlier and later examples.)

1865 *Punch* 4 Mar. 92/1 Pity poor Lucy! Obliged to go to the Monday Popular with Cousin Bess (from the country). **1894** [see *Brahmsian *a.* and *sb.*].

d. Short for *popular newspaper*: see sense 4 a above.

1952 [see sense 4 a above]. **1961** *Times* 11 Feb. 5/5 (Advt.), Choosing one's Sunday newspaper seems to have become a shade less straightforward in 1961. For forty years the alternative has had such a bonny simplicity about it: on the one hand the 'posh Sundays', on the other the populars. **1964** 'W. Haggard' *Antagonists* xviii. 169 The Press was besieging Nikola Mitrovic... He was hinting at women and money... The populars would run it hard. **1968** *Economist* 7 Sept. 67/2 If the decline of the populars continues, Fleet Street stands to lose a third of its present newspapers. **1976** T. Heald *Let Sleeping Dogs Die* vi. 110 Bognor..picked up the paper. It was one of the populars.

Popular Front. Also with lower-case initials. [tr. Sp. *frente popular*, F. *front populaire* in the same sense: see *front *sb.* 5 g.] An international political alliance of Communist, radical, and Socialist elements formed in 1935 and gaining power in France (1936–38), Spain (1936), and Chile (1938–42), although in Europe it was largely ineffective after 1938. Also *transf.*, of other radical or popular movements.

1936, etc. [see *front *sb.* 5 g]. **1936** *Age* (Melbourne) 5 May 11/7 The crowds last week were predominantly hostile to the Popular Front. **1937** 'G. Orwell' in *New English Weekly* 29 July 308/1 The worker and the bourgeois,..are fighting side by side. This uneasy alliance is known as the Popular Front. **1940** H. G. Wells *Babes in Darkling Wood* iv. iii. 380 The idea seems to be to make it the working credo of one world-wide popular front. **1942** E. Paul *Narrow St.* xxxi. 280 The Popular Front election, April 16 to 21, 1936, was the last held in France, as the Popular Front election in February of that same year was the last held in Spain. **1958** *Spectator* 6 June 721/1 A Popular Front drifting into Communism. **1960** C. Day Lewis *Buried Day* x. 219 The Spanish war began: the Popular Front was formed 'against fascism and war'. In Cheltenham the Party group sought to engage the local Labour Party in popular-front activities. **1963** *Listener* 14 Mar. 450/1 He [*sc.* Khrushchev] looks forward to the appearance of strong Popular Front movements, similar to those in the late nineteen-thirties. **1966** K. Martin *Father Figures* x. 205 Was it true that a Popular Front was the only hope of salvation? **1970** *Guardian* 25 Feb. 1/2 The 'hardline' guerrilla groups are led by the Popular Front for the Liberation of Palestine. **1971** I. Deutscher *Marxism in our Time* (1972) 291 The Popular Front was Stalinism's reaction against its own ultraleft follies through which it had smoothed Hitler's road to power. **1976** S. Hynes *Auden Generation* vii. 210 At the Albert Hall in February 1937..Harry Pollitt..spoke in support of the Spanish Loyalists and the Popular Front.

Hence **Popular Fronter**, one who supports the Popular Front; **Popular Fronting**, activity associated with the Popular Front; **Popular Frontism**, the principles or policies maintained by the Popular Front.

1938 *Nation* (N.Y.) 14 May 555/1 He [*sc.* Philip F. La Follette] wants no more to be tied to trade unionism, as the British progressives are, than he wants to be tied to popular frontism, as the French progressives are. **1940** *Economist* 13 July 36/1 The Russians were liquidating Popular Frontism at home. **1941** 'G. Orwell' in *Partisan Rev.* Mar.–Apr. 110 It was extremely amusing to watch the behaviour of orthodox Popular Front-ers, who were exclaiming dolefully 'It's going to be another Munich.' **1957** *New Republican* 7 Jan. 14/2 What kind of liberals will you find in the average large university? A handful of ADA people, most of them far from firebrands; *perhaps* one liberal of the sort who feels a nostalgic attachment to Popular Frontism. **1969** M. Steed in Henig & Pinder *European Pol. Parties* 157 There has been no suggestion that any formal links should be created between the fgds and the Communist Party... Whilst the popular fronting of 1966–68 was happily accepted by both sides.., it broke up in May 1969, when rival presidential candidates were chosen.

popularism. Add: **b.** = Populism a in Dict. and Suppl.

1961 *Sewanee Rev.* Autumn 519 French Egalitarianism had had only nominal influence in this country before the days of Popularism. **1962** *Listener* 5 Apr. 584/1 For a clearer understanding of what is happening we should be ready to play down these uneasy notions of right and left, and, instead, study British political attitudes in terms of republicanism and popularism.

popularist. Add: **a.** (Later *attrib.* examples.) **c.** *attrib.* or as *adj.*, concerning or appealing to the people generally, popular.

1922 *New Witness* 25 Aug. 120/2 The P.P.I. must now

be reckoned with as the most powerful political force in Italy... When one comes finally to examine the main points in the Popularist programme, one meets old friends often discussed in these pages. **1962** *Listener* 5 Apr. 585/2 The popularist fear of going into Europe is the fear of being swamped in another Holy Roman Empire. **1970** *New Yorker* 10 Oct. 150 What emerged was a popularist outlook (Hightower called it 'human') and the determination to dissolve painting and sculpture into broader aesthetic streams. **1970** *Guardian Weekly* 14 Nov. 3/4 There is no doubt that, after two years of passive and effacingly popularist administration, the President of All the People [*sc.* Nixon] tried to become President of Most of the People; a President who saw an opening to the..right.

popularity. Add: **8.** *popularity-hunting* (later example); **popularity contest,** a competition in which the popularity of the contenders is judged; freq. *transf.* and in allusive uses with reference (chiefly in negative contexts) to one's supposed popularity; **popularity poll** [*POLL *sb.*[1] 7 d], a poll taken from a section of a population in order to assess the popularity of a particular person or proposition in terms of the population as a whole; **popularity rating,** an assessment of popularity based on the findings of a **popularity poll.*

1941 B. SCHULBERG *What makes Sammy Run?* i. 15 I'm not running a popularity contest; I'm running a business office. **1952** *Manch. Guardian Weekly* 24 Apr. 8/4 This is a 'popularity contest' only; the results are not binding on the delegates of either party. **1959** R. CONDON *Manchurian Candidate* (1960) xvii. 211 Life isn't a popularity contest... I didn't ask them to like me. **1964** E. AMBLER *Kind of Anger* i. 16 You wouldn't win a popularity contest where he's concerned, and..he can be a vindictive old bastard. **1973** 'E. MCBAIN' *Hail to Chief* i. 15 The decisions I make ain't always popular, but..I'm not running no popularity contest. **1976** *National Observer* (U.S.) 1 May 4/5 Unless he can really blast a hole through this interest screen in the Democratic Party by winning handsomely in the primaries, not just in the popularity contests but in the delegate races as well, then I suspect he could be squeezed out at the convention. **1946** W. S. CHURCHILL *Victory* 162 Sir, I trust there will be no popularity-hunting at the public expense. **1938** 'E. QUEEN' *Four of Hearts* ix. 127 Three outstanding stars (selected..on the basis of the latest popularity poll conducted by Paula Paris for the newspaper syndicate). **1958** *Punch* 1 Jan. 50/1 Continuing to top the popularity poll for the masses was Princess Margaret. **1962** *Sunday Times* (Colour Suppl.) 10 June 3 A fact recognised in this year's *Melody Maker* popularity poll. **1972** *Country Life* 10 Feb. 347/3 Let us pray that they [*sc.* poodles] will never find themselves leading the popularity poll. **1979** J. WAINWRIGHT *Duty Elsewhere* lxiii. 176 Calling an assistant chief constable a flaming liar doesn't win popularity polls. *a* **1974** R. CROSSMAN *Diaries* (1977) III. 327 *The Times* has a poll showing a 20 per cent lead for the Tories, with a new popularity rating specially designed so that Ted Heath can be ahead of Harold Wilson. **1974** *Listener* 17 Jan. 70/1 The Japanese Prime Minister..enjoys an even lower popularity-rating..than President Nixon.

popularization. Add: (Later examples.) *spec.* (in sense 2 c of the vb.), the adapting of ideas or theories to the level of an educated but non-specialist public; freq. with derogatory connotations, the over-simplification of a subject to suit popular taste (cf. *POPULAR *a.* (*sb.*) 4 a). Also, the result or product of this process.

1926 WYNDHAM LEWIS *Art of Being Ruled* XIII. iv. 423 It is plainly the popularization of science that is responsible for the fever and instability apparent on all sides. **1951** M. MCLUHAN *Mech. Bride* (1967) 28/1 The lethal psychological and social effects..arise not from science but from its popularization. **1962** *Listener* 18 Jan. 119/1 Popularization is, then, a word with a moral identity... It implies..that the cases it describes are those where the subject is misrepresented by this treatment; where the truth of the matter has been diluted, if not falsified. **1973** *Nature* 23 Mar. 280/1 This book is more than an extraordinarily successful popularization. **1974** B. PEARCE tr. *Amin's Accumulation on World Scale* II. 591 Mandel places alongside a popularization of *Capital* a diatribe against the Soviet bureaucracy. **1977** M. COHEN *Sensible Words* 157 John W. Yolton..discusses Gildon's *Deist's Manual* (1705) as an important imitation and popularization of Locke's epistemology.

popularize, *v.* Add: **2. c.** (Earlier and later examples.) Also *absol.*

1833 J. S. MILL in *Monthly Repos.* VII. 266 The peculiar 'mission' of this age..is to popularize among the many, the more immediately practical results of the thought and experience of the few. **1916** G. B. SHAW *Pygmalion* 100 His [*sc.* Henry Sweet's] great ability as a phonetician..would have entitled him to high official recognition, and perhaps enabled him to popularize his subject, but for his Satanic contempt for all academic dignitaries and persons in general who thought more of Greek than of phonetics. **1923** *Times Lit. Suppl.* 4 Jan. 10/3 True-blue musicians; they knew their facts and.. looked at them steadily in order to check their theories, and they did not popularize.

d. To make (a word) generally known, *spec.* to use or encourage the use of (technical vocabulary) in general contexts or in everyday language.

1921 G. B. SHAW *Back to Methuselah* p. xliii, Why did not Erasmus Darwin popularize the word Evolution as effectively as Charles? **1926** [implied in *POPULARIZED *ppl. a.*]. **1965** E. GOWERS *Fowler's Mod. Eng. Usage* (ed. 2) 461/1 Our interest in our bodies has always made us prone to popularize medical terms.

popularized *ppl. a.* (later examples); **popularizer** (later examples).

1919 M. BEER *Hist. Brit. Socialism* I. I. vi. 80 Adam Smith and Abraham Tucker's populariser, Paley, either use and interpret natural law in a conservative sense or draw its social-revolutionary teeth. **1926** FOWLER *Mod. Eng. Usage* 444/2 A few examples of these popularized technicalities may be gathered together. **1934** H. G. WELLS *Exper. Autobiogr.* II. viii. 546 He..began writing books for the general reader and essays in natural history. He was a successful popularizer. **1951** M. MCLUHAN *Mech. Bride* (1967) 48/1 Professor Kinsey's book is a *carte blanche* for maximal genital activity. As popularized science, that is its entire drift. **1974** *Nature* 30 Aug. 754/1 The populariser of science, as he functions today, cannot disseminate the subtle ideas of science. **1978** *Ibid.* 31 Aug. 930/3 Popularisers have a duty to be scrupulous in matters of fact and clarity of presentation.

population[2]. Add: **2. c.** (Further examples.) Also of other entities.

1956 A. H. COMPTON *Atomic Quest* ii. 89 If the neutron population is increasing generation after generation, the reaction grows in intensity. **1968** *Brit. Med. Bull.* XXIV. 244/1 Much study has therefore gone into the effect of radiation on proliferating cell populations in various environments.

d. *Statistics.* A totality of objects or individuals under consideration, of which the statistical attributes may be estimated by the study of a sample or samples drawn from it.

1877 F. GALTON in *Nature* 12 Apr. 513/2 The number of pellets in each compartment represents the relative number in a *population* of seeds, whose weight deviates from the average, within the limits expressed by the distances of the sides of that compartment from the middle point. **1903** *Biometrika* II. 273 If the whole of a population were taken we should have certain values for its statistical constants, but in actual practice we are only able to take a sample, which should if possible be a random sample. **1922** *Phil. Trans. R. Soc.* A. CCXXII. 329 It is unfortunate that in this memoir no sufficient distinction is drawn between the *population* and the *sample.* **1939** D. D. PATERSON *Statistical Technique in Agric. Res.* i. 1 The sum total of all the units of any one kind is called, in statistical terminology, the population. **1970** *Jrnl. Gen. Psychol.* LXXXIII. 14 The experimenter notes that Ss used in this study had experienced only a brief period of hospitalization... Consequently, he cautions against the generalization of his findings to other neurotic and schizophrenic populations. **1977** *Accountants Weekly* 29 July 17/1 The tests built into the program ensured that sample data extracted for audit checks came from a complete population, a fundamental requirement in auditing.

e. *Genetics.* A breeding group of animals, plants, or humans; **population biology, genetics,** the branches of biology and genetics which treat such groups statistically. So *population biologist, geneticist.*

1889 F. GALTON *Nat. Inheritance* iv. 35 The science of heredity is concerned with Fraternities and large Populations rather than with individuals, and must treat them as units. **1949** C. STERN *Princ. Human Genetics* x. 168 Both fields, population genetics and pedigree genetics, are significant and both rest on the Mendelian analysis of inheritance. *Ibid.* 594 The genic constitution of the later populations will obviously depend on the genotypes of their second-generation ancestors. **1960** *Biol. Abstr.* XXXV. 1729/1 (*heading*) Data on ecology and population biology of mosquitoes. **1966** MACARTHUR & CONNELL *Biol. of Populations* p. x, Experiments performed by population biologists indicate another difference between population biology and other branches of science. **1966** R. ARDREY *Territorial Imperative* iv. 138 A population, in biology, is a reproductive community. More sharply stated, it is any group of individuals who have a modest probability, within any generation, of meeting and mating. **1968** R. C. LEWONTIN *Population Biol. & Evolution* 2 It is a problem of population biology to discover under what circumstances a one-to-one sex ratio is evolved. **1972** *Sci. Amer.* Jan. 100/3 He maintained four populations of *Drosophila* in the laboratory over a 48-month period. **1973** *Listener* 28 June 850/2 He [*sc.* A. Jensen] now knows a good deal more about population genetics than he did..in 1968. **1977** *Nature* 6 Jan. 26/2 The basic interests of the population geneticist of course lie in the realm of population dynamics, and the knowledge of allele frequencies is an essential prerequisite to further work. **1979** *Ibid.* 9 Aug. 455 (*heading*) Population biology of infectious diseases.

f. *Physics.* The (number of) atoms or subatomic particles that occupy any particular energy state.

1931 *Physical Rev.* XXXVII. 143 (*caption*) Illustrating the relation between spectral intensity distribution in the Compton line (left) and population of electron speed states (right). **1938** R. W. LAWSON tr. *Hevesy & Paneth's Man. Radioactivity* (ed. 2) viii. 88 The resulting gap in the atom, due to the incomplete population of the *K*-shell, may now be filled by the transition of an electron from the *L*-level into the *K*-level. **1961** [see *INVERSION 2 l]. **1971** *Sci. Amer.* June 22/1 By elevating more atoms to an upper energy level than exist at a lower level the absorption of excitation radiation produces an 'inverted' atomic population in the laser.

g. *Astr.* Either of the two groups into which stars can be approximately divided: those of *population I* are formed from the debris of other stars, those of *population II* are coeval with their galaxy.

[**1944** W. BAADE in *Astrophysical Jrnl.* C. 137 The stellar populations of the galaxies fall into two distinct groups, one represented by the..stars in our solar neighborhood (the slow-moving stars), the other by that of the globular clusters. Characteristic of the first group (type I) are highly luminous O- and B-type stars and open clusters; of the second (type II), short-period Cepheids and globular clusters.] **1951** *Astrophysical Jrnl.* CXIII. 413 Highly luminous stars of population I. **1952** C. PAYNE-GAPOSCHKIN *Stars in Making* iv. 74 The names 'Populations I and II' were originally given by Baade to the two groups of stars. As we shall see, they probably represent extremes rather than an absolute distinction. **1974** F. W. COLE *Fund. Astron.* xiii. 344/1 Two very different populations of stars can be recognized: population I consisting of the normal, metal-rich stars found in spiral arms of galaxies; and population II, the metal-poor stars found in globular clusters, as isolated stars in the galactic halo, and in the central galactic nucleus.

h. The general body of inmates in a prison, rehabilitation centre, etc. (see quot. 1950). Freq. in phr. *in population.*

1950 H. E. GOLDIN *Dict. Amer. Underworld Lingo* 162/2 *Population,* ..the general body of inmates as differentiated from convicts in trusty jobs, hospital patients, and occupants of punishment or psychopathic observation wings. **1953** W. BURROUGHS *Junkie* viii. 79 After eight days, you get a sendoff shot and go over in 'population'... You are allowed seven days to rest in population after medication stops. **1956** J. RESKO *Reprieve* (1959) III. xvi. 135 Our friends out in population took care of us. **1971** *Black Scholar* June 54/1 The officials told me that I would never be returned to the general population (Auburn) and advised me to put in for transfer to another institution. **1973** *Philadelphia Inquirer* (Today Suppl.) 7 Oct. 50/3 Sprague tried to block Soleni's move into general population. **1977** *New Yorker* 24 Oct. 68/2 Collectively, the inmates are referred to as 'population'.

4. *population census, control, cycle, distribution, drift, growth, increase, planning, policy, pressure, question, survey, theory, trend;* **population biology:** see sense 2 e above; **population curve,** a graph showing the variation of population with time; **population explosion,** a rapid or sudden marked increase in the size of a population; hence *population-explosive* adj.; **population genetics:** see sense 2 e above; **population inversion:** see *INVERSION 2 l; **population pyramid,** a roughly triangular figure on a level base, the width of which at any height is proportional to the numbers having an age proportional to that height.

1968 *Internat. Encycl. Social Sci.* XII. 369/1 In most advanced countries illiteracy has been almost eliminated, and therefore questions on literacy are no longer included in population censuses. **1931** J. S. HUXLEY *What dare I Think?* v. 166 Might it not have been better to have left the death side of nature's population-control to itself until we have some future policy for dealing simultaneously with birth? **1959** *New Statesman* 21 Mar. 401/1 Countries like India and Japan have made population-control a central feature in national policy, because they know that without it they are headed for disaster. **1973** J. M. WHITE *Garden Game* 117 War is becoming a necessary instrument of population-control. **1889** F. GALTON *Nat. Inheritance* 245 The population curve will..be a straight line. **1935** *Proc. Prehist. Soc.* I. 11 Advances of critical importance to humanity should be followed by such a multiplication as to be conspicuously reflected in the population curve. **1968** *N.Y. City* (Michelin Tire Corp.) 139 Long Island... The population curve is constantly rising. **1969** N. W. PIRIE *Food Resources* ii. 70 A few plant and animal species..go through fairly regular population cycles. **1968** R. A. LYTTLETON *Mysteries Solar Syst.* vi. 185 The density of finds does show some relation to the population-distribution. **1974** *Encycl. Brit. Macropædia* XVII. 67/2 The pattern of population distribution and density closely follows that of the rainfall pattern. **1964** *Ann. Reg. 1963* 22 The Minister of Housing and Local Government..was wrestling with the problems of population drift, regional planning, and slum clearance. **1977** *Modern Railways* Dec. 480/1 Population drift from the London area to central and north-east Essex necessitated a fundamental restructure of Great Eastern line services. **1953** *Population Bull.* Oct. 65 (*heading*) Latin America: area of population explosion. **1953** [see *EXPLOSION 4 b]. **1964** 'J. MELVILLE' *Murderers' Houses* vii. 116 Emily knew all about the Bomb and the Pill and could advocate one remedy for the declining Middle Classes and another for the Population Explosion. **1970** *Oxf. Univ. Gaz.* C. Suppl. VI. 5 A kind of documentary population-explosion, in fact. **1970** *Daily Tel.* 18 July 11/7 Population explosions in summer may result in up to 10 million aphides taking to the air each day from an acre. **1974** *Times* 21 Jan. 6 (*heading*) Leading the fight to head off the population explosion. **1967** *Punch* 3 May 637/3 This two-way flow, once started, would never stop; no government, much less any shipping company, could ever stop such a flow, population-explosive, travel-agency-prodded and democratic. **1927** J. S. HUXLEY *Relig. without Revelation* ix. 325 The study of heredity and population-growth. **1970** G. GERMANI in I. L. Horowitz *Masses in Lat. Amer.* viii. 295 With regard to the other Latin American states, it is clear that immigration made a crucial contribution to population growth. **1978** R. MITCHISON *Life in Scotland* vi. 108 Industrialization..was..the 'answer' to that population growth. **1931** J. S. HUXLEY *What dare I Think?* iv. 135 Population-increase cannot go on indefinitely. **1959** *New Statesman* 21 Mar. 401/1 In under-developed countries, excessive population-increase reduces the possibility of an economic break-through. **1974** *Times* 21 Jan. 6/2 The idea of population planning antagonized many countries. **1944** J. S. HUXLEY *On living in Revolution* xii. 131 It is very important that there should be a well-thought-out population policy for backward areas. **1974** *Times* 21 Jan. 6/5 Opposition to..population policies is led by countries with..large natural resources. **1931** J. S. HUXLEY *What dare I Think?* v. 165 Causing more babies to live and so creating greater population-pressure. **1969** *Times* 26 June 14/7 The migrations..could be a means of relieving the population pressure in a particular area. **1950** *Chambers's Encycl.* XI. 93/2 The age distribution in populations of plaice and other fish has been examined; and attempts have been made to study honey-bee colonies and wireworm populations from this point of view. All show, under natural conditions, the expected 'population pyramid', formed by large numbers of young ndividuals and gradually decreasing numbers of individuals of the higher age-groups. **1976** *Nature* 1 July 19/1 As a result of their high crude birth rate..the population pyramid has a relatively broad base; 51·8% are less than 20 yr old and 28·7% are less than 10 yr old. **1885** *Encycl. Brit.* XIX. 517/2 We cannot here deal with what is known as the population question'... The 'population question' is a question of conduct. **1911** G. B. SHAW *Getting Married* 116 St. Paul's reluctant sanction of marriage;.. his contemptuous 'better to marry than to burn' is only out of date in respect of his belief that the end of the world was at hand and that there was therefore no longer any population question. **1953** Population survey [see *ATTRACTANT]. **1966** *Economist* 17 Dec. 1253/3 Except in the matter of population theory, where he anticipated and influenced Malthus, Steuart had little or no effect on later economic thought in Britain. **1933** THOMPSON & WHELPTON (*title*) Population trends in the United States. **1950** THEIMER & CAMPBELL *Encycl. World Politics* 347/1 In the U.S.S.R., Eastern Europe and Latin America population trends are like those of the West in the later nineteenth century. **1976** J. S. MOORE *Goods & Chattels of our Forefathers* 9 The main population-trends can already be seen from a study of the data contained in the numerous ecclesiastical and private censuses taken in Gloucestershire in the early modern period.

populationist. Delete *nonce-wd.* and add later examples. Also, one who considers the population to be a significant element in a state's power.

1949 K. DAVIS *Human Society* 552 If the populationist stopped here, however, his work would have little to do with social science. **1968** *Internat. Encycl. Social Sci.* XII. 350/2 In Germany, Hermann Conring also attributed the power of states mainly to population. In England.. another confirmed populationist was William Petty, who founded the science of 'political arithmetic', or demography.

populism. Add: (Further examples.) Also *transf.*

1960 *Encounter* July 13 Russian Populism is the name.. of a widespread radical movement in Russia in the middle of the 19th century. **1969** [see *POPULISTIC *a.*]. **1972** *Time* 17 Apr. 31/1 Populism is a label that covers disparate policies and passions: among many others, New Deal reforms, consumer rage against business, ethnic belligerence. Often it is merely a catch phrase. Yet it describes something real: the politics of the little guy against the big guy—the classic struggle of the haves against the have-nots or the have-not-enoughs. **1973** *Black Panther* 21 July 3/2 The result was the defeat of western Populism and the further entrenchment of racism. **1976** T. EAGLETON *Crit. & Ideology* v. 166 Populism and theoreticism, in aesthetics as in politics, are familiar deformations of Marxist-Leninism. **1977** *Time* 3 Jan. 7/1 His creed combines traditionally antithetical elements of help-the-deprived populism and deny-thyself fiscal conservatism.

b. The theories and practices of the populist movement in French literature.

[**1929** L. LEMONNIER in *Revue Mondiale* 1 Oct. 281 (*title*) Du naturalisme au populisme.] **1930** —— in *This Quarter* Mar. 440 (*title*) Populism. *Ibid.* 443 At last, we hit upon the word 'populism'. It clearly expressed the fact that we meant to depict the people; it was not altogether a new word in French, inasmuch as it had been used to translate the name of the German political party *Volkspartei*, but it had never as yet been applied to any artistic, political or literary movement specifically French. Having then dubbed ourselves populists, we decided to write a manifesto. **1931** *French Rev.* IV. 473 Since the opening of the twentieth century, only three schools have counted [in French literature], unanimism, between 1908 and 1911, surrealism, about 1924, and populism in 1929. **1932** *Ibid.* V. 389 Populism is the antonym of 'snobisme'. **1934** F. WALTER tr. *Lemonnier's Populisme* in *PMLA* Mar. 356 Populism is a reaction founded on the realistic tradition and directed against the literature of analysis. **1934** *N. & Q.* 26 May 361/1 The beginnings of Populism, adumbrated somewhat obscurely in 1924, came out into shape in 1929 under the initiative of M. André Thérive and M. Léon Lemonnier. *Ibid.* 361/2 In Thérive's 'Le Baiser de Satan,' Populism has attempted what Naturalism shied from the historical novel.

populist. Add: **3.** A member of a group of French novelists in the late 1920s and early 1930s who placed emphasis upon observation of and sympathy with ordinary people.

[**1929** L. LEMONNIER in *Revue Mondiale* 1 Oct. 285 Tous ces romanciers viennent de se grouper et de se donner un nom: ils veulent être les *romanciers populistes.* Ils entendent le mot dans un sens très large.] **1930** [see *POPULISM b]. **1934** *PMLA* XLIX. 361 A sort of Tolstoyan sympathy is a cardinal virtue in the eyes of the Populists. **1934** *N. & Q.* 26 May 361/2 Eugène Dabit (a genuine proletarian), though a populist, begins somewhat to abandon the political and social neutrality.

4. One who seeks to represent the views of the mass of ordinary people.

1961 *Listener* 30 Nov. 897/2 They are not Populists or Poujadists. **1972** *New Society* 20 Jan. 131/1 LBJ was a true populist, as he recognised himself, remarking tartly (and justly enough) that it is 'the term some liberals reserve for Progressives who come from the southern and western parts of the nation'. **1977** *Time* 7 Mar. 7/1 Brogan questions whether Carter is a bona fide populist at all.

5. *attrib.* or as *adj.*

1893 [in Dict., sense 1]. **1898** *Nation* (N.Y.) 7 July 6/2 The Populist Governor abused his power by appointing as commissioners only men of his own party. **1924** *Glasgow Herald* 4 July 7 He [*sc.* the Russian intellectual] has lost much of his former 'populist' idealism, of his old worship of the people. **1928** [see *CENTRIST b]. **1931** *French Rev.* IV. 473 This paper will give an account of the rise and origins of the populist school. **1934** R. MICHAUD *Mod. Thought & Lit. in France* xi. 228 A so-called 'populist movement' was launched in 1929 by Léon Lemonnier and André Thérive, as a protest against the précieux and individualistic novel and as a return to the great naturalistic traditions of Zola. **1954** E. A. SHILS in Christie & Jahoda *Stud. Scope & Method of 'The Authoritarian Personality'* 45 A vein of xenophobia, populist, anti-urban and anti-plutocratic sentiment. **1955** H. PEYRE *Contemp. French Novel* ii. 47 Duhamel never made a speciality of the study of misery, as did the proletarian novelists and later a short-lived group of 'populist' novelists (Henri Poulaille, André Thérive, Eugène Dabit). **1961** *Listener* 7 Dec. 997/1 There is the ascending conception [of law and government], according to which the law-creating power may be ascribed to the community or people—the populist theory. **1968** W. SAFIRE *New Lang. Politics* 346/2 When the Populist candidate, General James B. Weaver, won 22 Electoral College and 1,029,846 popular votes in the 1892 election, many people..were fearful of impending revolution. **1969** R. BLACKBURN in Cockburn & Blackburn *Student Power* 190 A wholesale revision of classic liberal democratic theory to eliminate its dangerously populist tendencies and to accommodate the elitist features of contemporary capitalist society. **1974** M. B. BROWN *Econ. of Imperialism* xi. 275 Populist forms of government in the ex-colonial underdeveloped lands were overthrown mainly because they failed to develop their economies. **1976** *Survey* Summer–Autumn 15 There is little doubt that US policy..will be dominated by self-consciously populist politicians. **1977** *Time* 21 Mar. 53/3 Ironically, the very success of Carter's populist appeal may cause him special backlash problems.

populistic *a.* (further examples); **populi·stically** *adv.*

1969 D. MACRAE in Ionescu & Gellner *Populism* 162 That Ireland did not produce a full-fledged populism—as distinct from populistic themes that continue through De Valera to the present—is a paradox of European history. **1971** S. CAVELL *World Viewed* 54 A film like *Mr. Smith Goes to Washington*..suggests, populistically, ..that they are curable by the individual or mass goodness of the little people. **1976** *Times Lit. Suppl.* 16 Apr. 457/2 A man with his own blend of simple, populistic dignity and even honesty.

pop-up (pǫ·pʊp), *sb.* and *a.* [f. POP *v.*[1] + UP *adv.*[1]]. **A.** *sb.* **1.** *Baseball.* A ball which is hit softly up into the air and is easily caught.

1906 *Spalding's Offic. Base Ball Guide* 126 A trapped ball play was made when runners were on bases, and a 'pop-up' fly ball was expected to be caught. **1926** *Amer. Speech* I. 369/1 A 'pop-up', for an infantile attempt to hit, is beautifully characteristic of the contempt prompting its use. **1950** *Sun* (Baltimore) 6 Oct. (B ed.) 19/6 He hoisted four infield pop-ups. **1974** *Evening Herald* (Rock Hill, S. Carolina) 19 Apr. 7/1 Hager drew another intentional walk loading the bases but Holmes escaped the jam by getting Conner on a popup to third and Larry Hinson on a fly to right. **1978** *Time* 3 July 60/1 One of their catchers, Frank Mancuso, was a former lieutenant who had injured his back during parachute training; he could neither remain in the Army nor look skyward for a pop-up.

2. A pop-up toaster, trailer, etc.

1970 *New Yorker* 14 Nov. 49/3 Browned off like a piece of toast in a broken pop-up. **1976** *Times Lit. Suppl.* 6 Aug. 991 (Advt.), We manufacture jigsaw puzzles, pop-ups and other educational toys. **1978** *Sunday Sun-Times* (Chicago) 1 Jan. 122/1 Another popular RV type is the camping trailer, or 'pop-up'. **1978** *Detroit Free Press* 2 Apr. 17F/3, '75 Apache pop-up, slps 8, refrig, stove, heater, awning, exc cond.

B. *adj.* **a.** Designed to pop up or having a component that pops up. **b.** With a mechanism which causes something to pop up; esp. *pop-up toaster*: an electric toaster in which the sliced bread pops up when it is ready.

1934 in WEBSTER. **1959** C. OGBURN *Marauders* (1960) ii. 65 We shot off quantities of ammunition, mostly at informal or pop-up targets. **1959** 'E. MCBAIN' *Pusher* v. 42 The precinct house..did not boast chintz curtains or pop-up toasters. **1960** S. KAUFFMANN *If it be Love* I. vi. 90 An electric dishwasher and deep freeze and pop-up toaster. **1962** N. FREELING *Love in Amsterdam* I. 29 The pretty girl..flipped a pop-up file like those for telephone numbers. **1962** *Which? Car Suppl.* Apr. 55/1 The Austin A60 was the only car which did not have pop-up knobs..which show easily whether the doors are locked or not. **1963** S. MARSHALL *Exper. in Educ.* iv. 153 Every illustration is conceived and executed as a 'pop-up' scene. **1966** *Listener* 24 Nov. 755/1 This is a toaster of standard performance—the pop-up kind. **1972** *Times* 6 Dec. 22/6 A birthday card, with a pop-up centre. **1973** *Country Life* 19 July 151/3 For large lawns the most advanced system is the pop-up sprinkler..small spray nozzles which only appear above turf level when the water is turned on. **1975** *Evening News* 26 Apr. 4/1 London motorists may soon face..pop-up metal barriers ..to keep them off bus-only lanes. **1978** *Dumfries Courier* 20 Oct. 27/3 (Advt.), Hoover pop-up toaster in very good order, £8.50. **1978** *Times Lit. Suppl.* 1 Dec. 1400/3 Pop-up books are a different roaming ground for the imagination.

poral, *a.* (Further examples.)

1926 *Jrnl. Bot.* LXIV. 144 The poral outline is much like that of *Pseudonavicella.* **1961** D. M. PILLSBURY et al. *Man. Cutaneous Med.* ii. 49 In acne the sebaceous gland may atrophy as a result of concomitant poral occlusion.

porcelain. Add: **1.** (Examples of its use in *Dentistry.*)

1845 C. A. HARRIS *Princ. & Pract. Dental Surg.* (ed. 2) VI. i. 541 A want of resemblance to the other teeth, in colour, transparency, and animation, was the great objection, that was urged against the porcelain. **1863** *Trans. Odontol. Soc.* III. 228 The universal use of porcelain as a material of which to construct artificial teeth. **1911** G. H. WILSON *Man. Dental Prosthetics* viii. 311 The materials entering into dental porcelain are feldspar, silica, kaolin or clay, alkalies, and pigments. **1956** J. N. ANDERSON *Appl. Dental Materials* xxiv. 324 Today, porcelain is finding a resurgence of life, particularly in its application to crowns. **1965** *Brit. Dental Jrnl.* CXIX. 251/1 One of the main criticisms levelled at dental porcelain is the liability to fracture under low impact stress.

3. b. A variety of pigeon, having dark brown and cream plumage.

1855 [see *HYACINTH 3 b]. **1876** in R. Fulton *Illustr. Bk. Pigeons* xxv. 348 Porcelains..are closely allied to Suabians... These birds are of a nice rich brown.., the under parts being of an ashen tint.

5. *porcelain-blue* (earlier example); *porcelain-like* adj. (later examples); **porcelain enamel,** † (*a*) = GLAZE *sb.* 1; (*b*) = ENAMEL *sb.* 1 a; so **porcelain-enamelled** *a.*; hence **porcelain-enamel** *v. trans.*, **porcelain enamelling** *vbl. sb.*; **porcelain-kiln** = *porcelain oven*; **porcelain-paper** (examples); **porcelain tooth,** a false tooth made of porcelain.

1703 tr. *H. van Oosten's Dutch Gardener* II. xxxviii. 91 The Hyacinth that is handsom, must have a clear Porcelin, or China Blew, or near white Colour. **1883** *Jrnl. Chem. Soc.* XLIV. 397 (*heading*) Composition of porcelain enamels. **1921** *Chem. & Metall. Engin.* XXIV. 486/1 In 1860 the enameling of sheet iron was begun, and upon the advent of the drawing press and clay muffle in 1870 the process of porcelain enameling steel as we know it today developed into the enameling industry. **1924** E. G. BLAKE *Plumbing* II. iii. 40 Porcelain enamel is practically everlasting, does not chip with reasonable treatment, and can be kept perfectly clean with very little trouble. **1946** SIMONDS & BREGMAN *Finishing Metal Products* (ed. 2) xxxiii. 332 The compound word 'porcelain enamel' was made necessary by the wrong use of the word 'enamel' by manufacturers of paints. **1951** *Good Housek. Home Encycl.* 224/2 Porcelain enamel, being essentially a glass fused to a metal, has the properties of glass. **1955** INSLEY & FRÉCHETTE *Microsc. Ceramics & Cements* xi. 211 Porcelain enamel may be defined as an inorganic, glassy coating on a metal base, prepared by covering the preformed metal with a wet or dry powder coating of suitable composition and firing it for a few minutes to melt and smooth the surface. **1968** *Engineering* 26 July 171/3 Electron microbe examinations were made on a number of the magnesium-bearing alloys which had been porcelain enamelled without prior chromating treatments. **1969** *Sears Catal.* Spring/Summer 13 Two porcelain-enamel shelves. **1896** J. J. LAWLER *Amer. Sanitary Plumbing* 229 (*heading*) The porcelain-enamelled iron bathtub. **1935** H. R. SIMONDS *Finishing Metal Products* xxviii. 299 Some architects.. have been successful in making these buildings more attractive..by giving them new faces made of porcelain-enameled steel. **1975** *Specification* (ed. 76) II. 109/2 Cast iron porcelain enamelled baths continue to maintain pre-eminence at the luxury end of the market. **1921** *Chem. & Metall. Engin.* XXIV. 486/2 A temperature difference of more than 400 deg. F. (204 deg. C.) between the flue temperature and muffle temperature is not justifiable in the light of the latest developments in porcelain enameling ovens. **1968** *Engineering* 26 July 171/1 Since the end of the Second World War increasing attention has been given to the porcelain enamelling of aluminium, particularly in the fields of architecture and kitchen ware. **1893** E. A. BARBER *Pott. & Porc. U.S.* 258 It [*sc.* hard porcelain] is fired in biscuit at a low temperature, in the second story of the porcelain-kiln. **1908** *Westm. Gaz.* 29 June 2/4 Made of white, porcelain-like glass. **1964** S. DUKE-ELDER *Parsons' Dis. Eye* (ed. 14) xxvi. 378 In less severe cases a dense leucoma forms, porcelain-like in lime burns, and sight is lost. **1914** E. A. DAWE *Paper* 129 *Porcelain paper,* thick transparent paper of the nature of celluloid, made of well-beaten pulp. Used for Christmas cards and similar work. **1962** F. T. DAY *Introd. to Paper* 119/1 *Porcelain papers,* bulky variety of glazed, imitation parchment, similar to celluloid. **1845** C. A. HARRIS *Princ. & Pract. Dental Surg.* (ed. 2) VI. i. 540 The manufacture of porcelain teeth, did not for a long time promise to be of much advantage to dentistry. **1872** [in Dict., sense 4 a]. **1976** R. M. BASKER et al. *Prosthetic Treatm. Edentulous Patient* vi. 56 If the patient's masticatory habits have been responsible for an excessive amount of wear in a short period of time, porcelain teeth must be used if the succeeding dentures are to be serviceable for an adequate period.

porcelainic (pōəɹsĕlē·nik), *a.* [f. PORCELAIN + -IC.] = PORCELLANIC *a.*

1839 H. T. DE LA BECHE *Rep. Geol. Cornwall, Devon & W. Somerset* ix. 267 The fragments of them included in the greenstone of Kellan Head have a porcelainic appearance. **1971** *Materials & Technol.* II. v. 314 Ceramic ware of the porcelainic type was made in China from very early times.

porcellanic, *a.* Add: **b.** Characteristic or suggestive of porcelain.

1930 J. CANNAN *No Walls of Jasper* 29 His tooth brush dropped into its stand with the accustomed porcellanic chink.

porch. Add: **1. a.** (Later examples.)

1898 G. B. SHAW *Candida* I. 80 The parsonage is semi-detached, with a front garden and a porch. 1916 JOYCE *Portrait of Artist* (1969) 162 He pushed open the latchless door of the porch and passed through the naked hallway into the kitchen. 1919 G. B. SHAW *O'Flaherty V.C.* in *Heartbreak House* 167 The porch, painted white, projects into the drive. 1980 R. McCRUM *In Secret State* vii. 60 He returned to the porch, unlocked the front door and stepped inside.

c. A small platform outside the hatch of a spacecraft.

1969 *Daily Tel.* 14 July 16/5 Wearing their bulky suits and life-support packs, they will open the narrow hatch. Armstrong will squeeze himself out on to a small platform called the 'porch'. 1970 N. ARMSTRONG et al. *First on Moon* xi. 266 Armstrong: 'Yes. Got it... Okay, Houston, I'm on the porch.'

3. b. (Earlier and later examples.) Also *Canad.*

1832 J. P. KENNEDY *Swallow Barn* II. 41 Hafen Blok was regaling his circle of auditors in the porch at Swallow Barn. 1901 S. E. WHITE *Westerners* 251 Then there was the gambler, the faro man, who sat on the hotel 'porch'. 1916 H. L. WILSON *Somewhere in Red Gap* v. 195 Wilbur Todd had once endeavoured to hold her hand out on the porch at a country-club dance. 1925 F. SCOTT FITZGERALD *Great Gatsby* (1926) i. 14 The two young women preceded us out onto a rosy-colored porch, open toward the sunset, where four candles flickered on the table in the diminished wind. 1932 *Atlantic Monthly* Feb. 193/2 Broad porches ran the length of the house on both sides. 1948 *Manch. Guardian Weekly* 30 Dec. 13/1 President Truman has left the neo-Roman slabs of Washington to go home to Independence in Missouri, where he can feel more comfortable sitting on the back porch of an old frame house. 1968 *Globe Mag.* (Toronto) 13 Jan. 13/1 Raymond Souster would be the amiable fellow on the porch reminiscing with complacent nostalgia for lost times. 1978 C. MACLEOD *Rest you Merry* ix. 60 The student..had dumped the suitcases on the short walk in front of the brick house, and was studying the porch.

c. A small utility room attached to the back of a house. *N. Amer. dial.*

1916 *Dialect Notes* IV. 335 [Nantucket] *Porch*, an ell kitchen. 1929 *Amer. Speech* V. 124 'Piazzer' was the only term applied to a veranda [*sc.* in the dialect of Maine]. The 'porch' was a sort of extra shed-kitchen used as a laundry. 1969 in Halpert & Story *Christmas Mumming in Newfoundland* 211 The 'porch' is a small room at the rear of the house used for storing wood, hanging coats, cooking utensils, and so on. A door, which is always kept closed, leads from the porch into the kitchen.

6*. *Television.* In a video signal, either of the two periods of line blanking immediately before and after the line-synchronizing pulse; known respectively as the *front* and *back porch*.

1941 *Proc. IRE* XXIX. 307/1 The difference between 0·06*H* and 0·07*H*, namely 1 per cent of *H*, is the 'front porch' of the pedestal. 1953 AMOS & BIRKINSHAW *Television Engin.* I. ii. 32 The period of blanking level immediately following the line-sync signal..is termed the back porch. *Ibid.*, There is a brief period of blanking level occurring immediately before each line-sync signal. This is known as the front porch. 1965 *Wireless World* Aug. 389/1 The phasing of the oscillator is determined by the duration of the front porch of the composite video waveform, the flyback time of the line circuit and the tightness of lock. 1966 [see *line blanking* s.v. *LINE *sb.*² 32].

7. *porch chair, rail, roof*; **porch-climber** *N. Amer. slang*, a burglar; hence *porch-climbing* ppl. adj.

1908 *Sears, Roebuck Catal.* 753/2 Folding porch chair, made of wood frame with denim body. 1911 *Daily Colonist* (Victoria, B.C.) 25 Apr. 6/7 (Advt.), Porch and Verandah Chairs. There are no chairs more suitable for the porch or verandah than Sea Grass or Rattan. 1948 *Democrat* 22 Apr. 1/7 Porch and Lawn Chairs, Swings, Gliders and Metal Tables. 1900 ADE *More Fables* 218 He had a Chinaman for a Servant, because the Chinaman did not know he was an Author, but supposed him to be a Retired Porch-Climber. 1901 'J. FLYNT' *World of Graft* 27 The remaining third of Chicago's professional thieves are good, bad, and indifferent 'sneaks', 'porch-climbers', [etc.]. 1916 *Daily Colonist* (Victoria, B.C.) 27 July 6/3 Some well-intentioned citizens see a potential second-storey man or porch-climber in everyone who is not within doors after the stroke of midnight. 1927 *Scribner's Mag.* Feb. 180/1 The depredations of porch-climbers, safe-blowers,..and common thieves were a source of alarm. 1912 *Collier's* 28 Dec. 15/3 Beware of the beautiful ladies who have porch-climbing, safe-blowing pals. 1929 *Oxf. Poetry* 53 Brown meadow grass and cat-tails My banisters and porch rails— All these belonged to me. 1948 E. POUND *Pisan Cantos* (1949) lxxvi. 43 As the cat walked the porch rail at Gardone. 1869 'MARK TWAIN' *Innoc. Abr.* xliii. 448 The porch-roof is composed of tremendous slabs of stone.

porcupine, *sb.* Add: **1.** δ. (Later example in humorous use.)

1936 T. S. ELIOT *Coll. Poems 1909–1935* 147 How unpleasant to meet Mr. Eliot! With a bobtail cur In a coat of fur And a porpentine cat.

5. a. Substitute for def.: A small Australian monotreme, the echidna or spiny ant-eater, *Tachyglossus aculeatus*; (earlier and later examples).

1832 J. BISCHOFF *Sk. Hist. Van Diemen's Land* ii. 29 The native porcupine or echidna is not very common. 1843 J. BACKHOUSE *Narr. Visit Austral. Colonies* vii. 89 The Porcupine of this land..is a squat species of ant-eater, with short quills among its hair. 1924 *Truth* (Sydney) 27 Apr. 6 *Porcupine*, a rather large rodent with spiked quills, and which feeds chiefly upon bark, leaves and ants. 1944 *Living off Land* ii. 29 The spiny ant-eater (sometimes called porcupine) is a good food. 1970 W. D. L. RIDE *Guide Native Mammals Austral.* xii. 191 The most widespread Australian monotreme is the Echidna or Spiny-anteater which is called 'The Porcupine' by many country people.

6. porcupine ant-eater, substitute for def.: = sense *5a; (earlier examples).

1847 [see ECHIDNA]. 1860 G. BENNETT *Gatherings of Naturalist in Australasia* vii. 147 The Porcupine Anteater of Australia..and the Ornithorhynchus..form the only two genera of the order Monotremata.

Hence **po·rcupinal** *a.*, suggestive of a porcupine, prickly (in quot. *fig.*).

1846 R. FORD *Gatherings from Spain* xii. 139 The nerves tighten up into the catgut of an overstrung fiddle, getting attuned to the porcupinal irritability of the tension of the mind.

pore, *sb.*¹. Add: **4.** *pore-size, -space*; **pore pressure**, the pressure of pore water; **pore water**, water contained in pores in soil or rock.

1947 D. P. KRYNINE *Soil Mech.* (ed. 2) iv. 112 (*caption*) Analogy between (*a*) pore pressure in clay and (*b*) hydraulic uplift in a dam. 1969 C. R. SCOTT *Introd. Soil Mech. & Foundations* ix. 201 The stability of a retaining wall is adversely affected by large pore pressures in the soil behind it. 1977 A. HALLAM *Planet Earth* 64/3 Decreasing the pore pressure increases the resistance of the rock to fracturing. 1947 *New Biol.* III. 175 If a series of filters of known pore-size is used, the size of particles which just fail to pass a certain filter can be obtained. 1915 L. V. PIRSSON *Text-bk. Geol.* I. xvi. 388 The rocks are penetrated by cracks, crevices and jointing planes, and on a more minute scale there are the pore spaces between rock grains. 1975 *Nature* 17 Apr. 585/2 Usually the pore-space in a porous medium is visualised as a more or less complicated assembly of isolated or interconnected capillaries, and such porespace models are used in describing transport phenomena in porous media. 1936 *Proc. 1st Internat. Conf. Soil Mech.* III. 51 The ultimate deformations and conditions of failure of cohesive soils are governed mainly by the principal effective stresses, defined as the difference between the total principal stresses and the hydrostatic pressure of the porewater. 1943 K. VON TERZAGHI *Theoret. Soil Mech.* i. 15 When dealing with clays, we are seldom in a position to compute the pressure which develops in the pore water while the point of failure is approached. 1972 L. ZEEVAERT *Foundation Engin. for Difficult Subsoil Conditions* viii. 337 Upon dissipation of the excess pore water pressures, the soil tends to resume its initial elevation. 1977 *Offshore Engineer* June 35/2 The engineers are looking for tell-tale signs of soil fluidisation by large increases in pore water pressure caused by water trapped within the steel skirts and forced out beneath the skirt.

pored, *a.* (Later examples.)

1930 *Engineering* 28 Nov. 670/2 A wall built with Fletton bricks and very finely pored mortar. 1963 *Agra Univ. Jrnl. Res.* (*Sci.*) XII. 63 (*heading*) A note on the double pored dilepidid tape worms of some of the Indian carnivores. 1973 B. SHELMIRE *Art of Looking Younger* (1974) iv. 45 This cellular buildup causes the whole layer to become thicker and, in turn, makes the skin look coarse, leathery, and large-pored.

porge, *v.* Substitute for etym.: [ad. Judæo-Spanish *porgar*, Sp. *purgar* to cleanse, f. L. *purgāre* PURGE *v.*¹] (Later examples.) Also *absol.* **porger** (earlier example).

1773 J. R. MOREIRA *Kehilath Jahacob* 110/2 Porger of meat.—Purgadór. 1871 [see *KOSHER *v.*]. 1932 C. ROTH *Hist. Marranos* vii. 179 The children of Israel did not eat the sinew of the thigh; and it was customary..to 'porge' the leg before preparing it for food. 1973 *Jewish Chron.* 18 May 39/4 (Advt.), Shomer. Able to porge and knowledge of kashrus requirements for butchers and poulterers.

porgy. Add: **2.** *attrib.*, as *porgy boat, fleet, steamer*; *porgy-hunting* vbl. sb. (see quot. 1904).

1906 *N.Y. Even. Post* 18 Aug. (Saturday Suppl.) 1/2 The 'porgy' boats, dirty, snub-nosed..are far..removed in standing from their fellows. 1960 J. J. ROWLANDS *Spindrift* 211 The porgy boats are built and operated for just one purpose—fishing. 1914 W. D. STEELE *Storm* 191 For the first time that season the porgie fleet moved in around Long Point. 1904 *Scribner's Mag.* May 548 When we cruise about, hooking on to any job we can catch, and at any price we can get for it, that's porgy hunting. 1880 Porgy steamer [see *MACKERELING *vbl. sb.*]. 1914 *Oysterman & Fisherman* Jan. 7/3 The porgie steamer Long Island which..has been undergoing repairs.

porina (porəi·nă). *N.Z.* [mod.L. (F. Walker *List Specimens Lepidopterous Insects in Brit. Mus.* (1856) VII. 1572).] The larva of a moth formerly belonging to the genus *Porina*, now usually included in the genus *Oxycanus*, which damages grassland. Freq. *attrib.*

1929 W. MARTIN *N.Z. Nature Bk.* I. xvi. 153 The Porinas, Swifts, or Bull Moths... The subterranean larvae thus attacked [by fungi] have long been known as Vegetable Caterpillars. 1940 *N.Z. Jrnl. Agric.* Apr. 245/1 The Porina moth makes its first appearance in early October... It is the caterpillar..which causes the damage during the winter. *Ibid.* 246/1 Porina larvae feed almost entirely on surface leafage. 1950 *Ibid.* Apr. 357/1 Porina..and grass-grub are a serious hindrance. 1966 *Encycl. N.Z.* I. 319/1 The larval stages of the moths commonly called porina moths..are important pasture pests in New Zealand. They live in tunnels in the soil during the day and feed at night at the surface of the soil on grass foliage. 1969 [see *grass grub* s.v. *GRASS *sb.*¹ 13]. 1973 A. D. LOWE in G. R. Williams *Nat. Hist. N.Z.* viii. 198/2 The practice of closing paddocks for hay and seed crops frequently appears to have accentuated the porina problem.

porion (pōə·riǫn). *Anat.* Pl. **poria.** [f. Gr. πόρ-ος way through, passageway + *-ION².] (See quot. 1937.)

1909 in *Cent. Dict.* Suppl. 1920 H. H. WILDER *Lab. Man. Anthropometry* 47 *Porion*, the uppermost point in the margin of the auditory meatus. 1933 *Jrnl. R. Anthrop. Inst.* LXIII. 417 The poria [are] widely separated. 1937 *Amer. Jrnl. Physical Anthrop.* XXII. 485 *Porion*, a point on the upper margin of the external auditory meatus which according to Martin is vertically over the middle of the meatus, and according to Wilder is simply the uppermost point. 1970 *Monogr. Soc. Res. Child Devel.* XXXV. III. 48 As a rule, the two poria are instrumentally determined by contact of the upper margin of the rounded ear rods of the headspanner as they are inserted into the *S*'s external auditory meatus.

pork¹. Add: **2. b.** *U.S. slang.* Federal funds obtained for particular areas or individuals on the basis of political patronage. Cf. *PORK BARREL.

[1862 in D. W. Mitchell *Ten Yrs. in U.S.* xv. 271 To put myself in a position in which every wretch entitled to a vote would feel himself privileged to hold me under special obligations, would be giving rather too much pork for a shilling.] 1879 *Congress Rec.* 28 Feb. 2131/1 St. Louis is going to have some of the 'pork' indirectly; but it will not do any good. 1916 *N.Y. Even. Post* 12 May 8/2 'Pork' has hitherto stood for just one process, the parcelling out of Federal moneys for court houses, post offices, and waterways, not by States, but by Congressional districts. 1949 *Marshfield* (Wisconsin) *News-Herald* 19 July 4/3 That difference of more than $54,000,000 includes a lot of pork for individual senators. 1962 *Economist* 20 Oct. 252/1 Pork is the generic name for the tasty morsels of federal spending..which a member of congress likes to bring back to his constituents. 1964 D. M. BERMAN *In Congress Assembled* xii. 323 One of the first facts of congressional life is that it does not pay to antagonize the committee to which one will someday have to appeal for funds to support a local project. Such projects are commonly referred to as 'pork'.

c. Phr. *pork and beans* (Mil. slang), a name given to Portuguese soldiers serving in the war of 1914–18.

1919 *Athenæum* 8 Aug. 727/2 He [*sc.* the soldier] gave nicknames to the Overseas troops, as..'Chinks' for Chinese labourers..and 'Pork and Beans' for Portuguese. 1919 W. H. DOWNING *Digger Dial.* 39 *Pork-and-beans*, Portuguese soldiers. 1925 FRASER & GIBBONS *Soldier & Sailor Words* 228 *Pork and beans*, a nickname for the Portuguese troops serving on the Western Front.

3. *pork steak, trade*; *pork-packer* (earlier and later examples), *-packing* (earlier examples), *raiser, raising*; **porkburger**, a kind of hamburger made from pork; **pork-butcher**, (*a*) (earlier and later examples); (*b*) a shop-keeper who specializes in pork; so **pork-butchering** *vbl. sb.*, **-butchery**; **pork-eater** *Canad.*, a canoeman engaged on the run between Montreal and Grand Portage; also, by extension, any canoeman, esp. a new recruit; *obs.* exc. *hist.*; **pork house**, a business house trading in pork; **pork king**, a magnate in the pork trade; **pork-knocker, porknocker**, in Guyana (formerly British Guiana), an independent or casual prospector for gold or diamonds; hence **pork-knocking** *vbl. sb.*, the activity of a pork-knocker.

1939 *Amer. Speech* XIV. 154/2 *Porkburger*, ground pork, in other words, sausage! 1969 R. & D. DE SOLA *Dict. Cooking* 180/1 *Porkburger*, pork patty fried and eaten like a hamburger. 1807 SOUTHEY *Lett. from Eng.* III. lxiii. 182 The pork-butchers are commonly Jews. 1922 JOYCE *Ulysses* 59 The porkbutcher snapped two sheets from the pile, wrapped up her prime sausages and made a red grimace. 1925 W. DE LA MARE *Two Tales* 40 Yet to judge from some poets' faces, you might be easily justified in supposing they would have flourished better in the pork-butchering line. 1935 *Times Lit. Suppl.* 24 Oct. 673/1 [They] set a rabbinical winkle-seller on the road to fortune which leads to pork-butchery. 1793 J. MACDONELL *Diary* 5 July in C. M. Gates *Five Fur Traders* (1933) 94 Between two and three hundred yards to the East of the N.W. Fort beyond the Pork eaters camp is the spot Messrs David and Peter Grant have selected to build upon. 1801 A. MACKENZIE *Voy. from Montreal* p. xxvii, Of these, five clerks, eighteen guides, and three hundred and fifty canoe men, were employed for the summer season in going from Montreal to the Grande Portage, in canoes, part of whom proceeded from thence to Rainy Lake,.. and are called Pork-eaters, or Goers and Comers. 1823 J. FRANKLIN *Narr. Journey Shores Polar Sea* vii. 281 There is a pride amongst 'Old Voyagers', which makes them consider the state of being frost-bitten as effeminate, and only excusable in a 'Pork-eater', or one newly come into the country. 1829 J. McLOUGHLIN *Let.* 8 Dec. (1948) 69 By this opportunity I send you all you requested..and four Pork eaters. 1859 P. KANE *Wanderings of Artist* 34 The men who usually work this brigade of [Hudson Bay Company] canoes are hired at Lachine, and are called by the uncouth names of mangeurs du lard, or pork-eaters. 1953 *Beaver* Dec. 50 The provisions for the Crew were Pork & Biscuits; from which circumstance the young recruits were called 'Pork Eaters' to distinguish them from the old Winterers, who feed chiefly on 'Pemican'. **1969** E. W. Morse *Fur Trade Canoe Routes* I. ii. 23 The voyageurs plying the run between Montreal and Lake Superior were known derisively among the tougher breed wintering in the North West as 'pork eaters', *mangeurs de lard*. **1837** W. Jenkins *Ohio Gazetteer* 171 Eaton contains ..four pork houses. **1848** *Rep. Comm. Patents 1847* (U.S.) 527 The hogs are taken into the pork house from the wagons and piled up in rows. **1890** W. D. Howells *Boy's Town* 36 Cooper-shops where the barrels were made, alternated with the pork-houses. **1893** M. Elliott *Honor* 155 Gwendoline O'Shaunessey, the daughter of old O'Shaunessey the Western pork-king. **1930** R. Macaulay *Staying with Relations* xv. 222, I should like to go off with a president,..or a film or pork king. **1910** M. B. & C. W. Beebe *Our Search for Wilderness* vi. 187 The universal Guianian name for this type of independent miner is 'pork-knocker', the explanation being that by knocking the rocks to pieces, they find just enough gold to procure the pork upon which they live. **1930** *Times* 14 Mar. 5/3 The pork-knockers make a night of it before they go up into the bush. **1949** P. Hastings *Cases in Court* iii. 130 These gentlemen employed a number of natives who enjoyed the somewhat peculiar title of 'Pork knockers'. **1957** [see *inboard *a.*]. **1972** *Guardian* 1 Dec. 14/1 The famous gold and diamond prospectors of the interior (the so-called 'porknockers' whose name derives from their salt pork rations). **1974** H. MacInnes *Climb to Lost World* iii. 42 A couple of prospectors, or 'porknockers', were staying in the Park Hotel... They are called porknockers because salted pork was their staple diet; when they had a run of bad luck, they used to borrow, or 'knock' pork from their more prosperous friends. **1965** 'Lauchmonen' *Old Thom's Harvest* vii. 95 Winston, man, you better had go back to your pork-knocking. **1974** H. MacInnes *Climb to Lost World* xii. 221 We had some Brazilian natives with us... They..had come over for the diamond prospecting but, since the water had been too high for porknocking, they had agreed to work for us instead. **1838** *N.Y. Advertiser & Express* 7 Feb. 3/3 It is due to that enterprising class of citizens, the pork packers, that the error should be corrected. **1949** *Boston Sunday Globe* 26 June (Fiction Mag.) 2/1 These corporations were principally distillers, manufacturers of tobacco, and, especially, beef and pork packers. **1851** C. Cist *Sk. Cincinnati in 1851* 228 Pork and Beef Packing. **1870** *Trans. Illinois Agric. Soc. 1867–68* VII. 475 The only reliable statement of the pork-packing of the West we have any knowledge of. **1839** *Jrnl. Indiana Ho. Representatives* 8 Jan. 231 The scarcity..is likely to prove so mischievous to the interests of our pork raisers and dealers. **1872** *Trans. Illinois Dept. Agric. 1871* IX. 390 Dark, cold, damp Piggeries are a nuisance to any farmer or pork raiser. *Ibid.* 354 He had said that pork raising stood preeminent as a branch of stock raising in our State. **1880** G. T. Ingham *Digging Gold* 203 Is this the *honor* of Western pork-raisers? **1783** J. Woodforde *Diary* 8 Apr. (1926) II. 68 We had for Dinner..Mutton Stakes, Pork Stakes, Peas Soup. **1922** Joyce *Ulysses* 230 Master Patrick Aloysius Dignam came out of Mangan's..carrying a pound and a half of porksteaks. *Ibid.* 251 Master Patrick Aloysius Dignam..raised also his new black cap with fingers greased by porksteak paper. **1957** *Encycl. Brit.* XVIII. 245/2 Pork chops or steaks are usually browned in a hot skillet. **1851** A. O. Hall *Manhattaner* 13 Here, too, is modest beauty from Ohio (papa in the pork trade).

pork barrel. orig. and chiefly *U.S.* [Pork[1] 3.]

1. A barrel in which pork is kept. Also *fig.*, a supply of money; the source of one's livelihood.

1801 *Farmer's Almanack 1802* (Boston) sig. C2 *Better spare at the brim, than at the bottom*, is an old proverb, and should teach us to mind our pork and cider barrels. **1842** *Joliet* (Illinois) *Courier* 2 Feb. 3/1 Farmers can be accommodated with a very good Pork Barrel in exchange for Oats Butter or Wheat. **1861** *Harper's Mag.* Oct. 643/1, I came very near tumbling over a pork-barrel, and made a remark concerning obstructions in the street which was more forcible than chaste. **1863** *Frank Leslie's Illustr. Newspaper* 24 Jan. 277/3 We find that those who work honestly, and only seek a man's fair average of life, or a woman's, get that average... And thus we find that when an extraordinary contingency arises in life..we have only to go to our pork-barrel and the fish rises to our hook or spear. **1909** *Chambers's Jrnl.* Mar. 178/2 We had bought ten empty pork-barrels. **1946** S. Newton *Paul Bunyan* xxvii. 158 It was as big around as a pork barrel. **1978** M. Puzo *Fools Die* xi. 106 The Army Reserve of the United States was a great pork barrel. By just coming to a meeting for two hours a week you got a full day's pay.

2. *fig.* The state's financial resources regarded as a source of distribution to meet regional expenditure; the provision of funds (in U.S., Federal funds) for a particular area achieved through political representation or influence. Freq. *attrib.* or as *adj.*

1909 *Westm. Gaz.* 1 June 2/1 The Democratic Party.. has periodically inveighed against the extravagance of the administration, but its representatives in the Legislature have exercised no critical surveillance over the appropriations. They have preferred to take for their own constituencies whatever could be got out of the Congressional 'pork barrel'. **1913** R. M. La Follette *Autobiogr.* 60 It was on the so-called 'pork-barrel' bill for river and harbor appropriations. **1916** *N.Y. Even. Post* 12 May 8/2 The River and Harbor bill is the pork barrel par excellence, and the rivers and harbors are manipulated by Federal machinery and not by State machinery. **1926** R. Luce *Congress* 82 Undoubtedly there was once a 'pork-barrel', a metaphorical barrel from which legislators pulled out 'pork' to satisfy the ravenous appetites of greedy constituents. **1950** *Reader's Digest* Jan. 96/2 The Army Civil Functions appropriation bill—once known as the Rivers and Harbors bill and still called the 'pork barrel' bill—this year provided for 275 projects. **1950** *Sun* (Baltimore) 24 Aug. 4/3 The section of the bill is sometimes called the 'pork-barrel', and as it contains funds for projects in virtually every state, it is one that is the hardest to cut item by item. **1953** *Manch. Guardian Weekly* 11 June 10/4 We are shown..the way in which members of Congress..deal with the problem of public works (coarsely called the pork barrel). **1960** *Economist* 15 Oct. 266/2 It [*sc.* the Macmillan Government] has treated some nationalised industries almost as if they were its positive enemies, while a quite considerable pork-barrel has been opened up for a growing number of private firms. **1961** D. L. Munby *God & Rich Society* vi. 122 'Pork-barrel' politics, by which governments step in to help particular economic groups in the community. **1973** *Sat. Rev. Sci.* (U.S.) Mar. 29/3 Present fire allocations..have reached pork-barrel dimensions. **1976** H. Wilson *Governance of Britain* x. 172 In Westminster, the Government has complete control over expenditure... Thus, in Britain, 'pork barrel' expenditure is ruled out.

Hence **pork-barrelling** *vbl. sb.*, the process of providing regional funds by these means.

1967 *Economist* 14 Oct. 133/3 The one piece of regional pork-barrelling at last week's Labour party conference was the Prime Minister's promise that two aluminium smelters, using subsidised electricity, would be built, probably in development areas. **1974** *Camden* (S. Carolina) *Chron.* 22 Apr. 2/1 The commission needs stronger authority than it has in that field if legislative pork-barreling on higher education is to be kept to a minimum. **1976** *Guardian Weekly* 12 Sept. 7/5 Pork barrelling—the way Congressmen with political influence can obtain Federal funds for local projects. **1977** *N.Y. Rev. Bks.* 26 May 36/3 Such reallocation would sorely affect agricultural usage of the land and stimulate the construction of various water aqueducts, dams, and other projects currently denounced as mere congressional pork-barreling.

pork chop. [Pork[1].] **1.** (See Pork[1] 3 in Dict.)

2. An American black who accepts an inferior position in relation to whites. Chiefly *attrib.* *U.S. slang.*

1970 *Rep. 20th Ann. Round Table Meeting Lang. & Ling. Stud., Georgetown Univ.* 9 *CR*: Who can make magic? *Greg*: The son of po'—... I'm sayin' the po'k chop God! He only a po'k chop God! *Ibid.* 36 A *pork chop* is a Negro who has not lost traditional subservient ideology of the South..and the *pork chop God* would be the traditional God of the Southern Baptists. **1977** *N.Y. Rev. Bks.* 4 Aug. 35/1 This is the year of the Bionic Black, and porkchop nationalists have lost prestige.

Hence **po:rk-cho·pper** *U.S. slang*, a full-time union official (see quots).

1946 *N.Y. Times* 11 Aug. iv. 7/7 In the UAW, the rank and file call those who live by income derived from the union 'pork-choppers'. **1953** Berrey & Van den Bark *Amer. Thes. Slang* (1954) § 527/2 *Pork-chopper*, an official who is in the union for self-interested reasons. **1960** Wentworth & Flexner *Dict. Amer. Slang* 403/1 *Pork-chopper*, a political appointee, union official, or relative or friend of a politician, union officer, or the like, who receives payment for little or no work; one who is put on a payroll as a favor or as a return for past services. **1968** *Economist* 2 Nov. 30/2 They feel mostly contempt for the 'pork-chopper'—the former factory workers who have become full-time members of the union staff. **1977** *Time* 17 Jan. 32/3 Rank-and-filers have never considered him a 'pork-chopper', their term for a high-hat leader.

porker. Add: **1. b.** *fig.* A fat or porcine person.

1892 [see *Balzacian *a.*]. **1959** I. & P. Opie *Lore & Lang. Schoolch.* ix. 168 The unfortunate fat boy.., is known as: back end of a bus..porker, [etc.]. **1959** *Good Food Guide* 42 So many restaurants in the Thames Valley have been ruined by the expense-account porkers, who neither care what they pay nor know what they eat.

pork-pie. Add: **2.** (Further examples.) Now usu. applied to a kind of hat worn by men. Also *pork-pie cap*.

1888 C. M. Yonge *Beechcroft at Rockstone* II. xv. 41 There certainly was a figure in somewhat close proximity, the ulster and pork-pie hat being such as to make the gender doubtful. **1910** *Blackw. Mag.* Jan. 113/1 In the dreadful mustard-coloured uniform and pork-pie cap which the Government has ordained for these unusually fat servants. **1937** *Evening News* 12 Feb. 8/3, I seem to remember that porters at the entrances of big hotels once wore greatcoats reaching almost to their ankles and that each had a pork-pie cap with a peak and a little round button on top. **1940** Graves & Hodge *Long Week-End* xxi. 376 Low-crowned pork-pie hats were in fashion again. **1943** R. Chandler *Lady in Lake* xxi. 118 His blue pork-pie hat was set very square on his head. **1948** M. Allingham *More Work for Undertaker* xvii. 199 The inevitable green demob pork-pie sat a little too far back from his lined forehead. **1955** *Times* 16 Aug. 8/7 The men had white handkerchiefs on their faces, and wore raincoats and 'pork-pie' hats. **1968** R. Clapperton *No News on Monday* vi. 60, I..limped down the hot pavement with a straw pork pie tipped forward over my eyes. **1977** *New Yorker* 25 July 61/2 Lawford, the arrant individualist, sometimes showed up on the court wearing a pork-pie hat, a striped jersey, tight knickers, and long stockings.

porky (pōᵊ·ɹki), *sb.* Also **porcy**. Abbrev. of Porcupine *sb.*

1902 W. D. Hulbert *Forest Neighbors* 146 We found the Porky asleep in the sunshine. **1921** *Chambers's Jrnl.* May 290/2 An encounter in which 'Porcy' had the best of it. **1936** D. McCowan *Animals Canad. Rockies* xxvii. 235 A pair of shoes left carelessly outside a tent forms a tasty meal for a prowling Porky. **1956** W. R. Bird *Off-Trail in Nova Scotia* x. 267 They heard the familiar complainings of a 'porky' on the move.

Porlock (pǭ·ɹlǭk). The name of a town in Somerset, used allusively (see quot. 1816) in phr. *a person* etc. *from Porlock*, a person who interrupts at an inconvenient moment.

[**1816** Coleridge *Kubla Khan* in *Christabel* 53 At this moment he [*sc.* Coleridge] was unfortunately called out by a person on business from Porlock, and detained by him above an hour.] **1959** *Listener* 1 Jan. 37/3 All the incidental distractions—the telephone-bell, the Christmas carollers at the door, the gentleman or lady 'from Porlock' —to which one is subject.

porn (pǭɹn), **porno** (pǭ·ɹno), *a.* and *sb. colloq.*

A. *adj.* Abbrevs. of Pornographic *a.*

1952 N. Mailer *Man who studied Yoga* in *Advts. for Myself* (1961) 175, It is dirty, downright porno dirty, it is a lewd slop-brush slapped through the middle of domestic exasperations and breakfast eggs. **1963** 'D. Cory' *Hammerhead* ii. 21 Judging from the script..it might be just the *tiniest* bit porno. **1964** N. Freeling *Double-Barrel* v. i. 148 Looking at Miss Burger through binoculars was porno..anything porno is so hatefully sad. **1970** *Time* 16 Nov. 92 So busy are the makers of porn films in San Francisco that they have depressed the market for imported sex movies. **1972** J. Brown *Chancer* xv. 208 First, take the evidence. The joints, the photos, the porno magazines. **1972** *Screw* 12 June 19/1 This week I am reviewing the very best porn film ever made, so superior to others that it defies comparison. **1972** *New Yorker* 2 Dec. 164/2 They use their porno fantasies as part of the case they make for the slaughter of the whites. **1973** 'D. Halliday' *Dolly & Starry Bird* iii. 36 Jacko had put away his porn pictures. **1974** *Publishers Weekly* 18 Nov. 45/2 A teenage girl who had been trying to make the big time by performing at Beverly Hills orgies and doing porno films. **1976** *Daily Tel.* 13 Feb. 13/5 If only he would feed her, or take her to a porno movie—or even for a walk! **1978** S. Sheldon *Bloodline* xxii. 249 It's a porno film.

B. *sb.* **1.** Abbrevs. of Pornographer. *rare.*

1958 L. Durrell *Balthazar* vi. 144 'The old Porn himself!' (He had coined this nickname from the word 'pornographer'.) **1969** *Time* 5 Sept. 27 The right-wing National Democratic Party derides [Gunther] Grass as a 'porno', because his works are peppered with four-letter words.

2. Abbrevs. of Pornography. Also *attrib.* and qualified by *hard* or *soft* (cf. *pornography 2a).

1962 *John o' London's* 10 May 456/2 The central character and narrator, the Captain, is a seedy but not at all unsympathetic individual who makes a precarious living by writing 'porn'. **1964** *New Society* 13 Feb. 5/3 The stuff men pass round in barrack rooms as 'a nice bit of porn'. *Ibid.* 6/2 'There's nothing odd about our customers,' the porn shop assistant said. **1967** L. Deighton *London Dossier* 192 Books..divided into two main sections, straight 'porn' and sadism. **1968** *Punch* 31 July 144/1 Gavin, the Old Etonian ex-monk who is now one of London's most around publishers ('Not porno, love, the word's *engagé*, ha-ha-ha!'). **1969** R. Airth *Snatch!* ii. 21 Cognac, cigarettes, porn—small-time, Harry, small-time. **1970** *Guardian* 17 Jan. 10/1 However thin and tippling the Lennon lithographs..they were not pure tosh or porn. *Ibid.* 26 Nov. 4/4 The porno and sex wave crashes relentlessly on. **1972** *Daily Mirror* 12 Oct. 1 An all-out attack is to be mounted against the porn-pushers in Britain's High Streets. **1973** L. Meynell *Thirteen Trumpeters* i. 8 A large and flourishing porn shop. **1974** *Publishers Weekly* 4 Mar. 67/3 The condition of the cinema today (lousy stories, no real stars, too much porno). **1975** D. Lodge *Changing Places* ii. 96 Standing amid the alien porn of Soho. **1976** T. Heald *Let Sleeping Dogs Die* viii. 154 An elderly woman..looked up from the nudie magazine... More soft porn lay around her. **1977** E. J. Trimmer et al. *Visual Dict. Sex* (1978) xxiv. 274 Perhaps the institution of an Oscar for the best hard porn movie of the year might give the producers an incentive to quit conning their public. **1978** M. Puzo *Fools Die* xii. 130, I could write the soft-porn love stories for the top-of-the-line magazine. **1980** G. Greene *Dr. Fischer* xv. 108, I..sat for an hour before a soft porn film.

pornie (pǭ·ɹni). *slang.* [f. *porn *a.* and *sb.* + -ie.] A pornographic film.

1966 R. H. Rimmer *Harrad Experiment* (1967) 157 'What the devil are pornies?' Beth demanded. Jack grinned. 'Flickers a little on the pornographic side.' **1967** I. Hamilton *Man with Brown Paper Face* ii. 27 We're planning a pornie for the blue movie racket. **1975** *Publishers Weekly* 17 Feb. 80/3 A nice California kid until she was conned into filming pornies to pay off her lover's addict brother's connection.

porno-, comb. form of Pornography or Pornographic *a.*, prefixed to sbs. and adjs., as *porno-biography*, *-film*, *-movie*, *-photographer*; *porno-chic*, *-gothic* adjs. (also as sb.); **po·rnogram,** a pornographic short poem; **pornoma·nia,** a mania for pornography; **po·rnophile** a lover of pornography; **pornopho·bic** *a.*, having a horror of pornography (in quot. *absol.*); **Po·rnosec,** a name given to a department of the Ministry of Truth by George Orwell in his novel 'Nineteen Eighty-Four'; **pornoto·pia,** an ideal setting for the activities described in pornographic literature.

1970 *Sat. Rev.* (U.S.) 17 Oct. 32 The mildly lascivious may be grateful that he gives the longest plot summary of *Glenarvon* I know of, and prints the entire text of *Don Leon*, a not very titillating piece of pornobiography. **1971** *New Yorker* 11 Dec. 24 The Music Lovers—Ken Russell seems to have invented a new genre of pornobiography. In this film, Tchaikovsky is the chief victim of Russell's baroque vulgarity. **1973** *Times* 17 Feb. 12/8, I went to see *Deep Throat*, which is the big porno-chic movie of all time. **1969** *Truth* (Melbourne) 12 July 13/2 In these two countries [*sc.* America and England], there are something like 350 theatres and cinema clubs which feature and openly advertise movies under the name of pornofilms. **1968** *Tribune* 16 Feb. 11/1 So one must, I think acquit James Saunders of all but the technical responsibilities of adapting 'The Italian Girl', a pornogothick novel by Iris Murdoch, for the stage. **1975** *New Yorker* 19 May 23/1 *The Night Porter*—A porno gothic, set in Vienna in 1957 and veneered with redeeming social values. **1936** C. S. Lewis *Allegory of Love* vi. 251 He [*sc.* Dunbar] practises every form from satiric pornogram to devotional lyric. **1979** K. Bonfiglioni *After you with Pistol* xvi. 119 Death..lays on others the chore of hiding the pornograms, the illegal firearms, the incriminating letters. **1969** *Daily Tel.* 25 Apr. 20/3 Haven't we got a steadily increasing amount of violence, bigotry and gang warfare (to say nothing of..nihilism and pornomania)? **1969** *Truth* (Melbourne) 12 July 13/5 Pornomovies which are being shown in theatres in America, England and Western Europe known as sex houses. **1976** *Publishers Weekly* 16 Feb. 80/2 He comes in contact with porno movies and a girl who makes them. **1977** M. Drabble *Ice Age* i. 61 He'd been had up for offering bribes to council employees: the whole story had been ridiculous, tales of..call girls and twenty-pound notes, of tax evasion and pornomovies. **1960** *20th Cent.* May 434 The great social surveys ..are no diet for the pornophile. *a* **1966** E. Waugh in D. Pryce-Jones *Evelyn Waugh* (1973) xiv. 226 Will not this bit in the *Sunday Times* excite your pornophiles to fancy prices? **1973** *Austral. Humanist* xxvi. 4/2 Mary Whitehouse could provide fresh impetus for the pornophobic. **1965** *Listener* 3 June 837/1 A sequence of Gaby..untrussing for Pierre Louys in a room full of Oriental knick-knacks, then being somewhat primly caressed by the great pornophotographer. **1949** 'G. Orwell' *Nineteen Eighty-Four* i. 46 There was even a whole sub-section [*sc.* of the Ministry of Truth]—*Pornosec*, it was called in Newspeak—engaged in producing the lowest kind of pornography. *Ibid.* ii. 132 Pornosec, the sub-section of the Fiction Department which turned out cheap pornography for distribution among the proles. **1966** S. Marcus *Other Victorians* v. 216 The results..are to turn the novel in the direction of pornotopia—that vision which regards all of human experience as a series of exclusively sexual events or conveniences.

pornograph, *sb.* (*a.*) **2.** (Later examples.)

1955 M. Allingham *Beckoning Lady* vii. 109 Through the window, a line of bladders, now a trifle flabby, were.. visible. 'Listen.' Tonker seized the mouthgrip... Mr. Campion pulled himself together. 'It's horrible,' he said. 'A pornograph, Tonker.' **1967** *Spectator* 1 Dec. 683/1 A pornograph can be either verbal or visual, but the visual stimulus is generally more intense than the verbal one.

pornographic, *a.* Add: Hence **pornogra·phica,** pornographic literature or art; **pornogra·phical** *a.* (in quot. *fig.*); **pornogra·phically** *adv.*; **pornographico-** *comb. form*, as *pornogra·phico-devo·tional* adj.; **porno·graphize** *v. trans.*, to make pornographic in character.

1917 J. B. Cabell *Cream of Jest* ii. v. 65 The latest masterpiece of a pornographically gifted genius. **1921** *Times Lit. Suppl.* 10 Feb. 90/4 She introduced him to a coward, an alienist who was himself mad, a pornographically minded professor. **1939** A. Toynbee *Study of Hist.* V. 531 Apuleius's pornographico-devotional romance [*sc.* *Metamorphoses*]. **1966** *New Statesman* 16 Dec. 912/3 Within half a mile of Great Marlborough Street, shops with red neon signs offering 'Books' go on selling printed pornographica at eight quid a time. **1968** *Economist* 7 Dec. 79/3 Facing the exchange rate problem, he maintained, does not mean that 'pornographical financial thoughts are being harboured'. **1971** S. Cavell *World Viewed* xiii. 95 Godard perceives..that our tastes and convictions in love have become pornographized. **1973** J. Money in Zubin & Money *Contemp. Sexual Behavior* 414 *True Confessions* and *True Love* magazine stories are, in fact, the genuine pornography of women. So women have been allowed to enjoy themselves pornographically as much as they desire. **1978** D. Murray *Place Apart* ix. 199, I stood in the middle of the road being pornographically insulted.

pornography. Add: **2. a.** (Later examples.) Also qualified by *hard* or *soft*, with reference to *hard core* (b) s.v. *hard *a.* 22 b, *soft core* s.v. *soft *a.* 27, to denote pornography of a more, or less, obscene kind. Also *transf.*

1930 W. S. Maugham *Gent. in Parlour* xii. 64 Pornography rather than brevity is the soul of wit. **1968** *Sat. Rev.* (U.S.) 19 Oct. 23 In recent years the movies and television have developed a pornography of violence far more demoralizing than the pornography of sex, which still seizes the primary attention of the guardians of civic virtue. **1972** *Times Lit. Suppl.* 7 Jan. 12/2 Of course pornography should never be treated as if only its sexual aspects mattered—that is, as if no other kind of stimulus offered by the written word could be as socially or ethically significant. **1976** *Time* (Canada ed.) 5 Apr. 36/1 What pornography is can endlessly be debated. One rough definition: explicit books, films and other materials (including, by extension, performances) designed chiefly for sexual arousal. **1977** *Broadcast* 30 May 3/3 [Italian] 'pirate' TV stations which flourish on..'soft pornography'. **1977** *Lancet* 11 June 1241/2 A distinction could be drawn between erotic art (or soft pornography)..and hard pornography, which by connecting sex with violence, hatred, pain, and humiliation, stimulated gratification of sexual desire in deviant ways.

b. In *transf.* and extended uses.

1968 [see above]. **1977** *Listener* 17 Nov. 655/4 Turgid moralising..is the real English vice, the pornography of our day.

porny (pǭ·ɹni), *a. slang.* [f. *porn *sb* + -y[1].] Of, pertaining to, or characteristic of pornography; pornographic.

1961 S. Price *Just for Record* viii. 65 He had a real porny article... Not just dirty, mind you, but Art. **1967** [see *kinky *a.* B]. **1973** J. Wilson *Truth or Dare* i. 12 You make it sound like one of those porny books—'His hand caressed her silken knee' and all that rubbish. **1974** *Daily Tel.* 18 Oct. 16 A reduction in repeats, inane quizzes and cheap porny [television] programmes could do nothing but good. **1977** L. Meynell *Hooky gets Wooden Spoon* xiii. 157 Once he starts looking at those porny photos of his he can't think of anything else.

Poro (pǫ·ro). Also **poro, Porro, purra, Purrow.** [W. Afr.] The name of a secret tribal cult for men, based on circumcision and a school of initiation, which is widespread amongst tribes in Sierra Leone and Liberia, and is socially powerful; the head of such a tribal group; also *attrib.* Cf. *Sande.

1788 J. Newton *Thoughts upon Afr. Slave Trade* 15 The Purrow has both the legislative and executive authority. *Ibid.*, Everything belonging to the Purrow is mysterious and severe. **1803** T. Winterbottom *Acct. Native Africans Sierra Leone* I. viii. 135 They [*sc.* the Bulloms] have a superior, or head purra man, assisted by a grand council. **1925** T. N. Goddard *Handbk. Sierra Leone* iii. 57 Initiation into the Porro society takes place in youth. While boys remain in the Porro bush they are taught the arts and crafts of their tribe. **1930** R. P. Strong *Afr. Republ. Liberia* I. v. 83 The *poro* or presiding official of the society also uses signs to indicate the entrance to the bush school. **1954** E. Warner *Trial by Sasswood* (1955) ix. 161 The Loma have the most vigorous of Poro cults and are credited with having introduced the Poro into Liberia. **1962** C. Fyfe *Hist. Sierra Leone* xx. 571 Those who planned the rising had used the Poro as a cover to ensure secrecy. **1968** Harris & Sawyerr *Springs of Mende Belief* i. 1 The principal tribal cults, *poro* and *sande*... Poro..is made manifest by a series of rites and ceremonies depicting death to the early stages of life, and re-birth through resurrection to adulthood.

porocyte (pǫ·rosəit). *Zool.* [f. Gr. πόρο-ς Pore *sb.*[1] + -cyte.] In sponges, a cell containing a pore.

1898 E. A. Minchin in *Q. Jrnl. Microsc. Sci.* XL. 485 The especial functions and consequent peculiar form of the pore-cells, or porocytes, as they may be termed generally, ..enable us to regard the pore-cells as constituting a distinct class of cell-elements. **1932** Borradaile & Potts *Invertebrata* iii. 111 Other cells, known as porocytes, of a conical shape, extend through the jelly, having their base in the covering layer. **1940** G. S. Carter *Gen. Zool. Invertebrates* xix. 384 These pores pass through the substance of cells which surround them—the porocytes. **1966** *McGraw-Hill Encycl. Sci. & Technol.* II. 393/1 Cells called porocytes..pierce the walls [of calcareous sponges] at intervals and allow water to enter the central cavity.

porogamous (pǫrǫ·gămǝs), *a. Bot.* [f. as Porogamic *a.* + -ous.] = Porogamic *a.* So **poro·gamy,** fertilization of this kind.

1902 *Encycl. Brit.* XXV. 436/1 The pollen-tube normally reaches the apex of the embryo-sac through the micropyle (acrogamy or porogamy). **1905** I. B. Balfour tr. *C. E. von Goebel's Organogr. Plants* II. 615 The micropyle in all porogamous plants evidently conducts the pollen-tube. **1950** P. Maheshwari *Introd. Embryol. Angiosperms* vi. 183 The tube may enter the ovule either through the micropyle or by some other route. The former is the usual condition and is known as porogamy. *Ibid.* 184 Even in plants classed as porogamous, there are several modifications. **1965** Bell & Coombe tr. *Strasburger's Textbk. Bot.* 631 The pollen tube may reach the micropyle and hence the embryo sac by traversing the cavity of the ovule at a point where it is commonly filled with mucilage (porogamy, Fig. 757).

porokeratosis (pǫ:ro-, pōə:rokĕrătōu·sis). *Path.* [mod.L., ad. It. *porocheratosi* (V. Mibelli 1893, in *Giorn. Ital. delle Malattie Veneree* XXVIII. 340), f. Gr. πόρο-ς Pore *sb.*[1]: see *keratosis* s.v. *kerato-.] A skin disease in which the lesions are annular horny ridges enclosing an atrophic area and (in the rare classic form of the disease) usu. occur early in life on the hands and feet.

1893 tr. V. Mibelli in P. G. Unna et al. *Internationaler Atlas Seltener Hautkrankenheiten* xxvii. (1) 10/2 As regards the microscopic examination the case presents itself as a pathological fact *sui generis*, inasmuch as the principal alteration consists in hyperkeratosis of the sudoriferous ducts; and it is on this account that it deserves to be considered apart under the designation of 'Porokeratosis' which I propose provisionally as it has the merit of indicating clearly the anatomo-pathological significance of the alteration itself. **1899** *Allbutt's Syst. Med.* VIII. 478 In connection with these ringed nodules of the hands the peculiar disease known as Porokeratosis should be mentioned. **1943** *Arch. Dermatol. & Syphilol.* XLVII. 2 The extension of a lesion of porokeratosis is usually centrifugal, slow and insidious in onset, leaving a somewhat atrophic area in the center free of hair and glandular structures. **1960** J. Marshall *Dis. Skin* xxix. 777 Porokeratosis is a misnomer as the lesions are not, as Mibelli believed, related to sweat pores. **1967** *Arch. Dermatol.* XCVI. 611/1 This study of 31 patients presents disseminated superficial actinic porokeratosis (DSAP) as a distinctive and recognizable entity characterized by many uniformly small, minimal, annular, anhidrotic, keratotic lesions developing during the third or fourth decade of life on sun-exposed areas of skin. **1973** *Internat. Jrnl. Dermatol.* XII. 152/1 Our recent studies indicate that disseminated superficial actinic porokeratosis (DSAP) is a distinct entity which differs in many aspects from classic porokeratosis described by Mibelli and by Respighi.

Hence **po:rokerato·tic** *a.*

1943 *Arch. Dermatol. & Syphilol.* XLVII. 14 This consideration excludes the necessity of calling the lesion a nevus, in spite of the strong tendency of porokeratotic lesions to arrange themselves in linear and systematized configuration. **1972** *Brit. Jrnl. Plastic Surg.* XXV. 325 The tumours in both our cases were multifocal, and appeared to have arisen in the atrophic zone of the Porokeratotic lesion.

poromeric (pōəromeˑrik), *a.* and *sb.* [f. Poro(us *a.* + Poly)meric *a.*] **A.** *adj.* Applied to synthetic leather-like materials that are permeable to water vapour. **B.** *sb.* A poromeric material.

1963 *Boot & Shoe Recorder* 1 Oct. 117/3 Du Pont has coined a generic term for it [*sc.* 'Corfam']: 'poromeric', which means a 'microporous and permeable coriaceous sheet material'. **1964** *Times Rev. Industry* Mar. 23/2 Another new Du Pont development is Corfam, a 'poromeric' material which has brought a breakthrough in the manufacture of shoe uppers, since it 'breathes' like leather. **1966** *Chem. & Engin. News* 19 Dec. 13/1 Farbwerke Hoechst's subsidiary, Kalle, A.G., has a poromeric at the development stage. **1967** *Economist* 4 Nov. 544/3 Both Du Pont's and ICI's products are porous, or poromeric, as the trade chooses to say,..but Courtaulds' Quox is not, and is therefore only suitable for sandals. **1971** *New Scientist* 12 Aug. 370/2 The collagenous poromerics currently under development..are mostly in the form of a fibrous mat composed of intermingled collagen and synthetic fibres agglomerated by a polymeric bonding agent. **1978** *Times* 26 Apr. 12/2 The high quality poromeric synthetic materials..launched in the 1960s never fulfilled..expectations. *Ibid.* 12/4 The breakthrough..came with the poromerics..which, the makers claimed breathe like leather.

porometer (porǫ·mĭtəɹ). [f. Gr. πόρο-ς Pore *sb.*[1] + -meter.] An instrument for measuring the degree of porosity; *spec.* one for estimating the sizes of the stomata of leaves by measuring the rate at which air can be passed through them.

1911 Darwin & Pertz in *Proc. R. Soc.* B. LXXXIV. 137 We believe that a much more intimate knowledge of the *living* stoma and its movements would be necessary to prove his contention..that 'the regulatory function is almost *nil*'. With a view to testing the question we have designed an instrument which we propose to call a porometer. The idea is to estimate changes in the stomata by recording the change in the velocity of a current of air drawn through them in the living leaf. **1939** *Geogr. Jrnl.* XCIV. 124 The effect of the continuous illumination of the arctic summer in the stomatal mechanism of leaves was studied by porometers. **1970** *Nature* 25 July 377/2 The stomatal activity of fully hydrated..broad bean plants.. was investigated using a recording porometer attached to the second mature leaves from the apex. **1975** G. Anderson *Coring* iv. 77 The basic instruments [for core analysis] are the porometer for porosity measurements, the permeameter for permeability measurements, and the saturation retorts for saturation measurements.

poroporo (pǫ·ropǫro). Substitute for def.: A shrub, *Solanum aviculare*, belonging to the family Solanaceæ, native to Australia and New Zealand, and bearing violet-blue flowers followed by large orange berries; also called bullibulli or kangaroo apple. (Earlier and later examples.)

1853 J. D. Hooker *Bot. Antarctic Voy.: Flora Novæ-Zelandiæ* I. 182 Nat[ive] name [of *Solanum aviculare*], 'Poroporo' in the northern, and 'Kohoho' in the southern parts of the Islands. **1882** W. D. Hay *Brighter Britain!* II. 152 Among indigenous vegetable productions came.. the berries of poroporo..and other trees. **1921** H. Guthrie-Smith *Tutira* xxii. 216 At other times of the year kowhai and hill-flax..will provide nectar,..poroporo.. and other native plants, seeds and berries. **1965** [see *gunyang]. **1970** M. E. Fisher et al. *Gardening with N.Z. Plants* 112 The poroporo is a leafy shrub.

porosity. Add: Also, the degree to which a substance is porous (see quots.).

1939 *U.S. Dept. Agric. Yearbk. 1938* 1174 *Porosity, soil*, degree to which the soil mass is permeated with pores or cavities. **1971** *Gloss. Soil Sci. Terms* (Soil Sci. Soc. Amer.) 13/2 *Porosity*, the volume percentage of the total bulk not occupied by solid particles. **1975** G. Anderson *Coring* i. 2 Porosity is a measure of the space in a rock not occupied by the solid structure or framework of the rock. It is defined as the fraction of the total bulk volume of the rock not occupied by solids. *Ibid.*, A commercial oil-bearing sandstone can have varying porosities... The formation should contain at least 8–10% porosity before it can be considered commercially interesting.

porphin (pǭ·ɹfin). *Chem.* Also **-ine.** [a. G. *porphin* (Fischer & Halbig 1926, in *Ann. der Chem.* CDXLVIII. 194), f. *porph(yr)in* *porphyrin.] A synthetic, purple, crystalline solid, $C_{20}H_{14}N_4$, which has a macrocyclic aromatic molecule consisting of four pyrrole residues linked by —CH= groups, and from which the porphyrins are formally derived; now also = *porphyrin.

1926 *Brit. Chem. Abstr.* A. 963/1 The name 'porphin' is suggested for the parent substance of (II), containing no β-substituents. **1939** *Nature* 10 June 967/1 The chlorophyll molecule may be likened to a signet, or rubber stamp, the disk representing a so-called porphine ring. **1939** *Thorpe's Dict. Appl. Chem.* (ed. 4) III. 82/2 Porphin and the porphyrins..possess a characteristic type of absorption spectrum, and the power to form stable derivatives with metals, in which the two imino-hydrogen atoms are substituted, *e.g.* by a divalent metal atom. **1954** A. WHITE et al. *Princ. Biochem.* x. 201 Porphin was first synthesized by Hans Fischer and Gleim in 1935; the compound is not known to occur in nature. **1966** *Q. Rev. Chem. Soc.* XX. 211 When each of the four pyrrole rings of a porphin bears two different substituents A and B in the β-positions, then four isomers exist. **1968** I. L. FINAR *Org. Chem.* (ed. 4) II. xix. 797 Fleischer *et al.* (1965) have also examined porphin by X-ray analysis, and found the molecule is nearly planar, the observed small deviations from planarity not being large enough to be significant. *Ibid.*, Substituted porphins are known as porphyrins. **1973** *Jrnl. Amer. Chem. Soc.* XCV. 8506/2 The porphine used in this study was prepared by the acid-catalyzed condensation of pyrrole-2-carbinol in 10% acetic acid–xylene solution.

porphobilin (pǭɹfobəi·lin). *Biochem.* [a. G. *porphobilin* (Waldenström & Vahlquist 1939, in *Zeitschr. f. physiol. Chem.* CCLX. 191), f. *porph-yrie* *PORPHYRIA + -O + L. *bīl-is* BILE: see -IN[1].] Any of a group of red-brown pigments derived from porphobilinogen.

1939 *Chem. Abstr.* XXXIII. 8777/1 Boiling in acid destroys I by conversion to a red porphobilin (II) with a mol. wt. of 750 to 800. **1952** *Science* 2 May 496/2 Solutions of porphobilinogen obtained by the above method, after having been acidified to pH 4·0 and boiled for 30 min, gave rise only to porphobilin, a dark-brown pigment without characteristic absorption spectrum or any porphyrin characteristics. **1964** A. WHITE et al. *Princ. Biochem.* (ed. 3) xlii. 793 The urine darkens markedly on standing, because of the conversion of abnormal quantities of porphyrinogens and other heme precursors into porphyrins, porphobilins, and other unidentified pigments.

porphobilinogen (pǭɹfobəili·nŏdʒən). *Biochem.* [a. G. *porphobilinogen* (Waldenström & Vahlquist 1939, in *Zeitschr. f. physiol. Chem.* CCLX. 191), f. prec.: see *-OGEN.] A colourless, crystalline, substituted pyrrole, $C_{10}H_{14}N_2O_4$ (see quot. 1972), which in animals is a precursor of porphyrins and is excreted in the commoner forms of porphyria.

1939 *Chem. Abstr.* XXXIII. 8777/1 In acute porphyria the urine contains a colorless substance (porphobilinogen)..which is a pyrrole deriv. and is converted to uroporphyrin on standing. **1961** *Lancet* 22 July 175/2 The clinical signs disappeared quickly, but the patient continued to excrete rather a lot of porphobilinogen and uroporphyrin in the urine. **1964** A. WHITE et al. *Princ. Biochem.* (ed. 3) xlii. 790 Enzymic preparations utilizing porphobilinogen for porphyrin synthesis have been isolated from plant, bacterial, and animal sources. **1970** R. W. MCGILVERY *Biochem.* xxi. 496 The parent indole ring is made in the next step by the condensation of two molecules of 5-aminolevulinate to form porphobilinogen. **1972** *Stedman's Med. Dict.* (ed. 22) 1004/2 *Porphobilinogen*, ..2-aminomethyl-4-(2[1]-casboxyethyl)-3-carboxymethyl-pyrrole.

Hence **po:rphobili:nogenu·ria**, the presence of porphobilinogen in the urine.

1961 *Ann. Rev. Med.* XII. 265 The probable relationship between this syndrome [*sc.* toxic porphyria] and the consumption of seed wheat treated with hexachlorobenzene-containing fungicides is supported by the production of massive uroporphyrinuria and porphobilinogenuria in rats by mixing hexachlorobenzene with the food. **1970** PASSMORE & ROBSON *Compan. Med. Stud.* II. xxxi. 4/1 In hepatic porphyria of Swedish type, new methods of measuring aminolaevulinic acid and porphobilinogen enable subclinical cases to be detected. Such cases are said to have a low degree of expressivity by comparison with their relatives who have obvious clinical manifestations and readily detectable porphobilinogenuria.

porphyr-, porphyro-. Add: **po:rphyrobla·stic** *a. Petrol.* [ad. G. *porphyroblastisch* (F. Becke 1903, in *Compt. Rend. IX Sess. Congr. Géol. Internat.* (1904) II. 570): see -BLAST], applied to (the texture of) rock (usu. metamorphic) in which larger grains formed by recrystallization occur in a finer groundmass; so **po·rphyroblast**, one of these larger crystals; **po:rphyrocla·stic** *a. Petrol.* [ad. G. *porphyroklastisch* (F. Becke 1903, in *Compt. Rend. IX Sess Congr. Géol. Internat.* (1904) II. 570): see CLASTIC *a.*], applied to (the texture of) rock which has undergone dynamic metamorphism and in which larger grains remain in a finer groundmass; hence **po·rphyroclast**, one of these larger crystals; **porphyro·psin** *Biochem.* [*RHOD)OPSIN], any of a class of light-sensitive pigments found in the retinas of freshwater vertebrates, differing from rhodopsin in containing the aldehyde of vitamin A_2 rather than that of A_1 and in having a maximum absorption at a slightly longer wavelength.

1920 A. HOLMES *Nomencl. Petrol.* 188 *Porphyroblast*,.. a term given to the pseudo-porphyritic crystals of rocks produced by thermodynamic metamorphism. The corresponding texture is called *porphyroblastic*. **1926** G. W. TYRRELL *Princ. Petrol.* xvi. 270 When idioblasts form large crystals embedded in a fine-grained groundmass, like the phenocrysts of a porphyritic igneous rock, the term *porphyroblastic* is used to describe the texture. *Ibid.* 272 Maculose structure is that in which porphyroblasts of strong minerals such as andalusite, cordierite,.. etc., are well developed. **1966** *McGraw-Hill Encycl. Sci. & Technol.* VII. 11/2 The large crystals of some plutonic rocks are probably more properly classed as porphyroblasts. They may have formed essentially in solid rock by recrystallization aided by residual fluids from the solidifying magma. **1975** G. ANDERSON *Coring* ii. 31 Mottled dolomite is the result of incomplete dolomitization and exhibits itself as porphyroblasts in an altered calcareous matrix or as scattered patches of dolomite. **1920** A. HOLMES *Nomencl. Petrol.* 188 Porphyroclastic structure. **1926** G. W. TYRRELL *Princ. Petrol.* xvi. 272 The more resistant minerals..or rock fragments..may be less crushed, and may stand out in a pseudo-porphyritic manner from the finer material produced by the crushing of the softer constituents. This structure is called porphyroclastic. **1954** R. L. PARKER tr. *Niggli's Rocks & Min. Deposits* vi. 239 Porphyroclastic, with porphyroclasts. **1975** *Nature* 20 Feb. 598/2 Rocks of the anorthosite association *per se* are separated from an amphibolite facies gneiss complex..by clearly marked zones of blastomylonite and porphyroclastic gneiss. *Ibid.* 10 Apr. 489/2 Xenoliths with variable microscopic fabric patterns containing porphyroclasts seem to have suffered increasingly intense shearing stresses through progressive deformation. **1937** G. WALD in *Ibid.* 12 June 1017/1 The visual purple of freshwater fishes possesses different spectral properties. I shall refer to it as porphyropsin. **1962** K. F. LAGLER et al. *Ichthyol.* xi. 376 The retinas of fishes yield two kinds of light-sensitive pigments, rhodopsin and porphyropsin. **1975** *Compar. Biochem. & Physiol.* A. LII. 720/2 While terrestriality appears to act as a selective force for the predominance of rhodopsin, the function of the porphyropsin and mixed porphyropsin-rhodopsin systems remains obscure.

porphyria (pǭɹfi·riă). *Path.* [mod.L., f. *PORPHYR(IN + -IA[1].] Any of various metabolic disorders characterized by the excretion of abnormally large quantities of porphyrins.

1923 A. E. GARROD *Inborn Errors of Metabolism* (ed. 2) viii. 144 Pigmentation of the enamel is a rare phenomenon... Even in congenital porphyria it is evidently an exceptional sign. **1945** *Jrnl. Biol. Chem.* CLVII. 330 A complex mixture of pigments occurs in porphyria urine. **1969** MACALPINE & HUNTER *George III & Mad-Business* xii. 197 The galaxy of patients assembled in these pages is due to our method of selection and must not create the impression that porphyria is commoner among the great than the not so great. **1970** PASSMORE & ROBSON *Compan. Med. Stud.* II. xxxi. 10/2 The Swedish type of hepatic porphyria..may appear clinically only after administration of certain drugs, particularly barbiturates. **1975** *Victoria* (B.C.) *Times* 29 Apr. 14/3 Dermatologists..had been treating the man who lived in a soldiers' home for..porphyria.

Hence **porphy·ric** *a.*, of, pertaining to, or affected with porphyria; also as *sb.*, a person so affected.

1934 *Acta Med. Scand.* LXXXIII. 286 Hans Fischer.. has found a violet substance in the gallstones of the famous porphyric Petry. **1944** *Ibid.* CXVII. 8 A latent porphyric may suffer from another acute abdominal malady than a porphyric colic. **1974** *Nature* 9 Aug. 504/1 We noticed that skin lesions were provoked in porphyric rats, whose coats were shaved.

porphyrin (pǭ·ɹfirin). *Chem.* [a. G. *porphyrin* (Willstätter & Fritzsche 1909, in *Ann. d. Chem.* CCCLXXI. 33), f. *haemato-porphyrin* hæmatoporphyrin (s.v. *HÆMATO-), f. Gr. πόρφυρ-ος purple + *-in* -IN[1].] Any of a large class of deeply-coloured red or purple fluorescent crystalline pigments that are substituted derivatives of porphin, many of which occur widely in nature, both in the free state and as complexes with metals (as in the hæms).

1910 *Jrnl. Chem. Soc.* XCVIII. I. 127 The phyllins are converted by acids into the corresponding porphyrins, compounds which do not contain magnesium. **1939** [see *PORPHIN]. **1949** *Endeavour* VIII. 83/1 In both [*sc.* adult and fœtal haemoglobin], the prosthetic group (to which the oxygen becomes attached) is the same iron porphyrin compound. **1950** *Sci. News* XV. 95 Porphyrin is the coloured part of hæmoglobin minus the iron. Porphyrin is easily detected because it shows an intense red fluorescence when held before an ultra-violet lamp. **1961** *Lancet* 22 July 175/1 A deficiency in purine synthesis could result, during porphyria, from the increased formation of porphyrins. **1970** AMBROSE & EASTY *Cell Biol.* vii. 228 The biologically important compounds chlorophyll, haemoglobin, and the cytochromes all contain a common cyclic structure, called a porphyrin, which consists of four pyrrole rings linked by methine bridges (—CH═). **1974** *Sci. Amer.* Dec. 73/1 In chlorophyll the central cavity of the ring is occupied by a magnesium atom... Porphyrin rings in the blood protein hemoglobin and in the cytochromes contain an atom of iron instead.

Hence **po:rphyrino·pathy** (see quot. 1950).

1950 *Thorpe's Dict. Appl. Chem.* (ed. 4) X. 132/2 Porphyrinopathies, or diseases accompanied by abnormal porphyrin production or excretion. **1961** *Ann. Rev. Med.* XII. 258 In this review, the main porphyrinopathies will be listed using Waldenström's classification.

porphyrinogen (pǭɹfiri·nŏdʒən). *Biochem.* [a. G. *porphyrinogen* (Fischer & Bartholomäus 1913, in *Ber. d. Deut. Chem. Ges.* XLVI. 512), f. *porphyrin* *PORPHYRIN: see *-OGEN.] Any of the colourless, reduced derivatives of porphyrins in which the four pyrrole nuclei are linked by methylene groups, $—CH_2—$.

In quot. 1913 applied *spec.* to the first such compound to be prepared.

1913 *Jrnl. Chem. Soc.* CIV. I. 409 A colourless, crystalline reduction product, $C_{33}H_{42}O_4N_4$, of high molecular weight is obtained. This is termed porphyrinogen in view of its ready conversion into a red product having the spectroscopic properties of porphyrin. **1938** *Chem. Soc. Ann. Rep.* XXXIV. 384 Until this work was carried out, only three crystalline leuco-compounds of porphyrins, or porphyrinogens, were known, and none of these was derived from chlorophyll. **1955** *Endeavour* XIV. 135/1 It is possible that the porphyrins are not on the direct line of biosynthesis but are produced by reversible side reactions from closely related precursors, possibly the more highly reduced porphyrinogens. **1968** PASSMORE & ROBSON *Compan. Med. Stud.* I. xxvi. 7/2 Porphyrinogens are similar [to porphyrins] but in these compounds the pyrrole rings are linked by methylene ($—CH_2—$) bridges.

porphyrinuria (pǭːɹfiriniūə·riă). *Path.* [mod. L., f. *PORPHYRIN + -URIA.] The presence of excessive or abnormal porphyrins in the urine.

1916 *Chem. Abstr.* X. 1671 The term porphyrinuria is used in place of hematoporphyrinuria because the substance isolated from the urine is not identical with hematoporphyrin. **1944** *Jrnl. Amer. Med. Assoc.* 29 Jan. 287/1 The term porphyrinuria should be reserved to indicate those instances in which the porphyrins occurring naturally in the urine are present in amounts above the normal range, a condition which exists in a great variety of diseases. **1967** *Amer. Jrnl. Med.* XLII. 476/2 Marked porphyrinuria was an additional feature in this case, and the urine also consistently contained another brown pigment.

porphyrism (pǭ·ɹfiriz'm). *Path.* [ad. G. *porphyrismus* (H. Günther 1920, in *Deutsch. Arch. f. klin. Med.* CXXXIV. 257): see -ISM.] = *PORPHYRIA.

1923 A. E. GARROD *Inborn Errors of Metabolism* (ed. 2) viii. 139 In a more recent paper the same author puts forward the view that a constitutional anomaly, which he styles 'porphyrism', underlies acute and chronic cases alike. **1934** *Acta Med. Scand.* LXXXIII. 298 No signs of porphyrism in the family.

porphyry. Add: **5.** *porphyry-red, -smooth* adjs.; **porphyry-born** *a.*, born in the purple (see PURPLE *sb.* 2 d).

1964 AUDEN in *Listener* 1 Oct. 525/1 Neither of our Dads, like Horace's, Wiped his nose on his forearm, Neither was porphyry-born. **1963** A. LUBBOCK *Austral. Roundabout* 194 The range thrust its porphyry-red battlements into the forested valley. **1930** E. POUND *XXX Cantos* xvii. 78 And the cave salt-white, and glare-purple, cool, porphyry smooth.

porpoise, *sb.* Add: **1. b.** *porpoise beef* (earlier Canad. example), *-dive* v. intr.

1833 W. F. TOLMIE *Jrnl.* 21 Jan. (1963) 97 Ate some porpoise beef at breakfast. **1973** V. CANNING *Flight of Grey Goose* vii. 138 He..took a deep breath, and porpoise-dived down, swimming strongly.

2. (See quots.)

1929 F. C. BOWEN *Sea Slang* 105 *Porpoise, doing a*, said when a submarine dives down nose first at a sharp angle. **1931** *Times* 21 Aug. 7/1 It [*sc.* a seaplane] dropped back on to the water and then porpoised again, double the height of the first porpoise. **1961** F. H. BURGESS *Dict. Sailing* 74 *Doing a porpoise*, said of a submarine taking a sharp dive. **1963** *Amer. Speech* XXXVIII. 119 *Porpoise*, an undesired landing in which the airplane bobs up and down like a porpoise playing in the waves, caused by landing on the nose gear first.

porpoise (pǭ·ɹpəs), *v.* [f. the sb.] *intr.* To move like a porpoise; *spec.* **a.** Of an aircraft, esp. a seaplane: to touch the water or the ground and rise again. **b.** To move through the water like a porpoise, alternately rising above it and submerging.

1909 H. G. WELLS *Tono-Bungay* I. iii. 110 'Just as though an old Porpoise like him would ever make money,' she said... 'He'll just porpoise about.' **1919** *Rep. & Mem. Advisory Comm. Aeronaut.* No. 437. 6 The author has seen a machine..porpoise very badly in waves of only one to two feet high. **1930** P. WHITE *How to fly Airplane* xiv. 216 Sometimes, students fail to level off at all. This is an error which is bound to result either in a crash, or in a 'wheel' landing from which the plane will bounce or 'porpoise' quite high. **1931** [see *PORPOISE *sb.* 2]. **1939** G. H. JONES *No less Renowned* 46 The Coxswain and the Second Coxswain had their work cut out to prevent the vessel [*sc.* a submarine] from 'porpoising'. **1944** *Richmond* (Virginia) *Times-Dispatch* 21 Sept. 6/6 The Liberator [bomber]..touched the water at a speed of approximately 100 miles per hour, porpoised (bounced) once, and struck again tail-first. **1968** F. W. HOLIDAY *Great Orm of Loch Ness* v. 39 These objects were moving south-west... They were 'porpoising'—rolling under the surface and then reappearing. **1969** D. BAGLEY *Spoilers* vii. 206 I've set her [*sc.* a torpedo] to run at twelve feet. Any less than that an' she's likely to porpoise—jump in an' out o' the water. **1976** *Province* (Vancouver) 8 Mar. 1/3 From 500 feet there appeared an island full of seals and an ocean full of an enormous whale porpoising through his domain before diving out of sight. **1977** *Modern Boating* (Austral.) Jan. 34/2 With the trim..right out the boat begins to porpoise badly.

So **po·rpoising** *vbl. sb.*

1915 G. C. Loening *Military Aeroplanes* xi. 134 The latter condition, causing sudden changes in the angle of the bottom and its planing pressure,..gives rise to the disagreeable effect of 'porpoising'—a fore and aft rocking and jumping. **1920** L. Bairstow *Appl. Aerodynamics* ii. 55 Such phenomena as the depression of the bow due to switching on the engine and 'porpoising' are reproduced in the model with sufficient accuracy for the phenomena to be kept under control in the design stages of a flying boat. **1933** [see *hydrofoil 1]. **1974** P. Lovesey *Invitation to Dynamite Party* xii. 152 We have to steer by coming to the surface at intervals. It's a process known as 'porpoising'.

porridge, *sb.* Add: **3. a.** (Later examples.)

1972 *Listener* 18 May 662/2 Sometimes the programme has been a radio porridge, sometimes a shapely..necklace of sound, but never anything really remarkable. **1976** *Brit. Jrnl. Sociol.* XXVII. 36 On the other side of the great divide are the empiricists who..correlate vaguely-worded, interchangeable scales with each other and call the subsequent statistical porridge, alienation.

b. (Later examples.)

1870 *Scribner's Monthly* I. 154 While the engineers were floundering in the porridge at the west end, they wisely resolved to..sink a shaft to grade. **1966** H. Sheppard *Dict. Railway Slang* (ed. 2) 9 *Porridge*, sludge removed from drains.

c. A prison sentence; a term of imprisonment. *slang.*

1954 *Britannica Bk. of Year* 637/1 Several examples of underworld slang, probably of a date earlier than 1953, appeared in the newspapers. Thus, the reader learned that *Porridge* meant a term of imprisonment. **1955** D. Webb *Deadline for Crime* i. 16 He did his porridge quietly, peacefully, earned full remission and came out. **1958** F. Norman *Bang to Rights* iii. 171 Week excuses that's all you get, when you go away to do a bit of porridge. **1968** J. Wainwright *Edge of Extinction* 92 D'you think I'd forget the frigging jack 'ut sent me down for two years' porridge? **1972** J. Brown *Chancer* xiii. 169 You think I'm not sick of doing porridge too? **1977** 'E. Crispin' *Glimpses of Moon* xii. 236 His emotions at the prospect..of yet another dose of porridge were such that he was..incapable of thinking clearly.

4. *to keep* (etc.) *one's breath to cool one's (own) porridge* (later examples); *to make a porridge,* to blunder, to make a mess *of* something.

1883 R. Cleland *Inchbracken* xii. 92 If our young Captain has wance ta'en the notion, they may save their breath to cool their parritch, that would gainsay him. **1924** G. B. Shaw *Saint Joan* ii. 29 If you are going to say 'Son of St Louis: gird on the sword of your ancestors, and lead us to victory' you may spare your breath to cool your porridge. **1930** E. Pound *XXX Cantos* xxii. 99 He said He would save his breath to cool his own porridge. **1969** D. Clark *Nobody's Perfect* iii. 79 'Three months sounds like generous notice.' Hunt said soberly, 'For a man who has made a porridge, perhaps.' **1971** 'H. Calvin' *Poison Chasers* ii. 26 These boffins have made a porridge of this place. **1976** A. White *Long Silence* xi. 101, I knew I would make a porridge of explaining it.

5. *porridge bowl* (examples), *saucepan*; *-coloured* adj.

1902 Farmer & Henley *Slang* V. 258/2 *Porridge-bowl*.., the stomach. **1925** *Heal & Son Catal.: Table Wares*, Porridge Bowl..1/-. **1936** J. Buchan *Island of Sheep* ii. 25 Archie Roylance..looked up sympathetically from his porridge bowl. **1974** P. Lovesey *Invitation to Dynamite Party* ix. 110 A tin porridge-bowl..and a mug. **1977** 'J. Fraser' *Hearts Ease* xv. 166 You can go to that orphanage..stand in line and hold out your porridge bowl at breakfast time. **1949** E. Coxhead *Wind in West* i. 11 Grimy porridge-coloured upholstery. **1979** *Homes & Gardens* June 57/3 The village ground, with a guaranteed vicar in porridge-coloured flannels and a blacksmith in belted greys. **1926–7** *Army & Navy Stores Catal.* 150/1 Double milk or porridge saucepan..4 pt. 9/-. **1975** C. Fremlin *Long Shadow* iii. 24 A porridge saucepan soaking in the sink.

porridge, *v.* Add: **c.** *trans.*, to send to prison (*slang*). Cf. *porridge *sb.* 3 c.

1965 B. Knox *Taste of Proof* i. 27 Jean reckoned you blokes had porridged the wrong fella when you pulled in Frank for the Glen Ault job.

Porro, var. *Poro.

‖**porron** (porro·n). Pl. **porrones, porrons.** [Sp.] In Spain, a wine-flask with a long spout from which the contents are drunk directly.

1845 R. Ford *Hand-bk. for Travellers Spain* I. vi. 479/1 They are..drinking out of *Porrones*. **1936** *Burlington Mag.* June 301/1 An interesting fourteenth or fifteenth-century ancestor of the *porron* which is still used in Soho. **1968** K. Bird *Smash Glass Image* iv. 50 Francisco tilted the teapot-shaped *porrón* and ejected a stream of wine from the spout. It curved through the air..into his open mouth. **1972** 'D. Craig' *Double Take* x. 133 Porrón, that's what those wine bottles were called. Really, it should be a skin, in the true Spain. **1976** *Scotsman* 24 Dec. (Weekend Suppl.) 2/5 We..drink our modest bottle of vino corriente while the crowd below swill porrons and pigskins of the stuff which makes them very vocal indeed.

Porson (pǭ·ɹsən). The name of Richard *Porson* (1759–1808), English classical scholar, used (*a*) in the possessive to designate a metrical law formulated by him and governing Greek tragic trimeters (see quots.); (*b*) *attrib.* and *absol.* to designate certain founts of Greek type influenced by his handwriting.

(*a*) **1894** W. W. Goodwin *Greek Gram.* (ed. 2) v. 358 When the *tragic* trimeter ends in a word forming a cretic (—⏑—), this is regularly preceded by a short syllable or by a monosyllable... This is known as 'Porson's rule'. **1949** *Oxf. Classical Dict.* 565/2 The comic trimeter..is not bound by Porson's Law. **1962** H. Lloyd-Jones tr. *Maas's Greek Metre* 35 The rule..is known in this connexion as 'Maas's Law', as it is known as 'Porson's Law' with respect to the tragic trimeter and as 'Havet's Law' with respect to the tetrameter. **1973** A. H. Sommerstein *Sound Pattern Anc. Greek* 136 The iambic trimeter.. is governed in tragedy by, among other constraints, a rule known as Porson's Law. **1976** R. Pfeiffer *Hist. Classical Scholarship 1300–1850* xii. 160 Bentley had led the way in the scholarly treatment of Greek and Latin metre, and Porson was the first to make a further substantial advance; we may say that his claim to immortality is based above all on the rule called 'Porson's Law': that no word may end after a long *anceps* in the last iambus of the tragic iambic trimeter.

(*b*) **1894** *Amer. Dict. Printing & Bookmaking* 240/2 Greek type is cast by one foundry in New York... Some kinds now in use in the United States have been imported from England and from Germany... A heavy face, generally known as a Porson, is in use for headings and emphasis. **1927** D. H. Stevens et al. *Man. Style* (ed. 9) 269 Monotype Porson Greek. **1960** *Penrose Ann.* LIV. 38/2 Austin cut the Porson greek type in London.

Hence **Porso·nian** (-ōu·n-) *a.*, pertaining to or characteristic of Porson, his work, or the fount of Greek type named after him. Also *absol.* as *sb.*

1840 *Penny Cycl.* XVIII. 420/2 Porson's great reputation during his lifetime converted all the promising young scholars of the time into servile imitators of the great critic, and the 'Porsonian school of critics', as they have been termed, threw many impediments in the way of sound and comprehensive scholarship. **1896** *Dict. Nat. Biogr.* XLVI. 163/2 There was a reaction..against the Porsonian school. **1929** *N. & Q.* 13 Apr. 267/2 A stronger and more dignified type than the common current Porsonian. **1976** R. Pfeiffer *Hist. Classical Scholarship 1300–1850* xv. 179 In his editions of Greek tragedies he [*sc.* Hermann] may be said to rival Porson and the Porsonians or even surpass them.

port, *sb.*[1] Add: **1. c.** Phr. *port in a* (or *the*) *storm*, a refuge in difficulties or troubled circumstances (also in weakened senses); *spec.* in proverbial phr. *any port in a storm*, any refuge or escape (is welcomed) in adverse circumstances.

1749 J. Cleland *Mem. Woman of Pleasure* II. 133, I feeling pretty sensibly that it was going by the right door, and knocking desperately at the wrong one, I told him of it: 'Pooh, 'says he my dear, any port in a storm.' **1787** J. Cobb *First Floor* ii. ii. 51 Here is a door open, i' faith—any port in a storm, they say. **1821** Scott *Pirate* I. iv. 60 As this Scotsman's howf lies right under your lee, why, take any port in a storm. **1897** R. L. Stevenson *St. Ives* xxv. 188 'Any port in a storm' was the principle on which I was prepared to act. **1936** B. Adams *Ships & Women* x. 229 'How do you like Maggie Cuddeford?' she asked. I replied, 'Any port in a storm. I like you heaps better.' **1965** J. Porter *Dover Three* ii. 19 It was not quite the sort of company with which Dover would mix from choice but, as the jolly sailors say, any port in a storm. **1970** *Guardian* 7 Apr. 18/1 Midnight cries of scorn and indignation rang round the Commons, which was celebrating its return to work with a row over the Ports Bill... Well, any port in a storm these days. **1977** A. Morice *Murder in Mimicry* i. viii. 67 Henry and I moved on to our next port in the storm, which was a bar round the corner.

2. c. *port of entry*: a port by which people and goods may enter a country. Cf. *port *sb.*[3] 4 b.

1840 *Niles' Reg.* 23 May 188/1 Mr. King..reported a bill for the establishment of ports of entry in the states of Missouri and Arkansas. **1936** *Phytopathology* XXVI. 476 The suggested system of field inspection and certification ..will..relieve the port-of-entry inspection services of the sole responsibility of passing materials offered for import. **1977** *Arab Times* 13 Nov. 4/7 Ercan is not an internationally recognised port of entry into Cyprus. Only the Turkish state airline THY and the tiny Turkish Cypriot airline, KTHY use it.

d. *port of call*: a port visited by a vessel in the course of a voyage. Also *transf.*

1884 [see Call *sb.* 5 a]. **1919** W. T. Grenfell *Labrador Doctor* (1920) viii. 168 We..put down our helm..to avoid the wash... The last port of call was Henley, or Château, where formerly the British had placed a fort. **1980** J. B. Hilton *Anathema Stone* ix. 93 Waiting for me to be out of earshot..so that I would not know what was to be her next port of call.

6. a. *port-fog, -officer.*

1891 Kipling *Barrack-Room Ballads* (1892) 206 O the mutter overside, when the port-fog holds us tied. **1923** —— *Land & Sea Tales* 173 When the port-fog holds us Moored and helpless, a mile from the pier. **1901** *Chambers's Jrnl.* Aug. 522/2 The port-officer, and one or two Eurasian residents, came to the office..to interview us.

port, *sb.*[3] Add: **2. e.** *U.S.* An aperture in the body of an aircraft (see quots.).

1946 *Aeroplane Spotter* 21 Sept. 226/1 (*caption*) This photograph shows well the fabric covering the three machine gun ports in each wing. **1954** D. M. Desoutter *All about Aircraft* 415/2 Details of the armament and interior arrangements are sparse, but two large gun ports are visible in pictures. **1958** *N.Y. Times Mag.* 6 Apr. 68/4 The bombardier tightens the canvas over his ports. **1959** F. D. Adams *Aeronaut. Dict.* 128/1 *Port*, a circular window in the side of an aircraft fuselage, hull, or cabin, or a side aperture for a gun, a camera, etc.

3. b. (Earlier and later examples.)

1789 D. Davidson *Thoughts on Seasons* 169 They closed fast on every side—A *port* could scarce be found. **1811** J. Ramsay *Acct. Game of Curling* 10 Whether they will have to draw, strike, wick, or *enter a port*, they will seldom deviate an inch from their aim. [Note] To *enter a port*, is to make a stone pass through an opening made by two others lying opposite to one another. **1937** T. Henderson *Lockerbie* ix. 60 If ye mak' yersel' sma' ye'll can squeeze through the port. Here's the tee; noo canny. **1975** *Scotsman* 17 Mar. (Curling Suppl.) p. v/7 The whys and wherefores of shots made and lost, the backring take-outs, in-wicks, out-wicks and draws through narrow ports were all double Dutch.

4. Also, an aperture by which the mixture enters the cylinder or combustion chamber of an internal-combustion engine, or by which the exhaust gases leave it. (Further examples.)

1886 D. Clerk *Gas Engine* vii. 168 An exhaust valve, leading into the space by a port, is also actuated at suitable times from the secondary shaft. **1913** *Autocar Handbk.* (ed. 5) ii. 33 During the compression and firing strokes all four ports are out of line, so that the cylinder is completely closed. **1956** F. Preston *Pract. Car-Owner* i. 19/1 The upward stroke not only drives out burnt gas through an exhaust port in the cylinder wall but also draws in fresh mixture..through an inlet port. **1966** B. D. Power *High Vacuum Pumping Equipment* xi. 387 Conditions remote from the pumping port are being considered. **1967** L. Holmes *Odhams New Motor Man.* i. 34/1 Valves and a camshaft are not required, as there are ports in the cylinder walls which are uncovered by the moving pistons to let fuel mixture into and exhaust gas out of the cylinders. **1978** L. Pryor *Viper* (1979) ii. 25 Around the perimeter there are two ports. The fuel comes in one port, explodes between ports, then is expelled through the other port.

b. *Med.* = *portal *sb.*[1] 1 f Also *port of entry* (cf. *port *sb.*[1] 2 c).

1908 [see *cryptogenetic *a.*]. **1928** B. J. Leggett *Theory & Pract. Radiol.* II. vii. 220 Risk [of injury to surrounding tissues] becomes smaller the greater the number of fields or ports of entry. **1928** *Amer. Jrnl. Roentgenol.* XX. 135/2 It is not really necessary to have two separate ports for the useful radiation. **1936** B. J. M. Harrison *Textbk. Roentgenol.* iii. 50 Considering the physical conditions of the technique adopted, the milli-amperage, the kilovoltage..and the size of the area treated (port of entry). **1962** Ross & Moore in *Surg. Pract. Lahey Clinic* (ed. 3) 369 If successive biopsies are desired, the biopsy port is reopened by strong negative pressure applied on 'H' syringe for 5 seconds. **1977** *Radiologia Clinica* XLVI. 225 In order to obtain greater homogeneity of biological effects within the treatment volume, all prescribed ports should be used at each treatment session.

c. An aperture in any kind of container or vessel for the entry or egress of fluid.

1944 *Plastics* Jan. 18/2 In transfer moulding the material is placed in a heated pot from which it is forced through a narrow port into the actual mould. **1962** V. Grissom in *Into Orbit* 131 In the rush to get out before I sank I had not closed the air inlet port in the belly of my suit, where the oxygen tube fits inside the capsule. **1971** *Sci. Amer.* Sept. 222/3 A filter should be inserted between the inlet port of the compressor and the gas outlet of the laser.

d. An aperture in a loudspeaker enclosure.

1949 Frayne & Wolfe *Elem. Sound Recording* xxx. 627 Ports are provided at the front of the enclosure in order to utilize some of the back-radiated energy to reinforce the energy from the horn at the lower frequencies. **1975** G. J. King *Audio Handbk.* vi. 143 The box has two main apertures, one to accommodate the driver unit and the other, called the vent or port, which allows air to move in and out of the enclosure in sympathy with the air pressure changes inside.

e. (i) *Electr.* A pair of terminals where a signal enters or leaves a network or device, the current flowing into one terminal at any instant being equal to that flowing out of the other. Freq. *ellipt.* with preceding numeral adj.

1953 Wheeler & Dettinger in *Wheeler Monogr.* ix. 7 After considering many alternatives, the writer has adopted the term 'portal' or simply 'port' as the general designation of an entrance or exit of a network. A self-impedance becomes a 'one-port'. The usual transducer becomes a 'two-port' with one 'in-port' and one 'out-port'. The general network is designated a 'multi-port'. **1958** N. Balabanian *Network Synthesis* i. 9 The simplest network..is the one-terminal pair, or one-port. **1966** L. A. Manning *Electr. Circuits* xii. 256 A two-port network may be driven by either a voltage or a current source of input, and either voltage or current may be measured at the output. **1973** *Nature* 3 Aug. 264/1 The switching element was a four-port ferrite switch driven at 1 kHz. **1975** D. G. Fink *Electronics Engineers' Handbk.* iii. 43 A transistor is a two-port network, although it has three terminals. Connecting an extra wire to one of the terminals provides the extra terminal without violating any network laws.

(ii) A place where signals enter or leave a data-transmission system or a device in such a system.

1970 C. S. Carr et al. in *Proc. AFIPS Conf.* XXXVI. 592/2 We assume here that a process has several input-output paths which we will call ports. Each port may be connected to a sequential I/O device, and while connected, transmits information in only one direction. **1972** *Proc.*

IEEE LX. 1409/1 The combiner may have a fixed number of input ports to which the terminals are either always connected, or to which they may be connected, if not already occupied. *Ibid.* 1412/1 Each remote TYMSAT is capable of accommodating up to 31 simultaneous users... In addition, each CPU has 60 input ports, each corresponding to a different user. **1976** *U.S. Agric. Outlook 1977* (Nat. Agric. Outlook Conf., U.S.) 366 The University user can lease either a 10-character per second or a 30-character per second port. The monthly rate varies.., depending on the speed. **1976** *Rep. Computer Board of Managem., 1975–76* (University Coll., London, Computer Centre) I. 4 For several years we have had a single dial-up line, operating at only 1200 bands. This single port was heavily used.

6. port-light (see quot. 1927); **port-mouth,** delete † and add later examples; also *attrib.*

1926 *Chambers's Jrnl.* July 478/2 Portlights as fitted to deck cabins have some drawbacks. **1927** G. Bradford *Gloss. Sea Terms* 132/2 The usual round openings closed with glass for light and air are called ports. The glass is set in a hinged brass frame called the port light. **1908** *Animal Managem.* 140 Swimming mounted, requires a capable horseman, who should be a good swimmer himself. Before riding in, it is well to remove the portmouth bit if one is worn. **1965** C. E. G. Hope *Riding* v. 62 The best-known variety of the Pelham must be the British military bit, the *port-mouth universal, reversible.*

port, *sb.*[4] Add: **9.** esp. in phr. *at the high port*; also *transf.* and *fig.*

[**1918** E. S. Farrow *Dict. Mil. Terms* 294 *High port*, a position in bayonet training.] **1937** Partridge *Dict. Slang* 19/2 *At the high port*, at once; vigorously; unhesitatingly; very much: military; from ca. 1925. I.e. in fine style. **1956** D. M. Davin *Sullen Bell* II. vi. 148 'You seem very much at the high port,' Hugh said. 'I haven't seen you so bright since the evening you flung the smoke bomb into the Yank mess at Caserta.' **1970** *Daily Tel.* 28 Apr. 2/5 He began to climb the stairs with the gun at the 'high port' position. **1971** S. Mays *No More Soldiering for Me* xv. 153 He spun round with fists at the high port.

port, *sb.*[6] (*a.*) Add: **2. a.** Also used with reference to aircraft.

1917 R. B. Matthews *Aviation Pocket-bk.* vi. 164 The leading edges of the port and starboard top wing should be in a straight line. **1939** [see *flight engineer* s.v. *Flight *sb.*[1] 15]. **1948** [see *Assembly 1 c]. **1971** R. Dentry *Encounter at Kharmel* ii. 25 He had landed at Peshawar.. because the port motor was running too roughly to warrant continuing the flight. **1976** J. McClure *Rogue Eagle* iv. 69 The landscape sliding away beneath the port wing. **1977** *R.A.F. News* 27 Apr.–10 May 8/2 Then the port engine burst into flames.

b. *port-watch*: see quot. 1883.

1867 [see Larboard *sb.* (*a.*) B]. **1883** *Man. Seamanship for Boys' Training Ships R. Navy* (Admiralty) (1886) 5 The starboard watch work the starboard side of the deck, and the port watch the port side of the deck. **1953** C. S. Forester *Hornblower & Atropos* xvi. 228 Port watch wins!.. Starboard watch provides the entertainment tomorrow night!

port, *sb.*[7] Add: **a.** (Later examples.) Also, a drink of port; a glass used for port.

1907 *Yesterday's Shopping* (1969) 937 Table glass services... 12 Sherries... 12 Ports... 12 Clarets [etc.]. **1925** [see *Liqueur *sb.* 2]. **1938** G. Greene *Brighton Rock* III. i. 98 Give me another port. **1974** *Times* 5 Apr. 12/3 The goblet is £4.25... A claret is £3.15 and a sherry/port £2.95.

port (pōᵊɹt), *sb.*[10] *Austral.* colloq. abbrev. of Portmanteau *sb.*

1908 E. G. Murphy *Jarrahland Jingles* 82 Silently they packed their 'ports' and flitted to the West. **1915** J. P. Bourke *Off Bluebush* 122 They see a young chap with a 'port' on his back. **1928** J. Devanny *Dawn Beloved* ix. 107 'Get my working togs out of my port, will you?'.. Dawn..opened his old portmanteau and took out the things. **1934** T. Wood *Cobbers* xviii. 236 A dignitary festooned in silver lace opened the door and asked me if I had any more ports. in the brake. **1946** D. Stivens *Courtship Uncle Henry* 53 You take your port up and come back to the car. **1954** G. Dutton in *Coast to Coast 1953–54* 149 Well grab your ports, and I'll take you out to the huts. **1967** *Sunday Truth* (Brisbane) 17 Sept. 16/3 She went back to her hut and happily unpacked her ports. **1972** R. Magoffin *Chops & Gravy* 46 Roly grabbed his port..charged towards the bus.

port, *v.*[1] **1.** Delete † *Obs.* and add later examples.

1973 W. H. Hallahan *Ross Forgery* iv. 53 The skids.. had been ported into the press rooms. **1979** 'E. Peters' *One Corpse too Many* vii. 113 The boat..was of the light, withy-and-hide type that could be ported easily overland.

2. *port arms* (examples as *sb.*; also *attrib.*).

1918 E. S. Farrow *Dict. Mil. Terms* 462 *Port arms*, a position in the Manual of Arms. **1973** D. Barnes *See the Woman* (1974) I. 38 The..white-helmeted officers..stood with batons in a port-arms position, facing the crowd. *Ibid.* 81 Johnson held the shotgun at port-arms. **1974** D. E. Westlake *Help* (1975) xix. 128 The sentry..was still at port arms as though frozen in that position.

‖ **port-a-beul** (porʃt a biəl). *Sc.* Pl. (also used erron. as sing.) *puirt-a-beul.* [Gael., lit. 'music from mouth'.] 'A quick tune, gen. a reel-tune or the like, of Lowland Sc. orig. to which Gael. words of a quick repetitive nature have been added to make it easier to sing, now occasionally used as an accompaniment to dancing in the absence of instrumental music' (*Sc. Nat. Dict.*). Also *transf.* and *attrib.*

1901 K. N. MacDonald *Puirt-a-beul* 3 Puirt-a-beul, 'mouth-tunes', or 'tunes for dancing'. **1938** [see *mouth music* s.v. *Mouth *sb.* 21]. **1945** B. Fergusson *Lowland Soldier* 12 The burn's making ever its own port-a-beul. **1952** N. Mitchison *Lobsters on Agenda* viii. 94 The three from the Glen, Janet, Sheila and young Mrs Macrae, were trying over a port a beul, very lightly, a living breath of humming. **1957** *Scottish Stud.* I. 133 The *Puirt-a-beul* are popularly supposed to have originated as a result of the religious opposition to musical instruments such as the bagpipes and the fiddle, which was at its strongest in the middle of the nineteenth century. **1964** *Listener* 15 Oct. 595/2, I shall never forget.., in a Roman street, a childish jet of water dancing, like MacDiarmid's duck, to its own *port a beul.* c **1970** A. MacPhee *Story of Highland Bagpipe* (An Comunn Gaidhealach) 8 All Gaelic music and pipe tunes are not sad and plaintive. Merely listen to a good 'puirt-a-beul' (mouth-music) singer. **1974** *People's Jrnl.* (Inverness & Northern Counties ed.) 5 Jan. 13/2 Other lively numbers are 'Ta-Ra-Ra Bhoom Di-Ay', written in Gaelic when that rhythm was the fashion and 'Tha na Cailean Meallda', a swinging puirt-a-beul.

portability. Add: (Later examples.) Also *transf.* and *fig.* in the senses of *Portable *a.*

1955 *Sci. News Let.* 5 Mar. 160/1 Portable rink for outdoor ice skating makes this winter sport possible in some areas from April to November. Installed or dismantled in six days, the portability is achieved by more than eight and one-half miles of plastic piping. **1969** *Courier-Mail* (Brisbane) 19 May 11/4 Advocates of portability of superannuation benefits overlook the fact that private schemes have always been voluntary. **1970** A. Cameron et al. *Computers & Old Eng. Concordances* 24 Commenting on portability, I'm as great a sinner as anyone. **1972** *Sci. Amer.* Nov. 100/2 Nine-ounce portability and advanced computational capability. **1975** *Times* 14 Oct. 19/3 To make computer applications more independent of the manufacturer by developing 'software portability' (the ability to carry programmes, in effect, from one maker's machine to another). **1977** *Daily News* (Perth, Austral.) 19 Jan. 2/3 Seek long service leave after 10 years' continuous service, with 'portability' in the building industry and in the government.

portable, *a.* Add: **A. 1. a.** Also used to distinguish mechanical devices or electrical apparatus manufactured in forms smaller and lighter than normal, to enable them to be easily carried about.

1913 *Wireless World* Apr. p. xxxiv/2 The hon. secretary showed some model Marconi apparatus and a portable set. **1926** *Scribner's Mag.* Aug. 76/2 (Advt.), Portable receiving sets..now make it possible to carry this fine radio entertainment to summer camps and cottages. **1929** *Radio Times* 8 Nov. 444/1 What fun you can have with a portable gramophone. **1932** A. Christie *Peril at End House* ii. 31 There was a gramophone and..a portable wireless. **1937** E. Wharton *Ghosts* 22 In the middle of the carefully scoured table stood a portable wireless. **1951** *Catal. of Exhibits, South Bank Exhib., Festival of Britain* 128/2 Portable radio..mains or battery. **1961** *Lebende Sprachen* VI. 70/1 Portable typewriter. **1976** H. Nielsen *Brink of Murder* i. 11 The sportscast on the portable TV was in progress. **1977** *Wandsworth Borough News* 16 Sept. 17/4 To permit portable radios and accept the inevitability of dog mess, whilst stridently prohibiting children from cycling seems to reflect odd standards.

d. Of a building or the like: not of a permanent construction; capable of being dismantled and re-erected elsewhere.

1860 *Players* I. v. 39 (Advt.), Portable Theatres with scenery, Gas Fittings, &c. fitted up in town or country. **1955** [see *Portability]. **1968** *Globe & Mail* (Toronto) 3 Feb. 50/1 All have temporary lodging, two in portable halls and one in Woodbine Junior High School. **1972** [see *Modular *a.* 1 b].

e. *fig.* Of rights, privileges, information, etc.: capable of being transferred or adapted in changed circumstances.

1965 *Economist* 13 Feb. 671 Pension rights..should not be lost when an employee is sacked or moves to another firm; ideally they should be 'portable'. **1967** *Wall St. Jrnl.* 5 Jan. 2/3 (*heading*) Hoffa to seek portable pensions for teamsters moving into new jobs. **1970** A. Cameron et al. *Computers & Old Eng. Concordances* 22 The proposal never says..what care he's going to take to make sure that his work is portable, that his work really can be used by people at other institutions.

B. *sb.* That which is portable; *spec.* a piece of machinery that is portable (in sense 1 a above); usu. ellipt. for *portable camera, gramophone, radio, typewriter,* etc.

1883 J. Hay in *Century Mag.* Dec. 281/2, I don't doubt ..but what we could pay ourselves well for the job,—spoil the 'Gyptians, you know,—forage on the enemy. Plenty of portables in them houses, eh! **1918** C. Stone *Let.* 3 Apr. in C. Mackenzie *My Life & Times* (1966) V. 132 The gramophone (a Decca portable) is going again this evening after a fortnight's silence. **1926** *Wireless World* 26 May 16/1 (Advt.), For sale... Portables. **1930** T. E. Lawrence *Let.* 8 Jan. (1938) 677 An Italian bad-hat dashed me one of those electric gramophones... All the same that portable was good at Miranshah. **1931** B. Brown *Talking Pictures* v. 132 The Western Electric portable for sound-on-film. **1933** *Hearst's International* Mar. 101/2, I doubt if Mrs. Norris could type out a really good chapter on her rickety portable. **1952** M. Laski *Village* vi. 103 We've got an old portable we used to use for the farm correspondence... But she can't do touch-typing. **1957** *Practical Wireless* XXXIII. 530/2 Next comes the portable. It is probably here that it [*sc.* the transistor] finds its greatest application. **1960** *Life* 5 Dec. 8 (Advt.), This is the new Motorola portable—forerunner of all TV to come and gift idea of a lifetime. **1966** Auden *About House* 18 The Olivetti portable, The dictionaries (the very Best money can buy). **1973** *Times* 30 Oct. 32/9 (Advt.), Colour T.V. portables. **1976** J. Lee *Ninth Man* II. 201 He would steal some of these carbons. Sarah had a little portable at his apartment. He would retype them.

portacabin, var. *Portakabin.

portacaval (pōᵊɹtăkēⁱ·văl), *a. Surg.* Also **portocaval,** and with hyphen. [f. Portal *a.* (+ -o) + Cav(a + -al.] Applied to an anastomosis between the portal vein and one of the venæ cavæ, esp. an artificial one made so that blood in the former bypasses the liver.

1945 *Ann. Surg.* CXXII. 488 Every one of the ten cases of portacaval shunts..went through a successful postoperative convalescence. **1958** A. H. Hunt *Contrib. Study Portal Hypertension* xii. 99 The history of the modern operative treatment of portal hypertension begins with Ecle who suggested in 1877 that his portacaval anastomosis applied to human beings would provide the correct treatment for portal stasis. **1961** *Lancet* 19 Aug. 389/2 Portocaval anastomosis sometimes offers a way out of this quandary. **1968** Passmore & Robson *Compan. Med. Stud.* I. xxx. 47/1 The tributaries of the portal vein anastomose in certain sites with adjacent caval veins which return blood to the heart through either the superior or the inferior vena cava. Little blood passes through these porto-caval anastomoses in health. **1974** Marin & Ostrow in F. P. Brooks *Gastro-intestinal Pathophysiol.* vi. 205 Surgeons have expended much time and effort in attempts to reduce portal hypertension by bypassing the hepatic sinusoidal bed, especially with portocaval shunts.

Portagee, var. *Portuguee.

Portakabin (pōᵊ·ɹtăkæ:bin). Also **portacabin** [f. Porta(ble *a.* + *kabin* altered f. Cabin *sb.*] The proprietary name of a make of portable building. Cf. *Portable *a.* 1 d.

1963 *Trade Marks Jrnl.* 4 Dec. 1742/1 *Portakabin* B 851, 268. Buildings (not being fixed metal structures) and parts thereof included in Class 19. Portasilo Limited, Blue Bridge Lane, York..; Manufacturers. **1975** *Times* 23 Sept. 6/1 The Portakabin which served as his drawing office. **1977** 'R. Rostand' *Killing in Rome* xiii. 69 A large Portakabin, set on concrete blocks at the edge of the apron..the head office of Essex Air Ltd. **1979** *Jrnl. R. Soc. Arts* July 500/1 We created an artists' village—a collection of portacabins used in arctic oil exploration.

portal, *sb.*[1] Add: **1. d.** *Engin.* A rigid structural frame consisting essentially of two uprights connected at the top by a third member; orig. such a frame forming the end of a truss bridge.

1876 *Trans. Amer. Soc. Civil Engineers* V. 178 This bill of materials is calculated: chords, latticing, joint and reinforcing plates..85,912 pounds... Struts and portals.. 6,000 [pounds]. **1882** *Min. Proc. Inst. Civil Engineers* LXIX. 101 The Author [C. B. Bender]..believes it to be conducive to greater stiffness to put the material needed for knees and gussets into two effective end-portals and into the lateral top and bottom bracings. **1908** A. Tolhausen tr. *Böttcher's Cranes* VI. 245 The portal is to cover double railway lines of normal gauge. **1937** *Sunday Express* 14 Feb. 11/1 A series of vast concrete underground bridges, 'portals' they were called technically, were built. There were sixty in all, and each one bridged a railway tunnel under the earth and made a platform on which the building could be built. **1950** *Engineering* 31 Mar. 366/1 A simple portal structure built from broad-flanged beams may be used for spans up to about 40 ft. **1971** *Timber Trades Jrnl.* 21 Aug. 23/3 After the gale had been blowing for a whole week, the temporary bracing finally gave way and two portals were destroyed.

e. (The structural frame forming) the entrance to a tunnel.

1881 *Engineering* 25 Mar. 296/3 The geologist of the St. Gothard Tunnel..has been giving careful attention to the variations in the air currents between the two portals at Goeschenen and Airolo. **1909** J. W. Orrock *Railroad Struct.* iv. 85 The end portals for the tunnel consist of 12″ × 12″ posts..for a distance of 8 feet from the ends, with 12″ × 12″ timbers built over and across the end posts, to form retaining wall on top. **1941** Richardson & Mayo *Pract. Tunnel Driving* xxi. 364 Some kind of parapet over the portal is necessary to catch loose rocks rolling into the cut. **1971** K. G. Messenger *Flora of Rutland* 109/1 At the southern portal, the cutting is wider and deeper and it is obvious that it offered serious drainage problems to the engineers.

f. *Med.* Usu. *portal of entry* or *entrance* (or *entrance portal*), *portal of exit* (or *exit portal*). (*a*) The place where a micro-organism or drug enters or leaves the system. (*b*) The area of the body where a beam of radiation enters or leaves it. = *Port *sb.*[3] 4 b.

1910 *Jrnl. Amer. Med. Assoc.* 24 Sept. 1109/2 We have been led..to view the nasopharynx as the location in the body to be regarded with special suspicion as being the portal of entry of the virus. **1919** *Jrnl. Exper. Med.* XXIX. 380 Other portals of experimental infection were ..disclosed, such as the large nerves, subcutis, subarachnoid space, nasal mucosa, eye, and..the general blood. **1930** J. S. Friedenwald *Path. of Eye* xi. 227 An occasional individual contracting the infection in spite of having taken every conceivable precaution to protect against infection through all other known portals. **1931** *Jrnl. Amer. Med. Assoc.* 23 May 1756/1 If the portal is of limited area, the lateral scatter [of X-rays] is small. **1960**

A. L. SMITH *Carter's Microbiol. & Path.* (ed. 7) xii. 135/1 Pathogenic agents..have rather definite routes of discharge from the body, known as portals of exit, which, to a great extent, depend on the part of the body that is the site of disease. **1963** S. E. WEDBERG *Paramedical Microbiol.* xix. 410 Portal requirements limit the number of opportunities provided for pathogens to cause damage to tissues. **1966** A. A. DE LORIMIER in *Radiol. in World War II* (U.S. Army) iv. 86 Except for the portal of exit of the primary beam, the roentgen tube housing is impregnated with material possessing a protective equivalence of no less than 1·5 mm. of lead. **1973** FLETCHER & TAPLEY in G. H. Fletcher *Textbk. Radiotherapy* (ed. 2) i. 65/1 With a 22 Mev beam and a single homolateral portal, the skin reaction is minimal on the entrance side and is moderate on the opposite side. **1977** *Lancet* 8 Jan. 78/1 Disposable devices are now becoming available for prolonged controlled delivery of appropriate drugs at other portals of entry such as the eye and uterus.

g. *U.S. Theatr.* (See quots. 1947, 1959.)

1947 *Gloss. Technical Theatr. Terms* (Strand Electr. & Engin. Co.) 23 *Portal*, German and American terms for pros[cenium] opening. **1959** W. C. LOUNSBURY *Backstage from A to Z* 94 *Portal*, a gate, door, or entrance, usually downstage on either side of the stage. Portals may be scenery constructed for the play, or they may be a permanent part of the proscenium. In many theatres of newer design, portals are built to accommodate spotlights for sidelighting. **1978** *English Jrnl.* Dec. 44/1 'Gel the lights in the upstage right portal' are heard shouted across the auditorium.

4. portal bracing = sense 1 d above; also, the technique of using such a frame; **portal crane,** a crane mounted on a portal frame, so as to allow the passage of vehicles underneath; **portal frame** = sense 1 d above; **portal strut,** a horizontal member rigidly joining the tops of two uprights, esp. in a portal frame.

1881 *Trans. Amer. Soc. Civil Engineers* X. 164 Strong top lateral and portal bracing would greatly increase the strength and durability of the bridge. **1908** M. S. KETCHUM *Design of Highway Bridges* vii. 112 Portal bracing is placed at the ends of through bridges in the planes of the end-posts to transfer the wind loads from the upper lateral system to the abutments. **1928** W. A. MITCHELL *Civil Engineering* xvi. 479 The sway bracing at the entrance of the span..is called portal bracing. **1974** *Sci. Amer.* Feb. 95/1 The Crystal Palace was..the first [building] in which a light frame was made rigid against wind loads by the technique that came to be known as portal bracing. **1908** A. TOLHAUSEN tr. *Böttcher's Cranes* vi. 245 (*heading*) Hydraulic portal crane. **1958** *Times Rev. Industry* Oct. 20/3 No. 21 Quay at Alexandra Dock has been opened this year after being re-equipped with five 6/3 ton electric portal cranes. **1908** A. TOLHAUSEN tr. *Böttcher's Cranes* vi. 245 The portal or gantry frame.. shall be of built-up plates, and shall carry the platform on its top side. **1949** *Archit. Rev.* CVI. 287 The mullions in front of the portal frames are bright ultramarine. **1971** *Timber Trades Jrnl.* 21 Aug. 23/3 Each portal frame is constructed using 50mm (2in) nominal timber throughout. **1894** W. H. WARREN *Engineering Construction* xix. 294 The perpendicular distance between the end strut of the top lateral system and the intermediate portal strut. **1938** C. T. BISHOP *Structural Design* x. 194 Portal struts are used at the ends of through bridges to transmit top-lateral stresses to the abutments through the end posts acting as girders.

b. portal-to-portal *attrib., spec.* of workers' pay: pertaining to the time spent on the premises of one's place of work, for example in travelling to and from the entrance, changing, or washing, as distinguished from the time spent working. *U.S.*

1943 *Time* 25 Oct. 21/3 He emerged with proposed Contract No. 3: an intricate formula which cagily skirts any mention of increased hourly wages or 'portal-to-portal' pay. **1944** *Birmingham* (Alabama) *News* 27 Mar. 1/5 The Supreme Court ruled Monday that underground iron ore miners are entitled to 'portal-to-portal' pay for the time spent traveling between the mouth of the mine and the place where the ore is actually mined. **1948** *Ann. Reg. 1947* 231 Long-pending retrospective claims for portal-to-portal pay (*i.e.* pay for time spent inside factory gates but not actually on the job) were unequivocally disallowed. **1965** *McGraw-Hill Dict. Mod. Econ.* 385 Proponents of portal-to-portal pay insist that the worker should be paid for the time involved in necessary activities before or after actual on-the-job time on the ground that otherwise the work could not be done.

‖ **portal** (pǫɹtā·l), *sb.*[2] Also **portale, portales.** [ad. Sp. *portal*, pl. *portales*, porch, portico, piazza.] In S. America and the south-western U.S., a veranda, portico, or arcade.

1844 J. GREGG *Commerce of Prairies* I. 144 The only attempt at anything like architectural compactness and precision, consists in..buildings, whose fronts are shaded with a fringe of *portales* or *corredores*. **1892** C. F. LUMMIS *Tramp across Continent* 153 Outside, in the long *portal*, was enough blue, and red, and white corn to feed an army of horses. **1910** [see *MAJOR-DOMO c]. **1927** W. CATHER *Death comes for Archbishop* II. i. 51 Under this *portale* the adobe wall was hung with bridles, saddles [etc.]. **1927** *South Amer.* Nov.–Dec. 181/1 Our hall not being large enough, the *portales*—a large corridor with arches running down one side—was swept and tastefully decorated. **1948** *Southwest Rev.* Summer 245/2 What are now empty mule stalls then used to be the *portales* of a convent. **1973** D. HAMILTON *Intriguers* ix. 59, 'I..crawled to where I could watch the long porch outside the living room.'.. I said, 'Around these parts [*sc.* Arizona], that porch is known as a portal, ma'am. Accent on the last syllable.'

portal, *a.* Add: **2.** *portal system*, also, any other system of blood vessels which runs directly from one system of smaller vessels to another. (Examples.)

1930 *Jrnl. Anat.* LXV. 88 These vessels of the portal system lose their heavy neuroglial wrapping and open out into a network of very fine channels. **1974** M. HILDEBRAND *Analysis Vertebr. Struct.* xii. 262 In several places in the body (digestive organs, kidneys, hypophysis) blood that has passed a capillary bed elsewhere enters a second capillary bed before reaching the heart. The veins between two capillary networks constitute a portal system. **1974** D. & M. WEBSTER *Compar. Vertebr. Morphol.* xvi. 416 This is a renal portal system, filtering blood from the tail through a kidney capillary system before sending it to the [piscine] heart.

Portal (pōᵊ·ɹtăl). Name of Lord *Portal* (1885–1949), Minister of Works and Planning and First Commissioner of Works and Public Buildings 1942–4: **Portal house,** a steel-framed type of prefabricated house proposed in 1944. Also *ellipt.*

1944 *Archit. Rev.* Sept. p. lii/1 It is not clear whether the 250,000 [houses] will all be of the Portal ('Churchill') design which..is far from perfect of its kind. **1945** *Ann. Reg. 1944* 66 The Government had chosen the so-called Portal house of steel... The model Portal house..had been seen by about 30,000 persons. **1945** *Punch* 16 May 425/1 But my aunt was good for me when I was a child, and will possibly offer me accommodation if I cannot secure a Portal when I go home, so I suppose I must oblige her. **1948** A. M. TAYLOR *Lang. World War II* (rev. ed.) 158 *Portal houses*, proposed prefabricated houses for England, so called after Lord Portal, whose ministry was in charge of housing. Punch played up the name in jokes about 'crossing one's portal'.

‖ **portamento.** (Earlier and later examples.)

1771 C. BURNEY *Present State of Mus. France & Italy* 18 The French voice never comes further than from the throat; there is no *voce di petto*, no true *portamento* or direction of the voice, on any of the stages. **1926** *Amer. Speech* I. 500/2 Two Italian words, *glissando* and *portamento* are similar in meaning to the word 'smear', the principal difference being that the last-named is used [in trombone-playing] for a comic effect while the others are used for carrying the voice or sliding the fingers on the violin from one stop to the next. **1931** *Times Lit. Suppl.* 11 June 461/1 The notation of the tunes [in Bartok's *Hungarian Folk Music*] includes a number of signs to signify graces, quarter-tones, *portamento* and other of the folk-singer's idiosyncracies. **1961** C. BUNTING in A. Baines *Mus. Instruments* vi. iii. 142 The cellists were trying to..achieve the eloquence and directness of the human voice... There was felt a need to 'carry' the music (*portamento*) through the intervals without a break. **1971** *Guardian* 26 Aug. 10/1 Imrat..is a master of fluid portamento effects and of creating an illusion of sustained legato—obtained by pulling a sitar-string sideways across the frets. **1975** *New Yorker* 20 Jan. 86/3 She oscillated in portamento between the A on the staff and the C sharp above it, swinging pendulum-true. **1976** *Gramophone* Aug. 337/2 The sheer certainty of the vocal delivery is remarkable, with the singer's famous portamento much in evidence.

‖ **portantina** (pǫɹtantī·nă). [It.] = SEDAN CHAIR.

1758 M. W. MONTAGU *Let.* May (1967) III. 149 He hopes you took nothing ill, tho' you refused the Portantina. **1937** *Tablet* 11 Dec. 800/1 Carried in the *portantina*—the Sedan chair which he now invariably uses in the palace—the Pope passed through the *Salone Sistino* into the Sacred Museum.

portapak (pōᵊ·ɹtăpæk). [f. PORTA(BLE *a.* + PA(C)K *sb.*[1]] A portable system comprising a small television camera and a video tape recorder.

1974 *Cablevision* (Rediffusion) 10 Since October 1973 Jessica Stanley Clarke..has spent most of her time in Knowle West with one of the station's portapaks. *Ibid.* 12 The Youth Department had purchased a Sony portapak. **1974** *New Society* 26 Dec. 805/1, I showed them how to set up and operate the portapak. **1975** *Listener* 9 Jan. 40/1 The miniature and monochrome amateurism of the 'portapak' suitcase studio.

portasystemic, var. *PORTOSYSTEMIC *a.*

‖ **port de bras** (por də brā). *Ballet.* Pl. **ports de bras.** [Fr., lit. 'carriage of the arms'.] The act or manner of moving and poising the arms; also, one of a series of exercises designed to develop the graceful movement and poising of the arms.

1912 *Dancing Times* Aug. 449/2 Arms... The Port de Bras, and exercises thereon. **1920** *Ibid.* Dec. 181 In operatic dancing..certain exercises have been evolved..known as the side and centre practice, the ports de bras and the adage. **1922** BEAUMONT & IDZIKOWSKI *Man. Classical Theatr. Dancing* II. ii. 56 *Port de Bras* deals with the positions and movements of the arms. **1940** C. W. BEAUMONT *Diaghilev Ballet in London* ix. 203 The attention paid to such details..makes the dance a work of art and not a mere combination of steps and *port de bras* rendered by a woman in ballet costume. **1948** *Ballet Ann.* II. 68 The eight *ports de bras*, or exercises to develop the graceful movement and co-ordination of the arms. **1952** [see *ÉPAULEMENT]. **1958** *Times* 22 Aug. 6/3 So gracious and erect was her head held on her shoulders, so beautifully poised her *ports de bras*. **1963** *Times* 9 May 16/7 Her footwork proved exemplary... Her *ports de bras* were a little inelegant, sometimes giving a slightly gauche appearance to her line. **1975** *New Yorker* 18 Aug. 77/3 The grandeur of her carriage makes even a simple rhythmic port de bras, such as the one she does standing in a cluster of Wilis, an exciting dance experience.

‖ **port de voix** (por də vwa). *Mus.* [Fr., lit. 'carrying of the voice'.] A kind of appoggiatura (see quot. 1944).

1740 J. GRASSINEAU *Mus. Dict.* 182 *Port de voix*, a French term, which signifies the faculty and habitude of making shakes, passages, and diminutions, wherein the beauty of a song or piece of music greatly consists. **1876** STAINER & BARRETT *Dict. Mus. Terms* 364/2 *Port de voix* (Fr.), a kind of appogiatura combined with the Pincé. **1944** W. APEL *Harvard Dict. Mus.* 595/1 *Port de voix*,.. one of the most important French *agréments* of the 17th and 18th centuries. Essentially it is an upward-resolved suspension or appoggiatura... Usually..both appoggiatura and resolution are repeated, so that the ornament consists of four notes, the last three forming a *pincé*. **1978** *Early Music* Oct. 518/2 The *port de voix*, being firstly a connecting note and secondly a fluctuation of pitch, usually upwards, but also downwards, can be viewed as the most rudimentary form of decoration. **1979** *Ibid.* Jan. 22/1 When the *Port de voix* was shown as a rising grace note it could often be followed by a *pincé* without the need for a separate sign.

Port du Salut, var. *Port Salut* s.v. *PORT SALUT 2.

porte-. Add: *porte-bouquet* (earlier example); **porte-parole** (-parol) [F. *parole* word], a spokesman, a mouthpiece.

1839 C. SCHREIBER *Jrnl.* (1950) 93 The Ex-Chancellor.. took the nosegay in his hand, extricated it from the porte-bouquet..and instead of giving the flowers into Mr. Pamther's expectant hands, he smelt them himself. **1946** J. FLANNER in *New Yorker* 23 Mar. 74/2 Milch gave the appearance of being Göring's *porte-parole*. **1966** T. REESE *Story of Accusation* xi. 158 He is a lawyer. He is only a *porte-parole*.

ported, *a.*[1] Restrict *rare* to sense in Dict. and add: **2.** Having one or more ports or apertures; freq. in comb. with preceding numeral or adj.

1850 J. BOURNE *Catechism of Steam Engine* 67 Of the slide valve there are many varieties; but the kinds most in use are the D valve..and the three ported valve. **1884** *Engineering* 19 Dec. 566/2 The face on the cylinder is double ported. **1897** C. HURST *Valves* II. i. 98 The exhaust valves may assume the double-ported form. This type permits a considerable reduction of travel compared with the single-ported valve. **1952** H. F. OLSON *Musical Engin.* ix. 319 (*heading*) Phase inverter or ported cabinet. **1975** G. J. KING *Audio Handbk.* vi. 143 Because an aperture is an important part of the enclosure, the terms 'vented-box', 'ported' and 'tunnelled' are sometimes used to describe the system.

po·rted, *a.*[2] [f. PORT *sb.*[7] + -ED[2].] Supplied with port-wine.

1929 J. MASEFIELD *Hawbucks* 27 We're all dined and ported, thanks.

portée (pōᵊ·ɹtēi, ‖ porte). Also **portee.** [a. Fr. *portée* (in various senses), f. *porter* to bear, carry.] **1.** The importance or weight (of a theory, an argument, etc.); the (far-reaching) consequences (of an action or an event).

1894 A. LANG *Cock Lane* 9 It is with this majority, if they choose to find time, and can muster inclination for the task of prolonged and patient experiment, that the ultimate decision as to the *portée* and significance of the facts must rest. **1899** W. JAMES *Let.* 28 Jan. in R. B. Perry *Tht. & Char. W. James* (1935) II. 136 You seem to take my intention in the lecture to have had a wider *portée* than I ever thought of. **1904** H. JAMES *Golden Bowl* II. xxv. 10 She called it [*sc.* her action] names, the invidious, the grotesque attitude, holding it up to her own ridicule, reducing so far as she could the *portée* of what had followed it.

2. In hand-loom weaving, a specified number of threads grouped together to form the warp. Also *attrib.*, as *portee cross*.

1910 L. HOOPER *Hand-Loom Weaving* I. ii. 37 It only remains to take the group of eight threads *below* and *over* peg A in order to finish the first *portee*, as such a collection of threads warped in one round is called. *Ibid.* iv. 57 An excellent way of keeping account of the portees as they are warped is shown at fig. 27. *Ibid.* The fifty threads, taken all together, will pass above the first peg W, below the last one, then round it, and under the first, which completes the portee cross. **1954** H. J. BROWN *Hand-Weaving* v. 76 This second leash is called the portee cross. **1954** M. E. PRITCHARD *Short Dict. Weaving* 67 One portee makes two warp 'ends'. The word..dates back to the days of the Huguenot weavers in England, deriving from the French *portee*, meaning 'carried'. **1958** A. HINDSON *Designer's Drawloom* vi. 55 The portee, or grouped, crosses must not be split when they are spaced in the raddle. **1965** J. TOVEY *Technique of Weaving* II. 30/1 For convenience in keeping count of the number of threads warped, the ends of a strong yarn of a contrasting colour are crossed between groups of portées.

3. *Mil.* A self-propelled vehicle on which an anti-tank gun can be mounted. Also *attrib.* and in phr. ‖ *en portée* (aṅ) [Fr. *en* in].

1942 *Times* 22 Apr. 4/6 Finally, only two guns remained in action... Immediately afterwards one of these was destroyed and the portee of another was set on fire. **1944** *Return to Attack* (Army Board, N.Z.) 22 (*caption*) Anti-tank gun on portee at night. *Ibid.* 28/2 Portee anti-tank guns. **1948** R. FARRAN *Winged Dagger* viii. 141 It was a large command for a subaltern—ten armoured cars of mixed varieties, eight Bofors guns, a two-pounder portee and a tank. **1948** E. H. SMITH *Guns against Tanks* (N.Z. Dept. Internal Affairs) 3 The two-pounders were carried on the decks of specially constructed lorries, termed *portées*, which were fitted with ramps and winches to enable the guns to be quickly hoisted into place. Special fittings..enabled the trail and spade to be clamped firmly to the deck so that the gun, pointing over the rear of the *portée*, was ready for immediate action. *Ibid.*, Great attention should be paid to training the gun crews in fighting the two-pounders from the decks of the *portées*: that is, *en portée*. **1952** *Times* 30 Aug. 5/6 Through it the light vehicles of 7th Armoured Division, portees, carriers, and light tanks, began to pass across our front as they skilfully drew on the enemy. **1958** M. K. JOSEPH *I'll soldier no More* viii. 151 It was eight o'clock before they piled into the portee-waggon.

‖ **Porteño** (porte·nʸo). Also **porteño.** Fem. **Porteña.** [Sp.] A native or inhabitant of Buenos Aires, the capital of Argentina and (until 1884) of the province of Buenos Aires. Also *attrib.* or as *adj.*

1884 R. G. WATSON *Spanish & Portuguese S. Amer.* II. xviii. 274 The great majority of the people of *Buenos Ayres* were not..passive spectators... The colonial society opened its *salons* to the English officers, and the *Porteña* beauties were not displeased to number them amongst their admirers. **1904** C. E. AKERS *Hist. S. Amer.* ii. 37 The provincial representatives, whilst entertaining most vindictive feelings towards Rosas, had no real sympathy with the Porteños. *Ibid.* 39 He was to check *porteño* influence that the majority of the provinces joined hands against Mitre. **1910** *Encycl. Brit.* II. 472/1 The national army..assaulted the *porteños* posted before Buenos Aires. **1959** *Chambers's Encycl.* I. 580/2 The relatively wealthy and cultivated oligarchy of merchants and professional men, the *porteños*, who dominated Buenos Aires (which then meant both the present city and the present province of that name). *Ibid.* 581/2 Rosas was by birth a member of the *porteño* oligarchy. *Ibid.* 582/1 The *porteño* army under Bartolomé Mitre..was defeated and Buenos Aires was incorporated in the Confederation in 1859. **1973** G. M. D. HOWAT *Dict. World Hist.* 1212/1 *Porteño* municipal loyalty was clearly manifested in 1806–7, when..local leaders organized the defeat of the British expeditions. *Ibid.*, *Porteños* demanded free trade and free movement of European capital, technology, immigrants, and ideas. **1978** *Times* 4 Feb. 5/3 Rats..can be spotted worrying refuse bags in the streets... For the *Porteños*..have waited to the last moment to start installing the [refuse] compactors now required in large buildings.

portentious (pǭɹte·nʃəs), *a.* [Corruption of PORTENTOUS *a.*, infl. by PRETENTIOUS *a.*] Pretentious, pompous; portentous. Hence **porte·ntiously** *adv.*

1863 K. STONE *Jrnl.* 16 July in *Brokenburn* (1955) 227 The earth, the air, the sky, all are a dull dead grey. The sun seems to emit neither heat nor light, gleaming with a red glare like a blood-red moon... Some think it portenteous, a sign of great victories or defeats. **1937** in PARTRIDGE *Dict. Slang.* **1949** *Sun* (Baltimore) 21 Jan. 3/1 A portentious feature of this first telecast of a presidential inauguration was the use made of it in schools. **1956** *Ibid.* 20 Feb. (B ed.) 8/3 If you were lucky enough to have seen them, you witnessed a portentious enlargement of mankind's field of knowledge. **1958** *Times* 29 Oct. 3/1 A poem..was hammered home as a portentious statement containing the whole truth about the meaning, or meaninglessness, of life. **1962** *John o'London's* 15 Feb. 163/4 An Italian send-up of the portentious I.Q. flummery. **1975** *Publishers Weekly* 3 Mar. 64/2 Loving Ty whom she sees as somehow portentiously East Coast.

porter, *sb.*[1] Add: **3. porter's chair** (see quot. 1969).

1939 A. CHRISTIE *Ten Little Niggers* viii. 109 On the main terrace, Mr. Justice Wargrave sat huddled in a porter's chair. **1953** J. CARY *Except the Lord* xxxv. 152, I was able to assist her own efforts enough to get her into her usual armchair, one of those great leather chairs with a high domed back, which were called porter's chairs and were valued in farmhouses for their power of keeping out draughts. **1969** J. GLOAG *Short Dict. Furnit.* (rev. ed.) 532 *Porter's chair*, a high-backed armchair with wings raised to an arched hood, upholstered in leather, and placed in the hall of a town or country house, so that the porter or page boy on door duty could sit protected from draughts. Such chairs were introduced in the 16th century, and during the Georgian period were found in the entrance hall to every well-furnished house. **1972** N. MARSH *Tied up in Tinsel* viii. 195 He..sat down in one of two great porter's chairs that flanked the fireplace.

porter, *sb.*[2] Add: **1. d.** In full, *hospital porter*: a person employed by a hospital to convey patients and to carry out other general duties.

1950 G. B. SHAW *Farfetched Fables* III. 109 They offered me a job as hospital porter because I'm physically strong. **1964** D. FRANCIS *Nerve* vi. 64 The nurse came back with a stretcher trolley and two khaki-overalled porters... We waited outside in the hall, and saw them trundle Pip off towards the open lift. **1975** *Oxford Times* 7 Nov. 4/8 An Oxford hospital porter with a grudge against his employers used cheques he had stolen and forged..to obtain over £700 from banks in the city.

porter, *sb.*[3] (Later examples.)

1903 SOMERVILLE & 'ROSS' *All on Irish Shore* 73 Mrs Brennan added another spoonful of brown sugar to the porter that she was mulling in a saucepan on the range. **1919** G. B. SHAW *O'Flaherty V.C.* in *Heartbreak House* 179 And look at your fine new uniform stained already with..the porter youve been drinking. **1922** E. O'NEILL *Anna Christie* (1923) I. 6 Johnny draws the lager and porter and sets the big, foaming schooners before them. **1939** JOYCE *Finnegans Wake* (1964) III. 511 I've a big suggestion it was about the pint of porter. **1973** [see *PORTER-HOUSE 2].

b. *porter bar, -bottle, -pot* (earlier example).

1935 DYLAN THOMAS *Let.* July (1966) 157 One day a week I shall walk the miles to Glendormatie where there is a shop and porter bar. **1922** JOYCE *Ulysses* 42 A porterbottle stood up, stogged to its waist, in the cakey sand dough. **1807** SOUTHEY *Lett. from Eng.* I. viii. 90 A transparency..which represented a loaf of bread saying to a pot of porter, I am coming down; to which the porter-pot made answer, So am I.

porter, *v.*[2] Add: Also, (of any person) to carry from one place to another; = PORTAGE *v.*; **portering** *vbl. sb.* (later examples); also as *ppl. a.*

1927 *Glasgow Herald* 13 Aug. 8 This impressionable passenger thinks that it must be a rule of the railway portering brotherhood to make each footfall 'tell' to its uttermost. **1966** D. VARADAY *Gara-Yaka's Domain* xiii. 147 Tau decided to camp there..and..strengthen Cwgki and save himself the unwelcome bother of portering his riches. **1967** D. COOPER *Psychiatry & Anti-Psychiatry* v. 99 A member of the portering staff who witnessed the incident called a nurse who took her back to her ward. **1971** C. BONINGTON *Annapurna South Face* iv. 46 The Sherpas, who hold a monopoly in high-altitude portering, come from Sola Khumbu just opposite Everest. **1974** *Daily Tel.* 13 Dec. 14 We portered all the rapids. We did this because it would have been foolhardy for two relatively inexperienced canoeists to attempt them. **1977** J. I. M. STEWART *Madonna of Astrolabe* iii. 60 I've just been talking to a couple of young men who have been doing some portering for you. **1978** *Morecambe Guardian* 14 Mar. 29/7 (Advt.), Applicants should be fit and active as the work entails some portering and assisting the physiotherapists with the walking of elderly patients.

porterage, *sb.*[1] Add: **1.** Also, the manpower available for hire as porters.

1925 E. F. NORTON *Fight for Everest: 1924* 122 He went down with Bruce and Irvine that same day to Camp III, intent on investigating afresh with Bruce's aid the question of available porterage.

3. *porterage work* (later example).

1957 M. BANTON *W. Afr. City* ii. 31 Members of this tribe had started coming to Freetown to pick up a living by doing porterage work in the streets.

porterage, *sb.*[2] Delete *rare* and add: Also, the availability of the services of a porter or caretaker.

1975 *Country Life* 22 May (Suppl.) 48/1 Luxury flats.. 24 hour porterage. **1980** *Sunday Times* 20 Jan. 49/1 Purpose-built studio flat..CH, CHW, porterage.

porter-house. (Earlier and later examples.)

c **1758** S. FOOTE *Diversions of Morning* in T. Wilkinson *Wandering Patentee* (1795) IV. 239, I heard a goodish-looking well-dress'd man, that sat in the next box at the porter-house, affirm, that to his knowledge, if you proceeded to exhibit, you and your pupils would be all sent to Bridewell. **1786** *N.Y. Directory* 41 Norris Rich. porter-house, 3, Broad-street. **1939** JOYCE *Finnegans Wake* 405 He was immense, topping swell for he was after having a great time of it..in a porterhouse..if you want to know, Saint Lawzenge of Toole's, the Wheel of Fortune.

b. porter-house steak (earlier and later examples).

1842 C. MATHEWS *Career of Puffer Hopkins* xiii. 90 But I guess I'll take a small porter-house steak, without the bone. **1883** *Harper's Mag.* Aug. 462/2 A porter-house steak learned to expect him on the noon of every day. **1904** *Nation* (N.Y.) 31 Mar. 245 The picture was drawn of the country stepping up to the butchers' block and demanding porterhouse and sirloin steaks in abundance. **1959** [see *CHATEAUBRIAND]. **1979** W. H. CANAWAY *Solid Gold Buddha* xxiii. 148 Two porterhouse steaks.. washed down with three bottles of Rhône wine.

2. *ellipt.* A porter-house steak. Also *attrib.*

1854 *Harper's Mag.* Jan. 269/2 Will you have it rare or well-done? Shall it be a porter-house? **1908** G. H. LORIMER *Jack Spurlock* iv. 63 That [dream] in which the waiter is just taking the covers off a double porter-house, medium, with fresh mushrooms on top. **1911** [see *RARE *a.*[2] b]. **1958** V. P. JOHNS *Servant's Probl.* ii. 17 This is a juicy porterhouse neighborhood. **1973** G. BEARE *Snake on Grave* vii. 38 He would never pass up a pint of porter for a pound of Porterhouse.

po·rterless, *a.* [f. PORTER *sb.*[2] + -LESS.] Lacking a porter or porters.

1885 [see *GARE *sb.*[5]]. **1973** *Daily Tel.* 30 June 12/6 Here is my timetable: Arrive Weymouth Town Station shortly before midnight..; hump baggage up long, dark, porterless platform and hurl it bodily into waiting pantechnicon.

‖ **porteur** (portǒr). *Ballet.* [Fr., lit. 'one who carries'.] (See quot. 1957.)

1936 A. HASKELL in 'C. Brahms' *Footnotes to Ballet* 5 Taglioni (1821) was frail and ethereal, and..she shone so brightly that the male was soon degraded to the rôle of *porteur* from which Nijinsky finally rescued it. **1949** *Ballet Ann.* III. 93 With the advent of the Italian ballerina..ballet became even more a vehicle for the virtuosity of the female dancer backed by rows of pretty girls in the *corps de ballet*. The male dancer was..relegated to the position of *porteur*. **1957** G. B. L. WILSON *Dict. Ballet* 220 *Porteur*, Fr. lit. one who carries, a porter. A male dancer whose sole function is to lift the ballerina in supported leaps and similar movements. **1961** *Ibid.* (rev. ed.) 235 The male dancer in Western Europe was relegated to the rôle of a porteur during the half century preceding the coming of the Diaghileff Ballet and male dancing rôles were taken by the danseuse travestie.

portfolio. Add: **1. b.** The collection of securities held by an investing institution or individual; also, a list of such securities.

1930 *Economist* 4 Jan. 2/1 This fall is partly due to the banks' failure to secure any of last week's Treasury Bills, which is forcing them to replenish their portfolios in the market. *Ibid.* 11 Jan. 83/2 The more notable changes in the portfolio comprise an increase in the number of Chartered shares. **1948** *Ibid.* 3 Jan. 29/2 The banks last year took a hard knock on their gilt-edged portfolios. *Ibid.* 32/1 These examples demonstrate how important it is for the discount houses to keep their portfolios short. **1955** *Times* 3 June 10/3 The investment policy of the Company is under the constant review of the board and the portfolio periodically examined by a special committee of directors. **1967** [see *investment trust* s.v. *INVESTMENT 5 b]. **1967** *Listener* 5 Oct. 423 (Advt.), M & G General Trust Fund is a very big Fund (over £26m.) with a portfolio largely of British 'blue chips', plus a number of overseas stocks. **1969** J. ARGENTI *Managem. Techniques* 199 Just as an investor tries to select a portfolio of shares to give him a good return without too much risk, so the Board of a company tries to do the same thing when choosing a 'portfolio' of subsidiary companies. **1972** *Accountant* 17 Aug. 206/1 A valuation of the entire portfolio, the result to be incorporated in the current year's accounts. **1973** C. WILLIAMS *Man on Leash* (1974) 63 He was..buying more stock all the time. His portfolio was worth a million or a little over. **1978** *N.Y. Times* 30 Mar. D 1/2 Analysts said that institutions stepped up their stock purchases yesterday to dress up their portfolios before the end of the first quarter.

2. Also in phr. *without portfolio*, (of a government minister), not being in charge of a specific department of state. Cf. *Minister without Portfolio* s.v. *MINISTER *sb.* 3 c.

1891 W. FRASER *Disraeli & his Day* 370 At the time when Lord John Russell held office under Lord Aberdeen 'without portfolio', Disraeli made a very happy hit.

3. *portfolio capital, manager, official, policy, security, selection*; **portfolio investment,** the purchase of stocks and shares in a variety of companies.

1964 *Economist* 30 May 1015/1 Flows of portfolio capital. **1955** *Times* 29 July 5/2 It was a very complicated question because United States investment might be direct or it might be portfolio investment. **1965** *Guardian* 8 Jan. 1 (Advt.), Possibilities of portfolio investment in Australia. **1972** *Accountant* 23 Mar. 386/2 Last month Kingside negotiated a $4 million, seven-year, multi-currency loan facility with Lloyds and Bolsa International Bank primarily for the purpose of portfolio investment in the United States and Europe. **1969** *Times* 5 May (Wall St. Suppl.) p. vi/3 'Mutual funds are being bought as equity equivalents..and I'm frankly very worried about it,' said a portfolio manager for one of these funds. **1973** *N.Y. Law Jrnl.* 2 Aug. 3/3 Another bull market similar to the one that occurred following Thanksgiving 1971, says Kenneth Herlihy, portfolio manager of Philadelphia-based Decatur Income Fund. **1940** H. G. WELLS *Babes in Darkling Wood* IV. i. 322 They [*sc.* the Bolsheviks] only half-did the job, they cleaned up the site and then they jerry-built some unattractive sheds... A sort of mushroom growth of nasty little portfolio officials may have sprung up on the clearing. **1969** *Times* 5 May (Wall St. Suppl.) p. iii/3 Credit demanders and institutional investors may not yet be convinced that there are downside risks in the aggressive implementation of economic plans and portfolio policies. **1959** *Listener* 12 Feb. 272/1 American portfolio securities. **1965** H. I. ANSOFF *Corporate Strategy* (1968) ii. 30 While CIT [*sc.* capital investment theory] deals with selection of physical assets for the firm, portfolio selection concerns selecting securities, either for an individual investor or for an investment firm. **1969** J. ARGENTI *Managem. Techniques* 199 Portfolio Selection methods are very advanced mathematically. They are similar to Linear Programming..but include a means of balancing risks and returns.

port-hole. Add: Also **porthole. 1. b.** A small glazed window, often round, in the side of an aircraft or spacecraft.

1956 W. A. HEFLIN *U.S. Air Force Dict.* 395/1 *Porthole*, a naval term sometimes applied to a circular window in an aircraft. **1962** W. SCHIRRA in *Into Orbit* 33 They.. pointed out that they had already stuck on a periscope and a couple of small port-holes, but we all felt strongly that a pilot ought to have a clear, visual reference to his surroundings. **1968** *Listener* 27 June 827/1 Departure by air could involve hazards quite separate from the lurking fears..of being sucked, à la James Bond, out of a porthole. **1970** T. HUGHES *Crow* 13 It was cosy in the rocket, he could not see much But he peered out through the portholes at Creation. **1970** W. SMITH *Gold Mine* xxxii. 79 The Boeing began to roll forward. Manfred twisted his head against the neck rest and peered through the Perspex porthole.

2. c. *Austral.* and *N.Z.* An aperture in the wall of a shearing shed through which each shearer passes the sheep when shorn into his individual counting-out pen.

1882 ARMSTRONG & CAMPBELL *Austral. Sheep Husbandry* xv. 175 Upon the opposite side of the shearing board, 'port-holes', or small doorways, are made (one for each shearer), through which the sheep are turned when shorn. **1933** L. G. D. ACLAND in *Press* (Christchurch,

N.Z.) 30 Sept. 15/7 *Counting out pens.* Each shearer has his own and passes his sheep through a *porthole* into his, so that each man's tally may be counted. **1956** G. BOWEN *Wool Away!* (ed. 2) iii. 43 A lot of time and effort can be wasted in switching off and kicking sheep out the porthole. **1965** [see *CHUTE *sb.* 3 b].

d. *Archæol.* A hole in a slab or two adjacent slabs of stone, large enough to allow the passage of a body into a chambered tomb.

1940 *Proc. Prehist. Soc.* VI. 133 Problems associated with the nature and origin of portholes in megalithic tombs in Europe. **1954** S. PIGGOTT *Neolithic Cultures Brit. Isles* v. 136 The chamber entrance was formed by a 'porthole' made by hollowing the edges of two adjacent slabs to form an oval hole through which it is just possible to gain access to the burial chamber. **1958** G. DANIEL *Megalith Builders W. Europe* ii. 44 Port-holes occur in southern Iberia and in a small number of tombs in France and Britain, as well as in the Gallery Graves of southern Sweden. **1963** *Field Archaeol.* (Ordnance Survey) (ed. 4) 30 Space does not permit a description of all the variations of entrances true and false, forecourts, passages, portholes, different forms of chamber, horn features, revetments, etc.

4. (sense *2 d) *porthole cist, slab, stone.*

1939 V. G. CHILDE *Dawn European Civilization* (ed. 3) ix. 168 Forssander seems inclined to explain Pontic elements in Central Europe by a migration from the Caucasus of the makers of Globular Amphoræ who would also have brought the idea of the porthole cist and the pit-cave tombs. *Ibid.* xii. 206 A porthole stone often enhances the resemblance of a built tomb's doorway to the entry into a natural or artificial cave. The desire to emphasize the similarity has in fact been suggested as an explanation for the porthole stone's origin. **1970** BRAY & TRUMP *Dict. Archaeol.* 185 *Port-hole slab,* a stone slab with a circular hole, often, though not exclusively, forming the entrance to a chamber tomb. Sometimes the hole is square, or the entrance is made from two slabs set side by side with notches cut from their adjoining edges.

Hence **po·rt-holed** *a.*, provided with a port-hole or port-holes.

1938 *Antiquity* XII. 302 Some of these (e.g. Züschen, Fritzlar) have a portholed septal slab. **1940** *Proc. Prehist. Soc.* VI. 155 These figures should give the lie to the frequent assertion..that Britain is peculiarly rich in portholed tombs. **1969** *Daily Tel.* (Colour Suppl.) 11 Apr. 40/2 The port-holed headquarters of the National Maritime Union.

portia[1] (pōᵊ·ɹʃă). [f. Tamil *puarassu* flower-king.] In full, *portia tree.* An Indian name for *Thespesia populnea*, a tropical evergreen tree belonging to the family Malvaceæ and bearing yellow flowers.

1861 H. CLEGHORN *Forests & Gardens S. India* 197 It is usual to plant large branches of the portia..and banyan..trees in such a slovenly manner, that there is little probability of the trees thriving or being ornamental. **1881** J. S. GAMBLE *Man. Indian Timbers* 43 *T*[*hespesia*] *populnea* Corr...the Portia or Tulip Tree... A moderate-sized evergreen tree. **1921** R. S. TROUP *Silvicult. Indian Trees* I. 150 Tulip tree, portia tree... A small or moderate-sized evergreen tree of the coast forests of India and Burma. **1969** T. H. EVERETT *Living Trees of World* 237/1 The most important of this genus [sc. *Thespesia*]..is the Portia tree... Common along the coasts of tropical Asia and the Pacific Islands, this evergreen attains a height of 60 feet.

Portia[2] (pōᵊ·ɹʃă). The name of the heroine of Shakespeare's *Merchant of Venice* used as the type of a female advocate or barrister. Hence **Po·rtian** *a.*, pertaining to or resembling Portia.

1901 *Westm. Gaz.* 22 Jan. 12/2 The Paris Portia's First Success... Mdlle. Chauvan, the young lady barrister, made her first appearance yesterday in the Paris courts. **1909** *Ibid.* 17 Aug. 2/1 China..then took refuge in an interpretation of the letter of the Treaty which was quite Portian in its meticulousness. **1923** *Brewer's Dict. Phr. & Fable* (new ed.) 868/1 *Portia,* a rich heiress and 'lady barrister' in Shakespeare's *Merchant of Venice*... Her name is often used allusively for a female advocate. **1932** E. WEEKLEY *Words & Names* 33 *Portia,* which is good journalese for a lady barrister. **1977** J. MITCHELL *Half-Life* II. 39 Good Christ, they've brought back the people's Portia.

portico. Add: **3.** *attrib.* as *portico area;* **portico thief** = *cat-burglar* (s.v. *CAT *sb.*[1] 18 and 19).

1977 *N.Z. Herald* 5 Jan. 2-16/8 (Advt.), Portico area for outdoor entertainment. **1934** P. SAVAGE *Savage of Scotland Yard* xxiv. 260 Suspicion fell on half a dozen or more cat burglars—or portico thieves as they were officially called. **1938** F. D. SHARPE *Sharpe of Flying Squad* xxv. 254 Cat-burglars have existed since there have been houses to climb, but until comparatively recently they were always known by the more prosaic title of Portico Thieves.

porticus. Add: Pl. **porticus, porticuses. 1.** Delete *Obs.* and add later example.

1850 J. H. PARKER *Gloss. Terms Grecian, Roman, Italian, & Gothic Archit.* (ed. 5) I. 371 In the middle ages the word *porticus* was used for the *entrance porch* of a church, and for the *apses*... The structure over a tomb was termed *porticulus* and *porticus.* But *porticus* also retained its original sense of a long ambulatory... This porticus [by Cuthbert Tunstall at Durham] is a long gallery still in existence.

2. *spec.* in *Anglo-Saxon Archit.*, an aisle or transept on the north or south side of a church, containing a chapel.

1888 C. C. HODGES *Abbey of St. Andrew, Hexham* iii. 16 We may assume the word *porticus* to mean side chapels at the east and west ends of the aisles, as at Brixworth, on transepts, as at Norton, Stow, Sompting, and the church in Dover Castle. **1911** A. H. THOMPSON *Ground Plan Eng. Parish Ch.* ii. 35 A feature of the early cathedral and of St Pancras at Canterbury, was the projection of *porticus*, porches or side chapels, from the nave. These were entered by archways pierced in the centre of the lateral walls. **1936** A. W. CLAPHAM *Romanesque Archit.* i. 8 Early Anglo-Saxon building... The southern group of churches..are distinguished by a simple aisle-less plan with an apsidal chancel and a series of annexes called 'porticus' adjoining or surrounding the nave. **1959** H. M. TAYLOR in P. Clemoes *Anglo-Saxons* 142 From the earliest days the Saxon builders showed a fondness for separate chapels, or *porticus*, opening from the naves or chancels of their churches through comparatively small doorways. **1968** J. W. PARKER *Great Ch. of St. Mary, Stow in Lindsey* 11 What, we may ask, is the reason for the Saxon doorway into the transept? Did it lead to a porticus or chapel? **1971** D. M. WILSON *Anglo-Saxons* (rev. ed.) ii. 49 Various ancillary elements were added to this basic pattern—porches, porticuses, crypts, towers, western galleries and even, in the latest period, transepts. **1975** *Archaeologia Aeliana* III. 123 The church [of St. Peter, Bywell, Northumberland] formerly had *porticus* overlapping the junction of nave and chancel on the north and south. The roof-raggle of the north *porticus* is still visible. **1977** R. MORRIS in Binney & Burman *Change & Decay* 135/2 The digging of a trench around the base of a church to combat rising damp may destroy the remains of an Anglo-Saxon *porticus.*

portière. Add: (Earlier and later examples.) Also *fig.*

1843 *Ainsworth's Mag.* IV. 111 Her ladyship's cozy house refurnished with *portières* to all the doors. **1905** *Spectator* 7 Jan. 11/2 The waters go chasing down the cliffs in deep descending channels hung with curtains and *portières* of moss. **1909** *Chambers's Jrnl.* Oct. 664/2 The Cashmere dyes are fitted only for shawls and portières and tapestries for walls. **1927** F. B. YOUNG *Portrait of Clare* v. 524 A chair went over with a crash, the portière was ripped from its hanging. **1944** S. BELLOW *Dangling Man* 184, I sat down at a desk in a corner, near one of the portieres. **1975** *New Yorker* 11 Aug. 71/1 At the gala it was done against a black backcloth that opened into portières.

Hence **portiè·red** *a.*, furnished with a *portière.*

1923 F. L. PACKARD *Four Stragglers* v. 184 She turned her head a little, facing the portièred window beside the fireplace of the living-room in which they stood.

portiforium (pōᵊɹtifōᵊ·riŭm). Pl. **portiforia.** [a. med.L. *portiforium* portable breviary.] = PORTAS 1, PORTUARY.

1880, 1884 [see PORTUARY]. **1916** H. M. BANNISTER in C. H. Turner *Early Worcester MSS.* p. lx, The traditional title *Portiforium S. Oswaldi*..is clearly wrong, as that Saint's name appears by the first hand in its kalendar; it might justly be called the *Portiforium S. Wulfstani.* **1929** *Jrnl. Theol. Stud.* XXX. 174 In the library of Corpus Christi College..is preserved a book..known until recently as the *Portiforium* (or *Breviarium*) *Oswaldi. Ibid.* 175 The book..is a stout vellum volume... It is in fact almost a Breviary, or *Portiforium.* **1931** A. ESDAILE *Student's Man. Bibliogr.* vi. 200 On small breviaries, intended to be carried about and hence named 'portiforia', the chemise was at the head. **1956** *In Great Tradition* (Benedictines of Stanbrook) ix. 176 She [*sc.* Dame Laurentia McLachlan] had contributed..an article on the so-called *Portiforium Oswaldi*, an eleventh-century volume. **1974** *Bodl. Libr. Rec.* Dec. Dr. Emden's Register provides the information that John Neele, master of Holy Trinity College, Arundel, from 1484 until his death in 1498, bequeathed all his books at Arundel, with the exception of his bible and portiforium, to Magdalen College.

porting (pōᵊ·ɹtiŋ), *vbl. sb.* [f. PORT *sb.*[3] + -ING[1].] The arrangement, size, etc., of the ports in an internal-combustion engine.

1960 C. F. TAYLOR *Internal-Combustion Engine* I. vii. 238 (*caption*) Two-stroke engine porting. **1972** *Proc. Inst. Mech. Engin.* CLXXXVI. 746/2 The only cycle for which the porting requirements have compromised the rotor shape is the compressor-expander.

portion, *sb.* Add: **5. b.** *Judaism.* The section of the Pentateuch or of the Prophets appointed to be read on a particular Sabbath or Festival.

1892 I. ZANGWILL *Childr. Ghetto* II. 87 Reb Shemuel was already poring over a Pentateuch in his Friday night duty of reading the portion twice in Hebrew and once in Chaldaic. **1901** M. GASTER *Bk. of Prayer* I. 47 The Minister then reads the first section of the Parashá (Portion of the Law for the ensuing Sabbath). **1932** L. GOLDING *Magnolia St.* I. ii. 17 She should have kept Sam in..to say the week's portion out of the Pentateuch, to do his soul good. **1978** H. KEMELMAN *Thursday the Rabbi walked Out* x. 57 After the portion is read, you say another blessing..normally the Bar Mitzvah boy chants the portion from the Prophets, too. **1980** *Jewish Chron.* 15 Feb. 22/1 In next week's portion of the law, 'Terumah' (Exodus 25). *Ibid.* 39/4 Saturday, February 16 (Shevat 29). Portions of the Law (Torah)..*Parashat Shekalim*... Portion of Prophets (Haftara) [etc.].

portionable, *a.* Restrict †*Obs. rare* to sense in Dict. and add: **2.** Designating a woman endowed with a marriage portion or dowry.

1875 PALEY & SANDYS *Select Private Orations of Demosthenes* II. 162 'Orphan-sons or heiresses', meaning by the latter 'orphan-daughters' 'portionable-sisters'. **1910** *Blackw. Mag.* Aug. 200/1 Prût had carried off a portionable lady of the island on whom Sidd also had cast his eye.

Port Jackson (pōᵊɹt dʒæ·ksən). The name of the harbour of Sydney, Australia, used *attrib.* and *absol.* in the names of plants and animals native to the region, esp. **Port Jackson fig,** a small tree, *Ficus rubiginosa,* of the family Moraceæ; **Port Jackson (shark)**, a small bull-head shark belonging to the genus *Heterodontus,* esp. *H. portusjacksoni,* which is light brown with black markings; **Port Jackson (willow)** *S. Afr.*, a large shrub, *Acacia cyanophylla,* of the family Leguminosæ, which was introduced to South Africa from Australia and has become naturalized there.

1889 J. H. MAIDEN *Useful Native Plants Austral.* iv. 225 *Ficus rubiginosa*... 'Port Jackson Fig'... This fig, like other figs, exudes a juice when the bark is wounded. **1904** [see *ILLAWARRA]. **1954** *Coast to Coast 1953–54* 133 Today Ellen planted the Port Jackson Fig. **1965** Port Jackson fig [see *ILLAWARRA]. **1880** A. C. L. G. GÜNTHER *Introd. Study of Fishes* 716/3 (Index), Port Jackson Shark. **1932** *Nat. Geogr. Mag.* Sept. 369/2 There were sharks there in abundance—all sorts and sizes—..'gummies', 'angels', and 'Port Jacksons'. **1974** D. & M. WEBSTER *Compar. Vertebr. Morphol.* iv. 63 (*caption*) The jaws of a chondrichthyean, the Port Jackson shark, and of a teleost, the sheepshead. **1902** *Trans. S. Afr. Philos. Soc.* XI. 61 The value of Port Jackson bark on trees still standing..is worth 6s. per acre. **1950** *Cape Times* 12 Dec. 9/7 Great masses of *rooikrantz* and Port Jackson willow grow to within a few feet of the houses. **1959** *Ibid.* 27 Mar. 1/7 A man was shot dead at Durbanville last night after a 400-yard police chase at dusk through thick Port Jackson bush. **1973** PALMER & PITMAN *Trees S. Afr.* II. 731 Some Australian species, such as the aggressive and fast-spreading Port Jackson willow, *Acacia cyanophylla* Lindl., are cultivated in South Africa.

Portland[1]. Add: **Portland stone** (earlier and later examples); also *ellipt.*; also, applied to the colour of Portland stone.

1673 J. RAY *Observations Journey Low-Countries* 120 These figured Bodies were of very different Substances as to hardness..some soft Stone..others as hard as Portland Stone. *a* **1706** EVELYN *Diary* an. 1666 (1955) III. 459 All the ornaments, Columns, freezes, Capitels & projectures of massie Portland stone flew off. **1711** J. THORNHILL *Jrnl.* 21 May in *Proc. Suffolk Inst. Archæol. & Nat. Hist.* (1907) XIII. I. 35 Mr. Martin having cap'd his peers with Keitan stone & made Pedestalls of Portland, ye paving is genly Newcastle stone. **1869** *Bradshaw's Railway Manual* XXI. p. xxiv. (Advt.), Anticorrosion paint. White. Light Stone. Bath do. Cream Colour. Light Portland Stone. Drab or Portland do. **1963** *Times* 17 May 15/7 Viewed with a shaft of sunlight on it, the Portland stone is startlingly white.

portlandite (pōᵊ·ɹtlăndəit). *Min.* [f. PORTLAND[1] (see quot. 1933) + -ITE[1].] A form of calcium hydroxide that occurs naturally as minute hexagonal colourless plates and is a common product of the hydration of Portland cement.

1933 C. E. TILLEY in *Mineral. Mag.* XXIII. 420 The occurrence of $Ca(OH)_2$ as a well-defined species in the contact-zone of Scawt Hill [Co. Antrim] merits a new mineral name, and in view of its occurrence as a common product of hydration of Portland cement, and furthermore as crystals from this source have provided the first reliable physical and optical data on crystalline $Ca(OH)_2$, it is fitting that the mineral name should bear record of these facts. The name Portlandite is accordingly proposed. **1968** I. KOSTOV *Mineral.* 221 Periclase group... The calcium members are rare minerals: portlandite occurs in metasomatic deposits in limestones. **1977** *Sci. Amer.* Aug. 84 In a hardened cement this gel..occupies about 70 percent by volume of the hydrated material... The major part of the other crystalline products consists of calcium hydroxide (portlandite).

Portland Place (pōᵊ·ɹtlănd plēⁱs). The name of a street in London, applied allusively to the B.B.C., whose headquarters are there. Also *attrib.*

1937 D. L. SAYERS *Busman's Honeymoon* xvi. 324 Now, my little minstrels of Portland Place! Strike, you myrtle-crownéd boys! **1939** 'N. BLAKE' *Smiler with Knife* ii. 29 Bursting out..into Somerset folk-songs in perfect harmony and Portland Place accents. **1941** C. KING *Diary* 17 July in *With Malice toward None* (1970) 135 Walker had been spending the morning with the B.B.C... These birds from Portland Place..took his criticisms with a very bad grace. **1967** *Guardian* 16 Oct. 5/3 The most popular disc jockey..might almost have been born in Portland Place. **1974** C. HILL *Behind Screen* xxxi. 266 If it is interventionist to work for a more powerful..Board of Governors, then an interventionist chairman I was at Portland Place. **1977** T. JACKSON in *Rep. Comm. Future of Broadcasting* III. xiv. 227 Without the local stations Portland Place will be like a severed head.

portmanteau, *sb.* Add: **4. a.** *portmanteau manufacturer, -trunk* (later example).

1819 M. EDGEWORTH *Let.* 2 June (1971) 210 The boxes and small portmanteau trunk..have not arrived.

1885 *List of Subscribers, Classified* (United Telephone Co.) (ed. 6) 213 (*heading*) Trunk and Portmanteau Manufacturers.

b. (Further examples.)

1896 [see *BRUNCH]. **1972** *Amer. Speech 1968* XLIII. 201 He was particularly concerned with..*portmanteau forms* of the sort illustrated by *motel* for 'motor hotel'. **1973** *Sci. Amer.* Dec. 116/2 A more interesting blend, called a portmanteau word by Lewis Carroll, combines two words with similar meanings into one: 'instantaneous' and 'momentary' into 'momentaneous', 'splinters' and 'blisters' into 'splisters', 'shifting' and 'switching' into 'swifting' and 'edited' and 'annotated' into 'editated'. **1978** *Dædalus* Fall 93 But such names are more often nothing more than the portmanteau terms describing a group of contemporaries who come together for a few years and then go their own ways.

c. Applied *attrib.* to a general description or category, or to a word or expression which has a general or generalized meaning.

1909 *Daily Chron.* 18 Feb. 4/7 You may notice the same 'portmanteau' descriptions of persons wanted by the police. They would fit a dozen men in every hundred yards of London. **1949** [see *BAROQUE *a.* (*sb.*)]. **1955** *Times* 12 May 7/3 The phrase *Britanniarum omnium*, which had appeared on the coinage since 1902, was discontinued from the beginning of 1954. The words were a portmanteau expression designed as a free rendering in Latin of 'The British Dominions beyond the seas'. **1957** *Listener* 18 July 86/2 The Act of 1897..is one of those portmanteau measures under which a person can be charged with any action. **1960** [see *CASSEROLE 1]. **1960** *Times* 14 Oct. 15/6 Such portmanteau terms as 'sprays', 'seed dressings', and 'insecticides' have been used uncritically. **1962** *Listener* 19 Apr. 674/1 The concept, or rather the concepts, of 'culture'. This portmanteau word has been indispensable to intellectuals for 100 years at least.

d. portmanteau morph *Linguistics*, a morph which represents two morphemes simultaneously; also ellipt. *portmanteau*.

1947 [see *BIMORPHEMIC *a.*]. **1950** *Language* XXVI. 84 If we find it more convenient to regard these forms as single morphs, we must at least take them to be portmanteaus, and not completely arbitrary ones. **1953** C. E. BAZELL *Linguistic Form* 54 Furthermore this terminology renders superfluous the family of subtractive morphs, zero-morphs, and portmanteau-morphs. **1972** HARTMANN & STORK *Dict. Lang. & Linguistics* 180/1 *Portmanteau morph*, a single morph which stands for two morphemes. The best known example is French *au* |o| 'to the' which represents *à* + *le*.

portmanteau (poɹtmæ·nto), *v.* [f. PORTMANTEAU *sb.* 4 b.] *trans.* To combine. Also *intr.* for *pass.*

1902 *Westm. Gaz.* 28 May 2/2 We are amused at the attempt to portmanteau into one (as Lewis Carroll would say) the Education Bill and the Bread Tax. **1906** *Daily Chron.* 22 Mar. 6/7 Hotten's Slang Dictionary..has only two [words] for threepence—'thrums' and 'thrups'—neither of which will portmanteau with 'telegram' comfortably. **1967** G. F. FIENNES *I tried to run a Railway* v. 58 Chingford, Enfield, Hertford and Bishops Stortford (portmanteaud as the 'Chenford').

portmanto·logism. [f. PORTMANTEAU *sb.* 4 b + -OLOG(Y + -ISM.] = PORTMANTEAU *sb.* 4 b. Hence **portmanto·logist**, one who utters or studies portmanteau words.

1887 *Spectator* 9 Apr. 492/2 An allusion to the 'Torrible Zone' which is one of the most beautiful of portmantologisms. **1920** T. NICKLIN *Sounds of Stand. Eng.* 85 Sometimes we may surmise that these constructions are what may be called 'portmantologisms'. **1934** *Times* 16 Mar. 15/5, I wonder how many 'portmantologists' realize that the Russian language as spoken in the U.S.S.R. is resorting more and more to the invention of portmantologisms.

portmote. Add: Also **portmoot.**

1951 D. M. STENTON *Eng. Society Early Middle Ages* 177 The ancient borough court, the portmoot, was presided over by the reeve.

‖ **porto** (pōə·ɹto). [a. Pg. *pôrto* port wine.] **a.** = PORT *sb.*[7] **b.** In full *porto français*: an aperitif made from port; also *attrib.*

1847 DISRAELI *Tancred* I. i. 9 A capon in every platter, with some fountains of ale and good Porto. **1857** DICKENS *Dorrit* II. xxviii. 564 Bring Port wine! I'll drink nothing but Porto-Porto. **1926** R. FIRBANK *Concerning Eccentricities Cardinal Pirelli* vi. 65 All this Porto and stuff to keep awake make a woman liverish. **1935** SCHOONMAKER & MARVEL *Compl. Wine Bk.* iii. 88 The dark red Priorato of Catalonia, which was formerly sold as 'Tarragona Port', ..is annually shipped to France, where it forms the base of several well-known commercial *apéritifs*, and is liberally used in the manufacture of '*Porto français*'. **1951** R. POSTGATE *Plain Man's Guide to Wine* iii. 61 If he is with a Frenchman he can offer him 'un porto' which is like a cold and thin port, or 'un malaga français'... But he should not drink them himself. **1961** N. FROUD et al. tr. *Montagné's Larousse Gastronomique* 761/1 *Port, Porto,* Portuguese wine... Sweet and soft, and in France it is sometimes drunk as an aperitif. It is used in preparing sauces. **1970** N. FREELING *Kitchen Bk.* ii. 16 Porto, the invariable bourgeois apéritif. **1972** A. L. SIMON *Gazetteer of Wines* 194/2 Port, Porto or Vinho do Porto can only be produced in this area [*sc.* Douro]. **1974** S. COULTER *Château* I. xxii. 172 It was foie gras with porto jelly.

portocaval, var. *PORTACAVAL *a.*

‖ **portolano.** Add: Also **portolan** (pōə·ɹtolăn), which is now the usual form. Also *attrib.* and *Comb.*

1897 F. A. BATHER tr. *Nordenskiöld's Periplus* 18 The portolan-manufacturer or draughtsman used by preference gaudy and bright colours. **1898** *Geogr. Jrnl.* XII. 374 We then have..a Series of World-maps and Mediterranean portolans. **1935** *Ibid.* LXXXV. 105, 430 portolans dating from the fourteenth to the sixteenth centuries. **1941** *Antiquity* XV. 186 Portolan charts were intended for the use of mariners. **1972** *Daily Tel.* 12 Dec. 14/6 Dolphin Book Company, of Oxford, paid £7,000 for a complete Mediterranean portolan atlas signed Joannes Oliva and dated Messina 1582. **1978** *Nature* 1 June 409/1 For many the intriguing question remains: whether the keenly observant craftsmen-sailors of Northern Europe did not have a recorded lore of their own—effective but, like the portolan charts, tardily acknowledged by the churchmen?

Porto Rican: see *PUERTO RICAN *sb.* and *a.*

portosystemic (pōə:ɹtosiste·mik, -ī·mik), *a.* *Surg.* Also **porta-**, and with hyphen. [f. as PORTO-PYÆMIC *a.* + SYSTEMIC *a.*] Applied to an anastomosis between the portal vein and a systemic vein.

1962 *Lancet* 22 Dec. 1289/2 These studies have shown abnormalities of serum-I.L.A..in patients with portal hypertension and its associated portosystemic bypass. **1974** PASSMORE & ROBSON *Compan. Med. Stud.* III. xx. 21/2 Another site for porta-systemic anastomosis is in the territory of the junction of the inferior mesenteric and the inferior rectal veins. **1976** *Lancet* 11 Dec. 1268/2 An exploration was attempted..but was quickly abandoned because of massive blood-loss due to extensive portosystemic shunts and bleeding tendency.

portrait, *sb.* Add: **3. c.** *Typogr.* A format in which the height of an illustration or page is greater than the width; cf. UPRIGHT *a.* 5 c. Often used as quasi-*adj.* or quasi-*adv.*

1932 [see *LANDSCAPE *sb.* 1 c]. **1956** H. WILLIAMSON *Methods Bk. Design* iii. 16 The book is in fact taller than it is wide, and by analogy with the painter's method these proportions are sometimes called portrait. **1975** J. BUTCHER *Copy-Editing* 304 *Portrait*, (1) the shape of a book or illustration is referred to as 'portrait' when its height is greater than its width; (2) if a table is 'set portrait' it is set upright on the page and not turned to read up the page.

4. *portrait-group* (examples); **portrait-painter** (earlier and later examples); **portrait-painting** (earlier example; also *fig.*); hence as *ppl. a.*

1911 *Encycl. Brit.* XXII. 129/1 The magnificent portrait groups at Haarlem by Hals..must also be mentioned. **1937** *Burlington Mag.* Jan. 47/2 Concerning Cotes's portrait-group (represented by a colour plate), one may suspend judgment. **1970** *Oxf. Compan. Art* 452/1 He [*sc.* Gainsborough] also painted some small portrait groups in landscape settings. **1758** *N.Y. Gaz.* 21 Aug. 3/3 Thomas Milworth, Portrait Painter, Has removed to the House of Mr. Samuel Deall in Broad-street. **1780** J. WEDGWOOD *Let.* 21 Oct. (1965) 260 Methinks I would not be a portrait painter upon any condition whatever. **1959** *Observer* 29 Mar. 7/2 You have no idea what portrait painters suffer from the vanity of their sitters. **1765** T. H. CROKER et al. *Compl. Dict. Arts & Sci.* II. s.v. *Portrait*, We use the term portrait-painting, in contradistinction to history painting. **1821** H. C. ROBINSON *Diary* 2 Dec. (1967) 71, I have finished *Waverley*... Its merit lies in portrait and scene painting. **1842** DICKENS *Let.* 2 Apr. (1974) III. 179 My portrait-painting friend told me.

portrait, *v.* **1.** (Later example.)

1908 *Daily Chron.* 3 Apr. 4/4 We are not puffed and paragraphed and portraited in the papers.

portraitist. Add: (Later examples.) Also *fig.*

1976 *Amer. N. & Q.* XIV. 151/2 JEB [*sc.* James E. Buttersworth] was becoming an authentic ship portraitist, in response to demands from the owners of the shipping lines. **1977** V. S. PRITCHETT *Gentle Barbarian* viii. 119 Turgenev..is a portraitist who gives the surface of people.

‖ **portrait parlé** (portrę pārle). Pl. **portraits parlés.** [Fr., = spoken portrait.] A detailed description of a person's physical characteristics in mainly anthropometric terms, esp. one of a type used in the identification of criminals and developed by Alphonse Bertillon (see *BERTILLONAGE). Also *transf.*

1913 A. B. REEVE *Poisoned Pen* v. 141 Neither the 'portrait parlé' nor the ordinary photography nor any other system will suffice alone against the arch-criminal. **1940** N. MARSH *Surfeit of Lampreys* (1941) xiv. 205 Is this the B-b-Bertillion [*sic*] system?.. P-portrait parlé? **1956** H. T. F. RHODES *Alphonse Bertillon* xiv. 105 The *portrait parlé* is a derivative of the anthropometric system. **1963** T. TULLETT *Inside Interpol* iii. 35 One system is unique in police work and based on the Portrait Parle method of facial identification and the famous Bertillon system of measurement of certain key parts of the human frame. **1972** R. COBB *Reactions to French Revolution* iii. 67 *Portraits parlés* tell us perhaps more about the police..than about those to whom these visible passports were so painstakingly fixed. **1973** *Daily Tel.* 20 Dec. 7/3 He left an enormous volume of papers. Martin Gilbert has made of them not so much a biography as a *portrait parlé*. **1974** *Encycl. Brit. Macropædia* XIV. 671/2 Long before the birth of Christ, Egyptians used detailed word descriptions of individuals, a concept known today as 'portrait parle'.

portrayist (poɹtrēi·ist). *rare.* [f. PORTRAY *v.* + -IST.] = PORTRAYER.

1924 *Glasgow Herald* 25 Sept. 4 His considerable skill as portrayist and his narrative genius.

Port salut. Restrict † *Obs. rare* to sense in Dict. and add: **2. Port Salut** (por salü). [f. the name of a Trappist monastery, *Port du Salut* (also used), in Mayenne, N.W. France, where it was first produced.] A kind of soft pressed cheese.

1881 J. P. SHELDON *Dairy Farming* xxxv. 512 Cooked, heated, and pressed cheese... Gruyères français, Port du Salut, Rangiport. **1896** LONG & BENSON *Cheese* ii. 15 Camembert, Brie, Bondon, Neufchâtel, and Port du Salut, all..hail from France. **1902** *Encycl. Brit.* XXVII. 355/2 In France the pressed varieties of cheese with hard rinds include Gruyère..and Port Salut. **1935** [see *BEL PAESE]. **1942** E. PAUL *Narrow St.* iii. 22 Cheese was forthcoming (a Port Salut that increased my respect for the fat cook who did the daily marketing). **1951** [see *MAKE *v.*[1] 91 c (*b*)]. **1960** *Sunday Times* 17 Jan. 9/1 A full moon, the colour of Port Salut. **1966** P. V. PRICE *France* 283 There are..two sorts of cheese involved: *Port du Salut* is that made by the Trappist monks at Entrammes, near Laval... Other Trappists, however, and other cheese makers..are able to make and market a cheese under the name of *Port Salut*, which, unlike Port du Salut, is not a trademark. **1972** *Sat. Rev.* (U.S.) 24 June 77/3 French Trappist monks in northern Touraine have been making Port Salut cheese for 150 years.

port-si·der. *N. Amer. colloq.* [f. PORT *sb.*[6] (*a.*) + SIDER[2].] A left-handed person.

1926 *Amer. Speech* I. 369/2 They [*sc.* baseball players] are 'south-paws' or 'port-siders' or 'side-wheelers' when they are left-handed. **1945** *Record* (Philadelphia) 28 Oct. 8/2 We despair that portsiders will ever get their rights. **1946** *Sun* (Baltimore) 13 June 20/2 The firm had been printing check-books for Baltimore portsiders for nearly ten years. **1975** *Daily Colonist* (Victoria, B.C.) 30 July 2/1 The left-handers of my acquaintance. They're called southpaws, silly-siders and port-siders.

‖ **Portugaise** (portügę̄z). [Fr., = Portuguese.] **1.** *Cookery.* Chiefly in phr. *à la Portugaise*, designating food prepared in a Portuguese style. Also *attrib.* or as *adj.*

1845 E. ACTON *Mod. Cookery* xx. 548 *Arocē Docē* (*or Sweet Rice. A la Portugaise*)... This is quite the best sweet preparation of rice that we have ever eaten, and it is a very favourite dish in Portugal, whence the receipt was derived. **1889** A. B. MARSHALL *Cookery Bk.* v. 54 *Clear Soup à la Portugaise.* Prepare some French plums and leeks as below, mix them and add to them sufficient clear stock, boil up all together, and serve the soup very hot. **1907** G. A. ESCOFFIER *Guide Mod. Cookery* xvi. 489 *Poularde à la Portugaise.* Stuff the pullet with three-quarters lb. of rice, combined with five oz. of peeled and *concassed* tomatoes, cooked in butter. *Poêle* the pullet. Dish it; coat it with a Portugaise sauce..and surround it with a garnish of..tomatoes, stuffed with rice 'à la Portugaise'. **1929** G. VOISIN *French Cooking for All* iv. 53 *Sole à la Portugaise*... Butter a baking-dish, lay the fish in it, scatter over it a little chopped onion and cover with sliced tomatoes. **1931** A. DE CROZE *What to eat & drink in France* ii. 10 In French cookery 'Portugaise' means that chopped meat or forcemeat is used as a bed or cover with eggs or vegetables, shell-fish, or fish. **1953** J. CONIL *Haute Cuisine* x. 171 (*heading*) Tomato sauce or Portugaise. **1964** E. BOWEN *Little Girls* I. iv. 60 An eight-egg omelette, *portugaise*, had been contrived in the kitchen. **1970** SIMON & HOWE *Dict. Gastron.* 307/2 *Portugaise, à la,* culinary French name for a dish featuring tomatoes above all else, but usually also garlic and onions.

2. = **Portuguese oyster.*

1942 E. PAUL *Narrow St.* xxv. 221 The price tags on the turquoise green Portugaises and the flat grey Marennes of incomparable flavour would have caused a traffic jam a few years before. **1962** L. DEIGHTON *Ipcress File* xxxi. 200 Scallops and flat oysters and portugaise that looked like pieces of rock. **1966** P. V. PRICE *France: Food & Wine Guide* 40 There is the..*Portugaise*..with its bumpy, longish and deep shell. **1970** *Sunday Times* 18 Oct. 21/2 The big, fat *portugais* [sic] in their craggy misshapen armour. **1978** *Observer* (Colour Suppl.) 23 July 34/4 You can eat Pacific oysters, small as the Portugais [*sic*] in Paris.

Portugal. Add: **6. b. Portugal laurel,** substitute for def.: an evergreen shrub, *Prunus lusitanica*, native to Spain and Portugal; (later examples); **Portugal onion,** a variety of onion, esp. young seedlings of this variety used as spring onions; **Portugal oyster** = **Portuguese oyster*; **Portugal peach, quince** (earlier examples).

1914 W. J. BEAN *Trees & Shrubs Hardy in Brit. Isles* II. 241 In all but the coldest parts of Great Britain the Portugal laurel is one of the handsomest and most effective of evergreens. **1972** F. PERRY *Flowers of World* 262/1 The Portugal Laurel..makes a tree of 3–6 m (10–20 ft) with long-elliptic evergreen leaves and large racemes of dull white, heavily scented flowers. **1647** W. LILLY *Christian Astrol.* II. liv. 398, I..heavily complained to the woman for seven Portugall Onyons which I lost; she not knowing what they were, made pottage with them, as she said. **1783** J. WOODFORDE *Diary* 21 Nov. (1926) II. 107 Mr. Priest..made me this morning a Present of a fine String of the real Portugal Onions 20 in No. **1833** *Chambers's Edin. Jrnl.* 20 Apr. 96/2 A root of rye, size of a Portugal onion. **1845** E. ACTON *Mod. Cookery* iii. 97 The meat may then be stewed..with a Portugal onion. **1885** W. MILLER tr. *Vilmorin-Andrieux's Veget. Garden* 363 White Portugal

Onion... Bulb of a dull-white colour. **1890** J. R. PHILPOTS *Oysters* I. xxiv. 570 The Portugal oyster has appeared for the last two or three years in our markets. **1664** EVELYN *Kalendarium Hortense* in *Sylva* 72 August... Fruits in Prime... Portugal Peach, Crown Peach, Bourdeaux Peach. **1629** J. PARKINSON *Parad.* IV. xx. 589 The Portingall Apple Quince is a great yellow Quince... The Portingall Peare Quince is not fit to be eaten rawe like the former.

Portuguee (pōᵊɹtiŭgī·). *U.S.* Also **Portagee, Portugee.** Repr. a spurious 'singular' form of PORTUGUESE *a.* and *sb.*, this being regarded as a plural.

1830 J. F. COOPER *Water Witch* II. vii. 197 It being altogether unreasonable to suppose that a Portuguee should do what an Englishman had not yet thought of doing. **1860** *Atlantic Monthly* Dec. 735/1 Somehaow I caän't help mistrustin' them Portagee-lookin' fellahs. **1878** [in Dict. s.v. PORTUGUESE *sb.* 1]. **1880** *Harper's Mag.* Sept. 505/1 At one place was a 'Portugee' of the Western Islands. **1915** C. C. MARTINDALE *In God's Army* I. 181 China to a Portuguee was a forbidden land. **1975** J. GORES *Hammett* iii. 28 'Keep your eye on the Portagee,' said Hammett. But Dancing Frankie..put the Portuguese boy on the canvas for a six count with a roundhouse right that wasn't fooling.

Portuguese, *a.* and *sb.* Add: **A.** *adj.* **a.** (Later examples.) Also *spec.*, of or pertaining to Sephardic Jews whose ancestors came from Portugal.

1851 [see SEPHARDI]. **1866** GEO. ELIOT *Let.* 10 Aug. (1956) IV. 298 We looked about for the very Portuguese Synagogue where Spinoza was nearly assassinated... There are..three Portuguese Synagogues now [in Amsterdam]. **1902**, etc. [see *SPANISH *a.* 1 d]. **1937, 1960** [see *MANUELINE *a.*].

b. Portuguese oyster, a type of oyster, *Crassostrea angulata*, which has a bumpy, greenish shell and is native to Portugal although it is cultivated elsewhere, esp. in France; also *ellipt.*; **Portuguese parliament** *Naut. slang*, a discussion in which many speak simultaneously; hubbub.

1890 J. R. PHILPOTS *Oysters* I. xxv. 590 The mollusc known under the name of the Portuguese oyster does not belong to the same genus as our indigenous oyster. **1928** RUSSELL & YONGE *Seas* xiv. 301 Of recent years it [*sc.* the French oyster] has been almost completely ousted in the more southern beds by the Portuguese oyster. **1960** C. M. YONGE *Oysters* ix. 166 Some Portuguese oysters are ready for sale when only two years old. **1964** E. CLARK *Oysters of Locmariaquer* i. 4 The Portuguese oyster..has been gradually moving farther north. **1976** N. ROBERTS *Face of France* xiii. 139 The oysters of Arcachon..turn up as starters to the most modest meal, whether..the delicately flavoured 'flats' or the plumper but more commonplace Portuguese. **1897** 'F. B. WILLIAMS' *On Many Seas* 388 Of all the jabbering and wrangling and shouting to one another that I ever heard, that was the worst. It was like what sailors call a Portuguese Parliament. **1898** H. E. A. COATE *Realities of Sea Life* 133 They [*sc.* wild monkeys] could only be compared with the 'members of a Portuguese Parliament', where, according to Jack's idea, they are 'all talkers and no listeners'. **1962** GRANVILLE *Dict. Sailors' Slang* 90/2 *Portuguese parliament*, rowdy discussion in which everybody talks and nobody listens.

B. *sb.* **2.** (Earlier and later examples.)

1615 T. ROE *Jrnl.* 21 July in *Embassy to Court of Gt. Mogul* (1899) I. 19 The Enterpreters were certaine Magadoxians, that spake Arabique and broken Portuguese. **1882** W. W. SKEAT *Etym. Dict. Eng. Lang.* p. xviii, The other Romance languages..are Italian, Spanish, Portuguese, Provençal, Romansch, and Wallachian. **1933** L. BLOOMFIELD *Language* xxvi. 474 The descendants of runaway slaves who settled on the island of San Thomé off the coast of West Africa, spoke a creolized Portuguese. **1950** J. H. STEWARD *Handbk. S. Amer. Indians* VI. 168 It has been estimated that 15 percent of the vocabulary of Brazilian Portuguese is of *Tupí* origin. **1974** *Encycl. Brit. Macropædia* XV. 1031/2 Portuguese owes its importance largely to its position as the language of Brazil. **1980** G. GREENE *Dr. Fischer* viii. 47 Two letters in Portuguese were sent me to translate, although I knew no Portuguese.

portulaca. Add: (Later examples.) Also (erron.) **portulacca.**

1927 M. M. BENNETT *Christison* xi. 116 They ate portulacca to keep off scurvy. **1939** R. GODDEN *Black Narcissus* xix. 173 Lupins, delphiniums..and the portulaca she had grown to love in the plains. **1942** *E. Afr. Ann. 1941–2* 44/1 The indigenous portulaca found all round Nairobi with its masses of yellow flowers is very fascinating. **1953** *Arena* (Wellington, N.Z.) xxxv. 4 'And your lovely portulacca,' Hester said gently, 'I had forgotten you always grew it.' **1962** [see *CLEOME]. **1974** J. BERRISFORD *Window Box & Container Gardening* xix. 143 The annual portulacas..are suitable for seasonal use. **1978** *Detroit Free Press* 16 Apr. (Gardening Guide) 10/1 If you want to enjoy your garden in the evening, don't plant flowers such as day lilies, morning glories and portulacca that are closed at night.

portulace, -lack. Delete † *Obs.* and add later example of spelling *portulac*.

1911 C. E. W. BEAN *'Dreadnought' of Darling* xxvii. 234 They helped their provisions by eating a good deal of a shrub known as portulac.

port-wine. Add: **a.** (Later examples.)

1930 H. CRADDOCK *Savoy Cocktail Bk.* 192 Port Wine Sangaree..Port Wine..sugar..ice..nutmeg. **1968** *Daily Tel.* (Colour Suppl.) 13 Dec. 41/4 Portwine is being poured over chunks of ice.

b. *port-wine negus* (example); **port-wine magnolia** *Austral.*, an evergreen shrub, *Michelia figo* of the family Magnoliaceæ, native to temperate or tropical Asia and bearing scented reddish-brown or purple flowers.

1858 TROLLOPE *Three Clerks* III. ii. 38 Mrs. Davis was mixing port-wine negus as fast as her hands could make it. **1943** K. TENNANT *Ride on Stranger* viii. 86 At Lindfield there were port-wine magnolias. **1977** *Austral. House & Garden* Jan. 17/1 Check these and spray them too if necessary: Gardenia,..Port Wine Magnolia (Michelia), Crepe Myrtle, Flowering Quince.

port-winy *a.* (later examples); hence **port-wi·nily** *adv.*; **port-wi·ner,** an habitual drinker of port.

1908 *Daily Chron.* 20 Oct. 5/5 A magnificently Georgian figure in his court-robes, with a red wig and generally 'port-winey' make-up. **1909** R. W. SERVICE *Ballads of Cheechako* (1910) 54, I smoked and sat as I marvelled at the sky's port-winey glow. **1920** G. E. BUCKLE *Life Disraeli* V. ii. 67 Beauchamp..warned Disraeli that the High Church party other than 'the old port-winers' were holding aloof from the political contest. **1921** A. HUXLEY *Crome Yellow* ii. 8 There was the dining-room, solidly, port-winily English, with its great mahogany table. **1923** [see *CIGARY *a.*]. **1938** S. BECKETT *Murphy* 266 'A proper port-winer,' said the Coroner. 'The afterglow is unmistakable.'

pos. (Examples.)

1711 *Spectator* 4 Aug. 2/1 It is perhaps..speaking no more than we needs must, which has so miserably curtailed some of our Words, that..they sometimes lose all but their first Syllables, as in *Mob. reb. pos.* incog. and the like. **1716** [see Poz]. **1922** JOYCE *Ulysses* 418 Got a pectoral trauma, eh, Dix? Pos fact. **1930** [see *electron gun* (*ELECTRON² 2 b)]. **1969** 'R. CRAWFORD' *Cockleburr* II. vi. 126 'Are you sure you weren't spotted?' 'Pos.' **1977** *Hot Car* Oct. 99/4 (Advt.), Smiths electronic tacho (pos earth). **1979** *SLR Camera* Mar. 34/1 Having said that, there are of course the neg/pos experts who will tell you how to produce a 20 × 16 print from a quarter inch portion of a 35mm negative.

pos², var. *POSS *a.*

posada. Add: **1.** (Later examples.)

1931 P. GUEDALLA *Duke* IV. vii. 236 An obliging innkeeper rode twenty miles to tell him that Clausel was safely lodged in his *posada*. **1950** G. BRENAN *Face of Spain* iv. 95, I had not reached the posada till after midnight. **1955** *Times* 4 July 12/7 Dying in poverty in a lowly *posada* in Valladolid. **1965** *New Statesman* 7 May 734/1, I suppose it must have been Balzac who, when Cervantes' posadas and Fielding's coaching-inns were beginning to pall, discovered the potentialities of the boarding-house. **1966** *Listener* 4 Aug. 164/2, I was recently taken by my host in Mexico..to the ancient site of Teotihuacan,..and afterwards to lunch at a *posada* in the neighbouring village. **1974** C. LARSON *Matthew's Hand* xxvii. 161 He owns a *posada*—an inn.

2. In Mexico, each of a series of visits traditionally paid to different friends during the days before Christmas, representing Mary and Joseph's search for a lodging in Bethlehem.

1930 R. REDFIELD *Tepoztlan* vi. 128 There is time to rest now, and enjoy the Christmas *fiestas*... In many houses..the nine *posadas* are celebrated as they are celebrated all over Mexico... The matrons of the neighborhood have arranged in whose house will take place each of the nine fiestas. **1932** CHASE & TYLER *Mexico* x. 202 December 16. Christmas fiesta. Nine days. Posadas. Processions, rodeos, singing. **1959** *Listener* 24 Dec. 1105/1 These and other decorations will take a central place in the *posadas* which go on night after night for the twelve days before Christmas. The *posadas* are supposed to represent the vain search of Mary and Joseph to find a lodging in Bethlehem. **1978** *Tucson Mag.* Dec. 105/1 You may witness a real 'Las Posadas' celebration December 12 beginning at 7:30 p.m. The candle-lighted procession of Carrillo School children will begin at the school (400 South Main) and continue through one of the city's oldest neighborhoods, in emulation of the journey of Mary and Joseph seeking shelter. The 'inn' or posada for this evening's festivities will be the school itself, where refreshments will be served and a pinata will be broken.

posadaship (posā·dəʃip). [f. POSADA + -SHIP.] The position of the keeper of a posada.

1923 *Blackw. Mag.* Nov. 700/2 The details of how from posadaship she had fallen to this minute eating-house were slurred over.

‖ **posadero** (posadē·ro). [Sp.] In Spanish-speaking countries: an innkeeper.

1904 CONRAD *Nostromo* I. viii. 116 The posadero in Rincon swore that on calm nights..he could catch the sound in his doorway. **1912** W. G. LAWRENCE in T. E. Lawrence *Home Lett.* (1954) 423 After lunch..Juan the Posadero came out to talk with us.

pose, *sb.*⁵ Add: **4.** *N. Amer.* A resting place on a portage; the distance between two such rests. *Obs.* except *Hist.*

1793 J. MACDONNELL in C. M. Gates *Five Fur Traders* (1933) 96 The portage is full of hills is divided by the voyageurs into sixteen Poses or resting places. *c* **1840** D. THOMPSON *Narr. Explorations W. Amer. 1784–1812* (1916) xviii. 294 A Rest, or Pose, is the distance the cargo of a canoe is carried from place to place and then rest. **1858** *Porter's Spirit of Times* 30 Jan. 338/1 In crossing a long portage, they do not go through the whole distance with one load, but divide it into 'poses' or rests; and carry in succession each load to the first 'pose', and then carry them all to the second one, and so on, so that they can rest in walking back for the loads. **1933** C. M. GATES *Five Fur Traders* 97 Inasmuch as the same places were used as poses by all who passed, it came to be the common thing to measure the length of a portage by the number of poses along the trail. **1941** J. F. MCDERMOTT *Gloss. Mississippi Valley French 1673–1850* 126 The average length of a *pose* was about one-third of a mile. **1969** E. W. MORSE *Fur Trade Canoe Routes* I. i. 5 If the portage was more than half a mile (a ten-minute carry), the voyageur, in order better to distribute his loaded and unloaded periods, dropped his packs at what was known as a *pose*, and went back for the next load. *Poses* were about half a mile apart.

posé, *a.* Add: **2.** Composed, poised, self-possessed.

1858 QUEEN VICTORIA *Let.* 28 Apr. in R. Fulford *Dearest Child* (1964) 98 She..improves so much—is become so quiet and posée. **1862** CROWN PRINCESS OF PRUSSIA *Let.* 8 Apr. in R. Fulford *Dearest Mama* (1968) 50 Valerie..could hardly believe she was so young—so 'posée', quiet and self-possessed were her manners.

3. *Ballet.* Of a position, 'held', prolonged.

1949 A. CHUJOY *Dance Encycl.* 386/1 *Posé*, in ballet a poising of the body, made by stepping, with the knee straight, on to the pointe, or half-pointe; a ballet step 'held', such as an arabesque posé, for instance.

4. Adopted as a pose; = *POSED *ppl. a.*¹ c. *rare.*

1958 L. DURRELL *Balthazar* iii. 63 A world..which could afford to cultivate emotions *posées* by taste.

B. *sb.* **1.** *Ballet.* (See quots. 1949 and 1957.)

1927 [see *JETÉ]. **1930** CRASKE & BEAUMONT *Theory & Pract. Allegro in Classical Ballet* 42 (*heading*) Posé en avant... A *Jeté sur la pointe* is a slow movement employed in *adagio*, whereas a *posé* is a quick movement used in *allegro*, executed *pied à pointe* or *pied à trois quarts*. **1949** [see sense 3 above]. **1957** G. B. L. WILSON *Dict. Ballet* 220 *Posé* (*en avant, en arrière*), the poising of the body (forwards, sideways, or backwards) by stepping with a straight leg on to the full or half point. *c* **1973** J. CHOLERTON *Acrobatic Enchainements* (Assoc. Amer. Dancing) (ed. 7) 18 Present your Posé devant as near as possible to a Star. Do not confuse it with Posé en avant.

2. = *POSE *sb.*⁵ 4.

1931 G. L. NUTE *Voyageur* 46 The length of a portage was computed by voyageurs in a characteristic way. The canoe and goods were carried about a third of a mile and put down, or *posé*, two or more trips often being required to transport all the load to this point. Then, without resting, the men shouldered their burdens and went on to the next *posé*. And so on till all the *posés* had been passed. **1961** *Canad. Geogr. Jrnl.* July 5/2 He puts down his load at a set place known as a 'posé'. **1968** *Beaver* Autumn 9/2 We..made the traditional posés or rests after each half mile.

posed *ppl. a.*¹ Add: **c.** Assumed as a pose; deliberately adopted or put on.

1909 M. B. SAUNDERS *Litany Lane* I. iv. 43 There was also a nun-like acquiescence in her bearing, prim for her thirty-three years, and possibly a trifle posed.

‖ **pose plastique** (pōz plastī·k). Also **posé plastique.** [Fr., lit. 'flexible pose'.] A type of *tableau vivant*, freq. featuring near-naked women. Also *transf.*

c **1846** J. R. PLANCHÉ *Invisible Prince* (1852) v. 25 The figure..was alive and did both sing and speak... Ah! then it must have been a pose plastique!.. A pose plastique! what's that? **1857** DICKENS & COLLINS *Lazy Tour* v, in *Househ. Words* 31 Oct. 410/1 Poses Plastiques in the Grand Assembly Room..at seven and nine each evening. **1859** G. A. SALA *Twice round Clock* 77 The vast shop-fronts..offer a series of animated *tableaux* of *poses plastiques* in the shape of young ladies in morning costume, and young gentlemen..who are..'dressing' the shop window. **1862** H. MAYHEW *London Labour* Extra vol. p. xxxi, The demoralizing influence of low theatres, and the licentious corruptions of the Coal Hole and Posés Plastiques, might surely afford scope for rigorous prosecutions under the Society's auspices. **1893** *N. & Q.* 7 Jan. 5/1 In 1846 Nicholson was again back at the Garrick's Head, where he added to his usual attractions *poses plastiques* and *tableaux vivants*. **1903** *Rep. R. Comm. Alien Immigration* II. 307/2 in *Parl. Papers* (Cd. 1742) IX. 1 There were *poses plastiques*—there were girls half naked. **1963** P. FRYER *Mrs. Grundy* xxvi. 242 The men of the Victorian age were enthusiastic gazers at *poses plastiques* and *tableaux vivants* (the precise distinction between these is far from clear). **1969** V. G. KIERNAN *Lords of Human Kind* iv. 136 There was a vogue of *poses plastiques*, and tableaux such as 'The Sultan's favourite returning from the bath' were popular. **1974** H. R. F. KEATING *Underside* ii. 17 The poses plastiques inside, sir, you're very welcome to step in.

poseur. Add: (Earlier and later examples.) **poseuse** (earlier and later examples).

1872 B. JERROLD *London* xx. 174 'As one cannot go to bed in the middle of the afternoon—11.30 p.m.—it is necessary to go somewhere after the opera,' is the declaration of a well-known *poseur*. **1888** MRS. H. WARD *R. Elsmere* III. xliii. 260 *Poseuse*, schemer, woman of the world that she was. **1930** G. B. SHAW *Apple Cart* 57 If you let yourself be beaten by that trickster and poseur, never dare to approach me again. **1977** *Times* 18 Feb. 11/3 Eleanor Bron's disastrous Elena converts that passive enchantress into an assertive Bloomsbury *poseuse*. **1977** *Time* 8 Aug. 46/3 But his life as self-styled genius and unrepentant poseur continues to tantalize.

† **posh** (pǫʃ), *sb.*² *Obs.* [App. thieves' slang (cf. Romany *posh* half).] **1.** *slang.* Money; *spec.* a halfpenny; a coin of small value.

Eng. Dial. Dict. s.v. *posh* sb.⁴ provides evidence of *dial.* currency.

1830 *Sessions Papers Old Bailey, 1824–33* VI. 590/1 He had not got the *posh* (which means money) yet. **1839** H. Brandon *Poverty, Mendicity & Crime* 164/2 *Posh*—a stiver, lowest price of money. *Ibid.* 168 The paper makers get the tats and never tip the motts a posh. [*Translation*] Thieves who pretend to belong to paper mills get the rags and never pay the women a farthing. **1846** *Swell's Night Guide* 68 As I used to doss there sometimes, her nibs got sweet on me, and in course we did our reg'lars and the dossing mongary, lush and posh. **1859** Hotten *Dict. Slang* 76 *Posh*, a half-penny, or trifling coin. **1886** W. Newton *Secrets Tramp Life Revealed* 8 Posh..money of all kind. **1888** in Farmer & Henley *Slang* (1902) V. 261/1 They used such funny terms: 'brads', and 'dibbs', and 'mopusses', and 'posh'..at last it was borne in upon me that they were talking about money. **1892** M. Williams *Round London* 67 That sort of patter..is the thing to get the posh. **1905** *Daily Chron.* 2 Mar. 4/5 'But if I'd a brighfull o' posh,' she said, 'I wouldn't parker no wedge to you.'

2. *slang.* A dandy.

Perh. a different word.

[**1867** E. FitzGerald *Let.* 5 Jan. in T. Wright *Life E. FitzGerald* (1904) II. 81, I believe I have smoked my pipe every evening but one with Posh [*sc.* the nickname of FitzGerald's fisherman, Joseph Fletcher] at his house.] **1890** Barrère & Leland *Dict. Slang* II. 146/2 *Posh*,..a dandy. [**1892** G. & W. Grossmith *Diary of Nobody* 197 Frank..said..he had a friend waiting outside for him, named Murray Posh, adding he was quite a swell.] **1902** in Farmer & Henley *Slang* V. 261/1.

posh (pǫʃ), *sb.*³ [Etym. unknown.] Balderdash, rubbish, bosh.

1924 Galsworthy *White Monkey* ii. xii. 214 Was he a fool? Could he not let well alone? Pity was posh! And yet! **1953** A. Miller *Crucible* (1956) i. 20 Oh, posh!.. She took fright, is all. **1957** J. Kerouac *On Road* (1958) i. viii. 49 You're talking absolute bullshit and Wolfean romantic posh!

posh (pǫʃ), *a. slang.* [Of obscure origin, but cf. *posh *sb.*² The suggestion that this word is derived from the initials of 'port outward, starboard home', referring to the more expensive side for accommodation on ships formerly travelling between England and India, is often put forward but lacks foundation. The main objections to this derivation are listed by G. Chowdharay-Best in *Mariner's Mirror* (1971) Jan. 91–2.] Smart, 'swell', 'classy'; fine, splendid, stylish; first-rate. Also *absol.* as *sb.*

The pronunciation (pōᵘʃ), a supposedly 'posh' or facetious way of saying the word, is occasionally heard. Quot. 1903 may exemplify a different word.

[**1903** Wodehouse *Tales of St. Austin's* 37 That waistcoat..being quite the most push thing of the sort in Cambridge.] **1918** *Punch* 25 Sept. 204 Oh, yes, Mater, we had a posh time of it down there. **1923** Wodehouse *Inimitable Jeeves* vii. 72 Practically every posh family in the country has called him in at one time or another. **1925** W. Deeping *Sorrell & Son* ii. 22 Tips. Don't forget the tips. If a man's obliging—... It's a posh job. **1927** —— *Doomsday* xiv. 153 'You like it.' 'It's the poshest thing I've ever seen, old chap.' **1927** —— *Kitty* xxix. 372, I say—that's a posh show. **1927** *Daily Tel.* 24 May 9 It was a club in Ham-yard—not a very posh club. **1929** J. B. Priestley *Good Companions* ii. v. 391 I'd like to have..a very cosy car, small but frightfully posh. **1930** Auden *Poems* 63 To be posh, we gather, One should have no father. **1935** C. Day Lewis *Time to Dance* 32 For no silver posh Plane was their pigeon..But a craft of obsolete design. **1941** Baker *Dict. Austral. Slang* 56 *Posh, do the*, to spend lavishly, do something 'in style'. **1954** [see *ground *sb.* 11 b]. **1957** J. Osborne *Look back in Anger* i. 13 *Jimmy*: Haven't you read the other posh paper yet? *Cliff*: Which? *Jimmy*: Well, there are only two posh papers on a Sunday. **1958** K. Amis *I like it Here* viii. 98 This railway..though posher and faster, had often reminded him of the tram-like train. **1959** *20th Cent.* Nov. 377 At the time..none of the posh papers carried television reviews. **1970** [see *chez]. **1977** *Lancashire Life* Nov. 153/1 The poshest Granada Ghias..have electric windows. **1979** E. Cave *Blood Bond* i. iii. 35 Charles's penchant for the grand—the 'posh' as Tom would have called it.

posh (pǫʃ), *v.* [f. the adj.] *trans.* To smarten *up.* Freq. *refl.* and *pass.* Hence **po·shed-up** *a.*

1919 *War Slang* in *Athenæum* 22 Aug. 791/2 To 'posh up' was to make oneself look as smart as possible. **1932** D. L. Sayers *Have his Carcase* xv. 197, I don't get time to posh myself up of a morning. **1955** *Times* 29 June 12/5 Beautifully 'poshed-up' for this she is, though certainly she has never been allowed to look shabby overlong. **1959** *Oxf. Mail* 1 June 3/6, I knew most of that stuff has been stolen; I wanted to posh up my old car. **1967** R. Mackay *House & Day* 30 He was poshed up. That meant..a trip to the town. **1967** P. Purser *Twentymen* xvi. 104 We..had dined at a rotten, poshed-up Thames pub. **1968** T. Parker *People of Streets* 35 He'd..turn up at a big state ball all poshed up. **1975** J. McClure *Snake* iii. 45 Who goes to the trouble to posh himself up for the postman?

posh (pǫʃ), *adv.* [f. the adj.] In a 'posh' manner.

1957 *Listener* 7 Nov. 739/1 A device to enable you to 'write posh', as it were. You look up the 'vulgar' words, and against them you find the more elegant. **1961** P. Strevens *Papers in Lang.* (1965) xi. 130 The recent popularity of *My Fair Lady* led to another legend, that of phonetics as a system of teaching people to 'speak posh'. **1972** 'M. Innes' *Open House* ii. 20 A crowd of electricians might well take him for a cunning crook talking posh. **1979** R. Barnard *Posthumous Papers* iii. 33 Why do you sometimes talk Lancashire and sometimes talk posh?.. Not everyone can do the posh as well as you.

‖**po shan lu** (bo ʃan lū). Also **bo shan lu.** [Chinese.] A type of Chinese bronze censer, made during the Han dynasty and having the form of a mythical mountain of immortality.

1915 R. L. Hobson *Chinese Pott. & Porc.* I. ii. 12 Fig. 3 is an incense burner... It is a variation of the more usual 'hill censer' (*po shan lu*). **1954** S. H. Hansford *Gloss. Chinese Art & Archæol.* 13 *Po shan lu*, hill censer; censer shaped as a stem cup with cover in the form of a mountain peak. **1973** *Genius of China* 104/2 Bronze censer in the shape of a cosmic mountain *po-shan-lu*, held up by a man seated on a monster. **1978** *Nagel's Encycl.-Guide: China* 216 The *bo shan lu* or incense-burner with a conical lid suggesting the rocks on the island where the Taoist Immortals lived.

po·shness. *slang.* [f. *posh *a.* + -ness.] The state or quality of being 'posh'.

1931 C. Lithgow *Simple Sailor* xvii. 218 In his pet dark blue morning coat, with a gardenia in its buttonhole.., he was rather a splendid figure. No doubt whatever was there of 'his poshness'. **1960** C. S. Lewis *Studies in Words* vii. 179 'A general simplicity in our dress, our discourse, and our behaviour.' Sincerity (not affectation)? Plainness (not 'poshness')? The easy (not the hard)? **1965** M. Morse *Unattached* iv. 123 The real focus of dislike was the teachers' 'poshness', which the girls felt was often assumed in order to demonstrate that a social gap existed between teacher and pupil. **1978** R. Hill *Pinch of Snuff* xiii. 132 An extra element of 'poshness' was inherent in the 'Private Road' sign.

‖**posho** (pǫ·ʃo). *East Africa.* [Swahili, = daily rations.] **a.** Daily rations given to porters on safari. **b.** A kind of maize flour; a porridge made from this. Also *attrib.*

1892 M. French-Sheldon *Sultan to Sultan* v. 118 The method of dealing out rice, which is carried for *posho* or rations..is somewhat peculiar. *Ibid.*, Porters, carrying the heavy loads, are paid the least and receive the smallest *posho.* **1927** *Chambers's Jrnl.* XVII. 761/1 The safari boys were squatting round the cooking-pots, stirring their 'posho'. **1946** G. Hanley *Monsoon Victory* x. 106 In Africa they [*sc.* askaris] ate *posho*, which is maize flour cooked into a porridge. **1964** C. Willock *Enormous Zoo* ix. 157 He searched two fully occupied huts in the labour lines looking for *posho.* **1971** *E. Afr. Standard* (Nairobi) 13 Apr. 9/3 An Assistant Minister for Agriculture..was officially opening a posho mill. **1974** *Observer* (Colour Suppl.) 28 Apr. 45/3 Posho (ground corn on the cob)... It is cooked with water to make a kind of porridge. **1975** *Times* 17 Nov. 13/7 The [Ugandan] guards were already sharing their beans and posho and lumps of lean meat with me. **1977** H. Innes *Big Footprints* ii. i. 122 Sacks of maize flour they called posho.

posigrade (pǫ·zigrēid), *a. Astronautics.* [f. Posi(tive *a.* and *sb.* + *-grade*, after Retrograde *a.* and *sb.*] Of, pertaining to, or designating a small rocket that can be fired briefly to give forward thrust to a spacecraft.

1961 *Aeroplane* C. 152/1 Next, the three small 'posigrade' rockets on the blunt face of the capsule are fired to achieve separation from the booster. **1962** S. Carpenter in *Into Orbit* 53 This sends out an electrical impulse which explodes the bolts and fires the posigrade rockets that shove the capsule and booster apart. **1965** *Time* 24 Dec. 35 To change his elliptical orbit into a circle that reached closer to Gemini 7, he made several 'posigrade' burns. **1965** *World Bk. Year Bk.* 48/2 It was also necessary to take into account..another figure for the thrust of the small, posigrade rockets that give the spacecraft a gentle separation push away from the booster.

posish (pozi·ʃ). orig. *U.S.* Also **pozish.** Colloq. abbrev. Position *sb.*

1862 O. W. Norton *Army Lett.* (1903) 113 Snorting their impatience to 'get into posish', came the Monitor, the Galena and others. **1865** J. Pike *Scout & Ranger* i. 25 Some of the managers and their wives, feeling the importance of their 'posish', put on considerable 'style'. **1914** *Dialect Notes* IV. 130 What did I tell ya about standing—Oh what a pozish! **1923** Wodehouse *Inimitable Jeeves* xviii. 251, I wanted to find out the general posish of affairs. **1936** —— *Laughing Gas* xiii. 139 Well, you've gone and landed yourself in a nice posish. A dashed nice posish, I don't think. **1960** J. Grant *Come again, Nurse* x. 55 What's the coffee posish?

posit (pǫ·zit), *sb. Philos.* [f. the vb.] A statement which is made on the assumption that it will prove valid (see quots. 1949).

1949 Hutten & Reichenbach tr. *H. Reichenbach's Theory of Probability* ix. 373 A posit is a statement with which we deal as true, although the truth value is unknown. *Ibid.*, We do not say *B* will occur, but we posit *B*... The word 'posit' is used here in the same sense as the word 'wager' or 'bet'... We do not want to say..that it is true that the horse will win, but we behave as though it were true by staking money on it. **1953** W. V. Quine *From Logical Point of View* ii. 45 Physical objects, small and large, are not the only posits... The abstract entities which are the substance of mathematics are another posit in the same spirit. **1976** *Sci. Amer.* Mar. 119/3 He proposed a set of five posits about the structure of the world that he believed were sufficient to justify induction.

positing, *vbl. sb.* (Earlier and later examples.)

1854 Geo. Eliot tr. *Feuerbach's Essence Christianity* xxii. 213 This negativing of limits by the imagination is the positing of omniscience as a divine power and reality. **1967** *Listener* 5 Oct. 430/1 If subject does not respond to direct approach try seemingly more casual positings of kindred questions at the macro-level.

position, *sb.* Add: **I. 5.** *spec.* (*a*) the disposition of the limbs in a dance step (see also *first position* (b) s.v. *first C, *fourth position* s.v. *fourth C); (*b*) the posture adopted during sexual intercourse.

(*a*) **1778** *English Mag.* Feb. 59/2 A woman who was ignorant that her first curtsey should be in the third position. **1819** M. Edgeworth *Let.* 17 Apr. (1971) 199 She seems evermore as if she had the fear of the five positions before her eyes. **1884** D. Anderson *Compl. Ball-Room Guide* 10 *Second position*, put out right foot in a straight line with left heel, right heel about four inches from left heel. **1922** [see *à terre *adv.* and *adj. phr.*]. **1930** Craske & Beaumont *Theory & Pract. Allegro in Classical Ballet* 15 Lower the arms to the *fifth* position *en bas.* **1971** 'D. Halliday' *Dolly & Doctor Bird* xi. 143 Krishtof Bey rose to his feet..and struck the fifth position, brown arms outflung. **1979** A. Morice *Murder in Outline* iii. 26 Carefully placing his feet, right heel to left instep, in the number two position.

(*b*) **1883** tr. *Kama Sutra of Vatsyayana* ii. vi. 65 When the woman forcibly holds in her yoni the lingam after it is in, it is called the 'mare's position'. This is learnt by practice only. **1933** E. A. Robertson *Ordinary Families* vi. 112, I show de shentleman de twenty-seex poseetions of lof? **1969, 1971** [see *missionary *a.* 1 b]. **1974** W. Garner *Big enough Wreath* v. 60 My pa..always warned me about the Chinese position. **1976** *Sounds* 11 Dec. 4/1 Mickey Gallagher was being particularly adventurous one bedtime with his lady friend, and collapsed from Position Number 368 (look it up yerselves, you cheeky...) onto the floor and broke his wrist. **1977** *Times* 26 Mar. 12/5 There was actually—this was, maybe, 1938—a chapter on positions. Wow!

II. 7. b. *line of position* or *position line*: a line on which the observer is computed to be after having taken a bearing.

1863 W. Chauvenet *Man. Spherical & Pract. Astron.* I. viii. 428 Let the first observation give the position line *AA'* (Fig. 35), and let *Aa* represent, in direction and length, the ship's course and distance sailed between the observations. **1865** J. H. C. Coffin *Navigation & Nautical Astron.* (ed. 2) ix. 224 The nearer the body is to the prime vertical, the more nearly the line of position coincides with a meridian. **1919** G. C. Comstock *Summer Line* p. iii, The line of position, or Summer line, is generally recognized as the best method for fixing the ship's place by observation of the sun or stars. **1920** J. E. Dumbleton *Princ. & Pract. Aerial Navigation* i. 13 Owing to small errors three position lines will rarely intersect at a point, but a small triangle is formed known as a 'cocked hat'. **1962** *Flight Handbk.* (ed. 6) xiii. 292 One bearing gives a position-line; two or more are needed for a fix. **1974** K. Wilkes *Pract. Yacht Navigator* ix. 115/1 A position line from observation of a single identifiable object can be established by taking a compass bearing of it.

9. b. *spec.* in *social position.*

c **1832** J. S. Mill in F. A. von Hayek *J. S. Mill & Harriet Taylor* (1951) iii. 61 For a long time the indissolubility of marriage acted powerfully to elevate the social position of women. **1853** C. Brontë *Villette* II. xxviii. 293 Pedigree, social position, and recondite intellectual acquisition, occupied about the same space and place in my interests and thoughts. **1949** M. Mead in M. Fortes *Social Struct.* 18, I found it impossible to give an adequate sociological statement which did not include the specification of each actor in terms both of his social position and of his personality. **1971** P. J. Keating *Working Classes in Victorian Fiction* iii. 73 The physical and spiritual struggles inherent in their social position. **1976** G. Butler *Vesey Inheritance* vi. 176, I am a young woman of education and social position.

III. 10. position change *Genetics*, any change in the order of the genes along a chromosome; **position effect** *Genetics*, an effect on the phenotypic expression of a gene produced by a difference in its chromosomal position, esp. by its proximity to a mutant gene or to heterochromatin; **position-finding**, the process of ascertaining one's position or that of a distant object, esp. automatically by radio or similar means; usu. *attrib.*; **position line** (see *7 b); **position mark**, a mark made on a stone or other component part of a structure to indicate the position it is designed to occupy; **position paper** orig. *U.S.*, a written statement of attitude or intentions; **position play** *Chess* (see quot. 1960); **position player** (*a*) *Chess*, one who adopts position play; (*b*) *Austral. Football* (see quot. 1969); **position vector** *Math.*, a vector which defines the position of a point.

1937 *Nature* 30 Oct. 761/2 The primary structural change of inversion gives rise to secondary changes such as reduplication and deficiency. These are changes of 'balance', and rank with intra-genic changes and position changes as one of the three effective means of variation. **1952** C. P. Blacker *Eugenics* x. 245 These alterations of chromosome structure resulting from one or more breakages and recombinations have been called..position changes. **1930** *Jrnl. Genetics* XXII. 315 Since the addition of different deletions results in much the same effects, regardless of exactly where the breakage occurred, these are not 'position effects' caused by displacement of certain genes from others previously adjacent to them. **1952** Srb & Owen *Gen. Genetics* x. 201 In many ways, the numerous position effects described in the literature of genetics appear as a bewildering array of vaguely related phenomena. **1974** *Genetic Res.* XXIII. 291 Position effect variegation is now regarded as a general phenomenon but it is in *Drosophila* that by far the largest number of cases have been described. **1918** E. S. Farrow *Dict. Mil. Terms* 463 *Position finding system*, the term applied to the system used in determining the range and direction to any target from a battery or station. **1947** Crowther & Whiddington *Sci. at War* 57 Another position-finding system in which, however, the aircraft 'interrogates' by sending out pulses. **1959** A. Hardy *Fish & Fisheries* vii. 160 The deep-water trawlers have been getting larger, more powerful and more efficiently equipped with echo-sounding and position-finding apparatus. **1928** G. G. Coulton *Art & Reformation* viii. 145 An inspection..will convince us that the rare marks found otherwise than on the surface are not banker-marks, but position-marks. **1965** *Guardian* 4 Sept. 9/5 Republican leavers..got out an eleven-page policy statement, called a 'position paper'. **1972** Ld. Gladwyn *Mem.* xiii. 226 The idea was that all the political Under-Secretaries..should meet every so often and discuss what I suppose would now be called 'position papers'. **1977** *Time* 7 Mar. 13/1 Carter is just beginning to receive position papers from his advisers on what his policies should be. **1932** E. Lasker *Man. Chess* IV. 166/1 Whereas by combination values are transformed, they are proved and confirmed by 'position play'. Thus, position play is antagonistic to combination, as becomes evident when a 'combinative player' meets with his counterpart, the 'position player'. **1960** Horowitz & Mott-Smith *Point Count Chess* (1973) 356 *Position play* is a strategic move or plan as distinguished from a tactical (combination). **1969** Eagleson & McKie *Terminol. Austral. Nat. Football* III. 4 *Position player*, a variant for *placed man* [*sc.* a player who is allocated a fixed position on the field], recorded by four informants. **1961** C. C. T. Baker *Dict. Math.* 242 If *P* is the position of a point at any time, and *O* is a fixed point, the line *OP*, having length and direction, is a vector, and is denoted by $\overline{OP}$, or **OP**. If *P* is the point (x, y, z), the position vector is $\mathbf{R} = \mathbf{i}x + \mathbf{j}y + \mathbf{k}z$. **1969** Wade & Taylor *Contemp. Analytic Geom.* vii. 243 When we speak of a position vector it is to be understood that the vector has only one representative and that the initial point of this representative is at the origin.

position, *v.* **1. a.** (Later examples.)

1955 *Sun* (Baltimore) 12 Jan. 12/4 The straw is baled, elevated, and positioned on an accompanying truck. **1955** *Sci. Amer.* May 124/1 You first position the hairline of the slider over the caret between the first four balls (1, 2, 3, 4) and the second four (5, 6, 7, 8) in the bottom tier of this rule. **1959** *Listener* 5 Mar. 432/3 *Il Tabarro* was directed.. by Charles Rogers and produced (*i.e.* positioned, rehearsed dramatically, and so on) by Colin Graham. **1960** *Practical Wireless* XXXVI. 429/1 Beginners would be well advised to position the amplifier so that the underneath parts can be inspected while the power is on. **1967** *Times Rev. Industry* Feb. 90/3 Three two-jet engines positioned in much the same way as the British Trident. **1979** J. Wainwright *Tension* 62 Uniformed constables had been positioned to re-direct traffic.

positional, *a.* Add: (Further examples.) *spec.* (*a*) *Linguistics* = *isolating *ppl. a.* 1; (*b*) *Chess*, characterized by position play.

1908 T. G. Tucker *Introd. Nat. Hist. Lang.* 92 Languages which express grammar and modification of sense by position, without external or internal modification of the 'roots'..may be called *Inorganic* or *Positional*. *Ibid.* 93 The *Positional* languages include Chinese, Burmese, Anamese, and their group. *Ibid.* 117 The line of linguistic ease naturally taken by a language which finds the purely positional structure inadequate to it [*sic*] needs. **1929** *Times* 2 Nov. 6/7 Newman increased a run of 312.. to 349, and then missed a positional red winner. **1937** M. Euwe *Strategy & Tactics in Chess* 18 We call games such as the preceding one, in which strategy plays such an important part, *positional* games, in contrast to *combinative* games, in which the strategy is of minor importance. **1937** J. R. Firth *Tongues of Men* vii. 88 Three types of language structure: (i) Meanings indicated by words; relations by position... These were called *Isolating* and *Positional* Languages. *E.g.*, Chinese, English. **1937** *Language* XIII. 3 Not uncommonly, the same language has long consonants of different phonemic types; for example, English has long consonants both as positional variants and as geminate clusters. **1938** *Times Lit. Suppl.* 5 Mar. 157/2 It secured the dominance of the positional over the combinational school. **1945** *Diamond Track* (Army Board, N.Z.) 37/2 The Allied success..made the position of large forces of the enemy's positional infantry on our front most precarious. **1946** *Sunday Dispatch* 8 Sept. 6/2 There was no weakness in United, who played clever positional football. **1952** A. Cohen *Phonemes of Eng.* 90 'Positional diphthongs' are characterised by the preservation of the individual character of the component parts. **1960** C. Barnett *Desert Generals* III. ii. 103 The mentality of the army's senior and rising officers could not be similarly converted by decree to suit mobile armoured warfare. The stiff, positional war of the Western Front between 1914 and 1918 was the only..influence. **1964** R. B. Lees *Gram. Eng. Nominalizations* p. xli, Subcategorization is obviously a different kind of constraint on syntactic constituents from positional constraints in a tree or domination by a certain kind of node. **1970** *Nature* 12 Dec. 1121/1 In fact, the positional accuracy achieved is typically a small fraction of the vehicle stability. **1971** *Physics Bull.* July 397/2 Three instruments incorporating laser interferometers for calibration have been built at NPL. The first of these, for measuring the positional errors of the lines on precision scales and gratings, has been in use for several years. **1972** G. Green *Great Moments in Sport: Soccer* iv. 58 Cohen and Ray Wilson, the full backs, overlapping down the flanks ..as the whole side bamboozled Spain with mobile positional play. **1979** E. H. Gombrich *Sense of Order* ix. 243 Repetition devalues elements while isolation in the centre will emphasize them. In the 'field of force' we can observe the effects of 'positional enhancement'.

b. Special collocations: *positional goods* (Econ.): see quots.; *positional player* (Chess) = **position player* (a).

1976 F. Hirsch *Social Limits to Growth* iii. 27 The positional economy..relates to all aspects of goods, services, work positions, and other social relationships that are either (1) scarce in some absolute or socially imposed sense or (2) subject to congestion or crowding through more extensive use... If..positional goods remain in fixed supply while material goods become more plentiful, the price of positional goods will rise, as consumers' relative intensity of demand for them increases in terms of material goods. **1976** *Economist* 11 Dec. 129/2 Many of the things which are valued in our society are hierarchical. They are what Professor Hirsch calls 'positional goods'. **1977** *N.Y. Times Bk. Rev.* 13 Feb. 10/3 'Positional goods' —a house at the shore, tenure on the Harvard faculty, a Picasso on the wall. **1977** *Econ. Jrnl.* Sept. 574 Positional goods are defined as those to which access is a function of an individual's income relative to other people's. **1933** M. A. Schwendemann tr. *Reti's Masters of Chess Board* 4 Typical positional players like Steinitz and Rubinstein are of the opinion that this variation of the King's Gambit is in favour of White.

Hence **posi·tionally** *adv.*

1923 C. D. Broad *Sci. Thought* xi. 408 Some of these strands may be positionally uniform. **1961** *Times* 13 Feb. 4/1 The new open side wing forward, Rogers, was positionally at sea. **1964** *Amer. Speech* XXXIX. 35 The main adjective class is positionally any word that goes either as a prepositive or as a complement of a copulative. **1971** D. Crystal *Linguistics* 190 *The*..is positionally fixed, preceding the noun it modifies. **1975** *Nature* 31 Jan. 310/2 The molecules are positionally ordered but orientationally disordered and mobile.

positioner (pozi·ʃənəɹ). [f. Position *v.* + -er[1].] One who or that which positions; *spec.* a device or machine for mechanically moving an object into position and keeping it there.

1934 in Webster. **1957** E. B. Jones *Instrument Technol.* III. II. 133 The positioner also corrects for movements of the valve stem owing to unbalanced forces on the valve plug. **1969** *Engineering* 29 Aug. 216/1 A universal positioner,..with vertical table adjustment under full load, has been added to the range of manipulative equipment... Capacity is from 1 to 10 tons. **1972** *Physics Bull.* June 363/1 A micrometer stage is used to traverse the resistor under an RF probe which is held by a vertical positioner.

positive, *a.* and *sb.* Add: **A.** *adj.* **II. 5. c.** Functioning for the special purpose required; having or being a well-defined and effective action.

1903 *Sci. Amer.* 21 Feb. 134/1 Instead of depending on splash lubrication alone for oiling every part of the engine, positive oil feeds are led to each of the crankshaft bearings. **1938** L. V. W. Clark in A. E. Dunstan et al. *Sci. of Petroleum* I. IX. 434/1 Blow-out preventers of the first group have been..quite satisfactory for drilling in areas of normal pressure, but where higher pressures are encountered it becomes necessary for a positive control to be available. **1958** *Times* 1 July 6/6 The steering, which used to be somewhat indefinite, is now light and pleasantly positive in action. **1972** *Physics Bull.* Apr. 230/2 Minor but important details have been considered—the cable is five feet long and very flexible, the grip on the bench (with rubber ball feet) is positive. **1977** *Offshore Engineer* Apr. 27/2 The port has a step-down diameter which provides a positive stop during pipe pull-in. **1977** *Sci. Amer.* Aug. 106/1 The unassisted drum brakes are balanced and positive in action but require heavy foot pressure.

IV. 8. a. (Further examples.) Also, consisting in or characterized by constructive action or attitudes; see also *positive thinking* below.

1930 H. Crane *Let.* 22 May (1965) 351 The poem [*sc. The Bridge*]..is, I think, an affirmation of experience, and to that extent is 'positive' rather than 'negative' in the sense that *The Waste Land* is negative. **1961** *Oregonian* (Portland, Oregon) 24 Oct. 8 The Portland school board was asked..to take a positive stand towards developing ..more plans for the city's schools in event of attack. **1971** *Times* 15 Feb. 9/3 Ireland were the more positive side throughout and the same XV has been chosen for the game against Scotland. *Ibid.* 9/4 All the positive rugby after the interval came from Ireland. **1973** *Howard Jrnl.* XIII. 310 The opportunity to have a positive experience of learning may be very significant. **1976** M. Millar *Ask for me Tomorrow* (1977) xvi. 132 Please try to take a more positive attitude.

c. Designating a copy or likeness of an object with the same relief as that of the original, as opposed to the reverse relief of a mould.

1911 [see *negative *a.* 11 a]. **1931** [see *negative *sb.* 8 c]. **1940** [see *negative *a.* 11 a]. **1973** [see *negative *sb.* 8 b].

d. Psychol. *positive thinking*: the practice or result of concentrating one's mind affirmatively on what is constructive and good, thereby eliminating from it negative or destructive thoughts and emotions; also *attrib.*; *positive transfer*: the transfer of effects from the learning of one skill that facilitate the subsequent learning of another skill; *positive transference*: transference in which the feelings involved are of a positive or affectionate nature.

1916 C. E. Long tr. *Jung's Coll. Papers Analytical Psychol.* ix. 270 As long as it is a question of the so-called 'positive' transference, the infantile-erotic character can usually be recognised without difficulty. **1921** F. N. Freeman *Exper. Educ.* ii. 47 There is..positive transfer again from Set 3 to Set 4. **1924,** etc. [see *negative transference* s.v. *negative *a.* 8 c]. **1933** R. W. Bruce in *Jrnl. Exper. Psychol.* XVI. 351 There is a marked positive transfer in learning to make an old response to a new stimulus. **1953** N. V. Peale (*title*) The power of positive thinking. *Ibid.* i. 2, I listened to your speech tonight in which you talked about the power of positive thinking. **1959** N. V. Peale *Amazing Results of Positive Thinking* p. vii, By the application of positive thinking principles to their own life situations, they have mastered fear, healed personal relationships,..and gained strong new confidence. **1970** B. C. Mathis et al. *Psychol. Found. Educ.* iii. 83 If the experimental group is superior to the control group on B..positive transfer of training is said to have occurred. **1970** A. Janov *Primal Scream* xiv. 246 When the therapist is helpful and warm and offers a bit of advice, he is encouraging the 'positive' transference. **1974** *Country Life* 21 Nov. 1616/2, I believe that positive thinking can help one overcome many difficulties in life.

e. Pol. *positive neutralism* or *neutrality*: a policy adopted by some of the poorer and less developed countries of maintaining relations with each of the major powers while remaining neutral in regard to their rivalry (see quot. 1968). So *positive neutralist*.

[**1957** *Political Sci. Q.* LXXII. 266 A communiqué condemning the development of Power blocs in international affairs and urging neutralism as a positive way towards the establishment of international peace.] **1960** *Sunday Times* 28 Aug. 5/1 'We Africans are positive neutralists.'.. These phrases..have cropped up constantly in the speeches so far: 'positive neutralism' [etc.]. **1961** *NATO or Neutrality* (Fabian Soc.) iv. 20 A policy of positive neutrality would be of immense assistance in helping Britain establish good post-imperial relations with the new countries. **1968** P. Calvocoressi *World Politics since 1945* IV. xiii. 256 Neutralism and non-alignment, therefore, as distinct from neutrality, were the expression of an attitude towards a particular and present conflict: they entailed, first, equivalent relations with both sides and, secondly—in the phase called positive neutralism—attempts to mediate and abate the dangerous quarrels of the great.

9. c. *positive logic*: (*a*) [tr. G. *positive logik* (Hilbert & Bernays *Grundlagen der Math.* (1934) I. iii. 68)] (see quots. 1943, 1947); (*b*) circuit logic in which the larger or most positive signal is taken as representing 1 and the smaller signal 0.

1943 *Mind* LII. 49 Of other 'rudimentary systems' I mention only the so-called positive logic, which does not operate with negations. **1947** *Mind* LVI. 215 Rules 4.1 to 4.5 constitute the positive logic of compound statements, that is to say, they suffice for that part of propositional logic which is independent of negation. **1955** A. N. Prior *Formal Logic* III. ii. 258 This segment of Heyting's calculus forming what Hilbert and Bemays have called 'positive logic'. **1958** *Proc. IRE* XLVI. 1249 In the following discussion, positive logic is used. A binary '1' is defined as the most positive signal potential, and a binary '0' as the most negative. **1962, 1968** [see *logic *sb.* 3*]. **1974** D. A. Calahan et al. *Introd. Mod. Circuit Anal.* iii. 47/2 In theory, we must be told which type of logic, positive or negative, is assumed before we can determine the function of a logical device; in practice, positive logic is assumed unless otherwise specified. **1976** Belove & Drossman *Systems & Circuits for Electr. Engin. Technol.* xiii. 325 We shall use the positive logic convention whereby a relatively low voltage represents logical 0 and a relatively high voltage represents logical 1.

VI. 15. Other collocations: *positive discrimination*, the making of distinctions in favour of groups considered disadvantaged or underprivileged, esp. in the allocation of resources and opportunities; *positive electron*, a particle analogous to the ordinary negative electron but having a positive charge: orig. applied to the proton, now to the positron; *positive eugenics*, an attempt to encourage the birth of children to parents having qualities considered desirable to the community; *positive feedback* (see *feedback, feed-back *sb.* a); *positive pressure* (Med.), pressure greater than that of the atmosphere, used to force air or oxygen into the lungs intermittently to supplement or replace natural inspiration; freq. *attrib.*; *positive ray*, a stream of positively-charged ions which are produced in a gas discharge tube and move towards the cathode; *pl.* except when *attrib.*

1967 *Children & their Primary Schools* (Central Advisory Council for Educ.) I. v. 57 We ask for 'positive discrimination' in favour of such schools [in deprived areas] and the children in them, going well beyond an attempt to equalise resources. **1974** *Observer* 21 Apr. 14/6 Israeli educationists regard this as a challenge, and positive discrimination—in theory at least—has become an article of faith. **1977** *Film & Television Technician* Mar. 8/4 Ms Betty Lockwood, Chairman of the Equal Opportunities Commission, told a WEA seminar of trade union officials that positive discrimination inside unions and in training should be encouraged. That means discrimination in favour of either women or men, though in practice it is likely to mean women. **1978** *Daily Tel.* 28 Jan. 16 Camden Council's announcement that henceforth members of immigrant minorities, even when less qualified, will be preferred for employment to indigenous citizens will bring to the boil the simmering debate on what is euphemistically known as positive discrimination or affirmative action. **1900** Ld. Kelvin in *Phil. Mag.* L. 306 For atoms of electricity, which, following Larmor, I at present call electrons, it inevitably occurs to suggest a special class of atoms... A positive electron would be an atom which by attraction condenses ether into the space occupied by its volume; and a negative electron would be an atom which, by repulsion, rarefies the ether remaining in the space occupied by its volume. **1902** [see *ELECTRON[2]]. **1903** O. LODGE *Mod. Views on Matter* 12 The chief defect in the electrical theory of matter at present is that the *positive* electron, if it exists, has never yet been isolated from the rest of an atom. **1921** *Phil. Mag.* XLII. 307 So far as the writer can learn, the word proton was suggested by Rutherford for use in designating the hydrogen nucleus. This will also be designated as the positive electron in the present paper. **1932** *Science* 9 Sept. 238/1 Up to the present a positive electron has always been found with an associated mass 1,850 times that associated with the negative electron. **1964** M. GOWING *Britain & Atomic Energy, 1939–1945* 18 This positive electron, or positron as it is often called, was first found in..cosmic rays. [**1907** C. W. SALEEBY in *Sociol. Papers* III. 31 We must.. preserve the two-fold aspect of eugenics, the one positive—the encouragement of the better; the other negative—the discouragement of the worse.] **1909** —— *Parenthood & Race Culture* xi. 172 We must clearly divide our proposals, as the present writer did some years ago, with Mr. Galton's approval, into two classes: positive eugenics and negative eugenics. *Ibid.*, In regard to positive eugenics I ..cannot believe in the propriety of attempting to bribe into parenthood people who have no love of children. **1914** [see *negative eugenics* s.v. *NEGATIVE *a.* 8 c]. **1952** C. P. BLACKER *Eugenics* v. 111 The statement made [by Galton] in 1901 says that positive eugenics is more *important* than negative and that made in 1908 declares that negative eugenics is more *pressing* than positive. **1970** *Sci. Amer.* Mar. 107 Conceivably a changed social climate and increased knowledge will make it possible for positive eugenics to be practiced on man. **1972** P. B. MEDAWAR *Hope of Progress* 71 The case for 'positive eugenics', that is for constructive rather than merely remedial eugenics, is based on the model of stockbreeding. **1885** I. B. YEO tr. *Oertel's Respiratory Therapeutics* II. 607 (*heading*) Action of positive pressure on the surface of the thorax. **1909** *Arch. Internal Med.* III. 369 During positive pressure respiration, the so-called artificial respiration of laboratory procedure, the blood pressure falls during inspiration and rises during expiration. **1948** *Anesthesiol.* IX. 29 Positive pressure respiration decreases the venous return, and is in effect a way of applying tourniquets not only to all four extremities but also to the head and abdomen. **1970** *Jrnl. Pediatrics* LXXVI. 183 The indications for intermittent positive pressure ventilation were asphyxia on admission, a single asphyxial attack, [etc.]. **1903** J. J. THOMSON *Conduction Electr. through Gases* xvi. 522 On the view of the discharge given in Chap. xvi. there is a stream of positively charged molecules moving towards the cathode, causing this to emit cathode rays; if the cathode is perforated, part of this stream may pass through the holes, producing in the gas behind the cathode luminosity, forming in fact the Canalstrahlen, or positive rays as we may call them, if we think this view of their constitution sufficiently established. **1920** [see *mass spectrograph* s.v. *MASS *sb.*[2] 10 d]. **1922** GLAZEBROOK *Dict. Appl. Physics* II. 602/1 Positive rays were discovered by Goldstein in 1886 in electrical discharge at low pressure. **1955** C. G. DARWIN in W. Pauli *Niels Bohr* 9 Many elements in a positive-ray tube form temporary hydrides. **1968** M. S. LIVINGSTON *Particle Physics* ii. 20 Thomson's studies of the positive rays from ionized hydrogen gas were the first experiments in which the proton was isolated and identified as a particle.

16. Comb.: **positive definite** *adj. phr. Math.*, positive (formerly, positive or zero) in all cases; (of a matrix) having all its eigenvalues positive; hence **positive-definiteness**; **positive-going** *a.*, increasing in magnitude in the direction of positive polarity; becoming less negative or more positive; **positive-negative** *a.*, exhibiting both positive and negative characteristics.

1907 M. BÔCHER *Introd. Higher Algebra* xi. 150 A positive definite form is positive or zero for all real values of the variables. **1948** W. V. HOUSTON *Princ. Math. Physics* (ed. 2) vii. 120 The potential energy will be a quadratic expression in the coordinates that, if the equilibrium is stable, will be a positive definite expression. **1957** L. FOX *Numerical Solution Two-Point Boundary Probl.* vii. 179 If all the λ_r are positive, which is the case in many physical problems, and corresponds to some structure of the differential system corresponding to a positive-definite matrix *A*.., we can also assert [etc.]. **1970** G. SPOSITO *Introd. Quantum Physics* iii. 53 We further restrict this scalar product by stipulating that it be positive-definite: $(f, f) \geqslant 0$. **1968** FOX & MAYERS *Computing Methods for Scientists & Engineers* i. 6 The associated matrix may be 'general', or it may have special properties such as symmetry, with or without positive-definiteness. **1957** *Wireless World* Jan. 10/2 The area under the positive-going excursion is nearly equal to that under the negative-going excursion. **1979** *Sci. Amer.* Mar. 104/1 (*caption*) A positive-going (but not negative-going) shift in membrane voltage causes a brief outward gating current that coincides with the opening of the sodium channels. **1946** C. MORRIS *Signs, Lang. & Behavior* 82 Appraisors signify along a positive-negative continuum. **1964** E. A. NIDA *Toward Sci. Transl.* ii. 24 The differences between literal and free translating are, however, no mere positive-negative dichotomy, but rather a polar distinction with many grades between them.

positively, *adv.* Add: **3.** (Later examples.)

1961 C. E. VINCENT *Unmarried Mothers* x. 254 Her inability to resolve these various identity crises positively. **1972** *Jrnl. Social Psychol.* LXXXVII. 34 It has generally been assumed that level of fear is related positively to response in a potential panic situation.

5. Also *ellipt.*; *colloq.* used as an emphatic affirmative: yes, indeed.

1922 H. S. WALPOLE *Cathedral* II. ii. 188 She hasn't an idea in her head. I don't believe that she knows it's Jubilee Year. Positively! **1942** PARTRIDGE *Usage & Abusage* 4/2 Absolutely and *positively*... In slang their meaning is *yes* (popularized by a famous vaudeville duet between 'Mr. Gallagher and Mr. Sheehan').

positivism. Add: **1.** (Earlier and further examples.) Also, the name given generally nowadays to the view, held by Bacon and Hume amongst others (including Comte), that every rationally justifiable assertion can be scientifically verified or is capable of logical or mathematical proof; that philosophy can do no more than attest to the logical and exact use of language through which such observation or verification can be expressed. Also *ellipt.* for *logical positivism* (see *LOGICAL *a.* (and *sb.*) 7).

1847 J. D. MORELL *Hist. View Philos.* (ed. 2) I. I. i. 88 Let those who claim Bacon as the apostle of *positivism*, give us an interpretation of this whole division of his system. *a* **1866** J. GROTE *Exam. Utilitarian Philos.* (1870) 2 A way of thinking about morals, which may be roughly called by the name *Positivism*; by which I mean the line of thought which endeavours to construct a system of morals..from observation and experience of fact alone. **1934** W. M. MALISOFF tr. R. Carnap in *Jrnl. Philos. of Sci.* I. 16 In the following example we deal with the conflict of two theses..which correspond more or less to positivism and to realism. **1945** K. R. POPPER *Open Society* I. v. 59 Ethical positivism..maintains that..what is, is good. (Might is right.) **1961** M. ČAPEK *Philos. Impact Contemp. Physics* xvi. 297 The positivism prevailing amongst contemporary physicists, who insist on a consistent elimination of *all* unobservable factors. **1964** FODOR & KATZ in R. Klibansky *Contemp. Philos.* (1969) III. 303 We shall therefore examine the two dominant schools of thought in recent philosophy of language, ordinary-language philosophy and positivism. **1967** *Encycl. Philos.* VI. 415 Both share the general idea of progress, but whereas social positivism deduces progress from a consideration of society and history, evolutionary positivism deduces it from the fields of physics and biology. **1974** H. WANG *From Math. to Philos.* p. ix, The much publicized juxtaposition of logic with positivism (or empiricism or 'analytic' philosophy) has burdened logic with a guilt by association.

3. *Law.* A term derived from positive law (cf. POSITIVE *a.* 1) and applied to theories concerned with the enactment of law, the reaching of legal decisions, the binding nature of legal rules and the study of existing law; which postulate that legal rules are valid because they are enacted by the 'sovereign' or derive logically from existing decisions, and deny that ideal or moral considerations (such as those of natural law, or that a rule is unjust) should in any way limit the operation or scope of the law.

1927 M. R. COHEN in *Proc. 6th Internat. Congr. Philos., 1926* 469 (*title*) Positivism and the limits of idealism in the law. **1944** W. FRIEDMANN *Legal Theory* xv. 135 Positivism in jurisprudence comprises legal movements, poles apart in every respect. **1945** H. KELSEN *Gen. Theory Law* I. iii. 52 No sanction without a legal norm providing this sanction, no delict without a legal norm determining that delict. These principles are the expression of legal positivism in the field of criminal law. **1959** JOWITT *Dict. Eng. Law* II. 1366/2 *Positivism*, in international law, this means the method which attempts to present law as actually applied in State practice. **1961** H. L. A. HART *Concept of Law* i. 7 Some contemporary legal theory which is critical of the legal 'positivism' inherited from Austin. **1967** *Encycl. Philos.* IV. 419/1 The definition of law as the command of the 'sovereign' is no doubt the most prominent example of a form of positivism. *Ibid.*, Sometimes 'legal positivism' is used to refer to the view that correct legal decisions are uniquely determined by pre-existing legal rules. **1969** M. MORITZ in R. Klibansky *Contemp. Philos.* IV. 140 The author intends to give an empirical account of what is a legal order. He regards the distinction between natural law theory and legal positivism as being of secondary importance. **1971** *Mod. Law Rev.* XXXIV. VI. 632 Positivism regards law as a system of comprehensive and closely defined rules.

positivist. Add: (Further examples.) See also *logical positivist* s.v. *LOGICAL *a.* (and *sb.*) 7.

1892 [see *CRITICIST]. **1936** A. J. AYER *Lang., Truth & Logic* i. 23 Some positivists have adopted the heroic course of saying that these general propositions are indeed pieces of nonsense. **1958** G. J. WARNOCK *Eng. Philos. since 1900* 58 The Positivists were also engaged in linguistic analysis, officially without metaphysical ambitions; theirs was supposed to be the two-sided task, on the one hand of exposing the muddles of metaphysicians, and on the other hand of humbly clarifying the vocabularies of the scientist and the mathematician. **1971** J. H. HADDOX *Antonio Caso* 86 To the cowardly positivists frightened by the idea of 'mental anarchy' I say, no.

b. (Further examples.)

1934 *Philos. of Sci.* I. 16 In using the formal mode of expression the pseudo-problem 'What is a thing?' disappears, and therewith the opposition between the positivist and the realist answer disappears. **1943** W. G. HARDY *Some Semantic Theories* in *Cornell Univ. Abstr. of Theses* 56 Bridgman's operational theory of meaning amounts to a positivist demand that meanings be assigned according to the operations performed. **1960** J. O. URMSON *Conc. Encycl. Western Philos.* 324/1 In the twenties of the twentieth century Hume's positivist arguments were revived and strengthened. **1969** F. HALLIDAY in Cockburn & Blackburn *Student Power* 298 A bid to introduce IQ tests was made, but this positivist attack was repelled when students occupied the main building of the campus for two months. **1974** *Nature* 16 Aug. 609/1 Most philosophers of science, at least within the dominant positivist schools, take the Comtean view, of physics as the paradigmatic science. **1977** *New Yorker* 9 May 145/1, I suspect that we remain, in our hearts, medieval people: our assumptions are Aristotelian, not positivist or existentialist.

2. An adherent or supporter of legal positivism (see *POSITIVISM 3).

1927 M. R. COHEN in *Proc. 6th Internat. Congr. Philos., 1926* 469 It is therefore easy..to show that other positivists are full of hidden or unavowed natural law. **1971** *Mod. Law Rev.* XXXIV. VI. 631 Most positivists, and certainly Hart, would argue that legal rules can never be spelled out in terms of all the situations to which they might be relevant. **1973** I. M. SINCLAIR *Vienna Convention on Law of Treaties* v. 112 They [*sc.* the school of jurists led by Bynkershoek, Moser and Martens] did not wholly deny the role of natural law in filling gaps, but their emphasis on the constituent elements of positive international law gave them the title 'positivists'.

b. *attrib.* or as *adj.*

1923 R. POUND *Interpretations of Legal Hist.* iv. 78 The positivist ethnological interpretation [of legal history].. was given a comparative basis. **1944** W. FRIEDMANN *Legal Theory* xv. 135 The number and variety of positivist legal theories is as great as that of the sciences. **1963** S. I. SHUMAN *Legal Positivism* i. 11 Friedmann who speaks.. of 'Austin's positivist system'. **1976** *Howard Jrnl.* XV. I. 51 The change from a classical to a positivist approach to criminology..took the form of a belief in the biological and social causation of crime and the necessity for early prevention.

positivistic, *a.* **1.** (Further examples.)

1927 M. R. COHEN in *Proc. 6th Internat. Congr. Philos., 1926* 471 The same system of legal rights and duties may be expressible in positivistic or in idealistic language. **1935** [see *anti-metaphysical* s.v. *ANTI-[1] 3 b and c]. **1938** B. F. SKINNER *Behavior of Organisms* ii. 44 So far as scientific method is concerned, the system set up..is positivistic. It confines itself to description rather than explanation. **1956** J. O. URMSON *Philos. Analysis* viii. 119 It might be thought that such a characterization of positivistic analysis embodied an illegitimate nostalgia. **1961** M. ČAPEK *Philos. Impact Contemp. Physics* xvi. 297 A similar positivistic motive is conspicuously present in the minds of physicists dealing with the problems of determinism in quantum mechanics. **1975** *Sci. Amer.* Feb. 101/1 Thinkers of a mystical turn of mind..consider it the ..most fundamental of all metaphysical questions... Those of a positivistic, pragmatic turn of mind consider it trivial.

positiviˑstically, *adv.* [f. POSITIVISTIC *a.* + -LY[2].] In a positivistic manner.

1890 W. JAMES *Princ. Psychol.* I. vi. 177 Nevertheless, this formula which is so unobjectionable if taken vaguely, positivistically, or scientifically, as a mere empirical law of concomitance..tumbles to pieces entirely if we assume to represent anything more intimate or ultimate by it. **1935** *Mind* XLIV. 128 The difference between the subjective and the objective may be interpreted positivistically by the category of degree which rules the newer physics. **1946** R. G. COLLINGWOOD *Idea of Hist.* IV. ii. 182 The facts are positivistically conceived as isolated from each other. **1976** *Times Lit. Suppl.* 17 Dec. 1590/5 It is just such ordinariness that has so often been lost from psychology in its efforts to deal positivistically with isolated variables.

positon (pǫ·zitǫn). *Physics.* [f. POSIT(IVE *a.* and *sb.* + *-ON[1].] † **a.** Proposed as an alternative name for the proton. *rare*—[1]. *Obs.* **b.** [a. G. *positon* (P. Gruner 1935, in *Helvetica Physica Acta* VIII. 326.] = next.

1928 [see *NEGATON]. **1937** *Chem. Abstr.* XXXI. 2917/1 The following names are proposed for corpuscles of mass approx. 10^{-27} g. (present names in parentheses): nulliton (neutrino), positon (positron), negaton (electron). **1938**, etc. [see *NEGATON]. **1952** B. ROSSI *High-Energy Particles* i. 2 Positive electrons (or positons) are identical to negatons, except for their opposite sign of charge. **1956** *Nuclear Physics* I. 72 The word 'electron' applies to particles with an elementary charge of either sign. When it is desirable to emphasize the sign of the charge, the words 'positon' and 'negaton' are used. Thus the illogical phrase 'electron-positron pair' is replaced by 'electron pair', or..'positon-negaton pair'. **1960** *Ibid.* XVI. 683 (*heading*) Branching ratios of K capture to positon emission in non-unique first forbidden $2^- \to 2^+$ beta transitions. **1974** *Ibid.* A. CXXXII. 230 (*heading*) Electron capture to positon decay ratios and second-class currents.

positron (pǫ·zitrǫn). *Physics.* [f. POSI(TIVE *a.* and *sb.* + *ELEC)TRON[2].] The anti-particle of the ordinary (negative) electron, having the same mass and a numerically equal but positive charge.

1933 C. D. ANDERSON in *Science* 5 May 432/2 Experiments have been carried out which gave conclusive evidence that positrons are ejected from lead by the γ-radiation of ThC″. [*Note*] The contraction positron is here used to denote the free positive electron. **1933** *Times* 9 Dec. 9/3 The unit of heavy hydrogen, the deuteron, or deuton, as it has been called, bids fair to rival in interest its recently found cousins, the neutron and positron. **1934** *Discovery* May 123/2 It appears from investigations that the earth is being bombarded by streams of positrons and electrons of very high energy. **1946** *Ann. Reg. 1945* 356 The Bethe carbon cycle (in which carbon acts as a catalyst for the conversion of hydrogen into helium and positrons). **1958** *Spectator* 13 June 778/3 When the electron and the positron meet they annihilate each other. **1960** CHALMERS & QUARRELL *Physical Examination of Metals* (ed. 2) xvi. 765 Positrons, sometimes called 'positive electrons', result from proton–neutron transitions. **1968** C. G. KUPER *Introd. Theory Superconductivity* xii. 193 The conduction electrons and holes of semiconductor theory are closely analogous to the electrons and positrons of the Dirac theory. **1974** G. REECE tr. *Hund's Hist. Quantum*

Theory xv. 203 Not until the experimental observation of the positron..was the Dirac 'hole' theory generally believed.

Hence **positro·nic** *a.*

1948 I. ASIMOV in *Astounding Sci. Fiction* Feb. 44/2 If the field were a trifle stronger, the robot would never reach the technician concerned, since its positronic brain would collapse under gamma radiations—and then we would be out one expensive and hard-to-replace robot. **1957** —— *Naked Sun* (1958) ii. 32 He knew a positronic brain..nestled in the hollow of the skull. He knew that Daniel's 'thoughts' were only short-lived positronic currents. **1968** *Punch* 23 Oct. 592/2 Barbarella (Jane Fonda), a respected astronaut in 40,000 AD, is being briefed for her mission to find an important scientist from Earth who has disappeared among the planets with his great invention the positronic ray. **1974** I. ASIMOV in George & Humphries *Robots are Coming* 5 My positronic robot stories.

positronium (pǫzitrōu·niŏm). *Nuclear Physics.* [f. prec. + -IUM.] A short-lived neutral system, analogous to an atom, consisting of a positron and a negative electron bound together.

1945 A. E. RUARK in *Physical Rev.* LXVIII. 278/1 In 1937 I conceived the idea that an unstable atom composed of a positron and a negative electron may exist in quantities sufficient for spectroscopic detection. The name positronium is suggested. The spectrum of positronium would have lines at wave-lengths twice as great as the hydrogen lines. **1957** *New Scientist* 26 Dec. 28/3 When positronium is in free (i.e., near-vacuum) conditions, spectroscopic measurement shows that it has a lifetime of about one and a half ten-millionths of a second. **1966** *McGraw-Hill Encycl. Sci. & Technol.* X. 524/1 Positronium is of particular interest because it is the two-body system to which quantum electrodynamics is applicable, and its study has served as an important confirmation of the theory of quantum electrodynamics. **1970** [see *HYDROGENIC *a.* b]. **1976** *Science* 19 Nov. 826/3 If ψ were a bound system of two spin ½ particles, there could be excited levels with a spectrum similar to that of positronium (the system of electron and positron, bound to each other by the electromagnetic force).

posnjakite (pǫ·znyăkəit). *Min.* [ad. Russ. *poznyakit* (Komkov & Nefedov 1967, in *Zap. Vsesoyuz. Min. Obshch.* XCVI. 58): see quot. 1967 and -ITE[1].] A hydrated basic copper sulphate, $Cu_4(SO_4)(OH)_6{\cdot}H_2O$, that occurs as dark blue crystals similar to langite.

1967 *Mineral Abstr.* XVIII. 285/2 A new mineral..is named posnjakite in honour of E. W. Posnjak (1888–1949), well known for work on copper sulphates. **1970** *Mineral. Mag.* XXXVII. 740 (*heading*) Posnjakite from Cornwall. *Ibid.*, While examining and surveying the disused workings of the Drakewalls mine, Gunnislake, we have found specimens of the recently described species posnjakite in old stopes..above the deep adit level.

poss (pǫs), *a.* Also **pos.** Colloq. abbrev. POSSIBLE *a.* Chiefly in phrases *if poss, as soon as poss.*

1886–96 in Farmer & Henley *Slang* (1902) V. 260/1 While the public morals-shaper Thinks of writing to the paper To upset the show, if pos. **1909** *Punch* 3 Mar. 160/1 People tell me I ought to have all the amusement *poss* to prevent me from brooding, so I'm making an effort. **1916** A. HUXLEY *Let.* 30 June (1969) 104 Think over this and let us have it as soon as poss. **1959** P. BULL *I know Face* i. 27, I only came back with four ambitions in mind: to learn a little about acting (if poss.), [etc.]. **1972** D. FRANCIS *Smokescreen* ii. 30 'Why the rush?' 'Well, I don't know, darling. She just said, could we come as soon as poss.'

possess, *v.* Add: **I. 3. b.** *spec.* To have sexual intercourse with (a woman). Also *absol.*

This sense, suggested in private correspondence in 1969 by Professor W. Empson, may not have been intended by the writers themselves in some of the examples that follow.—Ed.

1592 KYD *Sp. Trag.* I. i. 10 By duteous seruice and deseruing love, In secret I possest a worthy dame. **1600** SHAKES *A.Y.L.* IV. i. 144 Now tell me how long you would haue her, after you haue possest her? **1680** ROCHESTER *Poems* 87 Mad to possess himself he threw, On the defenceless lovely Maid! *c* **1707** T. D'URFEY *Wit & Mirth* (1719) IV. 332 And tho' I let Loobies Oft finger my Bubbies: Who think when they kiss me, That they shall possess me. **1749** SMOLLETT tr. *Le Sage's Gil Blas* II. v. ii. 197 The four banditti expressed an equal desire of possessing the lady who had fallen into their hands, and talked of casting lots for her. **1876** *Romance of Lust* IV. 39 Her delight and surprise at finding the dear Egerton had equally desired to possess her. **1922** JOYCE *Ulysses* 72 Possess her once take the starch out of her. *Ibid.* 491 All the male brutes that have possessed her. **1961** *Partisan Rev.* XXVIII. 648 A conflict having to do with father-murder and the wish to possess the father's woman.

possessed, *ppl. a.* Add: **2. d.** *like all possessed*: with great force, vehemence, energy or spirit. *U.S.*

1833 S. SMITH *Life & Writings J. Downing* 209 [He] struck his fists together like all possessed. **1916** E. PORTER *Just David* 280 He danced and laughed and clapped his hands,..an' carried on like all possessed.

posse·ssingly, *adv.* [f. POSSESSING *ppl. a.* + -LY[2].] So as to possess or captivate (one); fascinatingly.

1927 *Observer* 11 Dec. 10/4 Miss Jenkins's diary..is nothing worth in itself, but how possessingly dramatised by the identity of her correspondent!

possession, *sb.* Add: **1. c.** *to take possession of*: see also TAKE *v.* 71. Conversely, *to give possession.*

1849 *Illustr. London News* 22 Dec. 406/1 Dan Sheedey and five or six men come to tumble my house; they wanted me to give possession. I said that I would not.

f. *U.S. colloq.* ellipt. for 'possession of narcotic drugs'.

1970 *N.Y. Times Mag.* 15 Feb. 19/1 John E. Ingersoll ..suggested that the penalty for simple possession for personal use be reduced to that of a misdemeanor. **1973** R. L. SIMON *Big Fix* x. 71 What's a few years in the cooler for possession. **1977** D. E. WESTLAKE *Enough!* i. 21 Her freak got busted on possession and went away for an extended rest.

8. possession order, an order made by a court of law directing that possession of a property be given to the owner.

1971 *Times* 24 June 3/8 Southwark council was granted possession orders against nine families squatting in eight properties in the borough in a High Court action. **1973** *Times* 11 Dec. 8/4 He granted a possession order to the GLC. The women took over the house..three weeks ago. **1977** F. BRANSTON *Up & Coming Man* ii. 17 Their large Edwardian semi-detached (three mortgages, possession orders pending on two of them).

possessionless, *a.* Delete *rare* and add further examples.

1898 A. P. ATTERBURY tr. *Sombart's Socialism & Social Movement in 19th Cent.* i. 9 Troops of possessionless workers..herded in great undertakings. **1938** DYLAN THOMAS *Let.* Dec. (1966) 211 We are..completely possessionless. **1944** I. ORIGO *Diary* 24 June in *War in Val d'Orcia* (1947) 224 It is a very odd feeling to be entirely possessionless. **1969** G. LEFF *Hist. & Social Theory* ix. 174 As defined by Marxism a class is a group which stands in a certain relation to the means of production, either as possessors or possessionless or as independent of either state.

possessive, *a.* Add: **2. a.** Also, showing a desire to possess or to retain what one possesses.

1924 E. O'NEILL *Desire under Elms* I. iv, in *Compl. Wks.* II. 164 Eben..stares around him with glowing, possessive eyes... It's purty! It's damned purty! It's mine! **1931** —— *Hunted* I, in *Mourning becomes Electra* (1932) 121 You know how possessive Vinnie is with Orin. She's always been jealous of you. I warn you she'll do everything she can to keep him from marrying you. **1958** P. GIBBS *Curtains of Yesterday* xx. 170 One of those possessive women who wants to grab everything within reach. **1977** C. STORR *Tales from Psychiatrist's Couch* x. 104 A classical case of the possessive Jewish Mum... She didn't like the boy to go out of the house without telling her.

possibilism (pǫ·sibiliz'm). [ad. F. *possibilisme*: see -ISM.] A possibilist doctrine or view; **a.** in *Politics*; **b.** in *Geogr.*

a. 1915 G. B. SHAW in *New Statesman* 23 Jan. 386/2 Having noticed that modern Secularism, Materialism, Rationalism: in short, Possibilism, have brought the minds of Mr Blatchford and Mr McCabe to a dead stop.. they [*sc.* the Chestertons]..have frankly embraced Impossibilism. **1954** G. D. H. COLE *Hist. Socialist Thought* II. xv. 248 Paul Brousse's Possibilism, which stressed the importance of reform within capitalism, was definitely unorthodox doctrine. **1974** tr. *Wertheim's Evolution & Revolution* iii. 376, I could not endorse possibilism if it claims that all solutions have equal chances of materializing.

b. 1925 H. BERR in Mountford & Paxton tr. *Febvre's Geogr. Introd. Hist.* p. xi, He [*sc.* Febvre] has found striking formulae in which to state the question precisely. Against the geographical determinism of Ratzel he sets the possibilism of Vidal de la Blache. **1951** G. TATHAM in T. G. Taylor *Geogr. in 20th Cent.* vi. 151 The development of Possibilism is closely linked with the writings of Vidal de la Blache and Brunnes in France. **1965** H. & M. SPROUT *Ecol. Perspective Human Affairs* v. 83 The doctrine called environmental possibilism, or simply possibilism, represents an historic reversal of perspective towards man–milieu relationships. **1974** KOLARS & NYSTUEN *Geogr.* xx. 375 The message of possibilism is that the environment offers not one, but many, paths for human activities and development.

possibilist. Add: **1.** (Further examples.)

1936 *Sat. Rev. Lit.* (U.S.) 15 Feb. 11/2 He [*sc.* Mazzini] was never what is called in modern phrase a 'possibilist'. He was..that most inspiring and most dangerous product of mankind, an 'idealist'. **1940, 1966** [see *GUESDIST]. **1973** *Times* 26 Nov. 15/2 The Labour Party would be irreparably split between its moderate possibilists and its left-wing extremists.

2. *Geogr.* One who emphasizes man's freedom of action in cultural development and minimizes the effects and restrictions of the environment. Also *attrib.* or as *adj.*

1925 MOUNTFORD & PAXTON tr. *Febvre's Geogr. Introd. Hist.* 20 We will not ask whether there are not really any cracks in the geographical edifice, and whether it is possible to follow at the same time..the 'determinists' after the manner of Ratzel, and what we may perhaps call the 'possibilists' after the pattern of Vidal. **1951** G. TATHAM in T. G. Taylor *Geogr. in 20th Cent.* vi. 155 Possibilists do not, nor have they ever claimed, that man can free himself from all environmental influences. *Ibid.*, Possibilist statements published during the last fifty years, make quite clear the contention that Nature does not drive man along one particular road. **1964** *Welsh Hist. Rev.* II. 275 He begins by disavowing any intention of arguing for geographical determinism and affirms his allegiance to the 'possibilist' school of geographers.

possibilistic (pǫsibili·stik), *a.* [f. prec. + -IC.] Of or pertaining to possibilism.

1965 H. & M. SPROUT *Ecol. Perspective Human Affairs* v. 83 A possibilistic analysis directs attention to those factors of the milieu that may affect the operational result. **1974** *Encycl. Brit. Micropædia* III. 912/3 Contemporary environmentalists recognize that physical surroundings are only part of a total environment that includes social and economic factors... Their approach is probabilistic, rather than deterministic or possibilistic.

possibility. Add: **4.** Special Comb.: **possibility theorem** = **impossibility theorem.*

1950 [see **impossibility theorem*]. **1961** J. ROTHENBERG *Measurement of Social Welfare* ii. 24 We shall give a sketch of Arrow's proof of the General Possibility Theorem. **1964** C. E. FERGUSON *Macroecon. Theory of Workable Competition* i. 10 (*heading*) The possibility theorem and rigorous proof of the competitive optimum.

possible, *a.* (*sb., adv.*) Add: **2. c.** *Philos.* Logically conceivable; that which, whether or not it actually exists, is not excluded from existence by being logically contradictory or against reason. Freq. in phr. *possible world*; also *attrib.* Also in gen. use, orig. with allusion to Voltaire's *Candide* (see quot. 1759).

1738 tr. *Bayle's Gen. Dict.* VI. 674/1 That cause must also be intelligent; for this world, which actually exists, being contingent, and an infinite number of other worlds being equally possible; the cause of the world must have considered all these possible worlds to pitch upon one. *Ibid.* 674/2 It will be true still..that there is an infinity of possible worlds. **1759** W. RIDER tr. *Voltaire's Candidus* i. 3 Pangloss read Lectures in Metaphisico-theologo-cosmolonigology. He demonstrated that there can be no Effect without a Cause, that in this best of *possible* Worlds, the Baron's Castle was the finest, and my Lady the best of all possible Baronesses. **1878** S. H. HODGSON *Philos. of Reflection* I. i. 79 There is then, beside our determinate world, a world indeterminate to us, but *possible* if there should be other modes of consciousness than ours, that is possible to our thought since we imagine its condition, and *actual* to those other modes, if they are actually existing. **1900** RUSSELL *Crit. Expos. Philos. Leibniz* v. 68 It may be well, for the sake of clearness, to enumerate the principal respects in which all possible worlds agree, and the respects in which other possible worlds might differ from the actual world. **1911** G. B. SHAW *Blanco Posnet* 299 The administrative departments were consuming miles of red tape in the correctest forms of activity, and..everything was for the best in the best of all possible worlds. **1914** —— *Misalliance* p. xlii, A life's work is like a day's work: it can begin early and leave off early or begin late and leave off late, or, as with us, begin too early and never leave off at all, obviously the worst of all possible plans. **1922** tr. *Wittgenstein's Tractatus* 127 Everything which is possible in logic is also permitted. **1924** A. HUXLEY *Little Mexican* 166 Next to the intimate and trusted friend, the perfect stranger is the best of all possible confidants. **1926** J. B. CABELL *Silver Stallion* xxvi. 112 The optimist proclaims that we live in the best of all possible worlds; and the pessimist fears this is true. **1928** R. LYND *Green Man* xviii. 147 It was impossible not to believe that this was the best of all possible worlds, for a world in which young men enjoy playing bad cricket is clearly a far happier place than a world in which young men would enjoy playing only good cricket. **1949** A. PAP *Elem. Analytic Philos.* ix. 177 Suppose there existed just one individual, *a*, that might be characterized by either one of the properties A, B and C. Then we can imagine the following 'possible worlds': (1) Aa. Ba. Ca [etc.]. **1966** R. F. ANDERSON *Hume's First Princ.* i. 3 (*heading*) Whatever is conceivable is possible. **1968** HUGHES & CRESSWELL *Introd. Modal Logic* iv. 77 This notion of one possible world's being accessible to another has at first sight a certain air of fantasy or science fiction about it. **1973** J. J. ZEMAN *Modal Logic* xv. 276 The system B,..whose possible world semantics involve an accessibility which is reflexive and symmetrical but not transitive. **1977** *Canad. Jrnl. Linguistics* 1976 XXI. II. 136 Now, we should be aware of the fact that the specific reading of (12) doesn't imply that the fish *a* which belongs to the set I (μ_1) of individuals in the possible world μ_1 belongs to the set I (μ_0) of individuals in the world μ_0 too.

3. (Later example.)

a **1817** JANE AUSTEN *Northanger Abbey* (1818) II. xiv. 273 The only offence against him of which she could accuse herself, had been such as was scarcely possible to reach his knowledge.

5. Delete *rare* and add further examples.

1929 A. HUXLEY *Let.* 26 Aug. (1969) 317 One is at 3500 feet in a rather primitive but quite possible little hotel. **1934** H. G. WELLS *Exper. Autobiogr.* I. vi. 313, I went the round of the scholastic agents,..and I answered many impossible and some possible advertisements. **1968** A. MUNRO in R. Weaver *Canad. Short Stories* (1968) 2nd Ser. 300 Leaving Miss Marsalles and her no longer possible parties behind, quite certainly forever.

B. *absol.* or as *sb.* **1. a.** Phr. *the art of the possible.*

The equivalent G. phr. *Die Politik ist die Lehre von Möglichen* is attributed to Bismarck (1867).

1969 D. C. HAGUE *Managerial Econ.* i. 12 Management, like politics, is the art of the possible. **1979** *Oxf. Dict. Quotations* (ed. 3) 84/2 Politics is the art of the possible. **1979** *Guardian* 31 Oct. 4/4 Britain's strong suit is jurisprudence. France's is the art of the possible.

b. (Later examples.)

1970 *Morning Star* 5 Mar. 2 Michael Parkinson looks at award-winning film possibles in 'Cinema' on Granada at

10.30 tonight. **1974** A. MORICE *Killing with Kindness* ii. 14 We were going to have a look at some boats... He'd marked one or two possibles in the local paper.

c. (Earlier and later examples.)

1792 H. MORE *Lett.* (1925) 175, I thought to have sent a line to Mr. T. but I have done my *possible* in writing for to-day. **1922** E. E. CUMMINGS *Let.* 26 Feb. (1969) 83 Dos's first words to me were a grim assurance that..his possible would be done to save The Chambre énorme from any similar fate.

d. A person who possibly may have done or may do something or attain some position; a possible candidate, member of a team, sexual partner, suspect, etc.

1915 J. BUCHAN *39 Steps* vii. 180 You're in no danger from the law of this land... they have dropped you from the list of possibles. **1923** *Daily Mail* 3 Mar. 13 C. L. Spackman..and H. J. Still as reserve backs are possibles. **1948** *Sporting Mirror* 21 May 13/3 Olympic 'possibles', especially those recognised to be in the first flight, are going to be in great demand everywhere. **1948** 'J. TEY' *Franchise Affair* xi. 117 He hadn't even thought of her when he sat down... She just wouldn't occur to any man as a possible. **1959** *Times Lit. Suppl.* 6 Nov. p. xx/4 Most of the presidential possibles in this year are college graduates. **1973** D. WESTHEIMER *Going Public* ix. 136 Some files they rejected..others they read through. A considerable stack of possibles began to mount. **1975** T. ALLBEURY *Special Collection* i. 4 They'd spent almost a month..checking..for suitable candidates. There had been three 'possibles'.

possie, pozzy[1] (pǫ·si, pǫ·zi). *slang* (orig. and chiefly *Austral.* and *N.Z.*). Also **possy, pozzie.** [f. POS(ITION *sb.* + -Y[6], -IE.] A position (orig. in sense 7c); the space a person occupies; a location; a place of residence; an appointment; an occupation. Hence as *v. trans.*

1915 T. SKEYHILL *Soldier Songs from Anzac* (1916) 15 'E climbs up stunted pine-trees, An' snipes away as us. But 'e never shows 'is pozzy. **1916** *Anzac Bk.* 10 The new sniper's pozzy down at the creek. *Ibid.*, *Pozzy* or *Possie*, Australian warrior's short for 'position' or 'lair'. *Ibid.* 102 His mates used to take a mean advantage of his good nature, and would shunt all the work, such as sweeping out the 'possie', or trenches, on to him. **1918** *Chrons. N.Z.E.F.* 25 Oct. 149/2 We were 'possied' some distance in rear of the front line. **1919** *Ibid.* 10 Jan. 284/2 In the small hours we reached our next 'possie'—a shell-torn gully near Pusieux. **1919** W. H. DOWNING *Digger Dial.* 39 *Possy*, position; place; dugout; home. **1925** A. WRIGHT *Boy from Bullarah* 99 Quick, get a pozzy with the machine. **1926** 'J. DOONE' *Timely Tips for New Australians* Gloss., *Possie*, a slang contraction of the word position which denotes a place. A job. *c* **1926** 'MIXER' *Transport Workers' Song Bk.* 70 You'll hear him in his bar-room 'possie', As a bloke comes in for a 'wet'. **1929** A. W. WHEEN tr. *Remarque's All Quiet on W. Front* v. 101 Then we change our possy and lie down again to play cards. **1934** *Bulletin* (Sydney) 3 Jan. 21/3 A bad set in a good possie will bring nothing save an occasional adventurous doe. **1937** N. MARSH *Vintage Murder* xxi. 238 Messing about on the scene of the crime... She's going to find herself in a very, very uncomfortable..pozzy, is Miss Caroline. **1941** *Coast to Coast* 204 S'pose you'll be after some easy stuff next time. A possie where there's a bit of fresh air. **1941** K. TENNANT *Battlers* xxvii. 301 Going to get a possie in the cannery? **1956** D. M. DAVIN *Sullen Bell* 47 'I've brought a picnic,' he said. 'So you watch out for a nice little pozzy while a good husband keeps his eyes on the road.' **1962** E. SALTER *Voice of Peacock* vii. 77 He couldn't have fallen into a possy like that by himself. **1970** P. WHITE *Vivisector* 620 Should have got here early—got us a good pozzy. Never be in the picture now. **1971** *N.Z. Listener* 19 Apr. 56/5 They found a possie in a bit of a trog and boiled-up.

possie, var. *POZZY[2].

possum, *sb.*[1] Add: **1. a.** (Further examples.)

1880 'MARK TWAIN' *Tramp Abroad* iii. 38 He cocked his head to one side, shut one eye and put the other one to the hole, like a 'possum looking down a pig. **1905** N. DAVIS *Northerner* 156 Falls ate his possum with the appetite which the ride in the cold air had given him. **1932** W. FAULKNER *Light in August* (1933) i. 19, I reckon it ain't any human in this country is going to dispute them hens with you, lessen it's the possums and the snakes. **1948** *Sat. Rev.* (U.S.) 29 May 4/2 The possum broke out of his cage. **1971** *Black World* Oct. 64/2, I suggested castor oil and fricassee possum in the milkshakes. **1975** E. WIGGINTON *Foxfire 3* 25, I wish I could get a good possum.

b. For (U.S. colloq.) read *colloq.* (orig. *U.S.*). (Earlier and later examples.)

1822 W. H. SIMMONS *Notices E. Florida* 40 After being severely wounded, they have been known to lie for several hours as if dead... Hence, the expression of 'playing possum' is common among the inhabitants, being applied to those who act with cunning and duplicity. **1924** [see *death-feigning* (*DEATH *sb.* 19)]. **1949** *Time* 5 Sept. 13/1 By last week, in the Senate investigation of Washington five-percenters, it became plain that John had been playing possum the whole time. **1961** G. H. COXE *Error of Judgment* iii. 26, I knew the only way I could beat you was to play possum, but it was a good try, kid.

c. (Further examples.)

1864 R. HENNING *Let.* 27 Nov. (1966) 184 Several [aborigines] were carrying possums which they had caught on their way. **1878** *Punch* 10 Aug. 59/2 Australian beef, and kangaroos—and 'possums, wombats, and ornithorhyncusses. **1901** M. FRANKLIN *My Brilliant Career* xxx. 258 There would be more life in trapping 'possums out on Timlinbilly. **1916** J. B. COOPER *Coo-oo-ee* xii. 174 'Tim' was pushing his cold nose into Jack's hand to coax him to open the back door to let him out to race round the hut to bark at the 'possums. **1928** 'BRENT OF BIN BIN' *Up Country* i. 6 'Possums when excited by the bark of dogs at the foot of trees where they have refuge will run up and down every branch in turn. **1941** I. L. IDRIESS *Great Boomerang* xiii. 93 His arm caught in a hollow limb reaching for possum or cockatoo's nest. **1959** *Post-Primary School Bulletin* (Wellington, N.Z.) XII. III. 22 A 'possum is born only sixteen days after the egg starts developing within the mother's body. **1966** J. K. BAXTER *Pig Island Lett.* 4 He sets his trap for possums And whistles to his dog. **1966** *New Scientist* 29 Sept. 713/3 Although still popularly known as possums to distinguish them from the opossums of the New World, the Australasian family has been given the apt name of Phalangeridae. **1970** *Southerly* XXX. 303 One night a possum broke into the kitchen, through a window left just slightly ajar. **1977** D. P. GILMORE in Stonehouse & Gilmore *Biol. Marsupials* x. 171 Today the possum is probably the most numerous mammal in New Zealand.

c*. *fig.* In various slang uses (see quots.).

1833 *N.Y. Mirror* 7 Sept. 80 *A 'possum*, the western phrase for a paltry fellow—a coward. **1900** *Dialect Notes* II. 51 *Possum*, a negro, or negress. **1943** BAKER *Dict. Austral. Slang* (ed. 3) 61 *Possum*, a 'ring-in'. **1945** —— *Austral. Lang.* vi. 130 Fools of one kind and another.. *flathead, possum, gammy*, [etc.]. *Ibid.* vii. 138 Thieves are described variously as..*dwelling dancers, stoops* and *possums*. *Ibid.* 142 *Jay* and *possum*, a trickster's victim.

c.** *like a possum up a gum-tree*: contented; (see also quot. 1898); *to stir* (or *rouse*) *the possum*: to stir up controversy, to liven things up. *Austral. colloq.*

See also GUM-TREE 2 in Dict. and Suppl.

1898 *Bulletin* (Sydney) 17 Dec. (Red Page), 'Like a possum up a gum tree' is not bad to express quickness or cleverness in doing anything. **1907** C. MACALISTER *Old Pioneering Days in Sunny South* 51 Sometimes..an ambitious carrier or drover would 'rouse the 'possum' by giving some long-winded ditty of the time. **1908** E. S. SORENSON *Squatter's Ward* 144, I mean to stir the 'possum in Sultan Susman from this out. **1941** BAKER *Dict. Austral. Slang* 56 *Like a possum up a gumtree*, completely happy, in the best of spirits and contentment. **1958** 'W. HENRY' *Seven Men at Mimbres Springs* (1960) viii. 94 They made 'more racket about it than six pickaninnies with a possum up a gum tree'. **1972** *Sydney Morning Herald* 31 Oct. 3 'I could be sitting in Parliament now without any great cost provided I forgot this idea of stirring the possum,' he said. **1976** *Courier-Mail* (Brisbane) 27 Mar. 18/2 Mr. Bob Hawke sees an opening to stir the possum and to step up union wage demands.

d. Also *possum beard, hunt* (also as *vb. intr.*), *hunting, rug* (earlier and later examples), *scalper, skin, snare, token*; **possum belly** *U.S. slang* (see quots.).

1928 'BRENT OF BIN BIN' *Up Country* xvi. 273 His 'possum beard and his slouch hat, out of which his mild blue eyes looked with incontestable simplicity. **1926** MAINES & GRANT *Wise-Crack Dict.* 12/1 *Possum belly* tent stake box carried under circus railroad cars. **1939** P. A. ROLLINS *Gone Haywire* 66 There was a sufficient supply of firewood in the 'cooney' or 'possum belly' (a baggy, dried cowhide fastened horizontally beneath the wagon box and used for carrying a reserve of fuel). **1973** *Amer. Speech 1969* XLIV. 207 *Possum belly*, livestock trailer with a drop frame to haul small animals underneath heavy cattle. **1841** *Spirit of Times* 17 July 235/1 A 'possum Hunt. **1900** *Congress. Rec.* 11 Jan. 784/1, I used to 'possum hunt. **1949** *Natural Hist.* May 223/1 According to song and story, most 'possum hunts end at the foot of a 'simmon tree. **1976** C. S. BROWN *Gloss. Faulkner's South* 154 An axe is a regular part of a possum hunt. **1840** *Southern Lit. Messenger* VI. 784/1 He is fond of possum, rabbit, and coon-hunting. **1873** J. H. H. ST.JOHN *Pakeha Rambles through Maori Lands* vii. 128 With a blanket, or better still, a 'possum rug,..the traveller may jog along very comfortably. **1942** C. BARRETT *On Wallaby* iii. 36 'Fifty quid,' he said reflectively. 'More than a possum rug's worth.' **1946** F. D. DAVISON *Dusty* 164 He was a possum scalper, now. **1911** C. E. W. BEAN *'Dreadnought' of Darling* xxix. 249 They did..sometimes sew themselves sort of elementary clothes out of possum skins threaded together with kangaroo tendons. **1966** 'J. HACKSTON' *Father clears Out* 13, I remembered the honey and the fruit, the rabbits, the possum-skins, the money—all the help my little world had given me. *Ibid.* 8 Before the dawn I went round possum snares. **1961** B. CRUMP *Hang on a Minute* 145 Well, a man could sell deerskins and possum tokens.

Possum (pǫ·sə̆m), *sb.*[2] Also **possum.** [f. the initial letters of *p*atient *o*perated *s*elector *m*echanism, after POSSUM *sb.*[1]] A proprietary name for any of various electronic devices, operated in different ways, which enable disabled persons to operate or control domestic fittings, machines, or other equipment.

1961 *New Scientist* 8 June 561/1 The basis of the device, which is known as 'Possum', is that a small steady suck or blow can operate a sensitive switch which, in turn, operates a rotary switch connected to a grid. The grid sets out letters, numbers and punctuation symbols. **1961** *Trade Marks Jrnl.* 12 July 918/1 *Possum*... All goods included in class 10 [*i.e.* surgical, medical, dental and veterinary instruments and apparatus, including artificial limbs, eyes, and teeth]. Reginald George Maling,..Aylesbury, Buckinghamshire; merchant. **1972** *Daily Tel.* 31 Oct. 18 Electronic devices with which severely disabled people can operate typewriters and other machines by mouth, finger or toe, possums..enable the handicapped to lead useful lives. **1974** *Listener* 25 Apr. 525/3 The Possum machine with which, by sucking and blowing into a tube, she can type, telephone, open the front door..or buzz for help. **1976** *Responaut* Autumn 13/2 My window on the world, apart from my eyes, is 15 inches by 7, the size of the tilting mirror attached to my respirator. Reflected through this I can see my two Possum indicators revealing the 21 electrical devices I am able to control.

possum, *v.* Add: Also *Austral.* **1.** (Further examples.)

1846 R. LEVINGE *Echoes from Backwoods* II. 32 'Possuming is become an idiom; a term signifying any one who is humbugging or deceiving. **1862** *Harper's Mag.* Dec. 99/2 So you see you must endure it to the end—fur thar's no possumin' thar. **1912** W. H. THOMAS in J. F. Dobie *Rainbow in Morning* (1965) II. 4 Now when that nigger comes to, if she's been possumin', she sho' will be hungry.

b. *trans.* To feign, to simulate.

1853 J. G. BALDWIN *Flush Times Alabama* 150 All this time I was possuming sleep..as innocent as a lamb.

2. (Further examples.)

1933 *Bulletin* (Sydney) 4 Jan. 11 A short-sighted young man went out 'possuming. **1942** C. BARRETT *On Wallaby* iii. 36 He may have done a bit of cyaniding and out of season possuming.

possy, var. *POSSIE, POZZY[1].

post, *sb.*[1] Add: **I. 4. c.** (Further *fig.* examples.) Phr. *first past the post*, used *attrib.* and *absol.* to designate the electoral system whereby the candidate with the largest number of votes, or the party with the largest number of seats, wins an election; *to pip on* (or *at*) *the post*: see *PIP *v.*[3] 1c.

1818 C. GRENVILLE *Let.* 19 Dec. (1920) 228 The 2nd Miss Morgan *expects* to marry Lord Rodney, if he does not again *jib at the Post.* **1921** E. O'NEILL *Emperor Jones* i. 161 Den de revolution is at de post. **1935** 'N. BLAKE' *Question of Proof* x. 197 'After all,' he continued, 'the Business-As-Usual slogan gets the British middle-class where they live—it has just the right combination of backs-to-the-wall bulldog courage and commercial *savoir-faire.* In this case it will leave its only rival—the respect-for-the-dead ballyhoo—at the post.' **1949** J. D. CARR *Below Suspicion* xvii. 208 'One of the things I like about you,' commented Butler,..'is the pellucid clarity of your style. Addison is nowhere. Macaulay is left at the post.' **1952** L. OVERACKER *Austral. Party System* viii. 221 At that time the 'first past the post' system of election was in use. **1958** C. P. SNOW *Conscience of Rich* v. 37 In strength of character we were about the same. In everything but natural gifts, he had so much start that I was left at the post. **1965** *Austral. Encycl.* III. 367/1 In 1892, Queensland became the Australian pioneer of one of the chief improvements on first-past-the-post, namely the alternative or contingent vote. **1966** *Encycl. N.Z.* I. 864/2 The..first-past-the-post electoral system. Under this system, which has been in operation for most of this century, minor parties are crushed. **1976** *Times* 20 Aug. 13/1 The existing electoral system, based on the 'first past the post' principle which has shown itself to be so anomalous at Westminster.

e. A goal-post.

1867 [see *POSTER[3]]. **1878** *Chambers's Encycl.* IV. 414/1 He will touch it down as near as he can to the goal, if possible between the posts. **1880** *Times* 15 Mar. 6/5 For some little time after this the English kept play in close proximity to their rivals' posts, causing the goal-keeper some anxiety. **1900** A. E. T. WATSON *Young Sportsman* 284 *Poster*,..a place kick which..would have hit the posts produced upward and rebounded into the field of play. **1972** G. GREEN *Great Moments in Sport: Soccer* xviii. 156 It ended with Nordahl turning Puis's chip to the near post against Wilson's upright, with the goalkeeper helpless. **1978** *Rugby World* Apr. 7/3 The Scots would..have been awarded a penalty try.., with the conversion being taken from in front of the posts, instead of from the more difficult position farther out.

f. A leg of a chair. *U.S.*

1902 W. N. HARBEN *Abner Daniel* 202 Something like a groan escaped Bishop's lips as he lowered the front posts of his chair to the floor.

IV. 8. b. *post and pan* (further examples); *post and panel* (further example). **j.** *post and beam*: applied to a mode of construction in which the framework consists of upright and horizontal beams.

b. 1954 S. PIGGOTT *Neolithic Cultures Brit. Isles* vi. 163 with the façade formed by orthostats ascending in height to the portals and originally linked by dry-stone walling in a 'post and panel' technique. **1975** *Country Life* 6 Feb. 319/3 Black and white timber and plaster work of the post-and-pan variety. **j. 1958** *Listener* 25 Sept. 459/1 The other structural method is the application of the simple post-and-beam technique to form a framed structure similar to that obtained by steel or reinforced concrete. **1978** *N.Y. Times* 30 Mar. c 8/2 The designer, Donald Davidson, assembled cedar slats post-and-beam style to make an armchair.

V. 9. *post-maker*; **post-mill** (later examples); **post-retained crown** *Dentistry* = *POST CROWN; **post-sitter** *Austral.* = *POST-BOY 3; **post time** *N. Amer.*, the starting time for a horse-race; **post-windmill** = *post-mill.*

1845 THOREAU *Jrnl.* 14 July in *Writings* (1906) VII. 365 A woodchopper, a post-maker. **1934** *Archit. Rev.* LXXVI. 165/3 The Post mill is the earliest known form of mill. The structure is box-like in shape and carries the machinery and the sails. Supporting this structure is a single upright post on which the mill revolves. **1968** J. ARNOLD *Shell Bk. Country Crafts* 169 The oldest mills, those in existence at the time of the Domesday book, were all post-mills. **1974** C. TAYLOR *Fieldwork in Medieval Archaeol.* 12 The circular mound on a hilltop may be a Bronze Age barrow, or it may be the base of a medieval post-mill, or it may be both. **1963** C. R. COWELL et al. *Inlays, Crowns, & Bridges* viii. 84 A post-retained crown is commonly indicated for a root-filled anterior tooth the natural crown of which has become discoloured. **1974** C. L. STURRIDGE in Harty & Roberts *Restorative Procedures Practising Dentist* ix. 141 In the front of the mouth a post-retained crown will be the treatment of choice if the tooth is non-vital. **1901** A. J. CAMPBELL *Nests & Eggs Austral. Birds* I. 106. The Brown Flycatcher or 'Post Sitter'..begins to breed [in] September or October. **1911**, etc. Post-sitter [see *POST-BOY 3]. **1941** *Sun* (Baltimore) 30 Aug. 13/1 Everything is in readiness for the opening of business about an hour before post time tomorrow. **1968** *Globe & Mail* (Toronto) 17 Feb. 42/1 (Advt.), Post time 7:45. **1931** *Times Educ. Suppl.* 19 Dec. (Home & Class-room Suppl.) p.iv/2 A Cambridgeshire post-windmill.. revolves in an artificial breeze to show wind-power. **1974** C. TAYLOR *Fieldwork in Medieval Archaeol.* vi. 119 A circular mound, discovered on the ground or from air photographs, can be proved to have been the site of a post-windmill if an old estate map depicts a windmill there.

post, *sb.*[2] Add: **I. 5. b.** (Further examples.)

1785 J. WOODFORDE *Diary* 11 Nov. (1926) II. 214, I.. put it [*sc.* a letter] into the Post myself. **1835** DICKENS *Let.* 4 May (1965) I. 60, I am in great haste having scarce time to get this letter in the Post. **1887** W. B. YEATS *Lett.* (1954) 54, I must finish to catch the post. **1921** G. B. SHAW *Back to Methuselah* II. 40 Excuse me, sir; but the letters must go to catch the post.

III. 8. c. (Earlier and later examples without the definite article.)

1789 J. WOODFORDE *Diary* 3 July (1927) III. 118 Received a Letter..desiring an answer by return of Post. **1792** F. BURNEY *Jrnl.* Aug. (1972) I. 225, I wrote her my good wishes, which she answered by return of post. **1980** ALEXANDER & ANAND *Queen Victoria's Maharajah* x. 183 The Maharajah replied by return of post.

V. 12. b. *post-carriage* (later example), *-girl*, *-packet*. **d.** *post-time* (earlier examples).

1872 *Argosy* XIV. 208 There was no railroad then. The ladies and the girls crammed themselves into a post-carriage from the Star. **1850** C. M. YONGE *Henrietta's Wish* v. 55 The post girl could take the jelly. **1944** *Coast to Coast 1943* 112 Living only for the next time the postgirl's whistle sent its shrill stab through her nerves. **1977** 'J. GASH' *Judas Pair* ix. 113 There were a couple of letters..on the doormat, so the post girl had called. **1819** KEATS *Let.* 12 Mar. (1958) II. 71 The sail of the Post-Packet to new york or Philadelphia. **1772** J. WEDGWOOD *Let.* 1 Sept. (1965) 133, I have been so long in these and other particulars this morning that post time is at hand. **1836** F. WITTS *Diary* 14 July (1978) 117 B., as usual, not appearing till nearly the luncheon hour and at post time, when I received a joint letter from my wife and Edward.

13. post-box (later examples); (*b*) a box to which post-office mail, newspapers, etc., are delivered; (*c*) any box where papers, etc., are left for collection; **post-bus**, a post-office vehicle which also carries passengers; also *attrib.*; **post-lady** = *post-woman*; **post-paid** *a.* (earlier and later examples); also *fig.*; **post-rider** (earlier example); **post-village** (earlier examples).

1954 J. COLLIN-SMITH *Scorpion on Stone* ii. 42, I say! I've been to the post-box. My papers have come. **1955** *Times* 3 May 5/4 Posting the letters at different post-boxes on the way. **1960** G. MARTELLI *Agent Extraordinary* v. 85 The *réseau* was entirely self-sufficient... There were no parachute drops, no wireless transmitters, no system of internal couriers or 'post-boxes'. **1963** *Times* 18 May 8/5 There were four other explosions in West-mount and one in the suburb of Pointe aux Trembles during the night, all in post boxes. **1964** L. LINTON *Of Days & Driftwood* iv. 27 The car was ready and able to take us beyond the post box for the first time in many days. **1968** 'S. JAY' *Sleepers can Kill* xv. 149 It's a post-box. The agents can deliver reports there, someone picks them up and sends them on. **1978** G. GREENE *Human Factor* III. iii. 126 Muller was on his own in a strange town, in a foreign land, where the post boxes bore the initials of a sovereign E II. **1960** *Guardian* 22 Feb. 6/4 Trains connect with post-bus services. **1968** A. MARIN *Clash of Distant Thunder* (1969) x. 80 'How did you get to Geneva?'.. 'By post bus from Bourg,' I said. **1972** *Times* 24 Oct. 5/4 Crundale, Kent... At 6 am the new Royal Mail Post bus began its morning run. **1975** *Scottish Field* Apr. 88/3 The inauguration of the 50th Scottish postbus is a milestone in an inspired scheme by the postal service to help those who live out in the wilds. **1975** *Oxford Times* 25 July 18/5 (*heading*) Postlady is dog's best friend!.. Mrs Kathy Hilsdon,..a postwoman for nearly 17 years. **1979** *Guardian* 30 Mar. 2/7 Elstead's postlady Mrs Pam Moss is confronted with one of the giant house numbers. **1653** T. BATEMAN *Let.* 13 Dec. in H. Ellis *Orig. Lett. Illustr. Eng. Hist.* (1827) 2nd Ser. III. 373 Post payd. **1689** in *12th Rep. R. Comm. Hist. Manuscripts* App. VII. 265 in *Parl. Papers 1889* (C. 5889) XLV. 533 Cannon bullets flew as fast as you could count them, and as soon as we took up their bulletts we sent them back again post paid. **1708** *Boston News-Let.* 11 Oct. 4/2 Whereas several persons do write upon their Letters Post paid ..without ever paying the Postage of the said Letters. **1762** GOLDSMITH *Life R. Nash* 117 This description.. must be sent in a letter post-paid. **1814** *Niles' Reg.* V. 369/1 Letters to the editor must be post-paid. **1926** *Scribner's Mag.* Sept. 24/1 (Advt.), Italian tooled cig-arette-cases are smart and light... Colors: brown, dark red and dark green. Postpaid. **1973** *Sci. Amer.* Oct. 118/3 The Math Shop..will supply postpaid (on prepaid orders) 100 plastic cubes. **1976** *Physics Bull.* Feb. 69/1 (Advt.), Price £6.50 postpaid. **1705** *Boston News-Let.* 19 Nov. 2/2 Strayed..a sorrel Mare... Whoever can give any true intelligence of her to..the Post-rider..shall be sufficiently Rewarded. **1827** A. SHERWOOD *Gazetteer Georgia* p. v, Post Village. **1847** H. HOWE *Hist. Coll. Ohio* 264 Allensville, Middleton, Oak Hill and Charleston are small post villages.

post, *sb.*[3] **2. d.** *post-trader* (earlier examples); **post exchange** *U.S.*, a shop at a military post where goods and services are available to military personnel and authorized civilians.

1871 *Republican Rev.* (Albuquerque, New Mexico) 1 Apr. 2/1 Indians stole Levinsky's buggy horses from the Post trader's corral. **1873** J. H. BEADLE *Undevel. West* xxv. 525 Mr. Lionel Ayres fills the position of Post Trader. **1892** *Ann. Rep. Secretary of War* (U.S.) I. 57 In February last, upon the ground that the term 'canteen' possibly conveyed to the public mind a meaning which, though foreign to the main purpose of the institution, has been for years associated in other armies with a place of conviviality and dissipation, the Secretary of War decided to change the name of such establishments to that of 'post exchange'. **1919** *Lit. Digest* 22 Nov. 70/2 The Y.W.C.A. hostess house has been turned into a post exchange. **1973** H. GRUPPE *Truxton Cipher* iii. 25 He added that he intended to remain in the Naval Reserve so as to retain his..post-exchange privileges.

post, *sb.*[5] **1.** Delete ?*Obs.* and add further examples.

1906 R. W. SINDALL *Paper Technol.* 21 The 'coucher', who transfers the wet sheet from mould to felt and builds up the pile or 'post' of alternate wet sheets and felts. **1965** ZIGROSSER & GAEHDE *Guide to Collecting Orig. Prints* iv. 64 When 144 sheets [of paper] have been formed, they and their protective pads (the stack being known as the *post*) are conveyed to a press to squeeze out more water.

post (pōust), *sb.*[11] U.S. slang abbrev. of POST-GRADUATE *sb.*

1900 *Dialect Notes* II. 51 *Post, n.*,.. 2. A post-grad-uate student. **1914** *Ibid.* IV. 134 It must be nice to be a *post*,—they have so many privileges. **1930** *Amer. Speech* V. 242 *Post*, post graduate.

post, *sb.*[12] *colloq.* (chiefly *U.S.*). [Abbrev. of POST MORTEM, POST-MORTEM *sb.*] An autopsy, post-mortem. Hence as *v. trans.*, to perform an autopsy on (someone).

1942 BERREY & VAN DEN BARK *Amer. Thes. Slang* § 534/2 *Post*,..post-mortem examination. **1961** *Amer. Speech* XXXVI. 145 The patient died last night and will be posted this morning. **1968** J. HUDSON *Case of Need* I. v. 41 The post hadn't been started. **1969** 'F. RICHARDS' *Risky Way to Kill* (1970) xii. 147 She died last night. Overdose, probably. They're doing a post. **1979** R. COOK *Sphinx* 177 They had no internal organs. Just a shell of a body. When a post is done the shell is only cursorily examined.

post, *v.*[2] Add: **4.** (Further example.)

1975 *Publishers Weekly* 10 Feb. 45/1 This poster was mailed to ABA members in the hope that they will post it.

5. e. To achieve, 'notch up'. *N. Amer.*

1949 *Richmond* (Virginia) *Times-Dispatch* 10 Oct. 13/5 William and Mary, which Saturday posted a 54-6 decision over the Keydets to tie North Carolina for the conference lead (each has a 2-0 record), has one remain-ing State battle. **1968** *Globe & Mail* (Toronto) 5 Feb. 18/9 John Armstrong of Oshawa posted the longest jump of 110 feet on his way to second place. **1972** *Time* 13 Mar. 48/3 In 1944 he [*sc.* a basketball pitcher]..posted the lowest earned run average in the major leagues. **1973** *Internat. Herald Tribune* 15 June 15/3 Wise, posting his eighth victory against three defeats, struck out four, walked three and retired 14 consecutive batters at one stretch. **1975** *New Yorker* 23 June 43/1 He won nineteen games for the Pirates and lost only eight, posting an earned-run average of 2.48.

f. To announce, publish. *N. Amer.*

1961 *Los Angeles Times* 21 June IV. 6/6 Gains of 2¼ were posted for Teleprompter and Republic Foil. **1962** *Economist* 19 May 697/2 Producer governments certainly cannot get better prices for their crude oil than those 'posted' by the companies controlled by the international groups there. **1973** *Time* 25 June 23/4 Companies that posted big price increases during Phase III will be audited. **1976** *Billings* (Montana) *Gaz.* 17 June 7-E/6 The stock market shook off Tuesday's spell of profit taking Wednesday and posted a modest gain in moder-ately active trading.

6. (Later U.S. examples.)

1967 *Boston Sunday Herald* 26 Mar. II. 9/1 Highway arteries have been posted, warning us that stiff fines will be imposed if we toss our leavings out of the car windows. **1976** *Billings* (Montana) *Gaz.* 30 June 8-A/1 We have posted all the bars and put up signs that make it clear that no drinking is allowed in any public place.

post, *v.*[5] Add: Also, *spec.* of bail money.

1974 *Observer* 7 Apr. 4/8 Immediately after posting five million francs..bail money..he took a private plane home from Geneva. **1974** *Progress* (Easley, S. Carolina) 24 Apr. 10/1 Arrested and charged with illegal possession and sale of piranha, the dealer posted bond and awaits trial which should come this week. **1978** S. BRILL *Teamsters* vi. 223 The other defendants flew in from around the country to plead innocent and post bail.

post, *Latin preposition*. Add: **post bellum** (earlier and later examples). Also *fig.*

1874 *Southern Mag.* XIV. 37 It [*sc.* Atlanta] looks so little like a *post-bellum* town. **1920** *Czecho-Slovak Trade Jrnl.* Apr. 5 The post-bellum difficulties..do not yet permit her to throb with full vigour and strength. **1940** BEERBOHM *Mainly on Air* (1946) 97 The future, the post-bellum period, is to be perfectly splendid. **1974** 'M. INNES' *Appleby's Other Story* xvi. 127 A *post-bellum* relationship. .. That was it. Mr Charles Carter..was no longer Miss Kenterell's quarry.

post coitum, after sexual intercourse; also as *sb.*; *spec.* with allusion to the proverb *post coitum omne animal triste est* (and variants) 'after sexual intercourse every animal is sad'. Also *transf.*

The phrase as such does not occur in classical Latin, but cf. [Aristotle] *Problems* 877 b 9 *διὰ τί οἱ νέοι, ὅταν πρῶτον ἀφροδισιάζειν ἄρχωνται, αἷς ἂν ὁμιλήσωσι, μετὰ τὴν πρᾶξιν μισοῦσιν*; 'Why do young men, on first having sexual intercourse, afterwards hate those with whom they have just been associated?'; Pliny *Nat. Hist.* x. lxxxiii. homini tantum primi coitus paenitentia 'man alone experiences regret after first having intercourse'.

1762 STERNE *Tr. Shandy* V. xxxvi. 126 The oily and balsamous parts are of a lively heat and spirit, which accounts for the observation of Aristotle, '*Quod omne animal post coitum est triste.*' [**1920** A. HUXLEY *Leda* 34 Some..Mount up on wings as frail and misty As passion's all-too-transient kiss (Though afterwards—oh, *omne animal triste!*)] **1928** *Jrnl. Morphol.* XLVI. 171 Embryos with six to ten somites are to be expected in the opossum about 8½ days post coitum. **1933** M. LOWRY *Ultramarine* iii. 158 Whether life was worth living or not was a matter for an embryo rather than a man. 'Post coitum omne animalia triste est. Omne? Supinus pertundo tunicam. **1959** *Listener* 15 Oct. 651/2 A remorseful attack of *post coitum triste*. **1966** C. M. BOWRA *Memories* xi. 246 Once Clark was visiting a college farm, and the party wit-nessed a bull servicing a cow. Clark..said, 'Blakeway, *omne animal post coitum triste*. There was, Blakeway, a firm of solicitors in London called Mann, Rogers, and Greaves.' **1967** *Listener* 12 Jan. 71/2 Elizabeth Sellars.. had to..register such stock emotions as there was time for—fear (lover dead *post coitum*?) and gratification (*post coitum* and dialogue apparently working). **1975** M. BRADBURY *History Man* i. 6 He is in that flat state of literary post coitum that affects those who spend too much time with their own lonely structures and plots. **1979** *Guardian* 13 June 9/5 If you think there's no post coitum triste in angling, try chatting up a tench fisher-man after he's spent a night by the lake.

post eventum = POST FACTUM.

1846 GEO. ELIOT tr. *Strauss's Life of Jesus* III. 166 Thus renouncing what is narrated..as composed *post eventum*. **1920** *Glasgow Herald* 13 July 6 Mr Asquith's post-eventum reproofs..leave us cold when we recall that ..he and his colleagues might have done much to make the preaching of their historic dogma on retrenchment an effective feature. **1958** *Listener* 25 Dec. 1092/2, I should have liked to put my oar, *post eventum*, into the argument. **1961** J. B. WILSON *Reason & Morals* i. 8 What seems to happen is that the philosopher arrives on the scene several centuries too late, and explains the advance of knowledge *post eventum*.

post festum = prec. (In quot. 1966 lit. 'after the festival'.)

1887 MOORE & AVELING tr. *Marx's Capital* I. i. 47 He begins, post festum, with the results of the process of development ready to hand before him. **1935** H. STRAU-MANN *Newspaper Headlines* ii. 55 It must be kept in mind that it is an interpretation *post festum*. **1958** W. STARK *Sociol. of Knowl.* 193 They [*sc.* derivations] are merely the accompaniments of action..the *post festum* rationalizations of human conduct which, in itself, is anything but rational. **1966** *New Statesman* 11 Nov. 718/3 The reference is to a mate in 17 which the problem's author very kindly meant to mark the 17th anniversary of this column some months ago... So let's 'celebrate' it, even though a bit *post festum*. **1970** B. BREWSTER tr. *Althusser & Balibar's Reading Capital* (1975) II. v. 122 It begins, *post festum*, with already established givens.

post partum (earlier and later examples); *post-partum depression* = *postnatal depression* s.v. *POSTNATAL *a.* Also *fig.*

1844 *Medico-Chirurg. Rev.* XLI. 267 On using the catheter, 36 hours post partum, Dr. Crosse found the uterus inverted in the vagina. **1846** *Northern Jrnl. Med.* IV. 1 (*heading*) Some suggestions regarding the ana-tomical source and pathological nature of post-partum hemorrhage. **1911** R. JARDINE *Delayed & Complicated Labour* xiv. 185 If the third stage of labour is properly conducted, post-partum hæmorrhage can be largely prevented. **1929** *Amer. Jrnl. Psychiatry* VIII. 767, I didn't study the infanticidal impulses of many women, because these impulses are more prominent in post-partum depressions. **1957** A. GUTTMACHER *Pregnancy & Birth* xvi. 250 'Post partum blues', beginning a day or two after delivery and lasting several days, are frequently encountered... Your doctor..can reassure you he has met postpartum blues..in people whose depression cleared up. **1959** N. MAILER *Advts. for Myself* (1961) 244, I was beginning to feel the empty winds of a post-partum gloom. **1974** *Publishers Weekly* 18 Mar. 44/3 The scary-funny business of bearing a baby and coping postpartum. **1976** *Dissertation Abstr. Internat.* B. XXXVI. 5793/1 Hostile attitudes toward mother figures predispose some women toward experiences of postpartum depression. **1977** *Lancet* 28 May 1126/1 A 31-year-old woman, 6 months post-partum, complained of fatiguability.

6. With English words and phrases. [Cf. *POST- B. 1 d.]

Usu. found in contexts where *after* would be equally appropriate and more agreeable.—Ed.

1965 *Listener* 16 Sept. 432/3 *Der Ferne Klang* is post-Wagnerian, and post just about everything else that was happening at the turn of the century. **1973** *Nature* 26 Jan. 273/1 Medium was replaced two days post plating and the number of foci determined on the third day. **1974** *Daily Tel.* 7 Jan. 13/3 Now, post the increase [in the price of oil],..future gold price prospects far outweigh individual share fundamentals. **1979** *Ibid.* 19 July 21/4 Post the Geneva meeting of Opec the OECD reckons that its 24 member countries..can expect average economic growth of only two p.c. over the next 12 months.

post-, *prefix*. Add: **A. 1. a.** (*a*) with verbs or pa. pples. *post-process* vb.; *post-stressed* ppl. a.; also, in nonce-wds. formed after verbs or pa. pples. in *ante-*: as *posticipated* (opp. to *anticipated*). **post-acce·lerate** *v. trans. Elec-tronics*, to accelerate (an electron or electron beam) after it is deflected in a cathode-ray tube; so **post-acce·lerating** *ppl. a.*; **postmultiply** *v.* (examples); **post-o·smicate** *v. trans. Biol.*, to postfix with a solution of osmium tetroxide; **post-preci·pitate** *v. trans.*, to deposit by post-precipitation (see b); *intr.*, to be so deposited; **post-produ·ce** *v. trans.*, to subject (film) to post-production (see b).

b. In *quasi*-adjectival relation to a sb.: *post-processing, -stressing.* In nonce-words formed after nouns in *pre-*: *postface* (later example), *postference, postmonition.* Also **post-accelera·tion** *Electronics*, in a cathode-ray tube, acceleration of the electron beam after its deflection; also **post-acce·lerator; post-ge·nitive** *Gram.*, a possessive noun following the noun it qualifies; cf. *post-possessive* below; **post-heat·ing** *vbl. sb.*, the heating of metal after welding, in order to relieve stresses; **postmultiplica·tion** *Math.*, multiplication by a postfactor; **postosmica·tion** *Biol.*, postfixation with a solution of osmium tetroxide; **post-posse·ssive** *Gram.*, a possessive pronoun following the noun it qualifies; cf. *post-genitive* above; **post-precipitation** *Chem.*, precipitation of a compound spontaneously following that of another for the same solution; **post-pro·cessor** *Computers* (see quot. 1977); **post-produ·ction,** film-production effected after the completion of shooting.

1946 *Proc. IRE* XXXIV. 433/2 The intensifier electrode or electrodes, sometimes called post-accelerating electrodes, provide acceleration after deflection. **1971** KLEMPERER & BARNETT *Electron Optics* (ed. 3) x. 397 Electrons may be deflected while they are of very small velocity, and they may be 'post-accelerated' later on to whatever speed is required. *Ibid.*, The spot size should not be increased by the post-accelerating field. **1940** *Philips Technical Rev.* V. 245 (*heading*) A cathode ray tube with post-acceleration. *Ibid.* 249/1 The strength of the lens increases with increasing post-acceleration voltage. **1971** KLEMPERER & BARNETT *Electron Optics* (ed. 3) x. 399 The best post-acceleration is effected by means of fine meshes. **1956** *Proc. IRE* XLIV. 665/2 Conventional post-accelerators, also called intensifiers, operate with conductive coatings of band or spiral shape, plated on the inside of the bulb. **1959** RIDER & USLAN *Encycl. Cathode-Ray Oscilloscopes* (ed. 2) i. 20/1 The beam..traverses the gap between the accelerator and post-accelerator areas. **1974** *Nature* 20 Sept. 262/1 In the postface (this must be one of the few nearly Latin words invented in the twentieth century!), Eugene Skolnikoff outlines the increasing involvement..of MIT in the field of science and public policy. **1877** SWINBURNE *Let.* 21 Apr. (1960) III. 326 To compare either with Shelley or Hugo for preference or postference, is purely absurd. **1922** E. KRUISINGA *Handbk. Present-Day Eng.* (ed. 3) II. i. 361 Nouns preceded by a definite article are not seldom used with a post-genitive. **1957** R. W. ZANDVOORT *Handbk. Eng. Gram.* II. ii. 105 The only case where an English genitive may be said to follow its headword is when it is the principal part of an *of*-adjunct to a preceding noun... The construction is known as the *post-genitive.* I gave him an old raincoat of my brother's. **1938** *Times* 4 Feb. 11/2 The post-heating process greatly improves an already satisfactory weld by allowing the metal at the weld to recover its original structure after the severe treatment given by the welding operation. **1966** C. R. TOTTLE *Sci. Engin. Materials* x. 224 Temperature gradients are reduced ..in welding by preheating the parent metal or post-heating immediately after welding. **1922** JOYCE *Ulysses* 663 The anticipated diamond jubilee of Queen Victoria ..and the posticipated opening of the new municipal fish market. **1938** S. BECKETT *Murphy* ix. 176 In the morning nothing remained of the dream but a postmonition of calamity. **1862** *Phil. Trans. R. Soc.* CLI. 312 Every matrix of the type $n \times n$ is equivalent (by post-multiplication) to one, and only one, of the reduced matrices included in the formula (62.). **1968** FOX & MAYERS *Computing Methods for Scientists & Engineers* v. 100 For the general eigenvalue problem we can perform virtually the same operation, though with post-multiplication included to preserve similarity. **1862** *Phil. Trans. R. Soc.* CLI. 312 These numbers will remain unchanged, when the given matrix is premultiplied by any unit-matrix, and post-multiplied by any matrix whatsoever. **1939** *Brit. Jrnl. Psychol.* XXIX. 302 After post-multiplying..by $\hat{e}'$ we get..[etc.]. **1978** *Nature* 20 Apr. 740/1 We are told, as though it were surprising, that pre- and post-multiplying a matrix by the matrix of its eigenvectors produces a diagonal matrix. **1965** *Jrnl. R. Microsc. Soc.* LXXXIV. 129 Sucrose was first used with formaldehyde in fixation for electron microscopy by Holt and Hicks.., who postosmicated the tissues that had been treated this way. **1971** *Nature* 2 Apr. 334/2 Random pieces of grossly normal thyroid tissue..were diced.., fixed in 1·5% glutaraldehyde.., post-osmicated, dehydrated and embedded in 'Araldite 502'. **1963** *Jrnl. Cell Biol.* XVII. 54/2 The final dense product could be easily referable to fine structure in sections of material embedded without postosmication. **1943** *Eng. Stud.* XXV. 103 The construction called by.. Curme 'double genitive', by Kruisinga 'post genitive', and, in the case of a pronoun (*a friend of mine*), 'post-possessive'. **1957** R. W. ZANDVOORT *Handbk. Eng. Gram.* III. ii. 140 The construction may be denoted as the post-possessive. a. I gave him an old raincoat of mine. He hated that pride of hers. b. It was no fault of theirs. **1936** KOLTHOFF & SANDELL *Textbk. Quantitative Inorg. Analysis* viii. 105 This second phase is therefore not coprecipitated but postprecipitated. **1939** A. I. VOGEL *Text-bk. Quantitative Inorg. Analysis* i. 148 Zinc sulphide is slowly post-precipitated. **1960** BELCHER & NUTTEN *Quantitative Inorg. Analysis* (ed. 2) x. 61 Examples of precipitates which tend to post-precipitate are zinc sulphide on mercury sulphide, and magnesium oxalate on calcium oxalate. **1932** I. M. KOLTHOFF in *Jrnl. Physical Chem.* XXXVI. 861 First of all, calcium oxalate precipitates and then on standing magnesium oxalate crystallizes out slowly. Therefore, we are not dealing here with a case of coprecipitation, but of post-precipitation, the crystals of calcium oxalate being not at all or only slightly contaminated by magnesium. **1963** G. SVEHLA tr. *Erdey's Gravimetric Analysis* I. iii. 183 Tin(IV) sulphide tends to carry down nickel, cobalt and iron ions from a hydrochloric acid containing solution by post-precipitation. **1977** *Sci. Amer.* June 9/2 (Advt.), With the HP 5420A, you can post-process measurement results using the four basic arithmetic functions. **1966** C. J. SIPPL *Computer Dict. & Handbk.* 278 The real-time system relieves the larger system of time consuming input and output functions as well as performing pre-processing and postprocessing functions, such as validity editing and formatting for print. **1967** *Economist* 12 Aug. 588/2 Molins, Ferranti and IBM have told the Ministry of Technology that they can jointly produce a post-processor for the Molins machine wi.hin twelve months flat. **1977** *Gloss. Terms Data Processing* (*B.S.I.*) VII. 2/1 *Postprocessor*, a computer program that effects some final computation or organization. **1976** *Broadcast* 12 Jan. 1/1 Bring in your film and we'll post-produce it on tape. *Ibid.* 1/2 Spend a day on post-production using time code computer editing. **1953** K. REISZ *Technique Film Editing* i. 49 A post-production break-down of the finished sequence. **1953** *Archit. Rev.* CXIII. 377/2 (*caption*) Auditorium spanned by post-stressed beams. **1965** *Language* XLI. 473 As many as five syllables occur prestressed, but only one syllable occurs post-stressed, except rarely when a postclitic follows a suffix. **1941** *Concrete & Constructional Engin.* XXXVI. 93/1 Dr. Abeles suggests stretching the hard steel wires after hardening and setting, which he calls 'post-stressing'. **1976** *Offshore Engineer* Mar. 26/3 The Kishorn structure departs from its smaller brothers by having a two-stage wall poststressing. The first stage will be stressed at the 15m high level, the remainder when the walls reach full height.

B. 1. a. With substantives, forming adjectives. *post-attack, -bop, -Christmas, -coition, -college, -contact, -crash, -creole, -election* (examples), *-experience, -flu, -game, -harvest, -holiday, -independence, -injury, -language, -lunch, -luncheon, -menopause* (also as *sb.*), *-midnight, -operation* (also as *adv.*), *-orgasm, -ovulation, -publication, -Reformation* (earlier and later examples), *-Renaissance, -revolution* (examples), *-school, -seizure, -Sputnik* (also as *adv.*), *-surrealist, -symbolist, -Watergate, -World War II.*

b. With adjs., or formed from *post* + a L. or Gr. sb. with an adjectival ending. *post-Aristotelian, -Cartesian* (further examples), *Chomskyan, -Darwinian* (examples), *-Hegelian, -Homeric* (earlier and later examples), *-Humian, -Jamesian, -Kantian* (earlier and later examples), *-Keynesian, -Marxist, -Nietzschean, -Saussurean, -Wagnerian; post-adolescent, -anæsthetic, -analytic(al), -atomic, -capitalist, -climacteric, -cognitive, -coital, -collegiate, -colonial, -conciliar, -conditional, -encephalitic, -epileptic* (earlier and later examples), *-eruptive, -experimental, -feudal, -industrial, -junctural, -marital, -menopausal, -orgasmic, -paroxysmal* (examples), *-pausal, -revolutionary* (later examples), *-romantic, -teenage*; adjs. formed as in senses 1 a and b above are occas. used *ellipt.* as *sbs.*; such adjs. may also have adverbial forms, as *post-coitally, -maritally.*

Also **postabo·rtal** *Med.*, occurring or performed after an abortion; **postabo·rtion** (also as *adv.*) *Med.*, (occurring or performed) after an abortion; **post-abo·rtum** (also as *adv.*) *Med.* [L. *abortus* abortion] = prec.; **post-abso·rptive** *Med.*, occurring after food has been absorbed into the body; **post-cenal** (further example); **post-co·nquest,** applied to periods after a conquest, *spec.* (with capital), after the Norman Conquest; **post-conque·stual, -Conquestual,** after the Norman Conquest; **post-consona·ntal, -consona·ntic,** after a consonant; hence **post-consona·ntally** *adv.*; **post-convu·lsive** *Path.*, subsequent to a convulsion; **postcy·clic, -ical,** occurring or operating after the termination of a cycle or cycles (esp. in *Transformational Gram.*); hence **postcy·clically** *adv.*; **post-defle·ction** *Electronics*, pertaining to or being acceleration of an electron beam after its deflection in a cathode-ray tube; **post-depositional** *Geol.*, occurring after the deposition of sediment; **post-eme·rgence,** occurring, performed, or applied after the emergence of seedlings from the soil; also *absol.*; **post-i·ctal** *Med.*, subsequent to a stroke or fit, esp. an epileptic fit; hence **post-i·ctally** *adv.*; **post-infe·ctious,** subsequent to an infection; *esp.* caused by an infection but arising after it has ceased; **post-lapsarian,** delete † *Obs.* and add: also *gen.*, after the Fall of Man; **postli·teral,** following a letter of the alphabet; **post-meio·tic** *Cytology*, occurring subsequent to meiosis; **post-mena·rchal, -mena·rcheal** *Med.*, of, pertaining to, or designating a girl who has menstruated; **post-metamo·rphic** *Geol.*, occurring or existing after metamorphism; **post-mi·neral,** occurring after the formation of a mineral deposit; **postneona·tal** *Med.*, pertaining to or designating the period between the end of the neonatal period, four weeks after birth, and the end of the first year of life; **post-no·minal,** following a substantive or a proper name; also *ellipt.* as *sb.*; **post-o·vulative, -ovula·tory** *Med.*, subsequent to ovulation; **post-pai·nterly** *Art* [cf. *PAINTERLY *a.*], of or characterized by a style of abstract painting that employs traditional qualities of colour, form, and texture; **post-pu·beral** = next; **post-pu·bertal,** subsequent to puberty; **post-pu·berty** *a.* = prec.; **postra·dical** *Philol.* following a root or root-word; also as *sb.*, a postradical element or word; **post-reprodu·ctive,** occurring after the period of life when a female can bear offspring; **post-tecto·nic** *Geol.*, occurring or existing after tectonic activity; **post-tonic** (further examples); **post-ve·rbal,** following a verb; hence **postve·rbally** *adv.*; **postvoca·lic** *Philol.*, following a vowel; hence **postvoca·lically** *adv.*

c. With sbs., forming sbs. *postcreation*; **post-a·rticle** *Gram.*, one of a set of words that can follow an article in a noun phrase; **post-climax** *Ecol.* [*CLIMAX *sb.* 4 b], the point in a plant succession at which development has continued beyond the balanced state of climax.

d. Adjs. of the type in sense B. 1 a above are sometimes used adverbially (cf. *POST *Latin prep.* 6), as *postabortion, -abortum, -operation, -Sputnik* above, *POSTFLIGHT *adv.*

1910 *Surg., Gynecol. & Obstetr.* July 55/1 Each case of post-partum or post-abortal infection must be studied individually. **1973** I. M. CUSHNER et al. in H. J. & J. D. Osofsky *Abortion Experience* vi. 147 This newer approach toward postabortal laparascopic sterilization..may very well lead to further reduction in the need for major surgical procedures in abortion. **1963** *Amer. Jrnl. Psychiatry* CXIX. 982/2 No known attempts to document statistically the incidence of post-abortion psychiatric illness have been found in American medical literature. **1973** E. C. PAYNE et al. in H. J. & J. D. Osofsky *Abortion Experience* xii. 272 In the first reported prospective study..a single postabortion interview took place during a period of 3 to 6 months after the procedure. In even more recent studies, women have been interviewed at a relatively specific time postabortion. **1910** F. J. TAUSSIG *Prevention & Treatm. Abortion* vi. 44 There was no fever or odor to the discharge, so that the diagnosis was clearly endometritis post-abortum due to decidual remnants. **1950** *Proc. Soc. Study Fertility* I. 26 (*heading*) The re-establishment of ovulation, post-partum and post-abortum. **1972** *Biol. Abstr.* LIII. 5727/2 The results of treatment of 2 groups of patients with post abortum acute insufficiency of the kidneys are discussed. **1919** *Proc. R. Soc.* B. XCI. 45 The energy expenditure during sleep may be assumed..to be only slightly smaller than that during complete muscular rest in the post-absorptive condition, *i.e.*, 12–14 hours after the last meal. **1972** *New England Jrnl. Med.* 5 Oct. 678/1 Recordings were made in the postabsorptive state between 9:30 a.m. and noon. **1936** *Jrnl. Pediatrics* VIII. 52 The change from the straight, boyish figure of the preadolescent girl to the more rounded, mature figure of the postadolescent girl. **1977** *New Yorker* 29 Aug. 19/2 The new false post-adolescent authority that needs to be blown away by somebody. **1910** *Practitioner* Feb. 253 The post-anaesthetic condition. *Ibid.* Mar. 361 Ether..rarely causes post-anaesthetic vomiting. **1965** J. POLLITT *Depression & its Treatm.* vi. 80 Patients should be carefully questioned about this to avoid the risk of post-anaesthetic vomiting. **1934** *Mind* XLIII. 136 [A sense of 'theory of knowledge'] is essentially a 'post-analytic' *evaluation*, not a description, of knowledge. **1927** J. LOEWEMBERG in *Jrnl. Philos.* XXIV. 5 Designating by 'pre-analytical', whatever is given *for* analysis, and by 'post-analytical', whatever is given *through* analysis, we wish to ascertain whether there is any possibility of assimilating to one another these two classes of data. **1934** WEBSTER, Post-Aristotelian. **1936** J. R. KANTOR *Objective Psychol. Gram.* viii. 100 The post-Aristotelian subjectivists divided the individual into soul and body. **1957** C. VEREKER *Devel. Polit. Theory* i. 40 This doctrine of equality, the emergence of which is sometimes held to be the distinguishing mark of post-Aristotelian social thought. **1965** N. CHOMSKY *Aspects of Theory of Syntax* ii. 107 Det→(pre-Article⌢*of*) Article (post-Article). **1971** Post-article [see *non-lexical* s.v. *NON- 3]. **1948** *Britannica Bk. of Year* (U.S.) 805/2 *Post-atom(ic)*, subsequent to the dropping of the atomic bomb. **1954** A. HUXLEY in *Encounter* Feb. 5/2 This..[temple] will be standing in the Western desert, an object, to the neo-Neolithic savages, of post-atomic times, of uncomprehending reverence and superstitious alarm. **1956** AUDEN & KALLMAN *Magic Flute* (1957) 58 The form of suite For piano in a Post-

Atomic Age. **1961** *Washington Post* 1 June 24 The speaker suggested that the desolation of a post-attack world would be too awful to face. **1964** Dentler & Cutright in I. L. Horowitz *New Sociol.* 424 Our discussion of the effects of a nuclear attack on the population makes it clear that the composition of the postattack population would be so different from that of today's population that this factor alone would make for differences in the postattack society. **1976** *Sci. Amer.* Nov. 33/3 In the immediate postattack period the fallout levels could vary greatly from one place to another. **1955** Keepnews & Grauer *Pict. Hist. Jazz* xix. 250 A young star who came along in the post-bop 1950s. **1977** *Rolling Stone* 5 May 24/2 Today his style is the antithesis of classic post-bop horn players like Coltrane. **1964** I. L. Horowitz *New Sociol.* 81 His critique of America could only be relevant and fruitful if it was made..with the projected hopes and ideals of a post-capitalist era. **1976** N. O'Sullivan *Conservatism* v. 122 The contemporary discussion about the nature of 'post-capitalist' (or 'post-industrial') society. **1931** *Times Lit. Suppl.* 10 Sept. 674/2 A particularly satisfying classification of the great seminal post-Cartesian theories of knowledge. **1963** *Ibid.* 1 Mar. 150/1 The general context of post-Cartesian thought. **1922** Joyce *Ulysses* 720 A temporary concussion caused by a falsely calculated movement in the course of a postcenal gymnastic display. **1970** *Jrnl. Linguistics* VI. 130 With a side glance at some post-Chomskyan developments. **1975** *Amer. Speech 1973* XLVIII. 154 According to the post-Chomskyan revisionist Charles J. Fillmore, however, 'there are reasons for questioning the deep-structure validity of the traditional division between subject and predicate'. **1959** *Encounter* Feb. 74/2 All these books are written with a light touch: just the thing for post-Christmas hang-overs. **1961** *Wall St. Jrnl.* 23 Jan. 2/2 Steel's post-Christmas production recovery is running out of steam. **1977** *Times* 21 Dec. 17/8 The post-Christmas clearance sale. **1897** A. D. L. Napier *Menopause* iv. 100 Of 500 post-climacteric cases, 36·5 per cent. had a return of hæmorrhage after the menopause had been established a year or more. **1973** E. A. Moscovic tr. *J. Botella-Llusiá's Endocrinol. of Woman* xvii. 364/2 The classic concept held that in postmenopausal woman estrogenic activity had been wiped out completely by the time woman entered the postclimacteric phase. **1916** F. E. Clements *Plant Succession* vi. 110 If a change of climate results in increased water-content..the sere..continues the development by replacing the climax and it may be termed the post-climax. **1928** *Jrnl. Ecol.* XVI. 26 Any well shaded ravine is occupied by *Picea albertiana* Stew. Br. which may be looked upon as a post-climax. **1964** V. J. Chapman *Coastal Vegetation* ix. 215 One must regard the Plantaginatum maritimi as either a post-climax or more properly as a..deflected climax. **1949** *Mind* LVIII. 220 A tendency to 'spatio-temporal scatter' is characteristic of paranormal cognition, the displacement manifesting itself as 'post-cognitive' or 'precognitive' telepathy. **1974** *Listener* 3 Jan. 22/3 If I make a 'correct' guess before the target has appeared..that's a pre-cognitive hit; if I get it right but several shots in arrears, that's post-cognitive. **1922** C. G. Child *Sterility & Conception* viii. 68 (*heading*) Postcoital tests for sterility. **1947** E. Hyams *William Medium* 34 Smoking a post-coital cigarette. **1975** B. Garfield *Hopscotch* ii. 26 'I'm distressed to see you so lackluster, old friend.' 'It's only post-coital *tristesse*.' **1968** M. R. Cohen in J. J. Gold *Textbk. Gynecol. Endocrinol.* xxv. 546 Ovulation timing..disclosed good mucorrhea at midcycle with excellent longevity of spermatozoa postcoitally. **1977** S. Schoenbaum *W. Shakespeare* (rev. ed.) vii. 85 A shotgun wedding boomed for the post-coitally chastened Will. **1953** N. Tinbergen *Herring Gull's World* xiii. 109 There is no post-coition display. **1893** 'Mark Twain' in *Century Mag.* Dec. 235/1 He..had finished a post-college course in an Eastern law school. **1973** *Jrnl. Genetic Psychol.* June 183 The relevance of undergraduate courses for meeting the demands of postcollege life. **1960** *Encounter* Nov. 26 A face-to-face group—the post-collegiate fraternity of the small suburbs. **1934** Webster, Post-colonial. **1959** *Daily Tel.* 12 Dec. 6/2 It was probably inevitable that India, in the full flush of post-colonial sensitivity, should fear that association with the America of that period might involve her unnecessarily in troubles which were little to do with Asia. **1969** *Times* (Uganda Suppl.) 15 Sept. p. i/5 Behind the imposing physical presence is a mind that has been described as one of the shrewdest in post-colonial Africa. **1974** 'G. Black' *Golden Cockatrice* iii. 57 If there's one thing worse than..rampant colonialism..it's post-colonial dictatorship. **1968** *Times* 24 Feb. 9/5 The post-conciliar attitude seems to draw attention..to the value of personal and social relationships. **1976** *Times* 9 Aug. 11/1 The post-conciliar church polishes characteristically pre-conciliar weapons. **1939** Joyce *Finnegans Wake* (1964) ii. 270 All them fine clauses in Lindley's and Murrey's never braught the participle of a present to a desponent hortatrixy,..from her postconditional future. **1922** E. Ekwall *Place-Names Lancs.* 1 The county of Lancaster developed out of the post-Conquest honour of Roger of Poitou. **1940** *Burlington Mag.* Aug. 56 Peruvian post-conquest tapestry work. **1959** E. A. Fisher *Introd. Anglo-Saxon Archit. & Sculpture* 94 Such post-Conquest Anglo-Saxon influence on art is outside the scope of this book. **1976** *Jrnl. Medieval Hist.* II. 1/1 The balance between French and English in post-Conquest England is still being discussed. **1920** *Contemp. Rev.* Dec. 898 The manuscript is post-conquestual. **1924** *Ibid.* Nov. 673 Welsh life in post-Conquestual days. **1934** Priebsch & Collinson *German Lang.* ii. i. 93 The position in the word (initial, post-consonantal, inter-vocalic). **1964** Y. Malkiel in *Archivum Linguisticum* XVI. 27 World-medial, postconsonantal *cl-*. **1953** K. Jackson *Lang. & Hist. Early Brit.* 470 (*heading*) IE. *gᵘ*. This became *b* in CC. initially except before *u*..; intervocally and preconsonantally, *g*; post-consonantally, *b*. **1969** *Word* XXV. 25 *Tana-dg-usim had-a-n* 'towards the village', *had-a-n* 'towards it or him,' the *-a-* being a postconsonantic variant of the post-vocalic *-*'. **1934** Webster, Post-contact adj. **1946** *Nature* 30 Nov. 769/2 Each article presents chronologically..the data available from earliest times onwards through four hundred years of contact with White civilization... post-contact change and the absorption of the tribes into European civilization are revealed and traced in as much detail as possible. **1907** W. A. Turner *Epilepsy* vi. 129 A third epileptic, whose post-convulsive symptoms were mainly of the nature of cataleptic rigidity and dementia. **1974** E. Niedermeyer *Compendium of Epilepsies* xi. 187 A post-convulsive sleep may ensue for a few hours. **1966** *Economist* 24 Dec. 1329/3 An effort to prevent post-crash injuries by fire. **1977** *Hongkong Standard* 12 Apr. 9/3 The prevention and control of both in-flight and postcrash fuel system fires and explosions. **1922** Joyce *Ulysses* 385 In woman's womb word is made flesh but in the spirit of the maker all flesh that passes becomes the word that shall not pass away. This is the postcreation. **1968** D. Decamp in *Lat. Amer. Research Rev.* III. 38 If any term is needed to distinguish the situation in Jamaica from that in Surinam and Haiti, then I suggest that we call Jamaica a *post-creole* community. **1977** *Language* LIII. 330 Speakers in a post-creole community are triply pressured: to avoid the basilect, to acquire the acrolect, and to vary the mesolect. **1967** J. Ross in *To Honor Roman Jakobson* III. 1672 If it cannot apply before the cycle, it must either apply in the cycle or after all cyclic rules have been applied—rules of this last type are called *post-cyclic*. *Ibid.* 1677 It is only if *pronominalization* is formulated as a post-cyclic rule that some constraint on forward pronominalization becomes necessary. **1971** J. W. Bresnan in *Language* XLVII. 276 One might think of ordering the NSR after the entire transformational cycle but before the postcyclic transformations. **1976** *Archivum Linguisticum* VII. 138 This obviously, would call for..an explicit formulation of the concept of 'transformation' one uses, that is whether one believes in prelexical, cyclic, precyclic, and postcyclic transformations. **1972** *Language* XLVIII. 310 Primary stress assignment must *precede* postcyclical transformations. **1972** *Ibid.* 301 It is preferable for a rule to apply postcyclically rather than cyclically. **1899** T. Veblen *Theory of Leisure Class* xi. 288 The ostensibly post-Darwinian concept of a meliorative trend in the process of evolution. **1939** *Mind* XLVIII. 528 In continuity with his previous books, Dewey is anxious to be a post-Darwinian Mill developing 'the science of evidence' in close connection with all the sciences. **1972** S. Hynes *Edwardian Occasions* 7 Much important Edwardian literature implies..a post-Darwinian, post-Hegelian way of looking at the linear shape of time. **1943** F. E. Terman *Radio Engineers' Handbk.* iv. 342 In the post-deflection arrangement the beam is deflected at low velocity. **1950** *Electronic Engin.* XXII. 461/1 Two main advantages..in the use of commercially available post deflexion accelerator (P.D.A.) cathode-ray tubes..are: (i) The attainment of higher screen brightness..and (ii) The problem of insulation in the glass pinch and the base are eased. **1959** Rider & Uslan *Encycl. Cathode-Ray Oscilloscopes* (ed. 2) i. 18/1 These post-deflection accelerating anodes are rings or wide bands of electrically conductive material painted on the inside surface of the envelope. **1971** Klemperer & Barnett *Electron Optics* (ed. 3) x. 398 Post-deflexion acceleration..appears to offer the means to increase the sensitivity. **1949** F. J. Pettijohn *Sedimentary Rocks* i. 7 Diastrophism plays the dominant role in controlling the production and deposition of a sediment—and to some extent its post-depositional history, also. **1965** G. J. Williams *Econ. Geol. N.Z.* xiii. 206/2 Post-depositional alteration is indicated by large chlorite plates that are discordant in relation to the foliation in schist pebbles. **1962** 'K. Orvis' *Damned & Destroyed* i. 9 His opinion would be the first post-election one I would hear. **1976** *New Yorker* 15 Nov. 204/2 Post-election surveys show that almost ninety per cent of the Republicans who voted backed the ticket. **1940** *Phytopathology* XXX. 334 Experience over a period of years with various chemical methods of damping-off control has emphasized the need for some soil disinfectant that will control both pre- and post-emergence damping-off. **1955** *Sci. News Let.* 2 July 10/3 There are three prescribed methods for fighting the weed war. They are known as pre-planting, pre-emergence and post-emergence. Pre-planting treatment is made on the soil before any seed is planted in the ground. Pre-emergence control is done after seeds have been sown, but before a desired plant pushes up through the ground. Post-emergence is designed to kill undesirable plants that exist in areas where plants are already growing. **1962** *Times* 12 Nov. 17/4 Another avenue of research which is leading to useful results is that involving pre-emergence spraying of cereal crops instead of the traditional post-emergence method. **1977** *Protecting World's Crops* (Shell Internat. Petroleum Co.) 8 Crop herbicides are often divided into pre-plant, pre-emergence and post-emergence products. **1928** E. F. Buzzard in H. French *Index Differential Diagnosis Main Symptoms* (ed. 4) 880 The tremor in post-encephalitic Parkinsonism closely resembles that of paralysis agitans. **1932** W. Boyd *Textbk. Path.* xxx. 812 Other postencephalitic conditions ..are narcolepsy and oculogyric crises. **1961** *Lancet* 23 Sept. 683/2 Since then, she has had postencephalitic epilepsy. **1971** G. W. Voeller in G. Birdwood et al. *Parkinson's Dis.* iii. 50 Fifteen years ago the post-encephalitic forms [of Parkinsonism] were predominant.., today, the idiopathic or arteriosclerotic forms predominate. **1875** J. H. Jackson in *W. Riding Lunatic Asylum Med. Rep.* V. 111 The automatism in these cases is not, I think, ever epileptic, but always post-epileptic. **1954** L. Fairfield *Epilepsy* i. 13 In some cases the post-epileptic deep sleep or 'coma', lasts an hour or more. **1936** *Discovery* May 148 (*heading*) Post-eruptive movements of the earth's crust. **1946** *Nature* 19 Oct. 560/1 Some powerful beneficial influence had been at work during the post-eruptive as well as the developmental period. **1964** *Economist* 31 Oct. 502/1 The needs of the 'post-experience' students and..immediate postgraduates. **1977** P. Strevens *New Orientations Teaching Eng.* viii. 90 In all types of occupational ESP a distinction emerges between *pre-experience* and *post-experience* courses. **1970** *Jrnl. Gen. Psychol.* Apr. 253 All Ss were asked in a post-experimental questionnaire to indicate the two words they thought earned them points. **1949** Koestler *Promise & Fulfilment* i. iii. 29 We are always apt to forget that nationalism is a product of a relatively recent, post-feudal European development. **1970** R. Stavenhagen in I. L. Horowitz *Masses in Lat. Amer.* vii. 267 The Spanish Conquest was..part of the political and economic expansion in post-feudal and mercantalistic Europe. **1918** A. Huxley *Let.* 25 Nov. (1969) 171 The whiskey bottle seems the only refuge from that post-flu depression. **1971** P. D. James *Shroud for Nightingale* v. 163 She had post-flu depression and she felt she couldn't cope with the baby. **1966** *Jrnl. Canad. Operational Res. Soc.* 114 *Analysis, post game*, use of data generated during a *game* or series of games to derive conclusions about the problems to which play was directed. **1976** *Springfield* (Mass.) *Daily News* 22 Apr. 39/1 When his club gets beaten 7–1 he is a post game press conference no-show. **1962** *Times* 20 Mar. 3/2 The study of post-harvest physiological changes in pasture plants. **1976** *National Observer* (U.S.) 25 Dec. 1/4 Last week the FAO council called for 'prompt action..on reducing post-harvest losses'. **1909** W. James *Pluralistic Universe* v. 184 Royce makes by far the manliest of the post-hegelian attempts to read some empirically apprehensible content into the notion of our relation to the absolute mind. **1964** P. Meadows in I. L. Horowitz *New Sociol.* 446 The Hegelians and the post-Hegelians (of either idealistic or materialistic breed). **1972** Post-Hegelian [see ***post-Darwinian**]. **1960** *Farmer & Stockbreeder* 5 Jan. 16/1 A post-holiday lull prevailed at most markets. **1976** H. Ferguson *Confessions Long Distance Acid Head* 52 Gordon..had brought back the usual amount of cigarettes and liquor, and another rare gift—the post-holiday feeling of exuberance. **1810** C. Lamb *Lett.* (1935) II. 97, I should suspect these personifications are the Translator's. They sound *post*-Homeric. **1959** *Encounter* July 46/1 This is the element of allegory or symbolism which so many post-homeric writers have found in the Lotus Eaters. **1909** W. James *Pluralistic Universe* v. 210 This being our post-humian and post-kantian state of mind, I will ask your permission to leave the soul wholly out of the present discussion. **1961** *Encounter* Jan. 16 The Humian and post-Humian side. **1941** Penfield & Erickson *Epilepsy & Cerebral Localization* (1942) ii. 19 The state in which an individual is deprived of, or released from conscious control, is called automatism. If it occurs following a seizure it may be called post-ictal automatism. **1961** *Lancet* 29 July 242/2, 36 hours later.. the E.E.G. showed no seizure activity, but there was general post-ictal disorganisation. **1972** M. Crichton *Terminal Man* iv. xi. 186 He's in a post-seizure state—post-ictal, we call it. **1959** *Brain* LXXXII. 152 Post-ictally the activity of the focus was very much reduced. **1975** *Electroencephalogr. & Clin. Neurophysiol.* XXXVIII. 601/2 Motor activity was observed to increase postictally concomitantly with the increase in EEG frequency and amplitude. **1961** *Middle East Jrnl.* Winter 3 The people were still experiencing post-independence let-down and suffering the after effects of poor harvests in 1957. **1976** *Times Lit. Suppl.* 13 Feb. 164/2 The post-independence state is even more centralized than the colonial one. **1947** *Partisan Rev.* XIV. 230 Industrial organization and the postindustrial state are here to stay. **1977** *Times* 21 Feb. 11/4 We are already laying the foundation for the post-industrial future. **1928** *Trans. Chicago Path. Soc.* XIII. 15 (*heading*) The pathology of post-infectious acute toxic encephalitis in children. **1946** A. B. Christie *Infectious Dis.* xiii. 108 Encephalitis of the so-called post-infectious type occasionally occurs after chicken-pox. **1974** S. L. Robbins *Path. Basis Dis.* xxxii. 1532/1 Injection of brain tissue and adjuvants..can set up a reaction in the central nervous system of experimental animals, which has a marked resemblance to post-infectious encephalomyelitis. **1951** Postinjury [see ***Kümmell's disease**]. **1976** *National Observer* (U.S.) 3 July 12/6 Whenever you injure a joint..there is a possibility of a permanent residual stiffness or postinjury arthritis. **1960** J. Bayley *Characters of Love* iv. 258 Both D. H. Lawrence and E. M. Forster use them [*sc.* symbolic patterns] in a discernibly post-Jamesian manner. **1959** E. P. Hamp in *Studia Linguistica* XIII. 34 Those post-junctural syllabics which did not themselves bear a primary. **1964** *Eng. Stud.* XLV. 385 Postjunctural pre-vocalic /ʃ/ began to be distributionally a spirant. **1843** Mill *Logic* I. i. iii. 79 His philosophical views are generally those of the post-Kantian movement, represented by Schelling and Hegel. **1946** *Nature* 7 Sept. 322/2 James Marsh..did much to acclimatize Kantian and post-Kantian philosophy in the United States. **1977** L. Houlden in J. Hick *Myth of God Incarnate* vi. 128 There is a strong element of post-Kantian consciousness in distinguishing the two approaches at all. **1960** *New Left Rev.* May–June 5/1 The more sophisticated elaboration of post-Keynesian evolutionary theory. **1975** *Times Lit. Suppl.* 18 July 811/3 Post-Keynesians who instinctively treat saving and investment as different activities. **1977** *Dædalus* Fall 61 Post-Keynesian and econometric studies in economics. **1946** C. Morris *Signs, Lang. & Behavior* ii. 47 The latter [*sc.* proprioceptive stimuli] are..not themselves language signs; since they are substitute signs synonymous with language signs they are properly called post-language symbols. **1950** *Eng. Stud.* XXXI. 63 What would the corrupt post-lapsarian variety of this attitude be? **1972** *Times Lit. Suppl.* 29 Dec. 1587/2 A prelude..to the deplorable history of postlapsarian man. **1953** *Archivum Linguisticum* V. 68 He [*sc.* Marr] indicates..labialization with a postliteral circle. **1958** J. Berry in J. A. Fishman *Readings Sociol. of Lang.* (1968) 742 Diacritically modified letters (i.e. 'simple' letters with e.g...postliteral circle or apostrophe). **1974** E. Ambler *Dr. Frigo* iii. 186 Saw patient while he was taking his post-lunch bed rest. **1959** N. Marsh *False Scent* (1960) ii. 59 A long gloomy post-luncheon talk. **1903** R. Whiteing *Let.* 9 Feb. in D. L. Moore *E. Nesbit* (1933) xi. 177 The love scenes, for such they are..though they are post marital. **1957** V. W. Turner *Schism & Continuity in Afr. Society* p. xviii, 'Uxorilocal' refers to the post-marital residence of a man in his wife's village. **1975** R. H. Rimmer *Premar Experiments* i. 111 They aren't fully aware of the impact that freer and open sexuality, premaritally and postmaritally, will have on human goals and values. **1949** G. B. Shaw *Buoyant Billions* i. 17 In your time the young were post-Marxists and their fathers pre-Marxists. **1963** M. H. Abrams in N. Frye *Romanticism Reconsidered* 29 It may be useful, then, to have a new look at the obvious as it appeared, not to post-Marxist historians, but to intelligent observers at the time. **1978** *Bull. Amer. Acad. Arts & Sci.* Jan. 35 He considers himself post-Risorgimento, post-Marxist. **1905** *Q. Jrnl. Microsc. Sci.* XLVIII. 490 In animals there are (normally) no post-maiotic divisions, whereas in plants there may be, and often are, a large number. **1905** [see *pre-meiotic* s.v. *PRE- B. 1]. **1934** L. W. Sharp *Introd. Cytol.* (ed. 3) xvi. 265 In certain cases evidence has been brought forward to show that the chromonema in each chromatid at the close of the second meiotic mitosis is already split 'in preparation for' the first postmeiotic division. **1973** *Genetical Res.* XXII. 285 A characteristic feature of recombination in *Sordaria brevicollis* is the relatively high proportion of recombination events which exhibit post-meiotic segregation. **1968** N. Vorys et al. in J. J. Gold *Gynecol. Endocrinol.* xi. 253 Postmenarchal ovarian hypersensitivity may cause short proliferative phases. **1937** Post-menarcheal [see *premenarcheal* s.v. *PRE- B. 1]. **1977** *Yearbk. Obstetr. & Gynecol.* 332 Their mean chronological age was 13·02 years and 11 were postmenarcheal. **1928** E. Novak in *Gynecol. & Obstetr. Monogr.: Cumul. Suppl. & Composite Index* 32 (*heading*) Postmenopausal bleeding with ovarian cancer. **1949** M. Mead *Male & Female* viii. 180 In Bali..the post-menopausal woman and the virgin girl work together at ceremonies from which women of child-bearing age are debarred. **1975** *Lancet* 5 July 7/2, 11 women were postmenopausal (by at least three years); their ages ranged from forty-eight to sixty-five years of age. **1925** *Practitioner* July 43 Post-menopause vulvitis is thus set up. **1975** *Acta Endocrinologica* LXXX. 262 Levels of plasma PRL rose with puberty and decreased during post-menopause and in elderly men. **1956** *Q. Jrnl. Geol. Soc.* CXII. 115 The gneiss..is transected by the Boyne Line.., and all the rocks appear to have suffered a certain amount of post-metamorphic shearing. **1965** G. J. Williams *Econ. Geol. N.Z.* vi. 66/1 Grindley (1963) noted that post-metamorphic folding in southern Westland was accompanied by axial-plane cleavage on mesoscopic shear folds. **1943** L. B. Lyon *Evening in Stepney* 18 Post-midnight hours, be born of costlier reverence. **1970** I. Petite *Meander to Alaska* ii. xi. 108 A ride..ending with a postmidnight ride back on a bicycle. **1907** *Technical Lit.* Sept. 189/1 It is important to look for evidence of recent or post-mineral faulting that may be connected with the secondary enrichment of the deposits. **1965** G. J. Williams *Econ. Geol. N.Z.* iii. 26/1 From the descriptions which are available the pattern of pre- and post-mineral faulting cannot be resolved in detail. **1958** *Jrnl. Amer. Med. Assoc.* 21 June 937/2 Infant deaths..may be divided into two groups—deaths of infants in the neonatal period (under 28 days) and those in the postneonatal period (28 days to one year). **1965** S. Peller in Glass & Eversley *Population in Hist.* V. 93 The difference between the rates for the ruling families and for the general population..was larger during the post-neonatal period of infancy than in the neo- or peri-natal period. **1973** Puffer & Serrano *Patterns of Mortality in Childhood* v. 76 The infant period is divided into neonatal (0–27 days of age) and postneonatal (28 days through 11 months). **1928** A. Huxley in *Vogue* 28 Nov. 122/3 A form which the critical intelligence of post-Nietzschean youth can respect. **1977** *N.Y. Rev. Bks.* 15 Sept. 41/1 To the post-Nietzschean Bloom, these are the essential qualities of human life under the shadow of belatedness. **1935** H. Straumann *Newspaper Headlines* ii. 51 As the word preceding it is a nominal, this position may more exactly be called *postnominal position*. **1952** *R.A.F. Rev.* Jan. 9/2 The use of the post-nominal letters 'T.D.' is peculiar to the Territorial Army. **1961** *Amer. Speech* XXXVI. 159 Finally certain postnominal modifiers, such as relative clauses. **1975** *Daily Tel.* (Colour Suppl.) 3 Jan. 11/3 In the higher ranks of the Forces and the Civil Service the appropriate title, or post-nominal letters, almost automatically follow appointment to a senior post. **1978** E. St. Johnston *One Policeman's Story* xii. 287 The third problem affecting Honours..was the right of any officer holding the Queen's Police Medal to put the initials, QPM, after his name. This is technically known as wearing 'post-nominals'. **1969** E. H. Pinto *Treen* 17 Operation Pegs... They are still used for plugging post-operation tubes. **1979** *Nature* 25 Jan. 327/3 The nodules were found in all rats by 6 months post-operation. **1973** S. Fisher *Female Orgasm* vii. 190 The judgments typically portrayed the orgasm and post-orgasm experience as having favorable..connotations. **1953** A. C. Kinsey et al. *Sexual Behav. Human Female* xv. 638 Sometimes, especially in youth, the post-orgasmic relaxation is hardly more than momentary. **1973** S. Fisher *Female Orgasm* ix. 290 How relaxed she feels during the postorgasmic state. **1923** *Amer. Jrnl. Physiol.* LXVI. 325 When a bird is killed for such post-ovulation stages care must be taken that a new ovulation stage is not initiated in the meantime. **1951** *Jrnl. Clin. Endocrinol.* XI. 937 Administration of chorionic gonadotropin was begun early in the postovulation period. **1933** *Amer. Jrnl. Anat.* LII. 610 The existence of a double uterine cycle explains the occasional appearance of intermenstrual post-ovulative bleedings. **1968** M. R. Cohen in J. J. Gold *Textbk. Gynecol. Endocrinol.* xxv. 543 During the postovulative phase. **1922** H. M. Evans in L. F. Barker et al. *Endocrinol. & Metabolism* II. vi. 581 In the postovulatory period it is the corpora lutea which are responsible for further marked changes which now regularly occur in the genitalia of some other mammals. **1975** *Biol. Reproduction* XII. 573 The cervical epithelium of postovulatory rabbits consists of ciliated cells and nonciliated cells with bulbous apical processes. **1965** *N.Y. Times Mag.* 21 Feb. 12/2 Post-painterly or 'hard-edge' abstraction cleaned up the gooey mess and substituted neatly defined geometrical shapes in chaste combinations. **1969** *New Yorker* 6 Dec. 184 At the Metropolitan, the largest displays are by so-called object-makers—'post-painterly' canvases; that is to say, smooth-surfaced, cool, and tending to blend with their setting. **1972** E. Lucie-Smith in Cox & Dyson *20th-Cent. Mind* III. xvi. 473 The man who formed a link between Abstract Expressionism and what came to be called 'post-painterly abstraction' was Morris Louis (1912–62). **1977** P. Johnson *Enemies of Society* xvi. 218 Morris Louis, by his own description a 'post-painterly abstractionist', simply painted streaks on the edge of the canvas, leaving the rest untouched. **1876** J. H. Jackson in *W. Riding Lunatic Asylum Med. Rep.* VI. 266 The temporary state of the patient immediately after the paroxysm—which will be called the post-paroxysmal condition. **1967** *Biol. Abstr.* XLVIII. 7986/2 (*heading*) Character of the clinical progress of adolescent rheumatism in post-paroxysmal period. **1966** W. S. Allen in C. E. Bazell *In Memory of J. R. Firth* 11 This difficulty could be met only by assuming that, except in post-pausal position, a high tone required a lower pitch to precede it. **1968** A. F. Fraser *Reproductive Behaviour in Ungulates* v. 75 A group of bulls which were in their first post-puberal year. **1886** *Buck's Handbk. Med. Sci.* III. 396/2 The post-pubertal falling off in growth is more rapid in girls than in boys. **1955** *New Biol.* XVIII. 32 It is possible that the post-pubertal mammal behaves like an insect imago.., and that the fundamental change which leads to eventual senescence has already taken place at puberty. **1978** *Homes and Gardens* Oct. 117/2 There are some effects of the pill which we know... Some girls suffer from post-pubertal amenorrhœa and do not conceive easily afterwards. **1943** Koestler in *Horizon* VII. 230 But that was still in his early period, a hang-over from adolescence, the nihilistic post-puberty pose. **1964** E. A. Nida *Toward Sci. Transl.* xi. 251 Incorporating postpublication corrections into subsequent printings. **1946** L. Bloomfield in H. Hoijer et al. *Ling. Struct. Native Amer.* 121 Some roots appear in *postradical* extensions... Most postradicals..have no clear meaning. **1958** *Archivum Linguisticum* X. 170 In some words Postradical..elements are recognized. **1850** *Dublin Rev.* Mar. 145 The elucidation of the post-reformation history of Ireland. **1964** P. F. Anson *Bishops at Large* i. 31 The post-Reformation *Ecclesia Anglicana.* **1978** R. Strong *And when did you last see your Father?* 153/2 The rise of the gentry and the establishment of a new post-Reformation aristocracy. **1941** *Listener* 19 June 882/2 The literature of post-Renaissance Europe. **1964** R. H. Robins *Gen. Linguistics* viii. 315 The post-Renaissance process of creating learned vocabulary from classical sources. **1978** D. Daiches *Edinburgh* ii. 43 The College..was from the beginning a post-Renaissance, post-Reformation university. **1900** *Q. Jrnl. Microsc. Sci.* XLIV. 3 Reproductive Period.—I have used this expression to denote the whole of that period in the life of a mammal.. during which its generative organs are capable of the reproductive function; and in contrast to the Pre-reproductive and Post-reproductive periods which severally precede and follow it, during which the generative organs are either not fully developed or are degenerative. **1963** *Lancet* 5 Jan. 2/1 As we reach the postreproductive years, a man's chance of dying is much greater than a woman's..so that at 60 a man has almost twice the likelihood of dying before 61 than a woman has. **1928** *Manch. Guardian Weekly* 7 Sept. 73/4 The Duce's personal implication in numerous ugly stories of the post-Revolution period. **1957** *Times Lit. Suppl.* 25 Oct. 685/3 Apart from a single passing reference to Zinoviev and Kamenev, Lenin, Trotsky, Stalin, Beria and Kruschev seem to be the only Bolsheviks named in the post-revolution chapters. **1938** *Burlington Mag.* June 270/1 Ducreux' post-Revolutionary studio. **1966** F. Schurmann *Ideol. & Organization in Communist China* p. xxxiii, Political centralization is one of the forms that post-revolutionary organization has taken. **1970** S. L. Barraclough in I. L. Horowitz *Masses in Lat. Amer.* iv. 155 Where land reform has been rapid..as was the case in post-revolutionary Mexico and Bolivia—some lines of production temporarily decreased. **1943** Y. Winters *Anatomy of Nonsense* 19 The method of the Post-Romantics, whether French Symbolists or American Experimentalists. **1947** A. Einstein *Mus. Romantic Era* xvii. 330 The post-Romantic period, when these musicians can be classified roughly according to their training in Germany or in Paris. **1965** *Times Lit. Suppl.* 25 Nov. 1063/2 Most readers..in this post-romantic age. **1949** Post-Saussurean [see *POST-BLOOMFIELDIAN *a.* and *sb.*]. **1977** *Language* LIII. 394 Each of these topics is divided in turn into three parts..the last one to post-Saussurean developments. **1934** Webster, Postschool. **1939** H. M. Miner *St. Denis* ix. 193 The young school child wants to have cards, ice skates, and a bicycle, because these amusements are those of postschool children. **1968** *Economist* 17 Aug. 17/2 The trendy thing for the past ten years has been to work on post-school education. **1975** *Language for Life* (Dept. Educ. & Sci.) xix. 278 Some schools do successfully guide their pupils to post-school opportunities. **1959** *Brain* LXXXII. 181 During the stage of post-seizure cortical hypoxia with flattening of the EEG loud sounds failed to produce spike responses in the strychninized animal. **1957** *N.Y. Herald Tribune* 25 Nov. 19/1 There is no doubt that post-Sputnik Washington is a different city and a different atmosphere. *Ibid.* 3 Dec. 24/1 He [*sc.* R. M. Nixon] has defeated the pinch-penny economizers, who, even post-Sputnik, are still in the..mood of providing too-little, too-late. **1977** *Dædalus* Fall 80 Many of the post-Sputnik educational programs were in fact based on this conclusion. **1938** Post-surrealist [see *muck-pot* s.v. *MUCK *sb.*[1] 5]. **1951** N. Rorem *Paris Diary* (1967) i. 7 She encouraged gaudy and exhibitionistic comportment..to give herself an identity with the post-surrealist gang she hung out with. **1952** Koestler *Arrow in Blue* xxiv. 224 But none of the existentialists, post-surrealists..had the guts to speak his opinion. **1953** S. Spender *Creative Element* i. 22 Writers on the Symbolists and Post-Symbolists.. note the tendency of a creative impulse which begins with a religious intensity. **1955** D. Davie in C. Tomlinson *Necklace* 1 Charles Tomlinson has taken note of the experiments and achievements of French symbolism. This does not mean that he belongs to the post-symbolist 'school' or the post-symbolist 'movement', if there are such things. **1958** J. Press *Chequer'd Shade* viii. 183 Whether the systematic employment of post-symbolist technique has weakened or strengthened poetry is likely to remain a matter of dispute. **1977** *Radio Times* 29 Oct.–4 Nov. 13/4 Nerval's sonnet sequences, *Les Chimères*..is now recognised as the source of all post-Symbolist and Surrealist poetry. **1938** *Mem. Geol. Soc. Amer.* No. 6. 108 The crystallization in such fabrics can be termed: pretectonic, posttectonic, or paratectonic with reference to the particular mineral that is under consideration. **1956** *Q. Jrnl. Geol. Soc.* CXII. 125 The well-known post-tectonic growth of andalusite in the eastern zone may have been accompanied by recrystallization which destroyed any incipient fabric. **1971** I. G. Gass et al. *Understanding Earth* xx. 296/1 These granites..are both syntectonic and post-tectonic. **1973** M. Amis *Rachel Papers* 22 Firstly, I assume I'm right in saying that teenage sex is quite different from post-teenage sex? **1976** *Sounds* 11 Dec. 40/2 Personally, I was in the throes of extreme post-teenage depression at the total unadventurousness of yer average British audience. **1953** K. Jackson *Lang. & Hist. Early Brit.* ii. 268 Syncope of the post-tonic penultimate syllable. **1973** A. H. Sommerstein *Sound Pattern Anc. Greek* v. 123 Post-tonic vowels (not just svarita vowels, but all vowels at any distance to the right of the accent in a word). **1934** Webster, Post-verbal. **1948** [see *COMPLEMENTATION]. **1965** N. Chomsky *Aspects of Theory of Syntax* 228 A somewhat different analysis of post-Verbal Adjectives in English. **1978** *Language* LIV. 85 The most unmarked order of adverbs in English is generally considered to be manner, place, and time in post-verbal position. **1971** *Ibid.* XLVII. 532 The principle involved is that the experiencer in certain types of sentences cannot be extracted if the complement sentence ends up postverbally. **1892** J. Wright *Primer Gothic Lang.* i. 10 Final postvocalic *g* and *g* in the final combination *gs* was probably a voiceless spirant. **1976** *Archivum Linguisticum* VII. 94 Icelandic words of the type *epli* being equivalent to those of the form *lappa* in having the quantitative peak on the post-vocalic consonant. **1964** R. H. Robins *Gen. Linguistics* iii. 101 In Scots English, /r/ occurs both prevocalically and postvocalically (*cart*, standard /ka:t/, Scots /kart/). **1895** G. B. Shaw in *Liberty* (N.Y.) 27 July 3/1 A post-Wagnerian reaction. **1965** *New Statesman* 7 May 736/1 The technical mêlée of.. early Renaissance polyphony and sensuous post-Wagnerian harmony. **1977** *Time* 14 Mar. 26/1 The post-Watergate Congress is in trouble with its constituents. **1978** *N.Y. Times* 30 Mar. B 5/1 Governor Carey's executive order and the city law were issued at a time of post-Watergate morality. **1957** K. Rexroth in *New World Writing* XI. 32 Many of the post-World War II abstract expressionists..look alike, and do look like accidents. **1970** I. L. Horowitz *Masses in Lat. Amer.* i. 5 This definition..strangely enough became the chief ideological tool of post-World War Two 'neo-Marxism'. **1979** *Dædalus* Winter 119 The successive discard, in the post-World War II world, of the totalitarian scheme.

2. In adjs. (rarely sbs.), chiefly *Anat.* and *Zool.* **post-alveo·lar,** behind the teeth-ridge; in *Phonetics* applied to a consonant articulated with the tongue against the back part of the alveolar ridge; **post-auri·cular,** behind the ear; **post-central** (further examples); hence **post-ce·ntrally** *adv.*; **postcra·nial,** situated posterior to the cranium; also as *sb. pl.*, the postcranial remains of an animal; hence **postcra·nially** *adv.*; **post-cri·coid,** posterior to the cricoid cartilage; **post-dental** (earlier and later examples); also as *sb.*; **post-humeral** (examples); **postpalatal,** also in *Phonetics,* applied to a consonant articulated with the tip or middle of the tongue against the hard palate; also *ellipt.* as *sb.*; **post-ve·lar,** behind or at the back of the velum; in *Phonetics,* applied to a consonant articulated with the tongue against the rear half of the velum or soft palate; also *ellipt.* as *sb.*

1932 D. Jones *Outl. Eng. Phonetics* (ed. 3) ix. 44 Post-alveolar: articulated by the tip of the tongue against the back part of the teeth-ridge. **1964** I. Dahl in D. Abercrombie et al. *Daniel Jones* 314 [c, ɟ] are post-alveolar. **1973** *Amer. Speech 1969* XLIV. 265 Heavy retroflexion is understood to be an *r* produced by passing the breath between the underside of the apex of the tongue and the postalveolar or prepalatal region. **1903** *Ann. & Mag. Nat. Hist.* XII. 342 *Mus hypoxanthus bacchante*... Fine hairs of ears rufous; no postauricular patch. **1934** F. Stark *Valleys of Assassins* ii. 193 The post-auricular length..is about one-third of the total length. **1977** *Proc. R. Soc. Med.* LXX. 399/1 Smaller defects in the centre of the face are therefore sometimes repaired with free grafts of full-thickness postauricular skin. **1959** Schvell & Jenkins in Saporta & Bastian *Psycholinguistics* (1961) 428/2 *Verbal aphasia,* resulting from lesions of the pre- and post-central convolutions. **1967** G. M. Wyburn et al. *Conc. Anat.* vii. 193 It..separates the precentral gyrus from the postcentral gyrus. **1968** *Brit. Med. Bull.* XXIV. 202/1 A normally responsive alpha rhythm at 7–8 cyc./sec. is present postcentrally, with slightly higher voltage on the right side. **1913** *Bull. Amer. Museum Nat. Hist.* XXXII. 563 The post-cranial skeleton. **1956** *Biologia* II. 231 The skull of the common lizard..has been described in detail previously... The present paper deals with its postcranial skeleton, i.e., the vertebral column, ribs, sternum, girdles and limbs. **1971** *Nature* 5 Feb. 407/2 It has been thought for some time that Miocene hominoids differed post-cranially from living hominoids, resembling instead the cercopithecoid monkeys. But careful examination of the post-cranials of *Limnopithecus*..and the European fossil *Pliopithecus* indicates that such non-hominoid structural features as they have are ceboid-like rather than specifically cercopithecoid-like. **1978** *Sci. Amer.* July 105/1 Anatomical studies..relating respectively to the birds' postcranial skeleton and their skull. **1971** Cappell & Anderson *Muir's Textbk. Path.* (ed. 9) xviii. 485/1 There is also the relationship between the iron-deficiency anaemia..and post-cricoid carcinoma in women. **1971** *Brit. Med. Bull.* XXVII. 34/1 Difficulty in swallowing is associated with a post-cricoid web of mucous membrane. **1899** W. Rippmann tr. *Viëtor's Elements of Phonetics* 77 As a rule the English sounds [in *thou, thin* etc.] are *postdental*, the narrowing being between the tongue point (with apical articulation) and the back of the front upper teeth. **1933**

[see *DOMAL *a.* 3]. **1933** BLOOMFIELD *Language* vi. 102 French speaks its [n] in postdental position. **1961** L. F. BROSNAHAN *Sounds of Language* vi. 138 The order of appearance of consonants is generally from back to front, in the order: glottal, velar, post-dental, palatal, labial, and labio-dental. **1906** J. B. SMITH *Explanation Terms Entomol.* 106 Post-humeral bristles: in *Diptera*, are usually two. **1961** Post-humeral [see *ACROSTICHAL *a.* 2]. **1899** W. RIPPMANN tr. *Viëtor's Elements of Phonetics* 142/1 Postpalatal stops, etc. = back stops, etc. *Ibid.* 67 The *gutturals* (more strictly: postpalatals or velars). **1902** [see *medio-palatal* adj. s.v. *MEDIO- 2]. **1925** [see *pre-palatal* s.v. *PRE- B. 3]. **1942** Post-palatal [see *medio-palatal* adj. s.v. *MEDIO- 2]. **1934** WEBSTER, Post-velar *a.* **1934** J. J. HOGAN *Outl. Eng. Philol.* i. 7 If the back-stops are made farther back than the normal series, they are called Post-Velars. **1942** BLOCH & TRAGER *Outl. Linguistic Analysis* ii. 16 Different points of articulation are designated by the terms *pre-velar*, *mediovelar*, and *postvelar* (or *uvular*). **1964** E. PALMER tr. *Martinet's Elem. Gen. Linguistics* ii. 50 A dorsal may also be..post-velar or uvular as in the initial sound of *rouge* in the Parisian pronunciation. **1966** M. PEI *Gloss. Linguistic Terminol.* 215 *Post-velar*, a consonant produced with the tongue farther back than the velar position, and the articulation against the rear half of the velum, or soft palate (Arabic *q*).

b. Rarely in *quasi*-adjectival relation to a sb. forming the second element: = occurring behind or posteriorly, as *POSTFIXATION *sb.* 1.

postable, *a.* Delete *rare*—⁰ and add example.
1926 *Glasgow Herald* 23 Mar. 9/1 The £40 limitation is wholly inadequate for jewellers and others, whose goods, though of 'postable' dimensions, are of considerable value.

postabortal, -abortion, -abortum, -absorptive: see *POST- B. 1 b. **post-accelerate:** *POST- A. 1 a. **post-acceleration, -accelerator:** *POST- A. 1 b.

postage[1]. Add: **6. postage meter** *N. Amer.* = *FRANKING MACHINE; hence *postage-metered* adj.
1927, 1961 [see *FRANKING MACHINE]. **1972** *Times* 18 May 27/1 Pitney Bowes..claims to be the world's largest producer and marketer of postage meters and mailing machines. *Ibid.*, It was 50 years ago that Walter H. Wheeler sold the British Post Office on the idea of postage metered mail. **1974** P. GZOWSKI *Bk. about This Country* 212 I'm sort of in the same position as the stamp-licker watching a postage meter being brought in the door.

postage stamp. Add: **a*.** Also *transf.* and *fig.*
1908 [see *DOD-]. **1930** R. GRAVES *Ten Poems More* 4 It is a large patch,..The postage-stamp of its departure,..closing in now To a plain countryside of less and less. **1971** M. TAK *Truck Talk* 121 *Postage stamp*, state permits in the form of a small decals that must be placed on a tractor. **1978** J. GORES *Gone, no Forwarding* vii. 42 Kearny began pacing the postage stamp of space behind his desk.

b. *postage-stamp-sized* adj.
1968 A. DIMENT *Gt. Spy Race* vi. 78 She wore nothing but the white, postage stamp-sized panties. **1968** 'R. RAINE' *Night of Hawk* viii. 38 A postage-stamp-sized moustache.

B. as *adj.*, used to denote something very small.
1962 *Housewife* (Ceylon) Feb. 33, I am certainly a veteran at providing the family with reasonably good food on a postage stamp budget. **1965** *New Society* 14 Oct. 5/3 Postage-stamp photos of smiling typists. **1968** J. WAINWRIGHT *Web of Silence* 137 A postage-stamp dance floor. **1971** R. BUSBY *Deadlock* iii. 32 Chrysanthemums were blooming in the postage stamp garden. **1973** 'R. MACLEOD' *Nest of Vultures* ii. 40 Spotlights were trained on a postage-stamp stage.

Hence **postage-stamped** *ppl. a.*, supplied with a postage stamp.
1942 PARTRIDGE *Usage & Abusage* 241/2 In the British Empire, a postcard may be already postage-stamped or it may require a postage stamp; in the U.S.A., it requires one, an already postage-stamped card being in the States a *postal card*.

postal, *a.* (*sb.*) Add: **b. postal ballot,** a method of voting by post; also *attrib.*; **postal card** (U.K. example); **postal code** = *POSTCODE; hence as *v. trans.*, to write a postcode on (a letter, etc.); **postal draft,** † (*a*) in 1914 the form used at Post Offices for the payment of Navy and Army Separation Allowances, later called 'allowance form'; (*b*) a draft or cheque drawn on the Postmaster General, introduced in Jan. 1925 for the payment of National Health Insurance benefits, and later extended to certain Government Departments; **postal note,** (*b*) *Austral.* and *N.Z.*, an order issued by a post office for any required sum and payable at any other post office; **postal order** (further examples); **postal trade,** trade in which orders are received and goods dispatched by post; **postal tube,** trade name for a cardboard tube designed to protect documents, plans, etc., during transmission by post; **postal vote,** a vote in an election, on a resolution, etc., submitted on a special form by post; so *postal voting* vbl. sb.
1945 *Times* 25 May 4/1 An elaborate procedure has been devised for checking all service votes so as to eliminate any proxy vote cast on behalf of a service voter from whom a postal ballot paper is received. **1973** A. BROINOWSKI *Take One Ambassador* i. 15 [The] returning officer for the elections..may be able to put his hand on a postal ballot paper for you. **1974** *Times* 12 Feb. 4/8 Union members should have the opportunity of electing their leaders by postal ballot. **1876** C. M. YONGE *Womankind* xix. 151 Do not come down to slap-dash notes and postal-cards. **1968** *Internat. List P.O.* (Universal Postal Union) (Eng. ed.) ii. 7 In recent years several countries have worked out postal codes designed to facilitate the sorting, routeing and delivery of mail. **1978** S. NAIPAUL *North of South* I. ii. 63 West 11..If we use only the postal code..they mightn't make the connection. **1969** P. WEST *Words for Deaf Daughter* v. 139 A two-page spread..sent postage-due, incorrectly postal-coded from some college. **1973** *Times* 17 July 11/5 The Post Office has published a booklet with the postal codes in it. **1929** *Post Office Guide* July 144 Remittances are made by certain Government Departments, etc., by means of Postal Drafts. **1885** *Victorian Year-Bk. for 1884–5* 481 Postal notes were first issued on the 1st January, 1885. **1926** *Austral. Encycl.* II. 318/1 In 1893 [in New South Wales] an inland and intercolonial parcels post was established and the postal-note system introduced. **1962** J. R. BERNARD in *Southerly* XXII. II. 98 A number of words compounded from standard words and attracting to themselves specific meanings are not treated at all in the dictionary. Among them are *bin-boy, bushfire, postal note,* [etc.]. **1973** *Bulletin* (Sydney) 25 Aug. 3 Enclosed please find my cheque/postal note. **1916** A. HUXLEY *Let.* c 12 July (1969) 106 Business first...this postal order, is *not* for you. ..au contraire, for me. **1974** *Encycl. Brit. Macropædia* XIV. 887/1 Postal orders were introduced in 1881. **1902** *Encycl. Brit.* XXV. 99/2 What is called in England 'postal trade', and in America 'mail order business', is growing very rapidly. **1894** *Country Gentlemen's Catal.* 166 Postal Pockets..Direction Labels, Postal Tubes. **1945** *Times* 25 May 4/1 There will be some inevitable duplication of postal and proxy votes. **1955** *Times* 11 May 14/4 Ministers in Argyll, who have been called to attend the General Assembly of the Church of Scotland in Edinburgh during the time they should vote in the general election, have been refused postal votes. **1971** *Oxf. Univ. Gaz.* 18 Feb. 671/2 More than fifty members of Congregation have required a postal vote on the resolution. **1974** *Times* 15 Jan. 2/6 An individual can claim a postal vote so long as he has moved from one local authority area to another. **1945** *Times* 25 May 4/1 Before these arrangements were made for postal voting by members of the forces a high proportion of them had appointed proxies. **1974** *Times* 15 Jan. 2/6 If an election is called..all claims for postal voting must be filed..a fortnight before election day.

postalize (pōu·stăləiz), *v.* [f. POSTAL *a.* (*sb.*) + -IZE.] To make like the postal system in respect of its fixed prices for delivery, regardless of distance. So **postaliza·tion.**
1893 *Review of Reviews* Oct. 394 Why not postalize Railway Traffic, and go as far as you like for 2½d? **1939** *Sun* (Baltimore) 19 Jan. 14/7 (*heading*) I.C.C. seeks order for investigating postalized rail fares. *Ibid.*, Chairman Marion M. Caskie..suggested today that the commission be given a mandate from Congress before investigating the Hastings plan for postalization of the railroads. **1950** *Economist* 16 Sept. 472/2 There is also some pressure for extending the system of 'postalisation' whereby United Kingdom consumers as a whole bear the transport charges. **1953** *Ibid.* 27 June 894/1 It takes a good deal of economic sophistication nowadays to see anything wrong with the principle of 'postalisation'—the principle of the postal service, that the consumers in thickly populated areas who can be served cheaply should subsidise the high-cost consumers elsewhere. **1966** *Ibid.* 17 Sept. 1166/1 This American gas expert, incidentally, would suggest selling to all boards at the same price, which might certainly interest the boards remote from Britain's east coast; but this idea of 'postalising gas' seems an ancillary frill on this argument.

postally (pōu·stăli), *adv.* [f. POSTAL *a.* + -LY[2].] For postal purposes; in the post; as far as postal matters are concerned.
1896 *Rep. Exhib. Sheffield Philatelic Soc.*, There were two letters postally used in 1768 and 1772. **1930** *Observer* 20 Apr. 15/5 It might..be better to show him our very latest additions to Whitehall—although they occur, postally at least, in that part of it called Charing Cross. **1970** *Daily Tel.* 17 Oct. 11/7 Those used for stamp duty, bills, receipts, licences and other fiscal purposes have *some* value, but it is very small indeed compared with the value of postally-used copies. **1972** *Police Rev.* 1 Dec. 1558/3 Neither was it acceptable to display mint (unused) stamps on the same page as those which had been postally used.

post-alveolar: see *POST- B. 2.

post and rail. (In Dict. s.v. POST *sb.*[1] 8 c.) Also hyphenated and in pl. **1.** A post and rail fence (see quot. 1823 in Dict.). Also, materials for post and rail fencing.
[**1641** *Rec. Colony & Plantation New Haven* (1857) 54 Fencing with..strong and substantiall posts and rales..nott above 18d.] **1778** 'J. H. ST. JOHN DE CRÈVECŒUR' *Sk. 18th-Cent. Amer.* (1925) 81 Our present modes of making fences are very bad... I have often observed whole lengths of posts and rails raised from the ground in the spring, and the labours of weeks thus destroyed. **1797** H. NEWDIGATE *Let.* 13 July in A. E. Newdigate-Newdegate *Cheverels* (1898) xiii. 184 As far as yᵉ Road is near the Cliff..there is a strong post & Rail all yᵉ Way. **1823** BYRON *Don Juan* VIII. lv. 138 So was his blood stirred..As is the hunter's at the five-bar gate, Or double post and rail. **1865** [see POST *sb.*[1] 8 c]. **1936** 'J. TEY' *Shilling for Candles* vii. 85 Flight fell with me at a post-and-rails last winter. **1959** J. VERNEY *Friday's Tunnel* xxxi. 292 The lane ended at the wood's edge in a broken post and rails.

2. *Austral. slang.* **a.** A wooden match.
a **1890** D. B. W. SLADEN in Barrère & Leland *Dict. Slang* (1890) II. 147/1 'Alf,' said a great friend of mine to a companion who was engaged with us on a shooting expedition down in Bulu-Bulu, one of the eastern provinces of Victoria, 'Have you got a match?' 'Only a post-and-rails,' was the deprecating reply, responded to with a patronising 'Never mind.' **1941** BAKER *Dict. Austral. Slang* 56 *Post-and-rails*,... (2) Wooden matches.

b. = **post-and-rail tea.*
1899 W. T. GOODGE *Hits! Skits! & Jingles!* 75 There is 'post and rails' and 'brownie' For yer breakfast now, yer know. **1904** T. PETRIE *Reminisc. Early Queensland* II. iv. 241 The tea then was all green tea, and very coarse, like bits of stick—indeed it was christened 'post and rails'. **1934** *Bulletin* (Sydney) 12 Sept. 9/2 A 'bark hut or log cabin will be erected' so that royalty may not get sunstroke while sipping his 'post-and-rail'. **1966** BAKER *Austral. Lang.* (ed. 2) iv. 85 Three old expressions are *ration tea,..post-and-rails* (also called *post-and-rail tea*) and *jack the painter*; the second is derived from the pieces of stalk and leaf floating on top.

c. [Rhyming slang for 'fairy tale'.] A lie.
1945 BAKER *Austral. Lang.* xv. 271 *Post-and-rail*, a lie (by rhyme on 'fairytale').

3. *attrib.* (sense *1), as *post-and-rail fence, fencing, paddock.*
1684 *Public Rec. Colony of Connecticut* (1859) III. 512 Great parte of my post and rayle fences being feched and burnt by the sowders. **1765** G. WASHINGTON *Diary* 6 Nov. (1925) I. 216 Sowing..19 Bushls. in ye large cut within the Post and Rail fence. **1850** H. C. WATSON *Camp-Fires of Revolution* 43 A party of our men..pulled up a post-and-rail fence. **1914** CONRAD *Chance* I. ii. 40 She had taken the trouble to climb over two post-and-rail fences only for the fun of being reckless. **1944** M. MORRIS in *Coast to Coast 1943* 85 Bare paddocks tufted with winter-whitened grass and endless post-and-rail fences regular as printed staves of music. **1973** E. EGLETON *Seven Days to Killing* xx. 210 The post-and-rail fence at the bottom of the yard. **1786** G. WASHINGTON *Diary* 18 Mar. (1925) III. 30 Post and rail fencing lately erected as yards for my Stud horses. **1944** E. DITHMACK in *Coast to Coast 1943* 26 Inside the post-and-rail paddock the leaves of the box-trees glittered. **1976** *Horse & Hound* 3 Dec. 70/4 (Advt.), Good stabling, grazing in post-and-rail paddocks in exclusive parkland setting.

b. Special Combs., as **post-and-rail tea** *Austral.*, strong, roughly made tea with stalks, etc., floating on the top.
1851 [see POST *sb.*[1] 8 c]. **1887** *All Year Round* 30 July 66 The tea so made [in a billy can] is naturally of rather a rough and ready description, and when the stalks and coarse particles of the fragrant leaf float thickly thereon, it is sometimes graphically styled 'post-and-rails' tea. **1936** A. RUSSELL *Gone Nomad* iv. 24 Flour, 'post and rail' tea (the cheapest kind), black sugar, salt and meat, were the only rations provided. **1959** H. P. TRITTON *Time means Tucker* i. 10/2 We got the jobs,..at a pound a week and tucker,..the tucker being mutton and damper, post-and-rail tea and brown sugar.

post-A·rmistice, *a.* [POST- B. 1 a.] Of or pertaining to the period immediately following the Armistice of 11 Nov. 1918.
1929 *Times* 22 July 15/2 The reckless capital flotation during the short-lived post-Armistice 'boom'. **1965** G. MCINNES *Road to Gundagai* iii. 48 When Terence sat at the keyboard to 'tickle the ivories', rip-roaring post-Armistice America with all its heady intoxication came vividly alive.

post-article, -auricular: see *POST- B. 1 c, 2.

po·stbase. *Linguistics.* [f. POST- B. 1 c + BASE *sb.*[1]] A derivational suffix.
1958 A. A. HILL *Introd. Linguistic Struct.* viii. 121 The other class of morphemes which can follow a base, we shall call postbases... Postbases, like suffixes, are non-initial. Since more than one postbase can be added to a single base, as in *boy-ish-ness*, a postbase must be described as a morpheme which can follow a base or another postbase. **1962** *Canad. Jrnl. Linguistics* VII. II. 94 This study shows that the morphophonemics of English words having post-bases ('derivational suffixes') of learned origin can be systematized by a comparatively small number of statements of wide application. **1967** *Ibid.* XIII. I. 22 OE adverbs also fall into subsets marked by comparative and superlative postbases.

post-Bloomfie·ldian, *a.* and *sb. Linguistics.* [f. POST- B. 1 b + the name *Bloomfield* (see below) + -IAN.] **A.** *adj.* Subsequent to the work of the American linguist Leonard Bloomfield (1887–1949), freq. applied *spec.* to American structural linguistics in the 1950s. **B.** *sb.* An American structuralist.
[**1949** J. R. FIRTH in *Archivum Linguisticum* I. 110 Slav linguistics..are certainly post-Saussurean and showing signs even in America of becoming post-Bloomfield.] **1961** F. W. HOUSEHOLDER in Saporta & Bastian *Psycholinguistics* 16/1 It would seem to a naive observer that the question 'what is the grammar for?' is an obvious one. Nevertheless, until recent years, no serious attempt to answer it seems to have been made by post-Bloomfieldian linguists. **1963** F. G. LOUNSBURY in J. A. Fishman *Readings Sociol. of Lang.* (1968) 63 The post-Bloomfieldian dogma in American linguistics has long

upheld the desideratum of exclusion of semantic considerations from linguistics. **1965** *Foundations of Lang.* I. 92 It remains quite clear that post-Bloomfieldian linguistics was preoccupied with accounting for the corpus of speech-utterances. **1966** A. A. HILL *Promises & Limitations Newest Type Gram. Anal.* 11 Post-Bloomfieldian structuralists produced rather remarkably few grammars. **1970** *Jrnl. Linguistics* VI. II. 287 Structuralist phonemics of the so-called Post-Bloomfieldians, for instance, is only a set of practical procedures. **1970** G. C. LEPSCHY *Survey Structural Linguistics* 11 'Structural linguistics' in a more limited sense (the post-Bloomfieldians). **1971** D. CRYSTAL *Linguistics* iv. 208 The term 'structuralism' was often used, in fact, in a narrow sense to refer to the kind of emphases which characterized post-Bloomfieldian linguistics (in a broad sense, of course, *all* linguistics is structural).

post-boarding, *vbl. sb.* [f. POST- A. 1 a + BOARDING *vbl. sb.*] The shaping of a garment by heating it on a form after it is dyed, rather than before. So **post-board** *v. trans.*

1952 *Dyeing of Nylon Textiles* (I.C.I.) xii. 135 When high-temperature post-boarding techniques are employed the scarlet and blue components..are not sufficiently fast to sublimation. **1963** MEITNER & KERTESS tr. *Schmidlin's Preparation & Dyeing Synthetic Fibres* ii. 39 After..setting..the stockings are dyed and subjected to post-boarding to impart the right type of handle. **1963, 1970** [see *PREBOARD *v.*].

post-boy. Add: **3.** *Austral.* = *Jacky Winter* s.v. *JACKY 3.

1911 J. A. LEACH *Austral. Bird Bk.* 121 Australian Brown Flycatcher, Jacky Winter, Post-boy, Post-sitter. **1931** N. W. CAYLEY *What Bird is That?* 64 Brown Flycatcher... Also called Peter-Peter, Post-boy, Post-sitter. **1969** [see *Jacky Winter* s.v. *JACKY 3].

postcard. Add: **2.** *attrib.*, as *postcard album, flower, -monger, -photograph, poll, portrait, stand, survey, system*; *postcard-size* adj.

1899 Postcard album [in Dict.]. **1907** *Yesterday's Shopping* (1969) 436c Post Card Albums. **1929** R. GRAVES *Poems* 21 Post-card flower of Kodak mud. **1938** *New Statesman* 13 Aug. 241/2 He can make his way..to..the Museums, outside which eager postcard-mongers will sell him views of Westminster Abbey and the Tower. **1920** T. P. NUNN *Education* x. 126 A postcard-photograph of a yacht. **1909** *Daily Chron.* 19 Mar. 1/6 There had been strong opposition..to the Sunday concerts, and a postcard poll was taken. **1907** *Yesterday's Shopping* (1969) 436c These Albums have been designed to hold the Post Card Portraits now so popular. **1926** *Paper Terminol.* (Spalding & Hodge, Ltd.) 21 Post Card size... Generally applied to a board measuring 22½ × 28 in., out of which 32 official post cards may be cut. **1973** R. BUSBY *Pattern of Violence* iv. 60 A handful of postcard-size prints. **1907** *Yesterday's Shopping* (1969) 428 Post card stand. **1948** *Shell Aviation News* No. 120. 5/3 The study is based on a post-card survey of about 17,000 aircraft owners, and shows that an estimated 9,800,000 hours were flown by non-scheduled aircraft in 1946. **1897** Post-card system [in Dict.].

b. Designating something picturesque, as *postcard land, sky, view.*

1958 *Spectator* 14 Feb. 204/1 A postcard land of blossom, and bridges humped over gurgling streams. **1959** *Woman's Own* 16 May 13/1 The shining sea. The postcard sky. **1959** *Listener* 12 Mar. 459/1 He [*sc.* Utrillo] was undoubtedly clever at enlarging, squaring-up, colouring and feeling his way into postcard views of paintable *motifs*. **1979** M. A. SHARP *Sunflower* v. 45 They were crossing the Triboro Bridge, with its postcard view of the city.

c. Special Combs., as **postcard beauty,** a fashionable beauty whose picture appeared on postcards which were collected by admirers.

1924 G. B. SHAW *Let.* in *To a Young Actress* (1960) 66, I think you will gravitate towards literature after a reign as a postcard beauty. **1958** *Sunday Times* 28 Sept. 4/7 She was included among the postcard beauties of her musical-comedy days.

po·stcard, *v.* [f. the sb.] **a.** *trans.* To communicate with or inform by postcard. **b.** *intr.* To send a postcard.

1910 *Westm. Gaz.* 2 Feb. 5/3 (Advt.), Patterns ready for sending by return post. Postcard us to-day. **1947** *Ki-grams* (Washington, D.C. Kiwanis Club) 6 Feb., Zeddie Blackistone post-cards about the flowers, the sunshine and golf at Palm Beach.

post-cart. (Further examples.)

1926 O. SCHREINER *From Man to Man* ix. 339 At half past four the postcart driver had inspanned his horses. **1949** L. G. GREEN *In Land of Afternoon* ii. 33 The old post-cart drivers used to halt between Ashton and Montagu.

post-centrally: see *POST- B. 2.

post-Chauce·rian, *a.* and *sb.* [POST- B. 1 b.] **A.** *adj.* After the lifetime of Chaucer; *spec.*, of a poet: writing after, and influenced by, Chaucer. **B.** *sb.* A post-Chaucerian poet.

1933 R. TUVE *Seasons & Months* ii. 70 One may see this Lydgatean influence in most of the poets of the 'post-Chaucerian' school. *Ibid.* iii. 71 English poetry from the time of Chaucer and the post-Chaucerians to that of the eighteenth-century pastoral. **1966** *Eng. Stud.* XLVII. 172 The foregoing are the only instances of post-Chaucerian *spiced conscience* that I have been able to discover. **1967** P. J. BAWCUTT *Shorter Poems of Gavin Douglas* p. xxx, Douglas must have been well read, not only in Chaucer and the post-Chaucerian poets of the fifteenth century, but in medieval Latin poetry.

post-Chri·stian, *a.* and *sb.* [POST- B. 1b.] **A.** *adj.* **a.** Subsequent to the lifetime of Christ, or to the rise of Christianity. **b.** Subsequent to the decline or rejection of Christianity.

1864 [see POST- B. 1]. **1888** T. K. CHEYNE et al. *Bible* (Variorum Teacher's ed.) (1893) Pref., The vowel-points merely represent a valuable, but still post-Christian, exegetical tradition. **1929** H. KEYSERLING *Amer. set Free* II. 583 This is not a pre-Christian, but a post-Christian state. **1945** *Downside Rev.* LXIII. 201 He exemplifies that paralysis from which post-Christian philosophy is suffering. **1956** K. CLARK *Nude* iii. 109 The yearning for another world had entered the post-Christian spirit. **1974** *Listener* 24 Jan. 121/3 Heliogabalus..reduced Rome to a kind of post-Christian Sodom and Gomorrah.

B. *sb.* A person in a nominally Christian society who has no professed religion.

1946 *Downside Rev.* LXIV. 117 Or we may have wondered for whom the book was written, for Mgr Knox addresses sometimes the post-Christian, sometimes the 'Sunday Mass' Catholic and sometimes his fellow priests. **1958** *Spectator* 4 July 10/3 A generation of men and women who have grown up completely outside institutional Christianity. They are not lapsed Christians... But neither are they formal agnostics. They are best defined as post-Christians. **1961** *Christian Century* 18 Jan. 80/2 Australian Catholics sincerely believe that their countrymen would be better off as Catholics than as post-Christians.

post-classic, *a.* Add: **b.** *spec.* Usu. with initial capital. Applied to that period (*c* 900 to 1520) of Meso-American civilization succeeding the Classic.

[**1956** J. E. S. THOMPSON *Rise & Fall of Maya Civilization* ii. 96 Burials have also been found in collapsed rooms at other sites, notably a burial with pottery of post-classical types at Copan.] **1965** R. F. SPENCER et al. *Native Americans* xi. 443/1 The Post-Classic period of Mesoamerican culture history essentially amounts to reorientation in Mesoamerican cultural foci... Many of the characteristics which are typical of the Post-Classic were present in the Classic Period. **1973** *Times* 26 July 18/4 Several pottery vessels..and the architecture of the house suggested connexions with the northern part of Yucatan in the Early and the Middle Postclassic periods. **1975** *Sci. Amer.* Oct. 73/2 The most neutral of scholars' terms for this period in Middle America is Last Post-classic; many simply call it 'the decadent period'.

post-classical, *a.* (Examples in *Mus.*)

1947 A. EINSTEIN *Mus. Romantic Era* xii. 167 But Bruckner did not write 'Post Classical' or Romantic church music in the style of Schubert. **1969** *Listener* 4 Sept. 320/1 In one week, between 4 and 10 September, the Proms give a most interesting perspective of post-classical symphonic development.

post-climax: see *POST- B. 1 c.

postclitic (pōᵘstˌkli·tik). *Linguistics.* [f. POST- A. 1 b + *CLITIC.] An unemphatic word stressed as part of the preceding word.

1963 BLOOMFIELD & NEWMARK *Linguistic Introd. Hist. Eng.* iv. 147 *The* is a proclitic in NE..and *one*, as in *a bad one* or *the green one*, is a postclitic. **1965** *Language* XLI. 473 As many as five syllables occur prestressed, but only one syllable occurs poststressed, except rarely when a postclitic follows a suffix.

post-cly·peus. *Ent.* [POST- A. 2 b.] In certain insects, the upper section of a divided clypeus.

1888 J. H. COMSTOCK *Introd. Entomol.* 10 When these [*sc.* two sclerites of the clypeus] are distinct they are designated as the ante-clypeus and post-clypeus respectively. **1926** R. J. TILLYARD *Insects Australia & N.Z.* i. 12 In others [*sc.* insects] the clypeus may be divided into two parts, an anteclypeus and a postclypeus. **1937** C. LONGFIELD *Dragonflies Brit. Isles* 13 In the *Anisoptera* the frons is the most prominent portion of the two, in the *Zygoptera* it is the postclypeus. **1957** RICHARDS & DAVIES *Imm's Textbk. Entomol.* (ed. 9) I. 19 In some insects the clypeus is partially or completely divided by a transverse suture into two sclerites—the post-clypeus and the ante-clypeus.

postcode (pōᵘ·stˌkōᵘd). Also with capital initial. [f. POST *sb.*² + CODE *sb.*¹] A series of letters or numbers, or both, allocated to postal areas to facilitate the automatic sorting and speedy delivery of mail. Also *attrib.* Hence **po·stcoding** *vbl. sb.*

1967 *Telegraph* (Brisbane) 18 May 3/1 The Post Office will allocate every city, town, suburb and small centre in Australia a four-figure postal location number called Postcode. Announcing this today, the Postmaster-General..said the Postcode system would enable the Post Office to handle the growing volume of mail more quickly, by taking full advantage of electronic mail coding equipment. **1968** *Times* 24 July 9/7 On the back of it is stamped the instruction 'Remember to use the postcode'. **1969** *Daily Tel.* 5 June 21/6 Postcoding is to be extended to cover all of Britain's 20,000,000 addresses instead of only 75 main centres. **1969** *Guardian* 9 Aug. 8/3 The first two letters of the Postcode route the letter to the distant mail-handling centre. **1971** *Sunday Times* (Colour Suppl.) 20 June 17 A postman at the letter-coding desk has each envelope put in front of him and types out its postcode on a keyboard at his fingertips. **1973** *Guardian* 7 Feb. 1/1 Postcodes are to be put on road signs. The experiment will start in the new town of Milton Keynes, Bucks.

post-common. (Later Hist. examples.)

1879 T. F. SIMMONS *Lay Folks Mass Bk.* 307 They were to kneel again during the post-common, as was the English name for the prayer after the communion. **1882** G. H. FORBES *Misale Drummondiense* 26 This Postcommon is found without any variation in Gerbert p. 294 b.

post-conquest(ual, -consonantal, etc., **-convulsive:** see *POST- B. 1. **postcranial(ly, -cricoid:** *POST- B. 2.

post crown. *Dentistry.* Also with hyphen and as one word. [f. POST *sb.*¹ + CROWN *sb.*] A prosthetic dental crown held in place by a post or wire sunk into the root of the tooth.

1905 G. EVANS *Pract. Treat. Artific. Crown-, Bridge-, & Porcelain Work* ii. 58 Each of these conditions causes fracture of roots carrying post or dowel crowns. **1936** J. R. SCHWARTZ *Cavity Prep. & Abutment Construction in Bridgework* xvii. 183 The earliest attempts to incorporate esthetics in the mechanical procedures of tooth restoration was the banded dowel, or postcrown, with a porcelain facing, presented by Dr. C. M. Richmond, many years ago. **1963** C. R. COWELL et al. *Inlays, Crowns, & Bridges* viii. 90 An effective temporary post-crown consists of acrylic resin on a preformed post or wire. **1974** L. J. LEGGETT in Harty & Roberts *Restorative Procedures for Practising Dentist* xvi. 216 A post crown is indicated, in a root-filled tooth, where there is insufficient bulk or strength in the remaining crown to support a jacket crown.

post-Cu·bist, *a.* and *sb. Art.* [POST- B. 1 b.] **A.** *adj.* Subsequent to Cubism. **B.** *sb.* A post-Cubist painter.

1927 R. H. WILENSKI *Mod. Movement in Art* 147 Imitations of..Post-Cubist art are not confined to actual works of painting. **1937** *Burlington Mag.* Dec. p. xx/1 Cubists and Post-Cubists. **1959** H. READ *Conc. Hist. Mod. Painting* v. 147 His post-Cubist development cannot be dissociated from the typical manifestations of Surrealism.

po·stcure, *sb.* (and *v.*). [f. POST- A. 1 b + CURE *sb.*¹] The action or process of further curing plastic (or an article of it) after fabrication, so as to complete the cure.

1957 B. A. DUMBROW *Polyurethanes* iii. 35 In a matter of minutes, the entire foam is produced in place and ready for post-cure, if such is necessary. **1958** D. J. DUFFIN *Laminated Plastics* iv. 75 It has been found advisable to place the part in a second oven at lower temperatures..to effect a postcure. **1967** *Electronics* 6 Mar. 324 The finished coating requires no post-cure, has very high cut-through temperature and superior resistance to high temperatures. **1968** *Encycl. Polymer Sci. & Technol.* IX. 18 A typical postcure..might involve 2 hr at 275°F, followed by 2 hr at 150°F.

So as *v. trans.*; **po·stcuring** *vbl. sb.*

1956 *Brit. Plastics* XXIX. 453/1 Post curing, for example, three hours at 80°C, will eliminate all residual peroxide and bring many laminates to a stable condition. **1964** SAUNDERS & FRISCH *Polyurethanes* II. vii. 115 Postcuring of the sponge was carried out for 1 hr. at 100°C. **1969** MONROE & CHITWOOD in G. Lubin *Handbk. Fiberglass & Advanced Plastics Composites* xiv. 325 If warpage is a problem, then the part must be post-cured on a post-cure fixture which holds the part to contour. **1975** A. T. RADCLIFFE in Whelan & Brydson *Devel. with Thermosetting Plastics* v. 61 The laminate should be initially cured at 50°C and subsequently postcured at 80°C.

postcyclic(al, -cyclically: see *POST- B. 1.

post-da·m, *v. Dentistry.* [f. POST(ERIOR *a.* and *sb.* + DAM *sb.*¹] *trans.* and *absol.* To construct a ridge along the upper posterior border of a palatal denture, which will press against the soft palate and form a seal. So **post-da·mming** *vbl. sb.*, the construction of such a ridge.

1910 J. W. GREENE *Clin. Course Dental Prosthesis* 47 We must have a way to post-dam, in such cases, without the patient's help. *Ibid.* 50 After you post-dammed its [*sc.* the impression's] rear end, it drops. *Ibid.*, You overstrained the palate in post-damming. **1945** F. W. CRADDOCK *Prosthetic Dentistry* iii. 56. Finally, the upper impression is post-dammed with a further addition of softened wax or compound across the posterior palatal edge. **1953** H. R. B. FENN et al. *Clin. Dental Prosthetics* v. 115 Post-damming is a means of increasing pressure over an area in order, either to control an impression material, or to improve peripheral seal.

Hence **post-dam** (also **post dam**) *sb.*, a ridge of this kind.

1932 E. H. MAUK in Turner & Anthony *Amer. Textbk. Prosthetic Dentistry* (ed. 6) iii. 133 Dr. J. Ewell Neal.. makes special reference to the notch or groove in the bone posterior to the tuberosity on each side where the quantity and character of the soft tissue are such as to tolerate, without injury, more 'post-dam' than was usually employed. **1940** M. G. SWENSON *Compl. Dentures* xiii. 167 The anterior line of the post dam area is determined by palpating in the mouth, in order to keep the post dam pressure on soft tissue. **1945** F. W. CRADDOCK *Pros-*

thetic Dentistry iii. 65 The post-dam extends from tuberosity to tuberosity and will generally be about $\frac{1}{8}$ inch wide and $\frac{1}{32}$ to $\frac{1}{16}$ inch deep. **1953** H. R. B. Fenn et al. *Clin. Dental Prosthetics* x. 277 Indirectly the post-dam seal influences phonation, for if it is inadequate the denture may become unseated during the formation of those sounds having an explosive effect. **1976** R. M. Basker et al. *Prosthetic Treatm. Edentulous Patient* ix. 110 This projection, the post-dam, compresses the palatal mucosa once the denture is placed in the mouth and thus creates a border seal.

post-date, *v.* Add: **2.** *trans.* To belong to a later date than (something).

1909 in Webster. **1955** [see *ferricrete]. **1971** *Daily Tel.* 5 Aug. 8/1 The mineral miracle, which post-dates his first visit to the Antipodes in 1965, has now made it clear that Australia has more to offer..than sun and surf. **1971** I. G. Gass et al. *Understanding Earth* i. 37 (*caption*) The granites post-date metamorphic rocks. **1971** *World Archaeol.* III. 170 The hearth must have post-dated the last use of the pit.

Hence **post-da·ting** *vbl. sb.*

1963 *N. & Q.* Jan. 16/2 (*heading*) A post-dating. **1968** *Times Lit. Suppl.* 11 Jan. 37/4 There are post-datings, that is, evidence for the later existence of words that OED supposes obsolete.

post-deflection, -depositional: see *post- B. 1.

postdiction (pōu·stdikʃən). [f. Post- A. 1 b + L. *dictiōn-em* a saying, speaking, after Prediction *sb.*] (The making of) an assertion or deduction about something in the past. So (as a back-formation) **postdi·ct** *v. trans.*, to assert or imply something about (something in the past or the present).

1940 J. Laird *Theism & Cosmology* v. 169 If, however, the future be indeterminate before it occurs, it cannot be fixed before it occurs. For there is nothing determinate to fix. Hence inferential prediction has quite a different status from inferential post-diction. **1952** *Mind* LXI. 40 Inductive sentences may also postdict a past event, *e.g.*..'It is probable that Caesar crossed the Rubicon.' **1960** *Commentary* June 487/1 The Gluecks' five-factor scale in effect *post*-dicted delinquency in the Boston boys from whom it was developed. *Ibid.*, Post-diction is easier than prediction. **1966** *Amer. Speech* XLI. 208 The auxiliary of prediction *will* combines with inflectional ending of postdiction *-ed* to produce a form, *would*. **1971** *Computers & Humanities* V. 192 Discriminant analysis of 30 content variables and 192 editorials..postdicted correctly the masthead of most editorials.

postdoc (pōustˌdɒ·k), *sb.* and *a.* Colloq. abbrev. of *post-doctoral *a.* and *sb.*

1970 *New Scientist* 21 May 368/3 In 1970 55 per cent of them are 'postdocs' as compared with 25 per cent in 1967. *Ibid.* 17 Dec. 519/3 Today the 'post-doc' appointment is referred to as a 'holding pattern'. **1971** *Ibid.* 27 Apr. 264/1 Meanwhile, the team has been enlarged by three new post-docs. **1974** *Nature* 8 Nov. p. xxix/2 (Advt.), Wanted. A postdoc in population biology interested in genetic structure of populations and species. **1978** *Ibid.* 18 May 182/1 [In the EMBL central laboratory] there is also a considerable number of 'fellows'—mainly post-docs who bring their own funds—and visiting scientists.

post-do·ctoral, *a.* [Post- B. 1 b.] Of, pertaining to, or for the purpose of advanced research by persons already holding a doctor's degree. Also as *sb.*, one who is undertaking or has undertaken a period of study or research subsequent to obtaining his or her doctor's degree.

1939 Webster Add., Postdoctoral *adj.* **1956** *Nature* 10 Mar. 456/1 As in Britain, there is considerable competition for the junior academic posts and post-doctoral fellowships. **1958** *Times* 8 May 2/3 (Advt.), Applications are invited for post-doctoral grants for research under the general direction of Professor R. N. Hazeldine. **1961** *Times* 26 Sept. 1/4 Postgraduate or post-doctoral work. **1966** *Rep. Comm. Inquiry Univ. Oxf.* I. 127 They [*sc.* junior research fellowships] are awarded to encourage individuals at the D.Phil. or immediate post-doctoral stage. **1971** *Nature* 10 Sept. 87/2 Physicists are the worst hit single group of scientists, with 2·9 per cent of the PhDs and 3·3 per cent of the postdoctorals out of a job. **1977** *Time* 14 Mar. 40/2 During his two-year stint as a post-doctoral fellow at the Max Planck Institute for Biochemistry near Munich, R.G., 27, impressed his boss as 'probably the most diligent man I've ever known'.

post-do·ctorate, *a.* [f. Post- B. 1 a + Doctorate *sb.*[1]] = *post-doctoral *a.*

1939 in Webster Add. **1957** [see *booster 2 d]. **1959** *Times* 17 Mar. 2/5 Applicants should be graduates (preferably post-doctorate).

post-e·cho. [Post- A. 1 b.] A faint repetition of a loud sound occurring in a recording soon after the original as a result of the accidental transfer of signals in a recording medium. Cf. *pre-echo.

1956 G. Slot *Hi-Fi from Microphone to Ear* xi. 151 The pre-echoes and post-echoes sometimes heard on gramophone records are usually due to this effect. **1962** *Times Lit. Suppl.* 19 Oct. 810/5 The vocal perspective is ingeniously varied to suggest the changing scene, but the fortissimo passages are occasionally marred by post-echo. **1977** *Gramophone* Mar. 1476/1 Each layer of tape tends to magnetize its recorded signal on to the adjacent layers during storage—in the process known as 'print-through'—to produce faint pre-echoes and post-echoes.

post-e·ditor. [Post- A. 1 b.] Someone who edits text that has been produced or processed by a machine.

1953 A. D. & K. H. V. Booth *Automatic Digital Calculators* xvii. 206 Reiffler suggests the use of a pre-editor who need not know the (*T.L.*) at all but who, reading his own language (our *F.L.*), eliminates from the text all such alternatives... In the same way a post-editor might be used to turn the translation into acceptable *T.L.* **1960** E. Delavenay *Introd. Machine Transl.* 121 For each Russian polysemantic word the machine has given alternative translations; the one selected by the post-editor has been given first. **1966** D. G. Hays in *Automatic Transl. of Lang.* (NATO Summer School, Venice, 1962) 146 Before text reaches the posteditor, it has been put through automatic dictionary lookup and automatic sentence-structure determination.

So **post-edit** *v. trans.*, to edit in such circumstances; **post-e·diting** *vbl. sb.*

1957 *Year's Work Eng. Stud.* 1955 41/2 His suggestions for mechanized translation involve a much heavier reliance upon 'post-editing' than experts at present feel they need to assume. **1960** E. Delavenay *Introd. Machine Transl.* iii. 29 He postulated the necessity both for pre-editing texts before translation and for post-editing them when translated. **1962** *Times Lit. Suppl.* 20 Apr. 268/3 The machine output will have to be 'post-edited', before submission of the finished product to the readers. **1971** *Computers & Humanities* VI. 45 A printer's computer tape would probably require some post-editing.

posteen, postīn. (Further examples of forms **poshteen, -tin.**)

1895 Kipling *Day's Work* (1898) 212 William, wrapped in a *poshteen*—silk-embroidered sheepskin jacket trimmed with rough astrakhan—looked out with moist eyes and nostrils that dilated joyously. **1910** *Encycl. Brit.* I. 314/1 Poshtins (sheepskin clothing) and the many varieties of camel and goat's hair cloth..are still the chief local products of that part of Afghanistan. **1961** P. Fleming *Bayonets to Lhasa* xi. 151 Saved from death by his thick poshteen. **1973** 'W. Haggard' *Old Masters* viii. 99 Bentinck was wearing moleskin trousers and..a sort of poshteen which would keep out the cold.

post-Einstei·nian, *a.* [Post- B. 1 b.] Subsequent to the work of Albert Einstein (see *Einstein); involving or pertaining to concepts developed later than the theories of relativity.

1938 S. Chase *Tyranny of Words* viii. 89 Bridgman develops various concepts for 'length' in post-Einsteinian terms. **1953** *Authentic Sci. Fiction Monthly* Apr. 137 With such rare exceptions as Bradbury, writers seem..to accept a relativity of moral standards which, while it may display a misleading harmony with the post-Einsteinian scientific outlook, is in fact simply a well of poison. **1973** B. Magee *Popper* vii. 97 Post-Einsteinian physics,..post-Freudian psychology,..post-Keynesian economics, ..post-Frege logic.

post-emergence: see *post- B. 1.

post-e·ntry, *a.* [Post- B. 1 a.] Occurring after entry; *spec.* applied to a closed shop in which new employees are required to join a union after appointment. Cf. *pre-entry *a.*

1964 [see *pre-entry *a.*]. **1972** H. Williamson *Trade Unions* (ed. 2) ii. 22 In a post-entry closed shop membership of a particular union is only insisted upon after the worker has been appointed. **1976** *Milton Keynes Express* 16 July 13/2 (Advt.), Clerical Assistant (Income Section). .. National conditions; superannuation; five day week; post-entry training facilities. **1978** R. Taylor *Fifth Estate* i. 18 Employers..have written post-entry closed-shop clauses into their collective agreements with unions.

poster[1]. **3.** (Earlier example.)

1797 H. Newdigate *Let.* 9 July in A. E. Newdigate-Newdegate *Cheverels* (1898) xiii. 181 A good dinner..was ready to come upon Table when y^e^ Posters arrived.

poster[2]. Add: **3.** *poster art, design, designer* (examples), *-designing, panel*; **poster colour** = next; **poster paint,** an opaque paint with a water-soluble binder such as is used on posters; **poster paper,** paper used in bills or posters; **poster session,** a meeting of scientists at which their work is represented by displayed pictures (see quot. 1977).

1920 Hardie & Sabin *War Posters* ii. 7 Poster art and pictorial art have essentially different aims. **1974** *Listener* 28 Feb. 283/3 Shostakovich's Twelfth Symphony. 'Poster art' it may be; but if so, some more Russian posters, please. **1925** *Studio* (Art & Publicity No.) Autumn (verso front cover), The 'Kingsway' Poster Colours..supplied in Tubes and Glass Pots. **1973** Poster colour [see *pop *a.* (*sb.*[8]) 3]. **1920** Hardie & Sabin *War Posters* ii. 14 The number of poster designs from his hand is at least fifty. **1970** *Oxf. Compan. Art* 900/1 English poster design in the 20th c. varies between the illustrative..and the work of great merit done for Shell-Mex. **1901** W. S. Rogers *Bk. of Poster* xix. 133 The standard of art-education amongst the poster designers is higher than in this country. **1935** [see **copy-writer*]. **1954** T. Eckersley *Poster Design* 7 The illustrations in this book are by leading poster designers. **1901** W. S. Rogers *Bk. of Poster* xix. 129 The scope of this work does not embrace the idea of treating the subject of poster designing at any great length. **1933** L. Richmond *Technique of Poster* p. v, Poster designing is a serious but most interesting art. **1939** W. Clemence *Man. Postercraft* xii. 92 Good quality flat poster paints, thinned with a little turpentine..blend well, are smooth of application, and dry in excellent time and condition. **1974** I. Murdoch *Sacred & Profane Love Machine* 103 She.. laid out his coloured pencils, his poster paints, brushes, water. **1929** *Encycl. Brit.* XVIII. 319/2 On the poster panels of to-day, in the United States, may be seen the work of Harrison Fisher. **1901** J. Beveridge *Paper-makers' Pocket Bk.* i. 26 German classification and sizes of papers..Affichenpapiere (thin poster paper). **1959** R. Hostettler et al. *Technical Terms Printing Industry* (ed. 3) 130/2 *Poster paper*,..papier pour affiches. **1976** *Physics Bull.* Aug. 335/3 Although it is clear that the technique derives from the scientific exhibition, the exact origin of poster sessions is unknown. **1977** *Sci. Amer.* Apr. 51/2 (Advt.), All contributed 'papers' are to be given in poster sessions, where from a visual display one decides whether to stop and exchange thoughts person to person.

poster[3] (pōu·stəɹ). *Rugby Football.* [f. Post *sb.*[1] + -er[1].] A ball that passes directly over the top of one of the goal-posts.

1867 *Routledge's Handbk. Football* 35 If the ball..rises directly over the end of one of the posts, it is called a *poster*, and is no goal. **1930** *Times* 14 Mar. 7/1 He played in three International matches, dropped a goal in two, and scoring [*sic*] a 'poster' in the other.

postered (pōu·stəɹd), *a.* [f. Poster[2] + -ed[2].] Depicted or described on posters; adorned or disfigured with posters.

1916 S. Kaye-Smith *Sussex Gorse* iii. 173 Rye electors were confronted with the postered virtues and vices of Captain Mackinnon (Radical) and Colonel MacDonald (Conservative). **1927** *Scots Observer* 7 May 9/2 The real blemishes of Glasgow are raw and postered gable-ends, untended waste grounds, [etc.].

posterior, *a.* and *sb.* (*adv.*) Add: **A.** *adj.* **1. b.** *Statistics.* Applied to the result of a calculation made subsequent to, and in consideration of, some observation(s); *posterior probability*, the probability that a hypothesis is true, calculated in the light of relevant observations. Opp. *prior *a.* (*adv.*) A. c.

1921 *Phil. Mag.* XLII. 387 Even if the prior probabilities of two laws with different domains are notably different, the effect of several verifications of each is able to make the posterior probabilities of the two laws practically equal to each other and to unity. **1931** H. Jeffreys *Sci. Inference* ii. 18 The posterior probability of p is the prior probability of p divided by the prior probability of the consequence. **1943** M. G. Kendall *Adv. Theory Statistics* I. vii. 179 A further difficulty arises if θ can lie in an infinite range, for then Bayes' postulate apparently leads to the conclusion that prior probabilities in any finite range are zero and hence so are posterior probabilities. **1972** A. W. F. Edwards *Likelihood* iv. 46 The posterior odds of two hypotheses on some data is equal to the product of the prior odds and the likelihood ratio. *Ibid.* iv. 48 In practice it is determined by the fact that both the prior and the posterior distributions of θ integrate to unity. **1977** *Lancet* 13 Aug. 339/1 If the sister of a hæmophiliac initially has two unaffected boys, the 'posterior' probability of her being a carrier falls from 1/2 to 1/5.

B. *sb.* **2. a.** Now usu. *sing.* The rump or backside (of a person). *colloq.*

1936 G. B. Shaw *Simpleton* Prologue ii. 27 He shoots his foot against the E.O.'s posterior and sends him over the cliff. **1976–7** *Sea Spray* (N.Z.) Dec./Jan. 90/1 (Advt.), It is soft so that a crewman winding the spinnaker sheet winch down aft can rest his posterior on it.

posterish (pōu·stəriʃ), *a.* [f. Poster[2] + -ish[1].] Characteristic or suggestive of a poster or posters. So **po·sterishness.**

1930 *Aberdeen Press & Jrnl.* 25 Apr. 6 Norah Neilson Gray still seems to us to be straying too much towards a sweet but too pretty posterishness in her work. **1931** *Times Lit. Suppl.* 25 June (Suppl.) p. vi/4 Several cover-designs achieve posterish attractiveness. **1947** *Sat. Rev. Lit.* (U.S.) 1 Mar. 30 Figures in a flat, cylindrical, posterish style. **1958** *Times* 15 Dec. 3/5 There is a painting in Sickert's posterish vein. **1967** *Listener* 16 Mar. 355/2 The formalized, abstracted figures have become posterish and realistic like those in a Soviet hero painting.

posterist (pōu·stərist). [f. Poster[2] + -ist.] A designer of posters; a poster-artist.

1901 W. S. Rogers *Bk. of Poster* p. v, If I may seem too enthusiastic on the side of Continental work, it is from no lack of sympathy with British posterists. **1968** *Times* 21 Dec. 20/4 The lack of sensitivity apparent in his academic studies..was almost an asset to a posterist. **1972** *Guardian* 19 June 11/4 The best known posterist of the period was John Hassall... His most famous design, 'Skegness is *so* Bracing', was..designed in 1909.

posterize (pōu·stəɹəiz), *v.* *Photogr.* [f. Poster[2] + -ize.] *trans.* To print (a photograph) so that there is only a small number of different tones. Also *absol.* Hence **po·sterized** *ppl. a.*, **po·sterizing** *vbl. sb.*

1943 C. I. Jacobson *Enlarging* (ed. 4) 278 Posterising Photographs... One method published by R. W. Wade, achieves something more than simple tone-separation. It does produce in addition, a 'posterised' picture, which is.. a picture in which all the elements are built up out of one or other of four tones only... The range of subjects suitable for posterising is practically unlimited. **1948** F. H. Smith *Photographs & Printer* 135 The photo-engraver can readily reproduce a photograph which has already been posterised. 1977 R. Hattersley *Photographic Printing* xviii. 132 Once you know how to make high-contrast negatives with Kodalith..it is relatively easy to posterize. *Ibid.* 133 With four or more tones a posterized print may not even look posterized. Instead it may look like an ordinary print with something just a wee bit odd about the tones.

Also **posteriza·tion**, the process of posterizing.

1950 O. R. Croy *Compl. Art of Printing & Enlarging* ii. 72 (*caption*) Posterization. The print consists only of three tones. 1977 J. Hedgecoe *Photographer's Handbk.* 245 Posterization or tone separation means turning a normal, continuous tone photograph into an image consisting of clearly distinguished areas of flat tone.

postero-. Add: (*a*) *postero-medial*; (*b*) also forming advs., as **posterolaterally, -ventrally.**

1959 *Bull. Mus. Compar. Zool. Harvard* CXX. 185 The segment anterior to Jacobson's organ no longer appears as a transverse slit in frontal section, but now runs anteromedially to posterolaterally. 1967 G. M. Wyburn et al. *Conc. Anat.* iv. 112/2 The great wing of the sphenoid terminating posterolaterally in the spine. 1901 *Proc. Zool. Soc.* I. 263 The characteristic features of this cavity.. are:—..(3) the characteristic position of its postero-medial wall, as seen from behind. 1967 G. M. Wyburn et al. *Conc. Anat.* i. 28/2 The duodenal papilla—on the postero-medial aspect is the situation of the opening of the bile duct. 1902 *Proc. Zool. Soc.* I. 89 The blue sides are margined posteroventrally with a black line. 1961 J. E. Collin *Empididae* I. 31 Middle femora with a comb-like row of tiny black bristles posteroventrally. 1974 D. & M. Webster *Compar. Vertebr. Morphol.* vii. 133 The external oblique muscle..runs anterodorsally to posteroventrally.

post eventum: see *post *Latin prep.*

post-existent, *a.* (Later example.)

1977 G. W. H. Lampe *God as Spirit* iii. 71 Luke was, in fact, unable to make a simple identification of the glorified, 'post-existent' Jesus with the Spirit in the Church.

post factum. Add: *adv. phr.* (Earlier and later examples.) Also as *adj.*

1692 Locke *Some Considerations Money* 12 Unless you intend to break in only upon Mortgages and Contracts already made, and (which is not to be supposed) by a Law, *post factum*, void Bargains lawfully made. 1927 *Mod. Philol.* Nov. 227 New locutions..constantly replace old ones, which, viewed *post factum*, would have been unintelligible, had they remained in use. 1949 Koestler *Insight & Outlook* p. vii, But textbooks are post-factum rearrangements of long and devious processes of inquiry. 1964 V. Nabokov *Defence* viii. 125 I'm very glad *post actum*..but..for the moment it somehow disturbs me. 1972 *New Yorker* 16 Jan. 28/2 Not wanting to use the police emergency number—911—in a post-factum situation.

post festum: see *post *Latin prep.*

po·st-final. *Linguistics.* [Post- B. 1 c.] In a word-final consonant cluster, a consonant following a main final consonant. Cf. *pre-final *sb.*

1933, 1965 [see *pre-final *sb.*].

postfix, *v.* Add: **2.** *Biol.* To fix again after a previous fixation; to treat with a second fixative.

1960 D. C. Pease *Histol. Techniques Electron Microscopy* iii. 49 The small blocks are washed..in the buffer, and then postfixed in buffered osmium tetroxide. 1969 *Jrnl. Cell Sci.* IV. 439 After perfusion blocks were cut from the cerebral cortex which were post-fixed by placing them without washing in a 2% solution of OsO_4. 1976 *Nature* 5 Aug. 494/2 The tissue was immediately fixed in collidine-buffered glutaraldehyde and after a short buffer rinse, postfixed in osmium tetroxide.

postfixa·tion, *a.* and *sb.* **A.** *adj. Biol.* [Post- B. 1 a.] Carried out or used after the fixation of tissue.

1958 J. R. Baker *Princ. Biol. Microtechnique* i. 30 The fixative..may be unsuitable for indefinite preservation... In such cases a post-fixation preservative may be used. 1961 *Jrnl. Biophysical & Biochem. Cytol.* XI. 492 (*heading*) Method for obtaining increased contrast in Araldite sections by using postfixation staining of tissues with potassium permanganate. 1966 R. Mahoney *Lab. Techniques Zool.* v. 285 (*heading*) Post-fixation preservatives.

B. *sb.* **1.** *Anat.* [*post- B. 2 b.] The state of a nerve of being postfixed (sense *2).

1953 G. A. G. Mitchell *Anat. Autonomic Nervous Syst.* xiv. 202 The sympathetic preganglionic fibres issuing from the cord are found chiefly in all the thoracic and upper two lumbar ventral nerve roots, although occasionally prefixation or postfixation may occur in association with coincident shifts of somatic nerves. 1957 *Ann. R. Coll. Surgeons England* XXI. 367 Table II shows that.. there is a much higher incidence of 'postfixation'.

2. *Biol.* [Post- A. 1 b.] Fixation of tissue that has already been treated with a fixative.

1963 *Jrnl. Cell Biol.* XVII. 28/2 For adequate post-fixation in osmium tetroxide of tissues fixed in the aldehydes ..the blocks were washed in buffered sucrose solution. 1967 *Jrnl. Cell. Sci.* II. 379 Post-fixation in osmium tetroxide was carried out for not less than 1 h. 1975 *Nature* 18 Dec. 613/2 Double fixation for blood cells with glutaraldehyde and osmium, followed by uranyl acetate postfixation, was also used.

po·stfixed, *ppl. a.* **1.** [f. Postfix *v.* + -ed[1].] Affixed at the end of or after a word, root, or stem.

1874 [in Dict. s.v. Postfix *v.*]. 1975 *Amer. Speech 1969* XLIV. 107 The endings of the English verbs have evolved in a continuing process from earliest Indo-European times, or perhaps more remotely from earliest Proto-Indo-European-Uralic-Altaic (at which time, one may surmise, they represented nothing more than postfixed pronominal forms).

2. *Anat.* [f. Post- A. 2 a + Fixed *ppl. a.*] Of a nerve: connected to the spinal cord relatively caudally. Cf. *prefixed, prefixt *ppl. a.* 3.

1892 C. S. Sherrington in *Jrnl. Physiol.* XIII. 635 A plexus and its trunks and branches will..be referred to as prefixed if containing spinal root-filaments attached to the cord further forward (headward) than are the root-filaments entering the corresponding trunks and branches of a converse class of plexus which will be referred to conversely as postfixed. 1931 *Proc. R. Soc.* B. CVII. 511 In animals with a 'post-fixed' sacral plexus this has been done by dividing extradurally the 6th and 7th post-thoracic dorsal roots... In animals with a normal or 'pre-fixed' sacral plexus only the 6th post-thoracic dorsal root has been divided.

3. *Biol.* [f. *postfix *v.* 2 + -ed[1].] Treated with a second fixative.

1968 *Jrnl. Cell Sci.* III. 579 The tissue elements in the glutaraldehyde-perfused and OsO_4 post-fixed cortex are separated by narrow extracellular spaces.

postflight, *a.* and *adv.* [Flight *sb.*[1]] **A.** *adj.* [Post- B. 1 a.] Existing or occurring after (a) flight. **B.** *adv.* [*post- B. 1 d.] After flight.

1970 N. Armstrong et al. *First on Moon* iv. 84 There was some suspicion, lingering in the postflight shock of the first Sputnik, that this was the road the Soviet Union had chosen. 1971 *New Scientist* 29 July 249/1 Postflight there was an important development... The cosmonauts.. suffered from severe orthostatic hypotension.

postfo·rming, *vbl. sb.* [f. Post- A. 1 b + Forming *vbl. sb.*] Shaping of thermosetting laminated plastic carried out upon reheating before setting is complete. So **post-fo·rmed** *ppl. a.*, **post-fo·rm** *v. trans.*

1945 *Metals & Alloys* XXI. 392/1 (*heading*) Post-formed laminated phenolic plastics. *Ibid.*, 392/2 The term of post-forming is generally used to designate the procedure by which this material is formed after the laminations have been heat-set. 1945 *Plastics* IX. 266/2 The first important reference to laminated plastics for hot post-forming was probably the announcement of 'Micarta 444' by the Westinghouse Electric and Manufacturing Co. of America. 1965 *Encycl. Polymer Sci. & Technol.* II. 53 To facilitate this postforming ability, a melamine-formaldehyde resin with an added plasticizer is used for impregnation. 1967 P. B. Schubert *Die Methods* II. ii. 53 (*heading*) Designing dies for postforming thermosetting laminates. 1970 *Interior Design* Dec. 753/1 The 78 feet long, chevron-shaped post office counter is entirely clad in postforming grade Formica laminate. 1971 P. Tooley *High Polymers* ii. 60 Polymethyl methacrylate..softens at about 120°C and becomes quite pliable at 160°C. This enables the sheet polymer to be 'post-formed' in the fabrication of smooth streamlined shapes such as windows. 1977 *Cleethorpes News* 27 May 6/7 (Advt.), Worth a second look are..the wide range of worktops in ceramics square and postformed laminates.

post-free, *a.* Add: (Examples.) Also as *adv.*, without postal charge.

1723 *Boston News-Let.* 7 Mar. 2/2 The Publisher... Desires them to send their Accounts Post-Free. 1743 Pope *Dunciad* I. 65 [*Note*] It was a practise so to give the Daily Gazetteer and ministerial pamphlets..and to send them *Post-free* to all the Towns in the kingdom. 1873 *Young Englishwoman* Apr. 202/2 Patterns sent post-free. 1929 *Times* 1 Nov. 16/6 The post-free price for copies ordered direct from the publisher is 5s. 9d. 1980 *Radio Times* 12–18 Jan. 10/1 (Advt.), Send for Littlewoods new catalogue... Post-free. No stamp needed.

post-Freu·dian, *sb.* and *a.* [Post- B. 1 b.] **A.** *sb.* Someone whose psychotherapeutic ideas or practice have developed and diverged from strictly Freudian doctrine; someone whose views have been influenced as a result of Freudian theory. **B.** *adj.* Subsequent to the impact and influence of Freudian ideas. Cf. *Freudian *a.* (*sb.*).

1938 *Essays & Stud. 1937* XXIII. 82 He [*sc.* Balzac] had little to learn of normal psychology from the post-Freudians. 1961 J. A. C. Brown (*title*) Freud and the post-Freudians. 1964 E. Becker in I. L. Horowitz *New Sociol.* 114 Mills has here failed to push on to a fully post-Freudian social psychology. 1966 *Listener* 13 Jan. 64/3 We should have no post-Freudian difficulties in reconciling patience, honour, and kindness with destiny, treachery, and retribution. 1973 *Times* 29 Dec. 12/6 Heavenly rewards hereafter make us post-Freudians suspicious. 1977 R. L. Wolff *Gains & Losses* i. 46 The emotional language frequent in nineteenth-century friendships between persons of the same sex..arouses thoughts in post-Freudian minds that sometimes were not present..in pre-Freudian minds.

postganglio·nic, *a. Anat.* [Post- B. 2.] Of a nerve of the autonomic nervous system: running from a ganglion to the organ which it innervates.

1897 [see *preganglionic *a.*]. 1908 *Jrnl. Physiol.* XXXVII. 139 Prof. Langley remarks that according to him all reflexes in the sympathetic system isolated from the spinal cord are such axon-reflexes either in pre- or postganglionic fibres. 1946 *Nature* 19 Oct. 556/1 Giant fibres which..are distributed, one in each postganglionic stellar nerve, to the mantle musculature. 1968 Passmore & Robson *Compan. Med. Stud.* I. xxiv. 88/2 Postganglionic fibres are unmyelinated. 1974 [see *preganglionic *a.*].

Hence **postganglio·nically** *adv.*

1967 [see *preganglionically *adv.*].

post-genitive: see *post- A. 1 b.

post-glacial, *a.* Add: Also as *sb.*, a post-glacial deposit or period; **post-gla·cially** *adv.*

1928 *Funk's Stand. Dict.*, *Post-glacial* n., a sedimentary deposit resulting from the retreat of a continental glacier. 1937 A. L. Du Toit *Our Wandering Continents* iv. 77 Over extensive areas the ice-front discharged into the ocean or else the sea lay not far away, as indicated by the marine post-glacials. 1949 *Bull. Geol. Soc. Amer.* LX. 1369/2 Some overlapping of ranges has taken place post-glacially, wherever reproductive isolation has gone far enough to permit it. 1957 J. K. Charlesworth *Quaternary Era* II. xliv. 1231 The Dogger Bank..was post-glacially dry land or a vast freshwater fen. 1975 J. G. Evans *Environment Early Man Brit. Isles* i. 8 We at present are in a period optimistically termed the Post-glacial, but which may be an interglacial.

post-grad (pō^u^stgræ·d), *sb.* and *a.* Colloq. abbrev. of Post-graduate *a.* (*sb.*).

1950 [see *grad[1]]. 1973 'D. Shannon' *No Holiday for Crime* (1974) vi. 93 Ron set up another one, one of the postgrad students. 1976 *Eastern Daily Press* (Norwich) 19 Nov. 9/6 (Advt.), Four Cambridge post-grads seek accommodation, Wymondham area. 1979 *Guardian* 26 Oct. 10/2 Best four years of your life..your postgrad days.

post-graduate, *a.* (*sb.*) Add: **A.** *adj.* (Further examples.) Also, *spec.* with reference to a second or further degree. Also *transf.* and *fig.*

1900 *Dialect Notes* II. 48 *P.G.* i.e. *post-graduate*, or *pretty girl*, n. 1. A post-graduate student. 2. A pretty girl. 1931 J. van Dernoot (*title*) Postgraduate contract bridge: advanced points for advanced players. 1952 A. Huxley *Let.* 12 Oct. (1969) 657 Let it be a post-graduate school. 1955 *Publ. Amer. Dial. Soc.* xxiv. 30 Only after they [*sc.* amateur adult criminals] have been exposed to the postgraduate curriculum of prison life do a few of them make possible recruits for the ranks of the professionals. 1965 *Nursing Times* 5 Feb. p. lxii (Advt.), *Post-graduate nurses*... Applications invited for this course from S.R.N.s..and Enrolled Nurses. 1974 *Times* 31 Jan. 3/2 Strong criticism of proposals to give loans to postgraduate students to supplement state grants. 1975 *Language for Life* (Dept. Educ. & Sci.) xxiii. 338 A form of teacher training which has shown a considerable expansion in recent years is the one-year course for graduates, leading to a post-graduate certificate of education. 1978 *Time* 3 July 48/1 Beatty is also a health-food enthusiast and, as Nichols notes, 'a postgraduate hypochondriac'.

B. *sb.* (Examples.) Also *transf.*, and loosely, one who has received a higher degree.

1900 *Congress. Rec.* 19 Feb. 1917/1 Now, the Senator is a senior, a post-graduate of great distinction of the academy of which he is now a member. 1904 M. E. Waller *Wood-Carver of 'Lympus* 178 Marking out the work for the post-graduates..has filled my time. 1932 *Daily Express* 20 Sept. 7/2 Able young post-graduates in America..have a love of knowledge. 1959 *New Statesman* 23 May 730/2 There is the 'grand tour' of the post-graduate, working off his money at the end of a year at Harvard or Princeton. 1972 *Daily Tel.* 22 Sept. 3/7 It..was the brainchild of John Fauvel, 24, a postgraduate in mathematics. 1975 *Physics Bull.* Mar. 129/3 By issuing in both cased and paperback editions, Macmillan have ensured that post-graduates should be able to afford it.

Hence **post-gradua·tion.**

1920 H. Crane *Let.* 14 Apr. (1965) 37 His last letter told of splenetic days following his post-graduation from Columbia.

post-heating: see *post- A. 1 b.

post-histo·ric, *a.* [f. Post- B. 1 b, after *prehistoric.*] Of, belonging to, or pertaining to, an imagined period beyond the close of recorded history or otherwise subsequent to the present historical period; also *transf.* Hence **po·st-history.**

1918 S. Graham *Quest of Face* i. 50 There never leaves his eyes the gleam of something beyond this time, the post-historic. 1953 S. Spender *Creative Element* 133 We live in an epoch without historic precedent, which may indeed be a kind of post-history. 1957 *Times Lit. Suppl.* 15 Nov. 689/3 When the scholars of post-historic China or India study English literature in the twentieth century. 1961 L. Mumford *City in Hist.* i. 4 His dehumanized alter ego, 'Post-historic Man'. 1977 *N.Y. Rev. Bks.* 27 Oct. 31/1 Benjamin's study of what might be called the post-history or the afterlife of works of literature has spurred the recent interest in the 'history of reception' among younger critics in Germany.

postholder. Add: **2.** [Reconstituted from native elements.] One who occupies a post or office; an official.

1976 *Cumberland News* 3 Dec. 32/7 (Advt.), Our Regional Officer..requires a person to look after the Carlisle office for a minimum of two months while the current postholder is away.

post-hole. Add: **1.** Also spec. *Archæol.*, a hole orig. dug to receive a wooden post and usu. packed with stones or clay to support the post. Also *attrib.* other than of implements, as *post-hole evidence, pattern.*

1932 *Times Lit. Suppl.* 28 July 542/3 The misprint 'portholes' for 'postholes'..should not betray the unwary reader into attributing too nautical a flavour to the Iron Age fort of Salmonsbury. **1936** *Discovery* Apr. 99/2 New house-sites were brought to light: some were of wattle-and-daub, and another with a compacted floor and post-holes was similar in plan to one discovered in 1934. **1962** H. R. LOYN *Anglo-Saxon Eng.* i. 43 Photography..and analysis of post-hole evidence have disclosed a series of royal halls. **1963** *Field Archaeol.* (Ordnance Survey) (ed. 4) 37 There are no stone settings or any indications of post-holes. **1971** *World Archaeol.* III. 120 Posthole patterns will be confused. **1977** *Antiquaries Jrnl.* LVII. 261 'Stakehole' is used here to mean the void made by the decay of timber post driven into the ground; 'posthole' means a larger hole excavated in order to insert a post.

2. A hole or well drilled to not very great depth.

1932 *Amer. Speech* VII. 269 [Language of California oil fields.] *Post-hole*, a shallow hole. *Post-hole territory*, shallow productive territory—i.e., in which the oil sands lie at depths up to 2500 feet, 'just under the grass roots'. **1965** G. J. WILLIAMS *Econ. Geol. N.Z.* ix. 133/1 The only published information directly relating to the ironsands represents the pioneering work of Nicholson, Fyfe (1958) who put down post-hole bores to depths of not more than 25 ft.

post-I·bsen, *a.* [f. POST- B. 1 a + the name of Henrik *Ibsen* (see *IBSENISM).] Subsequent to the life or works of Ibsen; influenced by the style or views (esp. concerning social reform) of Ibsen. Hence **post-I·bsenist** *a.*, pertaining to or characteristic of drama subsequent to, and influenced by, Ibsen; also as *sb.*, a developer of the methods or views of Ibsen.

1913 G. B. SHAW *Quintessence of Ibsenism* (Completed ed.) 199 The post-Ibsen playwrights. *Ibid.* 206 What I have called post-Ibsenist plays. *Ibid.* 209 The post-Ibsenists. **1919** —— *Heartbreak House* p. xxxvii, The most advanced post-Ibsen plays in the most artistic settings. **1930** E. POUND *XXX Cantos* xxviii. 131 So Loica went out and died there After her time in the post-Ibsen movement.

postical, *a.* For *Obs.* read *rare* and add later examples.

1940 *Chambers's Techn. Dict.* 666/1 *Postical*, relating to or belonging to the back or lower part of a leaf or stem. **1965** F. E. ROUND *Introd. Lower Plants* viii. 105 Branching may occur at the apex or it may be intercalary. In the former, new three-sided apical cells are formed by cleavage in the leaf of initial cells—usually in the ventral half, thus eliminating the ventral (i.e. postical) lobe of the leaf.

postiche, *a.* and *sb.* Add: **B.** *sb.* **c.** A piece of false hair worn as an adornment. Also *attrib.*

1886 C. E. PASCOE *London of To-day* (ed. 3) xl. 345 False tresses have been imported by cart-loads..and postiches and other mysteries of the toilette have been brought to that perfection to which competition so greatly conduces. **1908** *Westm. Gaz.* 21 Nov. 15/2 The postiches in use must be carefully manipulated to afford the exact size demanded. **1928** *Sunday Dispatch* 9 Dec. 8 The permanent wave has already given place to the permanent curl. And the little *postiches* (buns) which have made their appearance in Paris are being eagerly adopted. **1966** J. S. COX *Illustr. Dict. Hairdressing* 120/2 *Postiche clip*, a small, flat spring clip to which are attached small postiches; used to secure them to the growing hair of a head. **1970** J. G. VERMANDEL *Dine with Devil* i. 10 Try that big hat; it might be good for a waiflike effect, very ingenue. And the postiche with..what's that long white thing?

post-ictal(ly: see *POST- B. 1.

postie (pō̆u·sti). *slang.* Also **posty.** [f. POST *sb.*[2] + -IE, -Y[6].] A familiar name for a postman.

1871 S. S. JONES *Northumberland* 84/1 Tom Buglehorn, the postie,..when he cam wi' the letters. **1886** H. BAUMANN *Londinismen* 143/2 Posty. **1892** G. STEWART *Shetland Fireside Tales* (ed. 2) 227, I mind when I saw 'Posty' come, My heart began ta beat. **1898** [see *NUFF 1 b]. **1916** 'TAFFRAIL' *Pincher Martin* ix. 163 The marine postman..was delayed... ''Ere, posty!' shouted some one, 'got my *Dispatch?*' **1939** F. THOMPSON *Lark Rise* vi. 106 There was one postal delivery a day, and towards ten o'clock, the heads of the women..would be turned..to watch for 'Old Postie'. **1953** E. SIMON *Past Masters* II. 76 If Postie did not offer one a lift on the road—that could not be imagination. **1962** *Coast to Coast 1961–62* 73 They had a long run on outdoor workers at one stage, and it was often a cop or a postie. **1975** D. CLARK *Premeditated Murder* ii. 29 The postman would read the name rather than the number. So how did the posty..give Harte a card addressed..to Rencory? **1977** *S. Wales Guardian* 27 Oct. 6/2 He was missed by the upper valley residents on his transfer down to Ammanford, where he has been a 'postie' for the past 13 years.

postilion, postillion. Add: **6.** *postilion back* (earlier example).

1872 *Young Englishwoman* Dec. 651/2 A dress of olive-brown..had a basque bodice with a postilion back.

posti·l(l)ion, *v. slang.* [f. the sb.] *trans.* To insert and manipulate a finger in the anus of (a sexual partner) as a means of sexual excitement. Hence **posti·l(l)ioning** *vbl. sb.*

1888 tr. *Tableaux Vivants* xi. 95 The fair houri was postillioning me. **1969** G. LEGMAN *Oragenitalism* i. 90 Postillioning can best be done by the middle finger.

post-impre·ssionism. Freq. with capital initials. [POST- B. 1 c.] The theory or practice of the post-impressionist school in art; *spec.* a style of painting favoured in the early years of the twentieth century in which the artist sought to reveal the structural form of his subject without strict fidelity to its natural appearance; a movement or group of aims in art which constitutes a development away from impressionism.

1910 C. J. HOLMES *Notes on Post-Impressionist Painters* 11 The tradition of Post-Impressionism,..if any principles so youthful can be called a tradition, is the expression of personal vision. **1910** *Connoisseur* Dec. 315/2 The committee..wisely diluted the post-impressionism of the pictures in the entrance room by the inclusion of a dozen or more examples by Manet. **1932** *John o' London's Weekly* 30 Jan. 678/3 'Harbour of Gravelines' shows him [*sc.* Seurat] trying..to impose upon impressionism its missing sense of form. But that triumph goes to the two masters of post-impressionism, to Cezanne [*sic*] and Gauguin. **1948** R. O. DUNLOP *Understanding Pictures* iii. 20 This painter's name was, of course, Paul Cézanne, the unconscious founder of Post-Impressionism. **1957** *Observer* 3 Nov. 14/3 The deficiencies of Impressionism..were clear to many in the 1880s, and the term Post-Impressionism covers the often very different reactions of artists. **1972** S. HYNES *Edwardian Occasions* 10 Bloomsbury..supported Roger Fry's efforts to publicize Post-Impressionism. **1978** *Antiques & Art Monitor* 28 Oct. 11/3 A major exhibition entitled 'Post-Impressionism and Europe' is scheduled for the Royal Academy, London, next year.

post-impre·ssionist. Freq. with capital initials. [POST- B. 1 b.] An artist whose work exhibits one or more of the facets of post-impressionism; also *transf.* and *attrib.* or as *adj.* Hence **post-impressioni·stic** *a.*, characteristic of the post-impressionists.

1910 *Poster* in *Lett. R. Fry* (1972) I. Pl. 47 Grafton Gallery. Manet and the Post-Impressionists. **1910** C. J. HOLMES *Notes on Post-Impressionists* 10 In the first Post-Impressionist painters we have a reaction from the materialism which limited the original Impressionists to the rendering of natural effects of light and colour with the greatest attainable scientific truth. **1911** *Athenæum* 28 Jan. 104/3 Post-Impressionist Sculpture. **1913** A. E. HOUSMAN *Let.* 8 Mar. (1971) 129 An exhibition of post-impressionist undergraduate art, which is calculated to frighten the Germans. **1913** *Punch* 16 July 70/1 They grumble at the ladies' skirts, The Post-Impressionistic settings. **1914** H. HOLLEY (*title*) Creation: Post-Impressionist poems. **1922** C. BELL *Since Cézanne* 81, I can' think why you don't like it: its Post-Impressionist isn't it? **1928** [see *CUBISM]. **1934** C. LAMBERT *Music Ho!* III. 22 The post-impressionist harmonic experiments, the austerities and asperities of Stravinsky and Bartók. **1945** D. MACCARTHY *Memories* (1953) 181 'What was the exhibition to be called?'.. At last Roger [Fry], losing patience, said: 'Oh, let's just call them post-impressionists; at any rate, they come after the impressionists.' **1957** MANVELL & HUNTLEY *Technique Film Music* iii. 70 In each sequence décor is derived from the style of one or other of the post-Impressionist painters. **1974** *Impressionism* (R. Acad.) 53/1 Increasingly affected by Post-Impressionists 1909+, with rest of Camden Town Group. **1978** *Jrnl. R. Soc. Arts* CXXVI. 701/2 Mrs. Potter Palmer had been buying Impressionist and post-Impressionist paintings with great discernment almost a century ago.

post-infectious: see *POST- B. 1.

posting, *vbl. sb.*[1] Add: **I. 3.** Also, the (amount of) mail posted during a given period.

1909 *Daily Chron.* 30 Dec. 3/6 During the Christmas week of last year the postings in London alone totalled upwards of 70,000,000. **1971** D. POTTER *Brit. Eliz. Stamps* i. 14 Beginning with the Shakespeare set in 1964, special envelopes were..used. Stratford-on-Avon must have had one of their heaviest postings ever.

posting, *vbl. sb.*[2] Add: **2. b.** *posting-board.*

1838 *Actors by Daylight* I. 182 A pair or two of wooden posting-boards.

post-la·rval, *a. Zool.* [POST- B. 1 b.] Belonging or pertaining to those stages in the development of certain animals in which some larval characteristics may be retained, before the adult form is reached. So **post-la·rva,** an animal, esp. a fish, during this period of its development.

1898 *Proc. Zool. Soc.* 204 (*title*) On the early post-larval stages of the Common Crab. **1929** *Amer. Naturalist* LXIII. 160 Some..interesting discoveries..have resulted from the writer's investigations into the habits of young postlarval lobsters. **1942** *Copeia* 126 (*heading*) The occurrence of flounder post larvae in fish stomachs. **1962** K. F. LAGLER et al. *Ichthyol.* x. 313 Differences between postlarvae and adults in some fishes are so trenchant that they have resulted from time to time in taxonomic confusion. **1967** *Oceanogr. & Marine Biol.* V. 239 The postlarval development of Copepods similarly aroused Mazza's interest. **1972** *Aquaculture* I. 179 (*caption*) Third postlarval stage with 18 mm of total length. **1973** *Ibid.* I. 363 Postlarvae and juvenile siganids are attracted by artificial light at night.

postliteral: see *POST- B. 1.

postlude. Restrict *Mus.* to sense in Dict. and add: **a.** (Further examples.)

1947 A. EINSTEIN *Mus. Romantic Era* xiv. 187 The task..of supplying a commentary in the prelude and, particularly, the postlude. **1955** G. ABRAHAM in H. Van Thal *Fanfare for E. Newman* 26 The second version of the piano postlude to 'Schmerzen' was sent to Frau Wesendonk on a separate piece of paper. **1976** *Gramophone* Jan. 1229/1 Why the ties in the penultimate bar of the prelude and postlude of 'Pause'?

b. A written or spoken epilogue; an afterword, conclusion; an envoy.

1928 M. WILLIAMS *Catholicism & Mod. Mind* 339 (*heading*) Postlude: Easter in Gethsemani. **1934** *Punch* 2 May 503/2 Miss Bowen's 'postlude', a carefully reasoned essay in historical criticism, is a drastic and devastating but on many points convincing analysis of romantic legend. **1939** JOYCE *Finnegans Wake* (1964) 426 As the wisest postlude course he could playact, collaspsed [*sic*] in ensemble and rolled buoyantly backwards. **1959** *Times* 11 Sept. 16/6 Mr. Gerald Moore..whose little summarizing postludes to many of the songs..were miracles of concentrated wisdom. **1974** *Times* 15 Apr. 5/6 The rumpus was mostly caused by a very offensive postlude, spoken by one of the actors.

Hence **po·stlude** *v. intr.*, to supply a postlude; **postlu·dial** *a.*

1960 'A. BURGESS' *Doctor is Sick* xxi. 174 The psalmist ended, postluded. **1961** *Times* 10 Nov. 18/6 One of the poems is set twice: another has a preludial and postludial movement.

postman[1]**.** Add: **1. d.** In the possessive, as **postman's knock**: (*a*) a sharp knock or rap upon a door, typically made by a postman; (*b*) *transf.*, esp. a parlour game in which the participants in turn take the role of postman and deliver letters which are paid for by kisses.

1835 [see sense 1 b in Dict.]. **1837** DICKENS *Pickw.* xxix. 312 Sam Weller..was displaying that beautiful feat of fancy sliding which is currently denominated 'knocking at the cobbler's door', and which is achieved by skimming over the ice on one foot, and occasionally giving a two-penny postman's knock upon it, with the other. **1847** *Sporting Life* 11 Dec. 204/1 The *postman's knock*—a quick rat-tap, which only a postman can execute. **1873** C. M. YONGE *Pillars of House* III. xxxii. 199 A postman's knock made her start. **1927** W. E. COLLINSON *Contemp. Eng.* 12, I was interested to see the kissing-forfeit game of postman's knock under the guise of 'American post'. **1928** *Daily Express* 30 July 13/6 Rose's left glove was seldom out of his opponent's face, and he often brought off a punch which in the old days was called 'The Postman's Knock'. **1954** M. SHARP *Gipsy in Parlour* xii. 125 Postman's Knock found me..maladroit: to one pimply youth who called me out I presented such a face of scorn that he never kissed me.

postmaster[1]**.** Add: **3.** *Canad.* The master of a fur-trading post.

1832 in R. H. Fleming *Minutes Council Northern Dept. Rupert Land* (Hudson Bay Co.) (1940) 236 Post Masters Are a Class which ranks in the Service between Interpreters & Clerks. They are generally persons who while filling the office of common Labourers..were..raised from the 'ranks' and placed in charge of small Posts at Salys. from 35 to £45 p. Annm. **1953** A. R. M. LOWER *Unconventional Voy.* 33 The postmaster at Attawapiskat ..was minus the toes on his right foot.

postmaster general. Add: On 1 Oct. 1969 the office of postmaster general was abolished in Great Britain and responsibility for executing its functions was transferred to the newly constituted Post Office Board.

postmaster-generalship (earlier example).

1882 E. W. HAMILTON *Diary* 26 Nov. (1972) I. 365 In this list he had included..the Postmaster Generalship.

postmatu·re, *a.* [f. POST- B. 1 b; cf. PREMATURE *a.* in Dict. and Suppl.] **1.** *Obstetrics.* = *POST-TERM *a.*

1895 F. A. STAHL in *Amer. Jrnl. Obstetr. & Dis. Women* XXXI. 843, I take the liberty of suggesting the adoption of the term postmature labor to apply to labor which takes place after term. **1937** *Amer. Jrnl. Obstetr. & Gynecol.* XXXIV. 37 When pregnancy is prolonged by new corpora lutea or by progesterone, large postmature fetuses are produced. **1972** S. B. KORONES *High-Risk Newborn Infants* iv. 89 Approximately 75% to 85% of all deaths among postmature babies occur during labor.

2. Pertaining to or designating a person who is over the age of maturity.

1897 A. D. L. NAPIER *Menopause* iv. 79 In the post-mature woman it is partly in the early senile changes that we must look for a solution of the climacteric. **1941** J. S. HUXLEY *Uniqueness of Man* i. 19 A large proportion of the leaders of the community are always post-mature. **1971** *Biochim. & Biophys. Acta* CCXXXVI. 458 (*heading*) Evidence for progressive, age-related structural changes in post-mature human collagen.

Hence **postmatu·rely** *adv.*; **postmatu·rity,** the state of being postmature.

1902 *Jrnl. Obstetr. & Gynæcol.* II. 524 Neither the dimensions of the fœtus, nor the degree of development of his tissues and organs, nor the history of the pregnancy, can be taken as certain proof of postmaturity. **1933** *Jrnl. Pediatrics* II. 677 Similar factors of safety and stability seem to operate when the infant is postmaturely born, for in his behavior equipment he is advanced even though birth is postponed. **1937** *Amer. Jrnl. Obstetr. & Gynecol.*

XXXIV. 36 Kaern found that there was a definite relationship between postmaturity, excessive size of the fetus, and intrauterine death. **1941** J. S. Huxley *Uniqueness of Man* i. 18 Another point in which man is biologically unique is the length and relative importance of his period of what we may call 'post-maturity.' **1972** E. D. Morris in C. J. Dewhurst *Integrated Obstetr. & Gynaecol.* xxii. 383/1 Postmaturity can, in general, be said to be present when the pregnancy has continued so long beyond term that an extra risk to the foetus exists. **1977** *Lancet* 3 Dec. 1169/2 Labour was induced, often before term, for obstetric reasons..and also for post-maturity—which was defined as 40 weeks plus 7 days.

postmedial, *a.* Add: Also in *Linguistics* and *absol.* as *sb.*

1946 L. Bloomfield in H. Hoijer et al. *Ling. Struct. Native Amer.* 104 Suffixes appear in divergent forms, so that we set off accretive elements: premedials, post-medials, prefinals. **1958** *Archivum Linguisticum* X. 170 In some words Postradical, Medial, Postmedial, and Prefinal elements are recognized.

post-meiotic, -menarch(e)al: see *post- B. 1.

postme·nstrual, *a. Med.* [Post- B. 1 b.] Occurring after menstruation.

1885 *Brit. Med. Jrnl.* 14 Feb. 342/2 Taking the 'menstrual period' as lasting about four days, he marked off on his temperature-charts four days before the 'show' as the 'premenstrual period', and four days after as the 'post-menstrual period'. **1901** A. E. Giles *Menstruation* ii. 17 The metabolic changes may thus be summarised:..in the post-menstrual week, gradual return to the normal condition. **1922** Joyce *Ulysses* 411 The postmenstrual period. **1948** *Amer. Jrnl. Obstetr. & Gynecol.* LV. 38 In other regions the endometrium was of the usual postmenstrual type, and was covered with surface epithelium.

postme·nstruum. *Med.* [mod. L.: see Post- B. 1 c and Menstruum.] The stage of the menstrual cycle which follows menstruation.

1910 *Trans. N.Y. Obstetr. Soc. 1909–11* 229 They [*sc.* Hitchmann and Adler] divide the monthly cycle into four phases. The first phase, the postmenstruum, corresponds to the picture of the normal endometrium of our text-books. The glands are small and regular, round in cross-section. **1933** *Amer. Jrnl. Anat.* LII. 564 Jaeger.. and Blumenfeld..found conception most frequent in postmenstruum (63·6 per cent up to the fourteenth day). **1964** K. Dalton *Premenstrual Syndrome* iv. 23 Symptoms limited to the postmenstruum are extremely rare.

post-metamorphic, -mineral: see *post- B. 1.

postmito·tic, *a. Cytology.* [Post- B. 1 b.] After mitosis; *spec.* (of a cell) having ceased (reversibly or irreversibly) to display cell division. Also *absol.*, a cell which is unlikely or unable to divide again.

1942 E. V. Cowdry *Probl. Ageing* (ed. 2) xxiv. 628 The highly specialized cells, formed from the last differentiating intermitotics at the end of the series,..are 'end cells'. Their individual lives begin..after the last mitosis... In a word, they are postmitotics. *Ibid.* 631 The length of life of the majority of postmitotic nerve cells can be taken to be that of the body less one year. **1962** *Lancet* 27 Jan. 211/1 The granulocytes are post-mitotic and can be ruled out, and so we are restricted to the 'mononuclears'. **1968** H. Harris *Nucleus & Cytoplasm* v. 92 When all the nuclei in the heterokaryon enter mitosis together, post-mitotic reconstitution may produce a single large nucleus at one step. **1971** J. Z. Young *Introd. Study Man* xxii. 288 Errors in the hereditary instructions and their transcription may be of especial importance in post-mitotic cells.

post-mo·dern, *a.* Also post-Modern. [Post- B. 1 b.] Subsequent to, or later than, what is 'modern'; *spec.* in the arts, esp. *Archit.*, applied to a movement in reaction against that designated 'modern' (cf. *modern *a.* 2 h). Hence **post-mo·dernism, post-mo·dernist** *a.* and *sb.*

1949 J. Hudnut *Archit. & Spirit of Man* ix. 108 (*heading*) Post-modern house. *Ibid.* 119 He shall be a modern owner, a post-modern owner, if such a thing is conceivable. Free from all sentimentality or fantasy or caprice. **1956** A. Toynbee *Historian's Approach to Relig.* II. xi. 146 Our post-Modern Age of Western history. **1959** C. W. Mills *Sociol. Imagination* ix. 166 Just as Antiquity was followed by several centuries of Oriental ascendancy ..so now the Modern Age is being succeeded by a post-modern period. Perhaps we may call it: The Fourth Epoch. **1965** L. A. Fiedler in *Partisan Rev.* XXXII. 508, I am not now interested in analyzing..the diction and imagery which have passed from Science Fiction into post-Modernist literature. **1966** F. Kermode in *Encounter* Apr. 73/1 Pop fiction demonstrates 'a growing sense of the irrelevance of the past' and Top [*sic*] writers ('post-Modernists') are catching on. **1966** N. Pevsner in *Listener* 29 Dec. 955/2 The fact that my enthusiasms cannot be roused by..Churchill College.., does not blind me to the existence today of a new style, successor to my International Modern of the nineteen-thirties, a post-modern style, I would be tempted to call it, but the legitimate style of the nineteen-fifties and nineteen-sixties. **1977** *N.Y. Rev. Bks.* 28 Apr. 30/3 A process that culminates, by a curious but inexorable logic, in the post-modernist demand for the abolition of art and its assimilation to 'reality'. **1979** *Jrnl. R. Soc. Arts* Nov. 743/1 Many Post-Modern architects use motifs..in questionable taste. *Ibid.* 751/1 Post-Modernists have substituted the body metaphor for the machine metaphor, because so much research has shown that we unconsciously project bodily states into architecture. **1979** *Time* 8 Jan. 53/1 The nearest man Post-Modernism has to a senior partner is, in fact, the leading American architect of his generation: Philip Cortelyou Johnson. **1980** *Times Higher Educ. Suppl.* 7 Mar. 16/1 Postmodernism, structuralism, and neo-dada (formerly known as 'concrete poetry') all represent a reaction against modernism.

po:st-modifica·tion. *Linguistics.* [Post- A. 1 b.] The qualification or limitation of the sense of one word or phrase by another coming after. Also *attrib.* Hence **post-mo·difier; post-mo·difying** *vbl. sb.*

1962 R. Quirk *Use of English* xi. 181 In such units as *bravery of all kinds* or *bravery in the struggle against barbarism*, we meet..postmodification. **1965** *Language* XLI. 205 Deictic + head + post-modifier. **1970** *Eng. Stud.* LI. 404 The category noun modification is a large one (105 instances), almost half of them with postmodifying infinitives. **1975** *Amer. Speech 1971* XLVI. 224 A postmodification rule is necessary to transform relative clauses containing an infinitive, a prepositional phrase, or an adverb.

post mortem, post-mortem, *adv. phr.*, *a.*, and *sb.* Add: **B.** *adj.* (Further examples.) Also *transf.*

1909 *Westm. Gaz.* 8 June 5/1 M. Chauchard,..who is to sleep his last sleep..in a tomb which has cost nearly £4,000, has had many predecessors in post-mortem luxury. **1922** Joyce *Ulysses* 609 Her brandnew arrival is on her knee, *post mortem* child. **1962** *Gloss. Terms Automatic Data Processing* (*B.S.I.*) 45 *Post-mortem routine*, a diagnostic routine which may be used to indicate the contents of selected locations after a program has stopped. **1965** in Bessinger & Creed *Medieval & Linguistic Stud.* 54 What conception of the human spirit and its *post mortem* future is implied in our inscriptions? **1969** P. B. Jordain *Condensed Computer Encycl.* 389 Usually, when an unexpected or inexplicable difficulty is encountered, a postmortem dump is taken to record all available information about the failed state of a program: then a post-mortem analysis is made to discover the cause of the difficulty. **1979** R. Rendell *Means of Evil* 68 Doreen Betts's denial had..been.. a post-mortem white-washing of her mother's character.

C. *sb.* **2.** *transf.* A searching (and freq. recriminatory) analysis or discussion of a past event, as an examination or card-game. Cf. *inquest *sb.* 3 c.

In quot. 1844, a re-sit examination at Cambridge University.

1844 in Farmer & Henley *Slang* (1902) V. 264/1 I've passed the Post-mortem at last. **1907** R. Dunn *Shameless Diary of Explorer* ix. 111 Here in camp, we've been holding a post-mortem of the day. **1922** A. E. M. Foster *Light Side Auction Bridge* xxxvii. 155 The post-mortem fiend simply will not be denied. **1930** A. P. Herbert *Water Gipsies* viii. 82 'I knew,' he said at the family *post mortem* in the evening. 'I knew the colt had the legs of the field, if he only had the luck.' **1943** K. Tennant *Ride on Stranger* viii. 82 They drew in to the table and..began a family post mortem of the party. **1960** V. Jenkins *Lions Down Under* 114 The post-mortem at a team-talk in Timaru was a searching one. **1972** R. Markus *Aces & Places* 105 The post-mortem centred the blame on East for not ducking the jack of diamonds at trick two. **1974** L. Deighton *Spy Story* xii. 119 It's all right for you... You won't have to do the post-mortem with these guys.

Hence **post-morte·mity,** the state of death (*nonce-wd.*); **post-mo·rtemizing** *vbl. sb.*

1851 H. Melville *Moby Dick* III. ix. 67 At a certain juncture of this post-mortemizing of the whale. **1922** Joyce *Ulysses* 387 In the nights of prenativity and post-mortemity.

post-mo·rtem, *v.* [f. Post-mortem *a.*] *trans.* To subject to a post-mortem examination (in the senses of Dict. and Suppl.). Hence **post-mo·rteming** *vbl. sb.*

1871 M. Clarke *His Natural Life* (1874) III. xv. 291 'Strange that he should drop like that.'..'Yes, unless he had any internal disease... I'll *post-mortem* him and see.' **1900** *Jrnl. Compar. Path. & Therapeutics* XIII. 2 Hundreds of horses dead of horse-sickness had been post-mortemed by farriers and shoeing-smiths. **1910** H. G. Wells *Hist. Mr. Polly* iv. 105 You didn't, I suppose, Mr. Polly, think to 'ave your poor dear father *post-mortemed.* **1934** R. A. Knox *Still Dead* v. 67 The corpse..was taken up to the house and post-mortem'd and buried. **1971** D. E. Westlake *I gave at the Office* 123 If you people in the legal department manage to distill Truth from your post-morteming you'll be better than Solomon. **1977** N. Freeling *Gadget* I. 3 Who looks twice at a couple post-morteming a traffic scrape.

postmultiplication: see *post- A. 1 b.

postnatal, *a.* Add: *postnatal depression*, depression in a woman caused by a recent confinement, characterized by fatigue, irritability, and fits of crying. Hence **post-na·tally** *adv.*, after birth.

1927 *Jrnl. Anat.* LXI. 321 The two parts of which the foetal suprarenal is composed—the true cortex which persists post-natally and the foetal cortex which atrophies after birth—are generally considered to have a common origin. **1934** *Times Lit. Suppl.* 29 Mar. 222/2 The child.. contracts the actual disease only when post-natally brought into contact with the specific germ. **1966** *Ann. Rev. Med.* XVII. 221 The inhibition seems to disappear as the animal matures postnatally. **1973** *Guardian* 22 Feb. 13/2 Some 88,000 women a year were recently deemed in need of treatment for postnatal depression. **1978** J. Mann *Sting of Death* viii. 69 Anna Buxton was suffering severely from post-natal depression..a text-book case: Emmy was four months old.

postneonatal: see *post- B. 1.

post-Newto·nian, *a.* [f. Post- B. 1 b + Newtonian *a.* and *sb.*] Subsequent to the life or work of Sir Isaac Newton (1642–1727); *spec.* in *Physics* (see quots. 1964, 1973).

1865 Mill *Exam. Hamilton's Philos.* xxvii. 542 Applied mathematics in its post-Newtonian development does nothing to strengthen..these errors. **1963** N. Frye *Romanticism Reconsidered* 5 A post-Newtonian poet has to think of gravitation. **1964** *Astrophysical Jrnl.* CXL. 428 A post-Newtonian approximation, in which the effects of general relativity are treated as first-order corrections. **1973** *Nature* 31 Aug. 537/1 The only precise tests of the applicability of the theory of general relativity to the actual physical world are those long ago proposed by Einstein, and certain other tests proposed more recently that are closely related to Einstein's... They test the theory only to the so-called post-Newtonian approximation, roughly speaking to terms in $1/c^2$, where c is the speed of light. **1977** *Astrophysical Jrnl.* CCXVI. 914 The tidal radiation can be comparable to the radiation from post-Newtonian effects.

post-nominal: see *post- B. 1.

postno·tum. *Ent.* [f. Post- A. 2 b + Notum.] = Postscutellum.

1926 R. J. Tillyard *Insects Austral. & N.Z.* i. 18 In some cases..a short posterior sclerite is also developed, called the postnotum or postscutellum. **1964** R. M. & J. W. Fox *Introd. Compar. Entomol.* ii. 52 The notum continues forward to cover the posterior part of the next segment where it is termed the postnotum.

post-nu·clear, *a.* (*sb.*) [Post- B. 1 b.] **1.** *Phonetics.* Situated after a nucleus. Also *absol.* as *sb.*

1961 [see *internuclear *a.* 3]. **1961** Y. Olsson *On Syntax Eng. Verb* vii. 189 The variation between the post-nuclears *er* and *ee*..corresponds to a distinction between (2) and (1). **1968** *Language* XLIV. 80 Allotone 2..of the glide occurs in postnuclear syllables of the word. **1976** *Archivum Linguisticum* VII. 38 One feature both sub-classes share is their insistence that any non-nuclear occurrence be in prenuclear position rather than in tail (postnuclear) position.

2. Subsequent to the development or use of nuclear weaponry.

1963 *Economist* 7 Sept. 813/2 China was dreaming of a post-nuclear heaven. **1965** *Punch* 17 Feb. 259/3 Another post-nuclear society, this time dominated by farmers.

postnuptial, *a.* Add: Also, subsequent to mating (of animals).

1956 *Nature* 21 Jan. 143/1 Our experiment was begun on July 23..at about the estimated end of the post-nuptial refractory period and before the next season's spermatogenesis began.

post-oak. For *Quercus obtusiloba* substitute *Quercus stellata.* Also *attrib.* (Earlier and further examples.)

1775 B. Romans *Conc. Nat. Hist. E. & W. Florida* 18 The principal however are the following:..Virginian white oak... Dwarf white oak, or post oak. ***a* 1816** B. Hawkins *Sk. Creek Country* (1848) 19 The trees are post oak, white and black oak, pine [etc.]. *Ibid.* 20 Between these rivers, there is some good post and black oak land. **1836** D. B. Edwards *Hist. Texas* 46 They are protected.. by..post-oak ridges. **1892** J. C. Duval *Young Explorers* in *Early Times in Texas* II. ii. 14 About noon we came to a small stream bordered by a strip of post oak woods. **1906** 'O. Henry' *Four Million* 58 Joe Larrabee came out of the post-oak flats of the Middle West. **1945** B. A. Botkin *Lay my Burden Down* 263 They found the body of a white man hanging to a post oak. **1969** T. H. Everett *Living Trees of World* 118/2 The post oak..is widely distributed in dryish uplands from Massachusetts to Nebraska. **1975** *New Yorker* 5 May 101/1 All but six of the thirty-six holes are set off by themselves, framed by borders of post oak—a pretty tree that loses its large leaves in winter but retains its attractiveness because of the pleasing contortions of its branches.

Post Office, Post-Office. Add: Also with small initials. **2. b.** *transf.* A person who receives information and either transmits it or holds it for collection, esp. in espionage; also = *drop *sb.* 17 d. *slang.*

1885 E. W. Hamilton *Diary* 12 Apr. (1972) II. 835 M. Lessar suggests that Brett should be asked to be the post office of the Russian Embassy. Accordingly, Lessar goes to Brett, and hands him a Memorandum... Brett forwards the Memorandum here. **1919** J. Buchan *Mr. Standfast* vii. 148, I had got precisely what Blenkiron wanted, a post office for the enemy... I could see the juiciest lies passing that way to the *Grosses Hauptquartier.* **1935** A. J. Pollock *Underworld Speaks* 90/2 *Post office*, a person who receives or delivers letters to crooks. **1945** *Tee Emm* (Air Ministry) V. 55 Beware of becoming a 'post office', simply passing on everything that comes in, happy in the knowledge that there is a higher authority behind you. **1965** D. Williams *Not in Public Interest* vii. 133 It became evident in 1911 that the hairdresser's shop of Karl Gustav Ernst was being used as a 'post office' or clearing-house for German espionage agents in this country. **1974** T. Allbeury *Snowball* iv. 20 Just a low-grade courier, a dead letterbox and a post office.

2*. *U.S.* A parlour game in which the participants in turn act as postmaster or postmistress and pretend to deliver letters which are paid for by kisses. Cf. *postman's knock* (*POSTMAN[1] 1 d (*b*)).

The sense in quot. 1851 is uncertain.

1851 J. H. GREEN *Twelve Days in Tombs* 157 How often have the professors of Christianity violated all moral principles in the..game of Post-office, where we find stationed some beautiful sister as post mistress, whose duty it is to write the names of those from whom she thinks she can secure the postage. **1855** *Quincy* (California) *Prospector* 31 Mar. 2/1 We are astonished to see men and women who are looked upon as samples for the rising generation, join in such childish plays as.. 'Post office', &c. **1899** *Amer. Physical Educ. Rev.* 361 Those who select love games are at the dawn of adolescence. 'Drop-the-handkerchief' and 'post-office' are the two favorites of this group. **1904** C. S. DARROW *Farmington* 163 We had to keep still, and couldn't go outdoors, and had to play 'needle's eye' and 'post-office'. **1914** B. TARKINGTON in *Cosmopolitan* Mar. 489/2 'We'd have been playing "Quaker meeting", "clap in, clap out", or "going to Jerusalem", I suppose.' 'Yes, or "post-office" and "drop the handkerchief",' said Mrs. Schofield. **1949** *Sat. Even. Post* 12 Mar. 60/3 After a time this palled and they played Post Office.

3. *post-office directory*; also in the names of colours associated with various Post Office services, as *post-office green, red, yellow*; **post-office box** (*b*) = **post-office bridge*; **post-office bridge,** a portable self-contained form of Wheatstone bridge containing a large number of resistors which are selected by means of plugs; **post-office order** (earlier example); **post-office packet** *Hist.*, a packet-boat carrying mail for the Post Office; **post-office savings-bank,** add to def.: since 1 Oct. 1969, known as the National Savings Bank; hence *post-office savings(-bank)-book*.

1894 W. A. PRICE *Measurement Electr. Resistance* 81 Bridge ratios of 1000 and ·001 are available in addition to those in the Post Office box. **1914** *Phil. Mag.* XXVIII. 470 The resistances of the films of low resistance were measured by a post-office box in the ordinary way. **1965** G. A. G. BENNET *Electr. & Mod. Physics* viii. 129/2 A Wheatstone type network is connected up as shown ..with the galvanometer as one of the four resistances; a Post Office box would be suitable for this purpose. **1891** H. L. WEBB *Testing of Insulated Wires & Cables* vi. 38 A small clamp for holding the battery key down permanently would be a useful addition to a Post-office bridge. **1931** W. L. UPSON *Electr. Lab. Stud.* iii. 45 There is a second form of Wheatstone bridge known as the 'post-office bridge'. In this type there is no wire giving wide variability to the ratio of *B* to *A*, but there are fixed resistance coils so that the ratio may be made 1 to 1, 1 to 10, [etc.]. **1803** *Post-Office Annual Directory: London* 3 The Editors of the Post-Office Directory..present their most sincere and grateful Acknowledgements. **1852** DICKENS *Bleak Ho.* (1853) viii. 70 It appeared to us that some of them must pass their whole lives in dealing out subscription-cards to the whole Post-office Directory. **1963** *Ophthalmic Optician* 20 Apr. 408/1 If the hole exposes telephone services and cables, the perimeter will be lined with machinery painted in Post Office green. **1843** DICKENS *Let.* 30 Dec. (1974) III. 617 For a post office order there is no time. **1780** A. YOUNG *Tour in Ireland* I. 342 It is much to be wished, that there were some means of being secure of packets sailing regularly..; with the post-office packets there is this satisfaction. **1855** DICKENS *Holly Tree Inn* in *Househ. Words* Extra Christmas No., 15 Dec. 1/2 The Post-office packet for the United States was to depart from Liverpool. **1930** *Times Educ. Suppl.* 18 Jan. (Suppl.) p. iv/2 Red offers a fertile field for flights of descriptive fancy... Post Office red, and sealing wax red may be hackneyed words, but their tone is not in doubt. **1978** *Lancashire Life* Sept. 89/2 Newspapers, medicines, grocery orders—all are piled aboard the valley's post-office-red lifeline for delivery *en route*. **1861** *Act* 24 & 25 *Vict.* c. 14 Post Office Savings Banks..An Act to grant additional Facilities for depositing small Savings at Interest, with the Security of the Government for due Repayment thereof [17th May 1861]. Whereas it is expedient..to make the General Post Office available for that Purpose. **1885** *Encycl. Brit.* XIX. 572/2 The establishment of post-office savings banks was practically suggested in the year 1860 by Mr Charles William Sykes of Huddersfield, whose suggestion was cordially received by Mr Gladstone... Half a century earlier (1807) it had been proposed to utilize the then existing..money-order branch of the post-office for the collection and transmission of savings..to a central savings bank to be established in London. **1936** M. ALLINGHAM *Flowers for Judge* xi. 172 Mr. Campion turned over the battered cardboard-backed book... 'Post Office Savings Bank?.. Whose is it?' *Ibid.* xviii. 260 One day you find her Post Office Savings Bank-book. **1966** B. KIMENYE *Kalasanda Revisited* 21 His Post Office Savings book boasted the grand total of 600s. **1973** P. MOYES *Curious Affair of Third Dog* viii. 104 A Post Office savings book showing a balance of some ten pounds. **1976** *Scotsman* 15 Dec. 14/3 (Advt.), The Telecommunications showroom..is decorated internally in Post Office yellow, with relief panels throughout in silver.

post-offi·cial, *a.* and *sb.* [f. POST OFFICE, POST-OFFICE + -IAL, with play upon OFFICIAL *a.* and *sb.*] **A.** *adj.* Of or pertaining to a post office or its staff. **B.** *sb.* A post-office employee.

1938 DYLAN THOMAS *Let.* 31 Dec. (1966) 219, I don't know why your letter returned 'unknown', unless it was a post-official hint at the subsidence of my..reputation. *a* **1939** E. G. MURPHY in *Penguin Bk. Austral. Ballads* (1964) 209 For the Smiths rolled up..To drive the post-officials mad.

post-op (pōust,ǫ·p), colloq. abbrev. of *POSTOPERATIVE *a.* (*sb.*).

1971 E. CANDY *Words for Murder Perhaps* vii. 84, I can take temperatures and..make lovely beds for post-ops. **1974** *Country Life* 3–10 Jan. 58/3 Nursing Home...medical and post-op. patients. **1977** D. BENNETT *Jigsaw Man* 14 He felt he had been sawn in half. The post-op drugs took over.

posto·perative, *a.* (*sb.*) [POST- B. 1 b.] Occurring in or pertaining to the period following a surgical operation; having recently undergone an operation. Also as *sb.*, a person who has recently had an operation.

1889 in *Cent. Dict.* **1898, 1900** [in Dict. s.v. POST- B. 1 b]. **1925** E. HEMINGWAY *In our Time* (1926) 24 'I'm terribly sorry I brought you along, Nickie,' said his father, all his post-operative exhilaration gone. **1951** *Science* 19 Oct. 416/1 Prothrombin levels remained normal throughout the postoperative period in each animal. **1956** K. HULME *Nun's Story* x. 160 Sister Luke examined some of his post-operatives. **1962** *Lancet* 5 May 936/1 During the postoperative period he had a chest infection. **1973** R. HAYES *Hungarian Game* xiv. 332 They didn't want post-operatives to smoke. **1977** *New Yorker* 12 Sept. 114/2 Postoperative patients are always complaining about the quality of hospital food.

Hence **posto·peratively** *adv.*, after an operation.

1908 *Practitioner* Sept. 435 The nephrectomies shown to have a normal freezing point before operation invariably demonstrated post-operatively that the kidney, which was left, was functionally adequate. **1931** *Arch. Surg.* XXII. 552 The basal metabolic rate was not determined preoperatively or postoperatively. **1961** *Lancet* 26 Aug. 491/1 Why not give sedatives postoperatively by mouth instead of by injection. **1975** *Nature* 8 May 152/2 The occurrence of ptosis and miosis postoperatively was accepted as evidence that surgery had been successful.

post-osmicate, -osmication: see *POST- A. 1a, b. **post-ovulative, -ovulatory, -painterly:** *POST- B. 1.

postponable, *a.* Delete *rare*$^{-0}$ and add further examples.

1963 *Punch* 6 Feb. 206/1 So much of its expenditure is postponable. **1965** P. WYLIE *They both were Naked* I. iv. 189, I am in the middle of something. A novelette. Postponable, though. **1971** *Human World* Aug. 9 The accepted right and power of the country to decide by majority vote in free elections, not indefinitely postponable, that it has..had enough of the present government.

postpone, *v.* **2.** Delete † *Obs.* and add later example.

1874 H. J. ROBY *Gram. Latin Lang.* II. 351 Most prepositions are prefixed to the substantive; a few are always postponed; others are occasionally but rarely postponed in prose.

postponedly (pouˈstpōu·nėdli), *adv. rare.* [f. POSTPONED *ppl. a.* + -LY[2].] At a late time; belatedly.

1851 H. MELVILLE *Moby Dick* III. xxvi. 171 He was an old man who..had postponedly encountered that thing in sorrow's technicals, called ruin.

postpo·neless, *a. rare*$^{-1}$. [f. POSTPONE *v.* + -LESS.] That may not be postponed or averted.

c **1862** E. DICKINSON *Poems* (1955) I. 307 It's Coming—the postponeless Creature—It gains the Block—and now—it gains the Door.

postpose, *v.* Restrict † *Obs.* to sense b in Dict. and add: **a.** Now usu. *Gram.*

1930 T. SASAKI *On Lang. R. Bridges' Poetry* I. i. 7 Not a single adj. in '-able' or '-ible' is postposed in Bridges. **1962** R. QUIRK *Use of English* xiv. 241 To postpose an adjective as in 'the young man carbuncular'. **1978** *Studies in Eng. Lit.: Eng. Number* (Tokyo) 106 It is obvious that there are similarities..between the rule of extraposition which postposes the string *into the heavens* in (46b) and the one which postposes *into the clouds* in (42b).

Hence **postpo·sed** *ppl. a.*; **postpo·sing** *vbl. sb.*

1927 O. JESPERSEN *Mod. Eng. Gram.* III. i. 19 Postposed adjectives are not in general accord with colloquial English. **1972** W. LABOV *Language in Inner City* iv. 143 There are some postposed expressions which seem quite straightforward, even unmarked. **1975** *Language* LI. 815 Passivization..may involve not one but two transformational operations—subject postposing and object preposing. **1978** *Ibid.* LIV. 76 On the other hand, response-stance verbs, and verbs that are not stance verbs at all, do not allow such postposings.

postposition. Add: **2.** (Further examples.)

1928 H. POUTSMA *Gram. Late Mod. Eng.* (ed. 2) I. i. viii. 488 The influence of Latin Grammars makes itself felt in the post-position of the adjective. **1930** T. SASAKI *On Lang. R. Bridges' Poetry* I. i. 5 The postposition of two attributes joined together by means of 'and'. **1975** *Amer. Speech* 1971 XLVI. 226 Simple modifiers may appear in postposition in both English and German.

3. (Further examples.)

1925 GRATTAN & GURREY *Our Living Lang.* I. xiii. 83 Look at the word *at* in the following sentences:—..(*d*) These are the remarks they laughed at... We shall therefore avoid confusion of thought if we call it [*sc.* 'at'] a Postposition. **1976** J. S. GRUBER *Lexical Struct. Syntax & Semantics* II. iii. 343 In Japanese, there are some pieces of evidence..that postpositions, quantifiers, and other things which manifest left-branching..actually form one word.

Hence **postposi·tioning** *vbl. sb.*; **postpositional** *a.* (further examples); also *absol.* as *sb.*

1968 *Canad. Jrnl. Linguistics* XIV. I. 50 In this example we see that the head NP is identical to the object of the postpositional phrase. **1972** *Language* XLVIII. 390, I am suggesting that the morphemes which appear as postpositionals are really functionally like verbs. **1974** L. TODD *Pidgins & Creoles* ii. 15 In the Atlantic varieties plurality can be overtly marked by the postpositioning of *dem* immediately after the noun. **1975** *Language* LI. 797 The putative specified subject can never surface, either as a subject or as a postpositional object. **1976** J. S. GRUBER *Lexical Struct. Syntax & Semantics* I. iii. 67 It appears that we always have the form with *from* to the left, but for *in* and *on* post-positioning is possible or obligatory.

postpositive, *a.* (*sb.*) Add: **A.** *adj.* (Further examples.)

1930 T. SASAKI *On Lang. R. Bridges' Poetry* I. iv. 17 All these adjj. have been abundantly used through all the stages of English poetry... This fact appears partly to account for their frequent occurrence as postpositive attributes. **1936** *Amer. Speech* XI. 363/2 A discussion of the postpositive use of adjectives in such groups as *law ecclesiastical*. **1951** *Archivum Linguisticum* III. 24 Postpositive adjectives are in fact common in ON. **1963** [see *ENCLISIS]. **1978** *Language* LIV. 281 A particular clause-modifying particle has a fixed position, either clause-initial or 'post-positive'—i.e. placed (along with indefinites and enclitic personal pronouns) immediately after the initial item in the clause.

Hence **postpo·sitively** *adv.*

1961 R. B. LONG *Sentence & its Parts* xi. 256 Superlatives in *most* are now felt as compounds in which a modifying auxiliary pronoun has been united, postpositively, with a basic-form adjective head. **1964** *Amer. Speech* XXXIX. 36 Verbs contrast with adjectives by their ability to go postpositively.

post-possessive: see *POST- A. 1 b. **post-precipitate:** *POST- A. 1 a. **post-precipitation:** *POST- A. 1 b.

post-pri·mary, *a.* [POST- B. 1 b.] Of education or schools: subsequent to that which is primary. Of a pupil: receiving such education.

1919 *App. Jrnls. House of Representatives N.Z.* E. VI. 15 Suffice to say the main aim we have had in view is the bringing of the post-primary work into closer touch with the vocational needs of the pupils. **1926** *Rep. Consult. Comm. Educ. Adolescent* II. 36 Is it possible..to ensure that all normal children may pursue some kind of post-primary course for a period of not less than three, and preferably four, years from the age of 11+. **1929** *N.Z. Educ. Gaz.* 1 Mar. 36/1 The teaching of French pronunciation in our post-primary schools. **1930** *Times Educ. Suppl.* 18 Jan. 21/3 A post-primary course. **1961** J. K. HUNN *Rep. Dept. Maori Affairs* (N.Z.) 23 Maori indifference to post-primary and university education. **1975** *Language for Life* (Dept. Educ. & Sci.) xiv. 213 The Hadow Report urged that there should be no sharp division between infant, junior, and post-primary stages. **1977** *Daily Times* (Lagos) 27 Aug. 4/5 The education committee would help to propagate the importance of ideal family life by organising lectures for post-primary school pupils.

post-processor: see *POST- A. 1 b. **post-produce:** *POST- A. 1 a. **post-production:** *POST- A. 1 b. **post-puberal, -pubertal, -puberty, -radical:** see *POST- B. 1.

postreduc·tion. *Genetics.* [a. G. *postreduction* (Korschelt & Heider *Lehrb. der Vergleichenden Entwicklungsgeschichte der Wirbellosen Thiere* (Allgemeiner Theil) (1903) II. vi. 595): see POST- A. 1 b.] **a.** Reduction of chromosome number at the second of the two meiotic cell divisions, rather than at the first. Opp. *PREREDUCTION a.

1905 *Proc. Acad. Nat. Sci. Philadelphia* LVII. 188 To the idea of postreduction we can apply the criticism 'not proven'. **1915** *Jrnl. Morphol.* XXVI. 122 In regard to the question of pre- and post-reduction, I have evidence here that the first maturation division is the reduction division. **1921** L. W. SHARP *Introd. Cytol.* xi. 245 Such tetrads separate reductionally at the second mitosis (postreduction) rather than at the first (prereduction) in certain orthopterans.

b. Separation of homologous chromatids or genes at the second of the two meiotic cell divisions, rather than at the first. Opp. *PREREDUCTION b.

1934 L. W. SHARP *Introd. Cytol.* (ed. 3) xvi. 254 Disjunction in [meiosis] I is called 'prereduction'; that in II, 'postreduction'. **1950** *Adv. Genetics* III. 221 The prereductional or postreductional division of the heterozygous allele pair depends on its situation in the bivalent. Let us consider only the most common bivalent type, a bivalent with prereduction in respect to centromere, and provided with one chiasma. (In contradistinction to this, the Lecanium species have postreduction.) **1967** U. MITTWOCH *Sex Chromosomes* ix. 152 The sex chromosomes of *Apodemus* frequently exhibit postreduction, in contrast to most other mammals in which the X- and Y-chromosome show prereduction.

Hence **postredu·ctional** *a.*, involving or pertaining to postreduction; **postredu·ctionally** *adv.*

1905 *Proc. Acad. Nat. Sci. Philadelphia* LVII. 187 He is the solitary worker on the spermatogenesis of the Hemiptera who has taken the postreductional view. **1950** [see *POSTREDUCTION b]. **1950** *Adv. Genetics* III. 221 Since the number and situation of chiasmata, as a rule, varies even in the eggs of a single female, certain parts of a bivalent and consequently the gene pairs included in them may separate either prereductionally or postreductionally depending on the number and position of chiasmata.

‖**post rem.** *Philos.* [med.L. (Albertus Magnus) lit. 'after the thing'.] Used, often post-positively, of universals considered as concepts intuited from individual instances, as opposed to their having real existence either prior to the individual instance (see *ANTE REM) or only as experienced in individual instances (see *in re* (*c*) s.v. *IN *Latin prep.*).

1902 W. JAMES *Var. Relig. Exper.* 523 For religion generally..the word 'judgment' here means no such bare academic verdict or platonic appreciation as it means in Vedantic or modern absolutist systems; it carries, on the contrary, *execution* with it, is *in rebus* as well as *post rem*, and operates 'causally' as partial factor in the total fact. **1927** [see *ANTE REM]. **1931** S. BECKETT *Proust* 60 The Baudelarian [*sic*] unity is a unity 'post rem', a unity abstracted from plurality. **1941** E. C. THOMAS *Hist. Schoolmen* vi. 123 There remains a third aspect of Universals, generally described as Nominalist, which posits the Universal '*post rem*'. **1952** R. I. AARON *Theory of Universals* xii. 218 Nevertheless it [*sc.* the quality 'human'] is *post rem* and, to a certain degree, 'the workmanship of the mind'.

postreproductive: see *POST- B. 1.

postscript, *sb.* Add: **c.** Delete *rare* and add: Also, an additional or conclusory remark or action, an afterthought, a sequel.

1926 C. HAMILTON in *Hutchinson's Best Story Mag.* Nov. 16/1 'We are to keep each other company until my son returns,' she added. And as a postscript, 'It is his wish.' **1932** E. V. LUCAS *Reading, Writing & Remembering* ix. 153 *The Gentlest Art* led to an amusing postscript. A firm of drapers..sent me..a specimen of epistolary gentleness of the highest order. **1949** M. MEAD *Male & Female* xvi. 340 Some couples attempt a last child, for which there are..slang phrases—'little postscript', 'little frost blossom'. **1963** A. ROSS *Australia 63* iii. 76 Benaud, who fancies these kind of brief postscripts against weary bowlers, drove Statham and hooked Coldwell. **1965** *Listener* 23 Sept. 463/3 Would he have expanded during his sixty-odd extra years, or remained as much a postscript from the 'nineties as Max?

d. A short talk broadcast after a B.B.C. radio news bulletin.

They began in 1940 and were discontinued in 1944.

1940 *Radio Times* 18 Oct. 3/1 Priestley fans in this country..hear him only once a week, when he gives his Sunday-night postscript. **1943** *New Statesman* 20 Nov. 328 A sensible postscript by Barbara Ward. **1961** E. WAUGH *Unconditional Surrender* I. iii. 48 The BBC don't want to renew 'The Voice of Trimmer' Sunday evening postscripts. **1972** P. BLACK *Biggest Aspidistra* II. i. 95 The Postscripts began in March [1940], following the Nine O'clock News on the Home Service as a counter-attraction to Haw-Haw.

postscript, *v.* For *rare*—1 read *rare* and add: Also, to furnish as a postscript.

1970 D. MARLOWE *Echoes of Celandine* vii. 127 He remembered writing a letter to her... *Suddenly one realizes*, he had postscripted, *that there is a sadness.*

‖**post scriptum.** Also **postscriptum**, pl. **-ta.** [L. *post scriptum* (see POSTSCRIPT *sb.*).] = POSTSCRIPT *sb.* a and b. Also *attrib.* and as *adv. phr.*

1523, 1535, 1586 [see POSTSCRIPT *sb.* a]. **1853** MRS. GASKELL *Cranford* v. 91 In a post-scriptum note in his handwriting, it was stated that the Ode had appeared in the 'Gentleman's Magazine', December, 1782. **1899** C. J. C. HYNE *Further Adventures Capt. Kettle* x. 191 The letter ..ended in a post-scriptum tag. **1946** R. CAPELL *Simiomata* I. 11 Postscriptum.—While the April mutinies were Communist-inspired..they were not unprecedented. **1977** *Listener* 7 Apr. 447/3 A *postscriptum* has been pasted into the book registering Tambimuttu's disapproval.

post-sele·ction, *sb.* and *a.* **A.** *sb.* [POST- A. 1 b.] Selection, *spec.* natural selection, occurring subsequently. **B.** *adj.* [POST- B. 1 a.] Occurring after selection; of or pertaining to a time after selection.

1928 *Funk's Stand. Dict.*, *Post-selection*, natural selection carried on after the character of the animal has appeared. **1941** J. S. HUXLEY *Uniqueness of Man* ii. 56 Once the immigrants were established in the country, selection continued. This post-selection..must on the whole have encouraged and discouraged the same qualities favoured by pre-selection. **1946** *Nature* 7 Sept. 320/2 The main business of post-selection training for the Colonial Service will be carried out for the present in the Universities of Oxford, Cambridge and London. **1977** A. W. F. EDWARDS *Found. Math. Genetics* iii. 23 Starting at the point representing zygotic proportions before selection.., the population will move to the corresponding post-selection point.

post-Sta·lin, *a.* [POST- B. 1 a.] Of Russia or of Communism subsequent to the time of Stalin (died 1953); following the death of Stalin. Hence **post-Sta·linist** *a.*

1955 H. HODGKINSON *Doubletalk* 86 Mr. Molotov's colleagues in the post-Stalin leadership. **1958** *Times Lit. Suppl.* 17 Jan. 27/1 It is not clear how much of the post-Stalinist course in the Soviet Union would fall under the same condemnation. **1964** T. B. BOTTOMORE in I. L. Horowitz *New Sociol.* 365 The post-Stalinist Communist societies. **1965** *Language* XLI. 125 The Soviet discussions on structuralism and other linguistic debates of the post-Stalin era. **1974** tr. *Wertheim's Evolution & Revolution* 332 What characterizes the post-Stalin period is that what should have been a temporary compromise is increasingly being accepted as a lasting characteristic of Soviet society.

post-stre·tching, *vbl. sb. Building.* [POST- A. 1 b.] = *POST-TENSIONING *vbl. sb.* So **post-stre·tch** *v. trans.*; **post-stre·tched** *ppl. a.*

1941 *Concrete & Constructional Engin.* XXXVI. 78/2 Test results with structures post-stretched according to Mr. Hewett's method. **1946** *Ibid.* XLI. 147 Post-stretching is carried out against the hardened concrete, no immediate loss owing to elastic deformation of the concrete occurring, and that owing to shrinkage being reduced. *Ibid.* 195 The post-stretched mild steel reinforcement. **1949** P. W. ABELES *Princ. & Pract. Prestressed Concrete* xii. 92/1 Two kinds of transfer of prestress can be distinguished:—(a) instantaneous release of prestress by severing wires, previously tensioned independently of the members to be prestressed, a process which is called 'pre-tensioning' or 'pre-stretching', and (b) gradual release of the prestress by tensioning the wires directly against the hardened body of the member to be prestressed, a process which is called 'post-tensioning' or 'post-stretching'.

†**postsyna·psis.** *Cytology. Obs.* [POST- B. 1 c.] (See quots.)

1898 T. H. MONTGOMERY in *Zool. Jahrbücher: Anat. u. Ontogenie* XI. 20 The anaphase itself may be subdivided into 3 well marked periods: the early anaphase, the synapsis, and the postsynapsis. *Ibid.* 28 The postsynapsis, a term introduced here for the first time, is a well marked stage of the anaphase, distinguishable alike from the preceding synapsis as from the following telophase. **1911** *Jrnl. Morphol.* XXII. 753 My postsynapsis stage, equivalent to the diplotene.

postsyna·ptic, *a.* **1.** *Cytology.* [POST- B. 1 b.] Subsequent to meiotic synapsis.

1909 [see *PRESYNAPTIC *a.* 1]. **1912** *Jrnl. Exper. Zool.* XIII. 377 (*heading*) The post-synaptic spireme. Pachytene and diplotene. **1921** *Ann. Bot.* XXXV. 366 During the period when the mother-cells are in synapsis and the postsynaptic spireme stages, the tapetal cells vary greatly in appearance. **1931** *Cytologia* II. 353 Secondary association..is a post-synaptic phenomenon.

2. *Physiol.* [POST- B. 2.] Of, pertaining to, or designating a neurone that receives a nerve impulse at a synapse. Opp. *PRESYNAPTIC *a.* 2.

1937, 1965 [see *PRESYNAPTIC *a.* 2]. **1974** M. C. GERALD *Pharmacol.* v. 100 This interaction may produce one of two types of changes in the permeability of the postsynaptic membrane.

Hence **postsyna·ptically** *adv.*

1952 *Jrnl. Physiol.* CXVII. 115 The fact that a moderate dose of curarine abolishes 'external' as well as 'internal' miniature potentials, strongly indicates that they both arise 'post-synaptically', in the end-plate. **1973** *Nature* 8 June 355/1 Lead can only block postsynaptically in conditions in which the density of ACh-receptor complexes is much lower than it is during an end-plate potential. **1978** *Ibid.* 22 June 674/1 These neurones lie postsynaptically to high densities of nerve terminals shown by immunohistochemical techniques to contain somatostatin-like material.

post-sync(h (-siŋk), abbrev. of *POST-SYNCHRONIZATION, *POST-SYNCHRONIZE *v.* Hence **post-sy·nc(h)ed** *ppl. a.*; **post-sy·nc(h)ing** *vbl. sb.*

1960 O. SKILBECK *ABC of Film & TV* 98 *Post Synch.*, to make apparently Synchronous sound for existing Mute film with the aid of a Guide Track, Wild track or otherwise. **1962** *Movie* June 26/1 He wasn't helped there by the post-sync sound, which was often unrelated to what was on the screen. **1963** *Movie* Jan. 21/3 The post-synching of the Italian and French versions..was done without any reference to me. **1968** J. BINGHAM *I love, I Kill* xii. 160 Doing bits and pieces of reshooting and re-cording the dialogue, post syncing, as they call it. **1968** *Punch* 31 Jan. 153/2 'Post-synch' may be necessary for various reasons, perhaps because the sound track of an outdoor scene has been ruined by aircraft noise, perhaps because a foreign actor's speech is so thick as to call for a substitute voice. **1972** I. HAMILTON *Thrill Machine* xiv. 58 We could always post-sync the questions or re-cut the answers. **1978** *New York* 3 Apr. 68/2 He..plays the piano with self-dramatizing virtuosity that isn't helped by the poorly matched post-synced studio sound recording. **1979** D. LOWDEN *Budapesti 3* iii. 22 'So tell me what you want?.. A post-synch and dubbing theatre that'll take at least eight tracks?'.. He got them [*sc.* the letters] back, neatly typed..with the words 'dubbing tracks' and 'post-synch loops' intruding strangely in the text.

post-synchroniza·tion. *Cinemat.* and *Television.* [POST- A. 1 b.] The addition of a sound recording to the corresponding images of a film or video recording after the latter has been made. So **post-sy·nchronize** *v. trans.*; **post-sy·nchronizing** *vbl. sb.*

1933 A. BRUNEL *Filmcraft* 163 *Post-synchronise*, to add sounds, music or dialogue, after the mute film (pictorial image) has been shot. **1936** —— *Film Production* 177 For this purpose the artist, whose voice is to be used for post-synchronisation, is placed before a microphone in the studio and on to a screen is projected the scene to be post-synchronised. **1953** K. REISZ *Technique Film Editing* 275 This process involves getting the actors to speak the lines in synchronisation with the picture and is known as post-synchronising. Post-synchronisation is not used only to cover up faulty recording. *Ibid.* 276 In some Hollywood studios it has become common to post-synchronise most of the spoken lines. **1959** P. BULL *I know Face* v. 93, I.. said the two words. Two days later I was asked to post-synchronise them, as they were totally incoherent. **1960** D. WILSON *Television Playwright* 16 The advantage the director gains by retaking doubtful scenes..by the post-synchronizing of music and sound effects. **1965** *Wireless World* July 34 (Advt.), The PRO 70 for multi-channel recording and for dubbing, post-synchronising and transfer. **1968** *Punch* 31 Jan. 153/2 Dubbing is a specialised form of post-synchronisation.

post-tectonic: see *POST- B. 1.

post-te·nsioning, *vbl. sb. Building.* [POST- A. 1 b.] Strengthening of reinforced concrete by application of tension to the reinforcing rods after the concrete has set. So **post-te·nsion** *v. trans.*; **post-te·nsioned** *ppl. a.*

1948 *Concrete & Constructional Engin.* XLIII. 155 For post-tensioning there is no limitation of the size of the bars, but for pre-tensioning plain wires of 0·2 in. diameter are the largest that have been successfully employed. **1950** *Engineering* 13 Jan. 54/2 Adequate reasons exist to justify the claim that prestressed post-tensioned beams can successfully sustain the effects of fire. **1954** *Archit. Rev.* CXVI. 110 The gymnasium has a post-tensioned prestressed concrete frame and the changing rooms have load-bearing walls and precast concrete roof units. **1958** *Times Rev. Industry* July 25/1 Post-tensioning methods require relatively little capital expenditure. **1965** [see *PRE-TENSIONED *ppl. a.*]. **1974** LIN & ZIA in B. Bresler *Reinforced Concrete Engin.* I. vi. 302 The amount of concrete posttensioned at the job site in the U.S.A...is estimated to have been about 700,000 cu yd in 1972. **1976** G. S. RAMASWAMY *Mod. Prestressed Concrete Design* vii. 86 The member is post-tensioned after the concrete has sufficiently hardened.

postterm (pōᵘstˌtɜːm), *a. Obstetrics.* [POST- B. 1 a.] Born or occurring after a pregnancy that lasted significantly longer than normal.

1933 *Jrnl. Pediatrics* II. 677 There is a stable substrate of maturation..which tends to keep the underweight, the preterm and the postterm infant close to his normal maturity levels in the field of behavior. **1971** PIEROG & FERRARA *Approach to Med. Care of Sick Newborn* i. 7 The preterm infant is one born less than 38 weeks by gestational age from the first day of the last menstrual period; the postterm infant is one born 42 weeks or more from the first day of the last menstrual period. **1976** L. O. LUBCHENCO *High Risk Infant* vii. 163 There are relatively more infants who are large for gestational age in postterm deliveries than in term deliveries.

posttest (pōᵘ·stˌtest), *a.* and *sb. Psychol.* [f. POST- + TEST *sb.*[1]] **A.** *adj.* [POST- B. 1 a.] That comes after or is subsequent to a test. **B.** *sb.* [POST- A. 1 b.] A subsequent test designed to measure the effects of or changes since the initial test. Hence **postte·sting** *vbl. sb.*

1966 *Jrnl. Personality & Social Psychol.* IV. 175, 60 male and female college Ss were..tested..in a social pressure plus reinforcement session and again in a posttest reinforcement session 2 wk. later. **1966** J. S. BRUNER *Beyond Information Given* (1974) xviii. 321 This was followed by some training trials and then there was a posttest. **1972** *Jrnl. Social Psychol.* LXXXVI. 12 Endler ..observed posttest behavior consistent with his reinforcement schedules. **1973** *Jrnl. Genetic Psychol.* CXXIII. 90 The Ss were reassembled for the posttesting session, and the TAT and Test Anxiety Questionnaire were given. **1974** *Florida FL Reporter* XIII. 76/1 The recognition test of singular and plural SE forms was administered after the three-week training session and after the posttest.

Post Toasties. orig. *U.S.* Also with lower-case initials and sing. **Post Toasty, -ie.** The proprietary name of a breakfast cereal first marketed by Charles William *Post* (1854–1914), American manufacturer (cf. *POSTUM). Also *transf.* and *fig.*

[**1907** *Trade Marks Jrnl.* 2 Oct. 1941 *Toasties...* [Substances used as food or as ingredients in food]. Charles William Post,..London, England, and..Michigan, United States of America; manufacturer.] **1908** *Official Gaz.* (U.S. Patent Office) 31 Mar. 1177/2 *Postum Cereal Co. Limited*, Battle Creek, Mich. Filed 28, 1908. *Post Toasties...* Cereal Breakfast Foods. **1914** H. W. WILEY *1001 Tests of Foods* vi. 72 Many are the letters received in regard to the cereal breakfast foods, especially for children's use. One mother writes me: 'Two small youngsters are anxiously awaiting your opinion in regard to their favorite shredded wheat, grape nuts, and post toasties.' **1926–7** *Army & Navy Stores Catal.* 2/1 *Breakfast cereals*, Post Toasties—pkt. -/9. **1943** G. GREENE *Ministry of Fear* III. iii. 202 There was milk and post-toasties and bread and marmalade. **1945** L. SHELLY *Jive Talk Dict.* 31 *Post toasty*, corny character. **1950** A. WILSON *Such Darling Dodos* 134 Little pyramids of chocolate powder and post toasties..called 'Coconut Kisses'. **1969** *Listener* 22 May 732/1 They range from chilling glimpses of the world in the next century to golden, Post-Toastie pieces of life in which..the ancient decencies are reinforced. **1979** P. NIESEWAND *Member of Club* iv. 30 The economy-size box of Post Toasties on his breakfast table.

post-town. Add: **1.** Also, a town with its own postcode.

1973 *Guardian* 7 Feb. 1/1 The Post Office will recognise Milton Keynes as a separate post town on Monday.

po·st-treatment, *sb.* and *a.* **A.** *sb.* [POST- A. 1 b.] Treatment carried out subsequently. **B.** *adj.* [POST- B. 1 a.] Existing or occurring after treatment.

1946 *Genetics* XXXI. 375 Studies of hatchability of eggs deposited by females that had been inseminated by males treated with..2000 r of X-rays..suggest that the effect of posttreatment in reducing the frequency of chromosomal rearrangements is attributable to increased restitution. **1962** *Radiation Bot.* I. 132/2 Immediate ultraviolet post-treatments at 2967 Å..completely overcame 1 kr X-ray depression of embryo viability. **1967** E. CHAMBERS *Photolitho-Offset* xiii. 198 It is used mainly as a 'post treatment' after developing and before etching. **1972** *Gloss. Terms Timber* (*B.S.I.*) 25 *Post-treatment*, preservative treatment of ordinary plywood after it has been made. **1972** *Jrnl. Social Psychol.* LXXXVI. 84 Any differences in posttreatment attitude can therefore be attributed to the effects of the experimental treatment.

postulational (pǫstiŭlēⁱ·ʃənăl), *a.* [f. POSTULATION + -AL.] Of or pertaining to postulation; based on or involving deduction from a set of postulates.

1926 L. BLOOMFIELD in *Language* II. 153 Nevertheless, the postulational method can further the study of language, because it forces us to state explicitly whatever we assume. **1932** M. H. STONE *Linear Transformations in Hilbert Space* i. 2 The postulational treatment was carried through only recently by J. v. Neumann. **1933** L. S. STEBBING *Mod. Introd. Logic* (ed. 2) 506 A set of primitive propositions may be called 'a set of postulates', and the system thus constructed may be called 'a postulational system'. **1956** E. H. HUTTEN *Lang. Mod. Physics* iii. 75 The three laws of motion, together with the definitions, are given [by Newton] as a postulational system. **1961** E. NAGEL *Struct. of Sci.* v. 91 A familiar example of an abstract calculus is demonstrative Euclidean geometry developed in a postulational manner.

Hence **postula·tionally** *adv.*

1936 *Mind* XLV. 174 In general, if *x* is defined postulationally, any proposition containing *x* will *implicate* the postulational definition of *x*. **1966** H. V. GUENTHER *Tibetan Buddhism* vi. 89 The distinction between a 'coemergent belief in things' and a 'postulationally defined belief in things'..is concisely stated.

postulator. (Earlier and later examples.)

1863 tr. *Luquet's Life Anna Maria Taigi* 2 The undersigned Bishop of Hesebon, Postulator of the suit of the servant of God, Anna Maria Taigi. **1973** *Times* 2 Nov. 5/5 The required proof of two miracles is said to have brought to the postulator of the cause 'an embarrassment of choices'.

Postum (pōᵘ·stə̆m). orig. *U.S.* Also **postum.** [Pseudo-Lat. formation f. the name of Charles William *Post* (see *POST TOASTIES) + L. *-um.*] The proprietary name of a coffee substitute. Also *attrib.*

1895 *Official Gaz.* (U.S. Patent Office) 3 Dec. 1549/1, 27,402 *Food Drinks.* Postum Cereal Co., Limited, Battle Creek, Mich. Filed Oct. 7, 1895 *Postum Cereal.* Used since February 1895. **1912** [see *INSTANT *a.* 4 c]. **1922** *Hotel World* 15 Apr. 15/2 Choice of Coffee, Tea, Milk, Postum, Cocoa. **1962** *Flight Internat.* LXXXI. 871/1 Carpenter drank normal coffee instead of postum. **1967** *Listener* 21 Sept. 370/1 His frugal breakfast—perhaps a cup of Postum coffee and some biscuits. **1977** *New Yorker* 20 June 67/1, I will have a drink of Postum or coffee. **1978** J. CARROLL *Mortal Friends* v. vi. 572 None of that cappuccino stuff, Jack... See if they have Postum, will you?.. Well, lace it with a lot of milk, will you? Make it like American.

postural, *a.* Add: **1. c.** *postural integration*, 'some form of "body work", a term that applies to various specialized kinds of massage..that claim to bring about mental well-being through physical manipulation and body realignment' (private communication, Cyra McFadden, 15 Aug. 1979).

1977 C. McFADDEN *Serial* xviii. 42/1 She had like *mutated* over the years through Gurdjieff..Human Life Styling, postural integration, [etc.]. **1977** *Rolling Stone* 19 May 32/3 There was postural integration and the Alexander Technique and Aural Ecology and the Chiropractic Information Bureau and Rolfing and even one discipline called 'Prosperity Training'. **1979** *San Francisco Sunday Examiner & Chron.* (Sunday mag.) 26 Aug. 29, I used to do Gestalt therapy. I did body work, postural integration.

posturant (pǫ·stiŭrănt). *nonce-wd.* [f. POSTURE *v.* + -ANT[1].] One who adopts an intellectual or æsthetic posture; a poser.

1934 E. SITWELL *Aspects Mod. Poetry* i. 19 A school of American-Greek posturants..began to exude a thin stream of carefully chosen watery words.

posture, *sb.* Add: **1. b.** Among animals, a particular pose which is a signal of a specific pattern of behaviour.

1940 H. F. WITHERBY et al. *Handbk. Brit. Birds* II. 329 In terrifying posture feathers [of long-eared owls] are ruffled up. **1953** N. TINBERGEN *Herring Gull's World* ii. 7 Some of these movements and postures are not difficult even for the human observer to appreciate. **1962** *Symp. Zool. Soc.* No. 8. 71 A rat on the defensive in the upright posture does not look at its opponent. **1964** A. L. THOMSON *New Dict. Birds* 282/1 Behaviour by which the plumage is exposed to the sun by special postures seems to be widespread in birds. **1974** I. C. J. GALBRAITH tr. *Dorst's Life of Birds* I. ix. 175 The sexes may be recognized by certain postures characteristic of each mate.

3. Also, *spec.* a military or political attitude; a condition of armed readiness.

1962 *Listener* 29 Mar. 545/2 What is important about the Soviet posture is that the Soviet armed forces aim at flexibility. **1964** *Ann. Reg. 1963* 140 The public denunciations and rigidities of the cold war appeared to have been set aside in favour of more traditional diplomatic methods and more relaxed diplomatic postures. **1974** *Times* 5 Mar. 7/1 Renewed anxiety over Nato's conventional defences was expressed today..in the annual Pentagon 'posture' report to Congress. **1976** *National Observer* (U.S.) 1 May 16/3 DEA's mission is..to have foreign governments in a responsive posture.

Posturepedic (pǫstiŭɹpī·dik). *U.S.* Also **posturepedic.** [f. POSTURE *sb.* + ORTHO)PEDIC *a.*] The proprietary name of a Sealy mattress designed to give proper support to the relaxed body.

1952 *Official Gaz.* (U.S. Patent Office) 14 Oct. 289/2 Sealy, Incorporated, Chicago, Ill. Filed July 24, 1951. *Posturepedic.* The representation of the human figure is fanciful... For mattresses and box springs. Claims use since June 1, 1950. **1967** *N.Y. Times* 9 Apr. 63 Choose your Posturepedic at one of these fine sleep centers. **1976** *Laurel* (Montana) *Outlook* 23 June 19/5 (Advt.), Refinished walnut dining table, wooden high chair, posturepedic crib mattress. **1977** C. McFADDEN *Serial* xxxii. 71/1 He staggered down the hall to his Posturepedic.

posturing, *vbl. sb.* Add: **2.** Among birds, the use of particular poses as signals of specific patterns of behaviour.

1929 H. E. HOWARD *Introd. Study Bird Behaviour* i. 17 Posturing..is regarded as a manifestation of the affective aspect of the functioning of the sexual response. **1940** H. F. WITHERBY et al. *Handbk. Brit. Birds* I. 8 Display and Posturing.—Aerial evolutions..are a feature of courtship [of the raven]. **1953** N. TINBERGEN *Herring Gull's World* ii. 7 In general, the movements playing a part in posturing are based on flattening or raising of the plumage as a whole, on eye movements and on the attitude of head, neck and wings. **1973** R. A. HINDE in D. S. Farmer et al. *Avian Biol.* III. viii. 493 Ambivalent Posturing. Sometimes the bird adopts a posture that simultaneously expresses both tendencies.

post-velar: see *POST- B. 2. **post-verbal(ly:** *POST- B. 1.

post-Victorian, *a.* and *sb.* [f. POST- B. 1 b.] **A.** *adj.* Subsequent to the reign of Queen Victoria (died 1901) or the Victorian era (esp. in style or manners). **B.** *sb.* One who lives in the post-Victorian era.

1938 H. PALMER *Post-Victorian Poetry* p. ix, Because of the amount of space that has been taken up by the verse dating from 1900..the subject-matter seems to justify the selection of the title, *Post-Victorian Poetry.* **1960** *Times Lit. Suppl.* 24 June 400/2 Hulme was able to dress a post-Victorian change of mood in conceptual clothing which seemed..to fit. **1974** *Nature* 1 Mar. 86/2 Bowlby..offers a..less punitive approach to the child, than is generally taken..by the post-Victorians or the Freudians.

postvocalic(ally: see *POST- B. 1.

postvo·calized, *ppl. a. Philol.* [f. POST- A. 1 a + VOCALIZED *ppl. a.*] Followed (as a consonant) by a vowel.

1876 [see PREVOCALIZED *ppl. a.*].

po·st-war, *a.* (*sb.*) Also **postwar.** [f. POST- B. 1 a + WAR *sb.*[1]] **A.** *adj.* Of, pertaining to, or characteristic of, the period after a war (esp. those of 1914–18 or 1939–45); *post-war credit*, a system of additional personal taxation introduced by the British Government in 1941 to supplement wartime expenditure and repayable during the post-war period; a sum of money or promissory note associated with this scheme.

1908 *Daily Chron.* 16 July 5/1 There has been a reduction of some £2,000,000 since 1904–5, the first post-war year. **1915** *Political Q.* May 118 The plans outlined.. admit most easily of deviation into whatever may approve itself as the desired norm of post-war politics and economics. **1919** J. M. KEYNES *Econ. Consequences Peace* 84 Our hypothetical calculations leave us with post-war human requirements, on the basis of a pre-war efficiency of railways and industry. **1938** *Encycl. Brit. Bk. of Year* 22/1 The sheep population reached a post-war maximum in 1932. **1942** *Times* 9 July 2/3 (*heading*) Post-War Credit Certificates. *Ibid.*, The issue of over 9,000,000 certificates for post-war credit in respect of income-tax payments for the year 1941–42 has begun. **1959** *Daily Tel.* 9 Apr. 1/7 The Trades Union Congress yesterday welcomed the Chancellor's cuts in purchase tax and his proposals to speed up post-war credit payments. **1964** F. BOWERS *Bibliogr. & Textual Crit.* I. v. 34 Some resistance to accepting the validity of post-war pioneering studies. **1972** *Times* 9 Aug. 6/6, I propose..that repayment of post-war credits to people who have not been able to produce a certificate should begin on January 1, 1973. I envisage that this final stage of the repayment should be spread over the 12 months ending December 31, 1973. **1973** D. AARON *Unwritten War* III. vi. 103 Parkman did not attempt to predict the post-War fate of the Brahmin class.

B. *ellipt.* as *sb. U.S.* The period following a war.

1944 *Sun* (Baltimore) 18 July 8/7 They will glibly write ..of projects to be undertaken 'at post war'. **1945** *Time* 24 Sept. 15/2 Management-labor unity..must be continued in the postwar. **1947** *Partisan Rev.* XIV. 454 The tank driver of the War becomes the tractor driver of the Postwar.

posty, var. *POSTIE.

pot, *sb.*[1] Add: **1. e.** (Earlier and later examples.) Also, the pan of a close stool; a lavatory pan.

1598 FLORIO *Worlde of Wordes* 280/1 *Pitale*,..the pan or pot of a close stoole. **1915** *Dialect Notes* IV. 228 *Pot*,.. very common for *chamber*. **1954** A. S. C. Ross in *Neuphilol. Mitt.* LV. 42 U-speakers use ['džeri]..or *pot.* **1956** *New Statesman* 8 Dec. 740/2 The old woman on the next floor fighting over who choked the cawsy by pitching cinders down the pot. **1958** [see *ARTICLE 14 c].

h. A protuberant stomach, a paunch; = POT-BELLY 1.

1928 'BRENT OF BIN BIN' *Up Country* ii. 40 Mazere.. was happy that he could turn to manual work again himself, and felt the better for it. 'It's taking a little of the pot off me,' he would exclaim. **1929** KIPLING in *London Mag.* Dec. 631/1 Keede patted his round little pot. **1942** D. POWELL *Time to be Born* (1943) i. 22 At forty-eight.. he had no pot at all due to his Yogi exercises. **1952** [see *GUSSY *v.*]. **1959** *Encounter* Dec. 31/1 There was a time when I had a little professorial pot; later I was 'stout'..; then I became, I suppose, definitely pot-bellied. **1965** G. McINNES *Road to Gundagai* xiii. 222 The door opened carefully and revealed a tall man with a florid face, a large Roman nose,..and a big pot. **1973** 'D. JORDAN' *Nile Green* xxix. 129 His pot was hanging obscenely over the lip of a pair of scarlet bathing trunks.

i. (See quots.) *slang.*

1941 *Amer. Speech* XVI. 240 *Pot*, carburetor. **1945** BAKER *Austral. Lang.* viii. 160 Here is a brief list of indigenous Air Force language:..*pot*, a cylinder. **1961** PARTRIDGE *Dict. Slang* Suppl. 1230/1 *Pot*, n., a cylinder, esp. in one of the old rotary engines: R.F.C.–R.A.F.: 1914–18. They tended to split or to fly off. Hence, any aeroplane-engine cylinder. **1966** 'L. LANE' *ABZ of Scouse* 83 A pot is also a carburettor. *To tickle ther pot*: To prime a carburettor.

2. a. (Later examples.) Also allusively in *fig.* phr. *pot of gold* (see quot. 1895).

1895 *Brewer's Dict. Phr. & Fable* (new ed.) 1036/2 *Rainbow chasers*, problematical politicians and reformers, who chase rainbows, which cannot possibly be caught, to 'find the pot of gold at the foot thereof'. This alludes to an old joke, that a pot of gold can be dug up where the rainbow touches the earth. **1966** A. E. LINDOP *I start Counting* xxi. 266 Matron makes a pot of tea quite late at night and lets me go and have a cup with her. **1971** *Cape Herald* 15 May 14/1 Francis Lee, the Manchester City and England striker has hit the 'pot-of-gold' in more ways than one. **1974** 'E. LATHEN' *Sweet & Low* i. 11 The Japanese stock market..had been the legendary pot of gold at the end of some local rainbow. **1978** *Observer* 26 Mar. 11/7 The tendency has been to look at the North Sea in terms of its immediate isolated wealth, as a pot of gold. **1979** W. H. CANAWAY *Solid Gold Buddha* iii. 27 Miller.. made a pot of tea.

b. Also, a pot of tea.

1831 E. J. TRELAWNY *Adventures Younger Son* III. xxiii. 152 My wife always turned in three spoonsful,—one for I, one for her, and t'other for the pot. **1973** 'E. FERRARS' *Foot in Grave* ix. 166 The tea had got cold, so Christine made a fresh pot.

3. (Later *Austral.* examples.)

1943 [see *HANDLE *sb.*[1] 2 c]. **1966** G. W. TURNER *Eng. Lang. Austral. & N.Z.* viii. 163 In addition Sydney has a *pony* of five ounces.., Melbourne a *pot* of ten ounces (but a pot is eleven ounces in Brisbane), Adelaide a *butcher* (six ounces) and Perth a *big pot* (fifteen ounces, which would be a *schooner* in Sydney or a *pint* in Adelaide). **1973** *Parade* (Austral.) Oct. 35/1 'Oh, yes,' said the barman. 'We like their money, but we don't have middies, we sell pots.'

9. a. (Earlier example.)

1856 *Knickerbocker* XLVIII. 619 They had hauled down a big pot and intended henceforth to live as jolly as clams.

d. (Earlier and later examples.)

1880 HARDY *Trumpet-Major* I. viii. 135 When Festus put on the big pot, as it is classically called, he was quite blinded *ipso facto* to the diverting effect of that mood and manner upon others. **1885** *Punch* 12 Sept. 131/2 Oh, Yorkshire and Lancashire both are big pots. But Cricket's top honours again go to Notts. **1909** J. R. WARE *Passing Eng.* 28 Big pot (*Music-hall* 1878–82)... This phrase is probably one of the few that filter down in the world from Oxford, where, in the 50's it was the abbreviation of potentate. It referred to a college don, or a social magnate. **1947** 'A. P. GASKELL' *Big Game* 24, I don't feel at home with these big pots. **1979** R. RENDELL *Make Death love Me* iii. 29 Some general at the head of it. Some big pot who means business.

e. (Examples of sense in Dict.); also, orig. U.S., the betting pool in poker and other gambling games. Also *fig.* Cf. sense 9 b in Dict., *jack-pot* s.v. JACK *sb.*[1] 33 a in Dict. and Suppl.

1847 J. H. GREENE *Gambling Unmasked* (rev. ed.) 196 He won the first twenty '*pots*', that is to say, the stake [in poker]. **1856** G. W. BAGBY *Old Virginia Gentleman* (1910) 228 He has no great faith in 'cases', but believes in betting on three cards at a time, and has a special hankering for 'the pot' [in faro]. **1868** [see *KENO b]. **1878** [see *BULLET *sb.*[1] 6]. **1889** 'MARK TWAIN' *Speeches* (1923) 147 What is still more irregular, the man that loses a game gets the pot. **1890** J. P. QUINN *Fools of Fortune* II. ii. 194 In the

[faro] 'lay-out'..the six, seven and eight are called the pot. **1892** [see *CHIP *v.*[1] 8 b]. **1895** *Funk's Stand. Dict., Pot,*..5. *Card-playing,* (1) The amount of stakes played for; the pool. (2) In faro, the six, seven, and eight of the layout, collectively. **1935** *Encycl. Sports* 466/2 If no player opens there is a fresh deal, each player once more contributing to the pot, and so on until the pot is opened. **1951** *Amer. Speech* XXVI. 100/1 *Open the pot,* to make the first bet after the ante [in poker]. *Ibid.* 100/2 *Pot,* the total accumulation of all bets. It rests in the centre of the table, equi-distant from each player. **1963** *Richmond* (Virginia) *Times-Dispatch* 16 Dec. 19/2 When a poker player has absolute confidence in his hand he shoves into the pot every chip he has. **1971** *Black World* June 73/1 The sergeant put up the house, got the men into the game and took half the pot. **1977** I. SHAW *Beggarman, Thief* II. i. 118 'And if you succeed, then what?' he said. 'Russia takes the whole pot.'

f. *old pot*: see *OLD *a.* 1 c.

10. (Later examples of spelling *pott,* which is now usual.)

1890 in WEBSTER. **1911** *Encycl. Brit.* XX. 735/1 Writing papers. Pott..$12\frac{1}{2}\times15$. **1926** *Paper Terminol.* (Spalding & Hodge, Ltd.) 21 *Pott,* a standard size of printing paper measuring $15\frac{1}{2}\times12\frac{1}{2}$ in. (with slight variations). The term is derived from an ancient 'pot' watermark, which represented the Sangraal. **1962** F. T. DAY *Introd. to Paper* vii. 69 Sizes of paper in the United Kingdom centre round fifteen designations: Foolscap, Demy, Medium,..Pott, Elephant,..Eagle and Columbier.

11. (In *hopscotch.*) (Examples.) Also, the game itself or a part of the game. Also *local U.S.*

1866 W. GREGOR *Dial. Banffshire* 132 *Pot,*..the last division in the game of *hippin'-beds* [*sc.* hopscotch]. **1893–4** R. O. HESLOP *Northumb. Words* II. 549 *Pot,* the heading written at the top of the game called 'beds', or, locally, 'hitchey dabber'... To achieve it is to get 'pot'. **1895** *Funk's Stand. Dict., Pot..pl.* (Local, U.S.) (1) The game of hop-scotch. **1920** WEBSTER, *Pot*.., a piece of pottery or earthenware, as a marble or piece for playing hop scotch. **1936** *Glasgow Herald* 10 Nov., 'Hopscotch', however is an English name. We Scots called it 'peever',..or 'pot', or 'the beds'... In some parts of Scotland beds 7 and 8 were called 'the kail pats', and this may be one reason why the game is sometimes called 'pot'. Another explanation is that a piece of broken pot or earthenware was often used as a peever.

13. f. *to go to pot.* (Further examples.) For *vulgar* read *colloq.* Also, to deteriorate, to go to pieces.

1846 *Swell's Night Guide* 120/2 *Gone to pot,* become poor in circumstances, gone to the dogs. **1889** *Cornh. Mag.* July 46 For the potato is really going to pot... Constitutional disease and the Colorado beetle have preyed too long upon its delicate organism. **1910** E. M. FORSTER *Howards End* xxv. 205 Evie heard of her father's engagement when she was in for a tennis tournament, and her play went simply to pot. **1923** S. KAYE-SMITH *End of House of Alard* IV. 327 If we hung on now, still further crippled by death-duties, the land would simply go to pot. **1942** E. PAUL *Narrow St.* iv. 37 The Comédie Française.. went to pot artistically and remained a travesty of its former self until reorganized about 1938. **1953** E. SIMON *Past Masters* II. 81 Discipline's gone all to pot at the camp. **1956** W. GRAHAM *Sleeping Partner* 57 She could go in and clean up once in a while... The house wouldn't go to pot in a week or so. **1968** *Globe & Mail Mag.* (Toronto) 13 Jan. 11/3 Only a quarter of the Sames now depend on reindeer herding... Some of them, like some of Canada's native people, go to pot. **1979** *Truck & Bus Transportation* (Austral.) Apr. 65/2 It's [*sc.* the brake is] there to do its job, but it can throw a spanner in the works if the adjustment setting goes to pot.

k. *Austral.* and *N.Z. slang. to put* (a person's) *pot on*: to inform against, to tell tales; to destroy the prospects of. Cf. *POT *v.*[1] 6 b.

1913 A. J. REES *Merry Marauders* xi. 206 You ought to put the Liquor Party's pot on. **1919** W. H. DOWNING *Digger Dial.* 40 *Put his pot on*—Report him. **1928** W. S. SMYTH *Jean of Tussock Country* vi. 59 Dalton has put your pot on. **1935** DAVISON & NICHOLLS *Blue Coast Caravan* 178 He saw some blacks..standing on the platform under guard of a policeman. 'Hullo, what's up?' One of them replied, 'Aw, somebody's been putting our pot on.' **1948** *Landfall* II. 110 'Got a ten bob rise last week,' Duggan said. 'Funny that, you know,' Larry said. 'I been there about the same time as you, Tom, and I haven't had a rise yet. Wonder if Myers put my pot on.' **1957** V. PALMER *Seedtime* 119 There's an election coming on, and there's a chance I'll be dumped... This afternoon's work has probably put my pot on.

l. *to get off the pot* (and extensions): see quot. 1972. *coarse slang* (chiefly *N. Amer.*).

1961 PARTRIDGE *Dict. Slang* Suppl. 1269/2 *Shit or get off the pot!* A Canadian Army c.p. (1939–45), directed at a dice-player unable to 'crap out'. **1966** 'A. HALL' *9th Directive* x. 90 Get some definite information for me. Tell the Ambassador to get off the bloody pot. **1972** *Dict. Contemp. & Colloq. Usage* (Eng.-Lang. Inst. Amer.) 26/2 *Shit or get off the pot,* vulgar. A command that someone either complete an action in process or abandon the attempt and give someone else the opportunity to try. **1973** W. MCCARTHY *Detail* ii. 112 You've got forty-eight hours, that's all. Either get it, or get off the pot. **1974** *Farm & Country* 26 Mar. 4/2 To put it bluntly: the Ottawa politicians had better perform at once or get off the pot. **1977** 'J. LE CARRÉ' *Hon. Schoolboy* xii. 275 You better tell some of those limousine liberals back in Langley Virginia it's time for them to shit or get off the pot.

14. *pot-grown* adj.; **pot annealing** *vbl. sb.* = **box annealing*; also *attrib.*; hence **pot-anneal** *v. trans.*; **pot-bunker** *Golf,* an artificially constructed pot-shaped bunker; **pot-burial,** a prehistoric form of burial found in Crete (see quot.); **pot clay** (later examples); also (freq. with capital initials), a bed of this kind of clay near the base of the English coal measures; **pot courage** = *Dutch courage* s.v. COURAGE *sb.* 4 d; **pot cupboard,** a bedside cupboard designed to hold a chamber pot; **pot-drum** (see quot.); **pot-furnace,** (further examples); also, any furnace in which crucibles are heated; **pot-green** = POT-HERB; **pot-gut(s),** (*a*) = POT-BELLY 2; also, a pot-bellied animal; (*b*) = POT-BELLY 1; **pot-gutted** *a.* (later examples); **pot-lace** (examples); **pot-layering,** a method of propagating trees or shrubs in which a ball of soil, sometimes held within a split pot, is attached to a cut on a branch until enough roots have grown for the branch to be planted independently; **pot-licker, potlicker** *N. Amer.,* a mongrel dog; also *attrib.*; hence **pot-licking, potlicking,** toadying; **pot life,** the length of time that a glue, resin, or the like remains usable after preparation; **pot-line,** a line of retorts used for the electrolytic production of aluminium; **pot marigold,** the common marigold, *Calendula officinalis,* whose petals may be used to colour or flavour food; **pot marjoram,** substitute for def.: a small shrub, *Origanum onites,* whose leaves are used to flavour food; (earlier and later examples); **pot-mess** *Naut. slang,* a stew concocted from various scraps; *transf.,* a state of confusion or complete disorder; **pot rassler, rastler,** U.S. var. **pot-wrestler;** so **pot rassling, rastling** *vbl. sb.* (see quot.); **pot-sick** *a.,* (*b*) *nonce-use,* pot-bound; cramped or starved of nutrient; **pot stand,** a stand designed to hold pots or potted plants; **pot still** (earlier and later examples); so **pot-stilled** *adj.*; **pot-training** *vbl. sb.,* the training of a small child to use a chamber pot; hence (as a back-formation) **pot-train** *v.,* **pot-trained** *ppl. a.*; **pot-washings** *sb. pl.,* food removed from pots by washing; **pot-woman,** (*a*) a woman who sells pots; (*b*) *obs.,* a barmaid; (*c*) a woman who works at pottery; **pot-work** (earlier and later examples); **pot wrestler** (examples); (*c*) a chef; so **pot wrestling** *vbl. sb.*

1928 H. M. BOYLSTON *Introd. Metall. Iron & Steel* xv. 519 Tool steels are sometimes annealed in open-type furnaces of fairly small size, but in many cases are pot annealed. **1938** C. G. JOHNSON *Forging Pract.* 111 The steel is cooled very slowly either with the furnace..or cooled in a pot surrounded by heat insulating material (pot annealed). **1925** *Jrnl. Iron & Steel Inst.* CXII. 453 A newly designed installation for the drying of wire bundles..is..described, in which the chambers are heated with the waste gases from pot annealing furnaces. **1934** *Ibid.* CXXIX. 519 (*heading*) The heat conditions for the pot-annealing of steel hoops. **1909** *Westm. Gaz.* 30 Apr. 4/2 Had its original whins been forest-trees we should not now be digging pot-bunkers. **1963** *Times* 5 June 5/2 He..found a pot bunker and took seven which enabled Pirie..to halve. **1921** *Discovery* Feb. 33/1 A simpler form of burial, known as the 'pot-burial', was effected by trussing up the body, placing it under an inverted jar, and then burying it in the earth. **1860** E. HULL *Geol. Leicestershire Coalfield* (Mem. Geol. Survey) vi. 35 (*caption*) A. Loose breccia... B. Purple marl forming base of New Red Sandstone. C. Sandy shale. D. Coal 3 feet thick. E. Pot-clay, with rootlets stretching from the coal. **1913** *Geol. Derbyshire Coalfield* (Mem. Geol. Survey) viii. 124 Pot-clay suitable for the manufacture of stoneware occurs below a thin coal above the Alton seam. *Ibid.* 125 A bastard gannister, unsuited for use either as a pot-clay or as a gannister. **1939** tr. *E. N. Marais's My Friends the Baboons* vii. 81 Some were busy digging pot-clay from the hole with their hands while others were fashioning oxen and other animals from the clay. **1951** *Concealed Coalfield of Yorkshire & Nottinghamshire* (ed. 3) (Mem. Geol. Survey) iii. 13 The Coal Measures rest conformably on the Millstone Grit Series, the dividing line being placed, by international agreeement (Jongmans 1928, p. xliv), at the Pot Clay or *Gastrioceras Subcrenatum* Marine Band. **1968** M. A. CALVER in Murchison & Westoll *Coal* viii. 173 The Pot Clay fauna lacks the typical benthonic assemblage exhibited by the other kinds of marine band. **1806** C. WILMOT *Let.* 14 Oct. in *Russ. Jrnls.* (1934) II. 231 In a fit of *Pot Courage* no doubt he stroked his paunch & felt himself a Hero! **1867** E. CUST *Lives Warriors* II. I. 190 One of the best officers..became so drunk, that in his pot-courage he wrapped the napkin about his head, and.. went out in this guise into the trenches to attack the foe. **1794** T. SHERATON *Cabinet-Maker & Upholsterer's Drawing Bk.* III. 364 This left-hand drawer is..sometimes made very short, to give place to a pot-cupboard behind, which opens by a door at the end of the sideboard. **1973** *Country Life* 26 Apr. (Suppl.) 59/4 Late 18th century mahogany pot-cupboard. **1912** *Encycl. Relig. & Ethics* V. 90/1 The pot-drum is an earthenware vessel headed with a membrane. **1905** W. MACFARLANE *Lab. Notes Pract. Metall.* 11 (*heading*) Exercises in a crucible or 'pot' furnace. *Ibid.* 13 Gas coke is often good enough for a pot furnace. **1930** *Engineering* 18 Apr. 525/3 Sillimanite sieges in pot furnaces were more common. **1971** *Materials & Technol.* II. vi. 366 *Pot furnaces.* These are used for melting optical glass and other special glasses in quantities of up to half a ton at a time. **1742** W. ELLIS *Mod. Husbandman* July iii. 36 They proved..sweet Eating, when no other Pot Greens could be hardly got. **1972** *Sci. Amer.* Nov. 130/3 She studied our Southern cookbooks, too,..coming to the conclusion that 'distinctive features of Southern cooking are African in origin': gumbos and burgoo, hush puppies and pot greens, to begin with. **1915** W. L. HOWARD (*title*) Rest period studies with pot grown woody plants (Missouri Agric. Exper. Station Res. Bull. No. 16). **1946** G. A. R. PHILLIPS *Rock Garden* iv. 64 Pot grown plants may be planted with comparative safety at any time of the year. **1960** *Farmer & Stock-breeder* 9 Feb. 119/2 Start with small trees. In the case of *macrocarpa,* which are usually pot-grown, you could plant trees of $1\frac{1}{2}$–2ft. **1977** C. LLOYD *Clematis* vii. 114 Pot-grown clematis have the advantage of needing very little root disturbance in the process of planting. **1909** *Dialect Notes* III. 359 *Pot-gut, n.,* a pot-bellied person. *c* **1926** 'MIXER' *Transport Workers' Song Bk.* 72 She's seated in a motor With some 'pot-gut' by her side. **1926** G. FRANKAU *My Unsentimental Journey* xiv. 182 Those little squirrels they call 'pot-guts' scuttle fatly across the well-made road. **1942** BERREY & VAN DEN BARK *Amer. Thes. Slang* §429/2 *Fat person,*..pot-gut(s). **1951** R. CAMPBELL *Light on Dark Horse* 75 Then his old pot-guts would shake like a jelly. **1845** *Spirit of Times* 2 Aug. 267/1 *Ar* you a goin to tumtum all nite on that pot-gutted old pine box of a fiddle, *say?* **1909** *Dialect Notes* III. 359 *Pot-gutted, adj.,* pot-bellied. **1912** *Ibid.* 586 Look at that pot-gutted beer fly, will you. **1941** BAKER *Dict. Austral. Slang* 56 *Pot-gutted,* fat, paunchy. **1865** Pot lace [see *ANTWERP]. **1960** H. HAYWARD *Antique Coll.* 15/2 The style of pattern has given this [*sc.* Antwerp lace] the name of pot lace..from the substantial two-handled vase usually prominent in it. **1912** A. F. BROUN *Sylviculture in Tropics* II. iv. 146 'Pot-layering' is employed for branches which are either too high up a tree or too brittle to be bent into the ground. **1934** [see *air-layering* (*AIR *sb.*[1] II)]. **1961** *Amat. Gardening* 30 Sept. (Suppl.) 2/3 Air-layering. Also known as pot-layering... A means of rooting branches or shoots. **1932** V. RANDOLPH *Ozark Mountain Folks* 223 Jethro was splitting wood as I rode into his little clearing, heralded by a great number of pot-licker dogs. **1947** *Clarke County Democrat* (Grove Hill, Alabama) 30 Oct. 4/3 A hound is a hound, regardless of whether he is July, Red Bone, Walker, potlicker or just plain hush-puppy. **1948** W. FAULKNER *Intruder in Dust* (1949) i. 5 A true rabbit dog, some hound, a good deal of hound, maybe mostly hound, redbone and black-and-tan with maybe a little pointer somewhere once, a potlicker, a nigger dog. **1971** W. HILLEN *Blackwater River* ii. 10 One man was walking through the village with his three pot-lickers when they met a housecat. **1929** Potlicking [see *HOLE *v.*[1] 7]. **1968–70** *Current Slang* (Univ. S. Dakota) III–IV. 95 *Pot-licking, n.* Oversolicitous behavior... He made his way to the top only by *pot-licking.* **1945** H. BARRON *Mod. Plastics* viii. 199 When the hardener is mixed into the resin then the mixture has a very limited pot life. **1969** T. C. THORSTENSEN *Pract. Leather Technol.* xiv. 226 In this kind of finish the reactive components are usually mixed shortly before application, due to the limited pot life of the components. **1976** G. S. RAMASWAMY *Mod. Prestressed Concrete Design* vii. 86 The pot-life of the mixture was 20 to 25 minutes at an ambient temperature of 30°C. [**1936** *Industr. & Engin. Chem.* Feb. 148/1 Shutting down a 'line' of aluminum cells or 'pots'..is not a difficult or lengthy operation if properly performed.] **1951** *Economist* 29 Sept. 748/1 The drought had forced the huge hydro-electric installations on the Columbia River to reduce..power to the plants that provide aluminium. Already three 'potlines' have been closed down. **1957** *Times* 12 Nov. (Canada Suppl.) p. vi/5 The power is brought down on the other side of the mountain, 10 miles away, to feed the potlines located by the deep water estuary of the Douglas channel. **1965** *Wall St. Jrnl.* 25 Feb. 32/2 Aluminum Co. of America said it will install a third 33,000-ton-a-year potline for producing primary aluminum at its Warrick County, Ind. plant. **1814** J. GREEN *Address on Bot. U.S.* 41/2 *Calendula officinalis.* Pot Marygold, Common. **1883** *Encycl. Brit.* XV. 544/1 The pot-marigold..is the familiar garden plant with large orange-coloured blossoms. **1910** *Daily Chron.* 19 Feb. 9/6 Among the best annuals for town gardens are the..French and African marigolds..and the calendula or pot marigold. **1936** E. S. ROHDE *Herbs & Herb Gardening* ix. 128 Marigolds, including the old Pot Marigold.., have for some years been coming into favour again. **1966** G. B. FOSTER *Herbs for Every Garden* iii. 77 The petals of pot marigold were used to color butter, cheese, custards and sauces. **1597** Pot marjoram [see MARJORAM *a* γ]. **1629** J. PARKINSON *Parad.* II. cxxvi. 447 This kind of Marierome belongeth to that sort is called..In English Winter Marierome, or pot Marierome. **1936** E. S. ROHDE *Herbs & Herb Gardening* vii. 73 Pot Marjoram..is a larger and more branching plant than Sweet Marjoram. **1974** PAGE & STEARN *Culinary Herbs* 24 Pot Marjoram..is a dwarf shrub with erect densely hairy stems. **1914** 'BARTIMEUS' *Naval Occasions* xxiv. 238 What an awful pot-mess my cabin is in. **1916** 'TAFFRAIL' *Carry On!* 64 ''Strewth!', he murmurs under his breath, gazing at the littered floor in dismay... ''ere's a fine pot mess.' **1926** *Blackw. Mag.* Dec. 835/2 The resulting pot-mess vanished all too soon. **1961** F. H. BURGESS *Dict. Sailing* 163 *Potmess,* a mixture of any- and everything; a big heap; confusion. **1962** GRANVILLE *Dict. Sailors' Slang* 90/2 *Pot mess,* kind of stew very popular on the mess decks. **1942** BERREY & VAN DEN BARK *Amer. Thes. Slang* §460/15 Pot rassler *or* rastler, a *dishwasher.* **1968** R. F. ADAMS *Western Words* (rev. ed.) 234/2 *Pot rastler,* a logger's name for a dishwasher. **1942** BERREY & VAN DEN BARK *Amer. Thes. Slang* §819/1 Pot rassling, -rastling *or* wrestling,..*dishwashing or cooking.* **1872** HARDY *Under Greenw. Tree* I. II. iii. 157 Every morning I see her eyes mooning out through the panes of glass like a pot-sick winder-flower. **1907** *Yesterday's Shopping* (1969) 148/2 Pot Stands, triangular wood..each 0/3. **1947** [see *back-drop* (*BACK- B)]. **1971** *Cambr. Anc. Hist.* (ed. 3) I. II. xviii. 398 A biconical potstand has remote parallels at Büyük Güllücek, and in the Khirbet-Karak wares of the 'Amūq and Palestine. [**1799** *Rep. Comm. Distilleries Scotl.* in *Parl. Papers 1803* XI. 727/2 Private families distilled Whiskey for their own use; and the Still they used was a large pot, globular.] *Ibid.* 730/2 Suppose then that Fig. 5 represents an old fashioned Pot-Still. **1939** JOYCE *Finnegans Wake* 246 Ansighosa pokes in her potstill to souse at the sop be sodden enow and to hear to all the bubbles besaying. **1958** P. KEMP *No*

Colours or Crest viii. 150 A very small, wizened old man crouched over a crude pot-still..; on the ground beside him stood a number of small flasks filled with the clear spirit. **1965** Pot-stilled [see *MAO TAI]. **1972** J. GATHORNE-HARDY *Rise & Fall Brit. Nanny* viii. 265 It is actually physiologically impossible to pot train a child before the age of about six months. **1975** H. JOLLY *Bk. Child Care* I. xi. 179 You cannot truly pot train a baby before he is physically mature enough to exercise some control over his bladder and bowels. **1961** *Spectator* 17 Feb. 218 One-year-olds are pot-trained. **1966** 'K. NICHOLSON' *Hook, Line & Sinker* 11 Three sisters, the youngest only two and a half, and not fully pot-trained. **1960** L. DURRELL *Clea* II. ii. 126 Have you managed to annul your early pot-training? **1975** H. JOLLY *Bk. Child Care* I. xv. 217 If as a mother you never respond to your toddler's signals when he is about to wet his pants, he may give up trying to take the initiative himself and will probably be less co-operative with your efforts at pot training. **1912** C. N. MOODY *Saints of Formosa* ix. 195 They threatened to..feed her on the pot-washings with which the pigs are nourished. **1802** D. WORDSWORTH *Jrnl.* (1941) I. 182 We then went to the Pot-woman's and bought 2 jugs and a dish. **1918** *Pall Mall Gaz.* 29 June 5/4 A 'potwoman' at a public house applied for a summons for wages in lieu of notice. **1979** *Listener* 20 & 27 Dec. 854/4 The Thistle..had a three-cornered taproom. I once saw a pot-woman dance an impromptu fertility dance there. **1765** J. WEDGWOOD *Let.* 2 Mar. (1965) 29 This trade to our Colonies we are apprehensive of losing in a few years as they have set on foot some Potworks there already. **1902** A. BENNETT *Anna of Five Towns* xii. 328 Behind it..was a small, disused potworks. **1965** *Punch* 17 Feb. 244/1 The potworks expose their raw materials on their open marlbanks. **1860** BARTLETT *Dict. Amer.* (ed. 3) 335 *Pot-wrestler*, a scullion. Pennsylvania. **1873** *Kansas Mag.* Aug. 139/1 'Bullwhackers', .., 'pot-wrestlers' and 'ink-slingers' are but a few of the common pet English names a politician must use in addressing his audience, in order to show them he is sufficiently familiar with their language. **1889** FARMER *Americanisms* 434/2 *Pot-wrestler*, a Pennsylvanian equivalent of the English 'pot-wallopper'; a scullion. **1902** [see POTWALLOPER 2]. **1941** J. SMILEY *Hash House Lingo* 44 *Pot wrestler*, dish washer. **1947** *N.Y. Jrnl. American* 18 Mar. 17/4 The off-center meatball has been endorsed by the chefs of the old world. No less a pot-wrassler than the King's own glorified the chuckwagon croquette as the ambrosia of the parked gulp. **1942** Pot wrestling [see **pot-rassling*].

pot, *sb.*^{4} Add: **b.** *Rugby Football.* A dropped goal (see *DROPPED *ppl. a.* 1 a). *N.Z.*

1959 *N.Z. Listener* 24 July 6/4 Five potted goals—that was when a pot was worth four points.

pot (pǫt), *sb.*^{5} *slang* (orig. *U.S.*). [prob. f. Mexican Sp. *potiguaya* marijuana leaves; perhaps influenced by POT *sb.*^{1}; cf. *POD *sb.*^{2} 1 c.] **1.** = *MARIJUANA 1 a.

1938 [see *JAGGED *a.*^{2} b]. **1951** *N.Y. Times* 13 June 24/4 Progression from sneaky pete to pot to horse to banging. **1952** *Amer. Speech* XXVII. 28 Pot,..marijuana cigarettes... (Maurer, *potiguaya*, marijuana leaves after pods removed.) **1959** *Oxford Mail* 9 Nov. 1/6 The detectives invited their Greenwich Village pals to a big party..with poetry readings, bongo drums and plenty of 'pot' (marijuana) to smoke. **1961** N. MAILER *Advts. for Myself* 209 In Mexico, however, down in my depression with a bad liver, pot gave me a sense of something new. **1964** S. BELLOW *Herzog* (1965) i. 87 You have to do more than take a little gas, or slash the wrists. Pot? Zero! Daisy chains? Nothing! Debauchery? A museum word. **1965** *Punch* 22 Dec. 930/3 'Like a spot of pot, Jean?' he said. 'I never touch it,' I said archly. **1966** T. PYNCHON *Crying of Lot 49* iii. 63 'But we don't repeat what we hear,' said another girl. 'None of us smoke Beaconsfields anyway. We're all on pot.' **1968** *New Scientist* 22 Aug. 371/2, I am not defending the behaviour of these students and of course I don't agree with them that 'pot' is harmless. **1972** J. L. DILLARD *Black English* vii. 289 The teacher probably should not let illusions of knowledge about the ghetto tempt him into using sentences like *John and Mary are smoking pot.* **1973** [see *LSD^2]. **1975** D. LODGE *Changing Places* ii. 63 He took an extreme radical position on all such issues as pot, sex, race. **1977** *Jrnl. R. Soc. Arts* CXXV. 464/2 His son occasionally smokes pot.

2. *attrib.* and *Comb.*, as *pot liquor, smoke, -smoker, -smoking* vbl. sb. and ppl. a.; **pothead, pothead** (see *HEAD *sb.* 7 e); **pot party,** a party held for the smoking of marijuana.

1959, etc. [see *HEAD *sb.* 7 e]. **1974** *Times Lit. Suppl.* 1 Mar. 219/4 A girl..herself something of a pothead, who introduces Evans to the joys of the weed. **1970** C. MAJOR *Dict. Afro-Amer. Slang* 92 *Pot liquor*..; brew from marijuana seeds and stalks. **1967** *Boston Sunday Herald* 26 Mar. I. 40/8 Authorities said that as many as 25 teenagers attended drug sessions held twice a month at different Randolph homes by one group, and that others also held 'pot' parties. **1971** D. E. WESTLAKE *I gave at the Office* (1972) 219 The media have some leniency..as for instance when magazines stage pot parties. **1976** B. LECOMBER *Dead Weight* v. 68, I couldn't quite imagine even an Antiguan Customs officer suspecting Herr Ruchter of holding riotous pot-parties. **1978** J. KRANTZ *Scruples* iii. 66 An occasional pot party was as anti-establishment a gathering as he attended. **1966** T. PYNCHON *Crying of Lot 49* iii. 64 Their rising coils and clouds of pot smoke. **1967** *Guardian* 8 July 6/4 The bored pot-smoker looking for some better kick. **1971** *New Scientist* 11 Mar. 533/3 Pot smokers have a lowered sexual drive. **1976** H. NIELSEN *Brink of Murder* xi. 99 You must be calling on a pot smoker. Take me along? **1964** *Punch* 18 Mar. 413/1 'Pot-smoking' parties, gaming sessions. **1967** *Guardian* 3 Feb. 4/4 They said, there is no evidence of a direct link between pot-smoking and addiction to hard narcotics. **1970** G. F. NEWMAN *Sir, You Bastard* ii. 39 He didn't have the stereotype-copper look..but appeared more as one expected a pot-smoking nymphomaniac to look. **1977** *Rolling Stone* 13 Jan. 37/2 Kerr-McGee officials later quoted from the letter when they described Silkwood's pot-smoking proclivities to reporters.

pot (pǫt), *sb.*^{6} Colloq. abbrev. of POTENTIOMETER.

1943 C. L. BOLTZ *Basic Radio* iii. 56 Radio workers always refer to the 'pot'. **1948** *Electronics* July 120/2 The output voltage *z* of the multiplying pot is proportional to its angular rotation. **1953** R. BRETZ *Techniques Television Production* xix. 401 The first thing the student operator learns about the audio console is that the fader dials, or 'pots', in the middle of the panel each controls [*sic*] a separate source of sound. **1967** *Electronics* 6 Mar. 311/2 (Advt.), No matter what your pot requirements, they take a turn for the better when you contact Gamewell Division.

pot, *v.*^{1} Add: **II. 2. a.** (Further *fig.* example.) Also, to summarize, put into 'potted' form (see *POTTED *ppl. a.* 3 a).

1927 *Year's Work Eng. Stud. 1925* 42 After preliminaries, the matter is divided into: the effect of Function upon Sound..; of Emotion upon Sound..; and of *Gliederung*... The statistics and argument can hardly be 'potted' here.

c. To encapsulate (an electrical component or circuit) in a liquid insulating material, usu. a synthetic resin, which sets solid.

1950 W. W. STIFLER *High-Speed Computing Devices* xvi. 426 Tests..showed that it was possible to pot printed circuits in a special casting resin in such a fashion as to permit the plugging in of the complete subassemblies. **1962** F. I. ORDWAY et al. *Basic Astronautics* vi. 279 The plastics in which electronic components are potted usually contain bacteria. **1971** J. H. SMITH *Digital Logic* i. 5 The whole assembly is usually 'potted' into a block to form a module.

3. b. (Further examples.) Also, *pot off*, to transplant seedlings into individual pots; *pot on*, to move a plant from one pot into a larger one; *pot out*, to plunge potted plants into a bed in the open garden; *pot up*, to move seedlings or larger plants into pots.

1870 W. ROBINSON *Alpine Flowers for Eng. Gardener* I. 63 This is a better way than sowing in pots,..from which they require to be 'potted off'. **1916** M. HAMPDEN *Flower Culture* ii. 39 Now [*sc.* March] is the time for..potting up clumps of hardy plants from the garden. **1926** E. T. BROWN *Year in my Flower Garden* 58 Lift and pot roots of Solomon's Seal. **1950** *N.Z. Jrnl. Agric.* Aug. 167/1 When the leaves of the small plants touch each other in the boxes it is time to pot them up. **1950** O. SITWELL *Noble Essences* IX. vi. 139 The gentle gold of the industrial haze lay lightly on the rich beds of tulips, carnations or begonias, so neatly potted out. **1952** C. E. L. PHILLIPS *Small Garden* ix. 77 Nurselings in small pots are 'potted-on' into bigger ones when their roots have filled up the first one. **1958** *Listener* 12 June 982/2 They [*sc.* amaryllis plants] will throw off bulbils from the main bulb. These can be taken off and potted up. **1978** R. GORER *Growing Plants from Seed* v. 69 The seedlings are potted up separately in very small pots and progressively potted on.

5. c. (Earlier example.) Also, in *Rugby Football*, to score (a dropped goal). *N.Z.*

1862 W. B. CHEADLE *Jrnl. Trip across Canada* (1931) 48 Worked at harness-making & potted much money during term. **1959** [see *POT *sb.*^{4} b].

III. 6. b. *Austral. slang.* To hand (someone) over for trial, to inform on. Cf. *POT *sb.*^{1} 13 k.

1911 A. WRIGHT *Gambler's Gold* 138 Why should I pot the bloke? He done me a good turn, an' th' police is no good to me. **1916** J. B. COOPER *Coo-oo-ee* ix. 108 'Yer see,' he explained, 'they've got to try to hang some cove or else they'd lose their job. The more men they pot the better they're fixed in their jobs. See?' **1945** BAKER *Austral. Lang.* II. xi. 207 A few general expressions concerned with school life:..*to pot someone* or *to put someone's pot on*, to inform on. **1953** 'CADDIE' *Sydney Barmaid* xl. 230 What dirty swine has potted me?

IV. 8. (Examples.) Also freq. *intr.*

1914 R. FRY *Lett.* (1972) II. 377 Vanessa and I have been potting all day... We went when the potter wasn't there and got the man to turn the wheel. **1967** B. JEFFERIS *One Black Summer* (1968) i. 1 The grounds and buildings would be full of summer school students; doctors who longed to pot; dressmakers who yearned to try their hands at sculpture. **1968** *Canad. Antiques Collector* June 12/1 The Rockingham China Works..began to produce china (porcelain) in 1826. The factory ceased to manufacture towards the end of 1841. Many fine porcelain wares..were potted in this relatively brief period. **1971** J. WHITE *Left for Dead* 68 All I've got to do is to teach myself to pot... I've always been interested in making pottery. **1976** J. G. HURST in D. M. Wilson *Archaeol. Anglo-Saxon Eng.* vii. 323 Stamford ware is finely potted on a fast wheel and fired in a developed single-flue kiln.

V. 9. *colloq.* To cause (a baby or young child) to use a chamber-pot. Also *absol.*

1943 A. MEDLEY *Your First Baby* xviii. 180 With children who hardly wake up, perform with their eyes closed and drop off again, it is well worth while to pot them and to know that they will sleep dry and comfortable. **1948** B. GOOLDEN *Jig-Saw* ii. 9, I prefer them [*sc.* babies] house-trained... One feeds and pots automatically. **1957** H. CROOME *Forgotten Place* iv. 51 I'm not going to pot him or anything. I think early habit training is such a mistake. **1973** *Daily Tel.* (Colour Suppl.) 26 Oct. 7/2 She has poured the last coffee and sat back for the first time since potting the baby at 7.30 that morning.

‖ **potager** (pota3e). [Fr.: see POTAGERE.] = POTAGERE.

c **1786** T. BLAIKIE *Diary Scotch Gardener* (1931) 199 This garden..goes with a narrow stripe of potager to the point du jour where there is another potager. **1792** A. YOUNG *Trav. France* I. 99 There is a town, and a great *potager* to remove before it would be consonant with English ideas. **1885** H. JAMES *Little Tour in France* iii. 20 Your eye wanders over the neighbouring *potagers*. **1926** *Spectator* 9 Oct. 581/2 The herb garden..lost its supremacy to the *potager* or vegetable garden less than two centuries ago. **1958** L. DURRELL *Spirit of Place* (1969) 146, I calculate that with ten chickens and the excellent *potager* out there I shall just squeeze by. **1966** A. CHRISTIE *Third Girl* iv. 35 In England..you do not love your *potager* as much as you love your flowers. **1978** J. LEES-MILNE *Round the Clock* 55 The north garden..would be called the *potager*, were it in France. Vegetables, espaliers, roses and lawns were neatly compartmented.

potamoplankton (pǫːtămoplæ·ŋktǫn). [a. G. (C. Zimmer 1898, in *Biol. Centralbl.* XVIII. 522), f. Gr. ποταμό-ς river + PLANKTON.] Plankton found in rivers or streams.

1902 *Ann. Bot.* XVI. 584 These backwaters thus form a kind of transition from the typical Potamoplankton of the flowing river to the Heleoplankton of the ponds of the Thames valley. **1909** E. WARMING *Oecol. Plants* xxxviii. 161 Other subdivisions [of limnoplankton] may be recognized, such as potamoplankton, heloplankton, and probably several more. **1923** *Jrnl. Ecol.* XI. 209 Potamoplankton is the plankton of rivers. It is usually benthoplanktonic in character, but at times may show limnoplanktonic features. **1969** G. W. PRESCOTT *Algae* i. 17 Plankton of rivers is called potamoplankton.

pot and pan. [Rhyming slang for 'old man'.] One's father or husband.

1906 E. DYSON *Fact'ry 'Ands* xii. 153 How's yer ole pot-'n'-pan, Tutsie? **1935** A. J. POLLOCK *Underworld Speaks* 90/2 *Pot and pan*, the old man (otpay and anpay). **1938** L. ORTZEN *Down Donkey Row* 12 *Pot and Pan*, old man; meaning husband or father. **1945** BAKER *Austral. Lang.* 270 *Pot and pan*, old man. **1971** *National Times* (Austral.) 13 Dec. 20 From this handy guide you could soon establish the meaning of..'her pot and pan is in the bucket and pail'... Translated, it means '..her old man is in jail.'

potarite (pǫ̆tā·rəit). *Min.* [f. the name of the *Potaro* River, Guyana, where first found: see -ITE^1.] Palladium amalgam, occurring as brittle, silvery grains and nuggets and reported to consist of two distinct phases.

1925 *W. India Committee Circular* 22 Oct. 429/2 The second report deals with the occurrence of Palladium-Mercuride, a mineral new to science in British Guiana. Up to the present it has only been found in certain diamond-bearing gravels on the Potaro river; and so it was named 'Potarite'. **1928** *Mineral. Mag.* XXI. 397 He [*sc.* Sir John Harrison] proposed the name potarite (letter of April 3, 1925), but he did not himself record this name in print. **1960** *Amer. Mineralogist* XLV. 1094 Samples of PdHg which are identical with the mineral potarite may be prepared either by displacement of palladium from $Pd(NO_3)_2$ solution by mercury or by direct synthesis from powdered palladium and mercury in sealed evacuated tubes. **1968** I. KOSTOV *Mineral.* II. i. 95 Mercury group... Gold amalgam..and potarite (PdHg, tetragonal) with about 35% Pd, are rare representatives of the group.

potashery. (Earlier and later examples.)

1799 *Canada Constellation* (Niagara, Ontario) 8 Nov. 4/1 For field ashes, 9d. at the potashery, and 6d. if he goes for them. **1882** W. M. THAYER *From Log-Cabin to White House* 150 A pot-ashery was an establishment containing vats for leeching ashes, and large kettles for boiling the lye. **1930** *Canad. Hist. Rev.* XI. 39 The only buildings were..two saw-mills, a carding shop, a potashery, [etc.]. **1979** *Jrnl. R. Soc. Arts* Dec. 60/2 A syndicate of Liverpool-Manchester merchants..opened potasheries in New York and Philadelphia.

potassic, *a.* Add: **b.** *Geol.* Of a mineral or rock: containing an appreciable or a greater-than-average quantity of potassium, often as compared with sodium. Also applied to a metamorphic process in which such minerals are formed.

1903 W. CROSS et al. *Quantitative Classification Igneous Rocks* 227 The orthoclase may be considered as wholly potassic and reckoned as pure orthoclase. **1932** A. JOHANNSEN *Descr. Petrogr. Igneous Rocks* II. 63 The term orthorhyolite was originally suggested in 1919 for rhyolites whose only feldspar is potassic. **1967** *Amer. Mineralogist* LII. 828 The early part of the alteration sequence featured chiefly potassic metasomatism (biotite, potash feldspar), whereas the latter part was characterized by sodic metasomatism (aegirine, crocidolite). **1971** I. G. GASS et al. *Understanding Earth* i. 18/1 Two compositionally different feldspars, one more sodic and the other more potassic. **1974** P. G. HARRIS in H. Sørensen *Alkaline Rocks* VI. i. 434/1 The anomalous $^{87}Sr/^{86}Sr$ ratios of many suites of potassic rocks suggests..a multistage origin.

potassium. Add: **c.** Special comb.: **potassium-argon,** used *attrib.* to designate a method of isotopic dating, or results obtained from it, based upon measurement of the relative amounts in rock of potassium 40 and its decay (electron capture) product, argon 40.

1953 *Bull. Geol. Soc. Amer.* LXIV. 1473 (*heading*)

Potassium argon studies at the University of Toronto. **1955** *Ibid.* LXVI. 1711 (*heading*) Potassium-argon ages of metamorphic and igneous rocks from the Southern Appalachians. **1968** *Times* 3 Oct. 13/5 The duration of the various magnetic reversals is known from potassium-argon dating of land rocks. **1969** Bennison & Wright *Geol. Hist. Brit. Isles* xvi. 362 Earlier pleistocene deposits can only be dated, as yet, by the use of the potassium-argon method..which, because of the long half-life of potassium, is not suited to dating such relatively recent events. **1977** *Time* 7 Nov. 52/2 The age of a fossil can often be determined by analyzing the layer of rock or soil in which it was found and determining, often by the so-called potassium-argon method, just how old the layer is.

potato, *sb.* Add: **2. d.** δ. (Further examples in spellings *pratie, praty*.)

In quot. 1966 the use is *fig.*

1781 W. Dyott *Diary* 8 Sept. (1907) I. 5 In short, I think them [*sc.* the Irish recruits] calculated merely to eat potatoes, or 'pratys', as they call them. **1826** 'N. Nondescript' *The* — 15 Apr. 56 'I was just thinking,' said he in a whimpering tone, 'what we poor Irish would do, if we hadn't paraties.' **1830** *Constellation* II. 1/1 She took my advice, and doubling herself up in the blanket, was asleep before your Honour'd say praties. **1927** in C. Sandburg *Amer. Songbag* 463 O, I met her in the mornin' And I'll have yez all to know That I met her in the garden Where the praties grow. **1949** C. Graves *Ireland Revisited* vii. 82 Nobody uses the word 'begorrah,' and a potato is a 'spud' not a 'praty'. **1966** *Listener* 12 May 687/1 A sentimental domestic melodrama—what Irish audiences..call a 'pratie', or potato. **1972** *Islander* (Victoria, B.C.) 12 Mar. 8/1 We call them 'spuds'. The Irish affectionately call them 'praties' and they sometimes call mashed potatoes 'poundies'. **1973** *Times* 29 Aug. 7/6 Do you fancy some German sausage in the garden where the praties grow?

5. a. *hot potato*; (to drop something) *like a hot potato*: see *hot *a.* 12 a; *small potatoes* (further examples); also in sing. and in phr. *small potatoes and few in a* (or *the*) *hill*.

1836 D. Crockett *Exploits & Adventures Texas* ii. 25 This is what I call small potatoes and few of a hill. **1839** *Boston* (Mass.) *Morning Post* 23 July 1/1 The Conservatives in Maine have held a convention and nominated F. O. J. Smith, for Governor. S.P. (small potatos). **1880** [see *ham-fatter* s.v. *ham *sb.*[1] 3]. **1886** *Galaxy* 1 Oct. 272 Insignificant people are 'small potatoes, and few in a hill'. **1914** 'Bartimeus' *Naval Occasions* xiii. 101 In the beginning he was an Assistant Clerk—which is a very small potato indeed. **1923** Conrad *Rover* x. 160 Then indeed that corvette, the big factor of everyday life on that stretch of coast, would become very small potatoes indeed. **1926** M. J. Atkinson in J. F. Dobie *Rainbow in Morning* (1965) 80 He's a mighty small potato in my estimation. He's mighty small potatoes and few in a hill. **1927** H. T. Lowe-Porter tr. *Mann's Magic Mountain* II. vii. 787 If some first-class excitement doesn't come along every day, you pull a face as though you were saying: 'H'm, small potatoes *and* few in the hill!'. **1962** A. Buchwald *How much is that in Dollars?* 122 Mary Soo, by tradition but not contract, has the garbage concession of all United States Navy ships entering Hong Kong, which out here is no small potatoes. **1968** *Globe & Mail* (Toronto) 3 Feb. 7/6 When the conference gets around to 'other matters' on Wednesday, the current dispute over medicare should seem like small potatoes. **1973** H. Nielsen *Severed Key* iv. 49 'Morry Sacks is going to tell the law we found a million dollars on the beach?' 'No! Morry is too small potatoes.' **1974** *Publishers Weekly* 26 Aug. 300/2 A milieu where the crime is petty and municipal corruption small potatoes. **1976** *Gramophone* July 153/3 Serenus is small potatoes by CBS or RCA standards but its albums are tastefully produced and carefully annotated.

c. Also, (*the*) *clean potato*: a person or thing whose character or excellence is beyond reproach. Hence the phr. *not (quite) the clean potato* and vars., not completely sound or reliable; not (quite) the right or real thing.

1880 [in Dict.]. **1881** G. H. Gibson in *Bulletin* (Sydney) 16 Mar. 8 You weren't quite the cleanly potato, Sam Holt. **1890** 'R. Boldrewood' *Colonial Reformer* III. xxvii. 104 'Well,' said Mr. Cottonbush,..'it ain't quite the clean potato, of course [*sc.* to steal a neighbour's grass]; but if your sheep's dying at home, what can you do?' **1913** Galsworthy *Dark Flower* II. vii. 137 A suspicion he had always entertained, that Cramier was not by breeding 'quite the clean potato'. **1921** K. S. Prichard *Black Opal* xvi. 148, I ain't always been what you might call the clean potato. **1929** J. Masefield *Hawbucks* 165 We'll shake hands, clean potato, and be good friends. **1931** M. Franklin *Back to Bool Bool* 233 She was only the great-granddaughter of old Larry Healey of Little River, none so clean a potato, if rumour was correct. **1933** G. Heyer *Why shoot a Butler?* vi. 86 Not strictly the clean potato, is it?.. Guest in the man's house, you know. The Public School Spirit, and Playing for the Side, and all that wash. **1939** —— *No Wind of Blame* iv. 80 It isn't at all the clean potato. In fact, it's very dishonourable. **1941** Baker *Dict. Austral. Slang* 56 *A clean potato*, a free or unconvicted person, one with unblemished character. **1962** T. Ronan *Deep of Sky* 42 Some of the grand old pioneers and land-takers of history were not quite the clean potato.

d. A large or conspicuous hole in a sock or stocking through which the flesh shows.

1885 *Eng. Illustr. Mag.* June 616/1 The gladiators wore pasteboard helmets..and fleshings for legs and arms, with—what are vulgarly termed 'potatoes', that is, holes in the fleshings perceptible in many places. **1886** H. Baumann *Londinismen* 144/1 *Potatoes*, grosse Löcher in den Strümpfen. **1902** Farmer & Henley *Slang* V. 270/1 *Potato*,..used esp. for a heel through an undarned sock or stocking. **1949** D. M. Davin *Roads from Home* III. iv. 241 It was a mystery the way that Paddy went through his stockings... A great big potato staring out over the heel. **1973** *Country Gentlemen's Estate Mag.* Mar. 156/1 Gumboots..will hole a 'potato' like a cannon-ball in the heels of a new pair of socks in an afternoon.

e. In pl. *U.S. slang.* Money. Occas. in more specific use, dollars ('pounds' in quot. 1939).

1931 D. Runyon in *Collier's* 4 Nov. 8/2 'Listen, Sam,' I say, 'you have seven duckets, and we are only six, and here is a little doll who is stood up by her guy, and has no ducket, and no potatoes to buy one with, so what about taking her with us?' **1932** —— in *Collier's* 26 Mar. 7/4 Many citizens are figuring that maybe he suddenly discovers all his potatoes are counterfeit, because nobody can think of anything that will worry Sorrowful except money. **1933** *Sun* (Baltimore) 15 Sept. 1/2 Nobody gives fifteen thousand 'potatoes' to a party committee without wanting something. **1935** A. J. Pollock *Underworld Speaks* 90/2 *Potatoes*, money. **1939** Wodehouse *Uncle Fred in Springtime* i. 9 Was it conceivable..that any man, even to oblige a future brother-in-law, would cough up the colossal sum of two hundred potatoes? **1976** *National Observer* (U.S.) 8 May 14/2 Usually he [*sc.* a horse] runs with a price tag of about $3,500. With those kind of potatoes, it can be hard to get respect.

f. *Austral. slang.* Also in spelling *potater*. [Shortening of *potato peeler*, rhyming slang for *sheila.] A girl, a woman.

1957 D. Niland *Call me when Cross turns Over* ii. 69 Snow told him not to be a mug, the sheila had him in her sights because she thought he was a bit of all right. That would be the day, Locky retorted, when some bloody potater..had him stringing along with her. **1970** G. Greer *Female Eunuch* 266 Terms..often extended to the female herself. Who likes to be called..a *potato*? **1970** *Private Eye* 2 Jan. 12 He's been endeavouring to commit intimacy with your *potato*. **1971** *Ibid.* 2 July 16 As for this potato I must guide her footsteps back into the paths of righteousness.

6. a. *potato-croquette, -flour* (later examples), *-fritter, -harvest, -house, -land, -sack* (examples), *-soup* (earlier and later examples). **b.** *potato-chipper, -digger* (earlier and later examples), *-peeler* (examples), *-peeling* (further examples), *-planting*.

1895 *Montgomery Ward Catal.* 436/1 Potato Chipper, can be used as a..chopper for potatoes. **1951** *Catal. of Exhibits, South Bank Exhib., Festival of Britain* 52/1 Potato chipper; Thos. A. Nutbrown Ltd., Walker Street, Blackpool, Lancs. **1977** *Western Mail* (Cardiff) 5 Mar. 12/2 (Advt.), Hobart Potato Chipper, 40lb. per minute. Reconditioned. **1876** M. N. Henderson *Pract. Cooking* 194 Potato Croquettes. Add to four or five mashed potatoes..the beaten yolk of one egg. **1942** C. Spry *Come into Garden, Cook* iv. 38 The best croquettes in the world, *Potato Croquettes.* **1845** *Quincy* (Illinois) *Whig* 18 Dec. 2/5 A new potatoe digger was recently exhibited in operation at Salem, West Jersey. **1858** J. Brown *Let.* 13 May (1912) 160 And is the delightfullest of potato-diggers already digging? **1945** *Hardin* (Montana) *Tribune-Herald* 15 Feb. 2/4, I will sell at public auction..1 potato digger. **1906** U. Sinclair *Jungle* xi. 139 Potato-flour is the waste of potato after the starch and alcohol have been extracted; it has no more food value than so much wood. **1911** *Daily Colonist* (Victoria, B.C.) 4 Apr. 3/1 (Advt.), Potato Flour, Health Brand, packet 20c. **1845** E. Acton *Mod. Cookery* xix. 417 Potato fritters. (Entremets.) See directions for potato puddings. The same mixture dropped in fritters into boiling butter, and fried until firm on both sides will be found very good. **1966** P. V. Price *France* 308 Small sweetened potato fritters. **1808** E. Weeton *Let.* 1 Apr. (1969) I. 78 An uncommonly plentiful potatoe harvest. **1979** *Country Life* 2 May 1375 Mr Hurd works on the early potato harvest. **1791** W. Bartram *Trav. N. & S. Carolina* 192 The lowest or ground part is a potatoe house. **1861** C. M. Yonge *Stokesley Secret* vi. 89 There was a bonfire by the potato-house. **1921** *Proc. 3rd National Country Life Conf. 1920* (U.S.) 155 Potato houses..are isolated and located with special reference to the good of the products involved. **1970** S. Trueman *Intimate Hist. New Brunswick* iii. 56 The 'potato houses' looking like dwellings that have sunk so deep into the ground that they now consist mainly of high-peaked roofs. **1780** A. Young *Tour in Ireland* I. 344 Plough the potatoe land once or twice for barley. **1855** *Trans. Amer. Inst. City of N.Y. 1854* 168 Salt..will kill grubs, and may be used to advantage on potato land. **1965** K. H. Connell in Glass & Eversley *Population in Hist.* xvii. 428 The practice of letting farms by auction in a country [*sc.* Ireland] where land was almost the only resource encouraged tenants to outbid one another in the tribute they offered to acquire the right to potato-land. **1895** *Montgomery Ward Catal.* 436/1 The Peerless Potato Peeler. This is an entirely new and novel article for peeling and slicing potatoes. **1951** *Good Housek. Home Encycl.* 610/1 Potatoes should be peeled.. with either a special potato peeler or a sharp, short-bladed knife. **1961** *Which?* Mar. 61 (*heading*) Potato peelers. *Ibid.* 61/1 In this report, CA discusses five potato peeling devices on the market when our tests began. **1975** L. Gillen *Return to Deepwater* x. 178 She impatiently brushed them [*sc.* tears] away with the back of one hand before resuming her potato-peeling. **1885** A. Edwardes *Girton Girl* III. xiii. 221 The Seigneur..taking part in his potato-planting and his vraic harvest. **1951** R. Firth *Elem. Social Organiz.* iv. 142 To revert to the Irish peasantry..—there is a form of non-monetary co-operation..in tasks such as..potato-planting. **1859** G. A. Sala *Twice round Clock* 40 There are tall potato-sacks, propped up in dark corners. **1939** F. Thompson *Lark Rise* i. 4 A superannuated potato-sack thrown down by way of hearthrug. **1979** *Guardian* 28 Feb. 13/3 Ladies.. manage to knit passable potato sacks to cover their nether limbs. **1845** E. Acton *Mod. Cookery* i. 20 Potato soup. Mash to a smooth paste three pounds of good mealy potatoes..; mix with them..two quarts of boiling broth,.. add pepper and salt. **1861** Mrs. Beeton *Bk. Househ. Managem.* 76 *Potato soup*... When the potatoes are boiled, mash them smoothly..and gradually put them to the boiling stock [etc.]. **1960** *Good Housek. Cookery Bk.* (rev. ed.) 72/2 *Potato soup*... Peel and slice the potatoes and chop the onion and celery.

7. potato ball, (*a*) (examples); (*b*) also in *sing.* and *attrib.* (examples); **potato-beetle**[2], (*a*) (examples); substitute for def.: the Colorado beetle, *Leptinotarsa decemlineata*, a brown beetle with black spots and stripes which attacks the leaves of the potato and related plants; **potato bread** (earlier and later examples); **potato-bug,** (*a*) = *potato-fly*; (*b*) = *potato-beetle*[2]; (earlier and later examples); **potato-cake** (earlier examples); **potato chip,** (*a*) = *chip *sb.*[1] 2 b; (*b*) *U.S.* = **potato crisp* (see also quot. 1975); also (usu. with hyphen) *attrib.*; **potato clay,** a variety of clay used by the Hopi Indians in making pigments; **potato creeper** = **potato vine* (*b*); **potato crisp** (see *crisp *sb.* 7); **potato dumpling,** a dumpling whose ingredients include sieved cooked potatoes; **potato-eater,** a derogatory nickname usu. applied to an Irishman (see also quot. 1871); **potato failure** = **potato famine*; **potato famine,** a dearth of potatoes caused by crop failure; *spec.* (usu. with capital initials) that which occurred in Ireland in 1846–7; **potato flake** (usu. in *pl.*), (see quot. 1955); **potato-fly,** for *Lytta* substitute *Epicauta*; (examples); **potato hook** (examples); **potato latke** [*latke], a pancake made with grated potato; **potato masher,** a device consisting of a set of wires or a perforated flat plate (formerly, a solid wooden cylinder) attached to a handle, for mashing potatoes; also *transf.*, (*a*) in full **potato-masher grenade,** a type of hand grenade whose shape resembles that of a potato masher; (*b*) (see quot. 1945); **potato moth** *Austral.* = **potato tuber moth*; **potato-mouth** *v. trans.*, to mutter; also **potato-mouthed** *a.* = Mealy-mouthed *a.*; **potato onion,** substitute for def.: a variety of the common onion, *Allium cepa*, in which new bulbs are produced at the base; (examples); **potato pancake,** a pancake in which sieved mashed potato is the basic ingredient; also, = **potato latke*; **potato patch,** a plot of ground on which potatoes are grown; **potato peelings,** strips of the peeled skin of potatoes; **potato pie,** (*a*) (further examples); (*b*) (later example); **potato puff,** a kind of potato crisp in the form of a puff (see Puff *sb.* 5); **potato race** (examples); **potato rot** (earlier examples); **potato salad,** pieces of cold cooked potato mixed with salad dressing and other ingredients; **potato scone,** a scone made with sieved cooked potatoes; **potato set** = Set *sb.* 23 b; **potato stick,** a small crisp potato chip; **potato straw,** a very thin stick of potato, fried until crisp; **potato tuber moth,** the moth whose larva is the potato tuberworm; **potato tuberworm** *U.S.*, the pinkish-white caterpillar of the moth *Gnorimoschema operculella*; **potato-vine,** substitute for def.: (*a*) a potato plant, *Solanum tuberosum*; (*b*) one of several South or Central American climbing plants, esp. *Solanum jasminoides* or *S. wendlandii*, bearing blue or white flowers; (examples); **potato worm,** substitute for def.: = **potato tuberworm*; (examples).

1823 T. B. Hazard *Diary* 16 May (1930) 596/1 Planted a Potatoe Ball. **1824** M. Randolph *Virginia House-Wife* 120 Potato Balls. Mix mashed potatoes with the yelk of an egg, roll them into balls, [etc.]. **1845** E. Acton *Mod. Cooking* (ed. 2) xv. 304 English potato balls. **1846** *Jewish Manual, or Pract. Information Jewish & Mod. Cookery* v. 91 Potatoe balls are mashed potatoes formed into balls glazed with the yolk of egg, and browned with a salamander. **1850** *Rep. Comm. Patents: Agric. 1849* (U.S.) 198 In 1847, he planted a single potato-ball or apple; only one seed grew. **1877** *Rep. Vermont Board Agric.* IV. 33 Nature can make potato balls, but she couldn't make the Early Rose. **1912** M. B. Brown *Just Use-it-Up* vi. 140 Potato balls. **1948** *Good Housek. Cookery Bk.* II. 289 Scoop out the potato balls with a Parisian potato cutter. **1963** R. Carrier *Great Dishes of World* 213/2 Roll potato balls in flour and then in beaten egg. **1969** E. H. Pinto *Treen* 141 The hardwood handle with, at each end, a steel bowl with a hole in the base..is a potato ball maker, probably 18th-century. **1866** *Pract. Entomologist* I. 105/2 One day last week a gentleman left at our office a stalk from a potato hill, which was literally covered with the larva of the new potato beetle. **1868** *Amer. Entomologist* I. 44/1 It might perhaps be desirable.. to get people to call it [*sc.* the Colorado potato-bug] a 'potato-beetle'. **1876** *Times* 29 Aug. 6/5 The fact of its surviving in a letter posted at Listowel, Ontario, and delivered at Stranraer, Wigtonshire, N.B., shows that the potato beetle possesses great powers of endurance. **1906**

J. W. FOLSOM *Entomol.* xii. 382 From Colorado the well-known potato beetle..has worked eastward since 1840. **1931** Z. P. METCALF *Text-bk. Econ. Zool.* viii. 259 The Colorado potato beetle..often completely destroys whole fields of unsprayed potatoes. **1972** L. E. CHADWICK tr. *Linsenmaier's Insects of World* 165/2 The Colorado potato beetle..was imported accidentally into Europe from America. **1742** W. ELLIS *Mod. Husbandman* Sept. xxv. 119 *Potatoe Bread.* This Root has often been employed, like the Turnep, towards making Loaves of Bread in the scarce Times of Corn. **1915** *Chambers's Jrnl.* Oct. 661/2 There is a rather large group of words that have come at us with a rush, and cannot be classified,.. that fine phrase of Mr. Lloyd George's, 'the potato-bread spirit'. *c* **1950** *Mrs. Beeton's Bk. Househ. Managem.* xxx. 695 *Potato bread.*—The adhesive tendency of the flour of the potato prevents it being baked or kneaded without being mixed with wheaten flour or meal. **1799** E. DRINKER *Jrnl.* 2 Sept. (1889) 347 They call them [*sc.* a species of Cantharides] here..the Potato-Bug, being numerous on the potato tops. **1838** *Hesperian* (Columbus, Ohio) I. 42/1 This company, formed for the praiseworthy purpose of encouraging the growth of potatoe-bugs, and manufacturing potato-bug oil. **1864** *Trans. N.Y. State Agric. Soc. 1863* 798 Some have been discouraged from planting potatoes, the ravages of this potato-bug have been so great. **1865** *Pract. Entomologist* I. 3/1 The new Potato Bug is not what naturalists call a Bug, but a true Beetle. **1907** L. H. BAILEY *Cycl. Amer. Agric.* II. 524/1 The old-fashioned potato bug or blister-beetle..is combated in the same way as the Colorado potato-beetle. It is now rarely seen. **1908** *Springfield* (Mass.) *Republ.* 2 Sept. 14/6 Potato bugs on the rails..stalled eight trolly cars. **1949** *N.Y. Times Bk. Rev.* 5 June 14/2 It was settled that I should receive 1 cent per hundred for picking potato bugs. **1979** R. THOMAS *Eighth Dwarf* xxi. 210 The U.S. Constabulary..were swarming over the Opel plant ..like so many potato bugs. **1747** H. GLASSE *Art of Cookery* ix. 98 Potatoe-Cakes. Take Potatoes boil them ..mix them with Yolks of Eggs [etc.]. **1824** E. WEETON *Jrnl.* (1969) I. 33 Often I have..been obliged to live on potatoes and potatoe cakes for weeks. **1848** MRS. GASKELL *Mary Barton* II. xviii. 261 The potatoe-cakes she had made for her son's tea. **1878** *Amer. Home Cook Bk.* 67 Put around potato chips prepared as follows. **1886** [see *CHIP *sb.*[1] 2 b]. **1934** WEBSTER, *Potato chips*, thin slices of raw potato fried crisp in deep fat. **1955** *Sci. News Let.* 5 Mar. 153/3 Scientists at the Eastern Laboratory are also responsible for the potato-chip bar developed primarily as a 'high-calorie, high-density military ration with taste appeal'. The potato-chip bar takes up only one twentieth the space needed for an equivalent amount of ordinary potato chips. **1972** C. WESTON *Poor, Poor Ophelia* (1973) vi. 29 Two barefoot hippies were sharing a bag of potato chips. **1975** *N.Y. Times* 30 Nov. III. 1/2 The F.D.A. gave Procter & Gamble permission to go ahead with the use of the words 'potato chips' on its product... Its potatoes are dehydrated, then turned into a mush and pressed and fried. *Ibid.* 9 Their development went a long way toward solving a basic potato-chip problem... The natural chips are easily broken. **1898** *Internat. Folk-Lore Congr. World's Columbian Exposition 1893* I. 264 The corn having boiled about three-quarters of an hour, the pot is taken from the fire and its content poured upon the sieve, through which the purple-stained boiling water is strained upon the sumac berries. Some of the talc-like substance called potato-clay is then produced, and the operator puts a piece about the size of a walnut in his mouth, chewing it a little to soften it. **1925** H. F. MACMILLAN *Trop. Gardening & Planting* (ed. 3) 129 (*caption*) *Solanum wendlandii.* Giant Potato-creeper. **1928** K. GOUGH *Garden Bk. for Malaya* xii. 205 Several attractive flowering creepers, sometimes called 'Potato Creepers' belong to this large genus. **1929**, etc. Potato crisp [see *CRISP *sb.* 7]. **1940** GRAVES & HODGE *Long Week-End* xiv. 231 Potato crisps were a popular new food. **1970** *New Yorker* 26 Sept. 125/1 His mum..leaves him a florin..for some ginger pop and potato crisps. **1973** J. THOMSON *Death Cap* v. 72 A stiff little breeze blew the empty potato crisp packets across the paving-stones. **1976** W. TREVOR *Children of Dynmouth* v. 111 Having eaten two packets of bacon-flavoured potato crisps, he had purchased another tube of Rowntree's Fruit Gums. **1912** M. B. BROWN *Just Use-it-Up* vi. 139 Potato dumpling. This is a very well-known dish in North Germany. **1948** *Good Housek. Cookery Bk.* II. 284 *Potato dumplings* (to serve with Meat or Vegetable Casserole). **1972** *Sat. Rev.* (U.S.) 25 Mar. 52/1 Roast-goose with potato dumplings. **1974** 'D. CRAIG' *Dead Liberty* xvii. 100 Dravier asked for roast pork and potato dumplings. **1823** W. COBBETT in *Weekly Reg.* 9 Aug. 356 Never, in this country, will the people be base enough to lie down and expire from starvation under the operation of the *extreme unction*! Nothing but a *potatoe-eater* will ever do that. **1871** J. MACKENZIE *Ten Years North of Orange River* i. 16, I have heard 'potato-eater' employed by them (*sc.* Dutch farmers] as a contemptuous term for an Englishman! **1978** *Maledicta* II. 168 *Potato-eater*, anyone from Ireland, or of Irish descent, after the Irish dietary staple. **1845** E. S. CAYLEY *Lett. to Ld. John Russell* (1846) i. 9 The deficiency caused by the potato failure will be in some measure compensated by the unusually large crops of oats, barley, and beans. **1846** *Times* 7 Feb. 5/1 The extreme variety in the extent of the potato failure, and the..insulated subdivisions of land in which it prevails, lead us to..doubt whether any adjustment of public works can be made to meet the need wherever it may occur. **1846** *Illustr. London News* 12 Sept. 170/3 The hon. and learned gentlemen adverted in the first place to the potato failure. **1978** R. MITCHISON *Life in Scotland* vi. 112 If we compare the state of crofting families—sustained, in squalid poverty, through the potato failure of 1846 by their landowners—with the hardships of the..urban poor..in the early 1840's [etc.]. **1875** J. O'ROURKE *Hist. Great Irish Famine* vii. 196 To have met the Potato Famine with anything like complete success, would have been a Herculean task for any government. **1881** J. A. FROUDE *English in Ireland* (new ed.) III. p. xiii, The potato famine, and responsibility of England. **1970** R. LOWELL *Notebk.* 106 We're burnt, black chips knocked from the blackest stock: Potato-famine Irish-Puritan, and Puritan—gold made them smile like pigs once. **1974** P. LOVESEY *Invitation to Dynamite Party* ii. 27 He was an Irishman whose family emigrated at the time of the potato famine. **1955** *Sci. News Let.* 5 Feb. 89/3 To potato chips, French fries and home fries can now be added 'potato flakes', a new kind of dehydrated mashed potato... The flakes are made by drying cooked mashed potatoes on the rolls of a steam-heated double-drum drier. **1961** *Coast to Coast 1959–60* 165 A whole family of people..had spread a rug beside the path and were drinking coloured drinks from bottles and eating potato-flakes from bags. **1806** in R. B. Thomas *Farmer's Almanack for 1807*, The potatoe fly, or bug, appears about the first of July. **1832** W. D. WILLIAMSON *Hist. State Maine* I. 172 Potato Fly (looks like a Spanish Fly). **1854** E. EMMONS *Agric. N.Y.* V. 96 *Cantharidæ*...are at times abundant upon potato vines, whence they have acquired the name of potato fly. **1856** *Trans. Mich. Agric. Soc.* VII. 53 D. O. & W. S. Penfield..[exhibited] six Partridge's potatoe hooks. **1874** *Ann. Rep. Vermont Board Agric.* II. 551 Then with axes, potato hooks, and bog hoes, the turf was all peeled off. **1927, 1974** Potato latke [see *LATKE]. **1855** *Chicago Times* 16 Jan. 4/1 Butter moulds and stamps, ladles, rolling pins, potato mashers..at Hollister's Bazaar. **1895** *Montgomery Ward Catal.* 439/3 Tinned wire Potato Masher, wood handle. **1906** *Daily Colonist* (Victoria, B.C.) 26 Jan. 4/6 (Advt.), Kitchen utilities..Potato Masher, wood. Potato Masher, metal. **1915** J. WEBSTER *Dear Enemy* (1916) 238, I casually picked up the potato masher this morning while I was commenting upon last night's over-salty soup. **1919** H. G. PROCTOR *Iron Division* xii. 188 The German trench bombs were known..as 'potato mashers', because they are about the size of a can of sweet corn, fastened on the end of a short stick. **1925** FRASER & GIBBONS *Soldier & Sailor Words* 229 *Potato-masher grenade*, the name given a species of German hand-grenade, resembling in form a domestic potato-masher. **1929** F. A. POTTLE *Stretchers* (1930) x. 266 We saw bushels of potato-masher grenades, minenwerfer shells, and a machine gun belt of cartridges all of twenty feet long. **1929** W. T. SCANLON *God have Mercy on Us!* xxvi. 160 We had instructions on the use of every kind of grenade, including the German potato-mashers. **1945** L. SHELLY *Jive Talk Dict.* 31/1 *Potato masher*, drumstick. **1967** N. FREELING *Strike Out* 65 An old enamel saucepan,..and an oval metal affair with zigzag holes punched in it..he recognised it as a potato-masher. **1969** I. KEMP *Brit. G.I. in Vietnam* vi. 131 One..had begun to lob in grenades at us; these were of the 'potato masher' type, which sometimes failed to explode. **1969** E. H. PINTO *Treen* 141 Potato mashers were always turned from a single block,..like this one, they were often made *en suite* with a rolling pin..because in olden times, the pair was considered a lucky wedding gift. **1891** *Agric. Gaz. New South Wales* II. 158 Mr. A. Bragg..and Mr. T. B. Linley..have forwarded potatoes infested with the larvae or grubs of the potato moth. **1926** R. J. TILLYARD *Insects Austral. & N.Z.* xxviii. 426 The Potato Moth..is an introduced pest of potatoes, tomatoes and tobacco in both countries. **1965** *Austral. Encycl.* V. 88/2 The larvae of the potato-moth..tunnel in the leaf tissue. **1937** *Daily Express* 17 Mar. 6/4 Lewis, square, heavy-browed, stentorian, also potato-mouthed some words, seemed bothered by having to stick to text. **1930** J. DOS PASSOS *42nd Parallel* IV. 313 You know what we'd do if we had a man in the WhiteHouse instead of a yellow-bellied potatomouthed reformer...? We'd..clean this place up. **1845** J. C. LOUDON *Suburban Horticulturist* III. v. 661 The potato-onion may be planted in February. **1855, 1866** [see ONION *sb.* 2 a]. **1890** E. WATTS *Mod. Pract. Gardening* I. xiii. 68 The underground, or potato onion,.. is so called from its habit of increasing at the bulb. **1955** W. E. SHEWELL-COOPER *Complete Veg. Grower* x. 135 The Potato Onion..is more difficult to get hold of today. **1935** L. ZARA *Blessed is Man* I. iii. 103 She made him a heaping plateful of the fried potato pancakes so closely associated with this holiday [*sc.* Chanukah]. **1941** L. HELLMAN *Watch on Rhine* II. 76, I love a good potato pancake. **1960** *Good Housek. Cookery Bk.* (rev. ed.) 535/2 *Potato pancakes*... Put the mashed potato through a sieve if at all lumpy, add seasoning, and work the flour into it to make a smooth dough. **1962** S. V. THOMPSON *Let.* 30 Jan. in G. Marx *Groucho Lett.* (1967) 237 Mother thinks that with this you serve potato pancakes and onions with peas. True? **1978** *Detroit Free Press* 16 Apr. (Detroit Suppl.) 28/2 With that, they bring potato pancakes which are fresh and moist on the inside, with a good crusty exterior. **1794** E. DRINKER *Jrnl.* 25 June (1889) 229 John brought in a Mole he found in a potato patch he was laying out. **1807** *Salmagundi* 15 Oct. 331 Some.. enjoy the varied and romantick scenery of..potatoe patches and log huts. **1863** A. D. WHITNEY *Faith Gartney's Girlhood* xxii. 207 A hollow, beyond which were the cornfields and potato-patches. **1913** J. LONDON *Valley of Moon* 404 Hall put Billy to work on the potato patch—a matter of three acres which the poet farmed erratically. **1919** G. B. SHAW *O'Flaherty V.C.* in *Heartbreak House* 165, I..gave him for his mother a Volumnia of the potato patch rather than an affectionate parent from whom he could not so easily have torn himself away. **1972** R. ADAMS *Watership Down* xxxiv. 263 The cottager..shot him [*sc.* a rabbit] as he came through the potato-patch at dawn. **1875** TROLLOPE *Way we live Now* II. c. 314 If her future husband would consent to live on potatoes, she would be quite satisfied with the potato-peelings. **1959** I. & P. OPIE *Lore & Lang. Schoolch.* xiii. 295 Tales are told of..forcing a new boy into a box or dustbin half-filled with fish-heads, potato peelings..and making him stay there for an hour. **1975** *Sunday Times* 16 Nov. 44/3 My husband was having fun posting old tomatoes and potato peelings down the waste disposal. **1609** DEKKER *Guls Horne-Booke* i. 7 Potato-pies and Custards, stood like the sinfull suburbs of Cookery. **1728** E. SMITH *Compl. Housewife* (ed. 2) sig. A7[v] (*heading*) A Bill of Fare..For June... Second Course... Potato-Pye. **1842** *Ainsworth's Mag.* I. 2 A large remnant of a potato-pie in a brown earthenware dish. **1965** in P. Jennings *Living Village* (1968) 61 Weather permitting, potato pies are opened and the potatoes sold to the merchants. **1972** K. BONFIGLIOLI *Don't point that Thing at Me* xviii. 152 We took a cheap night flight to Blackpool... I had potato pie for supper. **1883** *Girls' Own Paper* 14 July 654/1 *Potato puffs.*—Chop..some cold meat or fish. Mash some potatoes and make them into a paste with an egg... Fold... Fry. **1972** *V.A.T.: Scope & Coverage* (H.M. Customs) 22 Any of the following when packaged for human consumption without further preparation, namely,.. potato sticks, potato puffs and similar products made from the potato. **1882** G. B. BARTLETT *New Games for Parlor & Lawn* 212 The Potato Race... This amusing out-of-door game requires a swift runner, with his feet well under control. **1946** *R.A.F. Jrnl.* May 167 The.. Inter-Command Sports Meeting will include the following events..:—potato race,..relay race. **1978** 'F. PARRISH' *Sting of Honeybee* i. 8 The potato race starts in three minutes. All entries to the collecting ring. *Ibid.* 9 The strange grey pony was not in the potato race. **1848** *Rep. Comm. Patents 1847* (U.S.) I. 136 The potato rot seems likewise to have been felt to a considerable extent among the common potato. **1854** B. P. SHILLABER *Life & Sayings Mrs. Partington* 43 A more disastrous havoc of potato rot has never since transpired than assailed her crops. **1861** MRS. BEETON *Bk. Househ. Managem.* 593 *Potato Salad*... Cut the potatoes into slices about ½ inch in thickness; put these into a salad-bowl with oil and vinegar [etc.]. **1877** E. S. DALLAS *Kettner's Bk. of Table* 399, I should weary the reader if I went on to sound the praises of the mustard and cress salad,..the potato salad, and the *salade de légumes.* **1952** B. MALAMUD *Natural* (1963) 185 Turkey, potato salad, cheese, and pickles. **1967** M. GILBERT *Dust & Heat* III. 246 He stopped..at a delicatessen store in Soho where he bought..a carton of cold potato salad. **1978** J. SYMONS *Blackheath Poisonings* I. 39 There was a tongue..a potato salad, a Russian salad and a green salad. **1885** A. EDWARDES *Girton Girl* I. vi. 136 Boiled mullet, hot potato scones, with other indigenous Guernsey dishes. **1931** D. L. SAYERS *Five Red Herrings* Foreword, We shall come back next summer to eat some more potato scones. **1973** *Perthshire Advertiser* 8 Aug. 17/6 Baking... Potato scones. **1972** Potato stick [see *potato puff* above]. **1895** M. RONALD *Century Cook Bk.* I. facing p. 82 (*caption*) Fluted knife for cutting potato straws. *c* **1950** *Mrs. Beeton's Bk. Househ. Managem.* xxx. 692 *Potato straws*... Slice the potatoes thinly, cut them into strips about 1½ inches long... Fry the straws..until crisp. **1892** *Insect Life* IV. 239 (*heading*) The Potato-Tuber Moth (*Lita solanella*). **1928** METCALF & FLINT *Destructive & Useful Insects* xvi. 481 Potato tuber moth..is very destructive to potatoes in warm dry regions. **1932** *Jrnl. Econ. Entomol.* XXV. 625 During the past nine years the potato tuber moth..has caused economic losses to potato growers. **1950** *N.Z. Jrnl. Agric.* Sept. 221/3 The district is not suited to the growing of late potatoes because from January onward the potato tuber moth is very active. **1939** METCALFE & FLINT *Destructive & Useful Insects* (ed. 2) xvi. 516 Potato tuberworm..is very destructive to potatoes in warm dry regions. **1960** *Jrnl. Econ. Entomol.* LIII. 868/1 The potato tuberworm, *Gnorimoschema operculella*.., has long been a pest of potatoes in California. **1774** P. V. FITHIAN *Jrnl.* 19 Sept. (1900) 257, I took a Walk thro' the Pumpkin & Potatoe Vines. **1870** *Amer. Naturalist* III. 92 The early frosts..nearly killed the potato vines. **1902** L. H. BAILEY *Cycl. Amer. Hort.* IV. 1680/2 *Solanum... jasminoides*, Paxt. Potato Vine (from the fl[ower]s.). Fine greenhouse climbing shrub. **1939** L. & J. BUSH-BROWN *America's Garden Bk.* xxiv. 807 Potato Vine. Solanum jasminoides. Annual... Star-shaped, white flowers. **1947** *Southern Folklore Q.* XI. 264 Proverbial remarks disparaging to a person's character [include]..this pronunciamento from central Mississippi: 'He ought to have been hung when a potato vine would hang him.' **1963** ROBERTSON & GOODING *Bot. for Caribbean* xxiii. 197 Climbers... Chalice Vine... Potato Vine (*Solanum wendlandii*). **1971** B. CLARK in E. L. Wardman *Bermuda Jubilee Garden* i. 6 There is a very wide selection to be made from..potato-vines (*Solanum seaforthianum* and *S. wendlandii*), and chalice-vines. **1977** P. MOYES *To kill Coconut* xv. 207 Henry was eating breakfast under an arbour of potato-vines and goat's foot. **1842** T. W. HARRIS *Treat. Insects Injurious to Vegetation* 226 Every farmer's boy knows the potato-worm. **1879** *Scribner's Monthly* Dec. 242/1 This white grub, which the farmers often call the 'potato worm' is..the strawberry's most formidable foe.

potato-ring. (Further examples.)

1901 *Chambers's Jrnl.* Feb. 103/2 Old Irish potato-rings are also much sought after by collectors; at recent sales they have sold for nearly £5 an ounce. **1907** *Daily Chron.* 1 June 4/5 Upon the tables were immense silver baskets and old silver potato rings filled with pink and red carnations. **1932** *Times Lit. Suppl.* 12 May 350/4 Certain characteristic features of Irish silver, notably the so-called 'potato' rings made in large numbers in Dublin from about 1760 to 1820. **1960** H. HAYWARD *Antique Coll.* 98/1 'Potato ring'... Circular silver dish or bowl stand with straight or incurved sides usually pierced and chased with pastoral or classical motifs. **1968** *Canad. Antiques Collector* Sept. 22/1 Delicate piercing [of silverware] might be suited to cake baskets, the so-called 'potato' rings, bottle coasters or the gallery of a tray. **1973** *Country Life* 8 Mar. 608/2 *Irish Silver in the Rococo Period* will..get out of his [*sc.* the average Englishman's] head that so-called potato rings have anything to do with potatoes... The fact is that such things are dish rings.

‖ **pot-au-feu** (potofö). [Fr., = pot on the fire.] A large cooking pot of a kind common in France; the soup or broth cooked in it, *spec.* the traditional French recipe associated with this. Also *attrib.* and *fig.*

1792 C. SMITH *Desmond* III. xxiii. 278 The pot *au feu* was brought forward to receive a supply of leeks. **1841** C'TESS BLESSINGTON *Idler in France* I. ii. 32 Our good hostess..served up a plentiful dinner, consisting of an excellent *pot au feu*, followed by fish, fowl, and flesh. **1868** C. M. YONGE *Chaplet of Pearls* I. xxiv. 311 To eat of the savoury mess in the great *pot-au-feu*. **1868** M. JEWRY *Warne's Model Cookery* 55/2 *Pot-au-feu*, the stock-pot. **1909** H. JAMES *Novels & Tales* XV. Pref. p. xvii,

We can surely account for nothing in the novelist's work that..hasn't, in that perpetually simmering cauldron his intellectual *pot-au-feu*, been reduced to savoury fusion. **1934** H. Hiler *Notes Technique Painting* iii. 183 A large glazed earthenware pot (*pot-au-feu*) which has not been used for any other purpose. **1948** 'J. Tey' *Franchise Affair* xvi. 188 The dish was a pot-au-feu chicken with all its vegetables round it. **1960** *News Chron.* 30 Mar. 6/5, I get out a vast blackened saucepan and make the old-fashioned, traditional French pot-au-feu. **1962** *Economist* 3 Nov. 485/2 This is an intimate family story, relating.. Saturday evening pot-au-feu dinners. **1975** [see *New England boiled dinner* s.v. *New England b].

Potawatomi (pǫtăwǫ·tǒmi), *sb.* Also **Pattawatami, Pottiwatomie, Poutouatami,** etc. [Native name.] **a.** A member of an Algonquian Indian tribe located in the Great Lakes region of the northern U.S.A., principally in Michigan and Wisconsin. **b.** The language of this people. Also *attrib.* or as *adj.*

1698 tr. *Hennepin's New Discovery* I. xxiii. 74 We sent afterwards three Men to buy Provisions in the Village with the *Calumet* or Pipe of Peace, which the Poutouatami's of the Island had given us. **1722** D. Coxe *Descr. Carolana* 48 The Nations who dwell on this River, are.. the Poutouatomis beforemention'd. **1789** *Deb. Congr. U.S.* 25 May (1834) 41 The treaties of Fort Harmar.. with the Sachems and warriors of the Wyandot,..Pattiwatima, and Sac nations. **1805** J. Wilkinson *Let.* 12 July in *Deb. Congr. U.S.* (1852) 10th Congr. 1 Sess. 575 All hopes of the speedy recovery of their prisoners from the hands of the Pattawatamies, being at an end. **1808** Governor Harrison *Let.* 14 Apr. in *Deb. Congr. U.S.* (1853) 12th Congr. 1 Sess. 1857 A young man from the Delaware towns came to inform me that a Pottawatomie Indian had arrived at the towns. **1835** [see *Kickapoo]. **1838** [see *long knife 1]. **1868** *N.Y. Herald* 31 July 5/4 The Senate..ratified treaties with the Potawatamies. **1877** L. H. Morgan *Anc. Society* ii. iv. 105 The Potawattamies have eight gentes of the same name with eight among the Ojibwas. **1927** L. Bloomfield in *Amer. Speech* II. 437/1 She knows only a few words of English, but speaks Ojibwa and Potawatomi fluently, and, I believe, a little Winnebago. **1933** —— *Language* 72 The Algonquian family covers the northeastern part of the continent and includes the languages of..the Great Lakes region (Ojibwa, Potawatomi..and so on). **1946** E. A. Nida *Morphol.* p.v, Linguists will readily recognize many of the problems as being drawn from Greek, Latin, French,..Potawatomi, Cherokee, and Navaho. **1965** *Language* XLI. 75 Pike and Erickson's work on Potawatomi..studies the field structures of certain lexical oppositions within given orders of Potawatomi verb affixes. **1972** *Ibid.* XLVIII. 847, 5 c [in a table of five-vowel systems] is given by Hockett for Potawatomi. **1978** *Maledicta* II. 233, I am told that the name [of Waukesha in Wisconsin] is from the Potawatomi word for 'fox'. **1979** *Tucson* (Arizona) *Citizen* 20 Sept. (Old Pueblo Suppl.) 3/1 The woman saw the 6-foot-4, 260-pound Potawatomi Indian walking down a Phoenix street.

pot-bellied, *a.* Add: (Further examples.) Also, = *pot-belly 2 b.

1899 [see *merchant *sb.* 4]. **1959** [see *pot *sb.*^{1} 1 h]. **1964** Mrs. L. B. Johnson *White House Diary* 21 May (1970) 143 Not only was the schoolhouse the same as the one at Fern, but there was a big pot-bellied stove inside. **1973** *Nation Rev.* (Melbourne) 31 Aug. 1455/4 He revealed an ancient potbellied stove. **1979** O. Sela *Petrograd Consignment* 5 A burly, pot-bellied Swiss.

pot-belly. Add: **2. b.** Used *attrib.* to designate a kind of domestic stove made in the shape of a barrel.

1973 L. Russell *Everyday Life Colonial Canada* vii. 76 About the middle of the nineteenth century a new kind of heating stove appeared, inelegantly known as the pot-belly stove. It was barrel-shaped, with a flat top on which a pot or kettle could be heated. **1976** *Columbus* (Montana) *News* 1 July 7/6 (Advt.), One..cast iron pot belly stove. **1976** *Morecambe Guardian* 7 Dec. 33/2 (Advt.), Wood burning or coke burning stove (pot belly type) preferably with chimney.

pot-boil, *v.* (Earlier example.)

1867 D. G. Rossetti *Let.* 22 Mar. (1965) II. 618, I have been pot-boiling to an extent lately that does not hold out much hope of estate buying.

pot-boiler. Add: **2. a.** (Earlier and later examples.) Also applied to musical compositions, plays, and films.

1864 D. G. Rossetti *Let.* 25 June (1965) II. 509 Small things and water-colours I never should have done at all, except for the long continuance of a necessity for 'pot-boilers'. **1915** W. S. Maugham *Of Human Bondage* . 256 You hear of men painting pot-boilers to keep an aged mother. **1934** C. Lambert *Music Ho!* v. 306 A certain number of works that were neither potboilers nor works of individual genius. **1973** *Times* 14 Mar. 18/7 In the next three years he directed five pot-boilers and did some screen writing. **1975** *Listener* 31 July 152/3 Ayckbourn's name could become associated with middle-brow, comedy potboilers. **1977** *Time* 10 Oct. 61/1 Condon works on his potboilers seven hours a day, seven days a week for ten weeks at a stretch.

pot-bound, *a.* (Later examples.)

1913 Mrs. G. De H. Vaizey *College Girl* v. 66 The red-brown earth..was too tempting to be resisted when she thought of her poor pot-bound plants at home. **1919** [see *aerotropism* (*aero-)]. **1925** W. Deeping *Sorrell & Son* vi. 56 You can get many a good hint from a man who dislikes you if you are not too pot-bound to soak it up. **1966** Rochford & Gorer *Rochford Bk. Flowering Pot Plants* i. 17 More frequent waterings will be required when the plant is pot-bound.

potch (pǫtʃ), *sb.* Also † **potsh.** [Origin unknown.] In full *potch opal.* Opal that has no play of colour and is of no value; also, a flat colour characteristic of this; *potch and* or *with colour* (see quot. 1971).

1897 *Jrnl. & Proc. R. Soc. New South Wales* XXX. 256 The dull, milky, and opaque stones are called 'potsh' by the miners. **1900** in J. S. Gunn *Opal Terminol.* (1971) 35 Demand for potch with color being active. **1902** *Chambers's Jrnl.* V. 494/2 'It's only potch, an' not worth a drink, the whole durned lot.'.. Occasionally I cut through seams of opal matrix carrying stones of beautiful red tints and sometimes of a peculiar blend of almost every colour. For all these Dan had but one contemptuous name, 'potch', which is the miner's term for inferior opal. **1912** *Empire Mag.* Nov. 282/1 A pocketful of 'potch-and-colour'—that is, 'potch' with a slight 'colour' of opal. **1921** [see *knobby *sb.*]. **1936** A. Russell *Gone Nomad* vii. 58 The value of a pocket varied according to the size, quantity and quality of the opal stones it contained... 'Potch' or immature opal could be found by the ton. **1940** [see *noodle *v.*^{2}]. **1958** M. D. Berrington *Stones of Fire* 24 'What's potch?'.. 'Opal crystal without fire. Looks something like pieces of crockery.' **1962** R. Webster *Gems* I. x. 189 The colourful precious opal is found in irregular patches in the thin veins of potch—the miners' term for opal which may be colourful but not showing the play of colour, or as they say 'not alive'—which fills the joints and bedding planes of the sandstone. **1971** J. S. Gunn *Opal Terminol.* 35 *Potch-and-colour, potch-with-colour,* opal potch with a slight colour of opal showing through. **1976** *Sci. Amer.* Apr. 94/3 The small amounts of precious opal are accompanied by an enormous quantity of valueless 'potch' opal, which looks like opal but shows no colour and is generally discarded by the miners... Electron microscopy shows that it usually consists of rounded particles of silica that are not well enough shaped, sized or ordered to form light-diffracting arrays.

potch (pǫtʃ), *v.* [ad. Yiddish *patshn,* ad. G. *patschen* to slap.] *trans.* To slap or smack; hence **potch** *sb.,* **po·tching** *ppl. a.*

1892 [see Poach *v.*^{2} 1 d]. **1966** R. H. Rimmer *Harrad Experiment* (1967) 150, I told you, Saul, Harry's not too old for a *potch* before he becomes a *paskudnick.* **1968** L. Rosten *Joys of Yiddish* 293 Don't be fresh or I'll potch you. **1969** K. Vonnegut *Slaughterhouse-Five* iv. 73 Her palm on his little jelly belly made potching sounds.

pot cheese. orig. and chiefly *U.S.* [f. Pot *sb.*^{1} 14.] A type of cottage cheese.

1812 'H. Bull-Us' *Diverting Hist. John Bull & Bro. Jonathan* xiv. 111 Tell me, thou heart of cork,..and brain of pot-cheese. **1859** Bartlett *Dict. Amer.* (ed. 2) 420 *Smear case,*..a preparation of milk..; otherwise called Cottage-Cheese. In New York it is called Pot-cheese. **1878** *Rep. Indian Affairs* (U.S.) 19 They learn to milk and make butter and pot-cheese, which they relish highly. **1935** *Colony of Connecticut* (Connecticut Board of Educ.) (Senate Doc. 53, 74th Congr., 1st Sess.) 12 Pot cheese, Dutch cheese, and bonnyclabber were the same. These were generally sweetened with maple sugar. **1964** W. Markfield *To Early Grave* xii. 245 She has eggs for me. *And* pot cheese. **1965** T. Fitzgibbon *Art Brit. Cooking* 133 Pot cheese is a type of cottage cheese made with sour milk and butter milk..cream and salt is worked in. It is rolled into small balls.

‖ **pot de chambre** (po də ʃɑ̃br). [Fr.] = Chamber-pot. Also *attrib.*

1777 P. Thicknesse *Year's Journey* I. i. 6 The priest put the present under the side of the bed..it was only a *pot de chambre.* **1891** A. T. Ritchie *Lett.* (1924) x. 220 The Dame du Palais..escorting the King to bed, carrying a sword, a lamp and a pot de chambre. **1894** G. N. Curzon *Probl. Far East* v. 140 The national implement of Korea, a circular brass pot, with a lid, but no handle, which..serves alternately as pillow, candlestick, ash-plate, spittoon, and *pot de chambre.* **1931** E. Waugh *Remote People* 65 A pedlar..with a bundle of bootlaces in one hand and an enamelled *pot de chambre* in the other. **1934** C. Lambert *Music Ho!* ii. 74 Those two symbols of an alien civilization, the top hat and the *pot de chambre.* **1938** L. Bemelmans *Life Class* 20 The *pot de chambre* humor of Regensburg. **1969** N. Freeling *Tsing-Boum* xxi. 146 It [*sc.* tea] arrived, in massive pot-de-chambre porcelain with little roses on it. **1972** 'I. Drummond' *Frog in Moonflower* ii. 47 Coffee in cups like *pots-de-chambre.* **1976** [see *routier^2 2].

Potemkin (pote·mkin). The name of Grigory Aleksandrovich *Potemkin* (1739–91), favourite of Empress Catherine II of Russia, used *attrib.* to designate the sham villages reputed to have been erected, on his orders, for Catherine's tour of the Crimea in 1787. Also *transf.* and *fig.*

1938 G. Soloveytchik *Potemkin* xiv. 283 Potemkin's detractors have asserted that he built whole sham villages, with cardboard houses and paste palaces..in order to create a false picture of progress and prosperity... The originator of these stories..was the Saxon diplomat Helbig, and the legend of 'Potemkin Villages'..as a synonym of sham owes its inception to him. **1954** Koestler *Invis. Writing* xi. 132 This was not a Potemkin village. It was something more curious. **1965** B. Pearce tr. *Preobrazhensky's New Econ.* 39 To lull the vigilance of..the working class, to keep it in the dark about the dangers which threaten it, and to weaken its will with Potemkin villages of childish optimism when it needs to continue to wage the heroic struggle of October. **1967** I. Marder *Paris Bit* i. 27 Paris is above all a city of façades, an enormous Potemkin village. **1973** J. Shub *Moscow by Nightmare* vii. 77 The new Kalinin Prospekt—the latest Potemkin Village of soaring glass and aluminium. **1974** *Guardian* 21 Mar. 3/8 It is good diplomacy ..to pretend that the EEC is a political entity... But don't expect serious decisions from a political Potemkin village.

potence^2. 5. (Later example.)

1978 *Erddig* (National Trust) 7 The building, shown on an estate plan of 1739, is complete with its potence (the revolving arm supporting the ladder needed to collect eggs and squabs) and several pairs of nesting fantails.

potency. Add: **1. c.** *Homœopathy.* The degree of dilution of a drug, taken as a measure of its efficacy (a high dilution being regarded as more efficacious).

[**1833** J. B. Gilchrist *Pract. Appeal* 54 Homœopathic medicines, extreme, attenuated, and minimissimised, acquire a potency in the inverse ratio of their attenuation and diminution.] **1846** C. J. Hempel *Homœopathic Domestic Physician* p. vii, Homœopathic drugs have now been potentialized up to the 200th and many of them up to 300th, 400th, 500th. etc., until the 2000th potency. **1906** *Homeopathic World* XLI. 109 From this tinctures of ever-augmenting potency (where disease is concerned) can be prepared. **1938** D. Shepherd *Magic of Minimum Dose* 4 *Nux vomica* has been a stand-by and valuable help in other cases of acute sinus trouble.., both in low potencies (1*x*) and high potencies. **1975** C. H. Sharma *Man. Homoeopathy* I. iv. 29 Whether the remedy has been chosen for you or you have chosen it yourself, always keep a careful record of what it is, the potency, frequency and quantity, and the symptoms which called for it.

d. Ability to have orgasm in sexual intercourse. Opp. Impotence 2 b.

[**1900** *Yale Med. Jrnl.* VI. 126 There are two forms of potency—the *potentia coeundi* and the *potentia generandi.*] **1901** F. R. Sturgis *Sexual Debility in Man* x. 293 My patient was..an ardent admirer of women, in whose company he indulged himself freely with perfect potency. **1929** G. R. Scott *Sex & its Mysteries* xii. 108 Anything which causes a lowering of the vitality is sufficient to induce impotence, hence the recommendation of meat, eggs and oysters for the generation of sexual potency. *Ibid.* 110 Nor does general disease affect woman's potency. **1939** G. V. Hamilton in E. V. Cowdry *Probl. Ageing* xvi. 469 The decline in sexual potency experienced by men during the ageing period. **1966** *Listener* 10 Mar. 352/1 It may..be true to say that young men use the car or motor-cycle as a potency symbol. **1977** E. J. Trimmer et al. *Visual Dict. Sex* (1978) xxii. 262 Sterility is inevitable if both testes are removed... Desire and potency may be lost, but this is not inevitable.

e. *Genetics.* The extent of the contribution of an allele towards the production of some phenotypic character. Also *attrib.*

1905 *Publ. Carnegie Inst.* No. 23. 59 From these cases it seems clear that the production of partial-rough young was due to some unusual potency of the gametes bearing the smooth character. **1916** *Proc. Nat. Acad. Sci.* II. 53 The appearance of gynandromorphism in certain crosses found its right explanation in the hypothesis of a quantitatively different behavior or a different potency of the male sex-factors in the different races. **1944** *Genetics* XXIX. 528 Using the morphological guide of bristle length..we might assign to gene b^o a potency of about 34, b^d a potency of 50,..and b^f of 54. *Ibid.*, A potency series was set by Stern (1929b) to represent the additive effects of bobbed alleles in *D*[*rosophila*] *melanogaster.* **1955** R. B. Goldschmidt *Theoret. Genetics* iii. v. 368 The potencies thus discovered..turned out to be of the orderly type, that is, acting like dosage and thus acting in different combinations in an orderly and parallel way.

f. *Pharm.* The strength of a drug, as measured by the amount needed to produce a certain response.

1933 *Med. Res. Council Special Rep. Ser.* No. 183. 25 An approximate estimate of the potency of a preparation can be obtained by administering a series of doses, each to a single animal. **1968** A. Goldstein et al. *Princ. Drug Action* v. 351 The essential attribute we seek in a drug is not potency, but efficacy at a safe dose. **1978** F. F. Cowan *Pharmacol. for Dental Hygienist* ii. 18 The position of graded dose-response curve along the dose axis is a measure of the drug's potency, i.e., how much of the drug it takes to produce a certain intensity of response... The maximum effect, or efficacy, of a drug is of greater clinical interest.

3. b. *Embryol.* A capacity in embryonic tissue for developing into a particular kind of specialized tissue or organ.

1908 F. R. Lillie *Devel. of Chick* 9 A very important property of primordia in many animals is their capacity for subdivision, each part retaining the potencies of the whole. **1926** J. S. Huxley *Essays Pop. Sci.* 263 The potency of forming limbs is confined to a definite area of the flank. **1958** B. M. Patten *Found. Embryol.* v. 108 If an area where a particular potency has been located is exposed in more detail, it is found that there is a certain central part of it from which practically all the explants exhibit the potency in question. **1968** C. W. Bodemer *Mod. Embryol.* ix. 139 During gastrulation the entire nervous system becomes limited in its potencies and can no longer develop into other structures.

5. *Math.* (See quot. 1959.)

1906 [see *factor *sb.* 6]. **1959** G. & R. C. James *Math. Dict.* 41/1 The cardinal number of a set is also called the potency of the set and the power of the set.

potent, *a.*^{1}: **3.** Substitute for def.: Capable of orgasm in sexual intercourse: applied chiefly to men. Opp. Impotent *a.* 2 b. (Further examples.)

1893 E. Martin *Impotence & Sexual Weakness* 74

He..took to himself a wife, and showed by subsequent events, that he was both potent and fertile. **1929** G. R. Scott *Sex & its Mysteries* xii. 110 So long as there is no disease or malformation of the genital organs a woman is potent until practically her dying days. **1975** L. B. Hobson *Examination of Patient* ix. 360 Sexual arousal, erection, and even ejaculation..are emotional as well as hormonal, and a man castrated in later life is still able to have sexual intercourse; that is, he remains potent. He is, however, sterile, since he produces no sperm.

potentia. (Further examples of phr. *in potentia*.)

1612 Jonson *Alchemist* II. iii. sig. E1 The Egg's.. a Chicken, in Potentia. **1674** N. Fairfax *Treat. Bulk & Selvedge* vi. 170 Gods bare Essence must be forthwith or actu, but his everlasting Essence..must be forth-coming or in potentia. **1797** *Encycl. Brit.* XV. 441/2 Potential, in the schools, is used to denote and distinguish a kind of qualities, which are supposed to exist in the body *in potentia* only. **1948** *Mind* LVII. 486 When I claim to *know* I simply make emphatic that I am logically committed, *in potentia*, in certain determinate ways. **1957** L. Durrell *Justine* I. 75 Life, the new material, is only lived *in potentia* until the artist deploys it in his work.

potential, *a.* and *sb.* Add: **A.** *adj.* **4. a.** (Further examples).

1945 *Language* XXI. 2 In English what may be called the potential mode of the verb is an overt category marked by the morpheme *can* or *could*. **1946** [see *handle *v.*[1] 1 b]. **1964** P. Healey in F. W. Householder *Syntactic Theory I* (1972) III. xv. 216 It will be noted that the Potential tense may occur in the Quote of the Saying sub-type.

5. a. Delete 'Now usually called simply *potential*' and add further examples of *potential function*.

1931 *Rev. Mod. Physics* III. 288 He..used several forms for the potential function; one in which the potential depended only upon central force fields..and others in which the potential was also a function of the apex angle. **1939** L. Bairstow *Appl. Aerodynamics* (ed. 2) vii. 320 The boundary conditions to be satisfied are easily deduced; a solid boundary must be a stream-line and along it ψ must be constant or $d\psi/ds$ zero. In the case of the potential function the condition takes the form that the normal velocity, i.e. $d\phi/dh$ must be zero. **1960** Houghton & Brock *Aerodynamics* xi. 267 The velocity potential and the stream function are combined in a new function called the complex potential function. **1967** N. M. Queen *Vector Anal.* vii. 66 An auxiliary function from which a given vector field **V** can be derived by a suitable differential operation is sometimes called a potential function for **V**; in particular, ϕ and **A** in equation (7.2) are known as the scalar and vector potentials for **V**.

c. *potential temperature* [tr. G. *potentielle temperatur* (W. von Bezold 1888, in *Sitzungsb. der K. Preuss. Akad. der Wissensch. zu Berlin* 1190)]: the temperature that a given body of gas or liquid would have if it were brought adiabatically to a standard pressure of 1 bar or 1 atmosphere.

1891 C. Abbe tr. W. von Bezold in *Mechanics of Earth's Atmosphere* xvi. 243 Von Helmholtz recognized the objection..and proposed that the word 'wärmegehalt' should be replaced by the evidently much more proper expression 'potential temperature'. When without gain or loss of heat it is adiabatically or pseudo-adiabatically reduced to the normal pressure. **1937** N. A. V. Piercy *Aerodynamics* i. 21 An atmosphere is stable when the potential temperature is greater, the greater the altitude. **1962** W. S. von Arx *Introd. Physical Oceanogr.* v. 128 In the very deepest part of the ocean such as in the trenches flanking island arcs, it can be shown that the potential temperature of the water is virtually uniform from the depth of the surrounding ocean floor to the bottom of the trench, even though the actual temperature increases somewhat with depth. **1967** P. Groen *Waters of Sea* vii. 290 At 3500 meters, where the temperature is 1·6°C, the potential temperature is only 0·3°C lower. Whereas strictly speaking the temperature is not invariable even if there is no heat exchange, the potential temperature is, if the water proceeds to other depths and is therefore subjected to a different pressure.

B. *sb.* **2.** (Further examples.) Also, resources that can be used or developed; freq. preceded by a defining word.

1941 *Sun* (Baltimore) 24 June 10/2 The vast armored power, mobile tactics and industrial potential of the Nazi armies have been exhibited and proved in the Low Countries, France and the Balkans. **1943** *Times* 10 Dec. 5/3 The whole war potential of the German Reich. **1958** *Spectator* 14 Feb. 196/1 Industrial potential has multiplied six times since currency reform. **1958** *Listener* 27 Nov. 897/1 Mr. Cooper managed to slip the theme of indifference and its potential into this play without breaking its back. **1959** *Ibid.* 23 July 122/2 There is thought to be enormous oil potential. **1965** *Ibid.* 1 July 22/3 All collections have a built-in boredom potential. **1969** H. MacInnes *Salzburg Connection* xx. 281 His record..has been excellent. His potential was high—very high. **1970** *Nature* 26 Dec. 1248/2 Although oceans and seas cover some 360 thousand km^2.., exploitation of their vast potential is only just beginning. **1978** *Observer* (Colour Suppl.) 12 Nov. 58/4 Children without these experiences..are likely to be handicapped in terms of the development of their full potential. **1979** *Country Life* 21 June 2047/3 This ever-perceived dark potential is surely part of the reason why the cat is the intellectuals' favourite beast.

4. a. (Further examples.) More generally, any function from which a vector field **F** can be derived by differentiation, esp. the scalar potential ϕ, where $\mathbf{F} = -\text{grad}\ \phi$, and the vector potential **A**, where $\mathbf{F} = \text{curl}\ \mathbf{A}$.

1873 J. C. Maxwell *Treat. Electr. & Magn.* II. III. ii. 27 (*heading*) The Vector-Potential of Magnetic induction. **1909** J. G. Coffin *Vector Anal.* vi. 173 We obtain $\mathbf{H} = .. \nabla \times \mathbf{Q}$... **Q** is called the potential due to the current distribution **q**, or the vector-potential belonging to the magnetic force **H**... The force vector **H** is obtained from the vector **Q** in a manner analogous to the way the force vector **F** is obtained from the scalar V, where..$\mathbf{F} = \nabla V$. **1933** H. B. Phillips *Vector Anal.* v. 102 When the potential is known the velocity can be obtained by differentiation. If a potential exists it is simpler to describe the motion by means of it rather than the velocity. **1966** *McGraw-Hill Encycl. Sci. & Technol.* X. 540/2 If the acceleration a satisfies a relation such as ..$\mathbf{a} = -\text{grad}\ \Phi$, the Φ is called an acceleration potential. **1971** W. Hauser *Introd. Princ. Electromagnetism* iii. 77 Vector function $\mathbf{F}_1$ is a curl-less vector function... It is therefore expressible as the negative gradient of a scalar function of position. We thus set $\mathbf{F}_1 = -\nabla\psi(\mathbf{r})$, where the function $\psi(x, y, z)$ is referred to as the scalar potential of $\mathbf{F}_1$. *Ibid.*, The divergenceless vector function $\mathbf{F}_2$ is..expressible as the curl of a vector function $\mathbf{A}, \mathbf{F}_2 = \nabla \times \mathbf{A}$, where **A** is referred to as the vector potential of $\mathbf{F}_2$.

b. Any of a group of thermodynamic functions mathematically analogous to electric and gravitational potentials, viz. the Gibbs free energy G (or ζ), the Helmholtz free energy A (or F or ψ), the enthalpy H (or χ), the internal energy U (or E or ϵ), and the chemical potential μ.

The Gibbs and the Helmholtz functions are given respectively by $G = U + PV - TS$ and $A = U - TS$, where U is the internal energy, P the pressure, V the volume, T the temperature, and S the entropy of the system. The chemical potential μ_i of a component i in a given phase is equal to $(\partial G/\partial m_i)_{P,T}$, where m_i is the quantity of the component present in the phase and the quantities of all other components remain constant.

1878 J. W. Gibbs in *Trans. Connecticut Acad. Arts & Sci.* III. 119 If we call a quantity μ_x, as defined by such an equation as (12), the potential for the substance S_z in the homogeneous mass considered, these conditions may be expressed as follows:— The potential for each component substance must be constant throughout the whole mass. *Ibid.* 149 If to any homogeneous mass we suppose an infinitesimal quantity of any substance to be added, the mass remaining homogeneous and its entropy and volume remaining unchanged, the increase of the energy of the mass divided by the quantity of the substance added is the potential of that substance in the mass considered... In the above definition we may evidently substitute for entropy, volume, and energy, respectively, either temperature, volume, and the function ψ; or entropy, pressure, and the function χ; or temperature, pressure, and the function ζ. **1917** G. E. Gibson tr. *Sackur's Textbk. Thermo-Chem. & Thermodynamics* vi. 178 The component I can go spontaneously from B to A if its chemical potential in A is less than its chemical potential in B. *Ibid.* 179 In chemistry it is usual to take the mol of each component as the unit of mass, and we may then define the chemical potential..of the component I in the solution A as the change in the thermodynamic potential of a very large mass of A when 1 mol of the component I is added to it without changing the temperature, the pressure or the masses of the other components. **1924** H. S. Taylor *Treat. Physical Chem.* I. ii. 67 The thermodynamic potential of all spontaneously occurring processes decreases. **1937** M. W. Zemansky *Heat & Thermodynamics* xvii. 321 If a substance is not present in a phase, it does not follow that its chemical potential is zero. The chemical potential is a measure of the effect on the Gibbs function when a substance *is* introduced. **1950** E. O. Hercus *Elem. Thermodynamics & Statistical Mech.* iv. 24 Two new thermodynamical quantities dependent only on the state of a system can be defined from the entropy. These are: Free Energy, $F = U{-}TS$. Thermodynamic Potential, $G = H - TS = U + pv - TS$. **1960** Hall & Ibele *Engin. Thermodynamics* x. 183 The stability of thermodynamic systems can be examined with reference to a set of quantities known as thermodynamic potentials. **1973** D. C. Kelly *Thermodynamics & Statistical Physics* viii. 147 The four thermodynamic potentials were invented to make thermodynamics 'easy'. Each potential is the natural energy variable for certain classes of physical processes.

c. Special Comb.: **potential barrier,** a region in a field of force in which the potential is significantly higher than at points either side of it, so that a particle requires energy to pass through it; *spec.* that surrounding the potential well of an atomic nucleus; **potential flow,** flow which is irrotational and for which there therefore exists a velocity potential; **potential gradient,** (the rate of) change of (electrical) potential with distance; **potential scattering** *Nuclear Physics*, elastic scattering of a particle by an atomic nucleus in which the scattering cross-section varies smoothly with the energy of the incident particle (cf. **resonance scattering*); **potential wall,** a region in a field of force in which the potential increases sharply; **potential well,** a region in a field of force in which the potential is significantly lower than at points immediately outside it, so that a particle in it is likely to remain there unless it gains a relatively large amount of energy; *spec.* that in which an atomic nucleus is situated.

1929 *Physical Rev.* XXXIII. 134 The particle in the internal region received energy sufficient to raise it over the potential barrier. **1931** G. Gamow *Constitution of Atomic Nuclei* ii. 37 How can such an α-particle get out from the nucleus if it has to cross on its way a potential barrier which is certainly higher than the total energy of the α-particle itself? **1966** H. J. Reich et al. *Theory & Applications Active Devices* iii. 64 An electron encounters a potential barrier in moving from left to right across the junction. **1973** V. Acosta et al. *Essent. Mod. Physics* xvi. 223 (*heading*) A beam of particles of kinetic energy E is incident on a potential barrier $V>E$ with a width of $OA = t$. **1937** N. A. V. Piercy *Aerodynamics* v. 140 Irrotational flow is often called potential flow. **1962** Walshaw & Jobson *Mech. of Fluids* viii. 211 'Potential' flows..neglect viscous actions and merely provide a framework of reference against which the behaviour of a real fluid may be compared. **1975** *Sci. Amer.* Nov. 85/1 An airfoil or a wing in steady motion through the air is a device by means of which circulation is created and maintained in the form of a vortex bound to the wing. This bound vortex is then superposed on the flow pattern that the wing profile would produce in an ideal fluid. The pattern is termed the potential flow. **1895** A. Daniell *Text-bk. Princ. Physics* (ed. 3) xvi. 585 This Electric Force on Unit Quantity, $\phi = (V_{\prime} - V_{\prime\prime}) \div d$, is the Potential-Slope or Potential-Gradient. **1931** *Discovery* July 212/1 Measurements of potential gradient have been made in balloons up to a height of nine kilometres. The gradient falls off rapidly, most of the positive charge being in the lower strata. **1963** E. V. Vernon in Zepler & Punnett *Electron Devices & Networks* i. 25 The potential gradient along the material is due to its ohmic resistance. **1973** R. Brown *Electricity & Atomic Physics* xii. 270 There is a potential gradient in the depletion layer, positive on the n side and negative on the p side, and this represents a potential barrier. **1937** Bethe & Placzek in *Physical Rev.* LI. 460/2 It amounts..to a scattering cross section $\sigma_1 = 4\pi R^2$... This part may be called potential scattering in the narrower sense. *Ibid.* 462/1 The total potential scattering is $\sigma_{pot} = (\sigma_1{}^{\frac{1}{2}} - \sigma_3{}^{\frac{1}{2}})$. **1955** A. E. S. Green *Nuclear Physics* xiii. 433 Within the category of elastic scattering we may distinguish two types of processes, namely, potential scattering and resonant scattering. **1971** B. L. Cohen *Concepts of Nuclear Physics* xiii. 331 Between the resonances in Fig. 13-7 we see the effects of potential scattering only. **1931** *Proc. R. Soc.* A. CXXXIII. 238 If this theory of the resonance levels is correct, it is difficult to reconcile the results of Pose, who finds quite sharp resonance levels in Al, with the results of experiments on α-particles of sufficient energy to pass over the top of the potential wall. **1973** V. Acosta et al. *Essent. Mod. Physics* xvi. 222 This situation may be treated in a simplified manner by using a thin potential wall—a potential barrier. [**1931** G. Gamow *Constitution of Atomic Nuclei* i. 18 The potential..must be more or less constant inside the nucleus and increase sharply at the boundary, the distribution forming a 'potential hole' of the shape shown.] **1935** *Physical Rev.* XLVII. 852/1 The positive valued parameters A and α are to be determined to fit the binding energies of the deuteron and the alpha-particle. Evidently A and $1/\alpha^{\frac{1}{2}}$ are directly proportional to the depth and breadth, respectively, of the potential well. **1952** Blatt & Weisskopf *Theoret. Nuclear Physics* ii. 49 Even very refined experiments at low energies do not suffice to determine more than an 'effective range' and 'depth' of the potential well, leaving the detailed shape completely indeterminate. **1972** DePuy & Chapman *Molec. Reactions & Photochem.* i. 1 Within this potential well the molecule can occupy any of a number of discrete vibrational energy levels.

potentialness. (Later example.)

1930 G. Greene *Two Witnesses* 135 The turning of potentialness into creative life.

potentiate, *v.* Add: **3.** *trans.* To increase the effect of (a drug or its action); to act synergistically with; also, to promote or enhance (a physiological or biochemical phenomenon). Also *fig.*

1917 T. Sollmann *Man. Pharmacol.* 96 Mansfield and Hamburger..believe..that ether potentiates chloral or morphine, by favoring the distribution of these agents in the nervous system. **1941** *Cancer Res.* I. 107/2 Numerous experiments have shown that various exogenous influences, each in itself carcinogenic, can 'potentiate' each other's influence by simultaneous action. **1962** *Lancet* 13 Jan. 112/1 He showed that cocaine potentiated the pressor action of adrenaline. **1969** D. Clark *Nobody's Perfect* iii. 109 Though the phenobarbitone had caused death, it had been potentiated by the alcohol. Without the alcohol he might have lived. **1973** R. G. Krueger et al. *Introd. Microbiol.* xix. 524/2 The membrane may serve to potentiate cell-virus association and thereby enhance infection. **1974** Hawkey & Bingham *Wild Card* xi. 107 What do you intend doing to potentiate the virus's cytolytic properties? **1977** *Observer* 21 Aug. 21/5 New York potentiates music the same way that alcohol potentiates certain pills.

potentiated *ppl. a.* (further examples); also **pote·ntiating** *ppl. a.* and *vbl. sb.*; **potentiation,** (*b*) the phenomenon whereby the simultaneous effect of two drugs or other agents may exceed the sum of their individual effects.

1914 J. T. Halsey tr. *Meyer & Gottlieb's Pharmacol.* xviii. 576 Honigmann's experiments with mixed narcosis with ether and chloroform or ether and alcohol apparently indicate a potentiation. **1917** T. Sollmann *Man. Pharmacol.* 96 When several drugs are administered together, each may act independently, as if it were present alone... In many cases, however, the combined action is greater or smaller than would be calculated (potentiated and deficient summation). **1941** *Cancer Res.* I. 107/2 The 'potentiation' seen in the simultaneous action of tumor-producing virus and other carcinogenic influence. *Ibid.*, The above-mentioned 'potentiating' influence of two different exogenous influences. **1958** *Bull. Math. Bio-*

physics XX. 1 Two drugs may act together synergistically or they may act antagonistically. The former action we shall refer to as positive potentiation; the latter as negative potentiation. **1970** I. MURDOCH *Fairly Honourable Defeat* I. xv. 165 Her body seemed to be weighted and pinned to the sloping bank by a potentiated force of gravity. **1971** P. HUSON *Devil's Picturebk.* ii. 64 Frequent use of a complex mnemotechnic system was believed to result in the enlivening or 'potentiating' of the imagination. **1974** *Aquaculture* IV. 410 Other workers..have also found the in vivo efficacy of a potentiated sulphonamide..to be far superior to sulphonamide, used alone, in the treatment of furunculosis. **1974** M. C. GERALD *Pharmacol.* iii. 63 Potentiation may result from two agents acting by different mechanisms or one drug facilitating the action of the other. **1975** *European Jrnl. Pharmacol.* XXXIV. 169 (*heading*) Potentiating effect of lithium chloride on aggressive behaviour induced in mice. **1977** *Amer. N. & Q.* XV. 83/1 These properties include curative power,.. potentiation,..and the prevention of decay or corruption.

potentiator (pote·nʃiˌēitəɹ). *Pharm.* [f. prec. + -OR.] An agent that increases the effect of a drug.

1955 *Sci. News Let.* 9 July 19/3 Animals that had just recovered from a barbiturate almost immediately went back into deep hypnosis when given chlorpromazine. This shows that it is a true potentiator, and not merely a prolonger of the action of the barbiturate. **1975** *Acta Endocrinol.* LXXIX. 511 (*heading*) Normal recognition of glucose as a potentiator in subjects with low insulin response and in mild diabetes.

potentiometer. a. Substitute for def.: A device for measuring potential difference or an e.m.f. by balancing it against a variable potential difference of known value produced by passing a known (usu. fixed) current through a known (usu. variable) resistance. (Further examples.)

1922 GLAZEBROOK *Dict. Appl. Physics* II. 611/2 A Weston cell having an E.M.F. of 1·0183 volts would be balanced across 10 coils and 0·183 of the total length of the slide wire, the pressure drop across each coil of the potentiometer being then 0·1 volt. **1935** TURNER & BANNER *Electr. Measurements* xi. 127 The Crompton type is one of the most widely used potentiometers; in this, instead of a continuous slide wire covering the whole voltage range, resistance coils are used with a selector switch. **1975** D. G. FINK *Electronics Engineers' Handbk.* xvii. 6 The constant-resistance potentiometer..uses a variable current through a fixed resistance to generate a voltage for obtaining a null with the unknown emf.

b. A voltage divider which is regulated by varying a resistance; also, *loosely*, a rheostat.

1910 G. W. PIERCE *Princ. Wireless Telegr.* xxvii. 324 The accurate adjustment of the local voltage is achieved by the use of a potentiometer. **1914** R. STANLEY *Text-bk. Wireless Telegr.* xvi. 221 Such an arrangement of battery and wire is called a potentiometer; by means of it we can obtain any voltage, to apply to our apparatus, from zero up to the full voltage of the battery. **1955** *Sci. Amer.* Aug. 96/2 Connect the power supply to the solution [in the ice-box dishes] through the carbon electrodes and adjust the potentiometer or tapped resistor to the prescribed potential of 200 volts. **1962** F. I. ORDWAY et al. *Basic Astronautics* ix. 375 The voltage in a current varies with the displacement of the mass by means of a potentiometer. **1966** *McGraw-Hill Encycl. Sci. & Technol.* X. 542/1 By using only the movable and one fixed connection, a potentiometer may be used as a rheostat. **1968** A. MARCUS *Electricity for Technicians* iv. 59 Such variable resistors are called rheostats or potentiometers.

2. *attrib.* and *Comb.*

1881 [in Dict.]. **1916** C. C. GARRARD *Electric Switch & Controlling Gear* iv. 261 Potentiometer-type regulators are used when it is desired to reduce the voltage applied to the terminals of the field coil to zero, as is the case, for example, with boosters. **1920** *Whittaker's Electr. Engineer's Pocket-bk.* (ed. 4) 434 These curves can be used for any potentiometer regulator which has a resistance 3½ times the field coil. **1922** GLAZEBROOK *Dict. Appl. Physics* II. 615/2 The total resistance of the potentiometer circuit remains unchanged whatever the setting of the dials. **1961** G. V. SADLER in G. F. Tagg *Pract. Electr. Engin.* III. 215 Special precautions must also be taken when potentiometer control is used on a crane whose d.c. supply is obtained from a static rectifier. **1962** G. A. T. BURDETT *Automatic Control Handbk.* ix. 4 Potentiometer pressure transducers are made in a number of forms. **1966** *McGraw Hill Encycl. Sci. & Technol.* X. 543/2 Potentiometer measurement of current is accomplished by passing current through a standardized resistor of appropriate value and measuring the potential difference across this resistor. **1979** *Sci. Digest* July 35/1 When potentiometer controls are used with microprocessor games the analog voltage due to the potentiometer must be converted into a digital quantity.

Hence **potentiome·tric** *a.*, of or pertaining to a potentiometer; employing, or obtained by means of, a potentiometer; *potentiometric titration*, a titration which is followed by measuring the change in potential of an electrode immersed in the sample solution; **potentiome·trically** *adv.*; **potentio·metry,** the technique of measurement with potentiometers, esp. in chemical analysis.

1915 *Jrnl. Chem. Soc.* CVIII. II. 307 (*heading*) Potentiometric arrangement for electrochemical investigations. **1926** KOLTHOFF & FURMAN *Potentiometric Titrations* viii. 151 Everyone who has had experience with the performance of potentiometric titrations knows that, near the equivalence-point especially,..the potential does not become constant immediately after the addition of the reagent. *Ibid.* xi. 247 Manganous salts may be titrated potentiometrically according to the Volhard-Wolff method. **1931** I. M. KOLTHOFF *Colorimetric & Potentiometric Determination of pH* vii. 129 (*heading*) Problems in potentiometry. **1946** L. MICHAELIS in A. Weissberger *Physical Methods Org. Chem.* II. xxii. 1052 Potentiometry consists of the measurement of the electromotive force of a galvanic cell composed of two half-cells one of which is a reference half-cell of known composition; and the other an electrode immersed in the solution to be investigated. **1966** ELVIDGE & SAMMES *Course Mod. Techniques Org. Chem.* (ed. 2) xxxiv. 284 Potentiometry makes possible the titration of very weak acids and bases. **1967** *Times Rev. Industry* Oct. 49/3 The length of the cable is then determined by a potentiometric method and may be indicated at any remote control position. **1972** GRUNWALD & KIRSCHENBAUM *Introd. Quantitative Chem. Anal.* xviii. 337 A silver–silver halide electrode is used for the potentiometric titration of a mixture of halide salts with silver nitrate. **1975** D. G. FINK *Electronics Engineers' Handbk.* x. 13 Potentiometric displacement transducers are widely used because of their relative simplicity of construction and their ability to provide a high-level output. **1978** *Nature* 17 Aug. p. ix/1 Finally the controller starts the titration to titrate the free iodine potentiometrically using sodium thiosulphate.

potentiostat (pŏte·nʃiostæt). [f. POTENTI(AL *a.* and *sb.* + -O + *-STAT.] A device used to regulate automatically the potential difference between electrodes in electrolysis.

1942 A. HICKLING in *Trans. Faraday Soc.* XXXVIII. 27 The electrical circuit of the device, which will subsequently be referred to as a 'potentiostat', is shown in Fig. 1. **1949** *Analytical Chem.* XXI. 497/1 The instrument...functions as a potentiostat in automatically maintaining the potential of a working electrode constant during an electrolysis. **1965** *New Scientist* 8 Apr. 99/1 These potentiostats..have a very rapid response to voltage fluctuations and now make the continuous control of commercial processes look very attractive. **1979** *Nature* 15 Mar. 239/1 The cinnabar electrode is connected to a platinum counter electrode and a potential of 0 V maintained between the two by means of a potentiostat.

Hence **potentiosta·tic** *a.*, under the control of or employing a potentiostat; with the potential difference between electrodes held constant; **potentiosta·tically** *adv.*

1955 *Chem. Abstr.* XLIX. 5166 The potentiostatic method was compared with other methods. **1961** *Trans. Symposium Electrode Processes* (U.S. Electrochem. Soc.) 164 An attempt was made to develop apparatus in which potentiostatic conditions could be achieved in a time short enough to study the growth and decay of metal monolayers at constant potential. **1967** tr. *K. J. Vetter's Electrochem. Kinetics* (*Theoret. Aspects*) ii. 364 The potentiostatically applied overvoltage must..be pure charge-transfer overvoltage at time $t = 0$. **1975** *Nature* 27 Mar. 322/2 Specimens held under potentiostatic control in the electrolyte were subjected to square wave strains in the range ±0·02 to ±0·05 at strain rates of $\sim$0·30 s^{-1}. **1976** *Ibid.* 19 Aug. 681/1 Anodisation could be accomplished both galvanostatically and potentiostatically.

potentize, *v.* Add: Hence **po·tentized** *ppl. a.* Also **po:tentiza·tion,** dilution of a drug in order to increase its power or efficacy.

1850 C. J. HEMPEL *New Homœopathic Pharmacopœia* I. 10 By the former, these successive developments of the original substance are called dynamizations, or potentizations; by the latter, attentuations. **1864** *Trans. Homœopathic Med. Soc. N.Y.* 56 The administration of potentized remedies. **1938** D. SHEPHERD *Magic of Minimum Dose* 7 The first law is the law of simillimum, which is followed by (2) the principle of the minimum dose, (3) the principle of potentization. **1972** D. V. TANSLEY *Radionics* viii. 80 To augment the violet one may add an ampoule of potentized onyx to the treatment. **1974** *Homoeopathy* June/July 87 Symptoms were noted when the drug was given in material and potentised doses. *Ibid.* 88 As the substance becomes more dilute with succeeding potentisations it becomes soluble.

potestas. Add: **4.** *Philol.* The phonetic or phonemic value of a letter in an alphabet.

1949 J. R. FIRTH in *Trans. Philol. Soc. 1948* 135 Each Arabic letter has..syllabic value, the value or *potestas* in the most general terms being consonant plus vowel, including vowel zero, or zero vowel. **1963** *English Studies* XLIV. 4 Thus if there is a contrast..between the North and elsewhere, then.. it is best treated as a contrast in graphemes irrespective of their phonemic 'value', or, to speak in more mediaeval terms, as a contrast in *figurae* irrespective of the *potestas* of each. **1967** R. H. ROBINS *Short Hist. Linguistics* iii. 56 Priscian worked systematically through his subject, the description of the language of classical Latin literature. Pronunciation and syllable structure are covered by a description of the letters (*litterae*), defined as the smallest parts of articulate speech, of which the properties are *nōmen*, the name of the letter, *figūra*, its written shape, and *potestās*, its phonetic value. **1972** H. BENEDIKTSSON *First Grammatical Treat.* iii. 90 He is willing to establish new letters with a value (*potestas*) of a combination of two consecutive letters.

‖**pot-et-fleur** (potˌeˌflör). [Fr., lit. 'pot and flower'.] A style of floral decoration using pot-plants together with cut flowers. Also *attrib.*

[**1960** V. STEVENSON in *Daily Tel.* 11 Feb. 11/2 There's a new mood afoot in flower arrangement—to combine cut flowers with indoor pot plants. I have been using this style of arrangement for ages, without finding a name for it. Can readers make any suggestions?] **1963** —— *Decorating with Flowers & Plants* vii. 71 When I wanted to describe this style of decoration about which I am writing, I invited the readers of the Woman's Page in the *Daily Telegraph* to coin a name... Our new style became pot-et-fleur, a term already recognized by the National Association of Flower Arrangement Societies of Great Britain, who have included a class in their national competition. *Ibid.* 73 You will have made your first pot-et-fleur arrangement. **1968** *Flower Arranger* Sept. 125 There were strong line arrangements in the tall slit windows behind the choir-stalls; soft arrangements, mostly *pot-et-fleur*, found here and there. **1972** *Jrnl. R. Hort. Soc.* XCVII. 375 Bonsai and pot-et-fleur are her two main techniques. **1978** T. TAYLOR *Flower Arranging* 66/1 A pot-et-fleur is a decoration that combines plants and cut flowers. The plants can be grown permanently and the flowers can be added from time to time.

pot fisherman. Add: (Examples of sense in Dict.); also, = *fish-potter* s.v. FISH *sb.*[1] 7.

1895 *Funk's Stand. Dict.* 1392/1 *Pot-fisherman*, one who fishes while floating buoyed up by an earthen pot, as on Asiatic rivers. **1970** *Times* 2 Sept. 10/5 A much brighter prospect has suddenly opened up for Guernsey's traditional pot fishermen, who looked as if they were doomed to go gradually out of business.

pot-head. Add: **2.** *Canada.* In full, *pothead whale.* = CA'ING-WHALE, *CAA'ING WHALE, *pilot-whale* s.v. PILOT *sb.* 6 in Dict. and Suppl.

1863 *Islander* (Charlottetown, Prince Edward Island) 14 Aug. 2/3 Large numbers of Potheads are in the Bay, which probably accounts for the squid panic. **1964** *Canad. Geogr. Jrnl.* Mar. 92/3 Entire herds of 40-foot pothead whales have been known to run aground on the beaches. **1979** *Monitor* (McAllen, Texas) 16 July 2A/1 More than 170 pothead whales beached themselves on Sunday.

3. *Electr.* An insulated connector used for making a sealed joint between conductors, esp. between insulated and uninsulated lines.

1901 W. J. HOPKINS *Telephone Lines* (rev. ed.) ii. 38 (*in figure*) Pot head splice. **1903** *Phil. Mag.* V. 327 The cables were brought out to pot-heads, and each wire terminated in a screw-cup. **1930** H. P. SEELYE *Electr. Distribution Engin.* xxvi. 497 The pothead usually consists of a cast-iron tank or pot into which the cable is inserted... The conductors pass through the pot and are either brought out through porcelain bushings, or are attached to conducting terminals fixed in the bushings. The pot is then filled with insulating compound. **1963** K. NEVILLE in D. Knight *100 Yrs. Sci. Fiction* (1969) 73 Ramon Lopez, one of the truck crew, was killed today hosing down a high-voltage pothead.

4. (See *POT *sb.*[5] 2.)

pother, *sb.* Add: **2.** (Later example of the form *pudder*.)

1956 AUDEN & KALLMAN *Magic Flute* I. iv. 32 (From within the temple comes the sound of singing).. What's that? What's that pudder? I shiver, I shudder.

pothery, *a.* Add: **1.** Also **puthery.**

1855 MRS. GASKELL *Let.* Feb. (1966) 332 It is so *puthery* here, I can hardly walk.

pot-hole. Add: Also **pothole, pot hole. 1.** (Earlier example.)

1826 T. L. MCKENNEY *Sk. Tour to Lakes* (1827) 54 The waters were once, in many places, some fifty feet above their present level; for their action upon the rocks is plainly seen in the pot holes, as the excavations are called, which are made by the action of pebbles upon the rocks.

3. *N. Amer.* A pond formed by a natural hollow in the ground in which water has collected. Cf. SLEW *sb.*[1] 1, SLOUGH *sb.*[1] 4. Also *attrib.*

1902 *Saskatchewan Hist.* (1956) IX. 31 In natural depressions of the soil..water had gathered and formed so-called 'pot-holes'—circular basins of a swampy nature, generally rather shallow. The 'potholes' usually have a heavy growth of wild hay. **1938** S. C. ELLS *Northland Trails* 85 It is a land of mysterious pot-hole lakes and ponds with neither inlets nor outlets. **1946** *Sun* (Baltimore) 5 July 11/3 Experimental planting of fish with airplanes gives promise for the 'back in there' pothole lakes and spring holes. **1955** R. P. HOBSON *Nothing too Good for Cowboy* (1956) vii. 69 The pothole meadows were still some five miles away from the spruce clump. **1962** *Daily Progress* (Charlottesville, Va.) 17 Aug. 4/2 Minnesota and the Dakotas..are dotted with innumerable small ponds called 'potholes'. **1963** *Globe & Mail* (Toronto) 13 Mar. 17/1 Show me the man who doesn't get the shivers when half-a-dozen greenhead mallards start side-slipping into the pothole in front of him.

4. A depression or hollow part forming a defect in the surface of a road or track. Also *pothole.*

1909 *Westm. Gaz.* 30 Aug. 1/3 We are also beginning to see how much our urban and suburban macadam roads suffer from artificial watering and constant scavenging, for all road engineers are agreed that the uneven surfaces and pot-holes..are practically confined to the districts where the water-cart reigns supreme. **1920** *Motor Cycle* 30 Sept. 384/2 On the outward journey the pot-holes between Edinburgh and Stirling seemed appalling. **1955** *Times* 5 July 5/7 On the other hand the springing makes rather heavy going of potholes like those caused by recessed manhole covers. **1972** 'J. & E. BONETT' *No Time to Kill* v. 52 The grey car turned onto a dirt road, slowed to a crawl as it met the potholes. **1978** *New York* 3 Apr. 100/4 The locals of D.C. 37 represent social-service workers, botanical garden employees, city engineers, pothole repairmen, hospital employees, [etc.]

5. *Austral.* A shallow hole dug in the

ground in prospecting for opal dirt (see *OPAL 4). Also *attrib.*
1940 I. L. IDRIESS *Lightning Ridge* 90 For a time I sank pot-holes alone then went mates with little Archie Campbell. **1967** —— *Opals & Sapphires* 112 Keep the find quiet until you have sunk more potholes to prove that it is worth while pegging out.

po·t-hole, *v.* Also **pothole.** [f. the sb.] **1.** *trans.* To produce pot-holes in.
1909 *Cent. Dict.* Suppl., *Pot-hole*, to produce in (a solid rock mass) a hole by the action of stones and silt whirled round in an eddy of water. **1975** *Nature* 20 Mar. 189/2 It was channelled and potholed by running water.

2. a. *trans.* To explore (pot-holes or the like). **b.** *intr.* To engage in pot-holing.
1970 *Observer* (Colour Suppl.) 25 Jan. 30/4 Its underworld labyrinth of elves and trolls consists of tunnels he potholed as a boy. **1970** *Times* 26 Oct. 4 They were with 10 others potholing on the Pennines at Casterton, near Kirkby Lonsdale.

po·t-holed, *a.* [f. as prec. + -ED².] Having pot-holes.
1933 AUDEN *Poems* (ed. 2) 43 By pot-holed becks. **1939** JOYCE *Finnegans Wake* 31 [He] had been meaning to inquire what, in effect, had caused yon causeway to be thus potholed. **1952** C. BARDSLEY *Bishop's Move* x. 114 It took the car of civilization away from the main road on to a bumpy, pot-holed track. **1960** I. CROSS *Backward Sex* i. 33 The lines of the tram tracks were pot-holed and rutted. **1976** *S. Wales Echo* 27 Nov. 6/3 People will have to go on putting up with a badly pot-holed road.

po·t-holer. Also **potholer.** [f. as prec. + -ER¹.] Someone who goes pot-holing.
1900 *Jrnl. Yorkshire Ramblers' Club* I. 134 The temptation to remain above ground certainly was very strong, and some of the pot-holers gazed rather wistfully after the men who, at the parting of the ways, left them for Ingleborough. **1908** *Pearson's Mag.* Mar. 282/1 To see a party of pot-holers on the warpath you would think, from the mass of spars and cordage, that they had got some idea..of an inland voyage into their heads. **1935** *Times* 27 July 13/4 At Derby to-day cave explorers and pot-holers from several parts of England will meet to found a British Speleological Association. **1957** *Times* 10 Dec. 10/5 (*heading*) Six potholers brought out. Rescuers work all day. Community singing in cave. **1973** D. ORGILL *Jasius Pursuit* xi. 107 This kind of cat-run, in the potholers' experience, often led to a larger chamber.

po·t-holey, *a.* [f. as prec. + -Y¹.] Having many pot-holes.
1921 *Blackw. Mag.* Nov. 641/2 We lurched along over a very pot-holey road. **1925** *Motor* 15 Dec. 1001/2 Some rough stretches of wavy and pot-holey surfaces. **1936** F. CLUNE *Roaming round Darling* x. 89 Road, neither pot-holey nor unholey for thirty-five miles.

po·t-holing, *vbl. sb.* Also **potholing.** [f. as prec. + -ING¹.] **1.** The exploration of underground pot-holes.
1899 *Jrnl. Yorkshire Ramblers' Club* I. 63 The sport of cave-hunting and pot-holing, apart from its scientific interest, has fascinations and charms peculiar to itself. **1908** *Pearson's Mag.* Mar. 280/1 Subterranean mountaineering, which is, in the vernacular, pot-holing, indisputably possesses a fascination of its own. **1925** *Jrnl. Fell & Rock Climbing Club* VII. 69 An afternoon's pot-holing..was the only mountaineering done. **1935** *Times* 27 July 13/4 The pot-holing clubs of Yorkshire and Lancashire have already joined to form a rescue organization. **1967** *Potholing & Caving* (Know the Game Ser.) 12/1 The words caving and potholing are used loosely to mean the same thing... Technically a cave is an underground system which may or may not be large enough to admit a human being... A pothole is a natural hole in the ground or a cave system, containing shafts or pitches. **1975** *Times* 9 Sept. 6/2 Mr Tony Harrison, aged 19, a member of Lancaster University's potholing team, has been killed in a fall, in a cave.

2. The formation of pot-holes.
1903 *Geogr. Jrnl.* XXI. 672 Of this [erosion] Mr. Ball thinks that at least two-thirds is accounted for by the pot-holing action. **1941** *Jrnl. Geomorphol.* IV. 71 (*heading*) Pot-holing of limestone by development of solution cups.

pot-hook, *sb.* Add: **2.** (Further examples.) Also *pl.* = SHORTHAND. *colloq.*
1846 *Swell's Night Guide* 128/1 *Pothooks and hangers*, short hand characters. **1937** PARTRIDGE *Dict. Slang* 653/1 *Pot-hooks and hangers*, shorthand. **1939** JOYCE *Finnegans Wake* 181 Instead of cluthoring those model households plain wholesome pothooks (a thing he never possessed of his Nigerian own) what do you think Vulgariano did but copy all their various styles of signature. **1957** R. S. HEINLEIN *Door into Summer* ii. 39 Darling, if this is a formal meeting, I guess you had better make pothooks. **1962** G. LAWTON *John Wesley's English* 239 His [*sc.* Wesley's] works are full of proverbs, pothooks, allusions, idioms, colloquialisms, and slang. **1963** C. MACKENZIE *My Life & Times* I. 156 From her I learnt to write pothooks and hangers and very soon to pass from pothooks and hangers to real letters.

b. *attrib.* Delete † *Obs.* and add later example (with reference to shorthand).
1914 W. OWEN *Let.* 2 Mar. (1967) 236 Thanks for the Catalogue of Pothook-books [Pitman's catalogue].

pot-housey, *a.* [f. POT-HOUSE + -Y¹.] Suggestive of or appropriate to a pot-house.
1872 HARDY *Under Greenw. Tree* I. i. viii. 105 If I strip by myself and not necessary, 'tis rather pot-housey, I own.

pot-hunt, *v.* [Back-formation f. POT-HUNTER.] *intr.* To hunt 'for the pot' (see POT *sb.*¹ 1 b); to be a pot-hunter.
1926 *Chambers's Jrnl.* July 418/1 You..prefer to pot-hunt—luckily for us, with six hefty Gurkhas and the servants to feed, as well as ourselves! **1936** AUDEN & ISHERWOOD *Ascent of F6* 46 When we were boys at school, I saw him..win the prizes... We are older now..But James..Must fill the last gap in his great collection And pot-hunt for his brother.

pot-hunter. Add: **2.** (Further examples.) Also *fig.*
1856 *Porter's Spirit of Times* 25 Oct. 126/1 It is disgusting to every lover of fair play to witness the ravages committed by the pot-hunter, who coolly murders the deer by torch-light from a dug-out or canoe. **1878** C. HALLOCK *Amer. Club List & Sportsman's Gloss.* p. ix/1 *Pot-hunter*, one who hunts or fishes for profit, regardless of close seasons, the waste of game, or the pleasure to be derived from the pursuit. **1905** 'O. HENRY' in *N.Y. World Mag.* 22 Oct. 8/1 He was an old man, with a slow and limping gait, so a pot-hunter of a newly-licensed chauffeur ran him down one day when livelier game was scarce. **1922** JOYCE *Ulysses* 158 Lady Mountcashel..rode out with the Ward Union staghounds... Uneatable fox. Pothunters too. **1936** *Sun* (Baltimore) 28 Feb. 11/5 Hundreds of ducks flying northward have been slaughtered. The chief offenders..are the so-called 'pot-hunters', who hunt for profit and rent duck blinds to sportsmen.

3. (Later examples.)
1912 A. BENNETT *Matador* 22 He used to be what they called a pot-hunter, a racing bicyclist. **1942** BERREY & VAN DEN BARK *Amer. Thes. Slang* § 636/21 *Contestant for a prize*, mug hunter *or* chaser, pot hunter.

4. One who finds or obtains objects of archaeological interest or value, esp. by unscientific or illicit methods, and for the purpose of private collection or profit.
1958 *N.Y. Times Mag.* 16 Feb. 48/3 This satisfaction.. is the big distinction between the new species of digger and the acquisitive 'pot hunter', that bane of archaeological scientists. Souvenir-hunting amateurs are still with us, of course. **1966** ROBBINS & IRVING *Amat. Archaeologist's Handbk.* v. 83 This chapter might carry the subtitle: 'Pothunters, beware!' A pothunter is a person who visits a site in order to find and hoard as many 'relics' as possible. **1967** L. DEUEL *Conquistadors without Swords* iv. 52 Museum collections all over the world owe most of their treasures to disreputable pothunters. **1973** *New Yorker* 24 Mar. 102/2 Stewart L. Peckham, chief archeologist of the Museum of New Mexico,..was distressed to find that almost all the major Mimbres sites..had been ravaged by pot-hunters.

pot-hunting. Add: (Further examples.) Also in sense corresponding to *POT-HUNTER 4.
1869 *Harper's Mag.* Jan. 157/1 This is regarded by many Plains men as a kind of pot-hunting, that is not entitled to the name of sport, and only to be resorted to for the purpose of securing the meat needed as food. **1946** L. P. HARTLEY *Sixth Heaven* ii. 47 I'm doing a bit of pot-hunting and have to attend classes and pow-wows. **1956** A. R. KING in *Amer. Antiquity* Apr. 423/2 Scientific archaeology carries more satisfaction than 'pot-hunting' and 'treasure troving'. **1973** *New Yorker* 24 Mar. 100/3 Poverty and desperation are extenuating factors in Bangladesh, but not in the United States, where pot-hunting is a weekend hobby of the more affluent. The rise in prices for American-Indian art..has had disastrous consequences for scholarship.

‖ **potiche** (pǫtī·ʃ). [Fr., in the same sense.] A large porcelain vase, usu. rounded in shape with bulging shoulders and a widish mouth freq. having a lid, originally produced in China during the Ming dynasty.
1895 in *Funk's Stand. Dict.* **1933** *Burlington Mag.* Nov. 202 (*caption*) Semi-Celadon Potiche of Chino-Sawankalōk Ware. **1935** *Ibid.* June p. xx/2 A royal potiche ornamented with a band of wave scrolls on the neck. **1960** H. HAYWARD *Antique Coll.* 226/2 *Potiche*, large broad-mouthed Chinese porcelain jar of 'baluster' shape, with cover; favoured from Ming..times. **1967** P. WHITE in *Coast to Coast 1965–66* 231 Answering back made her mistress rush at the *bibelots*, dust the *potiches* her maid neglected. **1972** *Trans. Oriental Ceramics Soc.* XXXVIII. 126 The jar of *potiche* form with broad base, short wide neck and low domed cover.

potichomanist (pǫtiʃǫ·mănist). *rare.* [f. POTICHOMANIA + -IST.] A person who practises potichomania.
1884 *Decorator's Assistant* 122 Potichomanists have found the art capable of greater results than the mere imitation of porcelain vases, by the introduction of glass panels [etc.].

‖ **potin**² (potæ̃). *rare.* [Fr.] A piece of gossip; a rumpus, a row.
1922 M. ARLEN *Piracy* II. vi. 111 He would hear of great dinners and dances and *potins.* **1938** G. ARTHUR *Not Worth Reading* vi. 86 No shred of evidence could ever be adduced to reinforce the *potin* that Fred Archer was the natural son of a peer. **1945** E. WAUGH *Brideshead Revisited* I. vi. 136 'What's going on?' 'Oh, just another boring family potin. Sebastian got tight again.'

potlatch. Add: **b.** (Earlier and later examples.) Also, an extravagant giving away or throwing away of possessions to enhance one's prestige or establish one's position. Also *attrib.*, *transf.*, and *fig.*
1865 C. C. LEIGHTON *Jrnl.* 30 Aug. in *Life at Puget Sound* (1884) 25 There was going to be a great *potlach* at the coal-mines, where a large quanitity of *iktas* would be given away,—tin pans, guns, blankets, canoes, and money... It seems that anyone who aspires to be a chief must first give a *potlach* to his tribe. **1902** H. L. WILSON *Spenders* xxx. 357 This life of idleness you been leadin'—one continual potlatch the whole time—it wa'n't doin' you a bit of good. **1916** [see *GIVE-AWAY 1]. **1934** R. BENEDICT *Patterns of Culture* (1935) vi. 202 A variant of this type of potlatch was that which was given upon the adolescence of the woman of highest rank. **1957** *Times* 12 Nov. (Canada Suppl.) p. v/3 Another change was the removal of the prohibition on potlatches and on some traditional religious ceremonies, an ironic measure, as they have now practically disappeared. **1965** H. KAHN *On Escalation* xiii. 270 'Potlatch' wars. Competitions in conspicuous consumption of resources or spectacular successes in such areas as space, economic growth, and 'showy' military systems are employed to gain prestige and influence events. **1969** *Times* 22 Sept. 14/3 Potlatch was an obligation to anyone caught out in a misdemeanour, or who had suffered loss of face through some mishap. Only by a parade of wealth or wild generosity or conspicuous waste could such a man regain his shattered image. **1970** *Globe & Mail* (Toronto) 26 Sept. 29/3 (Advt.), The game has become secondary to a potlatch ceremony called tailgate picknicking... This..requires that the host participants outdo their neighbours in the quality and variety of food and drink and the elegance of serving accessories. **1976** *New Yorker* 22 Mar. 44/3 But in September the potlatch ends and there is no one left but old men and women caring for babies whose parents cannot afford to keep them abroad.

po·tlatch, *v.* [f. the sb.] To give; *spec.* to establish one's name or position by the extravagant giving or throwing away of goods or by holding a feast, which entails some form of reciprocity or return.
1901 *Daily Colonist* (Victoria, B.C.) 6 Oct. 2/2 He had $120 coming to him, and he went to Mr. Landsberg and asked if he would potlatch one half of his wages to him and give the other half to the Duke. **1911** *Ibid.* 30 Apr. 8/3 The forty-one family heads of the Songhees band of Indians..had the pleasure of collecting the last of the moneys potlached to them by the provincial government. **1934** R. BENEDICT *Patterns of Culture* (1935) vi. 203 Potlatching for an heir on the North West coast. **1943** W. H. CHASE *Sourdough Pot* xxiii. 171 The deal was closed, the butter potlatched to her father. **1958** A. R. RADCLIFFE-BROWN *Method in Social Anthropol.* I. v. 123 Amongst the Tlingit..it is members of one moiety who potlatch against members of the other moiety. **1964** GOULD & KOLB *Dict. Social Sci.* 523/1 If..a person were humiliated by an accident which made him appear ridiculous, or if he were taken in war and made a slave, he or his relatives must *potlatch* in his name in order to reinstate him in public esteem.

potlatching. (Later examples.)
1964 GOULD & KOLB *Dict. Social Sci.* 523/1 Potlatching demanded reciprocity. **1975** H. WHITE *Raincoast Chron.* (1976) 182/1 There was incessant potlatching.

pot-lid. 1. (Later *Pottery* examples.)
1924 CLARKE & WRENCH *Colour Pictures on Pot Lids* i. 4 The collecting of pot lids and other Staffordshire pottery adorned with these pictures has gone on in a quiet way for some considerable time. **1957** MANKOWITZ & HAGGAR *Conc. Encycl. Eng. Pott. & Porc.* 181/1 Polychrome colour-printing on pottery was developed..from 1848..and was used extensively for the decoration of pot-lids. **1972** *Times* 7 July 14/7 These Staffordshire pot lids were a nineteenth-century packaging gimmick for products such as fish paste or cold cream.

po·tlikker, colloq. and dial. (chiefly *U.S.*) var. POT-LIQUOR; also *fig.*
1930 *Sun* (Baltimore) 17 May 1/3 Pot likker is the best way of preventing nearly all the diseases that we are heir to. **1932** *Ibid.* 8 Apr. 1/4 The Louisianian contended that the corn pone should be 'dunked' into the pot likker. **1950** *Amer. Speech* XXV. 230 *Pot likker*, the juice in which black-eyed peas are cooked. **1963** *New Statesman* 12 July 37/3 During the years when McCarthy's briefcase was a national badge of shame, Americans looked to Britain for an example of sanity and regard for civil liberties. The present anxiety may be unfounded, but some honourable Americans succumbed to the tempting potlikker of the loyalty issue with all its hazy innuendoes. **1974** *Black World* Jan. 53 The boiler at school threatening to blow/flannel gowns and slips Pot likker and cornbread/ bundles of kindling for the stove.

pot-liquor. (Earlier and later examples.)
1744 W. ELLIS *Mod. Husbandman* July xvii. 101 Mix fine Pollard with fresh Pot-liquor. **1909** *Dialect Notes* III. 359 *Pot-liquor*,..liquor from boiled greens or field peas and fat meat. **1931** *Sun* (Baltimore) 4 Mar. 12/7 Maryland pot liquor is the liquor left over in the pot after a boiling of ham and cabbage. **1949** C. HIMES *Black on Black* (1973) 277 They sat in the hot kitchen and ate greens and side meat and rice and..drank the pot-liquor with the corn bread.

po·t-ma:king, *vbl. sb.* The making of pots or pottery.
1767 J. WEDGWOOD *Let.* 26 July (1965) 58, I..am sorry to find the heat..was much more intense than can be made use of for Pottmaking. **1927** PEAKE & FLEURE *Peasants & Potters* 141 We think that they had picked up the art of agriculture, weaving and pot-making, etc. **1951** E. E. EVANS-PRITCHARD *Social Anthropol.* v. 101 A man who..fails in some enterprise, such as pot-making, through lack of skill is responsible for the penalties or failures his actions incur. **1957** P. WORSLEY *Trumpet shall Sound* vi. 115 Malasang, the centre of the pot-making industry, ceased production.

potman. Add: **2.** (Further examples.)

1898 G. B. Shaw *You never can Tell* II. 255 He's at the Bar... A potman, eh?... No, sir: the other bar. **1925** D. Garnett *Sailor's Return* 22 The next morning the potman came to the inn. **1936** Mencken *Amer. Lang.* (ed. 4) 243 *Barmaids* do the work, with maybe a *barman, potman* or *cellarman* to help. **1972** *Classification of Occupations* (Dept. Employment) II. 399/2 *Bar potmen* (wash glasses in licensed bar).

4. In various manufacturing processes: a man who attends to the filling, emptying, firing, etc., of pots (see quots.).

1874 J. A. Phillips *Elem. Metallurgy* 581 In order to desilverise by the aid of this arrangement, the potman sinks the ladle sideways to the bottom of the kettle. **1921** *Dict. Occup. Terms* (1927) §143 *Pot man* (alkali);.. charges shallow iron pans with salt and sulphuric acid, attends to firing, and supervises process until product is ready for salt cake furnace. *Ibid., Pot man* (lead); puts pig and scrap lead into pot and tends and feeds fire beneath it which melts lead [etc.]. **1932** *Amer. Speech* VII. 269 *Pot man,* the man who tends the boilers in which steam is generated for drilling.

potoroo. Substitute for def.: A small nocturnal marsupial belonging to the genus *Potorous*, esp. *P. tridactylus*, found in areas of dense vegetation in Australia; = Kangaroo-rat 1, *rat-kangaroo* s.v. Rat *sb.*[1] 7 e. (Later examples.)

1907 P. Fountain *Rambles of Austral. Naturalist* iv. 38 There are several local varieties of the potoroo. **1923** F. W. Jones *Mammals S. Austral.* 218 The remaining potoroos should be carefully protected. **1943** C. Barrett *Austral. Animal Bk.* xi. 100 The dark rat-kangaroo, known to the natives of Port Jackson as the potoroo,..is now a rare animal. **1965** *Courier-Mail* (Brisbane) 24 Aug. 13 The potoroo is one of the rarest native animals. **1970** W. D. L. Ride *Guide Native Mammals Austral.* 64 Potoroos apparently require the dense natural vegetation of their habitat for protection. **1975** *Nature* 8 May 141/2 The bones we exhibited included forms similar to those of living potoroos and phalangers.

pot-oven. Add: **2.** A kiln in which pottery is fired.

1878 L. Jewitt *Ceramic Art Gt. Brit.* xiii. 528 In his will, dated 29th of January, 1728..this Caleb Glover 'of Pott-ovens, pott-maker'..leaves all his 'working tools belonging to the trade of a potmaker, and the pot oven'. **1971** P. C. D. Brears *Eng. Country Pott.* 225 In 1798, John Morton & Sons assessed for their pot-ovens at Sinderhills.

pot-pie. (Later examples.)

1906 *Amer. Illustr. Mag.* Feb. 465/1, I was out huntin' for squirrels to make a potpie out of, for squirrel potpie's just lickin' good. **1933** M. de la Roche *Master of Jalna* ii. 16 From there came the appetising smell of chicken pot-pie. **1935** A. J. Cronin *Stars look Down* III. ix. 564, I know you've had no breakfast. Are you above eating a pit pot-pie? **1940** Mencken *Happy Days* iv. 59 The Rennert [Hotel] also offered an oyster pot-pie that had its points. **1975** *New Yorker* 20 Oct. 31/3 'He just bein' *prudent*,' said her father. 'Some of them non-needy chirrun might sneak in there and grab some of that chicken potpie.'

pot-plant. 1. (Earlier and later examples.)

1816 'A. Singleton' *Lett.* (1824) 63 The young Virginian ladies take pleasure in nurturing..and fostering their parlour pot-plants. **1870** W. Robinson *Alpine Flowers* I. 56 Our pot-plants are far before those of other countries. **1871** S. Hibberd *Amateur's Flower Garden* xiii. 240 Well-grown pot-plants..have a much brighter, a much more artistic and finished appearance, than plants of the same kinds equally well grown in the open ground. **1914** W. F. Rowles *Garden under Glass* xxii. 221 The loam..will be more suitable for the growth of the majority of pot plants. **1966** Rochford & Gorer *Rochford Bk. Flowering Pot Plants* i. 11 Flowering pot plants are usually regarded as expendable.

pot-pourri. Add: **2. a.** (Further examples.) Also *fig.*

1855 S. Whiting *Heliondé* 71 A couch, which..was made of pot-pourri, or some mixture of dried flowers peculiar to the Sun. **1911** D. H. Lawrence *White Peacock* II. ix. 344 The squire's lady has written a book filling these meadows and the mill precincts with pot-pourri romance. **1930** W. S. Maugham *Cakes & Ale* iv. 51 On little Chippendale tables stood large Oriental bowls filled with pot-pourri. **1960** R. Hemphill *Fragrance & Flavour* 79 If the pot-pourri becomes too dry add more salt, and if too moist add more orris root powder.

b. *transf.* A container designed to hold pot-pourri.

1770 J. Wedgwood *Let.* 20 Aug. (1965) 94 Or have an Auction..of Statues;..Lamps, Potpouri's [etc.]. **1960** R. G. Haggar *Conc. Encycl. Continental Pott. & Porc.* 381/1 Faience in the Swedish/Dutch style was made, that is useful pottery.., and ornamental pieces, (pot-pourris, tureens, etc.). **1971** L. A. Boger *Dict. World Pott. & Porc.* 268 *Potpourri*... In ceramics; the name is given to a container designed with a delicate perforated cover used to hold a mixture of potpourri. **1975** *Times* 19 Dec. 16/5 Among Minton's copies of Sèvres porcelain, a pair of *bleu-de-roi* ground pot-pourris and covers made £1,375.

3. a. (Earlier and further examples.) **b.** (Further examples.) **c.** Any diverse collection or assortment (of people or things).

1855 *Illustr. London News* 29 Dec. 755/2 The overture to the pantomime consisted of a *pot-pourri* of those popular tunes which the professors of the street-organ have been insisting on during the past year. **1866** G. H. Lewes *Let.* 1 July in *Geo. Eliot Lett.* (1956) IV. 282 There drink the sparkling water and lounge in the sun listening to the tolerable band performing overtures..pot-pourris and waltzes. **1894** G. B. Shaw in *Fortnightly Rev.* Feb. 256 My first Richard III..turned out to be a wild *pot-pourri* of all the historical plays. **1921** H. Crane *Let.* 25 Dec. (1965) 75 We have a houseful of indiscriminate relatives and it has been hard to collect myself for even this potpourri. **1946** *R.A.F. Jrnl.* May 151 We blue-printed it as a *pot-pourri* of comment and opinion on Service life and manners. **1971** *World Archaeol.* III. 193 All the work, except firing, takes place..amid the characteristic potpourri of tools, vessels, mats and clutter found in such household work areas. **1977** *Time* 28 Feb. 8/2 The election of December 1973 split the Folketing among a potpourri of ten parties. **1978** F. Maclean *Take Nine Spies* ii. 49 A *pot-pourri* from Franz Lehar's latest opera.

4. *pot-pourri jar* (earlier example), *vase.*

1889 *Daily Tel.* 8 Mar. 3/3 There are some,..to whom the 'Two Roses' come as fresh as a bright June morning, ..but some there are who,..will find instead merely a 'pot-pourri' jar full of dried rose leaves. **1875** E. Meteyard *Wedgwood Handbk.* 407 Pot-Pourri Vases. Decorated vessels for containing rose leaves and other scents were formerly much used. **1957** Mankowitz & Haggar *Encycl. Eng. Pott. & Porc.* 162/1 Less frequent are such pieces as.. pot-pourri vases. **1974** Savage & Newman *Illustr. Dict. Ceramics* 230 *Pot-pourri vase,* a vase, sometimes richly mounted in gilt-bronze, which is characterized by pierced decoration on the shoulder or cover, or both.

potrero (potrē·ro). [Sp., f. Potro.] **1.** In the S.W. United States and South America, a paddock or pasture for horses or cattle.

1848 J. A. Sutter *New Helvetia Diary* (MS.) 7 Mar., 6 Men have been sent from the Race, on acct. having no tools, employed them to get the small potrero repaired. **1886** T. S. Van Dyke *Southern Calif.* viii. 106 When, in the heat of day, one comes to some little *potrero* where pine-clad hills inclose a soft green meadow, [etc.]. **1892** *Dialect Notes* I. 193 *Potréro*, a pasture, generally for colts and young horses. Also a piece of land easily fenced in, situated in the bend of a stream or in a valley with a narrow pass for entrance. **1923** C. F. Saunders *Southern Sierras Calif.* iii. 105 Ahead in the sun lay the Devil's *Potrero*—a verdant, wild-flowery bowl rimmed around with mountains. **1931** *Times Lit. Suppl.* 19 Mar. 214/2 He was found to be capable of milking exceptionally large numbers of untamed cows, which were driven straight from a 'potrero' into a 'corral'. **1933** A. F. Tschiffely *Tschiffely's Ride* (1934) 5 Large herds of cattle grazing in the 'potreros' (paddocks). **1950** H. Backhouse *Among Gauchos* xiii. 117 It is customary to kill and skin the cattle in the *consumo potrero* or paddock reserved for cattle that are to be slaughtered. **1960** G. J. Butland *Lat. Amer.* xx. 287 This is the Uruguayan pastoral region *par excellence*; a land of cattle and sheep estancias with paddocks or *potreros* fenced and managed to secure the best seasonal use of the grass.

2. In the S.W. United States, a narrow steep-sided plateau or mesa.

1872 J. G. Bourke *Diary* (MS.) 3 Dec., Hills break away in potreros. **1880** A. F. Bandelier *Southwestern Jrnls.* (1966) I. 135 There are three ruins—one, on the Potrero de las Vacas, about one day's journey northwest. **1890** —— in *Papers Archaeol. Inst. Amer.* IV. 158 These cliffs appear like pillars or gigantic posts; hence their Spanish name 'Potreros'. The one forming the southern wall of the Cuesta Colorada gorge is an extensive plateau called Potrero Chato. **1940** E. Fergusson *Our Southwest* xix. 354 A potrero is a narrow ridge between canyons, and a saddle is a sag between peaks. **1953** B. P. Dutton *Hewett's Pajarito Plateau* (ed. 2) III. iii. 104 The long, narrow potrero bounding the canyon on the north is entirely cut out for a distance of nearly a mile, thus throwing into one squarish open park the width of two small canyons and the formerly intervening mesa. **1966** in A. F. Bandelier *Southwestern Jrnls.* Gloss. 397 *Potrero*, pastureland; in New Mexico, a tongue of high ground.

po·t roast. orig. *U.S.* [f. Pot *sb.*[1] + Roast *sb.*] A piece of beef or other meat cooked slowly in a closed container. Also *attrib.*

1881 F. E. Owens *Cook Bk.* 59 Pot Roast of Beef. Get a solid piece from the round [etc.]. **1897** *Altrurian Cook Bk.* 38 (*heading*) Mutton Pot Roast. **1920** [see *Hamburger 2]. **1929** E. Wilson *I thought of Daisy* iv. 232 The dinner was an admirable pot-roast, with onions, potatoes, and carrots. **1936** L. C. Douglas *White Banners* iii. 59 'We've had breast of lamb three times in the past two weeks.'.. 'Sorry,' said Hannah. 'I'll have a pot roast to-morrow.' **1955** Priestley & Hawkes *Journey down Rainbow* 23 They are taking your order for Navy Bean soup and pot roast. **1964** *House & Garden* Nov. 100/3 Normandy pot roast chicken. *Ibid.* 100/4 French pot roast lamb. **1966** T. Pynchon *Crying of Lot 49* iv. 82 Negroes carried gunboats of mashed potatoes, spinach, shrimp, zucchini, pot roast, to the long, glittering steam tables. **1973** G. Sims *Hunters Point* vi. 49 Can you stay for lunch?.. Only a pot-roast but..I make it fairly tasty. **1976** *National Observer* (U.S.) 6 Nov. 14/2 The scent of pot roast coming to a climax would drive me wild. *Ibid.*, Ma!.. I'm *starving* for a pot roast sandwich.

Hence **po·t-roast** *v. trans.*, to cook (meat) in this way; **po·t-roasted** *ppl. a.*; **po·t-roasting** *vbl. sb.*

1917 M. Green *Better Meals* ii. 15 *Pot roasting* is cooking in an iron kettle or earthen pot in a small amount of water, after meat has been quickly browned... Cook slowly until very tender, with or without vegetables. **1945** *ABC of Cookery* (Ministry of Food) ix. 35 Pot Roasting. This is cooking meat in a little fat in a saucepan with the lid on. **1951** N. M. Gunn *Well at World's End* xvi. 124 A solid round of cold pot-roasted venison. **1954** *Good Housek. Cookery Book* (rev. ed.) 134/2 Pot-roasted ham. *Ibid.* 553 You can boil, stew, braise, or pot-roast the meat or bird. *Ibid.*, Use the rack when pot-roasting or boiling. **1964** *House & Garden* Nov. 100/1 If he intended to pot roast, he left the lid empty. **1972** *Guardian* 9 Aug. 9/6 Pot roasting, as everyone knows, keeps juices in joints and splashes of fat off oven sides. **1979** *Country Life* 13 Sept. 806/4 Chicken pot-roasted in a case of sea salt.

po·t-shoot, *v. U.S.* [On analogy with Pot-shot *sb.*[1]] *trans.* and *intr.* To take a pot-shot at (someone); to take pot-shots. Also *fig.* So **pot-shooter; pot-shooting** *vbl. sb.*

1907 C. E. Mulford *Bar-20* xxi. 209 One hundred paces makes fine pot-shooting. **1913** —— *Coming of Cassidy* ii. 31 He..resolved that he wouldn't take chances with a man who would pot-shoot. **1921** —— *Bar-20 Three* xiv. 166 I'm leavin' town. I ain't got a chance among buildin's again' pot-shooters. **1934** *Sun* (Baltimore) 16 Jan. 20/1 A Blue Eagle which drew the fire..of two hunters..brought the pot-shooters momentarily into the toils of the law. **1945** *Ibid.* 28 Nov. 1/5 What opposition has been sounded against the Socialists' proposals and the Socialists' shortcomings has been a matter of pot-shooting instead of an organized campaign. **1969** *English Jrnl.* Dec. 1309 The young men who have enjoyed pot-shooting policemen for the past few summers.

pot-shot, *sb.*[1] Add: **1.** (Further *transf.* examples.) Also, a random blow or punch.

1907 C. E. Mulford *Bar-20* iii. 31 A pot shot at Hopalong sent that gentleman's rifle hurtling to the ground. **1938** *Sun* (Baltimore) 28 Jan. 1/5 He pleaded guilty to firing two 'pot' shots into the back of a loaded school bus. **1950** J. Dempsey *Championship Fighting* x. 49 A pot-shot with your right. **1965** C. D. Eby *Siege of Alcázar* (1966) iii. 70 A drunken *miliciano*..took a pot shot at him. **1979** 'A. Blaisdell' *No Villain need Be* iii. 50 Some nut..taking potshots at couples in cars.

2. *fig.* **a.** *U.S.* A piece of criticism or verbal attack, freq. one which is random or opportunistic. **b.** A random attempt.

1926 *Forum* (N.Y.) Nov. 757 But I don't think much of the pot-shot method of refutation. **1927** *Christian Century* 7 July 828 Let him take lusty potshots, though, at some poor, prostrate ghost of bygone years, and he is hailed as brilliant, erudite, and—curiously—daring! **1942** Berrey & Van den Bark *Amer. Thes. Slang* §179/2 Potshot, shot in the dark, *a wild guess.* **1943** *Commonweal* 30 Apr. 46 It is not just that Mr. Willkie is taking pot-shots at the British Empire—and please let's not swell up with anti-British self-righteousness. **1949** *Kenyon Rev.* XI. 582 It was a time when 'the intellect was at the tips of the senses' and so on. Admittedly these are literary phrases, therefore a kind of pot shot at the real point, but they seem to me good ones. **1955** *Newsweek* 7 Mar. 71 The tobacco industry is leaving no radioisotope unturned to counter medical potshots at its product and to bolster sales. **1955** *Times* 20 June 3/4 Thus certain canvases are both pot-shots at the subject and pot-shots at pictures. **1971** A. & A. Silverman *Case against having Children* vi. 189 All we have done here is to take potshots at the Myth of the Working Mother.

Hence **po·t-shot** *v. trans.* and *intr.*, to take a pot-shot at (a target), to take pot-shots; **po·t-shotter; po·t-shotting** *ppl. a.* and *vbl. sb.*

1904 P. Fountain *Gt. North-West* iv. 27 The breech-loader is the weapon of the dandy pot-shotter. **1918** E. Pound *Let.* 16 Dec. (1971) 143 And what the deuce of your punctuation?.. How much deliberate, and therefore to be taken (by me) with studious meticulousness?? How much the fine careless rapture and therefore to be pot-shotted at until it assumes an wholly demonstrable or more obvious rightness???? **1923** Kipling *Irish Guards in Gt. War* II. 60 Snipers were forbidden to pot-shot until they could see a man's head. **1927** *Amer. Speech* III. 29 Right hand pot-shotters. **1942** Berrey & Van den Bark *Amer. Thes. Slang* § 394/3 *Careless person*, ..potshotter. *Ibid.* 435/7 *Potshotter*, one who shoots without taking aim. **1943** I. Wolfert *Battle for Solomons* v. 63 However, it is likely that the battle which started as an old-fashioned 'better 'ole' kind of war has now got even more old-fashioned and become a ruthless, tracking, potshotting, Indian kind of war. **1947** Harlow & Black *Pract. Public Relations* 179 Competing companies will make it their business to 'pot-shot' both purchasing and supplying organizations. **1950** *Atlantic Monthly* Apr. 21 What is really disturbing is the constant potshotting of the administrative departments from Capitol Hill. **1954** M. Cowley *Lit. Situation* x. 178 At last he is likely to decide that the expenses are beyond his powers of computation; he will simply pot-shot at them, hoping that his guess won't be implausible. **1954** *Time* 28 June 36/3 After six years of marriage and nearly five of potshotting between their armed camps, they braced for the show-down. **1966** H. Waugh *Pure Poison* vi. 41 She goes for the lunatic theory—like a sniper just potshotting anyone. **1970** *National Rev.* (U.S.) 30 June 685/2 Like Tocqueville, Tyrmand potshots, hit and miss, the trivial and mundane, filling space between profound insights.

potstick. Add: (Later examples.) Also, a stick used for moving washing about in a pot.

1894 S. R. Crockett *Lilac Sunbonnet* xxvii. 225 She turns roon' wi' the pat-stick i' her haund. **1903** Somerville & 'Ross' *All on Irish Shore* 9 He..had, in addition, boiled the meal for the hounds with a knowledge of proportion and an untiring devotion to the use of the pot-stick which produced 'stirabout' of a smoothness and excellence that Miss Barnet herself might have been proud of. **1922** Joyce *Ulysses* 223 Maggy at the range rammed down a greyish mass beneath bubbling suds twice with her potstick and wiped her brow. **1961** F. G. Cassidy *Jamaica Talk* v. 86 To stir cooking food one uses a *pot-stick*.

potsy (pǫ·tsi), *sb.* *Northeast U.S.* Also potsie. [Etym. obscure, but cf. *pot *sb.*[1] 11.] **1. a.** The object thrown in the game of the same name. **b.** The name of a children's game similar to hopscotch.

1931 *Recreation* Mar. 672/2 *Potsy* is an adaptation of Hop Scotch, which now rivals its progenitor in popularity. The 'potsy' is a piece of tin, a rock or a puck. **1932** *Sun* (N.Y.) 26 Mar. 18/3 As any New Yorker will recognize, the potsy refers to the piece of tin can, doubled and redoubled and stamped flat with the heel, which is kicked from flagstone to flagstone of the sidewalk by the hopping, juvenile player of the game potsy. **1943** B. SMITH *Tree grows in Brooklyn* xiii. 100 Potsy was a game that the boys started and the girls finished. A couple of boys would put a tin can on the car track and sit along the curb and watch with a professional eye as the trolley wheels flattened the can... Numbered squares were marked off on the sidewalk and the game was turned over to the girls who hopped on one foot pushing the potsy from square to square. **1955** P. M. EVANS *Hopscotch* 5 Then you feel around and pick up your potsie without opening your eyes. **1956** S. BELLOW *Seize the Day* iii. 61, I sat down for a while in a playground.. to watch the kids play potsy and skiprope. **1963** T. PYNCHON *V.* v. 117 'What are you guys doing,' Profane said, 'playing potsy?'

2. The badge worn by a policeman or fireman.

1932 *Sun* (N.Y.) 26 Mar. 18/3, I recently bought a Sun which gave a vocabulary of firemen's slang, in which 'potsy' was the word for 'badge'. I have also found policemen and detectives who referred to their badges in this manner. **1936** *Baltimore News-Post* 18 Apr. 18/2 Most detectives in town never polish their gold badges (yellow potsys). **1948** MENCKEN *Amer. Lang.* Suppl. II. 750 *Potsy*, a fireman's badge. **1952** *N.Y. Herald Tribune* 24 Jan. 27/1 This boniface has been wearing his potsy as house dick for only a brief time. **1970** L. SANDERS *Anderson Tapes* xiii. 39 Ernie goes in the lobby and flashes his potsy.

Pott (pǫt). *Med.* The name of Sir Percivall Pott (1713–88), English physician, used in the possessive to designate phenomena described by him, as **Pott's disease**, a form of paraplegia caused by tuberculous disease of the spine (described in *Med. & Philos. Commentaries* (1779) VI. 318–24); **Pott's fracture**, a fracture of the fibula close to the ankle, of a type described by Pott (in *Remarks on Fractures & Dislocations* (1769) 57–64) and due to eversion of the foot; *loosely*, any fracture of the lower fibula.

1835 *Lancet* 12 Sept. 775/1 Patients attacked by Pott's disease frequently die of other affections before the former has made much progress. **1897** T. L. STEDMAN *20th Cent. Pract.* XI. 600 The symptoms of Pott's disease may be divided into those referable to the diseased vertebræ, to the affected nerve roots of the spinal cord, and to the spinal cord itself. **1974** C. B. T. ADAMS in R. M. Kirk et al. *Surgery* xiv. 286 Tuberculosis (Pott's disease..of the spine) or a pyogenic extrathecal abscess may also cause cord compression. **1849** *Proc. Path. Soc. Dublin* II. 13 Mr Robert W. Smith exhibited a remarkable specimen of Pott's fracture, taken from the body of a man, aet. 70, who had lately died in the hospital of the South Union Poor House. **1884** W. PYE *Surg. Handicraft* xiv. 209 It may be doubted whether a true Pott's fracture is ever so perfectly recovered from, that the movements of the ankle are quite free, and no deformity is noticeable. **1922** *Arch. Surg.* IV. 56 Pott's fracture, as described and pictured by himself, is a primary, nearly transverse, fracture of the fibula, attended by a subsequently produced 'partial dislocation' of the ankle joint internally. **1950** J. G. BONNIN *Injuries to Ankle* viii. 174 It has been denied by Ashurst (1922) and others that Pott's fracture, as Pott described it, ever existed... Pott's name is used more generally now to cover all fractures of the ankle by indirect violence. **1962** *Surgery* LI. 284/2, I believe that term to any and all fractures of the ankle due to external the term 'Pott's fracture' should be applied as a generic rotation violence.

potted, *ppl. a.* Add: **1.** (Further examples.)

1922 JOYCE *Ulysses* 368 Potted herrings gone stale. **1922** J. BUCHAN *Huntingtower* iv. 69 There was new milk..and most of the dainties which had appeared at tea, supplemented by a noble dish of shimmering 'potted-head'. **1953** *Special Sci. Rep.: Fisheries* (U.S. Dept. Interior: Fish & Wildlife Service) No. 104. 31 'Potted tuna' consisted of chunks of tuna mixed with potatoes and carrots. **1960** E. DAVID *French Provincial Cooking* 221 As an alternative to a home-made pâté, *rillettes*, which might be described as a kind of potted pork, are quite easy to make at home. **1977** *Observer* 12 June 19/4 'I'm so excited,' she said, her expression as glazed as potted shrimp.

2. (Later examples.)

1939 A. H. WOOD *Grow them Indoors* p. xi, In Carpaccio's..painting of St. Ursula's vision, two potted plants appear in the window of her room. **1976** *Times* 1 Apr. 11/4 The gorgeous store..collapsed amid a welter of potted palms and recriminatory statements.

3. *fig.* **a.** Of a piece of information, work of literature, or historical or descriptive account: put into a short and easily assimilable form; condensed, summarized, abridged. Also *transf.*

1883, 1901 [in Dict., sense 1]. **1909** F. GARDNER *Pure Folly* i. 4 Pélissier..in April, 1907..produced his first 'potted play', which he described as 'Baffles: a Peter-Pan-tomime.' Needless to say, the skit was a blend of the two plays 'Raffles' and 'Peter Pan'. **1921** —— *Days & Ways* xi. 193 *The Whip, Faust* and *The Chocolate Soldier* were the most popular..'potted plays'. **1929** *Morning Post* 2 Oct. 11/7 Previously such questions had merely served as an excuse for potted lectures on the iniquity of the British position. **1937** 'A. BRIDGE' *Enchanter's Nightshade* 32 Those little potted abstracts for the general reader. **1946** *R.A.F. Jrnl.* May 146 A potted history of the *Journal* from its infancy up to this final issue. **1957** *Listener* 24 Oct. 642/1 Even potted biographies are now usually written by experts. **1966** *Ibid.* 23 June 921/3 Photographs of all the county teams, a list of records, potted careers of most of the current players, [etc.]. **1975** *Physics Bull.* May 225/1 The first chapter..attempts to provide a very potted treatment of transport theory.

b. = *CANNED *ppl. a.* b.

1928 *Melody Maker* Feb. 133/2 The delightful art of piano-playing..is in immediate danger of being usurped by the 'potted' music of wireless and gramophone. **1928** T. E. LAWRENCE *Let.* 23 Apr. (1938) 595 Only gramophone music, but the potted stuff is very well, for people away abroad. **1949** F. MACLEAN *Eastern Approaches* I. ii. 29 It was then that I grasped that the cheering was potted, synthetic cheering, issuing from loudspeakers.. and conveniently obviating the need for unhygienic, insecure spectators.

4. Of pottery or porcelain, with defining adv.: (well, beautifully, etc.) fashioned or manufactured.

1902 *Encycl. Brit.* XXXI. 874/2 The ware is thin, light, beautifully potted, and of the utmost durability. **1969** *Canad. Antiques Collector* Mar. 22/2 The earlier wares of the Koryo period are thinly potted and covered with the well known celadon glaze. **1972** *Country Life* 3 Feb. 273/3 A pair of K'ang Hsi parrots..on the whole more agreeable (no pink) and I thought better potted.

5. a. *N. Amer. slang.* Drunk, intoxicated.

1924 P. MARKS *Plastic Age* xiv. 149 I'd 'a' been potted about half the time. *Ibid.* xviii. 202, I don't get potted regularly. **1925** *College Humor* Aug. 125/2 Did I *ever* tell you to go getting potted like you were last night? **1943** *Sun* (Baltimore) 14 Aug. 6/4 Awful calamity at the Park bird bath..when somebody discovered the birds were potted due to some members of the Mint Julep Association having emptied their julep glasses in the fountain. **1959** *Amer. Speech* XXXIV. 156 Gators never merely drink; instead, they *sop*... They may later be.. *potted*. **1974** J. DOWELL *Look-off Bear* 90 He was potted, plastered, stinko.

b. *U.S. slang.* Under the influence of marijuana (cf. *POT *sb.*[5]).

1960 WENTWORTH & FLEXNER *Dict. Amer. Slang* 404/2 *Potted adj.*,.. 2 Under the influence of narcotics, esp. marijuana. **1968** BUSBY & HOLTHAM *Main Line Kill* v. 48 The Jamaicans..didn't appear to be potted. **1968–70** *Current Slang* (Univ. S. Dakota) III–IV. 95 *Potted, v.* High on marijuana... I was *potted* out of my mind yesterday. **1972** *Dict. Contemp. & Colloq. Usage* 22/3 *Potted*..under the influence of marijuana.

6. Of an electrical component or circuit: encapsulated in an insulating material (cf. *POT *v.*[1] 2 c).

1947 *Plastics* July 71/2 Several practical applications of resin-potted circuits at the Bureau have given operation comparable to that of conventionally constructed devices. **1950** W. W. STIFLER *High-Speed Computing Devices* xvi. 427 Mass production of potted plug-in units depends upon the development of complex process controls. **1955** *Brit. Plastics* XXVIII. 418/1 Extreme care must be exercised in..the removal of even traces of atmospheric moisture from the surface of the potted components. **1967** *Electronics* 6 Mar. 193/4 (Advt.), Special Assemblies. Rectifier stacks, potted bridges, [etc.].

potter, *sb.*[1] Add: **2.** Also, in northern England, a vagrant, a kind of tramp or gypsy.

1867 *Q. Rev.* CXXII. 378 The 'potters', a kind of indigenous gipsies, often curiously bearing the names of the great Northern families. **1885** *Specimens Westmoreland Dial.* 38 A com at a potter tent int' green lonnin. **1899** *West Cumberland Times* 28 Jan. 3/2 He had known the piece of waste... He had seen potters camping on it... You mean tramps or gipsies?—Yes, something of that kind. **1972** *Times Lit. Suppl.* 3 Mar. 245/3 The travellers and vagrants—gypsies, 'potters', pedlars, beggars, Irish labourers looking for work—who haunted.. the roads of Lakeland.

3. potter's (or **potters'**) **rot**, silicosis or other lung disease caused by the continued inhalation of dust in a pottery.

1908 T. OLIVER *Dis. of Occupation* x. 307 As far back as the days of Ramazzini (1670), the lung troubles of the potters had been recognised and described. With the terms 'potters' rot' and 'potters' asthma' the public are quite familiar. **1966** WRIGHT & SYMMERS *Systemic Path.* I. x. 405/1 Soon after calcined flint was introduced in the manufacture of porcelain, at about the middle of the 18th century, 'potter's rot' made its appearance among the workmen. **1972** G. WIGG *George Wigg* viii. 161 Silicosis, known in Stoke as 'potter's rot', was a scourge in Dudley.

potter, *sb.*[3] (in Dict. s.v. POTTER *v.*). Add: (Further examples.) Also, a gentle stroll or saunter. Also *fig.*

1901 'L. MALET' *Hist. R. Calmady* III. v. 210 But Camp, who missing Richard, had followed his mistress out of the house for a leisurely morning potter, turned back sulkily. **1949** E. BOWEN *Heat of Day* xiv. 248 A potter through the boundary woods. **1955** M. ALLINGHAM *Beckoning Lady* v. 84 The prospect of a glorious potter about was too much for Amanda. **1966** O. NORTON *School of Liars* vi. 91 He'll have to go pretty steadily. No worries. No real work. A good potter for about a month. **1972** Q. BELL *Virginia Woolf* I. ii. 33 Leslie's favourite exercise was walking; he would sometimes go for what he called 'a potter', covering thirty miles or so.

potter, *v.* Add: **5. a.** (Further examples.)

1860 G. H. LEWES *Jrnl.* 26 Sept. in *Geo. Eliot Lett.* (1954) III. 349 To-day..I wrote some letters and pottered. **1922** JOYCE *Ulysses* 737 He prefers pottering about the house. **1947** W. S. MAUGHAM *Creatures of Circumstance* 94 Then he would turn his business over to his son and retire with his wife to a little house in the country where he could potter about till death claimed him at a ripe old age. **1977** *Times* 7 Dec. 12/3 Randall.. pottered about for 26 in 1¾ hours before giving a catch to gully.

b. (Further examples.)

1857 T. HUGHES *Tom Brown's School Days* I. ii. 32 Past the old church and down the footpath, pottered the old man and the child hand-in-hand. **1903** G. B. SHAW *Man & Superman* IV. 162 Mrs Whitefield, who has been pottering round the Granada shops, and has a net full of little parcels in her hand, comes in through the gate and sees him. **1918** GALSWORTHY *Five Tales* 272 He.. pottered in and out of his dressing-room. **1932** E. WAUGH *Black Mischief* vii. 257 The Envoy Extraordinary finished his second cup of coffee, filled and lit his pipe, and avoiding the social life of the lawn, pottered round by the back way to the Chancery.

pottery. Add: **4. pottery clay** = *pot clay* s.v. POT *sb.*[1] 14 in Dict. and Suppl., *potter's clay* s.v. POTTER *sb.*[1] 3.

1905 *Geol. N. Staffs. Coalfields* (Mem. Geol. Survey) xii. 224 (*heading*) Pottery clays, brick clays and marls. **1921** *S.W. Coalfield* (Mem. Geol. Survey) XIII. xii. 169 The isolated Bovey Tracey Beds of Devon, consisting in part of pottery clays..are supposed to have been laid down in a small, local lake-basin. **1962** W. STEGNER *Wolf Willow* IV. ii. 250 Floods of settlers..all figured in the dream, as did..oil, pottery clay, glass sand, and other.. resources.

pottiness (pǫ·tinės). [f. *POTTY *a.* + -NESS.] The state or condition of being potty.

1933 WODEHOUSE *Heavy Weather* iii. 47 It was not primarily his pottiness that led him to steal the Empress. **1935** D. L. SAYERS *Gaudy Night* v. 98 We shall all feel perfectly ghastly wondering..whether our own conversation doesn't sound a little potty. It's the pottiness, you know, that's so awful. **1957** E. HYAMS *Into Dreams* 250 He..got an impression of pottiness from the old politician's smile. **1974** *Times* 17 Jan. 7/8 The dementia of children who threw themselves upon them [*sc.* a pop group] in an orgy of enslaved pottiness. **1976** K. BONFIGLIOLI *Something Nasty in Woodshed* i. 15 This inability to see any flaws in oneself is a branch of pottiness.

potting, *vbl. sb.*[1] Add: **2.** (Further examples.)

1970 [see *MING b]. **1976** P. FLOWER *Crisscross* i. 6 How Sibyl loved it all: calling meetings..in between her potting.

3. c. *Woollen Manufacture.* (See quots.)

1920 J. M. MATTHEWS *Application of Dyestuffs* i. 66 An operation very similar to that of decatizing is known as potting. This is a treatment of woollen goods with steam and hot water for the purpose of producing a particular character of finish. **1927** HORSFALL & LAWRIE *Dyeing of Textile Fibres* ix. 275 Potting. This process is applied to fabrics of the faced type... The cloth is wound..on to a perforated roll which..is placed upright in a cistern in cold water. **1951** *Rev. Textile Progress* II. 329 Blowing..does not yield such good results as potting, *i.e.*, winding the cloth on a roller and heating it in water at about 160°F. for periods varying from a few hours to four days. **1961** BLACKSHAW & BRIGHTMAN *Dict. Dyeing* 137 *Potting*, a finishing process for wool cloths in which a roll of fabric is treated in water at 70–100°C. for several hours, then allowed to cool slowly, and finally immersed in cold water to set the fabric.

d. The act or process of abridging, condensing, or summarizing.

1909 *Daily Chron.* 20 Oct. 1/6 Drury Lane Dignity is down on Apollo Impudence for using the title of 'The Whip' in the 'potting' department of 'The Follies', and the seriousness of the whole business is expressed in Mr. Pelissier's startled cry to the British public: 'Hurry up! We have had a letter from Messrs. Hamilton and Raleigh's solicitors objecting to our burlesque of 'The Whip', so we may be locked up at any moment.' **1966** *Punch* 9 Oct. 521/3 The enormous subject is covered by rapid potting... The potting is efficient: the course of the 1914–18 War on the Western Front..is explained with much greater clarity than usual.

5. b. *dial.* The catching of lobsters in pots.

1971 *Nat. Geographic* Apr. 556/2 We were out potting. Potting? Lobstering, bringing in the pots.

6. b. *Billiards.* The act or process of knocking a ball into one of the pockets.

1909 in *Cent. Dict.* Suppl. **1935** *Encycl. Sports* 571/1 The practical application of this knowledge will make potting easy for many who find it inordinately difficult. **1950** *Hoyle's Games Modernized* (ed. 20) III. 340 The most successful [pool] player is not necessarily he who can 'pot' with the deadliest accuracy, but he who combines potting with effectively playing for position. **1956** E. GRIERSON *Second Man* iv. 59 Gilroy put an exquisite edge on his potting, though he did have a tendency to overdo it and go in off.

6*. Encapsulation of a circuit or component in an insulating material (cf. *POT *v.*[1] 2 c). Freq. *attrib.*

1947 *Plastics* July 57/1 During the war, exacting mechanical and electrical stability requirements of special electronic applications..necessitated the potting of the circuit components. **1955** *Rep. Progress Appl. Chem.* XL. 508 A typical potting resin comprises a mixture of 2:4-toluylene diisocyanate (20–40%), monomeric styrene (up to 10%), and castor oil, lactic acid being used as a catalyst. **1962** M. C. VOLK et al. *Electr. Encapsulation* i. 5 Potting is the simplest cavity-filling process. Procedure consists of positioning the component in its container ('pot'), adding encapsulant to fill the pot, then curing to polymerize or harden the encapsulant.

6.** The action or an instance of causing a baby or young child to sit on a chamber-pot.

1948 *Practitioner* Dec. 505 It is as well that the infant should suffer the experience of 'potting' quite early, and should come to appreciate that the environment reacts less encouragingly to random disposal of excreta than to its opposite. **1953** R. S. Illingworth *Normal Child* xxvii. 283 Provided that there is never a fight to keep the child on the chamber and the child does not resist, 'potting' is a harmless procedure. **1958** *Observer* 20 Apr. 8/4 Much else that controverts the views of Sir Truby King, and his 'Mothercraft' disciples, on early potting, bodily guilt, schedule feeding. **1960** *Guardian* 1 Apr. 7/1, I attended to the telephone, 'potting' of small child, and comforting child after fall. **1967** *Ibid.* 1 May 4/4 The job extends to getting the children up... No doubt the next 10 years will see minor changes—no more potting, for example. **1972** J. Gathorne-Hardy *Rise & Fall of Brit. Nanny* viii. 265 Nearly incessant potting..produces a high..quota of wins.

7. *potting bench, business, compost, -shed* (examples), *soil*; **potting-pot** (earlier example).

1874 *Gardeners' Chron.* 17 Jan. 95/3 A movable wooden tray, shaped like the top of a potting bench..will answer the purpose. **1935** A. G. L. Hellyer *Pract. Gardening* xxx. 185 (*caption*) The principal ingredients may well be stored in bins under the potting bench. **1766** J. Wedgwood *Let.* 15 Sept. (1965) 42 As our connections are to become extensive in the Potting business, it is absolutely necessary you should visit the Manufacture. **1916** M. Hampden *Flower Culture* ii. 38 Silver sand and old manure, chopped fine, may make up one part of the ordinary potting compost. **1971** P. D. James *Shroud for Nightingale* vi. 183 There were balls of green twine,..packets of seed,..a small plastic bag of potting compost and one of fertilizer. **1976** J. Berrisford *Backyards & Tiny Gardens* xv. 107 Bedding plants do well also in John Innes potting compost No. 2. **1739** E. Smith *Compl. Housewife* (ed. 9) 52 *Mackrel to pot*.. place them close in your potting-pots, and pour clarified butter on the top. **1874** *Gardeners' Chron.* 17 Jan. 95/3 The manure and compost yard should include a potting shed. **1902** W. B. Yeats *Where there is Nothing* (1903) I. 14 Come over here to the potting shed. **1907** E. Gosse *Father & Son* vii. 181 My Father would..bolt.. round the garden into the potting-shed. **1940** J. Betjeman *Old Lights for New Chancels* 48 Back down the Avenue, back to the pottingshed. **1976** *Derbyshire Times* (Peak ed.) 3 Sept. 18/1 (Advt.), Detached garage, well-established gardens to front and rear, potting shed. **1908** *Daily Chron.* 29 Feb. 9/1 This material [*sc.* manure from mushroom growing] is in excellent condition for mixing with potting soil as a fertiliser. **1936** *Forestry* X. 12 The potting soil used was a standard mixture.

potty (pǫ·ti), *a. colloq.* [f. Pot *sb.*[1] + -y[1].]

1. a. As a general term of disparagement: indifferent, feeble; petty, insignificant, esp. in *potty little*.

1860 Hotten *Dict. Slang* (ed. 2) 193 *Potty*, indifferent, bad looking. [*ed. 3* (*1864*), indifferent, bad looking,—said of a rotten or unsound scheme.] **1870** *Times* 12 Aug. 10/3 Then came a single, and then a catch from a 'potty' hit. **1899** E. Phillpotts *Human Boy* 72 It is such a potty little place, hardly worth calling a wood. **1904** Kipling *Traffics & Discov.* 270 'Think they'll take you an' your potty quick-firers? **1907** Galsworthy *Country House* III. iv. 246 We stand on our petty rights here, And our potty dignity there. **1927** Chesterton *Secret of Father Brown* v. 178 Who would, or could, have killed him up in that potty little place? **1930** —— *Four Faultless Felons* 236 It was within reasonable distance of revolution; not a potty little palace revolution. **1939** G. B. Shaw *Geneva* III. 57 What I think of the mob of bagmen from fifty potty little foreign states that calls itself a League of Nations. **1980** 'M. Innes' *Going it Alone* xx. 178 They've..smashed their way in. Just the idea I had with that potty little motor-mower.

b. Easy to manage, accomplish, or deal with; easy, simple.

1899 E. Phillpotts *Human Boy* 127 Ferrars..got regularly muddled over a potty question about Jacob. **1916** E. F. Benson *David Blaize* iv. 70 It was quite certain that Helmsworth would have won had not that ass Blazes..dropped the 'pottiest' catch ever seen. **1922** *Blackw. Mag.* July 55/2 It's potty on this scaffolding.., no end of cross-pieces to hold on to.

2. a. Crazy, mad; out of one's senses; eccentric, 'dotty'.

1920 *Cornh. Mag.* Jan. 7 Next day, at tea time, the producer of the comedy solemnly thanked Jess for saving a situation past praying for... In your potty part, you put 'em all to bed. How did you do it? **1921** *Chambers's Jrnl.* July 511/2 Pull yourself together. You'll be going potty if you don't get a move on. **1925** *Punch* 7 Jan. 7 Hear about Mary, Mums? Gone potty! Broke off her engagement 'cos her people disapproved. **1929** W. Faulkner *Sartoris* III. 170 Aunt Sally, a potty little woman. **1930** 'R. Crompton' *William the Bad* iv. 113 'I don't know what you're talking about,' she said. 'You seem to me quite potty today.' **1942** *Sun* (Baltimore) 25 July 8/1 Confronted, in the final scene, with the prospect of winning and wedding this incurably potty creature, he lets out an anguished yawp. **1952** [see *Baconian *a.* and *sb.* 2]. **1960** *Times* 21 Sept. 3/7, I realized Floss had put the boot in. I have been going potty about this. When I 'jumped' him we didn't mean to kill or hurt him. **1976** K. Bonfiglioli *Something Nasty in Woodshed* i. 19 Violet's mother..is, I suppose, either potty or an alcoholic. **1977** *Daily Mirror* 12 Apr. 17/1 He played the joyously potty day-dreamer.

b. Madly in love; mad *about*, gone *on* (someone or something).

1923 E. V. Lucas *Advisory Ben* xxxix. 206 I'm potty about her. **1926** *Punch* 8 Dec. 622/3, I suppose you're potty about the poor fish? **1928** 'R. Crompton' *William—the Good* ix. 228 'Hector's potty on her too,' said Ginger. **1930** A. P. Herbert *Water Gipsies* xx. 292 Jane..confessed to herself that she was mad about Mr. Bryan—just potty. **1975** *Reveille* 20 June 11/7 Women are potty about pans—they can't resist buying them.

Hence **po·ttily** *adv.*

1977 *Times Lit. Suppl.* 3 June 686/3 Contributors to anthologies can pursue minor themes more selectively, if occasionally pottily.

potty (pǫ·ti), *sb.* Also **pottie.** [f. Pot *sb.*[1] + -y[6].] A nursery word for a chamber-pot; occas. applied also to a lavatory.

1942 Berrey & Van den Bark *Amer. Thes. Slang* §84/14 *Chamber pot*,..potty. **1952** C. Hayes in S. Rogers *Children & Language* (1975) iv. 283 Don't flush the soap down the potty, dear. **1959** *Observer* 22 Mar. 21/5 Pram bedding, waterproof sheets, potties. **1960** S. Foot *Emergency Exit* ii. 20 Awful little bedside tables which.. have place for potty. **1960** *News Chron.* 20 Aug. 6/8 Granny soaking her corns and Baby..shaking his pottie. **1966** Auden *About House* 26 Lifted off the potty, Infants from their mothers Hear their first impartial Words of worldly praise. **1976** *Milton Keynes Express* 4 June 22/3 (Advt.), White baby bath and potty, £1.25.

2. *attrib.* and *Comb.*, as **potty-chair**, a child's commode; **potty-mouth** *U.S.* (see quot. 1968–70); **potty-seat** = **potty-chair*; **potty-training** *vbl. sb.*, the training of a child to use a chamber-pot; also *fig.*; hence (as a back-formation) **potty-train** *v.*; **potty-trained** *ppl. a.*

1961 Webster, Potty-chair. **1965** M. Shadbolt *Among Cinders* ii. 11 The only thing I really saw was a little kid's potty-chair. **1977** *Time* 19 Sept. 41/3 The junk in his basement, including 'one used potty-chair, a tricycle with no handle bars, one broken ski, an old doorknob and six bags of leaves'. **1968–70** *Current Slang* (Univ. S. Dakota) III–IV. 95 *Potty mouth, n.* A person who repeatedly uses foul language. **1976** *Time* 10 May 79/2 Potentially even more annoying is the widespread abuse of the channels—especially by so-called potty mouths using obscenities. **1961** L. Mumford *City in Hist.* Note to plate 10, Full of objects that bring the daily life near, from a clay sausage-griddle to a ceramic potty-seat with holes for the child's legs. **1974** E. Tidyman *Dummy* xiv. 195 He did go to school for a while, but..he wasn't potty trained at the time. **1978** F. Weldon *Praxis* xxii. 211 Justin was not, as they said in the nursery world, 'potty-trained'. **1958** R. Martin *Before the Baby—and After* xiii. 274 The number of modern young mothers who have erroneous views on 'potty' training is amazing. **1969** *New Scientist* 13 Mar. 31/1 There is no necessary link between outstanding cleanliness and tidiness and outstanding research work. Strict potty-training is not the key to the Royal Society. **1978** P. O'Donnell *Dragon's Claw* xii. 262, I expect you suffered from poor potty training as a baby.

potzer (pǫ·tsəɹ). *U.S. slang.* = *patzer.

1948 *Chess Rev.* Apr. 5/2 Immediately, spectators inquired, 'Didn't you see that win?' 'Yes,' was the impudent reply. 'But, with such a potzer, I draw when I will, not when he wills.' **1962** *Chess* 12 Mar. 190/1 When I meet these Russian potzers I'll put them in their place. **1966** *New Yorker* 12 Nov. 70/1 He was at work on what in the language of the park is called a 'potzer'—a relatively weak player with an inflated ego. **1970** J. Hansen *Fadeout* (1972) v. 41 'Do you..play chess, Mr... Brand.. stetter?' 'I'm what's called a potzer.'

pou, var. Pouw (in Dict. and Suppl.).

pouch, *sb.* Add: **1. e.** (Earlier example.)

1879 *Post Master General's Rep.* in *Parl. Papers 1878–9* (C. 2405) XXI. 197 The..number of pouches exchanged with these Travelling Post Offices..in 24 hours is now 1090.

f. = *diplomatic bag* s.v. *diplomatic *a.* and *sb.* A. 3.

1958 L. Durrell *Mountolive* vi. 140 When the Syrians want to be clever, they don't use a diplomatic courier; they confide their pouch to a lady, the vice-consul's niece. **1967** M. Childs *Taint of Innocence* iv. 240 He put the locked briefcase on Wyant's desk. 'Watrous said he thought you wouldn't mind sending it back to him by pouch.' **1968** D. Torr *Treason Line* 163 I've been down here for the past hour checking the airgrams for the Washington pouch. **1974** *Lebende Sprachen* XIX. 39/2 US *pouch*—BE/US *diplomatic bag.* Kuriersack, -tasche.

3. c. = *bag *sb.* 12 c.

1928 J. Buchan *Runagates Club* iv. 134 There were dark pouches under his eyes. *a* **1953** E. O'Neill *Hughie* (1959) 8 His blue eyes have drooping lids and puffy pouches under them. **1980** P. Harcourt *Tomorrow's Treason* I. ii. 37 Pouches under his eyes as if he hadn't slept.

pouch, *v.* Add: **1. c.** *Cricket.* To catch (the ball); also with the batsman as object.

1910 A. A. Milne *Day's Play* 114, I heard Slip call 'Mine' and he pouched the ball. **1963** *Times* 13 June 13/3 A series of pulls which ended with a catch at the wicket would appear in this form: 'After several cow-shots into the Great Beyond, Basher was neatly pouched by the timber-watcher.' **1970** *Times* 12 Jan. 7/7 Neither catch that Fletcher dropped was at all easy, but..Bobby Simpson or Philip Sharpe might well have pouched them both.

pouched, *a.* Add: **4.** *pouched mouse*, a small Australian marsupial resembling a mouse, belonging to the family Dasyuridæ, esp. the genera *Antechinus* and *Sminthopsis*; also called kangaroo-mouse.

1888 O. Thomas *Catal. Marsupialia in Brit. Mus.* 287 Little Pouched Mouse. Size rather small, general form murine. **1896** F. G. Aflalo *Sk. Nat. Hist. Austral.* II. 28 In some of the pouched mice, the tribal badge is either replaced by a mere fold of bristles or else entirely wanting. **1907** P. Fountain *Rambles Austral. Naturalist* vi. 60 The pouched-mouse varies its habits with its locality. **1942** C. Barrett *On Wallaby* iii. 40 There are perhaps a dozen kinds of pouched-mice, all Australian natives. **1970** W. D. L. Ride *Guide Native Mammals Austral.* viii. 112 Kowari, Byrne's Pouched Mouse, *Dasyuroides byrnei.* Central Australia..; desert associations and grasslands.

poudre (pudr'). *Canad.* [Fr. *poudre* powder.] Light, powdery snow, = *powder snow. *poudre day*, a day on which light, fine snow falls.

1791 E. P. Simcoe *Diary* 31 Dec. (1911) 71 There is little wind here, except with a snowstorm of fine snow. The French call it poudre or powdered snow, and to travel with that blowing in one's face is very disagreeable. **1873** W. F. Butler *Wild North Land* xiv. 152 The sun, which on one of these 'poudre' days in the North seems to exert as much influence upon the war of cold and storm as some good bishop in the Middle Ages was wont to exercise over the belligerents at Cressy or Poictiers.. muffled himself up in the nearest cloud and went fast asleep until the fight was over. **1901** G. Parker *Right of Way* 83 It was a goodly scene..the flowery tracery of frost hanging like cobwebs everywhere; the poudre sparkle in the air. **1951** W. O'Meara *Grand Portage* xxxiii. 214 It was a real 'poudre day'. Only a few inches of dry, fine snow lay on the prairie.

‖ **poudré** (pudre), *a.* Fem. **poudrée.** [Fr.] Powdered, *spec.* of the hair or a wig.

1827 Disraeli *Viv. Grey* III. v. vi. 104 A little old, odd-looking man, with a very *poudré* head, and dressed in a costume in which the glories of the vieille cour seemed to retire with reluctance. **1852** E. Ruskin *Let.* 24 Feb. in M. Lutyens *Effie in Venice* (1965) II. 278 Marmont poudré welcomed me. **1906** Beerbohm *Around Theatres* (1924) II. 243 Poudrée, she sings of Brittany; and in a crinoline she warbles of Parthenay. **1909** A. Lancastre Saldanha *Recoll.* iv. 34 My hair was exquisitely *poudré.*

‖ **poudreuse** (pudrøz). [Fr.] A lady's dressing table of a kind made in France in the time of Louis XV (see quot. 1966).

1929 V. Woolf *Let.* 5 May (1978) IV. 54 There are two pieces of furniture I must buy, so do mark them down—one a poudreuse, not necessarily in good condition. **1929** G. G. Gould *Period Furnit. Handbk.* vi. 82 *Toilette-coiffeuse*, especially for powdering, new in *Régence*; later popular as *poudreuse.* **1936** *Burlington Mag.* Aug. 88/2 *Berceuses* or *poudreuses* show the delicate outlines of the curved ornament of the French cabinet-makers. **1947** *Antique Dealer* Jan. 34 (*caption*) Louis XV Poudreuse by E. J. Gibrekyer. **1959** *House & Garden* Dec.–Jan. 27/1 The so-called *poudreuse* (dreadful word) with twin adjustable mirrors and pivoting cosmetic trays. **1960** *Times* 21 June 22/7 A Louis XV marquetry poudreuse. **1966** M. M. Pegler *Dict. Interior Design* (1967) 351 *Poudreuse*, a lady's powder or toilet table, often equipped with a mirrored lid in the center which lifts up. A Louis XV period innovation. **1973** *Country Life* 13 Dec. 32f (Advt.), An early 19th century Austrian mahogany poudreuse.

pouf[1]. Add: **2.** (Later examples.) Also *attrib.*

1906 *Queen* 28 Apr. p. viii/3 A quaint pouf sleeve. **1976** *State Jrnl.* (Lansing, Mich.) 11 July D 1/6 Designed with deep *pouf* sleeves. **1977** *New Yorker* 11 July 84/3 Noelle demonstrates her virginal contempt by choosing a white strapless evening dress with a pouf of fabric.

3. Now usu. a low stuffed or padded seat or cushion. (Further examples.)

1919 'C. Dane' *Legend* 32 Mrs Howe was in the chair... The Baxter girl crouched on the pouf. **1925** C. S. Taylor *Pract. Upholstery* xi. 96 The pouffe, or floor cushion, is much in favour. **1949** A. Christie *Crooked House* xiv. 106 Roger was astride a big pouffé [*sic*] by the fireplace. **1956** M. Shulman in *Good Housekeeping* July 51/2 You rented an apartment in Greenwich village and sat on a pouf. **1962** A. Sampson *Anat. Brit.* I. i. 22 Between the two sides is something which looks like a huge red pouff, with a back-rest in the middle of it: this is 'the Woolsack'. **1968** C. M. Vines *Little Nut-Brown Man* iii. 58 He held out the cutting towards me, down to where I was sitting on the pouffe, his thumbnail indicating a line of it. **1974** S. Coulter *Château* II. vi. 281 This little room..stuffed with Algerian poufs and cushions and ottomans.

pouf[2], var. *poof *sb.*[1]

pouf(f, poufter, varr. Poof *int.*, *sb.*[2] and *v.* in Dict. and Suppl., *poofter.

poughite (pōu·əit). *Min.* [f. the name of Frederick H. *Pough* (b. 1906), U.S. mineralogist + -ite[1].] An iron tellurite, $Fe_2(TeO_3)_2(SO_4)\cdot 3H_2O$, found as yellow orthorhombic crystals.

1968 R. V. Gaines in *Amer. Mineralogist* LIII. 1075 In 1944..Frondel and Pough mentioned a further new iron tellurite from Honduras... This mineral had first been observed by Dana and Wells in 1890 and thought to be tellurite... Its macroscopic definition [etc.]..enabled the author to establish its identity with material found at the Moctezuma mine in Sonora, Mexico. The name poughite is proposed for this new mineral. **1968** I. Kostov *Mineral.* 518 Poughite is orthorhombic..with perfect 010 cleavage.

poui (*pu*·i). Also pui. [Local name in Trinidad.] A tree belonging to the genus *Tabebuia*, of the family Bignoniaceæ, esp. *T. rosea*, the pink poui, and *T. serratifolia*, the yellow poui, native to the West Indies and Central America, and bearing terminal clusters of trumpet-shaped flowers; also, the wood of this tree.

1864 A. H. R. GRISEBACH *Flora Brit. W. Indian Islands* 787 *Tecoma serratifolia* Pony [*sic*]. **1924** RECORD & MELL *Timbers Trop. Amer.* II. 541 The 'pui' or 'poui'..is one of the best known timbers of Trinidad. **1939** R. C. MARSHALL *Silviculture of Trees of Trinidad & Tobago* 182 One frequently comes across patches of young poui in the forest. **1952** S. SELVON *Brighter Sun* i. 5 In April..pouis blossomed and keskidees sang for rain. **1962** *Times* 31 Aug. (Trinidad Suppl.) p. iv/4 The visitor will see some of the most lovely flowering trees and shrubs in the world—the bougainvillaea, the clear clean beauty of the yellow and pink poui. **1968** E. LOVELACE *Schoolmaster* I. i. 7 The poui is dropping rich yellow flowers. **1973** E. G. B. GOODING *Wayside Trees & Shrubs of Barbados* 94 The Yellow Poui was introduced into Barbados early this century.

Pouilly (pūiyi). Also with small initial. Any of various dry white wines produced in central France and named after villages called *Pouilly*, *spec.* (*a*) in full *Pouilly Fumé* (füme), that produced near Pouilly-sur-Loire in the Nièvre department; (*b*) in full *Pouilly-Fuissé* (fwīse), a white Burgundy produced near Pouilly-sous-Charlieu in the Mâcon region of the Loire department.

[**1814** M. BIRKBECK *Notes Journey through France* I. 29 Pouilly, [renowned] for its Vin Blanc.] **1833** C. REDDING *Hist. Mod. Wines* v. 160 Cosne is best known for its white wines called Pouilly, in considerable repute in Paris. **1924** D. H. LAWRENCE *Let.* 29 Oct. (1962) II. 816 Dinner at Coyoacán, and drank absinthe, gin, pouilly, chablis, beaune, port and whisky from beginning to end of an evening, and was not comforted. **1927** [see *MOULIN-À-VENT]. **1935** M. MORPHY *Recipes of All Nations* 104 The Pouilly comes from Saône-et-Loire: it is usually sold as Pouilly-Fuissé to differentiate it from the white wines of Pouilly-sur-Loire, sold as Pouilly-Fumé. **1942** E. PAUL *Narrow St.* i. 4 Noël pointed out to me once, over a bottle of Pouilly, that men and women, like gods, choose pets in their own image. **1952** W. PLOMER *Museum Pieces* 117 A cut of salmon, some wisps of chicken, a bottle of Pouilly. **1959** E. LINKLATER *Merry Muse* iv. 81 The fish and the Pouilly fumé were succeeded by a bevy of partridges and a tenderly decanted Léoville Poyferré of 1947. **1976** *Times* 20 Mar. 3/3 (Advt.), Mâcon Blanc, a dry, very fruity wine, typified by Pouilly-Fuissé and St. Véran.

Poujadism (pū·ʒādiz'm). Also with lower-case initial. [ad. Fr. *Poujadisme* (also used): see below.] The mainly reactionary and conservative political philosophy and methods advocated by Pierre *Poujade* (b. 1920), French publisher and bookseller, who in 1954 founded a movement for the protection of artisans and small shopkeepers (Union de Défense des Commerçants et Artisans), protesting chiefly against the French tax system then in force. Also in extended and allusive applications of similar movements acting in the interests of small-scale commercial enterprise.

1955 *Life* 18 Apr. 63/1 The mushrooming political strength of Poujadism last month forced Premier Edgar Faure's government to promise sweeping exemptions to the small shopkeepers. **1957** *Times Lit. Suppl.* 11 Oct. 607/2 The work of Chancellor Maupeou was undone..and what was no better than an aristocratic form of Poujadism grew in power of mischief. **1961** *Listener* 7 Sept. 337/1 France presents the contrast between a strongly proletarian industrial society and a peasantry that finds its sporadic expression in Poujadism or the recent Breton uprisings. **1964** *Economist* 1 Feb. 429/1 The ensuing process of concentration in commerce and industry..contributed to the political spread of *poujadisme* in the next few years. **1970** *Rev. Politics* XXXII. 174 Once organized Poujadism began its spread throughout France, it shared its founder's preoccupation with class defense. **1974** tr. *Wertheim's Evolution & Revolution* 149 Poujadism in France and the Farmers' Party in the Netherlands have..been openly conservative or even reactionary. **1976** *Times* 9 Feb. 13/4 The small business sector..is surely the very class which in other countries has..turned to 'poujadism'.

Hence **Pou·jadist**, an advocate or supporter of Poujadism; also *attrib.* or as *adj.*; **Poujadi·stic** *a.*

1957 *Observer* 27 Oct. 13/2 Miss S. is not irresponsible, not a Poujadist... But the spirit of Poujadism is awake... 'The Liberal vote is a "Poujadist", disgruntlement vote.' **1958** *Economist* 6 Dec. 867/1 Electing poujadists under the name of conservatives does not mean a change. **1960** *20th Cent.* Apr. 302 In France there is a strong Poujadist element; small shopkeepers, small factory owners, the depressed bourgeoisie. **1962** *Daily Tel.* 25 June 10/2 Unless Britain is going to become Poujadist in the full sense—that is, inimical to all politicians as such—then the electorate will have to accept the sense expressed by the Prime Minister. **1967** M. DOGAN in Lipset & Rokkan *Party Syst. & Voter Alignments* iv. 181 The Poujadistic social epidemic spread particularly in the small sleepy towns. **1972** *New Statesman* 28 Jan. 100/2 Another mass movement of angry shopkeepers, the Poujadist wave of the 1950s. **1977** *Guardian Weekly* 27 Feb. 8/3 The Poujadist Progress party, led by Mr Mogens Glistrup, the controversial Copenhagen tax-lawyer, is once again the second largest party with 26 seats.

‖**poule**² (pul). [Fr., = 'hen'.] **1.** *poule au pot*, in Gastronomy, a boiled chicken casserole. Also *fig.*

1884 N. LAKE *Menus made Easy* iv. 99 A fowl boiled and served with Bourgeoise sauce is called *Poule au pot*. **1930** M. T. & L. BONNEY *French Cooking for Eng. Kitchens* vii. 150 The Poule au Pot has as dignified a place on a menu as the Poussin. **1962** *Harper's Bazaar* Dec. 97/1 Chicken served as *poule au pot*. **1971** A. MIZENER *Saddest Story* xxxii. 433 An absolute monarchy committed to all Ford's favorite Tory doctrines—the *poule au pot* of the French peasant instead of the 'boiled fowls out of a pot that is no pot but a can' of American mass production.

2. *slang.* A girl or young woman, esp. one regarded as being promiscuous. Also *poule-de-luxe*, a prostitute.

1926 E. HEMINGWAY *Sun also Rises* iii. 14 The *poules* going by, singly and in pairs. **1937** [see *CHICHI *sb.*² and *a.*]. **1946** 'S. RUSSELL' *To Bed with Grand Music* vi. 87 All I know of the tricks used by poules-de-luxe. **1949** J. B. PRIESTLEY *Home is Tomorrow* 43 He is probably amusing himself somewhere with that little brown poule of his. **1955** D. BARTON *Glorious Life* i. 12 'If I had thought she would have understood,' said Swindlehurst, 'I would have called her to her face "the typing *poule*".' **1958** L. DURRELL *Mountolive* v. 102, I answer him in the voice of a *poule* from the Midi. **1976** *Times Lit. Suppl.* 24 Sept. 1213/3 Returns to France to find that his wife has remarried and that his daughter is in business as a *poule de luxe* and doing very well. **1979** *Ibid.* 23 Nov. 14/5 The archimandrite who regularly used the express between Sofia and Belgrade to entertain his *poules*.

poulet. Add: **2.** A chicken or a chicken dish, esp. in French Gastronomy.

The spelling in quot. 1840 represents a jocular anglicization.

1840 THACKERAY *Barber Cox* in *Comic Almanack* 213 Eating, for my share,..a pully bashymall, and other French dishes. **1861** MRS. BEETON *Bk. Househ. Managem.* xxi. 474 *Poulet aux cressons*... A fowl, a large bunch of water-cresses, 3 tablespoonfuls of vinegar, ¼ pint of gravy. **1894** G. DU MAURIER *Trilby* II. v. 111 A delightful little Franco-Italian pothouse near Leicester Square, where they had..a *poulet rôti*, which is *such* a different affair from a roast fowl! **1900** C. M. YONGE *Mod. Broods* xiii. 120 Here are eggs, and some milk..four *poulets*, such as they are. **1933** D. C. PEEL *Life's Enchanted Cup* viii. 87 She made a delicious *Poulet Marengo* with a suspicion of garlic in it. **1957** P. WILDEBLOOD *Main Chance* 53 The pressure cooker burst... It suddenly went off bang and threw bits of *poulet en cocotte* all over the place like confetti. **1978** *Chicago* June 218/2 Poulet Provençal ($6.50) comes with pearl onions, fresh mushrooms, olives, tomato purée.

‖**poulette** (pulet). [Fr. *poulette* young hen.] In full, *poulette sauce*. In French Gastronomy, a sauce made with butter, cream and egg-yolks.

1813 L. E. UDE *French Cook* 389 The *poulette* is made with a little *sauce tournée*, which you reduce, and next thicken with the yolks of two eggs, to which you add a little parsley chopped very fine. **1877** E. S. DALLAS *Kettner's Bk. of Table* 376 *Poulette Relish*..consists of shalots and mushrooms passed in butter, and served with chopped parsley in a Poulette sauce. **1907** A. ESCOFFIER *Guide Mod. Cookery* iii. 42 *Poulette Sauce.* Boil for a few minutes one pint of Sauce Allemande, and add six tablespoonfuls of mushroom liquor. Finish..with two oz. of butter, a few drops of lemon-juice, and one teaspoonful of chopped parsley. **1957** M. MCCARTHY *Memories Catholic Girlhood* viii. 204 Sweetbreads, with patty shells, and with a poulette sauce. **1977** ROSSANT & DAVIS tr. *Bocuse's New Cuisine* 330 *Poulette Sauce*..butter..flour..bouillon..mushroom.

Poulsen arc (pō͞u·lsĕn āɹk). [Named after its inventor, Valdemar *Poulsen* (1869–1942), Danish electrical engineer.] An arc discharge between a carbon electrode and a water-cooled copper electrode operated in an atmosphere of hydrogen or hydrocarbon vapour and a strong magnetic field in order to make possible the emission of waves short enough to be used for radiotelegraphy.

1906 *Electrician* 21 Dec. 375/1 The physical..circumstances of the Poulsen arc are rather forbidding. **1916** *Ibid.* 14 Jan. 535/2 In wireless telegraphy there has been a notable advance in the use of the Poulsen arc. **1931** [see *KEYING *vbl. sb.* 1]. **1949** W. R. MACLAURIN *Invention & Innovation in Radio Industry* iv. 60 The patents on the Poulsen arc were held by enterprises that were competing with Marconi.

poult (pult), *sb.*² [Shortening of POULT-DE-SOIE.] = POULT-DE-SOIE. Also, a similar fabric manufactured from man-made fibres. Also *attrib.*

1938 *Times* 7 July 22/1 A gown..with a bodice of white poult. **1951** *Good Housek. Home Encycl.* 199/1 Nylon Fabric is now available in many different finishes, such as tricot, net, poult. **1959** *Times* 21 Sept. 12/4 A short dress of coral-coloured poult. **1960** *Woman's Own* 9 Apr. 7/1 At a dance recently I wore my poult dress. **1970** *Trafford Spring & Summer Catal.* 276 See through lace sleeves and a 40 denier Nylon poult skirt.

poulter. 1. b. Delete † *Obs.* and add later examples.

1900 W. RALEIGH in W. E. Henley *Castiglione's Bk. of Courtier* p. xlv, The one-legged poulter's measure is not responsible for all the horrors of this. **1962** G. K. HUNTER *John Lyly* iv. 244 The case with 'fourteeners' or 'poulter's measure' is even more obvious. **1972** *Times Lit. Suppl.* 10 Nov. 1363/1 Poulter's measure (the form of verse with alternating lines of twelve and fourteen syllables).

poulterer. Add: **b.** *poulterer's measure*, = *poulter's measure* s.v. POULTER 1 b in Dict. and Suppl. Chiefly *Hist.*

1841 R. G. LATHAM *Eng. Lang.* v. 382 *Poulterer's Measure*,—Alexandrines and Service Measures alternately. Found in the poetry of Henry the Eighth's time. **1957** N. FRYE *Anat. Crit.* 263 There were some comparative failures, such as poulterer's measure.

poultice, *sb.* Add: **2.** *Austral. slang.* **a.** A mortgage.

1932 K. S. PRICHARD *Dark Horse of Darran* in *Kiss on Lips* 184 Mick Mallane..sayin' if the bank wanted his farm, poultice or no poultice, it'd have to go out and take it from him, and he'd be waitin' for 'm with his gun loaded. **1934** T. WOOD *Cobbers* xi. 134 Men talked about their blister, or their poultice, which means a mortgage, with complacency. **1958** *Coast to Coast 1957–1958* 137 When the farm was free of its 'poultice', her father had promised to hand over to Sam.

b. A (large) sum of money; a bribe.

1951 E. LAMBERT *Twenty Thousand Thieves* III. xii. 235 It's only two days to pay day and I've got a poultice in that pay-book of mine. **1957** 'N. CULOTTA' *They're a Weird Mob* (1958) v. 73 'Reckon 'e pulled 'im?' 'That's wot I reckon.'..'Yer can't prove ut.' 'Somebody slung in a poultice, I bet.' 'They're all crooked.' **1979** *Sun-Herald* 24 June 143 A bloke who made a poultice in recent weeks when he sold Rupert a quarter of a million Channel Ten shares.

poultry. Add: **4.** *poultry breeder*, *-fancier* (earlier example), *-house* (later examples), *-keeper* (examples), *meat*, *-raising* (examples), *-run*, *-show* (examples), *-yard* (earlier examples); **poultry-man** (later examples); also **poultry-woman.**

c **1882** W. COOK (*title*) Practical poultry breeder and feeder. **1976** *Evening Post* (Nottingham) 14 Dec. 6/6 Derbyshire police advises poultry breeders to have flood lighting as a deterrent. **1865** *Atlantic Monthly* June 661/2 My experiments with chickens have been attended with a success so brilliant that unfortunate poultry-fanciers have appealed to me for assistance. **1819** *Amer. Farmer* (Baltimore) I. 46 Respecting the cleansing of poultry-houses from vermin, or chicken-lice. **1921** *Proc. 3rd Nat. Country Life Conf. 1920* (U.S.) 155 No argument is necessary to justify poultry houses. **1942** C. MILBURN *Diary* 11 July (1979) 145 Mr Willoughby came later with a copy of the *Smallholder* and we looked at an advertisement for a 'Utility Poultry House'. **1867** L. WRIGHT (*title*) The practical poultry-keeper. **1935** *Discovery* Oct. 302/2 The poultry keeper and game preserver. **1960** *Farmer & Stockbreeder* 9 Feb. 123/3 Some poultry-keepers prefer to use no preventive drugs and to rely upon curative drugs, if and when an outbreak of coccidiosis occurs. **1976** *Newmarket Jrnl.* 16 Dec., He served on the committee of the allotments association and was an active gardener and poultry-keeper. **1889** *St. Landry Democrat* (Opelousas, Louisiana) 7 Dec. 2/5 Mr. Felch the well-known poultryman, has a Scotch collie dog. **1960** *Farmer & Stockbreeder* 9 Feb. 125/2 Mr. Thornber remembered that the poultryman slept for 21 days with the first mammoth they installed. *Ibid.* 16 Feb. 79/1 The amount of poultry meat marketed continued to shoot upwards. **1978** *Daily Tel.* 19 Sept. 19/7 Meat consumption in Britain is now at its lowest level since 1955—replaced largely by poultry meat. **1850** in D. J. Browne *Amer. Poultry Yard* 304 There is profit attending poultry raising, when undertaken on a moderate scale. **1870** 'MARK TWAIN' in *Buffalo Express* 4 June 2/3 From early youth I have taken an especial interest in the subject of poultry-raising. **1896** *Rep. Vermont Board Agric.* XV. 28 Poultry raising has of late years attracted the attention of the farmer. **1916** *Daily Colonist* (Victoria, B.C.) 23 July 8/5 There is room near every industrial centre in the province for many market gardens, poultry-runs, orchards and aviaries. **1930** R. CAMPBELL *Adamastor* 64 Heaven in which our senses swim, Aviary of aviators And poultry-run of seraphim! **1868** M. H. SMITH *Sunshine & Shadow in N.Y.* lxxiv. 597 He has gotten up baby-shows, poultry-shows, and dog-shows. **1873** F. KILVERT *Diary* 6 Aug. (1944) 223, I went..to Garth to attend the Garth Flower Show, Dog Show, Poultry Show, Bazaar and Athletic Sports, all in one. **1851** *Harper's Mag.* Apr. 662/2 The poultry-woman must be changed. **1748** RICHARDSON *Clarissa* I. ix. 52 You must remember the Green Lane..that runs by the side of the wood-house and poultry-yard. **1811** JANE AUSTEN *Sense & Sens.* III. vi. 114 The rest of the morning was..whiled away..in visiting her poultry-yard.

‖**pounamu** (po͵unamu). *N.Z.* Also 9 **punamu.** [Maori.] Nephrite.

[**1773** J. HAWKESWORTH *Acct. Voy.* II. II. vi. 400 This land..consisted of two Whennuas or islands..which he [*sc.* Cook] called Tovy Poenammoo; the literal translation of this word is, 'the water of green talc'.] **1835** W. YATE *Acct. N.Z.* (ed. 2) v. 271, I have put on board the Buffalo a mere pounamu and two garments. **1867** E. SAUTER tr. *F. von Hochstetter's New Zealand* xvii. 362 A magnificent Mere punamu, a battle axe..cut out of the most beautiful, transparent nephrite. **1905** W.B. *Where White Man Treads* 39 'Pounamu' (greenstone) was only to be found in the creeks of the inland ranges of the Middle Island. **1965** G. J. WILLIAMS *Econ. Geol. N.Z.* v. 45/2 Pounamu Ultramafics occur within the rocks of this area. **1973** *Times Lit. Suppl.* 9 Feb. 141/3 The repeated word of the title, *pounamu*, however translucent to New Zealanders, will be opaque to the English reader. It means 'greenstone', a New Zealand form of jade, evocative of a past when it was the prized material of axe and ornament.

pounce, *sb.*[2] Add: **3.** *pounce-bag* (examples), *-box* (later example), *pattern, pot.*

1855 W. WILLIAMS *Transparency Painting on Linen* 20 Pounce patterns..are formed of outlines perforated through the paper on which they are drawn, by a succession of small needle holes. *Ibid.* 27 The pounce-bag is made by tying a little fine, dry, black powder, in two or three squares of the muslin..used for painting on... The perforated pattern being placed on the cloth, the pounce-bag is lightly tapped on the surface, so as to force the powder..through all the perforations of the pattern. **1866** W. DAVIDGE *Footlight Flashes* xv. 146 A pack of cards, a piece of rosin, a flute case, a pounce, or sand box, and a newspaper printed in the German language. **1939** *Newsweek* 13 Mar. 37/3 And (using a 'pouncebag' filled with dry pigment) [the painter] rules the outline through the perforations onto the preliminary coat of mortar. **1957** MANKOWITZ & HAGGAR *Conc. Encycl. Eng. Pott. & Porc.* 181/2 *Pounce pot*, a small box with a perforated lid for perfumes; a powder box or jar; a pierced-topped jar for sprinkling powdered pumice used to dry ink (before the popularity of blotting paper). **1971** *Country Life* 29 July 263/1 The top [of an inkstand] is inset with an ormolu tray flanked by inkpot and pounce pot.

pounce, *v.*[3] **2.** (Further examples.)

1855 W. WILLIAMS *Transparency Painting on Linen* 28 If an accident..occur, it is only necessary to dust the powder off the muslin, to re-adjust the pattern, and again pounce in the design. **1960** B. SNOOK *Eng. Hist. Embroidery* 51 The design was either pricked and pounced and drawn with a clear black line, or it was printed from an engraving direct upon the linen.

pounced, *ppl. a.*[2] **1.** (Later example.)

1855 W. WILLIAMS *Transparency Painting on Linen* 28 The pattern being removed, the pounced design is secured by being traced with a soft black-lead pencil, and drawn in with a reed pen.

pouncer[2] (pau·nsəɪ). [f. POUNCE *v.*[3] + -ER[1].] A pouncing-tool; a pounce-bag.

1881 *Sylvia's Bk. Artistic Knicknacks* 371 Place the design on the canvas and pin it down; then take your pouncer, which is filled with fine charcoal or powdered colour, and dab..all over your perforated outline. The pouncer is..made by half-filling a thick muslin bag with charcoal or soot, and tying it tightly round. **1960** G. LEWIS *Handbk. Crafts* 16 Using a pouncer (a roll of felt) dipped into black pounce (powdered charcoal) for light materials..gently rub the powder through the perforations, then lift away the tracing.

pound, *sb.*[1] **I. 1. a.** For 'weight' read 'weight and mass'. (Further examples.)

1959 *Nature* 10 Jan. 80 To secure identical values for each of these units in precise measurements for science and technology, it has been agreed [by standards laboratories in many countries] to adopt an international yard and an international pound..: the international pound equals 0·453 592 37 kgm... The yard and pound units to be used in trade are the imperial units laid down in the Weights and Measures Act, 1878. *Ibid.* 81 With regard to the pound, the values currently in use..are: 1 imperial standard pound = 0·453 592 338 kgm.; 1 Canadian pound = 0·453 592 43 kgm.; 1 United States pound = 0·453 592 4277 kgm. There is evidence that the imperial standard pound has diminished by about 7 parts in 10 millions since 1846. **1961** [see *LB]. **1963** JERRARD & MCNEILL *Dict. Sci. Units* 109 In 1963 the pound was defined as being equal to '0·45359237 Kilogramme exactly' by the Weights and Measures Act... This pound is identical with the International pound adopted in 1959 by Standards Laboratories.

f. *pound of flesh*: also (with hyphens) as *attrib. phr.*

1958 *Listener* 13 Nov. 775/2 He is entirely consistent.. In the application of this pound-of-flesh attitude. **1963** AUDEN *Dyer's Hand* 228 *Pecorone* or other versions of the pound-of-flesh story.

g. *pound and pint* (Naut. slang), a sailor's ration as determined by the Board of Trade's Scale of Provisions. So *pound and pinter*, a ship on which rations were provided on this scale; *pound-and-pint idler* (see quot. *a* 1865). *Obs.* exc. *Hist.*

a **1865** SMYTH *Sailor's Word-bk.* (1867) 540 *Pound-and-pint-idler*, a sobriquet applied to the purser. **1902** W. RUNCIMAN *Windjammers & Sea Tramps* vii. 90 Their 'whack', or to be strictly accurate, the phrase commonly used was 'your pound and pint'. **1910** D. W. BONE *Brassbounder* 168 A pound and pint ruddy limejuicer. **1938** W. E. DEXTER *Rope-Yarns* v. 31 It seemed my lot to mostly sail in what we called 'hungry-gutted ships', 'pound and pinters'. **1952** 'SINBAD' *Sargasso Sam* xxviii. 211 Wot about tucker? We never come aboard this old wagon to eat deepwater muck. Looks like we're gettin' pound an' pint and no more.

h. [from *pound of lead*, rhyming slang for 'head'.] The human head.

1933 F. RICHARDS *Old Soldiers never Die* xiv. 180 We old hands often used to remark that when we did get hit it would either be a bullet through the pound or stop a five-point-nine all on our own.

II. 3. Since 1971, of the value of 100 new pence.

d. Also applied to units of currency originally valued at par with the pound sterling.

1949 *Britannica Bk. of Year* 364/2 On Aug. 17, 1948, a new Israeli pound..displaced the Palestine pound. **1955** *Ibid.* 141/1 Cyprus... Monetary unit: Cyprus pound (= £1 sterling). **1958** *Spectator* 15 Aug. 216/3 No one wanted to lend any money in terms of the Israeli Pound. **1975** *Times* 25 Nov. 7/1 The Israeli pound is officially fixed at seven to the dollar

f. Five dollars; a five-dollar note. *U.S. slang.*

1935 J. HARGAN *Gloss. Prison Lang.* 6 *Pound*, a five dollar bill. **1950** *New Yorker* 25 Feb. 76 A pound off of thirty-four-fifty would still leave twenty nine-fifty. **1970** H. E. ROBERTS *Third Ear* 11/1 Pounds, money; five dollars.

4. pound brush (earlier example); **pound-force** (pl. *pounds-force*), a unit of force equal to the weight of a mass of 1 pound avoirdupois, esp. under standard gravity; **pound note,** delete '(such as are issued in Scotland and Ireland)'; **pound-noteish** *a.* (*slang*), affected, pompous; **pound-weight** (pl. *pounds-weight*) = *pound-force* above.

1830 G. COLMAN *Random Rec.* I. ii. 35 My pictures are only sketches, and dabs of the pound-brush. **1896** T. W. WRIGHT *Elem. Mech.* ii. 62 The word pound has a.. variety of meanings. We speak of a pound weight, a pound force, and of a certain body itself as 'a pound'. **1909** J. M. JAMESON *Elem. Pract. Mech.* ix. 149 These two units of force, the pound force and the gram force are sometimes called Gravitational Units of Force. **1949** W. ERNST *Oil Hydraulic Power* i. 2 The pound force imparts 32·174 feet per sec[2] to the pound mass. **1961** [see *LB]. **1972** *Physics Bull.* May 285/1 The subsequent addition of small weights permits forces to be obtained directly in both tons-force and pounds-force. **1977** *Daily Tel.* 16 Dec. 2/3 As Britain moves towards complete metrication motorists will have to get used to checking their car tyre pressures in atmospheric bars instead of pounds force per square inch. **1936** J. CURTIS *Gilt Kid* vi. 63 Her pound-noteish voice both annoyed and amused the Gilt Kid. **1966** AUDEN *About House* 28 When we get pound-noteish ..send us some deflating Image. [**1871** J. C. MAXWELL *Theory of Heat* iv. 83 In all countries the first measurements of forces were made in this way, and a force was described as a force of so many pounds' weight or grammes' weight. **1877** W. H. BESANT *Treat. Hydromech.* i. 9 The unit of force is 750 lbs. weight.] **1891** J. G. EASTON *First Bk. Mech.* iv. 59 It is sometimes convenient..to speak of a force as of so many pounds weight. **1907** FRANKLIN & MACNUTT *Elem. Mech.* viii. 174 (*heading*) Values of the stretch modulus of various substances. (In pounds-weight per square inch.) **1936** A. W. HIRST *Electr. & Magn.* i. 4 A force of one pound-weight = 32·2 poundals. **1960** F. LAND *Lang. Math.* vi. 71 When I buy a pound of apples, the weight of the apples is 1 pound-weight..and its mass is 1 pound mass. **1976** *Daily Tel.* 4 Mar. 2/6 The Metrication Board..warned the Government that unless it introduced a sense of urgency into replacing feet for [*sic*] metres..and pounds weight for kilogrammes, then the target of 1980 for completion of the programme could never be met.

pound, *sb.*[2] Add: **1. d.** An enclosure in which vehicles impounded by the police are kept.

1970 P. LAURIE *Scotland Yard* iii. 75 Civilian cars that have been stolen or in accidents..stand in a pound nearby. **1970** *Globe & Mail* (Toronto) 25 Sept. 39/2 (Advt.), Permanent part time dispatcher for police auto pound, Saturday, Sunday and Monday nights. **1972** *Daily Tel.* 16 Mar. 17/6 The Vauxhall Viva had been towed to a pound because it was found parked on an urban clearway. **1974** *Times* 18 Feb. 17 I'm going to sell my car... No more police towing [it]..to a car pound.

6. pound-boat (examples); **pound-master** (earlier example); **pound net** (earlier and later examples).

1884 *Bull. U.S. Nat. Museum* No. 27. 700 Lake Erie pound boat... Their peculiar construction enables them to carry large quantities of fish in shallow water and to lift the bowl of the pounds without upsetting. **1891** *Rep. U.S. Comm. Fisheries 1887* 27 The pound-boat has two tall, tapering masts. **1792** *Southampton* (N.Y.) *Records* (1878) III. 335 John Cooper Samuel Cooper Henry Corwithe Poundmasters. **1865** *Michigan Gen. Statutes* (1882) I. 577 The penalties of this section shall not apply or work injury to persons who are the present owners of pound or trap nets. **1973** *Fisheries Fact Sheet* (Environment Canada Fisheries & Marine Service) No. 1. 4/3 Gill-nets and pound-nets are the chief gear.

pound, *v.*[1] Add: **2. a.** (Later examples.)

1908 *Smart Set* June 21/2 She stopped at the door of the house and pounded the knocker vigorously. **1951** *Amer. Speech* XXVI. 230/2 St. Joseph *pounds* Mansfield. **1960** M. SPARK *Bachelors* xii. 224 The typist in the corner listlessly pounded her silent machine. **1967** *Boston Sunday Globe* 23 Apr. 17/4 Air Force and Navy jets pounded North Vietnam in 118 missions Friday. **1968** *Globe & Mail* (Toronto) 5 Feb. 17/4 Detroit..pounded Minnesota North Stars 8–1. **1972** 'E. FERRARS' *Breath of Suspicion* vii. 101 I'll be working..pounding my typewriter.

d. phr. *to pound one's ear*: to sleep. *slang* (orig. *U.S.*).

1899 'J. FLYNT' *Tramping with Tramps* IV. 396 *Pound the ear*, to sleep. **1900** *Dialect Notes* II. 51 [College slang] '*Pound* one's ear, or one's pillow,' to sleep. **1907** [see *FLOP *v.* 2 c]. **1926** M. WALSH *Key above Door* xii. 128 'Only just awakened,' I admitted..'and how are my comrades in misfortune?'.. 'Still pounding their ears, no doubt.' **1927** C. SAMOLAR in *Amer. Speech* II. 290/2 To sleep is to *pound the ear*. I think this phrase originated with railroaders. Sleeping in a caboose on a fast-moving train actually consists of pounding one's ear. **1947** J. STEINBECK *Wayward Bus* xx. 300 Listen to the old bastard snore. He's pounding his ear.

e. To produce or turn *out* by 'pounding' a typewriter or the like.

1904 F. LYNDE *Grafters* v. 58 He sat down at the typewriter to pound out a letter to the general counsel, resigning his sinecure. **1941** B. SCHULBERG *What makes Sammy Run?* ix. 162, I was back in the old groove, pounding it out for the *Record* again. **1973** W. MCCARTHY *Detail* i. 48 He had just enough time to pound out two or three short paragraphs.

f. To walk upon; to cover (a distance or area) on foot; *spec.* of a policeman: to patrol (a beat). *colloq.* (orig. *U.S.*).

In quot. 1959 the use is *fig.* in punning allusion to the poetry of Ezra Pound (see *POUNDIAN *a.*).

1906 A. H. LEWIS *Confessions of Detective* iv. 44 It's worth while to pound a beat, when one has such kindly and appreciative superiors. **1909** 'O. HENRY' *Options* (1916) 30 I'm pounding the asphalt for another job. **1923** L. J. VANCE *Baroque* vi. 33, I won't get sent back to pound sidewalks for what I'm pulling off tonight. **1935** A. J. POLLOCK *Underworld Speaks* 91/1 *Pounding the pavement*, a prostitute soliciting men on the street. **1946** [see *KRIEGIE]. **1959** *Times Lit. Suppl.* 25 Sept. 546/5 An awful warning to any future translator tempted to indulge in the pleasures of what, metrically speaking, might be described as Pounding the beat. **1974** S. MARCUS *Minding Store* (1975) ii. 26 He personally pounded the pavements calling on fellow businessmen. **1978** J. GARDNER *Dancing Dodo* xxxiv. 270, I shall personally arrange for you to be back pounding the beat, in uniform.

poundage[1]**.** Add: **6. b.** A person's weight, esp. that which is regarded as excess.

1930 WODEHOUSE *Very Good, Jeeves!* iv. 93 Women who have anything to do with opera..always appear to run to surplus poundage. **1971** *Time* 5 Apr. 44/3 With his hair transplant and added poundage.

poundage[2]**.** Add: **2.** The keeping of cattle in a pound or enclosure; an enclosure in which cattle are kept.

1867 C. TOMLINSON *Cycl. Useful Arts* I. 3/2 [The slaughterman] only paying for the poundage of his beasts according to the requirements of his business. **1902** *Encycl. Brit.* XXXII. 644/1 The bye-laws usually provide..for the poundage to have floor-space sufficient for each animal.

pound-cake. (Earlier and later examples.)

1747 H. GLASSE *Art of Cookery* xv. 138 Pound Cake. Take a Pound of Butter..twelve Eggs..a Pound of Flour..a Pound of Sugar [etc.]. **1807** M. E. RUNDELL *New Syst. Domestic Cookery* 217 (*heading*) A good pound cake. **1942** B. ROBERTSON *Red Hills & Cotton* iii. 69 We liked..cornbread with chitterlings, ambrosia, stuffed eggs, pound cake. **1951** T. CAPOTE *Grass Harp* (1952) i. 12 Dolly, who lived off sweet foods, was always baking a pound cake. **1977** *Time* 24 Jan. 5/2 Pound cake will remain just that, no matter how many grams the ingredients weigh.

pounded, *ppl. a.*[1] Add: *pounded meat* (earlier and later examples); *spec.* (*U.S.* and *Canad.*) the flesh of buffalo or other game cut up, dried, and pulverized into powder to form the basic ingredient of pemmican.

1775 S. HEARNE *Jrnl.* 5 Sept. (1934) 177 One Cannoe came with some Dry'd & Pownded Meate. **1805** *Deb. Congress U.S.* 9th Congress 2 Sess. App. 1066 Buffalo robes, tallow, dried and pounded meat and grease. **1898** F. RUSSELL *Explor. Far North* 163, I saw large quantities of pounded meat, grease, and tongues eaten. **1922** *Beaver* Nov. 51/1 Pounded meat was made from the dried meat by beating it with flails until it became as small as desired and then stored away in bags. **1956** H. S. M. KEMP *Northern Trader* 93 The meat so acquired would either be dried, converted into pounded meat, or mixed with fat and cranberries and made up as pemmican.

pounder, *sb.*[2] Add: **2. b.** A policeman. *U.S. slang.*

1938 *New Yorker* 12 Mar. 38/2 Letting the sickly-sweet odor of burning marijuana into the street for the first passing pounder, or patrolman, to smell. **1970** C. MAJOR *Dict. Afro-Amer. Slang* 93 *Pounder*, a policeman or detective.

c. *Surfing slang.* (See quot. 1967.)

1967 J. SEVERSON *Great Surfing* Gloss., *Pounder*, an unusually hard-breaking wave. **1970** [see *GREENIE].

pounder, *sb.*[4] **2.** (Earlier and further examples.) Cf. SIX-POUNDER, TEN-POUNDER.

1684 [see FOUR C. 2]. **1747** [see NINE *a.* 5 b]. **1771** [see TWO IV. 1]. **1845** [see *one-pounder* s.v. *ONE B. 33]. **1862** *Rambler* Mar. 414 A large number of 100-pounder Armstrong guns. **1896** [see SEVEN C. 3]. **1915** A. D. GILLESPIE *Let.* 14 June in *Lett. from Flanders* (1916) 196 They started with 33-pounder bombs, like a big turnip with a long handle, and we watched them sailing through the air. **1915** C. MACKENZIE *Guy & Pauline* 264 'I know a man..who caught a four pounder with a bumble-bee.' 'I caught a six pounder at Oxford with a mouse's head myself.' **1977** F. PARRISH *Fire in Barley* ii. 25 He had sometimes seen very big trout here, three and four pounders. **1978** K. BONFIGLIOLI *All Tea in China* x. 127 The gunner ambled towards the long brass Armstrong 68-pounder.

Poundian (pau·ndiăn), *a.* [f. the name *Pound* (see below) + -IAN.] Of, pertaining to, or characteristic of the American writer and poet Ezra Pound (1885–1972) or his work; resembling or influenced by the style of Pound. Also *absol.* as *sb.*

1939 E. H. W. MEYERSTEIN *Let.* 4 Apr. (1959) 221, I never thought I should come round to Eliot as a poet. Here he has dropped his Poundian Babel-tongues. **1958** *N. & Q.* June 265/2 Sappho—a well-known source of Poundian inspiration. **1960** N. STOCK in *Agenda* June 1 The usual Poundian emphasis On medieval money and wages. **1965** *Times Lit. Suppl.* 25 Nov. 1070/4 Mr.

Charles Olson..can often be peculiarly irritating with his Poundian mannerisms. **1971** *Guardian* 27 May 9/6 His Poundian hankerings after aristocracy. **1975** P. FUSSELL *Gt. War & Mod. Memory* ix. 313 The reader in search of innovation will find it in..Jones's Eliotic and Poundian juxtapositions. **1976** *Times Lit. Suppl.* 23 July 926/5 In this new short book he is more a Poundian than a critic.

poundiferous (paundi·fĕrəs), *a. rare.* [f. POUND *sb.*³: see -FEROUS.] Accompanied by pounding.

1871 'MARK TWAIN' *Let.* 28 Jan. (1917) I. 183 A long, vociferous, poundiferous and vitreous jingling of applause announces the conclusion.

pounding, *vbl. sb.*¹ **4.** *pounding-mill* (earlier and later examples).

1785 T. JEFFERSON *Notes Virginia* vi. 43 A good situation on a creek for a pounding mill. **1849** C. LANMAN *Lett. from Alleghany Mts.* i. 17 The vein gold is brought to light by means of what is called a pounding mill. **1905** 'P. PENNINGTON' *Woman Rice Planter* (1913) 142 The cows and pigs are fed on the flour, a gray substance that comes from the grain as the chaff is removed in the pounding mill.

Poupart (pū·pāɹ). *Anat.* [The name of François *Poupart* (1661–1708), French surgeon.] *Poupart's ligament*: the inguinal ligament which extends from the anterior superior spine of the ilium to the pubic tubercle.

1756 P. POTT *Treat. Ruptures* i. 6 What is called Poupart's or Fallopius's ligament, is nothing more than the lower border of this tendon stretched from the fore part of the os ileum or haunch bone, to the pubis. **1804** A. COOPER *Anat. & Surg. Treatm. Inguinal & Congenital Hernia* xiv. 48 On examination, a fulness could be perceived above Poupart's ligament. **1844** A. COLLES in S. Mac Coy *Lect. Theory & Pract. Surg.* i. xx. 309 In the operation for femoral hernia you should always begin your first incision at least an inch above Poupart's ligament. **1910** *Practitioner* June 848 The opening in the peritoneum was closed and the operation was concluded by suturing Poupart's ligament..to the thickened part of the pectineal fascia. **1970** I. L. LICHTENSTEIN *Hernia Repair* vi. 72 Poupart's ligament will move when the patient strains, allowing a necessary resiliency to the body's exertion.

poupeton. Add: See also *PUPTON.

pour, *v.* Add: **1.** (Further examples.)

1881 MRS. J. H. RIDDELL *Senior Partner* II. x. 203 An old, old pug..took no notice of Mr. McCullagh or anything else, till Janey poured him out a glass of milk. **1909** E. BANKS *Mystery F. Farrington* 54 Pour me some tea, dear, and tell me about your play.

c. *spec.* with ellipsis of the name of the thing poured.

1906 W. S. MAUGHAM *Bishop's Apron* ix. 61/1 Mrs. Railing stirred the tea, put milk in each cup, and poured out. **1919** 'C. DANE' *Legend* 5, I used to pour out when interesting people came to tea. **1925** E. H. YOUNG *William* viii. 81 Lydia immediately got into a hammock. 'I can eat here, but..I can't pour out. Dora can do that.' **1930** A. BENNETT *Imperial Palace* lvi. 420 'Will you pour?' she asked... He poured out the tea. **1956** R. FULLER *Image of Society* ix. 226 'Shall I pour?' she asked. **1962** *Woman's Own* 31 Mar. 89/2, I think Alison should pour today. **1965** R. PETRIE *Running Deep* x. 115 'Miss Fairfield poured,' Ian reminded her. **1973** 'D. HALLIDAY' *Dolly & Starry Bird* iii. 43 'I shall pour,' Johnson said, and pushed a cup under my nose. 'Black coffee and Sambucca and good intentions.'

3. c. *to pour (on) the coal* (Aeronaut. slang), to cause an aircraft to accelerate; to pilot an aircraft at high speed. Also *transf.*

1937 E. C. PARSONS *Gt. Adventure* xix. 233, I poured coal into the old Hispano and lit out like a scared jack rabbit. **1944** T. H. WISDOM *Triumph over Tunisia* xxiii. 183 The bombs gone away, Jimmy put the nose down and poured on the coal to escape. **1961** J. M. FOSTER *Hell in Heavens* 58 He poured the coal to his plane and banked to avoid passing too close. **1971** M. TAK *Truck Talk* 122 *Pour on the coals*, to drive a truck at high speed.

pourable (pōə·ɹăb'l), *a.* [f. POUR *v.* + -ABLE.] That may be poured; that flows easily.

1946 *Nature* 2 Nov. 636/1 The experimental preparation used was..a dilution in water prepared..in proportions to give an easily pourable, miscible oil. **1957** V. J. KEHOE *Technique Film & Television Make-Up* 245 All Vinamold grades melt down to easily pourable liquids. **1959** *New Scientist* 22 Oct. 750/2 A thick syrup at room temperature, SAIB becomes pourable as the temperature is raised. **1970** *Sci. Jrnl.* May 19/1 Even with temperatures of −40°C the Astrolites did not freeze, remained pourable and were easily and safely handled.

pourboire. (Earlier and later examples.)

1817 H. C. B. CAMPBELL *Journey to Florence* (1951) 81 The expence of the *pour boire* at each of these places is very great... The people of the custom houses..regularly ask for it. **1963** [see *MANCIA]. **1964** *Economist* 6 June 1133/1 A *pourboire* in the shape of high rebates. **1979** *Times* 5 Dec. 14/3 Commissioners may acquire the much-coveted Cabinet boxes..if they pay for them... Until [1978]..the boxes were a kind of pourboire.

‖ **pour encourager les autres** (pur ãnkuraʒe lez ōutr'), *phr.* [Fr., 'in order to encourage the others', with reference to the execution of Admiral John Byng in 1757: cf. Voltaire *Candide* xxiii. 212 Il est bon de tuer de tems en tems un Amiral pour encourager les autres.] 'In order to encourage (or deter) the others', said of an exemplary punishment or sacrifice. Also *transf.* and in weakened senses.

1804 WELLINGTON *Disp.* (1844) II. 1032 The destruction of the band is complete, but I wished to hang some of their chiefs, *pour encourager les autres.* **1825** H. WILSON *Mem.* (ed. 2) II. 194 We talked a great deal. Hertford's subject was death, pour encourager les autres. **1896** G. B. SHAW *Let.* 29 Jan. (1965) I. 589, I am not alluding in any way to the 'Sign of the Cross' question, or to you. I have simply flicked the insect off the window pane in passing, *pour encourager les autres.* **1915** A. D. GILLESPIE *Lett. from Flanders* (1916) 118 We had another concert last night, and since some officer had to be the victim 'pour encourager les autres', I had to..sing them the Skye boat song. **1917** T. E. LAWRENCE in *Lett.* (1938) 235 This did not fall in with our ideas, since (pour encourager les autres) we wanted the news to get about that the Arabs accepted prisoners. **1963** *New Society* 21 Nov. 20/2 So *pour encourager les autres* the institute..has just published its conclusions. **1969** Y. CARTER *Mr. Campion's Farthing* xviii. 178 A cruel gesture, made, I suppose, *pour encourager les autres.* He committed suicide? **1973** 'M. UNDERWOOD' *Reward for Defector* viii. 71, I must be punished '*pour encourager les autres*'. **1977** *Rolling Stone* 30 June 69/3 He sent the old man away to prison all the same, *pour encourager*, as Voltaire bitterly put it in another context, *les autres.*

pouring, *vbl. sb.* Add: **b.** pouring cream, cream that flows readily; single cream.

1966 P. V. PRICE *France: Food & Wine Guide* 245 *Fontainebleau* is a very light cream cheese, often eaten with sugar and/or pouring cream. **1971** *Islander* (Victoria, B.C.) 13 June 8/1 Strawberries and cream go hand in hand..strawberries and pouring cream; strawberries and ice cream [etc.].

‖ **pour le sport** (pur lə spor), *phr.* [Fr., 'for sport'.] For fun, amusement, or sport.

1924 M. ARLEN *Green Hat* i. 6 A green hat, of a sort of felt..being, no doubt, one of those that women who have many hats affect *pour le sport.* **1936** A. CHRISTIE *ABC Murders* xix. 97 He kills, it would seem from his letters, *pour le sport*—to amuse himself. **1939** *Time* 22 May 10/2 He has never gained sufficient maturity to be anything more than a conscientious individualist 'pour le sport'. **1955** M. ALLINGHAM *Beckoning Lady* ii. 20 Mr. Magersfontein Lugg himself, garbed tastefully *pour le sport.* **1973** L. MEYNELL *Thirteen Trumpeters* ii. 22 Lucian had automatically made tentative exploratory investigations as to her readiness *pour le sport* and bedworthiness.

‖ **pour passer le temps** (pur pase lə tañ), *phr.* [Fr.] To pass the time; to amuse oneself.

1681 OTWAY *Souldiers Fortune* i. i. 3 Some little inconsiderable questions *pour posser* [sic] *le temps.* **1777** P. THICKNESSE *Year's Journey* II. lii. 153 The gay part of the French women love none, but receive all, *pour passer le tems.* **1823** SCOTT *Quentin Durward* I. p. xxiv, Although he admitted he read them *pour passer le temps*, yet..it was not without execrating the tendency. **1846** GEO. ELIOT *Let.* 5 Nov. (1954) I. 225, I wanted some kind of worship pour passer le temps. **1889** E. DOWSON *Let.* 1 Apr. (1967) 59, I still scribble occasionally—pour passer le temps, and devote most of my leisure to the French Renaissance. **1895** C. M. YONGE *Long Vacation* xiii. 128 'Yet you are helping on this concern.' 'True, but partly *pour passer le temps.*' **1976** M. BIRMINGHAM *Heat of Sun* ix. 158 Cynthia asked if she could go too: '*Pour passer le temps,*' she said... 'I love riding in cars at night.'

pour-point (pōə·ɹpoint), *sb.*² Also **pour point.** [f. POUR *v.* + POINT *sb.*¹] The temperature below which an oil is too viscous to be poured.

1922 T. G. DELBRIDGE in D. T. Day *Handbk. Petroleum Industry* I. 660 Pour point of a petroleum oil is the lowest temperature at which this oil will pour or flow when it is drilled without disturbance under certain definite specified conditions. **1936** W. L. NELSON *Petroleum Refinery Engin.* v. 48 Since 1929..the average specified pour-point for lubricating oils has been lowered from 30 to about 10°F. **1972** *Daily Colonist* (Victoria, B.C.) 3 Feb. 12/8 The reservoir has..a low sulphur content and a pour point of minus 55 degrees Fahrenheit. **1972** L. M. HARRIS *Introd. Deepwater Floating Drilling Operations* xvi. 171 Devices for heating and treating the emulsions are helpful, particularly, with high pour-point crudes.

‖ **pour rire** (pur rīr), *a.* (*adv.*) *phr.* [Fr., lit. 'in order to laugh'.] Of a kind or in a manner that causes amusement or derision, or suggests light-hearted or jocular pretence; not serious or in a serious manner.

1872 B. JERROLD *London* x. 92 The laugh is general.. over Smug who swept his own office once—and is no Liberal *pour rire.* **1884** *Sat. Rev.* 3 May 562/2 The author of a motion admits that it is only a motion *pour rire.* **1909** MRS. H. WARD *Daphne* III. ix. 219 'Then there was some local scandal?'.. 'Possibly. Scandal *pour rire*! Not a soul believed that there was anything..in it.' **1926** A. HUXLEY *Jesting Pilate* i. 115 Hereditary aristocracies still exist in the West—exist, but *pour rire.* **1931** *Times Lit. Suppl.* 5 Feb. 96/4 These and other essays in the book are full of those analogies *pour rire* and elegant verbal jokes that so delight us nowadays. **1942** J. LEES-MILNE in *Ancestral Voices* (1975) 65 The King washed up after dinner, or rather carried some glasses into the pantry and made a gesture of washing up, '*pour rire*'. **1946** A. L. ROWSE *Use of Hist.* 173 They all came over in a coach... The lady who descended from it..was got up to look like one of the *louche* ladies of the Restoration Court of Charles II. It was all *pour rire.* **1959** *Punch* 25 Mar. 411/2 A flight of facetious fancy, a suggestion *pour rire.* **1980** *Country Life* 28 Feb. 609/2 The jokes about such jargon as 'a fried-chicken taste that's lip-lickin' good' have long ceased to be *pour rire.*

‖ **pourriture** (puritūr). [Fr.: see POURITURE.] **a.** Rottenness, a person in a 'rotten' or unwell condition.

1890 E. DOWSON *Let.* 11 Feb. (1967) 136, I have a bad cold, leaden spirits, and in fine feel all round a pretty fair 'pourriture'.

b. *pourriture noble* [lit. 'noble rot': see *NOBLE *a.* 7 f]: a common grey mould, *Botrytis cinerea*, affecting grapes, which is deliberately cultivated to perfect certain French and German wines, and Tokay; the condition of being affected by this mould; also *ellipt.* as *pourriture.*

1911 *Encycl. Brit.* XXVIII. 722/2 The peculiar character of the Sauternes, for during the latter period of ripening a specific micro-organism termed *Botrytis cinerea* develops on the grape, causing a peculiar condition termed *pourriture noble* (German *Edelfäule*). **1924, 1935** [see *NOBLE *a.* 7 f]. **1951** R. POSTGATE *Plain Man's Guide to Wine* vi. 98 A full and scented wine, the product of the *pourriture noble.* **1963** *Times* 8 Feb. 12/5 Wines made from..over-ripe single grapes which are, in effect, sun-dried raisins, in a state of *pourriture noble*, or princely decay. **1966** P. V. PRICE *France: Food & Wine Guide* 175 Several great properties have begun to make dry wines again..by picking the grapes before the pourriture has started to form. **1972** *Country Life* 14 Dec. 1658/3 The *vin jaune* grapes are not harvested until November, by which time they have been withered by the *pourriture noble*..that affects Sauternes and the great sweet wines of Germany.

‖ **pour-soi** (pūrˌswa). *Philos.* [F., lit. 'for itself', 'for oneself'.] A phr. used by J.-P. Sartre in *L'Être et le Néant* (1943) to designate conscious, free being; being-for-itself; contrasted with *en-soi*, being-itself.

1947 *Jrnl. Philos.* XLIV. 720 The latter [*sc.* Heidegger], seeing the given always turning again into the abstract, concludes that human existence alone is *pour soi.* **1950** *Mind* LIX. 270 Sartre..in *L'Être et le Néant*..discusses the historical character of the *pour-soi.* **1962** *Listener* 30 Aug. 317/1 Sartre sees existence in the world as a polarity, a struggle for power. To survive, the *pour-soi* or individual consciousness has to reject and deny the *en-soi* of mere identity, of being what I have to be. **1964** C. SMITH *Contemp. French Philos.* ii. 33, I doubt if Sartre would agree that there can be any possibility of 'lucidly knowing' the *pour-soi.* **1966** A. MANSER *Sartre* iii. 45 Even though Sartre distinguishes between his approach and metaphysics..his division of being into two kinds, *l'en-soi* and *le pour-soi*, together with the question he asks in his introduction..seem to indicate that what follows can only be muddled and obscure. **1977** WARREN & PONSE in Douglas & Johnson *Existential Sociol.* 304 This tension between the *en-soi* and the *pour-soi* is common in gay liberation writings and experience.

‖ **pousada** (pōusā·dă). [Pg. *pousada* resting-place, f. *pousar* to rest.] An inn or hotel in Portugal, esp. one of a chain of hotels administered by the State. Also *attrib.*

1934 J. & C. GORDON *Portuguese Somersault* iv. 35 'Is there no such thing as a good *posada* [sic]?' asked Jo. 'Hotel?' said the cord porter. **1949** BRIDGE & LOWNDES *Selective Traveller in Portugal* vii. 115 Just outside the main gate of Elvas, with a fine view of the aqueduct, is one of the nicest of the Government *pousadas* or inns. **1954** G. HOGG *Portuguese Journey* 44 As we began to descend the hill into S. Tiago we passed the government pousada. **1967** *Guardian* 16 Dec. 9/2 Nights in pousadas will have to be rationed. But I have stayed in little *pensoes* and inns. **1972** *Times* 17 June (Portugal Suppl.) p. ii/4 The *pousada* restaurants cater for motorists. **1976** *Good Motoring* Jan.–Feb. 16/2 Hotel prices [in Portugal] vary enormously but the State-owned pousadas are good value.

pousse-café. Add: (Earlier and later examples.) Also *fig.*

1880 *Harper's Mag.* June 25/2 There is no easier way of solving a social problem than through the medium of a mild and fragrant cigar and a *pousse-café.* **1897** *N.Y. Dramatic Mirror* 27 Nov. 22/3 (Advt.), Weber and Fields' Music Hall..Next Burlesque, commencing Nov. 29, Pousse Cafe; or, the Worst Born. **1948** *Sun* (Baltimore) 1 Jan. 15/1 The sophisticate who goes to the tourist traps makes the barkeep unhappy by asking for fancy things like a pousse cafe (six different liqueurs which are poured gently to avoid mixing the colors). **1959** W. BURROUGHS *Naked Lunch* 72 Men and women in evening dress sip pousse-cafés. **1962** E. LANHAM *No Hiding Place* ii. 20 The sophisticated liqueurs of a pousse-café. **1965** *New Statesman* 24 Dec. 1011/2 The other glamour-hunter's night out was the Australian Ballet's *Raymonda*... It's tempting to be funny about..the interior of Rank's New Victoria, a storm in a pousse-café, sinking knee-deep in ice-cream kups and sweet-wrappings. **1973** *Anglican Theol. Rev.* (Evanston, Illinois) Sept. 35 In the position of Episcopalians in the sociological *pousse-café* of American life, such ecclesiastical Anglophilia was acceptable, even pleasant. **1977** *Time* 12 Sept. 46/3 Some striped jobs look like *pousse-café* or rugby sweaters gone south.

‖ **poussin** (pusæ̃). [Fr., a newly-born chicken.] In *Gastronomy*, a baby chicken. See also *petit poussin* s.v. *PETIT *a.* (*sb.*) 5.

c **1938** *Fortnum & Mason Price List* 72/1 Poussin and Green Peas—per head 5/6. **1957** 'P. QUENTIN' *Suspicious Circumstances* vi. 64 Lunch that day was so gourmet that I thought I would choke on it... Mother took little bird pecks at her Poussin Marie Louise or whatever it was. **1964** M. KELLY *March to Gallows* vii. 72, I looked at the menu card..saw the words *half poussin.* **1969** *Daily Tel.*

11 Jan. 14/2 In Dominica try 'mountain chicken'... Well, yes, I know it's a frog, but a special frog, tasting like *poussin* when grilled. **1974** *Times* 7 Mar. 13/5 Fresh *poussins*—small chickens four to eight weeks old are available.

Poussinesque (pusane·sk), *a.* [f. the name *Poussin* (see below) + -ESQUE.] Pertaining to or characteristic of the French landscape painter Nicolas Poussin (1594–1665) or his work; resembling or influenced by the style of Poussin.

1919 R. FRY *Let.* 9 Feb. (1972) II. 446 *La Jeune Parque* seems to me to have a quality of pure beauty—in the Miltonic Poussinesque direction that hardly any modern work possesses. **1934** *Burlington Mag.* Dec. 297/2 We hear nothing of Pierre Lamaire..whose variant of the Poussinesque landscape formula is yet quite a notable and personal one. **1944** *Ibid.* Aug. 186/2 It is no longer possible ..to point to individual figures as Poussinesque. **1955** *Times* 12 May 5/5 There is a brilliant little canvas by him of women bathing in a Poussinesque landscape. **1964** *Listener* 9 Jan. 57/1 The combination of rectilinear and diagonal movements in plane and inferred space..attains a complexity and variety of such a high order that we recognize it as 'Poussinesque'. **1979** *Basildon Park* (National Trust) 18 The Poussin-esque landscape by Francisque Millet (1642–79) on the west wall.

pou sto. (Later examples.)

1890 E. E. C. JONES *Elem. Logic* xi. 90 The interpretation of our proposition is liable to involve us in an infinite regress; we have no *ποῦ στῶ*. **1911** J. WARD *Realm of Ends* iii. 67 This is the physical basis which is supposed to furnish teleology with its indispensable *ποῦ στῶ*. **1963** W. SELLARS *Sci., Perception & Reality* iii. 89 It is here, rather than at the level of sense contents, that we find a *pou sto* for the apparatus of hypothetico-deductive explanation. **1967** *Philos. Rev.* LXXVI. 181 The self-stultifying form appears to be shorn of its *ποῦ στῶ*.

pout-net. (Later examples.)

1859 *Act* 22 & 23 *Vict.* c. 70 § 14 To kill Salmon in or from the River by means of any Pout Net, Rake Hook, or similar Engine. **1911** A. WARRACK *Scots Dial. Dict.* 425/2 *Pout-net*, a round net fastened to two poles, thrust under the banks of a river to force out fish.

pouty (pau·ti), *a.* *U.S.* [f. POUT *sb.*[2] or *v.*[1] + -Y[1].] Inclined to pout (said of a person or of the mouth); hence (as a personal attribute), sullen or petulant.

1863 'G. HAMILTON' *Gala-Days* 221 They never were tired when anything was to be done, or..peevish, or pouty, or 'offish'. **1897** R. M. STUART *In Simpkinsville* 23 This stove's ez dull-eyed and pouty ez any other woman ef she's neglected. **1912** R. A. WASON *Friar Tuck* 77 With a pouty look on his face, Tank sez: 'It's time we fixed up an' moved out into the dark.' **1971** C. FICK *Danziger Transcript* 44 Stella as in starlight was direct brown eyes and a pouty lower lip. **1976** 'O. BLEECK' *No Questions Asked* xiii. 147 She had a full red mouth that..might have looked kissable to some, but it looked only pouty to me.

pouw. Add: Also **pou, pow.** Cf. *GOMPAAUW, PAAUW, *PAUW. (Earlier and later examples.)

1798 A. BARNARD *Jrnl.* 13 May in A. W. C. Lindsay *Lives of Lindsays* (1849) III. 439, I..tied the *pow*, or wild peacock, to the waggon—a very fine bird indeed, of grave colours, but rich brown. **1858** [see *DIKKOP 1]. **1959** *Cape Argus Mag.* 3 Jan. 8/2 Even the beginner in bird lore would not look for..a pou in the Knysna forest. **1966** [see *NARTJIE].

poverty. Add: **III. 8. poverty-grass,** (*a*) substitute for def.: one of several North American grasses that grow on poor soil, esp. *Aristida dichotoma*; (earlier and later examples); **poverty level** = **poverty line*; **poverty line,** the estimated minimum income sufficient for obtaining the necessities of life; **poverty programme** *U.S.*, a programme or policy designed to alleviate poverty; **poverty shop** (see quots.); **poverty trap,** a situation in which an earned increase to a low income is offset by the consequent loss of means-tested state benefits.

1832 *Boston Even. Transcript* 30 Apr. 2/3 Fields..long given up to barrenness and poverty-grass, are now broken up in readiness to receive the grain. **1906** J. C. LINCOLN *Mr. Pratt* vi. 95 He owned the sheds and barn..and the beach grass and the poverty grass. **1939** H. H. BENNETT *Soil Conservation* xvii. 418 Scores of plants, known as weeds, enter into this far-reaching cover of volunteer vegetation: goldenrod, ragweed, poverty grass, [etc.]. **1973** H. MCCLOY *Change of Heart* iii. 23 The soil is still so sandy that only scrub pine, beach plum, bayberry bushes, and poverty grass grow wild there. **1976** *Billings* (Montana) *Gaz.* 27 June 12-G/1 Statistics for last year show that over five million persons past age 65, or one out of every six, live on a poverty level—defined as an income of under $46 a week for a single aged person or $57 for an aged couple. **1977** *Rolling Stone* 30 June 59/1 The poverty level varies according to family status. **1901** W. S. CHURCHILL in R. S. Churchill *Winston Churchill* (1969) II. Compan. I. ii. 108 Families who cannot provide this necessary sum, or who, providing it do not select their food with like discrimination are *underfed* and come below the 'poverty' line. **1901** B. S. ROWNTREE *Poverty* iv. 114 The recipients of charity are the poor, i.e. those who from causes 'primary' or 'secondary' are below the poverty line. **1904** [in Dict.]. **1932** *Discovery* June 181/2, 21 shillings in Charles Booth's time..[was] the income for an 'ordinary family' at or about the poverty line. **1941** *Economist* 19 Apr. 522/1 The most fortunate group were the old age pensioners of Group C, who might..have an income of 32s., but even this, though well above the poverty line, is nowhere near the human needs level. **1968** E. BRILL *Old Cotswold* vi. 89 He had little of the sharp business acumen that goes with the making of money on a big scale, but this is not evidence that he or his family were ever on the poverty line. **1973** *Observer* (Colour Suppl.) 19 Aug. 26/2 In 1960 about 11 per cent of the population..were living below the poverty line, defined as basic National Assistance rates plus 40 per cent. **1967** *Freedomways* VII. 104 A few years ago..it seemed as if there was a real promise of hope for the poor—both black and white—through the Poverty Program. **1970** *New Yorker* 29 Aug. 57/1 Some of the people..being in a position to welcome any kind of investment, even poverty-program investment..have decided Miller is entitled to his ideas. **1971** *Black Scholar* Apr.–May 10 Who subsist on such foreign aid programs as 'welfare' and 'poverty programs'. **1948** R. GLASS *Social Background of Plan* IV. ii. 161 Newport Road is famous for its 'poverty shops': fried fish shops, pawnbrokers and junkshops. **1956** J. M. MOGEY *Family & Neighbourhood* i. 10 It has become customary to call certain types of shops 'poverty shops': these are fried-fish shops, pawnbrokers, and junkshops. **1961** Poverty shop [see *fish and chips* s.v. *FISH *sb.*[1] 7]. **1972** *Daily Tel.* 21 Nov. 1/8 The idea was to prevent families falling into the 'poverty trap'—the situation in which a pay rise can mean the poor are worse off because they lose a disproportionate number of State benefits. **1973** *Guardian* 30 Mar. 6 The abolition of the 'poverty trap' called for the reintroduction of reduced tax rates for those near the threshold of tax. **1977** *Times* 23 Mar. 16/6 The 'poverty trap'..arises from the fact that the level of supplementary benefits judged to be the minimum.. acceptable can..total more than the personal allowance against tax.

poverty-stricken, *a.* (Earlier and later examples.)

1803 M. WILMOT *Let.* 1 Oct. in *Russ. Jrnls.* (1934) I. 55 Amidst such a multitude of titles a count or countess is often the merest poverty stricken low bread [*sic*] animal that ever was known. **1956** *Railway Mag.* Nov. 739/2 The original promoters of the Port & Pier Railway could hardly have visualised their poverty-stricken child playing such an important role as it was destined to do!

poverty struck, *a.* (Earlier example.)

1801 D. WORDSWORTH *Jrnl.* 29 Dec. (1941) I. 98 A miserable, poverty-struck looking woman.

pow (pau), *int.* orig. *U.S.* [Echoic.] The sound of a punch, blow, shot, or the like. Also *fig.*, used to denote the impact of an emotion or an idea. Also as *sb.*

1881 J. C. HARRIS in *Scribner's Monthly* June 244/1 He step en hit de hoss a rap—*pow!* De hoss 'uz dat s'prise at dat kinder doin's dat he make one jump, en lan' on his footses. **1914** B. TARKINGTON *Penrod* xxii. 207 Herman rubbed his smitten cheek. 'Pow!' he exclaimed. 'Pow-ee! You cert'ny did lan' me good one *nat* time.' **1931** *Technol. Rev.* Nov. 66/1 That class of comic-strip words like *zowie* and *pow*. **1955** H. KURNITZ *Invasion of Privacy* (1956) xxvi. 163 'A man hit him.' She went through the motion with both little fists. 'Pow!' **1961** J. HELLER *Catch-22* (1962) v. 42 He called me a wise guy and punched me in the nose..knocked me flat on my ass. Pow! Just like that. **1964** 'E. MCBAIN' *Ax* iv. 72 He got himself an axe someplace... Pow, good-bye janitor. **1968** L. DEIGHTON *Only when I Larf* i. 16 Imagine beating that typewriter.. for a hundred a week and all the pencils you can take home. Pow. Not me. **1970** G. GREER *Female Eunuch* 173 Perhaps they will not fall in love all at once but feel a tenderness growing until one day *pow!* that amazing kiss. **1970** [see *KER-]. **1976** *Leicester Chron.* 26 Nov. 16/3 In some cases that does not mean films which are more sanguinary, but poorly made action stuff with entire reliance on the pows and kerplunks.

powder, *sb.*[1] Add: **1. e.** = *POWDER SNOW.

1948 *Sun* (N.Y.) 30 Dec. 16 North Conway. 3 inch new powder. Skiing fair. **1973** P. A. WHITNEY *Snowfire* xii. 235 The average skier..didn't care for loose powder. But there was still powder on the steepest slope. **1973** R. HAYES *Hungarian Game* xliv. 257, I came here to ski and I'd hate to miss all this nice fresh powder. **1974** G. MOFFAT *Corpse Road* ii. 34 We had a light fall at Christmas ..just powder on frozen grass.

2. d. *in powder*, wearing hair-powder; also *out of powder*.

1792 LADY TEMPLETOWN *Let.* 11 June in A. E. Newdigate-Newdegate *Cheverels* (1898) vii. 103 M[r] Romney.. has acquitted himself well in respect to Lady Newdigate... The hair is of an agreable *duskiness* that is neither in nor out of powder. **1849** THACKERAY *Pendennis* I. xxiii. 219 Two superior officers in black..now in livery with their hair in powder. **1863** CROWN PRINCESS OF PRUSSIA *Let.* 11 May in R. Fulford *Dearest Mama* (1968) 211 We give a ball in powder tomorrow as this old Palais will have been up 100 years. **1874** L. TROUBRIDGE *Life amongst Troubridges* (1966) ix. 78 The day began hatefully by Grobee telling us that we were not to go to the Cresswells' dance in powder..what *possible* difference could it make to him whether we went with black hair or white. **1924** M. IRWIN *Still she wished for Company* xix. 233 Slovenly Lady Catherine Grey drove over, out of powder at four in the afternoon. **1954** H. ASHTON (*title*) Footman in powder.

g. Denoting other preparations in the form of a powder, chiefly in cookery, hygiene, perfumery, etc., and usu. as the second element of a Comb., as *baby powder, baking powder, curry powder, flea powder, insect powder, milk powder, soap powder, talcum powder, tooth powder, washing powder*, etc.: see under the headwords.

h. Slang phr. *to take a powder*: to depart, absent oneself; to abscond. See also *RUN-OUT 4. orig. and chiefly *U.S.*

1934 J. PROSKAUER *Suckers All* xxiv. 279 The smartest guy in the office took a walk out powder this morning. **1940** J. O'HARA *Pal Joey* 72 And take a powder out of here that day. **1941** R. CHANDLER in *Street & Smith's Detective Story Mag.* Sept. 25 Why are you taking a powder? **1954** 'N. BLAKE' *Whisper in Gloom* xvi. 220 'Where's the Yank?'.. 'Gone. He took a powder.' **1961** J. MACLAREN-ROSS *Doomsday Bk.* v. 65 Phoned four times—no reply. Seems as if..Passman's taken a temporary powder. **1972** 'H. HOWARD' *Nice Day for Funeral* iii. 39 If he'd dumped it [*sc.* a corpse] in the river..everybody was bound to think Frankie had taken a powder to dodge the grand jury. **1979** P. ABLEMAN *Shoestring* i. 14 The very minute that I first looked into her..eyes... Philip Marlowe took a powder and Shoestring, the womanless, took over.

3. b. Fig. phr. *to keep one's powder dry*, with allusion to the advice said to have been given by Oliver Cromwell to his troops: to adopt a practical or realistic policy; to act prudentially or cautiously, be on the alert.

[**1834** COL. BLACKER *Oliver's Advice* in E. Hayes *Ballads of Ireland* (1856) I. 192 The Pow'r that led great William, Boyne's reddening torrent thro',—In his protecting aid confide, and every foe defy—Then put your trust in God, my boys, and keep your powder dry. **1856** E. HAYES *Ballads of Ireland* (ed. 2) I. 191 There is a well-authenticated anecdote of Cromwell. On a certain occasion, when his troops were about crossing a river to attack the enemy, he concluded an address, couched in the usual fanatic terms in use among them, with these words —'put your trust in God; but mind to keep your powder dry'.] **1908** *Times Lit. Suppl.* 5 Nov. 383/1 In thus keeping his powder dry the bishop acted most wisely, though he himself ascribes the happy result entirely to observance of the other half of Cromwell's maxim. **1931** F. L. ALLEN *Only Yesterday* ii. 40 An inheritor of Theodore Roosevelt's creed of fearing God and keeping your powder dry. **1948** A. TOYNBEE *Civilization on Trial* x. 193 A 'Zealotism' tempered by a belief in keeping his powder dry. **1954** C. P. SNOW *New Men* ii. 17 It doesn't sound like business for this time. Still it won't do any harm to watch out and keep our powder dry. **1955** *Times* 6 Aug. 5/1 It is clear that M. Faure, to judge by what he did not say today, is keeping his powder dry. **1968** *Listener* 27 June 833/3, I seem to have been resigned most of my poetic life to the virtues of keeping one's powder dry rather than trying to fire the big guns.

5. a. *powder mark, scales, -smoke* (example); *powder-dry, -light* adjs.; (sense 2 d) *powder bowl; powder-dusted* adj.

1919 in G. Howell *In Vogue* (1975) 34/1 Porcelain powder bowls, for dusting powder. **1930** 'R. CROMPTON' *William's Happy Days* ix. 218 Powder bowls and dolls and cushions. **1972** *Daily Tel.* 10 Oct. 13 Today's young people hardly know what a rose-bowl is, and few possess a cut-glass powder-bowl for loose powder and feathery puff. **1934** T. WOOD *Cobbers* xvi. 215 They worked themselves powder-dry. **1942** W. FAULKNER *Go down, Moses* 100 The pale, powder-light, powder-dry dust of August. **1917** V. WOOLF *Mark on Wall* in *Two Stories* 20 The miniature of a lady with white powdered curls, powder-dusted cheeks, and lips like red carnations. **1937** D. & H. TEILHET *Feather Cloak Murders* i. 14 The revolver bullet left a clean hole when shot close, always with powder marks. **1975** G. LYALL *Judas Country* ix. 68 If I'd been faking a suicide, I'd've put the gun in a more obvious place. Anyway, can't you test his hand for powder marks? **1976** *Shooting Times & Country Mag.* 16–22 Dec. 30/1 Whereas almost every large, local gun-dealer stocks reloading machines, very few stock powder scales. **1905** T. COLLINS in Murdoch & Drake-Brockman *Austral. Short Stories* (1951) 16 The explosion came off, nearly smothering me with powder-smoke.

b. powder base = *foundation cream* s.v. *FOUNDATION 7 d; also (with hyphen) *attrib.*; **powder-burn,** a burn made by the hot gases emitted by a firearm; so **powder-burn** *v. trans.*; **powder cake,** a block of compressed face-powder; **powder chamber,** (*a*) (earlier example); **powder closet** *obs.* exc. *hist.*, a small room formerly used for powdering hair or wigs; **powder colour,** (*a*) an opaque water-colour in powder form; (*b*) (see quot. 1966); **powder compact** = *COMPACT *sb.*[2] e; **powder-house** (earlier and later examples); also *fig.*; so **powder-house-keeper; powder keg,** a small barrel or container for holding gun powder or blasting powder; also *fig.*; **powder magazine** (further examples); also *fig.*; **powder metallurgy,** the branch of metallurgy which is concerned with the production of metals as fine powders and their subsequent pressing and sintering into compact forms; hence **powder-metallurgical** *a.*; **powder metallurgist; powder paint** = **powder colour* (*a*); **powder pattern,** (*a*) *Cryst.* (see 5 c below); (*b*) a pattern indicative of the domain structure of a magnetized solid, formed when a colloidal magnetic powder is allowed to settle on it; **powder-post** (later example); **powder-post beetle,** a small brown beetle belonging to the family Lyctidæ, the larva of which bores tunnels in seasoned timber, reducing it to powder; **powder rag,** a piece of cloth used for applying face-powder; **powder slope**, a slope covered in powder snow.

1927–8 *T. Eaton & Co. Catal.* Fall & Winter 367 A greaseless Vanishing Cream, for use as a protective or powder base. **1932** [see *BASE *sb.*^{1} 11 b]. **1955** M. ALLINGHAM *Beckoning Lady* iv. 66 A good foundation of that powder-base stuff. **1972** *Vogue* 1 Mar. 52/1 An ideal powder-base—inimitable beneath modern make-up to ensure a flawless, perfectly matt finish. **1846** J. W. WEBB *Altowan* I. iv. 125 He might powder-burn the bear by the nearness of the shot. **1847** in H. Howe *Hist. Coll. Ohio* 99 In this struggle, Lytle..had..his face powder burnt. **1927** *Scribner's Mag.* Feb. 176/2 In the pursuit, the Rangers literally carried out their leader's orders to 'powder-burn' them. **1969** G. MACBETH *War Quartet* 72 With his gun One braised his leg three times. The doctor saw Powder-burns there, and left him. **1975** M. BABSON *There must be Some Mistake* xx. 182 You have gloves... Put them on now. The only powder burns must be found on those two that the police may re-enact the scene. **1961** 'A. A. FAIR' *Stop at Red Light* (1962) v. 82 Parts of a powder cake were on the floor, and bits of glass from the broken mirror. **1803** *Jrnl. Natural Philos.* IV. 251 As soon as the lever has arrived at the position N, the powder chamber P is exactly opposite the ball, and ready to be discharged against it. **1905** *Pall Mall Mag.* Dec. 746/1 Violante..lay dozing in the powder closet which opened out of Donna Carlotta's bedroom. **1927** *Daily Express* 12 Dec. 4 Methley Park..has one or two unusual features, however; and among these are some queer old powder closets. **1929** S. ERTZ *Galaxy* i. 11 The house contained a powder-closet for the dressing of ladies' hair in earlier days. **1980** *Country Life* 28 Feb. 609/1 The emergence of indecencies from the powder closet to the respectable page. **1862** *Illustr. Catal. Internat. Exhib., Industr. Dept., Brit. Div.* II. No. 5512 Colours prepared for missal-painting, and illumination in soluble powder-colour. **1913** R. FRY *Let.* 28 Dec. (1972) II. 376 Grind up your powder colours in water very stiffly and use with the yolks of eggs. **1963** S. MARSHALL *Exper. in Educ.* iii. 88 Powder colour has proved its worth. **1966** J. S. COX *Illustr. Dict. Hairdressing* 121/1 *Powder-colour*, colour rinses in powder form. **1927** [see *COMPACT *sb.*^{2} e]. **1937** D. L. SAYERS *Busman's Honeymoon* xv. 259 He laid a powder-compact aside on the what-not. **1978** *Cornish Guardian* 27 Apr. 32/4 The new president, Mrs. Tippitt, presented Mrs. M. Williams, the retiring president, with a powder compact. **1720** in *Mass. House of Representatives Jrnl.* (1921) II. 288 Daniel Powning, keeper of the Powder-House. **1848** *Knickerbocker* XVIII. 216 The powder house, the pound, the poor-house and the county-house, are all objects of notice to the traveller. **1928** *Manch. Guardian Weekly* 7 Sept. 181/4 The spark that fired this powder-house was a letter protesting against the 'constant criticism' of the methods of Lancashire cricketers. **1789** *Rec. Early Hist. Boston* (1886) X. 183 Foster Thomas, powder-house-keeper. **1855** W. G. SIMMS *Forayers* iii. 39 Sinclair..drew up an old powder-keg by a rope-hitch, which had been made about it. **1876** 'MARK TWAIN' *Tom Sawyer* xxxii. 323 It was the treasure-box..along with an empty powder-keg, a couple of guns in leather cases,..a leather belt, and some other rubbish. **1893** W. K. POST *Harvard Stories* 6 One reason why they do it..is to make you flare up, you little powder keg. **1945** *Richmond* (Va.) *News-Leader* 17 Sept. 7/2 (*heading*) Argentina's militarist regime believed sitting on powderkeg. **1972** *Publishers' Weekly* 24 Jan. 21 His stories weeks before the revolt warned of the powderkeg inside the prison. **1975** *Publ. Amer. Dial. Soc.* 1973 LIX. 47 *Powder keg*.., a round, metal container for blasting powder, usually of twenty-five pounds capacity. **1890** KIPLING *Departmental Ditties* (ed. 4) 98 You shouldn't take a man from Canada And bid him smoke in powder-magazines. **1933** J. BUCHAN *Prince of Captivity* II. ii. 196 Birkpool is..becoming a powder magazine. **1979** G. LATTA tr. *Jacquemard-Sénécal's Eleventh Little Nigger* II. iv. 94 The reunion of the four of them..would constitute a sort of powder-magazine: one spark and the magazine blows up. **1980** ALEXANDER & ANAND *Queen Victoria's Maharajah* i. 11 A lucky hit on the powder magazine. **1949** *Electronic Engin.* XXI. 88/1 The production of intricate structures is due to the fact that moulding powders are now made by powder-metallurgical processes. **1975** BRAM & DOWNS *Manuf. Technol.* iii. 79 Cemented carbides are a typical powder metallurgical product. **1949** C. G. GOETZEL *Treat. Powder Metall.* I. p. vii, The final chapter of Part One covers briefly the many uses for metal powders that are somewhat beyond the sphere of interest of the powder metallurgist. **1954** H. UDIN et al. *Welding for Engineers* iii. 39 This process of spheroidization of pores or inclusions has been of great interest to powder metallurgists. **1933** *Engin. & Mining Jrnl.* CXXXIV. 373/1 What is frequently referred to as 'powder metallurgy' had its beginnings at the turn of the century when the metals tungsten and molybdenum first became commercial commodities. **1959** *Listener* 12 Mar. 453/1 Coolidge in America developed the process now known as powder metallurgy, by which a bar of compressed tungsten powder was sintered at a temperature below the melting point of the metal. **1970** *New Scientist* 12 Nov. 325/1 Powder metallurgy is commonly used to make precision components, and to fabricate exotic materials. **1939** L. DE LISSA *Life in Nursery School* ix. 158 Powder paints are cheap and suitable and can be obtained in good colours. **1955** E. BLISHEN *Roaring Boys* I. 33 How should I learn to distinguish between different types of brush, to mix powder paint? **1973** *Galt Toys Catal.* 49 *Powder paint set*..mix up a small quantity with water as required. **1934** *Physical Rev.* XLVI. 227 (*caption*) Powder patterns with H normal to the surface. **1951** L. F. BATES *Mod. Magn.* (ed. 3) xii. 457 The main method of studying domain structure is undoubtedly the Bitter figure or powder pattern method. **1965** CRAIK & TEBBLE *Ferromagnetism & Ferromagnetic Domains* 308 The first stage in the preparation of colloids or suspensions for the powder pattern or Bitter figure technique, is the production of magnetite (Fe_3O_4) in a very finely divided state. **1927** *Bull. U.S. Dept. Agric.* No. 1490, 7 Powder post is that class of defects in which the larvae of insects reduce the wood fibers of seasoned or partially seasoned wood to a powderlike condition. **1905** *Yearbk. U.S. Dept. Agric.* 1904 387 (*caption*) Work of powder post beetle.. in hickory poles. **1911** *Technical Ser. Bureau Entomol., U.S. Dept. Agric.* XX. III. 111 (*title*) A revision of the powder-post beetles of the family Lyctidæ of the United States and Europe. **1928** *Forestry* II. 42 The sapwood..has been reduced to a finely powdered, floury condition—the characteristic damage that gives the name of 'powder-post beetles' to the *Lyctus* species. **1963** *B.S.I. News* Mar. 6/1 The third British Standard will describe a test for determining the toxicity of wood preservatives to the powder post beetle, *Lyctus brunneus*. **1975** G. EVANS *Life of Beetles* iv. 94 Lyctidae, the powder post beetles (e.g. *Lyctus* spp.), have larvae which produce a very fine powdery dust. **1904** 'O. HENRY' in *McClure's Mag.* Aug. 352/2 This stake comes in handier than a powder rag at a fat man's ball. **1906** —— *Four Million* (1916) 21 Delia finished her cry and attended to her cheeks with the powder rag. *a* **1911** D. G. PHILLIPS *Susan Lenox* (1917) II. ii. 33 Susan..safeguarded her nose against shine; she tucked the powder rag into the stocking. **1972** D. HASTON *In High Places* xi. 115, I could put this [failure] out of my mind swooping around the powder slopes.

c. With reference to the Debye-Scherrer method of X-ray crystallography (see *DEBYE), as *powder camera, diffraction, pattern, photograph, photography*.

1917 *Physical Rev.* X. 664 The powder photographs have an advantage..over ionization-chamber measurements, in that the intensities of reflection from different planes, as well as different orders, are directly comparable. **1924** R. W. G. WYCKOFF *Struct. Crystals* vi. 178 The spectrum lines which result from these reflections of monochromatic X-rays constitute a powder photograph. *Ibid.*, Such a powder pattern can be greatly simplified by filtering the X-rays to render them essentially monochromatic. *Ibid.*, The outstanding advantage of powder diffraction methods obviously lies in their ability to treat the many crystalline materials which do not grow large single crystals. *Ibid.* 185 A more extended description of these procedures is not justified because thus far they have found little application to powder photography. **1936** *Jrnl. R. Aeronaut. Soc.* XL. 411 The powder photograph is..a powerful means of recognising alloy phases. **1945** C. W. BUNN *Chem. Crystallogr.* v. 109 A powder camera consists essentially of an aperture system to define the X-ray beam, a holder for the specimen, and a framework for holding the photographic film. **1948** K. LONSDALE *Crystals & X-Rays* iii. 76 For powder photography monochromatic radiation is used..but the specimen is a mass of tiny crystals orientated in all directions. **1962** *Times* 4 Sept. 2/6 There are four X-ray generating sets and accessory equipment includes powder cameras. **1965** ADAMS & RAYNOR *Advanced Pract. Inorg. Chem.* xvii. 155 The intersection of a curved strip of film with these diffraction cones gives the familiar powder photograph, which consists of a series of curved lines. **1969** B. E. WARREN *X-Ray Diffraction* v. 67 Powder patterns are very often used for a precision measurement of the crystal axes.

powder, *v.*^{1} Add: **3. b.** (Further examples.) Phr. *to powder one's nose*, used also *euphem.* (with reference to a woman) for 'to go to the lavatory'.

1921 W. S. MAUGHAM *Circle* I. 28, I must powder my nose, Hughie. **1924** E. O'NEILL *Welded* II. 137 You'll want to go upstairs and powder your nose. **1927** S. ERTZ *Now East, now West* xvii. 261 She put no colour on her face,..which, if she powdered and didn't even redden her lips, always made people ask her if she were ill. **1930** A. BENNETT *Imperial Palace* lvi. 417 That's the bathroom and so on... You can hang your overcoat in there—and powder your nose. **1938** I. GOLDBERG *Wonder of Words* vi. 108 We are invited to wash our hands, or, if we wear dresses, to powder our noses. **1962** *Guardian* 5 Dec. 6/5 Useful information..about where to park..dine, stay overnight, and—for women—powder one's nose in comfort. **1969** R. T. WILCOX *Dict. Costume* (1970) 88/1 Venetian gentlemen also painted, powdered and patched. **1972** L. P. DAVIES *What did I do Tomorrow?* 72 I'll use your bathroom. To powder my nose, as nice girls say.

powder blue, *sb.* and *a.* Add: **1.** (Earlier example.)

1656 *Essex County, Mass. Probate Rec.* (1916) I. 233 Mace and Ribing, starch and poudarblu.

2. (Further examples.) Now also used of light blue shades.

1923 [see *CYCLAMEN c]. **1943** A. CHRISTIE *Moving Finger* xi. 130 A skin-tight powder-blue evening dress. **1967** *New Statesman* 28 July 110/3 Their powder-blue berets bob above helmets. **1970** *Cape Times* 28 Oct. 19/2 (Advt.), Rambler Rogue 1970, 12 800 miles, powder blue with black upholstery, executive's car. **1973** 'S. HARVESTER' *Corner of Playground* III. i. 170 A waxed red hat with a powder-blue band. **1978** *Jrnl. R. Soc. Arts* CXXVI. 352/1 Just as there are many different shades of blue, for example powder blue,..wedgwood blue and pacific blue, so there are many different nuances of piano tone.

3. *attrib.* or as *adj.* Applied *spec.* to a type of Chinese porcelain of the Ch'ing period having a ground of powder blue. Also as **powdered blue.**

1900 F. LITCHFIELD *Pott. & Porc.* vii. 114 The date of what is called 'powdered blue' china is said to be the Kang-he period (1661–1722). **1906** S. W. BUSHELL *Chinese Art* II. viii. 36 The finely pounded pigment is blown upon the raw body to produce, when glazed, a 'powder blue', or *bleu fouetté* ground. **1911** [see *KANG-HAI, KANG-HE, KANG-HI]. **1960** R. G. HAGGAR *Conc. Encycl. Continental Pott. & Porc.* 352/2 A powdered-blue ground colour of great depth and richness was introduced at Meissen porcelain factory before 1725. **1965** [see *K'ANG-HSI]. **1971** L. A. BOGER *Dict. World Pott. & Porc.* 270/1 *Powder Blue Ware*, in Chinese ceramics; porcelain of the Ch'ing period, especially of the K'ang Hsi reign, which is characterized by a beautiful and rather even ground of bright soft blue with a slightly clouded appearance.

4. *Comb.*, as *powder-blue-grey* adj.

1952 S. SPENDER *Learning Laughter* 30 Fields and fields of powder-blue-grey cornflowers.

powder-box. Add: **c.** (Later examples.)

1895 *Army & Navy Co-op. Soc. Price List* 172/2 Powder Boxes—Puff, ea. 7/5, 9/4, [etc.]. **1925** *Heal & Son Catal.: Glass*, Powder Box. Height 6 in. Price 9/6. **1949** *Dædalian Q.* Fall 26 Powder box, powder box, powder your nose, How many petals are in a rose? **1979** G. LATTA tr. *Jacquemard-Sénécal's Eleventh Little Nigger* I. v. 46 He was still clutching his powder-box and puff in his clenched hands.

powdered, *ppl. a.* Add: **7.** Applied to foods that have been reduced to the form of a powder by dehydration.

1889 in A. Davis *Package & Print* (1967) Pl. 69 Pancake flour—self-rising mixture—..powdered milk without butter fat, corn sugar, [etc.]. **1909** *Chem. Abstr.* 933 Powdered milks are made to contain varying amounts of fat by the removal of more or less fat cream before evaporation. **1917** *Official Gaz.* (U.S. Patent Office) 2 Jan. 363/1 The Cabell Company, Baltimore, Md... Velvet *Particular description of goods.*—Powdered Egg. *Claims use* since Sept. 1, 1916. **1917** *Bakers Rev.* Nov. 13 (Advt.), *Velvet* Powdered Egg, made from selected fresh hen eggs, is entirely and instantly soluble. **1919** *N.Y. Times* 14 Dec. III. 5/1 Dry eggs from China..include the white of egg, the yolk of egg, and powdered whole egg. **1925** T. M. RECTOR *Sci. Preservation Food* xii. 172 Hermetic sealing is not used in the preservation of eggs and egg products though there is certainly a field for it in 'powdered' egg. **1935** *Economist* 3 Aug. 226/2 As for powdered and condensed milk,..these imported milk products are going to be made artificially scarce. **1943** *Industr. & Engin. Chem.* XXXV. 1204/2 The losses of vitamin D in powdered whole egg during storage were studied at two temperatures, 15° and 98·6°F. **1953** *Ann. Reg.* 1952 153 The provision of powdered milk every day for over a million children. **1972** G. DURRELL *Catch me a Colobus* v. 84 Complan, a sort of powdered milk which we found was very useful for rearing baby animals. **1980** *Sunday Times* (Colour Suppl.) 20 Jan. 70/1, I have orange juice..then..a cup of powdered coffee.

powderize (paʊ·dəraiz), *v.* [f. POWDER *sb.*^{1} + -IZE.] **a.** = POWDER *v.*^{1} 3 b. *rare.* **b.** = POWDER *v.*^{1} 6.

a **1800** S. PEGGE *Anecdotes Eng. Lang.* (1803) 259 Many words will admit *-ize* for the termination. A Hair-Dresser powder*izes*, while a Chemist..pulver*izes* [etc.]. **1903** *Sci. Amer. Suppl.* 18 Apr. 22818/1 Only one thing can be done to lighten the task, and that is to powderize the soap when the mixed materials are still warm. **1978** *Nature* 20 Apr. 715/2 The material was powderised and partially attacked by a mixture of hydrofluoric and hydrochloric acids.

powderless, *a.* Add: **b.** Not employing powder.

1953 *Photoengravers Bull.* XLIII. 171 The key to powderless etching in the Dow etching development lies in the chemical composition of the bath. **1959** *Times* 14 Jan. 12/4 Another precision etching system, the Lithotex powderless etcher, is being manufactured in Britain. **1967** V. STRAUSS *Printing Industry* v. 217/1 Though conventional etching methods are still used.., they are progressively replaced throughout the industry by powderless etching. **1978** *Penrose Ann.* LXXI. 162 Powderless etching is still rare [in India] and electronic engraving extremely so.

powder-monkey. Add: **a.** Now also a term for a member of a blasting crew; = POWDER-MAN c. *U.S.*

1926 *Amer. Speech* II. 87/2 Dynamite is brought to the miner by the *powder monkey*. **1937** *Nat. Geogr. Mag.* Aug. 149/1 Hither and yon darted the 'powder monkeys', packing dynamite in the holes, shooting loose great masses of salt, which others broke up and loaded into trucks. **1939** W. FAULKNER *Wild Palms* 118 Suits from wop pick-and-shovel men and bohunk powder-monkeys and chink ore-trimmers. **1951** *Publ. Amer. Dial. Soc.* xv. 74 *Monkey* in various combinations has become a favorite term for handyman. There are *derrick monkeys, pump monkeys, boiler monkeys*, and *powder monkeys*. **1976** M. MACHLIN *Pipeline* xviii. 227 This time they wanted two powder monkeys, a couple of drillers..and four jobs for straight camp labor.

pow·der-room. [f. POWDER *sb.*^{1} + ROOM *sb.*^{1}] **a.** In Dict. s.v. POWDER *sb.*^{1} 5 b.

b. = *powder closet* s.v. *POWDER *sb.*^{1} 5 b.

1908 'F. DANBY' *Heart of Child* xv. 250 He liked to see.. his Staffordshire pottery en-niched in the quaint powder-room, opening out of the drawing-room. **1946** J. W. DAY *Harvest Adventure* xiv. 243 Look at the old drawings of Ockwells in Lysons' *Magna Britannica* [*sic*] and other works, and you will see that, a hundred years ago, the powder-room window was completely blocked up. **1966** M. M. PEGLER *Dict. Interior Design* (1967) 351 *Powder room*, originally a corner or small closet in the bedroom of an 18th-century house where one could go to have one's hair powdered.

c. A women's cloak-room or lavatory in a hotel or shop; *gen.* a lavatory. Also *attrib.*

1941 B. SCHULBERG *What makes Sammy Run?* xi. 272 She had just run into Laurette in the powder room. **1945** MENCKEN *Amer. Lang.* Suppl. I. 640 During the days of Prohibition some learned speak-easy proprietor in New York hit upon the happy device of calling his retiring-room for female boozers a *powder-room*. **1958** *Times Lit. Suppl.* 13 June 323/2 But there is too much of the language of powder-room chatter ('When Terry asked me to marry him, as I thought I hoped he would..') and platitude for her tale to gain and hold sympathy. **1959** D. DU MAURIER *Breaking Point* 219 The call-box was just opposite the ladies' powder room. **1977** *Time* 5 Dec. 68/3 While the play is laced with affectionately bantering humor and a gamy ration of powder-room candor, the characters are stereotypical.

powder snow. [f. POWDER *sb.*[1] + SNOW *sb.*[1]] A newly fallen, light, dry snow. Also *attrib.*

1929 F. SMYTHE *Climbs & Ski Runs* xi. 169 The *staublawine* or powder-snow avalanche is of little danger to the ski-runner. **1946** P. BOTTOME *Lifeline* xxiii. 253 He himself moved over the light powder snow like a soundless ghost. **1955** E. HILLARY *High Adventure* 159 High on the mountain a cloud of powder snow was being blown off the ridge. **1972** D. HASTON *In High Places* xi. 118 It was obvious what was happening—a huge powder snow avalanche was passing. **1974** *Listener* 17 Jan. 76/1 Nice sunshine, powder-snow skiing.

powdery, *a.* Add: **4. powdery mildew,** a parasitic fungus belonging to the family Erysiphaceæ, or the disease it causes in plants, characterized by a white, floury covering of conidia on the parts attacked.

1889 *Jrnl. Mycol.* V. 214 (*heading*) Powdery mildew of the bean. **1913** G. & I. MASSEE *Mildews, Rusts & Smuts* 36 The entire group [*sc.* Erysiphaceæ] is often spoken of as powdery mildews, on account of the dense masses of conidia that are produced, and rest on the white patches of mycelium, giving them the appearance of having been sprinkled with flour. **1936** *Jrnl. Agric. Res.* LII. 645 (*title*) The diurnal cycle of the powdery mildew *Erysiphe polygoni*. **1978** P. P. PIRONE *Dis. & Pests Ornamental Plants* (ed. 5) i. 9/2 Powdery mildews are fungi that grow superficially on the leaves and stems of their hosts.

Powellism (pau·ĕliz'm). [f. the name of John Enoch *Powell* (born 1912) + -ISM.] The political and economic policies advocated by J. Enoch Powell; *spec.* one of restricting or terminating the immigration of coloured people into the United Kingdom.

1965 *Economist* 17 July 217/1 In the past few months a new word has found its way into British politics: Powellism. **1968** *Guardian* 9 Sept. 6/1 Mr Enoch Powell's alternative..is a drastic move towards laissez-faire economics and a stopping of immigration. Powellism is gaining ground within the Conservative ranks. **1972** M. WILLIAMS *Inside Number 10* x. 254 Although we realized only too well that to dissociate Labour from Powellism was not a winner in electoral terms, it was decided unhesitatingly that Harold should leave no doubt about where the Labour Party stood on matters of race. **1973** C. MULLARD *Black Brit.* II. vi. 66 It [*sc.* the Institute of Race Relations] has remained on safe, non-controversial ground, arousing as much black scorn as Powellism. **1977** M. WALKER *National Front* v. 127 The ghost of Powellism in the parliamentary party is still not laid... Powellism, Young's own ambition to lead the Club, and the bitter debates on the EEC in 1971 were.. enough to account for the crisis.

So **Pow·ellist** *a.* and *sb.*; **Pow·ellite** *a.* and *sb.*

1965 *Economist* 5 June 1129/2 The Conservatives should not turn Powellite in opposition to an incomes policy. **1966** [see *blue-water school* s.v. *BLUE *a.* 13]. **1968** *Guardian* 26 Apr. 22/2 (*heading*) MPs' temperatures soar as Powellite sparks fly. **1968** *Manch. Guardian Weekly* 5 Sept. 12 The Conservatives..are likely for a year or two to be more Powellist in economics. **1968** *Peace News* 29 Nov. 8 Working-class Powellists..are not so much thinking like colonialists, but rather as aborigines. **1977** M. WALKER *National Front* iv. 90 The NF was deeply concerned that it had missed the Powellite boat, and that it was not expanding as it should. *Ibid.* iv. 93 Stories in the press about a split in the movement between Powellites and the rest.

Powellize (pau·ĕləiz), *v.* [f. the name of William *Powell*, of London, who invented the process + -IZE.] *trans.* To treat (timber) by boiling in a solution of sugar so as to preserve it and reduce shrinkage. So **Pow·ellized** *ppl. a.*; **Pow·ellizing** *vbl. sb.*

1903 *Sci. Amer. Suppl.* 5 Sept. 23139/1 The London city authorities..intend to repave the Strand thoroughfare with 15,000 Powellized blocks. **1913** *Chambers's Jrnl.* Aug. 621/1 Seeing that elm is plentiful and extremely low in price, Powellising should result in its more extended application. *Ibid.*, After being Powellised it becomes a very handsome and hard wood. **1929** *Encycl. Brit.* XXII. 222/1 Extensive tests carried out with Powellized sleepers on Indian railways give good results.

power, *sb.*[1] Add: **4. f.** Used with preceding adj. or sb. to designate a movement to enhance the status of the group specified or the beliefs and activities of such a group. See also **black power*, **flower power*, etc.

1970 'J. MELVILLE' *New Kind of Killer* ii. 32 I'm working to establish Parent Power right now. **1972** *Pride of Lions* (Columbia Univ.) Apr. 2/2 What is important is that you come out, have gay pride and leave the dance with a sense of Gay power. **1972** *Guardian* 17 May 12/1 Pupil power flexes its muscles in London today. The organisers have called on all London secondary schoolchildren to join them in a one-day general strike. *Ibid.* 19 Sept. 12/3 Three different types of reformers: the pupil power movement: the egalitarians: and the orthodox educational reformers. **1974** *Howard Jrnl.* XIV. 38 The growth of 'pupil power' and the increase in truancy. **1974** N. BAGNALL (*title*) Parent power. **1974** *Times* 7 Dec. 5/4 (*caption*) Mr Narayan: his hope lies in village power. **1975** *Times* 30 Dec. 8/8 The old form a powerful group—'grey power' to adopt Professor Wilensky's phrase.

6. c. *the powers that be* (after Rom. xiii. 1): the authorities concerned; the elements exercising social or political control. Also in sing.

1526 [see Dict., sense 6 a]. **1793** W. B. STEVENS *Jrnl.* 24 Feb. (1965) 70 The Selfishness and Timidities essential to his nature..make him cling to the Powers that be. **1814** SCOTT *Waverley* I. xix. 281 The cautious Baillie justly observed, that..the tenantry and villagers might become riotous in expressing their joy, and give offence to the 'powers that be', a sort of persons for whom the Baillie always had unlimited respect. **1886** KIPLING *Departmental Ditties* (ed. 2) 5 Potiphar Gubbins, C. E., Is dear to the Powers that Be. **1909** *Westm. Gaz.* 11 Jan. 12/4 Perhaps next year the powers that be may take a little more trouble to discover the talent that lies outside London. **1924** LAWRENCE & SKINNER *Boy in Bush* 15 He had to hear the end of a story against the powers-that-be. **1930** *Times* 25 Mar. 23/7 One can only express the hope that the Power-that-be in Nanking will realize the desirability for proceeding slowly and gradually. **1956** A. WILSON *Anglo-Saxon Att.* II. ii. 331 Donald's audience was not so large as it had been for the first lectures, but even now there was a fair number..those who had hoped that they might trap Donald into some mistake and earn a reputation for standing no nonsense from the powers that be. **1976** *Equals* Oct./Nov. 2/3, I feel that the powers-that-be have expected too much to happen too quickly.

7. (Earlier and later examples.) *By the powers!* (earlier example).

1490 JOHANNES DE IRLANDIA *Meroure of Wyssdome* (1965) II. 49 He had overcummyn all their powaris of myrknes. **1803** G. COLMAN *John Bull* I. i. 12 By the powers she's well enough. **1974** B. & R. HILL *Spirit in Stone* iii. 39 When his training period was over, he secretly painted his face in the way directed by his 'power' (i.e. spirit helper) and set out.

10. a. (Later example.)

1905 J. M. SYNGE *Shadow of Glen* 25 I'm thinking it's a power of men you're after knowing.

b. Delete *vulgar* and add later examples.

1938 B. L. BURMAN *Blow for Landing* 161 There's a power of music in an anvil. **1947** *Daily Mail* 22 May 3/4 There's a power of difference between farming now and when I was a lad. **1958** *People* 4 May 16/1 (Advt.), Hungry children do themselves a power of good when they polish off the sandwiches. *a* **1974** R. CROSSMAN *Diaries* (1975) I. 400 Two days at Prescote have done me a power of good.

11. d. *Math.* A property of a set that is the same for any two sets whose elements can be placed in a one-to-one correspondence and that in the case of a finite set is equal to the number of elements it contains; = *POTENCY 5.

1903 B. RUSSELL *Princ. Math.* xliii. 364 Power is synonymous with cardinal number. *Ibid.*, To prove that there are powers higher than the continuum. **1953** A. A. FRAENKEL *Abstract Set Theory* i. 79 The cardinal of the continuum, often called the power of the continuum. *Ibid.* iii. 306 Cantor and many of his successors..call cardinals in general by the neutral name of 'powers' (Mächtigkeiten). **1961** L. F. BORON tr. *Kuratowski's Introd. Set Theory & Topology* v. 61 The set of all odd natural numbers has the same power as the set of all even natural numbers. *Ibid.*, The open interval $-\pi/2 < x < +\pi/2$ has the same power as the set of all real numbers. **1968** H. SHARP *Mod. Fund. Math.* vii. 240 The power of a finite set is simply the number of elements in the set.

13. d. Motive power or heat (as contrasted with light) obtained from an electricity supply. Usu. *attrib.*

1896 R. ROBB *Electric Wiring* v. 82 Wires that carry current for running motors, or for furnishing power in distinction from light, are commonly called 'power-wires'. **1904** W. R. BOWKER *Dynamo, Motor & Switchboard Circuits* v. 96 (*caption*) Low-tension system for power and lighting. **1931** *Electrician* 13 Nov. 654/1 Where it is desired to instal power plugs in premises already lighted electrically a minimum of two 15A positions is demanded. **1941** E. WHITEHORNE *Elect. Wiring Specifications* vii. 98 (*caption*) Power wiring must serve specific loads and processes. **1958, 1975** [see *power point*, sense *18 below.]

14. (Further examples.) Also applied *concr.* to an engine that produces power.

1869 *Bradshaw's Railway Manual* XXI. 399 Indian Tramway..adapted according to local circumstances to cattle or locomotive power. **1953** BERREY & VAN DEN BARK *Amer. Thes. Slang* (1954) §82a/1 *Motor; engine*—1. chugger, coffee grinder, mill, percolator, power, stove. **1962** *Amer. Speech* XXXVII. 134 *Power*,..all the locomotives owned by a company. The expression is heard, 'The company has lots of power.' **1973** *Ibid.* 1969 XLIV. 245 A light engine crew moves *power* from one location to another. *Ibid.* 259 *Power*, 1: Number and type of locomotives on a train. 2: Locomotives available at a given time.

17. j. *more power to* (someone): good luck, may fortune favour (someone). See also *ELBOW *sb.* 4 g. Also *more power to one's arm.*

1842 S. LOVER *Handy Andy* ix. 89 'More power to you, Andy,' said the Squire. **1881** CARLYLE *Reminisc.* II. 321 More power to him! **1932** E. GLASGOW *Let.* 12 Jan. (1958) 112, I read and enjoyed and admired the articles by Allen Tate. They are fine and true. More power to him. **1948** 'J. TEY' *Franchise Affair* xvi. 187 Hooray! More power to him! I begin to like the boy. **1973** P. MOYES *Curious Affair of Third Dog* viii. 107 'I'm trying to find Griselda, you see.' 'In that case, more power to your arm.'

k. *power behind the throne*: one who exercises power behind the scenes while appearing to have no authority to do so.

[**1770** PITT *Speech* 2 Mar. in *London Museum* Apr. 249 A long train of such practices has at length unwillingly convinced me, that there is something within the court [in *Parl. Hist.* (1813) XVI. 843 something behind the throne] greater than the King himself.] **1866** MRS. LINCOLN in W. H. Herndon *Lincoln* (1889) III. 513, I told him [*sc.* Lincoln] once of the assertion I had heard coming from the friends of Seward, that the latter was the power behind the throne; that he could rule him. **1875** 'MARK TWAIN' *Old Times Mississippi* in *Atlantic Monthly* June 728/1 A power behind the throne that was greater than the throne itself. It was the underwriters! **1905** H. A. VACHELL *Hill* ix. 198 It was his habit to consult his wife in emergencies. The chief cutter..said that Amelia was the power behind the throne. **1931** W. HOLTBY *Poor Caroline* vii. 277 I'd been..generally working in the *background*, but then I *liked* to be the power behind the throne. **1973** J. WAINWRIGHT *Devil you Don't* 8 She'd been blinded..at the possibility of controlling such a man. Of being the power behind such a throne. **1977** *Time* 8 Aug. 43/2 Anderson..will become the real power behind the throne.

18. a. *power absorption, company, group, -holder, hunger, -impulse, -instinct, logic(s, -loss, -lust, -mania, -maniac, -monger* (later examples), *motive, -producer, relation, -seeker, -soul, structure, struggle, turret, -urge, vacuum, -worship.* **b.** *power approach, cart, craft, ditching, drill, hoist, mower, saw, shovel, -vehicle* (examples), *wringer.* **c.** *power lever.* **d.** *power-carrying, -craving, -generating, -handling, -losing, -loving, -seeking* (examples), *-sharing* (all may be used as adjs. or sbs.); *power-greedy, -hungry, -lusting, -mad, -thirsty* adjs. **e.** *power-crazed, -driven* (later examples), *-obsessed* adjs.; *power-driving, -farming* sbs. **f. power amplifier,** an amplifier designed to deliver an output of appreciable power into a load; **power-assisted** *a.*, employing some inanimate source of power to assist manual operation; applied esp. to brakes and steering in cars where power from the engine is so used; so **power-assi·stance,** (the equipment for) the application of power to assist manual operation; **power bandwidth** *Electronics*, the range of frequencies over which a device can deliver a certain power or a signal with distortion less than a certain value; **power base,** a source of authority or support; **power block,** (*a*) a group of allied states, or a great power with its allies and dependencies; (*b*) *Naut.*, a power-driven pulley used to haul in a seine; **power board,** (*a*) a board or panel containing switches or meters for an electricity supply; (*b*) chiefly *N.Z.*, the controlling authority for the supply of electricity in an area; an electricity board; **power brake,** a power-assisted brake (in a motor vehicle); **power broker** orig. and chiefly *U.S.*, one who exerts influence or affects the distribution of political power by intrigue; hence **power-brokering, power-broking** *vbl. sbs.*; **power buzzer,** an electrical vibrator used in the war of 1914–18 to generate telegraphic earth currents; **power cable,** a cable transmitting electrical power; **power car,** a railway carriage incorporating an engine; **power centre,** a locus of political authority; a powerful person or institution; so **power-centred** *a.*, concerned with the study, acquisition, or exercise of political authority; **power cut,** a temporary withdrawal or failure of the electricity supply; also *fig.*; **power density** *Nuclear Physics*, the power produced per unit volume of a reactor core; **power dive,** a dive made by an aircraft with its engine(s) providing thrust; also *transf.* and *fig.*; so **power-dive** *v. intr.*; **power-egg,** on an airship (rarely, an aeroplane), an ovate housing for an engine; **power élite,** a social or political group that exercises power; **power factor** *Electr.*, (*a*) the ratio of the actual power delivery by an a.c. circuit (or a component in it) to the product of the r.m.s. values of current and voltage; (*b*) as a property of an insulating material: the power factor under specified conditions of a capacitor made with this material as dielectric; **power failure,** a failure of a power supply, esp. the electricity supply; **power frequency** *Electr.*, a frequency in the range used for alternating currents supplying power (commonly 50 or 60 Hz); **power game,** a contest for authority or influence, esp. in politics; **power law,** a relationship between two quantities such that the magnitude of one is proportional to a fixed power of the magnitude of the other; **power level,** the amount of power being transmitted, produced, etc. (in some contexts measured relative to some reference level); **power line,** a conductor supplying electrical power, often spec. one supported by poles or pylons; **power-loader** *Mining*, a machine which loads coal on to a conveyor belt at the coal face; hence **power-loaded** *a.*; cf. *POWER LOADING *vbl. sb.*; **power-net,** a knitted stretch fabric used in women's underwear; **power oil,** oil brought up from a well and used on the spot as a source of power; **power-operated** *a.*, operated by power from an inanimate source; **power pack,** a unit for supplying power; *spec.* (*a*) one for converting an alternating current (from the mains) to a direct current at a different (usu. lower) voltage, and usu. comprising a transformer, rectifier, and capacitor; (*b*) (see quot. 1967); also *fig.*; **power package,** a self-contained source of power; **power pile** = *power reactor* below; **power play,** in sport, a concentration of players at a particular point; the style of play involving such concentrations; *spec.* in ice hockey, a group of players sent out against a depleted opposition; also *transf.*; **power point,** a point or socket (*POINT *sb.*[1] A. 19 e) from which electrical machinery or heaters can be operated; also *fig.*; **power pole,** a pole used to support an overhead power line; **power reactor,** a nuclear reactor designed principally as a means of producing power; **power response** *Electronics*, the way the output power of a device depends on the signal frequency; *spec.* the power bandwidth; **power seat,** a power-assisted reclining seat; **power series** *Math.*, a series of the form $\ldots + a'_2x^{-2} + a'_1x^{-1} + a_0 + a_1x + a_2x^2 + \ldots$, where the *a*s are independent of *x*; also, a generalization of this for more than one variable; **power set** *Math.*, the set of all the subsets of a given set; **power spectrum,** the distribution of the energy of a wave-form among its different Fourier components; **power steering,** power-assisted steering (in a motor vehicle); **power stroke,** in a piston engine, a stroke during which the piston is moved by the expansion of the gases in the cylinder; **power-system,** a set of political beliefs or institutions founded or dependent upon coercion; **power take-off** (equipment for) the transmission of mechanical power from an engine, esp. that of a tractor or similar vehicle, to another piece of equipment; **power tool,** an electrically powered tool; **power-to-weight** (or **power–weight**) **ratio,** the ratio of the power an engine or motor can produce to its weight (or the weight of the vehicle, etc., containing it); **power train** *Mech.*, the mechanism that transmits the drive from the engine of a vehicle to its axle; also, this together with the engine and axle; **power transformer** *Electronics*, a transformer designed to accept a relatively large power, esp. one connected to a mains supply or power line to provide power at a lower voltage to a circuit or device; **power transistor** *Electronics*, a transistor designed to deliver a relatively high power; **power tube** *Electronics* = *power valve* below; **power unit,** a device supplying, or controlling the supply of, power; a power plant; **power valve** *Electronics*, a valve designed to deliver a relatively high power; **power wire,** a wire transmitting electrical power.

1901 *Jrnl. Inst. Electr. Engin.* XXX. 405 If the phase difference..had been but 3½° instead of 7°, the power absorption would have been 1 H.P. and not 2 H.P. **1920** *Ibid.* LVIII. 896/1 The grid of the power amplifier is given a negative potential. **1923** *Radio Times* 28 Sept. 36 (Advt.), Standard loud speaker .suitable for public purposes when used with a power amplifier. **1961** G. A. Briggs *A to Z in Audio* 16 The final stage is the power amplifier designed to feed the loudspeaker with a few watts of audio power. **1970** J. Earl *Tuners & Amplifiers* ii. 51 The majority of power amplifiers have the push-pull output transistors driven direct from a pair of driver transistors. **1938** *Jrnl. R. Aeronaut. Soc.* XLII. 416 We may conclude, therefore, that, for the average pilot, the power approach (or the undershoot technique) is a feasible method of approaching and landing. **1959** *Times* 1 Sept. 12/2 One of the technical improvements in cars that has taken place unobtrusively during the past four years has been the provision of power-assistance for the brakes. **1970** *Commercial Motor* 25 Sept. 65/1 The steering was light even though power-assistance is not fitted. **1928** *Punch* 21 Mar. (verso front cover) (Advt.), The power-assisted brakes give absolute control over the car under all conditions. **1950** *Gloss. Aeronaut. Terms* (*B.S.I.*) I. 38 *Power-assisted control*, a flying control in which the force needed to move the surface is provided partly by electrical or hydraulic means and partly by the pilot's physical effort. **1959** *Observer* 1 Mar. 21/5 The power-assisted steering is one of the best I have tried; it spins back swiftly after sharp corners..and does not transmit severe road shocks. **1975** C. Nesbitt *Little Love & Good Company* xviii. 226 The size of the car I was learning in terrified me to begin with. It had power-assisted steering and I wasn't happy without gears. **1965** *Wireless World* Sept. 457/2 Power bandwidth is the curve of maximum output power (for the defined total distortion) versus frequency, plotted with logarithmic scales on both axes. **1977** *Gramophone* May 1773/2 The power bandwidth of the overall system (which is of course determined by that of the power amplifier) I found to be a little more restricted at its upper end than in some modern amplifiers. **1959** *Cambr. Rev.* 7 Feb. 311/2 This is clearly the altruistic formula for the egoistic power-base position just discussed. **1969** J. Mander *Static Society* i. 70 Mexico.. became the prey of rival *caudillos*, each with his geographically inaccessible power-base. **1976** *Encounter* June 79/2 Franco passed on without ever heeding the advice of his more intelligent supporters, who urged him to prepare his successor a power-base at the centre of the political spectrum. **1958** *Times Lit. Suppl.* 21 Nov. 675/2 The frontispiece showing the geographical arrangement of world power blocks. **1960** M. Sharcott *Place of Many Winds* ii. 37 The power block has come into use so that the men no longer have to pull the net by hand. **1904** *Electr. Rev.* (N.Y.) XLV. 444 The power-board is a handsome marble panel equipped with Weston ammeter and voltmeter arranged for taking readings. [**1918** *Statutes Dominion of N.Z.* 38 For every electric-power district there shall be an Electric-power Board.] **1938** R. Finlayson in D. M. Davin *N.Z. Short Stories* (1953) 242 The Power Board was brought to the pass at last of having to build a special concrete foundation for the poles. **1950** *N.Z. Jrnl. Agric.* Aug. 183/1 In New Zealand in the present [electricity] shortages there is an increasing tendency among power boards to adopt rationing. **1973** 'D. Halliday' *Dolly & Starry Bird* ii. 30 The power board is on the wall of the darkroom. **1977** *Daily Tel.* 26 May 19/1 (*heading*) Power board fined over fitter's death. **1896** G. Richmond tr. *Lieckfeld's Gas Engines* ii. 29 The simplest and oldest of the power brakes is that shown in fig. 3, 'The Prony Brake'. **1972** D. E. Westlake *Bank Shot* ii. 16 Kelp..stomped on the brake. It was a power brake, and the car stopped on a dime. **1961** T. H. White *Making of President 1960* ii. 52 None of the young men..could win the confidence of the aging back-room power brokers who wield such influence in the Democratic party. **1968** W. Safire *New Lang. Politics* 349/1 During his mayoral campaign and often after he was elected, Republican John Lindsay spoke scornfully, and often despairingly, of the 'power brokers' (a phrase coined by Theodore White) who ran New York behind the scenes. **1972** *Village Voice* (N.Y.) 1 June 12/5 He's not going to get the nomination in Miami without coming to some kind of arrangement with the power brokers. **1977** *Listener* 21 Apr. 498/3 Chiang Ching..embarked on a series of intimate relationships with Yenan's power-brokers. **1975** *N.Y. Times* 10 Apr. 29/1 He..argued that conventions were 'undemocratic' because they were subject to power-brokering instead of the will of the people. **1977** *Guardian Weekly* 6 Nov. 9/2 The last opportunity for him [*sc.* Tito] to preside over a gathering of all the political clans and employ his power-broking to ensure an orderly succession. **1922** *Encycl. Brit.* XXXII. 489/1 The power buzzer..was a powerful vibrator worked by the current from a 10-volt accumulator, and connected to inconspicuous earths of insulated wire which could..be buried 6 ft. deep... Detachments of troops isolated by the enemy could send out code signals which could be picked up by listening sets..at ranges up to 3000 yd. **1923** R. Stanley *Text-bk. Wireless Telegr.* (rev. ed.) II. xvii. 339 With a power buzzer of the 'Parleur' type on a 10-volt battery and a 100-yards earth base between the plates, in a fairly dry type of soil over chalk, good signals have been obtained over a range of 5 kilometres, the receiver being a 3-valve L.F. Amplifier connected to two earth plates 200 yards apart. **1905** Henry & Hora *Mod. Electr.* xi. 219 Tough paper forms an excellent insulating material for electric light and power cables. **1959** E. H. Clements *High Tension* xi. 182 One of Douglas's tall poles bearing the power-cable across the open forest. **1974** E. Ambler *Dr. Frigo* III. 241 The body was discovered..by workmen laying a power cable. **1977** *Mod. Railways* Dec. 492/1 Despite the apparently convincing case put forward for the positioning of the power car in the centre of the APT-P sets..it is reported that options are still open regarding the formation of any subsequent production trains. **1936** *Discovery* Nov. 356/1 The Union Pacific RR. has two twelve-car diesel-electric trains, of which the first two coaches are the power cars, each containing a 1,200 b.h.p. engine. **1946** *Nature* 5 Oct. 463/1 The 11,000 volt systems are in turn supplied by 33,000 volt or 66,000 volt systems, with proportionally higher power-carrying capacities. **1971** Power cart [see *green(s) fee* s.v. *GREEN *sb.* 17]. **1961** *Sunday Express* 19 Nov. 16 By one cunning dodge after another he has kept this one-time power centre of German militarism intact. **1962** M. McLuhan *Gutenberg Galaxy* 12 The Renaissance prince tended to become an exclusive power centre surrounded by his individual subjects. **1977** F. Young in J. Hick *Myth of God Incarnate* ii. 28 Cyril's attack on Nestorius is related to the political struggle between the ecclesiastical power-centres of Alexandria and Constantinople. **1960** *Encounter* Oct. 4/4 A party which deals with the real problems of real men and women will become immoral, power-centred. **1924** *Times Trade & Engin. Suppl.* 29 Nov. 239/1 With such an unusually large consumption of current,..the electric light, heat, and power companies can afford to sell power at a low cost. **1951** M. McLuhan *Mech. Bride* (1967) 136/2 This is a good record for the thousands of people who work in power companies. **1961** Bigelow & Otis *Manchester, Vermont* xii. 113 Manchester..had two competing power companies until 1904. **1977** J. Cleary *Vortex* i. 21 Get the power company out here... Shut off that power. **1936** *Discovery* Nov. 361/2 Part III is solely taken up by power craft. **1954** Fisher & Lockley *Sea-Birds* v. 126 The oceanic sea-birds have solved these problems of mobility by becoming sailplanes as well as power-craft. **1924** P. Radin tr. *Adler's Pract. & Theory Individual Psychol.* xix. 231 This, reduced to her line of power-craving, meant—'I must dominate everyone, draw everybody's attention to myself.' **1914** G. Frankau *Et Debellare Superbos* in *Poetical Wks.* (1923) I. 185 We grasped this sword for gain's sake, caste, nor king Power-crazed to his own people's ruining. **1952** M. Allingham *Tiger in Smoke* iv. 74 Teleprinters, radar..when we get a power cut the whole blessed police system is liable to go out of action. **1973** J. Wainwright *Touch of Malice* 97 It was a good clock—electric—and, apart from power cuts, it kept perfect time. **1953** W. E. Unbehaun *Hist. & Status Exper. Breeder Reactor* (U.S. Atomic Energy Comm. AECD-3712) 40 *Power density*, a measure of the power per unit of reactor core volume. **1955** *Proc. Internat. Conf. Peaceful Uses Atomic Energy* (United Nations) III. 238/2 The power density is highest in the seed with a value of better than 200 watts/cm³. **1967** *Technology Week* 23 Jan. 28/1 The *Phoebus 1 B* reactor..uses a new hydrogen pump developed by North American's Rocketdyne Div. that can handle 150 lbs. of hydrogen per second for studies of operations in the higher power-density range. **1942** *Tee Emm* (Air Ministry) II. 95 The value of power ditching is so great that the pilot should always ditch before fuel is quite exhausted. **1930** R. Duncan *Stunt Flying* vi. 55 In a power dive, terrific drag is exerted on the main planes with a downward pressure on the tail-plane. **1937** *Times* 14 Dec. 17/2 During these evolutions they [*sc.* Japanese bombers] 'power-dived' to within a very short distance above the Panay's decks. **1941** Steinbeck & Ricketts *Sea of Cortez* 163 The mosquitoes.. whooped and screamed and attacked, power-diving and wheeling up and diving again. **1954** *Ann. Reg. 1953* 373 Aeroplanes flew at increasing speeds, reaching the threshold of the speed of sound in level flight and much higher speeds in power dives from high altitudes. **1973** J. Wainwright *High-Class Kill* 24 Young Shaw had chucked himself over the guard-rail and power-dived into eternity. **1961** *Motor Cycle* 16 Mar. 334/1 Nowhere is a power drill more useful than in the garage. **1977** *36 Home Handyman Projects* (Austral. Home Jrnl.) 75/2 An economical way to buy a power drill and attachments is as a set by Black and Decker. **1898** A. G. Elliott *H. de Graffigny's Gas & Petroleum Engines* iv. 73 This motor.. has become especially famous for its application to power-driven road vehicles. **1935** *Discovery* Nov. 326/2 A new power-driven spray painting outfit which can be carried by hand and can be run from an ordinary lighting socket has recently been produced. **1967** Karch & Buber *Offset Processes* i. 4 Early Power-Driven Presses. In 1814, R. Hoe and Company built the first steam-operated press to be used for printing. **1978** J. A. Michener *Chesapeake* 693 Four of their power-driven boats lay off the point of Tilghman Island. **1907** *Jrnl. R. Agric. Soc.* LXVIII. 130 Seed dresser, for hand or power driving. **1916** *Aeroplane* 1 Nov. 802/1 There is quite a long distance separating these gondolas—or 'power-eggs', as the Naval Air Service calls them—from the forward car. **1931** *Flight* 16 Jan. 49/1 The revolution counters and oil-thermometers for the outboard engines are mounted on their respective power-eggs, clearly visible for the pilots. **1961** F. K. Mason *Hawker Aircraft since 1920* 292 The two Griffon prototypes..were to be..replaced by Griffon 61 'power eggs' at a later date, so becoming the Tempest IV. **1953** C. W. Mills *Veblen's Theory Leisure Class* p. xiv, The major change in national glamour, in which the debutante is replaced by the movie star, and the local society lady by the military and political and economic managers—the power elite. **1956** —— (*title*) The power elite. **1960** *News Chron.* 16 June 6/3 Behind the council lies the real power elite: The Federation of Economic Organisations. **1973** *Black Panther* 17 Mar. 7/2 The genocide, oppression, humiliation and repression this country's racist power elite has inflicted upon Native Americans, Black Americans also know. **1892** J. A. Fleming in *Jrnl. Inst. Electr. Engin.* XXI. 606 The ninth column gives a number which it is convenient to call the power-factor of the transformer at no load—it is the ratio of the true to the apparent watts. If the currents and pressures were simple sine functions, then the power-factor in that case would be the cosine of the angle of lag of primary current behind the primary terminal potential difference. **1912** *Ibid.* XLIX. 323 The power factor and conductance of dielectrics under alternating electromotive force of low voltage. **1930** *Engineering* 24 Jan. 97/2 It [*sc.* a generator] is rated at 30,000 kv.-a., at 80 per cent. power factor, generating at 13,900 volts, three-phase and 60-cycles, and running at 200 r.p.m. **1950** *Ibid.* 28 July 80/2 Power-factor measurements up to 250 kV root-mean-square can be made with a Schering bridge. **1967** M. Chandler *Ceramics in Mod. World* iv. 133 If [*sc.* zircon porcelain] has not only a low power factor, but also good electrical properties in general. **1933** *Newnes Mod. Motor Repair* 684/2 When power failure at high revs. occurs, get someone to speed up the engine and listen at the tail pipe. **1961** *Providence* (Rhode Island) *Jrnl.* 29 Nov. 22 The impact with the utility pole caused a brief power failure in the immediate area of the accident. **1967** 'T. Wells' *Dead by Light of Moon* (1968) i. 8 Hey! The whole street is dark... Must be a power failure. **1974** M. Babson *Stalking Lamb* xvii. 124 'Perhaps there is a power failure.' In the darkness, Sybilla sounded older. **1952** J. W. Day *New Yeomen of Eng.* xvi. 185 Substituting cheap modern power-farming for expensive hand and animal labour. **1971** *Power Farming* Mar. 7/1 It is just 50 years since one of the most significant innovations in the world of power farming first saw the light of day. **1950** *Engineering* 28 July 80/2 Equipment which will provide impulse voltages up to 1,400 kV peak, power-frequency voltages up to 250 kV root-mean-square, and direct current voltages up to 200 kV. **1967** M. Chandler *Ceramics in Mod. World* iv. 130 Although excellent for insulation at power frequencies, porcelain is far from being the ideal insulating material where high frequencies..are involved. **1958** *Spectator* 1 Aug. 175/3 The landowners..the officials.. and the womanisers..are all playing an elaborate and stylised power game under the eyes of their neighbours. 1970 [see *EXPO]. 1975 Guardian 20 Jan. 8/5 Britain's puny role in the East–West power game. 1956 H. SELIGMAN in A. Pryce-Jones New Outl. Mod. Knowl. 159 The future will bring stream-lined power-generating units of the type described. 1945 W. S. CHURCHILL Victory 26, I repulse those calumnies..that Britain..is a selfish, power-greedy..nation. 1941 WYNDHAM LEWIS Let. 31 May (1963) 290, I mean that of the big power-groups.. we are the inhabitants or controllers of the great ocean wastes. 1977 Listener 17 Feb. 223/2 Directors should be appointed for their competence, not because of the power group they represent. 1936 Discovery July 222/2 It is merely a question of the power-handling capacity of amplifier and loud-speaker. 1962 SIMPSON & RICHARDS Physical Princ. Junction Transistors viii. 174 The mesa transistor should also be competitive as far as power-handling capability and ease of fabrication are concerned. 1972 'G. BLACK' Bitter Tea (1973) ix. 139 A contractor's lorry..with a power hoist. 1927 A. HUXLEY Proper Stud. 29 Power-holders to whose material advantage it would have been to wield their power ruthlessly. 1971 T. W. ROBINSON Cultural Revolution in China i. 18 On the powerholders' side were those groups and individuals having a vested interest in maintaining the status quo. 1977 A. GIDDENS Stud. in Social & Polit. Theory x. 335 All power involves a certain 'mandate'.. which gives power-holders certain rights and imposes on them certain obligations. 1977 Dædalus Fall 87 Schools produce the docile work habits the capitalists desire and serve to provide a facade of meritocracy for what is in fact a perpetual class of power holders. 1935 HUXLEY & HADDON We Europeans ii. 37 The power-hunger of potentates. 1946 'G. ORWELL' James Burnham 17 He seems to assume that power-hunger..is a natural instinct. 1946 —— A. Koestler in Crit. Ess. 134 Spartacus, however, is not represented as power-hungry, nor, on the other hand, as a visionary. 1960 F. LAND Lang. Math. vi. 82 The power-hungry countries of the world are determined to remedy their situation. 1973 Listener 6 Sept. 307/3 There were ambitious, power-hungry men on both sides. 1936 WIRTH & SHILS tr. Mannheim's Ideology & Utopia iii. 124 Observing the mass-mind, especially its power-impulses and their functioning. 1938 B. RUSSELL Power ii. 21 Their power-impulses..seemed to themselves indubitably righteous. 1944 'G. ORWELL' in Horizon X. 240 No Orchids is aimed at the power-instinct. 1919 Phil. Mag. XXXVIII. 637 We know of no theoretical reason for supposing that the power-law will give a better approximate representation than any other law, e.g. a sine-law. 1968 Brit. Med. Bull. XXIV. 257/1 Davis & Zerlin..have suggested that..the amplitude of the averaged vertex response varies with the loudness of the stimulus according to a power law with an exponent of 0·4. 1977 Sci. Amer. Jan. 90/2 The inverse-square power-law spectrum of crater sizes on the moon has the property that if there are enough primary craters between one kilometer and 10 kilometers in diameter to cover an entire planet, there are also enough craters between 100 and 1,000 kilometers across to cover it. 1934 A. L. ALBERT Electr. Communication iii. 50 If the amount of noise cannot be reduced, the only alternative is to raise the power level of the speech or music being transmitted. 1945 H. D. SMYTH Gen. Acct. Devel. Atomic Energy Mil. Purposes viii. 85 The production goal..was set at a figure which meant that the pile should operate at a power level of 1000 kw. 1953 Language XXIX. 91 The human brain operates on a power-level of five watts. 1975 D. G. FINK Electronics Engineers' Handbk. I. 52 (heading) Power levels of speech. 1923 G. COLLINS Valley of Eyes Unseen xiv. 305 Luckily, I had just strength enough to reach up and touch the power-lever. 1951 M. MCLUHAN Mech. Bride (1967) 98/2 Her legs..are date-baited power levers for the management of the male audience. 1894 A. T. SNELL Electr. Motive Power iii. 91 For very heavy power lines, in which copper cables of about 19/16 s.w.g. are used, the stalks are forged of cast steel, sometimes galvanised. 1956 Nature 17 Mar. 536/2 At this remote desert location, interference due to artificial signals from electromagnetic devices and power-lines was negligible. 1970 T. HUGHES Crow 69 It was a naked power-line, 2000 volts. 1972 Daily Tel. 19 June 1/3 The aircraft narrowly missed plunging into a nearby reservoir and skimmed over power lines. 1943 Trans. Inst. Mining Engineers CII. 145 The point we are anxious about is whether there is mechanized machinery for taking big power-loaded outputs from such a dip as 1 in 6. 1963 Economist 12 Jan. 142/1 The industry raised its average percentage of power-loaded coal from 49 to 59 per cent between the two years. 1943 Trans. Inst. Mining Engineers CII. 40 The present development of the Meco-Moore power-loader differs from that of a few years ago. 1956 F. S. ATKINSON in D. L. Linton Sheffield 269 Intensive efforts are being made to replace the hand-loading of coal on to conveyors by mechanical power-loaders. 1946 KOESTLER Thieves in Night 296 It startles me that its up-to-date, stream-lined power logics should be accompanied by all this maudlin opera stuff. 1959 Times Lit. Suppl. 9 Oct. 575/3 Over large tracts of their lives the winds of the Hobbesian power-logic blow unchecked. 1951 H. ARENDT Orig. Totalitarianism i. 5 Persecution of powerless or power-losing groups may not be a very pleasant spectacle. 1922 GLAZEBROOK Dict. Appl. Physics II. 109/1 If the condenser has internal power loss,..the power factor..will not be zero. 1960 Farmer & Stockbreeder 1 Mar. 129/2 It sharply cuts power-loss in transmission and hydraulics. 1935 Mind XLIV. 94 Plutarch and Lucian, experienced in the ways of power-loving Rome. 1923 D. H. LAWRENCE Kangaroo xvi. 344 The land..invites parasites now... What would happen if the power-lust came that way? 1959 S. SPENDER tr. Schiller's Mary Stuart III. iv. 61 Your uncle, the power-lusting cardinal. 1962 Times 2 May 7/4 The power-mad politicians. 1976 B. BOVA Multiple Man xviii. 201 He was insane, sir. Crazy. Power-mad. 1971 New Scientist 20 May 434/1 Psychology students studying power-mania. 1963 Times 26 Jan. 11/3 It would be hard to see why.. even a power-maniac wanted to leave so charming an island. 1965 Punch 22 Sept. 443/2 Ropy little espionage agency, riddled with power-maniacs, sends courier to Europe to pick up important information. 1961 Guardian 16 Feb. 10/5 Intellectuals have been found flat on their faces for powermongers to walk over. 1977 Rolling Stone 19 May 41/2 Powermongers will undoubtedly find ways to obtain the requisite technology. 1955 P. MULLAHY in H. S. Sullivan Conceptions Mod. Psychiatry 243 The energy of the infant, or rather its manifestations in the power motive, become quickly modified or transformed. 1940 Sears, Roebuck Catal. Spring/Summer 929 Power mower. 1957 D. KARP Leave me Alone xiv. 192 The young boys in the development cheerfully cut grass with power mowers but disdained raking. 1970 R. LOWELL Notebk. 28 The lawns, the paths, the harbor—stitched with motors, Yawl-engine, outboard, power mower. 1978 J. A. MICHENER Chesapeake 836 In July he runs his power mower, pushing his lawn back year by year. 1950 Vogue (U.S.) 15 Nov. 150/2 (caption) Nylon power net pantie-girdle..for a smooth line under, say, tight velvet.. pants. 1952 Woman's Home Compan. Nov. 3 (Advt.), Sheer powernet corselette with the smooth fit of a glove. 1963 Times 17 Apr. 16/7 The company will manufacture power-net, fish-net, marquisette curtaining and other fabrics in the Natal area. 1969 Sears Catal. Spring/Summer 2 This bra-slip... The power-net frame: cool and smooth..a stretchy blend of nylon and spandex. 1963 Times 20 Mar. 15/6 The power-obsessed journalist. 1957 FORBES & O'BEIRNE Technical Devel. Royal Dutch/Shell iii. 256 For correct operation it was essential that the 'power oil' should be free from impurities and it was therefore necessary to wash it thoroughly above ground. 1972 L. M. HARRIS Introd. Deepwater Floating Drilling Operations xi. 108 The direct system has individual power-oil lines from the drill vessel to the individual functions on the subsea stack. 1917 W. G. RAYMOND Elem. Railroad Engin. (ed. 3) x. 129 In the automatic block system the signal at the entrance of each block is power-operated, usually electric. 1940 War Illustr. 5 Jan. 554/3 The 'Wellingtons'..with five separate machine-gun positions, including two in power-operated turrets. 1962 Lancet 1 Dec. 1155/1 Conventional prosthetic limbs may in fact be incapable of substantial development, but power-operated ones seem certain to become much more practical and effective. 1937 Jrnl. Inst. Electr. Engin. LXXX. 194/2 This is derived from two grid-controlled rectifier valves operated from a 'power pack' of the usual construction. 1942 Electronic Engin. XV. 285/3 The experimental model described, together with a power pack to permit operation direct from the 50 cycle mains, can be assembled on a box chassis measuring only 6½in. × 6½in. 1958 New Scientist 1 May 20/2 Its thickness is controlled by plating time and current, indicated by a graduated ampere-hour meter on the power 'pack'. 1967 Gloss. Mining Terms (B.S.I.) VIII. 21 Power pack, a motor-pump combination for producing power for hydraulic equipment. 1971 J. Z. YOUNG Introd. Study Man iv. 69 The mitochondria carry the respiratory enzymes, and are hence called the power packs of the cell. 1972 F. BRADBURY Hydraulic Syst. iii. 43 In a large plant..the control desk and the power pack may be separated by some distance or may be installed in separate machinery spaces. 1973 Houston Chron. 21 Oct. 3/1 (Advt.), Penske Road Race... It's big-time racing excitement in a box! With power pack, 2 cars and hand controls, 30-ft. of track. 1977 J. HEDGECOE Photographer's Handbk. 35 To produce more light a flash with a larger powerpack is needed. 1958 C. C. ADAMS Space Flight viii. 196 Auxiliaries. These include taxis and propulsion 'guns' for individual men in space suits, or reaction power packages attached like outboard motors to large objects. 1968 Listener 27 June 828/1 The power supply to this satellite was a 28 lb device called SNAP/9A. This power package contained as its energy source 17 kilocuries of Plutonium 238. 1945 H. D. SMYTH Gen. Acct. Devel. Atomic Energy Mil. Purposes vii. 70 The whole of a power pile..has to be enclosed in very thick walls of concrete, steel, or other absorbing material. 1961 Observer 26 Feb. 18/1 This is now well known as power-play, a form developed by the All-Blacks and Springboks from the simple logic of the decisiveness of forward domination. 1961 J. S. SALAK Dict. Amer. Sports 340 Power play (football), a play in which the offensive team concentrates blockers at one point. Ibid., Power-play (ice hockey), launched when a team has an extra man or is trailing in the final minutes, all players rushing into the opponent's zone, and putting on the pressure. 1968 Globe & Mail (Toronto) 5 Feb. 17/6 The North Stars lead the NHL in power-play goals with 37. Balon scored on the power play. 1973 L. MOSLEY (title) Power-play: the tumultuous world of Middle East oil 1890–1973. 1976 N.Y. Rev. Bks. 15 Apr. 34/2 The Church was making a last desperate power play (for which it is now paying dear) to keep its immigrant children in line. 1976 Washington Post 19 Apr. D3/2 Chicago got the first goal of the game, by Cliff Koroll on a power play. 1978 Dumfries Courier 13 Oct. 4/2 At No. 3 Donald Bogie, with a variation of power play and finesse, proved too much for an experienced opponent. 1951 M. MCLUHAN Mech. Bride (1967) 98/2 To the mind of the modern girl, legs, like busts, are power points which she has been taught to tailor. 1953 K. TENNANT Joyful Condemned xxxiii. 323 An iron was plugged in handily to a power point. 1958 C. WATSON Coffin scarcely Used ix. 86 Purbright watched for the power points. There was one in each of the large bedrooms. 1975 G. BURDETT Do your Own Home Wiring xiii. 124 An additional 13A power point can usually be supplied from a ring circuit in the form of a spur. 1978 Listener 2 Feb. 159/1 Surrealism..works that sprang into being simply by unplugging the power-points of the mind. 1959 M. SHADBOLT New Zealanders 174 They found it [sc. a car], bashed and tangled, at the foot of a slanting power pole. 1973 Black Panther 20 Oct. 11/2 The United Boeing severed two power poles. 1906 Chambers's Jrnl. 27 Oct. 765/2 The internal-combustion engine is coming..rapidly into favour as a cheap power-producer for almost every kind of work. 1909 Westm. Gaz. 19 Oct. 4/1 The overhead valve system of this wonderful power-producer is not uncommon to the engine employed in this firm's racing cars. 1946 Power reactor [see *BURN v.¹ 13h]. 1962 [see *CONVERTER 3f]. 1970 IEEE Trans. Nuclear Sci. XVII. I. 520 (heading) Silicon radiation detector monitors nitrogen 16 in a power reactor. 1958 New Statesman 9 Aug. 158/1 The meeting..symbolises the change in the power-relations of the Communist world. 1977 Dædalus Fall 66 In this approach it was stressed that the explanation of any institutional arrangement has to be attempted in terms of power relations and negotiations, power struggles and conflicts. 1962 R. F. GRAF Mod. Dict. Electronics 234/2 Power response, the frequency-response capabilities of an amplifier running at or near its full rated power. 1963 Wireless World July 354/1 The power response at 10W output is −3dB at 15 c/s and 15 kc/s. 1970 J. EARL Tuners & Amplifiers iii. 68 The latest 'quality' amplifiers ..boast a power response which is almost as good as the frequency response. 1975 Gramophone Nov. 953/3 Power response is taken to be the range of frequencies over which the amplifier can deliver at least half its rated power. 1960 McGraw-Hill Encycl. Sci. & Technol. XIV. 542/1 Bench or circular saws are the common woodworking type of power saw. 1969 in Halpert & Story Christmas Mumming in Newfoundland 107 A game of cards, the loan of a power-saw..can act as the favours that initially link two persons together. 1976 N. THORNBURG Cutter & Bone iv. 108 The car, a late-model Buick Century, seemed to have every possible piece of optional equipment, including power seats. 1946 'G. ORWELL' James Burnham 4 The English Puritans, the Jacobins, the Bolsheviks, were in each case simply power-seekers. 1979 P. ALEXANDER Show me Hero xxiii. 246 He was the perfect example of the power-seeker... He'd tread on anyone's face to get to the top. 1963 A. HERON Towards Quaker View of Sex i. 10 We see human energy that should be creative and loving deflected into activities that are coldly power-seeking. Ibid. iv. 41 Our tendencies toward aggression and power-seeking. 1977 P. JOHNSON Enemies of Society xii. 169 Marxism..has a methodology of power-seeking. 1893 A. R. FORSYTH Theory of Functions of Complex Variable iii. 56 Any one of the continuations of a uniform function, represented by a power-series, can be derived from any other. 1938 F. E. TERMAN Fund. Radio v. 136 for electrode voltages such that the instantaneous plate current never became zero, the characteristics of a tube could be expressed in forms of the following power series. 1968 P. A. P. MORAN Introd. Probability Theory iii. 135 $R(z)$ is a power series whose coefficients tend to zero. 1953 A. A. FRAENKEL Abstract Set Theory ii. 96 The set of all subsets of S may..be called the power-set of S. 1963 SELBY & SWEET Sets, Relations, Functions i. 18 Since A contained four elements, the power set 2^A was made up of 2^4 or 16 subsets, each subset an element of the power set. 1974 Encycl. Brit. Macropædia I. 521/1 The power set lattice.., defined by the inclusion relation on the power set $P(U)$ of all subsets of a set U, has important special properties not shared by lattices in general. 1972 Times 31 Oct. 15/3 It is safe to say that that kind of enforced power-sharing is practicable to the extent that the power to be exercised is circumscribed. 1973 Hansard Commons 20 Mar. 242/1 We have expressed positive views on many matters in the White Paper—for example,..on power sharing. 1978 P. COSGRAVE Margaret Thatcher ii. 34 It was widely believed that if there had not been a general election in February 1974 his Northern Ireland 'power-sharing' executive would have worked. 1940 Chambers's Techn. Dict. 669/1 Power shovel (or navvy), an excavator consisting of a jib carrying a radial arm to the end of which a large bucket or scoop is attached. The bucket makes a radial cut. 1966 McGraw-Hill Encycl. Sci. & Technol. III. 416/2 Power shovels are made which can be rapidly converted into a dragline, crane, or backhoe by changing booms and modifying the rigging. 1971 P. O'DONNELL Impossible Virgin iii. 57 Stacks of bricks, a concrete mixer, a power-shovel. 1922 D. H. LAWRENCE Aaron's Rod xxi. 311 Yield to the deep power-soul in the individual man, and obey implicitly. 1944 Bell Syst. Techn. Jrnl. XXIII. 282 The second part is devoted principally to the fundamental result that the power spectrum of a noise current is the Fourier transform of its correlation function. 1960 W. R. BENNETT Electr. Noise x. 208 Many important phenomena are found to have a power spectrum even though the Fourier transform itself does not approach a limit. 1972 T. H. G. MEGSON Aircraft Struct. xii. 427 It is assumed that gust velocity is a random variable which may be regarded for analysis as consisting of a large number of sinusoidal components whose amplitudes vary with frequency. The power spectrum of such a function is then defined as the distribution of energy over the frequency range. 1932 Automotive Industries 10 Dec. 739/2 The greatest need for power steering exists undoubtedly in connection with heavy trucks and buses. 1976 M. MAGUIRE Scratchproof xii. 182 She gunned the vehicle forward..as she swung the power-steering into a fierce lock. 1903 Work 9 May 218/2 Such engines have only one power stroke in every four. 1966 E. RUDINGER Consumer's Car Gloss. 113 Every other stroke (the down-stroke) of the piston is a power stroke which drives the engine; whereas in a four-stroke engine, there is only one power stroke in every four. 1950 D. RIESMAN et al. Lonely Crowd xi. 255 Even those intellectuals..who feel themselves very much out of power and who are frightened of those who they think have the power, prefer to be scared by the power structures they conjure up. 1977 Time 4 July 6/1 Brezhnev already ranked No. 1 in the Kremlin power structure and was accorded the diplomatic status due a chief of state nearly everywhere he went. 1961 Los Angeles Times 4 Aug. III. 4 Bitter echoes of the 1960 power struggle..are still audible in party circles. 1969 New Yorker 20 Sept. 110/1 A serious power struggle could take place in the North. 1978 Jrnl. R. Soc. Arts CXXVI. 669/2 The detention of the four leaders had deprived one main group in the power struggle for the succession of its principal leaders. 1943 J. S. HUXLEY Evolutionary Ethics vii. 59 A naked power-system cannot tolerate tolerance or face even intellectual opposition. 1970 C. FURTADO in I. L. Horowitz Masses in Lat. Amer. ii. 46 Allowing the landlord class to augment its share in aggregate income and to consolidate its position in the power system. 1929 Sears, Roebuck Catal. Spring/Summer 881 This power take-off and clutch pulley combined makes your Fordson tractor always ready for belt power. 1943 C. G. BARGER Automotive Mech. I. iv. 123 Power take-offs are used on such vehicles as dump trucks, fire engines, wreckers, and..allow the accessories to be operated by the power of the engine. 1957 P. H. WILKINSON Aircraft Engines of World 20 (Advt.), The

Lycoming 825-h.p. T53, featuring front-or-rear power take-off, is the world's first turbine designed specifically for helicopters. **1958** *Times* 1 July (Agric. Suppl.) p. viii/2 The mechanism of the trailer is driven with the power-take-off from the tractor and unloads at the rate of three tons in seven minutes. **1972** *Proc. Inst. Mech. Engineers* CLXXXIV. III. I. 284 Power take-off systems.. supplying the power to operate various truck-mounted equipment on tipping gear, garbage packers,..and many more applications. *Ibid.*, Power take-offs (PTOs) are necessary on most of today's trucks. **1951** H. Arendt *Orig. Totalitarianism* v. 141 Hobbes..proceeded from this insight to a plan for a body politic best fitted for this power-thirsty animal. **1959** *Sears, Roebuck Catal.* Spring-Summer 1299 Make your Drill a new power tool every time you change accessories. **1961** *Times* 3 Oct. (Computer Suppl.) p. ii/5 Muscles are replaced by machines or power-tools. **1971** *New Scientist* 27 May 529/1 Other batteries still in the development stage..include the silver oxide/zinc cell and the titanium battery, both currently under evaluation..for application in TV, portable powertools and possibly electric vehicles. **1937** *Times* 13 Apr. (Brit. Motor Suppl.) p. vi/4 It is of 4½ litres capacity, and the power-to-weight ratio is given at 4·2lb. a brake horse-power. **1971** *Engineering* Apr. 72 (Advt.), Reyrolle Hydraulics axial piston pumps and motors. Fixed or variable displacement, with excellent power-to-weight ratio (up to 2·8 hp/lb). **1943** C. G. Barger *Automotive Mech.* I. iv. 107 (*heading*) Power train. **1946** W. H. Crouse *Automotive Mech.* i. 24 The power train consists of a series of gears and shafts, which mechanically connect the engine shaft with the car wheels. **1966** *Economist* 10 Sept. 1040/2 Chrysler has gained substantial sales in the United States in the past four years since it began offering a 5-year, 50,000-mile guarantee for the 'power train' (engine-transmission-rear-axle) of its American-built cars. **1976** *National Observer* (U.S.) 2 Oct. 8/2 Auto manufacturers are reluctant to offer special-engine versions of all their models and power-train combinations. **1929** K. Henney *Princ. Radio* xvi. 403 A.-c. voltages are likely to be picked up by the cores of audio transformers if they are near power transformers carrying a.-c. currents. **1975** D. G. Fink *Electronics Engineers' Handbk.* vii. 17 Electronic power transformers normally operate at a fixed frequency. The most popular frequencies are 50, 60, and 400 Hz. **1959** K. Henney *Radio Engin. Handbk.* (ed. 5) x. 34 The increased ruggedness of the supply due to the inherently stable physical structure of the power transistor. **1974** G. A. G. Bennett *Electricity & Mod. Physics* (ed. 2) xiv. 271/1 Power transistors are made by the same techniques as other transistors; but the collector, in which most of the heat is dissipated, is fused onto a thick metal mounting plate forming one face of the unit. **1924** Moyer & Wostrel *Pract. Radio* vii. 103 The volume of sound may be increased by using a power tube of, say, 5 watts of electric power, in the last stage of amplification. **1975** D. G. Fink *Electronics Engineers' Handbk.* vii. 21 Power tubes, in contrast to receiving-type tubes, handle relatively large amounts of power, and..a major emphasis is placed on efficiency. The traditional division between the two tube categories is at the 25-W plate dissipation rating level. **1942** F. H. Joseph *Lett. home from Brit. at War* 44 Machine guns, rear power turret having four, front power turret two. **1907** H. Allen *Gas & Oil Engines* xiv. 307 A 4-cylinder engine,..having cylinders 8in. diam. and 8in. stroke, capable of running up to 800 revs. per minute, gives a power unit, when using petrol, of 100 b.h.p. **1908** S. H. Moore *Mech. Engin. & Machine Shop Pract.* xix. 421 Synchronous motors are best adapted for power transmission plants and for large power units of high voltage. **1918** G. Sherwood *Farm Tractor Handbk.* vii. 110 The machine [*sc.* a Fordson tractor] is merely a power unit and transmission gear *en bloc* mounted on two pairs of wheels, together with the simplest of control and steering arrangements. **1963** *Amer. Speech* XXXVIII. 120 The auxiliary power unit supplying electrical power to the KC-97 when it is on the ground. **1967** C. J. Freezer *Model Railway Terminol.* 8/1 The power unit is a device which converts the high-voltage mains current into low-voltage currents, often with several outputs. **1922** D. H. Lawrence *Aaron's Rod* xxi. 311 But the deep power-urge is not conscious of its aims. **1947** Koestler in *Partisan Rev.* XIV. 345 The best way to prolong the power-vacuum to the west of the Russian bloc..is to proclaim an independent British policy. **1976** *Times* 10 Sept. 1/1 (*heading*) Mao succession struggle. Death leaves power vacuum in China. **1919** W. D. Owen *Guide Study Ionic Valve* x. 38 Power valves need to be very hard otherwise the plate voltage would cause a discharge across the space. **1944** *Wireless World* June 163/2 Although power valves are used, they are only lightly loaded and HT volts and current are quite low. **1909** *Chambers's Jrnl.* June 341/1 Thompson in Edinburgh introduced the first power-vehicle running on india-rubber tires. **1916** *Ibid.* Feb. 83/1 The power-vehicle is also invaluable for communication between commanders and their units. **1831** *Engineering* 9 Jan. 58/3 Volumetric efficiency is important..in that it affects the power-weight ratio of an engine. **1950** *Times Rev. Industry* Sept. 25/2 The Swiss Federal Railways has improved the power-weight ratio of single-phase main-line types [of locomotives]. **1902** H. A. Foster *Electr. Engineer's Pocket-Bk.* 766 Special precautions of this kind must be taken where sharp angles occur, or where any wires might possibly come in contact with electric light or power wires. **1911** W. Aitken *Man. Telephone* xx. 409 All power wires from the fuse board are now usually laid up in lead-covered cables. **1938** R. Finlayson *Brown Man's Burden* 41 The new power wires... Ten thousand volts, ehoa! **1941** 'G. Orwell' *England your England* in *Lion & Unicorn* i. 17 Power-worship..has never touched the common people. **1921** *Electrician* 11 Mar. 304/2 In the United States where an electric ironing machine..costs about the same as a washing machine, some women use their power wringer as a cold mangle. **1957** *Observer* 1 Dec. 10/5 There is no national test for power wringers so test the safety release yourself before buying.

g. Designating alcoholic liquids of a grade suitable for generating mechanical power.

1919 *Rep. Interdepartmental Comm. Alcohol for Power* 4 in *Parl. Papers* (Cmd. 218) X. 117 Some sections of the community believe that the words 'industrial alcohol' refer to an inferior spirit for drinking purposes. We recommend, therefore, that all alcohol for power or traction purposes should be described as 'power alcohol'... This description has already been adopted in Australia. *Ibid.* 7 All sales..of power alcohol should be made on the basis of a certified percentage by volume of absolute ethyl alcohol, with a minimum of 90 per cent. at a temperature of 62 deg. F. **1920** *Act* 10 & 11 *Geo. V* c. 18 § 11 In this section the expression 'power methylated spirits' means any methylated spirits (other than mineralised methylated spirits) which are intended to be used in generating mechanical power. **1922** G. W. Monier-Williams *Power Alcohol* vii. 198 The conversion of the alcohol into power methylated spirits may be carried out only by an authorised methylator. **1934** *Proc. World Petroleum Congr. 1933* II. 693/2 It is quite a recent innovation to market a 'power' kerosine. **1939** *Sun* (Baltimore) 17 Apr. 13/3 Senator Gurney..estimated that if farm surpluses were used to make 'power alcohol' to be mixed with gasoline, 840,000,000 bushels of grain would be diverted to that purpose annually. **1940** S. Miall *New Dict. Chem.* 330/2 Power methylated spirit is absolute ethyl alcohol, 92 volumes; benzol, 5 volumes; crude pyridine, 0·5 volume, and crude naphtha, 2·5 volumes. **1955** *Know Your Tractor* (Shell Guide) ii. 27 The cost to the farmer of gasoline and power kerosine is very variable throughout the world. **1957** *Encycl. Brit.* I. 543/1 The use of power methylated spirits practically ceased during World War II. **1961** L. M. Miall *New Dict. Chem.* (ed. 3) 446/2 *Power kerosine*, a volatile kerosine of high anti-knock value, essentially a blend of aromatic hydrocarbons, used in tractor engines and usually called tractor vaporizing oil (T.V.O.). **1975** E. M. Goodger *Hydrocarbon Fuels* vii. 134 'Power kerosine' or 'tractor vaporising-oil' denotes a kerosine blend prepared for spark-ignition engines used in agricultural tractors, which is taxed at a lower rate than that of gasoline.

h. Applied to a sportsman who applies great muscular power to his style of play; also of the style of play itself.

1958 *Observer* 15 June 24/1 The machine-like rhythm and efficiency of her power tennis. **1959** *Times* 29 May 4/7 A power player, he went for every shot. **1959** *Sunday Express* 12 July 12/1 His splendid piece of power-running. **1969** *New Yorker* 14 June 44/3 Graebner could now probably explode one. He has what is almost a setup on his power side. **1973** *Black Panther* 25 Aug. 13/1 Henry Aaron will..establish himself unquestionably as the greatest power hitter in baseball history.

power, *v.* Restrict †*Obs.* to sense in Dict. and add: **2.** *trans.* To supply with power, esp. for propulsion. Also *fig.*

1898 W. F. Durand *Resistance & Propulsion of Ships* v. 326 (*heading*) Powering ships. **1929** *Chicago Tribune* 31 Jan. 3/8 His plane is a Travelaire, powered with a whirlwind motor. **1954** *Essays in Crit.* IV. 313 Creative activity is often..powered by the drive to accomplish. **1959** *Times* 29 June 12/7 The big traction engines that had powered the carousels. **1962** *Times* 25 Apr. 16/6 The incident..could have powered strong conflict between faith and sex. **1973** *Sci. Amer.* Feb. 102/3 It is the gravitational energy from the falling material, rather than the rotation, that probably powers the X-ray sources. **1976** *Billings* (Montana) *Gaz.* 30 June 3-E/3 Larvell Blanks and George Hendrick each belted two-run, first-inning homers Tuesday to power the Cleveland Indians to a 4–1 victory over the Milwaukee Brewers. **1977** 'A. York' *Tallant for Trouble* iv. 53 The police launch..was powered by two big Perkins engines.

3. *intr.* **a.** To move or travel with great speed or force.

1972 J. Mosedale *Football* ix. 129 The key play sent Nagurski powering toward the line. **1973** 'D. Rutherford' *Kick Start* ii. 46 The big bike solved all traffic problems for me, whether I was powering to the head of a two mile traffic jam or pulling it on to its stand on a yellow line. **1974** *Oxford Times* 20 Sept. 19/3 Derek Clarke powered in from the right and unleashed a superb shot. **1977** *Navy News* Aug. 38/1 At Mount Wise the following day, Civil Service powered to 256–5 off their 55 overs. **1978** *Daily Tel.* 20 June 13/2 For Michael Marshall ..diesel, electric and advanced passenger trains plainly have no appeal to compare with that of the majestic locomotives that powered along the track in the first half of the century.

b. To travel using an engine, esp. as an alternative or supplement to sail.

1975 *Daily Colonist* (Victoria, B.C.) 2 Apr. 21/2 We had to power most of the way, that's how little wind there was. **1976** 'F. Clifford' *Drummer in Dark* xv. 95 The Trident braked and powered round until it pointed down the long smeared runway. **1976** T. Heald *Let Sleeping Dogs Die* viii. 171 A seagoing cabin cruiser..was just beginning to power towards the narrow entrance to the cove.

So **pow·ering** *vbl. sb.*

1898 W. F. Durand *Resistance & Propulsion of Ships* v. 340 (*heading*) Powering by the law of comparison. **1899** *Engineering Mag.* Mar. 1011/1 It is in the powering of the two vessels that the great advance in marine engineering is most apparent. *Ibid.* 1011/2 The powering of the Oceanic is..about double that of the Great Eastern. **1976** R. Lewis *Witness my Death* i. 19 Coal and dust and slack for the powering of industrial furnaces.

pow·er-boat. Also **power boat, powerboat.** A motor-boat, esp. one with a powerful engine. Hence **pow·erboater,** one who travels by power-boat; **power boating,** travel by power-boat.

1908 R. W. Chambers *Firing Line* vii. 84 Every day.. the swift power-boats sped northward to the Inlet. **1932** *World Today* LIX. 254 (*heading*) Power boating. *Ibid.* 258/2 Craft built by the British Power Boat Company have, to date, secured the championships of the world. **1953** *Richmond* (Va.) *News Leader* 2 Sept. 24/7 From the Elizabeth River at Norfolk to Gibson Island in Maryland there'll be..more races for sailors and power boaters alike. **1966** *Listener* 28 July 144/2 That horrible vehicle, the power boat. **1971** 'E. Fenwick' *Impeccable People* xxi. 115 The powerboat owners suddenly became invisible... The local powerboaters..remained the most unpopular minority conceivable. **1975** *Times* 17 June 14/6 Power-boat racing is the preserve of those who have a great deal of..money. **1977** *Modern Boating* (Austral.) Jan. 71/3 Warren has set out to produce a book which will give a potential power boat buyer a complete idea of what leisure powerboating is all about.

pow·er-drive, *sb.* [f. Power *sb.*[1] + Drive *sb.*] **1.** (Equipment for) the driving of machinery by mechanical or electrical power. Also *fig.*

1952 B. Ulanov *Hist. Jazz in Amer.* (1958) xvii. 203 Lionel Hampton..added..a power-drive on vibes and drums all his own. **1960** *Farmer & Stockbreeder* 15 Mar. (Suppl.) 13 The rugged, reliable AEI 'Stayrite' Single-phase power-drive has been specifically developed for arduous farming applications. **1971** P. J. McMahon *Aircraft Propulsion* iii. 78 The normal transmission efficiency of a power drive is expressed as the ratio of power output to power input.

2. The impulse to exercise power.

1954 R. F. C. Hull tr. *Jung's Pract. of Psychotherapy* in *Coll. Wks.* XVI. i. 19 The first corresponds to Freud's pleasure principle, the second to Adler's power-drive, the desire to be on top. **1964** Gould & Kolb *Dict. Social Sci.* 483/1 Some modern definitions stress the fact of the power drive of parties. **1969** J. Mander *Static Society* vi. 180 The power-drive implied in this process is an ugly thing. **1979** J. Sherwood *Hour of Hyenas* ii. 23 You are very striking-looking, but..my power drive is far stronger nowadays than my sex drive.

powered, *a.* Delete 'chiefly in parasynthetic combinations' and add: Utilizing mechanical power for propulsion. (Further examples.)

1935 C. G. Burge *Compl. Bk. Aviation* 377/2 The introduction of powered flight in 1903. **1960** *Which?* Mar. 48/1 There are two main categories of lawnmower—hand-operated and powered. **1971** *Engineering* Apr. 65 (Advt.), Straddle carriers, powered bogies,..level luffing cranes. **1974** 'D. Craig' *Whose Little Girl are You?* i. 5 A display of powered model aircraft.

Powerforming (paʊ·əɹfǭɹmiŋ). Also with small initial. [f. Power *sb.*[1] + Re)forming *vbl. sb.*] The name of a process for reforming petroleum using a platinum catalyst. Hence **Pow·erformer,** an installation for this process.

1956 *Oil & Gas Jrnl.* 5 Mar. 62 A new catalytic-reforming process called Powerforming has been announced by Esso Research & Engineering Co. *Ibid.*, (*caption*) One of three Powerformers already operating is unit at left of picture at Carter's Billings refinery. **1958** W. L. Nelson *Petroleum Refinery Engin.* (ed. 4) xxi. 772 In catalytic reforming, only the platinum catalyst processes (Platforming,..Powerforming, Sovaforming, etc.) are sufficiently well defined to allow the prediction of yields. **1967** Bland & Davidson *Petroleum Processing Handbk.* iii. 32 The first commercial Powerforming installation was placed on-stream in July, 1955, at Baltimore, Md., by the Esso Standard Oil Co. **1969** *Daily Tel.* 30 Dec. 2/5 (*caption*) The fire..severely damaged one of the plant's two powerformers, used in the manufacture of top grade petrol.

powerful, *a.* Add: **A. 6.** (Earlier examples.) For *vulgar* read *colloq.*

1811 Byron *Let.* 25 June (1830) I. 249 For a long time I have been restricted to an entire vegetable diet,..so I expect a powerful stock of potatoes, greens, and biscuit. **1822** J. Woods *Two Years' Residence Eng. Prairie* 294, I also have got some beefs, and a powerful chance of corn.

7. *Comb.*, as *powerful-faced.*

1906 Rider Haggard *Benita* ix. 129 A clever powerful-faced man.

B. as *adv.* (Earlier and later examples.) For *vulgar* read *colloq.*

a **1822** in *Amer. Speech* (1956) XXXI. 270 *Powerful.* This word is much used by the middling and lower class of people in the interior of So: Carolina..: instead of saying a person is very strong, they would say, *he is powerful*; or *powerful strong.* **1832** W. Irving *Jrnl.* 10 Nov. (1919) III. 171 My gun is so powerful dirty. **1902** *Dialect Notes* II. 242 Powerful, adv. Very, as '*powerful* much'. **1927** *Amer. Speech* II. 362/1 Our lessons are all pow'eful hard to-day. **1942** *Morgantown* (W. Virginia) *Post* 26 Sept. 5 It does get powerful cold in those hills. **1977** F. Parrish *Fire in Barley* iii. 33 'Tes powerful hard t'temp me Mam's fancy. She d'play wi' her food, mos' times.

powerfulness. (Later examples.)

1961 *Chicago Rev.* Summer 94 Their art is an imitation of the inescapable powerfulness of this unknown and empty world. **1975** *Listener* 24 July 109/3 The powerfulness of Queenie Leavis's mind.

pow·erhouse. Also **power-house.** [f. Power *sb.*[1] + House *sb.*[1]] **1.** A building in which power is produced on a large scale for driving machinery or for generating electricity for distribution.

Quot. 1881 refers to a building containing steam engines for pumping water.

1881 *Harper's Mag.* Mar. 597/1 He found himself in the end at that 'Power House' of which he had heard..for many a year. **1890, 1895** [in Dict. s.v. POWER *sb.*^{1} 18 c]. **1901** *Chambers's Jrnl.* Mar. 206/1 In the centre of the power-house there is a raised desk, upon which are a series of press-buttons or keys. **1922** JOYCE *Ulysses* 238 The whirr of flapping leathern bands and hum of dynamos from the powerhouse urged Stephen to be on. **1922** D. H. LAWRENCE *England, my England* 175 Tall, ruined power-houses of tin-mines loomed in the darkness. **1964** LINSLEY & FRANZINI *Water Resources Engin.* xvi. 459 One of the world's largest underground plants is the Kemano powerhouse in Canada which has a generating capacity of 1,670,000 kw under a head of 2592 ft.

2. a. *fig.* A source of energy or inspiration; a strong person or animal; also a powerful group of people, e.g. a sports team. Also *attrib.*

1915 P. GEDDES *Cities in Evolution* xiii. 312 Before long, then, the School of Civics..must become a familiar institution in every city, with its civic library in rapid growth and widening use, and all as a veritable power-house of civic thought and action. **1916** J. BUCHAN (*title*) The power-house. **1941** *Sat. Even. Post* 1 Feb. 54/3 A thresher is one of the few powerhouses in the shark family. **1941** *Time* (Air Exp. Ed.) 15 Sept. 25/3 In the final, Powerhouse Kovacs was too much for Riggs in the first set, 7–5. **1943** *Amer. Speech* XVIII. 105 A hard hitter is known as a *distance hitter, power house, power hitter, slugger*, or *heavy sticker*. **1943** *Sun* (Baltimore) 20 Sept. 14/5 In the first two Saturdays of the young football season,..the mid-West and Duke again have their power-house elevens. **1952** *N.Y. World-Telegram & Sun* 29 Sept. 16/3 Michigan State, Maryland and Georgia Tech were supposed powerhouses. **1961** *Ann. Reg. 1960* 423 There continued to be no national powerhouse for [drama]. **1970** *Nature* 6 June 982/1 Although almost unreadable, it is a powerhouse of condensed factual information. **1974** E. TIDYMAN *Dummy* iii. 33 Strong? Jesus, yes. Not big, but a powerhouse. **1979** *Harvard Mag.* May–June 41 In 1972 the M.I.T. team, which had become the real powerhouse, somehow convinced the student government to give them $2,000 to go to England to play the English champions.

b. A strong hand in a card-game.

1932 *Amer. Speech* VII. 335 *Power house*, a very strong card hand. **1953** G. S. COFFIN *Acol & New Point Count* 34 The two clubs opening in Acol shows a rare powerhouse, the kind of hand you may expect to hold about once a month. **1958** *Listener* 11 Dec. 1012/2 A freak distribution resulted in South's power-house being useless against Four Spades doubled. **1967** P. ANDERTON *Play Bridge* iv. 28 An opening bid of 2 C. is reserved for the powerhouse and is forcing to game.

3. Applied *attrib.* or as quasi-*adj.* to loud or forceful popular music or performers of such music.

1942 BERREY & VAN DEN BARK *Amer. Thes. Slang* §578/10 *Powerhouse coda*, a strong finale. **1946** R. BLESH *Shining Trumpets* xii. 282 The hot-riff band is called in musicians' parlance a *powerhouse* band. **1952** B. ULANOV *Hist. Jazz in Amer.* (1958) xiv. 163 His brass was beginning to sound like the powerhouse sections of the swing bands. **1955** P. ROSSITER in A. J. McCarthy *Jazzbook 1955* 50 The first important revivalist group was formed ..in the early 'forties..led by..Lu Watters... The approach was powerhouse with a two trumpet, trombone and clarinet front line. **1968** *Blues Unlimited* Sept. 26 The powerhouse singing of types like Blind Roosevelt Graves. **1975** *New Yorker* 19 May 8/2 (Advt.), Powerhouse drummer Elvin Jones finishes up with his quintet on Sunday. **1976** *Leicester Trader* 24 Nov. 4/7 Argent's powerhouse rhythm section..have joined with John Verity who saw out the last days with the old band.

power loa·ding, *vbl. sb.* [f. POWER *sb.*^{1} + LOADING *vbl. sb.*] **1.** *Aeronaut.* The laden weight of an aeroplane divided by the total engine power.

1920 H. WOODHOUSE *Textbk. Appl. Aeronaut. Engin.* iii. 136 The lift loading of the machine per sq. ft. equals 8·3 lbs., and the power loading, 12·1 lbs. per h.p. **1927** *Observer* 12 June 17/3 The flights of the 'Horsley' have greater technical value than those wonderful American flights,..the 'Horsley' has an unprecedented high wing and power-loading. **1966** D. STINTON *Anal. Aeroplane* vii. 118 When power loading is used as a measure of merit for comparing different aircraft (W_0/P) lb/hp is used, where W_0 is the all-up-weight on take-off and *P* the sea level horsepower.

2. *Mining.* The loading of coal on to a conveyor belt at the coal face by means of a machine (cf. *power loader* s.v. *POWER *sb.*^{1} 18 f).

1943 *Trans. Inst. Mining Engin.* CII. 39 The films to be exhibited are shown by courtesy of the 'Power Loading' Committee, and illustrate the latest practice in power-loading in America. **1956** F. S. ATKINSON in D. L. Linton *Sheffield* 269 With thinner seams power-loading presents a difficult problem and progress has been slower. **1962** *Economist* 20 Jan. 243/1 Powerloading equipment tends to upset the whole work cycle of mining.

power-loom. (Later and *fig.* examples.)

1843 *Ainsworth's Mag.* IV. 95 A stoker to the power-loom in which are weaving the future destinies of mankind. **1941** J. MASEFIELD *In Mill* 6 More than a hundred power-looms were in full work. **1968** J. ARNOLD *Shell Bk. Country Crafts* xvi. 206 With the invention of the power-loom, in 1787, it became dominated by the machine.

pow·er plant. Also **power-plant, powerplant.** [f. POWER *sb.*^{1} + PLANT *sb.*^{1}] (An) apparatus or an installation which provides power; those parts of a machine, vehicle, or aircraft which provide power; an engine; a power station. Also *transf.*

1890 *Jrnl. Franklin Inst.* CXXIX. 270 Power Plant... Street-car work imposes a very variable load on the engines and dynamos... We require stronger engines than are needed for constant loads. **1897** E. K. SCOTT *Electr. Power in Workshops* 65 Messrs. Willans and Robinson are also laying down an extensive power plant for their new works at Rugby. **1909** *Westm. Gaz.* 4 May 4/1 The rigid dirigible..cannot be made to lift the weight of the power-plant necessary to render it independent of all winds. **1933** *Newnes Compl. Wireless* 595 (*heading*) Radio power plant. Notes on the uses, installation and servicing of rotary transformers, rotary converters, motor generators, and hand-driven generators. **1935** R. H. BAKER *Introd. Astron.* x. 209 Power derived from the waterfall, from the wind, and from fuel and food has its origin in the great power plant of the sun. **1942** W. FAULKNER *Go down, Moses* 207 They..would be back once more in the little lost county seats as barbers and garage mechanics..and power-plant firemen. **1964** [see *MITOCHONDRION]. **1967** *Jane's Surface Skimmer Systems 1967–68* 104/2 The powerplant is mounted at the aft end with an acoustic bulkhead and two crew rest rooms separating it from the main passenger cabin. **1973** *Nature* 16 Mar. 210/1 The remaining papers..covered gas turbine, steam and Stirling-cycle powerplants for vehicles.

pow·er-po:litics. [f. POWER *sb.*^{1} + POLITIC *sb.* 3, translating G. *machtpolitik* (f. *macht* might, power + *politik* politics).] Political action based on or backed by threats to use force. Hence **power-poli·tical** *a.*, pertaining to or characterized by power-politics; **power-politi·cian**, one who practises power-politics.

1937 G. M. YOUNG *Daylight & Champaign* 135 We shall all have to..learn to talk of power-politics and art-form antecedents and the literary-critical approach, as if we had been cradled in Marburg and reared in Michigan. **1939** WODEHOUSE *Uncle Fred in Springtime* xiii. 179 The Duke's decision..to mobilize his nephew Ricky and plunge immediately into power politics was one which would have occasioned no surprise to anybody acquainted with the militant traditions of his proud family. **1940** A. HUXLEY *Let.* 9 Oct. (1969) 460, I am engaged at the moment on a strangely apposite study of Père Joseph, collaborator of Richelieu, the most astounding case of a power politician who was also a religious mystic. **1942** L. B. NAMIER *Conflicts* 21 For centuries Vienna and Paris had been the centres of European power-politics. **1942** PARTRIDGE *Usage & Abusage* (1947) 355/1 Hitler was the *protagonist* of Nazism, with its power-political ideology. **1959** *Oxf. Mag.* 4 June 448/1 The abolition of compulsory Latin was a power-political move intended to pacify the jealous monoliths of America and Russia. **1961** J. WILSON *Reason & Morals* ii. 125 If I do not use human beings as ends in themselves..it..results in that political tyranny which tends to corrupt the power-politician or the brain-washer. **1973** J. BURROWS *Like an Evening Gone* ii. 31, I like that period... Besides—power politics of any age—it's a kind of adventure. **1977** *Church Times* 10 June 14/4 Even monasticism had been sucked into the power-political structure of the medieval Church.

Powhatan (pau·ˌætæn), *sb.* and *a.* [Native name.] **A.** *sb.* An Algonquian people of eastern Virginia; a member of this people; their language (now extinct). **B.** *adj.* Of, pertaining to, or characteristic of this people. Hence **Powhata·nic** *a.*

1608 J. SMITH *True Relation of Occurrences in Virginia* sig. D, With a lowd oration he proclaimed me A werowanes of Powhaton, and that all his subjects should so esteeme vs, and no man account vs strangers nor Paspaheghans, but Powhatans. **1612** W. STRACHEY *Trav. Virginia* (1953) I. i. 35 There was ever Enmity..between the High-and Low Country, going by the names of Monacans, and Powhatans. **1785** T. JEFFERSON *Notes Virginia* xi. 167 We are told that the Powhatans, Mannahoacs, and Monacans spoke languages so radically different, that interpreters were necessary when they transacted business. *Ibid.* 168 The territories of the Powhatan confederacy, south of the Patowmac comprehended about 8000 square miles, 30 tribes, and 2400 warriors. **1860** H. R. SCHOOLCRAFT *Hist. & Stat. Information Indian Tribes* V. i. 35 Their language was so diverse from the Powhatanic dialects, which were of the Algonquin group, that not a word could be understood without interpreters. *Ibid.* 36 The older ones among them, preserve their language in a small degree, which are the last vestiges on earth, so far as we know, of the Powhatan language. *Ibid.* 37 All the sympathies of Virginians were with the Powhatanic tribes. **1907** *Amer. Anthropologist* IX. 135 When the English landed at Jamestown in 1607, the Powhatan confederacy was a thing of recent origin. **1912** T. MICHELSON in *28th Ann. Rep. U.S. Bureau Amer. Ethnol. 1906–7* (*map legend*) Languages the exact position of which is uncertain... Powhatan, Weapemeoc, Secotan, etc. **1915** J. BUCHAN *Salute to Adventurers* xxiv. 334 A voice..spoke the Powhatan language, which I knew. *Ibid.* xxvi. 355, I found some Indians..and told one who spoke Powhatan the issue of the fight. **1953** WRIGHT & FREUND *Strachey's Trav. Virginia* I. 35 The Powhatans were an Algonquian tribe and their name, which first came from the name of a town near the present Richmond, was later applied to the chief Wahunsonacock and his confederacy. **1974** *Encycl. Brit. Micropædia* VIII. 170/1 In the 1970s an estimated 3,000 Powhatan were reported, largely scattered along the Virginia coast. **1977** *Language* LIII. 259/2 Siebert places these data in the framework of Eastern Algonquian, as reconstructed by Bloomfield, and provides an English–Powhatan lexicon of 263 words.

Powindah (pau·ˌindă). Also **Povindah, Powandah,** ‖**pāvendeh.** [Pashto, f. Pers. *parvinda* merchandise.] A nomadic trading tribe of Afghanistan; a member of this tribe. Also *attrib.*

1851 H. B. EDWARDES *Year on Punjab Frontier* I. ix. 454 The whole of the trade between India and Central Asia is carried on by periodical caravans, which cross and re-cross the soolimânee mountains every year. They are conducted by Afghan merchants, who are generally called Lohânees, but locally in the Dérajât Powinduhs, or Povindeuhs... Lohânee is not a name applicable to either the Kharotees or the Nâssurs, so I prefer calling them Powinduhs, a name which they all acknowledge. **1880** H. W. BELLEN *Races of Afghanistan* xi. 104 During the cold weather, the Povinda is to be seen in most of the larger cities of India. *Ibid.* 105 These Povinda clans, though classed as subdivisions of the Ghilji people, differ from them in one or two important respects. **1885** E. BALFOUR *Cycl. India* (ed. 3) III. 275/2 Considering the wild and independent life the Povindahs lead, they are marvellously orderly and well-behaved when dispersed in British territory, travelling from one end of India to another. **1888** H. G. RAVERTY *Notes on Afghánistán* 489 The Nâṣirs or Nâṣirís, as they are also called, are about the most numerous of the Powandah tribes, and possess no land whatever of their own. **1895** [see *MAHSUD]. **1920** *Blackw. Mag.* Oct. 445/1 Your car is halted at the boat bridge, to let the long Afghan powindah caravans pass. *Ibid.* 445/2 The powindahs are more often armed, each man's belt crammed with cartridges. **1934** AHMAD & AZIZ *Afghanistan* iii. 17 The Gomal pass.. is much used by Povindahs on their annual migration to their winter encampments on the Indus. **1953** J. MASTERS *Lotus & Wind* xii. 158 The man..was a Powindah horse-trader... When the Pushtu greetings were at last out of the way the Powindah said, 'Let us retire.' **1967** A. SWINSON *N.-W. Frontier* v. 104 Now the Powindahs.. are great clans of warrior merchants, Ghilzais and Kharotis as well as Powindahs proper. **1974** *Encycl. Brit. Macropædia* I. 169/1 A number of nomads (*pāvendehs*) cross the eastern frontier with their herds toward their summer pastures in Pakistan. **1978** 'M. M. KAYE' *Far Pavilions* xi. 177 They were only *Powindahs*—wandering, gipsy-like folk who live in tents and are always on the move.

powwow, pow-wow, pawaw, *sb.* Add: **3.** (Further examples.) *spec.*, a conference of senior officers. Also used occas. in general sense of 'bustle, activity'. For (Chiefly *U.S.*) read orig. *U.S.*

1893 'MARK TWAIN' in *Cosmopolitan* Sept. 629/1 Without the marring additions of human pow-wow and fuss and feathers and display. **1897** —— *Following Equator* xxxviii. 346 It all helps to keep up the liveliness and augment the general sense of swiftness and energy and confusion and pow-wow. **1925** FRASER & GIBBONS *Soldier & Sailor Words* 229 *Pow-wow*, a senior officers' conference, as, for instance, of a General with the Commanding Officers of units after a field-day or an operation. **1926** J. C. LINCOLN *Big Mogul* vi. 112 It seems there was a great pow wow, some wanted to wear one kind of thing and some another. **1930** G. MACMUNN *Behind Scenes in Many Wars* xiii. 239, I visited him here several times, and attended his rather interminable pow-wows and conferences. **1936** F. CLUNE *Roaming round Darling* xxii. 221 O'Hea and the bandmaster..had a private pow-wow. **1944** *Sun* (Baltimore) 17 May 18/2 Governor O'Conor..is conceded to be in control of proceedings at the Democratic pow wow. **1954** *Manch. Guardian Weekly* 28 Jan. 3/2 The associated lobbies that oppose the [St. Lawrence] seaway, the railroads, coal-owners, and Eastern port authorities, went into a round of emergency pow-wows. **1962** *Press* (Vancouver) Nov. 9 He turned up in London at a periodical pow-wow initiated by one Cyrus Eaton. **1977** *Time* 30 May 33/2 What had brought the Mob chiefs together was a series of powwows with New York City Mafia bosses about the new Mob power structure.

powwowing, *vbl. sb.* Add: (Later examples.)

1905 J. C. LINCOLN *Partners of Tide* i. 8, I cal'late there must have been some high old pow-wowin' in the old house, but..they fin'lly decided 'twas their duty to take the little feller to bring up. **1928** H. W. SHOEMAKER in *Publ. Pennsylvania Folk-Lore Soc.* I. iv. 15 He arrived at the Little Valley with the book and tried to raise dark Cathlin's spook by pow-wowing. **1938** A. HARK *Hex marks Spot* 52 Pow-wowing is a hidden but by no means secret art among the people of Pennsylvania. **1961** D. WALDO *Beat Drum Slowly* vii. 89 There's too much pow-wowing going on hereabouts.

Powysian (pōuˌi·siăn, pauˌi·siăn), *a.* and *sb.* Also †**Powisian.** [f. *Powys* (see below) + -IAN.] **A.** *adj.* Of or pertaining to the historical principality of Powys in east-central Wales, or its inhabitants or dialect. **B.** *sb.* **a.** An inhabitant of Powys. **b.** The dialect of Powys.

Powys was established as the name of a Welsh county in 1974.

1868 *Coll. Hist. & Archæol. Montgomeryshire* I. 426 Powis, *Pow isa is the low country*, a name still given by the peasants of Montgomeryshire to the plain of Shropshire, and indeed derived from that, the only level portion of the ancient Powisian dominions. **1880** *Ibid.* XIII. 42 The men of Argoed..uphold the *brother's* right, and acknowledge not a sister's claim to inheritance... Hence we find no Boadiceas, no Cartismanduas, no queens, among the Powysians. **1897** P. BARBIER *Age of Owain Gwynedd* (1908) i. 22 The death of Maredudd in 1132, and ..the steadily growing power of Gwynedd..tended much to the diminution of Powysian influence. **1910** A. JONES *Hist. Gruffydd ap Cynan* 89 It was the activity of the Powysian princes, and especially of Maredudd,..that made Powys the object of attack. *Ibid.* 180 Gruffydd.. threatened active hostility towards any Powysians who sought safety within his dominions. **1913** J. M. JONES *Welsh Gram.* 8 Powysian, the dialect of Powys, or North East and Mid Wales.

pox, *sb.* Add: **1. a.** (Later examples.) Now only *colloq.* and freq. used to designate any venereal disease.

1922 [see *LOCK *sb.*[2] 18]. **1930** *Amer. Speech* V. 392 *Pox*, any kind of venereal disease. **1930** BROPHY & PARTRIDGE *Songs & Slang 1914–18* 88 But now she's standing in the gutter, selling matches penny-a-box: While he's riding in his carriage With an awful dose of — [awful dose of pox *in* **1965** —— *Long Trail* 70]. **1968** [see *DOSE *sb.* 2 d]. **1969** *Coast to Coast 1967–68* 191 'Yah! Luther stinking swine! He had the pox!' Simon..had yelled in return 'Old bugger Pope pokes the nuns!' **1976** J. O'CONNOR *Eleventh Commandment* viii. 101 Wally.. strangled a prostitute for giving him a dose of the pox. **1977** *Sounds* 9 July 8/4 It's still potent diz bustin' rhino-stomp, a most touching lament to the pox, but it's not brash to an offensive level.

3. For † *Obs.* read *arch.* (chiefly *Lit.*) and add later examples.

1922 JOYCE *Ulysses* 392 But they can go hang..for me with their bully beef, a pox on it. **1941** V. WOOLF *Between Acts* 126 Hand me the mirror, girl. So. Now my wig... A pox on the girl—she's dreaming! **1963** *Sunday Times* 8 Sept. 29/3 Cool Shakespeare thrives in the sixth and phrases like 'Pox on't!' and 'Fie!' are in present usage. **1973** 'A. HALL' *Tango Briefing* xiv. 184 A pox on his grave repercussions, if he meant the whole thing'd blow up.. why couldn't he bloody well say so.

4. *poxfiend*; **pox-doctor** *slang*, a doctor specializing in the treatment of venereal diseases; phr. *got up like a pox-doctor's clerk* (and varr.), dressed smartly but in bad taste, overdressed; **pox-fouled** *a.*, infected with syphilis.

1937 D. JONES *In Parenthesis* v. 118 You feel the pack of the Ox-blood Kid—it's as light as the Rig'mentals—there's a whole lot of them that work it: the Pox-Doctor's Clerk, for one, the chitties, and types of scullion bummers up. **1949** PARTRIDGE *Dict. Slang* (ed. 3) 1141/2 *Pox doctor's clerk, like*—or *got-up like—a*, in a very smart civilian suit: Naval: C. 20. **1965** E. LAMBERT *Long White Night* xv. 136 They was all dressed like they was at Buckingham Palace and Foran was done up like a pox doctor's clerk. **1965** P. FERRIS *Doctors* iii. 57 They [*sc.* coloured doctors] can land a job in London as a pathologist or a pox-doctor, but that's about all. **1974** *Bulletin* (Sydney) 19 Jan. 13 Getting dressed up like Lord Muck and getting round kitted up like a flamin' pox doctor's clerk. **1922** JOYCE *Ulysses* 419 And snares of the poxfiend. *a* **1915** —— *Giacomo Joyce* (1968) 9 The pox-fouled wenches and young wives that, gaily yielding to their ravishers, clip and clip again.

pox, *v.* Delete *Obs.* and add: (Later examples.) Also *transf.* and *fig.*

1784 PRINCE WILLIAM *Let.* 23 July in P. Ziegler *King William IV* (1971) iii. 51 Oh, for..the pretty girls of Westminster..such as would not clap or pox me every time I fucked. **1802** G. GALLOWAY in *Admirable Crichton* 70 Tho' we were pox'd wi' poverty and law. **1846** *Swell's Night Guide* 45 These kens are tenanted by a blackguard.. school of pugging shakes, whose chief fame is in..poxing a swaddy. **1933** M. LOWRY *Ultramarine* i. 51 That boy got all poxed up to the eyeballs, voyage before last... Yes, he was poxed all away to hell. **1935** in *Sc. Nat. Dict.* (1968) VII. 225/1 When I wuz away for my breakfast my mate oot o' pure duvilment poxt the stone on me. **1961** 'F. O'BRIEN' *Hard Life* xiv. 115 Conditions on the canal bank are nothing short of a scandal with men and women going about there poxed-up to the eyes. **1968** *Amer. Speech 1967* XLII. 295 *Pox*, a general colloquial term for 'ruining or damaging stone through faulty handling, milling, or carving'. **1968** *Sc. Nat. Dict.* VII. 225/1 *Pox, v.*,..to botch (a job), ruin (a piece of work). **1970** G. F. NEWMAN *Sir, You Bastard* iii. 92 The car became expedient. He was poxed with running for trains, missing trains, and worse, catching trains crowded with sickly commuters. **1977** *Sat. Rev.* (U.S.) 23 July 15/2 Wilmington, Delaware, poxed at that time by 1,200 abandoned one- and two-story homes.

poxvirus (pǫ·ks,vəiərǝs). *Microbiol.* Also **pox virus.** [mod.L., f. POX *sb.* + VIRUS.] Any of a group of large DNA viruses that cause smallpox and various other epidermal diseases in vertebrates.

1941 *Amer. Jrnl. Vet. Res.* II. 102/1 There are many different strains of pox virus, some of them less pathogenic than others. **1962** [see *ARBORVIRUS]. **1973** R. G. KRUEGER et al. *Introd. Microbiol.* xix. 522/1 Poxviruses propagate rapidly in a wide variety of mammalian and embryo tissues *in vitro* producing cytopathic effects in 24–48 hr.

poxy (pǫ·ksi) *a.* [f. POX *sb.* + -Y[1].] Infected with pox; spotty; *fig.*, trashy, worthless. Also as a general term of abuse.

1922 JOYCE *Ulysses* 8 God knows what poxy bowsy left them off. **1950** M. PEAKE *Gormenghast* xxii. 149 Every poxy sunrise of the year, eh, that you burst out of the decent darkness in that plucked way? **1958** [see *MOOR *sb.*[1] 1 b]. **1959** I. & P. OPIE *Lore & Lang. Schoolch.* ix. 171 Other unfortunates are 'Spotty Dicks'..their friends call them: Bumps,..Crater face,..Pimple bonce, Poxie, and Scabby guts. **1968** BETHELL & BURG tr. *Solzhenitsyn's Cancer Ward* I. xix. 302 You know, that poxy-faced guy, the one with all the bandages. **1975** J. PIDGEON *Flame* i. 8 No more poxy weddings, no more bloody favours. **1976** J. O'CONNOR *Eleventh Commandment* ii. 31 The first tray..was full of poxy rings worth two or three quid. **1978** K. BONFIGLIOLI *All Tea in China* III. xi. 153 My poxy friend Peter.

‖ **poya** (pō̆·yă). [Sinhalese *pōya*, f. Skr. *upavasathá* fast day.] In full, *poya day*: a day on which the moon enters one of its four phases, observed as a day of special religious observance by Buddhists in Sri Lanka.

1853 R. S. HARDY *Man. Budhism* i. 22 When the dark póya, or day of the new moon, has come, the sun moves in one day the distance of 100,000 yojanas from the moon. *Ibid.* ii. 51 Today so many men have observed the póya (or sacred day). *Ibid.* v. 116 It was the póya day, when the prince..went to the public alms-hall to distribute the royal bounty. **1889** M. MONIER-WILLIAMS *Buddhism* XII. 316 These preachings are generally well-attended, especially on the four Poya days. **1910** tr. *Hackmann's Buddhism as Relig.* III. ii. 116 Real preaching (not only reading of the sacred text) is done in some temples on the so-called *poya* days, the four quarters of the moon, when lay people assemble in the *vihāras* to present their gift. **1913** L. WOOLF *Village in Jungle* ii. 40 If you had come last poya, Silindu, I could have given it. **1971** *Times Weekender* (Ceylon) 3 Oct. 9/2 He had obviously stoked up in anticipation of a dry Poya day ahead.

Poyning's Law. Delete 'See quot.' and add: Also (*correctly*) **Poynings' Law.** [f. the name of Sir Edward *Poynings* (1459–1521), Lord Deputy in Ireland, 1494–6.] The name given to a series of statutes, passed at Drogheda in 1494–5 and repealed in 1782, by which the Irish parliament was subordinated to the English Crown.

[**1612–13** in Coke *Fourth Part Institutes* (1644) lxxvi. 351 An Act made in the tenth year of H.7 called *Poynings Act.*] **1622** BACON *Henry VII* 138 But Poynings (the better to make compensation of the Meagernesse of his Seruice in the Warres, by Acts of Peace) called a Parliament; where was made that memorable Act, which at this day is called Poynings Law, whereby all the Statutes of England were made to bee of force in Ireland. **1656** [in Dict.] **1797** *Encycl. Brit.* IX. 327/2 During his administration was enacted the law known by the name of *Poyning's Law.* **1827** H. HALLAM *Const. Hist. Eng.* II. xviii. 719 This produced the famous statute of Drogheda in 1495, known by the name of Poyning's law. **1938** D. L. KEIR *Const. Hist. Mod. Brit.* vii. 434 By Poyning's Law, in 1495, the Irish Parliament itself made applicable to Ireland all statutes lately made in England, and acknowledged the right of the King to be informed of the causes for its summons and to approve, in his Council, all bills to be introduced when it met. **1973** B. BRADSHAW in B. Farrell *Irish Parliamentary Tradition* v. 69 Essentially Poynings' Law provided that a parliament could not be validly held in Ireland without the consent of the king..both to the convening of parliament and to the projected legislation.

Poynting (poi·ntiŋ). *Physics.* The name of John Henry *Poynting* (1852–1914), English physicist, used *attrib.* and in the possessive to designate concepts in electromagnetism, as **Poynting's theorem,** the theorem that the rate of flow of electromagnetic energy through a closed surface is equal to the integral over the surface of the Poynting vector; **Poynting('s) vector,** the vector product of the electric and magnetic field strengths at any point, which can often be interpreted as representing in magnitude and direction the rate of flow of electromagnetic energy.

1893 J. J. THOMSON *Notes Recent Res. Electr. & Magn.* p. xiii, Poynting's theorem. **1913** L. SILBERSTEIN *Vectorial Mech.* i. 45 The flux of electromagnetic energy, per unit time and unit area, *i.e.* the so-called Poynting-vector. **1962** CORSON & LORRAIN *Introd. Electromagn. Fields* xi. 399 The Poynting vector for sunlight is approximately 1·4 kilowatts/meter² at the surface of the earth. **1971** D. A. DUNN *Models of Particles* iii. 74 The usual form of Poynting's vector, which appears in Poynting's theorem and expresses the amount and direction of power flow, is invariant to a Lorentz transformation. **1976** D. E. SOPER *Classical Field Theory* x. 150 The energy current..and the momentum density..are given by the familiar Poynting's vector. **1977** *Daily Tel.* 14 Nov. 8 (Advt.), You'll find a complete range of ready-prepared programs for commonly-used calculations such as..field-strength and poynting vector due to electric dipole.

pozzolana, pozzuolana. Now also anglicized as **pozzolan (pozzulan, puzzolan).** Add to def.: **pozzolan cement,** a cement made from natural or artificial pozzolan, lime, and water.

1907 *Chem. Abstr.* I. 1078 (*heading*) Process of manufacturing limes, cements, and puzzolans. **1910** *Engineering News* LXIV. 597/2 The mixed Portland cement and puzzolan-cement is superior to Portland cement. **1918** R. PEELE *Mining Engineers' Handbk.* XLIII. 2217 Pozzulan cement proper is made by grinding hydrated lime and pozzulan, a volcanic material occurring near Naples. **1947** R. H. BOGUE *Chem. of Portland Cement* xxix. 520 Only when the chemical action is completely understood will it be possible to design a 'pozzolan' of ideal composition for any particular purpose. **1951** *Econ. Geol.* XLVI. 311 Pozzolans are natural and artificial siliceous and aluminous substances which are not cementitious themselves but which react with lime in the presence of water at atmospheric temperatures to produce cementitious compounds. **1971** *Materials & Technol.* II. ii. 106 Pozzolan cement is made by grinding together a cement (usually Portland cement) and a powdered siliceous material.

pozzolanic *a.* (later examples); hence also **po:zzolani·city,** the property of combining with lime in the presence of water to form a cement.

1927 F. L. BRADY *Introd. Building Sci.* xxi. 241 Mortars are used in England at the present day, which set by pozzolanic action. **1956** *Proc. Inst. Electr. Engin.* CIII. A. 225/1 Pulverized fuel fly ash from our power stations..has the pozzolanic property of setting with lime under water. **1960** *B.S.I. News* Jan. 15 'Pozzolanic portland cements' may contain up to twenty per cent. pozzolana but need not pass the test for pozzolanicity. **1972** *Daily Tel.* 29 Apr. 17 (Advt.), Manufacturers of pozzolanic cements and grouts.

pozzy[1]: see *POSSIE, POZZY.

pozzy[2] (pǫ·zi). *Army* and *Navy slang.* Also **possie, possy, pozi, pozzie.** [Origin unknown.] Jam, marmalade.

1916 *Daily Mail* 1 Nov. 4/4 'Pozzy' (jam). **1919** W. H. DOWNING *Digger Dial.* 59 *Pozi*, jam. 'Who puckeroed the pozi?' 'Who took the jam?' **1929** *Papers Mich. Acad. Sci., Arts & Lett.* X. 316/1 *Possie*, jam. This seems to be a variant of pozzi (or pozzy). **1962** GRANVILLE *Dict. Sailors' Slang* 91/1 *Pozzie* (*y*), jam or marmalade.

p-process: see *P III. 6.

practical, *a.* (*sb.*) Add: **A.** *adj.* **I. 1. b.** *spec.* of doors, windows, food, etc., forming parts of a theatrical or film set: operable; able to be used as in real life.

1933 P. GODFREY *Back-Stage* iv. 47 His [*sc.* the stage-carpenter's] doors and windows never open unless he has been told to make them 'practical'. **1960** O. SKILBECK *ABC of Film & TV* 98 *Practical.* Part, or fitting, of a Set which may have to operate exactly as though real; e.g. a door, tap, or light fitting. **1974** *Some Technical Terms & Slang* (Granada Television) s.v. *Practical*, Granada gave a 'practical' banquet in its play *The Dead.*

c. *Electr.* Applied to certain units (the ampere, volt, ohm, watt, coulomb, and farad) used for practical measurements, as contrasted with the absolute units of the C.G.S. system.

They are now part of the International System of Units.

1873 J. C. MAXWELL *Treat. Electr. & Magn.* II. IV. x. 244 The practical unit of electromotive force is called the Volt. **1882** *Nature* 24 Aug. 391/2 Instead of expressing electrical quantities directly in absolute measure, the [International Electrical] Congress has embodied a consistent system, based on the Ohm, in which the units are of a value convenient for practical measurements. In this, which we must hereafter know as the 'practical system', as distinguished from the 'absolute system', the units are named after leading physicists, the Ohm, Ampère, Volt, Coulomb, and Farad. **1886** J. D. EVERETT *Units & Physical Constants* (ed. 2) xi. 151 The practical unit of capacity is the Farad. It is defined as 10^{-9} of the C.G.S. electro-magnetic unit of capacity. **1904** *Jrnl. Inst. Electr. Engin.* XXXIV. 172 He suggested that the prefix *ab* or *abs* should be used with the names of the practical units (Volt, Ampere, Ohm, etc.) to form names for the corresponding C.G.S. electro*magnetic* units. **1932** [see *INTERNATIONAL *a.* (*sb.*) A. 1 c]. **1963** JERRARD & MCNEILL *Dict. Sci. Units* 12 Units based on this definition..are known as electromagnetic units (e.m.u.). The quantities defined by these units are generally of an inconvenient size for practical work so units, known as practical units, are used. The latter may be obtained by multiplying the e.m. unit by a suitable conversion factor. *Ibid.* 13 The inconvenience of having three systems of electrical units, ab units, stat units and practical units has been overcome by the introduction of the metre, kilogramme, second, ampere units (M.K.S.). In this system, the practical units have the same value as the theoretical ones.

3. (Later examples.)

1970 P. LAURIE *Scotland Yard* 292 *Practical*, the highest police compliment; particularly of a senior officer who can still distinguish between the formal processes of law and the realities of police work. **1972** *Police Rev.* 10 Nov. 1475/3 Dickens is on the side of the angels in applauding what we now loosely term 'good practical Police work'.

III. 6. *practical activity*, activity through which theory is realized and becomes actual; *practical attitude*, an attitude that is concerned with material facts and actual events; *practical criticism*, an analytical approach to literary criticism, advocated by I. A. Richards, which influenced and was further developed as *NEW CRITICISM; *practical nurse* chiefly *N. Amer.*, one who has completed a course of training in nursing practice but who is not a (state-)registered nurse; also *attrib.*; hence *practical nurse* v. trans., *practical nursing* vbl. sb.; *practical politics*, what actually takes place or is possible in political life, sometimes implying lack of moral principle (cf. *REALPOLITIK); hence *practical politician.*

1913 D. AINSLIE tr. *B. Croce's Philos. of Practical* II. i. 173 (*heading*) The practical activity in its dialectic. *Ibid.*, We shall no longer ask, therefore, whether the practical activity precede or follow knowledge. **1935** E. BURNS *Handbk. Marxism* xiii. 213 There, where speculation ends, with real life, real positive science therefore begins, the representation of practical activity, of the practical process of the development of men. **1963** T. BOTTOMORE tr. *Marx's Early Writings* 52 The criticism of the speculative philosophy of right does not remain within its own sphere, but leads on to *tasks* which can only be solved by *means of* *practical activity.* **1974** R. STEVENS *James & Husserl* 177 The intentional continuity between projects of meaning and their fulfillment in practical activity. **1883** F. H. BRADLEY *Princ. Logic* 20 Not only are the genuine characteristics absent from a mere practical attitude, but we find present there a quality which is absent from real judgment. **1902** W. JAMES *Var. Relig. Exper.* xi. 261 Our moral and practical attitude, at any given time, is always a resultant of two sets of forces within us. **1945** K. R. POPPER *Open Society* II. xxiv. 213 It may be better to explain rationalism in terms of practical attitudes or behaviour. **1962** MACQUARRIE & ROBINSON tr. *Heidegger's Being & Time* I. vi. 238 So this phenomenon by no means expresses a priority of the 'practical' attitude over the theoretical. **1970** C. A. VAN PEURSEN in J. M. Edie et al. *Patterns of Life-World* 148 Theoretical truth is of importance, but in no case does it present the origin of truth as such. The practical attitude of man, 'shunning what is harmful and pursuing what is apt to promote well-being', is of more importance. **1929** I. A. RICHARDS (*title*) Practical criticism: a study of literary judgment. **1958** *Oxf. Mag.* 13 Nov. 94/2 'Practical criticism' itself, as a term, is unsatisfactory... What on earth is the point of any sort of criticism if it isn't practical?.. In so far as it has a clear current sense, it means the analysis, apart from their literary context, of short passages of prose and verse. **1959** *Times Lit. Suppl.* 24 Apr. 241/3 It is not merely criticism; it is 'practical criticism' of a high order and of a kind which is too rarely found in France. **1972** *Ibid.* 3 Mar. 246/3 As for the assumptions involved in the identifying of me [*sc.* F. R. Leavis] with 'Practical Criticism', my first comment is that the formula isn't mine, and,..I have been known for my insistence, when having to use it, that 'Practical Criticism is criticism in practice'. **1977** *N.Y. Rev. Bks.* 15 Sept. 40/2 His practical criticism is not much concerned with the structure of an individual poem except as an embodiment of crisis. **1921** *Daily Colonist* (Victoria, B.C.) 1 Oct. 16/2 (Advt.), Situations Wanted—Female..experienced practical nurse, terms moderate. **1956** K. HULME *Nun's Story* vii. 104 Our practical nurses ..can stand only a four-hour shift, but our sisters take unlimited duty. **1964** MRS. L. B. JOHNSON *White House Diary* 24 Apr. (1970) 118 To my great delight we..saw a class in practical nursing, and I told them that the world was certainly waiting for their skills. So it is, as anybody who has tried to find a practical nurse for an elderly or ill member of the family can tell you. **1971** 'A. BLAISDELL' *Practice to Deceive* v. 68 Mrs. Carstairs would be back from practical-nursing her sister. **1979** W. KIENZLE *Rosary Murders* 20 One of the orderlies and one of the practical nurses..had enjoyed a quick roll in bed. **1812** *Deb. Congress U.S.* (1853) 12th Congress 1 Sess., App. 2210 There were two circumstances, inherent in this system of coercing Great Britain by commercial restrictions, which ought to have made practical politicians very doubtful of its result. **1961** *Times* 10 Jan. 8 The impression remains that the Liberal leader is still the diplomatist, more at home in the chancery, or the corridors of the United Nations, not the father figure, so necessary in Canadian leadership, or the practical politician, able to talk about sewage problems. **1796** *Rep. Comm. House of Commons* (1803) XIV. 38 With a view to such a knowledge of practical Politics, as may be desired from the History of our experimental Legislation. **1826** DISRAELI *Viv. Grey* I. II. xv. 217 'Hargrave', said his lordship, 'if you want any information upon points of *practical politics*'—that was his phrase..'there is *only one* man in the kingdom whom you should consult..and that's Stapylton Toad.' **1897** [see PRACTICAL *a.* 1 b]. **1919** F. HAMILTON *Vanished Pomps of Yesterday* i. 30 As the inventor of 'Practical Politics' (*Real Politik*), Bismarck had a supreme contempt for fluent talkers and for words. **1939** I. BERLIN *Karl Marx* iv. 74 It was his [*sc.* Marx's] first experience of practical politics: he conducted his paper with immense vigour and intolerance. **1961** N. P. STALLKNECHT in Stallknecht & Frenz *Compar. Lit.: Method & Perspective* vi. 121 We may..trace the notion of individual autonomy from its manifestation in religious practice and theological reflection through practical politics and political theory into literature and the arts.

B. *sb.* (Restrict 'in *pl.*' to senses in Dict.) **2.** (Earlier example.)

a **1737** M. GREEN *Spleen* (1936) 15 That tribe, whose practicals decree Small-beer the deadliest heresy.

3. An examination, course, or lesson devoted to practice in a subject. Also *fig.*

1934 in WEBSTER. **1955** *School Sci. Rev.* Nov. 38 For the practical paper, 93 per cent of candidates were successful —compared with 68 per cent who passed the theory, and of over 300 who passed the theory, only 7 failed the practical. **1961** *Times* 6 Nov. 14/2 Lieutenant Babington, straight out from England to take over a platoon..seems to have failed his practicals where discipline is concerned. **1966** *Rep. Comm. Inquiry Univ. Oxf.* II. 311 Nationally, the average for tutorials was much lower (1·7 hours against 6·3 hours at Oxford), while the national averages for lectures and practicals were about twice the Oxford figures. **1979** F. OLBRICH *Sweet & Deadly* xi. 125 He would get through this damned exam if it was the last thing he did... There would still be the practicals, of course.

practicalism. Add: Also, = PRAGMATISM 4; also, in Communist usage, excessive attention paid to practical matters resulting in the disregard of theory.

1898 W. JAMES *Philos. Concept. & Pract. Results* 5 The principle of practicalism.., as he [*sc.* C. S. Peirce] called it, when I first heard him enunciate it at Cambridge [Mass.] in the early '70s, is the clue..by following which ..we may keep our feet upon the proper trail. **1898** —— *Coll. Ess. & Rev.* (1920) 424 Now the principle of practicalism says that the very meaning of the conception of God lies in those differences which must be made in our experience if the conception be true. **1951** *Britannica Bk. of Year* 686/2 *Practicalism*, a Communist term for the fault of paying too much attention to practical problems of production, etc., and not enough to ideological propaganda. **1963** R. C. TUCKER *Soviet Political Mind* ix. 181 Krushchev..has been criticized by certain elements within the Soviet Communist Party for being insufficiently so [*sc.* theory-oriented]. He has rejected their charge of 'practicalism'.

practicality. 1. (Earlier and later examples.)

1828 MILL *Autobiogr.* (1924) 288 It is not for me to dispute the palm of practicality with these sage and cautious persons. **1961** E. BECKER *Zen* iv. 107 The 'marvelous person' that is supposed to result from Zen exhibits more Chinese practicality than Indian speculation. **1972** *Physics Bull.* May 303/1 If the physicist's numeracy is combined with his practicality and technical competence one sees that he can present a formidable challenge in this market traditionally the preserve of the arts graduate.

practicant. Restrict † *Obs. rare* to first sense in Dict. and add later examples.

1952 *John o' London's* 2 May 434/1 In..nutrition, we have known him as a brake on the over-enthusiasm of the practicants in that novel subject. **1974** *Spectator* 9 Nov. 591/3 Practicants of Transcendental Meditation.

practice. Add: **1. c.** *Philos.* The active practical aspect as considered in contrast to or as the realization of the theoretical aspect.

c **1898** C. S. PEIRCE *Coll. Papers* (1934) V. 412 Science, when it comes to understand itself, regards facts as merely the vehicle of eternal truth, while for Practice they remain the obstacles which it has to turn, the enemy of which it is determined to get the better. **1907** F. C. S. SCHILLER *Studies in Humanism* iv. 130 It seems necessary, therefore, to conceive 'practice' more broadly as *the control of experience*... The aim of the doctrine of the 'subordination' of 'theory' to 'practice'..is merely *voluntarism*. **1937** C. MORRIS *Logical Positivism* v. 67 Science has integrated and utilized all of the dimensions of meaning, and may be said to walk on the three legs of theory, fact, and practice. **1969** D. CAIRNS tr. *Husserl's Formal & Transcendental Logic* 32 The distinction is after all a relative one; because even purely theoretical activity is indeed activity—that is to say, a practice (when the concept of practice is accorded its natural breadth).

d. A Marxist term for the social action which should result from and complement the theory of communism. Cf. *PRAXIS 1 c.

1899 *Social-Democrat* III. 358 (*title*) Social-democratic theory and practice. ? **1924** *Communist Internat.* I. 49 The practice of the class struggle is fertilised by theory, and in its turn becomes the fruitful soil for theoretical study. **1925** N. BUKHARIN *Lenin as Marxist* 17 If Leninism in practice is not the same as Marxism, then we get just that separation of theory from practice which is specially harmful for such an institution as the Institute of Red Professors. **1966** P. HEATH tr. *Wetter's Soviet Ideology Today* I. vi. 139 It [*sc.* a theory] must issue, rather, in *correct* practice, i.e., in a practice that leads reality towards its *truth*. But the problem as to the criterion of truth is not thereby resolved. **1966** F. SCHURMANN *Ideology & Organization in Communist China* p. xlvi, By the time of Yenan, 'theory' had been canonized, and the Chinese Communists turned their attention to 'practice', namely organization and action. **1971** Z. A. JORDAN *Karl Marx* I. vi. 67 Concepts such as those of progress, of the historically restricted scope of social laws, of ideology and social engineering (practice in the Marxian terminology).

12. (sense 2 b) *practice direction, master*; (sense 3) *practice-crew, -dress, -room* (examples); **practice bar** *Ballet* = *BAR *sb.*[1] 13 d; **practice-curve**, a curve or graph showing the relation of practice to progress; **practice pad**, a non-resonant pad, usu. circular and made of rubber or the like, on which to practise the art of drumming; **practice wicket**, (see quot. 1934).

1938 N. STREATFEILD *Circus is Coming* viii. 132 Using the side of the steps as a practice bar and raising her right leg in an arabesque. **1946** —— *Party Frock* vi. 54 Sally was using the edge of the mantlepiece as a practice-bar. **1976** 'M. ALBRAND' *Taste of Terror* xiv. 78 An empty space, a practice bar, one wall mirrored. **1887** *Century Mag.* XXXIV. 178/2 Freshmen formed a practice crew of their own. **1924** R. M. OGDEN tr. *Koffka's Growth of Mind* v. 262 New configurations are also attributable to these lower centres; as is demonstrated by the fact that the practice curve improves by leaps which occur in learning new movements. **1956** B. R. BUGELSKI *Psychol. of Learning* xiv. 399 Learning curves are sometimes called 'practice' curves but about all that we can say for certain about such curves is that they will normally rise above a starting point if learning does take place. **1942** *Weekly Notes* 10 Jan. 19/1 (*heading*) Practice direction... The Judges of the Chancery Division have given the following direction: [etc.]. **1968** *Weekly Law Rep.* 24 May 815 (*heading*) Practice Direction (Divisional Court: Avoidance of Delay). **1977** C. HAMPTON *Criminal Procedure* (ed. 2) viii. 212 The Lord Chief Justice issued a practice direction in July 1967 explaining the procedure. **1934** A. P. HERBERT *Holy Deadlock* 192 The young ladies of the chorus were in 'practice-dress', their plump legs naked from their 'trunks' to their ankles. **1937** M. ALLINGHAM *Dancers in Mourning* iii. 39 Her short white practice dress. **1979** K. O'HARA *Searchers of Dead* xi. 116 A scrawny girl in a practice dress..chasséed below him. **1885** EMDEN & PEARCE-EDGCUMBE *Compl. Coll. Practice Statutes, Orders & Rules* 1147 (*heading*) Office Rules settled by the Practice Masters, 1880, 1881, 1882. **1890** *Law Rep.: Queen's Bench Div.* XXV. 243 The practice masters..have at some period between 1880 and 1888 issued a direction that 'writs of summons before the Judicature Acts came into force may be renewed without an order'. **1937** *Encycl. Court Forms & Precedents* I. 13 There are eight King's Bench Masters... They have also control of the Central Office and one of them sits daily to exercise this control and to give directions with respect to questions of practice and procedure relating to the business of the Central Office...[*Note*] The Master discharging this duty (called 'the Practice Master') takes *ex parte* applications and also gives advice to solicitors on points of practice and procedure. **1966** *Masters' Practice Directions, Tables & Forms* (Supreme Court of Judicature) 1 These directions shall..supersede any Practice Masters' Rule or Direction dealing with the same subject. **1968** *New Yorker* 18 May 56, I started playing drums in junior high. I got a practice pad and sticks and a Paul Yoder method book. **1972** *Down Beat* 16 Mar. 19/3 First of all, get a drum set, not a practice pad. Then play records. **1921** W. DE LA MARE *Crossings* 17 No more scales in that musty-fusty old practice-room! **1922** [see *BAR *sb.*[1] 13 d]. **1963** *Times* 11 June 15/3, 14 sound-proof practice-rooms. **1977** *New Yorker* 19 Sept. 54/3 A friend of Robin's, Roman Markowicz, popped out of a practice room and stopped us. **1980** *Early Music* Jan. 43/1, I agreed to come to the choir practice-room. **1871** 'THOMSONBY' *Cricketers in Council* 23 Your first lessons may well be solely in hitting. Go to your practice wicket, and endeavour to hit hard..every ball that is bowled to you. **1934** W. J. LEWIS *Lang. Cricket* 298 *Practice wicket*, a pitch with one wicket set up for the practice of batting or batting and bowling, usually in the nets.

practicism (præ·ktisiz'm). [f. PRACTIC(E + -ISM.] (See quot. 1957[1].)

1957 R. N. C. HUNT *Guide to Communist Jargon* xxxv. 121 Hence practicism is the tendency of party members to conduct their day-to-day work without regard to the theory which alone gives that work its justification and significance. **1957** *Economist* 26 Oct. 320/1 All the crimes in the jargon book of communist heresy—including such esoteric offences as 'practicism' (lack of clear revolutionary perspective).

pra·ctico-, combining form of PRAXIS or PRACTICAL *a.*: = practically.., practical and.., as in *practico-empirical, -social, -spiritual* adjs.; **practico-inert**, Sartre's term for his hypothesis that man's present freedom of action is limited as a result of the exercise of free choice, or praxis, by previous generations in their use of the material world.

1970 B. BREWSTER tr. *Althusser & Balibar's Reading Capital* (1975) II. iii. 83 All the visible phenomena and practico-empirical concepts produced by the economic world. **1966** A. MANSER *Sartre* xiii. 207, I want to say.. that all men are slaves in so far as their experience of life takes place in the realm of the *practico-inert* and in the exact measure in which this realm is originally conditioned by scarcity. **1975** B. COOPER tr. *Aron's Hist. & Dialectic of Violence* ii. 41 Alienation presupposes the moment of original freedom and translucid *praxis*. Otherwise, it would but remain the experience of the practico-inert, the activity-passivity that we live out each day, and could not be recognized as the experience of bondage. **1975** F. COPLESTON *Hist. Philos.* IX. xvii. 379 Man thus falls under the domination of the 'practico-inert' which he himself has created. Man makes the machine; but the machine then reacts on man, reducing him to the level of the practico-inert, to what can be manipulated. **1976** A. S. SMITH tr. *Sartre's Critique Dialectical Reason* 829 Practico-inert, matter in which past *praxis* is embodied. **1970** B. BREWSTER tr. *Althusser & Balibar's Reading Capital* III. 314 Ideology..is distinguished from a science not by its falsity, for it can be coherent and logical (for instance, theology), but by the fact that the practico-social predominates in it over the theoretical, over knowledge. *Ibid.* I. 54 In the 1857 *Introduction*, Marx writes.. 'practico-spiritual (*praktisch-geistig*) appropriation of this world'.

practicum (præ·ktikǝ̆m). *N. Amer.* [a. late L. *practicum*, neut. of *practicus*, Gr. πρακτικός practical, concerned with action. (Cf. G. *praktikum* practical training.)] A practical exercise; a course of practical training.

1904 T. F. HUNT *Cereals in Amer.* p. vi, The ideal condition involves a study of the plant in the field. Unfortunately..no systematic course of instruction can be planned that will conform with the season of crop growth and meet the exigencies of the weather. Practicums should be supplied that will as far as possible remedy this defect. **1938** KAINS & MCQUESTON *Propagation of Plants* 458 To carry out these practicums it is desirable..to have available a plot of ground of not less than one-half acre. **1973** *Arithmetic Teacher* Apr. 244/1 (Advt.), The second week will be a practicum involving children. **1974** H. L. FOSTER *Ribbin'* vii. 301 Practicum experiences involve various aspects of the community life, tutoring students, working with teachers and students, and participating in school activities. **1978** *Daily Colonist* (Victoria, B.C.) 27 Aug. 17/5 His desire for a kindergarten practicum caused a few problems..but it was arranged through the Sooke school district.

practolol (præ·ktǒlǫl). *Pharm.* [Etym. unknown.] A white powder, $C_{14}H_{22}N_2O_3$, that is similar to propranolol in its effect on the heart but has less effect on respiratory functions.

1969 *Lancet* 14 June 1221/1 The British Pharmacopœia has issued the following supplementary list of approved names... Practolol, 4-(2-Hydroxy-3-isopropylaminopropoxy)-acetanilide. *Ibid.* 2 Aug. 227/1 Practolol..was given to forty-seven patients who had cardiac dysrhythmias after myocardial infarction. **1976** *Nature* 12 Aug. 595/2 Practolol (40 mg kg^{-1}) a β_2 receptor blocking agent that does not enter the brain in significant quantity did not inhibit hyperactivity. **1976** *Lancet* 6 Nov. 984/1 Practolol therapy may be associated with various adverse reactions. *Ibid.*, Practolol ('Eraldin') tablets were withdrawn from general use on Oct. 1, 1975.

prad. Add: (Further examples.)

The examples are all Australian.

1882 *Sydney Slang Dict.* 10/2 He blew on Sam who

frisked a lobb and the same day came it on Joe for fencing the prad got on the cross. **1916** C. J. DENNIS *Moods of Ginger Mick* 27 'E sits there while I 'arness up me prad. **1930** *Bulletin* (Sydney) 17 Sept. 21/2 Our packhorses snorted suspiciously... The prads watched, all prick ears and snorts as the axe bit into the tree. **1933** *Ibid.* 27 Dec. 20 When it [*sc.* the rope] broke, the astonished prad plunged suddenly into the dam. Two doses of that remedy and he was a reformed animal. **1977** *Courier-Mail* (Brisbane) 31 Mar. 4/5 It would surely be more appropriate for the riding [for democracy] to be done on some business man rather than on a prad.

‖ **pradakshina** (prada·kʃinā). Also **pradakshna.** [Skr. *pradakṣiṇā*, f. *pra* in front + *dakṣiṇā* right.] In Hinduism and Buddhism, circumambulation of an object in a clockwise direction as a form of worship. Also *attrib.*

1810 E. MOOR *Hindu Pantheon* 327 The respectful ceremony of *Pradakshna*, which consists in circumambulating several times the..object..to be reverenced, keeping, with closed palms, the right hand and the face towards it. **1883** M. MONIER-WILLIAMS *Relig. Thought & Life in India* I. xii. 348 A pilgrim..sets out from the source of the Ganges,..and walks by the left bank of the river to its mouth..; then, turning round, he proceeds by the right side back to Gangotrī, whence he departed. This is called Pradakshiṇā. **1933** A. STEIN *On Anc. Central-Asian Tracks* iv. 61 The ceremonial circumambulation or *pradakshina* prescribed by Indian custom. **1956** R. PIERIS *Sinhalese Social Organization* II. 84 He then.. reverentially performs *pradakshiṇā* three times to the diagram. **1976** *Jrnl. R. Soc. Arts* CXXIV. 677/2 The apsidal temple in question could have been a temple for the Nāga cult, with the four-sided Nāga image..standing in the apse, placed there to be worshipped in the pradakṣiṇa way.

præcocial, *a.* Add: Also **precocial.** Insert in etym. after *præcocēs*: (C. J. Sundevall 1836, in *Kungl. Svenska Vetenskapsakademien Handlingar 1835* 70). Add to def.: also extended to refer to the young of other animals which are independent soon after birth. (Later examples.)

1932 J. S. HUXLEY *Probl. Relative Growth* iii. 90 The same reasoning applies to Ocypoda, whose young are similarly precocial. **1937** ALLEE & SCHMIDT tr. *Hesse's Ecol. Animal Geogr.* xxiii. 484 The young [of water-birds] are praecocial and very soon learn to forage for themselves. **1949** A. LEOPOLD *Sand County Almanac* I. 35 The hen plover is brooding the four large pointed eggs which will shortly hatch four precocial chicks. **1974** *Nature* 30 Aug. 732/2 The subject species, *Acomys cahirinus* (spiny mouse), is a murid rodent whose precocial infants possess functional motor and sensory capabilities within hours of birth. **1978** *Sci. Amer.* July 107/1 Reid has found that the contents of the kiwi egg are 61 percent yolk, a proportion half again as large as that found in the eggs of typical precocial birds.

prædella, erron. var. PREDELLA.

1926 *Trans. Scottish Ecclesiol. Soc.* VIII. II. 71 The sanctuary is, perforce, very small and the Holy Table..is placed directly against the wall... The single step Prædella is semi-circular, and is enclosed by a beautiful tudor rail.

Praedesque (prēⁱde·sk), *a.* [f. the name of W. M. *Praed* + -ESQUE.] In the manner or style of Winthrop Mackworth Praed (1802–39), poet, essayist, and writer of society verse. So **Prae·dian** *a.*; **Prae·dism,** the style of Praed's verse.

1865 *Dublin Univ. Mag.* II. 23 The best epigrams and Praedesque verses of the week. **1883** *Century Mag.* Feb. 595/1 Mr. Locker can write Praedesque poems. **1905** MRS. H. WARD *Marriage of W. Ashe* I. ii. 29 Meanwhile the outer room gathered to hear the recitation of some *vers de société*, fondly believed by their author to be of a very pretty and Praedian make. **1927** *Observer* 15 May 6 What he was thinking of was polite badinage, Praedism, and Horatian levity.

prædormital (prīdǭ·ɹmitǎl), *a. rare*⁻¹. [? f. PRÆ- + stem of L. *dormītiō* sleep + -AL.] = HYPNAGOGIC *a.*

1947 V. NABOKOV *Bend Sinister* 11 Suddenly, with the vividness of a prædormital image or of a bright-robed lady on stained glass, she drifted across his retina, in profile, carrying something.

præmunire, *sb.* **1.** (Later examples.)

1940 E. POUND *Cantos* lxx. 177 Treasons, felonies, new praemunires. **1961** E. F. JACOB *Fifteenth Cent.* VI. 253 In November, after consultation with the judges, writs under the statute of Praemunire were made out against Beaufort.

2. b. (Later hist. example.)

1902 J. GAIRDNER *Eng. Ch. 16th Cent.* viii. 141 Any subject henceforth bringing in bulls of excommunication was liable to a *præmunire.*

Prænestine (prəine·stīn, prī-), *a.* and *sb.* [ad. L. *Prænestīnus* f. *Præneste* Palestrina: see -INE¹.] **A.** *adj.* Of or pertaining to the ancient city of Præneste or its inhabitants.

1880 *tr. Woltmann & Woermann's Hist. Painting* I. iv. 88 The engraved metal caskets of the kind commonly known as Prænestine cistæ, because they have been found for the most part at Prænestê, the modern Palestrina. **1885** *Encycl. Brit.* XIX. 654/2 Præneste was chiefly famed for its great temple of Fortune and for its oracle, in connexion with the temple, known as the 'Prænestine lots' (*sortes Prænestinæ*). **1937** *Oxf. Compan. Classical Lit.* 163/1 As regards Latin writing, in the inscription on the Praenestine *fibula*.., probably of the 6th c.,..the direction is from right to left. **1939** L. H. GRAY *Foundations of Lang.* 332 The oldest record of Italic is a Praenestine fibula of the seventh century B.C., *Manios med fhefhaked Numasioi* 'Manius me fecit Numerio'. **1970** *Oxf. Classical Dict.* (ed. 2) 873/1 Praeneste has yielded the earliest specimen of Latin, whose peculiarities confirm Festus' statement..that Praenestine Latin was abnormal. **1976** *Archivum Linguisticum* VII. 60 Praenestine *fhfhaked* ..is an old reduplicated perfect remade into an aorist by the addition of *-t (> Early Latin *-d*).

B. *sb.* A native or inhabitant of Præneste.

1902 *Encycl. Brit.* XXXIII. 897/2 The Romans..were inclined to sneer at the pronunciation and idiom of the Prænestines. **1949** *Oxf. Classical Dict.* 726/1 Praenestines loyally resisted Pyrrhus..and Hannibal, and actually preferred their own status to that of Roman citizens.

Hence **Prænesti·nian,** the extinct Latin dialect spoken by the Prænestines.

1939 L. H. GRAY *Foundations of Lang.* 333 To the [Latino-Faliscan] group also belonged the closely similar Hernician and Prænestinian. **1954** [see *Latino-Faliscan* s.v. *LATINO-].

præses (prī·siz). [See PRESES.] **a.** Var. PRESES.

1763 BOSWELL *Jrnl.* 19 Jan. in *London Jrnl.* (1950) 155 It resembled a party's being worsted in the choice of praeses and clerk, at an election in a Scotch county. **1797, 1876** [in Dict. s.v. PRESES]. **1898** P. S. ALLEN *Let.* 10 Oct. (1939) 16 When the Praeses introduced me, the Bishop said..'You mustn't leave me alone with a man, who makes such bold proposals, President.'

b. An academic moderator.

1841 *Rules Compilation of Catal.* in *Brit. Mus. Catal. Printed Bks.* I. p. v/1 The respondent or defender in a thesis is to be considered its author, except when it unequivocally appears to be the work of the Praeses. **1853** C. C. JEWETT *Smithsonian Rep. Construction of Catal. of Libr.* The Respondent or defender in a thesis, is to be considered its author, except when it unequivocally appears to be the work of the Praeses. **1931** G. S. GORDON *Let.* 19 Dec. (1943) Is it possible that there *is* no such leisure for an academic official—whether Professor or Praeses—who has a conscience about the job he's paid for? **1967** *Anglo-Amer. Catal. Rules: Brit. Text* 27 Enter a dissertation written for defence in an academic disputation (according to the custom prevailing in European universities prior to the 19th century) under the praeses (the faculty moderator) unless the authorship can be well authenticated.

præsidial, var. PRESIDIAL *a.* and *sb.*

1918 C. G. ROBERTSON *Bismarck* v. 285 Bismarck persuaded the King of Bavaria to write to the King of Prussia, inviting him..to take the Imperial Crown and exercise as Emperor his Praesidial rights in the Confederation.

Præsidium: see *PRESIDIUM.

pragmatic, *a.* and *sb.* Add: **A.** *adj.* **6.** (Further examples.)

1907 W. JAMES *Pragmatism* iv. 136 The pragmatic value of the world's unity is that all these definite networks actually and practically exist. **1932** C. MORRIS *Six Theories of Mind* vi. 282 The pragmatic contribution to the theory of mind. **1948** *Mind* LVII. 358 These 'pragmatic paradoxes' as they have been called, are worth examination. **1964** A. W. BURKS in Moore & Robin *Stud. in Philos. C. S. Peirce* 2nd Ser. viii. 143 Peirce's pragmatic principle of meaning. **1971** G. PETROVIĆ in R. Klibansky *Contemp. Philos.* IV. 393 To the uninformed the pragmatic theory of truth seems identical with that of Marx.

b. *spec.* Relating to the practical interpretation of political or social issues. Cf. *PRAGMATISM 4 b.

1961 *Mem. & Proc. Manch. Lit. & Philos. Soc.* CIII. 58 This was an explicit pragmatic democratic philosophy of an older generation. **1964** *Listener* 29 Oct. 654/2 Isn't there a danger that this kind of practical, pragmatic socialism, taking problems as they come, is going to rob you of a long-sighted view into the future. **1966** *Times* 11 Mar. 8/6 Mr. Wilson replied..that his 'policy was already very socialist and very pragmatic'. **1970** *Bull. Inst. for Study of U.S.S.R.* Aug. 17 The technocrat is more or less content with any ideology provided that it does not hamper pragmatic development. **1976** *Howard Jrnl.* XV. I. 3 Taking into account an admission of guilt or willingness to compensate for damage should only be done on the grounds that it is to the advantage of society to have the offender admit his guilt or pay for the damage. This is a very pragmatic attitude.

7. *Linguistics.* Of or pertaining to pragmatics. Cf. sense B. 4 below.

1935 B. MALINOWSKI *Coral Gardens* II. IV. iv. 52 Since it is the function, the active and effective influence of a word within a given context which constitutes its meaning, let us examine such pragmatic utterances. **1953** C. E. OSGOOD *Method & Theory Exper. Psychol.* xvi. 699 The pragmatic dimension of semiotic, the relation between signs and their users or the effect of signs upon their users. **1957** C. CHERRY *On Human Communication* vi. 226 Statistical communication theory abstracts from the semantic and pragmatic aspects of the set of signs used. **1964** E. A. NIDA *Toward Sci. Transl.* iii. 36 There is a steady tendency for many terms to shift within the pragmatic area from an ethical response to an esthetic one. **1967** R. A. WALDRON *Sense & Sense Devel.* iii. 49 The attitudes to language dealt with in the last chapter came into conflict with tradition in the stress they lay upon the pragmatic functions of language.

B. *sb.* **4.** *pl.* const. as *sing. Linguistics.* The study or analysis of linguistic signs as they relate to the human user and his behaviour (see quot. 1937). Also *attrib.*

1937 C. MORRIS *Logical Positivism* 4 Analysis reveals that linguistic signs sustain three types of relations (to other signs of the language, to objects that are signified, to persons by whom they are used and understood) which define three dimensions of meaning. These dimensions in turn are objects of investigation by syntactics, semantics, and pragmatics. **1952** *Mind* LXI. 205 The 'pragmatics' group would say that 'points of view' are the business of philosophers. **1954** *Mind* LXIII. 360 The step..from descriptive pragmatics to descriptive semantics. **1964** E. A. NIDA *Toward Sci. Transl.* iii. 35 Pragmatics, in contrast to both semantics and syntactics, deals with the relation of symbols to behavior. **1969** I. I. REVZIN in R. Klibansky *Contemp. Philos.* III. 332 In this domain there has been a general shift of interest from syntactics (the first set-theoretical and generative models) to semantics (and possibly pragmatics). **1971** *Language* XLVII. 522 The philosophical dichotomy is between 'semantics' and 'pragmatics', roughly corresponding to reference and inference respectively. **1975** *Ibid.* LI. 37 Partee..expresses reservations about the place of the referential/attributive distinction in natural language, and sees the possibility of assigning it to pragmatics. **1978** *Sci. Amer.* Nov. 82/2 The grammar of language includes rules of phonology, which describe how to put sounds together to form words; rules of syntax, which describe how to put words together to form sentences; rules of semantics, which describe how to interpret the meaning of words and sentences; and rules of pragmatics, which describe how to participate in a conversation, how to sequence sentences and how to anticipate the information needed by an interlocutor.

pragmatical, *a.* Add: **5.** (Later example.)

1938 C. MORRIS in *Internat. Encycl. Unified Sci.* I. I. 68 The pragmatical factor which complements and completes the formal and the empirical factors.

6. Of or pertaining to pragmatics. Cf. *PRAGMATIC *sb.* 4.

1939 *Mind* XLVIII. 480 It is to be noted that 'pragmatical' as it occurs throughout this paper designates the relations holding between signs and their users or interpreters, and is not to be confused with 'pragmatic' or 'pragmatist'. **1942** R. CARNAP *Introd. Semantics* 10 Examples of pragmatical investigations are: a physiological analysis of the processes in the speaking organs..; a psychological analysis of the relations between speaking behavior and other behavior, [etc.]. **1946** C. MORRIS *Signs, Lang., & Behav.* 219 The present study has deliberately preferred to emphasize the unity of semiotic rather than break each problem into its pragmatical, semantical, and syntactical components. **1957** C. E. OSGOOD et al. in Saporta & Bastian *Psycholinguistics* (1961) 285/1 We may call the relation of signs to situations and behaviors..*pragmatical meaning.*

pragmatically, *adv.* Add to def.: Also, in a manner related to pragmatic philosophy, or to pragmatics.

1902 W. JAMES *Var. Relig. Exper.* xviii. 448 Pragmatically, the most important attribute of God is his punitive justice. **1909** —— *Pluralistic Universe* viii. 321 Pragmatically interpreted, pluralism or the doctrine that it is many means only that the sundry parts of reality *may be externally related.* **1933** *Mind* XLII. 246 Prof. Schlick's 'Causality in Everyday Life and in Recent Science' sets itself to discover the meaning of causality pragmatically, from its use. **1948** *Mind* LVII. 358 The fault is not a fault of logic in the sense that the definition is formally self-contradictory. It is merely pragmatically self-refuting. **1964** E. A. NIDA *Toward Sci. Transl.* iii. 46 Some Pentecostals respond 'pragmatically' to a passage of the Scriptures by engaging in shouting and dancing. **1969** C.-Y. CHENG *Peirce's & Lewis's Theories of Induction* xii. 129 Induction cannot be pragmatically significant in a *strong* sense.

pragmaticism. Add: **1.** (Further examples.)

1970 *Bull. Inst. for Study of U.S.S.R.* Aug. 17 Wiles also analyses the regimes in China and Cuba, where property relations are laid down by the Party: this, in his view, will inevitably lead to a kind of pragmaticism and finally to a bureaucracy bereft of ideological impetus. **1978** J. UPDIKE *Coup* (1979) vi. 230 The development of a plausible pragmaticism.

2. Substitute for def.: The name given by C. S. Peirce to his pragmatic philosophy, esp. to the doctrine that concepts are to be understood in terms of their practical implications.

1905 C. S. PEIRCE in *Monist* XV. 166 So then, the writer, finding his bantling 'pragmatism' so promoted, feels that it is time to kiss his child good-by and relinquish it to its higher destiny; while to serve the precise purpose of expressing the original definition, he begs to announce the birth of the word 'pragmaticism', which is ugly enough to be safe from kidnappers. **1934** C. HARTSHORNE et al. *Coll. Papers C. S. Peirce* V. p. v, Pragmaticism (Peirce's term to indicate his divergencies from other pragmatists) was thus Peirce's way of insisting that abstractions must give an account of themselves. **1946** B. RUSSELL in J. Feibleman *Introd. Peirce's Philos.* p. xv, Peirce's pragmatism (or pragmaticism, as he came to call it) is a very different doctrine from those of James and Schiller and Dewey. **1968** E. H. MADDEN in R. Klibansky *Contemp. Philos.* II. 33 Peirce's shift..to pragmaticism and the dispositional frequency theory.

pragmatism. Add: **4.** (Further examples.) Also, the philosophical method of inquiry of C. S. Peirce; = *PRAGMATICISM 2.

1902 C. S. PEIRCE in Baldwin *Dict. Philos. & Psychol.* II. 322/2 Synechism..is not opposed to pragmatism in the manner in which C. S. Peirce applied it, but includes that procedure as a step. **1928** T. S. ELIOT *For Lancelot*

Andrewes iv. 84 The great weakness of Pragmatism is that it ends by being of no *use* to anybody. **1946** B. Russell in J. Feibleman *Introd. Peirce's Philos.* p. xv, Pragmatism, for Peirce, was only a method; the truths which it sought to discover were absolute and eternal. **1967** *Encycl. Philos.* VI. 432/1 Pragmatism is a method of clarifying and determining the meaning of signs. **1971** G. Petrović in R. Klibansky *Contemp. Philos.* IV. 394 We have come a great distance..from the confusion of pragmatism with Marxism. **1974** K. R. Popper in P. A. Schilpp *Philos. K. Popper* I. 99 The tendency of English philosophers to flirt with nonrealistic epistemologies: phenomenalism, positivism,..sensationalism, pragmatism—these playthings of philosophers were in those days still more popular than realism.

b. *Politics.* Theory that advocates dealing with social and political problems primarily by practical methods adapted to the existing circumstances, rather than by methods which have been conformed to some ideology.

1951 A. B. Ulam *Philos. Found. Eng. Socialism* iii. 77 It is true that the Fabian movement and British socialism in general have been built upon foundations quite different from those of Marxism. We have here first of all a sturdy spirit of pragmatism. **1966** *New Left Rev.* Jan.–Feb. 25 Thompson at one point calls the Communist Party the 'alter ego' of the Labour and trade union Left. But he fails to see the implications of this; that the two are not so very different in nature, for they are united by a common pragmatism, which has led so often to a day-to-day accommodation. **1976** *Times* 2 Apr. 8/4 Your struggle with Adolf Hitler, when Britain cast overboard the philosophy of pragmatism, or utilitarianism—the philosophy of recognizing any group of gangsters, any puppets, as head of a country as long as they were in control of its territory. **1976** *Survey* Summer–Autumn 156 Now that Mao is dead there will no doubt be a sharp reaction towards 'pragmatism'.

pragmatist. Add: **2.** (Further examples.) Also, an adherent of historical pragmatism (cf. Pragmatism 3).

1892 W. Wallace tr. *Hegel's Logic* (ed. 2) 257 The motives which must be viewed by the pragmatist as really efficient. **1932** C. Morris *Six Theories of Mind* ii. 71 In this insistence that mind cannot be divorced from the world certain new realists and pragmatists are at one with the absolute idealists. **1937** —— *Logical Positivism* iv. 46 Two groups which at first sight might seem in opposition, namely: the pragmatists (or biological positivists), and the Wiener Kreis (the logical positivists).

b. (Later examples.)

1906 W. James in *Jrnl. Philos.* III. 337 (*heading*) Papini and the pragmatist movement in Italy. **1965** E. E. Evans-Pritchard *Theories Prim. Relig.* iii. 48 The emotionalist explanations of primitive religion which I have discussed have a strong pragmatist flavour.

pragmatistic, *a.* Add: (Earlier and later examples.) Hence **pragmati·stically** *adv.*

1906 W. James in *Jrnl. Philos.* III. 341 Subjective factors..are in *some* degree creative, then; and this carries with it..the admissibility of the entire Italian pragmatistic program. **1907** —— *Pragmatism* viii. 281 Concretely he means..just the pragmatistically unified and ameliorated world. *a* **1914** C. S. Peirce *Coll. Papers* (1958) VIII. II. ix. 247 But if this occasion did in actuality *not* arise, such habit of thought as the conditional proposition might produce would be a nullity pragmatistically and practically. **1961** *Proc. Aristotelian Soc.* LXI. 180 Basic concepts,..if chosen pragmatistically, would be like Quinian 'posits'. **1971** J. J. Shapiro tr. *Habermas's Toward Rational Society* v. 68 The successful transposition of technical and strategic recommendations into practice is, according to the pragmatistic model, increasingly dependent on mediation by the public as a political institution. **1974** R. A. Hocks (*title*) Henry James and pragmatistic thought.

pragmatize, *v.* Add: **2.** *intr.* To behave in accordance with, or give expression to, a doctrine of pragmatism.

1907 H. James *Let.* 17 Oct. in R. B. Perry *Tht. & Char. W. James* (1935) I. 428, I was lost in the wonder of the extent to which all my life I have (like M. Jourdain) unconsciously pragmatised. **1966** *New Statesman* 15 Apr. 537/1 The moment the election was won he [*sc.* Mr. Wilson] was 'pragmatising' around the place like a man possessed.

Hence **pragmatiza·tion,** the action or process of giving practical effect to theory.

1950 T. Wiesengrund-Adorno et al. *Authoritarian Personality* xvii. 726 It is precisely this pragmatization of politics which ultimately defines fascist philosophy.

‖**Prägnanz** (pre·gnants). *Psychol.* [G., = conciseness, definiteness: orig. used in this sense by M. Wertheimer 1923, in *Psychol. Forschung* IV. 317.] The tendency, noticed in experiments with Gestalts, for configurations to be given their most concise and clearly definable interpretations.

1925 *Amer. Jrnl. Psychol.* XXXVI. 359 How the configuration conforms to laws of simplicity, pregnancy or precision (Prägnanz), symmetry and the like. **1935** K. Koffka *Princ. Gestalt Psychol.* iv. 110 The principle was introduced by Wertheimer, who called it the *Law of Prägnanz.* **1938** *Mind* XLVII. 91 In this connection the criticism of Gestalt, and particularly of the Law of Prägnanz, implicit in certain experiments carried out by Thouless is very relevant. **1963** J. Mann *Frontiers of Psychol.* iv. 131 The basic nature of human data-receiving and processing equipment, which organizes perceptual data without the conscious awareness of consent of the perceiver. An example of such a tendency is the law of *Prägnanz.* **1971** *Sci. Amer.* Dec. 70/2 It should be evident by now that some principle of *Prägnanz*, or minimum complexity, runs as a common thread through most of the cases.

Prague (prāg). [Name of capital of Czechoslovakia.] **1.** Used *attrib.* in *Prague School* and various associated Combs. to designate the linguistic theories, primarily in relation to phonology, developed by or associated with members of the Prague Linguistic Circle (*Cercle Linguistique de Prague*), especially during the 1920s and 1930s.

1935 [see *morphonology]. **1936** *Eng. Stud.* XVIII. 159 Trnka is a member of the Cercle Linguistique de Prague, and his analysis may be described as an application to English of the principles of the so-called Prague phonological school. **1937** [see *phonology]. **1939** L. H. Gray *Foundations of Lang.* 61 The phoneme..is..regarded as..a point in the psychological pattern ('phonology'; Edward Sapir and the Prague school). **1959** [see *morpheme]. **1962** [see *neutralization 3]. **1964** E. Bach *Introd. Transformational Gram.* vi. 135 The parallel between such incompletely specified segments and the archiphonemes of the Prague school is evident. *Ibid.* vii. 143 Such widely differing schools of linguists as the Prague circle, glossematicians, and American structuralists have all concurred in insisting that languages should be studied as structures. **1964** M. A. K. Halliday et al. *Linguistic Sci.* 148 Modern theories in phonology were first developed by the 'Prague circle' founded by the Russian linguist N. S. Trubetskoy, whose work has been followed up by Roman Jakobson and many others. **1968** J. Lyons *Introd. Theoret. Linguistics* 126 The Prague school phonologists would say..that it is not the phoneme /p/ which occurs in the word *spot*, but the archiphoneme /P/. **1976** *Archivum Linguisticum* VII. 128 The different surface realizations are due to a different functional sentence perspective. This concept has been central in the Prague School since its foundation.

2. Prague ham, a type of smoked ham (see quot. 1931).

1931 C. L. T. Beeching *Law's Grocer's Man.* (ed. 3) 219/1 *Prague* hams (Pragerschinkers) are first salted in large vats and left in a mild brine for several months; they are smoked with beech wood and matured in cool cellars until marketed. **1959** W. Heptinstall *Hors d'Œuvre & Cold Table* II. 69 For a ham to be served hot, my preference goes to the Prague hams. They are..admirable for carving, also they have an exquisite flavour. **1961** *Harrods Food News* 4/2 Sliced Hams..Prague... lb. 12/-. **1976** T. Fitzgibbon *Food of Western World* 366/2 Prague ham..is served whole for a main course, either baked or boiled, and cold slices of it are often served as a first course.

So **Pra·guean, Pra·guian** *adjs.* and *sbs.*

1968 [see *marked *ppl. a.* 1 c]. **1972** *Language* XLVIII. 385 To use Praguean terminology, there are interlingual archiphonemes which allow, within a broad category, wide language-specific (hence speaker-specific) phonological variation for each content unit. **1973** *Ibid.* XLIX. 193 As Pragueans would put it, both writing and speech are signaling systems of the first order; in other words, one cannot dismiss writing as being the signaling system of the second order, a signal of a signal. **1974** *Trans. Philol. Soc. 1973* 64 As a result of neutralization the mark is dropped; what is left is the complex of distinctive features characterizing both members of the opposition, the *archiphoneme* in Praguian terminology.

prahu. Freq. spelling of Proa.

1821 J. Leyden tr. *Malay Annals* 148 Tun Talani and the mantri Jana Petra returned to their prahus. **1850** [in Dict. s.v. Proa]. **1932** W. S. Maugham *Narrow Corner* xv. 114 The harbour was far from crowded: there were only two junks, three or four large prahus, a motor-boat and a derelict schooner. **1964** K. G. Tregonning *Hist. Mod. Malaya* 104 They each gave up all right to levy dues upon *prahus* and other local craft. **1968** *Punch* 4 Dec. 802/2 A fishing *prahu* picked me up. **1977** *Borneo Bull.* 7 May 4/1 The healthy state of the regatta was illustrated this year by the number of racing prahus taking part.

praia (prai,ă). Also **praya.** [Pg.] A beach, a sea-shore; a river-bank; a water-front.

a **1865** Smyth *Sailor's Word-bk.* (1867) 541 *Praia*.., the beach or strand on Portuguese coasts. **1890** *Engineer* 24 Jan. 65/2 A more practical scheme is the proposed building of the whole river front of the city,..and the construction of a broad praya suitable for wheeled conveyances. **1893** Kipling *Seven Seas* (1896) 13 Hail, Mother! Hold me fast; my Praya sleeps Under innumerable keels to-day. **1933** P. Fleming *Brazilian Adventure* I. xv. 127 We had meant to camp that night on the sandbank (from now on all sandbanks will be referred to as *praias*). *Ibid.* 129 We slept that night on the praia, under a million stars. **1947** J. Bertram *Shadow of War* I. 11 Flags..streamed from the..roof-tops of grey Victorian company offices along the *praya.* **1963** J. Fleming *Death of Sardine* iii. 41 One day, when Trigoso Praia..was 'discovered' the road might be an important promenade but now it was tarmac and potholes.

‖ **praire** (prɛ̄r). [Fr.] The European clam, *Venus verrucosa*, or the North American hard-shell clam, *Mercenaria* (formerly *Venus*) *mercenaria*, which has been introduced to parts of Europe.

1878 P. L. Simmonds *Commercial Products of Sea* I. xii. 147 The 'paires doubles' [*sic*] (*Venus verrucosa*) or clams of the Mediterranean..are never as delicate in flavour as when freshly caught.] **1929** A. E. Housman *Let.* 27 Feb. (1971) 278 In the interesting menu of a Paris restaurant..there are *praires.* These may be among the shell-fish which I have eaten at Marseilles, but I do not remember them. **1960** [see *palourde]. **1971** M. McCarthy *Birds of America* 128 Sometimes I just have a dozen *praires* (which are cheaper than oysters)..for lunch. **1975** *Times* 31 May 7/3 A board..bearing praires, clovisses, Belan oysters, langoustines.

prairie. Add: Also 8, 9 **parara, pararie, praira,** 9 **praire, prairia. a.** (Further examples.) Also (*U.S. local*), a marsh, a swampy pond or lake.

1791 D. Bradley *Jrnl.* 19 Sept. (1935) 17 A prairia of two or three hundred acres where the grass or wild oats is 8 or 10 feet high and very thick. *Ibid.* 12 Oct. 22 Struck a large prairia in our course—found it impassable. **1794** W. Clark *Jrnl.* 1 Aug. in *Mississippi Valley Hist. Rev.* (1914) I. 421 An open..*Pararie*..handsomly interspersed with Small Copse of Trees. **1795** J. Smith in *Ohio Archaeol. & Hist. Q.* (1907) XVI. 380 We saw several pararas, as they are called. They are large tracts of fine, rich land, without trees and producing as fine grass as the best meadows. **1806** *New Eng. Republican* in *Massachusetts Spy* 16 July 1/5 A venerable Philosopher sitting in the middle of an immense Map, marked with vast praires, huge rivers, and mountains of salt. **1819** E. Dana *Geogr. Sk. Western Country* 37 The ore is dug from an open praira. *Ibid.* 108 There are two kinds of praira, the *river* and *upland.* **1834** D. Crockett *Narr. Life* xii. 85, I came to the edge of an open parara, and looking on before my dogs, I saw in and about the biggest bear that ever was seen in America. *c* **1834** H. Evans in *Chron. Oklahoma* (1925) III. 181 We could look and behold ..one continual large expanse of Pararie. **1916** *Dialect Notes* IV. 270 *Prairie, n.*, marsh. (Barataria Bay.) **1934** *Nat. Geogr. Mag.* LXV. 601 Shallow ponds, or 'prairies', with a tropical tangle of vegetation. **1942** M. K. Rawlings *Cross Creek* 51 We use the word 'prairie' in a special sense. We have no open plains, but around most of the larger lakes are wet flat areas thick with water grasses, and these we call our prairies. They are more nearly marshes, yet we save the word 'marsh' for the deep mucky edges of lake and river, dense with coontail and lily pads. **1951** *Collier's* 24 Nov. 16/3 The eastern half of the Okefenokee is open. There are 'prairies', or great fields of water from one to three feet deep, covered with white or yellow water lilies, purple bladderworts, [etc.]. **1958** S. A. Grau *Hard Blue Sky* iv. 234 'And they put the candles on squares of wood..and set 'em adrift... And the candles they draw Anton up from the bottom.'.. 'Such a big prairie to find a man in.'

b. *prairie country* (examples), *farm, fire* (earlier and later examples; also *fig.* and *attrib.*), *flower* (examples), *hay, madness, town*; **prairie bottom,** a low-lying expanse of prairie land; **prairie-breaking,** the use of a prairie-breaker; also, an area of land ploughed or broken by this means; **prairie buffalo** = *plains buffalo* s.v. *Plain *sb.*[1] 10; **prairie-buster** = *prairie-breaker*; **prairie clover** (earlier and later examples); **prairie coal** *N. Amer.*, dried cattle or horse dung used as a fuel; = *buffalo-chips* s.v. Buffalo 5; **prairie cock** = Prairie-chicken (in Dict. and Suppl.) or *sage-grouse* s.v. Sage *sb.*[1] 5 c; **Prairie Cree** = *Plains Cree; **prairie crocus** *Canada*, a blue- or mauve-flowered anemone, *A. patens*, native to northern Europe but naturalized in parts of Canada; **prairie fox** (examples); **prairie hare,** either of two North American hares, the varying hare, *Lepus americanus*, or the jack-rabbit, *L. townsendii*; **prairie hawk** (earlier and later examples); **prairie marmot** (earlier and later examples); **prairie owl,** either of two North American owls, the burrowing owl, *Speotyto cunicularia*, or the short-eared owl, *Asio flammeus*; **prairie oyster,** (*a*) (earlier and later examples); (*b*) calves' testicles cooked and eaten as a delicacy; **prairie pea,** a milk vetch belonging to the genus *Astragalus*, esp. *A. crassicarpus*, or its fruit; **prairie pigeon** (later example); **prairie plough** (earlier examples); **prairie plover** (earlier and later examples); **prairie potato** = *prairie-turnip*; **prairie province** (also with capital initials) *Canad.*, (*a*) the province of Manitoba, *obs.* exc. *hist.*; (*b*) *pl.* the area consisting of the provinces of Manitoba, Saskatchewan and Alberta; **prairie rattler** (examples); **prairie rattlesnake** (earlier and later examples); **prairie rose** (earlier and later examples); **prairie smoke,** a North American name for *Anemone patens*, a small perennial herb with blue flowers which is widely naturalized in prairie regions; also called pasque flower or crocus; **prairie snake** (example); **prairie snipe** (examples); **prairie soil,** soil of the kind characteristic of the North American prairies; *spec.* in *Pedology*, a soil that is marked by a deep, dark-coloured surface horizon with a high organic content, is subject to moderate leaching, and occurs under long grass in subhumid temperate regions; **prairie squint,** a squint produced by exposure to the bright light of a prairie; also *fig.*; **Prairie State** (earlier and further examples); **prairie turnip** (later examples); **prairie wagon** (examples); **prairie warbler** (earlier and later examples); **prairie wolf** (earlier and later examples); **prairie wool,** in Canada, the natural, undisturbed plant cover of prairie land, predominantly composed of grasses.

1819 T. Say *Jrnl.* 24 Aug. in E. James *Acct. Expedition Rocky Mts.* (1823) I. vii. 131 Our party encamped.. in a..beautiful and level prairie bottom. **1834** A. Pike *Prose Sk. & Poems* 12 It is bordered by a strip of timber, ..and on the outside of this, a prairie bottom..of exceeding rich land. **1868** *Rep. Iowa Agric. Soc. 1867* 139 On strong prairie-bottom it [*sc.* the Rio Grande bearded wheat] is liable to get down. **1861** *Trans. Illinois Agric. Soc.* IV. 37 The plows were running..too deep for ordinary prairie breaking. **1879** *Scribner's Monthly* Nov. 132/2 It is only by resorting to figures that one can reach a comprehension of the aggregate extent of these long, narrow, black strips of 'prairie-breaking'. **1886** P. G. Ebbutt *Emigrant Life Kansas* 45 Will Hopkins..used to do a good deal of prairie-breaking, having a twenty-four inch plough and six yoke of oxen. **1806** Lewis & Clark *Orig. Jrnls. Lewis & Clark Expedition* (1905) V. 80 A species of Lizzard called by the French engages prairie buffalo are natives of these plains as well as those of the Missouri. I have called them the horned Lizzard. **1859** H. Y. Hind *North-West Territory* xii. 105/1 That there are two kinds of buffalo appears to be still a matter of doubt; they are stated to be the prairie buffalo and the buffalo of the woods. **1951** F. G. Roe *N. Amer. Buffalo* iii. 47 The Red River hunt had had to travel increasingly long distances westward to find the ordinary Prairie buffalo. **1952** J. W. Day *New Yeomen of Eng.* viii. 94 On one tract..which was recently broken up, a very good job was made by a three-furrow prairie-buster hauled by a tracklayer. **1961** *Guardian* 8 Mar. 5/3 Open land in parks should be under planning control as protection against what are termed 'prairie busters'. **1857** A. Gray *First Lessons in Botany* 95 *Petalostemon*, Prairie Clover... Chiefly perennial herbs,.. [with] small flowers. **1870** *Amer. Naturalist* IV. 581 The prairie clovers..are among the most interesting of the leguminose species. **1939** *Nat. Geogr. Mag.* Aug. 247/2 Prairie clovers may be white, pink, purple, or violet. **1968** Peterson & McKenny *Field Guide Wildflowers Northeastern & North-Central N. Amer.* 252 Prairie-clovers have pinnate leaves and dense, longish pink or white flower heads on wiry stems. **1939** C. L. Douglas *Cattle Kings of Texas* 324 He could not bring himself to relish food cooked with 'prairie coal'. **1948** *Southwest Rev.* Summer 238/1 When the permanent settlers and their families came, this 'prairie coal' became the standard fuel. **1972** J. Minifie *Homesteader* vii. 51 As he walked he collected horse-dung for his cook-fire. Weathered 'prairie coal' makes a quick, hot fire. **1805** Lewis & Clark *Orig. Jrnls. Lewis & Clark Expedition* (1905) III. xviii. 123 Send out Hunters to shute the Prairie Cock a large fowl which I have only Seen on this river. **1846** J. W. Webb *Altowan* I. ii. 31 The prairie cock (a large species of grouse, of a pepper-and-salt colour, and long, pointed tail)..rose at their feet. **1876** J. Burroughs *Winter Sunshine* v. 115 The prairie hens or prairie cocks set up that low musical cooing or crowing. **1900** H. Garland *Eagle's Heart* 107 A belated prairie cock began to boom. **1806** *Deb. Congress U.S.* (1852) 9th Congress 2 Sess., App. 1136 The quality of the land is supposed superior to that on Red river, until it ascends to the prairie country, where the lands on both rivers are probably similar. **1848** E. Bryant *California* iii. 34 Our march was..through an undulating prairie-country. **1853** *Trans. Lit. & Hist. Soc. Quebec* IV. 298 The prairie country of the Saskatchewan is roamed over by countless herds of buffalo, also by the reindeer and the beautiful antelope. **1907** W. O. Lillibridge *Where Trail Divides* 152 The darkness that precedes morning has the prairie country in its grip. **1922** *Beaver* Oct. 15/1 During that time there had been two half-breed rebellions in the prairie country. **1946** J. T. Adams *Album Amer. Hist.* III. 261 Hay Burning Stoves were useful in this prairie country. **1883** E. Petitot in *Proc. R. Geogr. Soc.* V. 649 They occupied the country between the Savanois Indians on the east and the Grandes-pagnes (also called Prairie-Crees), on the west. **1913** F. W. Hodge *Handbk. Indians of Canada* (1971) 621/1 (Index) Plain Crees = Paskwawininiwug... Prairie-Crees = Paskwawininiwug. **1922** A. J. A. Stringer *Prairie Child* 304 Prairie-crocuses [are] soft blue and lavender and sometimes mauve. **1951** *Chambers's Jrnl.* Aug. 505/1 The mauve prairie-crocus, really an anemone, which pushes out of grass knolls as soon as the snow melts, is the first source of pollen. **1969** N. W. Parsons *Upon Sagebrush Harp* iii. 16 The land was ..blue with furry pasqueflower, or prairie crocus. **1838** H. W. Ellsworth *Valley of Upper Wabash* v. 49 A late and lamented brother of the writer, who had just finished a prairie farm. **1884** 'Mark Twain' *Huck. Finn* vii. 46 Hogs soon went wild in them bottoms after they had got away from the prairie-farms. **1886** P. G. Ebbutt *Emigrant Life Kansas* 198, I don't think Anderson had enough energy in him to start a prairie farm for himself. **1824** W. Owen in *Indiana Hist. Soc. Publ.* (1906) IV. I. 83 We then rode on to the prairie and rode twice through the prairie fire, which..moved very slowly. **1836** D. B. Edward *Hist. Texas* iv. 70 Why should there be any lack of timber, when by planting it.., and preserving it afterwards from the annual prairie fires..it would grow with such rapidity. **1852** A. Cary *Clovernook* 77 Stories of.. huge lights made by prairie fires. **1922** *Beaver* Oct. 17/2 One of the most..terrible sights of those early days was a stampede of hundreds of buffalo fleeing before a prairie fire. **1935** H. A. L. Fisher *Hist. Europe* I. xii. 144 The Moslem faith might have spread like a prairie fire through the Balkans. **1959** [see *back-fire *sb.* 1]. **1963** A. Heron *Towards Quaker View of Sex* iii. 27 'The prairie fire' view of homosexual contact—that..if it were allowed legally and morally everyone would turn to it. **1836** J. Hall *Statistics of West* iv. 56 The prairie-flower displays its diversified hues. **1873** *Newton Kansan* 22 May 3/2 The wild prairie flowers..are beginning to look beautiful. **1894** *Harper's Mag.* Aug. 422/1 To be sure there were patches of orange prairie flowers all about. **1922** H. L. Wilson *Merton of Movies* 69 Ain't I the little prairie flower, growing wilder every hour? **1839** Marryat *Diary Amer.* 1st Ser. I. xvii. 206 [In statistical table of furs] Prairie fox..5,000. **1846** R. B. Sage *Scenes Rocky Mts.* xxviii. 241 For several nights I had a constant visitor in the shape of a prairie-fox,—a creature about twice the size of a large red squirrel. **1876** J. Burroughs *Winter Sunshine* iv. 108 The prairie fox, the cross fox, and the black or silver-gray fox, seem only varieties of the red fox. **1948** A. L. Rand *Mammals E. Rockies* 107 Kit Fox. *Vulpes velox* (Also called Prairie Fox). **1840** E. Emmons *Rep. Quadrupeds Mass.* 58 *Lepus Virginianus*. Harlan. Prairie Hare... This species is common throughout the New England States, and is known generally as the White Rabbit. **1866** W. R. King *Sportsman & Naturalist in Canada* 32 The Prairie Hare..is one of the largest hares of the continent, weighing from seven to eleven pounds, and is of a grey colour tinged with yellow. **1917** H. E. Anthony *Mammals Amer.* 280/1 Although called the Prairie Hare, this species is found also on mountain slopes. **1817** E. P. Fordham *Jrnl.* 17 Dec. in *Personal Narr. Trav.* (1906) viii. 143 Saw some prairie hawks, blue bodies, ash coloured belly and wings, tipped with black. **1898** H. S. Canfield *Maid of Frontier* 201 With a swoop like the swoop of the prairie hawk down swooping for the quail, the Paint Horse was away. **1907** W. O. Lillibridge *Where Trail Divides* 259 Swift as the swoop of a prairie hawk..the man's arms were about her. **1835** A. Brunson *Jrnl.* 28 Oct. in *Wisconsin State Hist. Soc. Coll.* (1900) XV. 283 Here I fed myself, but could get nothing but Prairie hay & pumpkins for my horse. **1845** *Cultivator* II. 93 Without any kind of..comfort, except what they may gather from a poor supply of prairie hay. **1867** *Harper's Mag.* July 138/2 A little stable, near which were great stacks of prairie hay. **1878** J. H. Beadle *Western Wilds* xxviii. 433 First rate prairie hay, on which stock will keep fat all winter. **1880** D. Currie *Lett. of Rusticus* 6/2 They [*sc.* horses] are being fed with prairie hay. **1949** *Daily Oklahoman* 13 Feb. D. 4/4 More than 2,500 tons of the prairie hay used in the recent haylift operations to save icebound livestock in the western states were supplied by hay growers around Vinita, Okla. **1912** J. Sandilands *Western Canad. Dict.* 35 *Prairie madness*, the melancholia which attacks the lonely homesteader. **1973** H. Robertson *Grass Roots* iii. 53 The loneliness and isolation which contributed to emotional breakdowns known in the West as 'prairie madness'. **1826** J. D. Godman *Amer. Nat. Hist.* II. 114 The Prairie Marmot... Commonly called Prairie-dog. **1888** *Ipswich* (Mass.) *Chron.* 15 Sept. 2/4 Usually a country that is inhabited by prairie dogs, or more properly by prairie marmots, has a dry, thin atmosphere. **1979** *Jrnl. R. Soc. Arts* CXXVII. 171/2 The prairie marmot at Whipsnade has been seen elsewhere in the downs. **1846** R. B. Sage *Scenes Rocky Mts.* xii. 110 The prairie-owl and rattlesnake maintain friendly relations with these inoffensive villagers [*sc.* prairie-dogs]. **1860** C. W. Wilson *Mapping Frontier* (1970) II. 108 Nothing to disturb me but the melancholy note of the prairie owl. **1907** W. O. Lillibridge *Where Trail Divides* 13 He would have watched the movement of a coyote or a prairie owl, for the simple reason that it was the only visible object endowed with life. **1917** T. G. Pearson *Birds Amer.* II. 101 Short-eared Owl... Other Names.—Marsh Owl; Swamp Owl; Prairie Owl. **1958** *Publ. Amer. Dial. Soc.* xxx. 9 Prairie Owl and prairie dog owl, equally frequent names for the burrowing owl,..are expressions used by 23% of the Nebraska informants. **1883** J. F. Keane *On Blue-Water* xii. 167 We all jumped up and agreed unanimously to propose the last toast at once in the shape of a prairie oyster—an egg broken into a cup without smashing the yolk, the toast poured in on the top of it, and the whole taken at a swallow. **1912** 'Saki' *Chron. Clovis* 275 He hurriedly ordered another prairie oyster. **1920** [see *bromo-seltzer* s.v. *bromo-]. **1939** C. Isherwood *Goodbye to Berlin* 51 Would you like a Prairie Oyster? **1941** *Amer. Speech* XVI. 181 English slang metaphor also has its place, as..*prairie oyster* for the testicles of a steer, a food morsel considered dainty. **1955** W. Foster-Harris *Look of Old West* viii. 234 Prairie or mountain oysters were an unmentionable part of a male animal. **1960** *Spectator* 25 Nov. 878 A Prairie Oyster, which is the raw yolk of an egg slipped whole into a glass containing a tablespoon of Worcester Sauce and a dash of sherry, with a flick of red pepper. **1979** A. Jute *Reverse Negative* 26 His eyes were bloodshot. His prairie oysters must have lost their potency. **1848** E. Bryant *California* ii. 28, I observed, also, a plant producing a fruit of the size of the walnut, called the prairie-pea. **1870** *Amer. Naturalist* III. 162 One of the earliest flowers [of the Kansas plains] is the Prairie-pea. **1943** B. A. De Voto *Year of Decision* 155 They..made spiced pickles of the 'prairie peas'. **1937** *Nat. Geogr. Mag.* Aug. 200/1 The Eskimo curlew, or 'dough bird' or 'prairie pigeon', as it was called by the gunners, apparently rivaled the passenger pigeon in numbers prior to 1885. **1831** W. Sewall *Diary* 50 Apr. (1930) 136 Sat off with the team, and a prairie plow which came on late last night with instructions, to commence breaking prairie. **1840** *Cultivator* VII. 33/1 It may be amusing to eastern readers, to hear a description of a 'prairie plow'. **1861** *Trans. Illinois Agric. Soc.* IV. 392 The sod should be broken with a prairie plow. **1851** W. Kelly *Excursion to California* I. v. 83 A stand of prairie plover most opportunely made their appearance as we pulled up. **1940** E. T. Seton *Trail of Artist-Naturalist* xxxii. 299 The white-tailed longspurs, the prairie plover, were all gone, wholly routed by the plough. **1828** J. C. Beltrami *Pilgrimage in Europe & Amer.* II. xvii. 321 Everything appeared to me delicious, even some roots which they call prairie-potatoes, and which I had before thought detestable. **1848** E. Bryant *California* iv. 54 A root or tuber, of an oval shape, about one and one-half-inch in length..is called the prairie potato. **1891** *Canadian Indian* Mar. 168 The prairie potato..yields when dry a light, starchy flour, and is often cut into thin slices and dried for winter. **1917** H. Kephart *Camping & Woodcraft* II. xxi. 379 Potato, Prairie. Prairie turnip... Palatable in any form. **1876** J. C. Hamilton (*title*) The Prairie Province: sketches of travel from Lake Ontario to Lake Winnipeg. **1881** *Progress* (Rat Portage, Ontario) 12 Nov. 4/1 The editor of the Woodstock (Ont.) *Sentinel-Review*, proposes..to get up a huge excursion of marriageable girls in Ontario to proceed early next spring to the prairie province. **1908** M. A. Brown *My Lady of Snows* 221 The majority ruled, but the minority clamored from the prairie provinces. **1916** O. D. Skelton *Day of Sir W. Laurier* 97 The Winnipeg Board of Trade denounced the policy of 'crushing and trampling upon one hundred thousand struggling pioneers of the prairie province to secure a purely imaginary financial gain to one soulless corporation'. **1952** D. F. Putnam *Canad. Regions* 340/1 Manitoba, Saskatchewan and Alberta are known as the 'Prairie Provinces' because they include the Canadian section of the vast grass-covered interior plains of North America. **1959** *Manch. Guardian* 5 Aug. 4/4 Some of his [*sc.* Mr. John Diefenbaker's] friends in the prairie provinces think he has been clever to keep the Easterners out. **1965** *Globe & Mail* (Toronto) 5 Jan. B 5/1 All three Prairie provinces are particularly unhappy about the special incentives being offered to attract industrial enterprises. **1965** R. M. Hamilton *Canad. Quotations & Phrases* 130/2 The Prairie Province. From the title of the book which gave the phrase general circulation; after 1905 it was extended to include Saskatchewan and Alberta in 'The Prairie Provinces'. **1973** *Fisheries Fact Sheet* (Environment Canada Fisheries & Marine Service) No. 1. 4/3 The larger bodies of water in the Prairie Provinces. **1977** D. MacKenzie *Raven & Kamikaze* xi. 132 She'd come to England straight from a prairie-province university... Her father [was] a veterinarian in Saskatoon. **1878** J. H. Beadle *Western Wilds* 133 The only dangerous snakes are the little prairie rattlers, seldom over two feet long. **1948** *Chicago Tribune* 30 May 14 A prairie rattler coils to strike; its prey is a rabbit. **1977** *New Yorker* 6 June 47/2 One.. took up pentecostalism and died from shock while caressing a prairie rattler at a revival meeting back east in Tennessee. **1817** S. R. Brown *Western Gazetteer* 31 The only venomous serpents, are the common and prairie rattlesnake, and copper-heads. **1843** [see *Missisauga 2]. **1873** 'Mark Twain' & Warner *Gilded Age* 125 Prairie-rattlesnakes..never strike above the knee. **1948** *Natural Hist.* Apr. 187/1 An extensive campaign was waged against the prairie rattlesnake. **1961** C. H. Pope *Giant Snakes* (1962) 152 In the northern United States the prairie rattlesnake may not give first birth until it is four or even five years old. **1822** J. Woods *Two Years' Residence Eng. Prairie* 303 The prairie-roses, balm.. and sassafras-wood..have all powerful scents. **1946** E. B. Thompson *Amer. Daughter* 36 We gazed in awe upon the prairie rose, a delicate pink flower growing close to the ground, whose thorny stem belied its tender beauty. **1963** *Canad. Geogr. Jrnl.* Aug. 54/2 Later the hardy prairie rose makes its appearance and fills the air with its sweet scent. **1893** *Jrnl. Amer. Folk-Lore* VI. 136 *Anemone patens*, var. *Nuttalliana*... gosling, prairie smoke, crocus. **1952** *Sun* (Baltimore) 26 Feb. 10/7 The Pasqueflower..is a bluish open bell shaped wild flower of the prairies... Patches of the flower at a distance give the impression of a bluish haze. This gives rise to its more familiar name 'prairie smoke'. **1958** *Weekend Mag.* (Montreal) 7 June 38/1 Earliest of spring flowers, Manitoba's crocus grows so profusely in places that it looks like a low-lying mist. Hence its nickname: the 'Prairie smoke'. **1845** J. C. Frémont *Rep. Exploring Expedition* 12 A large prairie snake..was occupied in eating the young birds. **1851** W. Kelly *Excursion to California* I. v. 80, I shot a brace of prairie snipe. **1917** T. G. Pearson *Birds Amer.* I. 247 Upland Plover. *Bartramia longicauda*... [Also called] Prairie Snipe. **1817** S. R. Brown *Western Gazetteer* 66 The common field near the town contains nearly 5000 acres, of excellent prairie soil. **1876** *Trans. Illinois Dept. Agric.* XIII. 288 The prairie soils are usually darker, more crude, coarser and wetter than the woodland. **1910** C. G. Hopkins *Soil Fertility* vi. 79 The undulating prairie soils vary from a gray silt loam on light clay in the older areas, to a dark brown silt loam, in the later formations, and the common flat prairie soils vary with age from drab silt loam to black clay loam. **1928** C. F. Marbut in *Proc. & Papers 1st Internat. Congr. Soil Sci.* IV. 21 The podsolic and lateritic soils of category VI have been subdivided into 8 sub-groups consisting of Tundra, Podsols, Brown Forest soils, Red soils, Yellow soils, Prairie soils (dark colored humid soils), Laterites and Ferruginous Laterites. **1974** E. A. Fitzpatrick *Introd. Soil Sci.* vii. 116 In the U.S.A. and elsewhere there are prairie soils or brunizems which are similar to chernozems but they have a middle horizon with a clay maximum and are slightly less fertile. **1946** Auden *Under Which Lyre* in *Harvard Alumni Bull.* 15 June 707/1 The sophomoric Who face the future's darkest hints With giggles or with prairie squints As stout as Cortez. **1963** R. D. Symons *Many Trails* ix. 92 He wears a grey felt hat, beneath which his tanned face is puckered in the 'prairie squint'. **1842** *People's Advocate* (Carrollton, Illinois) 6 Aug. 4/5 Federal Coon Whiggery extinct in the Prairie State! **1852** Mrs. Stowe *Uncle Tom's Cabin* II. xlv. 316 Farmers of rich and joyous Ohio, and ye of the wide prairie states. **1861** O. J. Victor *Hist. Southern Rebellion* I. 166 Illinois, the 'Prairie State', then proved that she was as rich in her patriotism as in her soil and exhaustless resources. **1868** *Harper's Mag.* June 123/2 When he pronounced 'good-by' to the Prairie State, at the State line, he said, 'Behind the cloud the sun is shining still.' **1949** J. Monaghan *This is Illinois* 138 The nation began to hum the wonders of the Prairie State. **1963** R. I. McDavid *Mencken's Amer. Lang.* 691 Illinois has had many nicknames..but *Prairie State* and *Sucker State* are the only ones surviving. **1970** *Daily Progress* (Charlottesville, Va.) 24 May 4/1 Illinois is the Prairie state. **1855** A. M. Murray *Let.* 5 Sept. (1856) II. 290 About forty miles from Chicago we passed the first prairie town of Joliet. **1867** *Atlantic Monthly* Mar. 326/1 Chicago, for fifteen years after it began its rapid increase, was perhaps of all prairie towns the most repulsive to every human sense. **1908** Kipling in *Collier's* 28 Mar. 11/1 'If you go as far as Winnipeg, you'll see the finest hotel in all the world.' 'Nonsense!' he said. 'You're pulling my leg! Winnipeg's a prairie-town.' **1977** H. Osborne *White Poppy* viii. 68 A prairie town in a cowboy film. **1857** J. Palliser *Jrnls.* (1863) 38 The root..receives the name of the Prairie Turnip by the half-breeds, who, with Indians, use it as food. **1941** D. McCowan *Naturalist in Canada* 246 The Crees and the Blackfeet were glad to make a meal from the edible root of the Prairie Turnip. **1956** D. Leechman *Native Tribes Canada* 110 The prairie Indians also ate service berries, wild cherries, red willow berries, prairie turnips, bitter root, and wild rose haws. **1856** Prairie wagon [see *AMBULANCE 3]. **1867** W. H. DIXON *New Amer.* I. iii. 37 We find that our big Concord coach has been exchanged for a light prairie waggon. **1948** *Chicago Daily News* 10 Apr. 6/2, I have an idea that too much of the squirrel rifle and prairie wagon tradition still runs in the bloodstream of most Americans. **1811** A. WILSON *Amer. Ornithol.* III. 87 [The] Prairie Warbler..I first discovered in that singular tract of country in Kentucky, commonly called the Barrens. **1917** T. G. PEARSON *Birds Amer.* III. 150/1 The Prairie Warbler is not very common on the prairies. **1960** R. T. PETERSON *Field Guide Birds of Texas* 217 Prairie Warbler... This warbler wags its tail. **1804** LEWIS & CLARK *Orig. Jrnls. Lewis & Clark Expedition* (1904) I. ii. 108 A Prarie Wolf come [*sic*] near the bank and Barked at us this evening. **1898** H. S. CANFIELD *Maid of Frontier* 39 The long howl of the prairie wolf rose on the air and hung tremulant. **1948** *Daily Ardmoreite* (Ardmore, Okla.) 18 Apr. 14/7 There are practically only two distinct kinds of wolves in America—the large gray timber wolf and the coyote or prairie wolf. **1963** R. D. SYMONS *Many Trails* 121 The grey jackal of the plains.. we call in English the prairie wolf, but more often in corruption of its Aztec name, coyote. **1934** G. BETTANY *Valley of Lost Gold* 284 She loved..every blade of prairie wool. **1953** *Canad. Geogr. Jrnl.* June 245/1 The sheep crop the 'prairie wool'—that excellent hard forage composed of spear-grass, bunch-grass and buffalo-grass. **1970** [see *June grass]. **1973** R. D. SYMONS *Where Wagon Led* I. i. 13 The prairie grass was curled and dimpled—that's why they call it 'prairie wool'.

prairie-chicken. Substitute for def.: A North American grouse found in prairie regions and belonging to one of three species of the family Tetraonidæ, *Tympanuchus cupido, T. pallidicinctus*, or *Pedioecetes phasianellus*. Also *fig.* (Earlier and later examples.)

1840 *Picayune* (New Orleans) 13 Sept. 2/2 The travelling public will find..a fine table covered with white fish..and prairie chickens. **1949** *N. Dakota Hist.* Jan. 14 The 'coo' of the prairie chicken and the twittering of the meadowlark greet us. **1963** *Canadian Weekly* 30 Mar. 18/4 In 1945 the prairie chicken, or sharp-tailed grouse, by enactment was made an emblem of Saskatchewan. **1976** *National Observer* (U.S.) 3 July 10/6 He took Nicholson and his gang of cutthroats..and that cute little prairie chicken, Kathleen Lloyd, and made a damned good and entertaining movie. **1978** C. HARRISON *Field Guide Nests, Eggs & Nestlings N. Amer. Birds* 101 Greater Prairie Chicken... Nestling. Precocial and downy. Down pattern like that of the Lesser Prairie Chicken.

prairied, *a.* (in Dict. s.v. PRAIRIE.) (Later example.)

1930 H. N. SPALDING *From Youth to Age* 58 The happy cornlands of the prairied West.

prairie-dog. (Earlier and further examples.)

1774 J. R. PEYTON in J. L. Peyton *Adventures of my Grandfather* (1867) xii. 121 One of the singular and interesting sights on my route was the villages of the Prairie dogs. **1859** E. H. N. PATTERSON in L. Hafen *Overland Routes to Gold Fields* (1942) 110 Visited a prairie dog town this evening, which covers eighty acres. **1867** [see *LAY-OUT 2 b]. **1902** O. WISTER *Virginian* xvi. 176 There is a brown skunk down in Arkansaw. Kind of prairie-dog brown. **1914** B. M. BOWER *Flying U Ranch* 135 There ain't enough grass in our lower field to graze a prairie dog. **1932** S. ZUCKERMAN *Social Life Monkeys* ii. 23 Most writers describe the prairie dog of North America as an animal that lives in vast colonies. **1947** *Chicago Daily News* 20 Mar. 14/3 [They] make my book resemble a head of lettuce that has been gnawed by a pack of prairie dogs. **1961** *Maclean's Mag.* 29 July 23, I've seen me.. lying at the edge of a field in Saskatchewan spying on the prairie dogs. **1976** *Billings* (Montana) *Gaz.* 1 July 2-A/4 Flath contends, however, that the endangered black-footed ferret lives within prairie dog towns.

prairie-hen. (Earlier and later examples.)

1804 LEWIS & CLARK *Orig. Jrnls. Lewis & Clark Expedition* (1904) I. iv. 181 Capt. Lewis..Saw great numbers of Prarie hens. **1909** G. PARKER *Northern Lights* 336 A prairie hen rustled by with a shrill cluck. **1933** *Sun* (Baltimore) 15 Apr. 4/2 Dr. Gross considered the advisability of mating the heath hen with a Wisconsin prairie hen.

prairie schooner. For *U.S.* read *N. Amer.* and add earlier and further examples. Also *Austral. colloq.* (see quot. 1911[1]).

1841 E. R. STEELE *Summer Journey in West* 134 So much is this appearance acknowledged by the country people that they call the stage coach, a prairie schooner. **1847** T. WEED *Let.* in T. W. Barnes *Mem. T. Weed* (1884) II. 149 We found the road..occupied with an almost unbroken line of wagons, drawn generally by two yokes of oxen, bringing wheat to the city. These teams are called 'prairie schooners'. **1867** [see *DOUBLE-DECKER b]. **1904** [see SCHOONER *sb.*[1] 2]. **1911** C. E. W. BEAN *'Dreadnought' of Darling* vii. 67 An old white-bearded patriarch of a fellow that had once appeared in one of the up-river towns with a 'prairie schooner'—one of those big white-hooded sort of ambulance waggons which the travelling hawkers drive from homestead to homestead over the plains in the West. **1911** *Daily Colonist* (Victoria, B.C.) 21 Apr. 4/2 Last summer one Sunday morning on the Cariboo road a prairie schooner stood by the roadside. **1949** *Amer. Speech* XXIV. 259 Hordes of treasure seekers from regions east of the mountains crossed the plains in covered wagons, the ships of the desert of the early Western emigrants. Such wagons in various regions were known as..*prairie schooners*. **1955** W. FOSTER-HARRIS *Look of Old West* vi. 159 The prairie schooners, developed from the Conestoga were smaller but still too heavy and clumsy for mountain work or badly broken country. **1957** L. EISELEY *Immense Journey* 19, I slid over shallows that had buried the broken axles of prairie schooners. **1961** [see *CONESTOGA 2]. **1977** *Time* 14 Feb. 54/1 There it will begin tests that will culminate in flights that could do for space colonization what the prairie schooner and the railroads did for the settling of America.

prairillon. For *a* 1860 *Scenes Rocky Mts.* 172 (Bartlett) read **1846** R. B. SAGE *Scenes Rocky Mts.* 172, and add earlier example.

1843 J. C. FRÉMONT *Rep. Exploration* 60 We were posted in a grove of beech,..with a narrow *prairillon* on the inner side.

praise, *sb.* Add: **1. c.** A laudatory utterance; *spec.* = **praise poem*.

1861 tr. *Casalis's Basutos* II. xvii. 328 We often heard them recite, with very dramatic gestures, certain pieces... The natives called these recitations *praises*. **1901** G. M. THEAL *Rec. S.-E. Afr.* VII. 202 When the king goes out he is surrounded and encircled by these *marombes*, who recite these praises to him with loud cries, to the sound of small drums, iron and bells. **1929** *Bantu Stud.* (Johannesburg) July 201 We are concerned..with 'Izibongo' as the term denoting the 'Praises' of the Zulu Chiefs. **1937** G. P. LESTRADE in I. Schapera *Bantu-Speaking Tribes S. Afr.* xiii. 300 The tribal praise-poem reciter..makes a new praise from time to time. **1968** T. COPE *Izibongo: Zulu Praise-Poems* 51 The most primitive type of praise-poem is simply a collection of praises consisting for the most part of single lines or verses. **1970** R. FINNEGAN *Oral Lit. in Afr.* v. 111 The formalized praises which are directed publicly to kings, chiefs, and leaders, and which are composed and recited by members of a king's official entourage. **1979** G. FORTUNE in Hodza & Fortune *Shona Praise Poetry* 3 Fragments of the praises of individual kings of the Changamire dynasty have come down to us included in the clan praises of the Rozvi.

4. *praise-meeting* (examples), *-night*; **praise-house** *U.S.*, a small meeting-house for religious services; **praise-leader** *Sc.*, the leader of the singing in a church; **praise name,** in Africa, a name or title used in ceremonial contexts; a name applied to the subject of a praise poem; **praise poem,** a laudatory poem; *spec.* one of a genre belonging to the oral tradition of certain African peoples; so *praise poet, poetry*; **praise-reciter** = *praise poet* above; **praise song,** a laudatory song; *spec.* in Africa, = *praise poem* above; so *praise-singer, -singing*.

1862 H. WARE in E. W. Pearson *Lett. from Port Royal* (1906) 20, I went with him to the praise-house, where he has his school. **1867** *Nation* (N.Y.) 30 May 432/2 But the true 'shout' takes place on Sundays or on 'praise' nights..either in the praise-house or in some cabin. **1869** Praise-house [in Dict.]. **1920** C. JERDAN *Scottish Clerical Stories* xviii. 370 The minister.. looked down over the side of the pulpit and said to the praise-leader, 'Is David ill?' **1862** J. M. MCKIM in *N. Amer. & U.S. Gaz.* 14 July 1/8 When dey come to de praise meeting dat night dey sing about it. **1862** H. WARE in E. W. Pearson *Lett. from Port Royal* (1906) 36 He had been up to the praise-meeting by Uncle Peter's invitation. **1863** H. G. SPAULDING in *Continental Monthly* Aug. 195/1 The present opportunities for religious worship which the freedmen enjoy consist of their 'praise meetings'—similar in most respects to our prayer meetings. **1904** D. KIDD *Essential Kafir* ii. 91 If the trouble does not vanish..the people..say to the spirits, 'When have we ceased to kill cattle for you, and when have we ever refused to praise you by your praise-names?' **1932** C. FULLER *Louis Trigardt's Trek* vii. 79 Molamoso ruled the country... This refers, however, to Legadimane, whose family or 'praise name' was Molamoso. **1935** *Critic* (Cape Town) Oct. 2 The Tswana-speaking clan called the *BaRaMoseki* has as its praise-name the name *Mokwena* (from *kwena*, 'crocodile', the 'totem' of the clan), and every member of that clan is addressed as *Mokwena* on suitable occasions. **1968** T. COPE *Izibongo: Zulu Praise Poems* I. ii. 26 A clan name is the personal name of its founder, and personal names are essentially praise-names. **1979** G. FORTUNE in Hodza & Fortune *Shona Praise Poetry* 71 The praise name is the most frequently used construction in praise poetry... Structurally the praise name is a single noun or a single complex nominal construction, one of whose constituents is a class affix. **1864** H. WARE in E. W. Pearson *Lett. from Port Royal* (1906) 253 It was not praise-night. **1935** *Critic* (Cape Town) Oct. 4 A praise-poem..consists of a number of stanzas, following each other in different order in different versions of the same poem. **1957** S. EINARSSON *Hist. Icelandic Lit.* 44 Most scholars assume that skaldic poetry originated at the courts of kings, the poems being praise poems to celebrate the deeds of these kings. **1965** I. SCHAPERA *Praise Poems of Tswana Chiefs* 6 It is still.. common for someone to..recite praise-poems. **1977** *Amer. N. & Q.* XV. 148/2 The *Prothalamion* has not been sufficiently studied in the light of Horace's *Carmina*, several of which are praise-poems. **1979** G. FORTUNE in Hodza & Fortune *Shona Praise Poetry* p. x, The praise poems are written in the standard Shona orthography. **1935** *Critic* (Cape Town) Oct. 7 The old praise-poets had to compose in their heads, and had to remember as they went along. **1937** G. P. LESTRADE in I. Schapera *Bantu-Speaking Tribes S. Afr.* xiii. 296 Persons of but modest rank..compose their own praise-poems,..while those of higher status have theirs composed by..the praise-poets. **1965** I. SCHAPERA *Praise Poems of Tswana Chiefs* 5 There are..in every tribe some men who specialize in composing and reciting praises of chiefs... This they do not merely.. to establish..a personal reputation as a *mmôki* (praise-poet, praise-reciter), but also in the hope of reward. **1970** R. FINNEGAN *Oral Lit. in Afr.* v. 111 The 'praise names'.. often form the basis of formal praise poetry. **1971** *Listener* 2 Sept. 290/3 What is nowadays called 'bardic poetry' which is a genus of praise-poetry. **1977** *Westindian World* 3–9 June 13/4 It is sheer praise-poetry. **1979** G. FORTUNE in Hodza & Fortune *Shona Praise Poetry* 2 Praise poetry, especially of the more formal kind, is a mode of expression that is disappearing owing to urbanization and the replacement of traditional methods of education by schools. **1935** *Critic* (Cape Town) Oct. 7 A praise-reciter, whose business it is to know and remember praise-poems. **1965** Praise-reciter [see *praise poet* above]. **1954** M. F. SMITH *Baba of Karo* I. iii. 62 When you hear drumming, you hear the deep drum and you hear the praise-singers—you'll give them money! **1963** W. SOYINKA *Lion & Jewel* 61 And then I have to hire a praise-singer, And such a number of ceremonies Must firstly be performed. **1977** *Eastern Province Herald* (S. Afr.) 27 Apr., The installation of the new Chancellor.. was a dignified affair but it is difficult to understand what relevance a Xhosa praise singer had to the function. **1957** *Africa* XXVII. 26 (*title*) The social functions and meaning of Hausa praise-singing. **1886** Praise song [in Dict.]. **1928** W. C. WILLOUGHBY *Soul of Bantu* iv. 368 Praise-songs, which make up in glory for all they lack in veracity, are chanted upon occasion by the men whom they extol. **1957** *Africa* XXVII. 29 The District Head..may request that the praise-songs of title-holders who are his particular friends..should also be sung. **1970** P. OLIVER *Savannah Syncopators* 65 Bussani tribesmen in Upper Volta singing praise songs for the chief of the village of Yarkatenga.

praise, *v.* Add: **3. e.** *absol.* To express approbation; to bestow praise.

c **1386** CHAUCER *Parson's Tale* (1877, Ellesmere MS.) 473 Certes, the commendacioñ of the peple is somtyme ful fals and ful brotel for to triste. this day they preyse tomorwe they blame. **1609** SHAKES. *Sonnet* cvi. 13 For we which now behold these present dayes, Haue eyes to wonder, but lack toungs to praise. **1879** *Fortn. Rev.* I Apr. 507 So Molière is read or witnessed; we laugh and we praise. **1896** *Forum* (N.Y.) Mar. 1 Whether we praise lavishly or venture to blame, two perils threaten us.

4. b. Catch-phrase *praise the Lord and pass the ammunition* (see quots.).

1942 F. LOESSER (*song-title*) Praise the Lord and pass the ammunition. **1942** *Life* 2 Nov. 43 On the cover and above are pictures of Captain William A. Maguire, the man who inspired the best of this war's songs, *Praise the Lord and Pass the Ammunition*... Legend and the song written by Frank Loesser have it that..up jumped the sky pilot, gave the boys a look And manned the gun himself as he laid aside the Book, shouting 'Praise the Lord and pass the ammunition!'. **1943** *Sun* (Baltimore) 17 Sept. 10/5 The navy..named a 35-year-old chaplain from nearby Haddonfield, N.J., as the man who first used the phrase 'Praise the Lord and pass the ammunition' during the attack on Pearl Harbor. The chaplain, Lieut. Com. Howell E. Forgy, was on his first visit home in three years. **1948** A. M. TAYLOR *Lang. World War II* (rev. ed.) 159 *Praise the Lord and Pass the Ammunition*: attributed to a minister at Pearl Harbor... Real author of the phrase seems to have been Naval Lieutenant Howell Forgy, Presbyterian chaplain.

praiseach (prāʃa·χ). Also **praisseagh, prashack, prashagh, prashoge, prassia.** [Ir., f. L. *brassica* cabbage.] **a.** A porridge made from oatmeal, sometimes flavoured with vegetables. Also *fig.*, a mess, a collection of small pieces.

1698 J. DUNTON *Let.* in E. Maclysaght *Irish Life in 17th Cent.* (1969) 330 He chose rather to stay at home with Prashagh and Potatoes than hazard himself in France where he knew not that any such food grew. **1935** D. PIATT *Dialect in East & Mid-Leinster* 17/1 Praiseach... Secondary meaning: 'To make p. of a thing,' i.e., break in small pieces. **1969** C. CARFAX *Silence with Voices* viii. 51 Would I jam me wagon in the middle of a main road and wait to be made into *prashoge?*

b. The charlock, *Brassica arvensis*, or a related wild plant of the cabbage family.

1727 C. THRELKELD *Synopsis Stirpium Hibernicarum* s.v. Brassica, This is Praisseagh buigh in Irish, and grows plentifully in corn fields. **1859** *Ulster Jrnl. Archaeol.* VII. 278 In former times, when cabbages were not generally cultivated in Ireland, the wild kail (called in Irish *Praiseach*), was often made use of as a kitchen vegetable. **1880** T. MCGRATH *Pictures from Ireland* xi. 113 The growing oat crop struggles with the perennial thistle, dock, and prassia. **1904** N. COLGAN *Flora Co. Dublin* 22 *B[rassica] Sinapis*... Prashack. Yellow Weed. Charlock. **1943** D. A. WEBB *Irish Flora* 14 *B[rassica] arvensis*... Charlock, Praiseach... Tilled fields and waste places; common.

praiser. Add: **2. c.** *spec.* = **praise poet*. Cf. *MBONGO.

1904 D. KIDD *Essential Kafir* ii. 92 All chiefs keep a Court Praiser, whose business it is to go in front of the chief and sing his praises. **1937** G. P. LESTRADE in I. Schapera *Bantu-Speaking Tribes S. Afr.* xiii. 299 A praiser..may..alter the order..of stanzas. **1968** T. COPE *Izibongo: Zulu Praise Poems* I. ii. 26 When a man of distinction is rewarded for his services by the chief..he.. establishes a great kraal and appoints a personal praiser, who will collect..and perfect his praises, so that they constitute what we call a 'praise-poem'.

Prakrit. Add: Also 8 **Pracort.** (Earlier and further examples.) Also *attrib.* or as *adj.*

1766 J. CLELAND *Way to Things by Words* 88 The Pracort is the vulgar language, so called in contradistinction to the Sanscort. **1880,** etc. [see *MAHARASHTRI]. **1968** W. S. ALLEN *Vox Graeca* i. 14 In relatively ancient times this receives support from transcriptions into Prakrit (Middle Indian) on coins of the Greek kings of Bactria and India in the 1 and 2 c. B.C. **1971** [see *INDOLOGIST].

‖ **pralaya** (prala·yă). [Skr.] Dissolution, destruction of the world.

1922 JOYCE *Ulysses* 296 Questioned by his earthname as to his whereabouts in the heavenworld he stated that he was now on the path of pralaya or return but was still submitted to trial at the hands of certain bloodthirsty entities on the lower astral levels. **1954** G. S. Rao *Indian Words in Eng.* 134/1 *Pralaya*, destruction, esp. the destruction of the whole world at the end of a Kalpa. **1970** V. Mehta *Portrait of India* II. 62 We Hindus say that the universe has a *pralaya*, a death—a period of withdrawal for rest. We Madrasis have our *pralaya* all the time.

pralidoxime (prælidǫ·ksīm). *Pharm.* [f. *aldoxime* s.v. *ALDO- with arbitrary insertion of *p*, *r*, and *i* (from PYRIDINE).] (A salt of) the 2-hydroxyiminomethyl-1-methylpyridinium ion, $HO{\cdot}N{:}CH{\cdot}C_5H_4\overset{+}{N}{\cdot}CH_3$, which reactivates the enzyme cholinesterase and is used as an adjunct to atropine in the treatment of poisoning by certain cholinesterase inhibitors (as malathion and parathion).

1961 *Approved Names* (Brit. Pharmacopœia Comm.) 19 Pralidoxime Iodide, Picolinaldoxime methiodide, Protopam. **1965** *New Drugs* xlvi. 473/1 Pralidoxime chloride restores the depressed cholinesterase activity resulting from organophosphate poisoning. **1970** Passmore & Robson *Compan. Med. Stud.* II. xxxii. 2/2 Treatment of intoxication with carbamate or organophosphorus insecticides includes the use of atropine which antagonizes the muscarinic effects of acetylcholine and of pralidoxime, a cholinesterase reactivator. Pralidoxime is a quaternary ammonium compound (hydroxyiminomethyl-1-methylpyridinium) which is given slowly intravenously. **1974** M. C. Gerald *Pharmacol.* vii. 132 Normal cholinesterase activity is restored..when a cholinesterase reactivator, notably pralidoxime (2-PAM), is used as an antidote. **1978** *Daily Tel.* 23 Jan. 13/7 British soldiers and airmen are now equipped with pills which will enable them to survive three or four times the normal lethal dose of most nerve gases... The pills, produced from pralidoxime mesylate..are issued in batches for each 24 hours.

praline. Delete 'Chiefly *U.S.*' and add: The spelling *prawlin* is now *Obs.* (Earlier and further examples.)

1723 J. Nott *Cook's & Confectioner's Dict.* sig. B4 Almonds Fry'd, or Prawlins. **1770** Borella *Court & Country Confectioner* 40 We beg leave to use the words *praline* [etc.]. **1906** *Mrs. Beeton's Bk. Househ. Managem.* 1079 (*heading*) Chocolate pralines. **1913** [see *NOYAU b]. **1951** *People* 3 June 2/1 (Advt.), Crunchy wafers sandwiched with chocolate praline. **1971** A. R. Daniel *Bakers' Dict.* (ed. 2) 155/2 Praline sometimes consists of roasted blended whole almonds dipped in sugar boiled to the hard crack degree.

‖ **pralltriller** (pra·l,trilər). *Mus.* [G., f. *prallen* to bounce + *triller* trill.] (See quot. 1971.)

1841 J. Bishop in *Hamilton's Dict.* (ed. 13) 114 *Pralltriller* (German), a transient shake. **1876** Stainer & Barrett *Dict. Mus. Terms* 365/1 *Pralltriller*.., a transient shake. **1928** *Daily Express* 23 Feb. 3 What is a pralltriller?.. A musical ornament, performed by trilling the ornamented note with the note above it. **1971** *Everyman's Dict. Mus.* (ed. 5) 529/1 *Pralltriller* (Ger.), the rapid repetition of a note, with a note a degree higher in between.

pram[1]. Add: **a.** Later example of spelling *prame*.

1834 G. Crabbe in *Poetical Wks.* I. i. 9 Vessels of all sorts, from the large heavy troll-boat to the yawl and prame.

c*. A small sailing-boat. *U.S.*

1937 *Sun* (Baltimore) 31 July 11/8 In the pram class, Bucky Wilson..scored a surprise victory. **1956** *Ibid.* 11 Oct. 21/4 Hard luck forced Mary Sullivan and Henry White out of the competition when a boom broke on one of their prams. **1966** *Amer. Speech* XLI. 237 The smallest [sailboats] are called *Prams*, and they measure up to about 10 feet long.

d. *praam bow* (example of spelling *pram bow*).

1902 *Rudder* Apr. 208 The fore overhang [of the Meteor] is neither the old clipper stem nor the new pram bow.

pram[2]. For *vulgar* or *colloq.* read *colloq.* and add further examples of sense 1.

1916 G. B. Shaw *Pygmalion* v. 173 When I was a poor man and had a solicitor once when they found a pram in the dust cart, he got me off. **1955** *Times* 4 June 7/4 There are women who would not exchange a familiar pram with a quirk in its steering for the best new one that money could buy. **1963** [see *pram-park* below]. **1970** [see *pram-pusher* below].

3. *attrib.* and *Comb.*, as (sense 1) *pramful*, *pram-handle*, *-load*, *race*, *rug*; **pram-park**, (*a*) (see quot. 1963); (*b*) a space, area, etc., where prams may be left; **pram-pusher**, one who pushes a pram; *spec.* a young mother; so **pram-pushing** *ppl. a.* and *vbl. sb.*

1957 M. Frayn in *Granta* 9 Mar. 20/1 People said that an old woman had been arrested on the other side of the village, pushing a whole pramful of stolen goods along. **1977** F. Branston *Up & Coming Man* xv. 168 A young mum and a pramful of kids. **1934** Dylan Thomas *Let.* 15 Apr. (1966) 102 Mothers are resting their bellies on pram-handles. **1972** *Where* Oct. 273/3 Staff took to the post office two pramloads of the report-and-appeal. **1973** *Times* 28 Feb. (Suppl. on Victoria Centre, Nottingham) p. iv/6 A flying squirrel pushes a pramload (which is a nest) of birds. **1963** *Times* 3 May 15/7 In the House of Commons on Monday Sir Robert Cary asked how one gets a pram on a bus. In New Zealand they are carried in special pram-parks on the front of the radiators, where they seem to be safe, but nothing can be left inside, as they are hung wheels foremost. **1965** R. Rendell *To fear Painted Devil* xii. 136 We're going to have that extension done at last... A sun loggia... And a pram park! **1967** J. Wilson in L. Deighton *London Dossier* 35 Linguists wishing to meet *au pair* girls might do worse than to hang about the pram park inside Peter Jones department store. **1970** *Times* 23 Feb. 13/2 The scheme will include..seats and plants in the concourse, and a pram park. **1973** *Guardian* 3 Sept. 20 Pram parks should be provided inside shops. **1935** J. L. Hodson *Harvest in North* II. i. 39 Afe on yo' are nowt but skivvies and pram-pushers. **1963** *Guardian* 25 Jan. 8/7 The pram-pushers are always willing to discuss these, as a change from the inevitable baby-talk. **1970** A. Price *Labyrinth Makers* v. 64 Mothers bulldozing their way ahead with prams... Roskill adroitly slipped into the wake of one of the most aggressive pram-pushers. **1933** *Punch* 10 May 516/1 Possibly the pram-pushing girl's hat caught her eye. **1964** G. Butler *Coffin in Malta* vii. 198 Most husbands were competent nannies; he fully expected to do some pram-pushing himself. **1974** *Country Life* 7 Mar. 480/1 The pram-pushing Phil's anguished claim—'he's my son!' **1968** P. Jennings *Living Village* 123 In the scrapbook there is a very good colour photograph of a Boxing Day pram race. **1934** A. Thirkell *Wild Strawberries* ix. 196 Ivy, run and get the pram rug and put it round her.

‖ **prana** (prā·nă). [Skr.] In Hindu religion, the 'breath of life'; hence in extended uses, a life-giving force or inspiration; the breath, breathing. Also **pranayama**, regulation of the breath; breathing-control.

1830 H. T. Colebrooke in *Trans. R. Asiatic Soc.* II. 11 The term *práṅa*..properly and primarily signifies respiration, as well as certain other vital actions (inspiration, energy, expiration, digestion, or circulation of nourishment); and secondarily, the senses and organs. But, in the passages here referred to, it is employed for a different signification, intending the supreme Brahme. **1875** Monier Williams *Indian Wisdom* ii. 40 Highest of all stands Prāṅa or Life. As the spokes of a wheel are attached to the nave, so are all things attached to Life. **1930** F. Yeats-Brown *Bengal Lancer* v. 66 There was a *saddhu* at Puri who claimed to be able to resurrect sparrows..by breathing *prana* into them. **1938** S. Beckett *Murphy* 196 He..trusted he would be granted Prana to finish a monograph. **1955** E. Pound *Section: Rock-Drill* (1957) xciv. 92 Above prana, the light, past light, the crystal. **1956** E. Wood *Yoga Dict.* 25/1 The shorter unit of time often mentioned in Sanskrit philosophical literature, though not used in *prānāyāma* is called the second or moment (*kshana*), and is often considered to be one quarter of the time taken up in shutting an eye. *Ibid.* 123/1 *Prana*, that Vital Air which is..concerned with the health and strength of the heart and its work in the body. **1959** [see *ORGONE]. **1960** J. Hewitt *Yoga* v. 70 Prana, to the Yogi, means much more than mere breath. Prana is actually the power behind and within breath. The power of the atom is Prana. Thought is Prana... It pervades the whole universe. **1960** Koestler *Lotus & Robot* I. iii. 117 The Yogi then demonstrated the extraordinary power of his chest muscles—the result of pranayama. **1970** *Man, Myth & Magic* v. 146/3 The idea of an astral body is very old. Ancient Indian writings describe the eight *siddhis* or supernormal powers which can be acquired through a type of yoga called *Pranayama*. **1971** 'A. Hall' *Warsaw Document* xv. 185, I took a slow breath: the answer to panic is *prana*. **1979** W. H. Canaway *Solid Gold Buddha* xi. 76 He..did some *Pranayama*, and calmed himself, through the rhythmic breathing.

prance, *sb.* Add: **a.** (Further example.)

1898 F. P. Dunne *Mr. Dooley in Peace & War* 184 He has th' gait proper f'r half-past six o'clock th' avenin' befure pay-day. But 'tis not th' prance iv an American citizen makin' a gloryous spectacle iv himsilf.

Hence **prancy** *a.*, resembling or suggestive of a prance.

1961 *New Statesman* 26 May 828/3 The 'Bohemian Jive', a prancy affair, is now an essential part of the repertoire, whether you wear points or sandals. **1963** *New Yorker* 22 June 4 The trumpeting band of Emil Coleman and the prancy one of Mark Monte.

Prandtl (prænt'l). [Name of Ludwig *Prandtl* (1875–1953), German physicist.] *Prandtl number*: a dimensionless parameter used in calculations of heat transfer between a moving fluid and a solid body, equal to $c_p\nu/k$, where c_p is the heat capacity of unit volume of the fluid, ν is its kinematic viscosity, and k its thermal conductivity.

1933 W. H. McAdams *Heat Transmission* iv. 96 Prandtl number = 1/Stanton group. **1954** R. Stephenson *Introd. Nucl. Engin.* vi. 245 The ratio of the quantity of heat transferred by convection to the quantity of heat transferred by conduction is given by the value of the Prandtl number for the fluid. **1958** [see *NUSSELT]. **1974** F. M. White *Viscous Fluid Flow* ii. 84 Table 2-1 gives values of the Prandtl number for various fluids at 68°F. It shows that liquid metals have [a] very small Prandtl number, gases slightly less than unity, thin liquids somewhat higher than unity, and oils a very large value of *Pr*.

prang (præŋ), *sb.* *slang* (orig. *R.A.F.*). [etym. uncertain.] **1. a.** An accident in which an aircraft suffers damage; a crash-landing. **b.** A bombing-raid. Also *transf.* and *fig.*

1942 *Sun* (Baltimore) 7 Apr. 20/8 American flyers in the RAF Eagle Squadrons have introduced a new decoration. 'The Order of Prang'—but it never appears in official citations. 'Prang' is Eagle slang for crash. **1943** Hunt & Pringle *Service Slang* 53 'P/O Prune' is the title bestowed upon a pilot who has several 'prangs' on his record. **1945** Partridge *Dict. R.A.F. Slang* 45 *Prang*, a crash landing. (2) A bombing raid. **1946** G. Gibson *Enemy Coast Ahead* 105, I like high-level attacks..or else it must be the very low-level prang. **1948** G. Greene *Heart of Matter* III. i. 294 'There's no time like the present for a prang,' Bagster said, moving her firmly towards the bed. **1958** *Spectator* 16 May 614/1 The Prime Minister was questioned about the RAF's wizard prang on the Government's defence policy. **1979** N. Slater *Falcon* ii. 36 Tell him about your wizard prangs in the war.

2. An accident or collision involving a road vehicle; a car-crash.

1959 *Sunday Times* 1 Nov. 23/2 The grisly enormities of American stock-car racing, with an hysterical ghoul of a commentator who revelled in every prang. **1971** A. Diment *Think Inc.* ii. 26 Might have had a bad prang before they re-sprayed her.

prang, *v.* *slang.* (orig. *R.A.F.*). [etym. uncertain.] **1.** *trans.* **a.** To crash or crash-land (an aircraft); to damage (part of an aircraft) during a crash-landing. Also const. *down*.

1941 *Tee Emm* (Air Ministry) July 6/1 Do they give a grateful sigh and shut up shop when the last serviceable aircraft has been pranged against a hangar because its pilot would land towards obstacles? **1942** *R.A.F. Jrnl.* 18 Apr. 1 Gremlins..run down the nose of the machine and tip you up and you prang a prop. **1942** *Tee Emm* (Air Ministry) II. 143 By now he didn't give a darn—He pranged her down beside the barn. **1944** 'N. Shute' *Pastoral* v. 107 After so many operations it was an acute personal grief to him that he had pranged his Wimpey. **1977** *Belfast Tel.* 28 Feb. 9/1 (*caption*) The half of the propellor he is holding came off a Bristol fighter he 'pranged' in a schoolyard in 1925.

b. To bomb (a target) successfully from the air.

1942 [see *FINGER *sb.* 3a]. **1943** B. J. Hurren *Eastern Med.* 27 One can picture the..rage of the German and Italian air commanders..each verging on apoplexy that their chosen pilots should not be able to 'prang' a ship which presented a clear, long, visible deck target area of some 600 feet by 90 feet wide. **1952** M. Tripp *Faith is Windsock* v. 87 The Lancs broke off sharply at the last moment to prang Neuss. **1958** E. Hyams *Taking it Easy* I. i. 16 The RAF said they didn't know how to, they just know about pranging the Luftwaffe and the railway yard at Ham.

c. To involve (a road vehicle or other object) in an accident; to crash or 'smash up'; to collide with.

1952 E. F. Davies *Illyrian Venture* iii. 50 'What height would you like to be dropped at?' 'Would 800 feet suit you?'.. 'I think I can manage that without pranging the mountain.' **1966** T. Wisdom *High-Performance Driving* ix. 97 The driver may well have left his 'flasher' on many corners ago and is happily oblivious of the fact until you move off on his signal and 'prang' him. **1971** *Daily Colonist* (Victoria, B.C.) 26 Feb. 2/1 Recently my rather ancient Chevvy II got pranged from behind—nothing serious, just a smashed tail light. **1973** A. Mann *Tiara* ix. 79 Most of them don't drive... If they prang a car, there's always plenty of witnesses to say it's the priest's fault. **1976** *Islander* (Victoria, B.C.) 22 Aug. 11/1 We had pranged a rock getting out of Oak Bay.

2. *intr.* To crash or crash-land an aircraft. Also *transf.*

1943 P. Brennan et al. *Spitfires over Malta* ii. 55 The upwind end of the landing-path was a maze of bomb-holes... I was too brassed off to worry whether I pranged or not. **1961** 'J. Ross' *Last August* iii. 31 A wasp was pranging against the window. **1968** *Daily Express* 26 Feb. 4/1, I knew we were going to prang, but all I wanted to do was to make sure that we weren't killed or seriously injured.

3. *trans.* In extended uses: to break, to smash; to hit, to strike heavily (*against*). Also *fig.*

1942 J. Moore in *Observer* 4 Oct. 7/2 Now you talk..of pranging a date, meaning that you have left your popsy waiting outside the Unicorn while you continue to drink with the squadron in the Bull and Bush. **1943** Hunt & Pringle *Service Slang* 53 Jones pranged his arm at rugger to-day. **1946** *Slipstream* 38 Mind you don't prang yourselves against the table. **1948** Partridge *Dict. Forces' Slang* 147 He pranged the iron bedstead... He pranged his leg against the bedstead. **1977** F. Parrish *Fire in Barley* x. 99 He was holding a pitchfork. 'I thought I'd prang a rabbit.'

Hence **pranged** *ppl. a.*; **pra·nging** *vbl. sb.*

1942 *Air News* Oct. 4/1 'Pranging', by the way, is a new R.A.F. expression which means smashing things up—including one's own aeroplane. **1946** Brickhill & Norton *Escape to Danger* iii. 39 A couple of 109's hacked two Hurricane down near Montreuil on the 10th of June 1940, and Eric jumped from his pranged kite and ran for it. **1959** *Times Lit. Suppl.* 7 Aug. p. iii/3 Classic understating metaphors like 'having a party', 'falling in the drink', 'pranging', and so on, had their value in time of war. **1971** R. Dentry *Encounter at Kharmel* vii. 117 Looking for the wreckage of a pranged aircraft.

prankster (præ·ŋkstəɪ). orig. *U.S.* [f. Prank *sb.*[2] + -ster.] One who plays pranks; a hoaxer, a practical joker.

1927 *Amer. Speech* II. 245/1, *-ster* also, for a time, gave signs of being moribund... It is, however, found in a number of new formations... *prankster*, [etc.]. **1940** O. Nash *Face is Familiar* (1942) 14 There is at least one thing I would less rather have in the neighbourhood than a gangster, And that one thing is a practical prankster. **1951** *Mind* LX. 468 Suppose a prankster laid out some railroad tracks which..diverged in such a manner as to make them look parallel. **1957** C. Rice *My Kingdom for Hearse* i. 6 Some practical prankster had evidently left a dead horse in his nose. **1969** *Daily Tel.* 14 Nov. 36/4 Police admitted that it was an almost impossible task..to sift the bomb pranksters from the deadly serious ones. **1972** 'M. Yorke' *Silent Witness* III. 51 The key..had been turned on her... 'Some prankster, I suppose... It was a very childish trick.' **1977** *Time* 24 Jan. 37/1 Ken Waller, a not-too-merry prankster who steals bits of his opponents' costumes in order to upset their concentration before they go onstage to face the judges.

p'raps (præps), *adv.* Also **praps, p'r'aps, p'rhaps.** Repr. colloq. pronuncs. of Perhaps *adv.*

1835, 1837 [see Perhaps *adv.* (*sb.*) 1]. **1898** G. B. Shaw *Candida* I. 93, I did think you a bit of a fool once; but I'm beginnin' to think that praps I was be'ind the times a bit. **1912** Masefield *Widow in Bye St.* 24 We might go round one evening, p'raps. ? **1912** R. Fry *Lett.* (1972) I. 358 Don't leave this letter about... P'raps you'll *want* to burn it. **1955** N. Marsh *Scales of Justice* iv. 75, I know what they'll say about me. Not you, p'r'aps, but the others. **1974** 'P. B. Yuill' *Bornless Keeper* iv. 33 Praps we'd better both wait. **1976** D. Clark *Dread & Water* vi. 126 P'raps you'll tell me what you're gunna do about it?

prasad, prasada (prasā·d, -a). *Hinduism.* [Skr. *prasāda* lit. clearness, kindness, grace, Hindi *prasād.*] **1.** A propitiatory offering of food made to a god; food which is offered to an idol and then shared among devotees.

1828 H. H. Wilson in *Asiatic Researches* XVI. 83 A *Chamár*, oh king, ministers to the *Sálagrám*, and poisons the town with his *Prasád*. *Ibid.* 96 At noon, he halted and bathed the god, and prepared his food, and presented it, and then took the *Prasád* and put it in a vessel, and fed upon what remained. **1855** —— *Gloss. Judicial & Revenue Terms* 424/2 All castes may partake of the *Prasád* of any image. **1875** Monier Williams *Indian Wisdom* p. xxxvii, It is remarkable that the food offered to the gods, when appropriated and eaten by the priests, and the rice distributed by them to the people, are called *prasāda* (? = εὐχαριστία). **1913** J. N. Farquhar *Crown of Hinduism* ix. 381 In modern temples, the practice is to give every worshipper a portion of the food and of the water offered to the idol. The food is called *prasāda*, a grace-gift, and the water *tīrtha*, holy water. **1953** K. W. Morgan *Relig. Hindus* vii. 296 The food is first offered to the Lord and what is eaten is His praśāda. **1965** 'Lauchmonen' *Old Thom's Harvest* x. 132 East Indians..shared out prasad, mango..and rice. **1969** *Weekly Mail* (Madras) 26 July 7/5, 90 boys..became unconscious after taking 'prasad' at a religious function at Chakasigan village. **1979** D. Quinn *Fear of God* i. 52 The Indian said, 'Prasada, the remains are food offered to the Lord... The food is Krishna himself. You should eat it all.'

2. Divine grace or favour. Also *attrib.*

1895 E. W. Hopkins *Relig. India* xv. 429 The *prasāda* doctrine (of special grace) belongs to a much earlier literature. **1921** R. E. Hume *Thirteen Princ. Upanishads* 59 As regards speculative knowledge of Ātman, its apprehension by means of human knowledge is opposed by the doctrine of prasāda, or 'Grace', in Kaṭha 2.20. **1964** R. Antoine et al. *Relig. Hinduism* xxiii. 247 This divine grace: *anugraha, prasāda, puṣṭi, kṛpā*, is *the* means which habilitates the bhakta to the obtainment and practice of the bhakti.

praseodymium (prēⁱziǒdi·miǝm). *Chem.* [mod.L., f. G. *praseodym* (C. A. von Welsbach 1885, in *Monatshefte f. Chem.* VI. 490), f. Gr. πράσιος leek-green (f. πράσον leek) + G. *di)dym* Didymium: see -ium. Named in allusion to the colour of its salts and its isolation, with neodymium, from the supposed element didymium.] A metallic element, similar to iron in appearance, which is a typical lanthanide and forms leek-green compounds in which it has a valency of three (rarely four), some of which are used to impart a yellow colour to glasses and ceramics. Atomic number 59; symbol Pr.

1885 [see *neodymium]. **1905** Gooch & Walker *Outl. Inorg. Chem.* xix. 493 For more than fifty years the elementary character of didymium was accepted, until Auer von Welsbach, by a most laborious process of fractional precipitation of the double nitrate of didymium and ammonium, succeeded in isolating two distinctly different double nitrates..from which were prepared two different series of salts, of different elements, which were now named praseodymium and neodymium. **1922** T. M. Lowry *Inorg. Chem.* xxxiv. 672 Praseodymium also resembles cerium in forming a dioxide, PrO_2, when the nitrate is heated with potassium nitrate at 450°. **1950** *Thorpe's Dict. Appl. Chem.* (ed. 4) X. 183/2 All cerium-bearing minerals contain some praseodymium, e.g. cerite from Arendal (Switzerland) contains up to 8% of Pr_2O_3, monazite sand from Brazil, 5·5–6·2%. **1971** J. F. Liptrot *Mod. Inorg. Chem.* xxvi. 438 Lanthanum, cerium, praseodymium, neodymium and gadolinium may be obtained by reduction of their trichlorides with calcium at about 1000 °C. **1974** *Encycl. Brit. Micropædia* VIII. 179/2 Praseodymium is about one-third as abundant as lead and about a thousand times more plentiful than gold in the igneous rocks of the Earth's crust... Natural praseodymium is all stable isotope praseodymium-141.

prashack, prashagh, etc., varr. *praiseach.

prat, *sb.*[2] Delete *Rogues' Cant* and add: Also **pratt. 1. a.** Now usu. sing., the backside, rump. *slang* (orig. *Criminals'*).

1846 [see *nut *sb.*[1] 7 a]. **1914** Jackson & Hellyer *Vocab. Criminal Slang* 66 *Pratt*,..the human rear. **1952** R. Stout *Prisoner's Base* i. 3, I have had to spend most of my time recently sitting on my prat. **1959** E. Borneman *Tomorrow is Now* ix. 93 You gimme a pain in the royal pratt. **1972** D. Delman *Sudden Death* iii. 65 I'm a *shmo* about tennis, so if I fall on my prat a time or two you have to bear with me.

b. A hip-pocket. *U.S. Criminals' slang.*

1914 Jackson & Hellyer *Vocab. Criminal Slang* 66 *Pratt*.., a hip pocket. **1927** [see *prat-digging vbl. sb.] **1936** *Detective Fiction Weekly* 12 Sept. 93/1 In spite of the fact that a pocketbook may be removed most easily from a hip pocket known as a right or left 'pratt', the majority of men carry their money there.

2. A person of no account; a dolt, fool, 'jerk'. *slang.*

1968 M. Bragg *Without City Wall* xii. 130 He had been looking for the exact word to describe David and now he found it: *prat*. **1973** J. Wainwright *Pride of Pigs* 32 Harris was a bit of a pompous prat. **1974** N. Freeling *Dressing of Diamond* 204 Want to get an eyeful, do you, dirty-minded prat that you are. **1980** J. Wainwright *Eye of Beholder* 18 The pompous prat. The I-know-people-in-high-places nut.

3. *attrib.* and *Comb.*, as *prat-faced* adj.; (in sense *1 b) **prat digger,** a pick-pocket; so **prat-digging** *vbl. sb.*; **prat frisk,** the theft of a wallet from a hip-pocket; **prat-kick,** a hip-pocket; **prat leather,** a wallet kept in the hip-pocket; **prat poke,** a wallet stolen from the hip-pocket.

1935 *Amer. Speech* X. 19/2 *Prat-digger*, a pickpocket, one who exploits the *prat kick*. **1955** *Publ. Amer. Dial. Soc.* xxiv. 69 Others specialize in hip pocket work and are called *prat diggers*. **1908** J. M. Sullivan *Criminal Slang* 19 *Pratt digging*, stealing from the hip pocket. **1916** G. A. England *Pod, Bender & Co.* 291 It's a fact we've always been above such lays as pratt-digging. **1927** *Writer's Monthly* Nov. 390/1 The 'pratt'..is a trousers pocket. 'Pratt-digging' is stealing the 'pratt-leather' from the hip. **1976** U. Holden *String Horses* i. 17 They liked to kiss each other lightly.., push each other with taunts. 'You prat-faced les. Get off.' **1924** Prat frisk [see *prat poke]. **1896** I. K. Friedman *Lucky Number* 154, 'I dipped it from yer prat-kick.'.. 'I means I took her from yer back pocket,' answered the rogue blandly. **1955** *Publ. Amer. Dial. Soc.* xxiv. 125 The hip pockets are *prat kicks*. **1908** J. M. Sullivan *Criminal Slang* 19 *Pratt leather*, a pocketbook in the hip pocket. **1927** Prat leather [see *prat-digging vbl. sb.]. **1924** G. C. Henderson *Keys to Crookdom* 414 *Pratt poke*, purse kept in hip pocket. Pratt frisk—stealing such a purse, reefing a britch. **1955** *Publ. Amer. Dial. Soc.* xxiv. 115 When a wallet is taken from the hip pocket, it is known as a *prat poke*.

prat, *v.* Delete †*Obs.*, restrict *Sc.* to sense 1, and add: Also *Sc.* **pret. 1. b.** To lark about; to trifle, romp. Freq. const. *with.*

1728 A. Ramsay *Poems* (1953) II. 89 Some Beaus may snarl if we should prat. *a***1835** J. Affleck *Posthumous Poetical Wks.* (1836) 60, I never pretit onie where At midday, night or morn. **1851** A. Maclagan *Sk. from Nature* 153 As for her sons, their foes will find They're no to prat wi'! **1897** C.R. *Dunning Folk-Lore* 4 Thae brownies warna to prat wi'! They played gey pliskies whiles, an' did muckle mischeef.

2. To potter *about*; to fool around, to act in a silly or annoying manner. *slang.*

1961 Partridge *Dict. Slang* Suppl. 1231/2 *Prat about*, to potter, mess about. **1973** H. Miller *Open City* xvii. 187 Sit down and stop pratting about.

3. a. *intr.* To simulate coyness. **b.** *trans.* To feign rejection of (someone). *U.S. Blacks.*

1970 C. Major *Dict. Afro-Amer. Slang* 93 *Prat*, to play coy. **1972** 'I. Slim' in T. Kochman *Rappin' & Stylin' Out* 389 Pimping ain't no game of love, so prat 'em and keep your swipe outta 'em.

pratal, *a.* (Earlier and later examples.)

1847 H. C. Watson *Cybele Britannica* I. 65 The proposed series of terms runs thus:—1. Pratal.—Plants of meadows, or rich and damp grass-land [etc.]. **1932** G. C. Druce *Comital Flora Brit. Isles* 69 Meadow Crane's-bill. Pratal. British. Meadows, grassy road-borders.

‖ **Prater**[2] (prā·tǝɹ). [Ger., ad. It. *prato* meadow.] The name of a large wooded park in Vienna.

1803 C. Wilmot *Let.* 2 Aug. in *Irish Peer* (1920) 207 The Prater..is esteem'd the most magnificent public walk and drive in Europe. **1819** M. Wilmot *More Lett.* (1935) 20 The turn out in the Prater of a Sunday Eveᵍ is Magnificent. **1870** G. H. Lewes *Jrnl.* 10 Apr. in *Geo. Eliot Lett.* (1956) V. 89 Lytton then proposed that we should drive in the Prater. **1911** *Encycl. Brit.* XXVIII. 52/1 The Prater, a vast expanse (2000 acres) of wood and park on the east side of the city, between the Danube and the Danube Canal, is greatly frequented by all classes. **1938** W. J. Turner *Mozart* xvi. 312 One fine autumn day when they were sitting in the beautiful Prater, Mozart spoke of his approaching death. **1945** C. Isherwood *Prater Violet* 33 It is a warm spring evening in the Vienna Prater. **1974** A. Goddard *Vienna Pursuit* ii. 40, I.. made a stately circuit on the Big Wheel in the Prater.

pratfall (præ·tfǭl), *sb.* Chiefly *N. Amer. slang.* Also **prat(t)-fall.** [f. Prat *sb.*[2] + Fall *sb.*[1]] **a.** *Theatr.* A comedy fall; a fall on to the buttocks.

1939 N. Coward *Play Parade* II. 108 Don't do a prat-fall in your first routine. **1941** L. Rosten *Hollywood* 316 The Hollywood writers—graduates of the westerns.. masters of the chase, the 'pratt-fall'..—kept the movies moving. **1952** 'E. Box' *Death in Fifth Position* (1954) ii. 47 Some homicidal maniac..who enjoyed seeing ballerinas take fatal pratfalls. **1960** B. Keaton *Wonderful World of Slapstick* (1967) 96 Pop's pratfalls astonished Roscoe and everybody else. **1961** *Guardian* 27 Apr. 9/4 A more intelligent form of humour—away from the pratfall type of thing. **1977** *Time* 26 Dec. 49/1 Only Saturday-morning TV addicts could possibly endure the antics of *The World's Greatest Lover*, in which characters are forever shouting their lines, bulging their eyes and stumbling through pratfalls.

b. *transf.* and *fig.*

1953 R. Bradbury *Fahrenheit 451* (1954) i. 56 Life becomes one big pratfall. **1956** D. Karp *All Honorable Men* 174 That gentleman is in for a rude surprise some morning soon. I understand he handles government contracts. Another pratfall soon. **1971** *Guardian* 25 Nov. 17/2 Performers who write their own material often take enormous pratfalls. **1977** *Rolling Stone* 7 Apr. 43/1 Why has an important investigation so quickly degenerated into a series of pratfalls?

Hence as *v. intr.*, to fall on to the buttocks. Hence **prat-fallen, -falling** *ppl. adjs.* Also *fig.*

1940 *Time* 29 Jan. 41/1 The sight of Sonja (for the fourth time in her professional career) pratt-fallen. *Ibid.* 30 Dec. 30/1 Opera at the Met has a way of prattfalling between two stools. **1942** *Ibid.* 3 Aug. 74/2 On the way to the plate he prat-falls on the carefully laid-out row of bats in front of the dugout. **1972** *Listener* 6 July 22/1 The eloquent gamey pratfalling scapegoat. **1973** D. Lees *Rape of Quiet Town* iv. 55 As the tension built up..it was a piece of prat-falling comedy that saved me.

‖ **pratiquant** (pratikaṅ), *a.* (*sb.*) [Fr.] Making a practice of religious duties or observances; practising. Also *absol.* as *sb.*

1902 G. Arthur *Let.* Mar. in *Some Lett. from Man of No Importance* (1928) 140 If the King is not religious in the 'pratiquant' sense of the word, he has a very strong sense of religion. **1956** S. Bedford *Legacy* iii. iv. 154 Jules..says he couldn't marry someone who wasn't a Catholic... It isn't as though *he'd* ever shewed himself the least bit *pratiquant*. **1960** *Times* 27 Feb. 7/3 Fasting is an unhealthy habit; Communists tell the people of their Muslim lands. On the contrary, urge the new *pratiquants* in Turkey and elsewhere, it is astonishing how fitter you feel at the end of Ramadan. **1965** *New Statesman* 3 Dec. 890/2 After lapsing for 15 years, she had recently tried to become *pratiquant* again.

Pratt (præt). The name of Felix *Pratt* (1780–1859), Staffordshire pottery-manufacturer, used *attrib.* to designate a type of cream-coloured earthenware painted in high-temperature colours and widely produced in the late eighteenth and early nineteenth centuries. So *Pratt-type* adj., etc.

[**1912** F. Litchfield *Pott. & Porc.* (new ed.) vii. 195 The Pottery of Felix Pratt,..marked with the name *Pratt* and known as 'Pratt's ware', was in this district [*sc.* Fenton].] **1920** G. W. Rhead *Earthenware Collector* xi. 197 One of the most successful pieces of Pratt ware is the mug of 'Midnight Conversation' in the Hanley Museum. *Ibid.* A number of Pratt jugs have been known as Sunderland jugs. **1933** W. B. Honey *Eng. Pott. & Porc.* vii. 100 The so-called 'Pratt ware' was made by other Staffordshire potters as well as by those of Sunderland and other places in the North. **1957** Mankowitz & Haggar *Conc. Encycl. Eng. Pott. & Porc.* 182/2 *'Pratt' type*, wares made at the end of the eighteenth and beginning of the nineteenth centuries, decorated with a distinctive palette of high temperature colours. **1963** *House & Garden* May 68/2 The pottery pieces..are mostly Pratt-ware made either just before or just after the beginning of the nineteenth century, and are part of a collection of Pratt. **1967** *Times* 14 Mar. 21/7 (Advt.), English pottery and porcelain..including..a Prattware grotto group. **1974** *Country Life* 21 Feb. (Suppl.) 56 Six Pratt Pot-lids and some Pratt Ware. *a***1977** *Harrison Mayer Ltd. Catal.* 99/1 Pratt Type and Peasant enamel Wares... 20 Slides.

praty, dial. corruption: see Potato 2 d δ in Dict. and Suppl.

‖ **pratyahara** (pratʸāhā·ra). *Yoga Philos.* [Skr.] (See quots.)

1882 E. B. Cowell tr. *Áchárya's Sarva-Darśana-Samgraha* xv. 267 Now in this way, having his mind purified by the 'forbearances'..the devotee is to attain 'self-mastery'..and 'restraint' (pratyáhára). **1899** Max Müller *Six Syst. Indian Philos.* vii. 458 We can hardly doubt that these postures and restraints of breathing.. are helpful in producing complete abstraction (Pratyâhâra) of the senses from their objects, and a complete indifference of the Yogin towards pain and pleasure. **1942** D. D. Runes *Dict. Philos.* 248/1 *Pratyāhāra*,..withdrawal of the senses from external objects, one of the psychophysical means for attaining the object of Yoga. **1957** *Encycl. Brit.* XII. 251/2 The next step of *pratyāhāra* or the withdrawal of the senses from their natural outward functioning answers to what modern psychology calls introversion. **1960** J. Hewitt *Yoga* viii. 114 Sense-Withdrawal, called by the Yogis Pratyahara. **1976** *Canberra Times* 23 Aug. 2/8 The ability to transcend thought is acquired by the application of concentrated mind to a single point, pratyahara.

prawn, *sb.* Add: **I. 1. c. prawn cocktail:** see *cocktail 4; **prawn-fishing** = *prawning *vbl. sb.* 2; so *prawn-fisherman.*

1921 *Chambers's Jrnl.* Sept. 590/1 Numerous are the adverse comments I've heard on the prawn fisherman and his ways. **1924** *Blackw. Mag.* Apr. 489/2 Neither the Lydons nor anybody else could make me enjoy prawn-fishing on that high walk at Galway. **1978** R. Waddington *Catching Salmon* xi. 128 One cardinal principle.. applies to prawn-fishing. If in a stocked pool no fish takes or follows your bait in the first few casts, it is..useless to continue.

II. *transf.* and *fig.* **2.** See sense b in Dict. **3.** Applied to persons. **a.** Figuratively, or in a familiar manner. **b.** As a term of contempt: a fool, half-wit.

1845 Dickens *Let.* 27 Jan. (1977) IV. 253 By the time he had finished this third dinner, his eyes protruded infinitely beyond the tip of that feature [*sc.* his nose]. You never saw such a human Prawn as he looked, in your life. **1895** W. P. Ridge *Minor Dialogues* 207 Ah, I expect you're a saucy young prawn, Emma. **1937** Partridge *Dict. Slang* 657/1 *Prawn, silly*, a pejorative applied to persons. **1965** *Telegraph* (Brisbane) 5 July 8/4 Describing a fellow who was a bit eccentric, or one who was just plain nuts... Anyone would know what he [*sc.* an Australian] meant if he used the word..*prawn*.

c. In phr. *to come the raw prawn* (*over, with*, etc.): to attempt to deceive. *Austral. slang.*

1942 *Salt* 25 May 8 *Don't come the raw prawn*, don't try to put one over me. *c* **1948** S. L. Elliot in E. Hanger *Khaki, Bush & Bigotry* (1968) 36 The filthy rotten Crab, he'd better not come the raw prawn on us. **1951** Cusack & James *Come in Spinner* 306 Coupla bastards come the raw prawn over me on the last lap up from Melbourne and I done me last bob at Swy. **1959** E. Lambert *Glory thrown In* v. 41 Don't ever come the raw prawn with Doc, mate. He knows all the lurks. **1965** M. Shadbolt *Among Cinders* xxi. 202 Don't you come the raw prawn with me. **1970** *Private Eye* 16 Jan. 16 Don't come the raw prawn with me. Ozzie Barry and me are just good friends.

prawning (prǭ·niŋ), *vbl. sb.* [f. Prawn *v.* + -ing[1].] **1.** The action or process of fishing for prawn. Also *attrib.*

1886 [see Prawn *v.* in Dict.]. **1973** [See *open go* s.v. *open *a.* 22 c]. **1978** M. Gilbert *Empty House* xxiv. 219 Spades, buckets and prawning nets should be left in the porch. **1979** *Country Life* 24 May 1658/1 The Coquet..is a prawning and shrimping river.

2. Fishing for salmon using a prawn as bait.

1909 *Westm. Gaz.* 10 May 12/2 Prawning and spinning for salmon has begun on the Hampshire Avon. **1921** *Chambers's Jrnl.* Sept. 590/1 Prawning for salmon is looked down upon by many as being almost a form of poaching. **1931** E. Taverner et al. *Salmon Fishing* xxiii. 361 A rod, reel and line suitable for spinning will serve equally well for prawning.

praxeology (præksiǫ·lŏdʒi). Also **praxiology, praxo·logy.** [ad. F. *praxéologie* (L. Bourdeau 1882, in *Théorie des Sciences* II. vii. i. 463), or directly f. Gr. πρᾶξις action: see -ology.] The study of such actions as are necessary in order to give practical effect to a theory or technique; the science of human conduct; the science of efficient action. So **praxeolo·gical, -iological** *a.*; **praxio·logist**, one who studies practical activity.

1904 W. R. B. Gibson *Philos. Introd. Ethics* ix. 190, I say 'theory of experience' instead of theory of 'knowledge' or 'epistemology', in order to include the theory of action or 'praxology'. **1911** C. A. Mercier *Conduct & its Disorders* p. viii, Apart from the general advantage..of having a systematic knowledge of conduct as a whole; there are certain special advantages to be derived from a study of Praxiology, if I may so term it. **1944** *Philos. & Phenomenol. Res.* IV. 527 The theoretical science of human action, praxeology, and especially its hitherto best developed part, economics or catallactics. *Ibid.* 533 Praxeology does not employ the term *rational*. It deals with purposive behavior, i.e., human action. *Ibid.* 537 The technological and the praxeological methods. **1945** Z. Jordan *Devel. Math. Logic Poland* viii. 33/2 Kotarbinski's first published papers dealt with some problems of ethics and sociology, which were to supply the foundations of a general theory of action, called by him praxeology. **1961** T. Kotarbinski in *Methodos* XIII. 163 (*title*) The aspirations of praxiologists. **1962** E. Nagel et al. *Logic, Methodol. & Philos. of Sci.* 211 (*title*) Praxiological sentences and how they are proved. **1965** D. Wojtasiewicz tr. *Kotarbinski's Praxiology* i. 1 Considerations included in the present work come within the scope of praxiology—the general theory of efficient action. *Ibid.*, The praxiologist concerns himself with finding the broadest possible generalizations of a technical nature. **1966** Howard & Fox tr. *Aron's Peace & War* p. xviii (*heading*) Praxeology, the antinomies of diplomatic-strategic conduct. *Ibid.* i. 4, I must first define international relations, then specify the characteristics of the four levels of conceptualization which we call *theory, sociology, history, praxiology*. **1973** *Times Lit. Suppl.* 6 July 787/3 The synthesis of these two modes of knowledge he labels 'praxeological'. **1973** B. B. Wolman *Dict. Behavioral Sci.* 286/1 *Praxiology*, psychology viewed as the study of actions, and overt behavior... Any normative science, such as, e.g. education, social philosophy, ethics, etc., that sets norms and goals for human actions.

-praxia (præ·ksiă), comb. form repr. Gr. πρᾶξις action in some mod.L. terms, as *apraxia, *echopraxia, *parapraxia.

praxis. Add: **1. c.** A term used by A. von Cieszkowski in *Prolegomena zur Historiosophie* (Berlin, 1838), then adopted by Karl Marx *Zur Kritik der Hegelschen Rechtsphilosophie, Einleitung* in the *Deutsch-Französische Jahrbücher* (1844), to denote the willed action by which a theory or philosophy (esp. a Marxist one) becomes a social actuality. Also *attrib.* and *transf.*

This term, frequently translated as *practice, practical ability*, or *practical activity*, has been increasingly used since the 1960s, following the translation and availability of Marx's early writings.

1933 S. Hook *Towards Understanding K. Marx* ii. ix. 76 That is why Marx claimed that only in practice (*Praxis*) can problems be solved. **1936** —— *From Hegel to Marx* viii. 281 Practice (*Praxis*) was something much wider than *practicability*. It was selective behaviour... Marx's theory of the Praxis could explain what all other philosophers recognised but which they could not begin to account for, without writing fairy-tales, viz., how knowledge could give power. **1966** L. Dupré *Found. Philos. Materialism* viii. 216 But for Marx, praxis is more than a principle of consciousness: it is a prereflective unity of nature and consciousness which can be explicated in thought but not initiated. **1969** D. McLellan *Young Hegelians & Karl Marx* i. ii. 10 The main agent in this transformation was not to be thought, as in Hegel's philosophy, but will, which was the motive force for that synthesis of thought and action for which Cieszkowski coined the term, so influential later, of 'praxis'. **1971** R. J. Bernstein *Praxis & Action* (1972) p. xi, Marx.. went on to develop a thorough, systematic and comprehensive *theory of praxis*—a theory, which I shall argue, provides the key for understanding his basic outlook from his early speculations to his mature thought. **1974** *Times Lit. Suppl.* 31 May 582/5 'The embattled imagination' and 'maimed utopia', whose values are under threat in the praxis-obsessed intellectual climate of the Federal Republic. **1976** *Survey* Summer–Autumn 255 He ascribed to Marx, not a voluntarist doctrine as the negation of determinism, but a philosophy that conceived itself as historical praxis. **1978** *Daily Tel.* 23 Nov. 8/8 The new theology is seemingly based on the Marxian concept of praxis—the involvement of the oppressed in the historical processes of change.

d. Action that is entailed by theory or a function that results from a particular structure.

1953 E. L. Allen *Existentialism from Within* ii. 27 The Greeks did not speak of 'things' but of *pragmata*, implying that I have to do something (*praxis*) about them. **1962** Macquarrie & Robinson tr. *Heidegger's Being & Time* ii. iv. 409 What is decisive in the 'emergence' of the theoretical attitude would then lie in the *disappearance* of *praxis*. *Ibid.*, And just as *praxis* has its own specific kind of sight ('theory'), theoretical research is not without a *praxis* of its own. **1966** B. Haigh tr. *Luria's Human Brain & Psychol. Processes* i. 42 At first glance it may appear that lesions situated in very different parts of the brain may lead to a disturbance of praxis. **1968** J. M. Heaton *Eye* iii. 46 Thus, even at this early age, praxis has emerged, i.e. the activity of looking has become meaningful, an end in itself to the infant. **1970** E. Paci in J. M. Edie *Patterns of Life-World* 131 Since instruments are extensions either of the sensing body, or of the acting body, or of the body as organ of will and praxis, they represent a fusion of the self and nature in the body. **1972** Piccone & Hansen tr. *Paci's Function of Sci.* iii. xix. 360 Science loses its function and society hides the meaning of praxis through technistic ideology.

e. (See quot.)

1950 [see *lexis 1].

pray, *v.* Add: **5. b.** *spec.* To make a formal petition *for* (something); to move a prayer (Prayer[1] 5 in Dict. and Suppl.). Also *absol.*

1754 [in Dict.]. **1920** *Act* 10 & 11 *Geo. V* c. 67 §1 The Council shall..determine whether to issue the order as prayed for, or to issue the order with such modifications as may appear to be necessary. **1962** Hanson & Wiseman *Parliament at Work* viii. 211 The need for such an Order arose from the attempts of a group of Conservative backbenchers to 'harry the life' out of the Labour Government of 1950–51..by 'praying' into the small hours of the morning.

praya, var. *praia.

prayable, *a.* Restrict † *Obs.* to sense in Dict. and add: **b.** Of a prayer: that may be made.

1941 T. S. Eliot *Dry Salvages* ii. 10 The hardly, barely prayable Prayer of the one Annunciation.

prayed (prēid), *ppl. a.* [f. Pray *v.* + -ed[1].] In *prayed-for* adj., that is sought in prayer.

1867 C. E. Smith *Diary* 11 Mar. in C. E. S. Harris *From Deep of Sea* (1922) xvii. 224 Thank God for such a mercy! At last we are abreast of the longed-for, prayed-for Labrador. **1917** J. Masefield *Lollingdon Downs* 75 In the lonely silence I may wait The prayed-for gleam—your hand upon the gate. **1952** Dylan Thomas *Let.* 21 July (1966) 376 I'll wait in all morning for your prayed-for call.

prayer[1]. Add: **1. d.** Slang phr. *not to have* (or *have got*) *a prayer*: to have no chance.

1941 B. Schulberg *What makes Sammy Run?* vi. 92 Get..back to New York. You won't have a prayer around here. **1957** R. A. Heinlein *Door into Summer* ii. 46 'I'm going to give you some advice.'.. 'Well?' 'Do nothing. You haven't got a prayer.' **1968** E. B. White *Let.* 30 Dec. (1976) 574, I wish you luck. I don't think you have a prayer. **1973** A. Ross *Dunfermline Affair* 113 He went for me... He was a big lad, and strong, but he didn't have a prayer. An amateur up against a professional almost never does. **1977** *Time* 10 Oct. 9/3 Mitterrand was prepared to sign anything back in 1972, when his party did not have a prayer of coming to power.

5. (Later examples of *spec.* sense.) See also quot. 1958.

1937 *Hansard Commons* 4 June 1307, I undertake, if the House will allow the remaining Regulations to be passed now, to amend No 95 immediately, and the notification of the Amendment will, of course, be subject to a Prayer, just as the Regulations themselves are. **1946** *May's Treat. Parliament* (ed. 14) xiv. 286 The last item of this group consists of motions for the disallowance of statutory orders or regulations... These motions are usually in the form of addresses to the Crown praying for the annulment of orders or regulations and are hence commonly called 'Prayers'. **1958** Wilding & Laundy *Encycl. Parliament* 431 *Prayer*, a motion to annul a Statutory Instrument... Such motions count as Exempted Business..and are taken at the end of the day's sitting. They must be moved during the forty days after the order is laid on the Table, at the expiration of which it automatically becomes law. **1968** *Observer* 21 Apr. 3/3 The British Medical Association ..is arranging for a 'prayer' to be moved in Parliament. **1970** *Daily Tel.* 3 Nov. 2/6 Mr Enoch Powell, Conservative MP for Wolverhampton, South West, has a prayer down on the Commons Order Paper to annul the regulations. **1972** *Times* 23 Feb. 27/5 A..petitioner sought the direction of the court whether she might properly omit a prayer for costs from a petition which sought a decree of divorce. **1973** *N.Y. Law Jrnl.* 2 Aug. 5/3 Nowhere in this or any other document, has IBM denied the factual assertions, made by the United States, which are the basis for its prayer that IBM be held in contempt of court. **1975** J. P. Morgan *House of Lords & Labour Govt.* ii. 63 Where affirmative resolution is required both Houses must give their approval before such Orders can be passed; where an Order becomes effective unless a Prayer for annulment is carried by either House (the negative resolution procedure), the Lords again enjoy the same rights as the Commons.

6. a. *prayer-attitude, -life, service.*

1953 R. Knox *Off Record* xliv. 148 If one does a hop from Evangelicalism to the Church the difference is not so much one of doctrines as one of prayer-attitudes. *Ibid.* 150, I should find no difficulty in accepting the doctrine as doctrine, although it would make no addition to my own prayer-life. **1976** *Honolulu Star-Bull.* 21 Dec. F-2/3 Friends may call from 6 to 9 tonight at Dodo Mortuary, with prayer service scheduled for 7:30.

d. prayer bones *U.S.*, the knees; **prayer breakfast**, a breakfast during which prayers are offered; **prayer card**, a card used by a Member of Parliament for reserving a seat at prayers; **prayer chain**, a series of people each of whom receives a written prayer with an invitation to pass it or copies of it to others; **prayer circle**, a group of people who pray together; **prayer-cylinder** = Prayer-wheel; **prayer day**, a day in Parliament on which prayers (see sense 5 above) are heard; **prayer-flag**, in Tibet, a flag on which prayers are inscribed; **prayer-gong**, a gong calling people to prayer; **prayer-niche**, in a mosque, a niche in the centre of a sanctuary wall indicating the direction of Mecca; **prayer-nut**, in a chaplet, a nut-shaped bead which opens to form a diptych with reliefs; **prayer plant**, a perennial herb, *Maranta leuconeura*, belonging to the family Marantaceæ, native to Brazil, bearing irregular, three-petalled, white flowers, and often cultivated as a house plant for the sake of its shiny, variegated leaves; **prayer ring** = **prayer circle*; **prayer rug** (later examples); **prayer stool**, a stool for kneeling on while praying; **prayer ticket** = **prayer card*; **prayer-value**, efficacy or worth for prayer; **prayer-wall**, a wall on which prayers are inscribed; = *mani[2].

1926 *Amer. Speech* II. 362 *Prayer bones* (noun phrase), knees. 'Everyone get down on his prayer bones.' *a* **1944** J. Conroy in B. A. Botkin *Treas. Amer. Folklore* (1944) iv. 531 You've got to kneel down on your prayerbones... If you kneel down to save your poor old back, the little grains of sand eat into your prayerbones. **1970** C. Major *Dict. Afro-Amer. Slang* 93 *Prayer bones*, the knees. **1966** *New Statesman* 4 Mar. 285/2 The Republican governor of Oregon, is in the vanguard of a movement that sponsors 'prayer breakfasts' for politicians all around the world. **1969** *Listener* 28 Aug. 271/1 (*caption*) Billy Graham speaks at a Honolulu prayer breakfast. **1959** P. G. Richards *Hon. Members* iv. 75 No permanent reservation of seats is allowed... A Member who intends to be present at prayers at the start of a sitting can place a 'prayer card' on a bench; this card has to be obtained personally from an attendant at the House at any time after eight a.m. on the same day. **1975** *Daily Tel.* 16 Apr. 16 An interesting feature of the House of Commons before the Budget statement yesterday was the number of seats bearing Prayer Cards—reservations—on the Tory side. **1908** *Westm. Gaz.* 5 Oct. 4/1 Other ladies started prayer-chains to promote or defeat the different candidates' chances of victory. **1911** *Daily Colonist* (Victoria, B.C.) 11 Apr. 4/3 We have been requested to say something about the 'prayer chain' which is being worked again... We are told that in the time of Jesus it was said that whoever copied this prayer and sent it to nine persons would have great joy, and those who did not would have great sorrow. **1880** P. Deming *Adirondack Stories* 25 As a preliminary to the sermon, a prayer-circle was formed. **1894** I. L. Bishop *Among Tibetans* ii. 46 Prayer-cylinders which are turned by pulling ropes. **1897** *Geogr. Jrnl.* X. 35 A prayer-cylinder revolved by the wind. **1952** *Ann. Reg. 1951* 17 A motion..to cut off alcoholic refreshment after 10 p.m. on 'prayer days'. **1882** 'Shway Yoe' *Burman* I. xvii. 225 These prayer-flags..are made of paper, cut fancifully into figures of dragons, lizards, and the like, with embroidery-work round their edges. **1897** *Geogr. Jrnl.* X. 35 Groups of prayer-flags in memory of the dead are planted beside every village. **1936** [see *obo]. **1952** [see *chorten]. **1955** E. Hillary *High Adventure* 62 We sat down wearily in the snow beside a clump of Tibetan prayer-flags. **1905** E. F. Benson *Image in Sand* ix. 135, I adore theosophy, prayer-gongs, and letters from the ceiling. **1937** *Burlington Mag.* Oct. 193/2 The mihrab, or prayer-niche. **1971** *Country Life* 25 Feb. 426/1 The large construction..is an

Iranian prayer-niche in coloured tin enamel tiles (*faience*). **1937** *Burlington Mag.* Aug. 98/1 She holds a little silver chain, from which hangs..a 'prayer-nut' for a chaplet, in wrought silver. **1969** E. WILKINS *Rose-Garden Game* ii. 59 The..Chatsworth paternoster..has a terminal bead that is a little hinged box, which opens to show two miniature relief carvings... The prayer-nut is usually made of box-wood. **1953** J. HERSEY *Garden in your Window* iv. 57 The Prayer Plant, while a bit rare, is simple to grow. **1956** Y. FIELD *House Plants* iv. 97 The small maranta is a very beautiful foliage plant. Since this plant closes its leaves at night or almost curls them together it is known as the Prayer Plant. **1977** WARD & WELLSTED *Indoor Plants* 81/2 *Maranta leuconeura*... Prayer Plant, Rabbit's Tracks. This Brazilian plant has given rise to several spectacularly coloured foliage varieties. **1846** *Knickerbocker* XXVIII. 305 When a 'prayer ring' was to be formed, he announced it at the close of a sermon. **1904** Prayer-rug [see *KULAH[1]]. **1930** *Morning Post* 16 July 8/6 This fascinating old Koula Prayer Rug is believed to have been made for the Jewish Synagogue at Toledo. **1935** H. EDIB *Clown & his Daughter* xlviii. 277 Pembeh touched him on the shoulder and pointed to a prayer-rug spread at the threshold of the room. **1962** C. W. JACOBSEN *Oriental Rugs* 306 Tekke Prayer Rugs are available only from estates. **1979** *Guardian* 26 Oct. 15/2 The bearded Ayatollahs..[are] sweeping the most pressing problems under the prayer rug. **1908** *Daily Chron.* 6 Apr. 1/4 As they knelt upon the wooden prayer stool..they made no noise. **1924** J. E. MILLS *From Back Benches* ii. 9 Lady Astor..staked out the second row corner seat below the gangway, and, attending regularly.., secured her ticket from the attendant which 'booked' the seat, providing she attended prayers. All went well until Mr. Joynson Hicks, returning..after nearly a year's absence, deposited his 'prayer ticket' in.. Lady Astor's seat. **1906** W. R. INGE *Truth & Falsehood in Relig.* iv. 102 It does not satisfy those who really believe in the supernatural occurrences, which it is proposed to maintain in consideration of their 'prayer-value'. **1953** R. KNOX *Off Record* xliv. 149 It's no good contemplating becoming a Catholic unless you are prepared to accept doctrinal definitions which have, for you, no particular prayer-value. **1960** C. WINICK *Dict. Anthropol.* 562/2 *Mani wall* or *prayer wall*, a low long wall of mud and stone, covered with flat rocks, on which Tibetan characters are carved. Devout Tibetans walk with the mani wall to their right to get benefit from it. Such walls are frequently more than a quarter of a mile long. **1974** *Listener* 17 Jan. 76/2 As you walk up the trail, prayer-walls bisect the paths. The act of walking past the wall is a prayer in itself.

prayer-bead. Add: **1.** Also *gen.*, one of a string of beads used in prayer.

1975 R. P. JHABVALA *Heat & Dust* 61 The white sadhu ..had all his possessions with him—a bundle, an umbrella, prayer-beads, and a begging bowl. **1976** 'M. DELVING' *China Expert* iv. 47 He wore a string of Tibetan prayer beads around his neck. **1979** E. BERCOVICI *Wolf Trap* 145 Cotton pointed to the beads. 'What are those?' he asked pleasantly. 'Prayer beads,' the man answered, holding the strand out, trying to smile. 'Arab beads.'

prayerfully, *adv.* (Further examples.)

1962 *Friend* 16 Mar. 326/2 The decision, like all moral decisions, can only be taken, prayerfully, on the merits of the case by the individuals concerned. **1971** 'A. GARVE' *Late Bill Smith* ii. 49 She sipped a dry martini.., raising her glass prayerfully to the success of the cruise. **1973** *Daily Tel.* 3 Mar. 3/1 Before he died of starvation, David wrote..a touching letter to his parents..talking hopefully and prayerfully about his own situation. **1977** J. F. FIXX *Compl. Bk. Running* i. 5, It is to be prayerfully hoped, but not reasonably expected, that some political leader will find the gumption to blurt out the melancholy truth.

prayer-meeting. (Earlier and later examples.)

1780 *Arminian Mag.* III. 155 Some of these coming over to the prayer meetings at Wednesbury..were utterly astonished... Presently a prayer meeting was set up at Darlaston. **1817** W. SEWALL *Diary* 11 Jan. (1930) 7/1 Evening attended prayer meeting. **1928** J. BUCHAN *Runagates Club* xi. 298 It was the prayer-meeting, remember, which brought America into the War. **1954** D. S. DAVIS in *Ellery Queen's Mystery Mag.* June 27/1 Sue Thompson had..been..to Sunday prayer meeting. **1972** *News & Observer* (Raleigh, N. Carolina) 30 Dec. 4/3 Wednesday night prayer meeting..and the amen corner have gone with stewards who yelled out 'amen' during the sermon.

prayer-mill. (Earlier example.)

1832 J. BELL *Syst. Geogr.* V. 103 Prayer-mills, which are set in motion by wind or water.

pray-in: see *-IN *suffix*[3].

praying, *vbl. sb.* Add: **b.** *praying ground*; **praying flag-staff,** a staff bearing a prayer flag (see *PRAYER[1] 6 d); **praying machine** (earlier and later examples); also *transf.*; **praying mat** (earlier example).

1877 T. W. R. DAVIDS *Buddhism* 211 Everywhere in Tibet these praying flag-staffs meet the eye. **1935** Z. N. HURSTON *Mules & Men* I. ii. 39 He went way down in de swamp behind a big plantation to de place they call de prayin' ground, and got down on his knees. **1967** W. SOYINKA *Kongi's Harvest* 55 You must hurry or the confusion Will be worse than shoes before the Praying-ground at Greater Beiram. **1976** *Sunday Times* (Lagos) 26 Sept. 3/1 (*caption*) The scene at Obalende praying ground with the Lagos Chief..reading his address. **1826** S. STALLYBRASS *Jrnl.* 16 July in E. Stallybrass *Mem. Mrs. Stallybrass* (1836) iv. 203 An old man..was travelling sixty versts on foot, though not destitute of a horse, for the purpose of turning the *praying machine* for a week,.. in order to atone for past misconduct and drunkenness. **1879** *Good Words* 745/1 In the great temple there is a figure of Matreya, the coming Buddha... We..found ourselves before the top of the great praying machine, a revolving structure. **1972** C. STEPHENSON *Merrily on High* 185 Eastern [Orthodox] spirituality has tended to regard monks as primarily 'praying machines'. There has never been the tradition of 'scholar monks' which we have had in the west. **1869** 'MARK TWAIN' *Innoc. Abr.* li. 543 To step rudely upon the sacred praying mats.

praying, *ppl. a.* Add: **a.** (Later example.)

1931 F. L. ALLEN *Only Yesterday* iv. 80 The 'praying Colonels' of Centre College.

b. praying band = *prayer circle* s.v. *PRAYER[1] 6 d; **praying mantis** = *praying-insect*.

1883 *Century Mag.* Sept. 788/2 The Woman's Christian Temperance Union is the lineal descendant of the Woman's Crusade of 1874, whose first 'praying band' was led..by Mrs. Thompson. **1900** C. W. WINCHESTER *Victories of Wesley Castle* ii. 41 He had seen [him]..conducting a revival meeting with a praying-band, of which he was leader. **1937** *Sun* (Baltimore) (D ed.) 25 May 4/5 On the left sits a row of younger women—the 'praying band' or 'shout band'. **1895** Praying mantis [see MANTIS]. **1899** [see *mule-killer* s.v. *MULE[1] 5 c]. **1961** L. VAN DER POST *Heart of Hunter* xii. 161 My old coloured nurse Klara, who had a Bushman mother..showed me my first praying mantis. **1973** M. R. CROWELL *Greener Pastures* 40 They have established a cease fire, thanks to a praying mantis.

prazosin (prē·zosin). *Pharm.* [Arbitrary *pr-* (sometimes interpreted as representing *piperazine*), + AZO- + *-sin*.] A drug used (as the hydrochloride) in treating hypertension, being a vasodilator whose molecular structure incorporates quinazoline, piperazine, and furyl rings.

1970 *Jrnl. Clin. Pharmacol.* X. 417/1 These data suggest that prazosin hydrochloride is an efficacious agent for the therapy of ambulatory patients with arterial hypertension, particularly when a thiazide diuretic is given in concert. **1974** *Brit. Med. Jrnl.* 11 May 298/1 Prazosin is a new hypertensive drug thought to have a peripheral action involving direct relaxation of vascular smooth muscle and sympathetic blockade. **1978** A. S. NIES in Melmon & Morrelli *Clin. Pharmacol.* (ed. 2) vi. 200/1 Prazosin produces a number of side effects, the most prominent being weakness, dizziness, headache, palpitations and lack of energy... Postural hypotension occurring within two hours of the first few doses of prazosin has resulted in loss of consciousness in some patients.

pre-, *prefix.* Add: **A. I. 1.** With vbs., and ppl. adjs. and vbl. sbs. derived from them. *pre-address, -apprehend, -assemble, -audit, -book, -centrifuge, -clean, -coat, -compute, -cook, -decide, -dry, -film, -give* (*-given* ppl adj.; also *absol.* as sb.), *-grind, -incubate, -ionize, -know, -let, -lubricate, -machine, -own, -perceive, -plan, -polarize, -prepare, -pressurize, -publish, -qualify, -see, -separate, -soak, -think, -tune, -wash, -wear, -wrap, -write*; **prea·spirate** *Phonetics*, to aspirate (a sound) in advance of another sound; **pre-bai·ting,** the act or practice of accustoming vermin to harmless bait so that they will take poisoned bait more readily.

1912 W. OWEN *Let.* Aug. (1967) 152, I didn't bring your pre-addressed envelope. **1964** J. Z. YOUNG *Model of Brain* xii. 199 The particular classifying systems operating on any occasion are thus as it were pre-addressed. **1922** JOYCE *Ulysses* 713 What..causes, before rising preapprehended,..did Bloom..recapitulate? **1934** *Jrnl. Eng. & Gmc. Philol.* XXXIII. 191 The preaspirated tenues in Scotland are due to the same Norse substratum. **1976** *Archivum Linguisticum* VII. 95 All geminates are held to have once been preaspirated. **1960** R. W. MARKS *Dymaxion World of B. Fuller* 21/2 It is theoretically possible..to deliver a full-size, pre-assembled house by air. **1972** *Sci. Amer.* Oct. 118/2 The structure was prefabricated and preassembled in the carpentry shop complete with fans and electrical outlets. **1937** *Sun* (Baltimore) 2 Aug. 1/2 All pre-auditing shall be under the control of the executive branch of the Government. **1936** *Rep. Comm. Exper. Station* (Hawaiian Sugar Planters' Assoc.) 92 It would seem that a practice of prebaiting with unpoisoned cereal, followed by a heavy application of poisoned bait, should prove an effective means of control. **1944** J. S. HUXLEY *On Living in Revolution* x. 110 Careful study has now been made of the species [*sc.* the black rat], and this, with new methods of poisoning based on pre-baiting, is apparently providing the basis for effective control. **1973** *Times* 9 Mar. 14/1 In 1955 the anti-coagulant compounds, Warfarin and others, came on the market. No pre-baiting was needed with these. **1976** P. R. WHITE *Planning for Public Transport* vii. 149 The amendment also stipulated that minibuses only would be permitted, not for hire or reward, and that passengers would be pre-booked. *Ibid.* viii. 183 The period stipulated for pre-booking by rail appears unrealistic. **1976** *Nature* 15 Jan. 114/2 The homogenate was squeezed through nylon cloth and precentrifuged at 500g for 10 min after adjusting the *p*H to 8.0. **1954** *Sun* (Baltimore) 13 Apr. B23/4 Instead of picking around through a pile at the vegetable counter,..she can buy precleaned fresh produce of a uniform quality. **1937** *Discovery* Sept. 283/2 The press is..precoated with fresh kieselguhr. *Ibid.*, This precoating is done from a small vat. **1973** *Metal Finishing Jrnl.* XIX. 353 About 500,000 tonnes per year of pre-coated steel sheet was used in the UK for buildings. **1948** *Amazing Sci. Fiction* Sept. 146/1 The luminous track on the radar screen had scarcely deviated from the pre-computed path. **1956** *Jrnl. Assoc. Computing Machinery* III. 284 The method used..is to precompute between pass 1 and pass 2 this adjustment based on the count of each duplicated region. **1959** *Proc. Eastern Joint Computer Conf.* 170/1 Prior to the start of a given shut-down, a pre-computed schedule most applicable to the current situation is abstracted from a library of typical schedules. **1946** *Fortune* Apr. 200/2 A high-priced Restaurant carrying a sideline of precooked quick-frozen meals on plastic plates. **1964** E. BACH *Introd. Transformational Gram.* v. 92 Except with carefully 'precooked' data, there will be many conflicting ways of drawing rules together. *a* **1974** R. CROSSMAN *Diaries* (1975) I. 198 Very often the whole job is pre-cooked in the official committee to a point from which it is extremely difficult to reach any other conclusion than that already determined by the officials in advance. **1976** *Woman's Day* (N.Y.) Nov. 150/2 A step saver. No need to precook noodles. **1947** *Mind* LVI. 264 The meaning to be given to 'well-established' or to 'explanation', in history or the social sciences, cannot be pre-decided by a consideration of mathematics only. **1966** G. N. LEECH *Eng. in Advertising* i. 4 It is patently false that he writes according to a predecided formula. **1961** *Dairy Industries* Sept. 652 Particles of the product to be dried fall in counter current to slowly rising pre-dried air flowing at a rate of 0·05 to 1 meter per second. **1962** J. T. MARSH *Self-Smoothing Fabrics* xi. 171 The majority of the finishing ranges for the crease-resisting process..increase production and reduce costs by some form of partial pre-drying. **1960** D. WILSON *Television Playwright* 16 Does insistence on cinematic grammar imply that all television drama should be pre-filmed? **1969** J. ELLIOT *Duel* I. ii. 38 It was to consist of three fifty-minute programmes, all prefilmed. **1943** M. FARBER *Found. Phenomenology* xv. 506 The theory of pre-predicative experience, which 'pre-gives' the most primitive substrates in object-evidence, represents the first portion of the phenomenological theory of judgment. **1970** B. BREWSTER tr. *Althusser & Balibar's Reading Capital* (1975) III. iv. 297 In Marx's theory..a synthetic concept of time can never be a pre-given, but only a *result*. **1974** *Sci. & Society* XXXVIII. 395 The specific structure of 'unevenness' of the 'ever-pregiven complex whole' which is its existence. **1976** *Brit. Jrnl. Sociol.* XXVII. 296 The Rankean identification of history with pre-given past events. **1973** R. RENDELL *Some lie & Some Die* xiv. 121 He..smelt her grinding coffee beans—nothing pre-ground out of a packet for her. **1943** *Jrnl. Bacteriol.* XLVI. 383 One penicillin-containing set with and without glucose was allowed to preincubate uninoculated at 37°C., and a similar set at 2°C. **1977** *Lancet* 18 June 1310/1 The epithelial cells were not stained when tissue sections were preincubated in unlabelled α-B.T. before the standard reaction. **1940** *Jrnl. Appl. Physics* XI. 471/1 Then over the pre-ionized streamer channel the brilliant return stroke..follows at a speed of 10^{10} cm per second. **1979** *Nature* 7 June 477/3 For light ions, such long-distance propagation must be carefully arranged through a pre-ionised neutralising plasma channel, raising serious questions of possible propagation instabilities. **1867** J. S. MILL *Let.* 14 Feb. (1910) II. x. 76 Our freedom may be real though God preknows our actions. **1976** *Field* 30 Dec. 1292/2 (Advt.), Most of our beats are pre-let but we have one or two vacancies through late cancellation. **1961** *Motor Sport* Dec. 1003/1 In America Oldsmobile, Ford, Mercury, Lincoln, Plymouth, Dodge and Chrysler have adopted pre-lubricated chassis bearings. **1976** *Lebende Sprachen* XXI. 151/2 For further information about pre-lubricated bearings see Figure 1, Detail A. **1971** *Physics Bull.* July 406/3 Deep penetration welding using electron beams is becoming quite widely used for assembling pre-machined parts into complex assemblies as an economic alternative to forging, casting and mechanical fastening. **1977** *Offshore Engineer* Apr. 28/1 The system uses an internal clamp/welder to locate, clamp and make an inside root pass in about two minutes on a pre-machined pipe joint preparation. **1964** *Listener* 25 June 1030/3 Used cars are now referred to as pre-owned [in the U.S.A.]. **1970** M. PEI *Words in Sheep's Clothing* ii. 12 'Pre-owned' is described as the modern euphemism for 'second-hand'. **1977** *Caravan World* (Austral.) Jan. 3 (Advt.), 2 acres of pre-owned caravans and boats can be inspected. **1890** W. JAMES *Princ. Psychol.* I. xi. 444 In short, *the only things which we commonly see are those which we preperceive*, and the only things which we preperceive are those which have been labelled for us, and the labels stamped into our mind. **1934** WEBSTER, Preplan. **1948** *Times Rev. Industry* Aug. 18/3 Obviously continuous production must be pre-planned but thereafter is self-progressive. **1958** *Times* 11 Feb. 4/4 (Advt.), Preplanning the entire project ensures smooth continuity of operations and speedy completion. **1965** *Language* XLI. 92 Since this is not a preplanned book..there is a certain amount of repetition. **1976** *Daily Tel.* 13 Aug. 1/7 The positive anti-riot tactics, clearly pre-planned.., were introduced to counter any IRA organised trouble. **1977** J. M. JOHNSON in Douglas & Johnson *Existential Sociol.* viii. 231 None of the events described were anticipated or preplanned by the members in advance of their occurrence. **1949** *Jrnl. Acoustical Soc. Amer.* XXI. 199/1 The..temperature at which the output voltage falls to zero for a pre-polarized specimen. *Ibid.* 200/2 The voltage gradient necessary fully to pre-polarize varies with the time allotted to polarizing. **1957** E. G. RICHARDSON *Technical Aspects Sound* II. ii. 70 The tube is metallized on the inner and outer surfaces, pre-polarized radially, and the alternating current applied in the same direction. **1968** *Guardian* 16 Feb. 3/2 Pre-prepared dishes, such as fish and chips. **1978** *Guardian Weekly* 29 Oct. 12/3 The President didn't deliver pre-prepared phrases, but stayed close to events. **1945** *Jrnl. Amer. Chem. Soc.* LXVII. 157/1 A current is passed through previously pressurized acid water, and bubbles form in prepressurized water when it is quickly frozen. **1971** *Arch. Biochem. & Biophysics* CXLII. 325/2 The enzyme was prepressurized for 10 min. **1973** W. H. HALLAHAN *Ross Forgery* vi. 120 'A Lodging for the Night' —first published in a collection..under the title *The New Arabian Nights* in 1882..was not known to have been pre-published separately. **1977** *Lancet* 25 June 1350/2 He asserted..that an article whose contents had already received detailed attention in the papers and on the air had..been prepublished and forfeited its claim to entry as news in a medical journal. **1974** *Times* 27 Apr. 14/4 The drudgery of having to pre-qualify for [golf] tournaments. **1976** *Sunday Mail* (Glasgow) 28 Nov. 39/3 He finished in the top 25 last year, which ensured he doesn't have to prequalify this year for Turnberry in July. **1980** *Times* 29 Feb. 23 (Advt.), The Irrigation Department and the Electric Power Corporation invite qualified and experienced contractors..wishing to be pre-qualified as tenderers. **1931** JOYCE *Let.* 22 Aug. (1966) III. 227 You advised me to proceed against Roth... I did though I presaw the result. **1967** E. CHAMBERS *Photolitho-Offset* iii. 30 Pre-separated colour art work can be prepared using Bourges Colotone overlays. **1967** KARCH & BUBER *Offset Processes* iii. 64 Kits are useful in the preparation of pre-separated full-color process copy. **1919** *Science* 6 June 544/2 (*heading*) Presoaking as a means of preventing seed injury due to disinfectants and of increasing germicidal efficiency. *Ibid.* 545/1 The presoaked seeds are thoroughly wetted in the 1:80 solution..for ten minutes. **1974** *Indian Jrnl. Agric. Sci.* XLIII. 973/1 An experiment was laid out..in polythene bags with presoaked pupthene seeds in different N solutions. **1960** *20th Cent.* Sept. 242 This kind of talk is not formalized or pre-thought. **1966** 'A. HALL' *9th Directive* xii. 112 The Bureau..takes no action without the most serious pre-thinking. **1977** E. LEONARD *Unknown Man No. 89* xvii. 155 Pre-think your options. **1964** J. CARNOCHAN in D. Abercrombie et al. *Daniel Jones* 399 A series of pre-tuned reeds. **1974** HARVEY & BOHLMAN *Stereo F.M. Radio Handbk.* iii. 41 Within this narrow band it is possible to pre-tune the r.f. stage to 98 MHz. **1977** Pre-wash [see *PROGRAM, PROGRAMME *sb.* 2 g (i)]. **1976** *New Musical Express* 12 Feb. 40/1 (Advt.), Genuine 'Levi & Levi' type jeans, preworn and shrunk, just need patches. **1934** WEBSTER, Pre-wrap. **1959** *Times* 9 Mar. (Britain's Food Suppl.) p. vi/4 Pre-wrapped retail portions of natural cheese have been on the market for some years. **1963** *Economist* 29 June 1357/1 More and more cigars are..marketed pre-wrapped in large packs. **1951** DYLAN THOMAS *Let.* 12 Apr. (1966) 358, I would bring great packages of new poems to read, and much more pre-written prose to pad them in. **1969** *Computers & Humanities* IV. 106 This object code and a prewritten subroutine which searches the date item for the required elements becomes the Phase II control program.

2. With a sb. *pre-audit, -auditor, -censorship, -civilization, -coat, -evangelism, -excitation, -hearing, -incubation, -intimation, -knowledge* (later examples), *-negotiation, -oxygenation, -polarization, -pressurization, -publicity, -qualification, -rehearsal, -taste, -verbalization*; **pre-a·djunct** *Gram.*, an adjunct that precedes the word it modifies; also *attrib.*; **pre-aspira·tion** *Phonetics*, aspiration that precedes another sound; **preco·ntour** *Phonetics*, one or more unstressed syllables which precede the peak of a contour; **pre·pulse**, a preliminary pulse of electricity; **prerea·ction**, chemical reaction occurring before some other process; **pre-·rinse**, a preliminary rinse given to something before it is washed; **preseni·lity** *Med.*, premature senility; **pre-·soak**, (*a*) a soaking given prior to some subsequent process or treatment; (*b*) a liquid used for this; also *attrib.*; **pre-·wash**, a preliminary wash, used *spec.* as the name of a setting on an automatic washing-machine; also *attrib.*

1898 Pre-adjunct [see *head-word* s.v. *HEAD *sb.* 66]. **1914** O. JESPERSEN *Mod. Eng. Gram.* II. xiv. 331 There are some adjectives that are hardly ever used predicatively, and on the other hand some that are hardly ever used as pre-adjuncts. *Ibid.* 333 The averseness to pre-adjunct employment..has been transferred to other words beginning with an *a-* of a different origin. **1957** *Publ. Amer. Dial. Soc.* XXVIII. 123 *What, which, whose,* and *how* serve as pre-adjuncts: 1 What book?; 2 How far is it? **1945** S. EINARSSON *Icelandic* I. 1 Aspiration, a breath (ʰ) following or preceding (preaspiration) the stops *p, t, k*, is indicated by an ʰ. **1965** H. WOLTER in *Proc. 5th Internat. Congr. Phonetic Sci. 1964* 595 The auditory impression of the pre-aspiration is rather like an [h], although in connection with [t] it may sound like an [f]. **1976** *Archivum Linguisticum* VII. 91 Preaspiration is not, according to Liberman, a voiceless vowel, although it does cause the end of a preceding vowel to be devoiced. **1938** *Sun* (Baltimore) 2 Apr. 6/2 It retains the principle of pre-audit but it makes the pre-auditor amenable to Presidential authority. **1962** *Guardian* 6 Nov. 9/4 Today's issue was subjected to pre-censorship by the State Prosecutor's office. *a* **1974** R. CROSSMAN *Diaries* (1976) II. 663 The Lord Chancellor immediately replied that this would involve having pre-censorship all over again because if the licensees could be sued for libel then they would start controlling the plays. **1949** R. A. S. MACALISTER *Archæol. of Ireland* (ed. 2) p. x, It [*sc.* Ireland] has rendered to Anthropology the unique.. service of carrying a primitive European *Precivilization* down into late historic times. **1946** Precoat [see *filter aid* s.v. *FILTER *sb.* 5]. **1945** K. L. PIKE *Intonation Amer. Eng.* iii. 29 Immediately preceding the stressed syllable of a primary contour there oftentimes will be one or more syllables which are pronounced in the same burst of speed with that primary contour but which themselves are unstressed. These syllables may be called precontours, and depend for their pronunciation upon the syllables which follow them. They may constitute grammatically independent words,..or they may be parts of a word. **1962** B. M. H. STRANG *Mod. Eng. Struct.* 53 A contour may be preceded by one or more unstressed syllables forming a *pre-contour*; special meanings may be conveyed by varying the level of the pre-contour, but ordinarily it is spoken at pitch-level 3 unless the contour begins on level 3, which tends to lower the pre-contour. **1975** *Amer. Speech 1972* XLVII. 185 In many dialects, the medial consonant disappears in the precontour, as in *twenty-óne, United Státes.* **1968** F. A. SCHAEFFER *God who is There* v. ii. 143 Pre-evangelism must come before evangelism... The reason we have not been reaching many of these people is because we have not taken enough time with pre-evangelism. **1951** K. S. LASHLEY in Saporta & Bastian *Psycholinguistics* (1961) 186/2 Such contaminations might be ascribed to differences in the relative strength of associative bonds between the elements of the act, and thus not evidence for pre-excitation of the elements or for simultaneous pre-excitation. **1976** *Lancet* 30 Oct. 938/2 The electrocardiographic appearances in hypertrophic cardiomyopathy may erroneously suggest the presence of pre-excitation. **1934** WEBSTER, Prehearing. **1968** *Listener* 5 Sept. 315/3 The programmes were recorded in July and at a pre-hearing the impression was of an extension of current permissiveness rather than musical revolution. **1977** *Gramophone* June 95/3 On this disc the Cathedral choir,.. have given an opulent preview (or pre-hearing) of some of the music for the great day. **1943** *Jrnl. Bacteriol.* XLVI. 383 In the presence of glucose, preincubation of the sterile solutions caused a clear-cut reduction in penicillin inhibition. **1977** *Nature* 6 Jan. 58/2 Preincubation with increasing numbers of suppressor cells yielded successively less active supernatants. **1923** J. W. HARVEY tr. *Otto's Idea of Holy* xx. 171 This is nothing else than the pure *impulsion* to *redemption*, and the pre-intimation and anticipation of a boded 'good'. **1925** *Law Reports: Appeal Cases* 730 Expressing the matter in my own words, I would say that a threat is a pre-intimation of proposed action of some sort. **1962** *Science Survey* III. 290 For many of these fish, and certainly the majority of salmon, it is the first time the journey has been made and they can have no pre-knowledge of the route or the obstacles in front of them. **1979** G. SWARTHOUT *Skeletons* 177 Guiding myself through the gloom as much by preknowledge as eyesight. **1960** *Guardian* 22 June 9/1 The pre-negotiations may last some days. **1967** *Economist* 25 Nov. 834/1 The idea..was to slide covertly into pre-negotiations with Britain by the device of asking the commission to talk with the British about devaluation. **1961** *Lancet* 19 Aug. 405/2 If a short-acting muscle relaxant is also used, conditions for intubation are obtained more quickly. Preoxygenation of the patient is a wise precaution. **1961** C. F. GELL in H. G. Armstrong *Aerospace Med.* x. 145/1 Preoxygenation, or the breathing of 100 per cent oxygen at sea level, is a procedure that was utilized prior to high level flights in airplanes without pressurized cockpits or in the absence of pressurized suits. **1965** *Gloss. Aeronaut. Terms (B.S.I.)* XVII. 3 *Preoxygenation*, a process of breathing pure oxygen before flight in order to give protection against decompression sickness by eliminating nitrogen from the body tissues and fluids. **1950** *Industr. & Engin. Chem.* Feb. 264/2 An alternating stress..is applied parallel to the direction of polarization, and conversely, expansion and contraction in the direction of an electric alternating current field superimposed parallel to the prepolarization. **1953** *Jrnl. Acoustical Soc. Amer.* XXV. 294/2 Although polycrystalline barium titanate is basically an electrostrictive material, by prepolarization it assumes properties which make it very similar to piezoelectric materials. **1971** *Arch. Biochem. & Biophysics* CXLII. 327/2 For most of the enzymic activities the restoration or stimulation of activity by pressure was closely related to the amount of activity remaining during the prepressurization. **1963** *Times* 19 Feb. 12/4 The sum includes pre-publicity, brochures, and the specialist 'after-care'. **1969** *New Scientist* 23 Oct. 172/1 An unusual amount of prepublicity hinting at a good show. **1979** *Times* 1 Dec. 12/5 No lavish pre-publicity on the free plug circuit. **1978** *Nature* 2 Feb. 474/1 A 25–50-ms conditioning prepulse was used to determine the relationship between inactivation and membrane potential before and after glyoxal treatment. **1969** *Jane's Freight Containers 1968–69* 302/3 Pre-qualification of tenderers on an international basis for the wharf construction has been processed in liaison with the World Bank. **1979** *Daily Tel.* 19 Oct. 24 (Advt.), Kingdom of Swaziland Ministry of Works, Power and Communications. International invitation for tender prequalification. **1975** *Nature* 2 Oct. 368/2 Prereaction did not enable him to go leaner than 3·4% methane. **1978** *Ibid.* 12 Jan. 165/2 Preincubation of the antiserum with purified β_4-μ reduced all peaks to background level, whereas pre-reaction with BSA had no effect. **1962** A. NISBETT *Technique Sound Studio* vi. 106 Pre-rehearsals and perhaps pre-recordings of the complicated parts will be necessary. **1972** *Listener* 6 July 3/1 A good deal of pre-rehearsal often takes place away from the station, but WGBH can only offer one hour of studio rehearsal time. **1950** J. G. DAVIS *Dict. Dairying* 71 A jetting pre-rinse which raises the temperature of the bottle at the same time. **1963** *Which?* Feb. 50/1 It was easy to give a cold pre-rinse and it improved the washing performance. **1970** *Ibid.* Oct. 293/1 For most, there was a pre-rinse and a choice of two washing programmes, depending on how dirty the dishes were. **1900** DORLAND *Med. Dict.* 535/1 Presenility. **1902** *Brit. Med. Jrnl.* 16 Aug. 472/1 Another symptom of presenility is an early impairment of memory, especially of substantives. **1933** *Arch. Dermatol. & Syphilol.* XXVIII. 553 The cause of pseudoxanthoma elasticum is unknown... Jones, Alden and Bishop entertained the belief that since the disease is allied to the changes found in elastosis senilis, it is an evidence of presenility. **1972** *Albrecht v. Graefes Arch. f. klin. und exper. Ophthalm.* CLXXXIV. 314 Histologic changes in the corpus geniculatum laterale in older persons, presenility (Alzheimer's disease) and in senile dementia. **1919** *Science* 6 June 545/1 The disinfectant..must be applied at the end of the presoak period. **1920** *Jrnl. Agric. Res.* XIX. 371 A 6-hour presoak followed by a 6-hour treatment with formalin. **1969** *Chem. & Engin. News* 3 Feb. 16/1 Makers of enzyme-active detergents and presoaks compete strongly for a place in the..home laundry products market. **1976** *Chem. in Brit.* XII. 117/1 Proteases are incorporated into presoak and heavy duty washing powders and this is the major outlet for industrial enzymes. **1956** E. M. FORSTER *Marianne Thornton* 18 To look out through the high glass door, upon the magnificent Tulip Tree, became a ritual, and almost a pretaste of heaven. *a* **1974** R. CROSSMAN *Diaries* (1975) I. 329 We were a typical Labour Party gathering, which gave us a pre-taste of the Blackpool hotels when Conference starts in a few days' time. **1959** J. C. CATFORD in Quirk & Smith *Teaching of English* vi. 188 Conscious preverbalisation in L1, and translation into L2, may be entirely suppressed, but errors due to interference from L1 still keep breaking through. **1962** *Which?* Aug. 234/2 Up to 6 minutes pre-wash soak or 10 minutes washing. **1966** D. V. DAVIS *New Domestic Encycl.* iv. 131 If you have a fully-automatic washing machine, use the Pre-wash or Rinse programme. **1970** *Which?* May 143/2 The Bendix LTA had a pre-wash that could be included in the automatic cycle.

3. With an adj. *precombustible.*

1922 JOYCE *Ulysses* 657 Fanned by a constant updraught of ventilation between the kitchen and the chimney-flue, ignition was communicated from the faggots of precombustible fuel to polyhedral masses of bituminous coal.

II. 4. a. In adverbial relation to an adj. **precommissu·ral**, anterior to a commissure of the brain; **preoptic** (examples).

1896 *Q. Jrnl. Microsc. Sci.* XXXIX. 184 The cerebrum of Platypus..conforms to the mammalian type, yet numerous features—such as..the 'precommissural area'—indicate its close Saceropsidean affinities. **1900** A. HILL tr. *Obersteiner's Anat. Central Nervous Organs* (ed. 2) 429 A small portion of the fornix which streams on to the septum pellucidum (præcommissural fibres of Huxley) ought to be reckoned as fibres of association. **1953** G. A. G. MITCHELL *Anat. Autonomic Nervous System* viii. 99 A small fascicle of fornix fibres given off near the interventricular foramen passes downwards in front of the anterior commissure... In rabbits this precommissural fascicle ends in the medial and lateral septal nuclei and in the nucleus accumbens. **1971** J. Z. YOUNG *Anat. Nervous System Octopus Vulgaris* iv. 69 There is a direct connection between the rather enigmatic precommissural region and the anterior pedal lobe. **1889** *Cent. Dict.* VI. 4694/3 *Preoptic*, anterior with respect to optic lobes; pregeminal: specifically noting the anterior pair of the optic lobes or corpora quadrigemina of the brain. **1907** J. B. JOHNSTON *Nervous System Vertebr.* xviii. 297 Surrounding the preoptic recess is a layer of cells of very primitive character. **1970** *Jrnl. Anat.* CVII. 186 Evidence which indicates that the preoptic area is involved in the control of reproductive function.

B. I. 1. Also with (Eng. or other) sbs. directly forming sbs., as *pre-cancer, -climax, -delinquency, -menarche, -myelocyte*, etc. (below). Also *PREHOMINID, *PREPUBERTY, etc.

a. Formed on proper nouns (or their adjectives). *pre-Alfredian* (example), *-Arnoldian, -Augustinian, -Baconian* (examples), *-Caroline* [Charlemagne], *-Chaucerian* (example), *-Constantinian, -Copernican* (example), *-Darwinian* (examples), *-Galilean* (examples), *-Hitlerian, -Hitlerite, -Kantian, -Keynesian, -Linnæan, -Listerian, -Malthusian, -Mendelian, -Victorian* (examples); *pre-Celtic* (examples), *-European, -Fascist, -Greek* (example), *-Han, -Hispanic, -Nazi, -Saxon* (examples), *-Soviet, -Vedic.*

c. In pathological terms. *pre-cancerous* (earlier and later examples), *-epileptic, -malignant, -pathological, -symptomatic.*

d. Formed on other adjectives. *pre-capitalist, -capitalistic, -chemical, -cinematographic, -civilized, -coitional, -colonial, -conceptual, -conciliar, -copulative, -evolutionary, -experimental* (hence *-experimentally* adv.), *-feudal, -filmic, -industrial, -industrialist, -intellectual, -lexical, -literary, -matutinal, -modern, -orgasmic, -paroxysmal, -personal, -philosophical, -phonemic, -political* (examples), *-predicative, -prep, -preparatory, -primary, -rabbinical, -romanesque, -socialist, -telescopic, -theoretical, -tragic, -transformational*; freq. in *Gram.*, as *pre-accentual, -adjectival, -adverbial, -consonantal* (so *preconsonantally* adv.), *-infinitival, inflexional, -junctural, -pausal, suffixal, -syllabic.*

pre-a·dult, -adu·lt, prior to the attainment of adulthood; **pre-a·gonal, -ago·nic** *Med.*, occurring immediately before, or premonitory of, the death agony; **pre-agricul·tural** *Anthrop.*, that has not yet developed agriculture as a means of subsistence; **pre-analy·tic, -analy·tical**, preceding analysis; hence **pre-analy·tically** *adv.*; **pre-a·rticle** *sb. Gram.*, one of a set of words that can precede an article in a noun phrase; **pre-bacteriolo·gic, -lo·gical**, previous to the discovery of the relationship of bacteria to disease; **pre-ca·ncer** *sb. Med.*, a condition that implies an increased risk of the future development of cancer; cf. *pre-cancerous*, sense B. 1 c in Dict. and Suppl.; **prece·llular** *Biol.*, prior to the origin of cellular life; **pre-ci·vil**, prior to the development of social organization; **precli·max** *sb. Ecology*, the point in a plant succession at which development has ceased before the state of climax is reached; **preconvu·lsive** *Med.*, preceding a convulsion; **pre-cu·ltural**, pertaining to human existence prior to or independent of cultural development; **pre-deli·nquency** *sb.*, behaviour which is likely to result in (juvenile) delinquency; hence **pre-deli·nquent** *a.* and *sb.*; **pre-emerge·nt** = *pre-emergence* (sense B. 2 below); **pre-erythrocy·tic** *Biol.*, occurring or existing in the period between the entry of a malaria parasite into the body as a sporozoite and the subsequent entry into red blood cells of schizonts descended from the sporozoites; **pre-expone·ntial** *Math.*, occurring as a non-exponential multiplier of an exponential quantity; **prega·mic** *Cytology*, prior to the formation of gametes; **prega·strular** *Biol.*, prior to gastrulation; **pregeolo·gical**, occurring in, or pertaining to, the period of the earth's history earlier than the time of formation of the oldest known rocks; hence **pregeolo·gically** *adv.*; **pregra·mmar** *sb. Linguistics* (see quots.); **programma·tical** *Linguistics*, applied to an assumed period in linguistic communication prior to the existence of grammatical structure; **pre-i·ctal** *Med.*, preceding a stroke or fit, esp. an epileptic fit; **pre-Inca·ic** = *pre-Incarial*; **pre-La·tin**, designating (any of) the Italic languages older than Latin; **prelo·gic** *sb.*, a mode of thought that does not yet conform to logical reasoning (cf. *PRELOGICAL *a.*); **pre-meio·tic** *Cytology*, occurring before meiosis; that has not yet undergone meiosis; **premena·rche** *sb. Med.*, the premenarchal period in a girl's life; **premena·rchal, -mena·rcheal, -mena·rchial,** of, pertaining to, or designating a girl in the few years before the onset of menstruation; **pre-mo·ral**, pertaining to a stage of development prior to the personal acceptance of moral responsibility; hence **pre-mora·lity** *sb.*; **premy·elocyte** *sb. Anat.* = *MYELOBLAST; hence **premy:elo·cy·tic**; **preneopla·stic** *Med.*, before or prefatory to the development of a neoplasm; **pre-·noun** *sb. Gram.*, a word that generally precedes a noun and is in close syntactical relation to it; **pre-ovula·tory** *Med.*, before ovulation; **prepa·tent** *Med.*, applied to the period between parasitic infection of a host and the time when the parasite can be first detected; so **prepa·tency** *sb.*, the condition of an infected host during the prepatent period; **prepla·netary** *Astr.*, existing before the formation of planets; *spec.* constituting the material from which the planets were formed; **pre-pla·nting**, applied or performed before the crop is planted; also *absol.*; **preproinsulin** (prī·prō͵insiŭlin) *sb. Biochem.*, a precursor of proinsulin; **prepu·beral** = *pre-pubertal*; so **prepu·berally** *adv.*; **pre-pubertal** (further examples); hence **prepu·bertally** *adv.*; **pre-refle·ctive, -refle·xive,** prior to reflection or reasoning thought; **pre-relativi·stic**, before the theory of relativity was published (in 1905 and 1915); **pre-reprodu·ctive**, prior to the time when an individual becomes capable of reproduction; **preschizophre·nic**, of or pertaining to the period prior to the onset of schizophrenia; as *sb.*, a person showing symptoms similar to those observed prior to schizophrenia; so **preschizophre·nia** *sb.*; **prese·nile** *Med.*, occurring in or characteristic of the period of life preceding old age, esp. the two or three decades immediately before; **preso·lar, preste·llar** *Astr.*, not (yet) having formed a star or stars; **pre-stru·cturalist**, prior to the development of structural linguistics; **pre-systema·tic**, prior to the development of a formal system; so **pre-systema·tically** *adv.*; **preve·rnal**, pertaining to a season before or very early in spring.

1965 W. S. Allen *Vox Latina* v. 85 Pre-accentual loss in *disciplina*. **1965** N. Chomsky *Aspects of Theory of Syntax* iv. 148 Verbs are strictly subcategorized into Intransitives, Transitives, pre-Adjectival, pre-Sentence. **1977** *Word 1972* XXVIII. 94 From an Old Irish system of separate comparative and superlative suffixes, the language will have changed to a system of separate comparative and superlative preadjectival particles. **1902** *Buck's Handbk. Med. Sci.* (rev. ed.) IV. 527/2 The condition.. becomes manifest during the growing or preadult period. **1974** *Sci. Amer.* Sept. 127/3 A husband, a wife and their preadult children. **1977** *Bull. Amer. Acad. Arts & Sci.* Oct. 25 Since the goals of adults tend to reflect their preadult formative experiences, the changing assessment of progress as it is traditionally understood may prove to be essentially an integrational phenomenon. **1976** *Archivum Linguisticum* VII. 32 Absolute-final position is the norm for final position, with pre-adverbial positions as optional variants in sentences where non-sentence adverbials occur. **1900** *Buck's Handbk. Med. Sci.* (rev. ed.) I. 563/1 Immediately preceding death there is an intense congestion of the viscera which frequently results in an outpour of serum. This condition, when involving the peritoneal cavity, is termed pre-agonal ascites. **1974** L. Watson *Romeo Error* iii. 66 Professor Negovskii of the Soviet Academy of Medical Sciences calls them shock, preagonal state, agony and chemical death. **1886** *Buck's Handbk. Med. Sci.* II. 49/1 A sudden high elevation of temperature..after a chill in a previously apyretic case, means a complication, and not a fatal issue, but a hyperpyrexia without chill, and with a profuse sweat, is pre-agonic. **1927** *Contemp. Rev.* July 85 The moon to pre-agricultural society was the real magic. **1947** *Sci. Amer.* Sept. 47/1 The preagricultural population..must have been vulnerable to changes in climate..and to the disappearance of species of prey. **1975** J. G. Evans *Environment Early Man Brit. Isles* iii. 55 The mixed deciduous woodlands of pre-agricultural Britain. **1962** H. R. Loyn *Anglo-Saxon Eng.* ii. 79 The pre-Alfredian period is rich in reference to Anglo-Saxon saints and scholars. **1929** C. I. Lewis *Mind & World-Order* ii. 54 The acceptance of such preanalytic data as an ultimate epistemological category would..put an end to all worthwhile investigation. **1939** *Mind* XLVIII. 89 He holds that philosophy must begin with the pre-analytic data of experience as these are expressed in common-sense judgments. **1927** *Jrnl. Philos.* XXIV. 9 The given is for science a continual challenge, always remaining 'pre-analytical', in the sense of never condemning as bootless the task of more searching analysis. **1965** A. C. Danto *Analytical Philos. Hist.* x. 207 From the Deduction Assumption, together with our pre-analytical notion of explanatory *in*adequacy, we may..elicit the remainder of Hempel's Analysis. **1934** Cohen & Nagel *Introd. Logic* xix. 385 Analysis..may reveal many complexities in the pre-analytically simple object or concept. **1951** *Mind* LX. 550 Something which we knew pre-analytically to be true. **1886** C. M. Yonge *Chantry House* I. iii. 22 In those pre-Arnoldian times no lofty code of honour was even ideal among school-boys. **1965** Pre-article [see *post-article* s.v. *post- B. 1 c]. **1971** Pre-article [see *non-lexical* s.v. *non- 3]. **1959** J. Blish *Clash of Cymbals* iii. 72 'Pre-Augustinean time' came to be something that a historian could know all about, but a physicist, by definition, nothing. **1964** P. F. Anson *Bishops at Large* i. 44 Restoring the pre-Augustinian tradition in Britain. **1865** Mill *Exam. Hamilton's Philos.* xxiv. 469 Generality of the pre-Baconian type. **1953** K. Britton *J. S. Mill* v. 152 The enquiry into microscopic conditions was distinguished in pre-Baconian logic as the enquiry into *material causes*. **1902** *Buck's Handbk. Med. Sci.* (rev. ed.) IV. 391/2 It..was long ago expressed by Alexander von Humboldt.., to be sure, in pre-bacteriologic language. **1892** *Pall Mall Gaz.* 6 Feb. 2/1 He was educated in the pre-bacteriological era, and had little sympathy with modern developments of medical science. **1965** S. Peller in Glass & Eversley *Population in Hist.* v. 94 In the pre-bacteriological era, the survival rates for the ruling families were far ahead of those of the general population. **1938** Dorland *Med. Dict.* (ed. 18) 1129/2 *Precancer*, an abnormal growth which is likely to develop into cancer. **1963** *New Statesman* 19 July 71 Precancer means cells which, if left untreated, will eventually develop into invasive cancer. *Ibid.*, Microscopic studies of the cervical smears showed..five cases of pre-cancers. **1882** *Brit. Med. Jrnl.* 7 Jan. 5/1 (*heading*) The precancerous stage of cancer, and the importance of early operations. **1975** *Sci. Amer.* Nov. 78/3 Screening programs have an additional shortcoming: for every cancer they detect they reveal perhaps 10 other abnormalities, many of which seem to be precancerous. **1949** I. Deutscher *Stalin* vi. 194 It was, however, a formidable task to adjust their pre-capitalist, often pre-feudal and even nomad ways of life to the Marxist, Communist policies of the central Government. **1952** V. A. Demant *Relig. & Decline of Capitalism* i. 28 Spontaneous social co-operation such as is universal in pre-capitalist societies. **1974** B. Pearce tr. *Amin's Accumulation on World Scale* I. ii. 141 Non-European precapitalist societies were not fundamentally different from those of Europe. **1979** *China Now* Jan.–Feb. 22/1 Abrupt transformation of the feudal and pre-capitalist organizational structures. **1940** Wirth & Shils tr. *Mannheim's Ideology & Utopia* iii. 108 Two types of irrationalism..on the one hand, precapitalistic, traditionalistic irrationalism. **1959** *Brno Studies in English* I. 73 It would be unjust..to explain this preference for pre-capitalistic epochs merely as a means of escape. **1897** Pre-Caroline [see *half-uncial* s.v. *half- II. n]. **1934** Priebsch & Collinson *German Lang.* ix. 356 The oldest German or rather Latin–German MS...is written in a pre-Caroline minuscule. **1948** D. Diringer *Alphabet* 545 The pre-Caroline book-hand in North Italy. **1946** *Nature* 21 Sept. 406/2 A new..theory: that they [*sc.* bacteriophages] were the direct descendants of precellular stages in the evolution of living forms. **1974** *Proc. Nat. Acad. Sci.* LXXI. 286/2 (*heading*) An hypothesis for the initiation of precellular evolution. **1934** S. Robertson *Devel. Mod. Eng.* (1936) ii. 18 The pre-Hellenic inhabitants of Greece..were not Indo-European, nor were the Etruscans in Italy, the pre-Celtic peoples who inhabited Britain, or the Basques in Spain. **1953** K. Jackson *Lang. & Hist. Early Brit.* 342 The name may very well be pre-Celtic. **1977** *Word 1972* XXVIII. 29 A pre-Celtic layer is now hardly identified with certainty through faint indices. **1909** R. Bridges *Let.* 29 Oct. (1940) 74, I have never studied the pre-Chaucerian verse. **1973** P. A. Colinvaux *Introd. Ecol.* xxix. 416 He was able to undo the mischief that contact poisons had done and leave the plantations in the security of the pre-chemical age. **1974** M. Taylor tr. *Metz's Film Lang.* iii. 32 The most obvious pictorial juxtaposition, the most properly literary effect of composition, were, to hear him, prophetically precinematographic. **1957** C. Vereker *Devel. Polit. Theory* iii. 98 The metaphorical language used by political thinkers who posit a pre-civil social condition is usually designated contractual. **1960** C. S. Lewis *Studies in Words* 62 That pre-civil condition was described as *nature* or 'the state of *nature*'. **1953** S. Spender *Creative Element* 30 It also includes the whole universe, the unexplored, or uncivilized, or pre-civilized areas of the map. **1956** R. Redfield *Peasant Society & Culture* iii. 77 Having developed out of the precivilized peoples of that very culture. **1916** F. E. Clements *Plant Succession* vi. 110 As a consequence [of reduced water-content], development would cease before reaching the climax proper, and the potential community ..may be called the preclimax. **1929** Weaver & Clements *Plant Ecol.* xviii. 424 The prairie itself is a preclimax to the deciduous forest with higher rainfall. **1960** N. Polunin *Introd. Plant. Geogr.* xi. 331 There are instances in which an apparent climax constitutes in reality a preclimax. **1959** K. E. L. Simmons in D. A. Bannerman *Birds Brit. Isles* VIII. 218 The ceremonies are not 'pre-coitional' in that they do not lead immediately to mating. **1961** *John o' London's* 18 May 543/2 The pre-colonial history of Africa. **1975** A. Drummond *Thames Jrnls. Vicesimus Lush* 18 No mention appears to have been made of potential goldfields in pre-colonial New Zealand. **1956** J. S. Bruner et al. *Study of Thinking* iii. 50 It is curiously difficult to recapture preconceptual innocence... It is as if the mastery of a conceptual distinction were able to mask the preconceptual memory of the things now distinguished. **1967** *Sunday Times* 22 Jan. 10 Everyone tends to exaggerate the mutual isolation of pre-conciliar days. **1976** *Times* 9 Aug. 11/1 The post-conciliar church polishes characteristically pre-conciliar weapons of censure, interdict, suspension and excommunication. **1978** *Times Lit. Suppl.* 25 Aug. 944/2 A spiritual tangle of casuistry and superstition entirely typical of pre-Conciliar Catholicism. **1951** Trager & Smith *Outl. Eng. Struct.* I. 28 Most Northern Middle Western speakers have simple vowel before final or pre-consonantal *r*. **1965** W. S. Allen *Vox Latina* i. 43 Before it [*sc.* h]..the articles take their pre-consonantal rather than prevocalic form. **1976** *Archivum Linguisticum* VII. 163 He postulates the forms set down below, in which monophthongization would have been produced in pre-consonantal forms. **1953** K. Jackson *Lang. & Hist. Early Brit.* II. 470 (*heading*) IE [*sc.* Indo-European] *gu̯*. This became *b* in CC. [*sc.* Common Celtic] initially except before *u*..; intervocally and preconsonantally, *g*. **1966** *Amer. Speech* XLI. 260 [R], as in SG [*sc.* Standard German], a lenis post-velar fricative, occurring preconsonantally and finally. **1977** D. Cupitt in J. Hick *Myth of God Incarnate* vii. 138 Pre-constantinian Christian art was scarce, unofficial, of very poor quality and often somewhat ambiguous. **1907** W. A. Turner *Epilepsy* ix. 195 He regarded the pre-convulsive fall in alkalinity as a 'biochemical aura'. **1972** M. Verzeano in Petsche & Brazier *Synchronization EEG Activities in Epilepsies* 178 When the preconvulsive state is reached (d), the passages of circulating activity through the network are very rhythmic, very rapid, and involve a large number of neurons discharging at a very high rate. **1964** C. S. Lewis *Discarded Image* iii. 22 Casual statements about pre- Copernican astronomy in modern scientists who are not historians are often unreliable. **1973** M. Amis *Rachel Papers* 24 During the long pre-copulative session I glanced downwards. **1927** B. Malinowski *Sex & Repression in Savage Society* IV. i. 179 In a pre-cultural condition there is no medium in which social institutions, morals, and religion could be moulded. **1963** Auden *Dyer's Hand* 87 Politics in every advanced society is..not concerned with human beings as persons and citizens but with human bodies, with the precultural, prepolitical human creature. **1876–7** W. James in R. B. Perry *Tht. & Char. W. James* (1935) I. xxviii. 478 Pre-Darwinians thought only of adaptation. They made organism plastic to its environment. **1880** *Atlantic Monthly* Oct. 444/1 Pre-Darwinian philosophers had also tried to establish the doctrine of descent with modification. **1899** A. H. Yapp *Cuckoo* III. 189 In the case of the little birds and cuckoos we have had brought before us in the actions of the former what is decisively in the teeth of pre-Darwinian theory as of the Darwinian. **1921** G. B. Shaw *Back to Methuselah* p. viii, The pre-Darwinian age had come to be regarded as a Dark Age in which men still believed that the book of Genesis was a standard scientific treatise. **1932** Reckless & Smith *Juvenile Delinquency* vi. 168 (*heading*) Truancy as predelinquency. **1972** *N.Y. Law Jrnl.* 24 Oct. 4/8 California's Predelinquency Statute: A Case Study and Suggested Alternatives, by Robert L. Harris. **1951** Powers & Witmer *Experiment in Prevention of Delinquency* iii. 30 If the treatment group comprised only selected pre-delinquents..unhappy public relations might result. *Ibid.* v. 53 No boy who showed obvious pre-delinquent trends was excluded. **1977** M. Edelman *Polit. Lang.* iv. 69 Affluent adults may be 'predelinquent' or 'prepsychotic'; but it is not behavior that governs the connotations of these terms, but, rather, the statistical chances for a group and the belief that poor children are high risks. **1959** *Times* 21 Mar. 9/3 There is no small retail pack available yet of the pre-emergent weedkillers which are being tried extensively in commercial nurseries. **1928** L. J. J. Muskens *Epilepsy* vii. 257 The pre-epileptic headache..is little influenced by drugs. **1944** Huff & Coulston in *Jrnl. Infectious Dis.* LXXV. 237/2 For all the stages of the parasite [*sc.* *Plasmodium*] between sporozoite and erythrocytic trophozoite we shall use the term pre-erythrocytic stages. They are, of course, exoerythrocytic in the broadest meaning of the term. **1962** J. D. Smyth *Introd. Animal Parasitol.* vii. 87 (*caption*) Pre-erythrocytic schizonts of *Plasmodium cynomolgi* and *P. vivax* in parenchymal cells of rhesus monkey and man respectively; 7 days after mosquito inoculation. **1973** R. M. Pinder *Malaria* ii. 26 This process, which constitutes the pre-erythrocytic or primary tissue stage, takes from 8 to 12 days and is essential to allow the parasites to undergo the necessary metabolic adaptation for the change from life in a poikilothermic insect to that in a warm-blooded vertebrate. **1908** *Westm. Gaz.* 7 June 2/2 In India itself the idea and word 'Indian' hardly existed in pre-European times. **1971** *Black Scholar* June 35 We as black men are breaking loose..becoming once again the real black man in the full tradition of our pre-European forebears. **1890** W. James *Princ. Psychol.* II. xxviii. 647 By the pre-evolutionary naturalists, whose generation has hardly passed away, classifications were supposed to be ultimate insights into God's mind, filling us with adoration of his ways. **1923** *Proc. Soc. Exper. Biol. & Med.* XX. 371 (*heading*) The influence of nutrition during the pre-experimental period on the development of rickets in rats. **1971** *Jrnl. Gen. Psychol.* LXXXV. 157 During the pre-experimental period Ss were housed in group cages. **1970** *Ibid.* LXXXII. 47 It also suggests that pre-experimentally acquired tendencies..are important determinants of behavioral variability in experimental settings. **1966** D. G. Brandon *Mod. Techniques Metallogr.* iv. 182 Inclusion of the image term..leads to a correction factor, α, in both the pre-exponential and exponential terms. **1970** *Nature* 12 Dec. 1086/1 The Arrhenius expression is a frequently erroneous semiempirical formula, with the temperature independence of the activation energy *E* and the pre-exponential factor *A* becoming increasingly questionable as the reaction temperature range broadens. **1938** *New Statesman* 19 Feb. 276/2 It is possible..that the present Italy willingly accepts that German domination in Central Europe which sons of the pre-Fascist Italy spilled their blood to prevent. **1934** Webster, Pre-feudal. **1949** I. Deutscher *Stalin* vi. 195 It was..a formidable task to adjust their..pre-feudal and even nomad ways of life to the Marxist, Communist policies of the central Government. **1962** H. R. Loyn *Anglo-Saxon Eng.* iii. 105 In one respect the techniques of warfare in pre-feudal England led to an inferior status on the part of the smith. **1974** M. Taylor tr. *Metz's Film Lang.* v. 114 The *iconology* (likewise prefilmic) that organizes the denotation of those same objects. **1880** W. James *Will to Believe* (1897) 254 The spencerian philosophy of 'Force', effacing all the previous distinctions between actual and potential energy, momentum, work, force, mass, etc., which physicists have with so much agony achieved, carried us back to a pre-galilean age. **1952** *Mind* LXI. 417 He thinks biology is in a 'pre-Galilean' stage. **1934** *Anatomical Rec.* LX (Suppl.) 92 The most distinctive spindles are the first pregamic figures. **1953** R. Wichterman *Biol. of Paramecium* ix. 273/1 The four micronuclear products of the first pregamic division enter quickly upon the second pregamic division without a resting stage between them.. to produce eight micronuclear products. **1894** *Biol. Lect.* (Marine Biol. Lab., Wood's Holl, Mass.) II. 2 This consideration led some morphologists to insist on the need of a more precise investigation of the præ-gastrular stages, and the desirability of taking as a starting-point not the two-layered gastrula but the undivided ovum. **1970** *Annales Embryol. & Morphogénèse* III. 133 (*heading*) Competence and induction in the pregastrular chick blastoderm. **1882** Pregeological [in Dict.]. **1899** *Geogr. Jrnl.* XIII. 233 A map of the world in early Cambrian times might show the influence of these pre-geological incidents. *Ibid.* 234 If the ocean basins were not formed pre-geologically, but have grown from the changes that have occurred during the long ages of geological time, then we must seek for a cause that has acted continuously, and is acting to-day. **1971** I. G. Gass et al. *Understanding Earth* ix. 137/2 The event which caused the loss of the primary atmosphere must have occurred fairly early in the history of the planet, presumably in pre-geological time (over 3600 million years ago). Otherwise we would expect to find some record of it in the rocks. **1949** *Archivum Linguisticum* I. 121 Is there anything against speaking of 'pre-grammar' as one speaks of prehistory alongside history? **1966** M. Pei *Gloss. Linguistic Terminol.* 216 *Pre-grammar*,..research into the state of the language in its prehistoric stages, and of the grammatical categories which cannot be accounted for by logical analysis. [**1926** A. Sechehaye *Structure logique de la Phrase* i. 10 Il faut se souvenir de la différence..qui existe entre le langage prégrammatical et le langage organisé.] **1932** A. H. Gardiner *Theory of Speech & Lang.* II. iv. 220 Ries takes up the strange position that they [*sc.* sentences without verbs] are 'pre-grammatical, or better still extra-grammatical phrases'. **1937** J. Orr tr. *Iordan's Introd. Romance Linguistics* iv. 331 Every form of grammar has an individual origin, and has its source in some pre-grammatical or extra-grammatical act which in process of time is transformed into grammar. **1940** A. H. Gardiner *Theory of Proper Names* 12 This term [*sc.* 'name'] belongs to the pre-grammatical stage of thought. **1960** E. H. Gombrich *Art & Illusion* iv. 134 It was the Greeks who taught us to ask '*How* does he stand?' or even 'Why does he stand like that?' Applied to a pre-Greek work of art, it may be senseless to ask this question. **1958** W. Willetts *Chinese Art* I. iv. 206 Criteria establishing the pre-Han date of objects on which they appear. **1972** *Trans. Oriental Ceramics Soc.* XXXVIII. 13 This long survival of the most rudimentary of techniques..contributed to the style of hard-fired pottery of the last pre-Han centuries. **1919** *Proc. Soc. Antiquaries Scotl.* LIII. 24 There is no doubt that they were used as such by the pre-hispanic tribes. **1931** *Times Lit. Suppl.* 9 Apr. 281/1 Pre-Hispanic Art in Argentina. **1963** *Times* 9 Feb. 9/7 One of the greatest obstacles to the dispersal of the thick mystery which hangs over Peru's prehispanic past is the fact that the later civilizations apparently had no form of writing. **1978** *Guardian Weekly* 26 Feb. 18/3 The pre-Hispanic Caribbean. **1959** *Encounter* July 68/1 With a broad pre-Hitlerian gesture Napoleon destroyed her book. **1934** C. Lambert *Music Ho!* iii. 224 The earnest and thoroughgoing sense of sin that gave such a peculiar flavour to pre-Hitlerite night life. **1958** *Electroencephalogr. & Clin. Neurophysiol.* X. 223/2 As a rule, toward the end of the attack, the record is characterized by the return of the pre-ictal spike complex. **1969** W. Pryse-Phillips *Epilepsy* v. 17 Grand mal fits..may be preceded by pre-ictal symptoms such as tiredness, irritability, etc. **1963** *Times* 9 Feb. 9/7 In the Machu Picchu area, at San Pedro de Cacha, an intact group of thousands of Incaic and pre-Incaic tombs, some dating from about 1200 B.C., was found only a few weeks ago by the Peruvian archaeologist, Dr. Manuel Chavez Ballón. **1934** A. Huxley *Beyond Mexique Bay* 251 Karl Marx went out imaginatively into the revolutionary future, Ruskin and William Morris into the pre-industrial past. **1956** R. Redfield *Peasant Society & Culture* 71 He saw chiefly what had come into those villages from preindustrial Europe. **1969** G. Greene *Trav. with my Aunt* I. xiv. 136 Horses moved slowly along, dragging harrows. We were back in the pre-industrial age. **1977** P. Johnson *Enemies of Society* vii. 93 If there had been a powerful ecological lobby in eighteenth-century England..the Western world would still be condemned to pre-industrial living standards. **1957** O. R. McGregor *Divorce in England* iii. 75 The peasant or domestic worker's family of pre-industrialist days..was largely a self-sustaining economic unit. **1977** *Language* LIII. 330, I will outline B's analysis of the variation in the form of the pre-infinitival complementizer in Guyanese decreolization. **1939** L. H. Gray *Foundations of Lang.* 202 In this absence of declension we may..see another survival of the pre-inflexional stage. **1976** *Archivum Linguisticum* VII. 163 In this paper, having accepted a pre-inflexional phase of IE[*sc.* Indo-European],..he tries to reduce the processes which give origin to the alternations I am studying. **1964** *Language* XL. 255 In speech development of the child, we can..establish a preintellectual stage. **1977** H. G. Burger in B. Bernardi *Concept & Dynamics of Culture* 433 Up to a certain point in time, then, a child exercises two separate mental stages: pre-intellectual and prelinguistic. **1968** *Language* XLIV. 84 The border between words constitutes a potential pause point. The features manifested at this prejunctural spot are correlated with the difference between rapid speech forms and deliberate speech forms. **1972** *Ibid.* XLVIII. 411 Prejunctural *-j* is subsequently vocalized along with the fronting of stressed *-ō* to *-œ-*, which is unrounded in West Saxon. **1874** W. Wallace tr. *Hegel's Logic* 53 It was..the main question of the pre-Kantian metaphysic. **1947** *Mind* LVI. 164 It is doubtful whether any reader hitherto sunk in dogmatic slumber pre- or post-Kantian would be awakened by these rambling and inconclusive pages. **1951** W. H. Walsh *Introd. Philos. Hist.* vii. 141 Hegel saw the way the abstract conception of reason favoured by Kant and (in general) the pre-Kantian rationalists had been countered by the many philosophies of feeling. **1979** *Studies in Eng. Lit.: Eng. Number* (Tokyo) 172 Dr. Beer's present work..is a valuable attempt to explore Coleridge's poetic intelligence with all its pre-occupations coming from the poet's inborn interest in pre-Kantian Idealism and mysticism. **1959** *Ann. Reg. 1958* 88 The legislative assembly's rejection of measures to raise more local revenue illustrated some of the difficulties encountered in development—the pre-Keynesian thinking of many local leaders, [etc.]. **1960** *20th Cent.* Aug. 99 Old-fashioned, pre-Keynesian, *laissez-faire* liberalism. **1933** L. Bloomfield *Language* 373 Pre-Latin *[kolnis] 'hill' gives Latin *collis.* **1975** *Language* LI. 142 *S*-stem nouns like Pre-Latin **douk*+*es*+*i* are analogically re-analysed. **1957** C. La Drière in N. Frye *Sound & Poetry* II. 103 The concord is of natural, or at least prelexical or paralexical, *suggestion* of the sound with its conventional reference. **1971** *Language* XLVII. 319 The Lexical Insertion Rule can insert a predicate into a prelexical terminal string only if the lexical marking of the predicate is not distinct from the feature specification of the prelexical terminal string. **1976** *Archivum Linguisticum* VII. 127 The lexical decomposition of McCawley and others yields several closely related items which differ only in one or more prelexical elements. **1903** *Pop. Sci. Monthly* Jan. 211 A correspondent..wrote to ask if the garden would accept as a gift the large and important collection of pre-Linnean books that it had been his pleasure to accumulate. **1936** *Discovery* Mar. 85/1 There is a rich collection of botanical incunabula, old herbals, and other pre-Linnaean items. **1962** H. R. Loyn *Anglo-Saxon Eng.* vi. 286 Botanists exercise themselves..to give post-Linnaean forms to strongly pre-Linnaean Anglo-Saxon generalized plant names. **1928** *Daily Express* 23 Nov. 10/2 The idea of shutting out extremism by barring its representatives at the ports seems to us as obsolete as pre-Listerian surgery. **1951** White & Hynes *Med. Bacteriol.* (ed. 5) v. 53 In pre-Listerian days the surgeon's scalpel frequently conveyed infection from one patient to another. **1931** G. Stern *Meaning & Change of Meaning* 12 Pre-literary developments are best left aside at first..and ..research should be restricted to periods represented by written texts. **1941** F. Klaeber *Beowulf* (ed. 3) p. lxvi, Of especial interest are the *gefrægn*-formulas, which unmistakably point to the 'preliterary' stage of poetry, when the poems lived on the lips of singers, and oral transmission was the only possible source of information. **1967** *N.Y. Rev. Bks.* 23 Feb. 33/2 The study of technology or town-planning is the same for preliterary or literary societies. **1937** R. H. Lowie *Hist. Ethnol. Theory* (1938) xii. 219 Into the notions about the dead this logical factor does not intrude, hence prelogic here runs riot untrammeled. **1957** H. J. Uldall in Hjelmslev & Uldall *Outl. Glossematics* I. 4 All languages..are based on this participative prelogic. **1897** *Lippincott's Med. Dict.* 824/2 Premalignant. **1961** *Lancet* 29 July 250/2 It is suggested that there is a premalignant defect in the genes which control the development of the reticulo-endothelial system, and that the abnormal stem cells derived from these genes undergo further changes and become malignant. **1974** R. M. Kirk et al. *Surgery* iv. 56 Hereditary polyposis..of the colon is pre-malignant. **1920** E. Pound in *Lett. J. Joyce* (1966) III. 9 His misspent premalthusian youth. **1965** P. Goubert in Glass & Eversley *Population in Hist.* xix. 467 Results obtained by the second method [in the study of demography] apply to all 'pre-Malthusian' times. **1963** V. Nabokov *Gift* ii. 119 The river runs into the murk of the prematutinal twilight that still hangs in the gorges. **1905** *Q. Jrnl. Microsc. Sci.* XLVIII. 490 It is evident..that we may group the cells that are produced in the life cycle of an animal or plant into three categories, viz. Premaiotic, Maiotic, and Post-Maiotic respectively. *Ibid.*, The synapsis represents that series of events which are concerned in causing the temporary union in pairs of pre-maiotic chromosomes, previously to their transverse separation and distribution, in their entirety, between two daughter nuclei. **1972** *Genetical Res.* XX. 201 The sensitive stage lay between the last premeiotic mitosis and the start of DNA synthesis. **1956** *Amer. Jrnl. Obstetr. & Gynecol.* LXXI. 1319 The premenarchal girl who produces estrogen but in insufficient quantities to cause bleeding. **1975** G. S. Richardson in J. J. Gold *Gynecologic Endocrinol.* (ed. 2) v. 56/1 The premenarchal ovary is a polycystic ovary with an unscarred 'porcelain' surface. **1956** *Obstetr. & Gynecol.* XIII. 724 (*caption*) Newborn. Childhood. Premenarche. **1958** E. & E. R. Novak *Gynecol. & Obstetr. Path.* (ed. 4) xxxv. 601 (*heading*) Pre-menarche. **1937** *Human Biol.* IX. 27 The positive slope of the regression of chest-width upon chronological age is greater in the case of premenarcheal girls than in the case of post-menarcheal girls. **1943** *Jrnl. Pediatrics* XXII. 529 An early menarche is associated with..greater than average height and greater than average weight during the premenarcheal years. **1942** Mazer & Israel *Diagn. & Treatm. Menstrual Disorders* ii. 35 A study of 175 post-menarchial and 175 premenarchial girls. **1968** M. R. Abell in J. J. Gold *Textbk. of Gynecologic Endocrinol.* ix. 193 (*heading*) Premenarchial endometrium. **1902** W. Bateson *Mendel's Princ. Heredity: A Defence* 7 The cases are all examples of discontinuous variation: that is to say, cases in which actual intermediates between the parent forms are not usually produced on crossing. [*Note*] This conception of discontinuity is of course pre-Mendelian. **1941** J. S. Huxley *Uniqueness of Man* iv. 121 The picture of the hereditary constitution of human groups which can now be drawn in the light of modern genetics is very different from any which could be framed in the pre-Mendelian era. **1977** Kruskal & Mosteller *Representative Sampling* (Univ. Chicago Dept. Statistics) 11 The notion is like the old pre-Mendelian genetic idea of the homunculus. **1966** F. Schurmann *Ideology & Organization in Communist China* 3 Some writers assert that the economy in premodern societies is a subsystem of a larger social system. **1970** I. L. Horowitz *Masses in Lat. Amer.* i. 7 This concept equates 'mass' to forces in the old society (old in the sense of pre-socialist, rather than pre-modern). **1977** *Sci. Amer.* Oct. 96/1 Premodern medicine blamed such failures on sepsis. **1898** L. F. Ward *Outl. Sociol.* v. 112 The evolving intellect throughout all this long pre-social and pre-moral period was exclusively devoted to the egoistic interests of individuals. **1963** L. Kohlberg in *Vita Humana* VI. 13 The six developmental types were grouped into three moral levels and labelled as follows: Level I. Pre-Moral Level. **1973** M. E. Wood *Children* 26 Children are first amoral..than enter a pre-moral stage, when social and authoritarian factors are the main restraints. **1943** *Mind* LII. 19 The pseudo-morality of sanctions lacks the inward reality of morality. It is in fact a sort of pre-morality. **1916** Jordan & Ferguson *Textbk. Histol.* viii. 221 Myeloblast (Premyelocyte; Hemoblast, Mesameboid Cell; Primitive Blood Cell; 'Lymphocyte').—This is the parent blood-cell of bone-marrow. **1931** M. G. Wohl *Bedside Interpretation of Lab. Findings* caption facing p. 88 Abnormal leucocytes:..premyelocyte with beginning neutrophilic granules. **1964** W. G. Smith *Allergy & Tissue Metabolism* iii. 44 It is accepted that eosinophils are differentiated from the premyelocytes of the bone marrow. **1963** *Jrnl. Clin. Path.* XVI. 319 Among the acute leukaemias of the granulocytic group, acute premyelocytic leukaemia is distinguished by the severity of its haemorrhages, the frequency of hypofibrinaemia, a rapidly fatal course, and an unusual cellular hyperplasia. **1938** *New Statesman* 21 May 890/1 A record whose pre-Nazi date can be guessed from the fact that Fritz Busch conducts the Berlin State Opera Orchestra. **1972** P. Black *Biggest Aspidistra* I. iv. 41 *Brigade Exchange*, a war play..created by the pre-Nazi German radio. **1941** *Cancer Res.* I. 45/1 The object of these investigations was the study of the influence of irritation on the first manifestation of neoplastic transformation, which, in the case of the skin, represents the conversion of the preneoplastic thickened epithelium into a papilloma. **1978** *Nature* 13 Apr. 635/2 Electron microscopy has shown that during the latent period only preneoplastic changes resembling those of Bowen's disease are present in rat epidermis. **1946** L. Bloomfield in C. F. Hockett *Leonard Bloomfield Anthol.* (1970) 460 Particles (*prenouns*) appear before nouns in less variety than before verbs [in Algonquian]. **1966** G. N. Leech *Eng. in Advertising* ii. 14 The pre-noun is broken down into four chief secondary classes, determiner.. numeral..adjective..and a certain range of nouns, including proper names and words denoting substances. **1968** R. Kyle *Love Lab.* xviii. 233 Have you ever known an orgasmic woman who wanted to go back to a pre-orgasmic condition? **1976** *Spare Rib* Nov. 16/1, I was going to start by telling you how I came to join the pre-orgasmic group, but I suppose a lot of things preceded that step. **1980** *Time* 28 Jan. 90/1 Psychologists persistently refer to unresponsive women as 'pre-orgasmic'. **1935** *Anat. Rec.* LXIV. Suppl. No. 1. 52 The beginning of the pre-ovulatory enlargement coincides with the beginning of oestrus. **1975** Franchimont & Burger *Human Growth Hormone* II. iii. 175 During the first 10 days, FSH and LH fell and became stable at values similar to those encountered in the normally cycling female during the preovulatory period. **1899** Pre-paroxysmal [in Dict.]. **1907** A. W. Turner *Epilepsy* vi. 121 A form of pre-paroxysmal psychosis..is the feeling of good spirits and of exceptional well-being, which precedes the onset of an attack in some cases. **1977** *Lancet* 21 May 1095/1 Prepatency was documented in 35 patients who..started to excrete *Giardia.* The median prepatent period was 14 days. **1926** R. W. Hegner in *Q. Rev. Biol.* I. 399/1 The prepatent period extends from the time the infective parasites enter the body of the host until their offspring can be recovered by the usual laboratory methods. **1976** *Nature* 15 July 214/2 This highly virulent strain has a prepatent period of 8–14 d in mice. **1897** A. D. L. Napier *Menopause* iv. 78 For a variable period, usually about two years, the physiological economy is preparing for this pre-pathological change [*sc.* the climacteric]. **1977** M. Edelman *Polit. Lang.* v. 95 Ritualistic categorization further confuses feedback by defining a substantial proportion of the population as either pathological or pre-pathological. **1941** *Language* XVII. 225 A study of post-pausal and pre-pausal allophones reveals several recurrent differences between these and the corresponding allophones occurring elsewhere than at points of open juncture. **1973** A. H. Sommerstein *Sound Pattern Anc. Greek* v. 160 *Prepausal acute*: This phenomenon may well have nothing to do with the Acute-Grave rule; rather, it may be a feature of sentence intonation, viz. rise at end of phrase. **1948** J. L. Adams tr. *Tillich's Protestant Era* viii. 134 The dark ground of pre-personal being..is effective in every moment of our conscious existence. **1971** *Jrnl. Gen. Psychol.* LXXXIV. 257 The body, therefore, becomes man's expression in the world, the mirror of his being at the prepersonal and preobjective level. **1977** Fontana & van de Water in Douglas & Johnson *Existential Sociol.* iii. 126 For Merleau-Ponty, consciousness was basically the anonymous, prepersonal life of the body-subject. **1933** T. S. Eliot *Use of Poetry* 21 It is true also of the change from a pre-philosophical to a philosophical age. **1939** *Mind* XLVIII. 89 Mr. Loewenberg is a man with a mission: to rescue empiricism (*i.e.* pre-philosophical empiricism) from the empiricists. **1959** J. L. Austin *Sense & Sensibilia* (1962) vi. 55 Our ordinary, unamended, pre-philosophical manner of speaking. **1957** in *Amer. Speech 1972* (1975) XLVII. 222 To be safely pre-phonemic, let us begin with 1874, with Whitney's 'Elements of English Pronunciation', and observe what seemed important to him. **1960** H. M. Hoenigswald

Language Change viii. 73 The doctrine of gradual phonetic change may turn out to be a remnant from pre-phonemic days. **1968** R. A. Lyttleton *Mysteries Solar Syst.* ii. 54 Evidence seems to suggest that the meteorites do not represent original pre-planetary material but are a later product of the solar system. **1978** *Nature* 9 Feb. 504/1 The authors thus invoke another component—a pre-planetary disk which is accreting onto the central star. **1955** Pre-planting [see *post-emergence* s.v. *post- B. 1]. **1976** *Stillwater News* (Absarokee, Montana) 1 July 15/1 Whether pre-planting, post-plant or post-emergence herbicides are used depends upon type of crop, kinds of weeds and other conditions. **1963** Pre-political [see *pre-cultural* above]. **1977** *Jrnl. Politics* XXXIX. 7 Hobbes' resolutive-compositive method is an early and Rawls' original position a late example of the contractarian quest for political authority's pre-political foundations. **1943** Pre-predicative [see *pre-give*, sense *A. 1]. **1950** *Mind* LIX. 264 The first section of Husserl's book deals with what he calls 'pre-predicative' experience. **1971** *Jrnl. Gen. Psychol.* LXXXIV. 259 Merleau-Ponty..spoke more than previously of the interrelation of the predicative and prepredicative levels. **1975** Ld. Hailsham *Door wherein I Went* iv. 15 My formal education began at the age of five ..when I was sent to a pre-prep school in Rosary Gardens. **1960–1** *Where* Winter 16/1 *Pre-preparatory school*, an independent school for children under about 8. **1964** *Economist* 25 Apr. 356/1 Children do enjoy their pre-primary schooling. *Ibid.* 356/2 The pre-primary schools—voluntary to the age of five, then compulsory for one year. **1979** *Jrnl. R. Soc. Arts* CXXVII. 483/1 A task that continues uninterrupted from the pre-primary to the post-graduate class. **1975** *Nature* 11 Sept. 89/2 The existence of an analogous precursor to insulin, a preproinsulin, was strongly supported by the experiments of M. A. Permutt. **1979** *Ibid.* 21 June 675/1 The gene coding for preproinsulin II contained an additional intron of about 500 nucleotides between the region encoding amino acids 38 and 39 of the proinsulin II peptide chain. **1942** *Endocrinology* XXXI. 673 Prepuberal castration prevents the appearance of..physiological and behavioral reactions. **1949** *Radiology* LII. 112/1 The testes of normal chicks of this age are in the prepuberal state. **1977** *Yearbk. Obstetr. & Gynecol.* 329 Seventeen were prepuberal when leukemia was diagnosed. **1942** *Endocrinology* XXXI. 674 Male sexual behavior was shown by all 10 prepuberally castrated females. **1947** *Physiol. Rev.* XXVII. 275 Prepuberally castrated male chimpanzees show much more sexual activity than do similarly operated rodents. **1898** *Amer. Jrnl. Psychol.* IX. 257 The rate of growth.. decreases with fluctuations until about 10 years in girls and 12 years in boys, when the prepubertal acceleration sets in. **1932** S. Zuckerman *Social Life Monkeys* xvii. 267 Louttit holds that the nosing and circling activities of the prepubertal guinea-pig are part of its sexual responses. **1977** *Daily Colonist* (Victoria, B.C.) 19 Mar. 2/1 There may be some prepubertal girls using contraceptive pills 'to be sure'. **1978** *Bull. Amer. Acad. Arts & Sci.* Feb. 22 The eunuch or the prepubertal castrate does not develop the disease. **1937** *Nature* 3 Apr. 589/1 Prepubertally castrated male rats are not known to mate. **1942** *Psychosomatic Med.* IV. 190/1 (*heading*) Prepubertally castrated adults. **1977** *Sci. Amer.* Jan. 100/3 Samaritan religious tradition affords a kind of telescopic glimpse of the past: the ancient Judaism of pre-rabbinical times. **1978** S. H. Hodgson *Philos. of Reflection* I. i. ii. 107 The undistinguished unity of *primary*, pre-reflective, consciousness. **1932** *Mind* XLI. 116 We mean 'taking for granted', that state of pre-reflective unquestioning assurance. **1966** E. S. Casey tr. *Dufrenne's Notion of A Priori* 97 Pre-reflective thought experiences the *a priori* in the *a posteriori*. **1970** J. M. Edie *Patterns of Life-World* xviii. 339 Chomsky's.. own investigations lead us to what Merleau-Ponty termed the 'pre-reflexive' structures of experience. **1976** *Brit. Jrnl. Sociol.* XXVII. 360 Speaking can organize a separate mode of experience which is not simply a transmutation or decipherment of prepredicative thought. It has its own distinct phenomenological properties which exceed those of the prereflexive world. **1923** H. L. Brose tr. *Sommerfeld's Atomic Struct. & Spectral Lines* iv. 211 Coulomb's law is valid and likewise ordinary (pre-relativistic) mechanics. **1952** Koestler *Arrow in Blue* vi. 51 In pre-Relativistic days it was still just possible for the non-specialist to keep abreast of general developments in science. **1900** *Q. Jrnl. Microsc. Sci.* XLIV. 3 Reproductive period.—I have used this expression to denote the whole of that period in the life of a mammal, whether male or female, during which its generative organs are capable of the reproductive function; and in contrast to the Pre-reproductive and Post-reproductive periods which severally precede and follow it, during which the generative organs are either not fully developed or are degenerate. **1952** *New Biol.* XIII. 27 In ourselves the length of the prereproductive period of life has increased. **1977** J. L. Harper *Population Biol. of Plants* 231 The pre-reproductive period of trees is usually long. **1937** *N. & Q.* 6 Feb. 91/2 A pre-Romanesque church at Quintanilla de las Viñas. **1939** *Burlington Mag.* Mar. 110/1 Stone-sculptors of the pre-romanesque epoch lacked tradition and experience. **1907** H. M. Chadwick *Origin Eng. Nation* iv. 74 It is held that the remains..date from pre-Saxon times. **1962** H. R. Loyn *Anglo-Saxon Eng.* i. 7 Big rivers such as the Thames..preserve their pre-Saxon names. **1958** L. Bellak *Schizophrenia* i. 54 The pre-schizophrenic personality may be sociopathic, infantile,.. brilliantly highstrung. **1964** C. M. Thompson in M. R. Green *Interpersonal Psychoanal.* xxxiii. 315 So much for the outward picture of preschizophrenia. *Ibid.* 316 It is characteristic of the preschizophrenic that all true object relationships are impossible. **1965** A. F. Korner in B. I. Murstein *Handbk. Projective Techniques* ii. 29 Conversely, frank psychotics..often produce Rorschachs that reflect less of a schizophrenic process than do records of pre-schizophrenics. **1897** *Lippincott's Med. Dict.* 825/2 *Presenile*, occurring before old age: as, *presenile alopecia* or baldness. **1903** *Lancet* 22 Aug. 517/2 The patients in the severe cases are men as a rule in the pre-senile stage and they present well-marked cardio-vascular lesions. **1912** *Brit. Med. Jrnl.* 16 Nov. 1379/1 He has hitherto limited the term 'melancholia' to cases occurring at the climacteric and the pre-senile period of life. **1913** *Jrnl. Nervous & Mental Dis.* XL. 386 Further investigation of the types of mental makeup out of which an involutional depression may develop..may throw light on the peculiar combination of symptoms seen in the presenile psychosis. **1950** D. B. Kirby *Surg. of Cataract* x. 193/2 The presenile soft cataract up to the fourth decade may be handled by discission. **1976** F. Warner *Killing Time* i. vi. 17 Impaired mental and motor functions, presenile dementia, usually followed by death. **1962** E. Snow *Red China Today* (1963) lxxiii. 564 All three were born the 'year of the flood', 1949, and had no memory of a presocialist China. **1965** B. Pearce tr. *Preobrazhensky's New Econ.* 88 A country like the U.S.S.R...must pass through a period of primitive accumulation in which the sources provided by pre-socialist forms of economy are drawn upon very freely. **1973** *Sci. Amer.* Apr. 61/3 The molecules might be formed in the dense environs of a 'presolar nebula', that is, in the final phases of the collapse of a protostar into a self-luminous star. **1979** *Nature* 15 Feb. 556/1 According to the second model..the presolar grains condensed in a late supernova that triggered the collapse of the solar nebula. **1937** *Sci. & Society* I. 156 We have seen that pre-Soviet scholarship..had given a theoretical basis for the treatment of any language as potentially capable of developing any expressions required of it. **1949** M. Mead *Male & Female* xi. 230 In pre-Soviet Russia there seems to have been extraordinarily little valuation placed on women's child-bearing character. **1957** R. N. C. Hunt *Guide to Communist Jargon* xxiii. 81 Where pre-Soviet expansionist policy was concerned, the party line changed in the middle 'thirties. **1952** C. Payne-Gaposchkin *Stars in Making* (1953) ii. 43 Nebulae like the one in Orion must represent the primitive prestellar material. **1978** *Sci. Amer.* Apr. 112/1 The observational signpost for this prestellar stage is the emission by the cloud's many molecules of radio waves at wavelengths measured in millimeters. **1958** C. Rabin in *Aspects of Translation* 130 Pre-Structuralist works on grammar recognized this fact by separating the description of forms ('accidence') from the discussion of their meaning, which appeared as part of 'syntax'. **1961** *Brno Studies in English* III. 11 Cases.. were decidedly unknown to pre-structuralist study of language. **1933** L. Bloomfield *Language* 220 Some suffixes have *pre-suffixal stress*: the accent is on the syllable before the suffix. **1977** *Language* LIII. 10 If a German were to create a new word by adding the suffix *-ig* 'ish' to *Kind* 'child', the result would be [kindiç] with presuffixal *d* as in [kindər]. **1973** *Publ. Amer. Dial. Soc.* lx. 34 In such dialects, the /r/ is treated as if it were presyllabic, as an apical alveolar consonant. **1951** *Dorland's Med. Dict.* (ed. 22) 1212/1 *Presymptomatic*, existing before the appearance of symptoms. **1966** *New Society* 12 May 7/2 Donaldson's finding that one in six 'healthy' people has presymptomatic disease. **1978** *Nature* 9 Nov. 173/1 Bubbles moving in blood vessels have been successfully detected by the Doppler method in experiments confirming their significance and presymptomatic existence. **1951** N. Goodman *Struct. Appearance* i. i. 22, I use 'presystematically' for 'according to ordinary usage'. *Ibid.* 23 Care..must be exercised..when one word..has both a systematic and a presystematic use. For example, 'is a member of' is used in several different presystematic ways and also as the mere verbal reading of the systematic sign 'ϵ'. **1964** E. Bach *Introd. Transformational Gram.* v. 92 With..the free use of any presystematic knowledge of the language, we choose the analyses which maximize the independence of the classes set up. **1975** *Jrnl. Philos.* LXXII. 552 Presystematically, the physicalist ontological position is simply put: 'Everything is physical.' **1959** *Listener* 17 Sept. 429/1 The rings were unknown in pre-telescopic times. **1976** *Jrnl. R. Soc. Arts* CXXIV. 564/1 There were even observatories in pre-telescopic times. **1966** C. G. Hempel *Philos. Nat. Sci.* vi. 75 While the internal principles of a theory are couched in its characteristic *theoretical terms*.., the test implications must be formulated in terms..which are 'antecedently understood',..terms that have been introduced prior to the theory and can be used independently of it. Let us refer to them as *antecedently available* or *pretheoretical terms.* **1966** Y. Bar-Hillel in *Automatic Transl. of Lang.* (NATO Summer School, Venice, 1962) 8 So far, I have been using 'syntactic complexity' in its pretheoretical and unanalysed vague sense. **1968** A. J. Ayer *Origins of Pragmatism* 335 So far as anything can be, qualia are pre-theoretical. **1953** H. A. T. Reiche et al. tr. *Jaspers's Tragedy is not Enough* i. 31 Pre-tragic knowledge is rounded out, complete, and self-contained. **1957** N. Frye *Anat. Crit.* 210 The Greek *ananke* or *moira* is in its normal, or pre-tragic, form the internal balancing condition of life. **1960** H. Read *Forms of Things Unknown* xi. 177 From this point of view Stoicism is more complete; and above all that serene code of ethics achieved in ancient China—'the feeling of security without the shadow of tragedy, a natural and sublime humanity, a sense of being at home in this world, and a wealth of concrete insights', to quote Jaspers' own description of pre-tragic knowledge. **1965** N. Chomsky *Aspects of Theory of Syntax* 213 In the syntactic component of this (pretransformational) grammar, indices on category symbols were used to express agreement..but not subcategorization and selectional restrictions. **1973** *Word 1970* XXVI. 396 Yet perhaps all we have to do is to rephrase Cohen's distinction between *langue bébé* and *langue adulte* by calling the former 'pre-transformational language'. Then, there would still remain the necessity of explaining how..a child suddenly employs transformations. **1908** *Westm. Gaz.* 8 July 12/2 Translated from Pre-Vedic Sanskrit. **1935** G. K. Zipf *Psycho-Biol. of Lang.* (1936) iv. 160 In pre-Vedic Sanskrit, the accent might be on the last syllable. **1905** F. E. Clements *Res. Methods Ecol.* 321 Prevernal, pertaining to early spring. **1908** *Science* 7 Feb. 207/1 Overtopped by the autumnal, the sublayers are successively those of the serotinal, estival, vernal and prevernal. **1926** [see *aspect *sb.* 14]. **1960** N. Polunin *Introd. Plant Geogr.* x. 285 In temperate forests..the seasonal aspects are apt to be important—in particular the prevernal (i.e. before spring) one of herbs which flower before the shading tree-leaves expand. **1933** Blunden *Charles Lamb* 193 It was Lamb's instinctive utterance of indignation against the spirit of the pre-Victorians, the tendency to make a boudoir or a Persian heaven. **1964** D. Owen *Eng. Philanthropy* (1965) 5 Victorians and pre-Victorians agitated..for more efficient employment of..charitable trusts. **1973** M. R. Booth *Eng. Plays of 19th Cent.* III. 25 The materialism of the age, its social ambition and self-seeking drive..are topics not really explored in pre-Victorian comedy. **1979** 'J. Gash' *Grail Tree* i. 17 Ceramics and pre-Victorian tapestries.

2. a. With sbs. or phrases forming *quasi-*adjs. or attrib. phrases. *pre-Broadway, -cession, -Christmas* (examples), *-Civil War, -coition, -college, -computer, -consonant, -crusade, -development, dinner, -employment, -enclosure, -examination, -game, -Inca, increase, -independence* (examples), *-invasion, -jazz, -launch, -legislation, -liberation, -life, -London, -lunch, -machine, -market, -marketing, -oïdium, -ovulation, -pause, -phylloxera, -pottery, -qualificative, -radio, -recognition, -Reformation* (later example), *-relativity, -Renaissance* (examples), *-retirement, -revolution, -season, -seizure, -show, -sleep, -subject, -television, -theatre, -tour, -vowel, -work, -world.* **b.** With personal names. *pre-Hitler.* **c.** Adjs. of the type in 2 a, b above are sometimes used adverbially (cf. *pre *prep.*), as *pre-emergence* below, *pre-tax, *pre-war *advbs.*

pre-eme·rgence, occurring, performed, or applied before the emergence of seedlings from the soil; also *absol.* and as *adv.*; **pre-fla·me**, occurring in a gas flow before it reaches a flame.

The examples are arranged in alphabetical order and not, as in Dict., chronologically.

1977 *Times* 19 Nov. 13/3 The musical itself is definitely an oddity of the form, and comes here with less than triumphant pre-Broadway credits. **1920** *Chambers's Jrnl.* 13 Nov. 786/2 The natives obtained, individually or communally, land to which in the pre-cession days they could not have established a claim. **1925** T. Dreiser *Amer. Trag.* (1926) I. ii. xxvii. 338 Clyde..was invited by her to attend a pre-Christmas dance. **1976** *Morecambe Guardian* 7 Dec. 5/2 Getting party games organised is one of those pre-Christmas chores. **1961** *Georgia Rev.* Spring 10 In the pre-Civil War years, the South argued that the slave was not less humanely treated than the factory worker of the North. **1966** *Eng. Stud.* XLVII. 154 Professor Parry is at his best when he is dealing with New York, either the pre-Civil War capital or the tumultuous city of the 1920's. **1953** N. Tinbergen *Herring Gull's World* iv. 120 Head-tossing is the main part of the pre-coition behaviour. **1957** R. K. Merton *Student-Physician* 122 The greater intimacy between fathers and sons during the precollege years. **1960** *Farmer & Stockbreeder* 29 Mar. 39/1 (Advt.), Pre-College Student, not under 18,..to acquire sound agricultural background. **1976** *Sci. Amer.* Apr. 34/2 It was in this atmosphere that the National Science Foundation precollege curricula in biology and the social sciences became the focus of extended and bitter controversy. **1961** *Times* 3 Oct. (Computer Suppl.) p. viii/3 A most efficient system of manufacturing, restocking and transport had been devised in the pre-computer days. **1949** E. A. Nida *Morphol.* (ed. 2) ii. 20 The allomorphs are listed in a structurally corresponding fashion. First is given the preconsonant form and secondly the prevowel form. **1977** *Time* 7 Nov. 61/1 The message and the methods are modeled after those of Billy Graham, down to precrusade organization (by a staff of 17) and convert counseling. **1945** *Times* 29 June 5/6 Then there was at least a scheme in the pre-development stage to provide the V2 rocket with wings, which had great possibilities. **1942** C. Milburn *Diary* 25 Dec. (1979) 162 The sherry..was our pre-dinner appetiser. **1963** L. Deighton *Horse under Water* xiv. 60 We went back to H.K.'s for pre-dinner drinks. **1968** 'H. Pentecost' *Gilded Nightmare* (1969) i. iii. 46 The Trapeze Bar..is a predinner meeting place for the very rich. **1978** M. Gilbert *Empty House* x. 87 Roger ..was relaxing with his pre-dinner drink. **1940**, etc. Pre-emergence [see *post-emergence* s.v. *post- B. 1]. **1971** *Arable Farmer* Feb. 15/3 Tri-allate applied pre-emergence to wheat to control wild oat. **1977** J. L. Harper *Population Biol. of Plants* 112 In addition a 'safe site' is one from which specific hazards are absent—such as predators, competitors, toxic soil constituents and pre-emergence pathogens. **1942** *Amer. Rev. Tuberculosis* XLV. 643 The increasing adoption of preëmployment X-ray examination. **1949** H. C. Weston *Sight, Light & Efficiency* vii. 225 Whenever a pre-employment test..is applied the examinee should wear any glasses he is in the habit of wearing. **1971** *Flying* (N.Y.) Apr. 113/3 (Advt.), Airline employment test... Pre-employment tests. **1934** Webster, Pre-enclosure. **1945** H. J. Massingham in F. Thompson *Lark Rise to Candleford* p. ix, Intact from a pre-industrial and pre-Enclosure past. **1957** *Brit. Med. Jrnl.* 7 Sept. 551/2 Pre-examination strain can be defined as the condition wherein the nervous tension is of such a quality that it diminishes the efficiency of study and impairs the prospects of success. **1978** S. Allan *Inside Job* i. 17 She giggled nervously in the way Sheila remembered from pre-examination tension at school. **1924** *Colliery Guardian* CXXVII. 1443/2 Experiments show that contact with a heated surface may act in two ways: generally the ignition point is raised by the absorption of heat due to pre-flame combustion on a surface large enough to be only slightly affected itself. **1973** Boldt & Griffiths in J. P. Allinson *Criteria for Quality of Petroleum Products* v. 59 Amongst the main preflame products are the highly temperature sensitive peroxides and if these exceed a certain critical threshold concentration, the end gas will spontaneously ignite before the arrival of the flame front emanating from the sparking plug: this causes detonation or 'knocking'. **1951** *Time* 26 Feb. 78 C.C.N.Y., the heavy pre-game favorite each time, lost to Missouri (54–37), Arizona (41–38) and Boston College (63–59). **1976** *Billings* (Montana) *Gaz.* 17 June 1-H/5 Saturday's game at the Metra begins at 8:00 p.m., and pregame coverage goes on the air at 7:30. **1977** J. F. Fixx *Compl. Bk. Running* xxiii. 258 If at some football training tables the pregame meal is still steak, it is only because common sense is too often no match for tradition. **1938** E. Waugh *Scoop* I. iv. 74 A volume of pre-Hitler German poetry. **1960** *News Chron.* 4 May 5/6 Old Berlin songs that recalled carefree pre-Hitler days. **1908** *Encycl. Relig. & Ethics* I. 469/2 (*heading*) The pre-Inca people. **1950** J. H. Steward *Handbk. S. Amer. Indians* VI. 533 In both *Inca* and pre-*Inca* Coastal sites there is found..a good deal of cotton in the seed. **1974** *Encycl. Brit. Macropædia* XIV. 133/1 The dryness of the central and southern coasts has preserved the remains of a long succession of pre-Inca peoples. **1976** *Evening Post* (Bristol) 23 Apr. 21/2 (Advt.), Mini 850, antique gold, at pre-increase price. **1977** *Horse & Hound* 14 Jan. 44/3 (Advt.), New Rice eventer at pre-increase price, £666 on the road. **1960** *Daily Tel.* 9 July 6 The example of the Congo strengthens the case.. for taking every possible precaution in our own territories to maintain law and order in the tense pre-independence days. **1977** *Time* 15 Aug. 15/1 In preindependence days, Makarios battled the British with the legendary Colonel George Grivas. **1944** *Hutchinson's Pict. Hist. War* 27 Oct. 1943–11 Apr. 1944. 413 (*caption*) A U.S. officer pointing out a target to general Eisenhower during pre-invasion manoeuvres by an American Armoured Unit in England. **1967** *Freedomways* VII. 111 He knows the bombing and shelling and mining we are doing are part of traditional pre-invasion strategy. **1926** Whiteman & McBride *Jazz* vii. 157 The foreign market for American music in pre-jazz times was poor. **1934** C. Lambert *Music Ho!* III. 198 The melodic shape is clearly the most important factor in pre-jazz popular music. **1959** 'F. Newton' *Jazz Scene* iv. 68 Most of the material thus collected was 'pre-jazz'. **1963** *IEEE Trans. Product Engin. & Production* VII. IV. 39/1 The Surveyor spacecraft is subjected to several combinations of environment during prelaunch, boost, free flight, retro, landing and lunar operation. Vibration and shock are negligible during prelaunch operations because of careful handling. **1967** A. Battersby *Network Analysis* (ed. 2) 303 He then goes on to build up the pre-launch stock, advising M as soon as the required stock level has been reached. **1970** N. Armstrong et al. *First on Moon* ii. 45 The conversation..as always during a pre-launch breakfast, was studiedly casual. **1967** *Listener* 13 Apr. 481/1 What I should like to see is more consultation with Members of Parliament before legislation is prepared: what I call pre-legislation committees. *a* **1974** R. Crossman *Diaries* (1976) II. 528 A few weeks ago Roy Jenkins wrote me a long minute to say that he couldn't permit a pre-legislation committee on privacy. **1962** E. Snow *Red China Today* (1963) ii. 25 Near the Hsin Ch'iao I picked one [*sc.* a two-seater pedicab] up, pumped by a neatly dressed gray-haired gentleman who said he pulled a rickshaw at the old Peking Hotel in the 'pre-liberation' days. **1974** tr. *Wertheim's Evolution & Revolution* 287 In pre-liberation China religion in the Confucianist form was associated with the establishment. **1937** R. A. Wilson *Birth of Lang.* iv. 99 The formative energy which produced the tree must..have been latent in the pre-life matter. **1958** *Observer* 15 June 13/4 Scientists believe that pre-life processes may be occurring on the moon. **1962** F. I. Ordway et al. *Basic Astronautics* vi. 258 The search for evidence of extraterrestrial life, or at least prelife carbon compounds. **1967** J. B. Davis *Petroleum Microbiol.* ii. 19 There is no evidence of pre-life organic matter being incorporated in the sedimentary environment of geologic formations. **1959** P. Bull *I know Face* vi. 102 The Leeds incident occurred quite late in the pre-London tour. **1961** *Nottingham Even. Post* 28 July 12 The play is on its pre-London tour. **1962** G. Butler *Coffin in Oxford* iv. 64 They had..made a film..and had now moved.. to Oxford for the pre-London run. **1938** D. Kincaid *Brit. Social Life in India* xii. 276 The elderly gathered together in the clubs for pre-lunch drinks. **1955** A. Ross *Australia 55* 131 This was the first of four successive gloomy pre-lunch sessions for England. **1974** *Times* 4 Nov. 14/4 An appropriate pre-lunch appetizer. **1957** K. A. Wittfogel *Oriental Despotism* i. 13 Temperature and surface are the outstanding constant elements of the agricultural landscape. This was true for the pre-machine age; and it is still essentially true today. **1970** G. E. Evans *Where Beards wag All* xvi. 177 All, or nearly all, of the old terms connected with the pre-machine farming in the region are no longer used. **1963** *Wall St. Jrnl.* 9 Oct. 3/1 The council..proposed 'premarket' safety testing of cosmetics. **1977** *N.Y. Rev. Bks.* 14 Apr. 37/2 The modifications of law which constitute the subject of his book are elements of what Karl Polanya called the 'great transformation' from a pre-market to a market society. **1960** *Farmer & Stockbreeder* 5 Jan. 95/1 Results on farms throughout the country confirm the evidence of pre-marketing trials that Dictol will protect animals against husk. **1920** G. Saintsbury *Notes on Cellar-Bk.* i. 7 This was pre-oïdium and pre-phylloxera wine. **1922** *Proc. Soc. Exper. Biol. & Med.* XIX. 380 Coincident with ovulation in the pigeon there occurs an increase of the blood sugar to 25 per cent. or more above the pre-ovulation value. **1975** *Ann. Human Biol.* II. 325 Variations in the pre-ovulation interval are also indicated by the timing of mid-cycle hormonal peaks. **1974** M. K. Pope *From Latin to Mod. French* II. xvii. 222 The praepause form of the word, the one with sounded consonant, was retained very generally. **1953** *Language* XXIX. 419 There is agreement that there are pitch factors in at least two different kinds of pre-pause terminals ('terminal junctures'). **1920** Pre-phylloxera [see **pre-oïdium*]. **1957** R. Campbell *Portugal* 53 We may never hope to taste again the crowning glories of the best pre-phylloxera vintages. **1972** *Country Life* 25 May 1309/3 Christie's will sell over 100 small lots of mid-19th century port and pre-phylloxera claret. **1949** W. F. Albright *Archaeol. Palestine* iii. 62 In the pre-pottery Neolithic Age man took an important forward step in the Near East. **1960** K. M. Kenyon *Archaeol. in Holy Land* ii. 45 It may be inferred with a high degree of probability that this Pre-Pottery Neolithic A settlement of Jericho was based on a successful system of agriculture. **1977** G. Clark *World Prehist.* (ed. 3) ii. 51 Phases II and III of the Mesolithic period in the Levant, commonly termed 'Pre-pottery Neolithic A and B' in the literature. **1924** H. E. Palmer *Gram. Spoken Eng.* 183 (*heading*) Adverbs in the pre-qualificative position... These immediately precede the qualificative... They also precede any other adverb they may modify. **1946** R. Blesh *Shining Trumpets* (1949) x. 220 The first hot records..sold by the millions and, in those preradio days, disseminated jazz more rapidly.. than a score of travelling bands. **1949** Bruner & Postman in Bruner & Krech *Perception & Personality* (1950) 26 Differential availability [of response systems]..leads to certain characteristic 'normalizing' prerecognition responses in our incongruity experiments. **1970** *Jrnl. Gen. Psychol.* LXXXIII. 24 As a corollary of lower recognition thresholds with increased information, we can expect fewer prerecognition responses. **1929** Pre-Reformation [see *pre-Renaissance* below]. **1920** A. S. Eddington *Space, Time & Gravitation* ix. 149 Action is one of the two terms in pre-relativity physics which survive unmodified in a description of the absolute world. **1946** *Mind* LV. 161 A pre-relativity physicist could use the figure..by interpreting AM and TM as curves of velocity. **1929** T. S. Eliot *Dante* i. 19 A directness of speech which Dante shares with other great poets of pre-Reformation and pre-Renaissance times. **1976** R. Pfeiffer *Hist. Classical Scholarship 1300–1850* i. 21 There seems to be a slight shifting of emphasis to the advantage of the classics, inconceivable in pre-Renaissance times. **1961** A. Heron *Solving New Probl.* 21 Does the evidence obtained support a rationale for adapting a pre-retirement planning and preparation programme to the needs of older employees of different occupational levels? **1965** J. Pollitt *Depression & its Treatment* vii. 91 Older patients have greater difficulty than those of pre-retirement age in re-adjusting their lives after illness. **1976** *Evening Post* (Nottingham) 16 Dec. 2/6 Support for a pre-retirement course run by Gedling Borough Council was so good that plans for a second session are already in the pipeline. *a* **1902** S. Butler *Way of All Flesh* (1903) xiv. 63 The pre-revolution French peasant. **1939** H. Nicolson *Diary* 3 Apr. (1966) 394 Apparently many of their [*sc.* the Polish army's] guns are pre-Revolution guns of the Russian Army. **1978** N. Marsh *Grave Mistake* iii. 91 A pre-revolution Russian stamp that was withdrawn on the day it was issued. **1961** *Dallas Morning News* 10 Oct. 2–2 It looks as if coach Hank Stram's men will meet the Bills just as they are developing into the kind of team they were expected to be in pre-season reckonings. **1970** N. Armstrong et al. *First on Moon* vii. 144 In sports, the Houston Oilers are showing plenty of enthusiasm in their early preseason workouts. **1975** *Cricketer* May 27/2 D. J. Insole will be giving all first-class umpires a pre-season briefing. **1979** *N.Y. Post* 10 Aug. 17 In one of our most bizarre pre-season presidential campaigns, an incumbent President is being dismissed by both the opposition and large sectors of his own party as a non-person. **1926** Rows & Bond *Epilepsy* iv. 87 In the pre-seizure period the disturbances of consciousness often commence with a slight difficulty in the power of attention and pass through the stages of dreamy states and fugues to complete unconsciousness. **1966** *Jrnl. Neurol., Neurosurg. & Psychiatry* XXIX. 253/2 The E.E.G. appeared normal on all the pre-seizure tracings. **1926** *Glasgow Herald* 19 Oct. 9 Before the contests, there are whispers of excellent pre-show performances of competing cows. **1960** *Farmer & Stockbreeder* 2 Feb. 84/1 Sons of several famous bulls were in competition in the showyard and their fortunes were the subject of considerable pre-show speculation. **1964** *Language* XL. 269 Nobody has made a thorough study of presleep soliloquies before. **1970** N. Armstrong et al. *First on Moon* xiii. 333 We're standing by for an exciting evening of TV and a presleep report. **1924** H. E. Palmer *Gram. Spoken Eng.* II. 182 Adverbs in the pre-subject position. **1961** R. B. Long *Sentence & its Parts* xx. 471 No comma is used after pre-subject adjunct clauses functioning as clause markers in assertives. **1976** *Archivum Linguisticum* VII. 32 It looks like the same pre-subject position that we called I in the 'kernel' form of the sentence. **1965** *B.B.C. Handbk.* 28 Even though BBC radio's evening audience is much less than it was in pre-television days it is by no means inconsiderable. **1969** *Listener* 15 May 700/3 Sponsorship has entered into the scheme of things. So has advertising, which was never around in pre-television days. **1974** *Times* 17 Aug. 7/4 The older school of comedians, the pre-television comics. **1953** R. Fuller *Second Curtain* v. 74 The place was filling up: a few were eating pre-theatre meals. **1967** A. Bailey in L. Deighton *London Dossier* 49 This is really a lunch or pre-theatre restaurant, since it closes at 8.30 p.m. **1977** *Rolling Stone* 7 Apr. 30/2 Pre-tour jitters are an occupational hazard the McGarrigle sisters have avoided up to now. **1949** E. A. Nida *Morphol.* (ed. 2) ii. 16 Word-initial prevowel glottal stops. **1977** *Time* 26 Dec. 41/2 The message rings out, too, at the early morning pre-work prayer meetings held by businessmen. **1923** D. H. Lawrence *Birds, Beasts & Flowers* 99 Fishes, With.. their pre-world loneliness.

II. 3. In adjs. (also sometimes used as sbs.), chiefly *Anat.* and *Zool.* Also occas. with sbs. directly forming sbs., as *prealbumin. **prehy·oid,** in front of the hyoid bone; **premo·tor,** applied to the anterior part of the precentral area of the frontal lobe of the brain, which is concerned with the co-ordination of activities in the motor area immediately posterior to it; **pre·palatal** (further examples); *spec.* in *Phonetics,* of a consonant articulated with obstruction of the airstream immediately in front of the palate; **prepatellar** (earlier example); **prepatellar bursitis,** inflammation of the prepatellar bursa; = *housemaid's knee* s.v. Housemaid c in Dict. and Suppl.; **prespira·cular,** in front of a spiracle.

1949 I. F. & W. D. Henderson *Dict. Sci. Terms* (ed. 4) 351/1 *Prehyoid,* mandibulo-hyoid; *appl.* cleft between mandible and ventral parts of hyoid arch. **1974** D. & M. Webster *Compar. Vertebr. Morphol.* vii. 129 In living amphibians the hypobranchial muscles can be divided into a prehyoid and a posthyoid group. **1932** *Brain* LV. 534 In the baboon forced grasping appeared five to six days after removal of the motor and premotor areas. **1978** *Sci. Amer.* Oct. 52/2 (*caption*) The premotor area is involved in complex motor activity such as operating a typewriter. **1902,** etc. Pre-palatal [see *medio-palatal* adj. s.v. *medio- 2]. **1925** P. Radin tr. *Vendryès's Language* I. i. 23 We distinguish..the pre-palatals and the post-palatals. **1934** Priebsch & Collinson *German Lang.* II. i. 88 The *s* was more prepalatal. **1958** J. Berry in J. A. Fishman *Readings Sociol. of Lang.* (1968) 741 Is it better..that all related languages of southern Ghana write the prepalatal affricate 'tʃ' uniformly so, or (under cultural pressure of the trade language), '*ch*'? **1964** *Archivum Linguisticum* XVI. 22 The affricate *ch* [č] or the corresponding pre-palatal *x* [š]. **1973** *Amer. Speech 1969* XLIV. 265 An *r* produced by passing the breath between the underside of the apex of the tongue and the postalveolar or prepalatal region. **1977** *Word 1972* XXVIII. 248 Caballero..described the [ž] as a voiced prepalatal. **1882** C. B. Nancrede in J. Ashhurst *Internat. Encycl. Surg.* II. 717 (*heading*) Pre-patellar bursa. **1902** R. T. Frank tr. *Albert's Diagnosis Surg. Dis.* xxxiii. 370 Prepatellar bursitis requires but casual mention. A strictly circumscribed, elastic tense swelling directly in front of the patella is characteristic. **1927** W. C. Campbell *Orthopedics of Childhood* xii. 217 Pre-patellar bursitis is commonly due to excess kneeling. The symptoms are similar to those of bursitis elsewhere. **1964** *Australasian Post* 21 May 13, I rushed off in anguish and looked up prepatellar bursitis in a medical dictionary. It was.. housemaid's knee. **1902** *Nature* 16 Oct. 604/1 The last-mentioned [*sc.* the chorda tympani] is spoken of as..prespiracular in position. **1975** *Ibid.* 10 Apr. 483/3 Patterson confirms the homology between the spiracular groove of primitive actinopterygians..and the 'pre-spiracular groove' of rhipidistians.

pre (prī), *prep.* [A further development of *pre- B. 2c; cf. *post *Lat. prep.* 6.] = Before *prep.* 8.

Usu. found in contexts where *before* would be equally appropriate and more agreeable.—Ed.

1973 G. Sims *Hunters Point* xiii. 119 'Have you tried phoning David's friends in Los Angeles?'.. 'They are all pre my era and I don't know their names.' **1975** H. Kissinger in *Dept. of State Bull.* 6 Oct. 532 Pre my being in office; those decisions were made in the previous Administration.

pre-accentual: see *pre- B. 1d.

preach, *sb.*[2] Colloq. abbrev. of Preacher. *U.S.*

1968 D. Wilkerson *Hey, Preach—you're comin' Through!* 9 He grabbed my arm and blurted: 'Hey, Preach—you're comin' through!' **1969** C. F. Burke *God is Beautiful, Man* (1970) 96 Ananias..puttin' his hands on him like the preach down at the revival camp does.

preach, *v.* Add: **1. c.** Phr. *to preach to the converted*: to commend an opinion to those who already assent to it.

1867 Mill *Exam. Hamilton's Philos.* (ed. 3) xiv. 319 Dr. M'Cosh is preaching not only to a person already converted, but to an actual missionary of the same doctrine. **1916** G. Saintsbury *Peace of Augustans* iii. 144 One may be said to be preaching to the converted and kicking at open doors in praising..the four great novelists of the eighteenth century. **1971** *It* 2–16 June 14/4 The problem is as usual that one tends to be preaching to the converted —so the important thing is to make sure that people who don't know are informed.

preacher. Add: **4. preacher-man** *U.S. dial.,* = sense 1a.

1899 in H. Wentworth *Amer. Dial. Dict.* (1944) 474/1. **1913** H. Kephart *Our Southern Highlanders* xiii. 286 Everywhere in the mountains we hear of biscuit-bread.. preacher-man, granny-woman. **1977** *Times* 23 May 5/1 A nice, homespun preacherman who spoke with a Southern drawl.

preachify, *v.* Add: Hence **prea·chifying** *ppl. a.*

1916 W. Owen *Let.* 13 July (1967) 399 His dogmatic, pig-headed, preachifying, self-sufficient manners and domineering tone. **1978** J. Anderson *Angel of Death* vii. 70 I'm not a great admirer of..paternalistic, preachifying Christianity.

preaching, *vbl. sb.* Add: **3.** *preaching-place* (later examples), *-stand, -stole*; **preaching-cross** (later examples).

1845 A. Wiley in *Indiana Mag. Hist.* (1927) XXIII. 37 Many new neighbors were taken in as preaching places. **1848** *Wesleyan Missionary Notices* VI. 164/1 In my last I expressed a desire..to open a preaching-place in a mountain district [of Jamaica]. **1856** Mrs. Stowe *Dred* I. xxiii. 314 The assembly poured in and arranged themselves before the preaching-stand. **1857** P. Cartwright *Autobiogr.* viii. 85 We took in a new preaching-place at a Mr. Moor's. **1953** M. Powys *Lace & Lace-Making* vi. 67 A small piece of lace like a straight collar about seven inches long and one and a half inches wide could be used as a 'protective' for a preaching stole. **1959** C. L. Wrenn *Word & Symbol* (1967) 23 The association of the saintly first preachers of Christianity in religious memory with the 'preaching crosses', which the missionary first set up at his oratory, is a well-known feature of the early Celtic Church. **1960** *Church & People* Nov.-Dec. 182 Africans flocking to our Mission churches and preaching places. **1970** M. Swanton *Dream of Rood* 13 It is clearly a preaching cross. Its message is evangelical, stating the role of Christ in the world of men. **1972** *Country Life* 17 Feb. 408/1 One such building at Sare dedicated to Saint Francis Xavier has a most unusual statue in coloured wood showing the saint in cassock, surplice and preaching stole.

preaching-house. (Earlier example.)
1747 J. WESLEY *Jrnl.* 2 Nov. (1912) III. 321 Mr. J. Richards had just sent his brother word that he had hired a mob to pull down his preaching-house that night.

preachy, *a.* (Further examples.)
1955 A. HUXLEY *Let.* 29 May (1969) 748 If I seem to be smug and preachy, forgive me. **1966** *Word Study* Feb. 5/2 Getting so dogmatic, or preachy, or stuffy that our students rebel against us. **1978** *Time* 3 July 15/2 He is tiresomely preachy in his talks with non-Israeli leaders, repeating to the point of boredom his odd fact-and-fiction litany of Jewish biblical and legal rights, his self-justification for Irgun atrocities and his blend of self-righteous arrogance.

pre-Adamite, *sb.* and *a.* Add: **A.** *sb.* **4.** *N.Z.* An inhabitant of Canterbury Province before the settlement of 1850.
1930 L. G. D. ACLAND *Early Canterbury Runs* 1st Ser. i. 3 The old 'Pre-Adamites'..were those who had bought land from the New Zealand Company and settled here before the Canterbury settlers arrived. **1949** A. H. REED *Story of Canterbury* iii. 55 To the Hays and Sinclairs and other 'pre-Adamites'—as those few who had arrived before the 'Pilgrims' came jocularly to be called—these ships represented shops, schools, churches, roads and other amenities of which they had for so long been deprived. **1977** *N.Z. Herald* 8 Jan. 1-6/6 Any reader whose antecedents were among these 'Pre-Adamites', as they are called, is invited to send their names..to [address given].
B. *adj.* **1.** (Further example.)
1916 *Nature* 25 May 259/2 For imitation, a pre-Adamite simian character, plays no small part in the ostensible development, mental, moral, and otherwise, of gregarious folk.
pre-adamitism (later example).
1880 A. WINCHELL *Preadamites* p. iii, The central idea of the work is human preadamitism.

preadapt (prīădæ·pt), *v.* [PRE- A. 1.] *trans.* To adapt beforehand; *spec.* in *Biol.*, to adapt (an organism) for life in conditions not yet available to it. Hence **preada·pted** *ppl. a.* [in *Biol.* tr. F. *préadapté* (L. Cuénot *La Genèse des Espèces Animales* (1911) IV. 291)].
1849 [in Dict. s.v. PRE- A. 1.] **1915** *Eugenics Rev.* VII. 56 By being warm-blooded, mammals and birds are enabled to maintain their normal activity throughout a wide range of temperature, and they may therefore be said to be preadapted to all temperatures within that range. **1947** *New Biol.* III. 90 For the most part cave animals are drawn from groups habitually living in damp, dim places, such as under stones or at the bottoms of streams; they are, so to speak, preadapted to life in caves before they enter them. **1952** *Ibid.* XIII. 25 An animal adapted to living in a small isolated volume would be preadapted to captivity. **1969** J. M. WELLER *Course of Evol.* ix. 467 The evolutionary development..of these advanced and more complex feathers, whose original function was insulation, preadapted the very early birds for flight. **1970** T. H. EATON *Evolution* viii. 121 In retrospect we can say that some thecodonts were 'preadapted' in certain ways for the life of birds. **1976** *Sci. Amer.* Aug. 38/2 Such a trend, may, however, have helped to preadapt the Egyptians to a ready acceptance of food production later.
Hence **preˌada·ptive** *a.*, causing or characterized by preadaptation.
1915 *Eugenics Rev.* VII. 50 One can call indifferent or semi-useful, characters in a species which become evident adaptations on removal to a new habitat or on the acquirement of new habits, preadaptive or prophetic characters, or more briefly, preadaptations. **1944** G. G. SIMPSON *Tempo & Mode in Evol.* vi. 186 The direct development of adaptations in one environment may be preadaptive for another. **1969** J. M. WELLER *Course of Evol.* i. 20 Potentially preadaptive mutations..are likely to accumulate within a population as recessives.

preˌadapta·tion. [PRE- A. 2.] Adaptation beforehand; *spec.* in *Biol.* [tr. F. *préadaptation* (L. Cuénot *La Genèse des Espèces Animales* (1911) IV. 306)], the possession or acquisition by an organism of heritable features which adapt it to an environment or mode of life which only later becomes available to it.
1886 [in Dict. s.v. PRE- A. 2]. **1915** *Eugenics Rev.* VII. 56 Versatility is an attempt at universal preadaptation, indeed at complete independence of particular circumstances. **1934** *Biol. Abstr.* VIII. 289/2 'Preadaptation': the occupation of empty regions is made by neighbouring spp. already prepared in the sense of having a necessary and sufficient adaptation. **1942** *Tee Emm* (Air Ministry) II. 144 Wear the special pre-adaptation goggles which will provide you with your hour's synthetic night before you tackle the real one. **1953** G. G. SIMPSON *Major Features Evol.* vi. 188 The term 'preadaptation' has been applied to a great variety of real or supposed evolutionary phenomena, from the appearance of a small mutation with selective value in the population in which it occurs to the sudden appearance of a form monstrous in its parental population but miraculously, one might almost say, adapted to some quite different way of life. **1978** *Sci. Amer.* Sept. 51/1 If a favored mutation does appear, it can be viewed as exhibiting a 'preadaptation' to that particular environment: it did not arise as an adaptive response but rather proved to be adaptive after it appeared.
Hence **preˌadapta·tional** *a.*, pertaining to or characterized by preadaptation.
1940 R. GOLDSCHMIDT *Material Basis Evol.* iii. 151 A return of the subspecies at one extreme end toward the starting point could only be accomplished by retracing the steps of preadaptational mutation to its original condition. **1944** G. G. SIMPSON *Tempo & Mode in Evol.* vi. 188 The field naturalist..is not likely to be satisfied in such cases with the preadaptational axiom that animals enter a new environment simply because they can.

pre-address, see *PRE- A. 1. **pre-adjectival, -adjunct:** *PRE- B. 1d, A. 2.

preadmission. Add: **B.** *adj.* [PRE- B. 2.] Prior to admission.
1971 *Mod. Law Rev.* XXXIV. 642 The universities are to gain in both responsibility and autonomy..by assuming responsibility for pre-admission vocational training.

preˌadole·scent, *a.* and *sb.* [PRE- B. 1.] **A.** *adj.* **a.** Of a child: having nearly reached the beginning of adolescence. **b.** Of or pertaining to the two or three years before the beginning of adolescence.
1910 A. C. PERRY *Probl. Elementary School* x. 201 It is probably true that the preadolescent girl can pursue her school work side by side with the boy without the slightest danger. **1925** *Arch. Neurol. & Psychiatry* XIV. 215 Since the patient is usually preadolescent, a separation of the cranial sutures..is likely to be present. **1935** E. BOWEN *House in Paris* II. i. 81 His pre-adolescent mind. **1949** M. MEAD *Male & Female* xi. 232 The charming street-dance in which a little pre-adolescent girl dances to delight the men of the village. **1976** DEAKIN & WILLIS *Johnny go Home* vi. 85 Happier pre-adolescent family holidays.
B. *sb.* A preadolescent child.
1930 K. MCHALE *Pre-Adolescence* 3 Most people look upon the average pre-adolescent as one who has his second teeth..and who is not yet burdened with any difficult adjustments. **1951** *Child Devel.* XXII. 15 The opportunity to observe the play configurations of pre-adolescents was offered by the Guidance Study at the Institute of Child Welfare, University of California. **1960** *20th Cent.* Nov. 434 The idea of the unfallen, pre-adolescent has exercised an extraordinarily strong appeal. **1973** *Nature* 27 Apr. 582/3 A pabulum of romanticized science digested to gibberish for consumption by pre-adolescents.
Hence **preˌadole·scence,** the preadolescent period or stage of development.
1930 K. MCHALE *Pre-Adolescence* 3 The brain..reaches nearly maximum size during the years of pre-adolescence. **1949** E. B. HURLOCK *Adolescent Devel.* i. 4 Because boys mature slightly later than girls, we may regard their pre-adolescence as extending from 11 to 12½ or 13, early adolescence from 13 to 17, and late adolescence from 18 to 21 years. **1972** *Sci. Amer.* July 76/2 She was able to follow the same child from birth to preadolescence.

pre-adult, -adverbial, -agonal, -agonic, -agricultural: see *PRE- B. 1.

prealbumin (prīˌæ·lbiŭmin, -æ̆lbiŭ·min). *Biochem.* [PRE- B. 3 in Dict. and Suppl.; so called because it appears slightly in front of albumin during electrophoresis.] A plasma protein with an electrophoretic mobility slightly greater than that of albumin; *spec.* a tetramer in human blood which binds thyroxine and the retinol-binding protein.
1955 O. SMITHIES in *Biochem. Jrnl.* LXI. 634/2 The two components migrating more rapidly than the broad albumen zone are referred to as the pre-albumins$_1$ and $_2$ ($_1$ indicating the faster-moving component). **1959** *Nature* 3 Oct. 1067/2 (*heading*) Separation of prealbumins by starch gel electrophoresis. **1975** F. W. PUTNAM *Plasma Proteins* (ed. 2) I. ii. 72 Prealbumins have been described in other species such as the mouse; the molecular weight is only about 20,000 and the function is unknown. **1976** *Sci. Amer.* Sept. 58/2 When dietary protein intake is deficient, the two proteins that play a role in the transport of vitamin A (retinol-binding protein and prealbumin) are not made by the liver in adequate amounts.

pre-Alfredian: see *PRE- B. 1a.

preamble, *v.* Add: **II. 4.** (Later examples.) Also *transf.*
1951 W. SANSOM *Face of Innocence* iv. 45 She might think this was a trick of Harry's to get her away with him, to preamble the marriage-bed. **1980** *Time* 28 Jan. 90/1 Nouns continue to be overrun by the jargonaut: the New York *Times* demands stronger sourcing, meetings are preambled, situations are impacted.

pre-amp (prī·æmp), abbrev. of *PREAMPLIFIER.
1957 *Practical Wireless* XXXIII. 573/1 The pre-amp and output stages make use of highly efficient miniature valves. **1968** *Times* 29 Nov. (Sound of Leisure Suppl.) p. ii/2 The cost of stereo at its best is off-putting (a second matching speaker, stereo amplifier and pre-amp., stereo head, cartridge and stylus—your old turntable will still suffice). **1975** *Hi-Fi Answers* Feb. 81/1 (Advt.), Leak 12 watt mono valve amplifier, with Rogers pre-amp. £8. **1978** *Nature* 18 May 218/2 A preamp was mounted directly on the base of the detector (bias ~ 100V) and its output was fed to an amplifier.

preˌa·mplifier. [PRE- A. 2.] An amplifier designed to amplify a very weak signal (as from a microphone, pickup, or similar source) and deliver it to another amplifier for further amplification.
1935 *Television* VIII. 654/1 This pre-amplifier brought R4 signals up to consistent full loud-speaker strength. **1952** *Electronic Engin.* XXIV. 498/1 The low output signal obtained from a pick-up necessitates the use of a pre-amplifier. **1957** *New Yorker* 2 Nov. 95/2 Bogen RR550 DeLuxe FM-AM Receiver with built-in Preamplifier and Power Amplifier. **1965** *Wireless World* July 33 (Advt.), Transistor A.C. Microvoltmeter... Ideal as an oscilloscope preamplifier as it has a low noise level, low microphony, no hum and is independent of a mains supply. **1977** *Gramophone* June 117/1 Between the preamplifiers and the power amplifiers there are four Urei 527A ⅓-octave equalizers.

preˌa·mplify, *v.* [PRE- A. 1.] *trans.* To subject to a preliminary amplification; to amplify in a preamplifier. Hence **prea·mplified** *ppl. a.*
1959 *Geophysics* XXIV. 750 The reflected signal detected by the hydrophone is pre-amplified, passed through a variable passive filter, then amplified and printed on the recorder. **1978** *Nature* 13 July 135/1 After cell contact, lock-in amplifiers sample preamplified cell potentials..at selectable phase angles. *Ibid.* 14 Sept. 111/2 The signals were preamplified and detected by two automatic gain-controlled receivers.
Hence **preˌamplifica·tion,** the action or result of preamplifying.
1960 *Practical Wireless* XXXVI. 397/1 The amplifier has sufficient gain for many purposes with no pre-amplification. **1971** *Melody Maker* 13 Nov. 36/5 A new concept in sound engineering..is the Mark 3 Jam-Pak series, a unique idea in pre-amplification systems. **1977** *Rolling Stone* 13 Jan. 58/2 Most ribbon mikes produce lower output signals than most dynamic types and require more preamplification.

pre-anæsthe·tic, *a.* (*sb.*) *Med.* [PRE- B. 1.] **a.** Occurring before the introduction of anæsthetics into surgical practice.
1892 [in Dict. s.v. PRE- B. 1]. **1916** P. J. FLAGG *Art of Anæsthesia* I. 1 The pre-anæsthetic period ends and the anæsthetic period begins with the discovery of ether in 1842 and its general introduction in 1846.
b. Used or carried out as a preliminary to the induction of anæsthesia. Also as *sb.*, a drug so used.
1930 [see *NEMBUTAL]. **1934** *Current Res. Anesthesia & Analgesia* XIII. 169 (*heading*) Pernoston as a preanesthetic in surgery. **1957** S. M. BROOKS *Basic Facts Pharmacol.* ii. 76 The most popular preanesthetic is a combination of morphine and atropine. **1974** A. FREEMAN in Lichtiger & Moya *Introd. Practice of Anesthesia* xxvii. 334 A barbiturate combined with a narcotic and a belladonna alkaloid produces suitable preanesthetic sedation in most children over 1 year of age.
Hence **pre-anæsthe·tically** *adv.*
1952 V. J. COLLINS *Princ. & Pract. Anesthesiol.* vii. 64 His work indicated one of the primary objects in the use of morphine preanesthetically namely, depression of basal metabolic rate and oxygen consumption.

pre-analytic(al, -ally: see *PRE- B. 1.

pre-a·nimism. [PRE- B. 1 in Dict. and Suppl.] Primitive belief that certain powers exist in material objects. Cf. next.
1918 A. A. BRILL tr. *Freud's Totem & Taboo* (1919) iii. 152 We have practically no further knowledge of pre-animism, as no race has yet been found without conceptions of spirits. **1937** *Nature* 27 Nov. 923/1 Dr. Robert Ranulph Marett..is best known as an anthropologist, the formulator of the theory of preanimism in the study of primitive religion. **1956** E. E. EVANS-PRITCHARD *Nuer Relig.* xiii. 311 Many such origins have been propounded: magic, fetishism, manism, animism, pre-animism. **1963** S. FUCHS *Origin of Man & his Culture* xviii. 232 Andrew Lang maintained that pre-animism took two forms, that of magic and that of primitive monotheism.

pre-animi·stic, *a.* [PRE- B. 1.] Applied to a stage of religious culture, presumed to precede animism, at which the power or spirit attributed to a material object was believed to exist in the object.
1900 R. R. MARETT in *Folk-Lore* XI. 162 (*title*) Pre-animistic religion. *Ibid.* 170, I propose that we examine a few typical cases of Powers, which, beneath the animistic colour that..has more or less completely overlaid them, show traces of having once of their own right possessed pre-animistic validity as objects and occasions of man's religious feeling. **1918** A. A. BRILL tr. *Freud's Totem & Taboo* (1919) iii. 152 Our psychoanalytic view here coincides with a theory of R. R. Marett, according to which animism is preceded by a pre-animistic stage. **1949** KOESTLER *Insight & Outlook* xii. 175 Members of such very early, preanimistic types of society may be described as living in a state of original self-transcendence of consciousness. **1963** S. FUCHS *Origin of Man & his Culture* xviii. 232 It was soon necessary to assume a pre-animistic stage of religion.

pre-apprehend, -Arnoldian: see *PRE- A. 1, B. 1a.

pre-arrange, *v.* (Earlier example.)
1811 JANE AUSTEN *Sense & Sens.* III. vii. 133 With..the service pre-arranged in his mind, he offered himself as the messenger.

pre-article: see *PRE- B. 1. **preaspirate:** *PRE- A. 1. **preaspiration:** *PRE- A. 2. **pre-assemble:** *PRE- A. 1.

pre-asse·mbly, *sb.* and *a.* **A.** *sb.* [PRE- A. 2.] Preliminary assembly. Also *attrib.*

1958 *Engineering* 31 Jan. 140/2 From the fabrication shed the steel is moved over into the adjacent pre-assembly shed. *Ibid.* 140/3 The bulk of pre-assembly in the yard..is by welding.

B. *adj.* [PRE- B. 2.] Prior to assembly.

1977 *Design Engin.* July 37/3 This means that operations and parts are eliminated and that pre-assembly tolerances of components are relaxed.

preassure, *v.* (Earlier example.)

1697 J. SERGEANT *Solid Philos.* 294 Being pre-assur'd the Thing has more Modes in it than we know.

pre-ato·mic, *a.* [PRE- B. 1.] Existing or occurring before the utilization of atomic energy or atomic weapons; characteristic of such a time.

1914 H. G. WELLS *World set Free* iii. 141 Originally he had been something of a thinker upon international politics,..but the atomic bombs had taken him by surprise and he had still to recover completely from his pre-atomic opinions. **1945** R. A. KNOX *God & Atom* ii. 28 The ladder that is meant to climb heaven from our front door-step climbs it, instead, from a period world which only history recaptures for us. It is definitely pre-Atomic. **1945** *N.Y. Times* 12 Aug. 8 E/4 To talk about limited, almost parochial pre-atomic subjects, there is the important war of 1914–18. **1956** A. TOYNBEE *Historian's Approach to Relig.* 215 It [*sc.* the world] has already experienced two devastating pre-atomic wars in one lifetime.

pre-audit: see *PRE- A. 1, 2. **pre-auditor:** *PRE- A. 2. **pre-Augustinian:** *PRE- B. 1 a.

pre-auri·cular, *a. Anat.* [PRE- B. 3.] **1.** [ad. mod.L. (*sulcus*) *præ-auriculāris* (coined in Ger. by T. Zaaijer 1866, in *Natuurkundige Verhandelingen te Haarlem* XXIV. 28).] Designating a groove situated immediately anterior to the inferior margin of the auricular surface of the ilium, and better developed in the female than in the male.

[**1886** *Rep. Sci. Results Voy. H.M.S. Challenger* XVI. XLVII. 55 The most distinct examples of the sulcus præauricularis were found in the pelves of the Sandwich Island women.] **1897** *Lippincott's Med. Dict.* 822/2 Preauricular sulcus. **1911** *Anatomischer Anzeiger* XXXIX. 17 If now a dissection of the sacro-iliac joint is made in a woman, the praeauricular sulcus is seen to be entirely filled with ligamentous fibres. **1914** J. E. FRAZER *Anat. Human Skeleton* v. 132 The pre-auricular groove..is as a rule only found on female bones. **1974** *Amer. Jrnl. Physical Anthropol.* XLI. 381/1 The pre-auricular groove of the ilium is usually cited as one of the morphological features to be noted when sexing human pelves.

2. Situated in front of the ear(s).

1901 *Amer. Anthropologist* III. 38 Preauricular. **1934** *Jrnl. Anat.* LXVIII. 533 Pre-auricular fistulae and pre-auricular appendages..lie along the line of the first pharyngeal depression. **1970** *Amer. Jrnl. Ophthalm.* LXXII. 798 (*caption*) Pre-auricular lymph node showing secondary malignant melanoma.

pre-bacteriologic(al), -baiting: see *PRE- B. 1, A. 1.

prebiolo·gical, *a.* [PRE- B. 1.] Existing or occurring before the appearance of life; pertaining to the origin of life; = *PREBIOTIC *a.*

1960 *Science* 22 July 200/3 Calvin's experiments have been criticized on the basis that the prebiological atmosphere contained only a small proportion of carbon dioxide. **1971** I. G. GASS et al. *Understanding Earth* ix. 123 Concentration of these compounds by geological processes established reservoirs of prebiological food. *Ibid.*, A prebiological environment. **1973** C. SAGAN *Cosmic Connection* vii. 54 The search for prebiological organic chemicals on the Moon, on Mars, or on Jupiter is of great importance in understanding the steps leading to the origin of life.

So **prebio·logy,** the study of the origin of life, and of conditions before this; **prebio·logist,** a specialist in this.

1963 S. W. FOX in I. A. Breger *Org. Geochem.* ii. 40 The reaction mixture used represents..material which has significance in the context of prebiology, due particularly to the recent emphasis by Revelle..on carbon monoxide in the primitive atmosphere. **1971** I. G. GASS et al. *Understanding Earth* ix. 137/1 All the experimental evidence of prebiology points to the fact that the carbonaceous products were synthesized from gases. **1974** *Nature* 8 Mar. 180/1 Eight planetary astronomers..were assembled to meet ten practitioners interested in the origins of life (three exobiologists, two microbiologists, four chemical prebiologists and one palaeontologist).

prebio·tic, *a.* [PRE- B. 1.] = *PREBIOLOGICAL *a.*

1958 *New Statesman* 23 Aug. 214/2 The dust is prebiotic, that is, before the formation of life, but with all the biochemical elements, from which life originated, waiting to be 'organised' into a chemistry of reproduction. **1962** F. I. ORDWAY et al. *Basic Astronautics* vi. 250 Lightning.. may have originally been responsible for the creation of the first organic molecules from prebiotic molecules. **1968** *New Scientist* 29 Aug. 437/1 Studies on prebiotic synthesis—the way in which the chemicals of life may have originated on the primitive earth—generally have an esoteric ring to them. **1973** B. J. WILLIAMS *Evolution & Human Origins* vii. 94/1 It was a closed system containing only water, the gases assumed to be present in the prebiotic atmosphere, and an energy source.

preboa·rd, *v.* [PRE- A. 1.] *trans.* To shape by heating on a form before dyeing rather than after.

1940 *Rayon Textile Monthly* Apr. 59/1 Nylon, the new synthetic yarn..has added a new operation to the manufacture of stockings... It has been found necessary to 'set' the shape of the stocking before it is dyed... At first, various methods of 'pre-boarding', or 'setting', the stockings were tried. **1950** B. E. HARTSUCH *Introd. Textile Chem.* xi. 330 When full-fashioned nylon stockings are preboarded, they are mounted on metal forms of suitable shape, and these forms are heated externally with live steam for about 1 to 3 minutes. **1963** R. W. MONCRIEFF *Man-Made Fibres* (ed. 4) xliv. 660 The hosiery were seamed, pre-boarded 5 min. in 27 lb./in.² steam, scoured in 2 per cent sodium lauryl sulphate + 2 per cent caustic soda. They were dyed gold, finished with a standard resin emulsion hosiery finish, and postboarded dry at 200°C. **1970** *Ibid.* (ed. 5) xlvii. 809 The cycle of operations is normally (1) pre-board, (2) dye, (3) post-board, (4) dry.

Hence **preboa·rded** *ppl. a.*, **preboa·rding** *vbl. sb.*

1940 *Rayon Textile Monthly* Apr. 59/2 Various types of pre-boarding equipment. *Ibid.* 60/1 It is not necessary to lay the pre-boarded stocking out flat, as it still has to be dyed. **1953** K. H. INDERFURTH *Nylon Technol.* viii. 208 Placing the gray stockings onto the preboarding form.. must be carefully and accurately performed in order to ensure satisfactory fit, wearing qualities, and sales appeal. **1964** E. R. TROTMAN *Dyeing & Chem. Technol. Textile Fibres* (ed. 3) xxiii. 512 In the case of pre-boarding, the most convenient time for the operation is before scouring.

pre-book: see *PRE- A. 1.

Pre,bo·real, *a.* Also **pre-Boreal, preboreal.** [PRE- B. 1.] Applied to a European climatic period that followed the Arctic and preceded, or marked the transition to, the Boreal period, and was characterized by the spread of birch and pine forests. Also *absol.*

1924 *Jrnl. Linn. Soc.* (*Bot.*) XLVI. 497 (*caption*) Pollen-spectra... Holland (S.W. Sweden) (preboreal spectrum). **1934** *New Phytologist* XXXIII. 285 Erdtman suggests that it is partly on account of *P. montana* pollen that the pine maximum in many parts of the continent falls so much earlier than in England (i.e. in the Early Boreal or pre-Boreal). **1956** A. L. ARMSTRONG in D. L. Linton *Sheffield* vi. 101 The known [Mesolithic] moorland sites are usually upon patches of old land surface.., or in the eroded banks of streams and cloughs, where their pre-Boreal age is testified by remains of the Pennine forest lying in the peat above them. **1976** *Sci. Amer.* Feb. 94/2 Sometime between 8300 and 8000 B.C. the cold Late Dryas period was superseded by a warmer period known as the Preboreal. Pine and birch forest reinvaded the European plain from the south, and the reindeer herd, following the retreating tundra, moved off to the north and northeast.

pre-Broadway: see *PRE- B. 2 a.

Pre-Ca·mbrian, *a. Geol.* Also **pre-Cambrian, Precambrian.** [PRE- B. 1.] Of, pertaining to, or designating the time before the beginning of the Cambrian period and Palæozoic era, present-day rocks of which are marked by an almost complete absence of fossils. Also *ellipt.*, the Pre-Cambrian rocks or period.

1864 J. W. SALTER in *Geol. Mag.* I. 290 The author suggests that the syenitic trap of St. David's is a part of the old pre-Cambrian land. **1875** [in Dict. s.v. PRE- B. 1]. **1910** LAKE & RASTALL *Text-bk. Geol.* xvii. 292 Everywhere in the British Isles there is a marked unconformity between the pre-Cambrian and the later deposits. **1915** C. SCHUCHERT *Text-bk. Geol.* II. xxvii. 540 The result.. serves to make prominent the two most significant and distinctive features of the pre-Cambrian: (1) the wide-spread crustal revolutions,.. and (2) the profound depth to which erosion has planed. **1921** A. W. GRABAU *Textbk. Geol.* II. xxx. 198 (*heading*) Summary of the pre-Cambrian of the Canadian region. **1951** AUDEN *Nones* (1952) 71 That the red pre-Cambrian light Is gone like Imperial Rome Or myself at seventeen. **1959** *Times* 18 June (Queen in Canada Suppl.) p. xiii/2 The gnarled Precambrian surface of the Canadian Shield, the low hills of the Mackenzie valley are all foreign to the Yukon. **1969** E. W. MORSE *Fur Trade Canoe Routes of Canada* v. 57 At the upper end of Lac des Alumettes the voyageurs came.. into close contact with the granite of the Precambrian Shield, rising straight from the water. **1971** *Nature* 25 June 498/1 The Pre-Cambrian covers 85% of the total length of geological time and is the longest geological division. **1977** *Jrnl. R. Soc. Arts* CXXV. 406/1 Uranium deposits..occur in well defined provinces mainly in Precambrian terrain.

pre-cancer, -capitalist(ic): see *PRE- B. 1.

precarial (prĭkē̆ə·riăl), *a. rare.* [f. PRECARY *sb.* + -AL.] Of or pertaining to a precary.

1914 *Eng. Hist. Rev.* Jan. 137 It is also highly probable that precarial transactions were instrumental not only in the bringing together of ecclesiastical property, but also in utilizing it by means of dependent farms.

pre-Caroline: see *PRE- B. 1 a.

precast (prī·kɑst), *a.* [PRE- A. 1.] **a.** Formed by casting before being placed in position; composed of units so made. **b.** Pertaining to or involving such a process.

1914 C. E. FOWLER *Pract. Treat. Sub-Aqueous Foundations* xxvii. 553 The use of pre-cast piles for permanent construction at a reasonable cost is an ideal type. **1927** *Daily Express* 2 Mar. 3/6 The Concrete Products Association was formed yesterday to improve production..of 'pre-cast' units in building. **1932** DOWSETT & BARTLE *Pract. Formwork & Shuttering* ii. 28 A series of rolled steel filler joists arranged to carry a pre-cast floor. **1934** *Archit. Rev.* LXXV. 15/2 The floor is in pre-cast rose and green terrazzo tiles. **1960** *Times* 6 Oct. 7/4 It may be possible to make such roofs in plastic by precast methods. **1975** *Princ. Quality Concrete* (Portland Cement Assoc.) ii. 31 British engineers were experimenting with precast residential structures as early as 1905. Following World War II, precast construction became a permanent part of the European building trades.

precast (prīkɑ·st), *v.* [PRE- A 1.] *trans.* To cast (an object, or concrete) before it is placed in position. Also *absol.*

Some passive uses are not distinguishable from a predicative use of *precast* adj.

[**1929** W. C. HUNTINGTON *Building Construction* iii. 71 Concrete piles may be precast or cast-in-place.] **1938** WENTWORTH-SHIELDS & GRAY *Reinforced Concrete Piling* ix. 81 The use of concrete piles which, instead of being pre-cast, are made by forming a hole in the ground and filling it with concrete..is steadily extending. **1950** *Archit. Rev.* CVII. 333/3 A large contract, where much of the work can be precast at the site. **1956** *Nature* 4 Feb. 200/1 The art of precasting concrete has given rise to an established industry. **1974** A. HODGKINSON *AJ Handbk. Building Struct.* v. 167/2 The more difficult the in situ formwork problem, the easier is the decision to precast. **1975** *Princ. Quality Concrete* (Portland Cement Assoc.) ii. 31 Since its discovery concrete has been used to precast specialty items.

So **preca·sting** *vbl. sb.*

1938 C. E. REYNOLDS *Concrete Construction* xi. 484 Where unskilled labour and only a minimum of supervision are available pre-casting may allow the manufacture of the members to be localised and carried out under more convenient conditions. **1974** A. HODGKINSON *AJ Handbk. Building Struct.* v. 167/2 A quite different reason for precasting in certain parts of the UK is the local attitude of carpenters and steel fixers which may cause the contractor to limit absolutely the number of employees on site.

precative, *a.* **a.** (Further examples.)

1845 [see *ADHORTATIVE *a.*]. **1965** *Language* XLI. 12 *Jeșam* and *yeșam* represent full-grade precatives. *Ibid.* 520 A precative middle paradigm is given, but nothing is said about how middle precatives are formed.

precaution, *sb.* Add: **2.** *spec.* a precaution against conception in sexual intercourse; a contraceptive device. Usu. in *pl.*

1935 N. MITCHISON *We have been Warned* IV. 419 What did he do to you? Was it—rape?.. Was he using any precautions? **1941** [see *IT *pron.* 1 d]. **1968** B. RUSSELL *Autobiogr.* II. ii. 97 From the first we used no precautions. **1969** G. GREENE *Trav. with my Aunt* I. x. 98 If we didn't have a child together, it was purely owing to the fact that it was a late love. I took no precautions, none at all. **1975** T. HEALD *Deadline* vii. 168 Neither had taken any precautions... Miss Morrison was pregnant.

precautiously, *adv.* Delete *rare* and add later examples.

1921 A. DOBSON *Later Ess.* 163 A clever critic once observed of a popular novelist that few writers had better painted the inside of certain characters—adding *precautiously* 'so far as there is any inside'. **1922** JOYCE *Ulysses* 534 Bloom. (Reflects precautiously.) **1964** M. LANE *Night at Sea* xii. 212 Ben put his injured hand precautiously behind him.

precedent, *sb.* Add: **5.** *precedent-setting* adj.

1967 *Economist* 14 Oct. 160/3 In Boston an outspoken lawyer, in a precedent-setting challenge to the constitutionality of the Massachusetts laws against marijuana, is asking whether all the fuss over pot is really worth it. **1977** *New Yorker* 19 Sept. 50/2 Some people feel that the conductor was challenging the soloist and that she more than met the challenge, with the result that the last movement is taken at a precedent-setting speed.

precellence. For † *Obs.* read *rare* and add later examples.

Quot. 1958 contains a rendering of Henri Estienne's title *La Précellence du langage françois* (1579).

1958 *Times* 6 May 12/4 When he delivers the Sir Basil Zaharoff lecture on May 20, Professor Alfred Ewert..will take as his subject 'The precellence of the French tongue'. **1978** R. SYME *Hist. in Ovid* vii. 132 There was another side to the oratorical precellence of Messalla Corvinus. Some found him prolix and lacking in bite.

precellular: see *PRE- B. 1. **pre-censorship:** *PRE- A. 2. **pre-centrifuge:** *PRE- A. 1.

precept, *v.* Restrict † *Obs.* to senses in Dict. and add: **3.** *intr.* Of a local authority or similar body: to issue a precept; to make a demand *on* (a rating authority) for funds. Also *trans.*, to take by means of a precept. Cf. PRECEPT *sb.* 4 d. So **prece·pting** *ppl. a.* and *vbl. sb.*

1911 *Encycl. Brit.* XXII. 915/2 To distinguish the rate the name of the precepting authority is frequently added or the purpose for which it is levied specified. **1961** *Times* 30 May (I.C.I. Suppl.) p. xiv/3 The county council precepts 72 per cent of the rates. **1962** L. GOLDING *Dict. Local Govt.* 310 Authorities which have no rating powers are known as precepting authorities as they issue precepts, i.e., demands on the rating authority or authorities, specifying the amount required in the £ of rateable value to meet their financial requirements. Examples of precepting authorities are county councils.., joint boards, parish councils, burial boards, river boards and port health authorities. **1974** *Daily Tel.* 26 Apr. 2/2 Where percentage rises are especially high one cause is said to be the practice of some old water boards of covering a large part of their expenditure by precepting on the general rates. **1979** *Kensington & Chelsea Newslet.* Oct. 1/3 These precepting authorities are all affected by substantial salary and wage increases themselves, and they therefore are bound to precept upon local authorities a very much greater amount next year than they have in the past.

preceptee (prīseptī·). *U.S.* [f. *PRECEPT(OR + -EE[1].] One who is being trained by a preceptor. Cf. *PRECEPTOR 3.

1974 *Med. Times* (N.Y.) Dec. 62/2 The benefits for the preceptee are substantial. **1975** *Jrnl. Med. Educ.* May 471/2 The conference is designed to accomplish the following objectives:..discuss monitoring and evaluation methodologies appropriate for either daily preceptor–preceptee interaction or faculty–preceptorship interaction.

preceptor. Add: **3.** *spec.* A physician or specialist who gives a medical student practical training. *U.S.*

1803 [in Dict., sense 1]. **1837** R. DUNGLISON *Med. Student* ii. 126 The question;—what subjects the office-student should peruse during his first year... Generally.. the preceptor gives himself but little trouble. **1864** S. CHEW *Lect. Med. Educ.* p. x, Is it necessary to pay attention to Medical Auscultation? My old preceptor considered it wholly useless. **1912** *Cycl. Amer. Med. Biogr.* II. 316/1 On the death of his preceptor, Dr. A. Torrence, [he] succeeded to his practice. **1925** A. FLEXNER *Med. Educ.* v. 107 A mere boy, fresh from school, he attended his preceptor in his office and on his visits. **1937** J. T. FLEXNER *Doctors on Horseback* i. 9 Morgan apprenticed himself to an experienced doctor; there was no other way of studying medicine... Preceptors were limited to repeating what they had learnt from their own preceptors. **1948** *Jrnl. Hist. Med.* Winter 96 He swept out the office, cleaned the instruments, kept the accounts... After three years of this he would, if he had his preceptor's recommendation, appear before three members of the Board of Censors of the County Medical Society. **1959** HAMMOND & KERN *Teaching Comprehensive Med. Care* vii. 82 Each General Medical Clinic student was assigned to a preceptorial group... Two staff physicians were assigned to each group as preceptors. **1976** *National Observer* (U.S.) 16 Oct. 10/3 A third-year Michigan State student who has served under two preceptors.

preceptorship. Add: **b.** The position of one who is being trained by a preceptor (cf. *PRECEPTOR 3). *U.S.*

1970 *Vital Speeches* 1 Aug. 634 In any new graduate education program we might be well advised to emphasize again a preceptorship method of training. **1972** *Science* 27 Oct. 380/2 D.O. (Osteopathy) students begin serious clinical exposure early under preceptorships with D.O.'s in family practice. **1974** *Med. Times* (N.Y.) Dec. 62/1 Students attended medical school and also went through a preceptorship with an experienced physician. **1976** *National Observer* (U.S.) 16 Oct. 10/3 In this preceptorship program, as it's called, medical students spend from 4 to 12 weeks working in a rural or community doctor's office.

precess, *v.* Restrict † *Obs.* to sense defined in Dict. and add: **2.** *intr.* To undergo precession.

1892 A. M. WORTHINGTON *Dynamics of Rotation* xiii. 135 The application of the couple is said to cause the spinning wheel to 'precess'. **1902** *Jrnl. Inst. Electr. Engin.* XXXII. 83 The pull of gravity on a spinning-top does not make it topple over, but makes it precess. **1942** SYNGE & GRIFFITH *Princ. Mech.* xiv. 418 A disk, 6 inches in diameter, is mounted on the end of a light rod 1 inch long and spins rapidly. It precesses once in 15 seconds. **1957** *Endeavour* Oct. 185/2 In each of these levels the nucleus precesses about the direction of H_0, but maintains its correct orientation in the field. **1971** I. G. GASS et al. *Understanding Earth* vi. 90/2 The axis of figure starts to precess about the axis of rotation. **1973** [see *PRECESSION 3 c]. **1975** *Nature* 20 Feb. 590/3 When a single ^{3}He atom is placed in a magnetic field its nucleus.. precesses about the field direction in one of two permitted states, corresponding to two different energy levels. **1977** A. HALLAM *Planet Earth* 30/2 The satellites precess, or progressively change their orbiting path relative to the Earth's axis, due to these broad variations in the gravity field.

precession. Add: **3. a.** Now also used to denote the motion of the earth itself which manifests itself as the precession of the equinoxes. (Further examples.)

planetary precession, that part of the precession of the earth's axis caused by the gravitational attraction of the other planets.

1863 W. CHAUVENET *Man. Spherical & Pract. Astron.* I. xi. 604 The mutual attraction between the planets and the earth tends continually to draw the earth out of the plane in which it is revolving... The planetary precession is, then, the effect of a motion of the ecliptic upon the equator... The planetary precession does not affect the declination of stars, but changes their right ascensions, their longitudes, and their latitudes. **1913** S. E. SLOCUM *Theory & Pract. Mech.* vii. 430 (*heading*) Precession of the earth. *Ibid.*, An important case of regular precession is that furnished by the motion of the earth. **1926** H. N. RUSSELL et al. *Astron.* I. v. 141 The motion of the ecliptic pole produces..the planetary precession. **1939** SKILLING & RICHARDSON *Astron.* i. 16 Precession does not affect the position of the terrestrial poles upon the earth's surface. **1959** R. H. BAKER *Astron.* (ed. 7) ii. 59 The earth's precession is a slow conical movement of the earth's axis around a line joining the ecliptic poles, having a period of about 26,000 years. **1963** D. ALTER et al. *Pictorial Astron.* (ed. 2) xlvi. 211/2 This gradual north–south drift of the Southern Cross is a consequence of the precession of the earth, which produces a slow movement of the celestial pole among the stars on a circle with a radius of 23½°. **1971** BAKER & FREDRICK *Astron.* (ed. 9) ii. 49 It is the lunisolar precession that has been described... Planetary precession is the effect of other planets on the plane of the equator, so that its intersection with the ecliptic shifts slowly towards the east along the celestial equator. The result of the two precessions is the general precession.

b. The term is now applied to the motion of the body itself as well as to that of the axis of rotation. (Further examples.)

1907 FRANKLIN & MACNUTT *Elements Mech.* vii. 149 The torque required to produce precession of a spinning body depends upon the moment of inertia of the body and upon the angular acceleration which is involved in the continual change of direction of the axis of spin. **1942** *Tee Emm* (Air Ministry) June 56/1 He has a directional gyro—and should have some idea as to its rate of precession. **1958** *Engineering* 31 Jan. 132/3 If the weights are moved from one side of the point of balance to the other the direction of precession is reversed. **1962** F. I. ORDWAY et al. *Basic Astronautics* ix. 372 The antifriction motor..applies an additional torque in the direction of precession to compensate for friction in the bearings.

c. *spec.* The rotation of the spin axis of a nucleus, electron, etc., about the direction of a magnetic or an electric field.

1927 *Physical Rev.* XXIX. 395 Predicted and observed intensity relations for a number of band spectra are in agreement if we assume that σ is an electronic quantum number which is correlated with a precession about the internuclear axis. **1928** H. S. ALLEN *Quantum* xvi. 220 As the electron has a magnetic moment, its axis will experience a precession because of the couple due to its motion in the electric field. **1960** DICKE & WITTKE *Introd. Quantum Mech.* xii. 195 This torque produces a precession of the spin axis about the direction of the magnetic field; in other words, the particle acts like a gyroscope because of its spin angular momentum. **1965** *New Scientist* 1 July 36/3 This precession will alter the average area that the molecule presents to other molecules. **1973** O. HOWARTH *Theory of Spectroscopy* i. 14 The existence of precession explains why even a classical particle with a magnetic moment does not immediately align when put in a magnetic field. It precesses instead.

pre-cession: see *PRE- B. 2 a. **pre-chemical:** *PRE- B. 1 d.

‖**précieux** (presyö), *a.* [Fr.] = PRECIOUS *a.* 3. Also as *sb.* Cf. PRÉCIEUSE *sb.* (*a.*).

1891 M. S. VAN DE VELDE *French Fiction of To-day* I. iv. 109 A certain *précieux* hyper-refinement. **1939** *Burlington Mag.* Mar. p. xviii/1 The lives of other *précieux* in the stereotyped social and literary intercourse of the Salons. **1951** M. MCLUHAN *Mech. Bride* (1967) 63 Arno, Nash, and Thurber are brittle, wistful little *précieux* beside Capp. **1953** [see *BAROQUE *a.* (*sb.*)]. **1964** *Eng. Stud.* XLV. 111 As a *précieux* poet, the Duke [Orsino] is an accomplished master. **1969** *Listener* 8 May 637/1 There was point in A. C. Benson's defence in 1910 of 'The May Queen', that no *précieux* writer, with a care for his reputation, could have dared to write it... Certainly mid-19th-century literature was not *précieux*: it took risks.

precinct, *sb.* Add: **1. a.** (Further examples.)

1915 W. S. MAUGHAM *Of Human Bondage* xvi. 60 The precincts, with the exception of a house in which some of the masters lodged, were occupied by the cathedral clergy. **1956** *Newsweek* 9 Jan. 66/3 Just a few days before Christmas, nevertheless, the 230 tenants found eviction letters under their doors. In this way they learned that their proud precincts would be converted to house between 1,100 and 1,500 students by 1957. **1961** K. J. FRANKLIN *William Harvey* 59 He was offered an official residence in the precincts of Bart's.

b. (Further example.)

1921 L. STRACHEY *Queen Victoria* 415 For more than half a century no divorced lady had approached the precincts of the Court.

3. Also, a division of a city for the purpose of police control; *ellipt.*, = *precinct-house* (*b*), *-station* (see sense 5 below). *U.S.*

1864 [see **precinct station house*]. **1882** J. D. MCCABE *New York* xxiii. 374 The city is divided into thirty-five precincts, in each of which there is a station-house. **1894** P. L. FORD *Honorable Peter Stirling* 142, I had to go with them..to the precinct and speak to the superintendent. **1953** W. BURROUGHS *Junkie* (1972) ix. 90 They didn't find any junk on him so they took him to the third precinct to 'hold for investigation'. *Ibid.* x. 98 They drove back to the precinct and I was locked in. This time I was locked in a different cell. **1955** W. GADDIS *Recognitions* II. vi. 555 The case you reported to us as sadism and brutality reported by you to this precinct Tuesday December 20 at 10:17 A.M. resulted in false arrest. **1971** N. FREELING *Over High Side* III. 163 Watching..the cops from the ninety-ninth precinct, on the telly. **1974** *Amer. Speech* *1971* XLVI. 83 *Police station*, precinct.

4. A part of a town or community designated for a specific purpose; *spec.* one from which motor vehicles are excluded, esp. to allow pedestrians to shop in safety.

1942 H. A. TRIPP *Town Planning & Road Traffic* vii. 75 A great number of pockets will have been created, each of which will consist of a little local system of minor roads, devoted to industrial, business, shopping or residential purposes... Each pocket represents in its way a separate little community... The best term..seems to be 'precinct'. **1943** FORSHAW & ABERCROMBIE *County of London Plan* 51 Precincts are formed which can be maintained or re-planned as residential communities, business or industrial precincts. **1958** *Listener* 23 Oct. 643/1 The exclusion of wheeled traffic from the main shopping precinct. **1959** *Ibid.* 19 Mar. 509/2 The word 'precinct' implies an area free from through-traffic. *Ibid.* 22 Oct. 674/2 The Stevenage pedestrian precinct. **1961** L. MUMFORD *City in Hist.* ix. 276 In the original layout of the colleges in Oxford and Cambridge, medieval planning made its most original contributions to civic design: the superblock and the urban precinct divorced from the ancient network of alleys and streets.

5. *Comb.*, as (sense 3) *precinct caucus*, *level*; **precinct captain**, a leader of a political party in a precinct; **precinct court**, a court with jurisdiction over a precinct, subordinate to a county court; **precinct house**, (*a*) the headquarters of an election precinct; also *attrib.*; (*b*) a police station; **precinct sheet**, a register of eligible voters in a precinct; **precinct station** = *precinct house* (*b*) above; also **precinct station house**; **precinct worker**, one who promotes the interests of a political party in a precinct.

1954 B. & R. NORTH tr. *Duverger's Pol. Parties* I. i. 19 In the United States the caucuses formed at the county or city level co-ordinate the action of the *precinct-captains*. **1956** E. O'CONNOR *Last Hurrah* iii. 45 John, you'll see the precinct captains? **1977** *Time* 3 Jan. 38/2 Daley became a precinct captain at 21. **1976** *New Yorker* 24 May 118/2 In South Carolina precinct caucuses last night, the highest percentage of the votes—forty-seven per cent—was for 'Uncommitted'. **1704** in *N. Carolina Colonial Rec.* (1886) I. 605 Ordered that the Marshall bring forth the body of Tho: Evans to the next pr[e]cinct Court to answer the compl[aint]. **1943** L. E. PRICE in Boatright & Day *Backwoods to Border* 210 [Hooper] drove out to the precinct court in his rubber-tired carriage. **1863** *Rebellion Rec.* V. I. 77 The Mayor of Philadelphia..called upon all able-bodied men to assemble next morning at the precinct-houses of the election districts. **1899** T. HALL *Tales* 171 He did very well to copy off the entries in a precinct house register or to discover the important arrivals at the hotels. **1968** *Globe & Mail* (Toronto) 13 Jan. 25/5 Imagine committing a robbery half a block from a precinct house! **1972** *Village Voice* (N.Y.) 1 June 69/3 Up the street the team went, stapling on posters, casually strolling by the precinct house with the ladder. **1974** *Nation* (Barbados) 10 Mar. 3/5 Mr. Staines wrote his neighborhood precinct house asking that his thanks be passed on to the policeman. **1954** *Newsweek* 26 July 40/3 Latin America must be approached on the 'precinct level'. Labor leaders, teachers, local politicos must be convinced that inter-American cooperation will benefit the little groups. **1957** *Time* (Atlantic ed.) 20 May 13/2 Ike seems to find something distasteful in precinct-level party politics. **1974** *Union* (S. Carolina) *Daily Times* 23 Apr. 2/3 How do you catch the fraudulent? Would there ever be an updated precinct sheet to work from? **1936** J. STEINBECK *In Dubious Battle* ii. 12, I think I'll stop in at the precinct station. She might of got run over. **1975** *New Yorker* 16 June 114/2 The alleged beating two weeks earlier of a twenty-seven-year-old Chinese engineer inside the Fifth Precinct station. **1864** *N.Y. Herald* 4 Apr. 8/3 The body was removed to the Fourth precinct station house. **1952** *Time* 2 June 19/1 His deepest political instinct is party loyalty. From his start as a precinct worker and doorbell pusher in the wards of Cincinnati,.. he has been unmistakably Republican. **1976** *Washington Post* 19 Apr. B 2/3 More recently, Ray Krasnick, who headed the Tydings effort among precinct workers in Prince George's County, became Sarbanes' county coordinator.

precinctual (prīsi·ŋktiu,ăl), *a.* [f. PRECINCT *sb.* + *-ual*, perh. after *INSTINCTUAL *a.*] Of, pertaining to, or characteristic of a precinct.

1949 *Archit. Rev.* CVI. 144 The plan is clearly based on the precinctual theory, with interconnected squares, throughout which the pedestrian receives priority. **1960** *Guardian* 15 June 28/4 The road..'would be prejudicial to the precinctual character of the area'. **1965** *New Statesman* 30 July 146/1 There would be time to consider whether the Martin plan's obsession with 'enclosure' adds up to anything more than an unrevised residue of the *Architectural Review*'s 'Westminster Regained'—a precinctual proposal conceived at a time of positively prelapsarian innocence.

pre-cinematographic: see *PRE- B. 1 d.

precious, *a.* (*sb.*, *adv.*) Add: **6. e.** *precious coral*, a coral belonging to the order Antipatharia, forming branching colonies resembling plants.

1906 S. J. HICKSON in Harmer & Shipley *Cambr. Nat. Hist.* I. xiii. 352 The 'precious coral' occurs in the Mediterranean. **1935** TWENHOFEL & SHROCK *Invertebr. Paleontol.* iv. 113 The compound corallum may be in the form of.. bushy growths as in the precious corals. **1979** *Sci. Amer.* Aug. 115/3 The detritus feeders include the true sponges, the antipatharians ('precious corals') and the gorgonians (sea fans).

precipit, *a.* For † *Obs. rare* read *rare* and add later example.

1922 JOYCE *Ulysses* 743 Not acting with precipit precipitancy.

precipitable, *a.* Add: **b.** *precipitable water* (Meteorol.): the quantity of water vapour in an atmospheric column of unit cross-section, expressed as the depth it would have if condensed to a liquid or as the mass.

1928 *Mem. R. Meteorol. Soc.* III. 2 If m is the mass of water vapour in grams over each square centimetre of the base of the stratosphere we have $mg = 33$, *i.e.* $m = {\cdot}034$

gram. Thus the water vapour in the stratospherei s equivalent to ·34 mm. of precipitable water. **1971** *Nature* 23 Apr. 503/1 Schorn *et al.* have observed average water contents in the northern hemisphere [of Mars] of up to 25 μm of precipitable water.

precipitate, *v.* Add: **III. 5.** Also, to cause (dust or other particulate matter in a gas) to be deposited on a surface.

1911 *Jrnl. Industr. & Engin. Chem.* Aug. 543/2 Cotton-covered wire when used as a discharge electrode..proved far more effective in precipitating the sulphuric acid mists. **1912** *Jrnl. Franklin Inst.* CLXXIV. 263 Plants.. built for precipitating the fumes from copper smelters and the dust from cement plants. **1938** *Trans. Inst. Chem. Engineers* XVI. 40/1 The gas is..passed through an electrofitter of the dry type where the greater part of the dust is precipitated. **1975** S. MASUDA in A. R. Blythe *Static Electrification 1975* iii. 154 Particles charged by collision with unipolar ions emitted from the discharge electrode are driven by the coulombic force on to the collecting electrode, where they are precipitated.

precipitated, *ppl. a.* Add: **2.** Also, deposited from a state of suspension in a gas.

1938 *Trans. Inst. Chem. Engineers* XVI. 38/1 The precipitated dust falls into hoppers below each section of the plant. **1971** M. ROBINSON in W. Strauss *Air Pollution Control* I. 267 The decline of [migration velocity] w_e at.. higher gas velocities is usually accounted for by reentrainment of precipitated dust.

precipitating, *ppl. a.* Add: **6.** Also, causing precipitation from a gas.

1912 *Jrnl. Franklin Inst.* CLXXIV. 262 The brush form of discharge from points is only a good precipitating agent when the current of gas is small.

precipitation. Add: **III. 5.** Also, the removal and deposition of particulate matter from suspension in a gas; the separation of crystals of a solute phase from a solid solution (see also *precipitation hardening* below).

1908 F. G. COTTRELL *U.S. Patent 895,729* 2/1 The gases or vapors containing the suspended particles enter the precipitation chamber A through pipe B. **1912, 1920** [see *ELECTROSTATIC *a.*]. **1926** *Trans. Amer. Soc. Steel Treating* X. 718 The idea that the hardness of an alloy may be increased by the precipitation of a soluble constituent from solid solution was first advanced by Merica and his associates in a hypothesis to account for the age-hardening of duralumin. **1938** *Trans. Inst. Chem. Engineers* XVI. 37/2 It is unlikely that any new cement works will be designed without provision for dust separation by electrical precipitation. **1958** A. D. MERRIMAN *Dict. Metallurgy* 3/1 *Ageing*, a precipitation process, often submicroscopic, which occurs when a supersaturated solid solution is allowed to rest at atmospheric temperature after quenching. **1967** A. H. COTTRELL *Introd. Metallurgy* xx. 372 Cu-Be alloys soften rapidly by discontinuous precipitation at temperatures above about 300°C, but this can be prevented by the addition of about 0·4 wt per cent cobalt. **1974** *Encycl. Brit. Macropædia* IV. 161/1 Electrostatic precipitation is a method for the precipitation of fogs..: a high voltage is applied across the gas phase to produce electrical charges on the particles. These charges cause the particles to be attracted to the oppositely charged walls of the separator.

8. Special Comb.: **precipitation hardening** *Metallurgy*, hardening of an alloy by heat treatment that causes the precipitation from solid solution of crystals of a solute phase; a strengthening process utilizing this phenomenon.

1926 R. S. ARCHER in *Trans. Amer. Soc. Steel Treating* X. 719 It is proposed in this paper..to develop the general theory of what may be called 'precipitation hardening'. **1931** *Jrnl. Iron & Steel Inst.* CXXIV. 671 The binary iron-boron alloys were incapable of hardening by quenching and the precipitation hardening was hardly noticeable. **1957** *Technology* Oct. 291/2 Parts made from it [*sc.* a new stainless steel] are subjected to 'precipitation hardening', a method of heat treatment designed to give increased strength by precipitating an inter-metallic compound between the metal particles. **1973** J. G. TWEEDDALE *Materials Technol.* I. vi. 169 Precipitation hardening..is a three-part treatment (1) a solution treatment at elevated temperature to dissolve the solute (2) a quenching operation to trap the solute..(3) a precipitation or ageing treatment to develop the required size of precipitate.

precipitator. Add: **2. b.** Also *spec.* an apparatus for removing particulate matter such as dust or smoke from a gas by passing it between electrodes so that the particles acquire an electric charge and are attracted to an oppositely charged surface.

1919 *Jrnl. Amer. Chem. Soc.* XLI. 587 (*heading*) An electrical precipitator for analyzing smokes. **1958** *Engineering* 28 Feb. 274/3 Dust is extracted from the 'used' air by electrostatic precipitators. **1971** *Time* 7 June 61/3 Equip the plants' stacks with electrostatic precipitators and wet scrubbers that would cut air pollution by 99%.

precipitin. Substitute for def.: An antibody that on reacting with its antigen produces a visible precipitate. (Later examples.) Also *fig.*

1912 [see *IMMUNOLOGIST]. **1931** *Syst. Bacteriol.* (Med. Res. Council) VI. xiii. 424 Kraus named the substance present in the bacterial filtrate precipitinogen while the term precipitin was used to denote the hypothetical substance or antibody formed or set free in the animal body in response to injections of an antigen or precipitinogen. **1966** *Lancet* 24 Dec. 1397/1 Some natives in the Territory of Papua and New Guinea who have chronic lung disease also have in their sera precipitins against a soluble substance in the roofs of their huts. **1971** 'D. HALLIDAY' *Dolly & Doctor Bird* xiii. 192, I don't think any of us felt anything: we carried our own precipitins, for the moment, against fear and danger.

b. *attrib.*, as *precipitin reaction, technique*; **precipitin test**, a means of establishing the identity of a substance by testing whether it reacts with a particular precipitin; hence *precipitin testing* vbl. sb.

1958 *Immunology* I. 87 Quantitative studies of the precipitin and agglutination reactions. **1962** M. RABAEY in A. Pirie *Lens Metabolism Rel. Cataract* 310 Generally, α-crystallin has been the first lens protein which has been detected by means of precipitin techniques. **1905** F. C. WOOD *Chem. & Microsc. Diagnosis* I. ix. 255 Before applying the precipitin test to a suspected stain, the presence of blood should, if possible, be determined either by the formation of Teichmann's crystals or by the spectroscope. **1952** M. E. FLOREY *Clin. Applic. Antibiotics* I. ii. 31 They..found precipitin tests inconclusive and considered in consequence that the urticaria was not the result of an antibody-antigen reaction. **1976** *Lancet* 6 Nov. 985/1 Antibodiesto thyroglobulin were detected by a precipitin test in an Ouchterlony plate. **1971** *E. Afr. Standard* (Nairobi) 13 Apr. 9/8 This will form the basis of establishing precipitin testing for East Africa.

precipitinogen (prɪsipiti·nǒdʒěn). *Immunol.* Also † **preci·pitogen.** [f. prec. + *-OGEN.] A type of antigen which induces the production of a precipitin.

1904 G. H. F. NUTTALL *Blood Immunity & Blood Relationship* ii. 98 The immunifying substance, which they [*sc.* Obermayer and Pick] wrongly style 'precipitogen', as well as the precipitin they conclude are not albuminous. [*Note*] A misnomer..for the reason that it suggests a relation between precipitin and ('precipitogen') precipitable substances such as exists, for instance, between pepsin and pepsinogen, in other words that the 'precipitogen' is a forerunner of precipitin, which it is not. **1907** *Jrnl. Med. Res.* XVI. 173 Many or all of the other substances are assimilated more or less readily by the tissues, are neutralized in a relatively short space of time, and in some instances (precipitogens) definite reaction products to them may be formed. *Ibid.* XVII. 232 The complement, when incubated with antigen and low ($\frac{1}{10}$) dilution of immune serum, may..be absorbed through the union of precipitin and precipitinogen. **1931** [see prec.]. **1969** *Acta Path. & Microbiol. Scand.* LXXVII. 463 Some chemical properties of a group reactive precipitinogen from the *Fusobacterium* strain F1 have been investigated.

Hence **precipitinoge·nic** *a.*

1935 F. P. GAY *Agents of Dis. & Host Resistance* xxi. 418 Not all soluble proteins are precipitinogenic. **1970** B. G. F. WEITZ in H. W. Mulligan *Afr. Trypanosomiases* vi. 113 Cultivated trypanosomes are also agglutinogenic and precipitinogenic.

precipitron (prɪsi·pitrǫn). [f. PRECIPI(TATOR + *-TRON.] A kind of electrostatic precipitator.

1941 *Iron & Steel Engineer* Sept. 78 (*heading*) Precipitrons for the steel industry. **1975** E. B. CEADEL in Barr & Line *Ess. Information & Libraries* 45 It should not take him much time to find out what..services consultants mean by 'electrostatic precipitrons'.

précis, *v. trans.* Add: (Earlier and later examples.) Hence **précised** (prē̆·sīd) *ppl. a.*

1856 LD. CANNING *Let.* 2 Apr. in E. Fitzmaurice *Life 2nd Earl Granville* (1905) I. vii. 152 The lucid..way in which a heavy case is précis'd is admirable. **1916** *Daily Colonist* (Victoria, B.C.) 30 July 18/4 The main work of the Canadian War Records, that of compiling and precising the all-important diaries and appendices is, of course, in arrears. **1964** P. MACKESY *War for Amer.* ii. 60 The Ministerial viewpoint on the prospects offered by the advance from Canada is précised in CO 5/253, ff. 21–30. **1972** *Islander* (Victoria, B.C.) 9 Jan. 14/1 The new book Parsons on the Plains..is actually three books precis'd down and contained in one volume. **1977** C. HUSBAND in H. Giles *Lang., Ethnicity & Intergroup Relations* ix. 223 Headlines, as precised news values, represent an expression of 'constructed reality'.

precision. Add: **1. c.** *Statistics.* The reproducibility or reliability of a measurement or the like; used *spec.* to denote various measures or indices of this (see quots.). [The sense is due to W. Lexis, who used G. *präcision* (now *präzision*) (W. Lexis *Zur Theorie der Massenerscheinungen in der menschlichen Gesellschaft* (1877) ii. 25).]

1885 M. MERRIMAN *Textbk. Method of Least Squares* i. 1 The comparison of observations is necessary in order to determine the relative degrees of precision of different sets of measurements made under different circumstances. **1906** *Acta Univ. Lundensis* Ny Följd I. v. 7, *k* is called the measure of precision. **1911** G. U. YULE *Introd. Theory Statistics* xiii. 253 The reliability or precision of an observed proportion varies as the square root of the number of observations on which it is based. *Ibid.* xv. 304 The use of $\sqrt{2} \times \sigma$ (the 'modulus') as a measure of dispersion, of $1/\sqrt{2}\cdot\sigma$ as a measure of precision, and of $2\sigma^2$ as 'the fluctuation'. **1947** O. L. DAVIES *Statistical Methods in Res. & Production* 250 The normal distribution..is given by some writers the mathematical formulation: $he^{-h^2x^2}/\sqrt{\pi}$. The parameter *h* is then called the parameter of precision, but by comparison with the usual formula it is seen that this parameter is related to the standard deviation by the identity $h = 1/\sigma\sqrt{2}$. **1949** F. YATES *Sampling Methods for Censuses & Surveys* viii. 247 The relative precision of two different methods of sampling based on the same type of sampling unit may be defined as the reciprocal of the ratio of the sampling variances of the estimates given by the two methods when the same number of units are taken. **1957** KENDALL & BUCKLAND *Dict. Statistical Terms* 224 Precision is a quality associated with a class of measurements and refers to the way in which repeated observations conform to themselves; and in a somewhat narrower sense refers to the dispersion of the observations, or some measure of it, whether or not the mean value around which the dispersion is measured approximates to the 'true' value. In general the precision of an estimator varies with the square root of the number of observations upon which it is based. **1965** R. DEUTSCH *Estimation Theory* x. 154 Precision is a measure of how close the outcome of a measurement, or a sequence of observations, clusters about some estimated value of a specified parameter. **1965** D. V. LINDLEY *Introd. Probability & Statistics* II. v. 8 We shall call the inverse of the variance, the precision. The nomenclature is not standard but is useful. **1971** *Nature* 12 Feb. 484/1 An estimate of the precision (analytical reproducibility) of each K—Ar analysis is given as a ± value. **1974** *IEEE Trans. Instrumentation & Measurement* XXIII. 278/1 The desired precision of intercomparison was set at $\pm 0{\cdot}01\mu V$ (one part in 10^8). **1974** *Nature* 8 Nov. 137/1 Radioactive isotopic dates invariably include their precision, that is, the repeatability, yet most earth scientists still take these figures as measures of accuracy.

d. In numerical work, the fineness of specification, as represented by the number of digits given and distinguished from *accuracy* (the nearness to the true value).

1948 *Math. Tables & Other Aids to Computation* III. 286 Numbers are stored to a precision of 35 binary digits. **1956** G. A. MONTGOMERIE *Digital Calculating Machines* vii. 12 Precision can be expressed in two ways: we may say that a number is correct to so many decimal places or to so many significant figures. **1962** *Gloss. Terms Automatic Data Processing* (*B.S.I.*) 14 A result may have more precision than it has accuracy, e.g. the true value of π to eight decimal figures is 3·1415927; the expression π = 3·1415249 is precise to eight figures but accurate only to about five. **1970** H. A. RODGERS *Dict. Data Processing Terms* 81/1 Strictly speaking there is a difference of precision between 1,000 and $1. \times 10^3$; in the first case the low-order zeros are known to have that value while in the second case all that is known is the explicit digit and the multiplier. **1972** *Physics Bull.* Aug. 459/2 To precisions varying from 1 to 0·01 parts in a million, the value of $(2e/h)_J$ does not depend on whether the effects are observed in absorption or emission.

3. a. *attrib.* and *Comb.*, usu. implying an intended or actual precision of performance, execution, or construction.

1875 *Encycl. Brit.* III. 263/1 The theory of the common balance as we see it working in every grocer's shop, and.. of the modern precision balance. **1910** *Westm. Gaz.* 6 Jan. 4/2 Those wonderful American automatic precision tools that have played so conspicuous a part in almost every European factory. **1935** *Discovery* Jan. 9/1 Continuous knife-edges and continuous knife-edge bearings such as are now used in all precision balances. *Ibid.* Dec. 368/2 The optical outfits..consist of precision-made parts, the mere use of which teaches precision in working. **1937** *Ibid.* Apr. 112/1 These are real precision instruments,.. with lens of aperture F1·9 such as the old plate cameras never knew. **1939** *War Illustr.* 16 Dec. 440/3 The barrage ..gives London and other cities and vital points reasonable security from swooping raiders and precision-bombing. **1944** *Foundry* Feb. 116/1 Application of precision casting, utilizing either centrifugal or pressure methods, to the production of precision parts made from heat and corrosion resistant alloys is a recent development. **1950** *N.Y. Times Mag.* 27 Aug. 52/2 Strategic bombing as carried out by the American 8th and 15th Air Forces in Europe was 'precision bombing' directed, so far as operational accuracy permitted, against specific military targets. **1951** *People* 3 June 7/7 (Advt.), Just switch on that precision-built Arvin and discover for yourself how pleasant dry shaving can be. **1953** 'N. BLAKE' *Dreadful Hollow* 77 Yes, quite a precision-tool job. **1957** *Technology* Mar. 10/2 Other work includes..the repair of indicator gauges and other precision instruments. **1963** *New Yorker* 23 Nov. 23 (Advt.), What's low in upkeep, high in mileage,..precision-engineered with 42 hidden changes to date but looks the same every year? **1966** 'H. MACDIARMID' *Company I've Kept* viii. 187, I qualified as a precision fitter and obtained a job with a big general engineering firm. **1969** 'D. RUTHERFORD' *Gilt-Edged Cockpit* x. 172 We still think there's a market for individuality and a precision-built car. **1975** BRAM & DOWNS *Manuf. Technol.* i. 7 Gauge blocks are used as standards of measurement or reference in most precision-engineering works. **1976** J. VAN DE WETERING *Corpse on Dike* (1977) ii. 33 Mary kept her pistols in the drawer... 'Careful... They are precision instruments, both of them.'

b. Special Comb.: **precision approach radar,** a ground-based radar system used to follow accurately the approach of an aircraft and to enable landing to be supervised from the ground.

1950 *Electronics* Feb. 71/1 (*heading*) Airport surveillance and precision approach radar (GCA). **1956** *Electronic Engin.* XXVIII. 15/2 In practice, all airport radar requirements except precision approach radar..can be met. **1965** NAYLER & OWER *Aviation* xvii. 250/2 Ground Controlled Approach.., also known as Precision Approach Radar, gives the position of an approaching aircraft in elevation, azimuth, and range relative to the touch-down point on the runway.

precisionist, *sb.* and *a.* Add: **A.** *sb.* (Later examples.) Also *spec.* in *Art*: one of a group of U.S. artists of the 1920s who employed a smooth, precise technique in their paintings.

1960 *Art in Amer.* III. 33/1 Its [*sc.* Cubism's] effects still pervade the most recent work of the Precisionists. **1974** *Encycl. Brit. Micropædia* VIII. 185/2 The Precisionists did not issue manifestos, and they were not a school or movement with a formal program. *Ibid.*, The Precisionists' style greatly influenced the American Magic Realists and the Pop artists. **1978** *Verbatim* Winter 6/2 And I am certain that that great precisionist intended a true rhyme.

B. *adj.* Employing or exhibiting precision as an artistic technique.

1960 *Art in Amer.* III. 32/1 The Precisionist painting process is one of continual distillation and editing. **1978** *Chicago* June 62/1 Precisionist paintings, ranging from realistic to abstract. **1979** *Jrnl. R. Soc. Arts* Nov. 747/2 Even American or German architecture looks a bit thrown together when compared with the precisionist craftsmanship of his high-gloss aluminium detailing.

Hence **preci·sionism**, the style or technique of the precisionist painters.

1960 *Art in Amer.* III. 47 When Jefferson consciously reacted against the light, impermanent and provincial qualities of American building.. it was to another and more integral kind of 'precisionism' that he turned: to a precisionism of mass. **1978** S. F. YEH *Precisionist Painters* 10 The basis for Precisionism is to be found in Cubism.

pre-civil(ization, -ized: see *PRE- B. 1, A. 2. **pre-Civil War:** *PRE- B. 2a.

Pre-classic, *a. Archæol.* [PRE- B. 1.] Designating a period of Meso-American culture, about 1500 B.C. to A.D. 300.

1956 G. W. BRAINERD *Morley's Anc. Maya* (ed. 3) iii. 40 Maya history may be divided into three stages: (1) Pre-classic, extending from about 1500 B.C. to A.D. 317; (2) Classic, from A.D. 317 to 889; and (3) Postclassic, from 889 until 1697. **1967** L. DEUEL *Conquistadors without Swords* III. xv. 188 The emergence of an 'archaic age' in Mexican pre-history, now usually referred to as formative or pre-classic. **1970** BRAY & TRUMP *Dict. Archaeol.* 188/2 *Pre-classic* (*or Formative*) *period*, used in American archaeology for the period in which agriculture..formed the basis of settled village life. *Ibid.* 189/1 In the chronological sense..the Pre-classic period is usually taken to have ended c 300 AD. **1974** *Nature* 6 Dec. 472/1 The earliest occupation discovered belongs to the Real Xe phase of the Middle Preclassic Period... This cache was actually located beneath several preclassic floors.

pre-classical, *a.* Add: Also in extended uses.

1948 K. MALONE *Middle Ages* I. 28 The technic of adornment or elaboration was essentially the same in pre-classical and classical poetry. **1958** *Times* 15 Dec. 3/2 One of the first great pre-classical composers for whom general popularity seems surely destined is Monteverdi. **1976** *Observer* 16 May 1/2 He was the most brilliant and versatile of wind-players, starting as a classical bassoonist then branching out into the whole range of pre-classical wind instruments. **1978** *Early Music* Oct. 567/2 The cadenzas of the baroque and pre-classical eras were usually over a pedal point dominant rather than being the tonic six-four/dominant/tonic kind of the classical era.

preclean, -climax: see *PRE- A. 1, B. 1.

precli·nical, *a. Med.* [PRE- B. 1.] **1.** Of, pertaining to, or designating the first stage of a medical education, consisting chiefly of the necessary scientific studies without regular involvement with patients.

1930 A. FLEXNER *Universities* i. 14 Medicine stood almost still until the pre-clinical sciences were differentiated and set free—free to develop without regard to use and practice. **1948** F. ROBERTS *Med. Educ.* vii. 48 On entering the pre-clinical stage the student embarks on an intensive study of human anatomy and physiology. **1956** *Med. Press* 5 Sept. 225/1 In the more progressive medical schools it has been found of great benefit to give the pre-clinical student a series of specially selected clinical demonstrations. **1970** *Nature* 1 Aug. 431/2 In 1968–69 there were 6,017 pre-clinical and 7,024 clinical training places in medical schools in Britain. **1978** *Jrnl. R. Soc. Med.* LXXI. 373 The preclinical and paraclinical subjects that, it is widely accepted, comprise the early part of the European medical student curriculum.

2. Preceding the onset of recognizable symptoms that make a diagnosis possible.

1932 GAIGER & DAVIES *Vet. Path. & Bacteriol.* xvii. 277 The difficulty of diagnosing cases in the pre-clinical stage led to efforts to find a diagnostic agent for Johne's disease analogous to tuberculin for tuberculosis. **1943** *Brit. Jrnl. Tuberculosis* XXXVII. 98 How is the student of today going to prescribe tomorrow for the preclinical case diagnosed by mass-radiology? **1976** *Biol. Abstr.* LXI. 6389/1 (*heading*) Pulmonary cancer recognized in a preclinical phase of development.

3. Preceding clinical testing of a drug.

1962 *Folia Pharmacologica Japonica* 20 May 18* (*heading*) Consideration and some experiments of preclinical pharmacology of anti-cancer drugs. **1972** P. R. B. NOEL in Richards & Rondel *Adverse Drug Reactions* i. 3 The number of patients used..is not always very great and does not always exceed the number of animals used in the pre-clinical investigations.

precoat: see *PRE- A. 1, 2.

precocial, *a.* Now the usual spelling of PRÆCOCIAL *a.* (in Dict. and Suppl.).

precocious, *a.* Add: **3. b.** = PRÆCOCIAL *a.* (in Dict. and Suppl.).

1897 PARKER & HASWELL *Text-bk. Zool.* II. xiii. 382 The newly-hatched young may be..well covered with down and able to run or swim and to obtain their own food, in which case they are said to be precocious. **1970** R. A. & B. M. MAIER *Compar. Animal Behavior* ix. 193 Domestic chicks are precocious (well developed at hatching).

precog (prī·kǫg). Also **pre-cog.** [abbrev. of PRECOGNITION.] = PRECOGNITION 1. Also, one who predicts something; a person with precognition. Also *attrib.*, = PRECOGNITIVE *a.*

1966 *Listener* 19 May 727/2 It is generally recognized that 'pre-cog' dreams take place quite often; and with the knowledge which these dream researchers provide..it may be possible to obtain quite massive evidence of pre-cog dreaming. **1967** *Ibid.* 16 Mar. 359/3 Apart from the massive evidence of ESP in human life—what does the Professor say about 'pre-cog', I wonder—the abundance of ESP in nature must surely infuriate him. **1973** *Daily News* (N.Y.) 21 Aug. 53/1 Certain precogs prophesy the future with the buckshot approach, generalized predictions. **1977** *Sounds* 9 July 22/1 And as for the matter of whether the gent's armed with the sort of foresight Phillip K. Dick grants his 'precogs', you can just make up your own mind.

precognition. 1. (Later examples.)

1955 *Sci. Amer.* Oct. 116/3 The entire experimental series seemed to offer proof of some form of telepathy: 'pre-cognition' or 'post-cognition'. **1958, 1968** [see *EXTRA-SENSORY *a.*]. **1973** *Psychol. Abstr.* XLIX. 11/1 Telepathy and clairvoyance are seen as extensions of normal perceptual processes, precognition as the reverse of retrospective memory processes.

precognitive, *a.* (Later examples.)

1953 P. C. BERG *Dict. New Words* 127/2 *Precognitive telepathy*,..awareness by a percipient of images and ideas occurring at some future time in the mind of a subject or agent. **1974** *Sci. Amer.* June 118/2 One is more telepathic, more clairvoyant, more precognitive. **1975** *Physics Bull.* Mar. 125/2 The author has attempted to describe and briefly to discuss a number of cases claimed to show pre-cognitive happenings.

precognize, *v.* Now usu. with pronunc. (prī-kǫgnəiz). Delete *rare* and add later examples.

1956 A. J. AYER *Probl. Knowl.* iv. 187 There is a tendency for them [*sc.* non-philosophers] to think that if future events were precognized, they would have to exist already... To precognize something is to know, not what *is* happening, but what *will* happen. *Ibid.*, Unless the event really were future there would be no question of one's *pre*-cognizing it. **1970** A. CAMERON et al. *Computers & Old Eng. Concordances* 29, I don't foresee the solution that you are precognizing for the simple reason that I don't think there is enough demand for any computer to be built.

preco·ital, *a.* [PRE- B. 1.] Occurring or performed as a preliminary to sexual intercourse.

1935 H. M. & A. STONE *Marriage Manual* viii. 265 A long period of precoital play and a considerable prolongation of the sexual act are unsuccessful in bringing about a culmination for the woman. **1953** A. C. KINSEY et al. *Sexual Behav. Human Female* ix. 361 The pre-coital techniques in marriage are..the same. **1963** A. HERON *Towards Quaker View of Sex* Inadequacies of the love-partner during pre-coital play. **1971** 'V. X. SCOTT' *Surrogate Wife* 98 They engaged in very little precoital play. **1973** M. AMIS *Rachel Papers* 23 In normal circumstances, with her embarrassment in any kind of pre-coital conversation,..the stiff-limbed movements: you were a plaything of her unease.

Hence **preco·itally** *adv.*

1971 *Nature* 16 Apr. 433/2 Apocrine glands contribute to total body odour, but a smegma pheromone would be exposed precoitally with exposure of the glans.

precoition(al): see *PRE- B. 2a, 1d. **pre-college:** *PRE- B. 2a. **precolonial:** *PRE- B. 1d. **precombustible:** *PRE- A. 3.

pre-combu·stion. [PRE- A. 2.] In certain diesel engines, commencement of combustion of the charge before it is drawn into the main cylinder, in an adjacent small chamber; usu. *attrib.*, denoting (an engine equipped with) a chamber for this purpose.

1923 L. H. MORRISON *Diesel Engines* xx. 472 One of the first of the precombustion engines developed in the United States was the Western... The precombustion chamber is located in the cylinder head almost in line with the cylinder bore. **1932** *Mod. Diesel* v. 43 On the Continent the line of development appears to have been directed towards securing a steady and progressive burning of the fuel by a system of pre-combustion, the charge being ignited in a partially separated chamber from which the more or less controlled expansion then passes to the working cylinder. **1972** S. H. HENSHALL *Medium & High Speed Diesel Engines for Marine Use* iv. 75 Pre-combustion chamber hot member engines are characterized by their smooth running, complete combustion with clean exhaust and a tendency to high fuel consumption, together with difficulties in starting in very cold conditions.

precommissural: see *PRE- A. 4a.

pre-compre·ss, *v. Building.* [PRE- A. 1.] *trans.* To compress prior to some other treatment. Hence **pre-compre·ssion,** *spec.* the compressive force exerted in prestressed concrete by the reinforcing rods.

1936 *Structural Engineer* XIV. 259/1 A sketch of the great 10,000 tons press constructed for the laboratory for Buildings and Public Works,..Paris... It was constructed in concrete with only a light reinforcement, but pre-compressed by the tension given to the hooped wire. **1940** *Ibid.* XVIII. 629 In a pre-stressed girder the fact that the part..has been given a pre-compression equal to or exceeding the said tension, renders it impossible for fissures to appear under normal loading or even higher loading. **1946** *Concrete & Constructional Engin.* XLI. 191 In a cracked section of a prestressed member, the pre-compression is either reduced or totally annulled. **1969** *Civil Engin.* (Easton, Pa.) June 45/1 In the arch section, over-compression of the upper flange was prevented by precompressing the arches: the span was made 1in. shorter at each end with hydraulic jacks. **1974** LIN & ZIA in B. Bresler *Reinforced Concrete Engin.* I. vi. 303 Pre-stressing imparts a precompression to a concrete member in its tension zone so as to increase its cracking resistance. **1975** KONG & EVANS *Reinforced & Prestressed Concrete* ix. 196 The precompression in the concrete tends to reduce the diagonal tension.

pre-compute: see *PRE- A. 1. **pre-computer:** *PRE- B. 2a.

preconceptional, *a.* Delete *rare*[−1] and add further examples.

1933 *Jrnl. Amer. Med. Assoc.* 25 Nov. 1703/1 (*heading*) Preconceptional and prenatal influences affecting the new-born. **1957** C. T. JAVERT *Spontaneous & Habitual Abortion* xvii. 377 The author prefers to begin prenatal care on a preconceptional basis and has found this approach to be particularly effective in the management of habitual abortion patients. **1975** *Amer. Jrnl. Obstetr. & Gynecol.* CXXIII. 717/2 Preconceptional irradiation.. may impair the female reproductive capacity.

preconceptual, -conciliar: see *PRE- B. 1d.

preconde·nse, *v.* [PRE- A. 1.] *trans.* To condense (a starting material for a polymer) so as to form a stable, low-molecular-weight intermediate which is convenient to handle and can be fully polymerized at a later stage in a process. Also **preco·ndensate** [after *distillate, filtrate*, etc.], an intermediate of this nature. So **preconde·nsed** *ppl. a.*

1950 R. W. MONCRIEFF *Artificial Fibres* xxvii. 261 The formaldehyde and urea are pre-condensed, being allowed to react at room temperature for about five hours until the viscosity is 6 centipoises at 20°C. **1953** *Jrnl. Soc. Dyers & Colourists* LXIX. 44/2 The loss will be further accentuated by differences in molecular size of the pre-condensate, particularly when highly precondensed resins are used, as in some proprietary products. **1962** J. T. MARSH *Self-Smoothing Fabrics* xi. 159 These pre-condensates are probably methanol ureas which may be formed by condensing urea and formaldehyde either at room temperatures or by refluxing for a short time. **1971** S. A. HEAP et al. in H. Mark et al. *Chem. Aftertreatm. of Textiles* vi. 272 There is..a growing tendency for finishers to purchase precondensed 'resin' in liquid form. *Ibid.* 279 The conventional process for the application of urea–formaldehyde precondensates consists of impregnating, drying, curing to bring about resinification, and washing.

precondition, *sb.* (Further examples.)

1912 A. H. POWLES tr. *Bernhardi's Germany & Next War* 4 The conscious increase of our armaments is not an inevitable evil, but the most necessary precondition of our national health. **1923** J. W. HARVEY tr. *Otto's Idea of Holy* xi. 86 It sheds a colour..upon the life and practice that are its precondition. **1948** *Sunday Pictorial* 18 July 7/6 He cannot accept the lifting of the blockade as a pre-condition. **1974** tr. *Wertheim's Evolution & Revolution* 211 Among the psychological preconditions for a revolution.. one should include a feeling among relatively large groups that avenues towards emancipation are consistently blocked.

precondi·tion, *v.* [PRE- A. 1.] *trans.* To bring into a desired state or condition beforehand. Hence **precondi·tioned** *ppl. a.*, **pre-condi·tioning** *ppl. a.* and *vbl. sb.*

1922 JOYCE *Ulysses* 494 Self which it itself was ineluctably preconditioned to become. **1961** L. P. V. JOHNSON *In Time of Thetans* vii. 54 Second stage. Bringing reverence and servility to preconditioned humanity. **1967** *Jrnl. Compar. & Physiol. Psychol.* LXIV. 360 Significantly greater CERs..were shown by the preconditioned groups than by control groups. *Ibid.* 360/1 Sensory preconditioning (SPC) involves the pairing of two neutral stimuli, S_1 and S_2. Following this procedure a response is conditioned to S_2. **1969** *Jane's Freight Containers 1968–69* 420/3 The fibre-board unit load device should be preconditioned for 48 hours under these conditions prior to testing. **1971** *Homes & Gardens* Aug. 19 Frying pans and baking tins should then be lightly greased with oil or cooking fat to pre-condition the non-stick coating. **1974** *Psychol. Abstr.* LI. 572/2 The strength of resultant saccharin aversions was inversely related to preconditioning saccharin familiarity.

pre-Conquest, *a.* (Further examples.)

1922 E. EKWALL *Place-Names Lancs.* 172 The example seems to indicate that Over Wyresdale was in pre-Conquest time common land to the townships round the lower Lune. **1927** J. J. HOGAN *Eng. Lang. in Ireland* 27 There is preliminary matter about pre-Conquest Ireland, then *Conquest* follows with some omissions. **1957** K. A. WITTFOGEL *Oriental Despotism* iii. 51 In pre-Conquest Mexico the various forms of land and the obligations attached were carefully depicted in codices. **1960** S. CRUDEN *Scottish Abbeys* 54 To a small pre-Conquest church..there was added on the east a square choir with a rounded apse. **1975** 'S. MARLOWE' *Cawthorn Jrnls.* (1976) xi. 87 The inevitable merging of pre-Conquest and Spanish culture in Mexico.

preconscious, *a.* Add: (Earlier and later examples.) *spec.* in *Psychol.*, applied to memories and emotions existing at a deeper level than, or of a type different from, immediate memory or conscious thought, but which are accessible to and capable of being brought directly into consciousness; also *absol.* Cf. *FORE-CONSCIOUS *a.* (*sb.*) and quot. 1958.

1860 J. D. MORELL tr. *Fichte's Contrib. to Mental Philos.* iii. 43 It is not to be denied that all the apparently abnormal phenomena with which men are seized, in somnambulism, in vision,..and in ecstasy, spring out of the same spontaneous and preconscious region, from which all involuntary impulses and inspirations take their origin. **1867** H. MAUDSLEY *Physiol. & Path. of Mind* I. i. 15 The preconscious action of the mind, as certain metaphysical psychologists in Germany have called it. **1924** W. B. SELBIE *Psychol. Relig.* iv. 78 Consciousness, he [*sc.* Bergson] argues, only emerges when the individual becomes aware of his own mental states, and this allows for a preconscious or unconscious stage. **1925** J. RIVIERE tr. *Freud's Unconscious in Psycho-Anal.* in *Coll. Papers* IV. 25 We have now gained the conviction that there are some latent ideas which do not penetrate into consciousness... We may call the latent ideas of the first type preconscious. **1942, 1957** [see *FORECONSCIOUS *a.* (*sb.*)]. **1958** J. STRACHEY *Freud's Compl. Psychol. Wks.* XII. 262 In the 1925 English version, throughout the paper, 'foreconscious' was altered to 'preconscious', which has..become the regular translation of the German 'vorbewusst'. **1971** N. F. DIXON *Subliminal Perception* iv. 90 The problem is evidently one of confusing 'preconscious'—meaning antecedent physiological processes which do not have phenomenal representation—with the Freudian notion of 'a preconscious'. **1978** G. A. SHEEHAN *Running & Being* ix. 125 The preconscious..stores past preconceptions.

preco·nsciousness. [f. prec. + -NESS.] The state or condition of being preconscious; the preconscious part of the mind.

1930 W. EMPSON *Seven Types of Ambiguity* viii. 302 It is grasped in the pre-consciousness of the reader by a native effort of the mind. **1959** *Listener* 15 Oct. 624/1 This leads us to the idea of preconsciousness. That is the area of mental life in which everything we have experienced in the past, and can still remember, is stored. If consciousness is everything of which we are aware, then preconsciousness is everything which we can remember. **1970** *New Yorker* 26 Dec. 61 We learn of the 'hum' in the literal deeps of the poet's consciousness or pre-consciousness.

pre-consonant: see *PRE- B. 2 a. **pre-consonantal(ly), -Constantinian:** *PRE- B. 1. **precontour:** *PRE- A. 2. **pre-convulsive:** *PRE- B. 1. **precook:** *PRE- A. 1.

precoo·l, *v.* [PRE- A. 1.] *trans.* To cool prior to use or some further treatment. So **precoo·led** *ppl. a.*, **precoo·ling** *vbl. sb.* Also **precoo·ler,** a device for precooling.

1904 *Physical Rev.* XIX. 330 From the compressor, the air passes successively through an aftercooler; a separator;..and finally through a precooler charged with broken ice or snow—reaching the liquefier at a temperature of about 2°. **1911** *Power* 14 Nov. 755/2 The Atchison, Topeka & Santa Fé Railway Company has erected at San Bernardino, Cal., a combined ice-manufacturing and precooling plant. *Ibid.* 759/1 For icing the cars, upon the completion of precooling, or for such cars as are not precooled, the ice is handled by the endless-chain conveyor. **1912** *Ice & Refrigeration* Jan. 14/1 Under some conditions the plant intended only to precool fruits before they are loaded is most advantageous while..under other conditions car precooling after loading is preferable. **1926** *Spectator* 18 Sept. 412/1 By having a hermetically sealed compartment with the commodity pre-cooled, a low temperature is maintained until the box is opened at destination. *Ibid.*, After the cleaning the pre-cooling takes place. **1936** *Discovery* Apr. 104/1 The compressed helium is first pre-cooled by liquid nitrogen. **1958** A. LAURIE et al. *Commercial Flower Forcing* (ed. 6) xii. 328 The cases containing the bulbs are placed in storage in early October at 32 to 34 °F, where they remain until shipping, which is usually in late November. Lily bulbs handled this way are referred to as precooled bulbs in contrast to bulbs sent direct to the florist immediately after digging and grading. **1958** *Times* 23 June 2/6 The more promising development is the use of precooling plants on the farms, the object being to cool the fruit quickly as soon as it is picked but before it is finally packed. **1970** *Times* 4 Sept. (Aviation Suppl.) p. ix/9 Imperial Metal Industries' Marston Excelsior subsidiary will display a range of heat exchangers, including..a precooler for the Hawker Siddeley Nimrod. **1973** *Times* 22 Sept. 13/1 We buy a quantity of double nosed Golden Harvest pre-cooled daffodils..which are delivered in the first week of October.

pre-copulative: see *PRE- B. 1 d.

precordium[2] (prīkǭ·ɹdiəm). *Anat.* Formerly also præ-. [Sing. of PRÆCORDIA.] = PRÆCORDIA.

1892 A. E. SANSOM *Diagn. Dis. Heart & Thoracic Aorta* xvi. 128 On placing the hand over the præcordium, the observer may be sensible of a peculiar vibration occurring over a certain area and at a certain period of the heart's action. **1900** DORLAND *Med. Dict.* 533/1 *Precordium*, same as *precordia*. **1934** *Arch. Internal Med.* LIV. 341 Pulsations of the heart were felt 3·5 cm. below the epigastric notch, and sometimes a systolic thrill was felt over the precordium. **1962** *Lancet* 13 Jan. 104/2 A pericardial friction-rub was audible over the precordium, but blood-pressure was 140/70 mm. Hg and there were no signs of cardiac failure. **1970** W. DRESSLER *Clin. Aids in Cardiac Diagn.* v. 66 Fig. 24 is from a 31 year old man who showed a heaving systolic impulse in the left half of the precordium between the 2nd intercostal space and the 5th rib. **1977** J. T. WILLERSON in Willerson & Sanders *Clin. Cardiol.* 101/2 Inspection and palpation of the precordium in the patient with cardiac disease are valuable and important parts of the physical examination.

pre-crusade: see *PRE- B. 2 a. **pre-cultural:** *PRE- B. 1.

precu·re, *v.* [PRE- A. 1.] *intr.* Of a synthetic resin: to cure prematurely, making mechanical processing impossible. So **pre·cure** *sb.*, the premature curing of a synthetic resin; **precu·ring** *vbl. sb.*

1935 C. ELLIS *Chem. Synthetic Resins* I. xxviii. 612 Avoidance of precuring during drying is essential if the molding properties of the resin are to remain unimpaired. **1936** H. W. ROWELL *Technol. Plastics* xxiii. 170 Another form of pre-cure is due to mixing a batch of quick curing powder or already cured powder with one having a normal rate of cure. **1943** *Brit. Plastics* XV. 235/2 Precuring.. shows up on the underside of the moulding as a slight chalkiness, in which the outlines of individual moulding powder particles can be seen. **1952** J. DELMONTE *Plastics Molding* viii. 208 If preheating is carried much beyond this temperature, it [*sc.* a thermosetting resin] will begin to precure excessively and will lose its flow qualities. **1962** J. T. MARSH *Self-Smoothing Fabrics* xi. 172 Where the material is batched or plaited in a warm condition immediately after the stenter, there are dangers of what has been termed 'pre-cure' which it is essential to avoid where mechanical processing takes place before the final condensation, and which it may possibly be wise to avoid generally.

precursor. Add: **3.** *Biochem.* and *Chem.* A compound which precedes another in a metabolic pathway or a chemical synthesis, esp. a naturally occurring one.

1889 C. A. MACMUNN *Outl. Clin. Chem. Urine* iii. 36 Although we know it [*sc.* urea] is formed from proteids, we cannot trace it back through its precursors—the intermediate products of metabolism. **1890** L. C. WOOLDRIDGE tr. *G. von Bunge's Text-bk. Physiol. & Path. Chem.* vi. 102 This compound is doubtless the precursor of haemoglobin, for there is no considerable quantity of any other compound of iron in the yolk. **1948** *Jrnl. Biol. Chem.* CLXXII. 651 (*heading*) Homoserine as a precursor of threonine and methionine in *Neurospora*. **1960** [see *CRYPTOXANTHIN]. **1971** *Nature* 30 July 304/1 An important feature of the process is the maintenance of the high orientation in the acrylic precursor throughout the carbonization processes. **1977** *Sci. Amer.* July 40/2 Ozone and its precursor, atomic oxygen, are destroyed by catalytic reactions that depend on H and OH.

precu·t, *v.* [PRE- A. 1.] *trans.* To cut prior to some other operation. Also *absol.* So **precu·tting** *vbl. sb.*

1945 *Trans. Inst. Mining Engin.* CIV. 192 As with other types of loader which rely upon pre-cutting and blasting for the satisfactory preparation of the coal for loading, much difficulty was experienced. *Ibid.* 701 This roof can be a bad one if not properly controlled, and we felt we would not like to take the risk of pre-cutting and blowing coal, and thus removing all support. **1951** B. KELLY *Prefabrication of Houses* i. 4 There may be said to be various degrees of prefabrication, of which precutting might be one, the fabrication of panels another, [etc.]. **1960** J. SINCLAIR *Winning Coal* vii. 191 Two men pre-cut the face with an A.B. Fifteen Cutter. *Ibid.* 206 It may be preferable sometimes to pre-cut and load on the same shift with the separate cutter working about 40 yd ahead of the cutter-loader. **1961** M. BEADLE *These Ruins are Inhabited* (1963) xi. 160 The Co-ops are pre-cutting their meat and putting it in plastic film. **1964** A. NELSON *Dict. Mining* 343 *Pre-cutting*, a term used in machine mining where a coal-cutter makes a cut along the face in front of a cutter-loader.

Hence **precu·t** *ppl. a.*

1946 *Fortune* Apr. 244/2 Pease makes only wall, ceiling, and floor panels in the factory; roofs are built on the site from factory precut lumber by traditional methods. **1960** *Farmer & Stockbreeder* 29 Mar. 74/3 As the mower makes a new cut, the scatterer shakes up the pre-cut swath, thereby reducing the time necessary to make the hay. **1960** *Times* 29 Aug. 15/3 The Birmingham Co-operative Society has, for some time now, been selling pre-cut and prepacked meat. **1967** KARCH & BUBER *Offset Processes* iv. 112 (*caption*) Redi-Kut display letters are pre-cut and have a pressure-sensitive backing. **1974** *Encycl. Brit. Macropædia* XIV. 966/1 One of the earliest excursions into prefabrication was the adoption of precut framing lumber pieces for walls and partitions. **1976** *Sci. Amer.* Nov. 100/2 In the commonest form of stamping, a precut metal blank is formed in a mechanical press between a set of dies that have been carefully shaped to yield the desired part.

precut (prī·kʌt), *sb.* [f. the vb.] **a.** A cut made in something prior to some other operation on it. **b.** Something that has been precut.

1948 *Trans. Inst. Mining Engin.* CVII. 242 A long bottom jib was provided to give a pre-cut and so assist in the fracturing of the coal which is rather strong. **1960** J. SINCLAIR *Winning Coal* vii. 204 A middle pre-cut has been usefully employed where a floor tends to lift and break at the bottom of the coal. **1971** *Real Estate Rev.* Fall 49/1 They are to be distinguished from pre-cuts, which involve materials cut to proper size off-site and then conventionally constructed on site.

precy·stic, *a. Zool.* [PRE- B. 1.] Applied to protozoans that are preparing to encyst.

1926 C. M. WENYON *Protozool.* I. ii. 190 It may be that ..the precystic amœbæ..are produced by amœbæ living on the surface of the mucosa. **1938** *Archiv für Protistenkunde* XC. 405 The large majority of precystic *Colpoda* sink to the bottom to encyst. **1956** *New Biol.* XXI. 92 In preparation for this [encysting] the amoebae either digest or eject their inclusions and do not feed or grow, so that a generation of small amoebae with clear cytoplasm is produced—the precystic amoebae.

predacious, *a.* Add: **1.** Also, used of parasitic fungi which actually kill their hosts. Also *transf.* (Later examples.)

1908 C. ELIOT *Turkey in Europe* (ed. 2) iii. 73 The Turks never outgrow their ancestral character of predacious nomads. **1933** *Jrnl. Washington Acad. Sci.* XXIII. 140 Adhesion on hyphal tips..appears to be effective in the somewhat more feebly predacious activity of a fungus bearing solitary spores. **1936** *Mycologia* XXVIII. 307 (*heading*) A new predaceous fungus. **1946** *Ecology* XXVII. 257/1 The Chelonethida are of interest as predacious arachnids. **1964** R. M. & J. W. FOX *Introd. Compar. Entomol.* xiii. 372 Some predaceous species help to control other arthropods. **1971** R. C. W. BERKELEY in Hawker & Linton *Micro-Organisms* xii. 512 The activities of the predacious fungi have been much investigated in the hope that they could provide an effective means of controlling root parasitic eelworms.

predate, *v.*[1] **2.** (Later examples.)

1974 *Observer* (Colour Suppl.) 19 May 14/3 Houses that pre-date the introduction of noise controls and the airport itself. **1976** *Amer. N. & Q.* XIV. 98/1 Both poems predate the letters in the authorized edition of *The Letters of Junius* published in 1772. **1978** *N. & Q.* Dec. 532/2 Deeds of the Warren estates..provide instances in Lancashire which pre-date the above occurrence [of the name Diana] by at least three hundred years.

predate (prĭdē·t), *v.*[2] [Back-formation f. PREDATION.] **a.** *intr.* To seek prey. **b.** *trans.* Of a predator: to prey on, eat.

1974 *Trout & Salmon* Mar. 50/2 It is hoped that the stock of trout will predate sufficiently to minimise the problem [of coarse fish]. **1977** *Field* 13 Jan. 47/1 Man is a predator... To predate in person, instead of by proxy, is not unnatural. **1977** J. L. HARPER *Population Biol. of Plants* vi. 172 Wood pigeons (*Columba palumba*) cease to predate when the density of a food falls to a level at which the birds can no longer search quickly enough to pick up a sufficient quantity. **1977** *New Scientist* 27 Oct. 220/3 The eggs of many species of frogs are predated by many species of vertebrates and invertebrates.

predation. Restrict *Obs.* to sense in Dict. and add: **2.** *Zool.* The action of one animal preying upon another. Also *transf.* and *fig.*

1932 W. L. MCATEE in *Smithsonian Misc. Coll.* LXXV. No. 7. 144 Predation takes place much the same as if there were no such thing as protective adaptations. **1937** *Ann. Rep. Board of Regents Smithsonian Inst. 1936* 243 (*heading*) What is the meaning of predation? *Ibid.*, Predation has been shown..not to be, in a collective sense, an inexorable tax upon the luckless prey species. **1944** J. S. HUXLEY *On Living in Revolution* 61 The raids of the slave-making ants are not true war, but a curious combination of predation and parasitism. **1954** D. LACK *Nat. Regulation of Animal Numbers* xiv. 156 The small passerine birds cannot have been limited in numbers by predation. **1959** *Listener* 10 Dec. 1032/1 This predation of birds upon insects is of considerable practical importance. **1968** *Nature* 17 Aug. 694/1 Predation from vertebrates and the uncertainty associated with nests attached to palm leaves were certainly principal factors [in the death of *Scaphidura* chicks]. **1975** W. H. NESBITT in M. W. Fox *Wild Canids* xxvii. 395 They [*sc.* feral dogs] are a valuable part of the fauna by their sanitary predation activities. **1976** E. CURIO *Ethology of Predation* 1 Predation is an ecological factor of almost universal importance for the biologist. **1977** READER & CROZE *Pyramids of Life* 1. 30/1 In its continuous 'predation' on plants, the elephant tears branches from trees, pulls great tufts of grass and roots from the earth. **1977** *Times* 11 Feb. 17/3 New entrants to the shipping business are said to have little chance of surviving outside the conference network because of..the threat of predation (the practice of selling below cost to destroy competition).

predatism (pre·dătiz'm). *Biol.* [f. PREDAT(ION + -ISM.] Predation; the mode of life of a predator.

1930 R. A. FISHER *Genetical Theory Nat. Selection* vii. 157 Though the principle of Bates is excluded when two species are actually equally acceptable or unacceptable, to demonstrate such equality with sufficient precision to exclude differential predatism, and to demonstrate it with respect to the effectual predatory population, would seem to require both natural knowledge and experimental refinement which we do not at present possess. **1946** C. T. BRUES *Insect Dietary* vi. 243 Predatism..is a commonplace mode of sustenance among animals, including man himself. **1964** *Biol. Abstr.* XLV. 5426/2 (*heading*) A new occurrence of predatism in polychaete worms.

predative (pre·dătiv), *a. rare.* [f. L. *prædāt-*, ppl. stem of *prædārī* to plunder + -IVE, after *native, passive,* etc.] = PREDATORY *a.*

c **1925** D. H. LAWRENCE *Virgin & Gipsy* (1930) iii. 50 She [*sc.* the gipsy-woman] was..just a bit wolfish... 'Good-morning, my ladies and gentlemen,' she said, eyeing the girls from her bold, predative eyes.

predator (pre·dătəɹ). *Zool.* [f. L. *prædātor* plunderer (see PREDATORY *a.*); cf. mod.L. *Predatores* (W. Swainson in Swainson & Shuckard *On Hist. & Nat. Arrangement of Insects* (1840) II. iii. 115).] An animal that preys upon another.
1922 W. M. WHEELER *Social Life Insects* ii. 46 Species that behave in this manner are not true parasites, but extremely economical predators, because they eventually kill their victims. **1931** W. C. ALLEE *Animal Aggregations* xiv. 246 The struggle for existence between predators and their prey. **1945** J. STEINBECK *Cannery Row* xvii. 69 The little octopi..prefer a bottom on which there are many caves and little crevices..where they may hide from predators. **1959** W. TRAVIS *Beyond Reefs* viii. 165 We all adopted the lazy movements and slow rhythms of these big predators [*sc.* sharks]. **1971** *Nature* 1 Oct. 345/1 Predators also show a tendency to continue to select a given type of prey, even though other types may be..more easily available.
2. *attrib.* **predator–prey** *adj. phr.*, concerning the ecological balance between a predator and its prey.
1946 *Q. Rev. Biol.* XXI. 235/2 In equations depicting predator–prey interactions in lower vertebrates, loss types may substitute naturally for each other. **1968** *Times* 2 Oct. 12/6 This clearly has considerable implications for understanding predator–prey relationships.

predatory, *a.* **4.** (Further examples.)
1925 *Jrnl. Mammalogy* VI. 29 The larger predatory mammals..require for proper sustenance animal food in large quantities. **1970** R. A. & B. M. MAIER *Compar. Animal Behavior* vii. 116 Defenses against predators are necessarily less than completely effective; otherwise, predatory animals could not survive.
predatoriness (examples).
1963 *Times* 7 Mar. 13/2 The techniques of power, of political manipulation, of the predatoriness of officialdom, become even more insidiously efficient. **1979** *Listener* 30 Aug. 284/2 Poverty..makes public predatoriness irresistibly attractive.

pre-daw·n, *sb.* and *a.* **A.** *sb.* [PRE- B. 1 in Dict. and Suppl.] The period before daybreak. Also *fig.* **B.** *adj.* [PRE- B. 2.] Occurring before dawn; of or pertaining to the period before daybreak.
1946 D. C. PEATTIE *Road of Naturalist* i. 13 So now I woke, in the pre-dawn of the desert. **1951** *Jrnl. Geophysical Res.* LVI. 325 Between the post-twilight and pre-dawn, the intensity goes through a maximum which is partially localized to the north of our station. *Ibid.*, During the post-twilight period, an enhancement of intensity is observed in the western sky. In the predawn observations, no enhancement is noted in the eastern sky. **1963** J. LUSBY in B. James *Austral. Short Stories* 222 You felt the brittle pre-dawn tension of any war-time 'drome. **1965** G. MCINNES *Road to Gundagai* x. 178 The swirling pre-dawn mist lay wrapped about the feet of every illusion. **1973** G. HART *Right from Start* i. 30 On we went through October, 1970, the pre-dawn of the campaign. **1978** *Daily Tel.* 11 Nov. 11/1 A total eclipse of the sun at midday immersed the world..in semi-gloom, as in the pre-dawn.

predefine, *v.* Add: Hence **predefi·ned** *ppl. a.*
1929 R. BRIDGES *Testament of Beauty* IV. 124 But these philosophers..used the abstracted terms whereby they had pre-defined distinctions. **1976** *Brit. Jrnl. Sociol.* XXVII. 302 What is offered is not the theoretical construction of an object of study, but merely the systematization of predefined data. **1977** J. D. DOUGLAS in Douglas & Johnson *Existential Sociol.* i. 63 Even Goffman..has had little to say about the self except as a 'presenter' of predefined and learned social roles.

predelinquency, -delinquent: see *PRE- B. 1.

predeli·very, *a.* [PRE- B. 2.] Carried out in, or concerned with, the period preceding delivery of a baby.
1957 *Obstetr. & Gynecol.* IX. 633 (*heading*) Predelivery sedation with promazine. **1965** S. PELLER in Glass & Eversley *Population in Hist.* v. 91 Babies born out of wedlock had a perinatal mortality of 102, or 43 or 32 per 1,000.., depending on whether their mothers had been sheltered in the *pre*delivery maternity division of the General Hospital for 0–7, 8–28, or 29–56 days.

predesignate, *v.* Add: Hence **prede·signated** *ppl. a.*
1961 J. B. WILSON *Reason & Morals* ii. 109 People do not consciously adopt a language-game for a deliberate and predesignated purpose. **1973** *Nation Rev.* (Melbourne) 31 Aug. 1449/3 Fortnightly..aficionados of the Australian pit fowl gather at the predesignated meeting place.

predestinating, *ppl. a.* (Later example.)
1956 R. MACAULAY *Towers of Trebizond* xxi. 242 The predestinating Calvinists in the Celtic mountains.

predestination. Add: Hence **predestina·tionism,** belief in predestination or the system of thought it entails.
1901 G. H. HOWISON *Let.* 21 July in R. B. Perry *Tht. & Char. W. James* (1935) II. 221 *Of course* I don't reconcile predestinationism and capricious free-will. **1937** *Mind* XLVI. 287 The unsatisfactory answer offered by Leibniz to readers frightened by *his* Predestinationism.

predestinator. 2. Delete † *Obs.* and add later example.
1956 R. MACAULAY *Towers of Trebizond* xxi. 240 It is the Predestinators not the Pelagians who, as it says in the 9th Article, do vainly talk.
Hence **prede·stinatory** *a.* (*rare*) = PREDESTINATE *ppl. a.* 2.
1967 B. WRIGHT tr. *Queneau's Between Blue & Blue* xix. 203 If society gave me this predestinatory name, nature for her part provided me with peculiarly active grey matter.

predestine, *v.* Add: Hence **prede·stine** *ppl. a.* (*rare*).
1962 A. HUXLEY *Island* xiii. 204 These people are the propagandist's predestine victims.

predeterminative, *a.* Add: **2.** *Gram.* Having the quality of, or acting as, a predeterminer.
1961 R. B. LONG *Sentence & its Parts* ii. 42 In *only John* the adverb *only* is essentially predeterminative exactly as it is in *only the older children.*

predeterminer. Add: **2.** *Gram.* [f. PRE- B. 1 + *DETERMINER[1] 3.] One of a class of limiting expressions that precede the determiner. Also *attrib.*
1959 J. SLEDD *Short Introd. to Eng. Gram.* 116 The predeterminers, finally, are rather various but limited in number. **1961** *Amer. Speech* XXXVI. 159 It is customary to describe the English nominal as consisting of a sequence of constituents: predeterminers, determiners, adjectives, [etc.]. **1961** R. B. LONG *Sentence & its Parts* ii. 40 Predeterminer modifiers generally are adverbial in function, and mensurant, selectional, differential, conjunctive, or adjunct-like in force. **1964** [see *DETERMINER[1] 3]. **1965** O. THOMAS *Transformational Gram.* iv. 84 Like the other two classes of determiners, the predeterminers have a unique feature: they are invariably separated from the regular determiners by the word *of.* **1975** *Language* LI. 990 The articles are analysed with respect to..a class of modifiers sometimes known as predeterminers (*several, three,* etc.).

pre-development: see *PRE- B. 2a.

prediabe·tic, *a.* and *sb.* *Path.* [PRE- B. 1.] **A.** *adj.* Of, pertaining to, or designating a person in whom it appears that diabetes mellitus is likely to develop, but who does not exhibit its full symptoms. **B.** *sb.* A prediabetic person.
1921 *Jrnl. Amer. Med. Assoc.* 8 Jan. 79/2 A prediabetic stage in fat persons has been recognized. *Ibid.* 83/2 It is to the diabetic patient and his relatives that one can look most confidently for help in preventing diabetes... Such measures, however, are but general, and they will never suffice for the prediabetic. **1954** *Jrnl. Clin. Endocrinol.* XIV. 177 The high rates of fetal loss and the production of large babies are exemplified by the pregnancies of prediabetic women in the Cape Town region. **1962** H. ZAROWITZ in Ellenberg & Rifkin *Clin. Diabetes Mellitus* xi. 164 Because the hereditary potential for diabetes has been firmly established, this prediabetic state can occur at any time from birth to senescence. **1970** D. M. KIPNIS in Cerasi & Luft *Pathogenesis of Diabetes Mellitus* 46 Insulin sensitivity may be *increased* rather than decreased in prediabetics. **1976** *Billings* (Montana) *Gaz.* 27 June 1-B/5 Our baby will most likely be pre-diabetic (genetically disposed to diabetes, but not necessarily diabetic).
So **prediabe·tes,** the prediabetic state.
1937 *Endocrinol.* XXI. 195 'Prediabetes' in obesity is of interest because of its possible bearing on certain problems concerning the intermediate carbohydrate metabolism in obesity. **1964** *New Scientist* 27 Aug. 482/3 'Prediabetes', or the early stages, has been found in a surprisingly high percentage of the population.., and it is now known that definite changes can be detected before there is a noticeable rise in the blood sugar level. **1970** CAMERINI-DÁVALOS & COLE *Early Diabetes* IV. 256 Prediabetes is the condition of those persons who, because of a strong hereditary tendency, have a high probability for the later development of diabetes but in whom at the time of study, all tests of carbohydrate tolerance yield normal results.

predicability. (Later example.)
1965 F. SOMMERS in M. Black *Philos. in Amer.* 275, I shall use a reverse arrow to stand for the predicability relation between two terms.

predicant, *sb.* **1.** For 'Now *rare* or *Obs.*' read 'Now *Hist.*' and add later examples.
1816 T. J. HOWELL *Stranger in Shrewsbury* 130 The Dominicans, or Black Friars, were called in some places Jacobins, and in others Predicants. **1910** *Encycl. Relig. & Ethics* III. 176 The banishment of the pastors and the prohibition of public worship drove the people to private assemblies and the ministrations of lay preachers. Among the latter, who were known as 'predicants', François Vivens and Claude Brousson..were specially conspicuous. **1939** *Conc. Oxf. Dict. Eng. Lit.* 186/1 A monk of the order of the Predicants.

predicate, *sb.* Add: **1.** (Further examples.)
1903 B. RUSSELL *Princ. of Math.* I. iv. 45 We shall say that 'Socrates is human' is a proposition having only one term; of the remaining components of the proposition, one is the verb, the other is a predicate... Predicates.. are concepts, other than verbs, which occur in propositions having only one term or subject. **1962** A. MARTINET *Functional View of Lang.* ii. 44 *There was a riot, in the village, yesterday*... *There was* marks *the riot* as the predicate, i.e. as the element around which the others gravitate and in relation to which that function will be marked.
2. a. (Further examples.) Sometimes restricted to the main verb and its object or complement, to the exclusion of any adjunct. Also in *Logic* and *Math.*, freq. in wider use: an assertion or relation having one or more terms unspecified; a propositional function.
The generalization of *predicate* (G. *prädikat*) to include relations (many-place predicates) originated in Hilbert & Ackermann *Grundzüge der theoretischen Logik* (1928) 45: see quot. 1950.
1892 H. SWEET *New Eng. Gram.* I. 48 In language the logical connections between words extend over a wider area than the purely grammatical ones. Thus in such a sentence as *I came home yesterday morning*, the grammatical predicate to *I* is *came*, *home* and *yesterday* being grammatically connected with the predicate only, while *morning* is an adjunct to *yesterday* only. But in thought *yesterday* is as much part of the predicate as *came* itself, *came-home-yesterday-morning* being the logical predicate which, from a grammatical point of view may be regarded either as an extended predicate or a group-predicate. **1921** E. SAPIR *Language* ii. 37 The reduced sentence resolves itself into the subject of discourse—*the mayor*—and the predicate—*is going to deliver a speech.* It is customary to say that the true subject of such a sentence is *mayor*, the true predicate *is going* or even *is.* **1961** *Archivum Linguisticum* XIII. 81 The relative priority of such class concepts as noun and verb as against such as subject and predicate. **1968** J. LYONS *Introd. Theoret. Linguistics* viii. 334 *John killed Bill in Central Park on Sunday.* The subject is *John*; the predicate is *killed Bill*; and *in Central Park* and *on Sunday* are adjuncts.
1937 S. K. LANGER *Introd. Symbolic Logic* vii. 158 'Being white' has the properties of such a relation; any term, *a*, has it or does not have it, but since there is no second term we cannot say that *a* has this relation *to* any other. Such a relation of 'monadic' degree is called a predicate. *Ibid.* 159 The sole business of predicates in logic is to define classes. **1940** W. V. QUINE *Math. Logic* i. 27 'Is true' and 'is false'..are predicates by means of which we speak *about* statements. *Ibid.* 28 The verb 'implies'..is a binary predicate by means of which we talk *about* statements. **1943** *Trans. Amer. Math. Soc.* LIII. 42 Let us consider number-theoretic predicates, that is, propositional functions of natural numbers. **1950** tr. *Hilbert & Ackermann's Princ. Math. Logic* iii. 57 To the formula $x + y = z$ there corresponds a triadic predicate $S(x, y, z)$. The truth of $S(x, y, z)$ means that x, y, and z are connected by the relation $x + y = z$. [*Note*] Hitherto it has been customary in logic to call only functions with one argument place predicates, while functions with more than one place were called relations. Here we use the word 'predicate' in a quite general sense. **1965** HUGHES & LONDEY *Elem. Formal Logic* xxxix. 270 We shall..speak of the expressions, such as 'greater than' and 'between', which stand for two-place, three-place, etc., relations, as two-place, three-place, etc., predicates respectively. **1969** D. J. FOULIS *Fund. Concepts Math.* i. 14 Suppose that $P(x)$..becomes a proposition whenever x takes on any particular value in U. Then $P(x)$ is called a predicate or a propositional function, and the object variable x is called its argument. **1973** H. HERMES *Introd. Math. Logic* i. 40 In the statement *The crown jewels are kept in the Tower of London*, *The crown jewels* and *the Tower of London* can be understood as names for individuals and *are kept in* as a name for a predicate... *are kept in* is a name for a two-place predicate... *is tall* is a name for a one-place predicate.
3. *attrib.* and *Comb.*, as *predicate accusative, adjective, -centre* (*-centred* adj.), *clause, expression, marker, nominal, nominative, -part, -phrase, -position, -prefix, sentence, stress, -taking* adj., *term, variable, word*; **predicate calculus** [tr. G. *prädikatenkalkül* (Hilbert & Ackermann *Grundzüge der theoret. Logik* (1928) ii. 34)], any formal logic characterized by the use of existential quantifiers; cf. *propositional calculus* s.v. *PROPOSITIONAL *a.* b.
1887 W. W. GOODWIN *Greek Gram.* III. 194 The predicate nominative with the passive verbs of this class represents the predicate accusative of the active construction. *Ibid.* 196 The predicate adjective may be connected with its noun by the copula..or by a copulative verb. **1977** *Word* 1972 XXVIII. 79 In the following discussion I shall be concerned with predicate adjectives, except where otherwise noted. **1950** tr. *Hilbert & Ackermann's Princ. Math. Logic* p. ix, The terminology has been adapted to that of the *Grundlagen der Mathematik* by Hilbert and Bernays. For example, the term 'functional calculus' has been everywhere replaced by 'predicate calculus'. *Ibid.* iii. 67 We will now proceed, just as we did for the sentential calculus. to set up for the predicate calculus a system of axioms from which the remaining true sentences of the predicate calculus may be obtained by means of certain rules. **1955** A. N. PRIOR *Formal Logic* I. iv. 73 The calculus of predicational functions (often simply called the functional calculus, or the predicate calculus). **1966** *Mathematical Rev.* Jan. 7/1 (*heading*) Axiomatization of the infinite-valued predicate calculus. **1970** *Language* XLVI. 783 Whether grammatical or lexical-situational, all these relations are the linguistic counterpart of the predicate calculus. **1979** *Sci. Amer.* May 131/1 Could there exist an algorithm such that when it was given a statement written in precise mathematical language, it would report eventually whether the statement was true or false?.. For a powerful formalized language known as the predicate calculus it has been shown that no such algorithm exists. **1966** R. A. HALL *Pidgin & Creole Lang.* vi. 84 In the predicates of most pidgins and creoles, we find..virtually any type of free form or phrase, without any verb. Here are a few examples of nouns, pronouns, and adjectives as predicate-centers. *Ibid.* 85 Examples of other types of predicate-center include those containing adverbs or adverbial phrases. **1974** *Amer. Speech* 1970 XLV. 265 He differs from Becker in choosing a predicate-centered

approach in which the verb is the centra lelement. **1966** *Eng. Stud.* XLVII. 257 Grammatically *that*-clauses.. may also function as predicate clauses. **1957** G. RYLE in M. Black *Importance of Lang.* (1962) 154 Predicate-expressions also denote what they are truly predicable of. **1966** R. A. HALL *Pidgin & Creole Lang.* vi. 83 The predicate in many pidgins and creoles..is often set apart from what goes before, by some special syntactic marker. South Seas Pidgin English..has a 'predicate-marker' /i-/, which is normally used when the subject..is not of the first or second person. **1965** N. CHOMSKY *Aspects of Theory of Syntax* iv. 181 'Bill is a lawyer.' The Predicate-Nominal of the latter is not singular, in the base structure. **1887** Predicate nominative [see **predicate accusative*]. **1957** D. L. BOLINGER in *Publ. Amer. Dial. Soc.* XXVIII. 150 This resolves the subject vs. predicate-nominative ambiguity in plain hwQs. **1924** O. JESPERSEN *Philos. Gram.* 145 We might also use the terms 'subject-part' and 'predicate-part' instead of 'primary' and 'adnex'. **1965** N. CHOMSKY *Aspects of Theory of Syntax* ii. 102 The Place and Time Adverbials that are associated with the full Predicate-Phrase. **1955** A. N. PRIOR *Formal Logic* II. iii. 160 The Schoolmen also very freely substitute singular terms for general ones, in the predicate- as well as the subject-position. **1966** R. A. HALL *Pidgin & Creole Lang.* vi. 83 Haitian and the other Central American French-based creoles have a series of predicate-prefixes, which indicate negation..and tense. **1964** *Language* XL. 46 The sentences to be discussed.. have *is* as their main verb. They will be referred to as predicate sentences. **1934** PRIEBSCH & COLLINSON *German Lang.* I. iii. 60 We might term such stresses predicate stresses, for they indicate what is the logical (if not the grammatical) predicate. **1974** *Canad. Jrnl. Linguistics* XIX. II. 153 Not only is there a problem for the analyst of knowing when to..assign a predicate-taking adjective to an *easy* or *eager* deep structure. **1901** A. SIDGWICK *Use of Words* 157 Predicate terms depend on artificial distinction. **1954** I. M. COPI *Symbolic Logic* iv. 67 We write the symbol for its predicate term to the left of the symbol for its subject term. **1937** A. SMEATON tr. *Carnap's Logical Syntax of Lang.* III. 84 In Language II, there are..not only numerical variables.., but also predicate-variables..and functor-variables. **1955** A. N. PRIOR *Formal Logic* II. iii. 158 The nearest thing to a general term-variable in the functional calculus is the predicate-variable (ϕ, etc.). **1932** A. H. GARDINER *Theory of Speech & Lang.* iv. 216 The subject-word places before the listener a thing to which he is to direct his attention, and the predicate-word tells him what he is to perceive or think about it.

predicate, *v.* Add: **3.** For *U.S.* read 'orig. *U.S.*' and add later *transf.* examples.

1968 *Globe & Mail* (Toronto) 5 Feb. 2/2 Mr. Diefenbaker said the federal Government had erred by predicating the conference on a bill of rights. **1973** *Times Lit. Suppl.* 20 July 836/1 A new conception of reality is demanded, predicated on dissatisfaction with formalist literature and rooted in the here and now. **1975** *High Times* Dec. 96/2 Some of the agents admitted 'they viewed routes of advancement within the DEA to be open to them predicated on the numbers of arrests they made and the amounts of narcotics they seized'. **1977** *Listener* 30 June 867/2 Crime predicated on sexual disorder I distrust.

predica·tional, *a.* [f. PREDICATION + -AL.] Of or pertaining to predication.

1894 J. VENN *Symbolic Logic* (ed. 2) ii. 59 It..concluded, in the predicational form,—using 'is' instead of 'is identical with'. **1921** W. E. JOHNSON *Logic* I. xiv. 237 Giving added significance to the predicational factor by bringing out the relation of an adjective to its determinable. **1922** *Ibid.* II. iii. 56 A function is called predicational when the component that determines its form is the characterising tie, which unites two variants related to one another as substantive to adjective. **1953** K. BRITTON *J. S. Mill* vi. 194, I say 'This snow is white'... The predicational form of sentence indicates this connexion [between whiteness and the other qualities of snow]: whereas 'There is snow and noise' does not—it is not asserted that the snow is noisy. **1955** [see *predicate calculus* s.v. *PREDICATE *sb.* 3]. **1961** *Brno Studies in English* III. 15 The unwarranted assumption that any word taken by itself must possess an independent predicational function. **1978** *Language* LIV. 90 Quantification is often predicational (i.e. with adjectives) in Japanese.

predicatival (predikătəi·văl), *a.* [f. PREDICATIV(E *a.* + -AL.] Of, pertaining to, or constituting a predicate. Also *ellipt.* as *sb.*

1891 H. A. STRONG et al. *Introd. Study Hist. Lang.* xvii. 290 A similar vacillation occurs in cases of the predicatival noun or predicatival attribute. **1937** A. H. GARDINER in *Mélanges de Linguistique et de Philologie offerts à J. van Ginneken* 310 Predicatival examples are not very frequent, e.g. *She is very Boston, Surely that knock* (i.e. at the front door) *is John.* **1958** A. A. HILL *Introd. Ling. Struct.* xvi. 274 A verb consisting of an *-ing* form..will be defined as a predicatival rather than as a predicator.

predicative, *a.* Add: **1. a.** (Further examples.) Also, of, pertaining to, or constituting a predicate. Also *ellipt.* as *sb.*

1914 O. JESPERSEN *Mod. Eng. Gram.* II. xiv. 330 As a rule words that can be used as adjuncts (pre-adjuncts) can also be used in the same form as predicatives. **1925** E. KRUISINGA *Handbk. Present-Day Eng.* (ed. 4) II. I. 235 Predicative Participles... The simple present participle is very frequently used with the copula *to be,* to form what is called the progressive. **1925** GRATTAN & GURREY *Our Living Lang.* xxi. 129 The following typical examples of Qualifiers and Predicatives. **1930** in J. T. Hatfield et al. *Curme Vol. Ling. Stud.* 46 A noun or pronoun in the subjective case may take a great variety of predicative cases. **1932** *Eng. Stud.* XIV. 129 By starting from the full meaning of the finite (or as it is now called: predicative) member of the group, the author compels us to look for a discussion of the progressive, perfect, etc., in the sections on *to be, to have,* etc. **1932** W. L. GRAFF *Lang.* ix. 328 If we emphasize the relationship of the referential parts to one another, it is noted that the Greenlandic sentence consists of a noun and its attributes, whereas the English one is formed by a subject and its predicate. Hence the further division into attributive or possessive languages and predicative ones. **1933** O. JESPERSEN *Syst. Gram.* 25 Some languages have a special case, or even two special cases in which predicatives are put: shall we say that 'a teacher' is in the 'predicative' case in 'he is a teacher' and in the 'illative' in 'he became a teacher'? **1942** R. W. ZANDVOORT in *Eng. Stud.* XXIV. 2 Only 10 of these [*sc.* forms of *to do*] are finite (predicative) forms..; the rest are non-finite (non-predicative). **1959** M. SCHLAUCH *Eng. Lang. in Mod. Times* viii. 230 He [*sc.* Deutschbein] contrasts especially the predicative sentence, which may be complicated but is apprehended as an organic whole..and the attributive sentence. **1966** *Eng. Stud.* XLVII. 50 A discussion of intransitive verbs combined with a predicative 'apposition' (e.g. *he died young; he died an admiral*).

b. In various special collocations, as *predicative clause, syntagm,* etc.; *predicative adjunct, appositive* = *object complement* s.v. *OBJECT *sb.* 7.

1963 Predicative adjunct [see *OBJECT *sb.* 7]. **1963** F. T. VISSER *Hist. Syntax Eng. Lang.* I. ii. 182 Syntactical units of the type..'he died *a martyr*' consist of a subject, a predicate in the form of an intransitive verb, and an adjunct (called 'predicative adjunct' in this study)... Jespersen uses the term 'quasi-predicate'; Curme the term 'predicative appositive' and F. T. Wood..the term 'pseudo-complement'. **1964** E. PALMER tr. *Martinet's Elem. Gen. Linguistics* iv. 116 The syntagm *il y avait*..is not autonomous but independent. We shall call it a *predicative syntagm. Ibid.* 119 The predicate comprises a predicative moneme, accompanied or not by modifiers. The predicative moneme is the element around which the sentence is organized, the other constituent elements marking their function by reference to it. **1965** *Language* XLI. 136 What Šaxmatov called 'predicative-attributive relations'. **1966** *Eng. Stud.* XLVII. 50 Intransitive verbs combined with a predicative 'apposition' (e.g. *he died young*..). I should prefer this term to Visser's 'predicative adjunct'. *Ibid.* 262 It is permissible to..speak of subject clause, predicate clause, predicative clause.

2. = PREDICATORY *a.* I. *rare.*

1870 SWINBURNE *Let.* 19 Feb. (1959) II. 98, I trust you [*sc.* D. G. Rossetti] to 'cut close and deep'..if you find anything to pare away of the spouting or drawling, vociferous or predicative kind.

3. *Logic.* Of a function: of order only one greater than that of its argument of greatest order.

1906 B. RUSSELL in *Proc. London Math. Soc.* IV. 34 Norms..which do not define classes I propose to call *non-predicative*; those which do define classes I shall call *predicative.* **1910** WHITEHEAD & RUSSELL *Principia Math.* I. ii. 56 We will define a function of one variable as predicative when it is of the next order above that of its argument, *i.e.* of the lowest order compatible with its having that argument. **1936** *Mind* XLV. 498 The axiom of reducibility is adopted in *P*[*rincipia*] *M*[*athematica*]. This axiom moderates the second part of the theory by asserting that for every propositional function there is a formally equivalent one which is predicative, *i.e.*, has the lowest order compatible with its type. **1969** FEYS & FITCH *Dict. Symbols Math. Logic* v. 91 A property, of order only one greater than the order of what it applies to, is called by Russell a predicative property.

predicati·vity. [f. prec. + -ITY.] The fact or quality of predicating.

1963 W. V. QUINE *Set Theory* §36.265 This predicativity restriction obstructs Cantor's theorem. **1966** *Philos. Rev.* LXXV. 384 For each system in turn we examine the status of predicativity.

predicator. Restrict 'Now *rare*' to senses a and b and add further examples of sense c.

1958 [see *PREDICATIVAL *a.*]. **1961** [see *COMPLEMENT *sb.* 3 b]. **1966** *Amer. Speech* XLI. 204 All of the clauses here termed 'imperative' have as predicators verb forms which we can describe as present-tense subjunctives. **1966** G. N. LEECH *Eng. in Advertising* ii. 10 The elements of clause structure in English are:..P: Predicator (traditionally 'verb', but this term is needed for a class of word). **1969** *Eng. Stud.* L. 32 Clauses without a Predicator ..can assume the status of independent clauses.

predict, *v.* Add: **2. b.** *transf.* Of a theory, observation, etc.: to have as a deducible or inferable consequence; to imply.

1961 *Physical Rev.* CXXI. 1620 The theory predicts a linear dependence of M_{2p} on $[H_0/(T + \theta)]^2$, where θ is the experimentally determined Curie-Weiss constant. **1964** E. BACH *Introd. Transformational Gram.* viii. 186 General linguistic theory must provide a precise characterization of the way in which a theory can be said to 'predict' a given sentence. **1975** *Nature* 6 Feb. 442/1 Sensitivity to the taste of PTC predicts sensitivity to caffeine. **1976** *Sci. Amer.* July 39/3 The present isotopic ratios of neodymium therefore predict the total depletion in U-235. This calculation gives a result about 40 percent greater than the observed depletion. **1977** *Lancet* 24 Sept. 662/1 Running-water samples are perhaps closer to the water typically consumed in the home than are first-flush samples, and our results..indicate that they predict blood-lead more precisely.

4. To direct fire at with the aid of a predictor (sense *2).

1943 L. CHESHIRE *Bomber Pilot* iii. 57 They're predicting us now; looks like a barrage. **1952** M. TRIPP *Faith is Windsock* vi. 90 He saw a flak-burst below, then another, and another... 'Weave, Dig, the bastards are predicting us.'

predictability. (In Dict. s.v. PREDICTABLE *a.*) Add: (Further examples.) Also *attrib.*

1954 J. H. GREENBERG in H. Hoijer *Lang. in Culture* 4 Causality should not be confused with predictability. Perhaps only a predictability relation is discerned in some cases. **1955** *Bull. Atomic Sci.* June 227/3 The concept of predictability seems in some way related to the concept of pattern. **1972** *Archivum Linguisticum* III. 4 The imperfect subjunctive occurs consistently, with equal predictability, in the language of all characters, in all situations.

predictably (prĭdi·ktăbli), *adv.* [f. PREDICTABLE *a.* + -LY².] In a manner that can be or could have been predicted.

1914 J. H. SKRINE *Pastor Futurus* 88 The Pentecosts come back, as surely though not so predictably as the dawns. **1961** *Time* 13 Jan. 9/2 The British and French.. agreed to the setting up of a Communist state, North Viet Nam—which then, predictably, became a base for Communist operations. **1971** *Times* 25 Nov. (Canning Suppl.) p. ii/9 Metrication [of cans] is unlikely to be imposed, but economic pressures will probably hasten a voluntary change. Predictably, the International Organization for Standardization is busy on this and other metrication problems. **1975** *Times Lit. Suppl.* 24 Jan. 92/3 A full catalogue has been prepared by P. R. S. Moorey,..who has already made himself the undisputed master of this field... Predictably, the commentary..is authoritative and scholarly.

prediction, *sb.* Add: **3.** *attrib.* and *Comb.*, as *prediction paradox, study, table, value.*

1952 *Mind* LXI. 265, I hope Mr O'Connor will not mind my giving his paradox the new and somewhat more appropriate name of 'the prediction paradox'. **1950** S. A. STOUFFER *Measurement & Prediction* vi. 173 Each variable in a prediction study plays one of two possible roles. **1964** M. ARGYLE *Psychol. & Social Probl.* v. 70 Is it possible to work out a grand prediction table showing what treatment each individual should have? **1961** J. B. WILSON *Reason & Morals* iii. 144 Many scientists now use the prediction-value of scientific statements as virtually the only test of their truth.

predictionism (prĭdi·kʃəniz'm). [f. PREDICTION *sb.* + -ISM.] Belief in prediction or prophecy.

1919 P. H. OSMOND *Mystical Poets Eng. Church* vii. 215 He was a 'crank', dominated by extravagant notions—a victim of Predictionism and credulity. **1943** *Mind* LII. 200 The immediate issue is not Behaviourism but Predictionism, the doctrine which Professor C. I. Lewis so well sets out.

predictive, *a.* **a.** (Further examples.)

1908 *Westm. Gaz.* 9 May 4/4, I can see with prophetic eyes and hear with predictive ears a development of programme-music which may in the future militate somewhat against the dominant position of the opera. **1957** *Publ. Amer. Dial. Soc.* 1956 XXVI. 71 The results proved to be over 90% predictive. **1961** A. G. OETTINGER in *Proc. Symposia Appl. Math.* XII. 105 Predictive analysis yields a description of the syntactic structure of a sentence in terms consonant, although not identical, with old-fashioned parsing, immediate constituent theory.., or phrase-structure theory. **1964** E. A. NIDA *Toward Sci. Transl.* xii. 259 In contrast with this pass procedure is a 'predictive method'.., which more closely represents the mathematician's view of the language structure—one based on the expectations of what is to follow. **1966** I. RHODES in *Automatic Transl. of Lang.* (NATO Summer School, Venice, 1962) 206 Our method has become known as 'predictive analysis' and is based upon the universal habit on the part of the listener to *anticipate* the type of word which a speaker is about to utter. **1966** *Jrnl. Canad. Operational Res. Soc.* 117 *Predictive model,* a model used in a war game to predict the results of actions and interactions between opposing forces. **1972** *Jrnl. Social Psychol.* LXXXVIII. 145 Although the measures are required to compensate for educational disadvantage, they are also expected to have acceptable predictive validity in a system where all groups are competing for the limited further education places.

predictor. Add: **1. b.** *spec.* in *Statistics,* a variable whose value can be used in estimation; also *predictor variable.*

1950 S. A. STOUFFER *Measurement & Prediction* vi. 173 Each variable..can serve as a predictor. **1966** DRAPER & SMITH *Appl. Regression Analysis* iv. 104 There are many problems in which a knowledge of more than one independent (or 'predictor') variable is necessary in order to obtain better understanding and/or better prediction of a particular response. **1974** *Nature* 9 Aug. 466/1 Students' attitudes towards scientists were strongly related to only two of the predictor variables: deference and nurturance. **1975** *Sci. Amer.* May 97/1 Later species grew up in the shade of the pioneering species, and the numerical abundance of saplings in the understory proved to be a reasonable predictor of a species' success in reaching the canopy. **1977** *Canad. Jrnl. Linguistics* 1976 XXI. I. 21 Dashed lines are curves predicted on the basis of an additive model utilizing a multiple classification analysis.., which demonstrates the main effects of a given predictor (or independent variable).

2. *Mil.* An apparatus for automatically providing tracking information for an anti-aircraft gun from telescopic or radar observations.

1935 L. HART *When Britain goes to War* II. vi. 119 Greater progress has come through the invention of..the Vickers Predictor, whereby a combined calculation of the speed, course and height of the aeroplane is automatically made and electrically transmitted to the guns. **1936** *Sphere* 30 May 363 (*caption*) Operating the predictor, a delicate instrument for determining the range of enemy 'planes. **1941** *Ann. Reg. 1940* 69 The defenders adopted new tactics, gauging the path of the raiders by means of predictors instead of using searchlights. **1944** H. Hawton *Night Bombing* 92 Cologne's defences were massive, but with the sky thick with aircraft the searchlights were bewildered and the predictors confused. **1962** S. Pugh *Fighting Vehicles & Weapons* II. 74 The most satisfactory solution so far is this British-designed combination of Swedish Bofors 40 mm. power-operated, automatic light anti-aircraft gun, L.70, with a radar/predictor fire control equipment known as Fire Control Equipment No. 27 'Yellow Fever'. **1974** *Encycl. Brit. Macropædia* IV. 1048/2 The original electronic analogue computers arose from the needs of anti-aircraft artillery 'predictors'.

predigested, *ppl. a.* (Later *lit.* and *fig.* examples.)

1902 *Brit. Med. Jrnl.* 17 May 1199/1 In the case of the premature infant that is unable to suck, it has been found to be of advantage to pass predigested food directly into the stomach by means of a tube. **1922** 'K. Mansfield' *Let.* 17 July (1928) II. 229 What a relief it is to turn away from these little pre-digested books written by authors who have nothing to say! **1940** R. S. Lambert *Ariel & all his Quality* iv. 114 This paper [sc. *The Listener*] whose 'copy' comes to it predigested from other sources. **1975** *Country Life* 18 Dec. 1734/1 As early as 1789 Thomas Pitt, a Worcester chorister, published his pre-digested *Messiah*—ten anthems.

prediluvian, *a.* and *sb.* Restrict *rare* to the sb. and add further examples of the adj.

1928 V. G. Childe *Most Anc. East* i. 15 The Prediluvian kings' reigns are all incredibly long. **1931** C. Williams *Place of Lion* xvi. 277 Some incantation whereby the prediluvian magicians had controlled contentions among spirits. **1981** *Times Lit. Suppl.* 26 June 731/2 Their pre-diluvian fundamentalist faith.

pre-dinner: see *pre- B. 2 a.

prediscover, *v.* (Later example.)

1926 *Spectator* 3 July 18/2 The poet 'prediscovers' the Einstein theory.

pre-discovery. Add: **B.** *adj.* [Pre- B. 2.] Occurring or carried out before the discovery of something.

1946 *Nature* 9 Nov. 648/1 In the nomenclature of the time, these pre-discovery observations of Uranus are known as the 'ancient' observations. **1968** R. A. Lyttleton *Mysteries Solar Syst.* vii. 234 LeVerrier, in his discussion, included the pre-discovery observations of Uranus going back to 1690.

predisposition. Add: **1.** Also, a tendency in a person to respond or react in a certain way. (Further examples.)

1936 *Discovery* Aug. 254/1 All these effects..can be shown to result from psychological inhibitions and predispositions. **1949** C. I. Hovland et al. *Exper. Mass Communication* vii. 192 A person soon 'forgets' the ideas he has learned which are not consonant with his predispositions. **1973** G. A. Davis *Psychol. of Problem Solving* ii. 18 Habit and conformity are implicit in such..personality concepts as rigidity,..predisposition,..fear of the unknown and, on occasion, pigheadedness. **1980** *Sci. Amer.* Apr. 112/1 It is generally accepted that most animal characteristics are the product of an interaction between inherited predispositions and the environment.

predissocia·tion. *Physics* and *Chem.* [Pre- A. 2.] The passage of a molecule between a quantized vibrational and rotational state (above its ground state) and a dissociated state of the same energy that is not quantized, the occurrence of which results in certain bands in the spectrum of the molecule being diffuse instead of having the normal rotational fine structure. Freq. *attrib.*

1924 Henri & Teves in *Nature* 20 Dec. 895/1 The molecule can be modified in its internal structure: the atoms are driven apart, the bonds are weakened, the molecule becomes more reactive, and the rotational movements are no longer quantified. This first modification is a preliminary preparation of the molecule for its total dissociation, and it is necessary to introduce a new term for this change. We propose to denote it by the term predissociation of the molecule. **1930** *Physical Rev.* XXXV. 1028 (*heading*) Predissociation of diatomic molecules from high rotational states. **1944** Glasstone *Theoret. Chem.* iv. 188 In some cases the predissociation spectrum is followed by a region of continuous absorption but, in other instances, bands with fine structure are found on both long and short wave sides of the predissociation bands. **1962** P. J. & B. Durrant *Introd. Adv. Inorg. Chem.* vii. 222 Predissociation is commonly shown only in absorption, not in emission. **1966** Barnard & Mansell *Fund. Physical Chem.* ii. 96 A molecule undergoing pre-dissociation will dissociate within the time of one rotation and the rotational fine structure will tend to be lost in the gas phase spectrum. **1977** *Sci. Amer.* Feb. 95/1 Instead the molecule is disassembled at a lower energy through a phenomenon called predissociation.

Predmost (pre·dmǝust), *a.* Also **Předmost** (pǝʒe·dmost). [Anglicized form of the place-name *Předmost* near Brno (Brünn), in Moravia, Czechoslovakia.] Of, connected with, or relating to human or other remains, artefacts, etc., that evidence a Combe Capelle type of *Homo sapiens* of Upper Palæolithic culture, first excavated at Předmost between 1882 and 1894, and later at other sites, esp. in Central Europe and round the eastern Mediterranean; also *ellipt.* as *sb.* Hence **Predmo·stian.**

1916 H. F. Osborn *Men Old Stone Age* iii. 257 Such very primitive forms as the Brünn or Předmost race of Upper Palæolithic times. *Ibid.* iv. 349 All these sculptures of the mammoth have in common the indication of a very small ear—similar to that in the Předmost model. **1921** M. C. Burkitt *Prehistory* x. 130 The male statuette of Brünn, if it be of the age of Předmost and not more ancient, appears to be a prolongation of the Aurignacian artistic technique. **1927** Peake & Fleure *Hunters & Artists* v. 67 We may call it provisionally the Combe Capelle, or perhaps better the Predmost type by way of contrast with the Cro-Magnon type. **1931** *Times Lit. Suppl.* 23 Apr. 317/2 Sir Arthur Keith suggests that both the Cro-Magnons and the Predmostians are early Caucasians hailing ultimately from South-Western Asia. **1939** V. G. Childe *Dawn European Civilization* (ed. 3) i. 3 Mesolithic groups appear in general isolated and poorly equipped in contrast to Magdalenians or Předmostians. **1957** M. Bullock tr. *Boule & Vallois's Fossil Men* viii. 278 The long discussion of which these Predmost Men have been the object; their affinities are, above all, with the great Cro-Magnon race. **1960** W. Howells *Mankind in Making* xiv. 210 There you have *Homo sapiens.* And there you have the men of the present, and the men of the Upper Paleolithic. Some of the latter, like the Předmost skulls, had rather strong brow ridges. **1977** Brace & Montagu *Human Evol.* ix. 351 (*caption*) Předmost skull. Upper Paleolithic of Czechoslovakia.

prednisolone (predni·sǝlǝun). *Pharm.* [f. next with inserted *ol* (see -ol).] A synthetic steroid, $C_{21}H_{28}O_5$, which has similar properties and uses to prednisone, of which it is a reduced derivative.

1955 *Jrnl. Amer. Med. Assoc.* 21 May 166/1 Prednisolone (Meticortelone) and prednisone (Meticorten), two new synthetic steroids formerly known as metacortandralone and metacortandracin, have recently been recommended as effective in the treatment of rheumatoid arthritis. **1959** *Economist* 19 Dec. 1160/1 One of the five firms which produce the bulk of such drugs, charged chemists $17.90 for 100 tablets of prednisolone, under the brand name of Meticortelone. **1962** Harris & Gruber in A. Pirie *Lens Metabolism Rel. Cataract* 379 Of the steroids, prednisolone, either as its phosphate or as the alcohol, caused the greatest reduction in cation recovery. **1966** *Lancet* 24 Dec. 1382/2 He was given the usual measures for heart-failure and antibiotics, oxygen, and prednisolone 10 mg. t.d.s. to 'buy time'. **1974** Passmore & Robson *Compan. Med. Stud.* III. xviii. 98/1 Until the prednisolone takes effect the patient's distress should be relieved by bronchodilator drugs.

prednisone (pre·dnisǝun). *Pharm.* [Prob. f. *pregnadiene* (f. *pregna(ne + *diene) + *-isone*, after *cortisone.] A colourless, crystalline, synthetic steroid, $C_{21}H_{26}O_5$, resembling cortisone but possessing greater glucocorticoid activity, which is used as an anti-inflammatory agent and to depress immune responses, esp. in the treatment of rheumatoid arthritis.

1955 *Dis. Chest* XXVII. 515 Metacortandracin (Metacortin) used in this study and furnished by Schering Corporation, Bloomfield, New Jersey has been re-named Prednisone. **1955** [see *prednisolone]. **1959** S. Duke-Elder *Parson's Dis. Eye* (ed. 13) xiv. 150 Prednisone and Prednisolone, are often preferable for systemic administration since they are less liable to excite the unfortunate side-effects associated with cortisone. **1965** *Spectator* 1 Jan. 12/3 Prednisone is especially useful for easing the pain of aged arthritics. **1974** R. M. Kirk et al. *Surgery* iv. 58 Generalised disease responds to chemotherapy, usually with a combination of vincristine, mustine, procarbazine and prednisone in pulsed doses.

predominately, *adv.* Delete 'Now *rare*' and add later examples.

1961 *Christian Sci. Monitor* 17 Oct. 4/7 WWRL's [*sc.* a radio station's] colorful mobile unit, cruising predominately Negro neighborhoods. **1965** C. Walsh in J. Gibb *Light on C. S. Lewis* 110 He quickly gained a wide audience...it was predominately high-brow and middle-brow. **1970** [see *non-word]. **1973** *Yale Rev.* Spring 452 Other indications that the *Supplement* is predominately concerned with the modern..history of the English vocabulary. **1977** *Lancet* 6 Aug. 306/2 We were fascinated by the suggestion..that in San Francisco enteric diseases are predominately sexually transmitted.

pre-dry: see *pre- A. 1.

pre-e·cho. [Pre- A. 2.] **1.** A faint copy of a louder sound occurring in a recording shortly before the original as a result of the accidental transfer of signals in a recording medium.

1935 *Gramophone* June 42/2 It appears to be not 'an echo' in the strict sense of the word, but a 'pre-echo', as in all the examples I list below it occurs *before the actual recording grooves* are reached by the needle. **1956** [see *post-echo]. **1957** *N.Y. Times* 24 Feb. x. 15/1 Engineers say that a disk should not contain much more music than that;..the grooves will have to run too closely together with additional minutes;..there will be pre-echo, damage and results too ghastly to contemplate. **1962** *Times* 5 July 15/7 Prolonged storage [of tape] without rewinding..can cause 'print-through' (detectable as pre-echo on some discs). **1967** A. L. Lloyd *Folk Song in England* i. 21 The phenomenon of pre-echo on magnetic tape. **1976** *Gramophone* Sept. 445/3 It certainly avoids pre-echoes in silent bars immediately followed by fortissimi.

2. A foreshadowing or anticipation.

1948 *Mind* LVII. 375 Professor Raphael..commends Price's refutation of the 'naturalistic fallacy' (a pre-echo of G. E. Moore's). **1961** *Times* 29 May 12/7 Is this a mere pre-echo of *My Fair Lady?* **1975** *Listener* 20 Nov. 674/1 The most fascinating political pre-echo since the boy Harold Wilson had his photo taken on the steps of Number Ten. **1977** *Gramophone* July 187/2 What an extraordinary pre-echo of Brahms this second piece becomes in this performance.

pre-ecla·mpsia. *Path.* [Pre- B. 1.] A condition of pregnancy characterized by high blood pressure and some other of the symptoms associated with eclampsia, and formerly thought to be associated with toxæmia.

1923 *Jrnl. Michigan State Med. Soc.* XXII. 144/1 (*heading*) Toxemias of pregnancy including pre-eclampsia, eclampsia and nephritis. **1929** H. J. Stander *Toxemias of Pregnancy* 53 Pre-eclampsia is essentially eclampsia before the outbreak of convulsions and coma. **1955** H. M. Carey in I. Donald *Pract. Obstetr. Probl.* ix. 130 Pre-eclampsia classically is defined as the appearance, after the 28th week of pregnancy, of œdema, hypertension and albuminuria. **1974** Passmore & Robson *Compan. Med. Stud.* III. ii. xlii. 17/2 The term pre-eclampsia has also been used [for hypertension in pregnancy], on the basis that women who develop hypertension in late pregnancy may, unless treated, progress to the convulsive complication known as eclampsia. **1976** *Lancet* 18 Dec. 1341/1 Maternal pre-eclampsia, birth trauma, breech delivery, and disorders of hæmostasis have also been implicated in a disorder which predominantly affects immature male infants.

pre-ecla·mptic, *a.* and *sb. Path.* [Pre- B. 1.] **A.** *adj.* Characteristic of the state which precedes an eclamptic attack; of, exhibiting, or being pre-eclampsia. **B.** *sb.* A pre-eclamptic woman.

1899 J. C. Edgar in C. Jewett *Pract. Obstetr.* xxiii. 517 Symptoms of eclampsia may be classified as those of the prodromal period, or pre-eclamptic state, and those of the attack. **1924** de Wesselow & Wyatt *Mod. Views on Toxæmias of Pregnancy* viii. 90 It is practically certain that we are dealing with a pre-eclamptic. **1926** *Jrnl. Obstetr. & Gynæcol.* XXXIII. 21 The patient, 2-para, and seven months pregnant, was admitted for the pre-eclamptic signs of high blood-pressure, marked œdema and headache. **1960** Levitt & Altchek in Guttmacher & Rovinsky *Med., Surg., & Gynecol. Complications of Pregnancy* iv. 73/1 Clinically, the preeclamptic has more pronounced sodium and water retention than the normal gravida. **1962** *Lancet* 6 Jan. 7/1 Induction was performed in a patient with mild pre-eclamptic toxæmia. **1977** *Ibid.* 30 Apr. 923/1 Diabetic women in pregnancy often become pre-eclamptic.

pre-e·dit, *v.* [Pre- A. 1.] *trans.* To edit or sort as a preliminary to later editing; to prepare for computer processing by the addition or alteration of material. Hence **pre-e·dited** *ppl. a.*, **pre-e·diting** *vbl. sb.*

1934 Webster, Pre-edit, *v.* **1938** *Amer. Speech* XIII. 36 In pre-editing, an editor may have to consult recent books in the subject-field concerning a particular word. **1958** *N.Y. Folklore Q.* Autumn 245 The valuable *Frank C. Brown Collection of North Carolina Folklore* would have been much more valuable had Brown spent more time in arranging and pre-editing while he was alive. **1960** [see *post-edit *v.*]. **1968** *Amer. Documentation* Jan. 74/1 The documents are then returned to the DARE office for pre-editing and typing. **1970** A. Cameron et al. *Computers & Old Eng. Concordances* 49 The not-so-friendly blue giant grudgingly yielded up a trial-run concordance to 1,100 pre-edited lines out of the approximately 5,500 lines of the complete gospel text. **1973** *Amer. Speech 1969* XLIV. 192 The completed field records were..preedited and encoded. **1977** J. M. Smith in P. G. J. van Sterkenburg et al. *Lexicologie* 242 There is a need for some 'intelligent' pre-editing of input... Such pre-editing is time-consuming.

Hence **pre-e·ditor**, one who carries out pre-editing.

1934 in Webster. **1953** [see *post-editor]. **1958** *Aspects of Translation* 104 The pre-editor was to remove known ambiguities from the original text. **1960** E. Delavenay *Introd. Machine Transl.* 36 The role of the pre-editor would be to provide the machine with texts explicit from the graphio-semantic point of view.

pre-elect, *v.* **b.** Delete '*rare*' and add: Used *spec.* of the choice of heads of colleges and of certain classes of fellows in the universities of Oxford and Cambridge.

1977 *Daily Tel.* 28 Feb. 8/2 At Sidney Sussex, Cambridge, Miss A. P. Dowling, of Girton, has been pre-elected into a junior research fellowship. **1978** *Ibid.* 20 Jan. 14/4 At Christ's College, Prof. J. H. Plumb, Fellow of the College and Emeritus Professor of Modern English History, has been pre-elected to Mastership with effect from July 11, 1978.

pre-ele·ctric, *a.* [Pre- B. 1.] Occurring or pertaining to the time before the use of electricity, esp. in the making of gramophone records. Also *ellipt.*, a gramophone record not electrically recorded. Also **pre-ele·ctrical** *a.*

[**1908** *Westm. Gaz.* 29 Feb. 12/2 It was in pre-electric-light days, and I couldn't find the matches.] **1934** C. Lambert *Music Ho!* iv. 257 Recording will have improved on the present methods as much as the present methods have improved on the old pre-electric horn recording. **1947** *Penguin Music Mag.* May 58 The connoisseur, who has his collection of rare pre-electrical recordings carefully card-indexed. **1960** *Guardian* 8 Mar. 7/1 One has to listen to old pre-electrics with a 'creative ear'. **1968** *Listener* 22 Feb. 250/1 It is scored for..stereophonic tape.., pre-electric gramophone, percussion, [etc.]. **1977** *Gramophone* Feb. 1321/1 The first five records concern themselves almost entirely with pre-1930 (mostly pre-electric) issues.

preem (prīm), *sb.*^{2} and *v.*^{2} U.S. slang abbrev. of PREMIÈRE *sb.* or *v.* in Dict. and Suppl.

1937 *Amer. Speech* XII. 317/2 *Preem*, first showing. **1937** [see *ORK]. **1942** BERREY & VAN DEN BARK *Amer. Thes. Slang* §590/30 *Preem*, to present a premiere performance. **1945** [see *HYPO v.]. **1945** [see *PREMIÈRE v.]. **1948** *Variety* 25 Aug. 1/2 The mother-daughter act..has been bought by ABC and set for an Oct. 4 preem. **1952** *N.Y. Daily News* 5 Aug. 23c/5 A new hour-long radio show..which preems via ABC [network] Sunday, Aug. 17. **1961** A. BERKMAN *Singers' Gloss. Show Business* 70 *Preem* (Var.), theatre premiere.

pre-emergence, -emergent: see *PRE- B. 2, 1.

preemie (prī·mi). *N. Amer. slang.* Also **premie, premy.** [f. *PREM(ATURE *sb.* + -Y^6, -IE.] A premature birth; a baby born prematurely. Also *attrib.*

1927 *Amer. Speech* II. 314/1 A baby delivered prematurely is a 'premy'. **1942** BERREY & VAN DEN BARK *Amer. Thes. Slang* § 534/6 *Premie*, a premature birth. **1949** *N.Y. Times* 25 Sept. I. 75/2 Saving 75 per cent of the 'preemies' born. *Ibid.*, The dread eye diseases said to afflict 'preemies' are unfounded. **1968** *Trans-Action* Oct. 7/2 The prematures were more likely to be below their proper grade in school. Among white children..19·4 percent of the preemies were..in special classes. **1975** *Time* (Canada ed.) 19 May 57/1 The preemie's sense of security is further heightened by the recorded sound of a pregnant mother's heartbeat piped into the artificial womb. **1976** *Word 1971* XXVII. 61 The present-day premie nursery is the precursor of the prenatal assessment laboratory of tomorrow.

pre-e·mphasis. *Sound Recording* and *Broadcasting.* [PRE- A. 2.] A systematic distortion of a signal prior to transmission or recording, involving an increase in the relative strength of certain frequencies in anticipation of a corresponding decrease during reception or playback.

1940 *RCA Rev.* Jan. 359 The use of pre-emphasis circuit [*sic*] at the transmitter and a de-emphasis circuit at the receiver produces an overall gain in signal-noise ratio. **1942**, etc. [see *DE-EMPHASIS]. **1959** K. HENNEY *Radio Engin. Handbk.* (ed. 5) xxi. 35 Below 100 cycles the characteristic of the [disk] recorder system is made constant-velocity by electric means. This tends to give preemphasis to the low frequencies... Above 500 cps a preemphasis above a constant velocity is given to the high frequencies, especially over the noise frequency range. The necessary characteristic for reproduction is the inverse of this curve. **1977** *Gramophone* Mar. 1476/3 The most important of these is the 'breathing' or 'pumping' effect as residual noise is heard rising and falling in level as the expander alters system gain in response to sudden changes in signal level... High frequency pre-emphasis, followed by mirror-image de-emphasis, reduces the effects of breathing.

So **pre-e·mphasize** *v. trans.*, to subject to pre-emphasis.

1968 COOK & LIFF *Frequency Modulation Receivers* xiv. 490 Both the left (*L*) and right (*R*) channels are fed to 75-μ sec high-pass filters, where they are preemphasized. **1974** M. MANDL *Mod. Television Syst.* ii. 29 The higher audio-frequency range at the transmitter is preemphasized. **1977** *Gramophone* Mar. 1476/1 A dodge of this kind is universally employed in VHF/FM broadcasting, where high frequencies are boosted (pre-emphasized) at the transmitter and attenuated (de-emphasized) at the receiver.

pre-employment: see *PRE- B. 2a.

pre-empt, *sb.* Restrict *Austral. colloq.* to sense in Dict. and add: **2.** *Bridge.* A pre-emptive bid.

1939 N. DE V. HART *Bridge Players' Bedside Bk.* iii. 34 Macleod's pre-empt showed an obvious fear of both major suits, from which he was trying to shut us out. **1959** *Listener* 8 Jan. 84/2 It [*sc.* the hand] could qualify for the bolder pre-empt of *Four Clubs*. **1962** *Times* 11 July 7/1 Few players would fancy a pre-empt with a two-suiter and two primary controls. **1972** R. MARKUS *Common-Sense Bridge* II. 65 If everybody knows the strength and weakness of your pre-empts they can easily take the right counteraction. **1977** *Homes & Gardens* Feb. 17 There are two types of hand where you should respond Three No-Trumps in reply to a pre-empt.

pre-empt, *v.* Add: **1. b.** (Earlier and later examples.)

1855 L. OLIPHANT *Minnesota & Far West* 162 Wal, I guess, if you can find a corner that's not pre-empted, you may spread your shavings there [for a bed]. **1913** J. LONDON *Valley of Moon* II Many [tables and benches].. were already pre-empted by family parties. **1944** AUDEN *Sea & Mirror* in *For Time Being* 15 Two wonders as one vow Pre-empting all.

2. *Bridge.* **a.** *intr.* To make a pre-emptive bid.

1914 M. C. WORK *Auction Devel.* 313 It is the exceptional case in which it is advisable to preëmpt with an original No Trump. **1920** —— *Auction Methods Up-to-Date* v. 65 His only chance is to preëmpt so strongly that his first bid will hold the declaration. **1947** S. HARRIS *Fund. Princ. Contract Bridge* I. i. 17 When North preempts but does not make a game bid, it is important for South to remember that he must not increase the contract unless he holds three quick tricks. **1964** *Official Encycl. Bridge* 435/1 The third player is best placed to pre-empt. **1972** R. MARKUS *Aces & Places* 35 South opened the bidding with 1 ♠, West doubled and North.. pre-empted to 4 ♠, which became the final contract.

b. *trans.* To thwart (a player) by making a pre-emptive bid.

1964 *Official Encycl. Bridge* 435/1 The third player.. knows that he cannot pre-empt his partner. **1972** R. MARKUS *Common-Sense Bridge* II. 65 Here is a hand..to show how easily you can be pre-empted into a ridiculous contract.

3. To set aside (one thing in favour of another); to preclude (something); to prevent (an occurrence); to forestall (someone).

1965 *Sun* 6 Dec. 7/7 In American TV you never, never say that a serial has been killed in favour of a new serial. It is always pre-empted. What they really mean is that it has been cancelled and a right established for the next one. **1968** *Listener* 5 Dec. 768/1, I think the Nazi regime by its own grotesque vileness pre-empted fictional effort. **1976** 'A. HALL' *Kobra Manifesto* xvi. 217 He would kill me when the showdown came unless I could pre-empt him. **1977** *B.B.C. Radio 4 News 5 p.m.* 11 May (*recorded from oral evidence*) Federal rights pre-empt State rights. **1978** *Jrnl. R. Soc. Arts* CXXVI. 675/1 The targets serve to preempt such a situation arising.

Hence **pre-e·mpting** *vbl. sb.* and *ppl. a.*

1920 M. C. WORK *Auction Methods Up-to-Date* v. 61 With general strength, preëmpting is not necessary or advisable. *Ibid.* 63 A real preëmpting hand contains an unusual distribution of cards. **1965** H. KAHN *On Escalation* 287 It [*sc.* pre-emptive war] denotes an attack made because of a belief that the other side has determined to make an attack on the pre-empting party. **1967** *Listener* 2 Nov. 570/3 On the subject of 'pre-empting'—supplanting scheduled programmes in favour of special programmes of public interest—..he had some extremely interesting things to say.

pre-emption. Add: **1. b.** (Examples.) Also *concr.*, land so obtained or to be obtained.

1747 *First Rec. Baltimore Town* (1905) 21 Mr. Alexander Lawson applied also to enter his Preemption of making out Ground into the water. **1827** *United Empire Loyalist* (Toronto) 6 May 396/2 The first hundred purchasers of Town Lots, when they have erected a habitable house, will..be entitled to the pre-emption or privilege to purchase a Lot of Twenty-Five Acres..at..7s. 6d. per acre. *a* **1844** *Filson Club Hist. Q.* (1935) IX. 235 Each of these two men..had a pre-emption of 1400 acres. **1901** DUNCAN & SCOTT *Hist. Allen & Woodson Counties, Kansas* 582 Finding that the Indians would not settle on the Reserve, the Government, in 1860, had all of these lands offered for sale and opened to pre-emption. **1933** W. W. SPINKS *Tales Brit. Columbia Frontier* 110 Some of the land had already been pre-empted, and pre-emption amounted to an agreement by the government to sell the land to the pre-empter. **1968** R. H. PATTERSON *Finlay's River* 43, I see I have called it a homestead. Officially, in the books of the Land Registry, it is a pre-emption.

e. (Earlier examples.)

1780 in N. D. Mereness *Trav. Amer. Colonies* (1916) 643 Received a Letter and Preemption Warrant. **1784** J. FILSON *Discovery Kentucke* 37 The Settlement and preemption rights arise from occupation.

2. *Bridge.* The action of making a pre-emptive bid.

1961 *Times* 6 Dec. 8/3 A two-suiter is not built for preemption. **1962** *Times* 7 Mar. 3/6 A preemption in one of the minor suits is even less efficacious unless the hand has two tricks on the side. **1974** *Country Life* 26 Sept. 894/1 The hand is far too good for pre-emption. **1977** *Times* 17 June 12/1, I have been making notes of unsuccessful preemptions with their effect on subsequent bidding.

3. The action or an instance of setting aside or overriding something.

1978 *Nature* 20 Apr. 664/1 The issue of Federal preemption—Federal legislation that overrides state or local initiatives—lies at the heart of the current dispute. **1979** *Arizona Daily Star* 1 Apr. (Tucson T.V. Suppl.) 12/3 CBS hasn't treated this inspirational program very kindly. It's constantly being victimized by pre-emptions, time-slot changes and disappearances for up to three weeks at a stretch.

pre-emptioner (earlier examples).

1838 *Congress. Globe* 25th Congress 2 Sess. App. 142/3 Suppose a pre-emptioner was to go there and say, Mr. President, this house is too large for you; I..claim a preemption to part of this house. **1841** *Knickerbocker* XVII. 278 They amused themselves by calling the exclusives 'squatters', 'prëemptioners', etc. **1872** [see *HOMESTEADER].

pre-emptive, *a.* (*sb.*). Add: **2.** *Bridge.* Applied to a bid made with the expectation that it is high enough to prevent opponents from bidding normally and so obtaining adequate information.

1913 F. IRWIN *Auction High-Lights* 95 A preëmptive opening-bid in a major suit means that the bidder wants no information and wishes to play the hand at his own suit. **1916** 'BASCULE' *Adv. Auction Bridge* I. 77 To what extent does it pay to make what are known as preemptive, or 'shut-out' bids? **1923** *Daily Mail* 5 May 8 The supporting bid,..the pre-emptive raise, and 'the switch' assume a new value. **1932** *Daily Tel.* 8 Oct. 15/5 In using the term 'pre-emptive' I am not in any way ascribing the meaning of 'shut-out' to that word. **1947** S. HARRIS *Fund. Princ. Contract Bridge* I. i. 17 The most valuable preemptive bid..is an opening bid of four of a major suit or five of a minor suit. **1952** I. MACLEOD *Bridge* v. 62 (*heading*) Pre-emptive responses. **1973** *Times* 20 Oct. 11/3 You will find plenty of opportunities for preemptive opening bids.

3. Designating an attack on an enemy who is thought to be about to make an attack himself (see also quots. 1966, 1971). Also *transf.*

1959 *Listener* 31 Dec. 1140/1 The American Strategic Air Command..might be prevented by a Russian preemptive strike from ever getting the Sword out of its scabbard. **1966** SCHWARZ & HADIK *Strategic Terminol.* 108 *Pre-emptive strike*, armed attack motivated by the conviction that an enemy attack is under way or is irreversibly imminent. Also called 'forestalling blow' or 'anticipatory attack', the pre-emptive strike differs from a so-called 'preventive' strike or war in that [etc.]. A strike or war..is preventive if the enemy still has the option of desisting from his planned aggression. **1970** *Times* 9 Oct. 15/2 December 7, 1941, when the Japanese stabbed America in the back at Pearl Harbour—or as we would say in these cooler, more euphemistic times, made their pre-emptive strike. **1971** E. LUTTWAK *Dict. Mod. War* 156/1 *Pre-emptive attack*, an attack launched in the belief that an enemy attack has already entered the executive phase, i.e. that the decision has already been made. Unless the attack actually reduces or eliminates the effect of the imminent attack, it cannot be called pre-emptive. **1976** LD. HOME *Way Wind Blows* xii. 167 There was no doubt at all about the most effective deterrent—it was the 'Polaris' submarine; which, because it was virtually undetectable, was a genuine second-strike weapon which robbed the pre-emptive attack of all its former attraction. **1978** *Times* 25 Jan. 17/2 It may well be that a guillotine is necessary... But if it is to be justified as a pre-emptive strike [etc.].

B. *sb.* (Later example.)

1930 L. G. D. ACLAND *Early Canterbury Runs* 1st Ser. ii. 26 In eighteen months nearly all the run except the pre-emptives had gone.

pre-e·mptively, *adv.* [f. PRE-EMPTIVE *a.* + -LY^2.] In a pre-emptive manner.

1917 E. BERGHOLT *Royal Auction Bridge* II. 148 By declaring 'pre-emptively', up to the full strength of his hand, Z. will no doubt be able to prevent B. from directing A. what to lead. **1952** I. MACLEOD *Bridge* vii. 84 A double is for penalties unless..(3) The double is of a suit not above the level of three (and not at the three level bid preemptively). **1959** *Encounter* Nov. 17/1 It is..easier to imagine the Soviet Union striking pre-emptively than to imagine the U.S...doing the same thing. **1968** G. JONES *Hist. Vikings* IV. iii. 392 After the death of Knut the ancient West Saxon dynasty pre-emptively reinherited England. **1975** *Sci. Amer.* Oct. 8/2 Our past practice of preemptively deploying the latest strategic weapons our technology affords us has neither forced nor persuaded the U.S.S.R. to stop deploying strategic weapons increasingly threatening to our security.

pre-emptor. Add: Also **pre-empter. 1.** For *U.S.* read *N. Amer.* and add *Canad.* examples.

1860 *Brit. Colonist* (Victoria, B.C.) 12 Jan. 2/1 Preemptors run the risk of having to pay twice the amount required by the American government for wild land. **1933** [see *PRE-EMPTION 1 b]. **1962** G. NICHOLSON *Vancouver Island's West Coast* 265 A kindly Norwegian pre-empter.. assisted them in re-sawing and whittling the boards down to the proper dimensions by hand.

2. *Bridge.* One who makes pre-emptive bids.

1972 R. MARKUS *Common-Sense Bridge* III. 99 South.. overlooked the warning of the pre-emptor's bid and East's confident double.

preen, *v.*^{2} Add: **2. b.** For (? *catachr.*) read *fig.* and add further examples.

1907 G. B. SHAW *John Bull's Other Island* p. liv, Not so pitiable as the virtuous indignation with which Judge Lynch, himself provable by his own judgment to be a prevaricator, hypocrite, tyrant and coward of the first water, preened himself at its expense. **1926** W. & E. MUIR tr. *Feuchtwanger's Jew Süss* I. 7 The Catholics were preening themselves on the probable extinction of the Protestant line in Swabia. **1943** A. CHRISTIE *Moving Finger* xi. 131 These schools..seem to take a delight in turning out girls who preen themselves on looking like nothing on earth. They call it being sweet and unsophisticated. **1948** O. WALKER *Kaffirs are Lively* xi. 164 South Africa..sometimes preens itself on its lack of lynch-law. **1972** 'J. HERRIOT' *It shouldn't happen to Vet* i. 14 He had put one over on the young clever-pants vet and nobody could blame him for preening himself a little.

pre-enclosure: see *PRE- B. 2a.

pre-enginee·red, *ppl. a.* [PRE- A. 1.] Constructed from prefabricated units.

1958 *Times* 29 Mar. 5 (Advt.), APEE design to any specification pre-engineered buildings which can be erected speedily and economically by unskilled labour. **1974** *State* (Columbia, S. Carolina) 15 Feb. 9-B/7 (Advt.), Need men to erect pre-engineered buildings.

preen-gland (prī·n,glænd). *Zool.* [f. PREEN *v.*^{2} + GLAND^2.] = *oil-gland* s.v. OIL *sb.*^{1} 6e. Also called the uropygial gland.

1923 J. A. THOMSON *Biol. Birds* ii. 12 There is a striking paucity of skin-glands, for there is usually nothing but the preen-gland at the root of the tail. **1954** FISHER & LOCKLEY *Sea-Birds* viii. 190 This waxy oil..is similar in character to the oil from the preen-glands of birds. **1962** *Listener* 15 Nov. 807/2 It was noticed long ago that the bird rubs the beak on the preen gland which is situated on its back just in front of the tail. **1975** WALLACE & MAHAN *Introd. Ornith.* (ed. 3) iii. 84 The oil or preen gland (*uro-*

pygium) is a conical, bilobed structure, often with a tuft of tiny feathers that serve as a wick, located immediately in front of the tail.

pre-E·nglish, *a.* and *sb.* [PRE- B. 1 in Dict. and Suppl.] **A.** *adj.* **1. a.** Designating the period before settlement of English-speakers in the British Isles.

1922 E. EKWALL *Place-Names Lancs.* 26 We expect the name of such an important river (or at least its first el[ement]) to be of pre-English origin. **1922** F. KLAEBER *Beowulf* 190 The poet was interested in the old Anglian traditions—the only legends in *Beowulf* that are concerned with persons belonging to English (i.e., pre-English) stock. **1934** *Essays & Stud.* XIX. 157 *Ærgeweorc*..referring to constructions of the pre-English period. **1966** *Eng. Stud.* XLVII. 210 The oldest river-names are of pre-English origin.

b. Pertaining to a period before the adoption of a given word into English.

1960 C. S. LEWIS *Studies in Words* vi. 133 In modern English the two meanings are not at all related as parent and child. They can be explained only by the pre-English history of the word.

2. Prior to the emergence of the English language; *spec.* of or pertaining to the West Germanic or Anglo-Frisian dialect from which English developed.

1928 C. BERGENER *Contrib. Study Conversion of Adj. into Nouns in Eng.* 1 The conversion should have taken place in English, but for the sake of greater completeness also such cases have been included where the conversion was, or may have been, pre-English. **1933** *Mod. Lang. Notes* XLVIII. 383 For names not of English origin the authors..use..*pre-English*... The..term is a most unfortunate one, since it is ordinarily used in quite another sense, viz., to denote a word form in the hypothetical Germanic dialect out of which English developed. **1936** *Anglia* LX. 367 To the Langobardish *Laiamicho* answers a pre-English trisyllabic **Lāimikō* > **Laimikō*.

B. *sb.* The West Germanic or Anglo-Frisian dialect from which English developed. Also, English before written records.

1929 *Rev. Eng. Stud.* V. 179 A large and important group of writers and speakers..use *Anglo-Saxon* not in the sense 'Old English' but in the sense 'pre-English'. **1965** *Language* XLI. 34 The allophones of /g/..reveal..both [g] and [ʒ] in pre-English.

preening, *vbl. sb.* (In Dict. s.v. PREEN *v.*²) (Later examples.)

1890 E. COUES *Handbk. Field & Gen. Ornith.* II. iii. 129 Birds press out a drop of oil with the beak and dress the feathers with it, in the well-known operation called 'preening'. **1953** N. TINBERGEN *Herring Gull's World* iv. 41 Preening is a most vital occupation. **1975** J. A. G. BARNES *Titmice Brit. Isles* vii. 122 Preening must be considered almost as essential an activity as feeding.

preening (prī·niŋ), *ppl. a.* [f. PREEN *v.*² + -ING².] That preens (see PREEN *v.*² in Dict. and Suppl.); chiefly *fig.*, proud, self-confident.

1903 R. LANGBRIDGE *Flame & Flood* i. 2 The manner of Miss Lydia, as she nestled into repose upon the bench, was essentially that of the conquering fowl who, having winged her way out of the difficulties insurmountable until attained, looks back with preening self-congratulation on the terrors now safely left behind. **1959** *Times* 13 Jan. 10/6 The new, brightly preening *casa* built on the hillside by a wealthy Barcelona merchant. **1976** *Time* 27 Dec. 5/3 His preening charm and Irish good looks were also prominent in plays, films, television and supper clubs.

pre-e·ntry, *a.* [PRE- B. 2.] Prior to entry; *spec.* applied to a closed shop in which union membership is a prerequisite of appointment to a post. Cf. *POST-ENTRY *a.*

1941 [see *Air Training Corps* s.v. *AIR *sb.*¹ III. 3]. **1964** W. E. J. MCCARTHY *Closed Shop in Britain* ii. 52 On the most generous of estimates the number of workers affected by the pre-entry shop in all its forms is unlikely to be more than three-quarters of a million. This means that for every worker in a pre-entry shop there are four in post-entry shops. **1969** *Gloss. Aeronaut. & Astronaut. Terms (B.S.I.)* IV. 4 *Pre-entry streamtube*, the streamtube extending to the entry of a ducted body from infinity upstream. **1972** H. WILLIAMSON *Trade Unions* (ed. 2) ii. 22 In a pre-entry closed shop, membership of a union is essential before the man is appointed to a job. **1977** J. M. JOHNSON in Douglas & Johnson *Existential Sociol.* vii. 210 Because of my preentry preparations and personal contacts, I felt more or less at ease when I addressed a joint meeting of the social workers from the two CWS units to explain the purposes of the research. **1977** *Guardian Weekly* 25 Sept. 10/2 The pre-entry closed shop (that is the kind where you need a card to get a job).

pre-epileptic, -erythrocytic, -European: see *PRE- B. 1. **pre-evangelism:** *PRE- A. 2. **pre-evolutionary:** *PRE- B. 1d. **pre-examination:** *PRE- B. 2a. **pre-excitation:** *PRE- A. 2. **pre-experimental(ly, -exponential:** *PRE- B. 1.

pre-expo·sure. [PRE- A. 2.] A preliminary or premature exposure; *spec.* in *Photogr.*, one given uniformly to a sensitive film or plate in order to increase its sensitivity. So **pre-expo·se** *v. trans.*

1937 G. E. BROWN *Clerc's Photogr.* 582/1 (Index), Hypersensitizing, by pre-exposure. **1953** *Adv. Electronics* V. 76 In order to achieve high detectivity with photographic materials, it is necessary to pre-expose the negative uniformly in order to overcome the inertia of the material. *Ibid.* 77 Table VII shows..the density, *D*, of the film at optimum pre-exposure. **1967** E. CHAMBERS *Photolitho-Offset* v. 63 When double printing from positives, it is necessary to mask-out each positive in the areas where the other positive is required to print to prevent pre-exposure of the emulsion. **1972** P. PETZOLD *Effects & Exper. in Photogr.* (1973) 70/2 The film should be pre-exposed for only a few shots ... Further frames could be pre-exposed at higher or lower levels. **1979** *Nature* 24 May 341/2 Pre-exposure of human red blood cells..to dilutions of *Bufo marinus* serum followed by washing and resuspension in fresh buffer, caused a dose-dependent inhibition of subsequent ³H-ouabain binding to these cells. **1979** *SLR Camera* June 73/2 The only trouble with pre-exposing the shadows in this way is that they tend to lose density in the print.

pref (pref). Abbrev. of *preference* (*share*) s.v. PREFERENCE 8.

1898 *Weekly Official Intelligence* 5 Mar. 145/2 Kinloch (Chas & Co.) Ord., 4/;..Pref. 3/. **1927** *Financial Times* 10 May 1/3 Mexican Nat. 1st Pref. **1971** *Financial Mail* (Johannesburg) 26 Feb. 690/3 An alternative offer for MG's pref shares can be expected soon.

prefab (prī·fæb), *a.* and *sb.* *colloq.* Also **pre-fab.** [Abbrev. of *PREFABRICATED *ppl. a.*]

A. *adj.* Prefabricated. Also *transf.* and *fig.*

1937 *New Yorker* 27 Mar. 20 (*caption*) Darling, the Prefab Homes man was just here. **1944** *Archit. Rec.* Dec. 69/1 (*heading*) Expansible prefab house for postwar. **1958** *Times Lit. Suppl.* 21 Nov. 667/2 Wolsey's 'pre-fab.' chapel on the Field of the Cloth of Gold. **1962** J. PHILIPS *Dead Ending* (1963) II. iii. 77 That pre-fab bow tie. **1965** *New Scientist* 5 Aug. 326/2 Industrialized building is..a collection of developments. Some commentators make a division between 'light' and 'heavy', applying the former term to the progeny of the post-war 'prefab' systems, and the latter to such aids as pre-cast concrete sections of a ton or so each. **1966** T. PYNCHON *Crying of Lot 49* ii. 26 Barbed wire again gave way to the familiar parade of more beige, prefab, cinderblock office machine distributors, bottled gas works, [etc.]. **1973** C. BONINGTON *Next Horizon* xvii. 236 Neat rows of prefab huts, the homes of the Eskimoes. **1977** *Rolling Stone* 24 Mar. 58/2 The temptation to follow through with prefab notions of what that audience would like..was apparently too strong to resist.

B. *sb.* A prefabricated house or building; in Britain *spec.* a light, often single-storey house of the kind built in large numbers during and after the 1939–45 war when it was necessary to rehouse many people in a short time. Also *attrib.*

1942 *Time* 16 Mar. 77/3 This year 20% of all new houses may be prefabs. **1947** 'N. SHUTE' *Chequer Board* ix. 250 Any young couple might live in a prefab when they start off first. **1949** G. COTTERELL *Randle in Springtime* 112 She continued with complaints about the people living in the new pre-fabs that had been put up where a V1 had demolished some houses in the road. **1958** *Spectator* 24 Jan. 109/2 The Crystal Palace, the first prefab in the world. **1958** U. BLOOM *Abiding City* xii. 200 England..was rising from the ashes of the bombing, with the influx of pre-fabs springing up everywhere. **1959** *Times* 24 Sept. 15/2 Active youth clubs to keep the pre-fab element out of trouble. **1972** *Daily Tel.* 7 Dec. 16/2 The last 700 prefabs in London are to be demolished.

prefab (prī·fæb), *v. trans.* Colloq. abbrev. of *PREFABRICATE *v.* Hence **pre·fabbed** *ppl. a.*

1959 *Observer* 4 Oct. 21/6 Prefabbed to retail on both sides of the Atlantic, the Anglo-American telefilm serial is a celluloid bastard. **1959** *Encounter* Oct. 37/2 Pre-fabbed hand-crafts and papier-maché charm. **1973** 'J. MARKS' *Mick Jagger* (1974) 67 You're still growing up in a blues environment whether you've prefabbed it or whether it's natural.

prefabricate (prīfæ·brikēit), *v.* [PRE- A. 1.] *trans.* To manufacture (sections of a building or similar structure) in a factory or yard prior to their assembly on a site, esp. when they are larger or more complex than those considered traditional; also with the building as obj. Also *absol.* and *fig.*

1932 W. H. HAM in *Architecture* Apr. 187/1 We can prefabricate 90 per cent of a house in the factory, assemble it, and make it a permanent, attractive, useful home. **1939** *Christian Sci. Monitor* 3 Mar. 4/1 Practically every steel bridge is prefabricated, or put together in the back yard of the bridge builders before the pieces are taken apart, labeled and shipped for erection on the site. *Ibid.* 4/2 Ironwork firm, by prefabricating, makes sure that parts will join. **1941** *Times* (Weekly ed.) 23 Apr. 2 Four new plants now being erected in Nebraska, Oklahoma and Texas..will assemble annually 3,600 heavy bombers from parts pre-fabricated in automobile factories. **1944** *Hansard Commons* 7 Mar. 1906 In the most recent class of frigates at least 80 per cent. of the structure has been prefabricated. **1947** *News Chron.* 8 Apr. 2/2 The political structure which is being pre-fabricated with some success cannot be placed in position until its economic foundations have been laid. **1960** E. DELAVENAY *Introd. Machine Transl.* vii. 108 How far will it be possible to 'pre-fabricate', so to speak, this vocabulary, when preparing a programme of automatic translation, by establishing in advance a mixed vocabulary peculiar to such a translation? **1964** *Times Rev. Industry* Feb. 3/1 Five Clyde shipbuilding firms are at present prefabricating houses. **1965** R. B. WHITE *Prefabrication* III. vi. 300 The overall tendency to prefabricate has continued to make headway, particularly for buildings which form part of a national programme of expansion or modernization. **1974** *Sci. Amer.* Feb. 94/3 The Crystal Palace was the first great iron-framed building... It was also..the first for which the structural units were prefabricated.

prefa·bricated, *ppl. a.* [PRE- A. 1.] **1. a.** Of a building or similar structure: constructed by assembling a relatively small number of components which have been made elsewhere. **b.** Of a component of such a structure: made in a factory or yard prior to use elsewhere in construction.

1933 *Archit. Rev.* LXXIV. 49/2 There are a number of houses, one among them being actually of the new 'prefabricated' type. **1935** *Economist* 23 Mar. 679/1 Even the 'pre-fabricated' house, which is assembled from sections, quickly constructed, completely fitted with air-conditioning and domestic equipment..is not regarded as cheap enough to initiate the revival which is so sorely needed. **1944** *Archit. Rev.* XCVI. 30 Mr. Churchill says that we need 500,000 prefabricated houses for temporary homes in the first two years of peace. **1945** in R. W. Zandvoort et al. *Wartime English* (1957) 190 Little more than 100 yards away lie several prefabricated U-boat sections, all in an advanced state towards completion. **1951** 'J. WYNDHAM' *Day of Triffids* xvii. 298 The outbuildings are too small for our needs now—and I can't put up even prefabricated quarters singlehanded. **1959** *Listener* 17 Dec. 1072/1 Factories were built to manufacture prefabricated parts of buildings. **1963** N. MARSH *Dead Water* (1964) ii. 46 A large, prefabricated, multiple garage had been built. **1968** H. G. MILLER *Building Construction* iv. 34 These prefabricated sections, completely fitted with all doors and windows, are transported to the building site where the house can be quickly assembled on the prepared foundation. **1974** *Daily Tel.* 27 Nov. 9/1 So far about 10,000 tons of prefabricated sections of [the cruiser] Invincible have been assembled.

2. *transf.* and *fig.* Contrived, artificial.

1935 *Time* 7 Jan. 40/2 The youth is not having much success with his pre-fabricated recital. **1943** T. S. ELIOT *Reunion by Destruction* 12 The Church of South India is a pre-fabricated church. **1945** A. W. COYSH in *To start you Talking* ii. 30 The broadcast discussion is admittedly pre-fabricated. **1953** *Encounter* Oct. 14/1 This pre-fabricated public is made up not only of the more naïve party members..but also of fellow-travellers who read nothing but the pro-Communist press. **1963** [see *HAM *sb.*¹ B. 2].

prefabrica·tion. [PRE- A. 2.] The manufacture or use of prefabricated components.

1932 W. H. HAM in *Architecture* Apr. 195/1 Plaster.., down to ten years ago, prohibited any advanced thought along the line of prefabrication which would create economies worth while. **1946** *Sun* (Baltimore) 8 Feb. 4/2 Prefabrication seems to be the only solution to obtaining low-cost housing for veterans. **1952** J. B. SINGER *Plastics in Building* i. 25 Prefabrication, which at one time was only intended to bridge the gap in housing shortage, has been gradually extended to cover new fields. The use of factory-produced components is universally recognized as a means to rapid and economical building. **1960** I. CROSS *Backward Sex* 13 Albertville High School was a conglomeration of brick permanence and prefabrication. **1972** *Daily Tel.* (Colour Suppl.) 17 Nov. 79/2 For the upper ten storeys, standardisation and pre-fabrication were very extensively used.

prefabricator (prīfæ·brikēitəɹ). [f. *PREFABRICAT(E *v.* + -OR.] One who, or a business which, practises prefabrication.

1933 *Fortune* Apr. 54/3 Real-estate men offer house plus land for as little as $4,400. Against this new competition what have the prefabricators to show? **1940** *Reader's Digest* July 99 Gunnison Housing Corporation, largest of prefabricators, recently sold several factory-built houses in Springfield, Ill. **1949** *Archit. Rev.* CVI. 375/1 We find a degree and a habit of uniform standardization that no American prefabricator would even attempt to impose on his customers. **1965** R. B. WHITE *Prefabrication* I. i. 4 Foster Gunnison, pioneer prefabricator of New Albany, Indiana.

pre-fade (prī·fēid), *a.* and *sb.* *Broadcasting.* [PRE- B. 2.] **A.** *adj.* Performed or occurring before programme material is faded up for transmission. Of apparatus: used for such monitoring. **B.** *sb.* Monitoring of programme material prior to fading it up for transmission; an instance of this; also, a technical facility for such monitoring.

1941 *B.B.C. Gloss. Broadcasting Terms* 24 *Pre-fade listening.* (1) Listening to a programme output before it is faded up for transmission. (2) Technical facilities provided for this purpose. **1949** F. FELTON *Radio-Play* ii. 19 There is also a 'pre-fade' apparatus by which the operator can listen to the record in advance. **1962** A. NISBETT *Technique Sound Studio* viii. 150 Listening to this disc on prefade it is brought into step with disc one. *Ibid.*, After a quick prefade check, the disc is once again faded up. *Ibid.* ix. 160 In the case of a typical prefade (that used for the BBC's Radio Newsreel) it is known that the duration from a certain easily recognizable point to the end of the record is exactly 1′ 17″. So the record is started exactly 1′ 17″ from the end of the programme, but not faded up. **1968** R. MILTON *Radio Programming* 313 While you are giving a talk from the studio, the technician may listen to a part of the recording he will use next, to be sure it is the right one. He will do this by using his pre-fade monitor. **1975** G. ALKIN *TV Sound Operations* 126 Gram desks are provided with a 'pre-fade' output so that the operator can listen for the cue without fading it up, so that the output is not heard by the audience. *Ibid.*, The method of cueing in discs is to play the recording on pre-fade until the cue is heard and then stop the turntable.

prefa·de, *v.* *Broadcasting.* [f. the sb.] *intr.* To employ pre-fade listening. Also *trans.*, to monitor (programme material) before fading it up for transmission. Hence **prefa·ded** *ppl. a.*, **prefa·ding** *vbl. sb.*

1962 A. NISBETT *Technique Sound Studio* viii. 149 For professional disc work..it is valuable to be able to 'pre-fade' (i.e. listen before fading up) while the studio loud-speaker is being used to monitor the rest of the programme. *Ibid.* ix. 160 For the close of many radio programmes prefaded music is used. *Ibid.* 161 Vocal music is not usually suitable for prefading. **1971** T. C. COLLOCOTT *Dict. Sci. & Technol.* 929/1 *Prefading*, listening to programme material and adjusting its level before it is faded up for transmission or recording.

pre-Fascist: see *PRE- B. 1 a.

prefectly (prī·fektli), *a.* *rare.* [f. PREFECT, PRAEFECT *sb.* + -LY[1].] Characteristic of or befitting a prefect.

1927 J. ELDER *Thomasina Toddy* xxii. 218 Anne recognised them with her most prefectly twitch of the lips.

prefectorial, *a.* Add: **2.** Of or pertaining to a prefecture (sense 3).

1942 E. PAUL *Narrow St.* iii. 24 Hours of squinting in the dingy misplaced prefectorial light. **1963** *Times* 18 Feb. 8/3 As incumbent of the Lyons prefecture, a massive grey building typical of the 'prefectorial baroque'..he represents the central power of Paris.

prefer, *v.* **7. a.** For † *above* read *above* and add later example.

1883 G. MOORE *Mod. Lover* II. vi. 105 There was one place he preferred above all others.

preferability. (Later examples.)

1962 L. J. COHEN *Diversity of Meaning* vi. 160 The preferability of one conceptual form to another. **1975** *New Yorker* 21 Apr. 96/2 The manual went on to stress the actuarial preferability of drivers leading a stable life.

preferable, *a.* Add: **3.** = PREFERENCE 8. *attrib.*

1913 *Act* 3 & 4 *Geo. V* c. 20 §97 (1) Such preferable securities as existed at the date of the sequestration, and are not null or reducible.

preferee. (Later example.)

1977 *Navy News* Sept. 4/3 Inevitably, there are more sea billets than preferees on the one hand while there is strong competition among the preferees for the comparatively small number of shore billets.

preference. Add: **1. b.** *spec.*, under the system of preferential voting (see *PREFERENTIAL *a.* c), the naming or numbering of candidates in the order desired by the voter; hence, the position in that order assigned to any candidate by the voter.

1908 *Westm. Gaz.* 20 Aug. 2/1 Some 272 of Haynes's supporters had not used their preference and so their votes were put aside as exhausted. **1955** E. LAKEMAN *How Democracies Vote* iv. 88 The Returning Officer either awards the appropriate number of points for each preference and adds them up, or, if each voter is obliged to number every candidate, adds up the preferences each candidate thus receives. **1965** *Austral. Encycl.* III. 367/1 In 1910 it [*sc.* Western Australia] made the marking of preferences necessary to a valid vote. **1975** *Irish Times* 10 May 1/5, I cannot dictate how my preferences should be distributed. In a democracy that is the right of the electorate.

7. b. (Earlier and later examples.)

1852 MRS. GASKELL *Cranford* (1853) vii. 133 We were six in number; four could play at Preference, and for the other two there was Cribbage. **1908** R. W. CHAMBERS *Firing Line* ii. 20 That kills our four at Bridge... We'll have to play Klondike and Preference now. **1977** V. S. PRITCHETT *Gentle Barbarian* v. 80 At Spasskoy he [*sc.* Turgenev]..played chess and draughts and games of Preference.

c. *Bridge.* A bid or pass by a responder indicating in which of two or more suits bid by his partner he wishes to play.

1919 R. F. FOSTER *Foster on Auction* I. 96 This bidding invariably shows a two-suiter... If he prefers the spades, he can bid two spades to indicate his preference. **1927** M. C. WORK *Contract Bridge* iii. 42 That bid would be a forced take-out and would not announce strength, merely a preference. **1958** *Listener* 4 Dec. 965/3 If..partner is two-suited it will be enough to give a spade preference when he is able to demand it.

8. preference bid = sense 7c above; **preference voting** = *preferential voting* s.v. *PREFERENTIAL *a.* c).

1927 M. C. WORK *Contract Bridge* iii. 148 *Preference bid*, a bid made to show preference for one suit over another, rather than strength (in case partner has bid a two-suiter). **1934** G. F. HERVEY *Contract Bridge Dict.* 117 Y's bid is a preference bid showing that he prefers the hand to be played in Spades. **1908** *Westm. Gaz.* 20 Aug. 2/1 The local Labour Party is inclined to boycott preference voting and advocate its members to plump.

preferential, *a.* Add: **c.** *preferential ballot, voting*, a form of voting found in various systems of proportional representation in which candidates are numbered in order of preference by the voter; the use of the alternative vote (see *ALTERNATIVE *a.* 6).

1870 *Putnam's Mag.* June 717/1 Mr. Hare's scheme is one which..may be called that of *preferential* voting. It ascertains the quota by dividing the whole number of voters by the whole number of representatives... This method, which we have called that of preferential voting, is also called by the Swiss reformers that of the electoral quotient. **1908** *Westm. Gaz.* 20 Aug. 2/1 The State of Western Australia..is now attempting..preferential voting in a simple form. **1911** *Ann. Amer. Acad. Pol. & Social Sci.* XXXVIII. 760 The preferential ballot for cities is a plan to restore majority elections and true representative government. **1926** [see *alternative vote* s.v. *ALTERNATIVE *a.* 6]. **1955** C. R. ADRIAN *Governing Urban Amer.* iii. 61 During their heyday—the first and second decades of the present century—reformers sponsored other organizational and procedural changes: preferential voting, such as the Bucklin and Ware systems, which did not catch on, [etc.]. **1976** J. ROGALY *Parliament for People* vi. 71 Two less satisfactory forms of preferential voting are the 'second ballot', used in France, and the 'Alternative vote'.

d. *Anthrop.* Esp. in phr. *preferential marriage, mating*: the preference within a tribe or kinship group for marriage to take place between persons standing in a particular relationship to each other, such as cross-cousins. Cf. *PRESCRIPTIVE *a.* 4 b.

1909 *Cent. Dict.* Suppl., Preferential marriage. **1920** R. H. LOWIE *Primitive Soc.* (1921) ii. 16 Among the Kariera of Western Australia the acquisition of a bride is complicated by certain rules of preferential mating. That is, a man is..practically obliged to mate with a particular type of cousin or some more remote relative. *Ibid.* 35 Cross-cousin marriage, levirate, and sororate are by no means the only terms of preferential mating. **1943** E. J. & J. D. KRIGE *Realm of Rain Queen* ix. 145 We shall turn first to the preferential marriages. A marriage is obligatory or approved, or discouraged..according as it strengthens..or conflicts with the..edifice erected by the [payment of] cattle. **1968** R. NEEDHAM tr. *Lévi-Strauss's Elem. Struct. Kinship* (1969) p. xxx, Societies which advocate marriage between certain types of kin adhere to the norm only in a small number of cases..hence the idea of calling such systems 'preferential', a name which.. expresses the reality. **1971** —— *Rethinking Kinship & Marriage* p. lxviii, One should not ask whether a tribe has a prescriptive as opposed to a preferential marriage system.

e. *transf.* = *PREFERRED *ppl. a.* 5.

1926 *Carnegie Scholarship Mem.* XV. 378 Since the smaller crystals grown in flat strips had no preferential orientation, none could be expected in the smaller round crystals. **1955** T. L. RICHARDS in H. S. Peiser et al. *X-Ray Diffraction by Polycrystalline Materials* xxi. 469 Preferential crystal growth in a definite crystal direction. **1968** R. RIEGER et al. *Gloss. Genetics & Cytogenetics* 161 *Selective* or *preferential fertilization*, fusion of germ cells of different genotypes from one or both sexes in combinations having nonrandom frequencies. **1977** *Lancet* 9 July 92/2 The preferential production of the IgE and IgG4 classes might..be due to structural peculiarities in the sensitising allergens.

preferentially, *adv.* Add: **2.** To a greater extent or degree.

1926 *Encycl. Brit.* II. 886/1 In the case of brass, steel and aluminium alloys, certain types of chemical reagents which act preferentially upon the material in the crystal boundaries contribute to the occurrence of such fractures. **1935** TIPSON & STILLER in Harrow & Sherwin *Textbk. Biochem.* ii. 61 The tendency is for the primary hydroxyl group to be preferentially esterified. **1957** G. E. HUTCHINSON *Treat. Limnol.* I. xvi. 851 Several crop plants assimilated ammonia preferentially above *p*H 7. **1971** *Physics Bull.* Mar. 141/3 In an equilibrium reaction these elements with greatest binding energy per nucleon are formed preferentially. **1977** *Sci. Amer.* Jan. 39/3 The black hole will therefore preferentially emit particles with charge of the same sign as itself and so will rapidly lose its charge.

preferred, *ppl. a.* Add: **3. b.** Applied to a set of numbers or values forming an approximate geometrical progression and used to determine the officially recommended values of a dimension or other characteristic with which standard components should be made, so as to cover most efficiently the range of possible requirements.

1922 *Mech. Engin.* XLIV. 791/1 A careful study of manufactured articles shows that even when sizes are determined by utility or use value, the choice of size is largely arbitrary. It is therefore obvious that if certain numerical values are universally accepted as preferred values, and if they are so spaced and of such extent as to fit in with all requirements met in deciding on sizes to be used, the arbitrary choices may be so made as to yield sizes expressible in terms of these preferred numbers. **1936** *Proc. IRE* XXIV. 159 Preferred numbers are certain numbers that have been selected to be used for standardization purposes in preference to any others. **1962** S. HANDEL *Dict. Electronics* 269 Manufacturers and users of electrical and electronic components such as fixed resistors and capacitors find that there are advantages in standardizing component values and adopt preferred values so that each value differs from the preceding one by a constant multiplier. **1963** JERRARD & MCNEILL *Dict. Sci. Units* 110 Preferred numbers are conventionally rounded off terms in a geometrical progression whereby a tenth multiple of the initial term is obtained after a predetermined number of terms, viz: p, pq, pq^2, .. pq^{n-1}, pq^n, where p is the initial number, n is the number of terms and q a factor such that $q^n = 10$.

5. *transf.* That is exhibited or adopted by a natural system, object, or substance more commonly than, or to the exclusion of, other apparently possible properties or modes of development; *preferred orientation*, an orientation which crystals in a material tend to adopt or in which they tend to form, usu. because of applied stress.

1929 *Chem. Abstr.* XXIII. 1051 The detn. of the presence and the quant. description of preferred orientations in cryst. masses. **1954** R. L. PARKER tr. *Niggli's Rocks & Min. Deposits* v. 153 If the variable attribute (grain diameter, for instance) can be characterized both by size and by frequency, a mean size must first be determined. To this end the central or preferred value (modal value) in the distribution must be sought..or the value of the arithmetic mean..calculated. **1956** *Jrnl. Iron & Steel Inst.* CLXXXIII. 99/2 The Zn coating on galvanized wire shows no preferred orientation. **1956** *Q. Jrnl. Geol. Soc.* CXII. 123 A specimen from Logie Head.. shows no apparent preferred orientation of quartzes and the measurements are evenly scattered over the fabric diagram. **1962** E. S. GOULD *Inorg. Reactions & Struct.* (rev. ed.) iii. 64 The configuration with bond directions towards the corners of a regular octahedron..may be shown to be preferred. **1968** M. S. LIVINGSTON *Particle Physics* x. 171 In such a plot, broad peaks are frequently observed centred about specific values of energy. Such a preferred value of energy indicates a state of the system of two particles for which decay into the final products is more probable than for lower or higher values. **1971** *Nature* 4 June 306/2 The wind has a strongly preferred direction up and down the length of the steep-sided Loch. **1974** D. M. ADAMS *Inorg. Solids* v. 97 In Chapter 4 we saw that the relative sizes of the ions in a crystal could be related to preferred coordination arrangements.

‖ **préfet** (prefę). [Fr.] The chief administrative officer of a department of France; = PREFECT, PRÆFECT *sb.* 1 d.

1820 M. EDGEWORTH *Let.* 22 June (1979) 168 Mme Chéron whose son is Préfet I think of Toulouse or some Provincial town. **1861** TROLLOPE *Tales of All Countries* (ser. 1) 22 And the company are all talking to him as though he were the préfet. **1869** *Bradshaw's Railway Manual* XXI. 348 Directors: C. Bart, ex-Préfet, Paris. **1872** TROLLOPE *Golden Lion* xviii. 288 Colmar..has been accustomed to the presence of a préfet, and is no doubt important. **1908** O.E.D. s.v. *Prefecture* 3, A prefect or French *préfet.* **1942** 'A. BRIDGE' *Frontier Passage* vi. 102 They went off together to the *Préfecture* at Bayonne. .. Crossman's prestige..made access to the *Préfet* easy. **1958** *Listener* 18 Sept. 431/1 While there might be scoundrels like Darnand, such could be balanced by the courage of *préfets* like Bousquet. **1974** S. COULTER *Château* I. viii. 49 'You are invited to the Préfet's... A reception.'.. She was impressed; the Préfet was the chief officer of the department.

pre-feudal: see *PRE- B. 1 d. **pre-film(ic:** *PRE- A. 1, B. 1 d.

pre-·final, *sb.* and *a.* [PRE- B. 1.] **A.** *sb.* *Linguistics.* (See quot. 1933.) Cf. *POST-FINAL.

1933 L. BLOOMFIELD *Language* viii. 132 English final clusters consist of two, three, or four non-syllabics. One can describe the combinations most simply by saying that each cluster consists of a main final consonant, which may be preceded by a pre-final, which in turn may be preceded by a second prefinal; further, the main final may be followed by a post-final. **1965** *Amer. Speech* XL. 12 There is here no specification of finals with prefinals and post-finals.

B. *adj.* Preceding the final.

1957 *Publ. Amer. Dial. Soc.* XXVIII. 114 Each of the pre-final groups.

prefi·nished, *a.* [PRE- A. 1.] Of metal: coated or treated at the mill so as to make finishing by a subsequent manufacturer unnecessary.

1935 H. R. SIMONDS *Finishing Metal Products* v. 41 One manufacturer of tableware is..producing highly polished products from prefinished sheets. **1963** H. R. CLAUSER *Encycl. Engin. Materials* 550/2 Except for uniformity, a plain plated or painted surface looks the same whether it is made of prefinished metal or finished after fabrication. **1974** *Industr. Finishing* Oct. 10/1 Many types of coated or laminated strip product are in fact used in the construction of motor vehicles but in the present context a prefinished material is defined as one which only requires fabrication before it can be used in its final form.

So **prefi·nishing** *vbl. sb.*

1935 H. R. SIMONDS *Finishing Metal Products* v. 42 Lacquering and painting of sheets are an important part of the general prefinishing of raw materials. **1963** *Mech. World* CXLIII. 17/2 Rather than think in terms of functional or decorative coatings for pre-finishing,..it is probably more realistic to classify such pre-treatments as metallic or non-metallic.

prefi·re, *v.* [PRE- A. 1.] *trans.* To fire (pottery, clay, etc.) beforehand, *spec.* before glazing. Hence **prefi·red** *ppl. a.*, **prefi·ring** *vbl. sb.*

1944 E. ROSENTHAL *Porcelain & Other Ceramic Insulating Materials* I. viii. 203 Originally, pressed and other thin-walled articles were pre-fired at a temperature of between 800°–950°C. in order to give them the necessary mechanical strength so that they would not be deformed during the dipping process, but with the introduction of the aerograph for mass-production glazing pre-firing of the articles becomes superfluous. **1960** W. D. KINGERY *Introd.*

Ceramics xiii. 428 The fine structure in the grog (pre-fired clay)..consists of fine mullite crystals in a siliceous matrix. **1961** M. FRANCIS tr. *Salmang's Ceramics* viii. 210 The grog should also be pre-fired at the temperature at which the brick will subsequently be used, so as to prevent the texture of the brick loosening owing to after-shrinkage of grog grains. **1965** G. J. WILLIAMS *Econ. Geol. N.Z.* xx. 366/1 Some use has been made of these materials for refractories at Kamo, where the shrinkage is controlled by prefiring part of the mix.

prefix, *sb.* Add: **2. b.** A word placed at the beginning of the registered name of a pedigree animal, esp. a dog, to indicate the establishment in which it was bred.

1893 [see *AFFIX *sb.* 4]. **1922** R. LEIGHTON *Compl. Bk. Dog* 367 A Prefix or Affix shall constitute part of a name. **1954** [see *AFFIX *sb.* 4]. **1961** C. H. D. TODD *Popular Whippet* 139, I remember some lovely dogs that sailed under the Poppy prefix. **1976** C. COOPER *Newfoundland* i. 31 New names were coming to join those of established breeders, among them Lt-Col. Reid-Kerr with his Gleborchd prefix.

prefix, *v.* **1.** Delete 'Now *rare*' and add later example.

1977 *Daily Tel.* 23 Feb. 32/3 Would-be exporters can 'pre-fix' the subsidy at the present level by arrangement with the European Commission in Brussels.

3. b. *Biol.* To fix with the first of two consecutively used fixatives.

1963 *Jrnl. Cell Biol.* XVII. 32 It was found that material prefixed in glutaraldehyde or acrolein..and re-fixed in osmium tetroxide contained numerous dense particles of diffuse contours..occupying the glycogen areas. **1971** *Nature* 29 Oct. 622/2 Even when the final suspension was prefixed by adding osmium tetroxide, damaged liposomes were not seen.

5. (Later example.)

1898 *Phil. Trans. R. Soc.* B. CXC. 85 The skin and musculature of the arm of Man are somewhat prefixed as compared with *Macacus*.

prefixal, *a.* Delete *rare*⁻¹ and add later examples. Hence **prefi·xally** *adv.*, in the manner of a prefix.

1922 S. GREW *Art of Player-Piano* 86 The shorter note may be affined prefixally to the note after it. **1962** D. C. SWANSON in Householder & Saporta *Probl. Lexicogr.* 74 'Prefixal' is self-explanatory; 'co-valent' is used here (instead of non-prefixal) to refer to all other types collectively. **1964** E. A. NIDA *Toward Sci. Transl.* vi. 135 Once the verb root has been given, the selection of possible suffixes is more strictly determined than in Navajo, in which the prefixal formations do not, to the same extent, help the reader to predict either the sequence of prefixes likely to occur or the root likely to follow. **1971** *Language* XLVII. 396 Reflexive prefixal *t-* metathesizes with an immediately following sibilant and assimilates to the latter with respect to voice and pharyngealization. **1975** *Ibid.* LI. 618 The prefixal vowel in *prenatal* (but not in *pregnant*) is lengthened.

prefixation. I. 1. Delete *rare*⁻¹ and add later examples.

1957 *Archivum Linguisticum* IX. 101 Hypercharacterization..of a person..is the common denominator of a wealth of processes:..the spreading prefixation of *i(l)* to the 3d sing. in modern substandard French. **1975** N. CHOMSKY *Logical Struct. Linguistic Theory* viii. 235 Any complete verb phrase can be turned into a noun phrase by prefixation of 'to'. **1978** *Amer. Speech* LIII. 64 This last observation prompts Samarin to suggest that glossolalia may provide evidence for a universal tendency to prefer suffixation to prefixation.

II. [f. PRE- + FIXATION.] **2.** *Anat.* [PRE- A. 4 b.] The state of a nerve of being prefixed (see *PREFIXED, PREFIXT *ppl. a.* 3).

1953 [see *POSTFIXATION *sb.* 1].

3. *Biol.* [PRE- A. 2.] The initial fixation of tissue that is subsequently to be fixed with a second fixative.

1963 *Jrnl. Cell Biol.* XVII. 32 The particles appearing when osmium tetroxide was used after glutaraldehyde or acrolein prefixation were similar to those appearing in rat liver after potassium permanganate..fixation. **1974** *Nature* 20 Dec. 722/1 The present study takes advantage of several circumstances: (i) cells could be frozen without prefixation or cryoprotectants.

prefixed, prefixt, *ppl. a.* Add: The form prefixt is *Obs.* **3.** *Anat.* Of a nerve: connected to the spinal cord relatively cranially. Cf. *POSTFIXED *ppl. a.* 2.

1892, etc. [see *POSTFIXED *ppl. a.* 2].

prefixial (prīfi·ksiăl), *a.* [f. PREFIX *sb.*] = PREFIXAL *a.*

1975 *Verbatim* Dec. 13/2 'Bantu'..was coined in the 1850s by a philologist, Wilhelm Bleek, to characterize those peoples south of the Sahara speaking a group of related languages featuring prefixial concords, that is, a system in which the prefix is inflected to indicate grammatical case and number rather than, as in most western European languages, the suffix. **1976** *Archivum Linguisticum* VII. 136 Except for some prefixial combinations, the determinatum usually receives weak stress in English.

preflame: see *PRE- B. 2.

prefli·ght, *a.* [f. PRE- B. 2 + FLIGHT *sb.*¹] **a.** Of or pertaining to the time before powered flight. *rare.* **b.** Of or pertaining to the preparations for a flight, or for flying in general.

1922 *Encycl. Brit.* XXX. 44/2 Almost all altimeters in use are based on the pre-flight aneroid in which the trade convention was to assume everywhere an atmospheric temperature of 10° C. **1942** *R.A.F. Jrnl.* 27 June 4 American boys..are to be given pre-flight aviation training. **1962** A. SHEPARD in *Into Orbit* 98 Then I went through my final pre-flight medical. **1968** J. SANGSTER *Touchfeather* xviii. 205, I could just see his head at the flight deck window as he made some of his pre-flight checks. **1970** N. ARMSTRONG et al. *First on Moon* ii. 35 She had left the Holiday Inn two hours earlier to drive to the preflight examination area.

prefli·ght, *v.* [f. prec.]. *trans.* To prepare (an aircraft) for a flight.

1971 *Flying* (N.Y.) Apr. 40/3 A moron could..preflight and satisfactorily steer the 172. **1975** L. D. KUSCHE *Bermuda Triangle Mystery Solved* 98 Each plane had been..preflighted and held a full load of fuel. **1975** *High Times* Dec. 70/2 So you load up and preflight the plane. **1976** B. LECOMBER *Dead Weight* vi. 75 Simon..did want a flying lesson... I told him to pre-flight the Cherokee.

prefo·cus, *a.* and *v.* [f. PRE- A. 1.] **A.** *adj.* Of a bulb: constructed so that the lamp is automatically focused upon fitting of the bulb; also applied to parts of such bulbs, esp. the cap, which make possible the necessary accurate positioning of the filament during manufacture.

1944 (*title*) Dimensions of prefocus lamp-caps and lampholders (British Standards Institution). **1950** YOUNG & GRIFFITHS *Automobile Electr. Equipment* (ed. 4) vi. 181 Fine adjustment for the filament position is.. essential in order to take care of slight manufacturing discrepancies in the filament distance from the bulb cap unless, of course, the bulb is of the pre-focus type now prevalent in British-made headlamps. **1967** L. HOLMES *Odhams New Motor Man.* x. 238/1 For Continental towing, British cars must have their headlamps converted to dip to the right instead of to the left, and for this purpose special pre-focus bulbs can be obtained. **1970** *A.A. Bk. of Car* 162/4 The cut-away in the flange of a pre-focus bulb ensures that it is correctly located and focused. **1972** *Gloss. Electrotechnical, Power Terms* (*B.S.I.*) IV. iii. 17 *Prefocus cap*, cap..which enables the luminous element to be brought into a specified position relative to the cap during the manufacture of the lamp.

B. *v. trans.* To make or adjust so that a lamp will be automatically focused when a bulb is fitted. So **prefo·cused** *ppl. a.*, **prefo·cusing** *vbl. sb.*

1951 *Philips Technical Rev.* XII. 309/1 It is of great importance that when a new bulb is fitted into a headlight its filament comes to lie exactly in the right position. This is ensured by a pre-focusing of the filament in the factory with the aid of a special adjusting device. *Ibid.* 312 (*caption*) On the base can be seen two of the three studs with which the lamp is focused: they ensure that the axis of the lamp coincides with that of the reflector, the filament being 'prefocused' with respect to the studs. **1954** A. W. JUDGE *Automobile Electr. Maintenance* (ed. 3) viii. 209 In the case of recent American-type headlamps, 'sealed-beam' units are employed. These consist of a lens, bulb, and reflector unit built into one water-and dust-proof pre-focused unit. **1970** *A.A. Bk. of Car* 162/4 *Quartz-halogen bulbs.* These are obtainable for fitting into pre-focused units in place of ordinary bulbs. **1977** *Nature* 6 Jan. 92/1 The built-in lamp turret keeps four prefocussed lamps aligned, powered and ready to work.

preform, *v.* Add: *spec.* To form (plastic or other moulding material) into a shape, usu. one resembling a desired final shape, before some further processing. Also *absol.*

1936 H. W. ROWELL *Technol. Plastics* xx. 148 A 'tablet'..is made in a stock size of die and is not preformed to the approximate shape of the moulding. **1943** D. W. BROWN *Handbk. Engin. Plastics* i. 9 In order to reduce the size of the powder space required in moulds, the raw material is sometimes preformed into comparatively small pellets prior to being introduced into the mould. **1968** L. K. ARNOLD *Introd. Plastics* (1969) ii. 41 The powder may be preformed, that is, pressed into pellets or disks of convenient size to reduce bulk density and facilitate charging the mold. **1975** C. A. HARPER *Handbk. Plastics & Elastomers* xii. 36 There are..transfer-type presses that will automatically feed the powder, preform, preheat, transfer, and complete the molding cycle.

Hence **prefo·rming** *vbl. sb.*; also **prefo·rmer**, a press or similar device for preforming plastic.

1931 *Plastics & Molded Products* VII. 705 (Advt.), Trouble-free preforming and more economical production with Stokes single punch and rotary preform presses. **1952** J. DELMONTE *Plastics Molding* viii. 193 Standard single-punch preformers are illustrated in Figs. 2 and 3, and a rotary-type preforming machine is illustrated in Fig. 4. **1966** J. A. BRYDSON *Plastics Materials* x. 210 Preforming is carried out by compressing sieved powder that has been evenly loaded into a mould. **1968** *Encycl. Polymer Sci. & Technol.* IX. 26 Preformers are basically compacting presses; they may be mechanical, hydraulic, pneumatic, or rotary cam-type machines.

preform (prī·fǭɹm), *sb.* **1.** [f. the vb.] A moulded object which has to receive further processing to produce the final shape, which it usu. resembles.

1931 *Plastics & Molded Products* VII. 102 The test strip..is 7⅞ in. long by 1 in. wide and is molded from four preforms composed of a very soft grade of phenol-plastic compound. **1935** C. ELLIS *Chem. Synthetic Resins* II. lxviii. 1317 Tablets or preforms are made from the molding powder by applying high pressure..quickly and without heat. **1945** H. BARRON *Mod. Plastics* vii. 166 Preforms are employed where the use of fairly bulky moulding powder is a disadvantage. **1962** *Gloss. Terms Glass Industry* (*B.S.I.*) 33 *Preform*, a small glass product, normally employed in making glass-to-metal seals, formed by dry-pressing glass powder into shape in a die, the shape being fired to consolidate the glass particles into a non-porous component. **1968** *Encycl. Polymer Sci. & Technol.* IX. 26 It is easier for an operator to pick up a preform and place it in a mold cavity or transfer pot than to have to weigh a charge of granular material. **1970** *New Scientist* 12 Nov. 326/1 A precise quantity of [metal] powder is compacted and sintered so as to produce a preform which is approximately 85 per cent dense.

2. *Philol.* [PRE- A. 2.] A linguistic form reconstructed from later evidence.

1939 L. H. GRAY *Foundations of Lang.* i. 3 If..one has such a series as English (*he*) *bears*, Old Icelandic *berr*, Gothic *bairiþ*.., Old High German *birit*, Old Irish *berid*, Modern Irish *bheir*..,..one may, by comparing and contrasting these forms in accordance with phonetic correspondences.., determine why they are here alike, and there unlike, and may perceive how they can all be derived from an hypothetical pre-form. **1972** *Language* XLVIII. 409 There are two possibilities for reconstructing the gen. pl. preforms of the two attested nouns.

preformationist. Add: (Later examples.) Also *attrib.* or as *adj.*

1936 *Mind* XLV. 221 Boodin begins by explaining why he prefers to class the cosmological theories of Plato and Aristotle, notwithstanding certain preformationist tendencies especially in the thought of Aristotle, under the heading of creation theories. **1960** *New Biol.* XXXI. 119 As development proceeds, suitable conditions start the synthesis of a succession of new substances. This, at least, is the contemporary opinion; the Preformationists in the eighteenth century thought otherwise, but their point of view is hard to square with the atomic hypothesis. **1973** *Jrnl. Genetic Psychol.* CXXII. 326 Preformationist prejudices were so powerful that early embryologists..'saw' nonexistent miniature adults when viewing embryos through their microscopes. **1975** *Nature* 5 June 449/1 These findings fit well the expectations of the Preformationists. **1978** *Ibid.* 9 Nov. 125/1 Until this metaphor became available, the only alternative to a crude preformationist kind of innatism was a mysterious force such as Driesch's 'entelechy', which would allow the developing organism to survive the vicissitudes of the environment and the embryologist's knife.

preformed, *ppl. a.* Add: *spec.* of plastic or other moulding material (cf. *PREFORM *v.*).

1918 H. ABRAHAM *Asphalts* xxvi. 453 (*heading*) Preformed joints and washers. **1935** C. ELLIS *Chem. Synthetic Resins* II. lxviii. 1319 The charge may be used in any of three forms, powder, preformed tablets or sheets. **1943** D. W. BROWN *Handbk. Engin. Plastics* i. 9 In some cases..the shape of the article renders it impossible to use preformed materials. **1971** E. W. DUCK *Plastics & Rubbers* iv. 60 A pre-formed sheet of the plastic is heated and then brought on to the surface of the mould and drawn tight..by the application of a vacuum. **1977** *Gramophone* June 122/1 The enclosure is very substantially made.., being braced..and filled with pre-formed foam fittings.

pre-Freu·dian, *a.* [PRE- B. 1.] Of or characterized by attitudes, etc., that were commonly accepted prior to Freud's pioneer work in psychoanalysis.

1937 *Harper's Mag.* Nov. 563/1 With the tools of semantic analysis, the authors laid in ruin the towering edifice of classical philosophy... Psychology (pre-Freudian) emerged in little better repair. **1938** J. M. KEYNES *Two Memoirs* (1949) 100 It was not only that intellectually we were pre-Freudian, but we had lost something which our predecessors had. **1959** P. TOWNEND *Died o' Wednesday* x. 169, I had..accomplished very little, merely my duty..a matter that caused our ancestors in..pre-Freudian days no perplexity. **1970** *Eng. Stud.* LI. 489 Ward seems quite untempted by the call to psychological speculation, and the book is positively pre-Freudian. **1976** *Jrnl. R. Soc. Arts* CXXIV. 625/1 The Angst of the pre-Freudian and Freudian era.

prefrontal, *a.* (*sb.*) Add: **A.** *adj.* **b.** (Earlier example.)

1888 *Phil. Trans. R. Soc.* B. CLXXIX. 3 (*heading*) Results of experiments upon the prefrontal region of the hemisphere.

c. *prefrontal leucotomy, lobotomy*, lobotomy of the prefrontal part of the brain.

1936, etc. [see *LOBOTOMY]. **1937**, etc. [see *LEUCOTOMY].

prefulgence (prīfʊ·ldʒĕns). [f. as PREFULGENT *a.*] = PREFULGENCY.

1892 G. GISSING *Born in Exile* II. IV. iii. 227 In his most presumptuous moments he had never claimed the sexual prefulgence which many a commonplace fellow so gloriously exhibits. **1916** F. SWINNERTON *Chaste Wife* xxiii. 317 Too stupid to understand anything but physical prefulgence or absolute social convention.

preg (preg), *a.* Colloq. abbrev. of PREGNANT *a.*² 1 a.

1955 W. GADDIS *Recognitions* I. v. 172 She's preg, baby. **1962** E. O'BRIEN *Lonely Girl* xvi. 188 Are you preg?.. 'Cos if you are, you won't be able to cycle. **1967** *London Mag.* Aug. 10 A bit of news which may just interest you. I am P-R-E-G and not by Roy. **1968** *New Society* 22 Aug. 266/1 'She's pregnant' is now used in many classes ('preg, preggy, preggers', whatever class they belonged to, are now not much used).

pre-game: see *PRE- B. 2 a. **pregamic:** *PRE- B. 1.

preganglio·nic, *a. Anat.* [PRE- B. 3.] Of a nerve of the autonomic nervous system: running from the central nervous system to a ganglion.

1895 *Jrnl. Physiol.* XVIII. 280 (*heading*) Note on regeneration of præ-ganglionic fibres of the sympathetic. **1897** *Ibid.* XXII. 223 The regeneration of post-ganglionic fibres presents a somewhat similar problem to that we have considered in relation to the pre-ganglionic fibres. **1903** *Brain* XXVI. 5 The nerve fibres which leave the central nervous system are all pre-ganglionic fibres; they end in connection with nerve cells in the ganglia, and these give off post-ganglionic nerve-fibres which end in the tissues. **1946** *Nature* 19 Oct. 556/1 Single shocks at low intensity delivered to the preganglionic nerve excite a single giant fibre therein. **1972** [see *INTERMEDIOLATERAL *a.*]. **1974** M. C. GERALD *Pharmacol.* v. 93 Conversely preganglionic sympathetic fibers are generally short, with long postganglionic fibers arising from the ganglion to the innervated tissues.

Hence **preganglio·nically** *adv.*

1937 *Jrnl. Physiol.* LXXXVIII. 6 Nicotine..shortens and diminishes the *P* waves set up both antidromically and preganglionically. **1967** *Jrnl. Pharmacol. & Exper. Therap.* CLV. 37/1 The difference was statistically significant whether stimulation was carried out preganglionically or postganglionically.

pregastrular, -geological(ly): see *PRE- B. 1.

pregermina·tion. [PRE- A. 2.] The treatment of seed to start the process of germination before planting. So **prege·rminated** *ppl. a.*, having been subjected to such treatment.

1942 H. I. BALDWIN *Forest Tree Seed* 230 Pregermination:—Germinative processes set in motion, but completion impossible because of external factors. Seed coat may or may not be broken. **1959** *Times* 7 Dec. (Agric. Suppl.) p. viii/3 Pregermination of conifer seed is practised before sowing. **1978** *Countryman* Winter 117 A new planting technique which is taking off in quite a big way is 'the fluid sowing of pre-germinated seeds'.

preggers (pre·gəɹz), *a. slang.* [f. PREG(NANT *a.*[2] + *-ers*, as in *bonkers, crackers.*] = PREGNANT *a.*[2] 1 a.

1942 M. DICKENS *One Pair of Feet* vii. 115 Let anyone mention in her hearing that they felt sick, and it would be all over the hospital that they were 'preggers'. **1960** F. RAPHAEL *Limits of Love* I. iii. 38 'I'm preggers,' Susan said. **1964** *Times* 4 Feb. 7/3, I would only offer my seat to a woman if she were carrying a baby, if she were preggers, or if she were obviously infirm. **1968** [see *PREG *a.*]. **1971** R. DENTRY *Encounter at Kharmel* vii. 115 'There was a strong suspicion that one of the women was preggers.' 'Eh?' 'Up the duff, sir.' **1980** C. FREMLIN *With no Crying* ix. 50 Preggers! Well, what do you know?

preggo (pre·go), *a. Austral. slang.* Also prego. [f. PREG(NANT *a.*[2] + *-O[2].] = PREGNANT *a.*[2] 1 a.

1951 CUSACK & JAMES *Come in Spinner* 226 Guinea's face lighted with unholy glee. 'A Parker prego? Did I hear right?' **1965** P. WHITE *Four Plays* 94 'Can't resist the bananas.' 'Yeah. They say you go for them like one thing when you're preggo.' **1971** *Guardian* 27 May 13/7 Uncommon in print, but familiar in speech, is preggo (pregnant).

preggy (pre·gi), *a. slang.* Also **preggie.** [f. PREG(NANT *a.*[2] + -Y[1].] = PREGNANT *a.*[2] 1 a. Also *transf.*

1938 N. MARSH *Death in White Tie* v. 63 There was your bag, simply preggy with banknotes. **1961** S. PRICE *Just for Record* vi. 57 If poor little preggy Emily Nugent had lived I might never be where I am today. **1968** [see *PREG *a.*]. **1970** K. GILES *Death in Church* iii. 69 She looks preggie, pretty, polite and a little sloshed. **1976** *Star* (Sheffield) 30 Nov. 2/7 Final fling for noisy Parkers shows Michael and preggie June back in England.

pre-give, -given: see *PRE- A. 1.

pre-glacial, *a.* Add: Hence **pregla·cially** *adv.*

1875 *Q. Jrnl. Geol. Soc.* XXXI. 61 The small thickness of preglacially weathered rock that the brief stay of the ice at these high elevations enabled it to remove. **1903** *Jrnl. Geol.* XI. 675 To whatever state of maturity the valley development had attained preglacially, it was directly modified by the advent of the glacial epoch. **1963** D. W. & E. E. HUMPHRIES tr. *Termier's Erosion & Sedimentation* 411 A smooth preglacially eroded surface.

preglo·ttalized, *ppl. a. Phonetics.* [PRE- A. 1.] Preceded by a glottalized sound. Hence **preglo:ttaliza·tion.**

1964 E. J. A. HENDERSON in D. Abercrombie et al. *Daniel Jones* 419 Vichintana Chantavibulya..discovered that her pronunciation of the palatal semi-vowel in initial position is preceded by a weak glottal plosive... There is a similar pre-glottalized articulation of the labio-velar semi-vowel. **1965** *Canad. Jrnl. Linguistics* XI. 1. 32 Phonological feats are possible on a paralinguistic level that seem impossible on a linguistic one,..as pre-glottalized stops and nasals. **1968** B. S. ANDRÉSEN *Pre-Glottalization in Eng. Stand. Pronunc.* 10, I shall regard the glottal stop and the following labial/alveolar/velar plosive as one phonological unit, and refer to this as a 'pre-glottalized' voiceless labial/alveolar/velar plosive. The *use* of these phones will be referred to as 'pre-glottalization'. **1969** *Eng. Stud.* L. 317 Preglottalization can be compared to other articulatory modifications of sounds, e.g. velarization of l, as in [fæɫ]. **1977** *Language* LIII. 317 Except in sentence-initial position, *b d* are either preglottalized or prenasalized, and the processes occur in complementary distribution—word-internally, pre-glottalization is the norm. **1977** *Trans. Philol. Soc. 1975* 222 For Oromo *d* represents either an alveolar implosive or a preglottalized voiced alveolar plosive.

pregnance. Delete †*Obs.* and add: **1.** (Later example.)

1959 I. JEFFERIES *Thirteen Days* xi. 171, I rode off early..into the pleasant pregnance of the day.

2. = *PRÄGNANZ. (But see quot. 1974.)

1948 *Brit. Jrnl. Psychol.* June 181 How little we still know of the details of this process of adaptation, of its conditions and limitations, of its relation to..'the law of pregnance'. **1969** G. N. SEAGRIM tr. *Piaget's Mechanisms of Perception* vi. 305 Pregnance..is only a coercive effect produced..by a form whose elements..succeed in compensating any deformations which are present. **1974** R. ARNHEIM *Art & Visual Perception* (rev. ed.) ii. 67 To compound the confusion, translators have rendered the German *Prägnanz* with the English *pregnance*, which means very nearly the opposite.

pregnancy[1]. Add: **1. a.** Also *transf.*, with reference to appearance: bigness, swollen shape.

1950 *Manch. Guardian Weekly* 4 May 3/4 Since Packard abolished its regal proboscis and succumbed to the epidemic pregnancy of current American models [of automobiles].

5. Special Comb.: **pregnancy test**, a test to establish whether a woman (or female animal) is pregnant; so *pregnancy testing.*

1929 *Jrnl. Amer. Med. Assoc.* 25 May 1746/1 Their 'pregnancy test'..is based on the injection of urine into immature white mice. **1962** L. DAVIDSON *Rose of Tibet* 313 Forcible mating begun... Army doctors followed..to make pregnancy tests. **1977** *Private Eye* 13 May 22/2 (Advt.), *Pregnancy Test Service.* Send small sample of urine & fee £3 for *reliable & strictly confidential* results by first class return post (plain sealed cover). **1977** *Times* 21 June 5/8 Scientists yesterday carried out pregnancy tests on a Colorado beetle found at the weekend on a rose bush in a garden at Peacehaven, Sussex. **1938** *Amer. Jrnl. Obstetr. & Gynecol.* XXXV. 362 A review of the most recent work in pregnancy testing is presented. **1971** *Guardian* 15 Apr. 22/4 An instant pregnancy-testing service is to be promoted in chemists' shops.

pregnane (pre·gnēin). *Chem.* [ad. G. *pregnan* (A. Butenandt 1930, in *Ber. d. Deut. Chem. Ges.* LXIII. 660), f. *pregnan-diol* *PREGNANEDIOL (cf. -ANE).] A synthetic, crystalline, saturated, tetracyclic hydrocarbon, $C_{21}H_{36}$, which has two stereoisomeric forms and from which a group of steroids, including progesterone and pregnanediol, is formally derived; *spec.* the 5β-isomer.

1932 *Ann. Rep. Progr. Chem.* XXVIII. 237 On oxidation there was formed the saturated diketone, $C_{21}H_{32}O_2$, pregnandione, and by Clemmensen reduction of the latter A. Butenandt, F. Hildebrandt, and H. Brücher have obtained the corresponding hydrocarbon, $C_{21}H_{36}$, pregnane. **1936** *Zeitschr. für Kristallogr.* XCIII. 478 Pregnane forms platy crystals elongated along the *b* axis and showing generally the *c* face only. **1959** I. L. FINAR *Org. Chem.* (ed. 2) II. xi. 456 The molecular rotation of any steroid is considered as the sum of the rotation of the fundamental structure (which is the parent hydrocarbon cholestane, androstane, or pregnane) and the rotations contributed by the functional groups. **1960** L. T. SAMUELS in D. M. Greenberg *Metabolic Pathways* I. xi. 432 The two 21-carbon compounds are 5α-pregnane (allopregnane)..and 5β-pregnane (pregnane). **1971** M. F. MALLETTE et al. *Introd. Biochem.* xx. 778 Steroids are named as derivatives of the polycyclic hydrocarbons gonane, estrane, androstane, and pregnane.

pregnanediol (pre:gnēin-, pre:gnăndəi·ǫl). *Biochem.* and *Med.* Also **pregnandiol.** [ad. G. *pregnandiol* (A. Butenandt 1930, in *Ber. d. Deut. Chem. Ges.* LXIII. 660), f. L. *prægnan-s* pregnant + G. *di-* DI-[2] + *-ol* -OL; *cf.* *PREGNANE.] A crystalline steroid containing two hydroxyl groups, $C_{21}H_{36}O_2$, which is a product of the metabolism of progesterone and occurs in the urine during pregnancy.

1930 *Chem. Abstr.* XXIV. 2785 Pregnandiol is related to the sterols and gallic acid. **1934** *Jrnl. Biol. Chem.* CVII. 324 It also seems possible that our compounds may be related to pregnandiol. **1934** *Ann. Rep. Progr. Chem.* XXX. 216 Pregnanediol..is a physiologically inactive compound found in the urine during pregnancy. **1955** *Sci. Amer.* Jan. 55/3 In pregnancy urine there was found an inactive companion of estrone, called pregnanediol. Butenandt proved that pregnanediol was related to cholic acid, a component of bile, by breaking both down to a common product. **1961** *Lancet* 5 Aug. 277/2 The relationship between myometrial progesterone and pregnanediol in the urine is even less clearly defined. **1968** PASSMORE & ROBSON *Compan. Med. Stud.* I. xxxi. 13/1 Progesterone is reduced to pregnanediol, which is excreted as sulphate or glucuronide conjugates. **1976** *Path. Ann.* XI. 240 In 1946 Smith, Smith, and Hurwitz reported that stilbestrol administered to pregnant women increased urinary pregnanediol levels.

pregnenolone (pregnī·nǫlōun). *Biochem.* and *Med.* [ad. G. *pregnenolon* (Butenandt & Westphal 1934, in *Ber. d. Deut. Chem. Ges.* LXVII. 2085), f. *pregn-an* *PREGNANE + *-en* -ENE + *-ol* -OL + *-on* -ONE.] A synthetic steroid, $C_{21}H_{32}O_2$, which is a reduced derivative of progesterone and was formerly used in the treatment of rheumatoid arthritis.

1936 *Chem. Abstr.* XXX. 3036 Similar mixts. of III and I or III and pregnenolone (IV) met with in the prepn. of the hormone from stigmasterol can be sepd. in the same manner. **1955** *Jrnl. Amer. Med. Assoc.* 21 May 166/1 All the patients had received, at one time or another, gold salts, pregnenolone, antibiotics, [etc.]..that produced, at the most, only palliative relief. **1964** E. J. W. BARRINGTON *Hormones & Evolution* ii. 54 In this way cholesterol is thought to be transformed into progesterone, through the intermediary pregnenolone, by partial degradation of its side chain. **1967** *Martindale's Extra Pharmacopoeia* (ed. 25) 1543/2 Pregnenolone and pregnenolone acetate have been used in the treatment of rheumatoid arthritis..but their value has not been substantiated.

prego, var. *PREGGO *a.*

pre-gra·duate, *a.* [f. PRE- B. 1, after POST-GRADUATE *a.* (*sb.*).] = UNDERGRADUATE *a.*

1937 *Discovery* Sept. p. lxxxi/1 (Advt.), The Pregraduate courses extend over three or four years and lead up to an Associateship of one of the colleges, and a B.Sc. Degree of the University of London. **1977** *Proc. R. Soc. Med.* LXX. 377/1 The knowledge and skills required to practise independently were expanding the pre-graduate curriculum to bursting point.

pre-grammar, -grammatical: see *PRE- B. 1. **pre-grind:** *PRE- A. 1. **pre-Han:** *PRE- B. 1 a.

preha·rvest, *a.* [PRE- B. 2.] Occurring before a crop is ready to be gathered.

1934 in WEBSTER. **1948** *New Biol.* V. 62 Some varieties of apple, Beauty of Bath for example, tend to fall before they are fully ripe or of good eating quality. This is known as preharvest fruit drop. **1951** [see *HORMONE 2]. **1971** T. T. KOZLOWSKI *Growth & Devel. Trees* II. viii. 359 In apple, three normal periods of fruit drop occur... These include 'early drop'..and the preharvest drop.

pre-hearing: see *PRE- A. 2.

prehea·t, *v.* [PRE- A. 1.] *trans.* To heat prior to use or to some other treatment.

1898 *Engineering Mag.* XVI. 245 The gas is usually not preheated, but the gas producers are set close to the furnace, so that the initial heat..is not lost. **1937** *Discovery* May 155/1 The tool having been evenly preheated is transferred to the high heat chamber. **1958** LAMBERMONT & PIRIE *Helicopters & Autogyros* 201 The ram-jets are run on propane, which is preheated before being ducted to them. **1958** *Times* 27 Oct. 11/5 Preheat the oven to 420 deg. F. (Regulo 7) and lay the hare directly on the grid. **1975** *Nature* 2 Oct. 368/2 The mixtures were preheated by an external source.

Hence **prehea·ted** *ppl. a.*, **prehea·ting** *vbl. sb.* and *ppl. a.*; also **prehea·ter,** a device for pre-heating.

1898 *Engineering Mag.* XVI. 245 This method of preheating may follow either the regenerative or the recuperative system. **1910** *Encycl. Brit.* I. 445/1 What is called a 'preheater' is used to warm up the compressed air before it enters in the motor cylinder. **1911** A. REYNOLDS tr. *Dichmann's Basic Open-Hearth Steel Process* vii. 59 The second way of producing a steam-air gas with high hydrogen content, consists in the employment of superheated steam, or preheated air supply. **1931** HOFFERT & CLAXTON *Motor Benzole* viii. 221 An efficient preheater should be capable of raising the maximum flow of oil from the temperature at which it leaves the heat-exchange system to a temperature of at least 135°C. **1952** FUCHS & BRADLEY *Welding Pract.* II. iii. 65 Preheating of the parts being welded is always a help towards crack prevention. **1960** *Farmer & Stockbreeder* 15 Mar. (Suppl.) 11/1 Put the mixture into a greased and floured 6in cake tin and bake in a pre-heated fairly hot oven..for 1 hour. **1967** KARCH & BUBER *Offset Processes* ii. 20 After one minute in an open preheater press, a reinforcement mat and backing sheet are added. Then the entire assembly is heated and later bonded. **1976** *Woman's Weekly* 6 Nov. 74/1 (Advt.), In this article she looks at pre-heating underblankets.

prehend, *v.* Restrict *Obs. rare* to sense in Dict. and add: **b.** *Philos.* To apprehend with or without conscious formulation of the perceived object; to interact in time and space with an object or event. Cf. *PREHENSION 3 b. Hence **prehe·nded, prehe·nding** *ppl. adjs.*

1925 A. N. WHITEHEAD *Sci. & Mod. World* (1926) vi. 153 Then the enduring pattern is a pattern of aspects within the complete pattern prehended into the unity of A. **1927** AUDEN & DAY-LEWIS in *Oxf. Poetry* p. vi, Emotion is no longer necessarily to be analysed by 'recollection in tranquillity': it is to be prehended emotionally and intellectually at once. **1929** A. N. WHITEHEAD *Process & Reality* 56 The essence of an actual entity consists solely in the fact that it is a prehending thing. **1933** —— *Adventures of Ideas* xiv. 268 There are the physical and the mental poles, and there are the objects prehended and the subjective forms of the prehensions. **1938** C. D. BROAD *Exam. McTaggart's Philos.* II. I. 4 When a person has repeatedly prehended certain particulars as having a certain characteristic *C* he may 'form an idea of' that characteristic. **1945** R. G. COLLINGWOOD *Idea of Nature* III. iii.

173 An iron filing prehends the magnetic field in which it lies, that is it converts that field into a mode of its own behaviour, responds to it. *Ibid.* 174 A plant prehends the sunlight. **1947** *Mind* LVI. 97 In certain circumstances, when a person 'sees' a physical object, he visually prehends that physical object... In other cases what he visually prehends is, not the physical object.., but a particular which stands in a certain relation to the visum. **1959** W. A. CHRISTIAN *Interpretation of Whitehead's Metaphysics* i. 12 It has a subject (the prehending actual entity), an object or datum that is prehended, and a subjective form. **1971** J. B. COBB in D. Brown et al. *Process Philos. & Christian Thought* xii. 220 The new occasion prehends all the entities in its past.

prehensible, *a.* (Later example in sense b of prec.)

1947 *Mind* LVI. 101 This line has parts of two different kinds, visually prehensible and not visually prehensible.

prehensile, *a.* Delete 'Chiefly *Zool.*' and add later *gen.* examples. Also *fig.*

1945 R. HARGREAVES *Enemy at Gate* 23 Hungry, prehensile soldiers of fortune. **1959** *Listener* 15 Oct. 633/1 A prehensile readability. **1966** G. GREENE in *New Statesman* 25 Feb. 254/2 Martha was the plump and prehensile wife of a German correspondent who was suspected of strong Nazi sympathies. She was said to look after men's needs with a simple and indiscriminate fervour. **1976** *Time* 27 Dec. 52/3 Retailers have been eying Kong's potential with prehensile enthusiasm.

prehension. Add: **3. b.** *Philos.* Apprehension of something perceived that may or may not involve cognition; the interaction that exists between a subject and an entity or event.

1925 A. N. WHITEHEAD *Sci. & Mod. World* (1926) iv. 97 The word 'perceive' is, in our common usage, shot through and through with the notion of cognitive apprehension. So is the word 'apprehension', even with the adjective cognitive omitted. I will use the word 'prehension' for uncognitive apprehension: by this I mean apprehension which may or may not be cognitive. **1931** A. WOLF in W. Rose *Outl. Mod. Knowl.* xiii. 584 The 'interlockings' of actual occasions are called 'prehensions', and are conceived causally. Each actual occasion is generated from its prehensions of preceding occasions, and is prehended by succeeding occasions. **1938** C. D. BROAD *Exam. McTaggart's Philos.* II. I. 4, I propose to substitute the artificial term *Prehension* for 'perception' when used in McTaggart's extended sense. I think that this word avoids the objections to 'perception' and to 'acquaintance', which I have pointed out. **1945** R. G. COLLINGWOOD *Idea of Nature* III. iii. 173 Everything enjoys what he calls 'prehensions', that is to say, somehow absorbs what is outside itself into its own being. **1959** W. A. CHRISTIAN *Interpretation of Whitehead's Metaphysics* i. 12 A prehension is an operation in which an actual entity 'grasps' some other entity (actual or nonactual) and makes that entity an object of its experience. **1964** I. LECLERC in Reese & Freeman *Process & Divinity* 137 Form is the object of 'conceptual prehension', not of 'physical prehension'. **1971** V. LOWE in D. Brown et al. *Process Philos. & Christian Thought* i. 7 A prehension is not so much a relation as a relating, or transition, which carries the object into the makeup of the subject.

prehensive, *a.* Delete *rare* and add further examples. Also, pertaining to or involving prehension, esp. in sense 3 b. Also *fig.*

1886 J. SULLY *Teacher's Handbk. Psychol.* viii. 132 The discrimination and identification of the impression... This constitutes the first step in the process of perception. It may be marked off as the presentative or *prehensive* element. **1925** A. N. WHITEHEAD *Sci. & Mod. World* (1926) iv. 90 Things are separated by space, and are separated by time: but they are also together in space, and together in time, even if they be not contemporaneous. I will call their characters the '*separative*' and the '*prehensive*' characters of space-time. *Ibid.* 98 For Berkeley's *mind*, I substitute a process of prehensive unification. **1932** D. EMMET *Whitehead's Philos. of Organism* iv. 87 Actual entities are..described as 'prehensive occasions', that is to say, events or concrete facts of becoming. **1941** P. HUGHES in P. A. Schilpp *Philos. A. N. Whitehead* vi. 278 This activity of perceptual adaptation is a concrescence of prehensive processes, each of which has the quality of the act as a whole. **1966** *Punch* 13 Apr. 528/2, I shall propose to Longman to accept a work on the originality of Locke, Hobbes, and Hume, which will be as *pioneer* to a more prehensive work. **1974** *Nature* 6 Dec. 514/3 Limbless thalidomide children who carry out reaching and prehensive tasks with their mouths and teeth.

prehensiveness (further example).

1937 J. R. FIRTH *Tongues of Men* iii. 37 The very use of likeness and differences and the habitual comparison of ordered series of words assume the principle of 'interrelated prehensiveness' which may be called implication.

prehensorial (prīhĕnsōə·riăl), *a.* [f. PREHENSORI(UM + -AL.] = PREHENSORY *a.*

1903 *Proc. Zool. Soc.* I. 51 One cannot but wonder how the spider maintains a secure hold back downwards, especially when the powerful prehensorial legs of the first and second pairs are released.

pre-Hispanic: see *PRE- B. 1 a.

prehistorian. Delete *rare* and add further examples.

1936 *Discovery* Jan. 23/1 Its interest and importance are of equal..moment to prehistorian, archaeologist, and the student of religious beliefs. **1947** [see *distribution map* s.v. *DISTRIBUTION 9]. **1952** G. SARTON *Hist. Sci.* I. i. 6 Prehistorians have proved beyond doubt the existence of sophisticated cultures at very early times in many places. **1970** *Nature* 12 Dec. 1019/2 The very early carbon-14 dates..for the megalithic tombs of Brittany..have been regarded suspiciously by prehistorians. **1975** *Sci. Amer.* Feb. 41/3 A major French archaeological discovery that was declared fraudulent by many prehistorians in the 1920's has now regained credibility as a result of dating studies conducted at three independent laboratories. **1980** *Early Music* Jan. 85/1 Various groups of specialists: historians of theatre-décor, pre-historians of opera, analysts of court spectacle, experts on renaissance instruments.

prehistoric, *a.* Add: **a.** *prehistoric archæology*: the archæology of the prehistoric period.

1910 *Encycl. Brit.* I. 344/2 The more serious and cautious students of prehistoric archaeology. **1932** A. R. RADCLIFFE-BROWN in *Rep. Brit. Assoc. Adv. Sci. 1931* (Centenary Meeting) 143 Another field that lies within the general field of Anthropology as now organised is that of Prehistoric Archæology. **1935** *Chambers's Encycl.* I. 387/1 Prehistoric archæology has no dates. **1948** A. L. KROEBER *Anthropol.* (rev. ed.) xix. 843 How about relations to history—with which prehistoric archaeology so obviously intergrades that no real line of demarcation can be drawn? **1974** *Encycl. Brit. Micropædia* II. 838/1 Childe was professor of prehistoric archaeology at the University of Edinburgh.

b. *transf.* and *fig.* (chiefly *joc.*).

1859 GEO. ELIOT *Let.* 17 Aug. (1954) III. 133 Pug developes new charms... I think, in the pre-historic period of his existence, before he came to me, he had led a sort of Caspar Hauser life, shut up in a kennel in Bethnal Green. **1886** KIPLING *Departmental Ditties* (1888) 15 Delilah Aberyswith was a lady..With..a little house in Simla in the Prehistoric Days. **1886** 'MARK TWAIN' *Speeches* (1910) 185, I can see that printing-office of prehistoric times yet, with its horse bills on the walls. **1924** J. BUCHAN *Three Hostages* vii. 105, I obediently sampled an old hock, an older port, and a most pre-historic brandy. **1968** M. BRAGG *Without City Wall* x. 116 It's your success story which is jaded... It's been going on for centuries... Prehistoric! **1979** *Guardian* 12 June 23/2 Red and blue looked exactly the same to anyone watching on prehistoric black and white [television].

prehistorically *adv.* (further examples).

1974 *Verbatim* Dec. 1/1 Sulfur, iron,..and lead..were known to some peoples prehistorically. **1975** *Nature* 22 May 355/1 Wilkinson argues that 20th century studies on musk ox behaviour can be extrapolated back to predict the ways in which musk oxen could have been exploited prehistorically.

prehistory. Add: **b.** *transf.* Events or conditions leading up to a particular event, period, etc.

1931 N. MITCHISON in *Time & Tide* 25 July 893/1 Psychologists have come nearer to discovering its causes [*sc.* the causes of unhappiness] than politicians have, but they are mostly bad historians, inventing—as Freud has done—their pre-history to suit their theories. **1958** *Times Lit. Suppl.* 26 Dec. 746/5 The pre-history of the Civil War will not be found in the new position of the mercantile and industrial classes. **1960** K. AMIS *New Maps of Hell* (1961) i. 17 The prehistory of science fiction, up until 1914 or later, is admittedly as much British as American. **1974** *Encycl. Brit. Macropædia* X. 121/1 The latter third of the 19th century was a crucial point in the prehistory of jazz. **1977** *N.Y. Rev. Bks.* 27 Oct. 40/2 That is why the post-history of a work, the tradition it created, is as indispensable to the critic as its pre-history, its sources and the tradition it came from.

pre-Hitler: see *PRE- B. 2 b. **pre-Hitlerian, -Hitlerite:** *PRE- B. 1 a.

preho·minid, *sb.* and *a.* [PRE- B. 1 in Dict. and Suppl.] **A.** *sb.* A creature belonging to an anthropoid genus that is considered to be an evolutionary ancestor of the hominids. **B.** *adj.* Of or pertaining to a creature of this kind.

1939 *Nature* 7 Jan. 18/1 The human affinities of his [*sc.* R. Broom's] recently discovered relics of new types of fossil prehominids. **1948** *Proc. Prehist. Soc.* XIV. 30 Several authorities refer to the Chopper–Chopping-tool Complex of the Far East as having been developed by the Prehominid stock of mankind—members of the *Pithecanthropus* group. **1959** B. WALL tr. *Teilhard de Chardin's Phenomenon of Man* III. ii. 194 To call *Pithecanthropus* and *Sinanthropus* pre-hominids might suggest that they were not yet quite man. *Ibid.* 195 Those creatures which (however pre-hominid in cranial structure) are already clearly situated *above* the point of origin..of our human race. **1968** A. S. ROMER *Procession of Life* xviii. 290 Even if a pre-hominid wished to remain a tree-dweller, his living area would be much restricted unless he were able to venture out into the open. **1978** *Nature* 26 Oct. 744/1 Among living species, the pygmy chimpanzee..offers us the best prototype of the prehominid ancestor.

prehuman, *a.* Add: (Further examples.) Also as *sb.*

1883 A. WILSON in G. Allen et al. *Nature Studies* 105 That which the evolutionist and naturalist desire to know, is the nature of the forms which..must have connected the human root-stock with the pre-human root. **1932** S. ZUCKERMAN *Social Life Monkeys* ii. 24 There is no clear reason why the social behaviour of the 'pre-humans' should be considered to have been like that of apes rather than like that of monkeys. **1958** A. R. RADCLIFFE-BROWN *Method in Social Anthropol.* II. v. 181 It is reasonable to fix the real change from pre-human to human social life by reference to the beginnings of language. **1973** G. OLIVIER in M. H. Day *Human Evolution* 94 The possibility that man..may only have appeared very late, and that the other fossils, including *Pithecanthropus*, may be only pre-human hominids.

prehyoid: see *PRE- B. 3. **pre-ictal:** *PRE- B. 1.

pre-igni·tion. [PRE- A. 2.] Ignition of the fuel and air mixture in an internal-combustion engine before the passage of the spark.

1898 A. G. ELLIOTT *Gas & Petroleum Engines* iv. 88 This third engine has a vaporizer which..is so constructed that even if it became red-hot there would be no risk of pre-ignition. **1909** *Westm. Gaz.* 1 Apr. 4/1 The compression has been increased to the highest point compatible with safety in regard to freedom from pre-ignition. **1951** 'S. ABBEY' *Automobile Fault-Tracing* ii. 28 Pre-ignition and auto-ignition differ from detonation in that the incoming charge is ignited by an incandescent particle or surface before the sparking plug fires. **1970** *A.A. Bk. of Car* 50 Pre-ignition, like knocking, can cause extensive damage, as well as reduce engine power. **1977** I. M. CAMPBELL *Energy & Atmosphere* v. 108 Autoignition (also referred to as preignition, knock, or pinking) arises in an internal combustion engine largely on account of the finite velocity of flame propagation from the spark zone.

preimage (prī,i·mėdʒ). *Math.* [PRE- A. 2.] = *inverse image* s.v. *IMAGE *sb.* 7*.

1949 F. BLUM tr. *B. L. Van der Waerden's Mod. Algebra* I. i. 3 The element $\phi(a)$ is called the image of *a*, while *a* is an inverse image (pre-image) of $\phi(a)$. **1958** [see *INTO *adj.*]. **1975** N. CHOMSKY *Logical Struct. Linguistic Theory* ix. 317 *T* carries the elements of its domain into strings of $\bar{P}$ which differ from one another and from their preimages in the sense of condition C6.

pre-implanta·tion, *a.* *Biol.* [PRE- B. 2.] Occurring or existing between the fertilization of an ovum and its implantation in the wall of the uterus.

1945 W. J. HAMILTON et al. *Human Embryol.* v. 49 (*heading*) Pre-implantation period. *Ibid.* 50 The pre-implantation stages of the human ovum must be essentially the same as those of the monkey. **1968** *Nature* 9 Nov. 596/1 Mosaicism, extending to most tissues of the body in mice, was achieved by fusing pre-implantation embryos together *in vitro*. **1972** R. L. BRINSTER in Balin & Glasser *Reproductive Biol.* xx. 751 In the human, where the gestation period is 270 days, the pre-implantation period is still only 8 days.

pre-i·mpregnate, *v.* [PRE- A. 1.] *trans.* To impregnate (a material) with something prior to mechanical processing. So **pre-i·mpregnated** *ppl. a.*, *spec.* (*a*) of paper insulation: impregnated with oil and resin before use in electric cables; of a cable: containing such insulation; (*b*) of reinforcing material for plastics: impregnated with synthetic resin before fabrication; **pre-impregna·tion.**

1933 *Jrnl. Inst. Electr. Engin.* LXXIII. 353/2 The design conditions are extremely simple as the dielectric depends solely on the use of the pre-impregnated paper, the selection of gas-space dimensions, and the pressure of the gas. **1937** *Ibid.* LXXXI. 634/1 With proper attention to the physical properties of the impregnating medium, this pre-impregnation ensures the absolute definition of the gas spaces up to the maximum working temperature of the cable. **1958** *Times* 1 Dec. 2/5 Aeroplastics Limited ..have commenced production of their new process of preimpregnating glass fabric. **1958** D. J. DUFFIN *Laminated Plastics* iv. 73 Either a dry or preimpregnated glass reinforcement is now laid in the mold. **1960** *Jrnl. Inst. Electr. Engin.* VI. 694/1 The pre-impregnated cable does not suffer from this kind of trouble because the paper is dried and impregnated in sheet form before application to the cable. **1965** *Mod. Plastics Encycl. 1966* 628/1 A pre-impregnation step is frequently used, in which the reinforcing web is passed through a resin bath before lay-up. **1970** *Materials & Technol.* III. xii. 871 Mats or fabrics are pre-impregnated with resin by passing through baths containing a solution of the resin. The solvents are removed by drying and the material is worked into mouldings. **1971** *Nature* 30 July 305/2 These preimpregnated layers are then moulded together in the normal way under heat and pressure, and cured.

pre-Inca: see *PRE- B. 2 a. **pre-Incaic:** *PRE- B. 1. **pre-increase:** *PRE- B. 2 a. **pre-incubate:** *PRE- A. 1. **pre-incubation:** *PRE- A. 2. **pre-industrial** to **-intellectual:** *PRE- B. 1. **pre-intimation:** *PRE- A. 2. **pre-invasion:** *PRE- B. 2 a. **pre-ionize:** *PRE- A. 1.

preiotation (prī,ɔiotēⁱ·ʃən). [f. PRE- A. 2 + IOT(A (here standing for the palatal glide *y*) + -ATION.] In the Slavonic languages, the development of a palatal glide before a vowel. So **preiotiza·tion**; **preio·tized** *a.*, preceded by a palatal glide.

1877 A. H. KEANE tr. *Hovelacque's Sci. of Lang.* 281 The Lithuanian *este* becomes *jeste* in Church Slavonic; and this 'prëiotation', as it is technically called, is a leading feature of all the Slavonic tongues. **1883** W. R. MORFILL *Slavonic Lit.* i. 18 The difficulty of expressing the præiotised vowels is the same. **1887** —— in *Encycl. Brit.* XXII. 148/2 The addition of a *y* sound before vowels is one of the great characteristics of the Slavonic languages, called 'præiotization'. **1959** G. NANDRIŞ *Old Church Slavonic Gram.* 6 The Glagolitic letters for preiotized ę and ǫ are ligatures.

pre-jazz: see *PRE- B. 2 a.

prejudice, *sb.* Add: **1. c.** *to terminate* (*dismiss*, etc.) *with extreme prejudice*: to kill, to assassinate. Hence *termination with extreme prejudice. U.S. slang.*

1972 B. F. CONNERS *Don't embarrass Bureau* (1973) II. 99 'A few years ago when he wanted an agent..out of the organization he ended up dismissing him with extreme prejudice.' 'You mean he had him killed?'.. Ted nodded. **1974** W. GARNER *Big enough Wreath* x. 123 'There is no question of anyone killing anybody.' 'There is. I'm asking it... Terminate with extreme prejudice?' **1974** F. NOLAN *Oshawa Project* xvi. 105 Had he been taken out by his own people?.. He had seen some of those files with the brutal red block letters stamped diagonally across the page: *Terminate with extreme prejudice.* **1980** C. PINCHER *Dirty Tricks* i. 10 A 'termination with extreme prejudice', as the CIA called its assassination projects in those days.

pre-junctural, -Kantian, -Keynesian: see *PRE- B. I. **preknow:** *PRE- A. I.

prelanguage, *sb.* and *a.* **A.** *sb.* (Stressed *pre·language*.) **1.** [PRE- B. I in Dict. and Suppl.] A form of communication preceding the emergence or acquisition of language.

1940 BRYANT & AIKEN *Psychol. of Eng.* iv. 33 What we may call 'pre-language' consisted of meaningful cries used exclusively in context to express emotions, messages, [etc.]. **1973** C. F. HOCKETT *Man's Place in Nature* xxv. 382 The lines of development we have described slowly gave rise to a vocal-auditory communicative system very different from a close call system: to an open system that we shall call *prelanguage*. *Ibid.*, Prelanguage was not language. **1978** *Verbatim* May 15/2 Language was supposed to begin with grammar, and prelanguage was in no way relevant to the development of speech.

2. [PRE- A. 2.] A hypothetical antecedent language.

1966 E. P. HAMP in Birnbaum & Puhvel *Anc. Indo-European Dial.* 107 This prelanguage would have arisen in Dacia.

B. *adj.* (Stressed *prela·nguage*.) [PRE- B. 2.] Prior to the emergence of language.

1964 *Language* XL. 240 Various prelanguage stages of development.

prelapsarian, *a.* (Further examples.)

Quot. 1934 is taken by 'H. MacDiarmid' from an unknown source.

1934 'H. MACDIARMID' *Stony Limits* 65 'The buoyant Prelapsarian naturalness of a country girl.' **1949** AUDEN *Nones* (1952) 36 Her pallid affected heroes Began their hectic quest for the prelapsarian man. **1972** *Time* 22 May 32/2 Nature unspoiled, inhabited by prelapsarian man. **1977** *Daily Tel.* 24 Mar. 15/5 Glenda Jackson's evocation of poet Stevie Smith suggests a woman of prelapsarian innocence.

prelatial, *a.* Add: Also, that is a prelate.

1886 F. G. LEE *King Edward VI* iii. 142 Both as regards what the prelatial preacher said, and what he did not say, it appeared..unsatisfactory and..inadequate.

pre-Latin: see *PRE- B. I. **pre-launch:** *PRE- B. 2 a.

pre-law (prīlǭ·), *a.* (*sb.*) *U.S.* [PRE- B. 2.] Of or pertaining to subjects studied in preparation for a course in law. Also *ellipt.* as *sb.*

1961 in WEBSTER. **1971** *Mod. Law Rev.* XXXIV. 650 Their North American counterparts who have undertaken significant pre-law work in another discipline. **1976** *National Observer* (U.S.) 21 Feb. 16/1 (Advt.), Undergraduate prelaw program, premed, and other preprofessional offerings. **1976** *Billings* (Montana) *Gaz.* 17 June 3-B/1 (Advt.), [She]..plans to attend the University of Montana in Missoula to study pre-law. **1978** *Detroit Free Press* 5 Mar. 9/1 Career training offered at Madonna for deaf students includes..pre-law and education.

pre-legislation: see *PRE- B. 2 a. **pre-let:** *PRE- A. I. **prelexical:** *PRE- B. I d. **pre-liberation, -life:** *PRE- B. 2 a.

prelim (prɪli·m, prī·lim), colloq. abbrev. of PRELIMINARY *sb.* and *a.* **a.** (See note *s.v.* PRELIMINARY *sb.* b in Dict.) A preliminary practice, examination, contest, inquiry, or report. Also *transf.*, a student in a preliminary class. Also *attrib.*

1891 C. DAWSON *Let.* 19 Feb. in R. S. Churchill *Winston S. Churchill* (1967) I. Compan. I. v. 228, I was so glad to hear you had successfully passed the 'Army Prelim', allow me to congratulate you. **1901** *Daily News* 1 Apr. 5/6 We arrived at Putney, just in time to see Oxford come out for their 'prelim'. **1902** *Daily Chron.* 19 Dec. 5/2 The English public school boy goes north for months of special tutoring for his 'prelim.'; thereat, probably, to fail in his English paper. **1904** *Daily News* 28 Dec. 6 While yet in the preliminary class,..she..said, 'I want a canvas six feet long.' 'What does she want with a six-foot canvas?.. She's only a "prelim"!' **1923** L. J. VANCE *Baroque* xxvii. 173 A fight that'd make the Dempsey-Carpenteeyay bout look like a cooked prelim. **1928** *Collier's* 18 Aug. 25/2 You're nothin' but a has-been, staggerin' around like some prelim boy. **1958** *Times* 17 Oct. 3/5 The general college rule which stipulates that undergraduates who twice fail 'prelims' should be sent down or rusticated. **1965** D. FRANCIS *Odds Against* vi. 86 I'll put one of the boys on to it and let you have a prelim. Is it urgent? **1974** N. FREELING *Dressing of Diamond* 41 I've been waiting to hear from you to set a prelim afoot. **1977** P. COSGRAVE *Cheyney's Law* ii. 17 Tommy went to Cambridge... His prelims were only fair.

b. Usu. in *pl.* The preliminary matter of a book. Cf. *PRELIMINARY *sb.* c.

1927 *Observer* 18 Dec. 4 He tells..about signatures, prelims, end-papers, uncut and unopened pages, issues and imperfections. **1932** *Times Lit. Suppl.* 7 Jan. 13/2 When, with the 'prelims' of 'The Painted Veil', he [*sc.* W. S. Maugham] comes up against a more important bibliographical problem, his description is confused. **1957** *Ibid.* 1 Nov. 664/3 Besides a few corrections in the text there are some notes in pencil among the prelims..and in ink on the back endpaper. **1960** [see *BLAD *sb.*[2] 2 c]. **1976** *Indexer* Oct. 93/2 The index..should be provided by the publisher much as he provides prelims and jacket copy.

prelimen (prɪlǝi·mǝn). [f. L. *præ* before + *līmen* threshold.] A preliminary step.

1898 C. S. SHERRINGTON in *Phil. Trans. R. Soc.* B. CXC. 50 The requisite prelimen to the original aim of the inquiry [having been] carried through, the examination of certain spinal reflexes has been proceeded to.

preliminary, *sb.* Add: **c.** Usu. in *pl.* The preliminary matter of a book. Cf. *PRELIM b.

1888 C. T. JACOBI *Printers' Vocab.* 103 *Preliminary*, any matter coming before the main text of a work—title, preface, contents, etc. **1903** A. E. HOUSMAN *Let.* 12 Feb. (1971) 64, I don't quite know the meaning of 'the preliminary', but I enclose the dedication which is to follow the title page. **1977** *N. & Q. for Somerset & Dorset* Sept. 301 The list of abbreviations on p. 70 would have been more usefully placed in the preliminaries.

prelingual, *a.* Add: **a.** (Further examples.)

1924 R. M. OGDEN tr. *Koffka's Growth of Mind* v. 322 The behaviour of the child during his pre-lingual period. **1976** *Word 1971* XXVII. 132 What constitutes semantic salience for the pre-lingual child?

b. [PRE- B. 3.] Located in front of the tongue.

1953 *Archivum Linguisticum* V. 69 According to their articulating points Marr's consonants fall into labial, 'prelingual' (dentialveolar and palatal), and 'postlingual' (velar and ultravelar).

prelingui·stic, *a.* and *sb.* [PRE- B. I.] **A.** *adj.* = PRELINGUAL *a.* a.

1900 H. SWEET *Hist. Lang.* iv. 39 Even in the prelinguistic stage in which gesture predominated, there must have been some principles of order. **1901** [see *INNER *a.* 2 b]. **1919** M. K. BRADBY *Psycho-Anal.* x. 133 A dream does..sometimes belong to a pre-linguistic stage of mental experience. **1941** *Mind* L. 421 Mentality will vanish with the rest of our intellectual heritage if we revert to our pre-linguistic apehood. **1951** TRAGER & SMITH *Outl. Eng. Struct.* 13 Prelinguistic data are now available. **1963** ERVIN & MILLER in J. A. Fishman *Readings Sociol. of Lang.* (1968) 70 The prelinguistic sounds of deaf and hearing children are indistinguishable in the first three months. **1972** *Language* XLVIII. 487 The identification of a prelinguistic stage has for decades rested on the intuition that everything which precedes the first utterance identifiable as a word is non-linguistic. **1979** N. LASH *Theol. on Dover Beach* ii. 29, I am not suggesting that there is..any such thing as pre-linguistic or non-linguistic human experience.

B. *sb. pl.* [-IC 2.] The study of biological and physiological aspects of speech.

1949 [see *MICROLINGUISTICS *sb. pl.*]. **1953** *Internat. Jrnl. Amer. Linguistics Memoir* VIII. 28 'Prelinguistics' studies the physical and biological aspects of speech. **1959** M. JOOS in J. A. Fishman *Readings Sociol. of Lang.* (1968) 186 This line, along which he [*sc.* the linguistic analyst] can shift items into the 'past' or the 'future' as he moves from pre-linguistics towards metalinguistics. **1964** CRYSTAL & QUIRK *Syst. Prosodic & Paralinguistic Features in Eng.* ii. 27 Speech results from activities which create a background of voice set ('the idiosyncratic, including the specific physiology of the speakers, and the total physical setting'). This is in the area of 'prelinguistics'.

pre-Linnean, -Listerian, -literary: see *PRE- B. I.

preli·terate, *a.* [PRE- B. I.] Applied to social groups or cultures which have not acquired a form of writing. Also as *sb.*, a person belonging to such a group or culture. Cf. *NON-LITERATE *a.*

1925 E. FARIS in *Amer. Jrnl. Sociol.* XXX. 710 For some time the writer has been using..the term 'preliterate' to designate the peoples of the *sociétiés inferieures*, as Lévy-Bruhl calls them. *Ibid.* 712 Pre-literate man is... one in whose culture there is no written literature. *Ibid.*, Pre-literates do not have cities. **1933** A. R. RADCLIFFE-BROWN in *Encycl. Social Sci.* IX. 202/1 The confusion which has resulted in the attempt to apply to preliterate societies the modern distinction between criminal law and civil law can be avoided. **1957** *Antiquity* XXXI. 211 Rubbish deposited in superimposed layers by preliterate men. **1962** E. R. SERVICE *Primitive Social Organization* i. 8 Where an Arunta-like way of life is not yet significantly altered by modern influences it is a culture that is primitive, ancient, and preliterate. **1966** E. G. STANLEY *Continuations & Beginnings* 127 To understand the use of tags and set phrases, whole half-lines of verse used repeatedly, it is useful to know about some kinds of preliterate composition. **1967** *N.Y. Rev. Bks.* 23 Feb. 33/3 He writes about the last 8000 years of preliterate Europe, which means that he excludes Greeks and Romans. **1970** [see *NON-LITERATE *a.*].

Hence **preli·teracy,** the quality or state of being preliterate.

1957 G. CLARK *Archaeol. & Society* (ed. 3) i. 22 Clearly.. some difference of opinion is likely to exist as to precisely at what stage preliteracy gives way to literacy. **1967** *N.Y. Rev. Bks.* 23 Feb. 33/1, I wish I knew who invented the word 'preliteracy' to indicate the illiteracy of certain extinct or living cultures... Preliteracy points to literacy as the next step in human evolution... In the latter part of the nineteenth century illiteracy was still illiteracy—not preliteracy.

pre·load, *sb.* [PRE- A. 2.] A load applied beforehand; *spec.* (*a*) one in a bearing or machine part (see *PRELOAD *v.*); (*b*) the tension in heart muscle at the end of diastole.

1941 *Motor Commerce* July 25/3 Adjust the pinion assembly to the correct bearing pre-load of 12 to 17 in.-lbs., and lock the adjusting nuts in position by a lock-washer. **1954** *Sun* (Baltimore) (B ed.) 3 Nov. 36/4 This earth pile acts as a preload or surcharge on the subsoil... The preload or surcharge is to get a settlement of the earth before the towers are constructed. **1962** *Amer. Jrnl. Physiol.* CCII. 936/1 Theoretically, with no load on the muscle, the velocity of shortening is maximal... Experimentally, the closest one can approach such a condition with heart muscle is to use the smallest preload from which a contraction occurs that produces analysable data. **1970** *Circulation Res.* XXVI. 114/1 The muscle is prestretched to a certain initial length using a 'preload', P, and temporarily fixed at that length. **1971** J. J. GREGORY in Ayres & Gregory *Cardiol.* xii. 225 Just as ventricular function may be evaluated by change in afterload, interventions that alter preload may also be utilized to test myocardial function. **1971** *Power Farming* Mar. 71/1 Dynamic loading in a tightened bolt may vary from no stress at all to that exceeding the bolt's preload. **1972** H. E. ELLINGER *Automechanics* xxiii. 400 Pinion preload is sufficient to eliminate any end play in the pinion shaft and still low enough to prevent bearing damage. **1976** *Circulation* LIII. 298/2 In the intact heart it is impossible to completely separate preload from afterload.

preloa·d, *v.* [PRE- A. I.] *trans.* To load beforehand; *spec.* in *Engin.*, to design or make (a bearing or machine part) in such a way that there are internal loads independent of any working load (e.g. to reduce noise in operation).

1945 R. K. ALLAN *Rolling Bearings* x. 253 Another method..is to preload the bearings by axial adjustment. **1950** O. J. HORGER in M. Hetényi *Handbk. Exper. Stress Analysis* xi. 556 Seeger investigated the fatigue resistance of hollow shafts which were preloaded axially so as to produce compressive prestress below yield-strength value of the steel. **1952** C. H. DIX *Seismic Profiling for Oil* iii. 44 In some cases it is desirable to drill several shot holes, preload each one of them, and not plan to reshoot any of them. **1969** W. WRIGLEY et al. *Gyroscopic Theory* xiv. 324 When two ball bearings are preloaded against each other, the result is a much stiffer assembly. **1969** *Jane's Freight Containers 1968–69* 439 (*caption*) They are pre-loaded and sealed by shippers.

So **preloa·ded** *ppl. a.*, **preloa·ding** *vbl. sb.*

1936 *Brit. Pat.* 471,989, The object of our invention is to provide improved brake-operating mechanism which permits a pre-loaded spring to be used in conjunction with compensation between the brakes on the front and rear wheels of a vehicle for normal braking. **1941** *Automobile Engineer* XXXI. 180/3 Owing to the substantial design of the housing it has not been found necessary to employ pre-loading of the bearings. **1945** R. K. ALLAN *Rolling Bearings* x. 235 The primary object of preloading is to eliminate..radial and/or axial movements in a bearing when it is functioning in a machine. **1962** *John o' London's* 22 Feb. 182/2 The dice are, as it were, already pre-loaded. **1969** W. WRIGLEY et al. *Gyroscopic Theory* xiv. 324 Under the preloaded condition, the pair of bearings have axial and radial stiffnesses vs. load which are very nearly constant. **1971** B. SCHARF *Engin. & its Lang.* xii. 137 Preloading is frequently used in high precision work and in order to ensure noiseless running. **1976** ATTEWELL & FARMER *Princ. Engin. Geol.* xi. 826 Any pre-loading or the application of consolidation pressure must..start with the condition that the initial stresses applied to the soil are less than the existing shear strength of the soil.

pre-logic: see *PRE- B. I.

prelo·gical, *a.* [PRE- B. I.] Preceding or prior to logic or logical reasoning; chiefly in *Anthrop.*, applied to the thinking of persons or cultural groups which is based on myth, magic, etc. Also *transf.* and *absol.*

1893 C. S. PEIRCE *Coll. Papers* (1933) IV. I. iv. 62 The whole of the theory of numbers belongs to logic; or rather, it would do so, were it not, as pure mathematics, *prelogical*, that is, even more abstract than logic. **1923** L. A. CLARE tr. *Lévy-Bruhl's Primitive Mentality* ii. 91 To prelogical mentality, cause and effect present themselves in two forms, not essentially different from one another. **1926** —— tr. *Lévy-Bruhl's How Natives Think* I. ii. 78 By designating it [*sc.* the mentality of primitives] 'prelogical' I merely wish to state that it does not bind itself down, as our thought does, to avoiding contradiction. **1933** H. READ *Art Now* I. 34 Art conceived as a stage in the ideal history of mankind, as a pre-logical mode of expression, as something necessary and inevitable and organic. **1935** *Mind* XLIV. 544 Insistence on the alogical, or prelogical, character of the aesthetic consciousness. **1943** *Amer. Speech* XVIII. 220 The first stage of human development ..is that of the savage, prelogical mentality, with a one-valued semantics (or system of evaluations), in which.. 'everything is everything else' by 'mystic participation'. **1959** *Spectator* 11 Sept. 339/3 If we seek the pre-logical and oppose the march of intellect, we are the enemies of science..and the worshippers of myth. **1967** C. L. MARKMANN tr. *Fanon's Black Skin, White Masks* (1968) vi. 159 The prelogical thought of the phobic has decided that such is the case. **1977** G. W. Hewes in D. M. Rumbaugh *Lang. Learning by Chimpanzee* i. 28 Early language was also characteristically 'prelogical'.

pre-London: see *pre- B. 2 a. **pre-lubricate:** *pre- A. 1.

prelude, *sb.* Add: **2.** (Later examples of sense 'an introduction, preface (to a literary work)'.)
1889 *Mod. Lang. Notes* IV. 350 Grein's sixteenth Canto of the 'Christ'.., is a transitional passage... The whole passage forms a kind of interlude, while it is also a prelude to Part III. **1892** J. Earle *Deeds of Beowulf* p. xxiv, It is not easy to account for this Prelude, which really throws no light on the poem, nor in any way helps the narrative.

prelude, *v.* Add: **1. b.** (Further example.)
1915 J. Buchan *Nelson's Hist. War* II. ix. 34 Von Kluck preluded it [*sc.* an enveloping movement] by a heavy bombardment of Binche and Bray.
3. a. (Later example.)
a **1945** E. R. Eddison *Mezentian Gate* (1958) xxxix. 214 The musicians tuned their instruments, preluded and, when the murmur of talk was stilled.., struck up a cavatina.
Hence **prelu·dingly** *adv.*, in a prelusive manner. *rare.*
1932 J. Joyce in *New Statesman* 27 Feb. 261/1 Preludingly he conspews a portugaese into the gutter, recitativing.

Preludin (prĭli̯ū·din). *Pharm.* Also **preludin.** A proprietary name for phenmetrazine hydrochloride.
1954 *Trade Marks Jrnl.* 17 Mar. 270/1 *Preludin*... All goods included in class 1 [*i.e.* chemical products used in industry, science, etc.]. Albert Boehringer, [*et al.*].., trading as C. H. Boehringer Sohn, Ingelheim am Rhein.., Germany; manufacturers. **1955** *Official Gaz.* (U.S. Patent Office) 13 Sept. TM59/2 C. H. Boehringer Sohn, Ingelheim am Rhein, Germany..*Preludin*. For anti-depressant and anti-obesity drug. Use since April 1, 1954. **1955** *Chem. Abstr.* XLIX. 8566 (*heading*) Identification of Preludin (2-phenyl-3-methylmorpholine) and Ritalin..before and after passage through the body. **1957** *Brit. Med. Jrnl.* 5 Jan. 30/2 'Preludin', a new drug for controlling the appetite, is, I believe, gaining popularity among those who.. try to slim. It was discovered in 1953 and first marketed in Germany in 1954. **1959** [see *phenmetrazine]. **1960** *Spectator* 22 July 120/3 A few weeks ago we criticised the irrationality of the campaign then being waged by some newspapers against the pep-pill Preludin. **1970** Passmore & Robson *Compan. Med. Stud.* II. v. 39/1 Appetite suppressant drugs include phenmetrazine (preludin), chlorphentermine and diethylpropion (tenuate). Their value in this respect is limited and emotional dependence has been reported. **1974** M. C. Gerald *Pharmacol.* xv. 286 Phenmetrazine (Preludin) swept the market in Sweden after its introduction..in 1955. This drug..continues to be the abused drug of choice in Sweden. **1976** D. Hare *Teeth 'n' Smiles* i. 20 *Anson*: Is that heroin? *Peyote*: Preludin. *Anson*: Ah. Preludin is a fuck-pump... It enlarges your sexual capacity.

preludize, *v.* Add: (Earlier and later examples.)
1842 J. R. Planché *White Cat* 1. 9 The leader preludizes on the violin. **1978** *Gramophone* Feb. 1389/3 When at a recital Hans von Bülow had to follow a singer of whom he thought little he would sometimes sit at the piano and preludize for a moment or two on the passage from Beethoven's Ninth Symphony.

prelu:mirhodo·psin. *Biochem.* [Pre- A. 2.] An isomer of rhodopsin, stable only at very low temperatures, which is formed by the action of light on rhodopsin and changes spontaneously to lumirhodopsin.
1963 Yoshizawa & Wald in *Nature* 30 Mar. 1280/1 The intermediate was shown to be stable to about −140°, above which it forms lumirhodopsin. We shall call it prelumirhodopsin. **1968** A. White et al. *Princ. Biochem.* (ed. 4) xl. 904 After pre-lumirhodopsin is formed by the isomerization of one double bond, all subsequent steps proceed spontaneously. **1976** *Nature* 5 Feb. 424/2 The results of a picosecond study indicated that the formation of prelumirhodopsin when rhodopsin is irradiated probably involves a restricted change in the geometry of retinal rather than a complete isomerisation. *Ibid.* 22 Apr. 726/2 In the photolysis of the visual pigment rhodopsin the intermediate first observed is bathorhodopsin (formerly called prelumirhodopsin).

pre-lunch: see *pre- B. 2 a.

pre-lu·ncheon, *sb.* and *a.* **A.** *sb.* [Pre- A. 2.] A light mid-day meal preceding luncheon.
1873 C. M. Yonge *Pillars of House* II. xvi. 110 A preluncheon or nooning of cake and wine within an hour of the meal of the day.
B. *adj.* [Pre- B. 2.] Held or occurring before luncheon.
1975 *N.Y. Times* 29 Aug. 29/1 The four actors..did a jungle scream in unison for the press at a preluncheon cocktail party.

prem (prem), *sb.* and *a.* [Abbrev. of *premature *a.* or *sb.*] **A.** *sb.* A premature baby. **B.** *adj.* Premature; of or pertaining to premature babies.
1953 Baker *Australia Speaks* vi. 142 *Prem*, a hospital term for a premature baby. **1960** *News Chron.* 18 Mar. 8/6 Children's specialists are improving the outlook for 'prems'—frail, under-developed babies, some born too soon. **1961** *News of World* 23 Apr. 13 My last was three months prem. **1962** G. Butler *Coffin in Oxford* ix. 126 Father Mahoney was standing..at the end of the corridor by the nursery and 'prems' block. **1963** L. Diack *Labrador Nurse* xxix. 142 I've got a lovely prem. Four pounds. **1972** R. Lewis *Fool for Client* ii. 44 My daughter..was took bad in the night and they think the baby is going to be a prem. **1976** 'D. Halliday' *Dolly & Nanny Bird* iii. 41 The last time I heard her whisper like that, the incubator lights had cut out in a prem ward.

pre-machine: see *pre- A. 1, B. 2 a.

pre-ma·ke-ready. *Printing.* [Pre- A. 2.] (See quots.)
1948 R. R. Karch *Graphic Arts Procedures* x. 256 Premakeready includes those operations done in advance of placing the form on the printing press. **1964** *Gloss. Letterpress Rotary Printing Terms* (*B.S.I.*) 16 *Pre-make ready*, the operations relating to the obtaining of a good printing result which take place before the printing plates or formes go to the press. **1967** V. Strauss *Printing Industry* vii. 423/2 Pre-makeready is..that part of quality control in letterpress which deals with the printing-image carrier and has the purpose of reducing to a minimum the time spent for makeready of type forms on the press.

premalignant, -Malthusian: see *pre- B. 1.

pre-man, *sb.* and *a.* **A.** *sb.* [Pre- B. 1 in Dict. and Suppl.] (Stressed *pre·-man.*) A hominid or man-like creature that lived before the appearance of man, *Homo erectus* and *H. sapiens.* **B.** *adj.* [Pre- B. 2.] (Stressed *pre-ma·n.*) Occurring or belonging to the time before the appearance of man.
1921 H. G. Wells *Short Stories* (1927) 687 Men, our ancestors, had their first glimpse of the pre-men of the wilderness. **1947** *Sci. Illustr.* Sept. 60/1 Desert so devoid of life that it takes the visitor back to pre-man time on earth. **1953** J. S. Huxley *Evolution in Action* vi. 136 We can distinguish..three stages in the physical evolution of man. First, the deployment of the pre-men. **1971** J. Z. Young *Introd. Study Man* xxxiii. 457 Up to the stage that may be called pre-man (*Australopithecus*) the changes were gradual. **1977** *Time* 7 Nov. 48/1 Leakey has found more and better pre-man and early man fossils than any other anthropologist.

Premarin (prĭmēᵊ·rin). *Pharm.* Also **premarin.** [f. Pre(gnant *a.*[2] + Mar(e[1] + -in[1].] A proprietary name for a mixture of œstrogenic compounds obtained from the urine of pregnant mares and used in the treatment of various conditions, esp. those caused by or involving œstrogen deficiency.
1942 *Official Gaz.* (U.S. Patent Office) 21 July 498/1 Ayerst, McKenna & Harrison (United States) Limited, Rouses Point, N.Y...*Premarin*. For pharmaceutical preparations for the treatment of ovarian deficiencies. Claims use since Feb. 24, 1942. **1944** *Jrnl. Amer. Med. Assoc.* 19 Aug. 1098/2 Premarin.—An amorphous preparation containing the naturally occurring, water soluble, conjugated forms of the mixed estrogens obtained from the urine of pregnant mares. *Ibid.*, Premarin Tablets. **1956** *Trade Marks Jrnl.* 2 May 312/1 *Premarin*... Estrogenic preparations. Ayerst, McKenna & Harrison, Limited.., St. Laurent, Quebec, Canada; manufacturers and merchants. **1961** *Lancet* 2 Sept. 504/2 In these patients continued administration of premarin resulted in a suggestive, though inconclusive, improvement in mortality as compared with a comparable control group. **1977** *Ibid.* 19 Nov. 1063/1 A two to three fold increase in the incidence of ovarian cancer was recorded in women treated for menopausal symptoms with 'Premarin' (conjugated equine œstrogens) usually combined with stilbœstrol.

prema·rital, *a.* [Pre- B. 1.] Occurring before marriage.
1886 [in Dict. s.v. Pre- B. 1]. **1915** T. F. A. Smith *Soul of Germany* v. 97 During his pre-marital years he may form many such irregular acquaintanceships. **1937** A. Huxley *Let.* 17 Dec. (1969) 430 As to pre-marital continence, there is a great deal of evidence that this is important if there is to be higher education. **1951** M. McLuhan *Mech. Bride* (1967) 32/1 The tendency of the modern housewife, after a premarital spell in the business world, to embrace marriage and children but not housework. **1963** A. Heron *Towards Quaker View of Sex* i. 6 An increase in transient pre-marital sexual intimacies. **1976** *Drum* (E. Afr. ed.) Nov. 26/1, I think your girl is one of those sensible ones who do not like to indulge in pre-marital sex. **1980** 'R. Deacon' *Spy!* iii. 70 It was essential to cover up this pre-marital affair.
Hence **prema·ritally** *adv.*
1973 S. Fisher *Understanding Female Orgasm* ii. 34 Religiosity plays a role in how sexually active women are premaritally. **1975** R. H. Rimmer *Premar Experiments* (1976) i. 108 They aren't fully aware of the impact that freer and open sexuality, premaritally and postmaritally, will have on human goals and values.

pre-market(ing): see *pre- B. 2 a.

prematuration (premătiūrēⁱ·ʃən, prĭmætiurēⁱ·ʃən), *sb.* [f. Prematur(e *a.* (*adv.*) + -ation.]
1. The fact of making or becoming mature unnaturally early.
1909 *Westm. Gaz.* 3 Feb. 2/1 The systems followed in the schools of the leading civilised races of the world make for prematuration.
2. [after F. *prématuration* premature birth.] = Prematureness. *rare*⁻¹.
1977 A. Sheridan tr. *Lacan's Écrits* iv. 137 This is a point that I think I have myself helped to elucidate by conceiving the dynamics of the so-called *mirror stage* as a consequence of a prematuration at birth.

prematuration (prĭmætiurēⁱ·ʃən), *a.* [f. Pre- B. 2 + Maturation.] Occurring before maturation.
1919 T. H. Morgan *Physical Basis Heredity* xii. 142 Most of the eggs pass through this early prematuration stage in the larvæ and some of them may reach the maturation stage in the pupa. **1974** *Austral. Jrnl. Agric. Res.* XXV. 883 Only in one cultivar..could a difference in rate of development between samples be attributed with any confidence to pre-maturation cold acquisition.

premature, *a.* (*adv.*). Add: Also pronounced (premătiūᵊ·ɹ) in predicative use. **2. b.** *Obstetrics.* Born or occurring before full term (but usu. after the stage when the fœtus normally becomes viable).
1754 W. Smellie *Coll. Cases & Observations in Midwifery* II. xiii. 213 (*heading*) On the situation of the child during pregnancy, the signs of conception and premature labour. **1775** A. Hamilton *Elem. Pract. Midwifery* 122 When a woman miscarries in early Gestation, *this* they consider as an Abortion; but, if in the later Months, *that* they term a Premature Birth. **1800** *Med. Facts & Observations* VIII. 190 She has since borne six children by premature labour. **1840** [see *induction 9]. **1878** *Obstetr. Jrnl.* VI. 163 (*heading*) Case illustrating the viability of extremely small premature children. **1923** J. H. Hess *Premature & Congenitally Diseased Infants* iii. 40 Heat regulation is one of the least developed functions of the premature infants. **1924** C. Mackenzie *Heavenly Ladder* xviii. 244 The shock brought on a premature travail, and she was delivered of a boy in the Vicarage. **1969** D. Baird *Combined Textbk. Obstetr. & Gynæcol.* (ed. 8) xxxiii. 544 By international agreement a 'premature' infant has been defined as one weighing 2,500 g. (5½ lb.) or less at birth. **1973** *Sci. Amer.* May 27/2 Most of the mothers in the experimental group had had a premature baby (gestation period less than 38 weeks).
c. *premature ejaculation* (see quot. 1974); = *ejaculatio præcox.
1910 A. Abrams *Diagnostic Therapeutics* iii. 230 Occasionally onanism is followed by various grades of impotency (usually psychic) and premature ejaculation. **1925**, **1928** [see *ejaculatio præcox]. **1942** T. P. Wolfe tr. *Reich's Function of Orgasm* v. 138 Hysterical men suffer either from erective impotence or premature ejaculation. **1968** T. Wiseman *Quick & Dead* 140, I with my quick grin and premature ejaculations. **1974** Passmore & Robson *Compan. Med. Stud.* III. xxxv. 34/1 Partial impotence is common and may take the form of a failure to ejaculate or ejaculation before entry into the vagina or before orgasm is reached, i.e. premature ejaculation.
B. *sb.* *Obstetrics.* A child born before full term.
1900 in Dorland *Med. Dict.* **1923** J. H. Hess *Premature & Congenitally Diseased Infants* xiv. 313 In the premature especially the skin is delicate, lacking the horny layer. **1960** A. K. Geddes *Premature Babies* iii. 18 An irregular respiratory rhythm is normal for prematures.

premature (pre·mătiūᵊɹ), *v.* *Mil.* [f. Premature *a.*] *intr.* Of a shell or other projectile: to explode prematurely. Of a gun: to fire a shell that explodes prematurely. Hence **pre·maturing** *ppl. a.*
1916 'Boyd Cable' *Doing their Bit* v. 83 A shrapnel prematuring at the muzzle, and the bullets that should have gone lifting high and clear inside the case smashing, perhaps, into the open rear of a gun-emplacement or a battery a few hundred yards in front of the prematuring gun. **1918** G. Frankau *Judgement of Valhalla* 49 Behind, a cratered slope, with batteries Crashing and flashing, violet in the dusk, And prematuring every now and then.

prematurely, *adv.* Add: **b.** *spec.* in *Obstetrics.*
1812 *Medico-Chirug. Trans.* III. 137, I have however now before me, a list of *seventy-eight* labours occurring prematurely, either from the spontaneous action of the womb, or from accidental violence. **1902** *Brit. Med. Jrnl.* 17 May 1197/2 The dry mouth and the weak digestion, and the frequency of gastro-intestinal disorders in the prematurely born are matters of every-day observation. **1943** *Lancet* 9 Dec. 320/1 An infant, prematurely born, is, although in a normal stage of development, inadequately prepared to contend against the operation of external agents.

prematurity. Add: **3.** (Later examples.)
1927 *Times Lit. Suppl.* 10 Feb. 90/3 Our advice is to save this book for a dismally wet afternoon: tea will arrive with a startling prematurity. **1961** E. A. Powdrill *Vocab. Land Planning* iii. 45 The term 'prematurity' is used by planners, very often as a sort of delaying action in grounds of refusal. *Ibid.* 46 Thus, the term 'prematurity', used in the sense of preventing something from happening in advance of the proper time, also implies that at some future date the proposal could be approved.
4. *Obstetrics.* The birth of a baby before full term.
1875 *Trans. Edin. Obstetr. Soc.* III. 260, I have seen nothing to warrant me viewing prematurity—that is, at and after the seventh month—as necessarily convertible with debility. **1902** *Brit. Med. Jrnl.* 17 May 1196/2 In this contribution the type of prematurity which is considered is that of the infant expelled from the uterus at the seventh month of intrauterine life. **1937** A. Tow *Dis. of Newborn* iii. 63 More careful antepartum care has definitely lowered the incidence of prematurity. **1971** *Sci. Amer.*

Oct. 118/2 Prematurity from spontaneous abortion, affecting approximately one pregnancy in 10, is the main source of mortality.

pre-matutinal: see *PRE- B. 1 d.

pre-med (prī·me·d), *a.* (*sb.*[1]) Chiefly *U.S.* Colloq. abbrev. of *PREMEDICAL *a.* (*sb.*).

1962 E. SNOW *Red China Today* (1963) xxxv. 263, I finished my pre-med work in three years and won a scholarship to the American University in Beirut. **1971** 'S. RANSOME' *Trap 6* (1972) iii. 27 He's about to begin his premed courses and he's not sure whether he'll make it all the way through to his M.D. **1972** W. P. MCGIVERN *Caprifoil* (1973) xiii. 212 London told us you did a year of pre-med at Birmingham University. **1977** *Time* 28 Mar. 70/3 After high school Lily entered Detroit's Wayne State University as a premed student because 'I wanted to be a doctor'. **1978** *Detroit Free Press* 5 Mar. 9/1 Career training offered at Madonna for deaf students includes art, journalism, public relations, pre-med and pre-dentistry [etc.].

pre-med (prī·me·d, prī·med), *sb.*[2] Colloq. abbrev. of *PREMEDICATION. Also *attrib.*

1964 D. FRANCIS *Nerve* vi. 64 A brisk nurse told us he was going to the operating theatre within minutes and not to disturb the patient, as he had been given his pre-med. **1974** C. FREMLIN *By Horror Haunted* 110 The shaving, the marking-up, the pre-med injections. **1977** *Observer* 4 Sept. 22/1 You'll get a pre-med, a jab to make you drowsy, at about ten.

preme·dical, *a.* (*sb.*) Chiefly *U.S.* [PRE- B. 1.] Of, pertaining to, or designating subjects studied in preparation for a medical course. Also *ellipt.*, a premedical course of studies. Cf. *PRE-MED *a.* (*sb.*[1]).

1904 *Bot. Gaz.* XXXVII. 225 This general text-book of botany is written for premedical and pharmaceutical students in particular. **1928** *Brit. Med. Jrnl.* 1 Sept. 363/2 The elementary sciences, the pre-medical subjects of chemistry, physics, biology, and botany, are in the curriculum to familiarize the student with the structure and behaviour of the materials with which, and upon which, he will have to work. **1940** A. HUXLEY *Let.* 7 July (1969) 455 Matthew has got through his second year of pre-medical quite well. **1961** *Lancet* 26 Aug. 484/1 Major Titov's first question, on returning from Space recently, concerned his wife's premedical examination results. **1976** *New Yorker* 16 Feb. 41/3 They reserved their serious efforts for the medievalists, true scientists, linguists, prelaw and pre-medical students, other scholars.

preme·dicant. [PRE- A. 2.] A drug given as premedication. Also *attrib.*

1960 *Proc. R. Soc. Med.* LIII. 673/1 The sister in charge administered the premedicant combinations in rotation, leaving the anaesthetist and the assessor in ignorance of the drugs given to particular patients. **1964** *Brit. Jrnl. Anaesthesia* XXXVI. 703/1 When evaluating the effects of various premedicants, the authors were impressed with the very high incidence of pre-operative vomiting and nausea which occurred when pethidine 100 mg was given alone. **1971** PRYOR & MACALISTER *Gen. Anaesthetic & Sedation Techniques for Dentistry* ix. 60 The description of premedicant drugs earlier in this chapter should enable the anaesthetist to select appropriate combinations for any particular circumstance. **1977** *Lancet* 10 Dec. 1229/2 Anæsthetic premedicants include the minor tranquillisers (e.g., diazepam), major tranquillisers (e.g., droperidol), barbiturates, and opiates, but all possess undesirable side-effects.

preme·dicate, *v.* [PRE- A. 1.] *trans.* To give preparatory medication to, now esp. before anæsthesia. Hence **preme·dicating** *vbl. sb.*

1846 [in Dict. s.v. PRE- A. 1]. **1940** MACINTOSH & PRATT *Essent. Gen. Anæsthesia* x. 91 The dose of premedicating drug a patient will require can often be roughly gauged by his resistance to alcohol. **1972** *Nature* 15 Dec. 411/1 Before the injection..patients were premedicated with 100 mg of pethidine.

Hence **premedica·tion,** medication given prior to or in preparation for the main treatment; *spec.* a pre-anæsthetic. Cf. *PRE-MED *sb.*[2]

1926 *Surg., Gynecol. & Obstetr.* XLIII. 103/2 All patients received as a premedication half a gram of veronal and 2 centigrams of morphine. **1932** *Brit. Jrnl. Anaesthesia* IX. 41 For the purpose of this discussion, by *premedication* is understood a new conception of preanaesthetic medication, whereby the patient is rendered unconscious in his bed before the administration of the anaesthetic. **1965** J. POLLITT *Depression & its Treatment* iv. 57 If an emergency operation must be performed.., the combination of chlorpromazine..and a barbiturate..is effective as premedication.

premeditate, *v.* **1.** (Later examples.)

1929 S. LESLIE *Anglo-Catholic* xvi. 231 Your Aquin often premeditated modern theories, but he is generally truest..when his followers or commentators try their hardest to explain him away. **1965** K. SISAM *Struct. Beowulf* 3 *Beowulf*, with more lapses and more use of devices that help an improviser, has many of the marks of premeditated art.

pre-meiotic to **-Mendelian:** see *PRE- B. 1.

premenopau·sal, *a. Med.* [PRE- B. 1.] Of or pertaining to the years preceding the menopause.

1939 *Jrnl. Clin. Investigation* XVIII. 177/2 The pituitaries from premenopausal individuals were low in gonadotropic potency. **1944** *Jrnl. Clin. Endocrinol.* IV. 577/1 While anovulatory cycles may occur at any age, it seems certain that they are far more common in the premenopausal years than they are in younger women. **1956** C. F. FLUHMANN *Managem. Menstrual Disorders* xxv. 322 A series of 173 hospital patients over forty years of age with various types of abnormal uterine bleeding are illustrative of the 'premenopausal' period. **1975** *Lancet* 5 July 7/2, 6 women were premenopausal, with ages ranging from thirty-two to forty-four years.

So **preme·nopause,** the stage of a woman's life immediately preceding the menopause.

1941 MAZER & ISRAEL *Diagn. & Treatm. Menstrual Disorders* xxi. 308 A number of clinicians reported favorably on the use of testosterone propionate in cases of dysfunctional uterine bleeding, especially that of the premenopause. **1957** *Amer. Jrnl. Obstetr. & Gynecol.* LXXIII. 985 Since the average age of menopause in the American white woman is 46, it appears that age 40 would be the beginning of the premenopause. **1968** R. W. KISTNER in Astwood & Cassidy *Clin. Endocrinol.* II. vi. ix. 697 Effective treatment of the premenopause should.. produce regular, but not excessive, uterine bleeding.

preme·nstrual, *a.* [PRE- B. 1.] Occurring before menstruation; *premenstrual tension*, tension felt prior to menstruation. Also *transf.*

1885 [see *POSTMENSTRUAL *a.*]. **1928** *Jrnl. Amer. Med. Assoc.* 14 Jan. 109/1 With Premenstrual Tension.—This was shown by a considerable group of women and manifesting [*sic*] itself by extreme nervousness, symptoms of autonomic imbalance, irritability, psychic changes and a feeling of tremendous tension. **1943** *Amer. Jrnl. Dis. Children* LXV. 302 The premenstrual state persisted, and fifteen months later the child menstruated. **1954** G. I. M. SWYER *Reproduction & Sex* iv. 43 The 'premenstrual tension' of which some women complain. **1970** R. LOWELL *Notebk.* 72 Revolution, Drugging her terrible premenstrual cramps, Marches..to storm the city. **1974** J. COOPER *Women & Super Women* 11 Other occupations are.. smashing crockery from pre-menstrual tension. **1978** F. WELDON *Praxis* xxii. 203 You're hysterical. I expect you're pre-menstrual.

Hence **preme·nstrually** *adv.*

1931 *Arch. Neurol. & Psychiatry* XXVI. 1054 The blood of this patient showed twice the amount of female sex hormone that is normally found premenstrually. **1973** J. ZUBIN *Contemp. Sexual Behavior* viii. 160 Mean levels of hostility are highest premenstrually.

preme·nstruum. *Med.* [f. PRE- B. 1 in Dict. and Suppl. + MENSTRUUM.] The stage of the menstrual cycle which precedes menstruation.

1910 *Trans. N.Y. Obstetr. Soc. 1909–11* 229 In the third stage called by them [*sc.* Hitchmann & Adler] the premenstruum, the mucous membrane which is now thick and velvety, can be divided into a superficial, compact, and deeper, spongy layer. **1938** *Jrnl. Amer. Med. Assoc* 21 May 1722/1 During the premenstruum, the concentration of estrogen in the blood rises and affects the sympathetic nervous system. **1969** *Sunday Times* 14 Sept. 54/3 Crimes of violence by women, most often involving their own families, are more often committed during the premenstruum. **1977** *Lancet* 24/31 Dec. 1330/2 It is common knowledge that exacerbations of acne and skin allergies occur during the premenstruum.

preme·tallize, *v.* [PRE- A. 1.] *trans.* To convert (a dye) before use into a metal chelate form by treatment with a metal salt, usu. in order to improve fastness properties. Hence **preme·tallized** *ppl. a.*

1948 KIRK & OTHMER *Encycl. Chem. Technol.* II. 252 The formation of the metallic complex can be accomplished as an after-treatment, or the dye can be premetallized and applied to the fiber in the form of its soluble alkali salt. **1949** *Jrnl. Soc. Dyers & Colourists* LXV. 490/2 Ultralan Orange RS—This is a premetallised dye giving bright oranges when applied from strongly acid dyebaths, under which conditions the most level dyeings are obtained. **1963** A. J. HALL *Textile Sci.* ii. 82 Nylon can also be dyed with wool and cotton dyes (notably the acid wool dyes, pre-metallised dyes and direct cotton dyes). **1963** *Times* 31 May 19/6 The use of premetallised dyes for wool has also increased..despite the poor trading conditions in the textile printing industry.

premiation (prīmiēi·ʃən). *rare.* [f. as PREMIATE *v.*] Reward; the act of rewarding, a prize-giving.

a **1490** JOHANNES DE IRLANDIA *Meroure of Wyssdome* (1965) II. 53 And þocht euirilk man and ressonable creatur incontinent eftir þar deid and partyn furth of the waurld have certane knaulage of þar dampnacioun or premiacioun [etc.]. **1930** J. RITCHIE in *Scots College, Rome* iii. 93 We witnessed two great functions. The first was a premiation at the Gregorian University when..we saw John Joseph Dyer..marching up for his gold medals.

premie, var. *PREEMIE.

premier, *a.* and *sb.* Add: **B.** *sb.* **b.** (Further Canad. examples.)

This sense is now *obs.* in *Austral.* and *Canad.* usage: cf. sense B. c below and note *s.v.* PRIME MINISTER 3 b in Dict.

1883 *Brandon* (Manitoba) *Daily Mail* 29 Jan. 2/1 It says that several of those roughly classed as Ministerialists will in all probability vote 'no confidence' in the present Premier. **1916** A. BRIDLE *Sons of Canada* 14 It is of prime importance to remember how..so impersonal a figure ever came to be Premier of Canada.

c. *Austral.* and *Canad.* The chief minister of a State or Province.

1853 *Hamilton* (Ontario) *Gaz.* 3 Oct. 2/6 In the prosecution of this singularly dignified scheme—we shall say nothing of its abstract honesty—the Premier scruples not to employ the influence which his position invests him with. **1902** *Parl. Debates Austral. 1901–2* XI. 14528/2 Is it the case, as stated by the Premier of Queensland, that he (the Premier) has made repeated applications for a detailed statement of the receipts and expenditure of the departments transferred to the Commonwealth, and that such statement has not yet been supplied to him. **1917** N. MCNEIL in J. O. Miller *New Era in Canada* 197 Why did Honoré Mercier, as Premier of Quebec, place a reference to the Pope in the preamble of his Jesuits Estates Bill? **1929** M. DE LA ROCHE *Whiteoaks* xi. 151 Look at the situation in the Province of Quebec! There the women have no vote. 'We are Latins!' their Premier exclaims. **1930** W. K. HANCOCK *Australia* x. 209 In 1916 a Labour Premier of New South Wales..handed his resignation, not to the official head of the State, but to caucus. **1969** T. JENKINS *We came to Australia* I. ii. 30 Australia has a Prime Minister in the capital, Canberra, but..each of its six States has its own 'local' Prime Minister, known as a Premier. **1972** *Ann. Reg. 1971* 79 On 21 October the Progressive Conservative Party in Ontario under a new Premier, Mr William Davis, retained power with an increased majority winning 78 seats.

d. *U.S.* The Secretary of State. ?*Obs.*

1855 *N.Y. Herald* 22 Nov. 4/4 The casting vote between the Premier and the Kitchen is subject to the caprices and vacillations of the President, whose official position makes him supreme over both the action of the premier and the counsels of the Kitchen. **1878** *Harper's Mag.* Mar. 490/2 The diplomatic anteroom, where foreign dignitaries await audience with the Premier, is handsome in its appointments. **1886** E. ALTON *Among Law-Makers* vii. 68 The Secretary of State..is sometimes (though not accurately) referred to as 'The Premier'. **1905** *Washington Post* 21 Mar. 4 Elihu Root..is ideally equipped for the duties of the Department of State, but it is considered unlikely that he could be induced to return to the Cabinet, even as premier. **1925** W. H. SMITH *Hist. Cabinet U.S.A.* 28 He [*sc.* the Secretary of State] is frequently spoken of as the 'premier' of the cabinet, but there is no such title or designation known to our laws.

e. The Prime Minister of a country other than Great Britain or one of its colonies or a nation belonging to the British Commonwealth. Also used as a title prefixed to the surname of a premier.

1936 [see *MEIJI]. **1942** W. S. CHURCHILL *End of Beginning* (1943) 14 We sent Premier Stalin—for that I gather is how he wishes to be addressed..—exactly what he asked for. **1961** *N.Y. Times* 21 May IV. 1 Premier Khrushchev has made propaganda capital out of that fact. **1976** *Daily Tel.* 20 July 4/1 This is assumed to refer to some sort of demonstration similar to April's Peking riot by supporters of Teng and the late Premier Chou En-lai.

‖**premier cru** (prəmye krü). Also **premier crû.** Pl. **premier(s) crus.** [Fr., lit. 'first growth'.] A wine of the best quality. Also *transf.*, *fig.*, and *attrib.* Cf. *CRU, *GROWTH[1] 1 d.

1868 E. L. BECKWITH *Pract. Notes Wine* x. 47 The old, well-known *premiers crûs*, or first growths, retain their ancient and honoured places at the head of French wines. **1875** H. VIZETELLY *Wines of World* i. 13 Branne-Mouton, next-door neighbour to Château Lafite, and noted for its nutty aroma,..is deserving..of being ranked among the *premiers crûs*. **1928** P. M. SHAND *Bk. French Wines* ii. 58 Château Haut-Brion ranks..as the peer of the three great *Premiers Crus* of the Médoc. **1951** [see *CRU]. **1965** P. O'DONNELL *Modesty Blaise* i. 16 He has a wonderfully varied list of girl-friends. From *premier cru* to honest *vin du pays*. **1970** *Guardian* 21 May 13/1 The American demand begins at the top with the five Premiers Crus, and moves steadily down the 1855 classification of the Médoc wines. **1976** *Time* 20 Dec. 27 (Advt.), The best cognacs come only from the Grande and the Petite Champagne districts, the 'premiers crus' of the Cognac region. **1978** L. PRYOR *Viper* (1979) ii. 31 The Long Beach race..the United States' only true road race..lacks the *premier cru* quality of Monaco.

‖**premier danseur** (prəmye dɑ̃sœ̄r). Pl. **premiers danseurs.** [Fr., lit. 'first dancer'.] A leading male dancer in a ballet company. Cf. *PREMIÈRE DANSEUSE.

1828 [see *DANSEUR]. **1860** THACKERAY *Roundabout Papers* iii, in *Cornh. Mag.* May 634 Sir Alcide Flicflac (premier danseur of H.M. Theatre)! **1930** C. W. BEAUMONT *Hist. Ballet in Russia* VII. 49 Dutac was honoured with the position of *premier danseur* during the reign of Alexander I. **1930** —— tr. *Noverre's Lett. on Dancing & Ballets* 21 If he [*sc.* the *maître de ballet*] concentrate his attention on the *premières danseuses* and *premiers danseurs*, the action becomes tedious. **1938** A. L. HASKELL *Ballet* ii. 20 The field-marshal de Bassompière, [was] a *premier danseur* between campaigns. **1969** *Times* 11 Nov. 9/3 The vicissitudes of a *premier danseur* only half the size of his ballerina partner are worthy of consideration. **1973** R. HAYES *Hungarian Game* xxxv. 211, I watched a traffic cop directing sluggish cars like a *premier danseur* in a cattle pen. **1978** *Chicago* June 26/3 Jacques d'Amboise, premier danseur of the New York City Ballet, returns to choreograph a special number for the evenings.

première, *sb.* Add: Now also with pronunc. (pre·miēəɪ, *U.S.* prīmīə·ɪ). Also **premier, preemeer.** (Earlier and later examples.) Also *transf.*

1889 'F. LESLIE' *Let.* 9 Feb. in W. T. Vincent *Recoll. Fred Leslie* (1894) II. xxii. 81 It upset all of us and made us more nervous than a *première*. **1890** G. B. SHAW *Let.* 28 Feb. (1965) I. 244 This does not..include the expenses of the *première* at Amsterdam. **1915** *Sat. Even. Post* 9 Oct. 62/2 She always accompanies me to our premières. **1930** E. MANNIN *Confessions & Impressions* II. iv. 137 He complimented me on my literary *première* and told me to keep on writing. **1937** *New Republic* 19 May 48/1 Miss Gaynor [arrives] at another preemeer in smart mourning. **1941** *Commonweal* 10 Jan. 294/1 The movie première—pronounced pre-meer, with heavy emphasis on the second syllable—is a national phenomenon. **1957** *Times* 9 Sept. 11/4 Each season, when Balmain finally settles down to the production of a new collection of some 150 models, Ginette Spanier is sent away for three weeks' holiday, returning only a few days before the all-important *première*. **1968** S. Challis *Death on Quiet Beach* viii. 115 Fane was due to attend a late premier of his current movie. **1978** J. Anderson *Angel of Death* xiii. 144 'I'll be the only actress in the world who could do it justice.'.. 'I'll come to the premiere.'

première (pre·miēᵊɹ, prīmīᵊ·ɹ), *v.* Also **premier.** [f. prec.] *trans.* To present or perform (a play, film, programme, or the like) for the first time; to reveal (a new product). Also *absol.* and *intr.* for *pass.* Hence **premie·red, premiering** *ppl. adjs.*

1940 *Winchell Coll.* (Topeka, Kansas) *Jrnl.* 11 Dec. 4/6 There's irony in the request of Grinnell college's alumni that Frank Capra should premiere 'Meet John Doe' there. **1941** W. C. Handy *Father of Blues* v. 70 With..Gordon Collins, Lew Hall, all-time end men, premiering on the flanks, you'd feel a strange enchantment creeping over you. **1943** *Newsweek* 13 Sept. 101 Keepsakes, a new Sunday program..premièred on Blue Sep. 5, 8–8:30. **1945** G. Antheil *Bad Boy of Music* ii. 16 This symphony, my 'First Symphony', was later to be premiered in Berlin. **1945** Mencken *Amer. Lang.* Suppl. I. 387 A few of its [sc. *Variety*'s] characteristic inventions will suffice:..*to premier* (often shortened to *to preem*). **1952** 'E. Box' *Death in Fifth Position* (1954) i. 2 My company is going to première an important new ballet tonight. *Ibid.* vii. 181 By the time *Eclipse* was to be premièred, Ella had infuriated Miles..by threatening to leave the company. **1955** L. Feather *Encycl. Jazz* 141/1 He [*sc.* W. G. Fuller]..was co-composer and arr. of..*The Swedish Suite* premiered at Carnegie Hall '48. **1967** *N.Y. Herald Tribune Internat.* 11–12 Feb. 5/4 André Kostelanetz, who commissioned the work and premiered it 25 years ago, asked Mr. Lindsay to do the reading and will conduct the performance. **1973** *Times* 11 Apr. 12/7 In Frankfurt the Theater am Turm, which has premiered most of Peter Handke's plays, is run on similarly cooperative lines. **1975** *Publishers Weekly* 1 Dec. 62/3 He managed to keep the title in the public eye until the film premiered in December 1939. **1976** *National Observer* (U.S.) 10 Apr. 20/2 The premiere of a bizarre Scots drama, Menzies Mc Killop's *Future Pit*, now joined in repertory by a premiering trio of one-acters: Frank B. Ford's *Waterman*, Gladden Schrock's *Glutt*, and Michael Casales' *Cold. Ibid.* 16 Oct. 10/3 The ABC Evening News..premiered last week..and was notable in at least two respects. **1977** *Custom Car* Nov. 13/4 Saab premiered their long-rumoured Turbo 99.

‖**première danseuse** (prəmyę̄r dańsȫz). Also *ellipt.* **première.** Pl. **premières danseuses.** [Fr., fem. of *premier danseur.] A leading female dancer in a ballet company; a ballerina.

1828 [see *danseuse]. **1846** R. Ford *Gatherings from Spain* xxiii. 327 Egyptians, whose women are the premières danseuses on these occasions, in which [gipsy] men never take a part. **1867** *Galaxy* Aug. 441 The dancer who has passed the chrysalis ballet-girl stage, and is now a full-fledged, butterfly *première*. **1887** J. Payn *Holiday Tasks* 13 But here his eye wanders..from the photo of the *première danseuse* at the Frivolity Music Hall. **1890** G. B. Shaw *London Music 1888–89* (1937) 314 Many a *première danseuse* holds her position in spite of a neck and wrists which are, dancingly considered, dead as doornails. **1911** [see *ballerina]. **1930** [see *premier danseur]. **1942** L. Kirstein *Bk. of Dance* xiv. 319 The great..artist Vaganova,..frequently shines as its *première* [in the *Lac des Cygnes*]. **1974** *Sat. Rev. World* (U.S.) 19 Oct. 40/2 The *première danseuse étoile* of the Opéra in Paris. **1978** Ld. Drogheda *Double Harness* xx. 261 In 1919, she [*sc.* Ninette de Valois] was engaged as *première danseuse* for the season of international opera at Covent Garden.

premiership. Add: **1. b.** *U.S.* The office of Secretary of State. Cf. *premier *sb.* d. ? *Obs.*

1928 H. Minor *Story Democr. Party* 69 Madison had cabinet troubles, too. Monroe accepted the premiership in March 1811.

pre-mi·lking. [Pre- A. 1.] The removal of milk from a cow's udder before the birth of her calf.

1953 K. Russell *Princ. Dairy Farming* xiii. 157 Premilking can be done either by hand or machine. **1960** *Farmer & Stockbreeder* 5 Jan. 101/3 Too many concentrates before calving can result in pre-milking being necessary. **1970** W. H. Parker *Health & Dis. in Farm Animals* xiii. 167 Premilking..is a severe handicap to the calf.

premisal. Delete ? *Obs.* and add later example.

1912 *Catholic Encycl.* XIV. 75/1 Ethics may not be divided from psychology and theodicy, any more than from deductive logic. With the proper premisals then from the one and the other here assumed, we say that the Creator could not have given man a fixed nature, as He has, without willing man to work out the purpose for which that nature is framed.

premium. For 'Pl. **-iums,** formerly **-ia**' read 'Pl. **-iums, -ia**' and add: **3. a.** (Further examples.) *spec.*, a sum paid in addition to the rent on a leased property.

1859 Geo. Eliot *Let.* 19 Feb. (1954) III. 14 There was a house after my own heart at Mortlake..but it turned out to have a premium affixed to the lease, which made it too expensive. **1924** A. Christie *Poirot Investigates* iii. 71 'We've got a flat—at last!.. It's dirt cheap. Eighty pounds a year!'.. 'Big premium, I suppose?' **1966** *New Statesman* 21 Jan. 71/2 If railwaymen work genuinely longer or more difficult hours, and get overtime or shift premia in compensation, this is fair enough. **1966** *Economist* 29 Jan. 386/1 The case for higher night premia would be 'examined' in a later report, but he most definitely did not recommend them now. **1970** M. Greener *Penguin Dict. Commerce* 263 Very often when property is leased, the lessee, in addition to paying a rent for an agreed period, pays a lump sum. This is known as a premium, or sometimes as 'key money', and was once intended to avoid taxation and disguise the true rent. **1974** M. B. Brown *Econ. of Imperialism* viii. 177 Some foreign issues [of stocks] were certainly made more attractive because of the premiums at which they were issued.

b. *Comm.* (See quot. 1928.)

1928 *Funk's Stand. Dict.* II. 1956/3 *Premium*,..any object offered free to those who purchase goods to a certain value, as a set of books given free as an inducement to subscribe to a magazine. **1930** Lucas & Benson *Psychol. for Advertisers* xii. 204 $1,502,000,000 is spent annually on advertising. This is divided as follows: Newspapers..$690,000,000..Premiums, programs and directories..25,000,000. **1954** R. J. Schwartz *Dict. Business & Industry* 392/1 *Premium*, something given free or at a nominal price to induce an actual sale or to promote interest in a product. **1963** *Sunday Times* 17 Nov. 11/1 A rapidly-growing little specialist industry is growing round the 'take-a-plastic-daffodil-madam' school of retailing... A premium, in their jargon, can be anything given away or sold cheap to persuade people..to buy, stock, sample or re-order a product. **1974** *Encycl. Brit. Micropædia* VIII. 191/1 Until the 1900s the most popular premiums were pictures and trade cards.., which were collected and exchanged by enthusiastic consumers whose collections became quite valuable.

c. *Finance.* The excess of the forward price of a currency or a commodity over the spot price.

1933 B. Ellinger *This Money Business* x. 101 In normal times the difference between 'spot'—i.e. the rate for immediate delivery—and 'forward' rates depends on the rates of interest in the respective countries, but in abnormal times merchants may find a growing premium or discount on the forward rate over the spot rate. **1957** [see *forward *a.* 4]. **1971** R. F. Pither *Man. Foreign Exchange* (ed. 7) x. 138 Forward rates of exchange are quoted as a 'margin' or 'difference' against the 'spot' rate of the currency concerned, or as a 'premium' or 'discount' on the 'spot' rate, or they may be quoted 'outright'. **1978** R. G. F. Coninx *Foreign Exchange Today* viii. 111 Forward margins are referred to as *premiums* or *discounts*. *Ibid.* 113 With indirect quotations, premiums indicate that the home currency enjoys higher interest rates than the quoted currency.

6. a. (Further examples.)

1906 Galsworthy *Man of Property* xxiv. 295 When Mrs. MacAnder dined at Timothy's, the conversation.. took that wider, man-of-the-world tone current among Forsytes at large, and this, no doubt, was what put her at a premium there. **1932** *Time* 28 Mar. 30/2 The news put Philharmonic subscriptions back at a premium last week. **1974** *Times* 14 Mar. 11/2 Sadly, space is at a premium in most department stores.

b. *fig. to put* (or *place*) *a premium on* (something) and varr., to put a high value on something esp. as an inducement or incentive.

1907 G. B. Shaw *John Bull's Other Island* p. xvi, In short, our circumstances place a premium on political ability whilst the circumstances of England discount it; and the quality of the supply naturally follows the demand. **1911** —— *Getting Married* 142 Our democratic and matrimonial institutions..put a premium on want of self-respect in certain very important matters. **1933** J. W. N. Sullivan *Limitations of Sci.* iv. 132 The struggle for existence takes the place of the human breeder. Nature sets a premium upon certain varieties as compared with others. **1939** A. Huxley *After Many a Summer* i. xi. 147 He's been greedy and domineering, among other reasons, because the present system puts a premium on those qualities. **1959** [see *Pearl Harbour].

7. a. (sense *3 b) *premium promotion, selling*; **premium apprentice,** an apprentice who has paid a premium for instruction in his intended trade.

1927 F. H. Shaw *Knocking Around* vi. 54 My greatest efforts of all should be expended in an endeavour to ameliorate the lot of that hard-lying ocean Ishmael, the premium apprentice. **1979** *Jrnl. R. Soc. Arts* Dec. 36/2 When I left school,..I put in a happy period as a premium apprentice at the Sentinel Waggon Works at Shrewsbury. **1962** S. Strand *Marketing Dict.* 562 *Premium promotion*, the use of premiums (inexpensive gifts) in the promotion of the sale of products or services. **1974** *Encycl. Brit. Micropædia* VIII. 191/2 *Premium promotion*, an advertisement, often part of the product package, that induces prospective purchasers to buy the product by offering a free gift or a reduced price. **1966** *Lebende Sprachen* XI. 109/1 *Premium selling*, offering an item with the purchase of another product, either free or for a nominal additional payment, as an inducement to buy the product.

b. Passing into *adj.* Of a commodity, etc., esp. petrol: superior in quality and therefore commanding a higher price; of a price: such as befits an article of superior quality; higher than usual. orig. *U.S.*

1928 *National Petroleum News* 24 Oct. 115 (Advt.), This is our anti-knock gasoline, a premium motor fuel. **1931** *Economist* 5 Sept. 422/2 The profit to the garage on the sale of petrol..is now 2d a gallon on national 'commercial' grades and 2½d on national 'premium' grades. **1945** H. S. Bell *Amer. Petroleum Refining* (ed. 3) xviii. 278 The refiner cannot approach the desired knock rating of 80 for premium motor fuels..by simple skimming and thermal cracking except by a material reduction of the end point of his product. **1961** I. L. Horowitz *Philos., Sci. & Sociol. of Knowledge* v. 54 A world which pays a premium price for technological manipulation. **1965** *New Statesman* 23 Apr. 634/1 There were the garages selling the well-known, branded petrols, each in three main grades—Super, Premium and Regular. **1970** *Daily Tel.* 30 Jan. 19/1 All supersonic travellers would fly 'premium class' at a slightly lower rate than that paid at present by first-class passengers, but with the same comfort. **1977** *Listener* 1 Dec. 708 Qube (*sc.* U.S. cable television] has ten 'premium' channels where you pay per programme. **1979** *Guardian* 22 June 9/8 Trout will for some time still be a premium fish, selling at about £1 each.

premium bond. Also **Premium Bond.** [f. Premium + Bond *sb.*[1]] A debenture earning no interest but eligible for lotteries; *spec.* (in full *Premium Savings Bond*) since 1956, a British government bond not bearing interest but with the periodic chance of a cash prize. Also *attrib.* (See also *Ernie.)

[**1882** R. Bithell *Counting-House Dict.* 237 A number of Lottery Loans of the worst class have been started in some of the German States, and also in Austria... It would be impossible to get subscriptions to them to any great extent in this country if called by their proper name. The name of Premium-Loans..has therefore been substituted.., and the money that has been extracted from the pockets of unfortunate dupes by these means is enormous. **1908** *Westm. Gaz.* 29 Aug. 2/2 Two of the largest of these lotteries, the Panama and Congo premium-bearing loans, are two of the most scandalous pieces of finance which Europe has ever witnessed. Here is an exciting chance of winning a fortune by gambling; let us get the money somehow to buy half a dozen of the bonds, and work no more!] **1908** *Economist* 12 Sept. 477/2 The practical man in the street who knows anything about premium bonds is quite aware that they are in their nature and intention lotteries. **1918** *Ibid.* 19 Jan. 79/2 The report of the Select Committee on Premium Bonds.. concludes with the following paragraphs:— '..We do not, therefore, advise that an issue of Premium Bonds be made at the present time.' **1931** *Star* 8 May 6/3 Every trick—from premium bonds to guessing the number of beans in a bottle—seems to have been tried. **1940** Graves & Hodge *Long Week-End* v. 77 He [*sc.* Horatio Bottomley] was then launching new prize schemes—the Premium Bond Scheme of 1918, for example, to which his readers subscribed £90,000. Out of this he had agreed to pay £10,000 in prizes. **1956** H. Macmillan in *Times* 18 Apr. 5/2 Finally, I have something completely new for the saver in Great Britain—a premium bond. **1957**, etc. [see *Ernie]. **1957** *Observer* 25 Aug. 9/3 New National Savings reported last week totalled £26,689,000 (including £1,200,000 Premium Bonds and £2,566,000 accrued interest). **1958** *Times Lit. Suppl.* 15 Aug. p. x/3 He also prefers pools to premium bond gambling—in which a bloke can't choose his own combination of numbers, so how does one know that it's on the level? **1962** H. O. Beecheno *Introd. Business Stud.* xiv. 140 The Premium Savings Bond scheme has taken advantage of our national love of a gamble, holding out the possibility of a reward for the few much higher than other savings methods would give. **1974** *Guardian* 27 Mar. 1/1 Another £500,000 a month added to Premium Bond prizes.

premiumed, *a.* (in Dict. s.v. Premium). Add: Also, that has paid a premium.

1927 *Daily Express* 5 July 5/5 The trade may also be entered as a premiumed apprentice or as a beginner at a nominal wage.

premi·x, *v.* [Pre- A. 1.] *trans.* To mix beforehand.

1934 in Webster. **1966** *Gloss. Terms Internal Plastering* (*B.S.I.*) 17 A plaster in which a lightweight aggregate has been pre-mixed dry with a gypsum plaster to give a low density. **1966** *McGraw-Hill Encycl. Sci. & Technol.* V. 292/1 Gaseous fuels can be premixed with air or oxygen, in which case the mixture can be fed to a flame holder and burned in a very efficient manner. **1972** [see *premix *sb.*]. **1976** *Nature* 20 May 259/2 Rattlesnake venoms are neutralised also when premixed *in vitro* with either rattlesnake plasma or commercial antivenin.

Hence **premi·xed** *ppl. a.*, **premi·xing** *vbl. sb.*

1941 *Engineers' Digest* II. 417 (*heading*) Premixed combustion of gaseous fuel for steel finishing operations. *Ibid.*, Premixing provides accuracy of air to fuel-gas proportioning over the widest conceivable operating range. **1945** H. Barron *Mod. Plastics* vii. 163 (*caption*) Rotary premixing machines in which powdered phenolic resins (Novolak) is mixed with hexamethylenetetramine, wood flour, and colouring material. **1959** *Economist* 31 Jan. 431/2 A 'flexible' type of road carriageway base incorporating premixed water-bound macadam. **1960** *Farmer & Stockbreeder* 8 Mar. 75/1 The idea being that two different fertilizers can be applied at the same time without pre-mixing. **1963** A. M. Neville *Properties of Concrete* iv. 205 If instead of being batched and mixed on the site concrete is delivered ready for placing from a central plant it is referred to as ready-mixed or pre-mixed concrete. **1978** *Sci. Amer.* Apr. 155 In a premixed flame the gases are mixed prior to the burning and the rate of combustion depends on the flow rate.

premix (prī·miks), *sb.* and *a.* [Pre- A. 2.] **A.** *sb.* A mixture prepared beforehand; *spec.* (*a*) *Agric.*, a powder or granular preparation into which a drug or the like has been incorporated and which is mixed with animal feed to introduce the drug, etc., into it in suitably low concentrations; (*b*) synthetic resin to which various substances have been added to make it suitable for moulding; (*c*) (see quot. 1976).

1957 *Times* 2 Dec. (Agric. Suppl.) p. vi/4 A source of greater fear to those familiar with oestrogen effects is the inhalation of dust from a concentrated premix, which would present a definite hazard. **1960** O. SKILBECK *ABC of Film & TV* 98 *Premix*, when dubbing is likely to prove especially difficult, or when insufficient heads are available for the number of tracks involved, some tracks may be combined at a first premix stage and added to the remainder later. **1963** H. R. CLAUSER *Encycl. Engin. Materials* 519/1 The unsaturated resin is first mixed with fillers, fibers, and catalyst to provide a nontacky compound... The premix is molded at pressures of 150 to 500 psi and at temperatures ranging from 250–310 F. **1963** *Poultry Sci.* XLII. 1264/2 Premixes containing menadione sodium bisulfite complex (16 gm./lb.) were made employing soybean meal or corn as the carrier. **1967** SIMONDS & CHURCH *Encycl. Basic Materials for Plastics* 58/2 Premix is a damp, sometimes sticky variation of molding compound differing technically from so-called 'molding compound' only in the ratio of monomer which is used. **1971** *Farmer & Stockbreeder* 23 Feb. 25/1 Emtryl is available in two forms, as a soluble powder and as a premix. **1972** QUICK & LABAU *Handbk. Film Production* xviii. 201 In the event of an extremely complex mix, pre-mixes may be desirable. This is where a few of the tracks are mixed to a desired level and then that master track mixed with the remaining channels of information. The director makes decisions concerning whether or not to pre-mix his film. **1976** B. ARMSTRONG *Gloss. TV Terms* 71 *Premix*, a preliminary dub of certain sound tracks, usually music and effects, before the final mix.

B. *adj.* Premixed.

1963 H. R. CLAUSER *Encycl. Engin. Materials* 537/2 Premix molding materials are physical mixtures of a reactive thermosetting resin.., chopped fibrous reinforcement..and powdered fillers (usually carbonates or clays). **1968** P. I. SMITH *Plastics as Metal Replacements* i. 45 The manufacturer makes available to the moulder either conventional pre-mix compounds or pre-impregnated chopped strand glass mat all ready for moulding. **1975** *Petroleum Rev.* XXIX. 96/1 A semi-closed circuit deep sea diving breathing set, using air or a pre-mix gas. **1976** P. HILL *Hunters* xii. 176 A huge pre-mix concrete lorry was disgorging its load. **1977** *Evening News* 11 June 11/6 Producer and artist then live with these 'pre-mix' tapes for about two months.

premi·xture. [PRE- A. 2.] A mixture prepared beforehand.

1934 in WEBSTER. **1972** *Physics Bull.* Jan. 20/2 Two separate arrays of injector tubes are used to introduce premixtures of fluorine with helium and nitric oxide with carbon dioxide at the upstream end.

pre-modern: see *PRE- B. 1 d.

premo·dify, *v.* *Linguistics.* [PRE- A. 1.] *trans.* To modify (a word or phrase) by an immediately preceding word or phrase. So **premo·difying** *ppl. a.*; **premodifica·tion, premo·difier.**

1962 R. QUIRK *Use of English* x. 164 The premodification of nouns by nouns was a common feature of English before Germans studied science or America was discovered. **1966** G. N. LEECH *English in Advertising* xiv. 127 In advertising language, the interesting part of the noun group is the pre-modifying part... Noun groups with lengthy pre-modifications are italicised. *Ibid.* 128 Premodifiers which can have the designative, or categorising function are nouns, adjectives and compounds. **1972** *Language* XLVIII. 456 The relatively empty *do* [in the ungrammatical sentence *He had well done it*] does not permit a premodifier *well*, but with a richer verb premodification is normal, e.g. *He has well revealed the causes.* **1973** G. W. TURNER *Stylistics* iii. 81 Words preceding the head word in a group are conveniently called 'modifiers' (sometimes 'premodifiers'). **1976** *Amer. Speech 1974* XLIX. 82 It [sc. *much*] collocates with *like* in an affirmative sentence if it is premodified, hence *I like him very much.*

premonitory. B. (Earlier example.)

1834 *Knickerbocker* IV. 307 The premonitories seize me before I have time to run to the doctors for relief.

premonstrate, *v.* For † *Obs.* read *rare* and add later example.

1857 A. MATHEWS *Tea-Table Talk* I. 251 Marks, natural or acquired, premonstrate a talent for locomotion.

premonstration. For † *Obs.* read *rare* and add later example.

1920 E. H. BEGBIE *Mirrors of Downing St.* i. 9 His intuitions are amazing. He astonished great soldiers in the war by his premonstrations.

pre-moral(ity): see *PRE- B. 1.

premo·rbid, *a.* *Med.* [PRE- B. 1.] Preceding the occurrence of symptoms or disease.

1939 *Amer. Jrnl. Psychiatry* XCV. 1041 A number of factors were included: age, sex, physical build, premorbid personality..and permeability quotients. **1953** *Jrnl. Nerv. & Mental Dis.* CXVII. 516 The scale was used to evaluate each patient in..the following three areas: (a) the premorbid history; (b) possible precipitating factors; (c) signs of the disorder. **1969** *Jrnl. Amer. Med. Assoc.* 18 Aug. 1085/2 Marihuana may have a psychotogenic effect even in an individual with a healthy premorbid personality.

pre-mortem, *a.* Add: Also as *sb.* in *fig.* use.

1971 *Listener* 7 Jan. 18/1 'The death of the symphony orchestra' was discussed on Radio 4, in a kind of pre-mortem. **1972** F. WARNER *Lying Figures* III. 33 What of love? *Guppy.* A post-prandial pre-mortem.

premotor: see *PRE- B. 3.

premou·lt, *a.* and *sb.* *Zool.* **A.** *adj.* [PRE- B. 2.] Existing or occurring just before a change of plumage in birds or the shedding and replacement of the integument of insects, crustaceans, or reptiles. **B.** *sb.* [PRE- B. 1 in Dict. and Suppl.] A premoult stage or period.

1957 R. A. H. COOMBES in D. A. Bannerman *Birds Brit. Isles* VI. 312 (*heading*) The pre-moult migration of the sheld-duck. **1964** *Oceanogr. & Marine Biol.* II. 303 At moult [of the crab, *Carcinus maenas*], uptake of water, averaging 66·3% of the premoult weight, takes place. **1967** P. A. MEGLITSCH *Invertebr. Zool.* xvi. 681/1 The physiology of most of the body parts [of arthropods] is affected by premolt. **1973** *Nature* 9 Mar. 133/2 An insect does not enter premoult if its thoracic glands have been removed.

premultiplica·tion. *Math.* [PRE- A. 2.] Multiplication by a prefactor.

1862 *Phil. Trans. R. Soc.* CLI. 316 Let that matrix be reduced by premultiplication with a unit-matrix. **1972** *Computer Jrnl.* XV. 250/2 Pre- and post-multiplication is preserved.

premultiply, *v.* (Examples.)

1862 [see *post-multiply* vb. s.v. *POST- A. 1 a]. **1972** ROBERTS & SHIPMAN *Two-Point Boundary Value Probl.* viii. 223 If each side of (8.8.12) is premultiplied by the square partitioned matrix of order $n(m+1)$,..the following partitioned matrix is obtained. **1978** [see *post-multiply* vb. s.v. *POST- A. 1 a].

premunition. Restrict 'Now *rare*' to senses in Dict. and add: **3.** *Med.* [ad. F. *prémunition* (E. Sergent et al. 1924, in *Bull. de la Soc. de Path. exotique* XVII. 38).] (The production of) a resistance to disease due to the presence of the causative agent in the host in a harmless or tolerated state.

[**1924** *Tropical Dis. Bull.* XXI. 492 For absolute immunity the distinguishing term proposed is 'immunity'.. and for relative immunity, 'premunition' brought about by a process of 'premunition', with corresponding verb. (Unfortunately English words corresponding with 'premunition' and 'premunir' do not at present exist.)] **1934** T. W. M. CAMERON *Internal Parasites of Domestic Animals* IV. 218 In..premunition, removal of the latent infection may permit of re-infection. **1951** G. LAPAGE *Parasitic Animals* vii. 205 Some experts believe that the greater resistance of the negro race to human malarial parasites..is really premunition. **1971** P. C. C. GARNHAM *Progress in Parasitol.* vi. 101 Host and parasite eventually settle down together in the state of premunition. **1975** *Tropical Animal Health & Production* VII. 125 (*heading*) The premunition of adult cattle against Babesiosis.

premunity (prĭmiū·nĭti). *Med.* [f. PREMUN(ITION + -ITY, after *immunity.*] (See quot. 1938.) So **premu·ne** *a.*, exhibiting premunity.

1938 G. O. DAVIES *Vet. Path. & Bacteriol.* (ed. 2) vii. 145 Premunity denotes a state of resistance or tolerance to infection which only lasts so long as the infecting organism is present in the tissues of the host. **1948** U. F. RICHARDSON *Vet. Protozool.* i. 7 The more uniform 'premunity' of animals to protozoa in an infected area is mainly due to the more uniform exposure to infection and reinfection. *Ibid.* iv. 86 Infection derived from a premune animal is less severe than that from an active case.

premunization (prī:miunəizēⁱ·ʃən). *Med.* [f. PREMUN(ITION + -IZATION, after *immunization.*] The action or result of premunizing; premunition (sense *3).

1941 J. T. CUTHBERTSON *Immunity against Animal Parasites* iv. 49 Resistance to reinfection with the malarias of monkeys, birds, and dogs have all been shown to depend in part on premunization. **1975** *Tropical Animal Health & Production* VII. 126 Premunisation was effected by the injection of infected blood and control of the subsequent infection with drugs.

premunize (prī·miunəiz), *v.* *Med.* [f. PREMUN(ITION + -IZE, after *immunize*, as anglicization of F. *prémunir* (E. Sergent et al. 1924, in *Bull. de la Soc. de Path. exotique* XVII. 37).] *trans.* To introduce pathogens into (a host) so as to produce premunition. Hence **pre·munized, pre·munizing** *ppl. adjs.*

1925 E. SERGENT et al. in *Trans. R. Soc. Tropical Med.* XVIII. 384 We ask our British colleagues to..consider whether it is possible to give currency to the verb 'to premunize' and to Anglicize the word 'premunition'. **1934** T. W. M. CAMERON *Internal Parasites of Domestic Animals* II. 45 Immune animals..are premunized and may act as carriers. **1938** *Proc. R. Soc. Med.* XXXI. 1301 When a premunized host is superinfected..little apparent effect is produced. **1963** E. SERGENT in P. C. C. Garnham et al. *Immunity to Protozoa* iii. 44 A typical example of a premunizing vaccine is the antitubercular vaccine, BCG. **1975** *Tropical Animal Health & Production* VII. 125 Twenty-five cattle..were premunised with virulent *Babesia bigemina. Ibid.*, The results of haematological and serological immune responses of premunised cattle.. are reported.

premy, var. *PREEMIE.

premyelocyte, -cytic: see *PRE- B. 1.

prena·sal, *a.* and *sb.* **A.** *adj.* **1.** *Anat.* and *Zool.* [f. PRE- B. 3 + NASAL *a.*] (In Dict. s.v. PRE- B. 3.)

2. *Linguistics.* [f. PRE- B. 2 + NASAL *sb.*] Occurring before a nasal consonant.

1973 J. M. ANDERSON *Struct. Aspects Lang. Change* 137 Modifications in French, revolving around nasalization of prenasal vowels.

B. *sb.* *Linguistics.* [f. PRE- A. 2 + NASAL *sb.*] A prenasalized consonant.

1948 R. A. D. FORREST *Chinese Lang.* v. 93 The Heh-Miao..have rid their language of all compound consonants (except the prenasals). *Ibid.* 94 The irregular representation of the initials with prefixed homorganic nasals ('prenasals') is puzzling.

Hence **prenasa·lity**, the quality or state of being prenasalized.

1976 *Language* LII. 332 Another class of consonants involving nasality..argues against any solution to the problem of prenasality in which a single feature has the entire segment as its domain.

prena·salize, *v.* *Linguistics.* [PRE- A. 1.] *trans.* To pronounce (a consonant) with initial nasalization. Chiefly as pa. pple. or ppl. adj. Hence **prenasaliza·tion.**

1956 JAKOBSON & HALLE *Fund. of Lang.* iv. 43 Such relatively rare phonemes as the discontinuous nasals (the so-called prenasalized stops). **1961** WEBSTER, Prenasalization. **1973** J. M. ANDERSON *Struct. Aspects Lang. Change* 119 Some consonants..may become aspirated, pre-aspirated, glottalized, prenasalized, [etc.] **1976** *Language* LII. 331 Another class of segment is much more common..: this is the type generally described as 'prenasalized stops'. **1977** *Ibid.* LIII. 317 Prenasalization of these consonants, while common, is limited in the following ways: except in sentence-initial position, *b d* are either preglottalized or prenasalized, and the processes occur in complementary distribution.

prenatal, *a.* Add: (Further examples.) Also = *ANTENATAL *a.* 2.

1909 CHESTERTON *Orthodoxy* iv. 94 This proves that even nursery tales only echo an almost pre-natal leap of interest and amazement. **1909** *Westm. Gaz.* 19 Apr. 2/3 In some forgotten strange pre-natal world, Where rose-crowned summer smiled on placid seas. **1938** *New Statesman* 19 Feb. 298/2 Pre-natal clinics are increasing. **1960** C. MACINNES *Mr. Love & Justice* 207 Step up to the pre-natal clinic, darling. See what they have to say.

prenatally, *adv.* (further examples).

1953 R. LEHMANN *Echoing Grove* II. 73 Already midsummer dawn fainted pre-natally in the high uncurtained windows. **1965** *Science* 15 Jan. 306/3 This period of neural differentiation occurs prenatally in guinea pigs.. and during the 1st week of postnatal life in rats. **1976** *Lancet* 18 Dec. 1352/2 Of interest was the occurrence of measles prenatally in the mother of 1 patient..during the third trimester of gestation.

pre-Nazi: see *PRE- B. 1 a. **prenegotiation:** *PRE- A. 2. **preneoplastic:** *PRE- B. 1.

preneu·ral, *a.* and *sb.* *Zool.* [PRE- B. 3.] **A.** *adj.* In chelonians, applied to a skeletal element that lies between the nuchal bone and the neural bones. **B.** *sb.* A bone in this position.

1904 *Amer. Jrnl. Sci.* CLXVIII. 274 There is a preneural bone, whose anterior border has occupied a notch in the hinder border of the nuchal. **1957** *Bull. Mus. Compar. Zool. Harvard* CXV. 171 The very similar term 'pre-neural' has long been in use for an element that is immediately posterior to the nuchal. **1969** R. ZANGERL in C. Gans *Biol. Reptilia* I. vi. 333 Most of the Mesozoic genera retain some amphichelydian characters,..but.. the occurrence of a preneural is erratic. *Ibid.* 334 Preneural elements occur occasionally.

prenex (prī·neks), *a.* *Logic.* [ad. late L. *prae-nex(us* tied or bound up in front: see PRE- A. 1 and NEXUS.] Of or relating to a quantifier placed initially in a formula whose scope affects the whole formula; *spec.* in phr. *prenex normal form* (see quot. 1944).

1944 A. CHURCH in *Ann. Math. Stud.* XIII. 60 Thus we have that a w.f.f. is in prenex normal form if and only if all its quantifiers are initially placed, no two quantifiers are upon the same variable, and every variable occurring in a quantifier occurs at least once within the scope of that quantifier. *Ibid.* 61 Use of the prenex normal form was introduced by C. S. Peirce, although in a different terminology and notation. **1950** W. V. QUINE *Methods of Logic* (1952) IV. 226 Let us speak of a quantifier as prenex in a sentence when..it is initial..and its scope reaches to the end of the sentence. *Ibid.* 243 The prenex universal quantifiers..are dropped for ease in reading. **1951** *Jrnl. Symbolic Logic* XVI. 32 For any formula *F* of our *m*-valued formalization there is a formula *G* in prenex normal form which is weakly equivalent to *F*. **1965** HUGHES & LONDEY *Elem. Formal Logic* xli. 297 A wff in which all the quantifiers occur at the beginning, all are affirmative, and in which their scope extends to the end of the whole wff, is said to be in Prenex Normal Form. **1974** BOOLOS & JEFFREY *Computability & Logic* ix. 112 Thus..F_2 is in prenex form but F_1 is not; and since F_2 is a prenex formula logically equivalent to F_1, F_2 is a prenex form of F_1.

prenominal, *a.* Add: **b.** Preceding a substantive. Also as *sb.*

1961 *Amer. Speech* XXXVI. 163 Roughly speaking, the prenominal adjectivals will be only single, simplex (descriptive) adjectives. **1964** *Language* XL. 45 As a prenominal the genitive has two unique characteristics. **1965** *Ibid.* XLI. 283 Prenominal and postnominal modifiers. **1978** *Ibid.* LIV. 26 A prenominal numeral like *cinq* 'five' may be pronounced with a final consonant in all positions.

pre-noun: see *PRE- B. 1.

prenova (prīnōᵘ·vă), *a.* and *sb.* *Astr.* **A.** *adj.* [PRE- B. 2.] Preceding development of a star into a nova. **B.** *sb.* [PRE- B. 1 in Dict. and Suppl.] A star prior to its becoming a nova.

1939 D. B. MCLAUGHLIN in *Pop. Astron.* XLVII. 418 The pre-nova stage. During this portion of its life, the star is either constant or irregularly variable through a small range. **1943** *Publ. Observatory Univ. Michigan* VIII. 188 In the pre-nova state the star is very hot, probably 50,000° to 60,000° K. **1956** Z. KOPAL in A. Beer *Vistas in Astron.* II. 1499 (*heading*) Internal constitution of the pre-novae. **1957** C. PAYNE-GAPOSCHKIN *Galactic Novae* xi. 313 The pre-nova is regarded as a hydrogen-poor subdwarf with contraction the main source of energy. **1976** *Nature* 22 Jan. 172/3 First indications that the nova was unusual came when a search for the prenova on the Palomar Sky Survey plates showed no star at the nova's position.

prentice, *sb.* Add: **4.** *prentice-boy* (later examples), *-player; prentice-hand, -work*: later examples.

1839 C. J. LEVER *Confessions H. Lorrequer* vi. 47 A red-hot orangeman,..vice-chairman of the ''Prentice Boys'. **1852** DICKENS *Bleak Ho.* (1853) i. 1 Fog cruelly pinching the toes and fingers of his shivering little 'prentice boy on deck. **1898** Prentice hand [see *ELEVEN *a.* 2 c]. **1907** 'MARK TWAIN' *Christian Sci.* II. iii. 127 They seem to me to prove the presence of the 'prentice hand. **1980** *Times* 12 Jan. 10/6 Breaded scallops and fragile wun-tun came from an expert, not a prentice, hand. **1963** *Times* 7 May 8/7 How fine it would be to hear Sir John Gielgud on a stage where Edmund Kean was a prentice player. **1881** 'MARK TWAIN' *Prince & Pauper* xxii. 269 His frantic and lubberly 'prentice-work found but a poor market for itself. **1975** *Times Lit. Suppl.* 29 Aug. 963/1 It is unfair to print such academic prentice-work cheek by jowl with the work of experienced professionals.

pre-nu·clear, *a.* [PRE- B. 1.] **1.** *Phonetics.* That occurs before a nucleus.

1952 W. JASSEM *Intonation of Conversational Eng.* vi. 61 The distinctive feature of the prenuclear tunes is..the relation of the final tone of the tune to the initial tone of the following tune. **1961** [see *INTERNUCLEAR *a.* 3]. **1966** J. E. BUSE in C. E. Bazell *In Memory of J. R. Firth* 54 Of the four pre-nuclear classes, prepositions, determinatives and number particles are mutually exclusive with..the tense particles. **1976** *Archivum Linguisticum* VII. 38 One feature both subclasses share is their insistence that any non-nuclear occurrence be in prenuclear position rather than in tail (postnuclear) position.

2. Preceding the development of nuclear weapons.

1960 *Guardian* 14 Sept. 10/5 In the pre-nuclear age power was physical violence. **1965** *Economist* 11 Dec. 1181/1 Mr Kosygin's attitude is frightening because it is so stunningly out of date. It is pre-nuclear, pre-coexistence. **1968** *Punch* 10 Apr. 543/3 A strange, pre-nuclear atmosphere prevailed.

preobrazhenskite (prīˌobrăʒe·nskəit). *Min.* [ad. Russ. *preobrazhenskit* (Ya. Ya. Yarzhensky 1956, in *Doklady̆ Akad. Nauk SSSR* CXI. 1087), f. the name of P. I. *Preobrazhensky* (1874–1944), investigator of Russian salt deposits: see -ITE[1].] A hydrated magnesium borate found as nodules in salt deposits in Kazakhstan.

1957 *Amer. Mineralogist* XLII. 704 *Preobrazhenskite*... It occurs in colorless, lemon-yellow, and dark gray nodules in fine-grained halite-polyhalite rock. **1972** *Soviet Physics: Doklady* XVI. 519/1 The equation of preobrazhenskite so obtained corresponded to the chemical composition $3MgO.5 \cdot 5B_2O_3.4 \cdot 5H_2O$, but not $3MgO.5B_2O_3.4 \cdot 5H_2O$ as originally proposed. *Ibid.*, The most important crystal-chemical complex in the structure of preobrazhenskite comprises a set of infinite boron-oxygen chains perpendicular to the b axis with a new type of radical; the repeated link in each chain comprises four triple boron-oxygen rings..and two additional $BO_2(OH)_2$ tetrahedra.

preoccupied, *ppl. a.* **b.** (Examples.)

1842 *Rep. Brit. Assoc. Adv. Sci.* 113 The genus of birds, *Plectorhynchus*, being preoccupied in Ichthyology, is changed to *Plectorhamphus*. **1898** [see *BENTONITE]. **1913** [see *BALUCHITHERIUM]. **1967** J. R. & P. H. NAPIER *Handbk. Living Primates* III. 377 The subgeneric name *Lyonogale* is substituted for the preoccupied *Tana* Lyon.

pre-Œdipal (prīˌī·dipăl), *a.* *Psychoanalysis.* Also **preœdipal.** [f. PRE- B. 1 + *ŒDIPAL *a.*] That is prior to the onset of the Œdipal phase of development. Also **pre-Œ·dipus** *attrib.*

1932 *Internat. Jrnl. Psycho-Anal.* XIII. 282 Our insight into this early, pre-Oedipal, phase in the little girl's development comes to us as a surprise. **1958** *Ibid.* XXXIX. 516 (*title*) The preoedipal attachment to the mother. **1961** J. STRACHEY et al. tr. *Freud's Compl. Psychol. Wks.* XXI. 230 The phase of exclusive attachment to the mother, which may be called the pre-Oedipus phase, possesses a far greater importance in women than it can have in men. **1974** G. & R. BLANCK *Ego Psychol.* ii. 36 The beginning introjections, incorporations, and identifications are variously described in the literature as primitive, archaic forms of superego, or as..preoedipal super-ego.

pre-oïdium: see *PRE- B. 2 a.

pre-op (prī,ǫ·p), colloq. abbrev. of *PRE-OPERATIVE *a.* Also as *sb.*, ellipt. for *preoperative preparation* or the like.

1934 S. KINGSLEY in *Famous Plays of 1934* 159, I was kind of worried about that preop insulin. **1956** K. HULME *Nun's Story* x. 162 All pre-op medication given. **1972** M. CRICHTON *Terminal Man* I. v. 44 Pre-op patients..often didn't want to see people. **1976** 'R. GORDON' *Doctor on Job* iv. 34 The razor's a bit ropey. It's the one they use for the ward preops. **1977** *Lancet* 5 Feb. 301/2 His details are entered in the book for the agreed date, with comments such as 'very fat' or 'needs pre-op physio'.

pre-operation, *sb.* and *a.* Add: **A.** *sb.* **2.** A preoperational activity. **B.** *adj.* [PRE- B. 2.] Prior to a surgical operation.

1971 *Nature* 13 Aug. 456/1 For some time, it has been believed that young children are unable to form transitive inferences about quantity until they pass the stage of logical preoperations at about 7 yr old. **1976** J. SNOW *Cricket Rebel* 107, I relaxed as the pre-operation drugs took effect and I moved into another world. **1978** *Detroit Free Press* 16 Apr. D4/2 This way, except for a pre-operation visit, 'I just see them unconscious.'

preopera·tional, *a.* *Psychol.* [PRE- B. 1.] That precedes operational thought, usu. typified by the mental processes of children aged between 2 and 7. (Cf. *OPERATION 4 b.)

1953 MAYS & WHITEHEAD tr. *Piaget's Logic & Psychol.* ii. 12 Starting from the postulate that all logical problems arise in the first place from manipulations of objects, we can now say that this period is pre-operational. **1960** J. S. BRUNER *Process of Educ.* iii. 34 In this so-called preoperational stage, the principal symbolic achievement is that the child learns how to represent the external world through symbols established by simple generalization; things are represented as equivalent in terms of sharing some common property. **1964** LUNZER & PAPERT tr. *Inhelder & Piaget's Early Growth of Logic in Child* 291 Whether or not the co-ordination is complete, operations and pre-operational co-ordinations enter into the most diverse kinds of behaviour. **1975** M. D. SMITH *Educ. Psychol.* ii. 40 Pre-operational two to seven uses egocentric speech.

preoperative (priˌǫ·pĕrătiv), *a.* *Med.* [PRE- B. 1.] Given or occurring before a surgical operation.

1904 [in Dict. s.v. PRE- B. 1]. **1954** MARTIN & HYNES *Clin. Endocrinol.* (ed. 2) iii. 69 The use of pre-operative iodine or anti-thyroid drugs..adds further difficulty in the histological diagnosis of thyroidectomy specimens. **1957** *New Biol.* XXIV. 54 Without preoperative treatment with heparin there would be every likelihood of the blood clotting within the operated blood vessel. **1977** *Lancet* 25 June 1352/1 In preoperative preparation of the bowel most surgeons used neomycin for 1–3 days, or phthalylsulphathiazole for 3–10 days.

Hence **preo·peratively** *adv.*, before an, or the, operation.

1931 [see *POSTOPERATIVELY *adv.*]. **1957** *Ann. R. Coll. Surgeons* XXI. 368 The visual defect pre-operatively affected both eyes nearly equally. **1976** *Lancet* 27 Nov. 1205/2 All the patients feel well, and there have been no occlusive vascular episodes postoperatively. However, in the only patient (no. 2) whose electrocardiogram was abnormal preoperatively, no change has occurred.

pre-ordination. (Later example.)

1948 *Mind* LVII. 180 The well-worn antagonisms of the immanent and transcendent, of finite sinfulness and divine perfection and preordination, which centuries of theological brooding have failed to dissipate.

pre-orgasmic, -ovulatory: see *PRE- B. 1. **pre-ovulation:** *PRE- B. 2 a. **pre-own:** *PRE- A. 1. **pre-oxygenation:** *PRE- A. 2.

prep, *sb.* and *a.* For '*School* and *College slang*' read '*slang* (orig. *School* and *College*)' and add: **1. a.** (Further examples.) Also, lessons and exercises to be done by a pupil after school hours, either at school or as homework (see *HOMEWORK 2). Also *attrib.*

1900 *Dialect Notes* II. 51 (College Words and Phrases) *Prep*... Preparation. **1911** BEERBOHM *Zuleika D.* xxii. 313 With his elbows on the kitchen table..sat Clarence, intent on belated 'prep'. **1939** R. C. WOODTHORPE *Rope for Convict* v. 51 I've just remembered I haven't done the prep. he sent me. **1961** E. S. TURNER *Phoney War* vii. 28 At prep time, they were not allowed to use ink, for fear of damaging the art treasures on the walls. **1972** *Where* Sept. 237/3 The standard half-hour homework, or 'prep' as it is called in some schools, is purely notional. **1976** *Daily Times* (Lagos) 4 Sept. 19/2 (Advt.), Boarding with daily coaching, strict attention, and Prep Supervision for: Forms One to Five male and female in Lagos. **1977** J. I. M. STEWART *Madonna of Astrolabe* i. 8 Two of her boys..must be got home in time to be calmed down and persuaded to do their prep. **1979** *Homes & Gardens* June 97/2 There is a general shuffling, an air of impatience, boredom even, of the sort you find at prep. time in public schools.

b. Short for PREPARATION in various other senses. Also *attrib.*

1925 D. H. LAWRENCE *Let.* ? 17 Dec. (1962) II. 870 Tell Achsah, lest she make any preps for me. **1934** *Amer. Speech* IX. 237/2 The curtailed word or back-shortening *prep*... In this sentence, *The team had an intensive prep yesterday afternoon*, it has the same connotation as *drill* or *practice*. **1976** M. MILLAR *Ask for me Tomorrow* (1977) xvi. 127 A little too perfectly groomed, as if he'd just been given the full treatment in..a mortician's prep room. **1976** *Amer. Speech 1973* XLVIII. 204 He is given a *prep* 'surgical preparation'. **1977** *Hot Car* Oct. 69/1 (*caption*) Persevere with this as it is an important prep stage for the paint.

c. *Horse-racing.* A race that is a preparation for a more important event. *U.S.*

1944 *Sun* (Baltimore) 4 Mar. 9/4 A better-than-fair horse, which he..guided to second place..in the $7,500-McClennan, the widener prep won by Sun Again. **1975** *New Yorker* 15 Sept. 110/2 It isn't often that a hundred-thousand-dollar race is a prep for a two-hundred-and-fifty-thousand-dollar one. **1977** *Ibid.* 3 Oct. 112/1 Quiet Little Table..won the prep, running head-and-head down the stretch with Wise Philip and Jatski.

2. Restrict '*U.S.*' to sense b. **a.** (Earlier and later examples.) See also *PREPARATORY *a.* 2 a.

1895 J. L. WILLIAMS *Princeton Stories* 128 After awhile he found himself walking with the freshman way out toward the Prep. school. **1903** *Chicago Record-Herald* 7 June III. 1/1 A crowd of nearly 4,000 university, 'prep' school and grammar school rooters cheered from the bleachers. **1930** [see *FACT *sb.* 4 f]. **1934** C. LAMBERT *Music Ho!* v. 298 They are..as childish as the hidden rivers and prep school puns that adorn Joyce's *Anna Livia Plurabelle*. **1943** *Scrutiny* XI. 287 His [*sc.* Wodehouse's] humour is a cross of Prep-school and *Punch*. **1959** T. S. ELIOT *Elder Statesman* II. 63 You were expelled from your prep school for stealing. **1971** *New Yorker* 15 May 51/2 Dulwich College—what the English call a public school and we call a prep school. **1974** *Listener* 14 Mar. 339/3 The prep-school language and the note of petulance nicely convey the immaturity..of this band of heroes. **1976** *National Observer* (U.S.) 17 Apr. 10/4 It was not the Vietnam War that pinched the adolescent rush to prep schools.

b. (Examples.)

1899 A. H. QUINN *Pennsylvania Stories* 117 He was going to tell all those people, from the Governor down to the prep in the gallery, who came from his own old school, just what the College had done for *him*. **1948** *Chicago Daily News* 6 Dec. 23/4 (*caption*), 2 preps die in Oregon bush crash. **1978** *Maledicta 1977* I. 223 A stout prep who wore saucer-shaped glasses.

c. Short for *preparatory school.* Also *attrib.*

1895 J. L. WILLIAMS *Princeton Stories* 244 Charlie Symington was a well-built prep. boy who had been known to strike out three men with the bases full. **1924** H. DE SÉLINCOURT *Cricket Match* v. 158 To know whose call it is..was driven into me at the prep. **1927** W. E. COLLINSON *Contemp. Eng.* 21 My attendance at Dulwich College Preparatory School (the Prep.) coincided with the South African war. **1934** *Amer. Speech* IX. 237/2 In the following sentence the term refers to high schools, *Nebraska Preps Have Major Encounters this Week*. **1969** *Eugene* (Oregon) *Register-Guard* 3 Dec. 2D/1 The Eagles thought, to win the state B prep football title, they'd have to throw more than they did. **1976** *Honolulu Star-Bull.* 21 Dec. H-2/1 Going back to last Saturday's game, it was great to see just how far Russ Francis has come since his prep days at Kailua High.

prep (prep), *v.*[1] *U.S. slang.* [f. prec., sense 2.] *intr.* To attend a preparatory school, be a preparatory school student.

1915 *Dialect Notes* IV. 236 *Prep*, preparatory: used as a verb 'to attend a preparatory school'. **1920** F. SCOTT FITZGERALD *This Side of Paradise* II. 43 Where'd you prep? **1936** L. C. DOUGLAS *White Banners* xiv. 305 Thomas and this Colonel Livingstone had prepped together at this academy. **1967** *Boston Sunday Herald Mag.* 16 Apr. 8/2 What school do you go to?.. Where did *you* prep? **1977** *New Yorker* 23 May 91/1 A native of Peoria, Illinois, who prepped at Lawrenceville, Davis graduated from Princeton with highest honors in history.

prep (prep), *v.*[2] *slang* (orig. *U.S.*). [f. PREP *sb.* 1, or shortening of PREPARE *v.*] **a.** *trans.* To prepare (someone or something); to train (an animal) for racing; to prime (a witness); *spec.*, in hospital terminology, to prepare (a patient) for an operation. Also *absol.*

1927 *Amer. Speech* II. 313/1 Ask whether the 'ten-thirty appendectomy has been prepped yet?' For some reason a patient's abdomen is not shaved, it is 'prepped', that is, prepared for the surgeon. **1936** *Esquire* Sept. 160/3 *Little Lord Fauntleroy* and *Dodsworth* [*sc.* two films] have been 'prepping prod.' (preparing production) for some time. **1937** 'J. BELL' *Murder in Hospital* vii. 133 Macdonald started to prep him. *Ibid.*, She gave him his atropine for the operation when she had finished prep'ing the leg. **1943** *Sun* (Baltimore) 12 Oct. 16/5 (*heading*) Attention [*sc.* a horse] being prepped for New Orleans 'Cap. **1961** 'K. NORWAY' *Waterfront Hosp.* i. 19, I told Nurse David, 'Five minutes—we'll have to prep on the table.' **1965** *Eng. Stud.* XLVI. 461 *Prepster* 'one who is being prepped; trainee'. **1967** *Boston Sunday Herald* 14 May II. 3/1 Anyone planning to enter greyhound racing should know it costs close to $600 to prep each dog for the races. **1968** J. D. MACDONALD *Pale Grey for Guilt* (1969) xii. 145 Somebody prepped her pretty good, Sheriff. I might even have thought she saw somebody she sincerely mistook for me. **1969** I. KEMP *Brit. G.I. in Vietnam* v. 110 The gun-ships must have done a thorough job of 'prepping' the L.Z. because, apart from sporadic sniper fire,..we met no opposition there. **1972** M. GOLDBERG *Karamanov Equations* xxiii. 226 Have the nurse prep him... Neck, chest, and groin. **1975** *Globe & Mail* (Toronto) 18 Sept. 5/1 Looking as Tory as the advance men who precede the Premier to prep the crowd, he strolled through the market.

b. *intr.* for *refl.* To prepare oneself (for an event); to practise, to train (esp. in sport). *U.S.*

1934 *Amer. Speech* IX. 237/2 Verbal use of the word appears in *Beavers Arrive in Omaha to Prep for Husker Fray.* **1937** *Sun* (Baltimore) 22 Apr. 17/1 (*heading*) Track preps for Ky. Derby. **1941** *Ibid.* 3 July 16/1 The latter.. was prepping for the New Castle Handicap to be run on Saturday. **1949** *N.Y. Times* 4 Sept. v. 2/6 A pitcher, who had prepped earnestly for many years in the minors..was cut from the roster. **1972** *Newsweek* 10 Jan. 24/3 Mrs. Nixon has been prepping for the trip for weeks. **1977** *Time* 28 Nov. 66/1 Akers had prepped as a Royal assistant before moving into the head coaching job at Wyoming in 1975.

pre-pa·ck, *v.* [Pre- A. 1.] *trans.* To pack or wrap (an article, usu. of food) on the site of production or before retail. Also *fig.* So **pre-·packed** *ppl. a.*, **pre-pa·cking** *vbl. sb.* Also **pre-pa·cker.**

1928 *Daily Express* 23 Mar. 3/1 The public..would abandon bread altogether in favour of pre-packed foods, all of them comparatively expensive. **1931** J. W. Wingate *Man. Retail Terms* xv. 344 *Prepacking*, merchandise packed by the store in advance of sale. **1952** *Times* 6 Aug. 2/2 Describing the method of pre-packing butter in most machines, the report states that..the rate of delivery is between 60 and 80 packets a minute. **1957** *Times* 2 July (Agric. Suppl.) p. v/4 These requirements..have done much to encourage prepacking on the farm in units ready for retail sale without further wrapping or weighing. **1962** H. O. Beecheno *Introd. Business Stud.* ii. 14 Now we have the ability to pre-pack, preserve and store the vast majority of the goods available on the market. **1974** 'E. Anthony' *Malaspiga Exit* i. 14 The average pre-packed American beauty. **1976** C. Bermant *Coming Home* ii. iii. 149 The reasoning seemed to be pre-packed and clogged with clichés and slogans. **1976** *Milton Keynes Express* 23 July 23/3 (Advt.), Wholesale fruit and vegetable merchants and pre-packers of quality produce. **1977** *Oxf. Diocesan Mag.* July 14/2 We have exciting new concepts of mission—no longer seeing the Church as going out with a prepacked Gospel to sell.

pre-·pack, *sb.* [Pre- A. 2.] A container or wrapper in which an article (usu. of food) is enclosed on the site of production or before retail.

1957 *Daily Mail* 26 Sept. 8/5 Business is growing so fast that the sale of pre-packs is expected to increase by 70,000,000 a year. **1973** *Times* 1 Feb. 4/2 Prepacks containing 'A' grade eggs may be decorated with a red band. **1976** *Oxf. Consumer* Mar. 8/2 Prepacks of biscuits and shortbread must be marked with their weights if they weigh more than 50g.

pre-pa·ckaged, *a.* [Pre- A. 1.] Packaged on the site of production or before retail. Also *fig.* So **pre-pa·ckaging** *vbl. sb.* Also **pre-pa·ckage** = *pre-pack *sb.*

1944 R. E. Lee *Television* 179 Local stations will transmit pre-packaged variety shows. **1945** *Business Week* 18 Aug. 91 An ill-timed effort to market prepackaged frozen meat. **1947** *Printers' Ink* 3 Jan. 70 (*heading*) Produce marketers survey pre-packaging to stem competition from frozen foods. **1957** *Times* 2 July (Agric. Suppl.) p. vii/2 The growing popularity of pre-packaged foods, of self-service shopping, of refrigerators. **1960** *News Chron.* 22 Sept. 13/1 The pre-package industry was born. **1963** *Supermarket & Self-Service* (Johannesburg) Nov./Dec. 9/1 Place a mass display of pre-packaged cheese on a dump table in the middle of a side aisle. **1965** *Wireless World* July 345/2 (*heading*) Pre-packaged semiconductors for the retail market. **1966** *Rep. Comm. Inquiry Univ. Oxf.* II. 470 To establish a system of required lectures would..place a disastrous emphasis on prepackaged instruction. **1976** *Times* 1 May (Food Suppl.) p. iii/6 Prepackaging..has..been used for cuts of fresh meat.

preparation, *sb.* Add: **1. c.** (Further examples.)

1914 'I. Hay' *Lighter Side School Life* iv. 114 A prefect..awarded both signallers fifty lines for creating a disturbance in Preparation. **1971** *Black Scholar* Jan. 64/1 (Advt.), Teaching load each semester is 7 to 8 hours with two preparations.

6. (Further examples.)

1960 *Harper's Bazaar* Oct. 117/2 The..unfussy packaging of men's preparations. **1964** *New Statesman* 6 Mar. 354/1 In this country a doctor can prescribe from a list of about 5,000 'preparations', mostly mixtures of drugs. **1972** *Guardian* 7 Nov. 11/3 The Vichy preparations include complete ranges of cleansers, toners, moisturisers, night creams.

10. (sense 1 c) *preparation book*; (sense 8) *preparation sermon.*

1896 E. Turner *Little Larrikin* viii. 76 The diminution of the pile of preparation books. **1843** *Knickerbocker* XXI. 261 On the very day of the preparation sermon at Tinnecum, a number of young persons were assembled.

preparationist (prepărēi·ʃənist). *temporary.* [f. Preparation *sb.* + -ist.] One who favours naval and military preparedness.

1915 A. L. Lowell in *World's Work* (N.Y.) XXX. 719/1 The preparationists..fix their attention primarily on the means of securing the safety of our own land from injury by war. *Ibid.*, To the preparationists..the suggestion of a league to enforce peace ought to appeal as a means of doing on an international scale the thing they are seeking to do for the United States.

preparator. Delete *rare* and add further examples.

1884 *Science* 11 Apr. 443 While, however, the use of the photograph for outlines diminishes the labor of the artist about one-half, it increases that of the preparator. **1931** A. A. Morris *Digging in Yucatan* xvii. 267 A phenomenally skillful Japanese artist preparator who was then working for the American Museum of Natural History. **1937** *Nature* 2 Jan. 16/1 The [preservation] process was repeated once, and the bones were then ready for the preparators, who mended cracks and other deficiencies. **1938** *Times* 18 Jan. 15/5 In addition the Museum preparators have made use of skeletons already in the collection.

preparatory, *a.* **2. a.** (Earlier and further examples.) Also *U.S.*, applied to a (usu. private) school in which pupils are prepared for college entrance.

1822 M. Edgeworth *Let.* 23 Jan. (1971) 328, I have asked all your questions my dear mother about the preparatory school for Pakenham... Mr. Malthus and Dr. Batten declared that they should prefer having a boy sent to them from the Charter-House to having him from any lesser preparatory school. **1848** *Indiana Gen. Assembly Doc.* (1849) II. 279 Connected with the Institution is a flourishing Grammar School, which serves the double purpose of a Normal School and a Preparatory Department. **1851** C. Cist *Sk. Cincinnati in 1851* iii. 69 The Classes in the course of study in the Preparatory Department, are divided among the Adjunct Professors of Mathematics and Languages and the Professor of Modern Languages. **1879** *Scribner's Monthly* Dec. 207 The Johns Hopkins is seeking..to penetrate downward into the preparatory schools. **1903** *World's Work* (N.Y.) Sept. 3884/1 The preparatory school..take[s] boys from twelve to fourteen years of age to fit them in from three to six years for entrance to our best colleges. **1924** *Granta* 25 Apr. 361/2 At the age of eight, he arrived at his Preparatory School, 'The Wick', in Sussex. **1949** *Manch. Guardian Weekly* 20 Jan. 5/2 The son of a bishop, he went through a fashionable preparatory (that is, public) school. **1954** A. S. C. Ross in *Neuphilol. Mitt.* LV. 26 School-boys at their preparatory school..should be addressed as *Master*. **1963** [see *junior college* s.v. *junior *a.* (*sb.*) 5]. **1969** *Listener* 9 Jan. 41/3 Such a young man..can often command a tiny handout to tide him over by entering the profession of preparatory schoolmaster, purely as a temporary measure. **1972** *Lebende Sprachen* XVII. 35/2 US preparatory school—BE private secondary school. **1976** *Southern Even. Echo* (Southampton) (Advt. Suppl.) 6 Nov. 7/6 Resident matron required for January for Boys' Preparatory School.

prepare, *v.* Add: **1. e.** (Further examples.) Also, in extended sense, to be willing or determined *to do* something. *Be prepared*, the motto of the Scout and Guide organizations.

1902 G. B. Shaw *Mrs Warren's Profession* Pref. p. ix, Nor am I prepared to accept the verdict of the medical gentlemen who would compulsorily sanitate and register Mrs Warren. **1908** R. S. S. Baden-Powell *Scouting for Boys* i. 20 The badge..of the first class scout consists of a brass arrow head with the motto on it '*be prepared*'. *Ibid.* 48 The scouts' motto is founded on my initials, it is: *be prepared*. *Ibid.* 49 A scout..must Be Prepared at any time to save life. **1939** G. B. Shaw *Geneva* i. 13, I came here to place it before a body of persons of European distinction. I am not prepared to discuss it with an irresponsible young woman. **1948** E. Gowers *Plain Words* vi. 40 The recipient of a letter may feel better..if he is told that the Minister 'is not prepared to approve' than he would have done if the letter had said 'the Minister does not approve'. *Ibid.* 41 'The Board have examined your application and they are prepared to allocate 60 coupons for this production. I am accordingly to enclose this number of coupons.'.. *Prepared to allocate* should be *have allocated.* Since the coupons are enclosed, the preparatory stage is clearly over. **1961** New Eng. Bible *Acts* x. 47 Is anyone prepared to withhold the water for baptism from these persons? **1963** A. Christie *Clocks* xxvii. 229 What I say to you is: 'Be prepared.' And I don't mean it in the Boy Scout sense. **1972** J. Poyer *Chinese Agenda* (1973) xiv. 190 It's better to be prepared..that's what they taught us in the Boy Scouts. **1976** *Daily Tel.* 20 July 2/1 The Government was not prepared to fight for realistic exclusive zones for British fishermen.

prepared, *ppl. a.* Add: **b.** spec. *prepared core* Archæol. (see Core *sb.*[1] 5), *food*, *piano* (see quot. 1960).

1918 A. Huxley *Let.* 12 Aug. (1969) 160 Thirty-two quintals of sugar and prepared foods. **1946** *Mod. Music* Summer 205 *Four Sonatas* for prepared piano by John Cage were also heard. **1952** *Musical Q.* XXXVIII. 124 Cage's pieces for what he calls the 'prepared piano' offer an array of tightly organized little sounds of many colors. **1959** J. D. Clark *Prehist. S. Afr.* vi. 142 The characteristic technique of the Middle Stone Age times is the prepared core and specially prepared flake with thin section and faceted butt. *Ibid.* 157 The same basic prepared-core technique. **1960** *20th Cent.* Apr. 348 Cage, an American, is the originator of the 'prepared piano',..in which the pitch and timbre of certain notes are altered by attaching..metal, rubber, wood, etc., to the strings at various distances from the point at which the hammer strikes. **1964** H. Hodges *Artifacts* vii. 102 The core may be very carefully flaked in preparation so that ultimately one final blow will detach a flake tool of the required shape, and these prepared cores are generally the result of hammer, punch or pressure flaking. **1972** *Listener* 7 Sept. 292/3 Further rapid growth [is] expected in the prepared-foods trade. **1977** *Belfast Tel.* 24 Jan. 9/3 The same professionalism marked John Cage's sonata for prepared piano. For this another small grand piano had been fitted out in advance with an assortment of bolts, nuts and rubber wedges according to a carefully specified plan.

preparing, *ppl. a.* (Later example.)

1864 'E. Wetherell' *Old Helmet* I. i. 21 The other figures, the dark walls and ivy, the servants and the preparing collation, were only a rich mosaic of background for those two.

pre-paroxysmal: see *pre- B. 1 d.

pre-partum (prīˌpā·ɹtɒm), *a.* [L. phr., 'before birth', used *attrib.*] = *ante-partum *a.*

1858 R. Barnes *Physiol. & Treatm. Placenta Prævia* ii. 71, I believe these considerations present a rational explanation of a multitude of cases of præ-partum hæmorrhage, [etc.]. **1950** *Amer. Jrnl. Obstetr. & Gynecol.* LIX. 1116 In cases of prepartum bleeding, cesarean section to facilitate abdominal exploration was practically always necessary. **1978** J. Updike *Coup* (1979) v. 186 'My goodness, you're touchy these days.' 'Pre-partum blues,' he suggested.

prepatency, -patent, -pathological, -pausal: see *pre- B. 1. **pre-pause:** *pre- B. 2a.

prepay, *v.* Add: (Further examples.)

1899 A. E. W. Mason *Miranda of Balcony* xv. 216 He wires me..and prepays the reply. **1973** *Philadelphia Inquirer* (Today Suppl.) 7 Oct. 42/2 He'll be in to prepay.

prepaid *ppl. a.* (further examples); **prepayment** (further *attrib.* examples).

1926 C. Connolly *Let.* Sept. in *Romantic Friendship* (1975) 172, I..sent a prepaid wire. **1977** *Modern Railways* Dec. 465/2 Urgent introduction of a wide-ranging system of pre-paid bus tickets. **1906** Prepayment [see **coin-box*]. **1970** *Which?* Mar. 90/1 Fire meters had defective prepayment mechanisms. **1977** *Wandsworth Borough News* 16 Sept. 14/3 Cash from pre-payment meters, believed to be £107, was stolen from the home.

prepense, *a.* Add: **a.** (Further example of *malice prepense.*)

1923 D. H. Lawrence *Birds, Beasts & Flowers* 128 Full of malice prepense, and overweening.

c. (Further example.)

1919 W. B. Yeats *If I were Four & Twenty* in *Irish Statesman* 23 Aug. 212/1 For he [*sc.* Claudel] is prepense, deliberate.

preperceive: see *pre- A. 1. **prepersonal** to **-phonemic:** *pre- B. 1. **pre-phylloxera:** *pre- B. 2a. **preplan:** *pre- A. 1. **pre-planetary, -planting:** *pre- B. 1. **prepolarization:** *pre- A. 2. **prepolarize:** *pre- A. 1.

prepo·lymer. [Pre- B. 1 in Dict. and Suppl.] An intermediate in a process of polymerization which is convenient for manipulation and can be fully polymerized at a later stage in the process.

1956 *Mod. Plastics* July 111/3 If this thickening process is interrupted at the appropriate point, the prepolymer or sirup has about the same consistency as molasses (in June, not January!). **1962** *New Scientist* 25 Oct. 205/1 The state of polymerization of special synthetic fluids such as aviation turbine oils or polypropylene glycol (the latter a prepolymer used in the manufacture of polyurethane foams). **1971** *Penrose Ann.* LXIV. 23 The second [solventless ink] system uses liquid photo-sensitive pre-polymers which are polymerized and solidified immediately by exposure to high doses of ultra-violet light. **1978** *Sci. Amer.* June 107/1 The third method of consolidating stone is to treat it with organic monomers and prepolymers.

So **prepo:lymeriza·tion**; **prepo·lymerize** *v. trans.*, to convert (a monomer) into a prepolymer.

1949 B. L. Davies *Technol. Plastics* ix. 151 If the prepolymerization of the resin is carried too far, the flow in the mould is restricted so that only a limited range of mouldings can be produced. **1956** *Mod. Plastics* July 111/3 (*heading*) Prepolymerization. *Ibid.* 114/1 Thermosetting resins cannot be prepolymerized to any useful degree in this manner, since they set up to a firm gel at a relatively low degree of cure. **1967** Margerison & East *Introd. Polymer Chem.* iv. 200 If all traces of inhibitors..are not removed from the monomer, irreproducible rates of polymerization are often found; for this reason it is the practice to 'pre-polymerize' 1 or 2% of the monomer before use.

preponderously, *adv. rare.* [f. Preponderous *a.* + -ly[2].] To a preponderous degree; excessively.

1921 *Public Opinion* 5 Aug. 133/1 Is it a city or merely a village preponderously overgrown?

prepose, *v.* Restrict † *Obs.* to senses 1 and 3 and add: **2. a.** (Later examples.)

1946 O. Jespersen *Mod. Eng. Gram.* V. xv. 220 *Well to do* = 'well off, living in easy circumstances' is often preposed, generally written with hyphens: *a well-to-do farmer.* **1951** W. K. Matthews *Languages U.S.S.R.* iv. 53 Syntactically Altaic follows the rule of subordinating, in this case preposing, secondary to principal categories. **1971** *Language* XLVII. 276 The former [example] would result if the NSR preceded the postcyclic transformation which preposes *away.* **1975** *Ibid.* LI. 386 Truncated passives can be generated transformationally..by a rule which obligatorily preposes the underlying object..into underlying subject position. **1978** *Studies in Eng. Lit.: Eng. Number* (Tokyo) 106 It is obvious that there are similarities between the rule which preposes *higher into the heavens* in (46a) and the one which preposes, for example, *up into the clouds* in (42b).

preposed *ppl. a.*: delete † and add later examples. Also **prepo·sing** *vbl. sb.*

1888 *Trans. & Proc. Mod. Lang. Assoc. Amer. 1887* III. 39 It is a characteristic of Anglo-Saxon poetry..to introduce an idea with a pronoun... This preposed pronoun is noticed by all writers upon A.-S. style as frequently standing at the head of the sentence. **1928** O. Jespersen *Internat. Lang.* II. 153 Word-order with preposed subject (as in E[nglish] 'Are you ill?') cannot well be used in an I.A.L. **1970** B. M. H. Strang *Hist. English* v. 290 A strongly falling pattern overall, which has been less general in later English because of the increase in preposed weak particles. **1975** *Language* LI. 815 Passivization..may involve not one but two transformational operations—subject postposing and object preposing. **1976** J. S. Gruber *Lexical Struct. Syntax & Semantics* I. iii. 70 The preposing..seems to add emphasis to the phrase, changing the meaning slightly. **1978** *Language* LIV. 174 Bernard Mohan..presents some formulas and the results of a 'grammaticality' test..for various sentences with adverb-preposing or topicalization below and above a set of predicates. *Ibid.* 283 These failures are also significant facts about the speech of Achilles:..(d) Syntax: sentence length; clause length; preposed relative clauses.

preposition. 3. Delete *rare* and add further examples.

Now usu. hyphened in this sense.

1930 T. Sasaki *On Lang. R. Bridges' Poetry* 26 In French, where postposition, and not pre-position, of the adj. attrib. is the general rule. **1946** O. Jespersen *Mod. Eng. Gram.* V. xxi. 392 Historically, however, *for* was a subordinating conjunction, as shown (1) by the possibility of pre-position. **1961** *Moderna Språk* LV. 243 Another theory advanced by Jespersen is that some words cannot be freely used in pre-position because their signification demands a complement; thus *ashamed* (of something, to do something). **1963** F. T. Visser *Hist. Syntax Eng. Lang.* I. i. 19 The extreme scarcity, however, of examples, in Old English with pre-position of the clause..renders the correctness of this interpretation doubtful.

pre-position (prīpozi·ʃən), *v.* [Pre- A. 1.] *trans.* To position (esp. military equipment) in advance. So **pre-posi·tioning** *vbl. sb.*

1962 *Daily Tel.* 7 May 22/6 The area was selected as one where climatic conditions would provide the maximum test for seaborne military 'pre-positioning'... Stockpiling of military equipment, or as military experts call it, pre-positioning, has been accelerated in Europe. **1972** C. Johnston *Brink of Jordan* I. iv. 23 This gave the unsettling impression that they [*sc.* Saudi and Syrian forces] were simply pre-positioned there so as to ensure the best results for their countries in an eventual carve-up of Jordanian territory. **1979** *Sci. Amer.* Jan. 9/3 Indeed, our own proposals improve the quick-reaction defense of Europe by prepositioning more armor in Europe and rebasing most of the powerful combat air strength now held on the carriers to land bases in support of NATO.

prepositional, *a.* Add to def.: Formed with a preposition; serving as, or having the function of, a preposition. (Further examples.)

1940 C. C. Fries *Amer. Eng. Gram.* 130 The prepositional infinitive was made up of the preposition or function word *to* and the dative case of a verbal noun. **1961** R. B. Long *Sentence & its Parts* iii. 71 The prepositional adverbs *but* and *like* sometimes enter into subordinate clauses (then best regarded as interrogative in type) instead of preceding them and functioning as prepositions with declarative-clause objects. *Ibid.* viii. 185 Prepositional units used as subjects are assigned singular force. *Over the fence* is out. *To admit the truth* would be to endanger the whole enterprise. **1963** F. T. Visser *Hist. Syntax Eng. Lang.* I. iv. 390 This object is traditionally called 'the prepositional object';..it would be more correct to call it a 'direct object dependent on a prepositional group-verb'... Other terms for 'prepositional group-verbs' are 'phrasal verbs'..'group verbs'..'compound verbs'. **1965** N. Chomsky *Aspects of Theory of Syntax* ii. 101 It is well known that in Verb–Prepositional-Phrase constructions one can distinguish various degrees of 'cohesion' between the Verb and the accompanying Prepositional-Phrase. **1965** *Language* XLI. 158 Prepositional object: *John is looking at her* (actually this is not what is usually called a prepositional object, but the object of a prepositional verb-unit *look at.*). **1966** G. N. Leech *Eng. in Advertising* ii. 12 Prepositions are a class of words which occur in initial position in a type of adverbial group, the 'prepositional phrase'.

preposi·tionless, *a.* [f. Preposition + -less.] Lacking or without a preposition.

1956 A. H. Smith *Eng. Place-Name Elements* I. 6 The normal syntax demanded a prepositionless nominative. **1963** F. T. Visser *Hist. Syntax Eng. Lang.* I. iv. 328 To the general replacement..of the prepositionless complements by prepositional complements there are a few exceptions. **1965** *Language* XLI. 133 The subchapter on direct (i.e. prepositionless) verbal government includes.. 'The accusative of price, measure and quantity'. **1966** *Eng. Stud.* XLVII. 54 The traditional and vague term *direct object*..which corresponds to an OE complement in the accusative form and, later on, to a postverbal prepositionless stem-form.

prepotency. Add: **1. b.** *Psychol.* The quality inherent in a particular stimulus or response that makes it prepotent (cf. next).

1928 *Psychol. Rev.* XXXV. 420 What response the animal will make at a given moment depends upon the prepotency of the stimuli. **1953** B. F. Skinner *Sci. & Human Behav.* xiv. 220 When two responses are strong at the same time, only one can be emitted. The appearance of one response is called 'prepotency'.

prepotent, *a.* Add: **1. c.** *Psychol.* Applied to the effective stimulus and its response when stimuli with different, conflicting, responses occur together.

1906 C. S. Sherrington *Integrative Action Nervous Syst.* vi. 228 It is those stimuli which..are most fitted to excite pain which, as a general rule, excite in the 'spinal' animal..the prepotent reflexes. **1928** *Psychol. Rev.* XXXV. 420 The animal behaves as it does because a certain prepotent stimulus in the environment has forced it that way. **1948** W. McDougall *Introd. Social Psychol.* (ed. 29) 459 The 'prepotent reflexes' of sex, fear, and rage. **1953** B. F. Skinner *Sci. & Human Behav.* xiv. 220 The prepotent response does not, merely by virtue of its having been emitted, alter the strength of the dispossessed response. **1960** Hinsie & Campbell *Psychiatric Dict.* (ed. 3) 571/2 In general, nociceptive reflexes, such as the flexion reflex, are prepotent to all other types of reflex competing for the final common pathway.

pre-pottery: see *pre- B. 2a.

prepper (pre·pəɹ). *School* and *College slang.* [f. Prep *sb.* and *a.* 2 + *-er[1, 6].] **a.** *U.S.* A preparatory sports team or a member of such a team. **b.** A preparatory school (Preparatory *a.* 2 a).

1945 *Richmond* (Virginia) *Times-Dispatch* 10 Oct. 18/4 (*heading*) T[homas] J[efferson High School] leads off heavy slate for preppers. **1956** 'M. Innes' *Appleby plays Chicken* I. i. 16 My public school was..nothing to my prepper. **1962** 'R. Gordon' *Doctor in Swim* xi. 73 'Actually, I'm a stinks beak in a prepper,' he confessed. **1974** *Anderson* (S. Carolina) *Independent* 19 Apr. 5B/3 Audie Mathews, 6-4, of Chicago Heights, Ill., one of the nation's most coveted preppers, is reported to be considering North Carolina State, Illinois, Oregon, Purdue and UCLA. **1974** *Times* 29 Oct. 16/4 Cheam is demonstrably the oldest prepper in the business, having started in the Surrey suburb in 1645.

preppy (pre·pi), *a.* *U.S. School* and *College slang.* Also **preppie.** [f. Prep *sb.* and *a.* + -y[1].] Of, pertaining to, or characteristic of a pupil at a preparatory school (see *preparatory *a.* 2a); immature; (see also quot. 1980). Also as *sb.*, a pupil at a preparatory school. Hence **pre·ppiness.**

1900 *Dialect Notes* II. i. 51 *Preppy*, silly, immature. **1970** *New York* 16 Nov. 52/3 His first year as a preppie had left Junius feeling like a pound of plaster of Paris. **1971** M. McCarthy *Birds of Amer.* 10 When he finally did ask,..it was in a casual preppy voice. **1975** B. Meggs *Matter of Paradise* I. iii. 30 All you preppies had those funny names. *Ibid.* III. vi. 98 Bubbling along now in his keen preppie way. **1977** *New Yorker* 11 July 80/2 They are wearable, stylish, practical translations of the all-American look—of preppiness and of L. L. Bean. **1978** *N.Y. Times* 6 May 12/4 The pair of loafers my sons refuse to own because they're too preppy. **1980** W. Safire in *N.Y. Times Mag.* 30 Mar. 9 The word that sums up the rage of the fashion world is 'preppie'... Suddenly, neatness counts, the buttons are down, the sweaters and skirts are back.

pre-precipita·tion, *a.* *Metallurgy.* [Pre- B. 2.] Applied to phenomena occurring at or immediately before the onset of precipitation from solid solution in alloys, esp. the separation of submicroscopic particles from which crystals later develop.

1936 M. Cohen in *Metals Technol.* Oct. 14 (*heading*) Pre-precipitation behavior of the alloy. *Ibid.* 15 The resistance and dilation curves indicate knot formation even at 200°, although there is no pre-precipitation hardening at this temperature. **1949** J. E. Garside *Process & Physical Metall.* xii. 213 This process of age-hardening consists of two stages—(i) Pre-precipitation stage resulting in the formation of nuclei; (ii) Growth of the nuclei, first into particles of ultramicroscopic size, and then of microscopic size. **1959** B. Chalmers *Physical Metall.* viii. 391 The desirable results of precipitation are almost always obtained when a very large number of precipitate particles or pre-precipitation zones are formed. **1965** Hunsicker & Stumpf in C. S. Smith *Sorby Centennial Symposium Hist. Metall.* xviii. 287 In the face of mounting evidence the conviction became widespread that some sort of 'pre-precipitation' structure was developed at low temperatures and possibly at higher temperatures prior to and preparatory to actual precipitation.

pre-predicative: see *pre- B. 1d.

pre-preference, *a.* (Earlier example.)

1869 *Bradshaw's Railway Manual* XXI. 128 New capital..was created as a 4½ per cent. pre-preference or debenture stock, the first preference being made second.

pre-preg, *sb.* (*a.*) [f. *pre-(im)preg(nated *ppl. a.*] A fibrous material (e.g. glass or carbon fibres) that is pre-impregnated with synthetic resin for use in the manufacture of reinforced plastics. Freq. *attrib.* or as *adj.*

1954 R. H. Sonneborn *Fiberglas Reinforced Plastics* iii. 63 The pre-preg materials are fabrics or mats that are pre-loaded, using resin mixtures that are essentially the same as are used in standard molding operations. **1958** D. J. Duffin *Laminated Plastics* iv. 72 Although more expensive than standard materials, prepregs are widely used in the aircraft industry and elsewhere because of the considerable savings in time—and therefore labor—costs. **1965** *Mod. Plastics Encycl. 1966* 167/3 Pre-preg laminates are made by pre-impregnating glass cloth with a resin solution. **1969** *Sci. Jrnl.* Feb. 43/3 Prepreg is made by dripping numerous tows or groups of fibres in a dilute solution of resin in acetone and then laying them down side by side..on a firm flat surface. **1972** *Physics Bull.* Nov. 664/3 Fibre–polymer systems for the fabrication of composite parts are used either as prepregs, in which fibre and polymer are precombined and are ready for the fabrication operation, or as wet systems in which the dry fibre and the polymer are brought together during the moulding process.

Hence **pre·preg** *v. trans.*, to pre-impregnate with synthetic resin; **prepre·gged** *ppl. a.*; **prepre·gging** *vbl. sb.*

1964 Oleesky & Mohr *Handbk. Reinforced Plastics* II. iii. 77/2 Epoxy resins may be readily adapted to prepregging using glass fabrics or roving. *Ibid.* IX. ii. 545/1 The general specifications governing roving for filament winding also apply to roving to be prepregged. **1970** *Encycl. Polymer Sci. & Technol.* XII. 26 'Sheet molding compounds' is the term used by the Society of the Plastics Industry to identify these new reinforced, basically prepreged sheet compounds.

pre-prep(aratory: see *pre- B. 1d. **pre-prepare:** *pre- A. 1. **pre-pressurization:** *pre- A. 2. **pre-pressurize:** *pre- A. 1. **pre-primary:** *pre- B. 1d.

prepri·mate. [Pre- B. 1 in Dict. and Suppl.] An evolutionary ancestor of the primates, or an animal showing characteristics that are more highly developed in the primates.

1931 E. A. Hooton *Up from Ape* II. 67 Our arboreal pre-primate ancestors must have been very closely similar to the existing tree shrews of the Order Insectivora. *Ibid.* 69 When the insectivorous pre-primate became a hand-feeder and a manipulator of objects, it opened up for its descendants a new route of evolutionary progress. **1971** G. H. Bourne *Ape People* xiii. 322 The slope of the jaw seemed to be more like that of a modern preprimate known as the tarsier.

preprint, *sb.* Add: (Further examples.) Also *attrib.*

1929 E. C. Bingham *Some Defs. Rheology* 1 This paper is issued in preprint form primarily to stimulate discussion. **1955** J. A. Wheeler in *Niels Bohr* 174 A paper.. seen in preprint form through the kindness of the authors. **1961** D. J. Boorstin *Image* iv. 141 They [*sc.* scientists] now use the device of the 'preprint'. This is a version of an article made available *before* its 'publication'. **1970** *Nature* 26 Dec. 1356/2 We can show how well connected we are by giving references to a large number of preprints.

prepri·nt, *v.* [Pre- A. 1.] *trans.* To print in advance, *spec.* to print and issue (part of a work) before publication of the whole. Hence **prepr·inted** *ppl. a.*

1928 E. D. P. Evans (*title*) Meaning of minster in place-names. (Preprinted from the Philological Society's Transactions, 1925–28, part I.) **1958** *Practical Wireless* XXXIV. 72/2 It is provided with interchangeable paper on plastic shields which can be supplied either pre-printed or blank. **1964** *Economist* 11 July 165/1 The answer has been preprinted colour gravure. **1965** L. W. Beck *Stud. Philos. Kant* vii. 108 This paper..is preprinted here by kind permission. **1970** A. Davidson *Returns of Love* ii. 21 You pick up the little card which pops out of the slot, knowing that it's been pre-printed. **1977** *It* May 6/1 You can purchase books of 25 pre-printed slips at two pence per book.

prepro·cess, *v.* [f. Pre- A. 1 + Process *v.*[1]] *trans.* To subject to a preliminary processing. Hence **prepro·cessing** *vbl. sb.* Also **prepro·cessor**, a machine for preprocessing.

1964 *Ann. N.Y. Acad. Sci.* CXV. 568 The use of some analog equipment, such as filters, to preprocess data. **1965** *Proc. Internat. Fed. Information Processing Congr.* II. 329/1 (*heading*) ISODATA—a self-organizing computer program for the design of pattern recognition preprocessing. **1966** [see *post-processing* s.v. *post- A. 1 b]. **1967** E. R. Lannon in Cox & Grose *Organiz. Bibliogr. Rec. by Computer* IV. 83 In order to reduce errors..the system provides for a preprocessing and storage of a data base description..in secondary storage. **1967** *Computer Jrnl.* IX. 360/1 The preprocessor was..designed to translate these two dialects into a form acceptable to the Atlas compiler. **1970** A. Cameron et al. *Computers & Old Eng. Concordances* 68 Some preprocessing of the concordances is a desirable prerequisite to editing. **1976** *Nature* 29 Jan. 294/2 The three detected voltages were digitised, preprocessed and recorded on magnetic tape for later computer processing.

prepro·cessed, *ppl. a.* [Pre- A. 1.] Of food: processed before being offered for sale; needing little preparation.

1961 M. Beadle *These Ruins are Inhabited* (1963) viii. 107 Englishwomen..can't afford the extra cost of preprocessed food or commercial laundry charges. **1962** F. I. Ordway et al. *Basic Astronautics* xiii. 520 Fresh meat and vegetables under conventional refrigeration obviously cannot be considered. However, some preprocessed, small bulk, frozen foods are a possibility.

pre-production, *sb.* and *a.* **A.** *sb.* **1.** [Pre- A. 2.] (A) preliminary or trial production.

1938 *New Statesman* 20 Aug. 282/1, I have seen pre-productions, for the Festival, of this week's naturalistic plays. **1947** Crowther & Whiddington *Science at War* I. 49 The General Electric Company worked out a method of pre-production, by which small quantities of new valves could be produced by formerly unskilled women workers, while the problems of mass-production were being worked out.

2. [PRE- B. 1 in Dict. and Suppl.] Work prior to production; preparation for production.

1976 *Time* 20 Dec. 63/1 We're here in New York doing preproduction. **1979** D. LOWDEN *Boudapesti 3* xviii. 100 In films, 80% of scripts written never reached the stage of pre-production.

B. *adj.* [PRE- B. 2.] Prior or preliminary to (a) production.

1946 *Nature* 21 Dec. 897/2 An extremely active development department using a larger number of pre-production machines. **1959** *Times* 19 Feb. 2/4 Testing of valves up to pre-production stage. **1959** P. BULL *I know Face* iv. 66 Other pre-production costs included advance payment to producer. **1967** *Jane's Surface Skimmers Systems 1967–68* 133/1 The design team..is based in a factory at Zaporojie.., where all prototypes and pre-production engines..are developed and built. **1970** M. TORMÉ *Other Side of Rainbow* (1971) iii. 34 Nearly every television variety show operates in a three-phase pattern. First, there is a preproduction period in which songs are chosen, scripts are written, [etc.]. **1973** *Times* 12 Nov. 2/5 Noise measurements on the 02 preproduction aircraft had been disappointing. **1977** *Engin. Materials & Design* Aug. 17/1 The results obtained were comparable with those expected from a pre-production run of conventionally designed radiators.

pre-profe·ssional, *a.* and *sb.* [PRE- B. 1 in Dict. and Suppl.] **A.** *adj.* Prior or preliminary to professional training.

1948 *Mind* LVII. 387 University instruction in psychology should serve..as a preparation for other fields (*e.g.* law, medicine, engineering), in the form of pre-professional courses. **1975** *N.Y. Times* 28 Dec. IV. 12/4 New pre-professional (a currently popular term in education) programs, such as Mills's prelaw 'Administration and the Legal Process'.

B. *sb.* One who is training for a profession.

1970 *Jrnl. Gen. Psychol.* LXXXIII. 140 When I speak to audiences, I find that the myth is still believed firmly, even by preprofessionals. **1977** *Early Music* Apr. 263/1 The conference was designed to draw together professionals and college-age pre-professionals.

prepro·gram, *v.* Also preprogramme. [PRE- A. 1.] *trans.* To program (a computer or calculator) beforehand. Also *transf.* and *fig.* So **prepro·grammed** *ppl. a.*, **prepro·gramming** *vbl. sb.* (*U.S.* also **-gramed, -graming**).

1964 *Economist* 16 May 746/2 Ships operated entirely by pre-programmed computer are practicable. **1965** H. KAHN *On Escalation* viii. 166 Deterioration in international relations will provoke a pre-programed crash defense program. **1970** *Computers & Humanities* IV. 355 Produce a number of specific movies, then use the experience gained to develop appropriate software for combined interactive and preprogrammed modes of operation. **1971** J. Z. YOUNG *Introd. Study Man* p. viii, His brain may indeed be pre-programmed to operate in this way. **1973** P. EVANS *Bodyguard Man* xvii. 110 It was as though his thought-processes had been pre-programmed, as though this was a situation that he had foreseen. **1974** HAWKEY & BINGHAM *Wild Card* xv. 129 Because of the preprograming..all I have to do is transmit the starting instructions. **1977** J. D. DOUGLAS in Douglas & Johnson *Existential Sociol.* i. 60 Even the simplest of human activities, such as walking down the street, cannot be preprogrammed without danger of catastrophe. **1977** *Sci. Amer.* Apr. 94/1 (Advt.), A series of preprogrammed hand-held calculators that virtually revolutionized numerical data processing.

Hence as *sb.*, an already existing program.

1971 J. Z. YOUNG *Introd. Study Man* p. vii, The whole structure of our language and thought is limited by a preprogramme in the organization of the brain.

preproinsulin: see *PRE- B. 1.

prepster (pre·pstəɹ). *U.S.* [f. PREP *sb.* and *a.* 2 + -STER.] (See quot. 1965.)

1965 *Eng. Stud.* XLVI. 464 *Prepster* not only denotes a preparatory student in collegiate slang but also a trainee. **1974** *Sumter* (S. Carolina) *Daily Item* 22 Apr. 1B/1 His credentials—23 points per game and a fantastic field goal average of 80 per cent, plus nine rebounds per game and seven assists per outing as a senior—as a prepster.

prepsycho·tic, *a.* (*sb.*) *Psychol.* [PRE- B. 1.] Of or relating to symptoms, or to the period of time, prior to the onset of a psychosis. Also as *sb.* Hence **prepsycho·tically** *adv.*

1927 HENDERSON & GILLESPIE *Text-bk. Psychiatry* ix. 218 Are there certain pre-psychotic traits which indicate a severer grade of disturbance in the event of a psychosis developing? **1931** *Internat. Jrnl. Psycho-Anal.* XII. 298 (*title*) Ego defence and the mechanism of oral ejection in schizophrenia: the psycho-analysis of a pre-psychotic case. **1935** *Brit. Jrnl. Med. Psychol.* XV. 140 By 'prepsychotic' I mean someone who is showing ominous signs of an impending psychosis but who is not yet frankly psychotic. **1941** *Jrnl. Amer. Med. Assoc.* 16 Aug. 522/1 A severe hypotension, which existed prepsychotically as well as during the course of the psychosis, has been improved. **1959** H. NIELSEN *Fifth Caller* iii. 48 There was a tragic case—a man, prepsychotic, who needed expert attention. **1977** *Time* 4 Apr. 41/2 Tom Verlaine..delivers raw, jabbing vocals in a declamatory, prepsychotic style similar to Patti Smith's. **1977** *Lancet* 27 Aug. 449/1 There are no doubt prepsychotics who abuse alcohol.

prepuberal(ly, -pubertally: see* PRE- B. 1.

prepu·berty. [PRE- B. 1 in Dict. and Suppl.] The period of life preceding puberty, esp. the two or three years immediately before. Also *attrib.*

1922 R. T. FRANKS *Gynecol. & Obstetr. Path.* iv. 74 Prepuberty.—Practically it begins with the time at which 'budding into womanhood' is first noticed and ends with the onset of the first menstruation. *Ibid.* 75 In some instances..in which the menstruation is delayed or remains in abeyance, although ovulation occurs, the prepuberty and the puberty stage cannot be differentiated clinically. **1932** *Amer. Jrnl. Dis. Children* XLIII. 329 We firmly believe that there is a prepuberty rise in basal metabolism. **1941** *Jrnl. Pediatrics* XIX. 291 Adolescence lasts from the time of puberty until about 21 years. Today we are not discussing this whole subject, only certain phases of it and perhaps particularly that part of adolescence which we might call prepuberty and puberty. **1949** M. MEAD *Male & Female* xiii. 280 For the old institutionalized hostilities of..girls' tears and boyish pranks, the new pre-puberty dating pattern is being substituted. **1976** *Times* 1 Sept. (Fashion Suppl.) p. vii/1 All three categories of clothing—male, female and pre-puberty.

prepube·scent, *a.* [PRE- B. 1.] = *pre-pubertal* adj. s.v. PRE- B. 1 in Dict. and Suppl.

1904 G. S. HALL *Adolescence* I. p. x, Rousseau would leave prepubescent years to nature..and allow the fundamental traits of savagery their fling till twelve. **1932** R. F. FORTUNE *Sorcerers of Dobu* ix. 276 The pre-pubescent girls of his own age have lain with boys older than he. **1965** F. SARGESON *Mem. Peon* vi. 174 A pre-pubescent male was..demanding..that 'you leave my mother alone'. **1978** J. HYAMS *Pool* v. 61 This prepubescent midget has put me on the defensive.

Hence **prepube·scence** = *PREPUBERTY.

1916 *Arch. Internal Med.* XVII. 887 We may consider boys in the period of prepubescence as individuals of adult form but of small size, growing rapidly, and as yet scarcely influenced by the internal secretions of the sex glands. **1950** *Psychiatric Q.* XXIV. 495 It would appear that any study of attitudes towards death during prepubescence or adult life, would throw further light on the psychodynamics of human behavior. **1977** *N.Y. Rev. Bks.* 29 Sept. 13/1 During Baum's prepubescence the Civil War took place.

prepubic, *a.* **a.** (Further examples.)

1918 *Bull. Amer. Mus. Nat. Hist.* XXXVIII. 521 In the ornithischian dinosaurs the expanded prepubic process appears to have served as a base for a forward extension of the pubi-ischio-femoralis. **1934** *Anatomischer Anzeiger* LXXVIII. 44 The prepubic skeletal element [of *Ascaphus truei*] is cartilaginous. **1974** D. & M. WEBSTER *Compar. Vertebr. Morphol.* v. 102 In prototherian and metatherian (but not eutherian) mammals there is a fourth skeletal element on each side [of the pelvic girdle], called the marsupial or prepubic bone.

prepubis. Add: **1.** (Later example.)

1956 A. S. ROMER *Osteol. Reptiles* vii. 328 In this case [*sc.* the pterosaur skeleton] the majority opinion is that the true pubis is included in the plate and that this anterior element is a neomorph, a prepubis.

2. = *EPIPUBIS.

1931 G. K. NOBLE *Biol. Amphibia* x. 240 A prepubis may have been a primitive character of modern Amphibia. **1969** *Nature* 14 June 1091/1 Here I report the presence of the so-called marsupial bone (praepubis or epipubis) in the skeleton of *K[ryptobaatar] dashzevegi.* This bone has never before been found in fossil Multituberculata material. **1975** *Nature* 26 June 698/1 Marsupial bones (epipubes, prepubes) occur in Marsupialia, Monotremata and have also been found in Cretaceous Multituberculata.

prepublica·tion, *a.* and *sb.* [PRE- B. 2.] **A.** *adj.* Produced, issued, or occurring in advance of publication.

1922 F. SCOTT FITZGERALD *Let.* 6 Feb. (1964) 332 A pre-publication review which contained private information destined..to hurt the sale of my book. **1936** *Amer. Speech* XI. 171/1 The prepublication announcement and the blurb on the jacket of his recent book. **1964** F. BOWERS *Bibliogr. & Textual Crit.* III. iv. 78 It constituted a pre-publication state decided on before public sale could have offered any opportunity for objections. **1977** *Time* 13 June 60/2 Seldom has an anthology of critical essays aroused so much prepublication anxiety as Diana Trilling's *We Must March My Darlings.*

B. *sb.* [PRE- A. 2.] The action or fact of publishing beforehand; publication in advance.

1971 *Nature* 30 Apr. 547/3 In the opinion of the editor..an article about the paper that had appeared in *Medical World News* contained so much of its substance..as to constitute prepublication and disqualify its claims for space in a journal that aims to publish original material. **1975** P. HARCOURT *Fair Exchange* II. iii. 105 This book..where did you get it?..you realize it's pre-publication?

prepublicity, -publish: see *PRE- A. 2, 1.
prepulse: *PRE- A. 2.

prepu·nched, *ppl. a.* [PRE- A. 1.] Of a card or the like: having holes already punched in it. Of information: already stored or represented as a pattern of holes. So **prepu·nch** *v. trans.*

1953 *Proc. IRE* XLI. 1274/1 While at his desk the programmer may then assemble into a single deck of cards some prepunched library programs together with cards especially punched for the problem to be solved. **1957** *Practical Wireless* XXXIII. 705/1 Pre-punched holder plates take such focal components as valves, etc. **1964** T. W. MCRAE *Impact of Computers on Accounting* ii. 47 We are likely to see a great deal more of inter-business documentation in the form of machine-sensible input, such as sending a purchase order as a pre-punched card. **1965** *New England Jrnl. Med.* CCLXXII. 1211/2 The clerk..obtained a deck of data-processing cards that had been prepunched with the patient's file number.

prepupa (prīpiū·pă). *Ent.* [PRE- B. 1 in Dict. and Suppl.] An insect late in its larval development, during a relatively quiescent phase in which preparations for the transformation into a pupa take place; also, in certain beetles, a distinct instar preceding the pupa stage.

1925 A. D. IMMS *Gen. Textbk. Entomol.* 186 The prepupa represents a greatly abbreviated instar. **1955** P. A. BUXTON *Nat. Hist. Tsetse Flies* xi. 380 Generally speaking one measures the duration of life of the puparium in an inclusive way, from the time when the larva becomes immobile, through the life of prepupa and pupa, to the emergence of the adult. **1959** E. F. LINSSEN *Beetles Brit. Isles* II. 85 After the third moult..it [*sc.* a meloid beetle] turns into what is called a pre-pupa. **1975** *Nature* 17 Apr. 592/2 In such specimens..there is no visible response to background, whether the caterpillars or prepupae are exposed to long or short hours of daylight.

prepupal (prīpiū·păl), *a.* *Ent.* [PRE- B. 1.] Immediately preceding a larval insect's change into a pupa.

1906 J. B. SMITH *Explanation Terms Entomol.* 108 Prepupal: that stage in the larva just preceding the change to pupa. **1925** A. D. IMMS *Gen. Textbk. Entomol.* 185 A brief period of quiescence follows which marks the prepupal instar. **1933** *Jrnl. R. Hort. Soc.* LVIII. 233 The excellent photographs..illustrate the adult sawflies..and the larval, prepupal and pupal stages. **1971** BORROR & DELONG *Introd. Study Insects* (ed. 3) iv. 69/1 The other changes begin in the prepupal stage of the last larval instar.

preputial, *a.* (Later examples.)

1971 [see *FIXATIVE *sb.* 3]. **1976** *Lancet* 20 Nov. 1107/2 Culture of swabs from the preputial sac, and comparison with matched controls, suggested that the source of infection in boys is the prepuce or urethra rather than the bowel as in girls.

prequalification, -ative: see *PRE- A. 2, B. 2a. **prequalify:** *PRE- A. 1.

prequel (prī·kwĕl). [f. PRE- A. 2 + SE)QUEL *sb.*] A book, film, etc., the events portrayed in which or the concerns of which precede those of an existing completed work.

1973 *Britannica Bk. of Year 1972* 732/3 *Prequel,* a literary work whose narrative sequentially precedes that of an earlier work. **1977** *National Observer* (U.S.) 1 Jan. 1/4 Cammer..has just written a book, *Freedom from Compulsion*... He calls it a 'prequel' to his earlier book, *Up from Depression.* '"Prequel" is a word I coined', he explains. 'It's a sequel except it's on a subject that comes before.' **1977** *Globe & Mail* (Toronto) 17 Sept. 37/5 The Silmarillion, for which Tolkien coined the term Prequel, describes not only the creation of Middle Earth, but of the universe. **1979** *Films & Filming* Mar. 11 In this 'prequel' Tom Berenger stars as Butch Cassidy and William Katt as Sundance.

prerabbinical, -radio: see *PRE- B. 1d, 2a.

pre-Raph. (prīræ·f), *a.* (*sb.*) Colloq. abbrev. of PRE-RAPHAELITE *sb.* and *a.* (senses A. 1 and B. 1). Hence **pre-Ra·phly** *adv.*

1874 L. TROUBRIDGE *Life amongst Troubridges* (1966) 80 A new rage..painting the panels of the shutters of our bedrooms,..you can't think how pre-Raph. they look. Pale blue ground..and in each panel droops a flower, of course very pre-Raphly done. **1944** J. LEES-MILNE *Prophesying Peace* (1977) 54 These flowers are madly Pre-Raph. Do you suppose William [Morris] planted these? **1970** *Listener* 27 Aug. 291/2 The diaries of Laura Troubridge written when she was 'a madly Pre-Raph' young Victorian. **1975** *Times* 25 Sept. 13/5 William Gaunt's brilliant little 1940s book at that time contained all that most of us knew..about the Pre-Raphs.

pre-Raphaelism. (Earlier example.)

1852 GEO. ELIOT *Let.* 24–25 July (1954) II. 48 The British Q[uarterl]y..have one subject of which I am jealous—'Pre-Raphaelism in Painting and Literature'.

pre:-Raphaeli·tically, *adv.* [f. PRE-RAPHAELITIC *a.* + -AL + -LY[2].] In a manner suggestive of the pre-Raphaelites.

1895 G. B. SHAW *Let.* 1 Mar. (1965) I. 490 You are glad to..come back PreRaphaelitically to Giotto again. **1927** *Glasgow Herald* 7 July 4/6 The drabness of Arnold Bennett's pre-Raphaelitically accurate Five Towns.

pre-Raphaelitish, *a.* (Earlier example.)

1854 A. THACKERAY *Jrnl.* Feb. in H. Ritchie *Lett. A. T. Ritchie* (1924) v. 61 Mr. Millais was there, a tall good-looking Pre-Raphaeliteish young man.

pre-Raphaelitism. (Further examples.)

1974 J. CHRISTIAN *Pre-Raphaelites in Oxford* 5 In the history of Pre-Raphaelitism nowhere played a more important part than Oxford. **1978** *Bodl. Libr. Rec.* X. 52 In view of Oxford's strong connections with Pre-Raphaelitism, it is doubly gratifying to be able to record that the Bodleian Library has proved a comparatively rich quarry.

pre-ra·tional, *a.* [PRE- B. 1.] Intuitive, instinctive, based on mental processes more primitive than reason.

1903 C. A. STRONG *Why Mind has Body* xi. 274 Not reasoning, but some deep pre-rational instinct..is the basis of our belief in other minds. **1919** M. K. BRADBY *Psycho-Anal.* iii. 39 In our intuitive pre-rational unconsciously based convictions we shall rediscover the beliefs of primitive man. **1921** E. SAPIR *Language* ii. 39 We have been assuming that the material of language reflects merely the world of concepts and, on what I have ventured to call the 'pre-rational' plane, of images, which are the raw material of concepts. **1936** WIRTH & SHILS tr. *Mannheim's Ideology & Utopia* iii. 108 A mode of thought is thus created which conceives of history as the reign of pre- and super-rational forces. **1941** *Mind* L. 378 It is, however, pertinent to one central topic, morality as pre-rational, rational, and post-rational. **1948** P. TILLICH *Protestant Era* p. xxiv, The trend of the younger generation in Europe toward the vital and prerational side of the individual and social life. **1957** J. S. HUXLEY *Relig. without Revelation* (rev. ed.) iii. 52 This pre-rational phase of individual mental life.

prereaction: see *PRE- A. 2.

pre-rea·der. [PRE- B. 1 in Dict. and Suppl.] **a.** A book designed for students who cannot yet read. **b.** A person who cannot yet read. Also **pre-rea·ding** *ppl. a.* and *vbl. sb.*

1965 *Language* XLI. 548 There is no reason to believe that prereading training on Latin phonology would be of any benefit. **1966** J. DERRICK *Teaching Eng. to Immigrants* ii. 104 A set of pictures is published for use at this pre-reading stage. *Ibid.* v. 182 There is preparatory work even to this—work which may be called 'pre-reading' and which is aimed at familiarizing the pupils with the notion of reading and with some of the musculo-sensory activities that are involved in the whole process. *Ibid.* 183 Many elementary courses do in fact include a pre-reader or picture book which can be used with the class if pupils' copies are available. **1972** *Sci. Amer.* Dec. 114/3 Pre-readers will like the action just fine; small sophisticates in the early grades will find the challenge interesting. **1976** *Word 1971* XXVII. 501 This spontaneously developed ability of the prereader has been noted only sporadically.

prerecognition: see *PRE- B. 2a.

pre-reco·rd, *v.* [PRE- A. 1.] *trans.* To record for subsequent use, esp. in film-making and broadcasting. So **pre-reco·rded** *ppl. a.* (*prerecorded tape*, magnetic tape on which sound has been recorded prior to its sale); **pre-reco·rding** *vbl. sb.*

1937 M. STEINER in N. Naumburg *We make Movies* xiv. 233 Pre-recording means pre-scoring, pre-playing with an orchestra, piano, or whatever is required of the song or dance number to be used in the picture. **1941** *B.B.C. Gloss. Broadcasting Terms* 24 *Pre-Record* (*v. trans.*), to record a programme on a closed circuit for subsequent reproduction. **1954** *Newsweek* 11 Oct. 55/2 In TV, as in the movies, it is not unusual to pre-record musical numbers, but this is generally done a few days before the performance. **1958** *Sunday Times* 3 Aug. 3/6 Now that the station has bought a new record-player and gets all its music in prerecorded tapes, the personal touch is all but gone. **1962** *Times* 5 July 15/4 Pre-recorded tapes have been issued in some quantity in Great Britain. **1965** *Listener* 30 Dec. 1087/3, I can only say that pre-recording again ruined what might have been a delightful three-quarters of an hour. **1972** *Daily Tel.* 6 Jan. 1/2 Mr Wilson, Leader of the Opposition, visited a television studio yesterday morning to pre-record his contribution to the programme. **1978** *N.Y. Times* 30 Mar. B22/6 (Advt.), The synchronized cassette player lets you make perfect prerecorded presentations. **1978** *Lancashire Life* Sept. 131/1 Few people feel that the pre-recorded cassette is of comparable quality to the long playing record.

preredu·ction. *Genetics.* [ad. G. *praereduction* (Korschelt & Heider *Lehrb.der Vergleichenden Entwicklungsgeschichte der Wirbellosen Thiere* (Allgemeiner Theil) (1903) II. vi. 586): see PRE- A. 2 and REDUCTION.] **a.** Reduction of chromosome number at the first of the two meiotic cell divisions, rather than at the second. Opp. *POSTREDUCTION a.

1905 *Proc. Acad. Nat. Sci. Philadelphia* LVII. 186 He has to assume a complex axial metamorphosis, which is wholly unnecessary on the basis of a prereduction. **1915, 1921** [see *POSTREDUCTION a].

b. Separation of homologous chromatids or genes at the first of the two meiotic cell divisions, rather than at the second. Opp. *POSTREDUCTION b.

1934, etc. [see *POSTREDUCTION b].

Hence **preredu·ctional** *a.*, involving or pertaining to prereduction; **preredu·ctionally** *adv.*

1905 *Proc. Acad. Nat. Sci. Philadelphia* LVII. 187 He describes a prereductional division of the bivalent chromatin nucleolus. *Ibid.* 195 Whenever the heterochromosomes occur in pairs in the spermatogonia.. their univalent components become separated in the first maturation mitosis, *i.e.*, divide prereductionally. **1950** [see *POSTREDUCTION b]. **1950** [see *POSTREDUCTIONALLY *adv.*].

pre-reflective, -reflexive: see *PRE- B. 1.

pre-re·gistered, *ppl. a.* [PRE- A. 1.] Registered in advance, *spec.* in *Printing*, brought into alignment or coincidence beforehand (cf. REGISTER *v.* 4 b).

1967 KARCH & BUBER *Offset Processes* vi. 219 For multicolor work, cross-hair register marks sight the original material in precision-notched and pre-registered frames. **1973** *LSA Bull.* Mar. 24 The 13 countries with the largest numbers of pre-registered members (all with 20 or more)... The U.S.A...had 189 pre-registered participants.

preregistra·tion, *a.* and *sb.* **A.** *adj.* [PRE- B. 2.] Of or pertaining to the period of a doctor's training between qualification and registration (cf. *HOUSEMAN 6).

1922 *Brit. Med. Jrnl.* 2 Sept. 423/2 After January 1st, 1923, prospective medical students will also be required to pass a pre-registration examination in chemistry and physics. **1962** 'D. MARGERSON' *Med. as Career* x. 67 House officer posts, including the two obligatory pre-registration appointments, will usually take up eighteen months to two years. **1964** *Lancet* 5 Sept. 519/2 If..the two-year clinical course were followed by graduation and two years' preregistration house-appointments, hospitals in the 'network' would get preregistration doctors a year earlier than they do now. **1977** *Daily Tel.* 22 July 6 (Advt.), You'll get £2,636 to continue your normal medical studies. And £4,429 during your pre-registration period.

B. *sb.* [PRE- A. 2.] Registration in advance, *spec.* in *Printing*, the action of bringing into register in advance.

1967 E. CHAMBERS *Photolitho-Offset* vi. 68 Loading and pre-registration are carried out on a separate appliance, thereby enabling subjects to be prepared in advance. **1973** *LSA Bull.* Mar. 24 Pre-registrations for the Congress.

pre-rehearsal: see *PRE- A. 2. **pre-relativity:** *PRE- B. 2a. **pre-relativistic:** *PRE- B. 1.

pre-relea·se, *a.* (*sb.*) [PRE- B. 2.] **1. a.** Designating a period before the date fixed for release of a film.

1927 *Glasgow Herald* 15 Nov. 9/7 An amendment..providing that pre-release cinema shows should take place in provincial centres as well as in London was agreed to without a division. **1928** *Daily Express* 9 July 9 There is a pre-release presentation of Dolores del Rio in 'The Gateway of the Moon', at the Kensington Kinema. **1973** *Times* 11 May 2/6 The film..had only been booked for five prerelease test runs at cinemas in Leeds. **1976** L. ST. CLAIR *Fortune in Death* vii. 68 He's made..a Near East thriller. They wanted some pre-release publicity.

b. Of or pertaining to the period before release of a suspect or prisoner.

1958 F. NORMAN *Bang to Rights* III. 106 You have to atend [*sic*] what they call a prerelease course. **1959** *New Statesman* 7 Mar. 335/2, I am very glad that Critic called attention to the scheme for pre-release leave to selected prisoners. **1961** *Lancet* 22 July 204/1 Such measures as the open prison and the pre-release hostel were proving invaluable. **1971** R. CROSS *Punishment, Prison & Public* ii. 68 Attached to some prisons are pre-release hostels from which the inmates go out to daily regular work. **1976** *Newmarket Jrnl.* 16 Dec., The first mention of any possible charge relating to drink-driving came after he had given a blood sample and a pre-release breath test.

2. *ellipt.* as *sb.* A film or record given restricted availability before being generally released.

1929 *Sunday Dispatch* 13 Jan. 16/3 We, in London, have been privileged to view many pre-releases. **1978** *Sunday Times* 29 Jan. 43/3 'Top Ranking' started life in Britain as a status single, available only as an imported 'pre-release'.

pre-relea·se, *v.* [PRE- A. 1.] *trans.* To release beforehand.

1968 *Punch* 24 Apr. 589/1 There's a lot to be said for pre-releasing the decimal coinage at the lower end of the scale. *a* **1974** R. CROSSMAN *Diaries* (1975) I. 147 We had pre-released the news to the *Daily Express*, the *Guardian* and the *Evening Standard*. **1976** *Church Times* 2 Apr. 10/1 He persistently declines to extend to the Press that assistance (such as circulating in advance scripts of major speeches, or sticking to the text of speeches thus pre-released) which so greatly facilitates newspaper production.

pre-reproductive: see *PRE- B. 1.

prerequire, *v.* (Later example.)

1975 *Christian* II. 228 There are two levels of psychotherapy, the second prerequiring the first.

pre-retirement, -revolution: see *PRE- B. 2a.

pre-revolu·tionary, *a.* and *sb.* [PRE- B. 1 in Dict. and Suppl.] **A.** *adj.* **1.** Existing before a (particular) revolution.

1861 [in Dict. s.v. PRE- B. 1]. **1867** H. W. BEECHER in *N.Y. Ledger* 7 Sept. 2/3 Planted in 1646, it was more than a hundred years old when the pre-revolutionary excitements were taking place in Boston. **1874** T. B. ALDRICH *Prudence Palfrey* x. 166 Since the hanging of a witch or two in pre-revolutionary days, the office of sheriff there has been virtually a sinecure. **1936** *Burlington Mag.* Mar. 130/2 Baroque paintings of the pre-Revolutionary decades in France. **1961** *Times* 29 Dec. 11/1 Pre-revolutionary St. Petersburg. **1976** *New Yorker* 15 Nov. 213/1 Some extraordinarily rich evocations of pre-revolutionary village life in China.

2. Of a society or its condition: verging on social or political revolution.

1964 R. D. HOPPER in I. L. Horowitz *New Sociol.* xix. 313 In pre-revolutionary societies, there is formed a group that is marginal to the structure of political power and social prestige. **1972** 'H. BUCKMASTER' *Walking Trip* 85 It is a prerevolutionary situation I'm told by a white politician in Salisbury, and he thinks the next step is violence. **1974** *Listener* 24 Jan. 108/3 An artist in a pre-revolutionary situation concentrates upon actually producing art. **1975** A. BEEVOR *Violent Brink* vii. 165 England, the despair of Marx, seemed at last about to move into a pre-revolutionary situation.

B. *sb.* One who prepares the way for a revolution.

1937 *Times Lit. Suppl.* 1 May 323/2 Mr. Stephen Spender's 'The Destructive Element', with its presentation of Henry James as a master pre-revolutionary.

pre-rinse: see *PRE- A. 2. **pre-romanesque:** *PRE- B. 1d.

pre-Romantic, *a.* (*sb.*) *Mus.* and *Lit.* Also **pre-romantic.** [PRE- B. 1 in Dict. and Suppl.] Pertaining to or characteristic of the period before the Romantic Movement. As *sb.*, a composer or writer of that period.

1934 C. LAMBERT *Music Ho!* I. 57 Purcell, the most picturesque of the pre-Romantic composers. **1938** C. CONNOLLY in *New Statesman* 6 Aug. 223/1 The English pre-romantics..balanced their love of childhood by their hope of heaven. **1947** A. EINSTEIN *Mus. Romantic Era* xi. 134 One can find examples of it, particularly in the opera, even in pre-Romantic opera. **1959** *Brno Studies in English* I. 104 Bulwer attempted to follow in the steps of the great representatives of the English pre-romantic and romantic period, especially of William Godwin and Lord Byron. **1962** *Times* 16 Feb. 15/3 Mozart is observed..as the clever pre-romantic tune-spinner. **1963** N. FRYE *Romanticism Reconsidered* 9 It is obvious that in pre-Romantic poetry there is a strong affinity with the attitude that we have called sense... But the pre-Romantic structure of imagery belonged to a nature which was the work of God. **1978** D. GRYLLS *Guardians & Angels* iv. 112 In her treatment of parent-child relations Jane Austen is pre-Romantic. **1980** *Church Times* 25 July 6/4 The enormous revolution in literary taste which began in the 'twenties..demoted Spenser, the tribe of Ben Jonson, and the eighteenth-century pre-romantics.

pres: see *PREZ[1, 2].

‖ **pré salé** (pre sale). Also **pré-salé.** [Fr.] A salt meadow, *spec.* one on which sheep are reared; freq. used *attrib.* or *ellipt.* to designate the flesh of sheep reared on a salt meadow.

1839 F. A. KEMBLE *Let.* 21 July in *Rec. Later Life* (1882) I. 255 That peculiar close short turf which creates South Down and Pré Salé mutton. **1903** J. M. FALKNER *Nebuly Coat* i. 3 The low-lying meadows..where as good-tasting mutton is bred as on any *pré-salé* on the other side of the Channel. **1930** A. BENNETT *Imperial Palace* xxiii. 145 It was a man's menu... Turtle soup. Sole *Palace*. Pré-salé with two vegetables. **1935** M. MORPHY *Recipes of All Nations* 54 It is an error to imagine that French mutton and lamb are inferior to English meat. Their *pré-salé* is equal to any. **1966** P. V. PRICE *France: Food & Wine Guide* 48 The most vaunted type of lamb comes from flocks that feed on pastures by the sea, which gives the meat a special delicacy; this type is known as *pré salé* (salty meadow) and has an *Appellation Contrôlée*.

presanctify, *v.* Add to def.: Said also in some Anglican churches on Good Friday. (Earlier and later examples.)

1758 S. REDFORD *Important Inquiry* (ed. 2) App. 397 They offer up and shew the people the Sacrament reserved on those two solemn days, which they call the *imperfect* Mass, or the Mass of the *presanctified*. *a* **1773** A. BUTLER *Feasts Catholic Church* (1774) vi. iv. 355 This is called the 'Mass of the Pre-sanctified Mysteries, *Missa præsanctificatorum*'. **1839** *Penny Cycl.* XIV. 57/2 In the Greek or Constantinopolitan church three Liturgies are in use, those of Basil, Chrysostom, and the Liturgy of the Præ-sanctified. **1909** *Daily Chron.* 10 Apr. 5/4 At Westminster Cathedral yesterday morning the Mass of the Presanctified was solemnised in the presence of Archbishop Bourne. **1957** *Oxf. Dict. Chr. Ch.* 1101/1 In the Middle Ages all present at the Mass of the Presanctified received Holy Communion. **1965** C. E. POCKNEE *Parson's Handbk.* (ed. 13) 156 In some churches the Mass of the Pre-sanctified has been reintroduced with a general Communion from the reserved sacrament. **1978** C. JONES et al. *Study of Liturgy* 409 Communion from the reserved sacrament, the so-called Mass of the Pre-Sanctified.

presbycousis (prezbikū·sis). *Med.* Also **presby(a)cusis, -ac(o)usia** (-ăkū·ziă), **-kousis.** [mod.L., f. Gr. πρέσβυς an old man (cf. PRESBYOPIA) + ἄκουσις hearing (ἀκούειν to hear).] Loss of acuteness of hearing due to age.

1890 BILLINGS *Med. Dict.* II. 386/1 Presbykousis. **1892** F. P. FOSTER *Med. Dict.* IV. 2640/2 Presbycusis. **1896** *Syd. Soc. Lex.*, Presbycousis. **1900** *Lancet* 18 Aug. 538/2 To this last belonged the progressive deafness which came on between the ages of 40 and 50 years, and which had been called presbyacousia. **1911** STEDMAN *Med. Dict.* 703/1 Presbyacusia. **1958** *Times Rev. Industry* Aug. 13/1 Gradual blunting of auditory acuity with the increasing age of the worker..is known as 'presbycusis'. **1970** *Brit. Med. Jrnl.* 30 May 524/2 It is possible that the high level of everyday noise in industrial countries plays some part in the development of presbyacusis. **1976** *Listener* 2 Sept. 279/1 Presbycousis has not yet set in. Most people over 30, said Jeremy Bugler,..lose some of their hearing.

presbyope. Delete *rare*$^{-0}$ and add examples.

1880 L. Owen tr. *Giraud-Teulon's Elem. Treat. Function of Vision* ii. ii. 30 The presbyope presents himself generally under the following aspect: he has always enjoyed excellent distant vision... But he is drawing near to forty-five or fifty and begins to experience a certain difficulty in reading small type. **1900** C. H. May *Man. Dis. Eye* xxiv. 332 The presbyope is compelled to hold reading, writing, sewing, and other forms of near work farther away than the usual distance, making such efforts uncomfortable. **1937** *Jrnl. Optical Soc. Amer.* XXVII. 332/1 Presbyopes should invariably wear their reading correction (reading spectacles). **1974** *Nature* 25 Oct. 729/2 It is known that convergence can bring about accommodation; and it seems likely that in a presbyope, devoid of accommodative ability, convergence would still be accompanied by a central command for accommodation.

presbyteress. Restrict † *Obs.* to sense 1 in Dict. and add: **2.** (Later example.)

1901 J. Wordsworth *Ministry of Grace* v. 271 In these [*sc.* the 'Didascalia' and the 'Constitutions'] and similar books the elders Widows are sometimes mentioned under the title of *πρεσβύτιδες*, a name for which we have no nearer equivalent than the somewhat ambiguous and inexact 'Presbyteresses'... The Virgins, Widows and Presbyteresses have the first place among the women in church.

presca·ler. *Electronics.* [Pre- A. 2.] A scaling circuit employed to scale down the input to a counting or other scaling circuit so that it can deal with high counting rates.

1954 E. H. W. Banner *Electronic Measuring Instruments* xi. 277 When very short resolving times are essential, it is necessary to use a hard-valve pre-scaler in front of a scaler using these new tubes. **1967** *Electronics* 6 Mar. 152 (*caption*) The counter is used in pairs as a prescaler. **1972** *Physics Bull.* Feb. 114/1 A new high performance, low priced scaler timer for use in schools and technical colleges... It features a fast (1 μs) prescaler of integrated circuit construction with a bold two digit read out of counts. **1976** *CB Mag.* June 72/2 Because the VHF prescaler is built-in, the decimal point is placed properly on the display. **1977** *Design Engin.* July 81/3 A prescaler extends this range to 800 MHz.

preschizophrenia, -ic: see *pre- B. 1.

preschool, *a.* and *sb.* **A.** *adj.* [Pre- B. 2.] (Stress variable.) Of or pertaining to the time before a child is old enough for school.

1924 *Jrnl. Amer. Med. Assoc.* 5 Jan. 1/1 We weigh our preschool children nude on their birthdays. **1934** [see *attentive *a.* 1 b]. **1946** *Nature* 23 Nov. 737/1 They [*sc.* defects] develop during the pre-school age, and accurate knowledge concerning them is lacking. **1958** *Word* XIV. 170 In this experiment, preschool and first grade children ..were presented with a number of nonsense words. **1960** *Guardian* 29 Apr. 6/4 Dr Tizard suggested the opening of pre-school centres for mentally handicapped children. **1979** *Dædalus* Spring 76 Participation rates for mothers with children of preschool age increased from 18 to 27 percent between 1966 and 1976.

B. *sb.* [Pre- B. 1 in Dict. and Suppl.] (Stressed *pre·school.*) A kindergarten or nursery school for children of preschool age.

1934 in Webster. **1937** S. V. Benét *Thirteen o' Clock* (1938) 275 Nope, that doesn't work any more, what with pre-schools, automats and movies. **1958** *Word* XIV. 159 The oldest children at the Preschool were five years old. **1966** Bereiter & Engelmann *Teaching Disadvantaged Children in the Preschool* i. 3 This is a 'successful' preschool for disadvantaged children. **1977** *Caravan World* (Austral.) Jan. 67/3 Sue drops their young son at pre-school every morning.

Hence **pre-schoo·ler,** a child who is too young to attend school; a child who attends preschool; **pre-schoo·ling** *vbl. sb.*, the education of a preschool child.

1954 [see *-schooler]. **1958** *Word* XIV. 159 First graders did significantly better than preschoolers. **1965** *Economist* 4 Sept. 883/1 Even as pre-schoolers, these children do not lack experiences. **1971** *Daily Colonist* (Victoria, B.C.) 28 Aug. 18/1 Sesame Street, for preschoolers, to date has gotten few brickbats. **1972** *Guardian* 11 Aug. 12/1 Preschooling is the outstanding economical and effective device in the general approach to raising educational standards in EPAs. **1974** *Ibid.* 19 Mar. 20/2 The schools would be there to offer gipsy children preschooling opportunities. **1979** *Guardian* 5 June 11/3 Pre-schoolers should know their full name by 2½.

presciencelessness (pre·siĕnslĕsnĕs). *rare*$^{-1}$. [f. Prescience + -less + -ness.] The state or condition of lacking prescience.

1928 Hardy *Winter Words* 5 Led by sheer senselessness And presciencelessness Into unreason.

pre-score, *v.* [Pre- A. 1.] *trans.* To score or inscribe beforehand.

1977 *Engin. Materials & Design* Aug. 29/3 A diamond tool to scribe the fired material, or a system that prescores the ceramic alumina in its green state.

pre-sco·ring, *vbl. sb. Cinemat.* [Pre- A. 1.] The recording of a sound track in advance of the shooting of the film it is to accompany.

1937 *Jrnl. Soc. Motion Picture Engineers* XXIX. 356 We do not record songs or orchestras on the set... We record them in advance, usually before the picture goes into production. This we call pre-scoring. **1937** [see *pre-record *v.*]. **1948** E. Lindgren *Art of Film* i. ii. 31 The flexibility of sound-recording methods is well illustrated by the device known as pre-scoring. **1949** B. Woodhouse *From Script to Screen* vii. 111 The principle known as pre-scoring is used extensively.

prescree·n, *v.* [Pre- A. 1.] *trans.* To screen (in any sense) beforehand. Hence **prescree·ned** *ppl. a.*, **prescree·ning** *vbl. sb.*

1967 Karch & Buber *Offset Processes* v. 167 Although no claim is made that the use of this screen will improve the quality of the picture, this new technique will reduce the cost of prescreening the photographs and then stripping the half-tone negative into the flat. **1967** E. Chambers *Photolitho-Offset* xi. 174 With a prescreened film the contact screen is absent, and..the sensitivity of the film itself is varied in the form of a dot pattern. **1977** *Time* 20 June 48/2 The microwave detector could at the very least be used for pre-screening women—especially those under 35 who are ordinarily not encouraged to have mammograms unless they have a family history of breast cancer or symptoms of the disease. **1977** *Jrnl. R. Soc. Arts* CXXV. 241/1 Careful prescreening for human health hazards will have taken place. **1978** *New York* 3 Apr. 84/1 College Background Singles Only—Newsletter of pre-screened, higher quality singles events plus our own tennis and theatre parties.

prescribable (prĭskrəi·băb'l), *a.* [f. Prescribe *v.* + -able.] That can or may be prescribed; capable of being prescribed.

1967 *Economist* 25 Feb. 708/1 The Central Health Services Council's committee on the classification of proprietary preparations has laid down for doctors' guidance its views on when a food is a food and not a drug and therefore not prescribable. **1977** *Lancet* 24/31 Dec. 1360/1 Only a fraction of these are prescribable.

prescribe, *v.* Add: **2. c.** Delete † *Obs.* and add later examples.

1961 *Parthenon* (Marshall Univ., W. Va.) 10 Nov. 3/3 The '*Third Unabridged*' does not, of course, pretend to prescribe. It seeks, rather, to describe. **1978** *Amer. Speech* LIII. 70 Conceived as a modern dictionary that describes but does not prescribe, *Webster's Third New International Dictionary of the English Language* brought forth a deluge of adverse criticism and scathing reviews.

4. Delete † *Obs.* and add later example.

1919 K. Routledge *Mystery of Easter Island* viii. 116 As both the lifeboat and the cutter were carried in the waist of the ship when we were at sea, the space available for 'constitutionals' was prescribed.

prescribing *vbl. sb.* (earlier example).

1542 N. Udall *Erasmus's Apophthegmes* sig. N5^{v}, Signifiying, not to bee any prescribyng to the Romaines, how ferre thei ought to extend their empier.

prescription. Add: **I. 1.** (Earlier and later examples.)

1542 N. Udall *Erasmus's Apophthegmes* sig. f4^{v}, The moste parte of people is barred from offendyng, onely by prestripcions [*sic*] of lawes, but a philosophier accomptteth and vseth reason in stede of lawes. **1960** J. O. Urmson *Conc. Encycl. Western Philos.* 143/1 Moral judgements, on this view [*sc.* the prescriptivist's], share with imperatives the characteristic that to utter one is to commit oneself, directly or indirectly, to some sort of precept or prescription about actual or conceivable decisions or choices. **1963** *English Jrnl.* May 337/2 Note that this statement [from Sir James Murray's preface to the Dict.] contains not one word about fixing the language, about proscription or prescription of any kind. **1968** J. Lyons *Introd. Theoret. Linguistics* i. 43 It should be stressed that in distinguishing between description and prescription, the linguist is not saying that there is no place for prescriptive studies of language.

III. 6. *prescription charge, pad.*

1928 E. O'Neill *Strange Interlude* ii. 61 He..goes to the table and taking a prescription pad from his pocket, hastily scratches on it. **1961** *Daily Herald* 9 Feb. 9 Of the doubled prescription charge his argument was: 'It is ludicrous exaggeration to say that by and large a 2/os. charge is any more of a burden than a 1/os. charge was in 1949.' **1965** *Ann. Reg. 1964* 47 Medical prescription charges would be abolished (at a cost of £25 million a year) and pensions would be increased. *a* **1974** R. Crossman *Diaries* (1975) I. 35 Kenneth Robinson gave the case for abolishing prescription charges. **1975** M. Simpson *Chrome Connection* iii. 61 The indentations on the prescription pad bore witness to his complicity.

prescriptionist. (In Dict. s.v. Prescription.) Add: **b.** (Further example.)

1906 *Dialect Notes* III. 151 (*Arkansas*) Mr. H. B. Mayes has accepted a position as *prescriptionist* for James S. Robinson, one of the most prominent druggists of Memphis.

c. = *prescriptivist *sb.*

1954 *Mind* LXIII. 258 It would be correct to call him an ethical 'prescriptionist'. **1964** C. Barber *Ling. Change Present-Day Eng.* i. 8 In fact they become moralists or prescriptionists, intent on telling us how we ought to talk.

Hence **prescri·ptionism** = *prescriptivism 2.

1962 *Amer. Speech* XXXVII. 215 Long's expressed dissatisfaction with school grammars..as well as his impatience with common proscriptions like *everybody they* indicate his rejection of traditional prescriptionism.

prescriptive, *a.* Add: **1. a.** Now also *spec.* in *Linguistics.* (Opp. *descriptive *a.* 3 b: cf. *normative grammar* s.v. *normative *a.* b.)

1933 O. Jespersen *Essent. Eng. Gram.* i. 19 Of greater value, however, than this *prescriptive* grammar is a purely *descriptive* grammar. **1963** *English Jrnl.* May 338/1 An accurate description of the language as it is actually used, kept simple by the relative absence of variants.. will in itself serve prescriptive purposes. **1968** J. Lyons *Introd. Theoret. Linguistics* i. 43 Linguistics..is *descriptive*, not *prescriptive* (or normative). **1977** *Time* 4 Apr. 5/3 The point to be made to Ms. Spaak, the Académie Française and all other prescriptive-normative institutions that would like to see language spoken in a certain way: c'est impossible.

b. *Philos.* Having or implying an imperative force. Also *absol.*

1946 *Jrnl. Philos.* XLIII. 35 The issue is whether a definition shall be taken as prescriptive in empirical enquiry or used as a convenient tool constantly responsible to facts. A nominal definition is by definition prescriptive. **1951** [see *descriptive *a.* 3 a]. **1952** R. M. Hare *Lang. Morals* i. 2 If moral language belongs to the genus 'prescriptive language', we shall most easily understand its nature if we compare and contrast first of all prescriptive language with other sorts of language. **1961** I. L. Horowitz *Philos., Sci. & Sociol. of Knowl.* vii. 88 Whatever the ratio of descriptive and prescriptive elements in an ideology, it is clearly a different qualitative entity than either religion or science. **1963** R. M. Hare *Freedom & Reason* v. 72 If moral judgements were *singular* prescriptives.., there would be less difficulty. **1967** *Encycl. Philos.* II. 314/2 All the views of definition that have been proposed can be subsumed under three general types of positions... These three general positions will be called 'essentialist', 'prescriptive', and 'linguistic' types. **1976** T. D. Perry *Moral Reasoning & Truth* 176 Every moral statement is prescriptive in the sense that it entails a certain imperative.

4. (Earlier example.)

1765 Johnson *Preface* in *Plays of Shakespeare* I. p. vii, The Poet, of whose works I have undertaken the revision, may now begin to assume the dignity of an ancient, and claim the privilege of established fame and prescriptive veneration.

b. *Anthrop.* Applied to marriage traditionally considered obligatory between persons in certain categories of relationship to each other within a tribe or kinship group. (Cf. *preferential *a.* d.)

1958 *Amer. Anthropologist* LX. 75 Prescriptive marriage rules entail enduring affinal ties between groups. **1961** E. Leach *Rethinking Anthropol.* iii. 54 Needham.. claims to have demonstrated that a rule of prescriptive patrilineal cross-cousin marriage is an impossibility. **1968** R. Needham tr. *Lévi-Strauss's Elem. Struct. Kinship* (1969) p. xxxi, Exceptional cases apart, they do what they say they must, hence the reason for calling their marriage system 'prescriptive'. **1971** F. Korn in R. Needham *Rethinking Kinship & Marriage* 113 The terms can be consistently arranged in an asymmetric prescriptive terminology.

prescriptivism (prĭskri·ptiviz'm). [f. Prescriptive *a.* + -ism.] **1.** *Linguistics.* The practice or advocacy of prescriptive grammar; the belief that the grammar of a language should lay down rules to which usage must conform.

1954 *College English* XV. 395/1 Professor Bloomfield comes to the conclusion that what is taught in an English class must be some form of..prescriptivism, checked by the limits of fact as established by linguistics. *Ibid.* 395/2 Bloomfield defends prescriptivism first because it has social utility. That is, the public judges..our students by the language they use. **1957** *Eng. Lang. Teaching* XII. 1. 10 It is not for their prescriptivism as such that the older teaching grammars stand condemned. **1964** *Word* XX. 289 The charge of prescriptivism is also made against Chomsky. **1971** *Archivum Linguisticum* II. 54 We are probably all aware of the operation of even weaker collocational constraints as we search for the 'right' choice among, say, *achieve, accomplish, effect,*..etc. to associate with *plan* or *project* or *proposal*.., and a certain inescapable 'prescriptivism' informing language choices is perhaps worthy of note in passing. **1976** *Amer. Speech 1973* XLVIII. 264 Prescriptivism is wrong, the reader is told again.

2. *Philos.* The theory that (moral) judgements have prescriptive force akin to that of imperatives; freq. contrasted with *descriptivism 1.

1963 R. M. Hare *Freedom & Reason* ii. 16 Let me refer to the type of doctrine..as 'universal prescriptivism'. **1963** I. L. Horowitz *Power, Politics & People* 15 His [*sc.* Mills's] role in sociology as a contributor to its debates on descriptivism and prescriptivism. **1967** *Encycl. Philos.* II. 317/2 There are two main varieties of prescriptivism. The nominalist variety explains definitions as semantic rules for assigning names to objects, while the formalist variety regards definitions as syntactic rules for abbreviating strings of symbols. **1973** *Heythrop Jrnl.* XIV. 136 (*title*) Prescriptivism in theory and practice. **1976** T. D. Perry *Moral Reasoning & Truth* i. 33 Moore's famous doctrine of the 'naturalistic fallacy' which has been accepted in principle by three of the four major tendencies in analytical ethics: intuitionism, emotivism, prescriptivism.

prescriptivist (prĭskri·ptivist), *a.* and *sb.* [f. as prec. + -ist.] **A.** *sb.* An adherent or advocate of prescriptivism. **B.** *adj.* Of, pertaining to, or characteristic of prescriptivism.

1952 T. Pyles *Words & Ways Amer. Eng.* xi. 272 But he is likely not to see any reason why absolute uniformity, the desideratum of the prescriptivist, should be any particular concern of the student of language even if it were possible of attainment. **1959** *Aristotelian Soc. Suppl. Vol.* XXXIII. 167 It seems to me that only prescriptivist prejudice can deny that we have here a morality. **1960** J. O. Urmson *Conc. Encycl. Western Philos.* 143 To call a thing good is thereby to offer guidance about choices; and the same might be said of the other moral terms. Descriptivists, however, refuse to admit that this feature is part of the *meaning* of moral terms. Their principal opponents, who may be called 'prescriptivists', hold that it *is* part of the meaning. **1964** E. BACH *Introd. Transformational Gram.* v. 90 But the decision to edit..has nothing in common with the prescriptivist's zeal. **1967** *Encycl. Philos.* II. 317/2 The prescriptivist assimilates definitions to imperative sentences rather than to declarative sentences. **1973** *Heythrop Jrnl.* XIV. 139 His normative views are no more abitrary or relativist than those of any utilitarian, despite his non-naturalist and prescriptivist theory of meta-ethics. **1976** T. EAGLETON *Crit. & Ideology* v. 174 It is this purely prescriptivist morality.. which finds a later echo in the moral ideology of Kant. **1977** *Publ. Amer. Dial. Soc.* 1974 LXI/LXII. 8 The English teacher who..is suddenly bereft of her prescriptivist techniques and her substitution drills.

prescriptivity (prīːskripti·viti). [f. PRESCRIPTIVE *a.* + -ITY.] = PRESCRIPTIVENESS.

1963 R. M. HARE *Freedom & Reason* i. 6 The prescriptivity of moral judgements explains both why there should be thought to be a problem about moral freedom, and how to approach its solution. **1966** *Amer. Philos. Q.* III. 305/2 We questioned the 'prescriptivity' of the deduced conclusion of normative syllogisms. **1976** T. D. PERRY *Moral Reasoning & Truth* 9 When we point out to our interlocutor what other moral judgements his present judgement commits him to in view of its universalizability and 'prescriptivity' we shall often be able to force him to withdraw it.

prescriptorial (prīːskriptōə·riăl), *a. rare.* [f. PRE- B. 1 + SCRIPTORIAL *a.*] Existing before the use of writing.

1897 J. W. POWELL in *16th Ann. Rep. U.S. Bureau Amer. Ethnol. 1894–95* p. xcvi, The names are associative or symbolic in the vague fashion characteristic of prescriptorial ideation.

Presdwood (pre·stwud). Also **presdwood.** [Alteration of *pressed wood.*] (See quot. 1940.)

A proprietary name in the U.S.

1940 *Chambers's Techn. Dict.* 671/1 *Presdwood*.., tradename for a strong building-board having water-resisting properties. **1946** *Amer. Jrnl. Roentgenol.* LV. 198/2 The procedure was repeated using tempered presdwood phantoms. **1949** *Official Gaz.* (U.S. Patent Office) 5 Apr. 36/1 Masonite Corporation, Chicago... *Presdwood*... For fiberboard, insulating board, composite board, [etc.]... Claims use since Oct. 6, 1926. **1951** R. MAYER *Artist's Handbk.* v. 193 In the majority of instances Presdwood is superior to wooden panels.

pre-season, -seizure: see *PRE- B. 2a. **presee:** *PRE- A. 1.

presele·ct, *v.* [PRE- A. 1.] *trans.* To select in advance.

1864 [in Dict. s.v. PRE- A. 1.] **1910** *Proc. Amer. Inst. Electr. Engin.* XXIX. 189 The secondary switches are inserted between the line-switches and the first selectors in such a way that the primary line switches pre-select idle secondaries and the secondaries pre-select idle first selectors. **1941** J. S. HUXLEY *Uniqueness of Man* ii. 56 Immigrants were pre-selected for..the qualities making up the pioneer spirit. **1961** *Which? Reports on Cars* 7 The cars tested..are in no way pre-selected by the dealer or especially inspected by the manufacturer. **1974** *Country Life* 28 Nov. 1673/1 Four pushbuttons..can be set to pre-select any given four FM stations.

Hence **presele·cted, -sele·cting** *ppl. adjs.*

1910 *Proc. Amer. Inst. Electr. Engin.* XXIX. 184 A line switch always uses a pre-selected idle trunk instead of making a selection after a subscriber starts to call as the Strowger selector switches do. **1924** H. H. HARRISON *Introd. Strowger Syst. Autom. Telephony* i. 16 The combination of such pre-selecting switches with the trunking methods..made the large capacity exchange system a commercial possibility. **1933** AUDEN in *Rev. Eng. Stud.* (1978) Aug. 305 The pre-selected gear adjusted. **1962** J. RIORDAN *Stochastic Service Syst.* vi. 126 A. B. Clarke.. proposed..that the process be observed, in the stationary condition, for a preselected busy time τ. **1974** D. KYLE *Raft of Swords* iii. 19 A short-range missile..capable of being fired at pre-selected targets. **1977** *Offshore Engineer* June 60/3 A computer program..carried out a complete fatigue analysis of pre-selected joints of the tower.

presele·ction, *sb.* and *a.* **A.** *sb.* [PRE- A. 2.] Selection in advance; *spec.* the operation or use of a preselector.

1924 H. H. HARRISON *Introd. Strowger Syst. Autom. Telephony* 145/2 (Index), Pre-selection. **1930** W. K. HANCOCK *Australia* x. 207 Members of branches join with the unionists who live in the same area to choose by a pre-selection ballot the local party candidate, and to elect delegates to attend the State conference of the party. **1941** J. S. HUXLEY *Uniqueness of Man* ii. 55 Pre-selection was at work on the pioneers. The human cargo of the *Mayflower* was certainly not a random sample of the English population. **1948** R. V. POUND *Microwave Mixers* i. 28 Since most of the circuits..were designed for use in pulse-radar systems, preselection is achieved by means of the resonant TR cavity of the duplexer that precedes the converter. **1950** J. ATKINSON *Herbert & Procter's Telephony* (new ed.) II. xviii. 572/1 The trunking between the subscribers' lines and the 1st group selectors makes use of two stages of preselection by means of 10-outlet unidirectional mechanisms. **1957** *Railway Mag.* Nov. 758/2 Route-setting is used, with pre-selection facility.., the controls remaining stored until conditions allow of their becoming effective. **1962** *Lancet* 6 Jan. 23/2 All cases with chorioretinitis or cerebral calcification, were excluded. There was no other preselection. **1976** [see *PRESELECTOR a]. **1979** *Daily Tel.* 24 Sept. 4/8 Mr Bob Hawke, president of the Australian Council of Trade Unions and former President of the Australian Labour party, announced yesterday that he would be a contender for pre-selection for the safe Labour seat of Wills at the next Federal election.

B. *adj.* [PRE- B. 2.] Occurring before selection.

1977 *Daily Tel.* 7 Nov. 2 The Service's Ground Branch is most seriously affected, with one in three group captains nominated for command making it known at preselection stage that they are not interested in taking over their own stations.

presele·ctive, *a.* [PRE- A. 3.] That preselects or permits preselection.

1925 *Jrnl. Inst. Electr. Engin.* LXIII. 660/2 If there are switches with a large number of outlets the problem does not arise; neither would it arise if one could use preselecting outgoing secondary switches, i.e. switches which themselves found the line before it was wanted... Such a circuit will no doubt arrive and, when it does, outgoing switches of a pre-selective type will for 10-point switches ..completely sweep the board. **1930** *Engineering* 17 Oct. 498/3 The pre-selective device consists of an arrangement whereby the gear-control lever can be set for any gear, but the selected gear will not actually be engaged until a pedal is depressed. **1941** J. S. HUXLEY *Uniqueness of Man* ii. 54 Pre-selective influences are those which attract certain types into an environment and discourage others. **1955** *Times* 16 Aug. 2/6 The Conquest Century has the characteristic Daimler transmission, which comprises a fluid flywheel and a preselective epi-cyclic gearbox. **1971** B. SCHARF *Engin. & its Lang.* xvi. 234 More sophisticated overhead chain conveyors are provided with a mechanism by means of which any one of a number of discharge points can be preselected at any loading station. The material will then be automatically discharged or moved on to a side line... These conveyors are termed preselective overhead chain conveyors.

presele·ctor. [PRE- A. 2.] **a.** *Teleph.* A switch which when a subscriber lifts his receiver automatically connects the calling line to an idle trunk by a hunting action, independently of impulses produced by dialling; formerly also = *line finder* s.v. *LINE *sb.*[2] 32.

1912 J. POOLE *Pract. Telephone Handbk.* (ed. 5) xxxii. 535 The line-switch used by Siemens is a specially neat arrangement... It is called a 'pre-selector' by Messrs Siemens, and each switch is complete in itself. *Ibid.* 536 Secondary line-switches or pre-selectors are used in both systems to facilitate and economise the connections. **1921** W. AITKEN *Autom. Telephone Syst.* I. 3 A preselector is a switch that automatically selects an idle line of a group when the receiver is lifted. **1924** [see *HUNT *v.* 8*]. **1950** J. ATKINSON *Herbert & Procter's Telephony* (new ed.) II. xviii. 572/2 The 1st preselectors are arranged in groups, so that each group carries..an equal volume of traffic. The preselectors of one group are trunked via 2nd preselectors to a maximum of 100 1st selectors. **1976** T. H. FLOWERS *Introd. Exchange Syst.* iv. 89 The choice between preselection and line-finding is mostly a question of economics. The first needs one exchange switch, or exchange line, and the second one switch per cord circuit. The quantity of switches needed as line finders is thus much less than the quantity as pre-selectors, but whereas line finders must be full-sized exchange switches to achieve satisfactory traffic loading, pre-selector switches may have as few as ten contacts in the banks.

b. *Telecommunication.* A tuned circuit preceding the first mixer in a superheterodyne receiver; an analogous filter in a microwave receiver.

1930 *Electronics* Sept. 279/1 (*heading*) An improved preselector circuit for radio receivers. *Ibid.* 308/1 The essential features of this preselector are shown in Fig. 6. **1951** A. SHEINGOLD *Fund. Radio Communications* xv. 307 The preselector, when present, helps to maintain a favorable signal-to-noise ratio and minimizes interference effects. **1971** M. G. SCROGGIE *Found. Wireless & Electronics* xxii. 396 Because the i.f. amplifier is relied upon for most of the selectivity, the preselector tuning circuits do not have to be very sharp, so slight errors in gauging are not serious. **1975** D. G. FINK *Electronics Engineers' Handbk.* xxv. 72 Narrow-band filters in the receive path, often called preselectors, are built using mechanically tuned cavity resonators or electrically tuned YIG resonators. Preselectors can provide up to 80 dB suppression of signals from other radar transmitters in the same rf band but at a different operating frequency.

c. A gearbox that enables a driver to select the next gear at any time before the change is actually made (by means of a separate pedal). Usu. *attrib.*

1930 *Engineering* 17 Oct. 498/2 There is one cam for each gear, all mounted on a common shaft coupled to the pre-selector lever. **1935** *Economist* 7 Dec. 1144/1 It is a natural step from the power unit to the transmission, where most important developments have centred round such features as the fluid flywheel and the pre-selector gear. **1969** *Driving* (Ministry of Transport) xvi. 198 'Pre-selector' transmissions, mostly found on buses and coaches, have a lever by which the driver can select gears in advance, ready for later changes... No gear change takes place until a gear-change pedals is pressed and released. **1979** J. LEASOR *Love & Land Beyond* i. 13 An electrical gear change which could be used as an ordinary box or as a preselector.

pre-se·ll, *v. Comm.* [PRE- A. 1.] *trans.* To promote (a product) before it is available to the consumer; to persuade (the consumer) in advance to buy a product. Also *transf.* So **pre-se·lling** *vbl. sb.* and *ppl. a.*, **pre-so·ld** *ppl. a.*

1950 in WEBSTER Add. **1958** *Washington Post* 22 Sept. A2/1 Campaign organizers and the American Heritage Foundation public services advertising campaign has already done much to 'pre-sell' the public. **1959** *Times* 7 Apr. 14/4 It is the turn of the television programme to provide pre-sold material for cinema films. **1959** P. WOOD in S. Spender tr. *Schiller's Mary Stuart* 8 English audiences are far less indulgent to her than foreign ones, who are pre-sold on the pathos of her situation. **1960** *Times* 26 Oct. 4/2 Plays expanded from television originals are also, in a sense, pre-sold. **1961** *Economist* 11 Mar. 984/1 Others believed..that the 'pre-selling' of the major products by advertising direct to the consumer would have a much more potent effect when the barrier of the counter had been removed and she had nothing to do but pick them up. **1962** E. GODFREY *Retail Selling & Organization* iv. 33 Pre-sold goods. In some cases the preliminary stages of the sale will have been completed before the customer comes into the department, through advertising. **1967** *Guardian* 21 July 3/2 We deliberately avoided preselling the film to America. **1973** *Publishers Weekly* 30 Apr. 50/3 The recent January issue..was so relatively 'with it' that the entire issue was presold. **1977** *Daily Tel.* 2 Dec. 19/1 The interviews..have been pre-sold to the United States and other foreign countries.

presence. Add: **1. d.** The quality in reproduced sound that gives a listener the impression that the recorded activity is occurring in his presence (see also quot. 1950).

1950 *Audio Engin.* Sept. 33 In motion picture work presence refers to the lack of localization of the reproduced sound, so that the eye is beguiled into believing that the sound issues from the location the eye follows... A second use of the term *presence* indicates the degree of intimacy achieved... A third type of presence is detail presence, in which an auditor is able to pick out an individual instrument or soloist, and more or less easily follow its melodic line throughout the changing mass of sound. **1952** H. F. OLSON *Musical Engin.* vii. 262 The reverberation-frequency characteristic has a marked effect upon presence. Excessive reverberation in the low-frequency range reduces presence. A uniform directional pattern in the directivity characteristic of a loudspeaker enhances the presence. **1957** *IRE Trans. Audio* V. 106/2 If the need for great 'presence' calls for a very close microphone position, the reproduction may cause a solo instrument to sound much too large, and this can be corrected by attenuating the difference channel relative to the sum. **1958** *Proc. Inst. Electr. Engin.* CV. B. 609/1 The second observation concerns the critical nature of the frequency band in the region 2–4 kc/s... Deficiency in this band gives a distant impression; slight excess gives a forward quality, sometimes referred to as 'presence'. **1974** HARVEY & BOHLMAN *Stereo F.M. Radio Handbk.* v. 127 (*caption*) Curves showing prominence given to mid-range and bass frequencies by the presence control. **1976** G. ALKIN in J. Borwick *Sound Recording Pract.* xxiv. 364 Some types of Lavalier microphone have a non-linear frequency response which peaks in the 'presence' region (between about 4 and 6 kHz) to restore clarity of diction.

e. *Politics.* The maintenance by a nation of political interests and influence in another country or region; *spec.* the maintenance of personnel, esp. armed forces, on the soil of an allied or friendly state; *concr.*, armed forces stationed in this way. Also *transf.*, denoting the representation of a nation's interests at an event.

Cf. Fr. *présence*, in same sense as in quot. 1955.

[**1955** *Times* 4 Aug. 5/3 Times had changed, he said, and there was no longer any need for outmoded oriflamme to guarantee the *présence française*, or rather the *permanence française*, which could only exist 'if we respond to the wishes of the peoples oversea'.] **1958** *Spectator* 7 Feb. 176/2 The 'presence of France' must be maintained. **1961** *Listener* 21 Dec. 1058/1 As Britain and France step back on to the side-lines [in Africa], the United States steps forward to join them there. This new presence..was not at first easy for Britain to accept. **1963** *Ann. Reg. 1962* 319 An effective United Nations 'presence' in South West Africa. **1966** *Punch* 22 June 898/1 How small can a 'presence' be, of the sort we are going to maintain East of Suez?.. The Americans have a presence of 380,000 men in Vietnam alone, and regard that as barely enough. **1972** *Times* 18 Mar. 12/4 Setbacks in the Arab world that followed his liquidation of the guerrilla presence in Jordan. **1975** *Listener* 25 Sept. 390/1 They were known as the Trucial States. When the British presence was withdrawn in 1971, they became a federation called the United Arab Emirates. **1977** *Time* 10 Oct. 11/3 Working out a formula that would allow some Palestinian presence at Geneva was the focus all week long of intense bargaining.

5. a. Also *transf.*

1959 *Sunday Times* 18 Jan. 16/8 For a painter to have a presence is already an achievement. By 'presence' I mean the variously-definable something that bids a visitor pause and is one of the signs of greatness. **1977** 'E. ANTHONY' *Silver Falcon* vii. 135 The chestnut..had that indefinable quality known in the horse world as presence.

presenile, -senility: see *PRE- B. 1, A. 2.

presenium (prisī·niŏm). *Med.* [f. PRE- B. 1 in Dict. and Suppl. + L. *senium* feebleness of age.] The period of life preceding old age.

1926 *Lancet* 16 Oct. 820/2 Presenile Mental Disorders. In this article the term presenile is applied to mental disorders arising in the period of life beginning in the late 'forties and extending to the early 'sixties. This period includes the climacterium in women, and certain common mental disorders met with in both sexes during the years which precede the actual period of old age or senility. The more frequent clinical types of mental disorders that are encountered during the presenium are as follows. **1976** SMYTHIES & CORBETT *Psychiatry* vii. 132 Dementia occurring in the presenium demands thorough and complete investigation.

presensitiza·tion, *a.* and *sb.* **A.** *adj.* [PRE- B. 2.] Existing or occurring before sensitization.

1964 W. G. SMITH *Allergy & Tissue Metabolism* ii. 28 These responses rapidly returned to pre-sensitisation levels.

B. *sb.* [PRE- A. 2.] Sensitization beforehand.

1977 *Lancet* 27 Aug. 419/1 Data from patients whose serum had been tested for the presence of lymphocytotoxic antibodies before transplantation against a panel of at least 40 random lymphocyte donors were used in analyses of the effect of humoral presensitisation.

So **prese·nsitize** *v. trans.*, to sensitize beforehand; **prese·nsitized** *ppl. a.*

1963 *Lancet* 5 Jan. 45/1 In 2-month-old neonatally thymectomised C3H mice, an established Ak skin graft broke down within 12 days after the injection of lymphoid cells from C3H donors presensitised against Ak. **1967** KARCH & BUBER *Offset Processes* vi. 230 Presensitized plates are surface coated by the manufacturer and ready for exposure when removed from the original package. **1977** *Lancet* 27 Aug. 419/1 Recipients whose serum reacted against more than 5% of the panel members were regarded as being presensitised.

present, *a.* (*adv.*) Add: **I. 1.** *present company excepted* (and varr.), phr. used to indicate that a generalization does not apply to the hearers of it; (*to be*) *among those present*: to be present (at a function, etc.); to be in the vicinity; (orig. used in reports of social gatherings, etc.; hence in jocular use).

1793 J. O'KEEFFE *London Hermit* I. ii. 25 Sir, you should always except the present company. **1832** *Reg. Deb. Congress U.S.* 14 June 3530 Mr. C[layton] observed that the gentleman ought to remember that the present company is always excepted. **1846** DICKENS *Dombey* (1848) iii. 20 There's a Tartar within a hundred miles of where we're now in conversation, I can tell you, Mrs. Richards, present company always excepted too. **1913** F. L. BARCLAY *Broken Halo* vii. 92 'Present company excepted' is always understood, without being expressed, when sweeping generalities are being made. **1925** WODEHOUSE *Carry on, Jeeves!* iv. 84, I hopped out of bed pretty early next morning, so as to be among those present when the old boy should arrive. **1947** —— *Full Moon* vi. 111 There had unquestionably been mosquitoes among those present. **1975** G. MOFFAT *Miss Pink* iii. 54 Women never strike out for themselves... Present company excepted, of course.

present, *sb.*[2] Add: **2. e.** *a present from* (*Brighton* etc.): an inscription on a piece of souvenir pottery etc., bearing the name of the town in which it is sold; hence, a piece of pottery etc. so inscribed, a souvenir.

1852 DICKENS *Bleak Ho.* (1853) iv. 28 We found a mug, with 'A Present from Tunbridge Wells' on it. **1890** KIPLING *Courting of Dinah Shadd* 125 She gave me a drink out of a china mug wi' gold letters—'A Present from Leeds'. **1921** W. DE LA MARE *Mem. Midget* viii. 49 A gay little bumper of milk gilded with the enwreathed letters, 'A Present from Dover'. **1962** N. MITFORD *Water Beetle* 113 The china cabinet will contain Rose Pompadour Sèvres cheek by jowl with A Present from Bexhill. **1964** F. SINCLAIR *Three Slips to Noose* vii. 61 A small square room furnished with..china shepherds and presents from Clacton. **1974** J. STUBBS *Painted Face* i. 32 A small ashtray..inscribed *A Present from Brighton*.

present, *v.* Add: **I. 1. c.** Also *fig.*

1923 *Adelphi* Aug. 236 Osbert is a born impresario... Osbert 'presents' the [Sitwell] family, and does it with originality.

2. a. (Further example: cf. sense *9 b.)

1880 [see *PRESBYOPE].

4. c. Of a radio or television producer or broadcaster: to bring (a broadcast item) before the listening or watching audience, to introduce or announce (a programme). Of a performer: to perform (a song etc.).

1933 *Radio Times* 14 Apr. 120/1 Tonight Mr. James Agate 'presents' perhaps the greatest..star of this glittering series. **1961** *N.Y. Times* 30 Jan. 19 Ellie Mao, soprano, and Frederick Fuller, baritone, presented a program of folksongs entitled 'East meets West' in Carnegie Recital Hall last night. **1972** *Listener* 10 Aug. 187/2 The need felt by..the Presentation Department at Television Centre..to do something more than merely 'present' the evening's programmes. 'Presenting' means seeing that the programmes get on the air tidily and on time, smoothing over or explaining disaster, making announcements and trailing coming events. **1976** *Laurel* (Montana) *Outlook* 9 June 6/3 A solo, presented by Marilyn Parker, was accompanied by Mrs. Markegard.

5. (Later examples.) Also *absol.*

1976 *Daily Tel.* 20 July 3/2 How can anyone, any lawyer, present any case that is acceptable in common sense. **1976** *Dallas Morning News* 22 Sept. 10B/5 Learn to read, learn to listen, learn to think, learn to write, learn to present. *Ibid.*, Businesses have botched sales efforts mainly because their people..could not present their information in clear and 'selling' English.

9. b. Also more widely in *Med.*: of a condition: to be manifest, to occur. Of a patient: to present himself or appear for an initial medical examination. Cf. sense 2 b in Dict., and quot. 1880 in sense *2 a.

1925 *Boston Med. & Surg. Jrnl.* 23 July 179/1 A rather marked purplish hemorrhagic area presented about the wound. **1960** *Lancet* 16 Jan. 138/2 A patient presenting with an exacerbation of bronchitis was initially assigned by the doctor to one of three categories. **1972** *Nature* 8 Sept. 102/2 These complications may present as hypersensitivity reactions.., but most often they take the form of gastric erosions. **1976** *Lancet* 20 Nov. 1107/2, 73 boys who presented to their general practitioners..with symptoms of urinary-tract infection..were referred to a three-year prospective study. **1977** *Proc. R. Soc. Med.* LXX. 262/1 It is not unusual for patients to present in an eye department with symptoms associated with either poor accommodation or poor convergence.

presentable, *a.* Add: **4.** (Earlier and later examples.) Also *fig.*

1800 M. EDGEWORTH *Parent's Assistant* (ed. 3) VI. 147 Do send my *ooman* to me to make me *presentable*. **1801** —— *Belinda* I. iv. 132 Excuse me for showing you the simple truth; well dressed falsehood is a personage much more *presentable*. **1907** J. M. SYNGE *Lett. to Molly* (1971) 172, I will show it to you tomorrow if it is presentable enough. **1925** C. CONNOLLY *Let.* 23 Apr. in *Romantic Friendship* (1975) 72 He [*sc.* Maurice Bowra] is extremely presentable in any society. **1965** F. RAPHAEL *Darling* xix. 87 It was enough to be socially presentable. **1974** *Times* 19 Oct. 6/7 Bowra remarked that he had had his hair cut—'makes one more presentable'. The word 'presentable'.. was a very important epithet in the Bowra system of social terminology... Those who had 'unpresentable' pinned on them were remorselessly barred. **1979** A. MORICE *Murder in Outline* ii. 12 A group of more presentable-looking seniors granted the privilege of handing round the apéritifs.

presentation. Add: **III. 5. a.** (Later examples.) Also, a display or show (e.g. of slides) used esp. in advertising.

1972 G. BROMLEY *In Absence of Body* i. 13 'We've got the OOO-Frooty presentation tomorrow.'.. The presentation was to show the client proposals for a new [advertising] campaign. **1976** *National Observer* (U.S.) 12 June 3/4 Picnic lunches, public speeches, and presentations about Proposition 15 were to be the order of the day. **1976** J. H. SPENCER *Surgenor Campaign* i. 16 Cusack taking him through a slide presentation on their international capability: twenty-seven offices in fourteen countries.

c. In Broadcasting, the action or an instance of presenting a programme; also *ellipt.* for *presentation department* (see sense 10 below).

1941 *B.B.C. Gloss. Broadcasting Terms* 26 *Programme presentation.* (1) Action of presenting a sequence of programmes by means of a framework of microphone announcements... (2) Framework of microphone announcements in a sequence of programmes, its purpose being to supply continuity, to link programmes together, and to attract listeners. **1963** [see *NEWSPEAK]. **1968** *Listener* 22 Aug. 252/1 In bad periods of radio..language is usually what they [*sc.* programmes] are about, or, to call it by its new, pompous name, Presentation. **1968** *Radio Times* 28 Nov. 23/3 Television presentation by Nick Hunter. **1974** *Some Technical Terms & Slang* (Granada Television), *Presentation*, the department within Granada responsible for shape and coordination of the daily programme schedule. **1978** *Listener* 7 Dec. 762/4 The business of neat, informative presentation.

IV. 10. (in sense 4) *presentation binding, bowl, box, clock* (example), *copy* (earlier and later examples), *cup, drawing, pack, plate, silver, watch*; (in sense 1 b) *presentation dress*; (in sense 5 c) *presentation assistant, studio, suite*; **presentation department** (see quot. 1978).

1941 *B.B.C. Gloss. Broadcasting Terms* 24 *Presentation Assistant* (*abbrev.* P.A.), Broadcasting official immediately responsible for the smooth running of a sequence of programmes, and hence for co-ordinating the activities of programme producers, announcers, and engineers directed to that end. **1939–40** *Army & Navy Stores Catal.* 841 Books in presentation bindings. **1952** J. CARTER *ABC for Bk. Collectors* 139 *Presentation binding*, used variously for *gift binding* or *author's binding*. **1907** *Yesterday's Shopping* (1969) p. ii/2 Presentation bowls. **1973** L. COOPER *Tea on Sunday* ii. 30 Silver, some of it..presentation cups and bowls, shining behind shining glass doors. **1908** *Sears, Roebuck Catal.* 333/2 Alaska metal tableware set in a fancy presentation box. **1976** *Sunday Mail* (Glasgow) 28 Nov. 31/4 The two bigger boxes have ribbons and bows on them. We know there is a demand for the presentation box. That's why they are dearer. **1935** D. L. SAYERS *Gaudy Night* i. 17 A Presentation Clock was to be unveiled. **1803** SCOTT *Lett.* (1932) I. 182 Be so good as to disperse the following presentation copies with 'From the Editor', on each. **1938** [see *CANCELLANDUM]. **1978** A. WAUGH *Best Wine Last* xxiv. 304 There were a great many presentation copies, signed by brother and sister writers. **1973** Presentation cup [see **presentation bowl*]. **1978** *A–Z of BBC* (ed. 2) 163/1 Presentation Department is editorially responsible for supervising the transmission operation; for promoting programmes on the screen; for network identification..; for programme announcements and public service information,..; and for running the Television Duty Office. **1975** *Country Life* 20 Feb. 428 Among the drawings there are those, aptly christened by Johannes Wilde 'presentation drawings'. **1896** *Girl's Own Paper* 12 Dec. 161/1, I was borne off to the Court Dressmaker to choose the..presentation dresses. **1938** N. MARSH *Death in White Tie* viii. 83 He looked at the two photographs... One was of the Lady Mildred Potter in the presentation dress of her girlhood. **1976** *Shooting Times & Country Mag.* 9–15 Dec. 11/1 (Advt.), Supplied in presentation pack with supply of BB shot. **1867** C. L. EASTLAKE in *Queen* 15 June 470/1 If the pieces of 'presentation plate'..were only entrusted to art-workmen of sound education, we might hope for something better than the everlasting palm trees, camels and equestrian groups. **1967** N. FREELING *Strike Out* 40 Here on shelves was presentation silver..for Rob was the best bicycle champion Holland had had. **1960** *B.B.C. Handbk.* 40 It (*sc.* the Television Centre] will provide the service with..seven major production and two presentation studios. **1974** *B.B.C. Handbk. 1975* 264/2 The Television Centre houses separate presentation suites incorporating network control rooms, and studios for announcements and weather forecasts. **1931** M. ALLINGHAM *Police at Funeral* iv. 51 Presentation watch... The company gave him this watch.

presentational, *a.* Add: Also, of or pertaining to presentation in other senses. Also *absol.* (Further examples.)

1928 *Daily Tel.* 19 July 18/3 The intelligent theatres of New York..show an admirable sympathy both for good European drama and new forms of presentational art. **1929** A. N. WHITEHEAD *Process & Reality* II. iv. 170 Perception which merely, by means of a sensum, rescues from vagueness a contemporary spatial region, in respect to its spatial shape and its spatial perspective from the percipient, will be called 'perception in the mode of presentational immediacy'. **1942** S. K. LANGER *Philos. in New Key* iv. 97 The meanings given through language are successively understood, and gathered into a whole by the process called discourse; the meanings of all other symbolic elements that compose a larger, articulate symbol are understood only through the meaning of the whole... This kind of semantic may be called 'presentational symbolism', to characterize its essential distinction from discursive symbolism, or 'language' proper. **1958** C. H. WHITMAN *Homer & Heroic Tradition* vi. 107 It is by means of the image and the poetic symbol..that language is made presentational. *Ibid.* 127 If metaphor flags and facts prevail, the presentational is lost, and the poem sinks to prose. **1959** W. A. CHRISTIAN *Interpr. Whitehead's Metaphysics* iii. 54 For occasions of a relatively high grade of complexity, a contemporary region may be given in presentational immediacy. That is, the region may be perceived as the locus of sensa, and as the subject to mathematical relations. **1962** *Listener* 3 May 765/1 A personal style, an effective or original rhetoric, a brilliant presentational technique are cheerfully accepted in lieu of any real human adequacy. **1975** *Nature* 23 Oct. 723/1 An author with the technical knowledge and presentational skill of John Maddox needs no introduction. **1980** *Times* 24 May 14/3 It all was done for 'presentational' reasons..not merely to make the Americans feel good, but..to show solidarity.

presenta·tionally, *adv.* [f. prec. + -LY[2].] In a presentational manner; by means of or as regards presentation.

1934 *Mind* XLIII. 390 We have a number of unconscious sensations as elements in wholes in which they do not figure presentationally, but only as ingredients. **1954** *Mind* LXIII. 196 How does this internal occupation of the visual field itself come to occupy that field presentationally? **1958** C. H. WHITMAN *Homer & Heroic Tradition* vi. 105 Yet when we speak of the 'direct appeal' of an image or symbol, we mean that it appeals as an image of painting or sculpture appeals to the mind, that is, presentationally. **1979** *Guardian* 30 June 8/4 Presentationally speaking, as they say in the public relations business.

presentatively, *adv.* (Later example.)

1878 S. H. HODGSON *Philos. of Reflection* I. 172, I represent to myself what *I imagine* you to be feeling presentatively.

pre:sent-day·, *a.* [PRESENT *a.* (*adv.*) 10.] Current, contemporary; now in existence or in use; prevalent; living at the present time.

1887 [in Dict. s.v. PRESENT *a.* (*adv.*) 10]. **1902** in C. W. Cunnington *Eng. Women's Clothing* (1952) ii. 47 Present-day fashions require for the ideal figure an upright poise of the shoulders. **1925** I. A. RICHARDS *Princ. Lit. Crit.* 222 That Dante is neglected is due only indirectly to his present-day obscurity. **1926** D. L. SAYERS *Clouds of Witness* vi. 142 A present-day girl, who rushes about bareheaded in all weathers. **1930** *Times Educ. Suppl.* 31 May 245/3 Much of present-day British India never was under Mogul rule. **1934** *Amer. Speech* IX. 83/1 An invitation from Edward C. Ehrensperger to address the Present-Day English Section of the Modern Language Association of America. **1934** *Discovery* Nov. 309/1 There is a reversal back to negative phototropism, that is, they [*sc.* the termites] revert to the normal conditions of their present-day life. **1946** 'S. RUSSELL' *To Bed with Grand Music* v. 77 A pigskin bag at present-day prices. **1959** *Universities & Left Rev.* Spring 54/1 The passivity of the present-day working-class reader. **1967** E. SHORT *Embroidery & Fabric Collage* iii. 63 In present-day furnishing also there is a feeling for function as well as decoration. **1974** P. ERDMAN *Silver Bears* iii. 35 My family has an obligation not only to present-day Iran, but also to the Persia of the past. **1977** G. W. H. LAMPE *God as Spirit* ii. 51 Saul's sudden possession by the Spirit when he met a group of ecstatics coming down from a high place, preceded, like some of their present-day counterparts, by a musical group.

Hence **present-day·ness,** actuality, contemporaneity.

1963 *Times* 9 Jan. 11/3, 1960 doesn't view the eighteenth century as 1920 did—fashion and social economic state of society affect our attitude to the past, and it's the designer's job to bring out this present-dayness.

prese·ntedness. *Philos.* [f. PRESENTED *ppl. a.* + -NESS.] (See quot. 1951.)

1925 C. D. BROAD *Mind & its Place* v. 255 The premise ..might be derived from an uncritical jump from 'presentedness' to 'presentness'. **1933** *Mind* XLII. 307 It is part of the notion of a specious present that a certain characteristic, which we will call 'presentedness', has a maximum value at a certain point in it, and tails off to nothing in two opposite directions within it, *viz.* towards the point where the perceived past merges into the remembered past, and towards the point where the anticipated future merges into the perceived future. **1951** *Mind*

LX. 162 'Presentedness' seems to be Broad's name for the characteristic Hume called 'force and vivacity'. **1954** *Mind* LXIII. 33 Broad does not explain what he means by 'presentedness' beyond saying 'This is meant to denote a psychological characteristic.'

presentee² (prezĕntī·). *joc.* [f. PRESENT *a.* (*adv.*) in imitation of ABSENTEE.] One who is present. Hence **presentee·ism.**

1892 'MARK TWAIN' *Amer. Claimant* xxi. 211 There was an absentee who ought to be a presentee—a word which she meant to look out in the dictionary. **1931** H. WITHERS *Everybody's Business* ix. 161 Certainly he is an absentee.. —if he adopted the habit of dropping in at the works and making well-meant suggestions.., is it likely that his presenteeism would be helpful? **1943** *Nat. Liquor Rev.* July 4/2 The Kaiser Company's public relation officials discovered that the term 'absenteeism' irked the people who read it... The Kaiser Company..changed its policy and praised those who were on the job by using the term 'presenteeism'.

pre-se·ntence, *sb.* and *a.* **A.** *sb. Linguistics.* [PRE- B. 1 in Dict. and Suppl.] A construct that precedes or underlies the formation of a sentence.

1940 BRYANT & AIKEN *Psychol. of Eng.* iv. 33 These primitive 'pre-sentences' came to be broken up. **1965** *Language* XLI. 459 Let us call these sequences of morphemes presentences when they label nonsurface P-markers.

B. *adj.* [PRE- B. 2.] **a.** That occurs before a judicial sentence.

1957 *Encycl. Brit.* VI. 719/2 Under the federal rules of criminal procedure and the law of a few states, a pre-sentence investigation by the probation service and a report to the trial judge must be made. **1974** *Guidelines to Volunteer Services* (N.Y. State Dept. Correctional Services) 36 *Pre-sentence report*, a background investigation conducted by a probation department following an individual's conviction of a crime. **1979** *Arizona Daily Star* 1 Apr. A8/2 As Raymond said in a pre-sentence interview: 'My closest friends are my mother and my brothers. They're the only people I can trust.'

b. *Linguistics.* That occurs before a spoken or written sentence.

1965 N. CHOMSKY *Aspects of Theory of Syntax* ii. 102 Sentence Adverbials which form a 'pre-Sentence' unit in the underlying structure. *Ibid.* iv. 148 Verbs are strictly subcategorized into Intransitives, Transitives, pre-Adjectival, pre-Sentence, etc.

presenter. Add: **7.** One who presents or introduces a programme on radio or television.

1967 *Listener* 24 Aug. 249/2 A few words spoken into a camera by a presenter can smooth..an awkward script. **1974** *Radio Times* 16 Feb. 17/3 You and Yours. Presenter Lyn MacDonald. **1976** *Evening Times* (Glasgow) 1 Dec. 6/1 It's the fact that the Nationwide presenter made a quick dash by air from London to Abbotsinch and then on to Paisley.

presentiality. a. (Later examples.)

1911 tr. *Aquinas's Summa Theol.* I. xiv. 205 His glance is carried from eternity over all things, as they are in their presentiality. **1969** G. LEFF *Hist. & Social Theory* i. 18 Its presentiality takes precedence over all its other attributes.

presentiate, *v.* Add: (Later examples.) Hence **prese·ntiated** *ppl. a.*; **presentia·tion,** the act of rendering present.

1974 *Southern Calif. Law Rev.* XLVII. 800 If we say that the squirrel is futurizing the present, *i.e.*, preparing for the future, or presentiating the future, *i.e.*, bringing the future into the present, we are expressing an inaccurate anthropomorphism. *Ibid.* 802 The entire credit structure, including the monetary system itself, is founded on presentiation. Virtually no aspect of life in a modern society is left untouched by presentiation related to exchange. *Ibid.* 805 Because trouble is expected in a relation, efforts may be made in advance to deal with it transactionally, i.e., to eliminate it before it occurs through resolving the conflicts in advance, thereby turning what would have been relational into what is simply an allocated (presentiated) cost. **1976** *Jrnl. Econ. Issues* X. 15 Contracts 'presentiate' the future, or bring the future into the present where it is arranged. *Ibid.* 47 The transaction would be fully presentiated.

presentic (prĭze·ntik), *a. Gram.* [f. PRESENT *a.* (*adv.*) + -IC.] Pertaining to or characteristic of the present tense.

1964 H. S. SØRENSEN in *Eng. Stud.* XLV. (Suppl.) 81 As in the case of the incomplete perfect, grammarians have overlooked the fact that what is 'presentic' about the perfect is the point of reference, and nothing else. **1965** W. WINTER *Evidence for Laryngeals* 210 In B nonpresentic forms with an /a/ suffix were found in one and the same paradigm with presentic forms with an /n/ infix and no /a/ suffix.

presenting, *ppl. a.* (Further examples in *Med.*: cf. *PRESENT *v.* 9 b.)

1911 R. C. CABOT *Differential Diagnosis* 17 A 'presenting symptom', comparable to the 'presenting part' in obstetrics, may turn out to be of minor importance when we have studied the whole case. **1948** MARTIN & HYNES *Clin. Endocrinol.* iv. 96 Increasing weight may be the presenting symptom. **1960** R. D. LAING *Divided Self* vi. 111 All that could not find direct expression and open acknowledgement in her was condensed in her presenting symptom. **1973** *Times* 17 Oct. 14/4 The temptation to shoplift may be a presenting complaint in depressive illness or melancholia.

presentist, *sb.* (*a.*) Delete *rare* and add further examples. Also, one who has a bias towards the present or is influenced by present-day attitudes. Hence **pre·sentism.**

1927 [see *PASSÉISME]. **1956** *N.Y. Times Bk. Rev.* 8 Jan. 22/3, I think Mr. Nevins' review underscores the danger of 'presentism'; I suggest historians would strengthen their position by applying the chief test of their profession—perspective and caution in contemporary analyses. **1975** *Nature* 24 Apr. 729/3 Such history as is dealt with reads soundly, but it is often drawn from secondary sources and professional historians of science would judge it presentist and Whiggish. **1976** T. STOIANOVICH *French Hist. Method* i. 36 Even the attempt to understand the past in its own terms is 'presentist' to the extent that it is founded on what contemporary science and bias lead us to believe to have been its own terms. **1977** *Times Lit. Suppl.* 27 May 655/1 The author wants to explain how the world got to be the way it is at the start of the last quarter of the twentieth century. 'Presentism' accordingly governs the way he distributes attention.

presently, *adv.* Add: **2. a.** Revived in U.S. and to some extent in Great Britain.

1939 *Topeka* (Kansas) *State Jrnl.* 20 Feb. 12/1 Sunner is presently minister of interior and one of the outstanding leaders of the Falangists. **1943** *Time* 20 Sept. 25 They said Mussolini assured them he would return to power and re-establish the Fascist regime, comparing himself presently with Napoleon—the parallel being Napoleon's exile on Elba. **1945** *Richmond* (Virginia) *Times-Dispatch* 21 June 1/3 The one class of cadets presently at the academy. **1949** *Sun* (Baltimore) 9 Apr. 6/1 The members of the presently major coalition can hardly refuse to meet with the Mayor. **1957** G. MARX *Let.* 12 Apr. (1967) 213, I am presently building a house and doing my own show, but sometime within the next two months I'll make it. **1958** *Economist* 9 Aug. 433/1 It is entirely possible that Mr Macmillan..may now be getting greater commendation from the commentators of his generation than he will eventually get from historians; certainly the praise presently being heaped upon him seems to be..a consequence of the recent recovery in the Conservatives' fortunes. **1968** *Globe & Mail* (Toronto) 17 Feb. 52 (Advt.), We want a go-getter who is well established and presently calls on machinery, tool, and equipment supply firms. **1968** B. FOSTER *Changing Eng. Lang.* v. 215 This meaning of 'at present'..is one which once again has been reintroduced from across the Atlantic where it had also lingered on, with the result that it is now in good use in England. 'Warm air is presently moving north-east' reported a B.B.C. weather bulletin (20 May 1963). **1969** *Daily Tel.* (Colour Suppl.) 24 Jan. 8/4 Ivan Cooper, a Protestant and former Unionist,..and presently chairman of the Derry Labour Party, was elected chairman. **1971** *Nature* 2 July 23/1 The Caribbean area is a subplate presently attached to the South American plate. **1978** *N.Y. Times* 30 Mar. D14/5 (Advt.), GTE Sylvania is presently engaged in the research, design, development and production of high energy Lithium Battery power sources for use in highly specialized applications. **1978** *Dumfries Courier* 13 Oct. 2/5 Mr. William O'Brien, solicitor, Dumfries, for the accused, said Mr. Savage was presently unemployed, his last employment being a year ago.

pre-separate: see *PRE- A. 1.

‖ **presepio** (prese·pio). [It., f. L. *præsæpe* enclosure, stall: cf. PRÆSEPE.] A crib; a model of the manger in which Christ was laid.

1759 M. W. MONTAGU *Let.* 19 July (1967) III. 220 The devout people who spend 20 years in making a magnificent presepia [*sic*] at Naples. **1958** *Listener* 25 Dec. 1067/1 Every Italian family has its own *presepio*, as the crib is called. **1969** E. H. PINTO *Treen* 173/2 Presepio or Nativity figure tableaux have been and still are used in most parts of Christendom.

preservability. (In Dict. s.v. PRESERVABLE *a.*) Delete *rare* and add later examples.

1959 *Brno Studies in English* I. 11 This feature [*sc.* the documentary, preservable character of written utterances], which one may perhaps term 'preservability', has been appreciated by men since time immemorial. **1972** *Science* 22 Sept. 1067/1 Some biologic groups show fossil diversities closer to their actual diversities than do other groups because of inherent differences in preservability.

preservation. Add: **1. b. preservation order,** a legal obligation on an owner to preserve a building of historic interest or value.

1947 *Act* 10 & 11 *Geo. VI* c. 51 § 29 If it appears to a local planning authority that it is expedient to make provision for the preservation of any building of special architectural or historic interest in their area, they may for that purpose make an order (in this Act referred to as a 'building preservation order') restricting the demolition, alteration or extension of the building. **1953** *Act* 1 & 2 *Eliz. II* c. 49 § 11 The Minister may..make an order (in this Act referred to as a 'preservation order') placing under the more lasting protection of the Minister a monument with respect to which an interim preservation notice is in force. **1968** *Guardian* 13 Aug. 5/8 Residents of..Bridgnorth have won a battle to preserve the Crown Hotel..from being knocked down... A preservation order on the building has been confirmed by the Minister of Housing and Local Government. **1971** 'J. ASHFORD' *Bent Copper* iv. 27 Parkham Green village was justly famous for its ancient architectural beauty... The whole village was covered by a special preservation order. **1978** N. J. CRISP *London Deal* iv. 83 Those houses are the subject of preservation orders now.

preservationist (prezəɪvēi·ʃənist). [f. PRESERVATION + -IST.] An advocate of preservation, *esp.* one who advocates the preservation of historic buildings or antiquities. Also *attrib.* or as *adj.* Hence **preserva·tionism,** the practice or advocacy of preservation.

1927 *Blackw. Mag.* Sept. 314/1 The excuses made for her [*sc.* the peregrine falcon] by modern 'Preservationists' are altogether paltry. **1937** *Archit. Rev.* LXXXII. 50/1 We would not..do more than note in passing Raphael's plea for the preservation of antiquities and his appointment as controller of monuments by Pope Leo X. Distance has dimmed too much for us the true nature of Raphael and his kind as constructive artists, as opposed to the 'preservationists' of today, for us to risk such an appointment. **1957** *Observer* 10 Nov. 3/4 Town planning councils, preservationist maniacs and 'good taste' committees all came in for a drubbing. **1959** *Archit. Rev.* CXXVI. 205/2 Old houses in New Zealand have not yet acquired a period value. Preservationism is completely absent; too much so, one is inclined to say. **1960** *Guardian* 25 Feb. 1/2 A preservationist undergraduate..threatened to send 'Save Cowley Vicarage' telegrams. **1961** *Architect & Building News* 21 June 815/1, I hope the preservationists will not let up for a minute in their struggle to protect our dwindling countryside. **1973** *Times* 16 Oct. 2/5 In 1964 the London County Council wanted to demolish it, but a public inquiry ended in a victory for preservationists led by Sir John Betjeman. *a* **1974** R. CROSSMAN *Diaries* (1975) I. 623 She regarded it as pure sentimentalism and called it 'preservationism', a word of abuse. **1978** *Courier-Jrnl.* (Louisville, Kentucky) 16 Apr. D-4/1 Announcement of the discovery was delayed until recently ..because the mining concern..feared there would be a preservationist outcry.

preserve, *sb.* Add: **1. a.** (Later example.)

1839 J. D. HOOKER in L. Huxley *Life J. D. Hooker* (1918) I. 43 That Capt. Ross did *not* intend to treat me thus..I am sure, from his asking me to tell the quantity of preserves for animals required.

5. *attrib.* and *Comb.*, as (sense 2) *preserve-can, -dish, -jar, -pot.*

1882 W. D. HAY *Brighter Britain!* I. v. 138 There were empty preserve-cans, gallipots, and oyster-shells! **1856** M. J. HOLMES *'Lena Rivers* 108 The big preserve dish got broken. **1867** G. W. HARRIS *Sut Lovingood* 92 Preserve jars, vinegar jugs, seed bags, yarb bunches..all mix'd. **1885** E. P. ROE *Nature's Serial Story* xliii. 307 Racoons.. will uncover preserve-jars.., and with the certainty of a toper uncork a bottle and get drunk on its contents. **1969** R. & D. DE SOLA *Dict. Cooking* 183/2 *Preserve jar*, jar or pot for holding homemade preserves. **1854** THOREAU *Walden* 235 He goes to the mill-pond, she to her preserve-pot.

preserver. Add: **2. c.** = LIFE-PRESERVER 2.

1912 *Chambers's Jrnl.* Aug. 636/1 In the panic which is certain to ensue after a wreck even the handling of this preserver would be awkward in the narrow passages and gangways.

pre-se·rvice, *a.* [PRE- B. 2.] Of or relating to a period before a person or thing is ready for service (*spec.* national service) or use.

1928 [see *in-service* s.v. *IN *prep.* 17*]. **1944** W. TEMPLE *Church looks Forward* xix. 135 During the war, with the Pre-Service Units of various kinds, still more has to be done. **1948** *News Chron.* 24 Aug. 2/3 Britain's self-supporting Boy Scouts still find it easier to make recruits than do the Treasury-backed pre-Service cadet organisations. **1963** F. F. LAIDLER *Gloss. Home Econ. Educ.* 56 *Preservice training*, training given to a person before he/she enters an occupation. **1967** M. CHANDLER *Ceramics in Mod. World* v. 150 Short-term pre-service protection can be provided by coating such bricks with tar. **1974** H. L. FOSTER *Ribbin'* iv. 164 A few years ago I participated as a guest lecturer in a preservice education program for teacher aides in a large city.

preserving, *vbl. sb.* Add: **b.** (Further examples.) **preserving sugar,** a coarse kind of sugar used in the preserving of fruits.

1861 MRS. BEETON *Bk. Househ. Managem.* xxx. 758 In all the operations for preserve-making, when the preserving-pan is used, it should not be placed on the fire, but on a trivet. **1909** M. LITTLE *Cookery Up-to-Date* xi. 235 Weigh the apricots and to every pound of fruit add three-quarters of a pound of preserving sugar. **1916** *Daily Colonist* (Victoria, B.C.) 13 July 7/1 (Advt.), Preserving Kettles. Best grey enamel, 12 quarts, strong bail handle. **1921** *Ibid.* 30 Oct. 3/1 (Advt.), Preserving Quinces, 2 lbs. for 25¢. **1926** *Ibid.* 13 July 7/5 (Advt.), Preserving Crocks. For butter or eggs; four-gallon size, with cover. **1948** *Good Housek. Cookery Bk.* 667 If you intend to make jams, jellies and marmalades regularly, you would be well advised to invest in a good strong preserving pan. **1949** *Nat. Geogr. Mag.* XLVI. 193/2 [Watermelon] will cross with the so-called preserving melon, or citron, which is simply a hard, white-fleshed watermelon, good only for preserving. **1970** *Canad. Antiques Collector* July–Aug. 23/2 One of the first commercial potteries..to make.. preserving jars. **1972** K. STEWART *Times Cookery Bk.* xx. 265 Strawberry Jam... 4 lb strawberries 3½ lb granulated or preserving sugar. **1977** *Western Morning News* 30 Aug. 2/3 Attractive Sale of Furniture and Effects, including:..preserving pan.

pre-se·t, *a.* [PRE- A. 1.] Decided or determined in advance; (of apparatus, etc.) set in advance of its operation.

1934 *Practical Wireless* 10 Mar. 1127/2 (*heading*) Bank of pre-set condensers. **1946** *Jrnl. Inst. Electr. Engin.* XCIII. II. 426/2 Pressure switches..which close circuit on the pressure falling to a pre-set point, may be installed. **1954** *N.Y. Times Mag.* 29 Aug. 49/1 The pre-set missile is not guided; it is fired, like a shell, at a pre-determined trajectory. **1961** G. MILLERSON *Technique Television Production* iii. 23 (*caption*) Height is pre-set and not readily adjusted. **1966** D. G. BRANDON *Mod. Techniques*

Metallogr. 102 The specimen stage..will remain in a pre-set position sufficiently long to permit any area to be photographed with the full resolution of the instrument. **1973** *Country Life* 29 Nov. 1796 (Advt.), This ultra-modern..oven..switches off at a pre-set time. **1978** R. V. Jones *Most Secret War* xlv. 447 Graphite rudders that were placed in the main jet so as to deflect the stream of incandescent gases and thus turn the rocket on to a pre-set trajectory both in bearing and in elevation.

pre-se·t, *v.* [Pre- A. 1.] *trans.* To set or fix (apparatus) in advance of its operation; to settle or decide beforehand.

1946 *Sun* (Baltimore) 18 July 13/2 A pressure gauge.. can be preset to open at an altitude where there is enough oxygen for a man to breathe. **1958** *Engineering* 11 Apr. 468/3 Temperature controllers which can be remotely pre-set from the control room. **1960** [see *bias *a.*, *sb.*, and *adv.* B. 7]. **1962** D. Slayton in *Into Orbit* 68 You could preset the trainer for any kind of mission you wanted to fly. **1962** *Which?* May 148/1 The grinder was pre-set to give a certain particle size. **1977** *Gramophone* Feb. 1343/2 Under a sliding lid..are four similar controls for pre-setting your choice of 'instant' programmes.

prese·xual, *a.* [Pre- B. 1.] Preceding or not yet influenced by sexual activity or sexual awareness; pre-pubertal; also *Gram.*, not (yet) differentiated by natural gender.

1919 M. K. Bradby *Psycho-Anal.* iv. xii. 164 Because our own sexuality is associated with sense of guilt, to us innocence implies a pre-sexual state of mind. **1925** D. H. Lawrence *St. Mawr* 204 They [*sc.* pine-trees] hedged one in with the power..of the pre-sexual primeval world. **1927** B. Malinowski *Sex & Repression in Savage Society* i. ix. 77 The development of pre-sexual life at this stage also differs in Europe and Melanesia. **1949** *Archivum Linguisticum* I. 168 A syntactic peculiarity of old Bulgarian declension..discloses the existence of a presexual division of nouns into animate and inanimate. **1961** R. F. C. Hull tr. *Jung's Coll. Wks.* IV. 118 The necessity for this becomes really urgent when we ask ourselves whether the intense joys and sorrows of a child in the first years of his life, that is, *at the presexual stage*, are conditioned solely by his sexual libido. **1971** G. H. Bourne *Ape People* xi. 254 Presexual play in humans often involves the nibbling or biting of the earlobes.

preshow: see *pre- B. 2a.

preshri·nk, *v.* [Pre- A. 1.] *trans.* To shrink (fabric) prior to cutting or (a garment) prior to sale, so as to prevent shrinkage following washing or cleaning.

1936 G. G. Denny *Fabrics* (ed. 4) i. 104 A process for completely pre-shrinking cotton and linen fabrics. **1963** *Home Dressmaking* (B.B.C.) i. 4 Pre-shrink wool, cotton, silk fabrics, linings, interfacings, tapings, etc., before cutting. **1975** J. Labarthe *Elements of Textiles* vii. 301 There is no economy to any customer to buy cotton garments..unless these have been preshrunk by a dependable process. **1978** *Detroit Free Press* 5 Mar. d 9/1 Preshrink fabric and fringe, or it may shrink and pucker from steam.

Hence **preshru·nk** *ppl. a.*; also **preshri·nkage,** the process of preshrinking.

1942 G. G. Denny *Fabrics* (ed. 5) v. 191 Use of terms 'Full shrunk', 'Preshrunk', 'Shrunk'..prohibited if there is residual shrinkage left in the goods. **1951** *Good Housek. Home Encycl.* 251/1 All cloth..should be shrunk before cutting, unless it is guaranteed pre-shrunk. **1960** *Guardian* 9 May 4/6 Pre-shrinkage is one of the things the Irish are rather good about. *a* **1963** L. MacNeice *Astrol.* (1964) vii. 232 Astrology has been used to sell anything from pre-shrunk shirts to alcoholic drinks. **1975** J. Labarthe *Elements of Textiles* vii. 301 An..advantage given by a satisfactory preshrinkage process is that the strength of the fabric has been increased. **1978** *Detroit Free Press* 16 Apr. a14/4 (Advt.), Water-repellent nylon taffeta with pre-shrunk cotton flannel lining.

preside, *v.* **3.** (Later examples.)

1967 *Decision & Decision-Makers in Mod. State* (Unesco) 82 The council is presided by the President or the Vice-President. **1974** *Amer. Speech 1971* XLVI. 113 The meeting was presided..by Dean Pinero.

president, *sb.* Add: **2. f.** The priest or minister who presides at the Eucharist; the celebrant.

[**1867** M. Dods et al. tr. *Writings of Justin Martyr & Athenagoras* 63 There is brought to the president of the brethren bread and a cup of wine mixed with water. (*Note*) This expression may quite legitimately be translated 'to that one of the brethren who was presiding'.] **1945** G. Dix *Shape of Liturgy* v. 111 Justin says: '... Then the bread is 'offered' to the president and a cup of water mingled with wine.' **1971** *Order for Holy Communion* (Alternative Services Series 3) 30 The Breaking of the Bread. The president breaks the consecrated bread, saying [etc.]. *Ibid.* 31 The president and the other communicants receive the holy communion. At the administration the ministers say to each communicant, [etc.]. **1973** in *Mod. Eucharistic Agreement* 63 The eucharistic gathering and its president live their dependence on the one Lord and great High Priest. **1977** *Oxf. Diocesan Mag.* Aug. 17/2 The building now consecrated, the Eucharist began, with the Bishop of Oxford as president, and the Bishop of Reading, the Archdeacon of Berkshire, the Vicar and the Curate..as concelebrants.

g. At some sporting events, a referee, judge, or official in charge.

1961 F. C. Avis *Sportsman's Gloss.* 285/2 *President*, the senior judge in a group, as required at international show jumping competitions. **1971** L. Koppett *N.Y. Times Guide Spectator Sports* xiv. 210 The official in charge of [fencing] competition is called the 'president'. **1975** *New Society* 10 July 81/2 The 'president' (ie, ref) of a fencing match. **1976** *Sunday Tel.* 13 Mar. 36/6 Too few countries trouble to train presidents—officials who take charge of bouts.

presidential, *a.* Add: Hence **preside·ntialism,** the system or practice of presidential government; **preside·ntialist,** a supporter or advocate of such government.

1964 J. E. S. Hayward in *Parliamentary Affairs* XVIII. 35 *L'Express* drew the conclusion that the Opposition must accept Presidentialism and find a candidate for the next election. **1965** *Economist* 28 Aug. 787/3 Professor Burns himself is a convinced Presidentialist (and Democrat), and offers some concluding recommendations for reducing the four-party competition to two. **1973** W. G. Andrews in *Political Stud.* XXI. 311 The French constitutional structure has undergone radical change from parliamentarism towards presidentialism since 1958. **1974** *Times* 6 Nov. 14/6 If one begins to indulge in presidentialism after the South American pattern, then we shall have changed republics. **1975** *Government & Opposition* X. 28 The bipolarizing pressures inherent in a system of presidentialism based on election by universal suffrage have led to changes.

presiding, *ppl. a.* Add: **b.** *presiding judge* (U.S.); **presiding elder,** an elder who has charge of a district in the U.S. Methodist Church; **presiding officer,** an official in charge of a polling-station at an election.

1831 J. M. Peck *Guide for Emigrants* 258 There are three [Methodist] districts, over each of which is a presiding Elder. **1844** I. D. Rupp *He Pasa Ekklesia* 447 A presiding elder, though no higher as to order than an elder, has charge of several circuits and stations, called collectively a district. **1904** G. H. Lorimer *Old Gorgon Graham* ix. 186 The Doc...knew more Scripture when he was sixteen than the presiding elder. **1961** W. E. B. DuBois *Worlds of Color* ix. 137 He emphasized to the Presiding Elder the plan of giving up the old church and moving across the river. **1802** *Deb. Congress U.S.* 19 Jan. (1851) 117 The constant change of presiding judges..hung up the business. **1874** 'H. Churton' *Toinette* xxiii. 245 Geoffrey's counsel called the attention of His Honor, the Presiding Judge of the Court, to the fact. **1745** *Life & Adventures B.-M. Carew* vii. 86 By this Means no presiding Officer has it in his Power to make one more than two, which sometimes happens in the Elections amongst other Communities. **1872** *Act* 35 & 36 *Vict.* c. 33 sched. i. § 21 The returning officer shall appoint a presiding officer to preside at each station. **1978** D. Devine *Sunk without Trace* xviii. 170 Voting papers, to be valid, must have the official stamp embossed on them by the Presiding Officer at the time of issue to the individual voter.

Presidium (prĭsi·diŏm, -z-). Also **Præsidium.** [Russ. *prezidium*, ad. L. *præsidium*, garrison, f. *præsidēre* (see Preside *v.*).] The presiding body or standing committee in a Communistic organization, esp. in the Supreme Soviet. Also *attrib.*

1924 *Observer* 23 Mar. 13/5 In a second decree the Presidium of the Union C.E.C. decided to replace the sentence of ten years strict isolation passed on the Catholic Archbishop Ciepliak by the All-Russian C.E.C. by expulsion from the territories of the Union of Socialist and Soviet Republics. **1927** *Glasgow Herald* 10 Oct. 11 Mr Arthur Horner (South Wales), a member of the National Executive of the Miners' Federation, presided, and was supported by a presidium of 11. **1930** *Economist* 1 Nov. (Russian Suppl.) 1/2 The Central Executive Committee meets ordinarily about three times a year and, when it is not sitting, is represented by a small elected committee or Presidium, and by the Council of People's Commissaries, which is the executive organ. **1931** G. D. H. Cole in W. Rose *Outl. Mod. Knowl.* 727 The Congress [of Soviets]..is ..an occasional gathering of delegates, represented between sessions by a Præsidium. **1955** *Times* 9 May 10/3 The presidium of the Supreme Soviet yesterday annulled the Anglo-Soviet and Franco-Soviet treaties of alliance. *Ibid.* 14 July 6/6 The Praesidium, known in Stalin's day as the Politburo, is the highest policy-making body in the Soviet Union. **1958** *Spectator* 20 June 791/3 Khrushchev's last execution of a Præsidium member, in 1956, was kept quiet for a month or so. **1960** *Evening Bull.* (Philadelphia) 14 Dec. 13/6 A Russian official who made the mistake of referring to a member of the Presidium (the 14-member body that rules the Soviet Union) as a fool. **1968** *Listener* 1 Aug. 133/3 Dubcek started at the top with his bloodless revolution. First, he infiltrated the Party Praesidium, effectively the Party's ruling body, and excluded Novotny supporters in separate reshuffles. **1974** L. Deighton *Spy Story* xiii. 129 Madame Furtseva, the first woman to reach the Presidium of the Central Committee.

presie, var. *prezzie.

pre-sleep: see *pre- B. 2a. **pre-soak:** *pre- A. 1 and 2. **pre-socialist:** *pre- B. 1d.

pre-Socra·tic, *a.* and *sb.* *Philos.* Also **Presocratic, presocratic.** [Pre- B. 1.] **A.** *adj.* Of or relating to the period before Socrates (chiefly the sixth and early fifth centuries b.c.) when, in Greece, systematic enquiry into things and their causes began.

1871 [in Dict. s.v. Pre- B. 1]. **1892** J. Burnet *Early Greek Philos.* 2 The common practice of treating this younger contemporary of Sokrates [*sc.* Demokritos] along with the 'pre-Socratic philosophers' has obscured the true course of historical development. **1913** P. V. Cohn *Nietzsche's Compl. Wks.* (Index) XVIII. 117 The real philosophers of Greece pre-Socratic. **1957** Kirk & Raven *Presocratic Philosophers* p. vii, We have limited our scope to the chief Presocratic 'physicists' and their forerunners, whose main preoccupation was with the nature (physis) and coherence of things as a whole. **1964** C. S. Lewis *Discarded Image* iii. 37 The pre-Socratic philosophers of Greece invented Nature. **1974** *Nature* 8 Nov. 130/2 In the treatment of Greek science emphasis is laid upon the importance of the presocratic belief that causal relationships existed between natural phenomena. **1977** I. Murdoch *Fire & Sun* 33 Sexual love (Aphrodite) as cosmic power had already appeared in Presocratic thought in the doctrines of Empedocles.

B. *sb.* Any of the Greek philosophers of the sixth and fifth centuries b.c. who preceded Socrates (d. 399 b.c.).

1945 B. Russell *Hist. Western Philos.* (1946) i. xiii. 126 'The Good' dominated his [*sc.* Plato's] thought more than that of the pre-Socratics. **1957** Kirk & Raven *Presocratic Philosophers* 1 The Neoplatonist Simplicius,..who lived a whole millennium after the Presocratics, made long and evidently accurate quotations, in particular from Parmenides, Empedocles, [etc.]. **1972** E. Hussey *Presocratics* i. 1 What gives the group of Presocratics such unity as it possesses is..that all these men were involved in the movement of thought which led to the separation of science and philosophy from one another and from other ways of thinking. **1977** I. Murdoch *Fire & Sun* 51 Nor is he at all like the cosmic 'gods' of the Presocratics.

presolar: see *pre- B. 1. **pre-sold:** *pre-sell *v.* **pre-Soviet:** *pre- B. 1a. **pre-spiracular:** *pre- B. 3.

press, *sb.*[1] Add: **I. 5*.** *Psychol.* Something in the environment to which (a need in) the organism reacts (see quot. 1938).

1938 H. A. Murray *Explorations in Personality* ii. 40 A tendency or 'potency' in the environment may be called a *press*... For example, a press may be nourishing, or coercing, or injuring, or chilling,..or amusing or belittling to the organism. *Ibid.* 42 The endurance of a certain kind of press in conjunction with a certain kind of need defines the duration of a single episode. **1953** *Jrnl. Abnormal & Social Psychol.* XLVIII. 532/2 So we know *two* things about his narrators: their ambition and their most recent press. That press, as our hypothesis predicts, they projected directly into their..Tests. **1969** J. W. Getzels in Lindzey & Aronson *Handbk. Social Psychol.* (ed. 2) V. xlii. 501 There was no evidence that student press influenced the level of aspiration, at least so far as Merit students are concerned. **1973** *Jrnl. Genetic Psychol.* CXXIII. 87 Four slides were used to test for the presence of hostile press.

II. 6. b. In Gymnastics, a raising of the body by continuous muscular effort.

1901 *Health & Strength* Apr. 36/2 (*heading*) One arm body press... Lie flat on the ground..and with hand beneath centre of chest press the body up to arm's length. **1956** Kunzle & Thomas *Freestanding* i. 22 The presses to handstand are one of the best forms of strength training because at the same time the gymnast learns how to fight for and maintain a hand balance when the arms feel extremely tired.

c. *Weight-lifting.* A raising of a weight from the floor to shoulder-height followed by its gradual extension above the head.

1908 *Health & Strength Ann.* 93 Continental lifts differ considerably from those in practice in this country... The Continental 'Press' is a cross between the above [*sc.* the 'Push'] and the English 'Press'... The Continental 'Press' can only be distinguished from our 'Arm Press' by a slight side wriggle. **1914** *Ibid.* 83 Thomas Inch lifted 304½ lbs. (bent press) at Scarborough in December. **1925** F. G. L. Fairlie *Official Rep. VIIIth Olympiad, 1924* 255 Middle-weights... Two hands, Military Press: Galimberti (Italy), 214½ lb. **1928** *Health & Strength Ann.* 77 Lifters are urged to maintain themselves in a state of readiness on the three Olympic lifts, viz: 'Two Hands Clean and Military Press with Barbell', 'Two Hands Snatch', and the 'Two Hands Clean and Jerk with Barbell'. **1935** *Encycl. Sports* 704/2 There are swings, presses, snatches, jerks, all made with one hand, as well as two-hand and shoulder lifts. **1975** *Oxf. Compan. Sports & Games* 1099/1 At the 1924 Olympic Games the lifts were one hand snatch, opposite one hand jerk, two hands clean and press, two hands snatch, and two hands clean and jerk.

d. The action of pressing clothes.

1932 D. C. Minter *Mod. Needlecraft* 145/2 Muslin and lawn dresses usually require a final all-over press. **1957** J. Osborne *Look Back in Anger* i. 16 I'll give them a press while I've got the iron on. **1962** M. Duffy *That's how it Was* iii. 33 The girls would..run up something new..to wear the same evening with a quick press before they went out. **1975** Byfield & Tedeschi *Solemn High Murder* i. 6 'These things could do with a press if that's possible.' The smell of tropical mildew clung to the rumpled winter-weight clericals he handed the man.

e. In Basketball, any of various forms of close marking by the defending team. Also *transf.*

1961 J. S. Salak *Dict. Amer. Sports* 341 *Press* (basketball), a maneuver designed to hamper the offensive team's ability to move the ball toward their basket. There are many types of 'presses'. **1971** L. Koppett *N.Y. Times Guide Spectator Sports* iii. 86 The press itself creates openings for the offense. **1976** *Honolulu Star-Bull.* 21 Dec. h-1/5 A full-court press enabled Kalani to wipe out a 13-point third quarter lead. **1978** W. Safire *Political Dict.* 248 'Full-court press' became White House lingo in the late sixties... In politics, the term has come to mean a strenuous effort to get legislation passed probably because of its resemblance to 'all-out pressure'. In basketball, however, the phrase is used only to describe a defense.

13. e. Also *to go to press* (also *fig.*), *to read for press*.

1715 T. HEARNE *Let.* 2 Feb. (MS.), I find Mr. Urry's Chaucer advertised as being to go to ye Press in a little time. **1810** *Irish Mag.* III. 279/2, I shall, therefore..go immediately to press, be squeezed into the genteelest form I can. **1846** G. DODD *Brit. Manuf.* 6th Ser. 57 To read for press—that is, to search for the minutest errors. **1929** YEATS *Let.* 13 Sept. (1954) 768, I will work at it here and there... I should go to press with it next spring. **1933** [see *HOPE *sb.*[1] 4 a]. **1951** [see *BED *sb.* 6 c]. **1961** *Financial Times* 11 July 6 At the time of going to press..it is not possible to determine any very definite trend of trading at the present time.

h. *a good press*: see *GOOD *a.* 13. Hence *to have* (*receive*, etc.) *a good* (or *bad*, *mixed*, etc.) *press*: to be favourably (or unfavourably, divergently, etc.) commented on or criticized in current newspapers, journals, etc. Also *transf.*, to receive (favourable, etc.) publicity, to be (favourably, etc.) appraised in conversation or in literature.

1908 [see *GOOD *a.* 13]. **1913** R. FRY *Let.* Oct. (1972) II. 373 Has it [*sc.* an exhibition] been a success, and has there been any decent Press on it? **1915** [see *GOOD *a.* 13]. **1920** *Sat. Rev.* 10 July 26 Mr Austen Chamberlain has a very bad press. **1928** [see *GOOD *a.* 13]. **1932** *Statesman* (Calcutta) 2 Aug., It was the clearest case, for years, of how county cricket should not be conducted. Allom had a lively Press last Wednesday! **1934** H. G. WELLS *Exper. Autobiogr.* II. vii. 501, I wish I could hear at times of people still reading these three stories: they got, I think, a rather dull press. **1958** *Listener* 13 Nov. 769/1 Cromwell had rather a mixed press for his great day. **1961** P. KEMP *Alms for Oblivion* 1 In Britain General Franco had not enjoyed a good Press. **1967** *Observer* 26 Nov. 8/3 The Phoenicians had a largely hostile press from the Bible and from their rivals the Greeks and Romans. **1976** *Women's Report* Sept./Oct. 4/1 Chiswick Women's Aid has had a good press recently because the DHSS has withdrawn some of its grant money. **1977** *Sunday Times* 30 Jan. 38/1 Rape is enjoying a very educative Press from TV dramatists at the moment.

i. Usu. with *the*: used collectively for journalists, esp. reporters; also, of an individual reporter.

1926 in S. Bent *Ballyhoo* (1927) ii. 55 At least a half dozen times since the wedding the unfortunate composer has been badgered by the press until some such statement as 'we are very happy' has been wrung from him. **1949** 'J. TEY' *Brat Farrar* xii. 102 'He says he's a reporter,' Lana said... 'Oh, *no*!' Bee said. 'Not the Press. Not already.' **1951** M. DICKENS *My Turn to make Tea* iv. 45 'Here's the Press, Waldo,' his wife told him, 'come to put Marjorie in the *Post*.' *Ibid.* vii. 122 Sister..said that if I was The Press, Matron had deputed her to show me round. **1956** C. MACKENZIE *Thin Ice* x. 129 The dinners of the East Indiamen were held once a quarter without excessive formality and, what was more important for the speaker, without the Press. **1973** A. S. NEILL *Neill! Neill! Orange Peel!* II. 235 The Salvation Army damsel..came to a young man sitting alone. 'Are you saved?' 'Press,' he said. 'Oh, I beg your pardon,' and she moved hastily away. **1974** P. N. WALKER *Major Incident* viii. 95 As the police were desperately trying to clear the streets, the first of the press were trying to drive in. **1978** M. BUTTERWORTH *X marks Spot* II. i. 73 Arrange for the exhumation forthwith. Seal off Highgate Cemetery... No Press. No television.

IV. 14. (Further *attrib.* examples.)

1952 J. GLOAG *Short Dict. Furnit.* 374 *Press cupboard*, a large cupboard with a superstructure consisting of a shelf with smaller cupboards behind it..introduced during the second half of the 16th century. **1959** L. A. BOGER *Compl. Guide Furnit. Styles* xxii. 384 The name *press cupboard* was given in America to a form of cup-board resembling the English hall and parlor cupboard. **1970** *Canad. Antiques Collector* Jan. 29/1 A further kind of cupboard..was called a press, or press-cupboard, and was about the same general size and shape as a modern wardrobe. **1975** *Oxf. Compan. Decorative Arts* 651 *Press cupboard*, a large cupboard, sometimes confused with a court cupboard, which came into use in the latter half of the 16th c. and remained in fashion until the 18th c. It had the upper part recessed with contained cupboards and a shelf running in front of them.

V. 15. a. (*a*) *press-shop* (later examples), *-table*; (*b*) *press advertising*, *boss*, *camera*, *campaign*, *censor*, *censorship* (further examples), *club*, *freedom*, *interview*, *pass*, *photo*, *photograph*, *photographer*, *photography*, *ticket*.

1961 *Travel Topics* June 41/1 When one first thinks of press advertising, it conjures up the thought of taking space in the national dailies or Sunday papers. **1932** E. POUND *Let.* 18 Feb. (1971) 239 There is no reason why young England shd. pardon the ineffable polluters and saboteurs. What they have done to stifle literature in Eng., tho not so important as the press-bosses' stifling of economic discussion, is all of piece [*sic*]. **1948** A. L. M. SOWERBY *Dict. Photogr.* (ed. 17) 89 The typical Press camera consists of a frame containing the shutter, fitted at the back for plates in dark slides and with the lens carried on a flat panel supported at the four corners by struts and connected with the camera body by bellows. **1964** M. MCLUHAN *Understanding Media* xx. 200 The press camera contributed to radical changes in the game of football. **1974** *Encycl. Brit. Macropædia* XIV. 330/2 Press cameras are loaded with sheet film..for fast, handheld shooting; they are traditionally of folding-bellows design with a lens standard on an extendable baseboard. **1903** 'VIGILANS SED ÆQUUS' *German Ambitions* vi. 86 The German press campaign against our army in South Africa. **1951** M. MCLUHAN *Mech. Bride* (1967) 40/1 The working woman was put into adolescent short skirts and told in big press campaigns that the age-old tyranny of man was at an end. **1900** W. S. CHURCHILL *Let.* 1 May in R. S. Churchill *Winston S. Churchill* (1967) I. Compan. II. 1174 Wolverton is here, one of the press censors. **1940** L. DURRELL *Spirit of Place* (1969) 65 George Seferiades..chief foreign press censor, who is a remarkable poet and person. **1939** 'G. ORWELL' in *New English Weekly* 12 Jan. 203/2 The radio, press-censorship, standardised education and the secret police have altered everything. **1978** 'A. YORK' *Tallant for Disaster* vi. 93 Even the British have press censorship... What about all those D-notices and things? **1896** *Peterson Mag.* Mar. 311/1 The Pittsburgh Women's Press Club made a wise choice in selecting for a secretary Miss Marie de Sayles Coyle. **1967** L. T. BRAUN *Cat who ate Danish Modern* ii. 20 Why don't we meet for drinks at the Press Club? **1974** *Times* 18 Nov. 15/1 Advertisers threaten press freedom if they try to use their advertising power as a form of censorship. **1923** *Radio Times* 23 Sept. 18/3 Mr. J. W. Reith, the General Manager of the B.B.C...has managed to avoid..the usual press interviews. **1976** L. HENDERSON *Major Enquiry* viii. 47 The report of Shenton's press interview was given great prominence by the *Evening News*. **1914** *Automobile Topics* 6 June 303/1 Primary cause for protest was the method adopted by the Speedway management of distributing press passes. **1977** H. INNES *Big Footprints* II. i. 103 They weren't interested in my press pass or the fact that I was an American TV man. **1964** M. MCLUHAN *Understanding Media* xx. 200 A press photo of battered players in a 1905 game. *Ibid.*, The press photo coverage of the lives of the rich. **1980** R. MCCRUM *In Secret State* xviii. 168 The dashing whizz-kid of the press photos. **1944** M. LASKI *Love on Supertax* ii. 31 Suppose you wanted a really flattering press photograph and I knew someone who'd fake it up. **1974** 'J. LE CARRÉ' *Tinker, Tailor* xxiii. 196, I had with me the American press photographs of the arrest. **1922** M. ARLEN *Piracy* 7 Those young women of patrician and careless intelligence, whom it is the pet mistake of bishops, diarists, press-photographers, and Americans, to take as representing the 'state' of modern society. **1974** 'M. INNES' *Appleby's Other Story* v. 44 One has to think of the reporters and press-photographers. **1922** L. WARREN *Journalism* xxi. 230 In a book such as this it is quite out of the question to go into details concerning press photography. **1980** *Times* 3 Mar. 14/6 *Life*..was press photography for the press photographer at its most splendid. **1958** *Engineering* 11 Apr. 461/1 The current expansion programme, which includes the opening of a new press shop later this year and a new assembly building early in 1959. **1959** *Motor Manual* (ed. 36) i. 8 In the latest press shops, all the presses engaged in the production of one component are arranged in a long line, and are linked by roller conveyors. **1971** *Engineering* Apr. 20/2 Mounting of the equipment on the movable press-table is also easy. **1851** J. CHAPMAN *Diary* 10 July in G. S. Haight *Geo. Eliot & J. Chapman* (1940) 191 Spencer gave me a ticket for the Opera..and might have had an excellent place but for the vexing regulation that 'press tickets' must be exchanged which destroyed my chance of admittance. **1976** 'D. FLETCHER' *Don't whistle 'Macbeth'* 17 Some idiot in the box office had allocated press tickets for the first matinée instead of the first night.

b. (*b*) Operated by pressing, as *press-cock*, *switch*; (see also sense 16d below); also *PRESS-BUTTON *sb.* and *a.*, *PRESS-FASTENER, etc.

1932 *Jrnl. R. Aeronaut. Soc.* XXXVI. 854 The ideal starter..was a self-contained unit in which only one simple operation, such as pressing a press-cock, was required. **1892** E. J. HOUSTON *Dict. Electr. Words* (ed. 2) 424/2 *Pressel*, a press switch or push connected to the end of a flexible pendant conductor.

16. a. press-mould (see quot. 1974); so **press-mould** *v.*, **press-moulding** *vbl. sb.* **press-moulded** *ppl. a.*

1971 *Country Life* 27 May 1303/1 The [Staffordshire slipware] dish is press-moulded and is signed 'I.S.'. **1974** SAVAGE & NEWMAN *Illustr. Dict. Ceramics* 233 *Press-mould*, an absorbent mould made of lightly fired clay or plaster of Paris, and into which clay is pressed by hand to make such objects as small ornaments for relief or sprigged decoration. *a* **1977** *Harrison Mayer Ltd. Catal.* 95/2 A range of simple Press Moulds in 5 basic shapes. **1969** SPECK & SUTHERLAND *Eng. Antiques* 190/2 Press-moulded glass. **1958** H. WAKEFIELD in Edwards & Ramsey *Connoisseur Period Guides: Early Victorian Period* 100/2 It was the period in which the process of press-moulding was first developed for the production of dishes and other open shapes.

b. press attaché, a diplomat responsible for the dealings of an embassy with the press; **press baron**, a powerful newspaper owner, a newspaper magnate, esp. one who is a member of the peerage (see *BARON 2 b); **press boat**, a boat reserved for the use of reporters at a boat race or similar event; **press book**, (*a*) a volume of press cuttings; (*b*) a book printed at a private press, a type of fine book (see *FINE *a.* 12 d); **press-box** (earlier and later examples); **press card**, a document that authorizes a reporter to practise journalism, or one that gains him admission; **press clipping** orig. *U.S.* = *press cutting*; also *attrib.*; hence *press-clipper*; **press conference**, a meeting at which journalists and other representatives of the news media are given an opportunity to put questions to a politician, writer, etc.; also (*rare*) (with hyphens) as *v. trans.*; **press corps**, a group of reporters (usu. in a specified place); **press-corrected** *a.*, designating a text of which the proof sheets have been corrected before publication; **press correction**, (*a*) the act or process of correcting errors in a text during preparation for publication; (*b*) an error marked for correction; **press-corrector**, a proof-reader; **Press Council**, a body established in the U.K. in 1953 to raise and maintain professional standards among journalists; **press coverage**, the reporting (of an event) by the press; **press-cutter** = *press cutting agency*; **press cutting** (earlier and later examples); *press-cutting agency* (further examples), *album*, *book*, *bureau*, *people*; **press day**, (*a*) a day on which journalists are invited to an exhibition, a performance, etc.; (*b*) the day on which a journal goes to press; **press digest**, a digest or summary of press reports; **press kit**, a dossier prepared for journalists; **press notice**, a review in a newspaper or other periodical of a book, play, or the like; **press number**, a number at the foot of the page of an early printed book showing on which press or by which printer the page was printed (see quot. 1961); **press office**, an office within an organization or government department responsible for dealings with the press; **press-proof** (examples); **press release**, an official statement offered to newspapers for publication; **press-revise** (examples); **press run**, a spell of allowing a printing-press to run; the amount of printed material produced as a result; **press secretary**, a secretary who deals with publicity and public relations; **press show**, a performance given for the press, esp. a film shown to journalists before general release; also *attrib.*; so **press-show** *v. trans.*; **press stand**, a section of the tiered seats for spectators at racing or field events reserved for reporters; also *attrib.*; **press table**, a table reserved for journalists esp. in a court of law; **press time**, the time at which a newspaper goes to press; **press view**, a viewing of an exhibition by journalists before it is open to the general public.

1938 A. BARMINE *Mem. Soviet Diplomat* i. 16 When Krestinsky was at the Berlin Embassy, Stern had served for many years as his Press Attaché. **1980** 'R. DEACON' *Spy!* iii. 86 She had made a favourable impression with the press attaché. **1958** *Spectator* 20 June 794/3 The history of the rise in the peerage of the press barons..is one of the shoddiest episodes in the whole story of the press. **1975** *Times* 3 July 14/3 (*caption*) Press barons together; Lord Thomson shares a smile with..Lord Beaverbrook. **1870** D. J. KIRWAN *Palace & Hovel* xxiv. 363 By the side of the Press boat, the Umpire's boat..was anchored, many of the passengers wearing the rival colors. **1901** R. H. DAVIS in *Scribner's Mag.* Aug. 131/1 The press-boats buried their bows in the waters of the Florida Straits and raced for the cable-station at Port Antonio. **1897** A. BEARDSLEY *Let.* 6 Jan. (1971) 240, I quite forgot to return you the cuttings for your press book. I enclose them now. **1930** *Publishers' Weekly* 19 Apr. 2116/2 The past five years has seen keen collecting interest in Press books both early and modern. **1976** *Times Lit. Suppl.* 5 Mar. 271/3 There is also a large output of less sumptuous..books..produced by a host of part-time private presses, small publishers who commission fine books, and trade printers who..take time off to print a worthwhile book... It is to cover these books that the term 'press books' has been coined. **1889** *Sporting Life* (Philadelphia) 10 July 5/5 The upper stand ..will contain the seats for ladies and their escorts and the private boxes, not forgetting the press box. **1976** DEXTER & MAKINS *Testkill* 61 Festing followed me to the Press box and sat..in silence until the end of the game. **1934** *N.Y. Times* 20 Feb. 18/3 The number of press cards has been cut by 55 per cent. **1951** 'A. GARVE' *Murder in Moscow* iii. 41, I went on to see the head of the Soviet Press Department and collect my press card. **1976** *Times* 27 Feb. 15/2 The use of fake press cards by soldiers in Ulster puts genuine journalists in danger. **1903** *Everybody's Mag.* July 127/1 The press-clippers caught every reprint. **1903** *Christendom* Apr. p. ii (Advt.), United States Press Clipping Bureau. **1904** G. B. SHAW *Let.* 6 Apr. (1972) II. 416 PPS I subscribe to an American press clipping agency. **1942** D. POWELL *Time to be Born* (1943) i. 20 Julian fussed with some press clippings. **1975** *Language for Life* (Dept. Educ. & Sci.) xv. 232 The same is no less necessary for English, the 'materials' of which are duplicated sheets, press-clippings, files, photographs, and so on. [**1923** A. CECIL in *Cambr. Hist. Brit. Foreign Policy* III. viii. 628 [During the 1914–18 war] Lord Robert Cecil used to hold a kind of weekly reception for American journalists, when they were at liberty to question him on Foreign Affairs.] **1937** *Time* 1 Mar. 9/3 One afternoon Mrs. Roosevelt stole into the President's regular semi-weekly press conference to say good-by to her husband. **1953** *Manch. Guardian Weekly* 2 Apr. 7/4 Another general was soon to press-conference himself into the Presidency. **1958** *New Statesman* 15 Mar. 332/3 This programme..takes one of two forms: either it is a press-conference in which an eminent person is questioned by journalists in several countries, or it is a straight discussion between those taking part. **1976** *Eastern Even. News* (Norwich) 9 Dec. 1/5 'I don't believe anyone in this industry wants a dispute,' Sir Derek said at a Press conference during a visit to Bedlay Colliery, Lanarkshire. **1940** G. SELDES *Witch Hunt* i. 6 He came to Trier and used the American press corps. **1974** *Sunday Times* 21 July 1/3 A 200-strong international Press corps confined to the hotel by the island's [*sc.* Cyprus's] 24-hour curfew. **1964** F. BOWERS *Bibliogr. & Textual Crit.* v. ii. 139 Editors should choose the First Folio press-corrected reading..instead of the quarto and the uncorrected Folio reading. *Ibid.* I. iii. 19 A brief look at some problems of press-correction will illustrate with suitably neutral examples. *Ibid.*, Press-correctors do not deliberately introduce typographical errors in the copy. **1947** *Minutes of Evidence R. Comm. on Press* 12 Nov. 23/2 in *Parl. Papers 1947–8* (Cmd. 7330) XIV. 533 The proposal is that there should be a Press Council, something..approximating to the General Medical Council.., and that there should be punishments and rewards instituted in order to raise and preserve the standards of professional behaviour within the newspaper profession. **1953** *Times* 5 Nov. 4/2 The new Press Council had proclaimed deep concern at the unwholesome exploitation of sex by certain newspapers and periodicals. **1977** *Evening Post* (Nottingham) 27 Jan. 6/1 If a newspaper were genuinely hostile to the Labour Party and decided, as a result, that in future no reference would be made to it or its troubles and triumphs, there would be an excellent case for reporting the newspaper to the Press Council for failing to do its duty. **1957** J. Mitford *Poison Penmanship* (1979) 34 These examples represent only a very tiny sampling of press coverage of this part of the case. **1961** C. Willock *Death in Covert* iii. 71 All goes down to advertising. Whynne says we'll get it back twice over in press coverage. **1976** *Times* 27 Feb. 15/1 Documents from army sources critical of press coverage in Northern Ireland. **1901** G. Gissing *Let.* 30 Nov. in *G. Gissing & H. G. Wells* (1961) 200, I have never dared to subscribe to the press-cutters, for I remember..the day when a press notice meant a sneer which disturbed my work. **1898** G. B. Shaw *Let.* 24 Mar. (1972) II. 22 A sheaf of pamphlets & press cuttings. *a* **1916** 'Saki' *Infernal Parliament* in *Square Egg* (1924) 148 Pasting notices of modern British plays into a huge press-cutting book. **1922** A. E. Housman *Let.* 26 Oct. (1971) 206 The press-cutting agency sends me..more notices than I want to see. **1929** T. S. Eliot *Dante* iii. 63 He, Dante Alighieri, was an important person who kept press-cutting bureaux busy. **1936** 'G. Orwell' *Let.* 26 Aug. in *Coll. Ess.* (1968) I. 228, I don't know what sort of reviews it got in France—I only saw about two..the press-cutting people didn't get them. **1941** V. Nabokov *Real Life S. Knight* xi. 102 A press-cutting agency began to pepper him with samples of praise. **1942** 'M. Innes' *Daffodil Affair* I. 37 He has consulted his colleagues; assistants have been turning over press cuttings. **1967** 'E. Peters' *Black is Colour* iii. 53 Things like the press-cutting book and the photographs get into arrears very easily. **1967** J. B. Priestley *It's an Old Country* vii. 84 Magazines and paperbacks, jigsaw puzzles, photograph and press-cutting albums. **1923** A. Huxley *Antic Hay* vii. 103 It was Press Day. The critics had begun to arrive. **1956** J. Symons *Paper Chase* xiii. 99 'Press day. Very busy.' He waved the galleys. **1972** C. Fremlin *Appointment with Yesterday* xiv. 113 The Editor ringing up, more and more irate, as press day drew near. **1958** *New Statesman* 20 Sept. 368/3 The press-digest which the President and Mr Dulles receive from the US embassy in London. **1977** G. Markstein *Chance Awakening* xxv. 76 The press digest was lying on his desk. **1968** *Globe & Mail* (Toronto) 17 Feb. 1/8 The ad hoc committee of five had already quietly rented space in a downtown Ottawa office building and prepared a slick press kit. **1977** *New Yorker* 3 Oct. 36/2 Our advance word on this event [*sc.* the publication of a new encyclopaedia] came to us in the form of a fat press kit, stuffed with fact sheets and kind words about the work. **1888** 'Mark Twain' *Let.* 1 Oct. in C. Clemens *Mark Twain* (1932) iii. 49, I thank you ever so much for not forgetting to remember to send me the press notice. **1977** J. Aiken *Last Movement* i. 37 'What about your opening?'.. 'Big success. I'll show you our press notices.' **1895** *Funk's Stand. Dict.*, Press-number. **1949** *Harvard Library Bull.* III. ii. 198 (*title*) Press numbers as a bibliographical tool. **1961** T. Landau *Encycl. Librarianship* (ed. 2) 283/2 *Press number*, small figures which in books printed between 1680 and *c.* 1823 often appear at the foot of a page, sometimes twice in a gathering. The figures indicate on which press in the printer's workshop the sheet was printed or perhaps the identity of the worker. **1937** L. Hellman *Diary* 17 Oct. in *Unfinished Woman* (1969) viii. 87, I have been to the Press Office [in Valencia]..and paid a visit to Rubio, the Press Chief. *a* **1974** R. Crossman *Diaries* (1976) II. 269, I must send it straightaway across to the Press Office in Transport House. **1841** W. Savage *Dict. Art of Printing* 597 *Press proof*, a good impression of a sheet of a work, or of a job, to read it carefully by, and to mark the errors, previous to its being put to press. **1972** P. Gaskell *New Introd. Bibliogr.* 115 The third and final stage of proof correction was the press proof, when a forme or sheet was read for residual blemishes..just before the actual printing run was about to begin **1958** M. H. Saringulian *Eng.–Russ. Dict. Libr. & Bibliogr. Terms* 148/1 Press release. **1964** W. Markfield *To Early Grave* (1965) ii. 29 He sent out press releases, and the *Brooklyn Eagle* ran a small story. *a* **1974** R. Crossman *Diaries* (1975) I. 67, I therefore gave instructions that for one month all the press releases and all the actual letters to authorities written in my name on planning permissions and compulsory purchase orders should be sent to me. **1976** *Oxf. Diocesan Mag.* July 14/2 There must be the news angle to the press release which, of course, should be factual and not based on rumours or hearsay. **1888** C. T. Jacobi *Printers' Vocab.* 103 *Press revise*, the final proof for press or machine. **1960** G. A. Glaister *Gloss. Bk.* 324/1 *Press revise*, an extra proof from the corrected type when ready for machining. **1958** *New Statesman* 15 Mar. 328/2 Since there is no 'preventive censorship', a paper which incurs the wrath of the government risks losing its entire press-run, which is simply impounded and placed in the Reuilly Barracks. **1976** M. Ierley *Year that tried Men's Souls* III. 198 (*caption*) At the left is the page as it appeared when Publisher Benjamin Towne began his press run. **1959** J. Ludwig in *Tamarack Rev.* Summer 20 Eisenhower with that puzzled look which meant if his press secretary didn't say something fast he was a goner. **1967** H. P. Levy *Press Council* p. xiii, Sir Richard Colville, the Press Secretary to Her Majesty the Queen, kindly read the chapter on the Royal Family in typescript. **1976** P. Alexander *Death of Thin-skinned Animal* xv. 150 He..announced himself as the London correspondent of *Paris Match* and said he'd like to speak to Colonel Njala's press secretary. **1958** *Vogue* July 44 American horror films..are never press-shown and are a disappointment to connoisseurs. **1961** *John o' London's* 15 June 671/1 A hard-boiled press-show audience. **1962** *Ibid.* 2 Aug. 115/1 On my way to the press-show of *The Lion.* **1963** *Movie* Jan. 20/3, I don't think there are any plans for press-showing it. **1972** *Times* 3 June 7/3 In Rome..I started going to press shows. **1914** *Automobile Topics* 6 June 303/1 Incidentally each applicant was put through the third degree in order to establish his complete identity and right to the press stand privileges. **1915** G. Patten *Courtney of Center Garden* 53 Passing the press stand, Whip caught Chatterton's eye again. **1937** E. Rickman *On & off Racecourse* vi. 137 He would usually watch the racing from the press-stand. **1922** Joyce *Ulysses* 454 From the presstable, coughs and calls. **1974** F. Nolan *Oshawa Project* i. 1 By the time the speeches started, the general was drunk... Every correspondent at the press table..could see the signs. **1927** S. Bent *Ballyhoo* ix. 240 It may be timely..but the reasons for printing it are that there is a glut of space to be filled in advance of news press-time, and that it must be filled with bait which will give the paper 'attention value'. **1978** *Rugby World* Apr. 19/1 At press-time, Royal High were level on 14 points with Glasgow Academicals and Madras, each club having two games to play, but with only one of the sides to go up alongside Leith. **1890** G. B. Shaw *London Music 1888–89* (1937) 284 My ticket for the Press view at the Old Masters on Friday! *Ibid.* 368, I have been at the Royal Academy all day, 'Press-viewing' it. **1929** R. Fry *Let.* 27 Dec. (1972) II. 646, I may be able to wangle you one [ticket] for the Press view on Monday.

c. (sense *6d) **press cloth**, a piece of cloth placed between the fabric and iron while pressing; **press line**, a crease made by a pressing iron; **press mark**, a mark left on fabric by the impress of an iron; hence **press-mark** *v. trans.*; **press-pad**, a soft pad used in pressing clothes.

1918 M. J. Rhoe *Dress you Wear* xi. 127 Nearly all pressing is done over a damp press cloth. **1933** A. M. Miall *Home Dressmaking* vii. 51 You should have a second wet press-cloth ready, and change to it as soon as the first dries, to avoid scorching. **1964** *McCall's Sewing* viii. 118/1 Always use a press cloth to prevent shine when necessary to press on the right side of the garment. **1979** *Tucson* (Arizona) *Citizen* 20 Sept. 2B/3 A final pressing (with press cloth) from the right side will give your coat (and its hem) a brand-new look. **1947** C. Talbot *Compl. Bk. Sewing* xxxi. 208/1 Remove the sharp line by moving the seam back and pressing the sleeve under the seam, removing the press lines from the sleeve. **1948** H. Hall *Home Dress-Making Simplified* vii. 64 It is important to press-mark all the side seams of the waist, the shirt, and the sleeves, as these seams will be the fitting lines of the dress. **1948** E. L. Towers *Standard Processes in Dressmaking* xvi. 116 If press marks appear on the right side of the garment, hold the fabric in the steam of a kettle to remove them. **1974** J. Robinson *Penguin Bk. Sewing* I. ii. 44 If during making a few press marks..do show then remove these by steaming. **1924** W. D. F. Vincent *Cutters' Pract. Guide Overcoats* 73/1 A good plan when damping fronts, lapels and collar is to damp through a double piece of cloth from the back, the silk being face down on the soft cloth press-pad.

d. From the vb. stem (cf. sense 15 b in Dict. and Suppl.): **press fit** *Engin.*, an interference fit between two parts in which one is forced under pressure into a slightly smaller hole in the other; cf. *shrink fit* s.v. *shrink *v.* 17; hence **press-fitted** *a.*; **press-key**, a control or switch similar to a piano key, operated by pressing the end with the finger.

1888 *Lockwood's Dict. Mech. Engin.* 265 *Press fit*, a fitting of contiguous parts slightly tighter than a sliding fit.., to allow of the sliding parts being pressed together with a hydraulic press. **1902** *Internat. Libr. Technol.* III. § 22. 33 In a press fit, the internal piece..must be enough larger than the hole to insure the development of enough friction between the two pieces to hold it there securely when pressed home. **1971** B. Scharf *Engin. & its Language* xi. 111 Considerable effort is required to assemble the parts: this is reflected in the use of terms such as force, drive or press fit. **1970** K. Ball *Fiat 600, 600D Autobook* vi. 53/2 The side bevels embody the axle shaft slip joint cavities, the free bevels being mounted on a shaft press-fitted into the differential casing. **1976** *Gramophone* Dec. 1092/1 Tape transport is controlled by an array of press-keys all fitted with a non-slip tread to prevent finger slip.

press, *v.*[1] Add: **I. 1. a.** *to press the button*: see *button *sb.* 4b and cf. *press-button *sb.* and *a.*

c. *to press the flesh*: to greet by physical contact; *spec.* to shake hands. *U.S. slang.*

1926 Maines & Grant *Wise-Crack Dict.* 8/1 *Press the flesh*, shake hands. **1933** A. E. W. Mason *Sapphire* ii. 16 'Press the flesh,' said I, extending my hand. **1975** W. Safire *Before the Fall* vi. v. 436 The Soviet leader [*sc.* Brezhnev] surprised Kissinger..with his American political habit of 'pressing the flesh'—punching an arm, squeezing, back-patting. **1977** *National Observer* (U.S.) 22 Jan. 14/3 After the assassination of John Kennedy, some said no future President would be able to 'press the flesh'. But both Lyndon Johnson and Gerald Ford felt that personal appearances were integral to campaigning. **1977** *Time* 7 Nov. 31/2 Aides had to coax him into playing fewer tennis matches with celebrities..and spending more time pressing the flesh.

d. Also in Gymnastics, with various prepositions.

1956 Kunzle & Thomas *Freestanding* i. 25 From prone support jump up to a knee and elbow balance... From there learn to press up to handstand and then lower again. *Ibid.* 26 Use the ankles to bounce the body into the air again, pressing through with the toes to get the maximum impulse. *Ibid.* ii. 32 Straighten out with the knees, press off on to one leg and lower the trunk sideways. **1964** G. C. Kunzle *Parallel Bars* iii. 83 Do not neglect specific strength training, such as..pressing to handstand against the wall bars.

2. c. *intr.* In Golf and Tennis. (See quots. 1975, 1977.)

1910 *Encycl. Brit.* XII. 223/2 *Press*, to strive to hit harder than you can hit with accuracy. **1922** Wodehouse *Clicking of Cuthbert* vi. 132 Keep the head still.. don't press. **1975** *Oxf. Compan. Sports & Games* 423/1 To 'press' is to try to hit the ball too hard, usually with a resultant mis-hit. **1977** *Tennis World* Sept. 17/2 'Pressing' is trying too hard: a player is said to be pressing if his shots are over-eager or impatient.

4. a. *spec.* To smooth or flatten (fabric or clothes) with an iron or clothes press. Also with *out*.

1901 A. H. Rice *Mrs. Wiggs of Cabbage Patch* vi. 92 She pressed out Asia's best dress. **1908** M. H. Morgan *How to dress Doll* viii. 67 Sew the tucks firmly, then press them open. *a* **1911** D. G. Phillips *Susan Lenox* (1917) I. iii. 37 I'm going to wear my white dress with embroidery, and it's got to be pressed. **1928** A. Christie *Mystery of Blue Train* xxiv. 195 He found the imperturbable George pressing trousers. **1949** D. Smith *I capture Castle* xiv. 257 Your frock's quite a bit creased, miss... I could press it, if you like. **1957** C. MacInnes *City of Spades* I. ix. 68 At one time I pressed suits by day and worked in the Post Office by night. **1976** C. Dexter *Last seen Wearing* xvi. 123 The little woman at home cooking a meal for you and probably pressing your pants or something.

b. To dry and flatten (leaves, flowers, etc.) in order to preserve them.

1785 T. Martyn tr. *Rousseau's Lett. Elements Bot.* viii. 82 Your pile of plants and papers thus arranged, must be put into the press, without which your plants will not be flat and even; some are for pressing them more, others less. **1840** C. Fox *Jrnl.* 22 Mar. in *Memories Old Friends* (1882) vi. 75 Clara has been collecting flowers, and they have been together pressing many of them. **1930** R. Macaulay *Staying with Relations* ii. 20 'You see, I press... Do you enjoy pressing, Catherine?' 'Flowers, she means,' Benet explained. 'Isie likes to keep her verbs intransitive.' **1974** W. C. Cartner *Fun with Botany* 23 Plant specimens can be pressed and dried for further study... Lay out the fresh specimens between sheets of newspaper, and press the sandwich between two boards.

c. To make (a gramophone record), to record (a song, etc.). *colloq.*

1918 [see *matrix 4 c]. **1929** Wilson & Webb *Mod. Gramophones* xi. 253 The stampers which press records have to be kept at a certain temperature in order that the record material will flow properly. **1954** W. W. Johnson *Gramophone Bk.* 55 By 1929 one record manufacturer alone was pressing records at the rate of a million a week. **1968** P. Oliver *Screening Blues* 5 In the ensuing months more stores carried Race records, specially pressed for the Negro market. **1976** *Sunday Times* 21 Mar. 58/3 Island is coy about how many albums it is pressing.

II. 8. d. (Later example.)

1968 *Globe & Mail* (Toronto) 3 Feb. 10/1 About 2,000 enemy troops had pressed an attack there since Tuesday against a U.S.-advised Vietnamese garrison of about the same size.

III. 15. a. (Further examples.) Also with *on*. Freq. *fig.* and in colloq. phr. *to press on regardless*, to persevere despite the dangers or difficulties (see *regardless *a.* 1 c). Also as *adj. phr.*

a **1599, 1870** [in Dict.]. **1916** Joyce *Portrait of Artist* (1969) v. 243 And why were you shocked, Cranley pressed on in the same tone, if you feel sure that our religion is false and that Jesus was not the son of God? **1921** G. B. Shaw *Back to Methuselah* v. 266. After passing a million goals they press on to the goal of redemption from the flesh. **1930** *Flight* 23 Oct. 1177/2 Lord Thomson and his gallant crew would still have said press on, instead of crying halt, in airship development. **1948** Partridge *Dict. Forces' Slang* 147 *Press on, regardless*—or merely *press on*, to act keenly, to be efficiently busy. Hence, *press-on type*, an almost too keen person—applied mostly to 'operational types'. They press on, regardless of fog, flak, fighter opposition. **1950** G. Hackforth-Jones *Worst Enemy* iii. 212 Action was needed to stem this tide of defeatism. Head down was the way to progress through the blizzard. 'When in doubt, press on.' A good motto that. **1952** M. Tripp *Faith is Windsock* xiv. 209 The Vicar was laudatory: 'A magnificent press-on effort, old chap.' **1958** *Times* 18 Dec. 11/4 A few colourful wartime metaphors survive... A third and uncouth example, to press on regardless, stands for a dashing and stoical, if disillusioned, perseverance which continues to find a place in life today just as it did in the early days of the war. **1959** *Listener* 5 Mar. 428/2 While the scientists press on regardless, the humanists go on worrying. **1960** *Times Lit. Suppl.* 18 Mar. 182/1 What vitality the man must have had! And it is this vitality which Mr. Coulter's press-on-regardless manner succeeds very well in conveying. **1961** J. Dawson *Ha-Ha* i. 7 The other students..used to wave as they passed and cry: 'How goes it?' or 'Press on regardless.' **1968** *Listener* 15 Aug. 203/2 That kind of Irishman—admirable rather than safe: the kind I'd heard junior RAF men in the war refer to as 'a press-on type'. **1977** *Drive* May–June 54/2 Covering 40 miles for every gallon of 4-star fuel (even press-on drivers could manage at least 35 mpg).

17. (Later example.)

1811 J. Love *Let.* 29 Oct. (1840) 349 To press after attaining and communicating to others more of the beginnings and pledges of that glorious life which now we view at a distance.

press, *v.*[2] Add: **2. d.** Also in phr. *to press into service.*

1926 *Discovery* June 191/2 Bait, such as a meal-worm,

may be pressed into service [by the bird-photographer] to entice a bird on to some particular twig. **1935** *Yachting* Dec. 82/3 *Press into service*, a reminiscence of the press-gangs which caused the War of 1812 by stopping American merchantmen on the high seas and 'pressing' members of their crews into service in the British navy. **1961** NEW ENG. BIBLE *Mark* xv. 21 Simon, from Cyrene,..was passing by..and they pressed him into service to carry his cross. **1978** K. J. DOVER *Greek Homosexuality* ii. 97 They masturbate constantly..if no living being with a suitable orifice is available, but prefer horses, mules, or deer..; even the neck of a jar may be pressed into service.

press-. The stem of PRESS *v.*[1], used in combination with advbs. to form adjs. designating things that can be pressed *down, in, on,* etc. (See also *PRESS *sb.*[1] 15 b (*b*), 16 d.)

1903 *Work* XXV. 218/2 A treacle tin, washed out and dried, with a burner soldered in the press-in lid, will serve quite well if the experiments are conducted outside the house. **1936** A. RANSOME *Pigeon Post* xviii. 189 It was an ordinary tin of paint with a wire handle..and a press-in lid. **1962** L. S. SASIENI *Princ. & Pract. Optical Dispensing* viii. 203 The third type [*sc.* of bridge lining] (press-on or snap-on) is shaped roughly in the form of a half tube which presses on to, and snaps over, the metal bridge. **1963** *Rep. Comm. Inquiry Decimal Currency* viii. 68 in *Parl. Papers 1962–3* (Cmnd. 2145) XI. 195 The two main groups of cash registers are the 'press-in' key type and the 'press-down' key type. **1975** B. WOOD *Killing Gift* (1976) II. i. 48 A vacuum jar with a press-on lid.

press agency. [f. PRESS *sb.*[1] + AGENCY.] = *news agency* (*b*) s.v. *NEWS *sb.* (*pl.*) 6 c.

1897 H. MAXWELL *Sixty Years a Queen* VIII. 190 The British Government has no official or semi-official organ in the press. Official pronouncements are communicated.. to press agencies, and through them find their way into journals of all shades of politics. **1973** D. MAY *Laughter in Djakarta* ii. 35 He ought to make a further check on the news by going to the Indonesian press agency.

press agent. (In Dict. s.v. PRESS *sb.*[1] 16 b.) Add: (Examples.) Also, more widely, one employed by any person or organization to handle publicity.

1883 *Railway Age* 25 Jan. 46/3 On general principles.. we desire to observe that the associate press agent, or some one who makes Wichita conspicuous in the dispatches is an ass. **1902** W. H. CHANTREY *Theatre Accounts* ii. 28 Salaries... Press Agent and Bill Inspector 5-10-0. **1917** WODEHOUSE *Uneasy Money* x. 114 Roscoe Sherriff, her press agent. **1949** *Chicago Tribune* 9 Dec. 18/3 This was the first time that a press agent had hit on a truthful first page story in a month of Sundays. **1964** M. MCLUHAN *Understanding Media* xxi. 213 Today's press agent regards the newspaper as a ventriloquist does his dummy. **1977** *Time* 10 Oct. 61/1 A former pressagent, Condon, 62, boasts average book sales of 1.3 million.

Hence **pre·ss-agent** *v. trans.*, to advertise in the manner of or by means of press agents; **pre·ss-agented** *ppl. a.*; **press-agenting** *vbl. sb.*; **pre·ss-agentry**, the employment or activities of press agents.

1909 WODEHOUSE *Swoop* II. ii. 68 Come now, your Grand Grace, is it a deal? Four hundred and fifty chinking o'Goblins a week for one hall a night, and press-agented at eight hundred and seventy-five. **1913** *Writer's Mag.* Nov. 172/1 There is no 'side line' open to the young writer better than press agentry. **1920** W. T. TILDEN *Art of Lawn Tennis* 3, I shall be accused of 'press-agenting' my own book by this statement. **1926** *Daily Express* 6 Aug. 3/5 Even the Hohenzollerns know something about Press agentry. **1930** P. W. SLOSSON *Great Crusade & After* x. 271 The same press-agenting which helped make the reputation of a grand-opera star..was also at the service of a pugilist. **1933** *Nation* (N.Y.) 11 Jan. 43 He press-agented most of the striking new theories, from those of the Lombrosian criminology..on down to the neo-Nietzchean doctrines of Elie Faure. **1939** *Sun* (Baltimore) 22 Nov. 13/1 Mr. Frank Murphy, the present highly press-agented Attorney General. **1947** M. BERGER in R. de Toledano *Frontiers of Jazz* 100 Bunk indulged in some personal press-agenting. **1948** *Archit. Rev.* CIV. 89 The same press-agentry that ballooned the popularity of other stars in the field of jazz. **1959** *Time* (Atlantic ed.) 24 Aug. 45 A longstanding and well pressagented public 'feud'. **1973** E. BULLINS *Theme is Blackness* 9 Whether they will regard Black dramatic criticism seriously and not degenerate into professional press agentry. **1977** *Irish Press* 29 Sept. 10/2 Meanwhile back in Ireland we are faced with the usual problem of press agentry.

pre·ss-board. [f. PRESS *v.*[1] or *sb.*[1] + BOARD *sb.*] **1.** An ironing-board; *spec.* (see quot. 1939).

1849 G. G. FOSTER *New York in Slices* i. 14 The press-board has been placed across the back corner of the shop. **1896** J. C. HARRIS *Sister Jane* i. 17 I've got this press-board on my lap, or I'd fetch it myself. **1924** W. D. F. VINCENT et al. *Cutters' Pract. Guide Body Coats* 33/1 The seam should be placed straight on the press-board in front of you. **1939** M. B. PICKEN *Lang. Fashion* 116/2 *Press-board*, padded board, a small ironing board, used for pressing fabrics when sewing.

2. *Electr. Engin.* (Written **pressboard.**) A material consisting of compressed laminations of paper, used as a separator or insulator in electrical equipment; a piece of this.

1910 H. M. HOBART *Dict. Electr. Engin.* II. 415/1 *Pressboard*, sometimes termed *pressed board*, a fibrous material closely resembling press-spahn. **1926** A. P. M. FLEMING in J. A. Fleming *Electr. Educator* II. 1354/2 The manufacture of pressboards..is the same as for paper making so far as the production of pulp. **1952** J. P. CASEY *Pulp & Paper* II. xvi. 957 Pressboards made..in thicknesses ranging from 0·005 to 0·125 in. are used as a spacing and insulating medium. **1973** R. W. SILLARS *Electr. Insulating Materials* vii. 123 Pressboard is prepared from cotton rag fibres or from pulp processed like other electrical papers, but instead of drying out as a single layer, a number of wet layers are placed together, pressed in a hydraulic press and dried by heat.

pre·ss-button, *sb.* and *a.* [f. PRESS *v.*[1] or *sb.*[1] + BUTTON *sb.*] **A.** *sb.* **a.** = *PUSH-BUTTON *sb.*

1892 [see *PRESSEL]. **1977** *Gramophone* Nov. 959/3 To the right of the main tuning knob..are two press-buttons.

b. A fastener similar to a press-stud.

1907 *Yesterday's Shopping* (1969) 404/1 Pocket for powder, lined white silk, with puff, and press button fastening. **1917** M. A. SOUDER *Notion Department* xv. 122 There are two types of snap fasteners: those built upon the principle of the ball and pocket reinforced with a wire spring, properly designated as snap fastener, and those of a flatter and structurally weaker design of a ball and socket without this wire spring, called press buttons. **1933** *Archit. Rev.* LXXIV. 30/1 (*caption*) The upholstery is easily removable on the motor car press-button principle.

B. *adj.* **a.** = *PUSH-BUTTON *a.* a.

1958 *Oxford Mail* 23 Aug. 3/6 Very neat press-button catches are fitted on all doors. **1965** *Wireless World* July 34/1 (Advt.), Press-button operation.

b. = *PUSH-BUTTON *a.* b.

1948 *Daily Tel.* 23 Apr. 5/2 Lord Montgomery said although we heard much talk of 'press-button' warfare, scientists had not so far produced any new weapon that could justify the discarding of the present-day technique of land warfare. **1958** *Listener* 12 June 990/3 A press-button world. **1965** M. MCINTYRE *Place of Quiet Waters* i. 5 All this high-powered, press-button living is wrong. **1971** *Daily Tel.* 30 Jan. 3/4 It was joked about as obsolete and useless in the age of press-button warfare.

pressed, *ppl. a.*[1] Add: **1.** (Further examples.)

1850 E. DOBSON *Rudimentary Treat. Manuf. Bricks & Tiles* I. iii. 83 Pressed bricks..are prepared by putting the raw bricks one at a time, when nearly dry, into a metal mould, in which they are forcibly compressed by the action of a powerful lever which forces up the piston forming the bottom of the mould. This gives a very beautiful face to the brick. **1869** *Our Young Folks* V. 86 We are making pressed glass nowadays that is almost as clear and beautiful as blown. **1895** *Army & Navy Co-op Soc. Price List* 111/2 Pressed veal & ham (Blanchflower's). **1912** J. ARMSTRONG *Motor* 266, I expect to see the clutch and flywheel as pressed parts in the near future, while pressed-steel pistons and connecting-rods are most likely to become common. **1926** F. HURST *Appassionata* I. 10 Two empty pressed-glass perfume-bottles that had stood equidistant on that dressing-table ever since you could remember. **1935** H. C. BRYSON *Gramophone Record* ix. 212 As soon as the press is opened, the steam commences to circulate in the dies, so that the operator has to remove the pressed record speedily or it will adhere to the rapidly-warming die. **1955** *Sci. Amer.* Jan. 68/1 One result of these studies has been the discovery of two new kinds of magnetic materials, the ferrites and the pressed-powder magnets. **1955** *Railway Mag.* June 388/2 The floor..is built up of $1\frac{5}{16}$ in. thick boards..bolted to dove-tailed galvanised steel sheeting carried on pressed-steel floor members. **1968** *Radio Times* 28 Nov. 20/1 The week's 'Newly Pressed' pop records. **1976** *Country Life* 1 Apr. 814/1 Apart from the addition of a 'bib' spoiler, the Mexico has the normal pressed-steel front of the rest of the range.

2. *U.S. slang.* Well dressed.

1970 H. E. ROBERTS *Third Ear* 11/1 *Pressed*, to be very well dressed. **1972** T. KOCHMAN *Rappin' & Stylin' Out* 165 Being well dressed is..expressed kinetically ('pressed'), and..the term refers to a favored norm.

pressel (pres'l). [f. PRESS *v.*[1]]. A press-button switch; orig., one attached to a flexible pendant conductor. Also *pressel-switch.*

1892 T. O'C. SLOANE *Stand. Electr. Dict.* 434 *Pressel*, a press-button often contained in a pear-shaped handle, arranged for attachment to the end of a flexible conductor, so as to hang thereby. **1911** W. P. MAYCOCK *Electr. Wiring* (ed. 4) ii. 159 Instead of a cord pull-switch, one might connect an ordinary or two-plate ceiling-rose to the switch leads..and hang therefrom a 'pressel' or suspension or pendant switch..which is a convenient pattern for operating with one hand. **1916** G. FRANKAU *Guns* 21 And he hears, as he plays with the pressel-switch, the strapped receiver click on his ear that listens, listens. **1971** B. W. ALDISS *Soldier Erect* 79, I handed the microphone to Gor-Blimey. After some frigging about with the pressel-switch until he got things right, he spoke to Blue Spot. **1973** B. CALLISON *Web of Salvage* ii. 25 He released the pressel switch and the static came back.

presse-pâte (pre·s,pat). [Fr.] The section of a paper-making machine in which superfluous water is extracted from the pulp before it is formed into sheets or rolls. Also *attrib.*

1888 CROSS & BEVAN *Text-bk. Paper-Making* vi. 96 The presse-pâte system, originally adopted for the treatment of straw, has of late years been extensively applied to esparto. The presse-pâte consists of the wet end of a paper machine, and is furnished with sand-tables and strainers. **1937** E. J. LABARRE *Dict. Paper* 194/2 Presse-pâte..is a machine practically identical with the wet end of the paper-machine... It serves to extract 'loose' water from the (wood) pulp, which is allowed to accumulate on a press roll or round an iron rod, until a sheet or roll of wet board of sufficient thickness is obtained. **1963** R. R. A. HIGHAM *Handbk. Papermaking* ii. 62 The pulp may either be concentrated on deckers, or presse-pâtes, or left in slush form.

presser. Add: **1. a.** Also, one who presses wool into bales.

1911 W. H. KOEBEL *In Maoriland Bush* viii. 122 The 'presser' climbs inside the high, square, wooden structure that rises in the centre of the floor, in readiness to receive the fleeces. **1955** G. BOWEN *Wool Away!* vii. 95 Pressing wool is a simple straightforward job, but good pressers work without waste movement and without getting in each other's way. **1965** J. S. GUNN *Terminol. Shearing Industry* II. 9 *Presser*, a skilled man who presses the wool into bales so that they are not 'light on' (short in weight).

c. Also in *Glass-making.*

1962 *Gloss. Terms Glass Industry* (*B.S.I.*) 45 *Presser*, a worker who shapes glass by pressing in a mould by hand or by machine.

3. a. (Further example.)

1873 *Young Englishwoman* Mar. 150/2, I get the stitching as close as the width of space between the needle hole and the edge of presser.

5. presser-bar (*b*) (examples); **presser-eye** *Spinning*, an aperture or eye through which cotton yarn passes before being wound on the spindle; **presser-foot** (examples); also *attrib.*

1908 *Sears, Roebuck Catal.* 41/2 The presser bar is round and fitted with a presser bar adjuster by which the pressure on the goods is regulated. **1974** J. ROBINSON *Penguin Bk. Sewing* ii. 36/1 Presser Bar..Stitch Length Regulator. **1892** J. NASMITH *Students' Cotton Spinning* ix. 340 In short, the traveller performs the same function as the flyer eye in the throstle or the presser eye in the roving frame. **1895** *Montgomery Ward Catal.* 262/1 Parts for Old Style Low Arm Singer..Presser Foot. **1908** *Sears, Roebuck Catal.* 41/1 The presser foot has a very large under surface, which extends on both sides of the needle and holds any weight goods firmly in place over the feed. The forward part of the presser foot nearest the operator is curved upward so that foot will not catch in seams of fleecy materials. **1932** Presser-foot [see *HEMMING *vbl. sb.*[1] b]. **1961** *Which?* Nov. 277 (*caption*) Presser-foot screw..presser-foot lever. **1964** A. BUTLER *Teaching Children Embroidery* 29 Stitches with the presser foot, on ..a [sewing] machine with a zigzag attachment.

press-fastener. [f. PRESS *v.*[1] + FASTENER.] = *PRESS-STUD.

1926–7 *Army & Navy Stores Catal.* 664/3 Press fasteners ..in black or white, 1 dozen on card. **1956** *Good Housek. Home Encyl.* (ed. 4) 185/2 One side must be left open.., press fasteners or hooks and eyes being used to close it. **1960** *Mrs. Beeton's Cookery & Househ. Managem.* 145 Hooks and Eyes, Press Fasteners. **1976** J. WAINWRIGHT *Who goes Next?* 95 Racing gloves..fastened at the back of the wrist, with a good press-fastener.

press-gang, *sb.* Add: **1.** Also *transf.*

1771 C. BURNEY *Present State of Mus. France & Italy* 119 These boys are a kind of *press-gang*, who seize all other boys they can find in their way to the church, in order to be catechised. **1969** I. & P. OPIE *Children's Games* i. 18 In some places the press-gang think they will be successful if they demand, 'Join the ring or tell us your sweetheart's name.'

2. *joc.* A group of journalists; the press (PRESS *sb.*[1] 13 g).

1840 *Spirit of Times* 11 Jan. 535/1 In compliment to the 'Press gang' Messr. Prentice and Weissinger..were invited to occupy seats over the Judge's stand. **1859** L. WILMER *Our Press Gang* xxvi. 353 Our newspapers, in general are the organs of the mob, and..the Press Gang *itself* is..a mob of the worst kind. **1859** G. H. LEWES *Let.* 20 Apr. in *Geo. Eliot Lett.* (1954) III. 54 Nor have I any relations with the pressgang here..the Edinburgh papers might advantageously be employed in this matter. **1869** 'MARK TWAIN' *Lett. to Publishers* (1967) 27, I will attend to the Buffalo books for the press..did I tell you that I took dinner with the whole press gang yesterday? **1889** *Pall Mall Gaz.* 21 Oct. 4/3 Ask what you like, my good sir; don't you know I am one of the press gang myself? **1941** F. L. MOTT *Amer. Journalism* xxxv. 603 Many stories are told of the conviviality of the Chicago 'press gang' of the nineties, and from the legends which grew up..sprang the concept of the romantic sot of the newspaper office. **1975** H. WAUGH *Bride for Hampton House* (1976) i. 1 She..waved at the press gang when she took the big elevator to the newsroom floor.

pressie, var. *PREZZIE.

pressing, *vbl. sb.*[1] Add: **1.** (Further examples.)

a **1911** D. G. PHILLIPS *Susan Lenox* in *Hearst's Mag.* (1915) June 538/1 Susan finished her pressing and started to dress. **1960** *Vogue Pattern Bk.* Autumn 61 Careful pressing, at every stage in making clothes, helps to give your work that smooth professional finish. **1969** T. C. THORSTENSEN *Pract. Leather Technol.* xii. 192 This pressing of the oil removes some of the high melting point components and gives the oil a lower cold test. **1976** *Southern Even. Echo* (Southampton) 15 Nov. 15/5 The match was one of two halves, with Basingstoke doing all the pressing in the first.

2. b. An article formed or shaped in a press; *spec.* a gramophone record made by stamping a blank with a matrix.

1922 *Metal Industry* XX. 273/1 Many parts are now being manufactured as pressings which a few years ago would have been thought impossible. **1927** *Gramophone* Sept. 139/1 The new white label pressings arrived just in time for me to take them to Paris. **1952** GODFREY & AMOS *Sound Recording & Reproduction* v. 143 A vinyl pressing is superior to one made in shellac in that it is far less fragile. **1959** *Motor Manual* (ed. 36) 7 A pressing is produced by squeezing the sheet of steel between a die, securely anchored in the base of the press, and the punch which is forced into it at a pressure of 750 tons or more. **1959** *Times Rev. Industry* Nov. 46/2 Quantities of pressings and castings are required by makers of household equipment. **1962** *Times* 5 July 15/6 A master tape of a recent recording of music by Prokofiev and an ordinary commercial pressing of a disc made from it were started simultaneously. **1973** D. Westheimer *Going Public* v. 77 Lee..turned on the stereo. It was an LP pressing of some old John Kirby RPM singles.

3. *pressing cloth, machine* (earlier and later examples), *pad, plant, rag, room*; **pressing board** (b), an ironing board.

1969 E. H. Pinto *Treen* 151/1 (*heading*) Ironing and Pressing Boards. **1917** E. R. Hambridge *Simple Dress-making* iii. 65/2 Wring out the pressing cloth *very* tightly, and lay it on the fabric. **1974** Lippman & Erskine *Dress-making made Simple* iv. 59 A pressing cloth can be obtained pre-treated. **1825** *Austin Papers* (1924) II. 1028 We intend to send a gin and probably a pressing machine. **1940** *Chambers's Techn. Dict.* 671/2 *Pressing machine*, a machine in which the whole forming operation is carried out by pressing the plastic glass by a plunger forced into a die or mould. The machine may be operated by hand or it may be fully automatic. **1947** C. Talbot *Compl. Bk. Sewing* xxxi. 208/1 The rounded shaping of armhole and shoulder..must be protected in pressing. A tailor's cushion, a pressing pad, or a sleeve board will help. **1974** Lippman & Erskine *Dressmaking made Simple* vi. 87 Press..shaped parts over the tailor's pressing cushion/pad. **1958** *Manch. Guardian* 21 Jan. 6/6 Oriole Records Ltd... has its own pressing plant and..presses all Mr. Lonsdale's records for him. **1934** A. L. Hird *Princ. & Pract. Needle-work & Dressmaking* iv. 41 *Do not apply water directly* to any materials except wool and wool mixtures, but always by way of pressing rag or as steam. **1922** O. Mitchell *Talking Machines* vi. 70 When the discs pass into the pressing room the steel backing is laid upon a heated table with the mould upwards. **1937** F. Stark *Baghdad Sketches* 36 He was a tailor in his spare time, and he used the roof as a pressing room.

pressive, *a.* Add: **4. b.** *Psychol.* That pertains or relates to environmental press (see *press *sb.*^{1} 5*).

1938 H. A. Murray *Explorations in Personality* ii. 96 In emotional action it is the sudden, close, pressive situation that seems to 'do the work' by releasing energy in the motor centres of the interbrain.

press lord. Also with capital initials. [f. Press *sb.*^{1} + Lord *sb.*] A powerful newspaper owner, a newspaper magnate, esp. one who is a member of the peerage. Cf. *press baron* s.v. *press *sb.*^{1} 16b.

1930 *Economist* 30 Aug. 396/2 At the Labour Party Conference..resolutions will be discussed..putting forward claims, rather reminiscent of those of the Press Lords, that certain Labour interests should dictate how the Cabinet should be composed. **1932** *Ann. Reg. 1931* 23 The 'press lords', Lord Rothermere and Lord Beaverbrook, who had never abated their hostility to Mr. Baldwin, had once more opened a campaign against him, and in London at any rate they were not without a considerable following. **1947** *Sat. Rev. Lit.* (U.S.) 22 Feb. 15/2 Roy Howard still dresses and acts among the press lords like a police reporter. **1955** T. H. Pear *Eng. Social Differences* 22 Some Press-lords are wounded..or amused at the suggestion that increased circulation is one of their first aims. **1965** Auden *About House* (1966) 15 Only a press lord Could have built San Simeon. **1977** *Time* 17 Jan. 5/2 But the press lord from Down Under is no stranger to *Time* readers—or *Time* staffers.

pressman^2. Restrict † *Obs.* to sense 2 in Dict. and add **1.** Also *fig. rare.*

1978 *Church Times* 17 Feb. 11/4 In religious education there has been a constant battle waged to rise to the challenge of the 1944 Act and ensure that the subject is taught by qualified specialists rather than by willing amateurs or, worse, by reluctant press-men.

pressmanship. Add: **1.** Also, skill as a pressman.

1923 H. A. Maddox *Printing* ix. 106 Most printing is in the indifferent class and much good typography is marred by careless pressmanship. *Ibid.* x. 125 Printing from three-colour half-tone blocks demands a high standard of pressmanship.

press-mark. Add: (Further examples.) Now chiefly with reference to manuscripts and early books in old libraries. Also *attrib.*

1941 N. R. Ker *Medieval Libraries* p. xviii, Pressmarks are useful indications of provenance just in so far as they are distinctive. **1952** J. Carter *ABC for Bk.-Collectors* 141 Seymour de Ricci, in his *English Collectors of Books and Manuscripts*, shows how much can be learned from the study of press-marks by anyone concerned with the provenance of books. **1963** *Times Lit. Suppl.* 1 Mar. 160/3 A stock of the press-mark tickets used by Louis-Henri. **1971** *Eng. Stud.* LII. 351 The press-mark of the Leiden manuscript is not *Voss 106*, but *Voss. 106*, in which *Voss.* is an abbreviation of *Vossianus*.

Hence **press-mark** *v. trans.* and *intr.* (see quots. 1889 and 1895).

1889 *Cent. Dict.*, *Press-mark..*, *v.t.* and *i.* To place a press-mark on; also, to use press-marks. **1895** *Funk's Stand. Dict.*, *Press-mark*,..*vt.* & *vi.* To mark (a book) with characters showing the proper place in a bookcase. **1915** *Trans. Bibliogr. Soc.* XIV. 5 The Society's library..has been rearranged and re-pressmarked.

press officer. Also with capital initials. [f. Press *sb.*^{1} + Officer *sb.*] An official appointed by an individual or institution to handle publicity and public relations.

1919 J. Buchan *Mr. Standfast* xx. 366, I was about to make a rush for..one of the Press officers, who would.. be in the way of knowing things. **1941** *Whitaker's Almanack* 321/2 Colonial Office... *Press Officer*, A. Ridgway.. £800. **1949** H. Nicolson *Diary* 14 Jan. (1968) 163 One man..had asked Philip Jordan, as Attlee's Press Officer, to describe what the P.M. had had for breakfast that morning. **1959–60** A. Butler in *Parliamentary Affairs* XIII. 57 Journalists under great pressure make use of guidance from Press officers in Government departments when handling reports and Bills. **1961** *Times* 25 July 2/2 (Advt.), 'English Electric' require a Press Officer..to..be responsible for all press and public relations functions. **1969** A. G. Thomas in L. Durrell *Spirit of Place* 57 In 1939 Durrell..moved to Athens working first for the Embassy as an unestablished press officer. **1972** 'H. Carmichael' *Naked to Grave* v. 71 You would get all the information from the press officer which was currently available.

pressoreceptor (pre·sorĭsep tǫɹ). *Physiol.* Also with hyphen. [f. *presso-*, taken as comb. form of *pressure* + Receptor.] A proprioceptor which responds to changes in blood pressure.

1941 P. Bard *Macleod's Physiol. in Mod. Med.* xl. 576 (*caption*) Effects of electrical stimulation of nerves from pressoreceptors and chemoreceptors in the dog. **1943** *Physiol. Rev.* XXIII. 244 In man the diastolic pressure has been shown to rise during standing. This is a sign of increasing vasomotor tone. It is compensatory in nature until it encroaches too far upon pulse pressure. The reflexes originating in the vascular presso-receptors are responsible for this control. **1975** *Investigative Urology* XII. 465 We studied the influence of pressoreceptor stimulation on micturition reflex and urethral pressure profile.

presspahn (pre·sˌʃpān, pre·spān). *Electr. Engin.* Also **press-spahn.** [a. G. *preßspahn* (now *-span*) pressboard, orig. pieces of card for pressing clothes f. *preß-* (in comb.) pressed, pressing + *span* shred, splinter.] Pressboard (sense *2).

1904 *Electr. Engineer* 14 Sept. 412/2 Creasing 'fibre, presspahn, etc.,' destroys the glazed surface..and is.. likely to reduce its insulating value. **1913** Barr & Archibald *Design Alternating Current Machinery* ii. 39 Press-spahn, in thin sheets, is largely used for the insulation of low-voltage windings. **1938** W. T. MacCall *Electr. Engin.* I. iii. 38 Many special forms of paper and cardboard, such as presspahn,..are used for moderate pressures.

press roll^1. *Papermaking.* [f. Press *sb.*^{1} + Roll *sb.*^{1}] (See quot. 1940.)

1881 J. Dunbar *Pract. Papermaker* (ed. 2) 47 The author has tried a contrivance which effectually prevents the paper breaking at the press rolls. **1937** E. J. Labarre *Dict. Paper* 195/1 *Press rolls* are pairs of heavy rolls, termed 'first', 'second', and 'third' press rolls according to their order in the paper-machine, serving to press out the water from the web of paper. **1940** *Chambers's Techn. Dict.* 671/1 *Press rolls*.., heavy cylinders of the paper-making machine which press out moisture from the wet web. Before the last pressing, the web is reversed in order to remove felt-marks.

press roll^2. *Jazz.* [f. Press *sb.*^{1} + Roll *sb.*^{2}] A drum-roll (see Roll *sb.*^{2} 2) in which the sticks are pressed against the drum-head.

1934 [see *drag *sb.* 7 i]. **1939** W. Hobson *Amer. Jazz Music* iii. 53 A 'press roll', one of the many rhythmic patterns which have been used by jazz drummers for years. **1956** S. Longstreet *Real Jazz* 148 A press roll is played on snare drums. **1966** *New Yorker* 11 June 153/1 Barbarin, in addition to a marvellous press roll, in which his sticks come at one another low from opposite edges of the snare in fat blurs, like gulls after the same clam, uses a high hat [etc.]. **1977** *Ibid.* 9 May 51/1 He principally used..powerful, accented press rolls on his snare drum.

press-room^1. Add: **2.** (Later examples.)

1878 *Rep. Vermont Board Agric.* V. 79 At the end from the road were the press and wash rooms. **1966** P. V. Price *France: Food & Wine Guide* 164 Visitors see the pressroom..and the huge stone container for 13,000 litres of wine.

3. A room reserved for the use of reporters.

1902 *Evening Star* (Washington, D.C.) 16 Dec. III. 10/3 The press room at the District building is quite a center of interest. **1941** F. L. Mott *Amer. Journalism* xxxv. 607 President Theodore Roosevelt..provided a press room and telephones for the reporters. **1943** L. C. Wilson in F. L. Mott *Journalism in Wartime* 99 Merriman Smith, on the White House,..fills a notebook..and then he literally runs to the United Press telephone booth in the Press Room. **1952** F. L. Mott *News in Amer.* xiii. 137 The doors were opened, and there was a grand rush for the telephones in the press-room and for taxis and cars. **1973** *Guardian* 19 Apr. 1/6 The President's sudden appearance last night in the White House press rooms. **1976** *National Observer* (U.S.) 31 Jan. 1/1 The press room..is a bit boggling. It is really a complex of rooms, encompassing a Western Union setup, a Sports Comm., Inc., service.., a bank of dictation phones, a wall of releases and handouts, and eight long rows of tables..stacked with 125 typewriters. **1977** *Cleethorpes News* 6 May 7/2 She spent most of her time in the Press room before leaving through a small but enthusiastic crowd.

press-spahn, var. *presspahn.

press-stud. [f. Press *v.*^{1} + Stud *sb.*^{1}] A fastener made of metal, plastic, etc., used for joining two parts of a garment etc. together and consisting of two components, one with a short shank which is pressed into a corresponding hollow in the other. Also *attrib.*

1917 *Harrods Gen. Catal.* 1425/2 Press Studs, Black and White..2/9 per gross. **1928** *Daily Express* 19 Mar. 5/5 The chalk will leave an impression at exactly the correct place for the other half of the press-stud to be sewn. **1955** *Times* 29 June 12/4 A beautifully tucked skirt, complete even with a pink and white striped nylon petticoat kept in place by press studs attached to the dress. **1966** *Price List* (Olney Amsden & Sons Ltd.) 31 Press stud tape.. 22/6 doz. yards. **1974** *Drive* Autumn 32/2 Floor coverings used to be fixed by press studs. **1977** *Offshore Engineer* Apr. 74/2 The boot's normal strap and buckle fastening is backed up with a press-stud arrangement which allows the wearer to release it in two seconds.

pre·ss-up. [f. Press *v.*^{1} + Up *adv.*^{1}] An exercise in which the body is raised from a prone position by straightening the arms while keeping the hands and feet on the ground and the legs straight; (see also quot. 1961).

1947 J. Bertram *Shadow of War* 208 Press-ups are a fairly strenuous exercise at the best of times. **1955** M. E. B. Banks *Commando Climber* iii. 33 We went through the usual climbing exercises such as press-ups with the finger tips and not the palms of the hands. **1956** Kunzle & Thomas *Freestanding* i. 22 Start with the feet on the third or fourth wall bar and do press-ups as before. **1961** J. S. Salak *Dict. Amer. Sports* 341 *Press Up* (mountain climbing), an upward movement on rock completed by pressing down on the palms of the hands on large flat holds and ledges. **1967** *New Scientist* 28 Dec. 766/1 When we say that an athlete is 'fit', we generally mean that he can perform some arbitrary feat, like 50 press-ups, without getting unduly puffed. **1978** *Rugby World* Apr. 33/3 It's hard on the club coach who has to motivate players with whom he probably played and has to try to get one of his best friends to do another half-a-dozen sprints or extra press-ups.

pressure, *sb.* Add: **II. 6. b.** (Further examples.) Also stress, strain; in *Finance*, forces (*on* a currency) tending towards a change in its value.

1961 *N.Y. Times* 5 July 31 Throughout 'The Making of a President' Mr. White shows wonderfully well how the pressures pile up on candidates. **1964** *Ann. Reg. 1963* 203 Pressure on the peso..became so strong in May that the authorities could no longer resist it. **1976** *Times* 30 Mar. 4/4 Not that they do not want freedom; but it brings pressures and choices with which they find it hard to cope. **1976** *Howard Jrnl.* XV. I. 13 There may also be cases in which a period of detention is necessary as a respite from problems or pressures that will otherwise entrap the offender in greater trouble. **1977** A. Ecclestone *Staircase for Silence* v. 95 As a sensitive man he registered the pressures which were..shaping men to make choices which would carry them to such lengths.

c. (Earlier and later examples.)

1812 *Q. Rev.* May 159 At the end of the same session, the third bill, from the pressure of business, was given up without having come to a final hearing. **1911** D. H. Lawrence *White Peacock* III. v. 442 In spite of his pressure of business he had become a County Councillor. **1926** S. Jameson *Three Kingdoms* x. 292 She worked on with an aching heart on the evenings when pressure of business kept her in the office until it was too late even to see Sandy before he was in bed and asleep. **1938** R. C. Hutchinson *Testament* I. vi. 60 They were supposed to undergo examination every week, but that, from the pressure on the doctors' time, was often omitted. **1960** E. Stopp tr. *St. François de Sales's Sel. Lett.* 238, I can see that it is hopeless to wait for a better opportunity, since continual pressure of affairs seems to be my fate.

7. a. (Further examples.)

1949 *Sun* (Baltimore) 7 Feb. 8/2 There is no doubting the fortitude the Norwegians show thus far against Russian pressure. **1964** Gould & Kolb *Dict. Social Sci.* 530/2 [S. E. Finer] reserves the term pressure for those activities ..which amount to the 'application or threatened application of a sanction should a demand be refused'. **1966** *Listener* 19 May 713/1 The effects of the sort of social pressures described by Professor Sprott depend largely on the age of the person, the length of time they last, and their intensity. **1976** *Times* 30 Mar. 4/2 The Conservative Party should resist well intentioned pressures to spell out in detail what it would do when it won a general election.

b. *to bring pressure* (*to bear*: to exert influence to a specific end; *to bring* (or *put*) *pressure on* (someone): to urge or press (someone) strongly in order to persuade.

1864 W. Hardman *Let.* 21 Apr. in S. M. Ellis *Lett. & Mem. Sir W. Hardman* (1925) 172 Some pressure had evidently been brought to bear. **1897** Put pressure on [in Dict.]. **1908** A. F. Bentley *Process of Govt.* x. 208 We frequently talk of 'bringing pressure to bear' upon someone, and we can use the word here with but slight extension beyond this common meaning. Pressure, as we shall use it, is always a group phenomenon. **1912** T. Dreiser *Financier* xlv. 489 He thought once of going to Mrs. Cowperwood and having her bring pressure to bear on her husband. **1934** *Amer. Speech* IX. 11/2 *To put on the pressure* is to run the cards of a long suit in an effort to force the discard of cards which might otherwise win tricks. **1937** *Sun* (Baltimore) 22 July 1/5 Republic Steel Corporation officials and leaders of a local back-to-work movement and of a law and order league brought sustained 'pressure' on city officials of an Ohio town, seeking the use of force in reopening strike-bound mills. **1960** L. P. Hartley *Facial Justice* iii. 25 These dissidents brought pressure to bear on their Governments to leave the upper air alone. **1961** *Times-Picayune* (New Orleans) 1 Jan. II. 3 This might be done to arouse those who have been squeezed out by the trims to exert pressure on the Legislature, so it would be more receptive to a tax proposal later in the year.

IV. 9. a. *pressure drop, gradient.* **b.** *pressure transducer.* **d.** *pressure sensation.* **f.** *pressure-reducing, -retaining* adjs. **g.** other Combs.: *pressure-sensitive* adj.

1949 O. G. SUTTON *Sci. of Flight* i. 14 The solution of practical problems, such as the determination of the pressure-drop in pipes. **1964** J. C. CATFORD in D. Abercrombie et al. *Daniel Jones* 31 For normal voice the liminal pressure-drop across the glottis is of the order of 3 cm of water. **1918** *Meteorol. Gloss.* (Met. Office), *Gradient wind*, the flow of air which is necessary to balance the pressure-gradient. **1968** R. A. LYTTLETON *Mysteries Solar Syst.* i. 27 For a heated gas-cloud rotating round the sun, there can be a pressure-gradient perpendicularly away from the general equatorial plane of the distribution. **1934** WEBSTER, Pressure-reducing, adj. **1950** *Sci. News Let.* XV. 79 The liquids are displaced from the tanks by an inert gas. Nitrogen, stored under a high pressure and fed to the tanks through pressure-reducing valves, is commonly used for this purpose. **1971** B. SCHARF *Engin. & its Lang.* xii. 177 Pressure control valves may be pressure-reducing valves which maintain reduced pressure on the downstream side (i.e. after the valve), pressure-retaining valves which maintain the pressure on the upstream side, and indirect pressure control valves to maintain the pressure at a point other than in the line in which the valve is located. **1895** *Amer. Jrnl. Psychol.* VII. 81 *Druckempfindung*, pressure sensation. **1901** [see *CONTACT *sb.* 1 d]. **1932** *Mind* XLI. 363 Whenever I touch anything I have pressure-sensations with a characteristic local sign. **1937** *Jrnl. Exper. Psychol.* XX. 458 There were relatively more pressure sensitive spots on the dorsal side of the arm than on the ventral side. **1970** *New Yorker* 3 Oct. 108/3 Repair the damage with pressure-sensitive tape. **1949** *Jrnl. Sci. Instruments* XXVI. 327/2 (*caption*) Final form of electronic pressure transducer. **1956** *Nature* 25 Feb. 380/1 The time it takes for the wave to cover a known distance was measured by means of two barium titanate crystal pressure-transducers. **1963** H. K. P. NEUBERT *Instrument Transducers* iv. 348 Through the year the main application of piezoelectric pressure transducers has been the 'engine indicator' for use with internal-combustion engines, which employs quartz disks or piles of disks.

10. pressure arch *Mining*, a distribution of pressure over an excavation resembling that in a structural arch, caused by increased pressure on the side walls of the excavation, which act as abutments supporting the strata forming the roof; **pressure-boiler,** a boiler designed to withstand great pressure, for heating liquids above the normal boiling point; **pressure breathing** (see quot. 1965); **pressure broadening** *Physics*, pressure-dependent broadening of spectral lines caused by collisions of emitting molecules with their neighbours in a fluid: so **pressure-broadened** *a.*; **pressure cabin,** in an aircraft, an airtight cabin in which the air is maintained at a pressure safe and comfortable for the occupants; **pressure cable** *Electr. Engin.*, a paper-insulated cable that contains gas or oil under pressure within the outer sheath or pipe, in order to counteract the tendency of the oil to move away from the conductors in operating conditions and enable higher voltages to be used; **pressure chamber,** a chamber designed to hold material under pressure, or in which pressure can be applied; **pressure (die-)casting,** die-casting in which the metal is forced into the mould under pressure; a casting so made; so **pressure-cast** *a.*; **pressure drag** *Aeronaut.*, the drag on a moving body which results from the aerodynamic pressure distribution over its surface; form drag; **pressure flaking** *Archæol.*, the flaking of flint tools by applying pressure with a hard point; hence **pressure-flaked** *a.*, shaped in this way; **pressure-flaker,** a pointed bone tool used for pressure-flaking; **pressure flask,** a flask designed to withstand pressure greater than that of the atmosphere; **pressure hold** *Mountaineering*, a hold maintained by the exertion of sideways or downward pressure; **pressure hull,** the hull (or part of the hull) of a submarine which is designed to withstand the pressure of the sea when the vessel is submerged; **pressure jump** *Meteorol.*, a mobile zone of atmospheric disturbance, characterized by a steep pressure gradient and usu. marking a discontinuity in the height of an inversion layer; so *pressure-jump line*; **pressure lamp,** a portable oil or paraffin lamp in which the fuel is forced up into the mantle or burner by the air pressure in an enclosed reservoir, which is increased by pumping with a built-in plunger; **pressure line** = *pressure ridge*; **pressure microphone,** a microphone which responds to the instantaneous pressure of sound waves; **pressure mine,** a mine designed to be activated by the temporary reduction in hydrostatic pressure caused by a passing ship; **pressure pack, package,** a dispenser containing a substance, freq. an aerosol, under pressure; so **pressure-packaged** *ppl. a.*; **pressure-packaging** *vbl. sb.*; **pressure pad,** a pad designed to transmit or absorb pressure; **pressure pattern,** a pattern of prevailing atmospheric pressures; usu. *attrib.*, as *pressure-pattern flying*, denoting the use of air routes which enable aircraft to take advantage of the air currents associated with such patterns to economize on fuel or time; **pressure ridge** (further examples); **pressure saucepan** = *PRESSURE COOKER a; **pressure sore** *Med.*, a sore produced by continued pressure on a part of the body; **pressure stove,** a portable stove supplied with oil or paraffin under pressure; **pressure suit,** a garment that can be made airtight and inflated to protect the wearer against low ambient pressure (as in high-altitude flight); **pressure tank,** a tank in which a fluid, esp. fuel, is held under pressure; **pressure tendency** *Meteorol.* = **barometric tendency*; **pressure-tight** *a.*, (of a joint, container, or the like), tightly enough constructed to prevent the passage of a fluid under pressure; hence **pressure-tightness; pressure vessel,** a vessel designed to contain material at high pressures; esp. in a nuclear reactor, a vessel containing the reactor core immersed in the pressurized coolant; **pressure wave,** a wave consisting of a sudden change in pressure propagated through a medium; **pressure welding,** welding in which pressure is applied to the parts to be joined; welding brought about by pressure. Also *PRESSURE COOKER, *PRESSURE(-)FEED *v.* and *sb.*, etc.

1950 FERRARI & WARDELL in E. Mason *Pract. Coal Mining* I. ix. 145/2 Props and bars, chocks and cutter nogs, all of which can be withdrawn and reset, are used for carrying the weight of stone inside the pressure arch. **1958** A. NELSON *Methods of Working* iv. 32 A true pressure arch can only exist underground where two side abutments exist, each being strong enough to support its share of the load on the arch and also to provide the lateral thrust necessary for its stability. **1973** L. J. THOMAS *Introd. Mining* viii. 340 The recommendation of the committee was that stalls should be limited to three-quarters of the width of the pressure arch for stability, and that pillar width should be equal to stall width. **1891** S. P. SADTLER *Hand-bk. Industr. Org. Chem.* v. 179 Three grammes of substance are placed in a small beaker (preferably of metal), which is placed as one of several in a Soxhlet pressure-boiler, or the test is carried out in the Lintner pressure-flask,—and heated to the temperature of boiling water. **1952** A. HUXLEY *Let.* 20 May (1969) 644, I have had no return of my iritis and, thanks to the newly invented pressure-breathing treatment,..have practically eliminated the slight chronic bronchitis. **1965** *Gloss. Aeronaut. Terms* (*B.S.I.*) XVII. 3 *Pressure breathing*, a technique in which oxygen is supplied to the lungs at a pressure higher than the ambient barometric pressure. **1936** *Rev. Mod. Physics* VIII. 48/2 These pressure-broadened lines show the expected larger shifts and half-widths. **1970** A. F. HARVEY *Coherent Light* xxv. 1095 For most atmospheric phenomena the pressure-broadened line is appropriate. **1932** *Physical Rev.* XXXIX. 860 The pressure shift of spectral lines, unexplained by the usual theories of pressure broadening. **1967** W. R. HINDMARSH *Atomic Spectra* viii. 86 The three main causes of line-broadening are: the natural width of atomic energy levels..; Doppler width..; and collision, or pressure broadening. **1935** *Jrnl. R. Aeronaut. Soc.* XXXIX. 1045 Pressure cabins and/or free oxygen in the cabins are both being experimented with today. **1948** 'N. SHUTE' *No Highway* iv. 109 They..went into the rear fuselage, behind the pressure cabin. **1965** J. D. STORER *Behind Scenes in Aircraft Factory* iii. 33 A door in a normal pressure cabin would have to withstand an outward load of some seven tons. **1931** M. HOCHSTADTER et al. in *Jrnl. R. Soc. Arts* LXXX. 95 The utilisation of an impregnated paper cable..could be greatly increased if it were possible to get rid of the heterogeneity in the dielectric, or to render it harmless so far as the time-voltage curve and stability are concerned... It is possible to do this (a) By the use of a very thin impregnating oil and the provision of channels along the cable... (b) By radial compression of the cable in such a way that the radial 'breathing' is reversible at all temperatures, such vacuous spaces as tend to form being closed by the compression or the pressure in them raised to such an extent that no ionisation takes place. The latter alternative leads to the 'Pressure Cable'. **1966** *IEEE Trans. Power Apparatus & Syst.* LXXXV. 375 (*heading*) A few aspects of the general problem concerning tightness of connections formed by pressure cables. **1973** J. G. TWEEDDALE *Materials Technol.* II. ii. 41 A pressure-cast material is likely to be..more uniformly consistent in structure than other cast materials. **1979** MILLS & MANSFIELD *Genuine Article* iv. 71 'Beirut Sovereigns.' Untold numbers of these superb pressure cast forgeries now adulterate the market. **1922** *Proc. Inst. Mech. Engin.* I. 27 Pressure castings in iron though not yet out of the experimental stage, would..tend to eliminate holes due to occluded air or shrinkage. **1933** *Iron Age* 30 Nov. 18/1 Brass pressure castings are subject to porosity in the same manner that zinc and aluminum die castings are subject to porosity. **1973** J. G. TWEEDDALE *Materials Technol.* II. ii. 42 (*caption*) Systems for pressure casting. (a) Gravity pressure. (b) Gas pressure. (c) Mechanical pressure. (d) Centrifugal pressure. (e) Another system for using centrifugal pressure. **1915** *Jrnl. Chem. Soc.* CVIII. II. 820 A press is described..which by means of a lower cylinder with narrow holes bored vertically in it forces a molten solid out of the pressure chamber and so causes a sudden drop in pressure. **1934** *Jrnl. Cellular & Compar. Physiol.* V. 335 A pressure chamber was constructed which permits of viscosity measurements by the 'centrifuge method' at high hydrostatic pressures. **1966** *Lancet* 24 Dec. 1406/1 A small brass pressure chamber was constructed of about 20 ml. capacity. **1919** *Bull. Amer. Inst. Mining Engin.* Feb. 240 On fracture, the pressure die casting will be found to consist of a dense closely grained outer stratum and a porous inner stratum. **1933** *Machinery* XXXIX. 781/1 Pressure die-castings do not have a homogeneous structure, but, upon fracture, exhibit a dense fine-grained exterior and a coarser grained interior. **1973** J. G. TWEEDDALE *Materials Technol.* II. ii. 8 We have..injection moulding technologists concerned only with pressure-die-casting of thermo-plastic polymers. **1950** KUETHE & SCHETZER *Found. Aerodynamics* xii. 212 Two types of drag, form or pressure drag and skin friction, are evident in the flow of a viscous incompressible fluid past a body. **1959** F. D. ADAMS *Aeronaut. Dict.* 79/1 Inasmuch as pressure drag is a function of form, form drag and pressure drag are sometimes considered synonymous. **1961** H. H. KOELLE *Handbk. Astronaut. Engin.* v. 23 In ideal, inviscid, and incompressible two-dimensional flow there is no pressure drag. The sum of the pressure-force components in the free-stream direction is zero. **1934** *Geogr. Jrnl.* LXXXIII. 302 A knife of neolithic age, pressure-flaked from tabular chert. **1959** J. D. CLARK *Prehist. S. Afr.* vi. 161 Small pressure-flaked points shaped like equilateral triangles. **1954** S. PIGGOTT *Neolithic Cultures Brit. Isles* ii. 43 The same floor produced three antler tines, and Floor 58..another, associated with a heap of minute flakes, indicating their use as pressure-flakers. **1927** PEAKE & FLEURE *Hunters & Artists* 49 The new technique..includes a high finish by the process of pressure-flaking, that is to say the removal of small thin flakes by pressing near the edge with a bone tool rather than by striking with another stone. **1949** K. P. OAKLEY *Man the Tool-Maker* v. 29 Some of the tribes..dress spear-heads by pressure-flaking. **1959** J. D. CLARK *Prehist. S. Afr.* vi. 157 The finish is much finer and pressure flaking is frequently used. **1891** Pressure flask [see *pressure boiler* above]. **1967** *Oceanogr. & Marine Biol.* V. 188 Pressure flask for studying plants under a few atm. **1941** T. A. H. PEACOCKE *Mountaineering* iv. 46 Sideways pressure-holds, with the palms of the hands pointing down, should be used as much as possible. **1955** J. E. B. WRIGHT *Technique of Mountaineering* Pl. 10 (*caption*) Last man on Kern Knotts Crack using plimsolls for pressure holds for feet. **1975** W. UNSWORTH *Encycl. Mountaineering* 120/1 Pressure holds are holds where there is no grip as such and one relies on the friction of the rock. **1923** *Man. Seamanship* (Admiralty) II. 171 Situated on the pressure hull..is what is known as the 'diver's connection'. **1966** *McGraw-Hill Encycl. Sci. & Technol.* XIII. 211/2 The pressure hull, comprising all of the inner and part of the outer hull, is the strong hull that resists external sea pressure. **1974** L. DEIGHTON *Spy Story* xx. 210 The crash came like a sledgehammer pounded against the hollow steel of the pressure hull... Obviously some dire damage had been done to the submarine. **1950** M. TEPPER in *Jrnl. Meteorol.* VII. 21 It is proposed that a squall line might be considered as a disturbance generated by accelerations along the cold front and which travels along the warm sector inversion as a gravitational wave. It is recommended that any series of meteorological events similar to this mechanism be called a Pressure Jump Line. *Ibid.* 23/1 The leading edge of this pressure gradient, which shall be referred to as the pressure jump, is clearly defined on the maps, seems to undulate rather violently, and moves in a non-uniform manner. **1955** *Sci. News Let.* 12 Mar. 170/2 This squall line is also known as a pressure jump line, since a sudden rise in barometric pressure always accompanies it. **1963** E. R. REITER *Jet-Stream Meteorol.* iv. 271 We may..point out some..research work..which makes a pressure jump that travels as a gravity wave along the inversion between moist and dry air responsible for the formation of squall lines and tornadoes. **1967** *Oceanogr. & Marine Biol.* V. 42 Sudden rises in sea level..have been experienced occasionally at coastal locations with the passage over the sea of a moving squall line or pressure jump. **1939–40** *Army & Navy Stores Catal.* 279 'Tilley' lamps... A 'pressure' lamp. **1958** L. DURRELL *Balthazar* vii. 154 A whole encampment..had sprung up in the darkness, fitfully lit by oil and paraffin stoves, by pressure lamps and braziers. **1974** J. WAINWRIGHT *Hard Hit* 150 The white-hot mantle of the pressure-lamp. **1909** *Daily Chron.* 3 Sept. 1/2 Much of our hard work was lost in circuitous twists around troublesome pressure lines and high, irregular fields of very old ice. **1934** OLSON & MASSA *Appl. Acoustics* v. 93 If the response corresponds to the variations in pressure of the medium, it is termed a pressure microphone. **1966** *McGraw-Hill Encycl. Sci. & Technol.* VIII. 360/1 Pressure microphones are inherently nondirectional (omnidirectional), because pressure is a scalar and not a vector quantity. **1949** J. S. COWIE *Mines, Minelayers & Minelaying* viii. 162 The Germans, meanwhile, had played their last card, the 'Oyster' or pressure mine. **1957** *Encycl. Brit.* XV. 535/1 Since pressure mines are fired by the reduced water pressure produced by a ship passing over them, the best method of sweeping them is to simulate the passage of a ship by towing a large, expendable target over them. **1969** *New Scientist* 28 Aug. 421/2 In fairways that are not more than 100 or 200 feet deep, the pressure mines are a special hazard. **1958** HERZKA & PICKTHALL *Pressurized Packaging* (*Aerosols*) iv. 78 The first pressure packs marketed in Great Britain were packed in aluminium dispensers which monopolized the British market until the advent of the all-tinplate dispenser in 1955. **1959** *News Chron.* 30 June 6/5 The pressure-pack has no screw-cap and the dispensing valve automatically seals itself after use. **1966** HARRIS & PLATT in A. Herzka *Internat. Encycl. Pressurized Packaging* vi. 81 In the case of the pressure pack..the basic source of energy is provided by the propellant, which may be either compressed or liquefied gas. **1958** *Food Technol.* XII. 331/1 Results of one or both of the above mentioned methods will indicate whether the existing product is applicable to the pressure package. **1957** *Mod. Packaging* Dec. 156/2 Many foods that are pressure packaged cannot be subjected to heat without quality loss and thus must be refrigerated. **1959** *News Chron.* 30 June 6/3 A familiar product..is the pressure-packaged insecticide. **1957** *Mod. Packaging* Dec. 156/2 Most foods that have application to pressure packaging will require some sort of preservation treatment. **1912** *Machinery* 31 Oct. 148/2 The shell stripper..also acts as the spring pressure pad during the drawing operation. **1941** C. W. HINMAN *Pressworking Metals* vi. 75 The power of compression is adjusted by nuts beneath a pressure pad at the lower end of the casing. **1969** *Times* 7 Mar. 15/1 A group of research workers in California claims to have discovered a way of presenting visual information to blind people through an array of pressure pads which vibrate against the skin of their backs. **1979** B. FREEMANTLE *Charlie Muffin's Uncle Sam* xvi. 146 Battery-operated bells..rang if..anyone..stepped on one of the pressure pads..around the display cases. **1946** *Sci. News Let.* 2 Nov. 278/2 A new technique, 'pressure pattern flying', is now available to air pilots on the Atlantic route from Europe... This new technique consists in determining the shortest flight-time path to the destination by a series of late accurate reports..which locates pressure areas and enables a pilot to take advantage of the airflow circulating around them. **1954** *N.Y. Times* 6 June II. 31/2 During the past eight years Trans World Airlines pilots flying over the Atlantic..have mastered the techniques of getting maximum range from their planes by flying 'pressure patterns'. **1962** G. D. P. WORTHINGTON *Flight Planning* iv. 53 The study of pressure pattern flying and the increasing knowledge being obtained of jet streams has made it apparent that the shortest route is not always the quickest or most economical. **1913** I. COWIE *Company of Adventurers* xv. 264, I..was aroused every now and again by the cracking, rumbling and thunderous resounding of the ice as the cold took a firmer grip on it and upheaved it into pressure ridges. **1951** *Beaver* June 13 The entire ice-cover is criss-crossed by a network of pressure ridges. **1975** E. IGLAUER *Denison's Ice Road* ix. 230 Denison pointed to a pressure ridge, a wide band of broken ice, several feet high. **1951** *Good Housek. Home Encycl.* 229/1 For cooking a single dish for four or five persons, or a complete meal for one or two, a pressure saucepan will serve. **1889** *Buck's Handbk. Med. Sci.* VIII. 748/3 (Index), Pressure-sores. **1905** R. HOWARD *Surg. Nursing* ii. 23 In applying back splints to the leg and foot..the heel itself only rests lightly on the splint, otherwise a pressure-sore may occur. **1977** *Lancet* 10 Sept. 548/1 Chairfast patients consistently had a higher pressure-sore frequency than bedfast patients of a similar degree of helplessness. **1914** *Handbk. Amat. Camping Club* 51 The increasing popularity of the paraffin pressure stove, the best-known form of which is perhaps the 'Primus', is an indication that this form of kitchen range probably best fits the camper's bill. **1956** C. EVANS *On Climbing* viii. 129 For high altitudes, and extreme cold, it is possible to have a pressure-stove made with an extra large cup to hold more priming fuel. **1966** B. KIMENYE *Kalasanda Revisited* 31 The self-pitying thought, 'I might as well be dead', kept recurring in his mind as he pumped his pressure stove to boil a kettle of tea. **1936** *Flight* 1 Oct. 340/2 To enable the pilot to stand the extremely low pressure encountered at about 50,000ft..a special 'pressure-suit' has been produced. **1949** *Startling Stories* Sept. 125/2 The multiple layers of my pressure suit had made movement very difficult. **1962** J. GLENN et al. *Into Orbit* 244 G-suits are not to be confused with pressure suits (or, now, spacesuits) which the Astronaut wears during space flight to maintain atmospheric pressure at high altitudes. **1977** P. WAY *Super-Celeste* 58 The sudden expansion of his pressure suit turned his body into a heavy, rigid block... He was catapulted..into..the sky. **1862** *Electrician* 10 Jan. 115/2 (*heading*) Mr. Reid's pressure tank, used in testing cables during manufacture. **1917** 'CONTACT' *Airman's Outings* viii. 225 A small gravity tank for his machine, to be used when the pressure tank is ventilated by a bullet. **1929** F. P. GIBBONS *Red Napoleon* xii. 403 'Pressure tank hit,' Binney shouted. 'I'm dumping her.' **1962** *Sci. Survey* III. 85 Modern machines [*sc.* electrostatic generators] of this type, enclosed in steel pressure-tanks, have produced about 10 MeV. **1939** R. C. SUTCLIFFE *Meteorol. for Aviators* xvii. 218 The closest attention should always be given to the pressure tendencies. **1946** W. L. DONN *Meteorol.* vii. 118 The pressure tendency is the net change in pressure for the preceding 3 hours. **1970** F. W. COLE *Introd. Meteorol.* xiv. 323 While pressure, as such, is not a useful weather parameter, the change in pressure and the pressure tendency are both helpful in developing a forecast. **1946** *Nature* 21 Dec. 897/2 Pressurization of cabins for high-altitude flying now appears to be essential... This creates a fresh outlook on the body structure, which now has to be a pressure-tight shell. **1963** R. HAMMOND *Automatic Welding* ii. 85 Eight spot welds fix the spider to the rim, eliminating rivet holes and ensuring a pressure-tight joint. **1951** H. H. DOEHLER *Die Casting* xi. 458 (*heading*) Inspecting for pressure tightness. **1970** tr. *Zoebl's Fund. Hydraulic Circuitry* viii. 156 This type of plant is used for checking the pressure tightness of welded pipes. **1915** HAVEN & SWETT (*title*) The design of steam boilers and pressure vessels. **1960** *Practical Wireless* XXXVI. 298/1 X-ray photographs of the welds in the pressure vessel of a nuclear power station. **1962** *Newnes Conc. Encycl. Nucl. Energy* 707/2 For safety reasons the reactor is located inside a steel pressure vessel about 70 ft in diameter and 70 ft high. **1975** BRAM & DOWNS *Manuf. Technol.* ii. 60 If the product is a pressure vessel, very high-integrity welds are essential. **1949** O. G. SUTTON *Sci. of Flight* vi. 140 (*heading*) Pressure waves caused by moving bodies. **1956** A. H. COMPTON *Atomic Quest* iii. 212 The pressure waves in a metal strained far beyond the elastic limit. **1962** A. NISBETT *Technique Sound Studio* xi. 191 The water-tank artificial reverberation machine.., in which the sound is modulated on to a 80-kc/s carrier and fed via a piezo-electric element to produce pressure waves in the water-tank. **1975** T. ALLBEURY *Special Collection* iv. 18 He could feel the vibration in his ears, the pressure waves of the guns and bombs. **1926** STOUGHTON & BUTTS *Engin. Metall.* vii. 137 (*heading*) Electric heating for pressure welding. **1954** H. UDIN et al. *Welding for Engineers* iii. 34 Oxyacetylene pressure welding is accomplished by butting together under pressure the two pieces of metal to be joined and heating the junction by oxyacetylene torches. **1967** A. H. COTTRELL *Introd. Metall.* xxii. 435 In extrusion, the great pressure developed between the metal and the die can lead to sticking, due to pressure welding.

pre·ssure, *v.* orig. *U.S.* [f. the sb.] **1. a.** *trans.* To exert pressure on. Chiefly *fig.*, to urge or impel (someone *to do* something or *into* a situation or course of action); to drive or force (someone *out of* something). Also *absol.* (const. *for*), to exert pressure, to press. Hence **pre·ssured** *ppl. a.*, of work, affairs, etc.: urgent, pressing; of people: under pressure.

1939 R. CHANDLER in *Dime Detective Mag.* Jan. 103/2 I'm not trying to pressure you. **1944** *Sun* (Baltimore) 6 Oct. 7/3 You can't pressure the War Labor Board into action through strikes. **1951** L. Z. HOBSON *Celebrity* (1953) x. 140 It's too bad Gregory Johns is so set against public appearances, but even the studio isn't trying to pressure him. **1957** J. F. HORNER *Summary of Scientology* i. 10 Finally he was pressured into writing a popular treatise on Scientology. **1960** *Daily Mail* 12 May 10/6 Baldies can be 'pressured' into paying more than £200 for a course of treatment. **1961** S. RAVEN *Eng. Gentleman* III. iv. 170 Was Rufus trying to pressure him? asked Henry. Certainly not. Just trying to make him see things in a sensible way. **1963** *Economist* 12 Jan. 111/2 Preachers.. 'were pressured out of the pulpits they held'. **1968** P. OLIVER *Screening Blues* vi. 248 The imputation that the singers were pressured by the record companies which is frequently made, though probably having some measure of truth, is probably much overstated. **1971** H. CHEETHAM *Portrait of Oxford* xiii. 202 The trouble about an Oxford education..is that no-one..pressures you into working. **1971** C. BONINGTON *Annapurna South Face* iii. 32, I..was near to exhaustion from weeks of pressured work and worry. **1973** J. GOODFIELD *Courier to Peking* I. iii. 45 You personally have never pressured for unlimited resources. **1976** *Times* 8 July 2/5 He said the personalities of Joseph Markham and later Clive Mildoon began as fantasies, providing relief for the pressured and overburdened public figure of Mr John Stonehouse.

b. *trans.* To gain by bringing pressure to bear. *U.S.*

1944 *Sun* (Baltimore) 7 May 8/3 He intervened himself and pressured a better settlement for the unions. **1952** *Ibid.* 22 Mar. 6/4 Other strong unions will now immediately pressure comparable or greater gains for their own people.

2. *trans.* = *PRESSURIZE *v.* 1.

1961 in WEBSTER. **1979** *Daily Tel.* 8 June 2/1 The engine on the right would have continued to pressure the No. 3 [hydraulic] system under normal circumstances.

pressure cooker. [f. PRESSURE *sb.* + COOKER.] **a.** An airtight vessel in which food can be cooked in steam under pressure, so that a higher temperature is reached and the food is cooked more quickly.

1915 *Jrnl. Home Econ.* VII. 375 Why should the modern household more than the modern factory reject a tool of value? This question might well be asked concerning pressure cookers. **1919** *Delineator* Nov. 53/1 Of all modern household saving devices on the market to-day.. there is no one article which does more toward lessening household burdens..than the pressure cooker. **1937** H. W. TILMAN *Ascent of Nanda Devi* x. 111 Weight was saved by the abandonment of two pressure cookers..a cooker that cooks by steam under pressure and in which, I think, even a pair of boots would be made edible. **1950** F. SWINNERTON *Flower for Catherine* 57 Probably some tough old sheep, with lambs of her own, that I shall have to tenderize in the pressure cooker. **1951** *Good Housek. Home Encycl.* 229/1 Some pressure cookers have lids which seal internally, fitting under a rim. **1969** *Islander* (Victoria, B.C.) 5 Oct. 5/2, I had brought along my pressure cooker for speed, and soon I had this filled with the tasty ingredients for a stew.

b. *fig.* (freq. *attrib.*).

1954 KOESTLER *Invis. Writing* iv. 54, I had acquired it [*sc.* Russian]..by the same pressure-cooker method by which I had learnt modern Hebrew. **1958** *Spectator* 13 June 759/1 Strict curfews and a huge concentration of troops restored order, but the valve of the pressure-cooker was seen to be under enormous strain. **1968** MRS. L. B. JOHNSON *White House Diary* 18 Dec. (1970) 758 Every day of the last four years it seems to me she [*sc.* Mrs. Hubert Humphrey] has grown..and especially in the pressure cooker of a campaign. **1974** *Spartanburg* (S. Carolina) *Herald* 18 Apr. C4/1 With the season now almost four months old and the pressure cooker of the Masters just behind them, most of the game's top guns are taking a break. **1976** L. SANDERS *Hamlet Warning* (1977) iv. 36 Santo Domingo was a pressure cooker, ready to explode. **1976** *National Observer* (U.S.) 25 Dec. 6/5 An auction's pressure cooker atmosphere is no place for split second decisions involving tens of thousands of dollars.

Hence (*lit.* and *fig.*) **pressure-cook** *v. trans.* (also *absol.*), **pressure-cooked** *ppl. a.*, **pressure-cooking** *vbl. sb.*; also **pressure cookery**.

1940 *Sears, Roebuck Catal.* Spring/Summer 612 Your meals will taste better, too, because pressure cooking retains all the delicate flavors. **1950** *Mrs. Beeton's Bk. Househ. Managem.* 1155 (*heading*) Hay-box and pressure cookery. **1951** *Good Housek. Home Encycl.* 616/2 Pressure-cook for 25–30 minutes. *Ibid.* 618/2 Pressure cookery is the only safe method for the home sterilising of bottled and canned vegetables. **1958** *Listener* 2 Jan. 13/2 The Russians..avoid early specialisation or pressure-cooking in education. **1958** *Woman* 27 Sept. 4/3, I pressure-cooked it until the meat left the bone. **1960** *Farmer & Stockbreeder* 9 Feb. (Suppl.) 2/1 Nut and raisin pressure-cooked loaf cake is covered with a double thickness of greased paper. **1968** *Time* 11 Oct. 28 We concocted Chicago from one Bat for peace, Numerous Democratic toads, And a pressure-cooked American flag.

pressure-feed, *v.* and *sb.* [See FEED *v.* 7, 8c and FEED *sb.* 5.] **A.** *v. trans.* To supply (material, esp. fuel) by means of applied pressure. **B.** *sb.* Also **pressure feed.** A supply system in which the flow of material is maintained by applied pressure; the supplying of material in this way. So **pre·ssure-fed** *ppl. a.*, supplied with material in this way; utilizing a pressure feed.

1904 *Autocar* 6 Aug. 164/1 (*heading*) Carburetter. Pressure feed from the exhaust. *Ibid.*, The lubricator..is also pressure fed. **1906** W. W. BEAUMONT *Motor Vehicles* II. viii. 158 Pressure-fed lubrication is adopted for the engine and for the petrol feed. *Ibid.* xii. 206 Pressure feed is used, obtained by a shunt from the exhaust pipe to a distributing box. **1909** D. LEECHMAN *Carburetters* ix. 66 Petrol is maintained at a certain level..by means of a float and needle valve when the petrol is pressure fed. **1914, 1925** [see *GRAVITY(-)FEED *sb.*]. **1936** *Discovery* Sept. 299/2 The rocket motor of today with its..complicated system of pressure feeds, safety valves and dual liquid-fuel storage tanks, little resembles the old-style cardboard tube and gunpowder. **1961** H. H. KOELLE *Handbk. Astronaut. Engin.* xx. 16 Pump-fed systems are lighter than pressure-fed systems for all but the very shortest-duration requirements.

pressure group. [f. PRESSURE *sb.* + GROUP *sb.*] A group or association of people representing some special interest, who bring concerted pressure to bear on public policy. Also *attrib.* Hence **pressure groupism**, activity characteristic of a pressure group.

1928 P. H. ODEGARD *Pressure Politics* vii. 202 The character of pressure groups as of individuals can frequently be understood from the manner in which they spend their money. **1934** W. LIPPMANN *Method of Freedom* iii. 97 We come then to the conclusion that it is not the pressure groups as such which make it impossible for the state to act in the general interest..but pressure groups attached to and reinforced by political machines. **1936** A. HUXLEY *Eyeless in Gaza* xxii. 316 One joined the Party, one distributed literature, one financed pressure-groups. **1937** B. ZELLER *Pressure Politics in N.Y.* viii. 229 The outstanding feature of modern pressure group technique is the widespread use of propaganda channels. *Ibid.* ix. 263 This frequent and flagrant abuse of pressure group politics. **1941** W. TEMPLE *Citizen & Churchman* iii. 56 One American professor opened his reply with the words: 'It is obvious that the Church is a pressure-group.' **1953** WODEHOUSE *Performing Flea* 154 You can no longer put a negro on the stage unless you make him very dignified. Owing to the activities of the Negro pressure group, comic negro characters are absolutely taboo. **1954** *Encounter* Mar. 58/2 The illusion..that US opposition to the admission of Communist China to the UN is..an ephemeral, emotional attitude dictated by a nebulous pressure-group called 'The China Lobby'. **1959** *Oxf. Univ. Gaz.* 16 Mar. 795/1 It is an interesting aspect of the workings of pressure-group politics to see that in Australia and New Zealand it is the interests of the manufacturers which prevail, with both political parties, against the general good of those countries, which urgently require greater production and export of farm products. **1960** *Encounter* Jan. 39/2 Those literal-minded pressure-groups which haunt all public organs of opinion. **1966** *New Statesman* 13 May 683/1 Comment on this affair included, not surprisingly, accusations of pressure groupism and intolerance. **1971** P. GRESSWELL *Environment* 18 In a literate society, such pressure groups [*sc.* amenity societies] are a necessary adjunct to parliamentary democracy. **1978** *Dædalus* Spring 75 Almost equally annoying to scientists is the change in political attitudes; members of Congress now tend to look on them as just another selfish pressure group, and not as the wizards of perpetual progress.

pressure head. [f. PRESSURE *sb.* + HEAD *sb.*] **1.** The pressure exerted by a fluid, expressed as the height of a column of fluid which would produce that pressure by virtue of its weight (cf. HEAD *sb.* 17 a and b).

1907 WOODWARD & PRESTON tr. *Sorel's Carbureting & Combustion in Alcohol Engines* viii. 160 Let..*H* = pressure head on the liquid. **1974** J. A. FOX *Introd. Engin. Fluid Mech.* viii. 283 A velocity change of 1 ft/s can generate a pressure head of approximately 125 ft if it occurs rapidly enough.

2. *Aeronaut.* A pitot-static tube.

1930 *Aircraft Engin.* II. 95/2 The standard pressure head..consists of pressure and static tubes mounted parallel and near to each other. **1964** E. H. J. PALLETT *Aircraft Instrument Man.* ii. 11 Pressure heads now in general use are..electrically heated.

pressure jet. [f. PRESSURE *sb.* + JET *sb.*[3]] **a.** Used *attrib.* with reference to a type of oil burner in which the fuel is burned at a fine nozzle through which it is passed under pressure.

1911 W. H. BOOTH *Liquid Fuel* xiii. 212 The pressure-jet system will recover from 70 per cent. to 75 per cent. of the theoretical calorific value of the oil fuel used in actual practice. **1920** E. C. BOWDEN-SMITH *Oil Firing* iv. 90 In the pressure-jet burner great care must be taken to maintain a high temperature, or the burner may fail entirely. **1968** J. SLOME *Domestic Oil-Fired Central Heating* iii. 61 Pressure jet burners can make quite a considerable amount of noise.

b. A small jet engine mounted at the tip of a helicopter rotor blade and supplied with compressed air through a duct in the blade. Freq. *attrib.*

1950 *Jrnl. Helicopter Assoc. Gt. Brit.* III. 153 The pressure jet helicopter is..suitable for longer ranges. 1958 LAMBERMONT & PIRIE *Helicopters & Autogyros* 201 The XV-1 has a reciprocating engine..which acts by feeding air through tubes to small pressure jets at the tips of the three-bladed rotor during vertical flight.

pressure plate. [f. PRESSURE *sb.* + PLATE *sb.*] **a.** A plate for detecting or receiving pressure, *spec.* in an anemometer. **b.** A plate for applying pressure, *spec.* in a clutch.

1845 *Rep. Brit. Assoc. Adv. Sci. 1844* 24 A contrivance ..is affixed to the pressure plate, by means of which the fluid is deposited at a variable rate, but always depending on the force on the pressure plate at the time. 1856 *Ibid. 1855* 127 The force of the wind is ascertained by means of a circular plate having an area of four square feet, which is kept by the vane at right angles to the current of the wind... To this pressure-plate is attached a wire which communicates with a recording pencil. 1892 *Q. Jrnl. R. Meteorol. Soc.* XVIII. 174 It was not possible to obtain a perfectly distinct line from the pen of the Pressure Plate during a gale unless the paper moved at least 2 inches in each minute. 1921 J. V. WOODWORTH *Amer. Tool Making* xxvii. 445 The pressure on the foot treadle, which causes the pressure plate to clamp the can and lid against the chuck, also throws in the friction clutch which starts the work. 1958 *Newnes Compl. Amat. Photogr.* iv. 71 In a 35 mm. camera, the pressure plate should be examined carefully. 1963 D. H. MCINTOSH *Meteorol. Gloss.* (ed. 4) 16 In the pressure-plate anemometer, the deflexion of a flat plate placed in the wind is measured; its use is confined mainly to atmospheric turbulence measurement. 1976 *Horse & Hound* 3 Dec. 66 (Advt.), Superb rebuilt Land-Rovers fitted with..new clutch and pressure plate.

pressure point. [f. PRESSURE *sb.* + POINT *sb.*[1]] **1. a.** A point where pressure is supposed to stimulate or inhibit convulsions.

1876 [in Dict. s.v. PRESSURE *sb.* 10]. 1885 J. ROSS *Handbk. Dis. Nervous Syst.* 167 Pressure points are frequently observed in spasmodic affections. Pressure upon certain points puts a stop at times to the convulsion when present, and consequently these points may be called pressure-arresting points. In other cases the convulsions are brought on by pressure on particular points, and these may..be called pressure-exciting points. 1896 J. M. DA COSTA *Med. Diag.* (ed. 8) ii. 233 There are 'pressure-points' which when acted on will cause the convulsive movements to be arrested. 1910 J. L. SALINGER tr. T. Ziehen in A. Church *Dis. Nervous Syst.* 1082 The relation of the pressure-points is also noteworthy. Pressure upon these occasionally increases the severity of the attack, or may produce a new attack [of hysteria].

b. One of numerous small areas on the skin that are specially sensitive to pressure; also, a point at which pain is felt on pressure.

1882 *Amer. Jrnl. Med. Sci.* LXXXIV. 589 Dr. Meyer discovered a painful pressure-point at the upper part of the brachial plexus. 1891 W. STIRLING tr. *Landois's Text-bk. Human Physiol.* (ed. 4) II. xiv. 1018 The 'pressure-points'..lie much closer together, and are more numerous than the temperature-points. 1906 C. P. FLINT et al. tr. *Sahli's Diagnostic Methods* 758 The pressure sense is not scattered diffusely in the skin, but..depends upon localized organs. The projections of the latter upon the surface of the skin are called 'pressure points'. 1940 *Jrnl. Exper. Psychol.* XXVI. 516 This parallelism of the two kinds of sensation [*sc.* pressure and vibration] could not be proved for the pressure points. 1958 R. WARTENBERG *Neuritis, Sensory Neuritis, Neuralgia* xli. 406 In cases of neuralgia of the last intercostal nerve, typical pressure points, especially on the back, could always be found.

c. A point where an artery can easily be pressed against a bone to inhibit bleeding.

1909 R. HOWARD in *Sci. & Art of Nursing* III. xxii. 5 (*heading*) The main arteries and their pressure points. 1933 BAILEY & LOVE *Surg. for Nurses* xxix. 308 Pressure points..are situations in which large arteries are adjacent to bones, and so are easily compressed against the rigid underlying part. 1954 DIEHL & LATON *Health & Safety for You* iv. 46/1 (*caption*) Find the pressure point between the wound and the heart; press against the bone. 1973 *Guardian* 11 Apr. 11/4 He..sliced the top off his thumb. But he knew about pressure points.

d. A pressure sore, or a point where one is apt to develop owing to the pressure on it.

1929 E. L. ELIASON et al. *Surg. Nursing* xvi. 389 After the immediate effects of the operation have disappeared, a vigilant watch must be kept for the development of pressure points. 1941 K. D. KEELE *Mod. Home Nursing* iii. 43 Pressure points of the body have to be learnt. They are those parts which, being exposed to the brunt of bearing the weight of the body, get most wear. 1964 M. C. T. MORRISON *Basic Princ. Accident Surg.* xvi. 89 The patient should be nursed on pillows or foam rubber pads to distribute the pressure evenly over the whole of his back or side rather than on his 'pressure points'. 1969 BRAIN & WALTON *Dis. Nervous Syst.* (ed. 7) xiv. 630 The dressing should be well covered with adhesive plaster attached to skin some distance from the pressure points and changed every day.

2. *fig.* A person or thing that can be used by someone as a means of exerting pressure on another.

1975 T. ALLBEURY *Palomino Blonde* xv. 91 The girl.. is being used as a pressure point on him to give the details of his discovery to the Soviets. 1977 R. LUDLUM *Chancellor Manuscript* xv. 167 Hoover..will soon control the pressure points of the country. He'll be running it. 1978 *Internat. Relations Dict.* (U.S. Dept. State Library) 25/1 An international political strategy relating two or more issues in negotiations, and then using them as tradeoffs or pressure points, much as in a 'carrots and stick' technique.

pressure-test, *sb.* and *v. trans.* [f. PRESSURE *sb.* + TEST *sb.*[1]] **A.** *sb.* A test for pressure of any kind, or of ability to withstand or sustain pressure. **B.** *v. trans.* To subject to a test of this nature.

[1882 R. SENNETT *Marine Steam Engine* xxvii. 570 The water-pressure test should be double the working steam pressure, provided that during the examination no indication of weakness is observed.] 1888 W. C. UNWIN *Testing of Materials of Construction* xv. 479 It may be useful to examine if the rate of hardening in pressure tests can be expressed as simply as that in tension tests. 1897 [in Dict. s.v. PRESSURE *sb.* 9 b]. 1941 WYNDHAM LEWIS *Let.* 17 Oct. (1963) 300 No. 1 doctor said that if the [ocular] pressure-test gave a negative result, that then another cause must be looked for. 1957 *Sun* (Baltimore) 19 June 40/3 They were pressure-testing it with oxygen, after welding it, when the tank exploded. 1977 *Offshore Engineer* June 50/3 We pressure-tested flotation chambers to check water-tightness.

pressure treatment. [f. PRESSURE *sb.* + TREATMENT.] **a.** *Timber.* Impregnation of timber with a preservative fluid, such as creosote, under applied pressure.

1914 MOON & BROWN *Elem. Forestry* xii. 235 The Rueping, Card, Lowry and other more or less important processes are in common use but they are all variations of the same pressure treatment. 1942 H. D. TIEMANN *Wood Technol.* xvii. 258 Wood preservation against decay consists in impregnating wood, either by soakage or by pressure treatment, with antiseptic liquids. 1950 A. J. PANSHIN et al. *Forest Products* iv. 65 Practically all southern pine poles are given a full-length pressure treatment with creosote oil before being placed in service.

b. *Biol.* Subjection (of cells, organisms, etc.) to increased pressure.

1940 *Biol. Bull.* LXXVIII. 106 It is clear that the time relationships between nuclear and cytoplasmic division may be somewhat disturbed by pressure treatment. 1956 *Internat. Rev. Cytol.* V. 215 The cell is rendered incapable of performing the work of cleavage by any combination of temperature and pressure treatments that jointly weakens the gel structure to approximately the same degree. 1970 S. B. & A. M. ZIMMERMAN in A. M. Zimmerman *High Pressure Effects on Cellular Processes* viii. 183 Numerous vacuoles appear in the cell cytoplasm following decompression and may be representative of some damage caused by the pressure treatment.

Hence (as a back-formation) **pre·ssure-treat** *v. trans.* So **pre·ssure-treated** *ppl. a.*; **pre·ssure-treating** *vbl. sb.*

1936 *Jrnl. Cellular & Compar. Physiol.* VIII. 159 The Amoebae are placed in a centrifuge-pressure chamber which is so designed that the control and pressure-treated specimens are simultaneously centrifuged for a suitable period. 1938 HUNT & GARRATT *Wood Preservation* vi. 221 Untreated wood, exposed when pile heads are cut off to grade, may be pressure treated by a method developed by E. F. Hartman. 1950 A. J. PANSHIN et al. *Forest Products* iv. 66 One of the empty-cell processes is usually employed, unless customer specification for total retention of creosote is such that a full-cell pressure-treating process is required. 1960 *Farmer & Stockbreeder* 2 Feb. (Suppl.) 9/1 Concrete stanchions and pressure-treated timber trusses and purlins. 1963 H. R. CLAUSER *Encycl. Engin. Materials* 738/1 Pressure-treating operations must be conducted in plants with considerable equipment. *Ibid.*, Some of the American species are easy to pressure-treat, others are difficult to penetrate with any chemical. 1970 S. B. & A. M. ZIMMERMAN in A. M. Zimmerman *High Pressure Effects on Cellular Processes* viii. 187 The pressure-treated cells revealed a loss of Golgi complex and pinocytotic channels.

pressure tube. [f. PRESSURE *sb.* + TUBE *sb.*] **1.** A tube open at one or more points to a surrounding fluid whose velocity or pressure it is used to measure. Usu. *attrib.* in *pressure tube anemometer*.

1894 *Q. Jrnl. Meteorol. Soc.* XX. 186 Lately he had spent a good many hours by the side of Mr. Dines's pressure tube anemometer, watching the action of the pen in squalls of wind. 1920 G. TAYLOR *Austral. Meteorol.* viii. 77 The pressure and suction tubes..act together to move the float. 1970 R. W. LONGLEY *Elements Meteorol.* vii. 140 The record..came from a Dines pressure-tube anemometer which is able to measure rapid fluctuations in the wind.

2. A tube in which pressurized coolant or moderator is passed through the core in certain types of nuclear reactor.

1961 J. K. PICKARD et al. *Power Reactor Technol.* iv. 214 A graphite reflector can be used..which compensates for the loss of neutrons in the pressure tubes. 1968 MOORE & HOLMES in *Steam Generating & Other Heavy Water Reactors* (Brit. Nuclear Energy Soc.) 3/2 One of the important features of a pressure tube reactor is that not only can different materials be used for the moderator and coolant, but the operating conditions of these media can be selected quite independently to suit their functions.

pressurization (preʃəraizēi·ʃən). [f. as next + -ATION.] The action or result of pressurizing (*lit.* or *fig.*).

1937 *Jrnl. Aeronaut. Sci.* IV. 99/1 The problems of cabin pressurization will increase rapidly as wall pressure differentials of over 1300 lbs. per sq. ft. will maintain. 1946 *Nature* 21 Dec. 897/2 Pressurization of cabins for high-altitude flying now appears to be essential with the adoption of the gas turbine. 1958 'P. BRYANT' *Two Hours to Doom* 86 Have the pressurization..set for full. 1963 *Daily Tel.* 26 Apr. 14 A luncheon appointment between a publicity expert and an M.P. to discuss a particular interest appears suspect to Mr. Edelman as 'pressurization'. 1969 *Ibid.* 21 Nov. 2/3 A decompression explosion can also be ruled out as the plane was too low to need pressurisation. 1975 F. R. PALMER in W. F. Bolton *Eng. Lang.* ii. 44 The stop (or plosive) consonants..involve the pressurization of air pushed up from the lungs into the vocal tract. 1979 *Daily Tel.* 2 July 22/2 Cruel and critical but sympathetic pressurisation each day from the organising consultants.

pressurize (pre·ʃəraiz), *v.* [f. PRESSURE *sb.* + -IZE.] **1.** *trans.* To produce or maintain pressure artificially in (a container, closed space, etc., esp. an aircraft); to apply pressure to.

1944 *Aeronautics* Sept. 56/2 The fuselage will be pressurized so that at all altitudes cabin conditions will be equivalent to a height of 8,000 ft. 1958 *Times* 25 Jan. 9/2 This machine consists of a small electric compressor pump, which pressurizes the container to a pressure of 80 lb. to the square inch. 1958 *Times* 14 Aug. 9/7 This means she [*sc.* an undersea cargo ship] would have an empty space which must either be pressurized to balance the pressure of the sea, or made strong enough to withstand that pressure. 1970 *Nature* 18 Apr. 249/2 Before re-entry, the camera and payload section were sealed and pressurized to two atmospheres. 1972 *Daily Tel.* 11 Dec. 15/6 We returned from our first drive, pressurised the lunar module cabin and took our helmets off. 1975 *Sci. Amer.* July 52/3 The surface of the journal and the surface of the bearing are separated by a film of lubricant when the journal is turning rapidly enough to pressurize the wedge with lubricant.

2. To subject to moral or mental pressure or suasion; to urge or constrain.

1956 *Essays in Crit.* VI. 238 The best poems..have all these qualities together with a strict sense of form that pressurizes the colloquial idiom. 1964 *Listener* 26 Nov. 859/2 This is the move which concedes the initiative, since White is now able to gain space and pressurize the black squares on the king's side. 1970 N. BAWDEN *Birds on Trees* ii. 32 Charlie said we didn't want to pressurize him. 1973 'M. INNES' *Appleby's Answer* xiii. 116 Perhaps Bulkington has developed a quiet pressurising line on his young charges. 1978 *Guardian Weekly* 30 Apr. 15/3 U.S. officials are pressurising the Saudis to increase production capacity.

Hence **pre·ssurizing** *vbl. sb.*

1946 *Sun* (Baltimore) 16 May 6/3 Pressurizing enables passengers to enjoy the comfortable flying conditions of 8,000 feet while at a ceiling of 25,000. 1976 J. M. KELLY *Stud. Civil Judicature Roman Republ.* v. 130 The pressurizing of the defendant into surrendering the plaintiff's property.

pressurized (pre·ʃəraizd), *ppl. a.* [f. as prec. + -ED[1].] **1.** Containing, or made to contain, fluid under pressure. **a.** Of an aircraft cabin, spacesuit, etc.: designed to maintain an interior air pressure close to normal atmospheric pressure in a low-pressure environment.

1938 *Time* 23 May 33 Without pressurized cabins, planes now fly as high as 14,000 feet. 1945 *Times* 2 Oct. 2/4 It has a pressurized cabin which, up to a height of 20,000 ft., maintains a pressure inside the passengers' cabin equivalent to that at 8,000 ft. 1949 *Archit. Rev.* CV. 237/2 A very highly streamlined low-wing, four-motor monoplane, with tricycle undercarriage and pressurized cabin. 1951 A. C. CLARKE *Across Sea of Stars* (1959) 4 We could live comfortable for a month in our pressurised tractors. 1958 *Times* 28 Aug. 9/4 'Colonists' [on the moon] ..unable to quit their pressurized suits for a moment. 1962 F. I. ORDWAY et al. *Basic Astronautics* xiii. 516 (*caption*) First pressurized suit..was developed for Wiley Post and worn by him in 1934. 1975 D. LODGE *Changing Places* i. 3 They were protected from the thin, cold air by the pressurized cabins of two Boeing 707s.

b. Of an aerosol container or spray.

1955 *Industr. & Engin. Chem.* June 1198/1 Aerosol products are pressurized, self-spraying products that at the press of a valve button deliver an active ingredient in a fine spray (insecticides and room deodorants), a heavier spray (paints and enamels), a foam (shave creams), and newest among the applications, a dry powder. 1958 *Times* 24 Nov. 11/5 Helena Rubinstein has a new pressurized scent spray. 1961 *Lancet* 2 Sept. 506/1 It was decided to recommend that the surgical staff should use.. a pressurised powder spray of polybactrin. 1976 *Which?* Feb. 37/1 Technically, an aerosol is simply a fine spray. Most people use the word to describe the pressurised can that produces a spray.

2. Of a fluid: increased in pressure; *pressurized-water reactor*, a nuclear reactor in which the coolant is water at high pressure.

1953 *Chem. & Engin. News* 3 Aug. 3187/3 The AEC is continuing research and development work on the pressurized water reactor. 1957 E. HYAMS *Into Dream* III. vi. 236 As if the pressurized air contained some poison of the mind. 1958 *Times Rev. Industry* July 32/2 Pressurized fluid is fed to the power valve which..actuates the brake. 1960 *Economist* 22 Oct. 392/2 One important aspect of *Dreadnought* is that it gives British technicians a first experience of a pressurised water reactor. 1966 *McGraw-Hill Encycl. Sci. & Technol.* XI. 363/1 The sodium-cooled reactor originally installed on the submarine USS *Seawolf* has been replaced by a pressurized-water reactor. 1968 M. WOODHOUSE *Rock Baby* xviii. 182 Find out if there's still pressurized gas within the casing. 1977 *Sci. Amer.* June 46/1 The lower piston rests against the dividing plate, supported by a cushion of pressurized nitrogen gas.

3. *fig.* Of a person or situation: subject to pressure; under moral, mental, or social pressure or constraint.

1959 *Times* 30 Nov. 4/1 This age of pressurized competition. 1965 *Punch* 22 Sept. 425/2 This going out of London has made the job very pressurised. Weekends are hectic.

press-work. Add: **3. b.** The pressing or drawing of metal into a shaped hollow die; a piece of metal shaped by such means.

1896 O. SMITH *Press-Working of Metals* i. 14 In press-work the metal is sometimes heated as in forging, but in the great majority of cases it is handled cold. **1903** *Engineering* 16 Jan. p. v (Index), Press work for sheet metal. **1904** *Ibid.* 22 Jan. 132/3 We illustrate below a very remarkable specimen of 'press' work... The barrel shown ..has been drawn out of a steel-plate $\frac{1}{64}$th of an inch in thickness. **1941** C. W. HINMAN *Pressworking of Metals* i. 1 Today, it is a wonder how the past generation ever produced any satisfactory presswork. **1963** BIRD & HUTTON-STOTT *Veteran Motor Car* 82 This was a most remarkable piece of presswork and comprised a complete chassis..of deep-section side girders, upswept over the rear axle.

Hence as *v. trans.*, to shape (metal) in this way; usu. as *pres. pple.*; so **pre·ss-working** *vbl. sb.*

1896 O. SMITH (*title*) Press-working of metals. *Ibid.* v. 120 It is taken for granted that the materials employed for press-working..must be to some considerable degree in a malleable or ductile physical condition. **1941** C. W. HINMAN *Pressworking of Metals* vi. 62 (*heading*) Press-working nonmetallic materials. **1949** *Tool Engineers Handbk.* (Amer. Soc. Tool Engineers) lxxiii. 1058 Heated dies are used in the pressworking of brass and magnesium. **1958** EARY & REED (*title*) Techniques of pressworking sheet metal.

prestation. Add: **a.** (Further example.)

1973 *Proc. Gen. Board of Faculties Oxf. Univ.* CXXXIII. 568 The directive also lays down that in the case of provision ('prestation') of services [etc.]... This expression refers to a short visit to another country in order to provide services on a temporary or transient basis.

c. *Anthrop.* A gift, payment, or service that forms part of some traditional function in a society, given or due either to specific persons or to the group.

1889 W. R. SMITH *Lect. Relig. of Semites* xi. 403 The very idea of an execution implies a public function, and not a private prestation. *Ibid.* 413 Even in the theology of the Rabbins penitence atones only for light offences, all grave offences demanding also a material prestation. **1935** B. MALINOWSKI *Coral Gardens* I. vi. 204 Since the English language has a really unaccountable and intolerable gap, I am deliberately introducing here the word 'prestation' in the French sense, that is, of legally defined services to be tendered by one individual or group to another. **1951** *Jrnl. R. Anthrop. Inst.* LXXXI. 35/2 In Kachin type systems it is an exchange of women for gifts (prestations). *Ibid.* 51/1 The 'prestations'..may not only take on a variety of forms, they may have several quite different structural functions. **1954** I. CUNNISON in *Mauss's Gift* p. xi, There is no convenient English word to translate the French *prestation* so this word itself is used to mean any thing or series of things given freely or obligatorily as a gift or in exchange; and includes services, entertainments, etc., as well as material things. **1957** M. FORTES in R. Firth *Man & Culture* 178 Exogamy is evidently enforced without exception, as we should expect with a jural obligation that..is validated by prestations on both sides. **1967** F. BARTH in R. Firth *Themes in Econ. Anthropol.* 152 The rights of the cultivator as *user* as distinct from *owner* are expressed in the symbolic prestation of one pot of beer to the title holder after each harvest. **1968** R. NEEDHAM et al. tr. *Lévi-Strauss's Elem. Struct. Kinship* (1969) vi. 77 The *ufuapie* exchange prestations which are economic, legal, matrimonial, [etc.]. **1973** *Sci. Amer.* July 74/1 In general anthropologists have argued that the goods are a 'prestation', which has been defined as the act of paying in money or service what is due by law or custom.

Prestel (preste·l). The proprietary name of a computerized visual information system operated by British Telecommunications, by which data selected from one or more data bases may be made to appear on a television screen by dialling an appropriate telephone number.

1978 *Times* 28 July 17/7 A Post Office brain-child, originally called Viewdata and now known as Prestel.., is now operating in a test version in preparation for its full public launch. **1978** *Trade Marks Jrnl.* 6 Dec. 2689/1 *Prestel*... Electrical, electronic and electro-mechanical apparatus, instruments and installations; monitoring, control and data storage apparatus and instruments... The Post Office. **1979** *Observer* 11 Feb. 42 (Advt.), Even at this early stage, there are thousands of pages of information available to Prestel subscribers. It's a sign of the way television is moving from being a simple means of entertainment to a much more complex domestic information medium.

prestellar: see *PRE- B. 1.

prestige. Add: Also with pronunc. (prestī·dʒ). The pronunc. (pre·stidʒ) is no longer heard.

3. *attrib.* or quasi-*adj.* (not clearly distinguishable from some of the examples listed in sense 4 below). Cf. *PRESTIGEFUL *a.*, *PRESTIGIOUS *a.* 2.

1934 R. BENEDICT *Patterns of Culture* (1935) iv. 85 The Dionysian bent in the North American vision quest..did not usually have to make compromise with prestige groups and their privileges. **1937** *Time* 16 Aug. 34/2 The cinema has a special category for what it calls 'prestige pictures'. **1944** W. S. MAUGHAM *Razor's Edge* vii. 325 Though she didn't much care for them [*sc.* some modern paintings] she thought quite rightly that they would be a prestige item in their future home. **1949** L. P. HARTLEY *Boat* xi. 156 If only they could all put off their company manners and change into their old clothes! But no; this was a prestige occasion. **1953** *Time* 23 Mar. 104/2 A 'prestige production', in broadcasting circles, is a show that abounds in a specific type of intelligence. **1957** *Times Lit. Suppl.* 8 Nov. 674/1 Serious books, normally prestige ware, had overnight changed into consumer goods, so that both conscience and bank-balance slept tight. **1958** M. ARGYLE *Relig. Behaviour* viii. 85 Prestige suggestion, in which people change their opinion after being told that a prestige person holds a different one. **1961** D. JENKINS *Equality & Excellence* viii. 175 Too many expensively educated young women aspire to careers as secretaries or receptionists in 'prestige offices'. **1962** *Rep. Comm. Broadcasting 1960* 92 in *Parl. Papers 1961–2* (Cmnd. 1753) IX. 259 The occasional, highly-advertised prestige programme put on for the occasion of a Christian festival. **1967** *Word Study* Mar. 3/2, I do find it difficult not to blame Miss Prouty at least a little bit..for rejecting usages so widely current in the prestige dialect that they are sanctioned even by her own textbook. **1968** *Globe & Mail* (Toronto) 13 Jan. 37/2 (Advt.), Accommodation available in Toronto's finest small nursing home, central prestige location, single or double occupancy, with or without private bath. **1969** *Nature* 29 Nov. 840/1 The Soviet Union still..seems to treat all scientific and technological progress (from sputniks to fish-spotting and from television sets to trans-continental pipelines) as primarily 'prestige' achievements. **1971** E. JONES in J. Spencer *Eng. Lang. W. Afr.* 84 Yams are a kind of prestige crop and item of food in rural West Africa. **1974** *Times* 20 Sept. 1/4 Aston Martin, one of Britain's prestige car companies. **1977** *Irish Times* 8 June 13/6 (Advt.), Superb town residence in prestige location.

4. *Comb.*, as *prestige-object*, *-principle*, *-product*, *-structure*, *-value*, *-word*; *prestige-hunting*, *-ranking*, *-rating* vbl. sbs.; *prestige-bearing*, *-building*, *-conferring*, *-conscious*, *-marking* adjs.; **prestige advertising**, advertising with the principal aim of furthering the prestige of the advertiser (rather than increasing sales, etc.).

1958 P. SHORE in N. Mackenzie *Conviction* 39 I.C.I. is not alone in this kind of prestige advertising. **1959** *Manch. Guardian* 2 July 6/5, I doubt whether prestige advertising is important in recruiting university graduates. **1972** *Lebende Sprachen* XVII. 46/2 Prestige advertising. **1949** R. K. MERTON *Social Theory* II. v. 201 Pickpockets who.. delight in mastering the prestige-bearing feat of 'beating a left breech'. **1964** R. A. HALL *Introd. Linguistics* 21 Prestige-bearing persons. **1965** *Economist* 13 Nov. 723/1 A very different and very prestige-building new activity. **1961** D. JENKINS *Equality & Excellence* viii. 151 Those prestige-conferring occupations which used to be reserved for those 'of good family'. **1971** *Guardian* 25 Sept. 8/1 Prestige-conscious companies like IBM and Alcan. **1930** M. MEAD *Growing up in New Guinea* iii. 29 But this is neither child labour nor idle prestige hunting on the part of the parents. **1957** M. JOOS *Readings in Linguistics* 376/2 The dialects and idiolects of higher prestige were more advanced in this direction [of phonetic drift], and their speakers carried the drift farther along so as to maintain the prestige-marking difference against their pursuers. **1955** D. CHAPMAN *Home & Social Status* iii. 42 The piano, which was formerly the principal prestige-object. **1939** *Brit. Jrnl. Psychol.* Jan. 220 Concrete manifestations of the 'prestige-principle' at work. **1958** *Observer* 25 May 16/2 To-day 'culture' is being marketed as a prestige-product. **1955** T. H. PEAR *Eng. Social Differences* i. 29 How far does their [*sc.* adolescents'] prestige-ranking of occupations resemble that made by adults? **1957** YOUNG & WILLMOTT in 'C. H. Rolph' *Human Sum* vii. 140 An earlier national study of the prestige-ranking given to occupations by people who were predominantly non-manual workers. **1960** *New Left Rev.* Sept.–Oct. 3/1 The changing patterns of prestige-ranking. **1954** J. A. C. BROWN *Social Psychol. of Industry* v. 140 The worker may be..upset when he is moved to another job at the same pay, but with a lower prestige-rating. **1949** R. K. MERTON *Patterns of Influence* iv, in Lazarsfeld & Stanton *Communications Res.* II. 198 He begins his climb in the prestige-structure at a relatively high level. **1929** L. D. WHITE (*title*) The prestige value of public employment in Chicago. **1942** *Mind* LI. 170 Mathematics has indeed, a tremendous prestige value. **1958** *Listener* 21 Aug. 283/2 The two- or three-garage house, even the monster car itself, looked like losing its prestige value. **1967** E. SHORT *Embroidery & Fabric Collage* iii. 68 A good patchwork quilt has a prestige value in keeping with the labour that goes into the making of it. **1972** J. L. DILLARD *Black English* vi. 233 The prestige value of more expensive toys, bicycles, and athletic equipment. **1964** C. BARBER *Ling. Change Present-Day Eng.* ii. 25 There are many men of the professional classes who, far from practising the sounds of R[eceived] P[ronunciation] and the prestige-words of R[eceived] S[tandard], are deliberately refusing to do so. **1964** *Eng. Stud.* XLV. (Suppl.) 22 But very often there *is* a marked difference in tone between the foreign and the native terms, the former being felt as prestige-words, the latter as the plain terms.

prestigeful (prestī·ʒfŭl), *a.* [f. PRESTIGE + -FUL.] = *PRESTIGIOUS *a.* 2.

1956 C. W. MILLS *Power Elite* iii. 53 There is..an appreciation of the new for its own sake: that which is new is prestigeful. **1959** *Encounter* Aug. 71/1 The more or less prestigeful 'pure fields'. **1961** S. R. HERMAN in J. A. Fishman *Readings Sociol. of Lang.* (1968) 507 In the new environment he [*sc.* an immigrant] is often without the prestigeful status he enjoyed in his country of origin and he is very much in need of recognition. **1967** M. ARGYLE *Psychol. Interpersonal Behaviour* v. 93 The experimenter should be prestigeful, an attractive person of the opposite sex, or at any rate compatible. **1971** *Times Lit. Suppl.* 22 Oct. 1310/4 Bateson had his contributions refused publication by the prestigeful periodical *Nature*. **1974** R. A. HALL *External Hist. Romance Lang.* 22 Many scholars.. are inclined to follow the folk-lore of our Western European culture in ascribing the status of 'language' only to those types of speech which manifest the prestigeful features just mentioned.

prestigey (prestī·ʒi, prestī·dʒi), *a. colloq.* [f. PRESTIGE + -Y[1].] = *PRESTIGIOUS *a.* 2.

1963 *Spectator* 27 Sept. 385 Desires for prestigey bigness. **1968** J. BINGHAM *I love, I Kill* xi. 133 What you want is the serious actor bit. Something more prestigey. **1968** M. RICHLER *Cocksure* vi. 36 We're no more than a bauble..a prestige-y trinket.

prestiginous (presti·dʒĭnǝs), *a. rare*$^{-1}$. [f. PRESTIGE + *-in-* + -OUS, irreg. after *multitudinous*, etc.] = *PRESTIGIOUS *a.* 2.

1896 G. B. SHAW *Let.* 16 Mar. (1965) I. 614 A commercial and prestiginous success for Janet.

prestigious, *a.* Restrict 'Now *rare*' to sense in Dict. and add: Also with pronunc. (prestī·dʒǝs). **1.** (Further examples.)

1957 *Eng. Lang. Teaching* XII. 1. 5 Ogden, whose prestigious virtuosity in paraphrase had enabled him to work Basic English out. **1974** *Times Lit. Suppl.* 11 Jan. 32/3 For the period of nearly five years during which he remained as Prime Minister after the war he was..engaged in promoting policies which were actively disliked, or accepted reluctantly, by a majority of his supporters. This was the essential nature of the prestigious balancing act which he was constantly obliged to perform.

2. Having, showing, or conferring prestige (sense 2).

In this sense many prefer to use *PRESTIGEFUL *a.* or some other adjective.

1913 CONRAD *Chance* I. iii. 76 'You have had all these immense sums... *What* have I had out of them?' It was perfectly true. He had had nothing out of them—nothing of the prestigious or the desirable things of the earth. **1958** *Economist* 25 Oct. (Suppl.) 19/1 But then came a form of competition that the American automobile industry had never envisaged—a competition from other industries for the consumer's dollar spent on prestigious purchases. **1960** *Time & Tide* 8 Oct. 1179/1 The commercial [television] companies agreed—..to give ITN enough cash for its extremely prestigious and worthy coverage of the United Nations. **1963** *Listener* 18 Apr. 656/2 Once established in these prestigious places men leave only if they have to. **1967** G. STEINER *Lang. & Silence* 72 Recent French linguistic philosophy also assigns a special function and prestigious authority to silence. **1969** *Daily Tel.* (Colour Suppl.) 5 Sept. 32/1 Those hotels such as every prestigious capital needs. **1970** B. M. H. STRANG *Hist. English* 75 Of course, before 1770, not everyone was confined to the English of his town or village unless he hiked or hacked to another; many were exposed to the highly prestigious and influential written form. **1973** *Oxf. Univ. Gaz.* CIII. Suppl. 5. 33 The small but prestigious collection of German drawings in the Department. **1974** *Times* 27 Apr. 15/5 A career in pure science is still more socially prestigious, in Britain, than one in engineering or in applied science. **1975** *Physics Bull.* May 219/3 Halley was already quite distinguished, established as the Savilian Professor of Geometry at Oxford (a prestigious position).

prestigiously *adv.*, **prestigiousness:** further examples, corresponding to *PRESTIGIOUS *a.* 2.

1962 *Listener* 27 Dec. 1098/1 Art has become a commodity, albeit a highly prestigious one. But it is its very 'prestigiousness' that has brought upon its none too sturdy back the hordes of P.R.O.s and promoters. **1968** J. M. ZIMAN *Public Knowl.* vi. 118 He uses the standard technical words and phrases of the subject, not..to associate himself prestigiously with his would-be colleagues.

presto, *a.*[1], *adv.*[1], *sb.*[1] Add: **A.** *adj.* Also *transf.*

1952 A. CHRISTIE *They do it with Mirrors* i. 9 Everyone's life has a tempo. Ruth's was *presto* whereas Miss Marple's was..*adagio*. **1976** C. BERMANT *Coming Home* II. vii. 215, I was an andante being in a *presto* setting.

pre·stress, *sb.* and *a.* **A.** *sb.* [PRE- A. 2.] Tension applied to an object during manufacture or prior to some other treatment, usu. in order to counteract applied compressive loads (as in prestressed concrete).

1934 *Engineering News-Record* 13 Sept. 345/1 A prestress of 8,392 lb. per sq. in. **1940** *Structural Engineer* XVIII. 642/1 (*heading*) Diminution of the preliminary tensile pre-stress in steel by shrinkage and creeping. **1956** *Archit. Rev.* CXIX. 146/3 Strips of shuttering supported on props are necessary under the transverse diaphragms and these also support the precast units before the prestress is applied. **1967** *New Scientist* 10 Aug. 295/1 The higher the prestress applied, the higher the fatigue strength of the section. **1977** *Design Engin.* July 64/1 Forces depend on prestress, i.e. initial deflection of spring, as well as direction of motion.

B. *adj.* [PRE- B. 2.] Occurring before a stressed syllable.

1973 *Word 1970* XXVI. 98 In the traditional analysis long vowels occur only under stress... Therefore, no prestress vowel may be long. **1975** *Amer. Speech 1972* XLVII. 171 The sets of intersyllabic consonants and consonant clusters differ remarkably in different slots; for instance prestress /bh bt nk/ (as in *abhór*, *obtáin*, *enquíre*).

prestress (prīstre·s), *v.* [PRE- A. 1.] *trans.* To apply stress to (an object or material) prior to some other treatment; to introduce stress into (an object) during manufacture, so as to enable it more successfully to withstand applied loads; *spec.* with reference to reinforced concrete (cf. *PRESTRESSED *ppl. a.*).

1934 *Engineering News-Record* 13 Sept. 345/1 The idea of destroying the bond between steel rods inserted in concrete, and prestressing the rods in tension and the concrete in compression, is not new. **1936** *Structural Engineer* XIV. 252/1 The concreting operation is carried out in the usual manner, the only difference being that the longitudinal rods are pre-stressed. **1940** *Concrete & Constructional Engin.* XXXV. 330/1 Thin piano wires, of a strength of 350,000 lb. to 450,000 lb. per square inch, are prestressed to a stress equivalent to half that of yield point. **1967** *New Scientist* 10 Aug. 295/1 When the concrete is prestressed the steel is dynamically opposed to the applied load. *Ibid.*, Any series of units can be cast separately and then prestressed together to convert them into a monolithic whole. **1971** *Materials & Technol.* II. iv. 113 (*caption*) The vertical outer wall..was prestressed with Freyssinet cables.

So **prestre·ssing** *vbl. sb.*

1934 *Engineering News-Record* 13 Sept. 345/1 One advantage of the prestressing is to postpone the formation of cracks. **1940** *Structural Engineer* XVIII. 629 Notwithstanding the cost of the pre-stressing operations, this great saving in materials renders also pre-stressed designs very economical. **1953** *Sci. News Let.* 24 Jan. 63/2 In one phase of the study, it was found that prestressing doubled the ability of one aluminum alloy, used in the aircraft industry, to carry an external load. **1964** C. W. Glover *Structural Precast Concrete* xix. 328 The basic idea of pre-stressing is to induce in the unloaded members stresses that are contrary to the stress normally produced by loading. **1974** *Encycl. Brit. Macropædia* IV. 1078/1 The calculation of the initial tensile force required in the prestressing tendons to produce compressive stresses that will counteract the tensile stresses in the concrete.

prestre·ssed, *ppl. a.* [f. prec. + -ED[1].] Previously subjected to stressing; into which stress has been deliberately introduced during manufacture; *spec.* of concrete: reinforced by steel rods or wires which have been tensioned while the concrete is setting, so that after setting they tend to compress the concrete and thereby strengthen it.

1936 *Structural Engineer* XIV. 251/1 Two telegraph posts 40 ft. long,..one..in pre-stressed concrete, and the other..in ordinary reinforced concrete, were subjected to alternate stressing. **1948** *Concrete & Constructional Engin.* XLIII. 260 The resiliency and freedom from cracks of prestressed concrete make the material very suitable for railway sleepers and runways. **1955** *Times* 19 July 4/7 Huge pipes in cast iron, or spun iron, or prestressed concrete. **1963** Simonds & Church *Conc. Guide Plastics* (ed. 2) vii. 172 These prestressed laminated structures show strengths three to four times those of the unstressed fabric laminates. **1969** *Jane's Freight Containers 1968–69* 68/1 Crane—18-inch pre-cast, pre-stressed concrete piles; pre-stressed concrete deck. **1973** *Times* 14 Mar. 4/7 As Lancashire County Council's chief assistant in charge of bridges he designed about fifty, including..its first prestressed bridge.

pre-stre·tch, *v. Building.* [Pre- A. 1.] = *pre-tension *v.* Hence **pre-stre·tched** *ppl. a.*; **pre-stre·tching** *vbl. sb.*

1936 *Structural Engineer* XIV. 251/1 By inducing tension in the reinforcement one secures..a decrease of the tension produced in the concrete by the shearing process, or even its total suppression if the reinforcement is pre-stretched in two directions. **1941** *Concrete & Constructional Engin.* XXXVI. 93/1 M. Freyssinet's device with pre-stretched wires needs no anchorage for the manufacture of a long row of articles after one stretching operation. **1946** *Ibid.* XLI. 147 With pre-stretching the member has to remain in the mould until the stretching force, produced by tensioning of the reinforcement.., can safely be transmitted to the concrete. **1949** [see *post-stretching *vbl. sb.*]. **1965** E. C. Hiscock *Cruising under Sail* (ed. 2) v. 79 Terylene..is..more suitable for halyards and headsail sheets; but for those purposes Marlow Ropes Ltd. make a pre-stretched three-strand rope.

pre-structuralist, -suffixal: see *pre- B. 1.
pre-subject: *pre- B. 2a.

presumptive, *a.* Add: **3. b.** *Embryol.* Applied to undifferentiated tissue that becomes a specified part in the normal course of development.

1935 *Jrnl. Morphol.* LVIII. 432 Each presumptive mid-gut epithelial nucleus appropriates a portion of the vitellophage cytoplasm and thus are formed the definitive mid-gut epithelial cells. **1950** B. M. Patten *Early Embryol. of Chick* iv. 66 The sharpness of the boundaries between different presumptive areas..is an entirely artificial device. **1977** *Sci. Amer.* July 76/3 In the 1910's and 1920's Harrison and his colleagues demonstrated that in amphibian embryos the presumptive limb region (the region that will later produce a leg) behaves in many ways like a typical epimorphic field.

presupposition. Add: **3.** Comb., as *presupposition-free* adj.; **presuppositionless** *a.* (further examples); hence **presupposi·tionlessness.**

1966 *Jrnl. Philos.* LXIII. 699 (*heading*) Completeness theorems for some presupposition-free logics. **1972** *Jrnl. Symbolic Logic* XXXVII. 424 'Presupposition-free' here refers to the absence of presuppositions that there are individuals in the domain over which individual variables range. **1906** *Mind* XV. 281 There is no absolutely presuppositionless psychology. **1940** *Philos. Rev.* XLIX. 285 The idea of a presuppositionless philosophy. **1974** *Jrnl. Ecumenical Stud.* XI. 140 Presuppositionless appreciation of..convictions. **1976** *Word 1971* XXVII. 191 A presuppositionless analysis of a child's corpus will not have any theoretical import. **1940** M. Farber *Philos. Ess. in Memory E. Husserl* 44 The claim of presuppositionlessness has been made at various times.

presuppositional (prīsʊpŏzi·ʃənăl), *a.* [f. Presupposition + -al.] Of or pertaining to presuppositions.

1909 W. M. Urban *Valuation* i. 14 The method of psychological worth analysis we may..characterise as the Presuppositional Method. It begins with analysis of presuppositions. **1954** *Mind* LXIII. 154 Banishing all this presuppositional meaning. **1975** R. M. Kempson *Presupposition* iv. 74 Anomalies..arise for a presuppositional account with each logical connective. **1978** *Language* LIV. 494 McClaran's paper, 'Presuppositional aspects of Yucatec sentences', investigates the semantic and syntactic properties associated with Yucatec verbs bearing the suffixes *ik*, *Ak*, *il*, and *Al*.

pre-syllabic, -symptomatic: see *pre- B. 1.

presyna·ptic, *a.* **1.** *Cytology.* [Pre- B. 1.] Prior to meiotic synapsis.

1909 *Ann. Bot.* XXIII. 21 In common with Grégoire ('07), we may adopt, provisionally at least, the following scheme of phases for convenience of clearness in description. The prophases of division naturally fall into two periods, the pre-synaptic and the post-synaptic phases. **1912** [see *leptotene]. **1921** *Ann. Bot.* XXXV. 367 Fig. 5 represents a presynaptic pollen mother-cell.

2. *Physiol.* [Pre- B. 3.] Of, pertaining to, or designating a neurone that transmits a nerve impulse across a synapse. Opp. *postsynaptic *a.* 2.

1937 *Proc. R. Soc.* B. CXXII. 113 The response is erratic in that by no means every pre-synaptic stimulus yields a post-synaptic response. **1950** [see *hyperpolarize *v.*]. **1965** G. H. Bell et al. *Textbk. Physiol. & Biochem.* (ed. 6) xxxix. 796 In general the presynaptic fibre divides up into numerous fine branches which then end in greatly expanded terminals, presynaptic knobs, which make intimate contact with part of the membrane of the cell body or dendrites of the postsynaptic cell. **1979** *Internat. Rehabilit. Med.* I. 45/1 New evidence of the blocking of pain specific receptors..by morphine-like substances produced by presynaptic dendrites.

Hence **presyna·ptically** *adv.*

1971 *Nature* 12 Nov. 102/1 In the central nervous system, amphetamine releases presynaptically bound NE [*sc.* norepinephrine] or DA [*sc.* dopamine] and blocks their re-uptake. **1976** *Ibid.* 3 June 418/1 The fact that chlorpromazine also blocks α-adrenoceptors, possibly presynaptically located, may also contribute to the enhanced presence of catecholamines at the synaptic cleft.

pre-systematic(ally): see *pre- B. 1.

preta·pe, *v.* [Pre- A. 1.] *trans.* To prerecord using magnetic tape. So **preta·ped** *ppl. a.*, **preta·ping** *vbl. sb.*

1968 J. Philips *Hot Summer Killing* (1969) iii. ii. 151 The networks will be giving up commercial time. Pretaped shows are already prepared. **1972** *Listener* 6 July 3/1 Becton insists on live transmission... 'You are not really trusting people with the airtime if you insist on pre-taping.' **1972** W. P. McGivern *Caprifoil* (1973) viii. 144 He pre-taped a series of television speeches to camouflage his absence. **1973** *Sociometry* XXXVI. 103 Subjects listened to pre-taped instructions. **1976** *National Observer* (U.S.) 16 Oct. 6/2 They were a poor substitute for journalism, pretaped and all but tensionless.

‖ **prêt-à-porter** (prętapǫrte). [Fr., 'ready to wear'.] Phr. used *attrib.* and *absol.* to denote clothes that are sold in standard sizes ready for wear.

1957 *Punch* 16 Jan. 136/3 Gloves, scarves, jewellery, and *prêt-à-porter* clothes..all the fleeting frivolities..of the passing mode. **1958** M. Stewart *Nine Coaches Waiting* vi. 71 The young and lovely buy dresses *prêtes à porter*... Off the peg. **1959** *Guardian* 4 Dec. 6/3 The prêt-à-porter spring and summer shows are in full swing in Paris. **1967** *Times* 21 Feb. 9/2 As at the Paris prêt-à-porter fair, the Mary Quant stand was jampacked for the parades. **1973** *Sat. Rev. Arts* (U.S.) Jan. 84/3 The last two pieces contain an onslaught of information about the vigorous young designers and the boom of *prêt à porter*. There is worry that the heyday of French couture is over. **1977** *New Yorker* 11 July 79/1 The feverish search on Seventh Avenue for novelty and for sure profits has come to rival the showings of the Paris prêt-à-porter.

pre-taste: see *pre- A. 2.

pre·-tax, *a.* and *adv.* **A.** *adj.* [Pre- B. 2.] Designating gross assets, earnings, funds, or profits considered before the deduction of tax.

1963 *Times* 7 June 17/2 Group pre-tax profit is £124,000, £14,000 more than forecast, and after tax of £64,000 there is available to the holding company nearly £60,000. **1968** *N.Y. Times* 12 Jan. 38 They forecast a sales gain of 8 to 10 per cent but see an almost dramatic improvement in margins as pretax earnings rise 15 to 20 per cent above those of 1967. **1969** *Times* 2 May 28/5 Pre-tax profits are up from £810,000 to £930,000. **1977** *New Yorker* 29 Aug. 47/1 They'd give me five per cent of the pretax profit.

B. *adv.* [*pre- B. 2c.] Before the deduction of tax.

1976 *Daily Tel.* 17 Feb. 19 (*heading*) Lonrho advances 35pc pre-tax. *Ibid.* 16 July 17/1 It is encouraging to see a £4·57 million turnround to interim profits of £3·61 million pre-tax.

prete·ctal, *a. Anat.* [ad. mod.L. *prætectālis*, f. Pre- B. 3 + *tect(um + -al.] Lying in front of the tectum; of or pertaining to the pretectum.

1925 *Jrnl. Compar. Neurol.* XXXIX. 195 (*caption*) Horizontal section through the posterior commissure, showing the pretectal nucleus in relation to the other parts of the thalamus and midbrain. **1959** *Folia Psychiatrica et Neurologica Japonica* XIII. 268 The pretectal region is located between the posterior part of the thalamus and the tectum, equipped with admixture of cells of both thalamic and mesencephalic origin. **1973** *Brain Res.* LXIII. 360 The fact that two or three optic tract volleys were needed to evoke a response in the short ciliary nerve..indicates a low excitability of the pretectal neurones concerned.

Hence (as a back-formation) **prete·ctum,** the pretectal region of the brain.

1961 *Lancet* 9 Sept. 568/2 The disturbances in ocular motility and the radiological findings, led to the diagnosis of a small lesion in the pretectum. **1973** *Nature* 1 June 295/1 The control of pupil size..is known to be mediated by a reflex pathway through the pretectum.

pre-tee·n, *a.* orig. *U.S.* [f. Pre- B. 2 + Teen *sb.*[2]] Prior to one's teens; denoting the years of a child's life (usu. immediately) before the age of thirteen. Also *absol.* as *sb.* Hence **pre-tee·nager, pretee·ner,** a child (just) before the age of thirteen.

1960 V. Packard *Waste Makers* vii. 76 Even pre-teen boys' shoes were slated for obsoleting. They were being designed away from their 'sexless' look to a real 'nervous' look of flashy casualness. **1966** *N.Y. Times* 6 Jan. 33 Darlene [is] mother of two pre-teen children. **1966** *Economist* 10 Dec. 1144/2 One feature of nightlife on the Strip which the casual visitor is most likely to notice are the regular contingents of pre-teenagers, especially young girls of twelve and even less. **1967** *Atlantic Monthly* Jan. 77 The texts of many popular songs are so obviously coital that one wonders how they get on the radio and are sold openly to pre-teens. **1967** *Punch* 15 Mar. 377/2 Close behind the teen-age revolution, the emancipation of the pre-teens is gathering momentum... In North America the female pre-teen is already 'a knacky, switched-on dolly'. **1969** *Punch* 12 Mar. 384/3 By the time that the American child has reached the age of three, he is known as a sub pre-teener. **1970** *Daily Tel.* 8 May 17 The tendency is for children to experiment with cigarettes from as early as eight years old, and pre-teenagers are often regular smokers. **1972** J. L. Dillard *Black English* vi. 260 Twelve- and thirteen-year-old boys revealed the same type of half-funny, half-pathetic misinformation about sex which practically all preteens seem to have. **1972** *N.Y. Times* 3 Nov. 3/5 (Advt.), Both for preteen sizes 6 to 14. **1977** *Maclean's Mag.* 2 May 23/3 A mini crime wave involving gangs of teen-agers and pre-teens. **1978** *Church Times* 25 Aug. 6/2 An imaginative collection of prayers and poems for pre-teenagers.

pre-telescopic, -television: see *pre- B. 1d, 2a.

pretence, pretense, *sb.* Add: **7.** *attrib.* (in sense 5), passing into *adj.*, denoting something that is imitative or 'phoney'.

1941 *Punch* 17 Sept. 256/3 That lorry buzzing along High Street has got some pretence bombs and it's going to strew them about and we've got to pretend they have been dropped by the Blen. **1953** *Mind* LXII. 209 If I dream of a snake my dream must contain, if not a snake then an illusory or pretence snake.

pretend, *sb.* Restrict †*Obs. rare* to sense in Dict. and add: **2.** In (imitation of) children's use: the act of pretending in imagination or play (cf. Pretend *v.* 15b). Also *attrib.* passing into *adj.*, denoting a thing or action that is imitative or imaginary.

1888 F. H. Burnett *Sara Crewe* i. 28 One of her 'pretends' was that Emily was a kind of good witch, and could protect her. Poor little Sara! **1911** G. Stratton-Porter *Harvester* iii. 48 Not so indifferent after all... That was all 'pretend!' But she waited just a trifle too long. **1928** Barrie *Peter Pan* ii. 70 in *Plays*, Now that they know it is pretend they acclaim her greedily. *Ibid.* iv. 97 It is a pretend meal this evening, with nothing whatever on the table. *a* **1936** Kipling *Something of Myself* (1937) i. 10, I have learned since from children who play much alone that this rule of 'beginning again in a pretend game' is not uncommon. **1955** J. Masters *Coromandel!* 31 It's all pretend, Jason, isn't it? **1959** J. L. Austin *Sense & Sensibilia* (1962) vii. 72 The water in toy beer-bottles is not toy beer, but *pretend* beer. **1960** *Guardian* 3 May 2/1 All 'pretend' space outfits can be dangerous and should be banned. **1962** *Listener* 4 Jan. 20/2 A diminutive, waif-like figure, dressed in rags, with his pretend sword and his pretend gun. **1965** G. McInnes *Road to Gundagai* iii. 54 'It's only pretend,' she kept on saying. 'You mustn't be afraid of pretend.' **1974** W. Rees-Mogg *Reigning Error* 109 Gold is real money and paper is pretend money.

pretending, *ppl. a.* Add: Also (in senses 3d, 15b of the vb.), of a thing or action: imitative, imaginary; of a game, etc.: that involves pretence or imitation. Cf. *pretend *sb.* 2 above.

a **1901** C. M. Yonge *Autobiogr.* in C. Coleridge *C. M. Yonge* (1903) iii. 95 They were not perfect playmates, for they called all 'pretending games' falsehood. **1960** *Times* 27 Apr. 1/3 Only a proper castle, not an 18th/19th-century Gothic pretending one. **1965** *Vogue* Aug. 64 Pretendin' racoon, pretty as a picture.

‖ **prétendu** (pretaṅdü). ? *Obs.* Also fem. **prétendue.** [Fr.] An intended husband or wife; a fiancé(e).

1847 Thackeray *Van. Fair* (1848) xxxiii. 295 In reply to the exhortation of her daughter's *prétendu*, Mr. Pitt

Crawley. **1850** —— *Pendennis* II. i. 9 Lady Ann Milton, Mr. Foker's cousin and *prétendue*. *Ibid.* xx. 201 She has her mamma on one side, her *prétendu* on the other.

pre-tension (prīte·nʃən), *sb.*² [f. Pre- A. 2 + Tension *sb.*] Tension in an object applied previously or at an early stage of a process, e.g. that applied to the reinforcing steel in the manufacture of prestressed concrete.

1936 *Structural Engineer* XIV. 251/2 It is necessary to produce the pretension of the steel and to manufacture concrete of high resistance at a cost sufficiently low to allow one to preserve the greater part of the savings effected on the materials. **1941** *Concrete & Constructional Engin.* XXXVI. 74/1 Shrinkage, elastic deformation, and creep under stress reduce the pre-tension by 10 tons to 20 tons per square inch. **1976** G. S. Ramaswamy *Mod. Prestressed Concrete Design* i. 5 Inexpensive end anchorages are produced at the two ends of the bar to retain the pre-tension.

pre-tension (prīte·nʃən), *v.* [f. Pre- A. 1 + Tension *v.*] *trans.* To apply tension to (an object) prior to some other treatment, esp. incorporation in a structure.

1937 *Rep. Building Res. Board 1936* (Dept. Sci. & Industr. Res.) 99 In connection with some tests on a particular lightweight aggregate, four beams have been tested to determine the effect of pre-tensioning the tension reinforcement. **1949** P. W. Abeles *Princ. & Pract. Prestressed Concrete* ix. 63/2 A special process has been developed for the manufacture of hollow slabs in approximately 100 yd. long production lines, in which the wires are pre-tensioned in order to avoid any sag. **1973** *Sci. Amer.* Apr. 114/1 The output of work per cycle can be increased somewhat by pretensioning the fiber before it is immersed in the brine.

Hence **pre-te·nsioned** *ppl. a.*, **pre-te·nsioning** *vbl. sb.* (freq. *attrib.*).

1936 *Structural Engineer* XIV. 261/2 Thus, with two different steels, an effect was produced similar to that produced by M. Freyssinet's method of pre-tensioning. **1937** *Rep. Building Res. Board 1936* (Dept. Sci. & Industr. Res.) 98 The pre-tensioning apparatus is left in position until the concrete has hardened sufficiently to take the stresses induced in it. **1949** P. W. Abeles *Princ. & Pract. Prestressed Concrete* ix. 58/2 Precast articles having pre-tensioned steel are mainly applicable to slabs, sleepers, beams, [etc.]..where mass production is possible. **1964** C. W. Dunham *Adv. Reinforced Concrete* viii. 400 Pretensioned members can be used for other parts of a structure besides the floors and roof. **1965** *Economist* 5 June 1176/1 The first multi-storey prestressed concrete building in the world combining pretensioned, prestressed roof beams manufactured in the factory with post-tensioning on site using the Magnel system. **1971** J. R. Libby *Mod. Prestressed Concrete* xiv. 451 Pre-tensioning benches that can be moved from job site to job site have been used to a limited degree. **1975** Kong & Evans *Reinforced & Prestressed Concrete* ix. 196 In pre-tensioning, the tendons pass through the mould, or moulds for a number of similar members arranged end to end, and are tensioned between external end anchorages, by which the tension is maintained while the concrete is placed.

preter-, præter-, *prefix.* Add: **2. preter-se·nsuous** *a.* = *pretersensual* adj.

1963 V. Nabokov *Gift* iii. 172 If..he had had to answer before some pretersensuous court..he would scarcely have decided to say that he loved her.

preterist. 1. (Later example.)

1962 V. Nabokov *Pale Fire* 35 A preterist: one who collects cold nests.

prete·rm, *a.* and *adv. Obstetrics.* **A.** *adj.* [Pre- B. 2.] Born or occurring after a pregnancy that lasted significantly less than the normal time; *spec.* (see quot. 1977²).

1928 A. Gesell *Infancy & Human Growth* xv. 300 The pre-term child is viable even though he may have completed but three-quarters of his allotted uterine life-period. **1933, 1971** [see *post-term *a.*]. **1977** *Lancet* 11 June 1255/1 Cigarette smoking during pregnancy is associated with an increased proportion of pre-term deliveries. *Ibid.* 30 July 246/1 The terms 'prematurity' and 'immaturity', with their vague and multiple meanings, have been replaced by the precise terms 'low birthweight' (under 2500 g) and 'preterm' (less than 37 completed weeks).

B. *adv.* [*pre- B. 2c.] Before the end of the normal period of pregnancy.

1977 *Lancet* 9 July 87/1 We gave pregnant Sprague-Dawley rats 4 mg/kg indomethacin..and killed the fetuses at cæsarean section shortly pre-term.

prete·rminal, *a.* [Pre- B. 1.] Preceding that which is terminal.

1947 *Radiology* XLIX. 311/2 A similar preterminal course..is found with such toxic agents as the nitrogen mustards. **1965** N. Chomsky *Aspects of Theory of Syntax* ii. 84 A terminal string is formed from a preterminal string by insertion of a lexical formative. **1976** *Lancet* 4 Dec. 1253/2 Children with severe ketoacidosis in association with viral infections have symptoms and signs in the preterminal stage very similar to those of Reye's syndrome. **1977** *Navy News* June 39 (Advt.), Why not spend your pre-terminal leave with us and be introduced to the company.

prete·st, *v.* [Pre- A. 1.] *trans.* To test beforehand; *spec.* in *Psychol.*, to test in advance (the efficacy of questions or the methods of administration for use in a projected test). Hence **prete·sted** *ppl. a.*, **prete·sting** *vbl. sb.*

1949 C. I. Hovland et al. *Exper. Mass Communication* ii. 26 Qualitative pretesting consisted of face-to-face interviewing... After the first few interviews..the items were revised and pretested again. **1949** R. K. Merton *Social Theory* vi. 163 'Pre-testing' in social affairs is only a rough approximation. **1951** in M. McLuhan *Mech. Bride* (1967) 41/2 Columbia Broadcasting System uses Dr. Flesch's findings to pre-test radio scripts. **1969** N. A. Rosen *Leadership Change & Work-Group Dynamics* (1970) i. 20 Pre-testing, even on a small number of workers, would have led to communication among them. **1970** I. L. Horowitz *Masses in Lat. Amer.* i. 7 It further assumes that the masses have an historical mission and a pre-tested political direction. **1970** D. Goldrich et al. in *Ibid.* v. 176 The interview schedule had been pretested in Santiago. **1977** *Sci. Amer.* Apr. 25/1 The requirement does not apply to spherical tanks because they are built under conditions where the welds can be pretested for integrity.

pre-test, *sb.* and *a.* **A.** *sb. Psychol.* [Pre- A. 2.] An experimental test designed to assess the efficacy of questions or methods of administration intended for use in a projected test. Also occas., a preliminary or qualifying test. Also *attrib.*

1949 C. I. Hovland et al. *Exper. Mass Communication* ii. 26 The purpose of the quantitative pretest was the advance determination of the approximate distribution of answers to each question and the relationship between questions. **1966** J. S. Bruner *Beyond Information Given* (1974) xviii. 321 The experiment was carried out with six- and seven-year-olds and began with a pretest. **1970** *Jrnl. Gen. Psychol.* LXXXIII. 240 After the pretest, all rats were given Richter-type tests for 30 consecutive days. **1971** *Ibid.* LXXXIV. 99 Gross differences in motor performance..were reduced by training all Ss to asymptote during a pretest session. **1972** *Jrnl. Social Psychol.* LXXXVI. 14 The first, a pretest phase, was used to select 'high conformers'. **1973** *Jrnl. Genetic Psychol.* CXXII. 101 Their..pretest scores dropped significantly. **1976** *Columbus* (Montana) *News* 10 June 1/3 You have to have passed your 15th birthday and a pretest.

B. *adj.* (With hyphen.) [Pre- B. 2.] Existing before a test.

1960 *Farmer & Stockbreeder* 2 Feb. 76/1 The Board explains that daily gain on test has been introduced as a measurement of growth which is not complicated either by pre-test environment or the weekly slaughtering routine.

pretheatre, -theoretical: see *pre- B. 2a, 1d. **prethink:** *pre- A. 1.

pretonic, *a.* Add: Also *absol.* as *sb.*, = Pretone.

1953 K. Jackson *Lang. & Hist. Early Brit.* ii. 634 There is also..an *h-* prefixed to vowels; but in Brittonic there was not the same extension of this to pretonics not originally ending in *-s* in British that there was in Pr.I. **1973** *Archivum Linguisticum* IV. 24 This kind of system may be dealt with in the same way as the different pretonics of the individual tones.

Hence **preto·nically** *adv.*, as regards a pretone.

1953 K. Jackson *Lang. & Hist. Early Brit.* ii. 322 It [*sc.* a Latin pronunciation (ɑu)] is not reduced pretonically to *ǒ*; e.g. *awdur, cawlai.*

pre-tour, -tragic: see *pre- B. 2a, 1d.

pretrai·ning, *vbl. sb. Psychol.* [Pre- A. 1.] Training which takes place in advance of an experiment or test; also *attrib.* Hence (as a back-formation) **pretrai·n** *v. trans.*

1955 *Jrnl. Exper. Psychol.* L. 180 This pretraining has generally consisted of verbal paired-associates learning in which stimuli are the same as, or substitutes for, those of the motor task. **1957** J. S. Bruner *Beyond Information Given* (1974) i. 35 A subject is first given some pretraining, in one of four pretraining groups. **1959** *Psychol. Abstr.* XXXIII. 764/1 The stability of generalized expectancies (GEs) developed under 2 pretraining conditions and with differing frequencies of past reinforcement. **1971** *Nature* 9 July 124/2 Cats were pre-trained, using classical conditioning. **1973** *Jrnl. Genetic Psychol.* CXXII. 17 Children aged 2-½ to 5-½ were pretrained on two three-choice simple discrimination problems. **1974** *Psychol. Abstr.* LII. 1244/1 In Exp II..the type of response in pretraining..was varied.

pre-transformational: see *pre- B. 1d.

pretrea·t, *v.* [Pre- A. 1.] *trans.* To treat beforehand. Hence **pretrea·ted** *ppl. a.*

1934 *Jrnl. Physical Chem.* XXXVIII. 795 Comparing the form of the characteristic curve of the normally developed strip S with those of the strips that were pretreated with the iron citrate solutions..the latter are steeper. **1950** *Nucleonics* Mar. 48/1 It may be necessary to pretreat and purify the water before using it in the pile. **1956** *Nature* 21 Jan. 136/1 A variation of the relative concentrations..may account for the variation..of the shape of light curves observed in differently pretreated algae. **1963** *Mechanical World* CXLIII. 17/1 Of recent years the production of pre-treated metal surfaces has increased enormously. **1975** *Jrnl. Immunol. Methods* VIII. 383 Peritoneal macrophages..cultivated for 48 hr on glass pretreated with poly-L-lysine.

pretrea·tment, *sb.* and *a.* **A.** *sb.* [Pre- A. 2.] Treatment given beforehand. Also *attrib.*

1925 *Jrnl. Forestry* XXIII. 921 Within each pretreatment the seed experienced variations of that treatment. **1946** *Nature* 23 Nov. 748/2 Effective control was measured six weeks after treatment, all plots in this case having received pre-treatment with nitro-chalk seven days in advance of the weed-killer application. **1955** *New Biol.* XVIII. 88 Freshly excised grafts, after pre-treatment with 15 per cent glycerol in Ringer, were sealed off in glass tubes and frozen. **1961** *Times* 12 Apr. 17/6 The coil of steel is passed through chemical pre-treatment baths. **1973** *Times* 29 Oct. 20/7 Liquid wastes from all trade and industrial sources, broadly speaking, drain without pre-treatment in to the River Tees or into Tees Bay. **1978** *Jrnl. R. Soc. Arts* CXXVI. 686/1 The aim of pre-treatments is to increase the action of the adhesive bonding forces by eliminating greases, dirt and the oxides which exist on the surface.

B. *adj.* [Pre- B. 2.] Existing before treatment.

1961 *Lancet* 2 Sept. 499/2 This..gave an opportunity for estimation of the pretreatment level of serum-cholesterol. **1962** *Ibid.* 12 May 989/2 In 1 other patient infected with a proteus strain, organisms isolated during and after treatment were more resistant than the pre-treatment cultures. **1972** *Jrnl. Social Psychol.* LXXXVI. 84 The..pretreatment mean attitude score for the nine treatments is approximately equal.

pretrial, *sb.* and *a.* **A.** *sb.* (Stressed *pre·trial.*) [Pre- A. 2.] A preliminary hearing before a trial. Also *attrib. U.S.*

1938 E. J. Ellison in *Christian Science Monitor* 15 June (Weekly Mag.) 3/1 Why not have a special judge to clear out the legal underbrush, and call it a 'pre-trial'. *Ibid.* 3/2 Some two weeks before a case is scheduled for trial, the opposing parties appear before a pre-trial judge. **1938** *Daily Progress* (Charlottesville, Va.) 18 Aug. 4/1 The 'pre-trial' system was introduced in Detroit six years ago. **1970** *Daily Colonist* (Victoria, B.C.) 23 Apr. 10/1 Black Panther chairman Bobby Seale was accused at his pre-trial hearing of ordering the death of a Panther suspected of turning informer. **1971** *N.Y. Law Jrnl.* 23 Nov. 17/5 If case cannot be settled the Part I judge will assign the case to a pre-trial examiner, who will, with the aid of the attorneys, prepare the pre-trial order. **1976** *National Observer* (U.S.) 17 Jan. 2/2 The judge had ordered the papers not to print stories about a pretrial hearing for a murder defendant because the judge did not want prospective jurors to be influenced by arguments made at the hearing. **1978** *Chicago* June 116/3 Tom Sullivan sat at the defense table in the Hanrahan case, and he handled pre-trial matters for Kemer's co-defendant.

B. *adj.* (Stressed *pretri·al.*) [Pre- B. 2.] Of or pertaining to the period before a trial or trials.

1948 B. Vesey-Fitzgerald *Bk. Dog* 749 Whereas in pre-trial days the range [of sheepdog] was severely restricted, nowadays, as a result of trials, the scope for selection is nation-wide. **1971** *Times* 20 Mar. 11 Most have already spent more than a year in jail awaiting trial, and pretrial detention will be deducted from their sentences. **1978** *Times* 3 Nov. 17 (*heading*) Barristers' immunity from claims in negligence in pre-trial work narrowed. *Ibid.* 13 Nov. 7/8 Mr. Nazaryan, who has been in pre-trial detention for almost a year, is charged with anti-Soviet agitation and propaganda.

prettied: see *pretty *v.*

prettification (pri:tĭfikē¹·ʃən). [f. Pretty *a.* + -fication.] The fact or process of making pretty; prettifying.

1909 in Webster. **1920** *Times Lit. Suppl.* 23 Sept. 617/1 Such work is..the counterfeit of romance. It gives us, not a celebration of life, but a prettification of it. **1930** A. I. Nazaroff *Tolstoy* vi. 97 He is described very realistically, without the slightest trace of prettification or sugar-coating. **1966** *New Statesman* 23 Dec. 935/2 The sanctification of emotional impotence. The prettification of stultified tragedy. **1969** *Daily Tel.* 10 July 21/3 This [manner], together with some prettification of the action, deprived the play of the savagery that is surely there. **1978** *Listener* 20 July 76/3 The writer, Georgina Masson.. is up in arms over the prettification of the cemetery.

prettify, *v.* Add: Also **prettyfy.** Delete *colloq.* and add further examples. Also *fig.* Hence **pre·ttified** *ppl. a.*; **prettifying** *vbl. sb.* (further examples). Also **pre·ttifier,** one who prettifies.

1867 G. du Maurier *Let.* in D. du Maurier *Young George du Maurier* (1951) 273 Then D and I walked through the lovely Bois de Boulogne to the Mare d'Auteuil which has been brutally modernised and prettyfied. **1889** *Cent. Dict.*, Prettified. **1919** B. Tarkington *Let.* 14 June in *On Plays* (1959) 13 You know..why all the magazines *haf* to have the prettified girl cover. **1934** *Sun* (Baltimore) 2 Apr. 8/1 (*heading*) Prettifying war. *Ibid.*, These endeavors [to outlaw certain forms of warfare] are based on the assumption that we are making progress if somehow we can manage to prettify war. **1936** L. C. Douglas *White Banners* iii. 63 A man doesn't try to prettify himself very much, or make himself over to look different. He wants to be important for owning something rather than being something. **1955** *Times* 24 Aug. 7/4 To anyone who once heard a chanty at sea, such prettified verses, however musical, will always seem a travesty of their originals. **1960** W. Miller *Canticle for Leibowitz* xiv. 151 A place of majesty that overawed the would-be prettifiers. **1970** *Daily Tel.* 21 Feb. 8/5 The 19th-century weakness for prettifying the lives of great men. **1971** P. Gresswell *Environment* 89 Too much prettyfying is damaging enough but the bleak 'serviceable' attitude to details causes the more widespread damage... For this reason, many housing estates..are depressing. **1973** *Times* 30 Oct. 14/8 The Cubist works are prettified exercises in taste. **1976** *Early Music* Oct. 402/2 The *Dido* gathering should be suave and elegant but not prettified or frivolous.

pretty, *a.* (*sb.*) Add: **A. II. 3. a.** (Further examples.) Also *U.S.*

1878 J. H. Beadle *Western Wilds* xxiv. 387 A half-breed squaw, about as 'pretty' as a wild-cat struck with a club. **1891** 'Mark Twain' tr. *Hoffmann's Slovenly Peter* (1935, Ltd. Ed.) 25 'Try how pretty you can be Till I come again,' said she. 'Docile be, and good and mild.' **1938** *Amer. Speech* XIII. 6/2 *Pretty,*..good; fine; excellent. 'He was a real pretty ball player.'

b. (Further examples.) Freq. in negative contexts. Also in phr. *to say pretty things,* to speak consolingly or in a condescending manner.

1811 A. Constable *Let.* 28 Apr. in J. Constable *Corr.* (1962) I. 63 Uncle D.P.W. here for a pretty week. **1811** Jane Austen *Sense & Sens.* II. v. 80 It was not very pretty of him, not to give you the meeting. **1898** G. B. Shaw *Philanderer* IV. 140 *Paramore.* I can only admire you, and feel how pleasant it is to have you here. *Julia*... And pet me, and say pretty things to me! I wonder you dont offer me a saucer of milk at once! **1931** E. O'Neill *The Haunted* IV, in *Mourning becomes Electra* 246 Peter is coming, and I want everything to be pretty and cheerful. **1937** M. Allingham *Dancers in Mourning* iii. 43 Go out and say pretty things... We'll all back you up. **1957** P. Kemp *Mine were of Trouble* ii. 28, I have learnt something of that frantic advance on Toledo and the final battle. It is not a pretty story. **1973** *Black Panther* 8 Sept. 17/1, I slipped back..and observed some of these same officers... Their tactics weren't very pretty.

c. (*to come to*) *a pretty pass*: see *pass *sb.*[2] 7 a.

4. e. In phrases: (*as*) *pretty as paint, as a picture* (cf. *picture *sb.* 2 h), *as a speckled pup,* etc.

Most of the phrases are more or less restricted to the U.S.

1906 *Dialect Notes* III. 151 *Pretty as a speckled pup,*.. exceedingly pretty. **1909** *Ibid.* 359 *Pretty as a picture,*.. very pretty: often used of a fine specimen of fruit. **1922** E. V. Lucas *Genevra's Money* xvi. 112 Now, there's that girl—she's as pretty as paint. If I were the kind of feller that does these things I could make a fool of myself over her. **1926** M. J. Atkinson in J. F. Dobie *Rainbow in Morning* (1965) 88 As pretty as a speckled pup under a new-painted buggy; as pretty as a speckled hen; as pretty as a picture. **1927** *Amer. Speech* Dec. 169 To him 'pretty as a heart flush' was the supremely beautiful. **1927** E. O'Neill *Marco Millions* III. i. 141 Here! Let me get a good look at you! Why, you're still as pretty as a picture and you don't look a day older! **1936** N. Streatfeild *Ballet Shoes* vi. 77 Cook said it was as pretty as a picture, and Clara that it put her in mind of something off a Christmas card. **1976** *Time* 27 Sept. 39/2 Girls are variously 'ugly as homemade soap' or 'pretty as a speckled pup'.

5. b. (Later examples.)

1930 E. B. White *Let.* 4 July (1976) 93 The Pierce, after some brilliant road work, burned out a generator—which will cost me a pretty penny. **1978** L. Block *Burglar in Closet* i. 4 The attaché case..was a slim model in cocoa Ultrasuede that had cost someone a pretty penny.

B. *sb.* **a.** (Further examples.) Also as a form of address, with ellipsis of *my.*

1934 *Amer. Speech* IX. 288/2 *A pretty,* any good-looking girl. **1952** M. Allingham *Tiger in Smoke* xiv. 203 He's all right, pretty. He's all right now. **1972** [see LA, L.A. s.v. *L 7].

b. (Earlier and later examples.)

1736 *Boston News-Let.* 15 Apr. 2/2 (Advt.), Just arrived, and to be sold cheap, a choice variety of Haberdashery,.. Dutch Prettys, Silk Cane and Watch Strings, [etc.]. **1895** *Dialect Notes* I. 392 *Pretty,* a picture or similar article; a toy. **1927** W. E. Collinson *Contemp. Eng.* 54, I well remember the disgust we children felt at a lady (an English-woman) who..called a fancy cake a pretty! **1952** M. Allingham *Tiger in Smoke* viii. 130, I ought to keep that [miniature]. It must go down among the other pretties in the show table in the drawing-room. **1957** H. Croome *Forgotten Place* xx. 229 Scarves, handkerchiefs, nylons, pretties, were pushed aside, or sent flying. **1977** *Daily Mirror* 10 May 12/5 Perhaps the brisk sales of pretties in the shops now shows which way the wind is beginning to blow. **1977** J. Wambaugh *Black Marble* (1978) x. 225 Probably buying her pretties with what little money the kennel took in.

d. *ellipt.*, a pretty good sum (of money), a *pretty penny* (see sense A. 5 b in Dict.). *U.S.*

1851 G. Thompson *Diary* 28 Jan. in N. E. Eliason *Tarheel Talk* (1956) 138, I would not send her an ugly [valentine] for a pirty. **1909** G. Stratton-Porter *Girl of Limberlost* xxi. 393 I'd give a pretty to know that secret thing you say you don't. **1927** *Amer. Speech* II. 277/1 *I'll bet you a pretty,* I'll bet you a good deal. **1935** H. Davis *Honey in Horn* v. 46 I'll bet you a pretty he ain't got any [money]. **1941** W. C. Handy *Father of Blues* v. 69 I'd give a pretty to the ear that could forget them.

e. *Golf.* The fairway.

1907 *Westm. Gaz.* 13 Sept. 3/1 Often..he will get just as far as if he had been lying on the 'pretty'. **1909** *Ibid.* 11 Sept. 7/2, I happened upon Daniel Lambert..wielding a heavy mashie among the thistles that flourish along the pretty to the tenth. **1927** *Daily Tel.* 12 Feb. 10/5 When the ball went sailing down the pretty, straight and true, what a satisfaction it was to both of them.

D. b. pretty-by-night *U.S.* = *marvel of Peru* (Marvel *sb.* 6); **pretty-face (kangaroo, wallaby),** the whip-tailed wallaby, *Macropus parryi,* which is found in southern Queensland and northern New South Wales and has white markings on its head; **pretty please,** an emphatic or affected colloq. form of request.

1872 E. Eggleston *End of World* xxv. 169 She planted some pretty-by-nights in an old tea-pot. **1890** *Harper's Mag.* Jan. 282/1 Hollyhocks and larkspur and pretty-by-nights blossomed in the door-yard. **1911** C. Harris *Eve's Second Husband* 275 The 'pretty-by-nights' under the window..refused to consider the tragedy of Adam's unfaithfulness. **1931** W. N. Clute *Common Names of Plants* 135 The four o'clock..bears the name of pretty-by-night and lives up to it. **1947** M. Henry *Misty of Chincoteague* ix. 92 You kin cut a few of them purty-by-nights and some bouncin' Bess fer a centerpiece. **1887** W. S. S. Tyrwhitt *New Chum in Queensland Bush* viii. 145 The smaller kind [of kangaroo], known as pretty faces or whip tails,..are rather smaller and of a grey colour, with black and white on the face. **1911** W. H. D. Le Souëf *Wild Life Austral.* vii. 215 The most graceful of the Kangaroos..are locally called Pretty-face or Whip-tailed Kangaroos. **1943** C. Barrett *Austral. Animal Bk.* xi. 93 Its [*sc.* the whip-tail wallaby's] southern ally, often called 'pretty-face'..is among the most beautiful of all marsupials, with its slender, graceful body, its very long and slender tail, and white-and-grey face markings. **1970** W. D. L. Ride *Guide Native Mammals Austral.* v. 47 Whiptail, Pretty-face Wallaby... tail very long and slender, very marked white face-stripe. [**1891** R. T. Cooke *Huckleberries* 169 Say 'please' now—real pretty.] **1959** A. Sinclair *Breaking of Bumbo* v. 74 She was saying, *Please. Pretty please.* **1964** *Time* 28 Feb. 28/3 Can I, pretty please? **1966** 'T. Wells' *Matter of Love or Death* xii. 122 'I really can't.' I squeezed her hand. 'Not even if I say pretty please?' **1968** J. D. MacDonald *Pale Grey for Guilt* (1969) xv. 180, I guess you're not going to give it back just because I say pretty please with sugar. **1970** W. Smith *Gold Mine* xxxix. 105 Please, please, pretty please times three. **1973** C. Mason *Hostage* vii. 106 Say...'pretty please, with sugar on it.'

pretty, *adv.* Add: **1. b.** *pretty much,* almost, very nearly; approximately.

1806 D. Roe *Diary* 27 May (1904) 30 They got sum horsfish & that was pretty much all. **1861** [in Dict.]. **1873** [see *account *sb.* 9 c]. **1937** E. C. Vivian *Tramp's Evidence* vii. 90 Crandon goes to bed with the dicky-birds, pretty much. **1961** 'S. Gillespie' *Neighbour* vi. 93 Her flat was pretty much what he had expected. **1976** *Southern Even. Echo* 13 Nov. 12/7 The defendant.. 'pretty much on impulse' took the television.

2. a. For now *rare* and *illiterate* read *colloq.* and add further examples. *Spec.* in phr. *to sit* (or *be sitting*) *pretty,* to be comfortably placed or well situated; to be in a fortunate or advantageous position.

1864 Trollope *Can you forgive Her?* I. xxii. 173, I must go down. The Duchess of St. Bungay is here, and Mr. Palliser will be angry if I don't do pretty to her. **1891** J. Newman *Scamping Tricks* i. 2 We can talk pretty to each other. *Ibid.* vi. 46, I saw they were started on the road of mutual admiration, and travelling pretty, and that he meant calling again. **1902** *Free Lance* 5 Apr. 8/2 They must be spoken 'pretty' to, caressed, humoured, coaxed. **1921** M. Moore (*title of musical comedy*) Sittin' Pretty. **1924** Bolton & Wodehouse (*title of musical comedy*) Sitting Pretty. **1925** Wodehouse *Sam the Sudden* xv. 106 If you're American, we're sitting pretty, because it's only us Americans that's got real sentiment in them. **1932** —— *Hot Water* i. 32 We're sitting pretty. The thing's in the bag. **1932** S. Gibbons *Cold Comfort Farm* xvi. 223 It was nearly half past two, and everybody seemed sitting pretty for the sunrise. **1937** *Times Lit. Suppl.* 25 Dec. 970/2 This submerged Dickens, who would not 'play pretty' to any orthodoxy old or new, comes nearer to raising his head in the Christmas Books than in his longer works. **1939** 'N. Blake' *Smiler with Knife* xviii. 256 I'm sitting pretty for the moment, she thought; but [they]..will go over this district with a fine-tooth comb. **1947** *Times* 18 Nov. 2/3 Did he think the country was 'sitting pretty'? **1957** L. P. Hartley *Hireling* xi. 88, I shouldn't be sitting where I am, sitting pretty, to coin a phrase, if it wasn't for you. **1959** *Listener* 13 Aug. 239/1 At the moment the motor industry is 'sitting pretty'. **1967** O. Wynd *Walk Softly* xi. 182 Toba was still sitting pretty, at the most pausing for reassessment. **1972** *Driving* (Dept. of Environment) (ed. 2) 119 Always try to 'park pretty'; that is, squared up in the middle of the marked space. **1976** *Washington Post* 23 May G 2 (*heading*) In some cases, they're sitting pretty.

pretty (pri·ti), *v.* [f. the adj.] Freq. const. *up.* **a.** *refl.* To make (oneself) pretty; to make or dress (oneself) *up* to look attractive. **b.** *trans.* To make (something or someone) pretty or attractive; also used ironically, to spoil or injure. Also *absol.* Hence **prettied** (**up**) *ppl. a.*; **prettying** (**up**) *vbl. sb.*

1916 H. L. Wilson *Somewhere in Red Gap* ii. 70 All I think is that he's trying to pretty himself up for Nettie. **1932** *Sun* (Baltimore) 23 Aug. 4/4 The women [pilots] were sent up a new supply of cold cream today, which enabled them to 'pretty up' for their landing. **1935** M. M. Atwater *Murder in Midsummer* viii. 72 The nurse..thought her patient should have waked up to tears and moans, and here she was fussing about the set of the lavender knitted thing about her thin shoulders. Prettying up for company! **1939** R. Chandler *Big Sleep* xxii. 182 A low-voiced prettied-up rhumba. **1943** —— *Lady in Lake* (1944) viii. 50 She was gone a week and came back all prettied up. **1950** D. D. Paige in *Lett. E. Pound* p. xxv, The general aim has been to present a volume that can be read consecutively with as little eye fatigue as possible. The editor alone is responsible for these prettyings up. **1953** K. Tennant *Joyful Condemned* xxi. 203 They wanted ..plenty of time to pretty their hair. **1953** *Here & Now* (N.Z.) Oct. 5/2 Again, isn't it rather a sham to seal the roads along which she will travel and pretty up the buildings lining them. **1959** D. Niland *Big Smoke* II. vii. 160 He took the bottle from the bar and..smashed its end into a jagged, terrible weapon... He said, 'I'll pretty up your face, boy.' **1960** *Farmer & Stockbreeder* 19 Jan. (Suppl.) 1/3 I had made up my mind to marry Sue. The next night was our last night ashore and I had spent an hour and a half readying myself and prettying up. **1961** *John o' London's* 6 July 57/4 Even Jaques Becker.. can't resist both tarting and prettying up the Modigliani legend. **1969** *Sears Catal.* Spring/Summer 30 Smocking pretties the yoke and sleeves of this broadcloth dress with its ruffled stand-up collar. **1972** *Times* 29 Aug. 10/2 People pay a great deal of attention..to prettying their houses. **1974** 'M. Yorke' *Mortal Remains* v. iii. 154 Elsie's still prettying herself... She's been in the beauty shop all afternoon. **1979** J. Scott *Clutch of Vipers* vi. 91 The Chief Constable came in; looking..bull-shouldered in these prettied surroundings.

pretty-boy (pri·tiboi). Also without hyphen. [f. Pretty *a.* 4 + Boy *sb.*[1]] A foppish or effeminate man; a male homosexual. Also used ironically, a 'tough', a thug. Also *attrib.*

1885 *Daily News* 26 Jan. 3/7 The style termed by irreverent mashers the pretty-boy clip, the style sometimes called the upward drag, and the whim which ranges from a delicate fringe to furze-bush proportions, at first amazed and amused the neat Japanese damsels. **1898** R. Hughes *Lakerim Athletic Club* 241 Sawed-Off had sniffed scornfully that lawn-tennis was a game fit for nobody but girls and pretty boys. **1931** *Amer. Mercury* Nov. 353/2 *Pretty boys,*..the circus bouncers; strong-arm men. **1941** Baker *Dict. Austral. Slang* 57 *Pretty-boy,* an effeminate young man. **1946** G. Millar *Horned Pigeon* ix. 117 A pretty boy with wavy, brown hair flowing glossily over his round head... 'Who is it?' 'The *colonnello*'s bum-boy. A shit.' **1955** M. Allingham *Beckoning Lady* v. 71 The middle-aged pretty-boy face, complete with protuberant blue eyes and corrugated dark brown hair. **1956** 'E. McBain' *Cop Hater* (1958) xix. 157 Scar tissue hooded his eyes. He owned cauliflower ears and hardly any teeth. His name, of course, was 'Pretty-Boy Krajak'. **1968** M. Woodhouse *Rock Baby* xi. 111, I walked past pretty-boy... Close up, pretty-boy smelled worse than ever. **1970** E. R. Johnson *God Keepers* (1971) iv. 46 A man named Al Brunning, pretty-boy greaseball. **1973** M. Amis *Rachel Papers* 98 She was referring to the Beatles record (late-middle period—between pretty-boy rock and bleared occult) which had just come to an end. **1974** P. De Vries *Glory of Hummingbird* (1975) xi. 153 You're not cross-eyed..and your ears are pasted on straight. Not any pretty-boy, but probably photogenic.

prettyism. (Earlier example.)

1776 T. Anburey *Let.* 20 Nov. in *Trav. Interior Parts Amer.* (1789) I. 109 These *Enfant du Diable* [*sc.* skunks] differ from your *Enfant du Diable,* the London beaux, who have all their prettyisms perhaps, but are externally exhaling their pestiferous odours.

pretty-pre·ttiness. [f. Pretty-pretty *a.* + -ness.] The state or quality of being pretty-pretty; excess of prettiness.

1901 M. Beerbohm in *Sat. Rev.* 20 Apr. 500/2 For prettiness—even pretty-prettiness—in the right place I have as great a taste as anyone else. **1924** 'L. Malet' *Dogs of Want* i. 26 The coquettish little Cities of the Plain..and their cheap pretty-prettiness of countless hotels. **1931** *Observer* 6 Sept. 6/4 The revulsions into Sunday School pretty-prettiness are equally surprising. **1945** E. Bowen *Ivy Gripped Steps* in *Demon Lover* 130 His elder brother's jibes at his pretty-prettiness. **1960** Koestler *Lotus & Robot* II. vi. 165 A culture with a surface polish of utterly refined pretty-prettiness. **1965** *Observer* 17 Jan. 28/1 A yearning for the pretty-prettiness of the days when women were women.

pretty-pretty, *a.* and *sb.* Add: **A.** *adj.* (Earlier and later examples.) Also as *adv.*

1877 *Punch* 3 Feb. 47/2 To paint pretty-pretty, to compose namby-pamby, and perpetuate the modish and the monstrous. **1928** Galsworthy *Swan Song* I. xi. 80 Nothing pretty-pretty about that memorial—no angels' wings there! **1937** [see *arty-and-crafty *a.*]. **1952** L. T Stanley *Woman Golfer* 61 A 'pretty-pretty' swing may look nice, but it doesn't get you far. **1961** [see *bitchy *a.* 1]. **1962** 'K. Orvis' *Damned & Destroyed* xxi. 157 He just might sing pretty-pretty and tell you exactly what's cooking in Moss's fat head. **1973** *Times* 5 Oct. 13/1, I love the baby dresses and suits which are pretty without being pretty-pretty. **1980** A. Alpers *Life K. Mansfield* vi. 114 Some flabby fiction, and some pretty-pretty verse.

B. *sb.* (Further examples.) Also *sing.*, in absol. use.

1899 [see *chance *v.* 4 c]. **1929** W. Deeping *Roper's Row* xxxv. 401 But that was a monstrous argument to use, mush, the pretty-pretty, a kitten-faced sentimentality. **1934** C. Lambert *Music Ho!* v. 327 Prokofieff's third piano concerto..is curiously lacking in any sense of direction, oscillating disturbingly between the pretty-pretty and the ugly-ugly.

pre-tune: see *pre- A. 1.

pretzel. Add: **1.** (Earlier and later examples.) Also *fig.* and *attrib.*

1856 [see *blutwurst]. **1857** C. Kingsley *Two Yrs. Ago* III. ix. 271 After him came..like in *Struwelpeter,* Caspar, bretzel in hand. **1858** *Harper's Mag.* Aug. 327/1 Eating *pretzels* and drinking what is here called *bière de Bavière.* **1915** *Lit. Digest* 12 June 1443/1 Prunella's painting pretzels in Przemysl. **1932** E. Wilson *Devil take Hindmost* vii. 45 The pretzel man with his basket and the roast-chestnut man have come out again. **1933** R. L. Sutton *Arctic Safari* 24 The booby prize was a string of pretzels at least four feet long. **1933** *Sun* (Baltimore) 15 Aug. 8/7 In the old days your newest reporter would have been sufficiently cultured to know that one doesn't twist pretzels; one bends them. Hence the artisan or craftsman who performs the work is a pretzel bender. **1945** *Finito! Po Valley Campaign* (15th Army Group) 5 The air forces twisted the enemy's rail lines into pretzels of steel. **1961** Wodehouse *Ice in Bedroom* xvi. 128 You know as well as I do that Chimp Twist is as crooked as a pretzel. **1968** Mrs. L. B. Johnson *White House Diary* 7 Feb. (1970) 627

Little round tables with cokes and pizza, peanuts and pretzels. **1973** *Time* 25 June 11/3 Ervin Committee Member Lowell Weicker, dropped in for beer and pretzels. **1975** *New Yorker* 31 Mar. 29/2 She dumps an armful of immense pretzel stick cuttings into the pail. **1976** R. Cowper *Paradise Beach* in *Custodians* 71 He snatched her hands to his lips and set about them as if they were a pair of pretzels.

2. *Mus. slang.* (See quots.) Also *pretzel bender*.

1936 *Metronome* Feb. 61/2 *Pretzel*—French horn. **1936** *Amer. Mercury* May p. x/2 *Pretzel bender*—one who favors the French horn. **1945** L. Shelly *Jive Talk Dict.* 16 *Pretzel*, French horn. *Ibid.* 31 *Pretzel bender*, French horn player.

prevalence. 3. (Further examples.)

1839 *Ann. Rep. Registrar-Gen. England* 87 The prevalence of a disease..is expressed by the deaths in a given time out of a given number of living. **1857** T. W. Grimshaw et al. *Man. Public Health Ireland* xxvii. 298 From statistics [of small-pox]..it appears that its greatest prevalence is observed in May, the cases in that month being 13.7 per cent. of the total cases occurring in the year. **1961** M. Schorer *Sinclair Lewis* iv. viii. 471 He talked..about the prevalence of American slang in British speech. **1975** *Nature* 20 Mar. 168/3 Any successful preventative measure against leprosy will be shown by a fall in the number of new cases or in the incidence rate: the total number of cases (or 'prevalence' rate) will change much more slowly, because of the inclusion of patients who are already crippled.

pre-Vedic: see *pre- B. 1 a.

preveniently, *adv.* (Further examples.)

1974 *Times Lit. Suppl.* 29 Nov. 1343/1 Are they those misconceptions of the nature and role of poetry which this most preveniently resourceful essay in metaphysics would correct? **1977** G. W. H. Lampe *God as Spirit* iii. 74 God's Spirit works preveniently to bring a person to conversion. **1977** *Theology* LXXX. 192 Whenever and wherever there is response to the divine love, *there* that love is preveniently at work.

preventative, *a.* and *sb.* Add: **A.** *adj.* (Later examples.)

1936 W. H. S. Smith *Let.* 18 July in *Young Man's Country* (1977) ii. 16 My principal occupation was trying 'Bad Livelihood' cases. These are preventative cases for securing the good behaviour of criminals by taking a bond. **1939** *Ann. Reg. 1938* 93 Two new types of prison sentences were proposed. One was called 'corrective training'... The other was called 'preventative detention', and was to be for not less than two and not more than four years for persons over 30, but up to ten years on certain types of offenders with long criminal records. **1968** *Globe & Mail* (Toronto) 5 Feb. 10/8 A Democratic administration had gotten the United States deeply involved in Vietnam..by failing to apply 'preventative diplomacy'. **1973** *Black Panther* 21 July 8/3 The People's Free Health Clinic.. provides medical treatment and preventative care on a clinical level. **1976** *Oxf. Mission Q. Paper* July/Sept. 15 Many of the people are illiterate and it takes a lot of patient talking and convincing before they can see the benefits of preventative medicine.

B. *sb.* **c.** A contraceptive; = *preventive *sb.* c.

1901 J. A. Godfrey *Science of Sex* ii. vi. 257 The checks employed by women are more diverse in mechanical detail... Opinions differ greatly as to both the reliability and the physiological harmlessness of these forms of preventative. *Ibid.* 256 So long as the sheath remains whole, it is an absolute preventative. **1918** R. B. Armitage *Private Sex Advice to Women* x. 130 The use of 'contraceptives' or 'preventatives' is considered justified in certain cases. **1934** Dylan Thomas *Let.* Oct. (1966) 143 Do you believe in preventatives?

preventer. Add: **2.** (Further example.)

1920 *Chambers's Jrnl.* Mar. 208/1 A single set of hydrofoils under the bow, known as a preventer, helps to lift the boat when getting up speed, while checking any tendency to nose-dive.

3. b. (*a*) *preventer backstay* (later examples), *brace* (later example), *gasket* (later example), *guy* (later example), *sheet*.

1912 W. I. Downie *Reminisc. Blackwall Midshipman* ii. 22, I expect preventer backstays were practically a permanent part of her equipment during the trip. **1939** H. Hughes *Through Mighty Seas* x. 264 For the first time I saw preventer back-stays being rigged from the main top-gallant mast. **1867** G. E. Clark *Seven Years of Sailor's Life* xx. 203 We had the barque under a close-reefed main-topsail, and with preventer braces on the yard, flew on the waves. **1926** T. M. Hemy *Deep Sea Days* ii. 64 It was 'all hands wear ship'; then up aloft and change the preventer braces from one side to another. **1907** M. Roberts *Flying Cloud* xxxii. 304 Budd went aloft on the cro' jack-yard and passed a couple of preventer gaskets. **1923** *Man. Seamanship* (Admiralty) II. xi. 188 In the recent America Cup Races, both craft tried taking a preventer guy out to the weather crosstrees if the wind was light enough. **1867** G. E. Clark *Seven Years of Sailor's Life* xix. 191 The mainsail was furled, and preventer sheets put on the fore boom.

4. In full *blow-out preventer.* A heavy valve or assembly ('stack') of valves usu. fitted at the top of an oil well during drilling and closed in the event of a blow-out.

1916 A. B. Thompson *Oil-Field Devel. & Petroleum Mining* vii. 367 An apparatus which is largely employed with rotaries is what is called a 'Blow-out Preventer'. **1934** *Proc. World Petroleum Congr. 1933* I. 370/2 The main feature is a heavy rubber sleeve packer held in a container which is free to revolve in ball bearings inside the body of the preventer. **1962** *Economist* 15 Sept. 1046/2 The blow-out preventers and the drill bit itself can be lowered. **1972** L. M. Harris *Introd. Deepwater Floating Drilling Operations* x. 98 All preventers should have a pressure rating in excess of the maximum that could be expected on the wellhead. **1976** *Offshore Engineer* July 6/4 Shell has recovered, from 130m of water, the blow-out preventer (bop) stack which fell to the seabed while being lowered into position from the rig *Chris Chenery*. **1977** *Daily Tel.* 29 Apr. 2/1 They went to the gang boss and it was decided to rectify it when another driller noticed a small stream of mud running from the preventer's outlet.

preventionism (prĭve·nʃəniz'm). [f. Prevention + -ism.] A policy of prevention. So **preve·ntionist,** one who favours such a policy.

1918 A. Gray tr. *Grelling's Crime* II. ii. 109 All these questions..must simultaneously be answered in the affirmative, if the preventionists wish to justify their point of view. *Ibid.* 118 When preventionism suits their purpose, they speak of the right and the duty of the anticipated defence against future attack. **1978** D. Grylls *Guardians & Angels* ii. 66 The child-cruelty furore.. promoted sympathy for children's sufferings, and preventionists tended to deprecate not only cruelty but strictness.

preventive, *a.* and *sb.* Add: **A.** *adj.* **2.** spec. *preventive arrest, detention, maintenance, war.*

1639 Preventive war [in Dict.]. **1908** *Act 8 Edw. VII* c. 59 § 10 (1) Where a person is convicted on indictment of a crime,..and subsequently the offender admits that he is or is found by the jury to be a habitual criminal, and the court passes a sentence of penal servitude,..the court ..may pass a further sentence ordering that on the determination of the sentence of penal servitude he be detained for such period not exceeding ten nor less than five years,..and such detention is herein-after referred to as preventive detention. **1918** E. Pound *Let.* 15 Nov. (1971) 140 The wholesale preventive arrests surely prevented another rising... Similar preventive arrests would have prevented the Easter rising. **1932** *Rep. Dept. Comm. on Persistent Offenders* iv. 14 in *Parl. Papers 1931–2* (Cmd. 4090) XII. 553 Preventive Detention is a sentence intended for 'professional' criminals or criminals who definitely give themselves up to a career of serious crime. **1945** *Facts on File* 28 Feb. 70/2 Paris reports that the French police have released from 'preventive detention' P. G. Wodehouse, British novelist. **1948** H. Nicolson *Diary* 29 Nov. (1968) 155 A preventive war is always evil. **1953** B. V. Bowden *Faster than Thought* iv. 86 The technique of preventive maintenance..has considerably reduced the number of valve failures which occur while the machines are running. **1959** *Listener* 16 Apr. 674/1 Southern Rhodesian Government publishes a new preventive detention bill. **1963** *New Statesman* 22 Feb. 260/1 Preventive detention, a relatively humane experiment begun in 1908 and modified 40 years later, has been finally adjudged a failure and abolished. **1966** Schwarz & Hadik *Strategic Terminol.* 130 *Preventive war*, war initiated to prevent the enemy from making gains he might be expected to make if he were allowed to initiate the war, or that he might make without resorting to war if not forcibly opposed in good time. **1967** E. Duckworth in Wills & Yearsley *Handbk. Managem. Technol.* vi. 119 *Preventive maintenance*, a scheme for regular overhaul of equipment to prevent unexpected breakdown.

b. spec. *preventive medicine.*

[**1769** W. Buchan *Domestic Med.* ii. 531 Dr Mead recommends a preventive medicine.] **1870** *Food Jrnl.* I. i. 22 Preventive medicine received a great impulse by the labours of Coleman in relation to ventilation. **1881** [in Dict.]. **1926** *Eng. Rev.* Sept. 315 What preventive medicine can do is illustrated by the clearing up of the infective diseases of Panama. **1957** A. Huxley *Let.* 22 Feb. (1969) 818 If we could combine Krishnamurti with old Dr Vittoz's brand of psychotherapy..and a sensible diet, we would have solved the problem of preventive medicine. **1963** *Lancet* 19 Jan. 145/2 (*heading*) Statistical methods in clinical and preventive medicine.

B. *sb.* **c.** A contraceptive; = *preventative *sb.* c.

1822 F. Place *Illustr. & Proofs Princ. Population* v. 150 The proposals of Mr. Malthus, to persuade the poor that they have no right to eat.., as well as Mr. Godwin's infanticide, are..proposals to commence at the wrong end. The remedy alone can be found in preventives. **1901** E. B. Foote *Home Cycl.* iv. vii. 1137 To lessen the 'vicious employment of preventives' outside of marriage. **1911** R. Brooke *Let.* Mar. (1968) 292 The Church'll declare that God gave every man the Right-not-to-use-Preventives. **1943** R. Malkin *Marriage, Morals & War* 159 In 1940, when Lieutenant Colonel Gardner of the United States Army Medical Corps gave happy birth to the idea of a pamphlet explaining venereal diseases, which..would be sold together with a set of preventives and prophylactics. **1961** A. H. Nethercot *First Five Lives A. Besant* vii. 117 Before marriage, pure will power and moral determination were to be the only preventives. Physical preventives were..against the will of God.

preventorium (prĭventō°·riŏm). orig. and chiefly *U.S.* [f. Prevent *v.*, after Sanatorium.] An institution where preventive care is given to people at risk from tuberculosis or other diseases.

1907 W. Ewart in *Jrnl. Balneol. & Climatol.* XI. 155 The place for the 'Prevention-Sanatorium', or 'Preventorium', is the sea-coast. **1909** *Boston Even. Transcript* 10 Nov. (*heading*) To fight tuberculosis New York will have $700,000 preventorium. **1929** W. B. Tomson *Prevention of Tuberculosis* vii. 51 The preventorium stands out as the predominating instrument for prophylaxis and early treatment in childhood in America. **1930** *Aberdeen Press & Jrnl.* 21 Oct. 6/1 There are two preventoria in Aberdeen. **1936** *Dict. Amer. Biogr.* XVIII. 130/1 In 1909 he [*sc.* Nathan Straus] established in his cottage in Lakewood, N.J., the pioneer tuberculosis preventorium for children. **1953** H. R. Leavell in Leavell & Clark *Textbk. Preventive Med.* xvi. 497 'Preventoriums', where children from families with tuberculosis were sent and cared for..did not prove useful enough to justify their cost, and they were not taken over by government. **1968** *Awake!* 8 May 12/2 When I was eighteen, I had to spend some months in a preventorium.

preverb, *sb.* and *a.* *Gram.* **A.** *sb.* With pronunc. (prī·vɜːb). **1.** [Pre- B. 1 in Dict. and Suppl.] A particle or prefix preceding the stem of the verb.

1930 [see *Alfredian *a.*]. **1939** L. H. Gray *Foundations of Lang.* iii. 62 In English, many compound verbs borrowed from French consisting of a preverb (commonly, but erroneously, called a preposition..) and a base-word, and serving either as a noun..or as a verb, are distinguished in their use..by a difference of stress-accent. **1946** L. Bloomfield in C. F. Hockett *Leonard Bloomfield Anthol.* (1970) 460 Certain particles, *preverbs*, freely precede verb stems. **1951** *Archivum Linguisticum* III. 28 The early loss in NGmc of unstressed prefixes (*i.e.* mainly preverbs). **1967** C. J. Fillmore in *Glossa* I. 91 Many of the syntactic properties of the positive and negative adverbial elements called 'preverbs' have already been discussed.

2. [Pre- A. 2.] A verb which precedes another verb; an auxiliary verb.

1965 F. Behre in *Eng. Stud.* XLVI. 91 It is the content of the pre-verb that is qualified by *if* and not the pre-verb (*would, should, could, might*, etc.).

B. *adj.* With pronunc. (prīvɜ·ɹb). [Pre- B. 2.] Occurring before a verb. Also as *adv.*

1976 *Archivum Linguisticum* VII. 33 Essentially, then, medial position means non-initial, pre-verb position. **1976** *Amer. Speech 1974* XLIX. 82 The collocation of *much* with *prefer* applies only when *much* is preverb, as in *I much prefer a dry wine.*

preverbal (prīvɜ̄·ɹbăl), *a.* [Pre- B. 1.] **1.** Preceding the formulation of an utterance; prior to or present before the development of speech.

1931 G. Stern *Meaning & Change of Meaning* v. 115 A pre-verbal phase of 'gedankliche Gliederung' follows on the preliminary adjustment. **1938** I. Goldberg *Wonder of Words* ii. 28 Obviously there was what may be called a preverbal intelligence. **1957** C. E. Osgood et al. in Saporta & Bastian *Psycholinguistics* (1961) 287/1 The auditory effects of hearing 'hammer' do not produce behavior in any way relevant to *hammer* object in the pre-verbal child. **1978** Russell & Dewey in P. Moore *Man, Woman, & Priesthood* vii. 93 Mother-figures reign in the pre-verbal layers of personality laid down in infancy. **1979** *Nature* 13 Dec. 724/1 The stimulus comparison task..appears to have been carried out at a post-perceptual, pre-verbal level.

2. *Gram.* Preceding the verb. Also *absol.* as *sb.*

1948 [see *complementation]. **1958** *Archivum Linguisticum* X. 32 Or a post-verbal, counter to appearances, may vie with a preverbal. **1959** M. A. K. Halliday *Lang. of Chinese 'Secret Hist. Mongols'* vi. 88 The conditional is marked lexico-grammatically, by a system of adverbs; these, designated by position as 'preverbal' and 'final', occur either alone or in combination one with the other. **1972** J. L. Dillard *Black English* iv. 152 Abram.. is represented as using the pre-verbal durative particle *a* (*Your a gwine*). *Ibid.* v. 220 A preverbal *done* can be found as far back as Dunbar. **1977** *Word 1972* XXVIII. 147 The use of a preverbal particle in sentence initial position has recently become more common in the literary language.

preverbalization, -vernal: see *pre- A. 2, B. 1.

previable (prīvəi·ăb'l), *a.* [Pre- B. 1.] Before the stage when a fœtus has developed sufficiently to survive outside the womb.

1910 F. J. Taussig *Prevention & Treatm. Abortion* 2 Abortion is the pre-viable expulsion of the human ovum. **1936** —— *Abortion* iv. 81 The previable stage of pregnancy. **1945** *Jrnl. Obstetr. & Gynæcol.* LII. 35/1 The term 'pre-viable' has been proposed for the separate category of liveborn premature infants with a birth-weight of less than 2½ pounds. **1972** *Daily Tel.* 24 May 17/4 Research on pre-viable foetuses (those which may show some signs of life, but which have no hope of an independent existence) should be safeguarded further by limiting such work only to foetuses weighing less than 300 grammes (about two-thirds of a pound). **1978** *Church Times* 7 July 12/5 Difficult questions also arise over baptism, when a fully formed but pre-viable foetus is delivered by a legally procured abortion, still living but inevitably destined to die.

preview, *sb.* Restrict *rare* to sense 1 in Dict. and add: **2. a.** (Later examples.) Also, a foretaste, a glimpse.

1935 *Sun* (Baltimore) 4 Apr. 1/5 Voting,..held this week in Michigan, Illinois and Maryland, has left a somewhat mottled political picture as a 'preview' of the important Presidential contest which will take place next year. **1938** *Ibid.* 24 Jan. 6/3 His preview of the budget probabilities for the fiscal year now current. **1946** *War Report* (B.B.C.) 263 They were taking with them into captivity a preview of the wreckage of Hitler's Deutschland. **1956** W. H. Whyte *Organization Man* i. 10 The best place to get a preview of the direction the Social Ethic is likely to take in the future. **1959** *New Statesman* 31 Jan. 136/3 Mr Dene..was to be given a pre-view of army life on a special advance visit to Winchester Barracks. **1978** LaRosa & Tanenbaum *Random Factor* xii. 179 The morning of November 18 brought a preview of the winter to come.

b. (Occas. **prevue.**) *spec.* A showing or presentation of films, books, exhibitions, etc., before they are available to the public. Also *attrib.*

1922 *Opportunities in Motion Picture Industry* (Photoplay Research Soc.) 76 Where the studio employs a number of directors usually all of them sit in on the 'pre-views' that are given a film before it is actually ready for the final release. **1928** L. North *Parasites* 84 He attended a preview of a picture made by a small independent group of players. **1931** *Amer. Speech* VII. 74 Why should the word *trailer* be used to apply to a prevue of a motion picture? **1936** W. de la Mare in *J. Freeman's Lett.* p. xvii, That dubious puff, the pre-view, was not as yet in fashion. **1940** *Times* (Weekly ed.) 7 Aug. 17/3 A pre-view and mannequin parade of women's sportswear, coats, and costumes was held in London on Thursday. **1955** *Radio Times* 22 Apr. 42/2 (*heading*) Sport. Today's results and weekend pre-view. **1958** *Photoplay* Oct. 15 The first studio preview of *Stage Struck*. **1961** G. Millerson *Technique Television Production* i. 15 Picture monitors. These pre-view screens give a continuous view of what the three or more studio cameras and other video sources are seeing. **1977** *Rolling Stone* 13 Jan. 22/5 They finally came to a preview theater to see the 'Stairway to Heaven' segment.

preview, *v.* Restrict *rare* to sense in Dict. and add: **2. a.** *trans.* To show or present (a film, etc.) before its public presentation; to give a preview or foretaste of (something).

1928 L. North *Parasites* v. 66 We pre-view a picture every week. **1939** *Sun* (Baltimore) 26 Sept. 10/3 In some respects it promises to preview the World Series. **1950** Blesh & Janis *They all played Ragtime* i. 16 Such was the Negro's position in our society that it was inevitable that this rich new vein of music should be previewed for white America in whorehouses. **1951** *Newsweek* 27 Sept. 74/3 Euclid previewed a new line of vehicles which it is counting on to send its sales volume soaring. **1965** *Observer* 31 Jan. 23/5 The BBC did preview 'Culloden', but only on the same day that it was shown. **1966** *Listener* 15 Sept. 397/1 The first edition,..which previewed the Commonwealth Conference, merits only subdued congratulation. **1968** *Radio Times* 28 Nov. 33/1 William Douglas Home introduces his first television play—and previews his own edgy performance. **1977** *New Yorker* 6 June 108/1 His full-length opera 'The Voyage of Edgar Allan Poe', was 'previewed' in Minneapolis.

b. *intr.* Of a production, performance, etc.: to be previewed.

1978 *Tucson Mag.* Dec. 99/1 On the same afternoon, the TMA League's annual 'Christmas Fair' previews to members only. **1980** *Times* 11 June 9 Yet another massive stage project, now previewing at the Aldwych, where it officially opens on June 19. **1981** *Times* 26 Aug. 9/3 *Two Gentlemen of Verona* and *Titus Andronicus*, which start previewing tonight.

Hence **pre·viewer**; **pre·viewing** *ppl. a.*

1970 *Guardian* 6 Aug. 8/2 The previewing critics. **1970** *Globe & Mail* (Toronto) 25 Sept. 12/5 Some of the previewers yesterday were the photographer's grandmother, Mrs. Arthur S. King, Mr. and Mrs. J. A. Blackey, [etc.]. **1976** *National Observer* (U.S.) 23 Oct. 22/1 The previewers all have a common goal: to latch on to the money and fame that can be made on the billion-dollar-a-year lecture circuit.

previous, *a.* Add: **2. d.** (Further examples, including examples as *sb.*)

1885 *Ordinances Univ. Cambr.* 6 By Grace, 4 Apr. 1878, selected Candidates for the Civil Service of India who are Candidates for Honours are excused the Previous Examination. **1905** *Abol. Compulsory Greek* (Cambridge Univ.) 6 As regards the smaller and the local schools it may be pointed out that these are practically unaffected by the requirements of the Previous... In such schools the inclusion or exclusion of Greek in the regular curriculum does not depend on the Previous Examination. **1950** M. Marples *University Slang* 81 Soon after this date [*sc.* 1863] *Little-go* died out at Oxford, leaving the field to *Smalls*, and retired to Cambridge, where its official title, corresponding to *Responsions*, is *Previous*. **1979** *Jrnl. R. Soc. Arts* Oct. 706/2 As late as 1861, the subjects were little more than a repetition of the 'Previous' on a slightly larger scale.

e. *ellipt.* as *sb.* Previous convictions. *slang.*

1935 G. Ingram *Cockney Cavalcade* x. 168 He ain't got no 'previous', so you ought-a get bound over, didn't yer, Jack? **1970** G. F. Newman *Sir, You Bastard* i. 34 'Neither has any previous, Terry,' Burgess said. 'I thought perhaps the fella might have had a little bit,' he shrugged. **1974** E. Jones *Barlow comes to Judgement* 14 Sitting on the benches..were ten men... Nine of them had previous. The tenth had a clean record. **1977** 'M. Underwood' *Murder with Malice* v. 56 Anthony Rivings..five convictions for dishonesty..three other Rivings..all with previous.

prevoc·alic, *a.* Also (occas.) **prae-vocalic.** [Pre- B. 1.] Before a vowel; of or pertaining to the position before a vowel. Hence **prevoca·lically** *adv.*

1909 in Webster. **1934** M. K. Pope *From Latin to Mod. French* ii. xvii. 223 In educated speech throughout the sixteenth century final consonants, whether single or supported, were maintained when in prae-vocalic position in the phrase. **1943** A. L. Kroeber in *Univ. Calif. Publ. Linguistics* I. 30 The stops p, t, k are universal and stable. In the Arizona dialects they are less aspirated, prevocalically, than in other languages and have often been written b, d, g. **1949** *Language* XXV. 400 It is..improbable that *l* [in Umbrian] was treated differently before *į* and prevocalic *ī*. **1957** N. Frye *Sound & Poetry* 114 The two methods are even more sharply contrasted in the line endings of the two poets, where the frequencies of Spenser's prevocalic and Milton's postvocalic clusters are more than doubled. **1964** R. H. Robins *Gen. Linguistics* 101 In Scots English, /r/ occurs both prevocalically and postvocalically. **1966** [see *chest register* s.v. *Chest 10 b]. **1970** B. M. H. Strang *Hist. English* I. ii. 51 Dark *l* post-vocalically, and clear *l* pre- or inter-vocalically. **1976** *Archivum Linguisticum* VII. 164 Both to postulate an analogical extension of the pre-vocalic forms, since in the majority of the cases they do not even exist, and to assume lost vowels, is to beg the question.

pre-vowel: see *Pre- B. 2 a.

prevue, var. *Preview *sb.* 2 b.

pre-wa·r, *a.* and *adv.* **A.** *adj.* [Pre- B. 2.] Pertaining to or characteristic of the period before a war, esp. the wars of 1914–18 and of 1939–45.

1908 [O.E.D. s.v. Pre- B. 2]. **1908** *Daily Chron.* 24 Apr. 7/3 The Transvaal Government..are thoroughly honest—a great difference from the pre-war days. **1915** *Political Q.* May 90 The relations of the engineers (employers and workmen) were governed by two separate pre-war agreements. The earlier..made in 1911,..the second ..dated April 1914. **1917** [see *Foggy *a.* 5 b]. **1926** Galsworthy *Silver Spoon* iii. vii. 277 How stupid and pre-war! Why couldn't he, like her, be free, be supple, take life as it came? **1928** *Publishers' Weekly* 30 June 2617 The government of France has succeeded in stabilizing the franc at 25·52 to the dollar, approximately one-fifth of its pre-war ratio. **1938** *Encycl. Brit. Bk. of Year* 20/1 Tricycle undercarriages familiar in pre-war days, have been re-introduced in modernized form for greater safety in high-speed landings. **1942** E. Paul *Narrow St.* xxix. 260 What dealt our pre-war world its mortal blow was the supine cowardice and hypocrisy of so-called democrats. **1946** *R.A.F. Jrnl.* May 172 All the women were free..to resume their pre-war occupation... Already they have resumed their pre-war studies. **1958** *Listener* 6 Nov. 719/1 He [*sc.* Lord Montgomery] has severe and deserved strictures on the pre-war governments for their failure to bring the army up to date. **1975** *New Yorker* 28 Apr. 112/2 The Thai Nguyen steelworks now produces only pig iron, but planners hope that in two or three years it will regain its prewar capacity of a hundred and seventy thousand metric tons of steel annually. **1977** *Times* 22 Apr. 2/8 The pre-war, Spanish-style house has.. indoor swimming pool.

B. *adv.* [*Pre- B. 2 c.] Before a war, esp. the wars of 1914–18 and of 1939–45.

1920 *Econ. Conditions Central Europe* i. 12 Four million tons of coal were imported annually pre-war, mainly to Petrograd and Baltic ports. **1923** *Westm. Gaz.* 25 Aug. 4/5 The new tourist hails from districts and from classes which, pre-war, never dreamed of leaving England. **1928** *Daily Tel.* 4 Sept. 9/6 Some time pre-war there was a large contract out for tender from a foreign Government for water tanks. **1959** *Times Lit. Suppl.* 24 Apr. 288/4 The turnover of land is low, indicating a considerable decrease in distress sales as compared with pre-war. **1974** *Daily Tel.* 17 July 18 Pre-war, the 1933 Wimbledon final ..bears a similarity to this last championship.

pre-wash: see *Pre- A. 1, 2. **pre-wear:** *Pre- A. 1. **pre-work, -world:** *Pre- B. 2 a. **pre-wrap, -write:** *Pre- A. 1.

Prex. Add: (Earlier and later examples.) Also *transf.*

1828 *Yankee* (Portland, Maine) 16 July 232/1 Our Prex says this: You surely miss [etc.]. **1906** *N.Y. Even. Post* 11 June 6 If the various unpopular 'Prexes' would study the grounds of their unpopularity. **1942** Berrey & Van den Bark *Amer. Thes. Slang* § 854/10 Government officials and employees... Prex, Prexy, the President. **1967** H. Kemelman *Nine Mile Walk* 150, I was still officially a member of the faculty [of history] and as such was invited to the President's annual Christmas reception for the faculty. I accepted..because of past favours from Prex.

Prexy (pre·ksi). *U.S. slang.* Also **Prexie, p-.** [f. prec. + -y[6].] = Prex in Dict. and Suppl.

1871 L. H. Bagg *4 Years at Yale* 655 The title 'Prex'.. is oftener used alone to designate him [*sc.* the President] among the Seniors, the modified form of 'Prexy' is somewhat in vogue, in familiar talk. **1905** *N.Y. Even. Post* 1 Sept. 7 Scores of entering classes are lined up in chapel to listen to good advice from the dean or 'Prexie'. **1909** O. D. von Engeln *At Cornell* 58 The avenue is still, for Prexy is delivering his annual address in the Armory. **1929** *Publishers' Weekly* 22 June 2859/1 Professor Charles E. Merriam..has hobnobbed with politicians as well as prexies. **1948** *Variety* 25 Aug. 1/4 Madison Sq. Garden 'prexy' Gen. John Reed Kilpatrick. **1973** *Center City Office Weekly* (Philadelphia) 9 Oct. 3 Dr. Richard N. Harner, prexy of the Epilepsy Foundation, will appear in a taped interview with Frank Ford. **1974** *Cleveland* (Ohio) *Plain Dealer* 13 Oct. c. 13/1 While the NHL is controlled basically by the board of governors..the silver-haired prexy still wields a powerful stick when it comes to meting out fines and suspensions. **1979** *Honolulu Advertiser* 8 Jan. a. 3/1 Brokers at Stapleton Assoc. think they had more than their share of the breaks in '78. Prexy John Stapleton started things off by busting his leg on a ski trip.

prey, *sb.* Add: **4. b.** *bird of prey*: esp. a bird belonging to the order Falconiformes or Strigiformes. Also *attrib.* and *fig.* (Earlier and further examples.)

a **1398** Trevisa tr. *Bartholomæus Anglicus' De Proprietatibus Rerum* (1975) II. 1288 Most hote briddes of complexioun and colerik, as briddes of pray, haueþ þe vtter partyes ȝelowe. **1603** Shakes. *Meas. for M.* ii. i. 1 We must not make a scar-crow of the Law, Setting it up to feare the Birds of prey. **1899** W. E. H. Lecky *Democracy & Liberty* (ed. 2) I. p. xxii, He [*sc.* W. E. Gladstone] had a wonderful eye—a bird of prey eye—fierce, luminous and restless. **1920** H. E. Howard *Territory in Bird Life* vii. 269 A bird of prey would have more difficulty in approaching a flock unawares than it would have in approaching a single individual. **1956** D. A. Bannerman *Birds Brit. Isles* V. p. v, It is a sad fact that several of our most noble birds of prey can no longer be studied in what were once their native haunts. **1974** M. Bijleveld *Birds of Prey in Europe* i. 1 During the last two hundred years, the European continent has seen a period of intensifying persecution of the diurnal birds of prey.

prez[1] (prez). Also **pres** and with capital initial. Colloq. abbrev. of President *sb.*

1892 [see J.C.R. (*J III)]. **1936** *Esquire* Sept. 64/1 Mr. Roosevelt may be Mr. President to statesmen but he's the Prez to *Variety*. So is Harry Cohn, prez of Columbia Picts. **1942** Berrey & Van den Bark *Amer. Thes. Slang* § 183/4 *Pres,..prez*, president. **1956** *Washington Star* 7 Nov. a. 47 We should give the President our full support... Let's give three rousing cheers for the Pres! **1969** C. Burke *God is Beautiful, Man* (1970) 88 So this derty rat fink he says to the prez of the gang, Caiaphas, 'What's in it for me?' **1973** *Philadelphia Inquirer* (Today Suppl.) 14 Oct. 29/2 Reuben Malonado, 'prez' of the Royal Javelins, picked up an easy $150 a week. **1975** *N.Y. Times* 27 Feb. 20/5 'Look, there's the Prez,' one shouted when Mr. Ford came into view.

prez[2], **pres,** colloq. abbrevs. Present *sb.*[2]

1922 Joyce *Ulysses* 270 Accept my little pres. **1967** *She* Dec. 9/2 Perfect tree prez. for the husband of any wife who's fed up with having her best kitchen knives whisked away to the toolshed.

prezzie (pre·zi). *colloq.* Also **pres(s)ie,** (*rare*) **presee.** [f. prec. + -ie.] = prec.

1937 E. D. Metcalfe *Let.* 27 Jan. in F. Donaldson *Edward VIII* (1974) xxv. 312 The rest of the time will be spent shopping (buying presees for Wallis). **1961** J. Rose *At Cross* 141 Bella said 'I brought you quite a lot prezzies.' **1967** A. Diment *Dolly Dolly Spy* xiv. 184 We'll have the pressies first. **1975** *Australian* 24 Apr. 13 From..endeavours yesterday to discover what presents the Whitlams were taking overseas with them, we can inform you of the following piece of government policy: From this day forth no public announcements will be made about the nature of prime ministerial pressies. **1977** *Harpers & Queen* Dec. 164/2 A presie from Mummy. **1980** *Times* 12 Mar. 21/3 Beswick is chuffed by the reception from the shop floor. He is getting little prezzies from them.

‖**priamel** (prī,ā·məl). Also **Priamel.** Pl. **priameln.** [G., ad. L. *praeambulum*: see Preamble *sb.*] A kind of epigrammatic verse cultivated in Germany in the fifteenth and sixteenth centuries; also applied to a similar literary form in ancient Greek poetry.

1950 *Chambers's Encycl.* XI. 838/2 *Rosenplüt, Hans*.., recited epigrammatic poems (in a form known as the Priamel) at public ceremonies in honour of towns, princes or noblemen. [**1953** T. G. Rosenmeyer tr. *Snell's Discovery of Mind* iii. 48 Sappho makes use of the 'preamble', a species of folk poetry emphasizing one thing above the rest.] **1962** R. W. B. Burton *Pindar's Pythian Odes* viii. 106 The last sentence of the epode..is in the form of a Priamel or *praeambulum*, a series of parallel statements leading by stages to a climax, an extended form of paratactic simile of a type frequent in archaic poetry. **1976** *Oxf. Compan. German Lit.* 683/2 *Priamel*, a minor poetic form, cultivated in the 15th c. and 16th c., in which, after a preparatory cumulative build-up, a comic or witty *pointe* forms the final line... The chief exponent of Priameln is Hans Rosenplüt. **1976** *Classical Q.* XXVI. 194 The first line is a priamel, the three terms of which are all applicable to Peleus, who is to be the subject of the myth that follows.

priapulid (prəi,æ·piulid), *sb.* and *a.* [f. mod.L. name of class or phylum *Priapulida*, f. generic name *Priapulus* (J. B. P. A. de M. de Lamarck *Hist. Nat. Animaux sans Vertèbres* (1816) III. 76), diminutive form of Priapus: see -id[3].] **A.** *sb.* A marine unsegmented worm belonging to the class Priapulida, found in mud at the bottom of cold seas. **B.** *adj.* Of, pertaining to, or designating an animal of this kind.

1906 H. Theel in *Kungl. Svenska Vetenskapsakad. Handlingar* XL. iv. 5, I am now going to give a summary review of those Priapulids..which pass their life in the northern and arctic seas. **1916** A. Huxley *Burning Wheel* 36 Your heaven's so, With a path leading up to it past a row Of votary Priapulids. **1951** L. H. Hyman *Invertebrates* III. xiii. 184 The priapulids are animals of modest size, up to 8 cm., and drab coloration. *Ibid.* 194 The priapulid larvae live in the bottom muck along with the adults. **1967** *New Scientist* 14 Sept. 547/2 In the case of the priapulids..a plausible explanation for their pentamery is not so hard to furnish. **1979** *Sci. Amer.* July 114/1 The mud supported an active group of burrowing invertebrates, with priapulid worms predominant.

pricasse, var. *Prikaz.

price, *sb.* Add: **I. 1. f.** *colloq.* A high price.

1920 'K. Mansfield' *Bank Holiday* in *Athenæum* 6 Aug. 166/1 He likes to watch..her puzzled eyes lifted to his: 'Aren't they a *price*!'

5. (Further examples.) Freq. in phr. *at a price.*

c **1647** Clarendon *Hist. Rebellion* (1703) II. vii. 189 So much enamoured on Peace, that he would have been glad, the King should have bought it at any price. **1849** Thackeray *Pendennis* I. xiii. 118 He's too young for you ..and..poor as Job. Can't have him at no price, can she Mr. Bo? **1859** B. Jerrold *Wit & Opinions D. Jerrold* 155 We love peace, as we abhor pusillanimity; but not peace at any price. **1873** C. M. Yonge *Pillars of House* I. xi. 230 Mr. Froggatt says he would not go at any price. **1923** R. Fry *Let.* 29 Apr. (1972) II. 533 The British public won't have me at any price. **1928** A. Christie *Mystery of Blue Train* xxi. 172 I'm going to leave you... I can't stand my father-in-law at any price. **1934** G. B. Shaw *On Rocks* Pref. 177, I am not offering you the truth at a price for my own profit. **1961** L. Mumford *City in Hist.* xvii. 544 The machines..that would lend themselves to decentralization in a life-centered order, here become either a means to increase congestion or afford some slight temporary palliation—at a price. **1974** J. Pope-Hennessy *R. L. Stevenson* viii. 151 Louis Stevenson had stipulated..that he would not at any price stay in a hotel..but wished to live in a house. **1978** 'W. Haggard' *Poison People* iv. 144 It's..illegal to hold it [*sc.* gold] in quantity. I don't say bullion can't be found at a price.

5*. *what price —?*: what is the value or use of —?, what is the likehood of —? Freq. merely an expression of contempt: 'so much for —'.

1893 P. H. Emerson *Signor Lippo* xiv. 52 What price you, when you fell off the scaffold? **1895** H. W. Nevinson *Neighbours of Ours* iii. 73 What price the little backstairs Dook? **1899** R. Whiteing *No. 5 John St.* ix. 94 What price grammar? It don't seem to teach people to keep a civil tongue in their 'ead. **1905** E. Nesbit *Oswald Bastable* 93 Oswald now thought that politeness was satisfied..so he said: 'What price treasures?' **1907** G. B. Shaw *Major Barbara* II. 245 *Bill* (cynically..) Wot prawce Selvytion nah? **1914** C. Mackenzie *Sinister St.* II. IV. ix. 1114 It's all very nice for you to be so calm. But what price its being my watch that's lost, not yours, old sport? **1920** D. H. Lawrence *Women in Love* i. 10 'What price the stockings?' said a voice at the back of Gudrun. **1930** R. Lehmann *Note in Music* VII. 301 But what price jaunts on Sundays—eh? **1959** M. Gilbert *Blood & Judgement* xvi. 164 Quick work... What price the law's delays. **1973** 'B. Graeme' *Two & Two make Five* iv. 31 What price himself to replace Perkins, he asked himself with cynical amusement. **1977** *New Scientist* 12 May 336 (*heading*) What price Australian uranium?

V. 14. *price-boom, -boost, control* (so *price-controlled* adj.), *freeze, hike, -level, -maintenance* (examples) (so *price-maintain* vb. trans., *-maintained* ppl. adj.) *raiser, range, -regulation, review, rise, -wave*; *price-conscious, -sensitive* adjs.; **price-cutting** (further examples); hence (as a back-formation) *price-cut* vb. intr. and trans.; also *price cut* sb.; *price-cutter* (later examples); **price discrimination**, the action of charging different prices to different customers for the same goods or services; **price-earnings ratio** (see quot. 1965); **price elasticity** (see quot. 1971); hence *price-elastic* adj.; **price-fixing**, the action of introducing a fixed or standard price for something esp. by agreement between manufacturers; also *attrib.*; hence (as a back-formation) *price-fix* vb. trans., *price-fixed* ppl. adj.; **price-gouging**, the action of increasing prices by large amounts at once; **price index**, an index showing the variation in the prices of a set of goods, etc., since a chosen base period; also (with hyphen) *attrib.*; **price leader** orig. *U.S.*, a dominant firm that determines the prices within an industry; hence *price leadership*; also *price-leading* ppl. adj.; **price-list** (examples); **price movement**, a fluctuation in price; **price ring**, an association of traders formed to control certain prices; **price-slashing**, price-cutting by large amounts; so *price-slasher*; **price stop**, a ban on price increases; **price support**, assistance in maintaining price levels regardless of supply or demand; **price system** (see quot. 1968); **price tab** *U.S.*, a bill; **price-tag** (earlier and later examples); also *fig.*; hence as *v. trans.* and *price-tagging* vbl. sb.; **price ticket** = *price-tag*; **price war**, intense competition among traders by price-cutting.

1928 *Britain's Industr. Future* (Liberal Industr. Inquiry) IV. xx. 268 The rapid industrial slump which followed the price-boom of 1919–20. **1961** *Wall St. Jrnl.* 23 Jan. 2/2 A price-boost might well be delayed until mid-summer. **1974** *News & Press* (Darlington, S. Carolina) 25 Apr. 8/6 Both business men and consumers are fearful that the lifting of economic controls will set off new waves of price and wage boosts. **1961** *Wall St. Jrnl.* 4 Oct. 1 Farmers aren't as price conscious as last year, so we can get more money on a sale. **1963** *Economist* 20 July 281/1 The price-conscious professional classes. **1974** *Country Life* 28 Nov. 1662/1 From the price-conscious north I have news of good stocking fillers. **1914** *Automobile Topics* 12 Dec. 321 (*caption*) Ford loses price control suit. **1936** *Discovery* Apr. 128/1 He waxes..mildly indignant over price-control of new metals by monopolies. **1944** *Sun* (Baltimore) 6 Oct. 13/5 Price control clinics, manned by officers and enlisted men, to hear reports from GIs on instances of overcharging, were ordered established. **1955** T. H. Pear *Eng. Social Differences* 184 The freeing of both tea and coffee from price-control. **1974** *Listener* 3 Oct. 422/3 The attempted price controls..have been far too severe. **1948** *Hansard Commons* 5 Mar. (Written Answers) 105 Mr. J. Morrison asked..What are the wholesalers' and retailers' margin of profit allowed on ..such household goods as are price controlled. **1976** *Sci. Amer.* Nov. 138/2 Of its two million citizens more than 12,000 were dead of the flu and its concomitant pneumonia by the middle of November, against a macabre background of military embalmers and a price-controlled quick-coffin industry. **1925** *Wireless Dealer* I. II. 259/1 The retailer who is given a big discount must not price-cut to the public. **1928** *Publishers' Weekly* 30 June 2596 If turnover is secured by price cuts which decrease the normal profit [etc.]. **1957** *Chem. & Engin. News* 1 Apr. 28/2 In the chemical industry it is impossible to tell in advance whether a price cut may at some time in the future 'tend substantially to reduce competition'. **1964** *Financial Times* 31 Jan. 1/2 The..Adsega supermarket chain..has been price-cutting cigarettes. **1965** *Mod. Law Rev.* XXVIII. v. 554 The assumption of the publishers was that 'best sellers' would be price-cut. **1967** *Economist* 4 Mar. 845/1 The steady erosion of prices that followed the arrival of the price-cutters. **1969** D. C. Hague *Managerial Econ.* iv. 89 Even if several firms do follow the price cutter..price cutting may still be attractive. **1929** *Times* 2 Nov. 7/5 That could only be done with the abolition of the suicidal policy of price-cutting and competition. **1962** E. Godfrey *Retail Selling & Organization* i. 6 Price-cutting and the widespread introduction of supermarkets have made competition very difficult to meet. **1974** 'G. Black' *Golden Cockatrice* ii. 32 I'll fight a price-cutting war by matched price-cutting. **1957** Clark & Gottfried *University Dict. Business & Finance* (1967) 276 When the purpose or result of such *price discrimination* is to reduce competition or to injure competitors, either of the seller or the buyer, it is illegal under the anti-trust laws. **1969** D. C. Hague *Managerial Econ.* iv. 83 We were considering a special case of price discrimination... We supposed that the producer was in the most favourable of all situations and could charge a different price to each individual consumer. **1974** *News & Courier* (Charleston, S. Carolina) 25 Apr. 17-C/2 White failed to show International was guilty of breach of contract and price discrimination. **1961** *Dallas Morning News* 9 Apr. IV. 1 Foods, which long had been considered 'recession resistant' but hardly dynamic stocks, have been acting like growth stocks, going to higher price-earnings ratios. **1965** *McGraw-Hill Dict. Mod. Econ.* 390 *Price-earnings ratio*, the current market price of a company's stock expressed as a multiple of the company's per-share earnings. It is computed by dividing the annual per-share earnings of a company into the market-value of its stock. For example, if company A's stock is selling at $100 per share and the company earned $5 per share, the price-earnings ratio is 20. **1968** *Newsweek* 25 Nov. 91/2 Other stocks may continue to show solid earnings growth but then they become overexploited. Investors simply bid too high for them. This shows up in the price-earnings ratio. **1972** *Observer* 22 Oct. 15/3 A couple of dark clouds... One is the sky-high price-earnings ratio of your stock. **1964** *Economist* 15 Feb. 620/2 The argument that books are price-elastic. **1967** *Times Rev. Industry* Mar. 16/1 This company clearly believes that shoe demand is price elastic. **1976** P. R. White *Planning for Public Transport* vi. 127 Weekend and day return fares..relate to trips such as shopping and visiting friends, demand for which is more price-elastic. **1952** T. W. Hutchinson tr. *Schneider's Pricing & Equilibrium* i. 23 We can measure the reaction of the quantity demanded to changes in price, when all other prices and income remain constant, by the price elasticity. **1971** J. A. Perrow *Econ.* i. 17 Price elasticity may be defined as the responsiveness of demand for a good to a small change in its price. **1976** P. R. White *Planning for Public Transport* viii. 157 The non-business market. Here, the time and price elasticities are almost the reverse. **1949** *Time* 25 July 24/2 In the past, prices had been held down by a combination of price fixing and subsidies. Bread was price fixed, so were cooking oils [etc.]. **1933** K. T. Langguth *Financial Dict.: Eng.–German* 186 Price-fixed. **1949** *Consumer Reports* Aug. 344/1 Places to buy price-fixed merchandise at less than the established price. **1971** 'E. McBain' *Hail, Hail, Gang's all Here* ii. 183 That apartment's price-fixed... If he gets out, they can put a new tenant in and legally raise the rent. **1920** *Argus* (Melbourne) 4 June 6 Competition will reduce prices in time, but price-fixing..will only arrest the tendency to cheapness. **1930** *Economist* 15 Feb. 352/2 Rationalisation must also be distinguished from price-fixing associations or cartels. **1965** *Spectator* 26 Feb. 251/1 The price of whisky and gin was slashed following the end of price-fixing. **1973** *Country Life* 29 Nov. 1773/3 This 20-year-old price-fixing procedure [for Champagne] comes to an end in 1975. **1958** *Times Rev. Industry* Feb. 106/2 Those whose task it was to determine relaxations of the price-freeze. **1978** Ld. Hailsham *Dilemma of Democracy* xix. 122 Inflation has led to a demand either for a price freeze, or a wage freeze or both. **1967** *Guardian* 5 Aug. 7 Negro housewives..are the victims of price-gouging in the neighbourhood shops..owned by whites. **1974** *Aiken* (S. Carolina) *Standard* 22 Apr. 1-B/2 Each wage demand that is not balanced against productivity and each incident of price gouging motivated by greed help perpetuate the inflation cycle. **1977** *Times* 8 Aug. 42/3 This week the agency will open an investigation of alleged price gouging on fuel oil used in home heating; one consumer group is claiming the FEA permitted oil companies to overcharge by $2 billion last year. **1948, 1968** Price hike [see *hike *sb.* 2]. **1977** *Rolling Stone* 24 Mar. 16/2 Industry spokespersons tend to cite increased costs on every level when explaining the dollar price-hike. **1886** Price index [see *index *sb.* 9 e]. **1930** *Economist* 5 Apr. 763/1 The Economist price index has fallen during the past two years much more heavily than price indices in certain other countries on the gold standard. **1930** W. K. Hancock *Australia* ix. 184 The Statistician's price-index numbers. **1954** M. Beresford *Lost Villages* vi. 183 It cannot be said that our price-indexes are yet near perfection. **1954** E. H. Carr *Interregnum* 77 A price-index issued by the labour section of the Moscow Soviet for the calculation of wages in Moscow. **1973** Price index [see *index *sb.* 9 e]. **1936** A. R. Burns *Decline of Competition* iii. 77 The United States Steel Corporation is more frequently classified as a price leader than any other American corporation. **1962** *Economist* 13 Jan. 151/2 The International Nickel Company of Canada..is the acknowledged price leader. **1936** A. R. Burns *Decline of Competition* iii. 76 Price leadership exists when the price at which most of the units in an industry offer to sell is determined by adopting the price announced by one of their number. **1979** *Internat. Jrnl. Sociol. of Law* May 133 For price leadership to work, the price leader must have close to the largest share of the market. **1961** *New Left Rev.* July–Aug. 5/2 In Italy, each of the industrial sectors is dominated by a single, price-leading firm. **1927** Bowley & Stamp *Nat. Income 1924* 58 On account of the change in price-level, we should substitute a comparative level of £9,500, [etc.]. **1940** *Economist* 13 Jan. 53/1 Voluntary negotiation..can only result in a welter of independent wage decisions in different industries, each bearing a different relation to the general price level. **1972** *Accountant* 19 Oct. 485/2 Differences between financial statements prepared along the alternative bases of current-value and price-level accounting. **1872** *Young Englishwoman* Dec. 662/3 Will you be so kind as to send a price-list of the combs and hair-pins. **1915** W. Owen *Let.* 8 Jan. (1967) 313 What my friend advised me to do is to get price-lists and samples from England immediately. **1973** *Sat. Rev. Society* (U.S.) May 68/1 A list of catalogs or 'price lists', of items stocked by the Government Printing Office. **1960** *Guardian* 10 Dec. 9/6 The intending signatories agreed..that they would price maintain their vehicles. **1964** *Financial Times* 31 Jan. 1/2 More price-maintained lines would be added to their lists of reductions. **1968** *Times* 29 Nov. p. iv/4 Since they are still price-maintained it is not possible for retailers to cut prices, though in recent years budget labels have emerged. **1930** *Economist* 13 Sept. 483/1 The price-maintenance scheme is ultimately financed by the Reich. **1965** *Mod. Law Rev.* XXVIII. v. 552 Fifty years have now passed since the head of a well-known department store, in opposing enactment of a general price-maintenance law, told a Congressional Committee [etc.]. **1969** D. C. Hague *Managerial Econ.* xiv. 297 Is there a well-established (and legal) tradition of price maintenance? **1934** *Discovery* Sept. 245/2 They [*sc.* the farmers] have the advantage of being able to hear things that should be known at once to them: such as price movements, weather reports, harvest conditions and prospects. **1948** G. Crowther *Outl. Money* (rev. ed.) iii. 95 This is one way in which price movements have a direct causal effect on the level of production and employment. **1965** J. Meuvret in Glass & Eversley *Population in Hist.* xxi. 517 Here again, however, price-movements can afford some illumination. **1906** 'Mark Twain' *Autobiogr.* (1924) II. 24 That congregation's real estate stands at a low figure. What they are anxious to have now..is a price-raiser. **1965** *Punch* 7 July 2/1 George Brown's challenge to price-raisers to justify themselves. **1925** *Ladies' Home Jrnl.* May 146/2 Price ranges from 25c to 45c. **1937** M. Hillis *Orchids on your Budget* (1938) iii. 46 Another good rule is not to attempt to have everything come within the same price range. **1973** D. Westheimer *Going Public* i. 15 The fact that so much of your business is in the lowest price-range has its positive side... You'll find your bread-and-butter business is in the lower price-range. **1919** J. M. Keynes *Econ. Consequences Peace* vi. 225 The effect on foreign trade of price-regulation and profiteer-hunting as cures for inflation is even worse. **1935** *Economist* 12 Oct. 704/1 This shortage..is largely a consequence of planning and price-regulation. **1959** *Chambers's Encycl.* XI. 195/2 Price-regulation was in existence in Babylonia as early as the middle of the third millennium B.C. **1960** *Farmer & Stockbreeder* 22 Mar. 78/3 On Wednesday, representatives of the Branch met seven Conservative M.P.s at the House of Commons..when there was a long and useful discussion about many aspects of the White Paper and the Price Review. **1969** *Times* 6 Jan. 7/7 In spite of occasional controversy, especially before annual price reviews, the overall impression one gets of the past 10 years is one of fair stability. **1928** *Britain's Industr. Future* (Liberal Industr. Inquiry) II. viii. 97 The majority of cartels and price rings fall under the category of Trade Associations.. and not under that of Public Companies or Corporations. **1957** *Observer* 1 Dec. 1/4 This is no moment..for a price ring designed to keep prices up, or restrictive principles to prevent them going down. **1965** M. Hilton tr. J. Meuvret in Glass & Eversley *Pop. in Hist.* xxi. 511 The price-rise..can be explained..by bad harvests. **1977** *Times* 4 Oct. 15/2 Price rises are still at an unacceptable level. **1966** *Economist* 3 Dec. 1046/1 In the price-sensitive group of semi-manufactures, the bigger impact was on imports of textiles, paper and, above all, iron and steel. **1976** *Scotsman* 24 Dec. 3/7 Dunford and Prudential were justified in passing on information of a 'price-sensitive' character to their institutional shareholders, as potential underwriters. **1964** *Punch* 11 Mar. 377/3 John Bloom.. is a notorious price-slasher. **1930** *Publisher's Circular* 14 June 793/3 The economic and cultural consequences of reckless price-slashing. **1940** *Economist* 28 Dec. 799/1 The 'price-stop order', designed to prevent war-time increases in prices, has been reinforced several times by stricter penalties; but it has not been possible to prevent some rise in prices. **1950** *Ann. Reg. 1949* 244 A price stop was placed on certain essential commodities. **1949** *Sun* (Baltimore) 10 Sept. 11/4 Corn from this year's crop is expected to move into Government hands under price-support programs to join more than 400,000,000 bushels remaining there from the 1948 crop. **1957** M. Swan *Brit. Guiana* 95 Price support has come in the form of the Commonwealth Sugar Agreement. **1965** J. L. Hanson *Dict. Econ.* 326/1 *Price Support.* The U.S. Government's method of giving assistance to farmers. Prices are fixed well above the equilibrium level and so output cannot be completely disposed of on the market, the U.S. Government agreeing to purchase at the fixed prices any surpluses resulting from this policy. **1962** M. McLuhan *Gutenberg Galaxy* 118 Complex markets, price-systems, and commercial empires. **1968** P. A. S. Taylor *Dict. Econ. Terms* (ed. 4) 85 *Price system.* This is an economic system in which prices are determined by the forces of the market. **1974** *Encycl. Brit. Macropædia* XIV. 1004/2 A price system weighs the desires of consumers in terms of the prices they are willing to pay for various quantities of each commodity or service. **1949** *Sun* (Baltimore) 12 Sept. 1/8 A big victory for labor in the board's belief that companies should pick up the price tab on pensions. **1881** *Harper's Mag.* Sept. 587/1 Untying a little green price tag from the handle of the umbrella. **1942** D. Powell *Time to be Born* (1943) iv. 97 Vicky was uncomfortably aware of Miss Finkelstein's eagle eye putting price tags on her suit, her hair, her shoes. **1951**

Sport 30 Mar. 7/2 When I remember what a record transfer-fee price-tag did to Bryn Jones.., I can only sympathise with you. **1961** L. van der Post *Heart of Hunter* II. viii. 123 Though no price-tag could be put on them [*sc.* protected animals], we knew our lives would be immeasurably poorer without them. **1971** C. Fick *Danziger Transcript* (1973) 20 Your uniform smells as though the price tags are still on it. **1972** *Countryman* Winter 61 These faceless experts make an attempt to price-tag the social benefit of forestry. **1974** W. Foley *Child in Forest* II. 159 She price-tagged them by instinct. **1977** *Offshore Engineer* July 14/2 The NEB says that 'the project is likely to incur a 20–30% cost overrun' on the $8,000 million price tag it currently sees as realistic. **1972** *Straits Times* (Malaysian ed.) 23 Nov. 6/5 Encik Khir chaired the meeting which was held to resolve the problems facing shopkeepers over price-tagging. **1977** *Daily Times* (Lagos) 11 Jan. 17/2 Given the low level of enlightenment in the country, the intransigence of Nigerians to any government directive, price tagging was born with a lot of problems which have so far retarded its success. **1934** *Archit. Rev.* LXXVI. 27/2 A well-lettered price-ticket, decorative value apart, is more desirable than a label covered with hieroglyphics. **1957** P. Worsley *Trumpet shall Sound* viii. 159 Natives..tore the price-tickets off the goods. **1930** *Economist* 22 Mar. 652/2 Experience shows that this group invariably emerges from a price-war with a stronger hold on the oil markets than before. **1969** D. C. Hague *Managerial Econ.* iv. 74 A market which is free from the dangers of occasional, or continual, price cutting or even major price wars. **1977** *Times* 6 Aug. 3/1 A tea price war began yesterday as packers ordered cuts after auction prices fell. **1891** G. Clare *Money-Market Primer* 89 At all times some semblance of agreement is traceable between the respective price-waves.

price, *v.* Add: **1. d.** *to price out of the market*: to eliminate (oneself or another) from commercial competition through prohibitive prices; to charge a prohibitive price for (goods or services) or to (the customer). Also simply *to price out*: to charge a prohibitive price to.

1938 *Sun* (Baltimore) 3 Jan. 8/3 Building material dealers and manufacturers, and to a less extent building labor, not only priced themselves out of the market but also priced the country out of an anticipated increase of $2,000,000,000 of national income. **1946** *Ibid.* 10 Aug. 4/1 Our price policies in the past..have had a tendency to price our export commodities out of the world market. **1946** *Your Investments* Sept. 9 Many consumers were being priced right out of the market..by the accelerated rise in living costs. **1947** *Daily Progress* (Charlottesville, Va.) 4 June 1/3 Government support prices for peanuts are so high that 'it forces peanut butter up so far as we are being priced out of the market'. **1949** *Sun* (Baltimore) 28 Jan. 10/1 Earlier support plans have simply priced cotton out of the world market. **1955** *Times* 15 June 3/1 The country should realize that we could be easily priced out of international markets. **1958** *Spectator* 14 Feb. 201/1 As for the story that we should have been 'priced out of our export markets', time has shown that this does not happen so easily as pessimists predict. **1971** *Guardian* 6 Sept. 9/8 Swiss exports may be pricing themselves out of world markets. **1975** *Times* 4 Sept. 2/1 In an effort to price out [football] hooligans..most Saturday concessionary fares are being ended. **1977** *Guernsey Weekly Press* 21 July 1/6 His members were very concerned about the risk of being priced out of the market.

e. *to price up*: to increase the price of.

1943 *Our Towns* (Women's Group on Public Welfare) ii. 58 The shop then prices up the goods in order to cover.. the commission. **1976** N. Roberts *Face of France* xxv. 227 The [champagne] trade started pricing up its wares to restrain demand.

price-current. Add: Also *pl.* **prices-current** (occas. used for the sing.).

1815 *Niles' Reg.* IX. 3/2 This account of the *selling prices* of the several stocks mentioned, is taken from the *public prices current* of the two places. **1839** *Southern Lit. Messenger* V. 38/2 There are no daily papers..no prices current—no reports from the stock market. **1856** *Trans. Mich. Agric. Soc.* VII. 533 A glance at our 'prices current' might suffice to satisfy the most incredulous. **1965** J. L. Hanson *Dict. Econ.* 326/1 *Prices Current*, a price list showing the prices ruling at a certain date.

priceless, *a.* Add: **3.** *colloq.* Amusing, absurd, ludicrous; delightful.

1907 *Punch* 23 Jan. 59 Lady Bountiful: Oh, dear Miss Smith, *do* send me some of your priceless little sketches for my rummage sale on the 26th. **1914** D. O. Barnett *Let.* 19 Nov. (1915) 11 There was a priceless 'drunk' here the other day when I was on guard... He made the most magnificent remarks en route and so did the chaps who were carrying him. **1921** G. B. Shaw *Back to Methuselah* II. 87 What a priceless humbug old Lubin is! **1924** D. Moore *Fen's First Term* xii. 127 She had been a 'priceless idiot'. **1925** 'R. Crompton' *Still—William* xi. 201 'I do hope I remember all this when I wake up,' said the Toreador, 'it's too priceless.' **1978** S. Naipaul *North of South* I. i. 29 The European..burst out laughing... 'Can you imagine how they must have..rolled their eyes? Absolutely priceless.'

pricelessness (earlier example); **pri·celessly** *adv.*

1879 Trollope *Eye for Eye* II. i. 13 There came a day in which the pricelessness of the girl he loved sank to nothing. **1910** G. Murray tr. *Euripides' Iphigenia in Tauris* 62 Brother, and home, and sister pricelessly Beloved. **1934** G. B. Shaw *On Rocks* I. 222 You see, what makes your diagnosis so pricelessly funny to me is that as a matter of fact my life has been a completely intellectual life, and my training the finest intellectual training in the world. **1977** J. B. Hilton *Dead-Nettle* vi. 61 Frank, you are pricelessly sweet.

pricey (prəi·si), *a. colloq.* Also **pricy.** [f. Price *sb.* + -y[1].] Expensive, high-priced. Also *comb.*

1932 'C. L. Anthony' *Service* III. ii. 101 I've got the day off to-day—been up to a sale to see about a show-case. But I couldn't touch it. It was a very pricey article. **1944** *World's Press News* 31 Aug. p. iii/1 (*heading*) 'Pricy' at second hand... The advertiser offered 4s. 6d. for each issue of *Vogue* ten days after publication. The price of *Vogue* is 3s. **1953** D. Whipple *Someone at Distance* xxvii. 243 'Pricey, I know,' continued Mr. Pye. 'But worth it, Madam.' **1957** *Economist* 19 Oct. (Suppl.) 10/1 The 'pricier' models like the Ford Zodiac or the Vauxhall Cresta. **1962** M. Procter *Devil in Moonlight* xi. 114 It's pricey... It might cost you a lot of money. **1971** *Daily Tel.* 19 Aug. 2/5 Meat has become a very pricey business for most households. **1976** W. H. Canaway *Willow-Pattern War* xvii. 174 A pricey-looking transistor radio. **1978** *SLR Camera* Aug. 88/1 It can..be fitted with a motor drive unit, but not with the wide variety of viewing heads and viewing screens available for the more pricy sisters in the catalogue.

prick, *sb.* Add: **14.** Also, an early kind of knitting-needle. Cf. *knitting-prick* (Knitting *vbl. sb.* 3).

[**1707** *Rec. Convention R. Burghs Scotl.* (1880) I. 431 For the better improvement of stocking manufactures it is thought fitt that for hereafter all prick stockings may be made of three plyed wosten and of due proportione.] **1838** W. Howitt *Rural Life Eng.* I. III. iii. 309 They knit with crooked pins called pricks. **1969** E. H. Pinto *Treen* 304 Bow curved needles, made from wire sharpened both ends..and known as pricks, were commonly used for 'bump' or coarse knitting.

17. a. (Further examples.) For (Now *low.*) read *coarse slang.*

1680 Rochester *Poems* 14 But though St. James has the honor on't, 'Tis consecrate to Prick and Cunt. **1744, 1763** [see *bollock 1]. **1896** A. Beardsley *Let.* c 3 Dec. (1970) 223 Yes *everything* is phallic shaped except Symons's prick. **1922** Joyce *Ulysses* 424 Trinity medicals... All prick and no pence. **1965** W. Young *Eros Denied* xiv. 132 You know, the young men's pricks seem to be getting bigger and bigger. It must be the Welfare State. **1971** 'A. Burgess' *MF* iii. 39 His nakedness and limp prick..were now properties of the changing room. **1976** 'E. McBain' *Guns* (1977) ii. 38 Jocko had..a very small pecker... Blood on the bulging pectorals, tiny contradictory prick.

c. As a vulgar term of abuse for a man.

1929 *Amer. Speech* IV. 343 *Prick*, one in authority who is abusive or unjust. **1934** H. Miller *Tropic of Cancer* 110 Jesus, what I'd like is to find some rich cunt—like that cute little prick, Carl. **1935** J. T. Farrell *Guillotine Party* 193 That's what I think of you, Merton..you're a p...k! **1937** Partridge *Dict. Slang* 659/1 *Prick*... An offensive or contemptuous term (applied to men only). **1961** P. Kemp *Alms for Oblivion* ii. 40 Winn drafted a bitter reply, concluding with the *cri-de-coeur*: 'Uncomplaining gravest difficulties here but how long oh how long must we continue to kick against the pricks in your office.' **1967** 'E. Trevor' *Freebooters* xi. 124 We don't like bein' pushed around by an incompetent prick of a commanding officer. **1971** B. W. Aldiss *Soldier Erect* 52 Don't you call *me* a cunt, you Midland prick, you, or I'll sort you out! **1973** J. Wainwright *Devil you Don't* 25 John Smith said: 'Some men have big pricks.' 'Some men *are* big pricks.' **1978** M. Puzo *Fools Die* xi. 115 They have good jobs, big futures. And the pricks won't even do their service.

18. Delete ?*Obs.* and add later examples.

1975 B. Meyrick *Behind Light* iv. 57 Normally Pa had thirty or so good leaves left to make rolled 'pricks' as a change from pressing into wads. *Ibid.*, Soon our back pantry was full of thick hanging 'pricks' of twisted and rolled tobacco. **1977** *Navy News* Feb. 6/6 The hair on the nape of the neck was bound in yarns..and called a perique. In my days we rolled leaf tobacco in a similar way and called the result a 'prick', just modern spelling of an old word.

21. prick-farrier *Services' slang*, a medical officer; **prick punch** (later example); **prick-shooting**, shooting at the 'prick' or target; **prick-stitch** (see quots.); so **prick-stitch** *v. trans.* and *intr.*, **prick-stitching** *vbl. sb.*; **prick-sucker** *coarse slang*, a fellator or fellatrix; **prick-teaser** *coarse slang* = *cock-teaser* (*cock *sb.*[1] 23); also **prick-tease** *sb.*; hence (as back-formations) **prick-teased, prick-teasing** *ppl. adjs.*

1961 Partridge *Dict. Slang* Suppl. 1232/1 *Prick(-)farrier*, a medical officer: R.A.F. regulars': since ca. 1928. **1971** S. Kerry *Doctor's Cabin* iv. 48 'Meet Doc Kerry, our prick farrier.' They both laughed. 'No offence meant,' said Johnny. 'It's just a vulgar Naval term for a surgeon.' **1921** *Daily Colonist* (Victoria, B.C.) 2 Oct. 26/5 A chalk mark is good, but a prick punch makes a mark that will not rub out. **1801** T. Roberts *Eng. Bowman* 241 Of Prick-shooting..the marks used in this kind of shooting have..consisted either of a small circular piece of white paper, fixed to a post..; or of a target. **1887** W. Butt *Ford's Archery* (rev. ed.) 138 This prick-shooting next became known as the paper-game. **1924** W. D. F. Vincent et al. *Cutters' Pract. Guide Body Coats* 62/1 Hunting Coats are generally finished with plain seams, and have the front edges seamed and prick-stitched. **1928** A. S. Bridgland *Mod. Tailor* II. xviii. 242 *Prick-stitch.*—This stitch is employed to give either strength or appearance, and consists in alternately passing the needle straight up and down through the material, the stitch itself being either a back or a side-stitch. **1933** J. E. Liberty *Pract. Tailoring* iii. 18 *Prick-stitch.* This is exactly similar to side-stitch but is made by two actions, one upward, the other downward, the stitch actually being pricked alternately through the material which would be too thick for side-stitching. *Ibid.* v. 54 Prick back over the felling and along the seam for not quite ¼ in., then prickstitch parallel to the felling up to the top of the welt and to the same width. *Ibid.* vii. 100 To obtain the desired result, it will need to be prick stitched. **1955** —— *Ibid.* (ed. 2) v. 56 The usual D tack, with a little addition of a short row of prickstitching midway between the flap seam and the top edge of the jetting. **1964** *McCall's Sewing* xiii. 239/2 *Prick stitching.* Take short half-back-stitches in which only two or three threads of the fabric are picked up. Pull each stitch tight. **1968** J. Ironside *Fashion Alphabet* 83 *Glove-stitch*, also known as 'prick' stitch. Stitch used for hand glove-making and sometimes for sewing very heavy materials and leather. The thread is taken through one layer of material and then the other. **1868** *Index Expurgatorius of Martial* 21 Cotilus, the prick-sucker,..is shown to be the filthiest of men. **1974** *New Direction* IV. iv. 5/4 From then onward she became an ardent prick-sucker. **1977** E. J. Trimmer et al. *Visual Dict. Sex* (1978) ii. 31 A girl who works her way through several partners without actually having intercourse will become known as a '*prick-tease*'. **1975** D. Durrant *With my Little Eye* viii. 74 Prick-teased boys had up for rape. **1961** Partridge *Dict. Slang* Suppl. 1232/1 *Prick-teaser*, a late C. 19–20 variant of *cock-teaser*. **1971** R. Busby *Deadlock* i. 8 He laughed..and pulled her roughly across the seat. 'A prick teaser, are we?' **1978** F. Norman *Dead Butler Caper* v. 32 That Gloria's a right prick teaser. She'll con 'im somethin' rotten. **1967** 'P. Loraine' *W.I.L. One to Curtis* i. 16, I supplied..an empty house..for whatever prick-teasing kind of a party they wanted to throw. **1972** J. Mann *Mrs. Knox's Profession* iv. 24 He shouted after her: 'Prick-teasing bitch.'

prick, *v.* Add: **1. a.** Also, to wound or disable (a game bird) by shooting. Cf. *pricked *ppl. a.* 1 c.

1900 'Blagdon' *Shooting* 89 Too often, when cover is deficient and birds are consequently difficult to approach, there is a tendency to take long shots at birds which are really beyond sporting range, with the result that a large number of birds are 'pricked', or slightly wounded, without being brought to bag. **1916** *Shooting Don'ts* 39 Don't 'brown' into a covey. To be continually killing more than one bird at a shot will make you suspected. It results in a waste of birds, on account of the number that get 'pricked', and die.

22. (Further examples.)

1789 *Ann. Agric.* XI. 51 My first parcel [of seeds] was pricked in upon a small garden bed. **1913** J. Weathers *Twentieth-Cent. Gardening* vii. 67 Annuals sown under glass are first of all 'pricked out' into other pots or boxes when large enough to handle. **1935** A. G. L. Hellyer *Pract. Gardening* v. 46 Seeds..should not be very close together unless it is certain that time will be available to 'prick' them out. **1952** C. E. L. Phillips *Small Garden* vi. 55 When the youngsters have developed their first pair of true leaves, prick them off into other boxes or pots. **1977** 'E. Peters' *Morbid Taste for Bones* i. 8 He was content to help Brother Cadfael prick out early lettuces.

28. b. *prick out*, to come into view as specks or points.

1930 R. Macaulay *Staying with Relations* xx. 305 By two o'clock a few stars had pricked out, tiny candles shaking between the drifting gloom of clouds.

prick-eared, *a.* Add: **1.** (Later examples.) Also, of corn or wheat.

1922 Blunden *Shepherd* 81 From the young corn the prick-eared leverets stare At strangers come to spy the land. **1940** C. Day Lewis tr. *Virgil's Georgics* I. 25 The dangers of showery spring, When the prick-eared harvest already bristles along the plains. **1946** L. B. Lyon *Rough Walk Home* 11 Prick-eared, he lurks To leeward, patiently bold.

pricked, *ppl. a.* Add: **I. 1. c.** Of a game bird or part of a bird: wounded or disabled by shooting. Also *transf.*

1937 *Discovery* Dec. 385/1 Wounded or pricked birds left about the place are numerous. **1940** N. M. Sedgwick *Young Shot* v. 45 The guns should carefully mark where game falls,.. where..a bird with a pricked wing comes down. **1952** *Chambers's Jrnl.* Apr. 212/1 Thereafter, for days, a salmon was seen constantly to move in the one place, and gradually I became certain that it was one and the same fish that had twice been lost. Never did any of us visit the Island but there it was, rolling up every few minutes as so often a pricked fish will. **1958** R. Waddington *Grouse* ix. 105 Very high grouse mean many pricked birds and the moor in general is the sufferer.

3. (Later examples.)

1820 M. Edgeworth *Let.* 20 Dec. (1971) 226, I think the pricked map upon the whole better out and have seen the proof sheets and left it out. **1880** in L. Higgin *Handbk. Embroidery* 107 Designs..on pricked paper. **1900** F. Jackson *Hist. Hand-Made Lace* 216 *Pricked*, the term used in pillow lace-making to denote the special marking out of the pattern upon parchment. **1927** 'R. Crompton' *William—in Trouble* v. 119 Half a dozen Italian stamps.. turned out..to be 'pricked' and useless for collections. **1933** *Burlington Mag.* Jan. 43/1 There are pricked designs for figures which can be identified on vestments still existing. **1967** *Daily Tel.* 1 Feb. 13/2 Making lace borders, using a pricked parchment pattern, and placing pins in the holes, which control the completed stitches.

II. 8. *pricked-out*, of seedlings, planted out in a bed after being moved from the trays or boxes in which the seeds were germinated.

1938 G. Greene *Brighton Rock* IV. 154 The small pricked-out plants irritated him like ignorance. **1975** *Country Life* 13 Feb. 388/3 Space the pricked-out seedlings at seven by four.

pricker. Add: **4. a.** Phr. *to get* (or *have*) *the pricker*: to become (or be) angry. *Austral.* and *N.Z. slang.*

1945 Baker *Austral. Lang.* vi. 121 A man in a temper is said. .*to have the dingbats, the pricker* or *the stirks.* 1955 D. Niland *Shiralee* 102 You've got the pricker properly, eh? You'll knock him into next week, will ya? 1959 G. Slatter *Gun in my Hand* viii. 91 You'll come a gutzer son I ses... Got the pricker with me.

pricking, *vbl. sb.* Add: **1. b.** Phr. *pricking of* (or *in*) *one's thumbs*, used in various constructions with allusion to quot. 1605 in Dict.: an intuitive feeling or hunch; a premonition, a foreboding.

1935 'G. Orwell' *Clergyman's Daughter* i. 43 'I had a feeling I was going to meet you to-day.' 'By the pricking of your thumbs, I presume?' 1946 D. C. Peattie *Road of Naturalist* v. 52, I stood then on the back platform of the flying *Overland* with the knowledge that I had got into new terrain, not easily to be mastered, pricking in my thumbs. 1966 E. Palmer *Plains of Camdeboo* vi. 92 There should have been a pricking in our thumbs the morning we went to see the fossils, but we had no warning at all.

6. b. In *Palæography*, the piercing of a series of holes on a leaf to assist with the ruling of lines; a set of such holes.

1908 E. Johnston *Writing & Illuminating* (ed. 2) vi. 110 The writing line dots are pricked through all the sheets by means of a fine awl or needle... See also *methods of ruling without pricking.* 1912 E. M. Thompson *Introd. Gk. & Lat. Palaeogr.* 55 In earlier MSS. these prickings are often found near the middle of the leaf. 1971 T. A. M. Bishop *English Caroline Minuscule* p. xii, In English MSS. written after c. 900 the prickings for horizontal ruling are found only in outer lateral margins. 1973 *Bodl. Libr. Rec.* IX. 12 Prickings with an awl had been made along outer bounding-lines of four bifolia simultaneously with hair-sides up. 1976 *Codicologica* I. 78 Other aspects of the medieval book: the nature of parchment, ink, pricking, and ruling.

8. (Later examples.)

1935 A. G. L. Hellyer *Pract. Gardening* v. 47 Pricking out should be done as soon as it becomes necessary. 1952 C. E. L. Phillips *Small Garden* vi. 53 Pricking out simply means lifting the seedlings from this nursery bed. .and replanting them more widely somewhere else. 1976 *Abingdon Herald* 9 Dec. 5/2 A heating cable will enable you to carry on plants after pricking out.

10. pricking-iron *Saddlery* (see quot. 1960); **pricking-up** *Basketry* (see quot. 1912).

1904 P. N. Hasluck *Saddlery & Harness-Making* (1962) II. i. 18 Fig. 32 shows a tool used in stamping the lines preparatory to stitching. These tools vary in width from three teeth, which are used only for round points and scalloped work, to twenty-four teeth for straight lines... (*caption*) Fig. 32.—Pricking-iron. 1946 N. Wymer *Eng. Country Crafts* v. 47 From the start he was taught to keep his needle-holes as equidistant as possible, the length he must make each stitch being marked off for him on his leather by means of a pricking-iron. 1960 G. E. Evans *Horse in Furrow* xvi. 206 On the cart-trace *back* decorative sewing. .was the rule. A *pricking iron*—a chisel-shaped implement with points or teeth at regular intervals on the blade—was first used to mark out the pattern and to ensure that the stitches were uniformly placed. 1975 J. H. L. Shields *To handmake a Saddle* x. 42 The end to be stitched is then pricked with a No. 4 pricking iron. 1912 T. Okey *Introd. Art of Basket-Making* 153 *Pricking up*, turning up the stakes after their insertion in the bottom with the point of the shop-knife to form the framework of the sides of a basket. 1959 D. Wright *Baskets & Basketry* vi. 136 *Pricking-up*: turning up of willow stakes over the point of the knife after they have been inserted into the base. 1960 E. Legg *Country Baskets* 93 The turning up of the stakes is done rather differently than with cane, the *pricking up* method being adopted.

prickle, *sb.*[1] Add: **6. b.** (Earlier example.)

1875 *Encycl. Brit.* I. 897/1 The cells. .next in order are polygonal, and not unfrequently possess pointed processes or prickles projecting from them, hence the name, *prickle cells*, employed by Schultze.

9. prickle-cell (earlier and later examples).

1875 Prickle-cell [see *6 b]. 1962 Blake & Trott *Periodontology* ii. 17 This epithelium consists of a few layers of prickle cells. 1974 R. M. Kirk et al. *Surgery* v. 72 Histologically the tumour is of the prickle-cell layer, invading the deeper tissues, and later spreading to the regional lymph glands.

prickly, *a.* Add: **1. b.** (Earlier and later examples.) Also, of persons: quick to react angrily, touchy.

c 1862 E. Dickinson *Poems* (1955) II. 490 His pretty estimates Of Prickly Things. 1935 N. Mitchison *We have been Warned* iv. 340 Would you mind particularly if the C.P. were involved. .? They're a nasty, prickly lot. 1943 A. Ransome *Picts & Martyrs* i. 11 It's Mother she's getting at, not us... She's prickly with disapproval. 1950 *Listener* 9 Nov. 482/1 Hence the prickly suspicions of the new China's relations with the Western Powers. 1957 R. Watson-Watt *Three Steps to Victory* cxxiv. 453, I was probably being needlessly prickly. 1975 *N.Y. Times* 2 Apr. 37/2 They were self-conscious gentry, prickly of their privileges and independence. 1980 T. Morgan *Somerset Maugham* iii. 168 Janet Vale of the *Morning Telegraph* found him prickly.

3. prickly ash, substitute for def.: one of several North American shrubs or trees whose aromatic bark is used medicinally, including those belonging to the genus *Zanthoxylum*, esp. *Z. americanum*, of the family Rutaceæ, and the angelica tree, *Aralia spinosa*, of the family Araliaceæ; (earlier and later examples); **prickly Moses** *Austral.*, one of several species of *Acacia* bearing prickles, esp. *A. verticillata*, *A. juniperina*, or *A. pulchella*; **prickly poppy**, substitute for def. s.v. Poppy *sb.* 3: an annual or perennial herb belonging to the genus *Argemone* of the family Papaveraceæ, native to North or Central America, esp. *Argemone mexicana*, a widespread weed of tropical and subtropical regions; **prickly rhubarb** = *Gunnera.

1709 J. Lawson *New Voy. Carolina* 101 Prickly-Ash grows up like a Pole. 1743 J. F. Gronovius *Flora Virginica* II. 150 *Aralia*... Gambriar and Prickly-ash. 1778 J. Carver *Trav. N.-Amer.* 393 The chief...prepared for him a decoction of the bark of the roots of the prickly Ash. 1860 M. A. Curtis *Bot.* 91 Prickly ash. (*Aralia spinosa*)... The berries. .are thought by some to be also a valuable remedy for the bite of a rattlesnake. 1899 M. Going *Field, Forest, & Wayside Flowers* 74 Prickly-ash, and hackberry. .are thus unsystematic in their mode of conducting their affairs. 1931 M. Grieve *Mod. Herbal* I. 70/1 The Prickly Ash. .is a small North American tree. *Ibid.* 71/2 The name Prickly Ash has also been given to *Aralia spinosa*. ., the Prickly Elder, or Angelica Tree. 1938 M. K. Rawlings *Yearling* xxix. 379 She. .made him a tonic of prickly ash and poke-root and potassium. 1975 M. C. Davis *Near Woods* ii. 27 A clumped prickly ash had found a home among sandstone boulders. 1887 *Australian* Apr. 9/3 An expedition was now made into the scrub for fishing rods... I cannot recommend 'snap-scrub' for a rod, nor that awful thing which our philosopher called 'prickly moses'. 1965 *Austral. Encycl.* VII. 276/1 Prickly Moses, a corruption of 'prickly mimosa' applied to several species of wattle. 1724 P. Miller *Gardeners & Florists Dict.* I. s.v. *Argemone*, Argemone is a sort of Poppy, and some call it the prickly Poppy. 1760 [see Poppy *sb.* 3]. 1869 *Amer. Naturalist* III. 163 The Prickly Poppy (*Argemone*) looks now like a common thistle. 1898 A. M. Davidson *Calif. Plants* 112 The prickly poppy will send out great white flowers with crumpled petals and a great many yellow stamens. 1977 Lewis & Elvin-Lewis *Med. Bot.* ii. 31/2 Prickly poppies are widely distributed in weedy habitats in temperate and tropic regions. 1895 W. Robinson *Eng. Flower Garden* (ed. 4) 501/2 Gunnera (Prickly Rhubarb).—South American plants remarkable for large and handsome foliage, somewhat resembling that of gigantic Rhubarb. 1900 *Century Bk. Gardening* 98/2 Gunneras are called 'Prickly Rhubarbs', and the big leaves are not unlike those of a large Rhubarb. 1952 A. G. L. Hellyer *Sanders' Encycl. Gardening* (ed. 22) 217 Gunnera (Prickly Rhubarb)... Hardy herbaceous perennials. First introduced mid-nineteenth century.

prickly pear. (Earlier and further examples.)

1612 W. Strachey *Trav. Virginia* (1849) I. x. 119 Here is a cherry-redd fruict both within and without. .which wee call the prickle peare;. .they beare a broad, thick, spungeous leafe, full of kernells. 1672 W. Hughes *Amer. Physitian* 38 Most call it the Prickle-Pear Bush, and the fruit the Prickle-Pear. 1725 H. Sloane *Voy. Jamaica* II. p. vi, Tab. VIII Shews. .the sort of Prickly Pear, thought in Jamaica to be that particular kind of Opuntia, whereon feeds the small Worm or Beatle, from whence comes in Cochineel. 1739 P. Delegal in *Georgia Hist. Soc. Coll.* (1840) I. 188 The islands in Georgia are full of the prickly pear shrubs which feed flies. 1836 J. Hildreth *Dragoon Campaigns Rocky Mts.* xvi. 141 It was covered with the prickle-pear. 1917 *Nature* 20 Sept. 57/2 The prickly pear cactus (*Opuntia tuna*) has become extensively naturalised [in Hawaii]. 1925 T. S. Eliot *Poems 1909–1925* 98 Here we go round the prickly pear Prickly pear prickly pear... At five o'clock in the morning. 1956 C. Mackenzie *Thin Ice* iii. 36 We left Tangier about an hour before sunrise, riding through plantations of prickly pear. 1974 V. Nabokov *Look at Harlequins* (1975) I. iii. 12 We walked round the house, skirting prickly-pear shrubs. 1978 G. D. Rowley in V. H. Heywood *Flowering Plants of World* 65/1 Opuntias (prickly pears) are grown commercially in parts of Mexico and California for their large juicy fruits.

prick-madam. (Later examples.)

1955 G. Grigson *Englishman's Flora* 182 Prick-madam was the name used [for the yellow stonecrop] in the sixteenth and seventeenth centuries. 1978 *Verbatim* May 2/2, I have never grown *stonecrop*; now that I know it as prickmadam I am tempted to try.

pricy, var. *Pricey *a.*

pride *sb.*[1] Add. **I. 3. b.** Phr. *pride and prejudice*; occas. *prejudice and pride.* Cf. Prejudice *sb.* 3.

1610 J. Hall *Sixt Decade of Epistles* v. 42 Lay downe first, all pride and preiudice, and I cannot fear you. 1647 J. Taylor *Liberty of Prophesying* xii. 185 Epiphanius makes pride to be the onely cause of heresies. .Pride and Prejudice cause them all, the one criminally, the other innocently. 1650 —— *Holy Living* iv. 323 There is in it [*sc.* anger] envy and sorrow, fear and scorn, pride and prejudice, [etc.]. 1758 *Idler* 13 May 41/2 The prejudices and pride of man. 1758 C. Lennox *Henrietta* II. 48 The triumph of virtue over pride and prejudice. 1769 H. Brooke *Fool of Quality* IV. 292 Reason, and the workings of nature had begun to get the better of pride, and prejudice, in the peer. 1782 F. Burney *Cecilia* V. x. x. 379 The whole of this unfortunate business. .has been the result of Pride and Prejudice. 1782 Cowper *Hope* in *Poems* I. 170 Now truth perform thine office, waft aside The curtain drawn by prejudice and pride. 1796 R. Bage *Hermsprong* I. xxxi. 204 But the tender interest they had in each other was torn asunder by pride and prejudice; and this pride and this prejudice, she feared, had been infused into the tender mind of Miss Campinet. 1813 Jane Austen (*title*) Pride and prejudice.

5. b. pride-of-California, a perennial wild pea with pink or violet flowers, *Lathyrus splendens*, native to California; **pride of China, pride of India,** add: = Margosa, Neem (in Dict. and Suppl.); (earlier and later examples).

1785 G. Washington *Diary* 13 June (1925) II. 383 Next 3 rows of the Seed of the Pride of China. 1803 J. Davis *Trav. U.S.A.* 79 The mocking-bird. .was warbling, close to my window, from a tree called by some the Pride of India. 1834 J. J. Audubon *Ornith. Biogr.* II. 191 They . .feed voraciously on. .the berries of the pride of India. 1835 J. H. Ingraham *South-West* II. 101 The 'pride of China',—the universal shade-tree in the south-west. 1893 *Harper's Mag.* Apr. 756/2 This causeway broadened into a sandy street under huge pride-of-India trees, whose branches met overhead. 1895 'F. Franceschi' *Santa Barbara Exotic Flora* 64 *Lathyrus Splendens*, appropriately called 'the pride of California',. .has made its appearance in our gardens quite lately. 1949 *Bull. Hist. & Philos. Soc. Ohio* VII. 71 A tall conical envelope of straw. .protected the Pride of China, a tree brought from New Orleans. 1970 W. Smith *Gold Mine* xxvii. 63 The moonlight came in through the window, playing shadow pictures through the branches of the Pride of India tree onto the wall. 1976 *Hortus Third* (L. H. Bailey Hortorium) 638/2 *Lathyrus*...*splendens* Kellogg. Pride-of-California... somewhat shrubby.

II. 12. Delete † and substitute for def.: A group of lions forming a social unit. (Later examples.)

1929 *Times* 30 Sept. 12/6 Owing to the dry weather a pride of 16 lions, including females and cubs, concentrated on the Kajiado road. .less than 20 miles from Nairobi. 1940 V. Pohl *Bushveld Adventures* x. 218 Presently we distinguished outlines of several other forms beyond the one we now knew to be the leader of the pride. 1964 C. Willock *Enormous Zoo* v. 75 We found the pug-marks of a pride of lion. 1975 *Sci. Amer.* May 54/2 The social unit of the lion—the pride—is a long-lasting entity. *Ibid.* 55 (*caption*) A typical pride usually includes two or three adult males, from five to ten adult females and a number of cubs.

15. *pride-swollen* adj. (earlier and later examples).

1598 Marston *Scourge of Villanie* x. sig. H3, These pride-swolne dayes. *a* 1846 B. R. Haydon *Autobiogr.* (1927) i. 10 His large, red, pride-swollen, big-featured face.

pride, *v.* **4.** (Later example with *for.*)

1850 D. M. Craik *Olive* I. v. 71 How Elspie then prided herself for the continual tutoring which had made the image. .an image of love.

prideful, *a.* Add: Also *N. Amer.* **a.** (Later examples.)

1900 *Century Mag.* Dec. 293 The doctor's stately and prideful wife. 1945 R. Hargreaves *Enemy at Gate* 64 A prideful, unbending spirit was in no mood to bow a compulsory knee without a fight for it. 1956 B. Chute *Greenwillow* v. 64 He's prideful, and that's a sin, but he's been good to me. 1974 G. M. Fraser *McAuslan in Rough* 159 When that veteran has not only learned his political science at Govan Cross but is also a member of an independent and prideful race. 1974 R. Helms *Tolkien's World* iv. 73 The true heroism in this situation was. .the endurance of his men, forced by his prideful act to exhibit their loyalty to the death. 1977 *Time* 28 Feb. 23/1 He also was continuing to have his problems with prickly, prideful Senator Robert Byrd.

b. (Later examples.) Also, meriting a feeling of pride.

1939 *Sun* (Baltimore) 19 Oct. 11/3 She was very prideful of this, and when she finished Bill. .went over and congratulated her. *a* 1967 A. Ransome *Autobiogr.* (1976) i. 19, I was practising day in day out the simpler conjuring tricks that were to lead me to the prideful moments of a professional magician who, before vast audiences, should produce rabbits out of a hat. 1968 *Globe & Mail* (Toronto) 17 Feb. 28 They find they can now choose from a prideful list for entertaining. .or just revel in that greatest joy of all. .a leisurely candlelit dinner with fine wines and matching service. 1978 J. Carroll *Mortal Friends* I. v. 56 Collins was aware of the pleasure, the prideful pleasure, Brady was taking in his words.

pridefully, *adv.* (Later examples.)

1947 S. J. Perelman *Westward Ha!* (1949) x. 123 His new ball-point fountain pen, which he had been exhibiting pridefully all morning. 1977 *Time* 14 Feb. 56/3 A play that will most appeal to people of the sort he has so wickedly satirized—the pridefully literate.

priderite (prəi·dĕrəit). *Min.* [f. the name of R. T. *Prider*, 20th-c. Australian geologist, who made a study of the suite of rocks from which the first identified sample was taken: see -ite[1].] A lustrous black titanate of potassium and barium that is optically similar to rutile and occurs as rectangular prisms and plates.

1951 K. Norrish in *Mineral. Mag.* XXIX. 496 (*heading*) Priderite, a new mineral from the leucite-lamproites of the West Kimberley area, Western Australia. *Ibid.* 500 The formula of priderite is approximately $(K, Ba)_{1.33}(Ti,Fe)_8O_{16}$. 1960 *Jrnl. Geol. Soc. Austral.* VI. 72 Priderite, a potassium titanate. ., is the mineral which was earlier referred to as rutile. 1968 *Mineral. Mag.* XXXVI. 869 The priderite bearing rocks are alumina-deficient and alkali-rich but sodium-poor.

priest, *sb.* Add: **I. 2. b.** *priest-in-charge* (see quot. 1977).

1941 A. Thirkell *Northbridge Rectory* iii. 59 At St. Sycorax, where he was priest-in-charge, a title which gave him deep pleasure, he indulged in a perfect orgy of incense and vestments. 1963 *Times* 4 Feb. 12/4 In the summer. .he will become priest-in-charge of Titsey. .in the Southwark diocese. 1976 *Oxf. Diocesan Mag.* July 18/2

Stanford Dingley is not typical of rural parishes, in that, though very small, it has had its own priest, though not actually resident, for the last 20 years—a rector, a curate, and now a priest-in-charge. **1977** MACMORRAN & ELPHINSTONE *Handbk. Churchwardens* (new ed.) vi. 61 The unbeneficed clergy..fall into two classes: first, ministers in charge of benefices which for the time being lack the services of any incumbent (generally called 'curates-in-charge' or 'priests-in-charge'): and secondly, assistant curates, viz. clergymen appointed to assist incumbents within their parishes. **1979** *Guardian* 31 Oct. 10/7 Actually he isn't even a vicar. He's just a priest in charge who's been there about eighteen months.

III. 10. a. *priest-king* (later examples), *-ruler*.

1898 R. BROWN in R. M. Dorson *Peasant Customs* (1968) I. 168 The majestic figure of the Priest-king of Uru-salim. **1920** H. G. WELLS *Outl. Hist.* III. xix. 124/2 The beginnings of organized war, first as a bickering between villages, and then as a more disciplined struggle between the priest-king and god of one city and those of another [in Mesopotamia]. **1928** A. EVANS *Palace of Minos* II. II. 774 The remains of the remarkable painted relief of the personage wearing a plumed lily crown and collar, in whom we may with good reason recognize one of the actual Priest-Kings of Knossos. **1939** J. D. S. PENDLEBURY *Archaeol. Crete* iv. 249 One [chariot] drawn by winged griffins contains two female figures, one of whom.. has a headdress resembling in some ways that of the Priest King. **1958** *Times Lit. Suppl.* 24 Jan. 42/2 But he [*sc.* Charlemagne] was not a priest-king. **1978** *Listener* 28 Sept. 402/4 Were not priest-kings adored just because they were victims, in the sense that they were sacrifices for the people? **1920** H. G. WELLS *Outl. Hist.* III. xvi. 94/2 There [in the Euphrates-Tigris valley] flourished the first temples and the first priest-rulers that we know of among mankind.

priested, *ppl. a.* (In Dict. s.v. PRIEST *v.*) **a.** (Later example.)

1916 JOYCE *Portrait of Artist* (1969) v. 221 A priested peasant, with a brother a policeman in Dublin and a brother a potboy in Moycullen.

priesteen (prī·stī:n). [f. PRIEST *sb.*; see *-EEN².] Anglo-Irish diminutive of PRIEST *sb.*

1907 J. M. SYNGE *Playboy of Western World* I. 23 'It isn't fitting,' says the priesteen, 'to have his likeness lodging with an orphaned girl.' **1912** JOYCE *Let.* 19 Aug. (1966) II. 304 Can your friend in the sodawater factory or the priesteen write my verses? **1922** —— *Ulysses* 212 The quaker's pate godlily with a priesteen in booktalk.

priestess. Add: **3.** *Comb.*, as *priestess-queen* (after *priest-king*).

1920 H. G. WELLS *Outl. Hist.* III. xix. 114/1 The Sumerians allowed much more freedom and authority to women than the Semites. They had priestess-queens, and one of their great divinities was a goddess, Ishtar.

‖ **prikaz** (prika·z). Also **pricasse, prikas.** Pl. **prikazy.** [Russ.] In Russia: an office or a department, esp. in the central administration (now only *hist.*); an order or a command.

a **1725** C. WHITWORTH *Acct. Russia* (1758) 61 The Court..was very numerous and magnificent, being filled on solemn occasions by the *Bojars*, or privy Counsellors, with all the officers of each Pricasse. **1854** R. G. LATHAM *Native Races Russ. Empire* xii. 165 The *Prikas* is a kind of *Divan* or *Council*, consisting of two Kirghiz and two Russian assessors. **1886** *Encycl. Brit.* XXI. 105/1 He [*sc.* Kotoshikhin] served in the ambassador's office (*posolski prikaz*), and when called upon to give information against his colleagues fled to Poland about 1664. **1905** *Contemp. Rev.* Feb. 155 No law, ukaz, prikaz, can be decided upon except on the report of a Minister. **1917** [see *COLLEGIUM]. **1952** S. HARCAVE *Russia* iv. 58 Administrative offices (*prikazy*) were set up as new problems arose. **1963** N. V. RIASANOVSKY *Hist. Russia* xviii. 212 The authority of a prikaz extended over a certain type of affairs, such as foreign policy in the case of the ambassadorial prikaz. **1971** J. S. RESHETAR *Soviet Polity* vi. 217 Collegium decisions can be carried out only by an order (*prikaz*) issued by the minister because the collegium as such has no authority.

prim, *a.* Add: **c.** *prim-lipped* adj.

1926 J. MASEFIELD *Odtaa* xix. 318 A prim-lipped man, with the look of a 'spoiled priest',..seemed to be in charge of the guard. **1953** E. S. GRENFELL in C. K. Stead *N.Z. Short Stories* (1966) 74 The old man turned a..prim-lipped face to the parson.

prima². Add: **b.** Short for *PRIMA BALLERINA, PRIMA DONNA.

1930 T. KARSAVINA *Theatre St.* xiv. 183 From a group in the first wing, a sanctum reserved only for primas, an infuriated figure rushed up to me. **1951** GREEN & LAURIE *Show Biz* 571/1 *Prima*, prima donna. **1968** J. M. WHITE *Nightclimber* xv. 97 Her voice lacked the sheer power needed to make a real impression in the bigger operahouses. In central and eastern Europe, nevertheless, she always enjoyed the reputation of an undisputed prima.

‖ **prima ballerina** (prī·mă balərī·nă, bælər-). Pl. **prime ballerine, prima ballerinas.** [It., lit. = first female dancer.] **1. a.** A ballerina of the highest rank; the leading ballerina of a ballet company. Cf. *BALLERINA, *PREMIÈRE DANSEUSE.

1900 J. T. GREIN in *Sunday Special* 23 Sept. 2/2 Curiously enough for many years the London public has failed to do justice to the prima ballerina. **1912** J. E. C. FLITCH *Mod. Dancing & Dancers* iv. 62 At the Alhambra ..the dancing of the *prime ballerine*, almost all of whom were foreign, left little to be desired. **1918** D. H. LAWRENCE *Let.* 12 Jan. (1962) I. 536, I dreamed you were a sort of *prima ballerina*—which is the translation of a cinema star, I suppose. **1921** *Dancing Times* June 709 Lydia Lopokova has made a welcome re-appearance..as prima ballerina of the Diaghileff Company. **1955** *Times* 19 May 3/7 The transformation of Mephistopheles into the *prima ballerina* Mephistophela is thoroughly Heinesque. **1958** *Times* 13 Sept. 10/5 Her Giselle was a fragile, vulnerable creature, excessively shy, and bearing no mark of the *prima ballerina*. **1976** P. HARCOURT *Dance for Diplomats* iii. 30 He paid homage to his *prima ballerina* and the *corps de ballet*.

b. prima ballerina assoluta [It., lit. = absolute], a prima ballerina of outstanding excellence.

1870 T. A. BROWN *Hist. Amer. Stage* 33/2 She made her *debut* as prima ballerina assoluta in the Teatro Regio in Ancona. **1904** A. BENNETT *Great Man* xvii. 181 The glimpse which Henry had of the *prima ballerina assoluta* in her final pose..caused him to turn..to Geraldine to see whether she was not shocked. **1915** M. E. PERUGINI *Art of Ballet* xxxii. 272 With Signorina Maria Bordin..as *prima ballerina assoluta*..the production achieved instant success. **1928** *New Statesman* 31 Mar. 793/1 Tilly Losch (*prima ballerina assoluta* of the Vienna Opera-house). **1957** G. B. L. WILSON *Dict. Ballet* 37 Only twice in the history of the Imperial Th. was the additional title of 'prima ballerina assoluta' bestowed—on Pierina Legnani and on Mathilde Kschessinska. **1975** *New Yorker* 26 May 31/1 She..said that the Bolshoi's former prima ballerina assoluta, Galina Ulanova, was now one of its most valued teachers. **1978** LD. DROGHEDA *Double Harness* xxi. 300 She would inherit the position of *prima ballerina assoluta*, with her name standing alone at the top of the list of dancers.

2. *transf.* and *fig. spec.* an important or self-important person; something which has leading status in its particular field.

1954 *Economist* 11 Sept. 1/1 A prolonged attack of stage fright has repeatedly postponed the entrance of the new fighters..into squadron service with the RAF and the new *prima ballerina*, the supersonic P.1 fighter, has not turned up this week at rehearsals. **1964** M. CLIVE *Day of Reckoning* viii. 71 Any old lady..could turn..her daily round into a sort of sacred ballet, herself the prima ballerina. **1975** N. LUARD *Robespierre Serial* xvi. 146 I'm right with you however our prima ballerina responds. But what the hell are you going to tell him?

Primacord (prəi·măkǭɹd). *Mil.* Also **primacord.** [f. PRIMER *sb.²* + CORD *sb.¹*] A proprietary name in the U.S. for a type of detonating fuse consisting of a core of high explosive in a textile and plastic sheath.

1937 *Official Gaz.* (U.S. Patent Office) 23 Feb. 699/2 The Ensign-Bickford Co., Simsbury, Conn... *Primacord.* For detonating fuse. Claims use since Dec. 11, 1936. **1950** [see *CORDTEX]. **1959** *N.Y. Times Mag.* 31 May 38/2 One crew has its primacord all set to blow a big obstacle. **1972** *Daily Colonist* (Victoria, B.C.) 27 Feb. 30/1 Police.. warned parents..that 1,000 feet of primacord—an explosive detonating cord used to trigger dynamite—had gone missing.

primacy. Add: **1. b.** *Psychol.* The predominance of certain impressions, esp. first impressions, over subsequent or derived ones, in the mind or memory; also *attrib.*, as *primacy effect, principle.*

1896 M. W. CALKINS in *Psychol. Rev. Monogr. Suppl.* I. II. 35 Ordinary self-observation has..enumerated frequency, recency, vividness.., and primacy (the earliest position in a definite series of events) as the factors of interest. **1913** C. E. SEASHORE *Psychol. in Daily Life* v. 151 Familiar illustrations of the secondary or quantitative laws are (1) the law of primacy: other things being equal, the first impression will be the most effective. **1926** R. M. OGDEN *Psychol. & Educ.* xii. 199 Primacy is popularly expressed by the statement that 'first impressions are lasting'. **1931** *Psychol. Rev.* XXXVIII. 217 The law of primacy has also been suggested on the basis of experimentation, and this has been contrasted with recency. **1953** C. I. HOVLAND et al. *Communication & Persuasion* iv. 117 Experimental psychology for a long time postulated a Law of Primacy and a Law of Recency. **1959** LAMBERT & FILLENBAUM in Saporta & Bastian *Psycholinguistics* (1961) 457/1 The European cases in most instances fail to support either a primacy or a habit strength principle. **1971** *Sci. Amer.* Aug. 85/1 The increased probability of recall for the first few words in the list is called the primacy effect.

prima donna. Add: **1.** (Further examples.) Also **prima donna assoluta** [It., lit. = absolute], a *prima donna* of outstanding excellence.

1782 W. BECKFORD *Let.* 5 Apr. in J. W. Oliver *Life William Beckford* (1932) v. 110 Our Prima Donna, Miss Fawkener..has real talent. **1855** GEO. ELIOT in *Fraser's Mag.* LII. 50/2 He will..interpolate no *cantata* to show off the powers of a *prima donna assoluta*. **1938** *Oxf. Compan. Mus.* 749/2 The term *Prima Donna Assoluta* ('absolute first lady') is sometimes used to make perfectly clear the position of the *very* most important woman member of an opera company. **1958** *Listener* 14 Aug. 250/2 A singer who is hailed as a *prima donna assoluta*. **1976** S. GALATOPOULOS (*title*) Callas: prima donna assoluta.

2. *transf.* and *fig.* A person of the highest standing in a particular field or activity; one who behaves in a self-important or temperamental manner. Also as *v. intr.*

1834 [see *ANGERIAN *a.*]. **1846** *Swell's Night Guide* 36 Here also hang out some of the prima donnas of the flags and curbs, some of the small fry of 80, Quadrant. **1861** B. HEMYING in H. Mayhew *London Labour* (1862) Extra vol. 215/1 Two classes of prostitutes come under this denomination—first, kept mistresses, and secondly, prima donnas or those who live in a superior style. **1877** A. MACMILLAN *Let.* in C. Morgan *House of Macmillan* (1943) vii. 117 It is clear that our *Prima Donna* must be paid on a different scale from the others. **1936** *Amer. Mercury* May p. x/2 *Prima donna*, the first-class gripe artist; a temperamental [jazz] musician. **1938** *Times Lit. Suppl.* 639/3 We see her [*sc.* Madame de Stael]..as the 'prima donna', exacting, torrential and exasperating. **1940** E. HEMINGWAY *For whom Bell Tolls* xiv. 181 Stop prima-donnaing and accept the fact. **1943** *Sun* (Baltimore) 24 Sept. 14/2 A willingness to merge his identity with that of the journal of which he was a part. He was no prima donna. **1948** D. CECIL *Two Quiet Lives* II. 146 The most trivial points..were enough to produce a violent explosion of prima donna temperament. **1970** S. ELLIN *Bind* iv. 22 You've been putting on a prima donna act for the last hour. What's it all about? **1970** 'B. MATHER' *Break in Line* ix. 117, I felt no resentment... It was going to be hairy enough without any prima-donnaing on my part. **1973** C. BONINGTON *Next Horizon* ix. 140 He had invited Royal Robbins..to be chief [climbing] instructor, and the two men, both prima donnas in their own right, could not have offered a greater contrast. **1976** BOTHAM & DONNELLY *Valentino* iv. 34 Di Valentina was rapidly becoming the prima donna of the Manhattan cabaret set. **1978** *Jrnl. R. Soc. Arts* CXXVI. 537/2 The industrial designer tends often to adopt the rôle of catalyst rather than that of a prima-donna in his relationship with his colleagues in the development team.

Hence **prima do·nna-ish** *a.*, **prima do·nnaism, prima-do·nnaship.**

1889 *Scottish Art Rev.* II. 114 Miss Macintyre..is still too young and amateurish to make it possible to predict whether she will be..spoiled by her early prima-donnaship. **1961** A. WILSON *Old Men at Zoo* i. 25 It..served to increase my dislike for their unusual touchy, prima donna-ish relationship. **1969** P. DICKINSON *Pride of Heroes* I. 16 Pibble had taken a prima-donna-ish dislike to the stationmaster. **1970** C. F. HOCKETT *Leonard Bloomfield Anthol.* p. xiv, We can still know..his reaction to the pettishness, the prima-donnaism, the neglect of already accumulated experience, and the antiscientific bias that have all too often characterized our discussions. **1973** 'B. MATHER' *Snowline* vi. 73 He is apt to get prima donna-ish when he is out of temper. **1980** *Daily Tel.* 14 Jan. 12 We hope that he will go on being equally modest and lazy, cocking a snook at the prima-donna-ish antics of some chess masters while continuing from strength to strength.

prima facie. Add: **A.** *adv.* (Further examples.)

a **1676, 1797** [see *DOLI CAPAX]. **1900** [see *EN BLOC]. **1955** *Times* 5 May 4/1 If the right given to the tenant was an asset, it was something which *prima facie* would on his death pass to his personal representative. **1971** *Mod. Law Rev.* XXXIV. 693 The recommendation was prima facie *unlawful*.

B. *adj.* (Further examples.) Also *ellipt.* as *sb.*

1916 G. B. SHAW *Androcles & Lion* p. lx, An objection from an average stockbroker constitutes in itself a *prima facie* case for any social reform. **1955** *Times* 1 July 6/5 The Magistrate..said that on the girl's evidence there was plainly a *prima facie* case. **1978** P. LOVESEY *Waxwork* 153 If anyone can supply the *prima facie* evidence that her husband was involved, it's her. **1980** N. FREELING *Castang's City* xxv. 169 You've nothing for a *prima facie*... Any lawyer could knock it down.

primal, *a.* Add: **1. b.** *Psychol.* Relating or pertaining to such needs, fears, behaviour, etc., as form the origins of emotional life, esp. as in Freud's theory that, in the hypothesized murder of the dominant father who possesses the females in a primal horde, lies the unconscious origin of the Oedipus complex and the beginning of conscious emotions.

1918 A. A. BRILL tr. *Freud's Totem & Taboo* iv. 218 If the totem animal is the father, then the two main commandments of totemism..agree in content with the two crimes of Oedipus..and also with the child's two primal wishes whose insufficient repression..forms the nucleus of perhaps all neuroses. **1934** R. MONEY-KYRLE tr. *Róheim's Riddle of Sphinx* i. 81 All this forms a 'religion' in which the infantile primal fantasies recur in a projected form. **1950** J. STRACHEY tr. *Freud's Coll. Papers* V. 229 Parricide, according to a well-known view, is the principal and primal crime of humanity. **1961** R. FLIESS *Ego & Body Ego* III. v. 301 (*heading*) Primal hate against the eldest brother. **1968** M. HARRIS *Rise of Anthropol. Theory* xvi. 425 In this fashion, the primal patricide, helped along by hereditary memory traces in the 'racial unconscious', gave rise to the Oedipus complex, nuclear family, incest taboo, [etc.]. **1969** P. A. ROBINSON *Freudian Left* 109 Freud had in fact asserted that the primal-crime hypothesis was not to be understood as a simple statement of fact. **1970** A. JANOV *Primal Scream* v. 55 It is when we force the neurotic patient to feel, rather than act out his primal fears that we can help him understand the feelings that are terrorizing him. **1973** D. NICHOLSON-SMITH tr. *Laplanche & Pontalis's Lang. of Psycho-Anal.* 332 If we consider the themes which can be recognised in primal phantasies..the striking thing is that they all have one trait in common: they are all related to origins. *Ibid.* 334 This anticathexis..is unlikely to derive from the superego, whose formation is subsequent to primal repression. **1976** N. THORNBURG *Cutter & Bone* i. 7 He was.. indistinguishable from the evangelists and fire-worshippers, the pornographers and primal screamers. **1977** *Undercurrents* June–July 16/1 Another group is that at Atlantis near Burtonport, Co. Donegal, who practice self-sufficiency and primal therapy. *Ibid.* 26/1 Tim Eiloart discusses the development of the treatment, its basic methods, and the attitude of primal therapists to other forms of psychiatric treatment. **1978** *Listener* 19 Oct.

499/1 In America, one of the best-known of the therapies which claim to help you relive those early traumas is primal therapy.

c. Special collocations (sense *1 b): *primal father*, the dominant male, possessing all the females, assumed to have existed by some theories of the origins of social life; *primal horde*, a conjectured original form of human group; *primal law*, the conjectured law of nature whereby human beings originally lived, esp. under the dominance of the male; *primal scene*, a Freudian term for the first time that a child is emotionally aware of his parents copulating.

1918 A. A. Brill tr. *Freud's Totem & Taboo* iv. 245 An ideal could arise having as a content the fullness of power and the freedom from restriction of the conquered primal father, as well as the willingness to subject themselves to him. **1934** R. Money-Kyrle tr. *Róheim's Riddle of Sphinx* iv. 179 All human institutions are regarded as foundations of the primal father. **1918** A. A. Brill tr. *Freud's Totem & Taboo* iv. 246 The family was a reconstruction of the former primal horde and also restored a great part of their former rights to the fathers. **1934** R. Money-Kyrle tr. *Róheim's Riddle of Sphinx* iii. 171 What is the relation between the ontogenic conception of culture and the primal horde theory. **1969** P. A. Robinson *Freudian Left* 98 Verbal communication is the only vehicle of traditional continuity we know of; but, *ex hypothesi*, the primal-horde epoch must have been over before the development of speech. **1903** J. J. Atkinson (*title*) Primal law. *Ibid.* i. 210 The following thesis, however, on the genesis of primal law in human marriage, treats of a *conjectural* series of events in the ascent of man. **1925** J. Strachey tr. *Freud's Infantile Neurosis* in *Coll. Papers* III. v. 510 We will proceed with the study of the relations between this 'primal scene' and the patient's dream. **1955** M. Klein et al. *New Directions in Psychoanal.* xiii. 327 When, in this emotional state, he covers his eyes with his hand he is, I think, reviving the young infant's wish never to have seen and taken in the primal scene. **1957** M. McCarthy *Memories Catholic Girlhood* viii. 204, I conceived an aversion to apricots..from having watched her with them, just as though I had witnessed what Freud calls the primal scene. **1973** D. Nicholson-Smith tr. *Laplanche & Pontalis's Lang. of Psycho-Anal.* 335 Should we look upon the primal scene as the memory of an actually experienced event or as a pure phantasy? **1977** A. Sheridan tr. *Lacan's Écrits* iii. 96 The Wolf Man never managed..to integrate his recollection of his primal scene into his history.

primalism (prəi·măliz'm). *rare.* = Primality.

1904 Chesterton *G. F. Watts* 145 This indescribable primalism, which we have noted as coming out in the designs, in the titles and in Watts' very oil-colours.

primality. Restrict *rare* to sense in Dict. and add: **2.** *Math.* [f. Prime *a.* + -al + -ity.] The property of being a prime number.

1919 L. E. Dickson *Hist. Theory Numbers* I. xvii. 397 A test for the primality of $2^n \pm 1$. **1958** *Computer Jrnl.* I. 101/1 It proved possible to test for primality a series of numbers of the form $2^k - 1$. **1975** *Nature* 16 Oct. 544/1 They added that A. Ferrier, using a desk machine, had just demonstrated the primality of another large number.

‖ **prima materia** (prəi·mă matīə·riă). [L., = first matter. Cf. Gr. ἡ πρώτη ὕλη.] = *materia prima.

1906 W. B. Yeats *Poems, 1899–1905* p. xii, I know I have been busy with the Great Work, no lesser thing than that, although it may be the Athanor has burned too fiercely, or too faintly and fitfully, or that the *prima materia* has been ill-chosen. **1919** D. H. Lawrence *Phoenix II* (1968) 232 From the conjunction of fire and water within the living plasm arose the first matter, the Prima Materia of a living body, which, in its dead state, is the alchemistic Earth. **1954** R. F. C. Hull tr. *Jung's Coll. Wks.* XVI. ii. iii. 189 The refining of the *prima materia*, the unconscious content, demands endless patience, perseverance..and ability on the part of the doctor. **1969** K. Minogue in Ionescu & Gellner *Populism* 209 Nationalism has supplied them with a vocabulary suitable to their self-assertion expressing their claim to be unique and valuable, rather than simply indistinguishable *prima materia* fit for the inevitable process of industrialization.

primaquine (prəi·mă-, prī·măkwīn). *Pharm.* [f. Prima² + Quin(olin)e.] A synthetic quinoline derivative which is used (in the form of an orange-red crystalline phosphate) in the treatment of malaria; 8-(4-amino-1-methylbutylamino)-6-methoxyquinoline, $C_{15}H_{21}N_3O$.

1949 *Jrnl. Amer. Med. Assoc.* 3 Sept. 26/2 The Malaria Study Section, Laboratory of Tropical Disease, National Institutes of Health..suggested the term 'primaquine', to distinguish the compound from 'pentaquine' and 'isopentaquine'. **1960** *Times* 11 Nov. 17/1 Primaquine, one of the newer and most efficient drugs for the treatment of malaria. **1962** *Lancet* 1 Dec. 1133/1 An erythrocyte defect similar to that found in primaquine sensitivity. **1965** *New Scientist* 19 Aug. 440/1 Medical officers at the Walter Reed Army Research Institute in Washington..report that the anti-malarial drugs, chloroquine and primaquine..are proving less and less effective. **1973** B. J. Williams *Evolution & Human Origins* iv. 65/2 Such hemolytic reactions also occur in persons with G6PD deficiency ion response to certain drugs, including some antimalarials (receiving the terms 'primaquine sensitivity', etc.). **1974** M. C. Gerald *Pharmacol.* iv. 77 Of the 15,000 compounds ..screened as substitute antimalarials, only two, chloroquine and primaquine, were found to be superior to quinine. **1978** *Nature* 22 June 627/1 The antimalarial drugs selected for the WHO list are chloroquine, primaquine, pyrimethamine and quinine.

primarily, *adv.* Add: Also increasingly, following Amer. usage, with pronunc. (prəimēə·rĭli).

primary, *a.* and *sb.* Add: **A.** *adj.* **I. 3. a.** (Further examples.)

1899 Middleton & Chadwick *Treat. Surveying* I. v. 170 The methods..are not so complicated, or so minutely accurate, as those employed in dividing up a 'grand' or primary triangulation. **1920** W. N. Thomas *Surveying* xiii. 382 On the Ordnance Survey the first framework of triangles set out over the country constituted the 'Principal' or 'Primary' triangulation. **1923** Glazebrook *Dict. Appl. Physics* III. 571/2 For precision of definition, it is essential that there shall be one, and only one, material standard to represent each of the fundamental units. This is called the primary standard, and is preserved under the strictest conditions of custody, used only at very rare intervals, and then solely for purposes of comparison with the corresponding secondary standards. **1945** R. A. Knox *God & Atom* iii. 41 St. Thomas..distinguished God as the Primary Cause from those secondary causes to which we attribute this or that effect in our daily experience, and taught that the influence of the Primary Cause was present everywhere, conspiring with the secondary cause to produce the effect. **1966** *McGraw-Hill Encycl. Sci. & Technol.* XIV. 441/1 In 1907, the International Union for Cooperation in Solar Research adopted the value 6438·4696 A as the primary standard for the wavelength of red radiation from cadmium measured relative to the meter. **1973** *Nature* 12 Jan. 146/3 The time interval between publication in a primary journal and the appearance of the corresponding abstract. **1973** *Sci. Amer.* Dec. 65/2 The tangle that springs up where the forest has been felled is the first stage in the growth of a 'substitute forest'. In more formal terms it is an early stage in the development of a 'secondary forest', which will replace the cleared 'primary forest'. **1975** J. B. Harley *O.S. Maps* ii. 18 A succession of local central meridians were as a result brought into use before the associated tertiary triangulations could be adjusted to the primary triangulation of Great Britain.

II. 4. b. (Later examples.)

1914 M. Drummond tr. *Haberlandt's Physiol. Plant Anat.* i. 61 More often..it [*sc.* the middle lamella] also comprises the primary thickening layers. **1943** *Bot. Rev.* IX. 125 Current concepts of the origin of primary vascular tissues..are much confused. *Ibid.* 129 'Procambium' has come to mean specifically the vascular meristem from which primary xylem and phloem are derived. **1953** K. Esau *Plant Anat.* iii. 39 The primary walls have primary pit fields. *Ibid.* iv. 77 If these cells [that give origin to the meristem] are the direct descendants of the embryonic cells..the meristems are called primary. **1971** F. C. Ford-Robertson *Terminol. Forest Sci.* 41/1 The primary (cell) wall..is the wall of the meristematic cell modified during differentiation.

d. *primary age*, used *attrib.* of children receiving or ready to receive primary education; also *ellipt.* as *primary*; *primary education*, add to def.: now formally applied in Great Britain to the education of children between the ages of five and eleven years; *primary school* (later examples).

1908 A. Ruhl *Other Americans* x. 173 In the gymnasium four little primary girls were imitating..the gestures of the elocution teacher. **1944** *Act* 7 & 8 *Geo. VI* c. 31 § 8 It shall be the duty of every local education authority to secure that there shall be available for their area sufficient schools—(*a*) for providing primary education, that is to say, full-time education suitable to the requirements of junior pupils. *Ibid.* § 7 The statutory system of public education shall be organised in three progressive stages to be known as primary education, secondary education, and further education. *Ibid.* § 9 For the purpose of fulfilling their duties under this Act, a local education authority shall have power to establish primary and secondary schools. **1956** H. M. Pollard *Pioneers Popular Educ. 1760–1850* xxi. 265 Kay-Shuttleworth recommended that particular attention be paid to the large primary schools which had grown up..in The Hague [etc.]. **1958** K. Lovell *Educ. Psychol. & Children* xvi. 198 The primary school child like the pre-school child has his fears and anxieties. **1963** Barnard & Lauwerys *Handbk. Brit. Educ. Terms* 151 *Primary education*,..comprises full-time education suitable to the requirements of junior pupils (*i.e.* pupils under twelve). **1964** Curtis & Boultwood *Introd. Hist. Eng. Educ.* (ed. 3) viii. 184 All normal children..may be transferred at the age of 'eleven plus' from the primary or preparatory school to one type or another of secondary school. **1964** D. Holbrook *Eng. for Rejected* 54 How inefficient of the primary school to suppose that Joan has 'no imagination'. **1972** *Jrnl. Social Psychol.* LXXXVI. 167 The first study cited presents highly similar results for black and white primary-age subjects. **1976** *Times* 27 Apr. 14/7 It is impossible to generalize about English primary schools: some are progressive, informal, unauthoritarian, while others are strictly traditional. **1978** *Nagel's Encycl.-Guide: China* 316 *Primary Schools* take children from 7 to 13. For these six years, they learn little more than Chinese and arithmetic.

e. *primary assembly, meeting* (earlier examples); *primary election* (examples); also *primary caucus*.

1792 *Ann. Reg. 1789* [214/2] The primary elections had for some days been carried on in the different districts of Paris. *Ibid.* [215/1] The inhabitants of every district in France, preparatory to the election of delegates, hold what is called a primary assembly, where they choose a prescribed number of electors who are to act for the whole in the choice of a representative. **1801** *Spirit of Farmers' Museum* 61 The Editor of the Gazette of the United States..notices the 'Primary Assemblies' of our towns. **1821** *Massachusetts Spy* 11 Apr. 3/3 This was all the *hocus-pocus* of a primary caucus. **1829** *Niles' Reg.* XXXVI. 363/2 The battle is in reality fought in the primary meetings, and not on the day appointed by law for the election. **1835** C. P. Bradley *Biogr. Isaac Hill* 54 The freemen of the State were called upon to give at their primary elections, an expression of their opinion. *a* **1850** T. Ford *Hist. Illinois* (1854) 88 Personal politics..were carried from the primary elections into the legislature. **1885** *Century Mag.* Apr. 825 Nine out of ten of our wealthy and educated men..are really ignorant of the nature of a caucus, or a primary meeting, and never attend either. **1961** *Atlanta Constitution* 4 Nov. 1 An investigation of Atlanta's recent primary election produced 'no evidence' that any irregularities took place. **1974** *Hartsville* (S. Carolina) *Messenger* 22 Apr. 6-A/1 This is the first time in the state's history that the Republican Party decided to nominate its candidates in a primary election, rather than by the convention method.

f. *primary spermatocyte* (Zool.), a spermatocyte which will undergo meiosis to yield further spermatocytes.

1896 E. B. Wilson *Cell* iii. 122 The primary spermatocyte first divides to form two daughter-cells known as spermatocytes of the second order or sperm-mother-cells. Each of these divides again..to form two spermatids or sperm-cells. **1927** *Jrnl. Exper. Zool.* XLIX. 463 The darkly colored pycnotic primary spermatocytes..are the most conspicuous cells in the germinal epithelium. **1960** W. B. Crow *Synopsis of Biol.* viii. 40 In the grasshopper each primordial germ cell divides eight times producing $2^8 = 256$ cells... The cells finally formed by such division are called primary spermatocytes; they undergo the reduction division.

g. *primary endosperm nucleus* (Bot.), the (usu. diploid) nucleus formed in an ovule by fusion of the two polar nuclei; also, the (usu. triploid) nucleus formed by fusion of a sperm nucleus with these nuclei.

1899 *Bot. Gaz.* XXVII. 58 The polar nuclei may fuse to form the primary endosperm nucleus. **1950** Robbins & Weier *Bot.* ix. 205/2 The nucleus resulting from this triple fusion is called the primary endosperm nucleus. **1960** W. B. Crow *Synopsis of Biol.* viii. 42 The immotile male nuclei..are carried to the embryo-sac wherein one fertilizes the ovum... The other nucleus usually in angiosperms fuses with the primary endosperm nucleus, itself the product of fusion of two polar nuclei, so that triple fusion occurs, the triploid nucleus provided dividing up to form the nuclei of the endosperm. **1974** G. W. Burns *Plant Kingdom* xx. 487/1 One sperm passes to the egg, uniting with it to form the zygote, and the other combines with the two polars, producing the primary endosperm nucleus.

h. Designating an earthquake P wave (see *P III. 3).

[**1912** *Nature* 5 Sept. 4/2 The usual seismographic record shows three chief groups of disturbances, due respectively to the longitudinal and transverse waves through the core..and to the superficial waves round the crust. These ..are complicated and supplemented by reflections of the deep waves at the surface, and sometimes by twin earthquakes caused by the primary.] **1919** *Proc. R. Soc. Edin.* XXXIX. 161 Tables familiar to all seismologists, in which times of transit of the primary and secondary waves are expressed in terms of the arcual distances of the stations of observation from the..epicentre. **1955** *Sci. Amer.* Sept. 56/3 In 1897 R. D. Oldham of England identified on seismograms three main types of seismic waves: (1) primary (P) waves, which are compression-and-expansion waves like those of sound; (2) secondary (S) waves, which vibrate at right angles to the direction of travel, as light waves do; (3) surface waves, which appear in the upper 20 miles or so near the earth's surface. **1968** R. A. Lyttleton *Mysteries Solar Syst.* ii. 56 The velocity of the primary waves.. is always essentially faster than that of the secondary waves.

i. *primary road* = *main road* s.v. Main *a.* 8 b.

1956 R. Braddon *Nancy Wake* xviii. 215 They had frequently to cross primary roads. **1974** *State* (Columbia, S. Carolina) 27 Feb. 18-A/1 There are roads (even primary roads) which look impressive on a map but which fade away into mystery on the ground.

6. f. Add defs.: (i) Orig. applied to compounds regarded as being derived from any of four molecules (water, ammonia, hydrogen chloride, and hydrogen, by replacement of one hydrogen atom by an organic radical. This sense survives in mod. use with respect to ammonia derivatives, *spec.* amides (but see quots. 1965), amines, and ammonium salts, and is extended to analogous derivatives of other elements, esp. phosphorus. [The sense is due to Gerhardt & Chiozza, who used F. *primaire* (*Compt. Rend.* (1853) XXXVII. 88).]

1854 *Q. Jrnl. Chem. Soc.* VI. 195 The amides thus produced, which we shall call primary amides, represent a molecule of ammonia in which 1 atom of hydrogen is replaced by the negative radicals. **1888** Bloxam *Chem.* (ed. 6) 586 The amides, like the amines..may be primary, secondary, or tertiary accordingly as one, two, or three atoms of H in the NH_3 group has been replaced. **1889** G. M'Gowan tr. *Bernthsen's Text-bk. Org. Chem.* 119 Just as amines are derived from ammonia, so from phosphuretted hydrogen, PH_3, are derived primary, secondary, and tertiary phosphines by the exchange of hydrogen for alcoholic radicals. **1938** G. H. Richter *Textbk. Org. Chem.* xiv. 230 The reduction of compounds that contain a $>C=N-$ linkage also produces primary amines. **1962** Cotton & Wilkinson *Adv. Inorg. Chem.* xx. 392 The phosphines are less basic than amines of the same type, but for phosphines the order is tertiary > secondary >

primary, whereas for amines it is commonly irregular but usually with primary > tertiary. **1965** *Nomencl. Org. Chem.* (I.U.P.A.C.) C. 176 The generic name 'amine' is applied to compounds NH_2R, NHR^1R^2, and $NR^1R^2R^3$, which are called primary, secondary, and tertiary amines, respectively. *Ibid.* 188 Compounds containing one, two, or three acyl groups attached to nitrogen bear the generic name 'amide'. When only one acyl group is attached to a nitrogen atom, the generic name 'primary amide' may be used; when two acyl groups are so attached, the generic name 'secondary amide' may be used; and when three acyl groups are so attached, the generic name 'tertiary amide' may be used. *Ibid.* 190 *N*-substituted primary amides $R^1—CO—NHR^2$ and $R^1—CO—NR^2R^3$. [*Note*] These compounds have been called, respectively, secondary and tertiary amides, but this usage is not recommended.

(ii) Subsequently applied to organic compounds (except amines, etc.: see (i) above) in which the characteristic functional group is located on a saturated carbon atom which is itself bonded to not more than one other carbon atom. [Applied orig. to alcohols by H. Kolbe, who used G. *primär* (*Ann. d. Chem. u. Pharm.* (1864) CXXXII. 102).]

1864 *Chem. News* 26 Nov. 260/1 Primary alcohol. **1888** MORLEY & MUIR *Watts's Dict. Chem.* (rev. ed.) I. 100/1 In the primary alcohols the carbon-atom joined to the hydroxyl is connected immediately with only one other carbon atom. **1929** L. A. COLES *Introd. Mod. Org. Chem.* xii. 140 Methyl and ethyl alcohol are the two most important members of the primary alcohol series. **1968** J. MARCH *Adv. Org. Chem.* ix. 866 Primary alcohols or aldehydes can be converted directly to nitriles by air oxidation in the presence of ammonia, a strong base..and a copper complex.

(iii) Applied to a saturated carbon atom which is bonded to only one other carbon atom; also, bonded to or involving a primary carbon atom. Of an ion or a free radical: having (respectively) the electric charge or the unpaired electron located on a primary carbon atom.

1903 WALKER & MOTT tr. *Holleman's Text-bk. Org. Chem.* I. 46 A carbon atom which is only linked to one other carbon atom is called primary. **1926** H. G. RULE tr. *J. Schmidt's Text-bk. Org. Chem.* 70 When a carbon atom is combined in such a manner that only one of its four valencies is satisfied by carbon, it is termed a primary carbon atom. **1951** I. L. FINAR *Org. Chem.* iii. 31 A primary carbon atom is one that is joined to one other carbon atom. **1968** J. MARCH *Adv. Org. Chem.* ix. 866 Primary amines at a primary carbon can be dehydrogenated to nitriles. **1972** DEPUY & CHAPMAN *Molec. Reactions & Photochem.* iv. 46, 2,2-Dimethylcyclohexanone..cleaves to give the tertiary alkyl radical rather than the primary alkyl radical. **1972** NORMAN & WADDINGTON *Mod. Org. Chem.* ix. 116 A tertiary carbonium ion is a relatively more stable species than a primary carbonium ion..and is formed much faster. **1972** S. J. WEININGER *Contemp. Org. Chem.* v. 106 The secondary $(—CH_2—)$ carbon-hydrogen bonds..of propane are more easily broken than the primary $(—CH_3)$ carbon-hydrogen bonds of ethane.

g. *Electr.* Substitute for entry: (i) Orig. of an electric current: supplied directly by a cell or battery, as opposed to an induced current. Now, with reference to any device utilizing electromagnetic induction, esp. a transformer: of, pertaining to, or carrying the input electrical power.

1837 M. FARADAY in *Ann. Electr., Magn., & Chem.* I. 176 The conducting power of the connecting system A B D was sufficient to carry all the primary current. *Ibid.* 177 These experiments establishing..a distinction between the primary or generating current and the extra current, led me to conclude that the latter was identical with the induced current described..in the first series of these researches. **1862** *Electrician* 21 Feb. 183/2 In the primary wire of the induction coil, the 'return' or 'extra' current is an effect which is equally objectionable. *c* **1865** [in Dict.]. **1893** G. KAPP *Dynamos* xvii. 435 Such an apparatus is known as a transformer, the coil through which we send the alternating current being called the primary or driving coil. **1896** F. BEDELL *Princ. Transformer* i. 3 The primary electromotive force..is equal to the product of the number of primary turns, and the rate at which the magnetic flux in the magnetic circuit is changing. **1929** A. T. DOVER *Electr. Traction* (ed. 2) x. 281 The primary winding..has tappings to give 1000, 800, and 220 volts. **1938** KERCHNER & CORCORAN *Alternating-Current Circuits* vii. 193 The primary current could thus be made to lead or lag the primary voltage by adjusting the degree of coupling between the two transformer windings. **1963** WILLIAMS & PRIGMORE *Electr. Engin.* x. 333 In the open-circuit test ..the rated voltage..is applied to the primary terminals of the transformer. **1971** H. A. ROMANOWITZ *Introd. Electr. Circuits* xxii. 491 When a transformer is used to deliver energy at a higher voltage than that at which it is received, the primary winding is the one with the small number of turns and the larger wire in its coils.

(ii) Of a cell or battery: in which the chemical reaction that generates the current is irreversible, and which therefore cannot store electrical energy applied to it.

1882 *Engineer* 19 May 365/2 The distinction between a primary and a secondary battery is in no sense an important one when we are considering either as the producer of a current. **1886** R. WORMELL *Electr. in Service of Man* 427 The primary battery gives out a current of electricity, and the secondary acquires a condition which gives it also in turn the power of producing an electric current. **1922** GLAZEBROOK *Dict. Appl. Physics* II. 59/2 Polarisation is one of the difficulties encountered in all primary cells. **1971** H. A. ROMANOWITZ *Introd. Electr. Circuits* ii. 36 The wet cells and dry cells just described, which are not rechargeable, are classified as primary cells.

h. Applied to the testes and ovaries as sexual characters essential to reproduction and determined directly by the genetic sex, without hormonal intervention; sometimes the sexual ducts and organs are included, as essential to reproduction though developing as a result of hormonal influence (these are otherwise classed as either accessory or secondary characters). Cf. *SECONDARY *a.*

1871 DARWIN *Descent of Man* I. viii. 253 With animals which have their sexes separated, the males necessarily differ from the females in their organs of reproduction; and these are the primary sexual characters. *Ibid.* 254 Unless..we confine the term 'primary' to the reproductive glands, it is scarcely possible to decide which ought to be called primary and which secondary. **1894** H. ELLIS *Man & Woman* ii. 18 When we are dealing with Man it is perhaps most convenient to set aside as primary the sexual glands..and the organs for emission and reception in immediate connection with these glands. **1926** J. R. BAKER *Sex in Man & Animals* ii. 26 The primary sexual characters are..the testes and ovaries. The accessory sexual characters are the obviously useful sex characters other than the testes and ovaries, such as the vas deferens ..and the vagina... The secondary sexual characters are those which seem not to be directly concerned in reproduction, such as beards, antlers, and crests. **1948** C. D. TURNER *Gen. Endocrinol.* viii. 263 The primary sex characters are the gonads... Ducts and glands involved in the transmission of gametes or developing zygotes are known as the sex accessories. **1960** B. I. BALINSKY *Human Embryol.* xvi. 432 The primary sex characters distinguishing a male from a female animal are the sex glands—the testis and the ovary, respectively. By secondary sex characters are meant the distinctions between the sexes other than the presence of sex glands. These..fall into two groups: the organs which are essentially necessary for reproduction,..and organs or characters..such as the spurs and comb in the cock, the beard in man, [etc.]. **1977** E. J. TRIMMER et al. *Visual Dict. Sex* (1978) xxii. 262/1 A boy castrated before puberty will fail to develop the primary and secondary sexual characteristics of a normal male that would otherwise be stimulated by hormones produced by the testes.

i. *Geol.* Of a mineral: that is an original constituent of the rock. Of a rock: whose constituents have undergone no alteration since formation. Usu. applied *spec.* to minerals and rocks that have crystallized from magma.

1886 J. GEIKIE *Outl. Geol.* xiii. 151 It is the primary or original constituents of a rock which ought to determine its species, but these are often replaced by secondary minerals, and thus it is not in all cases possible to say what were the primary minerals. **1905** —— *Struct. & Field Geol.* iii. 37 Those rock-constituents which crystallised out from the magma are termed primary or original, to distinguish them from another group of minerals which are of later origin than the rocks in which they occur. **1914** J. PARK *Text-bk. Geol.* xii. 191 A primary mineral or rock constituent is one that is developed during the cooling of the molten magma, or, in the case of sedimentary rock, that appeared among the original constituents. **1921** *Trans. Geol. Soc. S. Afr.* XXIV. 116 In some varieties..a titaniferous lime-iron garnet comes in, together with primary calcite. **1931** A. JOHANNSEN *Descr. Petrogr. Igneous Rocks* I. ii. 28 The primary minerals of the igneous rocks are comparatively few in number... The feldspars, the pyriboles, the micas, quartz, olivine, and the feldspathoids are practically all. **1966** READ & WATSON *Beginning Geol.* xii. 147/1 In this environment, the primary minerals..are no longer stable, and they give place to new minerals and fabrics more in harmony with the new conditions. **1971** B. W. SPARKS *Rocks & Relief* iv. 132 A relatively small class of primary calcareous rocks, known as carbonatites, are [*sic*] associated in some areas with alkaline igneous rocks.

j. *Sociol.* Esp. as *primary group*: a term for the sort of direct and informal relationships that an individual forms by reason of family or environmental associations which are considered basic to social life and culture (see esp. quots. 1933 and 1971).

1894 SMALL & VINCENT *Introd. Study of Society* III. ii. 183 (*heading*) The primary social group: the family. **1909** C. H. COOLEY *Social Organization* iii. 23 By primary groups I mean those characterized by intimate face-to-face association and coöperation... They are primary..chiefly in that they are fundamental in forming the social nature and ideals of the individual. **1933** —— et al. *Introd. Sociol.* iv. 55 If human nature belongs, then, to men in association what kind or degree of association is required to develop it?.. Are there simple forms of association..? It appears that there are, and we shall call them *primary groups*. *Ibid.*, A primary group may be defined as a group of from two to possibly fifty or sixty people..who are in relatively face-to-face association for no single purpose, but merely as persons rather than as specialized functionaries. **1950** E. A. SHILS in Merton & Lazarsfeld *Continuities in Social Res.* 25 The primary group, they say, 'served two principal functions in combat motivation: it set and emphasized group standards of behavior and it supported and sustained the individual in stresses he would not otherwise have been able to withstand.' **1971** Z. BARBU *Society, Culture & Personality* ii. 34 E. Farris rejects the criterion of face-to-face association and specifies that intimate relationships, together with group consciousness, *esprit de corps*, and the feeling of 'we' constitute the main characteristics of a primary group. On the other hand E. A. Shils considers primary groups as identical with what other writers call informal groups, i.e. more or less spontaneous gatherings based on some kind of mental affinity.

k. *Physics* and *Astr.* Of, pertaining to, or designating radiation that is not produced by other radiation but may itself produce other (secondary) radiation; of cosmic rays: originating outside the earth's atmosphere.

1900 J. S. TOWNSEND in *Proc. Cambr. Philos. Soc.* X. 218 The apparatus shown..was used to determine the relative intensities of the secondary radiations given out by different bodies, and the intensity of the secondary radiation compared with that of the primary radiation which excites it. **1921** J. SCOTT-TAGGART *Thermionic Tubes* i. 23 When the primary or original electron attains a velocity sufficiently high to break off electrons from the gas molecule, it will leave the latter positively charged. **1938** R. W. LAWSON tr. *Hevesy & Paneth's Man. Radio-activity* (ed. 2) v. 61 The number of secondary electrons corresponding to each incident primary electron depends on the velocity of the primary electron. **1944** *Ann. Reg. 1943* 361 Results which they regarded as..confirming that the main part of the primary cosmic ray radiation does not consist of electrons. **1946** *Electronic Engin.* XVIII. 75/1 An electrode will emit primary electrons when its temperature is raised sufficiently to overcome the work function of the material of which it is made. **1959** K. HENNEY *Radio Engin. Handbk.* (ed. 5) vii. 15 Secondary emission may be obtained by electron bombardment of pure metals... In this case a part of the energy of the bombarding or primary electron is transferred to one or several conduction electrons of the solid. **1973** SMITH & JACOBS *Introd. Astron. & Astrophysics* xviii. 459 The fact that positrons..are only one-tenth as numerous indicates that these electrons are primary particles, and not secondaries like the light nuclei. This conclusion is based on the fact that more positrons than electrons are produced when primary cosmic rays collide with interstellar atoms.

l. *primary poverty*, lack of means to buy the basic necessities of life.

1901 B. S. ROWNTREE *Poverty* p. viii, Families whose total earnings are insufficient to obtain the minimum necessaries... Poverty falling under this head I have described as 'primary' poverty. **1909** M. F. DAVIES *Life in Eng. Village* II. xii. 140 An estimate has been made of the minimum cost at which food, fuel, dress, household sundries, and house-room..can be obtained..and it has then been seen how many families were below this standard, or in primary poverty. **1936** R. C. K. ENSOR *England 1870–1914* xiv. 515 The number of people found by Rowntree in 'primary' poverty in 1901 was 15·46 per cent. of the wage-earning class in York. **1960** *Guardian* 25 Feb. 3/6 Primary poverty was uncommon..although 130 fathers were out of work. **1964** M. LASKI in S. Nowell-Smith *Edwardian England* iv. 173 Primary poverty, that is to say,..conditions where the family income..is insufficient to maintain health and working efficiency.

m. *primary succession* (Ecol.) = *PRISERE.

1905 F. E. CLEMENTS *Res. Methods Ecol.* iv. 241 Primary successions..arise on newly formed soils, or upon surfaces exposed for the first time, which have in consequence never borne vegetation before. **1932** FULLER & CONARD tr. *Braun-Blanquet's Plant Sociol.* xiii. 235 The Anglo-American school distinguishes between primary successions or sequences of communities which originate independently of men and secondary successions. **1952** P. W. RICHARDS *Trop. Rain Forest* xii. 269 The successions or seres leading to the establishment of stable climax Rain forest are classified..into primary successions or priseres starting on soil not previously occupied by plants ..and secondary successions or subseres. **1961** HANSON & CHURCHILL *Plant Community* v. 151 (*caption*) Primary succession on sand and gravel. **1973** P. A. COLINVAUX *Introd. Ecol.* vi. 77 The successions so far discussed are all primary successions, that is to say they are supposed to proceed by pioneering new sites.

n. *primary industry, production*, the husbandry or use of raw materials, as in agriculture, forestry, fishing, mining, etc.; *primary produce, products*, the fruits of these activities; *primary producer*, one engaged in such industries; *primary-producing* adj., that produces or is the source of raw materials.

1930 *Economist* 8 Feb. 290/1 Our exporting manufacturers will be faced with lessened purchasing power in the hands of primary producers overseas. **1935** *Ibid.* 12 Jan. 57/2 Our own index of the dollar prices of primary products shows a rise of fully 20 per cent. **1941** BAKER *N.Z. Slang* v. 38 We were gaining [1880–1900] a footing in world markets for our primary produce. *Ibid.* vii. 60 [The] social and economic existence [of Australia and New Zealand] is largely dependent upon primary production—upon the soil. **1950** *N.Z. Jrnl. Agric.* Jan. 3/1 The basis of New Zealand's economic standards is the country's primary industries. There has been an inclination to overlook the fact that in the economic structure of New Zealand agriculture must always be the cornerstone. *Ibid.* Aug. 99/1 It has been a particularly interesting experience to attend in my capacity as Minister of Agriculture..and to see in action the machinery of the several bodies that administer the interests of different sections of primary producers. **1956** T. BALOGH in A. Pryce-Jones *New Outl. Mod. Knowl.* IV. 506 Political influence in primary-producing countries was secured by concluding bulk-buying agreements. **1959** A. H. MCLINTOCK *Descr. Atlas N.Z.* 44 In common with other exporters of primary products, New Zealand representatives have, at international conferences, drawn attention to the serious effects produced by protective barriers established at unrealistically high levels. **1965** S. T. OLLIVIER *Petticoat Farm* xi. 160 The primary produce from New Zealand went to feed other countries. **1966** G. W. TURNER *Eng. Lang. Austral. & N.Z.* iv. 85 In both Australia and New Zealand, a land naturally infertile by English standards has been made to yield products which have made the term 'primary industry' synonymous with farming, by the application of scientific agriculture. **1974** M. B. BROWN *Econ. of Imperialism* iv. 94 The extraction by the United States and by other developed countries of minerals and primary products from the whole world would not be regarded by classical economists as any sort of plunder. **1974** *Globe & Mail* (Toronto) 12 Oct. 8/3, 37 per cent of Quebec's labor force is employed in primary industry (mining, forestry, etc.) and manufacturing. **1975** *Listener* 11 Sept. 322/3 Indexing of the export prices of primary-producing countries against the rise in prices of the goods *they* need to import. **1976** *Oxford Times* 12 Mar. 11/1 The role of a University Department of Agricultural Science is..to provide graduates who can..become leaders in the field of primary production. **1977** *Herald* (Melbourne) 18 Jan. 4/1 On the talks so far, the Primary Industry Minister, Mr. Sinclair, probably sums up best by saying that he is 'relatively happy'.

o. *primary air*, air admitted to the fuel in a furnace or burner at or before the earliest stage in its burning.

1931 *Engineering* 9 Jan. 39/3 The primary air and coal enter at the side of the burner through a long, narrow port. **1932** *Discovery* Aug. 248/1 The 'primary air' or 'bottom air' entering from beneath the fuel bed..meets the incandescent coke, and immediately the oxygen disappears and is converted into carbon dioxide. **1971** E. R. Norster *Combustion & Heat Transfer in Gas Turbine Syst.* 91 The earlier Python engine had a 'vaporizing' tubular-type chamber, the fuel being pre-mixed with some primary air before being fed tangentially into a swirl chamber.

p. *primary constriction* (Cytology), a chromosomal constriction associated with the centromere.

1932 C. D. Darlington *Rec. Adv. Cytol.* 495 *Primary* or *attachment constriction*, that always associated with the spindle attachment. **1937** *Ibid.* (ed. 2) 575 *Primary* or *centric constriction*, that always associated with the centromere. **1957** C. P. Swanson *Cytol. & Cytogenetics* v. 112 The localized centromere produces the primary constriction. **1969** Brown & Bertke *Textbk. Cytol.* xviii. 344/1 This 'constriction' associated with the centromere is often loosely called the centromere, or kinetochore, but more exactly it is the primary constriction.

q. *Ecol.* Forming part of the lowest trophic level in a community, either as a producer or as a consumer that feeds on a producer; of or pertaining to a producer.

[**1893** W. K. Brooks in *Mem. Biol. Lab. Johns Hopkins Univ.* II. 148 A few forms are so predominant that..we may regard the great primary food-supply as made up of two simple protozoa, Globigerina and the Radiolarians, and some five or six unicellular plants.] **1934** *Q. Rev. Biol.* IX. 163/1 In connection with..his phrase ('primary food supply') which I have undertaken to use, Brooks gives..a meaning somewhat more comprehensive than that which I prefer... It suits my purpose better to confine the usage to the microscopic plants equipped with chlorophyll and capable of manufacturing carbohydrates from raw materials. **1940** *Ibid.* XV. 48/2 The various primary animals (phytophages) of a formation are often independent of each other. **1953** E. P. Odum *Fund. Ecol.* iv. 82 In speaking of productivity, it is important to distinguish between the basic or primary productivity..and consumer or secondary productivity. **1956** *Limnology & Oceanogr.* I. 116/1 The diagram shows how some streams may be fertile in having high total respiratory metabolism and yet possess little primary productivity. **1969** B. K. Sladen in Sladen & Bang *Biol. of Populations* vii. 92 The knapweed plants were the producers, and nine animal species were primary consumers eating the knapweed plant. *Ibid.* 93 The productivity of the producers, the photosynthetic plants, must be greater than that of the primary consumers. **1971** M. Alexander *Microbial Ecol.* xvi. 410 Aquatic algae are typically primary organisms in that their energy is obtained from sunlight. **1976** S. B. Chapman in *Methods in Plant Ecol.* iv. 161 Primary production is the production of organic matter by photosynthesis. *Ibid.*, Gross primary production, the total amount of organic matter produced (including that lost in respiration) over a given period of time. *Ibid.*, Net primary production, the amount of organic matter incorporated by a plant or an area of vegetation (gross primary production minus the loss due to respiration) over a given period of time.

r. *Psychol.* Relating to abilities or traits which, through factor analysis, appear basic to other aspects of intelligence or personality.

1938 L. L. Thurstone *Primary Mental Abilities* p. vi, These subsequent studies have had the advantage of some orientation about the first seven primary factors as landmarks... It is probably better to find the principal landmarks in the cognitive and conative primary traits by means of group procedures. *Ibid.* vi. 92 The tests will be improved by making them relatively pure measures of the primary abilities. **1958** K. Lovell *Educ. Psychol. & Children* iii. 58 Thurstone has termed these primary mental abilities and claims that they are found both in very young children and in adults. **1965** R. B. Cattell *Sci. Analysis of Personality* iii. 60 Several 'primary abilities' were also involved, such as numerical, spatial, verbal, and logical abilities. **1969** H. J. & S. B. Eysenck *Personality Struct. & Measurement* 328 We have seen that while primary factors emerge in considerable profusion, these seldom if ever agree precisely with those postulated by Cattell and Guilford. **1970** L. J. Bischof *Interpreting Personality Theories* (ed. 2) vi. xii. 464 In his current work, Cattell calls the source traits Primary Personality Factors. With few exceptions, the Primary Personality Factors are bipolar or dichotomized. **1972** *Jrnl. Social Psychol.* LXXXVI. 187 Disputes about the number and nature of primary personality factors in questionnaire data are still rife.

s. *primary structure* (Aeronaut.), those parts of an aircraft whose failure would seriously endanger safety.

1939 *Aircraft Engin.* Feb. 66/1 The primary structure of the main plane is erected in a wall jig. **1959** F. D. Adams *Aeronaut. Dict.* 132/1 Elements not a part of the primary structure include cowlings, fairings, windshields, etc. **1964** J. E. D. Williams *Operation of Airliners* ix. 133 To ensure that throughout the operational life of the aircraft the possibility of disastrous fatigue failure is remote, the primary structure must either have an extremely long probable life or be designed to fail safely.

t. Of radar: transmitting radiation for targets to reflect, not requiring any generation of signals by targets.

1945 R. Watson-Watt in *Nature* 15 Sept. 323/2 Primary radar is that form of radar which 'does not require the co-operation of the object to be located'. **1960** T. J. Morgan *Radar* xii. 137 The measurement of the wind direction and velocity was carried out by means of direction finding stations, then later by primary radar. **1963** R. S. H. Boulding *Princ. & Pract. Radar* (ed. 7) xxii. 470 In secondary radar as distinct from normal (or primary) radar, the target plays an active part in the operation of ranging and position finding.

u. *primary stress*, the principal stress in a word (see Stress *sb.* 8). Also *attrib.* So *primary-stressed* adj., (of a word or syllable) carrying a primary stress.

1951 Trager & Smith *Outl. Eng. Struct.* i. 36 There must be a stress phoneme whose characteristic is maximum normal loudness, which we may call *primary stress.* **1964** G. L. Trager in D. Abercrombie et al. *Daniel Jones* 267 When a clause begins with the primary-stressed syllabic, there are only two pitches. **1968** Chomsky & Halle *Sound Pattern Eng.* 34 We note that primary stress falls on the prefix if the stem is monosyllabic. *Ibid.* 114 The other..vowels..have never received primary stress at any stage of their derivation. **1971** *Eng. Stud.* LII. 349 From recorded readings we know that the unnatural stress-patterns which result can be emended by a prolongation of the first of two primary-stressed syllables. **1972** *Language* XLVIII. 328 In simple declarative sentences ending in a predicate, primary stress is often most naturally placed on the subject. *Ibid.* 331 Surface structure alone is insufficient to determine primary-stress placement.

v. *primary structure* (Biochem.), the sequence of amino-acids forming the chain structure of a protein or polypeptide, as opposed to the three-dimensional configuration and arrangement of the chains.

1952 K. U. Linderstrøm-Lang *Proteins & Enzymes* 58 The presence of intrahelix as well as interhelix bonds may justify a classification into secondary (intrahelix) and tertiary (interhelix) structures, as distinct from the primary structure of the simple β-chain. **1964** G. H. Haggis et al. *Introd. Molecular Biol.* iii. 48 The peptide chains coil up, and fold back on themselves, to form a complex three-dimensional molecular structure, and..the determination of sequence, or primary structure, is only the beginning of a description of the protein molecule. **1970** R. W. McGilvery *Biochem.* viii. 150 Any disruption of protein structure that does not involve the primary structure ought to be self-healing once the cause of the disruption is removed. **1974** *Nature* 29 Nov. 351/2 Let us now discuss the effect of natural selection on secondary or tertiary structure, as natural selection acts through these higher order structures and not on primary structure.

B. *sb.* **4.** (Further examples.)

1967 E. Short *Embroidery & Fabric Collage* i. 14 If the three primaries are placed on a white background the reverse will happen. **1972** *House & Garden* Feb. 70/2 The most successful rooms are those using vivid primaries. **1979** *Guardian* 13 June 12/5 Cellular cotton shirts come in all pastels and primaries.

5. (Earlier and later examples.) Also, a primary circuit, current, etc.

1837 M. Faraday in *Ann. Electr., Magn., & Chem.* I. 200 The renitency encountered in the conductors will necessarily exercise a due influence in lessening the force of secondary currents, but cannot be made available as a cause of the comparative atony which these currents, by the initial impulses of the primary, invariably display. **1896** F. Bedell *Princ. Transformer* i. 2 The alternating current transformer..consists simply of two independent circuits, a primary and a secondary, wound independently upon a common core of laminated soft iron. **1931** B. Brown *Talking Pictures* iii. 36 Modulation of the voltage is accomplished through a transformer, the primary of which is supplied with the speech recording current coming from the microphone, via the amplifiers. **1938** Kerchner & Corcoran *Alternating-Current Circuits* vii. 182 Circuit 1, energized by means of an alternating potential difference, is called the primary. **1967** M. F. Buchan *Electr. Supply* vi. 156 Consider now what happens if the secondaries are connected in delta, whilst the primaries are star-connected to a 3-wire supply.

6. (Earlier and later examples.) Add to def.: now usu. = *primary election*, one at which candidates for political office in the U.S.A. are chosen.

a **1861** T. Winthrop *Life in Open Air* (1863) 147 'Boys,' said he,..'when I accepted the office of Orator of the Day at our primary and promised to bring forward our resolutions in honor of Mr. Wade.' **1868** *All Year Round* 19 Sept. 351/2 He is 'powerful' in 'primaries', where he votes early and often for his favourite candidates. **1900** B. C. Clark in *Mod. Eloquence* X. p. xvii, Those of you who remember as I do the times that tried men's souls will not, I hope, forget their humble servant when the primaries shall be held. **1908** *Contemp. Rev.* Apr. 404 Other Western States have passed similar laws for direct primaries. **1930** *Economist* 7 June 1267/1 They have nominated Mr. Franklin Fort, a 'dry' Congressman, as his opponent in the Republican 'primaries'. **1966** *Listener* 25 Aug. 289/3 He could be freed from this bondage either by a system of primaries in which the field of choice were extended to others beyond the narrow range of committed party workers or through the introduction of the alternative vote. **1967** *Boston Herald* 1 Apr. 1/1 George C. Wallace, Jr., said Friday that he was thinking of entering the New Hampshire presidential preferential primary next March 12. **1976** *Times* 26 Feb. 15/2 Sitting Presidents need to do far more than escape disaster in the primaries, which are popularity contests among their own party's voters.

8. *Physics* and *Astr.* A primary ray or particle, esp. a primary cosmic ray.

1923 *Physical Rev.* XXII. 243 The emission is comprised in part of electrons whose speeds are not appreciably less than that of the primaries. **1932** *Ibid.* XLI. 545 The average number of secondaries per primary is about 100 in iron and 230 in lead. **1942** J. D. Stranathan *'Particles' of Mod. Physics* xii. 488 Many of the primaries and many of the large number of secondaries formed high in the atmosphere are unable to penetrate the entire atmosphere. **1956** *Spaceflight* Oct. 27/1 The charged cosmic ray primaries..consist of approximately 80 per cent. protons, 18 or 19 per cent. alpha particles, and the remainder heavier nuclei. **1959** K. Henney *Radio Engin. Handbk.* (ed. 5) vii. 15 If all the energy brought into the body by the bombarding primary could be transformed into the energy required for the emission of secondary electrons, the ratio δ would be very high. **1974** *Encycl. Brit. Macropædia* V. 203/1 The discovery in meteoritic crystals of particle tracks produced by primaries heavier than iron.

9. *Gram.* In Jespersen's terminology, a word or group of words (normally a noun or a noun-phrase) of primary importance in a phrase or sentence. Cf. *Adjunct *sb.* 5b, *Subjunct.

1924 O. Jespersen *Philos. Gram.* vii. 97 We may, of course, have two or more coordinate adjuncts to the same primary: thus, in *a nice young lady*, the words *a*, *nice*, and *young* equally define *lady.* **1928** —— *Internat. Lang.* II. 97 When adjectives are made into primaries, we have the endings already considered. **1928** *Mod. Lang. Rev.* XXIII. 143 After a chapter on clauses as 'primaries', about 150 pages are devoted to a thorough survey of relative clauses. **1935** [see **noun-equivalent*]. **1940** *Eng. Stud.* XXII. 88 *Primary, secondary* and *tertiary*, intended to connote.. *headwords, attributes* and *adjuncts*, the terms representing their relative importance or ranks within the sentence, headwords coming first. **1959** M. Schlauch *Eng. Lang. in Mod. Times* viii. 221 In this system [of Otto Jespersen's] a leading term, for instance a noun subject, is a primary.

primate, *sb.*[1] Add: **4.** (Usually with pronunciation prəi·mēɪt.) Substitute for def.: A mammal belonging to the order Primates, which includes man, apes, monkeys, and several groups of prosimians. Also *attrib.* (Examples.)

1898, 1899 [see Primates *sb. pl.*]. **1906** E. Ingersoll *Life of Animals* 7 The higher the Primate in the scale of organization the more perfectly are its fore limbs and hands adapted to seizing and handling objects. **1929** R. M. & A. W. Yerkes *Great Apes* i. 2/1 No infrahuman primate, least of all the great ape, has been thoroughly domesticated. **1967** J. R. & P. H. Napier *Handbk. Living Primates* p. v, Animal behaviour, ecology and genetic biology..today dominate basic research trends in primate biology. **1977** Rainier III & Bourne *Primate Conservation* p. xviii, All authors of this book agreed that the royalties earned should be used to further primate conservation.

primatology (prəimătǫ·lǒdʒi). [f. Primate *sb.*[1] 4 + -ology.] The study of primates.

1941 J. F. Fulton in T. C. Ruch *Bibliographia Primatologica* I. p. xi, Dr. Ruch has followed Linnaeus in adopting the term 'primate', and in the title of his bibliography he has introduced a new and useful derivative 'Primatology'. **1942** Ruch & Fulton in *Science* 9 Jan. 47/1 It is only within the past decade or two that the study of the primates as a distinct zoological group has come into sufficient stature to warrant separate designation—'primate biology' or if you will, 'primatology'. **1956** *Nature* 17 Mar. 505/2 Duckworth had very wide interests in anatomy, teratology, primatology, anthropology, archaeology and general natural history. **1967** *Guardian* 20 Oct. 6/3 With the growth of primatology we are increasingly aware how unusual are man's problems in dealing with his fellows. **1973** *Sci. Amer.* Jan. 11/1 Geza Teleki ('The Omnivorous Chimpanzee') is completing work for his Ph.D. in primatology at the University of Georgia. **1976** *Primate Eye* VII. 1 In this issue of Primate Eye, we are including a number of reviews of books in the field of primatology.

Hence **primatolo·gical** *a.*, of or pertaining to primatology; **primato·logist**, one who studies primates.

1945 M. F. A. Montagu *Introd. Physical Anthropol.* ii. 11 Dead primates enable the primatologist to make detailed studies of their anatomy. **1949** *Antiquity* XXIII. 126 One of the few technical treatises on man's embryology that is anthropological and primatological in its orientation. **1957** L. Eiseley *Immense Journey* 105 Primatologists may therefore be forgiven their fumblings over great gaps of millions of years from which we do not possess a single complete monkey skeleton. **1973** *Nature* 18 May 175/2 A general section on the radiation of the placental mammals, placing primate evolution in its proper perspective—a perspective which is far too readily forgotten in many modern primatological studies. **1977** *Ibid.* 20 Oct. 654/3 He launched an attack on primatologists..for the way they have generally discussed the adaptive significance of social behaviour.

primavera. (Later example.)

1953 R. Chandler *Long Good-Bye* xv. 95 The table of polished primavera.

prima vista. 2. (Examples.)

1845 [see Transpose *v.* 7]. **1974** *Listener* 14 Feb. 218/2 The London Symphony Orchestra..is still full of excellent players who can read almost everything *prima vista.*

prime, *sb.*² Add: **I. 1. b.** *Linguistics.* A simple, indivisible linguistic unit.

1959 F. W. HOUSEHOLDER in *Word* XV. 231 (*title*) On linguistic primes. **1961** —— in Saporta & Bastian *Psycholinguistics* 19/1 We must recognize at least two kinds of linguistic units: (1) *ultimate units*, or *primes*, out of which other more complex units may be constructed. **1963** J. LYONS *Structural Semantics* ii. 11 The lexeme is a formal unit of grammatical analysis, established distributionally. It may or may not be a 'prime',..though it frequently is for Greek. **1964** E. BACH *Introd. Transformational Gram.* v. 58 Each *level* of a linguistic theory comprises..a set of *primes* (i.e., atoms or indivisible elements). **1965** N. CHOMSKY *Aspects of Theory of Syntax* 222 Each level *L* is a system based on a set of primes (minimal elements—i.e. an alphabet). **1975** —— *Logical Struct. Linguistic Theory* iii. 105 If *a* and *b* are (not necessarily distinct) primes of L, we can form a⌢b and b⌢a as new elements of L.

2. d. (Further examples.)

1917 D. W. PAYNE *Founder's Man.* p. xi, The prime mark ′ above a number means minutes or linear feet. **1964** *Amer. Jrnl. Physics* XXXII. 264/2 The prime (′) here indicates ordinary differentiation of a function of a single variable. **1973** A. H. SOMMERSTEIN *Sound Pattern Anc. Greek* iii. 91 A Roman numeral followed by a prime indicates that the convention in question is intended to *replace* the Chomsky-Halle convention of the same number. **1976** *Physics Bull.* May 191/2 We would like to draw the attention of readers to the equation $(B_0)_t = B_0 - D'M$ (our prime) appearing in the last column.

5*. Colloq. abbrev. of PRIME MINISTER (sense 3). Cf. PRIME *sb.*¹ 10.

1916 A. HUXLEY *Let.* May (1969) 99 The Prime received suddenly one morning a letter..'Dear Mr. A[squith]'. **1924** GALSWORTHY *White Monkey* I. ii. 14 Didn't he think that the cubic called 'Still Life'—of the Government, too frightfully funny—especially the 'old bean' representing the Prime?

5.** *Cycling.* An especially difficult stage in a long-distance cycle race.

1959 *Observer* 31 May 32/4 Weatherlaw was the first 'prime'—a specially marked stretch of hilly road which gives the first three men to the summit a bonus of money and time. **1961** *Times* 7 June 5/6 Pewter tankards being offered as prizes at the town primes along the route. **1975** *Oxf. Compan. Sports & Games* 235/1 On mountainous stretches certain summits are designated as *primes*.

5*.** Short for **prime rate*.

1973 *Business Week* 10 Feb. 19 The all-out struggle over the prime. **1977** *Offshore Engineer* July 19/3 Citibank's current prime is 6¾%. **1978** *Daily Tel.* 25 Nov. 19/2 At 11·5 p.c., the prime now stands at its highest level since October 1974.

prime, *a.* Add: **3. b.** *Broadcasting.* Pertaining to or associated with the largest audience of the day. See also *PRIME-TIME 3.

1959 *Times Lit. Suppl.* 6 Nov. p. xxxi/5 John Fischer, the editor of *Harpers*,..asks for an autonomous authority empowered to produce programmes of exceptional merit, financed by a levy on the income of the broadcasters, who will also be under an obligation to transmit these programmes in the cherished prime-viewing hours. **1961** WEBSTER s.v., Prime television time. **1976** *Broadcast* Dec. 15/3 We have to go through the routine again slap in the middle of prime listening time on a Saturday morning. **1977** *Times* 7 Dec. 19/1 It is seldom that anyone gets handed such a quantity of prime television time to do what he likes with.

4. a. *prime rib*, best rib of beef, i.e. one of the first two ribs in the forequarter. Also *attrib.*

1960 E. DAVID *French Provincial Cooking* 335 To satisfy customers, butchers bone, trim and tie up secondary cuts of meat..and sell them at a small amount less than, say, sirloin or prime ribs. **1973** D. BARNES *See the Woman* (1974) II. 195 I'll buy us a prime-rib dinner. **1973** *Listener* 19 Apr. 501/1 A landscape of luscious rib roasts, lamb chops, shell steaks, T-bone steaks, sirloin steaks, fillet mignon, prime ribs, veal piccata and so on. **1978** *Chicago Tribune Mag.* 2 Oct. 8/2 The 25-cent hot beef special is now a $2.75 prime rib sandwich, served with salad and potato.

b. *spec.* used of land, the position of real estate, etc.

1634 [in Dict.]. **1850** *Househ. Words* 3 Aug. 433/1 Sir Roger Rockville..was the last of a very long line... His first known ancestor came over with William, and must have been a man of some mark,..for he obtained what the Americans would call a prime location. **1961** J. D. ADAMS in *Webster* s.v., Prime farming land. **1976** *Western Mail* (Cardiff) 27 Nov. 17/2 (Advt.), A charming detached Freehold four-bedroom residence built in 1935,..in a prime residential area. **1977** *Grimsby Even. Tel.* 24 May 4/9 (Advt.), A thriving newsagents, tobacconist, sweets and general business situated in a prime position in a growing village close to Grimsby. **1978** *Church Times* 1 Sept. 4/1 It may still occupy a prime site on a busy thoroughfare.

8*. *Astronautics.* Originally designated to take part or be used in a space mission, esp. in *prime crew*, the original person or persons selected to man a spacecraft.

1965 *Life* 3 Dec. 48 Pete Conrad, who spent a week in space, is the prime crew. **1970** N. ARMSTRONG et al. *First on Moon* iii. 63 At 4:30 A.M. the transfer vans arrived—one prime, one backup. **1970** R. TURNILL *Language of Space* 13 Every manned space flight, American or Russian, has a back-up crew, to replace the prime crew in the event of illness or death.

9. a. prime cost, the direct cost of something, not including discounts, expenses involved, etc.; **prime (interest, lending) rate**, the lowest rate of interest offered on bank loans at a given time and place.

1718 C. HITCHIN *Receivers & Thief-Takers* 11 For instance, suppose you steal Goods to the value of twenty Pounds prime Cost. **1732** R. JOHNSON *Let.* 6 Oct. in *Cal. State Papers, Amer. & W. Indies* (1939) 231, I have examined what dutys are payd in this Province on English European ships or goods, and there is only 2½ *p.c.* our currency upon the prime cost of goods from Europe in general. **1775** in *15th Rep. R. Comm. Hist. Manuscripts* App. VI. 297 in *Parl. Papers 1897* (C. 8551) LI. 1 Vessels have come from Hispaniola, and sold gunpowder to the Provincials at prime cost. **1890** A. MARSHALL *Princ. Econ.* I. VI. vi. 519 This is the Prime cost which a manufacturer has commonly in view when, trade being slack, he is calculating the lowest price at which it would be worth his while to accept an order. **1925** S. E. THOMAS *Elem. Econ.* xiii. 168 The excess is 'dumped' on foreign markets at a price just sufficient to cover prime cost, or even below prime cost. **1938** BOWERS & ROWNTREE *Econ. for Engineers* (ed. 2) xiii. 258 Prime costs, according to accounting procedure, are direct labor and materials expenses alone... Many economists, however, define prime costs as all *avoidable* costs, so that a plant shutdown would eliminate all prime costs. **1944** A. CAIRNCROSS *Introd. Econ.* xvi. 199 Normally, some surplus over prime or variable costs will be earned. **1953** STONIER & HAGUE *Textbk. Econ. Theory* v. 110 'Variable', 'prime' and 'direct' costs represent all those costs which can be altered in the short run as output alters. **1962** S. STRAND *Marketing Dict.* 573 *Prime cost*, the cost of a product involving labor and all the parts that go into making it. **1978** J. KELLOCK *Elements of Accounting* x. 175 The value of rejected materials or by-products will be credited to the cost of raw materials purchased or deleted from the prime cost. **1958** *Wall St. Jrnl.* 29 Dec. 8/3 The 'prime' rate was thus brought back to within a half percentage point of the 4½% rate which was in effect from August, 1957... The 'prime' rate is the interest banks charge their biggest borrowers with the best credit status. **1970** *Daily Tel.* 4 Mar. 19 Several reductions in 'prime lending rate' by small American banks, are not likely to lead to cuts by major American banks for at least a fortnight. **1972** *Bankers Mag.* (Boston, Mass.) Winter 45/1 Many bankers have turned critical on the concept of a prime rate. **1973** *N.Y. Law Jrnl.* 26 July 3/3 Better-quality construction loans with a takeout were being made at the beginning of the year at a spread of about three points over the prime rate. **1978** S. BRILL *Teamsters* vi. 252 Glick's Las Vegas loans were given at a time when he was far from being a candidate for a prime rate.

prime, *v.*¹ **4.** Delete *local* and add later examples. Also *fig.*

1930 *Engineering* 11 Apr. 473/1 Special arrangements for priming the pumps are not required, as the latter themselves exhaust all the air automatically during the first few revolutions, when the engine is being started on compressed air. **1973** L. RUSSELL *Everyday Life Colonial Canada* v. 64 The..shaft had a piston with a leather diaphragm, which had to be wetted ('primed') by pouring a little water into the pump. **1977** T. SHARPE *Gt. Pursuit* xiii. 124 Significance is all... Prime the pump with meaningful hogwash.

b. *Aeronaut.* To inject fuel into (the cylinders of an aircraft engine) to facilitate starting. Also *intr.*, or with the engine as *obj.*

1915 G. A. BURLS *Aero Engines* i. 20 L is a cock, or tap, communicating with the 'combustion chamber'..and may be used to 'prime' the chamber with a few drops of petrol. **1927** V. W. PAGÉ *Mod. Aircraft* (1928) xiv. 571 Prime engine by injecting a small quantity..of gasoline through each priming cock. **1931** M. M. FARLEIGH *Princ. & Probl. Aircraft Engines* x. 166 The cylinders should then be primed with fresh gasoline in the case of extreme sub-zero climatic conditions. **1939** *Aero Engines* II. 256 Do not prime excessively,..one stroke of the priming pump usually being found sufficient for a hot engine. **1941** A. W. JUDGE *Aircraft Engines* II. xi. 395 If the engine had been properly primed with mixture it was possible to start it by means of the starter magneto alone. **1977** D. BEATY *Excellency* vi. 80 He primed the engines, pressed the starter button, heard the propeller creak round.

c. *fig.* Cf. *PUMP PRIMING *vbl. sb.*

1959 *Conferences & Exhibitions* Mar. 23/2 The aim is to introduce a trade to a fair in which it has not exhibited before by 'priming the pump'. **1963** *Times* 26 Jan. 12/1 He was understandably slow to prime the pump when a quick success in the Brussels negotiations might have given enough extra, uncontrollable impetus to start an inflation.

7. *Biol.* and *Med.* To treat (an animal or tissue) so as to induce a desired susceptibility or proclivity.

1943 *Jrnl. Endocrinol.* III. 273 Excellent results were obtained with rabbits..primed by five daily injections of 2 mg. of AP61B or AP118B. *Ibid.*, Of eleven rabbits primed with five daily doses of 1 mg. only four accepted the buck. **1963** *Rec. Progress Hormone Res.* XIX. 674 In the latter effect, the body is in a true sense 'primed' for new biological activity. **1967** *Science* 17 Nov. 939/3 The 30 mice anesthetized with ether were exposed for 30 seconds to atmosphere containing 5 ml of ether per 1 liter of air; half of these were acoustically primed 10 seconds later. **1971** *Nature* 24 Dec. 456/1 In guinea-pigs primed with DNP-OA, injection of allogeneic lymphoid cells stimulates synthesis of antibodies to both hapten and carrier. **1975** *Jrnl. Compar. & Physiol. Psychol.* LXXXIX. 214/2 At 16 days postnatally, 18..mice were acoustically primed by a 30-sec exposure to the sound produced by an electric bell.

primed *ppl. a.*, (*b*) *Biol.* and *Med.*, rendered susceptible; prepared; (cf. sense 7 above).

1943 *Jrnl. Endocrinol.* III. 273 In considering the question of inducing superovulation from the primed ovary, the first question arising is whether the ovulation-producing act of mating is sufficient to cause ovulation in a greater than normal number of follicles. **1960** *Proc. Soc. Exper. Biol. & Med.* CIV. 589/2 The primed mechanism responds to the second stimulus of the protein, but the resulting antibody is apparently specific for certain particular loci on the protein surface. **1967** *Science* 17 Nov. 940/1 Biochemical examinations of primed and nonprimed mice may reveal whether differences in oxidative phosphorylation..are associated with changes in audiogenic seizure susceptibility. **1975** *Behavior Genetics* V. 328 In an attempt to determine the increase in susceptibility due exclusively to acoustic priming, the seizure severity scores from the nonprimed..mice of a concurrently run study..were subtracted from the severity scores of the primed, non-cross-fostered mice of the present study.

prime, *v.*³ Delete 'Now only *dial.*' and add: **2.** *U.S.* To pull off the lower leaves of tobacco plants.

1792 J. POPE *Tour S. & W. Terr. U.S.* 63 [The Creeks] scarcely ever weed, hill, prime, top or succour their Tobacco. **1963** H. GARNER *Best Stories* 167 Taking suckers first make [*sic*] it better to prime after. *Ibid.* 168, I thought of the rows upon rows still to be primed of sand leaves, the lowest leaves on the plant.

primed (praɪmd), *a.* [f. PRIME *sb.*² + -ED².] Having the symbol ′ as a superscript.

1927 *Proc. R. Soc.* A. CXIII. 630 We shall make it a rule always to use..primed or multiply primed letters such as ξ' and α'' to denote parameters, representing matrix rows and columns. **1944** C. PALACHE et al. *Dana's Syst. Min.* (ed. 7) I. 13 Projection values are primed, and polar values unprimed. **1968** *Amer. Jrnl. Physics* XXXVI. 1105/1 He obtained $F' = l^2(1, \gamma, \gamma)F$ and $a' = l(\gamma^3, \gamma^2, \gamma^2)a$, for the force and acceleration transformed to the instantaneous (primed) rest frame of the electron.

prime mo·ver. [f. PRIME *a.* (*adv.*) + MOVER¹.] **1.** (See MOVER¹ 3. Further examples.)

1972 *Science* 26 May 892/3 Jamie L. Whitten,..a prime mover in the passage 18 years ago of Public Law 566. **1973** *Amer. Speech 1969* XLIV. 293 Concerning the origin of the jargon, Adams..relies on the theories of his informants... Their views focus on the probable ages of the originators: teenagers or adults or an intermediate group of 'prime movers'. **1973** *Nature* 17 Aug. 467/1 Both of them have been prime movers, in the period of forty years covered, in securing the establishment of ethology as a separate, respectable and inevitable branch of animal biology. **1977** *Jrnl. R. Soc. Arts* CXXVI. 40/2 Maria Grey, 'prime mover' of this enterprise, would have been the first to wish to have associated with her the men and women who helped in the work.

2. (See MOVER¹ 2 b. Further examples.)

1967 R. WHITEHEAD in Wills & Yearsley *Handbk. Managem. Technol.* iv. 55 Up to almost the present time engineering has been concerned with the study of prime movers—heat converted into usable energy. **1971** *Sci. Amer.* Sept. 37/3 By the 16th century the waterwheel was by far the most important prime mover. *Ibid.* 152/3 The piston engines in the nation's more than 100 million motor vehicles have a rated capacity in excess of 17 billion horsepower, or more than 95 percent of the capacity of all prime movers (defined as engines for converting fuel to mechanical energy). **1974** *Petroleum Rev.* XXVIII. 783/2 Primary production equipment, comprising gas/oil separators and forwarding pumps with gas turbine prime movers.

3. A towing vehicle; *spec.* (see quot. 1963).

1938 T. J. HAYES *Elem. Ordnance* xix. 677 Artillery prime movers are used to tow artillery. **1945** *Finito! Po Valley Campaign* (15th Army Group) 51 A German convoy of two 170 mm cannon pulled by prime movers. **1962** *Exhib. Brit. Military Vehicles* 128 This vehicle is a development of the tractor 30 ton 6×4 G.S...for semi-trailer F.V. 12002 which it will replace in the service as prime mover for the 50 and 60-ton semi-trailer tank transporters. **1963** *Dict. U.S. Mil. Terms* (U.S. Dept. Defense) 171 *Prime mover*, a vehicle, including heavy construction equipment, possessing military characteristics, designed primarily for towing heavy, wheeled weapons and frequently providing facilities for the transportation of the crew of, and ammunition for, the weapon. **1969** *Age* (Melbourne) 24 May 61/9 (Advt.), Commer semi trailer outfit complete, 61 mod., petrol motor, prime mover and 34 ft. semi trailer... $2000. **1976** *Daily Times* (Lagos) 22 Sept. 15/1 Those above eight tonnes but not articulated prime movers i.e. with trailers now cost ₦35. **1977** 'D. RUTHERFORD' *Return Load* ii. 28 He had..invested a legacy..in a Leyland prime mover... Like most owner-drivers he made a practice of hiring the semi-trailers which, when hitched to the tractor, made up the complete articulated vehicle.

primer, *sb.*¹ Add: **2. d.** *N.Z.* (With pronunc. pri·məɪ.) One of the primer classes, covering the first years of instruction in a primary school; also, a child in a primer class.

1928 *Syllabus of Instruction for Primary Schools* (N.Z. Dept. Educ.) 55 In all schools teachers of Primer classes will use 'Physical Exercises and Games for Infants'. *Ibid.*, Where there are three teachers: Primers do infant work; Squad I, Tables 1–36; [etc.]. **1947** 'A. P. GASKELL' *Big Game* 92 There was Micky, her [*sc.* the teacher's] smallest primer, a little wizened creature with sad eyes. **1957** J. FRAME *Owls do Cry* xxviii. 125 He is in primer three at school. **1963** N. HILLIARD *Piece of Land* 191 It seemed no time since he'd been in the primers. **1963** B. PEARSON *Coal Flat* i. 8 She had taught in the primers of his school when he was in Standard six.

primer, *sb.*² Add: **2. b.** *Biochem.* A molecule that serves as a starting material for a polymerization (see quot. 1976). Freq. *attrib.*

1954 CANTAROW & SCHEPARTZ *Biochem.* xvii. 391 A 'primer' of branched polysaccharide, the main linkages of which are α-1,4, is essential for the action of animal phosphorylase. **1963** *Proc. Nat. Acad. Sci.* XLIX. 533 (*heading*) Formation of DNA-RNA hybrids with single-stranded DNA as primer. **1965** M. W. Neil *Vertebr. Biochem.* (ed. 2) xii. 182 Polysaccharide synthesis involving the addition of uridine diphosphate-bound units to a primer chain is widespread in nature, and is the mechanism whereby such macromolecules as cellulose, chitin, starch and the mucopolysaccharides, in addition to glycogen, are elaborated. **1976** Conn & Stumpf *Outl. Biochem.* (ed. 4) xviii. 507 Primer, in biochemistry, refers to the initial terminus of a molecule onto which additional units are added to produce the final product. **1977** D. E. Metzler *Biochem.* xv. 903/2 The enzyme displays many of the properties expected of a DNA-synthesizing enzyme. It requires a template strand of DNA as well as a shorter primer strand.

c. *Physiol.* (See quots. 1963, 1975.) Freq. *attrib.*

1963 Wilson & Bossert in *Recent Progress Hormone Res.* XIX. 674 We propose to distinguish the releaser effect, involving the classical stimulus-response mediated wholly by the central nervous system, from the primer effect, in which the endocrine and reproductive..systems are altered physiologically. *Ibid.* (*caption*) The pherome may be the primary stimulus causing a quick behavioral response (releaser effect), or it may act more slowly and indirectly by altering the physiology and 'priming' the animal for a different behavioral repertory (primer effect). **1971** *Nature* 16 Apr. 432/2 Pheromonal primer effects are near-universal in social mammals, including primates. **1975** *Ibid.* 20 Nov. 194/2 The action of pheromones is commonly divided into two classes..: chemical 'releasers' of specific acts of behaviour, and 'primers' which seem to act initially on the endocrine system.

3. Delete † *Obs.* and add later examples.

1937 *Times* 13 Apr. (Brit. Motor Suppl.) p. xiii/1 Before colour can be applied the body undergoes a number of preparatory stages, being thoroughly washed down with an acid cleaner and afterwards with hot and cold water, and dried off in preparation for the first coat of primer. **1958** *Listener* 14 Aug. 251/2 If the patches are touched in with primer and undercoat you will not run into any trouble. **1969** W. R. R. Park *Plastics Film Technol.* vi. 156 An effective primer works better with a thick coating. **1976** *Southern Even. Echo* (Southampton) 11 Nov. 8/3 These were then given a 'primer' coat of lime plaster—almost like white-wash—and the geometrical designs painted on.

5. *Aeronaut.* = *priming pump* s.v. *priming *vbl. sb.*[1] 8.

1923 *Gloss. Aeronaut. Terms* (Brit. Engin. Standards Assoc.) 48 *Engine primer*, a device for supplying fuel to the induction pipe or combustion chambers to facilitate starting. **1932** Chatfield & Taylor *Airplane & Engine* (ed. 2) x. 225 In automobiles this temporary excess of fuel for starting is supplied by means of the choke but for airplane engines a primer is usually used. **1939** *Aero Engines* II. 256 Always turn off the primer after use.

prime-time. Restrict † *Obs.* to senses in Dict. and add: **3.** *Broadcasting.* (Except in *attrib.* use usu. as **prime time.**) The time of day when an audience is expected to be at its largest; a peak listening- or viewing-period. Also *attrib.* and *absol.*, prime-time television. Also *transf.*

1964 *Variety* 2 Dec. 31/3 For the first time in years, WNBC-TV has copped the number one rating position in prime time, in the highly competitive N.Y. market. **1966** [see E.S.T. s.v. *E. III]. **1971** *Daily Tel.* 13 Feb. 15/7 A 2p coin will buy three minutes time for local calls in prime time and six minutes at night and weekends. *Ibid.* 17 Apr. 19/3 The average [commercial local radio] station should aim to sell some 17,500 minutes of prime time in an average year at an average rate of £10 per minute. **1973** R. Stout *Please pass Guilt* (1974) xiv. 143 That ad would have made a wonderful five-minute spot... She would have been glad to pay for prime time—say ten o'clock. **1976** *Billings* (Montana) *Gaz.* 18 June 12-D Jaclyn Smith is one of the gals who's huckstered in TV commercials a committee studied along with prime-time programs to determine the image given women on the small screen. **1977** *New Yorker* 10 Oct. 124/2 The Grand Central Racquet Club..charges the highest fee I know of for renting either of its two courts—forty-five dollars an hour in prime time. **1978** G. Vidal *Kalki* vii. 179 Wasn't Kalki blown to bits before our very eyes on prime-time?

primeur. Add: **a.** (Later examples.) **b.** New wine.

1913 E. Wharton *Custom of Country* II. xii. 172 A bill burdened by Undine's reckless choice of *primeurs*. **1924** R. Fry *Let.* 2 July (1972) II. 555 They raise three crops a year of *primeurs*. **1937** W. Fortescue *Sunset House* vi. 118 She prides herself upon her *primeurs*, being a scientific gardener. **1950** *Vogue* Aug. 100/4 Intellectuals..spend a lot on:..Exotic food (but not *primeurs*). **1968** A. & G. Sainsbury *France & her People* i. 19 In Brittany are places..with a mild climate which has made them famous for the production of *primeurs*, the early fruit and vegetables. **1973** *Times* 15 Dec. 11/3 A wine can be called 'Primeur' if it is offered for drinking before the date when the wines made in the normal way and bearing a vintage date are put on the market. **1975** *Harpers & Queen* May 34/2 Beaujolais is the success of the century,..even the new *primeur*..now brought over to be tasted at two months old. **1978** *Chicago* June 206/2 The Wassermans discuss the continuing tendency to produce Rhône reds—wines to be aged for as long as 30 years—in the *primeur* fashion.

primevalness. (Example.)

1971 D. Crystal *Linguistics* ii. 49 What evidence there was about language-history..militated against acceptance of even the most basic assumptions used in the arguments about primevalness.

primidone (prai·midōun). *Pharm.* [f. *p(y)rimid(ine + *-di)one.] A white, crystalline pyrimidine derivative, $C_{12}H_{14}N_2O_2$, which is an anticonvulsant used esp. to treat *grand mal* and psychomotor epilepsy. Cf. *Mysoline.

1953 *Brit. Med. Jrnl.* 5 Sept. 540/1 The introduction of primidone ('mysoline'; 5-phenyl-5-ethylhexahydropyrimidine-4:6-dione) as an anticonvulsant drug some two years ago. **1958** [see *Mysoline]. **1961** *Lancet* 9 Sept. 569/1 He was treated with primidone..and benzhexol hydrochloride..with striking reduction in the frequency of the seizures. *Ibid.* 569/2 He was discharged on primidone therapy. **1974** M. C. Gerald *Pharmacol.* xi. 214 Among the safest and most effective drugs are..primidone (Mysoline) and diphenylhydantoin for psychomotor seizures.

priming, *vbl. sb.*[1] Add: **7*.** In the sense of Prime *v.*[1] 4 (in Dict. and Suppl.). Cf. *pump priming *vbl. sb.*

1888 *Lockwood's Dict. Mech. Engin.* 266 *Priming*,.. (2) the priming of a force pump is the expulsion of the air from the water space, in order that the water shall enter into the partial vacuum thus produced... (3) The fetching of a lift pump by pouring liquid into the bucket in order to produce sufficient vacuum to enable it to draw. **1928** A. L. Dyke *Aircraft Engine Instructor* 217 The idling system also contains an air bleed which serves the.. purpose of..contributing to the operation of the priming device. **1931** M. M. Farleigh *Princ. & Probl. Aircraft Engines* x. 166 When..continued priming of the cylinders fails to bring about any combustion, the ignition should be checked carefully both for quality of spark and the time of its occurrence. **1969** W. T. Ingram et al. *Gloss. Water & Wastewater Control Engin.* 247 *Priming*,..the action of starting the flow in a pump or siphon.

7.** *Biol.* and *Med.* (See *prime *v.*[1] 7.)

1943 *Jrnl. Endocrinol.* III. 270 Pituitary extracts were administered by a series of subcutaneous injections for the purpose of stimulating the follicles ('priming'). **1963** *Recent Progress Hormone Res.* XIX. 673 New external stimuli following the priming are required to release the altered behavior patterns. **1967** *Science* 17 Nov. 939/2 Acoustic priming appears to be ineffective before the age of 14 days, corresponding to the normal onset of hearing in mice. **1975** *Behavior Genetics* V. 324 This failure of the 17-day-old albino mice to exhibit as great a change in seizure severity as a result of acoustic priming might have been due to their innately elevated auditory thresholds. **1978** *Nature* 5 Jan. 10/1 Production of interferon can also be modulated in other ways; pretreatment of cells with small amounts of homologous interferon before addition of an interferon inducer often increases the yield, a phenomenon termed 'priming'.

8. priming pump *Aeronaut.*, a small pump in an aircraft for priming its engine.

1932 R. Mahachek *Airplane Pilot's Man.* vi. 49 On large engines the choke is replaced by a priming pump which injects fuel directly into the intake system. **1942** D. M. Crook *Spitfire Pilot* 79, I..gave the priming pump a couple of strokes, and pressed the starter button.

priming (prəi·miŋ), *vbl. sb.*[3] *U.S.* [f. Prime *v.*[3] + -ing[1].] The action of removing the lowest leaves, or other layers of leaves, from a tobacco plant; also, the leaves removed.

1899 M. L. Floyd *Cultivation of Cigar-Leaf Tobacco* 14 The first priming, which means the first four leaves taken from the stalk, also the last priming, which means the last four or six leaves taken from the top of the stalk, are kept separate. **1904** E. Glasgow *Deliverance* 166 The very primings ought to be as good as some top leaves. **1938** *Daily Progress* (Charlottesville, Va.) 21 Oct. 5/1 Following the change from 'stalk cutting' to 'priming' (cutting of separate leaves for curing in bundles), less heat was required.

priming (prəi·miŋ), *ppl. a. Biol.* and *Med.* [f. Prime *v.*[1] + -ing[2].] That primes (see *prime *v.*[1] 7).

1930 *Amer. Jrnl. Physiol.* XCII. 129 The first test consisted of 'priming' injections of two rat units of purified extract into all animals. **1940** *Anat. Rec.* LXXVII. 1 Four to 6 month old rabbit does of medium-sized strains were injected subcutaneously..with a priming dose of the gonadotropic material. **1975** *Behavior Genetics* V. 324, 24 hr after the priming exposure the pigmented mice show an identically large increase in audiogenic seizures, whereas the albino mice have a lesser increase.

primitive, *a.* and *sb.* Add. **A.** *adj.* **I. 1. b.** Applied to behaviour or mental processes that apparently originate in unconscious needs or desires and have not been affected by objective logical reasoning.

1910 *Amer. Jrnl. Psychol.* XXI. 115 The following investigation of children's spontaneous constructions and primitive activities is made in the hope..that a clearer, saner insight into the child's nature and needs may follow. **1919** M. K. Bradby *Psycho-Anal.* iii. 28 The mind is unevenly developed, and what is relatively primitive co-exists with what is advanced without completely harmonising with it. **1923** L. A. Clare tr. *Lévy-Bruhl's Primitive Mentality* 32 If then, primitive mentality avoids and ignores logical thought, if it refrains from reasoning and reflecting, it is not from incapacity to surmount what is evident to sense. **1924** *Brit. Jrnl. Med. Psychol.* IV. 32 Synthetic or intuitional conceptions of the unconscious, based on analogies with primitive notions and behaviour. **1962** M. Gabain tr. *Piaget's Moral Judgment of Child* ii. 189 It is not nearly so natural as one would think for primitive thought to take intentions into account.

2. b. *Anthrop.* That relates to a group, or to persons comprising such groups, whose culture, through isolation, has remained at a simple level of social and economic organization.

[**1781** Gibbon *Decl. & F.* III. xxxviii. 638 From this abject condition, perhaps the primitive and universal state of man.] **1903** C. S. Myers in *Rep. Cambr. Anthropol. Exped. Torres Straits* II. ii. 143 Stories which travellers relate about the remarkable capacity possessed by primitive peoples for distinguishing faint sounds amid familiar surroundings, cannot be accepted as evidence of an unusually acute hearing. **1920** R. H. Lowie *Primitive Society* (1921) i. 12 The knowledge of primitive society has an educational value that should recommend its study. **1938** R. Bunzel in F. Boas *Gen. Anthropol.* 333 There are ..certain primitive societies where the accumulation of wealth is considered undesirable. **1954** R. Firth in *Inst. Primitive Society* ii. 15 As I (and I think most of my colleagues) use it, 'primitive' is little more than a technological index—a shorthand term for a type of economic life in which the tool system and level of material achievement is fairly simple: little use of metals; no complex mechanical apparatus; no indigenous system of writing. **1963** *Brit. Jrnl. Sociol.* XIV. 21 Many books by social anthropologists have titles which include the word *primitive*. When we use this word..we refer to a low level of technology which limits social relationships to a narrow range. **1976** J. Friedl *Cultural Anthropol.* viii. 316 The primitive economy is one that is controlled exclusively by the local community.

II. 4. b. Applied to a parent language at an early, unrecorded, or reconstructed stage of its development into a group of dialects or languages.

1878 T. L. K. Oliphant *Old & Middle Eng.* i. 13 The Primitive Aryan *katvar* changes to the Gothic *fidwor* (our *four*). **1895** Kellner & Bradley *Morris's Hist. Outl. Eng. Accidence* (rev. ed.) iii. 30 The Teutonic languages differ much more from Primitive Aryan in the consonants than in the vowels. **1898** Primitive Germanic [used s.v. Germanic *a.* 2]. **1914** H. C. Wyld *Short Hist. Eng.* ii. 32 Parent, or Primitive Germanic, was divided into three great branches. **1920** *Trans. Philol. Soc. 1916–20* 129 (*heading*) Primitive Slavonic. **1933** L. Bloomfield *Language* i. 13 If a language is spoken over a large area,.. the result will be a set of related languages... We infer that..the Germanic (or the Slavic or the Celtic)..have arisen in the same way; it is only an accident of history that for these groups we have no written records of the language, as it was spoken before the differentiation set in. To these unrecorded parent languages we give names like *Primitive Germanic* (*Primitive Slavic, Primitive Celtic*, and so on). [*Note*] The word *primitive* is here poorly chosen, since it is intended to mean only that we happen to have no written records of the language. German scholars have a better device in their prefix *ur-* 'primeval'. **1972** M. L. Samuels *Linguistic Evol.* 2 The alternation corresponding to *stand–stood* was regular in the Indo-European system, and so with that corresponding to *seek–sought* in Primitive Germanic.

5. b. (Further examples.) *primitive cell*, the smallest unit cell of any particular lattice, having lattice points at each of its eight corners only; *primitive lattice*, a lattice generated by the repeated translation of a primitive cell.

1931 *Zeitschr. f. Kristallogr.* LXXIX. 501 The cell chosen is..not necessarily the primitive, i.e. smallest cell, as such a cell would often demand a description in oblique and inconvenient axes. But it is always either the primitive cell or a one- or three-face-centred or a body-centred cell. **1932** *Ann. Rep. Progr. Chem.* XXVIII. 263 *P* stands for primitive lattice. *Ibid.*, The rhombohedral lattice is designated by *R*, and the hexagonal by *C* or *H* according as the crystallographic axes coincide with or are perpendicular to the primitive translations of the lattice. **1945** C. W. Bunn *Chem. Crystallogr.* vii. 223 In a set of symbols characterizing a space-group, the first is always a capital letter which indicates whether the lattice is simple (*P* for primitive), body-centred (*I* for inner), side-centred (*A, B*, or *C*), or centred on all faces (*F*). **1966** *McGraw-Hill Encycl. Sci. & Technol.* III. 595/1 The three primitive cells of the cubic lattices are, respectively, a cube, a rhombohedron with a plane angle of 109° 28′, and a rhombohedron with an angle of 60°. The two rhombohedra are extremely inconvenient to handle; consequently, the body-centered and face-centered cubes are adopted in their stead. **1974** D. M. Adams *Inorg. Solids* ii. 12 In general it is convenient to work with the cell of highest symmetry and this is not necessarily primitive.

c. Applied to any root of an integer n such that the least power to which the root can be raised to yield unity modulo n is the totient of n.

1837 J. Hymers *Treat. Theory Algebraical Equations* x. 193 If r be one of the roots and a be a primitive root of the prime number n..it is proved..that all the roots of this equation may be represented by r, r^a, [etc.]. **1916** G. A. Miller et al. *Theory & Applic. Finite Groups* xv. 308 For any prime p, it is shown in the theory of numbers that there exists a primitive root g of p such that $1, g, g^2, .., g^{p-2}$, when divided by p, give in some order the remainders $1, 2, 3, .., p-1$. **1972** J. E. & M. W. Maxfield *Discovering Number Theory* viii. 65 A primitive root (mod m) exists for $m = 2, 4, p^a$, and $2p^a$, where p is an odd prime and a is a positive integer. There is no primitive root for other values of m.

d. *Group Theory.* [tr. G. *primitiv* (S. Lie *Theorie der Transformationsgruppen* (1888) I. xiii. 221).] Applied to a substitution group whose letters cannot be partitioned into disjoint proper subsets in a way that is preserved by every element of the group.

1888 *Amer. Jrnl. Math.* X. 300 A group in the plane is primitive when with each ordinary point which we hold, no invariant direction is connected. **1897** W. Burnside *Theory of Groups of Finite Order* ix. 177 A simple group can always be represented in primitive form. **1933** L. P. EISENHART *Continuous Groups of Transformations* ii. 80 The group of motions in the euclidean plane is primitive. **1968** D. PASSMAN *Permutation Groups* i. 14 Let G be a transitive permutation group of prime degree. Then G is primitive.

e. *Logic* and *Math.* [tr. It. *primitive* (G. Peano 1897, in *Atti della R. Accad. delle Sci. di Torino* XXXII. 568).] Applied to concepts and propositions that serve as the basis of a deductive system and are not further defined or demonstrated; *primitive recursive* (see *RECURSIVE *a.* 2a).

1903 B. RUSSELL *Princ. Math.* p. xi (*heading*) Two indefinables and ten primitive propositions in this calculus. **1910** WHITEHEAD & RUSSELL *Principia Math.* I. I. i. 95 Following Peano, we shall call the undefined ideas and the undemonstrated propositions primitive ideas and primitive propositions respectively. **1922** tr. *Wittgenstein's Tractatus* 121 The possibility of crosswise definition of the logical 'primitive signs' of Frege and Russell shows by itself that these are not primitive signs and that they signify no relations. **1932** LEWIS & LANGFORD *Symbolic Logic* i. 23 Thus it is proved that these primitive ideas and postulates for logic are the only assumptions required for the whole of mathematics. **1952** P. GEACH tr. *Frege's Philos. Writings* 161 The same happens for the formula $a = b$. In some cases its meaning can be assumed as a primitive idea, in others it is defined. **1959** M. BUNGE *Causality* ix. 233 Neither Aristotle nor his followers seem to have been aware of the *logical* necessity of admitting..a set of unexplained or primitive concepts and ideas in order to avoid reasoning in a circle. **1970** E. DUCKWORTH tr. *Piaget's Genetic Epistemol.* 7 Simultaneity, then, is not a primitive intuition; it is an intellectual construction.

f. Applied to those *n*th roots of unity of which the *n*th power, but no lower power, is unity.

1916 G. A. MILLER et al. *Theory & Applic. Finite Groups* xvii. 325 For $p^s = 9$, the six primitive ninth roots of unity are $\rho, \rho^2, \rho^4, \rho^5, \rho^7, \rho^8$ and are the roots of $x^6 + x^3 + 1 = 0$. **1971** E. C. DADE in Powell & Higman *Finite Simple Groups* viii. 274 We conclude that *F* contains a primitive *e*th root of unity.

10. *Primitive Baptist*: in the U.S.A., a member of a loosely organized secession of conservative character from the Baptist Church; also *attrib.*

The *Primitive Methodist Connexion* (after 1902 known as *Primitive Methodist Church*) united in 1932 with the United Methodists and Wesleyan Methodists to form the Methodist Church. The *Primitive Methodist Church, U.S.A.*, remains however a separate denomination.

1851 T. A. BURKE *Polly Peablossom's Wedding* 143 Brethren Crump and Noel were both members of the Primitive Baptist Church. **1856** in N. E. Eliason *Tarheel Talk* (1956) 288 Was recived by examinytion on the primitive baptis faith. **1872** Z. N. MORRELL *Flowers & Fruits* vi. 72 There was also an organization calling themselves 'Primitive Baptists', on the Colorado River. **1933** *Sun* (Baltimore) 24 Aug. 6/4 Elder A. J. Harrison..was elected head of the Ketockin Association, Old School, Primitive Baptists. **1948** *Daily Ardmoreite* (Ardmore, Okla.) 15 July 14/1 The Washita Valley Primitive Baptist association will meet at the Primitive Baptist church here, July 22. **1972** J. S. HALL *Sayings from Old Smoky* 144 Dave Reagan said of the Primitive Baptists, 'They are just like yellow jackets. They'd 'cruit [recruit] up in summer, and in winter they'd all die out'.

11. *Art.* **a.** Applied to the art and artists of pre-Renaissance western Europe.

[**1843** A. DE MONTOR (*title*) Peintres primitifs.] **1847** LD. LINDSAY *Sk. Hist. Christian Art* II. ii. 93, I strongly suspect an ancestral relation between them [*sc.* the frescoes of the Baptistery at Parma] and the primitive and interesting school of Bologna. **1857** G. SCHARF *Handbk. Paintings by Anc. Masters* (Art Treasures Exhib., Manchester) 5 Ottley,..an earnest student of the earlier periods of Italian art, had formed a small, but very authentic, collection of primitive works. **1923** J. GORDON *Mod. French Painters* ix. 94 In the early Italian primitive painters, and, indeed, in primitives of every order, we find beneath the artists' learning the foundations laid upon what may be called folk painting. **1927** R. FRY *Flemish Art* I. 24 This realization of space implies a sense of colour as a plastic function which is also almost entirely absent in primitive Flemish art. **1932** KONODY & LATHOM *Introd. French Painters* i. 3 What is known as primitive French painting is a hybrid art, composed of Italian, French, Spanish and German elements in varying proportions. **1970** *Oxf. Compan. Art* 925/1 Within the European context art historians and connoisseurs have used the term 'primitive' for early phases within the historical development of painting or sculpture in the various European countries.

b. Executed by one who has not been trained in a formal manner. Also, imitative of an early style suggesting lack of formal training. Of an artist: without formal training. Cf. *NAÏF *a.* 1b, *NAÏVE *a.* 1c.

1942 J. LIPMAN *Amer. Primitive Painting* 5 The critic..has come..to evaluate primitive art positively rather than negatively. *Ibid.* 7 The primitive artist typically allowed himself free rein in depicting pose, gesture..and background. **1952** M. MCCARTHY *Groves of Academe* (1953) viii. 148 On the walls were dark paintings of the first presidents, clergymen and theologians, a primitive engraving showing William Penn and the Indians. **1957** Primitive painting [see *NAÏVE *a.* 1c]. **1962** W. GAUNT *Everyman's Dict. Pictorial Art* I. 12 A native development [in U.S.A.] of great interest in the eighteenth and nineteenth centuries was that of a 'primitive' or folk art, practised by sign painters and other craftsmen and amateurs. **1964** J. SUMMERSON *Classical Lang. Archit.* v. 39 Laugier's primitivism..certainly appealed to him [*sc.* Sir John Soane] but he was prepared to go much further than Laugier in..inventing a 'primitive' order of his own. **1967** Primitive portrait [see *mourning-piece* s.v. *MOURNING *vbl. sb.*[1] 5]. **1976** *Sunday Times* (Colour Suppl.) 8 Feb. 7/3 Beryl Cook, seaside landlady and primitive painter, talks to Allen Saddler. **1978** I. MURDOCH *Sea* 126 Hartley and Fitch were sitting stiff and upright, like a married pair rendered by a primitive painter.

12. *primitive accumulation* (Econ.): in Marxist theory, the original accumulation of capital, supposedly derived from the expropriation of small producers or smallholders, from which capitalist production was able to start; hence *primitive socialist accumulation*: the accumulation of capital which would be needed to start socialist production, also to be derived from the expropriation of small producers, smallholders, or peasants.

1887 MOORE & AVELING tr. *Marx's Capital* II. VIII. xxvi. 736 The whole movement..seems to turn in a vicious circle, out of which we can only get by supposing a primitive accumulation..preceding capitalistic accumulation. *Ibid.*, This primitive accumulation plays in Political Economy about the same part as original sin in theology. *Ibid.* 738 The so-called primitive accumulation..is nothing else than the historical process of divorcing the producer from the means of production. **1935** E. BURNS *Handbk. Marxism* xvi. 258 The so-called primitive accumulation of capital consisted in this case in the expropriation of these immediate producers. **1950** A. ERLICH in *Q. Jrnl. Econ.* LXIV. 69 This formative period of modern capitalism..had now to find its counterpart in 'primitive socialist accumulation' which was assumed to serve as midwife in the same way for the socialist society of the future. **1959** *Listener* 29 Oct. 726/1 Trotsky proposed to carry through this Draconian programme, of what he called 'primitive socialist accumulation' without Stalin's terrible methods. **1965** B. PEARCE tr. *Preobrazhensky's New Econ.* 67 If we partly exclude the operation of the law of value..we must accordingly replace its regulatory action by another law, inherent in planned economy at its present stage of development—the law of primitive socialist accumulation. **1967** I. DEUTSCHER *Marxism in our Time* (1972) 242 It was out of the question that a country like this should be able to achieve socialism in such circumstances. It had to devote all its energies to 'primitive accumulation', that is, to the creation under state ownership of the most essential economic preliminaries to any genuine building of socialism.

B. *sb.* **I. 1. b.** (Later examples.) Also *transf.*, someone uncivilized, uncultured.

1924 *Brit. Jrnl. Med. Psychol.* IV. 35 The primitive has in many ways a contact with his environment of a refinement and subtlety that is more than a match for civilized brains. **1926** L. A. CLARE tr. *Lévy-Bruhl's How Natives Think* 13 Primitives... By this term, an incorrect one, yet rendered almost indispensable through common usage, we simply mean members of the most elementary social aggregates with which we are acquainted. *a* **1936** KIPLING *Something of Myself* (1937) vii. 184 Out of the woods..came two dark and mysterious Primitives. **1967** [see *CHARLEY, CHARLIE 8]. **1972** *Buenos Aires Herald* 2 Feb. 7/1 The primitives fight for their territories and economic planners insist that the vast region must be opened. **1977** M. COHEN *Sensible Words* iii. 122 The newly emphasized methods of linguistic analysis include studying the language of children and 'primitives'.

4. a. (Further examples.) Also, a naïve painter; also *transf.* of artists working in another medium. **b.** (Further examples.) Also *attrib.* Also *transf.* of other art forms.

1907 R. FRY *Let.* 5 Mar. (1972) I. 282 A great Ferrarese altarpiece... The effect will be fine in our Primitive room. **1910** E. SINGLETON *Art of Belgian Galleries* i. 17 The Last Supper is one of the most profound and best-painted works of the Fifteenth Century; and if one were to make a list of five or six supreme masterpieces of the Flemish Primitives, this would have to be included. **1922** C. BELL *Since Cézanne* 51 One definitely artistic gift..many children do possess..is a sense of the decorative possibilities of their medium. This gift they have in common with the Primitives; and this the *douanier* possessed in an extraordinary degree. **1923** [see *PRIMITIVE *a.* 11a]. **1932** F. F. SHERMAN *Early Amer. Painting* p. xv, Numerous dealers in antiques..offer them for sale..as 'primitives'. Primitives they certainly are not... They are worthless as works of art or of antiquity. **1934** *Musical Q.* Apr. 214 The Primitives stem from Moussorgsky, through Debussy and the *Sacre.* **1947** G. GREENE *19 Stories* 155 The first season of 'primitives' [*sc.* films] was announced (a highbrow phrase). **1951** R. FIRTH *Elem. Social Organiz.* v. 163 When we talk..of the Italian primitives..we are referring..to art that is distinguished primarily by being earlier in time, though it..also bears the character of lack of sophistication. **1952** O. KALLIR in A. M. Moses *Grandma Moses* p. xv, Grandma Moses is called a 'primitive'. Each of her pictures shows plainly that its author has had no art training. **1958** *Listener* 21 Aug. 269/2 The school of the 'primitives', represented by John Osborne, Sheelagh Delaney, and..Bernard Kops. **1959** E. POUND *Thrones* ci. 78 Hs'uan Tsung, 1389 natus, painted kittens, and Joey said, 'are they for real' before primitives in the Mellon Gallery. **1964** MRS. L. B. JOHNSON *White House Diary* 20 Jan. (1970) 56 There was also a little American Primitive—just made you merry to look at it. **1974** P. DE VRIES *Glory of Hummingbird* (1975) iii. 39 We respected the artist's [*sc.* a writer's] reluctance to show portions of work not in sufficiently polished form because we felt..that here was a true primitive. **1976** *Sunday Times* (Colour Suppl.) 8 Feb. 22/1 Most of all, her paintings are funny. You can't say that about many primitives. **1977** *Jrnl. R. Soc. Arts* CXXVI. 35/2 The Flemish Primitives..would superimpose the dark colours and leave the pale colours transparent.

II. 6. (Later examples.) Also, = *PHONETIC *sb.*

1814 J. MARSHMAN *Elem. Chinese Gram.* 36 If we then add the 214 elements to the 1689 primitives, we shall have one thousand nine hundred and three characters producing nearly the whole language. **1874, 1907** [see *PHONETIC *sb.*]. **1909–10** L. BLOOMFIELD in C. F. Hockett *Leonard Bloomfield Anthol.* (1970) 1 Derivative nouns and verbs also stand..in a definite ablaut relation to their primitives. **1975** *Language* LI. 969 It. *bozz-ello*..is an authentic derivative from *bozza*; while *bosel, bossel, bozel* in Renaissance French is a cluster of completely isolated forms lacking a primitive—a situation which reflects on the grammatical status of *-el.*

8. *spec.* a complete primitive (see Dict., this sense). (Examples.)

1885 A. R. FORSYTH *Treat. Differential Equations* i. 8 The relation, which exists between the variables themselves without their differential coefficients and which is the most general one possible, is called sometimes the general solution, and sometimes the primitive, of the differential equation. **1929** T. C. FRY *Elem. Differential Equations* ii. 27 This relation includes every possible solution of the differential equation. It is called the general solution or primitive. **1969** B. SPAIN *Ordinary Differential Equations* i. 9 Obtain the differential equations corresponding to the primitives..$y = c \log x$..[etc.].

9. *Logic* and *Math.* A primitive concept or proposition (see *A. 5e). Also in extended use.

1950 *Jrnl. Symbolic Logic* XV. 130 Hence ϕ and μ as defined above will suffice as the sole primitives for the arithmetic of positive integers. **1960** G. BERGMAN *Meaning & Existence* ii. 44 It is not required that an improved language be interpreted by interpreting separately all, or even any, of its primitives. **1964** M. BLACK *Compan. Wittgenstein's Tractatus* 25 We find Wittgenstein..constantly returning to the theme of the 'logical indefinables' or the 'logical primitives'. **1964** R. H. ROBINS *Gen. Linguistics* iv. 133 Many linguists are prepared to accept these terms [*sc.* *contrast* and *distinctive*] as primitives, i.e. as requiring no further definition within linguistics. **1975** *Language* LI. 621 We are not yet in a position to characterize seriously the semantic representation of roots. My guess is that we are not yet aware of the majority of semantic primitives. **1975** M. A. SLOTE *Metaphysics & Essence* iii. 41 This notion of (an) experience, like the other notions we have been using as primitives, is not just an arbitrary primitive with which to attempt the definition of the concepts we wish to define. **1976** J. S. GRUBER *Lexical Struct. Syntax & Semantics* II. i. 260 Interpretive semantics is valuable only for those functions which a logical calculus entails, and for this it must operate on trees of semantic primitives.

primitivism. Add: **1.** (Further examples.) Also, a belief in the desirability of a 'return to nature'; an exaltation of simplicity or of irrationalism; the practice of primitive art.

1934 A. HUXLEY *Beyond Mexique Bay* 257 To introduce a salutary element of primitivism into our civilized and industrialized way of life. **1938** *Burlington Mag.* June 302/2 Far more primitivism has been attributed to him [*sc.* Rousseau] than is actually justified. **1939** J. CHARLOT *Art from Mayans to Disney* xi. 86 Political cartoons reminiscent of Monnier and Grandville, which are not flavoured at all by the primitivism of his [*sc.* Posada's] later work. **1947** A. EINSTEIN *Mus. Romantic Era* ix. 95 What formal primitivism, after Beethoven! **1950** E. H. GOMBRICH *Story of Art* xxvii. 440 This Primitivism advocated by Gauguin became perhaps an even more lasting influence on modern art than either Van Gogh's Expressionism or Cézanne's way to Cubism. **1951** *Essays in Crit.* I. 97 The term 'Back to Nature' covers the many and varied forms of primitivism. **1952** J. SUMMERSON *Sir John Soane* 17 Soane's 'primitivism'..is formalized at Bentley Priory (1798). **1958** H. R. HITCHCOCK *Archit. in 19th & 20th Cent.* 450/2 'Primitivism' in painting and sculpture has been of recurrent importance since the days of the Fauves and the Expressionists; a comparable primitivism in architecture has been much rarer, except for Gaudí. **1969** *Daily Tel.* 10 Feb. 10/4 He [*sc.* Thomas Mann] puts the German character on the operating table..: the loneliness, the smug provincialism, the Wagnerian primitivism, the eroticism. **1976** *Survey* Summer–Autumn 107 Khrushchev was only comprehensible if one began by accepting his Marxist primitivism.

primitivist (pri·mĭtivist), *sb.* and *a.* [f. PRIMITIVE *a.* + -IST.] **A.** *sb.* A believer in primitivism (sense 1); an advocate of the superiority of primitive customs or of primitive art; a person who uses obsolete methods or techniques. **B.** *adj.* Of or pertaining to primitivism or to the primitive, esp. in art; irrational, opposing scientific development.

1926 W. R. INGE *Lay Thoughts* 204 So the Utopians are usually primitivists. They glorify the noble savage, who runs wild in woods. **1934** *Musical Q.* Apr. 213 Three currents are left in the wake of the Modern Movement—Primitivist, Classicist, Popularist. **1949** B. WILLEY in *Ideas & Beliefs of Victorians* (B.B.C.) 43 Perhaps as Rousseau and other primitivists had urged, civilisation was a monstrous aberration, and men were happier and better when fresh from the hands of God or Nature in some primeval Eden. **1952** J. SUMMERSON *Sir John Soane* 33, I mentioned earlier the 'primitivist' element which is so important a factor in the Soane style. **1961** *Times* 7 June 17/3 All the rather flashy vitality and 'primitivist' imagery of his old manner have been discarded. **1975** *Nature* 20 Mar. 219/1 Attacked by the new school of linguistics and cognitive epistemology as an ignorant primitivist, Skinner not only maintains his position but makes it more dogmatic. **1977** *Times Lit. Suppl.* 15 July 874/3 Nothing but primitive commonplaces: without laws, private property or rulers, the Indians 'live according to nature'. It is a primitivists' fantasy world characterised by the observance of natural moral practices. **1977** D. WATKIN *Morality & Archit.* I. ii. 25 He [*sc.* Viollet-le-Duc] has..a related 'primitivist' notion that Roman and

Renaissance architecture lost contact with the pure fount of Greek truth, and is thus morally and stylistically in questionable taste.

Hence **primitivi·stic** *a.*

1943 [see *ISOLATIONISTIC *a.*]. **1948** L. SPITZER *Linguistics & Lit. Hist.* 210 Claudel can sing..not only 'Georgica', as did Vergil in a primitivistic mood. **1958** H. R. HITCHCOCK *Archit. 19th & 20th Cent.* iv. 60 Soane's Dulwich Gallery of 1811–14, outside London, is likewise built of common brick and has similarly primitivistic detailing. **1959** *Encounter* Nov. 76/1 A kind of atavism, an inability to think..in any but primitivistic terms. **1972** M. BRADBURY in Cox & Dyson *20th-Cent. Mind* III. xii. 343 Golding's universe is normally a-social or perhaps presocial, primitivistic at its core and yet also conscious that it is only through *knowing* our primitivism that we will find our innocence.

primitivize (pri·mĭtivəiz), *v.* [f. PRIMITIVE *a.* + -IZE.] *trans.* and *intr.* To render primitive; to impute primitiveness to; to simplify; to return to an earlier stage. So **primitiviza·tion, pri·mitivizing** *vbl. sb.* and *ppl. a.*

1942 Primitivisation [see *OVERINCLUSION]. **1955** *Times* 18 May 8/6 It does not bring about a primitivizing or animalizing of the human, but rather it celebrates man at his human best. **1959** *Encounter* May 50/2 Mr. Logue is a primitivizing poet. **1968** D. LAWTON *Social Class, Lang. & Educ.* iii. 23 'Cultural deprivation' or absence of external stimulation resulted in a 'primitivization' of an individual's behaviour. **1969** D. DAUBE *Roman Law* iii. 168 A common failing of modern research into ancient law is the inclination to primitivize the sources, to press the naive side of any statement or custom and overlook the element of sophistication which is often quite strong. **1971** *Jrnl. Gen. Psychol.* LXXXIV. 208 In psychology the term 'regression' refers to a primitivization of behavior, a 'going back' to a less mature way of behaving which the individual has 'outgrown'. **1976** T. STOIANOVICH *French Hist. Method* 146 Since the impairment of an existing superstructure provokes economic primitivization, staunch support develops in favor of a viable new superstructure.

primmy (pri·mi), *a. rare.* [f. PRIM *a.* + -Y[1].] Tending to primness.

1879 [see *GOVERNESSY *a.*].

‖ **primo** (prī·mo), *a.* and *sb.* [It., = first: cf. PRIMA[2].] **A.** *adj.* Used in some phrases, chiefly musical, as **primo basso**, chief bass singer (example *fig.*); **primo buffo**, chief male comic singer or actor; **primo tenore (assoluto)**, chief tenor singer (of outstanding ability); **primo uomo**, singer of the chief male part; (see also quots.).

1740 J. GRASSINEAU *Mus. Dict.* 183 *Primo*, the first; this word is often abridg'd, P°, I°..and added to other words, as *Primo canto,—the first treble.* **1801** BUSBY *Dict. Mus.*, *Primo* (Ital.). First: as *Primo Violono* [sic], first violin; *Primo Flauto*, first flute. **1826** M. KELLY *Reminisc.* I. 48 The celebrated Genaro Luzzio was the primo buffo, and the principal female, La Coltellini, was delightful, both as a comic actress and singer. **1848** GEO. ELIOT *Let.* 8 June (1954) I. 266 Dear Quartett of Friends—I may still say so, though I fear your primo basso has departed. **1855** —— in *Fraser's Mag.* July 50/2 He will write no *part* to suit a *primo tenore.* **1876** STAINER & BARRETT *Dict. Mus. Terms* 366/1 *Primo*, (*It.*) First (masc.), as *tempo primo*, at the original pace or time; *violino primo*, first fiddle; *primo buffo*, chief comic actor or singer; *primo musico* and *primo uomo*, principal male singer in the opera. **1880** GROVE *Dict. Mus.* II. 509/1 It was *de rigueur* that the First Man (*Primo uomo*) should be an artificial Soprano. *Ibid.* 514/1 The chief, or *Buffo* group, consisted of two Female Performers..and three Men, distinguished as the *Primo Buffo*, [etc.]. **1889** G. B. SHAW *London Music 1888–89* (1937) 166 His dignity as *primo tenore assoluto.* **1938** *Times Lit. Suppl.* 28 May 370/3 What the *primo uomo* was to the eighteenth-century opera..the man with the stick is to the symphony concerts. **1955** E. DENT in H. Van Thal *Fanfare for E. Newman* 86 The first half of the nineteenth century..was the triumph of the *prima donna* over the *primo uomo*, the *castrato* hero of the eighteenth century, though she soon had to face her rival in the *primo tenore.*

B. as *sb.* **1.** *Mus.* In a pianoforte duet, the upper part; the pianist who plays this part.

1792 J. A. K. COLIZZI *Three Duets for Two Performers on the Harpsichord or Piano Forté* 3 Primo. **1883** GROVE *Dict. Mus.* III. 30/2 In pianoforte duets, *Primo* or 1mo is generally put over the right-hand page, and then means the part taken by the 'treble' player. **1954** K. DALE *19th-Cent. Piano Mus.* xii. 284 Swirling cadenzas of scales in demisemiquavers for performance by *primo. Ibid.* 286 The playing of six quavers in a bar by *primo* against four by *secondo* throughout the whole of the trio section cannot have been altogether easy for the young performer. **1965** *Listener* 1 July 33/3 Britten's rhythmic control as *secondo* balancing and counteracting Richter's natural genius as *primo.* **1964** G. READ *Mus. Notation* xviii. 298 For four-hand music on one instrument, the two parts are placed on facing pages..the first player (*primo*; top part) reads from the right-hand page.

2. (With capital initial.) A title given to an official of the Royal Antediluvian Order of Buffaloes.

1879 *Buffalo* 16 Jan. 3/3 Yours fraternally, Primo James Dewsbury. *Ibid.* 5/1 Primos who..have been elevated to the position of Knights of the Order of Merit. **1928** *Daily Express* 2 Aug. 9/5 Mr. J. C. E. Cartwright.., Grand Primo of England, inaugurated the Croydon and District Provincial Grand Lodge... The Grand Primo of the new lodge is Mr. L. R. N. Percy. **1966** *R.A.O.B. Centenary, South Yorkshire, 1866–1966* (Royal Antediluvian Order of Buffaloes), Of the 17 Provincial Grand Primos..only two have been taken from us by the call of the reaper.

primoge·niturist. *rare.* [f. PRIMOGENITURE + -IST.] One who believes that the right of succession or inheritance belongs to the first-born.

1976 I. MURDOCH *Henry & Cato* I. 7 His father, a rigid primogeniturist, had left everything to..the elder son.

primordial, *a.* Add: **1. b.** *primordial soup*: see *SOUP *sb.*

4. a. *primordial meristem* = *promeristem* (PRO-[2] 1 in Dict. and Suppl.).

1925 EAMES & MACDANIELS *Introd. Plant Anat.* iii. 41 The youngest cells in a region of growing plant body in which the formation of new organs or parts of organs is taking place constitute a promeristem, or primordial meristem. **1943** *Bot. Rev.* IX. 142 The limits between primordial meristem cells at the apex and procambium cells below are vague.

primordiality. (Earlier and later examples.)

1874 W. WALLACE tr. *Hegel's Logic* 297 The cause therefore appears as passing into its correlative, and to be losing its primordiality in the latter. **1977** J. A. FISHMAN in H. Giles *Lang., Ethnicity & Intergroup Relations* i. 17 Primordiality denotes both primacy, in the sense of a presumably original essence, as well as primitivism or irreducibility.

primordium. Add: **b.** (Examples.) In *Embryol.* = *ANLAGE.

1875 BENNETT & DYER tr. *Sachs's Text-bk. Bot.* II. 531 In Primulaceæ..five protuberances (primordia) appear on the receptacle above the calyx, each of which grows up into a stamen. **1898** A. WILLEY in *Nature* 25 Aug. 390/1 The word that commends itself to me [for the German 'Anlage']..is primordium. **1908** F. R. LILLIE *Devel. of Chick* 8 The ovum is the primordium of the individual, the ectoderm the primordium of all ectodermal structures,.. the first thickening of the ectoderm over the optic cup the primordium of the lens, etc. **1935** *Jrnl. Morphol.* LVIII. 425 The primitive mesenteron..consists of a single layer of squamous epithelium dorsal to the attachments of the cardiac primordia, and two layers ventral to them. **1965** BELL & COOMBE tr. *Strasburger's Textbk. Bot.* 115 The primordia of the leaves arise at the apex from the outer layers of cells. **1978** M. J. T. FITZGERALD *Human Embryol.* ix. 75 At the end of the fifth week the primordia of the hands and feet are already apparent.

primp (primp), *a.* [f. the vb.] Smart, neat, prim.

1835 *Fraser's Mag.* July 17 Your primp wizand faces. **1903** *N.Y. Times* 26 Sept. 4 (Advt.), All-weather coats they are—just as primp, good-fitting and handsome as a man could wish to wear. **1931** *Aberdeen Press & Jrnl.* 19 Feb., Scotia's leed has mony a kin', Tae fit baith primp an' pliskie. **1966** J. S. COX *Illustr. Dict. Hairdressing* 122/1 *Primp*, smart, neat.

primp, *v.* Delete *dial.* and add: **1.** (Further examples.) Also *refl.*

1914 R. FROST *North of Boston* 103 Lord, if I were to dream of everyone Whose shoes I primped to dance in! **1945** J. STEINBECK *Cannery Row* viii. 47 A Lee cousin primped up slightly wilted heads of lettuce the way a girl primps a loose finger wave. **1959** *Numbers* Feb. 30 Primping yourself up like a damned quean. **1965** F. KNEBEL *Night of Camp David* xiv. 232 She came willingly enough, after primping her hair and smoothing her charcoal linen dress. **1974** 'A. HAIG' *Peruvian Printout* 45 When Heinrich..came back..Shirley even forgot to primp herself.

b. (Earlier and later examples.) Also const. *up*.

1887 *Harper's Mag.* Mar. 544/1 When you was primping so, I thought all the time it was for Mrs. Rainwater. **1901** W. N. HARBEN *Westerfelt* iv. 49 Ef you want to primp up a little an' bresh that hoss-hair off'n yore pants, go in yore room. **1937** *Daily Tel.* 31 Aug. 12/4 It [*sc.* the women's dressing-room of an American flying-boat] is described as containing 'mirrors and leather-covered stools for primping'—which I take to mean such running repairs as passengers find necessary. **1939** N. COWARD *Words & Music* in *Play Parade* II. 120 In tropical heat Nobody who's sweet, survives We powder and primp And try to be sympathetic. **1977** *Daily News* (Perth, Austral.) 19 Jan. 6/4 (*caption*) Dorothy Hamill, 1976 Olympic figure skating champion, primps before making her New York debut with the Ice Capades at Madison Square Garden.

c. *intr.* To make tidying or smoothing movements. *rare.*

1881 I. M. RITTENHOUSE *Maud* (1939) 1 Eva..pulled down her basque, 'primped' at her hair,..and looked expectantly towards the door.

3. *trans.* and *intr.* To move (oneself or another person) fussily or mincingly.

1951 W. SANSOM *Face of Innocence* xiii. 184 She primped us over to Roddy with all the posturing, like a dove stamping out its love-dance, of one person meeting another. **1953** J. MASTERS *Lotus & Wind* vii. 89 She opened the door..and primped along the passage. The skirt clung so tightly around her thighs that she had to hobble. **1977** *N.Z. Listener* 15 Jan. 46/4 The comedians pranced and primped with Ronnie Corbett.

primped *ppl. a.*: also **primped-up; primping** *vbl. sb.* (later examples).

1935 Z. N. HURSTON *Mules & Men* (1970) I. vi. 126 Tain't no use in you gittin' yo' mouf all primped up for no hoein' and rakin' out of me, Bertha. Call yo' grandson and let him do it. **1959** *News Chron.* 11 Aug. 6/4 Adolescence..is early enough to begin real primping. **1963** *Listener* 28 Mar. 570/1 One had the primped-up stage, gorgeous to the eye. **1977** *New Yorker* 16 May 108/2 When the course is closed to play and the green-keeping staff is giving it a final primping for the opening round.

primrose, *sb.* (*a.*) Add: **6. b.** A commercial soap of a yellowish colour. In full, *primrose soap.*

1796 M. EDGEWORTH *Parent's Assistant* (ed. 2) II. 127 A fresh assortment of..Primrose Soap. **1907** *Yesterday's Shopping* (1969) 39/2 *Soaps* (*Plain*). Pale Primrose (Army & Navy) bar about 3 lb. 0/9. The Royal Primrose (J. Knight's) bar about 3 lb. 0/9½. **1909** H. G. WELLS *Tono-Bungay* III. i. 265 We had added to the original Moggs' Primrose several varieties of scented and super-fatted. *c* **1938** *Fortnum & Mason Catal.* 56/2 *Soaps, Household..* Primrose Royal..per bar 1/3.

7. *primrose yellow* (further examples); *primrose-coloured* (earlier example), *-vested* adjs.; **primrose soap**: see sense 6b above.

1788 *Gazetteer* 12 May 2/3 The train was a primrose coloured goffree'd crape spotted with blue crape in relief. **1922** JOYCE *Ulysses* 195 Primrosevested he greeted gaily with his doffed Panama as with a bauble. **1907** *Yesterday's Shopping* (1969) 478/2 Oil Colours..Primrose yellow..Raw sienna. **1954** T. S. ELIOT *Confid. Clerk* I. 32, I thought a primrose yellow would be cheerful. **1978** *Vogue* 1 Mar. 128 Shirtdress..primrose yellow with Peter Pan collar.

8. Primrose Day (earlier example); **Primrose League** (further examples); so **Primrose Leaguer.**

1884 E. W. HAMILTON *Diary* 21 Mar. (1972) II. 581 Mrs. G...carried a splendid bouquet of primroses,..to show that the 'Primrose Leaguers' have no title to appropriate the flower to themselves. *Ibid.* 19 Apr. 597 'Primrose Day'. Were I an admirer of Lord Beaconsfield, I should be furious that his memory should be so ridiculed. **1912** CHESTERTON *Manalive* II. ii. 240, I have faced many a political crisis in the old Primrose League days at Herne Bay. **1923** J. M. MURRY *Pencillings* 146 Disraeli..was a far more remarkable man than the most enthusiastic Primrose Leaguer has ever imagined. **1959** B. & R. NORTH tr. *Duverger's Pol. Parties* (ed. 2) I. i. 66 The Primrose League, an organization distinct from the party proper, aimed at social mixing. **1975** R. TAYLOR *Lord Salisbury* viii. 134 He told the Primrose League in a memorable speech: 'You may roughly divide the nations of the world as the living and the dying.'

B. as *adj.* (Earlier and later examples.)

1788 *Gazetteer* 12 May 2/3 An immense panache of white, blue and primrose feathers. **1815** in R. W. Chapman *Jane Austen's Pride and Prejudice* (1923) 398 Primrose sandals, and white kid gloves. **1931** [see *JUMPER *sb.*[2] 3 c]. **1976** *S. Wales Echo* 25 Nov. 27/4 (Advt.), Bathroom/w.c., half-tiled in Primrose, matching Primrose suite.

primrose, *v.* **a.** (Further examples.)

1928 *Daily Express* 10 Mar. 5/3 There are few of the many who enjoy the country who will be able to resist primrosing. **1941** E. BOWEN *Look at Roses* 122 This afternoon..we'll go primrosing. **1967** 'L. BRUCE' *Death of Commuter* viii. 82 'I'm going to take her primrosing tomorrow,' he told Carolus. 'In Langley Wood'. **1973** J. THOMSON *Death Cap* vi. 88 To go bird's-nesting, or blackberrying or primrosing.

primrosy, *a.* Add: **c.** *fig.* (Cf. *primrose path* s.v. PRIMROSE *sb.* (*a.*) 7.)

1908 E. V. LUCAS *Over Bemerton's* xx. 202 His duty always lies along the primrosiest path.

primuline (pri·miulīn). *Chem.* Also **Primuline.** [f. PRIMUL(A + -INE[5].] A synthetic yellow dyestuff which is the sodium salt of the sulphonic acid derivative of primuline base (see below) and is used in the dyeing of cotton. The dye may also contain other analogous salts.

1887 *Dyer & Calico Printer* VII. 101/1 A new series of colours..are just now being brought out by Brooke, Simpson, & Spiller (Limited). These colours, the discovery of Mr. A. G. Green, promise to compete successfully with the direct cotton colours at present in the market. The basis of the series is a compound, to which the name of primuline has been given. **1919** E. DE B. BARNETT *Coal Tar Dyes* 108 Primuline dyes cotton in bright yellow shades, but these are too fugitive to be of any value. **1950** *Thorpe's Dict. Appl. Chem.* (ed. 4) X. 215/1 The sodium salts of the sulphonic acids of the higher thionated *p*-toluidines (primuline bases) were first manufactured..in 1887 under the name of 'Primuline' and employed for the production of so-called 'ingrain colours' by ..diazotising and developing upon the fibre. **1968** E. N. ABRAHART *Dyes* v. 135 Among the direct dyes C.I. Direct Red 70..employs Primuline as diazo component and Schäffer's acid as coupling component.

2. Special Combs.: **primuline base,** a yellow thiazole derivative, $C_{21}H_{15}N_3S_2$, which is obtained when *p*-toluidine is heated with sulphur and is an intermediate in dye manufacture; *loosely*, any of the related compounds also formed by this process; **primuline red,** a red dyestuff obtained from primuline base by diazotization followed by coupling with β-naphthol.

1889 *Jrnl. Chem. Soc.* LV. 228 The product is not homogeneous, but consists of about 50 per cent. of a base, $C_{14}H_{12}N_2S$,..40 per cent. of primuline-base, and 10 per cent. of unaltered paratoluidine. **1913** *Thorpe's Dict. Appl. Chem.* (ed. 2) IV. 385/1 These more condensed bases ('primuline bases') were obtained in larger amount by increasing the proportion of sulphur to 4½–5 atoms to 1 mol. amine. **1961** COCKETT & HILTON *Dyeing of Cellulosic Fibres* v. 156 Primuline Base may be sulphonated to give the monosulphonic acid, the sodium salt of which is the yellow dye Primuline, a direct dye for cellulosic fibres. **1968** E. N. Abrahart *Dyes* v. 135 The sulphurization products of *p*-toluidine, primuline base and dehydrothio-*p*-toluidine are used..in the manufacture of some valuable cotton dyes. **1900** *Jrnl. Soc. Chem. Industry* 30 Apr. 345/1 Primuline Red is obtained by dyeing with Primuline, diazotising, and developing with β-naphthol. **1917** *Jrnl. Soc. Dyers & Colourists* XXXIII. 140/1, I replied by pointing out the greater fastness of Primuline Red compared to Benzopurpurine.

primus, *a.* and *sb.* Add: **A.** *adj.* **1.** *primus inter pares* (further examples); also fem. *prima inter pares*.

1909 Webster, Prima inter pares. **1919** M. Beer *Hist. Brit. Socialism* I. ii. v. 162 He could be their self-sacrificing father and teacher, their authoritative adviser and leader, but never the *primus inter pares*. **1961** *Times* 12 Oct. 18/1 But this is a ballet in which Dame Margot is but *prima inter pares*. **1973** *Times* 20 Oct. 13/5 Herr Schneiderhan did not attempt to stand out as a virtuoso but attacked his solos as *primus inter pares*, playing with and to his accompanying strings. **1979** *Guardian* 5 May 21/3 Mrs Thatcher..becomes..*primus inter pares* in that quaint and English system known as Cabinet Government.

B. *sb.* **2.** Also **Primus.** The proprietary name of a make of pressure stove or lamp, usu. burning paraffin; *loosely*, any pressure stove. Freq. *attrib.*

1904 *Outing* Mar. 698/1 At last we found and packed with rucksacks, small kerosene cans, Primus stove, etc. **1904** *Railway Mag.* XIV. 45/1 A ¾ in. scale locomotive is more expensive to construct, and needs a 'Primus' burner. **1907** *Athenæum* 12 Oct. 436/2 Robinson with great efforts made the 'Primus' work, and then burnt the stew with it. **1910** *Trade Marks Jrnl.* 22 June 989 Primus... Stoves. Aktiebolaget B.A. Hjorth & Co..., Stockholm, Sweden; manufacturers. **1910** *Official Gaz.* (U.S. Patent Office) 5 July 246/2 Aktiebolaget B.A. Hjorth & Co., Stockholm... *Primus*. **1933** E. A. Robertson *Ordinary Families* iii. 53 It was asking too much of anyone's stomach to expect primus cookery. **1944** M. Laski *Love on Supertax* i. 11 Have you ever tried..to light a primus stove?.. The methylated spirits flare up... You must frantically pump paraffin through to the burner. **1951** G. Millar *White Boat from England* ii. 16 We had several gadgets for the primus, including a pyramidal toaster. **1973** J. Stranger *Walk Lonely Road* xiv. 108 Coffee, thick and strong and sweet, brewed over a Primus. **1974** O. Manning *Rain Forest* iii. i. 254 Simon folded back the flaps of a large, square tent... A primus lamp hung from the roof.

prince, *sb.* Add: **I. 3. b.** A person with power or influence; a magnate. *U.S.*

1841 J. S. Buckingham *America* III. 427 Capitalists and merchants [of Boston]..are here called 'princes'. **1884** *Century Mag.* Sept. 796 At a shady end of the veranda, are seen the railroad king,..the bonanza mine owner, the Texas rancher, and the Pennsylvania iron prince. **1904** [see *baron 2b]. **1976** T. Gifford *Cavanaugh Quest* (1977) viii. 137 He was a perfect reflection of the typical Minneapolis power broker, though somewhat better dressed than the grain barons and the department store princes and computer tycoons.

c. An admirable or generous person. *colloq.* (chiefly *U.S.*).

1911 H. B. Wright *Winning of Barbara Worth* xvi. 252 Yes sir, gents, I'm here to tell you that that there man, Jefferson Worth, is a prince—a prince. Let me tell you what he done for me. **1939** I. Baird *Waste Heritage* v. 69 Hep ain't like other guys, he's a prince. **1951** J. D. Salinger *Catcher in Rye* iii. 31 He's crazy about *you*. He told me he thinks you're a goddam prince. **1966** J. Cleary *High Commissioner* viii. 164 'You have a lot of time for him, haven't you?' 'They don't come any better. He's a prince, you know?'

IV. 11. prince's pine, (*b*) (earlier and later examples).

1807 F. Pursh *Jrnl. Bot. Excursion* (1869) 15 Pyrola umbellata calld here Princess [*sic*] pine. **1818** A. Eaton *Man. Bot.* (ed. 2) 203 *Chimaphila..umbellata*, (prince's pine, bitter wintergreen). **1884** [see Pipsissewa]. **1954** C. J. Hylander *Macmillan Wild Flower Bk.* 280 Pipsissewa... Also known as Prince's Pine, this is a trailing and somewhat woody perennial.

12. *Prince of Wales check*, a large check pattern; *Prince of Wales('s) feathers*: (*a*) see Feather *sb.* 8; also *ellipt.* and *fig.*; (*b*) = *crape-fern* (*crape *sb.* 3b); *Prince of Wales knot* (see also quot. 1978); *Prince Rupert's drop* (further example).

1958 P. Mortimer *Daddy's gone a-Hunting* vii. 35 A tall, thin man in Prince of Wales check. **1959** *Sunday Express* 21 June 14/3 Prince of Wales check trousers. **1960** *News Chron.* 11 July 6/5 The Prince of Wales check Sudan cotton in grey and black. **1972** *Vogue* Feb. 73 Prince of Wales check wool tent coat. **1882** T. H. Potts *Out in Open* 108 T[*odea*] *superba*, 'the glory of the west'. How great the impression made by its marvellous beauty, may be assumed from the number of familiar names.. bestowed upon it, as the Royal fern, the King's fern, Prince of Wales' feather. **1919** T. Wright *Romance of Lace Pillow* ix. 82 Other patterns were the *Prince of Wales's Feathers*. **1933** *Flight* 29 June 626/2 And a final break-up in a 'Prince of Wales Feathers', were other manoeuvres which held the spectators literally spellbound. **1944, 1951** [see *crape-fern]. **1958** C. Freeman *Pillow Lace in E. Midlands* 46 The names given to the various patterns often refer to some element of the design. .. Other favourites were..Prince of Wales's Feathers [etc.]. **1966** H. Sheppard *Dict. Railway Slang* (ed. 2) 9 *Prince of Wales*, blowing off steam by engine. **1971** D. J. Smith *Discovering Railwayana* x. 58 *Prince of Wales*, short for Prince of Wales' feathers, a plume-like emission of steam. **1977** Binney & Burman *Change & Decay* 143/2 (*caption*) Lea, Wiltshire; St. Giles. Bell of 1622, with Prince of Wales feathers. **1977** *R.A.F. News* 22 June–5 July 1/1 The manœuvre takes the nine Gnats up into a Prince of Wales feathers, with eight aircraft trailing white smoke and the leader trailing red. **1897** *Sears, Roebuck Catal.* 222/2 Illustration No. 2205 shows the De Joinnile [necktie] as worn with an ordinary finger ring. No. 2206 shows it tied in a Prince of Wales knot. **1971** *Guardian* 3 Aug. 9/3 Broad kipper ties..tied in loose Prince of Wales knots, were featured by many Paris houses. **1978** 'K. Blake' *Professionals 1: Where Jungle Ends* iii. 39 His Prince of Wales knotted tie in rich brown. **1862** Ruskin *Unto this Last* iv. 145 Nay, boiled bulbs they might have been—glass bulbs—Prince Rupert's drops, consummated in powder..for any end or meaning.

Prince Albert. **1.** The name of Prince Albert Edward, afterwards King Edward VII, used *attrib.* and *absol.* to designate a kind of frock coat or suit made fashionable by him. orig. *U.S.*

1884 I. M. Rittenhouse *Maud* (1939) 270, I ran out and ushered Mr Lyons in, gotten up to kill in his Prince Albert coat. **1890** [see *jimswinger]. **1895** *Montgomery Ward Catal.* 273/1 Prince Albert Suits. **1897** Kipling *Day's Work* (1898) 221 A man in a black Prince Albert, without a collar, came up. **1903** S. Clapin *New Dict. Amer.* p. viii, If a Londoner is fortunate enough to cross the Atlantic,.. but is unfortunate enough to have to buy a frock-coat..he must call it a 'Prince Albert'. **1919** *Ladies' Home Jrnl.* July 19/2 Instinctively I looked about him for revolvers. There were none, not even the slightest bulge at the hips of the Prince Albert coat he wore. **1927** *Scribner's Mag.* Feb. 164/1 Antone was dressed for a call, having donned a shiny Prince Albert coat over his collarless shirt. **1941** W. C. Handy *Father of Blues* vii. 91 Glittering young devils in silk toppers and Prince Alberts. **1967** C. O. Skinner *Madame Sarah* viii. 147 Amid the..city coats, Prince Alberts and pin-striped trousers, Sarah looked vainly for a single woman. **1972** H. Kemelman *Monday the Rabbi took Off* xv. 103 Others [*sc.* Chassidim]..favored a Prince Albert, which because it was warm, they kept open.

2. The name of Prince Albert, the Prince Consort, used in *pl.* to designate foot- or toe-wraps worn by tramps, sailors, etc., inside boots; the boots themselves. *Austral.*

1893 K. Mackay *Out Back* (ed. 2) ii. v. 191 With bent shoulders..they 'mouched' along,..showing glimpses of brown, unwashed skin above the frayed edges of their 'Prince Alberts', the toes of their bluchers gaping wide. **1903** 'T. Collins' *Such is Life* (1937) i. 52 Unlapping from his feet the inexpensive substitute for socks known as 'prince-alberts'. **1924** *Truth* (Sydney) 27 Apr. 6 *Prince Alberts*, rags or bandages used by a swagman or sundowner around his feet in place of socks. **1945** Baker *Austral. Lang.* 105 *Prince Alfreds* or *Prince Alberts* as synonyms for *toe-rags*. These terms developed from the malign suggestion that the Prince Consort was so poor when he came to England to marry Queen Victoria that he wore toe-rags instead of socks. *Ibid.*, Rough lace-up boots were also known as *Prince Alberts* in Queensland in the closing years of last century. **1958** J. Bisset *Sail Ho!* v. 48 These foot-wraps were known in British ships as 'Prince Alberts'.

Prince Charming. [Partial tr. F. *Roi Charmant*, the name of the hero of the Comtesse d'Aulnoy's *L'Oiseau Bleu* (1697). In English the name first appears as that of the hero of Planché's *King Charming* or *Prince Charming*, and was later adopted for the hero of various fairy-tale pantomimes, *esp.* the *Sleeping Beauty* and *Cinderella*.] A fairy-tale hero; the lover every girl dreams of; a perfect young man.

[**1850** *Times* 27 Dec. 5/2 Lyceum... Then followed the principal attraction of the evening, in the shape of a new and original fairy extravaganza, in two acts, entitled *King Charming; or, the Blue Bird of Paradise*. *Ibid.*, We would particularly notice..the final scene of the restoration of King Charming.] **1855** *N.Y. Daily Times* 25 Dec. 4/3 The burlesque of 'King Charming'..The legend is taken from the Countess D'Aulnoy's fairy tale of 'L'Oiseau Bleu', and relates to the adventures of the wonderful *Prince Charming*, an immortal monarch, gifted with perpetual youth. *Ibid.* 4/4 Mrs. H. C. Watson as *Prince Charming* scarcely did herself justice. **1862** *Welcome Guest* 4 Jan. 152/3 They tell me I am good looking, but I don't believe it; although the young ladies of my acquaintance, who are too bold for me, call me 'Prince Charming'. **1913** W. J. Locke *Stella Maris* xv. 205 Love she had heard of, the love of Prince Charming for Princess Rose. **1920** [see *backfisch]. **1929** E. Wilson *I thought of Daisy* v. 286 When Prince Charming comes along, he's always just a great, big, strong, clean-limbed American. **1931** G. C. D. Odell *Ann. N.Y. Stage* VI. 427 A holiday frippery, Planché's King Charming, or, the Blue Bird of Paradise, ushered in, on Christmas Eve [1855], a success that lasted, without interruption, until January 12th. *Ibid.* 450 [Laura Keene] hired the unlucky Metropolitan theatre..and advertised the opening for December 24th, with Two Can Play at that Game and Prince Charming... The Broadway Theatre on the same evening produced King Charming, as it called Planché's extravaganza... Prince Charming was not played at Miss Keene's..some miscreant had so slashed the chief scene of Prince Charming that the play could not be given. **1936** R. C. K. Ensor *England 1870–1914* vii. 215 He [*sc.* Rosebery] had come to the front as the Prince Charming of politics—young, handsome, rich, eloquent, candid, and popular. **1939** J. Curtis *What Immortal Hand* iii. 36 She had not the slightest wish to marry anybody from Lowdham Street... No, she wanted some kind of Prince Charming like they had in the pictures. **1939** Wodehouse *Uncle Fred in Springtime* xv. 225 There was a look in her eyes that made me think right away that she was feeling he was her Prince Charming. **1945** G. Endore *Methinks the Lady* (1947) ii. 27 And your Prince Charming? You met him at Mona's? **1960** E. Eliot *They all married Well* xiii. 201 Virginia Bonynge was too pretty..to be forever scorned by *all* the Prince Charmings who abounded in London. **1961** *Guardian* 17 May 6/1 Like most other English schoolgirls, I spent many an hour dreaming... Prince Charmings used to come and carry me off on white chargers. **1975** *Radio Times* 9 Jan. 43/2 They are destined to find their Prince Charmings at a commercial fair in Rochefort. **1976** *Daily Mail* 25 Mar. 22/1 We all know.. the story of Cinderella... Our hero is a progressive Prince Charming who doesn't mind the privilege and protocol provided he can marry the girl of his choice. *Ibid.*, Way back in the days of Dr Kildare, Richard Chamberlain must have been every girl's idea of Prince Charming. **1977** *Christian* IV. 124 The beast has by the kiss of love become the Prince Charming who, far from having to be shut away, is now the very life and soul of what I am.

prince consort: see Consort *sb.*[1] 3, Prince *sb.* 6.

princely, *a.* Add: **1. b.** *princely states*, the states of India that were ruled by native princes before the Indian Independence Act of 1947. Also (*rare*) in *sing.*

1952 *Columbia Lippincott Gazetteer of World* 835/2 By Jan. 26, 1950, when India became a sovereign republic, all acceding princely states had been brought within the constitutional framework. **1959** *Listener* 19 Mar. 497/2 The Princely States..have disappeared. **1967** Singha & Massey *Indian Dances* iv. 59 Both the South Indian Princely States and the Madras High Court recognized their rights and status. **1975** *Times* 29 Aug. 12/1 The map of India..was redrawn to incorporate the former princely states. **1980** H. R. F. Keating *Murder of Maharajah* xviii. 225 Here is a simple District Superintendent of Police..invited to a princely state because a murder has been committed.

prince's feather. b. (Earlier and later examples.)

1712 J. Mortimer *Whole Art Husb.* II. 166 [see quot. 1721 in Dict.]. **1883** W. Robinson *Eng. Flower Garden* 14/1 Prince's Feather, Love-lies-bleeding... Among annuals none are more in want of judicious use and appreciation than these. **1925** E. Glasgow *Barren Ground* i. xi. 134 A narrow path led between rows of log cabins, each with its patchwork square of garden, and its clump of gaudy prince's feather or coxcomb by the doorstep. **1974** M. Allan *Plants that changed our Gardens* i. 41 Prince's Feather..grows up to 5 ft tall and has flower plumes of deep crimson.

princess. Add: **5. b.** Used as a form of address to a woman or girl. *colloq.*

1924 J. Buchan *Three Hostages* xviii. 254, I have waked you from sleep, my princess. Therefore so far it is good. **1968** J. Symons *Man whose Dreams came True* i. v. 42 'This is celebration night, Princess.' He had called her Princess the whole evening. **1969** A. Laski *Dominant Fifth* iii. 120 Ah come on, princess, you're being morbid. **1970** J. Aiken *Embroidered Sunset* i. 7 It was one of Uncle Wilbie's pleasantries to address Lucy as Princess. **1972** R. Ludlum *Osterman Weekend* i. 12 Hey, Princess—get your brothers out and help your mother with the smaller bags.

7. *princess ring, princess (tele)phone.*

1962 M. & G. Gordon *Journey with Stranger* (1963) iii. 28 If you want a good bargain in princess rings, go down New Road in Bangkok. **1973** —— *Informant* iii. 13 She was..constantly twisting a princess ring from Thailand. **1966** B. Glemser *Dear Hungarian Friend* viii. 139 She.. picked up the azure blue Princess telephone, and said, 'Hello?' **1969** D. E. Westlake *Up your Banners* (1970) xxxi. 210 We had to go next door and use Mrs. Lupowitz' Princess phone, a skittering pink beast that traveled all over its waxed table..whenever anybody tried to dial it. **1972** G. Baxt *Burning Sappho* ii. 42 He'd been watching Pat circling her gold princess phone for ten minutes. **1973** *Sat. Rev. Society* (U.S.) Mar. 70/1 Colored phones and such models as the lighter and smaller 'Princess' and the 'Trimline' (with the dial mechanism in the handset). **1976** M. Machlin *Pipeline* ii. 29 Brandon opened the chest and removed a brown princess telephone from it.

8. princess dress (earlier and later examples); also *princess cut, line, tunic.*

1867 in A. Adburgham *Shops & Shopping* (1964) xi. 119 Princess breakfast dress. **1872** *Young Englishwoman* Oct. 541/1 A long princess-tunic. *Ibid.* 546/1 A lovely Princess dress, with cape. **1877** in A. Adburgham *Shops & Shopping* (1964) xvi. 178 The Princess cut. **1960** C. W. Cunnington et al. *Dict. Eng. Costume* 172/1 *Princess dress*,..a style popularly associated with the Princess of Wales when *c.* 1878–80 it was very fashionable. **1964** *McCall's Sewing* i. 5/1 A narrow centre panel, often seen in a princess-line dress, will add height. **1968** J. Ironside *Fashion Alphabet* 25 *Princess*, a line which follows the curves of the body..darted for shape but with no seam at the waistline. **1973** *Times* 15 Nov. 1/3 The wedding dress was in pure white silk in the traditional *Princess* line.

‖ **princesse lointaine** (prænses lwɑ̃tɛ̃n). [Fr., lit. 'distant princess', title of a play by E. Rostand (1868–1918), based on a theme of the poetry of the 12th-cent. troubadour Jaufré Rudel.] An ideal but unattainable woman. Also as *attrib. phr.*, aloof, unapproachable.

1921 W. J. Locke *Mountebank* viii. 96 The woman who could satisfy all his romantic imaginings was the Princesse

Lointaine. **1934** A. THIRKELL *Wild Strawberries* xi. 238 Pierre had sat with Agnes, feeling like Geoffroy Rudel with the Princesse Lointaine. **1940** A. CHRISTIE *Sad Cypress* I. i. 17 That little air of yours—aloof—untouchable—*la Princesse Lointaine.* **1949** R. HARVEY *Curtain Time* 127 Papa was the romantic and the mystic, following the gleam of the fiercer bass, the more golden walleyed pike, and sailing in search of a muskelunge, as if for some *princesse lointaine.* **1957** L. DURRELL *Bitter Lemons* 97, I had seen her..driving about the hills with the same *princesse lointaine* expression. **1962** I. MURDOCH *Unofficial Rose* xxxiii. 314 He had loved Lindsay as the enticing but untouchable *princesse lointaine.* **1969** M. DRABBLE *Waterfall* 42 She lay there, the unachievable *princesse lointaine.* **1976** P. QUENNELL *Marble Foot* iv. 162 Constant's *princesse lointaine* was the Chinese film-actress Anna May Wong.

Princeton-First-Year. Applied to a form of male homosexual activity in which partners achieve orgasm by intercrural friction.

1969, 1971 [see *plain sewing* s.v. *PLAIN *a.*[1] and *adv.* C.c]. **1980** *Times Lit. Suppl.* 21 Mar. 324/5 'Princeton-First-Year' is a more condescending version of the term 'Princeton Rub'; that is, *coitus contra ventrem.*

Princetonian (priːns,tōᵘ·niăn), *sb.* and *a.* [f. *Princeton* (see below) + -IAN.] **A.** *sb.* A student or graduate of Princeton University, New Jersey, U.S.A. **B.** *adj.* Of or pertaining to Princeton University.

1876 (*title of newspaper*) The Princetonian. **1896** J. BARNES (*title*) A Princetonian. A Story of undergraduate life at the College of New Jersey. **1898** J. W. ALEXANDER *Princeton* 5 These two renowned and useful organizations ..[are] exclusively Princetonian. *Ibid.* 26 Some cynical Princetonian has said that nothing less than two armies and a revolution could drive a son of Old Nassau to a New England college. **1928** [see *old-line* s.v. *OLD D. 3]. **1949** *Cavalier Daily* (Univ. of Virginia) 22 Oct. 4/2 Staffers of the Daily Pennsylvanian visited the Princetonian offices following the Penn-Princeton football game. **1971** M. MCCARTHY *Birds of Amer.* 192 The languid voice of a Princetonian major in government studies. *Ibid.* 193 The ultra-WASP Princetonian, who bore the curious name of Silvanus Platt. **1977** *New Yorker* 23 May 88/1 Thus ringingly begins an 'Alumni Primer' that is distributed to each Princetonian during the summer following his.. graduation from that hallowed institution.

principal, *a.* and *sb.* (*adv.*) Add: **A.** *adj.* **1. a.** *principal boy*, the leading male role in a pantomime, usu. played by a woman; *principal girl*, the leading female role in a pantomime.

1893 H. E. MCLELLAND *Jack & Beanstalk* 11 She's Jill, our 'principal girl', the gallery's joy. *Ibid.*, So it's only natural, as I'm the principal boy! **1897** G. B. SHAW *Our Theatres in Nineties* (1932) III. 24 Why..is the 'principal boy' expected to be more vulgar than the principal girl? **1900** [in Dict.]. **1901** R. J. BROADBENT *Hist. Pantomime* xxi. 224 Towards the close of the 'fifties ..the character of Harlequin began to be played by women, the origin of what is now known as the 'principal boy'. **1910** BARONESS ORCZY *Lady Molly* ix. 236 The little actress looked ready to cry... 'I am principal boy at the Grand,' she explained. **1925** M. W. DISHER *Clowns & Pantomimes* xvii. 317 This obsession with barbaric splendour was shown in Harris's choice of 'principal boys'. **1932** D. L. SAYERS *Have his Carcase* xv. 201 Airy-fairy-Lilian they used to call me when I was principal boy in old Rosenbaum's shows. **1962** *Oxford Mail* 24 Dec. 6/6 In 1947 he met his wife in pantomime at Lincoln. 'She was the principal girl, Maid Marion. I was just one of the bad robbers.' **1969** *Listener* 2 Jan. 18/1 Gone are the good days when principal boys were girls. **1971** *Petticoat* 17 July 28/1 He..was wearing a pink voile shirt with principal-boy sleeves. **1975** *Times* 2 May 11/3 The greatest of pantomime principal boys, Dorothy Ward.

11. *principal component*, one of the components of a set of statistical data (regarded as points in a multi-dimensional space) which contribute most strongly to its variance; freq. *attrib.* (in *sing.* or *pl.*), designating a method of analysis which involves finding the principal component and removing the variance due to it, and repeating this successively; *principal ideal*, an ideal whose elements can be generated by multiplying some particular member of the ring by each member (including itself) in turn; *principal quantum number* (Physics), the quantum number symbolized by *n* (see *N I. 4 b); *principal stress*, each of the three purely tensile or compressive stresses acting in mutually perpendicular directions into which any combination of stresses acting at a point can be resolved.

The examples are arranged in alphabetical order (in Dict. they are arranged chronologically).

1933 H. HOTELLING in *Jrnl. Educ. Psychol.* XXIV. 421 We..determine the components, not exceeding *n* in number, and perhaps neglecting those whose contributions to the total variance are small. This we shall call the method of principal components. **1963** SOKAL & SNEATH *Princ. Numerical Taxon.* vii. 195 Two different methods of factor analysis are customarily practiced: the principal components method is largely employed by British factor analysts. **1968** *Brit. Med. Bull.* XXIV. 236/2 Examples of the use of the older established techniques of principal components analysis..and factor analysis..rather than taxonomic analysis, predominate in the literature. **1969** A. P. DEMPSTER *Elem. Contin. Multivariate Anal.* vii. 136 The principal component analysis of a given sample relative to a given reference inner product over variable-space consists of finding the eigenvalues and eigenvectors of the sample covariance inner product relative to the reference inner product. The eigenvalues found in this way will be called sample principal components of total variance relative to the chosen reference inner product or, more briefly, principal components. **1937** A. A. ALBERT *Mod. Higher Algebra* (1938) xi. 255 Every two quantities of a principal ideal ring have a greatest common divisor. **1965** J. J. ROTMAN *Theory of Groups* iv. 66 A principal ideal domain is a domain in which every ideal is a principal ideal. **1970** D. M. BURTON *First Course in Rings & Ideals* ii. 19 An ideal (*a*) generated by just one ring element is termed a principal ideal. **1922**, etc. Principal quantum number [see *N I. 4 b]. **1973** J. G. TWEEDDALE *Materials Technol.* I. ii. 23 A specific maximum possible number of orientations of orbital pattern, each pattern being completely occupied if two electrons are in it, is possible for each mode, the number being determined by the relevant Principal Quantum Number. **1858** W. J. M. RANKINE *Man. Appl. Mech.* I. v. 94 The three conjugate normal stresses are called principal stresses, and their directions, principal axes of stress. **1922** GLAZEBROOK *Dict. Appl. Physics* I. 803/2 The intensity of greatest shearing stress at any point is equal..to one-half the algebraic difference of the greatest and least principal stresses. **1944** A. HOLMES *Princ. Physical Geol.* vi. 78 The various types of faults depend on the relationships between the three principal stresses.., assuming of course, that..the stress difference is sufficient to bring about fracture and movement. **1971** I. G. GASS et al. *Understanding Earth* xix. 272/1 Making certain other reasonable assumptions about the shear fracture character of the fault, it is possible to derive..the direction of the maximum principal stress.

12. *Surveying.* = PRIMARY *a.* 3 a in Dict. and Suppl.

1790 *Phil. Trans. R. Soc.* LXXX. 248 The first set [of Secondary triangles] consists of thirty-five, whereby the relative distances of so many points have been determined from certain stations of the principal series. **1795** *Ibid.* LXXXV. 490 (*heading*) Of the selection of the angles constituting the principal triangles, and the manner of reducing them for computation. **1847** W. YOLLAND *Acct. Measurement of Lough Foyle Base* VII. 113 From the commencement of the Irish Survey, in 1825, secondary objects required for breaking up the principal triangulation into a smaller network..were regularly observed at the same time as observations were made of the principal stations. **1920** [see *PRIMARY *a.* 3 a].

13. *Seismology.* Applied to the most intense shock or earthquake occurring in a sequence.

1899 C. DAVISON *Hereford Earthquake Dec. 17, 1896* iv. 199 The principal shock was also registered by magnetographs at Kew. *Ibid.* 200 The principal earthquake was felt by several persons in the Isle of Wight. **1902** *Q. Jrnl. Geol. Soc.* LVIII. 374 The focus of this shock was evidently close to the northern end of the focus of the first and principal shock. **1938** L. D. LEET *Pract. Seismol.* ix. 295 Davison has cited several well-studied cases..where the range of audibility of after-shocks increased progressively and systematically, giving evidence of decreasing depth of foci following the principal shock. **1965** A. HOLMES *Princ. Physical Geol.* (ed. 2) xxv. 893 The principal shock, which generally lasts only a few seconds, or at most, and rarely, a few minutes, may be preceded by fore-shocks and is invariably followed by a series of after-shocks.

B. *sb.* **1. a.** (Further examples.)

1827 S. RODMAN in B. Swan *New Bedford in 1827* (1935) 3/2, I visited the High School, Wm. Johnson, principal. **1833** *Century Mag.* XXX. 780/1, I am, sir.. permitted to be the Principal of the Canterbury, (Conn.) Female Boarding School. **1949** *Lubbock* (Texas) *Morning Avalanche* 23 Feb. I. 10/6 Price was named to the position of principal of the new school. **1973** *N.Y. Law Jrnl.* 30 July 13/7 Petitioner, a probationary assistant principal in James Wilson Young High School, resigned in writing on Feb. 13, 1973 (effective June 29, 1973) after being pressed to do so by both the District Principal (Mr. Covell) and the Assistant District Principal (Mr. Pecorale) of the School District. **1974** *Hartsville* (S. Carolina) *Messenger* 22 Apr. 1-A/4 Dr. Black pointed out that students who presented certificates to their principals in September, 1973 will not need another one.

e. A rank in the Civil Service.

1890 A. E. HOUSMAN *Let.* 9 Oct. (1971) 27 The Administrative Principal, Mr Webb, has to-day taken up the comparison of Trade Mark applications. *Ibid.* 28 The position as Principal held by Mr Webb would give him a status not justified..by length of service. **1915** F. G. HEATH *Brit. Civil Service* xxii. 230 The salaries are as under: Twelve Analysts (Second Class), £160 by £15 annually to £350;..one Deputy Principal, £700 by £25 to £800; and one Principal Chemist, £1200, and after five years.., £1500 per annum. **1951** T. A. CRITCHLEY *Civil Service Today* ii. 38 Under these high officials..are the assistant secretaries, in charge of divisions, and principals, in charge of sections. **1951** *Posts in Civil Service for University Graduates* 9 The Principal's day to day work is not confined to his desk. **1967** *Times Rev. Industry* Feb. 100/2 The full time staff is small... Of these five are 'principals' —as the Civil Service calls executives.

f. A fully-qualified practitioner or partner in a professional business.

1968 *Economist* 13 Apr. 41/1 A young man can..become a principal in general practice..after four to five years' training..plus a year's pre-registration service—in hospital. **1972** *Accountant* 26 Oct. 502 (Advt.), Principals with the responsibility for training newly articled clerks should ensure that the best course of action for their newly articled clerks is to enrol with the Metropolitan College. **1975** *Law* (Employment Service Agency: Careers and Occupational Information Centre) 8 The principal with whom he has served his articles or apprenticeship may offer him an opening.

2. a. (Later examples.)

1962 H. O. BEECHENO *Introd. Business Stud.* xiii. 117 Whereas an agent is not normally allowed to relend his principal's money at interest..a bank is allowed to do this. **1976** *Times* 22 Apr. (Baltic Exchange Suppl.) p. i/9 The Baltic is unusual in being open both to middle men and principals.

f. A leading performer in a drama or entertainment.

1936 N. STREATFIELD *Ballet Shoes* xiv. 212 The production was on a very large scale... The principals became unduly important. **1961** *Times* 20 June 16 The three principals are admirable: as Danila, Mr. Yuri Soloviev gives a tremendous performance; he has a prodigious technique in leaps and turns. **1971** *Morning Star* 28 June 4 Steve Hodson and Gillian Blake, the two principals in Yorkshire TV's new children's series. **1976** *National Observer* (U.S.) 8 May 20/3 To add to my discomfort, I found the voices of the principals, Michael Cristofer and Tyne Daly, distinctly unpleasant.

‖ **principessa** (printʃipe·să). [It., f. med.L. *principissa* (see PRINCESS *sb.*)] An Italian princess. Also *attrib.*

1823 LADY BLESSINGTON *Jrnl.* 27 July in E. Clay *Lady Blessington at Naples* (1979) 38 The Principessa Partanno is..no longer in her *première jeunesse.* **1861** C. M. YONGE *Young Step-Mother* xxiii. 333 He should go and marry the Principessa Bianca, a foreigner and Papist. **1945** E. WAUGH *Brideshead Revisited* I. ii. 50 The Principessa Fogliere gave a ball and Lord Malton was not asked. **1963** *Times Lit. Suppl.* 11 Jan. 21/3 The increasingly angular principessa who adores him. **1967** P. E. H. DURSTON *Mortissimo* (1968) iii. 27 The most elegant little *principessa* in the Villa Borghese. **1973** 'D. JORDAN' *Nile Green* xxxiii. 159 The princess..smiled, a weary principessa smile. **1979** N. SLATER *Falcon* i. 22 The pretty principessas would be storming the Embassy gates.

principium. Add: **1. c.** *principium individuationis*: the principle through which an entity is differentiated from matter, or being from non-being. (Cf. INDIVIDUATION 1 *note.*)

1694 LOCKE *Essay Hum. Und.* (ed. 2) II. xxvii. 179 'Tis easie to discover, what is so much enquired after, the *principium Individuationis*, and that 'tis plain is Existence it self, which determines any sort of Being to a particular time and place incommunicable to two Beings of the same kind. **1739** HUME *Treat. Hum. Nature* I. IV. 349 In order to justify this system, there are four things requisite. *First,* To explain the *principium individuationis.* **1883** F. H. BRADLEY *Princ. Logic* 265 It was shown above.. that space and time-relations are no *principium individuationis*; for they fall within the *what*, and do not make the *this*. **1947** *Horizon* Feb. 150 But above this layer of all-embracing 'identification' Sorge reappears as *principium individuationis*, isolating a person and stimulating his intellect into the frightful awareness of his nakedness and his fate. **1965** *Listener* 2 Sept. 344/1 Something.. must divide us from other people, there must be some kind of *principium individuationis.*

principle, *sb.* Add: **5. c.** *first principle*: a primary proposition, considered self-evident, upon which further reasoning or belief is based; freq. in *pl.*

In some quots. influenced by sense 3 in Dict.

1638 [see PRINCIPLE *sb.* 10 a]. **1690** LOCKE *Essay Hum. Und.* I. ii. 10 Those (as they are called) first Principles. **1701** J. NORRIS *Ideal World* I. ii. 75 As much above the Possibility as the Necessity of Demonstration, in one Word, a very first Principle. **1785** [see PRINCIPLE *sb.* 7 a]. **1817** COLERIDGE *Biog. Lit.* I. xii. 253 Philosophy in its first principles must have a practical or moral as well as a theoretical or speculative side. *Ibid.* 260 Those original and innate prejudices..which to all but the philosopher are the first principles of knowledge. **1871** B. JOWETT tr. *Plato's Dialogues* I. 711 And this is the reason why every man should expend his chief thought and attention on the consideration of his first principles: —are they or are they not rightly laid down? **1934** *Times Lit. Suppl.* 19 July 497/2 It is to Coleridge's search for first principles in literature that appeal is made. **1961** *Cambr. Daily News* 10 Feb. 7 Once you have absorbed the first principles in art.

7. c. Also in phr. *on general principles*, freq. in weakened sense: in general, for no specified reason, from a settled motive.

1894 SOMERVILLE & 'ROSS' *Real Charlotte* II. xxi. 90 She had no particular dislike for Francie..but on general principles she was pleased that discomfiture had come to Miss Fitzpatrick. **1898** R. HUGHES *Lakerim Athletic Club* 246 Pretty wanted to punch his head on general principles, but decided it would be better to beat him at tennis. **1914** *New Republic* 26 Dec. 15/1 In one Spanish village he was locked up on general principles, because the King happened to be passing through town that day. **1930** J. C. RANSOM *God without Thunder* II. viii. 173 It is like the flattery of the man who flatters us on general principles. **1938** 'G. GRAHAM' *Swiss Sonata* 87 Vicky will be held responsible for it just on general principles, and that will be that.

d. Phr. *in principle*: theoretically; in general but not necessarily in individual cases.

1820 G. CANNING in C'tess of Airlie *Lady Palmerston* (1922) I. vi. 102 So objectionable does it appear to them in principle as well as in practice. **1859** PALMERSTON in P. Guedalla *Palmerston Papers* (1928) 117 The First Method would evidently be the best in Principle. **1874** GEO. ELIOT *Let.* 15 July (1956) VI. 67, I am thoroughly opposed in principle (quite apart from any personal reference to myself) to the system of *contemporary* biography. **1932** *Ann. Reg. 1931* 295 These [proposals] were rejected by Washington, but the latter made a counter-proposal: that France accept the scheme 'in principle', and leave to a conference of technical experts those practical modifications which she desired. **1951** J. CORNISH *Provincials* 102 Still, we were loggers; we had won in principle. **1963**

RICHARDSON & TOYNBEE *Thanatos* 87 When we say that we know a thing it involves us in saying that it is, at least in principle, verifiable by the senses.

principled, *ppl. a.* Add: **4.** Based on or guided by (technical) principles or rules; not arbitrary or *ad hoc*.

1968 P. M. POSTAL *Aspects Phonol. Theory* iii. 47 The one principled way to make such a choice independently of the grammar..is to pick one of the several representations which eliminate *all* phonetically predictable features. **1970** *Canad. Jrnl. Linguistics* XVI. I. 3 Both factions agree on what constitutes the natural domain of linguistics:..the principled explanation of sound-meaning relations in languages. **1972** *Language* XLVIII. 301 It is interesting that there is a principled basis for choosing, in certain types of circumstances, a rule with a global environment over a corresponding non-global rule plus an ordering statement. **1978** *Ibid.* LIV. 410 As there is no principled way to prevent base rules from generating intransitive prepositions in any PP position, 5c could be base-generated, given E's base rules.

pring (priŋ), *sb.* [Echoic.] The sound made by a bell.

c **1921** D. H. LAWRENCE *Phoenix II* (1968) 183 She heard a loud prrring-prrring of a bicycle-bell.

pring (priŋ), *v.* [Echoic.] *intr.* To make a sound like a bell.

1927 *Scots Observer* 30 Apr. 10/4 The bell of no. 13 was pringing lustily.

pringling (pri·ŋgliŋ), *ppl. a.* [f. PRINGLE *v.* + -ING^2.] That pringles, or causes a prickly sensation.

1896 A. CONAN DOYLE *Uncle Bernac* i. 7, I..pressed my lips upon the wet and pringling gravel. **1923** C. MORLEY *Where Blue Begins* i. 5 In the golden light and pringling air he felt excitable and high-strung.

pri·ngling, *vbl. sb.* [f. the vb.] A prickly and tingling sensation.

1956 P. WENTWORTH *Silent Pool* xli. 214 Young Watson felt a pringling at the back of his neck.

prink, *v.*^{3} (Later examples.) Also, to walk daintily or with precise movements.

1962 M. BALDWIN *Death on Live Wire & On stepping from Sixth Storey Window* 11 Uncle Cyclops Had one eye To bulge at ankles prinking past. **1962** J. ONSLOW *Bowler-Hatted Cowboy* xiii. 124 In the morning a doe with her twin fawns had passed us, stopping to nibble at the willow bushes as she prinked down the hill.

prinkle (pri·ŋk'l), *sb. Sc.* [Origin obscure.] A young coal-fish, *Pollachius virens*.

1832 P. BUCHAN *Secret Songs of Silence* (MS.) 177 The laddie and the lassie, Gaed out to gather prinkle, O. **1903** G. SIM *Vertebrate Fauna of 'Dee'* 238 In the young stages, the names of 'Prinkle', 'Gerrick', 'Poodlie', are given [to the coal fish]. **1943** W. S. FORSYTH *Guff o' Waur* 54 Wupp it weel wi' curly 'oo', The prinkles to confoun'. **1972** *Which?* May 135/1 Saithe..may be called coal fish, coley, and a whole host of local names from cooth to prinkle.

Prins (prins). *Chem.* The name of H. J. *Prins* (1889–1958), Dutch chemist, used *attrib.* to designate the condensation of an olefin with formaldehyde or other aliphatic aldehydes in the presence of a dilute mineral acid.

1944 *Jrnl. Chem. Soc.* 296 Under the conditions of the Prins reaction, a normal, acid-catalysed addition to the olefinic linking occurs. **1970** *Tetrahedron Lett.* I. 37 (*heading*) The isolation and synthesis of a novel tetracyclic ether from East Indian sandalwood oil. A facile intramolecular Prins reaction.

print, *sb.* Add: **I. 3.** *esp.* = *finger-print* s.v. *FINGER *sb.* 15.

1924 P. MACDONALD *Rasp* vi. 88 But how to explain the finger-prints? And Deacon did not know of those prints. **1929** 'G. DAVIOT' *Man in Queue* ii. 18 Attached..was a report from the finger-print department. There was no trace of these prints in their records. **1936** A. CHRISTIE *Cards on Table* xxii. 215 Handled it with gloves,..and..the last prints would be those of Mrs. Benson herself. **1938** N. MARSH *Artists in Crime* v. 66 If you come across any keys, try them for prints. **1952** E. GRIERSON *Reputation for Song* xxi. 170 They *will* take his prints. **1957** F. & R. LOCKRIDGE *Tangled Cord* (1959) xiii. 170 Harry here gets to thinking maybe he touched something and left prints. **1975** J. MCCLURE *Snake* viii. 113 The drinking vessels had been cleaned of any prints, and the wash basin..given a thorough rub-over. **1980** P. G. WINSLOW *Counsellor Heart* ii. 32 While the print man was working Capricorn had a few words with..the Divisional Surgeon.

5. (Later examples.) Also *attrib.*

1909 [see *CREAMERY 1 b]. **1955** J. G. DAVIS *Dict. Dairying* (ed. 2) 153 The cream..goes through either a box moulder for packing into 56 lb. boxes or a pat moulder for wrapping 1 lb. and ½ lb. prints. **1963** M. MCCARTHY *Group* ix. 194 Libby was scandalized by the amount of fresh print butter Polly mixed in..*plus* brandy and sherry. **1972** E. WIGGINTON *Foxfire Bk.* 188 When it [*sc.* a mould] is filled, push down on the handle of the mold, which acts like a piston, thus releasing the 'print' of butter.

6. (Earlier and later examples.) Also, a pattern printed on fabric.

1756 E. HOLYOKE in G. F. Dow *Holyoke Diaries* (1911) 16 Put Prints out to whiten. **1825** E. WEETON *Let.* 22 Apr. in *Jrnl. of Governess* (1969) II. 352 When you open the parcel..you will find the print which I have procured for you: there are two patterns, a yard each. **1917** *Harrods Gen. Catal.* 1409/2 Best English Prints, for Servants' Dresses. **1957** M. B. PICKEN *Fashion Dict.* 264/1 *Print*, fabric stamped with design by means of paste dyes used on engraved rollers, wood blocks or screens. **1964** *McCall's Sewing* i. 7/1 Like stripes, prints also can be used to create desirable effects. *Ibid.* vii. 108/1 First check to see if the print has a regular directional pattern. **1972** *Vogue* June 94 Mandarin coat and slit dress of matching print. **1976** *Times* 25 Mar. 11/3 Made in pure silk chiffon, it was chosen from a range of evening dresses in many prints and colours. **1976** *Guardian* 2 Apr. 4/1 Detail from Nympheus: a hand blocked print on linen copied from an 11th century Chinese painted silk, now in the British Museum.

II. 7. Used without *in* or *into*.

1932 E. V. LUCAS *Reading, Writing & Remembering* iii. 69, I have no recollection that the article ever reached print. *Ibid.* vi. 121, I publish it here for the first time—it has waited only forty-five years for print. **1934** H. G. WELLS *Exper. Autobiogr.* I. vi. 356 This success whetted my appetite for print and I sent Harris a further article.. which he packed off to the printers at once. **1950** *Science News* XV. 7 There is one fundamental reason why free-lance articles so rarely see print. **1970** G. F. NEWMAN *Sir, You Bastard* viii. 204 He knew that the fray with James would make some print. **1977** *Time* 14 Mar. 31/1 Nor is it likely that a British version of the Pentagon papers or the Watergate scandals would ever have seen the light of print.

9. Restrict †*Obs.* to sense in Dict. and add: **b.** *in the print*, in the printing trade.

1973 L. HEREN *Growing up Poor in London* ii. 39 For our mother, only a minimum of education was required to ensure a good safe job in the print. *Ibid.* viii. 193 For her [*sc.* his mother] a good job in the print and a house in Bromley or Beckenham meant security, respectability and keeping yourself to yourself.

11. a. (Later examples.)

1942 D. POWELL *Time to be Born* (1943) iv. 80 A few names, if sufficiently in the public prints, naturally did stick. **1961** R. M. WILLIAMS in D. N. Barrett *Values in America* iii. 74 The criticisms levelled against higher education in the public prints. **1973** *Daily Tel.* (Colour Suppl.) 30 Nov. 7/2 The popular prints are interested in Parliament only when something dramatic blows up, or when an MP, possibly overworked, makes an ass of himself.

b. Also in general use.

1928 *Daily Mail* 25 July 18/5 Prints of the Memorandum and Articles of Association can be inspected at any time.

13. In mod. use applied to (*a*) a (usu. positive) photographic picture produced on an opaque medium for direct viewing (as opposed to a transparency); (*b*) a positive copy of a motion picture (on a transparent medium).

(*a*) **1915** [see *colour transparency* s.v. *COLOUR *sb.*^{1} 17 b]. **1939** MACK & MARTIN *Photogr. Process* ix. 304 It is the final objective of the photographic process to produce a positive image (either a transparency or a paper print). **1958** C. L. THOMSON *Colour Films* 39 Transparencies as a basis for prints have the advantage that the printer knows in advance that the colour photograph is a successful one, and will therefore produce an acceptable print. **1970** C. B. NEBLETTE *Fund. Photogr.* xxi. 299 Ektachrome paper is designed for making color prints from transparencies on Ektachrome and Kodachrome film. **1978** *Sci. Amer.* Apr. 110 (*caption*) In this negative print made with the 48-inch Schmidt telescope on Palomar Mountain the nebulas appear black.

(*b*) **1912** F. A. TALBOT *Moving Pictures* viii. 87 The majority of cinematograph manufacturing establishments undertake to develop negatives, and to supply positive prints ready for projection. **1914** J. B. RATHBUN *Motion Picture Making* ii. 29 The light of the projector passes through the transparent positive print and traces the image on the screen. **1942** *Sun* (Baltimore) 23 Feb. 10/7 Lou Fonseca, director of the American League's motion picture, 'The Ninth Innings', said today that a number of prints of the film are now available for clubs, schools and other organizations. **1973** H. GRUPPE *Truxton Cipher* (1974) xiv. 141 The movie was a..bad Western... The print was on its sixth tour through the Atlantic Fleet, and ..the worse for wear. **1978** R. HILL *Pinch of Snuff* xii. 125 They made a film I'm interested in... I'd like to find out how many prints there were.

13*. A signal on magnetic tape produced by print-through.

1950–1 *B.B.C. Quarterly* V. 250/2 On playback..the comparatively high-level prints resulting from storage are replayed at their initial level. **1958** H. G. M. SPRATT *Magn. Tape Recording* iii. 110 The strength of the print rises rapidly immediately the reel has been wound up and then, with the rate of increase falling, tends towards an ultimate limiting value. **1962** A. NISBETT *Technique Sound Studio* iv. 84 The erasure is more marked on the small printed signal than on the main body of the recording (the print being reduced by perhaps 16 dB, as against 3 dB off the main signal).

15. a. print chain, an endless chain of printing types in some printers; **print-maker, -making** (as sense 12); **print order,** an order for a certain number (of an issue of a book, paper, etc.) to be printed; **print room** (examples); **print run** = *RUN *sb.*^{1} 20 d; **print-script,** a style of handwriting that imitates typography; **print train** = *print chain* above; **print wheel,** a disc having printing types round its rim that can be brought into position by rotation of the disc.

1967 R. BREGZIS in Cox & Grose *Organiz. Bibliogr. Rec. by Computer* V. 119 The cards are printed out by an IBM 1401 computer using a print chain with an expanded set of 101 characters. **1972** *Computers & Humanities* VII. 97 High quality printout, suitable for publication purposes and from an extended print chain with a large character set, is highly desirable. **1928** M. DOBSON *Block-Cutting & Print-Making by Hand* ii. 4 There are..many terms peculiar to the craft of print-making. *Ibid.* xx. 176 He who would be his own print-maker will really find no great obstacle in the way. **1961** *Times* 18 May 17/5 The work of 27 Soviet print-makers..and..almost our first view of current artistic activity in Russia. **1965** ZIGROSSER & GAEHDE *Guide to Collecting Orig. Prints* i. 4 Print-making is a democratic form of art, for it enables not one but many persons to own and enjoy the same work of art... Every medium has both utilitarian and aesthetic functions. This is especially true of printmaking. **1977** J. TREVALYAN in S. Turner *Handbk. Printmaking Supplies* 8 Today printmaking has grown into a vast and profitable business... When several printmakers meet together their talk is almost always where can this or that be bought. **1953** POHL & KORNBLUTH *Space Merchants* (1955) ii. 13 The first issue comes out in the fall, with a print order of twenty million. **1971** M. RUSSELL *Deadline* vii. 75 There's a 15,000 extra print order. Some newsagents sold out by ten yesterday. **1979** J. SHERWOOD *Hour of Hyenas* iii. 32 The only subject discussed was the money value of various contracts and the size of the resulting print order. **1849** *Index to Add. MSS. Brit. Mus. 1783–1835* p. iv, A certain number also of manuscripts..have long since been transferred to the Print Room. **1862** GEO. ELIOT *Let.* 17 May (1956) IV. 34 We..went to the Printroom of the British Museum to see Italian portraits of 15th cent. **1901** A. WHITMAN *Print-Collector's Handbk.* x. 132 Six officials have presided over the destinies of the Print Room. **1921** E. J. SULLIVAN *Art of Illustration* xxxvii. 252 Push past the unpretentious and silent swing door to the Print Room. **1956** HAYDEN & BUNT *Old Prints* p. viii, He will pass from our modest book to the masterpieces in the Print Rooms of the British and the Victoria and Albert Museums. **1970** B. ALLEN *Print Collecting* vi. 97 The little blue card..entitles him to be a regular visitor to the Print Room. **1975** *Language for Life* (Dept. Educ. & Sci.) xxi. 311 These books..cannot always command the large print runs of text books. **1979** *Bookseller* 23 June 2836/1 This compilation..sold out of its first print-run rapidly. **1979** *Times* 19 Dec. 12/4 Increasingly..books with a strong American end are being entirely printed in the United States, with a proportion of the print run bought for the United Kingdom. **1922** *Print Script* (Board of Educ.) 5 During the last few years the movement in favour of 'print-script' has spread so widely in the schools of this country that a wish has been expressed that the experience of the Board's Inspectors should be made available to the general public. **1932** A. J. FAIRBANK *Handwriting Man.* Introd., Of the problems arising in the schools today.., one..is how to adapt the handwriting which has been named 'print-script'..so that there may remain in the revised model nothing to hinder the tempo at which an adult writes. **1955** P. RUDLAND *From Scribble to Script* 6 A comparatively recent innovation in the teaching of handwriting is what is known as *print-script*... Print-script originated from an address on penmanship given by Edward Johnston at the Annual Conference of Teachers in 1913. **1959** J. C. GAGG *Beginning Three R's* xii. 82 It would seem that print-script is.. the most useful first style for slower children. **1975** *Language for Life* (Dept. Educ. & Sci.) xi. 185 Some teachers believe that a print-script should be used. **1970** *Computers & Humanities* IV. 247 Lest one despair of limitation in the number of possible escape codes, it should be pointed out that the standard IBM print train for the 360 line of computers permits 240 characters and to date (August 1969) only 174 are used on the extended set now planned by the Library of Congress for catalog card printing in all Roman alphabets. **1941** T. J. RHODES *Industr. Instruments for Measurement & Control* iv. 144 The multiple-point recording potentiometer is achieved by substituting a print wheel for the recording pen and by equipping the potentiometer with a motor-driven selector switch synchronized with the print wheel. **1961** L. W. HEIN *Introd. Electronic Data Processing* xiii. 255 Print wheel 1 will be used to print the first letter of the name, and wheel 120 will be used for the cents position of the net pay figures on the stub. **1970** A. CAMERON et al. *Computers & Old Eng. Concordances* 39 We had print wheels made; we never even got to fitting them on the machine.

b. print journalism, writing, reporting or writing for newspapers (as opp. television); so *print journalist*; **print medium** (usu. pl., **media**), newspapers (as opp. broadcasting); **print union,** a trade union for printers (also *printing union* s.v. *PRINTING *vbl. sb.* d).

1975 *Listener* 1 May 578/3 Michael Barratt can be taken to task for unwittingly imposing the techniques of popular print journalism on television reportage. **1977** *Listener* 1 Dec. 708/1 Eric Sevareid..has done for television what Walter Lippman did..for print journalism. **1971** *Ibid.* 25 Nov. 711/3 Some other print journalists—the editor of the *Evening Standard* is one—have chosen to break the solidarity of press and television to suggest that television's standards have been lower. **1973** *Time* 25 June 15/3 It will be the print journalists' and historians' task to review and criticize. **1975** *Listener* 10 Apr. 463/3 The camera simply recorded..the cycle of a diplomatic issue in a way no print journalist could ever hope to describe. **1968** *Globe & Mail* (Toronto) 13 Feb. B3/1 The message..is accentuated in print media advertising. **1972** *Guardian* 29 Jan. 11/5 The print media..claim..that they are being discriminated against. **1978** *Verbatim* Feb. 1/1 Part of the responsibility for our bent language rests with the print media. **1959** *Daily Tel.* 22 July 1/5 Print unions reject hours and pay offer. **1975** *Times* 7 Aug. 1/4 (*heading*) Print unions' ultimatum to 'Observer'. **1980** *Times* 13 Aug. 1/7 The unexpectedly strong reaction among other print unions brings a new dimension into the dispute over machine managers' pay. **1976** *New Yorker* 13 Sept. 103/3 (Advt.), Print writing is tougher than television writing.

print, *v.* Add: **II. 6. b.** *to print out*: to produce in or as a print-out.

See also 14 c below.

a **1884** KNIGHT *Dict. Mech.* Suppl. 722/1 The sending operator prints out his message in plain letters at the distant end of the line, whether the receiving operator is at the instrument or not. **1953** *IRE Trans. Instrumentation* June 68 This Binary Outscriber indicated that it would adequately perform its required task: that of rapidly printing-out the memory contents. **1955** *IRE Trans. Electronic Computers* IV. 2/2 The typewriter can operate directly upon information received from the accumulator and alphanumeric translator and print out a completely general format. **1957** *IRE Trans. Instrumentation* Sept. 194/1 A Flexowriter prints out the character that was stored in the interim flip-flop storage registers. **1969** *Listener* 10 July 44/3 In the case of the two computers, of course, the actual difference could be shown by printing out their programmes. **1977** *Sci. Amer.* Sept. 23/1 (Advt.), Results are displayed to hospital personnel and printed out as reports.

8. b. (Later examples.)

1912 *Englishwoman* July 73 The line block will print well on paper on which the delicate shades of the half-tone would be lost. **1971** D. Potter *Brit. Eliz. Stamps* ix. 95 On rare occasions the embossed stamp appears albino, when the colour has failed to print through lack of ink. **1979** *SLR Camera* June 41/1 For the other cases which will not print on these medium grade papers you'll have to use harder or softer grades to produce a result that even approaches the satisfactory.

d. With pass. force: to appear in print; to be printed.

See also quot. 1775 in sense 6 in Dict.

1930 *Sat. Rev. Lit.* (U.S.) 2 Aug. 21/2 The *Return* began printing in *Collier's*. **1953** *Northampton Dioc. Mag.* Autumn 11 The spoken word rarely prints satisfactorily. **1973** M. Russell *Double Hit* xviii. 132 The newsvendors' stands stood untended: the first editions were still printing.

11*. Of magnetic tape or a recorded signal: to give rise to print-through. Also *trans.*, to transfer (a signal) as a result of print-through.

1950–1 *B.B.C. Quarterly* V. 245/2 After a certain time, ..measure the level of the signal printed on to the erased slip. **1952** *Appl. Electronics Ann. 1951* 43/2 Trouble.. occurs sometimes with the programme 'printing' from one layer to another of the reel. **1958** J. Tall *Techniques Magn. Recording* iii. 33 Homogeneous tape was..favored until a few years ago in some parts of Europe and is still used occasionally there. It is subject to one major fault..: it 'prints' excessively.

III. 14. a. Also, to produce (a print) of a motion picture or from a transparency.

1915 J. B. Rathbun *Motion Picture Making* ii. 36 In printing the positive film from the negative, the teeth of the sprockets in the printing machine pass through both films, holding them in perfect register. **1931** B. Brown *Talking Pictures* x. 229 The usual method in printing is to mask the sound track space on the unexposed film and then print off the picture. *Ibid.* 243 While printing cinema films is similar in principle to ordinary photographic work, it is carried out on entirely different lines, due to the enormous length of the negative. **1974** *Encycl. Brit. Macropædia* XII. 549/2 From this optical negative the sound track can be printed photographically on the exhibition release prints. Sometimes the release prints are printed as positives directly from the final magnetic track, rather than from a negative made from this track.

b. (Further example.)

1929 R. H. Goodsall *Beginner's Guide Photogr.* vii. 37 A piece of printing paper is placed in contact with the negative and the light allowed to pass through the latter... Where there is little or no deposit on the negative it prints dark.

c. *to print out* (intr.): to produce an image (or, of an image, to appear) without chemical development. Also *trans.*, to print without development.

See also 6b above.

1882 *Rep. Brit. Assoc. Adv. Sci. 1881* 595 The author has 'printed out' the spectrum on chloride of silver. **1902** *Encycl. Brit.* XXXI. 703/2 Considerable use is also made of ready-prepared platinotype paper, sensitized with salts of platinum and iron, which can be printed out entirely or only partly printed and developed with potassic oxalate. **1906** R. C. Bayley *Compl. Photographer* xiv. 175 In order that P.O.P. may be sufficiently sensitive to be usable at all, and give a rich image by printing out, it is not sufficient that it should contain silver chloride only. **1913** Hind & Randles *Handbk. Photomicrogr.* xiv. 230 The paper is printed-out in daylight until all detail is visible, then developed in potassium oxalate solution. **1948** *Rep. Progress Physics* XI. 255 When exposures are increased by a factor of 10^7 to 10^8 the photographic material 'prints out'; it darkens visibly due to a process of reduction of the emulsion grains. **1953** *Phil. Mag.* XLIV. 223 This [exposure to radiation] caused silver to print-out internally both in strained crystals and in crystals which had been annealed. **1963** John & Field *Textbk. Photogr. Chem.* ii. 26 Emulsions of this type..were coated on paper, to give 'printing-out papers', so called because the image printed out directly. **1965** *Photogr. Jrnl.* CV. 285/2 A positive image is 'printed out', that is, it becomes visible without chemical development.

d. *trans.* To produce a positive print from (a negative or transparency).

1913 F. A. Talbot *Pract. Cinematogr.* vii. 93 An enterprising amateur who had an excellent negative handed it over to a topical-film firm to print and circulate. **1929** R. H. Goodsall *Beginner's Guide Photogr.* vii. 37 When the negative has been developed, washed and dried..it is ready to be printed. **1940** G. G. Quarles *Elem. Photogr.* x. 133 When a number of negatives are to be printed at one time, it is well to sort them into piles according to contrast. **1974** C. Swedlund *Photogr.* ix. 221/2 Contact printing was the original method of printing negatives, and it remains the process most typically used for negatives of such size..that their images do not require enlargement.

e. *to print down* (trans.): to transfer a photographic image from (a negative) to a printing plate.

1923 F. T. Cockett *Photo-Litho. & Offset Printing* 30 The seccotined worsted will adhere to the base glass and to the cut edges of the negatives so that the whole series can be printed-down in one operation. **1944** J. C. Tarr *Printing To-day* ix. 106 The negatives are printed down on to the metal vacuum frames. **1967** E. Chambers *Photolitho-Offset* iv. 48 Further treatment would result in a grey dot formation which would prove unsatisfactory for printing-down to metal.

f. *to print in* (trans.): to transfer (an image on a negative) to another negative that has already been exposed once; to produce an additional image on (an exposed negative); also *absol.*

1929 R. H. Goodsall *Beginner's Guide Photogr.* viii. 51 This is one method by which clouds may be printed-in. The foreground negative is exposed first, partially developed, and then returned to the easel and the sky portion printed in from another negative while the foreground is screened by a card. **1956** *Focal Encycl. Photogr.* 910/2 To print in large areas, such as a sky, a plain card is used to shade the remainder of the image. **1958** *Newnes Compl. Amat. Photogr.* 1 The man who spends joyful evenings printing in clouds. **1976** M. J. Rosen *Introd. Photogr.* v. 119/2 For printing in small areas of the print, the typical tool is an opaque mask of light cardboard or plastic with a small hole in it. To print in, the print first is given its normal exposure.

15*. [f. *print *sb.* 3.] **a.** *trans.* To test (an object) for finger-prints.

1938 N. Marsh *Death in White Tie* xv. 163 We'd better print the brandy-glass. **1951** A. Hocking *Death disturbs Mr. Jefferson* ii. 24 Austen said to the policeman: 'Print all the rest of the stuff, will you?' **1967** 'D. Shannon' *Rain with Violence* (1969) iii. 39 The lab men had printed the patent leather tote bag. **1971** 'L. Egan' *Malicious Mischief* (1972) i. 9 Dick Hunter, who had just been made Detective again..was printing the kitchen door.

b. To record the finger-prints of (a person).

1952 J. Steinbeck *East of Eden* I. 484 Ever been mugged or printed? **1955** D. W. Maurer in *Publ. Amer. Dial. Soc.* xxiv. 147 He is *printed* (his fingerprints taken) and *mugged* (photographed). **1957** C. MacInnes *City of Spades* ii. xiii. 192 The screws can print you in the nick at Brixton. **1970** G. F. Newman *Sir, You Bastard* viii. 232 He had been charged, printed, and provisionally questioned.

15.** To make (a printed circuit or component).

1946 *Business Week* 23 Feb. 19/2 (*caption*) Developed for proximity fuses, radio circuits 'printed' on ceramic plates are space savers adaptable to miniature pocket receivers. **1946** *Wireless World* Oct. 349/1 The connections are printed on the panels, the 'ink' being a solution of silver, which is dried, baked on and finally varnished over. *Ibid.*, Even the resistors are printed by the use of appropriate solutions. **1956** *Appl. Electronics Ann. 1955–56* 46/1 It is now possible to print a complete piece of electronic equipment except for the larger components. **1958** *Daily Mail* 8 Sept. 8/2 Using modern techniques of etching and engraving, a wiring circuit is actually 'printed' on to a flat base. **1966** *McGraw-Hill Encycl. Sci. & Technol.* X. 596/1 Resistive inks are composed of various forms of carbon with a resin binder..and a solvent vehicle. This mixture is applied through a stencil to form a rectangular pattern..and then baked... Resistive elements printed in this manner have wide tolerance limits. **1973** Dokter & Steinhauer *Digital Electronics* vi. 227 What is printed is not generally the whole circuit but merely the wiring connections.

printability (pri:ntăbi·liti). [f. Printable *a.* + -ity.] **a.** Of type, a block, a plate, etc.: capacity to produce print. **b.** Of paper: capacity to take print. **c.** Of language, statements, etc.: suitability or fitness to be printed. Also *attrib.*

1967 E. Chambers *Photolitho-Offset* iv. 43 The positives are printed-down by the deep-etch method of plate-making which creates a plate with firm hand dot fringes of good printability, sharpness and long press-life. **1969** *R. & E. Coordinator* (Res. & Engin. Council Graphic Arts Industry) Apr. 8/1 A meter and a modified IGT Printability Tester are used to measure the drying time..of quick drying inks into paper. **1971** *Scholarly Publishing* II. 361 The first experimental paper, both sized and unsized, substantially exceeded the minimum specifications ..and was found to have good printability as well. **1979** M. Russell *Touchdown* i. 18 His only difficulty would be to stay within the limits of printability.

‖**printanier** (præntãnye), *a.* (*sb.*) Also **printanière.** [F. *printanier*, lit. 'of springtime' (*printemps*), f. L. *primus* first + *tempus* time.] Made from or garnished with spring vegetables. Also as *sb.*

1861 Mrs. Beeton *Bk. Househ. Managem.* 78 (*heading*) Potage printanier, or spring soup. **1867** Trollope *Claverings* I. xix. 237 There's just a little soup, printanière; yes, they can make soup here. **1897** *Sears, Roebuck Catal.* 15/1 Soups..French Bouillon, Julienne, Printanier, Vegetable [etc.]. **1907** *Yesterday's Shopping* (1969) 19/1 *Soups*..Printanière—½ lb. tin 0/5½. *c* **1938** *Fortnum & Mason Price List* 57/1 *Soups*..Printanier—per tin 1/–. **1965** *House & Garden* Dec. 84/2 *Printanier*, neatly.. diced very young vegetables, sometimes cooked in with the dish, but mainly used for garnishing.

printed, *ppl. a.* Add: **2. b.** Used of a writer.

1893 W. G. Collingwood *Life & Work J. Ruskin* I. v. 56 He was quite an artist; and a printed poet!

c. printed matter, paper, leaflets, papers, cards, circulars, etc., that are printed, not written. So **printed-matter mail,** a cheaper rate of postage than that for ordinary mail.

1876 in *Jrnl. R. Soc. Arts* (1976) May 343/1, I am directed by the Council of this Society respectfully to draw your Lordship's attention to the anomaly which exists with reference to the conveyance of printed matter by the post, owing to the distinction which the Post-office makes between the book post and the newspaper post. **1897** *Post Office Guide* July 375 The Articles which are entitled to be sent at the rate applicable to *Printed Papers* are mostly impressions or copies obtained upon paper, parchment, or cardboard, by means of printing, lithography, engraving, photography, or any other mechanical process easy to recognize... Besides these articles, there are some others which are admitted, though not really printed matter, as, for instance, manuscripts intended for the press (when sent with the proofs of the same), papers impressed for the use of the blind, and cardboard drawing models stamped in relief. **1918** *Ibid.* July 9 The expression 'Printed Paper' means a packet not exceeding 2 oz. in weight which consists of or contains one or more of the following articles or documents, that is to say:—..Books..Sketches..Maps.. [etc.]. **1929** H. Crane *Let.* 6 Sept. (1965) 345 My old landlady..had thought they were 'printed matter' and had failed to forward them. **1929** D. H. Lawrence *Let.* 9 July (1962) II. 1163, I will address them..by registered printed-matter mail. **1957** C. Brooke-Rose *Languages of Love* 32 Two newspapers and three letters for her lay on the hall table. One was only printed matter, and one an unsealed invitation. **1959** *Spectator* 14 Aug. 181/1 Printed matter is not much read by the non-Communists or the uncommitted. **1967** *Economist* 15 July 238/3 With the inevitable rise in the price of newspapers..and the probable ending of resale price maintenance on confectionery and even tobacco, newsagents will be keener than before to sell printed matter.

4. Also *printed-out* (see *print *v.* 14c).

1934 *Jrnl. Optical Soc. Amer.* XXIV. 316/1 Weigert found that if shorter exposures than were required to produce a printed-out image were given..the image rendered visible by suitable development was dichroic. **1976** K. I. & R. E. Jacobson *Imaging Syst.* ii. 55 The colour of the printed out silver is usually reddish purple.

5. *printed circuit,* an electric circuit in the form of a flat sheet of insulating material bearing thin conducting strips and components, usu. mass-produced by a method that involves printing the circuit design on the sheet using a stencil or photograph of it; so *printed circuitry, wiring;* also applied to individual components made by such processes.

1946 *Business Week* 23 Feb. 19/2 On the back of the plate are solder spots that connect through holes in the plate with the 'printed' circuit. **1946** *Sci. News Let.* 2 Mar. 133 'Printed wire', the new development that reduces wiring radio circuits to a two-dimensional lithographic process. **1946** *Wireless World* Oct. 349/1 (*heading*) Printed 'wiring'. **1952** *Electronic Engin.* XXIV. 129/1 A major disadvantage of printed circuits has been the difficulty of incorporating satisfactory resistors. **1956** *Mod. Plastics* XXXIII. 223/2 Use of printed circuitry in 1955..increased in electronic computers, industrial control units, servo-mechanisms, and similar equipment. **1958** *Daily Mail* 8 Sept. 8/2 Research men working with printed circuits have evolved a way of reducing the thickness of the copper foil which carries the current from five-thousandths of an inch..to half a thousandth of an inch. **1966** *McGraw-Hill Encycl. Sci. & Technol.* X. 596/2 Printed capacitors are fabricated as part of the conductor circuit pattern when a high dielectric constant ceramic..is used as the circuit base material. Conductive patterns are screened on opposite sides of the circuit base to form the capacitor. **1970** J. Earl *Tuners & Amplifiers* vi. 141 The vast majority of tuner-amplifiers are now transistored, the designs being based on printed circuit boards..and sometimes integrated circuits. **1971** *Engineering* Apr. 30/1 The introduction of solid-state electronics and printed circuitry to vending machinery has minimized the number of separate electrical relays required. **1977** *Gramophone* Nov. 960/3 Normally these would flex the board during transit, with the possibility of cracking the printed wiring.

6. Produced by print-through (sense *1).

1950–1 *B.B.C. Quarterly* V. 245/1 In an investigation of accidental printing, one of the main difficulties is in measuring printed signals which are more than 50 db lower in level than the recorded signal, but are closely spaced about it on the tape. **1962** A. Nisbett *Technique Sound Studio* iv. 84 (*caption*) Wavelength of original and printed signal.

printer. Add: **1. a.** (Further example.)

1966 J. & P. Dixon *Photography* i. 18 A good printer is of tremendous value to a studio. Without seeing the original subject he can take the negative and produce prints of superb quality.

2. a. (Earlier and later examples.) Now usu. short for *teleprinter.

1859 T. P. Shaffner *Telegr. Manual* xviii. 273 The apparatus comprises two essential mechanisms, the 'Transmitter' or 'Compositor', and the 'Receiver' or 'Printer'. **1928** A. Williams *Telegraphy & Telephony* ii. 36 (*caption*) A specimen of the printing done with the Creed printer. **1960** I. Fleming *For your Eyes Only* 26 Anything you have to say I'll put straight on the printer to London. **1972** R. Busby *Reasonable Man* xviii. 161 Williams flicked the telex message... 'When this came up on the printer it jogged my memory.'

d. *Photogr.* and *Cinemat.* An apparatus for producing positive prints from negatives.

1912 F. A. Talbot *Moving Pictures* viii. 82 This is the Williamson printer. **1940** G. G. Quarles *Elem. Photogr.* x. 135 The actual darkroom technique of making the exposure will depend upon the type of printer available.

The simplest..is the simple hinged-back printing frame. **1951** R. SPOTTISWOODE *Film & its Techniques* viii. 196 The step printer (whether of the contact or optical type) is much like a camera or projector. The printing and printed films are pulled down one frame at a time..and held in front of a frame-sized aperture while exposure takes place. **1974** L. LIPTON *Independent Filmmaking* ix. 371 The highest quality masters are made with optical and contact step printers, although continuous contact machines are also used.

e. *Computers.* A device which produces a printed record of the input or output of a computer of which it is part or to which it is connected.

1946 *Math. Tables & Other Aids to Computation* II. 103 The static outputs of a total of 80 decade counters and 16 PM counters are connected to the printer. **1949** E. C. BERKELEY *Giant Brains* viii. 137 The recorder consists of a printer, a reperforator, and a tape transmitter... The printer is a regular teletypewriter connected to the machine. **1962** *Communications Assoc. Computing Machinery* V. 477/2 Routines intended for line-at-a-time printers do not yield optimal output for typewriters. **1974** 'A. HAIG' *Peruvian Printout* 37 The high-speed printer in the New York computer room was still for a moment... Howard and Sam walked round the backs of the printers lifting the boxes of printout on to a rubber-wheeled trolley. **1975** T. ALLBEURY *Special Collection* xix. 135 Their addresses were typed up on the fast printer in 3·4 seconds.

4. a. printer-slotter, a machine used for printing on cardboard or other packaging materials.

1954 *TAPPI* Feb. 144A/1 Another..development which appears very near is a printer-slotter arranged to handle aniline inks. **1957** *Ibid.* Nov. 190A/2 A completely new design Langston printer-slotter is currently available in three sizes... This machine is of a split or opening construction so arranged that a two-color press can be easily converted..into a press of three, four, or even more stations. **1968** *Globe & Mail* (Toronto) 13 Jan. 48/2 (Advt.), Corrugated box printer-slotter operator. Call Mr. Cherry.

printergram (pri·ntəɪgræm). [f. *TELE)-PRINTER + TELE)GRAM.] A telegram transmitted by telex.

1932 *Telegraph & Telephone Jrnl.* Oct. 2/2 Printergrams are charged for at the same rate as phonograms. **1942** CROOKS & DAWSON *Dict. Typewriting* (ed. 4) 268 Telex subscribers..have the advantage of being able to send and receive inland or overseas telegrams directly to and from the Post Office and/or the cable companies who are also on Telex. Telegrams handled in this manner are known as 'Printergrams'. **1976** [see *PHONOGRAM 3].

printery. Add: Also *Austral.* and *Afr.* **1.** (Later examples.)

1921 MENCKEN *Amer. Lang.* (rev. ed.) 187 *Printery*.. appeared very early, and..has been reinforced by many analogues, e.g., beanery, bootery [etc.]. **1943** K. TENNANT *Ride on Stranger* x. 102 The Order owned..a share in a printery. **1969** *Sydney Morning Herald* 24 May 1/7 Mr Newton..watched the search for several minutes before announcing: 'I'm bored with this. I'm off to the factory (a printery he operates in Canberra).' **1973** *New Journalist* (Austral.) July–Aug. 6/2 The licence of 3KZ is owned by Industrial Printing and Publicity Co. Ltd. This began as a Labor printery. **1975** B. GARFIELD *Hopscotch* xxii. 226 An *Evening Standard* van..returning to the printery from its last delivery. **1979** V. S. NAIPAUL *Bend in River* xiv. 229 We didn't have many printeries in the town.

printing, *vbl. sb.* Add: **a.** (Later examples.)

1966 *Listener* 1 Sept. 301/2 In the United States they have far greater fingerprinting output than we have.. though they have not quite universal printing. **1970** O. DOPPING *Computers & Data Processing* xv. 234 In programming editing operations for printing, it is essential to consider how the form will look to the user.

b. Also, the total number of copies (of a book) printed at one time; an impression.

1928 *Publishers' Weekly* 26 May 2117 A best selling novel... Four large printings were necessary before publication. **1933** *Morning Post* 7 July 14/7 (Advt.), 7 printings in 5 weeks. *Peter Abelard.*

c. *printing out*: the production of an image without chemical development (cf. *PRINT *v.* 14c); *printing-out paper* (abbrev. *P.O.P.), a printing paper capable of being used for this.

1891 W. E. WOODBURY *Gelatino-Chloride of Silver Printing-Out Process* ii. 6 One of the principal advantages of the chloride emulsion paper is its ability to give good prints from weak negatives—superior, in fact, to any that could be obtained by other printing-out processes. **1902** *Encycl. Brit.* XXXI. 703/2 The most notable change in recent years is the supersession of albuminized papers by papers coated by machinery with emulsions of silver haloids in gelatine, the chloride being used for most of the printing-out papers,..while the bromide forms the basis of most of the developable papers. **1904** [in Dict., sense d]. **1918** J. R. ROEBUCK *Sci. & Pract. of Photogr.* vi. 127 Photographers generally still rank prints on printing out paper ahead of prints on developing paper, but the former requires more time and labor, so that they have gone largely out of general use. **1939** [see *printing paper* (sense d below)]. **1968** H. ASHER *Photogr. Princ. & Pract.* (1970) viii. 230 Printing-out papers are not normally stocked by dealers but they are still obtainable. **1976** K. I. & R. E. JACOBSON *Imaging Syst.* ii. 54 One of the oldest systems.. uses printing out papers which produce visible images of good photographic quality directly on exposure to a strong light source..without the need for development or any other amplification process. *Ibid.* 55 Exposure to light of lower intensity for longer periods..causes these internal latent images to act as centres for the printing out of silver.

c*. = *PRINT-THROUGH 1.

1949 S. J. BEGUN *Magn. Recording* v. 98 Impregnated mediums exhibit 'printing' to an objectionable extent. **1950–1** *B.B.C. Quarterly* V. 248 (*caption*) Records of printing at various frequencies. **1962** A. NISBETT *Technique Sound Studio* iv. 84 (*caption*) Printing depends on the thickness of the tape base layer, as well as temperature and physical shock.

d. *printing industry*; **printing-frame** (further example); **printing paper** (*a*) (earlier example); (*b*), delete '(also *printing-out paper*, abbrev. P.O.P.)' and see sense c above; (further examples); **printing union** = *print union* s.v. *PRINT *sb.* 15b.

1858 Printing-frame [see *ACCELERATOR b]. **1976** *Times* 23 Mar. 1/5 The union said in a letter to the printing industries committee that the question had not arisen because of the dispute at Barnsley. **1806** R. SUTCLIFF *Trav. N. Amer.* (1811) xiv. 258 The mill..is..employed in making writing and printing paper. **1939** MACK & MARTIN *Photogr. Process* ix. 313 Silver halide printing papers may be divided roughly into two classes, *viz.*: printing-out papers ('P.O.P.') in which the reduction of the halide to metallic silver is completed by the action of the light, no development being required; and developing-out papers ('D.O.P.') in which the latent image formed by exposure is subsequently developed. **1968** G. L. WAKEFIELD *Introd. Photogr.* viii. 146 A printing paper is coated with a sensitive emulsion similar to that on a film but much slower and generally sensitive only to blue light. **1976** M. J. ROSEN *Introd. Photogr.* v. 117/1 Photographic printing papers are manufactured in a variety of contrast grades. **1976** *Times* 23 Mar. 1/5 The union asked other printing unions to follow its example and refuse to take part in joint meetings or federated chapels (office branches) where the institute was represented.

printing, *ppl. a.* (Earlier and later examples.)

1841 WRIGHT & BAIN *Brit. Pat. 9204* In Sheet 3 we exhibit a side view,..of an electro-magnetic printing telegraph. **1849** *Rep. Brit. Assoc. Adv. Sci.* Notices & Abstr. 133 A colloquial and also a printing telegraph are used. **1929** *Bell Syst. Techn. Jrnl.* VIII. 267 Commercial telegraph operation..is carried on almost exclusively by two well known methods, manual morse and printing telegraph. **1940** *Chambers's Techn. Dict.* 674/2 *Printing telegraph*, a telegraph system in which the received signals are translated and operate a printing machine, giving a readable message. **1968** *Gloss. Terms Offset Lithogr. Printing* (*B.S.I.*) 28 *Printing pressure*, the pressure applied at the point of contact between two printing surfaces to transfer ink from one surface to the other. **1971** *Gloss. Electrotechnical, Power Terms* (*B.S.I.*) III. iii. 7 *Printing telegraphy*, any method of telegraph operation in which the received signals are automatically recorded as printed characters.

printing-house. Delete 'Now only *Hist.*' and add later examples. *Printing House Square* (examples in allusive use).

1861 B. MORAN *Jrnl.* 3 Dec. (1949) II. 917 *The Times*, is filled with such slatternly abuse of us and ours, that it is fair to conclude that all the Fishwives of Billingsgate have been transferred to Printing House Square. *a* **1910** 'MARK TWAIN' *Autobiogr.* (1924) II. 285 Orion severed his connection with the printing-house in St. Louis. **1938** H. NICOLSON *Diary* 9 Sept. (1966) 358 Colin Coote.. says that *The Times* leader urging the Czechs to surrender their fringes was written by Leo Kennedy and merely glanced at by Geoffrey Dawson. He is appalled by the lack of responsible guidance in Printing House Square. **1951** S. JENNETT *Making of Bks.* iii. 48 In some printing houses one of the boxes in the case is set aside for the reception of defective or battered types. **1956** C. COCKBURN *In Time of Trouble* vi. 88 *Is, indeed, anyone, anywhere, truly worthy of* The Times? This was the awfully solemn thought which..sometimes oppressed Printing House Square. **1964** F. BOWERS *Bibliogr. & Textual Crit.* III. i. 64 McKerrow..once remarked that some contradictory pieces of evidence could be reconciled most easily by the hypothesis that the entire printing-house had adjourned to the nearest pub and got drunk. **1978** *Times* 18 Apr. 17/7 Surely you cannot be so short-sighted in Printing House Square as to..believe..as you grandly state in a recent leading article. **1979** *N.Y. Rev. Bks.* 25 Oct. 44/4 The great printing houses became nodal points in a semi-secret network of cultural communications.

printing-office. (Earlier examples.)

1733 B. FRANKLIN *Poor Richard* (title-page), Printed and sold by B. Franklin, at the New Printing-Office. **1802** *Monthly Mag.* XIV. 347/2 This portrait is done by the letter-engraver who executed in wood for the printing-office of Fust.

pri·nt-out. [f. vbl. phr. *to print out* (*PRINT *v.* 14c, 6b).] **1.** *Photogr.* Used *attrib.*, = *printing out* (*PRINTING *vbl. sb.* c).

1899 P. N. HASLUCK *Bk. Photogr.* 184/1 Something may be done in the development of print-out papers. **1929** *Proc. 7th Internat. Congr. Photogr. 1928* 23 (*heading*) Parallelism between photo-electric conductivity effects and direct print-out effects. **1930** O. WHEELER *Photogr. Printing Processes* iii. 28 While daylight is still commonly employed for exposure in print-out processes, artificial light..is often used commercially. **1939** MACK & MARTIN *Photogr. Process* v. 175 If an emulsion receives a very great exposure, the halide is reduced directly by the light without the aid of a developer. This print-out effect was the only means of producing a photograph in the very earliest days of photography. **1965** *Photogr. Jrnl.* CV. 285/2 A special kind of print-out paper has been in use for data recording for some years. **1973** W. THOMAS *SPSE Handbk. Photogr. Sci. & Engin.* vi. 407 Sufficient exposure of an emulsion to light causes visible darkening without development (a print-out image).

2. (A sheet or strip of) printed matter produced by a computer or other automatic apparatus; the production of such matter. Also *fig.*

1953 *IRE Trans. Instrumentation* June 68 An hour's operation includes some 40 print-outs of the complete memory. **1957** *Ibid.* Sept. 193/2 The reading system consists of a film reader, control and decoding section, and print-out equipment. *Ibid.* 194/1 A stepping switch is caused to step to the next position at the end of each character print-out. **1961** *Aeroplane* CI. 573/2 In addition to the automatic print-out unit for the recording of positional information, an optional addition to the data presentation unit is a computer to convert the slant range and elevation co-ordinates into ground range and height data. **1966** 'C. E. MAINE' *B.E.A.S.T.* vi. 79 Synøve and.. Wetherby..were standing by one of the print-out machines, reading a long sheet of paper as it emerged. **1969** *New Scientist* 1 May 238/2 Everyone should be entitled to a print-out of the information in the data bank in regard to him. **1971** K. GOTTSCHALK in B. de Ferranti *Living with Computer* iv. 31 The drafting and print-out of leases, wills and forms used in lawyers' offices to eliminate repetitive work. **1974** *Ellery Queen's Mystery Mag.* Nov. 148/1 We could use computers at this end too, to run through possible letter combinations and produce the necessary printouts almost at once. **1979** M. BABSON *Twelve Deaths of Christmas* xvii. 87 Sod your computers, *I'm* getting the printout from the marrow of my bones.

print-shop. Add: **1.** (Further examples.)

1778 *English Mag.* Feb. 59/1 Notwithstanding the many satirical exhibitions at the print-shops, of grown gentlemen learning to dance..there are many arguments that may be used in defence of this genteel exercise. **1897** A. BEARDSLEY *Let.* 13 Apr. (1970) 302 The book and print shops [in Paris] are an evergreen joy to me.

2. *U.S.* A printing-office or printery.

1921 *Amer. Printer* 5 Nov. (*heading*) Visit to an old Oxford printshop. **1961** R. L. DUNCAN *Voice of Strangers* IV. iii. 246 He went into the print shop, where Fletcher had just finished cleaning the press. **1970** *Eng. Stud.* LI. 164 His quarrel with Sir John Cheke.., the exegetic controversy with Edward Lee, the question of Henry VIII's divorce were all reflected in the books pouring out of Basle's printshops. **1977** C. MCCARRY *Secret Lovers* xiii. 170 Each afternoon he sent Joëlle to collect the typescript from the printer; she took it back to the print shop every morning.

print-through (pri·ntþrū). Also **print through.** [f. vbl. phr. *to print through.*] **1.** The accidental transfer of recorded signals to adjacent layers in a reel of magnetic tape. Freq. *attrib.*

1956 R. E. B. HICKMAN *Magn. Recording Handbk.* ii. 24 The print-through is..dependent upon the output level of the original signal. **1958** H. G. M. SPRATT *Magn. Tape Recording* iii. 110 The ratio of the level of the original signal to that of the last echo before and the first echo after that signal is termed the print-through or transfer ratio. **1962** *Times* 5 July 15/7 Dangers to tape..arise from prolonged storage without rewinding, which can cause 'print-through' (detectable as pre-echo on some discs). **1975** *Hi-Fi Answers* Feb. 76/2 To be sure no print through is occurring it would be a good idea if you were to rewind each tape in your collection at least once in six months to redistribute the tape in the reel and minimise any print through effect.

2. *Printing.* (See quot. 1961.)

1961 R. F. BOWLES *Printing Ink Manual* xi. 349 Another factor which has a marked effect on the quality of the print is the degree of 'print through' which is visible. 'Print through' is the degree to which the print is visible on the reverse side of the sheet, and is the combination of 'show-through' and 'strike-through'. **1973** L. C. YOUNG *Materials in Printing Processes* ix. 121 When the printing on one side of a paper can be seen through the paper, this print-through may either be due to show-through or strike-through... Normally the vehicle only penetrates a short distance into the sheet, but even this will have the effect of reducing the printing opacity, so making print-through more likely.

prion. Insert in etym. after 'mod.L.': (Comte B. G. E. de la V. Lacépède *Tableaux Méthodiques des Mammifères et des Oiseaux* (1799) 14). Substitute for def.: A small saw-billed petrel belonging to the genus once so called, now included in the genus *Pachyptila* of the family Procellariidæ and found in southern seas. (Examples.)

1848 J. GOULD *Birds Austral.* VII. 54 (*heading*) Dove-like Prion. **1862** *Proc. Zool. Soc.* 125 In form and colouring it is precisely similar to the other *Priones*. **1901** A. J. CAMPBELL *Nests & Eggs Austral. Birds* II. 917 Mr Travers frequently found these Prions caught in the branches of scrubby trees. **1937** *Discovery* May 141/2 The prion is a ghost. A fluttering thing of pale grey-blue and white. **1959** *New Biol.* XXIX. 112 Some small bird species such as the prions owe their survival to the fact that they are only active at night, thereby avoiding the skuas' attack. **1972** K. SIMPSON *Birds in Bass Strait* 71/2 The Dove or Antarctic Prion is perhaps one of the most numerous of all southern seabirds.

prior, *a.* Add: **a.** *prior charge*, in *Finance*: see quots. 1968, 1974. Also (with hyphen) as *attrib. phr.*

1877 *Encycl. Brit.* VII. 15/1 The Companies Clauses Act, 1863, part iii., which makes debenture stock a prior charge on the undertaking, and gives the interest thereon priority of payment over all dividends or interest on any shares or stock of the company. **1930** *Economist* 22 Mar. 653/1 Foreign bonds, industrial prior-charge stocks and even industrial preference shares shared in the general tendency, though to a less conspicuous extent. *Ibid.* 29 Mar. 695/2 Gilt-edged stocks and well-secured industrial debentures and prior charges. **1968** JOHANNSEN & ROBERTSON *Managem. Gloss.* 105 *Prior charges*, all types of debentures, preference shares and other stocks ranking for payment of interest or dividend in precedence to the ordinary shares. **1974** *Terminol. Managem. & Financial Accountancy* (Inst. Cost & Managem. Accountants) 62 *Prior charge capital*, those classes of share and loan capital, the holders of which have a claim on the profits and assets of a business before the ordinary shareholders.

c. *Statistics.* Applied to the result of a calculation made in ignorance of, or previously to, some observation(s); *prior probability*, the probability that a hypothesis is true calculated without reference to certain relevant observations. Opp. *POSTERIOR *a.* 1 b.

1921, etc. [see *POSTERIOR *a.* 1 b]. **1977** *Sci. Amer.* May 126/3 With this valuable extra information, which statisticians call a 'prior distribution,' it is possible to construct a superior estimate of each player's true batting ability.

priorate. Add: **1. a.** Also, the (term of) office of a prioress.

1925 C. S. DURRANT *Link betw. Flemish Mystics & Eng. Martyrs* I. x. 150 The Priorate of Mother Salome has ever been looked back to as a time when [etc.].

priorite (prəi·ǒrəit). *Min.* [ad. G. *priorit* (W. C. Brögger 1906, in *Skr. udgivne af Vidensk.-Selsk. i Christiania* (*Mat.-Nat. Kl.*) I. vi. 111), f. the name of G. T. *Prior* (1862–1936), British mineralogist: see -ITE¹.] A mixed oxide, chiefly of niobium, titanium, and yttrium, with traces of several other elements, which occurs as black or dark brown orthorhombic crystals.

1907 *Jrnl. Chem. Soc.* XCII. II. 886 Another mineral of this series is one from Swaziland, South Africa, analysed by G. T. Prior..; for this, the name *priorite* is proposed. Blomstrandine and priorite are isomorphous and are respectively dimorphous with polycrase and euxenite. **1944** C. PALACHE et al. *Dana's Syst. Min.* (ed. 7) I. 796 Priorite was found originally at Urstad on the island of Hitterö in southwest Norway. **1966** *Amer. Mineralogist* LI. 156 Only two well-established Ce–Y rare-earth mineral series are known for which names have been assigned to the end members: 3. aeschynite–priorite series [;] 4. britholite–abukumalite series. **1968** I. KOSTOV *Mineral.* 254 Euxenite group... The chief members of the group are euxenite.., priorite ((Y, Th)(Nb, Ti)$_2$O$_6$).

prioritize (prəi,ǫ·rĭtəiz), *v.* orig. *U.S.* [f. PRIORITY + -IZE.] **a.** *trans.* To designate as worthy of prior attention, to give priority to (in the sense of *PRIORITY 2). **b.** *trans.* To determine the order in which (items) are to be dealt with, to establish priorities for (a set of items). Also *absol.*

A word that at present sits uneasily in the language. —Ed.

1973 T. H. WHITE *Making of President 1972* xii. 325 The storefront operators in the counties that Malek had 'prioritized' had identified independents, wavering Democrats and 'don't knows'. **1975** R. BURNS *Alvarez Jrnl.* 47 But in the meantime I've got to prioritize the operations, and the priority standard is the probability of conviction. **1977** *Time* 14 Mar. 28/2 From then on toward midnight, he tries, in his own words, 'to prioritize'. **1977** *Daily Colonist* (Victoria, B.C.) 15 May 33/5 A special committee had been struck.. to prioritize their recommendations and to report. **1981** *Times* 3 Feb. 13/6 In the Nato headquarters.. we are well used to prioritizing our targets.

Hence **prio:ritiza·tion; prio·ritized, prio·ritizing** *ppl. adjs.*

1977 *Financial Times* 24 Dec. 3/6 It has two meanings, depending on whether one is doing the prioritization, or having it thrust upon one. **1977** *Time* 14 Mar. 28/2 Prioritizing takes him into the Oval Office to talk each day with the President and to drop in on.. Vice President Mondale. **1978** *Verbatim* Feb. 1/2 A teacher in Mill Valley has drawn up a 'prioritized list of all components of the school program'.

priority. Add: **1. b.** *Taxonomy.* The claim of the first validly published Latin name to be taken as the correct one for any given organism.

1842 *Rep. Brit. Assoc. Adv. Sci.* 109 We have no hesitation in adopting as our fundamental maxim, the 'law of priority', viz... The name originally given by the founder of a group or the describer of a species should be permanently retained. **1928** D. B. SWINGLE *Textbk. Systematic Bot.* vii. 68 By agreement botanists do not go back of Linnaeus' 'Species Plantarum' (1753) to establish priority in the publication of names. **1953** E. MAYR et al. *Methods & Princ. Systematic Zool.* xi. 213 It would be unfair.. to blame all name changes on the law of priority. **1963** DAVIS & HEYWOOD *Princ. Angiosperm Taxon.* viii. 291 Enough information should be given to indicate why a name has not been adopted if it appears to have priority over the accepted name.

2. Also, the right to precede others or to receive attention, supplies, etc., before others. Hence *transf.*, an interest having a prior claim to consideration; often in *pl.* or preceded by a qualifying word, as *first, high, top priority*.

1917 *Times* 10 Mar. 6/4 The Minister of Munitions.. has issued an important Order under the Defence of the Realm Act as to priority of war work... During the last 12 months the Ministry of Munitions has been administering a scheme which ensured for war work and for work of national importance priority over all other work in regard to labour and materials. **1922** *Encycl. Brit.* XXXII. 147/1 The Priorities Committee undertook whenever necessary to administer priorities in the production of all raw materials and finished products. *Ibid.* 835/1 The labour needs of employers in war industries were graded as entitled to 'Super-Priority', 'First' or 'Second Class Priority', or as not deserving special treatment. **1940** *Economist* 18 May 893/1 How far can we tap reserves of skill for war work by the full mobilisation of this class of man power and its allocation, according to an infrangible schedule of priorities, exclusively to war and export manufacture? *Ibid.* 24 Aug. 236/2 There was no priority at all until June of this year, and since then there has only been a general Priority of Production Direction which went no further than to notify to industry two short lists of very broad categories of munitions. **1941** *New Statesman* 26 Apr. 429/2 First priority is being given to dairy cattle. **1944** *Daily Tel.* 23 Sept. 2/2 The obvious remedy for that would be to make civil aviation priority No. 1 at the Ministry. **1948** 'N. SHUTE' *No Highway* ii. 49, I think this trip to Canada is top priority of anything that's going on at Farnborough today. **1949** G. COTTERELL *Randle in Springtime* iv. iii. 213 I'm going into furnishing, see. Anything you've got to have dockets and priorities for. Lino, stair carpets. **1958** *Listener* 11 Sept. 368/1 The Minister had to explain that their area did not have early priority. **1960** M. SPARK *Ballad of Peckham Rye* iii. 42 She came up with an estimate and said 'priority'... I said, 'Excuse me, Miss Coverdale, but I've got two priorities already.' **1968** *Highway Code* 37 (*caption*) Give priority to vehicles from opposite direction. **1969** *Morning Star* 29 Jan. 1/1 Improvements.. are much less than could be achieved if the Government got its priorities right. **1970** G. F. NEWMAN *Sir, You Bastard* iv. 122 There was a priority on at the Yard, all detectives were being called back. **1972** A. ULAM *Fall of Amer. Univ.* v. 211 He would couple this frankness with a plea to the young not to give up, to work within the system, for with reordered priorities this country might still be saved and might even be worth saving. **1977** *Listener* 26 May 682/2 There will be questions of social priorities involved.

5. In sense 2, passing into *adj.* (Further examples.)

1917 *Times* 10 Mar. 6/4 (*heading*) National work. Important priority scheme. **1922** *Encycl. Brit.* XXX. 818/2 Trades specified in a priority list drawn up with reference to the relative urgency of the industrial requirements of the country. **1934** T. E. LAWRENCE *Let.* 8 Apr. (1938) 795 She.. has no one aboard now to get her priority treatment. **1942** *Times* (Weekly ed.) 2 Dec. 15 Various priority and freight rationing schemes are in operation. **1946** K. TENNANT *Lost Haven* (1947) xvi. 248 Young Len's working for the mill, ain't he? And that's a priority job. **1960** O. MANNING *Great Fortune* xiii. 153 This young man might have been granted a priority flight over Europe. **1967** *Guardian* 10 Jan. 4/4 Measures should be taken to increase the ratio of teachers to children in educational priority areas. **1976** *Broadcast* Dec. 1/3 The achievement of a shorter working week for weekly paid staff is a priority objective.

priorly, *adv.* Delete *rare* and add earlier and later examples.

1779 R. BAKER *Remarks Eng. Lang.* (ed. 2) 94 It seems a wonder that we have no such word as *priorly*. It would be naturally formed from *prior*, and would be very useful. **1965** *Amer. Psychologist* XX. 1007/2 After a certain point in human evolution, the only means whereby man could fill his evolutionary niche was through the cultural transmission of the skills necessary for the use of priorly invented techniques, implements, and devices. **1970** *Jrnl. Gen. Psychol.* LXXXII. 207 It states that organisms respond to discrepancies between contemporaneous stimuli and some internalized average of other inputs, experienced priorly or as context.

Priscol (pri·skǫl). *Pharm.* Also **priscol.** A proprietary name for *TOLAZOLINE.

The trade-mark registration in the U.S. is no longer active (see next, quot. 1949).

1938 *Trade Marks Jrnl.* 18 May 604/2 Priscol... All goods included in class 3 [*i.e.* chemical substances prepared for use in medicine and pharmacy]. Society of Chemical Industry in Basle.., Basle, Switzerland; manufacturers and merchants. **1938** *Official Gaz.* (U.S. Patent Office) 14 June 247/2 Society of Chemical Industry in Basle... *Priscol* for preparation having an action on the circulation of the blood. Claims use since May 6, 1936. **1945** *Federation Proc.* IV. 114/1 Although priscol, 15 mgm., was adrenolytic in relation to blood pressure, it was not adrenolytic or sympatholytic in respect to the cervical sympathetic functions studied. **1956** LD. AMULREE in A. Pryce-Jones *New Outl. Mod. Knowl.* 222 On the theory that the confusion [in senile dementia] is increased by a shortage of oxygen within the brain, priscol and other vaso-dilators have been used without any definite improvement in the patient's condition. **1968** W. C. BOWMAN et al. *Textbk. Pharmacol.* xxix. 763 Tolazoline (Priscol) exhibits a wide range of pharmacological activity in addition to its antiadrenaline action.

Priscoline (pri·skǫlīn). *Pharm.* Also **priscoline.** [f. *PRISCOL + -INE⁵.] A proprietary name in the U.S. for *TOLAZOLINE.

1949 *Jrnl. Amer. Med. Assoc.* 21 May 272/2 Since this paper was written, the name priscol has been changed to priscoline. **1950** *Official Gaz.* (U.S. Patent Office) 22 Aug. 996/2 Ciba Pharmaceutical Products, Inc., Summit, N.J... *Priscoline*... For preparations having an action on the circulation of the blood. Claims use since Mar. 15, 1949. **1966** W. F. BARKER *Peripheral Arterial Dis.* vi. 85 Priscoline is perhaps one of the most widely used drugs in peripheral vascular occlusions.

prisere (prəi·sīəɹ). *Ecol.* [f. PRI(MARY *a.* + *SERE *sb.*²] A sere that began on an area not previously occupied.

1916 F. E. CLEMENTS *Plant Succession* ix. 182 Within the same climax, seres are classified as primary and secondary, i.e., as priseres and subseres. **1926** TANSLEY & CHIPP *Study of Vegetation* ii. 19 We distinguish a sere beginning on bare soil.. as a primary sere, or prisere. **1939** A. G. TANSLEY *Brit. Islands & their Vegetation* x. 218 Any concrete example of succession, i.e. any definite series of communities leading to a climax, is called a sere, and the complete succession from bare habitat to climatic climax is a primary sere or prisere. **1960** N. POLUNIN *Introd. Plant. Geogr.* xi. 324 The complete sere just indicated is a primary sere (prisere), beginning on a bare substratum without organic material. **1977** A. S. COLLINSON *Introd. World Vegetation* vi. 103 Where plants begin their succession on virgin territory.. the process is termed a primary succession or prisere.

‖ **prisiadka** (prĭsya·tkă). Also **prisjádka, prisyadka.** [Russ.] A dance-step in which the male dancer squats on his heels and kicks out each leg alternately to the front. Also used for the dance itself. Cf. *KAZACHOK.

1938 B. SCHÖNBERG tr. *Sachs' World Hist. of Dance* i. 28 Wilder still are the Bavarian *Schuhplattler* and the Ukrainian *prisjádka* with their heel stamping. *Ibid.* 30 The squat-fling dance is still the possession of many European peoples... In the Ukraine it is known by the term *prisjádka*. **1972** *Daily Tel.* 14 Aug. 6/9 They.. burst out into wild Ukrainian dancing with every possible variation of the squatting step 'prisyadka'. **1977** J. WAMBAUGH *Black Marble* (1978) xii. 292 'I don't care if I'm six feet tall,' Valnikov said, squatting on his haunches, trying some prisiadka kicks that put him temporarily on his ass.

prism. Add: **7. prism-binocular(s)**, binoculars containing two pairs of triangular prisms, introduced so as to shorten the apparatus and improve the stereoscopic effect.

1901 *Brit. Optical Jrnl.* Sept. p. iv (Advt.), Busch's Prism Binoculars... The lightest and most portable Prism Binocular on the market. **1919** *Jane's Fighting Ships* 59 adv., Bausch & Lomb Optical Co... Field Glasses (Stereo Prism Binocular). **1957** *Encycl. Brit.* III. 583/2 Ernst Abbe took the matter up *de novo* in 1893 when he designed prism binoculars and telescopes. His constructions were the forerunners of the modern prism binocular.

prison, *sb.* Add: **1. d.** In *Roulette* and related board-games: a position on the board where bets are held in abeyance until the next round of play; *spec.* in phr. *to put* (a stake) *in prison.*

1867 *Bohn's Hand-Bk. Games* 346 The punters may.. have their stake moved into the middle semicircles of the colour they then choose, called 'la première prison', the first prison, to be determined by the next event, whether they lose all or are set at liberty. **1940** WODEHOUSE *Eggs, Beans & Crumpets* 32 When Zero turns up.. stakes on the even chances aren't scooped up—they are what is called put in prison. **1977** P. ARNOLD *Encyl. Gambling* 247/1 *Prison*, a convention whereby a stake on the even-money chances at roulette is left on the table, or 'put in prison' when zero appears, to be either retained by the bettor or lost according to the next spin.

e. *prison-without-bars* (colloq.): an open prison (*OPEN *a.* 2 c).

1948 *Manch. Even. News* 10 Nov., The former governor of Britain's 'prison-without-bars' at Loudham Grange. **1952** 'J. HENRY' *Who lie in Gaol* v. 69, I heard a great deal of the many advantages I would enjoy at the prison-without-bars at York; in fact it was looked upon as a form of heaven by most of the prisoners [at Holloway]. **1959** 'H. CARMICHAEL' *Stranglehold* vi. 58 A solicitor who was doing time at the prison-without-bars.

3. a. (*a*) *prison chaplain, -clock, -discipline* (earlier example), *guard, library, officer, pallor, reform, -wall* (later examples; also *fig.*), *warder, yard.* (*c*) *prison camp* (examples), *farm, hospital.* **b.** *prison-keeper* (earlier example), *visitor; prison-visiting* sb. **c.** *prison-grey, -like* (later examples) adjs. **d. prison haircut** = *prison-crop*.

1925 *Scribner's Mag.* Oct. 386/1 The scene is a Turkish prison-camp during the recent war. **1978** *Lancashire Life* Nov. 150/1 (Advt.), Mr. P——, a Pole who arrived in England in 1947 after.. escaping from a German prison camp. *a* **1902** S. BUTLER *Way of All Flesh* (1903) lxv. 293 He might experimentalise advantageously upon the viler soul of the prison chaplain. **1910** *Encyl. Brit.* V. 851/2 Prison chaplains are appointed by the home secretary. **1972** N. MARSH *Tied up in Tinsel* iii. 78 The prison chaplain gave a short, civilized sermon. **1898** O. WILDE *Ballad of Reading Gaol* 18 The prison-clock Smote on the shivering air. **1818** T. F. BUXTON *Inquiry Prison Discipline* 137 Having.. described two.. opposite modes of prison discipline, I would suggest.., that a comparison of these is the most certain criterion of their respective merits. **1834** J. S. MILL in *Monthly Repos.* VIII. 590 Has not a notion grown up within a few years, (we believe a very false one), that the increased mildness of prison-discipline has made our gaols.. places where the prisoner is actually too comfortable, and too well off? **1961** *Atlanta Constitution* 4 Nov. 1 The jury praised the administration and operation of the Atlanta Police Department, the Fulton Tax Commissioner's Office, the Bellwood and Alpharetta prison farms, [etc.]. **1968** *Listener* 15 Feb. 210/1 As remarkable.. is the improvement he has brought about in his year in charge of the smaller prison farm, Tucker. **1975** C. WESTON *Susannah Screaming* (1976) iii. 39 Delgado made a break from the prison farm where he had been sent after a period of good behavior in a federal cellblock. **1956** 'H. MacDiarmid' *Stony Limits & Scots Unbound* 90 A flash of sun in a country all prison-grey. **1961** W. T. Ballard *Night Riders* i. 15 Two wore the uniform of prison guards, three the striped suits of convicts. **1970** G. Jackson *Let.* 10 June in *Soledad Brother* (1971) 40, I am being tried in court right now..for the alleged slaying of a prison guard. **1977** *Time* 12 Dec. 47/3 With only good time remaining as a route to early release, the potential for abuse by prison guards would be heightened as well. **1974** *Times* 17 Aug. 7/1 A snotty little nervous kid with a prison hair-cut. **1933** J. Buchan *Prince of Captivity* II. i. 178 You would spend some weeks in a prison hospital till they patched you up. **1943** F. Thompson *Candleford Green* ix. 142 Such a journey..and a prison hospital..at the end of it. **1978** P. G. Winslow *Coppergold* 48 He fell a victim to influenza..was taken to the prison hospital. **1855** Dickens *Dorrit* (1857) I. i. 4 The prison-keeper appeared carrying..a basket. **1967** H. Pinter *Night School* in *Tea Party & Other Plays* 101, I was running the prison library. **1979** K. Bonfiglioli *After You with Pistol* vi. 31 He gets a nice job in the prison library but *horrid* things happen to him in the showers. **1839** E. A. Poe in *Burton's Gentleman's Mag.* Oct. 206 This prison-like rampart formed the limits of our domain. **1916** D. H. Lawrence *Amores* 77 The town Glimmers with subtle ghosts Going up and down In a common, prison-like dress. **1944** A. L. Rowse *Eng. Spirit* xxxv. 244 That sepulchral, prison-like building. **1970** P. Dickinson *Seals* ii. 53 Many criminals..are really only happy..when..their day is shaped by a prison-like discipline. **1907** B. Thomson *Story of Dartmoor Prison* xxi. 260 The better class of men came to realize that prison officers were their friends rather than their enemies. **1961** *Observer* 9 Apr. 22/8 He refers to prison officers as prison warders, a title abandoned something like thirty years ago. **1978** P. Lovesey *Waxwork* 79 It is quite impossible to conduct a conversation through an iron grille with two prison officers at my client's shoulder. **1935** A. J. Cronin *Stars look Down* II. xx. 446 He sat there with his prison pallor upon him. **1977** *New Yorker* 24 Oct. 141/1 He squints into the unaccustomed sunlight..and..suffers from a case of prison pallor. **1890** W. Booth *In Darkest Eng.* I. ix. 74 Once the work of Prison Reform is taken in hand by men.. who are in full sympathy with the class for whose benefit they labour. **1972** A. Roudybush *Sybaritic Death* (1974) vii. 67 His original project had been to devote his activities to the cause of prison reform. **1838** H. Martineau *Retrospect of Western Travel* I. 224, I trust that the practice of prison-visiting will gain ground. **1973** L. Cooper *Tea on Sunday* i. 21 Barry Slater, the unfortunate legacy of Alberta's spell of prison visiting. **1837** H. Martineau *Society in Amer.* II. III. iv. 285 Every prison visitor has been conscious, on first conversing privately with a criminal, of a feeling of surprise at finding him so human. **1975** N. Freeling *What are Bugles blowing For?* xv. 88 Vera made a good prison visitor. **1855** Trollope *Warden* xvi. 248 No convict, slipping down from a prison wall, ever feared to see the gaoler more entirely than Mr. Harding did to see his son-in-law. **1898** O. Wilde *Ballad of Reading Gaol* 16 The weeping prison-wall. **1951** M. Kennedy *Lucy Carmichael* I. vii. 62 Rickie peeped for a moment over the prison walls of his own depression. *a* **1902** S. Butler *Way of All Flesh* (1903) lxiv. 286 The prison warder..sent for the doctor. **1914** *Prison Officers Mag.* Nov. 450/2 For the past four years the majority of the Irish Prison Warders have favoured us with their confidence and support. **1928** [see *wardering *vbl. sb.*]. **1961** [see *prison officer* above]. **1978** M. Butterworth *X marks Spot* 179 With two escorting prison warders as witnesses. **1642** in *Rec. Early Hist. Boston* (1877) II. 70 The Constables are appointed..to take care for the building a salt peter howse in the prison yarde. **1776** *Jrnls. Continental Congress U.S.* (1906) IV. 121 Resolved, That the said J. Connolly be allowed..to walk in the prison yard or hall. **1851** J. J. Lancaster in *Rep. Sel. Comm. Passengers' Act* 142 in *Parl. Papers* XIX. 1 Those in Millbank [*sc.* a London military hospital] are drawn up in the prison-yard or wards. **1856** Dickens *Dorrit* (1857) II. vi. 383 They prowled about..in the old, dreary, prison-yard manner. **1963** N. Marsh *Dead Water* (1964) v. 126 She ..walked aimlessly..as if the garden were a prison yard.

prisoner[2]. Add: **1. a.** *prisoner of conscience*, one who is detained or imprisoned because of his or her political or religious beliefs.

1961 *Amnesty* 11 July 2/1 What are the facts we need? There are thousands of them and each one is a human being, a prisoner of conscience behind bars because of his political views or religious beliefs. **1962** *Time to keep Silence* (Amnesty International), Prisoners of Conscience are of two distinct sorts—those prepared to suffer persecution because they have the courage of their convictions, and those who are prisoners of their own conscience because they lack the courage of their convictions. When the latter become the former, all of us will be free. **1970** *Times* 20 Apr. 6/5 A great many prisoners of conscience, it claims, are sent with or without trial 'to the so-called special psychiatric hospitals'. **1977** *Guernsey Weekly Press* 21 July 6/6 A prisoner of conscience is a person who is detained because of his political, racial or religious beliefs.

b. prisoner's dilemma (see quot. 1957); **prisoner's friend** *Armed services*, an officer who represents a defendant at a court martial.

1957 Luce & Raiffa *Games & Decisions* v. 95 We turn now to a different example of a non-zero-sum game. This one is attributed to A. W. Tucker... The following interpretation, known as the prisoner's dilemma is popular: Two suspects are taken into custody and separated. The district attorney is certain that they are guilty of a specific crime, but he does not have adequate evidence to convict them at a trial. He points out to each prisoner that each has two alternatives: to confess to the crime the police are sure they have done, or not to confess. If they both do not confess..he will book them on some very minor trumped-up charge..and they will both receive minor punishment; if they both confess they will be prosecuted, but he will recommend less than the most severe sentence; but if one confesses and the other does not, then the confessor will receive lenient treatment for turning state's evidence whereas the latter will get 'the book' slapped at him. **1963** *Jrnl. Abnormal Psychol.* LXVI. 308/2 Trust of the other person plays a critical role in determining choices made in Prisoner's Dilemma games. **1977** A. W. Tucker *MS. letter* (*copy in O.E.D. files*), The Prisoner's Dilemma is my brain child. I concocted it at Stanford in early 1950 as a catchy example to enliven a semi-popular talk on Game Theory... My example became known by the 'grapevine', but I did not publish it. **1914** 'Bartimeus' *Naval Occasions* xxi. 198 The Prisoner's Friend then gave evidence. **1972** J. Potter *Going West* 191 He was prisoner's friend to you in that spot of unpleasantness during the war.

2. a. *prisoner of war* (further examples). Freq. abbrev. *P.O.W.*, *POW* (see P II). Also *attrib.*, esp. in *prisoner(s) of war camp*. Hence *prisoner-of-wardom* nonce-word.

1922 C. E. Montague *Disenchantment* x. 146 To 'take it out of' German prisoners of war. **1922** *Encycl. Brit.* XXXII. 163/1 The inspection of prisoners-of-war camps by the accredited representatives of the protecting State. **1944** [see *kriegie]. **1946** *Encycl. Brit. Bk. of Yr.* 605/1 (*caption*) Japanese inmates of a prisoner of war camp on Guam. **1961** *Times* 7 June 17/1 A Union prisoner-of-war camp. **1974** *Times* 4 Mar. 9/4 (*heading*) Prisoner-of-wardom. **1974** [see *Oflag].

pri·sonful. [-ful.] As much or as many as a prison will hold.

1911 G. B. Shaw *Getting Married* 173 If a prisonful of thieves were asked what induced them to take to thieving, [etc.]. **1922** A. Bennett *Lilian* II. ii. 66 Only the malice of a prisonful of women could have seriously asserted her to be older than Felix.

prisonize (pri·z'nəiz), *v.* [f. Prison *sb.* + -ize.] *trans.* To cause (a person) to adapt himself to prison life. Chiefly in *pass.*: to adapt to the attitudes and social behaviour of prison life, esp. at the expense of one's 'normal' personality. Hence **pri:soniza·tion**, the fact or process of becoming adapted to prison life and unfitted for the outside world.

1940 D. Clemmer *Prison Community* xii. 299 As we use the term Americanization to describe a greater or less degree of the immigrant's integration into the American scheme of life, we may use the term *prisonization* to indicate the taking on in greater or less degree of the folkways, mores, customs, and general culture of the penitentiary. *Ibid.* 300 First offenders..'wise up', as the inmates say, or in other words, by association they become prisonized. **1963** T. & P. Morris *Pentonville* vii. 169 Prisonization may be defined as the continuous and systematic destruction of the psyche in consequence of the experience of imprisonment, and the adoption of new attitudes and ways of behaving..which may frequently make it impossible for the individual to act successfully in any normal social role. *Ibid.* 170 While the majority of inmates become 'prisonized' in some aspects, few are wholly prisonized. *Ibid.*, A certain type of prisonized man whose behaviour forms the hard core of inmate subculture. **1972** E. Heffernan *Making it in Prison* i. 7 The 'outlaw' has been found to be the most highly 'prisonized' in terms of loyalty to the inmate code. *Ibid.* ii. 32 If any category may be considered 'new' to prisonization, it is the professional, with shorter sentence length..and fewer total years in an institutional atmosphere. **1973** Cull & Hardy *Fund. Criminal Behavior & Correctional Syst.* viii. 147 He found that those inmates who were farthest from release..were the most prisonized. **1975** D. Duffee *Correctional Policy & Prison Organization* iii. 35 The counter-suggestion was made that prisonization is just an institutional form of deprivation felt by the lower class, uneducated, and black offenders most of their lives.

priss (pris). *U.S. colloq.* [Back-formation from next.] One who is prissy; a prim girl; an effeminate man, a 'pansy'.

1923 G. McKnight *Eng. Words* iv. 61 Youthful impatience with anything or anybody that interferes with a good time is expressed by such names as *kill-joy*, *frost*, *wet-blanket*... To these may be added, from the language of girls,..*poor potato*,..*cuckoo*, *old priss*, *old Jane*. *Ibid.* 62 If she [*sc.* a girl] is unpopular, she is..a *priss*, a *tomato*, a *chunk of lead*, a *drag*. **1942** Berrey & Van den Bark *Amer. Thes. Slang* §825/32 *Priss*, a girl who objects to 'necking'. **1975** A. Bergman *Hollywood & LeVine* (1976) ii. 23, I..was led to my room by an elderly priss named Roy. He told me I looked the rugged type. **1976** *National Observer* (U.S.) 16 Oct. 10/3 Randall..is television's consummate comedy priss, his overelocution and self-righteousness maddeningly funny.

prissy (pri·si), *a.* (and *sb.*) *colloq.* (orig. *U.S.*). [Perh. blend of Prim *a.* and *sissy.] Precise and over-particular; prim, priggish, or prudish, esp. in a supposedly effeminate way. Also *Comb.* and as *sb.*

1895 J. C. Harris *Mr. Rabbit at Home* iv. 40 Once, when I was courting, I spoke of a sitting hen, but the young lady said I was too prissy for anything. **1905** *Dialect Notes* III. 91 *Prissy, adj.* Precise, nice, over-particular. 'She's awful *prissy*.' Rare. **1925** A. Woollcott in 'L. Carroll' *Alice's Adventures in Wonderland* p. viii, The extraordinary contrast between the cautious, prissy pace of the man and the mad, gay gait of the tale he told. **1927** *Amer. Speech* II. 362/1 *Prissey*.., a boy who acts like a girl. 'Don't be such a prissey, Jim.' **1927** D. Marquis *Archy & Mehitabel* xxiv. 107 Some strait laced prune faced bunch of prissy mouthed sisters of uncharity. **1929** W. Faulkner *Sound & Fury* 49 He don't like that prissy dress. **1932** E. Hemingway *Death in Afternoon* xvii. 205 He should redeem..the prissy exhibitionistic, aunt-like, withered old maid moral arrogance of a Gide. **1948** M. Gilbert *They never looked Inside* xii. 177 She reminded him instantly of one of Walt Disney's prissy little rabbits. **1952** A. Wilson *Hemlock & After* I. ii. 36 He was disgusted at the precise, prissy tones in which he heard himself saying, 'It's lovely to be in the country.' **1957** *Listener* 2 May 722/1 His work is haunted by a disagreeable, sickly, prissy *art nouveau* rhythm. **1963** *Guardian* 28 Mar. 1/3 The rather prissy manner in which Dr Beeching has chosen to announce his determination to make us turn into a new economic man. **1968** *Times Lit. Suppl.* 28 Nov. 1327/1 The prissy, petit-bourgeois level of Robespierre. **1973** B. Broadfoot *Ten Lost Years* xxi. 244 We weren't quite as prissy as this New Generation thinks we were. **1975** L. Gillen *Return to Deepwater* viii. 140 Good grief, you little prissy, you've been kissed before, certainly!

Hence **pri·ssified** *a.*, **pri·ssily** *adv.*; **pri·ssiness.**

1934 Webster, Prissily,.. *adv.*—prissiness, *n.* **1957** *Observer* 15 Sept. 13/2 When it aspires to epigram, the dialogue falls into a quaint, soggy prissiness. **1958** *Spectator* 22 Aug. 246/2 Little girls prissily painted a still-life of oranges. **1963** P. M. Hubbard in *Mag. of Fantasy & Sci. Fiction* Jan. 8/1 He had a slightly prissified voice. **1976** *Listener* 15 July 58/1 The blackcurrant eyes, the prissily pursed mouth. **1976** 'J. Ross' *I know what it's like to Die* xxvi. 161 An accountant's clerk of terrifying prissiness.

pristane (pri·stēⁱn). *Chem.* [ad. G. *pristan* (Y. Toyama 1923, in *Chem. Umschau auf d. Gebiete d. Fette, Oele, Wachse u. Harze* XXX. 186/1), f. L. *prist-is*, Gr. πρίστ-ις saw-fish, (*loosely*) shark; see -ane.] A saturated hydrocarbon, now known to be 2,6,10,14-tetramethyl pentadecane, $C_{19}H_{40}$, which occurs in the liver oils of certain sharks and related species and is a colourless oil solidifying below about 30° C.

1923 *Jrnl. Chem. Soc.* CXXIV. i. 890 The pure hydrocarbon, which is named pristane, has the following characters:..b.p. 158°/10 mm.,..296°/760 mm., without decomposition. **1963** *Nature* 20 July 284/1 It is estimated that pristane constitutes about 1·1 per cent of the total paraffin fraction of crude wool wax. **1965**, **1971** [see *phytane]. **1975** *Sci. Amer.* June 94/3 Pristane is also found in some marine organisms, whereas phytane almost never appears except in organisms that have been contaminated by petroleum.

pristine, *a.* Add: Now usu. with pronunc. (pri·stīn).

2. In various *transf.* and extended senses: having its original condition; unmarred, unspoilt. Of a natural object, physical feature, or the like: unspoilt by human interference, untouched; virginal, pure. Of a manufactured object: spotless, pure in colour; fresh, good as new. Hence, in weakened sense: brand-new, newly-made. orig. *U.S.*

These transferred uses, though now increasingly common, are regarded with disfavour by many educated speakers.

1923 W. Stevens *Harmonium* 59 The responsive man, Planting his pristine cores in Florida, Should prick thereof. **1940** W. Faulkner *Hamlet* III. i. 180 The furious cold rain..galloped on in tearful and golden laughter across the glittering and pristine earth. *Ibid.* IV. i. 298 This time the Justice raised one hand, in its enormous pristine cuff, toward her. **1942** —— *Go down, Moses* 166 He felt the old lift of the heart, as pristine as ever, as on the first day. **1951** *Everywoman* May 68/2 (Advt.), Has a slim waist, full skirt and a pristine white detachable collar. **1955** *Bull. Atomic Sci.* Apr. 119/2 The endeavor to retain the pristine secrecy of atomic energy information. **1967** S. Attanasio tr. *Hohendorf's Life & Times of Goethe* 44 Christiane was a short, attractive brunette, with a pristine mouth and round cheeks. **1974** *BP Shield Internat.* Oct. 28/4 The value of Lake Sibaya as a pristine system cannot be overemphasised. **1975** *Times* 11 Aug. 4/5 Gone the cluttered spike, the chatter of teleprinters; his habitat now is the pristine, air-conditioned new building on the Barbican promenade of Lazard Brothers. **1976** *Milton Keynes Express* 25 June 44/1 (Advt.), The quality of the coachwork can only be described as in pristine condition. **1977** *Gramophone* May 1725/2 (Advt.), All records and tapes obtained through DLR, including budget labels, are factory fresh, unconditionally guaranteed, pristine products.

Hence **pri·stinely** *adv.*

1899 *Westm. Gaz.* 16 May 2/3 This indignant Tory thinks that what would be pristinely beautiful as Dollis Hill would be newly ugly as Gladstone Park. **1972** *Bookseller* 3 June 2456/2 Roughly half the books mentioned are not published within that week. It is only the populars who insist on having something pristinely fresh, published that day. **1975** F. King *Needle* ix. 48 A Bentley like that one, though it would be a shame to damage and stain something so pristinely beautiful.

‖ **Prisunic** (prizünik). [Fr., lit. 'sole price'.] One of a chain of multiple stores (in France) in which a cheap class of goods is sold (orig. all at the same price).

1965 R. Postgate *Plain Man's Guide to Wine* (ed. 2) ii. 39 The '*Prisunic*' and other French shops which sell every-day wines. **1967** J. Porter *Chinks in Curtain* ii. 23 A few messy looking shops. A Prisunic. Oh dear! I plodded on. **1970** *Guardian* 19 Dec. 3/5 The old couple set up house in the doorway of the prisunic down the road. **1971** *Ibid.* 30 Oct. 3/7 The..grocer says he is still feeling the draught from the *prisunic* and..may decide to go.

prisyadka, var. *PRISIADKA.

privacy. Add: Also with pronunc. (pri·văsi). **1. b.** The state or condition of being alone, undisturbed, or free from public attention, as a matter of choice or right; freedom from interference or intrusion. Also *attrib.*, designating that which affords a privacy of this kind.

1814 J. CAMPBELL *Rep. Cases King's Bench* III. 81 Though the defendant might not object to a small window looking into his yard, a larger one might be very inconvenient to him, by disturbing his privacy, and enabling people to come through to trespass upon his property. **1890** WARREN & BRANDEIS in *Harvard Law Rev.* IV. 193 (*title*) The right to privacy. *Ibid.* 196 The question whether our law will recognize and protect the right to privacy..must soon come before our courts for consideration. **1901** G. B. SHAW *Capt. Brassbound's Conversion* II. 252 Well, I am afraid I want a little privacy, and, if you will allow me to say so, a little civility. **1933** *Post Office Electr. Engineers' Jrnl.* XXVI. 224/1 Overseas radio telephone services operated by the Post Office are provided with privacy equipment on all channels where the necessary deciphering equipment is provided at the distant end. **1940** *Chambers's Techn. Dict.* 752/2 *Secrecy* (or *privacy*) *system*, modification of speech-frequencies within the speech-band, so that during transmission from a radio transmitter to a receiver the signal is unintelligible and cannot be tapped. *a* **1953** E. O'NEILL *More Stately Mansions* (1964) II. iii. 130 Can I never have a moment's privacy in my own home? **1965** [see *PRIVATE *a.* (*sb.*) 2 f (*a*)]. **1970** R. K. KENT *Lang. Journalism* 106 *Privacy, right of*, the right of a citizen not to have details of his life explored in the press... The right of privacy also prevents the use of a person's name or picture in an advertisement without his permission. **1975** R. H. RIMMER *Premar Experiments* III. 233 In the meantime, you can live in one of Premar's privacy rooms. **1976** *Billings* (Montana) *Gaz.* 27 June 5-D/5 (Advt.), There's also a large patio with privacy fence and a double attached garage, all on a nicely landscaped half acre. **1977** *Chicago Tribune* 2 Oct. XII. 21/1 (Advt.), Huge patio deck with privacy fence and decorator touches. **1978** I. MURDOCH *Sea* 375 When Titus appeared I decided to go outside to avoid interruption and ensure privacy.

private, *a.* (*sb.*) Add: **2. a.** *private individual, person* (further examples).

1673 J. RAY *Observations Journey Low-Countries* 305 When the Gallies are at home those [slaves] that belong to private persons are permitted to lodge in their Masters houses. **1885** *List of Subscribers, Classified* (United Telephone Co.) (ed. 6) 233 (Advt.), The Birkbeck Bank opens Drawing Accounts with trading firms and private individuals. **1930** G. B. SHAW *Apple Cart* p. xviii, Socialists have said to me that they were converted by seeing that the nation had to choose, not between governmental control of industry and control by separate private individuals [etc.]. *Ibid.* p. xix, We cannot do this as private persons. It must be done by the Government or not at all. **1931** M. ALLINGHAM *Look to Lady* xiv. 150 When publicity is fatal..then the private individual has to get busy on his own account. **1960** N. MITFORD *Don't tell Alfred* iii. 41 If my husband were a private person, none of this would matter. **1975** N. FREELING *What are Bugles blowing For?* xi. 67, I find it miserable. Everyone so callous... But I'm just a private individual. **1978** *Verbatim* Sept. 1/1 In certain circles, it has become popular to the point of irritation to characterize every eremitical, dyspeptic, close-mouthed selfish crank as a *private person*.

c. *private member* (earlier and later examples). Hence *private member's bill*, a bill introduced in Parliament by a private member.

In quot. 1606 *private member* means 'not a member of the Privy Council'.

1606 *House of Commons Jrnl.* 13 May I. 308/2 Petitions heretofore delivered by the Privy Council:... 28 *et* 43 *Eliz*... Last Session, by Mr. Hare, a private Member. **1835** *Mirror of Parliament* 25 Feb. 69/2 In the last Session, Wednesday was usually devoted to Bills brought in by private Members of Parliament... The Chancellor of the Exchequer.—Nobody is more sensible than I am of the extent to which the country is often indebted to private Members, who undertake the management of public Bills. **1852** DISRAELI *Ld. George Bentinck* xxvii. 580 Instead of experiencing the usual and almost inevitable doom of private members of parliament and having his statements shattered by official information, Lord George Bentinck on the contrary was the assailant and the successful assailant of an administration on these very heads. **1908** J. REDLICH *Procedure House of Commons* I. II. iii. 173 This, it was complained, was done systematically, and the result had been to destroy all chance of private members' bills being carried. **1930** *Daily Express* 6 Nov. 19/2 It was a private members' day, on which neither Government policy nor the fate of the Government came up for discussion. **1939** W. I. JENNINGS *Parliament* vii. 180 Many private members' Bills are 'inspired' by interests outside. **1950** *Erskine May's Law of Parl.* (ed. 15) xiv. 287 Private Members' *bills* have precedence on Friday up to the Friday before Good Friday. **1964** ABRAHAM & HAWTREY *Parl. Dict.* (ed. 2) 31 *Private member's bill*, a public bill introduced by a private member... It must be carefully distinguished from a private bill. **1969** *Listener* 10 July 37/2 Seldom is a government prepared to offend many of its supporters in Parliament and the country by making itself responsible for contentious reforming measures. Private members' legislation is therefore a necessity. **1976** H. WILSON *Governance of Britain* x. 171 Any Private Member's Bill, such as those which under Standing Orders can be introduced for a limited period of the year under a procedure of balloting for priority, must if a penny of public expenditure is involved carry with it the cachet of 'Queen's recommendation signified'.

d. (Later example.) Also *private trade, trading.*

1671 in *Publ. Hudson's Bay Rec. Soc.* (1942) V. 5 That Capta. Guillam & all others..bee examined what private trade hath bin by them. **1821** G. SIMPSON *Jrnl.* 8 Jan. in *Ibid.* (1938) I. 212 Chastellan & Lamallice..are renewing their old practice of carrying on Private Trade with the Indians. **1929** *Times* 26 Feb. 17/5 He courageously scrapped his own Bolshevist economic theories in 1921 and reinaugurated private trading. **1965** B. PEARCE tr. *Preobrazhensky's New Econ.* 97 At the present moment the State Bank hardly grants any credits to private trade and industry. **1979** *Guardian* 12 Nov. 7/1 Most trading skills, shops and trucks remain in the hands of private traders. Private trading is not illegal.

f. *private detective, investigator*, a detective who is engaged privately and is not a member of an official police force. Also (orig. *U.S.*) in *colloq.* and *slang* collocations, as *private dick* (*DICK *sb.*[6]); *private eye* (*EYE *sb.*[1] 3 d); also (with hyphen) *attrib.*; hence as vb. intr. and *private-eyeing* vbl. sb.

(*a*) **1868** TROLLOPE *He knew he was Right* (1869) I. xix. 150 'The man was a policeman once.' 'What we call a private detective.' **1873** G. LENING *Dark Side N.Y. Life* 59 A jealous wife engages a private detective to watch her husband. **1898** F. REMINGTON *Crooked Trails* i. 19 He rode a Spanish pony..and arrested Polk, his guide, and two private detectives, whom Polk had bribed to set him over the Rio Grande. **1905** CHESTERTON *Club of Queer Trades* i. 40 Though only a private detective myself, I will take the responsibility. **1936** A. CHRISTIE *ABC Murders* v. 38 'Then you're not—anything to do with the police, sir?' 'I am a private detective.' **1940** R. CHANDLER *Farewell, my Lovely* iii. 21 Philip Marlowe, Private Investigator. One of those guys, huh? **1965** D. FRANCIS *Odds Against* v. 71 The one thing people want when they employ private investigators is privacy. **1974** V. GIELGUD *In Such a Night* ii. 17 Giacomo told me of your reputation as a private investigator. **1975** J. WAINWRIGHT *Square Dance* 173 You'd be surprised how professional..some of the better provincial private detective agencies are.

(*b*) **1912** A. H. LEWIS *Apaches N.Y.* vi. 128 But w'at wit' th' stores full of private dicks a booster can't do much. **1938** R. CHANDLER in *Dime Detective* June 23/1 We don't use any private eyes in here. So sorry. **1939** —— *Big Sleep* xviii. 127 Ohls pulled a chair up and sat down and said: 'Evening, Cronjager. Meet Phil Marlowe, a private eye who's in a jam.' **1946** E. O'NEILL *Iceman Cometh* I. 14 Yuh remember dey used to send down a private dick to give him the rush to a cure, but de lawyer tells Harry nix, de old lady's off of Willie for keeps dis time and he can go to hell. **1952** WODEHOUSE *Pigs have Wings* i. 20 'You mean she's a sleuth?..' 'Substantially that, miss. I gather that she leaves the rougher work to her subordinates.' 'Still she's a genuine private eye.' **1962** [see *gum-shoe* s.v. *GUM *sb.*[2] 9]. **1964** WODEHOUSE *Frozen Assets* vi. 119, I imagine private-eye-ing is one of those things where you've either got the knack or you haven't. **1971** B. MALAMUD *Tenants* 25 He felt in the house,..a presence other than himself. Nothing new but who now? Private Eye snooping for one cause or another? **1974** E. AMBLER *Dr. Frigo* II. 98 Isn't all research private-eye work, Doctor? **1975** J. HONE *Sixth Directorate* IV. v. 176 That's not what I'm here for—to carry on your private eyeing for you. **1979** G. SWARTHOUT *Skeletons* 231 She had offered to marry me again..if I would private-eye for her.

g. *private army*, an army not recruited by the State; a mercenary force. Also *transf.* and *fig.*

1941 W. TEMPLE *Citizen & Churchman* ii. 25 Anything like a 'private army' is a contradiction of the civilized state. **1950** V. PENIAKOFF *Private Army* Part IV (*title*) Popski's private army. **1959** M. GILBERT *Blood & Judgement* ix. 95 The police were a private army. **1964** GOULD & KOLB *Dict. Social Sci.* 482/2 *Factions, cliques..private armies, lobbies, pressure groups*..are terms which, like *party*, denote voluntary associations to influence government. **1968** *N.Y. Times* 23 July 41 (*heading*) Norman Mailer enlists his private army to act in film. **1968** 'J. WELCOME' *Hell is where you find It* i. 15 The security and secret services, so called, had recently..been shaken up and amalgamated... We were an off-shoot, a semi-amateur show, a private army. **1969** D. BAGLEY *Spoilers* v. 60 'Some of my patients had been cutting up ructions at the Howard Club. Johnny didn't like it.' 'And you had to take your own private army to back you up?' **1979** J. RATHBONE *Euro-Killers* ii. 27 Their riot sticks..infuriated him—he hated private armies.

h. *private developer* (see *DEVELOPER f).

1961 *Kentish Times* 28 July 10 There is little land left in the urban district, with its Green Belt setting, for either Council or private developer. **1965** *New Society* 26 Aug. 6/1 A modern civic centre to be built by a private developer under council guidance. **1970** *Guardian* 17 Aug. 5/2 The private developer is in a better position to judge the demands for development than the planner. **1972** *Country Life* 25 May 1330/1 Berkshire has given planning permission for some 18,000 houses, of which private developers build less than 3,000 new houses a year. **1975** *Times* 30 Aug. 13/5 How many private developers are interested in urban renewal?

3. b. *private parts* (earlier and later examples). Also *transf.* and *fig.*

1785 GROSE *Dict. Vulgar T.*, *Commodity*, a woman's commodity; the private parts of a modest woman, and the public parts of a prostitute. **1853** *Law Jrnl. Rep.* XXXI. III. 123/1 What do you mean in law by exposing his *person*? The indictment should have been for exposing his *private parts*. *a* **1930** D. H. LAWRENCE *Last Poems* (1932) 157 The reddened limbs..and the half-hidden private parts. **1959** I. & P. OPIE *Lore & Lang. Schoolch.* vi. 96 It may be a verse in which the private parts are mentioned, as in the baby-washing songs of Tiny Tim. **1969** *Listener* 27 Feb. 282/1 He has an objection to 'showing his private parts' to the reader; and to this modesty, as much as to his dreadful loquacity, must, alas, be ascribed his failure to produce the great autobiography that one might have expected from him. **1971** *Farmer & Stockbreeder* 23 Feb. 30/1 Major Ogilvie recalls some mothers feeling embarrassed at having to see the 'private parts' of an animal's body—like teats and udders—being handled by a man.

4. a. Also, as a sign or notice indicating that a room or the like is private. (Further examples.)

a **1911** D. G. PHILLIPS *Susan Lenox* (1917) II. xi. 285 The frosted glass door marked 'Private'. **1973** 'D. CRAIG' *Bolthole* i. 15 He saw a wide staircase with a tasselled rope across it and a Private sign. **1973** G. MITCHELL *Murder of Busy Lizzie* xv. 177 My sitting-room is the one marked PRIVATE.

c. *private play, theatre* (earlier examples), *theatrical* (earlier and later examples); also *attrib.* or as *adj.*; **private bar** = *lounge bar* s.v. *LOUNGE *sb.* 4; also *ellipt.*; **private bath(room)**, a bath(room) set aside for private use, usu. one attached to a room in a hotel or guest house; **private beach,** a beach that is privately owned, esp. by a hotel for the use of guests; **private box** (see BOX *sb.*[2] 8); **private business** *Eton College slang*, extra tuition; **private collection,** a collection (of paintings or the like) in private possession; **private development,** development (sense *3 d) undertaken by a private individual or company; **private hotel,** a residential hotel or boarding house which receives guests only by private arrangement; **private inquiry,** work undertaken by a private detective (see sense 2 f above); hence **private inquiry agency, agent; private joke,** a joke understood only by oneself or a privileged few; **private motoring,** motoring in a privately owned vehicle; so **private motorist; private view** (earlier examples).

1909 G. B. SHAW in *Nation* 28 Aug. 787/2 Mr. Chesterton..sees in every public-house a temple... He enters ostentatiously, throws down all the shields and partitions that make the private bar furtive. **1910** H. G. WELLS *Hist. Mr. Polly* viii. 259 The policeman...put his head inside the Private Bar, to the horror of every one there. **1953** K. TENNANT *Joyful Condemned* xxxiv. 340 The gossip of the Private Bar. **1963** N. MARSH *Dead Water* (1964) i. 15 There was only one other woman in the private beside Jenny. *Ibid.* ii. 55 'I want another drink. Anyone join me?'.. He made towards the old private bar. **1972** M. GILBERT *Body of Girl* xii. 107 She was in here.. just after we opened. She came into the private bar. **1975** A. HUNTER *Gently with Love* xxxiii. 132 Come into the private—I would not have you leave without a crack. **1825** E. WEETON *Jrnl.* 14 June (1969) II. 384, I like to bathe alone, and a private bath is just to my taste. **1906** 'O. HENRY' *Four Million* 47 The double front room with private bath. **1910** *Bradshaw's Railway Guide* Apr. 1148 Bedrooms with private bath and telephone. **1974** *Country Life* 21 Mar. 692/3 (Advt.), My bedroom, with its own tv and private bath. **1910** *Bradshaw's Railway Guide* Apr. 1148 Suites of rooms with private Bathrooms. **1961** *Sphere* 6 May 212 A new 1st-class hotel, the Hibiscus, with private beach, opens this summer. **1975** S. BRETT *Cast* iii. 24 Marius's got a villa down the South... It's a lovely place. Private beach. **1632,** etc. Private box [see BOX *sb.*[2] 8]. **1829** [see *FAMILY *sb.* 9 c]. **1897** KIPLING *Let.* 1 June in C. E. Carrington *Rudyard Kipling* (1955) x. 254 We went to the Lyceum... Irving put a private box at our disposal. **1979** *Country Life* 9 Aug. 393/2 The top floor will contain 30 private boxes. **1900** J. S. FARMER *Public School Word-Bk.* 158 *Private-business*,.. extra work with the tutor. **1979** D. NEWSOME *On Edge of Paradise* ii. 87 Half-an-hour's preparation for his Private Business lecture on Napoleon. **1899** R. FRY *Let.* Oct. (1972) I. 174 He took me to an amazing private collection, full of marvellous drawings and sculptures all looking far better for being in a private place. **1979** R. COX *Auction* i. 24 There were several Memlings in Austrian private collections. Stefan Zweig owned one. **1961** *Recreation* Dec. 531/1 Areas should..have room around the edges to protect the values of the area from encroachment by private developments. **1971** 'D. HALLIDAY' *Dolly & Doctor Bird* ii. 19 Coral Harbour is a private development in one of the moneyed quarters of New Providence Island. **1975** *Times* 30 Aug. 13/5 Impressions of the results of the last boom period for private development are still..fresh. **1857** G. H. LEWES *Jrnl.* 11–18 May in *Geo. Eliot Lett.* (1954) II. 326 We went to *Dingley's Private Hotel*—very comfortable. **1910** *Bradshaw's Railway Guide* Apr. 1012/2 Cullen's private hotel and family boarding house. **1936** [see *CATCH *v.* 40]. **1960** L. DAVIDSON *Night of Wenceslas* i. 8, I had really borrowed the money from old Imre, who lived in the same private hotel. **1962** BULL & RICHARDSON *Hotel & Catering Law* (rev. ed.) iii. 37 This chapter is concerned with premises which are not conducted as 'inns', that is with private premises as distinct from public premises. It is convenient to refer to such premises as 'private hotels', this term also including guest houses, boarding-houses, apartment houses, and similar places. *Ibid.*, The private hotel proprietor reserves to himself the right to pick and choose his guests, and does not hold himself out as willing to receive anyone who calls. He makes a separate contract, either written or verbal, with his guests. **1970** C. WHITMAN *Death out of Focus* x. 153 It was a typical private hotel bedroom. **1972** *Times* 1 Apr. 14/1 The very words 'boarding house' are out. Now it is 'guest house' at the very least, and possibly even 'private hotel'. **1874** M. CLARKE *His Natural Life* III. xxii. 331, I dabbled a little in the Private Inquiry line of business. **1892** Private inquiry agency [see *inquiry, enquiry 4]. **1897** A. Morrison *Dorrington Deed-Box* ii. 98 Your respectable talents will be devoted to the service of Dorrington & Hicks, private inquiry agents. **1922** Private inquiry agent [see *inquiry, enquiry 4]. **1948** 'J. Tey' *Franchise Affair* x. 106 We cannot expect you to turn yourself into a private inquiry agent on our behalf. **1973** R. Lewis *Of Singular Purpose* v. 113 All solicitors use private enquiry agents... They are often ex-policemen. **1974** 'M. Innes' *Appleby's Other Story* xxiii. 181 Miss Kentwell works for a private enquiry agency..of the highest repute. **1949** E. Coxhead *Wind in West* i. 19 She answered it [*sc.* an advertisement]..for a sort of private joke. **1978** J. McNeil *Consultant* v. 68 Susan had learned..not to ask for explanations of Webb's private jokes. **1974** *Country Life* 2 May 1050/1 The restrictions on private motoring caused by the higher cost of petrol. **1976** *Times* 3 Aug. 2/1 Between 1964 and 1974 passenger traffic increased by 40 per cent, private motoring growing by nearly 65 per cent, rail staying level and bus traffic declining. **1926** *Daily Chron.* 13 May 4 (*caption*) Private motorists made themselves popular by giving lifts to people who would otherwise have had to walk long distances. **1975** *Times* 18 June 4/5 The Egon Ronay *Guide to Transport Cafés*..should also be of help to the economy-minded private motorist. **1790** F. Reynolds *Dramatist* I. 12 Whence arises the pleasure at an Opera, a private Play, or a Speech in Parliament? **1794** C. Mathews *Let.* 3 Aug. in A. Mathews *Mem. Charles Mathews* (1838) I. 100, I left England without calling on Wayte, to whom I am indebted for a few articles; among which are the dresses for the private play. **1868** P. Fitzgerald *Life David Garrick* I. vi. 158 It was once determined to get up a private play..and the parts were cast in a moment. **1784** W. Hayley (*title*) Plays of three acts written for a private theatre. **1807** E. Weeton *Let.* 18 Nov. (1969) 50 She..was never outshone in elegance of movement at a Ball, out-performed at a private Theatre. **1787** J. Powell (*title*) The narcotic & private theatricals. **1818** Keats *Let.* 23 Jan. (1931) I. 96, I began an account of a private theatrical—Well it was of the lowest order, all greasy and oily. **1914** G. B. Shaw *Fanny's First Play* 153 The end of a saloon in an old-fashioned country house..has been curtained off to form a stage for a private theatrical performance. **1837** Dickens *Pickw.* xxviii. 289 A select two or three,..were being honoured with a private view of the bride and bridesmaids, up stairs. **1840** —— *Old C. Shop* xxix. 254 Miss Monflathers,..at the head of the head Boarding and Day Establishment..condescended to take a Private View with eight chosen young ladies. **1847** E. Gray *Let.* 28 Apr. in M. Lutyens *Ruskins & Grays* (1972) iv. 33 John [Ruskin] is going to a private view of the Royal Academy.

d. Used with reference to medical treatment and facilities for which fees are charged to the patient instead of being provided by the state or a public body; from 1946 in the United Kingdom *spec.* of treatment and facilities outside the *National Health Service* (see *national *a.* 5), as *private bed, nursing, patient*, etc. Also *ellipt.*

1754 W. Smellie *Midwifery* II. xxvi. 437, I attended a private patient. **1801, 1843** [see sense 6 in Dict.] **1860** F. Nightingale *Notes on Nursing* vi. 38, I have often seen the private nurse go on dusting..while the patient is eating... The above remarks apply much more to private nursing than to hospitals. *Ibid.* 39 Generally, the only rule of the private patient's diet is what the nurse has to give. **1914** A. Bennett *Price of Love* xii. 256 In those days of State health insurance all doctors were too busy..to be of assistance to private patients. **1934** P. Bottome *Private Worlds* xii. 114 They stood in a small private room off the ward, and looked down at the moaning woman on the bed. **1935** D. L. Sayers *Gaudy Night* ix. 191 He's in a private ward, so you can get in any time. **1942** M. Dickens *One Pair of Feet* vii. 110 Sister Adams..told me that I was to..go on day duty on the Private wards. *Ibid.* 115, I went on cutting bread savagely and the Private Nurse stirred milk with pursed lips. **1942** [see *dog's body 2]. **1943** G. Greene *Ministry of Fear* II. ii. 150 It's a very charming nursing-home and I'm a private patient. **1946** *Act* 9 & 10 *Geo. VI* c. 81 §5 The Minister may allow any medical practitioner..on the staff of a hospital providing hospital and specialist services to make arrangements for the treatment of his private patients either at their hospital or at any other such hospital. **1946** P. Bottome *Lifeline* ii. 33 Ours is not a state-run affair..but a private hospital. **1956** P. Scott *Male Child* I. i. 26, I spent most of April in a private nursing home. **1960** C. Watson *Bump in Night* i. 15 He lay in a small private ward of Chalmsbury General Hospital. **1961** *Ann. Reg. 1960* 9 There had been a demand that 'private patients' who relieved the finances of the health service by paying their own doctor should get free access to N.H.S. drugs. **1967** M. Sharman *Face of Danger* i. 7 They..walked out of the private wing of the hospital. **1967** P. Willmott *Consumer's Guide Brit. Social Services* vi. 158 Private beds amount to little over one per cent of the total number of beds in use. *Ibid.*, Financial help towards the cost of private treatment is provided by several provident associations. **1969** B. Turner *Circle of Squares* iv. 27 Poor Flisch had a private room. **1971** *Guardian* 1 July 6/5 Hospital laboratory technicians..will refuse to carry out tests on private patients. **1972** P. Johnson *Offshore Islanders* vi. 400 Labour ministers lacked the will to impose a salaried service on the medical profession... Private practice, private beds in hospitals, private health insurance were permitted. **1976** W. J. Burley *Wycliffe & Schoolgirls* iii. 67 She was a staff nurse..and chucked up her job to go into private nursing. **1976** N. Leigh-Taylor *Doctors & Law* iv. 35 The Government has announced that it intends..to abolish private treatment in N.H.S. hospitals.

e. *Teleph.* and *Telegr.* (i) Applied to (*a*) a line that is permanently for the exclusive use of the subscriber or is not connected to the public network; (*b*) a number that is ex-directory; (*c*) a number at a private address rather than business premises.

1878 *Telegr. Jrnl.* VI. 51/1 The regulations concerning the despatch and receipt of telegrams, the tariffs for the same, and for the renting of private wires. **1885** *List of Subscribers* (United Telephone Co.) p. vii, The Charge for Private Lines is at a fixed annual rental, payable in advance, varying with the situation and the distance apart of the points connected. **1911** W. Aitken *Man. Telephone* xxiii. 476 Private Lines..are lines not having exchange service. **1924** J. Buchan *Three Hostages* xvi. 235 This must be a private telephone..of which only his special friends knew the number. **1933** D. L. Sayers *Murder must Advertise* viii. 129 He was not in the telephone-book, but his private number would doubtless be on the telephone-clerk's desk. **1940** *War Illustr.* 16 Feb. p. ii/1 Taking the final proof of his commentary on the foreign news of the day to the 'private wire' room, to be telegraphed or telephoned to Manchester. **1942** A. Christie *Body in Library* vi. 59, I had a private line put in connecting my bedroom with my office. **1969** N. Freeling *Tsing-Boum* xiii. 95 Good morning. Police Judiciaire!.. I'm at a private number in Marseilles; will you..clear me a direct line. **1972** L. Moir tr. *Simenon's Maigret & Flea* ii. 34 You'll know where to find me. My private number's in the book. **1974** *Encycl. Brit. Macropædia* XVIII. 95/1 Private-line systems for data communications have come into widespread use in the past decade. **1974** D. Gray *Dead Give Away* vii. 72 Cyril decided on a nap in his study, where he had a private line, on which he could ring Nina. **1976** H. MacInnes *Agent in Place* xxiii. 241 Tony..dialled Bill's number—not his private line, just the ordinary one. **1976** T. H. Flowers *Introd. Exchange Syst.* i 11 Picture telegraphy.. is possible over the telephone service lines but difficulties discourage small users and encourage large users of such services to rent private circuits not subject to switching.

(ii) *spec.* of an exchange: serving private lines; *private branch exchange*, an exchange on private premises by which private lines may be connected to the public network.

1891 J. Poole *Pract. Telephone Handbk.* vii. 124 Fig. 102 represents a type of switch-board which was designed by the writer in 1881 for the use of private telephone exchanges. **1905** *Ann. Rep. Amer. Telephone & Telegr. Co. 1904* 6 There is an enormous increase in the number of private branch exchanges in hotels. **1911** W. Aitken *Man. Telephone* xxi. 416 No hotel or warehouse of any standing is now considered complete without a private branch exchange connected to the 'Central' by a number of circuits. **1943** A. L. Albert *Fund. Telephony* viii. 170 A private branch exchange or *PBX* in a large store, hotel, manufacturing plant, or to serve a college campus. **1974** *Encycl. Brit. Macropædia* XVIII. 94/1 Typical automatic switching systems in operation include the step-by-step system, used..for local exchanges and private branch exchanges.

(iii) Describing components in a telephone exchange which belong to a circuit whose potential indicates the condition of a particular subscriber's line and enables its condition to be ascertained without interfering with calls in progress; esp. in *private wire* (see quot. 1969).

1906 J. Poole *Pract. Telephone Handbk.* (ed. 3) xxx. 486 When a current is started and stopped through the 'private' magnet, the end of the side-switch arm slips under the outer tooth. **1919** R. Mordin *Strowger Automatic Telephone Exchange* i. 23 The whole arrangement of fixed contacts is called the connector bank; the upper half the private bank, and the lower the line bank. The moveable contacts are termed respectively the private wiper and the line wiper. **1927** C. W. Wilman *Man. Automatic Telephony* vi. 55 This wire is comparable with the test wire in a manual system inasmuch as it indicates whether a particular line is free or busy... It is..known as the private line (because it prevents intrusion on a busy trunk). **1969** S. F. Smith *Telephony & Telegr. A* vi. 153 A third wire is therefore provided on all connexions through the exchange, the potential of which indicates the condition of the circuit. This avoids intrusion on calls in progress and is called the private wire, usually abbreviated to '*P-wire*'.

5. b. *private bank* (see Bank *sb.*[3] 7a); hence *private banker, banking*; *private car*, (*a*) *U.S.*, a privately owned and used railway carriage; (*b*) a motor car owned and used privately, as distinct from a commercial vehicle; *private family* (earlier example); *private income*, an income derived from private sources, as investments, property, etc; an unearned income; *private means*, income derived from private sources (cf. *private income* above); *private press*, a printing and publishing house of limited resources and output, often operated for the owner's personal satisfaction rather than profit, and usually issuing small editions of books designed to meet higher standards of production than those of commercial publishers; *private residence* = *private house*; *private room*, a room in a club, hotel, etc., that may be hired for private use (see also sense 5d below); *private school* (further examples); also, a school that is independent of a State system of education (see *independent *a.* 5d); *private service*, domestic service in a private house.

1714 in A. McF. Davis *Tracts Currency Massachusetts Bay* (1902) 115 Which does most of all import them, the Publick or the Private Bank? **1802** M. Edgeworth *Let.* 1 Dec. (1979) 43 Private banks never issue any notes. **1978** M. Birmingham *Sleep in Ditch* 120 My mother wanted me to be a banker..in one of the small, distinguished private banks. **1837** in W. L. Mackenzie *Life & Times M. Van Buren* (1846) 178 The Bills of the banks of this State only shall be circulated as Money by private bankers. **1978** P. Noyes *Who is Simon Warwick?* viii. 104 A house which only a private banker could possibly have described as a cottage. **1836** in W. L. Mackenzie *Life & Times M. Van Buren* (1846) 176 If the fetters are knocked off by the repeal of the Restraining Law, private banking associations may be formed. **1954** *Econ. Hist. Rev.* VII. 167 A tentative sketch of some developments in London private banking is offered. **1897** Kipling *Capt. Cour.* ix. 186 Send 'Constance', private car, here, and arrange for special [train]. **1926** *Brit. Gaz.* 12 May 1/3 There were few private cars on the roads and nearly every vehicle was labelled 'Food only'. **1938** E. Ambler *Cause for Alarm* xiv. 232 We had to wait for a private car and a van to pass. **1979** B. Peterson *Peripheral Spy* ii. 34 It really must be important when Col. Petrovich waited for you with his private car. **1873** C. M. Yonge *Pillars of House* IV. xlix. 385 Between his private income and the endowment he would be able to keep up..a staff of Curates. **1910** A. Bennett *Clayhanger* IV. ii. 470 It's a good thing she has a private income of her own. **1923** J. M. Murry *Pencillings* 86 No one really pays much attention now to the subtle problems which tormented Henry James, simply because no one would earn any gratitude by solving them. Even the attempt to solve them calls for a private income. **1941** 'G. Orwell' in *Partisan Rev.* VIII. 496 Nearly all [Home Guard] commands are held by retired colonels, people with 'private' incomes or, at best, wealthy business men. **1952** M. Laski *Village* iii. 65 Because she's got a private income no one ever expected her to go out and take a job. **1971** G. Household *Doom's Caravan* ii. 53 He was a bachelor with a private income. **1862** Mrs. J. B. Speid *Our Last Years in India* vi. 149 In the case of married military men, under the grade of field officer, I cannot see, unless they have private means..how they can escape involvement. **1976** C. Bermant *Coming Home* II. ii. 131, I was without connections and without private means. **1834** J. Martin *Bibliogr. Catal. Bks. Privately Printed* p. v, The second portion of the work, consisting of an account of the publications from literary clubs, and private presses. **1900** *Library* I. 407 Since the days when Horace Walpole started as a master-printer at Strawberry Hill quite a number of book-lovers have amused themselves with the management, and occasionally with the actual working, of a private press. **1922** D. B. Updike *Printing Types* II. xxii. 215 The types of the Kelmscott, Doves, and other English private presses were from his [*sc.* E. P. Prince's] hand. **1934** H. Waddell *Let.* in M. Blackett *Mark of Maker* (1973) xii. 112 The man who is secretary of the Pilgrim Trust (Tom Jones)..runs a very luxurious private press, for which he wants me to do a translation. **1955** S. H. Steinberg *Five Hundred Years of Printing* iii. 217 It was pleasure in fine printing, or at least in printing according to personal taste, rather than commercial success that made kings and nobles set up private presses in the seventeenth and eighteenth centuries. **1968** *Times* 30 Jan. 13/3 (Advt.), First editions and private press books, including the Shakespeare Head Press *Homer*, 1930–31. **1978** *Times Lit. Suppl.* 15 Sept. 1024/1 Some private presses eventually extended their operations so much that their work is more properly described as commercial. **1885** *List of Subscribers, Classified* (United Telephone Co.) (ed. 6) 8 Any Subscriber who pays £20 a year for an Exchange connection can..have his Private Residence joined up with the system. **1974** P. Lovesey *Invitation to Dynamite Party* iii. 34 'There was a second explosion..at Sir Watkin Wynn's residence.' 'A private residence? What have they got against Sir Watkin Wynn?' **1824** Scott *Redgauntlet* III. vii. 197 Walking into the inn, [he] demanded from the landlord breakfast and a private room. **1847** C. Brontë *Jane Eyre* I. xi. 172 When I asked a waiter if any one had been to inquire after a Miss Eyre, I was answered in the negative; so I had no recourse but to request to be shown into a private room. **1879** Trollope *John Caldigate* II. xviii. 251 'I suppose I can have a private room here, at noon to-morrow?' asked Caldigate, turning to the woman at the bar. **1920** 'Sapper' *Bull-Dog Drummond* 7 Have we ever had staying in the hotel a man called le Comte de Guy?.. Has he ever fed here, or taken a private room? **1974** J. Gardner *Return of Moriarty* 87 A private room had been booked for Moriarty and his guest,..at the Café Royal. **1875** Trollope *Prime Minister* (1876) I. i. 6 He had been at a good English private school. **1914** C. Mackenzie *Sinister St.* II. III. iii. 547, I don't think it is snobbishness... It's a throw back to primitive life in a private school. **1944** Private school [see *independent *a.* 5d]. **1945** *Guide to Educ. Syst. Eng. & Wales* (Min. of Educ.: Pamphlet No. 2) 59 *Private school*, independent school owned by a private individual or group of individuals. **1969** T. Jenkins *We came to Australia* I. iii. 41 There are both State and private schools. **1976** C. Bermant *Coming Home* II. iii. 154, I was a teacher in one of those private schools, which was basically a very expensive..crammer for the sons of oil sheiks. **1934** D. L. Sayers *Nine Tailors* 139 Deacon was a waiter in some club... He wanted to try private service. **1953** A. Christie *Pocket Full of Rye* v. 36 She'd been in private service first and after that in various cafés. **1978** M. & N. Ward *Home in Twenties & Thirties* 38/1 There was..an inexorable reduction in the number of people engaged in private service.

6. b. *private account*, a bank account relating to one's personal (as opposed to business) assets; *private call*, a personal telephone call to or from one's place of work; *private life*, a person's domestic or personal (way of) life, as distinct from that relating to employment, official position, etc. (freq. with a notion of sense 3).

1924 'Sapper' *Third Round* i. 34 [The cheque] is drawn on my private account. **1973** A. Behrend *Samarai Affair* viii. 84 He compiled a list of every individual connected with the case... Thus:..Bank Manager, Hartley's private account. **1942** E. Waugh *Put* *out More Flags* i. 52 There's a ridiculous woman on the line saying is this a private call? **1974** 'J. Le Carré' *Tinker, Tailor* xi. 84 The misuse of unlisted Circus telephones for private calls. **1526** R. Whytford *Martiloge* f. cxxxiv, He resygned his crowne, & lyued a holy pryuate lyfe. **1843** Dickens *Mart. Chuzz.* (1844) xvi. 193 A full account of the Ball..with the Server's own particulars of the private lives of all the ladies that was there! **1886** Kipling *Departmental Ditties* (ed. 2) 22 He heliographed his wife Some interesting details of the general's private life. **1943** J. B. Priestley *Daylight on Saturday* xxii. 169 Her own private life, now in ruins, insisted upon claiming her attention, and she could not pretend to herself that it was less important than the private lives of all the other women in the factory. **1973** A. Behrend *Samarai Affair* viii. 81, I was speaking of Mr Gosling as a pilot of course... I know next to nothing of Mr Gosling's private life.

7. b. *private notice question* (see quot. 1964).

1871 *Hansard Commons* 27 Feb. 941, I wish to ask some questions of the Prime Minister, of which circumstances prevented me from giving any other than a private Notice to him. **1913** *Ibid.* 21 Jan. 225 Private notice question... May I ask the Chancellor of the Exchequer a question of which I have given him private notice. **1929** G. F. M. Campion *Introd. Procedure of House of Commons* iv. 126 Private Notice Questions are of two kinds: (a) those of an urgent character, and (b) non-urgent. **1931** *Daily Express* 13 Oct. 12/2 A private notice question can cause more flutter in the Civil Service than any other of the few instruments of torture left in the hands of back-bench members. **1964** Abraham & Hawtrey *Parl. Dict.* (ed. 2) 168 On specially urgent matters, 'private notice questions' may be asked after the end of the time allotted by the standing orders to questions for oral answer. A member who wishes to avail himself of this privilege must give notice of the terms of his question to the minister and to the Speaker not later than twelve o'clock on the day on which he is to ask it. **1976** S. Lloyd *Mr Speaker, Sir* iii. 88 The Speaker also has power under the Standing Orders to allow what are called Private Notice Questions (I will refer to them from now on as P.N.Q.s), ones which in his opinion are of an urgent character and relate either to matters of public importance or to the arrangement of business.

c. *private secretary*: see Secretary *sb.*[1] 2; *private secretaryship*, the office or post of private secretary.

1773 R. Jephson *Let.* 2 Mar. in D. Garrick *Private Corr.* (1831) I. 530 Our friend Tighe is much engaged in his office of Private Secretary to the Lord Lieutenant, but is getting better health and more strength every day. **1814** Jane Austen *Mansf. Park* II. xvii. 155, I would rather find him private secretary to the first Lord than any thing else. **1869** Trollope *Phineas Finn* II. lxv. 232 The Duke of St. Bungay was at work as a Private Secretary when he was three-and-twenty. **1880** E. W. Hamilton *Diary* 25 Apr. (1972) I. 3 Horace Seymour and Henry Primrose are the two between whom the other private secretaryship lies. **1891** W. Fraser *Disraeli & his Day* (ed. 2) 42 Mr Algernon Greville became, some years afterwards, Private Secretary to the Duke. **1930** J. B. Priestley *Angel Pavement* v. 207, I can't bear those private secretary jobs. Yours is one of them, isn't it? **1954** K. Amis *Lucky Jim* iv. 48 Our influencial friend will shortly be declaring his private secretaryship vacant. **1974** R. Ingham *Yoris* i. 1 You'll be this chap's private secretary, so you'll get to know everything.

d. *private law* (see quot. 1923).

1773 J. Erskine *Inst. of Law of Scotl.* i. 9 Public law is that which hath more immediately in view the public weal... Private is that which is chiefly intended for ascertaining the civil rights of individuals. The private law of Scotland is to be the proper subject of this treatise. **1923** W. J. Byrne *Dict. Eng. Law* 519/2 Private or civil law deals with those relations between individuals with which the State is not directly concerned; as in the relations between husband and wife, parent and child,.. contracts, torts, trusts, legacies. **1932** H. F. Jolowicz *Hist. Introd. Roman Law* i. 5 The charge from republic to empire did not make any immediate difference to private law. **1969** D. Daube *Roman Law* iii. 152 The basic structure..is still largely dominated by the criminal trial; but the cases discussed have shifted to lesser crimes and even near to private law. **1973** I. M. Sinclair *Vienna Convention on Law of Treaties* iv. 86 The potentially misleading nature of private law analogies.

e. *private international law* (see quots.)

1834 J. Story *Commentaries Conflict of Laws* i. 9 The jurisprudence, then, arising from the conflict of the laws of different nations, in their actual application to modern commerce and intercourse, is a most interesting and important branch of public law... This branch of public law may be fitly denominated private international law, since it is chiefly seen and felt in its application to the common business of private persons. **1861** R. Phillimore *Commentaries Internat. Law* IV. p. iii, This volume is devoted to the consideration of *Jus Gentium—Private International Law*, or *Comity*: that is, strictly speaking, the law which ought to govern the legal relations of individuals not being the subject of the State which administers the law. **1938** G. C. Cheshire *Private Internat. Law* (ed. 2) i. 22 The expression 'Private International Law', coined by Story in 1834,..and used on the Continent by Foelix in 1838,..has been adopted by Westlake and Foote and most French authors. The chief criticism directed against its use is its implication that the subject forms a branch of International Law. There is, of course, no affinity between Private and Public International Law. The latter comprises those universally accepted customs which are recognized by States in their public relations with each other; the former consists of rules which the Courts of each territorial jurisdiction follow when a dispute containing some foreign element arises between private persons. **1962** J. F. McMahon in *Brit. Year Bk. Internat. Law 1961* 326 The European Economic Community Treaty..devotes two of its articles to what it calls 'approximation of laws'... This gradual approximation of law, however, will have to take place both in the field of legislation and in the jurisprudence of the courts. The Court of the European Communities is not itself concerned with private international law and that question has only been invoked on one occasion before the Court.

f. *private treaty* (see quot. 1973).

1858 *Estates Gaz.* 16 Aug. 16/1 (Advt.), To be sold, by private treaty, a substantial and well-built house. **1922** V. Sackville-West *Heir* i. 19 Are we to try for auction or private treaty? Personally I think the house at any rate will go by private treaty. **1957** D. H. D. Alexander in *Auctioneers & Estate Agents* (Chartered Auctioneers' & Estate Agents' Inst.) 99 Almost all general urban practices depend..upon the commissions earned on the sale of houses and properties whether such sales are by private treaty or auction. **1973** Westland & Rodway *Place of your Own* i. 11/2 In Scotland..houses are more often sold 'by private treaty'. This way, the owner places a reserve, or 'upset' price on the property and invites those interested to make offers, in writing, by a specified date. On that date, the offers are examined, and the property will usually go to the highest bidder. An offer made this way is binding by law, unless you withdraw it before it is formally accepted... Some properties in England and Wales are offered for sale on these terms. **1979** *Irish Times* 28 Sept. 23/1 One of the very few [houses] that well justifies its private treaty price tag of over three-quarters of a million pounds.

g. *private war*: a war fought by a restricted number of participants from personal or private motives. Also *transf.*

1866 C. M. Yonge *Dove in Eagle's Nest* I. p. vi, An offended nobleman, having sent a *Fehdebrief* to his adversary, was thenceforward at liberty to revenge himself by a private war. **1894** Kipling *Jungle Bk.* 85 A wolf who obeyed the orders of this boy who had private wars with man-eating tigers was not a common animal. **1948** G. V. Galwey *Lift & Drop* vii. 196 Operating a war of his own against the gang and the Law. **1973** J. R. L. Anderson *Death on Rocks* x. 175 If there's a senior police officer on the spot..it will help... You and Simon may feel that you have a private war against Potterton, but this is more than a private war. **1974** 'G. Black' *Golden Cockatrice* xi. 194 A killing that was one incident in the continuing private war the Russians and the Chinese have been waging against each other.

h. *private company*: a company whose membership and transfer of shares are limited by law.

1908 *Act* 8 *Edw. VII* c. 69 §121 For the purposes of this Act the expression 'private company' means a company which by its articles—(*a*) Restricts the right to transfer its shares; and (*b*) Limits the number of its members..to fifty; and (*c*) Prohibits any invitation to the public to subscribe for any shares or debentures of the company. **1928** *Act* 18 & 19 *Geo. V* c. 45 § 55 If any company, being a private company, alters its articles in such manner that they no longer include the provisions which..are required to be included in the articles of a company in order to constitute it a private company..the company shall, as on the date of the alteration, cease to be a private company. **1928** *Britain's Industr. Future* (Liberal Industr. Inquiry) ii. vii. 84 The most important existing legal distinction is between Public Companies..and Private Companies, limited to not more than 50 shareholders. **1948** *Act* 11 & 12 *Geo. VI* c. 38 §31 If at any time the number of members of a company is reduced, in the case of a private company, below two,..and it carries on business for more than six months while the number is so reduced, every person who is a member of the company during the time that it so carries on business..shall be severally liable for the payment of the whole debts of the company contracted during that time. **1961** T. E. Utley *Occasion for Ombudsman* ii. 18 The recent case of the Esso Petroleum Bill, when a private company sought powers of compulsory purchase.

i. *private world*: a private 'realm' within which one moves or lives; = World *sb.* 10.

1921 A. Huxley *Crome Yellow* xiii. 128 He determined to retire absolutely from it [*sc.* the great world] and to create..at Crome a private world of his own. **1958** *Listener* 19 June 1024/1 Never has the private world of the thwarted male been so shamelessly exposed to view. **1976** S. Hynes *Auden Generation* ix. 296 The private world of love is threatened by public violence.

j. *private sector*: that part of an economy, industry, etc., which is free from direct state control. Usu. with *the*.

1952 T. Surányi-Unger *Compar. Econ. Syst.* iii. 59 Coordination of freedom and planning obviously influences the formation of private and public sectors within the whole economic structure... The compromising countries still reveal larger private than public sectors. Their *private sectors* are relatively much larger than those of the countries under Eastern planning. **1965** J. L. Hanson *Dict. Econ.* 327/2 *Private sector*, that part of the economy which is left to private enterprise. **1971** *Guardian* 22 July 11/3 Sooner or later there will develop a new set of ideas about the private sector in education. **1980** *Illustr. London News* Mar. 19/1 The extension of the steel strike into the private sector.

k. *private language*: a language which can be understood by the speaker only, esp. in *Logic* involving the query whether such a concept can have meaning. Also *loosely*, a language shared by a privileged few.

1953 G. E. M. Anscombe tr. *Wittgenstein's Philos. Investigations* i. 94 Sounds which no one else understands but which I '*appear to understand*' might be called a 'private language'. **1955** L. P. Hartley *Perfect Woman* xiii. 121 Why should you understand my private language? **1964** *Amer. Philos. Q.* I. 20/1 A private language is one of which it is not merely the case that it is not understood by anyone other than the speaker, but more that it is logically impossible that it should be understood by anyone other than the speaker. **1979** D. Francis *Whip Hand* xiv. 173 The reins felt alive, carrying messages... A private language, shared, understood.

l. *private-label*: used *attrib.* to denote a product manufactured by a particular company for sale through its own retail markets; cf. *own-label* s.v. *own *a.* 4a.

1961 *Economist* 11 Mar. 984/1 There are the usual 'private-label' teas, flour, butter, and dried cereals, fruit and pulses; besides these, private label jams and biscuits are quite common and several companies market their own canned peas, soups, canned fruit and canned vegetables; there is even a private-label pine essence. **1971** *Guardian* 9 June 13/2 Supermarkets' private label brands were selling at around 1s. 10d., while the major manufacturers were sometimes cutting their prices by as much as 1s.

10. b. (Further examples.)

1859 Geo. Eliot *Let.* 10 Apr. (1954) III. 43 The letter is marked 'private'. **1971** A. Price *Alamut Ambush* x. 125 The letter?.. He said it'd be a bit much to open it because it was marked 'private'.

16. Delete † *Obs.* and add later examples.

1876 'Mark Twain' *Tom Sawyer* xxxv. 272 I'll smoke private and cuss private. **1883** —— *Life on Mississippi* iii. 54 They all drunk more than usual—not together, but each man sidled off and took it private, by himself. **1905** [see *case *sb.*[2] 6c].

B. *sb.* **7.** (Examples.)

1940 C. McCullers *Heart is Lonely Hunter* ii. iv. 155 He's so fat he hasn't seen his privates for twenty years. **1955** P. Bowles tr. *Beckett's Molloy* 77 She..thrust her stick between my legs and began to titillate my privates. **1979** 'E. McBain' *Calypso* v. 49 The dancer..wiped the black man's glasses over what the Vice Squad would have called her 'privates'.

9. Short for *private school*.

1925 C. Connolly *Let.* 6 Apr. in *Romantic Friendship* (1975) 64, I met quite a nice small boy who is at my private. **1932** N. Mitford *Christmas Pudding* v. 81 At my private..we had a most handy little cemetery for the fathers, just behind the cricket pav. **1940** —— *Pigeon Pie* iv. 80 It is exactly like one's private here. **1965** *Listener* 22 July 128/1 What private were you at?

private enterprise. [Private *a.* (*sb.*) 4c, 5.] A business or other commercial activity that is privately owned and free of direct state control; such concerns collectively. Also *attrib.*

1844 [see Enterprise *sb.* 1b]. **1859** Mill *On Liberty* v. 191 When private enterprise, in a shape fitted for undertaking great works of industry, does not exist in the country. **1888** E. Bellamy *Looking Backward* xxii. 331 Credit..was the only means you had for concentrating and directing it [*sc.* capital] upon industrial enterprises. It was in this way a most potent means for exaggerating the chief peril of the private enterprise system of industry by enabling particular industries to absorb disproportionate amounts of..disposable capital. **1905** H. G. Wells *Kipps* i. ii. 32 The same national bias towards private enterprise and leaving bad alone..now indentured him firmly into the hands of Mr. Shalford of the Folkestone Drapery Bazaar. **1927** *Melody Maker* Sept. 931/1 The present massacre of private enterprise on the exhibiting side of the [cinema] trade. **1930** *Economist* 5 July 14/2, 53,983 houses were built by private enterprise. **1935** *Discovery* Mar. 63/1 In these days, when even established private enterprise meets with official disapproval, it was hardly to be expected that so universal a service as television could escape semi-official monopoly. **1948** 'J. Tey' *Franchise Affair* xiv. 149 The Larborough firm had..replaced the windows... But they, of course, were Private Enterprise. **1958** *New Statesman* 1 Nov. 577/2 The man who at last can get a mortgage may not care if public money is being doled out to him through private-enterprise building societies. **1961** J. Heller *Catch-22* (1962) xxi. 210 Bombing his own men and planes had therefore really been a commendable and very lucrative blow on the side of private enterprise. **1973** 'D. Jordan' *Nile Green* xxviii. 126 He must be offering the Egyptians a sort of gadget—on the side, a private-enterprise extra. **1975** *N.Y. Times* 17 Oct. 4/2 Despite three decades of Communist rule, pockets of private enterprise in Poland have not only survived but are also showing signs of a modest renaissance.

So **private enterpriser**, an advocate of or participant in private enterprise.

1896 G. B. Shaw in *Labour Leader* 19 Dec. 443/2 The public bodies under Socialism could watch the results of private enterprise... Under the present system we pay the successful private enterpriser too well. **1904** —— *Common Sense of Municipal Trading* vii. 57 Free competition between private enterprisers. **1952** *N.Y. Times Mag.* 20 July 13/2 From the days of Jefferson and Jackson..it [*sc.* the Democratic Party] has drawn to its ranks..the immigrant and the private enterpriser in conflict with the 'money interests'. **1956** 'A. Gilbert' *Riddle of Lady* iii. 43 A nice chap, thought Crook, a private enterpriser. **1965** *Economist* 5 June 1163/2 An old-fashioned bureaucracy more afraid of the change that the planners may bring than even the private enterpriser.

privateer, *sb.* Add: **2.** (Later *fig.* example.)

1836 Dickens *Let.* 1 Nov. (1965) I. 188, I perceive that 'Bells Life'—'The Carlton Chronicle', and some other Weekly papers, are in the habit of re-publishing my sketches from the Chronicle verbatim... Some remonstrance in the paper might have the effect of inducing the Privateers at all events to acknowledge the source from which they derive the Articles.

3*. An advocate or exponent of private enterprise.

1940 *Amer. Guardian* 5 Apr. 4/3 It is the general policy of the privateers never to reduce their rate unless forced to do so by public competition in the shape of municipally or federally owned [electric power] plants. **1965** *Spectator* 19 Feb. 223/1 These two engaging privateers

..are concerned not so much with steel as with the general pattern of British politics. **1979** *Arizona Daily Star* 22 July C 10/1 As a privateer, Serrano drove himself to the races and for the last half of the series even served as his own mechanic.

privateness. Delete 'Now *rare*' and add later examples.

1922 E. R. Eddison *Worm Ouroboros* xv. 212 I'll walk apart, madam,..if thou wouldst have privateness to deliver thy mind. **1939** 'G. Orwell' *Coming up for Air* iv. vi. 276 The privateness of all those lives! **1941** —— *Lion & Unicorn* 15 What it does link up with..is the addiction to hobbies and spare-time occupations, the *privateness* of English life. **1941** E. R. Eddison *Fish Dinner* vi. 92 He let go her hands and stood..as if withdrawn for the moment into some inside privateness of deliberation.

privatism (prəi·vǎtiz'm). [f. Private *a.* + -ism.] An inclination or tendency to be private (in various senses); the use or advocacy of personal or private ideas, institutions, etc. Hence **privati·stic** *a.*, **privati·stically** *adv.*

1948 C. S. Lewis in Williams & Lewis *Arthurian Torso* ii. vi. 188 'Privatism.' This occurs when the poet writes what the reader, however sensitive and generally cultivated he may be, could not possibly understand unless the poet chose to tell him something more than he has told. **1970** *Time* 28 Dec. 6 Few observers of the U.S. scene foresaw that political passions on the campuses would become muted in a new emphasis on 'privatism'. **1970** C. A. Reich *Greening of Amer.* x. 284 'Human nature' was not necessarily always privatistic, grasping, competitive, materialistic. **1971** J. J. Shapiro tr. *Habermas's Toward Rational Society* vi. 121 Student activists are less privatistically oriented to professional careers and future families than other students. **1971** *Atlantic Monthly* Nov. 119, I cannot say in blanket fashion whether this Mao myth is 'good or bad'... The 'privatistic' alternative, anyway, in a country with *per capita* income perhaps one twentieth of America's, is not a glittering one. **1977** *Times Lit. Suppl.* 2 Sept. 1054/2 Self-interest—what Dr Kammen euphemistically calls 'privatism'—and secularism were strong. **1978** T. Honoré *Tribonian* 37 They were trained largely in private law..and imperial constitutions, let alone criminal and public law, had little part to play in legal education. The privatistic outlook of these men is likely to be reflected in the output of constitutions.

privatization (prəi:vǎtəizēi·ʃən). [f. Private *a.* + -ization.] **1.** The policy or process of making private as opposed to public, *spec.* the advocacy or exploitation by the State of *private enterprise; = *denationalization 2.

1959 *News Chron.* 28 July 2/6 Erhard selected the rich Preussag mining concern for his first experiment in privatisation. **1960** *Ibid.* 22 Apr. 11/5 Complete privatisation was opposed by the Socialists..because they feared..the little man selling out his shares to the big capitalists. **1970** *Observer* 25 Jan. 1/6 He foresaw 'privatisation' of many sectors of industry now in public ownership. **1970** J. Cotler in I. L. Horowitz *Masses in Lat. Amer.* xii. 440 If rural marginality allows for the..privatization of State power, the political sphere demands..a new line of social integration. **1976** *National Observer* (U.S.) 1 May B6/3 The contrast between then and now measures the tendency toward privatization and withdrawal of our commitments from the open, public arena that has occurred during the course of the Twentieth Century. **1976** *Globe & Mail* (Toronto) 12 Dec. 5/7 Privatization in the handing over of elements of the public service to the private sector is threatening the livelihoods of thousands of public servants. **1977** *Ibid.* 20 Jan. 6/1 The Government published a working paper..which set out some possibilities..including this: 'The possibility of the private sector providing goods or services that are now provided through government enterprise and programs.' The government, it seemed was toying with the idea of 'privatization'. **1979** *New Statesman* 6 July 14/3 This political formula of controlled privatisation depends on not too many people finding the stringent limits on expression spiritually intolerable.

2. The act or process of regarding as personal or separate, *spec.* the concept of an institution, activity, discipline, etc., seen in terms of its relation to the individual rather than to society generally or to a part of society.

1968 *Listener* 6 June 720/1 On these two points, the privatisation of death, and the loss of any sense of an appropriate length of life, I have contrasted contemporary English society with alien cultures—Celtic or African. **1969** J. H. Goldthorpe et al. *Affluent Worker in Class Struct.* iv. 96 Our findings would indicate as the most probable concomitant of these workers' orientation to work and of their present type of employment what we have earlier referred to as *privatisation*—a process, that is, manifested in a pattern of social life which is centred on, and indeed largely restricted to, the home and the conjugal family. **1972** *Clergy Rev.* Mar. 209 Despite our privatization of God, we are all sharers in spiritual matters. **1973** *Times Lit. Suppl.* 26 Oct. 1307/2 To buy things like that secondhand car which initiates the simultaneous privatization and social extension of their life-style. **1974** J. I. M. Stewart *Gaudy* iii. 40 He had carried with him all the privatization of experience that characterizes bourgeois life. **1975** *Amer. Anthropologist* LXXVII. 260 While the stress on language and on intersubjectivity is fine, the privatization of anthropology, its ultimate inability to issue in a set of explanatory propositions, is disastrous. **1976** Nichols & Armstrong *Workers Divided* 20 We also seek to indicate..what is sometimes called 'privatization'..: a nuclear family-based separation from community. **1976** *Jrnl. Church & State* XVIII. 209 (*title*) Does Church–State separation necessarily mean the privatization of religion? **1978** *Times Lit. Suppl.* 17 Feb. 194/4 The modern 'privatization' of religion owes more to constitutional developments than to Christianity having become 'controversial'. **1979** E. Norman *Christianity & World Order* vi. 80 To regard Christianity as being..concerned primarily with the relationship of the soul to eternity, is these days denounced within Christian opinion as a 'privatization' of religion.

privatize (prəi·vǎtəiz), *v.* [f. Private *a.* + -ize.] **1.** *trans.* To regard as personal or separate, *spec.* in the sense of *privatization 2.

1969 W. Glen-Doepel tr. *Metz's Theol. of World* v. 109 The societal dimension of the Christian message was not given its proper importance but, implicitly or explicitly, treated as a secondary matter. In short, the message was 'privatized' and the practice of faith reduced to the timeless decision of the person. *Ibid.* 114 It is impossible to privatize the eschatological promises of biblical tradition: liberty, peace, justice, reconciliation. Again and again they force us to assume our responsibilities towards society. **1972** *Biblical Theol. Bull.* Feb. 47 Because of their transcendental, existentialistic, personalistic drift these theologies have privatized and presentialized the Christian message. **1977** *Times Lit. Suppl.* 8 Apr. 441/4 Few of his dockers were 'privatized' in the sense in which that term was used by Goldthorpe and his colleagues in their Luton study. **1979** E. Norman *Christianity & World Order* vi. 80 The modern politicized Christians also 'privatize' religion.

2. To make private as opposed to public, *spec.* of the State, to assign (services, industries, etc.) to *private enterprise; = *denationalize *v.* 2 b.

1970 *New Society* 5 Feb. 222/3 Is the Office of Health Economics trying to hint that the best place to start totally privatising the National Health Service is at eye level? **1972** *Daily Tel.* 10 Feb. 16 Some local government services (water, refuse collection, fire-fighting, sea-side amenities, art galleries, museums) could be 'privatised', as well as national health services and State schools. **1976** *Globe & Mail* (Toronto) 12 Dec. 7/2 The House might want to address itself to the question whether we want the Crown corporations to continue to be involved in business or whether they should all be privatized. **1979** *Ibid.* 24 May 7/5 Mr. Clark intends to proceed with his promise to 'privatize' Petro Canada.

Hence **pri·vatized** *ppl. a.*

1973 Goldthorpe & Lockwood in *Sociol. Rev.* II. 154 At this point we may return to our earlier distinction between the 'privatised' and the 'socially aspiring' worker. **1968** *Brit. Universities Ann.* 95 Until recently, the values of the entertainment industry, and the demand for purely 'privatised' standards of morality gave the young little to act collectively about. **1969** R. Blackburn in Cockburn & Blackburn *Student Power* 195 Condemned to a trapped existence in anonymous private or public bureaucracies, 'industrial' man is promised the domestic joys of a 'privatized' existence. **1971** J. J. Shapiro tr. *Habermas's Toward Rational Society* ii. 13 The adult role anticipated at the university..is therefore unsuited for supporting a privatized orientation bound to career and advancement. **1976** *Spare Rib* Dec. 4/3 As long as most people live in nuclear family-type set-ups..babysitting will remain a 'privatised', individual act. **1978** A. Brittan (*title*) The privatised world. *Ibid.* v. 121 The 'privatised self' is explicable in terms of developments in the class structures of western societies.

privilege, *sb.* Add: **2.** (Later N. Amer. examples.)

1968 *Globe & Mail* (Toronto) 13 Feb. 32/7 (Advt.), Kennedy Rd.—Steeles, home privileges, parking, 1–2 girls. *Ibid.*, $20. wk. Gentlemen 18–25. Good meals, lunches, privileges. Nova Scotian family. **1972** *New Yorker* 22 July 48/1 Hillside homesites..with ocean beach privileges. **1976** J. Lee *Ninth Man* 57 Thirty dollars a week... But you get icebox privileges. All my tenants get icebox privileges.

8. *privilege leave* (earlier and later examples.)

1883 Kipling *Let.* 14 Aug. in C. E. Carrington *Rudyard Kipling* (1955) iv. 53 Privilege leave..gives you the pleasant duty of enjoying yourself in a cool climate for thirty days and being paid £20 for that duty. **1980** J. Ditton *Copley's Hunch* ii. ii. 138 Anybody who escapes from enemy hands is entitled to leave—over and above the ordinary ration of privilege leave.

privilege, *v.* Add: **1. c.** *trans.* *R. C. Ch.* To make (an altar) privileged.

1844 *Orthodox Jrnl.* 6 Jan. 3/2 The high altar was privileged by Gregory XIII.

d. In *pa. pple.* Entitled *to* (a special right).

1856 Mrs. B. G. Ferris *Mormons at Home* xii. 199 A few who call themselves physicians..are privileged to a seat in this important assemblage.

privileged, *ppl. a.* Add: **d.** *Eccl.* Applied to days in the Church's calendar which are placed in the highest category of importance, or one of the higher categories (e.g. as regards the precedence they take when two feasts or observances coincide).

1877 J. D. Chambers *Divine Worship in Eng.* v. 85 Sundays..are distinguished..into Principal Privileged, Greater Privileged, Minor Privileged, Inferior Semi-privileged or ordinary Sundays. *Ibid.* 87 The Privileged Sundays, according to the present Anglican Rite, appear, beside the Principal Double Festivals and their Octaves, to be the First Sunday in Advent, Passion Sunday and Palm Sunday, and Sunday within the Octave of the Ascension. The Privileged Ferials: Ash Wednesday, the Four Days before Easter, the Vigils, Fasts and days of Abstinence above enumerated. **1953** *Anglican Services* v. 56 Ordinary (or lesser) Sundays..give way..to feasts or the privileged Octave days of feasts of Our Lord. *Ibid.* 57 Ferias are of three classes, Privileged, greater, and ordinary. *Ibid.* 61 Octaves are of three kinds, privileged, common, and simple.

Privy-Councilship. [-ship.] = Privy-Counsellorship.

1910 *Blackw. Mag.* Sept. 422/1 Even Privy Councilship does not turn nonsense into sound argument.

‖**Prix de Rome.** (prī də rǫm). [Fr., = prize of Rome]. In full *Grand Prix de Rome.* One of a group of prizes awarded annually by the French Government, established by Louis XIV in 1666 for competition by young painters and sculptors, extended in 1720 to include architects, and in 1803 to include musicians and engravers. The winner of the first prize in each category is entitled to a period of study in Rome; also, the winner of a *prix de Rome.*

1879 Grove *Dict. Mus.* I. 233/2 In 1828 he [*sc.* Berlioz] took the second, and at last, in 1830,..the first prize—the 'Prix de Rome'. **1884** R. & E. Holmes tr. *Berlioz' Autobiogr.* I. xxii. 113 The intention of the Government, in establishing the Prix de Rome, was, first, to bring forward year by year the most promising among the young French composers; secondly, to enable them, by means of a pension, to devote themselves entirely for five years to the study of music. **1889** F. F. Buffen *Musical Celebrities* 53 At the age of nineteen Gounod succeeded in gaining the second 'Prix de Rome' for his cantata, 'Marie Stuart et Rizzio', and in 1839 took the 'Grand Prix' with his composition of 'Fernand'. **1905** J. Webster *Wheat Princess* i. 10 Allow me to present Monsieur Benoit, the last *Prix de Rome*—he is the man to paint your ghost. **1906** W. J. Locke *Beloved Vagabond* (1907) xvi. 204 'You a *Prix de Rome*, Master?' 'Yes, my son, in Architecture.' He was clothed in a new and sudden radiance. To a Paris art student a *Prix de Rome* is what a Field Marshal is to a private soldier. **1957** *Observer* 29 Dec. 11/5 The Master had trained as an architect, won the Prix de Rome. **1968** 'S. Jay' *Sleepers can Kill* xv. 153 Oh, well, there goes the Prix de Rome. He put the charcoal down. **1972** *Guardian* 22 July 9/6 John Skeaping ..was living in Rome, having won the Prix de Rome for sculpture.

‖**prix fixe.** (prī fīks). [Fr., lit. = fixed price.] A meal served in a hotel or restaurant at a fixed price, a table d'hôte meal (cf. *à la carte); the menu offered at such a meal. Also *attrib.*

1883 R. L. Stevenson in *Magazine of Art* VI. 274/2 You taste the food of all nations in the various restaurants; passing from a French *prix-fixe*, where every one is French, to a roaring German ordinary where every one is German. **1930** A. Bennett *Imperial Palace* xiv. 82 Prevent customers who prefer the *prix-fixe* from choosing more expensive things than the price will stand. **1933** 'G. Orwell' *Down & Out* vii. 59 A *prix fixe* restaurant where we went for dinner. **1966** P. V. Price *France: Food & Wine Guide* 33 In the majority of restaurants there will be at least one *prix fixe*, a fixed price menu, offering several courses. **1973** *Guardian* 28 May 3/4 In Chantilly..there is *crème chantilly* with everything. But ..you wouldn't believe how the *prix fixe* can expand. **1975** *Times* 20 Dec. 10/7 The *prix-fixe* menus..averaged now 25 francs.

prize, *sb.*[1] Add: **3. c.** *glittering prizes.*

1875 F. Arnold *Our Bishops & Deans* I. v. 286 There are certain glittering prizes which are the great attractions to these. **1923** Ld. Birkenhead in *Times* 8 Nov. 7/4 The world continues to offer glittering prizes to those who have stout hearts and sharp swords. **1976** F. Raphael (*title*) Glittering prizes. **1977** A. Clarke *Let. from Dead* ix. 104 Just keep your trap shut..and remember the glittering prizes. **1978** *Broadcast* 3 Apr. 9/3 Party political broadcasts are not the glittering prizes that once they seemed to be... The public are bored by them.

4. a. (*a*) *prize essay, poem* (later examples); now also *fig.* (as adj.) describing undesirable qualities: outstanding, unrivalled, complete, utter. (*b*) *prize pig* (later example).

1831 *Edin. Rev.* LIII. 556 The world..is pretty well agreed in thinking that the shorter a prize-poem is, the better. **1856** C. M. Yonge *Daisy Chain* ii. xviii. 548 He.. had written the best prize poem ever heard at Oxford. **1857** Geo. Eliot *Let.* 22 May (1954) II. 329 Meditations about a new book..when the Prize Essay has reached a second edition. **1933** Blunden *Charles Lamb* 21 George Richards, whose Oxford prize-poem delighted Byron. **1952** E. O'Neill *Moon for Misbegotten* i. 63 *Hogan.* All prize pigs, too! I was offered two hundred dollars apiece for them. **1956** K. Tillotson *Matthew Arnold & Carlyle* 139 Arnold opens non-committally, using a technique of evasion common in prize-poems. **1976** *Southern Even. Echo* (Southampton) 13 Nov. (Suppl.) 5/3 The final episode finds Katy..accused of writing to a young man regarded as a prize flirt. **1978** M. Tripp *Wife-Smuggler* v. 58 I've been made a fool, a prize bloody fool. **1980** E. G. Wilson *John Clarkson* iv. 46 A Cambridge prize essay was bound to have a good circulation.

b. *prize-giving* (examples); **prize-book** (earlier and later examples); **prize-roll**, a roll or list of prize-winners.

1839 C. Sinclair *Holiday House* xii. 274 Being the

best scholar there [*sc.* at school], he might..receive a whole library of prize-books. *c* **1909** D. H. LAWRENCE *Collier's Friday Night* (1934) i. 4 Then on the next shelf prize-books in calf and gold. **1905** E. M. FORSTER *Where Angels fear to Tread* v. 124 Fortunately the school prize-giving was at hand. **1955** E. BLISHEN *Roaring Boys* II. 100 Prize-giving..didn't flow naturally out of what had gone before, as it does in a grammar school. **1973** R. PARKES *Guardians* vii. 124 There they all were, droning away..as though at some Kafkaesque prize-giving. **1912** *Chambers's Jrnl.* May 329/1 A medal can be verified occasionally if the prize-roll or some other collateral document is extant.

prize, *sb.*³ Add: **3.** *prize ship* (earlier example); **prize-master** (earlier and later examples).

1760 in *Essex Inst. Hist. Coll.* (1911) XLVII. 125 He put a Prize Master (as he called him) and three more of his Hands on board the Sloop. **1916** in *Outlook* (N.Y.) 9 Aug. 823/2 Prizes cannot be brought into the waters of the United States for the purpose of laying up by a prize master. **1931** *Times Lit. Suppl.* 16 July 555/3 For his conduct as a prizemaster in the captured Genéreux..he was advanced to commander. **1937** C. S. FORESTER *Happy Return* I. vii. 80 Gerard, whom he had left on board as prizemaster, had served in a Liverpool slaver. **1710** *Boston News-Let.* 26 June 2/2 On the said day arrived Her Majesties Ship the Feversham..with Col. Hunter, our Governour, and with him a Prize ship of 300 Tons.

prize, *sb.*⁴ Add: **3. prize-beam,** a beam used in packing tobacco.

1800 W. TATHAM *Hist. & Pract. Ess. Tobacco* 52 As all tobacco must be in due case when it is put into the hogshead, so must the prize-beam retain its depressed position until two distinct ends are attained, to wit, that of giving a compact consistency to the cake [etc.].

prize, *v.*³ Add: **2.** (Earlier and later examples.)

1724 H. JONES *Present State Virginia* 40 [They] by Degrees *prize* or press it with proper Engines into great Hogsheads. **1902** *U.S. Dept. Agric. Farmers' Bull.* No. 60. 17 The leaves..are tied into hands and bulked down for a short time, after which they are 'prized' into hogsheads.

b. To pack (persons) into a narrow space.

1799 W. BECKFORD *Let.* 16 Aug. in J. W. Oliver *Life W. Beckford* (1932) x. 269 Assure Lady Heard that she shall not be worn to death with seeing Sights,..nor prysed into rumbling Carriages.

prizeman. Add: Hence **pri·zewoman.**

1940 *Horizon* Jan. 61 Miss Pitter, a Hawthornden prizewoman.

prize-money. Add: **a.** (Earlier example.)

1749 *New Hampsh. Probate Rec.* (1916) III. 733, I give to Doctor Robert Ratsey all my Waidges, Prize money, [etc.].

b. [f. PRIZE *sb.*¹] Money awarded as a prize or as prizes.

1934 in WEBSTER. **1961** *N.Y. Times* 24 Jan. 23 He won the Masters, the United States Open and a record $80,738 in prize money. **1973** M. AMIS *Rachel Papers* 194, I was entering a national under-21 short-story competition, sponsored by one of the colour magazines. With the prize-money we might just have a few days in Paris ourselves.

prizer². Add: **b.** A prize-winner.

1846 E. COPLESTON *Let.* 9 Dec. in W. J. Copleston *Mem. E. Copleston* (1851) 188 My delight was not a little heightened, by seeing my horned countrymen of North Devon among the 'prizers'.

prize-ring. (Earlier example.)

1822 *Sunday Times* 20 Oct. 4/2 Bill Cropley, one of the heroes of the prize-ring, but now a hard-working coal-heaver.

prizewoman: see *PRIZEMAN.

pro, *Latin prep.* Add: **A.** *prep.* **2. pro bono publico.** (Later examples.) Now freq. used as a signature to an open letter (as to a newspaper).

1914 'I. HAY' *Lighter Side School Life* vii. 194 Fiery old gentlemen write..to say that in their young days boys were boys and not molly-coddles. Old friends like *Materfamilias, Pro Bono Publico,*..rush into the fray... There is quite a riot of pseudonyms. **1922** JOYCE *Ulysses* 306 Someone..ought to write a letter *pro bono publico* to the papers about the muzzling order for a dog the like of that. **1973** G. BEARE *Snake on Grave* viii. 40 He would..write a letter to *The Times* which he would sign 'Pro Bono Publico'. **1977** *New Yorker* 12 Sept. 133/1 A politician who speaks for an important industry is considered very much pro bono publico.

4. pro forma. Also with hyphen and as one word. (Further simple and *attrib.* examples.) *pro-forma invoice*, an invoice sent to a purchaser in advance of the ordered goods, so that formalities may be completed (see also quot. 1965); also *absol.* as *sb.*, an official form for completion; a pro-forma invoice.

1827 W. BOLLING in *Virginia Mag. Hist. & Biogr.* (1935) XLIII. 240 Then called proforma at Mr. Robertson's to see my sister. **1858** P. L. SIMMONDS *Dict. Trade Products* 303/2 *Pro-forma-account*, a model or sketch account; a pattern bill of particulars. **1895** *Funk's Stand. Dict., Pro forma*,...as a matter of form; as, a *pro forma* invoice. **1928** BLUNDEN *Undertones of War* ii. 19 He rejoiced in inventing new Army Forms, which he called 'pro forma's'... Some of them were such that one's best information could not find a heading in them. **1930** M. CLARK *Home Trade* 100 An order may be received from an unknown person or firm... In such cases a pro forma invoice may be dispatched. **1945** *Ann. Trop. Med. & Parasitol.* XXXIX. 226 A senior member of the nursing staff..checked that the patient took the tablet and recorded each dose given and taken on a *pro-forma*. **1959** *Punch* 27 May 705/1, I do not know in precisely what form the Department of Meteorology of the Imperial College of Science is asking for information about hail, but at the very least there should be a 'proforma' with columns headed. **1965** J. L. HANSON *Dict. Econ.* 329/2 *Pro-forma invoice*, a commercial document with three main uses: (i) A polite request for payment when a supplier is unwilling to allow his customer credit; (ii) With goods sent on approval, becoming an ordinary invoice if the goods are retained; (iii) When goods are sent to an agent to be sold; (iv) In foreign trade when goods are exported on consignment, informing the importer of the expected prices of the goods. **1977** *Wandsworth Borough News* 16 Sept. 2/2 A pro-forma for all organisations..should contain a sentence encouraging applicants to think of any aspect of their work which might not be covered by the form. **1978** *Jrnl. R. Soc. Med.* LXXI. 413 Details of the illness were recorded on a proforma.

10. pro tempore. (Further examples of the abbreviated form *pro tem.*)

1835 DICKENS *Let.* ?30 Oct. (1965) I. 85 Through the stupidity of Frisby who was in attendance pro: tem: Frank Ross 'dropped in' to my writing room. **1886** [see *GADGET]. **1913** *Sat. Even. Post* 4 Oct. 47 It was proper that Sergeant Bagby, in his capacity as host *pro tem.* should do the..explaining. **1955** *Times* 12 May 11/6 One feels that this is only a capital *pro tem.*, making do until the kingdom reaches some new turning-point in its fortunes. **1974** 'E. LATHEN' *Sweet & Low* xv. 146 Would you be willing to take charge of our cocoa trading—on a pro-tem basis?

B. *sb.* **1. a.** (Later examples.)

1835 E. FITZGERALD *Let.* July in *FitzGerald to his Friends* (1979) 18 But then I get a settled home, a good companion, and the other usual pro's that desperate people talk of. **1969** V. E. FRANKL in Koestler & Smythies *Beyond Reductionism* 419 All the protesters are actually anti-testers, they have no 'pro', no positive alternative to offer, but they are fighting against, rather than struggling for something.

C. *prep.* For, in favour of. **D.** *adj.* or quasi-*adj.* **a.** Favourable, positive, supportive; favourably disposed.

1837 H. MARTINEAU *Diary* in *Autobiogr.* (1877) II. iv. 109 In the morning I am *pro*, and at night..*con* the scheme. **1961** *Dallas Morning News* 17 Feb. I. 5 We're getting more 'pro' letters than 'con' on horse race betting. **1966** 'W. COOPER' *Mem. New Man* I. iv. 49 'In touch' was a phrase everybody used... They used it in a pro sense; being in touch was most desirable. **1974** R. HARRIS *Double Snare* v. 32 It's nice of you to be so pro the idea—I don't feel pro or against.

b. *pro-attitude* (Philos.), an attitude such as approval, pleasure, satisfaction, etc., which is the normal reaction to all things considered ethically good.

1935 C. A. CAMPBELL in *Mind* XLIV. 298 All usages of the term 'good' signify at least this common feature in that to which goodness is attributed, *viz.*, that it is the object of what may perhaps least misleadingly be called a *pro*-attitude. **1939** W. D. ROSS *Foundations of Ethics* xi. 284 This attractive character, or..the fact that we have a pro-attitude towards them, seems to be all that is common to these three kinds of thing that are habitually called good. **1947** A. C. EWING *Def. of Good* ii. 68 A slightly different view would be that to call anything 'good' is to say that it is the object of some 'pro attitude' on the part of most people... I use 'pro attitude' to cover desiring, liking, seeking, choosing, approving, admiring, etc. **1949** *Mind* LVIII. 90 The *ground* of a pro-attitude lies..in the concrete factual characteristics of what we pronounce good. **1964** A. EDEL in I. L. Horowitz *New Sociol.* 224 We may omit here the internal operation of general values, in the sense of obligations and pro-attitudes not peculiar to social science—regard for truth, objectivity and impartiality, [etc.]. **1967** G. R. GRICE *Grounds of Moral Judgement* i. 9 Wanting, for Nowell-Smith is one of many pro-attitudes, and..it is fair to say that his use of the term 'pro-attitude' conceals distinctions of importance.

pro, pro., *abbrev.* Add: **2. a.** In the sense of PROFESSIONAL *sb.* 2.

1866 *Sporting Life* 17 Oct. 4/4 County matches..are also the true source of our supply of professionals of ability, for you rarely hear of a good 'pro' until he has played for his county. **1885**, etc. [in Dict.]. **1902** C. J. C. HYNE *Mr. Horrocks, Purser* 124 'I tell you the man's not a theatrical.'.. 'Never knew any pro. yet bring either honour or profit to any boat,' said the Purser. **1932** *John o' London's* 25 June 426/1, I spent all my holidays practising in tournaments and having coaching from a pro. **1951** 'J. TEY' *Daughter of Time* xvii. 209 One wouldn't expect an amateur to walk into the Yard and solve a case that had defeated the pro's. **1960** [see *GOY]. **1965** *New Statesman* 7 May 712/1 Randall is essentially a pro in the tradition of technician editors, able, almost apolitical. **1975** J. SYMONS *Three Pipe Problem* xvi. 158 They're not pros, how long do you think they'll stand up under questioning?

b. *attrib.* or as *adj.* in the sense of PROFESSIONAL *a.* 4, esp. in sporting uses.

1932 A. J. MORRISON *New Way to Better Golf* ii. 25 The pupil..did not recognize me as the handy man of the pro shop and a former caddy. **1949** *Times Digest* (Richmond, Va.) 26 Nov. 10/4 Riggs was enthusiastic about the crowds which his pro tennis stars have been drawing. **1961** *Boxing News* 20 Oct. 10 Next live pro item will be the Maurice Cullen–Guy Gracia bout from Newcastle on November 13. **1970** *Washington Post* 30 Sept. D1/1 Baseball needs such finishes in order to provide some counter-interest to college and pro football, already moving into high gear. **1975** C. JAMES *Fate of Felicity Fark* II. 20 These *Krauts* are all pro athletes in disguise. **1978** S. BRILL *Teamsters* vi. 236 Three former pro football players were partners. **1978** *Rugby World* Apr. 51/3 New Zealander Ken Bousfield, a Sydney player, rejected a league offer of over £17,000 for three years at the end of last season. But this year, he has turned pro with Penrith.

c. pro('s) shop, a (work)shop run by the resident professional at a golf club.

[**1905** H. VARDON *Compl. Golfer* iv. 39 The proper place for him [*sc.* the beginner] to go is the professional's shop which is attached to the club of which he has become a member. Nearly all clubs have their own professionals, who are makers and sellers of clubs.] **1932** [see sense 2b above]. **1937** H. LONGHURST *Golf* 3 An extremely high standard of business morality obtains among professional golfers. A novice may enter a pro's shop [to buy clubs], a chicken ready for the plucking, and yet come out with all his feathers on. **1953** J. TURNESA *Low Score Golf* ii. 13 Let's leave the pro shop and go over to the lesson tee. **1964** D. LANGDON *How to play Golf & stay Happy* iii. 27 Palmer..rushed back to the pro's shop after a disastrous round of 76, slammed his driver into the vice and filed away the club face. **1976** T. GIFFORD *Cavanaugh Quest* ii. 31 The members' golf committee had allowed Billy to live in the room over the pro shop.

3. Abbrev. of (*professional*) *prostitute*. Cf. *PROFESSIONAL *sb.* 2b.

1937 in PARTRIDGE *Dict. Slang*. **1941** B. SCHULBERG *What makes Sammy Run?* ix. 247 He treats all women like pros. **1950** [see *BAG *sb.* 16*]. **1968** H. C. RAE *Few Small Bones* II. i. 79 She's a semi-pro actually... She works in a garage..during the day, but at night she ...entertains. **1976** 'E. MCBAIN' *Guns* iv. 95 Benny already had himself two girls..experienced pros who were bringing in enough cash every week to keep him living pretty good.

pro-, *prefix*¹. Add: **II. 4. b.** *pro-element, -infinitive, -name, -sentence, -syllable, -verb* (further examples), *-vicariate, -word*; **pro-form** *Linguistics*, a pronoun or other lexical unit substituted for a longer expression. **c.** *pro-infinitival, -syllabic* adjs.

1975 N. CHOMSKY *Logical Struct. Linguistic Theory* x. 560 'So' is introduced as a pro-element standing for the verb phrase in such sentences as 'John saw him and so did I'. **1964** KATZ & POSTAL *Integrated Theory Ling. Descr.* iv. 83 We stipulate in the general theory of linguistic descriptions that the dictionary entry of every pro-form (i.e., every form dominated by the constituent Pro) must contain the semantic marker (Selector). **1969** *Canad. Jrnl. Linguistics* XIV. 49 In this structure the head noun is a pro-form which is of the *du* class. **1976** *Analysis* XXXVI. 80 Proforms and modified proforms, upon given occasions of their use, get their semantic content from their antecedents. **1905** O. JESPERSEN *Growth & Struct. Eng. Lang.* viii. 208 Another recent innovation is the use of *to* as what might be called a pro-infinitive instead of the clumsy *to do so*: 'Will you play?' 'Yes, I intend to.' 'I am going to.' **1940** —— *S.P.E. Tract* LIV. 153 This leads to the possibility of using an isolated *to* as a 'pro-infinitive': Will he sing? Yes, he wants to. **1934** J. J. HOGAN *Outl. Eng. Philol.* III. xiv. 136 The modern 'pro-infinitival' *to*, as in *I want to*. **1964** *Eng. Stud.* XLV. 88 *To* here stands..for *to tell me*, or *to do so*, for which reason Jespersen calls it a 'pro-infinitive'. **1765** J. ELPHINSTON *Princ. Eng. Lang. Digested* II. viii. 184 Instead of a name or noun repeated, a pro-name or pronoun. **1972** *Language* XLVIII. 461 To answer the question *Did he do it?*, one requires an element that will affirm or deny. It may appear alone, and in that case will carry the sentence intonation, accent and all. Such a single answer-word might be *Unquestionably*. It may also appear at the end of a pro-sentence, e.g. *He did it unquestionably*. **1976** *Analysis* XXXVI. 83 The antecedent of the modified prosentence 'it is false', is the quoted sentence together with the quotes. **1948** J. R. FIRTH in E. P. Hamp et al. *Readings in Linguistics II* (1966) 185 In certain of its prosodic functions the neutral vowel might be described temporarily as a pro-syllable. However obscure or neutral or unstressed, it is essential in *a bitter for me* to distinguish it from *a bit for me*. In contemporary Southern English many 'sounds' may be pro-syllabic. **1956** *Archivum Linguisticum* VIII. 123 Structurally the difference [between ij and ɛr] is that of a vocalic phoneme followed by a junctional prosody and a consonantal phoneme preceded by a prosyllabic prosody. **1924** O. JESPERSEN *Philos. Gram.* vi. 83 We should get a class of substitute words which might be divided into pro-nouns, pro-adjectives, pro-adverbs, pro-infinitives, pro-verbs..but it could hardly be called a real grammatical class. **1976** J. S. GRUBER *Lexical Struct. Syntax & Semantics* II. i. 267 For the other occurrences of pro-verbs, the nature of the semantic category common to both the pro-verbs and the verbs embedded in them is more obscure. **1881** *Dublin Rev.* July 173 The districts of Lake Tanganyika, and the Victoria Nyanza have already been created Pro-Vicariates Apostolic. **1965** *Language* XLI. 393 We can define a set of proword substitutions which are similar to various types of zeroing.

5. a. *pro-abortion, -abortionist, -Allied, -Ally, -American* (further example), *-Arab, -Axis, -Boche, -Boer* (earlier example), *-British* (examples), *-business, -Communist, -Fascist, -German, -Israeli, -Nazi, -Soviet, -West, -Western, -Zionist*; **pro-kno·ck** *a.* and *sb.*, (a substance) tending to cause knocking when present in the fuel burnt in an internal-combustion engine; **pro-li·fe** *a.*, in favour of the maintenance of life; *spec.* against inducing abortion; hence **pro-li·fer**, someone with these views. **b.** Also in comb. with a sb. (or verb-stem) + -ER; *pro-Britisher, -marketeer* [*MARKETEER 3]. **c.** *pro-Arabism, -Germanism, -Sovietism.*

1976 Pro-abortionist [see *pro-lifer* below]. **1976** *National Observer* (U.S.) 31 Jan. 5/3 If Carter can appeal successfully to both proabortion and right-to-life Democrats, we might as well hand him the nomination now. **1977** *Lancet* 2 July 48/2 Pro-abortionists are left, therefore, with familiar Parliamentary tactics of filibustering to try to prevent progress. **1919** W. S. CHURCHILL in M. Gilbert *Winston S. Churchill* (1977) IV. Compan. I. 536 None of the pro-Allied Russian Governments would meet them. **1915** H. MUENSTERBERG in *Fatherland* 22 Dec. 347/1 The psychological equation of his personality makes him a pro-German in all that is best in him, and only his temper and his perpetual desire to be with the masses made him a pro-Ally. **1916** *Lit. Digest* (N.Y.) 1 Jan. 3/2 He has been trapt into the nets of those who wove the pro-Ally newspaper opinion in this country. **1916** MRS. BELLOC LOWNDES *Let.* 29 May (1971) 72 In America it has been rejected by one set of publishers as pro-German—by another as pro-Ally. **1971** D. E. WESTLAKE *I gave at the Office* (1972) 159 They were revolutionaries who were pro-American, which is very rare in the world today. **1920** G. BELL *Let.* 12 Sept. (1927) II. xviii. 499 It is only quite recently that I have realized how prominent a place I have occupied in the public mind here as the pro-Arab member of the administration. **1973** 'D. RUTHERFORD' *Kick Start* ix. 186 The Russians..are openly pro-Arab. **1959** *Daily Tel.* 2 Nov. 10/2 Traditional pro-Arabism influenced us. **1938** *New Statesman* 25 June 1054/1 After he [*sc.* M. Imrédy] had made a speech to this effect, M. de Kánya hastened to deliver his pro-Axis speech of June 1st. **1942** *Times Rev. Year 1941* 3 Jan. p. i/2 One result of their [*sc.* the Germans'] intrigues was a *coup d'état* in Iraq, where on April 3 Raschid Ali and a group of military malcontents expelled the Regent and set up a pro-Axis government. **1915** *National Rev.* Apr. 169 A pro-Boche Government would have been bundled out 'neck and crop' last August. **1923** KIPLING *Irish Guards in Gt. War.* II. 160 Some pro-Boche agent in the far-off lands where it was purchased. **1896** *Daily News* 22 Apr. 5/1 If it were indeed a necessity of the situation to be pro-Boer or pro-British..then as Britons we should be for the British, we admit. **1927** H. DOBBS in *Lett. Gertrude Bell* II. 543 The so-called pro-British sections of the populations. **1980** P. VAN GREENAWAY *Dissident* vii. 148 A man, if he is anti-Soviet, must therefore be pro-British..and *vice versa.* **1927** *Leader* 31 Dec. 517/1 That was unexpected talk to what in Ireland is called a Chamber of Commerce—Chambers whose members are mostly pro-Britishers and Shoneens. **1975** HUNT & SHERMAN *Econ.* (ed. 2) xii. 155 A large amount of probusiness propaganda. **1978** *New York* 3 Apr. 34/3 It might also provide Kennedy with a pro-business image for a presidential campaign. **1950** *New Yorker* 6 May 96/2 The pro-Communist *Lettres Françaises* is the best literary weekly in Paris. **1976** 'M. BARAK' *Secret List H. Roehm* iii. 35 The establishment of a pro-communist spy ring. **1937** DUCHESS OF ATHOLL in Koestler *Spanish Testament* 6 A so-called 'Radical Government', reinforced later by members of Señor Robles' pro-Fascist party. **1940** 'G. ORWELL' in *World Rev.* (1950) June 28 The government..are subjectively pro-Fascist. **1914** R. BROOKE *Let.* 3 Sept. (1968) 613 The intellectuals..are mostly pacifists and pro-Germans. **1915** KIPLING *Let.* 12 Aug. in C. E. Carrington *Rudyard Kipling* (1955) xvii. 433 Munthe..tells me of all his grief..to find that Sweden is so—not pro-German but afraid of Russia. **1938** E. PHIPPS *Let.* 9 Jan. in M. Gilbert *Winston S. Churchill* (1976) V. xliv. 894 Van's displacement.. would be represented as a victory for the pro-Germans in England. **1964** *Times Lit. Suppl.* 12 Nov. 1018 He [*sc.* Frank Harris] spent the 1914–18 War in the United States, where he wrote pro-German propaganda. **1914** W. B. YEATS *Tribute to Thomas Davis* (1947) 12, I am not more vehemently opposed to the Unionism of Professor Mahaffy than I am to the pro-Germanism of Mr. Pearse. **1940** *Tablet* 4 May 421/1 The pro-Germanism of expedience which was once practised by certain politicians. **1975** J. CROSBY *Affair of Strangers* iv. 33 French policy.. is far more pro-Arab than the French people are. The French people..would be pro-Israeli. **1927** *Jrnl. Inst. Petroleum Technologists* XIII. 301 Amyl nitrate and nitrite..according to Midgley are pro-knock. **1928** *Ibid.* XIV. 188 They might have some indications..as to how the pro-knock worked as against the anti-knock in that particular type of flame propagation. **1953** E. M. GOODYER *Petroleum & Performance in Internal Combustion Engines* viii. 189 Ignition accelerating materials are those which act as pro-knocks in spark-ignition engine fuels, and include organic peroxides, nitrates, nitrites, and various sulphur compounds. **1973** K. OWEN in Hobson & Pohl *Mod. Petroleum Technol.* (ed. 4) xv. 596 Monomethylaniline..acts as an anti-knock agent in its undecomposed form but..if it is decomposed too early in the combustion cycle it can even have a pro-knock effect. **1961** G. SMITH *Business of Loving* xvii. 284 Benny divides people into.. the life-enhancers and the life-diminishers; he is a believer in the first, a leader of the pro-life party. **1978** *Dædalus* Spring 155 Its eleven members include only five scientists, one of whom was known for his prolife position. **1979** *Time* 30 July 6 As the oldest of eleven children (all married), I'd like to point out our combined family numbers more than 100 who vote only for pro-life candidates. **1976** *National Observer* (U.S.) 31 Jan. 5/2 Carter.. had misled proabortionists and prolifers. **1976** *Observer* 24 Oct. 9/1 Anti-abortion forces have been organising to overturn the decision [of the U.S. Supreme Court]... The pro-lifers, as they prefer to call themselves, can no longer be written off as a lunatic fringe. **1979** *Time* 30 July 6 Pro-lifers have children, pro-choicers do not. **1961** *Economist* 2 Dec. 877/1 Mr Heath's speech may legitimately be criticised by pro-marketeers. **1976** H. WILSON *Governance of Britain* 10, I had to be aware of.. the balance between committed pro-marketeers and committed anti-marketeers. **1936** *New Yorker* 29 Feb. 24/3 Ernst Röhm, who in 1928 had written a pro-Nazi autobiography. **1974** G. JENKINS *Bridge of Magpies* vii. 113 Her husband was the boss of the pro-Nazi underground movement. **1950** L. FISCHER in Koestler et al. *God that Failed* 225 This I did not understand in the years when I was pro-Soviet. **1977** *Listener* 21 Apr. 499/3 Mao's pro-Soviet opponents. **1950** L. FISCHER in Koestler et al. *God that Failed* 224 My years of pro-Sovietism have taught me that no one who loves people and peace should favour a dictatorship. **1952** *Sun* (Baltimore) 6 Feb. 1/5 The Soviet claims..treated such 'neutralism' on the part of United Nations members as pro-Sovietism. **1958** 'A. BRIDGE' *Portuguese Escape* iii. 44 One of the real stars is pro-West, and arranged with our man in Hungary to bring him along. **1976** *Billings* (Montana) *Gaz.* 17 June 2-G/1 Kenya, the only pro-West nation on the East African coast. **1934** WEBSTER, Pro-Western. **1965** H. KAHN *On Escalation* i. 24 It [*sc.* the United States] could have invaded Iraq in 1958 to restore a pro-Western government. **1980** P. VAN GREENAWAY *Dissident* v. 123 Is it possible for a man to be pro-Western *without* being anti-Soviet? **1949** KOESTLER *Promise & Fulfilment* I. ii. 13 'Somehow we like the Arabs'..confessed a sincere and pro-Zionist Englishman. **1971** D. MEIRING *Wall of Glass* viii. 65 The idea that Jew could kill Jew in Palestine for political reasons was the more intolerable the more pro-Zionist you were.

pro-, *prefix*². Add: **1. proaccelerin** (-ækse·lĕrin) *Biochem.*, a relatively labile procoagulant present in the blood; **proa·ctivator** *Biochem.*, a precursor of the activator of a compound; **probasi·dium** *Bot.* [ad. F. *probaside* (P. Van Tieghem 1893, in *Jrnl. de Bot.* VII. 80)], in some fungi, a part of a basidium, or an early stage in its development, in which nuclear fusion takes place; **probio·tic** *a.* = *PREBIOLOGICAL, *PREBIOTIC *adjs.*; **proca·rcinogen**, a substance that is not directly carcinogenic itself but is converted in the body into one that is; so **proca:rcinoge·nic** *a.*; **procoa·gulant** *sb.* and *a.* *Biochem.*, (of or pertaining to) any substance that promotes the conversion of the inactive prothrombin to the clotting enzyme thrombin; **proconve·rtin** *Biochem.* [CONVERT *v.*], a relatively stable procoagulant present in the blood; **proery·throblast** *Med.* [ad. It. *proeritroblasti* (A. Ferrata *Morfologia del Sangue* (1912) v. 232)], the earliest recognizable precursor of the red-cell series, characterized by a large nucleus with nucleoli and by basophilic cytoplasm; **proestrus,** var. *proœstrum* below in Dict. and Suppl.; **proethnic** *a.*: see as *main entry; **pro:fibrinoly·sin** *Biochem.* = *PLASMINOGEN; †**proga·mete** *Biol.*, a structure able to give rise to one or more gametes; **prohe·terocyst** *Biol.*, an incipient heterocyst; **proho·rmone** *Physiol.*, a natural precursor of a hormone; **proi·nsulin** (pro,i·n-) *Biochem.*, the natural precursor of insulin; **promeristem** (later examples); **pro:mitocho·ndrion** *Cytology*, an inactive form of mitochondrion; **promy·elocyte** *Med.*, a cell intermediate in development between a myeloblast and a mature myelocyte; so **promy·elocytic** *a.*; **pro·œstrum,** also **proestrus, proœstrus;** (further examples); **propla·stid** *Cytology*, a small unspecialized plastid, able to differentiate into a plastid of any type characteristic of the species; **prosecre·tin** *Physiol.*, a supposed precursor of secretin; **prothe·ca** [THECA], in Foraminifera, the primary wall; **protri·chocyst** *Zool.* [ad. G. *protrichocyste* (B. M. Klein 1928, in *Arch. f. Protistenkunde* LXII. 210)], an undeveloped trichocyst.

1951 P. A. OWREN in *Proc. 3rd Internat. Congr. Internat. Soc. Hematol.* 379, I wish to propose the terms proaccelerin and accelerin instead of Factor V and Factor VI, because ..these factors constitute the system which is responsible for the acceleration of thrombin formation. **1966** *McGraw-Hill Encycl. Sci. & Technol.* II. 266/1 The intereactions of tissue thromboplastin, calcium ions, and several proteins of plasma, including proaccelerin..and proconvertin, result in the conversion of prothrombin into a proteolytic enzyme, thrombin. **1956** T. ASTRUP in *Blood* XI. 783 In blood, human milk, tears, and in other body fluids enzymatically acting activators of plasminogen are also found, or can be produced. The production of activating agents in these cases is caused by the transformation of a precursor (a proactivator). **1973** *Jrnl. Clin. Invest.* LII. 2591/2 Conversion of highly purified plasminogen proactivator to plasminogen activator was shown to result in the generation of chemotactic activity. **1928** C. W. DODGE tr. *Gäumann's Compar. Morphol. Fungi* xxv. 415 This enlarged hyphal cell which..forms the first stage of the basidium..is called [the] probasidium. **1979** I. K. ROSS *Biol. Fungi* vi. 156 In the spring, each cell of the teliospore [in *Puccinia graminis*] functions as a probasidium and produces a thin-walled metabasidium. **1954** *New Biol.* XVI. 44 We have as yet no basis for confidence about the probiotic state. **1971** J. Z. YOUNG *Introd. Study Man* xxvi. 372 A probiotic soup of amino-acids, ribose, four purine and pyrimidine bases, and a source of high-energy phosphate. **1963** *Clin. Pharmacol. & Therapeutics* IV. 111/1 A compound requiring metabolic activation is one which when administered to animals is very likely not carcinogenic by itself ('procarcinogen') but requires transformation in the host to become a 'proximate' carcinogen—a sort of lethal synthesis. **1975** *Pharmacol. Basis of Cancer Chemotherapy* 129 (*heading*) Procarcinogens and their bioactivation. **1944** *Jrnl. Exper. Med.* LXXX. 121 The papers dealing with the 'cocarcinogens' show clearly that the substances thus designated do not cause neoplastic changes but act either by enabling the real carcinogens to reach susceptible cells or by promoting the formation of growths. They are in other words procarcinogenic. **1976** *New Scientist* 9 Dec. 586/2 Cigarette smoke..contains procarcinogenic polynuclear aromatic hydrocarbons which are broken down by enzymes in the lungs. **1958** LANDABURU & SEEGERS in *Amer. Jrnl. Physiol.* CXCIII. 178/1 Other factors support the production and enzyme function of thrombin, and these we call procoagulants. **1960** *Nature* 26 Mar. 930/2 The control of prothrombin activation is by a group of anticoagulants and procoagulants functioning in dynamic equilibrium. **1962** W. H. SEEGERS *Prothrombin* ix. 202 There is a procoagulant effect noticeable in whole blood or plasma following the alimentary intake of certain kinds of fats. **1971** R. S. SHEPARD *Human Physiol.* xiv. 243/2 (*caption*) Intermediates of prothrombin activation may result in the formation of a number of other procoagulants as well as anticoagulants. **1976** *Nature* 22 Apr. 711/2 It has been shown that human fibroblasts contain a potent procoagulant activity called 'tissue factor' (TF). **1951** P. A. OWREN in *Proc. 3rd Internat. Congr. Internat. Soc. Hematol.* 383 This substance acts as the limiting factor for prothrombin conversion and I have thus chosen to give it the name proconvertin. **1976** *Nature* 17 June 621/2 The coagulation of blood is envisaged as a complex but ordered succession of processes, and at least four of the many factors (prothrombin, proconvertin, Christmas factor and Stuart factor) are known to be dependent on vitamin K. **1927** A. PINEY *Rec. Adv. Hæmatol.* ii. 29 It is obvious that the adherents of the monophyletic school will be of opinion that the red corpuscle is derived from the primitive stem cell (hæmocytoblast). They contend that all sorts of transitions can be found between large non-hæmoglobiniferous cells (pro-erythroblasts) and the mature, fully hæmoglobiniferous corpuscle. **1962** *Lancet* 27 Jan. 208/2 A continuous morphological spectrum of cells was evident, indicating many transitional forms between what appeared to be typical small lymphocytes and myeloblasts or proerythroblasts. **1969** HAYHOE & FLEMANS *Atlas Haematol. Cytol.* (1970) I. 7 The proerythroblast is not itself the functional stem cell serving as a self-maintaining progenitor of the normoblast series. **1947** E. C. LOOMIS et al. in *Arch. Biochem.* XII. 1 We suggest the following names for the compounds: 1). Fibrinolysin ... 2). Profibrinolysin—the inactive form or precursor of fibrinolysin. This compound is the proenzyme form from serum or plasma activated by streptokinase, organic solvents and other enzyme activators. **1958** *Observer* 14 Dec. 4/3 A precursor, profibrinolysin, is present in the blood and is changed to fibrinolysin by natural agents released when needed. **1968** A. WHITE et al. *Princ. Biochem.* (ed. 4) xxxi. 733 The proteolytic enzyme, plasmin (fibrinolysin), ordinarily exists in plasma as the inactive precursor..plasminogen (profibrinolysin). **1892** *Q. Jrnl. Microsc. Sci.* XXXIII. 6 In my terminology I have used the word[s]..gametogonium and progamete to express, from slightly different points of view, a cell which divides to form gametes, or (rarely) passes into the state of a gamete. *Ibid.* 54 In most cases of so-called 'parthenogenesis' of Metazoa only one polar body is formed, and the ovum, rather a progamete than an oosphere, segments and develops directly. **1904** *Proc. Amer. Acad. Arts & Sci.* XL. 231 The zygospores are abundant between the gills of the host, and the progametes arise at times from branches of the same hypha. **1970** *Nature* 14 Nov. 686/1 A close pattern of heterocysts and presumptive heterocysts ('proheterocysts') is apparent. **1973** *Jrnl. Cell Sci.* XIII. 641 In the presence of ammonia, heterocyst development is affected, so that a pattern consisting largely of proheterocysts, rather than mature heterocysts, is formed. **1935** *Amer. Jrnl. Physiol.* CXII. 511 Many of the published opinions concerning the prohormone have been made from incidental observations, rather than from directed experiments planned to give information concerning its existence or properties. **1970** *Proc. Nat. Acad. Sci.* LXVII. 1637 Unlike the islet cell, which stores hormone primarily in the form of insulin, the parathyroid may store its hormone as the prohormone, with conversion taking place when the gland is stimulated. **1977** *Lancet* 25 June 1341/2 Vitamin D is a pro-hormone which only becomes active on transformation to its 25-hydroxy derivative, a process that is subject to pronounced but poorly understood constraints. **1916** E. A. SCHÄFER *Endocrine Organs* xvii. 128 Provisionally, it will be convenient to refer to this hypothetical autacoid as *insuline.* It must, however, be stated that it has yet to be determined whether the active substance is present as such in the pancreas or whether it exists there as *pro-insuline*, which becomes elsewhere converted into the active autacoid. **1967** D. F. STEINER et al. in *Science* 26 Apr. 700/2 The labeling data reported here support our earlier interpretation that component *b* is a precursor in the biosynthesis of insulin. It might be less cumbersome, therefore, to designate this material 'proinsulin'. **1969** *Nature* 15 Nov. 696/1 Proinsulin has little or no biological activity, but is present in the circulation and produces insulin-like effects when injected into normal animals. **1970** *Jrnl. Clin. Investigation* XLIX. 506/2 At present data concerning the biological activity of human proinsulin are not available. **1925** EAMES & MACDANIELS *Introd. Plant Anat.* iii. 41 Promeristems gradually become differentiated. **1953** K. ESAU *Plant Anat.* iv. 78 The initiating cells and their most recent derivatives are often distinguished, under the name of promeristem. **1976** BELL & COOMBE tr. *Strasburger's Textbk. Bot.* (rev. ed.) 89 Primary embryonic tissues are those which are derived ontogenetically directly from the tissue of the embryo, and they are referred to as primordia or promeristems. **1969** CRIDDLE & SCHATZ in *Biochem.* VIII. 323/2 Since the term 'proplastid' is well established.., the mitochondria-like particles from anaerobic yeast cells were correspondingly termed 'promitochondria'. **1974** *Nature* 15 Mar. 258/2 Such mitochondria as yeast promitochondria do not contain all the carriers of the respiratory chain and possess an enhanced resistance to anaerobiosis. **1925** Strong & Elwyn *Bailey's Textbk. Histol.* (ed. 7-vi. 142 The myelocytes are the most abundant develop) mental forms of marrow... The most immature are known as promyelocytes, the fully matured as metamyelocytes. **1977** *Lancet* 15 Oct. 806/2 Cytoplasmic vacuolation, similar to that in erythroblasts, occurs in promyelocytes in the bone-marrow of alcoholics. **1957** L. K. Hillestad in *Acta Medica Scand.* CLIX. 189 This paper deals with three cases of a special type of acute myelogenous leukemia... The white blood cell picture in the peripheral blood resembles that of the more chronic forms of leukemia, as it is dominated by promyelocytes and myelocytes with very few myeloblasts. A logical name for this type of leukemia is *acute promyelocytic leukemia.* **1973** *Brit. Jrnl. Haematol.* XXIV. 255 Acute promyelocytic leukaemia..is now recognized as a distinct clinical and pathological entity, classically characterized by..replacement of bone marrow by abnormal myeloblasts and promyelocytes. **1923** *Amer. Jrnl. Anat.* XXXII. 306 Through its action on prooestrus and ovulation the corpus luteum indirectly inhibits those growth processes which are initiated by the maturing follicles. **1923** Proestrus [see *metœstrus]. **1937** *Nature* 4 Dec. 950/1 It can no longer be affirmed that the procœstrus of the lower mammal corresponds simply to the menstrual flow of the human female. **1966, 1973** Proestrus, prooestrus [see *metœstrus]. **1976** *Sci. Amer.* July 52/2 In the normal estrous cycle of the rat the pituitary secretes large amounts of luteinizing hormone..in the afternoon of proestrus, approximately 30 hours after the initial increase in estradiol secretion by the ovaries. **1922** L. F. Randolph in *Bot. Gaz.* LXXIII. 345 Since these bodies have been found to occur as a constant feature of the cytoplasm of meristematic cells in maize, and inasmuch as they have been found to be definitely concerned with the formation of chloroplasts, the term 'proplastid' will be used for such bodies. **1934** L. W. Sharp *Introd. Cytol.* (ed. 3) iv. 69 The differentiated plastids seen in mature tissues may be traced back to plastid primordia, or proplastids in the young cells of the meristem or embryo. **1967** Kirk & Tilney-Bassett *Plastids* xiv. 497 It may be generally true that whenever a chloroplast-containing plant cell has to start dividing, the chloroplasts revert to proplastids to facilitate the plastid division that must take place if plastid numbers in the cell are to be maintained. **1902** Bayliss & Starling in *Jrnl. Physiol.* XXVIII. 331 The distribution of 'prosecretin', as we have proposed to call the mother-substance, corresponds ..precisely with the region from which acid introduced into the lumen excites secretion from the pancreas. **1935** *Amer. Jrnl. Physiol.* CXII. 511 In this study we have.. attempted to obtain concrete evidence concerning the existence of prosecretin. **1962** R. A. Gregory *Secretory Mech. Gastro-Intestinal Tract* xii. 157 Bayliss & Starling originally supposed that it [*sc.* secretin] might exist in the form of an active precursor 'prosecretin' from which secretin was liberated by acid hydrolysis. This view was later abandoned. **1945** M. F. Glaessner *Princ. Micropalaeont.* v. 108 The protheca or primary wall consists of a layer of clear transparent calcite (diaphanotheca), and a thin dark outer rind-like film (tectum). **1963** K. A. Allen tr. *Pokorny's Princ. Zool. Micropalaeont.* I. vi. 236 In some of these forms [of Foraminifera] there is only a single undifferentiated layer, the protheca. **1933** G. N. Calkins *Biol. Protozoa* (ed. 2) iv. 135 The trichocysts at rest are capsules filled with a densely staining..substance... They appear to be connected with the silver line system and..are here represented by granules when the trichocysts are undeveloped. In such granular form they are sometimes called 'protrichocysts'. **1965** *Jrnl. Cell Biol.* XXVII. 67 The structures containing the amorphous material are variously referred to as protrichocysts, mucoid trichocysts, mucigenic bodies, or secretory ampules. **1972** M. S. Gardiner *Biol. Invertebrates* xix. 850/2 Electron micrographs reveal that the stripes contain refringent granules, considered protrichocysts, which are..blue in *S[tentor] coeruleus*, giving this species its beautiful color.

2. prode·lta *a.* and *sb.*, *Geol.*, (the part of a delta) lying underneath and beyond the sloping front of a delta; so **prodelta·ic** *a.*; **profi·lmic** *a. Semiotics* [ad. F. *profilmique*: cf. E. Souriau in *Revue Internationale de Filmologie* (1951) II. vii–viii], happening or situated in front of a camera; **proneu·ral** *a.*, of the first bone in a turtle's carapace, situated in front of the neural bones; also *absol.*

1940 E. S. Hills *Outl. Structural Geol.* i. 4 The bottom-sets or prodelta clays represent the finer detritus spread out over the floor of the sea or lake in which the delta was formed. **1963** D. W. & E. E. Humphries tr. *Termier's Erosion & Sedimentation* xi. 227 This bed is, perhaps, comparable to that formed on a prodelta. **1969** Bennison & Wright *Geol. Hist. Brit. Isles* xiv. 319 The high percentage of silt in the clays has led to a comparison with some modern pro-delta sediments. **1975** Hobson & Tiratsoo *Introd. Petroleum Geol.* ii. 32 The sediments of the delta front, pro-delta and continental shelf are organically fairly rich. **1968** Murchison & Westoll *Coal* v. 89 The seaward advance of delta-fronts and prodeltaic muds, silts and sands. **1974** *Nature* 8 Feb. 344/2 Interbedded sheets and lenses of moderately well sorted prodeltaic and littoral sands. **1973** P. Willemen in *Screen* Spring/Summer 13 Profilmic events should be divided into signifying reality and into non-signifying reality (eg on one level, a city is a signifying reality, a mountain range is not). *Ibid.*, In the cinema one 'sections' the profilmic reality. **1974** M. Taylor tr. *Metz's Film Lang.* iii. 33 That great artist..manages to have beauty, which has been pitilessly rejected from every 'profilmic' occasion. **1952** A. Carr *Handbk. Turtles* i. 36 Along the mid-line twelve of the bones of the carapace are arranged in a row. In front is the proneural bone (usually known as the nuchal). **1967** P. C. H. Pritchard *Living Turtles of World* 10 The foremost bone in the turtle shell..is large; it is called the proneural or nuchal bone. Behind the proneural comes a midline row of eleven or fewer bones, called neurals.

proa, prahu. Add: (Further examples.)

The length of these boats is now often in excess of thirty feet (see quot. 1977).

1923 [see *ballahou, ballahoo]. **1957** P. Worsley *Trumpet shall Sound* vii. 133 The officer..stayed put, only to see the prophet himself arrive in a beflagged prau. **1971** *Walkabout* (Austral.) Nov. 55/1 On Groote Island.. there are many cave paintings. Some depict Indonesian praus from Macassar. **1973** *Daily Tel.* 2 Oct. 19/6 Cento II, a 31ft proa with a 15ft outrigger and carrying 250 sq. ft of sail was also being repaired. **1977** *Austral. Sailing* Jan. 26 For your reporter and for the new Crossbow II, described as a twin masted proa 73 ft overall, this was the highpoint of the fifth annual week of sailing speed trials.

pro-abortion(ist): see *pro-[1] 5 a. **pro-accelerin, -activator:** see *pro-[2] 1.

proa·ctive, *a. Psychol.* [f. Pro-[2] 1 + Active *a.* 2.] Of a mental effect from a previous situation which is active in a subsequent activity, esp. in learning theory, as *proactive inhibition, interference*, the inhibition of or interference with learning caused by effects that remain active from conditions preceding that learning.

1933 Whiteley & Blankfort in *Jrnl. Exper. Psychol.* XVI. 852 Objective results..indicate..a somewhat inhibitive influence of the various sets upon learning, and under similar conditions of prior and later learning, they suggest what might be called a *proactive inhibition.* However, perhaps the term *proactive inhibition* might better be reserved to designate the detrimental influence of a condition introduced prior to learning upon a subsequent recall, thus differentiating it from..retroactive inhibition. **1940** *Amer. Jrnl. Psychol.* LIII. 174 By proactive inhibition is meant either (a) the retardation of the learning of an activity when some other activity has occurred as a prior condition (sometimes called negative transfer), or (b) the fact of poorer retention of an activity when some other activity has occurred as a prior condition to the original learning of that activity, than when a period of comparative rest preceded the original learning. **1943** *Mind* LII. 360 Then we find that remembering is functionally dependent on..what happens *before* learning (proactive inhibition). **1951** *Brit. Jrnl. Psychol.* Mar.–May 39 It seems unlikely that proactive inhibition would have no permanent effect on the learning of the interpolated series.. retroactive and pro-active processes are essentially interactive processes. **1967** Hilgard & Atkinson *Introd. Psychol.* (ed. 4) xii. 324/2 Proactive inhibition plays a very important role when 'experienced' subjects are used in an experiment. **1971** E. Saltz *Cognitive Bases of Human Learning* vi. 204 Most studies of interference are some variation of one of the following three experimental paradigms: (*a*) proactive interference, (*b*) proactive inhibition, or (*c*) retroactive inhibition.

pro-Allied, -Ally: see *pro-[1] 5 a.

pro-am, *a.* (*sb.*) [f. Pro *abbrev.* + Am(ateur 2.] Of a sport or other activity: practised by or open to both professionals and amateurs (see also quot. 1951). Also *ellipt.* as *sb.*, one who takes part in such activities; a pro-am event.

[**1931** *N.Y. Times* 26 May 34/2 (*heading*) Kinder-Hevener..lead the Pro-Amateurs with 71.] **1949** *Sun* (Baltimore) 12 Mar. 22/1 In the pro-am division, Cross teamed with Al Jamison, professional from Quantico, Va., for one of the 63's. **1951** Green & Laurie *Show Biz* 571/1 *Pro ams*, professional amateurs, those pseudo-tyros who constantly appeared on so-called amateur radio and vaudeville programs. **1968** *N.Y. Times* 11 July 46 They send helicopters to take me from one pro-am to another. **1970** *Times* 13 Feb. 13/3 Since turning professional in 1968 Oosterhuis has won only..one pro-am event. **1976** *Billings* (Montana) *Gaz.* 24 June 1-D/7 Pate..practiced Tuesday in light rain and played in a proam Wednesday.

pro and con. Add: **A.** *adv. phr.* **b.** (Further example.) Also in form *pro-or-con.*

1964 A. Edel in I. L. Horowitz *New Sociol.* 236 At what point do we find science passing into an internal influence in having purposes or pro-*and*-con attitudes? *Ibid.*, The role of social science parameters in having purposes and pro-or-con attitudes can best be grasped by focusing on the very concepts of having a purpose and holding an attitude.

B. *sb. phr.* (Further example of *sing.*)

1923 Galsworthy *Captures* 59 The house rocked with pro and con.

D. Used as *prep. phr.*

1895 W. Stevens *Let.* 4 Aug. (1967) 6 Nor have I any suggestions pro and con anything in particular.

pro-Arab: see *pro-[1] 5 a. **pro-Arabism:** *pro-[1] 5 c. **pro-attitude:** *pro *Latin prep.* D. 1 b.

proavis (pro,ē¹·vis). Pl. **-aves** (-ē¹·vīz). [f. Pro-[2] + L. *avis* bird.] A hypothetical animal forming an evolutionary link between fossil reptiles and fossil birds. So **proa·vian** *a.*, of or pertaining to an animal of this kind; also as *sb.*

1907 F. Nopcsa in *Proc. Zool. Soc.* I. 235 An effort to condense these hypothetical changes into a drawing is given in text-fig. 82, which might..be called a 'Pro-Avis'. **1910** W. P. Pycraft *Hist. Birds* ii. 37 It is to the earlier Jurassic formations..that we must look for traces of the pro-avian types. *Ibid.* 38 What these 'pro-aves' were like we can only dimly surmise. **1926** G. Heilmann *Orig. Birds* iv. 191 The term Proavian or Proavis covers a form intermediate between reptile and bird. *Ibid.* 192 Before starting to reconstruct the proavian skeleton, we must try to gain a clear understanding of the particular peculiarities..that would lead on to the bird. **1962** J. C. Welty *Life of Birds* xxiii. 481/2 Heilmann attempted the reconstruction of a hypothetical, missing-link 'proavian'. **1974** I. C. J. Galbraith tr. *Dorst's Life of Birds* I. xvi. 301 An intermediate hypothetical being [between reptiles and birds] has had to be erected and named *Proavis.* *Ibid.* 301 It is really more appropriate to imagine a series of proaves.

pro-Axis: see *pro-[1] 5 a.

probabilify (prǫbăbi·lifəi), *v.* [f. L. *probābil-is* Probable *a.* + -ify.] *trans.* To give probability to; to give (some proposition) reasonable grounds for being true. So **probabilifica·tion**, the action or process of rendering probable; hence **probabilifi·able, probabilifica·tory** *adjs.*

1936 H. H. Price *Truth & Corrigibility* 9 It is probabilification which will chiefly concern us. *Ibid.* 16 Some parts of the total body of evidence either imply or probabilify other parts. *Ibid.* 18 A system where the mutual support..is only of the probabilificatory kind. **1949** W. Kneale *Probability & Induction* I. 11 Some conjunctions containing *A* would not probabilify *B* to the same degree or even at all. *Ibid.*, Admittedly the notion of probabilification requires further elucidation. **1953** *Mind* LXII. 455 Probabilifiable by sense-perception. **1966** A. Flew *God & Philos.* vii. 148 A traveller's tale not probabilified by any promising theory. **1973** J. L. Mackie *Truth, Probability & Paradox* v. 213 Equivalent contraposition does not hold even for probabilification between propositions.

probabilism. Add: **3.** The name given to theories in various fields, freq. contrasted with deterministic or possibilistic theories, which claim that the governing laws are not invariant, but state only probabilities or tendencies.

1952 O. H. K. Spate in *Geogr. Jrnl.* CXVIII. 419 It does not seem certain that 'possibilism' as often understood.. is the automatic alternative to a vigorous environmentalism. There may be a middle term, which one might call 'probabilism'. **1955** *Psychol. Rev.* LXII. 209/2 As Mises has pointed out in dismissing probabilism in physics, macrolaws have their origin in differential equations. **1956** E. Brunswik in K. R. Hammond *Psychol. E. Brunswik* (1966) xvii. 509 The statistical mechanics and quantum theory, being of a microscopic character, has little to do with the probabilism of functional psychology. **1965** H. & M. Sprout *Ecol. Perspective* vi. 107 A familiar version of behavioral model, derived largely, one suspects, from classical economics, might be called 'common-sense probabilism'. **1970** L. J. Cohen *Implications of Induction* i. 17 Some of Popper's arguments against Carnap are examples of anti-probabilism at this level. **1970** *Jrnl. Gen. Psychol.* LXXXIII. 108 Heider..focused on this region and his assumptions are similar to Brunswik's with regard to probabilism, multiple mediation, and vicarious functioning.

probabilist. Add: **2.** More generally, one who holds any theory of probabilism (cf. *probabilism 3). (Example.)

1965 H. & M. Sprout *Ecol. Perspective* vi. 107 The common-sense probabilist assumes that the individual applies his environmental knowledge rationally to the choice of ends achievable.

3. An expert or specialist in probability theory.

1973 *Nature* 1 June p. i/1 (Advt.), Forty-six leading probabilists are represented.

B. *adj.* = *probabilistic *a.* 2.

1960 E. Delavenay *Introd. Machine Transl.* vi. 93 Linguists who become automatic translation programmers will have to be trained on probabilist methods. **1970** L. J. Cohen *Implications of Induction* i. 29 The attack mounted here against probabilist theories of inductive syntax.

probabilistic, *a.* Add: **2.** Pertaining to or expressing probability; subject to or involving chance variations or uncertainties.

1951 *Philos. of Sci.* XVIII. 216 The recognition of the probabilistic character of environmental cue–object and means–end relationships through replacement of the traditional absolute right–wrong alternatives..by cues or means of lower statistical validity. **1957** N. Chomsky *Syntactic Struct.* ii. 17 The development of probabilistic models for the use of language (as distinct from the syntactic structure of language) can be quite rewarding. **1965** C. H. Springer et al. *Adv. Methods & Models* i. 11 Models which are based on the mathematics of statistics and probability, into which we introduce the uncertainties which usually accompany our observations of real events, are called probabilistic models. **1966** C. G. Hempel *Philos. Nat. Sci.* v. 65 Many important laws and theoretical principles in the natural sciences are of probabilistic character. **1972** *Computers & Humanities* VII. 17 His lengthier treatment of two stochastic models notes that probabilistic stylistics is somewhat more advanced than deterministic approaches. **1978** *Sci. Amer.* Feb. 131/3 The strict determinism of classical mechanics is abandoned in the quantum theory and is replaced by a probabilistic interpretation of measurements at the microscopic level.

Hence **probabili·stically** *adv.*, in a probabilistic manner; in terms of probabilities.

1955 *Science* 11 Nov. 910/1 Not only perception but also thinking and valuing are fruitfully conceived as only in some degree probabilistically valid achievements. **1965**

Language XLI. 201 Between the total workings of such a determinate system..and the sound a speaker produces there is a layer of indeterminacy that can only be handled probabilistically. **1975** *Nature* 17 July 166/2 Equations such as (2) and (3) can provide very simple examples of fully deterministic systems whose dynamics are best described probabilistically. **1978** *Sci. Amer.* June 99/2 The processes that govern the placing of telephone calls are so complicated that it is more fruitful to view them probabilistically than to do so deterministically.

probability. Add: **1. b.** (Further example.)
1835 DICKENS *Let.* 14 Dec. (1965) I. 105, I shall not in all human probability be home before Wednesday Week.

3. Also, used of quantities which are derived logically by inferential or inductive reasoning, when mathematical concepts may be inapplicable or insufficient. (Further examples.)
1764 T. BAYES in *Phil. Trans. R. Soc.* LIII. 376 The probability of any event is the ratio between the value at which an expectation depending on the happening of the event ought to be computed, and the value of the thing expected upon it's [*sic*] happening. **1939** *Internat. Encycl. Unified Sci.* I. VI. vi. 48 (*heading*) Probability as a unique logical relation. **1949** HUTTEN & REICHENBACH tr. *H. Reichenbach's Theory of Probability* p. v, Philosophical analysis was the starting point for a new mathematical construction of the calculus of probability. **1951** S. S. STEVENS *Handbk. Exper. Psychol.* 44/2 Russell once told his lecture audience that 'probability is the most important concept in modern science, especially as nobody has the slightest notion what it means'. **1975** A. R. WHITE *Modal Thinking* iv. 68 The common philosophical confusion of probability with estimates of probability.

4. *attrib.* and *Comb.*, as *probability amplitude, calculus, field, function, generating function, judgement, measure, proposition, relation(ship), statement, value, wave*; **probability curve,** a graph of a probability distribution; **probability density,** a probability distribution that is a continuous function; **probability distribution,** a function whose integral over any interval is the probability that the variate specified by it will lie within that interval; **probability paper** (see quot. 1933); **probability sample,** a sample whose members are chosen randomly; **probability space,** a space each point of which is an outcome and has a probability associated with it; **probability theory,** a branch of mathematics that deals with quantities having random distributions.
1936 *Physical Rev.* XLIX. 520/2 Let a_s denote the probability amplitudes of states in which the neutron is free and in a state *s*. **1944** H. REICHENBACH *Philos. Found. Quantum Mech.* xvii. 84 Since the probabilities are derived always as the squares of complex functions, these latter functions are sometimes called probability amplitudes. **1970** I. E. MCCARTHY *Nuclear Reactions* I. iii. 74 The probability amplitude description of a quantum process is a very simple one. **1940** *Mind* XLIX. 265 While scientists apply the probability-calculus with great success to, *e.g.*, microphysics, biology and vital statistics, philosophers are still not unanimous as to the right interpretation and 'meaning' of probability. **1971** *Times Lit. Suppl.* 1 Oct. 1180/4 The mathematics of Xenakis's highly sophisticated techniques derived from the probability calculus are no more discernible by the human ear than are the mathematics of the rudimentary chance operations favoured by John Cage. **1893** Probability curve [see *NORMAL *a.* 2 e]. **1914** [see *probability paper* below]. **1964** M. MCLUHAN *Understanding Media* v. 52 Some computer that translates our least gesture into a new probability curve. **1939** H. JEFFREYS *Theory of Probability* i. 24 We shall usually write this briefly $P(dx|p) = f'(x)dx$, dx on the left meaning the proposition that *x* lies in a *particular* range *dx*. $f'(x)$ is called the probability density. **1961** POWELL & CRASEMANN *Quantum Mech.* ii. 59 The fundamental postulate..states that the quantity $\psi^*\psi = |\psi|^2$ is to be interpreted as a probability density for a particle in the state ψ. More precisely,..in a measurement of the position of the particle, the probability $P(\mathbf{r})d\mathbf{r}$ of finding it in a volume element $d\mathbf{r} = dxdydz$ at a point $\mathbf{r}$ is proportional to $|\psi(\mathbf{r})^2|d\mathbf{r}$. **1968** P. A. P. MORAN *Introd. Probability Theory* ii. 68 When $f(t)$ is continuous, $f(t)dt$ can be regarded as the probability that *X* lies in the range $(x, x+dt)$ when *dt* becomes small. $f(t)$ is then known as the probability density of the distribution. **1937** H. CRAMÉR *Random Variables & Probability Distributions* ii. 11 The use here made of the terms *probability function* and *distribution function* corresponds to the terminology of Kolmogoroff. **1944** H. REICHENBACH *Philos. Found. Quantum Mech.* xxiv. 111 The specification of these values is therefore replaced by the statement of their probability distributions. **1970** G. A. & A. G. THEODORSON *Mod. Dict. Sociol.* 314 A probability distribution gives the probable frequency of occurrence of each category or class interval..of a given variable. **1940** *Mind* XLIX. 272 The definition of randomness as 'Nachwirkungsfreiheit' is wholly inadequate for the purpose of characterising a probability-field. **1965** R. C. JEFFREY *Logic of Decision* vii. 103 A probability field is a collection of propositions which contains the denial of any proposition that it contains, and which contains the conjunction and the disjunction of any pair of propositions that it contains. **1906** *Acta Univ. Lundensis* I. v. 8 The values of the probability function $\phi(x)$ are most conveniently tabulated by Sheppard. **1974** H. FRANK *Introd. Probability & Statistics* ii. 40 A probability function is defined as a function $Y=f(X)$ such that *X* is a random variable and *Y* is the set of probabilities associated with *X*. **1949** *Jrnl. R. Statistical Soc.* B. XI. 217 The recurrence relation for the probability-generating function $\Pi_{r+1}(z)$ for the entire population in the $r + 1$th generation is obtained by substituting $G(z)$ for *z* in $\Pi_r(z)$. **1968** P. A. P. MORAN *Introd. Probability Theory* ii. 79 We consider the probability generating function obtained by multiplying (2.62) by z^k and summing over the possible values. **1914** C. D. BROAD *Perception* ii. 150 The correct probability is always that relative to the knowledge of the person who makes the probability-judgment. **1934** *Philos. Rev.* XLIII. 133 The given experience of the moment of knowing is the basis of a probability-judgment concerning the experience. **1954** L. J. SAVAGE *Found. Statistics* iii. 33 Let me say precisely what is meant..by a probability measure. **1971** *Sci. Amer.* Aug. 95/1 Mathematical probability is based on a special function that assigns to each subset *A* of a given set Ω a positive real number that represents the probability that a point selected 'at random' from the set Ω will actually be in *A*. This function is called a 'probability measure' on the set Ω, and we shall denote it by *m*. **1914** A. HAZEN in *Trans. Amer. Soc. Civil Engineers* LXXVII. 1549 Probability Paper.—The practical difficulty with the plotting on Fig. 1 is the great curvature of the lines showing the required storage. This difficulty is so great as to make the method unsatisfactory in most cases; but it has been removed by using paper ruled with lines spaced in accordance with a probability curve, or, as it is otherwise called, the normal law of error. **1933** *Med. Res. Council Special Rep. Ser.* No. 183. 9 A special form of graph paper known as 'probability paper' has been prepared, on which the ordinates represent a scale of percentages so spaced that the actual distances on the paper are proportional to the corresponding values of the normal equivalent deviation. On 'logarithmic probability paper' the scale of ordinates is identical with that on ordinary probability paper, but the scale of abscissae is logarithmic. **1958** E. J. GUMBEL *Statistics of Extremes* i. 29 If the theory holds, the observations plotted on probability paper ought to be scattered closely about the straight line. **1914** C. D. BROAD *Perception* ii. 150 This is not as much objectivity as is wanted for probability-propositions. **1922** tr. *Wittgenstein's Tractatus* 111 There is no special object peculiar to probability propositions. **1921** J. M. KEYNES *Treat. Probability* i. 4 If a knowledge of *h* justifies a rational belief in *a* of degree *α*, we say that there is a probability-relation of degree *α* between *a* and *h*. **1965** P. CAWS *Philos. of Sci.* xxxiv. 261 If premise and conclusion are both known, some probability relation may be established between them. **1955** O. KLEIN in W. Pauli *Niels Bohr* 102 The basic ideas of quantum theory, where the causal relationship between events is replaced by a probability relationship. **1955** F. C. MILLS *Statistical Methods* (ed. 3) xix. 659 A probability sample is one for which the inclusion or exclusion of any individual element of the population depends on the application of probability methods, not on personal judgment, and which is so designed and drawn that the probability of inclusion of any individual element is known. **1972** *Jrnl. Social Psychol.* LXXXVIII. 208 Field interviewers.. administered the Rokeach Value Survey to a national probability sample of 1489 American adults. **1968** J. B. JOHNSTON et al. *Sets, Functions, & Probability* v. 163 We shall now describe how a probability space can be associated with certain chance phenomena in the real world. **1975** I. STEWART *Concepts Mod. Math.* xvii. 247 Axiomatic probability theory works entirely in terms of probability spaces. **1930** J. LAIRD *Knowl., Belief & Opinion* xvii. 376 According to this view, probability-statements are statements of proportions in very large series. **1939** E. NAGEL *Princ. Theory of Probability* iv. 23 Probability statements are on a par with statements which specify the density of a substance; they are not formulations of the degree of our ignorance or uncertainty. **1941** *Mind* L. 48, I shall here refer to the contrast between two very well-known types of probability-theory. **1962** *Listener* 15 Nov. 793/1 In psychological research, too, probability theory plays an essential part because many of the variables can be measured only approximately. **1974** P. ERDMAN *Silver Bears* ii. 16 At M.I.T... he had become fascinated with the probability theories of..John von Neumann and Oskar Morganstern [*sic*]. **1922** W. E. JOHNSON *Logic* II. xi. 251 Mill's position is paradoxical, since he apparently attributes a higher probability-value to a law, merely on the ground of its width. **1940** *Mind* XLIX. 267 From a purely mathematical point of view there would be no obstacle to the choice of series of the above kind as fields of measurement for probability-values. **1942** *Electronic Engin.* XV. 149/1 The term wave is commonly used in a very wide sense, to cover almost everything from a heat wave to the probability waves of modern physics. **1956** E. H. HUTTEN *Lang. Mod. Physics* v. 186 Physicists have sometimes spoken of the 'probability wave'; but this phrase must not be taken literally.

probable, *a.* (*sb.*) Add: **A.** *adj.* **3. e.** Now chiefly U.S. Law. *probable cause,* reasonable cause or grounds (for making a search or preferring a charge).
a **1676** M. HALE *Historia Placitorum Coronæ* (1736) II. xviii. 150 They are not to be granted without oath made before the justice of a felony committed, and that the party complaining hath probable cause to suspect they are in such a house or place, and do shew his reasons of such suspicion. And therefore I do take it, that a general warrant to search in all suspected places is not good, but only to search in such particular places, where the party assigns before the justice his suspicion and the probable cause thereof, for these warrants are judicial acts, and must be granted upon examination of the fact. **1789** J. MADISON in *Congress. Reg.* I. 428 The rights of the people to be secured in their persons, their houses, their papers, and their other property from all unreasonable searches and seizures, shall not be violated by warrants issued without probable cause, supported by oath or affirmation, or not particularly describing the places to be searched, or the persons or things to be seized. **1811** *U.S. Circuit Court Rep.* (1827) 37 What, then, is the meaning of the term 'probable cause'? We answer, a reasonable ground of suspicion, supported by circumstances sufficiently strong in themselves to warrant a cautious man in the belief, that the person accused is guilty of the offence with which he is charged. **1850** *Calif. Sup. Court* I. 11 The offence which.. there is probable cause to suppose he has committed. **1878** *U.S. Rep.* XCVII. 646 If there was probable cause of seizure, there was a reasonable cause. If there was a reasonable cause of seizure, there was a probable cause. **1927** *Ibid.* CCLXXV. 106 The liquor was obtained by a search and seizure instituted without warrant or probable cause. **1937** N. B. LASSON in *Johns Hopkins Stud. Hist. & Pol. Sci.* LV. II. iv. 125 In the searching of automobiles.. no warrant but only the existence of probable cause is necessary to constitute the search a reasonable one. **1954** *Fed. Reporter* (1955) CCXXII. 556/1 An 'anonymous tip' to officers..was not 'probable cause' for arrest without warrant. **1976** *Washington Post* 14 Dec. A18/2 Why should the United States, without even a whisper of probable cause, be bugging a dependent ward that had been formally delivered into its care by the United Nations?

f. *probable error*: the difference between the mean of a distribution and the first or third quartiles, i.e. an error of such a magnitude that larger and smaller errors are equally likely.
It has now been largely superseded as a measure of accuracy or consistency by the standard error.
1812 *Phil. Mag.* XXXIX. 241 All that can be gained is, that the errors are as trifling as possible—that they are equally distributed—and that none of them exceed the probable errors of the observation. **1854** *Amer. Jrnl. Sci. & Arts* XVII. 396, I have calculated..the amount of probable error in the determinations of many of the atomic weights. **1872** THOMSON & TAIT *Elem. Nat. Philos.* I. iii. 113 The probable error of the sum or difference of two quantities, affected by independent errors, is the square root of the sum of the squares of their separate probable errors. **1886** *Proc. R. Soc.* XL. 66 Throughout this discussion the technical term 'probable error' has been used; it may in every instance be replaced by Mr. Galton's very apt name 'quartile'. **1889** F. GALTON *Natural Inheritance* v. 58 The term Probable Error is absurd when applied to the subjects now in hand, such as Stature, Eye-colour, Artistic Faculty, or Disease. I shall therefore usually speak of Prob. Deviation. **1903** *Biometrika* II. 273 Unfortunately custom has not taken this standard deviation as the measure of the goodness of the sample, but the whole theory having developed from the normal curve, the probable error instead of the standard deviation has been chosen, i.e. ·67449 × standard deviation. **1938** D. C. BARTON in A. E. Dunstan et al. *Sci. of Petroleum* I. VIII. 369/2 Determinations of relative gravity with a probable error of ±10 or even ±5 tenth milligal are of value in geophysical prospecting. **1968** R. A. LYTTLETON *Mysteries Solar Syst.* iii. 104 The value of approximately $0{\cdot}08 \times 10^{12}$ dyn cm^{-2}..suggests a radius as large as 2770 km, which exceeds the quoted observed value by a little more than twice the probable error.

B. *sb.* Restrict † *Obs.* to sense in Dict. and add: **b.** One who will probably, though not certainly, be successful; a likely candidate, competitor, etc.; *spec.* a member of the supposedly stronger team in a trial match (opp. to *POSSIBLE *sb.* 1 d).
1906 *Pall Mall Gaz.* 23 Jan. 2 The last two 'probables' are untried men as far as Parliament is concerned. **1909** *Westm. Gaz.* 28 May 12/3 All probables ran. **1976** *West Lancs. Evening Gaz.* 8 Dec. 18/1 Fylde lock Bill Beaumont is one of four Lancashire players included in the Probables team for the first England trial at Twickenham on December 18. **1977** R. LUDLUM *Chancellor Manuscript* xxxii. 349 'What have you found out about our four candidates?'..'One..I'd say a probable.'

c. *Mil.* An aircraft recorded as probably shot down. Also, a submarine probably destroyed.
1940 in *Winged Words* (1941) 27 They were the new Heinkel 113s... We got..three or four of what we call 'probəbles'. **1940** W. S. CHURCHILL in D. McLachlan *Room 39* (1968) vi. 131 At least 5 probables [*sc.* submarines] have occurred since the beginning of new year. **1944** *Sat. Even. Post* 22 July 73/3, I chalked him up with only a probable, because I did not see it crash. **1955** C. S. FORESTER *Good Shepherd* II. 278 Out of his escort force he had lost a destroyer... But he had sunk two probables and a possible. **1977** L. DEIGHTON *Fighter* v. 278 The RAF announced that..584 aircraft 'were probably destroyed'... One assumes that half the probables were downed.

probableness. Delete † *Obs.* and add later example.
1951 J. S. BRUNER in Blake & Ramsey *Perception* v. 128 The higher the 'probableness' or likeness to English of our nonsense words, the less the amount of stimulus information (in terms of length of exposure) necessary for recognizing them correctly.

proband (prōᵘ·bǎnd). [ad. L. *proband-us,* gerundive of *probāre* to test, examine.] An individual chosen as a propositus because of the presence of some trait whose inheritance is to be studied. Also *attrib.*, as *proband method, test.*
1929 *Resumptio Genetica* IV. 296/1 (Index), Proband. **1931** E. & C. PAUL tr. *Baur's Human Heredity* xi. 501 A graphic representation of the parents, grandparents, great-grandparents, etc., of the individual from whom an investigation starts (such a person is called a proband) is known as that person's ancestral table. *Ibid.* 508 The proband method is wrongly supposed to be difficult to apply. **1940** HINSIE & SHATZKY *Psychiatric Dict.* 431/2 The practicable statistical method of probands in the study of selective population groups..is called the proband method. **1962** *Lancet* 29 Dec. 1341/2 Seven probands had a first-degree relative who had been treated with an antidepressant drug while under hospital care for a depressive illness. **1967** *Economist* 9 Dec. 1065/4 It is said that the Proband test effectively screens disease carriers in an endemic herd, and that once foreign buyers got used to it they would still want British pedigree ani-

mals. **1977** *Jrnl. Med. Genetics* XIV. 125/2 The same balanced translocation was found in the proband's sister, in 5 of 6 sibs of the mother and in 2 children of one of them.

Pro-Banthine (prōubæ·npīn). *Pharm.* Also **Probanthine, probanthine.** [f. PRO(PYL + *Banthine*, a proprietary name for methantheline bromide, a related compound (see quot. 1954).] A proprietary name for *PROPANTHELINE.

1953 *Official Gaz.* (U.S. Patent Office) 17 Mar. 571/1 G. S. Searle & Co., Skokie, Ill... *Pro-Banthine*... For medicinal agent for the treatment of abnormal conditions of the gastro-intestinal system in tablet and ampoule form. Claims use since July 31, 1952. **1953** *Trade Marks Jrnl.* 29 Apr. 358/2 Pro-Banthine... Pharmaceutical preparations in the form of tablets or ampoules for the treatment of gastro-intestinal disorders. G. D. Searle & Co..., Village of Skokie, State of Illinois, United States of America; manufacturers. **1954** [see *PROPANTHELINE]. **1955** *Radiology* LXIV. 331/1 Probanthine (15 mg.) should be given intramuscularly one hour before the examination to reduce pancreatic secretion to a minimum and to lower the concentration of enzymes in the juice. **1958** J. H. BURN *Lect. Notes Pharmacol.* (ed. 5) 28 Methantheline (Banthine) and propantheline (Probanthine) are used to relieve the pain of gastric and duodenal ulcers. **1967** H. BECKMAN *Dilemmas in Drug Therapy* 300 In Pro-Banthine you have pure anticholinergic action and in Donnatal there is this action plus the sedative effect of the contained phenobarbital. **1969** I. KEMP *Brit. G.I. in Vietnam* vii. 154, I was told I had a 'pyloric spasm'—in the upper intestine—and given tablets of probanthine, which at last eased the pain.

probasidium: see *PRO-[2] 1.

probate, *v.* Add: **3.** *U.S.* To place (a convicted person) on probation. Hence **pro·bated** *ppl. a.*, of or pertaining to a sentence of probation.

1961 in WEBSTER. **1972** *N.Y. Times* 3 Nov. 42/1 [He] was given a 10-year probated sentence. **1977** *Time* 19 Sept. 38/2 That was when he announced that 'whether women like it or not, they are sex objects' as he set free on a probated sentence a 15-year-old youth who had raped a 16-year-old coed in a high school stairwell.

probation. Add: **I. 3.** Used in the U.K. by Criminal Courts for certain adult offenders. (Further examples.)

1921 E. RUGGLES-BRISE *Eng. Prison Syst.* ix. 108 The principle of conditional conviction is common to most penal codes... It may take the form..of judicial reprimand, or of being bound over to be of good behaviour, or of probation. **1969** F. FINLAY *Boy in Blue Jeans* xix. 218 I'm amazed to hear you got probation. *Ibid.* 219 Within weeks of being put on probation Christopher left the hostel and he was sacked from his job. **1971** R. CROSS *Punishment, Prison & Public* i. 20 Probation is essentially the suspension of punishment conditional on there being no further offence for a period during which the offender is placed under personal supervision. *Ibid.* iii. 110 It leads one to wonder whether magistrates might not make more use of probation and less of imprisonment. **1973** *Howard Jrnl.* XIII. 346 He applies crisis theory to probation, and rightly suggests that there is scope for short-term probation.

III. 5. *probation officer* (examples); **probation order,** a court order committing an offender to a period of probation; **probation report,** a probation officer's report on an accused person submitted to a court before sentence is passed, a social inquiry report; **probation service,** probation and after-care service, a function which carries responsibility for the oversight of probationers and the care of accused persons and discharged prisoners.

1906 *Rep. N.Y. Probation Comm.* i. 8 The duties of the probation officer were to inquire into the previous history of any defendant when so directed by the court. **1909** *Westm. Gaz.* 1 Apr. 2/1 Section 107 of the Act contains a most useful conspectus of the substitutes for imprisonment which are at the disposal of the Court. They are.. discharging the offender and placing him under the supervision of a probation officer. **1922** H. H. GODDARD *Juvenile Delinquency* 78 Finally she was brought to the Bureau [in Ohio] September 1918, by the probation officer to see if we could give any advice. **1930** *Morning Post* 8 Aug. 10 The Home Secretary has decided to introduce an experimental scheme for training full-time probation officers. **1975** *Howard Jrnl.* XIV. II. 28 Such work should also be familiar to the reporting probation officer if he is to be of real value to the sentencing court. **1921** E. RUGGLES-BRISE *Eng. Prison Syst.* ix. 109 The extent to which Probation Orders are applied varies to a great extent in different parts of the country. **1948** *Act* 11 & 12 *Geo. VI* c. 58 § 3 Where a court by or before which a person is convicted of an offence..is of opinion that having regard to the circumstances, including the nature of the offence and the character of the offender, it is expedient to do so, the court may, instead of sentencing him, make a probation order, that is to say, an order requiring him to be under the supervision of a probation officer for a period to be specified in the order of not less than one year nor more than three years. **1969** *Listener* 26 June 908/3 Each probation officer has around 60 cases at a time (most in Wales and fewest in London; women probation officers, dealing with female offenders, have a smaller case-load). Out of these, he can expect about six or seven to be so successful that the probation order can be cut short. **1978** J. B. HILTON *Some run Crooked* ix. 91 The Bench..made a probation order: and Harbutt listened like a model penitent. **1973** J. PATRICK *Glasgow Gang Observed* iv. 39 The probation report offered this summary of Dick at the age of fourteen. **1977** *Wandsworth Borough News* 16 Sept. 17/2 [He] was remanded in custody for probation reports. **1958** *New Statesman* 11 Oct. 479/3 It is fair to say..that even if the probation service can ever carry this added burden, it is likely to be found..that the rehabilitative part of the work calls for welfare workers with a special kind of training not hitherto given to probation officers in this country. **1972** *Times* 19 Dec. 3/6 For the first time since the probation service was set up in 1907, officers in inner London yesterday went on strike.

probationary, *a.* Add: **1.** (Further examples.)

1922 *Act* 10 & 11 *Geo. V* c. 30 § 40 Such of those persons as..are serving a probationary period preliminary to establishment. **1963** T. & P. MORRIS *Pentonville* iv. 78 Once he has successfully completed his one-year period of probationary service, the prison officer is in effect a prison officer for life. **1964** A. SWINSON *Six Minutes to Sunset* iv. 54 He passed the Indian Civil Service examinations from Wren's and like most of his class spent two probationary years at Balliol and a third to get his degree. **1971** *Guardian* 8 Feb. 7/7 Introduction of a probationary licence for a period of one year after passing the test.

2. (Further examples.)

1926 *N.Z. Educ. Gaz.* 1 Dec. 202/2 Teachers selected for service as probationary assistants must understand they are still under training. **1963** B. PEARSON *Coal Flat* iii. 47 There was her routine of school, and her relations..with Miss James the probationary assistant. **1964** M. BANTON *Policeman in Community* ii. 17 On the Friday he has instructed a number of new recruits (probationary constables) to parade at the station at 6 a.m.

probationer. Add: **b.** (*e*) *Lord Probationer*, a newly appointed Scottish judge before he undergoes his trial and takes the oath. *Obs.* (*f*) *N.Z.* A teacher during his first year in a school after training at a teachers' training college.

e. 1799 *Edin. Weekly Jrnl.* 22 May, William Macleod Bannatyne, Esq. having gone through his trials as Lord Probationer, took the oaths and his seat on the Bench by the title of *Lord Bannatyne*. **1838** W. BELL *Dict. Law Scotl.* 176 The form of trial [for new judges]..consists in the presentee, or Lord Probationer as he is called, hearing and reporting, and delivering an opinion on certain of the causes depending in court. **1910** *Pall Mall Gaz.* 26 Apr. 3/5 He appears again in the First Division, and the junior judge reports to the judges of that court the judgments the Lord Probationer has pronounced.

f. 1921 *N.Z. Educ. Gaz.* 1 Dec. 21/1 Central classes for the instruction of pupil-teachers, probationers, and uncertificated teachers in science and in drawing and handwork may..be established by an Education Board. **1922** *Ibid.* 1 June 62/2 Pupil-teachers and probationers may not attend any classes in hygiene established for uncertificated teachers. **1963** B. PEARSON *Coal Flat* i. 8 You were here [*sc.* at this school] before, as probationer, weren't you?

probative, *a.* Add: **2.** (Further examples.)

1971 *Jrnl. Gen. Psychol.* LXXXIV. 222 A theorem deducible only from the conjunction of axioms as their only implicate is, therefore, most probative of the theory that contains them. **1972** *Mod. Law Rev.* XXXV. I. 73 The views of the majority have been treated as the most probative, if not the dispositive, factor. **1975** *Sci. Amer.* May 118/1 A new argument for credibility seemed to have emerged when one of the troubled men underwent a polygraph test, which at best is hardly fully probative.

probatively *adv.* (further example); also **pro·bativeness,** the quality of affording proof.

1971 *Jrnl. Gen. Psychol.* LXXXIV. 222 Theorems differ in their degree of probativeness of a theory. **1973** *N.Y. Law Jrnl.* 20 July 2/2 Movant has failed to probatively demonstrate that respondent has willfully failed and refused to comply with the judgment of the court.

probatory, *a.* Add: **1.** (Further example.)

1970 *Internat. Jrnl. Cancer* V. 311/1 Samples of tumours or normal tissue were obtained by probatory excision.

3. (See quot.)

1924 P. S. ALLEN in *Library* Mar. 255 The manuscripts are identified in the catalogue by the first words of the second leaf, the 'probatory words'.

probatum. **2.** **probatum est** (further examples).

1831 M. EDGEWORTH *Let.* 20 Jan. (1971) 474 Mother in law gave Fanny..the best receipt for a poultice that ever was (probatum est). **1884** G. MEREDITH *Let.* 17 Sept. (1970) II. 745 All material conquest follows self-conquest... *Probatum est.*

probe, *sb.* Add: **2. c.** Any small device, esp. an electrode, which can penetrate or be placed in or on something for the purpose of obtaining and relaying information or measurements about it, or of exciting radiation in it.

1924 *Physical Rev.* XXIV. 597 Potential distribution and ion concentration were investigated by Langmuir's modified probe method. **1938** *Proc. IRE* XXVI. 1534 The electric field intensity was measured by a small probe with a crystal detector, followed by an audio-frequency amplifier and a copper-oxide meter. **1943** F. E. TERMAN *Radio Engineer's Handbk.* iii. 260 Just as waves can be set up in space by straight wires and loops, so can the wave-guide modes be excited by electric probes and loops. **1965** *Wireless World* July 31 (Advt.), A completely new transducer..utilizes the variation in capacitance between its probe and the object under investigation to provide an electrical signal. **1971** *Sci. Amer.* Dec. 76/1 W. L. Bretz in our laboratory designed and built a small probe that could record the direction of airflow at strategic points in the respiratory system of ducks. **1972** *Physics Bull.* Jan. 23/3 In its basic form the pulse echo apparatus..comprises a heavily damped piezoelectric transducer source, often called a probe, which is placed on the surface of the sample under test. **1977** *Sci. Amer.* Aug. 63/1 [On the ocean floor] temperature gradients are determined by plunging a long cylindrical probe several meters into the soft sediment and measuring the temperature at one-metre intervals with fixed thermistors.

d. *Aeronaut.* and *Astronautics.* (i) A tube fitted to the nose or wing of an aircraft in order to fit into a drogue towed by another and convey fuel from it in aerial refuelling.

1949 *Flight* 11 Aug. 178/2 Either the tanker or the aircraft to be refuelled..could be fitted with the 'probe'. **1950** C. H. LATIMER-NEEDHAM *Refuelling in Flight* 186 On the nose of the fighter aircraft, a horizontal tubular member, or probe, approximately 4 ft. in length, is fitted, and this is aimed by the pilot at the trailing drogue so that as the fighter closes with the tanker the probe enters the drogue and thus makes contact. **1966** [see *DROGUE 3]. **1978** *Aeroplane Monthly* Jan. 35/1 This sub-variant incorporated the necessary 'plumbing' to permit in-flight refuelling, achieved with the aid of a probe of gigantic proportions.

(ii) A projecting device on a spacecraft designed to engage with the drogue of another craft during docking.

1969 *Times* 23 May 1/3 Ground control told the astronauts that it suspected that the ring, which serves as a mount for the docking probe, had slipped by about three degrees. **1970** N. ARMSTRONG et al. *First on Moon* iv. 80 The command module had at its top a 'probe', a triangularly shaped assembly with a pencil-like point. **1970** R. TURNILL *Lang. of Space* 34 Three tiny capture latches on the nose of the probe provide the first steadying link, and then the command module crewman fires a gas bottle which thrusts the two together so that 12 docking latches snap shut to complete the process.

e. A small, usu. unmanned, exploratory spacecraft (other than an earth satellite) for transmitting information about its environment; also, a rocket or an instrument capsule for obtaining measurements in the upper atmosphere.

1953 *Jrnl. Brit. Interplanetary Soc.* XII. 73 The probe will arrive at Mars nine months after opposition. **1958** *Observer* 17 Aug. 1/6 From then on the probe will be on its own for about 59 hours, coasting through space, gradually slowing down under the pull of the earth's gravity. **1959** F. D. ADAMS *Aeronaut. Dict.* 132/1 *Probe*,..3. An instrumented research rocket, or its payload, for penetrating the upper atmosphere or beyond. **1967** *Technol. Week* 23 Jan. 2/2 (Advt.), Motorola command receivers are ready to prove themselves again and again..in high altitude probes ..and in a multitude of new tactical applications. **1968** *Times* 15 Nov. 8/5 The Russian probe was not able to measure the lower 25 kilometres of the Venusian atmosphere. **1970** R. TURNILL *Lang. of Space* 122 A second spacecraft..is intended to go into orbit around Saturn, and drop off at least one probe. **1977** *Nature* 8 Sept. 98/3 The 11 instruments on board include television cameras, infrared and ultraviolet spectrometers, charged particle detectors, magnetometer and plasma wave detectors and, for the first time on an interplanetary probe, radio wave detectors.

4. b. *fig.* A penetrating investigation. Also in other transferred senses of the vb.

1903 *Christendom* 9 May 151/1 Few words are commoner in newspaper headlines than 'probe', which is newspaper English for an investigation of alleged abuses. **1930** *Amer. Speech* VI. 119 Probe started in junk yard blaze. **1945** *Ann. Reg. 1944* 307 With an obbligato of court injunctions, Congressional 'probes', Gallup polls,..the case dragged on. **1948** I. BROWN *No Idle Words* 99, I have just seen an inquiry into a fatal explosion in a factory described as a Blast Probe. **1959** *Listener* 31 Dec. 1140/2 Such conventional forces should be capable of performing all the functions for which the troops of Nato are at present organized: to deal with frontier incidents, to distinguish between local probes and deliberate sustained attack. **1962** A. HUXLEY *Island* xi. 177 Slanting down through chinks in the green vaulting overhead, the long probes of sunlight picked out here a row of black and yellow water jars, there a silver bracelet. **1962** *Listener* 15 Mar. 477/3 The results of the so-called Berlin probe—the recent meetings between Mr Gromyko and the American Ambassador in Moscow—have been 'no wickets and no runs'. **1971** J. B. CARROLL et al. *Word Frequency Bk.* p. vii, The AHI Corpus is..a highly informative probe of what might be called the American school lexicon. **1980** R. MCCRUM *In Secret State* iv. 26 Would Hayter start an internal probe into the background to the Lister business?

4*. *fig.* *Spec.* in *Nuclear Physics*, applied to a particle which can be used to penetrate nuclei, atoms, etc., and reveal their internal structure.

1955 C. G. DARWIN in W. Pauli *Niels Bohr* i. 5 The α-particle was always Rutherford's favourite. He could see that its great mass and its great energy made it the most effective of all probes to show what was in the atom. **1971** S. KAUFMAN in L. C. L. Yuan *Elem. Particles* iv. 160 Extremely high-energy..projectiles are required to produce the mass equivalent of these strange particles and to provide probes of short enough wavelength to 'see' any internal structure. **1972** DEPUY & CHAPMAN *Molec. Reactions & Photochem.* v. 78 Quenching is another useful probe for determination of mechanism. **1974** I. E. MCCARTHY *Nuclear Reactions* I. i. 6 The invention of accelerating machines promised new probes, for example protons, deuterons, and even heavier ions. **1975** SPIRO & LOEHR in Clark & Hester *Adv. Infrared & Raman Spectroscopy* I. iii. 135 To manipulate the composition of the sample, Oseroff and Callender employed a 'pump' laser beam, to establish the photo-stationary state, coaxial with a 'probe' beam, which produced the Raman spectrum. **1975** *Nature* 5 June 459/1 This effect in α-phenylethylamine was first noticed by Hug *et al.*, who realised that it originated in the two degenerate asymmetric deformations of the methyl group and could function as a new probe of chirality.

5. probe-and-drogue, used *attrib.* with reference to (i) a method of aerial refuelling (see 2d (i) above), or (ii) a method of docking spacecraft (see 2d (ii) above); **probe microphone** (see quot. 1955); also (*colloq.*) **probe mike.**

1951 *Engineering* 27 Apr. 491/1 In the probe-and-drogue system, the tanker trails a hose..to the end of which is attached a conical metal drogue..with the open end facing rearward. **1959** *Times* 8 Sept. 4/2 The range of the Vulcan V bomber will be increased significantly by the use of the probe and drogue aerial refuelling system. **1970** R. TURNELL *Lang. of Space* 34 *Docking tunnel*... So called because it contains the interlocking probe and drogue system for linking up the two craft in space. **1955** *Gloss. Acoustical Terms* (*B.S.I.*) 24 *Probe microphone*, a microphone or device incorporating a microphone for measuring sound pressure at a point in a sound field without significantly altering by its presence the sound field in the neighbourhood of the point. **1976** K. BENTON *Single Monstrous Act* iii. 37 'What is it?.. A probe mike?' 'That's it... It's shaped like a spike.' **1979** 'J. LE CARRÉ' *Smiley's People* (1980) xxi. 257 They'd like to run a couple of probe mikes into the ground floor.

probe, *v.* Add: **2.** (Further examples.) Cf. *PROBE *sb.* 4b.

1884 *N.Y. Weekly Tribune* 12 Mar. 1/2 The Senate Committee did not probe the Public Works Department in vain. **1915** C. MACKENZIE *Guy & Pauline* 228 If he could only probe by some remark a generous impulse. **1953** *Manch. Guardian Weekly* 5 Mar. 3/1 The press exhaustively probed the unpublished agenda and was then kept..firmly out of earshot. **1977** F. BRANSTON *Up & Coming Man* xiv. 150 Headlines were mostly variations of 'CID probe M-Way Rolls death mystery'.

4. (Further examples.)

1887 M. CORELLI *Thelma* II. iv. 66 Lady Winsleigh.. had..the cleverness to probe into Thelma's nature and find out how translucently clear and pure it was. **1906** G. MEREDITH *Let.* 5 Apr. in *Amer. N. & Q.* (1973) XI. 69/2 'Beauchamp's Career' does not probe so deeply, but is better work on the surface. **1923** *Times Lit. Suppl.* 4 Jan. 9/3 The only instrument by which his *fin-de-siècle* soul.. could probe to something solid to live by. **1959** *Listener* 14 May 827/1 If an aggressor were to try a probing action it's just as likely that he would probe on the sea, or even under the sea, as on land or in the air. **1962** *Ibid.* 5 July 3 (*heading*) Anthony Crosland and Donald MacRae probe into the state of the nation.

probing *vbl. sb.*, **prober** (further examples).

1948 I. BROWN *No Idle Words* 99 They [*sc.* sub-editors] are probers to a man. **1954** L. MACNEICE *Autumn Sequel* 75 The probing mind begins to fail the prober. **1958** *Listener* 20 Nov. 822/2 If the probing [of the moon] is carried out recklessly..then the extra-terrestrial bodies will be contaminated. **1970** *Times* 26 Feb. 4/6 Rescue workers today delved with probing rods into a mass of snow. **1974** *State* (Columbia, S. Carolina) 15 Feb. 1-A/4 (*heading*) White House refuses material for probers.

probenecid (prōᵘbe·nĭsid). *Pharm.* [f. PRO(PYL + BEN(ZOIC *a.* + *-e-* + A)CID *a.* and *sb.*] A white, crystalline, bitter-tasting powder which is a uricosuric agent used esp. to treat gout; *p*-(di-*n*-propylsulphamoyl)benzoic acid, $(C_3H_7)_2NSO_2 \cdot C_6H_4COOH$.

1950 *Ann. Internal Med.* XXXIII. 18 Benemid. [*Note*] Sharp and Dohme's trademark for p-(di-n-propylsulfamyl)-benzoic acid. This drug has been tentatively given the generic designation 'probenecid'. **1953** *Proc. Soc. Exper. Biol. & Med.* LXXXII. 604/1 Probenecid has been shown to inhibit reversibly the renal tubular secretion of a number of organic acids, such as penicillin.., phenolsulfonphthalein.., and para-aminohippuric acid. **1963** *Lancet* 5 Jan. 54/2 People with these vague aches associated with uric-acid blood-level elevation have responded well to colchicine intravenously as initial treatment and probenecid daily. **1974** A. HENRY in R. M. Kirk et al. *Surgery* xv. 305 Acute attacks [of gout] are controlled by colchicine or phenylbutazone, while uricosuric agents such as probenecid keep the plasma uric level down and must be continued throughout life.

probertite (prōᵘ·bəɹtəit). *Min.* [f. the name of Frank H. *Probert* (1876–1940), U.S. mining engineer + -ITE[1].] A hydrated borate of sodium and calcium, $NaCaB_5O_9 . 5H_2O$, which is found as colourless, monoclinic crystals at a number of locations in California.

1929 A. S. EAKLE in *Amer. Mineralogist* XIV. 427 The new borate..occurs as one of the minerals of the kernite deposit in the Kramer District, Kern County, California, and the name 'probertite' is proposed for the mineral, in honor of Frank H. Probert, Dean of the Mining College, University of California, to whom the writer is indebted for specimens, photos and notes of its occurrence. **1949** *Amer. Mineralogist* XXXIV. 19 Probertite..is monoclinic, has a radiating prismatic habit, perfect (110) cleavage and specific gravity of 2·141. **1964** NIES & CAMPBELL in R. M. Adams *Boron, Metallo-boron Compounds & Boranes* iii. 93 Hot concentrated borax liquors can be prepared in which the calcium content frequently is manyfold its equilibrium value, and when it finally deposits from these hot solutions it is usually in the form of probertite, $NaCaB_5O_9 \cdot 5H_2O$.

probing, *ppl. a.* (Further examples.)

1909 *Daily Chron.* 10 Aug. 7/2 He answered probing, keenly-put questions with dogged determination not to betray himself. **1962** F. I. ORDWAY et al. *Basic Astronautics* v. 187 Contact devices..either require direct contact with the surface in making the measurements or are located in a probing craft on, or in the atmosphere of, the world under examination. **1962** *Daily Tel.* 11 June 12/5 The probing talks between Russia and the United States on Berlin. **1972** *Jrnl. Social Psychol.* LXXXVI. 158 His reasoning is assessed by a series of predetermined probing questions that are administered with each situation.

probiotic: see *PRO-[2] 1.

probit (prōᵘ·bit). *Statistics.* [f. PROB(ABILITY + UN)IT.] The unit which forms the scale into which percentages may be transformed so that data evenly distributed between 0 and 100 per cent become normally distributed with a standard deviation of one probit.

1934 C. I. BLISS in *Science* 12 Jan. 38/1 These arbitrary probability units have been called 'probits'. **1947** D. J. FINNEY *Probit Analysis* iii. 20 The probit of the proportion *P* is defined as the abscissa which corresponds to a probability *P* in a normal distribution with mean 5 and variance 1. **1967** J. M. RENDEL *Canalisation & Gene Control* ii. 27 This distance from the mean measured in standard deviations is called a 'probit'.

b. *attrib.*, as *probit line, unit;* **probit analysis,** the technique of using probits in statistical analysis.

1947 D. J. FINNEY *Probit Analysis* i. 6 The statistical treatment of quantal assay data has been much aided by the development of probit analysis. **1956** *Nature* 25 Feb. 356/2 In general, high resistance is associated with flat probit/regression lines. The probit lines for resistant strains are nearly always flatter than for normal strains. **1958** *Immunology* I. 225 On transforming the per cent haemolysis into probit units and plotting these results against the reciprocal of the corresponding serum dilution, a linear relationship was obtained. **1968** *Brit. Med. Bull.* XXIV. 248/1 An analysis of variance is given, from which it can be seen, for instance, whether a fit by a set of parallel probit lines is justified. **1975** *Jrnl. R. Statistical Soc.* C. XXIV. 259 Probit analysis of dose-response curves and surfaces.

problem. Add: **3. c.** As the second element in various *Combs.* and collocations describing (*a*) a supposedly insoluble quandary affecting a specified group of people or a nation; (*b*) a real or imagined chronic personal difficulty, as *credibility, drink, health, weight problem.*

1950 M. HAY *Foot of Pride* vi. 161 The ship struck a mine..and all on board, save one, were drowned. A senior official of the British Immigration Office..impulsively expressed his relief that this particular Jewish problem had been solved. **1957** [see *JEWISH *a.* 1]. **1965** L. HUGHES in *Negro Digest* Sept. 57/1, I know I am The Negro Problem. **1969** 'J. MORRIS' *Fever Grass* iv. 44 She had the body of a ballet dancer with a weight problem. **1970** D. BAGLEY *Running Blind* iv. 83 He had a drinking problem at one time and decided to cut it out. **1971** 'A. GARVE' *Late Bill Smith* i. 15 'Sugar?' 'No, thanks. I've a waistline problem.' **1974** E. AMBLER *Dr. Frigo* I. 41 If Villegas had a health problem which could be helped by a change of climate [etc.]. **1977** *Grimsby Even. Tel.* 24 May 7/1 [He] told the court he had a drink problem and asked to be given a chance. **1978** S. BRILL *Teamsters* ii. 48 As a convicted bank robber, the inmate has a credibility problem.

d. In various colloq. phrases, as *no problem,* simple, easy, 'the question does not arise'; *that's your* (*his*, etc.) *problem,* used to disclaim responsibility or connection.

1963 *Amer. Speech* XXXVIII. 271 *No sweat* means 'no problem'. **1967** M. KENYON *Whole Hog* xxii. 217 'Don't you think he just might bring out the acid and the humane killer again? For me?' 'That's your problem.' **1973** M. AMIS *Rachel Papers* 117 Finally, every time I emptied my glass, he took it, put more whisky in it, and gave it back to me, saying 'No problem' again through his nose. **1976** L. SANDERS *Hamlet Warning* (1977) xxiii. 207 'Shouldn't we tell the hotel people what to do with the debris?'.. 'That's their problem.' **1977** C. FORBES *Avalanche Express* xi. 116 'If I catch you fooling around I'll break your arm.' 'No problem,' John assured him easily.

7. (*a*) *problem analysis, -game, paper, -programmer, -situation, skin, -solution, -tackler; problem-free, -ridden* adjs.; (*b*) *problem book, column, letter, page, picture, play* (further examples); (*d*) 'in which problems of a personal or social character are manifested', as *problem case* (CASE *sb.*[1] 8), *child, family, parent;* **problem-oriented** *a. Computers,* (of a computer language) devised in the light of the requirements of a certain class of problem; **problem-solver,** one who finds solutions to difficult or perplexing questions or situations; hence **problem-solving** *sb.*, the action of finding solutions to such problems; also as *adj.*, applied to behaviour, mental processes, equipment, etc., involved in or related to this activity; **problem tape** *Computers,* a magnetic tape containing the numerical information for a problem.

1969 J. ARGENTI *Managem. Techniques* 200 (*heading*) Problem analysis. **1931** F. M. FORD *Let.* 14 Mar. (1965) 200 It might have an enormous sale as a problem book. **1937** 'L. Q. ROSS' *Educ. Hyman Kaplan* 2 Here was a student who might, unchecked, develop into a 'problem case'. **1949** KOESTLER *Promise & Fulfilment* III. iv. 328 A large number of the immigrants of recent years are psychological problem cases. **1920** J. TAFT in *Proc. Nat. Conf. Social Work* 63 The placing and replacing of a problematic child..is also costly... The problem child is such a costly, nagging, persistent proposition that..we are forced to bring intelligence to bear upon his case. **1944** H. G. WELLS *'42 to '44* 83 What can one forecast from America, the great problem-child of humanity? **1964** M. ARGYLE *Psychol. & Social Probl.* ix. 123 Another group, which includes problem children and psychopathic delinquents, have had discipline that was too strict and harsh. **1977** D. BEATY *Excellency* iv. 50 We're the bankrupt problem child of the E.E.C. **1974** M. CECIL *Heroines in Love* ix. 213 The problem columns of all the new magazines. **1937** W. DE B. HUBERT in C. P. Blacker *Social Problem Group?* vi. 122 It is not at present known with certainty what proportion of families showing *both* mental defect and social problems..contribute to the total number of problem families. **1958** *Sunday Times* 26 Jan. 18/6 The number of hospital admissions is six times greater in the case of children from problem families. **1977** P. JOHNSON *Enemies of Society* xiv. 191 It means more 'problem families' and so more crime. **1964** P. WORSLEY in I. L. Horowitz *New Sociol.* 385 There is no 'problem-free' solution. **1921** H. E. PALMER *Princ. Language-Study* xiii. 145 Many types of puzzles and problem-games are practically identical with mathematical problems. **1970** O. NORTON *Dead on Prediction* i. 7 Whenever a man picks up a woman's magazine he *always* turns to the problem letters. **1961** *Computer Jrnl.* IV. 217/1 In most if not all of the current computer program languages—called 'problem-oriented languages'—the programmer must be concerned in some degree with how his program will be handled either on a specific computer or on a class of computers with specific characteristics. **1967, 1970** [see *machine-oriented* adj. s.v. *MACHINE *sb.* 10]. **1973** C. W. GEAR *Introd. Computer Sci.* viii. 319 These statements are part of what we call a Problem Oriented Language because they provide a language in which the problem can be described, but in which the method of solution is not described. **1974** M. CECIL *Heroines in Love* viii. 192 The problem page ('Why when I have this beautiful home..do I feel the need for something more?'). **1919** *Granta* 1 May 4/2 The solutions of the problem paper in the Mathematical Tripos. **1961** *Economist* 2 Dec. 909/3 Short 'problem papers' on points of specific difficulty may be either inspired by the staff or requested by a government office or an outside group. **1932** A. S. NEILL (*title*) The problem parent. *Ibid.* i. 9 There is never a problem child; there is only a problem parent. **1956** A. G. MCRAE *Hill called Grazing* x. 104 Problem children, if you like, though I prefer to think of them as the offspring of Problem Parents. **1962** *Listener* 7 June 976/2 The issue of the problem-parent and the uncomprehending home. **1910** *Punch* 30 Mar. 219 (*caption*) The problem picture. **1979** G. MACDONALD *Camera* xiii. 180/2 As the [nineteenth] century advanced social realism in Britain did not mature... Instead middle-class dilemmas were explored in 'problem pictures' with titles like 'The Confession',.. 'The Prodigal Daughter', etc. **1941** G. HEYER *Envious Casca* iv. 53 A problem-play, is it? **1957** V. BRITTAIN *Testament of Experience* (1979) iii. 96 My chief passion was for work..and my fourth for intellectual drama and 'problem' plays. **1970** R. E. C. HOUGHTON *Shakespeare's Measure for Measure* 5 The very term 'problem plays' is loose and ambiguous—were they problems to their author, or are they only problems to the modern critic?.. The most intelligible use of the term would be for a play primarily concerned to present a moral problem. **1970** O. DOPPING *Computers & Data Processing* xix. 305 Those who design programming systems..are sometimes called system programmers. In contrast, the user's normal programmers are sometimes called problem programmers or application programmers. **1924** R. GRAVES *Mock Beggar Hall* 59 A disturbing problem-ridden affair demanding the comments of a moralist. **1950** *Mind* LIX. 385 The problem-situation involving rational argument and discussion. **1978** J. DUNN in Hookway & Pettit *Action & Interpretation* 169 There is no doubt much redundancy and not a little error of one kind and another in agents' characterisations of their problem situations. **1970** *Cape Times* 28 Oct. 3/2 (Advt.), A daily cleanser for problem skins. **1956** J. KLEIN *Study of Groups* 192 (*heading*) Cooperative versus solitary problem-solution. **1899** J. MILNE *Romance of Pro-Consul* xvi. 173 He [*sc.* Sir George Grey] was the problem-solver called in late. **1929** R. FROST *Let.* 6 Jan. (1964) 194, I don't believe in myself as a problem-solver. **1974** *Times* 31 Aug. 4/6 Practical problem-solvers can contribute much to education. **1979** *Dædalus* Summer 148 Pragmatism..is a fairy tale of energies magically released..into what Dewey called the 'situation', jointly apprehended by the problem-solvers involved. **1931** *Psychol. Rev.* XXXVIII. 337 Problem-solving by insight is regarded..as qualitatively different from problem-solving on the basis of trial and error. **1964** *Language* XL. 237 Most problem-solving situations involve concept evocation rather than the formation of new concepts. **1966** A. BATTERSBY *Math. in Managem.* i. 15 A computer is said to have applied a problem-solving programme to the proposition that the base angles of an isosceles triangle are equal. **1978** *Amer. Poetry Rev.* July/Aug. 38/4 Every once in a while the problem-solving yields to an almost basking, sunny Calvinism. **1979** *Yale* Apr. 4/2 Man is a problem-solving animal. **1963** *Times* 29 Jan. 9/4 Contributing to a Forum, colliding politely at a Meeting Point, joining in the domestic Parliament of a Woman's Hour, onward the problem-tacklers go. **1948** *Math. Tables & Other Aids to Computation* III. 9 It was intended that the routine tapes should contain all the orders, the table tapes should contain numerical information of a general nature, comparable to function tables used in manual computing, and the problem tape should contain numerical information specific to the problem being solved. **1956** G. A. MONTGOMERIE *Digital Calculating Machines* x. 213 The input tapes are of three kinds. First the problem tape containing the numerical information for a set of data and also, usually, some instructions.

problematic (prǫblĕmæ·tik), *sb. Sociol.* [f. PROBLEMATIC *a.* 1.] Something that constitutes a problem, or an area of difficulty in a particular field of study.

1957 R. K. MERTON *Social Theory* (rev. ed.) II. 127 Working out its problematics, i.e., the principal problems (conceptual, substantive and procedural). **1969** R. BLACKBURN in Cockburn & Blackburn *Student Power* 194 The dialectical approach to the same problematic adopted by such writers as Isaac Deutscher and Herbert Marcuse enabled them to obtain a more lasting insight into the dynamic of Soviet society. **1971** *Catholic Q.* XXXIII. 439 Essays..sharing the common problematic of attempting to situate the language of faith within language as a whole along the lines indicated by modern linguistic analysis. **1977** R. H. BROWN in Douglas & Johnson *Existential Sociol.* ii. 77 A humanistic sociology investigates the problematics of feeling and meaning.

pro·blemless, *a.* [f. PROBLEM + -LESS.] Devoid of or unaffected by problems; presenting no problems.

1924 *Public Opinion* 3 Oct. 320/1 Jowett went serenely on his way—apparently problemless. **1967** *Lingua* XVII. 55 As far as word classes are concerned, problemless or 'regular' hypotheses about little-known languages are always very suspicious! *a* **1970** E. STARKIE in J. Richardson *Enid Starkie* (1973) IV. x. 80 The advantages... The problemless life. It was sacrificing nothing.

pro-Boche: see *PRO-¹ 5a.

proboscidal, *a.* Add: Also *fig.*

1922 JOYCE *Ulysses* 456 He assumes the avine head, foxy moustache and proboscidal eloquence of Seymour Bushe.

pro-Britisher: see *PRO-¹ 5b. **pro-business:** *PRO-¹ 5a.

proby, probie (prōᵘ·bi). *colloq.* [f. PROB(ATIONER + -Y⁶, -IE.] A probationer; *spec.* U.S., a fireman undergoing probation.

1899 L. BECKE *Old Convict Days* ii. 42 For a proby (probationer) you're a plucky one. I won't report you. **1946** *Richmond* (Va.) *News Leader* 25 Jan. 11/4 There are times when the 'probies' (students at the probationary firemen's school) must think [etc.]. **1969** *Publ. Amer. Dial. Soc.* LII. 30 *Proby*, a man on probation because he is new on the force [*sc.* the Denver Fire Department]... 'John is still a proby.'

procainamide (prokē¹·nămaid). *Pharm.* Also **procaineamide.** [f. **procaine amide.*] An amide, $NH_2C_6H_4{\cdot}CONH{\cdot}CH_2CH_2N(C_2H_5)_2$, which is formally derived from procaine (an ester), and is used in cardiac therapy (esp. to control arrhythmia) in the form of a hydrochloride, a white hygroscopic solid.

1954 *Lancet* 8 May 957/1 It is now established that procainamide is superior to quinidine in the treatment of ventricular tachycardia. **1954** *Brit. Pharmaceut. Codex* 610 Procainamide Hydrochloride is *p*-amino-N-(2-diethylaminoethyl)-benzamide hydrochloride and may be prepared by treating the NN-diethylethylenediamine with *p*-nitrobenzoyl chloride, and reducing the nitro-compound obtained. **1971** L. SCHAMROTH *Disorders Cardiac Rhythm* lvii. 326/2 Follow-up therapy may be carried out with oral procainamide: 250 to 500 mgm 4 to 6-hourly. **1979** *Sci. Amer.* Dec. 52/1 Procainamide, which is administered to counteract irregular rhythms of the heart, must be given to most patients every three hours in order to provide blood levels near the therapeutic range.

procaine (prōᵘ·kēin). *Pharm.* Also **procain.** [f. PRO-¹ + CO)CAINE.] The synthetic compound 2-diethylaminoethyl *p*-aminobenzoate, $NH_2C_6H_4{\cdot}COO{\cdot}CH_2CH_2N(C_2H_5)_2$, which is used as a local anæsthetic, usu. in the form of its hydrochloride, a white, crystalline solid. Cf. *NOVOCAIN.

1918 *Jrnl. Amer. Med. Assoc.* 23 Feb. 537/2 Procaine is the official name of the product introduced as novocaine. **1919** *Ibid.* 6 Sept. 757/2 Procain is employed largely in infiltration anesthesia. **1940** H. A. MCGUIGAN *Appl. Pharmacol.* 536 The activity of procaine is increased by the addition of 0·25 per cent sodium bicarbonate or 0·50 per cent potassium sulfate to the solution injected. **1951** A. GROLLMAN *Pharmacol. & Therapeutics* xvii. 324 Procaine is relatively non-toxic, being destroyed rapidly by the liver. **1958** *Daily Mail* 24 July 5/7 He thought it contained procaine to help her fibrositis. **1962** H. HEATH in A. Pirie *Lens Metabolism Rel. Cataract* 364 The actions of some drugs, e.g. zoxazolamine, pentobarbital and procaine, are potentiated in the scorbutic state. **1976** H. FERGUSON *Confessions of Long Distance Acid Head* 7 Apart from cannabis, I have used barbiturates,..morphine, cocaine, procaine, ritalin, even apomorphine once.

b. Special Combs.: **procaine amide** = *PROCAINAMIDE; **procaine penicillin,** an insoluble salt of procaine and benzylpenicillin, which is an antibiotic used in the form of a suspension in oil and which releases penicillin slowly after intramuscular injection.

1950 *Jrnl. Pharmacol. & Exper. Therapeutics* XCVIII. 21/2 (*heading*) The action of procaine amide..on ventricular arrhythmias. **1963** V. SCHRIRE *Clinical Cardiol.* xix. 348 Procaine amide should be used in preference to intravenous quinidine. **1968** I. L. RUBIN et al. *Treatm. Heart Dis. in Adult* x. 240 Procaine amide is administered intravenously as the drug of choice in the treatment of ventricular tachycardia. **1947** *Proc. Staff Meetings Mayo Clinic* XXII. 567 The preparation is a procaine salt of penicillin G (duracillin) which was prepared in the research laboratories of Eli Lilly and Company. Procaine penicillin G is a crystalline, nonpyrogenic substance which is prepared by combining one molecule of procaine base..with a molecule of penicillin. **1949** FLOREY & JENNINGS in H. W. Florey et al. *Antibiotics* II. xxxvii. 1220 The first accounts of trials with procaine penicillin in man all mentioned the freedom of patients from local or general toxic effects. **1961** *Times* 27 Mar. 5/4 The fungicidal activity of the antibiotic procain penicillin. **1967** *Martindale's Extra Pharmacopœia* (ed. 25) 1007/2 Procaine penicillin is administered by intramuscular injection to create a depot from which penicillin is slowly liberated.

procaineamide: see *PROCAINAMIDE.

procarbazine (prokā·ɹbăzīn). *Pharm.* [f. PRO(PYL + CARB(AMIC *a.* + HYDR)AZINE, formative elements of the systematic name.] A hydrazine derivative whose hydrochloride is used in the treatment of some neoplastic diseases, esp. Hodgkin's disease; *N-p*-isopropylcarbamoylbenzyl-*N′*-methylhydrazine, $C_{12}H_{19}N_3O$.

1965 *Brit. Med. Jrnl.* 18 Dec. 1473/1 (*heading*) Natulan (procarbazine) combined with radiotherapy in management of inoperable malignant melanoma. **1974** R. M. KIRK et al. *Surgery* iv. 58 Hodgkin's disease (Lymphadenoma)... Generalized disease responds to chemotherapy, usually with a combination of vincristine, mustine, procarbazine and prednisone in pulsed doses. **1977** *Lancet* 14 May 1041/2 Of all cytotoxic drugs the teratogenicity of the alkylating agents is particularly well-documented; these, and procarbazine too, are best avoided at all stages of pregnancy if possible.

procarcinogen(ic): see *PRO-² 1.

procaryon, etc., varr. PROKARYON, etc.

‖ **procédé** (prosede), *sb.* [Fr.] Manner of proceeding; method, procedure, process.

1872 GEO. ELIOT *Let.* 14 Mar. (1956) V. 256, I altogether abominate that *procédé* of M. Forgues and others who undertake to trim and abridge. **1935** *Scrutiny* IV. III. 285 The characteristic *procédé* may be seen in this extract from the second section of his [*sc.* Santayana's] essay on Russell. **1962** *Listener* 15 Nov. 832/3 All the familiar *procédés* of opera have vanished, whether set numbers or Wagnerian leading-motives.

procedural (prosī·diŭrăl), *a.* [PROCEDURE + -AL.] Of or pertaining to procedure. Hence **proce·durally** *adv.*

1889 F. W. MAITLAND in *Pol. Sci. Q.* IV. 506 Our collections include a few documents which bear no legislative authority, namely..a few procedual [*sic*] formulas. **1908** R. POUND in *Illinois Law Rev.* Nov. 232 The necessity of patient cutting away by the courts of an *abatis* of procedural obstacles in order to attack the substantive points before them. **1919** H. A. L. FISHER *Stud. Hist. & Politics* 52 It includes a reform of the civil, penal, and procedural codes. **1938** *Mind* XLVII. 529 Prof. Schilpp is capable of lapsing into revolting phrases like 'procedurally formal'; but this gives no proper indication of his style, which is on the whole vigorous and beautifully clear. **1947** *Daily Tel.* 13 Dec. 1/1 Mr. Marshall, although sure that M. Molotov's words were 'not seriously designed for consumption here, but for another audience', said that such procedural methods 'do not inspire respect for the Soviet Government'. **1963** J. PRESCOTT *Case for Hearing* vi. 89 We'll make the girl a ward of court... Any quick and procedurally easy application to the magistrates' court for permission to marry would be out. **1968** *Brit. Med. Bull.* XXIV. 252/2 A computer can be used to take procedural decisions during the test itself. **1978** *Nature* 13 July 104/3 Now at least it seems as if the commission is leaning over backwards to be procedurally fair.

procedure. Add: **1. e.** *Computers.* A set of instructions for performing a specific task.

1946 *Ann. Computation Lab. Harvard Univ.* I. iv. 98 There are many coding routines..which occur so frequently as to make standard coding procedures of real value. This chapter includes..certain of the longer procedures. **1954** *IRE Trans. Electronic Computers* III. 15/1 Specialized procedures, formed from combinations of basic procedures,..are needed to achieve higher speeds of operation for special purposes. **1965** *Data Processor* Oct. 22/3 A procedure is a block of instructions designed to perform a specific function such as the calculation of overtime pay in a payroll application... Procedures share common elements with different programs. Seldom-used procedures can be held in auxiliary storage and called into the main storage only when required. **1970** O. DOPPING *Computers & Data Processing* xix. 315 Subroutines are called procedures in Algol. A number of standard functions are obligatory among these procedures, ..but in addition to these the programmer may write his own procedures.

process, *sb.* Add: **1. c.** Used in *Philos.*, esp. in and with reference to the work of A. N. Whitehead (1861–1947), to designate the course of becoming rather than being.

1926 A. N. WHITEHEAD *Relig. in Making* iii. 114 In this fusion of ground with consequent, the creative process brings together something which is actual and something which, at its entry into that process, is not actual. The process is the achievement of actuality by the ideal consequent, in virtue of its union with the actual ground. In the phrase of Aristotle, the process is the fusion of being with not-being. **1949** O. LEE *Existence & Inquiry* 11 Because the world seen as process was very different from what it had been before, a new theory of inquiry was needed to deal with it. Dialectic was the answer first proposed—a logic of process. **1964** E. E. HARRIS *Found. of Metaphysics in Sci.* xxii. 451 Samuel Alexander, J. C. Smuts, Lloyd Morgan and Henri Bergson..expounded theories of process and evolutionary pluralism. Whitehead..like Hegel, attempted to reconcile pluralism with monism and process with holism. **1977** *Theology* LXXX. 187 The world is a dynamic totality of events..hence it is a process, *from* the given past *through* the present.. and *towards* a future.

5. b. *Social Sciences.* The continuing interaction of human groups and institutions, esp. as observed and studied through its effects in social, political, cultural, etc., life, with the aim of finding underlying patterns of behaviour in the data available, freq. contrasted with the study of such aspects of society through its structures. Also *attrib.*

1887 MOORE & AVELING tr. *Marx's Capital* I. I. i. 12 The different proportions in which different sorts of labour are reduced to unskilled labour as their standard, are established by a social process that goes on behind the backs of the producers, and, consequently, appear to be fixed by custom. **1898** E. A. ROSS in *Amer. Jrnl. Sociol.* III. 860 Everything that is being done to bring to light the processes of socialization and control contradicts the easy-going theory that actual society is a spontaneous product due to the social instincts of man. **1902** L. F. WARD in *Ibid.* VII. 761 Ratzenhofer shows the precise *modus operandi* of the whole process of social assimilation. **1928** [see *EDUCATIONAL *a.* 2]. **1939** *Jrnl. Psychol.* VIII. 389 The question may be raised whether any light upon this situation can be obtained by examining the *process* of personality development for leads to..more satisfactory methods and procedures. **1951** R. F. BALES *Interaction Process Anal.* p. iii, An attempt to formulate some of the basic structural characteristics and dynamic processes one would expect to find in small groups. **1954** *Amer. Anthropologist* LVI. 398 In *synchronic* studies of national character, we are discussing not the origins of the culture or the society, but the process of learning of identifiable human beings living within that society at a given period. **1958** *Pol. Stud.* VI. 243 The term 'process' seems to enter social and political discourse today in two different ways: it can be used widely or it can be used more specifically. *Ibid.* 248 Here I think we probably find a plausible separate use for this process notion—to refer to an isolable complex of interactions between procedural rules..and the internal and external relations of various kinds of social groups. **1960** *Amer. Anthropologist* LXII. 18 The recent advances in the structural-functional approach are impressive..compared to the lag and the disagreements over how to conceptualize cultural processes. **1969** K. CAUTHEN *Science, Secularization & God* v. 165, I have already declared myself in favor of a metaphysical philosophy based on the process model argued so persuasively by Whitehead and Hartshorne. **1971** R. F. MURPHY *Dialectics of Social Life* i. 31 The study of 'process' and 'dynamics' is thus not as processual and dynamic as we would like to believe, for it commonly approximates a seriation of structures through time.

6. c. (*d*) A method of straightening and styling the hair by chemical means; *transf.* hair thus treated; the chemicals which effect this. *U.S. Blacks.*

1964 L. HAIRSTON in J. H. Clarke *Harlem* 288 Sonny rubbed the process in so thick with his rubber gloves, it started stingin' a little t'rough the heavy layer of grease he packed in my scalp. *Ibid.* 293 By Friday my process 'd need retouchin'. **1967** *Trans-Action* Apr. 8/1 Time may pick up when a familiar car cruises by and a few dudes drive down to Johnny's for a 'process' (hair straightening and styling). **1970** E. OFARI in *Black Scholar* Oct. 49/2 Draper apparently has never heard of cadillacs, processes, chitterlings, the blues. **1972** B. G. COOKE in T. Kochman *Rappin' & Stylin' Out* 64 The 'process' of hair straightening is now considered demeaning; most black brothers have abandoned it.

d. A linguistic operation or change.

1954, etc. [see *ITEM *sb.* 2d]. **1964** R. H. ROBINS *Gen. Linguistics* v. 212 Different forms of the paradigms are then described as the result of processes, vowel change.. etc. applied to the root form. (*Process* in this use is a descriptive term; it has nothing to do with historical processes in time or with changes in the forms of the language through the years.) **1974** R. QUIRK *Linguist & Eng. Lang.* v. 92 Educated opinion here is well-informed about the 'existing processes' of English.

12. a. (Examples referring to individual cells.)

1893, etc. [see *DENDRON]. **1977** *Sci. Amer.* Aug. 108/2 In the nervous system a network of nerve cells with elongated processes communicate with one another by secreting neurotransmitters, which traverse the tiny gap between two nerve cells.

13. a. (sense *1c) *process motif, theism, -thinker, thought, view*; (sense 6c) *process block* (further examples), *department, embossing, -engraver* (examples), *engraving, lens, -maker, photography, plate* (examples), *print, -printer, reproduction*; also with reference to a kind of colour printing in which a continuous and wide range of colours is produced by superimposing half-tones in each of three or four different colours; as *process colour, ink, printing*; with reference to industrial processes, esp. continuous ones, as *process cost, engineer, engineering, industry, operation, plant, sheet, work* (further example); *process-type* attrib.; (sense *6d) *process approach, model, morpho-*

phonemic; **b. process annealing** *Metallurgy*, heat treatment applied to an alloy after cold working to prepare it for further cold working; **process black,** a black ink suitable for use in process work; **process butter** (see quots. 1902, 1906); **process camera,** a camera specially designed for taking photographs for use in process work; **process chart,** a diagram showing the sequence and sometimes the time and place of the different stages in an industrial or commercial process, or the different activities performed by an employee; **process cheese,** cheese made by melting and blending (and often emulsifying) other cheeses; also *fig.*; cf. **processed cheese*; **process control,** the regulation and control of the physical aspects of an industrial process, esp. automatically by instruments; freq. *attrib.*; hence **process controller; process heat,** heat supplied or required for an industrial process; so **process heating** *vbl. sb.*; **process philosophy,** philosophy based on the theory of process (sense *1c); **process projection** *Cinemat.*, projection on to the back of a translucent screen, the other side of which is used as a background for ordinary filming; **process schizophrenia,** endogenous schizophrenia that does not seem connected with environmental causes; hence **process schizophrenic; process shot** *Cinemat.* (see quot. 1973); **process steam,** steam supplied or required for an industrial process other than power generation; **process theology,** theological theory based on the concept of process (sense *1c); hence **process theologian; process water,** water used in an industrial process; **process worker,** one who works in process printing or in an industrial process.

1936 *Metals Handbk.* (Amer. Soc. Metals) 211 *Process annealing*, heating iron base alloys to a temperature below or close to the lower limit of the critical temperature range followed by cooling as desired. **1977** R. B. Ross *Handbk. Metal Treatm.* 322 The purpose of Process annealing is to remove work hardening prior to further cold work. **1972** W. P. Lehmann in *Language* XLVIII. 266 Recent grammatical study has led to a preference for a process approach in linguistic analysis. **1907** *Yesterday's Shopping* (1969) 471/1 *Process black*..for use in drawings intended for process reproduction. **1964** E. Chambers *Camera & Process Work* xv. 208 The ink manufacturers make inks suitable for proofing, these are usually sold under such names as half-tone black, process black or press black. **1888** C. T. Jacobi *Printers' Vocab.* 104 *Process blocks*, illustrations in relief produced by any mechanical process. **1925** Process block [see *letter-press 1]. **1899** *Jrnl. Franklin Inst.* CXLVII. 94 (*heading*) Renovated or process butter. **1902** Leffmann & Beam *Select Methods of Food Analysis* 370 So-called 'process' or 'renovated' butter, made by rendering old or inferior samples, purifying the fat, coloring, salting, and molding it, is now a familiar commercial article. **1906** L. L. Van Slyke *Mod. Methods of testing Milk & Milk Products* i. 18 Renovated or process butter is the product made by melting butter and reworking, without the addition or use of chemicals or any substances except milk, cream or salt. **1911** Simmons & Mitchell *Edible Fats & Oils* iv. 44 The preparation of 'process' butter from stale or unsaleable genuine butter. **1895** *Photogr. Jrnl.* XIX. 313 In the construction of a process camera rigidity and parallelism and ability to stand wear and tear have to be carefully studied. **1967** Karch & Buber *Offset Processes* v. 141 The lithographic plate is usually produced from a negative which is made with the process camera. **1974** J. Craig *Production for Graphic Designer* 72 The first step in making a printing plate is to photograph the copy..using a special camera, called a process camera. **1941** Colvin & Stanley *Running Machine Shop* vi. 256 Process charts can also be made to follow the operator instead of the part or product. **1968** B. Yuill *Supervision Princ. & Techniques* xxi. 240 The layout must be carefully planned by using such techniques as materials and man process charts, which show the proposed courses of materials and the movement of manpower through the plant. **1977** P. E. Hicks *Introd. Industr. Engin. & Managem. Sci.* iv. 63 Whereas analysis was restricted only to operations and inspections in using the operation process chart, the flow process chart includes additional consideration of moves, delays, and storages. **1926** T. R. Pirtle *Hist. Dairy Industry* i. 110 The development of the process or packaging cheese business is one of the outstanding accomplishments of the cheese industry in recent years. **1951** M. McLuhan *Mech. Bride* (1967) 24/1 These wondrous totalitarian techniques for making the public into process cheese. **1972** *Federal Register* XXXVII. 11722/3 The amendments..will have the effect of providing for optional use of buttermilk in pasteurized process cheese food. **1926** F. B. Wiborg *Printing Ink* xx. 241 *Process color inks.* These inks are made exclusively for the purpose of printing pictorial subjects... Special process inks are made for this class of printing. **1951** R. G. Radford *Letterpress Machine Work* II. xii. 134 The majority of experienced process colour printers prefer the Miehle two-revolution machine. **1968** *Heidelberg News* Sept. 4/3 Only use process colour when it is justified. Four colour work is seen at its best, has most impact, alongside black and white. **1931** *Electronics* Oct. 144 (*heading*) Electronic oscillators for industrial process control. **1945** D. P. Eckman *Princ. Industr. Process Control* x. 202 Many simple controllers serve in industrial process control as safety devices to protect process equipment from overloads of temperature or pressure. **1967** *Economist* 8 Apr. 162/2 It would make a great difference to the market for, and the cost of, industrial process control if engineers could make headway in designing standardised sections of process control instruments, etc., that could be assembled, building-block fashion, at the client's plant. **1977** *Sci. Amer.* Sept. 122/3 A small process-control computer monitors the temperature, directs the insertion and withdrawal of the wafers and controls the internal environment of the furnace. **1951** *Proc. Inst. Electr. Engineers* XCVIII. ii. 609/1 The output signal of the process controller is transmitted to the regulating unit, which adjusts the physical quantity upon which the controlled quantity depends in order to restore it to the desired value. **1955** *Automatic Control* (1957) ii. 26 Process controllers supervise the manufacture of plastics, synthetic fibers, drugs, the whole range of products of the chemical industry. **1926** S. I. Levy *Introd. Industrial Chem.* ii. 47 The process cost sheets reveal clearly the great importance of chemical efficiency. **1974** *Terminol. Managem. & Financial Accountancy* (Inst. Cost and Managem. Accountants) 21 *Process cost centre*, a cost centre in which a specific process or a continuous sequence of operations is carried out. **1967** *Times* 18 Jan. 16/4 There are restrictive practices in the industry, particularly in the machine room and process department. *Ibid.* 16/7 *Process department*, prepares photographs and line drawings as plates. **1968** *Guardian* 29 Feb. 11/2 Joe Balfour's work wasn't good enough for process department, so he was transferred to assembly. **1931** R. R. Karch *Printing & Allied Trades* xvii. 166 Thermography is known as 'raised letter' printing, and 'process embossing'. **1948** —— *Graphic Arts Procedure* i. 7 Imitation engraving is known by several names, among which are *raised-letter printing, process embossing.* **1935** *Proc. Inst. Production Engineers* XIV. 158 Process and rate department (under chief process engineer). **1948** W. H. Schutt *Process Engin.* i. 1 The process engineer must visualize exactly how the article should be made and what equipment, tools, and floor space are required. **1960** *McGraw-Hill Encycl. Sci. & Technol.* X. 642/2 Process specifications are set by process engineers (as distinguished from product engineers) and cover just how processes are to be controlled. **1948** W. H. Schutt (*title*) Process engineering. **1980** *Jrnl. R. Soc. Arts* May 326/2 'Design for Production' is a discipline which involves both product and process engineering. **1923** H. A. Maddox *Printing* x. 126 Process engravers usually adapt their filters to certain ink standards. **1951** R. G. Radford *Letterpress Machine Work* II. xii. 127 Discoveries..have made it possible for the process engraver to make a set of three- or four-colour half-tone plates by photo-mechanical means. **1894** *Amer. Dict. Printing & Bookmaking* 464/1 *Process printing or engraving*, a method by which engravings are made by the aid of photography. **1965** *Listener* 23 Sept. 462/3 The year was 1872, when..*Punch's* tentative introduction of process engraving first heralded the disappearance of the laborious procedure of reproducing line drawings by wood engraving. **1933** E. Molloy *Newnes Engin. Pract.* III. 794/2 The faster the machine..ran, the greater the amount of steam that would be available for process heat. **1947** O. Lyle *Efficient Use of Steam* xx. 597 The two principal uses of process heat are for the heating of water or watery solutions and for the evaporation of water. **1971** *Materials & Technol.* II. xii. 751 Steam generators which raise steam for process heat operate from 15 to about 150 p.s.i. **1926** S. I. Levy *Introd. Industr. Chem.* iii. 65 (*heading*) Process heating by steam. **1971** *Materials & Technol.* II. xii. 751 Steam has found considerable employment as a heat carrier for process heating. It can easily be ducted from a boiler to the vessel or column wherein the processes take place. **1951** *Industr. & Engin. Chem.* Dec. 2695 (*heading*) Quality control in the process industries. **1926** Process ink [see *process colour* above]. **1974** J. Craig *Production for Graphic Designer* 109 Because process inks are transparent, it is the light reflected from the paper's surface that supplies the light to the ink. **1902** *Encycl. Brit.* XXXI. 696/2 In the 'Process' lens, Series V. *f*/8, the combination is adjusted to secure identical size and sharpness of each colour-image in three-colour process work. **1961** Process lens [see *colour correction* s.v. *colour *sb.*[1] 18]. **1900** *Fortn. Rev.* Jan. 65 Engraving..as a profession, and as a means of obtaining fame, has entirely died out; the engraver nowadays is a process-maker. **1972** W. P. Lehmann in *Language* XLVIII. 267, I should like to propose that support for a process model of language has been provided by recent typological studies. *Ibid.* 269 In a process-model grammar of language, nominal modifiers are introduced by embedding. **1977** *Trans. Philol. Soc. 1975* 23 The earliest generative ('process morphophonemic') solution I know of to this problem is that of Bloomfield (1933, §13.9). **1967** C. Michalson *Worldly Theol.* i. 19 Daniel Day Williams..was the first theologian to bring the process motifs into combination with other theological traditions. **1958** *IRE Trans. Industr. Electronics* VII. 23/1 Process operations are characterized by the continuous and cyclic handling of large liquid, gas, and bulk flow streams. **1941** W. M. Urban in P. A. Schilpp *Philos. Whitehead* 319 The general group of modern philosophies which are called process philosophies, philosophies, which, in Bergson's terms, find more of reality in becoming than in that which becomes. **1949** B. M. Loomer in D. Brown et al. *Process Philos. & Christian Thought* (1971) 76 The second criticism..runs to the effect that process philosophy, being a kind of naturalism and consequently predisposed in favour of continuity of explanation, neglects the discontinuous qualities of existence. **1960** *Times Lit. Suppl.* 15 Apr. p. xv/2 Dr. Pittenger's Christology seems to be the product of a combination of panentheism, process philosophy, and Christian existentialism. **1971** D. Brown et al. *Process Philos. & Christian Thought* p. v, In recent years, however, process philosophy has come to mean especially, though not exclusively, the philosophy of Alfred North Whitehead and his intellectual descendants, most notably Charles Hartshorne. **1940** *Jrnl. Soc. Motion Picture Engineers* XXXIV. 252 The origination of a combination of projectors superimposing identical prints of the same background on the screen simultaneously compounded the light delivery of a single machine and therefore greatly expanded the scope of background process photography. **1970** C. C. Ammonds *Printing: Basic Sci.* x. 158 Correction for two colours in the achromatic lens is adequate for the simpler forms of color photography, but for process photography..much greater correction is necessary. **1928** C. S. Darling *Exhaust Steam Engin.* ix. 188 It is..possible in a process plant to obtain useful heat from the condenser of a turbine. **1894** *Amer. Dict. Printing & Bookmaking* 460/2 A number of photographers and printers..hope that they can print direct from process plates. **1931** R. R. Karch *Printing & Allied Trades* xvi. 162 Four-color process plates are used in printing most of the magazine advertisements in color. **1965** Zigrosser & Gaehde *Guide to Collecting Orig. Prints* iv. 71 All prints made by photomechanical methods are called process prints. **1901** *Edin. Rev.* Apr. 551 A few..were found ready to submit their work to the uncertainties and vagaries of the process-printer. **1931** R. R. Karch *Printing & Allied Trades* xvi. 161 *Process printing.* By the use of three transparent colors, red, yellow, and blue, illustrations may be printed that contain all the colours of the rainbow. **1962** L. M. Larsen *Industr. Printing Inks* ii. 33 With the coming of process printing..it has been necessary to use high color strength inks. **1974** J. Craig *Production for Graphic Designer* 105 Four-color process printing is the method used to reproduce full-color continuous-tone copy. **1939** *Jrnl. Soc. Motion Picture Engineers* XXXII. 589 Developments in process projection equipment and technology. **1951** A. Cornwell-Clyne *Colour Cinematogr.* (ed. 3) vii. 583 Process projection, called in Britain 'background projection', a somewhat more precise description, assumed great importance economically in ratio to the continuous rise in the cost of film production. *Ibid.*, Process projection, as a technique, was evolved for the purpose of dispensing with the necessity of location photography. **1977** *Times Lit. Suppl.* 29 Apr. 525/3 There are eight steel engravings after Turner, reproduced absolutely facsimile—line for line. This is close to the edge of possibility in process reproduction. **1962** *Psychol. Bull.* LIX. 329/1 Process schizophrenia involves a long-term progressive deterioration..with little chance of recovery. **1967** Hilgard & Atkinson *Introd. Psychol.* (ed. 4) xxi. 536/2 They hypothesized that process schizophrenia..might be caused by some sort of brain damage..; consequently process schizophrenics might respond..in a manner similar to patients with diagnosed brain damage. **1935** *Proc. Inst. Production Engineers* XIV. 165 Process sheets are drawn up showing the operations to be performed on each component in their correct sequence. **1953** J. J. Rose *Amer. Cinematographer Hand-bk. & Ref. Guide* (ed. 8) 150 Process shots have been the means of saving studios considerable production time and expense in filming scenes for pictures having a foreign locale. **1960** K. Amis *New Maps of Hell* ii. 61 Slow-motion process shots of newts. **1973** D. A. Spencer *Focal Dict. Photographic Technol.* 492 *Process shot*, studio film shot in which a still or moving background is rear projected on to a translucent screen in front of which the action takes place—also called transparency process. **1924** *Power Engineer* XIX. 454/2 In view of the scattered nature of the works, it is not advantageous to attempt to collect condensed process steam. **1954** E. Molloy *Power & Process-Steam Plant* i. 4 Breweries require large amounts of process steam. **1963** A. Jaganmohan tr. *Shlyakhin's Steam Turbines* xi. 160/1 Back-pressure turbines are used..where both electrical energy and process steam are required at the same time. **1972** D. A. Pailin in Cox & Dyson *20th-Cent. Mind* III. iv. 130 Process theism cannot deal adequately with the nature of God's actuality. **1974** M. Wiles *Remaking of Christian Doctrine* vi. 110 For the process theologian there is no essential problem about the transcendent God's activity in the world. **1977** *Theology* LXXX. 187 The North American process theologians would say..the world is a dynamic totality of events..and not of things. **1971** D. Brown et al. *Process Philos. & Christian Thought* p. vi, When process theology is talked about in American (and to some extent British) theological schools today, Bergson, Berdyaev and Teilhard may be in the background, but the work of Whitehead, Hartshorne, Ogden and Cobb is primarily in mind. **1975** *Times Lit. Suppl.* 15 Aug. 926/2 Process theology, in which God is in a state of *becoming*, has been shown to be anything but Christian. **1977** F. Young in J. Hick *Myth of God Incarnate* ii. 42 Evolutionary theology and process theology are not foreign to the Christian tradition. **1977** *Theology* LXXX. 189 There is, in Whitehead, Hartshorne, and other process thinkers, a full recognition of the reality of natural evil as well as of moral evil and man's sinfulness. **1972** D. A. Pailin in Cox & Dyson *20th-Cent. Mind* III. iv. 123 Charles Hartshorne..has been the leading exponent of the 'process' view of God... Whitehead is the father of process thought. **1966** *McGraw-Hill Encycl. Sci. & Technol.* X. 642/1 Processes have..been classified into continuous or process-type operations, as in an oil refinery, and intermittent (or repetitive) or manufacturing-type operations. **1972** Process view [see *process thought* above]. **1928** *Rep. Water Pollution Res. Board 1927–8* 9 In some factories..alternative methods are employed by which the production of process water is avoided. **1949** G. E. H. Lewis *Factory Steam Plant* iii. 46 Where process water heating is not feasible the air preheater merits consideration. **1978** *Environmental Conservation: Chemicals* (Shell Internat. Petroleum Co.) 2 This has been achieved mainly by segregating contaminated process water from the usually much larger volume of uncontaminated storm and cooling water, and..by re-using and recycling process water. **1924** C. A. Suckan *Supervision & Maintenance of Steam-Raising Plant* v. 77 Where steam is used for process work such as boiling. **1908** C. T. Jacobi *Printing* (ed. 4) xxiv. 251 The process worker will have arranged his screens at..angular distances for the respective colours. **1974** *Nature* 15 Feb. 421/1 In England the death of a 71 year-old former process worker at ICI is being investigated in order to establish whether or not it was caused by long exposure to the fumes of the monomer.

process, *v.*[1] Add: **3. a.** (Further examples.) Also, to operate on (data) (cf. *data processing* s.v. *datum 3). Also *fig.*

1948 A. Toynbee *Civilization on Trial* 84 The form in which this culture has been 'processed' for export. **1957** *B.B.C. Handbk.* 47 The News Bureau..selects and processes news and other items of urgent information for transmission by teleprinter to the news departments. **1958** *Newnes Compl. Amat. Photogr.* 283 Pakolor film can be processed by the user. **1959** *Times Lit. Suppl.* 27 Feb. 109/3 Mr. Morgan presents a deliberately narrowed vision of life, where every detail is 'processed' to fit. **1960** E. DELAVENAY *Introd. Machine Translation* 122 Language data are indeed processed not only with translation in mind but with the aim of obtaining the widest and deepest penetration of such facts as the relationships between words. **1968** *Brit. Med. Bull.* XXIV. 189/2 Only data which can be explicitly formulated..can be processed by a computer. **1968** *Listener* 4 July 17/3 Rock music is the most efficient medium of creative expression. A song can be composed, processed and broadcast round the world in a week. **1970** *Daily Tel.* 20 May 2/4 The heart of the system is a computer which processes radio signals and continually plots the airliner's position on a moving chart. **1971** *Nature* 11 June 344/1 It may take two months for this volume of vaccine to be processed. **1972** *Language* XLVIII. 271 The right hemisphere of the human brain can also process oral symbols for concrete nouns. But only the hemisphere with a specialized speech center can process verbs. **1976** P. HILL *Hunters* v. 43 We're processing the statements that have already been taken.

b. To subject (a person) to a process, as of registration, examination, or analysis. orig. *U.S.*

1935 *Sun* (Baltimore) 16 Apr. 4/1, 900 applicants were put through medical examinations and transported to army camps to be 'processed'. **1945** H. L. MENCKEN *Amer. Lang.* Suppl. I. 417 *To process*, now threatens to take its place in the language alongside *to contact*... The New Dealers gave it a much wider range..widening it to include human beings among its objects. It has since been adopted..both in its older sense of doing something to inanimate materials and in its new sense of mauling and manipulating God's creatures. **1948** D. SOIBELMAN *Therapeutic & Industr. Uses of Music* vi. 132 One physician has reported that, since installing music in his waiting room, he has found the average time taken to process a patient reduced by..one-half. **1954** *Manch. Guardian Weekly* 23 Dec. 15/3 All Chinese students..including those whose cases are still being processed, are completely free to travel anywhere in the United States. **1959** *Times Lit. Suppl.* 27 Mar. 173/2 Maupassant, Lautrec, Gauguin—one by one the wild boys are being expertly processed, attractively jacketed, to emerge as items suitable for ticking off on library lists. **1977** *Detroit Free Press* 11 Dec. 21-A/2 Officials at the center said 12 victims were processed there.

processed *ppl. a* (further examples); *processed cheese* = *process cheese* s.v. *PROCESS *sb.* 13 b; **processing** *vbl. sb.* (further examples); also *attrib.*

1912 *U.S. Dept. Agric. Yearbk. 1911* 387 Processing consists in heating the cans to a sufficiently high temperature to insure the preservation of their contents. **1918** THOM & FISK *Bk. Cheese* vi. 84 *Processed cheeses.* Cheese of any group may be run through mixing and molding machines and re-packaged in very different form from that characteristic of the variety... The possible variations are numerous. **1933** *Sun* (Baltimore) 15 July 1/6 He accordingly proclaimed August 1 as..the date upon which the processing tax should become operative. **1936** *Discovery* May 157/1 A well-prepared wood or esparto paper can be more permanent than a carelessly processed rag paper. **1958** *Newnes Compl. Amat. Photogr.* 280 Use a film for which processing kits are available. **1958** *Times Lit. Suppl.* 29 Aug. 478/4 It is instructive, if unedifying, to follow the tergiversations and admire the polemical acrobatics of various practitioners of the art of literary processing, notably of that arch-processor V. Yermilov. **1960** Processed pea [see *garden-pea* s.v. *GARDEN *sb.* 6]. **1964** L. DEIGHTON *Funeral in Berlin* xxxviii. 231 His processed cheese sandwiches. **1966** A. YOUNG in *Spero* I. ii. 19 He sat behind me in Homeroom, sportshirt, creased pants, shiny black pointy-toed stetsons, jacket, processed hair. **1972** *Daily Tel.* 29 Apr. 12/1 The fully-automated, processed tourist rarely visits Genoa. **1977** B. PYM *Quartet in Autumn* vii. 63 Fresh vegetables..would be better than processed peas. **1977** J. HEDGECOE *Photographer's Handbk.* 70 (*caption*) Various types of processing drum are made for color prints. **1979** *SLR Camera* Jan. 43/1 The catalogue almost swells at the seams with such goodies as processing drums, colour analysers, printing filters, [etc.].

process, *v.*[2] Add: **1.** (Further examples.)

1902 *To-Day* 20 Aug. 113/1 Neither Barnum nor the new Lord Mayor will be able to process this year. **1912** A. HUXLEY *Let.* 23 June (1969) 46 On the Bismarck Tower a bonfire was lighted and 1000 odd students processed from the tower to the University. **1953** H. NICOLSON *Diary* 4 July (1968) 242 We process in robes to the City Hall where there are many graduands. **1962** G. MOORE *Am I too Loud?* xxxiii. 254 The vision of our young and beautiful Queen processing slowly up the aisle in her gorgeous robes is never to be forgotten. **1971** K. THOMAS *Relig. & Decline of Magic* iii. 63 They also involved processing across the field with cross, banners and bells to drive away evil spirits and bless the crops.

2. *trans.* To lead or carry (a person, etc.) in procession; to traverse (an area) in procession.

1959 *Times* 10 Dec. 14/7 The Lord of Miracles is solemnly processed all round the city. **1968** D. M. SMITH *Mod. Sicily* lii. 484 The flagellants then processed the streets as they had done in 1647 and 1773. **1974** D. AVERY *Not on Queen Victoria's Birthday* vii. 117 Most of the families left their feasting to attend the sermon in the church under the impression that the saint was to be processed afterwards.

Hence **proce·ssing** *vbl. sb.* and *ppl. a.*

1920 *Blackw. Mag.* Dec. 712/2 The bowings and curtseyings and processings and workings of the Puddispor congregation could have told anybody *that!* **1959** *Antiquity* XXXIII. 19 A single row of processing animals. **1977** *Gramophone* May 1724/2 So we must be prepared for ..the shuffling of processing feet, the coughing and the tramping of the congregation.

processable (prōu·sĕsăb'l), *a.* [f. PROCESS *v.*[1] + -ABLE.] That can be processed. Hence **pro:cessabi·lity**, the capacity to be processed.

1956 *Industr. & Engin. Chem.* May 930/1 Processing studies of Adiprene B urethane rubber have resulted in an understanding of a number of the factors required for processability. *Ibid.* 932/1 They become progressively tougher and more viscous while remaining 'processable' even in an advanced state of scorch. **1965** J. R. SCOTT *Physical Testing of Rubbers* ii. 45 Examples of this empirical approach to the problems of measuring processability are the procedures developed in the U.S.A. for the wartime synthetic rubber program. **1967** COX & GROSE *Organiz. Bibliogr. Rec. by Computer* vii. 183 This may help us in problems of transmission of machine processable cataloguing data. **1971** P. M. HUBBARD *High Tide* ii. 24, I was a sort of raw material, which had not proved as processable as they had hoped.

processer, var. *PROCESSOR.

procession, *sb.* Add: **1. c.** (See also quot. 1937.)

1937 PARTRIDGE *Dict. Slang* 661/1 *Procession*, as applied to a race, esp. a boat-race (above all, one in which there are only two crews), implies 'an ignominious defeat'. **1958** *Times* 22 Sept. 14/2 Although she [*sc.* the British yacht] made up half a minute..it was obvious that..it could not now be anything more than a procession.

d. *Cricket.* A rapid succession of batsmen; a batting collapse.

1891 W. G. GRACE *Cricket* iii. 76 West Gloucestershire [scored] 6 only. Only nine overs were bowled, and it was a most inglorious procession. **1927** M. A. NOBLE *Those 'Ashes'* 210 The Civil Service first innings was almost a procession. They were able to make only 59. **1977** *Times* 17 Jan. 7/1 The Australian procession started when Turner was caught by Majid off Sarfraz for 11.

processional, *a.* Add: **b.** (Later example.) Also, traversed by a procession or processions.

1906 H. BEGBIE *Priest* viii. 124 The sound of a heavy step approaching from the processional aisle on the south caught her ear. **1942** *Country Life* 9 Oct. 695/1 (*caption*) Processional way to Buckingham Palace from Victoria Station. **1973** *Times* 15 Oct. 4 Thieves broke into St Albans Abbey, Hertfordshire, on Saturday night and stole..the silver gilt top of a processional cross.

processionally, *adv.* (Further examples.)

1851 G. B. PAGANI *Life of Rev. A. Gentili* III. ix. 190 Father Gentili commenced the custom of going processionally on Sundays and singing the Litany of the Holy Name of Jesus, from the chapel at Gracedieu all the way to Osgothorpe. **1895** 'MARK TWAIN' in *N. Amer. Rev.* July 10 There were now three bullets in that one hole—three bullets imbedded processionally. **1936** G. B. SHAW *Simpleton* II. 59 (*stage directions*) Kanchin and Janga enter processionally, reading newspapers. **1960** R. W. MARKS *Dymaxion World of B. Fuller* 8/1 In Fuller's special argot, however, 'regenerative' means 'multi-orbital, cyclic, processionally concentric'—a definition which itself requires definition.

processioner. 4. (Earlier examples.)

1731 *Bristol Parish* (Va.) *Vestry Bk.* (1898) 59 Order'd that George Tucker be Prosessioner in the Stead of Robert Tucker junr who is Lame and cannott Officiate as prosessioner. **1795** in L. P. Summers *Ann. Southwest Va.* (1929) 463 The said Processioners to examine their business the first day of February next. **1828** W. BOLLING in *Va. Mag. Hist. & Biogr.* (1938) XLVI. 321 Attended the processioners around my lines..to the upper line between Dr. Watkins and myself.

processor (prōu·sesəɹ, *U.S.* prǫ·s-). Also **processer.** [f. PROCESS *sb.* + -OR.] **a.** A person who performs a process. **b.** A machine or system which performs a process. Cf. *microprocessor* s.v. *MICRO- 1.

1909 M. B. SAUNDERS *Litany Lane* ii. 10 Her tragic face..was already being 'blocked' for the night's press in many a rushing 'processor's' den. **1934** *Planning* I. xx. 5 Various industries handling agricultural products between the first processor and the consumer have recently been turned over to the N R A. **1948** *Times* 2 Mar. 2/3 [The] film processor..was sentenced to 21 months' imprisonment. **1959** *Times* 9 Mar. (Britain's Food Suppl.) p. xviii/1 Processors of Vegetable Oils for the Biscuit and Margarine Industries. **1960** *Farmer & Stockbreeder* 5 Jan. 53/2 It would provide the foundation on which producers and processers could develop quality and reduce costs. **1962** *Times* 9 Oct. (Uganda Suppl.) p. v/4 African processers have invested considerable sums in permanent salting vats. **1977** *New Yorker* 29 Aug. 62/2 Any program that runs on the system can access any information physically accessible to the (central) processor. **1978** *Homes & Gardens* Oct. 140/1 Food processors, or kitchen machines..are food choppers and slicers with some abilities at mixing.

processual, *a.* Restrict *Roman Law* to sense in Dict. and add: **b.** Pertaining to a social or linguistic process.

1957 R. K. MERTON *Social Theory* (rev. ed.) ix. 316 An instructive processual analysis of the formation of subgroups. **1958** WILLEY & PHILLIPS *Method & Theory in Amer. Anthropol.* 5 In the context of archaeology, processual interpretation is the study of the nature of what is vaguely referred to as the culture-historical process... It implies an attempt to discover regularities in the relationships given by the methods of culture-historical integration. **1960** *Amer. Anthropologist* LXII. 19 How processual analysis might be more systematically related to structural analysis. **1970** *Antiquity* XLIV. 28/1 In both these works..historical activities tend to be viewed as being essentially descriptive, while the ultimate aims of archaeology are characterized as being processual, that is to say, concerned with the formulation of general rules of cultural behaviour. **1971** [see *PROCESS *sb.* 5 b]. **1977** *Word 1972* XXVIII. 295 Since understanding sentences, and generating others, in the language described implies constant switches from process to system and from system to process..he will have to find the most reasonable compromise between the requirements of systematic and processual simplicity.

prochlorperazine (prǫkloɹpe·răzīn). *Pharm.* [f. PRO(PYL- + CHLOR- + *PI)PERAZINE.] A pale yellow viscous liquid which is used, usu. in the form of one of its salts, as a tranquillizer; 2-chloro-10-[3-(4-methylpiperazin-1-yl)-propyl]phenothiazine, $C_{20}H_{24}ClN_3S$.

1958 *Psychiatric Res. Rep.* IX. 23 Proc[h]lorperazine treatment of psychotic patients was begun at Longview Hospital in November, 1955. **1959** *Jrnl. Amer. Med. Assoc.* 16 May 361/1 Caffeine and sodium benzoate seems to be an effective and rapidly acting antagonist to the toxic manifestations of prochlorperazine. **1977** *Lancet* 9 July 94/2 Dizziness and vomiting can be avoided by intravenous prochlorperazine 12·5 mg given 5 min before the mexiletine injection.

prochromosome (prōukrōu·mǭsōum). *Cytology.* Also with hyphen. [ad. G. *prochromosom* (J. B. Overton 1905, in *Jahrb. f. wissensch. Bot.* XLII. 126): see PRO-[2] and *CHROMOSOME.] One of the densely staining heterochromatic masses seen in certain interphase nuclei, frequently associated with centromeres; = *CHROMOCENTRE.

1906 *Proc. R. Soc.* B. LXXVII. 557 These bodies correspond in fact exactly to what in 1904 we have already described as the Anlagen of the premaiotic chromosomes in the corresponding cells in the testes of Periplaneta, and there can be no doubt that they represent also the structures subsequently alluded to as prochromosomes by Overton, Miyake, and Strasburger in the same stage in certain mono- and dicotyledonous plants. **1907** *Ann. Bot.* XXI. 335 In certain plants there is a tendency of the chromatin to form lumps or masses in the resting condition, in which there is often a general uniformity in size, and when the number of such lumps approaches the number of somatic chromosomes, each mass has been looked upon by some as representing a prochromosome, or the centre of organization of a chromosome. **1934** [see *EUCHROMOCENTRE]. **1965** A. K. & A. SHARMA *Chromosome Techniques* viii. 205 The number of prochromosomes may be equal to, or if fused, less than, the number of chromosomes in the complement. **1969** BROWN & BERTKE *Textbk. Cytol.* i. 8/2 Flemming (1882) illustrated stained nodes in the nuclear network... Overton named them *prochromosomes* in 1905 and 3 years later Baccarini called them *chromocenters*; both names are still in use.

procidence. Add: Now usu. as mod.L. **procidentia.** Freq. distinguished from *prolapse* or restricted to the more severe kinds (see quots.).

1607 TOPSELL *Four-f. Beasts* 388 Another disease called *Procidentia ani*, that is to say, the falling out of the fundament. **1829** S. COOPER *Good's Study of Med.* (ed. 3) V. 146 If the descent [of the uterus] be only to the middle of the vagina, it is called *relaxatio uteri*; if to the labiæ, *procidentia*; if lower than the labiæ, *prolapsus*. The distinction is of trifling importance. **1888** A. H. N. LEWERS *Pract. Text-bk. Dis. Women* viii. 113 When the uterus has partly, or wholly passed the orifice of the vulva, the case is called one of 'procidentia'. *Ibid.* 114 In extreme cases of procidentia the whole uterus lies outside. **1903** J. P. TUTTLE *Treat. Dis. Anus* xvii. 667 Procidentia..is practically always applied to those cases in which all the coats of the bowel descend. **1956** H. E. BACON et al. *Proctology* xviii. 215 The difference between prolapse and procidentia lies in the coats of the bowel involved. *Ibid.* 218 Protruding through the anal orifice, procidentia is diagnosed from a series of circular folds irregularly placed. **1974** PASSMORE & ROBSON *Compan. Med. Stud.* III. xxviii. 62/2 In third degree prolapse (procidentia) the whole uterus lies outside the introitus.

procidentia: see prec.

Procion (prōu·siǫn). A proprietary name for any of a large class of reactive dyestuffs based on 1,3,5-triazine and covering a wide range of colours. Usu. *attrib.*

1956 *Trade Marks Jrnl.* 23 May 424/1 *Procion*... Dyes, dyestuffs and colouring matters, none being for laundry or toilet purposes. Imperial Chemical Industries Limited, ..London, S.W.1; Manufacturers and Merchants—10th February 1956. **1957** *Listener* 18 July 73 (Advt.), Polythene, for instance,..bright and fast new dyes like the 'Procion' range... They're all I.C.I. discoveries, you know. **1957** *Official Gaz.* (U.S. Patent Office) 23 July TM 129/1 *Procion*... For dyes, dyestuffs, and colouring matters. **1971** R. L. M. ALLEN *Colour Chem.* xiii. 205 Procion dyes provide a complete range of shades in both the M and H series. **1974** *Sci. Amer.* Jan. 41/1 The branching patterns of a cell can be traced by injecting the fluorescent dye Procion yellow or by stimulating and then recording from its axons in roots and connectives. **1976** *Nature* 25 Mar. 338/2 Procion dye was injected intracellularly by iontophoresis to determine axonal morphology of one or two cells in a particular brain.

Proclian (prǫ·kliăn), *a.* Also **Pro·cline** (-ləin). Of or relating to Proclus (A.D. ?410–85), a neo-Platonist philosopher and head of the Athenian school after Plutarch and Syrianus, his views, or works.

1912 F. von Hügel *Eternal Life* vii. 118 We find in Eckhart a..scientific, still predominantly Proclian, thirst for intellectual utter simplicity and clearness. **1951** *Mind* LX. 417 The Proclian *Liber de causis*. **1967** I. P. Sheldon-Williams in A. H. Armstrong *Cambr. Hist. Later Greek & Early Med. Philos.* 477 The Procline Neoplatonism had worked out those implications. *Ibid.*, The enemies were..the Procline theology based on polytheism, and the Procline theurgy deriving from the belief in a supernatural power inherent in the phenomenal world.

procli·max. *Ecol.* [f. Pro-² 1 + *climax *sb.* 4 b.] (See quot. 1938.) Also *attrib.*

1934 F. E. Clements in *Jrnl. Ecol.* XXII. 45 For those cases in which the community is modified and held for a more or less indefinite period in some other condition, the term 'proclimax' is suggested. **1938** Weaver & Clements *Plant Ecol.* (ed. 2) xviii. 480 Proclimax is a general term which includes all the communities that simulate the climax to some extent..but lack the proper sanction of the existing climate. It thus includes subclimax, preclimax, and postclimax, as well as disclimax. **1951** *Jrnl. Ecol.* XXXIX. 81 The pro-climax communities of Mediterranean cliffs..develop directly from the crustose-lichen stage. **1975** R. H. Whittaker *Communities & Ecosystems* (ed. 2) iv. 182 These may be termed 'subclimaxes', or 'proclimaxes' of various sorts, in Clements' treatment.

Procline: see *Proclian *a.*

proclisis (prō·klisis). *Gram.* [mod.L., f. Gr. πρό forward + κλίσις, f. κλίνειν to lean.] Pronunciation as a proclitic; the transference of stress to a following word.

1893 J. Clark *Man. Linguistics* vi. 158 The existence of proclisis, which naturally is lifted in emphatic positions, οὐ freeing itself at the end of a sentence. **1955** *Archivum Linguisticum* VII. ii. 135 The facts of enclisis and proclisis in Polish are generally on the same lines as in Czech. **1964** *Language* XL. 276 Since he objects to the application of the idea of proclisis as well as enclisis, he keeps to the terms 'anteposition' and 'postposition' in referring to the placing of the pronoun with respect to the verb.

proclitic, *a.* and *sb.* Add: **A.** *adj.* (Further example.)

1973 A. H. Sommerstein *Sound Pattern Anc. Greek* ii. 11 Prepositions, being proclitic, are separated from the following word by a single # boundary.

Procne: see *Progne.

procoagulant: see *pro-² 1. **pro-Communist:** *pro-¹ 5a.

proconsul. Add: **3.** (See quot.)

1939 *Sunday Times* 8 Jan. 13/1 A pro-Consul..is a resident member of a British trading community abroad, generally a shipping agent or merchant of repute.

4. Usu. with initial capital. [A. T. Hopwood 1933, in *Ann. Mag. Nat. Hist.* 10th Ser. XI. 98.] An extinct ape belonging to the genus so called, known from Miocene fossil remains discovered in East Africa by Louis Leakey (1903–72) in 1932.

1933 *Jrnl. Linn. Soc.: Zool.* XXXVIII. 457 It would seem that the dentition of *Proconsul* is more primitive than that of the chimpanzee. **1954** *New Biol.* XVII. 12 The remains of fossil apes are especially abundant [on Rusinga Island in Lake Victoria],..of which the most famous has been *Proconsul*. **1962** *Listener* 5 Apr. 589/1 This animal, which has been named Proconsul, existed approximately 25,000,000 years ago. **1973** J. Bronowski *Ascent of Man* i. 38 A classical find made by Louis Leakey goes by the dignified name of *Proconsul*... (The name *Proconsul*..was coined to suggest he was an ancestor of a famous chimpanzee at the London Zoo in 1931 whose nickname was Consul.) **1977** A. Hallam *Planet Earth* 284 Proconsul, an animal about the size of a small baboon, is known from a good skull, jaws and some limb bones.

proconsulate. b. (Later example.)

1933 G. Arthur *Septuagenarian's Scrap Bk.* 243 The soldier whose proconsulate was extended for over two years and who was then wistfully asked if he would not come back again.

proconsulship. (Later example.)

1976 *Church Times* 25 June 11/4 The only absolutely firm date in the whole of the New Testament is the proconsulship of Gallio, shown by an inscription to have begun in the early summer of 51.

proconvertin: see *pro-² 1.

procreator. (Later example.)

1975 *Way* Suppl. xxv. 12 In the sexual union, man and woman under God become procreators.

procrypsis (prokri·psis). *Zool.* [f. Pro- (cf. Procryptic *a.*) + Gr. κρύψις concealment.] Protective colouring in animals.

1920 G. D. H. Carpenter *Naturalist on L. Victoria* 196 Procryptic colouring conceals its wearer from danger, causing it to resemble either the general surroundings or some particular part thereof (Special Procrypsis). **1933** *Discovery* Nov. 357/2 The resemblance of creatures to their environment..technically termed Procrypsis. **1946** *Nature* 24 Aug. 278/1 Is resemblance to part of a dead ant to be sharply separated from resemblance to a whole, living ant? To a Darwinian, one is an example of special procrypsis, while the other is pseudoaposematic. **1977** M. Tweedie *Insect Life* ii. 74 We see among them [*sc.* insects] the first stages of the type of adaptation commonly known as camouflage, but among biologists as cryptic adaptation or procrypsis.

procto-. Add: **proctoscope, -scopic** *a.* (earlier examples); **procto·scopy,** use of, or examination with, a proctoscope.

1896 *Mathews' Med. Q.* III. 203 A little practice in Kelly's method teaches the operator how to carry the end of the proctoscope away from the prostate. *Ibid.* 208 The proctoscopic mirror faces the operator. *Ibid.* 332 A central aperture, which..escaped my own digital perception..and was not discovered until subsequently revealed by proctoscopy. **1977** *Lancet* 21 May 1085/1 The diagnosis of inflammatory bowel disease was..confirmed at proctoscopy.

proctology (prǫktǫ·lŏdʒi). [f. Procto- + -logy.] The branch of medicine concerned with the anus and rectum or (with some writers) with the anus and the whole colon.

1899 *Trans. Ohio State Med. Soc.* 257 Thos. Chas. Martin M.D. Cleveland. Teacher of Proctology in the Cleveland College of Physicians and Surgeons; Proctologist to the Cleveland General Hospital. **1929** W. E. Minor *Clin. Proctology* iv. 37 Some years ago I adopted a terminology which recognizes only one type of hemorrhoid. I find this solution very acceptable and helpful to the student of proctology. **1956** H. E. Bacon et al. *Proctology* p. ix, The late Joseph M. Mathews defined proctology as the science that treats of surgical diseases of colon, rectum and anal canal. **1959** K. Zimmerman in R. Turell *Dis. Colon & Anorectum* II. lviii. 1195 The practice of 'office proctology', or 'ambulant proctology', was for many years in the hands of charlatans. **1976** *Times* 29 Apr. 18/4 The section of proctology of the Royal Society of Medicine held their annual dinner at 1 Wimpole Street, yesterday evening.

Hence **proctolo·gic, proctolo·gical** *adjs.*; **procto·logist,** an expert or specialist in proctology.

1899 *Trans. Amer. Proctologic Soc.* I. p. v, Article I. The name of this Association shall be the *American Proctologic Society*. Article II. Its object shall be the cultivation and promotion of knowledge in whatever relates to Disease of the Rectum and colon. **1899** *Ohio State Jrnl.* 8 June 3/1 A new national medical association to be known as the American Proctological society was organized yesterday. **1899** Proctologist [see above]. **1907** *Proctologist* I. 1 No medical work..is complete, today, that does not deal fully and explicitly with proctological diseases. **1926** L. J. Hirschman *Handbk. Dis. Rectum* (ed. 4) 7 As efficient diagnostic and therapeutic service should be rendered to the proctologic patient as to any other. **1950** J. P. Nesselrod *Proctology* ii. 54 Proctologists are not yet in full accord..with regard to the extent of their field. **1959** K. Zimmerman in R. Turell *Dis. Colon & Anorectum* II. lviii. 1195 Many..proctologic conditions may be treated in the office. **1964** *Punch* 26 Aug. 307/2 Proctologists, who are admired as working in a gold mine. **1971** *Dis. Colon & Rectum* XIV. 8/2 Barium-enema examination and proctologic evaluation were requested. **1979** *Guardian* 9 Jan. 8/5 Mr Carter's own proctological history. **1980** S. Stein *Resort* i. 14 Politicians are assholes attended by proctologists.

procto·rially, *adv.* [f. Proctorial *a.* + -ly².] In a proctorial capacity; in the manner of a proctor.

1883 H. S. Holland in S. Paget *H. S. Holland* (1921) iii. iv. 290 You speak of a deeper sense of the power of evil—I have felt it proctorially. **1971** F. R. Leavis in *Human World* Aug. 5 As for myself and Cambridge, I haven't to complain that I suffered..proctorially enforced oppression.

Proctor (prǫ·ktəɹ). The name of Robert George Collier *Proctor* (1863–1903), English bibliographer, used *attrib.* or in the possessive in **Proctor method** = *Proctor('s) order*; **Proctor number,** the number assigned to an early printed book in Proctor's *Index*; **Proctor('s) order,** a system of classifying early printed books geographically and chronologically, first used in the *Index to the Early Printed Books in the British Museum* (1898–1938) begun by Proctor.

[**1903** *Library* IV. 195 Proctor's 'Index'..is arranged under towns and countries in chronological order.] **1904** A. W. Pollard in *Library* V. 22, I think it was Baer of Frankfurt who first gave the author the pleasure of seeing a 'Proctor number' quoted side by side with that of Hain. **1931** M. R. Stilwell *Incunabula & Americana* 22 In the majority of instances, it will be found that Proctor's order prevails in whatever place-entry bibliography one may wish to consult. **1934** A. Esdaile *National Libraries of World* i. 18 Incunabula..gathered by Robert Proctor into one room..and arranged by order of countries, towns, presses, and date, an arrangement now often called 'Proctor order'. **1952** J. Carter *ABC for Bk.-Collectors* 143 *Proctor's order*, the classification of early printed books, on scientific typographical principles, by country, town and printer. **1955** *N. & Q.* May 229/1 Henry Bradshaw..arranged the books in what he called his natural history method in bibliography; it meant the arrangement and classification of them as natural objects are classified. This arrangement is now popularly known as the Proctor method. **1961** T. Landau *Encycl. Librarianship* (ed. 2) 291/1 *Proctor order*, system of classification of incunabula named after the arrangement in R. G. C. Proctor's Index of early printed books in the British Museum. **1967** Cox & Grose *Organiz. & Handling Bibliogr. Rec. by Computer* 137 Since the end of the last century it has been customary to catalogue incunables in 'Proctor Order'.

proctotrupid (prǫktotrū·pid), *a.* and *sb. Ent.* Also **Procto-, -trypid.** [f. mod. L. family name *Proctotrupidæ*, f. generic name *Proctotrupes* (P. A. Latreille *Précis des Caractères génériques des Insectes* (1796) 108), f. Procto- + Gr. τρυπ-ᾶν to bore: see -id³.] **A.** *adj.* Of, pertaining to, or designating a proctotrupid. **B.** *sb.* A small wasp belonging to the family Proctotrupidæ or the superfamily Proctotrupoidea, which include parasitoids of insects and spiders.

1869 [in Dict. s.v. Procto-]. **1891** [see *chalcid *a.* and *sb.*]. **1932** Riley & Johannsen *Med. Entomol.* xxiv. 422 In California a little proctotrupid..invades houses in numbers in the fall. **1932** E. Step *Bees, Wasps, Ants Brit. Isles* 184 The wings are much simpler..in the Chalcids and Proctotrypids. **1972** L. E. Chadwick tr. *Linsenmaier's Insects of World* 300/2 Equally small and also at home in the water are a few proctotrupids.

proctotrupoid (prǫktotrū·poid). *Ent.* [f. mod.L. name of superfamily *Proctotrupoidea*: see prec. and -oid.] = *proctotrupid *sb.*

1954 Borror & DeLong *Introd. Study of Insects* xxix. 716 The proctotrupoids are not as common as the chalcids or ichneumons. **1971** R. R. Askew *Parasitic Insects* viii. 155 The great majority of proctotrupoids are endoparasites.

procumbent, *a.* Add: **3.** *Zool.* Of a tooth: lying along the jaw.

1874 T. C. Jerdon *Mammals of India* 62 Upper middle incisors distant; lower ones procumbent. **1902** *Encycl. Brit.* XXX. 506/1 In the lower jaw there is a single pair of procumbent incisors, followed by several small teeth representing the canine and early premolars. **1977** Roonwal & Mohnot *Primates S. Asia* 41 It holds small fruit in both hands while chewing, and larger food, such as an unpeeled banana, is chipped with its procumbent lower incisors. **1978** *Nature* 17 Aug. 663/1 Diplodocids had elongated tapering snouts with delicate, procumbent teeth for selecting smaller plant parts.

procuracy. Restrict †*Obs.* to other senses in Dict. and add: **1. a.** (Later example.)

1978 *Jrnl. R. Soc. Arts* CXXVI. 672/2 The rôle, function and powers of public security organs, the procuracy and the courts are more closely defined.

procurator. 2. a. For †*Obs.* read '*Obs.* except *Hist.*' and add later examples.

1897 Addis & Arnold *Cath. Dict.* (ed. 5) 761/2 The procurators or official agents of monasteries of nuns should not hold office more than three years. **1909** B. Ward *Dawn Cath. Revival* I. 55 The procurator [at Douay] was Rev. Gregory Stapleton, who had held that office since 1773. **1931** J. Clayton *St. Hugh of Lincoln* v. 35 The procurator was guest master... Other visitors to the Grande Chartreuse claimed the procurator's time... They loved him, Hugh the procurator, for the gracious speech and courteous treatment.

procurement. Add: **3.** *Mil.* The action or process of procuring equipment and supplies. Freq. *attrib.*

1957 [see *logistical *a.* 4]. **1958** *Times Rev. Industry* Mar. 9/2 Strategic materials on the active stockpiling list had reached their procurement priority levels by the middle of last year. **1966** *Amer. Speech* XLI. 300 It receives the plans and decisions of the Secretary of Defense and Secretary of the Air Force, and its own Chief of Staff, and translates them into training, logistic, and procurement programs. **1966** *Electronics* 17 Oct. 103 It is this growth in avionics complexity that is making military procurement officers insist on built-in test capability. **1977** *R.A.F. News* 30 Mar.–12 Apr. 10/4 It is then the task of the operational requirements staff to define the parameters in a detailed operational requirement which..is passed to the Procurement Executive who put it to industry to see how it can best be met.

procureur. Add: **c.** = Procurer 4.

1910 *Times* 29 Apr. 14/1 The procureurs (the cant name is 'ponce') at work in this country are mostly foreigners. **1979** W. J. Fishman *Streets East London* 52/2 Lodging houses infested by thieves, *procureurs* and prostitutes.

‖ **procureuse** (prokürö̈z). [Fr.] = Procuress 2.

1930 E. Waugh *Vile Bodies* vi. 105 What a coarse face..she looks like a *procureuse*. **1968** C. Cooper *Thunder & Lightning Man* iv. 52 Does she condone it?.. Is she just an old *procureuse*? **1977** 'R. Player' *Month of Mangled Models* vii. 123 She's only a common procureuse dressed like a duchess.

procurrent (prokɒ·rĕnt), *a. Ichthyol.* [ad. L. *procurrent-*, *procurrens*, pres. pple. of *procurrere* to run forward.] Of a fish's fin: having rays that are almost parallel.

1902 Jordan & Evermann *Amer. Food & Game Fishes* 538 Procurrent (fin). With the lower rays inserted progressively further forward. **1931** J. R. Norman *Hist. Fishes* iii. 72 True spines are never developed in this [caudal] fin, but rudimentary or procurrent rays resembling spines may be found at the base of the lobes.

procurvature. [f. Pro-² + Curvature.] = Procurvation.

1903 R. I. Pocock in *Ann. & Mag. Nat. Hist.* XI. 411 The species described by Keyserling as *Trechona pantherina* appears to me to be the female of *auromitens*, in spite of a less procurvature of the anterior line of eyes.

procuticle (prokiū·tik'l). [f. PRO-[2] + CUTICLE.] The inner, thicker layer of the cuticle of an arthropod, situated below the epicuticle and comprising the exocuticle (if present) and the endocuticle.

1951 A. G. RICHARDS *Integument of Arthropods* xvi. 148 The term procuticle is proposed for the embryologically original (parent) chitin-protein fraction. *Ibid.* 149 The procuticle may remain seemingly unchanged in soft transparent cuticle and soft areas.., in which case the fully formed cuticle is said to consist of epicuticle and endocuticle... Or the outer portion of the procuticle may become hardened and darkened by sclerotization, giving an outer dark exocuticle and an inner transparent endocuticle. **1959** W. ANDREW *Textbk. Compar. Histol.* iii. 91 It [*sc.* the cuticle of arthropods] presents a great diversity of structure but in general may be divided into an outer part without chitin, the 'epicuticle', and an inner part with chitin, the 'procuticle' or 'endocuticle'. **1962** GORDON & LAVOIPIERRE *Entomol.* ix. 53 The procuticle confers on the integument amongst other properties those of hardness and strength and is the real skeletal support of the body of the insect. **1967** [see *EXOCUTICLE a]. **1976** C. P. FRIEDLANDER *Biol. Insects* i. 16 When first secreted the entire procuticle is in the endocuticle condition; subsequently a large proportion of it is hardened.. to form the exocuticle.

procyonid (prōu·si͵ǫnid), *sb.* and *a.* [f. mod.L. family name *Procyonidæ*, f. generic name *Procyon* (G.C.C. Storr *Prodomus Methodi Mammalium* (1780) 35): see PROCYON.] A mammal belonging to the family Procyonidæ, which includes racoons and pandas. Also as *adj.*, of, pertaining to, or resembling an animal of this kind.

1909 *O.E.D.*, Procyonid. **1910** H. F. OSBORN *Age of Mammals* iv. 288 This [*sc.* the Lower Miocene] is the first geological appearance of the characteristically American family of raccoons, or procyonids. **1921** *Proc. Zool. Soc.* 419 The genus [*Ailuropoda*] is neither Ursid nor Procyonid. **1941** *Geol. Ser. Field Mus. Nat. Hist.* VIII. 33 (*title*) A new procyonid from the Miocene of Nebraska. **1964** E. P. WALKER *Mammals of World* II. 1179/2 Most procyonids travel in pairs or family groups. **1973** *Nature* 28 Sept. 218/2 Its [*sc.* the giant panda's] closest affinities are with the ursids (bears) or procyonids (raccoons). **1978** T. A. VAUGHAN *Mammalogy* (ed. 2) xii. 217/1 Procyonids are of modest size, weighing from less than a kilogram to about 20 kg.

procyonine (prōu·si͵onīn), *a.* [f. mod.L. subfamily name *Procyoninæ*: see prec.] (Earlier and later examples.)

In Dict. s.v. PROCYON.

1869 [see *ARCTOID *a.* (*sb.*)]. **1921** *Proc. Zool. Soc.* 418 If the tooth in *Ailuropoda* is not Ailurine or Procyonine, it is certainly not Ursine.

prod, *sb.*[1] Add: **1. b.** *N. Amer. colloq.* (Further examples.)

1910 B. EDWARDS in H. A. Dempsey *Best of Bob Edwards* (1975) v. 96 The old man was on the prod. **1947** B. A. DE VOTO *Across Wide Missouri* 26 Not only the Arikaras but the Blackfeet were on the prod. **1962** [see *ONERY, ONNERY, O'N'RY].

2. b. *Founding.* Any of a number of pointed projections, intended to hold the loam, on the flat metal base used for preparing a loam mould.

1888 *Lockwood's Dict. Mech. Engin.* 267 The pyramidal or conical points cast on loam and core plates for the retention of the loam are termed prods. **1889** J. G. HORNER *Pract. Iron Founding* viii. 103 A plate..is cast, studded over with 'prods' to hold the loam which is swept over its face. **1923** —— *Mod. Ironfoundry* vii. 65 Prods are cast on many loam mould plates. Generally, they occur on one side only, and the pattern prods are mounted in a strip of wood, provided with a handle.

Prod (prǫd), *sb.*[3] and *a.* Also **prod.** An Anglo-Irish colloq. abbrev. of PROTESTANT *sb.* 2a and *a.* 1. Cf. *PROT *sb.* and *a.*

1942 E. BOWEN *Seven Winters* 51 She spoke of 'Prods' (or, extreme, unctuous Protestants) with a flighty detachment that might have offended many. **1961** *Spectator* 28 Apr. 599 He was a 'Mick', I was a 'Prod' but we found no difficulty in being friends although we differed in faith. **1970** M. KENYON *100,000 Welcomes* ii. 14 A long-hair student, or a Prod, or similar riff-raff. **1974** *Irish Democrat* Dec. 7/2 This is..about O'Brienism, which is based on the fearful symmetry that taig is taig and prod is prod and never the twain shall meet. **1977** P. CARTER *Under Goliath* iii. 15 Most of the kids were in tough Prod gangs, like the Tartans... They always seemed to..tell if you were as hard-line Prod as they were.

Proddy (prǫ·di), *a. colloq.* (chiefly *Anglo-Irish*). Also **proddy.** [f. *PROD *sb.*[3] and *a.* + -Y[6].] Protestant. Also *Comb.*, as (children's slang) *Proddy-hopper, -woddy*; **Proddy Dog** (opp. *Cat*: Catholic).

1954 W. K. HANCOCK *Country & Calling* i. 50 And they would sing: *Proddy Dog, Proddy Dog, Sitting on a well, Up comes the Devil And pulls him down to hell.* Then we and the Catholic boys would pelt each other with cowdung. **1958** I. CROSS *God Boy* 165 Proddy-hopper, proddy-hopper, go to hell. **1959** I. & P. OPIE *Lore & Lang. Schoolch.* xvi. 344 In Ireland, both north and south, Catholics are 'Cathies' and Protestants 'Proddy-woddys'. *Ibid.*, In Staines..R.C. children call the Protestants 'Old Proddy Dogs'... They still call them 'Proddy Dogs' at Ilford. **1961** *Spectator* 28 Apr. 603 In other streets Papist and Proddy schoolboys could pass in peace. **1968** T. PARKER *People of Sheets* 60 We always divided up into the same two sides, The Cats and The Proddy Dogs. **1975** G. SEYMOUR *Harry's Game* v. 76 Nice safe little billet.. in a nice Proddy area... I'm not going..to sit on my arse in Proddyland.

prodelision. (Further examples.)

1933 *Trans. Philol. Soc. 1931–32* 32 They would point to the patent phenomena of adaptation or assimilation of the two sounds to one another..and also to the facts of elision, prodelision, and crasis (in the case of vowels), that is, of coalescence. **1968** W. S. ALLEN *Vox Graeca* iv. 96 Much rarer than elision is the process of 'prodelision' in which it is the short initial vowel of the second word that is lost after a final long vowel or diphthong.

prodelta(ic): see *PRO-[2] 2.

prodigiosin (prodidʒiōu·sin). *Biochem.* [a. G. *prodigiosin* (E. Kraft *Beiträge zur Biol. des B. Prodigiosus* (Dissertation, Würzburg, 1902) 37, following suggestion by K. B. Lehmann), f. mod.L. *prōdigiōs-us* marvellous, PRODIGIOUS (former specific epithet of the bacterium now called *Serratia marcescens*): see -IN[1].] A dark red crystalline pigment with antibiotic properties which is produced by certain bacteria of the genus *serratia* and has a molecule ($C_{20}H_{25}N_3O$) consisting essentially of three pyrrole rings linked to a central carbon atom.

1914 *Chem. Abstr.* VIII. 2894 Prodigiosin, the pigment of *B[acillus] prodigiosus*, is more sol. in alc. than in water. **1950** A. H. CORWIN in R. C. Elderfield *Heterocyclic Compounds* I. vi. 320 Tripyrrylmethanes are also of some interest because of the fact that they are leuco bases of tripyrrylmethane dyes, one of which, prodigiosin, has been isolated from a natural source. **1968** A. ALBERT *Heterocyclic Chem.* (ed. 2) v. 234 Pyrroles are well represented in Nature. Apart from the many porphins and related tetrapyrroles.., there is the bacterial pigment prodigiosin, and the antibiotic netropsin. **1971** *Jrnl. Antibiotics* XXIV. 636 Prodigiosin..is the bright red pigment of *Serratia marcescens* and was probably responsible for many medieval 'miracles' involving the appearance of blood stains on the Holy Host.

prodigiosity (prodidʒiǫ·sĭti). [f. L. *prōdigiōs-us* PRODIGIOUS + -ITY.] **1.** A person or thing of enormous size; a monster.

1895 G. MEREDITH *Amazing Marriage* II. xxxvi. 407 We're none of us 'fifty feet high, with phosphorous heads', as your friend..says of the prodigiosities.

2. A marvellous quality or performance.

1910 W. J. LOCKE *Simon* vi. 77 He had fallen in love with her when she had first taken Marseilles captive with the prodigiosities of her horse Sultan.

prodnose (prǫ·dnōuz), *sb.* [f. PROD *v.* + NOSE *sb.*] An inquisitive person, a noseyparker; *spec.* a detective.

1934 DYLAN THOMAS *Let.* 11 May (1966) 126 Singing as loudly as Beachcomber in a world rid of Prodnose. **1965** *Spectator* 12 Feb. 213/2, I shall be greatly disappointed if some prodnose does not get a PhD thesis out of these pages in 2065. **1968** V. C. CLINTON-BADDELEY *My Foe Outstretch'd* vi. 103 He was sensitive about his reputation as an amateur prodnose. **1973** D. ROBINSON *Rotten with Honour* 97 I'll tell you why, you squalid prodnose. **1976** *Listener* 5 Aug. 135/2 Were the other lonely prodnoses with clipboards, operating in the dark, copying me? Or was I, daunting thought, the only pollster operating in the entire nation?

prodnose (prǫ·dnōuz), *v.* [f. prec.] *intr.* To pry; to be inquisitive. So **pro·dnosing** *vbl. sb.*

1958 *Spectator* 3 Oct. 430/1 At this time [*sc.* the 1940s] the social virtue of prodnosing..was still at a fairly harmless stage of development. **1969** *Daily Tel.* (Colour Suppl.) 31 Oct. 20/1 It is perhaps high time that the industrial psychologists who are encouraged to prodnose into most things got to work on the Press.

prodromal, *a.* Add: **2.** Now usu. with pronunc. (prodrōu·mal).

produce, *sb.* Add: **6.** *produce broker* (earlier example), *trade* (earlier example).

1851 C. CIST *Sk. Cincinnati in 1851* 143 Forwarding and Commission merchants and Produce brokers. **1872** *Rep. Vermont Board Agric.* I. 161 B. F. Rugg, who was then engaged in the produce trade,..undertook to carry out a plan for controlling the Boston butter market.

produce, *v.* Add: **1. b.** (Earlier and later examples in the sense 'to bring (a performer or performance) before the public'.) Now also *spec.* to administer and supervise the production of (a film or broadcast programme). Also *absol.*

1836 DICKENS *Let.* 25 Aug. (1965) I. 171 A farce in two acts..to be produced at the Saint James's Theatre on the first of October. **1897** G. B. SHAW in *Sat. Rev.* 13 Feb. 170/1 Like all plays under Mr. Barrett's management, 'The Daughter of Babylon' is excellently produced. **1912** F. A. TALBOT *Moving Pictures* 329 The Hepworth Manufacturing Company..recently has produced several powerful and excellent film-plays. **1923** *Radio Times* 28 Sept. 23/3 The whole production produced and directed by Mr. R. E. Jeffrey, who has adapted this well-known play for wireless transmission. **1935** E. F. DYER *Producing School Plays* ii. 24 If he [*sc.* the producer] finds no inner meaning there is either something wrong with him or with the play which he has chosen to present; either he is not a suitable person to produce the play, or the play is unworthy of production. **1937** 'M. INNES' *Hamlet, Revenge!* I. i. 17 I'm producing. And I've built a sort of Elizabethan stage. **1940** C. P. PURDOM *Producing Plays* i. 2 Any one who knew anything of the theatre could recognize a play produced by Mr. Granville-Barker. **1966** *Listener* 6 Oct. 515/2, I think it was over-ambitious of Mr Wheeler to produce and write the script, yet one cannot belittle his success in presenting very clearly the broad scope of his subject. **1971** N. K. PARROTT in J. R. BROWN *Drama & Theatre* iv. 87 *Othello* got produced, mainly because somebody wanted to do it and convinced enough other people to join him in presenting it.

3. b. Also *absol.*

1976 'A. GARVE' *Home to Roost* ii. 26 She had naturally expected to start a family... There was no apparent physical reason why we shouldn't produce.

e. *absol.* To produce the goods, money, results. *slang.*

1970 G. F. NEWMAN *Sir, You Bastard* viii. 226 Ring me. And you'd better produce. **1977** *New Yorker* 24 Oct. 64/3 One queen's 'husband' asked her to 'produce' for four of his friends and stabbed her when she declined.

producer. Add: **1. b.** The person who produces a dramatic performance, film, or broadcast programme.

1891 SCOTT & HOWARD *Life E. L. Blanchard* I. 213 Though he was a clever actor, he rose to greater fame as what we should now call a stage-manager or producer of plays. **1896** G. B. SHAW in *Labour Leader* 19 Dec. 443/4 Our extraordinary clever producer of Ibsen would get enormously rich. **1909** *Westm. Gaz.* 30 Apr. 5/2 Mr. Louis Calvert's appointment as stage manager, or, according to the more modern term, 'producer' of the so-called Millionaires' Theatre in New York, may be reckoned a high compliment. **1911** D. S. HULFISH *Cycl. Motion-Picture Work* II. 95 The producer is in charge of the studio. **1912** F. A. TALBOT *Moving Pictures* 329 There is every indication that the British producers are making up headway. **1915** *Times* 26 Nov. 11/4 The English film-producers of all branches are rapidly proving that..the hustle of the American 'producer', and the mobile features..of the foreign actor are not essential. **1925** *Scribner's Mag.* Sept. 283/2 The great Delando, most resourceful of the Broadway producers, put down the last act of 'The Republic'. **1933** *Radio Times* 14 Apr. 72/2 It will be interesting to see how the producers handle a 'spectacular' show of this kind. **1938, 1944** [see *DIRECTOR 1 g]. **1949** A. HUXLEY *Ape & Essence* 24 Titles, credits and finally..the name of the *producer*. **1961** G. MILLERSON *Technique Television Production* 190 The producer may be the business-head of the programme, responsible for organization, finance, policy, etc., while his director is concerned with interpretation, staging and directing its production. **1973** *Radio Times* 26 July 55/1 The producer [in TV] has overall charge of the production.. and it is he who marshals the resources of the BBC to make sure the production is appropriate to the play and to the series of which the play is part. **1976** M. MAGUIRE *Scratchproof* iv. 51 Sam Goldwyn used to say that a producer shouldn't get ulcers, he should give them.

c. *producer-in-chief.*

1939 M. SPRING RICE *Working-Class Wives* i. 13 Men ..are the recognised producers-in-chief. **1976** *S. Wales Echo* 23 Nov. 6/6 He is also producer-in-chief of a series of plays for Granada which will be shown in Britain.

2. (Earlier example.)

1784 ADAM SMITH *Wealth of Nations* (ed. 3) II. IV. viii. 515 The interest of the consumer is almost constantly sacrificed to that of the producer.

3. *gas producer*, substitute for def.: a furnace for producing fuel gas by passing a current of air and usually steam through hot solid fuel so that incomplete combustion occurs; *producer gas*, gas so produced, used as a low-grade but inexpensive fuel and consisting chiefly of nitrogen and carbon monoxide with smaller amounts of hydrogen and carbon dioxide. (Further examples.)

1902 *Encycl. Brit.* XXVIII. 595/1 In all the attempts to make water gas up to that date the incandescence of the fuel had been obtained by 'blowing' so deep a bed of fuel that carbon monoxide and the residual nitrogen of the air formed the chief products, this mixture being known as 'producer' gas. **1939** *Times* 28 Mar. 11/2 Fuel costs favoured the producer gas engine compared with the oil or petrol engine. **1941** *Thorpe's Dict. Appl. Chem.* (ed. 4) V. 368/1 In the Thwaite cupola producer.., where a dry-air blast..is employed, it is usual to add a certain proportion of limestone to the fuel charge in order to form a liquid slag with the ashes. **1967** M. CHANDLER *Ceramics in Mod. World* ii. 81 If producer gas or heavy oils are used..it is necessary to have a muffle throughout the length of a kiln.

4. *Ecol.* Any organism or part of an organism that produces the organic compounds it needs from simple substances such as water, carbon dioxide, or nitrogen. Freq. *attrib.*

1941 *Q. Rev. Biol.* XVI. 395/1 In the marine plankton the plant type of life is sometimes called 'producer' and the animal type 'consumer' plankton. *Ibid.* 397/1 Certain important groups of producer plankton..were absent from the neighbourhood of the poles. *Ibid.*, The hotter regions..favor the more catabolic types of metabolism among the producers by a general increase of vital velocities. **1942** *Ecology* XXIII. 400/2 In the language of community economics introduced by Thienemann ('26), autotrophic plants are producer organisms, employing the energy obtained by photosynthesis to synthesize complex organic substances from simple inorganic substances. **1953** E. P. ODUM *Fund. Ecol.* ix. 223 Considering the fresh-water environment as a whole, the algae are the most important producers. **1976** T. C. EMMEL *Population Biol.* i. 21 The first trophic level in ecosystems is represented by green plants and comprises the producers (or autotrophs). **1978** *Sci. Amer.* Mar. 102/2 These rodents derive energy directly from the primary producers (leaves, shoots, seeds and buds), from other consumers (invertebrates in the forest litter and occasionally birds' eggs and young) and from decomposers (fungi).

5. *attrib.* and *Comb.*, as *producer-exhibitor, -novelist, -retailer*; **producer goods** (see quot. 1956); **producer-oriented** *a.*, interested in or favouring the producer of goods rather than the consumer.

1920 *Stage Year Bk.* 52 It became increasingly certain, however, that the main body of exhibitors was opposed to the producer-exhibitor. **1951** *Manch. Guardian* 14 May 4/2 It is, of course, extremely difficult to give a coherent picture when you are showing objects..that include producer goods, consumer goods, and transport. **1956** J. C. SWAYNE *Conc. Gloss Geogr. Terms* 114 *Producer goods*, goods used to make other goods. **1969** *Listener* 13 Feb. 219/2 The producer-novelist David Thomson gave us a good example in *From Oblivion to Obscurity* (Third Programme), by another novelist, with previous radio successes, F. C. Ball. **1962** *Times* 18 Oct. (Walter Thompson Suppl.) p. ii/3 Monopolists and critics of advertising..are fundamentally producer-oriented. **1964** M. MCLUHAN *Understanding Media* (1967) II. xxxi. 333 Nearly all of our technologies since Gutenberg have been ..not producer-oriented, but consumer-oriented. **1938** *Daily Tel.* 16 Feb. 14/6 Finally, it is said that compulsory pasteurisation would threaten the economic existence of the small producer-retailer. **1960** *Farmer & Stock-breeder* 5 Jan. 87/2 Producer-retailers with over 50 head of poultry will again be required to contribute ½d per dozen.

produ·cership. [f. PRODUCER + -SHIP.] The position or function of a producer.

?**1924** G. B. SHAW *To a Young Actress* (1960) 65 You are not within five years hard work of being good enough for Comisarjevsky, whose producership I have made a condition of my consent to the Parisian Pygmalion. **1926** *Spectator* 1 May 796/1 By a judicious system of African producership and land ownership peace has prevailed. **1933** V. A. DEMANT *God & Man & Society* iii. 70 The only unassailable standard of producership is the fulfilment of the real demands of the whole body of consumers. **1960** *Times* 16 Mar. 10/4 By 1944 [Dr. Rennert] had risen to the chief producership of the Berlin Städtische Oper.

producing, *ppl. a.* (Further examples.)

1884 *U.S. Tenth Census* X. 13 'Shale oil' was found at a depth of 751 feet, and in November, 1871, producing sand was struck at 1,110 feet. **1920** *Stage Year Bk.* 51 One or two of the bigger and better producing firms had begun to look higher. **1927** *Petroleum Devel. & Technol. in 1926* (A.I.M.E. Petroleum Div.) 202 Where it occurs, naturally no complete travel from the injection well to the producing wells is had. **1932** *New Yorker* 23 July 2/2 (Advt.), Rockland Producing Company 'Death Takes a Holiday': Fri., July 22. **1976** *Daily Tel.* 3 Dec. 5/5 So far..most of Mexico's producing wells have been on land or in the relatively calm and shallow waters of the Gulf of Mexico.

product, *sb.*[1] Add: **1. a.** Also, more widely, applied to other mathematical entities (as events, matrices, permutations, sets, tensors, vectors, etc.) obtained by certain defined processes of combination of two or more entities, the processes not necessarily being commutative and the entities combined not necessarily being of the same kind (cf. *SUM *sb.*[1]). (Further examples.) Cf. *inner product* s.v. *INNER *a.* (*sb.*[2]) 1 k, *outer product* s.v. *OUTER *a.* (*sb.*[1]) 3.

1892 F. N. COLE tr. *Netto's Theory of Substitutions* ii. 23 The substitution which results from the successive application of two or more substitutions we call their product. **1913** C. E. CULLIS *Matrices & Determinoids* vi. 158 If *A* and *B* are any two matrices, the product AB is defined below to be a certain third matrix which is completely known when *A* and *B* are known. **1941** COURANT & ROBBINS *What is Math.?* ii. 110 By the 'intersection' or 'logical product' of *A* and *B* we mean the set consisting only of those elements which are in *both A* and *B*. **1962** B. D. SECKLER tr. *Gnedenko's Theory of Probability* i. 22 The event consisting in the simultaneous occurrence of *A* and *B* will be called the product, or intersection, of the events *A* and *B* and will be denoted by *AB*. **1965** BIRKHOFF & MAC LANE *Survey Mod. Algebra* (ed. 3) vii. 188 Show that tensor products are distributive on direct sums. **1965** PATTERSON & RUTHERFORD *Elem. Abstract Algebra* ii. 35 Defining the product of two permutations in this way, we obtain a binary operation in the set of all permutations... It is not commutative. **1972** A. G. HOWSON *Handbk. Terms Algebra & Anal.* ii. 11 The Cartesian product, $A \times B$, of two sets *A* and *B* is defined to be the set of all ordered pairs (*a*, *b*) of elements from *A* and *B* respectively. *Ibid.* xxxiv. 172 The vector product is *not* associative.

3. a. Now freq. that which is produced commercially for sale. Also *collect.*, merchandise, esp. gramophone records.

1928 S. R. HALL *Mail-Order & Direct Mail Selling* xx. 373 To build up a successful mail-order business, one must first have or create the article or products that have mail-order possibilities. **1950** A. TACK *Sell your Way to Success* viii. 113 Work out the sales points around your product. **1976** *Street Life* 7–20 Feb. 22/3 Some records can be sold like soapflakes, but the majority are not purely 'product'. **1977** *Time* 12 Dec. 68/2 More product, to borrow the record-company jargon, from the pianist who burst out of Russia two years ago and has been a one-man industry ever since.

b. The value of goods produced, esp. *gross national* (or *total annual*) *product* (see *GROSS *a.* 6c).

1888 E. BELLAMY *Looking Backward* xxii. 314 The total annual product of the nation..would not have come to more than three or four hundred dollars per head. **1962** *Listener* 29 Mar. 548/1 There is a fixed proportion of the gross national product which can be spent on defence. **1966** *Ibid.* 17 Mar. 374/1 [We could] keep our defence expenditure between five and six per cent of gross national product.

6. *attrib.* and *Comb.*: (in sense 1) *product event, integral, measure, space*; (senses 2–4) *product design, division, group, launch, line, mix, morpheme, nucleus*.

1959 *Listener* 21 May 885/1 A blackboard in the product design section. **1980** *Jrnl. R. Soc. Arts* May 335/2 There is no doubt that the four companies..have put a lot of effort into product design. **1970** *Financial Times* 13 Apr. 14/3 The new structure of the British Steel Corporation consisting of product divisions is generally considered to be one of two logical management systems for a modern business of international proportions. **1968** P. A. P. MORAN *Introd. Probability Theory* i. 2 Given any two events, A_1 and A_2, we define a 'product' event denoted by A_1A_2 which occurs if any events E_i occur which belong to both A_1 and A_2. **1957** *Which?* Autumn 2 In the United States and the Scandinavian countries, there are independent organisations that issue reports, regularly or occasionally, each dealing with the brands widely available in one product-group. **1962** E. GODFREY *Retail Selling & Organization* i. 7 The Nielsen Survey..showed that in three product groups—coffees, soft drinks and toilet soaps—50 per cent of all grocery shops offered one or more items below list price. **1968** P. A. P. MORAN *Introd. Probability Theory* vi. 290 Expressions such as (6.40) are known as 'product integrals'. This is a mathematical concept which is related to a product of a number of factors in the same way that an integral is related to a sum. **1976** *Times* 22 Apr. 11/4 They were for use in explaining to salesmen, dealers and executives a product launch, a new marketing philosophy or some new twist in internal communications. **1969** *Time* 17 Jan. 52 The company has greatly broadened its product line, introducing seven new models in the past two years. **1980** *Jrnl. R. Soc. Arts* May 325/2 It has over 400 product lines and thousands of variants. **1950** W. FELLER *Introd. Probability Theory* I. v. 91 Independence of trials means product measure. **1968** P. A. P. MORAN *Introd. Probability Theory* iv. 194 ϕ is the 'product measure' generated by the separate measures on the n one-dimensional spaces. **1953** F. G. MOORE *Manuf. Managem.* v. 85 Valid comparisons of over-all figures sometimes become almost meaningless because variations in the 'product mix'—the quantities of different items produced—occur continually. **1965** H. I. ANSOFF *Corporate Strategy* (1968) i. 18 Strategic decisions are..concerned.. specifically with selection of the product-mix which the firm will produce. **1970** O. DOPPING *Computers & Data Processing* xxii. 365 Product mix is an economically important problem which can in many cases be handled by computer. **1965** *Language* XLI. 365 The sentences would have no string structure at all if transformations combined morphemes from separate elementary sentences into novel product-morphemes (portmanteau blends). **1931** G. GAMOW *Constitution of Atomic Nuclei* iii. 63 The particle (α or β) ejected from the nucleus No. 1 may leave the product-nucleus No. 2 in an excited state. **1963** Product nucleus [see **delayed neutron*]. **1968** E. T. COPSON *Metric Spaces* viii. 134 The product space $X \times T$ is an $(m+n)$ dimensional Euclidean space. **1968** P. A. P. MORAN *Introd. Probability Theory* i. 10 The space of all such events is known as the product space of the two spaces.

7. Special Combs.: **product champion,** a person entrusted with the promotion of a product or idea; **products liability,** a manufacturer's legal responsibility to the consumer for his product or products; **product moment,** of a set of pairs of statistical data, the sum of the products of the elements of each pair; freq. *attrib.* (with hyphen), designating a correlation coefficient (symbol *r*) calculated from this, equal to the covariance divided by the geometric mean of the variance; cf. *PEARSON b, *CORRELATION 1 c.

1969 *Observer* 2 Nov. 12/7 'Product champions' are appointed to help push new ideas through the natural opposition within a big company. **1976** *Jrnl. R. Soc. Arts* CXXIV. 725/1 We welcome ideas from serious-minded enthusiasts or 'product champions'. **1972** *Guardian* 12 Aug. 10/5 American judges and legislators have created..a completely new set of rights known as product liability law. The dramatic effect of this is to make the manufacturer..strictly liable to the ultimate consumer. **1976** *National Observer* (U.S.) 23 Oct. 11/2 Kerry Choi, head of product-liability research for the Association of Trial Lawyers of America..says most of the cases he handles for member attorneys involve inadequate warnings. **1978** *Rep. R. Comm. Civil Liability & Compensation for Personal Injury* I. v. xxii. 255 Products liability must be considered in the context of public concern to protect the interests of the consumer. **1904** *Drapers' Company Res. Mem.* (Biometric Ser.) I. 32 We shall obtain by the method of mean square contingency satisfactory results, *i.e.*, values close to the coefficient of correlation as found by product moment or four-fold division methods. **1904** *Amer. Jrnl. Psychol.* XV. 78 The method of 'product moments' is valid, whether or not the distribution follow the normal law of frequency, so long as the 'regression' is linear. **1918** *Biometrika* XII. 87 We are now in a position to set down the algebraical values of the product-moment coefficients. **1925** R. A. FISHER *Statistical Methods* vi. 146 Such an estimate is called the correlation coefficient, or the product moment correlation, the latter term referring to the summation of the product terms, *xy*, in the last equation. **1930** M. EZEKIEL *Methods Correlation Anal.* viii. 127 The value $\Sigma(xy)$ is sometimes called the product moment. **1951** PADEN & LINDQUIST *Statistics for Econ. & Business* xiv. 231 The use of the mean x/σ_X, y/σ_Y product for this purpose was first proposed by the English statistician Karl Pearson and is therefore called the Pearson product-moment coefficient of correlation. **1972** *Jrnl. Social Psychol.* LXXXVII. 33 Pearson product-moment correlations were calculated between fear ratings and intensity of escape attempts. **1972** E. LUKACS *Probability & Math. Statistics* iv. 90 In the bivariate case one also has a mixed moment (product-moment) of second order.

production. Add: **I. 1. b.** (Earlier and later examples.)

1784 ADAM SMITH *Wealth of Nations* (ed. 3) II. IV. viii. 515 Consumption is the sole end and purpose of production... The mercantile system..seems to consider production and not consumption, as the ultimate end and object of all industry and commerce. **1817** D. RICARDO *Princ. Pol. Econ.* xx. 444 The cost of production, and therefore the prices of various manufactured commodities, are raised to the consumer by one error in legislation. **1887** MOORE & AVELING tr. *Marx's Capital* I. II. vi. 147 In order that a man may be able to sell commodities other than labour-power, he must of course have the means of production, as raw material, implements, &c. **1933** S. HOOK *Towards Understanding K. Marx* xi. 120 For Marx it is the relations of production, not the forces of production and not the conditions of production, which are the basis of the cultural superstructure. **1964** S. M. MILLER in I. L. Horowitz *New Sociol.* 300 We need sustained economic growth, high production, and high employment in order to solve many of the problems of the unemployed and the poor today in America. **1977** *Undercurrents* June–July 23/1 First, to infiltrate the key institutions, including 'the means of production' (The People's Warehouse).

II. 3. c. The action or process of producing a stage play, film, or other performance. Also, the performance itself.

1894 [in Dict., sense 3 a]. **1925** *Scribner's Mag.* July 7/1 Jesse Lynch Williams has been..preparing a play for production in New York in the fall. **1928** BARRIE *Peter Pan* p. viii, I remember writing the story of *Peter and Wendy* many years after the production of the play. **1932** *New Yorker* 11 June 52/2 Wherever she appears.., as a telephone operator in some big, showy production—a breath of humanity sweeps over the screen. **1937** *Printers' Ink Monthly* May 40/2 *Production*, the building, organizing and presenting of a radio program. **1942** *N. & Q.* 12 Sept. 161/1 'Business of the Stage' denotes the movements, groupings, vocal inflections, etc., of the players, which are settled at rehearsal. The modern term is 'Production'. **1949** *Radio Times* 15 July 15/2 *'The Dilettanti'* by Thomas Love Peacock. Adapted for broadcasting... Production by Noel Iliff. **1952** GRANVILLE *Dict. Theatr. Terms* 101 *In production* (of a play), *in* rehearsal and general preparation for *production*. A *dark* theatre sometimes has a notice stating that 'this theatre is closed; a new play is *in production*'. **1962** A. NISBETT *Technique Sound Studio* 267 *Production*, compilation, and studio direction, etc., of a programme. **1976** M. MAGUIRE *Scratchproof* ii. 30 Loose talk..can ruin a production before it even gets off the ground.

d. *fig.* An unnecessarily elaborate performance; a fuss, commotion, drama. Freq. in phr. *to make a production* (*of*, *out of*, etc., something).

1941 B. SCHULBERG *What makes Sammy Run?* vii. 128 Something tells me that when our blast comes, it will really be a production. **1959** R. CONDON *Manchurian Candidate* (1960) ix. 131 You make a production out of it like I was involved somehow in your life. **1962** M. & G. GORDON *Journey with Stranger* (1963) xi. 74 The simplest tasks at home became productions when travelling. **1967** S. WOODS *Case is Altered* ix. 107 You've made rather a production of this, Inspector. **1974** R. BUTLER *Buffalo Hook* ii. 15 Why should there be this big production over a cargo..that's covered by insurance anyway.

V. 7. a. (Further examples.)

1929 T. H. BURNHAM *Engin. Econ.* xv. 192 Production control necessitates a system of records and charts which indicate at a glance whether the planned production is being adhered to, or if departure therefrom is occurring, at what stage the divergence is arising. **1938** E. AMBLER *Cause for Alarm* i. 17 He's afraid of the production figures falling off. **1941** B. SCHULBERG *What makes Sammy Run?* xi. 283 Production costs have been too high. **1943** J. B. PRIESTLEY *Daylight on Saturday* viii. 52 If our lads was fightin' like 'ell..yer'd see them production figures take a high jump. **1951** R. FIRTH *Elem. Social Organization* iv. 136 The organization of production tends to be based not merely on a system of cash rewards... A production relationship is often only one facet of a social relationship. **1957** *Technology* Mar. 8/1 Then he goes into the production shops, where he gains experience of the many aspects of aircraft construction. **1958** J. F. MAGEE *Production Planning & Inventory Control* i. 1 A manager necessarily thinks of problems in production planning in terms of people and their responsibilities. **1962** A. BATTERSBY *Guide to Stock Control* x. 89 In striving for the shop-floor efficiency associated with long manufacturing runs, the Production Manager will always be tending to drive stock levels upwards. **1966** *New Statesman* 20 May 753/1 (Advt.), Book Publishers invite applications..for the post of production controller to supervise the production of a section of their Home Education list, from manuscript to bound copy. **1970** O. Dopping *Computers & Data Processing* xxii. 364 The most common problem in production planning in a workshop is to determine the sequence in which different operations, pertaining to different orders, should be placed in the different machine groups. **1975** *North Sea Background Notes* (Brit. Petroleum Co.) 7 Production licences..give the licensee exclusive rights over a specific area to explore for and produce hydrocarbons. **1975** *Petroleum Economist* Aug. 309/1 The Hamilton Brothers facility involved developing a production riser as a technical innovation. **1976** *Scotsman* 24 Dec. 13/7 (Advt.), Experience of production control within a high volume fabrication and pressing shop would be a distinct advantage. **1977** *Observer* 24 Apr. 1/6 The rig crew was about to install a safety valve on the top of a production pipe. **1978** P. Sutcliffe *Oxf. Univ. Press* iv. x. 166 Frowde..acquired great expertise and used it to good effect in producing his own books. He was his own production manager, firm and clear in his instructions to Hart.

b. In *Broadcasting* and *Cinemat.* (sense 3c), *production assistant, clerk, director, editor, manager, staff, team*; also *production control, control room*.

1960 D. Davis *Gram. Television Production* 77 *Production Assistant* (*P.A.*), the director's personal assistant on a programme. **1969** W. Rutherford *Gallows Set* i. 18 In one group were the members of the film crew. In the other..were..the most senior director..[and] Anne, his production assistant. **1972** *Listener* 21 Dec. 852/1 Sequence of calls before a shot. Production Assistant: 'Quiet. Going for a take. Standing by'. Director: 'Right'. **1963** *Movie* Apr. 11/1 Production clerk at R.K.O., then second assistant director. **1961** G. Millerson *Technique Television Production* i. 15 Some networks prefer to have separate rooms for production control. *Ibid.*, Through the window of the production control room we can see the studio below. **1937** *Printers' Ink Monthly* May 40/2 *Production director*, individual in charge of the radio studio programs. **1961** G. Millerson *Technique Television Production* i. 15 Facing these monitors sit the production director and his assistant. **1972** Production editor [see *make-up editor* s.v. *make-up 6]. **1938** *Times* 7 Jan. 13/6 Beside him [*sc.* the producer] sits the production manager, whose functions are similar to those of a stage manager in a theatre. **1959** W. S. Sharps *Dict. Cinematogr.* 121/1 *Production manager*, in filming this post is often held by the Assistant Director and he is responsible for ensuring that everything and every person concerned in production is available at the right place at the right time. **1973** *Listener* 22 Nov. 727/1 In..the film-within-the-film, the wife of the production manager..sits sourly knitting on set. **1962** A. Nisbett *Technique Sound Studio* 246 *Control cubicle* (*BBC*), the soundproof room equipped with control desk..which is occupied by production and operational staff. *Ibid.* 10 Although each member of the production team is concentrating on his own job, this is geared to that of the team as a whole. **1974** *Listener* 27 June 820/2 My wanting to make this series of documentaries..aided by my production team's talents as film makers.

c. Special Combs.: **production brigade**, in communist countries, a unit within a commune required to meet specified agricultural production figures; **production engineering**, the planning and control of the manufacturing processes, plant, and equipment involved in the production of any manufactured product; so **production engineer**; **production line**, a line (*line *sb.*[2] 19c) along which things undergo successive stages of production; **production number**, a spectacular song or dance in a musical show or revue; **production platform**, a platform (sense *8d) used in the production of oil or gas from the sea bed; **production reactor**, a nuclear reactor designed to produce fissile material; **production relations**, in Marxist theory the social relations arising from and essential to the process of production, as those between the controllers of the means of production (raw materials, land, machinery, etc.) and the labour force; **production run**, a run (Run *sb.*[1] 19c) for the purpose of the routine production of a product; **production-sharing** (see quot. 1963); **production testing**, testing under the conditions that would prevail during production; hence **production-test** *v. trans.*; **production well**, a well from which oil or gas is actively being produced.

1962 E. Snow *Red China Today* (1963) lix. 453 About management? It is in the hands of the production brigade. **1978** HuaKuo-Feng in *Peking Rev.* 10 Mar. 22/1 In some cases the cadres arbitrarily demand grain and money from the commune, production brigade, production team or commune members or even requisition labour power. **1920** *Engin. Production* Mar. 128/3 As a production engineer it has frequently been necessary for me to select machines suitable for the intensive manufacture of various components. **1921–2** (*title*) Proceedings of the Institution of Production Engineers. **1940** E. J. H. Jones *Production Engin.* i. 3 From the schedules thus compiled, it is possible for the production engineer to ascertain whether sufficient plant will be available for the work in hand. **1946** G. Galle in *Philips Resistance Welding Handbk.* ii. 41 Production engineers should be careful to watch that the seam welder is not overloaded. **1966** S. Beer *Decision & Control* i. 7 Tests have been run in the works to see whether one kind of machine tool is better than another. The purchasing department says that *A* is better than *B* because it is cheaper to buy. The production engineers say that *B* is better than *A* because it produces a better job. **1920** *Engin. Production* Nov. 467/2, I look forward to the time when the curriculum of our universities shall include lectures on production engineering. **1921–2** *Proc. Inst. Production Engineers* I. 39 The name calls up visions of conveyors, elevators, and all such gear, which is by no means the only part of production engineering. **1956** *Nature* 4 Feb. 200/1 The art of precasting concrete has given rise to an established industry producing staple things like blocks, tiles, floor beams and parts for small structures, where problems are in the nature of factory production-engineering. **1966** *McGraw-Hill Encycl. Sci. & Technol.* X. 640/1 Production engineering as a planning activity takes place between product design and the planning of the over-all manufacturing process. **1978** R. V. Jones *Most Secret War* xl. 377 The superiority of American production engineering was often a powerful—even vital—aid. **1935** T. H. Burnham *Engin. Econ.* (ed. 3) II. viii. 245 Many nice problems arise as to when it is economic to break up a group system and lay down a special production line. **1943** J. S. Huxley *TVA* xii. 112 One, two, and three bedroom houses were built on outdoor production lines and distributed to various communities. **1958** *Listener* 27 Nov. 903/1, I suggest one of those 'production-line' chickens, which is big enough for four. **1964** M. Argyle *Psychol. & Social Probl.* viii. 107 A production line must go at the speed of the slowest man. **1971** *Daily Tel.* 14 Aug. 7/4 The nauseating 'production line' feeling experienced in so many crematoria. **1975** *N.Y. Times* 8 Oct. 3/1 The new telescope is to be a production-line 25-meter model..and has been chosen to keep costs to a minimum. **1936** *Metronome* Feb. 61/2 *Production number*, show tune. **1959** *Listener* 12 Nov. 845/3 One production number, danced in silhouette against a changing background, marked an exciting advance in presentation. **1967** Wodehouse *Company for Henry* v. 98 One of those big production numbers so popular in revue, where the whole strength of the company let themselves go in uninhibited dance. **1964** *Oil & Gas Jrnl.* 12 Oct. 104/1 Offshore Louisiana suffered its worst battering in history from Hurricane Hilda... The industry must decide what to do about multiwell production platforms that have been sheared off and sunk. **1976** *Scotsman* 27 Dec. 6/1 The order from Brazil for a production platform from the McDermott yard at Ardersier. **1956** Production reactor [see *converter 3f]. **1966** *McGraw-Hill Encycl. Sci. & Technol.* XI. 359/1 Water is used as a coolant in the United States production reactors, whereas in the United Kingdom gas cooling has been the basis for most designs. **1950** T. H. Marshall *Citizenship & Social Class* ii. 108 The essential factor in this theory is the conception of these production-relations as forces determining the life-situation of individuals. **1973** C. D. Kernig *Marxism, Communism & Western Society* VII. 36/1 In the historico-materialist view of history..it is assumed that revolutions arise out of a state of conflict between production and production relations. **1979** G. A. Cohen *Karl Marx's Theory of Hist.* ii. 31 A production relation binds at least one person(s)-term and at most one productive force(s)-term, and no other type of term. **1967** D. Goch in Wills & Yearsley *Handbk. Managem. Technol.* 146 Compared with the standard usage of 3 lb of moulding powder per unit, the production run required an additional 30 lb. **1973** J. Leasor *Host of Extras* i. 22 Many people think that the Ford Model T had the longest production run of any car—eighteen years. Rolls beat them on this..by being in production with the Silver Ghost for nineteen consecutive years. **1963** *Economist* 8 June 1046/1 The concept that the Indonesians prefer is one of 'production-sharing', under which the contractor takes over existing or potential development, brings in his capital equipment to carry it out, and has as his reward a share of what is produced, processed and sold. **1975** *Petroleum Economist* Sept. 348/1 The Lebanese government has invited bids from interested oil companies for offshore acreage on a production-sharing basis. **1960** *Farmer & Stockbreeder* 19 Jan. Suppl. 41/1 It should provide a means of production-testing individual hens. **1975** *Petroleum Economist* Aug. 286/1 An exploratory well was production tested in June last year at rates of 4 200 b/d of condensate and 23 million cubic feet per day of gas. **1975** *Offshore* Sept. 75/2 While the well was not production tested, Shell indicates it could be a major discovery and Amoco calls it 'potentially significant'. **1934** *Proc. World Petroleum Congr. 1933* I. 359/1 (*heading*) The tubing of production wells under pressure. **1976** *Offshore Engineer* Mar. 6/4 At present only one production well is operating; depending on final assessment of reserves, from four to six wells will be used.

d. Designating a vehicle or appliance made in the ordinary course of production, as opposed to one made for testing or other special purposes.

1961 *Motor Sport* Dec. 1002 This talented designer has shown quite outstanding genius in placing another production B.M.C. engine across the front of his Mini. **1971** 'D. Rutherford' *Clear the Fast Lane* 39 The usual changes needed before a production car is ready for rallying. **1972** *Lebende Sprachen* XVII. 136/2 Six Jetstream prototypes are to be built before production aircraft begin to emerge within the next few months. **1974** *Encycl. Brit. Macropædia* XII. 567/2 Stock-car racing, limited to American production-model passenger cars with suitable modifications, began at Langhorne, Pennsylvania, on July 4, 1939. **1974** *Guardian* 26 Mar. 32/4 Disabled drivers' tricycles should be replaced with modified production cars. **1978** *Gramophone* Mar. 1642/2 A raffle for the first ever production model Quad Electrostatic loudspeaker.

productional (prodʌ·kʃənăl), *a.* [f. Production + -al.] Of, pertaining to, or resulting from production.

1931 *Economist* 7 Feb. 285/2 In comparison with its 'productional' programme the Government's 'distributional' programme has been very modest. **1961** G. Millerson *Technique Television Production* 11 You will find here..several controversial hypotheses, for which the author must be held responsible (dynamic composition; aural composition; productional rhetoric). **1961** E. Wilson *Shaw on Shakespeare* 255 Shaw denounced script cuts and productional schemes which distorted the plays and destroyed their integrity.

productionism (prodʌ·kʃəniz'm). [f. Production + -ism.] A doctrine based upon the importance of production.

1930 *Times Lit. Suppl.* 23 Oct. 858/1 They [*sc.* some plays] may be unreadable..because the author was obsessed by the theory of 'productionism' and..contributed nothing of substance or of design but only a few wisps of straw. **1963** J. S. Huxley in *New Scientist* 27 June 713/2 In the USSR we have an analogous situation that may be called 'productionism' largely to keep up with and beat the USA in industrial efficiency.

productionize (prodʌ·kʃənəiz), *v.* [f. Production + -ize.] *trans.* To produce for general use; to put into production. So **produ·ctionized** *ppl. a.*; **produ·ctionizing** *vbl. sb.*

1937 *R. Air Force Q.* VIII. 102 Generally, an experimental military aircraft..attains speeds on tests which are not equalled by the subsequent '*productionized*' craft in the service. **1939** *Neuphilol. Mitt.* 137 Productionize, vb. **1957** *Times Survey Brit. Aviation* Sept. 15/7 There may well be less chance of reducing costs by 'productionizing'. **1961** *Flight* LXXX. 431/2 Ferranti are 'productionizing' the MoA moving-map display. **1970** *Sci. Jrnl.* May 37/2 A parallel programme inside the factory was devoted to productionizing the equipment.

productive, *a.* (*sb.*) Add: **A.** *adj.* **1. c.** *Med.* Of a cough: that raises mucus or sputum.

1923 *Radiology* I. 168/2 At the time of examination ..she had a persistent and slightly productive cough. **1965** *Brit. Jrnl. Industr. Med.* XXII. 194/1 Those who smoked, and more particularly those who had a productive cough, had lower ventilatory capacities and lower forced expiratory ratios than the remainder.

3. Also, esp. in Marxist theory, as *productive forces*.

1907 L. Boudin *Theoretical System K. Marx* ii. 26 The basis of the structure [of society] is a given state of the development of the productive forces of society. **1909** E. Untermann tr. *Marx's Capital* III. xv. 293 The means, this unconditional development of the productive forces of society, comes continually into conflict with the limited end, the self-expansion of the existing capital. **1927** E. & C. Paul tr. Lenin in D. Ryazanoff *Karl Marx* 123 At a certain stage of development, the material productive forces of society come into conflict with the ..property relationships within which they have hitherto moved. **1973** C. D. Kernig *Marxism, Communism & Western Society* VII. 36/1 The concept 'productive forces' is very important for the Marxist interpretation of revolution... Designated as 'productive forces' are working people, means of production..developed and employed by people and, in addition, the means of labour (raw materials, natural resources) that are consumed.

productivity. Add: **1. b.** *Ecol.* The rate of production of biomass.

1908 J. Johnstone *Conditions of Life in Sea* ix. 179 It is much more difficult to attempt..estimations of the productivity of a sea area, than merely to attempt to ascertain the mass of life at one particular time. **1934** *Q. Rev. Biol.* IX. 175/2 Along the Southern California coast the greatest productivity is..within fifty miles of shore. **1953** E. P. Odum *Fund. Ecol.* iv. 82 It is important to distinguish between the basic or primary productivity on the one hand and consumer or secondary productivity on the other. **1960** N. Polunin *Introd. Plant Geogr.* xv. 478 There is insufficient data as yet to compare the vegetational productivity of different climatic zones. Thus although some tropical inland waters may be more prolific as producers of plant or animal life than some extra-tropical ones, others are practically barren. *Ibid.* xvi. 520 The average productivity of similar land and ocean *areas* appear to be roughly comparable over the year, being said to be of the order of three tons of dry material per acre. **1970** W. D. Russell-Hunter *Aquatic Productivity* xii. 226 This primary productivity of the oceans..amounts to considerably more than half of the primary productivity of the entire world.

c. *Econ.* The rate of output per unit of input, used esp. in measuring capital growth, and in assessing the effective use of labour, materials, and equipment. Also *transf.*

1899 J. B. Clark *Distrib. Wealth* iv. 49 We have said that the *specific* productivity of labor fixes wages... In like manner, the *specific* productivity of capital fixes interest. **1930** *Economist* 18 Jan. 107/2 Still, if productivity has risen high, profits have not followed suit. **1936** J. M. Keynes *Gen. Theory Employment* xi. 138 Many discussions of this subject seem to be mainly concerned with the physical productivity of capital in some sense. **1947** *Amer. Econ. Rev.* May 402 We must try to distinguish as sharply as possible between increase and decrease of productivity caused by larger or smaller output volume—volume productivity increase—and the increase and decrease of productivity caused by real improvement of production or organization—real productivity increase. **1955** *Sci. Amer.* July 35/1 Machinery prices being similar for the managements of all the plants, productivity was a direct function of the average hourly earnings of production workers. **1957** *Introd. Work Study* (Internat. Labour Office) i. 5 *Productivity*..is..the arithmetical ratio between the amount produced and the amount of the resources used in the course of production. **1962** *Daily Tel.* 15 Nov. 1/4 The pace at which our productivity is increasing is too slow, and we hope this National Productivity Year will ginger things up a bit. **1965** H. Wilson in *Oxf. Times* 3 Dec. 16/2, I think I may claim the responsibility for introducing the word 'productivity' to Whitehall, and I'm not proud of it. **1970** *Physics Bull.* July 291/1 The 'productivity' of the Council has also edged up, with the subject boards considering more courses at fewer meetings. **1976** A. W. A. PETERSON in T. S. Barker *Econ. Struct. & Policy* v. 107 The model of production..assumes that industrial investment brings about higher labour productivity as a result of the introduction of more modern equipment.

2. *attrib.* and *Comb.*, as (sense *1c) *productivity agreement, deal, measure, team.*

1978 *Cornish Guardian* 27 Apr. 12/7 An active participant in the introduction of the Company Productivity Agreements. **1970** G. GREER *Female Eunuch* 243 By playing upon..discontent with wage freezes and productivity deals, an adroit Tory can convert the working class to the most arrant conservatism. **1977** *Navy News* Dec. 18/1 The opinion that in industry some 'spurious productivity deals' are now being drawn up has been voiced in a letter received from a PO. **1959** J. W. KENDRICK *Wages, Prices, Profits & Productivity* (Amer. Assembly, Columbia Univ.) ii. 39 The most commonly used productivity measure is 'output per man-hour'. **1953** *Britannica Bk. of Year* 638/2 A team of experts appointed to study methods of increasing production assumed the title of Productivity Team.

‖ **produit net** (prodwi net). [Fr., lit. 'net product'.] In the politico-economical doctrine of the Physiocrats, the amount of the excess of the value of agricultural products over the cost of their production. (Cf. PHYSIOCRAT.)

1792 A. YOUNG *Trav. France* I. xxii. 559 By pursuing the jargon of the *produit net*, and making it variable, instead of fixed, every species of inconvenience and uncertainty has arisen. **1885** *Encycl. Brit.* XIX. 360/1 The real annual addition to the wealth of the community consists of the excess of the mass of agricultural products (including..metals) over their cost of production. On the amount of this 'produit net' depends the wellbeing of the community. **1931** M. DOBB in W. Rose *Outl. Mod. Knowl.* xvi. 598 The essential definition of 'productive' as creative of surplus or *produit net.* **1965** SELDON & PENNANCE *Everyman's Dict. Econ.* 53 Cantillon's contention that only agricultural enterprises yield a surplus over the costs of production gave rise to the Physiocrats' concept of 'produit net'.

pro-element: see *PRO-[1] 4b.

proembryo. Insert at beginning of etym.: [a. G. (M. J. Schleiden *Grundzüge der Wissenschaftlichen Botanik* (1843) II. III. 52).] Delete 'the *suspensor* of Phanerogams' and 'Now little used'. Add: In seed plants, the group of cells formed by the early divisions of the zygote after fertilization; also, a young embryo. Also *attrib.* (Further examples.)

1862 F. CURREY tr. *Hofmeister's On Germination of Higher Cryptogamia & Fructification of Coniferæ* xvi. 441 The breaking up of the pro-embryo of the Coniferæ into a number of independent suspensors is a phenomenon of the most peculiar kind. **1919** F. O. BOWER *Bot. Living Plant* xvii. 274 The very first division of the zygote stamps the polarity of the pro-embryo. **1950** D. A. JOHANSEN *Plant Embryol.* xii. 76 The young proembryo completely fills the archegonium in *Torreya taxifolia.* **1964** H. J. DITTMER *Phylogeny & Form in Plant Kingdom* xxiv. 587 Embryonic development in this plant [*sc.* tansy mustard] begins with a series of transverse divisions of the zygote forming a chain of proembryo cells. **1978** *Nature* 2 Feb. 441/1 Frequently only two seedlings germinate from a single seed and this suggests that only a small proportion of proembryos reach maturity.

proembryonic *a.* (later example).

1957 H. C. BOLD *Morphol. Plants* xxvii. 522 All of the proembryonic cells descended from the zygote may begin to develop into embryos.

proenzyme (pro͵e·nzəim). *Biochem.* [f. PRO-[2] 1 + *ENZYME.] The inactive precursor of an enzyme; = ZYMOGEN.

1900 in DORLAND *Med. Dict.* **1902** C. A. HERTER *Lect. Chem. Path.* viii. 254 The glandular cells from which they [*sc.* enzymes] come apparently do not hold them in any considerable quantity, but contain substances called proënzymes, from which they are produced. *Ibid.*, These proënzymes, pepsinagen and rennet zymogen. **1976** *Nature* 22 Jan. 235/2 Plasminogen is the plasma proenzyme which, on conversion to its active form, plasmin, is considered responsible for lysis of fibrin deposits resulting from physiological or pathological activation of the coagulation cascade.

proerythroblast: see *PRO-[2] 1. **pro-estrus,** var. *pro-œstrum* s.v. PRO-[2] 1 in Dict. and Suppl.

pro-e·thnic, *a.* [PRO-[1] and [2].] **1.** (See PRO-[2] 1.) (Further examples.)

1906 J. H. MOULTON *Gram. N.T. Gk.* I. ix. 221 The Greek participle..represents the proëthnic participle. **1935** G. K. ZIPF *Psycho-Biol. of Lang.* iv. 162 The shift in accent which took place in almost every Indo-European dialect after the pro-ethnic parent language broke up into its dialects.

2. Favouring the Gentiles, as opp. to the Jews. *rare.*

1920 R. HARRIS *Testimonies* II. ii. 13 Propagating by testimonies a Gospel which is at once pro-ethnic and anti-Judaic.

Hence **pro-e·thnically** *adv.*

1920 R. HARRIS *Testimonies* II. ii. 16 As it is written: Father of many nations (ἐθνῶν) have I set thee... The extract from Genesis turns on the use of the word ἐθνῶν, and the words are used pro-ethnically.

proette (prōᵘe·t). [f. PRO *abbrev.* + *-ETTE.] A female professional golfer.

1968 *Maclean's Mag.* Sept. 39 For obvious reasons, the LPGA objects to its members being called 'pro' golfers, and is trying to popularize the description 'proettes'. **1969** *Sunday Times* 5 Oct. 20 Even a lady 'proette' has lost the US Women's Open through signing for a correct total but a 5 and a 4 when she meant a 4 and a 5. **1971** *Time* 28 June 41 And while no proette has ever topped $50,000 for a season, Jack Nicklaus for one has picked up that much in a single tournament. **1975** *Auckland* (N.Z.) *Star* 18 Jan. 35 Two Australian proettes started the second round of the Benson & Hedges $7000 women's golf classic..today in fine style... New Zealand proette Marilyn Smith..turned in 37.

pro:-Europe·an, *sb.* and *a.* [PRO-[1] 5a.] **A.** *sb.* One who favours or supports Europe or other European countries; *spec.*, a supporter of (British membership of) the European Economic Community. **B.** *adj.* Favouring or supporting Europe or other European countries; *spec.*, supporting (British membership of) the European Economic Community.

1944 *Sun* (Baltimore) 8 July 6/4 An even more rhetorical appeal was issued on the same day by the *PPF*.. ('pro-European'). **1962** *Guardian* 10 July 18/7 The Liberals alone have a consistently pro-European tradition. **1963** *Ann. Reg. 1962* 35 The pro-Europeans in the country were a majority of the under-45s, of the over-£25 a week men.., and of those educated past the age of 16. **1969** *Time* 4 July 23 Maurice Schumann, 58, Minister of Foreign Affairs, combines impeccable Gaullist credentials with a pro-European outlook. **1970** *Manch. Guardian Weekly* 4 Apr. 8 A strongly pro-European speech from Mr Roy Hattersley, the Minister of Defence. **1971** *New Yorker* 3 July 64 The highly uncertain future if Britain does not go into Europe has not yet been adequately explained or understood, according to some anxious pro-Europeans. **1979** *Guardian* 28 Apr. 32/2 A tougher line on Europe may upset the more pro-European wing of her party.

prof (prɒf). Also † *U.S.* **proff.** (Colloq.) abbrev. of PROFESSOR 4. Also *attrib.*

1838 *Yale Lit. Mag.* Feb. 144 For Proffs and Tutors too, Who steer our big canoe, Prepare their lays. **1859** G. H. LEWES *Jrnl.* 14 July in *Geo. Eliot Lett.* (1954) III. 116 At Berne I called on Prof. Schiff. **1888** [see PROFESSOR 4b]. **1916** H. L. WILSON *Somewhere in Red Gap* ii. 74, I bet Wilbur thinks the prof is awful old-fashioned, playing with his fingers that way. **1933** AUDEN *Dance of Death* 8 With profs. from Germany. **1949** H. WADMAN *Life Sentence* 16 Prof, how are you? You don't look a day older. **1967** O. WYND *Walk Softly* iv. 42 It's certainly not the local practice at prof level. Heads of departments come near to be living gods. **1975** C. FREMLIN *Long Shadow* x. 79 You were at the reception desk, phoning up to the Prof.'s room. **1979** L. MEYNELL *Hooky & Villainous Chauffeur* xi. 150 Don't call me *Prof*; it's an abbreviation I find particularly distasteful.

pro-Fascist: see *PRO-[1] 5a.

‖ **proferens** (profe·renz). *Law.* Pl. **proferentes** (profere·ntiz). [L., pres. pple. of *proferre* to offer, adduce.] The party which proposes or adduces a contract or a condition in a contract. Also in phr. *contra proferentem*, or *-es*, used of legal decisions made 'against the proposer(s)', with reference to the maxim *verba cartarum fortius accipiuntur contra proferentem*,' the words of contracts should be interpreted most forcibly against him who adduces them'.

[*a* **1626** BACON *Elem. Common Lawes Eng.* (1630) I. 11 *Verba fortius accipiuntur contra proferentem.* This rule that a mans deedes and his words shall be taken strongliest against himselfe,..is..a rule drawn out of the depth of reason. **1766** BLACKSTONE *Comm.* II. xxiii. 380 That the deed be taken most strongly against him that is the agent or contractor, and in favour of the other party. '*Verba fortius accipiuntur contra proferentem.*'] **1927** *Times Law Reports* 3 June 528/2 At the least the expression was ambiguous and must be construed *contra proferentem.* **1935** *Lloyd's List Law Rep.* 9 May 306/1 In this case the underwriters were not the *proferentes.* **1947** J. CHARLESWORTH *Law of Negligence* (ed. 2) xxix. 617 The Court of Appeal held that the word..was ambiguous and must be construed *contra proferentem.* **1971** R. A. PERCY *Charlesworth on Negligence* (ed. 5) xvi. 670 On the first point, Mackinnon J. and the Court of Appeal held that the word 'indemnify' was inapt to exclude a claim by the plaintiffs, and at least was ambiguous and must be construed *contra proferentes.* **1974** E. R. H. IVAMY *Marine Insurance* (ed. 2) xxiii. 349 He saw no reason for coming to the conclusion that the insurers were the *proferentes.*

profesh (profe·ʃ). *slang.* Abbrev. of PROFESSION 6; applied *spec.* to the theatrical profession. Also *U.S.*, the body of professional tramps.

1901 J. LONDON *Let.* 6 Dec. (1966) 126 Wyckoff is not a tramp authority... Wyckoff only knows the working-man... The profesh are unknown to him. **1907** —— *Road* 236 The profesh are the aristocracy of The Road. **1914** E. PUGH *Cockney at Home* 192 'Mr. Alexander,..being a hartist in his profesh, which there's only one thing as keeps him off the London stage at this present moment, and that is—' 'Eggs!' **1936** WODEHOUSE *Laughing Gas* xviii. 192 We're most of us in the profesh downstairs.

profess, *v.* **1. 1. a.** (Later examples.)

1939 A. CLARKE *Sister Eucharia* i. 8 The day she was professed a year Ago. **1975** *Anglo-Saxon Eng.* IV. 140 If the manuscript was a gift to William of St Calais around 1083 when the first monks were professed at Durham, it is written in a script..that would have been familiar to the new bishop.

profession. Add: **III. 6. e.** Applied allusively and *euphem.* to PROSTITUTION 1.

1888 KIPLING *In Black & White* 78 Lalun is a member of the most ancient profession in the world. **1914** C. MACKENZIE *Sinister St.* IV. ii. 862 There's only Miss Carlyle who's in the profession and comes in sometimes a little late. **1922** A. WOOLLCOTT *Shouts & Murmurs* ii. 57 The Actor and the Streetwalker... The two oldest professions in the world—ruined by amateurs. **1936** *Times Lit. Suppl.* 18 Apr. 338/4 Blackham has attempted a comprehensive survey of the activities of womankind from 'the oldest profession' to the magistracy.

professional, *a.* (*sb.*) Add: **A.** *adj.* **II. 3.** *professional* (*middle*) *class*, members of the learned and skilled professions regarded collectively. Freq. (with hyphen) *attrib.*

1888 [in Dict.]. **1919** G. B. SHAW *Heartbreak House* p. viii, Just as Ibsen's intensely Norwegian plays exactly fitted every middle and professional class suburb in Europe. **1960** C. DAY LEWIS *Buried Day* 131 The professional-class families. **1965** M. MORSE *Unattached* ii. 74 Social class (professional-middle to lower working class). **1979** G. ST. AUBYN *Edward VII* i. 29 Gibbs had been brought up as a member of the professional Middle Class.

4. a. (Earlier and further examples.)

1798 in *Deb. Congress U.S.* (1852) 10th Congress 1 Sess., App. 2741 The solemn air and dictatorial manner of a professional schoolmaster. **1836** *New Sporting Mag.* July 198 On this point I heard a remark from one of the professional [cricket] players. **1883** W. JAMES *Let.* 13 Jan. in R. B. Perry *Tht. & Char. W. James* (1935) I. 611 [S. H.] Hodgson is..a *gentleman* to his finger tips and a professional philosopher as well. **1946** *Mind* LV. 149 But is this work to bear fruit only in the narrow and specialised fields that professional philosophers inhabit? **1968** P. MCKELLAR *Experience & Behav.* xi. 277 Such a person might..be a professional philosopher who gets on well with other people in parties and other social situations.

b. (Earlier example.)

1851 J. PYCROFT *Cricket Field* iv. 56 The chief patronage..was..in London. There the play was nearly all professional: even the gentlemen made a profession of it.

c. Disparagingly applied to one who pursues relentlessly an activity or belief that is regarded with disfavour; inveterate, habitual, ruthless.

1879 *Cornh. Mag.* Oct. 414 It is one of the misfortunes of the professional Don Juan that his honour forbids him to refuse battle. **1937** *Time* 18 Jan. 75/2 Chekhov was a strong supporter of Zola and the Dreyfusards, Suvorin was a professional anti-Semite. **1978** J. KRANTZ *Scruples* vi. 167 The 'extra man' invited to sit next to her at dinner was either a homosexual or a professional leech who dined out every night by mere virtue of being unmarried and mildly presentable.

d. Reaching a standard or having the quality expected of a professional person or his work; competent in the manner of a professional.

1926 C. CONNOLLY *Let.* 8 May in *Romantic Friendship* (1975) 124, I think one must be pretty professional to succeed [as a writer]. **1945** 'A. GILBERT' *Black Stage* iv. 56 'This chap's got his head screwed on all right,' exclaimed Goodier. 'Looks like the professional touch to me.' **1969** M. BUTTERWORTH *Vanishing Act* xi. 124 The old and tried method of bulk-carrying—by crew members of ships and aircraft who do it on a regular, professional basis, and know all the angles—is safest and best. **1973** D. FRANCIS *Slay-Ride* ix. 100 The cutting edges had been sharpened like razors and the point would have been good as a needle. A professional job: no amateur could have produced that result with a few passes over a carborundum. **1979** *Daily Mail* 31 Jan. 9/6 The average [career] adviser in schools was strictly an amateur... But those responsible for guiding university students into the right jobs were highly professional.

e. Of technical equipment: of a type or standard used by professionals.

1955 *Brit. Communications & Electronics* II. 48/2 Professional recording equipment ranges from the fixed studio equipment, through mobile apparatus, down to portable machines. **1965** *Wireless World* Sept. 460/1 An important thing to check, especially in professional audio amplifiers, is the stability margin. **1971** *Hi-Fi Sound* Feb. 67/2 A professional pickup—a studio or lab component—may well be robust and dependable, but not a candidate for top hi-fi systems, in which tracking weights are at their lowest. **1975** G. J. KING *Audio Handbk.* x. 222 Professional machines operating at 38 or 76 cm/s may adopt essentially constant-current recording over the primary bandwidth.

B. *sb.* **2. b.** *spec.* A prostitute. Cf. *PROFESSION 6e.

1861 [see *AMATEUR 2]. **1973** 'D. JORDAN' *Nile Green* xxvii. 121 'I'm not a professional,' she said, too coolly, 'and he's not precisely my type.' **1977** *Listener* 17 Feb. 215/1 The girl he offers a client in order to clinch a deal ..is already a professional.

C. *Comb.*, as *professional-looking* adj.

1936 A. HUXLEY *Eyeless in Gaza* vi. 64 She [*sc.* a model ship] was so professional-looking. **1980** J. CARTWRIGHT *Horse of Darius* v. 67 Dieter had..prepared a very professional-looking salad.

professionality. (Earlier example.)

1861 *Economist* 27 Apr. 456/1 The pungency is given.. by that additional flavour of professionality.

professionalize, *v.* Add: **1.** (Further examples.)

1947 *Mind* LVI. 393 In the third period..philosophy has been professionalized. **1954** [see *LUBRITORIUM]. **1974** *Nature* 11 Jan. 122/3 Steeds 'professionalises' the subject so that a research student with the aid of this book should be able to make intelligent use of anisotropic elasticity.

Hence **profe·ssionalized** *ppl. a.*; **professionalizing** *vbl. sb.* (further examples); also as *ppl. a.*; **professionalization** (further examples).

1923 G. B. SHAW *Perfect Wagnerite* (ed. 4) 152 Wagner was not only the highly professionalized royal conductor of Dresden..: he was also the author of the saying that music is kept alive..on the cottage piano of the amateur. **1958** *Oxford Mag.* 20 Feb. 290/1 The increased professionalisation of sport. **1959** B. WOOTTON *Social Sci. & Social Path.* ix. 287 The history of this rapid growth of professionalization, and of the splintering of generalized welfare work into numerous highly specialized professions, is an interesting story. **1969** H. PERKIN *Key Profession* i. 20 The professionalization of university teaching..turned even more on the reform of Oxford and Cambridge. **1972** *Science* 12 May 645/1 The professionalizing of forestry created a community of interest between private and public policy makers. **1973** L. HOLCOMBE *Victorian Ladies at Work* i. 19 There was a raising of the status of the workers in teaching and nursing, this 'professionalization' being..distinctive..of the period. **1975** *Language for Life* (Dept. Educ. & Sci.) xxiii. 341 Language should become a well-established option in Dip. H.E. courses and..institutions selecting for a professionalising year should look upon it as an important qualification for acceptance. **1977** *N.Y. Rev. Bks.* 14 Apr. 38/3 The bar became increasingly professionalized—which meant that lawyers and judges were drawn from higher social classes. **1977** R. HOLLAND *Self & Social Context* ix. 265 The relation between sociology and psychology in the United States and Britain, both as disciplines and as *professionalising* disciplines. **1979** *Dædalus* Spring 15 They also believe in the 'professionalization' of sociology.

professionize, *v.* For *rare*$^{-1}$ in Dict. read *rare* and add: **2.** *trans.* To turn (an activity) into a profession.

1920 *Christian World* 23 Sept. 14/1 They professionized the study and diverted literature from its true and best purpose.

professor. Add: **II. 4. d.** A schoolmaster, a personal tutor; *spec.* a secondary school headmaster. Chiefly *U.S.*

1903 *Dialect Notes* II. v. 326 *Professor*, a male teacher. This abuse of the word 'professor' seems to have grown up in the country districts recently. It is now applied indiscriminately to any schoolmaster. **1940** W. FAULKNER *Hamlet* I. iii. 65 He's going to be the new school professor next year... Or so they claim. **1972** *Buenos Aires Herald* 4 Feb. 13/5 (Advt.), Spanish. Perfect accent, very clear pronunciation with experienced professor.

5. a. (Further examples.)

1816 *Sussex Weekly Advertiser* 22 July, Mr. Lambert, professor of Cricket, has published the whole art of playing. **1954** F. C. AVIS *Boxing Ref. Dict.* 87 *Professor*, a familiar name for a boxing coach.

b. (Earlier and later examples.)

1774 in C. S. R. Hildeburn *Century of Printing* (1886) II. 182 Catalogue of New and Old Books, to be sold by Auction, by Robert Bell, Bookseller and Professor of Book-Auctioneering, on Monday, the Seventh of February, 1774. **1848** W. C. MACREADY *Diary* 9 Dec. (1912) II. 415 At James's Hotel, where I dined, the landlord introduced me to *Professor* (!) *Risley*—the balancer and posture-master; *of course* I shook hands with him, etc.! **1896** C. H. SHINN *Story of Mine* 56 They were never out of sight of pilgrims—Irishmen with wheelbarrows,..'professors' with divining rods and electric 'silver detectors'. **1927** *Amer. Speech* III. 27 Most of those who insist on being given the title 'professor' are quacks or fakers of some kind... The title 'Professor' is now applied more often jocularly than seriously. **1972** *Times* 30 May 2/8 Their [*sc.* performing fleas] trainer, 'Professor' Len Tomlin, was 'too upset' last night to speak about the tragedy which had struck his troupe of 15 performers.

professor (profe·səɹ), *v.* Also with initial capital. [f. the sb.] *trans.* To address (a person) as 'professor'.

1893 W. JAMES *Let.* 8 July (1920) I. 345 Both you and Angell, being now colleagues and not students, had better stop Mistering or Professoring me. **1901** —— *Let.* 16 June (1920) II. 148, I professor-ed you because I had read your name printed with that title in a newspaper letter. **1908** —— *Let.* 28 July (1920) II. 308 Dear Bergson,—(can't we cease 'Professor'-ing each other?)

professoriat (prǫfesō^{ə}·riăt). [f. L. *professōrius* belonging to a public teacher (see PROFESSOR) + *-AT.] **a.** ≐ PROFESSORIATE 1. **b.** = PROFESSORIATE 2. Also *fig.*

1860 [see PROFESSORIATE 2]. **1933** *Sun* (Baltimore) 19 Dec. 1/2 Privately, they express complete distaste for the program, contempt for the 'professoriat'. **1978** *Encounter* Feb. 62/1 In this essay Davie's learning, verbal intelligence, scrupulousness, and his sense of how a poet actually works, combine to do credit to a text and, incidentally, to the Professoriat.

profibrinolysin: see *PRO-^{2} 1.

proficiency. Add: **3.** *attrib.* and *Comb.*, as *proficiency certificate, level, test*; **proficiency badge** *Scouting and Guiding*, a badge worn to mark achievement in a given test of skill or endurance; **proficiency pay** *Mil.*, increased pay given in respect of proficiency.

1921 *Daily Colonist* (Victoria, B.C.) 10 Apr. 9/4 It is proposed to further consider the proficiency badges which a Two Star Wolf Cub can obtain. **1970** *Policy, Organisation & Rules of Scout Assoc.* II. 25 The Cub Scout proficiency badges are designed to give advanced training in the twelve areas referred to. **1970** G. F. NEWMAN *Sir, You Bastard* 259 Sneed still held the proficiency certificate for using people. **1977** P. STREVENS *New Orientations Teaching of English* viii. 91 *Proficiency level*, particularly the distinction between *beginners* and *non-beginners*. **1909** *Westm. Gaz.* 24 Apr. 2/3 £450,000 is the charge for the service or proficiency pay of British soldiers. **1918** E. S. FARROW *Dict. Mil. Terms* 473 *Proficiency pay*, in the British service, extra pay, varying from 3d. to 6d. daily, issuable to soldiers of cavalry, artillery, infantry and school of musketry, according to conditions laid down in the Royal Warrant. **1960** D. D. EISENHOWER in *Public Papers of Presidents of U.S. 1960–1961* 49 Additional longevity pay of career personnel,..an increased number of men drawing proficiency pay. **1918** E. S. FARROW *Dict. Mil. Terms* 473 *Proficiency test*, in target practice, the annual test conducted to determine the proficiency of organizations in collective marksmanship.

profile, *sb.* Add: The pronunc. (prō^{u}·fəil) is now usual. **1. b.** A biographical sketch or character study (common in journalistic use since *c* 1920); a summary description or report.

a **1734** R. NORTH in J. L. Clifford *Biogr. as an Art* (1962) 31 As for the many sketches or profiles of great men's lives, pretended to be synoptical or multum in parvo, we are sure there is nothing we look for in them. **1840** DICKENS *Let.* 26 Nov. (1969) II. 158, I have gone through your two profiles, and marked them in pencil here and there. **1925** *New Yorker* 21 Feb. 9 (*heading*) Profiles. **1927** *Observer* 23 Oct. 6/2 No man can better give a thumbnail sketch of..a personality intimately known. In this volume we have glimpses of a few political personages... But novel 'profiles' of writers whom he has known are not to be found. **1930** H. CRANE *Let.* 21 Nov. (1965) 357 One assignment is a 'profile' of Walter Teagle, president of Standard Oil (N.J.). **1942** *Observer* 29 Nov. 1/4 M. Maisky, the Russian Ambassador, is the subject of the 'Profile' on page 7. **1952** M. STEEN *Phoenix Rising* v. 112 He's the big guy..who does the profiles in the Saturday edition. **1959** *Economist* 20 June 1096/2 He is the author of 'Profiles in Courage', a prize-winning and best-selling work of popular history. **1962** *Listener* 7 June 1004/1 A film profile of Julian Bream. **1975** *Language for Life* (Dept. Educ. & Sci.) xiv. 217 We have in mind a profile which would include diagnostic information and examples of written work. *Ibid.* xvii. 249 More reliable and productive would be a detailed profile of every child's strengths and weaknesses. **1976** *Liverpool Echo* 6 Dec. 1/5 United States President-elect Jimmy Carter was today examining profiles of 70 possible candidates for Cabinet and other senior posts.

2. Also, *in lost profile* (see *PROFIL PERDU).

1967 W. AMES *Prince Albert & Victorian Taste* xi. 139 The Duke..is seen in lost profile, with just enough of his nose and chin showing to be unmistakable.

3. a. (Further examples.) In *Physical Geogr.*, the outline of part of the earth's surface as seen in a vertical section along a straight line or a line following the course of a valley or river; *profile of equilibrium*, the profile of a graded river or stream; a profile such that the velocity is just sufficient to transport all the load supplied to it from above; also, an analogous profile of a beach, such that the amount of sediment deposited is balanced by the amount removed.

[**1841** A. SURELL *Étude sur les Torrents des Hautes-Alpes* i. 2 Quand on relève le profil en long du thalweg, on obtient..une courbe sensiblement continue, dont la pente s'élève, ou, si l'on aime mieux, dont la tangente s'approche de la verticale, à mesure qu'on approche du col. *Ibid.* iv. 18 Le profil longitudinal forme une courbe continue, convexe vers le centre de la terre.] **1868** *Min. Proc. Inst. Civil Engineers* XXVII. 549 The longitudinal profile of the irrigation canal, leading out of such a river should be..a regular inclined plane. *Ibid.*, The profile course of a river ..described a curve, concave to the horizon throughout, but more inclined near its source than elsewhere. **1894** *Jrnl. Geol.* II. 77 The profile of a consequent stream may for a time possess unequal slopes at its subsequent falls, but it soon attains a tolerably systematic curve of descent. *Ibid.*, Following certain French writers, the profile of the stream when this balanced condition has been reached has been called the profile of equilibrium. **1902** *Jrnl. Geol.* X. 1 (*heading*) Development of the profile of equilibrium of the subaqueous shore terrace. **1924** *Q. Jrnl. Geol. Soc.* LXXX. 581 There is little indication of the U-shaped transverse profile which is so characteristic of the Towy valley near Nant Stalwyn. **1944** A. HOLMES *Princ. Physical Geol.* xiv. 292 Along a shore of submergence the slope of the initial surface may be either steeper or gentler than that of the ideal profile of equilibrium. **1950** *Geol. Mag.* LXXXVII. 430 Fig. 1 represents the profile (perpendicular to the fold-axis) of part of the quarry face. **1952** M. L. BEGEMAN *Manuf. Process* (ed. 3) xix. 488 (*caption*) Milling profile of a locomotive side rod. **1954** W. D. THORNBURY *Princ. Geomorphol.* xviii. 476 (*caption*) Comparison of topographic profiles across North America and the South Atlantic basin. **1961** L. E. DOYLE *Manuf. Processes & Materials* xxxiv. 755 An optical comparator.. offers one way of checking the profiles and positions of gear teeth. **1964** V. J. CHAPMAN *Coastal Veg.* viii. 194 The beach profile is often such that it allows the waves to break close in-shore at high tide. **1968** R. W. FAIRBRIDGE *Encycl. Geomorphol.* 871/2 During the last glacial period of the Pleistocene, mean sea level was lowered by about 100 meters or more. River valleys cut down towards a new profile of equilibrium. **1969** D. J. EASTERBROOK *Princ. Geomorphol.* vi. 131 Below its junction with the Platte River, the profile of the Missouri River steepens because of the entry of gravel from the Platte. **1972** M. G. CROSS *Oceanogr.* i. 14 A profile of the ocean bottom under the ship's track is drawn by a recorder. **1976** S. JUDSON et al. *Physical Geol.* xiii. 311/2 The long profile of a stream from its headwaters to its mouth is..steepest in its upper reaches.

c. The shape of a wave.

1902 *Encycl. Brit.* XXXII. 579/2 Mr Froude made the assumption that the profile of the wave was a curve of sines. **1952** R. W. DITCHBURN *Light* iv. 81 A wave of irregular profile may always be regarded as the sum of a series of simple harmonic waves. **1959** E. PULGRAM *Introd. Spectrogr. of Speech* ii. 33 The profiles of waves A and C are so different from one another that one cannot help wondering whether, apart from pitch, they really represent the same tone. **1975** E. HECHT *Schaum's Outl. Theory & Probl. Optics* i. 1, $g(x+vt)$ is a solution of the wave equation corresponding to an arbitrary profile $g(x)$ propagating in the negative x-direction. *Ibid.* 2 Show that $f(x-vt)$ is a progressive wave moving in the positive x-direction with an unchanging profile.

e. *transf.* A characteristic personal manner; an attitude, a policy (of a country, government, etc.). *low profile*: see *LOW *a.* 23.

1961 *Musical Amer.* May 14/1 In all of Prokofieff's music..we find his profile—his 'signature'—his craftsman's attitude. **1962** *Listener* 11 Jan. 105/2 Marschner's application of a powerful declamatory style lends Heiling an extraordinary dramatic profile. **1970** *Guardian* 16 Dec. 10/2 The United States..has repeatedly committed itself to keeping its profile low. **1972** *Times* 30 Mar. 2/1 The most complicated question is the profile the Army should adopt at the start of Ulster's 'marching season'. **1972** *Guardian* 12 Apr. 14/1 The British profile during the present crisis in Vietnam has been as low as could be conceived. *Ibid.* 24 May 13/6 There is only one realistic way to deal any sort of worthwhile blow at the IRA... This is to 'raise the profile' very briefly in one..area. **1978** S. BRILL *Teamsters* ix. 323 Jackie expanded his base and his profile by joining civic groups.

4. d. *Soil Sci.* The set of horizons of which a soil is composed, as displayed in a vertical cross-section down to the parent material.

1906 E. W. HILGARD *Soils* x. 165 (*caption*) Soil profiles illustrating differences in soils of humid and arid regions. **1923** *Soil Sci.* XVI. 95 In this scheme of soil classification, the soil profile includes the whole thickness, upon which the soil-forming processes have operated, from the surface down to the parent rock or geologic substratum. The importance of a separation of a profile into its natural divisions is emphasized. **1927** N. C. COMBER *Introd. Sci. Study of Soil* xiii. 144 Areas in which the profiles are essentially alike are grouped together and the characteristic profile is given a definite name. **1946** L. D. STAMP *Britain's Struct. & Scenery* xi. 94 Over a large part of Highland Britain..there has been insufficient time for the weathering of rocks and the formation of a complete profile. **1954** W. D. THORNBURY *Princ. Geomorphol.* iv. 80 Some soils have profiles that could not have developed under a single set of soil-developing controls, but consist of a younger profile developed under existing topographic and climatic conditions superposed upon an older profile formed under different conditions. **1976** M. D. GIDIGASU *Laterite Soil Engin.* xx. 512 In well-developed laterite profiles, the laterite horizon ranges in texture from gravelly soils to laterite rock.

e. *Geol.* A representation of the form of the interface between strata obtained from measurements made at points lying on a straight line; also, the line itself; *to shoot a profile*, to make such measurements.

1929 *Colorado School of Mines Q.* Mar. 108 For a number of potential profiles covering the ground, lines of equal resistivity may be drawn in plan view, instead of equipotential lines. **1929** *Trans. Amer. Inst. Mining & Metalling Engineers* LXXXI. 597 To delimit a newly discovered dome and determine the depth to the top of the cap..profiles are shot by the refraction method. **1931** [see *PROFILING *vbl. sb.* 3]. **1940** C. A. HEILAND *Geophysical Explor.* ix. 499 In a new area a profile is first shot to determine the normal sequence of beds. *Ibid.* x. 736 The survey..is of interest because of the excellent correlation possible between resistivity profiles. *Ibid.* 739 Fig. 10-71 shows resistivity-depth curves for a dipping vein taken along three profiles, laid out 15° off strike, at increasing distances from the outcrop. **1949** *Geophysics* XIV. 57 (*heading*) Airborne magnetic profile above 40th parallel, eastern Colorado to western Indiana. **1950** *Bull. Amer. Assoc. Petroleum Geologists* XXXIV. 1384 The slope of a time-distance curve plotted from a profile across the dome usually showed salt velocity. **1960** M. B. DOBRIN *Introd. Geophysical Prospecting* (ed. 2) v. 86 Figure 5-13 shows two sample refraction records shot from opposite directions, each made with a spread of 22 detectors spaced 300 ft apart along a profile in line with the shots. **1977** *Nature* 3 Nov. 23/2 (*caption*) Seismic and magnetic profiles from locations indicated in Fig. 1. Vertical scale for the seismic profiles is in seconds of two-way travel time.

f. The outline formed on a graph or chart by joining the scores that a person has obtained in tests for various personality traits, esp. in order to provide a quantified result easily comparable with the results of others or of the norm; a similar type of diagrammatic representation of measured individual attributes for purposes of comparison. Also *transf.*

1932 Darrow & Heath in K. S. Lashley *Stud. Dynamics of Behavior* 68 By repetition and comparison of tests on the same person, we find a tendency for the shape of the profile to be characteristic of a given individual. **1940** T. L. Kelley *Talents & Tasks* 28 The full line is the profile of an individual, and the dotted line that of the average participant in the type of job being considered. **1946** *Jrnl. Clin. Psychol.* II. 23/1 Several recent articles have discussed the usefulness of the Minnesota Multiphasic Personality Inventory in various clinical situations ..and one has dealt with the problem of test profiles. **1948** *Eng. Stud.* XXIX. 109 Two variables are considered of prime importance in identifying specific patterns of tone in speech: the shape of the curve of speech melody, and the position of the principal stress on that curve. A given combination of shape and stress-position will be referred to as a profile. **1957** R. B. Cattell *Personality* ix. 366 The definition of a profile as a set of ordered measurements (corresponding to the mathematical definition of a vector quantity) applying to a single case. **1960** J. B. Carroll in Saporta & Bastian *Psycholinguistics* (1961) 342/1 Métraux's..'profiles' of speech development include descriptions of the tendency of the child to verbalize with regard to his own and others' behavior. **1973** *N.Y. Law Jrnl.* 24 July 4/4 To be sure, Ruiz-Estrella did fit the hijacking profile, but no one contends that this statistical survey..can come close to supplying traditional probable cause for a search. **1973** *Times* 26 July 8/2 Mr. Ehrlichman said that the need for a psychiatric profile of Dr. Ellsberg had prompted the decision to break into the office. **1974** *Physics Bull.* Nov. 505/1 Abstracts would be sent selectively to subscribers..according to their interest 'profiles'. **1977** *Language* LIII. 186 Given that we have participants of particular socio-economic profiles—but not taking their individuality into account—and given the specific situation, these are the choices which are most expected.

g. *Astr.* (A diagram of) the way the intensity of radiation varies with wavelength from one side of a line in a stellar spectrum to the other.

1933 *Proc. Nat. Acad. Sci.* XIX. 642 (*caption*) Schematic profiles of lines in the spectrum of a nova expanding with constant high velocity. *Ibid.*, The predicted profile of a star with an effectively transparent radiation shell, ejecting matter symmetrically with respect to two hemispheres. **1953** L. H. Aller *Astrophysics* p. v, The abundance of calcium may be determined from the profile of the '*K*' line in the solar spectrum. **1957** *Encycl. Brit.* XXI. 1951/1 The profiles of faint lines are strongly affected by the resolving power of the spectrograph. **1971** *Nature* 15 Jan. 214/1 He was one of the first to measure intensity profiles of the Fraunhofer lines in the solar spectrum and to attempt to explain these by theoretical models.

h. (A diagram of) the way a quantity varies along a line, esp. a vertical line through the earth or atmosphere; more widely, any graph in the form of a line.

1953 *Jrnl. Geophysical Res.* LVIII. 519 Five temperature profiles are obtained which represent stratospheric conditions over New Mexico during October 1952. **1955** *Sci. Amer.* Sept. 168/2 If we took gravity readings all over the earth and corrected them to sea level, we would have a gravity profile of the geoid. This profile undulates. **1963** G. L. Pickard *Descriptive Physical Oceanogr.* vi. 97 Temperature/depth or salinity/depth profiles..are usually drawn as the first stage in examining oceanographic data. **1970** *Sci. Jrnl.* Apr. 50/3 The measurement of temperature profiles within the atmosphere from satellite heights. **1971** I. G. Gass et al. *Understanding Earth* v. 85/2 (*caption*) Crustal temperature–depth profiles, as a function of heat flow and surface radioactivity. **1972** *Nature* 25 Feb. 417/1 Oxygen isotope profiles through the entire depth of the ice sheets of Greenland and Antarctica..provide an excellent record of climatic changes. **1977** *Lancet* 29 Oct. 932/1 The area irradiated by the transducer was calculated from beam profiles obtained by scanning a piezoelectric probe hydrophone through the centre of the beam, parallel to the transducer face. **1978** *Nature* 20 Apr. 725/1 PAS staining of the modified bovine receptors revealed a radically different profile and showed the presence of at least four major peaks with molecular weights in the region of $3{\cdot}9 \times 10^4$, 5×10^4, $1{\cdot}25 \times 10^5$ and $1{\cdot}8 \times 10^5$.

i. *Astronautics.* A particular sequence of accelerations undergone by a space rocket in flight; the plan of a space flight as regards the nature and duration of successive trajectories.

1962 K. A. Ehricke *Princ. Guided Missile Design* I. vii. 774 (*caption*) Constant thrust acceleration profile with and without intermediate coast period. **1962** R. C. Duncan *Dynamics Atmospheric Entry* i. 16 The functional phases of the direct-entry profile are: 1. Orbital phase... 2. Departure phase... 3. Free-fall phase... 4. Approach phase... 5. Landing phase. **1966** *Electronics* 3 Oct. 131 In the Mercury and Gemini programs, and in hypothetical mission profiles, the crew's time usually limits the number of adjustments that can be made in an experiment. **1972** *Jrnl. Spacecraft & Rockets* IX. 259 (*heading*) Thrust profile shaping for spin-stabilized vehicles.

7. (Earlier example.)

1824 J. Decastro *Mem.* 43 The master carpenter had forgot to saw off one of the unpainted pieces of profile belonging to a wing.

8. *profile picture, study, writer*; **profile chart** *Ecol.* = **profile diagram*; **profile cut,** a method of cutting a diamond in which it is sliced into thin plates that are polished on one side, finely grooved on the other, and bevelled on the edge; also *attrib.* as *adj.*; **profile diagram** *Ecol.*, a representation of a vertical section through a forest, showing the outlines of the individual components of the vegetation; **profile drag** *Aeronaut.*, that part of the drag on an aerofoil or aircraft which arises directly from its profile and from skin friction, i.e. those parts of the drag which are not attributable to lift; **profile grinding** *Engin.*, grinding in which the wheel extends the whole width of the work and is given a profile which when viewed at right angles to the axis of rotation is the negative of the one it is desired to produce on the work; so **profile-grind** *v. trans.*, **-ground** *ppl. a.*; also **profile grinder,** a machine for this; **profile paper** (earlier example); **profile shot,** a photograph or view of the human face in profile; **profile stage property** = sense 7.

1926 Tansley & Chipp *Aims & Methods in Study of Vegetation* iv. 65 Profile charts record diagrammatically the vertical relations of the vegetation..as seen in profile or 'elevation'. **1965** P. J. Fisher *Jewels* vi. 83 Normally, for the conventional brilliant cut, an octahedral diamond crystal is sawn into two halves... For the new profile cut the same crystal is sawn into four plates. **1970** R. Webster *Gems* (ed. 2) xx. 378 The Profile cut allows considerably greater area of visible diamond than a brilliant cut of similar size. Viewed from above a Profile cut diamond resembles a row of baguettes joined by a common table facet. **1976** 'D. Craig' *Faith, Hope & Death* xxii. 156 Good stuff, like profile-cut diamonds. [**1933** Davis & Richards in *Jrnl. Ecol.* XXI. 369 The stratification is very irregular and ill-marked, as can also be seen from the diagrammatic profile in Fig. 6.] **1952** P. W. Richards *Trop. Rain Forest* ii. 24 Because the direct observation of the stratification of the Rain forest usually offers insuperable difficulties, Davis & Richards..adopted the device of constructing profile diagrams to scale from accurate measurements of the position height and width and depth of crown of all the trees on narrow sample strips of forest. **1974** Mueller-Dombois & Ellenberg *Aims & Methods Vegetation Ecol.* viii. 148 Profile diagrams can be used to illustrate details in vertical spacing of species. **1922** *Flight* XIV. 692/2 Prandtl calls this increment of the drag at given lift by the trailing vortex system the 'induced drag', and the drag of the wing of infinite aspect ratio and of the same section he calls the 'profile drag'. **1936** *Jrnl. Aeronaut. Sci.* IV. 13/2 The covering of cellulose acetate may be highly polished to lower the profile drag. **1979** *Nature* 20–27 Dec. 778/3 These calculations take into account the effects of lift (or, in aeronautical jargon, 'induced drag') and of the power needed to overcome direct air resistance ('profile drag'). **1941** *Automobile Engineer* XXXI. 169/3 (*caption*) Profile grinding a helical gear by the Maag gear grinding process. **1956** *Ibid.* XLVI. 348/2 The floor-to-floor time was 12 minutes, or 6 minutes per gear. To profile grind at such rates a reasonable standard of gear preparation is necessary. **1950** C. R. Hines *Machine Tools for Engineers* xi. 234 Profile or contour grinders. These grinders are similar to pantograph milling machines. **1968** S. Tolansky *Strategic Diamond* viii. 67 (*caption*) Shaped profile grinder roller for making ceramic spark plug. **1975** Bram & Downs *Manuf. Technol.* i. 31 Microscopes are incorporated in suitable machine tools such as profile grinders. **1917** T. R. Shaw *Precision Grinding Machines* x. 155 (*heading*) Profile and form grinding. **1956** *Automobile Engineer* XLVI. 347 (*heading*) Faster profile grinding of spur gears. **1968** S. Tolansky *Strategic Diamond* viii. 66 Profile grinding is used extensively and ubiquitously for both large and small components which require to be of exact size or have complex shape. *Ibid.* 67 In spite of the hardness of the carbide profile grinding wheels and rollers they soon wear and lose both accurate outline and..accuracy in dimensions. **1941** *Automobile Engineer* XXXI. 168/3 In some cases the gears are hobbed and in others pinion type profile ground cutters are employed. **1874** 'Mark Twain' *Gilded Age* xvii. 160 He plotted the line on the profile paper. **1793** J. Woodforde *Diary* 25 Nov. (1929) IV. 80 They were so kind as to bring us a profile Picture of our late worthy friend Mr. DuQuesne. **1967** P. A. Whitney *Silverhill* iii. 48 He could not photograph me properly. Someone less skilled had taken over, but profile shots were not the same. **1968** L. Deighton *Only when I Larf* ii. 24 He swung round to give me a profile shot. **1972** I. Hamilton *Thrill Machine* viii. 34 She always managed to turn slightly this way or that to give Joe a profile shot. **1854** A. C. Mowatt *Autobiogr.* xvii. 308, I suppose you will send some profile stage properties to my room. **1959** *N. & Q.* Feb. 84/1 An initial profile-study gives some biographical facts. **1978** *Rugby World* Apr. 36/2 Being wholly inarticulate on any aspect of Rugby, I decided it might be wiser to confine my questioning to Gareth's second enthusiasm which, according to a generation of profile-writers, is fishing.

profile, *v.* Add: **1. b.** To compose or present a profile (sense *1 b) of (a person). Also *transf.* orig. *U.S.*

1948 *Word Study* Apr. 3/1 A student publication at Wayne wrote: 'Pan Profiles Russell Beggs' *Panorama.*' **1959** J. Thurber *Years with Ross* v. 85 Ross..took..the flagpole sitter..and profiled him. **1967** *Times Rev. Industry* Oct. 12/2 In February when the *Review* profiled Mr. Len Neal..he spoke enthusiastically of his department. **1970** T. Lupton *Managem. & Social Sci.* (ed. 2) iv. 98 Ways of measuring and 'profiling' the many structural characteristics of organizations. **1974** *Observer* 24 Mar. 29 (*caption*) Anthony Sampson profiles Mrs Katherine Graham, whose newspaper exposed the Watergate scandal. **1979** *Tucson* (Arizona) *Citizen* 20 Sept. 7B/3 Hugh Downs hosts a magazine format show. Tonight, disco star Donna Summer is profiled.

c. To summarize or register (information).

1971 *Nature* 19 Mar. 153/2 The user constructs a list of words and phrases (search terms) that summarize (profile) his information requirements. **1975** *New Yorker* 12 May 93/1 Electrical wires from the model power plants..ran over to a control room, where electronic equipment could absorb the findings of a hundred and twenty instruments that profiled, among other things, hull pressures, mooring forces, and six degrees of freedom of motion.

2. (Examples in *Engin.*) Cf. *profiling *vbl. sb.* 2.

1905 J. Horner *Engineers' Turning* xv. 294 Fig. 368 is a tool in its holder used for profiling ball handles, as used on lathes, and other machine tools. **1953** G. S. Schaller *Engin. Manufacturing Methods* xix. 340 (*caption*) Vertical rotary-head milling machine profiling a vertical surface. **1973** J. G. Tweeddale *Materials Technol.* II. vi. 146 Side-cutters are often profiled axially to cut a specific shape.

3. *intr.* To present one's profile to view; *spec.* in *Bullfighting*, to stand in profile in preparation for a charge.

1932 E. Hemingway *Death in Afternoon* 347 Profiling with more style, his kills would gain greatly in emotion. **1957** A. MacNab *Bulls of Iberia* xv. 205 To get it to charge he has to profile on the contrary horn, making it feel sure it will catch him each time. **1973** *Black World* Sept. 84 Ever get tired of people posturing, Posing and profiling? **1974** F. Nolan *Oshawa Project* ii. 14 He'll be over here.. profiling for the newsreels.

4. *trans.* To measure or investigate the profile (sub-senses of *4) of. Cf. *profiling *vbl. sb.* 3.

1932 *Physics* II. 174 One of the earliest applications of the seismograph was its use in profiling salt domes. **1960** *Econ. Geol.* LV. 204 Sometimes the geologist wants to profile a particular stratigraphic horizon..instead of the land surface. **1972** *Physics Bull.* Feb. 85/1 The Clarendon Laboratory at Oxford..has improved still further its original method of profiling the atmosphere from a satellite. **1978** *Nature* 5 Jan. 49/2 Side-scan sonar has been used..to profile icebergs, by lowering a sonar transducer vertically..from the side of a boat.

profiler (prō^{u}·fəiləɹ). [f. Profile *v.* + -er^1.]

1. A profile machine.

1904 *Electr. World & Engin.* 19 Mar. 581/2 (*heading*) Motor driven profiler. **1927** *Daily Tel.* 11 May 18/3 (Advt.), Gear cutters, Profilers, Radials, &c. **1957** W. H. Armstrong *Machine Tools for Metal Cutting* vii. 156 The distinguishing feature of a profiler is a profiling unit that is mounted on a spindlehead which may be fed transversely. **1963** Jones & Schubert *Engin. Encycl.* (ed. 3) 1007 Most of the profilers used at the present time are hand-operated, so far as the feeding movements are concerned.

2. An instrument for measuring profiles, esp. of strata of rock or the sea bed.

1959 *World Oil* Apr. 107/2 A versatile new marine exploration device..has been applied recently to problems in connection with petroleum exploration... Known as the..continuous seismic profiler, the technique essentially is a continuous sound reflection device. **1969** J. W. Mavor *Voyage to Atlantis* v. 104 We carried five basic instrument systems. First, a sonar system..to measure depth. Three instrument systems, the seismic profiler, the magnetometer and the gravimeter. Finally, [etc.]. **1972** J. G. Dennis *Structural Geol.* xvi. 368 Most present-day profilers work with sound sources such as high voltage sparks or air guns. **1973** *Nature* 22 June 455/2 Seismic reflexion profiler data reveal a distinct basement ridge. **1975** *McGraw-Hill Yearbk. Sci. & Technol.* 291/2 Velocity shears top to bottom are given by a free-falling electromagnetic profiler... The instrument measures minute voltages induced by the flow of sea water in the Earth's weak magnetic field. **1978** *Nature* 7 Dec. 601/2 Temperature profiles were taken from the RV Oceanographer with the microstructure profiler (MSP), a winged instrument which falls freely through the water measuring temperature, pressure, and conductivity.

profiling (prō^{u}·fəiliŋ), *vbl. sb.* [f. Profile *v.* + -ing^1.] **1.** The drawing of profiles.

1888 [in Dict. s.v. Profile *v.*].

2. *Engin.* The shaping of a part, orig. by means of a tool guided by a template or pattern. Freq. *attrib.*, esp. in *profiling machine* (= *profile machine* s.v. Profile *sb.* 8).

1892 [in Dict. s.v. Profile *v.*]. **1950** C. R. Hine *Machine Tools for Engineers* ix. 155 (*caption*) Four-spindle vertical Hydrotel milling machine with automatic 360-deg profiling attachment. **1957** [see *profiler 1]. **1967** A. Battersby *Network Analysis* (ed. 2) 377 This measure is likely to utilize the drilling machine inefficiently, because of the odd bits of time spent in waiting for successive small batches from the profiling machine.

3. *Geol.* and *Physical Geogr.* [f. Profile *sb.*] The measurement or investigation of profiles, esp. of strata; *spec.* by means of measurements made at points lying on a straight line.

1929 *Trans. Amer. Inst. Mining & Metall. Engineers* LXXXI. 598 Mapping structures..by means of refraction profiling. **1931** F. H. Lahee *Field Geol.* (ed. 3) xxiii. 680 Field work may be conducted according to one of three main plans: (1) fan-shooting or fanning by the refraction method; (2) profile shooting, or profiling by the refraction method; and (3) profiling by the reflection method. **1938** B. McCollum in A. E. Dunstan et al. *Sci. of Petroleum* I. viii. 396/2 In most cases..the profiling of this very shallow boundary cannot be successfully carried out at the present time by reflection. **1963** J. B. Hersey in M. N. Hill *Sea* III. iv. 65 Continuous refraction profiling should prove especially valuable in the study of unconsolidated sediments in deep water. **1968** R. W. Fairbridge *Encycl. Geomorphol.* 1227/2 Sub-bottom acoustic profiling..has demonstrated many wave-cut terraces partly hidden beneath a thin veneer of late Holocene sediments. **1977** R. J. Rice *Fund. Geol.* viii. 141 Profiling. A third approach to the analysis of hillslope forms is by measurement of representative profiles.

profilmic: see *pro-^{2} 2.

profilograph. Add to def.: = *PROFILOMETER 2. (Examples.)

1941 *Jrnl. Amer. Ceramic Soc.* XXIV. 229 The closest approach to this was a profilograph which had been constructed by Abbott at the University of Michigan and a somewhat similar device which had been built in Germany by Schmaltz. These instruments used a diamond stylus mechanically mounted on a mirror in such a way that movements of the diamond point in a direction normal to the surface of the material could be magnified by an optical lever system and the results recorded on a photographic film. **1963** *Engineering* 20 Sept. 360/1 The Bump-cutter employs 110 12 in diameter saw blades impregnated with natural diamonds. The design principle is based on a profilograph with the cutting head mounted on a 16 ft long frame supported by drive wheels at the rear and steering wheels at the front. **1976** ATTEWELL & FARMER *Princ. Engin. Geol.* x. 751 Unless joint surfaces are sufficiently exposed..to lend themselves to profilograph examination, it is difficult to see how a reduction factor can be applied.

profilometer. 1. Substitute for def.: Any instrument or device for measuring the profile of the face. (Example.)

1939 *Jrnl. Amer. Med. Assoc.* 18 Nov. 1903/2 A description of Dr. Joseph Safian's profilometer is found in his book 'Rhinoplastic Surgery'.

2. Any instrument for measuring or recording the roughness of a surface; *spec.* (*a*) one in which a fine stylus is drawn over a metal surface; (*b*) one consisting of a wheeled frame for travelling along a road.

1937 *Metal Cleaning & Finishing* May 426 During the past two years, a new instrument called the 'Profilometer' has been developed. This instrument supplements the earlier work in this field, and enables roughness measurements to be made rapidly with a portable instrument. **1938** *Times* 26 Nov. 9/4 The profilometer—designed and constructed at the Road Research Laboratory—has been used to measure the riding qualities of a number of experimental sections. This 16-wheeled machine compares irregularities in the surface by integrating the vertical rise and fall in profile of the road above a given datum, the results being recorded as 'inches per mile'. **1949** G. SCHLESINGER *Factory* xi. 219/1 Generally the Profilometer provides only 'average' readings..determining the roughness of the surface without producing conclusions as regards the waviness. **1958** H. M. SHERRARD *Austral. Road Pract.* xvi. 302 The profilometer consists of a wheel resting freely on the road surface whose vertical movement is traced on a ribbon of paper, thus giving a profile of the road. **1966** R. ASHWORTH *Highway Engin.* xii. 254 The profilometer consists of a 16-wheeled articulated carriage arranged so as to support the recording gear at a constant height above the continuously arranged level of the road surface at these 16 wheel points. **1976** [see PROFILOMETRY below].

Hence **profilo·metry**, the use of such an instrument; **profilome·tric** *a.*

1971 T. F. J. QUINN *Applic. Mod. Physical Techniques Tribol.* i. 32 This 'microscopic' approach must involve the use of as many methods of surface examination as possible. The more conventional methods of optical microscopy..and surface profilometry..are often too coarse for this approach. **1975** D. F. MOORE *Princ. & Applic. Tribol.* ii. 15 The profilometric, cartographic, and photogrammetric measurement techniques..deal with a complete representation of surface roughness. **1976** J. HALLING *Introd. Tribol.* ii. 21 The most usual method for the study of surface geometry is profilometry. In the profilometer a very fine diamond stylus..is drawn over the surface irregularities... The vertical movement of the stylus..is measured and amplified, usually electronically, so that the recorded output provides a picture of the actual surface.

‖**profil perdu** (prǫfīl pẽrdü). Also **profile perdu.** [Fr.] (See quot. 1959.) Also *attrib.*

1959 P. & L. MURRAY *Dict. Art* 257 *Profil perdu*, (Fr. lost profile) is that view of a head in which the profile is lost because the whole head is turned so far away that only the outline of the cheek is visible. By extension, the *profil perdu* of any object is what is seen of it when it is more than half turned away from the spectator. **1961** *Times* 14 Feb. 6/6 Rubens and Velasquez repeat the idea with back views, profile or *profile-perdu* heads. **1967** E. WYMARK *As Good as Gold* xv. 214 She..stood gazing down the street, her figure a *profil perdu* against a grey sky.

Profintern (prǫ·fintəɹn). [Russ. *Profintérn*, f. *Krásnyĭ* Intern*atsionál* Prof*soyúzov* Red International of Trade Unions, after *Komintérn* *COMINTERN.] An international organization of left-wing Trade Unions, founded in 1921 and dissolved in 1937.

1928 R. W. DUNN *Soviet Trade Unions* vi. 65 Through its delegates in the Red Trade Union International (Profintern) to participate in the international labor movement. **1938** *Encycl. Brit. Bk. of Yr.* 335/1 The Red International of Labour Unions ('Profintern') was founded at Moscow in 1921 under the auspices of the Third International to work for the reorganization of the Trade Union movement throughout the world on militant and revolutionary lines. **1949** I. DEUTSCHER *Stalin* 401 Parallel with the Comintern, the *Profintern* (the International of the Red trade unions) had opposed itself to the so-called Amsterdam International. **1958** *Economist* 1 Nov. 424/2 The fact that A. Lozovsky, who had vanished previously, is also reported as dead in 1952 suggests that the former head of the International of Red Trade Unions (Profintern) may also have been a victim of the anti-Jewish drive. **1977** *N.Y. Rev. Bks.* 26 May 26/4 Nikolsky was a representative of the Profintern, the Trade Unions International.

profit, *sb.* Add: **7. a.** *profit economy, -monger* (further example), *-mongering* (example), *plan, -planning*; *profit-bearing, -conscious* (hence *-consciously* adv.), *-hungry, -linked* adjs.; (obj. genitive) *profit-maximizer*; *profit-cashing, -generating, -making* (further examples), *-maximizing, -seeking,* sbs. and adjs.; (instrumental, etc.) *profit-motivated, -oriented* adjs.

1918 W. S. CHURCHILL *Let.* 10 Sept. in M. Gilbert *W. S. Churchill* (1975) IV. vii. 145 The lives they have saved and the prisoners they have taken have made these 18,000 men the most profit-bearing we have in the army. **1945** *Richmond* (Va.) *Times-Dispatch* 5 May 12/3 Profit-cashing by those who desired a clean slate over the week-end stalled numerous leaders. **1960** *Farmer & Stockbreeder* 1 Mar. 149/2 (Advt.), Every profit-conscious egg producer must have Evans Maxilay and Topscore strains. **1976** *Western Mail* (Cardiff) 22 Nov. 8/4 A number of their most profit conscious private sector industries. **1972** *Physics Bull.* June 366/3 Profit-consciously,..the company will normally supply the crawler only as part of its contract inspection service. **1943** *Sun* (Baltimore) 8 Feb. 3/2 The 'profit economy' has not always been equal to the demands of war. **1970** R. STAVENHAGEN in I. L. Horowitz *Masses in Lat. Amer.* vii. 242 Sol Tax describes the Panajackel Indians' economy as being a 'penny capitalism'..because they are oriented towards a profit economy. **1976** *National Observer* (U.S.) 14 Aug. 4/1 Profit-generating factors seem to have existed on Sundays in the Big Apple. **1939** *Sun* (Baltimore) 18 Aug. 6/1 The profit-hungry Celanese Corporation of America..is creating a public resentment. **1972** *Accountant* 12 Oct. 447/3 (*heading*) Profit-linked share incentive schemes. **1973** *Times* 31 Oct. 1/1 (*heading*) Government puts limit on profit-linked rises in Phase Three changes. **1953** E. SMITH *Guide Eng. Traditions & Public Life* 76 'Public Schools'..are not conducted for the purpose of profit-making. If there should be any excess of income over expenditure it is used for improvements in the school. **1974** *Times* 15 Oct. 5/2 A straightforward profit-making job with very few public benefits. **1968** *Listener* 28 Mar. 403/1 A pure profit-maximiser would already be attacking these hindrances to profit if he could. **1961** *Southern Econ. Jrnl.* Oct. 163/1 Where the industry's product price has been kept below the 'profit-maximizing' and 'entry-limiting' prices due to fears of public reaction. **1968** *Listener* 4 Apr. 437/2 So much for constraints of profit-maximising. **1977** *Dædalus* Fall 92 Larger and larger fractions of the GNP are being produced in sectors..that are clearly not competitive profit-maximizing sectors. **1961** *Spectator* 2 June 808 The profitmongers have an uncanny nose for threats. **1884** W. MORRIS in *Justice* 17 May 2/2 Ugliness is but a part of the bestial waste of the whole system of profit-mongering, which refuses cultivation and refinement to the workers. **1973** *Listener* 14 June 805/1 The public's distrust of..endorsements, knowing them to be profit-motivated and not spontaneous. **1978** W. GARNER *Möbius Trip* ii. 57 The tatty commercialism of profit-motivated research. **1976** *Nigerian Chron.* 18 Aug. 7/4 Government has recently decided to grant full autonomy in personnel matters to all profit-oriented parastatals. **1979** *Arizona Daily Star* 5 Aug. E3/4 'I think we need a president who is more profit-oriented,' he said. **1967** D. GOCH in Wills & Yearsley *Handbk. Managem. Technol.* 158 *Profit plan*, profit target based on a predetermined rate of return required from the invested funds represented by the fixed assets and working capital employed in carrying on a business activity. **1964** E. C. D. EVANS (*title*) Profit planning and the measurement of return on capital employed. **1927** M. SADLEIR *Trollope: a Comm.* 148 The profit-seeking [of the Great Exhibition]..lay behind the pious ejaculations of an inspired Press. **1949** I. DEUTSCHER *Stalin* ii. 27 The evils of modern profit-seeking industrialism. **1965** H. I. ANSOFF *Corporate Strategy* (1968) iii. 37 It would seem..that profit-seeking, or maximization of profit, would be the natural single business objective.

b. profit foul *U.S. Basketball*, an intentional or 'professional' foul committed to prevent one's opponents from scoring (? *Obs.*); **profit margin,** the margin that remains in a business operation when the costs involved are deducted from profits, usu. considered as a percentage of the capital employed (cf. MARGIN *sb.* 2b, quot. 1866); **profit(s) motive** (usu. with *the*), the incentive that the possibility of making profits gives to individual or free enterprise; **profit-sharing** (further examples); also as adj.; **profit squeeze,** the diminishment in profit margins due to costs rising relatively faster than selling prices with insufficient compensation from increased sales; **profit-taking** (further examples); so *profit-taker*.

1952 *Sun* (Baltimore) 15 Jan. 17/3 Veteran Coach Murray Greason..criticized today what he termed wide-spread use of the 'profit foul' in basketball. **1926** *Encycl. Brit.* III. 225/2 Various measures were taken during the War to restrict profiteering, especially in belligerent countries. These included the fixing of maximum prices, and in some cases of profit margins at each stage of production and distribution. **1974** *Guardian* 25 Mar. 22/6 The discount stores operate on narrow profit margins. **1976** B. WILLIAMS *Making of Manchester Jewry* iii. 67 The general move was in the direction of mass sales at a low profit margin. **1931** PATTERSON & SCHOLZ *Econ. Probl. Mod. Life* (ed. 2) ii. 37 The profits motive represents the modern crystallization of the economic force of self-interest. Hence, production is guided by market value and turns toward the production of luxuries for which there is an effective demand. **1936** J. M. KEYNES *Gen. Theory Employment* xxiii. 335 In conditions in which the quantity of aggregate investment is determined by the profit motive alone, the opportunities for home investment will be governed..by the domestic rate of interest. **1947** A. E. WAUGH *Princ. Econ.* xxxvi. 863 A society that used coercion instead of the profit motive would not need to establish such institutions as those of free enterprise and free contract. **1975** *Verbatim* May 3/2 Never forget that the profit motive can sometimes be used to a customer's advantage. **1900** *Econ. Rev.* X. 239 (*heading*) Two profit-sharing concerns. **1920** M. BEER *Hist. Brit. Socialism* II. IV. xiv. 292 Profit-sharing and Industrial Co-partnership schemes have been re-examined. **1949** *Here & Now* (N.Z.) Oct. 11/2 Far from being the predatory capitalist, he offers himself as the profit-sharing employer. **1975** *Times* 14 Jan. 14/1 Only 22 per cent of the sample belonged to profit sharing or bonus schemes related to the profits the company makes. **1979** *West Lancs. Even. Gaz.* 28 May 11 (Advt.), The company offers an attractive starting salary, operates a profit-sharing scheme and other benefits. **1958** *Wall St. Jrnl.* 8 Dec. 1/6 The outstanding feature of 1959 may be a further profit squeeze. **1969** J. ARGENTI *Managem. Techniques* iii. 11 If margins fall, profits fall, unless the company can somehow increase sales volume—and that is not easy. This phenomenon is known as 'the Profit Squeeze' and most companies today are feeling its effects. **1552** Profit taker [see sense 7a in Dict.]. **1968** *Economist* 5 Oct. 78/1 What does seem to have arrived is the day of the profit-taker. **1980** *Times* 5 Jan. 19 The profit takers pulled out of gold. **1928** *Daily Mail* 25 July 18/3 In the Electrical group Bournemouth and Pooles eased on profit-taking. **1976** *Birmingham Post* 16 Dec. 9/10 Stocks settled for a small gain after two rally attempts were stalled by profit-taking.

c. *pl.*, as **profits tax,** a tax on business profits, *spec.* that levied on company profits, as *excess profits tax* (*EXCESS *sb.* 6b).

1920 [see *corporation tax* s.v. *CORPORATION 7]. **1938** *Ann. Reg. 1937* 38 The Chancellor..was urged from many quarters to withdraw the profits tax and meet his requirements from a further increase in the income tax. **1947** *Western Daily Express* 14 June 1 The increased profits tax was criticized at the annual meeting of the Association of British Chambers of Commerce. **1958** *Times* 7 Jan. 15/1 The effect on capital allowances for profits tax purposes of new plants coming into operation. **1974** *Times* 17 Apr. (Ontario, Manitoba & Saskatchewan Suppl.) p. iv, Both provinces have imposed a special 'windfall profits' tax to prevent developing companies from profiting unduly from share increases in the world price of their products.

profitability. Delete *rare* and add: (Further examples.) Also, the state of being profitable; the capacity to make a profit. Also *attrib.*

1924 J. STAMP *Current Probl. Finance & Govt.* 11, I may venture to say that we have almost reached a limit of profitability along the old lines of deductive reasoning. **1931** *Economist* 26 Sept. 548/2 In so far as an industry's profitability is improved the weight of its fixed interest charges is lessened. **1961** *Listener* 2 Nov. 691/2, I am not frightened by profits; no one should ever be frightened of profits. Profitability is the only measure of success. **1964** *Daily Tel.* 15 Feb. 9/2 (*heading*) Guthrie starts BOAC drive for profitability. **1969** *Times* 6 Jan. 7/8 But for foot-and-mouth disease, production would certainly have risen considerably and the price position would already have caused alarm among producers near the profitability margin. **1979** *Jrnl. R. Soc. Arts* CXXVII. 617/1 There is a direct connection between profitability and survival.

profiteer (prǫfitīə·ɹ), *sb.* [f. PROFIT *sb.* + -EER; cf. Fr. *profiteur* (*de guerre*).] One who profits; *spec.* one who seeks to make excessive gain, as by the extortionate sale of necessary goods. Also as second element in *war profiteer*.

1912 *Athenæum* 21 Dec. 756/3 The fundamental unfairness of the relations between the wage-earner and the 'profiteer'. **1914** *Englishwoman* Nov. 94 The tricks of the armament profiteers are fresh in the public mind. **1918** W. OWEN *Let.* 10 Aug. (1967) 568 All the stinking Leeds & Bradford War-profiteers. **1942** W. S. CHURCHILL *End of Beginning* (1943) 130 If there are any would-be profiteers of disaster who feel able to paint the picture in darker colours, they are certainly at liberty to do so. **1952** A. POWELL *Buyer's Market* ii. 137 In the twilight world of undergraduate conversation..a kind of stage 'profiteer' or 'tycoon': a man of Big Business and professionally strong will. **1975** *New Yorker* 21 Apr. 134/3 There have already been reports of some killings in several cities, where government police, tax collectors, war profiteers,..have been among the targets previously announced. **1976** *Economist* 16 Oct. 15/2 The radicals also had..strong support among ex-Red Guards and other profiteers of the 1960s cultural revolution. **1980** *Times* 9 May 15/4 Dante ..puts profiteers next door to sodomites in the Seventh Circle of Hell.

profiteer (prǫfitīə·ɹ), *v.* [f. prec.] **a.** *intr.* To practise profiteering; to be a profiteer.

1916 *New Age* 17 Feb. 361/1 The companies are..not only removed from the common temptation to profiteer, but are guaranteed a practically fixed income. **1920** R. MACAULAY *Potterism* II. iii. 94 She had merely profiteered out of it all, and had a good time. **1928** R. CAMPBELL *Wayzgoose* i. 20 Journalists are..profiteering on the brains of sheep.

b. *trans.* To obtain (money) by profiteering; to exploit (a person) financially. *rare.*

1923 S. KAYE-SMITH *End of House of Alard* I. 12 He wouldn't lend us any of the money he profiteered out of those collapsible huts. **1928** *Sunday Express* 3 June 13/1 Aren't we being profiteered here?

profiteering (prǫfitīə·riŋ), *vbl. sb.* [f. as prec. + -ING[1] (see note).] The action or fact of seeking to make an excessive profit, as by providing necessities at extortionate prices. Also *attrib.*

Quot. 1814 is apparently an independent and isolated formation. The word was revived in the early twentieth century by A. R. Orage and others.

1814 *Guernsey Star & Gaz.* in *New Age* (1919) 21 Aug. 278/2 The extortionate profiteering that is being practised by the tradesmen in the public market. **1914** *New Age* 27 Aug. 391/2 England is at war upon profiteering. *Ibid.* 15 Oct. 561/2 The profiteering braggadocio..of 'City Man' and his confederates. **1919** *Act* 9 & 10 *Geo. V* c. 66 (*title*) An act to check profiteering. *Ibid.* §8 This Act may be cited as the Profiteering Act, 1919. **1922** W. J. Locke *Tale of Triona* vi. 56 'A dog and a rose and a glass of wine,' said she, 'are a woman's due for amusing a man. But a motor-car is profiteering.' **1939** A. Thirkell *Before Lunch* xii. 307 He said he'd take a hundred more for it than he gave. No, no, I said... No profiteering. I'll give what you gave. **1976** F. Zweig *New Acquisitive Society* II. v. 112 Profiteering could also cover excessive or illegitimate rents. **1978** P. Boardman *Worlds of Patrick Geddes* ix. 307 The mainsprings of the Financial Age were ..the perfection of profiteering-techniques.

profiterole. Delete †*Obs.* and add: Also **profiterolle.** Now *spec.* a small hollow case of choux pastry usu. filled with cream and served with chocolate sauce.

1884 F. J. Deliee *Franco-Amer. Cookery Bk.* 131 Range the profiteroles in pyramid form in the centre. **1889** A. B. Marshall *Cookery Bk.* xiv. 315 *Chocolate profiteroles*... Make a choux pastry..and force it out from the bag on to a dry baking tin in shapes about the size of a small button mushroom. **1906** *Mrs. Beeton's Bk. Househ. Managem.* lxii. 1667 *Profiteroles* (Fr.), a kind of light cake, baked in hot ashes, and filled with cream or custard. **1949** N. Mitford *Love in Cold Climate* II. vi. 264 Chocolate profiterolles with real cream. **1960** F. Raphael *Limits of Love* I. x. 129 Between dances, Andrew and Julia ate.. chocolate profiteroles and hot sausages. **1972** *Daily Tel.* (Colour Suppl.) 25 Aug. 42/3, I had three puddings (40p plus each); first profiteroles which were a credit to the pâtissier, Patrice.

profiting, *ppl. a.* (s.v. Profit *v.*) (Later example.)

1908 *Daily Chron.* 3 Oct. 5/4 So many profiting interests are concerned that there can be little doubt as to the ultimate formation of a syndicate.

proflavine (profle̅ⁱ·vīn). *Pharm.* Also **-in** (-in). [f. Pro-² + Flavine in Dict. and Suppl.] A yellowish-brown crystalline solid, 3,6-diaminoacridine, $C_{13}H_{11}N_3$, which is used, in the form of an orange-red hydrated sulphate, as an antiseptic.

1917 C. H. Browning in *Brit. Med. Jrnl.* 16 June 825/1 The Medical Research Committee's Department of Biochemistry and Pharmacology has..continued to give us valuable aid, especially by providing an experimental supply of 'proflavine'. *Ibid.* 21 July 71/1 The name 'proflavine' has been suggested to us by the Medical Research Committee. **1917** *Lancet* 3 Nov. 676/1 Proflavine..is..a preliminary product in the manufacture of acriflavine or flavine. **1945** *Times* 7 Aug. 10/2 Other interesting items included 24,000,000 hypodermic tablets, 40,000,000 acriflavine and proflavine tablets. **1958** *Nature* 11 Oct. 983/1 Proflavin, although not interfering with synthesis of deoxyribonucleic acid in phage-infected cells, inhibits the maturation of phage progeny particles. **1970** Passmore & Robson *Compan. Med. Stud.* II. xviii. 41/1 Acridine dyes, e.g. proflavine, acriflavine, are more active than aniline dyes against Gram-positive bacteria, and are also active against Gram-negative bacilli. **1971** D. J. Cove *Genetics* x. 137 The starting point of these studies was a 'phage strain which carried an *rII* mutation induced by the acridine proflavin.

profluence. **2.** Restrict †*Obs.* to sense a in Dict. and add: **b.** (Later example.)

1950 M. Peake *Gormenghast* lxxi. 392 The windows.. appeared to be sprinkled over the green façades..with an indiscriminate and wayward profluence that gave no clue as to how the inner structures held together.

pro-form: see *pro-¹ 4b.

profundal (profʊ·ndăl), *a.* and *sb. Ecology.* [ad. G. *profund* Profound: see -al.] **A.** *adj.* Applied to the region of the bed of a lake lying below the thermocline. **B.** *sb.* The profundal region of a lake bed.

[**1928** K. E. Carpenter *Life in Inland Waters* viii. 180 Modern workers usually prefer to recognise a 'sub-littoral zone'.., ending at about 50 metres in lakes of the plain type.., and below this a 'profound' or 'deep-water' region.] **1931** *Ecol. Monogr.* I. 233 In fresh-water lakes few animals have proved themselves capable of living in that unusual habitat, the anaerobic profundal zone of the lake bottom. *Ibid.* 245 In Third Sister Lake the three major benthic zones have the following approximate extent: littoral, 0–3 m.; sublittoral, 3–10 m.; profundal, 10–18 m. **1957** G. E. Hutchinson *Treat. Limnol.* I. xv. 818 Enabling the animals of the profundal benthos to live not merely under conditions of low oxygen and high CO_2 tension. **1961** *Ekol. Polska* A. IX. 352 A total of 2300 samples was taken from the profundal of Lake Tajty. **1965** B. E. Freeman tr. *Vandel's Biospeleol.* i. 9 The profundal regions of lakes..constitute an environment similar to the subterranean media. **1972** *Oikos* Suppl. No. 14. 5 In the profundal of a eutrophic lake the environment is relatively homogeneous and the species diversity low compared with the littoral.

prog, *sb.*³ Add: (Earlier and later examples.) prog *v.*³ (earlier and later examples).

1890 Barrère & Leland *Dict. Slang* II. 152/2 *Proggins* (university), proctor. **1892** *Granta* 13 Feb. 196/1 [Proctor] What do you mean by this, Sir? You have been following me about for the last ten minutes... [Freshman] Oh—er—I only wanted to see you proggins some one! **1935** D. Sayers *Gaudy Night* xii. 255 The Proggins was just coming..round the corner of Broad Street. **1935** N. Mitchison *We have been Warned* iv. 428 'I warned him he might get progged.'.. 'We might make the progs feel a bit awkward!' **1945** G. B. Grundy *Fifty-Five Years at Oxford* iv. 55 He did not care a — for all the — proggins in the kingdom. **1965** *Guardian* 6 May 5/3 This evening may be the last..on which undergraduates can be progged. *Ibid.* 5/5 The progs have chased and chased us Up and down the town.

prog (prǫg), *a.* and *sb.*⁴ *slang.* Also **Prog.** Abbrev. of Progressive *a.* (*sb.*) in Dict. and Suppl.

1958 'N. Blake' *Penknife in my Heart* vii. 91 The Lanes, his hosts, were a prog. couple. **1965** *N.Y. Times* 1 June 33 The 'progs' or progressives believe Tewkesbury lives too much in the past. **1968** *Listener* 29 Aug. 280/2 Chaps like us..who don't believe in change, do far more for the Church than a thousand bloody progs like Pope John. **1971** *Progress* (Cape Town) May 1/1 (*heading*) Prog. expansion programme. *Ibid.* 1/2 (*heading*) Swing to Progs in North Rand. **1977** *Guardian Weekly* 11 Dec. 7/1 Liberal-minded South Africans cheered their favoured Progressive Federal Party... Much applause for the gains of the 'progs', as they are locally termed.

prog (prǫg), *sb.*⁵ *slang.* Abbrev. of *programme *sb.* 2e.

1975 *Listener* 11 Dec. 790/1 Nice to have you with us on the prog, we say, don't we, fans?

prog, *v.*¹ **2.** (Further U.S. dial. examples.)

1935 Z. N. Hurston *Mules & Men* I. vi. 128 We proaged thru the woods that was full of magnolia, pine..and many kinds of trees whose name I do not know. **1949** 'J. Nelson' *Backwoods Teacher* vi. 63 He took a stick and progued around in the hole. **1949** *Sun* (Baltimore) 9 June 10/6 A progger..is a fellow that goes progging for frogs.

progamete: see *pro-² 1.

progeny. Add: **6.** *attrib.* and *Comb.*, as **progeny test**, an assessment of the genetic value of an individual made by examining its progeny; so **progeny-test** *v. trans.*, to assess in this way; **progeny-tested** *ppl. a.*, **progeny-testing** *vbl. sb.*

1918 Babcock & Clausen *Genetics in Relation to Agric.* xv. 293 We find that the progeny test of individual plants was first used by Le Couteur and Shirreff. But it was Louis de Vilmorin who first gave special attention to the value of the progeny test (1856). **1932** [see **performance test*]. **1953** Srb & Owen *Gen. Genetics* xxiii. 501 The wisdom of using sires proved good by progeny tests and by careful observations on relatives has become evident to almost all breeders. **1960** *Farmer & Stockbreeder* 8 Mar. 101/2 A.I. organizations are in a favoured position, because they deal with large numbers, and can progeny-test many bulls. **1971** *Ibid.* 23 Feb. 13/3 The Milk Marketing Board's Warren Farm progeny tests..could hardly be called a tremendous success. **1972** *Country Life* 6 Jan. 53/1 Extensive progeny testing of A1 bulls is carried out... By the use of egg transfer it should be possible to produce large numbers of calves from potential bull-breeding females and to progeny test them. **1944** *Jrnl. Agric. Res.* LXIX. 471 Use of progeny-tested dairy sires would be a little more likely to increase the rate of improvement. **1974** *Country Life* 12 Dec. 1853/1 This not only offers the advantage of the progeny-tested sire as compared with the crossing bull, which is what the farmer has to use at present, but a shorter and more concentrated calving season for the stockman. **1933** *Amer. Naturalist* LXVII. 502 Progeny testing in poultry breeding can be used in evaluating the breeding potentiality of either sire or dam. **1970** Progeny testing [see **performance testing*]. **1977** *Jrnl. Agric. Sci.* LXXXVIII. 129/1 We can calculate the expected response to selection for various types of progeny... We may also be able to choose between the use of different types of family or between, say, family selection and a progeny-testing programme.

progeria (prodʒīə·riă). *Path.* [mod.L., f. Gr. προγήρ-ως prematurely old + -ia¹.] A fatal disease of children characterized by symptoms usually associated with senility.

1904 H. Gilford in *Practitioner* Aug. 210 The name progeria, for which I am indebted to Mr. James Rhoades and Professor Arthur Sidgwick, is not only a far better word [than micromegaly], but is a true description of the distinguishing features of the two cases. *Ibid.* 217 The name progeria..has been given in recognition of the senile characters which form such a conspicuous feature of the disease from the beginning. **1927** *Times* (Weekly ed.) 28 Apr. 475/2 Cases of premature senility in children (goblins) described as progeria, the persistence in an adult (ateleioses) of child characters (elves). **1957** L. Eiseley *Immense Journey* 108 The cause of this curious disease, known as progeria, or premature aging, is totally unknown. **1969** *Guardian* 13 Jan. 2/3 A post-mortem examination will be carried out on..a 9-year-old girl who died of a disease that gave her the physical characteristics of a 90-year-old woman. Norma..was the second member of her family to be suffering from progeria.

Hence † **proge·rian** *sb.*, a person with progeria; also *attrib.*; **proge·ric** *a.*, of or being a person with progeria.

1913 *Lancet* 1 Feb. 305/1 Progerians pass from a delayed childhood into a premature old age. *Ibid.* 306/1 The total length of the progerian face from nasion to chin is only 84 mm. **1914** *Boston Med. & Surg. Jrnl.* 16 July 110/2 Progerians are usually dwarfs. **1933** R. W. B. Ellis tr. *Aperl's Infantilism* vii. 73 (*caption*) Mould of the upper and lower jaws in the same progeric patient as in figs. 11 and 12. **1945** *Amer. Jrnl. Dis. Children* LXIX. 276/2 The conditions..are postulated for the progeric patient..during the period from 2 to 6 years of age, when most of his subcutaneous fat vanished. **1976** *Nature* 22 Apr. 713/1 With factor VII-deficient plasma, both normal and progeric cells showed a markedly prolonged clotting time.

pro-German, -ism: see *pro-¹ 5a, c.

progestational (prodʒeste̅ⁱ·ʃənal), *a.* [f. Pro-² 1 + Gestation + -al.] Relating to, promoting, or being part of the physiological preparations for pregnancy; applied *esp.* to substances whose physiological effects resemble those of progesterone; *progestational proliferation*, proliferation of the endometrium in preparation for pregnancy.

1923 G. W. Corner in *Physiol. Rev.* III. 467 It seems preferable to avoid the suggestion of falsity or imitation inherent in the prefix *pseudo* [in *pseudopregnancy*], by using the terms progravid, progestational. **1928** *Amer. Jrnl. Physiol.* LXXXVI. 78 Sections taken through the middle of the uterine horn showed that no progestational proliferation had taken place in these animals. **1929** *Ibid.* LXXXVIII. 326 It is possible that there is an antagonistic relation between oestrin and the progestational substance. **1932** *Ibid.* C. 111 The production of a progestational endometrium in the uterus of a castrate rabbit. **1944** [see *progestin]. **1948, 1949** [see *gestagen]. **1954** [see *hydroxyprogesterone]. **1960** *Times* 19 Jan. 3/5 (Advt.), Applicants should have had considerable experience in steroid chemistry, and be well acquainted with recent work on gonadotropic, oestrogenic and progestational hormones. **1970** *Sci. Jrnl.* June 26/2 The ovaries produce ova and the oestrogenic and progestational hormones, mainly oestradiol and progesterone, which are concerned with the development and maintenance of the attributes of femaleness, including sexual receptivity and the inception of pregnancy. **1974** *Fertility & Sterility* XXV. 575/1 A special uterine reaction to the luteal hormone (progestational proliferation) was identified in the adult rabbit.

Hence **progesta·tionally** *adv.*, as regards progestational activity or state.

1948 W. H. Pearlman in Pincus & Thimann *Hormones* I. 441 Corticosterone..(progestationally inactive in the Clauberg test). **1958** *Jrnl. Clin. Endocrinol. & Metabolism* XVIII. 350 The highest point of formation of progestationally effective substances in the corpus luteum appears to be between the seventh and eighth day following ovulation. **1968** R. W. Kistner in Astwood & Cassidy *Clin. Endocrinol.* II. vi. ix. 680 If an endometrial biopsy..reveals 'progestationally immature endometrium',..one tablet daily..can be prescribed.

progesterone (prodʒe·stěrōᵘn). *Physiol.* [ad. G. *progesteron* (W. M. Allen et al. 1935, in *Klin. Wochenschr.* 17 Aug. 1182/1), blend of *progestin and its G. synonym *luteosteron* (K. H. Slotta et al. 1934, in *Ber. d. Deut. Chem. Ges.* LXVII. 1271), f. Luteo-, repr. *corpus luteum*: see *-sterone.] A female steroid sex hormone, $C_{21}H_{30}O_2$, which is secreted by the *corpus luteum* and also made synthetically, and is responsible for the cyclical changes in the uterus in the latter part of the menstrual cycle and also necessary for the maintenance of pregnancy. Also *attrib.* and *Comb.*

1935, etc. [see *progestin]. **1949** [see *gestagen]. **1957** *Times* 2 Dec. p. vi/2 When P.M.S. is used in conjunction with a steroid hormone progesterone it will bring maiden sheep into season to produce an extra crop of lambs in their second summer (six months earlier than normal). **1958** [see *gestagen]. **1961** L. Martin *Clin. Endocrinol.* (ed. 3) ix. 229 Owing to its feeble progesterone-like action,..large doses must be given. **1965** Lee & Knowles *Animal Hormones* ii. 20 As the corpus luteum matures, increasing amounts of progesterone are produced which depress the output of LH and LTH. **1966** [see *diosgenin]. **1968** *Times* 11 Nov. 10/8 Udry and Morris suggest that of the two ovarian hormones, oestrogen tends to increase the likelihood of human sexual activity, and progesterone to decrease it. **1974** *Daily Colonist* (Victoria, B.C.) 25 Aug. 26/2 By 1954, Chang and Pincus had found two progesterone hormones that worked. The birth-control pill was born. **1974** *Fertility & Sterility* XXV. 575/2 The following trivial names are used in this paper:.. progesterone (pregn-4-ene-3,20-dione). **1979** *Jrnl. R. Soc. Arts* CXXVII. 417/2 It was possible to inhibit ovulation in experimental animals with progesterone.

progestin (prodʒe·stin). *Physiol.* [f. Pro-¹ 5 + Gest(ation + -in¹.] **a.** Progesterone, esp. an unpurified preparation of it. **b.** = *progestogen, *gestagen.

1930 W. M. Allen in *Amer. Jrnl. Physiol.* XCII. 174 We have as yet proposed no name for this hormone of the corpus luteum... In so far as we are acquainted with its physiological behavior, its chief action lies in its ability, by alteration of the endometrium, to aid gestation in the castrated rabbit; and for this reason we wish to propose for it the name *progestin*, i.e., a substance which favors gestation. **1935** [see *androsterone]. **1935** W. M. Allen et al. in *Nature* 24 Aug. 303/2 Heretofore, two different names have been used in the literature for this hormone (progestin, luteosterone). For the sake of international uniformity, we agree to use..the name *progesterone* for the pure hormone. **1936** *Jrnl. Amer. Med. Assoc.* 23 May 1809/1 The Council adopted the following terms: (1) *progesterone* to indicate the chemically pure substance..(2) *progestin* as a general term to indicate the substance (and other chemically allied substances..in case any such compounds are subsequently discovered) without reference to the state of chemical purity. **1944** J. HOFFMAN *Female Endocrinol.* xli. 711 The term *progestin* is applied to crude extracts of corpus luteum tissue which possess progestational activity. The name progesterone describes the crystalline form of the luteal hormone. **1945** H. BURROWS *Biol. Actions of Sex Hormones* xxi. 389 More than one substance having the same kind of action as progesterone is known, and a generic name is therefore convenient. The author has used the term 'progestin' to denote chemical compounds having a biological action comparable with that of progesterone. [*Note*] 'Progestogen' has been suggested as an alternative generic name. *Ibid.* 390 The corpora lutea of the ovary are the chief natural source of progestin... The placenta is another source. **1961** J. ROCK in C. A. Villee *Control of Ovulation* xii. 228 The two artificial steroids are called 'progestins' because of the fact that their action resembles that of progesterone. **1966** *New Scientist* 15 Dec. 620/1 The synthetic progestins which are contained in all oral contraceptive tablets were in fact introduced for the wrong reason. **1976** *Sci. Amer.* Feb. 32/2 The steroid hormones..include the male sex hormones (collectively called the androgens), the female sex hormones (the estrogens and the progestins) and the hormones secreted by the cortex.

progestogen (prodʒe·stǒdʒen). *Physiol.* Also **progestagen.** [f. as prec. + -O + -GEN; the variant spelling may reflect the influence of *GESTAGEN.] = *GESTAGEN.

1941 DORLAND & MILLER *Med. Dict.* (ed. 19) 1171/2 *Progestogen*, a general term for any substance possessing progestational activity. **1945** [see *PROGESTIN]. **1962** *Lancet* 12 May 1012/1 In those premature labours where relaxation of the cervix precludes uterine contractions, such measures as cervical suture and the administration of progestogens can prevent disaster. **1968** PASSMORE & ROBSON *Compan. Med. Stud.* I. xxxvii. 11/1 The principal ovarian hormones..fall into three broad functional categories, oestrogens, progestagens and androgens. *Ibid.* 14/2 A more useful pharmacological definition of a progestagen is a substance which induces secretory changes in an oestrogen-primed endometrium. **1968** *Times* 28 Nov. 14/4 Most oral contraceptive pills contain both a progestogen and an oestrogen. **1977** *Lancet* 21 May 1101/2, 7 women.. used low-dose progestagen pills.

Hence **progestoge·nic** *a.* = *PROGESTATIONAL *a.*

1949 H. E. NIEBURGS *Hormones in Clin. Pract.* viii. 176 The progestogenic preparations are mainly employed for the prevention and treatment of habitual and threatened abortion. **1969** *Sunday Times* 14 Sept. 54/3 The remedy may be a change to a more 'progestogenic brand' [of oral contraceptive]. **1973** *Nature* 9 Mar. 88/1 Administration of sex hormones or their analogues, whether androgenic, oestrogenic or progestogenic, can produce temporary remission in about one-quarter to one-third of patients with advanced breast cancer. **1977** *Lancet* 19 Nov. 1085/1 Evidence is accumulating to indicate that it is principally the œstrogenic and not the progestagenic component of combined oral-contraceptive preparations which causes the acceleration of blood-clotting.

proglacial (proglē·sĭal, -ʃăl), *a. Geomorphol.* [f. PRO-² 2 + GLACIAL *a.*] Situated or occurring just beyond the edge of an ice-sheet or glacier.

1937 WOOLDRIDGE & MORGAN *Physical Basis Geogr.* xxii. 393 The term 'extra-morainic' has been proposed to cover all such lakes, but they are evidently not literally extra-morainic in every case, and the term 'pro-glacial' is preferable. **1957** G. E. HUTCHINSON *Treat. Limnol.* I. i. 89 During the early stages of deglaciation, proglacial lakes collected between the Cary Moraine and the receding ice. **1970** R. J. SMALL *Study of Landforms* xi. 395 His reconstruction of pro-glacial drainage conditions. *Ibid.*, The waters of the lakes escaped, either into adjacent lakes or away from the pro-glacial zone altogether. **1972** R. J. PRICE *Glacial & Fluvioglacial Landforms* (1973) vii. 185 As the glacier front moves down-valley the former proglacial fluvioglacial deposits are overridden by the ice.

prognathously (prǫgnæ·þəsli). *adv.* [f. PROGNATHOUS *a.* + -LY².] In a prognathous manner; with the jaw prominent or protruding.

1974 N. GORDIMER *Conservationist* 226 A jaw of fine teeth... Set rather prognathously, in the forward-jutting rounded arc that, in life, would make a wide white-toothed smile. **1976** T. SHARPE *Wilt* xiv. 146 He smiled prognathously.

Progne. Add: Also in Gr. form **Procne. 1.** (Later examples.)

1956 E. POUND tr. *Sophocles' Women of Trachis* 41 As Progne shrill upon the weeping air, 'Tis no great sound. **1980** 'A. T. ELLIS' *Birds of Air* 125 'You seem very cheerful,' she snapped... 'Oh, I am,' said Mary.. Procne to mute Philomela grieving for her Itys, she thought.

prognostical, *a.* (*sb.*) Restrict † *Obs.* to B and add: **A.** *adj.* (Later examples). *rare.*

1894 H. LATHAM *Service of Angels* 40 Is it prognostical? Is it proleptic? **1924** KEYNES in *Econ. Jrnl.* XXXIV. 316 We come to something more prognostical of Alfred in a little device of William Marshall's latter days.

prognostically, *adv.* (Later examples.)

1911 *Amer. Jrnl. Med. Sci.* CXLI. 644 Studying one's cases prognostically. **1977** *Lancet* 4 June 1199/2 H.D.L. is much more important prognostically.

progradation (prōgrădē·ʃən). *Physical Geogr.* [f. next + -ATION.] The seaward advance of a beach or coastline as a result of the accumulation of river-borne sediment or beach material.

1909 W. M. DAVIS in *Geogr. Jrnl.* XXXIV. 303 There is good reason for regarding the action of the streams in terracing or degrading the former valley floors as the cause of the progradation of the strand-plain. **1937** WOOLDRIDGE & MORGAN *Physical Basis Geogr.* xxi. 332 Progradation may result from the extensive deposition of river alluvium, as in deltas. **1967** *Oceanogr. & Marine Biol.* V. 130 Brothers (1954) concluded that dune formation during subsequent periods of shoreline progradation added great quantities of sand to the foreland around Auckland. **1971** *Nature* 10 Sept. 91/2 The virtual elimination of shelf seas, during a prolonged phase of tectonic stability and peneplanation following rapid build-up of evaporites and progradation of coastal plain sediments.

prograde (prōᵘ·grēⁱd), *a.* [f. PRO-¹ 1 + RETRO)GRADE *a.* and *sb.*] **1.** *Petrol.* Of a metamorphic change: resulting from an increase in temperature or pressure. Opp. *RETROGRADE *a.* 3e.

1967 K. G. COX et al. *Introd. Pract. Study Crystals* x. 200 The volatile constituents, H_2O and CO_2, are expelled from the rocks with rising temperature and cease to be available for the formation of low-temperature minerals (usually rich in H_2O and CO_2) when the temperature declines at the end of prograde metamorphism. **1977** A. HALLAM *Planet Earth* 174 The metamorphism of sedimentary rocks..involves the production of water vapor, carbon dioxide and other gaseous substances... This type of metamorphism is called prograde metamorphism, and takes place principally in response to increasing temperature.

2. *Astr.* From west to east; anticlockwise as seen from north of the ecliptic; = DIRECT *a.* 3. Opp. RETROGRADE *a.* 1a.

1969 *Nature* 19 July 243/2 Once in a prograde orbit, the tides on the Earth would begin to push the Moon outwards to its present position. **1977** *Ibid.* 3 Mar. 15/3 The overhead motion of the Sun relative to an observer fixed on the surface [of Venus] is prograde with a speed of about 4 m s^{-1}.

prograde (progrē·ⁱd), *v. Physical Geogr.* [f. PRO-¹ 1 + RETRO)GRADE *v.*] **a.** *intr.* Of a shore or shoreline: to undergo progradation.

1909 W. M. DAVIS in *Geogr. Jrnl.* XXXIV. 303 After having maturely retrograded the cliffs, the waves have prograded the strand-plain. The strand-plain broadens a little opposite each valley, for now that the shore-line is prograding, the rivers have opportunity of building their deposits forward. **1929** H. MEREDITH *East Anglia* ii. 63 Its beach progrades in inverse proportion to the retrograding of the Ness itself. **1954** W. D. THORNBURY *Princ. Geomorphol.* xvii. 443 Beach features are particularly ephemeral forms along a retrograding shore line, but along a shore line that is advancing seaward or is prograding they may be semipermanent. **1967** *Oceanogr. & Marine Biol.* V. 123 Thus valley train material extending seaward off Alaska has prograded almost to the headlands. **1978** *Nature* 17 Aug. 655/1 During the Campanian, fluvial, deltaic and coastal plain systems prograded eastwards across marine strata such that by the end of the Campanian (~69 Myr BP) the area of marine deposition was greatly restricted.

b. *trans.* To cause to prograde.

1909 [see sense a]. **1919** D. W. JOHNSON *Shore Processes* v. 223 Just so long as the current aggrades (builds up) the seabottom offshore, the waves will prograde (build forward) the shore. **1939** REVELLE & SHEPARD in P. D. Trask *Rec. Marine Sediments* IV. 279 The coarse material carried to the sea by rivers may temporarily prograde the shore, forming deltas. **1968** R. W. FAIRBRIDGE *Encycl. Geomorphol.* 133/1 Marine Deposition Coasts. These are another type of Secondary coasts that have been prograded by waves and currents.

Hence **progra·ded** *ppl. a.*, **progra·ding** *vbl. sb.* and *ppl. a.*

1910 *Jrnl. Geol.* XVIII. 166 The prograding of the shore beyond the headland. **1918** *Trans. & Proc. N.Z. Inst.* L. 215 Some of the material is thrown up on the beach, so that the shore-line advances seawards, leaving a prograded strip of new land. **1919** D. W. JOHNSON *Shore Processes* v. 223 Following Davis we may call any shore which is experiencing such a long-continued advance into the sea, a prograding shore, and distinguish it from the more usual retreating or retrograding shore. The prograding of a shoreline..may continue for a few years, a few centuries, or many thousands of years. **1940** *Geogr. Jrnl.* XCVI. 261 Occasional deep lows, locally called pits and containing water, are scattered about amongst the shingle. They were usually found during rapid prograding to the lee of bends. **1968** R. W. FAIRBRIDGE *Encycl. Geomorphol.* 895/2 (*caption*) Prograded spit, Whananaki Inlet, Northland, New Zealand. **1978** *Nature* 12 July 131/1 The environment was interpreted as a prograding tidal estuary where shelf deposits pass upwards into fields of migrating dunes and megaripples.

program, programme, *sb.* Add: These two forms have become established as the standard N. Amer. and British spellings respectively, with the exception that *program* is usual everywhere in connection with *Computers*. This latter distinction is followed in this article and throughout the Suppl. in editorial matter. **2. a.** (Further examples.)

1936 G. GREENE *Gun for Sale* iii. 107 They sat two programmes round at the cinema. **1975** *Cricketer* May 41/3 (Advt.), Immediate cash paid for all programmes up to 1960. £5 minimum pre-war cup finals. **1976** *Globe & Mail* (Toronto) 16 Feb. 17/1 This was the season's final program in the Toronto Symphony's Young People's Concerts series.

b. Also *transf.*, a planned series of activities or events.

1941 *Bull. Amer. Assoc. Petroleum Geologists* XXV. 1256 Past successes enable us now to look ahead to a difficult but orderly exploration program, rather than a frenzied, inefficient scramble for immediately needed oil. **1949** SHURR & YOCOM *Mod. Dance* 3 The fallacy of this statement became increasingly apparent as personal contact with, and participation in, teacher education programs in the colleges and universities increased. **1955** *Science* 25 Nov. 1005/2 The satellite program..is already underway. **1961** BERKNER & ODISHAW *Sci. in Space* i. 15 An orderly scientific program [of space research] cannot be conducted if the unreliability associated with new vehicles is always present. **1976** *Liverpool Echo* 7 Dec. 17/9 On the Wirral the West Cheshire programme was reduced to three games. **1977** *Nature* 11 Aug. 487/2 A joint programme to provide a set of soil structure standards..has been under way for five years at the Universities of Warsaw and Moscow.

c. *Mus.* A sequence of objects, scenes, or events intended to be suggested by a musical composition or used to determine its structure.

1854 H. F. CHORLEY *Mod. German Mus.* II. 306 There is no parroting such a programme..to an opera as the overture to 'Leonora'. **1883** GROVE *Dict. Mus.* III. 34/2 There is a growing tendency amongst critics and educated musicians to invent imaginary 'programmes' where composers have mentioned none. **1944** W. APEL *Harvard Dict. Mus.* 605/1 In the final analysis, there are two types of program music: that which is good music regardless of the program; and that which is poor music even with a 'good' program. **1962** *Listener* 15 Mar. 489/3 While the majority of his piano pieces bear explanatory titles, in his symphonies he was far more reticent as to the underlying programme. **1974** *Encycl. Brit. Micropædia* VIII. 231/3 Only in the so-called Romantic era, from Beethoven to Richard Strauss, is the program an essential concept.

d. = *dance programme* s.v. *DANCE *sb.* 7.

1899 A. E. W. MASON *Miranda of Balcony* iv. 40 He compared programmes with Miranda... Four dances must intervene before he could claim her. **1913** MRS G. DE H. VAIZEY *College Girl* xxvii. 369 The three programmes were filled to the last extra. **1949** N. MARSH *Swing, Brother, Swing* iii. 42 Her coming-out ball had been here... She felt the cord of her programme grow glossy under the nervous pressure of her gloved fingers. **1976** *Times* 11 June 14/6 Guests carry around little programmes to remind them who they are dancing with.

e. *Broadcasting.* (i) A broadcast presentation treated as a single item for scheduling purposes, being broadcast between stated times and without interruption except perhaps for news bulletins or advertisements.

1923 *Radio Times* 28 Sept. 1 From November 14th last year..we have..transmitted roughly 1,700 distinct evening programmes. **1933** *Ibid.* 14 Apr. 72/2 In the programmes for Friday next, you will find particulars of *Looking In*, first television review. **1946** *B.B.C. Year-bk.* 62 About 120 new programmes..are put on the air every week. *Ibid.*, Such famous programmes as 'Itma', 'Music Hall', and 'Workers' Playtime'. **1962** A. NISBETT *Technique Sound Studio* i. 17 Certain topical and miscellany programmes..go on the air in the form of a mixture of live and recorded segments. **1976** *Times* 21 May 2/8 Since the programme I have had about a dozen other nasty telephone calls.

(ii) A radio service providing a regular succession of programmes on a particular frequency.

1939 R. MACAULAY *Lett. to Sister* (1964) 96 I've just read the debate on B.B.C. in Hansard... The fact is we *can't* get on without 2 programmes. **1939** [see *HOME *a.* 2e]. **1945**, etc. [see *LIGHT *a.*¹ 19b]. **1946** *B.B.C. Year-bk.* 51 The Director-General promised that within ninety days of the end of hostilities in the West, the BBC would provide its listeners in the United Kingdom with two full-scale alternative programmes. *Ibid.*, It is the aim of the Home Service to provide the home programme of the people of the United Kingdom. **1968** *B.B.C. Handbk.* 48 The popular music programme on 247 metres became Radio 1. The Light Programme, on 1500 metres and VHF, became Radio 2. The Third Network, which embraces the Music Programme, the Third Programme, Study Session and the Sports Service, became Radio 3. **1980** *Times* 31 July 15/3 Radio 3 used to be the most civilized and broad-ranging programme in the world.

f. *Electronics.* Also *programme signal.* A signal corresponding to music, speech, or other activity.

1935 NILSON & HORNUNG *Pract. Radio Communication* viii. 356 The program fed into the mixer does not always come directly from a microphone. **1948** A. L. ALBERT *Radio Fund.* xiv. 569 The frequency deviations of a program signal in frequency-modulation can be made, and is made, quite large... If the program has a wide frequency deviation, but noise does not, the signal-to-noise ratio of the output of a discriminator will be high. **1954** MOLLOY & PANNETT *Radio & Television Engineers' Ref. Bk.* IV. 12 It is necessary at times to compress the programme from a range of 50 to 22 db. **1959** K. HENNEY *Radio Engin. Handbk.* (ed. 5) xxi. 7 Program signals have very complex wave shapes. **1970** J. EARL *Tuners & Amplifiers* iv. 77 The amplifier..must process the programme signal (e.g. the signal from the pickup, radio tuner, tape recorder or whatever). **1977** *Gramophone* Nov. 937/1 The 2760 copier unit completes the system.. and has automatic end-of-tape sensing and erasure of programme.

g. (i) A sequence of operations that a machine can be set to perform automatically.

1945 J. P. ECKERT et al. *Description of ENIAC* (PB 86242) (Moore School of Electr. Engin., Univ. of Pennsylvania) 1 The intended use of the ENIAC is to compute large families of solutions all based on the same program of operations. **1954** *Amer. Machinist* 25 Oct. 136/1 The operator..sets a combination of switches calling for table movements equivalent to blueprint dimensions, or a 'program', then presses a starting button. **1962** E. BRUTON *Automation* vi. 74 An automatic washing machine may be designed to wash for four minutes, empty, and spin-dry for ten. This is its programme. It can be 'programmed' in other ways. **1970** *Which?* Oct. 293/1 For most, there was a pre-rinse and a choice of two washing programmes, depending on how dirty the dishes were. **1972** *Daily Tel.* 11 Jan. 11/2 There's a Westinghouse electric clothes-dryer..which takes 12 lb of clothes and has five drying programmes: auto-dry, wash 'n 'wear, time dry, air fluff and low heat. **1977** *Times* 9 July 21/4 The ability of modern machines to offer merely rinse and dry programmes for clothes that have been prewashed by hand.

(ii) *Computers.* A series of coded instructions which when fed into a computer will automatically direct its operation in carrying out a specific task. Also *transf.*

1946 *Nature* 20 Apr. 527/2 Control of the programme of the operation of the machine [*sc.* ENIAC] is also through electrical circuits. **1947** *Math. Tables & Other Aids to Computation* II. 358 An important limitation upon programming is that the machine must adhere to a prescribed linear course of operation. It cannot at any point choose between two subsequent programs on the basis of results already obtained. **1950** *Phil. Mag.* XLI. 256 The problem of constructing a computing routine or 'program' for a modern general purpose computer which will enable it to play chess. **1953** *Proc. IRE* XLI. 1245/1 A large family of high-speed, large-scale, stored-program, digital computers have been built. *Ibid.* 1247/1 This conditional instruction makes it possible for the programmer to write programs which take different courses of action depending upon the results of previous computation. **1960** *Times* 4 Oct. (Computer Suppl.) p. v/3 To prepare this sequence of instructions, or program (a spelling now adopted in computer terminology), the programmer will have broken down an operation into its simplest elements. **1971** *Times Lit. Suppl.* 4 June 635/2 Were accurate estimation of the merits of such positions possible, the next world chess champion could quite conceivably be a computer programme. **1972** *Sci. Amer.* Mar. 42/3 Computer instructions are so complicated that programmers are often baffled when they look at programs they have written but have not seen for several months, and a third party usually finds them inscrutable. **1972** R. M. LEE *Short Course Basic Fortran IV Programming* i. 8 Programs are written in one of the many user-oriented languages, such as FORTRAN, and then translated into machine language... The translation is done by the computer. **1974** *Sci. Amer.* Oct. 105/1, I have described the timing and the characteristics of the coordination of the eye-head movements that are elicited by the appearance of a visual target, and have presented our evidence for the conclusion that the programs for eye-head coordination are not present in the central nervous system in their entirety. **1977** W. S. DAVIS *Operating Syst.* v. 58 Before any program can be run, it must first be set up (cards loaded in the card reader, the printer loaded with..paper.., tapes and disk packs mounted, and so on).

h. *Psychol.* and *Educ.* In human and animal learning, a series of step-by-step questions or tests (freq. designed to be used in a teaching machine operated by the learner) aimed at the establishment of learning patterns through the stimulus of rewarding correct responses or behaviour at each step.

1950 B. F. SKINNER in *Psychol. Rev.* LVII. 207/2 Such a set was randomized in a program of reinforcement repeated every hour. In changing to this program from the arithmetic series..the pigeons were soon able to sustain a constant rate of responding under it. **1958** —— in *Science* 24 Oct. 971/2 The machines themselves cannot be adequately described without giving a few examples of programs. **1961**, etc. [see *LINEAR *a.* 3c]. **1962** *Listener* 17 May 855/2 The drawback to a multiple choice programme..is that plausible wrong answers must be presented to the student, and he may remember these instead of the correct ones. **1967** COULTHARD & SMITH in Wills & Yearsley *Handbk. Managem. Technol.* xi. 204 Two types of programme are currently in use: 1. The linear programme—which repeats a statement just made, omitting a key word or words, and requires the trainee to remedy the omission... 2. The intrinsic programme—which provides an explanation of a key point in the subject and asks the trainee to select the correct answer to a question from several alternative answers. **1976** W. B. KOLESNIK *Learning* x. 226 The program can be used in grades one through twelve in the area of language, arts, mathematics, [etc.].

4. *programme-book, -card* (further examples), *-making* (examples; also in senses other than 2b), *note, -seller* (examples), *vendor*; (sense *2e) *programme content, director, editor, engineer, item, -maker* (see also sense in Dict.), *planner, planning, staff, time*; (sense *2g) *program step, tape, testing*; **programme boy, girl,** a boy or girl employed to sell programmes at a place of entertainment; **programme-building,** the selection of items for a concert or for a period of broadcasting; so **programme-builder; programme chairman** *U.S.*, one who arranges the programme of events or the agenda for a particular event for a society, etc.; **programme company,** a company authorized to make programmes and advertisements for broadcasting on British commercial television; **programme contractor** = **programme company*, so **programme-contracting** *a.*; **program(me) control,** (*a*) = *PROGRAMMER 3; (*b*) control of or by a program(me); **program(me) controller** = *PROGRAMMER 1c, 3; **program counter** *Computers*, a register in the control unit of a computer which contains the address of the next instruction to be executed, this number being increased by one each time unless an instruction to do otherwise occurs; **programme girl**: see **programme boy*; **programme junction** *Broadcasting* (see quot. 1941); **program library** *Computers* = *LIBRARY[1] 2*; **programme line** *Telecommunications* (see quot. 1940); **programme movie** = **programme picture*; **programme music** (earlier and later examples); **programme pencil,** a small pencil for filling in a programme-card at a dance, etc.; **programme picture,** a cinema film made relatively cheaply and intended to be shown as part of a programme that includes another film as the main feature; **program register** *Computers* = *control register* s.v. *CONTROL *sb.* 5; **programme service** *Broadcasting*, a service consisting in the regular broadcasting of radio or television programmes for reception by the public; **programme symphony,** a symphony with a programme (sense *2c).

1954 *Grove's Dict. Mus.* (ed. 5) VI. 943/2 Philip Hale's long series of notes for the Boston Symphony Orchestra made the programme-books of that orchestra valuable historic documents. **1976** *New Yorker* 9 Feb. 102/3 The wretched program book gave no texts—only excerpts from the Woolf cycle, and translations of the rest. **1921** *Dict. Occup. Terms* (1927) § 889 Programme boy, girl, seller. **1928** *B.B.C. Handbk.* 73/2 The programme builders believe that..the 60,000 hours of programmes will receive the liveliest and most general approval..by the application of a common-sense policy. **1947** *Penguin Music Mag.* Dec. 27 Every programme-builder should know the symphonic repertoire from A to Z. **1961** *Listener* 21 Dec. 1088/3, I don't know what was in the mind of the programme-builder of the concert given by the B.B.C. Symphony Orchestra. **1928** *B.B.C. Handbk.* 74/1 The best method of explaining the details of programme building is to follow a week's programmes from their first beginnings to the day on which they are broadcast. **1935** *Discovery* Sept. 277/1 It may be left safely to the B.B.C., whose experience and standards of programme building..may be relied upon to result in presentations in line with public approbation. **1948** *Penguin Music Mag.* Feb. 93 Mr. Barbirolli's extraordinary skill in programme-building. **1957** *Encycl. Brit.* IV. 208/2 It is principally under the headings (5) and (6).. that radio has created expression forms peculiar to itself, and in most other respects program-building is creative only in the sense that the program-builders can build combinations of suitable music and speech around one or another central idea. **1948** *Penguin Music Mag.* June 135 The Orchestra's first programme-card was several degrees more adventurous than any before it. **1961** *U.S. Nat. Bureau Standards Rep. Fiscal Year 1961* 57 The Bureau contributed to the planning and success of the Symposium through the efforts of..Dr. C. M. Herzfeld, Program Chairman. **1976** *Billings* (Montana) *Gaz.* 27 June 5-E/3 She is a past president, program chairman and secretary of the chapter. **1958** *New Statesman* 22 Mar. 375/3 As each programme-company in turn began broadcasting in the regions, the tale was always the same: of viewers with a choice, most chose the ITV channel most of the time. **1962** *Rep. Comm. Broadcasting 1960* 1 in *Parl. Papers 1961–2* (Cmnd. 1753) IX. 259 Independent television comprises not only the ITA but also the programme companies, which have at various dates since 1954 been appointed by the ITA. **1968** *Listener* 11 July 84/3 What are called the programme companies, in ITV, are set up in the first instance as contractors on the basis of the advertising franchise in their area. **1958** *New Statesman* 20 Dec. 880/1, I am not sure that I agree that the effect of the competition on the programme-content is as superficial as they seem then to have found. **1964** M. MCLUHAN *Understanding Media* (1967) xxviii. 293 Like the radio that it still provides with program content, the phonograph is a hot medium. **1968** *Listener* 29 Aug. 285/3 There is now hardly a significant publication, from the weekly reviews to the mass-selling dailies, which does not have equity in one or other of the programme-contracting companies. **1954** *Act* 2 & 3 *Eliz. II* c. 55. § 2 The programmes broadcast by the Authority shall..be provided not by the Authority but by persons (hereafter in this Act referred to as 'programme contractors') who, under contracts with the Authority, have, in consideration of payments to the Authority.., the right and the duty to provide programmes or parts of programmes to be broadcast by the Authority. **1958** *New Statesman* 5 July 1/2 With commercial success and popular support behind them the existing programme contractors, and those who would like to become programme contractors, are in a much more powerful position than they were when ITV was an untried gamble. **1962** *Rep. Comm. Broadcasting 1960* 166 in *Parl. Papers 1961–2* (Cmnd. 1753) IX. 259 The [Independent Television] Authority's power to control the companies, once they are appointed programme contractors, is illusory and negligible. **1945** J. P. ECKERT et al. *Description of ENIAC* (PB 86242) (Moore School of Electr. Engin., Univ. of Pennsylvania) B-5 The simplest procedure for handling the problem is to devote one multiplier program control to each of the n multiplications. **1951** M. MCLUHAN *Mech. Bride* (1967) 21/1 The president of the National Broadcasting Corporation ridiculed the proposal to separate business control from program control. **1953** *Proc. IRE* XLI. 1271/2 (*heading*) Program control of external units. **1957** D. M. CONSIDINE *Process Instruments & Controls Handbk.* IX. 78 The operation of a tire vulcanizer, on a completely automatic timed basis, is an example of program control. **1977** *Design Engin.* July 15/3 Eight parallel latched outputs are available as binary, BCD, or as a 7-segment-plus-decimal-point output under program control. **1957** D. M. CONSIDINE *Process Instruments & Controls Handbk.* IX. 78 By controlling sequence, intervals, and rates of change, a program controller may encompass all the operations in a complete industrial process. **1961** *Times* 4 Aug. 2/3 Independent Television in Wales..now invite application for the following key posts:... Programme Controller. In this position, experience of Television production, a knowledge of Welsh, and broad interests over the whole field of entertainment are essential. The Controller in Cardiff will plan and budget all programmes, and must know how and where to produce or acquire material. **1967** F. W. CLARKE *Installing Small Pipe Central Heating* vi. 37 Where a boiler supplies hot water and serves the heating, the various jobs required of it can be simply co-ordinated by a programme controller. This turns the heating or the hot water on and off at selected times, as set on the clock. **1976** C. BERMANT *Coming Home* II. iv. 161, I returned to Granada and sent a memo to the programme controller. **1946** *Math. Tables & Other Aids to Computation* II. 102 Counters are used not only for arithmetic purposes, but also as a part of the programming circuits which determine when and how a given unit shall perform. Each unit whose operations consume more than one addition time has such a program counter. **1962** HUSKEY & KORN *Computer Handbk.* XVI. 29 In the case of a jump instruction, the address for the next instruction to be fetched comes from the address part of the present instruction... The state of the program counter must be changed to agree with this address so that it will count on from the new starting point. **1977** *Design Engin.* July 15/3 There are four parallel inputs, a testable sense input, three bi-directional control flags for use as inputs or outputs, a program counter, a two-word stack for nested subroutine calls, and an instruction-decode programmable logic array. **1961** G. MILLERSON *Television Production* i. 15 He may operate the buttons and faders for video switching himself, but most networks consider the programme director too preoccupied with the many other aspects of production, and delegate this job to another person. **1972** *Listener* 6 July 2/1 Michael Rice, the Programme Director, asked one of his people..to lead the production team. **1929** *Radio Times* 8 Nov. 387/3 Broadcast reading has only been tried half-heartedly. The programme editors still suffer from ..fear of not pleasing everybody all day long. **1949** *Ibid.* 15 July 41/3 He returned to the BBC as a programme engineer. **1962** Programme engineer [see *BALANCE *sb.* 14 b]. **1905** *Daily Chron.* 13 Feb. 9/3 An interesting story of a medical student's love for a programme girl..was told. **1918** [see *CLOAK-ROOM b]. **1921** [see **programme boy*]. **1979** G. LATTA tr. *Jacquemard-Sénécal's Eleventh Little Nigger* I. v. 47 The programme girls..persuaded her to swallow a considerable amount of whisky. **1962** Programme item [see **programme planning*]. **1941** *B.B.C. Gloss. Broadcasting Terms* 25 *Programme junction*, brief interval between the end of one programme and the beginning of the next, used for switching operations whereby transmitters are linked to, or detached from, the network concerned. **1975** *Listener* 23 Oct. 532/2 There was internal machinery to see that there were common programme junctions. **1960** *Ann. Rev. Automatic Programming* I. 93 (*heading*) MERCURY autocode: principles of the program library. **1977** R. E. HARRINGTON *Quintain* xii. 139 Sanderson gave me the constants and I just ran the program. I didn't even write it. He got it from the program library. **1940** *Chambers's Techn. Dict.* 676/2 *Programme* (or *program*) *line*, a transmission line, of superior propagation characteristics, for relaying broadcasting programmes. **1944** *Proc. IRE* XXXII. 601/1 A key located to the left of the VU meter should be used to connect this meter to the outgoing program line. **1929** *Radio Times* 8 Nov. 393/1 There are people who..abuse the programme-makers! **1977** *Broadcast* 13 June 5/2 Programme makers could..put their ideas to the empirical test by means of a pilot programme. **1904** W. JAMES *Let.* 1 Jan. in R. B. Perry *Tht. & Char. W. James* (1935) II. 201 Münsterberg has the most extraordinary power of schematization and program-making. **1949** *Penguin Music Mag.* Feb. 19 That almost perfect example of programme-making, *Music in Miniature*. **1980** *Listener* 3 Jan. 21/1 Industrial disputes [in broadcasting] took up more time than programme-making. **1935** *Movie Mirror* Dec. 106/1 Dropping into the theater, prepared for a regular program movie, my interest was caught after the first few feet and worked up to a fever pitch at the final reel. **1879** GROVE *Dict. Mus.* I. 232/2 Berlioz was one of the most uncompromising champions of what, for want of a better name, has been dubbed 'programme music'. **1954** C. S. LEWIS *Eng. Lit. in Sixteenth Cent.* I. ii. 139 Disorder in life rendered by disorder in art. This is in poetry what 'programme music' is in music. **1923** M. R. WERNER *Barnum* 319 And then in Barnum's program notes each year appeared this notice. **1942** E. BLOM *Music in England* ix. 149 Ella also wrote his own programme notes. **1958** 'E. DUNDY' *Dud Avocado* I. vii. 136 I'd never seen a ballet whose story I was able to follow even when the programme-notes were in English. **1965** *Listener* 25 Nov. 874/1 The relevance of the play to the 'thirties in Britain and also to Radio in Europe Week was so admirably condensed in a programme note in *Radio Times* by the producer, Douglas Cleverdon, that it does not seem worth labouring. **1978** *Daily Tel.* 20 Jan. 13/1 To 25 years' experience before the camera can be added (I learn from the programme note) some recent experience as a director in the theatre. **1895** *Montgomery Ward & Co. Catal.* Spring & Summer 115/2 'Programme' Pencils, round, enameled in colors with gilt tip and ring. Suitable for use in lady's memorandum book. **1921** E. N. HULL *Sheik* i. 9 She hesitated, tapping her programme-pencil against her teeth. **1928** *Sunday Dispatch* 19 Aug. 14/2 A 'programme' picture is a film which costs from £6,000 to £8,000 or thereabouts, and cannot be called a 'super'. **1935** *Movie Mirror* Dec. 38/3 Your Reviewer Says: An average program picture, but Velez fans will want to see it for sure. **1956** Programme planner [see *B.B.C.]. **1961** A. WILSON *Old Men at Zoo* ii. 92 The television engineers and programme planners with whom the office now seemed filled. **1974** *Guardian* 23 Jan. 1/5 If the [TV] close-down had been at 10.30 there would have been more room for manoeuvre by the programme planners. **1940** R. S. LAMBERT *Ariel & all his Quality* iii. 77 Charles Siepmann..was promoted to..Director of Programme Planning. **1962** *Rep. Comm. Broadcasting 1960* 159 in *Parl. Papers 1961–2* (Cmnd. 1753) IX. 259 What particular 'time slots' each [TV company] is to occupy, and with what programme items... That is to say, the overall programme planning. **1948** *Gloss. Computer Terms* (Mass. Inst. Technol. Servo-mechanisms Lab. Rep. R–138) 8 *Program register*, the part of the computer used for holding orders after they are extracted from storage but before they are carried out. **1956** Program register [see **control register*]. **1962** R. V. OAKFORD *Introd. Electronic Data Processing Equipment* iii. 37 Information (normally instructions) can be transferred to the program register in the control unit from general memory or from the arithmetic (process) unit. **1921** Programme seller [see **programme boy*]. **1977** M. BABSON *Lord Mayor of Death* v. 45 Here comes the programme seller. **1940** L. R. LOHR *Television Broadcasting* ii. 23 Television transmitters have been in operation from time to time in Philadelphia, Schenectady,.. and Bridgeport, but none of these had established a program service for the public at the time of writing. **1962** A. NISBETT *Technique Sound Studio* i. 17 The next link is a continuity suite where the entire programme service is assembled. **1940** R. S. LAMBERT *Ariel & all his Quality* ii. 43 Programme and administrative staff had not been divided into watertight..categories. **1977** *Listener* 28 Apr. 540/2 There has been a planned increase of programme staff, facilities and output. **1950** *High-Speed Computing Devices* ix. 157 The Type 604 can perform 60 program steps, or operations, per card; a program step includes any one of the four arithmetic operations, or a number transfer. **1956** [see *COMMAND *sb.* 1 d]. **1978** *Sci. Amer.* Feb. 29/2 (Advt.), Because of this dual capability, it can..identify which program step a system was executing at the time of malfunction. **1934** C. LAMBERT *Music Ho!* III. 162 Nationalism..destroys both the aristocratic quality of the eighteenth-century abstract symphony and the individualist quality of the nineteenth-century programme symphony. **1962** *Listener* 29 Nov. 941/2 The third symphony..was suggested by visits to Mycenae and Venice. Programme symphonies are even more out of fashion than the normal type, but I can only say that I tried to express the emotions aroused in me by the places rather than to paint pictures of them. **1948** *Math. Tables & Other Aids to Computation* III. 126 We can have on the first section of the program tape.. the program for arranging the data in order by age. **1964** C. DENT *Quantity Surveying by Computer* iii. 26 In other cases the data tape is read in under control of the instructions (stored in the memory by the program tape), the data being worked on as it is read in. **1959** J. JEENEL *Programming for Digital Computers* viii. 393 In program testing one usually employs certain techniques especially developed for this purpose. **1964** F. L. WESTWATER *Electronic Computers* ix. 140 The coding is tested on the computer... (This is called 'program testing'.) **1957** *Practical Wireless* XXXIII. 529/2 Fewer programmes.. would enable the BBC to..reject the dross which is still allowed programme time. **1977** M. BABSON *Lord Mayor of Death* xii. 82 Programme vendors..were..shaking their heads regretfully at would-be customers.

program, programme, *v.* (The note s.v. *PROGRAM, PROGRAMME *sb.* applies equally to the vb.) Add: **1.** (Further examples.)

1912 A. BENNETT *Jrnl.* 16 Feb. (1932) II. 44 On Wednesday morning at 7 a.m. as 'programmed' a week ago, I began 'The Regent'. **1949** *Archit. Rev.* CVI. 375/1 Let us.. consider a country like Japan where, after wholesale destruction, four million minimum dwellings are now being programmed. **1956** *Sun* (Baltimore) (B ed.) 24 Sept. 10/2 Senator Scott found..that 75 per cent of the soil bank outlay of $261,000,000 programmed for 1956 was to be spent in twelve mid-Western farm states. **1970** *Daily Tel.* 30 Jan. 2/4 He tried to programme her day into housework and study, but with four children and a pile of nappies it did not work. **1977** *Gramophone* Feb. 1308/1 The items are programmed in a quite interesting way, the fireworks of Liszt's *Hungarian Rhapsody* No. 2 being followed by the cool renunciation of Satie's *Gymnopédie* No. 1. **1979** *Church Times* 25 May 14/5 When the ceremonies and speeches were over, the General..was programmed to leave the gathering and walk along the red carpet to his car.

† **2.** *intr.* To write programme notes. *Obs. rare.*

1889 G. B. SHAW *London Music in 1888–89* (1937) 243 He programmed in a pat-the-young-man-on-the-back style.

3. *trans.* and *intr.* To broadcast. *U.S.*

1937 *Amer. Speech* XII. 101 *To program* means..to broadcast. **1967** *Boston Sunday Herald* 26 Mar. II. 8/2 (Advt.), Personalities are an important ingredient in today's radio, and WCOP provides warm, personable, well established people—they program 24 hours a day with your listening pleasures in mind. **1969** *N.Y. Rev. Books* 2 Jan. 17/3 We can program twenty more hours of TV in South Africa next week to cool down the tribal temperature raised by radio last week. **1978** *Chicago* June 22/1 CSO does not program enough contemporary music.

4. a. To express (a task or operation) in terms appropriate to its performance by a computer or other automatic device; to cause (an activity or property) to be automatically regulated in a prescribed way.

1945 J. P. ECKERT et al. *Description of ENIAC* (PB 86242) (Moore School of Electr. Engin., Univ. of Pennsylvania) B-4 In this fashion, problems involving numbers of multiplications far in excess of 24 can be programmed. **1949** *Nature* 22 Oct. 684/2 The problem must be programmed, that is, it must be split up into a series of simple operations which the machine can perform. **1952** *Phil. Mag.* XLIII. 1245 When a mathematician assembles the set of orders required to work out the solution of a problem he is said to be programming this problem for the machine. **1955** *IRE Trans. Industr. Electronics* II. 3/1 Industry needs more flexible methods of programming machine cycles to achieve automatic operation of machine tools in limited-quantity production. **1958** *Times Rev. Industry* Feb. 52/2 The Burroughs Typing Sensimatic has unmatched flexibility. The control unit permits each job to be individually programmed. **1962** G. A. T. BURDETT *Automatic Control Handbk.* XIX. 2 The engineer must programme the operations which the machine is to carry out. Preferably this programming, i.e. planning in advance and in sequence all the steps of the required operations, should involve the minimum of human effort and..a computer may be used. **1971** *Sci. Amer.* Apr. 71 Evidently an annual cycle of feeding and fasting is also programmed in the animal. **1973** A. PARRISH *Mech. Engineer's Ref. Bk.* XIX. 15 If feeds and speeds are programmed such that the spindle motor is producing its maximum horse power, any hard spots in the work piece can result in stall. **1977** *Sci. Amer.* Sept. 187 (*caption*) Typical task for a traveling-wire EDM is cutting gear teeth... When a slow and complex series of cuts is programmed, it can run unattended for 60 hours.

b. To incorporate (a property) *into* a computer or other device by programming.

1972 CARR & MIZE *MOS/LSI Design & Application* viii. 233 The uniqueness desired within the master PLA chip is often programmed into the master chip by changing only the gate mask. **1977** D. BAGLEY *Enemy* XV. 121 He's installed a scad of microprocessors in that control board... He could program his timetables into them. **1977** *Nature* 11 Aug. 571/3 This book..deals with the problem of programming 'common sense' into a computer.

5. a. To cause (a computer or other device) automatically to do a prescribed task or perform in a prescribed way; to supply with a program. Also *absol.*

1945 J. P. ECKERT et al. *Description of ENIAC* (PB 86242) (Moore School of Electr. Engin., Univ. of Pennsylvania) B-1 The problem of programming the ENIAC. *Ibid.*, We then wish to program the first accumulator to transmit its contents twice into the second one. **1947** *Proc. IRE* XXXV. 761/1 When an accumulator is programmed to transmit subtractively, it will transmit, not the number it holds, but the complement of the number it holds. **1950** *Phil. Mag.* XLI. 256 (*heading*) Programming a computer for playing chess. **1961** K. AMIS *New Maps of Hell* i. 33 Here an airborne device, programmed to detect and forestall aggressive intentions, ends by prohibiting most kinds of human action. **1962** *Lancet* 8 Dec. 1215/2 The Pegasus computer can be programmed to punch out the desired results on standard teleprinter tape. **1973** *Daily Tel.* 8 Jan. 13 (Advt.), What you get for £505. 1. Full central heating and domestic hot water... 5. Time switch to programme the boiler. **1973** *Sci. Amer.* Sept. 87/1 Cardiographic instruments can be programmed to sound an alarm if an alarming event occurs. **1976** M. M. MANO *Computer System Archit.* ii. 74 For small quantities it is more convenient to use a programmable ROM, referred to as PROM... Each cell in a PROM incorporates a link that can be fused by application of a high current pulse. A broken link in a cell defines one binary state and an unbroken link represents the other state... This allows the user to program the unit in his own laboratory..to achieve the desired relationship between input address and output data. **1976** *Physics Bull.* Dec. 535/3 The operation is computer controlled so that the mirrors can be programmed to follow a particular source round the sky.

absol. **1954** *Amer. Machinist* 25 Oct. 134/2 Tool Engineers..will have to learn a new approach to tooling. Instead of designing massive fixtures or intricate mechanical controls, they will 'program'. **1958** *Oxf. Mag.* 29 May 470/1 It is not difficult to learn to program..backed by regular university lectures in numerical analysis and computing. **1966** *Sci. Amer.* Sept. 72 The ability to write a computer program will become as widespread as the ability to drive a car. Not knowing how to program will be like living in a house full of servants and not speaking their language. **1977** *Daily Tel.* 14 Nov. 8 (Advt.), To program, just read down the column, making the appropriate keyboard entries as you go!

b. *fig.* To train to behave in a predetermined way.

1963 *Language* XXXIX. 455 He succeeded in programming the live bees that crowded around the imitation insect to head in a prescribed direction to seek and find nectar. **1966** L. JONES in A. Chapman *New Black Voices* (1972) 459 We have always been separate, except in our tranced desire to be the thing that oppressed us, after some generations of having been 'programmed'.. into believing that our greatest destiny was to become white people! **1967** *Freedomways* VII. 131 The black student is being educated in this country as if he were being programmed in white supremacy and self-hatred. **1968** *New Scientist* 19 Dec. 653/1 To what extent can astronauts, environmentally be-suited, rigidly programmed, and electrically guided to their destination, be said to resemble the courageous explorers of the past? **1975** A. PRICE *Our Man in Camelot* iv. 71 Your cover is perfect... You were trained and programmed for just such an operation as this. **1976** J. ROSS *I know what it's like to Die* ii. 12 Violent death programmed him to action in a predetermined routine; his reflexes conditioned by his training.

6. *Psychol.* and *Educ.* To form into a teaching programme (*PROGRAM, PROGRAMME *sb.* 2 h).

1958 B. F. SKINNER in *Science* 24 Oct. 976/2 When material is adequately programmed, adjacent steps are often so similar that one frame reveals the response to another. **1971** PITTENGER & GOODING *Learning Theories in Educ. Practice* iii. 91 Programming complex behavior requires careful planning and sequencing of material.

7. *intr. Astronaut.* Of a spacecraft: To perform a scheduled and automatically controlled manœuvre.

1958 *Daily Progress* (Charlottesville, Va.) 11 Oct. 1/5 He said the first stage appeared to have 'programmed'—started curving on its trajectory to the northeast—higher than it should. **1962** M. CAIDIN *Man-in-Space Dict.* 156/2 *Programming*, movement of a booster vehicle through assigned trajectory maneuvers in flight, as when a booster launches from a vertical position, then programs over toward horizontal flight. **1962** J. GLENN in *Into Orbit* 189 'We're programming in roll OK,' I said.

programmable (prōu·græmăb'l), *a.* and *sb.* Also (*rare*) **programable.** [f. PROGRAM, PROGRAMME *v.* + -ABLE.] **A.** *adj.* Of an apparatus or an operation: capable of being programmed. Also *fig.*

1959 *Times Rev. Industry* May 36/2 The investigating team..designed a 'push-button office'... Such an arrangement would..be a data processing system..not based on a ..programmable computer. **1965** M. FRAYN *Tin Men* ix. 51 Filling up a football coupon is another job which a computer could easily be programmed to do... We have a range of variables which can be identified in advance and manipulated according to predetermined rules. It's programmable. **1967** COX & GROSE *Organization & Handling Bibliogr. Rec. by Computer* II. 46 With a system such as I have described all the elaborate mechanical and studio devices used to compose pages and flats are now replaced by programmable operations generated by algorithm from simple input instructions. **1971** *Sci. Amer.* Aug. 100/1 (Advt.), Others know us as a computer company: more than 10,000 own our programmable calculators and computers. **1972** CARR & MIZE *MOS/LSI Design & Application* viii. 232 (*caption*) Programable logic array (PLA) contains multiple ROMs and flip-flop feedback elements for sequential logic elements. **1979** *Nature* 13 Sept. 131/2 The laser frequency..and data recording were controlled by a programable calculator. **1979** B. PETERSON *Peripheral Spy* vi. 157 Predictable, hell! I'm programmable, that's what. Just like a godamned computer.

B. *sb.* A programmable calculator.

1975 *New Scientist* 27 Feb. 506 New handheld programmables will appear in 1975–76 not unlike the HP-65 at as little as £85. **1977** *Sci. Amer.* Apr. 94/2 (Advt.), All our hand-held and portable programmables incorporate HP's special RPN logic system.

Hence **pro:grammabi·lity**, the property of being programmable.

1966 *Jrnl. Assoc. Computing Machinery* XIII. 369 (*heading*) Use of multiwrite for general programmability of search memories. **1975** *Daily Tel.* 17 July 7 (Advt.), Programmability overcomes both limitations—and makes a calculator vastly more powerful. **1977** *Sci. Amer.* June 79/1 Programmability transformed the slick slide-rule calculator into an advanced scientific machine.

programmatic, *a.* Delete *rare* and add further examples (corresponding to various senses of 'programme').

1904 G. S. GORDON *Let.* 25 Oct. (1943) 4 Pardon this very egotistical and programmatic letter dear Molly. **1935** *B.B.C. Ann.* 81/2 Announcements relating to B.B.C. policy in every respect—programmatic, engineering, or other—are issued. **1937** *Proc. Prehistoric Soc.* III. 265 There is no shortage of programmatic declarations, of resumés of problems and aims. **1941** *Mind* L. 395, I may fitly use these programmatic statements as my text on which to hang the main reflections. **1947** *Proc. IRE* XXXV. 757/1 Both digital and programmatic information must be stored: the machine must be able to remember both the numbers that are operated on and the instructions for performing the operations. **1958** *Listener* 27 Nov. 861/1 No new Pope ever makes what might be called a programmatic speech giving the policies he intends to follow. **1971** S. HERRICK *Astrodynamics* I. vii. 176 Programmatic or program-assisted singularities are destructive bits of sub-programming.. of which two are noteworthy. **1974** *Listener* 24 Jan. 121/3 A symphonic poem along Straussian programmatic lines. **1977** M. GOUDER in J. Hick *Myth of God Incarnate* iv. 65 In the programmatic opening paragraph of Acts, Luke designates the advance of the church as being in four stages. **1979** *Dædalus* Summer 105 Even the most apparently blithe comedies are far more programmatic than a haphazard jumble of anecdotal detail.

Hence **programma·tically** *adv.*, in the manner of a programme or programme music; in accordance with a programme; with regard to a programme.

1947 A. EINSTEIN *Music in Romantic Era* xi. 126 Spohr wrote a 'Characteristic Tone-Painting in the Form of a Symphony'..which makes use of a poem as the starting-point for revivifying programmatically the traditional form of the symphony. **1952** *Word* VIII. 97 Still other American linguists are programmatically rejecting the strict asseverance of meaning from sound and the exclusion of meaning from linguistic science. **1971** S. HERRICK *Astrodynamics* I. vii. 179 Programmatically or computationally, especially with automatic, automaton machinery, there is a great difference. **1974** *Times Lit. Suppl.* 29 Mar. 344/5 Beardsley's admirable drawing and programmatically tortured lettering. **1978** *Nature* 23 Feb. 785/3 The book..offers to approach flow phenomena programmatically in the framework of a general dynamic theory.

programmed (prōu·græmd), *ppl. a.* [f. PROGRAM, PROGRAMME *v.* + -ED[1].] **1.** Predetermined or controlled by a program (see *PROGRAM, PROGRAMME *v.* 4a, 5a, *sb.* 2g). Also *transf.*

1947 *New Republic* 23 June 15/3 The machine, having been properly briefed.., will perform its programmed task. **1953** *Proc. IRE* XLI. 1235/1 A significant new concept in non-numerical computation is the idea of a general-purpose programmed computer—a device capable of carrying out a long sequence of elementary orders analogous to those of a numerical computer. **1958** *Engineering* 28 Feb. 263/2 After taking off vertically..the vehicle veered to the south-east along its programmed trajectory. **1959** E. M. GRABBE et al. *Handbk. Automation, Computation & Control* II. iv. 13 Programmed checks..consist of the verification of the correctness of the system operation by means of special procedures introduced by the system user. **1964** M. MCLUHAN *Understanding Media* (1967) iii. 46 In the new electric Age of Information and programmed production. **1966** P. O'DONNELL *Sabre-Tooth* xviii. 241 Willie nodded, taking the cue and moving into his role like a programmed robot. **1967** D. WILSON in Wills & Yearsley *Handbk. Managem. Technol.* 45 In addition to the validation of input data, internal programmed controls are usually included during computer processing. **1972** M. CRICHTON *Terminal Man* 106 The programmed machine could exceed the capabilities of the programmer. **1974** E. AMBLER *Dr. Frigo* III. 155, I am not referring to the immediate tactical success, but to.. the programmed success of the future. **1978** G. A. SHEEHAN *Running & Being* ii. 27 It stripped off those layers of programmed activity and thinking.

2. *Psychol.* and *Educ.* Presented in the form of a teaching programme (*PROGRAM, PROGRAMME *sb.* 2h), or employing such a programme.

1958 B. F. SKINNER in *Science* 24 Oct. 975/3 Immediate feedback encourages a more careful reading of programmed material. **1962** *Listener* 23 Aug. 273/2 Hundreds of thousands of Americans..are now being taught by machine, and by what are termed programmed texts. **1963** *Guardian* 15 Jan. 6/1 'Earth in Orbit'..is a geography book with a difference. It is the first programmed textbook of English origin. **1967** *Punch* 22 Mar. 407/2 The shades of Mr. Chips, let alone Dr. Arnold, have long ago fled before an influx of black-maned technicians panning stealthy TV cameras over programmed learning machines. **1967** COULTHARD & SMITH in Wills & Yearsley *Handbk. Managem. Technol.* 204 Programmed learning is already extensively used in this country in schools (teaching mathematics and the sciences), in the armed services, by the airlines, and in companies with extensive training programmes for salesmen, technicians, etc. **1968** *Brit. Universities Ann.* 10 Experiments in programmed teaching have been going on in several institutions notably at Bradford. **1970** W. S. SAHAKIAN *Psychol. of Learning* x. 187 Programmed instruction is designed so that maximal reinforcement ensues by successfully controlling environment. **1974** *Nature* 22 Mar. 300/1 (Advt.), The reader will find that his understanding of the concepts of the subject and his confidence in using them are both developed rapidly as he works through the programmed problems.

programmer (prōu·græməɹ). Also (*rare*) **programer.** [f. PROGRAM, PROGRAMME *sb.* or *v.* + -ER[1].] **1.** One who programmes, in various senses, as: **a.** (In Dict. s.v. PROGRAM, PROGRAMME *v.*) **b.** One who devises a course of programmed instruction. **c.** One who plans or chooses programmes for broadcasting. **d.** One who arranges something according to a programme.

1890 [in Dict. s.v. PROGRAM, PROGRAMME *v.*]. **1958** *Science* 24 Oct. 971/1 The machine itself..is a labor-saving device because it can bring one programmer into contact with an indefinite number of students. **1966** *Listener* 27 Jan. 147/2 It is one of the unwritten laws of programming that even if the same-only-different is to be served up it must be loudly proclaimed to be different; that at least convinces the programmers. **1966** *Punch* 27 July 146/1 It was Baden Powell who revolutionised the process of growing up... Even his most grudging admirers must admit that he was an improvement on witch doctors and tribal elders as a programmer of boys' spare time. **1975** J. DE BRES tr. *Mandel's Late Capitalism* vii. 236 The only means at the disposal of late capitalist economic programmers for the correction of actual development when they deviate from predictions, is State intervention in the economy. **1977** *Daily Tel.* 2 Dec. 16/6 Using a computer device..they can let the programmers know, while the show is in progress, that they are unhappy with what they are viewing as television entertainment. If they are in the majority, it will be taken off the air and replaced by something else. **1978** *Detroit Free Press* 2 Apr. 1C/1 One programer at ABC believes that the show will help ABC's image among those who for religious or other reasons, hold ABC and TV in general responsible for moral decay.

e. *spec.* One who writes computer programs.

1948 *Math. Tables & Other Aids to Computation* III. 45 Magnitudes of numbers at each step have to be studied by the programmer..to avoid exceeding capacity in other operations. **1951** *Electronic Engin.* XXIII. 140/1 Most machines print the results of computations at the will of the programmer by means of some electromechanical device. **1958** *Oxf. Mag.* 29 May 469/1 Numerical analysts and programmers are in great demand in the laboratories of government and industry. **1968** N. CHAPIN *360 Programing in Assembly Lang.* vi. 139 A compiler program causes the computer to accept as input the source program the programer has written... The computer translates the source program..and produces the object program. **1974** *Maclean's Mag.* (Toronto) Jan. 44/3 As any programmer will tell you, a computer is merely as good as the data fed into it. **1980** R. MCCRUM *In Secret State* iii. 12 Quitman was not a trained programmer, but he had been given the standard course in basic computer access methods.

2. = *programme picture* s.v. *PROGRAM, PROGRAMME *sb.* 4.

1936 *Movie Mirror* Feb. 118/2 *Frisco Waterfront*... A better-than-average programmer that brings Rod La Rocque back to American films. **1939** *Motion Picture Herald* 11 Nov. 56/1 Very ordinary programmer. It is so simply told as to fail to arouse much for or against criticism. **1974** *Radio Times* 14 Feb. 9/3 When..Montgomery directed this Guadalcanal actionflick, everybody hoped it would certainly be a handsome cut above its other gun-toting rival *Guadalcanal Diary* made in 1943 without the benefit of real locations or scriptwriters. Instead the result was a routine action programmer with Cagney in rather restrained mood.

3. A device that automatically controls the operation of something in accordance with a prescribed programme; in quot. 1945 a part of an early electronic computer analogous to the control unit of later ones.

1945 J. P. ECKERT et al. *Description of ENIAC* (PB 86242) (Moore School of Electr. Engin., Univ. of Pennsylvania) B-2 The use of the master programmer is being stressed since it is the mechanism in the ENIAC which enables one to link the simple sequences of instructions given the other units of the computer into a complex whole. **1962** J. GLENN in *Into Orbit* 143 During the powered phase of flight..an electronic programmer inside the Atlas would guide it along the prescribed path. **1968** *McGraw-Hill Yearbk. Sci. & Technol.* 59 Until the mid-1950s this automation was in the form of special machines with mechanical programmers (cams, levers, and stops, operating in conjunction with powered lead screws) or tracer mechanisms, which cause the cutting tool to follow a path described by simultaneously moving a 'feeler' over a model of the part to be made. **1968** *Which? Guide to Central Heating* 73/1 A programmer is basically a more versatile time switch, which gives you independent control over your room heating and water heating. **1973** *Daily Tel.* 4 Dec. 11/4 If you go out for a few hours turn down the room thermostat or adjust your boiler programmer.

programming (prōu·græmiŋ), *vbl. sb.* Also (*rare*) **programing.** [f. PROGRAM, PROGRAMME *sb.* or *v.* + -ING[1].] †**1.** The writing of programme notes. *Obs. rare.*

1889 G. B. SHAW *London Music in 1888–89* (1937) 243 Sir George patronized everyone in his programming days.

2. *Broadcasting.* The choice, arrangement, or broadcasting of radio or television programmes.

1940 L. R. LOHR *Television Broadcasting* p. ix, The first [part] deals with television in relation to the public, that is, the programing of a television service. **1951** *Broadcasting* 15 Oct. 84/2 ZIV is delighted that NBC has taken this step..because better programming is good for the entire industry. **1958** B. ULANOV *Hist. Jazz in Amer.* xviii. 226 WNEW, the New York radio station that has proved most adventurous in its programming of popular music. **1960** *News Chron.* 21 Sept. 6/3 Peak-time programming was reduced to the familiar diet of quizzes. **1964** M. MCLUHAN *Understanding Media* (1967) v. 63 TV caused drastic changes in radio programming. **1973** *Guardian* 16 Mar. 10/1 'Complementary programming', the principle on which BBC-2 now gives you a serious programme while BBC-1 has a light one. **1976** *Broadcast* 29 Mar. 10/2 The five station types are defined by size and programming capability.

3. Planning carried out for purposes of control, management, or administration, esp. in economics.

1943 *Sun* (Baltimore) 1 July 14/2 The President transferred from Mr. Jones' RFC to Mr. Wallace's BEW full control over the programming of imported strategic materials. **1959** *Listener* 21 May 884/2 The design of controls, the programming of production methods, and so forth. **1967** E. DUCKWORTH in Wills & Yearsley *Handbk. Managem. Technol.* 117 Operational research in general has to do with the programming function in industry and all the methods described will be found to apply to the programming problems. **1975** J. DE BRES tr. *Mandel's Late Capitalism* vii. 237 There is undoubtedly a certain reciprocal effect, of a both technical and economic character between planning of production and accumulation within individual companies and programming of the economy as a whole.

4. The operation of programming a computer; the writing or preparation of programs; *programming language* = *LANGUAGE *sb.* 1d.

1945 J. P. ECKERT et al. *Description of ENIAC* (PB 86242) (Moore School of Electr. Engin., Univ. of Pennsylvania) B-1 An elementary programming procedure. **1947** *Electronic Engin.* XIX. 107/1 It remains to show how the automatic sequencing of operations—or programming—is achieved. **1949** *Math. Tables & Other Aids to Computation* III. 376 The most time-consuming factor occurring in the use of the ENIAC is the 'programming' (i.e. setting up the machine for a specific problem). **1954** *Sci. News* XXXIV. 60 The 'programming' of calculations to be done by computors is lengthy and tedious. **1959** *Computer Bull.* II. 81/1 This committee held three meetings starting on 24 January 1958 and discussed many technical details of programming language. **1962** *Lancet* 8 Dec. 1215/1 The final stage of programming must therefore consist in the translation of the flow diagram into actual coded orders which the machine can understand. **1967** *Economist* 8 Apr. 162/1 Programming schools are sprouting up everywhere. **1968** N. CHAPIN (*title*) 360 programing in assembly language. **1977** *Sci. Amer.* Sept. 236/3 Most of the programming languages in service today were developed as symbolic ways to deal with the hardware-level concepts of the 1950's.

5. *Psychol.* and *Educ.* The preparation and organization of the material necessary to a course of programmed instruction.

1954 B. F. SKINNER in *Harvard Law Rev.* XXIV. 96 In addition to the advantages which can be gained from precise reinforcement and careful programming, the device will teach reading at the same time. **1969** [see *LINEAR *a.* 3c]. **1976** W. B. KOLESNIK *Learning* vi. 124 The method of instruction most closely identified with the concept of learning-as-conditioning is commonly referred to as programming. *Ibid.* 125 While programming does sometimes involve the use of mechanical or electronic equipment, it need not do so.

programmist (prōu·græmist). Also **programist.** [f. PROGRAM, PROGRAMME *sb.* + -IST.] One who writes programme notes.

Found only in the writings of G. B. Shaw.

1888 G. B. SHAW in *Star* 26 Nov. 2/3 The usual Dvorakian dressing of Bohemian rhythms and intervals which give the analytical programmists an opportunity of writing about 'national traits'. **1889** —— *How to become Mus. Critic* (1960) 144 Mr Joseph Bennett, the programist, says of the symphony:—'It has been described by the composer as a "little" work.' **1896** —— *Our Theatres in Nineties* (1932) II. 244 The average programmist would unblushingly write, 'Here the composer..has abruptly introduced the dominant seventh of the key of C major into the key of A flat.'

progress, *sb.* Add: **7.** *progress clerk, committee, department, man, manager, payment*; **progress chaser,** an employee responsible for ensuring that work is done efficiently and to schedule (cf. *CHASER[1] 7); hence **progress-chasing**; **progress report,** an interim report on progress made to date.

1939 *Daily Tel.* 18 Dec. 12/6 (Advt.), Progress chasers wanted for aircraft work. **1943** J. B. PRIESTLEY *Daylight on Saturday* vii. 41 Even my friend Mona takes to it [*sc.* factory work] better than I do. You know she's a progress chaser now, don't you? **1977** *Lancashire Life* Mar. 49/1 The imminent threat of war found Arthur Lowe, progress chaser with Fairey Aviation, joining the Duke of Lancaster's Own Yeomanry in Manchester. **1943** J. B. PRIESTLEY *Daylight on Saturday* viii. 52 Doesn't matter what we do here—progress chasing and.. all the rest of it—we can't keep 'em to the high level. **1971** R. LEWIS *Fenokee Project* i. 10 Pete dealt with the progress chasing on outstanding contracts. **1921** *Dict. Occup. Terms* (1927) § 939 *Progress clerk*,..traces and pushes forward work in its various stages from operation to operation until it is ready for delivery... Keeps a record of output, etc., in works. **1942** A. P. JEPHCOTT *Girls growing Up* iv. 77 A progress clerk..is conscious of the superiority of her life over that of a girl who does a petty routine job all day. **1974** *Evening News* (Edinburgh) 8 Oct. 11/4 (Advt.), *Progress clerk*, £1600 plus, have you previous experience in electronics? **1914** E. T. ELBOURNE *Factory Admin. & Accounts* II. 39 (*heading*) *Progress Committee*—under Works Manager. **1925** C. L. BOLLING *Commerc. Managem.* x. 148 The managerial staff or 'progress department' will put into operation the plans of the advisory staff. **1932** S. E. THOMAS *Commerce* xxvii. 394 It is the duty of the Progress Department to follow up the various processes, to prepare job cards, material charts, etc. **1922** Progress man [see *CHASER[1] 7]. **1957** C. SMITH *Case of Torches* ii. 26 The small offices.. where the engineers and draughtsmen and progress men pored..over their columns of figures. **1925** C. L. BOLLING *Commerc. Managem.* x. 152 Each job undertaken is notified to the progress manager. **1932** S. E. THOMAS *Commerce* xxvii. 388 The executives under the works manager may include..a *Progress Manager*, who sees that the plans of the production manager or of the planner are carried into effect and that no unnecessary delays take place as the work passes from one process to another. **1959** *Wall St. Jrnl.* 12 June 3/1 The change will affect companies that receive 'progress payments'—funds advanced by the Government, usually monthly, to help offset a company's costs as it carries out major contracts. **1977** *Herald* (Melbourne) 17 Jan. 2/6 The company had obtained nearly $120,000 in progress payments but had completed only one contract in that period it was alleged. **1929** SAUNDERS & ANDERSON *Business Reports* iv. 43 Progress report is another report which may be limited to time, place, and handling of data similar to the informational report. **1943** J. B. PRIESTLEY *Daylight on Saturday* xxv. 189 Cheviot was now frowning hard at the progress reports on his desk. **1972** 'E. FERRARS' *Breath of Suspicion* iii. 38 So, if I see her again, you want a sort of progress report.

progress, *v.* Add: **6.** (Further examples.) Also, *spec.* to cause (work, etc.) to make regular progress towards completion.

1954 'N. SHUTE' *Slide Rule* 184, I was chiefly occupied.. in progressing the design and construction of the factory at Portsmouth. **1965** E. GOWERS *Fowler's Mod. Eng. Usage* (ed. 2) 479/2 *Progress*... *Prŏ'grĕs* is usual for the transitive verb, now much used in the manufacturing and building industries in the sense of pushing a job forward by regular stages. **1976** *Southern Even. Echo* (Southampton) 16 Nov. 13/2 (Advt.), Purchasing Administrator to work in busy spares section. Placing and progressing orders. **1978** *Observer* 12 Feb. 12/3 Welders to be trained to make more tack items to allow them to progress their own work to completion.

progression. Add: **10.** *Spectroscopy.* A series of regularly spaced lines or bands in a spectrum which arise from transitions to or from a series of energy levels having consecutive quantum numbers.

1926 *Physical Rev.* XXVIII. 638 In other words we suppose that the absorption bands whose stimulation is associated with these series all belong to a single *n'* progression. **1949** P. PRINGSHEIM *Fluorescence & Phosphorescence* ii. 136 If all excited molecules of a vapor are in one definite vibrational level *v'* of an electronic state *T'*, they can return from there to all existing levels *v"* of the ground state and thus produce an emission spectrum in which the lines corresponding to *v"* = 0, 1, 2.. form a regular 'progression'. **1965** R. N. DIXON *Spectroscopy & Struct.* vi. 129 When an electronic spectrum is studied in absorption at moderate temperatures most of the molecules in the lower state will be in the vibrational level with *v"* = 0, and the vibrational structure will consist of one series of bands, corresponding to consecutive values of *v'*. Such a series is called a progression. The bands are labelled *v'–v"*. Thus the absorption series 0–0, 1–0, 2–0, 3–0..is a progression in the upper state vibration frequency. **1976** *Chem. Physics Lett.* XLI. 289/2 The Raman spectrum is completely dominated by an intense band at 316 cm^{-1} and its associated overtone progression.

progressism (prō͞u·grĕsiz'm). [f. PROGRESS *sb.* + -ISM.] = PROGRESSIONISM.

1921 R. BOSANQUET *Meeting of Extremes in Contemp. Phil.* 206 Men do not, under the influence of such progressism, admit that some one or more climaxes of the finite may have been attained in the past. **1922** W. R. INGE *Outspoken Ess.* 2nd Ser. 26 The 'Progressism' of much modern thought is a poor substitute for this belief in the substantial reality of the eternal values.

progressive, *a.* (*sb.*) Add: **A.** *adj.* **2. b.** (Earlier and later examples.) Also of games other than cards.

1875 W. B. DICK *Amer. Hoyle* (ed. 10) 56 There is another variety to be met with occasionally, which may be styled 'Progressive Jack-Pots'. **1885** C. M. SEAVER (*title*) Standard guide to progressive euchre. **1886** I. M. RITTENHOUSE *Maud* (1939) 366 So we had a jolly little time, playing progressive euchre, and indulging in some music. **1888** A. RANDALL-DIEHL *Two Thousand Words* 169 *Progressive euchre*, a game of cards in which a player starts at one table, among the several scattered about the room. If he wins at the first table, he passes on to the next, and is credited with one game. If he wins again, he moves forward one table. **1903** R. BROOKE *Let.* 27 Dec. (1968) 5, I am going to have quite a gay time this week—progressive whist, fancy dress-balls etc. **1904** *Bridge & Progressive Bridge* 25 Progressive Bridge... The Rules of Bridge apply except that no account is taken of games or rubbers. **1906** *Daily Colonist* (Victoria, B.C.) 1 Jan. 15/1 Mrs. Piggott entertained a number of her lady friends..progressive five hundred being the amusement. **1907** *Yesterday's Shopping* (1969) 361/1 At Home. Progressive Hearts — o'clock. R.S.V.P. Progressive Bridge ..Progressive Whist. **1926** R. MACAULAY *Crewe Train* II. v. 118 Do you enjoy whist?.. We have very nice progressive drives on Wednesday nights. **1963** M. KENDON *Ladies' College Goudhurst* 20 In 1905 the girls were asked..for an evening of Progressive games.

c. progressive assimilation, in Philol. the process whereby a sound is modified by or harmonized with one closely preceding it.

1915 G. NOËL-ARMFIELD *Gen. Phonetics* ix. 32 If the first sound carries its influence forward the assimilation is said to be progressive. **1934** M. K. POPE *From Latin to Mod. French* II. i. 64 Assimilations and dissimilations may be either *regressive* or *progressive*, i.e. a sound may be modified in anticipation of a sound following, or the articulatory position of one sound may modify the pronunciation of a later one. **1939** L. H. GRAY *Foundations of Lang.* iii. 68 Assimilation may..be either *progressive*, when the first phoneme modifies the second,..or *regressive*, when the second modifies the first. **1964** C. BARBER *Ling. Change Present-Day Eng.* iii. 63 A historical example of *progressive* assimilation is seen in words like *watch*.., where the rounded vowel..is the result of the influence of the preceding w. **1977** *Canad. Jrnl. Linguistics 1976* XXI. I. 124 Chapter 5..shows..the action of progressive and regressive assimilation in triggering errors.

d. *progressive proofs* (see quot. 1960).

1932 PLACE & CLUNES *Letterpress Printing* xiv. 247 *Block-Maker's Progressive Proofs.* The colour sheets of 'progressives' provided by the process block-maker must be followed with absolute exactitude. **1948** R. KARCH *Graphic Arts Procedures* vii. 221 The two preceding pages show 'progressive proofs' and the final result of four-color process printing. **1960** G. A. GLAISTER *Gloss. of Bk.* 331/1 *Progressive proofs*, the proofs made in colour-printing as a guide to shade and registration. Each colour is shown separately and imposed on the preceding ones.

e. Psychol. *Progressive Matrices* (see *RAVEN).

1939 *Brit. Jrnl. Med. Psychol.* XVIII. 16 Progressive Matrices (Sets A, B, C, D and E 1938) obtainable from Messrs H. K. Lewis & Co. **1948** *Psychometrika* XIII. 36 In Sets E and D of the Progressive Matrices, the speed with which certain details are perceived seems to be important for the solution. *Ibid.* 41 The Progressive Matrices are loaded in several factors, plus a factor common to all of them. **1954** A. ANASTASI *Psychol. Testing* x. 261 The Progressive Matrices Test, developed in England by Raven..should also be included... This test, designed as a measure of Spearman's *g* factor, requires primarily the eduction of relationships within abstract material.

3. e. *Educ.* Of teaching methods, types of schools, etc.: aiming to develop individual capability and character in children rather than to achieve standardized results.

1839 tr. A. Necker de Saussure (*title*) Progressive education. **1910** CHESTERTON *G. B. Shaw* 185 Shaw has always made this one immense mistake (arising out of that bad progressive education of his), the mistake of treating convention as a dead thing. **1924** *Progressive Education* Apr. 3 The Progressive Schools are increasing rapidly. **1943** [see *ESSENTIALIST *adj.*]. **1946** E. HODGINS *Mr. Blandings builds his Dream House* (1947) 22 The creative, anarchistic, and sexual freedoms of a progressive school. **1959** *Listener* 5 Feb. 244/1 A man who tries to exercise authority in the manner of a sergeant-major will get short shrift in a progressive school. **1967** *Guardian* 14 Oct. 8/4 The Progressive Education Association founded..in 1915, had done its work so well that it was dissolved in 1955. **1976** *Listener* 29 Apr. 526/1 Anxious children did particularly poorly in a progressive classroom.

f. Of taxation: (see quot. 1902).

1889 G. B. SHAW *Fabian Ess. Socialism* 193 The Radical progressive income taxers singing together, and the ratepaying tenants shouting for joy. **1902** *Encycl. Brit.* XXXIII. 197/2 The question whether the burden of taxation should not be *progressive*—the proportion of the sum taken by the state from the tax-payers increasing with the wealth of the individual. *Ibid.* 199/1 A general system of progressive taxation. **1976** *National Observer* (U.S.) 21 Aug. 3/2 By using the progressive income-tax structure, state and local governments are placing the burden back on those hardest hit by raising regressive local taxes. **1978** *Times* 18 July 15/5 Progressive taxation is imposed in this country in order to moderate the unequal distribution of income.

g. *progressive kiln*, a long kiln through which timber to be dried is slowly passed on trucks.

1920 A. L. HOWARD *Manual of Timbers of World* 397 In all progressive kilns the timber is piled on trucks, and moved at regular intervals through zones of varying temperature and humidity. **1971** *Timber Trades Jrnl.* 14 Aug. 26/1 Small mills naturally use compartment kilns for export drying, but a progressive kiln will now pay off at 6om³ per day and offers lower consumption of heating fuel and electricity.

h. *Gram.* = *EXPANDED *ppl. a.* 2b.

1924 H. E. PALMER *Gram. Spoken Eng.* II. 149 Tenses composed of the verb (bi:) and the Ing-form are called *Progressive Tenses.* **1932** *Jrnl. Eng. & Gmc. Philol.* XXXI. 252 The creation of the progressive form resulted from the desire to express the idea of progressive action, action going on: 'He *is writing* a letter to his mother.' **1946** *Trans. Philol. Soc. 1945* 130 The distinction between the 'terminate' and the 'progressive' aspects of the verb, e.g. *I go/am going, do you go/are you going?* **1957** R. W. ZANDVOORT *Handbk. Eng. Gram.* I. ii. 36 What was said.. of the imperfective or durative aspect of the present participle also applies to its predicative use, as in *The ships were sailing out of the harbour.* This construction..is known as the *Progressive*, because it usually denotes an action or an activity as in progress. **1959** *Brno Studies in English* I. 13 Mod E progressive tenses must be regarded as marked counterparts of the simple tenses. **1965** N. CHOMSKY *Aspects of Theory of Syntax* ii. 64 *Frighten* is a Transitive Verb..; it takes Progressive Aspect freely.

i. Of music: modern, experimental, innovatory, avant-garde; used with reference to several distinct musical developments, as *progressive jazz, pop, rock*, etc.

1947 *Down Beat* 13 Aug. 1/4 Stan Kenton next month returns to the band business... First recordings will be for an album to be titled Concert in Progressive Jazz. *Ibid.* 19 Nov. 1/5 Stan..abhorred references to his music as 'jazz', himself using the descriptive phrase 'progressive jazz'. **1950** S. KENTON in *Metronome* July 23/1 In modern and progressive jazz and bebop there is such an urge today for new harmonic sounds..that the music has suffered. **1952** B. ULANOV *Hist. Jazz in Amer.* xiii. 141 The movement that is variously labeled 'progressive' or 'modern' or 'new' jazz is a New York movement. **1958** in P. Gammond *Decca Bk. Jazz* xvii. 213 June Christy.. might have persuaded the band to swing instead of exploiting these weary, 'progressive' jazz harmonies so thoroughly explored by Stravinsky some forty years ago. **1959** 'F. NEWTON' *Jazz Scene* vi. 117 Leading 'progressive' players like the pianist Lennie Tristano. **1963** R. I. McDAVID *Mencken's Amer. Lang.* 744 It [*sc.* funk] also designates progressive bop containing a strong blues element which marks its Negro origin. **1970** E. LEE *Music of People* vii. 147 A new style has arisen, usually called 'progressive pop', which is of such musicality that it has been heralded by some critics as a new form of art music. **1975** *New Yorker* 21 Apr. 7/1 (Advt.), Headhunters, a progressive disco-jazz quintet created in Herbie Hancock's image. **1977** *It* May 26/3 Patti wrote this heavy condemnation of 'progressive' rock radio as we hear it now.

4. a. (Further examples.)

More recently in South Africa, designating several political parties committed to a policy of multi-racialism; also, freq. a name or term adopted by radical, left-wing, or communist parties.

1930 W. K. HANCOCK *Australia* viii. 163 The area to be developed was also within constituencies held by the Country Progressive party, on whose support the Victorian Government was dependent. **1954** *Manch. Guardian Weekly* 16 Sept. 3/3 The ludicrous and largely Communist-dominated 'Progressive Party' campaign of 1946. **1955** *Treatm. Brit. P.O.W.'s in Korea* (H.M.S.O.) 4 The 'progressive' view—the Communist view—was the only one allowed. **1969** A. G. FRANK *Latin Amer.* xxii. 269 Concerned and progressive people everywhere scrutinize these..laws, and often criticize them. **1971** *Progress* (Cape Town) May 5/4 There had been talk of a split for a long time; the Press had even coined the term the 'Progressive Group' of the United Party. **1976** R. WILLIAMS *Keywords* 207 Nearly all political tendencies now wish to be described as progressive, but..it is more frequently now a persuasive than a descriptive term.

b. Characterized by (the desire to promote) change, innovation, or experiment; avant-garde, advanced, 'liberal'.

1908 H. G. WELLS *War in Air* ii. 35 It was always a very rhetorical and often trying affair, but in these progressive times you have to make a noise to get a living. **1949** 'J. TEY' *Brat Farrar* i. 11 The great house in the park was a boarding-school for the unmanageable children of parents with progressive ideas and large bank accounts. **1953** M. McCARTHY *Groves of Academe* i. 4 In a progressive community where the casserole and the cocktail and the disposable diaper reigned. **1956** [see *LABOUR *sb.* 2c]. **1974** *Howard Jrnl.* XIV. 99 The Rev. W. D. Morrison, whose outspoken views in the 1890s led to the most progressive document on prison reform since the writing of John Howard himself. **1976** *Church Times* 27 Aug. 6/5 There was something either in those particular temperaments or in the 'progressive' ethos, that militated against contentment.

5. *Comb.*, as *progressive-minded* adj.

1955 KOESTLER *Trail of Dinosaur* 206 The worshippers of tyranny and terror usurp the rightful place of a truly progressive party and cunningly direct the energies of the progressive-minded into 'anti-Fascist' crusades. **1975** A. BERGMAN *Hollywood & Le Vine* v. 60 A bad time for progressive-minded people.

B. *sb.* **1.** (Further examples.)

1921 J. R. HORNADY *Bk. of Birmingham* ii. 27 In the North we divide; there you will find Republicans, Democrats, Progressives, Independents, and so forth. **1954** *Britannica Bk. of Year* 638/1 Awareness of Communist thought produced the word..*Progressive*, a Communist sympathizer. **1955** *Treatm. Brit. P.O.W.'s in Korea* (H.M.S.O.) 15 'Progressives' were soon given a major rôle to play as mouthpieces of Communist propaganda. **1958** *Listener* 4 Dec. 941/1 The true Progressive was essentially urban and middle class. **1970** *Cape Times* 28 Oct. 1/1 The United Party has been a bit bitter about the Progressives, believing that they should not exist. **1971** *Rand Daily Mail* 4 Dec. 1/1 Mr. Bill Carr's decision to seek election to the Johannesburg City Council as a Progressive is more than just a coup for that particular party. **1976** *Times* 7 Aug. 12/2 When progressives seem to behave like theological scrap merchants, swopping bits and pieces in the ecumenical marketplace according to their fancy, clucking noises of disapproval are heard from the Vatican.

2. *pl.* Shortened from *progressive proofs* (sense *A 2d).

1923 H. A. MADDOX *Printing* x. 125 A final set of colour proofs (progressives) is prepared for the guidance of the printer. **1932** [see sense *A 2d].

3. One who favours, advocates, or practises progressive (sense *A. 3e) educational methods.

1936 H. G. WELLS *Anat. Frustration* viii. 73 The 'natural virtue' schools of such educational 'progressives' as Neill and his associates. **1944** H. CROOME *You've gone Astray* xvi. 168 You may know the true progressive..by the fact that he calls children not boys and girls, but 'kids'. **1961** CURTIS & BOULTWOOD *Short Hist. Educ. Ideas* (ed. 3) xx. 578 Pleas by the Progressives for activity methods, informal learning, and the encouragement of self-discipline and initiative. **1969** M. ASH *Who are Progressives Now?* i. 23 Of still greater gall to the old-style progressive at the Dartington Colloquy..was the pervasive belief of some others present, that by a well-meant concession to the independent progressive schools a niche could be found for them in the State system as recipients of..difficult children. **1976** *Times* 26 Apr. 13/3 In the past the debate between traditionalists and progressives in education has often taken place on the abstruse and abstract plane of educational philosophy.

4. *Gram.* Shortened from *progressive form, tense*, etc. (sense *A. 3h).

1961 R. B. LONG *Sentence & its Parts* v. 127 The point of view is internal, as with all progressives. **1965** N. CHOMSKY *Aspects of Theory of Syntax* 216 Such Verbs as *own*..occur freely with or without Progressive. **1978** *Language* LIV. 418 Half of his discussion of imperfectivity (32–40) is devoted largely to an examination of the English progressive in which it is clear that he is arguing from form to meaning, rather than the reverse.

progressivism. (Further examples.)

1961 CURTIS & BOULTWOOD *Short Hist. Educ. Ideas* (ed. 3) xx. 581, 1938..marked the final withdrawal of the pragmatist group from identification with progressivism. **1978** *Church Times* 17 Mar. 9/1 One might cite William Golding as representative of those intellectuals who were brought up to Wellsian rationalism and progressivism.. and then rejected it. **1979** *Daily Tel.* 12 Oct. 5/1 Mr Amin [President and Prime Minister of Afghanistan] did not refer to Communism or Socialism in his speech but stressed that the constitution would be based on 'progressivism', the word commonly used by Communists in parts of Asia where Communism is still frowned upon.

progressivist. Add: **a.** (Further examples.)

1945 K. R. POPPER *Open Society* I. iv. 39 Had he [*sc.* Plato] been a progressivist, he might have hit at the idea of a classless, equalitarian society. **1959** *Times* 23 Sept. 13/6 The younger composers..are indistinguishable in outlook from the vanguard of our English progressivists.

b. *attrib.* or as *adj.*

1969 *Daily Tel.* 13 Nov. 14/3 A favourite progressivist argument..is that people who are most vehemently against something are often the very same people who are unconsciously most inclined to it themselves. **1977** D. WATKIN *Morality & Archit.* III. ii. 94 According to the progressivist view, anything which reminds one 'of the past' is regarded as a vice.

proguanil (prōgwā·nil). *Pharm.* [f. PRO(PYL + *BI)GUAN(IDE + *-il.*] A bitter-tasting synthetic compound, 1-*p*-chlorophenyl-5-isopropylbiguanide, $C_{11}H_{16}ClN_5$, which is used, in the form of its white crystalline hydrochloride, in the prevention and treatment of malaria. Cf. *PALUDRINE.

1949 *Brit. Med. Jrnl.* 15 Jan. 88/2 (*heading*) 'Paludrine' (proguanil) in prophylaxis and treatment of malarial infections caused by a West African strain of *P. falciparum.* **1956** *Nature* 25 Feb. 368/1 Further mosquito infectivity experiments have confirmed that, in patients carrying gametocytes of a proguanil-resistant strain of *P. falciparum*, anopheline mosquitoes can be infected from a person taking 0·4 gm. proguanil daily. **1961** *New Scientist* 20 Apr. 119/1 It was found that if a strain of *P. gallinaceum* was transmitted serially from chick to chick, and the birds were treated with gradually increasing doses of proguanil, the organisms became highly resistant to its action. **1970** PASSMORE & ROBSON *Compan. Med. Stud.* II. xx. 20/1 Proguanil (paludrine) acts on the malaria parasite both in the blood and in the liver, probably by interfering with the reduction of folic acid. **1977** *Times* 5 July 7/6 Protection is easy: one of the antimalarial drugs such as proguanil should be taken.

proheterocyst: see *PRO-[2] 1.

prohibited, *ppl. a.* Add: *prohibited area*, a region which only authorized persons may enter.

1940 *Hansard Commons* 5 Mar. 195 *Mr. Woodburn* asked the Secretary of State for War whether, in his designation of a part of Scotland as a prohibited area, he has considered the repercussions of this decision on the Scottish tourist industry. **1948** E. POUND *Pisan Cantos* (1949) lxxxiii. 126 Bein' aliens in prohibited area. **1961** F. H. BURGESS *Dict. Sailing* 164 *Prohibited area*, an area marked on a chart, where anchoring, trawling, or fishing etc., may be forbidden by authority. **1964** G. LYALL *Most Dangerous Game* vi. 48 The convictions for flying in prohibited areas.

prohibition. Add: **4.** Now usu. with reference to the restrictions on the manufacture and sale of intoxicating drinks in the United States (1920–33) under the Volstead Act.

1925 W. J. BRYAN *Mem.* 186 His views on the initiative and referendum and prohibition had not altered. **1927** *New Republic* 21 Sept. 109/1 The Republicans have been laboring night and day to keep prohibition from becoming an issue in the campaign. **1931** M. F. FURNESS *Mem. Sixty Years* xix. 246 We of course heard much talk of Prohibition, and also saw a good deal of its absence. **1966** C. M. BOWRA *Mem. 1898–1939* viii. 212 Maurice had been in the United States during the fantastic boom of the twenties. This was also the period of prohibition, which made it a matter of prestige and honour to drink too much, especially hard liquor. **1970** *Nature* 19 Sept. 1186/2 For that matter the laws [in the U.S.A.] against marihuana have become so widely abused as to appear to many as a new Prohibition.

6. *prohibition amendment, candidate, era, law, state, system*; **prohibition party** (examples).

1883 *Harper's Mag.* Dec. 162/1 The prohibition amendment was defeated [in Ohio]. **1877** *Ibid.* Dec. 146/1 R. Pitman..Prohibition candidate for Governor. **1909** G. F. PARKER *Recoll. Grover Cleveland* (1911) 71 In addition, something over 300,000 votes had been cast for the Prohibition and the Greenback candidates. **1922** S. LEWIS *Babbitt* xiii. 174 He was blind and deaf from prohibition-era alcohol. **1968** *N.Y. City* (Michelin Tire Corp.) 32 The area later became famous as the 'speakeasy belt' during the Prohibition era. **1884** *N.Y. Weekly Tribune* 20 Aug. 7/1 The platform..means specifically that the prohibition law shall be enforced. **1949** *Daily Oklahoman* 13 Feb. D.2/2 A petition will be circulated calling for repeal of the state's liquor prohibition law. **1869** in D. L. Colvin *Prohibition in U.S.* (1926) iv. 73 We adopt the name of the National Prohibition Party, as expressive of our primary object. **1948** *Time* 12 Jan. 13/1 The Prohibition Party has nominated a candidate for President ever since its formation in 1869. **1892** *Outing* Dec. 209/1 They have no beer here: North and South Dakota are prohibition states. **1949** *Time* 10 Oct. 27/3 The state's church-going United Drys..were fiercely proud of living in a prohibition state. **1877** *Harper's Mag.* Dec. 146/2 He argues..the prohibition system a success.

prohibitionism. (Further example.)

1915 *N. Amer. Rev.* Dec. 948 All the speakers agreed that the bad saloon did more harm to the liquor trade than prohibitionism.

prohibitiveness. (Earlier example.)

1891 T. HARDY *Let.* 15 July (1978) I. 240 The late Lord Lytton..abolished prohibitiveness as between himself & the mass of the thinking public..by consenting to paper covers at 2s/-.

prohibitory, *a.* Add: **3.** *Gram.* = PROHIBITIVE *a.* 3.

1925 G. R. DRIVER in A. S. Peake *People & Bk.* 97 Since *lû* and *lâ* implied a precative and a prohibitory sense respectively, there was no risk of confusion between these forms.

prohormone: see *PRO-[2] 1. **pro-infinitive, -infinitival:** *PRO-[1] 4 b, c. **proinsulin:** *PRO-[2] 1. **pro-Israeli:** *PRO-[1] 5 a.

project, *sb.* Add: **5. b.** *Educ.* An exercise in which pupils are set to study a topic, either independently or in co-operation, from observation and experiment as well as from books, over a period of time.

1916 D. SNEDDEN in *School & Society* 16 Sept. 420/2 Some of us began using the word 'project' to describe a unit of educative work in which the most prominent feature was some form of positive and concrete achievement. **1919** J. A. STEVENSON in *School Sci. & Math.* Jan. 57 A project is a problematic act carried to completion in its natural setting. **1924** *Progressive Education* I. 72 A distinguishing earmark of a project, then, is the whole child responding to a situation; it is child activity. **1938** *New Statesman* 8 Jan. 46/2 *New Schools for Old* shows us the changes now being introduced into American public school methods of education. Children are encouraged to cope with the practical problems of life, and emphasis laid upon the 'project' or collective enterprise. **1942** B. CLEMENTS et al. *Projects for Junior School: Teachers' Bk.* i. 5 When working out a project the teacher gives help only when and where necessary, since the basic principle of modern teaching is child activity and teacher guidance. **1959** *Housewife* June 16 Cristy, who in one crowded summer, enjoys a library reading project, a visit to a Kansas farm and a course in baby care. **1961** CURTIS & BOULTWOOD *Short Hist. Educ. Ideas* (ed. 3) xx. 580 Not only were large-scale projects on such topics as 'Conservation' and 'Pan-Americanism' undertaken by many schools—often all the schools of an area—as part of the curriculum, but, in addition, community service by school children became common. **1965** *Nursing Times* 5 Feb. 191/1 By etymological definition, a project is a plan, scheme or design. Educationally, it refers to any exercise in which students gather their own information on a subject, arrange it and present it in an interesting form. **1976** P. DICKINSON *King & Joker* i. 19 Can I do next term's project on it [*sc.* a toad]?

c. *N. Amer.* A government-subsidized block of houses or apartments available at low rents. *housing project*: see *HOUSING *sb.*[1] 7.

1932 *Amer. City* Aug. 82/1 (*heading*) Federal Aid Now Offered for Low-Cost Housing and Slum-Clearance Projects. *Ibid.* 82/2 All housing projects should be large-scale developments. **1958** *Hearings Housing Act 1958* (U.S. Congress, Comm. Banking & Currency) 7 July 78 There is new thinking now to break up the projects and even though they are slum sites or urban redevelopment sites, to build scattered on the site. **1966** *Listener* 29 Sept. 454/1 Jim lives in one of a group of fifteen-storey-high buildings that make up a project, a city-owned housing estate. A family can rent an apartment cheaply in a project if it has a low income. Officially intended to replace the slum neighbourhoods of ten years ago, the projects are stark, anonymous, all-brick slums now. **1968** *Globe & Mail* (Toronto) 3 Feb. 3/4 A 2,000-unit high-rise and low-rise project. **1975** *New Yorker* 29 Sept. 43/3, I lived in a project then. The floors were so new they didn't have to be covered with anything.

d. A co-operative enterprise, often with a social or scientific purpose, but also in industry, etc.

1952 D. RIESMAN in *Antioch Rev.* Dec. 426 Professor John R. Seeley is now engaged in directing a large research project. **1952** AUDEN *Nones* 61 Thou shalt not worship projects nor Shalt thou or thine bow down before Administration. **1965** H. I. ANSOFF *Corporate Strategy* ii. 17 CIT uses long-term profitability over the lifetime of the project as the yardstick for evaluation. **1966** T. PYNCHON *Crying of Lot 49* iv. 88 When they grew up they..got stuck on some 'project' or 'task force' or 'team' and started being ground into anonymity. **1969** J. ARGENTI *Managem. Techniques* v. 26 Major projects call for the co-ordination of large numbers of machines, sub-contractors, finance, local authorities, design staff and so on. **1974** *Howard Jrnl.* XIV. 37 One aspect of a larger collective project being undertaken by members of the Centre for Contemporary Cultural Studies on 'mugging'.

8. *attrib.* and *Comb.* (sense 5), as *project approach, area, book, engineer, house, housing, manager, method, officer, work.*

1973 *N.Y. Law Jrnl.* 4 Sept. 5/6 We are endeavoring to try appropriation cases on a project approach. **1961** *Economist* 2 Dec. 935/3 It means accepting—as in India—the idea of a 'project area' in which all the means of modernisation will be made to converge. **1976** *Billings* (Montana) *Gaz.* 20 June 3-B/1 We joined Montana Federation of Women's Clubs because it offers prizes in all sorts of project areas. **1947** A. EINSTEIN *Mus. Romantic Era* xiii. 181 The scheme for the composition of such a work is found in Schumann's 'project-book'. **1976** *Columbus* (Montana) *News* (Fair Bk. Suppl.) 10 June 18/1 Those exhibiting must have the project books up to date and be enrolled in the project and unit in which they are exhibiting. **1931** F. L. EIDMANN *Econ. Control Engin. & Manuf.* iv. 45 In plants where the engineering projects are large,..it has been found that a very good way of handling the work is to assign one engineer to the task of 'living' with the job from start to finish... This engineer is known as a 'project engineer' in some organizations. **1973** *Times* 12 Nov. 28/8 Let us see the professionals all take a greater share of responsibility if a project is to be a success instead of leaving it to the 'jack of all trades'—the project engineer. **1967** G. JACKSON *Let.* Nov. in *Soledad Brother* (1971) 139, I thought most blacks..understood..that these places were built with us in mind, just as were the project houses, unemployment offices, and bible schools. **1970** D. GOLDRICH et al. in I. L. Horowitz *Masses in Lat. Amer.* v. 182 Those invaders who could qualify by 'normal' criteria for project housing would receive it. **1973** *Black Panther* 14 Apr. 7/3 Her application for project housing was refused by the Chattanooga Housing Authority. **1965** *Guardian* 31 Mar. 11/3 The truth lies..in the person of what is usually known as the project manager. **1976** *Southern Even. Echo* (Southampton) 10 Nov. 19/6 Conder, based at Winchester, are also acting as the project managers. **1916** J. C. MOORE in *School Sci. & Math.* Nov. 688 The project method in science is nothing new, though the name often calls forth an attack... The story of every great invention is the story of a project. **1925** W. H. KILPATRICK *Foundations of Method* xxi. 346 'You defend then the term 'project method'?'.. 'If it be thought of as a purposeful way of treating children in order to stir the best in them and then to trust them to themselves as much as possible, yes, I approve it.' **1943** H. READ *Educ. through Art* vii. 233, I am aware that serious criticisms have been made of the project method of teaching, but they seem to be based on a formless type of project. **1953** CURTIS & BOULTWOOD *Short Hist. Educ. Ideas* xvii. 476 After the Great War of 1914–18 Dewey's problem method was reinterpreted by W. H. Kilpatrick as the project method. **1968** H. I. ANSOFF *Corporate Strategy* 1 Dr Ansoff worked for the RAND Corporation as a project officer. **1973** R. HAYES *Hungarian Game* xxxi. 183 Generally speaking, sir, agents administer *things*, while Project Officers administer *people.* **1941** *Manch. Guardian Weekly* 14 Mar. 214/4, I..discover 'underlying object of fostering project work on citizenship'. **1958** *Sunday Times* 15 June 4/8, I want more, not less, practical mathematics in junior schools..and suitably graded mathematical project work in secondary schools.

project, *v.* Add: Also *South. U.S. dial.* **projeck, projick. II. 6. d.** *South. U.S. dial.* To wander, saunter, stroll (*around*); to trifle, mess, play *with*.

1828 J. HALL *Lett. from West* 290 A man who goes into the woods..has a..great deal of *projecking* to do, as well as hard work. **1845** W. T. THOMPSON *Chron. Pineville* 107 You see what comes of your projectin' about town, when you ought to be gwine home. **1848** —— *Major Jones's Sk. Trav.* 62, I didn't know whether he was projeckin' with me or not. **1891** 'O. THANET' *Otto the Knight* 66 Quality liked projeckin' roun' de kitchin. **1893** H. A. SHANDS *Some Peculiarities of Speech in Mississippi* 51 *Projicking*, a word used by negroes and illiterate whites to mean *fooling, trifling*; as, 'If you don't stop your projickin' with me, I'll lick you.' **1906** F. LYNDE *Quickening* 135 Don't you know you oughtn't to go projecting around in the woods all alone? **1929** W. FAULKNER *Sound & Fury* 10 Don't you start no projecking with Queenie. *Ibid.* 67 Is you been projecking with his graveyard? **1957** *Daily Progress* (Charlottesville, Va.) 5 Feb. 8/1 It beats all get-out how some people are always tinkering and 'projecking' on how to do things different from the way most people do them.

9. c. To cause (an image) to be visible on a screen situated at a distance. Also *absol.*

1865 *Rep. Brit. Assoc. Adv. Sci. 1864* II. 98 The impressive character of the image projected [by a magic lantern], being often stereoscopic in aspect. **1902** *Encycl. Brit.* XXVII. 95/2 In the magic lantern an electric lamp or limelight..projects, through an objective lens, the successive images of the film upon a distant screen. **1935** *Television Today* II. 599/2 (*heading*) Projecting the cathode-ray oscillograph picture. **1946** R. LEHMANN *Gipsy's Baby* 57 Leisure employs me..as a kind of screen upon which are projected the images of persons. **1964** *Photogr. Jrnl.* CIV. 152/1 Microfilm images..can be projected directly on to printing plates. **1969** *Focal Encycl. Film & Television Techniques* 378/1 The projection cathode ray tube..produces a very bright picture which can be projected with a suitable optical system. **1979** D. MEIRING *Foreign Body* ii. 30 Now it's film time... We'll project on the wall, just to the left of the bar.

d. To cause the image(s) on (a photograph, film, or slide) to be visible on a screen.

1896 R. W. PAUL *Brit. Pat. 4686*, My invention relates to an improved apparatus for producing representations of moving scenes, figures or objects by projecting onto a screen..by means of..suitable projecting apparatus, a series of photographic pictures of such scenes... In order to give a definite position to the picture on the film which is to be projected I prefer to employ the following mechanism. **1912** F. A. TALBOT *Moving Pictures* ix. 91 The film to be projected is carried upon a spool mounted on an arm or bracket above the mechanism. **1949** KIDD & LONG *Filmstrip & Slide Projection* 8 Often miniature slides can be projected in the standard projector (some of which project both miniature slides and filmstrips). **1962** L. DEIGHTON *Ipcress File* xv. 87 If they had to have a major here to project the film it might just be worth watching. **1971** L. B. HAPPÉ *Basic Motion Picture Technol.* i. 37 Corresponding prints could..be projected by similar anamorphic lenses to show a picture filling a very wide screen. *Ibid.* 39 The proportions of the new Cinemascope format when projected were 8 units wide by 3 high.

10. b. To attribute (an emotion, state of mind, etc.) to an external object or person, esp. unconsciously. Also *absol.*

1923 J. S. HUXLEY *Ess. Biologist* iv. 167 Certain neurotic types project their depression so as to colour everything that comes into their cognizance a gloomy black. **1925** A. & J. STRACHEY tr. *Freud's Coll. Papers* III. 458 It was incorrect of us to say that the perception which was suppressed internally was projected outwards; the truth is rather..that what was abolished internally returns from without. **1939** *Jrnl. Psychol.* VIII. 409 It appears that the subject projects similar patterns or configurations upon widely different materials. **1960** E. E. CUMMINGS *Let.* 30 Jan. (1969) 266 Indeed this correspondent can't help suspecting yourself of what the psychoanalysts call 'projecting'. **1966** I. G. SARASON *Personality* xii. 181 A defense mechanism through which an individual unconsciously projects his own undesirable characteristics to others than himself. **1975** K. R. SCHERER et al. *Human Aggression & Conflict* iv. 116 The subjects were projecting their needs into their imagery.

c. To convey to others, esp. by one's manner and actions (a positive image of one's personality or attributes). Usu. *absol.*

1955 *Psychiatry* XVIII. 217/2 The self-evaluation projected by his clothes and manner. **1957** *Economist* 12 Oct. 130/1 This matter of 'projection' is taken very seriously. 'He simply doesn't project' can be as final a dismissal of political aspiration as the fact that a man is known to have beaten a whole series of wives. **1959** *Encounter* Sept. 50/2

Competing with the roar of the machines..the actors struggle to project. **1960** *News Chron.* 28 July 4/5 Unable to 'project' publicly, in private he deploys considerable private charm. **1967** M. ARGYLE *Psychol. Interpersonal Behaviour* iii. 55 If a person behaves unpleasantly, or in some other way fails to live up to the image he has projected, equilibrium is disturbed.

III. 12. a. *pass.* = next sense.

1902 J. M. BALDWIN *Dict. Philos. & Psychol.* II. 414/2 The radiations taken together are called the 'projection system', the lower centres being projected upon the cortex. **1925** *Jrnl. Neurol. & Psychopath.* VI. 5 We draw the conclusion that the upper part of the retina in apes is projected on the medial side of the corpus geniculatum externum. **1926** *Brain* XLIX. 2 The nasal part of the retina is always projected laterally to the temporal half [of the external geniculate body].

b. *intr. Physiol.* Of an area or organ of the body, or its nerves: to have or be nerve fibres extending *to* an area. Also const. *upon*.

1936 *Jrnl. Compar. Neurol.* LXIV. 37 The anterior thalamic nuclei project to a small part of the orbital surface of the frontal lobe. *Ibid.*, The nucleus ventralis posterior, projects entirely upon the cortex of the central sulcus and the postcentral convolution. **1951** T. C. RUCH in S. S. Stevens *Handbk. Exper. Psychol.* iv. 125/2 The ablation of a cortical area truncates the axons running to it, and the locus of the resulting retrograde degeneration establishes which thalamic nucleus projects to the particular area ablated. **1975** D. H. FORD *Anat. Central Nerv. Syst.* vii. 83 The white matter of the [spinal] cord..consists of association fibers..which connect adjacent levels of the cord, longer association bundles which project up or down the various funiculi to interconnect further segments of the cord, or very long projection systems which project to supracord levels or which enter the cord from higher levels. **1978** *Sci. Amer.* July 38/1 These fibers usually branch repeatedly and may project to distant parts of the nervous system or leave the nervous system to innervate effector tissues.

projectile, *a.* and *sb.* Add: **A.** *adj.* **5.** *Literary Criticism.* (See quots.)

1929 I. A. RICHARDS *Pract. Criticism* 357 Aesthetic or 'projectile' adjectives..raise several extraordinarily interesting questions... In so far as they register the projection of a feeling into an object they carry a double function. **1949** BROOKS & WARREN *Fund. Good Writing* x. 351 What I. A. Richards calls 'projectile' adjectives: that is, adjectives which function, not so much to give an objective description, as to express the writer's or speaker's feelings... The '*miserable* wretch' may actually be smiling happily. The woman who has just been called 'a *great little* wife' may be large or small.

projecting, *vbl. sb.* (Later examples.)

1959 *Times Lit. Suppl.* 16 Jan. 39/1 *Introduction to Cine*..starts off the complete beginner and takes him as far as editing and projecting. **1960** E. H. GOMBRICH *Art & Illusion* xi. 385 We prefer suggestion to representation, we have adjusted our expectations to enjoy the very act of guessing, of projecting.

projection, *sb.* Add: **IV. 6. b.** *Math.* Any homomorphism from a vector space or the like into a part of itself such that each element of the part is mapped on to itself; also, a homomorphism from a group into a quotient group.

1942 *Amer. Jrnl. Math.* LXIV. 115 The study of groups which have projections on abelian groups. **1950** *Bull. Amer. Math. Soc.* LVI. 488 The systematic use of these injection and projection homomorphisms is at the heart of our formulation of the duality phenomena. **1976** D. E. CHRISTIE *Basic Topology* vii. 191 An indispensable tool for products is the projection, a function from the product to one of the factors.

7. b.

I. *Orthomorphic*: also called *CONFORMAL; IV. *Zenithal*: also called *azimuthal*; VII. Another conventional projection is the *two-point equidistant*, showing accurately the distances from every point to each of two chosen points. Other projections named after their inventors are *Albers'*, a conical equal-area projection with two standard parallels; and *Clarke's*, projected from a centre outside the globe onto a diametrically opposite plane. Projections may be *interrupted*, so that the representation is not convex but lobate or partly dissected; and *transverse*, representing a globe rotated through a right or other angle from its conventional orientation.

1910 J. I. CRAIG *Theory Map-Projections* v. 45 (*heading*) Transverse conical projection... This projection is of no practical importance. *Ibid.* 53 (*heading*) Zenithal or azimuthal projections. *Ibid.* 55 Lambert's equivalent azimuthal projection. **1910** *Encycl. Brit.* XVII. 656/1 (*caption*) Clarke's perspective projection for a spherical radius of 108°. **1912** A. R. HINKS *Map Projections* i. 6 There is a class of projections sometimes named azimuthal, from the fact that the azimuths, or true bearings, from the centre of the map, of all points, are shown correctly. *Ibid.* 7 The objection to the term *azimuthal* is that it is hard to pronounce, and several writers have followed German in calling always this class of projection *zenithal*. *Ibid.* iii. 26 Albers' conical equal area projection. **1922** C. CLOSE in *Ordnance Survey Prof. Papers* No. 5. 6 (*heading*) Two-point equidistant projection. **1927** J. A. STEERS *Introd. Study Map Projections* vi. 152 (*heading*) 'Interrupted' projections. **1969** G. C. DICKINSON *Maps & Air Photographs* i. 9 Distances..can be shown correctly from one, or two, but no more, chosen points on certain special projections. [*Note*] The zenithal equidistant and the two-point equidistant projections respectively. *Ibid.* 17 If a map can be broken in some areas that do not matter—the oceans if map is needed mainly for continental areas, or vice versa—and the meridians gathered together at several 'central' meridians the good qualities of the 'central' areas are more widely spread. Fig. 4F shows such an interrupted sinusoidal projection. *Ibid.* 20 Let us try projecting it [*sc.* the globe] onto a flat sheet of paper touching the globe, at the north pole to begin with, and furthermore see what happens when we move the source of light... The results from a group of projections known collectively as zenithal or azimuthal projections. *Ibid.* 24 If in relation to the parallels, the words 'their true distance apart' in the preceding specification is [*sic*] replaced by 'spaced so that the area between them is the same as that on the globe' we get Alber's projection. *Ibid.* 25 Suppose we want to make a transverse Mercator's projection based on (say) 90°W. and not the equator.

d. *Econ.* A forecast based on present trends.

1952 *Economist* 30 Aug. 526/1 The FBI's figure.. amounts almost exactly in total to a direct projection of the sharp upward trend in consumption during 1950 and 1951. **1962** *Listener* 16 Aug. 235/1 When this work has reached the stage of placing the various national projections alongside one another, the foundations of planning will have been laid. **1969** *Times* 4 Sept. 7 The eminent thinker acknowledges that economic performance is not conclusive but insists that it furnishes the basic structure and framework of power. Here is his G.N.P. projection for 1980. **1976** *Time* 27 Dec. 48/2 Among those who doubt the Carter projections are the members of Time's Board of Economists.

8. a. *spec.* The process of projecting (an image on) a film or transparency on to a screen for viewing.

1896 R. W. PAUL *Brit. Pat. 4686*, I prefer to employ the following mechanism,..causing the film to be propelled instantaneously a small amount, after which it remains still for projection of the picture. **1912** F. A. TALBOT *Moving Pictures* ix. 99 This second lens is used for the projection of lantern slides. **1953** L. J. WHEELER *Princ. Cinematogr.* vi. 193 Both lanterns must be accurately trained on the screen to give the appearance of continuous projection. **1976** *Times* 22 Apr. 11/3 Amplified sound, music, lighting, slide projection, videotape, all the tools of the professional chatterbox will be deployed to tempt conference organizers.

b. *Mus.* The projective quality of sound; acoustic penetration. Also *transf.* of an instrument.

1977 *Gramophone* Dec. 1045/1 So fine was the earlier recording that the later one..is not necessarily an improvement, even if the sound has slightly more clarity and projection. **1977** *Oxf. Times* 16 Dec. 16 The Allegri Quartet..tested the viola and cello in exchanged positions. The increased projection of the viola was remarkable.

9. b. *Psychoanal.* The unconscious process or fact of projecting one's fears, feelings, desires, or fantasies on to other persons, things, or situations, in order to avoid recognizing them as one's own and so as to justify one's behaviour. Also in more general use.

1909 PETERSON & BRILL tr. *Jung's Psychol. of Dementia Praecox* iv. 87 By the method of outward projection they frequently place the responsibility on some foreign agency. **1923** J. S. HUXLEY *Ess. Biologist* iv. 167 This projection, or interpretation of external reality in terms of one's self, is a curious and almost universal attribute of the human mind. **1924** J. RIVIERE tr. *Freud's Defence of Neuro-Psychoses* in *Coll. Papers* I. ix. 180 In paranoia the reproach is repressed in a manner which may be described as *projection*; by the defence-symptoms of distrust directed against others being erected. **1938** G. W. ALLPORT *Personality* vi. 173 There is likewise a complementary form of projection whereby a person does not attribute his own frame of mind to others but rather one that justifies and explains his own frame of mind to himself. **1944** *Horizon* IX. 169 His [*sc.* Lenin's] fanatical hatred of the Bourgeoisie of which, in analytical terms, the Russian revolution was merely a 'projection'. **1950** T. S. ELIOT *Cocktail Party* I. ii. 59 The man I saw before, he was only a projection—I see that now—of something that I wanted. **1966** R. D. LAING et al. *Interpersonal Perception* ii. 16 Projection refers to a mode of experiencing the other in which one experiences one's outer world in terms of one's inner world. **1966** *Listener* 5 May 653/2 Rogozhin.. who tries to win Nastasya with money, and ends by murdering her, can be seen to be a projection of Myshkin's urge to power and destruction. **1975** K. R. SCHERER et al. *Human Aggression & Conflict* iv. 117 Perhaps through the mechanism of complementary projection, they perceived the students to be particularly hostile, dangerous, and intent on overpowering the soldiers. **1976** SMYTHIES & CORBETT *Psychiatry* xv. 271 Projection means the attribution to external agencies of one's own psychological conflicts.

c. The conveying of a positive image of one's personality to others by one's manner and actions.

1955 *Times* 10 May 3/7 Attack, boldness, and what actors call 'projection' of the artist's personality, are undeniably all there. **1957** [see *PROJECT *v.* 10 c].

9*. *Physiol.* and *Psychol.* The process whereby a stimulus is perceived as being located at a point other than where the sensation or perception occurs (see quots.).

1887 G. T. LADD *Elem. Physiol. Psychol.* II. vi. 387 The law of eccentric projection is generally stated thus: Objects are perceived in space as situated in a right line off the ends of the nerve-fibres which they irritate. **1890** W. JAMES *Princ. Psychol.* II. xvii. 41 The other cases of translocation of our sensations are equally easily interpreted without supposing any 'projection' from a centre at which they are originally perceived. *Ibid.* 42, I conclude.. that there is no truth in the 'eccentric projection' theory. **1892** VAN LIEW & BEYER tr. *Ziehen's Introd. Physiol. Psychol.* iv. 77 By 'eccentric projection' we understand the fact that a sensation produced by the stimulation of the nerve-*trunk* instead of the nerve-*ends* is regularly attributed to irritation of the peripheral ramifications of the nerve. **1902** J. M. BALDWIN *Dict. Philos. & Psychol.* II. 358/2 *Projection*, the spatial objectivation of objects in sense perception... This usage is vague and descriptive, varying from the mere recognition of a spatial datum to the hypothesis of the spatial projection of states at first purely 'inner' and unspatial. It is also complicated with the hypothesis..that nervous projection.., to the periphery, sometimes extends out in lines at right angles to the sensitive surface. *Ibid.*, *Projection* (*nervous*, or '*eccentric*'), the property of the nervous system whereby stimulations are referred to the periphery of the body or to the end-organs. **1972** *Encycl. Psychol.* III. 47/1 *Projection, eccentric*, the introspective observation that sensory experiences are usually localised outside the body at the same position as the stimulus object... Thus the blue is seen as on the sky rather than in the retina.

9.** *Physiol.* The spatial distribution, in the brain, or other parts of the central nervous system, of the points to which nerves or nerve impulses go from any given area or organ; const. *on*, *upon*, *to* the receiving part; also *concr.*, a tract of projection fibres.

1924 *Scand. Sci. Rev.* X. 18 [This case verified my supposition..that every limited lesion of the calcarine cortex causes a corresponding limited blind spot in the visual field, or, that there exists a mathematical projection of the peripheral retina in the calcarine cortex.] *Ibid.* 37 The projection of the retina on the calcarine cortex. **1925** *Jrnl. Neurol. & Psychopath.* VI. 3 It is very probable that the projection of the retina on the primary centres in the ape is similar to that in man. **1934** *Proc. R. Soc.* B. CXV. 504 Although the existence of the cortico-pontine fibres has long been recognized.., there has as yet been no solution of the problem of their distribution in the pons and projection on the cerebellum. **1936** *Jrnl. Compar. Neurol.* LXIV. 7 The thalamic projection to the frontal cortex has occasioned much discussion. **1938** J. F. FULTON *Physiol. Nerv. System* xv. 335 In addition to the corticospinal projections, the cerebral cortex in the higher forms gives rise to a vast extrapyramidal projection passing to many subcortical levels. **1951** T. C. RUCH in S. S. Stevens *Handbk. Exper. Psychol.* iv. 136/1 The projection of the body surface upon the posteroventral nucleus of the thalamus was worked out in greater detail. **1973** W. J. S. KRIEG *Synoptic Functional Neuroanat.* 4/2 In the pons..the cortical projections are broken into bundles, and many fibers form connections to the cerebellum here.

V. 10. *projection dynamics, phenomenon, screen, surface*; **projection booth, box** = *projection room* below; **projection-fibre,** substitute for def.: a nerve fibre connecting one part of the central nervous system with another, esp. the cortex with the brain stem or spinal cord; (further examples); **projection lens,** the objective lens in a film or slide projector, which projects an enlarged image into space; **projection printing** *Photogr.*, printing in which an optical system is placed between the negative and the printing paper, so that enlargement or reduction of image size is possible; hence **projection printer,** an apparatus for this; **projection room,** a room in a cinema or film studio designed to contain the projector and its operators, through windows in the wall of which the film is projected; **projection rule,** in *Transformational Grammar*, a rule, based on underlying phrase markers, for combining lexical senses of words so as to predict their semantic role in a given sentence; **projection system,** add: in mod. use, a system of projection fibres; (earlier and later examples); **projection test** = *projective test* (see *PROJECTIVE *a.* 5b); **projection welding,** resistance welding in which welding is effected at one or more projecting points of contact previously formed in the components by pressing; so **projection weld** *sb.* and (with hyphen) *v. trans.*, **-welded** *ppl. a.*; also **projection welder,** an apparatus for projection welding.

1929 F. GREEN *Film finds its Tongue* xviii. 249 Out in the theatre, sitting in the audience, is an Observer. He has a telephone that leads to the projection booth. **1968** *Globe & Mail* (Toronto) 17 Feb. 45 (Advt.), Recreation area consisting of large family room with..projection booth and screen for home movie entertainment. **1934** S. CHESMORE *Behind Cinema Screen* ix. 85 In modern theatres the projection box is roomy..and well lit. **1966** P. O'DONNELL *Sabre-Tooth* iv. 67 The projection box was equipped with a kershaw filmstrip and slide projector. **1953** C. E. OSGOOD *Method & Theory in Exper. Psychol.* vi. 229 (*heading*) Projection dynamics in perception. **1920** S. W. RANSON *Anat. Nerv. System* xviii. 297 Many of the fibers of the medullary white center connect the cerebral cortex with the thalamus and lower lying portions of the nervous system. These are known as projection fibers, and may be divided into two groups according as they convey impulses to or from the cerebral cortex. **1970** L. J. A. DIDIO *Synopsis of Anat.* xix. 437/2 White matter of the cerebral hemispheres... It is composed of myelinated nerve fibers that may be divided into three groups: projection fibers, commissural fibers, and association fibers. *Ibid.*, Projection fibers are those that establish either ascending or descending connections between the cerebral cortex and structures outside the telencephalon. **1917** C. N. BENNETT *Guide to Kinematogr.* ix. 131 A secondary effect is often produced through the additional length of focus of the projection lens. **1962** *Which?* Mar. 68/1 The slide is put into a slide carrier in the projector and slid in front of a lamp and behind a projection lens.

1962 HENDERSON & GILLESPIE *Text-bk. Psychiatry* xii. 294 When a failure of repression occurs the paranoid symptoms develop as projection phenomena. **1940** LUCAS & DUDLEY *Making your Photographs Effective* xi. 168 The apparatus required for projection printing consists of the projection printer, or enlarger,..and the easel. **1965** M. J. LANGFORD *Basic Photogr.* xviii. 324 The term 'enlarger' although common usage, is deceptive. 'Projection printer' is the more accurate description of an optical device to give prints both larger and *smaller* than the original negative. **1923** *Brit. Jrnl. Photogr.* LXX. 350 The remaining factor in contact printing is the distance between the light and the negative... The question of printing distance operates equally in projection printing. **1974** A. FEININGER *Darkroom Techniques* II. 51 Unlike contact printing, ..projection printing allows a photographer a considerable amount of control as far as the final appearance of the print is concerned. **1914** R. GRAU *Theatre of Science* iii. 48 The fixture and office furniture are of massive mahogany and plate glass and the projection room is the last word in luxurious splendor. **1930** *Aberdeen Press & Jrnl.* 29 Mar. 7/4 A fire occurred in the projection room of the Swan Cinema. **1975** *Language for Life* (Dept. Educ. & Sci.) xxv. 425 Almost a quarter of the schools had a projection room. **1962** KATZ & POSTAL *Integrated Theory Ling. Descr.* iii. 64 The set of projection rules of a semantic component is..an unordered set. Each rule applies when the conditions of its application are met, and no two rules apply in the same case because no two rules have the same conditions of application. **1964** FODOR & KATZ *Struct. Lang.* xix. 493 A semantic theory must contain two components: a dictionary of the lexical items of the language and a system of rules (which we shall call *projection rules*). **1965** N. CHOMSKY *Aspects of Theory of Syntax* iv. 154 The projection rules must now be adapted to detect and interpret conflicts in feature composition. **1966** J. J. KATZ *Philos. Lang.* iv. 153 A system of *projection rules* that provide the combinatorial machinery for projecting the semantic representation for all supraword constituents in a sentence. **1977** *Language* LIII. 93, I assume..that semantic representations are complex objects, related to different aspects of syntactic structure by means of 'projection rules', or 'interpretive rules', of different types. **1946** KOESTLER *Thieves in Night* 170 You are fond of people..as projection-screens for your own feelings. **1954** —— *Invisible Writing* xxvi. 276 My emotions were self-centred, and those who inspired them served merely as projection-screens. **1890** W. JAMES *Princ. Psychol.* I. ii. 59 The entire cortex being, according to him [*sc.* Munk], nothing but a projection-surface for sensations, with no exclusively or essentially motor part. **1876** *Quain's Elem. Anat.* (ed. 8) II. 565 First projection system..between the convolutions above and the cerebral ganglia..corresponds for the most part to the corona radiata. **1890** A. HILL tr. *Obersteiner's Anat. Central Nerv. Organs* 168 Through the fibres of this system sense-pictures are projected on the perceptive cortex, and..the cortex..reflects outwards again the states of stimulation, information with regard to which is transferred to it by means of sensory nerves. The whole of these conducting paths Meynert, therefore, terms a 'projection system'. **1958** M. ARGYLE *Relig. Behaviour* ix. 104 The orthodox [church members] scored higher on ego-defensiveness and dependency measured by various projection tests. **1962** *Listener* 11 Jan. 62/2 Achievement motivation as measured by the projection test in which children were asked to write stories about pictures. **1967** M. ARGYLE *Psychol. Interpersonal Behaviour* i. 18 In 'projection tests' subjects are asked to tell a story about people shown in rather vaguely-drawn pictures... There is considerable doubt over the validity of such projection tests, and they cannot be said to provide very good predictions. **1950** HIPPERSON & WATSON *Resistance Welding* iii. 86 Projection welds may be made with a great variety of projection shapes and sizes. *Ibid.* 88 Unequal thicknesses of sheet may be projection welded. **1961** J. A. OATES *Welding Engineer's Handbk.* xxiii. 249 In cases where the projection welds have to be made on a narrow flange it is an advantage to use an elongated projection. **1980** L. M. GOURD *Princ. Welding Technol.* xi. 167 Reinforcing rings are frequently projection-welded around holes in sheet-metal tanks. **1950** HIPPERSON & WATSON *Resistance Welding* i. 25 A few typical projection welded applications..are shown. **1980** L. M. GOURD *Princ. Welding Technol.* xi. 166 (*caption*) Examples of projection-welded details. **1946** *Philips Resistance Welding Handbk.* i. 15 Owing to the number of spots, projection welders are of a higher kVA. than normal spot welders. **1968** ROMANS & SIMONS *Welding Processes & Technol.* v. 39 The majority of projection welders are operated by compressed air. **1918** HAMILTON & OBERG *Electric Welding* iii. 119 The welding of sheet metal is not restricted to one spot at a time, as any reasonable number of welds can be made at one operation by the method known as 'point-' or 'projection-welding'. **1975** BRAM & DOWNS *Manuf. Technol.* ii. 63 In projection welding the component is shaped to provide localised current flow, concentrating the welding heat at the areas of projection.

proje·ctional, *a.* [f. PROJECTION *sb.* + -AL.] Of, pertaining to, or connected with projection (in various senses).

1899 *Phil. Trans.* B. CXCI. 298 The large system of fibres just described above is probably both an associational and projectional system. **1949** *Mind* LVIII. 76 If the term 'God' is really non-significant, Findlay's earlier description of the religious attitude should be translated into emotive or projectional terms.

proje·ctionist. [f. as prec. + -IST.] One who operates a film projector.

1922 A. C. LESCARBOURA *Cinema Handbk.* vii. 285 One reel must serve for a large number of projectionists. **1938** *Times* 23 May 11/1 A suggestion that the cinema projectionists' dispute in London and the home counties might be extended. **1958** X. FIELDING *Corsair Country* viii. 167 The projectionist is making the final adjustments to his Heath Robinson apparatus. **1969** B. PATTEN *Notes to Hurrying Man* 14 This is the projectionist's nightmare: A bird finds its way into the cinema..smashes into a screen. **1973** J. WAINWRIGHT *Pride of Pigs* 158 They usually employed a lad—the 'second projectionist', so-called—to carry the reels to and from the projection room. **1977** *Western Morning News* 30 Aug. 11 (Advt.), Classic Entertainment Centre. We have an immediate vacancy for a Senior projectionist. Experience on 'Kalee 21' essential.

projective, *a.* Add: **2. d.** *projective plane*, that two-dimensional manifold which may be regarded as a spherical shell with all pairs of antipodal points identified; it is an example of a *projective space*, a space which may be regarded as obtained by taking a vector space of the next higher dimension, identifying all vectors which are multiples of one another, and omitting the origin.

1900 Projective plane [in Dict., sense 2 a]. **1910** VEBLEN & YOUNG *Projective Geom.* I. iv. 97 Any such space we call a properly projective space. **1942** *Amer. Jrnl. Math.* LXIV. 137 A satisfactory analytic theory may be developed for every projective plane in which Desargues' Theorem is valid. **1960** HILTON & WYLIE *Homology Theory* iii. 133 The real projective space *Pn* may be defined as the image of the *n*-sphere *Sn* under identification of all pairs of antipodal points. **1962** B. H. ARNOLD *Intuitive Concepts Elem. Topology* iii. 71 A projective plane can be considered as a disk and a Möbius strip whose edges are joined. **1964** C. E. SPRINGER *Geom. & Anal. Projective Spaces* vi. 150 A projective space is orientable if the dimensionality of the space is odd and nonorientable if it is even. **1975** I. STEWART *Concepts Mod. Math.* xiii. 199 This is exactly what is happening in the projective plane: going round once things get twisted; going round twice brings them back to normal.

5. b. *Psychol.* Of or pertaining to the projection of unconscious feelings, fears, fantasies or desires; esp. of tests designed to reveal unconscious elements of personality by responses to words, pictures, etc. Also *ellipt.* as *sb.*

1895 J. M. BALDWIN *Mental Devel. in Child* vi. 120 All of them [sc. stages of attitude] belong in the 'projective' stage of the child's sense of self, *i.e.*, they all go to furnish data which he afterwards appropriates to himself as 'subject'. **1939** *Jrnl. Psychol.* VIII. 404 No attempt has been made to provide a complete review of all the projective methods now being used. **1954** L. BELLAK *TAT & CAT in Clin. Use* p. x, The T.A.T. in common with all the other projective tests, is still far from being a properly established instrument. **1956** A. I. HALLOWELL in B. Klopfer et al. *Devel. Rorschach Technique* II. xiv. 476 Rorschach theory, as well as that underlying other projective tests, has been based on the general assumption.. that 'every subject's responses..are *determined* by psychological attributes of that subject'. **1966** I. G. SARASON *Personality* xii. 180 The ideas behind projective techniques have been largely psychoanalytic. **1971** *Jrnl. Gen. Psychol.* LXXXIV. 321 The clinician using the auditory method is now able to consider stimulus properties when evaluating projective material. **1976** L. R. AIKEN *Psychol. Testing & Assessment* (rev. ed.) viii. 223 Questionnaires and projectives are useful, but the most popular psychometric device for determining attitudes is an attitude scale.

7. *projective verse*, a term invented by C. Olson (1910–70), American poet and poetical theorist, to describe a brand of verse propelled by its inherent energy and composed according to a system of poetic values in which structure, lay-out, and breathing have an importance not accorded them in traditional forms. Hence *projective poet*, etc. Also *ellipt.*

1950 C. OLSON in *Poetry New York* III. 15 *Projective verse* teaches, is, this lesson, that that verse will only do in which a poet manages to register both the acquisitions of his ear *and* the pressures of his breath. *Ibid.* 20 Which gets us to..the degree to which the projective involves a stance toward reality outside a poem [etc.] *Ibid.* 22 Eliot ..has only gone from his fine ear outward rather than, as I say a projective poet will, down through the workings of his own throat to that place where breath comes from, where breath has its beginnings, where drama has to come from, where, the coincidence is, all art springs. **1962** E. MOTTRAM in *London Mag.* Dec. 71/1 Projective or open verse is a 'stance towards reality' as it brings the verse into being—'some simplicities that a man learns if he works in *open*, or what has been called *composition by field*, as opposed to inherited line, stanza, over-all form, what is the "old" base of the non-projective'. **1962** *Listener* 27 Dec. 1102/1 Of the 'projective verse' school, Ginsberg and..Edward Dorn seem to me remarkable talents. **1963** *Ibid.* 7 Mar. 435/3 A poet I liked very much is Robert Bly. In versification he is not 'projective', but in tone and attitude he is. **1967** *Book Week* (Washington Post) 19 Mar. 6/1 Here what he [*sc.* Olson] calls the Projective Open or Field verse (as opposed to the systematic Closed Forms of the past) is put to work, using *line, syllable, breath*, as principles he has preached. His one theme is energy—how a man's energy is expended in history and in space.

projector. 4. b. Substitute for def.: An apparatus containing a source of light and a system of lenses for projecting on to a screen an enlargement of an image or a slide, film, or opaque surface. (Examples.)

1912 F. A. TALBOT *Moving Pictures* 135 In colour work the projector requires a special type of shutter. **1915** W. H. CHANTREY *Theatre Accounts* (ed. 2) 78 Cinematograph projectors should be fitted with two metal film-boxes of substantial construction. **1926** *Encycl. Brit.* II. 961/2 In June 1895 Thomas Armat of Washington.. arrived at the principle of the modern projector, a device in which the film, moving intermittently, has periods of rest and illumination in large excess of the period of movement. **1962** *Movie* Oct. 12/3 The flickering blue light of the projector in the viewing theatre sequence. **1964** M. MCLUHAN *Understanding Media* (1967) xxix. 311 The present dissociation of projector and screen is a vestige of our older mechanical world of..separation of functions. **1977** J. HEDGECOE *Photographer's Handbk.* 312 Projectors for 35 mm transparencies and smaller are now usually magazine loaded.

5. *Comb.*, as *projector lamp, -man.*

1962 *Which?* Mar. 74/1 Projector lamps are expensive. **1972** *Gloss. Electrotechnical, Power Terms (B.S.I.)* IV. iii. 15 *Projector lamp*, lamp in which the luminous element is so mounted that the lamp may be used with an optical system projecting the light in chosen directions. **1927** *Observer* 17 Apr. 3 The picture is..'ridden in'—that is, the orchestra work up to an appropriate climax, and at a given bar the projector-man 'makes his throw'.

projicient. Restrict †*Obs.* to sense in Dict. and add: (prodʒi·ʃ¹ĕnt). **B.** *adj.* Concerned with an individual's perception of his surroundings.

1904 *Nature* 8 Sept. 465/1 [Reporting C. S. Sherrington.] In presence of the arcs of the great projicient receptors and the brain there can be few receptive points in the body the activities of which are totally indifferent to one another. **1927** J. H. PARSONS *Introd. Theory Perception* vii. 143 The projicient senses—vision.., hearing.., and smell—in the head segments provide those sensations which occupy the focus of the perceptual pattern, the field of attention. **1954** *A.M.A. Arch. Neurol. & Psychiatry* LXXII. 472 On the other hand, the admonitions from the group representative are apprehended largely by visual and auditory means; the authority figure is very much more clearly defined by 'projicient' modalities, and, we guess, is always clearer to the individual.

So **projicience** (prodʒi·ʃ¹ĕns), projicient activity or ability.

1906 C. S. SHERRINGTON *Integrative Action Nervous Syst.* ix. 324 It is in the leading segments that we find the 'distance-receptors'. For so may be called the receptors which, acting as sense-organs, initiate sensations having the psychical quality termed projicience. **1927** J. M. PARSONS *Introd. Theory Perception* ii. 7 At a somewhat higher level there is evidence of response to radiation of shorter wave-length—light, and perhaps ultra-violet radiation. As soon as this occurs the germ of projicience is found. **1931** *Brit. Jrnl. Psychol.* XXII. 143 Many, if not most, of the stimuli, to which man and the higher mammals respond through projicience, cannot be adequately described without using qualitative terms. **1949** A. GESELL et al. *Vision* xii. 196 This ability is a topographic discrimination, an elementary form of projicience.

prokaryon (prōᵘkæ·ri,ǫn). *Biol.* Pl. **prokarya.** [f. Gr. προ- PRO-² + κάρυον nut, kernel; cf. *PROKARYOTE.] The structure in a prokaryote which contains the genetic material; the prokaryotic 'nucleus'.

1957 E. C. DOUGHERTY in *Jrnl. Protozool.* IV. Suppl. 14/1 For the moneran nucleus I propose *prokaryon*.., and for that of higher organisms, *eukaryon*... From these derive..the nouns *prokaryosis* and *eukaryosis* and their corresponding adjectives, *prokaryotic* and *eukaryotic*.., denoting, respectively, 'the condition of possessing prokarya or eukarya'. **1969** BROWN & BERTKE *Textbk. Cytol.* vi. 96/1 The more or less central region of indeterminate shape and no bounding membrane is sometimes called the nucleus but more properly the prokaryon.

prokaryote (prōᵘkæ·riǫt). *Biol.* Also **-caryote.** [a. F. *procaryote* (É. Chatton 1925, in *Ann. des Sci. Nat.: Zool.* VIII. 76), f. as prec. + Gr. -ώτ-ης.] A prokaryotic organism. Opp. *eukaryote.*

1963 *Cold Spring Harbor Symp. Quantitative Biol.* XXVIII. 1/1 The distinction of *eukaryotes* which possess a characteristic chromosome nucleus and *prokaryotes* where the nuclear equivalent does not show any chromosome-like structures, is not bounded by a nuclear envelope, and does not divide by mitosis. **1967** KIRK & TILNEY-BASSETT *Plastids* xi. 364 This theory..makes it unnecessary to explain the separate evolution of photosynthetic ability in the prokaryotes (organisms such as bacteria and blue-green algae, with no separate membrane-bounded nucleus, or other organelles) and the eukaryotes (higher organisms, including algae and higher plants, with chromosomes inside a membrane-bounded nucleus, and other membrane-bounded organelles). **1969** LOEWY & SIEKEVITZ *Cell Struct. & Function* (ed. 2) i. 4 The genetic information in procaryotes, at least in the organisms studied so far, is located on a single chromosome that consists of a circular double strand of DNA and that lacks the basic proteins called histones. **1976** W. C. SCHEFLER *Biol.* xiii. 242/1 Procaryotes therefore have a very simple structure, which leads biologists to believe that a division of living organisms into these two basic cellular types occurred long before the evolutionary development of plants and animals as distinct groups. **1976** *Sci. Amer.* Sept. 167/2 No plant or animal is able to fix nitrogen, only prokaryotes: organisms, including bacteria and blue-green algae, that have no cell nuclei.

prokaryotic (prōᵘkæri,ǫ·tik), *a.* *Biol.* Also **-caryotic.** [f. as prec. + -IC.] Having no nuclear membrane in its cell; belonging to the group of organisms so characterized, which comprises bacteria and blue-green algæ. Opp. *eukaryotic.*

1957 [see *PROKARYON *a.*]. **1969** [see *CONIDIUM]. **1974** *Taxon* XXIII. 246 Cells with a general organization between entire prokaryotic and eukaryotic cells have not been found. **1976** *Sci. Amer.* Feb. 35/2 Bacteria are prokaryotic cells, that is, their genetic material is distributed throughout the cytoplasm. **1976** W. C. Schefler *Biol.* xiii. 242/1 Procaryotic cells..lack mitochondria, chloroplasts, an endoplasmic reticulum, Golgi bodies, and lysosomes.

proke, *v.*[1] **2.** (Later examples.)
1843 N. Macleod *Crack aboot Kirk* (ed. 2) I. 2 If a man has a sair leg or a sick body ye needna keep prokin' at him and roarin' in his lug a' day that he's no weel. **1914** P. MacGill *Children of Dead End* xxi. 149 I'm sick of prokin' in the gutters here. **1941** E. R. Eddison *Fish Dinner* xiv. 261 The plague that sat dozing in her mouth's corner proked at him swiftly.

prokinesis (prō^{u}kəinī·sis, -kɪn-). *Zool.* [ad. G. *prokinetik*, f. Gr. πρό Pro-[2] + κῑνητικ-ός moving: see Kinetic *a.* (*sb.*) and *kinesis.] A process, found in some birds and lizards, by which the upper bill or jaw may be raised relative to the cranium by rotation about a hinge anterior to the eyes.
1962 T. H. Frazzetta in *Jrnl. Morphol.* CXI. 287/2 It is here advocated that..Hofer's 'prokinesis' be modified to designate any kinetic joint anterior to the eyes. **1964** *Ibid.* CXIV. 3/1 The basic avian condition is prokinesis from which rhynchokinesis evolved. **1964**, etc. [see *rhynchokinesis]. **1973** *Nature* 11 May 73/1 Prokinesis and rhynchokinesis may have evolved independently in neognathous and palaeognathous birds, or rhynchokinesis may have evolved from some form of prokinesis.
So **prokine·tic** *a.*
1960 *Q. Rev. Biol.* XXXV. 219/2 In view of the fact that there are so many differences in the actual operation of kinesis in the various orders [of birds], I doubt if the terms pro- and rhyncho-kinetic actually are morphologically meaningful. **1964** *Jrnl. Morphol.* CXIV. 4/2 The prokinetic condition is the most widespread and apparently the primitive condition in the class Aves. **1974** P. J. K. Burton *Feeding & Feeding Apparatus in Waders* ii. 35 An important feature of rhynchokinesis is that the pivots about which the two jaws move are relatively much further apart than in prokinetic species.

pro-knock: see *pro-[1] 5a.

prolactin (prolæ·ktin). *Physiol.* [f. Pro-[1] + Lact(ation + -in[1].] A gonadotrophic polypeptide hormone which promotes lactation.
1932 O. Riddle et al. in *Proc. Soc. Exper. Biol. & Med.* XXIX. 1211 We..have identified this same hormone, which we shall here call 'Prolactin' as the hitherto undefined pituitary principle which is essential for lactation in mammals. **1941** *Nature* 11 Jan. 44/2 The activity was at first ascribed to a single hormone of the pituitary which was called prolactin. Very recent work has gone to show that this activity is, in fact, due to the co-operation of two separate hormones of the anterior pituitary—prolactin and glycotropin. **1952** [see *lactogen]. **1974** *Sci. Amer.* Sept. 53/3 There is probably a role for a third gonadotropic hormone of the pituitary, prolactin, in maintaining the steroid-producing function of the corpus luteum for its usual 14-day life span, but there is some doubt whether this is true in humans. **1979** *Jrnl. R. Soc. Arts* CXXVII. 416/2 We know that the blood prolactin level is directly related to suckling frequency.

prolactinoma (prolæktinō^{u}·mă). *Med.* [f. prec. + *-oma.] A tumour that produces excessive quantities of prolactin.
1975 S. Franks et al. in *Hormone Res.* VI. 273 Pituitary tumours causing disorders of reproduction are almost without exception 'prolactinomas'. **1977** *Lancet* 9 Apr. 779/2 The incidence of prolactinoma in patients with pituitary tumours is likely to vary in different endocrine clinics.

prolamine (prō^{u}·lămīn, -in). *Biochem.* Formerly also **prolamin.** [f. *proline with inserted *-am* (f. Amide).] Any of a class of proteins which occur in the seeds of cereals and are characterized by solubility in a 70–90 per cent solution of alcohol and insolubility in water.
1908 T. B. Osborne in *Science* 2 Oct. 422/1 Prolamins.. form a unique and sharply differentiated group of proteins which occur in quantity in the seeds of cereals... I propose this name for the group which heretofore has been simply called alcohol-soluble proteins. The name refers to the relatively large proportion of proline and amide nitrogen which they yield on hydrolysis. **1921** *Monthly Bull. Agric. Intelligence & Plant Dis.* XII. 400 The only well-defined proteins found in oats are a venaline,..and a prolamine soluble in alcohol, and belonging to the same group as the gliadin of wheat. **1931** E. C. Miller *Plant Physiol.* ix. 518 The prolamins..are known to occur only in the seeds of cereals. *Ibid.*, The glutelins and prolamins are collectively termed 'glutens'. **1938** *Thorpe's Dict. Appl. Chem.* (ed. 4) II. 493/1 Prolamines (gliadins) are present only in small quantities in the inner endosperm of rice. **1971** *Sci. Amer.* Aug. 36/3 The nutritional proteins in corn kernels are classified in four categories according to solubility: (1) albumins, soluble in water; (2) globulins, soluble in saline solutions; (3) prolamines, soluble in moderately strong alcohol.

prolan (prō^{u}·læn). *Physiol.* [a. G. *prolan* (B. Zondek 1929, in *Zeitschr. f. Geburtshülfe u. Gynäkologie* XCV. 363), f. L. *prōl-ēs* progeny: see -an.] The name given to what was formerly thought to be one female sex hormone but is now known to comprise both follicle-stimulating hormone (*prolan A*) and luteinizing hormone (*prolan B*).
1931 *Biol. Abstr.* V. 1357/2 The hormone of the anterior lobe of the pituitary body, called prolan, is an activator of the ♀ sex gland. **1936** *Brit. Med. Jrnl.* 28 Mar. 628/2 Prolan preparations are also found to be effective here [*sc.* in habitual miscarriage from no apparent cause]. **1966** Rowlands & Parkes in A. S. Parkes *Marshall's Physiol. of Reproduction* (ed. 3) III. xxv. 51 This gonadotrophic material, called Prolan by Aschheim and Zondek, was at first thought to be of hypophysal origin. **1971** *Path. Biol.* XIX. 1119 Estimation of..prolan B at concentrations lower than the threshold of immunological activity during various pathological conditions is rendered possible.

prolapsed, *ppl. a.* Add: Also *fig.*
1926 S. Baldwin *On England* 111 We see the sentences of the ancients clean run like athletes and fit for their work as compared with the prolapsed and slovenly figures of so much of our own diction.

prolately, *adv.* (Earlier example.)
1866 B. H. Kennedy *Public School Latin Primer* 110 The Infinitive stands... 4. Prolately, after Prolative Verbs and Adjectives.

prolating (prō^{u}le^{i}·tiŋ), *vbl. sb.* [f. Prolate *v.* + -ing[1].] Increase or extension.
1919 *Empire Rev.* 256 The loss of wealth, high taxation, the dislocation of trade and industry with their attendant evils, labour unrest and the prolating of unemployment.

prola·tively, *adv.* [f. Prolative *a.* + -ly[2].] As a prolative infinitive.
1888 B. H. Kennedy *Rev. Latin Primer* 163 The Infinitive of a Copulative Verb used Prolatively is followed by a Complement in the Nominative.

prole (prō^{u}l), *sb.* and *a.* Freq. *derogatory.*
A. *sb.* Abbrev. of Proletarian *sb.*
1887 G. B. Shaw *Let.* 21 Oct. (1965) I. 176 We call the working men proles because that is exactly what they are. **1939** 'G. Orwell' *Coming up for Air* i. ii. 18 There's a lot of rot talked about the sufferings of the working class. I'm not so sorry for the proles myself. **1939** Joyce *Finnegans Wake* (1964) 39 The doubles of Perkin and Paullock, peer and prole. **1949** 'G. Orwell' *Nineteen Eighty-Four* ii. 209 The dumb masses whom we habitually refer to as 'the proles', numbering perhaps 85 per cent of the population. **1954** Koestler *Invisible Writing* iii. xxi. 238, I know that these little Proles can't help being what they are—dumb, callous, primitive. **1958** *Observer* 11 May 15/2 Even the boatswain, a 'good prole' who doesn't believe in unions or democracy, is afraid to take the helm. **1967** J. Potter *Foul Play* i. 11 Make way there, you proles. **1975** I. Murdoch *Word Child* 10 'I'm fed up with hearing the proles binding about the price of meat,' said Freddie. **1977** J. I. M. Stewart *Madonna of Astrolabe* x. 138 In the Blunderville heyday the Mumfords were the next things to proles.
B. *adj.* Abbrev. of Proletarian *a.* c.
1938 'G. Orwell' *Let.* 20 Apr. in *Coll. Ess.* (1968) I. 314 As to the great proletarian novel, I really don't see how it's to come into existence. The stuff in *Seven Shifts* is written from a prole point of view, but of course as literature it's bourgeois literature. **1949** —— *Nineteen Eighty-Four* i. 12 A woman down in the prole part of the house suddenly started kicking up a fuss. **1959** *News Chron.* 21 Oct. 3/1 She came from prole roots in St. Pancras. **1963** *Listener* 7 Feb. 263/1 Excellent radio actresses like Gladys Young, for whom our prole dramatists write no parts nowadays. **1969** 'H. Calvin' *Chosen Instrument* x. 132 Superior journalists..would think it Victorian and prole to know shorthand. **1977** *Times* 20 Apr. 12/2 What has happened in England is that..the proles, or to be exact the prole élite, have seized the power.

prolet- (prō^{u}le·t). Abbrev. [after Russ. *prolet-* in *proletkul't* for *proletárskaya kul'túra* proletarian culture] of Proletarian *a.* and *sb.*, as in *prolet-art, -cult,* (*-kult*), *-cultist, -cultural* adj., used to designate cultural activities (esp. such as were started in Russia after 1917) which supposedly reflect or encourage a purely proletarian ethos.
1921 E. & C. Paul *Proletcult* ii. 19 Proletarians who are alive to their class interest..will insist upon Independent Working-Class Education, upon proletarian culture, upon Proletcult. **1921** *Glasgow Herald* 28 Dec. 11 There is little proof that there has been general misrepresentation, and it is general misrepresentation that the prolet-cultist wants. **1922** *Ibid.* 4 Jan. 5 One cannot imagine any greater stimulus to the 'Prolet-Cultural' movement. **1931** H. G. Wells *Work, Wealth & Happiness of Mankind* (1932) xv. 732 From the Proletarian springs 'Prolet-art', for example, among the first fruits of the new spirit. It is art without individuality. **1943** E. M. Almedingen *Frossia* ii. 84 Frossia told her about *Coppelia* at the neighbouring Proletcult. **1961** *New Left Rev.* May–June 27/2 The follies of *proletcult*, the stridency and crude class reductionism which passed for Marxist criticism. **1963** A. Hartley *State of England* ii. 26 The *Proletkult* of a philosopher such as Sartre is purely intellectual. **1967** *Oxf. Compan. Theatre* (ed. 3) 952/2 *Trades Unions Theatre*, Moscow..was created in 1932 from the Proletcult Theatre, started after the October Revolution by Sergei Eisenstein. **1974** Moore & Parry *Twentieth-Cent. Russ. Lit.* (1976) ii. 24 The magazine *Proletarskaya kul'tura* incorporated the name of the movement, which itself became, in shorthand, *Proletkul't.* **1976** T. Eagleton *Crit. & Ideology* v. 165 Such purely gestural, shamefaced materialism will provoke..the reaction of those who press their questioning of the intrinsic élitism of literature and its aesthetics to neo-*proletkult* limits.

proletaire. b. (Earlier example.)
1833 J. S. Mill *Let.* 2 Feb. in *Wks.* (1963) XII. 140 Those of the St. Simonians who retain their connection with the Pere Suprême and with each other, have made themselves *prolètaires.*

proletarian, *a.* and *sb.* Add: **A.** *adj.* **c.** (Further examples.) Also as *proletarian revolution*: the stage of political development predicted by Marx when the proletarians would overthrow capitalism.
1903 G. B. Shaw *Man & Superman* v. 196 We have been driven to Proletarian Democracy by the failure of all the alternative systems. **1925** tr. *Lenin's Proletarian Revolution* i. 11 Almost a third of this pamphlet..is devoted by this windbag to a twaddle which must be very agreeable to the bourgeoisie, as it..obscures the question of the proletarian revolution. **1934** C. Lambert *Music Ho!* iv. 248 The sleeves themselves are rolled up in the most approved proletarian fashion. **1935** W. Empson *Some Versions of Pastoral* 3 It is hard for an Englishman to talk definitely about proletarian art. **1966** *Guardian* 13 Dec. 8/2 [China] The example of the great proletarian cultural revolution. **1973** C. D. Kernig *Marxism, Communism & Western Society* VII. 238/1 The proletarian revolution becomes an act of human emancipation or the self-realization of man after his self-alienation. **1975** *Chinese Econ. Stud.* VIII. iv. 3 Countless proletarian heroes have suddenly emerged. **1976** *Times* 28 Sept. (China Suppl.) 10/3 Under the banner of 'proletarian internationalism' ideological motives seem to be distinguishable features of Chinese aid. **1977** *China Now* June 4/1 Tachai is an expression of the proletarian revolution China is in the midst of today (in contrast to the democratic revolution between 1949 and 1966). **1978** *Times Lit. Suppl.* 1 Dec. 1402/5 Sociologists and realistic novelists—including proletarian novelists—find it difficult if not impossible to describe the texture of this world.
B. *sb.* (Earlier and later examples of mod. sense.)
1870 *On the War* (Internat. Working-Men's Assoc.) 4 Mindful of the watchword of the International Working-men's Association: *Proletarians of all countries unite*, we shall never forget that the workmen of *all* countries are our *friends* and the despots of *all* countries our *enemies.* **1966** D. Wilson *Quarter of Mankind* i. 7 The peasant, not the urban proletarian, is the central character in China's drama. **1969** A. G. Frank *Latin Amer.* (1970) xxiii. 360 The rural and slum proletarians..tend to be quite near-sighted and to see only the land and the jobs which they want but don't have.

proletarianism. (Later examples.)
1918 *Nation* (N.Y.) 7 Feb. 131/2 Fidelity to the cause of international proletarianism..must stay the hands of the Bolshevik peace negotiators. **1975** D. Francis *High Stakes* v. 75 If politicians..searched diligently amongst their antecedents for proletarianism and denied aristocratic contacts..who was I to spoil the fun?

proleta:rianiza·tion. [f. Proletarianize *v.* + -ation.] The fact or process of rendering or becoming proletarian (sense c).
1920 *19th Cent.* Sept. 445 If State agriculture in Russia comes to be on a larger scale, will there not be a sort of proletarianisation of the peasants? **1936** 'H. MacDiarmid' *Lucky Poet* (1943) iii. 145 The line we advocate ..will..greatly speed up the proletarianization of Scottish Arts and Letters. **1948** C. S. Fox tr. *Röpke's Civitas Humana* iii. vi. 140 Proletarianisation means..that human beings have got into a highly dangerous sociological and anthropological state which is characterised by lack of property, lack of reserves of every kind.., by economic servitude, uprooting, massed living quarters, militarisation of work..; in short, by a general devitalisation and loss of personality. **1961** L. P. Hartley *Two for River* 45 The appalling vulgarity of that town! Nowhere has the proletarianization of the English race gone so fast, or so far. **1966** F. Schurmann *Ideology & Organization in Communist China* i. 40 Given the unilinear development of history, the process of world-wide proletarianization is inevitable. **1974** *Daily Tel.* 24 May 3/2 The initiative for getting rid of the oak tables came from one or two students keen to promote the 'proletarianisation' of the college. **1977** P. Johnson *Enemies of Society* xiv. 190 The proletarianization of the British middle class, that leading creator and custodian of western civilization, is one of the most significant social changes of our times.

proletarianize, *v.* Add: (Further examples.) Hence **proleta·rianized** *ppl. a.*; **proleta·rianizing** *vbl. sb.*
1921 tr. *Rathenau's New Society* 60 To many it is not agreeable to picture to themselves the aspect of a thoroughly proletarianized country. **1937** 'C. Caudwell' *Illusion & Reality* vi. 115 Proletarianise the craftsman to the level of a labourer or machine-minder. **1949** 'M. Innes' *Journeying Boy* i. 6 The lower stratum of the intellectual class was being proletarianised. **1957** M. McCarthy *Mem. Catholic Girlhood* i. 40 The peculiarly fatigued, dusty, proletarianized character of American municipal entertainment. **1962** *Guardian* 9 Mar. 7/2 Many of the most important American cities..have become increasingly proletarianised in the worst sense. **1965** D. E. C. Eversley in Glass & Eversley *Population in Hist.* ii. 66 A fall in the death rate..accelerated the proletarianizing process. **1966** D. Wilson *Quarter of Mankind* iii. 37 The middle class has become a captive collaborator with the Communist Party, having to work for its own downfall in the interests of a reconstructed, proletarianized nation. **1974** *Daily Tel.* 15 Jan. 14/3 Now officially referred to..as 'Mr Tony Benn'. So the..process by which the man who was once called Viscount Stansgate has tried so determinedly to proletarianise himself is almost complete

1974 B. PEARCE tr. *Amin's Accumulation on World Scale* I. 27 Analogous to this process is the mobilizing of the internal colonial reserves, as with the proletarianizing of blacks in the United States. **1979** *Jrnl. R. Soc. Arts* CXXVII. 354/2 The proletarianizing of the north-east coast.

proleta·rianly, *adv.* [f. PROLETARIAN *a.* and *sb.* + -LY².] According to proletarian views.

1931 *Time & Tide* 3 Oct. 1130 This *rentier* has been unfeeling enough to practice what is capitalistically called virtue, but is proletarianly known as vice; *he has saved money!*

proletariate, -at. Add: The usual spelling is now *proletariat.* **2. a.** *fig.* (Further example.)

1881 *Nature* 24 Feb. 387/1 First..was the Sparrow, the most impudent proletariat—I had almost said Social democrat, because the whole world today has that bad word in the mouth.

b. (Earlier and later examples.) *dictatorship of the proletariat*: the Communist ideal of proletarian supremacy following the overthrow of capitalism and preceding the classless state.

1856 GEO. ELIOT in *Westm. Rev.* X. 75 The Proletariat, or those who are dependent on daily wages. **1886** tr. *Marx's Manifesto of Communists* 8 The small middle class, the artisans, merchants, mechanics, shopkeepers, and farmers, are all doomed to fall into the ranks of the Proletariat, because their small capital cannot compete with that of the millionaire, and..their skill is depreciated by new modes of production. Thus the Proletariat recruits from all classes of population. **1920** M. BEER *Hist. Brit. Socialism* II. III. vi. 120 O'Brien's was the policy of a relentless class war by a proletariate that was absolutely unable to convert its votes into political power. **1927** H. LASKI *Let.* 20 Nov. in *Holmes–Laski Lett.* (1953) II. 998 Did I tell you that I have traced the origins of the famous 'Dictatorship of the Proletariat' to Babeuf? **1937** E. ST. V. MILLAY *Conversation at Midnight* ii. 69 The dictatorship of the proletariat, though not yet present and in this room, is a fact! **1941** *New Statesman* 19 Apr. 407/1 Unluckily the proletariat are even more conservative in their food than the bourgeoisie. **1964** P. G. CASANOVA in I. L. Horowitz *New Sociol.* 71 Mills..could not believe that Marx's view that the proletariat was the force of history could be applied to the United States of 1960. **1972** W. LEONHARD in C. D. Kernig *Marxism, Communism & Western Society* II. 429/2 The term 'dictatorship of the proletariat' was probably coined in 1837 by Auguste Blanqui. *Ibid.* 434/1 After Stalin's death..a change again took place in the Soviet presentation of the dictatorship of the proletariat. **1976** T. EAGLETON *Crit. & Ideology* ii. 58 In nineteenth-century England..there were sound political reasons why the proletariat should be excluded from literacy, but sound religious reasons why it should not be.

proletariza·tion. [f. F. *prolétaire* PROLETAIRE + -IZE + -ATION.] = *PROLETARIANIZATION. Also **pro·letarize** *v. trans.*; **pro·letarized** *ppl. a.*

1918 *Times* 19 Aug. 5/6 We are drifting towards the complete proletarization of the official classes. **1920** E. ANTONELLI *Bolshevist Russia* I. iii. 80 The theory of 'proletarizing' the peasants was never abandoned. **1952** GERTH & MARTINDALE tr. *Weber's Anc. Judaism* I. ii. 56 Indebted or landless, hence, proletarized Israelites. **1968** P. B. AUSTIN *On being Swedish* xiii. 86 The sinister cleavage between highbrow and lowbrow, the proletarization of the soul which lies at the root of so many of the western world's spiritual and even material ills, is here virtually unknown. **1975** *Daily Tel.* 15 Aug. 12 The real aim is the proletarisation of society.

prolidase (prōᵘ·lidēⁱz, -s). *Biochem.* [f. *PROL(INE + IM)ID(O- + *-ASE.] A proteolytic enzyme which hydrolyses peptide bonds formed with the nitrogen atom of proline or 4-hydroxyproline.

1937 BERGMANN & FRUTON in *Jrnl. Biol. Chem.* CXVII. 191 We should like to call this enzyme *prolidase* in order to indicate that in the substrates of this enzyme the proline nitrogen is present as imido nitrogen. **1951** *Adv. Enzymol.* XII. 220 Prolidase is specifically activated by Mn^{++}. **1976** *Metabolism* XXV. 504 Prolidase is an important enzyme in completely degrading collagen to free amino acids. Prolidase is present in human intestinal mucosa.

pro-life, -lifer: see *PRO-¹ 5a.

proliferate, *v.* Add: **1. b.** Also more widely: to give rise to an increasing number of offspring, to reproduce prolifically.

1926 *Socialist Rev.* Apr. 33 Those who..have neither the time to care for their children's moral well-being, nor the space which is necessary to ensure their physical welfare, proliferate, unchecked. **1955** *Sci. Amer.* May 32/3 Normal man carries throughout life a host of microbes which now and then start proliferating and cause disease.

d. *gen.* Of things, happenings, etc.: to increase greatly in numbers; to be(come) rife.

1961 *Daily Tel.* 19 Jan. 12/3 There was more than a suspicion that the system which had gradually evolved over the years was not able to produce the highest quality in British football—a quality which becomes more and more indispensable as international matches proliferate. **1972** *Sci. Amer.* Feb. 13/3 Indeed, microwave devices may proliferate as much as television sets have proliferated. **1976** *National Observer* (U.S.) 21 Aug. 6/6 In recent years, cut-rate sporting goods have proliferated to appeal to the less fussy adventurer.

2. b. To produce (esp. nuclear weapons) in large quantities.

1971 *Nature* 24 Dec. 493/2 Both superpowers continue to proliferate nuclear weapons. **1974** *Daily Tel.* 24 June 1/2 The Government strongly supports international agreement not to 'proliferate' nuclear weapons.

proliferating, *ppl. a.* (Further examples.)

1964 *Time* 4 Dec. 21/1 In Europe, U.S. diplomats are still trying to promote a multilateral nuclear fleet (MLF) as an alternative to proliferating national forces. **1967** *Economist* 25 Feb. 698/2 Indeed, the case for Britain (and France) going non-nuclear would become more persuasive after the signing of the treaty than it would in a treaty-less, proliferating world. **1968** *Ibid.* 13 Apr. 41/1 Those who struggle on in the hospital service, taking the necessary diplomas of the proliferating specialist colleges.

proliferation. Add: **1. c.** *transf.* Enlargement or extension; an increase in number (*of*); now esp. of nuclear weapons.

1920 H. G. WELLS *Outl. Hist.* II. 641/2 The British and French were at first the leading peoples in this great proliferation of knowledge. **1955** *Sci. Amer.* May 88/2 With the proliferation of cults came a tendency to worship privately without the intercession of priests. **1966** *Listener* 4 Aug. 177/3 One of the most noticeable results of setting up a Royal Commission has been the proliferation of proposals for legal solutions to industrial relations problems. **1966** SCHWARZ & HADIX *Strategic Terminol.* 89 *Proliferation*, in the context of nuclear strategy the increase of the number of states possessing independent national control over nuclear weapons, by the acquisition and development of the necessary technological capacity and industrial capabilities. **1967** *Observer* 5 Mar. 13/5 The issue is whether proliferation of bombs can be prevented without fettering peaceful nuclear developments. **1972** *Sci. Amer.* Feb. 15/3 Most of the problems are related to the fact that a large proliferation of microwave devices would make heavy demands on part of the electromagnetic spectrum. **1976** *National Observer* (U.S.) 21 Aug. 5/3 Is the United States' role..so dominant in the nuclear field that we could stop proliferation if our own policies were strict and consistent?

proliferative, *a.* (Examples of general use.)

1952 W. D. JACOBS *William Barnes* ii. 16 Words of the Anglo-Saxon vocabulary and their proliferative quality. **1969** E. BISHOP *Compl. Poems* 83 Our problems Becoming helplessly proliferative.

proliferator (proli·fĕrēⁱtəɹ). [f. PROLIFERATE *v.* + -OR.] One that proliferates; *esp.* one that advocates or engages in the production of nuclear weapons.

1974 *Nature* 31 May 397/2 If the present nuclear countries had busied themselves more over nuclear arms control in the past 5 years, they would have a better moral platform from which they could harangue proliferators.

proliferent (proli·fĕrĕnt), *a. nonce-wd.* [f. as PROLIFEROUS *a.*: see -ENT.] Prolific.

1922 JOYCE *Ulysses* 377 Solicitude for that proliferent continuance.

prolificacy. (Later examples.)

1926 V. A. RICE *Breeding & Improvement of Farm Animals* v. 61 'Prolificacy' implies especially frequent or numerous production. **1962** G. MACEWAN *Blazing Old Cattle Trail* i. 3 A strong point about the longhorns was their prolificacy. **1971** *Farmer & Stockbreeder* 23 Feb. 24/2 Mr. Doane's recipe for increasing prolificacy of a flock included selection of rams with sex drive and fertility.

prolifically, *adv.* (Further examples.)

1915 C. S. JONES *Hohenzollerns* 167 He had for many years sought to win the favour of the great Frederick by writing prolifically on agriculture. **1947** O. BARFIELD in *Ess. presented to Charles Williams* 113 We owe them all to tarning, a process which we find prolifically at work wherever there is poetry.

proline (prōᵘ·līn). *Biochem.* Formerly also **prolin.** [ad. G. *prolin* (Fischer & Suzuki 1904, in *Ber. d. Deut. Chem. Ges.* XXXVII. 2843), contraction of *pyrrolidin* *PYRROLIDINE.] A colourless, crystalline amino-acid, pyrrolidine-2-carboxylic acid, $C_5H_9NO_2$, the lævorotatory form of which is a constituent of most proteins.

1904 *Jrnl. Chem. Soc.* LXXXVI. I. 917 (*heading*) Derivatives of prolin. *Ibid.*, The proline used was derived from gelatin. **1911** *Jrnl. Biol. Chem.* IX. 205 Prolin is ordinarily determined in the ester hydrolysis by alcoholic extraction of the amino-acids whose esters boil below 90° at less than 1 mm. pressure. **1913** *Ibid.* XIII. 513 Proline, when added to blood used for perfusing a surviving dog's liver, leads to no increase in the normal formation of acetoacetic acid, nor is the acetoacetic acid excretion of glycosuric animals markedly increased by the administration of proline. **1946** *Nature* 5 Oct. 474/2 All the proline residues appear to be situated at points roughly one third and two thirds along the length of the molecule. **1954** A. WHITE et al. *Princ. Biochem.* vii. 109 Proline is present in all proteins which have been studied. **1973** BIGGS & WOODSON *Clin. Biochem.* iii. 38 All amino acids—with the exception of proline, which has an imino group—have an amino group on the α carbon.

prolix, *a.* **1. a.** Delete †*Obs.* and add later example.

1973 M. AMIS *Rachel Papers* 8 Mother's was a prolix and generally rather inelegant parturition.

Prolixin (proli·ksin). *Pharm.* A proprietary name in the U.S. for fluphenazine hydrochloride, $C_{22}H_{26}F_3N_3OS.HCl$, a phenothiazine derivative used as a tranquillizer.

1959 *Dis. Nervous System* XX. 170/2 The fluphenazine used in this study was supplied..under the trade name Prolixine [*sic*]. **1960** *Official Gaz.* (U.S. Patent Office) 1 Mar. TM 8/2 Olin Mathieson Chemical Corporation, New York... *Prolixin.* For central nervous system depressant preparations. First use Sept. 18, 1959. **1972** A. GOTH *Med. Pharmacol.* (ed. 6) xix. 217 The phenothiazine anti-emetics include chlorpromazine (Thorazine), fluphenazine dihydrochloride (Prolixin; Permitil), perphenazine (Trilafon), [etc.]. **1973** *Black Panther* 23 June 13/2 Do these drugs include Prolixin, a powerful mood stabilizer which includes side effects in from 50 to 100% of the cases that include pseudo-Parkinson's Disease—painful tremors and rigidity, restlessness ('the prolixin shuffle'), muscle contractions, spasms of the back, neck and throat, [etc.]?

prolly (prǫ·li), *adv.* Representation of a colloq. pronunciation of 'probably'.

1962 J. D. MACDONALD *Key to Suite* vii. 112 The girls have dresses on today. I guess you prolly noticed. **1969** K. GILES *Death cracks Bottle* iv. 37, I don't know wot 'appen to it. The mice prolly. **1976** N. THORNBURG *Cutter & Bone* i. 29 'Some big old buck nigger prolly do it,' Ronnie said.

prolly, var. *PROLY *sb.* and *a.*

proloculus (prolǫ·kiŭləs). *Zool.* Also *erron.* **proloculum.** [f. PRO-² 1 + LOCULUS.] In Foraminifera, the first chamber formed by the zygote.

1928 J. A. CUSHMAN *Foraminifera* ii. 12 The initial chamber in the foraminifera is known as the proloculum. **1935** TWENHOFEL & SHROCK *Invertebr. Paleontol.* ii. 36 The zygote secretes a small shell around itself, the proloculum of the microspheric shell. **1952** R. C. MOORE et al. *Invertebr. Fossils* ii. 40/2 The size of the proloculus of megalospheric forms varies considerably in certain species. **1975** *Nature* 18 Sept. 208/2 In random thin sections these seem to arise from a cluster of small chambers or from a large initial chamber which may be the proloculus.

prolong, *sb.* Restrict † *Obs.* to sense in Dict. and add: **2.** A prolongation.

1905 *Electrochem. & Metall. Industry* III. 9/1 This product..is a by-product with the European smelters, who use sheet-iron 'prolongs' on the condensers to collect it.

prolongability (prolǫŋăbi·lĭti). [f. PROLONGABLE *a.* + -ITY.] Capacity to be prolonged or lengthened.

1950 D. JONES *Phoneme* 183 'Prolongability'..is an infallible criterion for determining which type of length a vowel or diphthong has.

prolongedly (prolǫ·ŋĕdli), *adv.* [f. PROLONGED *ppl. a.* + -LY².] At length, extensively, over a long period.

1934 F. ROLFE *Desire & Pursuit of Whole* xxiv. 268 Crabbe plastered a double-handful of the glutinous rice, firmly and prolongedly, over the sot's face. **1972** G. JONES *Kings, Beasts, & Heroes* p. xvii, The *Beowulf* poet's business is with a non-divine hero of wondertale descent whom he associates closely, constantly, and prolongedly with the antecedents of northern tribal history.

prolongingly (prolǫ·ŋiŋli), *adv. rare*—¹. [f. PROLONGING *vbl. sb.* + -LY².] At length, prolongedly.

1851 H. MELVILLE *Moby Dick* III. xlii. 243 A voice that prolongingly moulded every word.

proluse (prolⁱū·z), *v. nonce-wd.* [Back-formation from PROLUSION.] *intr.* To give an introductory discourse; to prolusionize.

1917 KIPLING *Diversity of Creatures* 330 This they permitting, he, emboldened thus, Prolused of humankind promiscuous.

proly (prǭᵘ·li), *sb.* and *a.* Usu. *derogatory.* Also **prolly.** [f. PROLETARIAN *a.* and *sb.*] **A.** *sb.* = *PROLE *sb.*

1959 J. CARY *Captive & Free* 84 Hooper, son of a lorry driver, who worked his way through the grammar school to a varsity, had, like many of his type, a great contempt for the class from which he had sprung. He called it the prolies. He thought of a proly as a born slave and parasite. **1969** E. MCGIRR *Entry of Death* iii. 64 The politicians say that the prollies prefer to sit back and wait..rather than take direct haction. **1970** K. GILES *Murder Pluperfect* viii. 166 Our Lady might have been..loving the prolies.

B. *adj.* Of working-class origin; = *PROLE *a.* Also in phr. *prolier-than-thou*, after *holier-than-thou* (see *HOLY *a.* 5c).

1971 *Listener* 2 Sept. 311/3 This 'prolier than thou' account. **1972** C. DRUMMOND *Death at Bar* iii. 69 It was one thing..for people of decent family and quite another for prolly sergeants. **1977** *Time Out* 28 Jan.–3 Feb. 3/3 The prolier-than-thou sectarianism of the new convert to Marxism is all too evident in her letter.

prom (prǫm). *colloq.* [Abbrev. of PROMENADE *sb.*] **1.** *U.S.* = *PROMENADE *sb.* 2c.

1894 D. MORROW in H. Nicolson *Dwight Morrow* (1935) 41, I have..been invited over to the Smith Junior Prom. **1899** A. H. QUINN *Pennsylvania Stories* 170 All you children can get tickets of me for the Senior Prom right now. **1914** G. ATHERTON *Perch of Devil* i. 74 The Prom is anything but an exclusive affair. **1924** [see *DRAG *v.* 1e]. **1930** P. W. SLOSSON *Great Crusade* (1931) xii. 342 Dancing was a universal convention, and the formal balls, 'proms' and 'hops' became extremely expensive affairs. **1956** [see

*JUMP *sb.*[1] 1 d]. **1972** T. P. McMAHON *Issue of Bishop's Blood* (1973) vii. 88 A girl..who went into a decline because she hadn't been invited to the Junior Prom at Santa Clara University. **1977** I. SHAW *Beggarman, Thief* I. vi. 76 Girls who..went..to the proms at which he played the trumpet in the band.

2. = *promenade concert* (s.v. PROMENADE *sb.* 4b); *the Proms*, the Henry Wood Promenade Concerts, now given annually at the Royal Albert Hall, London (also in *sing.*).

1902 *Free Lance* 4 Jan. 358/1 There is never one of the programmes at the Proms..unworthy of the..most cultured music lover. **1913** H. WALPOLE *Fortitude* II. i. 180 A walk or two and going into the gallery at Covent Garden once or twice and the Proms sometimes. **1927** *Morning Post* 16 Aug. 6/7 (*heading*) Mozart's music at the 'Proms'. **1930** *Daily Express* 8 Sept. 6/2 Faces are certainly funny things—as you remarked when we went to the 'Prom.' at the Queen's Hall the other night. **1944** *Times* 10 June 5/4 While the L.S.O...has continued in the path it designed for itself..the Proms have continuously evolved. **1945** *Ann. Reg. 1944* 369 A concert in celebration of the fiftieth anniversary of the first 'Prom'. **1955** *Times* 19 Aug. 2/5 During his lifetime Henry Wood used the Proms as a stamping ground for new music. **1958** *Times* 20 June 3/6 This year is Puccini's centenary and, for the first time in a Prom, a whole act from one of his operas is included. **1973** *Listener* 14 June 810/1 Henry Wood decreed that the nine symphonies of Beethoven should be the backbone of the Proms. **1976** *Ibid.* 8 Apr. 440/1 The word 'Prom' no longer has anything to do with promenading: it means something like the Albert Hall Proms—young people of the student class enjoying high culture in a spirited, informal manner.

3. = PROMENADE *sb.* 2a in Dict. and Suppl.

1909 J. A. GLOVER-KIND *I do like to be beside Seaside* (1970) (song) 4, I do like to stroll upon the Prom, Prom, Prom. **1910** *Bradshaw's Railway Guide* Apr. 1142/2 Charmingly situated on the West Prom., directly facing the Sea. **1925** *Glasgow Herald* 18 July 8/7 A scrap of conversation overheard on the 'prom' of a well-known resort. **1953** *Manch. Guardian* 21 Dec. 7/8 (Advt.), Southport.—Clifton Hotel, Prom.: A.A., R.A.C.: 86 bedrooms, lift, garage. **1973** P. LOVESEY *Mad Hatter's Holiday* i. 7 Moscrop joined the general movement in the direction of the West Pier..one of a long parade of freshly-arrived visitors taking that first bracing turn along the prom.

4. *attrib.* and *Comb.*, as (sense 1) *prom dress*, *girl*, *night*; (sense 2) *prom concert*, *-goer*.

1973 'S. HARVESTER' *Corner of Playground* II. iii. 93 She had queued to see ballet at Covent Garden, gone to Prom concerts, visited art galleries. **1976** *National Observer* (U.S.) 26 June 17/4 Prom dresses, cheers, put-downs, yearbook inscriptions...we remember them all. **1978** *Detroit Free Press* 5 Mar. (Spring fashion Suppl.) 19 (Advt.), The prom dress is back... In a big, beautiful way. **1894** *Outing* XXIV. 68/2 For two days..in January the room is crowded with 'Prom' girls and their escorts. **1947** *Penguin Mus. Mag.* II. 37 There is one body of Promgoers who..are seen and heard too much,..a source of continual irritation to the serious Promenader. **1971** *Guardian* 26 Aug. 10/1 Tonight promises to be an adventurous evening for Prom-goers. **1974** *State* (Columbia, S. Carolina) 3 Mar. 6-F (Advt.), Sugarplum styles—beribboned with satin or velvet, strewn with flowers..to make your prom night unforgettable.

promarketeer: see *PRO-[1] 5b.

promastigote (promæ·stigōut), *a.* and *sb.* *Zool.* [erron. f. Gr. πρό (? taken as opp. Gr. α-, in *amastigote*) + μαστιγ-, μάστιξ whip (used to render FLAGELLUM) + -ωτης (see -OT[2] and -OTE).] (Applied to) the flagellated form assumed by parasitic protozoans of the genus *Leishmania* when carried by arthropods.

1971 *Jrnl. Parasitol.* LVII. 626/2 Promastigote (leptomonad) flagellates..were from 2 strains [of *Leishmania hertigi*]... Body width frequently tapering rather abruptly.., similar to some promastigotes of *L. adleri*. **1974** *Nature* 7 June 588/1 Examination of the promastigotes of *L. hertigi* immediately revealed cytoplasmic inclusions of a type which had not been observed in any of our previous studies. **1976** *Ibid.* 19 Aug. 689/1 We present evidence that transformation from the mammalian (amastigote) stage of *L. donovani* to the insect and/or culture (promastigote) stage is inhibited by host hamster spleen homogenates.

promazine (prōu·măzīn). *Pharm.* [f. PRO(PYL + M(ETHYL + *-azine* (f. AZ(O- + -INE[5]).] The compound 10-(3-dimethylaminopropyl)phenothiazine, $C_{17}H_{20}N_2S$, which is used (in the form of its white crystalline hydrochloride) as a tranquillizer.

1956 *Jrnl. Amer. Med. Assoc.* 5 May 45/1 Treatment with promazine satisfactorily relieved the withdrawal symptoms of acute alcoholic intoxication in all patients who remained in the hospital for the complete course of therapy. **1958** *Martindale's Extra Pharmacopœia* (ed. 24) 398 Promazine has actions similar to those of chlorpromazine. It has been used for its tranquillising effect in psychotic conditions, especially those associated with hyperactivity, in acute alcoholism and delirium tremens, and in the withdrawal symptoms of drug addiction. **1965** J. POLLITT *Depression & its Treatment* iv. 46 Admission to hospital for continuous narcosis may be necessary. This may be induced by four-hourly doses of barbiturates, but these should give way as soon as possible to phenothiazine derivatives such as chlorpromazine or promazine. **1971** [see *PROMETHAZINE].

promenade, *sb.* Add: **2. a.** Now most freq. a paved walk raised alongside the beach at a seaside resort.

1892 B. POTTER *Jrnl.* Mar. (1966) 234, I was disappointed with the Hoe. It is exactly like the grounds of the Naval Exhibition, broad asphalt promenades, cigar kiosks, and even the lighthouse all complete. **1899** P. E. AMY *Beautiful Jersey* 69/2 *Promenades.* The chief of these is the Esplanade, a marine promenade, practically a continuation of Albert Quay. **1938** G. GREENE *Brighton Rock* I. i. 5 The ghost train diving between the grinning skeleton [sic] under the Aquarium promenade, the sticks of Brighton rock, the paper sailors' caps. **1939** *Blackpool Official Guide*, Blackpool's promenades cover the whole seaboard of seven miles in length. *Ibid.*, There is no other seafront which combines such a variety of scenery as Blackpool's famous promenade. **1958** J. BETJEMAN *Coll. Poems* 117 Prepare for an evening of dancing and cards And forget the sea-breeze on the dry promenades. **1977** *Lancashire Life* Dec. 57/1 Along the promenade at that point there were cannons at intervals.

b. *spec.* A gallery at a music-hall, frequented by demi-mondaines and their followers.

The two most notorious promenades were at the Empire and the Alhambra music-halls in Leicester Square.

1863 *Observer* 18 Jan. 6/2 The Alhambra, of all the music halls, is the one least entitled to use the name... The balcony is converted into a promenade for loose women and the simpletons who run after them. **1899** BEERBOHM *Around Theatres* (1953) 32 We bought two seats... We passed, on our way to them, into the far-famed Promenade. **1906** A. BENNETT *Whom God hath Joined* i. 20, I saw the great Charlie the other night..in the promenade at the Empire. **1914** C. MACKENZIE *Sinister St.* II. IV. ii. 870 Michael reached the Orient Palace of Varieties, and.. joined the throng of the Promenade. *Ibid.* 872 On the Promenade where it was quite certain that every woman had a history to account for her presence there, how utterly living had quenched life. **1915** KIPLING in *Nash's Mag.* Oct. 133/1 He was as communicative as—as a lady in the Promenade. **1918** A. BENNETT *Pretty Lady* i. 2 Behind the audience came the restless Promenade, where was the reality which the stage reflected. **1964** C. MACKENZIE *My Life & Times* III. 236 A flash tart who frequented the promenades of the Empire or the Alhambra. **1979** R. BLYTHE *View in Winter* iv. 182 The wonderful Empire in Leicester Square..the promenade there..was frequented by the first-class ladies of the town.

c. A ball or dance at a school or college. *U.S.*

1887 *Lippincott's Mag.* Aug. 298 The most important society event of the year is the Junior Promenade. **1905** *N.Y. Herald* 22 Jan. 10 The fair guests invited to the Junior Promenade, the great event of the college year. **1933** *Fortune* Aug. 90/3 True jazz..is even losing its great popularity at college promenades. **1972** *Lebende Sprachen* XVII. 35/2 US promenade—BE school dance, college dance.

d. *Dancing.* (See quots.) Also *promenade position*.

1953 K. AMBROSE *Beginners, Please!* vi. 43 When a pivot is made on one leg (as in Figs. 5–6–7..) the movement is termed a *promenade*. **1956** J. C. MILLIGAN *101 Scottish Country Dances* 28 *Promenade for three couples* is a formation, not a method of progression. **1957** G. B. L. WILSON *Penguin Dict. Ballet* 222 *Promenade*, (1) a slow turn on one foot while the body is held in a set position, such as an arabesque; (2) a slow turn in a pas de deux when the danseuse, on point, is turned round by her partner. **1967** CHUJOY & MANCHESTER *Dance Encycl.* 747/1 *Promenade position*, in ballroom dance, a couple in closed position moving sideways to the left, with the side of the foot leading. **1968** J. C. MILLIGAN *Introd. Scottish Country Dancing* 51 Promenade can be done by two, three or four couples. It is done in both reel and strathspey time and takes eight travelling steps.

3. Short for *promenade deck*: see sense 4a.

1845 *Knickerbocker* XXV. 61 On the upper deck the engineers and sailors, ladies, emigrants and gentlemen, sat side by side upon the single seat which ran all round the promenade. **1873** W. D. HOWELLS *Chance Acquaintance* i. 1 On the forward promenade of the Saguenay boat ..Miss Kitty Ellison sat. **1974** 'G. BLACK' *Golden Cockatrice* iv. 74, I..went up one deck..going out on to the open promenade which was empty.

4. a. *promenade deck* (earlier and later examples); **b. promenade band** (further example); **promenade concert**, add to def.: or at which a proportion of the audience stands; (earlier and later examples).

1893 *World* 11 Oct. 23/2 Long before the run of a successful Savoy opera is over Sir Arthur's melodies are dinned into our ears by every promenade band and street piano. **1839** DICKENS *Let.* 9 Feb. (1965) I. 640 Kate at the Promenade Concert. **1921** *Daily Colonist* (Victoria, B.C.) 24 Mar. 4/1 It should combine the features of a convention hall with the facilities for holding promenade concerts at which at least 3,000 persons can be accommodated. **1954** *Grove's Dict. Mus.* (ed. 5) IX. 357/1 On 30 June 1944 the Promenade Concerts were closed down..on account of flying bombs, but they were replaced on 1 July by broadcasts from Bedford. It was there that Wood conducted his last performance on 28 July. **1962** *Listener* 2 Aug. 189/3 The programme engineer at the Promenade Concerts noticeably reduced the volume of cheers at the conclusion of Mahler's Third Symphony. **1829** *Amer. Traveller* (Boston) 14 Apr. 2 The engraving above, exhibits what may emphatically be termed a *Land Barge*.. with a cabin, berths, &c. below; a promenade deck, awning, seats, &c. above. **1931** M. DE LA ROCHE *Finch's Fortune* vi. 114 He strode out with the best of them on the promenade deck. **1973** 'D. MARINER' *Beaufort Dossier* x. 177 The promenade deck was really a broad passage... Its roof was the..boat-deck overhead.

promenade, *v.* Add: **2.** (Earlier and later examples.)

1818 T. BROWN *Brighton* II. i. 22 Their more fortunate comrades *promenade* Hyde Park, or the Mall. **1977** *Lancashire Life* Aug. 33/2 Promenade Blackburn's bustling modern centre today, and you might find anxiety over a new town rival puzzling.

promenader. Add: **b.** *spec.* One who attends a promenade concert; *esp.* one who stands.

1889 G. B. SHAW in *Star* 19 Aug. 2/4 With the floor.. hidden by a crowd of promenaders too closely packed to promenade. **1918** A. BENNETT *Roll-Call* I. ii. 36 Promenaders promenaded in and out of the corridor. **1959** *Listener* 29 Oct. 716/1 Even the Promenaders..do not respond joyfully to a reduction in the large share of familiar classics. **1966** K. S. SORABJI in 'H. MacDiarmid' *Company I've Kept* ii. 65 That archetype of the 'democratic' audiences, the Promenaders. **1977** *Times* 23 July 14/6 There was general enthusiasm among the young promenaders for the English flavour of this year's jubilee season.

prometaphase (prōu·me·tăfēiz). *Cytology.* [f. PRO-[2] + *metaphase* s.v. *META- 4.] The stage in mitotic or meiotic nuclear division, following prophase and preceding metaphase, during which the spindle is formed and the chromosomes become oriented towards it.

1931 W. J. C. LAWRENCE in *Cytologia* II. 361 The degree of repulsion gradually diminishes and diakinesis is abruptly terminated by the sudden converging of the chromosomes on the centre of the nucleus. This stage (pro-metaphase) is very brief and is characterised by the secondary association of a number of the bivalents. **1969** BROWN & BERTKE *Textbk. Cytol.* xix. 404/1 Evidence at prometaphase and anaphase seems to indicate that the centromere is 'pulled' toward the pole or poles, the arms of the chromosome apparently passively following along.

promethazine (prome·þăzīn). *Pharm.* [f. PRO(PYL + METH(YL + *-azine* (f. AZ(O- + -INE[5]).] A bitter-tasting antihistamine compound, 10-(2-dimethylaminopropyl)phenothiazine, $C_{17}H_{20}N_2S$, which is used chiefly as an anti-emetic and a sedative, usu. in the form of its hydrochloride, a white powder.

1951 *Lancet* 26 May 1143/2 'Avomine' (promethazine 8-chlorotheophyllinate) is a safe and effective remedy for seasickness. **1959** *Which?* July 69/2 All that is certain is that hyoscine, meclozine, cyclizine and promethazine do act to prevent travel sickness, and all have some side-effects **1961** *Lancet* 23 Sept. 688/1 To control shivering a mixture of promethazine hydrochloride 50 mg., pethidine 50 mg., and chlorpromazine 50 mg. was made up to 20 ml. 2–4 ml. of this mixture was administered intravenously as required. **1971** B. R. JONES *Pharmacol.* iii. 15 Post-operative vomiting is reduced by including in the premedication an intramuscular injection of either an antihistamine such as Promethazine ('Phenergan') or a tranquillizer of the phenothiazine type such as Promazine.

promethea (promī·þiă). [L. *Promēthea*, fem. of adj. *Promētheus*: see PROMETHEUS.] In full, *promethea moth*. The North American silk moth, *Callosamia promethea*, of the family Saturniidæ.

1889 *Cent. Dict.* s.v. Prometheus. **1901** M. C. DICKERSON *Moths & Butterflies* 119 Late in fall and winter we may find brown cocoons containing the chrysalides of the Promethea moth swinging from the branches of the wild cherry. **1905** V. L. KELLOGG *Amer. Insects* xiv. 422 The promethea-moth.., light reddish brown in female, and blackish and clay colour in male.., is perhaps the most abundant of all these giant moths. **1909** G. STRATTON-PORTER *Girl of Limberlost* xv. 300 He found a splendid Promethea on a lilac in a corner. **1949** *Nat. Hist.* Feb. 80/2 The Cecropia and Promethea have their wings wrapped around their bodies. **1954** BORROR & DELONG *Introd. Study of Insects* xxvi. 507 The promethea moth, *Callosamia promethea* (Drury), is sometimes called the spice-bush silk moth. **1972** SWAN & PAPP *Common Insects N. Amer.* 268 Promethea moth... Canada to Florida, west to the Great Plains.

Prometheanism (promī·þiăniz'm). [f. PROMETHEAN *a.* + -ISM.] Conduct or policy resembling that traditionally ascribed to Prometheus.

1957 N. FRYE *Anat. Crit.* 157 Patterns of the 'Romantic agony', chiefly sadism, Prometheanism. **1976** M. J. LASKY *Utopia & Revolution* (1977) xi. 412 He [*sc.* Locke] disdained the incendiaries of the age with their fiery images, and deplored the whole tradition of Prometheanism.

prometheus. 2. a. Substitute for def.: = *PROMETHEA. (Examples.)

1889 in *Cent. Dict.* **1972** SWAN & PAPP *Common Insects N. Amer.* 265 Efforts to reel or card the fibers of the Prometheus and Polyphemus cocoons have not been successful.

promethium (promī·þiŏm). *Chem.* orig. -eum. [mod.L.: see PROMETHEUS and -IUM.] An artificially produced metallic element (traces of which have subsequently been found in nature) which is a lanthanide whose longest-lived isotope has a half-life of about 18 years. Atomic number 61; symbol Pm. Cf. *ILLINIUM.

1948 MARINSKY & GLENDENIN in *Chem. & Engin. News* 9 Aug. 2348/2 We propose, therefore, the name 'prometheum' (symbol Pm) for element 61 after Prometheus, ..who stole fire from heaven for the use of mankind... This name..symbolizes the dramatic way in which the element may be produced in quantity as a result of man's harnessing of the energy of nuclear fission **1949** *Sun*

(Baltimore) 22 Sept. 21/4 An element 500 times 'hotter' than radium is being studied... It is promethium, one of the rare earth metals. **1955** T. D. O'BRIEN et al. in Sneed & Brasted *Comprehensive Inorg. Chem.* IV. vi. 184 Promethium comes between neodymium and samarium in the lanthanide series. It has an oxidation number of +3 and possibly +4. **1959** SEABORG & VALENS *Elements of Universe* 126 Promethium was discovered as a result of its artificial production in the atomic reactor. *Ibid.*, Promethium nitrate is a rather undistinguished-looking powder. **1976** COTTON & WILKINSON *Basic Inorg. Chem.* xxvi. 450 Promethium occurs only in traces in U ores as a spontaneous fission fragment of ^{238}U. Milligram quantities of pink $^{147}Pm^{3+}$ salt can be isolated..from fission products in spent fuel of nuclear reactors.

prometryne (prōᵘ·mĕtrəin). *Agric.* Also -tryn (-trin). [f. PRO(PYL + ME(THYL + -*tryne* (f. TRI(AZI)NE).] A herbicide, 2,4-bis (isopropylamino)-6-methylthio-1,3,5-triazine, $C_{10}H_{19}N_5S$, which is usu. employed in the form of a wettable powder against annual grasses and broad-leaved weeds.

1961 *B.S.I. News* July 28 Common names for pesticides... Prometryne. 4,6-bisisopropylamino-2-methylthio-1,3,5-triazine. **1968** *Weed Control* (Nat. Acad. Sci., Washington) x. 181 Prometryne..has..a melting point of 118°C, and a solubility of 48 ppm in water. It is highly soluble in many organic solvents. **1971** *Arable Farmer* Feb. 15/3 Resistance of..peas to prometryne..occurs as a result of such metabolic conversions within the plant. **1976** J. R. PLIMMER in Kearney & Kaufman *Herbicides* (ed. 2) II. xix. 925 Granular formations of prometryn did not cause vapor damage to cotton plants exposed to their vapor.

Promin (prōᵘ·min). *Pharm.* Also **promin.** A proprietary name in the U.S. for a glucoside derivative of 4,4′-diaminodiphenyl sulphone, $C_{12}H_{12}N_2O_2S$, which has a bacteriostatic action and has been used esp. to treat leprosy.

1937 *Official Gaz.* (U.S. Patent Office) 29 June 1008/2 Parke, Davis & Company, Detroit... *Promin.* For p-amino-benzene-sulfonamide used in treatment of streptococcic infections. Claims use since April 16, 1937. **1939** *Canad. Med. Assoc. Jrnl.* XL. 319/1 The following compounds have been investigated: p-aminobenzene sulphonamide (sulphanilamide),..a glucoside derivative of 4:4′ diamino diphenyl sulphone (promin). **1948** *Call-Bulletin* (San Francisco) 12 Apr. 3/6 Diasone and two companion drugs, promin and promizole, have shown promise against both tuberculosis and leprosy but they have some disadvantages. **1958** *New Scientist* 11 Sept. 798/2 Eventually it was found by Dr. John Lowe in 1948 that the simpler parent compound—diamino diphenyl sulphone..(now called dapsone) was more active than promin. **1971** W. H. JOPLING *Handbk. Leprosy* vi. 52 Dapsone..had the advantage over Promin of being much cheaper and of being suitable for oral administration (Promin has to be given intravenously).

prominence, *sb.* Add: **3. b.** *Phonetics.* The degree to which a sound or syllable stands out from its phonetic environment.

1929 I. C. WARD *Phonetics of Eng.* xiv. 135 The effect of prominence is produced by the very intimate combination of length, stress, pitch, and inherent sonority of sounds. **1949** C. E. BAZELL in *Travaux du Cercle Linguistique de Copenhague* V. 83 When two features..are simultaneous in overt order, no distinctions of prominence (e.g. syllabic/asyllabic) can be made. **1950** D. JONES *Phoneme* 137 Prominence is an effect perceived objectively by the hearer. It is thus quite a different thing from stress which is a subjective activity on the part of the speaker. *Ibid.* 144 It is a natural tendency of English people and speakers of other stress languages to attribute all prominences to stress alone. **1962** A. C. GIMSON *Introd. Pronunc. Eng.* 219 Among the vowels prominence increases as the vowel becomes more open. *Ibid.* 221 Sound qualities also contribute to an impression of prominence but mainly through the characteristic relationship of certain qualities with unaccented syllables and others with accented syllables. **1973** *Word 1970* XXVI. 62 Not every syllable given accentual prominence in the sentence is a rhythmic accent with temporal prominence.

prominent, *a.* (*sb.*) **B.** *sb.* **1. b.** Delete † *Obs. rare* and add later N. Amer. examples.

1948 *Sun* (Baltimore) 19 June 3/2 Hillcrest Country Club, a favorite among movie prominents, was blown up today by an accumulation of gas. **1975** *Maclean's Mag.* (Toronto) 15 Dec. 62/2 Several prominents such as John Diefenbaker and Joey Smallwood pushed for a reprieve.

promiscuous. Add: **2. b.** Now esp.: indiscriminate in sexual relations (cf. PROMISCUITY 2).

1900 [in Dict.]. **1924** C. CONNOLLY *Let.* Dec. in *Romantic Friendship* (1975) 32, I am not promiscuous but I can't be loyal to an icicle. **1937** A. HUXLEY *Let.* 17 Dec. (1969) 430 Where it is 'done' to attach a great deal of importance to the achievement of promiscuous satisfaction..there..will the amount of attention given to other matters decline. **1949** *Times Lit. Suppl.* 21 Oct. 680/2 She was promiscuous in her favours, and did not at once become his alone. **1955** G. GREENE *Quiet American* II. ii. 130 One starts promiscuous and ends like one's grandfather, faithful to one woman. **1978** S. HERZEL in P. Moore *Man, Woman, & Priesthood* viii. 119 It is precisely because men *can* compartmentalize that they are more easily promiscuous than women.

6. b. (Earlier examples.)

1826 DISRAELI *Vivian Grey* II. xii. 170, I do wish you'd come in some day quite promiscuous. **1827** *Ibid.* III. viii. 115 It's remarkable wrong to tax 'em all promiscuous. **1875** SWINBURNE *Let.* 5 Nov. (1960) III. 82 It turned up promiscuous when at last wanted after ten years.

promise, *sb.* Add: **4. a.** (Further examples.)

1886 E. G. WHITE *Hist. Sk. Foreign Missions Seventh-Day Adventists* 281/2 They should be ready to counsel and instruct those who have newly come to the faith, and who give promise of possessing ability to work for the Master. **1919** T. S. ELIOT *Poems*, Grishkin is nice.. her friendly bust Gives promise of pneumatic bliss. **1971** *Daily Tel.* 17 June 3/3 To police he showed 'promise' of becoming a sophisticated criminal.

5. *promise-breaking* (examples), *-keeping* (later example).

1842 DICKENS *Let.* 22 Mar. (1974) III. 146 You.. have set me down, I know, as a neglectful, erratic, promise-breaking and most unworthy person. **1940** *Mind* XLIX. 231 Utilitarians have tended rather to overestimate the disastrous consequences of promise-breaking. *a* **1974** R. CROSSMAN *Diaries* (1975) I. 249 From the point of view of the electorate this technical promise-keeping is quite unimportant.

promise, *v.* Add: **3. a.** (Later examples.)

1904 L. T. MEADE *Love Triumphant* II. ix. 192 If anything could induce me to promise myself to a man..it would be to Cedric Vershoyle. **1967** C. POTOK *Chosen* xii. 200 My father promised my sister to the son of one of his followers when she was two years old.

5. b. Delete 'Now *arch.* or *dial.*' and add later examples.

1963 J. KENNAWAY *Bells of Shoreditch* I. i. 12 He said, 'I promise you, you're looking very well.' **1969** [see *GHASTLY *a.* 1 b].

promised, *ppl. a.* Add: *promised land* (later examples).

1920 WODEHOUSE *Jill the Reckless* (1922) x. 142 The rank and file of the profession were greeted, like Moses on Pisgah, with a fleeting glimpse of the promised land, consisting of a large desk [etc.]. **1965** *Amer. N. & Q.* Apr. 128/2 Nearly 100 songs tell about travel around the Horn and across the Plains to the promised land, life in California..and the great joy of going home. **1972** D. DAKIN *Unification of Greece* 268 Just when the promised land seemed to be within their grasp, the Greeks... suffered ignominious defeat. **1975** J. CLEARY *Safe House* vi. 250 The farmers..had headed west to the Promised Land of California.

promissory, *a.* **1. b.** (Further examples.)

1882 [see AGENT *sb.* 4]. **1911** *Oklahoma Session Laws* (3rd Legislature) 216 If any such promissory note or assessment is not paid when due, action may be brought thereon. **1960** G. DURRELL *Zoo in my Luggage* iii. 79, I paid him the two shillings, and then wrote out a promissory note for the other five shillings. **1972** *Times* 18 Feb. 20/5 In 1963 UDT..accepted a number of promissory notes.

promitochondrion: see *PRO-² 1.

promizole (prōᵘ·mizōᵘl). *Pharm.* Also **Promizole.** [f. *PROMI(N + *THIA)ZOLE.] A bacteriostatic agent, 2-amino-5-*p*-aminobenzenesulphonylthiazole, $C_9H_9N_3O_2S_2$, formerly used to treat leprosy and tuberculosis.

Formerly a proprietary name in the U.S.

1944 *Proc. Staff Meetings Mayo Clinic* XIX. 26 Promizole is the trade name of 4,2′-diaminophenyl-5′-thiazole-sulfone [*sic*]. **1944** *Official Gaz.* (U.S. Patent Office) 11 Apr. 191/1 Parke, Davis & Company, Detroit... *Promizole.* For chemotherapeutic agent for the treatment of bacterial infections. Claims use since Dec. 23, 1943. **1948** [see *PROMIN]. **1964** P. FEENY *Fight against Leprosy* xvi. 147 From every continent there was coming a steady stream of literature about the effects of promin, diasone, sulphetrone and one more weapon that had been added to the arsenal, promizole.

Prommer (prǫ·məɹ), *colloq.* Also **prommer.** [f. *PROM 2 + -ER¹.] One who attends a promenade concert (*esp.* at the Royal Albert Hall); a promenader.

1947 *Penguin Music Mag.* May 36 Even in 1932 a Prommer could follow a score without digging his elbow into someone every time he turned a page. **1960** *Times* 30 July 9/1 (*heading*) Prommers Stay for Gerhard. **1969** *Listener* 12 June 836/3 Traditionally, of course, your average Prommer is a catholic music-lover..who jolly well doesn't care who sees him enjoying himself on Saturdays. **1972** *Guardian* 14 Aug. 8/1 A regular Prommer who couldn't make it this particular night and is..listening at home. **1975** *Times* 19 Sept. 9/8 The finale was a young man's reading, and seemingly much to the liking of the even younger prommers.

promo (prōᵘ·mo), *a.* and *sb. colloq.* [Abbrev. of *PROMOTIONAL *a.*, *PROMOTION 2 a.] **A.** *adj.* = *PROMOTIONAL *a.* **B.** *sb.* Publicity, advertising; *spec.* a promotional trailer for a television programme. *Comb.*, as **promo man,** a promotion man, publicity organizer.

1963 *Amer. Speech* XXXVIII. 156 Other stump words or clipped forms such as *info.*.and *promo.* **1966** *Sat. Rev.* (U.S.) 12 Feb. 8/3 'Will Robin escape?... Will Batman arrive in time to save him? The worst is yet to come!' And sure enough, minutes later on came the second of this trilogy—*The Blue Light.* What a promo! **1971** D. E. WESTLAKE *I gave at the Office* (1972) 11, I did promo voice-overs for the new TV shows. **1972** *Village Voice* (N.Y.) 1 June 46/1 A slightly agitated promo-man-about-town stopped me one day recently as I was crossing Sheridan Square. **1973** *Publishers Weekly* 10 Sept. 54 (Advt.), With big national TV promo by the author.. Robert Rosefsky is really doing a terrific job of promoting his book on TV. **1974** *Some Technical Terms & Slang* (Granada Television), *Promo*, a short promotional trailer for a programme. **1976** *New Musical Express* 17 Apr. 22/4 Despite promo pics that make them look like 12-year-olds, their 'charisma' is more David Cassidy style. **1978** *Advertising Age* (Chicago) 16 Oct. 19 (*heading*) Oxford promo is publicity happening.

promote, *v.* Add: **I. 1. c.** *Sport* (chiefly *Assoc. Football*). To transfer (a team) to a higher division of a league (see *PROMOTION 1 d).

1924 *Times* 5 May 6/6 Bristol City,..promoted a year ago, return to a lower division. **1949** *Times* 25 Apr. 6/2 (*heading*) Swansea Town promoted.

d. *Curling.* To move (another stone) forward by striking.

1937 T. HENDERSON *Lockerbie* 58 He left the stone alone..deeming it safer play to promote the Minister's stone.

e. *Bridge.* To establish (a relatively low card) as a winner; to secure (a trick) by this action.

1959 *Listener* 31 Dec. 1178/3 A further spade lead will promote the nine of diamonds. *Ibid.*, The fifth heart will promote one of North's trumps. **1962** *Ibid.* 12 Apr. 662/2 The defence would take two rounds of clubs and play a third club, promoting a trick for West's nine of hearts.

2. a. *spec.* To further the sale of (an article) by advertising or other modes of publicity; to publicize (a venture, person, etc.). Also *absol.*

1930 *Publishers' Weekly* 31 May 2732/2 The books all to be individualized in appearance and fully promoted. **1965** *Melody Maker* 3 Apr. 7/3 With the group over here to promote their latest recording,..they could well make the chart. **1971** D. POTTER *Brit. Eliz. Stamps* x. 117 These packs are heavily promoted, with full-page colour advertisements in the national press. **1976** *National Observer* (U.S.) 30 Oct. 9/3, I love chocolate-chip cookies, and I love to promote.

c. *Chem.* To increase the activity or effectiveness of (a catalyst) by addition of another substance; to act as a promoter of (a catalyst) or in (a catalytic reaction). *Loosely* (passing into 2 a), to initiate, catalyse.

[**1920** *Jrnl. Physical Chem.* XXIV. 243 When more than one of the components are themselves catalysts a difficulty presents itself in choosing between 'promoter' and 'promoted'.] **1930** N. K. ADAM *Physics & Chem. of Surfaces* viii. 280 Many reactions go on at the surface of charcoal. It is a good catalyst for promoting halogenations. **1936** R. H. GRIFFITH *Mechanism of Contact Catalysis* iii. 82 The fact that a substance may act as a poison to a catalyst, and yet itself be promoted by that catalyst, is obviously quite possible. **1940** GLASSTONE *Textbk. Physical Chem.* xiii. 1128 On an ordinary iron catalyst one atom only in 2,000 appears to be able to catalyze the reaction between nitrogen and hydrogen, but when suitably promoted the proportion of active points is increased ten-fold. **1946** *Chem. Abstr.* XL. 4876 The catalytic action is promoted by a smaller quantity of BF_3. **1947** *Jrnl. Polymer Sci.* II. 41 The presence of small amounts of relatively high molecular weight mercaptans greatly promotes the copolymerization reaction. **1967** R. W. LENZ *Org. Chem. Synthetic High Polymers* x. 270 *N,N*-Dimethylaniline promotes the spontaneous decomposition of benzoyl peroxide, and this combination can be used to initiate polymerization reactions at low temperatures. **1975** P. H. EMMETT in Drauglis & Jaffee *Physical Basis for Heterogeneous Catalysis* 21 Why then is a K_2O-Al_2O_3 promoter better than Al_2O_3 alone in promoting an iron synthetic ammonia catalyst?

IV. 8. *slang* (orig. *U.S.*). To borrow or obtain (usu. illicitly). Also to exploit (someone) *for* material advantage.

1930 *Amer. Mercury* Dec. 457/1 *Promote*, to steal. 'We got to promote a boat to run the stuff in.' **1934** J. M. CAIN *Postman always rings Twice* 97 If I hadn't been there, and begun promoting him for something to drink that afternoon, maybe he'd be here now. **1941** *Argus* (Melbourne) *Week-End Mag.* 15 Nov. 1/4 In Army parlance to arrange something is always to 'tee up'; just as to borrow something is to 'promote' it. **1942** Z. N. HURSTON in A. Dundes *Mother Wit* (1973) 226/1 You skillets is trying to promote a meal on me.

promoted (promōᵘ·tėd), *ppl. a.* [f. PROMOTE *v.* + -ED¹.] That has been promoted; furthered, advanced. **1.** *Chem.* Of a catalyst: containing or influenced by a promoter (sense *1 d).

[**1920:** see *PROMOTE *v.* 2 c.] **1927** *Jrnl. Amer. Chem. Soc.* XLVIII. 2821 In the case of pure iron and promoted iron catalysts for ammonia synthesis, oxygen is the type of poison which seemed best suited for such a study. **1968** E. K. RIDEAL *Concepts in Catalysis* vi. 120 Promoted iron catalysts used in the ammonia synthesis are generally prepared by reduction in hydrogen at 500°C of a mixture 95% Fe_3O_4 plus 4–5% Al_2O_3 plus 0–1% K_2O. **1975** P. H. EMMETT in Drauglis & Jaffee *Physical Basis for Heterogeneous Catalysis* 18 The carbon monoxide chemisorption indicates that about 50 percent of the singly promoted (Al_2O_3 the only promoter) catalyst is usually covered with promoter.

2. In other senses of the vb.

1962 *Listener* 6 Dec. 975/3 A splendid, and splendidly promoted, mixture of Baedeker, gazetteer, and travellers' tales. **1977** *Cleethorpes News* 6 May 31/1 Two fine individual performances destroyed promoted Cromwell-Drewery on their Premier debut.

promotee (promō^u^tī·). [f. PROMOTE *v.* + -EE¹.] One who is or has been promoted.

1958 E. H. CARR *Socialism in One Country* I. I. iii. 110 The railways, whose staff adopted..an unwelcoming.. attitude to promotees. **1966** *Punch* 2 Feb. 174/3 Crimes of local importance have to be handled at higher and higher levels to provide something for the promotees from *Z Cars* to do. **1977** *Hongkong Standard* 12 Apr. 8/1 This promotion causes the promotee to lose money on the deal.

promoter. Add: **I. 1. d.** *Chem.* A less active additive which increases the activity of a catalyst; more generally, a substance which improves a catalyst in some way. Also, a substance used as an initiator in a catalytic polymerization reaction.

1911 J. Y. JOHNSON *Brit. Pat.* 19,249 6 Very much better yields can be obtained in the synthetical production of ammonia from its elements if there be employed, as the catalytic agent, iron in admixture with certain bodies as hereinafter explained... These bodies my foreign correspondents [*sc.* Badische Anilin & Soda Fabrik, Germany], for the sake of brevity, term 'promoters'. **1927** *Jrnl. Amer. Chem. Soc.* XLVIII. 2826 The results show that the predominant effect of promoters of the type alumina and potassium aluminate is to increase the number of catalytically active atoms relative to the total number of metal atoms present. **1930** N. K. ADAM *Physics & Chem. of Surfaces* viii. 241 Many promoters are simply refractory supports for a metallic catalyst. **1961** J. N. ANDERSON *Appl. Dental Materials* (ed. 2) xxiv. 251 When these promoters meet the benzoyl peroxide in the polymer, they start a chain of events similar to that which occurs when heat is applied. **1963** P. H. PLESCH *Chem. Cationic Polymerization* iv. 149 The patent literature contains a great many combinations of a metal halide and a co-catalyst (often called promoter, especially in American patents), most of which are substances which can combine with the metal halide to form a protonic acid. **1970** G. ODIAN *Princ. Polymerization* vii. 464 The reactive cyclic ether used as a component of the catalyst system is referred to as a promoter (or a cocatalyst). **1971** *Sci. Amer.* Dec. 52/3 It has been found that iron plus a few percent of the oxides of potassium and aluminum, which are known as promoters, give a longer-lived catalyst and one with greater resistance to impurities in the feed stream.

e. One who organizes or actively supports a sporting event, entertainment, etc., esp. for profit.

1936 [see *football pool* s.v. *FOOTBALL 4]. **1950** *Sport* 7–11 Apr. 22/3 This would involve the full co-operation of sports promoters and the B.B.C. **1951** *Sunday Pictorial* 21 Jan. 16/3 He's a promoter's dream and has sold £450 worth of tickets for this outing. **1956** B. HOLIDAY *Lady sings Blues* (1973) xxii. 180 If it had been left to the management and promoters, I could have shot myself long ago. **1964** *Melody Maker* 28 Nov. 3 Deejays and promoters must stop being idiots. **1971** *Daily Tel.* 27 May 2/6 The Isle of Wight County Council last night rejected all three farm sites proposed by Richard Roscoe, a promoter, for staging a pop festival.

f. *Med.* An agent that causes tumour promotion (*PROMOTION 2d) (see quot. 1978).

1947 *Brit. Jrnl. Cancer* I. 390 Dibenzanthracene is undoubtedly a potent Initiator, but a weak Promotor; benzpyrene is moderately potent both as Initiator and Promotor; croton oil, on the other hand, is exceptionally potent as a Promotor, but quite useless as an Initiator. **1969** *Progress Exper. Tumor Res.* XI. 50 When the initiating agent is given..to mice and this is followed by repeated skin application of the promoter after a lapse of as much as 380 days, tumors arise within 32–42 days from the beginning of promoting treatment. **1970** [see *PROMOTING *ppl. a.* 2b]. **1976** *Maclean's Mag.* (Toronto) 27 Dec. 22/3 These carcinogens don't usually cause cancer unless they mix with other agents called promoters. **1978** *Nature* 20 July 271/1 Tumour promoters are compounds which are not carcinogens but which can induce tumours in mice treated with a subcarcinogenic dose of a chemical carcinogen.

g. *Genetics.* An essential part of an operon, situated between the operator and the structural gene(s), at which transcription starts. [The sense is due to F. Jacob et al., who used F. *promoteur* (*Compt. Rend.* (1964) CCLVIII. 3128).]

1967 C. R. WOESE *Genetic Code* iv. 93 The operator locus comprises both the modulation sequence and the punctuation for tape-reader attachment. Jacob and his associates..have more recently adduced evidence for the existence of the latter, which they call *promoter*, by a study of deletions. **1971** D. J. COVE *Genetics* xi. 163 Mutations in the promoter region lead to a reduction in the rate of messenger synthesis from the whole operon. The promoter is thought to be the region for the attachment of the DNA-dependent RNA polymerase, the enzyme responsible for transcription. **1975** *Nature* 13 Mar. 118/1 The promoter has been loosely defined as the site on the DNA where the RNA polymerase recognises some signal which allows it to bind tightly and initiate transcription.

II. 3. a. For † *Obs.* read '*Obs.* exc. *Hist.*' and add: *β.* (Later example.)

1955 W. W. GREG *Shakespeare First Folio* iv. 150 The Act may well have been a dead letter except for action by professional promooters.

III. 4. (Earlier and later examples.)

1699 *Edin. Gaz.* 26–29 June, Munday last being the Day appointed for the publick Graduation..Mr. William Scot..Promoter for this year declam'd an Elegant Harangue. **1858** *Min. Univ. St. Andrews* (MS.), XVII. 415 The Senatus appoint the ex-Rector to act in the meantime as pro-Rector and Promotor. **1962** *Aberdeen Univ. Rev.* Autumn 313 The other graduands who have obtained First Class Honours are called up, one by one, by the Promotor.

promoting, *vbl. sb.* Add: **2. b.** *Chem.* The action of *PROMOTE *v.* 2c.

1936 R. H. GRIFFITH *Mechanism of Contact Catalysis* iii. 82 The most useful oxides, to give the promoting effect with ion-oxide catalysts, were of the unreducible type, and would give spinels of the same cubic symmetry as Fe_3O_4. **1947** *Jrnl. Polymer Sci.* II. 42 Aliphatic mercaptans in the buradiene-styrene recipe with persulfate as catalyst exert a strong promoting effect upon the copolymerization.

promoting, *ppl. a.* Add: **2. b.** *Med.* That causes tumour promotion (*PROMOTION 2d).

1944 *Jrnl. Exper. Med.* LXXX. 101 (*heading*) The initiating and promoting elements in tumor production. **1966** *Lancet* 31 Dec. 1457/2 Nevertheless, should such initiated skin be subsequently treated with a promoting agent (not itself carcinogenic), the train of events leading to cancer is again accelerated so that a visible tumour appears at the initiated site. **1970** *Cancer Res.* XXX. 312/1 It is generally agreed that promoting agents cause epidermal hyperplasia.., but not all hyperplastic agents have been shown to be promoters. **1976** [see *PROMOTION 2d].

promotion. Add: **1. c.** *Curling.* The positional advancement of a stone by striking. Cf. *PROMOTE *v.* 1d.

1897 *Encycl. Sport* I. 261/1 A canny, or quiet, draw is expected from the lead, and it is better that his stone, when spent, should be short of the tee, where it is in the way of promotion. **1937** T. HENDERSON *Lockerbie* ix. 57 Ye're a graun' curler. That yin's in the wey o' promotion.

d. *Sport* (chiefly *Assoc. Football*). Reallocation of a team to a higher division of a league on the basis of final position in a league table after a season's play.

1907 *Times* 15 Apr. 11/3 Notts Forest and Chelsea have now made themselves certain of promotion. **1949** *Times* 25 Apr. 6/2 Swansea Town assured themselves of promotion to the Second Division. **1965** [see *INJECT *v.* 2]. **1967** *Listener* 17 Aug. 223/3 'Millwall must be certainties for promotion': thus Bill Nicholson, one of the two or three most analytic club managers in England.

e. *Boxing.* The organization or staging of a contest; a contest staged.

1951 *Sport* 7–13 Jan. 14/4 This show is but the first of the season at Streatham but will be the forerunner of many more value-for-money promotions at the South London hall. **1958** F. C. AVIS *Boxing Ref. Dict.* 87 *Promotion*, the organization of a boxing contest. **1962** *Listener* 27 Sept. 466/2 The odd-looking circular building would be just the place for boxing promotions.

f. *Phonetics.* The intensification of normal stress levels in verse; an instance of this.

1956 S. CHATMAN in *Kenyon Rev.* XVIII. 424 What I have called 'metrical tension' can conveniently be described as 'promotions' or 'suppressions' of the stress levels of normal non-verse speech under the pressures of the abstract metrical pattern. **1973** *Word 1970* XXVI. 55 These examples, from Prator, illustrate suppression and promotion respectively.

g. *Bridge.* The action of promoting a card or trick (see *PROMOTE *v.* 1e).

1959 *Listener* 31 Dec. 1178/2 The problem is to prevent North..from winning a second trump trick by promotion. **1964** *Official Encycl. Bridge* 633/2 *Trump promotion*, the creation of trump tricks through forcing the premature use of the trump cards of the opposition.

h. *Transformational Gram.* The translation of material from an embedded to a main sentence.

1968 R. W. LANGACKER *Lang. & Struct.* II. v. 128 A permutation rule that we will call Not Promotion is an interesting example that accounts for a subtle type of ambiguity in negative sentences. **1973** P. SCHACHTER in *Language* XLIX. 19 The derivation of both constructions involves the *promotion* of material from an embedded into a matrix sentence.

2. a. *spec.* The furtherance of the sale of something by advertisement or other modes of publicity. Also *transf.*

1925 C. MORLEY *Thunder on Left* ix. 112 He spoke of the Elevated Railroad's limited appropriation for promotion, of the peculiar problems of transportation publicity. **1928** *Publishers' Weekly* 26 May 2169 Promotion cannot be done without waste... But the idea back of the new mergers is the idea of outlets, of promotion, of selling more goods. **1932** *Ibid.* 7 May 1945/2 A free gift offer in a full page Book-of-the-Month Club promotion. **1958** *Listener* 23 Jan. 148/1 Sir Miles [Thomas]..began his business career as an adviser to Mr. W. R. Morris..on 'sales promotion'. **1962** *Advertisers' Rev.* 26 Oct. 17/2 Price-reductions were easily preferred to all other types of promotion... Other types of promotions considered effective were sample offers, banded offers and free gifts. **1969** *Morning Star* 20 Nov. 5 Heather..had to show a good knowledge of BEA as well as poise and charm. She will represent the airline in promotions and conferences. **1976** *National Observer* (U.S.) 13 Nov. 9/4 Some industry observers say one of those promotions could be trading stamps, although they cost four times as much as a game promotion and require a long-term commitment from a store. **1980** *Bookseller* 12 Jan. 194/1 (Advt.), Evans Brothers Limited require a Publicity Controller to deal with the promotion of their Adult and Children's Trade Books. Applicants should..be capable of dealing with all aspects of book promotion and advertising. *Ibid.* 194/3 The successful candidate..will have experience in organising direct mail promotions, preparing catalogues, leaflets and adverts, [etc.]

c. *Chem.* The action of *PROMOTE *v.* 2c.

[**1920** *Jrnl. Physical Chem.* XXIV. 263 Such an example of auto-catalysis..is to be distinguished from simple auto-catalysis, in which a reactant or product has a direct catalytic effect on the reaction. Here the specific effect of the product is on the catalyst... From the point of view of promoter action such a term as 'auto-activation' or 'auto-promotion' would be more appropriate.] **1926** *Jrnl. Chem. Soc.* 1817 (*heading*) Promotion with iron. **1940** GLASSTONE *Text-bk. Physical Chem.* xiii. 1128, 1 per cent. of ceria gives the optimum promotion for the catalytic action of thoria on the combination of oxygen and hydrogen. **1968** E. K. RIDEAL *Concepts in Catalysis* v. 97 The V–O stretching frequency ν = 1025 cm^{-1} is shifted to longer wavelengths by promoters such as alkaline sulphates, where the order of activity in promotion is Cs>Rb>K>Na.

d. *Med.* The furtherance of neoplastic growth following its initiation by a carcinogen; the conversion of latent tumour cells into active, malignant ones; (see quot. 1964¹).

1944 *Jrnl. Exper. Med.* LXXX. 121 Non-Specific Promotion.—It seems certain that many agents and influences which have no actual carcinogenicity will be found to stimulate the multiplication of latent neoplastic cells. **1964** *Progress Exper. Tumor Res.* IV. 209 Cocarcinogenesis is not synonymous with tumor promotion, since promotion inherently denotes a specific step in the sequence of events leading to skin tumor formation. Conversely, cocarcinogenesis describes a situation in which response to a carcinogen is increased by a second factor introduced concurrently with the carcinogen, with no implication of impact at a specific step in tumor formation. *Ibid.* 226 Apparently, there is a threshold for the amount of croton oil that must be used in each application in order to achieve promotion. **1976** *Brit. Jrnl. Cancer* XXXIV. 660/1 The events related to tumor promotion are understood better since the isolation and chemical characterization of active promoting agents by Hecker (1968) and Van Duuren (1969).

6. (sense *1d) *promotion contender, rival; promotion-challenging, -chasing, -seeking* sbs. and adjs.; (sense *2a) *promotion campaign, kit, man, scheme, stunt*; **promotion bar,** a notional barrier imposed to restrict a person's promotion above a certain level unless certain specified requirements are met; **promotion sheet,** a record of an employee's service showing his claim to promotion or increased pay.

1973 C. MULLARD *Black Britain* II. iv. 43 Besides overt racism employers operated a promotion bar. **1962** *Listener* 19 July 116/1 The distributors were rash in putting it [*sc.* a film] on without a promotion campaign. **1972** *Oxf. Mail* 15 Feb. 12/6 Carlisle are in their customary promotion-challenging position. **1977** *Sunday Express* 30 Jan. 31/8 Big Brian Joicey grabbed two goals to earn Barnsley a well-deserved victory over promotion-chasing rivals Bournemouth. **1978** *Rugby World* Apr. 19/1 At the time of writing they still had three matches left to play, including games against fellow promotion contenders Jedforest and Selkirk. **1964** *Bookseller* 2 May 1783/1 The Society of Young Publishers reports that the half-way mark has been reached in their appeal for £1,000 towards the production of 'promotion kits' for mailing to 2,000 booksellers and 1,000 libraries throughout the country. **1958** *Spectator* 25 July 138/1 Given a really good labour-saving idea, the British are not so reluctant to try it as many high-powered promotion men would have us believe. **1977** *Rolling Stone* 19 May 14/4 Bennett formerly worked as a Beatles promotion man. **1977** *News of World* 17 Apr. 24/7 It was just as well that most of Brighton's promotion rivals faltered yesterday. **1925** C. MORLEY *Thunder on Left* xx. 250 The children had found some deceptive promotion scheme advertised in a cheap magazine. **1958** *New Statesman* 26 Apr. 548/1 Some people seem to think that there is something bogus about these promotion schemes and that their cost would be better applied in making a permanent price reduction. **1976** *Norwich Mercury* 10 Dec., The mark of a promotion-seeking team is to win when playing badly. **1909** *Daily Chron.* 23 Mar. 1/4 The manipulation of their promotion sheets, with the object of postponing the payment of justly earned increased salaries, was one of the grievances of the strikers. **1955** W. GADDIS *Recognitions* II. ii. 372 It was all fixed up about this guy who jumped out a window... It's something for a TV promotion stunt.

promotional (promō^u^·ʃənăl), *a.* [f. PROMOTION + -AL.] Promotive; of or pertaining to promotion (usu. sense 2 in Dict. and Suppl.) or promoters; relating to advertising.

1922 *Universalist Leader* 13 May 4 Experience has disclosed that emotional contributions are promotional of the very poverty we had felt moved to alleviate. **1926** *Publishers' Weekly* 22 May 1675/1 As a further promotional step the..Company is displaying a letter commenting on its service. **1935** *Sun* (Baltimore) 10 Jan. 11/5 Consolidated Gas picked up more than a point on hopes of an amicable adjustment of its rate controversies with the regulatory authority through adoption of a 'promotional' schedule of charges. **1950** *Sport* 22–28 Sept. 14/1 A promotional 'war' seems certain over the privilege of staging a fight with Lee Savold. **1959** *Sociometry* Sept. 273 Some effects of promotional frustration on employees' understanding of, and attitudes toward, management. **1960** W. TAPLIN *Advertising* i. 12 Some of the ideas involved in advertising..the complex of promotional activities of which they form part. **1963** *Guardian* 2 Feb. 12/7 What about that for promotional literature? **1978** *Incorporated Linguist* Summer 60/3 Nearly twenty years ago, a totally unknown mineral water gained national fame in France through a relatively inexpensive and brilliant promotional campaign relying solely on the slogan '*Bébé aime Charrier*' originally spelt 'B.B.' thus capitalizing instantaneously on the tempestuous Bardot–

Charrier romance. **1980** *Bookseller* 12 Jan. 165/2 His publishers' promotional machinery was faultlessly efficient.

promotor. Restrict †*Obs.* to sense in Dict. and add: **2.** *Chem.* = *PROMOTER 1 d.

1931 *Chem. Abstr.* XXV. 428 The influence of various other promotors and protectors in hydrogenation is studied. **1976** J. PETRÓ in Szabó & Kalló *Contact Catalysis* II. v. 60 Additives which have a favourable effect on the operation of catalysts are termed promotors (activators).

3. Var. *PROMOTER 1 f. *rare.*

promovable (prōᵘmū·văb'l), *a.* [f. PROMOVE *v.* + -ABLE.] = PROMOTABLE *a.*; esp. in phr. *removable and promovable* (cf. PROMOTABLE *a.*, quot. 1887), of Sc. and Ir. magistrates.

19th- and 20th-century examples of PROMOVE *v.*, etc., may be found in *S.N.D.*

1920 W. O'BRIEN *Evening Memories* xiii. 216 Two paid magistrates removable and promovable at the caprice of Dublin Castle.

prompt, *sb.* Add: **II. 2. b. prompt corner,** the prompter's corner off-stage; **prompt entrance** (see quot. 1952); **prompt script** = PROMPT-BOOK; **prompt-side,** substitute for def.: the side of the stage where the prompter takes up his position, usu. on the actor's left (*U.S.*, on the right); (earlier and later examples); **prompt table,** the table on which the prompter rests his book; **prompt-word,** a word spoken by a prompter (in quot. *transf.*).

1933 P. GODFREY *Back-Stage* i. 17 A good stage-manager is never far from the prompt corner. **1967** *Listener* 21 Sept. 370/3 When the moment came, I was standing in the prompt corner with..the stage-director. **1886** M. MACKINTOSH *Stage Reminisc.* ii. 25 It would give him a better chance with the audience to sing it from the 'prompt' entrance. **1890** B. HALL *Turnover Club* xx. 187 One evening he was standing in the 'prompt entrance' with a prominent actress who was starring at the house then. **1952** GRANVILLE *Dict. Theatr. Terms* 143 *Prompt entrance*, that way on to the stage from the prompt corner which is for the use of the stage management. **1920** WODEHOUSE *Jill the Reckless* (1922) xiv. 210 The assistant stage-director bent sedulously over the footlights.. shading his eyes with the prompt script. **1824** R. HUMPHREYS *Mem. J. Decastro* 30 A thunder-drum, which now stands on the prompt side of the theatre. **1963** C. MACKENZIE *My Life & Times* I. 90 The next thing I remember is sitting on my nurse's knee in the front of the dress circle of the Cork Opera House on the right-hand side, or as an actor would say, on the prompt side. **1844** J. COWELL *Thirty Years passed among Players* II. ii. 59/2 Every book or manuscript they have an opportunity to place upon a prompt-table. **1967** *Listener* 21 Sept. 369/2 He caught sight of Trebel..lurking by the prompt table. **1918** A. QUILLER-COUCH *Foe-Farrell* 176, I knew..that I must break his fate to him. I even gave him the prompt-word. 'Homelike', I suggested.

prompt, *a.* (*adv.*) Add: **A.** *adj.* **4.** *Nucl. Physics.* Of a neutron or gamma ray: emitted within a small fraction of a second as the direct result of a fission, as distinct from radiation due to the decay of fission products.

1947 M. DEUTSCH in C. Goodman *Sci. & Engin. of Nucl. Power* I. ii. 84 The average total kinetic energy of the two fission fragments from U^{236} is about 160 Mev. In addition, the prompt neutrons have kinetic energies totaling about 5 Mev. If the energy of excitation of the fission fragment immediately after its formation is insufficient to cause neutron emission, the nucleus may lose energy by the emission of prompt gamma rays. **1950** [see **delayed neutron*]. **1962** H. D. BUSH *Atomic & Nuclear Physics* vii. 140 'Prompt' γ-rays are also observed due to the excitation of the primary fission products. **1973** *Physical Rev.* VII. C. 1180/1 In Table 1 the energy emitted per fission event in the form of prompt-γ radiation and the number of γ rays per fission are given for a number of energy intervals above 0·14 MeV. **1974** S. E. HUNT *Fission, Fusion & Energy Crisis* vi. 53 Reactors are operated so that if they relied on the neutrons emitted instantaneously on fission, on so-called 'prompt' neutrons, alone, the fission chain reaction would be subcritical, i.e. the reaction would die away.

B. *adv.* **b.** Promptly; soon.

1910 W. M. RAINE *Bucky O'Connor* ii. 23 The reverend gentleman..had this diverting experience so prompt after he was wishing for it.

C. prompt-critical *a. Nucl. Physics,* critical even when the effect of delayed neutrons is neglected and prompt neutrons alone are considered; hence **prompt-criticality.**

1954 R. STEPHENSON *Introd. Nucl. Engin.* ii. 64 When the *k* for a U^{235} reactor is exactly equal to 1·0073, there is sufficient reactivity to maintain the chain reaction by means of the prompt neutrons alone, and the reactor is said to be prompt critical. **1956** S. GLASSTONE *Princ. Nucl. Reactor Engin.* iv. 242 The rapid increase in the flux when the reactivity exceeds the prompt-critical value would make the reactor difficult to control, and special precautions must be taken that this condition does not arise in reactor operation. **1973** D. R. INGLIS *Nucl. Energy* IV. 120 Plutonium has only about one-third as many delayed neutrons as does uranium (about 0·23 percent of neutrons are delayed), and this provides only a narrow margin for adjustments below a prompt critical condition. **1954** R. STEPHENSON *Introd. Nucl. Engin.* vii. 269 This is the condition for prompt criticality. **1974** S. E. HUNT *Fission, Fusion & Energy Crisis* vi. 53 Prompt criticality would be even more serious in a fast reactor of the Dounreay type than in the more usual thermal neutron reactors, since the neutrons do not need to be slowed down between one generation of fissions and the next.

prompter. Add: **2. b.** Also *Comb.* in possessive, as **prompter's bell, box, copy, table** = *prompt-bell, -box, -copy, *table* s.v. PROMPT *sb.* 2 b.

1812 C. MATHEWS *Let.* 20 Jan. in A. Mathews *Mem. Charles Mathews* (1838) II. viii. 187, I..never did believe (nor will I, till I hear the prompter's bell) that Drury would be played in next winter. **1895** W. ARCHER *Theatr. World 1894* 369 Where, at the stroke of the prompter's bell, a new world is revealed to the delighted sense. **1775** F. ABINGTON *Let.* in *Private Corr. D. Garrick* (1835) II. 32 Begging leave to sit in the prompter's box. **1870** E. L. BLANCHARD *Diary* 23 Mar. in Scott & Howard *Life E. L. Blanchard* (1891) II. 381 Adelphi; Byron's new four-act drama of *The Prompter's Box: A Story of the Footlights and the Fireside.* **1770** A. MURPHY *Let.* 20 Sept. in *Private Corr. D. Garrick* (1831) I. 399 Having the prompter's copy in my drawer for above two years past. **1834** W. C. MACREADY *Diary* 10 June (1912) I. 152, I came up and was first at rehearsal; from the prompter's table I wrote a hasty note to R. Price. **1889** J. L. TOOLE *Reminisc.* I. i. 29, I was sitting at the prompter's table, when I heard a voice at my elbow.

promptive, *a.* (Further example.)

1955 W. FAULKNER *Fable* 384 The third man..said,.. just diffident and promptive, as you address someone.. who may have temporarily forgotten your need or forgotten you: 'Paris'.

promptuary, *sb.* (*a.*) **A.** *sb.* **1.** Delete ? *Obs.* and add later example.

1977 'E. CRISPIN' *Glimpses of Moon* xi. 222 He looked.. like a gorilla at large in an unguarded banana promptuary.

promyelocyte, -cytic: see *PRO-² 1. **pro-name:** *PRO-¹ 4 b.

pronase (prōᵘ·nēⁱz). *Biochem.* [f. *PRO(TEI)-NASE.] A purified preparation of proteinase from cultures of the bacterium *Streptomyces griseus.* (A proprietary name in the U.S.)

1960 *Jrnl. Biochem.* (Japan) XLVIII. 600 The above mentioned, excellent proteolytic activity of *Streptomyces griseus* protease is expected to develop many new industrial and scientific applications, in cooperation with the success in commercial production of this enzyme. [*Note*] Partially purified *Streptomyces griseus* protease is put on the market from the Kaken Chemical Co., Ltd., in the trademark of '*Pronase*'. **1962** *Science* 2 Nov. 594/1 The zona pellucida may be removed from all stages of the mouse egg by digestion with pronase. **1963** *Official Gaz.* (U.S. Patent Office) 22 Jan. TM132/2 California Corporation for Biomedical Research, Los Angeles, Calif... *Pronase* for highly purified proteinase prepared from *Streptomyces griseus* culture broth. First use May 9, 1961. **1976** *Ann. Rev. Microbiol.* XXX. 163 Ribonuclease digestion of a phenolic extract containing the antiviral factor resulted in complete loss of activity, whereas treatments with trypsin or pronase did not lessen antiviral activity.

pronatalist (pronēⁱ·tălist), *a.* and *sb.* Also **pro-natalist.** [f. PRO-¹ 5 a + NATAL *a.*¹ and *sb.* + -IST.] **A.** *adj.* Of or pertaining to the encouragement of large families, esp. by the state; in favour of or advocating large families. **B.** *sb.* A pronatalist person.

1938 *Mod. Law Rev.* II. 102 The suppression of abortion was part of the policy of the *Alliance Nationale pour l'Accroissement de la Population Française*, founded by J. Bertillon in 1896. (Three months after this had been founded, Paul Robin set up his counter organisation, '*La Ligue de la Régénération Humaine*', for advocating birth-control and attacking the pro-natalists. *Ibid.* 105 In most countries and at most periods there have been pro-natalist policies directed at encouraging marriage and the raising of large families.) **1953** *Population Stud.* VII. 39 Even the most ambitious of French pro-natalists admit to-day that policy must be directed to encouraging the birth of a third and possibly a fourth child, rather than concentrating on the large family. **1974** *Encycl. Brit. Macropædia* XIV. 818/2 Taken as a whole, Europeans in the Middle Ages were pronatalists. **1974** *Sci. Amer.* Sept. 125/3 Between the 1930's and the 1950's there was..an increase in pronatalist intervention by the [U.S.] Government, particularly through the tax structure. **1976** *Nature* 4 Nov. 7/1 More and more governments are reversing pro-natalist policies and instituting family planning programmes. **1979** *Jrnl. R. Soc. Arts* CXXVII. 415/1 Some countries are still avowedly pro-natalist.

So **prona·talism,** advocacy or encouragement, esp. by the state, of large families.

1938 *Mod. Law Rev.* II. 105 The semi-official (e.g. municipal) encouragement of birth-control in the first half of the nineteenth century was severely shaken by the Franco-Prussian war, which was followed by an intensive pro-natalist campaign. Similarly, a further impetus to pro-natalism was given during the last war, and the policy is now an official one. **1974** D. V. GLASS in H. B. Parry *Population* I. v. 73 Japan, too, in spite of its high Gross Reproduction Rate, included pronatalism in its imperialist policy.

pronate, *ppl. a.* (Further *literary* example.)

1938 S. BECKETT *Murphy* ii. 24 He raised his left hand..and seated it pronate on the crown of his skull.

pro-Nazi: see *PRO-¹ 5 a.

prone, *sb.* Delete 'Now rare' and add: Also ‖**prône.** **2.** (Further examples.) Also prayers, exhortations, etc., attached to the sermon.

[**1763** C. CORDELL *Divine Office for Use of Laity* I. p. vi, The prayers, publications, and familiar instructions used at the Parish-Mass, on Sundays..either immediately after the Gospel, or before the Lavabo are called in France the Prône, from a Greek word signifying the Nave of the Church.] *a* **1773** A. BUTLER *Moveable Feasts Catholic Church* (1774) I. v. 78 A Person who besides Morning and Evening Prayers has devoutly attended High-mass with a Prone or Sermon. **1860** F. C. HUSENBETH *Life Monsignor Weedall* iii. 50 These sermons were called by the French name of *Prones*... In these *Prones*, however, no one surpassed Mr. Weedall. **1912** A. FORTESCUE *Mass* vii. 295 The Prayers of the Faithful..became the *prône*, commands to pray for all classes of people, living and dead, which are still given out before the sermon. **1915** F. E. BRIGHTMAN *Eng. Rite* II. 1037 The Bidding of the Bedes has not stood alone, but has formed part of a group of vernacular devotions, instructions, and notifications, attached to the Sermon, and known as the 'Prone'. **1937** W. DOUGLAS *Church Mus. in Hist. & Pract.* v. 120 The most powerful [urge] was that toward the use of the vernacular. Both in England and in Northern Europe..this tendency had brought about a series of vernacular public devotions called the Prone, in connection with the Sermon at High Mass. It contained a bidding prayer for intercessions, a confession and absolution, the Creed, the Lord's Prayer, and the Ten Commandments with explanation, and the Church notices. **1968** F. E. VOKES in *Studia Evangelica* V. 146 The so-called 'Prone', the vernacular instruction in the Mass. **1972** J. G. DAVIES *Dict. Liturgy & Worship* 76/2 The association between the sermon and the intercessions which is found in some of the Reformed churches is probably derived from their association in the prone. **1978** D. H. TRIPP in C. Jones et al. *Study of Liturgy* II. III. xi. 255 The normal Sunday worship was to be a preaching-service, based on the medieval prone.

prone, *a.* Add: **6. c.** Const. *absol.* with preceding sb. (usu. with hyphen).

1926, etc. [see *ACCIDENT *sb.* 10 b]. **1973** J. M. WHITE *Garden Game* 47 They were fundamentally good boys..but they were also violence-prone. **1974** *Times* 18 Oct. 16/4 The traditionally drought-prone areas. **1975** *Publishers Weekly* 25 Aug. 287/2 This tale of a wayward bus line founded by the author's failure-prone father.

proneural: see *PRO-² 2.

prong, *sb.*² Add: **2. c.** (Earlier examples of U.S. sense.)

1725 in *Amer. Speech* (1940) XV. 300 To a Gum on the sound side of the north prong of the Spring Swamp. **1784** G. WASHINGTON *Diary* 25 Sept. (1925) II. 311 Carpenters Creek, a branch of Jackson's..which is the principal prong of James River. **1834** J. M. PECK *Gazetteer Illinois* III. 217 It [*sc.* Crawford's Creek] enters the south prong of Bear creek.

pronghorn, *sb.* Add: **2.** [f. PRONG *sb.*² + HORN *sb.*] A projecting stabbing implement (in context a gas lamp). *nonce-wd.*

1922 JOYCE *Ulysses* 439 The navvy..gores him with his flaming pronghorn.

pronk (prǫŋk), *v. S. Afr.* [Afrikaans, to show off, strut, prance, ad. Du. *pronken* to strut.] *intr.* Of springbok: to leap in the air, to buck, esp. as an alarm-signal. Hence **pro·nking** *vbl. sb.*

1896 F. V. KIRBY *In Haunts of Wild Game* ii. 49 He quickly settles down into a long 'rocking-horse' canter, or else goes 'pronking' away, as the Boers style it. **1915** *Chambers's Jrnl.* Nov. 703/1 When a whole troop of these antelopes are thus leaping..'pronking', or 'pranking', as the Boers call it. **1957** R. CAMPBELL *Portugal* v. 90 Both the mules..began to rise off the ground as if the earth were red-hot, like springboks 'pronking', with all four feet at once, arching their backs. **1966** E. PALMER *Plains of Camdeboo* ix. 154 Every hunter in the past had his theory as to why springbuck pronk, just as every Karoo farmer has today. **1971** *Sunday Mail Family Section* (Brisbane) 10 June 6 The beautiful springbok.. gives a spectacular alarm signal... It springs into the air, back arched, displaying a crest of pure white hairs. This is called 'pronking'.

pronk (prǫŋk), *sb. slang.* [Origin uncertain: cf. Du. *pronker* fop.] A weak or effeminate person, a softie; a crank, fool, mug.

1959 C. MACINNES *Absolute Beginners* 25 Here the pronk half rose in his ballet tights and saluted. *Ibid.* 33 No one is going to..try to blackmail me with that crazy old mixture of threats and congratulations that a pronk like you falls for. **1972** L. HENDERSON *Cage until Tame* iv. 28 Whoever this pronk Durant was he had a lot to learn. **1976** —— *Major Enquiry* xv. 102 This pronk reckons he can..point out the right one [*sc.* car] with a hazel twig.

pronograde (prōᵘ·nogrēⁱd), *a.* [f. L. *prōn-us* PRONE *a.* + *-gradus* going, walking: see GRADE *sb.*] Moving on all fours.

1902 [see *ORTHOGRADE *a.*]. **1918** F. WOOD-JONES *Probl. Man's Ancestry* 22 The likeness [to man] still further diminished in the lemurs, and in the general run of pronograde quadrupedal mammals it reached a minimum. **1971** F. S. HULSE *Human Species* (ed. 2) vii. 168 For moving or standing in a pronograde position, that is, on all fours, a somewhat tube-shaped pelvis is quite adequate. **1978** *Nature* 14 Dec. 706/1 A narrow trochlea with pronounced anteromedial and posterolateral borders such as is characteristic of cercopithecoid monkeys (and many other pronograde quadrupedal mammals).

pronominal, *a.* (*sb.*) Add: **A.** *adj.* **2.** (Further examples.) Also, characterized by the presence of a pronoun.

1924 O. Jespersen *Philos. Gram.* 303 There are two kinds of questions; 'Did he say that?' is an example of one kind, and 'What did he say?' and 'Who said that?' are examples of the other. Many names have been proposed for these two kinds: yes-or-no question or categorical question *v.* pronominal question [etc.]. **1928** H. Poutsma *Gram. Late Mod. Eng.* (ed. 2) I. vii. 381 *Sweet*..distinguishes them as general and special questions; Kruisinga..as disjunctive and pronominal questions. **1931** G. Stern *Meaning & Change of Meaning* xi. 332 German *etcetera*..may mean 'podex, crepitus ventris, devil, cacare', etc. This might be called a pronominal use. **1960** E. Delavenay *Introd. Machine Transl.* 120 Prepositions require further programming..as do pronominal verbs (s'améliorer). **1965** B. Collinder in Bessinger & Creed *Medieval & Linguistic Stud.* 28 Adolf Noreen distinguished between *expressive* and *pronominal* sememes. **1978** *Language* LIV. 369, I also argue that the pro-predicates have an especially close resemblance to 'pronominal determiners' like the italicized portions of the following.

B. *sb.* (Further example.)
1971 *Language* XLVII. 169 The prefixes of the inflectional category include aspects such as *si-*..and *yi-*.., modals such as *ni-*..and *di-*.., and pronominals such as *yi-*..and *i-*.

pronominalize *v.* (further examples); hence **prono·minalized, prono·minalizing** *ppl. adjs.*
1961 *Amer. Speech* XXXVI. 163 These are reducible identically to the pronominalized *each one, this one*..or finally all the way to *it*. **1971** *Language* XLVII. 527 The indefinite article, when truly indefinite (when pronominalized by *one*), introduces a noun in a qualitative rather than an identifying sense. **1975** *Archivum Linguisticum* VI. 78 The subject of *ofereode* is pretty clearly the (unhappy) result of the situation outlined in the stanza; the genitive, which has been pronominalized, referring to the situation itself. **1977** *Language* LIII. 97 The pronominalizing languages present in surface more of the logical structure of restrictive relative clauses than do the non-pronominalizing languages. **1978** *Amer. Speech* LIII. 31 In colloquial English, *they* can be said to pronominalize a [+ human, + III] antecedent of undetermined sex, regardless of number.

pronominalization (pronǫ:minălaizē¹·ʃən). [f. Pronominalize *v.* + -ation.] The process or fact of replacing (a noun or noun phrase) by a pronoun. Also *attrib.*
1961 *Amer. Speech* XXXVI. 163 The optional deletion of the modifier..occurring in the grammar after the pronominalization. **1965** N. Chomsky *Aspects of Theory of Syntax* iii. 145 Sameness of reference requires reflexivization of the second Noun Phrase (this is also true of pronominalization). **1970** *Language* XLVI. 172 The essence of the pronominalization rule adopted..is that any noun phrase..may be expressed as a pronoun. **1971** J. P. Thorne in A. J. Aitken et al. *Edin. Stud. Eng. & Scots* 59 The rules governing pronominalisation require either that the pronoun occurs in the deep structure of the sentence or that the deep structure contains two identical noun phrases, in which case a transformational rule rewrites one of them as a pronoun in the surface structure. **1979** *Trans. Philol. Soc.* 58 Hankamer (1971)..has argued that pronominalization is a special instance of deletion.

pronosophical (prǭ"nosǫ·fikăl), *a.* *nonce-wd.* [f. Gr. προνοέω to foresee + *-sophical* as in *philosophical.*] Having the wisdom of foresight; previsionary.
1922 Joyce *Ulysses* 425 Stephen: Gesture..would be a universal language, the gift of tongues rendering visible.. the first entelechy, the structural rhythm. Lynch: Pronosophical theology. Metaphysics in Mecklenburg street!

pronotum. Add: (Later examples.) **pronotal** *a.* (examples).
1904 *Proc. U.S. Nat. Mus.* XXVII. 389 The pronotum [of *Ceratophyllus multispinosus*] has two rows of few weak bristles. *Ibid.* 395 *Ceratophyllus alaskensis*...Male: Head flattened on top as usual. Pronotal ctenidium of 22 spines. **1925** A. D. Imms *Gen. Textbk. Entomol.* ii. 665 In many species [of flea] the pronotum carries a row of stout spines forming the pronotal comb. **1947** C. A. Hubbard *Fleas Western N. Amer.* iv. 38 Taxonomically the only portion which has any great significance is the pronotum and the absence or presence on it of the pronotal comb or ctenidium. **1959** Southwood & Leston *Land & Water Bugs Brit. Isles* iii. 17 Head and pronotum [of the juniper shieldbug] with concolorous puncturation except sometimes near the pronotal angles. **1972** Swan & Papp *Common Insects N. Amer.* xii. 123 The head [of lace bugs] is often covered with a hood, the pronotum extended on the sides like another pair of wings. *Ibid.* xxiii. 655 Genal and pronotal spines absent [in the human flea].

pronoun. Add: **b.** *Comb.*, as *pronoun-form, -object.*
1933 L. Bloomfield *Language* xvi. 269 Among the substantives are some pronoun-forms which, by over-differentiation, do not serve as actors: *me, us, him, her, them, whom.* **1973** *Word* 1970 XXVI. 81 In the first-person plural, the subject pronoun-form functions as an indirect object: *They give me the money.* **1957** R. W. Zandvoort *Handbk. Eng. Gram.* i. v. 78 *To do* is used as a notional verb, chiefly in its non-finite forms and with a neuter pronoun-object (*something, nothing, this, that, it, what?* etc.). **1963** F. T. Visser *Hist. Syntax* I. iv. 425 The period of transition from Old to Middle English is characterised by a considerable number of remarkable changes in the form of most of the reflexive pronoun-objects.

pronounal, *a.* (Further example.)
1961 R. B. Long *Sentence & its Parts* ii. 39 Inflection for the possessive is fundamentally a nounal or pronounal variety of inflection.

pronto (prǫ·nto), *a.* *Mus.* [a. It. *pronto* ready, prompt, f. L. *promptus* quick: cf. next.] (See quots.)
Quot. 1740 represents quasi-*adv.* use.
1740 J. Grassineau *Mus. Dict.* 184 *Pronto*, readily, quick, nimbly, without loss of time. **1908** L. J. De Bekker *Stokes' Encycl. Mus. & Musicians* 517/2 *Pronto, It.* Quick, ready. **1938** *Oxf. Compan. Mus.* 759/1 *Pronto* (It.) 'Ready', 'prompt'. So *Prontamente*, 'promptly'.

pronto (prǫ·nto), *adv. colloq.* (orig. *U.S.*). [a. Sp. *pronto*, f. as prec.] Quickly; promptly, straight away.
1850 L. H. Garrard *Wah-to-Yah* ix. 134 Bent told him to *vamos, prento!* (go quick). *Ibid.* xi. 162 Me be off prento. *Ibid.* xvii. 225 Esta—'here'—said she...Vamos—prento, por el rancheros—'go quick for the rancheros.' **1911** H. B. Wright *Winning of Barbara Worth* v. 96 All we have to do with it is to push for Rubio City pronto. **1926** J. Black *You can't Win* vi. 66 If we was in the city I'd take fifty cents of it purty pronto. **1934** R. Macaulay *Going Abroad* ii. 26, I bring zem wizout fail; pronto, right away. **1938** E. Bowen *Death of Heart* iii. v. 405 I'm going to take you right back—now, pronto, at once. **1948** 'N. Shute' *No Highway* v. 128 Will you.. get Honey back here, pronto? **1952** M. Allingham *Tiger in Smoke* x. 165 When the war ended you were slung out pronto. **1966** *Listener* 22 Dec. 927/3 He finished up by saying that there would be a punitive expedition pretty pronto if the stuff was not returned. **1976** P. Cave *High Flying Birds* iii. 33 You tell that bastard to come and see me... Pronto.

Prontosil (prǫ·ntosil). *Pharm.* Also **prontosil.** [G., proprietary name.]. **1.** A proprietary name for a reddish-brown crystalline bacteriostatic dye, 2′,4′-diaminoazobenzene-4-sulphonamide, $C_{12}H_{13}N_5O_2S$, which was the first of the sulphonamide drugs to be known and was given (usu. orally) in the treatment of a wide range of bacterial infections; formerly also called *Red Prontosil.*
1936 *Proc. R. Soc. Med.* XXIX. 313 Advice will be given of a new class of substances, which have an actual chemotherapeutic action in streptococcal infections (prontosil, prontosil S). **1936** *Trade Marks Jrnl.* 15 July 874/2 Prontosil... A medicated dye preparation for human use in the prevention and treatment of Streptococcus infections. Bayer Products, Limited. **1937** *Lancet* 13 Mar. 626/1 Trefouël and others..have shown that the soluble red azo-dye Prontosil Soluble (for injection) and the almost insoluble orange azo-dye Red Prontosil (oral) are bactericidal only after reduction to sulphanilamide. **1938** F. B. Young *Dr. Bradley Remembers* viii. 437 Some German, it seemed—it was always the Germans in those days—had compounded a new synthetic drug..marketed under the name of Prontosil. **1938** *Times* 8 Dec. 18/5 The new drug, prontosil, the value of which in treating human puerperal fever was clearly established at the Queen Charlotte's Hospital isolation blocks and research laboratories. **1942** *Endeavour* July 122/2 The origin of these and other developments of bacterial chemotherapy was the synthesis by Mietzsch and Klaren of the drug known as prontosil, and the disclosure of its therapeutic properties by Domagk. **1965** *Listener* 10 June 847/1, I can remember helping to make some quinine ampoules for the treatment of a young wife who was dying in her first pregnancy. They were useless. A few years later a proprietary drug called 'Prontosil' came to us, and by giving tablets of that by mouth we began to cure puerperal fever. **1972** 'J. Herriot' *It shouldn't happen to Vet* (1973) xxi. 143 Just a suggestion, James..I honestly think that the situation calls for a little Prontosil.

2. Special Combs. (none now current): **Prontosil Album** [L. *album*, neut. of *albus* white], a name for sulphanilamide; **Prontosil Red** or **Rubrum** [L. *rubrum*, neut. of *ruber, rubrus* red] = sense 1; **Prontosil soluble** (see quot. 1958).
1937 *Lancet* 27 Feb. 510/1 From the 12th to the 29th the patient also received one tablet of Prontosil Album by mouth every six hours. **1958** *Martindale's Extra Pharmacopœia* (ed. 24) 1250 Proprietary preparations of sulphanilamide were formerly marketed in Great Britain under the names Prontosil Album (Bayer Prod.) and Streptocide (Evans Medical Supplies). **1938** *Brit. Med. Jrnl.* 8 Jan. 104/2, I have obtained successful results in the treatment of erysipelas and acute dermatitis by using as a local application prontosil red, 7½ grains being dissolved in 1 oz. of distilled water. **1938** *Lancet* 10 Sept. 647/1 The new rule..will apply not only to sulphanilamide but to related substances including products sold under the following names:..Prontosil rubrum.., Prontosil Soluble, [etc.]. **1959** Evers & Caldwell *Chem. of Drugs* (ed. 3) ix. 114 Prontosil rubrum is broken down in the body to 4-aminobenzenesulphonamide. **1964** Ariëns & Simonis in E. J. Ariëns *Molecular Pharmacol.* I. 77 One of the bioactivations first recognized as such was that of Prontosil Rubrum.., the compound found by Domagk..to be effective in the protection of mice against bacterial infections. **1936** *Lancet* 11 July 107/2 There seems to be some risk of toxic reactions associated with the administration of Prontosil (soluble) intravenously. *Ibid.* 5 Dec. 1323/2 When prontosil soluble was substituted for the sulphonamide, there was no bactericidal effect. **1958** *Chambers's Techn. Dict.* 1017/2 Prontosil-soluble, which has greater antibacterial effect [than Prontosil] and is more soluble, is the disodium salt of 4′-sulphonamido phenylazo-7-acetylamino-1-hydroxy naphthalene-3·6-disulphonic acid.

pronuba. Add: **2.** [C. V. Riley 1872, in *Nature* 26 Sept. 444/1.] In full, *pronuba moth.* A small white North American moth of the genus formerly so called, now usually included in the genus *Tegeticula*, esp. the yucca moth, *T. yuccasella*, which pollinates yucca plants.
1872 *Nature* 26 Sept. 444/1 The larva of *Pronuba* eats through the Yucca capsule in which it fed, enters the ground and hibernates there. **1905** V. L. Kellogg *Amer. Insects* xvi. 577 (*caption*) Pronuba-moth depositing eggs in ovary of Yucca. **1929** Robbins & Rickett *Botany* xxvi. 437 Without the *Pronuba* moth the *Yucca* would not produce seeds. **1946** D. C. Peattie *Road of Naturalist* ii. 24 The smoky little Pronuba moths..come to the blossoms, mate there, hover and hide and perform small extraordinary rites without which no Joshua tree would stand and brandish arms at heaven.

pronunciamento. Add: (Earlier and later examples.) Also *attrib.*
1835 *Morning Courier & N.Y. Enquirer* 23 Nov. 2/2 It is not..a question of a *pronounciamiento* in favor of federalism or centralism, or who shall govern. **1906** R. Fry *Let.* 20 Nov. (1972) I. 273 The Trustees..will pass some sort of resolution accepting my *pronunciamento.* **1929** *Times* 1 Nov. 17/4 The worst result of the Spanish doctor's pronunciamento is likely to be a regular cult of conscientious and laboured irregularity. **1939** H. G. Wells *Holy Terror* iv. iii. 439 The pronunciamento bosses of those little old republics there used to be in South America. **1951** E. Paul *Springtime in Paris* xi. 202 Then came Zhdanov's pronunciamento in Russia condemning jazz as degenerate and unfit for proletarian amusement. **1968** R. Hargreaves *Bloodybacks* x. 265 Although there was anything but unanimity of sentiment and opinion among the inhabitants of the Thirteen Colonies, the Congressional *pronunciamento* had committed them to continued resistance. **1972** *Daily Tel.* (Colour Suppl.) 10 Nov. 18/1 The political revolution consisted largely of intimidation, arbitrary rule..and windy *pronunciamientos.* **1975** *New Yorker* 20 Jan. 61/3, I wish he had prevailed on the author to drop a few samples of the writer-hero's more high-flown, phony-eloquent pronunciamentos.

pronunciation. Add: **6.** *attrib.* and *Comb.*, as **pronunciation key**, a list of symbols providing a guide to pronunciation; **pronunciation-spelling**, the spelling of words in accordance with their usual pronunciation; an instance of this.
1962 C. L. Barnhart in Householder & Saporta *Probl. in Lexicogr.* 174 Two great scholars..said that the pronunciation key was of no importance whatsoever; they felt that any key that used symbols consistently was adequate. **1966** *Random House Dict. Eng. Lang.*, (*heading*) Pronunciation Key. **1944** H. J. Uldall in E. P. Hamp et al. *Readings in Linguistics II* (1966) 149 If there have been cases of spelling-pronunciation, there have also been cases of pronunciation-spelling. **1953** K. Jackson *Lang. & Hist. in Early Brit.* i. ii. 70 If the spelling..depended on tradition alone..there would be far more cases of pronunciation-spellings betraying lenition than the few which do exist. **1979** *Amer. Speech* LIV. 33 There are no spelling pronunciations in the corpus, although there are pronunciation spellings like the British *cuppa* and *pinta*, as in *cup of tea* and *pint of milk.*

proœmium. (Later examples of var. form.)
1826 *Hansard Commons* 25 Apr. 590 The whole of the authorities..formed a very dry proemium to the proposal with which it [*sc.* the bill] terminated. **1933** R. Tuve *Seasons & Months* i. 11 Both analogues and influences may be found for the 'alma Venus' of Lucretius' proemium.

pro-œstrus, var. *pro-œstrum* s.v. Pro-² 1 in Dict. and Suppl.

proof, *sb.* Add: **I. 1. a.** (Further examples.)
1927 A. H. McNeile *Introd. to N.T.* 13 He therefore makes no use of proof-texts, and no suggestions that Christianity is the real and 'fulfilled' Judaism. His sole 'proofs' are the actual words and deeds of the Master and the effects which they produced. **1945** R. Knox *God & Atom* iii. 42 In the long run, you felt, the first three Proofs stood or fell by the value of the causality argument.

II. 10. b. For † *Obs.* read *Hist.* and add later example.
1956 W. S. Churchill *Hist. Eng.-Speaking Peoples* I. ii. i. 126 They..were clad in proof, but..they cast aside their ring-mail.

11. c. The aeration of dough by leaven before baking. Cf. *prove *v.* 1 g.
1903 Kipling *Five Nations* 23 There is no proof in the bread we eat or rest in the toil we ply. **1961** *Sunday Times* 5 Feb. 30/4 You knead it [*sc.* the dough] again, but this time for a few minutes only—just to 'knock out the proof', as the bakers say.

III. 13. b. Delete † *Obs.* and add further examples.
1948 C. Abel *Business of Photogr.* xxxix. 357 Ownership of the proofs submitted by a portrait photographer

to a customer has long been a matter of argument in the profession. **1960** MORTENSEN & DUNHAM *How to pose Model* (ed. 3) xii. 152 As soon as you have picked out the proofs that you want to make into prints, destroy *all* the others.

14. (Earlier and later examples of current sense.)

1889 J. ATKINS *Coins & Tokens of Possessions & Colonies of Brit. Empire* 5 Proofs exist of both these pieces. **1920** *Brit. Numismatics Jrnl. 1918* IV. 131 The same artist issued proofs either for a sixpence or a farthing. **1969** *Times* 21 July p. v/4 Proofs (special coins struck from highly polished dies mainly for collectors) have been issued for this denomination. **1977** *Times* 5 May 20/2 Jubilee crown proofs are in silver.

IV. 18. a. (sense 4) *proof-test* vb.; (senses 12–14) *proof coin, copy, -correcting* (earlier example), *correction* (further examples), *-corrector, impression* (later example), *stage, state* (example).

1949 W. H. SHELDON *Early Amer. Cents 1793–1814* I. 39 *Proof* coins were never struck for circulation... Proofs were first used as presentation pieces. **1969** *Coin Investor* 18 Jan. 3/1 The difference between a proof coin and a brilliant uncirculated one is that a proof coin has been specially struck on a highly polished die. **1976** *National Observer* (U.S.) 17 Jan. 17/4 (Advt.), Highly sought after by collectors, Proof coins are the ultimate expression of the minting art. Dies and solid gold blanks are polished by hand to a mirror finish. **1806** SCOTT *Let.* Oct. (1932) I. 327, I would like to see them in the proof copy in case any minute alterations may yet occur to me. **1975** A. POWELL *Hearing Secret Harmonies* ii. 66 He held under his arm what looked like the proof copy of a book. **1850** W. M. THACKERAY *Let.* June in H. Ritchie *Lett. A. T. Ritchie* (1924) iii. 29 Then comes printing and proof correcting & so forth. **1940** *Chambers's Techn. Dict.* 677/2 *Proof corrections*, additions or emendations to a proof. They should be made in ink, and clearly indicated in the margin. **1978** *Hart's Rules for Compositors & Readers* (ed. 38) 34 (*heading*) Proof-correction marks. **1928** L. P. SMITH *Words & Idioms* 162 We are becoming more and more the slaves of schoolmasters and proof-correctors. **1932** A. E. HOUSMAN *Let.* 19 June (1971) 322 On p. 32 the proof-corrector has again given directions for making a change which ought not to be made. **1910** *Connoisseur* Oct. 93/1 How to distinguish Proof Impressions. **1895** F. M. FORD *Let.* (1965) 8 You may tell Longmans that W.M.R. had offered to revise my chapters as they go to Press wh. is better than in the proof stage I shd. think. **1966** N. NICOLSON in H. Nicolson *Diaries & Lett., 1930–1939* 118 The name had to be altered again..at proof-stage. **1910** *Connoisseur* Oct. 93/2 To such a man even the names of the various proof states must be a source of bewilderment. **1951** *Sun* (Baltimore) 30 Jan. 5/3 Their major purpose..is to proof-test some slide-rule work being done by nuclear physicists and weapons experts.

b. proof-glass (examples); **proof load** *Mech.*, a load which a structure must be able to bear without exceeding specified limits of deformation; *loosely*, proof stress; **proof-read** *v. trans.*, to read (printer's proofs) and mark errors for correction; hence **proof-read** *ppl. a.*; **proof-reader** (earlier example); **proof-reading** *vbl. sb.* and *ppl. a.* (examples); **proof-slip** *Typog.* = PROOF-SHEET; **proof strain** *Mech.*, the strain produced by the proof stress; *loosely*, proof stress; **proof strength** (earlier example); **proof stress** *Mech.*, the stress required to produce a specified permanent deformation of a material or structure; **proof theory** (see quot. 1942); hence **proof-theoretic** *a.*, of or pertaining to proof theory; **proof-theoretically** *adv.*, in a proof-theoretic manner.

1765 H. JACKSON *Ess. Brit. Isinglass* 73 We likewise advise them to a serious Perusal of our new-invented *Proof-glasses*. **1848** *Knickerbocker* XVIII. 380 With what profound deliberation he drew his proof-glass from the bung-hole of a brandy-pipe. **1858** W. J. M. RANKINE *Man. Appl. Mech.* II. iii. 287 The toughness of the bar, or the extension corresponding to the proof load. **1930** *Engineering* 21 Feb. 241/2 This working load is equivalent to one-half the proof load, which again is almost one-half the ultimate strength of the chain. **1973** A. PARRISH *Mech. Engineer's Ref. Bk.* xii. 5 A 'proof load' is a specified load which a lifting appliance shall withstand without showing permanent set exceeding a specified amount or showing other defect. **1933** G. STEIN *Autobiogr. Alice B. Toklas* v. 139 A good many years later Jane Heap said that she had never appreciated the quality of Gertrude Stein's work until she proof-read it. **1937** W. FOLLETT in *Atlantic Monthly* Jan. 49/1 *The New York Times*..is..the most nearly proofread of the larger metropolitan dailies. **1951** L. HELLMAN *Autumn Garden* I. 14 His publishers..want the manuscript... I'll have to proofread it with him tonight. **1964** F. BOWERS *Bibliogr. & Textual Crit.* IV. iv. 126 The automatic assumption is surely wrong that every forme of cheap commercial printing was necessarily proof-read. **1966** 'H. B. TAYLOR' *Triumvirate* xx. 115 The galleys of proofread type. **1976** *Times Lit. Suppl.* 2 July 813/4 It is smoothly written, although no better illustrated than Professor Donohue's survey..and far less well proofread. **1855** I. C. PRAY *Mem. J. G. Bennet* 41 From this post he was transferred to that of a proof-reader in the printing-house of Wells & Lilly. **1852** GEO. ELIOT *Let.* 15 June (1954) II. 36 Between theatre-going and proof-reading, my spiritual eyes are burning as dim and bleared as gas-lights. **1937** W. FOLLETT in *Atlantic Monthly* Jan. 49/2 Such a thing it is to be equipped, or cursed, with the proofreading eye. **1977** *Early Music* Oct. 470/2 Manuscripts..*A* and *B* show more evidence of proofreading. **1883** 'MARK TWAIN' *Lett. to Publishers* (1967) 162 You must glance through all the proof-slips..for..I have added footnotes and other stuff which you have not seen. **1967** COX & GROSE *Organiz. & Handling Bibliogr. Rec. by Computer* v. 118 The material along with the worksheet and the LC proof slip or the Title II card..is then routed to the Catalogue Department... All books for which there are proof slips or Title II depository cards are processed. **1858** W. J. M. RANKINE *Man. Appl. Mech.* II. iii. 273 Resilience or Spring is the quantity of mechanical work required to produce the proof strain. **1862** [see *proof stress* below]. **1888** J. G. HORNER *Lockwood's Dict. Mech. Engin. Terms* 268 A proof strain would in all cases be short of that which would have a crippling effect. **1811** *Niles' Reg.* I. 311/1 The same process repeated until the ley has acquired proof strength. **1862** W. J. M. RANKINE *Man. Civil Engin.* II. i. 226 Resilience, or Spring..is the quantity of mechanical work required to produce the proof-stress on a given piece of material, and is equal to the product of the proof strain, or alteration of figure, into the mean load which acts during the production of that strain; that is to say, in general, very nearly one-half of the proof load. **1935** *Discovery* Apr. 112/2 By the use of aluminium alloy with a ·1 per cent. proof stress of 17 tons per square inch instead of the 15 tons per square inch alloy now used, the hull weight of such a [flying] boat could be kept as low as 12½ per cent. of the total weight. **1962** *BSI News* June 12/1 Qualities of steels determined by the ratio of the 0·2 per cent proof stress at elevated temperatures to the minimum tensile strength at room temperature. **1952** S. C. KLEENE *Introd. Metamath.* xiv. 213 The proof-theoretic equivalents provability and irrefutability refer only to the enumerable infinity of formal proofs... The set-theoretic notions are actually equivalent to the proof-theoretic ones. **1967** —— *Math. Logic* 118 The proof-theoretic approach to the predicate calculus. **1952** —— *Introd. Metamath.* xiv. 425 The axioms are 'consistent' proof-theoretically. **1967** —— *Math. Logic* 118 We now develop some of the further results proof-theoretically. **1942** D. D. RUNES *Dict. Philos.* 255/2 *Proof theory*. The formalization of mathematical proof by means of a logistic system..makes possible an objective theory of proofs and provability, in which proofs are treated as concrete manipulations of formulas (and no use is made of meanings of formulas). **1969** *Listener* 10 July 44/2 The analogy he was using was one with proof theory in logic, where from initial axioms and rules of inference you can produce true theorems—rather like doing geometry exercises in school. **1979** *Sci. Amer.* Oct. 138/3 For this purpose Hilbert introduced a new theory called proof theory, or metamathematics, in which meaningful statements about the meaningless signs and configurations of the axiomatic system could be formulated.

proof, *v.* Add: **1. c.** To aerate (dough) by the action of yeast before baking. Cf. *PROVE *v.* 1 g.

1875 *Encycl. Brit.* III. 253/2 After this laborious process the finished dough is covered over for some time.. during which fermentation again begins, and the mass is 'proofed'. **1972** *Countryman* Autumn 45 There were three ovens, one above the other, in our bakehouse. The bottom one was small and used only for proofing buns and certain cakes.

d. = *proof-read* vb. s.v. *PROOF *sb.* 18 b.

1960 *Times* 16 Feb. 6/1 Bristol set its own papers and printed and proofed them in the city. **1974** R. C. DENNIS *Conversations with Corpse* viii. 70 Arenas was reading a pink report, making occasional corrections of grammar or punctuation... He handed me the pages he had already proofed. **1979** A. EASSON *Elizabeth Gaskell* i. 44 William also proofed much of her work.

Hence **proofed** *ppl. a.*; **proo·fing** *vbl. sb.*

1902 Proofed, proofing [see PROOF *v.* 2]. **1909** *Westm. Gaz.* 3 Sept. 5/2 Dr. Bartsch, of the Royal Proofing Office at Great Lichterfelde, communicates the result of experiments he has made in disinfecting large quantities of books with hot air. **1940** *Chambers's Techn. Dict.* 678/1 *Proofed tape*, cotton cloth coated with a rubber compound, wrapped round rubber-insulated cables. **1953** *News Chron.* 2 June 2/2 Squatting..in the light-weight (six pound) proofed cotton nylon tents. **1957** *Times* 20 Dec. 19/2 The moth-proofing of wool, the rot-proofing of jute, the mould-proofing of paint. **1958** *Times Lit. Suppl.* 18 Apr. 214/5 We are told nothing about the special proofings of the *Second World War* volumes. **1976** H. WILSON *Governance of Britain* viii. 157 The Conservative leader is fairly well proofed against trouble with the [party] machinery. **1977** *Broadcast* 13 June 7/2 There were.. only ten days between the signature of the Report and its proofing and publication.

Prooshian (prū·ʃăn), *a.* and *sb.* Also **Prooshan, Prooshun, Proosian.** Joc. var. PRUSSIAN *a.* and *sb.*

1837 [see PRUSSIAN *a.* 2 b]. **1843** DICKENS *Mart. Chuz.* (1844) xix. 239 Some people..may be Prooshans; they are born so, and will please themselves. **1871** F. C. BURNAND *More Happy Thoughts* (ed. 2) xxix. 214 The Gay Prooshians have no end of ships. **1878** W. S. GILBERT *H.M.S. Pinafore* II. 28 For he might have been a Roosian, A French, or Turk, or Proosian, Or perhaps Itali-an! **1899** KIPLING *Stalky & Co.* 128 'My word!' said M'Turk,.. 'The Prooshian Bates has an infernal straight eye.' **1914** R. BROOKE *Let.* 24 Aug. (1968) 611 To Hell with the Prooshians. **1922** JOYCE *Ulysses* 324 The Prooshians and the Hanoverians.

proot (prŭt), *int.* [Etym. obscure]. A command to a donkey to move faster. Hence **proot** *v. intr.* To cry proot. Cf. PROO *int.*

1879 R. L. STEVENSON *Trav. with Donkey* 18 [He] taught me the true cry or masonic word of donkey-drivers, 'Proot!' *Ibid.* 20 'Proot!' seemed to have lost its virtue. I prooted like a lion, I prooted mellifluously like a sucking-dove; but *Modestine* would be neither softened nor intimidated. **1950** L. G. GREEN *In Land of Afternoon* ix. 132 One expert driver..encourages his mules by yelling the principal parts of Greek verbs... The word of command '*Proot!*', which appears to have come from France with the Huguenots, is more commonly heard.

prop, *sb.*[1] Add: **1. g.** *Rugby Football.* One of two outside front-row forwards who support the hooker in a scrummage.

1950 B. H. TRAVERS *Let's talk Rugger* iii. 50 In a 3-4-1 scrum the wing forwards have to push the front-row props towards the hooker all the time. **1959** *Sunday Times* 15 Mar. 40/7 Later in the half, Wood the Irish prop, was hauled back for a five-yard scrum when many people thought he had forced his way over for a try. **1960** E. S. & W. J. HIGHAM *High Speed Rugby* 154 In order to achieve a well-balanced and fairly comfortable scrum, it is desirable to pair off the two props and the two locks so that they are, as nearly as possible, of the same length of body and the same length of leg. **1971** [see *LOCK *sb.*[2] 11 c]. **1977** *Western Morning News* 1 Sept. 10/7 Perhaps the most significant move, however, is the inclusion of Nigel Redgrave, another to rejoin Albion..at loose head prop.

4. prop forward *Rugby Football*, = sense 1 g above; **prop-free front** *Coal-mining* (see quot. 1967); **prop-root** [tr. G. *stützwurzel* (K. Goebel *Organographie der Pflanzen* (1901) II. 479)], a root springing from the base of a plant above ground level, providing extra support; **prop-word** (see quot. 1892).

1951 *Sport* 30 Mar.–5 Apr. 6/3 The greatest surprise of the whole 26 is the omission of Bill Hopper, the young Leeds prop forward. **1978** *Rugby World* Apr. 33/2 Mayer belonged to a by-gone age in that, despite his size, he always was scrupulously fair on the field, and the revolution in prop-forward scrummage techniques over the past few years, to some extent, passed him by. **1956** F. S. ATKINSON in D. L. Linton *Sheffield* xiv. 270 Much pioneer work has been done in the coalfield to the north-east of Sheffield and in Nottinghamshire to develop a new method of mining at the coalface, known as the 'prop-free front' system. With this method a strong, flexible scraper-chain conveyor, called an armoured conveyor, is installed in the space between the nearest roof supports and the face of coal being worked... To maintain intact the roof between the vertical supports and the wall of coal, cantilever bars are used which are supported by the props behind the conveyor. **1967** *Gloss. Mining Terms* (*B.S.I.*) XI. 11 *Prop-free front*, a system of supports in a longwall face in which props are not normally set between the conveyor and the coal. The roof above and in advance of the conveyor is supported by cantilever bars set on props on the goaf side of the conveyor. **1905** I. B. BALFOUR tr. *Goebel's Organogr. Plants* II. 277 A series of transitions..leads us from the soil-roots to those which spring from the base of the stem of many Monocotyledones, and which soon entering the soil serve as prop-roots. **1938** FRITSCH & SALISBURY *Plant Form & Function* x. 109 These prop-roots serve the purpose of augmenting the somewhat feeble primary root-system. **1953** K. ESAU *Plant Anat.* xvii. 474 Others [*sc.* roots] serve mainly as supporting organs, such as the prop roots in the mangrove plants and, on a smaller scale, in the grasses and sedges. **1976** NORSTOG & LONG *Plant Biol.* vi. 165 A conspicuous feature of the majority of the trees [of the tropical rain forest]..is their smooth, thin, lichen-covered bark and their flaring buttresses or, in the case of some smaller trees, stilt-like prop roots. **1892** H. SWEET *New Eng. Gram.* I. 66 Another way of using the adjective without its noun in English is to substitute the unmeaning noun-pronoun *one* for the noun, the inflection of the noun being transferred to the prop-word, as we may call it. **1914** O. JESPERSEN *Mod. Eng. Gram.* II. 248 The reason why the word *one* has been chosen to fulfil the role of a prop-word is chiefly to be sought in the frequent and quite natural use of *one* (by itself) to take the place of a substantive just mentioned. **1934** *Language* X. 370 We call *drinking* in one employment a participle, in another a gerund, *one* now a numeral, now a prop-word, now a pronoun. **1965** *Eng. Stud.* XLVI. 59 A careful survey of the propword 'one' question.

prop, *sb.*[2] Add: **2. b.** A diamond; a valuable piece of jewellery. *Criminals' slang.*

1914 JACKSON & HELLYER *Vocab. Criminal Slang* 66 *Prop*... General circulation amongst pickpockets and looters. A diamond stud originally, now comprehending diamonds in any sense... Example: 'Any heel gun can get a breech poke, but it takes an A1 claw to grab a prop.' **1925** *Flynn's Mag.* 7 Mar. 191 *Prop*, a large diamond. **1931** [see *GROIN *sb.*[2] 3*]. **1971** S. HOUGHTON *Current Prison Slang* (MS.) 17 *Prop*, nice piece of jewellery.

3. *Comb.* (all ? *Obs.*), as **prop-getter, man, -nailer** *Criminals' slang*, one who steals props (sense 2); a pickpocket.

1901 'J. FLYNT' *World of Graft* 220/2 *Prop-getters*, thieves who make a specialty of 'lifting' scarf-pins. **1931** *Police Jrnl.* Oct. 505 *A prop getter*, a thief who steals scarf-pins. **1935** *Amer. Speech* X. 19/2 *Prop man*, a pickpocket or *snatcher* who lifts stickpins containing valuable stones. **1862** H. MAYHEW *London Labour* Extra vol. 25 'Prop-nailers', those who steal pins and brooches. **1886** H. BAUMANN *Londinismen* 146/1 Prop-nailer.

prop, *sb.*[5] Abbrev. of PROPRIETOR.

? **1880** in W. Whitman *Daybks. & Notebks.* (1978) I. 157 Herman Beckurts—prop: Denver *Tribune*. **1913** W. T. ROGERS *Dict. Abbrev.* 157/1 *Prop...*, proprietor. **1956** H. GOLD *Man who was not with It* III. xxviii. 264 The prop. on this busy corner was with it and for it. **1974** A. ROSS *Bradford Business* 15 A painted board..said *Redlands Hotel—props. K. & G. Lyall*. **1980** *Guardian* 25 July 12/8 At Porters..(the Viscount Newport prop.—and head waiter on a busy Thursday evening).

prop, *sb.*[6] *colloq.* [f. PROP(ELLER.] **1.** A propeller, esp. on an aircraft.

1914 *Flight* 10 Jan. 43/2 He made a fine glide from 650ft., making a perfect landing with the 'prop' stationary. **1918** E. M. Roberts *Flying Fighter* 239, I crashed into a hedge, smashed my prop to bits, and then the machine landed on its nose in the next field. **1931** *Daily Express* 13 Oct. 15/3 A smiling young man jumped back from the roaring prop. **1935** C. S. Forester *Afr. Queen* viii. 139 Must 'a' just 'it a rock with the tip of the prop. **1969** G. Macbeth *War Quartet* 33 We ran, Clumsy in fleece and leather, to the field, Hearing the props whirl. **1974** L. Deighton *Spy Story* xix. 202 The propellers came to a standstill... For a moment the sub became unstable... Then the props picked up speed.

2. *attrib.* and *Comb.* **a.** Simple *attrib.*, as *prop swinger*; in the sense 'propeller-driven', as *prop bomber, plane, trainer.*

1975 *New Yorker* 8 Sept. 25/2 Man's most sophisticated machines of war were sent to hover..over the towns and villages of the Plain of Jars: light spotter planes at 2,000 feet; prop bombers, gunships, and flareships at 5,000 feet; [etc.]. **1965** J. V. Pacilio *Discovering Aerospace* 50 The aircraft engineer would say that a prop plane 'loses its efficiency' at this speed. **1973** *Black Panther* 13 Oct. 14/2 All prop planes were..supposed to land on Runway 31-Right. **1936** F. Clune *Roaming round Darling* xiii. 117 The quartet of 'prop swingers' and 'contracters' departed hopefully for the aerodrome. **1974** *Daily Tel.* (Colour Suppl.) 19 Apr. 15 They make jet trainers and prop trainers.

b. Special Combs.: **prop-fan,** (an aircraft engine incorporating) an airscrew having broad blades swept back from a direction perpendicular to the rotation axis; **prop-jet** = *turboprop; **prop-shaft,** a propeller shaft, esp. of a motor vehicle; **prop wash,** a surge or wash of air created by the action of a propeller; also *transf.*

1970 Metzger & Ganger *Results of Initial Prop-Fan Model Acoustic Testing I* (NASA N 71-25785) 1 In order to explore the low noise potential of a Prop-Fan as an aircraft propulsion system, a noise survey was conducted. *Ibid.* 3 The test item consisted of a 21-inch diameter, 12-bladed, manually adjustable pitch, shrouded Prop-Fan model with 22 fixed pitch recovering vanes. **1977** *Jrnl. R. Soc. Arts* CXXV. 352/1 Propeller developments in the guise of so-called prop fans are being studied in the USA. Uninstalled performances as good as those for low pressure ratio fans are estimated at high subsonic speeds. **1977** *New Scientist* 1 Dec. 567/1 The propfan..has eight thin, swept-back blades which allow it to turn at high speeds without encountering the compressibility problems associated with conventional propellers. *Ibid.* 567/2 On a flight from New York to Miami the propfan airliner would take several minutes less than its turbofan counterpart, because of reduced climb and descent times. **1946** P. H. Wilkinson *Aircraft Engines of World* II. 264 Most of the atmospheric jet engines now in production or under development for use in piloted aircraft are turbojets or propjets. **1963** *Engineering* 1 Nov. 560/3 The Dart was the first propjet engine to go into commercial service. **1971** *Flying* Apr. 2/1 (Advt.), The MU-2F and MU-2G outperform competitive prop-jets simply because they are the only propjets in their category designed to utilize a low-drag high-speed wing. **1972** *Daily Colonist* (Victoria, B.C.) 5 Mar. 16/1 The pilot of a Mohawk Airlines propjet which crashed..apparently knew he would not make it to the airport runway. **1964** C. Barber *Ling. Change Present-Day Eng.* iv. 87 *Prop-shaft*..'propellor shaft'. **1965** *Listener* 17 June 914/3 Telemetering devices which can measure the vibration in a wheel or a prop-shaft. **1976** *Drive* Jan.–Feb. 78/1 Propshaft vibration is an occasional nuisance cured only by diligent garage detective work. **1941** *Amer. Speech* XVI. 168/1 *Prop wash,* an expression of disbelief. (Air Corps.) **1944** *U.S. Air Services* May 16/1 All we could feel was the breathing of tightly packed men..and the animal shudder of the glider as it swung into the prop wash and swung out again. **1958** L. Wolff *Low Level Mission* 19 The prop-wash blasts of the four engines would interfere with other planes to the rear. **1977** *Observer* 28 Aug. 21/4 The pilot climbed aboard... The diminutive figure.. waved bravely in the prop-wash.

prop, *sb.*[7] *Criminals' slang.* Abbrev. of Property *sb.* used in *Comb.*, as **prop game,** the practice of defrauding householders into paying exorbitant prices for unnecessary house repairs; **prop man,** one who perpetrates such a fraud. (See also Props *sb. pl.* in Dict. and Suppl.)

1966 *Evening Echo* (Bournemouth) 20 Apr. 15/1 The 'prop game' appeared to be..unique to Leeds, something that has cropped up in the last two and a half years. **1966** *Guardian* 13 Dec. 5/4 Gangs operating from Leeds are known as 'the prop men' because the racket began in Leeds when so-called property repairers made exorbitant charges after the gales of February, 1961. **1967** N. Lucas *CID* viii. 97 The 'prop game'..was a method by which men obtained money from old people by posing as officials.

prop, *v.*[1] Add: **1. b.** In various humorous and ironic phrases. Usu. with *up.*

1908 Wodehouse & Westbrook *Globe By The Way Bk.* 34 As regards Boarding-The-'Bus and Propping-The-Public-House-Wall, the issue is perhaps more open. But here again I look to see the representatives of the old country well to the fore. **1938** G. Heyer *Blunt Instrument* x. 196 There's a couple propping the wall up at the end of the street. You know the style: kissing and canoodling for the past hour. **1950** 'J. Tey' *To love & be Wise* xi. 133 You'll find him propping up the counter of the post-office. **1965** *Listener* 7 Oct. 539/1 He was to be seen almost every night propping up the left end of the bar in the Wheatsheaf. **1973** J. Pattinson *Search Warrant* ii. 37 A solitary man was propping up the bar. **1978** B. Priestley *Island Emperor* iii. 25, I lay in the sun and..I propped up Niki's bar.

4. For *Australian* read 'orig. *Austral.*' and add further examples. Also *transf.*

1928 'Brent of Bin Bin' *Up Country* 171 How they raced and propped and wheeled on desperate courses bristling with pitfalls. **1946** *Sun* (Baltimore) 4 Oct. 16/4 Tacato Briar was unprepared for break and propped coming out of gate. **1954** *Ibid.* 10 July 9/3 Sans Egal went to the front at once and opened a lead of some six lengths along the backstretch. However, when he entered the final straightaway, he attempted to 'prop' and lost much of his lead. **1969** T. Keneally *Survivor* 70 Seconds later a university sedan, driven by George the university guard, wheeled fast in through the gate and propped at the front of the house. **1970** P. White *Vivisector* 602 The present mob might have trampled Rhoda underfoot if it hadn't suddenly realized she was something beyond its experience, so it propped, and divided.

propædeutic, *a.* and *sb.* **B.** *sb.* **1.** (Earlier example.)

1798 A. F. M. Willich *Elem. Crit. Philos.* 19 In the mean time Kant's system, or rather his elementary *Propedeutic* for a system, acquired still greater reputation.

propædia (prōᵘpī·diă). [ad. Gr. προπαιδεία: see Propaideia.] An introductory volume of the 15th edition of the *Encyclopædia Britannica* (published in 1974) in which information is presented in the form of short outlines. (Cf. *macropædia, *micropædia.)

1974 [see *micropædia]. **1974** *Times* 12 Jan. 12/1 The first volume, propaedia, will be introductory, setting forth a classification of all knowledge into 10 parts, each with a long essay.

propagand, *sb.* (Earlier and further examples.)

1795 W. Cobbett *Bone to gnaw for Democrats* 13 Citizen David, painter to the Propagande, has represented Liberty under the form of a Dragon. **1806** 'C. Caustic' *Democracy Unveiled* (ed. 3) I. 75 Vile propagands in every city Make smooth the path of French banditti.

propagand (prǫpăgæ·nd), *v.* [Back-formation from Propaganda.] *trans.* and *intr.* = Propagandize *v.* in Dict. and Suppl.

1901 *Westm. Gaz.* 11 Jan. 2/2 Being free to 'propagand' he has not hesitated to do so. **1923** *Ibid.* 16 May 8/1 Russia was spending large sums out of her Secret Service in order to propagand in the East against British interests. **1935** N. Mitchison *We have been Warned* II. 208, I expect he'll propagand me a lot. **1938** E. Hemingway *Fifth Column* (1939) 171 That typical French *ivresse* that you were propaganded to believe did not exist. **1948** W. Fortescue *Beauty for Ashes* xii. 77 Would I consent to be a voluntary speaker and 'propagand' on platforms?

Hence **propaga·nded** *ppl. a.*; **propaga·nding** *vbl. sb.* and *ppl. a.*

1920 R. Frost *Let.* 19 Sept. (1972) 94 Good luck with the propaganding. **1937** F. P. Crozier *Men I Killed* xii. 268 They discuss it in awed whispers, well away from the propaganding microphones of the B.B.C. **1958** *Times Lit. Suppl.* 24 Oct. 604/2 Faulty reasoning..and unfelicities like 'propaganding' are a few of the obstacles it [*sc.* a book] presents. **1968** *Economist* 31 Aug. 45/1 The fear-bound and self-propaganded Kremlin leaders. **1971** F. R. Leavis in *Human World* Aug. 9 To see it [*sc.* the present government] replaced by one that has an alternative party-backing, representing a proclaimed and propaganded different policy and programme.

propaganda. Add: **2. a.** (Earlier examples.)

1790 J. MacPherson Let. 27 Sept. in A. Aspinall *Corresp. George, Prince of Wales* (1964) II. 98 All Kings have..a new race of Pretenders to contend with, the disciples of the propaganda at Paris or, as they call themselves, Les Ambassadeurs de genre humain. **1797** *Gentl. Mag.* Aug. 687 The Propaganda, a society whose members are bound, by solemn engagements, to stir up subjects against their lawful rulers.

3. The systematic propagation of information or ideas by an interested party, esp. in a tendentious way in order to encourage or instil a particular attitude or response. Also, the ideas, doctrines, etc., disseminated thus; the vehicle of such propagation.

1908 Lilley & Tyrrell tr. *Programme of Modernism* 102 The Church..soon felt a need of new methods of propaganda and government. **1911** G. B. Shaw *Blanco Posnet* 324 Though we tolerate..the propaganda of Anarchism as a political theory..we clearly cannot.. tolerate assassination of rulers on the ground that it is 'propaganda by deed' or sociological experiment. **1929** G. Seldes *You can't print That!* 427 The term propaganda has not the sinister meaning in Europe which it has acquired in America... In European business offices the word means advertising or boosting generally. **1938** R. G. Collingwood *Princ. Art* ii. 32 Where a certain practical activity is stimulated as expedient, that which stimulates it is advertisement or (in the current modern sense, not the old sense) propaganda. **1957** R. N. C. Hunt *Guide to Communist Jargon* 132 The Soviet Government not only has an elaborate machinery for conducting such propaganda abroad..but also does the same at home through the press, radio, films etc. **1974** *Anderson* (S. Carolina) *Independent* 23 Apr. 4A/6 CIA went on employing propaganda fronts long after anybody except professionals on both sides was paying any attention to the propaganda. **1976** A. J. Russell *Pour Hemlock* xiv. 166 White propaganda, the truth; gray, a composition of half-truths and distortions; or black, a pack of lies.

4. *attrib.* and *Comb.*, as (sense *3) *propaganda campaign, chief, film, fund, leaflet, poster, raid, technique, war, warfare.* (See also sense 2 b in Dict.) **propaganda machine,** an organization responsible for the dissemination of propaganda.

1937 Koestler *Spanish Testament* vi. 133 One of the most effective propaganda campaigns launched by the rebels was that relating to the alleged shooting of hostages by the Madrid Government. **1974** *Encycl. Brit. Macropædia* XV. 39/2 Today several hundred more or less scholarly books and thousands of articles shed substantial light on the psychology, techniques, and effects of propaganda campaigns, major and minor. **1942** *Short Guide Gr. Brit.* (U.S. War Dept.) 1 The first and major duty Hitler has given his propaganda chiefs is to separate Britain and America. **1950** Koestler in *God that Failed* 27 The absurdity of a propaganda-chief who only reads his own paper. **1973** D. May *Laughter in Djakarta* x. 161 It's a propaganda film..anti-neo-colonialism. **1978** Cadogan & Craig *Women & Children First* x. 224 According to widely shown propaganda films, the most adept German spy was bound to give himself away eventually through mispronunciation. **1842** *Communist Chronicle & Communitarian Apostle* I. v. 77 The propaganda fund shall be devoted to the propagation of the doctrines of communism. **1947** F. Frenaye tr. *C. Levi's Christ stopped at Eboli* (1948) xvii. 162 When their ship came back to Trieste from Odessa, Communist propaganda leaflets were found on board. **1978** A. Waugh *Best Wine Last* xv. 178 The propaganda leaflets that our aeroplanes scattered behind the German lines. **1948** Propaganda machine [see *machine *sb.* 8]. **1972** H. MacInnes *Message from Malaga* ii. 35 A propaganda machine is only as effective as people are stupid. **1978** F. Maclean *Take Nine Spies* iv. 153 The Russians only responded with counter-blasts from their own propaganda machine. **1945** *New Yorker* 31 Mar. 52/1 A propaganda poster pasted on the remaining walls. **1979** *Listener* 1 Nov. 604/3 English [war] propaganda posters are bland alongside those of America, Holland or Sweden. **1934** *Ann. Reg. 1933* I. 181 On July 1 occurred the first of a series of propaganda raids by German aeroplanes over the Austrian frontier, when leaflets abusing the Dollfuss Government were dropped. **1927** H. D. Lasswell (*title*) Propaganda technique in the World War. **1975** *New Yorker* 21 Apr. 133/1 The Communists are taking full advantage of their highly developed propaganda techniques. **1838** tr. *Recoll. Caulincourt, Duke of Vicenza* I. iv. 74 The English Cabinet was well aware that a propaganda war was impossible as long as Russia should continue allied to France. **1974** D. Seaman *Bomb that could Lip-Read* vi. 49 The I.R.A...are already winning the propaganda war, the one that finally matters. **1979** *Guardian* 22 Feb. 6/1 The [Russian] propaganda war against China continues to intensify. **1942** *R.A.F. Jrnl.* 18 Apr. 31 Propaganda warfare in the field was used.

propaganda (prǫpăgæ·ndă), *v.* [f. the sb.] *trans.* = Propagandize *v.*

1921 J. F. Porter *Sir Edward Elgar* 10 Elgar..never attempted to propaganda his work. **1949** H. L. Mencken in *Philologica: Malone Anniversary Stud.* 317 There is..a desire to get rid of circumlocution and the waste of words, as in..to propaganda, to steam-roller, to belly-ache.

propagandic. For *rare*—[0] in Dict. read *rare* and add examples.

1939 W. Fortescue *There's Rosemary* xxxix. 242 Next morning I studied my newspaper to see if my propagandic statistics had been faithfully recorded and was aghast to see, in 'leaded caps', a paragraph headed *The Baby fizzled.* **1946** L. Krey in W. S. Knickerbocker *20th Cent. English* 409 Just such grossly indecent or propagandic publications as often yield fabulous returns.

propagandism. Add: (Earlier examples.)

1800 *Aurora* (Philadelphia) 8 May 3 A war undertaken by the coalesced power against the system of *Propagandism* by which they have been menaced. **1807** *Weekly Inspector* (N.Y.) 28 Mar. 75/1 We have ever been disposed to attribute the wonderful success of the French, since their revolutionary era, to *Propagandism* or, in other words, to the poison of their principles, circulated by their emissaries; and corrupting the *mind* of the nations they proposed to attack.

propagandist, *sb.* (*a.*) Add: **A.** *sb.* **1.** (Earlier and later examples.)

1797 Burke *Two Lett. on Conduct of our Domestick Parties* 109 How can I help it if this Royal propagandist will preach the doctrine of the rights of men? **1929** J. Fineberg tr. *Lenin's What is to be Done?* in *Coll. Wks.* IV. II. 147 A propagandist..must present 'many ideas', so many indeed that they will be understood as a whole only by a (comparatively) few persons. **1942** *Sun* (Baltimore) 12 Jan. 8/1 The rumors have been fostered by Hitler's propagandists. **1976** *Daily Tel.* 20 July 3/1 Dr Goebbels, the Nazi propagandist, could not have invented a more vilifying tag than that of the Black Panther.

B. *adj.* (Earlier examples.)

1824 D. Webster *Speech on Greek Revolution* 5 It may be easy to call this resolution *Quixotic,* the emanation of a crusading or propagandist spirit. **1833** *Blackw. Mag.* June 933 Portugal..has been abandoned..to the revolutionary spoliation and propagandist arts of France.

propagandistic *a.* (further examples); **propagandistically** *adv.* (further example).

1941 G. G. Scholem *Major Trends in Jewish Mysticism* viii. 306 Men of tireless literary and propagandistic activity. **1957** I. Asimov *Earth is Room Enough* (1960) 19 Such propagandistic lies were not uncommon. **1976** *New Yorker* 26 Jan. 66/3 Kim Il Sung figures he has made enough headway, even propagandistically, at the United Nations for the moment. **1977** *N.Y. Rev. Bks.* 23 June

4/2 There was no such propagandistic cause as anti-communism to impel those peach-cheeked youngsters to wage a war against an enemy caught up in the thrall of a fanatical, even suicidal nationalism.

propagandize, *v.* Add: **a.** (Further example.) Also, to subject (a person) to propaganda; to encourage to a belief thus.

1928 *Observer* 11 Mar. 13/4 A crowd of the peasants.. tries to 'propagandize' an American soldier. **1933** *Sun* (Baltimore) 3 Oct. 12/1 Those who have only money enough..should not be propagandized into spending beyond their means. **1938** *Daily Tel.* 7 Jan. 12/4 They had too much common-sense to be propagandized. **1969** *Wall St. Jrnl.* 14 Feb. 1/6 South Korea..propagandizes its citizens heavily. **1974** tr. *Sniečkus's Soviet Lithuania* 31 The Party..propagandised Marxist-Leninist theory and intensified the ideological training of its members.

b. (Further examples.) Also, to disseminate propaganda.

1967 *Cold Spring Harbor Symp. Quant. Biol.* XXXII. 7/2 Being honest, I always have to mention when I am propagandizing against cigarettes—that 80% of heavy cigarette smokers do *not* die of lung cancer. **1974** K. Millett *Flying* III. x. 335, I propagandize and make coffee. **1977** *New Yorker* 6 June 137/1 He propagandized for wilderness preservation as well as urban amenity.

Hence **propaga·ndizing** *ppl. a.* and *vbl. sb.*

1855 J. D. Howard in *N. Amer. Rev.* LXXX. 5 The early conquests of the Saracens, then, are to be ascribed ..to the propagandizing spirit of their new faith. **1860** *Even. Jrnl. Tract* No. 13. 2 What class of men north and south did Mr. Fillmore represent? The old Whig or Clay party south who had no sympathies with the slave propagandising element of the Democratic party. **1927** S. Bent *Ballyhoo* iii. 87 The propagandizing of screened officials. **1978** *N.Y. Times* 30 Mar. B2/1 Here is a perfectly legal industry..based on the commercial exploitation and propagandizing of something that is illegal. **1979** *Country Life* 8 Nov. 1687/4 'Folk song' is a silly, sentimental, misleading and propagandising concept.

propagate, *v.* Add: **4.** (Examples of the active voice.)

1973 *Sci. Amer.* Feb. 73/2 Internal waves propagate energy through the body of a stratified fluid in much the same way that energy is propagated by waves at the surface. **1975** *Nature* 8 May 157/1 The flagellum of this organism propagates waves both distally and proximally in common with other trypanosomes.

b. *refl.* for *passive.*

1880 [see *cathode ray* s.v. *cathode c]. **1908** tr. *Suess' Face of Earth* III. iv. i. 4 Some kind of wave propagating itself freely through the crust of the earth.

c. *intr.* for *passive.* To be propagated, to travel.

1943 F. E. Terman *Radio Engineers' Handbk.* III. 255 Waves of a variety of types may propagate down a wave guide. **1957** J. J. Stoker *Water Waves* x. 374 In practically all of this book we assume that the medium in which waves propagate is water. **1966** C. R. Tottle *Sci. Engin. Materials* vii. 168 Griffith in 1920..proposed that glass possessed many fine cracks in the surface, which could propagate through the material and cause failure. **1967** *Oceanogr. & Marine Biol.* V. 31 The elevation ζ may be specified as a function of position and time, representing an external surge propagating into the sea area. **1969** *Sci. Jrnl.* Dec. 44/3 In a waveguide the microwave energy propagates down the inside of a hollow conductor. **1971** *Nature* 3 Dec. 292/2 When a laser beam propagates through a mixture of gases. **1974** *Sci. Amer.* Jan. 38/3 In the nerves of both higher and lower animals it is the cell membrane that..enables the nerve impulse to be set up and to propagate. **1977** *Nature* 21 July 203/2 The proton is knocked out of the nucleus and could be observed propagating freely after the collision.

propagating *ppl. a.* (examples of the sense 'travelling').

1971 *Sci. Amer.* June 22/1 The energy stored in the inverted population is then available to amplify a propagating light wave at a particular frequency. **1972** *Ibid.* Jan. 18/3 The muffling of seismic signals might be achieved by conducting the test in an underground material where a comparatively small fraction of the energy of the explosion would appear in a propagating seismic wave. **1973** *Physics Bull.* Nov. 657/3 It may be helpful to consider first the ways in which propagating gravitational waves are like electromagnetic waves.

propagation. Add: **7.** *Chem.* In a chain reaction, the step or series of steps in which product molecules are formed or polymer chains lengthened, but which is self-perpetuating by virtue of the regeneration or relocation of reactive centres; e.g. in polymerization, reaction of a radical with a molecule of monomer to form a longer radical. Freq. *attrib.*

1928 *Proc. R. Soc.* A. CXXII. 621 The conditions which govern the propagation of the stable reaction chains. **1940** *Ann. Rep. Progr. Chem.* XXXVI. 74 When an active molecule possesses such a long lifetime, the rate of formation and destruction of these centres plays no part in the rate of polymerisation, which is then solely determined by the velocity of the propagation reaction. **1950** *Thorpe's Dict. Appl. Chem.* (ed. 4) X. 88/1 This is followed by the propagation stage, in which successive additions of monomer molecules occur, maintaining an odd electron, characteristic of a free radical, at the end of the growing chain. **1964** J. M. Crabtree et al. tr. *V. N. Kondrat'ev's Chem. Kinetics of Gas Reactions* ix. 613 The chain propagation processes involving HO_2 radicals are important in the so-called slow oxidation of hydrogen which occurs.. at relatively high pressures. **1973** K. J. Saunders *Org. Polymer Chem.* i. 10 This new radical then adds further monomer molecules in rapid succession to form a polymer chain. In this propagation the active centre remains, being continuously relocated at the end of the chain.

8. *attrib.* and *Comb.*, as *propagation tray*; **propagation coefficient, constant,** or **factor** *Physics*, the coefficient of the distance in an equation representing the propagation of a wave (quot. 1943 represents an equivalent def.); **propagation function** *Physics*, = *propagator 3.

1943 *Gloss. Terms Telecommunications (B.S.I.)* 7 *Propagation coefficient, propagation constant,* the natural logarithm of the vector ratio of the steady-state amplitudes of a wave at a specified frequency, at points in the direction of propagation separated by unit length. **1911** J. A. Fleming *Propagation Electr. Currents* ii. 68, *P* is a complex quantity and therefore may be written in the form $\alpha + j\beta$. It is called the Propagation constant of the line. **1963** R. W. Ditchburn *Light* (ed. 2) ii. 28 The wavelength..is denoted by λ. An associated constant $\kappa = 2\pi/\lambda$ is called the wavelength constant (or propagation constant). **1976** G. R. Olhoeft in R. G. J. Strens *Physics & Chem. of Minerals & Rocks* 262 All of the material properties (other than geometric boundary conditions) which are important to the description of the propagation of an electromagnetic wave (or lack of propagation) are described in the propagation constant by the quantities μ, ϵ, and σ. **1958** Condon & Odishaw *Handbk. Physics* IV. vii. 108/2 The solution is a plane wave..varying periodically in time with the frequency $\nu = \omega/2\pi$ and advancing in the $+x$ direction through space with a complex propagation factor $\gamma = j\omega\sqrt{\epsilon^*\mu^*} = \alpha + j\beta$. **1949** *Physical Rev.* LXXVI. 770/1 Many of the properties of the integrals are analyzed using formal properties of invariant propagation functions. **1970** J. Schwinger *Particles, Sources, & Fields* iii. 145 Considering spin 0 particles and their real scalar sources,..we examine the effect of adding an additional weak source $\delta K(x)$. It is given by $\delta W(k) = \int(dx)\delta K(x)\phi(x)$, where $\phi(x) = \int(dx')\times \Delta_+(x-x')K(x')$. This combination of source and propagation function, measuring the effect of pre-existing sources on a weak test source, is the *field* of the sources. **1977** *Grimsby Even. Tel.* 31 May 9/5 A hundred small cannabis plants in propagation trays, plus smoking pipes and an LSD tablet were found.

propagator. Add: **1. c.** (Later examples.) Also, a small box with a transparent lid and a base that can be heated, for germinating seeds or raising seedlings.

1914 W. F. Rowles *Garden under Glass* i. 16 The propagator itself may consist of a box..covered by loose sheets of glass. **1950** E. J. King *Propagation of Plants* iii. 29 A propagator is a small frame built inside a heated greenhouse in such a way as to give even higher temperatures than those in the main part of the house. **1971** *Daily Tel.* 13 Feb. 7/3 A week or two lost in raising seeds in a heated greenhouse, or electric propagator in the home, is not a matter of extreme urgency. **1976** *Abingdon Herald* 9 Dec. 5/2 A small propagator..enables one to raise seeds at any time. **1979** *Garden* CIV (Advt.), Humex Mono-top Propagator. Pick of the bunch—the electrically heated propatray base surmounted by an.. enclosure with sliding doors for easy access.

d. The male copulative organ; the penis. Now *arch.*

1670 J. Ogilby *Africa* 451 Lastly, they have little Bellies, broad Feet, long Toes, and furnish'd, as most of the Blacks upon the Guinee Coast, with large Propagators. **1971** *Black Scholar* June 12/1 Setting foot on the shores of West Africa in 1550, the Englishman was struck by the African's religion..and his 'Propagator', which he perceived monstrous.

3. *Physics.* An algebraic function that is taken as representing the propagation of a particle on the sub-atomic scale, esp. between its space–time points of creation and annihilation.

1951 *Physical Rev.* LXXXIV. 1233/1 G' (1,2), the 'quantum propagator', is a function of $(x_{\mu 1}x_{\mu 2})$ not containing any Dirac operators. **1958** *Ibid.* CXII. 1417/1 A coincidence arrangement appears capable of testing the electron propagator at distances approaching the nucleon Compton wavelength, which is comparable with our present limit on the photon propagator. **1973** J. A. Reissland *Physics of Photons* vi. 186 If the effect of a perturbation $H'(t)$ is to create a particle at position $\mathbf{r}'$ at time t', the function (6.19) traces the propagation of that particle until it is removed at $\mathbf{r}$ at a time t. Hence the term 'propagator' for the one-particle Green's function $G(\mathbf{r},t;\ \mathbf{r}',t') \equiv i\eta(t-t')\langle a(\mathbf{r},t)a^+(\mathbf{r}',t')\rangle$ where $a^+(\mathbf{r}',t')$ creates a particle at $\mathbf{r}',t'$ and $a(\mathbf{r},t)$ destroys it at $(\mathbf{r},t)$. **1974** *Physics Bull.* May 191/2 Propagators (or Green's functions) have been much used by physicists.

propagule. Restrict *rare* to sense in Dict. and add: **2.** A seed, spore, or other product of a plant which is disseminated to form a new individual; also, occasionally used as a name for the products of asexual reproduction in certain lower animals. Hence **propa·gular** *a.*, of or pertaining to a propagule.

1905 F. E. Clements *Res. Methods Ecol.* iv. 241 Dormant seeds and propagules are abundant. **1959** *New Biol.* XXVIII. 80 Extrinsic barriers between breeding populations..effectively prevent or check gene flow because they are not crossed by adults, or by seeds, pollen, or other 'propagules'. **1965** Bell & Coombe tr. *Strasburger's Textbk. Bot.* 204 Propagules may consist of single cells (spores), groups of cells (gemmae), or entire organs or complexes of organs (bulbils). **1967** *Oceanogr. & Marine Biol.* V. 494 Several hydroids are particularly adapted.. to ensure asexual reproduction by means of propagular stolons whose brittle and curved extremities can catch a neighbouring leaf. **1969** *New Scientist* 20 Nov. 402/1 Any fungal propagules landing on its surface will be killed. **1974** *New Phytologist* LXXIII. 981 Wallace pointed out that the small propagules of Compositae..allowed that family to gain an early footing on islands. **1977** *Nature* 3 Nov. 48/2, I report here that the marine red alga *Centroceras* produces missile-shaped propagules which are carried away by ocean currents.

propamidine (propæ·midīn). *Pharm.* [f. Prop(ane + Amid(e + -ine[5].] A diamidine with bactericidal and fungicidal properties which is used, usu. in the form of its isethionate (a white, hygroscopic powder), in dressing minor wounds or burns; 1,3-di(4-amidinephenoxy)propane, $CH_2[CH_2 \cdot O \cdot C_6H_4 . C(NH)(NH_2)]_2$.

1941, 1951 [see *pentamidine]. **1964** W. G. Smith *Allergy & Tissue Metabolism* iv. 56 Mast cell degranulation will account for the histamine liberating activity of compound 48/80. This is also true of the histamine releasing properties of..propamidine. **1976** 'J. Herriot' *Vets might Fly* (1977) ii. 20 Lord Hulton was a devotee of May and Baker's Propamidine Cream and used it for all minor cuts and grazes in his cattle.

propane. Add: **2.** *attrib.*, as *propane gas.*

1974 *Janet Frazer Catal.* Spring/Summer 458/4 Portable refrigerator... Suitable for use with Butane or Propane gas. **1979** 'J. Ross' *Rattling of Old Bones* iii. 25 The propane-gas lamps..were flooding the cupboard with hissing white light.

propanediol (prōᵘ:pēⁱndəi·ǫl). *Chem.* [f. Propane + Di-[2] + -ol.] = *propylene glycol* s.v. *propylene 2; also, a derivative of this.

1894 G. M'Gowan tr. *Bernthsen's Text-bk. Org. Chem.* (ed. 2) 206 Propylene glycol is known in two isomeric forms, viz.: (*a*) Tri-methylene glycol† or β-Propylene glycol,..(*b*) α-Propylene glycol‡. [*Note*] † 1-3-Propanediol. ‡ 1-2-Propane-diol. **1952** *Jrnl. Pharmacol. & Exper. Therapeutics* CV. 452 The 1,3-propanediol ethers have greater protective action in electroshock seizures than the corresponding position isomers of the 1,2-propanediol series. **1966** *McGraw-Hill Encycl. Sci. & Technol.* XIV. 16/2 According to basic chemical structure, four categories of tranquilizers are delineated: phenothiazines..; rauwolfia derivatives..; propanediols, for example, meprobamate or Miltown; diphenylurethanes. **1976** *Ann. Rev. Microbiol.* XXX. 421 A clear example of evolution to reverse function in the laboratory is the evolution of propanediol catabolism through recruitment of enzymes normally involved in L-fucose and L-lactate metabolism.

propanidid (propæ·nidid). *Pharm.* [Arbitrarily f. Propan(e.] A colourless or yellowish oily liquid which is given intravenously in solution as a short-acting anæsthetic; propyl-4-diethyl-carbamoylmethoxy-3-methoxyphenylacetate, $C_{18}H_{27}NO_5$.

1964 *Brit. Jrnl. Anaesthesia* XXXVI. 655/1 The new intravenous narcotic propanidid..displays a biphasic action on ventilation consisting of stimulation followed by depression. **1965** *Med. Jrnl. Austral.* 21 Aug. 329 Propanidid is a unique, short-acting intravenous anæsthetic agent with many interesting features—in particular, its mode of inactivation. **1971** Pryor & Macalister *Gen. Anaesthetic & Sedation Techniques Dentistry* x. 63 Propanidid has made a tremendous contribution towards making the induction of anaesthesia pleasanter for the patient and working conditions easier for the dental surgeon.

propanol (prōᵘ·pănǫl). *Chem.* [f. Propan(e + -ol.] Either of the isomers of propyl alcohol; sometimes *spec.* normal propyl alcohol, 1-propanol (cf. *isopropanol* s.v. *iso- b).

[**1892** *Proc. Chem. Soc.* 16 June 128 Citric acid, on this system, would be named propanoltrioic acid or simply propanoltri-acid.] **1894** G. M'Gowan tr. *Bernthsen's Text-bk. Org. Chem.* (ed. 2) 92 Normal propyl alcohol. [*Note*] 1-Propanol. *Ibid.* 93 Secondary propyl alcohol. [*Note*] 2-Propanol. **1926** H. G. Rule tr. *Schmidt's Text-bk. Org. Chem.* I. 111 Propyl alcohol, propanol, C_3H_7.OH. Both of the theoretically possible structural isomerides of this formula are known. **1951** I. L. Finar *Org. Chem.* I. iv. 62 Propylene, propene, C_3H_6, may be prepared by heating propanol or *iso*-propanol with sulphuric acid. **1964** N. G. Clark *Mod. Org. Chem.* viii. 140 Two isomeric propanols sxist, of which the primary alcohol is less important. **1964** J. C. Matthews *Mod. Chem. Course* xxv. 302 Add 20–25 drops of ethanol or propanol slowly with shaking.

propantheline (propæ·nþēlīn). *Pharm.* [f. Prop(yl + *x)anth(ene + -*el* (f. E(thy)l) + -ine[5].] A white, bitter-tasting powder, $C_{23}H_{30}NO_3Br$, which is a quaternary ammonium bromide derived from xanthene, and is a parasympatholytic agent used esp. for treating the symptoms of peptic ulceration. Also *propantheline bromide.* Cf. *Pro-Banthine.

1954 *Brit. Jrnl. Pharmacol.* IX. 218 (*heading*) A comparison of the peripheral parasympatholytic and autonomic ganglion blocking activities of methantheline ('Banthine') and propantheline ('Pro-Banthine') with atropine and hexamethonium. *Ibid.* Propantheline (2'-di*iso*propylaminoethyl xanthene-9-carboxylate methobromide) is the isopropyl analogue of methantheline and differs from it only in degree of activity.., its actions being qualitatively similar. **1955** *Lancet* 10 Sept. 526/2 Propantheline bromide can be used to relieve colic, whether due to spasm of the sphincter or associated with biliary reflux and pancreatitis. **1958** [see *PRO-BANTHINE]. **1970** O. L. WADE *Adverse Reaction to Drugs* ii. 13 Atropine or propantheline in the doses required to reduce gastric motility and gastric secretion in the treatment of peptic ulcer may cause unpleasant dryness of the mouth or blurring of vision. **1977** *Lancet* 26 Nov. 1134/1 The effects of propantheline bromide on the eyes should be considered when the drug is used in the treatment of hyperhidrosis.

propassion. (Later examples.)
1875 H. E. MANNING *Internal Mission of Holy Ghost* xiv. 392 In our Divine Lord there were no passions... We say indeed, that there were in Him pro-passions. **1876** —— *Glories of Sacred Heart* ix. 266 All those pro-passions, as they are called—because the Church never speaks of passions when it speaks of the Sacred Heart.

propellent, *a.* and *sb.* Add: Now usu. spelt **-ant. A.** *adj.* (Further examples.)
1919 R. H. GODDARD in *Smithsonian Misc. Coll.* LXXI. II. 6 This enables high chamber pressures to be employed..and also permits most of the mass of the rocket to consist of propellant material. **1945** *Soap & Sanitary Chemicals* Apr. 125/3 Methyl chloride is an excellent propellant gas for aerosols to be used against insects out of doors.

B. *sb.* **a.** (Further examples.)
1917 W. S. CHURCHILL in M. Gilbert *Winston S. Churchill* (1977) IV. Compan. I. 125 What proportion of our total explosive or propellant output could be based upon 10 million gallons of whiskey? **1931** L. H. MORRISON *Amer. Diesel Engines* v. 129 The explosion of these lighter parts of the fuel provides the propellant whereby the remainder of the fuel is injected into the engine cylinder in a finely atomized condition. **1936** W. S. CHURCHILL in *Second World War* (1948) I. 538 By ammunition is meant projectiles (both bombs and shells) and cartridge-cases containing propellent. **1939** W. BEVERIDGE *Blockade & Civilian Population* 8 Fats, broadly speaking, are all directly convertible into munitions, because they can be used, and are very largely used, in making propellants. **1966** *McGraw-Hill Encycl. Sci. & Technol.* V. 153/1 Besides black powder, which is mainly used in sporting rifles, the common gun propellants are either nitrocellulose or a mixture of nitrocellulose and nitroglycerine.

b. A substance that is used (alone, or reacting with another) as a source of the hot gases that provide the thrust in a rocket engine. Cf. *FUEL *sb.* 2*c, *OXIDIZER 1, *MONOPROPELLANT *sb.* and *a.*
1919 R. H. GODDARD in *Smithsonian Misc. Coll.* LXXI. II. 67 Let us assume, for case (a) (many small secondary rockets), as well as for case (b) (large secondary rockets), that the ratio of mass of metal to mass of propellant is the minimum reasonable amount that can be expected. **1948** M. J. ZUCROW *Princ. Jet Propulsion & Gas Turbines* xii. 467 The propellants employed in a rocket motor may be a solid, two liquids (fuel plus oxidizer), or materials containing an adequate supply of available oxygen in their chemical composition (mono-propellants). **1955** *Times* 29 June 16/3 Some five years ago we faced a difficult decision as to the most suitable propellents for the type of rockets which we were developing. **1957** *Spaceflight* I. 51/1 A propellant can be either fuel or oxidizer. **1967** *New Scientist* 21 Sept. 594/2 Project officials ordered a series of critical tests to determine just how much propellant would be available for use after the main retrorocket had been fired. **1974** *Sci. Amer.* Aug. 7/1 (Advt.), Launch weight of the spacecraft was only 1,108 pounds, including 66 pounds of propellant and 122 pounds of science instruments.

c. The compressed fluid in an aerosol container or the like that causes its contents to be ejected.
1945 *Soap & Sanitary Chemicals* Apr. 127/1 Nitrous oxide also has a pressure too high for it to be practical as a propellant. **1957** H. R. SHEPHERD in E. Sagarin *Cosmetics Sci. & Technol.* xxxvi. 804 While some aerosol cosmetics are made with a single propellent, it is customary to use a mixture or a solution of propellents. **1966** *McGraw-Hill Encycl. Sci. & Technol.* V. 279/1 In the small first-aid water fire extinguisher, a propellant must be provided. Usually this is carbon dioxide. **1973** *Daily Tel.* 21 Aug. 15/7 The propellent in the anti-perspirant caused freezing in the lung tissues resulting in loss of oxygen and death. *Ibid.* 15/8 A variety of compressed or liquified bases are used in aerosols and technically known as propellents. Most are halogenated hydrocarbons, which are also refrigerants, and sniffing of such propellents is a recognised form of drug abuse in Britain and the United States. **1978** *N.Y. Times* 30 Mar. 62/3 The nitrous-oxide cartridges are made for use as the propellant in restaurant-sized equipment for whipping cream and non-dairy toppings.

propeller. Add: Also propellor. **3. a.** (Further example.)
1980 *Daily Tel.* 22 Aug. 2/3 SMM Engineering..has won an £800,000 order..for a propellor and a bow steering unit for an 80,000-ton tanker.

c. A device on an aeroplane analogous to a ship's propeller in form and function; now always, an airscrew (formerly, a pusher as opposed to a tractor).
1842 W. S. HENSON *Brit. Patent 9478* 2 In the place of the movement or power for onward progress being obtained by movement of the extended surface or plane, as is the case with the wings of birds, I apply suitable paddle wheels or other proper mechanical propellers. **1843** G. CAYLEY in *Mechanics' Mag.* 8 Apr. 278/1 The broad horizontal rudder, or tail, H, capable of being turned on its hinge to any angle,..gives the power of ascent and descent when the propellers are used. **1853** —— *Let.* 22 June in J. L. Pritchard *Sir George Cayley* (1961) 263 When perfected this toy [*sc.* Chinese flying top] furnishes a very beautiful specimen of the action of the screw propeller in air. **1871** *English Mechanic* 27 Jan. 448/2 Through the instrumentality of the hollow bladed screw-propeller.. shall we..be enabled to sustain and propel the mechanism which we shall construct, in and through the atmosphere. **1888** H. MIDDLETON *Brit. Patent 9725* 5 Propellors and supporters for flying machines consisting of curved flexible wings with ribs. **1894**, etc. [see *airscrew* s.v. *AIR *sb.*[1] B. III. 6]. **1908** H. G. WELLS *War in Air* viii. 271 She..swept down to the water..and came..rolling and..writhing.., halting and then coming on again, with her torn and bent propeller still beating the air. **1917** R. B. MATTHEWS *Aviation Pocket-bk. 1917* iv. 93 An airscrew is described as a tractor when placed in front of the main planes, and as a propeller when fitted behind. **1928** *Trans. Inst. Mining Engineers* LXXVI. 110 A considerable amount of research-work has been carried out on screw propellors in wind-tunnels. **1937** J. H. YOUNGER et al. *Airplane Maintenance* xv. 298 A propeller develops thrust by its reaction on a mass of air, which it pushes backward. **1968** MILLER & SAWYERS *Technical Devel. Mod. Aviation* vi. 205 The advantage of the turboprop stems essentially from the greater efficiency of the propeller than the jet as a means of propulsion at low speeds and for take-off. **1977** D. ANTHONY *Stud Game* vi. 38 A lounge decorated with..an ancient propeller Lindbergh might have used.

5. *propeller efficiency*; *propeller-driven* adj.; **propeller fan,** a fan that produces a flow of air parallel to the axis of rotation of its impeller; *esp.* one with the impeller unenclosed or in a very short casing that does not restrict the air flow; **propeller shaft,** a shaft transmitting power from an engine to a propeller or to the driven wheels of a motor vehicle; **propeller turbine** = *TURBOJET; usu. *attrib.*
1953 D. O. DOMMASCH *Elem. Propeller & Helicopter Aerodynamics* iii. 69 The development of the turbo-prop engine has made flight at high subsonic Mach numbers possible for propeller-driven aircraft. **1973** *Black Panther* 13 Oct. 14/2 They had steered 553 in behind a small propeller driven plane. **1909** *Westm. Gaz.* 4 Mar. 4/2 Propeller efficiency also constitutes one of the most serious drawbacks to the experimenter. **1897** *Proc. Inst. Mech. Engineers* 469 The propeller fan was for volume of air without compression, the centrifugal for volume with compression. **1937** C. KELLER et al. *Theory & Performance Axial-Flow Fans* i. 1 In axial-flow or propeller fans the air or gas flows essentially in an axial direction through the fan. **1950** T. H. F. HOLMAN et al. *Textbk. Heating & Ventilating* vi. 77 Fans are of two main types, the propellor fan..and the centrifugal fan. **1966** W. C. OSBORNE *Fans* ii. 47 Larger propeller fans of up to 24 ft (7·5 m) or more in diameter are often really axial flow fans in very short casings, since such a design is mechanically more satisfactory. *Ibid.*, Large 'propeller' fans are commonly used on cooling towers. **1970** M. G. LUFF *Air Conditioning* viii. 261 In terms of ventilation and air conditioning there are three main types of fan, the propeller fan, the axial flow fan and the centrifugal fan. **1839**, etc. Propeller shaft [in Dict.]. **1913** A. E. BERRIMAN *Aviation* iii. 24 In monoplanes the propeller-shaft is ordinarily on a level with the middle of the body. **1945** P. H. WILKINSON *Aircraft Engines of World* 345 The drive shaft..drives the two concentric propeller shafts for the two contra-rotating propellers through planetary spur reduction gears. **1962** *Which? Car Suppl.* Oct. 143/1 New propellor shaft coupling. **1973** *Daily Tel.* 13 July 13 (Advt.), There's no ugly propeller shaft tunnel in the floor of the car to spoil the stretch of deep-pile carpets. **1945** *Jrnl. R. Aeronaut. Soc.* XLIX. 196/2 Perhaps the large blower of the jet or propeller turbine unit may encourage the study of boundary layer control possibilities of higher maximum lift coefficients. **1951** *Engineering* 6 July 8/1 The propeller-turbine engine could be expected to improve appreciably in power output and specific weight as combustion temperatures were increased from current values. **1968** MILLER & SAWYERS *Technical Devel. Mod. Aviation* vi. 183 (*heading*) Propeller turbines succeed with the Viscount. *Ibid.*, The propeller-turbine engine was of more immediate interest to the airlines than the jet, and by 1950 the idea of fitting it to existing airplanes like the DC-6 and Constellation was becoming widely accepted in the United States.

propelling, *vbl. sb.* and *ppl. a.* Add: **b.** *ppl. a.* Also in *Comb.*, as *propelling pencil*, a mechanical pencil containing a screw by which the lead may be projected and retracted.
1895 *Montgomery Ward Catal.* 185/1 Men's Propelling and Repelling Pencil..takes full size and length of lead. **1933** D. L. SAYERS *Murder must Advertise* x. 169 If Bredon really wanted a propelling pencil he ought to get an Eversharp. **1955** S. BECKETT *Molloy* 136 Between my fountain-pen and my propelling-pencil. **1962** L. DEIGHTON *Ipcress File* xi. 71 Murray used a propelling pencil with changeable coloured leads. **1976** M. BUTTERWORTH *Remains to be Seen* ii. 15 Silver propelling-pencil poised over the page.

propensely, *adv.* Add: **3.** Favourably, readily. *nonce-use.*
1922 JOYCE *Ulysses* 409 If I had poor luck with Bass's mare, perhaps this draught of his may serve me more propensely.

proper, *a.* (*adv.*, *sb.*) Add: **I.** *adj.* **2. c.** *Physics.* (See quot. 1924.) [tr. G. *eigen(zeit)* proper (time) (H. Minkowski 1908, in *Nachr. von der k. Ges. der Wissensch. zu Gottingen* (Math.-phys. Klasse) 103).]
1916 *Monthly Notices R. Astron. Soc.* LXXVI. 704 The element *ds* integrated along the geodetic line gives $s = \int ds$. This is what Minkowski calls the proper-time of the material particle. **1923** *Proc. R. Soc.* A. CII. 530 Where *m* and $(-e)$ are the 'proper mass' and charge of the electron respectively. **1924** A. S. EDDINGTON *Math. Theory Relativity* i. 34 Quantities referred to the space-time system of an observer moving with the body considered are often distinguished by the prefix proper- (German, *Eigen-*), e.g. proper-length, proper-volume, proper-density, proper-mass = invariant mass. **1942** P. G. BERMAN *Introd. Theory Relativity* iv. 41 Whenever the two events can be just connected by a light ray which leaves the site of one event at the time it occurs and arrives at the site of the other event as it takes place, the proper time interval τ_{12} between them vanishes. **1952** C. MØLLER *Theory of Relativity* iv. 137 While q^0/c^2 expresses the source density of proper mass, we see that the source density for relativistic mass is $((\mathbf{f}.\mathbf{u}) + q)/c^2$. **1964** W. G. V. ROSSER *Introd. Theory Relativity* iii. 102, l_0..is the length of the fish measured in the coordinate system in which it is at rest; l_0 is called the proper length of the fish, whilst l..is the length of the fish measured in an inertial reference frame relative to which the fish is moving with uniform velocity. **1970** *Nature* 17 Oct. 272/1 Proper mass (equivalently, rest-mass, proper energy, or rest-energy) is the most important Lorentz-invariant scalar associated with any system.

3*. *Math.* and *Physics.* Used in collocations as a translation of G. *eigen* own, proper, characteristic.

a. Applied to a vibration or oscillation: = *NORMAL *a.* 2 c.
1873 *Proc. London Math. Soc.* IV. 258 The problem of determining the proper tones of any spherical cavity bounded by rigid walls. **1909** *Westm. Gaz.* 4 Sept. 10/1 All elastic bodies, including metals, when made fast at one end, vibrate when subjected to a shock from outside. The vibrations so caused are what are known as proper vibrations. **1962** S.-I. TOMONAGA *Quantum Mech.* I. i. 16 It was possible to arrange the proper oscillations in order by giving each of them an integral number *s* which has the physical meaning that $(s-1)$ is the number of nodes of the oscillation.

b. = *EIGEN-, as *proper function* = *EIGENFUNCTION; *proper value* = *EIGENVALUE.
1930 RUARK & UREY *Atoms, Molecules & Quanta* xv. 526 Such an aggregate of E values is often referred to as a 'spectrum of characteristic values', or 'proper values'. **1935** PAULING & WILSON *Introd. Quantum Mech.* iii. 58 The functions $\psi_s(x)$ which satisfy Equation 9-8 and also certain auxiliary conditions..are variously called wave functions or eigenfunctions (Eigenfunktionen), or sometimes amplitude functions, characteristic functions, or proper functions. **1938** [see *EIGENVALUE]. **1958** [see *LATENT *a.* i]. **1975** GRAY & ISAACS *New Dict. Physics* 574/1, ψ must always be finite... The integral of $|\psi|^2$ over all space must be equal to 1... Wave functions obtained when these conditions are applied are called proper wave functions and form a set of characteristic functions of the Schrödinger wave equation. These are often called eigenfunctions and correspond to a set of fixed energy values in which the system may exist, called eigenvalues (proper values).

II. 5. c. *Math.* (i) Applied to any subset (subgroup, etc.) that does not constitute the entire set.
1906 W. H. & G. C. YOUNG *Theory of Sets of Points* iii. 16 A set which is contained entirely in another set is called a component of the latter set, and, if there are points of the latter set not belonging to the former set, it is said to be a proper component of the other. **1937** R. D. CARMICHAEL *Introd. Theory of Groups of Finite Order* i. 28 A subgroup of *G* which is not identical with *G* is called a proper subgroup of *G*. **1953** A. A. FRAENKEL *Abstract Set Theory* i. 21 A subset of *S* which is different from *S*, is called a proper subset. **1965** B. MITCHELL *Theory of Categories* i. 6 If the monomorphism $\alpha: A' \rightarrow A$ is not an isomorphism, we shall call A' a proper subobject of *A*.

(ii) Applied to a subgroup (subring, etc.) that does not constitute the entire group, and has more than one element.
1953 W. LEDERMANN *Introd. Theory of Finite Groups* ii. 31 Every group *G* has two trivial or improper subgroups, namely, *G* itself and the group which consists of the unit element by itself $(I^2 = I)$; all other subgroups are called proper subgroups. **1965** PATTERSON & RUTHERFORD *Elem. Abstract Algebra* ii. 39 A subgroup of *G* other than *G* or *E* is called a proper subgroup. *Ibid.* iii. 100 Every non-zero ring has two ideals, namely the ring itself and the subset consisting of 0 alone. Any ideal which is not one of these two is called a proper ideal.

III. 10. c. *proper Bostonian*: = *BRAHMIN b. Also *attrib.* or as *adj.*
1947 C. AMORY (*title*) The Proper Bostonians. *Ibid.* i. 12 Outside observers have claimed to be able to tell the Proper Bostonian male by waistcoat, and the Proper Bostonian female by hat. **1956** C. W. MILLS *Power Elite* iii. 58 Proper Bostonians and proper San Franciscans.. would be genuinely embarrassed..[by] cheap publicity. **1969** A. LASKI *Dominant Fifth* v. 180 Daughter of a not particularly wealthy and certainly not Proper Bostonian American. **1973** R. L. SIMON *Big Fix* i. 10 Her proper Bostonian background, the old shipping family back on Lewisburg Square. **1977** J. CLEARY *High Road to China* vii. 231 She was only a mild rebel: there was still too much of the Proper Bostonian in her.

B. *adv.* **1.** Also, correctly, in a genteel manner (of speech).
1915 *Dialect Notes* IV. 188 Talk proper before your teacher. **1952** M. ALLINGHAM *Tiger in Smoke* ii. 41 Per-

haps she'll 'ave another go at teachin' me to speak proper, pore soul. **1966** F. SHAW et al. (*title*) Lern yerself Scouse. How to talk proper in Liverpool. **1980** *Listener* 22 May 665/1 He has not learnt how to talk proper.

properdin (propə·ɪdin). *Phys.* [f. L. *prō-* PRO-[1] + *perd-ere* to destroy (see PERDITION) + -IN[1].] A protein found in the blood and concerned with the body's response to infection.

1954 *Science* 20 Aug. 279/1 This protein, tentatively named *properdin*.., acts only in conjunction with complement and Mg++ and participates in such diverse activities as the destruction of bacteria, the neutralization of viruses, and the lysis of certain red cells. Properdin is a normal serum constituent and differs from antibody in many respects, particularly in its lack of specificity and in its exact requirements for its interactions. [*Note*] Hans Hirschmann..suggested this name. **1963** C. J. C. BRITTON *Whitby & Britton's Disorders of Blood* (ed. 9) xiv. 356 Properdin levels are low in acute leukæmia. **1975** SPRAGG & GIGLI in Mathieu & Kahan *Immunol. Aspects Anesthetic & Surg. Pract.* vi. 116 Properdin has been highly purified as a distinct protein with a molecular weight of 223,000 daltons.

properly, *adv.* Add: **6.** *Math.* So as to form a proper subset or a proper subgroup (see *PROPER *a.* 5c).

1965 E. SCHENKMAN *Group Theory* iv. 125 If Π is a set of primes, a Sylow Π-subgroup of a group *G* is a Π-subgroup of *G* not properly contained in any Π-subgroup of *G*. **1968** E. T. COPSON *Metric Spaces* i. 6 The set *A* is..properly contained in *B* if every member of *A* belongs to *B* and there is at least one member of *B* which does not belong to *A*. **1971** E. C. DADE in Powell & Higman *Finite Simple Groups* viii. 326 The group *H*..is properly contained in *G*.

Propertian (prǫpə·ɪʃ[i]ăn), *a.* [f. L. *Propertius* (see below) + -AN.] Belonging to or characteristic of Sextus Aurelius Propertius, Latin elegiac poet of the first century B.C., or his poetry.

1871 J. R. LOWELL *My Study Windows* 217 Goethe, who was classic..in his 'Hermann and Dorothea', and at least Propertian in his 'Roman Idyls', wasted his time.. on the mechanical mock-antique of an unreadable 'Achilleis'. **1918** E. POUND *Let.* 22 Nov. in *Lett. J. Joyce* (1966) II. 424, I hope my Propertian ravings will amuse you. **1930** W. S. MAUGHAM *Cakes & Ale* xiv. 161 Love lyrics and elegies in the Propertian manner. **1974** *Classical Q.* XXIV. 96 The verb of the first clause is rendered in English by the pluperfect. The Propertian passage displays a structural similarity.

propertied, *a.* **3.** Delete *nonce-use* and add later example.

1909 M. E. ALBRIGHT *Shakesperian Stage* 147 The Elizabethan stage..was little more than a union of the old *sedes* and *plateæ* of the moralities, or the propertied and unpropertied stages of the interludes.

property, *sb.* Add: **2. d.** *ellipt.*, shares or investments in property.

1964 *Financial Times* 3 Mar. 19/5 There was a little more interest in Properties, sentiment being helped by last Friday's Gallup poll. **1977** *Evening Post* (Nottingham) 24 Jan. 16/9 Properties ran into profit-taking with Haslemere 176p, MEPC 62p, Land Securities 161p, and Stock Conversion 161p on offer.

e. A person (esp. one engaged in show business) regarded as a commercial asset, esp. in phr. *hot property* (cf. *HOT *a.* 6a, 9b), a success or sensation, a 'hit'. *colloq.*

1958 J. BLISH *Case of Conscience* xiv. 153 Signor Egtverchi is now a hot property... Suddenly..he is worth a lot of money. **1969** *Rolling Stone* 28 June 22 The Hagers, potentially hot property, now have Record One **1980** M. GILBERT *Death of Favourite Girl* xii. 114 Katie was a big property by then and..naturally I was ready to talk about her.

5. e. *Linguistics.* An intrinsic aspect or function.

1953 C. E. BAZELL *Linguistic Form* iii. 38 The acoustic and articulatory property-complexes are 'genuine' aspects of the phonemes. **1962** E. F. HADEN et al. *Resonance-Theory for Linguistics* iv. 49 Every entity in language has a Property and a Form... The Property of each entity is internal to it, corresponding to its function in the complex of which it is a part. **1965** N. CHOMSKY *Aspects of Theory of Syntax* iv. 160 In any given linguistic system lexical entries enter into intrinsic semantic relations of a much more systematic sort than is suggested by what has been said so far. We might use the term 'field properties' to refer to these..aspects.

8. a. *property account, developer, -holder* (earlier example), *-owner* (earlier and later examples), *right, speculator, value; property-based, -owning* adjs.; **property bond,** a share or bond in property; **property mark,** a mark indicating ownership; **property qualification** (earlier example); **property tax** (earlier and later examples).

1869 *Bradshaw's Railway Man.* XXI. 417 *Expended*... Property accounts—materials..[$]139,463. **1974** *Terminol. Managem. & Financial Accountancy* (Inst. Cost & Managem. Accountants) 58 *Real or property account*, the record of an asset, (e.g. buildings, plant and equipment, cash, etc.). **1957** K. A. WITTFOGEL *Oriental Despotism* 2 The modern property-based system of industry. **1974** tr. *Wertheim's Evolution & Revolution* 27 Only one of the filiation lines leads to social progress, namely the one passing through the 'property-based', 'multicentered', or ..'open' society. **1970** *Daily Tel.* 17 Jan. 22/3 The considerable expansion of property values since the war.. is the great selling point for property bonds, compared with other investment plans. **1972** *Accountant* 12 Oct., Property bonds..reflect the value of the property owned by the property fund without being subject to the vagaries of the stock exchange. **1970** *Harper's Bazaar* Oct. 76/1 Property developers..wreaked vandalism upon the cities and countryside of England. **1977** M. WALKER *National Front* v. 125 A property developer called Roy Bramwell. **1824** *Deb. Congress U.S.* (1856) 18th Congress 1 Sess., App. II. 3129 The memorial of the..property-holders of the city of Baltimore. **1899** *Amer. Anthropologist* Oct. 601 Property marks are used very frequently by the Eskimo tribes of Alaska. They occur almost exclusively on weapons used in hunting, which, after being dispatched, remain in the bodies of large game. **1865** *Harper's Mag.* July 154/2 It is the nightmare of property-owners. **1941** W. TEMPLE *Citizen & Churchman* v. 75 What are the rights of property-owners in respect of the property which they own? **1979** C. E. SCHORSKE *Fin-de-Siècle Vienna* ii. 46 The property owners of the inner city..feared the competition of vast new housing construction. **1923** *Spectator* 19 May 837/2 It remains to state as clearly as may be what means lie ready to develop a property-owning democracy. **1978** *Countryman* LXXXIII. 37 (*title of poem*) Towards a property-owning democracy. **1807** *Deb. Congress U.S.* 16 Nov. (1852) 916 The Constitution of the United States requires no property qualification in the elected. **1942** W. TEMPLE *Christianity & Social Order* ii. 27 Men are sinful, so property-rights are needed, not so much for the satisfaction of the rich as for the protection of the poor. **1968** *Listener* 27 June 847/1 A friend likened it [*sc.* a vacuum cleaner] to a property speculator's cocktail cabinet. *a* **1974** R. CROSSMAN *Diaries* (1975) I. 46 Nobody in a Labour Cabinet is going to object to an action which is extremely popular outside London and which will only ruin property speculators. **1808** in *57th Rep. R. Comm. Hist. Manuscripts* 139 in *Parl. Papers* 1902 (Cd. 931) LIII. 1 How do the farmers with you talk of the *Property Tax*? **1978** *N.Y. Times* 30 Mar. B6/3 The legislative leaders and Governor Carey agreed today to..offer low-income taxpayers, particularly the elderly, a property-tax protection program. **1914** *Proc. 6th Nat. Conf. City Planning* (U.S.) 102 Suddenly he finds his property values injured..because someone has chosen to construct a small retail store. **1979** V. S. NAIPAUL *Bend in River* vi. 109 The big recent rise in property values in the town.

b. Now also *Cinemat.* (*b*) *property manager, truck, wagon, woman, workshop*; **property-plot** (example); **property-room** (earlier examples). See also *PROPERTY BOX 2.

1959 W. S. SHARPS *Dict. Cinematogr.* 121/2 *Property manager*, the person responsible for obtaining, storing and supplying all the inanimate items required for a set. **1933** P. GODFREY *Back-Stage* iv. 44 The property-plot is a detailed list of every article of furniture and every other stage accessory used throughout the play. **1784** J. BYNG *Torrington Diaries* (1934) I. 176 In the property room is a profusion of wigs, and truncheons. **1829** H. FOOTE *Compan. Theatres* 38 In the line with the flies, over the auditory, are carpenters' shops, property-rooms, store-rooms, &c. **1961** BOWMAN & BALL *Theatre Lang.* 280 *Property truck*, a wagon offstage on which properties can be placed until needed. **1963** *Movie* May 19/3 He sat in the back of the property truck writing the ending. **1895** *McClure's Mag.* V. 55/1 The baggage-wagons and the property-wagons have stopped near the dressing-rooms. **1808** *Monthly Pantheon* I. 692/2 His wife was (in the technical language of the theatre) a dresser and property-woman. **1829** H. FOOTE *Compan. Theatres* 38 Beneath it is the *printing-office*; and over it are property workshops.

pro·perty box. *Theatre.* [f. PROPERTY *sb.* + BOX *sb.*[2]] †**1.** A seated compartment (BOX *sb.*[2] 8) which may be privately rented. *Obs.*

1812 *Dramatic Censor 1811* 53 And Ladies Carlisle and Jersey rent Property boxes, which reduces the number of Ladies seceders to fourteen. **1828** J. EBERS *Seven Yrs. King's Theatre* ix. 243 In this year (1825) and the preceding one, the terms existing in the property-boxes expired.

2. A box (BOX *sb.*[2] 1) in which stage properties are stored.

1864 P. PATERSON *Glimpses Real Life* 3 Richard's truncheon we knew was in the property-box. **1890** B. HALL *Turnover Club* ii. 28, I met on the rocks, with a 'property-box', A gloomy theatrical man.

propertyless, *a.* Add: (Earlier and later examples.) Also *ellipt.* as *sb.*

1822 W. COBBETT *Cottage Econ.* 107 They were formerly the sons and daughters of small farmers; they are now the progeny of miserable property-less labourers. **1886** [in Dict.]. **1912** BELLOC *Servile State* I. 16 Two classes of free citizens, the one capitalist or owning, the other propertyless or proletarian. **1941** R. HUMPHREYS *Latin Amer.* 20 For the Indian and the propertyless, independence meant not new freedom but new masters. **1977** *Dædalus* Summer 72 They predicted, in Hegelian fashion, an abolition of private property and class ownership of the means of production by a regenerated communism among the propertyless masses.

Hence **pro·pertylessness,** the state of being propertyless.

1964 M. MCLUHAN *Understanding Media* xxxiii. 357 Hence the specter of joblessness and propertylessness in the electric age.

prophage (prōᵘ·fēⁱdʒ). *Biol.* [Contraction of F. *probactériophage* (Lwoff & Gutmann 1950, in *Ann. de l'Inst. Pasteur* LXXVIII. 734): see PRO-[2] and *PHAGE.] The form which a temperate phage has in a lysogenic bacterium: it is incorporated into and replicates with the bacterial genome, and is only potentially lytic.

1951 [see *INDUCE *v.* 4e]. **1955** *Sci. Amer.* Apr. 93/1 Some prophages control the production of substances by their hosts (e.g., diphtheria toxin) or have other important effects on them. **1969** A. M. CAMPBELL *Episomes* vi. 81 Prophage insertion is a special kind of recombination process. **1973** R. G. KRUEGER et al. *Introd. Microbiol.* xviii. 507/1 The evidence suggested that the virus resided in a novel state as a prophage and that the presence of the prophage or phage genome in the cell rendered the cell immune to vegetative replication of other similar temperate phage particles by the same mechanism that limited its own vegetative replication.

propham (prōᵘ·fæm). [f. PRO(PYL + PH(ENYL + CARB)AM(ATE.] Isopropyl *N*-phenylcarbamate, $C_6H_5{\cdot}NH{\cdot}CO{\cdot}O{\cdot}CH(CH_3)_2$, a white crystalline substance used as a selective herbicide to control weeds among crops, esp. during germination.

1955 *Proc. Brit. Weed Control Conf. 1954* I. 183 The almost complete failure of the more insoluble propham, CIPC and CMU to give control of wild oats may also be connected with the inability of the material to reach the wild oats at the critical time at Site I, where TCA was successful. **1958** *Weed Control Handbk.* (Brit. Weed Control Council) i. 19 For the control of wild oats in sugar beet and peas, propham has given results comparable with those obtained with trichloroacetic acid when applied in the same way—before the final seed-bed cultivations. **1973** ASHTON & CRAFTS *Mode of Action of Herbicides* xiii. 202 Propham is rapidly broken down by micro-organisms in the soil; such degradation is promoted by warmth and moisture. For this reason propham has proved most useful in cool season crops.

prophase. Substitute for entry in Dict.: **prophase** (prōᵘ·fēⁱz). *Cytology.* [ad. G. *prophase* (E. Strasburger 1884, in *Arch. f. mikrosk. Anat.* XXIII. 250): see PRO-[2] and PHASE.] The first stage in a mitotic or meiotic nuclear division, preceding prometaphase, during which the chromosomes become visible and shorten and the nuclear envelope disappears. Also *attrib.* or as *adj.*

Prophase of the first meiotic division is divided into *LEPTOTENE, *ZYGOTENE, *PACHYTENE, *DIPLOTENE, and *DIAKINESIS, in that order.

1884 *Jrnl. R. Microsc. Soc.* IV. II. 714 In both [plants and animals] we find that in the 'prophases' of nuclear division cytoplasm is collected at the future poles of the cell-nucleus. **1887, 1898** [in Dict.]. **1903** *Bot. Gaz.* XXXV. 250 The first division in Salamandra is characterized by a long period of growth of the cell and nucleus during the prophase..; the first longitudinal fission taking place during the prophase and the second during the metaphase or anaphase. **1911** *Q. Jrnl. Microsc. Sci.* LVII. 27 The most important difference between the pre-meiotic and meiotic prophases is the entire absence in the former of any appearance of fusion of chromatin threads, such as takes place in zygonema. **1931** E. B. FORD *Mendelism & Evolution* I. i. 18 Blocks of genes cross over together, as would be expected if, in fact, this phenomenon is due to the twisting of the chromosome threads round each other during the prophase of the reduction division. **1948** R. A. R. GRESSON *Essent. Gen. Cytol.* v. 33 (*caption*) Prophase chromosome to show arrangement of chromosomes. **1957** C. P. SWANSON *Cytol. & Cytogenetics* iii. 49 Prophase is said to be initiated at the moment when the chromosomes become visibly distinct. **1970** AMBROSE & EASTY *Cell Biol.* ix. 296 In late prophase..the spindle dissolves and the asters move apart.

Hence **propha·sic** *a.*

1913 *La Cellule* XXIX. 311 The first indication that the prophasic changes have begun is seen in the breaking down of the anastomoses along the lines between the heavier portions of the reticulum. **1929** *Bot. Gaz.* LXXXVIII. 376 In the latter case the visible division of the chromonema would always be prophasic. **1951** H. C. BOLD in G. M. Smith *Man. Phycol.* xi. 225 The Florideae furnish a conspicuous exception in that the spermatium nucleus is usually described as in a prophasic condition at the moment of union.

prophet, *sb.* Add: **II. 5. c.** (Earlier examples.)

1843 *Ainsworth's Mag.* III. 220 What's to win the Derby?.. What say the prophets? **1862** *Times* 31 Dec., Prophets, tipsters and welshers—the parasites of the ring.

III. 6. c. *prophet-like* (example).

1857 G. H. LEWES *Biogr. Hist. Philos.* (ed. 2) II. 319 Now grave, prophetlike, and impassioned.

propho (prǫ·fo). *slang* (orig. *U.S.*). [f. PROPH(YLAXIS + *-O[2].] Prophylaxis of venereal disease. Also *attrib.*

1919 L. L. LINCOLN *Company C, 11th Engineers* 37 In his efforts to get away with it he paid many visits to 'Doc. Propho'. **1921** J. DOS PASSOS *Three Soldiers* IV. 202 That's one thing you guys are lucky in, don't have to worry about propho. **1925** —— *Manhattan Transfer* III. i. 281 Just my propho kit. **1959** J. BRAINE *Vodi* vii. 115 Jack..had pointed out that there were no propho stations in Civvy Street.

prophylactic, *a.* and *sb.* Add: **B.** *sb.* **b.** A condom.

Condoms were formerly used more for their prophylactic properties against venereal disease than for their contraceptive properties.

1943 [see *PREVENTIVE *sb.* c]. **1950** 'D. DIVINE' *King of Fassarai* xviii. 143 'What were you doing before this?' 'Handin' out prophylactics in Baltimore.' **1964** G. MCDONALD *Running Scared* v. 73 Prophylactics made them [*sc.* women] more willing... People could have intercourse..without restraint. **1972** C. POTOK *My Name is Asher Lev* III. x. 259 Along the..beach lay..beer cans, bits of paper, a prophylactic. **1975** *Listener* 27 Nov. 728/3 The GI wore his packet of prophylactics in his cap and propositioned every woman in sight.

prophyll (prōᵘ·fil). *Bot.* [f. PRO-² + Gr. φύλλ-ον leaf.] **1.** Now the usual form of *prophyllon* (PRO-² I). (Examples.)

1905 I. B. BALFOUR tr. *Goebel's Organogr. Plants* II. 382 Prophylls are characterized first of all by their position. We find them..usually in pairs at the base of the lateral shoots. **1921** J. SMALL *Textbk. Bot.* vii. 75 The first few leaves on a lateral branch are described as prophylls. There are commonly two, and they may be spiny..or just small and simpler than the other leaves... The latter prophylls are usually called bracteoles. **1953** K. ESAU *Plant Anat.* xvi. 413 The first cataphylls on a lateral shoot are called prophylls. **1976** BELL & COOMBE tr. *Strasburger's Textbk. Bot.* (rev. ed.) 131 These first leaves of the side shoot, which are frequently of simple form.., are termed prophylls.

2. = *PROTOPHYLL.

1971 D. W. BIERHORST *Morphol. Vascular Plants* ii. 24/2 This [*sc.* the protocorm] is a parenchymatous moss bearing..a number of avascular, leaflike structures ('prophylls').

propinquitous, *a.* Add: For *nonce-wd.* read *rare* and add further examples.

1941 *Cold Spring Harbor Symp. Quant. Biol.* IX. 155/1 The tendency to propinquitous union. **1974** R. ADAMS *Shardik* xxviii. 234 Let us just step outside for a stroll in some nice, lovely place with no propinquitous walls or bushes.

propio-, propion-. Add: **propiola·ctone,** a pungent, colourless, liquid β-lactone, $CH_2{\cdot}CO{\cdot}O{\cdot}CH_2$, which is used as a disinfectant; also **β-propiolactone; propionyl** (earlier example).

1917 *Chem. Abstr.* XI. 2577 Propiolactone..was prepd. by treating an aq. soln. of $CH_2ICH_2CO_2Na$ with $AgNO_3$ and stirring the resulting ppt. for 15–25 min. **1952** *Chambers's Jrnl.* Apr. 255/2 Treating natural wool with a chemical called propiolactone increases its diameter and density without appreciable effect upon its surface properties. **1966** *McGraw-Hill Encycl. Sci. & Technol.* I. 463/2 β-Propiolactone works best at high humidities and is active even below 10° C. **1850** *Phil. Trans. R. Soc.* CXL. 129 The existence of a series of bases of the formula $C_nH_{n+1}N$, *i.e.* bases containing formyl, acetyl, propionyl (metacetyl), butyryl, &c., appears to be still doubtful.

propionic, *a.* **1.** (Earlier example.)

1850 [see *PROPYL].

propitiative (propi·ʃiˌătiv), *a. rare.* [f. PROPITIATE *v.* + -IVE.] Tending to propitiate; propitiatory, conciliatory.

1928 *Observer* 19 Feb. 17/2 Where the majority of passengers have to travel in a brutalising congestion, the sight of half-empty 'firsts' next door is not propitiative.

proplastid: see *PRO-² I.

propodus (prǫ·podŏs). *Zool.* [f. PRO-² + Gr. πούς, ποδ- foot.] = PROPODITE.

1945 T. H. SAVORY *Spiders Brit. Isles* (ed. 2) 196 The propodus ends in a large claw and often a pair of smaller accessory claws. **1976** *Nature* 11 Mar. 136/1 Among the factors affecting the strength of a crab's master claw is the cross-sectional area of muscle in the manus (that part of the propodus behind the apposing fingers).

proportional, *a.* and *sb.* Add: **A.** *adj.* **1.** *proportional counter,* an ionization chamber in which the voltage between the electrodes is great enough to produce gas amplification but not so great that the output pulse ceases to be proportional to the initial ionization; so *proportional counting; proportional limit* (Mech.), the maximum stress to which a body or material can be subjected without a departure from the proportionality of stress and strain.

1906 *Proc. R. Soc.* XII. 427 Bars tested in torsion to some stress below the elastic limit (proportional limit of bar) and the direction of torsion reversed immediately. **1937** *Rev. Sci. Instruments* VIII. 254 (*heading*) Properties of the proportional (Geiger-Klemperer) counter. *Ibid.* 255/1 The proportional or Geiger-Klemperer counter which is operated in a range of potential below discharge but above the region of ionization by collision has been used in several series of experiments, notably where the detection of protons in the presence of gamma-radiation is required. **1939** *Rev. Mod. Physics* XI. 213/2 With the gases mentioned, stable proportional counting and freedom from extremely critical voltage control can only be achieved with the aid of high gain amplifiers. **1950** D. H. WILKINSON *Ionization Chambers* vi. 157 With simple precautions as to the allowed region of initial ionization the proportional counter becomes a precision instrument, and may be used as an accurate measure of particle energy. **1950** E. E. WAHLSTROM *Introd. Theoret. Igneous Petrol.* v. 115 Both the elastic limit and the proportional limit vary with the time through which the stress is applied. **1958** FAIRES & PARKS *Radioisotope Lab. Techniques* xi. 111 In order to obtain the high electric fields required to produce gas amplification, the proportional counter usually takes the form of a metal cylinder, having a fine wire, insulated at its ends, stretched along its length. **1961** G. R. CHOPPIN *Exper. Nuclear Chem.* xi. 186 This fact and the sensitivity to impurities make Geiger-Müller counting less attractive than proportional counting. **1971** *Nature* 16 Apr. 448/1 Several investigators have measured the diffuse cosmic X-ray intensity in the 1/4 keV band by means of rocket-borne gas proportional counters. **1972** MALLOWS & PICKERING *Stress Anal. Probl. S.I. Units* ii. 37 It is common..to use the proportional limit, elastic limit, and yield stress as alternatives for one another in design calculations: since they are usually close to one another, this is quite acceptable.

2. b. *proportional representation,* a system of parliamentary representation based on numerical (rather than regional) divisions of the electorate, *spec.* one by which each party is represented in proportion to the numerical strength of the vote it receives, usually by means of a method of transferable vote (see TRANSFERABLE *a.* in Dict. and Suppl.).

1870 *Putnam's Mag.* June 720/1 When once the theory of proportional representation is reduced to practice..it will assert its superiority. **1873** MILL *Autobiogr.* vii. 302 The two greatest improvements which remain to be made in Representative Government... One of them was Personal, or, as it is called with equal propriety, Proportional Representation. **1884** [see sense 2 in Dict.]. **1909** [see TRANSFERABLE *a.*]. **1917** H. G. WELLS in *Times* 30 Mar. 7/5 The essential point to grasp is that Proportional Representation is not a novel scheme, but a carefully worked-out remedy for universally recognized ills. **1940** F. A. HERMENS *Democracy & Proportional Representation* 1 There are few devices of democratic government on which opinions differ so sharply as on proportional representation. **1952** [see *GAULLIST *a.* and *sb.*]. **1963** J. GRIMOND *Liberal Challenge* xi. 314, I believe ..that the best solution might be to keep the present system for the Commons but introduce proportional representation for a second chamber. **1976** *Scotsman* 24 Dec. 4/3 A series of amendments to provide for the Scottish and Welsh assemblies to be elected by proportional representation were tabled yesterday.

proportionalism. 2. (Further example.)

1954 B. & R. NORTH tr. *Duverger's Pol. Parties* II. iii. 377 In all three P.R. replaced a modified majority system (second ballot in Switzerland and Norway, some features of proportionalism in Denmark).

proportionality. Add: **1. b.** *limit of proportionality* (Mech.) = **proportional limit.*

1888 W. C. UNWIN *Testing of Materials of Construction* iii. 65 Between A and B a sensible, but slight, curvature appears in the diagram, and a sensible, though small, deviation from proportionality begins to appear in the stresses and strains. Bauschinger calls the point A the limit of proportionality. **1930** *Engineering* 3 Jan. 31/1 The figures for limit of proportionality..were obtained from stress-strain diagrams. **1971** B. SCHARF *Engin. & its Lang.* iv. 22 The following values may be obtained by means of a tensile test: limit of proportionality..; yield stress..; proof stress [etc.].

c. *constant* or *factor of proportionality* (also *proportionality constant, factor*): the constant ratio of one variable to a second to which it is proportional.

1919 *Smithsonian Misc. Coll.* LXXI. II. 9 The cross section, S, should obviously be as small as possible; and this condition will be satisfied at all times, provided it is the following function of the mass of the rocket (M—m), $S = A\,(M-m)^{\frac{2}{3}}$, where A is a constant of proportionality. **1937** *Rev. Sci. Instruments* VIII. 255/1 These are all connected with..proportionality between resultant electrical impulse and initial ionization per particle. The proportionality factor should not depend much upon the kind of particle entering the counter. **1955** J. LINDHARD in W. Pauli *Niels Bohr* 188 Accordingly, ω and the average excitation potential become proportional to Z, i.e. $\hbar\omega = I = Z.I_0$. However, it was found difficult to calculate the proportionality constant I_0. **1962** F. I. ORDWAY et al. *Basic Astronautics* x. 396 The proportionality factor C_F, called thrust coefficient, is a result of the expansion of the combustion gases through the nozzle.

2. A formula affirming the proportionality of two or more quantities.

1954 A. DRESDEN tr. *van der Waerden's Science Awakening* vi. 176 The proportionality $a{:}b{::}c{:}a$ means that $na > mb$ implies $nc > md$, and $na = mb$ implies $nc = md$, and $na < mb$ implies $nc < md$, no matter how the integers m and n are chosen. **1976** *Nature* 27 May 301/2 The luminosity of a star of solar mass satisfies the approximate proportionality $L \propto G^7M^5 \propto t^2$.

proposal. 1. Restrict †*Obs.* to sense in Dict. and add: **b.** *Philos.* (See quots.) *rare.*

1932 W. E. JOHNSON in *Mind* XLI. 1 (*title*) Probability: the relations of proposal to supposal. *Ibid.* 5 Any statement of implication, whether formal or material, may be translated into the language of probability by taking the implicans as supposal and the implicate as proposal. **1944** *Mind* LIII. 98 Following Johnson I shall call the proposition on the left of the solidus the 'proposal' and that on the right of it the 'supposal'.

3. c. An offer or tender. Now *U.S.*

1748 [in Dict., sense 3 a]. **1914** *Chicago Tribune* 8 May 14 Sealed proposals plainly marked on the outside 'Proposals for coal'..will be received at the Indian Office. **1935** H. W. HORWILL *Dict. Mod. Amer. Usage* 244/1 *Proposal* is sometimes used in Am. in the sense of *tender.*

propose, *v.* Add: **3. e.** Also with *for* and (more usually) *to.* (Further examples.)

1855 THACKERAY *Newcomes* II. xiii. 127 Perhaps neither of them will propose for her. **1872** A. C. STEELE *Broken Toys* II. xxv. 167, I am going to Vere Court tomorrow to propose for Nella Vere. **1911** G. B. SHAW *Getting Married* 227 *Sykes.* When her blood boils about it ..she doesnt care what she says. *Reginald.* Well: you knew that when you proposed to her. **1928** E. O'NEILL *Strange Interlude* IX. 341 Ned's just proposed to me. I refused him, Charlie. **1931** H. WALPOLE *Judith Paris* II. 311 She had been amazed when the handsome young Pomfret Herries had proposed for her in marriage. **1978** T. SHARPE *Throwback* iii. 19 Mr Flawse..took a swig of brandy to steady his nerves. The bloody woman was proposing to him.

proposita (prōᵘpǫ·zită). [L., fem. of *prōpositus:* see *PROPOSITUS.] A female propositus.

1970 *Jrnl. Med. Genetics* VII. 180/2 The proposita.. presented as a profoundly retarded, 21-year-old girl with poor posture. **1976** *Nature* 15 Jan. 139/1 A study of 12 different blood group systems in the proposita and her parents failed to exclude paternity.

proposition, *sb.* Add **6. a.** *spec.* in *U.S.,* a constitutional proposal.

1921 *Congress. Rec.* 21 Feb. 3537/1 If this particular proposition were a law, and the Federal Trade Commission were given the authority that is herein provided, they would protect the country and the people in it by proper license. **1979** *Tucson Mag.* Jan. 25/1 Today's mad, mad world of Proposition 13 and other horrors. **1979** *Time* 13 Aug. 24/1 County officials hope the mistake will work in their favor, on the somewhat shaky grounds that the absurdity of Proposition .004 will defeat it.

7. a. An enterprise or project submitted for consideration or action; a matter, problem, or undertaking which requires attention; also with respect to ease or difficulty of performance, etc., as an *easy, serious, tough proposition* and with regard to likelihood of (commercial) success, as *business, mining proposition.* orig. *U.S.*

1877 R. J. BURDETTE *Rise & Fall of Mustache* 258 For a long time the good lady held out stoutly against the chicken proposition. **1893** *Scribner's Mag.* June 756/1 'Arn't you ashamed to tell me this?' 'Of course I am, but that isn't the proposition just now.' **1896** ADE *Artie* xviii. 168 I'm goin' against a tough proposition. **1902** O. WISTER *Virginian* ii. 19 The biggest tobacco proposition for five cents got out yet. *Ibid.* xviii. 214, I saw over in a fenced meadow..what he was pleased to call 'the proposition'. Proposition in the West does, in fact, mean whatever you at the moment please. **1906** *Daily News* 24 Jan. 12/3 Later on it was found that the Main Reef series of gold-bearing rock dipped into this property, which became an attractive mining 'proposition', as the slang phrase goes. **1909** S. E. WHITE *Rules of Game* III. ix. 181 We're the only two business propositions in this country. **1929** *Daily Express* 7 Nov. 2/5 Every industry I want to nationalize must be a business proposition. **1932** E. WILSON *Devil take Hindmost* viii. 70 Care of the worker is a money-saving proposition. **1941** *Strand Mag.* June 140/2 All I know is that I've got to find her. The question is, how? And it won't surprise you to hear that it appears to me to be a pretty stiff proposition. **1958** *Economist* 26 July 271 Once the basic capital expenditure has been made on a machine and microphone, this is definitely an economic proposition.

b. *transf.* of persons.

1901 *Tit-Bits* 27 July 416/2 He was a pretty smooth proposition himself. **1908** C. E. MULFORD *Orphan* xiv. 178 I'd rather have him with me in a mix-up than against me. He's the coolest proposition loose in this part of the country at any game. **1915** T. BURKE *Nights in Town* 19 He is educated..to regard himself as, in the Broadway phrase, a serious proposition. **1925** C. E. MULFORD *Cottonwood Gulch* vii. 92 Knife fighters are bad propositions. **1979** 'H. HOWARD' *Sealed Envelope* v. 74 Soon as I discovered she was an easy proposition I dropped out. I don't go for a twist who sleeps in anybody's bed.

8. *Comb.,* as (sense 4) *proposition-forming* adj.

1955 A. N. PRIOR *Formal Logic* III. iii. 261 We may define in terms of 'ε' another proposition-forming operator. **1968** HUGHES & CRESSWELL *Introd. Modal Logic* ii. 23 'It is necessary that' is thus a (monadic) proposition-forming operator on propositions.

proposition (prǫpozi·ʃən), *v.* orig. *U.S.* [f. the sb.] **1.** *trans.* To make or present a proposition to (a person). (Sometimes with unfavourable connotations.)

1924 H. C. WITWER *Love & Learn* x. 275, I finally got Ike sold on the idea that my plan was a good thought and he departed to proposition Hershel. **1927** *Collier's* 24 Dec. 36/4 He propositioned her to use his lodge at Big Bear [Lake] for her party. **1935** A. J. POLLOCK *Underworld Speaks* 91/2 *Propositioned,* asked to join in an unlawful undertaking. **1938** *Amer. Speech* XIII. 194 One need be very little of a purist to recoil from the current expression 'I *propositioned* him', meaning, of course, 'I made a proposition to him'. **1947** E. ANDREWS *Hist. Scientific Eng.* xiv. 252 It makes us more tolerant today when we hear a businessman speak of 'contacting' a customer or, worse yet, of 'propositioning' him. **1949** *Chicago Tribune* 10 Dec. 12/5 Count that day gained in which A sofomore sonny Won't proposition pop For movie money! **1949** 'J. TEY' *Brat Farrar* iii. 20 I'm propositioning you... What is wrong with the proposition? **1967** *Punch* 28 June 949/2 While being propositioned by Lord Beaverbrook about becoming the film critic of the *Evening Standard,* I nervously filled in a yawning silence by telling this anecdote **1978** J. A. MICHENER *Chesapeake* 660 [They] sailed up·

river to the landing of a farm owned by an old man.., and there they propositioned him: 'You ain't gonna have much more use for your long gun... We aim to buy it.' **1979** *Dædalus* Summer 46 The deputy..proceeds to proposition her with a debased contract.

2. To request sexual favours from (a person); to solicit.

1936 J. G. COZZENS *Men & Brethren* I. 139 There's no real reason to be embarrassed because your clerical collar keeps you from feeling free to proposition every woman you meet. **1946** 'P. QUENTIN' *Puzzle for Fiends* iii. 23 You ..had him proposition you in a canoe? **1949** K. MALONE in Kirby & Woolf *Philologica* 317 *To proposition*, at least in the field of amour, is not only distinct from *to propose*, but in a sense antithetical to *propose*. **1953** W. BURROUGHS *Junkie* vi. 60, I remember once he told me how he'd been propositioned by a queer who offered him twenty dollars. **1963** T. PYNCHON *V.* xi. 328 The girls were professional and tried for a while to proposition Fausto and Dnubietna. **1974** M. GILBERT *Flash Point* xii. 105 This girl stopped me, by asking me for a cigarette... There was no question of me propositioning her or annoying her. **1975** *New Yorker* 4 Aug. 25/1 In Hyde Park, that black whore had propositioned him as he walked from work toward the Tube.

propositional, *a.* Add: **a.** (Further examples.) *spec.* applied to speech and language in which statements and assertions occur.

1874 J. H. JACKSON in *Med. Press & Circ.* 14 Jan. 21/1 But if *I* have to say, 'Gold is yellow', I have to revive the words, and I have to put them in propositional order. **1879** —— in *Brain* I. 312 A speechless patient may retain the word 'no', and yet have only the interjectional or emotional, not the propositional, use of it; he utters it in various tones as signs of feeling only. **1892** *Mind* I. 10 There are *five* independent laws, which are necessary and sufficient for propositional synthesis. **1922** tr. *Wittgenstein's Tractatus* 45 The sign through which we express the thought I call the propositional sign. *Ibid.* 51 An expression is thus presented by a variable whose values are the propositions which contain the expression... I call such a variable a 'propositional variable'. **1926** H. HEAD *Aphasia* I. iii. 39 Occasionally he can not only use 'yes' and 'no' correctly, but can even repeat them. Here, then, we have propositional speech and voluntary utterance. **1932** LEWIS & LANGFORD *Symbolic Logic* ix. 267 In elementary functions only propositional variables occur. **1935** WEISENBURG & MCBRIDE *Aphasia* x. 277 When propositional speech is negligible, spoken expression may nevertheless be frequent. **1943** W. G. HARDY in *Cornell Univ. Abstr. of Theses* (1944) 57 Richards..now concerns himself with the educative values of propositional analysis. **1947** H. REICHENBACH *Elem. Symbolic Logic* 179 The recursive definition of the term 'propositional expression'. **1955** A. N. PRIOR *Formal Logic* I. iii. 50 We introduce the symbol 'o' as a propositional *constant*, to stand..for some arbitrarily chosen proposition. **1957** J. EISENSON in L. E. Travis *Handbk. Speech Path.* (1959) xii. 438 When linguistic symbols are used to communicate a specific idea or to elicit a specific response, we are dealing with propositional speech. **1968** N. RESCHER *Topics in Philos. Logic* v. 51 The most satisfactory course is to base the logic of belief (and of assertion) upon a propositional analysis, rather than one articulated in terms of sentences, inscriptions, utterances, or the like. **1973** J. J. ZEMAN *Modal Logic* p. v, The book..contains a detailed development of non-modal propositional logic. **1976** *Listener* 9 Dec. 743/1 The capacity for propositional speech—the synthesis of words into statements that, by their form, give extra meaning to those words. **1977** *Word 1972* XXVIII. 223 In propositional speech (both in forming constructions and in understanding them), the patient had difficulty sorting out relationships between more than two critical items.

b. In special collocations, as *propositional attitude*, an attitude which can vary expressed towards a proposition that does not vary; *propositional calculus*, a calculus which formalizes the basic truth-functional operations possible in logical propositions and gives notation, indicating conjunction, disjunction, negation, etc., to their sentential connectives; *propositional connective*, a connective which is used as a logical operator in propositions; *propositional function* (see quot. 1910 and cf. *PREDICATE *sb.* 2a).

[**1904** B. RUSSELL in *Mind* XIII. 509 Belief is a certain attitude towards propositions, which is called knowledge when they are true, error when they are false.] **1939** *Mind* XLVIII. 479 When we disbelieve, then doubt, and finally believe a proposition, it must be the *same* proposition toward which we have these different attitudes; that is, propositions must be invariant under change of propositional attitude. **1940** B. RUSSELL *Inquiry into Meaning & Truth* xi. 204 A negative basic proposition thus requires a propositional attitude, in which the proposition concerned is the one which, on the basis of perception, is denied. **1966** W. V. QUINE *Ways of Paradox* xv. 189 Striving and wishing, like believing, are propositional attitudes and referentially opaque. **1969** J. HINTIKKA *Models for Modalities* iii. 87 (*heading*) Semantics for propositional attitudes. **1903** B. RUSSELL *Princ. Math.* ii. 12 It is not with such entities that we are concerned in the propositional calculus, but with genuine propositions. **1938** *Jrnl. Symbolic Logic* III. 83 Chapter 2 supplements the propositional calculus, in effect, with the Boolean algebra of one-place predicates. **1959** *Ibid.* XXIV. 97 Gödel proves the non-existence of a finite matrix characteristic for the intuitionist propositional calculus IC. **1966** *Mathematical Rev.* XXXI. 4/1 Since the main results are existential, a really conclusive solution requires a narrow meaning of 'propositional calculus'. **1973** J. J. ZEMAN *Modal Logic* ii. 7 Our first task will be..to set down some propositional calculi. Many systems discussed later will be presented as extensions of the propositional calculus. **1938** *Jrnl. Symbolic Logic* III. 84 A deductive system is presented which involves..the propositional connectives, and prediction and quantification with respect to individuals. **1952** S. C. KLEENE *Introd. Metamath.* iv. 73 In particular, $\supset$, &, $\vee$, $\neg$ are propositional connectives, and operators of the forms $\forall x$ and $\exists x$ are quantifiers..these six are logical operators. **1974** *Jrnl. Philos. Logic* III. 202 The propositional connectives concern statements. **1903** B. RUSSELL *Princ. Math.* ii. 13 Where there are one or more real variables, and for all values of the variables the expression involved is a proposition, I shall call the expression a *propositional function*. **1910** WHITEHEAD & RUSSELL *Principia Math.* I. i. 15 Let ϕx be a statement containing a variable x such that it becomes a proposition when x is given any fixed determined meaning. Then ϕx is called a 'propositional function'; it is not a proposition, since owing to the ambiguity of x it really makes no assertion at all. **1943, 1969** [see *PREDICATE *sb.* 2 a]. **1974** *Jrnl. Philos. Logic* III. 196 A predicate, or propositional function, is a statement-valued function, i.e. a function that maps objects of some kind into statements (propositions).

Hence **proposi·tionalist,** someone who is concerned with the logic of propositions; **propositionally** *adv.* (earlier example).

1879 *Brain* II. 215 Then propositionally 'yes' and 'no' give assent or dissent to anything whatever. **1952** *Mind* LXI. 61 The spurious character of our propositionalist's argument becomes evident. **1970** W. V. QUINE *Philos. of Logic* i. 3 The propositionalist by-passes differences between languages.

propositionize, *v.* Delete *rare* and add further examples.

1878 *Brain* I. 312 Loss of speech is therefore the loss of power to propositionise. It is not only loss of power to propositionise aloud (to talk), but to propositionise either internally or externally. **1920** *Ibid.* XLIII. 119, I believe that under the uncouth word 'propositionizing' is included what I understand by 'symbolic thinking'. **1921** *Brit. Jrnl. Psychol.* XI. 185 There are some aspects of the loss of function in aphasia which are not strictly comprised under the heading of 'propositionising'. **1955** R. JAKOBSON in H. Werner *On Expressive Lang.* 77 The patient fails to operate with contiguity, while operations based on similarity remain intact. Thus he [*sc.* an aphasic] loses the ability to propositionize. **1956** —— in Jakobson & Halle *Fund. Lang.* II. iv. 71 The impairment of the ability to propositionize, or generally speaking, to combine simpler linguistic entities into more complex units, is actually confined to one type of aphasia.

‖ **propositum** (prōupǫ·zitŏm). *Philos.* [L., neut. of *prōpositus*: see next.] The first premise of a syllogism; an argument, principal theme or subject propounded.

1858 A. DE MORGAN *On Syllogism* (1966) 83, I see great difference in the *propositum* between 'This house was built by Jack' and 'This is the [or even *a*] house that Jack built'. **1913** [see *JUDICATUM]. **1920** S. ALEXANDER *Space, Time, & Deity* II. 249 'Proposition' contains a reference to language, and 'propositum' would be a better, though a pedantic name.

propositus (prōupǫ·zitɒs). Pl. **propositi.** [a. L. *prōpositus*, pa. pple. of *prōpōnere* (see PROPONE *v.*).] An individual who was the first member of a family to come to the notice of a researcher, and through whom investigation of a pedigree began. Cf. *PROBAND, *PROPOSITA.

1926 *Eugenics Rev.* XVIII. 248 ☛ Points to the Propositus or central figure in the pedigree. **1939** *Brit. Jrnl. Psychol.* XXX. 9 When propositi are separated into groups of comparable mental grade, defect is seen to be more common among relatives of simpletons than among relatives of idiots. **1956** *Nature* 7 Jan. 40/1 The factor was transmitted to them by the paternal grandmother (generation II) of the propositus. **1961** *Lancet* 19 Aug. 437/2 We have collected the details of 107 sibships; the propositi attended our clinics. **1977** *Ibid.* 3 Sept. 504/1 The propositus (family C) presented with pituitary insufficiency.

propoxur (propǫ·ksūəɪ). [f. PROP(YL + OX-I + UR(ETHANE.] An insecticide having a long-lasting ability to produce rapid incapacitation of affected insects; *o*-isopropoxyphenyl-*N*-methylcarbamate, $CH_3\cdot NH\cdot CO\cdot O\cdot C_6H_4\cdot O\cdot CH(CH_3)_2$.

1964 *Zeitschr. f. Angewandte Zool.* LI. 332 Deposits on filter paper of..carbamates (carbaryl and propoxur), prepared up to 105 days ago, were repeatedly applied to imagines of five different strains of house-flies (Musca domestica). **1977** *Time* 12 Sept. 56/3 Health authorities are now using more of other insecticides, such as Malathion and propoxur to kill DDT-resistant mosquitoes.

propoxyphene (propǫ·ksifīn). *Pharm.* [f. PROP(IO- + OXY- + -*phene* (f. PHEN-, PHENO-).] A mild narcotic analgesic, chemically related to methadone, which is given orally (usu. as the hydrochloride, a whitish powder) esp. in cases of chronic or recurrent pain, its effects being similar to but weaker than those of codeine; (+)-α-4-dimethylamino-3-methyl-1,2-diphenylbut-2-yl propionate, $(CH_3)_2N\cdot CH_2\cdot CH(CH_3)\cdot C(C_6H_5)(CH_2\cdot C_6H_5)\cdot O\cdot CO\cdot CH_2CH_3$.

1955 *Arch. Internat. de Pharmacodyn.* CIV. 165 The analgesic activity of Propoxyphene has been demonstrated in patients with chronic pain. **1957** *Jrnl. Amer. Med. Assoc.* 29 June 966/2 Propoxyphene is a new synthetic analgesic with the effectiveness of codeine but having less undesirable gastrointestinal side-effects. *Ibid.* 969/2 Since the preparation of this article, the Council on Drugs of the American Medical Association has changed the generic name of propoxyphene hydrochloride to dextro propoxyphene hydrochloride. **1974** M. C. GERALD *Pharmacol.* xiv. 272 In recent years propoxyphene has been among the most frequently prescribed drugs. **1976** *National Observer* (U.S.) 28 Aug. 3/1 The drug agency has suggested that the Justice Department's Drug Enforcement Administration (DEA) rule that propoxyphene-containing products be added to the list of the Controlled Substances Act's 'Schedule IV' drugs. This would mean that physicians must renew prescriptions for Darvon and similar drugs every six months.

proppy (prǫ·pi), *a.*^{2} *Austral. colloq.* [f. PROP *v.*^{1} + -Y^1.] Of a horse: tending to prop (PROP *v.*^{1} 4) or stop suddenly in mid-stride, faltering; also of other animals. Hence **pro·ppily** *adv.*

1945 BAKER *Austral. Lang.* 70 Another extension is the adjectival use of *proppy* for a horse that jibs and plays up when ridden or driven. **1951** H. G. LAMOND in Murdoch & Drake-Brockman *Austral. Short Stories* 213 Both [dogs] walked proppily on tiptoes. **1969** *Australian* 24 May 35/5 King's Delight had a bruised sole on the near fore, and Clare said the horse was proppy in his action.

propraetorship. (Later example.)

1824 J. H. NEWMAN in *Encycl. Metrop.* (1845) X. 280/1 From the period of his Consulate to his Proprætorship in Cilicia.

propranolol (propræ·nǒlǫl). *Pharm.* [f. PRO(PYL + *PR(OP)ANOL with reduplication of final -OL.] The compound 1-isopropylamino-3-(1-naphthyloxy)-2-propanol, $C_{16}H_{21}NO_2$, which is a *β*-adrenergic blocking agent used mainly (in the form of a colourless crystalline hydrochloride) in the treatment of cardiac arrhythmia.

1964 *Brit. Med. Jrnl.* 19 Sept. 720 (*heading*) Effect of propranolol (Inderal) in angina pectoris: preliminary report. **1965** J. H. BURN *Lect. Notes Pharmacol.* (ed. 8) 10 When propranolol is given, a patient performs a given amount of work at a lower heart rate and he can perform a greater amount of work without feeling pain. **1972** *Lancet* 16 Sept. 565/2 In our clinical experience, propranolol is effective in the treatment of heroin dependence. **1974** *Sci. Amer.* June 62/3 This complex series of events can be turned off by propranolol, a drug that prevents the noradrenaline from combining with the beta adrenergic receptor. **1980** *Brit. Med. Jrnl.* 29 Mar. 885/1 We have..investigated the effect of giving higher doses of a non-selective beta-blocker (propranolol)..to patients with suspected myocardial infarction.

proprietariat (proprəiĕtēə·riăt). *nonce-wd.* [f. PROPRIETARY *a.*, after *proletariat*.] The propertied class.

1896 G. B. SHAW *Rep. Fabian Policy* 4 It [*sc.* the Fabian Society]..does not believe that the moment will ever come when the whole of Socialism will be staked on the issue of a single General Election or a single Bill in the House of Commons, as between the proletariat on one side and the proprietariat on the other. **1928** —— *Intelligent Woman's Guide Socialism* 223 The Proletariat and the Proprietariat face each other. **1950** —— *Far-fetched Fables* 86 The feudal proprietariat is all for well policed private property.

proprietary, *sb.* and *a.* Add: **B.** *adj.* **1. a.** (Further examples.) *proprietary name* or *term*, a word or phrase over which a person or company has some legal rights, esp. in connection with trade (as a trade mark).

1911 *T. Eaton & Co. Catal.* Spring & Summer 175 (*heading*) Proprietary Medicines. **1921** W. A. CRAIGIE *Let.* 18 Feb. (Oxf. Dict. files), We have expressly recognized that it [sc. *Vaseline*] is a proprietary term. **1924** *Pocket Oxf. Dict.* 932/1 *Vaseline*... Proprietary term introduced in 1872 by R. A. Chesebrough. **1930** *Engineering* 7 Mar. 304/1 These stock, or proprietary, engines are made by..specialists. **1930** *Economist* 22 Nov. 957/1 The Economic Council was unable to agree as to whether the undertaking by retailers selling proprietary articles to charge the price fixed by the manufacturers..should be prohibited. **1933** *O.E.D.* (new impr.) s.v. *Vaseline*... A proprietary term, introduced by R. A. Chesebrough in 1872. *Ibid.* Suppl. s.v. *Ferozone*... Proprietary name. **1958** *New Statesman* 28 June 822/2 Many [doctors]..tend to prescribe a well-advertised proprietary brand because they have no time to consult their list for a cheaper standard preparation. **1972** *Physics Bull.* Aug. 489/2 'Freon' is the proprietary name for Du Pont's brand of the fluorinated derivatives of hydrocarbons used as refrigerants and aerosol propellants. **1974** *Islander* (Victoria, B.C.) 4 Aug. 10/1 By the mid-18th century, more than 200 so-called 'proprietary medicines' were being sold in Britain and in the American colonies.

b. *proprietary company* = *private company* s.v. *PRIVATE *a.* 7h. *Austral.*

1896 *Companies Act* (Victoria, Austral.) § 2 'Proprietary Company' means a company..which..(a) has not more than twenty-five members or shareholders; (b) does not receive deposits, except from its members or shareholders..; (c) does not use its title without the addition thereto immediately before the word 'limited' of the word 'proprietary'. **1973** R. N. PURVIS *Purvis on Proprietary Companies* i. 8 A public company must have at least three directors, whereas a proprietary company need have only two.

proprietous (pro͵prəi·ėtəs), *a.* [f. PROPRIETY + -OUS.] Characterized by (extreme) propriety or punctilious behaviour. Also *Comb.* Hence **propri·etously** *adv.*

1844 *Ainsworth's Mag.* VI. 228 An elderly person, whose proprietous grey silk dress..conveyed the idea of a distant relative. **1845** *Ibid.* VII. 498 The rows of canvass-covered proprietous-looking [bathing] machines. **1882** 'L. MALET' *Mrs. Lorimer* I. v. 120 My dear, I feel a little stifled when I think of you guarded by these proprietous and unimaginative dragons. *Ibid.* vi. 132 Mrs. Mainwaring had lost for a moment that proprietous self-command and calm dignity of demeanour, which..were certainly liable to keep most people at a very respectful distance from her. **1913** D. H. LAWRENCE *Sons & Lovers* viii. 181 He must see a girl home from the skating rink—quite proprietously—and so can't get home. **1974** R. B. PARKER *Godwulf MS* i. 9 The elevator that took me to the fourth floor was covered with obscene graffiti that some proprietous soul had tried to doctor into acceptability. **1979** *Verbatim* Autumn 1/1 In Marvin Pope's exhaustive scholarly study of *The Song of Songs*, the Bride's vivid description of her passion for the Bridegroom as 'my bowels were moved for him'—striking in its proprietous King James context (5:4)—is rendered 'my inwards seethed for him.'

propriety, *sb.* Add: **7.** Also, *to play propriety*, to ensure correct moral behaviour, act as a chaperone.

1836 [in Dict.]. **1877** V. LUSH *Jrnl.* 13 Feb. (1975) 187, I invited a few of the Choir here after practice, with Mrs Scott and Mrs Lloyd to play propriety and we had a very jolly evening. **1925** I. SMITH *Marriage in Ceylon* 137 Angela..had felt it would not be 'the thing' to accept hospitality of the man who in a few days' time would be her husband without someone to 'play propriety'.

proprioceptor (prōᵘ·prioseptǫ̈ɹ). *Physiol.* [f. L. *propri-us* own, PROPER + -O + RE)CEPTOR.] Any sensory structure which receives stimuli arising within the tissues (other, usually, than the viscera); *esp.* one concerned with the sense of position and movement of a part of the body. Cf. *EXTEROCEPTOR, *INTEROCEPTOR.

1906 [see *EXTEROCEPTOR]. **1927** HALDANE & HUXLEY *Animal Biol.* i. 24 The receptor organs are those parts of the living organism which are specially sensitive to the changes going on around them. Some of them are affected by the changes going on inside the body in muscles and joints and in the organ of balance (proprioceptors), others by the changes taking place in the world outside (exteroceptors). **1938** *Jrnl. Exper. Biol.* XV. 112 The campaniform sensilla will act as proprioceptors for the palps. **1940** FRAENKEL & GUNN *Orientation of Animals* iv. 37 In the knee-jerk the stimulus is translated by the proprioceptors in the leg, goes to the central nervous system and is there, so to say, reflected back to the leg, where it is translated into effect or action. **1964** J. Z. YOUNG *Model of Brain* xv. 242 Proprioceptors are probably present [in octopus arms] but it is not clear how they could appropriately signal the position of the arms. **1974** D. & M. WEBSTER *Compar. Vertebr. Morphol.* x. 200 The most studied proprioceptor is the muscle spindle.

So **proprioce·ption**, the reception of information by proprioceptors and its interpretation; **proprioce·ptive** *a.*; **proprioce·ptively** *adv.* (*rare*).

1906 C. S. SHERRINGTON *Integrative Action of Nervous Syst.* iv. 130 Since in this field the stimuli to the receptors are given by the organism itself, their field may be called the proprio-ceptive field. *Ibid.* ix. 349 The supposition that the organ [*sc.* the cerebellum] is the chief co-ordinative centre or rather group of centres of the reflex system of proprio-ception. **1927** HALDANE & HUXLEY *Animal Biol.* v. 123 Proprioceptive organs may affect the consciousness. Thus we can tell how much our knee is bent even with our eyes shut, owing to the joint-organs, or how great a weight we are holding, owing to the muscle-organs. **1958** S. H. BARTLEY *Princ. Perception* xiv. 315 Kinesthesis and the vestibular sense have been called proprioception, since they have something to do with end results originated by the activity of the body itself. **1961** L. F. BROSNAHAN *Sounds of Language* i. 15 Articulations which are similar..must require greater precision of execution.. in order to keep the resulting speech sounds distinct, both proprioceptively and auditorily. **1968** *New Scientist* 7 Nov. 315/1 Proprioceptive information..describes such things as the tension in the muscles and the location and movement of the parts of the limb. **1977** *Lancet* 5 Nov. 977/1 He had..absent vibration sense, and very reduced proprioception in the lower limbs.

proprio-spinal (prōᵘ·prio͵spəinăl), *a. Anat.* Also as one word. [f. as prec. + SPINAL *a.*] Situated wholly within the spinal cord.

1904 C. S. SHERRINGTON in *Nature* 8 Sept. 461 (*caption*) Proprio-spinal neurones. *Ibid.* 463/1 We..arrive at the following reflex chain for the scratch reflex: (i.) The receptive neurone... (ii.) The long descending propriospinal neurone.., from the shoulder segment to the grey matter of leg segments. **1920** H. HEAD *Studies in Neurol.* II. III. 504 If these proprio-spinal paths have been destroyed, or their functions abolished, the mass-reflex may appear in its complete form even though some sensation and voluntary movement are still present below the level of the lesion. **1959** *Brain* LXXXII. 614 We have retained the name 'fasciculi proprii' for the fibres under review, as there is no suitable English equivalent. Sherrington's name 'proprio-spinal fibres'..might be suggested. But it seems to us that a name which includes the term 'spinal' is undesirable. **1974** *Exper. Brain Res.* XXI. 188 Our results show that long propriospinal fibres stimulated a few segments caudal to the cervical enlargement.

props, *sb. pl.* Add: **1. a.** (Earlier examples.)

1841 *Spirit of Times* 16 Oct. 396/2 There we subsisted by *spouting*, not Shakespeare, but our dresses and props. **1854** E. L. BLANCHARD *Diary* 22 Nov. in Scott & Howard *Life E. L. Blanchard* (1891) I. 125 Go to Drury; see props.

b. A familiar name for a property-man or the props department.

Quot. 1831 may be an example of *PROP *sb.*[5]

1831 P. EGAN *Show Folks* 23 'Good Houses' now to make him right, The *Treasury* to swell: The Actors [*sic*] need—the *Props* delight—And '*All's well, that ends well!*' **1889** [in Dict.]. **1902** PATTERSON & BATEMAN *By Stage Door* 192 While he was 'Props' he was discharged..for not yelling 'fire!' at the right time. **1921** GALSWORTHY *Six Short Plays* 128, I want 'Props'. *Ibid.* (*stage-direction*) 'Props' goes out through the French windows. **1933** P. GODFREY *Back-Stage* iv. 48 No self-respecting 'Props' will spend a penny on new materials if odd scraps will serve. **1976** M. MAGUIRE *Scratchproof* ii. 23 What do you think of our tack-room interior? Have props done a good job?

c. as *sing.* a stage property.

1911 C. POLLOCK *Footlights* 257 By-play with small articles, rehearsed twenty times, is blundered over when the player finds the 'prop' actually in his hands. **1961** M. CATTO *Mister Moses* iii. 80 The stage had been set—it awaited the last theatrical prop. **1976** *Early Music* Oct. 394/1 Each tableau, step, gesture, prop and lighting-cue must arise from necessity and have its effect at once. **1978** *Listener* 23 Mar. 366/3 Ronnie Barker's face..is,.. as with all true comedians, his best prop.

2. *transf.*

1898 A. M. BINSTEAD *Pink 'Un & Pelican* vi. 146 And when at last the day came for him to go, he 'collected his props', as he called getting his belongings together, most reluctantly. **1926** *Publishers' Weekly* 10 July 120/1 Woodard-Clarke's [window-display]..took a middle course between the painted background route and the 'props' of nature. The clear blue sky was conveyed by blue cloth of chiffon-like texture. **1948** M. GILBERT *They never looked Inside* iii. 35 Have a cigarette? They are part of the office props. **1976** S. BARSTOW *Right True End* III. xiv. 224 A shot of me standing on a stone pier beside a whelk-stall, holding a huge crab by one claw. It must have been dead, lent to me as a prop by some kindly stall-holder.

3. *attrib.* and *Comb.* **a.** *props department, girl, man*; **props room** = *property room* s.v. PROPERTY *sb.* 8b. **b.** Formed with the *sing.*, as *prop boy, girl, man*; **prop basket** = *PROPERTY BOX 2; **prop table** (see quot. 1964); **prop wagon**, a property wagon (see quot.).

1952 GRANVILLE *Dict. Theatr. Terms* 144 It is the traditional boast of an old actor that he was born in a *prop basket* in the prompt corner. **1935** *Motion Picture* Nov. 38 Colman, who was off in a corner talking with a prop boy, heard her. **1960** K. A. OMMANNEY *Stage & School* v. xv. 413 All movable articles are stored in the props department. **1970** R. LEACH *Theatre for Youth* I. v. 43 Masks properly belong to the props department. **1964** E. CRAMPTON *Handbk. Theatre* 260 These tables are the direct responsibility of the prop-girl. **1977** S. BRETT *Star Trap* iii. 31 There's always the stage staff... Nothing like a warm little props girl to comfort a chap. **1942** BERREY & VAN DEN BARK *Amer. Thes. Slang* § 605/12 *Property man*,..prop man. **1951** in H. DOWNS *Theatre & Stage* II. 818/2, I once knew a 'props' man who was..a marvel. **1971** *Esquire* July 88/3 We were watching the prop men lug the elephant tubs and the chimp- and lion-act furniture. **1978** M. PUZO *Fools Die* xxviii. 323 Script-girls, secretaries, studio accountants, cameramen, propmen, the technical crews, the actors and actresses, the directors and even the producers. **1957** Props room [see *BALLOON *sb.*[1] 6c]. **1977** C. WOOD *James Bond* xii. 103 This place..was like the props room of a folded theatrical company. **1939** BURRIS-MEYER & COLE *Scenery for Theatre* xiii. 390 Prop table, left. **1964** E. CRAMPTON *Handbk. Theatre* 260 *Prop tables*, tables set in the wings ..for properties to be taken on and brought off-stage during a performance. **1927** *Hollis St. Theatre Progr.* (Boston) 19 Sept. Gloss., *Prop wagon*, wagon for transporting paraphernalia and equipment used on carnival.

propugnaculum. (Earlier example.)

1773 BOSWELL *Jrnl. Tour Hebr.* 10 Sept. (1785) 198 Before it the ocean roars, being dashed against monstrous broken rocks; grand and aweful *propugnacula*.

propulsion. Add: **3.** *attrib.*, as *propulsion-jet, -system*; **propulsion gun**, a hand-held device that an astronaut can cause to eject a jet of compressed gas so as to propel him in space.

1958 C. C. ADAMS *Space Flight* viii. 196 Auxiliaries. These include taxis and propulsion 'guns' for individual men in space suits, or reaction power packages attached like outboard motors to large objects. **1965** *Life* 18 June 26/2 White himself used a camera attached to his propulsion gun, and McDivitt operated another at his window inside. **1935** BALMER & WYLIE *After Worlds Collide* i. 14 The earth around the huge metal cylinder had been melted by the blasts of its atomic propulsion-jets. **1961** *Amer. Speech* XXXVI. 170 In the years after 1919, he [*sc.* Robert Esnault-Pelterie] had taken the initiative in stimulating studies on propulsion systems for interplanetary travel. **1966** *Electronics* 14 Nov. 16/3 In addition, four panel discussions will bring together the nation's top men in the fields of space policy and launch and propulsion systems.

propyl. Now also with pronunc. (prōᵘ·pəil). Delete first sentence of def. and substitute: Either of two isomeric radicals, $CH_3{\cdot}CH_2{\cdot}$-CH_2— (*1-propyl, primary* or *normal propyl*) and $(CH_3)_2CH$— (*2-propyl, secondary propyl* or *isopropyl*); sometimes *spec.* the normal form. (Earlier and later examples.)

1850 *Phil. Trans. R. Soc.* CXL. 127 Substances of the formula $C_{18}H_{13}N$ will also be obtained..by fixing upon aniline the radical (propyl) belonging to the missing alcohol of propionic acid* (metacetic acid). [*Note*] *A more appropriate name for metacetic acid, proposed by Dumas, Malaguti and Leblanc.., as it is the *first* acid of the series $C_nH_nO_4$ that exhibits the character of a *fatty* acid. **1887** MOORE & AVELING tr. *Marx's Capital* I. i. 18 Butyric acid is a different substance from propyl formate. Yet both are made up of the same chemical substances, carbon (C), hydrogen (H), and oxygen (O), and that, too, in like proportions—namely, $C_4H_8O_2$. **1950** *Thorpe's Dict. Appl. Chem.* (ed. 4) X. 223/1 *n*-Propyl radical is formed by exposing the vapour of di-*n*-propyl ketone to ultra-violet light at 2 mm. pressure. **1951** I. L. FINAR *Org. Chem.* I. viii. 122 All aldehydes can be made to undergo the Cannizaro reaction by treatment with aluminium ethoxide. Under these conditions the acid and alcohol are combined as the ester,..*e.g.*..propionaldehyde gives propyl propionate.

pro:pylthiou·racil, any propyl derivative of a thiouracil; *spec.* 6-*n*-propyl-2-thiouracil, $C_7H_{10}N_2OS$, an antithyroid substance used to combat thyrotoxicosis.

1945 *Jrnl. Clin. Endocrinol.* V. 424/1 The compounds 6-ethylthiouracil and 6-*n*-propylthiouracil are among a group which are approximately ten times as active as thiouracil when tested in rats. *Ibid.* 424/2 It seemed fitting to test the effectiveness of ethylthiouracil and propylthiouracil in human beings suffering from hyperthyroidism. **1961** *Lancet* 23 Sept. 688/2 On 2 of these patients there was subsequent difficulty in management with a lack of the usual responsiveness to propylthiouracil. **1975** B. CATZ *Thyroid Case Stud.* 13 The dose of propylthiouracil taken daily was 600 mg.

propylene. Add: **2.** Used *attrib.* or in *Comb.* in the names of derivatives: **propylene glycol,** either of two isomeric liquids, $CH_2OH{\cdot}$-$CHOH{\cdot}CH_3$ and $CH_2OH{\cdot}CH_2{\cdot}CH_2OH$; *spec.* the 1,2-glycol (the former), which has a wide variety of uses, chiefly as a solvent or carrier, as a constituent of antifreeze, and in the food and perfume industries; **propylene imine** (also **pro:pylen(e)i·mine**) [ad. G. *propylenimin* (Gabriel & Ohle 1917, in *Ber. d. Deut. Chem. Ges.* L. 815)], a synthetic, colourless, highly inflammable liquid, $CH_3{\cdot}CH{\cdot}CH_2{\cdot}NH$, which is widely used industrially, freq. in polymerized form and esp. as a binding agent with dyes and adhesives, and in the manufacture of plastics, paper, etc.

1885 MORLEY & GREEN in *Jrnl. Chem. Soc.* XLVII. 132 From the aqueous portion of the distillate 140 grams of propylene glycol (boiling at 185–195°) can be obtained by fractional distillation. **1926** *Jrnl. Biol. Chem.* LXVIII. 416 It was..desired to convert propylene glycol into β-hydroxybutyric acid by a set of reactions which would not involve carbon atom (2). **1951** I. L. FINAR *Org. Chem.* I. xvii. 329 Lactic acid..may be prepared: (i) By oxidising propylene glycol with dilute nitric acid. **1966** *Kirk–Othmer Encycl. Chem. Technol.* (ed. 2) X. 649, 1,2-Propylene glycol, $CH_3CHOHCH_2OH$, is a colorless and odorless liquid with a slightly sweet taste. **1917** *Jrnl. Chem. Soc.* CXII. I. 564 β-Bromopropylamine and β-bromo*iso*propylamine.. both yield β-bromo*iso*propylamine, this result being explicable by the intermediate compound being propylenimine. **1944** *Jrnl. Org. Chem.* IX. 133 Propylenimine was prepared from 2-amino-1-propanol. **1966** *Kirk–Othmer Encycl. Chem. Technol.* (ed. 2) XI. 527 Ethylenimine and propylenimine are colorless mobile liquids with a strong ammoniacal odor. **1971** *Nature* 16 Apr. 460/2 Propylene imine is an important chemical intermediate with a variety of applications in the production of polymers, coatings, adhesives, textiles and paper finishes.

propylidene (propi·l-, propəi·lidīn). *Chem.* [ad. F. *propylidène* (E. Reboul 1876, in *Compt. Rend.* LXXXII. 30): see PROPYL and *-IDENE.] The bivalent radical CH_3CH_2CH=; usu. *attrib.*, esp. in names of derivatives of this.

1876 *Jrnl. Chem. Soc.* XXIX. I. 894 Propionic aldehyde is treated with phosphoric chloride, and forms a propylidene dichloride homolog[o]us with ethylidene dichloride; its formula is CH_3—CH_2—$CHCl_2$, and it boils at 85°–87°. **1903** A. J. WALKER tr. *Holleman's Text-Bk. Org. Chem.* I. 146 Propylene chloride, $C_3H_6Cl_2$,..is not identical with the reaction-product obtained by treating acetone with phosphorus pentachloride..nor with that from propionaldehyde, $CH_3{\cdot}CH_2{\cdot}CHCl_2$ (propylidene chloride). **1951** I. L. FINAR *Org. Chem.* I. iv. 49 General methods of preparation of the olefins... By the action of zinc dust on methanolic solutions of *gem*-dihalogen derivatives of the paraffins.., *e.g.*, propylene from propylidene bromide. **1976** *Chem. Physics Lett.* XXXVII. 220/2 The barrier to conversion of propylidene to propylene is greater than in C_2H_4.

propylitization (prǫ:pilitəizē̆ⁱ·ʃən). *Petrol.* [f. PROPYLIT(E + -IZATION.] The hydrothermal alteration of an igneous rock to propylite.

1903 A. GEIKIE *Text-bk. Geol.* (ed. 4) II. 812 The solutions ..in their progress..induce chemical and mineralogical changes in the surrounding rocks which thus undergo various transformations, being sometimes weakened by the removal of certain constituents, as in propylitization and kaolinisation. **1965** G. V. WILLIAMS *Econ. Geol. N.Z.*

viii. 87/1 The mineralization is a typical Tertiary andesitic propylitization of which there is evidence from Te Puke..in the south to Great Barrier Island in the north. *Ibid.*, They found..that zones of intense propylitization (containing known gold-bearing veins) are detectable electrically.

propyne (prōᵘ·pəin). *Chem.* [f. PROP(ANE + *-YNE.] A gaseous, unsaturated hydrocarbon, CH_3—C⋮CH, which resembles acetylene, from which it is formally derived by replacing a hydrogen atom by methyl; allylene.

1931 *Jrnl. Chem. Soc.* 1610 The names of hydrocarbons containing the triple linking will end in *yne, diyne*, etc... Examples: Propyne, heptyne. **1935** *Jrnl. Amer. Chem. Soc.* LVII. 1089/2 The gaseous product of the reaction, propyne, was not determined quantitatively, but was identified through the fact that it formed a silver salt with ammoniacal silver nitrate solution. **1969** M. JULIA in H. G. Viehe *Chem. of Acetylenes* v. 341 Acetylene itself with photolyzed diazomethane..gave propyne and allene. **1975** GUTSCHE & PASTO *Fund. Org. Chem.* viii. 208 Treatment of propyne with water (in the presence of mercuric ion..) yields 2-propenol, which immediately rearranges to..acetone.

pro-rate, *v.* Add: Also **prorate.** **a.** (Earlier and later examples.)

1860 *Congress. Globe* 21 Dec. 180/1 The amendment.. requires this company to pro-rate passenger fare with all railroad companies or lines which terminate either at Alexandria, Washington or Baltimore. **1921** *Oil & Gas Jrnl.* 1 July 3/1 (*heading*) Are runs to be prorated? **1926** J. ISE *U.S. Oil Policy* xii. 116 California oil was cutting deeper into the eastern markets all the time, and in July [1923] some of the pipe-line companies in the eastern fields started to prorate runs. **1963** J. MITFORD *Amer. Way of Death* v. 66 In all likelihood, idle time of employees is figured in and prorated as part of the 'man-hours'. **1978** *Time* 3 July 37/3 San Jose businessman Larry Whitaker ..said he would pro-rate his own $18,921 property tax cut among his 150 California employees.

Hence also **pro-ra·ted** *ppl. a.*, **pro-ra·ting** *vbl. sb.*

1911 F. E. WEBNER *Factory Costs* 212 On the other hand, there is no possible way of entirely avoiding a prorating or averaging of expense. **1921** *Oil & Gas Jrnl.* 1 July 3/1 In order to conserve space in the containers there may be instituted in the near future a prorating program. **1967** *Boston Sunday Globe* 23 Apr. 24 (Advt.), A pro-rated portion of the purchase price.

proration (prorē¹·ʃən). [f. PRO-RATE *v.* + -ION.] The action or an instance of prorating; *spec.* allocation of the permitted production of oil or gas between competing operators, fields, etc.

1923 *Oil Weekly* 22 Sept. 12/1 The Eastern fields and those of the Middle West are without proration problems. **1931** *Economist* 20 June 1324/2 Oil proration, copper curtailment agreements, and railroad mergers indicate the swing of the pendulum. **1954** R. CASSADY *Price Making in Petroleum Industry* vii. 114 Under a proration scheme.. a sort of floor is placed under prices by limiting the amount of oil to be withdrawn on a basis of the needs of the market. **1957** *Times* 11 Dec. 16/5 The Pembina Oilfield is subject to strict proration; but all the wells have produced the maximum allowable since they were completed. **1960** *Economist* 15 Oct. 264/1 The ideas of a petroleum exporters' cartel, miscalled 'international proration'..are not inherently unfeasible. **1971** *Nature* 28 May p. viii/1 (Advt.), Only a Wang 100 can do side calculations, analyses, prorations and serve as an adding machine.

Hence **prora·tioning** *vbl. sb.* in the same sense.

1948 E. V. ROSTOW *National Policy for Oil Industry* iii. 21 In 1932, the Supreme Court declared prorationing legal. **1959** DE CHAZEAU & KAHN *Integration & Competition in Petroleum Industry* vii. 163 Prorationing to market demand has clearly brought about orderly marketing of crude oil with much fewer and less extreme price changes. **1960** *Guardian* 15 Oct. 7/5 The Organisation of Petroleum Exporting Countries..would..try to keep prices stable by regulating production (the system known to the industry as 'pro-rationing'). **1962** W. A. LEEMAN *Price of Middle East Oil* ix. 230 In effect the Venezuelans proposed a system of world-wide 'prorationing', similar to the arrangements already established in Texas, Louisiana, Oklahoma, and a number of other states.

proroguing, *vbl. sb.* (Later example.)

1937 G. FRANKAU *More of Us* vi. 69 And, as he donned those shoes Shoemaker Lobb webs From toe to heel with best bespoken broguing, This house of lords seemed ripe for his proroguing.

pros (prǫs), var. *PROSS.

1905 *Sessions Paper* 8 Feb. 556 She is only a *pros.*; you know her. **1972** J. MILLS *Report to Commissioner* 104 I'm a pros, man, I shoot up in my thighs.

‖**prosa** (prōᵘ·ză). *Eccl.* Pl. prosae. [L.] = PROSE *sb.* 2. Cf. *PROSULA.

1801 T. BUSBY *Dict. Mus.*, *Prosæ*, certain hymns used in the Romish church consisting of rhyme without measure. **1907** [see *PROSULA]. **1929** *Exultet Roll* (Brit. Mus.) 5 In the South of Italy, at least from the early part of the tenth century till the thirteenth, a custom existed of writing out this prosa..on a separate roll distinct from the other services of the day. **1957** N. FRYE *Anat. Crit.* 275 The emergence of the 'prosa' out of the sequence in medieval music. **1970** P. EVANS *Early Trope Repertory of St. Martial de Limoges* i. 9 Both the prosa and the prosula are basically literary in their conception. The prosa is created by adding a text to the pre-existent melismatic sequentia which follows the Alleluia.

prosauropod (prosǭ·ropod), *sb.* and *a.* *Palæont.* [ad. mod.L. name of infraorder *Prosauropoda* (F. von Huene 1920, in *Zeitschr. für Induktive Abstammungs- und Vererbungslehre* XXII. 211), f. PRO-² 1 + mod.L. *Sauropoda*: see SAUROPOD *a.* and *sb.*] **A.** *sb.* A dinosaur belonging to the infraorder Prosauropoda, which includes herbivorous, usually bipedal, saurischians. **B.** *adj.* Of or pertaining to an animal of this kind.

1951 C. C. YOUNG in *Palaeontologia Sinica* CXXXIV. 88 For the sake of convenience we may discuss the prosauropods together. **1962** E. H. COLBERT *Dinosaurs* iv. 80 The prosauropods quickly developed to become the dinosaur giants of their day. **1965** *Proc. Linn. Soc.* CLXXVI. 211 Each of the two prosauropod families transferred from the Carnosauria..bears..a striking resemblance to one of two existing prosauropod families. **1971** E. C. OLSON *Vertebr. Paleozool.* II. viii. 354 Some genera..among animals often classed as prosauropods were intermediate in structures related to gait, being only partially quadrupedal. **1978** *Nature* 17 Aug. 662/1 Prosauropods probably could feed tripodally—supporting their weight on the hindlimbs and stout tail.

proscenium. Add: **3.** *proscenium box* (earlier examples), *curtain, drop, opening.*

1828 J. R. PLANCHÉ *Paris & London* (1830) I. v. 24 (*stage direction*) A Diagonal View of the Stage of the Odeon is seen through the wings—the proscenium boxes, L. **1849** THACKERAY *Pendennis* I. xiv. 124 One of the illustrious patrons of the Museum Theatre, and occupant of the great proscenium-box, was..the Marquis of Steyne. **1829** *Harlequin* 20 June 46 The only drop below the proscenium curtain was the very fine pierced forest limbs, which every frequenter of Drury Lane Theatre must recollect. **1975** C. HOGGET *Stage Crafts* i. 14 Pelmet for proscenium curtains should overhang reveals to allow curtains to open fully. **1827** T. DIBDIN *Reminisc.* II. 115 One artist offered to paint me a proscenium drop (as we call the painted cloth which falls between the acts). **1889** *Theatre* XIII. 292 The proscenium opening is formed by groups of columns on either side of the first proscenium box. **1974** *Encycl. Brit. Micropædia* VIII. 244/1 The proscenium opening was of particular importance to the realistic playwrights of the 19th century.

prosciutto (proʃū·to). Also (erron.) **prosciuto.** [It., 'ham'.] Italian spiced ham. Also (pleonastically) *prosciutto ham.*

c **1938** *Fortnum & Mason Price List* 39/2 Proscuitto [*sic*] (Hors d'Œuvre Sliced Ham)..3/9. **1945** E. WAUGH *Brideshead Revisited* I. iv. 90 Melon and prosciuto on the balcony. **1952** V. CANNING *House of Seven Flies* iii. 53 Charlie had ventured too far in search of black market *vino, prosciutto* and anything else he could lay his hands on. **1960** I. FLEMING *For Your Eyes Only* 153, I shall have melon with prosciutto ham. **1964** MRS. L. B. JOHNSON *White House Diary* 6 May (1970) 131 We had a gourmet lunch, beginning with prosciutto and melon. **1965** *Guardian* 4 Aug. 6/4 *Prosciutto* ham was among the delicacies on the buffet table. **1967** 'J. CROSS' *To Hell for Half-a-Crown* xv. 190 She had fixed melon with *prosciutto.* **1977** C. MCFADDEN *Serial* xx. 46/2 Kate..sauntered up to a vantage point in front of the prosciutto.

prose, *sb.* Add: **4. a.** Also, a dull, prosy person. *colloq.*

1844 DICKENS *Mart. Chuz.* xxxvii. 439, I verily believe you have said that fifty thousand times, in my hearing. What a Prose you are!

6. *prose book, work*; **prose fiction,** the genre of fictional narratives written in prose; **prose-poem** (earlier examples); **prose sense,** the meaning of a poem as it can be paraphrased in prose; **prose style,** characteristic manner of writing in prose.

1940 DYLAN THOMAS *Let.* 13 May (1966) 248, I do not want to write another straight prosebook yet. **1841** Prose-fiction [see PERFECT *a.* 4 a]. **1848** MILL *Pol. Econ.* I. II. xiv. 467 The most successful writer of prose fiction (Scott). **1919** V. WOOLF in *Times Lit. Suppl.* 10 Apr. 189/2 It is for..[the historian of literature] to ascertain whether we are now at the beginning, or middle, or end, of a great period of prose fiction. **1957** *Encyl. Brit.* XVI. 573/2 Dickens, perhaps the most remarkable genius in the history of English prose fiction. **1842** POE in *Graham's Mag.* Jan. 69/1 Criticism is *not*..an essay, nor a sermon, nor an oration,..nor a prose-poem. **1850** C. KINGSLEY *Alton Locke* I. ix. 139 That great prose poem, the single epic of modern days, Thomas Carlyle's 'French Revolution'. **1947** C. BROOKS *Well Wrought Urn* xi. 182 The 'prose-sense' of the poem is not a rack on which the stuff of the poem is hung. **1852** THACKERAY *Esmond* III. iii. 88 His [*sc.* Addison's] prose style I think is altogether inimitable. **1906** R. BROOKE *Let.* 10 May (1968) 51 This effort has..worked..havoc in my carefully elaborated prose-style. **1959** G. D. PAINTER *Proust* I. viii. 115 His [*sc.* Proust's] prose style was..faded and artificial. **1976** N. FREELING *Lake Isle* xiii. 120 Someone, presumably..has been phoning somebody. A prefect to judge from the prose style. *c* **1827** MILL *Speech* in *Adelphi* (1924) I. 692 The very small number of good prose works which have been published for many years past, except indeed novels. **1934** J. JOYCE *Let.* 1 June (1966) III. 306, I work every day alone at my big long wide high deep dense prosework. **1978** W. WHITE *Whitman's Daybks. & Notebks.* I. p. xxiii, Every name of a person, place, book, poem, prose work, or a 'situation' in Whitman's life and times that seemed to me to call for annotation, I have annotated.

prosecretin: see *PRO-² 1.

prosecute, *v.* **6. d.** (Further examples.)

1865 *Chambers's Encycl.* VII. 799/1 If a person is murdered, some one of the relatives naturally prosecutes. **1901** G. B. SHAW *Capt. Brassbound's Conversion* III. 286 The counsel for the prosecution can proceed to prosecute. The floor is yours, Lady Waynflete. **1966** *Listener* 9 June 828/1 Even when the police prosecute, committal for trial cannot be left entirely to their discretion. **1971** *Reader's Digest Family Guide to Law* 743/1 A private individual has the right in most cases to follow the same procedure, even if the police have decided not to prosecute.

prosecuting *ppl. a.* (earlier and later examples).

1832 *Jrnl. Indiana Ho. Representatives* 6 Dec. 33 Duly elected Prosecuting Attorney of the 2d Judicial Circuit. **1912** M. NICHOLSON *Hoosier Chron.* 180 The Republican prosecuting attorney of Ranger County joined with the local bank in certifying Miles's probity. **1959** *Granta* 6 June 33/2 'Where were you?' shouted the bluff prosecuting counsel. **1976** *Daily Mirror* 16 July 9/2 Prosecuting authorities are now more sensitive to the need to investigate suspicions of corruption.

prosecutorial (prǫsĭkiūtōᵊ·riăl), *a.* [f. PROSECUTOR + -IAL.] Of or pertaining to a prosecuting official or his duties. Also *transf.*

1973 *N.Y. Law Jrnl.* 19 July 1/8 To our minds the participants' attempt to set up a federal crime for which these defendants stand convicted went beyond any proper prosecutorial role. **1975** *Columbia Law Rev.* LXXV. 130 Prosecutorial discretion is the power held by an agency or official charged with enforcement of the law to exercise selectivity in the choice of occasions for the law's enforcement. **1978** *N.Y. Times* 30 Mar. B3/5 The Midtown Enforcement Project has received a Federal grant..to bring innovative enforcement and prosecutorial methods to the area from 30th Street to 60th Street from river to river. **1978** *Listener* 29 June 848/1 His closely-argued, mercilessly prosecutorial book.

proselyting, *vbl. sb.* (Later examples.)

1931 H. F. PRINGLE *Theodore Roosevelt* II. xiii. 456 Mrs. Storer went on with her proselyting. **1948** *Richmond* (Va.) *Times-Dispatch* 13 Feb. 30/1 San Francisco..was guilty of one of the worst cases of out-and-out..proselyting and subsidizing yet seen.

pro-sentence: see *PRO-¹ 4b.

proseology (prozǫ·lŏdʒi). *colloq. rare.* [f. PROSE *sb.* + -OLOGY.] Prolix, turgid, or confusing prose.

1909 *Daily Chron.* 19 July 3/4 To plough through all the extracts from journals, letters, &c., which form the book needs not a little patience and sticking power. Doubtless, those who can get beneath all this proseology will find much to excite them. **1968** *Economist* 29 June p. xi/2 The usual, easy proseology reviling the accursed folk or crying the beloved country.

pro shop: see PRO* *abbrev.* 2c.

prosimian, *a.* and *sb.* (Examples.) Substitute for defs.: **A.** *adj.* Of, belonging to, or designating prosimians. **B.** *sb.* A mammal belonging to the suborder Prosimii, a group of primitive, mostly arboreal primates, which includes lemurs, lorises, galagos, and tarsiers.

1925 *Bull. Geol. Soc. China* IV. 142 In some area intermediate between the Oriental and Ethiopian regions the centre of prosimian dispersal was located. **1945** *Bull. Amer. Mus. Nat. Hist.* LXXXV. 181/2 It seems quite possible that New World and Old World monkeys arose independently from Eocene prosimians... Their prosimian ancestors, if distinct, must have been closely allied. **1959** *New Scientist* 10 Dec. 1175/1 Professor Schultz considers that the very important exploratory function of the hands of simians superseded the tactile sense of the prosimians (such as the lemurs). **1966** [see *HIGH *a.* 6d]. **1972** T. A. VAUGHAN *Mammalogy* vii. 117 (*caption*) Hands and feet of some prosimian primates. **1974** *Sci. Amer.* Apr. 127/1 The prosimians and the tenrecs, unlike any other mammals, respond sharply to external temperature. **1977** P. NAPIER *Lemurs, Lorises & Bushbabies* i. 9 The lemurs, lorises and bushbabies are called prosimians.

prosiopesis (prǫsĭopī·sis). *Gram.* [f. Gr. προ- before + σιώπησις taciturnity, f. σιωπᾶν to be silent.] Jespersen's term for ellipsis of the beginning of a grammatical structure in speech.

1924 O. JESPERSEN *Philos. Gram.* x. 142 The subject must generally be expressed, and those few cases in which it is omitted, may be explained through prosiopesis, which sometimes becomes habitual in certain stock exclamations like *Thank you.* **1927** —— *Mod. Eng. Gram.* III. 226 *It* is occasionally left out through prosiopesis. **1935** H. STRAUMANN *Newspaper Headlines* 41 Whether such sentences should be considered as incomplete or elliptic or as aposiopesis and prosiopesis is a question of terminology. **1966** G. N. LEECH *Eng. in Advertising* viii. 78 One marginally casual feature of advertising language is the occurrence of what..has been termed prosiopesis.

prosiphonate, *a.* (Examples.)

1935 TWENHOFEL & SHROCK *Invertebr. Paleont.* ix. 378 Prosiphonate ones [*sc.* septa] are found in Mesozoic forms [of cephalopod]. **1952** R. C. MOORE et al. *Invertebr. Fossils* ix. 371/1 In late Paleozoic and Mesozoic ammonoids, this structure [*sc.* the siphuncle] is mostly confined to immature stages, and forward-pointing septal necks appear in submature whorls. This condition is described as prosiphonate. **1970** R. M. BLACK *Elements Palaeont.* viii. 86 Short septal necks encircle the siphuncle where it passes through the septa; the septal necks project forwards (prosiphonate) in the later formed septa of Mesozoic ammonites.

‖ **prosit** (prō·sit), *int.* [L., usu. through Ger., 'may it benefit'.] Used to wish good health, success, etc., esp. as a toast in German-speaking countries.

1846 R. FORD *Gatherings from Spain* xv. 182 '*Muchas gracias, buen provecho le haga á usted*', 'Many thanks—much good may it do your grace', an answer which is analogous to the *prosit* of Italian peasants after eating or sneezing. **1916** J. BUCHAN *Greenmantle* iii. 40 He filled us two long tankards of very good Munich beer. '*Prosit*,' he said, raising his glass. **1930** AUDEN *Poems* 12 Thanks. Prosit! **1937** E. AMBLER *Uncommon Danger* x. 131 Vodka ..should be poured straight down the throat. I will show you. *Prosit!* **1944** W. LOWRIE tr. *Kierkegaard's Attack upon 'Christendom'* 170 For one who belongs essentially to the criminal world..the taking of an oath is no more than saying 'Prosit' to one who sneezes, or adding Esq. to a letter. **1951** F. BROWN *Murder can be Fun* ii. 24 'Prosit!' said Tracy. They drank. **1973** WILSON & MICHAELS tr. *M. Bar-Zohar's Third Truth* v. 73 Schneider said '*Prosit*,' and lifted his glass.

prosocial (prōᵘsōᵘ·ʃăl), *a. Social Psychol.* Also **pro-social.** [f. PRO-¹ 5 + SOCIAL *a.*] Of or pertaining to the type of behaviour that is automatically loyal, sometimes in a rigid and conventional manner, to the moral standards accepted by the established group; freq. contrasted with antisocial or asocial types of response.

1961 R. R. SEARS in *Jrnl. Abnormal Psychol.* LXIII. 471/2 Prosocial aggression is aggression used in a socially approved way for purposes that are acceptable to the moral standards of the group. **1972** *Jrnl. Social Psychol.* LXXXVI. 223 The subjects who made more flexible, asocial moral judgements felt less concern about doing well..than those who were more conventional and prosocial. **1973** PATTERSON & COBB in J. F. Knutson *Control of Aggression* 176 The analysis of stimulus control for prosocial responses required that the interaction involve two persons who had not interacted with each other during the preceding eighteen months. **1977** *New Society* 5 May 244/2 Little work has been done on measuring the positive effects of 'prosocial' programmes which may help correct the imbalance in British television of, on average, four violent 'incidents' an hour.

prosodeme (prǫ·sodīm). *Linguistics.* [f. *PROSOD(IC *a.* 2 + *-EME: cf. F. *prosodème.*] A prosodic feature with phonemic status; a suprasegmental phoneme. Hence **prosode·mic** *a.*

1940 *Language* XVI. 249 The discussion of the vowel systems is thoroughly confused by the lack of separation between segmental and prosodic phonemes, so that one never knows whether, say, a long and a short vowel pair consists of two vowel phonemes or of a single vowel with two different prosodemes of quantity. **1945** *Ibid.* XXI. 283 He says that there are two prosodemes of vowel quality. **1949** *Ibid.* XXV. 282 Any significant sound feature whose overlap of other features is temporally correlated to syllabic contour should be called a prosodeme, and should be treated by itself in a manner appropriate to its special nature. **1955** *Archivum Linguisticum* VII. II. 134 The Polish accent..being separated from the end of the word which it indicates by its position, by the intervention of another prosodeme. **1964** L. S. HULTZÉN in D. Abercrombie et al. *Daniel Jones* 85 The treatment is primarily at prosodemic level. **1971** D. CRYSTAL *Linguistics* iv. 184 Contrastive units in suprasegmental phonology were sometimes called prosodemes, or prosodic phonemes.

prosodic, *a.* Add: **2.** *Linguistics.* Of or pertaining to suprasegmental features of pitch, juncture, stress, etc. Also, of or pertaining to prosodies (*PROSODY 2*); esp. *prosodic analysis*, the type of linguistic analysis associated with J. R. Firth and his followers, which employs as fundamental concepts the phonematic unit (see *PHONEMATIC *a.* b) and the prosody.

1940 *Language* XVI. 31 There are a number of vowel phonemes, each of which may be accompanied by either short quantity or long quantity, these being prosodic phonemes. **1942** BLOCH & TRAGER *Outl. Linguistic Anal.* 41 We now turn our attention to those modifications of the segmental bounds to which we have given the names of *quantity*, *accent* and *juncture*... The methods of analysis are in principle the same for these prosodic features as for segmental phonemes... The product of the analysis will be an inventory of what may be called the *prosodic* or *suprasegmental phonemes.* **1949** J. R. FIRTH in *Trans. Philol. Soc. 1948* 136 The prosodic diacritica included tone, voice quality, and other properties of the sonants. **1952** A. COHEN *Phonemes of Eng.* 19 Other elements of speech, such as length, stress, or pitch, which according to the terminology of Prague are called prosodic features or 'suprasegmental phonemes' in American usage. **1955** *Bull. School of Oriental & Afr. Stud.* XVII. 134 The difference in theoretical basis between the prosodic approach and the phoneme theory is reflected firstly in the setting up of a total *system* to account for the phonetic material presented here, and secondly in the stating of that system not in relation to the *syllable* but to the *word.* **1957** *Proc. Univ. of Durham Philos. Soc.* I. Ser. B (Arts) I. 3 The aim of prosodic analysis in phonology is.. a phonological analysis in terms which account take [*sic*] not only of paradigmatic relations and contrasts, but also of the equally important syntagmatic relations and functions which are operative in speech. **1968** J. LYONS *Introd. Theoret. Linguistics* iii. 131 By virtue of their occurrence in words of one prosodic class rather than another, they are realized phonetically in different ways. **1971** *Archivum Linguisticum* II. 68 The mainspring of prosodic analysis in phonology was the recognition of phonetic features whose domains extended beyond those of the (more practical) phoneme. **1974** R. QUIRK *Linguist & Eng. Lang.* i. 20 His [*sc.* Dickens's] characters' speeches are..repeatedly accompanied by instructions as to tempo, stress, pitch, rhythm, and other prosodic features.

prosodically, *adv.* Add: **b.** With regard to prosodic features (*PROSODIC *a.* 2).

1949 *Trans. Philol. Soc. 1948* 144 The Danish glottal stop is..best considered prosodically as a feature of syllabic structure and word formation. **1964** M. A. K. HALLIDAY et al. *Linguistic Sciences* iii. 69 The vowel phoneme /iː/, is prosodically marked: it is characterized by the movement of the tongue towards a certain position, rather than by its attainment of a fixed position for a fixed segment of time. **1973** *Nature* 13 Apr. 481/1 The early utterances of the child which consist of only single morphemes are nevertheless 'sentences' since they are prosodically marked and because they are productively used.

prosody. Add: **2*.** *Linguistics.* In the theories of J. R. Firth and his followers: a phonological feature having as its domain more than one segment.

Prosodies include the class of 'suprasegmental' features such as intonation, stress, and juncture, but also some features which are regarded as 'segmental' in phonemic theory, e.g. palatalization, lip-rounding, nasalization.

1949 J. R. FIRTH in *Trans. Philol. Soc. 1948* 129 We may abstract those features which mark word or syllable initials and word or syllable finals or word junctions from the word, piece, or sentence, and regard them syntagmatically as prosodies, distinct from the phonematic constituents which are referred to as units of the consonant and vowel systems. **1951** *Bull. School of Oriental & Afr. Stud.* XIII. 945 The prosodies abstracted by these treatments have included not only aspiration but also, e.g. yotization, labiovelarization, rhotacization, affrication, friction, and voice. **1957** *Proc. Univ. of Durham Philos. Soc.* I. Ser. B (Arts) I. 3 *Prosodic analysis*..makes use of two types of element, Prosodies and Phonematic Units... Phonematic units refer to those features or aspects of the phonic material which are best regarded as referable to minimal segments, having serial order in relation to each other in structures... Structures are not, however, completely stated in these terms; a great part..of the phonic material is referable to prosodies, which are, by definition, of more than one segment in scope or domain of relevance, and may in fact belong to structures of any length. **1964** R. H. ROBINS *Gen. Linguistics* iv. 161 The relevant phonetic data may be assigned to such different categories of prosody as sentence prosodies, sentence part prosodies, word prosodies, syllable prosodies, and syllable part prosodies. **1966** J. T. BENDOR-SAMUEL in C. E. Bazell *In Memory of J. R. Firth* 31 There are three word prosodies: nasalization, yodization, and the absence of nasalization and yodization. **1968** [see *PHONEMATIC *a.* b]. **1971** *Archivum Linguisticum* II. 68 In phonology, too,..the Firthian view was to reject the phoneme in favour of a syntagmatic concept, which was termed—perhaps not too happily—the 'prosody'.

prosopagnosia (prǫ:sopægnōᵘ·siă). *Med.* [mod.L., ad. G. *prosopagnosie* (J. Bodamer 1948, in *Arch. f. Psychiatrie* CLXXIX. 6), f. Gr. πρόσωπ-ον face, person + ἀγνωσία ignorance.] An inability to recognize a face as that of any particular person.

1950 *Q. Cumulative Index Medicus* XLIV. 125/2 Agnosia in recognition of physiognomy (prosopagnosia). **1953** *Brain* LXXVI. 542 There is still to be considered the seeming contradiction between the patient's severe prosop-agnosia and his better achievements in the perception of Snellen's types, in time reading and counting of fingers. **1976** *Lancet* 30 Oct. 967/1 She can read N6 slowly and complains of inability to recognise faces (prosopagnosia): people are recognised by their voices. **1979** *Sci. Amer.* Sept. 162/3 The lesions that cause prosopagnosia are as stereotyped as the disorder itself.

prosopography. Restrict † *Obs.* to sense in Dict. and add: **2.** [tr. mod.L. *prosopographia.*] A study or description of an individual's life and career; hence, historical inquiry, esp. in Roman hist., concerned with the study of (political) careers and family connections; a presentation of evidence relating to this study.

The German word *prosopographie* is attested at an earlier date than the English form, but with less specific methodological implications.

1929 R. M. DAWKINS *Sanctuary of Artemis Orthia at Sparta* x. 292 Account has been taken of the lettering, the formulae, and the prosopography. **1934** R. SYME in *Jrnl. Roman Stud.* XXIV. 80 Of recent years prosopography, as it may conveniently be called, has been the object of a heightened interest coincident with the detailed study of the development and working of the imperial administration. **1954** A. MOMIGLIANO in *Cambr. Jrnl.* Mar. 345 He [*sc.* M. I. Rostovtzeff] was lucky in being born early enough to escape the present ridiculous adoration of so-called prosopography (which, as we all know, claims to have irrefutably established the previously unknown phenomenon of family ties). **1959** A. G. WOODHEAD *Study Gk. Inscriptions* iv. 47 A prosopography for the Argolid.. and another for Macedonia..mark the beginnings of similar coverage for other parts of Greece. **1961** *Encounter* Jan. 40/1 The technique which..has come to be known as *prosopography*: 'the study of personalities'. **1968** L. DURRELL *Tunc* ii. 62 A queer sort of prosopography reigns over this section of time. **1969** H. B. A. PETERSSON *Anglo-Saxon Currency* iv. 71 *Prosopography*, the comparative study of the personnel charged with the minting of a coinage. **1970** *Times Lit. Suppl.* 13 Nov. 1326/4 Arthur Schlesinger, Jr., takes Mr. Powell as an exponent of 'prosopography', a term borrowed from the ancient historians. A prosopographer investigates 'the common background characteristics of a group of actors in history by means of a collective study of their lives'. **1971** A. H. M. JONES et al. (*title*) The prosopography of the later Roman Empire. **1973** *Proc. Brit. Acad.* LVII. 429 The third and very important and permanent by-product of [A. H. M.] Jones's needs is the *Prosopography of the Later Roman Empire*... The other scholars who have brought the *Prosopography* into being will in the end have done the major part of the huge task, but Volume I at least will stand as a particular and lasting monument to Jones. **1973** *Jrnl. Interdisciplinary Hist.* III. 543 (*heading*) The Prosopography of the Tudor University. *Ibid.* 544 On the theme of prosopography (or collective biography), the argument has tended to revolve around two distinct but related issues: the social status and numbers of those attending the universities. **1975** *Anglo-Saxon Eng.* IV. 168 Dolley..infers from prosopography that the missing first element of the moneyer's name on this cut-halfpenny is not *Ægel-* but some form of *Leof-*. **1976** *Times Lit. Suppl.* 18 June 734/4 He [*sc.* C. E. Stevens] had a preoccupation..with 'gutting the source'..and so likewise, whether their field be history (social, political, military or economic), historiography or prosopography, do the contributors whose work is assembled here to do him honour.

Hence **prosopo·grapher**, one who undertakes or is concerned with prosopography; **prosopogra·phic(al)** *a.*, denoting the method of historical inquiry which makes use of prosopography; **prosopogra·phically** *adv.*, in a prosopographical manner; as regards prosopography.

1930 *Antiquity* IV. 526 During the period from the 4th. century to the Roman rehandling of the site a series of dedicatory inscriptions, mostly of the latter 1st. and 2nd. century A.D., accumulated. These Mr. Woodward describes with much prosopographic detail. **1933** R. SYME in *Classical Q.* XXVII. 144 A mistake or a change of name must be assumed—or else we must believe that the grandfather received a second consulate from Augustus... The whole question has a more than prosopographical value. **1939** —— *Roman Revolution* p. viii, The index is mainly prosopographical in character. *Ibid.* p. ix, Many of them are bare names..and most of them will be unfamiliar to any but a hardened prosopographer. **1940** A. MOMIGLIANO in *Jrnl. Roman Stud.* XXX. 77 Prosopographical research has the great virtue of reaching individuals or small groups, but does not explain their material or spiritual needs: it simply presupposes them. **1954** *Antiquity* XXVIII. 127 The essay on prosopographical method is a useful introduction. **1959** A. G. WOODHEAD *Study Gk. Inscriptions* iv. 46 This prosopographical study is particularly valuable for the social historian, but it may have its bearing on a variety of problems. *Ibid.* 47 Ptolemaic Egypt is prosopographically served by the *Prosopographia Ptolemaica.* **1961** *Encounter* Jan. 40/2 Namier found his métier as the pioneer applier of the prosopographical technique. **1961** DOLLEY & SKAARE in R. H. M. Dolley *Anglo-Saxon Coins* 70 We believe that there is both epigraphical and prosopographical evidence to warrant a division of the coinage of Æthelwulf into four distinct phases. **1967** A. N. SHERWIN-WHITE *Racial Prejudice in Imperial Rome* II. 53 Finally the sons of successful procurators become senators. This is a familiar tale in this prosopographical age. **1970** Prosopographer [see above]. **1971** *Dædalus* C. 55 The attitude toward the workings of politics taken by the early prosopographers appears to owe little to the writings of political theorists. *Ibid.* 66 The monks have also been studied prosopographically. **1971** A. H. M. JONES et al. *Prosopography of Later Roman Empire* I. p. v, The project of a prosopographical dictionary of the Later Roman Empire was originated by Theodor Mommsen. **1973** *Times Lit. Suppl.* 23 Feb. 209/4 A prosopographical register of some 779 wealthy individuals who lived in Athens during the sixth, fifth, or fourth centuries. **1975** D. W. S. HUNT *On Spot* ix. 176 While I am in the prosopographical vein I shall imitate Plutarch by completing the other leaf of the diptych with a portrait of Lieutenant-Colonel Emeka Odumekwu Ojukwu, the Military Governor of the Eastern Region.

prosopon (prǫ·sōᵘpǫn). [a. Gr. πρόσωπον face.] **1.** *Theol.* A conception or external presentation of one of the three Persons of the Trinity; = HYPOSTASIS 5.

1900 J. S. BANKS *Devel. Doctrine in Early Church* I. vii. 101 John of Damascus..says, Father, Son, and Spirit are one God or one substance (*ousia*, nature, essence), but not one person (*hypostasis, prosopon*). **1932** A. C. MCGIFFERT *Hist. Christian Thought* I. xii. 238 As creator and governor God is called Father, as redeemer he is called Son, as regenerator and sanctifier he is called Holy Spirit. But it is one and the same God, one and the same divine person, who acts in all these ways. The difference is not in being or person, but in function or activity. Each of these functions or activities—Father, Son and Spirit—was called by Sabellius prosopon (πρόσωπον), the Greek word of which the Latin translation is persona. The word means not person but face, and was used for the mask worn by actors in the theatre or for the part they played. **1936** G. L. PRESTIGE *God in Patristic Thought* iii. 55 Christ, who was called the prosopon of God with no less assurance (if with less frequency) than He was called God's Word or Wisdom. **1950** [see *ALLOGENOUS *a.*] **1969** *Dict. Christian Theol.* 279/1 *Prosopon* is a term used as an alternative to *Hypostasis*..to express the plurality of the Godhead. **1973** J. A. T. ROBINSON *Human Face of God* vii. 215 The prosopon, the face or person, of the Son is henceforth the faces of men and women.

2. Outward appearance or aspect.

1947 AUDEN in *Amer. Scholar* XVI. 406 Even the dinner waltz..is a voice that assaults International wrong,..Completely delivering to the sick, Sad, soiled prosopon of our ageing Present the perdition of all her rage.

pro-Soviet, -ism: see *PRO-[1] 5 a, c.

prospect, *sb.* Add: **II. 8. d.** A person or thing considered to be suitable for a particular purpose, *spec.* a potential or likely purchaser, customer, client, etc.

1922 S. LEWIS *Babbitt* vi. 68 He drove a 'prospect' out to view a four-flat tenement in the Linton district. **1922** *Glasgow Herald* 19 Dec. 8/8, I consider my bull calves excellent prospects for next season's fairs. **1926** *Publishers' Weekly* 16 Jan. 161/2 What the newspaper advertisement is for is to carry your helpful suggestions to the people who would be logical prospects for you. **1927** *Observer* 27 Nov. 11/1 There are thousands of 'prospects' who simply will not decide about a car until they have seen the new Ford. **1932** *New Yorker* 9 Apr. 32 She naturally considered her friends her best prospects. **1958** LICKORISH & KERSHAW *Travel Trade* v. 149 To define your market, use this check-list: Is the price of your service..right for the likely prospects?.. How often are the prospects likely to buy your service? *Ibid.* vii. 236 The ultimate purpose of both paid advertising and 'editorial' publicity is to increase the number of prospects who will buy the tickets and tours offered by the travel trade. **1967** N. FREELING *Strike Out* 49 A bank manager..would certainly regard her as a good prospect for a mortgage. **1973** R. C. DENNIS *Sweat of Fear* ix. 60 He told them he had a prospect looking at the house now. **1976** *Daily Mirror* 16 July 5/5 Carter men even checked the health and mental stability of the final six vice-presidential prospects.

e. A selected victim of a thief or pickpocket; a dupe.

1931 'D. STIFF' *Milk & Honey Route* viii. 91 Always approach a male prospect from the rear. *Ibid.* ix. 103 It is seldom that as he approaches one prospect after another he is not moved as much by speculative curiosity as by the need of sustenance. **1937** [see *lemon-game* s.v. *LEMON *sb.*[1] 7].

IV. 10. a. (Further example.)

1975 *Offshore* Sept. 73/1 Finding oil and natural gas at prospect Cognac off the Louisiana coast, whether the field turns out to be large or not, is an important reminder of what this offshore exploration business is all about.

V. 11. (from sense 2) *prospect-hunter.*

1803 D. WORDSWORTH *Jrnl.* 27 Aug. (1941) I. 271 The ferryman...would often say, after he had compassed the turning of a point, 'This is a bonny part,' and he always chose the bonniest, with greater skill than our prospect-hunters and 'picturesque travellers'.

prospecting, *vbl. sb.* Add: **II. 2. a.** (Earlier examples.)

1848 W. COLTON *Jrnl.* 18 Oct. in *3 Yrs. in Calif.* (1850) xxi. 292 Half their time is consumed in what they call prospecting; that is, looking up new deposits [of gold]. **1849** C. T. JACKSON in *Ex. Doc. 31st U.S. Congress 1 Sess. House* No. 5. 457 It is obvious that the shallow pits now sunk on the vein [of copper] show only its surface, and that they can only be regarded..as mere superficial explorations, or '*prospecting diggings*', as they are called in the west.

b. *prospecting camp, dish, pan, shaft* (earlier example), *trip.*

1851 in *Occasional Papers Univ. Sydney Austral. Lang. Res. Centre* (1966) No. 9. 19 The sediment which is composed of dirt, small stones and the particles of Gold which appear at and in the different compartments at the bottom are now emptied thro' two plugholes into a.. tin dish, called a prospecting pan. **1869** *Overland Monthly* Mar. 279/1 Over one of the hoisting shafts there is a large wooden bucket with a rope and rude windlass such as you might see on the prospecting shaft of the poorest miner. **1880** *Cimarron News & Press* 22 July 2/2 New Mexico ought to become one vast prospecting camp for the next five years. **1931** V. PALMER *Separate Lives* 183 Men..had been trickling in from the prospecting-camps and copper-shows of the dry country. **1944** F. CLUNE *Red Heart* 62 He now knew how to twirl a prospecting dish. **1948** P. JOHNSTON *Lost & Living Cities Calif. Gold Rush* 52/2 A number of miners disappeared while on prospecting trips, leaving no trace of their fate.

prospective, *a.* and *sb.* Add: **A.** *adj.* **4. b.** *Gram.* Denoting a tense of a verb which is present in form but implies a future action or state.

1931 O. JESPERSEN *S.P.E. Tract* XXXVI. 528 This leads to the use of *is going to* with an infinitive as what may be called a prospective present, and *was going to* as a prospective past. **1963** L. R. PALMER *Interpretation of Mycenaean Gk. Texts* 51 On the 'prospective' form *e-ke-qe*, which I formerly interpreted phonetically as a future, see p. 190. *Ibid.* 190 The facts thus suggest that the addition of the particle *-qe* to the verb gives it 'prospective' force.

B. *sb.* **3.** *in prospective* (further example).

1978 *Times Lit. Suppl.* 20 Jan. 69/5 Its rather curious title 'Mankind in Prospective' perhaps accords with the book's New World spelling—has 'prospective' already evolved into a noun there?

prospectively, *adv.* **1.** (Earlier example.)

1826 J. S. MILL in *Wks.* (1967) IV. 75 The few who watch prospectively the signs of future supply and demand.

prospectus. Add: (Earlier and further examples.) Also, a description or account of the activities of a school or other educational institution.

1765 D. GARRICK *Let.* 27 Jan. in R. B. Peake *Mem. Colman Family* (1841) I. v. 136, I could be glad that something was put into the St James's Chronicle..for my friend Monnet. You have seen his prospectus by this time. **1823** COGSWELL & BANCROFT (*title*) Prospectus of a school to be established at Round Hill, Northampton, Massachusetts. **1832** F. TROLLOPE *Domestic Manners* II. xxx. 163 Whilst at New York, the prospectus of a fashionable boarding-school was presented to me. **1937** *Discovery* Jan. p. ii/1 (Advt.), Boys' Preparatory School... Boarders only; six graduate staff, entire charge if required. Prospectus on request. **1980** *Times* 15 July 5/2 (Advt.), Tuition by post. Free prospectus... Wolsey Hall, Oxford.

prospe·ctusless, *a.* [f. PROSPECTUS + -LESS.] Of a company or its shares: for which no prospectus has been issued.

1898 *Westm. Gaz.* 26 Oct. 8/1 It is a lesson to those who deal in prospectusless shares... We said we should not buy the shares until some official prospectus has been issued. *Ibid.* 11 Nov. 8/1 It is not a sound business principle to buy the shares of a prospectusless company. **1907** *Sat. Rev.* 20 Apr. 486/1 We are by no means opposed to prospectusless companies, thinking that when the public are not asked to subscribe, there is no reason why the public should be informed of the details of other people's business. **1928** *Daily Mail* 9 Aug. 18/1 A good deal of interest has been aroused..by our references yesterday to statements published by prospectusless companies.

‖ **Prospekt** (prǫ·spekt). Also with small initial. [a. Russ. *prospékt.*] In the Soviet Union: a long, wide street; an avenue, a boulevard. Cf. PROSPECT *sb.* 3 b.

1866 *Chamber's Encycl.* VIII. 427/2 About ten of the other streets of the city [*sc.* St. Petersburg] are distinguished for their grandeur, though none of them equals the Nevski Prospekt. **1966** L. DEIGHTON *Billion-Dollar Brain* xxvi. 274 There were signs of a thaw. All along the Prospekt the huge drainpipes were groaning. **1979** O. SELA *Petrograd Consignment* 105 Petrograd..was a tedious panorama of featureless white. Sleds slipped noiselessly along the *prospekts*.

prosper, *v.* **1. c.** (Later examples.)

1731 P. MILLER *Gardeners' Dict.* s.v. Phaseolus. In the West-Indies it [*sc.* the pigeon-pea]..will thrive on barren land which has been worn out, where scarcely any thing else will prosper. **1946** D. C. PEATTIE *Road of Naturalist* iii. 34 Nature out of her vast variety has provided forms that prosper even there [*sc.* in Death Valley].

‖ **prosphora** (prǫ·sfǫrǎ). [a. Gr. προσφορά.] A religious offering, esp. the bread offered for use in the Eucharist (see quots.).

1874 GLADSTONE in *Contemp. Rev.* Oct. 676 Uniting the humble and unworthy *prosphora* with the one full perfect and sufficient Sacrifice, to offer it upon the altar of the heart. **1945** G. DIX *Shape of Liturgy* v. 111 The Greek terminology is throughout the pre-Nicene period quite clear... The communicant 'brings' (*prosenegkein*) the *prosphora*; the deacon 'presents' it or 'brings it up' (*anapherein*); the bishop 'offers' (*prospherein*) it. **1957** *Oxf. Dict. Christian Church* 1115/1 *Prosphora*.., in the E. Church, the altar bread. **1961** D. ATTWATER *Christian Churches of East* I. 224 *Prosphora*.., the Byzantine altar-bread, like a small loaf or cake.

pross (prǫs). A slang abbrev. of PROSTITUTE *sb.* 1 a. Cf. *PROS.

1937 in PARTRIDGE *Dict. Slang.* **1942** BERREY & VAN DEN BARK *Amer. Thes. Slang* § 507/2 *Prostitute*,..pross. **1969** C. BURKE *God is Beautiful, Man* 55 You heard that you should go out on a date with a pross, but I tell you, you better not even think about it. **1973** J. SEABROOK *Loneliness* 75 She's been hanging round the Cherry Tree—that's the pub where all the old prosses go—and she's been going down there since she was thirteen. **1975** J. F. BURKE *Death Trick* iii. 48 'Why is the man naked?' 'He was tricking with a pross.'

prossie (prǫ·si, -zi). *slang* (orig. *Austral.*). Also **prossy, prozzy.** [f. prec. + -Y[6], -IE.] = prec.

1941 BAKER *Dict. Austral. Slang* 57 *Pros, prossie*, a prostitute. **1942** BERREY & VAN DEN BARK *Amer. Thes. Slang* § 507/2 *Prostitute*,..pross, prossy. **1945** B. NAUGHTON in C. Madge *Pilot Papers* I. 102 The average prossy is very soft-hearted at the bottom of her. **1961** H. S. TURNER *Something Extraordinary* vii. 144 She reserves her whole-hearted contempt for the 'prossies'. Prostitution is wrong. **1971** F. RAPHAEL *Who were You with Last Night?* 74 A shipmate of mine had this gag... 'What's in a prossy's telegram?' Answer, 'Come at once.' **1971** J. WAINWRIGHT *Dig Grave* 107 Gawd! A prozzy with pretentious tastes in T.V. drama.

prostacyclin (prǫstǎsəi·klin). *Biochem.* [f. as next + CYCL(IC *a.* + -IN[1].] A derivative of prostaglandin $F_{1\alpha}$ which is generated by the arterial walls from prostaglandins and is an anti-coagulant and vasodilator.

1976 R. A. JOHNSON et al. *Prostaglandins* XII. 915 The chemical structure of prostaglandin X..from prostaglandin endoperoxides, is 9-deoxy-6,9α-epoxy-Δ^5-PGF$_{1\alpha}$... The trivial name prostacyclin is proposed for [this]. **1977** *Lancet* 1 Jan. 18/1 Fresh rings of arteries and veins obtained from surgical specimens generated an unstable substance, prostacyclin (prostaglandin X..) which is a potent inhibitor of platelet aggregation. **1979** *Nature* 6 Sept. 14/3 Many papers dealt with the newly discovered prostacyclin. Because of its vasodilator and platelet anti-aggregating properties it has already been tested for treatment of peripheral artery diseases. **1980** *Brit. Med. Jrnl.* 29 Mar. 939/3 The enhanced platelet release reaction in patients with poor prognosis may be related to decreased prostacyclin activity.

prostaglandin (prǫstǎglæ·ndin). *Biochem.* [a. G. *prostaglandin* (U. S. von Euler 1935, in *Klin. Wochenschr.* 17 Aug. 1183/1), f. G. *prosta(ta* or Eng. PROSTA(TE *sb.* (*a.*) + GLAND[2] + -IN[1].] Any of a group of closely related unsaturated, oxygenated, cyclic fatty acids which occur in seminal fluid and many tissues in male and female mammals and have numerous marked physiological effects (notably the contraction of smooth muscle, esp. that of the uterus). Cf. next.

1936 U. S. VON EULER in *Jrnl. Physiol.* LXXXVIII. 233 In secretion and extracts from the prostate and seminal vesicles of man and the vesicular gland of the sheep a pharmacodynamically highly active substance, prostaglandin, has been demonstrated. **1957** *Acta Chem. Scand.* XI. 1086/1 We have succeeded in obtaining one 'prostaglandin' factor (PGF) in crystalline form. **1960** *Ibid.* XIV. 1693 (*heading*) The isolation of prostaglandin F from sheep prostate glands. **1965** *Sun* 2 Nov. 11/1 It is thought that prostaglandins may work by acting on the woman's reproductive muscles, so helping the process of conception. **1970** *New Scientist* 3 Sept. 468/1 All 14 of the closely related prostaglandins discovered so far occur naturally in minute amounts in the human body. **1971** *Daily Tel.* 15 Oct. 2/2 An extra dose of prostaglandins is being tried as a 'once-a-month' pill for women, but a deficiency of prostaglandins in semen has been associated with infertility. **1973** J. R. WEEKS in Kahn & Lands *Prostaglandins & Cyclic AMP* 2 The prostaglandins are among the most potent substances known, acting in some systems at concentrations of 0·01 ng/ml *in vitro.* **1977** *Martindale's Extra Pharmacopoeia* (ed. 27) 1328/2 An important source of prostaglandins is the cortex of a Gorgonia coral, *Plexaura homomalla* or sea whip, from the Caribbean. **1979** F. H. STEWART et al. *My Body, my Health* i. 17 Researchers suspect that prostaglandin released by the uterus may play a role in menstrual cramps.

prostanoic (prǫstǎnōᵘ·ik), *a. Biochem.* [f. prec. after *heptanoic acid* (cf. *-OIC).] *prostanoic acid*: the 20-carbon carboxylic acid from which the prostaglandins are formally derived, the molecule of which consists of a saturated five-membered ring to which a saturated chain of eight carbon atoms and one of seven are attached at adjacent positions, the shorter chain ending with a carboxyl group; 7-(2-octylcyclopentyl)heptanoic acid.

1963 *Jrnl. Biol. Chem.* CCXXXVIII. 3563/2 Recent isolation of additional prostaglandins..have necessitated introduction of a new nomenclature for this class of compounds. This is being based on the trivial name prostanoic acid for the parent C_{20} acid. **1970** *New Scientist* 3 Sept. 468/2 Prostanoic acid..itself has no hormone-like action. **1972** *Lancet* 4 Nov. 5 (Advt.), All natural prostaglandins contain 20 carbon atoms and have the same basic carbon skeleton—prostanoic acid.

prostatism (prǫ·stēⁱtiz'm). *Med.* [ad. F. *prostatisme*, f. *prostat-e* PROSTATE + *-isme* -ISM.] Any condition due to disease of the prostate gland, esp. difficulty in urination.

1900 DORLAND *Med. Dict.* 540/1 *Prostatism*, a morbid state of mind and body due to prostatic disease. **1904** *Boston Med. & Surg. Jrnl.* CL. 451/2 The frequent, painful, feeble and usually incomplete emptying of the bladder seen in elderly men, which we term prostatic obstruction or prostatism, is not dependent on any single lesion of the prostate. **1920** *Ibid.* CLXXXII. 79/1 Prostatism is the best word I know to express that condition which results from obstruction to urination at the bladder neck due to adenomatous or sclerotic changes in the glands of the prostate itself, or of the posterior urethra. **1956** V. F. MARSHALL *Textbk. Urol.* iv. 61 An abnormally small prostate can cause prostatism, usually by fibrosis. **1977** *Jrnl. Urol.* CXVII. 70/1 Most patients have symptoms commonly referred to as prostatism, which include hesitancy, deterioration in the urinary stream, post-micturition dribble, urgency, frequency and nocturia.

prosthesis. Add: In *Surg.* usu. pronounced (prǫsþī·sis). **2. b.** (Pl. prostheses.) An artificial replacement for a part of the body.

1900 in DORLAND *Med. Dict.* **1926** T. G. ORR *Mod. Methods Amputation* vi. 90 These prostheses, while excellent, are not so practical for use in civil life because they are usually not available. **1945** THOMAS & HADDAN *Amputation Prosthesis* vii. 262 If the leg amputee is to be a successful member of society he must first learn to walk and travel on his prosthesis. **1959** *New Scientist* 10 Dec. 1181/2 (*caption*) A plastic prosthesis has been inserted and blood flow restored. **1959** L. SMITH *One Hour* (1960) v. 66 Her hand touched the empty trouser leg... It was before I had learned to use the prosthesis. **1976** *Evening Post* (Nottingham) 15 Dec. 22/3 (Advt.), Had a mastectomy? We offer a discreet and efficient fitting service. Stockists of the Camp Tru-life Prosthesis. **1977** D. FRY *Homo Loquens* x. 140 Everyone understands the need for supplying prostheses to, say, a thalidomide baby at the earliest possible opportunity.

prosthetic, *a.* Add: **2.** (Further examples.)

1966 *Lancet* 31 Dec. 1447/1 Prosthetic valve replacement avoids this complication, but a mechanical valve cannot grow with the patient. **1977** C. SAGAN *Dragons of Eden* viii. 205 Perhaps some day it will be possible to add a variety of cognitive and intellectual *prosthetic* devices to the brain—a kind of eyeglasses for the mind.

3. *Biochem.* Applied to a non-protein group forming part of or combined with a protein, e.g. in an enzyme. [This sense is due to A. Kossel (1892), who used G. *prosthetisch* (*Arch. f. Anat. u. Physiol.* (*Physiol. Abt.*) (1893) 157).]

1898 J. A. MANDEL tr. *Hammarsten's Text-bk. Physiol. Chem.* (ed. 2) ii. 48 The nucleoproteids..may be considered as combinations of a proteid nucleus with a side chain, which Kossel calls the prostetic [*changed to* prosthetic *in ed.* 4 (1904)] group. **1932** *Science* 10 June 615/2 It is of fundamental importance to decide whether the activity of insulin is a function of the whole molecule or of a prosthetic group, non-proteid in composition, which is attached to the protein complex. **1939** *Nature* 25 Nov. 886/2 It is now known also that vitamin B_1, including its pyrophosphate derivative, is identical with the prosthetic group of the enzyme carboxylase. **1954** K. J. LAIDLER *Introd. Chem. Enzymes* v. 94 The cytochromes are therefore complete enzymes in themselves, their prosthetic groups being successively reduced and oxidized during the course of a biological oxidation. **1964** G. H. HAGGIS et al. *Introd. Molecular Biol.* iii. 42 The total structure of a protein molecule often includes, in addition to its peptide chains a component of different chemical constitution, known as a prosthetic group. The haem component of haemoglobin is an example of a group of this kind. **1973** R. G. KRUEGER et al. *Introd. Microbiol.* vii. 238/1 Prosthetic groups are usually permanently attached to the enzyme, having been built into the enzyme when it was synthesized.

B. *sb. pl.* The branch of surgery concerned with the replacement of defective or absent parts of the body by artificial substitutes.

1894 in G. M. GOULD *Illustr. Dict. Med. & Biol.* **1911** G. H. WILSON *Man. Dental Prosthetics* Pref., This book has been written in response to the oft-repeated request by teachers and members of the dental profession for a concise modern text-book on Dental Prosthetics. **1963** *New Scientist* 28 Nov. 525 Here is only one more instance of a remarkable flowering of techniques..ranging from prosthetics to chromosomal manipulations, which have tremendous potential for good, but also allow a mockery of nature.

prosthetist (prǫ·sþĭtist). *Surg.* [f. PROSTHET(IC *a.* + -IST.] One who designs and fits prostheses.

1902 *Buck's Ref. Handbk. Med. Sci.* (ed. 2) V. 513/2 Napoleon..certainly made many cripples and should be hailed as the patron saint of prosthetists. **1924** D. D. CAMPBELL *Full Denture Prosthesis* x. 235 It scarcely need be observed that no prosthetist, sure of his method of securing central occlusion, will avail himself of such a mechanical aid. **1953** H. R. B FENN et al. *Clin. Dental Prosthetics* xix. 453 (*caption*) If this type of denture is to be successful it requires absolute accuracy on the part of both the prosthetist and the technician. **1970** M. VITALI in G. Murdoch *Prosthetic & Orthotic Pract.* xiii. 531 The prosthetist..could not say when the pylon is going to be ready for delivery but it has helped a lot to understand some of the problems of the amputee.

prosthion (prǫ·sþiǫn). *Anat.* [Neut. of Gr. πρόσθιος foremost (f. πρόσθεν before, in front): cf. *-ION[2].] The lowest or the most forward point of the maxilla between the two central incisors.

1925 *Biometrika* XVII. 55 If there be two points used, the prosthion and the alveolar point..then the computation of the angles and sides of the fundamental triangle of the skull becomes impossible. **1933** *Jrnl. R. Anthrop. Inst.* LXIII. 42 Some modern craniometricians speak of the prosthion and the alveolar point as if they were coincident. **1937** *Amer. Jrnl. Physical Anthrop.* XXII. 486 Prosthion has..been generally used to designate both the most forward and the lowest points, in accordance with the measurement being taken. The distinction is made, however, by Buxton and Morant, who call the most forward point prosthion and the lowest the alveolar point. **1937** [see *NASION]. **1974** MOORE & LAVELLE *Growth of Facial Skeleton in Hominoidea* iv. 196 Up to the stage of eruption of the first permanent molar, the face of the orang utan is growing strongly downwards and forwards. Subsequently, the face begins to tilt so that the prosthion, instead of moving downwards and forwards, moves forwards and somewhat upwards.

prosthodontia (prǫsþodǫ·ntiă). *Dentistry.* [f. as next + -IA[1].] Prosthodontics.

1917 F. A. PEESO *Crown & Bridge-Work* viii. 151 (*heading*) Relations of prosthodontia and orthodontia. **1934** F. W. FRAHM *Princ. & Technics Full Denture Construction*, p. xiv, The term 'prosthetic dentistry', or 'prosthodontia', may..be defined as an account of methods for the replacement of any lost or missing parts of the dental organism by artificial substitutes. **1947** H. H. HORNER *Dental Educ. Today* ix. 266 The School of Dentistry..offers graduate courses in orthodontia, prosthodontia, and oral surgery.

prosthodontics (prǫsþodǫ·ntiks), *sb. pl. Dentistry.* [f. as next + -IC; cf. *ORTHODONTICS *sb. pl.*] The branch of dentistry concerned with the design, manufacture, and fitting of artificial replacements for teeth and other parts of the mouth; prosthetic dentistry.

1947 H. H. HORNER *Dental Educ. Today* ix. 266 Postgraduate and refresher courses are offered in orthodontics., prosthodontics.., [etc.]. **1977** M. M. HUDIS *Dental Lab. Prosthodontics* p. xv, The basic concepts will be developed so that they may be integrated into the total concept of prosthodontics. **1978** *Who's Who* 1495/2 Formerly Professor and Chairman of the Prosthodontics Department, University of Southern California.

prosthodontist (prǫsþodǫ·ntist). *Dentistry.* [f. PROSTH(ESIS + Gr. ὀδοντ-, ὀδούς tooth + -IST.] One who practises prosthodontics.

1917 F. A. PEESO *Crown & Bridge-Work* viii. 151 Quite frequently when the services of an orthodontist has been employed the coöperation of the prosthodontist is necessary to complete and render his work permanent. **1934** F. W. FRAHM *Princ. & Technics of Full Denture Construction* vi. 74 The prosthodontist should avail himself of the use of the very best appliances and technics that will help him to develop and adapt the very finest that is possible in the construction of dentures. **1977** *Daily Colonist* (Victoria, B.C.) 21 May 34/3 'I don't like to go to the dentist myself,' says Dr..Tregaskis..dental professor and prosthodontist.

prostie, var. *PROSTY.

Prostigmin (prosti·gmin). *Pharm.* Also **-ine** (-īn), and with small initial. A proprietary name for neostigmine (s.v. *NEO- 1 b).

1931 *Trade Marks Jrnl.* 11 Nov. 1500/2 Prostigmin... Chemical substances prepared for use in medicine and pharmacy. The Hoffmann–La Roche Chemical Works Limited... London. **1935** *Times* 9 Mar. 9/4 Later, using a drug known as prostigmin, she obtained much better results in the treatment of a severe case of myasthenia. **1946** *Official Gaz.* (U.S. Patent Office) 19 Mar. 327/1 *Prostigmin.* For medicinal preparation... Claims use since Apr. 29, 1931, in the form 'Prostigmine'; and since Nov. 8, 1931, on the mark as shown. **1956** LD. AMULREE in A. Pryce-Jones *New Outl. Mod. Knowl.* II. 217 The use of prostigmine in the treatment of myasthenia gravis and of the extract of thyroid and of its synthetic substitute thyroxin in the treatment of diseases of the thyroid, are further examples of the way in which modern therapy can overcome hitherto irremediable diseases. **1961** *Lancet* 2 Sept. 512/1 Various unsuccessful regimens were tried, including a diabetic diet, acetylcholine derivatives, and prostigmine. **1967** H. BECKMAN *Dilemmas in Drug Therapy* 47/1 In sinus and nodal tachycardia, neostigmine (Prostigmin) may occasionally effect a conversion to normal rhythm. **1974** M. C. GERALD *Pharmacol.* vii. 132 Such reversible inhibitors,..neostigmine (Prostigmine), for example, act for several hours after a single dose.

prostisciutto (prǫ:stiʃū·to). *nonce-wd.* [Blend of PROSTITUTE *sb.* and *PROSCIUTTO.] A female prostitute regarded metaphorically as an item on a menu.

1930 S. BECKETT *Whoroscope* 1 What's that? A little green fry or a mushrooming one? Two lashed ovaries with prostisciutto?

prostitute, *ppl. a.* and *sb.* Add: **B.** *sb.* **1. c.** A man who undertakes male homosexual acts for payment; usu. *male prostitute.*

1948 [see *male prostitute* s.v. *MALE *a.* 1 e]. **1958** L. DURRELL *Balthazar* vii. 157 A magnificent-looking male prostitute whose oiled curls hung down his back and whose eyes and lips were heavily painted. **1967** *Listener* 1 June 718/2 Few of them ever told me what they were in for, though in the case of Ralph, a male prostitute known to the wing as Suzanne, it was only too obvious. **1975** *Daily Tel.* 24 July 3/6 Many of the boys became male prostitutes.

2. b. Delete 'Now *rare*' and add further examples.

1889 G. B. SHAW *Let.* 31 Aug. (1965) 223 The radical who writes conservative articles is considered a prostitute. **1980** C. FITZGIBBON *Rat Report* vi. 122 You damned us.. for turning scientists into military prostitutes.

prostitution. Add: **1. d.** Of men: the undertaking of homosexual acts for payment.

1886 R. F. BURTON *Terminal Ess.* in *Arabian Nights' Entertainments* X. 242 According to Gomara there were at Tamalipas houses of male prostitution. **1975** P. MCCUTCHAN *Very Big Bang* xiii. 122 Porn, poncing, male prostitution—you name it, the court'll send you down for it. **1975** *Times* 21 June 2/3 Runaway boys..were procured for a male prostitution ring by offers of food and shelter.

prosty (prǫ·sti). *U.S. slang.* Also **prostie.** Abbrev. of PROSTITUTE *sb.* 1 a. Cf. *PROSSIE.

1930 *Bookman* Dec. 397/2 These song writers exploit motherhood into a mania, and go Rotary about any old half-baked, klux-ridden Dixie backwash. They make love in kindergarten terms, turn Sunday-school superintendent about prosties whom they term 'faded roses' or 'butterflies', and otherwise trade on primitive mass ideas. **1941** [see *HOPPY *sb.*[2]]. **1951** GREEN & LAURIE *Show Biz* 571/1 *Prostie*, prostitute. Variety's sensitized way of describing female characters comparable to those in early Mae West plays. **1972** G. BAXT *Burning Sappho* vii. 128 The prostie in the orange wig. **1976** J. HAYES *Missing* i. 29 If she was a prostie, he couldn't afford her fee.

‖ **prosula** (prō·sulă). *Eccl.* Pl. **-æ.** [mod.L., dim. of L. *prosa* *PROSA; see -ULE.] (See quots.)

1907 ORME & WYATT tr. *Wagner's Introd. Gregorian Melodies* xiv. 245 A second kind of trope, which also goes back to Tutilo, resembles the Sequences, and is often like them called *Prosa*, or, when of lesser extent, *Prosula.* **1958** W. APEL *Gregorian Chant* iii. 433 Twenty-five of the Offertoires..are further amplified by the addition of a *prosula*..that is, a new text appended to the end of a verse, usually the last. *Ibid.*, The music for the *prosula* or, as we would say, for the trope, is identical with the closing passage of the verse. **1970** [see *PROSA]. **1975** *Anglo-Saxon England* IV. 134 A Kyriale, beginning imperfectly with part of the prosula to the *Kyrie eleison* entitled *Clemens rector. Ibid.* 135 A number of Kyries do not have prosulae.

prosy, *a.* **1.** (Earlier examples.)

1814 JANE AUSTEN *Let.* 9 Sept. (1952) 402 The scene with Mrs. Mellish, I should condemn; it is prosy & nothing to the purpose. **1823** SCOTT in *Ballantyne's Novelist's Library* V. p. lxxxvi, Perhaps, to be circumstantial and abundant in minute detail, and in one word, though an unauthorized one, to be somewhat *prosy*, is one mode of securing a certain necessary degree of credulity in hearing a ghost-story.

pro-syllable, -syllabic: see *PRO-[1] 4 b, c.

Prot (prǫt), *sb.* and *a.* Also **prot.** A colloq. abbrev. of PROTESTANT *sb.* 2 a and *a.* 1; *spec.* opp. to *Catholic* (freq. in derog. or contemptuous use). Cf. *PROD *sb.*[3] and *a.*

1725 J. THORNTON *Let.* in *Dublin Rev.* (1916) Apr. 318 Sir George Brown, I hear, is got to Gant, there be-moaning his folly in having tied himself up to an old Prot, who cunningly settled all she had out of his reach. **1737** R. CHALLONER *Let.* 15 Sept. in *Recusant Hist.* (1970) X. 351 Our Prelate here, has..absolutely refused to consent to the Parties being married first by a Priest and then by a Prot. minister. **1843** M. EDGEWORTH *Let.* 3 Dec. (1971) 599 The average salary of the Irish priest is £290 per Annum and average of Prot—£120 or £130. **1900** C. M. YONGE *Mod. Broods* v. 50 Oh, she is a regular old Prot.. almost a Dissenter. **1900** M. CREIGHTON *Let.* 16 Nov. (1904) II. 454 The position was 'I would meet you if I could: but I am not going to be bullied by a handful of Prots.' **1937** AUDEN & MACNEICE *Lett. from Iceland* xiii. 204, I know a Prot Will never really kneel, but only squat. **1955** E. POUND *Section: Rock-Drill* (1957) lxxxvi. 24 Yes yr/ Holiness, they are all of them prots. **1971** B. SLEIGH *Smell of Privet* x. 87 'You must never say cup, always chalice. Don't be such a Prot, my dear!' I had no idea what a 'Prot' was, but vowed to myself I would never be one again. **1977** P. WAY *Super-Celeste* 100 Back in Belfast..there were Prot bombs and Catholic bombs and SAS bombs.

protactinium (prōᵘtækti·niə̆m). *Chem.* Also **protoactinium** (prōᵘ:toˌækti·niə̆m). [mod.L., coined (as *protactinium*) in Ger. (Hahn & Meitner 1918, in *Physik. Zeitschr.* XIX. 211/1) see PROTO- and *ACTINIUM 2. So named because the principal isotope produces actinium by radioactive decay.] A radioactive metallic element of the actinide series, which occurs in small quantities as a decay product in uranium ores, and whose longest-lived isotope has a half-life of about 33,000 years. Atomic number 91; symbol Pa.

The spelling *protactinium* is that adopted by the International Union of Pure and Applied Chemistry.

1918 *Jrnl. Chem. Soc.* CXIV. II. 346 Assuming that 8% of the uranium atoms disintegrating produce 'protoactinium', the quantity in the 73 mg. is that in equilibrium with 86 grams of uranium. **1919** *Chem. Abstr.* XIII. 1181 Protactinium is one of the 5 new radioactive elements occupying a place in the periodic table hitherto vacant. **1934** *Nature* 8 Sept. 386/1 The protoactinium was precipitated with zirconium as phosphate in the earlier stages, partly freed from zirconium by fractional crystallization and precipitated together with tantalum. **1934** *Times* 13 Sept. 9/4 The successful isolation of protactinium, the parent element in the actinium series of radioactive changes, was announced yesterday. **1959** *New Scientist* 17 Dec. 1264/3 From 60 tons of waste material from the production of uranium from its ores, chemists at Windscale have with some difficulty extracted 100 grammes of protactinium. **1962** COTTON & WILKINSON *Adv. Inorg. Chem.* xxxii. 906 Protactinium as ^{231}Pa.. occurs in pitchblende, but even the richest ores contain only about 1 part Pa in 10^7. The isolation of protactinium..is difficult, as indeed is the study of protactinium chemistry generally, owing to the extreme tendency of the compounds to hydrolyze. **1970** J. W. GARDNER *Atoms Today & Tomorrow* vi. 99 The decay chain proceeds from thorium (atomic number 90) via protactinium (atomic number 91) to uranium. **1973** PHILLIPS & MILNER in J. C. Bailar et al. *Comprehensive Inorg. Chem.* V. 79 Protactinium is the third member of the actinide series, but it possesses many of the properties of the Group V elements in its chemical reactions... The stable valency state in solution is Pa(V), and the existence of Pa(IV) is also possible.

protagonist. Add: **1, 2.** Also *pl.*, the leading characters in a play, story, contest, etc.; the most prominent or most important individuals in a situation or course of events.

Fowler's classification of the plural as an absurd use (*Dict. Modern English Usage* p. 471; maintained in Sir E. Gowers' second edition, p. 489) may be challenged on the grounds that derivation from Greek πρῶτος *first*, does not preclude a plural form, and limitation to the singular is strictly relevant only in the context of ancient Greek drama.

1671 [in Dict.]. **1930** D. L. SAYERS *Strong Poison* viii. 109 I'm getting a certain amount of light on the central figures in the problem—what journalists like to call the protagonists. **1950** G. B. SHAW *Shakes versus Shav* 135 Living actors have to learn that they too must be invisible while the protagonists are conversing, and therefore must not move a muscle nor change their expression. **1952** *Sunday Times* 6 July 4/8 The soliloquy is a special problem on the screen but in 'Julius Caesar' there are only two of them, both short. Mr. Mankiewicz has told me that he hopes to use an intimate technique, giving importance above all to the characters of the protagonists. **1962** L. Auchincloss in I. Howe *Edith Wharton* 35 The change..comes with the infiltration of the other protagonists of the drama, the Spraggs, the Wellington Boys, the Gormers, [etc.]. **1976** *Times* 29 Oct. 1/1 Strong opposition to more cuts in public expenditure were voiced at a meeting of the Cabinet on Tuesday. The protagonists were Mr Crosland..Mr Shore..and Mr Benn.

¶ **3.** [Through confusion of sense 2 with Pro-[1] 5a.] A proponent, advocate, or supporter (of a cause, idea, etc.).

In this use the notion of 'a leading personage' is not implied. In some contexts there is ambiguity between this sense and sense 2.

1935 *Hansard Commons* 4 June 1718/2 My right hon. Friend the Member for Epping and others on the right have come out in this House as the protagonists of self-determination. **1935** A. P. Herbert *What a Word!* iv. 99, I heard with horror..that the word 'protagonist' is being used as if it were pro-tagonist—one who is *for* something, and opposed to ant-agonist, one who is against it. **1952** *Times* 2 Apr. 5/4 As a protagonist, in and out of Parliament and especially in the county of Sussex of the fullest use of land for food production, I feel impelled to reply to my friend Miss Nancy Price's letter..and to defend the town council of Worthing. **1961** L. R. Klein et al. *Econometric Model of U.K.* iv. 122 Professor Robbins, a firm protagonist of the importance of the influence of demand over the period. **1972** *Observer* 15 Oct. 39/6 In practical terms, I wish I thought that, in 1975, we shall read..alongside *protagonist*, not just '*also:* proponent' but '*also, improperly:* proponent'. **1974** *BSI News* Sept. 12/3 Over the last few years the relative merits of the pascal and the bar have been discussed interminably... Protagonists of the pascal do not think its magnitude of any relevance to its choice. **1975** *Times Lit. Suppl.* 22 Aug. 939/2 Kōkan was..an unabashed protagonist of the technical superiority of Western civilization. **1979** *Jrnl. R. Soc. Arts* CXXVII. 334/2 A protagonist of and expert on the Added Value concept.

Hence ¶ **prota·gonism** *rare*, the defence or advocacy of a cause, idea, etc.

1909 *N.Y. Even. Post* 27 Nov. 6 The principal character..is gradually drawn into a protagonism of common sense, candour, and progress. **1937** *Mind* XLVI. 511 This method, the validity of which depends upon the progressive series of experiments developed in the *Phenomenology*, is dramatic; it requires the experimenter to be protean in his factitious protagonism.

Protagorean (protægǒri·an), *a.* and *sb.* [f. *Protagoras* (Gr. Πρωταγόρας) the name of a Greek philosopher of the 5th century B.C. + -an.] **A.** *adj.* Of or pertaining to Protagoras or his philosophy. **B.** *sb.* An adherent or admirer of the philosophy of Protagoras. Hence **Protagore·anism**, the Protagorean philosophy.

1678 R. Cudworth *True Intell. Syst.* i. 10 The Protagorean Philosophy made all things to consist of a Commixture of Parts (or Atoms) and Local Motion. **1845** *Encycl. Metrop.* II. 614/1 The need of such a measure, he asserts, in opposition to the Protagorean notion of man being the measure of all things, which he treats as a silly truism. **1887** *Encycl. Brit.* XXII. 236/1 Socrates rested his scepticism upon the Protagorean doctrine that man is the measure of his own sensations and feelings. *Ibid.*, In the review of theories of knowledge which has come down to us in Plato's *Theætetus* mention is made..of certain 'incomplete Protagoreans'. **1907** *Hibbert Jrnl.* Jan. 439 A Protagorean treatise of the fifth century B.C. **1921** T. R. Glover *Pilgrim* 176 The idea of Christian charity has been perverted,..to mean a Protagorean acceptance of the equal value of all opinions. **1932** *Times Lit. Suppl.* 21 Apr. 282/2 It supplies the key to the interpretation of the refined Protagoreanism which the author avows. **1954** *Essays in Crit.* IV. 55 There Arnold figures as a Protagorean sceptic. **1958** *Times Lit. Suppl.* 17 Jan. 26/2 For Professor Guthrie this is a genuine outline of Protagorean thought.

protalus (protēi·lŏs). *Physical Geogr.* Also **pro-talus.** [f. Pro-[2] + Talus[1].] A rocky ridge or lobe on the lower edge of an existing or former snow-bank, composed of frost-fractured boulders and other debris that have slid or rolled over the snow from a talus or scree higher up the slope, or been transported by solifluction from the talus. Usu. *attrib.*, as *protalus lobe, rampart.*

1934 K. Bryan in *Geogr. Rev.* XXIV. 656 The word 'nivation' is the name of a process of excavation around snowbanks described by Matthes. The use of the same word for these ramparts of blocks is likely to prove misleading, and the reviewer suggests that 'protalus rampart' would be appropriate for the features. **1962** *Prof. Papers U.S. Geol. Survey* No. 324. 61/2 Many deposits thin downslope to a featheredge, but in the mountains some terminate in a lobate mass bearing one or more arcuate ridges in which the fragments tend to be oriented imbricate to the slope... Such protalus lobes appear to have flowed slowly forward as a unit, presumably by solifluction. **1970** R. J. Small *Study of Landforms* xi. 378 The disintegrated material may slide across the bank of firn below, and accumulate to give moraine-like piles of debris ('pro-talus') running approximately parallel to the headwall. **1976** *Scottish Geogr. Mag.* XCII. 182 An excellent example of a protalus rampart occurs in Wester Ross 10 km south-east of Gairloch. *Ibid.* 184 The protalus complex lies at the foot of a scree slope that rises through a vertical height interval of 100–200 m.

protamine. Substitute for entry in Dict.: **protamine** (prǭu·tămīn). *Biochem.* and *Med.* Also † **-in** (-in). [ad. G. *protamin* (F. Miescher 1874, in *Verhandl. d. Naturforsch. Ges. in Basel* VI. 153): see Proto- and Amine.] **1.** Any of a class of basic proteins of relatively low molecular weight which occur combined with nucleic acids in the sperm of many species of fish, and which have the property of countering the anti-coagulant action of heparin; orig. *spec.* that obtained from the salmon.

1874 *Jrnl. Chem. Soc.* XXVII. 794 Nuclein occurs in the salmon roe in the form of an insoluble compound with the new base protamine, the latter constituting no less than one-fourth of the weight of the roe. **1896** *Ibid.* LXX. i. 582 The names *salmine* and *sturine* are suggested by [*sic*] the two protamines. **1902** *Encycl. Brit.* XXXI. 724/1 These Protamins..take up water and yield the bases above referred to. **1928** W. V. Thorpe tr. *Kossel's Protamines & Histones* ii. i. 2 Increasing knowledge of the hydrolysis products of the protamines confirmed Kossel's view..that the protamines belonged to the protein group and were the most elementary type of this..class of compounds. **1954** A. White et al. *Princ. Biochem.* ix. 195 The protamines are relatively small and simple proteins, deficient in many amino-acids and extremely rich in arginine. **1970** R. W. McGilvery *Biochem.* xxvi. 653 The effects of heparin can be reversed by giving protamine, the highly basic small protein associated with nucleic acids in fish sperm. **1971** D. R. Williams *Metals of Life* iii. 27 The threshold between polypeptides and proteins is arbitrarily set at MW 5000 since the smallest physiologically active polymers, the protamines (found in spermatozoa), have molecular weights commencing at this value. **1973** B. A. Brown *Hematol.* iv. 132/1 At the completion of surgery, protamine is administered in order to neutralize the effects of the heparin.

2. *attrib.* and *Comb.* **a.** In various combs., as *protamine-insulin, protamine-zinc(-insulin)*, denoting suspensions of insulin with a protamine, and usu. also zinc chloride, which have greater stability and a more prolonged hypoglycæmic action than insulin alone.

1935 C. L. Heel tr. N. B. Krarup (*title*) Clinical investigations into the action of protamine insulinate. **1936** *Canad. Public Health Jrnl.* XXVII. 157/2 In the preparation of protamine insulin for injection, a suitable quantity of protamine, buffered with sodium phosphate, is added to regular insulin. **1936** *Canad. Med. Assoc. Jrnl.* XXXV. 240/1 The other solution contained a buffer phosphate, 1 c.c. of which, when added to the protamine-zinc-insulin complex, adjusted the reaction so that the hydrogen-ion concentration..was identical with that of blood. **1956** *Nature* 4 Feb. 223/2 Robinson and Fehr were able to estimate the percentage of insulin in protamine insulin by using the upper phase from a butanol/acetic/water..mixture as a chromatographic solvent. **1960** M. Spark *Bachelors* vii. 100 Protamine zinc for more prolonged coverage throughout the evening and the following night. She needs 80 units. **1962** H. Burn *Drugs, Med. & Man* xiv. 148 While the maximum time of action of insulin alone was six hours, that of protamine-insulin was 12–18 hours, and finally that of zinc-protamine-insulin was 24–30 hours.

b. protamine sulphate, a salt of a protamine and sulphuric acid, given as an aqueous solution to neutralize the anti-coagulant effect of heparin; **protamine titration,** a test of the clotting ability of blood in which blood is first made incoagulable with heparin and then titrated against protamine sulphate until clotting occurs; a value so obtained.

1936 *Jrnl. Pharmacol. & Exper. Therapeutics* LVIII. 80 After standing 4 or 5 days the precipitated protamine sulfate has settled and is removed by centrifugation. **1962** *Listener* 3 May 769/2 Certain mixtures of large molecules—for example, mixtures of starch, gelatin, and protamine sulphate—will form drops which have great stability. **1971** S. I. Rapaport *Introd. Hematol.* xxiv. 311 One-tenth volume of 1 per cent protamine sulfate is added to plasma, and the plasma is examined for a precipitate after 15 minutes at 37°C. **1949** J. G. Allen et al. *Jrnl. Lab. & Clin. Med.* XXXIV. 473 (*heading*) A protamine titration as an indication of clotting defect in certain hemorrhagic states. **1949** *Jrnl. Amer. Med. Assoc.* 30 Apr. 1251/1 The blood..showed an increased protamine titration when the prothrombin level was normal or near normal, when fibrinogen levels were not abnormal and when fibrinolysin was not grossly disturbed. **1973** B. A. Brown *Hematol.* iv. 132/1 The protamine titration..is used to estimate the minimum required dose of protamine.

protan (prǭu·tæn), *sb.* (*a*). *Ophthalm.* [f. *protan-* in *protanomaly, *protanopia, etc.] A protanomalous or protanopic person. Also as *adj.*

1944 D. Farnsworth in *Inter-Society Color Council News Let.* lvi. 8 There are 3 or more types of Anomaly (chromatic imbalance). 1. n. Protan; adj. Protanous: reduction of red-bluegreen discrimination relative to interesting axis. **1962** *Lancet* 15 Dec. 1269/1 The former includes protan and deutan defects with 3 or more alleles at each locus, and the latter includes true hæmophilia and Christmas disease. **1968** [see *Ishihara]. **1974** *Nature* 23 Aug. 653/1 It is highly probable that there are at least two gene loci involved in each of four X-linked diseases: colour blindness (protan and deutan), haemophilia (A and B), muscular dystrophy (Duchenne and Becker), and retinal degeneration (retinoschisis and Norrie's disease).

protandrous, *a.* Add: [ad. G. *protandrisch* (F. H. G. Hildebrand *Die Geschlechter-Vertheilung bei den Pflanzen* (1867) 17).] **1.** (Earlier and later examples.)

1870 A. W. Bennett in *Jrnl. Bot.* VIII. 317 (*heading*) Protandrous. **1965** Bell & Coombe tr. *Strasburger's Textbk. Bot.* 602 Many apparently protandrous flowers..were borne in the axils of the dead leaves.

2. *Zool.* = Proterandrous *a.* 2.

1897 Parker & Haswell *Textbk. Zool.* I. vi. 285 A few forms [of Nematoidea] are hermaphrodite, but, instead of having a double set of reproductive organs, as in Platodes, organs of the ordinary female nematode type are present, and the gonads produce first sperms and afterwards ova. Such animals are said to be protandrous (male products ripe first). **1929** *Amer. Naturalist* LXIII. 571 The lengths of males [of *Pandalus danae* Stimpson] indicated that they were in two year-groups... On the other hand the females seemed to belong to a third year-group... This appeared to suggest that the form under consideration was protandrous. **1973** *Nature* 5 Oct. 262/2 Both protandrous and protogynous hermaphroditism have been reported in fishes, and there is some evidence that smaller and younger specimens of *U*[*mbra*] *limi* are predominantly males, while larger and older individuals are mostly females.

protandric *a.* (examples in the sense of *protandrous *a.* 2); **protandry** (examples in *Zool.*).

Delete *a* **1882** *Nature* (Annandale).

1870 [see *protogyny]. **1887** *Bergens Museums Aarsberetning* vii. 29 It may not be amiss to draw a comparison between the protandric hermaphroditism of Myxine and the hermaphroditism of the few other hermaphroditic vertebrates known. **1892** J. A. Thomson *Outl. Zool.* 632/2 (Index), Protandry of Myxine. **1932** *Proc. 6th Internat. Congr. Genetics* II. 26 Several of the oviparous species show a large percentage of intersexuality when young, with a strong tendency toward protandry. *Ibid.* 27 This species is regularly protandric, each young animal producing many thousands of sperm balls. **1951** [see *gonochoric* adj. s.v. *gono-]. **1970** *Nature* 11 July 189/2 Gross examination of gonads in larger males and smaller females showed no evidence of protandry. **1975** *Ibid.* 15 May 221/2 He considered it likely that *A. equina* is a protandric hermaphrodite which mainly self-fertilises and retains larvae within the parent.

protanomal (prǭu·tănǫ·măl). *Ophthalm.* [ad. G. *protanomale* (W. A. Nagel 1907, in *Zeitschr. f. Psychol. und Physiol. d. Sinnesorgane: Abt. II* XLII. 67), f. Gr. πρωτ- Prot- + G. *anomal* anomalous.] A person with protanomaly.

1915 J. H. Parsons *Introd. Study Colour Vision* ii. iii. 183 Of the partial protanopes (protanomal, Nagel) Donders and König do not record any case, v. Kries one only, whereas Nagel, Guttman, and Abney and Watson record a considerable number. **1973** *Jrnl. Optical Soc. Amer.* LXIII. 236/1 In Fig. 2, the red primary is assigned a value of 637 nm for normals and deuteranomals, and 629 nm for protanomals.

Hence **protano·malous** *a.*, having protanomaly; also *absol.*

1911 *Amer. Jrnl. Psychol.* XXII. 370 It is now customary..to distinguish two groups of anomalous trichromates, upon the analogy of the two groups of dichromates,—the red-anomalous or protanomalous trichromates, whose sensitiveness to red is below normal, and the green-anomalous or deuteranomalous trichromates, whose sensitiveness to green is below normal. **1938** [see *protanomaly]. **1965** *Science* 9 July 186/1 The protanomalous subject can match all colors of the spectrum with mixtures of three hues but requires more red in each mixture than the normal subject. **1975** *Sci. Amer.* Mar. 172/3 Some have considered that the protanomalous need more red in their mixture because, although they have normal cone pigments, the red signals are too weak.

protanomaly (prǭu·tănǫ·măli). *Ophthalm.* [f. prec. + -y[3].] A form of anomalous trichromatism marked by a reduced sensitivity to red and subnormal discrimination between red, yellow, and green hues.

1938 *Proc. Physical Soc.* L. 674 As the results for only one protanomalous observer are given, it is impossible to talk of any stages of protanomaly except by comparison with the results for the deuteranomalous observers. **1946** W. D. Wright *Res. Normal & Defective Colour Vision* xxiv. 297 Anomalous trichromatism is subdivided into three corresponding groups—protanomaly, deuteranomaly and tritanomaly—from the fact that each group has characteristics intermediate between those of the trichromat and the corresponding dichromat. **1973** *Vision Res.* XIII. 2033 The condition of anomalous trichromacy thus includes the categories of simple and extreme protanomaly and simple and extreme deuteranomaly.

protanope (prǭu·tănǭup). *Ophthalm.* [ad. G. *protanop* (J. von Kries 1897, in *Zeitschr. f. Psychol. und Physiol. d. Sinnesorgane* XIII. 248), f. Prot- + Gr. priv. ἀν- + ὤψ, ὠπ- eye, face.] A person with protanopia.

1908 *Psychol. Bull.* V. 298 When red and blue are mixed to match blue-green the protanope requires a relative excess of red in his purple mixture; and in similar determinations with red and yellow the protanope may demand five times as much red as the deuteranope. **1924** tr. J. von Kries in *Helmholtz's Treat. Physiol. Optics* II. 402 In order to have brief descriptive terms for the relation that has been found to exist here, without expressing any theoretical bias, the writer suggests the names *protanopes* and *deuteranopes* to describe the two kinds of dichromats, that is, persons who lack the first component or the second component, respectively, of the normal visual organ. **1953** *Jrnl. Physiol.* CXXI. 565 The protanopes confuse red with green and are characterized by a very low sensitivity to light of long wavelengths. **1959** [see *DICHROMAT, DICHROMATE *sb.*[2]]. **1971** *Vision Res.* XI. 1034 Protanopes are deficient in some red-sensitive cone pigment that is present in normal eyes.

protanopia (prǫtănōᵘ·piă). *Ophthalm.* [mod. L., f. prec. + -IA[1].] A form of dichromatic colour-blindness marked by an insensitivity to red and an inability to distinguish between red, yellow, and green hues.

1902 J. M. BALDWIN *Dict. Philos. & Psychol.* II. 371/1 In..the so-called red-blindness, the red end of the spectrum is shortened, and the maximum brightness is further towards the green (protanopia). **1923** L. C. MARTIN *Colour* x. 146 In complete protanopia or deuteranopia we have the spectrum consisting (broadly speaking) of two parts of differing hue separated by a grey or white. **1950** *Jrnl. Optical Soc. Amer.* XL. 46/2 If the scores at either +5 or −5 are incorrect the subject has complete red-green color deficiency, i.e. either protanopia or deuteranopia. **1974** *Ophthalmic Res.* VI. 281 Colour discrimination as tested with the Ishihara plates and Nagel anomaloscope..was typical for protanopia.

Hence **protano·pic** *a.*

1908 *Psychol. Bull.* V. 298 Certain individuals..make their mixtures much redder, and other individuals much greener than the average. Here again we must distinguish between a protanopic and a deuteranopic subtype. Investigations since Rayleigh's pioneer publication have shown that the former sub-type is much more numerous than the latter. **1973** *Vision Res.* XIII. 1762 The reduction in gradient of the deuteranopic isochromatic line through the blue-green and purple region suggests an explanation of why some deuteranopes cannot distinguish either the protanopic or the deuteranopic diagnostic figures in the Ishihara test.

protargol (prōᵘtā·ɹgǫl). *Med.* [a. G. *protargol* (A. Neisser 1897, in *Dermatologisches Centralblatt* I. 5), f. *prot-eïn* PROTEIN + L. *arg-entum* silver; cf. -OL.] A substance made from protein and various compounds of silver, used as a mild antiseptic and a stain.

1898 *Boston Med. & Surg. Jrnl.* 25 Aug. 194/2 In the few cases of purulent ophthalmia that have been treated with protargol the length of the course of the disease has apparently only been slightly shortened, but the severity of the attack has been decidedly lessened. **1907** J. H. PARSONS *Dis. Eye* xxix. 580 In more severe cases.. protargol, 15 to 20 per cent., should be rubbed into the margins of the lids with a stumpy camel's hair brush. **1938** *Stain Technol.* XIII. 154 Protargol exhibits an isoelectric point roughly about pH 4, at which acidity it is precipitated, hence it might be expected to behave somewhat like a dye by having its selectivity altered by variation of pH of the staining mixture. **1976** *Acta Zool.* LVII. 117 The figures demonstrate the close connection between the surface cilia as shown by SEM [*sc.* scanning electron microscopy] and the subsurface kinetosomes revealed by the protargol impregnations.

protarsal (protā·ɹsăl), *a. Ent.* [f. PROTARS(US + -AL.] Of or pertaining to the protarsus.

1902 R. I. POCOCK in *Proc. Zool. Soc.* II. 391, 2nd leg with superior basal and anterior apical femoral spine, three inferior apical protarsal spines..and one inferior medium tarsal spine.

protasis. Add: **2.** (Earlier and later examples.)

a **1568** ASCHAM *Scholemaster* (1570) 57 He began the Protasis with *Trochaijs Octonarijs.* **1961** *Listener* 5 Oct. 527/2 For a good deal of his new novel one might as well be reading the protasis of a fair-to-middling detective story.

3. (Earlier and later examples.) Also *fig.*

1588 W. KEMPE *Educ. Children* sig. G.4 ᵛ, Only the protasis or first part of our similitude is attributed but to Cato, for want of a like similitude garnished with like authoritie. **1904** [see *if-clause* s.v. *IF *conj.* (*sb.*) 10]. **1922** JOYCE *Ulysses* 704 Positing what protasis would the contraction for such several schemes become a natural and necessary apodosis? **1971** *Language* XLVII. 81, I use the term 'conditional sentence' to cover the entire complex sentence consisting of a protasis and an apodosis.

protea. In etym., for 'Linnæus 1737' substitute 'Linnæus *Hortus Cliffortianus* (1737) 29'. Substitute for def.: An evergreen shrub or small tree of the genus so called, belonging to the family Proteaceæ, usually native to southern Africa or Australia, and bearing cone-like heads of small flowers with prominent bracts. Also *attrib.* (Further examples.)

1770 R. WESTON *Universal Botanist* I. 221 Cape Protea or Silver-tree. **1804** H. ANDREWS *Botanists Repository* V. tab. cccxlix, From the great number of the divided leaved Proteas, we are led to conjecture, that they are as numerous as those with entire leaves. **1901** L. H. BAILEY *Cycl. Amer. Hort.* III. 1438/2 Proteas are tender shrubs which are among the most attractive and characteristic plants of the Cape of Good Hope. **1951** [see *DISA]. **1972** J. BURMEISTER *Running Scared* 13 Their daughter had been chosen to present a protea, South Africa's unlovely national flower, to the President. **1972** PALMER & PITMAN *Trees S. Afr.* I. xxiv. 503 The close-set protea leaves may yield as important a source of food to sugarbirds and sunbirds as do the flowers.

Protean, *a.* (*sb.*) Add: Now freq. with pronunc. (prōᵘtĭ·ăn). Also **protean. A.** *adj.* **1. c.** Of a theatrical performer: characterized by the ability to take several parts in the same piece; quick-change; also *transf.* of such a performance. orig. *U.S.* Cf. sense B 1b in Dict.

1897 *Daily Tel.* 10 Mar. 4/5 Few will deny that Leopoldi Fregoli..is..alert, versatile, neat in his business, quick as lightning in his changes, and..the best 'protean' entertainer that the oldest playgoer has ever seen. **1909** WEBSTER, *Pro'te-an*... 3..*Theat.* Noting an actor who plays different parts in a play; hence, noting a performance of this kind. *Slang.* **1952** GRANVILLE *Dict. Theatr. Terms* 145 *Protean act*, an act performed by a: *Protean entertainer*, a lightning-change artiste. An impersonator. **1961** BOWMAN & BALL *Theatre Lang.* 282 Protean actor, protean artist. Hence protean act, protean drama, etc.

d. Of animal behaviour: unpredictable, following no obvious pattern.

1959 CHANCE & RUSSELL in *Proc. Zool. Soc.* CXXXII. 67 We therefore propose the term 'Protean Displays'. The mythical Proteus frustrated would-be captors by constantly changing his shape, so that they had nothing systematic to which to react. *Ibid.* 68 Protean displays involve rapid, sudden transitions, as one obvious component of their confusing effect. **1967** *New Scientist* 13 July 96/2 The term protean behaviour was coined to cover behaviour that is sufficiently unsystematic to prevent the predator from predicting in detail the positions, actions or both, of the prey. **1970** *Nature* 6 June 968/1 We have surveyed the occurrence of such protean behaviours and defined them as behaviours which are sufficiently unsystematic in appearance to prevent a reactor predicting in detail the position and/or actions of the actor. *Ibid.*, The erratic nature of a protean display defeats anticipation by the predator.

protease. Add to def.: a proteinase or peptidase. (Earlier and later examples.) [First formed as F. *proteinase* (G. Malfitano 1900, in *Ann. de l'Inst. Pasteur* XIV. 420).]

1903 *Ann. Bot.* XVII. 237 There is at present evidence that enzymes which digest proteids (proteases) occur.. in certain lowly Algae, in some fungi, and in various Phanerogams. **1923** [see *PEPTIDASE]. **1931** [see *PROTEINASE]. **1949** ABRAHAM & HEATLEY in H. W. Florey et al. *Antibiotics* I. ii. 85 This can happen..by the secretion of destructive exocellular enzymes such as penicillinase, protease, or peptidase. **1962** A. SPECTOR in A. Pirie *Lens Metabolism Rel. Cataract* 330 An endopeptidase called *β*-protease..will attack lens protein in acid pH and a second enzyme, the *α*-protease,..attacks the breakdown products produced by the endopeptidase. **1973** ZEFFREN & HALL *Study of Enzyme Mechanisms* ix. 168 Chymotrypsin is one of several proteolytic enzymes or proteases which function collectively in the mammalian small intestine. **1976** *Path. Ann.* XI. 380 This may be related in part to the presence of protease inhibitors in connective tissues.

protect, *v.* Add: **1. a.** Also *absol.*

1894 E. FAWCETT *New Nero* ii. 26 Music..was always an expression of..that soulless and mysterious will-to-live, which for ever creates, protects, and perpetuates. **1934** W. B. YEATS tr. *Sophocles' Oedipus at Colonus* in *Coll. Plays* 543 *Theseus*... If God sent you hither, you need no protection of mine, but God or no God my mere name will protect.

c. To attempt to preserve (a threatened plant or animal species) by preventing collecting, hunting, etc.; to restrict access to (land valued for its wild life or its undisturbed state).

1893 *Zoologist* XVII. 390 If a particular species were declining, and were known to frequent a particular place, the County Council should..be called upon to protect that restricted area. **1935** *Discovery* Oct. 304/1 To protect a bird proved..to be noxious simply brings bird-protection into contempt. **1969** F. N. HEPPER in J. Fisher et al. *Red Bk.* 360/1 The need to protect plants for their own sake is becoming increasingly accepted by those in authority.

2. (Earlier examples.)

1789 *Deb. Congress U.S.* 9 Apr. (1834) 106 [Measures] calculated to encourage the productions of our country, and protect our infant manufactures. **1825** J. S. MILL in *Westm. Rev.* III. 415 The various classes of manufactures are protected from foreign competition.

4. c. To provide (an electrical device or machine) with safeguards against too high a current or voltage.

1875 *Telegr. Jrnl.* III. 60/2 Lightning protectors invented to protect telegraph lines. **1888** D. SALOMONS *Managem. of Accumulators & Private Electric Light Installations* (ed. 3) II. ii. 97 Put a safety fuse in every switch and wall plug... Every lamp is protected in this way..against accidental short-circuits. **1935** MONSETH & ROBINSON *Relay Syst.* xiii. 458 The first zone..is protected by an instantaneous balanced-beam impedance element. **1975** D. G. FINK *Electronics Engineers' Handbk.* VII. 27 Two types of fast-blow fuses are used to protect power-tubes.

5. *Chem.* **a.** To prevent the alteration or removal of (a particular group or part of a molecule) in a reaction, by first causing it to form an unreactive derivative from which the original structure can later be regenerated.

1889 G. M'GOWAN tr. *Bernthsen's Text-bk. Org. Chem.* 352 When it is wished to prepare the mono-nitro-compounds, the aniline must again be 'protected', either by using its acetyl compound or by nitrating in presence of excess of concentrated sulphuric acid. **1929** MITCHELL & HAMILTON *Biochem. Amino Acids* i. 90 In other words, the chloracetyl group, introduced to protect the amino group of the amino acid is, after it has performed its protective function, itself transformed into an amino acid group. **1951** I. L. FINAR *Org. Chem.* I. xi. 203 If the synthesis requires reaction with one halogen atom only, the most satisfactory procedure is to 'protect' the other halogen atom by ether formation and subsequently decompose the ether with concentrated hydrobromic acid. **1964** N. G. CLARK *Mod. Org. Chem.* vi. 90 By forming the dibromide..the double bond is 'protected' from the ensuing reaction, and may be restored later to the compound by zinc treatment. **1971** D. R. WILLIAMS *Metals of Life* ix. 134 Freeman *et al.* have found that the amide bonds in simple peptides which are usually easily hydrolysed to give amino acids again are protected by transition metal ions, the best protectors being copper (II) and nickel (II).

b. To render (a hydrophobic sol) inert to the flocculating action of small concentrations of an electrolyte.

[**1903** *Jrnl. Chem. Soc.* LXXXIV. I. 135 The capacity of colloidal solutions to protect a colloidal solution of gold against the precipitating action of an estimated quantity of sodium chloride is expressed as the gold number.] **1909** J. ALEXANDER tr. *Zsigmondy's Colloids & Ultramicroscope* iii. 77 Another colloid which protects the nascent colloidal gold was discovered by Faraday, and called by him 'jelly'. **1939** *Thorpe's Dict. Appl. Chem.* (ed. 4) III. 287/2 A quartz suspension protected by gelatine will possess the cataphoretic velocity and isoelectric point of gelatine. **1966** GUCKER & SEIFERT *Physical Chem.* xxii. 665 A lyophobic sol is often stabilized by addition of a lyophilic sol, which is then termed a protective colloid. An example is gelatin, which protects the silver bromide sol used in photographic emulsions.

protectant, *a.* Delete †*Obs. rare*—[1] and add examples of the sense: protecting (esp. plants) against disease.

1943 *Phytopathology* XXXIII. 627 (*heading*) The slide-germination method of evaluating protectant fungicides. **1954** *Jrnl. Econ. Entomol.* XLVII. 462 (*heading*) Protection of stored shelled corn with a protectant dust in Indiana. **1977** *Protecting World's Crops* (Shell Internat. Petroleum Co.) 2 Protectant fungicides, if applied before the disease occurs, kill or inhibit the development of fungal spores or mycelia (strands of fungus) before they can damage plant tissues.

B. *sb.* An agent that protects, esp. a plant against disease.

1935 *Jrnl. Pomol. & Hort. Sci.* XIII. 262 The effects of the wetting agents..upon the biological activities of the protectant..have to be determined. **1940** *Phytopathology* XXX. 2 Synthetic organic chemicals developed by the Crop Protection Institute were efficient, non-injurious seed protectants for combating damping-off in Lima beans. **1960** *New Scientist* 4 Aug. 344/1 Removal of the dark green colouring matter present in crude preparations of pyrethrum markedly increased its stability in sunlight, and further improvement was achieved by the addition of..a number of antioxidants... The data suggest that these compounds act primarily as protectants for pyrethrin II and cinerin II, whereas the absence of 'chlorophyll' pigments enhances the stability of pyrethrin I and cinerin I. **1975** *Nature* 22 May 329/1 It is clear that as a protectant, sclareol is highly specific for rust fungi.

protected, *ppl. a.* Add: **a.** (Further examples.) Now also, receiving legal immunity or exemption.

1926 *Brit. Gaz.* 12 May 2/6 The London Central Meat Market, at Smithfield, is now a protected area, and barriers have been drawn across all the approaches. **1942** *Ann. Reg. 1941* 27 Now they [*sc.* men above the reservation age] were to be reserved only if engaged on what was called 'protected work', i.e. work which the Government recognised as of national importance. **1944** *Manpower* (Ministry of Information) 112 Firms were divided into 'protected' and 'unprotected' establishments, according to the urgency of the work they were doing. **1956** J. C. SWAYNE *Conc. Gloss. Geogr. Terms* 114 *Protected state*, a territory, e.g. Brunei, Kuwait, under a ruler who receives the protection of another state. The protecting state controls foreign affairs, but has no jurisdiction over internal matters. **1968** 'C. AIRD' *Henrietta Who?* vii. 64 You're a protected tenant... No one can make you leave. **1975** 'J. BELL' *Victim* i. 12, I took in my second lot of tenants. Protected tenure. **1978** *Country Life* 20 July 148/3 Jersey has no statutory list of protected buildings as has existed in Britain for the last three decades.

b. Of a species whose survival is threatened: affected by laws preventing collecting, hunting, etc.

1930 J. S. HUXLEY *Bird-Watching & Bird Behaviour* vi. 115 The National Trust and the Royal Society for the Protection of Birds..are..paying watchers to see that protected birds are not shot or robbed of their eggs. **1936** *Discovery* Feb. 34/2 Any local authority may now, on application to the Ministry [of Agriculture] take the bird [*sc.* the little owl] off the protected list. **1959** E. F. LINSSEN *Beetles Brit. Isles* I. 156 In an effort not to bring about its [*sc.* the Great Silver Beetle's] total destruction, naturalists refrain from publishing records regarding its distribution... It should be treated as a 'protected' species and left alone. **1976** *Hortus Third* (L. H. Bailey Hortorium) 798/1 In most cases it is better to leave these plants to live where they are native and protected than to move them to gardens. **1978** *Vole* Dec. 18/1 It seemed like every damn animal on this planet should be a protected species.

protecting, *ppl. a.* Add: **a.** (Earlier examples of *protecting duty.*)

1785 *Daily Universal Reg.* 1 Jan. 2/3 The Protecting Duties, so generally called for in Ireland. **1820** *Ann. Reg.* 73/2 The American timber being of an inferior quality to that from the Baltic, required a protecting duty.

b. *spec.* in *Chem.*, applied to a group introduced into a molecule in order to protect a feature of that molecule in a reaction. (Cf. *PROTECT *v.* 5a.)

1947 *Nature* 12 Apr. 500/1 The use of another protecting unit easily removed by hydrolysis in combination with the carbobenzoxy method would considerably extend the use of the latter. **1952** L. J. Desha *Org. Chem.* (ed. 2) xiii. 246 Finally, the protecting acetyl group is removed by hydrolysis. **1968** I. L. Finar *Org. Chem.* (ed. 4) II. xiii. 584 This enamine can react with another amino-acid, and the protecting group is removed by mild bromination.

protection. Add: **1. c.** Freedom from molestation obtained by paying money to a person who threatens violence or retribution if payment is not made; hence protection money itself. Also in other extended uses.

1860 [implied at *protection-rent* below]. **1903** *Independent* 15 Jan. 148/2 I'm sure that no one man knows all ends of this business of 'protection'. **1930** *Economist* 25 Oct. 754/1 A gangster would take it upon himself, say, to organise the selling of fish in one district in Chicago... The fishmonger who did not care for protection would find his shop bombed. **1938** G. Greene *Brighton Rock* II. i. 78 I've got protection. You be careful. **1938** F. D. Sharpe *Sharpe of Flying Squad* xix. 202 A man offered to sell 'protection' to the bookmakers—at a price. **1962** D. Francis *Dead Cert* ix. 106, I..asked the owners straight out if they were paying protection. **1977** 'W. Haggard' *Poison People* III. iv. 123 A man whose prosperous business had kicked at increasing demands for protection and had therefore finally gone to the wall.

d. An attempt to preserve certain animals, plants, or undisturbed areas of land by enforcing rules governing access, collecting, hunting, etc.

1880 *Act* 43 & 44 *Vict.* c. 35 It is expedient to provide for the protection of wild birds of the United Kingdom during the breeding season. **1894** W. H. Hudson *Lost Brit. Birds* 1 It was thought best to leave out any species represented by at least three or four pairs that have some measure of protection afforded to them when breeding. **1895** G. S. Anderson in Roosevelt & Grinsell *Hunting in Many Lands* 377 (*heading*) Protection of the Yellowstone National Park. **1930** J. S. Huxley *Bird-Watching & Bird Behaviour* vi. 115 Protection has brought the bittern back to breed and boom in Norfolk. **1936** *Discovery* Sept. 293/1 From time to time the moose is overhunted in some districts, but after a few years' protection they come back again. **1952** H. L. Edlin *Changing Wild Life of Brit.* v. 71 The Harriers, typical hawks of the marshes, became very rare, but under protection a few continue to nest. **1969** F. N. Hepper in J. Fisher et al. *Red. Bk.* 360/2 The I.U.C.N. itself has taken the principal lead in this field by initiating a scheme for the protection of plant species.

e. *Electr. Engin.* The action or result of *protect *v.* 4c.

1890 Slingo & Brooker *Electr. Engin.* xvii. 725 The way in which it [*sc.* the cut-out] affords this protection is by automatically disconnecting the circuit when the current..exceeds a certain predetermined limit. **1920** *Whittaker's Electr. Engineer's Pocket-Bk* (ed. 4) 428 Merz-Price protection may operate by a balance of voltages or a balance of currents. The former is used for the protection of cables, and the latter for the protection of transformers and alternators. **1962** *Newnes Conc. Encycl. Electr. Engin.* 612/1 The fuse forms the basis of most small, simple distribution-system protection, combining overcurrent protection and fault isolation. **1977** R. W. Smeaton *Switchgear & Control Handbk.* xxvi. 27 The proper choice of protection is based on equipment size, application reliability, shutdowns, probability of faults, and economics.

f. *Chem.* The action of *protect *v.* 5a and b.

1909 J. Alexander tr. *Zsigmondy's Colloids & Ultramicroscope* xviii. 185 The origin of the protection of the gold can be most simply explained by the assumption that specific attractive forces bring about a union of the ultramicrons of metal and protective colloid. **1939** *Thorpe's Dict. Appl. Chem.* (ed. 4) III. 287/1 The protection of sols is of great importance and has been practised empirically since ancient times. **1947** *Nature* 12 Apr. 500/1 The use of the carbobenzoxy reagent for protection of amino-groups in the course of peptide synthesis has.. some limitations. **1951** I. L. Finar *Org. Chem.* I. xii. 215 'Protection' of the double bond is conveniently carried out by the addition of bromine which is subsequently removed by zinc dust in methanolic solution. **1958** J. W. Mullin in Cremer & Davies *Chem. Engin. Pract.* VI. xi. 459 Protection is effected by a number of lyophilic molecules which envelop a lyophobic particle and cover it with a monomolecular layer.

g. *Bridge.* (See quot. 1967.)

1952 I. Macleod *Bridge* vii. 88 Naturally, if there is an element of protection about your bid,..partner will realize that you may be quite a bit weaker. **1958** *Listener* 30 Oct. 709/3 This is a situation in which I cannot look for protection. **1967** *Bridge Players' Encycl.* 393/2 *Protection*, reopening with a bid or double when the opposing bidding has stopped at a low level.

h. *Mountaineering.* (See quot. 1971.)

1966 C. Bonnington *I chose to Climb* iii. 46 There was no protection and it was now necessary to pivot round on one's toes to grasp the smooth, square-cut edge of the bulge. **1971** —— *Annapurna South Face* Gloss. 323 *Protection*, quantity and quality of running belays used to make a pitch safe to lead.

4. (Earlier examples.)

1789 *Deb. Congress U.S.* 15 Apr. (1834) 150 He conceived it the duty of the committee to pay as much respect to the encouragement and protection of husbandry ..as they did to manufactures. **1820** *Hansard Lords* 26 May 579 Let your lordships consider..what would be the effect..if the existing system of protection were abolished, and a fixed duty..were substituted.

5. protection forest, a forest whose purpose is to provide a dense cover of vegetation which helps to inhibit erosion and conserve water; **protection money,** money paid to secure protection (sense *1c); **protection racket,** an illegal scheme for the levying of protection money; † **protection rent** = **protection money*.

1889 W. Schlich *Man. Forestry* I. i. 47 Already in the middle ages so-called 'Protection Forests' existed. **1928** R. S. Troup *Silvicultural Syst.* ix. 116 To afford protection against erosion, landslips, and avalanches in mountainous regions, to conserve the water-supply in catchment areas and to prevent floods; forests maintained for such purposes are termed 'protection forests'. **1974** Longman & Janík *Trop. Forest* vi. 123 Forest reserves are also particularly appropriate in steep terrain to prevent erosion and rapid run-off of water in catchment areas, and these have been recognised for many years as 'protection forests'. **1923** *Nation* (N.Y.) 24 Oct. 449 The men that help unload get $1 a case, and the revenue officers $2 protection money. **1934** R. Graves *I, Claudius* xx. 289 Shopkeepers in the town and farmers in the country had to pay secret 'protection-money' to the local captains; if they refused to pay there would be a raid at night by masked men, their house would be burned down and their families murdered. **1972** T. Lilley *'K' Section* vi. 29 The opium dens and brothels closed. The coffee-shops that now refused to pay protection money. **1937** E. Ambler *Uncommon Danger* x. 149 His business then was intimidating shopkeepers—the 'protection racket', as it is called now in America. **1954** T. S. Eliot *Confidential Clerk* II. 62 Colby doesn't need your protection racket So far as I'm concerned. **1976** D. Daiches in D. Villiers *Next Year in Jerusalem* 275 The characteristics of a Chicago gangster tale: a leader organizing a protection racket, violent measures taken against those who refuse protection money. **1860** *Leisure Hour* 19 July 460/2 In return for black-mail or protection-rent, they shared the property of those who paid it, and engaged to defend it from aggressions.

protectionism. Add: (Earlier and later examples.)

1852 *Punch* 31 July 53/1 If a steam-boat does accidentally 'put in' with a few voyagers, it is met, in the first place, by a spirit of Protectionism and high prices in the shape of pier dues. **1945** K. R. Popper *Open Society* I. vi. 97 What I demand from the state is protection..for my own freedom and for other people's... [This] view..may be called 'protectionism'. **1955** *Times* 4 June 5/1 The Canadian Government's decision to amend the Customs tariff—the changes are due to come into effect today—has a suggestion of protectionism. **1969** *Listener* 14 Aug. 201/1 This protectionism..was originally intended to stave off the intrusions of the American cinema. **1977** *Time* 30 May 51/1 In times of recession, nations inevitably turn toward protectionism as a means of shielding jobs from the threat of foreign goods.

protective, *a.* (*sb.*) Add: **A.** *adj.* **1. a.** (Later examples.)

1938 *Encycl. Brit. Bk. of Year* 467/1 The term 'protective foods' was originally applied to milk and green leaf vegetables, because they made good the deficiencies commonly found in human diets... It has come to include.. foodstuffs..which protect the body against disturbance in structure or function of its organs and parts..which protect, in short, against 'disease'. **1940** *Topeka* (Kansas) *State Jrnl.* 19 Apr. 1/8 De Geer in his broadcast declared The Netherlands would resist with arms any attempt by a foreign power to extend protective help to her. **1944** J. S. Huxley *On living in Revol.* xiii. 139 Agriculture..can be devoted mainly to providing protective foodstuffs. **1955** *Gloss. Terms Radiol.* (*B.S.I.*) 67 *Protective material*, material which is used to provide protection against ionizing radiation. **1974** *Times* 2 Feb. 18/7 The Inland Revenue accepts that in certain trades the employee has to supply his own tools, protective clothing, etc. *a* **1977** *Harrison Mayer Ltd. Catal.* 4/1 Always wear suitable protective clothing.

b. *protective coloration, colouring,* an animal's colouring that blends with its habitat, enabling it to conceal itself. Also *fig.*

1892 F. E. Beddard *Animal Coloration* iii. 86 A South American bittern..affords an excellent instance of the advantages which result from a protective coloration. **1918** G. H. Thayer *Concealing-Coloration in Animal Kingdom* ii. 25 We have..Obliterative Coloration, and Mimicry, as the two main principles of Protective Coloration. **1934** *Proc. Nat. Acad. Sci. Washington* XX. 559 (*heading*) Does protective coloration protect? **1937** Koestler *Spanish Testament* II. 372, I was able to observe..what direct biological forces this process of protective coloration exerts. Guilty or innocent, the prisoner changes form and colour, and assumes the mould that most easily enables him to secure a maximum of those minimal advantages possible within the framework of the prison system. **1941** A. Christie *Evil under Sun* x. 183 Protective colouring is your line. Remain rigidly non-active and fade into the background! **1949** N. Mitford *Love in Cold Climate* iii. 30 As far as my fellow guests were concerned, I was clearly endowed with protective colouring;..I might just as well not have been there at all. **1957** T. W. Kirkpatrick *Insect Life in Tropics* viii. 214 This instance of protective coloration is unlike most others. **1977** B. Colloms *Victorian Country Parsons* xi. 211 To avoid trouble he became over-anxious to please and grew adept at assuming protective colouration [*sic*]. **1979** *Books & Bookmen* Jan. 16/1 One strand of English (and American) poetry, the strand that reflects nineteenth-century bourgeois values at their most unequivocal, can only survive by adopting the protective colouring of a game.

c. *Electr. Engin.* Providing protection against too high a current or voltage.

1896 R. Robb *Electric Wiring* v. 171 All conductors.. must be provided near the point of entrance to the building with some protective device which will operate to shunt the instruments in case of a dangerous rise in potential, and will open the circuit and arrest an abnormal current flow. **1922** [see *bias *v.* 5]. **1962** *Newnes Conc. Encycl. Electr. Engin.* 612/1 A great variety of protective equipment is marketed for distribution systems because of its influence on capital expenditure on such items as switchgear. **1976** *Billings* (Montana) *Gaz.* 6 July 3-D/1 A protective relay adjacent to a Kemmerer, Wyo., power plant was blamed Monday for the Fourth of July electrical black-out that darkened most of Utah. **1978** *Gramophone* Apr. 1796/3 There is also a mains voltage adjuster and twin 2.5A protective mains fuses.

2. a. (Earlier example.)

1820 *Ann. Reg.* 771/1 The protective or restrictive system.

c. *protective arrest, custody,* the detention (of a person) either allegedly or truly for his own protection.

[**1933** R. Bernays *Special Correspondent* xliii. 222 Jews, Socialists, pacifists, Liberals—anyone who has engaged in political agitation or is believed to be hostile to the New Germany—are incarcerated without trial and for an indefinite period. The German name is *Schutzhaft* (protective detention), the idea being that they are asylums..for men who otherwise might suffer grievous bodily harm for their political opinions at the hands of their infuriated countrymen.] **1935** S. Lewis *It can't happen Here* xv. 154 It was blandly explained..that they were merely being safeguarded. Sarason did not use the phrase 'protective arrest'. **1936** *Sun* (Baltimore) 17 Feb. 8/3 He is declared to have been placed under protective custody. Now this phrase is a deliberate steal from the vocabulary of Nazi Germany, its purpose being to cast a pall of dignity around the proceeding when Brown Shirts take an opponent into a Brown House for the purpose of beating him with a rubber hose. *Ibid.*, 'Protective arrest' sounds better than 'ganging up' and gives the impression that the State in its beneficent wisdom is protecting somebody when the only need for protection is protection against the protectors. **1940** *Topeka* (Kansas) *State Jrnl.* 8 May 3/1 When I was asked to take some letters..I agreed readily thinking they might be an open sesame for sleeping quarters. They were—under British 'protective arrest' in Spillum. **1940** C. V. Wedgwood *William the Silent* vii. 192 He was even forced to take monks and priests into protective custody —and it really was protective custody, though the catholics represented it as plain imprisonment. **1947** P. Woodruff *Wild Sweet Witch* 7 The Deputy Commissioner of the day did take a man into protective custody to prove he was not the panther. **1964** N. Marsh *Dead Water* iii. 79, I wish I could put you under protective custody. **1973** 'D. Shannon' *No Holiday for Crime* viii. 128 Pat's reformed pusher ready to tell all sitting safe in protective custody.

3. *Chem.* **a.** Having the quality or property of protecting a sol (cf. *protect *v.* 5b); *spec.* in *protective colloid*, a lyophilic colloid whose presence in small quantities protects a lyophobic sol.

1906 *Jrnl. Soc. Chem. Industry* 31 May 484/1 To insure the satisfactory production of bright deposits it is in all cases essential to employ clear, well filtered solutions. The authors explain the observed phenomena by supposing that the bright deposit is formed by causing the metal to retain its amorphous condition and preventing it from becoming crystalline. The mutual protective effect of colloids upon one another..is probably the chief factor. **1909** J. Alexander tr. *Zsigmondy's Colloids & Ultramicroscope* 77 Lobry de Bruyn (1898), characterized gelatin jelly as a protective colloid (Schutzkolloid). **1939** *Thorpe's Dict. Appl. Chem.* (ed. 4) III. 287/1 Zsigmondy showed that the sharp colour change from red to blue displayed by gold sols under the influence of electrolytes could be used as a means of obtaining a quantitative comparison of the protective action of different colloids. **1950** E. K. Fischer *Colloidal Dispersions* vi. 247 In the manufacture of colored pigments, protective colloids aid in keeping the particle size small. **1960** [see *peptization]. **1967** G. P. A. Turner *Introd. Paint Chem.* xi. 160 If the protective colloids are not truly compatible with the film-former, gloss will be reduced and the film weakened.

b. = *protecting *ppl. a.* b.

1932 *Chem. Abstr.* XXVI. 5072 The method of synthesizing peptides which consists in stabilizing the amino group of 1 acid with a protective group R, then so altering the CO_2H group as to enable it to couple with a 2nd amino acid and removing the group R after the coupling has been effected. **1968** I. L. Finar *Org. Chem.* (ed. 4) II. xiii. 582 Bergmann (1932) introduced carbobenzoxy chloride as an amino protective group, and this appears to be the most widely used method of protection.

B. *sb.* Also, a contraceptive sheath.

1971 *It* 2–16 June 23/3 (Advt.), Protectives by post:.. Durex Gossamer Doz. 50p. **1977** *Lancet* 15 Oct. 811/1 Although the condom, or male protective, is marketed primarily as a method of contraception, some stress is laid both by the manufacturers and by the medical profession on its value as a prophylactic against sexually transmitted diseases.

protector, *sb.* **1. a.** Add to small-type note: Also, *Protector of the Poor*, a term of respect formerly used in British India, as by Indian servants to their masters.

1890 Kipling in *Macmillan's Mag.* June 149/2 The news does not come from my mouth, Protector of the Poor. **1894** —— *Jungle Bk.* 165 'Was it to help thee steal green corn?..'Not green corn, Protector of the Poor—melons', said Little Toomai. **1910** *Blackw. Mag.* Feb. 167 They sent him to Lord Caerlaverock, for the ex-viceroy loved to be treated as a kind of consul-general for India. But this Protector of the Poor proved a broken reed. **1911** F. H. Burnett *Secret Garden* iv. 25 The native servants.. in India..called them [*sc.* their masters] 'protector of the poor' and names of that sort. **1952** J. Masters *Deceivers* ix. 99 Protector of the Poor, at first cockcrow the villain called for a lotah for purposes of nature.

b. (Further examples.)

1867 G. H. Selkirk *Guide to Cricket Ground* ii. 33 *Pads*, leg guards and protectors for the abdomen. **1898** *Sci. Abstr.* I. 240 (*heading*) Telephone line protectors. **1922** *Lillywhites' Sports Requisites* 7 Wicket-keeping Sundries. Palmer's Abdominal Protectors. **1934** *Jrnl. Inst. Electr. Engineers* LXXIV. 236/2 Protectors are connected to every open-wire Post Office line.

d. (*a*) A man who keeps a mistress; (*b*) a man who looks after a prostitute in return for her earnings, a pimp. Cf. Protection 1 b.

1905 [see *man's woman* s.v. *man *sb.* 21]. **1938** F. D. Sharpe *Sharpe of Flying Squad* x. 116 Prostitutes and their protectors were roped into the stations by the dozen. **1954** *Britannica Bk. of Year* 637/2 A group of criminals making a living from organized prostitution was referred to as a Vice-Ring, the leader of such a group being a Vice-Chief..or—with reference to the prostitutes controlled by him—a Protector.

e. One by whom protection from harassment is assured or who collects protection money. Cf. *protection 1 c.

1933 H. G. Wells *Shape of Things to Come* ii. 153 The man who wanted to be left alone in peace..was pressed to pay his tribute to the gang. Or he would not be left in peace. And even if his particular 'protectors' left him in peace, there might still be other gangs about for whom they disavowed responsibility and with whom he had to make a separate deal. **1977** J. Wainwright *Nest of Rats* iii. 15, I was wise enough to choose my own 'protector'.

protectorate, *sb.* Add: **2. c.** (Earlier example.)

1844 *Times* 30 July 4/5 Queen Pomane [of Tahiti] had been forced to accept the 'Protectorate' of the French flag.

3. (Earlier and later examples.)

1860 E. B. Andrews in G. E. Metcalfe *Gt. Brit. & Ghana* (1964) 285/1 The Protectorate on this side of the Volta. **1871** *Act* 34 *Vict.* c. 8 Whereas the inhabitants of certain territories in Africa adjoining Her Majesty's settlements of Sierra Leone, Gambia, Gold Coast, and Lagos, and the adjacent protectorates. **1921** *Brit. Year Bk. Internat. Law 1921–2* 114 Virtually colonies; constitutionally foreign soil—that is the definition of 'protectorates': juridical monsters. **1923** *Publ. Permanent Court Internat. Justice* B. iv. 27 The extent of the powers of a protecting State in the territory of a protected State depends, first, upon the Treaties between the protecting State and the protected State establishing the Protectorate, and, secondly, upon the conditions under which the Protectorate has been recognised by third Powers as against whom there is an intention to rely on the provisions of these Treaties. **1955** *Sci. Amer.* Mar. 60/2 The protectorate borders on the vast jungle belt of central Africa in which yellow fever is endemic. **1961** L. van der Post *Heart of Hunter* i. vii. 110 Although Lobatsi was in a British Protectorate the railway itself belonged to Southern Rhodesia.

4. *protectorate land, law.*

1936 *Discovery* June 189/1 Nigeria is in the peculiar state of having both mandated and protectorate lands within its boundaries. **1961** L. van der Post *Heart of Hunter* i. vii. 112 The provincial commissioner..would have up the station-master and draft instructions to ensure that the station was run in the spirit as well as the letter of Protectorate Law.

protectorist (prote·ktŏrist). *Hist.* [f. Protector *sb.* + -ist.] = Protectorian *sb.*

1913 J. Willcock *Life Sir H. Vane* xvi. 275 About half the members of the Commons were Protectorists or supporters of the constitution prescribed in *The Petition and Advice.*

protectrice. For †*Obs.* in Dict. read 'Now *rare*' and add later example.

1974 J. Flint *Cecil Rhodes* v. 105 Lobengula...had imagined that Queen Victoria was now his ally and protectrice.

protegulum (prote·giulŏm). *Zool.* [mod.L., f. Pro-[2] 1 + L. *tegulum* covering.] In brachiopods, the embryonic form of the shell.

1891 C. E. Beecher in *Amer. Jrnl. Sci.* XLI. 344 All brachiopods, so far as studied by the writer, have a common form of embryonic shell, which may be termed the protegulum. **1904** *Amer. Jrnl. Sci.* CLXVII. 283 The protegulum of this species [sc. *Stropheodonta perplana*] is nearly circular. **1935** Twenhofel & Shrock *Invertebr. Paleont.* viii. 269 Growth proceeds around the protegulum, mainly along the anterior and lateral margins of the two valves. **1959** L. H. Hyman *Invertebrates* V. xxi. 531 Each valve begins as a minute plate, the protegulum, presumably composed of periostracum. **1973** P. Tasch *Paleobiol. Invertebrates* vii. 263/2 The outer surface of the mantle flaps (lobes) became white and smooth, indicating initial shell formation (protegulum).

proteiform, *a.* (Earlier and later examples.)

1793 *Critical Rev.* IX. 183 Pathologists have, within these last years, differed greatly respecting the cause of this Proteiform disease [*sc.* gout]. **1944** S. Putnam tr. *E. da Cunha's Rebellion in Backlands* ii. 84 The proteiform mestizo of the seaboard.

protein. Add: Now pronounced (prōᵘ·tīn).

It seems likely that in proposing the word *protéine* Mulder was adopting a suggestion made to him by Berzelius: see *Nature* (1951) 11 Aug. 244.

c. (Further examples.)

1917 *Nature* 15 Feb. 471/2 Just as the protein supply in meat may be compensated for by the greater utilisation of the protein-rich pulses. **1925** C. H. Browning *Bacteriol.* iii. 46 Instead of adding peptone a useful procedure is to digest the minced meat at the commencement by pancreatic extracts containing the protein-splitting ferment trypsin, which produces peptone bodies in the mixture and yields a very suitable basis for nutritive medium. **1928** *Physiol. Rev.* VIII. 418 If, as is stated by Mathews.., Fischer was induced to turn his attention to protein chemistry by Kossel, the debt science owes this great biochemist is beyond estimation. **1946** *Nature* 19 Oct. 556/2 Estimations are made on protein-free filtrates, prepared by adding to 0·2 c.c. serum, 11 c.c. water and 0·5 c.c. of each of the Folin-Wu reagents. **1953** *Amer. Naturalist* LXXXVII. 255 The heterogeneity which is the dismay of the protein chemist attempting to solve purification problems may be the very basis for his existence as a human being. **1956** *Nature* 28 Jan. 190/1 Although reticulocytes have practically their full complement of hæmoglobin, evidence from amino-acid incorporation studies suggests that these cells..still have protein-synthesizing capacity. **1960** *Farmer & Stockbreeder* 9 Feb. 110/2 (Advt.), Lobolettes are protein-packed, rich in energy and fully fortified with vitamins, minerals and trace elements. **1961** *Lancet* 29 July 258/1 These figures may be explained by the presence of one or more insulin antagonists..or by protein-binding of the insulin in the blood. *Ibid.* 5 Aug. 284/1 Rona and Takahaski first demonstrated..that.. the plasma-calcium consisted of a diffusible fraction and a non-diffusible protein-bound fraction. **1972** J. Maddox *Doomsday Syndrome* iii. 75 Protein deficiency is still a serious cause of stunted development..among poor people even in advanced societies. **1979** *Arizona Daily Star* 5 Aug. (Parade Suppl.) 14/3 Protein-rich foods such as meat, dairy products and nuts should be eaten.

d. Special Combs.: **protein plastic,** a plastic in which protein is the chief component; *esp.* a casein plastic; **protein shock** *Med.*, a disturbed state produced by the parenteral introduction into the body of a foreign protein; also, protein therapy; **protein therapy** *Med.*, the production of protein shock for therapeutic purposes.

1936 Sturken & Woodruff *U.S. Patent 2,040,033* 1/1 Our invention relates to the production of protein plastics which may be cured in the mold without the necessity of a prolonged cure in formaldehyde solution or formaldehyde vapor. In the past, protein plastics such as casein have found many uses in the light plastics field. **1943** H. R. Fleck *Plastics* iv. 82 The two most widely known and industrially important protein plastics are those formed from casein..and those formed from the proteins present in soya beans. **1969** *Encycl. Polymer Sci. & Technol.* XI. 696 The term 'protein plastic' is specifically interpreted commercially to mean casein plastic. **1917** *Jrnl. Exper. Med.* XXVI. 699 The mechanism of recovery following the so called 'protein shock therapy'. *Ibid.* 705 By means of the protein shock, antibody-rich fluids (serum) are forced into the lymph channels. **1935** F. P. Gay *Agents of Dis. & Host Resistance* lxiii. 1506 Symptomatic disturbances during protein shock are an increased pulse rate, sweating, decreased blood pressure, increased peristalsis, increased lymph flow and lymph volume, and a mobilization of the serum enzymes. **1964** S. Duke-Elder *Parsons' Dis. of Eye* (ed. 14) xiv. 149 In certain aspects the response to cortisone resembles that to fever therapy by 'protein shock'. **1917** *Jrnl. Amer. Med. Assoc.* 8 Sept. 766/2 The application of foreign protein therapy to the acute, subacute and chronic arthritides. **1940** B. I. Comroe *Arthritis* xv. 195 Substances..now employed for non-specific protein therapy include bacterial vaccines. **1967** *Biol. Abstr.* XLVIII. 7122/1 (*heading*) The use of protein therapy for gastric and duodenal ulcers.

proteinase (prōᵘ·tīnēⁱz, -s). *Biochem.* [a. G. *proteinase* (Grassmann & Dyckerhoff 1928, in *Zeitschr. f. physiol. Chem.* CLXXIX. 41): see Protein and *-ase.] Any enzyme that hydrolyses proteins to smaller polypeptides.

1929 *Chem. Abstr.* XXIII. 615 Plant proteases... The proteinase and the polypeptidase of yeast. **1931** *Biochem. Jrnl.* XXV. 256 In their main conclusions these authors agreed that green malt contains (1) a protease or proteinase (to adopt the nomenclature of Grassmann) which appears to attack..crystalline egg-albumin..and (2) at least one peptidase which attacks the dipeptide leucylglycine. **1941** *Adv. Enzymol.* I. 76 Pepsin, trypsin, and chymotrypsin represent the three best recognized proteinases. **1963** *Biochem. Jrnl.* LXXXVI. 100/1 The purified proteinase probably liberated peptides from a boiled sample of α_2-crystallin, and it seems probable that the lens proteinase is an endopeptidase. **1970** Passmore & Robson *Compan. Med. Stud.* II. xviii. 33/1 Potent bacterial proteinases and collagenases decompose muscle tissue and collagen.

proteinoid (prōᵘ·tīnoid), *sb.* (*a.*) *Biochem.* [f. Protein + -oid.] A protein-like polypeptide or mixture of polypeptides obtained by heating a mixture of amino-acids. Also *attrib.* or as *adj.*

1956 S. W. Fox in *Amer. Scientist* XLIV. 353 Evidence that proteinoids can be formed by heating one or two amino acids has now accumulated. *Ibid.* 354 The appearance of aspartic acid after hydrolysis is part of the evidence for a proteinoid product. **1968** *New Scientist* 4 Apr. 41/1 When Sidney Fox first discovered this form of amino acid condensation ten years ago, he was immediately attracted by the idea that these quasi-proteins—or proteinoids,..might represent the first evolutionary step ..that led to the true proteins. *Ibid.* 41/2 Perhaps the most striking similarity that proteinoids bear to true proteins..is that..they act like enzymes. **1971** *Nature* 7 May 42/1 In contrast to the plausible explanations for proteinoid formation, there seems to be no satisfactory concept for the genesis of polynucleotide templates in the presumed conditions of the primitive Earth. **1977** A. Hallam *Planet Earth* 236 (*caption*) Cell-like structures called 'proteinoid microspheres' have been produced by evaporating organic chemicals on hot lava beds.

proteinosis (prōᵘtīnōᵘ·sis). *Path.* [mod.L., ad. G. *lipoid)proteinose* (E. Uhrbach in J. Jadassohn *Handb. der Haut- und Geschlechtskrankheiten* (1932) XII. 336): see Protein and -osis.] The abnormal accumulation or deposition of protein in tissue.

1937 *Arch. Dermatol. & Syphilol.* XXXV. 357 A subsequent microscopic examination revealed the tinctorial and cellular features of lipoid proteinosis. **1954** *Ann. Internal Med.* XLI. 163 Lipoid proteinosis is a peculiar abnormality of fat deposition characterized by the appearance of white or yellow plaques and nodules in the skin and mucous membranes, producing hoarseness due to vocal chord involvement. **1958** *New England Jrnl. Med.* 5 June 1123 (*heading*) Pulmonary alveolar proteinosis. **1961** *Lancet* 30 Sept. 733/2 A man aged 36 gave a 2-year history of increasing breathlessness with diffuse shadowing on the chest radiograph. 15 months after the onset of symptoms a lung biopsy..showed that he had pulmonary alveolar proteinosis. **1974** *Arch. Dermatol.* CX. 594/2 This finding suggests that lipid accumulation in lipoid proteinosis lesions is not due to a primary defect in lipid metabolism, but could be due to secondary adherence to glycoproteins.

proteinuria (prōᵘtinⁱūᵊ·riă). *Med.* [mod.L., ad. F. *protéinurie* (L. Hugounenq 1901, in *Lyon Médical* CXVI. 87): see Protein and -uria.] The presence of abnormal quantities of protein in the urine.

1911 *Jrnl. Physiol.* XLII. 238 It seemed important to determine how far an individual suffering from so grave a disturbance of protein metabolism as this condition of proteinuria betokens, could be in nitrogenous equilibrium. *Ibid.* 241 Of some significance is the fact that the excretion of creatin appears to be characteristic of Bence-Jones proteinuria. **1976** *Acta Med. Biol.* XXIV. 9 These patients with symptomless persistent proteinuria appear to constitute a distinct clinical group which is characterized by normal renal function..and a more favorable prognosis.

Hence **proteinu·ric** *a.*, of, pertaining to, or suffering from proteinuria.

1932 *Dorland's Med. Dict.* (ed. 16) 1042/2 Proteinuric. **1969** *Metabolism* XVIII. 556/1 A polypeptide exhibiting diabetogenic and anti-insulin properties has been isolated from the urine of 33 of the 35 proteinuric diabetic patients. **1977** *Lancet* 21 May 1108/2 Groups divided up according to whether they remained normotensive or developed mild pre-eclampsia or proteinuric pre-eclampsia as defined by Nelson.

protension. Delete *rare* and add: **2.** (Later example.)

1890 W. James *Princ. Psychol.* II. xx. 222 In the case of protension or mere farness it [*sc.* the neural process] is more complicated.

3. (Further example.)

1935 *Philos. of Sci.* II. 236 In a similar reaction against Wundtian atomism Külpe also added duration (protension) to the list.

b. (With spelling **protention,** after G. *protention* (E. Husserl 1922 in *Jahrb. f. Philos. u. phänomenol. Forsch.* I. iii. ii. § 77.145), perh. infl. by *retention 2 c.) In Phenomenology, extension of the consciousness of some present act or event into the future. Hence **prote·ntional** *a.* Cf. *retention 2 c.

1931 W. B. Gibson tr. *Husserl's Ideas* iii. ii. 216 The same holds good, according to the naïvely natural view, in respect of *anticipation*.., or previsional expectation. At first there comes in the immediate '*protention*' (as we might put it). *Ibid.* 237 Continuous changes in an opposite direction: 'after' corresponding to 'before', a protentional continuum corresponding to the retentional. **1941** *Philos. & Phenomenol. Res.* II. 341 These expectations—Husserl calls them..'protentions'—belong, of course, to our present acting. **1966** A. Gurwitsch *Phenomenol. & Psychol.* ix. 149 The notions of protention and particularly of retention are at the center of the Husserlian theory concerning the experience of time. **1974** D. Carr *Phenomenol. & Probl. of Hist.* iv. 103 It is the act conceived as the living present, with its horizons of retention and protention, which is 'responsible' for the original or primary givenness of anything.

protensity. Delete *rare*—⁰ and add examples.

1915 G. F. Stout *Man. Psychol.* (ed. 3) ii. i. 212 In all sense presentations we can discern Quality, Intensity, and Protensity or Duration. **1920** S. Alexander *Space, Time, & Deity* II. 130 The 'protensity' of sensation is nothing but its continuance, that is, again, a continuous repetition of the sensation in time. **1935** *Philos. of Sci.* II. 236 The four classical attributes of sensation are quality, intensity, extensity and protensity. **1964** Jakobson & Halle in D. Abercrombie et al. *Daniel Jones* 99 The tense/lax opposition should..be..viewed as a separate, 'protensity' feature which..corresponds to the quantity features in the prosodic field. **1972** *Language* XLVIII. 31 This difference between laxness diphthongization and all other types is a simple consequence of the fact that laxness is a protensity feature.

protention. See *protension 3 b.

proteo- (prōᵘti,o-), comb. form of Protein; **proteocla·stic** *a.* [see Clastic *a.*] = Proteolytic *a.*; **proteoglycan** (-gləi·kæn) (see quot. 1969); **proteoli·pid, -ide,** a complex that contains protein and lipid moieties and is insoluble in aqueous media but soluble in organic solvents; cf. *lipoprotein* s.v. *lipo-. Also Proteolysis, etc.

1929 I. F. & W. D. Henderson *Dict. Sci. Terms.* (ed. 2) 260/2 Proteoclastic. **1959** W. Andrew *Textbk. Compar. Histol.* v. 195 The granular amoebocytes or granulocytes of the oyster carry out intracellular digestion by means of sucroclastic, lipoclastic, and proteoclastic enzymes. **1969** Hascall & Sajdera in *Jrnl. Biol. Chem.* CXLIV. 2384/2 We refer to this fraction, which is a basic building block for the cartilage matrix, as proteoglycan subunit. Because of the selectivity of the techniques used in its purification we presume that it contains only covalently bound protein. The second component is a glycoprotein fraction. [*Note*] The term 'proteoglycan' is used to describe macromolecules which consist primarily of polysaccharide which is presumed to be bound covalently to the small amount of protein present. 'Glycoprotein' is used to indicate a macromolecule which is primarily protein, but which contains covalently bound saccharide. **1974** *Sci. Amer.* May 67/1 It does appear, however, that the wet surfactants on the ocean, which are known to be glycoproteins and proteoglycans, are reasonably good carriers of phosphate, of various organic molecules, of the scarcer ions of seawater and of heavy metals. **1977** *Lancet* 4 June 1190/2 The major proteins of cartilage are proteoglycan..and type-II collagen. **1950** Folch & Lees in *Federation Proc.* IX. 171/2 (*heading*) Brain proteolipides, a new group of protein-lipide substances soluble in organic solvents and insoluble in water. **1971** [see *lipoprotein* s.v. *lipo-]. **1976** *Nature* 25 Mar. 348/1 The L-glutamate binding proteins of insect and crustacean muscle are hydrophobic proteins (that is, proteolipids) extractable with organic solvents.

proteolytic, *a.* Add: Hence **proteoly·tically** *adv.*, as regards or by means of proteolysis or proteolytic enzymes.

1903 *Ann. Bot.* XVII. 613, I have further succeeded in preparing a proteolytically active glycerin-extract from the roots. **1970** *Nature* 12 Dec. 1097/1 Plasmin..proteolytically degrades fibrin and fibrinogen preferentially to other substrates. **1978** *Ibid.* 21 Sept. 182/2 One current speculation is that the two forms of fibronectin may be the same gene product, but the surface form is proteolytically processed to the slightly smaller plasma form.

proter (prōᵘ·təɹ). *Biol.* [a. F. *proter* (Chatton & Lwoff 1936, in *Arch. Zool. expér. et gen.* LXXVIII. 85), f. Gr. πρότερος in front.] In ciliate protozoa, the anterior of the two organisms formed by transverse fission. Cf. *opisthe.

1950 A. Lwoff *Probl. Morphogenesis in Ciliates* xi. 73 In ciliates of the *Leucophrys* type, the proter and the opisthe are modelled in the anterior and posterior parts of the parent. **1961** Mackinnon & Hawes *Protozool.* iv. 222 At binary fission..the oral structures then go to the anterior daughter, or proter.

protero-. Add: **Proterozoic** *a.* (examples of *absol.* use).

1905 Chamberlin & Salisbury *Geol.* I. i. 17 In these four great series of sedimentary rocks there are, here and there, intrusions of igneous rocks, and in some places the sedimentary beds have been metamorphosed into crystalline rocks by heat and pressure. This is particularly true in the lowest of these series, the Proterozoic, where a large part of the sediment is metamorphosed, and where there is much igneous rock. **1971** *Nature* 25 June 498/1 The establishment of global subdivisions for the Upper (Late) Pre-Cambrian, or the Proterozoic, is particularly important. **1977** A. Hallam *Planet Earth* 189 The Proterozoic was, compared with the Archaean, dominantly a period of crustal reworking.

proterogenesis (prǫtĕrodʒe·nĕsis). *Biol.* [mod.L. (coined in Ger. by O. H. Schindewolf 1925, in *Neues Jahrb. f. Min., Geol. und Paläont.* LII. B. 337): see Protero- and -genesis.] The anticipation of future evolutionary development in the early stages of an organism's life. Hence **pro:terogene·tic** *a.*, **-gene·tically** *adv.*

1938 *Rep. Brit. Assoc. Adv. Sci.* 79 Among the examples quoted by Schindewolf in support of the principle of proterogenesis is one drawn from the cephalopod family the *Clymendiæ* which lived during the Devonian period. It consists of a number of genera and species in which, at one end of the series, the shell has the normal type of spiral coil..with an almost circular outline throughout development. In the next member of the series the innermost portion of the spiral has a triangular outline. In other members of the series the latter form of outline finds every degree of expression up to one in which it prevails at all stages of growth, including the adult. The series as it stands may be quoted in support of either the proterogenetic or the tachygenetic view, according to which end of the series is taken as the starting point. Schindewolf adopts the former. *Ibid.* 82 Trend characters, on the other hand, arise either cœnogenetically or deuterogenetically and proceed proterogenetically or tachygenetically towards later or earlier stages in life-history respectively in successive generations. **1947** A. M. Davies *Introd. Palæont.* (ed. 2) iv. 139 In some cases this change is contrary to the rule of palingenesis, since the youthful whorl-shape foreshadows the adult whorl-shape of forms that come later in time... This reverse sequence to that of palingenesis is termed proterogenesis or cænogenesis, and has been observed in other animal phyla, particularly in the Graptolites. **1947** H. H. Swinnerton *Outl. Palæont.* (ed. 3) x. 195 The significance of the inner capricorn whorls in alimorphs may accordingly become anticipatory or recapitulatory, proterogenetic or palingenetic according to which view is adopted. **1966** Davis & Langerl tr. *Hennig's Phylogenetic Systematics* iii. 228 The theory of the 'early ontogenetic origin of types' assumes a special place in discussions of the origin of higher categories or new types. Equivalent or nearly equivalent are the concepts of 'proterogenesis' (Schindewolf), paedomorphism (Garstang), and—as Wettstein 1942 emphasizes—the designations diametagenesis.., fetalization.., and neomorphosis.

proteroglyph (prǫ·tĕroglif). *Zool.* [ad. F. *protéroglyphe*, mod.L. *Proteroglypha* (A. H. A. Duméril 1853, in *Mem. Acad. Sci.* XXIII. 415), f. Protero- + Gr. γλυφή carving.] A venomous snake belonging to a group characterized by grooved fangs in the front of the mouth. So **proterogly·phous** *a.*

1895 Proteroglyphous [in Dict. s.v. Protero-]. **1896** *Proc. Zool. Soc.* 616 In the Proteroglyphs adapted to life in the sea, a similar series of modifications takes place. **1956** L. M. Klauber *Rattlesnakes* II. xi. 715 The front-fanged snakes whose fangs are permanently erect are referred to as proteroglyphs. **1965** R. & D. Morris *Men & Snakes* viii. 177 With the sea-snakes and the cobras, we come to a condition known as Proteroglyphous. Here there has been a reduction in the structure of the upper jaw, the front region having disappeared, bringing the poison fangs to the fore... These are the so-called 'fixed-front-fang' snakes. **1969** A. Bellairs *Life of Reptiles* I. v. 193 According to this hypothesis the viperids would have had a separate ancestry from the proteroglyphs (elapids and sea snakes).

protest, *sb.* Add: **4. c.** In Adlerian psychology, a personal, perhaps unconscious, dissent or attempted dissociation from one's self or circumstances; esp. *masculine protest* (see quots. 1917 and 1972).

1917 Glueck & Lind tr. *Adler's Neurotic Constitution* (1921) iii. 49 The dynamics of the neurosis can therefore be regarded (and is often so understood by the neurotic because of its irradiation upon his psyche) as if the patient wished to change from a woman to a man. This effect yields in its most highly colored form the picture of that which I have called the 'masculine protest'. **1939** H. Orgler *A. Adler* v. 128 The second little theft was carried out as a protest against his being released on parole. **1972** H. Papanek in Freedman & Kaplan *Interpreting Personality* iii. 127 The term 'masculine protest' refers to the attitude of a boy or girl who is raised in a patriarchal culture, in which the real man is respected and admired and the feminine role connotes submissiveness and immaturity.

d. The expressing of dissent from, or rejection of, the prevailing social, political, or cultural mores.

1953 S. A. Brown in A. Dundes *Mother Wit* (1973) 40/2 We go then to what is called the New Negro Movement, then to..Social Protest. **1967** *Listener* 8 June 752/3 Mr Woodcock..traces the development of protest from the first tramps of *Down and Out in Paris and London* to the final achievement of Big Brother. **1968** *Ibid.* 4 July 22/3 Unlike many American authors of his generation, he has [not]..the rather breathy enthusiasm of those who have jumped alongside the youthful millions on the bandwagon..of Protest. **1975** A. Powell *Hearing Secret Harmonies* ii. 72, I was watching a programme..dealing with protest, counterculture, alternative societies.

5. *attrib.* and *Comb.* **a.** Demonstrating or representing a protest against a specific action or proceeding, as *protest banner, button, camp, group, meeting* (further examples), *movement, rally, strike*; designating a literary or artistic medium which seeks to register or portray dissatisfaction with a given event, style, etc., as *protest art, literature, music, poetry, song*; also *protest-singer, -singing*; (sense *4 c) *protest mechanism*; also *protest-oriented* adj. **b.** Special combs.: **protest march** = *march *sb.*⁴ 1a; hence as *v. intr*; also **protest marcher; protest vote,** a vote placed with a minor faction and considered to represent a protest against the policies of a greater; so **protest voting.**

1973 S. Henderson *Understanding New Black Poetry* 16 Not 'protest' art but essentially an art of liberating vision. **1976** *Milton Keynes Express* 18 June 3/3 Their threat to swamp the area with protest banners had been lifted at the last minute. **1972** *Sat. Rev.* (U.S.) 27 May 6/2 A large protest button, reading: 'Memorial Day, 1969, 35,000 GI's dead in Vain. No More.' **1968** 'O. Mills' *Sundry Fell Designs* i. 9 This..must be her eleventh protest camp, not counting non-overnight demonstrations in Trafalgar Square but counting the Aldermaston marches. **1961** B. R. Wilson *Sects & Society* 1 The sect, as a protest group, has always developed its own distinctive ethic. **1973** *Freedom* 1 Sept. 4/1 The various 'protest' groups had lost interest in The Bomb. **1960** *Times Lit. Suppl.* 5 Feb. 77/1 Mr. Klaus Roehler's stories..invite automatic comparison with other outcrops of post-war protest literature. **1975** *Listener* 16 Jan. 69/1 A..flood of protest literature which circulated through the underground channels of *samizdat*, or clandestine publishing. **1959** 'M. Derby' *Tigress* iv. 151 What was he..doing in Ceylon? Leading a hydrogen bomb protest march? **1963** *Economist* 9 Nov. 550/2 The people were protest-marching. **1966** C. Achebe *Man of People* i. 4 Protest marches and demonstrations were staged up and down the land. **1967** *Punch* 8 Nov. 699/1, I see an army with banners, protest-marching up and down Charing Cross Road. **1976** *Eastern Even. News* (Norwich) 9 Dec. 3/1 The meeting held at the Hippodrome theatre after a protest march with banners through the town centre. **1960** *Guardian* 12 Oct. 8/5 Sir Edgar Whitehead..failed to..speak to the patient thousands of protest marchers. **1976** J. Wainwright *Bastard* v. 74 The leather-stampers [*sc.* policemen] who stroll alongside the protest marchers. **1920** *Challenge* 21 May 45/1 Adler..has shown how this protest mechanism is responsible for neurotic manifestations of another kind. **1939** L. MacNeice *Autumn Jrnl.* vii. 30 In the sodden park on Sunday protest Meetings assemble. **1965** S. T. Ollivier *Petticoat Farm* x. 137 The Richards brothers.. called a protest meeting of all suppliers. **1909** *Westm. Gaz.* 5 Nov. 5/2 A protest movement is being organised in Belgium against the interference of England in the internal policy of Belgium, especially in regard to the Congo question. **1974** tr. *Wertheim's Evolution & Revolution* iv. 114 In such a case, it should not be called a counterpoint any more, but a social protest movement. **1969** *Listener* 5 June 806/1 Can he [*sc.* Bob Dylan] have forgotten entirely the horrors that gave such a fine edge to his protest music? *Ibid.* 6 Feb. 163/3 Mr Desmond Bird spoke of our 'protest-oriented' society. **1973** S. Henderson *Understanding New Black Poetry* 25 There has been, despite denials, some protest poetry in the sixties. **1960** *Guardian* 11 July 5/3 A protest rally was held in Trafalgar Square. **1977** W. H. Manville *Good-bye* ii. 16 A lot of show-biz people were going to sing and tap-dance at a last-ditch protest rally. **1968** *Guardian* 19 Sept. 9/4 Brave new causes for brave new protest singers. **1969** *Listener* 5 June 805/3 Bob Dylan's *Nashville Skyline* LP completes his recent renunciation of the rebellious, CND-orientated protest-singer image in favour of that of a fun-loving country boy. **1966** *Punch* 19 Jan. 70/2 Anyone tired of protest singing must have been cheered to learn that a group in California ..is rapidly climbing the charts with seventeenth-century songs. **1953** J. Greenway *Amer. Folksong of Protest* 3 Protest songs are unpleasant and disturbing. **1966** *Punch* 9 Feb. 208/2 The rise of the protest songs seems to be doing something for the audibility of lyrics. **1979** *Oxford Times* 21 Dec. 15 What happened to protest songs? Well, here's one, asking: 'Do you find it attractive to be radio-active?' **1974** T. Allbeury *Snowball* xxii. 138 A million workers were due to vote on protest strikes. **1973** *Irish Times* 2 Mar. 9/3 In the event, West Mayo threatened a protest vote. **1976** *Times* 3 Feb. 7/5 A substantial part of the [French] communist vote is a protest one. **1948** in M. McLuhan *Mech. Bride* (1967) 6/6 A blank ballot is the only means of protest voting.

protest, *v.* Add: **1. d.** *trans.* With direct speech as obj.

1903 E. Childers *Riddle of Sands* v. 48 'I'm not boring you, am I?' he said suddenly. 'I should think not,' I protested. **1919** V. Woolf *Night & Day* xii. 154 'But I do read De Quincey,' Ralph protested 'more than Belloc and Chesterton.' **1952** M. Laski *Village* xvi. 218 'But it's quite a good idea,' protested Martha. **1976** B. Freemantle *November Man* iii. 36 'And why the hell not?' he protested.

7. a. Also const. *at*.

1947 Partridge *Usage & Abusage* 46/1 The following from a newspaper placard, *The Daily Worker*, Feb. 6, 1938,—40,000 protest at food prices. **1969** *Daily Tel.* 22 Apr. 29 Conservatives protested angrily..at the Government's failure to announce new contribution rates.

b. *trans.* To protest against (an action or event); to make the subject of a protest. Chiefly *U.S.* Cf. 2c in Dict.

1904 *Brooklyn Eagle* 5 June **5/6 Many of the students are much incensed at the judges and will probably protest the decision. **1927** E. G. Mears *Resident Orientals on Pacific Coast* i. 6 The Peking Foreign Office has regularly protested acts of injustice and violence. **1930** C. Johnson *Negro in Amer. Civilisation* xx. 297 They are protesting the disposition of public school officials to ignore vocational training for Negro youth. **1944** *Sun* (Baltimore) 22 July 2/1 For Hitler it was sufficient that this former chief of staff resigned in 1938 to protest Hitler's march into Austria. **1951** *Newsweek* 27 Sept. 74/3 The residents of Follanshee..have protested the sale, claiming it would throw 2,441 persons out of work. **1956** [see *heel *sb.*¹ 11]. **1966** H. Kemelman *Saturday Rabbi went Hungry* ii. 15 For one thing, I protest their having been singled out. They were pushed and one of them fell. **1977** H. Fast *Immigrants* II. 82 Dan protested naming the child after Jean's mother. **1978** *Dædalus* Summer 188 They protest the brutal simplicities, the unilinearity and determinism of the great cruel myths of modernization.

Protestant, *sb.* and *a.* Add: **A.** *sb.* **I. 2. a.** (Further examples.)

1864 J. H. Newman *Apologia pro Vita Sua* vii. 425 If Protestants wish to know what our real teaching is,..let them look, not at our books of casuistry, but at our catechisms. **1900** C. M. Yonge *Mod. Broods* v. 50 You seem to me like the Roman Catholic child, who said there were five sacraments, there ought to be seven, but the Protestants had got two of them. **1938** O. C. Quick *Doctrines of Creed* II. xiii. 134 Neither Thomistic orthodoxy nor the modernism of the Liberal Protestants can take such an interpretation seriously. **1955** R. Macaulay *Let.* 5 Feb. in *Last Lett. to Friend* (1962) 190 It is this tendency to rule out Protestants (including Anglicans) from the Church of Christ that is so tiresome and silly. **1962** C. Quin tr. *E. Amand de Mendieta's Rome & Canterbury* viii. 183 After the Reformation movement had led to a vigorous reaction among Protestants against excessive devotion to the Virgin Mary, Roman Catholic theologians have always regarded the defence of the legitimacy of such devotion as one of their chief tasks. **1966** D. E. Jenkins *Guide to Debate about God* iii. 65 Protestants have tended not to be very concerned about the collapse of reason in relation to awareness of God. **1973** *Ann. Reg. 1972* 376 In Northern Ireland the most sinister development was sectarian assassination; 81 Catholics and 40 Protestants.

b. (Further examples.) Also, a Low Church member of the Church of England.

The name continues to be disfavoured by many Anglicans (see also sense c below).

1834 J. H. Newman *Let.* 30 July (1891) II. 59 The word Protestant does not, as far as I know, occur in our formularies. It is an uncomfortable, perplexing word, intended to connect us..with the Protestants abroad. We are a 'Reformed' Church, not a 'Protestant'. **1874** J. H. Blunt *Dict. Sects* 447/2 High Churchmen of modern times.. have..objected to the designation of Protestant as being (1) one of too negative a character to express at all justly the principle of Catholic resistance to the uncatholic pretensions and practices of Rome: and (2) as being a name which is used by so many sects as to be inclusive even of heresy. **1913** C. MACKENZIE *Sinister St.* I. II. vi. 239 'Finding out for yourself,' echoed Chator with a look of alarm. 'I say, you're an absolute Protestant.' 'Oh, no I'm not,' contradicted Michael. 'I'm a Catholic.' **1933** G. FABER *Oxf. Apostles* iii. 73 They [*sc.* the Tractarians] were hostile to Roman pretensions..but they claimed the same title of Catholic..and they loathed the title of Protestant only less than that of Dissenter. **1960** *Daily Tel.* 15 Nov. 12/8 Surely Canon Lionel Lydekker is mistaken when he writes that the original meaning of Protestant was 'protesting against any tampering with the Holy Catholic Faith'. *Ibid.*, Canon Lydekker's definition of 'Protestant' is in line with 18th-century usage when, in this country, it meant Anglican, as distinct from Nonconformist, just as on the Continent it still means Lutheran as distinct from Calvinist (or 'reformed').

c. A member of a nonconformist or non-episcopal Church.

1958 M. ARGYLE *Relig. Behaviour* xii. 157 By Protestants we mean to refer to the main 'nonconformist' denominations such as Methodists, Presbyterians and Baptists. **1963** AUDEN *Dyer's Hand* 350 In New England Protestants of Anglo-Scotch stock consider themselves a cut above Roman Catholics and those of a Latin race. **1977** R. L. WOLFF *Gains & Losses* 8 Dissenters or Nonconformists, Protestants of many varying sects, who dissent from the Church of England.

B. *adj.* **1. a.** (Further examples.) *spec.* designating (*a*) Christian belief and principles outside the Communion of Rome (now the most common sense); (*b*) a nonconformist or non-episcopal Church (cf. sense A. 2c above).

(*a*) **1861** C. M. YONGE *Young Stepmother* xxix. 448, I wonder if the omnibus is too protestant to leave a parcel at the convent. **1930** T. PARSONS tr. *Weber's Protestant Ethic* i. 35 Business leaders and owners of capital, as well as the higher grades of skilled labour, and even more the higher technically and commercially trained personnel of modern enterprises, are overwhelmingly Protestant. *Ibid.* iii. 80 The conception of the calling thus brings out that central dogma of all Protestant denominations which the Catholic division of ethical precepts into *præceptia* and *consilia* discards. **1935** E. GILL *Lett.* (1947) 342 Prudishness is more typically the vice of the protestant puritan. **1940** R. NIEBUHR *Christianity & Power Politics* i. 18 This is the issue upon which the Protestant Reformation separated itself from classical Catholicism. **1954** B. GRIFFITHS *Golden String* vii. 114 When his mother heard that it would be necessary for him to attend a Protestant service, she had replied that she would rather go to the workhouse with her eleven children than submit to that. **1958** B. PYM *Glass of Blessings* xiv. 164 It was absurd to have this suspicious Protestant attitude towards convents. **1960** *Daily Tel.* 10 Nov. 14/7 The Rev. John Castle asks: 'Where in her formularies is the Church of England described as "Protestant"?' The answer is (albeit singly and solely) in the Coronation Service. Whether or no the contention that the oath then taken by the Sovereign regarding the 'Protestant Religion' is merely one imposed by the State without the fiat of the Church, is beside the point. **1965** C. E. POCKNEE *Parson's Handbk.* (ed. 13) i. 7 These quotations from well-known Roman Catholic writers are sufficient to disprove the idea that there is something 'protestant' or anti-Roman in the custom of bowing as the normal act of reverence. **1976** *Listener* 29 Apr. 526/2 'The Good Lord' may have Protestant connotations, which would be inappropriate in translating ['le Bon Dieu' in] a Catholic poem. **1976** *Times* 28 Sept. 2/1 Mr. Mason, Secretary of State for Northern Ireland, yesterday made a determined attempt to win the hearts and minds of Ulster's disgruntled population, Roman Catholic and Protestant, by pledging himself to tackle their serious economic ills.

(*b*) **1864** J. H. NEWMAN *Apologia pro Vita Sua* v. 248 They [*sc.* Anglican Bishops] were..fraternizing..with Protestant bodies, and allowing them to put themselves under an Anglican Bishop, without any renunciation of their errors. **1942** J. BAILLIE *Invitation to Pilgrimage* x. 71 Some of the lesser Protestant sects, Quaker, Methodist, and others,..tended to be 'perfectionist'—sometimes even to a greater degree than Mediaeval Catholicism has ever been. **1954** R. MACAULAY *Let.* 19 Aug. in *Last Lett. to Friend* (1962) 166 Conversions.. from the unlovely Protestant churches. **1963** AUDEN *Dyer's Hand* 350 In New England..the most respectable Protestant denominations are the Congregationalists and the Unitarians. **1973** *Times* 16 Apr. 1/7 He will meet Roman Catholic, Anglican and Protestant church leaders, and Mr Whitelaw, Secretary of State for Northern Ireland. **1977** R. L. WOLFF *Gains & Losses* 13 Those who were more Protestant than the legally established Church of England had their own troubled history.

b. Protestant ascendancy, the Anglo-Irish ruling class in Ireland, which has been Protestant since the Reformation, as opp. the native Irish who remained Roman Catholic; also *transf.*; **Protestant Episcopal** (later examples); hence **Protestant Episcopalianism, Episcopalism; Protestant ethic**, the ethical outlook towards business enterprise which, according to Max Weber's analysis, first evolved in protestant Europe through the teachings of Calvin that to be successful through hard work was a person's duty and responsibility; also **Protestant work ethic.**

1827 Protestant ascendancy [see sense 1 a in Dict.]. **1875** F. ARNOLD *Our Bishops & Deans* I. iii. 148 What idea of Protestant truth was conveyed to the Roman Catholics by the favourite phrase 'Protestant ascendancy'? **1922** R. DUNLOP *Ireland from Earliest Times* v. 129 The Treaty of Limerick marks the beginning of a new period known as that of the Protestant Ascendancy. **1936** R. M. DOUGLAS *Irish Bk.* 138 He [*sc.* the Catholic Irishman] was 'loyal', and..became an informer, a policeman, or a soldier serving the Protestant ascendancy. **1966** C. M. BOWRA *Memories 1898–1939* xii. 272 His mother, an O'Reilly, was a true daughter of the Protestant Ascendancy. **1977** *Herald* (Melbourne) 17 Jan. 7/3 The neglect of the Castle Hill uprising reflects the prejudices of the Protestant ascendancy in Australia. **1857** *Church Rev.* Jan. 562 The Protestant Episcopal is representative—republican; but not democratic. **1920** *Catholic World* Sept. 777 The best they can offer now as a way out of the hated 'Protestant Episcopal' is 'Protestant Catholic' church! **1961** *N. & Q.* June 236/2 His thesis is that the name 'Protestant Episcopal', though historically justifiable, is a liability to the missionary efforts of American Anglicans and should be replaced by 'The American Episcopal Church'. **1977** *Time* 10 Oct. 37/1 Social relations executive of the Protestant Episcopal Diocese of Massachusetts. **1956** R. MACAULAY *Towers of Trebizond* i. 14 My aunt had inherited..strong prejudices against..all American religious bodies except Protestant Episcopalianism. **1836** *Southern Lit. Messenger* II. 282 In regard to Protestant Episcopalism in America, it may be safely said that, prior to this publication of Dr. Hawks, there were no written memorials extant. [**1904** M. WEBER in *Archiv. f. Sozialwissenschaft und Sozialpolitik* XX. 1 (*title*) Die protestantische Ethik und der 'Geist' des Kapitalismus.] **1926** R. H. TAWNEY *Relig. & Rise of Capitalism* 320 Both 'the capitalist spirit' and 'Protestant ethics'..were a good deal more complex than Weber seems to imply. **1930** T. PARSONS tr. *Weber's Protestant Ethic* iii. 89 We thus take as our starting-point in the investigation of the relationship between the old Protestant ethic and the spirit of capitalism the works of Calvin, of Calvinism, and the other Puritan sects. **1944** *Social Res.* Feb. 61 Weber's original intention in *The Protestant Ethic* must be seen against the background of his time. **1956** W. H. WHYTE *Organization Man* I. i. 6 The organization man.. needs..something that will do for him what the Protestant ethic did once. **1968** C. ARMSTRONG *Balloon Man* xii. 146 She was tough. In her own way, Protestant ethic or whatever, she was. **1977** *Listener* 7 Apr. 455/1 Infant prodigies..are the ultimate denial of the Protestant Ethic —hard work can produce lesser rewards than sheer talent. **1980** *Country Life* 24 Apr. 1283/3 Mrs Smith had the Protestant work-ethic in the very marrow of her bones.

Protestantism. Add: **1.** (Further examples.)

1862 J. H. NEWMAN *Lett.* 28 June (1970) XX. 216, I do hereby profess *ex animo*..that Protestantism is the dreariest of possible religions; that the thought of the Anglican service makes me shiver. **1864** —— *Apologia pro Vita Sua* v. 181, I held a large bold system of religion, very unlike the Protestantism of the day, but it was the concentration and adjustment of the statements of great Anglican authorities. **1930** T. PARSONS tr. *Weber's Protestant Ethic* 27 We are dealing with the connection of the spirit of modern economic life with the rational ethics of ascetic Protestantism. **1938** O. C. QUICK *Doctrines of Creed* ii. 12 While the error of scholasticism was to tie down Christianity to a particular philosophy, the error of much modern Protestantism has been to disparage philosophy altogether. **1952** P. TILLICH *Courage to Be* v. 114 Protestantism..was established as a strictly authoritarian and conformist system, similar to that of its adversary, the Roman Church of the Counter-reformation. **1964** A. WATTS *Beyond Theol.* vi. 155, I am not speaking of modern 'liberal Protestantism', but of that 'old-time Bible religion'. **1974** *Encycl. Brit. Macropædia* XV. 136/2 Providence..may also be experienced as personal guidance. This latter phenomenon is common..in some forms of Protestantism in which generally each person is expected to have a private experience of divine guidance. **1976** B. GRIFFITHS *Return to Centre* xv. 106 Protestantism opened the Bible to the private interpretation of every man. **1976** *Times* 13 Aug. 13/6 What gives them their weight and validity is their promulgation by the *magisterium* and surely it is this authority that the traditionalists are ready to defy. Is not this nearer to the heart of Protestantism? **1977** B. COLLOMS *Victorian Country Parsons* xii. 228 William Kingsley was a broadminded parson whose sermons and services were suitable for most brands of Protestantism.

2. (Later example.)

1948 F. W. DILLISTONE in M. Warren *Triumph of God* iii. 80 The energy of young Protestantism was bound to be poured out in the effort to consolidate its own position within the hostile environment by which it was surrounded.

Protestantization (prǫ:tèstăntəizē^1·ʃən). [f. PROTESTANTIZE *v.* + -ATION.] The action or fact of rendering Protestant; conversion to Protestantism.

1880 W. JAMES in *Atlantic Monthly* Oct. 447/2 After Charles IX. and Louis XIV., no general protestantization of France. **1977** S. SCHOENBAUM *Shakespeare* v. 54 Further forays into Protestantization followed.

protester. Add: **2. c.** An opponent of the established order, esp. one who actively remonstrates over an issue of public importance; a demonstrator.

1960 *Times Lit. Suppl.* 1 Jan. 3/2 Those cold-water apartments where hipsters and protesters..try to go their own way. **1968** *Listener* 4 July 22/3 Absolutely and actively in sympathy with the protesters over most issues, he can ..trace out the roots of their discontents. **1971** 'E. LATHEN' *Longer the Thread* vii. 65 Thatcher..would not believe..that homicide investigations came to a halt whenever youthful protesters threatened to act up. **1976** 'R. B. DOMINIC' *Murder out of Commission* v. 41 Protesters picked up some pretty strange habits during the Vietnam War.

proteus. Add: **3. b.** [Adopted as the name of a genus by J. N. Laurenti in his *Synopsis Reptilium* (1768) 35.] = *OLM. (Earlier and later examples.)

a **1829** H. DAVY *Consolations in Travel* (1830) iv. 190 The same infinite power..has given the Proteus to the deep and dark subterraneous lakes of Illyria,—an animal to whom the presence of light is not essential. **1902** BASKETT & DITMARS *Story of Amphibians & Reptiles* vii. 48 *Proteus*..lives in a cave in Austria. **1965** B. E. FREEMAN tr. *Vandel's Biospeleol.* iii. 23 *Proteus* represents a veritable giant amongst the European cave fauna, because it reaches a length of 30 cm.

prothallial, *a.* Add: (Later examples.) *spec.* applied to a small cell formed at an early stage in the development of the male gametophyte of certain gymnosperms, or a similar structure in certain pteridophytes.

1892 *Ann. Bot.* VI. 214 Judging from the obvious continuity of the dividing wall with the lateral walls of the prothallial chambers..there can hardly exist a doubt that the two cavities result from a primary transverse division of the cell. **1910** COULTER & CHAMBERLAIN *Morphol. Gymnosperms* vi. 277 The appearance of two evanescent vegetative (prothallial) cells is a feature only of the Abietineae. **1929** ROBBINS & RICKETT *Botany* xxii. 326 Two are very small cells (prothallial cells) which die and disintegrate almost as soon as formed. **1965** BELL & COOMBE tr. *Strasburger's Textbk. Bot.* 593 In the originally unicellular microspore (pollen grain) [of *Pinus*] one or two (or sometimes more) small cells are formed at a particular spot just inside the wall; these prothallial cells often degenerate after a time. **1969** F. E. ROUND *Introd. Lower Plants* xi. 132 The microspore divides within the spore wall to form a single 'prothallial' cell and an antheridial initial cell. **1973** A. CRONQUIST *Basic Bot.* xvi. 262 The prothallial cell [of *Selaginella*] is considered to be an evolutionary vestige of the body of the gametophyte.

prothallium. Add: (Later examples.) Also, a homologous structure in the development of certain gymnosperms.

1892 J. B. FARMER in *Ann. Bot.* VI. 213 (*title*) On the occurrence of two prothallia in the embryo sac of *Pinus*. **1935** C. J. CHAMBERLAIN *Gymnosperms* xiii. 309 In some heterosporous pteridophyte ancestor [of the conifers], the prothallium (gametophyte) became included within the spore..and finally disappeared entirely.

prothallus. Add examples referring to gymnosperms.

1940 *Chambers's Techn. Dict.* 680/1 The term prothallus is extended to cover homologous stages in the life-cycle of Gymnosperms. **1965** K. R. SPORNE *Morphol. Gymnosperms* i. 19 Cell-walls are being laid down between the nuclei of the female prothallus, a process which, in most gymnosperms, continues until the whole of the prothallus becomes circular.

protheca: see *PRO-^{2} 1.

prothesis. 3. (Later examples.)

1968 P. M. POSTAL *Aspects Phonol. Theory* vii. 144 The Prothesis rule is that which inserts an [i] in the front of verbs containing less than one vowel. **1976** *Language* LII. 307 Evidence for prothesis in Spain dates from the Vulgar Latin of the 2nd century.

prothetely (proþe·təli). *Ent.* [ad. G. *prothetelie* (H. J. Kolbe 1903), in *Allgemeine Zeitschr. f. Entom.* VIII. 1), f. Gr. προθεῖν to run before + τέλος end: see -Y^3.] In certain insect larvæ, the development of one part of the body, esp. the wings, at a faster rate than that of the rest. Hence **prothete·lic** *a.*, of or pertaining to this type of development.

1934 FOLSOM & WARDLE *Entomol.* (ed. 4) iii. 169 As a rare abnormality a holometabolous larva may possess two pairs of true external wing-pads... The phenomenon is termed prothetely. **1940** R. GOLDSCHMIDT *Material Basis of Evolution* iv. 283 The actual working of this timing mechanism can be inferred from cases of so-called prothetely, where a single larval organ, e.g. wings or antennae, metamorphoses alone. *Ibid.* 284 (*caption*) Head of prothetelic caterpillar of *Lymantria dispar* with pupal antennae. **1960** H. OLDROYD tr. *Jeannel's Introd. Entomol.* iv. 83 (*caption*) Prothetelic larva of *Tenebrio molitor*.. showing rudiments of wings. *Ibid.*, Prothetely. Quite often when bred artificially, but more rarely in nature, insect larvae may have rudiments of wings, which have matured at a greater rate than the rest of the body. **1978** *Nature* 23 Mar. 350/2 They..obtained morphogenetic effects (precocious-prothetelic adults after administration to young instars) only in Heteroptera.

prothrombin (proþrǫ·mbin). *Phys.* [a. G. *prothrombin* (A. Schmidt *Zur Blutlehre* (1892) xii. 202), f. Gr. πρό PRO-^{2} + θρόμβ-ος clot, THROMBUS: see -IN^1.] A protein formed in the liver and normally present in blood, whose conversion into thrombin is an essential part of the clotting process.

1898 E. A. SCHÄFER *Text-bk. Physiol.* I. 160 A fibrin ferment (thrombin), or its precursor (prothrombin), producing the formation of fibrin from fibrinogen. *Ibid.*, The fibrin ferment is sometimes spoken of as 'thrombin', and the nucleo-proteid material in the plasma from which it is produced is then termed 'prothrombin'. **1912** J. G. MCKENDRICK *Princ. Physiol.* viii. 117 The theory at present in vogue is that when blood is shed there is at once the death of many colourless cells. These contain a protein called pro-thrombin, which, in turn, produces an enzyme known as thrombin. **1936** [see *hypoprothrombinæmia* s.v. *HYPO- II]. **1946** [see *oxalated* ppl. a. s.v. *OXALATE *v.*]. **1957** *Sci. News* XLIV. 31 In the presence of ionized calcium, of a further globulin component of the plasma, and probably of other factors, thromboplastin converts prothrombin, by what must be a relatively minor change in its molecule, to thrombin. This last substance now reacts directly with fibrinogen, changing it to fibrin. **1974** R. M. KIRK et al. *Surgery* ii. 10 Vitamin K analogue, 10 mg intramuscularly each day, replaces the deficiency but if there is concomitant liver damage, prothrombin is not synthesised. **1976** [see *proconvertin* s.v. *PRO-[2] 1].

b. *attrib.*, as **prothrombin time**, the time taken for blood or plasma to clot when an excess of a calcium salt and possibly other natural components of the clotting mechanism (besides prothrombin) are added.

1935 *Amer. Jrnl. Med. Sci.* CXC. 505 By omitting the addition of excess thromboplastin, but otherwise following the directions of the method outlined for the determination of prothrombin, one determines the clotting time of recalcified plasma, which for normal plasma is from 90 to 130 seconds. This method is still commonly called Howell's Prothrombin Time. **1957** A. J. QUICK *Hemorrhagic Dis.* ii. 44 The prothrombin time of normal human plasma is consistently 12 seconds, whereas when measured by the two-stage test, it varies from 244 to 452 units. **1972** *Daily Colonist* (Victoria, B.C.) 1 Feb. 2/1, I am on anticoagulants and have a prothrombin time test taken weekly to determine dosage.

protic (prōᵘ·tik), *a. Chem.* [f. PROT(ON in Dict. and Suppl. + -IC.] Of a liquid, esp. a solvent: possessing protons whose binding is sufficiently loose for them to participate in protonation; hydrogen-bonded.

1944 *Jrnl. Physical Chem.* XLVIII. 53 In all protic solvents, protons enter strongly into any consideration of acid-base properties. **1965** PHILLIPS & WILLIAMS *Inorg. Chem.* I. xv. 556 Similarly, in other 'protic' solvents a special role is played by substances producing H^+ ions, or the characteristic anion of the solvent (e.g. NH_2^- in NH_3, F^- in HF, and HSO_4^- in H_2SO_4). **1973** E. J. KING in Covington & Dickinson *Phys. Chem. Org. Solvent Syst.* iii. 333 We first distinguish two broad classes [of solvent] based on dielectric constant. In solvents of high dielectric constant, often referred to loosely as polar solvents, ion-pairing is minimal, even negligible in dilute solutions... By contrast, in solvents of low dielectric constant, loosely called non-polar solvents, ion-pairing is important and acid strength depends on the choice of standard base... Each broad class in turn is sub-divided into hydrogen-bonded and non-hydrogen-bonded solvents. The term *protic* is frequently used for the first sub-division, *aprotic* for the second. **1975** *Nature* 3 Jan. 40/1 These reactions show that molecular nitrogen can be reduced at a single metal site in a protic medium with negligible discharge of dihydrogen or displacement of dinitrogen by hydride ligands.

protide (prōᵘ·təid). *Biochem.* Also **-id** (-id). [a. F. *protide* (G. Bertrand 1923, in *Bull. de la Soc. de Chim. biol.* V. 102), f. *protéine* PROTEIN: see -IDE.] A generic term for a protein, peptide, or amino-acid. Hence **proti·dic** *a.*

The scheme of nomenclature proposed by Bertrand met with little favour among English-speaking scientists (see *Chem. & Engin. News* (1952) 5 May 1910). *Protide* is now to be found almost exclusively in translations or abstracts from French.

1936 A. P. MATHEWS *Princ. Biochem.* xxii. 215 The International Union of Pure and Applied Chemistry suggested that the proteins be called 'protides' in consonance with the 'glucides' and 'lipides'. **1958** (*title*) Protides of the biological fluids. *Ibid.* p. v, Some biochemical constituents of protidic nature or origin in the living animal are considered in a further nine original papers. **1962** *Biol. Abstr.* XXXIX. 948/1 (*heading*) Study of the protidic fraction of Digitaria exilis. **1973** *Compar. Biochem. & Physiol.* B. XLV. 225 (*heading*) Protides of the Mustelidae: comparative study of plasma lactate dehydrogenases. **1975** *Biol. Abstr.* LX. 4700/2 Some data..suggest that the initiation of growth is strictly dependent in [*sic*] nutritional factors (mainly protids). **1977** *Lancet* 10 Dec. 1242/2 The 26th colloquium on protides of the biological fluids will be held in Bruges on May 1–5.

protist. Add etym.: [f. mod.L. *Protista*, f. G. *protisten* (E. Haeckel *Generelle Morphologie der Organismen* (1866) I. 203): see PROTISTA *sb. pl.*] (Later examples.)

1905 J. MCCABE tr. *Haeckel's Evol. Man* I. vi. 98 In the case of the protists, the entire organism usually consists of a single autonomous cell throughout life. **1926** C. M. WENYON *Protozool.* I. I. 4 A typical Protist consists of a small portion of cytoplasm and a nucleus. **1965** B. E. FREEMAN tr. *Vandel's Biospeleol.* vi. 62 Not a single free-living aquatic protist can be considered as a true cavernicole. **1975** *Nature* 7 Aug. 467/2 These [phytoflagellates] were the ancestors of all plants, and..of non-photosynthetic protists and animals.

protistan, *sb.* (Example.)

1940 [see *METACHRONAL *a.*].

protistology (prōtistǫ·lǒdʒi). [f. PROTIST, PROTISTA *sb. pl.* + -OLOGY.] The study of organisms included in the Protista. Hence **protisto·logist**, one who studies protists.

1911 J. A. THOMSON *Introd. Sci.* iv. 110 It might also be convenient to have a special science of Protistology for the minute and simple organisms which seem to hesitate between plant and animal life. **1911** *Q. Jrnl. Microsc. Sci.* LVI. 396 Cytologists and protistologists alike have been content..with assuming that the Bacteria are a group of simple organisms. **1926** C. M. WENYON *Protozool.* I. I. 4 It is safer to regard them all as one large group, the Protista, the study of which is known as Protistology. **1951** *John o' London's Weekly* 17 Aug. 501/2 A scholar..may spend his days at the microscope and read only treatises on protistology. **1965** B. E. FREEMAN tr. *Vandel's Biospeleol.* vi. 61 The disappearance of pigments in *Euglena* placed in darkness is a common occurrence, well known to protistologists. **1973** *Microscopy* XXXII. 325 He [*sc.* Georges Deflandre]..was soon deep in studies of protistology (the biology of unicellular organisms).

protium (prōᵘ·tiǒm). *Chem.* [mod.L., f. Gr. πρῶτ-ος first + -IUM.] The 'normal', most abundant isotope of hydrogen, having only a proton in the nucleus and forming at least 99·98 per cent (by volume) of naturally occurring hydrogen; symbol ^{1}H (also H^1). Cf. *DEUTERIUM, *TRITIUM.

1933 [see *DEUTERIUM]. **1936** *Nature* 12 Dec. 1021/1 Several attempts have been made to determine the ratio protium–deuterium (^{1}H:^{2}H) in ordinary water, and the results mostly fall into two groups, either near 5500 or near 9000. **1957** G. E. HUTCHINSON *Treat. Limnol.* I. iii. 211 Hydrogen has two stable isotopes, H^1, sometimes called protium, and H^2 or D, usually called deuterium. **1972** *Nature* 31 Mar. 202/1 Of late, both Cornforth and Arigoni have developed techniques for the solution of this problem based in the chemical synthesis of CH_3^- groups containing one atom each of the three hydrogen isotopes, protium, deuterium and tritium. **1975** *Physics Bull.* May 211/1 In the case of the neutron diffraction experiments D_2O was used instead of H_2O as deuterium is a better coherent scatterer than protium.

proto-. Add: **1.** (*a*) *proto-chemistry* (later example), *-culture*, *-history*, *-music*, *-novelist*, *-phoneme*, *-poet*, *-scientist*; **protocu·ltural** *a.*, belonging to such origins as can be surmised of human cultural development; † **pro·togram** *Obs.*, an acronym; **protograph** (further example); † **protogra·phic** *a. Obs.*, acronymic; **proto-histo·rian**, (*a*) (see sense 1 (*a*) in Dict.); (*b*) one who studies proto-history; **proto-histo·rical** *a.* = *proto-historic* adj.; **pro·to-literate** *a.*, characterized by the most primitive kind of writing; **proto-scienti·fic** *a.*, belonging or relating to primitive science, or to an early stage in scientific development; **pro·tosyntax** (see quot. 1940); hence **protosynta·ctical** *a.*; **protosynta·ctically** *adv.*; **pro·totheme** (see quot. 1897); **proto-typographer** (further examples).

1976 *Times Lit. Suppl.* 12 Nov. 1418/2 The development of alchemy and proto-chemistry [in China]. **1961** A. I. HALLOWELL in S. L. Washburn *Social Life Early Man* 237, I suggested that the level of development represented by cultural adaptation can be focused more sharply in evolutionary perspective if we hypothecate a protocultural phase in hominid evolution. **1976** *Sci. Amer.* Oct. 104/2 The difference is not necessarily related to the confinement of our troop but may simply reflect protocultural differences. **1971** R. M. & F. M. KEESING *New Perspectives Cultural Anthropol.* 48 There must have been 'protomen' with 'protoculture'. **1924** *Glasgow Herald* 27 Sept. 4 'Anzac' is one of the first programs to which the war gave birth. It is used..to describe anything pertaining to the 'Australian and New Zealand Army Corps'. **1933** H. WENTWORTH *Blend-Words in Eng.* 3 Words formed from the initials of other words—called *letter words* ..and *protograms* (F. H. Vizetelly)—are fewer. **1974** *Bible Translator* July 317 According to Russian biblical scholarship these basic sections are..(1) the protographs of the Septuagint and the New Testament [etc.]. **1924** *Glasgow Herald* 27 Sept. 4 The great majority of words of the protographic type have been coined within the last decade. **1949** *Proc. Prehist. Soc.* XV. 196 That difficult problem so often shirked by prehistorian and proto-historian—the mechanics of cultural diffusion. **1928** V. G. CHILDE *Most Anc. East* viii. 176 The implements of the protohistorical period were almost entirely of metal. **1950** A. HUXLEY *Themes & Variations* 54 That Golden Age of Peace, which not long since was regarded as a mere myth, but is now revealed by the light of archaeology as a proto- and pre-historical reality. **1920** R. R. MARETT *Psychol. & Folk-lore* xi. 249 The value of proto-history, as it is sometimes termed. **1947** H. C. E. ZACHARIAS (*title*) Protohistory. An explicative account of the development of human thought from Palaeolithic times to the Persian monarchy. **1980** *Encounter* May 66/1 We—the workers in British protohistory during the last 30 years—have suffered corporately from inadequate preliminary education, leading to the mental counterparts of asthma, myopia and strabismus. **1942** DELOUGAZ & LLOYD *Pre-Sargonid Temples* i. 123 The architectural history of the Sin Temple bears out..the subdivision of the Early Dynastic period into three and the Proto-literate into at least two distinct phases. **1971** Proto-literate [see *pictographic* adj. s.v. *PICTOGRAPH]. **1963** AUDEN *Dyer's Hand* 474 A music which sounds remarkably like primitive proto-music. **1977** *Rolling Stone* 21 Apr. 41/3 Ultimately, *14 Canons* is a unique type of protomusic—a series of potentially extendible alchemical exercises. **1976** *Times Lit. Suppl.* 19 Nov. 1459/4 Bunyan's humanity and his raciness and his humour and everything that makes him a proto-novelist. **1960** H. M. HOENIGSWALD *Lang. Change & Ling. Reconstruction* xii. 132 If a split affects the same proto-phoneme in each daughter language, the partial likeness between the sets of correspondences is impaired. **1974** R. W. WESCOTT in *Language Origins* 116 Only eight proto-phonemes (which are more nearly equivalent to contemporary morphophonemes than to contemporary Phonemes) appear in all five of their formulations. The eight are p, t, k; m, n; y, w; e. **1963** AUDEN *Dyer's Hand* 34 Whatsoever Adam called every living creature, that was..its Proper Name. Here Adam plays the role of the Proto-poet. **1934** WEBSTER, *Protoscientific*, adj. **1968** M. BUNGE in R. Klibansky *Contemp. Philos.* II. 4 In the underdeveloped (protoscientific) disciplines, fact-collecting passes for the sole respectable occupation. **1978** *Sci. Amer.* Jan. 69/1 Overshadowed by scholasticism, the work of the protoscientists was ignored or treated as heresy, and its proponents endured ridicule and some persecution. **1940** W. V. QUINE *Math. Logic* vii. 292 The part of syntax which omits membership will be called protosyntax... Protosyntactical definability is intended not as an approximation to constructivity, but as something more inclusive. The notion of a non-theorem, e.g., is protosyntactically definable, yet presumably not constructive. **1943** *Mind* LII. 272 A restricted portion of the syntax (that which omits membership) is distinguished by the label 'protosyntax'. **1964** *Amer. Philos. Q.* I. 265/1 The entire construction is done..within Quine's protosyntax. **1897** Prototheme [see *deuterotheme* s.v. *DEUTERO-]. **1905** *N. & Q.* III. 176/1 These protothemes in familiar intercourse, or even on more serious occasions, often received the termination *-a*, *Seax*, for instance, becoming *Seaxa*. **1931** *Library* XII. 109 This volume is printed with the type of Johannes de Salsburga and Paulus de Constantia, the prototypographers of Barcelona. **1976** *Times Lit. Suppl.* 22 Oct. 1328/2 Thanks to Caxton, England had a native prototypographer who worked with patriotic gusto in the national language.

2. a. (Further examples.) Also in *Philol.*, forming sbs. and adjs. designating the earliest attested or hypothetically-reconstructed form of a language or family of languages (cf. *PRIMITIVE *a.* 4b). (The list that follows represents only a selection of possible items.) *proto-Algonquian*, *-Aryan*, *-Athapaskan*, *-Australian*, *-Australoid*, *-Austronesian*, *-Corinthian* (further examples), *-Gallo-Romance* (also *-Romanic*), *-Germanic*, *-Greek* (further examples), *-Hattic*, *-Indo-European*, *-Italic*, *-Malay*, *-Medic*, *-Polynesian*, *-Romance*, *-Semitic* (examples), *-Slavonic*. Also with geographical names and sbs., as *proto-Atlantic*, *-Nile*, *-ocean*, *-Thames*; and with astronomical names, as *proto-earth*, *-Jupiter*, *-sun* (hence *protosolar* adj.). Also *protocloud*, *-cluster* in *2b, *PROTO-CONTINENT, *PROTOGALAXY, *PROTOPLANET, *PROTOSTAR. **proto-Hi·ttite**, the language of the Hattian people, philologically unrelated to Hittite.

1939 L. BLOOMFIELD in C. Hockett *Bloomfield Anthol.* (1970) 352 Our basic forms are not ancient forms, say of the Proto-Algonquian parent language. **1974** *Canad. Jrnl. Linguistics* XIX. 145 As was mentioned above, Proto-Algonquian palatalization came down into Fox pretty much unscathed. **1904** G. S. HALL *Adolescence* II. xviii. 657 The Todas of India, whom some call proto-Aryans. **1938** PARTRIDGE *World of Words* iv. 126 The Latin may be traced to an Aryan original; but the proto-Aryan form.. was caused by some accidental circumstance. **1964** M. E. KRAUSS in *Internat. Jrnl. Amer. Linguistics* XXX. 118 (*title*) Proto-Athapaskan-Eyak and the problem of Na-Dene: the phonology. **1966** J. T. WILSON in *Nature* 13 Aug. 676/1 It is proposed that, in Lower Palaeozoic time, a proto-Atlantic Ocean existed so as to form the boundary between the two realms, and that during Middle and Upper Palaeozoic time the ocean closed by stages. **1972** *Sci. Amer.* Nov. 62/3 In Devonian times an order of jawless freshwater fishes, cousins to the orders that once flourished on opposite sides of the proto-Atlantic, inhabited the streams of the region that is now the European and Asiatic flanks of the Urals. **1918** *Phil. Trans. R. Soc.* B. CVIII. 382 This fossil human skull of a not yet adult Proto-Australian presents..the general picture of a cranium similar in all respects to the cranium of the Australian of to-day. *Ibid.*, The Proto-Australian is, in some very important features, to be sharply differentiated from Neanderthal man. This is nowhere more clearly seen than in the palate and teeth. **1923** R. B. DIXON *Racial Hist. Man* IV. ii. 374 The Australian population thus appears to be made up almost entirely of two types, the Proto-Negroid and Proto-Australoid, of which the former is concentrated in the north and northwest, the latter in the south and southeast. **1959** Proto-Australoid [see *GERONTOMORPHIC *a.*]. **1963** G. B. MILNER in C. Mohrmann et al. *Trends in Mod. Linguistics* 68 Dempwolff had found a sufficient body of evidence to justify his setting up a Proto-Melanesian language..as he had reconstructed a Proto-Polynesian language, both of which he regarded as ultimately descended from Proto-Austronesian. **1976** *Language* LII. 221 The systematic reconstruction of Proto-Austronesian..phonology and lexicon was first attempted by Otto Dempwolff. **1932** *Times Lit. Suppl.* 8 Sept. 622/4 Corinth, where the Protocorinthian style forms a natural transition between the Geometric and the Orientalizing. **1973** *Univ. Oxf. Ann. Rep.* 1970–71 8 Publications: 'A Protocorinthian Dinos and Stand'. **1969** *Times* 18 July 6/4 The proto-earth may have swept up from the dust cloud much more silicate material than it now possesses. **1977** A. HALLAM *Planet Earth* 18/2 Most probably, the Moon formed from a dense atmosphere, generated by the high temperatures of solid-particle accretion at the surface of the proto-Earth. **1950** *Language* XXVI. 9 A concrete example of how this type of intermediate reconstruction can be done and what it gives us can be seen in the phonological system of Proto-Gallo-Romance. **1964** *Ibid.* XL. 32 If Provençal should turn out to belong to it, 'Proto-Gallo-Romance' is the obvious choice. **1946** *Stud. in Philol.* XLIII. 463 Then with a similarly acquired statement of Proto-Provençal, we can formulate Proto-Gallo-Romanic. **1934** PRIEBSCH & COLLINSON *German Lang.* iv. 236 The Proto-Italic and Proto-Germanic peoples. **1960** *Amer. Speech* XXXV. 227 From pre-Scandinavian or Proto-Germanic to Old and Modern Icelandic. **1964** *Language* XL. 294 Next he reviews the history of the problem of the Proto-Germanic long stops. **1972** *Ibid.* XLVIII. 407 Proto-Germanic, which should be based on the internal reconstructions of the individual dialects. **1959** T. BURTON-BROWN *Early Medit. Migrations* iii. 66 There were established, from at least as early as the end of the Third Millennium, some kind of 'proto-Greek' people. **1964** E. PALMER tr. *Martinet's Elem. Gen. Linguistics* v. 149 Tsakonian is a proto-Greek dialect. **1968** W. S. ALLEN *Vox Graeca* i. 30 It may be mentioned that in Proto-Greek, and still preserved in Mycenaean, there was a series of 'labio-velars'. **1933** E. H. STURTEVANT *Compar. Gram. Hittite Lang.* i. 29 There seems to be no need for the cumbrous terms 'Proto-Hattic' or 'Proto-Hittite'. **1948** D. DIRINGER *Alphabet* v. 89 Some scholars call them 'Proto-Hattic' or 'Proto-Hittite'. **1924** A. H. SAYCE in *Jrnl. R. Asiatic Soc.* 245 Proto-Hittite is the name given by Dr. Forrer to the prefixal language, examples of which are found in the cuneiform texts of Boghaz Keui. **1952** O. R. GURNEY *Hittites* vi. 122 The name Proto-Hittite has been widely adopted in order to avoid confusion with the official Hittite, but is somewhat misleading, since it suggests an earlier stage of Hittite, whereas it is a language totally unrelated to the latter. The name Hattian is preferable. **1947** R. S. WELLS in *Word* III. 15 Linguists have reconstructed large parts of the vocabulary of Proto-Indo-European. **1955** W. P. LEHMANN in *Language* XXXI. 355 (*title*) Proto-Indo-European Resonants in Germanic. **1960** *Amer. Speech* XXXV. 227 Specific laryngeal problems in Proto-Indo-European phonology. **1979** *Amer. Speech 1978* LIII. 266 We have virtually no evidence for the earlier history of Proto-Indo-European forms. **1968** *Language* XLIV. 269 On the evidence of Latin, Oscan, and Umbrian, Proto Italic still had the phrasally prior final consonants that have disappeared in Proto-Romance. **1976** *Archivum Linguisticum* VII. 62 Oscan *-tt-* represents a proto-Italic cluster *-ky-. **1976** *Sci. Amer.* May 113/1 James B. Pollack and his co-workers..suggest that exactly the same process would have taken place within the miniature solar system of the Jovian satellites, with the proto-Jupiter the source of the heat. **1909** A. C. HADDON *Races of Man* 18 *Indo-Chinese, Parcæans* or *Southern Mongols*:..Those members who spread into the East Indian Archipelago are often called Oceanic Mongols, but a better term is Proto-Malays; and it is from these the true Malay is derived. *Ibid.* 14 The broadening of the head is probably due to an early mixture with a Proto-Malay stock. **1947, 1958** Proto-Malay [see *JAKUN]. **1964** W. A. HAMID in W. Gungwu *Malaysia* III. xii. 179 The Proto-Malays are the tribes to be found in the interior forests among the foothills of the Malay archipelago. **1877** A. H. SAYCE in *Trans. Philol. Soc. 1875–6* 136 In Protomedic and Susianian..the initial is similarly always dropped in the plural of the verb. **1880** —— *Introd. Sci. Lang.* II. x. 321 The Protomedic group of languages to which Accadian belongs, in the Ural-Altaic family. **1894** Protomedic [see *MEDIC *sb.*[2]]. **1972** *Sci. Amer.* Apr. 116/1 Primate forms found in fossil forest beds deposited 35 million years ago beside the proto-Nile. **1975** *Nature* 29 May 376/1 Young rift oceans (proto-oceans) are commonly the site of large scale evaporite deposition. **1930** R. PAGET *Human Speech* vii. 145 Several other gesture-words from Proto-Polynesian. **1973** *Amer. Speech 1970* XLV. 118 The reconstruction of some proto-Polynesian forms. **1949** *Archivum Linguisticum* I. 151 The Proto-Romance consonant clusters... We use this term, instead of the vague..'Vulgar Latin'. **1978** *Language* LIV. 182 There is no discussion of proto-morphophonemics, which might conceivably have raised the issue of umlaut in Proto-Romance. **1948** D. DIRINGER *Alphabet* 214 The proto-Semitic alphabet. **1969** *Word* XXV. 115 The Proto-Semitic consonant system is generally assumed to have had a voiced velar stop phoneme */g/ as established by a set of correspondences throughout the Semitic family. **1920** *Trans. Philol. Soc. 1916–20* 128 In Proto-Slavonic all final consonants fell out. *Ibid.* 130 Beside the palatalization there is another sweeping tendency in Proto-Slavonic phonology. **1951** *Archivum Linguisticum* III. 205 The work is a succinct presentation of Protoslavonic morphology. **1975** *Nature* 11 Sept. 91/1 S. Ramadurai.. argued that carbonaceous chondrites contain interstellar graphite grains from the protosolar nebula. **1978** *Ibid.* 16 Mar. 239/2 Further conditions which must be satisfied are ..penetration of this element into the protosolar cloud. **1974** *Sci. Amer.* Mar. 51/3 At a distance of perhaps 20 million miles from the protosun, a fifth of the way to the present orbit of the earth, a very few nonvolatile materials could have condensed into solid particles. **1969** BENNISON & WRIGHT *Geol. Hist. Brit. Isles* xv. 346 The consequent drainage pattern developed on the eastwards-tilted Mesozoic rocks included the proto-Thames.

b. proto-bi·face *Archæol.*, an early form of biface; **pro·tocell**, a body postulated as ancestral to the cell; **protocerebrum**, (*b*) the anterior segment of the brain of an arthropod; **pro·tocloud** *Astr.*, a protogalactic cloud; **pro·tocluster** *Astr.* = prec.; **protocneme** (prō^u·toknīm) *Zool.* [Gr. κνήμα tibia; cf. CNEMIAL *a.*], one of six pairs of primary mesenteries which are found in corals of the order Scleractinia; **protodo·lomite** *Min.*, a mineral with a composition near that of dolomite, $CaMg(CO_3)_2$, but an imperfect crystal structure; **protodynastic** *a.* (further examples); **protoe·nstatite** *Min.*, an artificial, high-temperature form of the magnesium silicate $MgSiO_3$; **protofi·bril** *Biol.*, a filament of protein that is a component structural element of a fibril or *spec.* of a microfibril; **protofi·lament** *Biol.*, a filament of protein, about 5 nanometres in diameter, a group of which constitute a microtubule; **protohu·man** *sb.* and *a. Anthrop.*, (pertaining to or being) one of the man-like prehistoric creatures from which man is held to have evolved; **pro·tolife**, inanimate existence representing a late stage in the evolution of life; **pro·tolith** *Petrol.* [Gr. λίθ-ος stone] (see quot. 1972); **protoli·thionite** *Min.* [ad. G. *protolithionit* (F. Sandberger *Untersuchungen über Erzgänge* (1885) ii. 169): cf. LITHIONITE], a variety of zinnwaldite containing a higher proportion of lithium and a lower proportion of iron; **protomerite** (earlier and later examples); **proto-Neoli·thic** *a. Archæol.*, belonging to or characteristic of the earliest Neolithic period; also *absol.* as *sb.*; **protonephri·dium** *Zool.* [mod.L., coined in Ger. by B. Hatschek *Lehrb. der Zool.* (1889) II. 160: see NEPHRIDIUM], in certain invertebrates, esp. flatworms, an excretory system made up of solenocytes opening into ducts leading to pores in the exterior surface; also, a larval nephridium of this type; so **protonephri·dial** *a.*; **pro:toperithe·cium**, in some fungi, an ascogonium from which have grown out one or more trichogynes, some of which develop into part of a perithecium if spermatization occurs; hence **pro:toperithe·cial** *a.*; **protopetro·leum** [mod.L., coined in Ger. by C. Engler 1897, in *Ber. d. Deut. Chem. Ges.* XXX. 2360], an intermediate product in the formation of petroleum from organic debris; **pro·topheno-menon** *Philos.*, a primary phenomenon; **protophloem**, add: [a. G. *protophloëm* (E. Russow 1873, in *Mém. Acad. Impér. Sci. St.-Pétersbourg* 7 sér. XIX. 4]; (further examples); **pro·topod** *a. Ent.* [ad. It. *protopodo* (A. Berlese 1913, in *Redia* IX. 127)], of an insect larva, lacking abdominal segmentation and limbs; **protopro·teose** *Biochem.*, any of a class of proteoses that are soluble in water and dilute salt solutions and are formed during gastric secretion; **protosco·lex** *Zool.*, a vesicle formed from the germinal layer of a hydatid cyst and capable of development into a scolex or a secondary cyst; **pro·tostele** *Bot.* [STELE 2], a simple type of stele in which a central core of xylem is surrounded by a cylinder of phloem: hence **protostelic** (-stī·lik) *a.*; **pro·totheca** *Zool.* [THECA], a cup-shaped basal plate which is formed at the start of the development of a colony of stony corals; **pro·totroch** *Zool.* [Gr. τροχός wheel], a pre-oral ciliated ridge encircling the body of the trochosphere larva of certain invertebrates, including polychæte worms and some annelids and molluscs; **protovermi·culite** *Min.*, a mineral similar in composition to vermiculite but containing more water, and found as large yellow or brown scales; **protoxylem**, add: [a. G. *protoxylem* (E. Russow 1873, in *Mém. Acad. Impér. Sci. St.-Pétersbourg* 7th Ser. XIX. 3)]; (further examples).

1975 *Nature* 7 Aug. 470/2 Some protohandaxes may have one face made entirely of cortex, so not all of these artefacts can be called protobifaces and the term protohandaxes is preferable. **1976** *Ibid.* 8 July 104/2 Other tool forms, such as..protobifaces..occur with less frequency. **1965** S. W. FOX *Orig. Prebiol. Syst.* 372 The explanation has been extended to permit us to visualize a spontaneous synthesis of protein-like material sufficiently similar to yield a protocell which could spontaneously include ATP-splitting ability. **1974** PONNAMPERUMA & GABEL in Carlile & Skehel *Evolution in Microbial World* 407 Oparin does not in any way imply that the coacervates he and his associates have studied were the actual precursors of the protocell. **1977** A. HALLAM *Planet Earth* 236 Carbonaceous meteorites also contain organic spheres, and mineral grains coated with organic sheaths, that have been likened to 'protocells'. **1897** *Q. Jrnl. Microsc. Sci.* XL. 261 Viallanes has shown, by his very careful researches on the structure of the adult brain.., that it consists in insects of three segments... The first or protocerebrum, including the optic centres, corresponds to the first segment in Peripatus. **1969** *New Scientist* 10 July 56/2 It is generally known that the regulating clock mechanism of insects lies in the protocerebrum. **1970** *Nature* 31 Oct. 412/1 A protocloud formed at that time would initially expand with the Universe, but at a reduced rate. **1971** *Proc. Internat. School of Physics 'Enrico Fermi'* XLVII. 336 The density fluctuations associated with protoclusters—and *a fortiori* protogalaxies—would be too small to be detected. **1976** *Nature* 11 Nov. 114/2 Four stages might usefully be distinguished: (1) the creation of a massive protocluster cloud; (2) the separation of individual protostars from such a protocluster cloud; [etc.]. **1900** Protoeneme [see *metacneme* s.v. *META- 4]. **1916** H. S. PRATT *Man. Common Invertebr. Animals* 138 The gullet is joined with the body wall by all of the protocnemes. **1940** L. H. HYMAN *Invertebrates* I. vii. 589 These original twelve septa, which arise as couples, are called protocnemes. **1956** J. W. WELLS in R. C. Moore *Treat. Invertebr. Paleont.* F 333/2 When the first 6 mesenteric pairs (comprising 12 protocnemes) have developed the embryonic period [of scleractinians] is terminated. **1955** GRAF & GOLDSMITH in *Bull. Geol. Soc. Amer.* LXVI. 1566 These poorly ordered near dolomites, or protodolomites, also have been observed to form during the rapid cooling of dry periclase-calcite assemblages through the dolomite stability field. *Ibid.* 1567 In view of their relatively narrow compositional range, it appears probable that protodolomites have a relatively high degree of short-range Ca–Mg order, rather than being merely metastable, disordered, high-magnesium calcites. **1967** *Oceanogr. & Marine Biol.* V. 151 The deficiency of magnesium in the Red Sea brine might be caused by dolomitization of the carbonate rocks (some evidence of which is found in the presence of crystals of protodolomite in the core from the Discovery Deep). **1902** *Nature* 6 Nov. 14/2 [Professor E. Smith] intends to give a full account of the structure of the brain in the predynastic and protodynastic Egyptians. **1962** S. E. FINER *Man on Horseback* vii. 89 These are the traditional monarchies where the ideals of nationality, liberty, equality and popular sovereignty have not yet penetrated. Another and better description is perhaps the proto-dynastic societies, societies where allegiance is owed to the dynasty. **1977** G. CLARK *World Prehist.* (ed. 3) v. 236 There can be no doubt of the existence precisely at the period of transition from the Predynastic to the Protodynastic or Archaic period of Egyptian history of innovations that stemmed from Mesopotamian sources. **1939** *Jrnl. Amer. Ceramic Soc.* XVIII. 110/1 Constitution of steatite... On heating to 800°, talc lost its H_2O and was transformed into protoenstatite. **1962** *Ibid.* XLV. 156/2 The rate of the metastable inversion of protoenstatite to clinoenstatite during cooling is very sensitive to particle size. **1965** L. BRAGG et al. *Crystal Struct. Minerals* xii. 236 The detailed shape and relative positions of the silicate chains depend on the relative positions of the Mg atoms and their surrounding, octahedrally coordinated, oxygens. In protoenstatite the chains are fully extended, whereas in enstatite and clinoenstatite they are slightly different in shape and not fully extended. **1961** FILSHIE & ROGERS in *Jrnl. Molecular Biol.* III. 785 It can be observed..that a high concentration of lead has entered each microfibril and become bound to preferred sites, revealing a composite structure consisting of filamentous subunits relatively unstained by lead (henceforth to be referred to as protofibrils) each of the order of 20 Å in diameter. **1966** *New Scientist* 24 Feb. 480/2 Protofibrils, some 20 angstroms wide, may be observed to occur in a regular array, and it is widely accepted that they aggregate around an annulus, with perhaps nine outer protofibrils and two further protofibrils inside. **1971** *Nature* 22 Jan. 253/1 Wood fibres are hollow tubes composed of layers of cellulosic protofibrils embedded in a matrix of hemicellulose and lignin. **1971** *Proc. Nat. Acad. Sci.* LXVIII. 1766 If we assume a protofilament arrangement of monomeric subunits..in a microtubule, it becomes apparent that a homofilament microtubule can be constructed only if the number of protofilaments is even (i.e. 12 or 14 in the usual model) while a heterofilament microtubule always results if an odd number (11 or 13) of protofilaments are assembled. **1977** *Jrnl. Protozool.* XXIV. 4/1 Microtubules..can be thought of as protofilaments that are end-to-end polymers of dimers which are then bound together to form a tube with an open lumen. **1910** *Daily Chron.* 9 Apr. 6/2 The Oceanic negro is far removed from primitive man, but.. he inherits, as we all do, but happily in a lesser degree, the savage instincts of the proto-human. **1954** L. C. EISELEY in W. L. Thomas *Current Anthropol.* 69/1 We have.. stumbled into the world of essentially cultureless or almost cultureless proto-human types which are diverse in form because they represent evolution still at work upon the parts of the body. **1954** W. LA BARRE *Human Animal* iv. 83 The linearity of man, his relative hairlessness, his clothing, and his culture-based carnivorousness suggest that the proto-humans, like the anthropoids, were warm-climate-adapted animals. **1971** R. M. & F. M. KEESING *New Perspectives in Cultural Anthropol.* 45 Sharing must be viewed as a crucial protohuman innovation. **1978** *Sci. Amer.* Apr. 94/1 Excavation of these protohuman sites has revealed evidence suggesting that two million years ago some elements that now distinguish man from apes were already party of a novel adaptative strategy. **1966** *Palaeogeogr., Palaeoclimatol., Palaeoecol.* II. 54 The formation of cobionts and protolife through inorganic photosynthesis stopped at the beginning of this period of transition. **1977** A. HALLAM *Planet Earth* 236/1 The stromatolites are universally regarded as the remains of true life: the earlier microscopic fossils may well also represent the remains of blue-green algae, but it is perfectly probable that they represent some form of primitive protolife. **1972** *Gloss. Geol.* (Amer. Geol. Inst.) 571/2 *Protolith*, the unmetamorphosed rock from which a given metamorphic rock was formed by metamorphism. Syn: *parent rock*. **1974** *Nature* 15 Mar. 199/1 This investigation attempts to decipher the premetamorphic age of the protolith of a recrystallised breccia from Apollo 16. **1892** *Dana's Syst. Min.* (ed. 6) VI. 627 *Protolithionite*, a lithium-iron mica from the granite of the Erzgebirge, Fichtelgebirge, etc. Color dark. Optically nearly uniaxial... Sandberger regards it as the source of the zinnwaldite, hence the name. **1959** *Amer. Mineralogist* XLIV. 1297 It is a lithium-iron mica, closely related to zinnwaldite and containing a large amount of the protolithionite component of the lepidolite series. **1885, 1921** Protomerite [see *EPIMERITE]. **1962** J. D. SMYTH *Introd. Animal Parasitol.* vi. 73 In some forms [of gregarines], the protomerite is drawn out into a specialised region for attachment. **1921** R. A. S. MACALISTER *Text-bk. European Archaeol.* I. x. 549 A culture independent of any of those which we have now considered, namely the 'Protoneolithic' Campignian. **1924** [see *ASTURIAN *a.* and *sb.*]. **1931** *Antiquity* V. 520 Menghin distinguishes a Protoneolithic, and a Mixoneolithic, in the latter of which the Neolithic arts found their full expression. **1960** C. WINICK *Dict. Anthropol.* 440/2 *Protoneolithic*, in some classifications, the lower, or early, Neolithic era, consisting of the Campignian and Ertebole cultures. **1895** Protonephridial [see *protonephridium* below]. **1963** R. P. DALES *Annelids* v.98 The metanephridial funnels or protonephridial solenocytes lie in the coelomic fluid. **1895** E. S. GOODRICH in *Q. Jrnl. Microsc. Sci.* XXXVII. 479 The nephridia of the Planarians..are formed of a main duct, which branches out into fine tubules ending blindly internally in flame-cells; they do not develop beyond this 'protonephridial' condition—protonephridium of Hatschek. **1900** *Ibid.* XLIII. 742 For its [*sc.* the nephridium's] closed representation..and for closed 'head-kidneys', the term Protonephridium might, perhaps, be used with advantage. It is the name proposed by Hatschek for the closed nephridia of the Platyhelminths. **1930, 1967** [see *metanephridium* s.v. *META- 4]. **1949** A. S. ROMER *Vertebrate Body* ii. 19 The excretory organs [of Amphioxus]..are tiny tubes (protonephridia) of a type found in certain invertebrates. **1978** L. C. OGLESBY in P. J. Mill *Physiol. Annelids* xiv. 619 In only one group, the Rotifera, is there direct evidence that the protonephridia serve an osmoregulatory role. **1955** G. M. SMITH *Cryptogamic Bot.* (ed. 2) I. xii. 450 If appropriate spermatidia or conidia are not available for the trichogynes, there is no further development beyond the protoperithecial stage. **1976** *Ann. Rev. Microbiol.* XXX. 98 Nutritional control is important for the initiation of protoperithecial development and conidiogenesis. **1941** *Bot. Rev.* VII. 396 A haploid mycelium or a multicellular trichogyne of *Neurospora sitophila*.., through which nuclei of opposite sex are passing *en route* to the ascogonium in a proto-perithecium, where they are destined to take part in the formation of the first pair or pairs of conjugate nuclei. **1974** *Nature* 24 May 383/1 In *N[eurospora] crassa*, protoperithecia have been induced to develop into fruiting bodies, albeit sterile. **1909** *Econ. Geol.* IV. 625 Engler thus enumerates the various stages which in his opinion occur in the formation of petroleum from organic matter:..4. Formation of liquid hydrocarbons and violent reaction with 'cracking' into light or gaseous products = formation of protopetroleum. **1938** B. T. BROOKS in A. E. Dunstan et al. *Sci. of Petroleum* I. 52/1 Accordingly it might be expected that protopetroleums in transition stages will be found in geologically recent strata in the form of solid or semi-solid material. **1973** R. E. CHAPMAN *Petroleum Geol.* ii. 32 There is general agreement that the main source of petroleum is the organic matter buried with a fine-grained sediment (usually a clay); and that diagenesis of this organic matter leads to a 'protopetroleum' which, before or during migration, becomes modified by the physical and chemical environment—particularly by increasing temperature during burial—until it eventually becomes petroleum. **1953** G. E. M. ANSCOMBE tr. *Wittgenstein's Philos. Investigations* I. 167 Our mistake is to look for an explanation where we ought to look at what happens as a 'proto-phenomenon'. That is, where we ought to have said: *this language-game is played*. **1966** *Amer. Philos. Q.* III. 7/1 We should look simply at what is said as a proto-phenomenon. **1902** Protophloem [see *metaphloem* s.v. *META- 4]. **1953** K. ESAU *Plant Anat.* xii. 286 The primary phloem may be divided into protophloem and metaphloem. **1965** Protophloem [see *metaphloem* s.v. *META- 4]. **1925** A. D. IMMS *Gen. Textbk. Entomol.* 179 In the protopod phase metamerism is incomplete, the abdomen being imperfectly differentiated. **1934** FOLSOM & WARDLE *Entomol.* (ed. 4) iii. 172 The protopod larva is characterized by a lack of differentiation of the internal and external organs. **1969** R. F. CHAPMAN *Insects* xx. 400 Among the parasitic Hymenoptera the first instar larva hatches as a type known as a protopod larva. **1891, 1916** Protoproteose [see *heteroproteose* s.v. *HETERO-]. **1936** A. P. MATHEWS *Princ. Biochem.* xxii. 221 'Proto-proteoses', precipitated by half saturation of their solutions by ammonium sulphate. **1971** *Exper. Parasitol.* XXX. 233/1 Protein synthesis in larval *Echinococcus granulosus* protoscolices occurs by the pathway involving amino acyladenylates and amino acyl-tRNA as intermediates. **1976** *Lancet* 9 Oct. 811/2 Since the Lebanese also eat raw liver a hydatid of the tonsil might arise from implantation of a protoscolex in a tonsillar crypt. **1901** L. A. BOODLE in *Ann. Bot.* XV. 705 A centrally placed solid stele (protostele), consisting of a central mass of xylem..surrounded by a continuous ring of phloem. **1919** F. O. BOWER *Bot. Living Plant* xxi. 330 Generally in young sporelings there is a simple stele of a type called a 'protostele', having a solid xylem-core, and phloem surrounding it. **1957** H. C. BOLD *Morphol. Plants* xxiii. 446 The most primitive genera and the juvenile stages of most others have stems that contain protosteles. **1975** J. D. HAYNES *Botany* xxii. 331 The stele of most members of this group [*sc.* lycopods] is a protostele. **1902** *Encyl. Brit.* XXV. 413/2 There is good reason to suppose that the protostelic condition is primitive in evolution. **1957** H. C. BOLD *Morphol. Plants* xxiii. 447 Internally the roots are exarch and protostelic. **1904** H. M. BERNARD in *Ann. Mag. Nat. Hist.* XIII. 4 The parent colony of a calicle rises out of a basal cup—the Prototheca.. The term 'prototheca' was suggested to me in conversation by my friend Prof. Jeffrey Bell. **1906** S. J. HICKSON in Harmer & Shipley *Cambr. Nat. Hist.* I. xiv. 386 The calicoblasts form..a skeletal plate at the aboral end of the coral embryo, which becomes turned up at the edges to form a shallow saucer or cup. This cup is called the 'prototheca'. **1935** TWENHOFEL & SHROCK *Invertebr. Paleont.* iv. 78 The embryonic skeleton of a typical coelenterate has the shape and appearance of a little, hollow, conical cup and is known as the prototheca. **1897** A. T. MASTERMAN in *Q. Jrnl. Microsc. Sci.* XL. 291 There are three prominent ciliated bands, the preoral (or prototroch), the collar-band..and the trunk band. **1904** *Amer. Naturalist* XXXVIII. 500 Cells arising from the first quartette..make up a cell row which very probably forms at least a part of the second ciliated band on the head of the adult, in a position corresponding with that of the prototroch of the annelid larva. **1932** BORRADAILE & POTTS *Invertebrata* vii. 207 A band of cilia round the base [of the Pilidium larva] constitutes the prototroch. **1959** *Q. Jrnl. Microsc. Sci.* C. 89 The ectoderm of the mouth region [of the pre-adult *Scoloplos armiger*]..includes transitorily the prototroch cells. **1978** K. S. RICHARDS in P. J. Mill *Physiol. Annelids* ii. 48 In the prototroch the compounding of cilia helps to eliminate such lateral stresses. **1877** *Proc. Acad. Nat. Sci. Philadelphia* 269 Professor Geo. A. König described a micaceous mineral from Magnet Cove, Ark., to which he gave the name Protovermiculite... The mineral occurs in large foliated plates, loose in the soil. **1948** *Amer. Mineralogist* XXXIII. 656 Protovermiculite from Magnet Cove, Arkansas. Large golden yellow scales. **1902** *Phil. Trans. R. Soc.* B. CXCV. 135 The protoxylem is separated from it [*sc.* the pith] by a large mass of primary metaxylem. **1974** *New Phytologist* LXXIII. 979 The helically thickened protoxylem..is stretched during the elongation of the axis.

c. More widely, prefixed to adjs. and sbs. designating an original, early, or undeveloped form of an artistic or political movement, as *proto-Baroque*, *-Cubist* adjs., *-Fascism* (hence *-Fascist* sb. and adj.), *-Marxian* adj., *-Renaissance* (also *attrib.*), *-romantic* adj.

1935 *Burlington Mag.* Apr. 159/1 Why are the artists working about the year 1800 gothic-manneristic, classicistic, proto-Baroque, high Baroque? **1977** *Dædalus* Summer 2 Titian's removal of the Virgin..to the right side of the worshipers in his Pesaro Madonna—once considered a protobaroque stylistic invention. **1979** *Jrnl. R. Soc. Arts* Nov. 767/2 If I can use the historical analogy again, with sixteenth-century Italy, the proto-Baroque or Mannerist period, which seems to have had the same kind of doubts and plu[r]alism characteristic of our age. **1959** H. READ *Conc. Hist. Mod. Painting* v. 156 The metamorphic *Three Dancers* is in fact a turning point in Picasso's art almost as radical as was the proto-cubist *Demoiselles d'Avignon*. **1938** *New Statesman* 19 Feb. 302/1 It [*sc.* racism] is proto-Fascism, based on mysticism on the one hand, and pseudo-biology on the other. **1945** H. READ *Coat of Many Colours* i. 3 Lucian, one of those romantic exiles who brought some light and liberty into a proto-fascist world. **1959** —— *Conc. Hist. Mod. Painting* iv. 119 Anarchists.., proto-fascists in some cases, the Dadaists, adopted Bakunin's slogan: destruction is also creation! **1973** *Black Panther* 28 Apr. 8/3 The danger in a 'professional' national police force is the same as that of a volunteer army. In both we find an elitist, racist, proto-fascist orientation and esprit. **1977** M. WALKER *National Front* i. 15 Proto-fascist, crypto-fascist,..quasi-fascist; the sub-groups..multiply and do little to impose meaning on the confusion. **1969** P. A. ROBINSON *Freudian Left* 168 Portrait of Hegel as loyal son of the Enlightenment and proto-Marxian critic of the European social order. **1909** *Cent. Dict.* Suppl., *Proto-Renaissance*.., a revival movement in art and literature preceding the Renaissance proper, especially that which began in the reign of the Emperor Frederick II. (1194–1250). **1911** *Encycl. Brit.* XX. 468/1 A 'Proto-Renaissance', the characteristic of which was a fresh interest in surviving remains of classical antiquity. **1942** N. PEVSNER *Outl. Europ. Archit.* iv. 61 The Tuscan Proto-Renaissance of S. Miniato..i.e., the architecture of Florence in the 11th century, and nothing else. **1945** *Burlington Mag.* Jan. 23/2 Such, however, was the popular 'proto-Renaissance' in our country. **1948** N. PEVSNER *Outl. Europ. Archit.* (rev. ed.) v. 82 Of Romanesque or Proto-Renaissance connections there are here none left. **1963** *Times Lit. Suppl.* 26 Apr. 312/4 'Proto-Renaissance' Romanesque 'antique' models. **1947** A. EINSTEIN *Mus. Romantic Era* viii. 81 Many of the traits in Mozart's works can be considered 'Romantic' or proto-romantic. **1971** *Country Life* 12 Aug. 392/1 The drawings are large in scale..and far removed from the experimental, proto-romantic work that we associate with Brown.

protoactinium, var. *PROTACTINIUM.

proto-Algonquian: see *PROTO- 2 a.

protoanemonin (prōᵘto‚ăne·mǒnin). *Chem.* [Coined in Japanese as *purotoanemonin* (Asahina & Fujita 1920, in *Jrnl. Pharmaceut. Soc. Japan* XL. 3): see PROTO- and ANEMONIN (cf. quot. 1920).] A poisonous, vesicant, pale yellow oil, which is isolated from many plants of the family Ranunculaceæ, and is an unsaturated lactone, $CH_2{=}C{\cdot}CH{=}CH{\cdot}CO{\cdot}O$, having bacteriostatic and fungistatic properties.

1920 *Chem. Abstr.* XIV. 1384 The sharp, oily substance volatile with steam obtained from *Ranunculus scleratus* L., consists in the main of the mother substance of anemonin, and has been given the name *protoanemonin*, which under spontaneous union of 2 mols. passes into anemonin. **1949** H. W. FLOREY et al. *Antibiotics* I. xiv. 605 Protoanemonin ($C_5H_4O_2$) was obtained as a pale yellow irritating oil. It solidified to give anemonin within a few hours at room temperature but was stable at 5°C. in 1 per cent. aqueous solution. **1958** *New Biol.* XXVI. 44 All three species [of buttercup] contain a glycoside 'ranunculin' which is readily broken down in damaged tissues to give glucose and an unsaturated lactone—protoanemonin. This lactone is poisonous and blistering, and makes *R. bulbosus* and *R. acris* very unpalatable to stock. **1972** *Science* 5 May 512/2 Lesser in toxicity are the vitamin antagonists such as protoanemonin..and amino acid antagonists such as mimosine.

proto-Aryan to **-Austronesian:** see *PROTO- 2 a. **proto-Baroque, -biface:** *PROTO- 2 c, b.

protobiont (-bəi·ǫnt). *Biol.* [f. Gr. πρωτο- PROTO- + βιοντ-, pres. pple. stem of βιοῦν to live, f. βίος life.] A small drop of fluid surrounded by a membrane, hypothesized as ancestral to living cells.

1964 A. SYNGE tr. *Oparin's Chem. Origin of Life* iii. 61 The droplets would come to contain a constantly increasing concentration of the corresponding catalysts when the mass of the droplet increased as it grew by polymerising the monomers of the surrounding medium. Such coacervate droplets with an improved organisation are still only hypothetical but, for convenience of discussion, we shall refer to them in what follows by the provisional name of 'protobionts'. **1970** A. L. LEHNINGER *Biochem.* xxxiv. 782 Oparin..has suggested that the first cells, which he called protobionts, arose when a boundary or membrane formed around one or more macromolecules possessing catalytic activity, presumably proteins. **1971** *Sci. Amer.* May 30/1 Judging from the various forms of life we know today, the first protobionts were probably microscopic in size and single-celled in structure. **1978** *Ibid.* Sept. 65/1 To Oparin the reproductive machinery and DNA are only the ultimate biochemical subtleties that turned metabolically competing protobionts into living cells.

protocell, -cerebrum: see *PROTO- 2 b. **protochemistry:** PROTO- 1 in Dict. and Suppl.

protochlo·rophyll. *Biochem.* [a. G. *protochlorophyll* (N. A. Monteverde 1893, in *Acta Horti Petropolitana* XIII. 210): see PROTO- and CHLOROPHYLL.] A naturally occurring photo-active precursor of chlorophyll.

1894 *Jrnl. R. Microsc. Soc.* 702 The same author [*sc.* Monteverde] finds, in etiolated leaves, besides xanthophyll and carotin, a pigment to which he gives the name *protochlorophyll*. It displays a distinct red fluorescence. **1928** *Science* 7 Dec. 570/2 Protochlorophyll is not a decomposition product of some other organic substance, as leucophyll, but is a pigment which develops without the influence of light and changes photochemically into chlorophyll upon exposure to light. **1951** *Ann. Rev. Plant Physiol.* II. 131 Protochlorophyll is a pale greenish pigment containing two hydrogen atoms less than chlorophyll. **1956** E. I. RABINOWITCH *Photosynthesis* II. xxxvii. 1759 Up to 90% of the protochlorophyll, accumulated in the dark, are quantitatively converted, within a minute or less of moderately strong illumination, into chlorophyll *a*. **1976** *Photochem. & Photobiol.* XXIV. 555 We now extract cells with acetone... Protochlorophyll is obtained by extracting this solution with petroleum ether..and extracting this petroleum ether fraction with 80% acetone to remove substances which interfere with subsequent chromatography.

protocho·rdate, *sb.* and *a.* *Zool.* [ad. mod.L. *Protochordata* (F. M. Balfour *Treat. Compar. Embryol.* (1881) II. xii. 27), f. PROTO- + *CHORDATE *a.* and *sb.*] **A.** *sb.* A small marine animal belonging to one of the subphyla Hemichordata or Cephalochordata, which form a group considered to be related to ancestors of the vertebrates, and are characterized by a dorsal nerve cord, a notochord, and gill slits. **B.** *adj.* Of, pertaining to, or resembling an animal of this kind.

1894 A. WILLEY *Amphioxus & Ancestry of Vertebrates* v. 242 Of the free-living protochordates, the lowest type of organisation is undoubtedly presented by the *Enteropneusta* (Hemichorda). *Ibid.* 282 There is no *a priori* reason for doubting that the Vertebrate mouth is completely homologous with the Protochordate mouth. **1918** H. F. OSBORN *Orig. & Evol. Life* viii. 246 The principal.. secretory glands..doubtless had their beginnings among the ancestors (protochordates) of the vertebrated animals. **1933** L. A. ADAMS *Introd. Vertebrates* i. 17 All these modern protochordates are small and live in the sea. **1951** C. K. WEICHERT *Anat. Chordates* ii. 12 The animals included in this category [*sc.* Acrania] are believed to show similarities to the ancestors of the chordates and for this reason are sometimes called the protochordates. **1978** *Nature* 5 Jan. 61/2 Attention has focused on the protochordate endostyle since the demonstration that certain of its cells could bind iodine.

protocloud to **-cneme:** see *PROTO- 2 b.

protococcoid, *a.* Add: (Example.) Also **protococcoi·dal** *a.*

1965 F. E. ROUND *Biol. Algae* i. 3 The unicells may be sub-divided into non-motile (Protococcoidal), 'amoeba'-like (Rhizopodial) and motile cells (Flagellate). **1967** M. E. HALE *Biol. Lichens* iii. 45 The common protococcoid algae are soon killed off by the fungus.

protocol, *sb.* Add to etym.:

The word has now entered the general vocabulary of English in senses *5 b, c.

2. a. Also *fig.*

1923 A. HUXLEY *Antic Hay* xii. 184 The parting kiss.. was already in the protocol, as signed and sealed before her departure by giggling Molly.

c. [In Gr. sense.] The first sheet of a roll of papyrus, bearing the manufacturer's official mark; this mark itself.

1885 *Encycl. Brit.* XVIII. 233/1 The first sheet of a roll was named πρωτόκολλον... On the Arab conquest of Egypt in the 7th century, the manufacture was continued, with the substitution of Arabic in marking the protocol. **1905** W. E. CRUM *Catal. Coptic MSS. Brit. Mus.* 181 Upon the 1st *selis*, above the Coptic text, is part of the protocol in large Kufic characters. **1912** E. M. THOMPSON *Introd. Gk. & Lat. Palaeogr.* 25 After their conquest of Egypt in the seventh century, the Arabs continued the manufacture of papyrus and also affixed protocols to their rolls.

d. *Protocols of the (Learned) Elders of Zion*: a spurious publication of Russian origin purporting to describe Jewish plans for the domination of the world. Also, *Protocols of Zion*.

1920 (*title*) The Jewish peril: protocols of the Learned Elders of Zion. **1921** *Times* 16 Aug. 9/6 The so-called 'Protocols of the Elders of Sion' were published in London last year under the title of 'The Jewish Peril'. **1937** H. G. WELLS *Star-Begotten* vii. 128 These Reds—Moscow—Bernard Shaw—New Dealers—Atheists—Protocols of Zion, all of that—mere agents. **1941** —— *You can't be too Careful* v. i. 238 You can study how the new pogromism was revived in that curious and impudent forgery, *The Protocols of the Elders of Zion*. **1974** *Jewish Chron.* 20 Dec. 15/4 The antisemitic Protocols of the Elders of Zion have gone through more editions in Arabic than any other language. **1979** O. SELA *Petrograd Consignment* 142 Wasn't he desperate to read the Protocols of the Elders of Zion again; wasn't another pogrom all he lived for.

e. *Philos.* A statement which forms an essential part of a person's description of something experienced or perceived; a basic statement that can be verified or assessed.

1936 *Mind* XLV. 275 N[eurath] expresses Protocol-propositions in the form 'Charles's protocol (there is a table in the room perceived by Charles)'. **1956** J. O. Urmson *Philos. Analysis* viii. 121 Protocols are direct reports of the given and are justified with reference to the given... I choose between the possible protocols 'This is red' and 'This is green' by seeing which correctly reports experience. **1965** P. Caws *Philos. Sci.* xi. 74 A set of protocol sentences..constitutes a *protocol*.

3. (Further examples.) *spec.* the detailed record of the procedure and results in a scientific experiment; hence, experimental procedure.

1887 *Amer. Jrnl. Psychol.* I. 136 The protocol here is admirable, taken on the spot by Mr. Birchall and printed in full, and Mr. Guthrie is very positive in stating that there were a large number of 'complete successes'. **1910** *Amer. Jrnl. Physiol.* XXVII. 36 The protocols of the experiments above discussed follow. **1923** [see *intratracheally* adv. s.v. *INTRA-]. **1929** I. A. Richards *Pract. Crit.* 4, I lectured the following week partly upon the poems, but rather more upon the comments, or protocols, as I call them... I asked each writer to record on his protocol the number of 'readings' made of each poem. **1947** *Ann. Rev. Microbiol.* I. 357 The data are not given, but from the protocols it appears probable that the hemagglutinin persists while toxicity and infectiousness are lost. **1961** *Lancet* 22 July 213/2 Not only the urinary but also the fæcal porphyrin excretion must be considered. Protocols of published cases [of porphyria] frequently lack this vital information. **1973** *Jrnl. Genetic Psychol.* CXXII. 192 Each *S*'s protocol was scored in terms of the number of responses to critical items which indicated a preference for balance. **1976** *Amer. Speech 1974* XLIX. 12 The phonetic transcriptions and marginal notes made from that record and entered in the workbooks are a protocol, and they are regarded as working notations. **1977** *Lancet* 9 Apr. 805/1 The most common treatment protocol appears to have been a series of 6 treatments (range 1–30) at a dose of 250 (range 100–400) roentgens per treatment.

5. a. Also used of analogous departments in other countries.

1975 M. Sinclair *Long Time Sleeping* xii. 150 'I wonder when was the last time we refused to accept an Ambassador?' 'I'll ask Protocol in the morning.' **1980** J. Hone *Flowers of Forest* I. 13 His job..had been in Protocol... It was his function to control liaison..between our own and other allied intelligence services.

b. An official form of procedure and etiquette in affairs of state and diplomatic relations; the observance of this.

1945 in Webster Add. **1949** *Washington Post* 22 Mar. 1/3 He [*sc.* President Truman] felt that it would not be good protocol for him to be away hobnobbing with an Englishman out of office at the very time that the man now in charge of Britain's foreign affairs is in Washington. **1953** *Economist* 12 Dec. 799/1 Alleged breaches of diplomatic protocol at the Bermuda conference. **1957** *Listener* 5 Sept. 337/2 Dr Adenauer..chatted gaily and frankly... Protocol and affairs of state were set aside. **1980** J. Cartwright *Horse of Darius* iii. 46 Our sovereign is coming here... The protocol is very important. Who comes to visit. How we keep in touch with Tehran.

c. In extended and general uses, any code of conventional or proper conduct; formally correct behaviour.

1952 *Daily Express* 27 Mar. 4/3 He punctuates his work with a gay laugh..and a first-name informality with colleagues... Not that protocol is in danger. For behind his exuberance is a tough grasp of ceremonial and what is due. **1954** W. Faulkner *Fable* 18 The old generalissimo turned, his two confreres..flanking him in rigid protocol. **1954** *Times* 27 Nov. 6 The ceremony was taking its course in accordance with academic protocol. **1959** *Woman's Own* 20 June 37/2 Prince Edward and Princess Alexandra had a childhood as free from protocol as their mother's had been. **1971** B. W. Aldiss *Soldier Erect* 20 That sort of American approach was even harder to master than the Ancient British protocol but, once mastered, it gave positive results.

7. a. (sense *2c) *protocol sheet*; (sense *5a) *protocol department, section*.

1912 E. M. Thompson *Introd. Gk. & Lat. Palaeogr.* 24 Among the Romans the protocol-sheet was inscribed with the name of the Comes largitionum..and with the date and the name of the place where it was made. **1958** L. Durrell *Mountolive* vi. 133 Then, turning, he completed his devoirs to the Protocol section. **1977** 'S. Leys' *Chinese Shadows* (1978) viii. 182 Masses can always be arranged by appointment: one should apply at the Protocol Department in the Ministry of Foreign Affairs.

b. *spec.* in *Philos.* (sense *2e), as *protocol language, proposition, sentence, speech, statement*.

1933 *Philosophy* VIII. 98 Carnap then considers the 'protocol language'. Scientific evidence is derived from protocol propositions that describe our perceptions, feelings, thoughts, etc. *Ibid.*, Finally, Carnap develops the thesis that protocol speech is part of physical speech. **1935** *Analysis* II. 59 The form of protocol statements cannot be found, but must be fixed by a convention. **1937** A. Smeaton tr. *Carnap's Logical Syntax of Lang.* v. 317 The statement of the protocol-sentences is the affair of the physicist who is observing and making protocols. **1965** P. Caws *Philos. of Sci.* xi. 73 A protocol sentence must be such that a decision as to its empirical truth or falsity can be reached after a finite number of observations.

‖**protocolaire** (prǫtokǫlēr), *a.* [Fr.] Characterized by a strict regard for protocol; formal, ceremonial.

1934 'A. Bridge' *Ginger Griffin* xviii. 232 But of course James wouldn't—he's too *protocolaire*. **1958** *Spectator* 24 Jan. 101/1 Less *protocolaire* than Trooping the Colour. **1962** T. Zinkin *Caste Today* 29 Occasionally there are festivals or private ceremonies... On those occasions, as in the most protocolaire of royal banquets, the place and part to be taken by each are known to all. **1975** N. Freeling *What are Bugles blowing For?* xxiii. 137 A list..of engagements..ranging from the unavoidable to the purely *protocolaire*. **1979** H. Wilson *Final Term* viii. 161 Duncan Sandys..said that even in pre-Amin days he had always insisted on the title 'Britain' despite protocolaire objections.

protocolar (prō^{u}·tokǫlăɹ), *a. rare.* [f. Protocol *sb.* + -ar^{1}: cf. prec.] Of, pertaining to, or characterized by (a) protocol; formal, *protocolaire*.

1905 *Truth* 22 June 1589/1 To some extent it [sc. *The Mikado*] is protocolar, but one must not for that think it an empty form. **1960** *News Chron.* 12 Apr. 6/7 The Canadian Prime Minister, found himself in the peculiar protocolar position of sending a message of sympathy..at the same time as he was sending a vigorous protest.

protocolic, *a.* For *nonce-wd.* read *rare* and add later example.

1969 *Punch* 8 Jan. 60/3 It..cuts out all your time-consuming Ambassadorial summonses, stern notes..and general argy-bargy in protocolic triplicate.

pro·tocone. *Zool.* [f. Proto- + Cone *sb.*^{1}] An inner cusp on the front corner of a mammalian upper molar tooth.

1888 H. F. Osborn in *Amer. Naturalist* XXII. 1072 (*table*) Proposed terms... Protocone... Protoconule... Protoconid. **1896** *Proc. Zool. Soc.* 573 In the deciduous 4th premolar [of *Centetes*] likewise the protocone develops first. **1922** [see *deuterocone* s.v. *DEUTERO-]. **1933** A. S. Romer *Vertebr. Paleont.* xii. 248 A single cusp is found at the inner apex; this was originally believed to represent the original reptilian cone and hence is called the protocone. **1968, 1971** [see *METACONULE]. **1976** *Nature* 5 Aug. 464/2 The upper first deciduous molar displays spatial dominance of the protocone.

protoconid (-kō^{u}·nid). *Zool.* [f. prec. + *-id^{5}.] A cusp on a mammalian lower molar tooth corresponding to the protocone on an upper molar.

1888 [see prec.]. **1896** *Proc. Zool. Soc.* 568 In the lower molar [of *Gymnura*] the protoconid evidently develops fast. **1907** [see *deuteroconid* s.v. *DEUTERO-]. **1933** [see *METACONID]. **1971** W. D. Turnbull in A. A. Dahlberg *Dental Morphol. & Evolution* ix. 168 (*caption*) The eocristid and its associated primary cusp, the protoconid or eoconid..are shown. **1976** *Nature* 5 Aug. 464/2 There is a spatially dominant protoconid with a large flat buccal face, a lingually facing anterior fovea, and an inferiorly projecting mesiobuccal enamel line.

pro·tocontinent. *Geol.* [f. Proto- + Continent *sb.*] = *supercontinent. Hence **pro:tocontine·ntal** *a.*

1958 L. King in *Continental Drift* (Univ. of Tasmania) 13 Recent studies..suggest once more the validity of continental drift, with two proto-continents Laurasia and Gondwana. **1968** *Sat. Rev.* (U.S.) 2 Mar. 48 (*caption*) The hegira of the Indian subcontinent about 60,000,000 years ago is suggested on the above map of earth's proto-continent. **1977** *Sci. Amer.* Mar. 104/2 As long as the fairly coherent supercontinent could move in relation to its adjacent ocean floor, the ocean floor could have been subducted, partially melted and chemically differentiated to manufacture typical continental crust at the leading edge of the protocontinent. **1978** *Nature* 10 Aug. 547/1 The protocontinental tectosphere produced in island-arc environments or along the active margins is probably thin, chemically heterogeneous and poorly consolidated.

protoconule (-kō^{u}·niul). *Zool.* [f. *Protocon(e + -ule.] An intermediate cusp between the protocone and the paracone of a mammalian upper molar tooth.

1888 [see *PROTOCONE]. **1905** [see *METACONULE]. **1933** A. S. Romer *Vertebr. Paleont.* xii. 248 Between protocone and paracone there is often a smaller cusp, the protoconule. **1968** R. Zangerl tr. *Peyer's Compar. Odontogr.* 187 Intermediate cusps occurred along the trigon, a protoconule between protocone and paracone and a metaconule between protocone and metacone.

pro·tocorm. *Bot.* [ad. F. *protocorme* (M. Treub 1890, in *Ann. Jard. Bot. Buitenzorg* VIII. 30), f. Proto- + Corm^{2}.] A tuber-like body produced in the seedling stage of certain pteridophytes and orchids which grow in association with mycorrhiza. Also *attrib.*

1891 F. O. Bower in *Proc. R. Soc.* L. 267 The sporophyte [of *Phylloglossum*] consists of two parts:—(i) the protocorm, with its protophylls and roots, and (ii) the strobilus. **1905** I. B. Balfour tr. *Goebel's Organogr. Plants* II. 232 The chief mass of the seedling [of orchids] is formed of the 'protocorm'. **1938** G. M. Smith *Cryptogamic Bot.* II. vii. 180 A massive globose structure (the protocorm)..grows through the gametophyte. **1959** S. Shushan in C. L. Withner *Orchids* iii. 53 Continued enlargement of the embryo, which can henceforth be called the protocorm, results in either a smooth or irregular globular mass of cells. **1962** K. R. Sporne *Morphol. Pteridophytes* iv. 64 The protocorm might well be regarded as a derivative and retrograde development. **1967** *New Scientist* 14 Sept. 551/1 By subculturing every few weeks, protocorm formation may be kept going indefinitely. **1977** J. Arditti *Orchid Biol.* 211 Within 4–6 months, a mass of protocorms is formed.

proto-Cubist: see *proto- 2c. **proto-cultural, -culture:** *proto- 1.

pro:to-di·asystem. *Linguistics.* [f. Proto- + *diasystem* (1954), f. Gr. διά through + System.] A hypothetical reconstruction of the system of linguistic relationships in a proto-language (see also quot. 1969).

1964 *Word* XX. 376 If I use the term proto-language for a reconstruction and proto-dialect for the real speech, my implication is that the reconstruction is in fact a proto-diasystem. **1968** *Language* XLIV. 485 Proto-languages are to be understood as proto-dia-systems, with over-all sets of correspondences between related linguistic structures. **1969** S. P. Durham *Computer in Reconstruction of Proto-Diasystem: Franco-Provençal* I. i. 14 Since a diasystem is a combination into one single descriptive statement of the features of several dialects viewed horizontally, a proto-diasystem can be considered a combination into one single statement of the features of several dialects viewed vertically, that is, historically. **1972** *Computers & Humanities* VII. 6 A corpus of about 1000 words, chosen from eleven villages, provided a concordance to suggest a reconstruction of the Franco-Provençal proto-diasystem and a tentative phonology.

protodolomite to **-filament:** see *proto- 2a, b, c.

pro·to-form, *sb.* (and *a.*) *Linguistics.* [f. Proto- + Form *sb.* 5c.] A hypothetical form of a word or part of a word from which actual words have been derived. Also *attrib.* or as *adj.*

1964 *Language* XL. 145 We must use different symbols to represent the proto-forms. **1965** *Canad. Jrnl. Linguistics* X. 94 Reconstruction of proto-form phonological shapes. **1965** *Language* XLI. 305 There is no reason to assume stress on a first syllable of the proto-form. **1976** *Archivum Linguisticum* VII. 63 Both of these assumed proto-forms might appear surprising in view of the dearth of direct evidence in Latin texts and inscriptions.

pro·togalaxy. *Astr.* Also with hyphen. [f. Proto- + Galaxy *sb.*] A vast mass of gas, not yet formed into stars, postulated as a preliminary stage in the evolution of a galaxy.

1959 *Astrophysical Jrnl.* CXXX. 43 These nuclei had already originated before the protogalaxy condensed into stars. **1969** *Monthly Notices R. Astron. Soc.* CXLV. 417 The central part of the cloud begins to collapse, and the collapsing region gradually grows until it eventually includes almost the entire mass of the proto-galaxy. **1977** *Sci. Amer.* Oct. 43/3 Shapley's work laid the foundation for the present view that the globular clusters were formed 10 to 13 billion years ago during the gravitational collapse of the protogalaxy, a vast cloud of gas consisting of hydrogen and helium.

Hence **protogala·ctic** *a.*, of, pertaining to, or being a protogalaxy.

1969 *Monthly Notices R. Astron. Soc.* CXLV. 407 We assume for simplicity that the proto-galactic material consists of pure hydrogen. **1977** *Sci. Amer.* Oct. 44/2 As the protogalactic cloud contracted local regions of higher density became self-gravitating and condensed within a relatively short time into globular star clusters.

proto-Gallo-Romance, -Romanic: see *proto- 2a.

protogenic (-dʒe·nik), *a.*^{2} *Chem.* [f. Proto(n in Dict. and Suppl. + *-genic.] Of a solvent (or solute): having a tendency to protonate most solutes (or solvents). Opp. *protophilic *a.*

1931 N. F. Hall in *Chem. Rev.* VIII. 194 The protogenic and protophilic character of very weak acids and bases is largely masked by the overwhelming prominence of the similar properties of water. **1940** Glasstone *Text-bk. Physical Chem.* xii. 958 For convenience solvents are divided roughly into three categories according as the molecules are (*a*) proton acceptors, i.e., basic, or protophilic, (*b*) proton donors, i.e., acidic, or protogenic, or (*c*) neither donors nor acceptors, i.e., aprotic. **1969** R. G. Bates in Coetzee & Ritchie *Solute-Solvent Interactions* ii. 51 The four classes of solvents, 'amphiprotic', 'protogenic', 'protophilic', and 'aprotic', are not clearly restrictive and the proper classification of many solvents is in doubt. **1973** E. J. King in Covington & Dickinson *Physical Chem. Org. Solvent Syst.* iii. 333 Formic acid is an obvious example of an acidic or protogenic solvent, but it has weak basic properties too.

pro:to-geome·tric, *a.* Also **proto-Geometric** and as one word. [f. Proto- + *geometric *a.* d.] Designating the period preceding the Geometric Age in Greece, or the pottery attributed to this period, contemporaneous with the collapse of Mycenæan civilization on the mainland and the period of cultural decline that followed it (*c* 1100–*c* 900 B.C.).

1926 *Cambr. Anc. Hist.* IV. xvi. 580 Between the flourishing of the Creto-Mycenaean civilization, and the geometric period proper, there lies a long period which has been named, not very happily, the proto-geometric: a period of cultural decay. **1933** *Jrnl. Hellenic Stud.* LIII. 162 Cremation first appears in connexion with the proto-Geometric style in pottery. **1939** J. D. S. Pendlebury *Archaeol. Crete* iv. 243 This type of tomb, square with a circular vault above, continues in Lasithi and the neighbourhood into Proto-geometric times. **1950** H. L. Lorimer *Homer & Monuments* i. 42 Simple as the proto-Geometric culture is, it marks a period, not of decline, but of renascence. **1953** *Antiquity* XXVII. 75 The Protogeometric iron sword of about 30 inches long, when new, was quite as effective for cutting as for thrusting. **1961** *Oxf. Mag.* 16 Feb. 232/1 The earliest Proto-geometric wares found at Smyrna can be dated about 1000 B.C. **1973** J. Boardman *Greeks Overseas* (ed. 2) i. 3 The finds in Athens cemeteries show that after a very short while, probably by about 1050 B.C., the new 'Protogeometric' style of vase-painting had been evolved from the debased Mycenæan forms.

proto-Germanic to **-Greek:** see *proto- 1, 2a.

protogynous, *a.* Add: [ad. G. *protogynisch* (F. H. G. Hildebrand *Die Geschlechter-Vertheilung bei den Pflanzen* (1867) 17).] (Earlier and later examples.)

1870 A. W. Bennett in *Jrnl. Bot.* VIII. 320 *Chlora perfoliata*..is protogynous. **1909** J. R. A. Davis tr. *Knuth's Handbk. Flower Pollination* III. 221 The flowers [of *Bartsia alpina*] in Greenland were found by Warming to be feebly protogynous, the anthers dehiscing soon after the maturation of the stigma. **1973** *Nature* 23 Mar. 275/2 Some cross-pollination may occur because the flowers are protogynous and have some insect visitors.

2. *Zool.* = Proterogynous *a.* 2.

1931 F. A. E. Crew in W. Rose *Outl. Mod. Knowl.* 285 In quite a number of forms protandrous..or protogynous..hermaphroditism is the rule, it being usual for an individual first to function as a female or male, and then, later, as a male or female. **1973** *Nature* 12 Oct. 333/1 This system is an illustration of the phenomenon of social determination of phenotype, which includes social control of sex reversal in protogynous fishes.

protogyny. (Earlier and later examples.)

1870 A. W. Bennett in *Jrnl. Bot.* VIII. 315 The terms Protandry and Protogyny used by Hildebrand to express, in the one case the development of the stamens before the pistils, in the other case the development of the pistil before the stamens, are so convenient and expressive that I have adopted them in this paper. **1940** *Nature* 30 Mar. 485/2 Protandry, protogyny, special floral arrangements and other devices could also be listed. **1972** *Science* 12 May 601/2 In these plants, dioecism, protandry, protogyny..are common.

protohæm, -heme (prōᵘ·tohīm). *Biochem.* [a. G. *protohäm* (H. Fischer et al. 1931, in *Zeitschr. f. physiol. Chem.* CXCV. 21): see Proto- and *hæm, heme.] A ferrous chelate derivative of a protoporphyrin; *spec.* = *hæm, heme a.

1931 *Chem. Abstr.* XXV. 2157 By using a technic which excludes the possibility of oxidation, etioheme, protoheme, mesoheme and meso-ester heme were obtained cryst. from the corresponding porphyrins. **1963** R. P. Dales *Annelids* iv. 88 In haemoglobin the haem is the red protohaem, in chlorocruorin it is the green chlorocruorohaem. **1963** C. H. Doering tr. *Karlson's Introd. Mod. Biochem.* ix. 183 Peroxidases oxidize substrates by employing H_2O_2 as an oxidizing agent. Depending on their origin, they may contain either a red heme (protoheme or closely related ones) or a green heme. **1970** R. W. McGilvery *Biochem.* xxi. 499 The normal product of porphyrin synthesis is protoheme IX, which is quickly bound by globin peptides and protected from oxidation.

proto-Hattic to **-Jupiter:** see *proto- 1, 2a, b.

pro·to-language. *Linguistics.* [f. Proto- + Language *sb.*] A hypothetical parent language from which actual languages or dialects have been derived.

1948 W. F. Twaddell in *Language* XXIV. 139 Our reconstruction of a proto-language is theoretical and partial. **1950** H. M. Hoenigswald in *Ibid.* XXVI. 357 We may refer to Meillet's rule that in reconstructing the vocabulary of a proto-language we need the testimony of three, rather than two, independent witnesses. **1955** *Orbis* IV. 428 Many distinguished linguists have expressly declared that the assumption of a uniform proto-language conflicts with all we know about languages actually observed. **1964** *Word* XX. 376 The reconstructed proto-language is a formula, a statement on relationships, albeit in a diachronic rather than synchronic direction, and does not therefore represent, at least not necessarily, a genuine speech form that ever existed. **1977** R. Williams *Marxism & Lit.* I. ii. 25 In one area this movement was 'evolutionary' in a particular sense: in its postulate of a proto-language (proto-Indo-European) from which the major 'family' had developed.

protolife: see *proto- 2b.

protolingui·stic, *a.* [f. Proto- + Linguistic *a.*] Descriptive of communication or signs which are understood without the use of verbal language (see quot. 1964); of communication, etc., from which language is presumed to have developed. Also, relating to the study of proto-language. Hence **protolingui·stics** *sb. pl.*

1964 *Discovery* Oct. 32/3 Those [*sc.* symbols]..which are commonly translated into or from ordinary language; and those which are not so translated—like clothes, architectural design and furniture... We are concerned here with symbols of this latter kind and with behaviour to which a meaning is attached when it occurs in a specific setting. In both these kinds of strictly non-verbal communication we are dealing with messages which are not para-linguistic, but proto-linguistic. **1975** M. Critchley in E. H. & E. Lenneberg *Foundations Lang. Devel.* I. I. 6 One point must..be kept well to the fore when ruminating upon this topic of protolinguistics. From an anatomic, physiological angle, speech is a parasitic function. **1976** R. W. Wescott in *Ann. N.Y. Acad. Sci.* CCLXXX. 104 As used here, the term 'protolinguistics' will mean the analytic and comparative study of protolanguages. *Ibid.* 115 Some protolinguistic problems, finally, are due almost exclusively to lack of information. **1978** *Sci. Amer.* Apr. 104/3 If, as I suppose, the hominids under observation communicated only as chimpanzees do or perhaps by means of very rudimentary protolinguistic signals, then the observer might feel he was witnessing the activities of some kind of fascinating bi-pedal ape.

proto-literate, -lith: see *proto- 1, 2b.

protoli·thic, *a. Archæol.* [f. Proto- + Gr. λίθος stone, after *neolithic*, etc.] **1.** A term introduced by the American ethnologist W. J. McGee to designate a type of primitive stone implements formerly in use amongst the Seri Indians of eastern Mexico (see quots.).

1897 *Amer. Anthropologist* X. 326 In this stage of development (called *protolithic* after McGee) stone implements come into more or less extended use in connection with implements of shell, tooth, etc. **1898** W. J. McGee in *17th Ann. Rep. Bur. Amer. Ethnol. 1895–6* I. 295 None other so well represents protolithic culture.

2. Belonging to the earliest stone age: eolithic.

1931 *Antiquity* V. 518 In the new terminology three major divisions are recognised, the old Lower and Middle Palaeolithic being grouped together as 'Protolithic', the Upper Palaeolithic and Mesolithic as 'Miolithic', the 'Neolithic' continuing as usual though now including the old Aeneolithic. **1962** A. D. Krieger in Jennings & Norbeck *Prehist. Man in New World* 29 Menghin..employs six culture stages applied to both Old and New World, namely, (1) Protolithic (2) Epiprotolithic, (3) Miolithic, (4) Epimiolithic, (5) Neolithic, and (6) Chalcolithic. The first two are more or less equivalent to Lower Paleolithic as used by Old World archeologists... Menghin is careful to avoid any suggestion that such stages in the New World are of an age equal to those of the Old World; even his Protolithic in America may be no more than twenty thousand years old.

protolithionite: see *proto- 2b.

protologue (prōᵘ·tolǫg). *Taxonomy.* Also **protolog.** [f. Proto- + -logue.] The description and other details accompanying the first publication of the taxonomic name of a plant or animal.

1905 Schuchert & Buckman in *Science* 9 June 900/1 For the sake of accuracy we suggest that the original description by words (type-description) be called the protolog. **1939** *Jrnl. Bot.* LXXVII. 206 A 'protologue' is the printed matter (description etc.) accompanying the original publication of a name or epithet. **1957** W. T. Stearn *Linnaeus's Species Plantarum* xiii. 126 For each Linnaean species all the constituent elements in Linnaeus's protologue must be taken into consideration. **1970** *Watsonia* VIII. 43 The entire protologue reads as follows.

protology. Restrict †*Obs. rare*—⁰ to sense in Dict. and add: **2.** (protǫ·lŏdʒi). The study of or enquiry into origins. Hence **protolo·gical** *a.*, that pertains to what is original or primitive.

1903 *21st Ann. Rep. Bur. Amer. Ethnol. 1899–1900* 138 In the quaint protology, or science of first things, of the Iroquois things are derived from things through transformation and evolution. **1937** *Proc. Prehist. Soc.* III. 188 When man began to control his environment to a greater extent, 'things' became for him imbued with 'force', and in this way arose the magical and protological conception of the world. **1974** *Archiv für Rechts- und Sozialphilosophie* LX. 385 We have found that the learning of basic logical principles and methods via protological calculus has also a didactic advantage. **1977** M. Goulder in J. Hick *Myth of God Incarnate* iv. 75 In place of the primitive eschatology, the stress would now fall on protology.

protolytic (-li·tik), *a. Chem.* [f. Proto(n in Dict. and Suppl. + *-lytic.] Applied to a reaction or process in solution which consists in the transfer of a proton from one molecule to another, one of the molecules usu. being of the solvent; also applied to the solvent itself. Also **proto·lysis**, a protolytic reaction; proton transfer in solution.

1931 N. F. Hall in *Chem. Rev.* VIII. 191 Acid-base or protolytic reaction may be defined by the general equation..A⇌B + ⊕ (acid⇌base + proton). **1934** *Chem. Abstr.* XXVIII. 5740 Acids and bases are designated [by J. N. Brønsted] 'protolyte' and their reaction 'protolysis'. **1959** I. M. Kolthoff in Kolthoff & Elving *Treat. Analytical Chem.* I. I. xi. 411 It is clear that a base can be of any charge type, its charge being one less positive than that of its conjugate acid, for example, $Al(OH)_2^+$, NH_3, HCO_3^-, CO_3^{-2}. Its reaction with an acid solvent is called a protolysis reaction and no distinction is made between a dissociation (NH_3 in water) and hydrolysis (cyanide in water). **1968** V. Gutmann *Coordination Chem. in Non-Aqueous Solutions* i. 6 Acids and bases are defined as proton donors and proton acceptors respectively and acidbase reactions are regarded as being due to proton transfer reactions (protolysis). **1969** T. R. Blackburn *Equilibrium* ii. 66 If a solvent is both appreciably acid and appreciably basic (as water is), it will have a measurable autoprotolysis constant. Such solvents are called protolytic.

‖**protoma** (prǫ·tŏma). Pl. **-æ, -as.** [mod.L., ad. Gr. προτομή Protome.] = Protome in Dict. and Suppl.

1931 *Antiquity* V. 330 Fragments of horns and ears of the stone protomas of the bulls forming the capitals. **1953** *Proc. Prehist. Soc.* XIX. 45 From Ghar Dalam there are two protomae of animals, in the same ware, and having a similar decoration to the pottery described above.

proto-Malay, -Marxian: see *proto- 2a, c.

protome. Delete *rare* and add: Now *spec.* the forepart of an animal represented decoratively, as in (ancient) sculpture.

1886 A. J. Evans in *Jrnl. Hellenic Stud.* VII. 14 The horse's head, or protomê, as is well known, is introduced generally in a sunken square. **1933** C. Seltman *Greek Coins* v. 60 The device of the foreparts of two lions facing one another. The son..replaced one of the half-lions by the forepart of a bull, and at first the two *protomes* were back to back. **1942** *Antiquity* XVI. 356 But there is one motive, the bull's protome, that does seem really distinctive of the Halaf style. **1972** *Scripta Hierosolymitana* XXIV. 41 A Greek artist conceived the strange idea of..combining two traditional elements..by uniting a lion *protome* with a swinging handle. **1978** W. A. P. Childs *City-Reliefs of Lycia* 13 The lintel was decorated with four winged bull-protomes.

proto-Medic: see *proto- 2a.

protomer (prōᵘ·tŏməɹ). [ult. f. Gr. πρῶτος first + *-mer.] **1.** *Chem.* [f. Proto(n or *proto(tropy.] Any prototropic tautomer.

1923 [see *prototropy]. **1968** *Jrnl. Amer. Chem. Soc.* XC. 1575/2 Analysis of the protomer stabilities in terms of relative chemical binding energies is risky. **1979** C. Roussel et al. in J. V. Metzger *Thiazole & its Derivatives* II. vii. 379 Protic solvents stabilize more the form giving the stronger hydrogen bond: so the mercapto protomer..should become apparent in the ultraviolet spectra recorded in ethanol.

2. *Biochem.* [f. Prot(ein.] Any of the protein subunits of which an oligomeric protein is built up.

1965 J. Monod et al. in *Jrnl. Molecular Biol.* XII. 89 The identical subunits associated within an oligomeric protein are designated as protomers. *Ibid.* 106 Within oligomeric proteins the protomers are in general linked by a multiplicity of non-covalent bonds, conferring both specificity and stability on the association. **1970** *Nature* 28 Nov. 828/1 By definition a protomer constitutes one primitive cell. **1980** *Biophysical Chem.* XI. 49/1 The treatment has been extended to include aggregated structures containing from two to five protomers, thus encompassing almost the whole spectrum of oligomeric proteins likely to be encountered.

Hence **protome·ric** *a.*

1923 *Jrnl. Chem. Soc.* CXXIII. 828 The two forms of the ion are tautomeric..; but they yield protomeric hydrides, and isomeric derivatives with radicles such as methyl and ethyl. **1968** *Jrnl. Amer. Chem. Soc.* XC. 1575/1 In the cases of the heteroaromatic isomers, the protomeric equilibrium has been..found to favor the amide in solution. **1974** *Nature* 24 May 316/1 The accumulation of data on the protomeric units of several synthetases. **1979** R. Barone et al. in J. V. Metzger *Thiazole & its Derivatives* II. vi. 20 When the electronegativity of the substituent borne by the amino group increases, the protomeric equilibrium is expected to be shifted towards the imino structure.

protomerite: see *proto- 2b. **protomusic:** *proto- 1.

proton. Add: **2.** *Physics.* A stable sub-atomic particle which has a positive charge numerically equal to that of the electron, forms a part (or in the commonest isotope of hydrogen the whole) of all atomic nuclei, and is a baryon with a mass of 938·3 MeV (1836 times that of the electron), spin of ½, and isospin of ½; it is now usu. regarded as a particular state of a nucleon. [Perh. suggested by, if not derived from, the name of William *Prout* (1785–1850), English chemist and physician, who suggested that hydrogen was a constituent of all the elements.]

1920 *Engineering* 17 Sept. 382/3 Sir Ernest [Rutherford], replying, said that..a clear nomenclature was certainly wanted; the term 'prouton' for [*read* or] 'proton' might be suitable for the H nucleus. **1922** J. Mills *Within Atom* ii. 13 The hydrogen atom is composed of only one proton and one electron. **1926** *Nature* 9 Oct. 526/2 Recourse was had to passing fairly large amounts of hydrogen—up to one litre—through heated palladium, in the hope that at the moment of exit a fraction of the protons and electrons would combine to form the helium nucleus. **1942** J. D. Stranathan *'Particles' Mod. Physics* xi. 416 By firing alpha particles through a cloud chamber filled with nitrogen, it has been possible to photograph the track of the proton leaving the nitrogen nucleus. **1955** *Sci. News Let.* 10 Sept. 170/1 The number of protons in the nucleus determines the kind of matter the atom forms, whether hydrogen, uranium, iron, carbon or any other. **1962** H. D. Bush *Atomic & Nucl. Physics* iii. 62 Isotopes will occur where atomic nuclei have the same number of protons but differing numbers of neutrons. **1968, 1972** [see *NEUTRON]. **1979** *Nature* 7 June 483/2 A novel prediction of many such grand unified models is that baryon number is not absolutely conserved; so the proton may actually decay!

3. Special Comb. (all for sense *2): **proton accelerator,** a particle accelerator designed to acclerate protons; **proton acceptor, donor,** a substance or species which is able to accept protons from, or give them up to, a substrate; also *proton donator*; so *proton-accepting, -donating* ppl. adjs.; **proton gradiometer,** a rod with a proton magnetometer at each end, which may be stood on the ground in a vertical position to measure local variations in field strength at ground level due to features just below the surface; **proton magnetometer,** a magnetometer in which the magnetic field strength is determined from the frequency of the voltage induced by the precession of protons in hydrogen atoms (e.g. in water) following the removal of a stronger magnetic field applied to orient the protons; **proton-precession magnetometer** = prec.; **proton synchrotron,** a synchrotron designed to accelerate protons.

1947 Proton accelerator [see *BEVATRON]. **1961** LIVINGSTON & BLEWETT *Particle Accelerators* xiii. 438 The synchrocyclotron, which has been so successful as a proton accelerator in the 100- to 700-Mev range, requires a solid-core magnet. **1969** *Times* 5 Feb. 13/6 Four new particles of matter have been discovered in two independent experiments using the proton accelerators at Brookhaven..and at the European Nuclear Research Centre. **1925** *Jrnl. Chem. Soc.* CXXVII. I. 1383 All prototropic changes appear to involve..(i) the removal of a proton from one part of a molecule to some outside basic or proton-accepting component of the system, and (ii) the addition to another part of the molecule of a proton..from some acidic or proton-donating component of the system. **1966** GUCKER & SEIFERT *Physical Chem.* xix. 537 Many a neutral molecule is amphiprotic because it has an ionizable proton and a proton-accepting oxygen or nitrogen atom. **1925** *Jrnl. Chem. Soc.* CXXVII. I. 1378 We..regard the acid as a proton donator and the base as a proton acceptor. **1940** GLASSTONE *Text-bk. Physical Chem.* xii. 958 It is unlikely that free protons exist to any extent in solution, and so the acidic or basic functions of any species cannot become manifest unless the solvent molecules are themselves able to act as proton acceptors or donors, respectively: that is to say, the medium itself must have basic or acidic properties. **1953** L. C. JACKSON tr. *Ketelaar's Chem. Constitution* 85 A base, according to Brönsted, is a proton-acceptor just as an acid is a proton-donor. **1973** A. W. ADAMSON *Textbk. Physical Chem.* xii. 544 NH_3 is a much better proton acceptor than is H_2O. **1925** Proton-donating, donator [see *proton-accepting, acceptor* above]. **1940, 1953** Proton donor [see *proton acceptor* above]. **1977** HELMPRECHT & FRIEDMAN *Basic Chem.* vii. 149, H_2SO_4 is a more effective proton donor and a stronger acid than HSO_4^-. **1960** M. J. AITKEN in *Archaeometry* III. 38 Previous articles..have described the use of the proton *magnetometer* for archaeological prospecting. The proton *gradiometer* is a development which not only has advantages in operation, but is also less complex and therefore cheaper to construct. *Ibid.* 39 With the two-bottle system of the proton gradiometer all these large-scale effects are avoided for they affect both bottles equally. **1970** *Oxf. Univ. Gaz.* C. Suppl. VI. 25 Comparative surveys using proton gradiometer, pulsed magnetic induction, and soil conductivity meter. **1959** Proton magnetometer [see *EYE *sb.*[1] 3 g]. **1961** *Antiquaries' Jrnl.* XLI. 44 In an attempt to locate these burials..a survey with proton magnetometer followed by selective excavation was organized. **1975** *New Yorker* 12 May 58/3 With a proton magnetometer, the geologists began aeromagnetic surveys to develop a general view of the region's geological structure. **1976** W. M. TELFORD et al. *Appl. Geophysics* iii. 136 The important advantages of the proton magnetometer are that it measures absolute field strength and that its sensitivity (~1γ) is higher than any of the instruments considered so far. The fact that it requires no orientation or levelling makes it very attractive for marine and even more for airborne operations. **1958** *Jrnl. Geophysical Res.* LX. 880 The proton-precession magnetometer has been successfully adapted..for measuring the horizontal and vertical components of the earth's magnetic field. **1971** I. G. GASS et al. *Understanding Earth* xvi. 236/1 Fluxgate and proton-precession magnetometers were developed to measure magnetic fields to one part in 10^5. **1947** *Proc. Physical Soc.* LIX. 677 (*heading*) Theory of the proton synchrotron. **1966** *Daily Tel.* 25 Nov. 26/3 Nimrod, a proton-synchrotron, is essentially a circular racetrack, round which bursts of sub-atomic particles are repeatedly accelerated until they approach the speed of light. **1975** *McGraw-Hill Yearbk. Sci. & Technol.* 208/2 The collision of protons of energy 28 GeV from the CERN proton synchrotron with a metal target yielded..charged pions and kaons.

protonate (prōu·tǫnēit), *v. Chem.* [f. PROTON in Dict. and Suppl. + -ATE[3].] **a.** *trans.* To transfer a proton to (a molecule, group, atom, etc.), a co-ordinate bond being formed to the proton. **b.** *intr.* To receive a proton in this way. So **pro·tonated** *ppl. a.*, having received a proton; bonded to an additional proton; **pro·tonating** *vbl. sb.*

As used by Pitzer (quot. 1945), *protonated* had a slightly different, more restricted sense, being applied to the two bonds (each with a bridging hydrogen atom) which link the boron atoms in the electron-deficient compound diborane, B_2H_6.

1945 K. S. PITZER in *Jrnl. Amer. Chem. Soc.* LXVII. 1127/1 Let us call it a proton containing double bond or, shorter, a protonated double bond. **1951** *Jrnl. Amer. Chem. Soc.* LXXIII. 3647/2 With the carbinols..the fact that one *p*-amino grouping was never protonated is consistent with the view that only one of the rings is involved in resonance interactions. **1958** *Ibid.* LXXX. 3715/1 Compounds such as tri-*p*-aminophenylmethanol..when dissolved in sulfuric acid form stable carbonium ions in spite of the strong electron-withdrawing groups present in the form of protonated amino substituents. **1966** SMITH & CRISTOL *Org. Chem.* xlii. 795 Pyrrole..does protonate in the presence of very strong acids with the destruction of the aromatic sextet. **1969** T. R. BLACKBURN *Equilibrium* ii. 66 Any acid stronger than the hydronium ion will simply protonate water molecules to produce an equal quantity of H_3O^+. **1972** COTTON & WILKINSON *Adv. Inorg. Chem.* (ed. 3) v. 176 Even protonated carbonic acid, or more properly, the trihydroxycarbonium ion, $C(OH)_3^+$..has been observed in solutions of carbonates or bicarbonates in $FSO_3H\text{–}SbF_5\text{–}SO_2$ solutions at −78°. *Ibid.* 182 Fluorosulfuric is one of the strongest of pure liquid acids. It is commonly used in presence of SbF_5 as a protonating system. **1975** *Nature* 30 Oct. 823/2 Calculations..show that this spectral shift can be associated with the formation of the protonated $C{=}N^+$ bond.

protonation (prōutǫnēi·ʃən). *Chem.* [f. prec. + -ION.] The action or result of protonating.

1948 *Jrnl. Biol. Chem.* CLXXV. 249 The effectiveness of the positively charged ammonium group in preventing appreciable protonation of the carboxyl group of the L-leucine cation in 100 per cent sulfuric acid can be appreciated when it is remembered that both acetic acid and monochloracetic acid are completely ionized in this solvent. **1958** *Jrnl. Amer. Chem. Soc.* LXXX. 3715/1 If one of the benzene rings in diphenyl- or triphenylmethanol is replaced by a pyridine ring, protonation of the nitrogen atom would be expected to decrease the stability of the carbonium ion produced in sulfuric acid. **1970** *Nature* 25 July 370/1 The double helix denatures abruptly at both low and high *p*H because of protonation of amine groups near *p*H 3 and ionization of hydroxyl groups near *p*H 11·5. **1976** *Sci. Amer.* June 43/3 The release and uptake of protons by intact cells was clearly different from the change in protonation observed during the photoreaction of isolated purple membrane.

† **protone** (prōu·tōun). *Biochem. Obs.* [ad. G. *proton* (A. Kossel 1898, in *Zeitschr. f. physiol. Chem.* XXV. 174), f. *pro(tamin* PROTAMINE + *pep)ton* PEPTONE.] Any of various peptone-like substances produced as the primary products of hydrolysis of protamines.

1898 [see *HEXONE 1]. **1916** A. P. MATHEWS *Physiol. Chem.* iv. 136 It has been suggested by Taylor that the protamine, salmin, may be made up of these tri-peptides, or protones, united as follows. **1928** A. T. CAMERON *Textbk. Biochem.* viii. 115 According to Kossel protamines are hydrolysed first into protones which are compounds containing two radicals of arginine..united with one of alanine, or serine, or proline, or valine.

protonemal, *a.* (examples), **protonematal** *a.* (further examples).

1875 BENNETT & DYER tr. *Sachs's Text-bk. Bot.* II. 318 These latter [leaves] then put forth protonemal filaments, which produce first of all a flat pro-embryo; and upon this finally new leaf-buds arise. **1938** G. M. SMITH *Cryptogamic Bot.* I. ii. 135 The protonematal initial develops into a green filament (the primary protonema), also differentiated into nodes and internodes. **1958** *Nature* 19 Apr. 1139/2 In the course of studies on protonematal regeneration and growth in the moss *Splachnum ampullaceum* (L.) Hedw., the effect of gibberellic acid on the growth of the protonemata was also tested. **1969** F. E. ROUND *Introd. Lower Plants* viii. 101 The protonemal stage is..generally ignored in the description of liverworts.

proto-Neolithic to **-nephridium:** see *PROTO- 2 b.

protonic (protǫ·nik), *a.*[2] [f. PROTON in Dict. and Suppl. + -IC.] **a.** Of, pertaining to, or characteristic of, a proton or protons.

1929 A. N. WHITEHEAD *Process & Reality* 127 Each proton is a society of protonic occasions. **1932** E. MOLLOY *Compl. Wireless* 113/1 If..an atom happens to lose one or more of its planetary electrons..some of the protons become unbalanced, and there is a surplus of protonic force. **1953** R. B. BRAITHWAITE *Scientific Explanation* 93 Hydrogen atoms behave..as if they were solar systems each with an electronic planet revolving round a protonic sun. **1961** G. R. CHOPPIN *Exper. Nuclear Chem.* i. 1 The existence of nuclei means, therefore, that there must also be another force present which is strong enough to counterbalance the protonic repulsion and hold the nucleons together. **1976** *Nature* 23 Sept. 298/2 It is important at each step to vary the *p*H of the aqueous buffered component to keep the protonic activity of the solvent constant.

b. *Chem.* Of an acid, solvent, etc.: possessing a proton which can be used in protonation. Of a hydrogen atom in a molecule: available for use in protonation; possessing some positive charge.

1951 *Jrnl. Polymer Sci.* VI. 518 If we use this value for both the methyl and butyl salts in the protonic solvents, we obtain the *B* values given in..Table VIII. **1953** AUDRIETH & KLEINBERG *Non-Aqueous Solvents* ii. 28 Why should not any protonic solvent, capable of undergoing limited self-ionization into hydrogen ion and some base-analog ion, serve as a parent substance of a system of acids, bases, and salts? **1966** PHILLIPS & WILLIAMS *Inorg. Chem.* II. xxxiii. 563 Organometallic compounds undergo typical reactions with compounds which contain protonic hydrogen, i.e. which act as acids towards them... Of these reactions, hydrolysis is one of the most important. **1968** [see *HYDRIDIC *a.*]. **1969** T. C. WADDINGTON *Non-Aqueous Solvents* i. 8 In terms of Brønsted-Lowry or protonic acids, the strongest acid in a solvent is the protonated form of that solvent and the strongest base the deprotonated form.

Hence **proto·nically** *adv.*

1979 *Science* 7 Dec. 1157/2 The semifluid bimolecular lipid membrane and the plug-through complexes form a condensed, continuous nonaqueous (protonically insulating) sheet that acts as the osmotic barrier and separates the aqueous proton conductors on either side.

proto-Nile: see *PROTO- 2 a.

protonmotive (prōu:tǫnmōu·tiv), *a. Physics* and *Biochem.* Also **proton motive.** [f. PROTON in Dict. and Suppl. + MOTIVE *a.*] Of, pertaining to, or characterized by the movement of protons in response to an electric potential gradient; *protonmotive force*: a force analogous to the electromotive force, which acts on the proton gradient across cell membranes and comprises the sum of the electric potential difference and the pH gradient across the membrane.

1966 P. MITCHELL in *Biol. Rev.* XLI. 494 The operation of the proton-translocating ATPase and o/r chain systems in an ion-tight membrane would create both a pH differential and a membrane potential, conveniently described together as a protonmotive force..by analogy with electromotive force. **1977** HALL & BAKER *Cell Membranes & Ion Transport* iv. 79 The energy derived from the proton gradient (the proton motive force) may be used to drive oxidative phosphorylation. **1978** *Nature* 7 Sept. 14/3 Bonner suggested that a modified protonmotive ubiquinone cycle satisfies the kinetics of cytochrome interactions. **1979** *Science* 7 Dec. 1153/3 The first protonmotive device conceived by man was the electromotive hydrogen-burning fuel cell, invented by William Grove in 1839. **1980** *Federation Proc.* XXXIX. 1706/1 According to Mitchell's chemiosmotic hypothesis, a protonmotive force..energizes the synthesis of ATP by a proton-translocating ATPase.

protonosphere (protǫ·nǒsfīəɪ). [f. as prec. + -O + SPHERE *sb.*] (See quot. 1960.)

1960 F. S. JOHNSON in *Jrnl. Geophysical Res.* LXV. 578/1 The name protonosphere is adopted here to describe the ionized medium above about 1800 km where protons are the principal ionized constituent, the name ionosphere being reserved for the lower region consisting of heavier atmospheric ions, such as atomic oxygen. **1973** *Q. Jrnl. R. Astr. Soc.* XIV. 197 Estimates of the flux of ionization into and out of the protonosphere. **1975** *Physics Bull.* July 338/3 (Advt.), There are vacancies for three Research Students, to commence in October 1975 and work for the degree of PhD... 2. Ionosphere and protonosphere by satellite radio transmissions.

Hence **pro:tonosphe·ric** *a.*

1971 *Radio Science* VI. 849/1 The observed fluxes must be lower limits to the total protonospheric fluxes, since H^+ ions may also be differing from the protonosphere and contributing to the *F*-region via charge exchange below 800 km. **1978** *Nature* 2 Feb. 428/1 Temporal changes of protonospheric content are indicative of the filling and draining of this region.

protonotary, prothonotary. Add: **5.** *Comb.* **prothonotary warbler,** an American warbler, *Protonotarius citrea,* of the family Parulidæ, distinguished by a deep yellow head and breast, green back, and blue-grey wings.

1783 J. LATHAM *Gen. Synopsis Birds* II. II. 494 Prothonotary W[arbler]... This inhabits Louisiana, where it has obtained the name of *Protonotaire.* **1811** A. WILSON *Amer. Ornithol.* III. 72 Prothonotary Warbler... They are abundant in the Mississippi and New Orleans territories, near the river. **1874** E. COUES *Birds of Northwest* 47 Prothonotary Warbler... This species..only reaches the lowermost Missouri. **1977** *Daily Tel.* 24 Jan. 10/4 Bird-watchers..already know what a prothonotary warbler is.

protonovelist, -ocean: see *PROTO- 1, 2 a.

protopathic, *a.* Add: **2.** *Neurology.* In the theory that there are two (or three) sets of nerves and sensory receptors supplying the skin, the epithet of the coarser and more primitive sensibility (involving pain and temperature) and of the parts of the nervous system on which it is based.

1905 H. HEAD et al. in *Brain* XXVIII. 106 The position of the point stimulated cannot be recognised and each stimulus causes a widespread radiating sensation... To this form of sensibility we propose to give the name 'protopathic'. **1912** J. G. MCKENDRICK *Princ. Physiol.* xiii. 224 If a sensory nerve to an area of skin is divided, sensibility may return if the ends unite. The sensations that return first have been termed protopathic, and depend on heat, cold, and pain spots. **1920** [see *EPICRITIC *a.*]. **1942** *Brain* LXV. 110 Head's protopathic and epicritic fibres..come to grief when they make contact with the hard facts of anatomy. **1951** W. L. JENKINS in S. S. Stevens *Handbk. Exper. Psychol.* xxx. 1172/1 Also abandoned for the lack of experimental confirmation are Head's proposal of a dual system of four epicritic and four protopathic skin senses [etc.]. **1958** *Ann. N.Y. Acad. Sci.* LXXIV. 30 Return of protopathic sensibility commences about six weeks following section of the sensory nerves and is completed within six months. **1974** M. & D. WEB-

STER *Compar. Vertebr. Morphol.* xii. 278 The often unmyelinated protopathic fibres..arise from small cell bodies in the dorsal root ganglia. **1977** *Lancet* 11 June 1271/2 Head, in his model of the protopathic and epicritic nervous system,..introduced the notion of processing of sensory input at the level of entry into the central nervous system.

protope·ctin. *Biochem.* [ad. G. *protopektin* (A. Tschirch-Bern 1907, in *Ber. d. Deut. Pharm. Ges.* XVII. 242): see PROTO- and PECTIN.] = PECTOSE.

1908 *Chem. Abstr.* II. 431 (*heading*) On pectin and protopectin. **1922** *Biochemical Jrnl.* XVI. 704 The soluble pectin probably develops from an insoluble pectic substance contained in the cell wall... This insoluble pectin corresponds to the protopectin of Fellenberg, and to the pectose of earlier investigators. **1951** Z. I. KERTESZ *Pectic Substances* iii. 55 Protopectin is now believed by some to represent very large (and therefore water-insoluble) pectinic acid molecules. **1962** S. M. SIEGEL *Plant Cell Wall* i. 16 The constitutional differences between protopectin and the other pectic substances remain unclear. Empirically, the protopectins are distinguished by their insolubility, and, in general, by a higher molecular weight. **1973** J. J. DOESBURG in L. P. Miller *Phytochemistry* I. x. 272 In most plant tissues, the pectic substances are present in the form of water-insoluble protopectin. Ripe fruits are the main exceptions having a part present in soluble form, which is formed from protopectin during the ripening process. **1976** BELL & COOMBE tr. *Strasburger's Textbk. Bot.* (rev. ed.) 64 Protopectin can..be regarded as a cementing substance holding the cells of a tissue together.

Hence **protope·ctinase** [*-ASE] (see quots.).

1927 *Bot. Gaz.* LXXXIII. 331 Protopectinase.—The term applied to the enzyme which hydrolyzes or dissolves protopectin, with the resultant separation of the plant cells from each other, usually spoken of as maceration. *Ibid.* 338 Various strains of potatoes, of a wide range of mealiness, were used as test tissue for protopectinase activity, with the idea that the most mealy might have middle lamellae most easily hydrolyzed by the enzyme. **1951** Z. I. KERTESZ *Pectic Substances* xiv. 335 Until a few years ago it was believed that protopectinase is distinct from the enzyme which hydrolyzes the 1,4 glycosidic linkages in pectinic acids... However, there is now a growing tendency toward the view that the two enzymes (protopectinase and pectin-polygalacturonase) are identical. **1973** J. J. DOESBURG in L. P. Miller *Phytochemistry* I. x. 281 In the past a specific enzyme, protopectinase, was thought to produce soluble pectic material from protopectin... Since there is no adequate proof of the existence of such a specific enzyme..it is believed that the action of 'macerating' enzymes is exerted by one or more of the pectic enzymes mentioned hereafter.

protoperithecium to **-phenomenon:** see *PROTO- 2b.

protophi·lic, *a. Chem.* [f. PROTO(N in Dict. and Suppl. + *-PHILIC.] Of a solvent (or solute): having a tendency to remove a proton from most solutes (or solvents). Opp. *PROTOGENIC *a.*[2] Also **pro·tophile** (*rare*), such a substance.

1930 N. F. HALL in *Jrnl. Chem. Educ.* VII. 787 The terms *protophilia* and *hydrophilia* have been proposed to describe the tendency of a molecule to unite with proton, and it would seem that some such word as *protophile*, forbidding as it is, would arouse less prejudice than the term *base* used in such a broad and subversive manner. *Ibid.* 792 Next there is the basic strength, or protophilic tendency of the solvent. **1931, 1940** [see *PROTOGENIC *a.*[2]]. **1953** AUDRIETH & KLEINBERG *Non-Aqueous Solvents* ii. 33 Amphiprotic solvents occupy a position intermediate between those of marked protophylic [*sic*] character, such as ammonia and the amines, and those of distinct protophobic character, such as acetic and hydrogen fluoride. **1969** [see *PROTOGENIC *a.*[2]]. **1973** E. J. KING in Covington & Dickinson *Phys. Chem. Org. Solvent Syst.* iii. 334 Ethanolamine and dimethyl sulphoxide are basic or protophilic solvents.

protophloem, -phoneme: see *PROTO- 2b, 1.

pro·tophyll. *Bot.* [f. PROTO- + Gr. φύλλ-ον leaf.] In club-mosses, a structure resembling a leaf produced on the upper surface of the protocorm or tuber.

1891 F. O. BOWER in *Proc. R. Soc.* L. 267 The sporophyte [of *Phylloglossum*] consists of two parts:—(i) the protocorm, with its protophylls and roots, and (ii) the strobilus. **1902** *Encycl. Brit.* XXXII. 74/1 The plant [sc. *Phylloglossum*] is produced by tubers, which resemble the protocorm in bearing first a number of protophylls. **1938** G. M. SMITH *Cryptogamic Bot.* II. vii. 180 From the upper surface of the protocorm arise a few to many erect, conical outgrowths (protophylls) which are leaf-like in function. **1962** K. R. SPORNE *Morphol. Pteridophytes* iv. 64 Further protophylls appear in an irregular manner.

pro·toplanet. *Astr.* [f. PROTO- + PLANET *sb.*[1]] A large diffuse body of matter in a solar or stellar orbit, postulated as a preliminary stage in the evolution of a planet.

1949 *Astrophysical Jrnl.* CIX. 309 A simple model is therefore considered first, consisting of two spherical masses ('protoplanets') in near contact, located inside the gaseous disk surrounding the sun. **1952** H. C. UREY *Planets* i. 13 First, a spherical or irregular cloud must rapidly collapse to a flat disk... Second, the disk of gas would break up into a Kolmogoroff spectrum of turbulent eddies... Finally a system of protoplanets, one for each of the planets, would be left at the appropriate distance from the sun. **1971** I. G. GASS et al. *Understanding Earth* ix. 135/2 This conclusion suggests..that a considerable degree of fractionation had already taken place in the protoplanet before it condensed into a solid body. **1974** *Sci. Amer.* Mar. 57/3 The second compositional class would have consisted of protoplanets formed just after the metallic iron-nickel alloy condensed out of the solar nebula.

Hence **protopla·netary** *a.*, of, pertaining to, or being a protoplanet.

1962 *Lancet* 13 Jan. 89/1 Meteorites are generally assumed to have originated by the disruption of protoplanetary bodies in the region now occupied by the asteroids. **1977** *Nature* 13 Oct. 584/1 When the cloud collapses and a new hot star is created in its centre, the flattened protoplanetary disk formed from the remnants of the cloud continues to be cold.

protoplasm. Add: Before von Mohl coined the word in this sense it had been used (also in Ger.) with a slightly different meaning by J. E. Purkinje (*Uebersicht der Arbeiten und Veränderungen der schlesischen Ges. für vaterländische Kultur 1839* 82).

protoplasmal, *a.* (Example.)

1885 W. S. GILBERT *Mikado* 1. 7, I can trace my ancestry back to a protoplasmal primordial atomic globule.

protoplast[1]. Add: **2. b.** The living contents of a cell; *esp.* in recent usage, a living cell whose cell wall has been removed or destroyed.

1884 *Rep. Brit. Assoc. 1883* 536 When the protoplast is in its normal position lining the cell wall, this core of protoplasm filling the pore would offer great resistance to a bodily passage of the cell sap. **1895** *Jrnl. Microsc. Soc.* 563 For the protoplast of the Cyanophyceæ and Schizomycetes the author proposes the term *archiplast*. **1925** E. B. WILSON *Cell* (ed. 3) i. 22 Cytosome and nucleus taken together form a living unit or protoplasmic system that is often spoken of as the protoplast (Hanstein) or sometimes as the energid (Sachs). **1953** C. WEIBULL in *Jrnl. Bacteriol.* LXVI. 690/2 The spherical bodies obtained by lysis in sucrose will be designated as 'protoplasts'. **1970** AMBROSE & EASTY *Cell Biol.* viii. 271 The outer wall and capsule in many bacteria can be digested away by enzyme treatment leaving the protoplast, which is surrounded by a membrane still retaining the main permeability characteristics of the original bacterium.

protopod to **-Polynesian:** see *PROTO- 2b, 1, 2a.

protopo·rphyrin. *Chem.* [a. G. *protoporphyrin* (Fischer & Lindner 1925, in *Zeitschr. f. physiol. Chem.* CXLII. 147): see PROTO- and *PORPHYRIN.] Any of a group of fifteen isomeric porphyrins, $C_{34}H_{34}N_4O_4$, in which the porphin nucleus has four methyl, two vinyl, and two propionic acid substituents; one isomer (*protoporphyrin IX*) occurs widely in living organisms, notably as hæm (its ferrous chelate derivative).

1925 *Chem. Abstr.* XIX. 1714 The esters of ooporphyrin, Kämmerer's porphyrin, Papendieck's porphyrin and CO_2- and HCl-porphyrins are identical... The name 'proto-porphyrin' is proposed for all of these. **1937** *Jrnl. Biol. Chem.* CXVIII. 521 Probably the most important porphyrin in nature is protoporphyrin IX... There are fifteen possible isomers of this compound, but this one..is the only one so far demonstrated in nature. **1961** *Lancet* 26 Aug. 450/2 This man..produced no abnormal quantity of uroporphyrin but excessive amounts of protoporphyrin which were localised mainly within his circulating red cells. **1964** A. WHITE et al. *Princ. Biochem.* (ed. 3) xlii. 792 A common pathway exists for the synthesis of heme and of chlorophyll leading to formation of protoporphyrin IX... Insertion of iron into the latter results in heme formation. In plants, in addition to synthesis of heme, magnesium is inserted into protoporphyrin IX to form magnesium protoporphyrin, which is converted in plastids to chlorophyll. **1975** *Nature* 26 June 706/1 The prosthetic group of haemoglobin has a protoporphyrin structure (ferrohaem) in which the ion atom is ionically bound.

Hence **pro:toporphy·ria** *Med.*, the presence of protoporphyrin in the red blood cells.

1956 in *New Gould Med. Dict.* (ed. 2) 975/1. **1961** I. A. MAGNUS et al. in *Lancet* 26 Aug. 451/2 The absence of uroporphyrin clearly distinguishes this syndrome from congenital porphyria. It seems to be a hitherto undescribed erythropoietic condition for which we suggest the name 'erythropoietic protoporphyria'. **1975** *Sci. Amer.* July 73/1 Investigators can easily induce these typical symptoms without serious consequences in patients suffering from mild forms of erythropoietic protoporphyria, so that the disease is one of the few of its kind where the action spectrum for a direct effect of light has been studied in detail. **1977** *Proc. R. Soc. Med.* LXX. 572/2 Erythropoietic protoporphyria (EPP) is a disorder, usually of autosomal dominant inheritance, in which large amounts of protoporphyrin are found in erythrocytes.

protoproteose to **-solar:** see *PROTO- 1, 2a, b, c.

pro·tosome. *Genetics.* [f. PROTO- + *-SOME[4].] The larger of two particles which together were postulated to constitute a gene; cf. *EPISOME. (No longer current.)

1931, 1966 [see *EPISOME a].

pro·tostar. *Astr.* [f. PROTO- + STAR *sb.*[1]] A contracting mass of gas in which nucleosynthesis has not yet begun, representing an early stage in the formation of a star.

1954 H. ALFVÉN *Orig. Solar Syst.* xii. 188 This condensation may have taken place from a 'protostar' of the type considered by Spitzer and others. **1972** *Sci. Amer.* Aug. 49/3 It has been suggested that protostars are formed when some of the gas and dust associated with the spiral arms of the galaxy piles up into clouds. **1976** [see *OBSERVATIONALLY *adv.*]. **1977** J. NARLIKAR *Struct. Universe* ii. 27 Such a cloud contracts as a whole, but subsequently breaks up into smaller subunits or 'protostars' when instability develops in the system.

Also **protoste·llar** *a.*, of, pertaining to, or being a protostar or protostars.

1973 *Nature* 17 Aug. 425/1 Conditions are therefore appropriate for the formation of solid planets if the nature of the protostellar body is such that dispersal of the particulate matter does not take place soon after its formation. **1975** *Ibid.* 6 Feb. 393/2 The initially low metal abundance could radically alter both the cooling of the gas required for protostellar collapse and the mechanisms which limit the greatest mass which can condense into a star. **1976** *Astron. Jrnl.* LXXXI. 1092/2 There is..a cluster of protostellar objects..southwest of M17 at the apparent edge of fragment B.

protostele to **-syntax:** see *PROTO- 1, 2a, b.

protota·xic, *a. Psychol.* [f. PROTO- + TAX(IS + -IC.] Applied to a hypothetical first or basic stage of experiencing or receiving impressions; also, related to a primal type of experience. See also *PARATAXIC, *SYNTAXIC *adjs.*

1945 P. MULLAHY in *Psychiatry* VIII. 183/2 Prototaxic symbolization seems without reference to an ego, to 'I' or 'me' because the infant has no, or only a rudimentary, self. **1953** H. S. SULLIVAN *Interpersonal Theory of Psychiatry* (1955) ii. 28 These modes are: the prototaxic, the parataxic, and the syntaxic. I shall offer the thesis that these modes are primarily matters of 'inner' elaboration of events. *Ibid.* 29 The prototaxic mode, which seems to be the rough basis of memory, is the crudest..the earliest, and possibly the most abundant mode of experience. **1969** A. NEEL *Theories of Psychol.* xx. 247 The first stage he [*sc.* Sullivan] called the prototaxic. **1972** L. SALTZMAN in Freedman & Kaplan *Interpreting Personality* vi. 176 (*heading*) Prototaxic mode of experience. **1975** J. C. GOWAN *Trance, Art & Creativity* ii. 24 The prototaxic mode is notable for the scary, hair-raising aspect of the numinous.

proto-Thames to **-theme:** see *PROTO- 1, 2a, b.

protothetic (-þe·tik). *Logic.* [ad. G. *protothetik* (S. Leśniewski 1929, in *Fundamenta Math.* XIV. 4), f. Gr. πρωτο- PROTO- + θετικός fit for placing, positive, f. θετός, ppl. adj. of τιθέναι to set, place.] A type of propositional calculus on the basis of which Leśniewski developed his system of logic (see quots. 1945, 1955). Also **protothe·tics** *sb. pl.* in the same sense.

1940 *Jrnl. Symbolic Logic* V. 83 Protothetic involves not only propositional variables..but also truth-function variables. **1945** Z. JORDAN in *Polish Sci. & Learning* VI. 24/2 Lesniewski's system consists of three parts. The first of them, called Protothetic, corresponds to what is known as the 'calculus of equivalent statements'..or the 'theory of deduction', together with that of the apparent variable. It makes use of one axiom and of one logical constant only. **1946** [see *MEREOLOGY]. **1955** A. N. PRIOR *Formal Logic* III. iii. 293 The basis of Leśniewski's logic is the 'protothetic', i.e. propositional calculus enriched with functional variables and quantifiers,..and on this he builds two further disciplines called 'ontology' and 'mereology'. **1963** O. WOJTASIEWICZ tr. *Łukasiewicz's Elem. Math. Logic* iv. 92 The sentential calculus can be extended by the introduction of variable functors and what are called *quantifiers*. One such system, containing the sentential calculus, is S. Leśniewski's *protothetics*. **1974** *Jrnl. Philos. Logic* III. 231 The extended propositional calculus which serves as a basis for this theory is not full protothetic.

prototroch: see *PROTO- 2b.

prototroph (prōᵘ·totrōᵘf, -trǫf). *Genetics.* [f. as next.] A strain (usu. of bacteria or fungi) which can grow on the simplest medium necessary for the growth of its species, without supplementary nutrients.

1946 RYAN & LEDERBERG in *Proc. Nat. Acad. Sci.* XXXII. 172 We propose to designate as a prototroph any strain which has the nutritional requirements of the 'wild type' from which it was derived irrespective of how it became prototrophic. **1952** *Genetics* XXXVII. 720 The occurrence of prototrophs, thus selected, from platings of thoroughly investigated auxotroph parents has been taken as *prima facie* evidence of crossing. **1958** *Heredity* XII. 269 Bursts of white, prototrophic cells frequently arise from colonies of certain strains of red, adenine-requiring yeasts. The occurrence of prototrophs appears to result from back-mutation at the locus for adenine requirement. **1975** J. B. JENKINS *Genetics* viii. 311 Prototrophs are cells that can grow on minimal medium.

Hence **pro·totrophy**, the state of being a prototroph.

1952 *Genetics* XXXVII. 720 The methionineless stock is, fortunately, so stable that back mutations to prototrophy are undetectable under the conditions of crossing experiments. **1974** *Nature* 8 Feb. 387/1 *E. coli* strain H/r 30 R requiring arginine was used for measurement of mutation to prototrophy. **1975** *Ibid.* 26 June 736/2 It was impossible to grow the population for long periods without reversion to prototrophy.

prototrophic (-trōu·fik, -trǫ·fik), *a.* [f. Gr. πρωτο- (see PROTO-) + τροφ-ή nourishment + -IC.] **1.** *Bot.* [ad. G. *prototroph* (A. Fischer *Vorlesungen über Bakterien* (1897) v. 47).] = *autotrophic* adj. s.v. *AUTO-[1].

1900 A. C. JONES tr. *Fischer's Struct. Bacteria* v. 48 A better classification would be to divide the bacteria, according to their mode of life, into three biological groups, prototrophic, metatrophic, and paratrophic. *Ibid.*, Prototrophic species are those which either require no organic compounds at all for their nutrition (nitrifying bacterium), or which, given the smallest quantity of organic carbon, can derive all their nitrogen from the atmosphere (bacteria of root-nodules). With them may be classed..sulphur and iron bacteria. **1923** F. O. BOWER *Bot. Living Plant* (ed. 2) xxviii. 430 On the basis of nutrition Bacteria have been classified into three groups: (i) Prototrophic, those which require no organic compounds at all for their nutrition. These are represented by the nitrifying Bacteria which live in open nature, in the soil, and are never parasitic. (ii) Metatrophic... (iii) Paratrophic. **1940** *Nature* 26 Oct. 541/2 If virus was the first form of life, it ought to be possible to find prototrophic viruses which feed on inorganic materials.

2. *Genetics.* Being a prototroph.

1946 [see *PROTOTROPH]. **1952** *Genetics* XXXVII. 721 Prototrophic stereomycin-sensitive (S^s) stocks were crossed to S^r (streptomycin-resistant) auxotrophs by plating the parents on minimal-streptomycin agar. **1958** [see *PROTOTROPH]. **1978** *Nature* 29 June 753/2 When complementary auxotrophs of opposite mating type are conjugated and plated on minimal medium (MM), several types of prototrophic colonies grow up.

Hence **prototro·phically** *adv.*

1978 *Nature* 20 Apr. 731/1 These cells..now grow prototrophically at a reduced rate identical to that of the spermidine-deficient cells.

prototropy (protǫ·trŏpi, prōu·totrǫpi). *Chem.* [f. PROTO(N in Dict. and Suppl. + Gr. τροπή turn, turning.] Tautomerism in which the forms differ only in the position of a proton; migration of a proton from one part of a molecule to another.

1923 T. M. LOWRY in *Jrnl. Chem. Soc.* CXXIII. 828 Prototropy, or the reversible change of protomers, which differ from one another in the position of a proton or hydrogen nucleus. **1953** C. K. INGOLD *Structure & Mechanism in Org. Chem.* v. 219 Proton migration is considered always to depend on proton-transfer processes..and is of such outstanding importance, that it is usually designated by the special name prototropy. **1964** N. G. CLARK *Mod. Org. Chem.* xv. 296 The behaviour of ethyl acetoacetate is another example of the phenomenon of tautomerism, in particular of prototropy.

Hence **prototro·pic** *a.*, of, pertaining to, or exhibiting prototropy.

1925 *Jrnl. Chem. Soc.* CXXVII. 1382 Prototropic changes, which involve only the migration of a proton, are catalysed both by acids and by alkalis, like the hydrolysis of an ester. **1947** *Nature* 11 Jan. 68/1 Dislocation of α-hydrogen in glutamic acid can be interpreted as due to reversible condensation of the amino-group with the carbonyl in the prosthetic component of aminopherase to form a prototropic system. **1953** C. K. INGOLD *Structure & Mechanism in Org. Chem.* x. 579 When 2-hydroxypyridine, or α-pyridone, as it is usually named after its prototropic tautomer, is alkylated..the formed quaternary ammonium ion passes into its anhydro-base, the N- alkyl-α-pyridone. **1976** *Nature* 6 May 15/1 Ganellin showed that dynamic structure-activity relationships are capable of analysing quite complex situations, such as relative ionic populations in a prototropic equilibrium mixture.

prototype. Add: **b.** *spec.* That of which a model is a copy on a reduced scale.

1920 *Flight* 8 Jan. 57/2 Anyone can make a model resembling a full-size prototype that won't fly; this is not a scientific model. **1924** H. GREENLY *Model Railways* i. 6 *Tonnage coefficient* is the scale equivalent of the weight of a train or loco. in tons actual of the particular prototype. **1942** *Model Railway News* Jan. 24/2 Were the Americans to enter the British market (i.e. the market based on British prototypes) the story would..be different. **1955** E. A. STEEL *Model Mech. Engin.* i. 1 The working model must be an engineering job. A model locomotive is built to the scale of 1½ in. to the foot or one-eighth the size of a prototype of similar design. **1967** C. J. FREEZER *Model Railway Terminol.* No. 18. 2/2 On the prototype the gauge is always expressed in feet and inches, or metric measurements. In the model it can be similarly expressed, but..it is customary to use numbers or letters to describe the gauges. **1975** *Railway Modeller* Jan. 18/1 An hour or two beside a main line..can provide one with quite a collection of short trains suitable for modelling. A study of prototype railway magazines is another prolific source.

2. *Electr.* A basic filter network (usu. having series and shunt reactances in inverse proportion) with specified cut-off frequencies, from which other networks may be derived to obtain sharper cut-offs, constancy of characteristic impedance with frequency, etc. Freq. *attrib.*

1923 *Bell Syst. Technical Jrnl.* II. 28 Mid-series and mid-shunt sections derived from prototypes other than the 'constant-*k*' wave-filter..are other possible units. **1932** W. L. EVERITT *Communication Engin.* vii. 170 The fundamental data required for a filter are the pass band or, in the case of a low-pass filter, the cut-off frequency, and the impedance into which it is to work. From these data the prototype is computed. **1962** *Newnes Conc. Encycl. Electr. Engin.* 298/2, *m*-Derived Sections. These are 'derived' from the prototype sections above... The result is to introduce resonance into the shunt arm and/or antiresonance into the series arm,..so that the attenuation rises much more steeply. **1977** M. H. KLAYTON *Fund. Electr. Technol.* xviii. 578 This band-pass filter is another form of the constant-*k* prototype circuit. The same elements can be rearranged to form a constant-*k* prototype band-suppression filter, sometimes called a wave trap.

3. The first full-size working version of a new vehicle, machine, etc., or a preliminary one made in small numbers so that its performance and methods of mass-production can be evaluated. Freq. *attrib.*

1932 *Flight* 26 Feb. 170/1 The A.B. 20 was actually begun as a three-engined machine, like its prototype the D.B. 70. **1935** C. G. BURGE *Compl. Bk. Aviation* 261/1 The first experimental machine of a new type is usually made by a special department in the factory... This first or 'prototype' machine is, to a large extent, hand-made. **1939** *Flight* 28 Dec. 530*a*/1 Of these one or two, such as the Ha 138 flying boat, may have been put into production, but in the main the machines are 'prototype only'. **1948** J. S. MURPHY *Production Engin.* ii. 20 The previous model forms an ideal basis for the prototype, and experimental work can be carried out under practical conditions. **1948** 'N. SHUTE' *No Highway* i. 16 That was the prototype Reindeer, the one we had here for the trials. **1955** *Times* 10 Aug. 8/4 The American figures assumed the large-scale development 15 to 20 years hence of types of reactor now at the prototype stage. **1964** *Jrnl. Geophysical Res.* LXIX. 2399/1 The development of a prototype lunar transponder..demonstrates the feasibility of designing future transponders for hard landings on the moon. **1970** P. H. HILL *Sci. Engin. Design* iii. 47 When entering the experimental stage of the design process..one should first deal with the mock-up, then the model, and finally the prototype after the mock-up and model have proven the real worth of the design. **1978** *Daily Tel.* 7 Apr. 2/5 Three camels from Longleat Wildlife Park..were driven 80 miles to Reading..where the prototype of the camel-milking machine..had been set up.

prototypic, *a.* (Further examples.)

1926 *Physiol. Rev.* VI. 322 The author..advanced the view that the blood plasma of Vertebrates and Invertebrates with a closed circulatory system is..but a reproduction of the sea water of the remote geological period in which the prototypic representatives of such animal forms first made their appearance. **1963** A. FARRER in Mascall & Box *Blessed Virgin Mary* 28 A change which is prototypic of our own adoption, and the breaking of our bondage. **1965** LD. NORTHBOURNE tr. *Schuon's Light on Anc. Worlds* iv. 76 Semi-divine beings, the prototypic and normative personages whom earthly man has to imitate in all things. **1974** H. ASHLEY *Engin. Anal. of Flight Vehicles* i. 7 During the first decade of powered flight, 1903–1913, configuration was going through rapid, somewhat haphazard evolution. There were therefore many deviations from the prototypic arrangement outlined in Section 1.2, e.g., the Wright Flyers..employed antisymmetric warping of the wing structure for roll control.

prototypical, *a.* (Further examples.)

1964 GOULD & KOLB *Dict. Social Sci.* 257/1 Fads, unlike fashions, may occur even in simple societies which have merely prototypical class systems. **1967** D. COOPER *Psychiatry & Anti-Psychiatry* i. 19 In the popular mind the schizophrenic is the prototypical madman. **1978** J. SACKS in P. Moore *Man, Woman, & Priesthood* iii. 30 The claim of Korah was the prototypical denunciation of chosenness in the name of equality. **1979** *Amer. Speech 1978* LIII. 281 The prototypical instances of interruption are perhaps those in which the interrupting material is semantically connected to what is interrupted.

prototypically, *adv.* (Further example.)

1957 H. READ *Tenth Muse* xxx. 281 An attempt to find in architecture a new universal art..represented proto-typically by Greek architecture and later by Byzantine architecture.

prototyping (prōu·totəipiŋ), *vbl. sb.* [f. PROTOTYPE + -ING[1].] The design, construction, or use of a prototype. Freq. *attrib.*

1951 *Chem. Age* LXV. 833/1 Prototyping of machines, instruments, and of chemicals is an essential step in this development. *Ibid.* 833/2 Prototyping may also prove of value in the estimation of costs. **1965** *Economist* 13 Nov. 738/1 Means for using the accumulated facts are to be developed through such techniques as experimentation, prototyping, intervention and micromodelling. **1976** HILBURN & JULICH *Microcomputers/Microprocessors* i. 4 Most microprocessor manufacturers have development systems, sometimes called prototyping systems, available for the designer. **1977** *Sci. Amer.* Sept. 99/2 (Advt.), There's room for eight plug-in options such as a prototyping board for experimenting with interfaces to other equipment.

prototypographer to **-xylem:** see *PROTO- 1, 2 b.

protozoology. Add: (Further example.) Hence **pro:tozoolo·gical** *a.*, of or pertaining to protozoology; **protozoo·logist**, an expert or specialist in protozoology.

1906 *Nature* 29 Nov. 117/2 When the protozoologist has worked out his life-histories and obtained his results, then the medical man steps in and carries off the honey to the medical hive. **1922** *Daily Mail* 17 Nov. 1 (Advt.), Botanical, zoological and protozoological work. **1944** L. E. H. WHITBY *Med. Bacteriol.* (ed. 4) vii. 90 The most commonly used preparations in protozoological work are Leishman's stain and Siemsa's stain. **1956** *New Biol.* XXI. 88 Probably more is known of *E. histolytica* than of any other amoeba, and what is revealed is not only of practical importance to medical science but is of the greatest interest to protozoologists. **1971** *Daily Tel.* 18 June 25 (Advt.), A Protozoologist..is required to join a team responsible for the maintenance and supply of free living protozoa and to assist in the research programme of the Centre. **1972** *Nature* 3 Mar. 44/2 Most of his 500 publications deal with protozoological problems. **1974** *Ibid.* 3 May 89/3 In former times protozoology was considered to be a suitable subject by which students could be introduced to biology.

protracted, *ppl. a.* **1. a.** (Earlier and later examples of *protracted meeting.*)

1832 *Patriot & Farmer's Monitor* (Kingston, Ontario) 10 Apr. 2/6 It is now required of the Episcopal Methodist preachers, to make the public acquainted with their motives for establishing Protracted Meetings. **1925** W. J. BRYAN *Mem.* 17 A protracted meeting held in a Christian Church. **1948** *Chicago Tribune* 21 Nov. VII. 1/7 Loafers' Glory..acquired that name years ago when a protracted meeting was held in the little log schoolhouse.

protrichocyst: see *PRO-[2] 1.

protriptyline (protri·ptilīn). *Pharm.* Also (*erron.*) **protryptiline, protryptyline.** [f. PRO(PYL + TRI- + *he*)*ptyl* (s.v. HEPTANE) + -INE[5].] A tricyclic antidepressant, 5-(3-methylaminopropyl)dibenzo[*a, e*] cycloheptatriene, $C_{19}H_{21}N$, given as the hydrochloride, a white bitter-tasting powder.

1963 *Amer. Jrnl. Psychiatry* CXX. 594/1 In an attempt to evaluate a derivative of amitriptyline, MK-240 (protryptyline), where the 'sleepiness' was removed by a change in the chemical formula, the drug was studied in 61 patients with various types of depression. **1965** *Psychosomatics* VI. 346/1 Protriptyline is at least five times as active as amitriptyline against depressive reactions. **1966** *Canad. Med. Assoc. Jrnl.* XCIV. 1220/1 Protryptyline gave chemical results that compared favourably with those of antidepressants of established value. **1978** *Nature* 23 Mar. 330/1 The tricyclic antidepressant drugs which are tertiary amines..were more potent inhibitors than those which are secondary amines (desmethylimipramine, nortriptyline, protriptyline).

protrusively, *adv.* (Later example.)

1975 H. THOMSON *Occlusion* ix. 156 The whole procedure is repeated for the outgoing movements beginning at intercuspal position and moving laterally on each side and then protrusively.

protuberance. 2. b. (Earlier example.)

1869 *Jrnl. Franklin Inst.* LVII. 317 The first protuberance which I observed, is represented by Fig. 1. Above an intensely luminous peak-shaped mass, rising from the border of the sun, is spread a cloud-like formation.

protu·beranceless, *a.* [f. PROTUBERANCE + -LESS.] Without a protuberance; flat, regular.

1954 W. FAULKNER *Fable* 353 The entire earth one unbroken machined de-mountained dis-rivered expanse of concrete paving protuberanceless by tree or bush or house.

proud, *a.* (*sb., adv.*) Add: **I.** *adj.* **2.** (Further U.S. examples.)

1938 M. K. RAWLINGS *Yearling* viii. 69 Be proud things come so bountiful. *Ibid.* xv. 163 I'd be proud to eat breakfast before I go. **1949** H. HORNSBY *Lonesome Valley* xxiii. 302 I'm just as proud to see you..as if you was one of my own young 'uns! **1951** H. GILES *Harbin's Ridge* x. 99, I was sure proud Granny was there that day.

II. 7. d. (Later example.)

1970 *Country Life* 1 Oct. 856/1 Your case is the same as that of the farmer who sows his winter wheat too early; by the time the cold weather arrives the crop is 'proud'—too lush and forward.

9. (Further examples.)

1960 R. C. BELL *Board & Table Games* vii. 172 The inlay pieces..were fitted into them [*sc.* recesses], leaving an excess standing proud. **1971** P. AUDEMARS *Stolen like Magic Away* vi. 92 The exposed rails of the track..stand proud and quite high above the flints. **1974** *Good Motoring* July/Aug. 18/2 The horn push, sited right across the central spoke of the steering wheel, is well proud of the spoke and this gives rise to occasional, accidental blasts.

E. *Comb.* **a.** *proud-arsed, -crested* (later example), *-lidded, -necked, -plumed, -visaged.* **b.** *proud-arching, -fed, -pied* (later allusive example).

1919 A. HUXLEY in *Coterie* Sept. 61 The swan's proud-arching opulent loveliness. **1952** AUDEN *Nones* 56 When the proud-arsed broad-shouldered break and run. **1944** BLUNDEN *Shells by Stream* 57 And look, those birds with perfect ease, Proud-crested. **1929** —— *Near & Far* 37 A proud-fed but a puny rill. **1948** C. DAY LEWIS *Poems 1943–47* 88 Palpable calm, visible reticence, Proud-lidded water. **1934** T. S. ELIOT *Rock* ii. 75 Yet they walk in the street proudnecked, like thoroughbreds ready for races. **1912** C. MACKENZIE *Carnival* xlii. 373 When April pauses to survey her handiwork, assuming in the contemplation of the proud pied earth the warmth and maturity of midsummer. **1949** BLUNDEN *After Bombing* 9 With a sounding proud-plumed company By a glittering sea. **1844** J. R. LOWELL in *Graham's Mag.* July 15 Though these proud-visaged hopes, once turned to fly, Hurl backward many a deadly Parthian dart.

Proustian (prū·stiăn), *sb.* and *a.* [f. the name of Marcel *Proust*, French writer (1871–1922), + -IAN.] **A.** *sb.* An admirer or imitator of Proust.

1919 R. FRY *Let.* 28 Oct. (1972) II. 464 I've..got Proust's second volume... I forget whether you are a Proustian or not. **1928** *Sunday Express* 26 Feb. 5/2 If you desire to be a Jurgenist you must toil at Jurgenism as the Proustian toils at Proustery. **1936** A. HUXLEY *Eyeless in Gaza* xiv. 183 You're a Proustian, I take it? **1958** *Times* 6 Mar. 13/5 Proustians will be glad to have these 'moves on the chess-board of Time' in a volume that stimulates endless new ideas. **1973** *Listener* 2 Aug. 155/3 An ardent Proustian who was trying to persuade me to.. plunge into the full 12-volume *fleuve*.

B. *adj.* Of, pertaining to, or characteristic of Proust, his writings, or his style.

1926 A. HUXLEY *Jesting Pilate* I. 139 The decaying relics of feudalism..form the stormy background to the Proustian comedy. **1929** [see *IMITATION 5]. **1931** *Times Lit. Suppl.* 2 Apr. 274/2 The Proustian distinction between 'involuntary memory'..and 'voluntary memory'. **1936** L. P. SMITH *Reperusals & Re-Collections* ii. 23 An immense leisurely, true novel, written with a Tolstoyan or Proustian amplitude, which allows space for an immense copiousness of detail and for infinite digressions. **1943** J. LEES-MILNE *Ancestral Voices* (1975) 186 Lady Crewe believes no relationship, no emotion, no motive to be straightforward, and suspects everything and everyone. This is truly Proustian. **1958** *Spectator* 10 Jan. 51/1 Too often the adjective 'Proustian' evokes a kind of decadent Barsetshire. **1976** A. POWELL *Infants of Spring* viii. 123 A lack of interest for individuals in what might be called the Proustian sense was perhaps characteristic, too, of the whole of the Arts Society.

Hence **Prou·stery** *nonce-wd.*, a Proustian manner; **Proustia·na**, memorabilia of Proust.

1928 Proustery [see PROUSTIAN *sb.* above]. **1965** *Guardian* 20 Dec. 6/5 She invited me to her home to see her Proustiana. **1973** *Times* 4 Oct. 17/2 Considering the volume of Proustiana..it requires an artist's skill to pick out the white stones of this life and work.

prove, *v.* Add: **A. 2.** *pa. pple.* (Further examples of the form **proven.**) Now common in the U.S.

1916 *Nat. Real Estate Jrnl.* (U.S.) 15 Mar. 110/2 Time has proven the jurisdiction of our creation for we have advanced with a knowledge and better understanding of ourselves and our profession. **1927** E. O'NEILL *Marco Millions* II. i. 106, I believe that what can be proven cannot be true. **1931** C. KELLY *U.S. Postal Policy* iv. 81 How little he understood the will of the American people is proven by their unyielding demand for this service. **1934** *Dict. Amer. Biogr.* XIV. 531/1 He had already proven himself a bold operator in various speculative fields. **1943** W. ROUGHEAD *Art of Murder* 131 Our national nostrum, 'Not Proven'..a verdict which has been construed by the profane to mean 'Not Guilty, but don't do it again'. **1944** *Scots Mag.* Aug. 387 That his volume had a very large circulation for some generations is proven from a statement quoted by Stevenson. **1957** B. & C. EVANS *Dict. Contemp. Amer. Usage* 399/1 The participle *proven* is respectable literary English. In the United States it is used more often than the form *proved.* In Great Britain *proved* is used more often and *proven* sounds affected to many people. **1959** I. EPSTEIN *Judaism* xviii. 201 This doctrine of resurrection..cannot be proven philosophically. **1963** L. HUGHES in *Liberator* July 4/1 Savages have proven a point. **1971** *Sci. Amer.* July 5 (Advt.), The MGB's 1798 c.c. twin-carb engine is proven time and again in competition. **1976** *Brit. Jrnl. Sociol.* XXVII. 315 Many of its specific predictions have been proven wrong by the course of events over the last century. **1979** *Economist* 11 Aug. 74/1 If it means a form (or rather, forms) of involvement that seem profitable to employees and employers alike, both can be proven right. **1980** *Daily Tel.* 18 Mar. 15/3 As yet..chloracne is the only disorder proven to result from human contact with olioxin.

B. I. 1. a. (Further example.)

1881 'MARK TWAIN' *Prince & Pauper* xxv. 198 He seized Miles by the arm, dragged him to the window, and began to devour him from head to foot with his eyes.. stepping briskly around him and about him to prove him from all points of view.

d. For *Coal-mining* read *Mining* and add further examples.

1869 *Trans. N.Z. Inst.* II. 368 At Coromandel..the [gold-bearing] lodes have been 'proved' to a depth of over 300 feet from the surface. **1883** J. BRADSHAW *N.Z. as it was & Is* xii. 178 In the Coromandel and Thames goldfields, reefs have been 'proved' to a depth of over 600 feet below the sea level. **1978** *Nature* 6 Apr. p. xix/1 The Steeple Aston Borehole (1970–1971) proved Jurassic, Upper Coal Measures, Upper Devonian and igneous intrusive rocks. **1979** *Jrnl. R. Soc. Arts* Jan. 84/2 Figure 1 shows the extent of the coalfield under the land and also shows that about 10 kilometres of coal measures under the sea have been proven.

f. *Homœopathy.* [tr. G. *prüfen* (Hahnemann).] To give (a drug) to healthy persons to ascertain the symptoms it produces.

[**1833** C. H. DEVRIENT tr. *Hahnemann's Organon of Healing Art* 216 Employ those medicines whose pure effects have been proved upon a healthy person in the manner best suited to the cure of diseases homœopathically.] **1843** *Brit. Jrnl. Homœopathy* I. 160 It is essential that a preparation precisely similar to that proved should be always employed. **1910** *Encycl. Brit.* XIII. 645/2 To ascertain the curative virtues of any drug it must be 'proved' upon healthy persons—that is, taken by healthy individuals of both sexes in a state of health in gradually increasing doses. **1974** *Homoeopathy* June/July 93, I got Nelsons to potentise fulmar oil, and I wanted it proved, but no one would cooperate.

g. *intr.* Of dough: to become aerated by the fermentation of yeast prior to baking; to rise. Also of yeast: to cause such aeration.

1854 C. TOMLINSON *Cycl. Useful Arts* I. 181/1 The whole of the flour is..left about an hour..to *prove.* **1854** A. E. BAKER *Gloss. Northamptonshire Words & Phrases* II. 139 In making a cake, if it rises well, 'it *proves* well'. A baker will often say 'It is good yeast, it *proves* so well'. **1909** MRS. BEETON *Cookery Bk.* (new ed.) 265/2 Knead well, and leave dry, cover over with a clean cloth, and let it prove for 1½ hours. **1911** JACK & STRAUSS *Woman's Bk.* 214/2 After shaping the loaves, place them on a baking-sheet..and set them to prove for fifteen or twenty minutes. **1923** W. G. R. FRANCILLON *Good Cookery* (ed. 2) xxi. 386 *Currant loaf*...Set to prove. Then bake in a quick oven for about fifteen minutes. **1959** *Woman* 14 Mar. 21/1 Put the dough to rise and prove in a warm but not too hot place. **1972** *Guardian* 30 June 11/3 Form the dough into a ball... Cover with a clean cloth and stand in a warm place to prove.

II. 7. c. *refl.* To evince proof of one's abilities or prowess.

1961 *She* Mar. 38 But no one could help him, in his agonising struggle to save them—and prove himself. **1964** *Harper's Mag.* Dec. 95/1 A third such student, Caesar, came from a Latin-American country where a man is expected to prove himself by having many affairs, and a mistress after marriage. **1973** *Times* 1 Dec. 13/6 You have to prove yourself to your father, don't you?

8. d. *to prove too much*, to pursue an argument too far; to establish by argument a proposition so inclusive as to yield unhelpful results.

1791 J. MACKINTOSH *Vindiciæ Gallicæ* iv. 215 To this I answer, *first*, that such reasoning will prove too much, and that, taken in its proper extent, it impeaches the great system of morals, of which political principles form only a part. **1801** T. JEFFERSON *Let.* 9 Sept. in Koch & Peden *Life T. Jefferson* (1944) 565 It may be objected that this proves too much, as it proves you cannot enter the ship of a friend to search for contraband of war. **1870** J. H. NEWMAN *Gram. of Assent* vi. 153 The theory to which I have referred cannot be carried out in practice. It may be rightly said to prove too much. **1893** 'L. CARROLL' *Sylvie & Bruno Concluded* iii. 41 But surely that involves the logical fallacy of *proving too much?*

12. a. For *U.S.* read *N. Amer.* and add earlier and later examples.

1867 A. D. RICHARDSON *Beyond Mississippi* xi. 138 He does not see the land again until ready to 'prove up' which he may do after thirty days. Then he revisits his claim. **1878** J. H. BEADLE *Western Wilds* ii. 43 My wife proved up on her Cherokee blood. **1921** *Daily Colonist* (Victoria, B.C.) 11 Mar. 12/5 Proved up, with hard work, a wild and forest covered homestead. **1958** J. G. MACGREGOR *North-West of 16* v. 67 They also had to bring fifteen acres under cultivation and to erect some sort of abode. (Carrying out these obligations and getting title to the land was termed 'proving up'.) **1963** G. H. THOMSON *Crocus Country* xix. 124 The homesteaders, however, were obliged to fence so many acres before they could 'prove up' or be given the patent to their land. **1969** *Islander* (Victoria, B.C.) 16 Nov. 12/2 Mr. James Foulds, widower, proved up on his homestead..in 1910 or thereabouts. **1977** *New Yorker* 11 July 37/2 He tried to educate people in the responsibilities of living on public estate, so they could stay within the rules, legalize their occupancy, prove up.

b. = sense 1 d. Also *absol.* orig. *N. Amer.*

1921 *Daily Colonist* (Victoria, B.C.) 13 Oct. 2/4 Several claims staked up and down the channel from the discovery have proved up in a similar manner. **1926** *Ibid.* 17 Jan. 35/5 The richest mineralization that has been proved up in the whole district. **1975** *Offshore* Aug. 87/2 The company is aiming to prove up about 20 trillion cubic feet of the fuel to justify an initial transmission line to southern markets. **1977** *Bulletin* (Sydney) 22 Jan. 42/1 It frequently takes as much as 10 to 12 years from an initial discovery to prove up a viable mine, arrange finance and forward sales-contracts.

13. prove out, to establish (something) as correct or workable; to test (a system or process) exhaustively. Also *intr.* for *refl.* orig. *U.S.*

1959 *Wall St. Jrnl.* 13 May 14/2 Fishermen are pondering the commercial possibilities of pollock... If pollock proves out, the trawlers could stay closer to U.S. shores. **1964** D. F. GALOUYE *Counterfeit World* xii. 98 Of all the metaphysical concepts..mine was the only one open to final verification. It could be proved out conclusively. **1967** *Electronics* 6 Mar. 28 (Advt.), We'll run a sufficient number of samples to prove out the process. **1969** *Daily Mail* 15 Jan. 5/7 The Moon is a convenient body on which to prove out our systems and programmes. **1972** *Daily Tel.* (Colour Suppl.) 10 Nov. 10/1 A duration of 50 to 60 hours was required really to prove out the plane. **1976** N. THORNBURG *Cutter & Bone* iv. 102 If your hundred-to-one chance proves out, and Wolfe actually is the one.

proved, *ppl. a.* Add: **2.** (Further examples.)

1941 A. TARSKI *Introd. Logic* I. vi. 118 Statements established in this way are called *proved statements* or *theorems.* **1965** B. MATES *Elem. Logic* vi. 97 We may wish to use previously proved theorems.

proven, *ppl. a.* Add: **1.** (Later examples.) In some uses passing into sense 2 ('tested, approved, shown to be successful').

1963 *Automobile Engineer* LIII. 231/1 One..well known manufacturer is experimenting with an automatic stepped ratio transmission based upon proven principles. **1964** *Archivum Linguisticum* XVI. 125 A few relatively recent histories of the language..continue to repeat seemingly contradictory, debatable and even erroneous statements on this subject as if they were proven facts. **1968** *Globe & Mail* (Toronto) 17 Feb. B6 (Advt.), We seek an ambitious, mature university graduate possessing a proven sales background preferably in pharmaceutical sales. **1975** *Daily Tel.* 27 Nov. 29/1 (Advt.), Applicants should possess..a proven success record within a national consumer goods environment. **1976** *Sunday Times* 8 Feb. 66/3 (Advt.), The ideal candidate will above all have a proven profitable track record as a manager. **1977** T. M. BERNSTEIN *Dos, Don'ts & Maybes of Eng. Usage* 181 The form *proven* is used as an attributive adjective..and particularly in certain technical locutions, such as 'a *proven* oil field'.

2. Also (of a person, etc.) in wider use.

1942 W. FAULKNER *Go down, Moses* 144 Boon and the negroes..ran the coons and cats, because the proven hunters..scorned such other than shooting..to test their marksmanship. **1961** *Sunday Express* 8 Oct. 30 Game little *Angazi* is a proven mudlark. **1968** *Globe & Mail* (Toronto) 17 Feb. B6 (Advt.), An outstanding opportunity exists for a proven manager to join a new management team.

provenance. Add: **a.** (Earlier example.)

1785 E. SHERIDAN *Jrnl.* (1960) 61 Miss Anstruther as I before mention'd Elegant, fashionable in her appearance, but nothing of that *provenance* in her manner that caught me so much in Miss Brook.

b. The history or pedigree of a work of art, manuscript, rare book, etc.; *concr.*, a record of the ultimate derivation and passage of an item through its various owners.

A distinction is often drawn between the 'origin' and the 'provenance' of an article, as in quot. 1960.

1926 J. BUCHAN *Dancing Floor* I. vi. 111 If I knew the provenance of the manuscript, I might be able to understand it better. **1946** 'M. INNES' *From London Far* ii. x. 146 That aspect of the history of art which collectors call provenance? Who owned the picture last..and who before that. The ideal is to trace it right back to the studio. **1947** A. CHRISTIE *Labours of Hercules* xi. 220 Sir Reuben would have purchased a Renaissance goblet, *provenance* unspecified. **1960** E. A. LOWE *Eng. Uncial* 21 A Canterbury origin is probable, Canterbury provenance is certain. **1966** *Listener* 10 Feb. 207/1 At gallery number three on Madison Avenue I was introduced to a man who asked if I had a *provenance* or any sort of papers for the picture. **1967** J. N. BARRON *Lang. Painting* 156 *Provenance*, a history or pedigree of a painting: the establishment of the identity of successive owners since its execution. Also included would be all published documents, catalogues, and journals that contain references to the painting, along with reproductions, exhibitions, and sales records, as well as correspondence, especially of the artist, in which mention of it may be made. **1974** A. PRICE *Other Paths to Glory* II. ix. 223 'He was only interested in where it came from, eh?' *Provenance.*

c. *Forestry.* The location in which tree seed is collected. Also, seed from a specific location.

1933 *Empire Forestry Jrnl.* XII. 198 The problem of seed origin embraces both the geographical location where the seed was collected..and the genetic character of the mother trees... In European literature the term 'provenance'..has come to be used for the first phase of the problem. **1942** H. I. BALDWIN *Forest Tree Seed* iii. 29 Provenance is of tremendous significance to the outcome of plantations. **1956** M. L. ANDERSON tr. *Köstler's Silviculture* iii. 89 The first experimental planting, with thirty different provenances of pine, had been carried out as early as 1821. **1970** H. L. EDLIN *Collins Guide to Tree Planting & Cultivation* vi. 100 The true origin of each stock is called its provenance. *Ibid.* 101 A second generation of the same stock would still have that provenance.

Hence **pro·venanced** *a.*, provided with a record of provenance; established as to origin.

1939 *Nature* 20 May 848/2 Only adequately provenanced objects should be collected; only so can we hope to map, ultimately, the cultural regions of pre-industrial Britain. **1971** J. MANN *Charitable End* iii. 27 Most of it's [*sc.* an art collection is] not provenanced, you know. **1975** *Numismatic Chron.* 198 (*heading*) Some provenanced finds of Crusader bezants.

Provençal, *a.* and *sb.* Add: Also 8– Provençale. **A.** *adj.* **1.** (Further examples.)

1650 [see *PICARD *adj.*]. **1771** [see *LANGUEDOCIAN *a.* and *sb.*]. **1936** A. W. CLAPHAM *Romanesque Archit.* iv. 78 A not uncommon feature of the Provençal apse is its polygonal external form. **1971** *Guardian* 16 Feb. 9/3 A quilted skirt in fine wool Provençal print.

2. Designating a style of cookery characteristic of Provence, typically containing rich savoury ingredients.

1841 THACKERAY in *Fraser's Mag.* June 720/1 You know what a *Provençale* sauce is?.. A rich, savoury mixture, of garlic and oil. **1966** *Harrod's Food News* Sept. 2/2 Individual Scampi Provençal—per carton 9/6. **1974** *Times* 23 May 7/6 Try my favourite Provençal mixture with tomatoes, herbs and anchovies.

B. *sb.* **2.** (Earlier and further examples.)

1642 J. HOWELL *Forraine Travell* x. 124 The French have three dialects, the Wallon..the Provensall..and the speech of Languedoc. **1792** [see *CATALAN]. **1964** *Archivum Linguisticum* XVI. 34 Occitan—or Provençal, as it is more usually known—was one of the major European literary languages... *Provençal* is ambiguous, referring as it does both to the language as a whole and to one particular dialect, that of Provence. **1977** *Listener* 28 July 118/1 The verbal texts..are sung in the original Provençal.

3. *Cookery.* (See quots.)
1960 *Times* 5 Sept. 13/5 *Provençale*, a dish which contains tomatoes, garlic and peppers. **1977** *Time* 28 Nov. 31/3 Particularly recommended are..*provençales* (with garlic, tomatoes and herbs, served somewhat like a pizza).

Hence **Provença·lism**, an idiom or mode of expression typical of the Provençal language; **Provençalist**, a student of Provençal language and literature.
1934 *Times Lit. Suppl.* 30 Aug. 587/1 Mr. W. P. Shepard, himself no mean Provençalist. **1958** Provençalism [see *CATALANIST]. **1975** *Times Lit. Suppl.* 12 Sept. 1023/4 A brilliant essay..that Provençalists ignore at their peril. **1978** *Language* LIV. 428 The Berlin school was spearheaded by K. A. F. Mahn, who, as a Provençalist, became something of a rival of Raynouard and Diez.

Provence. Add: *Provence rose*, the cabbage rose, *Rosa centifolia*, or a variety of it, esp. one bearing fragrant red flowers, or a hybrid produced by crossing *R. centifolia* and *R. gallica*; also, a flower of one of these plants. (Further examples.)
Substitute for note: There is a long-established confusion between Provence and Provins roses, reflected in quots. 1597 and 1905 (in Dict.). Quot. 1578 in Dict. probably refers to the Provins rose: cf. *province rose* s.v. *PROVINCE 10.
1597 GERARD *Herball* III. i. 1801 The Damaske Rose is called..of some *Rosa provincialis*, or Rose of Provence. **1707** J. MORTIMER *Whole Art Husbandry* I. xviii. 477 The Red Provence Rose, whose Branches and Leaves are bigger and greener than those of the common Red Rose. **1817** *Repository of Arts* (Ackermann) Jan. 53/1 A.. bonnet..ornamented with Provence roses and fancy flowers. *a* **1821** KEATS *Cap & Bells* in R. Monckton-Milnes *Life Keats* (1848) II. 219 She..wetted three or four White Provençe rose-leaves with her faery tears. **1837** T. RIVERS *Rose Amateur's Guide* 2 It is therefore very probable that it [*sc. Rosa centifolia*] was called the Provence Rose from growing more abundantly in that province. *Ibid.*, Hybrid roses, between this [*sc. R. centifolia*] and *Rosa gallica*, are called Provence Roses by the French amateurs of the present day. **1847** C. M. YONGE *Scenes & Characters* xxv. 301 Those are some Provence roses for Miss Weston. **1848, 1869** [see *GALLICA]. **1909** R. G. KINGSLEY *Roses* iii. 39 The Moss Rose,.. originally a sport from the common Provence or Cabbage Rose, was also introduced into England from Holland in 1596. **1955** G. S. THOMAS *Old Shrub Roses* xii. 139 *Rosa gallica* (the 'French Rose' or 'Rose of Provins'). The title Provins is also found in the old name, *Rosa provincialis*, but must not be confused with the Provence Rose, *Rosa centifolia*. **1978** J. HARKNESS *Roses* xiii. 180 These old roses [*sc.* centifolias] have mostly been known by three common names: Cabbage roses, Provence roses and Cent-feuilles.

provender, *v.* Add: **3.** *intr.* To partake of provender; to feed *on*. *rare.*
1819 KEATS *Let.* 9 June (1931) II. 376 Infidel Rooks do not provender with Elisha's Ravens. **1891** C. GRAVES *Field of Tares* IV. vi. 241 Leaving the iron horse provendering on coal and water..we follow the footsteps of the man with the black valise.

provenience. Add: Now chiefly *U.S.* (and to some extent *Canad.*). Elsewhere *provenance* is the more usual form. (Further examples.)
1955 J. R. HULBERT *Dicts. Brit. & Amer.* 54 It would be redundant and space consuming to give two pronunciations and indicate their provenience every time a word containing an *r* in this position turned up. **1968** P. M. POSTAL *Aspects Phonol. Theory* iv. 71 Thus in English the gross divisions seem to correspond to the Germanic, Romance, and Greek provenience of forms. **1978** *Maledicta 1977* Winter 133, I am concerned here particularly with some lexical reflections of the dislike of foreigners, as those reflections appear in English, although they are certainly not all of English provenience. **1978** *New York* 3 Apr. 81/2 Why should the hero's hypertrophic sense of smell—heightened to the point where, blindfolded, he can ferret out olfactorily the exact provenience and writing thickness of a ballpoint pen—be the means for his blowing up the world?

pro·venly, *adv.* [f. PROVEN *ppl. a.* + -LY[2].] In a proven manner.
1887 G. B. SHAW *Let.* 27 May (1965) 170 The provenly heroic Annie Besant. **1967** *Times Rev. Industry* July 33/2 The uncommitted clearing banks are staying firmly on the sidelines until the industry has provenly made its way. **1972** *Daily Tel.* 30 Dec. 18 The otter is provenly beneficial to fishing. **1975** *Ibid.* 30 Aug. 11/2 The doctor concerned was fully trained and provenly competent.

prover. Add: **I. 1. d.** *Homœopathy.* A healthy person on whom the effect of a drug is tested. Cf. *PROVE *v.* 1 f.
1843 *Brit. Jrnl. Homœopathy* I. 162 The prover should choose a period when he is in the best of health. **1848** C. J. HEMPEL tr. C. Hering in *Jahr's New Manual* I. p. viii, Every lover of homœopathy must bestow the most unbounded praise and admiration on the Austrian provers. **1902** *Encycl. Brit.* XXIX. 312/2 The manifestations of drug action thus produced are carefully recorded, and this record..after being verified by repetition on many 'provers', constitutes the distinguishing feature of the homœopathic materia medica. **1931** J. E. BARKER *Miracles of Healing* vii. 102 It may seem easy to match the symptoms of a patient with a drug producing the same symptoms in healthy provers who have experimentally taken it. In reality this is exceedingly difficult. **1974** *Homoeopathy* June/July 89 After taking the thirty powders the provers have a rest for a month, and then have a further thirty powders.

proverb, *sb.* Add: **1. c.** (Earlier example.)
1743 in A. D. Candler et al. *Georgia Rec.* (c 1913–16) XXIII. 513 He had then recourse to his Usual Salve, (well known, to all persons at Savannah with whom he converses, even to a proverb) That He was Seventy Years of Age, His Memory decayed, etc.

5. (Examples.)
1855 *Home Games for People* 104 *Proverbs.* One of the party is sent out of the room: the rest busying themselves with thinking of a proverb..to be discovered by him on his return. **1867** 'AUNT CARRIE' *Popular Pastimes for Field & Fireside* 188 *Proverbs.* The company select some one to leave the room; those remaining agree upon a proverb [etc.]. **1879** 'L. HOFFMANN' *Drawing-Room Amusements & Evening Party Entertainments* ii. 50 Proverbs. This is another 'guessing' game. **1895** *Montgomery Ward & Co. Catal.* Spring & Summer 236/3 Proverbs. The old standard game revised, consisting of 100 cards containing the best proverbs. **1910** W. OWEN *Let.* 27 Dec. (1967) 66 We have been playing games (e.g. Proverbs, Memory Tray, etc.) this evening. **1975** *Way to Play* 257/2 *Proverbs...* It is sometimes called hidden proverbs, or guessing proverbs.

6. *proverb card* (later examples).
1966 S. MANN *Collecting Playing Cards* vii. 141 *Proverb Cards*, containing pleasant Devices, suited to the most witty English Proverbs. Made c. 1700... The value is indicated by a single suit-mark at top right. **1977** *Jrnl. Playing-Card Soc.* Nov. 44 There seem to be two packs of Proverb cards that could conceivably be the one referred to by Lenthall.

proverbial, *a.* (*sb.*) Add: **A.** *adj.* **1. a.** Also *absol.*
1961 *N. & Q.* Feb. 76/2 The description given certainly enlightens the reader as to a number of characteristics of the proverb, but equally certainly leaves him doubtful about where the proverbial leaves off.

2. (Later examples.) Also used with allusive force to introduce a word or expression that is familiar as (part of) a proverb or catch-phrase.
1924 *Argosy* 27 Sept. 463/1 In the more than proverbial nick..of time. **1928** W. A. WOLFF *Trial of Mary Dugan* xxiv. 282 Like the proverbial man from Missouri, I have to be shown. **1931** H. ASHBROOK *Murder of Steven Kester* xv. 225 The whole thing is rather ideal—the proverbial house party, a murder, everyone under suspicion. **1937** M. ALLINGHAM *Dancers in Mourning* viii. 108 White Walls normally contained an excitable household... This morning..the proverbial monkey-wrench had landed squarely in the middle of the brittle machinery. **1976** J. SNOW *Cricket Rebel* 19 Having bowled a short ball at a batsman during one match he sarcastically patted the pitch almost in front of my feet. This is the proverbial red flag to a fast bowler. **1976** 'D. FLETCHER' *Don't whistle 'Macbeth'* 212 The proverbial penny had dropped... It certainly made me very uncomfortable.

proverbialism (earlier and later examples); also = PROVERBIALITY a.
1832 W. MOTHERWELL in A. Henderson *Scottish Proverbs* p. xiv, Zachary Boyd, Rector of Glasgow University, has ..given quite a cento of common proverbialisms. **1935** *Times Lit. Suppl.* 14 Dec. 854/4 We pick them [*sc.* proverbs] up every now and then from great men's epigrammatic sayings and above all from books... This aspect of modern proverbialism should not be ignored. **1976** *Hiroshima Stud. Eng. Lang. and Lit.* XXI. 72 His resort to such proverbialisms indicates his dependence on the world of experience.

pro-vicariate: see *PRO-[1] 4b.

provident, *a.* Add: **1.** *Provident Society* (examples). Also *Provident Club.*
1858 M. TUCKETT *Diary* 12 Nov. (c 1975) 18 We betook ourselves to the Polytechnic where a stall awaited us, in the sale for the Provident Society. **1869** *Bradshaw's Railway Manual* XXI. App. 98 The United Kingdom Railway Officers' and Servants' Association, and Railway Provident Society. **1968** A. BRYANT *Hist. Brit. United Provident Assoc.* 2 During the 'twenties and 'thirties many Provident Clubs became linked with particular hospitals. **1973** P. GOSDEN *Self-Help* vi. 49 During the first half of May, 1836, petitions were received by the Commons from a number of societies in South Lancashire... These included..the Provident Society of Salford. **1978** P. SUTCLIFFE *Oxf. Univ. Press* II. xii. 63 He started a provident club for medical aid and a clothing club.

provide·ntialism. [f. PROVIDENTIAL *a.* + -ISM.] The belief that events are predestined, whether by God or by fate.
1927 J. S. HUXLEY *Relig. without Revelation* 18 The release of God from the anthropomorphic disguise of personality also provides release from that vice which may be termed Providentialism. **1934** H. G. WELLS *Exper. Autobiog.* I. v. 264 The ultimate adoption of the Five Year Plan and its successor has been the completest change over from the providentialism of Marx to the once hated and despised method of the Utopists. **1954** C. S. LEWIS *Eng. Lit. in 16th Cent.* I. ii. 148 His [*sc.* Fabyan's] philosophy of history is a simple Providentialism which leaves him completely agnostic about second causes.

providentialness. (Later example.)
1903 E. WHARTON *Sanctuary* I. i. 10 The sense of general providentialness on which Mrs. Peyton reposed.

province. Add: **I. 2. a.** *spec.* in recent use, Northern Ireland.
1972 *Ann. Reg. 1971* 26 A horrifying escalation of violence in the Province. **1977** [see sense 10 below].

5. (Earlier example.)
1789 *Ann. Agric.* XI. 293 All the animation, vigour, life, and energy of luxury, consumption, and industry, which flow with a full tide through this kingdom, wherever there is a free communication between the capital and the provinces.

6. a. Also, an area containing a distinctive group of animal or plant communities. (Earlier and later examples.)
1847 H. C. WATSON *Cybele Britannica* I. 14 Eighteen 'Provinces', or groups of counties, have been marked out on the map; and..they will be found more natural sections of the island than are the counties themselves. **1860** *Q. Jrnl. Geol. Soc.* XVI. p. xxxv, Thus natural provinces are constituted, each including a considerable number of forms peculiar to itself. **1932** FULLER & CONARD tr. *Braun-Blanquet's Plant Sociol.* xiv. 355 The province is.. characterized by at least one climax community. **1947** R. GOOD *Geogr. Flowering Plants* ii. 38 This classification divides the floras and floristic units of the world first into kingdoms, then into regions.., and finally into provinces. **1957** P. DANSEREAU *Biogeography* i. 54 Each area (the provinces here) holds a more or less heterogeneous residue of the units that have fared variously in the course of its total history. **1973** J. W. VALENTINE *Evolutionary Paleoecol. Marine Biosphere* iii. 74 The regions that constitute distributional units of organisms are called biogeographical regions or provinces (biotic provinces, faunal provinces, floral provinces, and so on). **1974** *Sci. Amer.* Apr. 83/3 The marine faunas today are partitioned into more than 30 provinces, among which there is in general only a low percentage of common species.

b. In full *petrographic* or *petrographical province.* An area of igneous rocks that appear to have been formed during the same period of igneous activity, presumably from the same magma. [cf. G. *geognostisch bezirk* (H. Vogelsang 1872, in *Zeitschr. d. deutsch. geol. Ges.* XXIV. 525).]
1886 J. W. JUDD in *Q. Jrnl. Geol. Soc.* XLII. 54 There are distinct petrographical provinces, within which the rocks erupted during any particular geological period present certain well-marked peculiarities in mineralogical composition and microscopical structure, serving at once to distinguish them from the rocks belonging to the same general group, which were simultaneously erupted in other petrographical provinces. **1886** F. RUTLEY in *Ibid.* XLII. 96 Lavas of totally distinct characters are poured out from the same vent, so that the use of the term 'petrographic province' seemed to be of rather doubtful propriety. **1910** LAKE & RASTALL *Text-bk. Geol.* xiii. 230 The occurrence of chemical peculiarities running through all or nearly all the igneous rocks of a province shows that they are not all brought together by chance, but that there must be some real relationship between the different types. **1941** *Amer. Jrnl. Sci.* CCXXXIX. 542 (*heading*) Compositions (less anorthite) of the salic portions of residual magmas in New Zealand petrographical provinces. **1954** H. WILLIAMS et al. *Petrography* i. 10 The markedly potassic, lencitic lavas of the region around Rome and Naples..form a petrographic province. **1962** P. T. BRONEER tr. *Beloussov's Basic Probl. in Geotectonics* xxxii. 657 At first it was thought..that different geographic areas were characterized by the predominance of different magmas. This was the origin of the study of petrographic provinces.

c. In full now *physiographic province.* An extensive region all parts of which have a broadly similar geology and topography and which differs significantly from adjacent regions.
1893 J. W. POWELL in *14th Ann. Rep. U.S. Geol. Survey, 1892–3* I. 71 One of the results of this interpretation is the recognition of geologic provinces... The geologic province is the unit of past geography; throughout each the successive deposits represent a definite chronologic sequence, and throughout each there may generally be found definite, consistent, and mutually corroborative series of records of geologic events. **1895** B. WILLIS *Northern Appalachians* (Nat. Geogr. Monogr. I. No. 6) 197 The plains were the homes of the most populous Indian tribes... The ranges of the mountains..were a barrier to intercourse long after the several topographic provinces had come under one national government. **1914** *Ann. Assoc. Amer. Geographers* IV. 85 The confusion will be worse when the plotting of census and other statistics by physiographic provinces has become common. **1936** *Bull. Amer. Assoc. Petroleum Geologists* XX. 1278 (*caption*) Outline map of Mexico showing principal physiographic provinces. *Ibid.* 1297 Although geologists and travellers subdivide the mountainous area of Chiapas into several sections, differing in their topographic and geologic aspects, nevertheless, their related and combined features can be taken as a whole to form one large province. **1974** *Physics Bull.* Oct. 430/2 Another striking feature of the Mercurian surface is the asymmetry in distribution of the major physiographic provinces (also a characteristic of the moon and Mars).

† **d.** *Soil Science.* In full *soil province.* (See quots.) *Obs.*
1909 *Bull. Bureau of Soils* (U.S. Dept. Agric.) No. 55. 26 The complete scheme of classification, so far as perfected by the Bureau of Soils, also provides for the grouping of these series..into thirteen great soil provinces, as shown in the map. **1913** *Ibid.* No. 96. 7 A soil province is an area having the same general physiographic expression, in which the soils have been produced by the same forces or groups of forces and throughout which each rock or soil material yields to equal forces equal results. **1924** F. E. BEAR *Soil Managem.* iv. 30 Province refers to a large land area in which either the mode or the source of origin, or both, of the soil have been quite similar throughout. Thus the Glacial and Loessial Province of the Bureau of Soils includes the en-

tire land area in the United States over which the glacial processes were most important in the formation of the original soil.

e. = *oil province* s.v. *OIL *sb.*[1] 6e.

1926 [see *oil province* s.v. *OIL *sb.*[1] 6e]. **1933** *Bull. Amer. Assoc. Petroleum Geologists* XVII. 1107 The earliest..trap to form in many American petroleum provinces was a reservoir rock which was wedged out and overlapped by an impervious cap rock. **1966** *McGraw-Hill Encycl. Sci. & Technol.* X. 61/2 Underground occurrences of petroleum may be classified as pools, fields, and provinces. **1971** *Daily Tel.* 29 Dec. 5/3 This huge oil yield from the northern 'province' of the North Sea will have important consequences for this country.

III. 8. (Earlier example.)

1690 LOCKE *Essay Hum. Und.* IV. xx. 362 They seemed to me to be the three great Provinces of the intellectual World, wholly separate and distinct one from another.

IV. 10. province rose = *Provins rose* s.v. *PROVINS or *Provence rose* s.v. PROVENCE in Dict. and Suppl.; also *absol.*; **province-wide** *a.*, extending throughout or pertaining to a whole province.

1597 GERARD *Herball* III. i. 1802 The greate Rose..is generally called the greate Province Rose. **1629** J. PARKINSON *Paradisi in Sole* cix. 413 Some Gentlewomen have caused all their damaske stockes to be grafted with province Roses, hoping to have as good water, and more store of them. *Ibid.*, The flowers are..of a sent not so sweete as the damaske Province. **1731** P. MILLER *Gard. Dict.* s.v. Rosa. The Damask, Province, and Frankfort Roses grow to the Height of seven or eight Feet. **1964** P. WORSLEY in I. L. Horowitz *New Sociol.* 380 Government intervention in province-wide infrastructural fields, such as air-ways, bus-lines, insurance etc. **1977** *Belfast Tel.* 22 Feb. 8/8 The old Loyalist merry-go-round of..province-wide protests and rallies for the converted are discarded.

provincial, *a.* and *sb.* Add: **A.** *adj.* **2. a.** Specifically of Canada.

1795 *Quebec Gaz.* 8 Jan. 3/1 Clerk of the Provincial Court for the District of Three Rivers. **1849** J. E. ALEXANDER *L'Acadie* I. 35 It was found necessary to intermingle the newly arrived regulars with the Glengarry light infantry, a provincial corps. **1878** *Herald* (Ottawa) 24 Jan. 1/4 Two whiskey informers..were under the protection of the Provincial Police. **1965** *Globe & Mail* (Toronto) 10 Mar. 1/6 Provincial police said the single-engined plane..struck the lines with its undercarriage. **1968** *Ibid.* 3 Feb. 11/1 He said his department is seeking to have provincial services extended to Indians. **1976** *Telegraph-Jrnl.* (St. John, New Brunswick) 12 Aug. 1/1 He will recommend a *provincial* tax hike.

4. a. Also *provincial theatre.*

1867 *Harper's Mag.* Dec. 96/1 The provincial theatres compare favorably with those of London. **1952** GRANVILLE *Dict. Theatr. Terms* 145 *Provincial theatre*, the stage outside London.

c. *spec.* Of a university other than the older universities of Oxford and Cambridge (or other than that of Oxford only).

1914 C. MACKENZIE *Sinister St.* II. III. ix. 688 It was still natural to regard Cambridge as a provincial university, and to take pleasure in shocking the earnest young Cambridge man with the metropolitan humours and airy self-assurance of Oxford. **1955** *Ann. Reg. 1954* 351 *Lucky Jim*..was an example of the work of the new 'provincial school' about which there was much talk in the year. **1958** *Times Lit. Suppl.* 17 Jan. 30/4 Talk of..'the red-brick intellectuals', though no Movement founder-member had done more than *teach* at one of the provincial universities. **1966** C. M. BOWRA *Memories 1898–1939* xiii. 320 In the United States the academic profession had ties all over the country and was not divided as in England into Oxford and Cambridge on the one side and 'provincial' universities on the other. **1978** *Encounter* July 8/1, I studied at an English provincial university.

5. (Further examples.)

1813 M. EDGEWORTH *Let.* 6 Apr. (1971) 10 He..speaks excellent language but with a strong provincial accent which at once destroys all idea of elegance. **1863** TROLLOPE *Rachel Ray* I. vi. 118 Mrs. Rowan perceived at once that Mrs. Tappitt was provincial,..but she was a good motherly woman. **1899** J. MCCARTHY *Reminisc.* II. xxxv. 252 Rather tall, very angular, surprisingly awkward..with a rough provincial accent and an uncouth way of speaking. **1909** A. W. EVANS tr. *A. France's Penguin Island* VII. ix. 312 Provincial women, since they wear low heels, are not very attractive, and preserve their virtue with ease. **1954** C. S. LEWIS *Eng. Lit. in 16th Cent.* I. i. 68 Scotch poetry had already a considerable achievement behind it and was by no means a local or provincial department of English poetry.

7. b. Delete *erron.* Substitute for def.: Epithet of the Provins rose (see *PROVINS).

B. *sb.* **2. a.** (Further examples.)

1916 JOYCE *Portrait of Artist* (1969) 48 If the minister did it he would go to the rector: and the rector to the provincial: and the provincial to the general of the jesuits. **1960** [see *DEFINITORY *sb.*]. **1973** *Franciscan* XV. 168 The Community Retreat conducted by Brother Luke, the American Provincial.

4. c. In Canada: a member of a provincial police force.

1936 W. B. MOWERY *Paradise Trail* 4 On his flight across the provinces he had..slipped out of several tight squeezes with the Provincials. **1952** H. GARNER *Yellow Sweater* 143 One of the Provincials took me upstairs. **1963** J. N. HARRIS *Weird World Wes Beattie* xi. 137 The provincials were extremely dubious about trying to find a weapon in the depths of Lake Muskoka in March.

5. (Later examples.)

1913 C. MACKENZIE *Sinister St.* I. II. v. 210 She used to laugh and tell him he was a regular old 'provincial'. **1954** C. S. LEWIS *Eng. Lit. in 16th Cent.* I i. 83 Until we have trained ourselves to feel that 'gudeman' is no more rustic or homely than 'husband' we are no judges of Douglas as a translator of Virgil. If we fail in the training, then it is we and not the poet who are provincials.

9. (Further examples.)

1961 *Listener* 31 Aug. 325/1 His thoughts about Beckford and Beckett, Jouhandeau and Camus, the *anti-roman* and the English provincials. **1973** *Times* 2 July 15/6 The London papers stood out for a long time after the provincials had joined with him.

provincialate. (Further examples.)

1911 A. BRENNAN *Life St. Lawrence of Brindisi* xviii. 179 During his Provincialate the Friars of Piedmont..renewed their petitions. **1930** T. S. WESTBROOK *Glimpses Catholic Eng.* 70 During the Provincialates of Agnellus..and of his successor Albert of Pisa..the brethren at Oxford lived in the strictest poverty. **1960** J. B. DOCKERY *Christopher Davenport* viii. 121 During the Provincialate of Sancta Clara the community were well clothed. **1976** *Oxford Times* 3 Dec. 13/3 For the Jesuit student, as later for all his religious brethren during his Provincialate, he came as a breath of fresh air.

provincialism. Add: **3.** (Earlier example.)

1770 *Monthly Rev.* XLII. 180 His language..is, moreover, frequently debased with certain provincial*isms.*

4. *Ecol.* The development of biogeographical provinces. Cf. *PROVINCE 6a.

1969 *Spec. Papers Geol. Soc. Amer.* No. 119. 1 Provincialism increased by the addition of the Malvinokaffric Province. **1975** *Nature* 22 May 353/2 Why should the early Devonian faunas exhibit more provincialism, for instance, than those of the late Silurian.

provinciality. Add: **2.** *Ecol.* The restriction of the distribution of a plant or animal community to a particular province or group of provinces. Cf. *PROVINCE 6a.

1969 *Spec. Papers Geol. Soc. Amer.* No. 119. 3 The waxing and waning of provinciality displayed by Lower Devonian invertebrate faunas can be viewed in another way. **1971** J. G. JOHNSON in *Amer. Jrnl. Sci.* CCLXX. 257 Degrees of faunal resemblance..can be measured by a Provinciality Index (PI) consisting of a weighted ratio of common and endemic genera. **1976** *Nature* 24 June 695/1 It is noteworthy that an abrupt increase in phyletic rate commonly coincides initially with the brief upsurge in cladogenetic rate accompanying major provinciality increase.

provincializa·tion. [f. PROVINCIALIZE *v.* + -ATION.] A making or becoming provincial; conversion into a province.

1924 *Glasgow Herald* 16 Sept. 7 In a vigorous speech [he] emphasised the provincialisation and Indianisation aspect of the Report. **1967** A. N. SHERWIN-WHITE *Racial Prejudice in Imperial Rome* 1. 24 Critognatus contrasts Roman imperialism, as revealed by the permanent exploitation and provincialization of southern Gaul (Gallia Narbonensis) unfavourably with the former temporary devastation of the country by the Cimbri. **1976** *Northern Miner* (Toronto) 19 Aug. 6/1 The government of Saskatchewan took the first step in the provincialization of the potash industry.

provi·ncialized, *ppl. a.* [f. PROVINCIALIZE *v.* + -ED[1].] Made, or having become, provincial; having become a province.

1955 *Times* 23 June 11/6 A country which had felt itself neglected and provincialized under the Danish and, especially, the Swedish connexion. **1974** *Sci. Amer.* Apr. 85/3 A widespread, soft-bodied fauna of low diversity gave way to a slightly provincialized, skeletonized fauna of somewhat higher diversity.

proving, *vbl. sb.* Add: **1. b.** *Homœopathy.* The testing of a drug (see *PROVE *v.* 1f).

1843 *Brit. Jrnl. Homœopathy* I. 291 In the provings of the insoluble substances, such as calcarea, silica, &c., the symptoms produced by the first doses are rarely experienced..in the subsequent ones. **1881** *Encycl. Brit.* XII. 126/2 The record of such provings constitutes a large part of the literature of homœopathy. **1905** J. H. CLARKE *Homœopathy Explained* xvi. 122 There is always this check in homœopathy—the provings can be tested in practice. **1936** H. A. ROBERTS *Princ. & Art of Cure by Homœopathy* i. 16 The results of such investigation would enrich the homœopathic materia medica by completing provings of some of the older remedies, and by bringing out provings of new remedies. **1975** C. H. SHARMA *Man, Homoeopathy & Natural Med.* i. 16 Before a homoeopathic remedy can be used by a physician, it has to go through a series of 'provings'.

4. b. *N. Amer.* The action of establishing a claim. Also with *up*. Cf. PROVE *v.* 12.

1958 J. G. MACGREGOR *Northwest of 16* v. 67 They also had to bring fifteen acres under cultivation and to erect some sort of abode. (Carrying out these obligations and getting title to the land was termed 'proving up'.)

6. *attrib.* (Further examples.)

1944 *Air News Yearbk.* II. 188 Poland and Norway represented the 'proving ground'. **1948** 'N. SHUTE' *No Highway* i. 28 They did a whole lot of proving flights over the route before they put it into regular operation. **1959** *Listener* 15 Jan. 147/2 And, finally, proving time: once you have reconstituted the yeast and made a dough, carry on with your normal timing. **1971** M. LEE *Dying for Fun* ix. 55 All over his desk were scattered invitations—art galleries, press conferences..air trips and proving flights. **1975** *Harpers & Queen* May 27/1 The other day, I and my dough came to be separated at a crucial point in the 'proving' process. **1979** *Nature* 8 Feb. 430/1 Scientists have used astronomy as a proving ground for theories of gravity ever since Newton explained the sizes and shapes of the planetary orbits.

Provins (prǫvæ̃ns). The name of a French town, thirty miles east of Melun, used attrib. to designate a variety of *Rosa gallica*, formerly known as *Rosa provincialis*, the apothecary's red rose, which has long been cultivated there. Cf. *province rose* s.v. *PROVINCE 10.

1837 T. RIVERS *Rose Amateur's Guide* 11 In France, this [sc. *Rosa gallica*] is called the 'Provins Rose'. **1902** JEKYLL & MAWLEY *Roses for Eng. Gardens* ii. 13 These two names, Provence and Provins, for two classes of garden rose..are so much alike... Provence is the Cabbage Rose (*R. centifolia*); Provins is *Rosa gallica*, the garden kinds being mostly striped. **1955** C. C. HURST in G. S. Thomas *Old Shrub Roses* ix. 61 The Provins Roses were also much appreciated in India and in England. **1978** J. HARKNESS *Roses* xiii. 173 It [sc. *Rosa gallica officinalis*] is also known as the Apothecary's Rose, a reference to its uses in medicine, and as the Provins rose, because that French town specialized in making conserves and medicine from it.

provirus (provəiə·rǒs). *Biol.* [f. PRO-[2] + VIRUS, after *PROPHAGE.] The form which a DNA or RNA virus has when incorporated into, and able to replicate with, the DNA of a host cell.

1952 *Physiol. Rev.* XXXII. 419 Most of the cells perpetuate the potentiality of producing virus, although the virus itself is rarely detectable in them. For this reason, such cells are considered as infected with a provirus, a perpetuating, but immature and nonlytic agent. **1953** S. E. LURIA *Gen. Virol.* xiv. 277 We may suppose that in the recovered plant the virus is mainly in a condition (provirus) similar to the prophage. **1964** *Proc. Nat. Acad. Sci.* LII. 323 It has been suggested that the provirus of Rous sarcoma virus-infected cells is composed of DNA. **1970** *Nature* 5 Sept. 1023/1 It is widely believed that cells transformed with Rous sarcoma virus (RSV) contain a DNA transcript of the viral RNA, the so-called 'provirus'.

Hence **provi·ral** *a.*

1969 C. D. DARLINGTON in C. W. M. Whitty et al. *Virus Dis. & Nervous Syst.* 137 Diseases such as Kuru and Scrapie having combined genetic, cytoplasmic and pro-viral components. **1976** *Nature* 15 July 190 (*heading*) Proviral sequences of baboon endogenous type C RNA virus in DNA of human leukaemic tissues.

provision, *sb.* Add: **7.** (Earlier and later examples of West Indian sense.)

1808 J. STEWART *Acct. Jamaica* 100 Ground provisions (as they are called), or roots... These roots, or ground provisions, are so productive (particularly the yam), [etc.]. **1827** [see *ground-provisions* s.v. GROUND *sb.* 18 a]. **1955** *Caribbean Q.* IV. I. 51 A large number of the contractors used these payments to acquire small plots of land in which they planted cocoa, provisions, and later, nutmeg trees. **1965** 'LAUCHMONEN' *Old Thom's Harvest* i. 11 Bet we can grow some whopping good crop of provision on that piece of land, Pa.

10. *provision basket* (example), *book, dealer* (further example), *farm, farmer, house, importer, man, pit, shop, store, trade* (earlier example), *train, wagon*; **provision pay** (earlier example).

1876 'MARK TWAIN' *Tom Sawyer* xxviii. 268 The gay throng filed up the main street laden with provision baskets. **1922** *Beaver* Apr. 9/2 A record of the provisions stocked, with their weight or quantities, was entered as they were received in the 'Provision Book', in which was also entered the allowances as they were given out. **1877** *Harper's Mag.* Jan. 284/2 They sold some grapes and apples and pears to the provision dealer in exchange for beef and chicken. **1958** J. CAREW *Black Midas* i. 9 At the back of the village were rice-fields, small provision farms..and wild-cane reeds. **1953** E. MITTELHOLZER in *Caribbean Anthol. Short Stories* 41 Hoolcharran had begun as a provision farmer, and lived in a mudhouse. **1798** W. TOMISON *Jrnl.* 2 Feb. in A. M. Johnson *Saskatchewan Jrnls. & Corr.* (1967) 108 The rest employed bringing ice for the provision house. **1804** J. ORDWAY in *Jrnls. Lewis & Ordway* (1916) vi. 166 We continued building, raised a provision & Smoak house 24 feet by 14 f. **1903** *N.Y. Times* 15 Oct. 1 Deacon Cotten..was dickering with representatives of meat and provision houses for supplies. **1885** *List of Subscribers, Classified* (United Telephone Co.) (ed. 6) 174 Provision importers. **1872** *Boston* (Mass.) *Ordin.* (1873) 193 The vehicles of market or provision men. **1683** *Rec. East Hampton, N.Y.* (1887) II. 131 For his Wages hee is to be payd the some of thirty five pound in probision pay. **1887** *Courier-Jrnl.* (Louisville, Kentucky) 3 Feb. 7/4 Within a very few minutes after the opening the crowd in the provision pit increased. **1854** M. S. CUMMINS *Lamplighter* xv. 115 Willie accompanied them as far as the provision-shop. **1796** *Boston* (Mass.) *Directory* s.v. *Fletcher*, Provision store. **1830** *Reg. Deb. Congress U.S.* 11 May 429/2 The provision trade of the West. **1896** *Harper's Mag.* Apr. 764/1 Blücher..found that he had captured..all the enemy's hospital outfit, his field-smithies, and his provision-train. **1765** R. ROGERS *Jrnls.* p. viii, I tarried till August 26th, and was then ordered with 100 men to escort the provision-waggons. **1925** G. STUART *40 Yrs. on Frontier* I. 97 Three days were consumed in getting together the equipment of men and horses with provision wagons and everything necessary.

provision, *v.* Add: **a.** (Further examples.) Also *refl.* **b.** (Further examples.) Also with *up*.

1903 R. BEDFORD *True Eyes* viii. 48 Why didn't you provision from home? **1928** *Daily Express* 11 Aug. 4/6 The main thing to remember in going to the islands is to provision-up for your stay well ahead. **1941** *Pitman's Business Educ.* Oct. 152 Without access to overseas supplies of oil, Germany has attempted to provision herself by the seizure of Rumania and by the invasion of Russia. **1973** *Animal Behaviour* XXI. 306/2 We suspect that the females were provisioning separate cells.

provisional, *a.* (*sb.*) Add: **A.** *adj.* **1. a.** (Further examples.) *Provisional Government*: now *spec.* a government set up to rule until constitutional self-government can be established; *Provisional I.R.A.*: the unofficial wing of the Irish Republican Army instituted in 1970; *provisional* (*driving-*)*licence*: a licence issued to a learner-driver; *provisional order*: (see quot. 1963).

1848 *Act* 11 *& 12 Vict.* c. 63 s. x They shall make a Provisional Order under their Hands and Seal of Office. **1870** *Act* 33 & 34 *Vict.* c. 1 §2 Any Select Committee of the House of Commons to which any Bill for confirming Provisional Orders has been referred in relation to any Provisional Order therein contained may examine witnesses upon oath. **1916** WELLS & MARLOWE *Hist. Irish Rebellion of 1916* ix. 47 At the Post Office was established the Headquarters of the 'Provisional Government of the Irish Republic'. **1931** *R.A.C. Guide 1931–32* 34 To enable an applicant suffering from a disability to learn to drive a motor vehicle of any special construction ..the Licensing Authority may..grant him a provisional licence for a period of three months. **1963** J. F. GARNER *Administrative Law* iii. 42 Provisional orders are made by a Minister of the Crown under the authority of a statute, and they are therefore sometimes described as a form of delegated or subordinate legislation, but they have no legal force until they have been included (usually by way of reference in a schedule) in a Provisional Orders Confirmation Act. **1965** J. CH'ÊN *Mao & Chinese Revolution* (1967) I. viii. 172 Under the Constitution, the Provisional Soviet Government was elected with Mao as its chairman. **1970** TIERNEY & MACCURTAIN *Birth Mod. Ireland* 131 Pearse then stepped out on to the portico and read the Proclamation of the Provisional Government of the Irish Republic. **1970** *Times* 9 Apr. 12/2 The recent formation of a 'provisional' I.R.A. Council. **1971** S. A. DE SMITH *Constitutional & Administrative Law* xv. 342 Provisional orders, which do not have legal effect till confirmed by Act of Parliament and are therefore not a form of delegated legislation at all. **1973** *Times* 11 Oct. 2/5 Mr McMorrow had been active in the Provisional IRA in Londonderry. **1974** *Guardian* 22 Mar. 8/7 The Environment Department has turned down a plea for stricter eyesight tests for people applying for their first provisional driving licence. **1976** *Burnham-on-Sea Gaz.* 20 Apr. 24/4 Mrs —— told the court that she only held a provisional licence and this had now expired. **1978** *Times* 6 Mar. 2/6 Under the Provisional IRA's new structure, each active service unit is largely self-contained, and in contact only with the central command.

B. *sb.* **3. a.** One whose tenure of office is of a temporary nature; a provisional governor.

1848 A. H. CLOUGH *Let.* 26 Feb. in J. Bertram *N.Z. Lett. of T. Arnold* (1966) 78 Will the army and Nationals rally around this government, or allow the people to set up their Provisionals. Inasmuch as the Provisionals are all in the Ministry, I suppose they may please themselves.

b. A member of the Provisional I.R.A.

1971 *Guardian* 11 Aug. 1/5 Some senior members of the IRA Provisionals, known to have been in Belfast recently, have..arrived. **1974** *Listener* 14 Mar. 323/1 The Provisionals' traditional method of discipline: putting a gun barrel behind a man's knee and blowing off his knee cap.

‖**provisorium** (provizōə·riŭm). [Ger.] A provisional or interim measure or condition.

1957 *Listener* 28 Nov. 867/1 Since it has not been possible to reach such understandings subsequently.. the provisorium flowing from these circumstances has endured. **1963** *Economist* 3 Aug. 428/1 Bonn was not a 'provisorium' but a 'transitorium'.

provitamin (prōu·vitămin). *Biol.* Also **pro-vitamin.** [a. G. *provitamin* (Windhaus & Hess 1926, in *Nachr. von der K. Ges. d. Wissensch. zu Göttingen* (1927) 175): see PRO-² and *VITAMIN.] A substance which is converted into a vitamin within an organism. (Freq. with following capital letter indicating relationship to a specific vitamin.)

1927 ROSENHEIM & WEBSTER in *Lancet* 5 Feb. 306/2 These observations suggest that the provitamin (we propose to use this convenient term, suggested by Prof. Windhaus, for the parent substance of vitamin D) is destroyed by bromine. **1943** *Endeavour* Apr. 73/2 It became evident that, though the diets of the tropical natives were often deficient in the calcifying vitamin,.. they really had ample supplies because of the action of sunlight on the provitamin. **1952** *New Biol.* XIII. 40 Doubling the number of chromosomes in pure yellow corn caused a 40% increase in the carotenoid pigment content, including the active provitamin A fraction of the carotenoids. **1971** *Nature* 22 Jan. 255/2 Vitamin D..is produced in the skin when ultraviolet radiation is absorbed by the pro-vitamin 7-dehydrocholesterol. **1976** H. CAMPION et al. in B. E. C. Nordin *Calcium, Phosphate & Mineral Metabolism* xii. 445 The two principal provitamins D, ergosterol..and..7-dehydrocholesterol..are formed in vivo by two very similar routes.

provo[1], **provoe.** Add: Also with capital initial. **1.** (Later example.) Also *transf.*, a provost-cell.

1779 *New-Jersey Jrnl.* (Chatham, N.J.) 13 Apr. 3/1 The other two are safely lodged in the provo of the continental troops. **1832** W. DUNLAP *Hist. Amer. Theatre* iv. 43 The Jail, then called the provo, where American prisoners suffered for asserting the rights of their country, scowled on the east. **1865** W. REID in *Cincinnati Daily Gaz.* 13 Dec. 1/3 He was boasting of his success with the 'cussed free niggers'. 'We've got a Provo' in our town that settles their hash mighty quick. He's a downright high-toned man, that Provo', if he is a Yankee.

2. *Comb.*, as **provo-marshal**: cf. PROVOST-MARSHAL.

1919 G. B. SHAW *Peace Conference Hints* vii. 102 The estimate of military crime which any statistician can give..without consulting a provo-marshal. **1934** —— *Too True to be Good* II. 50 Offences which cannot be stated on a charge sheet and dealt with by the provo-marshal.

provo, Provo[2] (prōu·vo). [a. Du. *provo*, abbrev. of F. *provocateur.*] A member of a group of young Dutch agitators of anarchist persuasion, whose policy was to provoke the authorities; the Dutch anarchist group or movement. Also *attrib.*

1966 *Times* 15 June 1/5 For several weeks there has been unrest in Amsterdam. Young men and women calling themselves 'provos', from the French *provocateur*, who reject any authority or discipline, have gathered in certain parts of the city to provoke police intervention. **1967** *Listener* 19 Jan. 83/2 A somewhat riotous group of youngsters, who called themselves Provos, organized themselves and started to prove the validity of their organization's name by provoking the authorities. **1967** J. EASTWOOD *Little Dragon from Peking* x. 97 Hitchhikers, *autostops*, *Blousons noirs*, provos from Amsterdam. **1968** *Listener* 22 Feb. 233/1 Police action against a Provo demonstrator when Princess Beatrice of the Netherlands was married in 1966. **1970** *New Yorker* 8 Aug. 50/3 One of the most interesting aspects of Provo, the Dutch movement that was among the first and brightest of the radical movements of the last decade, was that it blossomed forth with a number of responsible civic ideas. **1976** J. VAN DE WETERING *Corpse on Dike* v. 58 You look funny..but you don't look like a hippie or a provo or a bird-of-protest.

provo, Provo[3] (prōu·vo, prǫ·vo). *colloq.* [abbrev. of PROVISIONAL *a.* (*sb.*).] A member of the Provisional I.R.A. Also *attrib.* or as *adj.*

1971 *Guardian* 14 Aug. 9/7 In their bombing campaign the Provos seem to have hit on a policy..described as being the best way to bring down Stormont. **1972** *New Yorker* 19 Feb. 52/2 There are still no more than a few thousand I.R.A. men, Provo or Official, in the Six Counties. The Officials have less than half as many members as the Provos. **1973** *Daily Tel.* 27 Jan. 1/2 IRA men who recognise courts are automatically disowned by the Provos. **1976** *Church Times* 26 Nov. 5/2 The march squelched on to a new rallying point as a mob of Provo IRA thugs had barred the way into Falls Park. **1977** *Cork Examiner* 8 June 16/2 The Provos also claim that two soldiers were killed in a bomb explosion in West Belfast.

provocable, *a.* (Later example.)

1850 A. H. CLOUGH *Let.* 3 Jan. in J. Bertram *N.Z. Lett. of T. Arnold* (1966) 188 There is a great blessing..in being set down among uncongenial people—for me at least who am over provocable.

‖**provocateur** (provǫkatōr). [Fr., = 'instigator, provoker'.] One who provokes a disturbance; an agitator; an *agent provocateur.* Also *attrib.*

1922 U. SINCLAIR *They call me Carpenter* xxvii. 94 The poor devils who went on strike were locked out of the factories..and their policies bedevilled by provocateurs. **1925** L. TROTSKY *Whither England?* v. 99 It must also thoroughly understand that the strike will fail to be immediately defeated only if it is able to offer the necessary resistance to the strike-breakers, provocateurs, Fascisti, etc. **1934** C. STEAD *Seven Poor Men of Sydney* iv. 112 What y' raisin' 'ell for; where y' come from? You're a *provocateur.* **1940** 'G. ORWELL' *Inside Whale* 142 To say 'I accept' in an age like our own is to say that you accept..submarines, spies, provocateurs, press censorship, [etc.]. **1956** A. L. GOODHARD in A. Pryce-Jones *New Outl. Mod. Knowl.* 581 The most important task..is the final extirpation..of all the remnants of these *provocateur* fabrications. **1961** C. COCKBURN *View from West* vi. 67 It looked much as though there might have been some *provocateurs* at work. **1974** T. P. WHITNEY tr. *Solzhenitsyn's Gulag Archipelago* I. I. viii. 319 The trial of the provocateur R. Malinovsky. **1976** 'J. DAVEY' *Treasury Alarm* i. 13 So you want me to..tell you if he's a genuine bloated capitalist or some sort of provocateur.

provocation. Add: **III. b.** *attrib.* **provocation test** *Med.*, a test to ascertain whether or not a person is alive.

1966 *Lancet* 31 Dec. 1466/2 On Oct. 12, 1965, patient was anæsthetized with halothane for a few minutes as a provocation test. **1971** *Essentials from Rep. Organtranspl.* (Netherlands Red Cross) 12 Provocation-tests and the best possible recording techniques should be used.

provocative, *a.* and *sb.* Add: **A.** *adj.* **2.** (Later examples.) Now limited to sexual contexts.

1933 [see *EXOTIC A. 2 b]. **1960** [see *BEEHIVE 1 c]. **1980** I. ST. JAMES *Money Stones* I. vii. 24 Her provocative teasing looks.

provocator (prǫ·vǒkeɪtəɹ). [ad. Fr. *provocateur.*] A provoker or challenger; = *PROVOCATEUR.

1896 W. LE QUEUX *Secret Service* iv. 79 From Paris 'flying brigades' of spies and provocators are sent out. **1913** *Amer. Yearbk. 1912* 392/2 This..has caused a reawakening of the revolutionary movement..the old Terrorist wing having practically disappeared..on account of the exposure of the activity of Eugene Azeff and his staff of police spies and provocators within its ranks. **1918** A. GRAY tr. *Grelling's Crime* II. ii. 132 If even the creator of the defensive Entente of 1904 was regarded as a dangerous provocator, [etc.].

‖**provodnik** (prəvɒdnʸi·k). [Russ.] In the U.S.S.R.: **a.** A guide. **b.** An attendant or guard on a train.

1888 J. C. MURRAY tr. *S. Maimon's Autobiogr.* xviii. 148, I was once seized as a prowodnik myself. **1927** *Contemp. Rev.* June 729 Two *provodniks*, or train attendants, looked after our coach. **1936** P. FLEMING *News from Tartary* ii. 23, I went back to my compartment and found the provodnik. **1976** *National Observer* (U.S.) 21 Feb. 7/2 A provodnik is shaving in one of the two lavatories at the height of the morning rush.

provolone (prǫvolōu·ni). [It., f. *provola* cheese made from buffalo's milk.] An Italian smoked cheese, often made in a variety of shapes, as spherical, pear-shaped, etc. Also *attrib.*

1946 A. SIMON *Conc. Encycl. Gastron.* IX. 22/1 *Provelone*, an all-the-year-round Italian cheese. **1952** S. KAUFFMANN *Philanderer* (1953) xii. 198 Madeline had gone shopping..to get him the anise and java ring and provolone that he loved. **1967** *Boston Sunday Globe* 23 Apr. (Advt. Section) 7/2 For color and flavor contrast add some sliced Swiss cheese, Italian Provolone. This last is light in color, sharp, tangy, cuts without crumbling, and has an agreeable flavor. **1968** V. & M. PETTITT *Len Deighton's Continental Dossier* 25 *The Basilicata*—a rather remote wild area where Romans caught bears for the Colosseum... Specialities: Provolone cheese, Aglianico di Vúlture—a full red wine. **1975** *New Yorker* 4 Aug. 20/3 Authentic Philadelphia hoagies, which are sort of submarines made of Genoa salami, cooked salami, provolone, capicola, lettuce, tomato, olive oil, and assorted spices. **1978** *Detroit Free Press* 16 Apr. (Detroit Suppl.) 7/1 The house specialty ($1.25–$6.50) is made from eight kinds of Italian luncheon meat, salamis, provolone cheese, Italian bread and sweet peppers.

provost guard. *U.S.* A body of soldiers acting as military police under a provost-marshal; also, the quarters used by these.

1778 *Jrnls. U.S. Continental Congress* (1908) X. 74 About thirty [officers] who have been confined in the provost guard and in the most loathsome gaols. **1864** O. W. NORTON *Army Lett.* (1903) 212 Company K is provost guard and river patrol. **1883** SWEET & KNOX *On Mexican Mustang through Texas* xlii. 595 We may be caught by the provost-guard, and put in the bull-pen. **1887** G. B. MCCLELLAN *McClellan's Own Story* iv. 69 These..I at once brought to the city and employed as a provost-guard.

pro-West, -Western: see *PRO-¹ 5 a.

prowl, *v.* Add: **2. d.** *Criminals' slang* (in U.S.). To examine, search, or inspect (a place or person), esp. before committing a robbery; to 'case'; to rob.

1914 JACKSON & HELLYER *Vocab. Criminal Slang* 67 *Prowl*, noun... An expeditionary investigation; a survey in transit; a search of the person or of a place in the sense of '*frisk*'; a burglary; a sneak; a saunter. Also used as a verb in the same senses. **1926** J. BLACK *You can't Win* xi. 136 I'd rather 'prowl' one of them than any business man. *Ibid.* xx. 318 He magnanimously suggested that I 'prowl the joint' he lived in. **1938** in *Amer. Speech* XIII. 158/1 Store is prowled. **1943** R. CHANDLER *Lady in Lake* xii. 71, I went back to the kitchen and prowled the open shelves above and behind the sink. **1977** 'M. INNES' *Honeybath's Haven* xv. 137 Some sort of sneak-thief had conceivably been prowling the dead man's property.

prowl, *sb.* Add: **a.** *on the prowl* (further examples); now freq. in search of an amorous partner.

1922 JOYCE *Ulysses* 600 A figure of middle height on the prowl, evidently, under the arches saluted again, calling: *Night!* **1946** *Sun* (Baltimore) 3 July 4/5 That big cat..is reputedly on the prowl again. **1959** W. BROWN *Cry Kill* iii. 31 Not a beauty like Lola Stuart, but good enough to catch the eye of any guy on the prowl. **1966** *N.Y. Times Bk. Rev.* 27 Mar. 35/1 Including his memorable encounters with an emancipated American college girl on the prowl. **1972** F. WARNER *Lying Figures* II. 9 Out on the prowl tonight, lover-boy? **1973** 'E. PETERS' *City of Gold & Shadows* iii. 45 A normal minor wolf on the prowl, with..an eye cocked for congenial company.

b. *Comb.*, as **prowl car** orig. *U.S.*, a police patrol car having a radio link with headquarters; **prowl dog** = *guard dog* s.v. GUARD *sb.* 18 in Dict. and Suppl.

1937 *Sun* (Baltimore) 6 Sept. 2/7 The man..climbed into the rear seat of our prowl car. **1953** H. CLEVELY *Public Enemy* xxix. 229 There's a prowl car outside... You were followed here. **1963** J. JOESTEN *They call it Intelligence* IV. xix. 188 A prowl car, manned by Western police, providentially arrived on the scene. **1967** N. LUCAS *C.I.D.* xi. 169 The presence of one of the Austin vans in the area had not passed unnoticed by the alert crew of a Berkshire County Police wireless prowl car.

1971 *Islander* (Victoria, B.C.) 16 May 11/1 Meantime another prowl car pulled into the yards. **1971** *Southerly* XXXI. 71 A prowl car told us to switch our parkers on. **1974** W. Garner *Big enough Wreath* xii. 163 We got patrols. We got prowl dogs.

prowler. Add: (Further examples.) Also, a burglar, a sneak thief.

1912 D. Lowrie *My Life in Prison* i. 5 Inadvertently we had left the back door open one night and a nocturnal prowler had taken advantage of it. **1926** J. Black *You can't Win* xix. 295 What a fox he is, to roll his money up in the curtain... What chance would a prowler have of finding his money? **1955** H. Kurnitz *Invasion of Privacy* (1956) xv. 99 It was Zorn's first ride in a police car. The radio chattered endlessly..of prowlers, burglars, rapists. **1976** *Flintshire Leader* 10 Dec. 1/7 Many of them are elderly or handicapped and live in fear of prowlers, car accidents and falls on uneven pathways.

proword: see *pro-[1] 4 b.

prox., abbrev. of Proximo.

1881 G. B. Shaw *Let.* 14 July (1965) 39 After the 1st prox. my address will be 37 Fitzroy Street W. **1935** A. P. Herbert *What a Word!* iii. 64 There must be millions of our citizens who have not the least notion what is meant by your *inst., prox.,* and *ult.* **1962** *Daily Tel.* 10 Dec. 12/7 'Inst', 'prox' and 'ult', which even today are scattered broadcast.

proxemics (prǫksī·miks). *Sociol.* [f. Prox(imity + *-emics*; cf. *emic *a.*] The study of the spaces that people feel it necessary to set between themselves and others as they vary in different social settings, or between different social groups or cultures; also the study of the feeling for space between people as it is manifested in aspects of culture such as the planning of houses or towns, in language, etc.

1963 E. T. Hall in *Amer. Anthropologist* LXV. 1003 Proxemics, the study of how man unconsciously structures microspace—the distance between men in the conduct of daily transactions, the organization of space in his houses and buildings, and ultimately the layout of his towns. **1969** *Guardian* 29 Sept. 7/2 Though territoriality and its effects has been studied for many years now in connection with animal life, Dr Hall is..the first person to link the concept direct with human beings and..has coined a purely human word for it: proxemics. **1974** *Language Sciences* Aug. 32/3 Ever since Edward Hall.. made public the results of his research on man's use of space, the interrelated observations and theories of which he calls proxemics, [etc.]. **1976** U. Eco *Theory of Semiotics* 10 *Kinesics and proxemics*: the idea that gesturing depends on cultural codes is now an acquired notion of cultural anthropology.

Hence **proxe·mic** *a.*, of, relating or pertaining to proxemics.

1963 E. T. Hall in *Amer. Anthropologist* LXV. 1003 (*title*) A system for the notation of proxemic behavior. **1965** [see *kinesic *a.*]. **1971** *Times Lit. Suppl.* 4 June 653/4 In man 'proxemic' behaviour ranges from the distance two people maintain while engaged in conversation or the way a group of people arrange themselves, to architecture and city planning. **1976** J. F. Kess *Psycholinguistics* vi. 145 A detailed notational system for proxemic behaviors along a number of dimensions.

proximal, *a.* (*sb.*) Add: **A.** *adj.* **2. c.** *Dentistry.* Of, pertaining to, or being opposing surfaces of adjacent teeth in the same arch.

1908 G. V. Black *Work on Operative Dentistry* II. 3 Cavities occurring in the proximal surfaces of the teeth are called proximal cavities. **1944** S. Hemley *Fund. Occlusion* vi. 150 The teeth in the same arch in the adult dentition are normally in proximal contact with each other on both the mesial and the distal surfaces. **1963** C. R. Cowell et al. *Inlays, Crowns, & Bridges* iv. 35 The restoration covers the incisal edge of the tooth as well as the affected proximal surface. **1975** G. T. Charbeneau *Princ. & Pract. Operative Dentistry* xi. 262/1 The annoyance of food impaction between such teeth with an open proximal contact will be the initial concern of the patient.

3. *Psychol.* Applied to the stimuli immediately responsible for a perception or sensation.

1935 K. Koffka *Princ. Gestalt Psychol.* iii. 80 The table..can be called a stimulus for our perception of a table;..the excitations to which the light rays coming from the table give rise are called the stimuli for our perception. Let us call the first the distant stimulus, the second the proximal stimuli. **1955** F. H. Allport *Theories of Perception* v. 147 The gestaltists point out the necessary differences between the proximal stimulus-pattern and the percept,..and attribute the 'way things look' to the organizing forces of the brain-field. **1971** *Jrnl. Gen. Psychol.* LXXXV. 3 A relation between the various aspects of perception and the proximal and distal stimuli is clearly revealed in almost all experiments.

proximate, *a.* **2.** (Examples of *proximate analysis.*)

1831 [see Analysis 3]. **1857** W. A. Miller *Elem. Chem.* III. i. 6 The separation of wheat flour into starch, sugar, gluten, ligneous fibre, and oily matter, affords an instance of proximate analysis. **1951** Campbell & Gibb *Methods of Analysis of Fuels & Oils* i. 1 The proximate analysis of coal, which is carried out on coal ground to pass a 72 B.S. sieve and air-dried, involves the direct determination of (*a*) moisture, (*b*) volatile matter, and (*c*) ash, the remainder, the so-called 'fixed carbon', being obtained by difference. **1971** M. F. Mallette et al. *Introd. Biochem.* ix. 314 The crude lipid of the proximate analysis found on..certain food labels refers to the nonvolatile material derived by weighing the residue after evaporation of the extraction solvent.

proximity. Add: **2.** *attrib.* **proximity fuse,** a detonator in a missile that employs radar to operate it automatically when within a predetermined distance of a target; so **proximity-fused** *a.*

1945 *Sci. News Let.* 6 Oct. 214/1 The proximity fuze, a tiny radio set device in the nose of the projectile, is rated as the U.S.A. No. 2 secret weapon. **1956** A. H. Compton *Atomic Quest* 53 Applications of radar in the form of the 'proximity fuse' were critically important in bringing victory [in World War II]. **1972** *Guardian* 11 Jan. 11/2 In the Chinese campaign in Hongkong..the guerrillas eventually produced bombs equipped with photo cells, magnetic and proximity fuses, and vibration detectors that would set off the charge if you so much as looked at it. **1978** R. V. Jones *Most Secret War* xliv. 427 The new proximity-fused shells.., although originally a British invention, had been developed and engineered in America.

proxy, *sb.* Add: **III. 6. a. proxy form,** a form on which a proxy vote is registered; **proxy sitting** *Spiritualism,* a sitting arranged with a medium and attended by one person at the request of another, usu. unknown, person who hopes for news of someone recently dead; **proxy war** *U.S.*, a war limited in scale or area, instigated by a major power which does not itself become involved.

1930 *Economist* 6 Sept. 453/2 Accordingly they may, and should, use the company's money for the printing and postage of proxy forms. **1927** N. Walker *Bridge* III. iv. 139, I had known about practically nothing that was mentioned in the two previous proxy Leonard sittings. **1933** *Proc. Soc. Psychical Res.* XLI. cxxx. 139 (*title*) A consideration of a series of proxy sittings. **1948** *Mind* LVII. 393 Telepathy is again invoked as the source of supernormal material: a well-worn hypothesis, which fails to cover the data obtained by proxy-sittings, cross-correspondences and so forth. **1962** C. D. Broad *Lect. Psychical Res.* xv. 352 The essentials of a proxy-sitting are the following. The experimenter..receives in writing from some person, often a complete stranger to him, a few distinctive facts about a certain recently deceased individual... The specified facts are such as would suffice to enable the experimenter to recognize with some probability that the medium was referring to the individual in question. **1955** *N.Y. Times* 9 Jan. 8E/5 A threat that the United States would instantly retaliate with atomic weapons against the heart of the Communist world if the Commies started another proxy or brush-fire war. **1978** *Amer. Polit. Sci. Rev.* Sept. 971/2 Proxy wars, as the Athenians discovered in trying to rule their empire indirectly, are extremely costly.

b. *Petrol.* and *Min.* Applied to a mineral that proxies another.

1931 [see *proxy *v.* 2]. **1949** F. H. Hatch et al. *Petrol. Igneous Rocks* (ed. 10) I. ii. 69 These Al''' atoms which function as silicons are 'proxy Al's', and each unit contains two of these. **1965** A. W. G. Whittle in G. J. Williams *Econ. Geol. N.Z.* x. 150/2 It is probable that an appreciable amount of 'proxy-nickel' was leached during the hydrothermal alteration of the pendotites to serpentinites.

proxy, *v.* Restrict *rare* to sense in Dict. (s.v. Proxy *sb.*) and add: **2.** *Petrol.* and *Min.* *trans.* To occur in place of, esp. in a crystal lattice. Also *intr.*, const. *for.* Hence **pro·xying** *vbl. sb.*

1922 A. Johannsen in *Jrnl. Geol.* XXX. 640 The [German] author says a 'gabbro tendency' is shown, and that diallage is proxied by an amphibole of similar chemical composition. **1925** *Amer. Jrnl. Sci.* CCIX. 313 It is not possible for Br atoms to proxy for Na atoms in halite; they can occupy only places of Cl atoms. **1931** A. Johannsen *Descr. Petrogr. Igneous Rocks* I. 189 'Proxy-minerals' is a translation of the German words *stellvertretende Gemengteile*, used by von Leonhard [in 1823] for minerals which take the place of other minerals in a rock; i.e., proxy them but do not replace them in the sense of molecular replacement... Thus if a certain type rock contains biotite, and another is like it in every way except that the dark mineral is hornblende, then in the latter the hornblende proxies biotite, and hornblende is the proxy-mineral. **1946** *Amer. Mineralogist* XXXI. 423 In tetrahedral positions Al proxies part of the Si. *Ibid.* 424 Other variables in the chemical composition [of the montmorillonite group of minerals] are..the proxying of OH by F as in the micas. **1963** W. A. Deer et al. *Rock-Forming Minerals* II. 353 The richterite..has an unusually high content of titanium some of which may proxy for silicon in tetrahedral positions.

pro-Zionist: see *pro-[1] 5 a.

prozone (prōu·zōun). *Immunol.* [Contraction of *pro*-agglutinoid *zone*, f. Pro-[1] + *agglutinoid + Zone *sb.*] The range of relative quantities of precipitin (or agglutinin) and antigen within which the expected precipitation (or agglutination) fails to occur when they are mixed; the mixture so produced, usu. containing antibody in excess. Freq. *attrib.*

[**1914** H. Zinsser *Infection & Resistance* vi. 162 In the study of agglutinin and precipitin reactions, phenomena exactly analagous to the Neisser-Wechsberg effect have been noticed, in the case of the agglutinins, the so-called 'pro-agglutinoid' zone being a case in point.] **1916** *Jrnl. Immunol.* I. 6 The fourth line in this table represents the so-called prozone in which excess of precipitinogen inhibits precipitation. **1934** Zinsser & Bayne-Jones *Textbk. Bacteriol.* (ed. 7) xvi. 222 The specificity of the prozones is demonstrable in two ways. In the first place, bacteria that have been subjected to the action of serum showing such a prozone, without being agglutinated, will no longer agglutinate when subsequently emulsified in a potent agglutinating serum. Again, absorption of a prozone serum with the homologous bacteria will remove the prozone. **1964** D. F. Gray *Immunol.* xi. 114 The 'constant antibody' precipitin reaction illustrates a phenomenon of diagnostic importance that may occur in agglutination tests, viz. the prozone, in which antigen: antibody aggregation is interfered with in the presence of an excess of antigen or of antibody. **1970** Passmore & Robson *Compan. Med. Stud.* II. xxii. 15/2 The prozone phenomenon..is probably due to the stabilizing effects of high protein concentration on the particles; the protein coating increases the net charge of the particles and brings about increased electrostatic repulsion between individual particles, thus opposing the efforts of the antibody molecules to link them together.

prozzy, var. *prossie.

Pru (prū). Colloq. abbrev. of *Prudential Assurance Company*; *esp.* in phr. (*the*) *man from the Pru*, a representative of the Company who calls regularly at private houses to collect life insurance premiums (see quot. 1963).

1927 W. E. Collinson *Contemp. Eng.* 111 The best known English company, the Prudential, is often called the Pru. **1961** C. Cockburn *View from West* ii. 19 To what extent..is our entire view of life..determined by what is told us by the Men from the Pru? **1963** *Times* 24 Apr. 12/3 The Prudential Assurance Company has discontinued the issue of life insurance policies paid by weekly premiums. This does not mean that 'the man from the Pru' will no longer be calling from door to door: all new 'industrial' life policy premiums will ordinarily be collected every four weeks instead of weekly. **1973** A. Behrend *Samarai Affair* xiii. 141 She..said with no more emotion than if addressing a man from the Pru, 'My husband's told me what you've come for.' **1978** *Guardian Weekly* 15 Jan. 21/3 Next year I hope the Cottesloe [Theatre] will offer us, like the man from the Pru, a definite policy.

prude (prūd), *v.* [f. the sb.] *intr.* To conduct oneself in the manner of a prude; to act prudishly. Hence **pru·ding** *vbl. sb.*

1737 H. Carey *Musical Century* 13 Crowds of coxcombs thus deluding, Cringing, chatt'ring, ogling, flatt'ring By coquetting and by pruding, All are victims to my art. **1850** C. M. Yonge *Henrietta's Wish* x. 151 'Pruding,' said Beatrice, 'showing openly that you like it to be observed how prudent and proper you are.' **1923** V. L. Silberrad *Lett. Jean Armiter* ix. 194 Girls aren't brought up in cotton wool nowadays as you were. We do as we jolly well like! It's no good preaching and pruding.

prun- (prūn). *Chem.* [f. Prun(us.] A formative element used in the names of several substances which occur in trees of the genus *Prunus*, as **pru·nase** [*-ase], an enzyme which hydrolyses *β*-glucosides (notably prunasin), liberating glucose, and occurs chiefly in bitter almonds and yeast, as well as in the fruit of several *Prunus* species; **pru·nasin** [f. prec. + -in[1]], a crystalline substance found in a number of trees, notably the bird cherry, *P. padus*; the racemic form of a glucoside of the nitrile of mandelic acid, $C_6H_5{\cdot}CH(CN){\cdot}OC_6H_{11}O_5$; **pru·netin** [*-etin], a colourless crystalline isoflavone derivative, $C_{16}H_{12}O_5$, which is the monomethyl ether of prunetol and occurs combined as glycosides in the wood and bark of several trees; **pru·netol** [f. prec. + -ol] = *genistein; **pru·nitrin** [*-trin* prob. after Dextrin], a colourless crystalline glucoside of prunetin.

The quotations follow in chronological order.

1910 H. Finnemore in *Pharmaceutical Jrnl.* XXXI. 604/1 This aqueous solution was shaken with ether, which at once precipitated a nearly colourless, semi-crystalline product, consisting mainly of a new dihydric phenol, $C_{16}H_{12}O_5$, to which the name prunetin is assigned. *Ibid.*, Prunetin contains a single methoxy group, and when demethylated by boiling with hydriodic acid yields the corresponding trihydric phenol, prunetol, $C_{15}H_{10}O_5$. *Ibid.*, Further treatment of the aqueous solution yielded a colourless glucoside which when hydrolysed gave prunetin, and was obviously the mother substance of that phenol, and to which the name prunitrin is accordingly given. **1912** H. E. Armstrong et al. in *Proc. R. Soc.* B. LXXXV. 360 It appears to be desirable to assign a distinct name in future to the enzyme in 'emulsin' by which the resolution of the simple cyanophoric glucoside is effected; as it occurs very generally in the various species of Prunus, we propose to term it Prunase; also it will be convenient to use the name Prunasin in speaking of the glucoside (d-mandelonitrile glucoside) which, hitherto, we have termed Fischer's glucoside. **1918** Perkin & Everest *Natural Org. Colouring Matters* vii. 205 Prunetin,..colourless needles, melting-point 242°, dissolves in alkalis with a slight yellow colour. **1936** W. Stiles *Introd. Princ. Plant Physiol.* v. 106 The prunasin is now hydrolysed by means of prunase into glucose and mandelonitrile. **1940** *Thorpe's Dict. Appl. Chem.* (ed. 4) IV. 283/1 This *β*-glucosidase is also called prunase and latterly, *β*-phenylglucosidase. **1956** I. L. Finar *Org. Chem.* II. vii. 244 The enzyme zymase hydrolyses amygdalin into one molecule of glucose and a glucoside of (+)-mandelonitrile (this compound is identical with prunasin, a naturally occurring glucoside). **1959** N. Campbell in E. H. Rodd *Chem. Carbon Compounds* IVB. viii. 925 Genistein (prunetol), 5:7:4′-trihydroxyisoflavone, $C_{15}H_{10}O_5$, colourless needles,.. occurs along with luteolin in dyers broom. *Ibid.*, Prunetin, ..genistein 7-methyl ether,..is isolated from the bark of a wild cherry related to *Prunus emarginata*..and the commercial timber muninga (*Pterocarpus angolensis*). *Ibid.* 926 Prunitrin, prunetin 4′-glucoside..occurs in *Prunus Serotina* L. and is synthesised by methylating sophoricoside. **1976** *Nature* 15 Apr. 604/1 The ecological success of bracken is partly..because of its ability to synthesise various secondary compounds which deter predators and phytopathogens. These compounds include the cyanogenic glycoside, prunasin, toxic because on enzymatic hydrolysis HCN is released.

prune, *sb.* Add: **1. d.** *slang* (orig. *U.S.*). A disagreeable or disliked person; a simpleton; spec., *Royal Air Force*, the personification of stupidity and incompetence (also, as a fictitious title, *P.O. Prune*). Hence **pru·nery**; **pru·nish** *a.*

1895 W. C. Gore in *Inlander* Dec. 112 *Prune*, one who is disagreeable, and irritable. **1941** Baker *Dict. Austral. Slang* 57 *Prune*, a simpleton, fool. **1942** *Tee Emm* (Air Ministry) II. 67 All because the Prunes of the Air Force *will* ignore the existence of A.A. Danger Areas. **1942** *Observer* 4 Oct. 7/2 The Royal Air Force has adopted him [*sc.* P.O. Prune] now, and an official magazine is devoted to the purpose of trying to cure him of his prunery! *Ibid.*. One day, I think, in some solemn dictionary Prune will become immortal. **1942** T. Rattigan *Flare Path* I. 30 They call me P.O. Prune—he's a character in The Training Manual—sort of crazy, good-tempered, half-witted sort of bloke..and I—well, I kind of act P.O. Prune for them. *Ibid.* II. i. 53 He's not quite so prunish as he lets on. **1943** C. H. Ward-Jackson *Piece of Cake* 49 *Prune, Pilot Officer*, a fictitious character who behaves as every officer should not, created by Squadron Leader Anthony Armstrong and the artist RAFF (L.A.C.W. Hooper)... Prune was created to teach pupils and other flying personnel how things should not be done. **1944** 'N. Shute' *Pastoral* ii. 35 He wished..that he knew what it was that worried her, whether it was some prune that she had left at her last station. **1961** G. Smith *Business of Loving* viii. 201 Snap out of it, you moonstruck old prune. **1963** *Listener* 28 Feb. 392/3 No horse-play, no gremlins: in Mr Barr's script the Prunes have all been turned into serious-minded Prisms. **1970** *Women Speaking* Apr. 5/1 If a man doesn't like a girl's looks or personality, she's a.. prune, lemon. **1978** J. Krantz *Scruples* xiii. 368, I think she's a bit of a prune.

3. (Further examples.)

1922 Joyce *Ulysses* 690 A sofa upholstered in a prune plush. **1976** *Vogue* Jan. 74/1 Prune silk crepe de chine with tiny white print.

4. (Further examples.) Also adj. phrs. *prunes and prismy, pruny and prismy.*

c **1909** D. H. Lawrence *Collier's Friday Night* (1934) i. 8 She says this in a very quaint 'prunes-and-prisms' manner, with her chin in the air and her hand extended. **1922** Joyce *Ulysses* 365 Say prunes and prisms forty times every morning, cure for fat lips. **1931** *Time & Tide* 4 July 802/2 A tougher-minded generation than ours may find it altogether too prunes-and-prismy. **1940** G. D. H. & M. Cole *Counterpoint Murder* v. 50 She's forty if she's a day, and all pruny and prismy. **1979** *Daily Tel.* 22 Nov. 14/7 She regales us with an amusing chronicle of Lady Lytton's attempts to find a congenial companion among the straightlaced Indian Civil Service wives, whose 'prunes and prisms' expressions she found most off-putting.

5. *prune-orchard, -rancher, -whip; prune-coloured, -dark* adjs.; **prune-brandy,** an alcoholic beverage prepared from prunes; **prune-juice,** also, nonsense *U.S. slang*; **prune picker** *U.S. colloq.*, a Californian.

1895 M. Pemberton *Impregnable City* vi. 41 Drink that, and when you've drained the bumper, we'll have some prune brandy. **1872** *Young Englishwoman* Nov. 595/1 A hat of duck-green turquoise is trimmed with prune-coloured velvet. **1923** *Blackw. Mag.* Oct. 499/2 The foothills..were covered with a shadow over which prune-coloured clouds hung. **1941** L. MacNeice *Plant & Phantom* 64 With prune-dark eyes, thick lips, jostling each other. **1957** J. Kerouac *On Road* (1958) iii. iv. 199 Here we were dealing with the pit and prunejuice of poor beat life. **1965** Wodehouse *Galahad at Blandings* x. 170 We decided that a big Society wedding was a lot of prune juice and we wanted no piece of it. **1921** *Chambers's Jrnl.* Mar. 173/1 Prune-orchards do not need irrigating. **1918** L. E. Ruggles *Navy Explained* 112 *Prune picker*, a native of California. So called because of the abundant prune crops. **1929** *Papers Mich. Acad. Sci., Arts & Lett.* X. 316 *Prune picker*, a Californian. **1921** *Chambers's Jrnl.* Mar. 174/2 With proper pruning and cultivation the prune-rancher has an assured..living. **1942** 'R. West' *Black Lamb & Grey Falcon* II. 26 Their coffee-brown beauty which fastidious nostrils, secretive lips and eyes like prune-whip made refined and romantic.

prune, *v.*² Add: **3.** (Further examples.)

1836 J. H. Newman in *Brit. Mag.* X. 137 Prune thou thy words. **1925** B. Beetham in E. F. Norton *Fight for Everest, 1924* 368 Bow to the inevitable, countenance what you deem to be reasonable, but prune early with a firm pencil anything excessive. **1970** *Railway Mag.* Oct. 546/1 The locomotive-hauled stock of British Railways has been drastically pruned in recent years.

b. Also with *out*.

1955 *Bull. Atomic Sci.* Mar. 94/2 Undoubtedly, these will be pruned out in the next edition. **1973** *Sci. Amer.* June 93/3 Shannon therefore proposed that the computer should not consider all possible moves from each position but should prune out the most obvious of bad moves.

pruner. Add: **2.** A tool used for pruning trees or shrubs.

1895 *Montgomery Ward Catal.* Spring & Summer 391/3 This pruner, being made with the shear cut, will work with double the ease of any other pruner. *Ibid.*, Waters' Improved Tree Pruner. **1916** L. H. Bailey *Pruning Man.* vi. 192 (*caption*) Double-lever and single-lever pole pruner. **1949** E. Hyams *Not in Our Stars* xiii. 160 The long-arm pruner had tired his arms and shoulders. **1971** *Country Life* 14 Oct. 955/3 My arm aches from using the sickle, and the heavy pruner. **1975** E. Wigginton *Foxfire 3* 26 Got to where I couldn't press the pruners enough to cut a big limb.

pruning, *vbl. sb.*² Add: **1.** (Later examples.)

1941 P. P. Pirone *Maintenance of Shade & Ornamental Trees* v. 58 Proper and systematic pruning helps trees better to withstand adverse environmental conditions. **1972** G. E. Brown (*title*) The pruning of trees, shrubs and conifers.

2. (Later examples.)

a **1930** D. H. Lawrence *Last Poems* (1932) 289 Humanity needs pruning. **1969** *Listener* 6 Mar. 322/1 It is a surprise to find the *Lyric Symphony*..a highly charged, expansive outpouring in seven longish movements of which the first three could themselves do with some pruning. **1970** T. Lupton *Managem. & Social Sci.* (ed. 2) ii. 47 A drastic alteration of working practices and some pruning of manpower. **1971** *Nature* 16 July 206/2 If a second edition is prepared, the editors would do well to perform some judicious pruning.

prunus. Add to etym.: adopted by Linnæus (*Hortus Cliffortianus* (1737) 186) as the name of a genus. **1.** Also, a tree or shrub belonging to this genus, esp. one of many varieties of cherry cultivated for the sake of their ornamental, pink or white flowers. (Later examples.)

1901 L. H. Bailey *Cycl. Amer. Hort.* III. 1445/2 It is an important point in the growing of these grafted Prunuses to remove all sprouts from the stock as soon as they appear. **1945** J. Betjeman *New Bats in Old Belfries* 22 Pinkly bursts the spray Of prunus and forsythia across the public way. **1966** *New Statesman* 7 Jan. 25/2 The evergreen prunus we call cherry-laurel. **1972** *Countryman* Summer 48 The old prunus on the lawn..immediately caught my eye.

prurience. 3. (Later examples.)

1926 H. W. Fowler *Mod. Eng. Usage* 473/1 *Prurience, -cy.* There is no differentiation; *-ence* is recommended. **1974** C. Ricks *Keats & Embarrassment* i. 15 Prurience, pruriency, and prurient came fully into their modern meaning (from 'itching') in the eighteenth century.

prurient, *a.* Add: **3.** (Further example.) Also *absol.* or as *sb.*

1911 G. B. Shaw *Blanco Posnet* 334 The farcical comedy which has scandalized the critics in London..is played to the respectable dress circle of Northampton with these same jests slurred over so as to be imperceptible by even the most prurient spectator. **1969** *Punch* 29 Jan. 159/1 We've had the prudes and the prurients, the 'Love-Outs' and the love-ins, sex without marriage and marriage without sex. **1974** C. Ricks *Keats & Embarrassment* i. 15 The prurient is characterized by a particular attitude..of cherishing, fondling or slyly watching.

prurit. For †*Obs. rare*⁻¹ read *rare* and add later example.

1953 S. Beckett *Watt* 182 A diffuse ano-scrotal prurit.

prurition (prūri·ʃən). *rare*⁻¹. [f. Prurit(us + -ion.] = Pruritus.

1922 Joyce *Ulysses* 695 He scratched imprecisely with his left hand, though insensible of prurition, various points and surfaces of his partly exposed..skin.

prushun (prʊ·ʃən). *U.S. slang.* [Origin obscure.] A boy who travels with a tramp and begs for him.

1893 *Century Mag.* Nov. 106/1, I once knew a kid, or prushun, who averaged in Denver nearly three dollars a day. **1899** 'J. Flynt' *Tramping with Tramps* 396 *Prushun*, a tramp boy. An 'ex-prushun' is one who has served his apprenticeship as a 'kid' and is 'looking for revenge', *i.e.*, for a lad that he can 'snare' and 'jocker', as he himself was 'snared' and 'jockered'. **1907** J. London *Road* (1914) 235 If he travels with a 'profesh', he [*sc.* 'a road-kid'] is known possessively as a 'prushun'. **1927** *Dialect Notes* V. 459 The tramp lives in idleness while the boy goes about begging food for both. Many continue as *prushuns* until middle life, and when their master dies are left helpless.

prusik (prʊ·sik), *a.* *Mountaineering.* Also (*erron.*) **prussik**, and with initial capital. [f. the name of Karl *Prusik*, Austrian mountaineer.] Used to designate a method invented by Dr. Prusik of ascending a climbing rope by means of two separate continuous loops, each attached to it by a special knot (*Prusik knot*) which tightens when weight is applied and slackens when it is removed, thus enabling the loop to be moved up the rope. Also *ellipt.* as *sb.* Hence as *vb.*, to climb with the aid of prusik loops or similar devices; **pru·siking** *vbl. sb.*

1937 E. A. M. Wedderburn *Alpine Climbing* vi. 101 By employing the Prusik method he [*sc.* a man who has fallen] may be able to get himself out of a crevasse unaided... He first attaches the middle-sized loop of cord to the climbing rope as high as he can reach with a Prusik knot.., passes it through his waist loop, [etc.]. **1946** J. E. Q. Barford *Climbing in Brit.* v. 68 The Prusik Knot or Friction Hitch. This is a new and very useful hitch which is used for attaching a subsidiary rope or sling to the main rope. **1955** M. Banks *Commando Climber* v. 83 We.. moved on carefully, realising that, despite Prussik slings, rescue operations are extremely difficult. **1956** C. Evans *On Climbing* vii. 105 Each person in the party should have two Prusik loops (nine-foot lengths of Italian hemp cord spliced to make a rope ring). **1959** H. Merrick tr. *Harrer's White Spider* 199 It is..obvious that Longhi was unfamiliar with the 'Prusik-knot' technique. *Ibid.* 200 It would not have taken Longhi half an hour to 'Prusik' himself by his own efforts up to the overhang. **1968** [see *Jumar]. **1972** D. Haston *In High Places* i. 8 He can use a special wrap-around knot to attach himself to the rope. This is called a prusik knot, after its German inventor. *Ibid.* ix. 103 Mike and I prussiked up in two hours to the high point. *Ibid.* xi. 120 A carry from Camp IV, up the overhanging prussiks, along the horizontal horrors of the ice ridge and up the never-ending icefields above. **1977** *Guardian Weekly* 20 Mar. 19/2 Two of the instructors.. help to provide a wide variety of experience in the arts of prusiking, abseiling, and all the necessary techniques, to both the advanced specialist and to schoolchildren.

Prussian, *a.* and *sb.* Add: **A.** *adj.* **1.** (Earlier example.)

Prussian binding (see quot. 1882), *collar* (see quot. 1955).

1565 R. Shacklock tr. *Hosius's Hatchet of Heresies* (*title-page verso*), Fixing his eye on Prussian grounde, He sawe holy Hosius makyng this boke. **1880** *Queen* 19 June (Advt.), Sun umbrella cover..bound Self, Scarlet, Green, or Blue Prussian Binding. **1882** Caulfield & Saward *Dict. Needlework* 412/2 *Prussian bindings.* These are designed for the binding of mantles, dressing-gowns, and waterproofs... They consist of a silk face and cotton back, having a diagonal twill. **1932** D. C. Minter *Mod. Needlecraft* 113/1 Neaten the bottom of a fitting sleeve with lute ribbon or Prussian binding. **1955** J. E. Liberty *Pract. Tailoring* (ed. 2) xi. 211 The Prussian or Double collar, is made to button up to the neck and has a small stand. There are variations of this type, from the style very like the double linen collar worn with a tie, to that where the fall lies flatter on the fronts and does not fit so closely to the stand, 2 to 3½ in. fall, as on uniforms. **1968** J. Ironside *Fashion Alphabet* 52 *Prussian collar*, a fairly high-standing turned-down collar, as on military great-coats.

2. a. Prussian blue. (Further examples.) Also *ellipt.*

1835 [see *Antwerp]. **1911** O. Onions *Widdershins* iv. 154 The daylight had gone, but I knew that 'Prussian' would be about the colour for the eyes. **1940** [see *Antwerp].

d. A variety of pea with large, bluish seeds. Also *ellipt.*

1804 J. Gardiner *Amer. Gardener* 43 Spanish morottos, rouncivals, prussians, green and white, marrowfats, and other large late peas are the kinds to sow this month. **1824** J. C. Loudon *Encycl. Gardening* (ed. 2) iii. viii. 618 The egg, the Moratto, the Prussian blue, and the Rouncivals, ..are all very fine eating peas. **1832** J. Tod *Annals Rajast'han* II. 765, I never saw finer crops of Prussian-blues,..cauliflowers, celery, and all that belongs to the kitchen-garden. **1915** *N. & Q.* 6 Nov. 370/1 Prussian blues are a particular description of peas. Those and Marrowfats were in my early days considered the best varieties of that vegetable.

B. *sb.* **1.** (Earlier examples.)

1554 W. Prat tr. *Discr. Aphrique* sig. B6ᵛ, The Germaynes, Italyons, Spanyardes, Frenchemen, Scottes, Iryshmen, the Danes, Liuones Prussiens. **1565** R. Shacklock tr. *Hosius's Hatchet of Heresies* f.2ᵛ This agrement of fayth..floryshed among..the Germanes.. Catholyke Russians, Prussians, or Masouians.

2. = *Old Prussian *sb.* b.

1888 J. Wright tr. *Brugmann's Elem. Compar. Gram. Indo-Gmc. Lang.* I. 11 The Baltic division consists of Prussian, Lithuanian, and Lettic. **1972** W. B. Lockwood *Panorama Indo-European Lang.* 139 A catechism, in Prussian and German, was twice printed in 1545.

Prussianism. Add: (Further examples.) Also, the militaristic concepts and disciplinary methods regarded as typical of the Prussian system. Hence **Pru·ssianist** *a.*

1915 *Chambers's Jrnl.* Oct. 664/2 Then we are getting.. 'Prussianism', 'Prussianization',.., with all their meanings. **1916** A. Huxley *Let.* 31 Mar. (1969) 95 One discusses too the collapse of English civilisation, whose rapid decay under the sinister influence of Prussianism is everywhere apparent. **1922** Prussianist [see *goose-step]. **1942** *R.A.F. Jrnl.* 2 May 6 Yet there *is* discipline... It is all done without Prussianism. **1944** F. A. Hayek *Road to Serfdom* 7 It was the prevalence of socialist views and not Prussianism that Germany had in common with Italy and Russia. **1945** K. R. Popper *Open Society* II. xii. 27 Hegel..became the first official philosopher of Prussianism. **1978** *Christian* V. 18 Pope Leo XIII decided..to come to terms with both French Republicanism and Prussianism.

Prussianize, *v.* Add: (Later example.) Also *intr.*, to act in a manner regarded as typical of Prussians. **Prussianized** *ppl. a.*, **Prussianizing** *vbl. sb.*, **Prussianization:** later examples.

1909 *Q. Rev.* CCX. 664 A similar policy pursued in a neighbouring territory—the attempted prussianisation of the inhabitants of Prussian Poland. *Ibid.*, Since his [*sc.* Bismarck's] time there has been a steady attempt to prussianise them. *Ibid.*, So far, the prussianising policy had wholly failed. **1915** [see *PRUSSIANISM]. **1927** 'IXION' *Further Motor Cycle Reminisc.* 82 The victim [of the practical joke] occupied a minor official position, by dint of which he Prussianized rather too freely. **1963** *Times Lit. Suppl.* 18 Jan 45/2 The Poles in Prussia's eastern provinces were not only devout Catholics but also Polish patriots who..offered stubborn resistance to Bismarck's Prussianization policy. **1976** *Listener* 19 Feb. 202/1 After 60 years, some Hanoverians, especially the military, had become Prussianised.

Pru·ssianly, *adv.* [f. PRUSSIAN *a.* + -LY².] In a manner regarded as typical of Prussians.
1917 *Daily Chron.* 26 July 2/5 People don't shove quite so selfishly, don't scowl at each other so Prussianly. **1932** BLUNDEN *Face of England* 72 He stumped, yet more Prussianly, into the pavilion. **1979** F. MORTON *Nervous Splendour* i. 7 Helmet Prussianly spiked.

prussic, *a.* (Examples of *prussic acid* used *attrib.* and *fig.*)
1860 MRS. GASKELL *Let.* ?28 June (1966) 912 The thunder yesterday gave me a dreadful headache so I had to..have my prussic acid medicine made up. **1927** D. H. LAWRENCE *Mornings in Mexico* 12 Such a suave, prussic-acid sarcasm.

Prussification (prʌsifikēⁱ·ʃən). [f. PRUSSI(AN *a.* + -FICATION.] = PRUSSIANIZATION. So **Pru·ssify** *v. trans.* = PRUSSIANIZE *v.*
1898 *Daily News* 21 Jan. 4/5 The Bill to increase the fund for the Prussification of the Polish provinces of the kingdom. **1904** *Daily Chron.* 23 Nov. 4/6 His proposal was successfully opposed by the other kingdoms as tending to the Prussification of the new empire. **1924** *Contemp. Rev.* Mar. 301 The Russians were trying their hardest to russify, and the Prussians were trying their hardest to prussify their Polish provinces.

pry, *v.*² Add: (Further examples.) Also *fig.*
1896 C. M. SHELDON *His Brother's Keeper* iii. 66 We managed to pry out of him that he had seen you and Eric go down the ladders. **1921** E. O'NEILL *Diff'rent* II. 245 It was always like pryin' open a safe for me to separate him from a cent. **1926** *Harper's Mag.* Feb. 363/1, I stood rooted to the spot and you could not have pried me away. **1927** S. ERTZ *Now East, Now West* ii. 21 He walked about the decks..hand in hand with Cleve, whenever that friendly child could be pried loose from some new and fascinating acquaintance. **1933** D. GARNETT *Pocahontas* v. 46 Holding out his clenched fist for her to pry his fingers open. **1947** S. BELLOW *Victim* (1948) i. 14 Philip pried off the caps on the handle of a metal cabinet in the kitchen. **1954** T. S. ELIOT *Confidential Clerk* I. 18 She's come to pry some cash from the money-box. **1968** J. AIKEN *Whispering Mountain* iii. 64 Owen's teeth were pried open and the neck of the bottle forced between them. **1976** *Time* 20 Dec. 1/2 When Watergate raised questions about the integrity of the Executive Branch, Congress appointed an independent prosecutor to pry out all the facts. **1978** C. TOMLINSON *Shaft* 14 As if this place could be pried out of now.

Przewalski (prəʒəvæ·lski). Also **Prejevalsky, Przevalsky.** The name of N. M. *Przewalski* (1839–1888), Russian explorer, used *attrib.*, *ellipt.*, and in the possessive to designate a wild horse, *Equus przevalskii*, collected by him in 1876 in Central Asia, its native land, and named after him by I. S. Poliakov in 1881 (*Izvestiya Imper. Russ. Geogr. Obshchestva* XVII. 1).
1881 *Ann. Mag. Nat. Hist.* VIII. 16 (*heading*) Prejevalsky's Horse. **1884** *Nature* 21 Aug. 391/2 Przevalsky's wild horse has warts on its hind-legs as well as on its fore-legs. *Ibid.*, Nor has Przevalsky's horse any dorsal stripe. **1928** *Daily Tel.* 3 Jan. 5/1 Of the numerous arrivals at the zoo during the past year, the following are amongst the rarest or most valuable:..a Prejevalski's wild horse,.. and two Komodo monitor lizards. **1951** G. G. SIMPSON *Horses* iii. 17 It is usually said that the only living true wild horse..is the central Asiatic race or subspecies called Przewalski's horse. **1969** J. FISHER et al. *Red Bk.* 101/1 Przewalski's horse..is the sole surviving species of wild horse. *Ibid.*, 101/2 The Przewalski horse can be mistaken for the kulan, or Mongolian wild ass. **1972** *Guardian* 22 May 7/3 (*caption*) A young Przewalski filly. Only about 30 of these Mongolian wild horses are..left in the mountains of China. **1973** *Daily Tel.* 23 Aug. 14 The Przewalski, whose primitive characteristics include a hog mane and mealy muzzle, is the only true horse now living in a wild state in the Gobi Desert, where it is almost extinct.

ps-. In words beginning thus the only pronunc. current is that with initial (s); the indication of an alternative (ps) in the following main entries would be misleading and is accordingly not shown.

psalm, *sb.* Add: **3.** *psalm-singing* adj. (earlier and later examples); **psalm-singer** (later examples). Both words frequently have somewhat derogatory connotations.
1818 'A. BURTON' *Adventures J. Newcome* 254 *Psalm-singer*, an epithet of the greatest possible contempt. **1908** J. M. SULLIVAN *Criminal Slang* 17 *Psalm singer*, a prison trusty; an informer. **1909** *Daily Chron.* 15 Dec. 5/5 Cromwell, the greatest ruler England ever had, was, with his glorious Ironsides, a Psalm-singer. **1818** 'A. BURTON' *Adventures J. Newcome* 59 Ye skulking, d—d psalmsinging crew! **1909** *Daily Chron.* 15 Dec. 5/5 In our war with the Boers we found Psalm-singing Dutchmen more than a match for our troops. **1964** Psalm-singing [see *Bible-banging* ppl. adj. s.v. *BIBLE III].

psaltery, *sb.* Add: **1.** Also, a modern imitation of this.
1901 W. B. YEATS *Let.* 20 July (1954) III. 354 Dolmetsch has interested himself in the chanting..and has made a psaltery for Miss Farr. It has 12 strings. **1975** *Gramophone* Oct. 709/1 The psaltery heard here is a bigger instrument than those we see in old paintings... It has seventy-three strings..and is played with both hands, the instrument lying flat on a table.

psaltery, *v.* For † *Obs. rare*⁻¹ read *rare* and add later example.
1903 G. B. SHAW *Let.* 11 June in *Florence Farr, Shaw, Yeats* (1946) 17 Are you too busy psalterying to copyright my new play at the Bayswater theatre?

psammic (sæ·mik), *a. Ecol.* [f. Gr. ψάμμ-ος sand + -IC 1.] Inhabiting areas of sand or gravel.
1938 J. R. CARPENTER *Ecol. Gloss.* 222 *Psammic*, concerning communities on sand or gravel. **1965** B. E. FREEMAN tr. *Vandel's Biospeleol.* vii. 69 The banks of rivers and lakes contain numerous psammic Rotifera.

psammite. Delete *rare* and add: In later use, a sediment or sedimentary rock composed of medium-sized particles (now commonly defined to be between 1/16 mm and either 2 or 4 mm diameter); also, a metamorphic derivative of a sandstone. (Further examples.)
1882 A. GEIKIE *Text-bk. Geol.* 154 (*heading*) Gravel and sand rocks (psammites). **1933** *Geogr. Jrnl.* LXXXI. 158 If the water table approaches the surface evaporation takes place, causing a concentration of the salts carried down. These salt-sand crusts are psammites. **1962** READ & WATSON *Introd. Geol.* I. v. 260 (*heading*) The psammites: sand, sandstone, greywacke, arkose. **1977** A. HALLAM *Planet Earth* 174 Meta-sandstones are sometimes called psammites.

psammitic *a.* (further examples); also, derived by metamorphism from a sandstone.
1882 A. GEIKIE *Text-bk. Geol.* 87 *Psammitic*, or sandstone-like, composed of rounded grains, as in ordinary sandstone: when the grains are larger (often sharp and somewhat angular) the rock is *gritty*, or a grit. **1910** *Q. Jrnl. Geol. Soc.* LXVI. 377 They may be conveniently divided into (1) a Psammitic Group, consisting chiefly of flaggy quartz-felspar granulites..; and (2) a Pelitic Group, consisting chiefly of garnetiferous mica-schists (or gneisses) which are often coarse and quartzose. **1921** G. W. TYRRELL in *Geol. Mag.* LVIII. 501 It is suggested that the terms *psammitic* and *pelitic* might usefully be restricted to the hard metamorphic rocks which have been changed beyond the limits implied by the corresponding Latin terms [sc. *arenaceous* and *argillaceous*]. **1956** E. W. HEINRICH *Microsc. Petrogr.* iv. 99 Psammitic and pelitic rocks may be further subdivided on the basis of mineralogical composition. **1959** *Trans. R. Soc. Edin.* LXIII. 554 In a series of psammitic and slightly calcareous pelitic schists, such as those of Morar, there is great difficulty in discovering the metamorphic grade in relation to that of other areas. **1962** READ & WATSON *Introd. Geol.* I. ix. 539 Psammitic gneisses commonly form massive pinkish rocks composed principally of quartz and feldspar.

psammo-. Add: **psa·mmophile** *sb.* and *a. Bot.* [a. F. *psammophile* (J. Thurmann *Essai de Phytostatique* (1849) I. xiii. 268): see *-PHIL, -PHILE], (a plant) thriving best in sandy soil; **psammophi·lic** *a.* = *psammophilous* adj.; **psammophilous** *a.* (further examples); **psa·mmophyte,** a plant characteristic of sandy habitats; **psa·mmosere** *Ecol.* [*SERE *sb.*²], a plant succession having its origin on sand.
1888 F. A. LEES *Flora W. Yorkshire* 69 Others [*sc.* plants]..are quite as much psammophiles, if their stations be any guide. **1901** C. MOHR *Plant Life Alabama* 131 The slender, wiry culms of this grass..render the species one of the most striking types of psammophile plants. **1973** M. A. SLEIGH *Biol. Protozoa* xi. 264 These psammophilic forms [of Protozoa] have been studied by J. Dragesco. **1888** F. A. LEES *Flora W. Yorkshire* 78 (*heading*) Arenaceous soils and psammophilous species. **1909** E. WARMING *Oecol. Plants* lxviii. 263 The fourth formation, composed of large dune-grasses, is much more psammophilous than halophilous. **1961** R. D. MANWELL *Introd. Protozool.* xv. 305 Some species [of Sarcodina] appear to be restricted to beach sands... Such species are said to be 'psammophilous'. **1903** W. R. FISHER tr. *Schimper's Plant-Geogr.* II. i. 80 The formations of the sandy sea-shore and of dunes serve as excellent examples of the vegetation of psammophytes. **1909** E. WARMING *Oecol. Plants* lxix. 264 *Triticum junceum*..is one of the halophilous psammophytes that begin the production of dune. **1973** F. DI CASTRI in di Castri & Mooney *Mediterranean Type Ecosystems* ii. 22 The psammophyte *Ambrosia chamissonis* was remarkably similar in the coastal fringe of Chile and western North America. **1916** Psammosere [see *lithosere* s.v. *LITHO-]. **1929** WEAVER & CLEMENTS *Plant Ecol.* iv. 74 The differences of hardness and stability result in very dissimilar seres. These are distinguished as (rock) lithoseres and (sand) psammoseres, respectively. **1964** V. J. CHAPMAN *Coastal Vegetation* vi. 150 The dune succession..is quite clearly a prisere, and since it develops on sand it is often known as a Psammosere.

psammoma. Add: Hence **psammo·matous** *a.*, of or pertaining to a psammoma.
1919 J. EWING *Neoplastic Dis.* xx. 309 In other tumors of nerve-trunks the structure is that of typical perivascular endothelioma as occurring in the dura mater, and psammomatous changes may appear in them. **1974** *Radiology* CXIII. 34/2 The second characteristic of psammomatous calcification is its diffuse extent throughout the abdomen due to serosal and omental implants.

psepho-, comb. form of Gr. ψῆφος pebble, used esp. in terms relating to voting (cf. PSEPHISM).

psephocracy (sɪfǫ·krăsi). *rare.* [f. prec. + -CRACY.] The form of government which results from election by ballot; representative government. So **pse·phocrat,** an elected ruler, or an adherent or supporter of government by election.
1966 *New Statesman* 15 Apr. 531/1 How then did Britain..become a democracy?.. It never did... What we do have is representative government, or the rule of the ballot-box, or (in one word) psephocracy. *Ibid.*, 531/2 Psephocracy on the British model has been extended, thanks to the advice of British psephocrats, to a couple of dozen nations. **1970** *Sci. Jrnl.* Feb. 27/1 The present system [of government] is more of a leadership than a referred system—the so called 'psephocracy'.

† **psephograph** (sī·fograf). *Obs.* [f. *PSEPHO- + -GRAPH.] A machine for the automatic recording of votes.
1906 *Westm. Gaz.* 18 Dec. 7/2 The machine, of which a young Italian, Signor Boggiano, is the inventor, and which is known as the 'Psephograph', or vote-recorder, has the appearance of an upright box. **1907** *Daily Chron.* 11 Mar. 6/2 The plebiscite taken by means of the vote recording psephograph..has resulted as follows:— For the Tunnel, 3,212; against, 812.

psephology (sɪfǫ·lŏdʒi, sef-). [f. *PSEPHO- + -OLOGY.] The study of public elections, and statistical analysis of trends in voting; *loosely*, the prediction of electoral results.
1952 D. E. BUTLER *Brit. Gen. Election of 1951* 1 It.. seems appropriate to preface this book with a discussion of why elections merit study and an examination of how much has been..learnt from psephology... I am indebted to Mr. R. B. McCallum for the invention of this word to describe the field of research in which he is so eminent a pioneer. It is derived from ψῆφος—the pebble which the Athenians dropped into an urn to vote. **1952** *Economist* 4 Oct. 18 (*heading*) British psephology. **1957** *Ibid.* 21 Sept. 917/2 Even with the present degree of Liberal revival in the country, prudent (as distinct from roseate) psephology suggests that the only new seats the Liberals might pick up [etc.]. **1958** *Times* 6 Nov. 6/5 (*heading*) Material for psephology—Chichester figures anxiously awaited. **1973** *Guardian* 25 May 12/2 Even with the aid of psephology, it remains difficult to detect what precisely turns votes.
So **psepholo·gical** *a.*, **psepholo·gically** *adv.*; **psepho·logist,** a political scientist who specializes in the study of elections; an electoral analyst or commentator.
1952 *N.Y. Herald Tribune* 8 Aug. (Late City Ed.) 12/3 He [*sc.* R. B. McCallum] suggested I [*sc.* D. E. Butler] call myself a psephologist. **1952** *Daily Express* 30 Sept. 4/3 (*heading*) Psephologically speaking: you may vote for a good-looking party. **1955** D. E. BUTLER *Brit. Gen. Election of 1955* p. v, Acknowledgements..Mr. R. B. McCallum and Mr. H. G. Nicholas, my psephological mentors, gave me much valuable help. **1958** *New Scientist* 27 Mar. 32/1 The next General Election should provide the first opportunity modern Britain will have seen of testing a little-known and much neglected psephological law. **1958** *Times* 6 Nov. 6/5 The psephologists at Central Office and Transport House will be.. ready to read into the results of Chichester, and all the other by-elections pending, sinister or cheering evidence. **1962** *Times* 16 Mar. 13/2 Psephologically, and even more psychologically, it [*sc.* the Orpington by-election] is in a class by itself. **1964** *Time* 4 Nov. 3 By 9 p.m., when Vermont had plopped into the Democratic column and television's psephologists flatly declared Johnson the winner, the answer became obvious: very, very, big. **1969** *Daily Tel.* 9 Sept. 17/6 If psephological calculations mean anything, enough votes will be mustered by Spain to secure an adverse vote against Britain. **1977** *Oxford Times* 29 Apr. 10/2 Whatever happens next Thursday will be psephologically interesting. **1977** *Times* 25 July 8/4 The repercussion of this estrangement (the psephological importance of which has yet to be fathomed) was felt in the economy. **1977** *Time* 21 Nov. 28/2 Psephologists will be sorting out the particulars for months to come, but one trend was clear in last week's off-year election returns: a solid vote for sanity.

pseud (siū̆d), *a.* (*sb.*) *colloq.* [f. the Gr. stem ψευδ- false, or as a shortening of PSEUDO quasi-*adj.* or PSEUDO-.] = *PSEUDO quasi-*adj.* B. Also *absol.* as *sb.* *Pseuds'* or *Pseud's Corner*, used of the pretentious or insincere generally (with allusion to the use in quot. 1968²).
1962 *Spectator* 26 Oct. 656 Present-day trend-setters, pseud as they come. **1964** *Ibid.* 20 Mar. 379/1 The pseuds and intellectual craze-mongers seem to have dropped *cinéma-vérité* almost as quickly as they took it up. **1968** *Jazz Monthly* Apr. 28/2 As well as being the creator of an avant-garde film on human buttocks, Miss Ono has a long list of other achievements which must put her in the running for the title of Pseud of the Century. **1968** *Private Eye* 22 Nov. 3/3 (*heading*) Pseuds' Corner. **1971** *Guardian* 21 Oct. 14/2 Woodstock, the drug scene, the race war, Vietnam... The genre is familiar, and the path through it can verge dangerously close to Pseud's Corner. **1973** P. DICKINSON *Green Gene* I. i. 20 A few big firms..which.. don't mind spending a bit on a pseud paper which makes people..think it's all not so bad as all that... It's a real pseud. **1976** *Listener* 25 Mar. 362/2 His ability to ad lib flowery prose with panoramic views overlooking Pseud's

Corner. **1977** *Ibid.* 7 Apr. 447/1 A dreamy piano solo, recalling both Beiderbecke's 'In a Mist' and (I know this sounds pseud) early Schoenberg. **1980** *Oxford Times* 11 Jan. 13/1 Both strike me as the slightly pseud face of rock 'n' roll.

pseudandry: see *PSEUDO- 2a. **pseud-entity:** see *pseudo-entity* s.v. *PSEUDO- 2a.

pseudepigram (siūde·pigræm). *nonce-word.* [f. *pseud-* (see PSEUDO-) + EPIGRAM, punning on *pseudepigraph.*] A pretended epigram.

c **1905** F. ROLFE *Nicholas Crabbe* (1958) viii. 60 The frolicsome Thorah screamed pseudepigrams everywhere.

pseudergate: see *PSEUDO- 2a.

pseudery (siū·dəri). *colloq.* [f. *PSEUD *a.* (*sb.*) + -ERY.] An affected or pompous manner of expression, usu. with intellectual pretensions; an example of this.

1972 *Guardian* 24 Feb. 10/3 There's nothing like an overt piece of pseudery to make one feel all lilywhite. **1975** *Daily Tel.* 30 Aug. 6/2 In another paper, a psychiatrist solemnly reported his finding that 'in general fat people do not go to university'... These farragoes of improbable pseudery..tend to be prefaced by an enormously portentous address. **1976** *Broadcast* 12 Jan. 9/3 Capital's Sunday pseudery gets the boot. **1978** *Daily Tel.* 19 Jan. 12/6 Best of all is Mr Ward's pithy dismissal of the sort of supernatural pseudery that has enthralled the credulous since the beginning of time.

pseud-idea: see *pseudo-idea* s.v. *PSEUDO- 2a.

pseudish (siū·diʃ), *a. colloq.* [f. *pseud-* (see PSEUDO-) or *PSEUD *a.* (*sb.*) + -ISH[1].] Of architecture: imitative and exaggerated. Of other arts: affected, spurious. Also *ellipt.* as *sb.* Hence **pseu·dishness** = *PSEUDERY.

1938 O. LANCASTER *Pillar to Post* 66 Pseudish. This style which attained great popularity both in this country and in America (where it was generally known as Spanish-colonial), is actually our old friend Pont Street Dutch with a few Stockholm trimmings and a more daring use of colour. **1945** *Archit. Rev.* XCVII. 165/1 The Georgian Movement slid into Pseudish, but the ideal—of chaste simplicity—remained. **1972** *Jazz & Blues* Nov. 30/3 Other contributions are getting dangerously pseudish. **1975** *Times Lit. Suppl.* 28 Nov. 1429/2 This style, which surely earns Betjeman's label 'pseudish'. **1976** *Listener* 23 Dec. 814/1 Better, perhaps, than the pseudish silences that have been creeping over telly art in the past year. **1978** *Punch* 6 Sept. 374/1 We're accustomed to pseudishness in Arts Council catalogues.

pseudo, quasi-*adj.* (*sb.*, *adv.*) Restrict †*Obs. rare* to senses in Dict. and add: Now usu. with pronunc. (siū·do). **B.** *adj.* Pretentious, insincere, sham, affected, meaningless; having aspirations beyond true worth. Also *absol.* as *sb.*, a pretentious or insincere person. Pl. **pseudoes, pseudos.**

Now used independently of its relation to the combining form PSEUDO- which characterizes the senses in Dict.

1945 *Archit. Rev.* XCVII. 110/1 The flamboyant, the vulgar, the monumental and the 'pseudo' have had their day. **1958** *Times* 11 Dec. 6/2 The whole conception was 'pseudo'. **1959** K. TYNAN in J. Feiffer *Sick Sick Sick* (ed. 2) Introd., The real Bohemians of Greenwich Village as well as the pseudoes. **1959** K. R. POPPER *Logic Sci. Discovery* ii. 51 Nothing is easier than to unmask a problem as 'meaningless' or 'pseudo'. **1962** *John o' London's* 19 Apr. 371/1 So all the pseudos flocked in. **1964** J. SYMONS *End of Solomon Grundy* III. ii. 150 That's the trouble with the country to-day, too many pseudo people in it... This garage trouble, now, it comes from the pseudos like that man Grundy. **1967** *Observer* (Colour Suppl.) 28 May 14/2 The undiscriminating, arty chat of a campus pseudo. **1977** *Time* 18 Apr. 1/1 Intellectuals all over the world, real or pseudo, proudly proclaim that 'democracy' won.

pseudo-. Add: Now usu. with pronunc. (siūdo). **1. a.** *pseudo-antithesis, -argument, -art, -artist, -book, -communism, -communist, -conversation, -criticism, -definition, -democracy, -difficulty, -emotion, -fact, -folk* (in examples *attrib.*), *-Freud, -grammar, -historicity, -history, -intellectual, -knowledge, -language, -life, -linguistics, -literature, -logic, -moralist, -morality, -mystic, -mysticism, -need, -objectivity, -passive, -passivization, -philosopher, -philosophy* (earlier and later examples), *-principle, -procedure, -proverb, -question, -religion, -simplicity, -theology, -thesis, -word.*

The examples are given here in an alphabetical sequence for convenience of location.

1949 KOESTLER *Insight & Outlook* xi. 169 The biological approach..makes these appear..as a typical pseudoantithesis. **1943** *Mind* LII. 139 The methodological unification here attempted..helps to eliminate pseudo-arguments. **1977** *Theology* May 173 That 'many people would prefer' to do something is an alarmingly Benthamite pseudo-argument. **1960** *Encounter* Mar. 83/1 The dull air of *acedia* that hangs over the mass pseudo-arts. **1934** DYLAN THOMAS *Let.* Dec. (1966) 147 This is the quarter of the pseudo-artists. **1928** D. H. LAWRENCE *Let.* 1 Apr. (1932) 718 That was very nice of you, to send me that little pseudo-book full of red gold. **1945** KOESTLER *Yogi & Commissar* III. iii. 225 The spreading of Russian pseudo-communism over Europe can be stopped only by a true socialist movement. **1948** *Civil & Mil. Gaz.* (Lahore) 11 Apr. 1/1 Nineteen workers of the Lahore Mint, suspected to be Communists or pseudo-Communists, were arrested. **1926** D. H. LAWRENCE *Glad Ghosts* 30 The pseudo-conversation was interrupted. **1951** N. FRYE in D. Lodge *20th Cent. Lit. Crit.* (1972) 423 The literary chit-chat which makes the reputations of poets boom and crash in an imaginary stock exchange is pseudo-criticism. **1956** J. H. WOODGER tr. *Tarski's Logic, Semantics, Metamath.* 285 The sentences under (2), clearly related to the axiom of reducibility of *Principia Mathematica*, can be called pseudodefinitions in accordance with the proposal of S. Leśniewski. **1965** *Language* XLI. 37 Looked on as a theory, traditional grammar consists of primitive notions only. Its definitions are pseudodefinitions, mere embellishments. **1960** KOESTLER *Lotus & Robot* I. v. 161 The result is a pseudo-democracy in a political vacuum. **1977** M. EDELMAN *Polit. Lang.* vii. 130 One of the few psychiatrists to examine such meetings as political phenomena concludes that the self-government is in fact 'pseudodemocracy'. **1905** W. JAMES *Ess. Radical Empiricism* (1912) xi. 254 Closely connected with this pseudo-difficulty is another one of wider scope and greater complication. **1963** J. LYONS *Structural Semantics* ii. 18 A pseudo-difficulty created by posing a pseudo-question. **1949** KOESTLER *Insight & Outlook* xv. 206 The scientist..dismissed them with a shrug as pseudoemotions and purely conventional attitudes. **1938** R. G. COLLINGWOOD *Princ. Art* iv. 61 He would not have based his theory on a pseudo-fact. **1972** S. FISHER *Female Orgasm* (1973) xv. 390 A tremendous volume of pseudofact is being transmitted to people of all age levels about the nature of sexual response. **1962** *Times* 25 July 13/1 The reach-me-down pseudo-folk poetry. **1976** A. MURRAY *Stomping Blues* xi. 212 No less pretentious..are those pseudo-folk blues musicians. **1951** M. LOWRY *Let.* 25 Aug. (1967) 252 You might call it pseudo-Freud and the philosophy of 'nothing but'. **1963** *Times Lit. Suppl.* 31 May 391/2 The mystique is Victorian home-life made..intellectually respectable by pseudo-Freud. **1927** L. BLOOMFIELD in C. F. Hockett *Leonard Bloomfield Anthol.* (1970) 190 Prescientific notions about language, with the dismal study of pseudo-grammar, still prevail in our schools. **1935** *Mind* XLIV. 407 For the general public of Goethe's day (including Goethe himself and other imaginative writers) the concept 'Hellenic' was as little historical as is that of 'Aryan' for the modern Nazis;.. like it, it entailed a terrific parade of pseudo-historicity. **1958** T. F. T. PLUCKNETT *Early Eng. Legal Lit.* i. 11 Then there is the pseudo-historicity of our law. **1880** A. H. SAYCE *Introd. Sci. of Lang.* II. ix. 239 An attempt was made to extract a pseudo-history from the Greek myths. **1946** R. G. COLLINGWOOD *Idea of Hist.* 180 Meyer's great merit lies in his effective criticism of the openly positivistic sociological pseudo-history fashionable in his time. **1973** B. J. WILLIAMS *Evolution & Human Origins* iv. 48/2 These taxonomies were used, in turn, to construct pseudo-histories. **1938** *Sun* (Baltimore) 16 Apr. 8 Attacks on the profit motive by many of the pseudo-intellectuals who have supported and colored so much of the Administration's policy in the past. **1977** P. JOHNSON *Enemies of Society* xvi. 218 The fatuous Mary Wimbush, the pseudo-intellectual. **1842** W. NEWNHAM *Reciprocal Influence of Body & Mind* ii. 24 That pseudo-knowledge..would leave its possessor without a single ray of duty. **1957** C. DAY LEWIS *Poet's Way of Knowledge* 16 If you like to think of science as 'knowledge', and poetry as at best some kind of 'pseudo-knowledge', no one can stop you, but you will be thinking in terms unacceptable to many scientists to-day. **1979** *Dædalus* Spring 15 The critics accuse the positivists of surreptitiously..transforming a pseudo-knowledge into a power which..can only be exerted 'in the interests of the dominant class'. **1960** Pseudolanguage [see *INTERLANGUAGE *sb.*]. **1978** *Amer. Speech* LIII. 61 Samarin suggests that glossolalia is on the same continuum as actual language and is closely related to other kinds of 'pseudolanguage' which can be produced by any sufficiently uninhibited person who is merely playing with language-like sounds. **1942** F. BROWN in *Unknown Worlds* Mar. 6/2 A formula for giving pseudolife to inanimate objects. **1978** G. A. SHEEHAN *Running & Being* ii. 32 His solution..is not to impersonate the achiever... This would be a pseudolife. **1962** H. A. GLEASON in Householder & Saporta *Probl. in Lexicogr.* 86 The reaction to popular pseudo-linguistics. **1964** M. A. K. HALLIDAY et al. *Linguistic Sci.* i. 6 Workers in other fields have gone on working with their own do-it-yourself pseudo-linguistics, being content..with inexact observations and *ad hoc* categories. **1972** *Language* XLVIII. 438 It is indicative of Arens' conservatism and his appreciation of neo-Humboldtian pseudo-linguistics in Germany that he should expand this last chapter. **1944** *Mind* LIII. 185 He therefore can only distinguish 'true literature' (the expression and communication of an experience) from 'pseudo-literature' (*e.g.* advertisement, propaganda, pot-boiling, Collingwood's 'magic' and 'entertainment'). **1964** *Listener* 9 Jan. 61/1 How can John Raymond in *The Sunday Times* deal with seven volumes of verse in just over 1,000 words?.. He can afford to generalize and chat, and in this way he provides a kind of pseudo-literature. **1960** K. AMIS *New Maps of Hell* i. 21 Time travel..is inconceivable, but..an apparatus of pseudo-logic..is set up to support it. **1964** A. WYKES *Gambling* ii. 50 The Victorian pseudo-moralists who screamed..of the dangers of drink and gambling were for the most part unthinking pleasure-stiflers. **1943** *Mind* LII. 19 This is the morality of obedience at its best and surest. Doubtless it is easily confused with the pseudo-morality of sanctions. **1961** *Encounter* Feb. 78 Hugh Kingsmill described Lawrence as 'a pseudo-mystic'. **1964** P. F. ANSON *Bishops at Large* ix. 344 The pseudo-mysticism propagated by Mrs Besant and leading members of the Theosophical Society. **1960** *Commentary* June 472/2 The continual creation of pseudo-needs as a basis for production. **1979** *Time* 8 Jan. 72/3 Lasch detects narcissism nearly everywhere, in the buzz words of the 'human potential' movements, in the 'pseudo needs' created by advertisers for restless consumers. **1946** KOESTLER in *New Writing & Daylight* VII. 82 Novels date more than drama and poetry. The reason for this is the novel's pseudo-objectivity. **1973** MATIAS & WILLEMEN tr. M. Cegarra in *Screen* Spring/Summer 185 The pseudo-objectivity of the film. **1964** *Language* XL. 77 Smx$_2$ marks indefinite voice, or pseudopassive. **1965** N. CHOMSKY *Aspects of Theory of Syntax* ii. 104 It is now possible to account for 'pseudo-passives', such as 'the proposal was vehemently argued against',..by a slight generalization of the ordinary passive transformation. *Ibid.* 106 Where 'on the boat' is a V[erb]-Complement in 'John decided on the boat' (meaning 'John chose the boat'), it is subject to pseudopassivization by the passive transformation. **1828** DISRAELI *Voy. Capt. Popanilla* iv. 35 A state of existence which has puzzled many pseudo philosophers. **1842** W. NEWNHAM *Reciprocal Influence of Body & Mind* 159 It is also employed by many pseudo-philosophers as a convenient term. **1966** *Eng. Stud.* XLVII. 154 In the mid-twentieth century the typical Bohemian has become the beatnik poet or pseudo-philosopher. **1817** JANE AUSTEN *Sanditon* (1925) vii. 92 It were Hyper-criticism, it were Pseudo-philosophy to expect from the soul of high toned Genius, the grovellings of a common mind. **1897** Pseudo-philosophy [see *IRRATIONALIST]. **1879** W. JAMES in *Mind* IV. 337 Illusory simplification..is made by invoking some sham term, some pseudo-principle, and conglomerating it and the data into one. **1964** M. A. K. HALLIDAY et al. *Linguistic Sci.* vii. 218 Where he has learned..such a sheer quantity of linguistic material..testing all of it becomes a 'pseudo-procedure'; it just cannot be done. **1965** *Language* XLI. 206 Scholastic pseudo-procedures of discovery. **1949** KOESTLER *Insight & Outlook* vii. 101 A similar pseudo-proverb is, 'He never works between meals'. **1934** R. CARNAP *Unity of Sci.* 40 The danger may arise of being diverted by the material mode of speech into considering pseudo-questions. **1947** D. RYNIN *Johnson's Treat Lang.* 353 On this assumption, 'Is everything known to God?' is for us not a genuine question, but a pseudo-question. **1963** Pseudo-question [see *pseudo-difficulty* above]. **1927** A. HUXLEY *Proper Stud.* 220 There is a powerful religion, or rather pseudo-religion, of sexual purity. **1956** R. C. ZAEHNER in A. Pryce-Jones *New Outl. Mod. Knowl.* 66 The modern pseudo-religions the most obvious of which was Hitlerism. **1969** *Daily Tel.* 24 Apr. 20/3 The pseudo-religion of Social Justice. **1931** E. SAPIR in *Amer. Mercury* XXII. 205/2 The simplicity of English in its formal aspect is..really a pseudo-simplicity or a masked complexity. **1951** M. MCLUHAN *Mech. Bride* (1967) 141/2 It is the weak and confused who worship the pseudosimplicities of brutal directness. **1940** C. S. LEWIS *Let.* 17 Jan. (1966) 176 You will presently see both a Leftist and a Rightist pseudo-theology developing. **1961** 'F. O'BRIEN' *Hard Life* x. 75 His talk is always full of 'ifs' and 'buts', rawmaish and pseudo-theology. **1977** *Rolling Stone* 30 June 62/2 There has also been the startling growth of psychological technology: all the encounter groups and how-to manuals, all the new therapies and analyses, all the pseudotheologies and gurus and disciplines. **1935** R. CARNAP *Philos. & Log. Syntax* 21 All these philosophical theses are deprived of empirical content, of theoretical sense; they are pseudo-theses. **1963** —— in P. A. Schilpp *Philos. of R. Carnap* 51, I argued in detail that the thesis of materialism was just as much a pseudo-thesis as that of idealism. **1951** S. ULLMANN *Princ. Semantics* II. 59 In view of the hybrid nature of particles, it might be convenient to label them *pseudo-words.* **1954** *Archivum Linguisticum* VI. 18 Ullmann..speaks of 'pseudo-words' which would have no full semantic status.

b. *pseudo-American, -antique, -divine, -Elizabethan, -existing, -Georgian, -historic(al), -infantile, -intellectual, -Marxist, -medical, -medieval, -mystical, -philosophic(al), -psychological, -religious* (later examples), *-revolutionary, -romantic* (later examples), *-sophisticated, -Spanish, -technical* adjs.

The examples are also given here in an alphabetical sequence for convenience of location.

1938 Pseudo-American [see *KIDDO]. **1964** C. BARBER *Present-Day Eng.* ii. 20 English pop-singers have developed a special pseudo-American accent of their own. **1936** *Burlington Mag.* May 219/2 The Byzantine pseudo-antique character. **1959** Pseudo-antique [see *KATHAREVOUSA]. **1950** D. GASCOYNE *Vagrant* 33 To be with God, and not pseudo-divine Scorn-inspired self-deceivers. **1946** BLUNDEN *Shelley* 205 One of the endless pseudo-Elizabethan or at least post-Elizabethan compositions. **1956** Pseudo-Elizabethan [see *MIMSEY *a.*]. **1904** B. RUSSELL in *Mind* XIII. 353 False propositions, according to Meinong, are the non-subsisting, merely pseudo-existing objectives of erroneous judgments. **1905** E. WHARTON *House of Mirth* I. i. 7 Its marble porch and pseudo-Georgian façade. **1936** J. BUCHAN *Island of Sheep* vii. 125 The house was..a pseudo-Georgian edifice of red brick with stone facings. **1919** M. BEER *Hist. Brit. Socialism* I. I. v. 51 The soul of moral philosophy was *ius naturale*, which is..pure ethics in a pseudo-historic guise. **1905** O. JESPERSEN *Growth & Struct. Eng. Lang.* x. 246 That pseudo-historical and anti-educational abomination, the English spelling. **1927** W. E. COLLINSON *Contemp. Eng.* 7 Pseudo-infantile forms like pinny (pinafore). **1977** D. MORRIS *Manwatching* 185 The pseudo-infantile woman displays pouted lips, wide-open eyes, and child-like body postures. **1944** KOESTLER in *Horizon* Mar. 173 The pseudo-intellectual hangers-on whose primary motive is.. neurosis pure and simple. **1956** A. S. C. ROSS in M. Black *Importance of Lang.* (1962) 99 To say *Miss Austen* instead of *Jane Austen* is either precious or pseudo-intellectual. **1938** *Ann. Reg. 1937* 197 M. N. Pokrovsky... His 'school' is now persecuted as holding pseudo-Marxist, anti-Leninist and therefore unscientific conceptions. **1945** H. READ *Coat of Many Colours* xliv. 219 If Balzac had followed the advice of our pseudo-Marxist critics, he would have made his works subservient to his political theories. **1908** *Jrnl. Amer. Med. Assoc.* 28 Nov. 1860/2 Among the pseudo-medical institutions that have been investigated and closed through fraud orders by the Post-office Department was a Cincinnati concern known as the Epileptic Institute. **1977** *Gay News* 24 Mar. 18/3 Old pseudo-medical myths die hard. **1978** J. UPDIKE *Coup* (1979) iii. 108 Some..calibrated diet whose pseudo-medical niceties were catered to even in the depths of our famine. **1883** Pseudo-medieval [see *HIGH *a.* 6a]. **1967** E. SHORT *Embroidery & Fabric Collage* iv. 117 Too often a designer who happily experiments with plant forms and animals will, when confronted with the human figure, resort to the hackneyed, pseudo-medieval figure in the nebulous draped garment which is so often seen in church work. **1933** *Mind* XLII. 184 It is indeed to the Greeks, or at any rate to Plato, that this argument, not inconsistently with its quasi-Kantian, Christian or Hebraic (and some will say, pseudo-mystical) flavour, harks back. **1960** KOESTLER *Lotus & Robot* II. xi. 245 The rest is pseudo-mystical verbiage. **1961** *Encounter* Feb. 78 This credo is expressed in pseudo-mystical terms. **1914** J. LONDON *Let.* 26 Mar (1966) 418, I have played with philosophy, expositing the power of mind over matter... While this is..pseudo-philosophic, nevertheless it will make it most palatable to ..the folk who will read it. **1922** C. BELL *Since Cézanne* 82 We shall then be armed..against the portentous 'Ist', whose parthenogenetic masterpiece we are not in a state to relish till we have sucked down the pseudo-philosophic bolus that embodies his eponymous 'Ism'. **1933** M. OAKESHOTT *Experience* IV. 243 A psychology which is not scientific certainly exists, and certainly would not be superseded by a science of psychology... Nevertheless, such a psychology..would be a pseudo-philosophical form of experience. **1940** *Mind* XLIX. 99 The encumbrance of these largely parasitic philosophical and pseudo-philosophical ideas. **1946** *Mind* LV. 360 When we ask what in fact constitutes the order or form of the vegetative realm or any below the highest one, the answer is given in terms derived from human experience and purpose. Or else it is a worse answer in pseudo-mechanical, pseudo-psychological terms, like 'vital force'. **1964** *Eng. Stud.* XLV. 419 Professor Bodelsen's work..eschews..the flights of pseudo-psychological fancy of the gaudier school of criticism. **1938** *Burlington Mag.* Jan. 44/1 Even in old Siena..there were, not only pagan painters, but also pseudo-religious artists ..who substituted prettiness for piety. **1943** K. MANNHEIM *Diagnosis of our Time* vii. 102 It is not a matter of chance that both Communism and Fascism try to.. superimpose a pseudo-religious integration. **1957** J. S. HUXLEY *Relig. without Revelation* iii. 59 Only in high civilisations does art become emancipated from religious or pseudo-religious domination. **1978** *China Reconstructs* Nov. 5/1 Their pseudo-revolutionary line and its counter-revolutionary aims are being thoroughly criticized. **1979** *Dædalus* Winter 132 This leads them sometimes..to become unexpected allies..of pseudorevolutionary, violent minorities. **1927** R. H. WILENSKI *Mod. Movement in Art* 29 The degenerate romantic and pseudo-romantic art of the nineteenth century. **1961** D. G. JAMES *Matthew Arnold* i. 26 We may call it 'Romantic' if we like; it is better to call it pseudo-romantic or even sentimental. **1977** *Time* 19 Sept. 11/1 Against such alienation, the pseudo-romantic exploits of Andreas Baader and Ulrike Meinhof hardly needed ideological underpinnings to strike a responsive chord. **1935** W. G. HARDY *Father Abraham* 134 Abraham saw a quiet, controlled, secretive man with that indefinable air of assurance which travel imparts—considerably different, indeed, from the pseudo-sophisticated Lugal of argumentative days but yet recognizable. **1960** A. L. HENCH in *Amer. Speech* XXXV. 73 One of my brighter students recently asked me..why I had used the word *sophisticated* to praise a literary critic... The student said he understood the word meant 'artificial', 'adulterated', 'tarnished', even 'slightly corrupt'... I told him that of course the word sometimes was used to mean 'artificial' or 'false' but that I thought persons who used it this way actually meant *pseudosophisticated*. **1928** H. CRANE *Let.* 31 Jan. (1965) 315 The perfect labyrinth of 'villas'—some pseudo-Spanish, some a la Maya. **1964** H. KÖKERITZ in D. Abercrombie et al. *Daniel Jones* 143 In America, *Don Quixote* and *Don Juan* have assumed a pseudo-Spanish pronunciation. **1945** *Mind* LIV. 185 The philosopher..must be particularly conscious of the pitfalls of language, and especially of all pseudo-technical and emotive language. **1964** P. STREVENS in D. Abercrombie et al. *Daniel Jones* 120 They all commonly bear the same pseudo-technical label.

2. a. pseuda·ndry [Gr. *ἀνήρ, ἀνδρ-* man], the use by a woman of a male pseudonym; **pseude·rgate** *Zool.* [a. F. *pseudergate* (Grassé & Noirot 1947, in *Compt. Rend.* CCXXIV. 219): see *ERGATE], in certain genera of termites, a blind, wingless member of the colony, carrying out some of the functions of the workers; **pseud-idea**: see *pseudo-idea* below; **pseu·do-a:cid** *Chem.* [tr. G. *pseudosäure* (A. Hantzsch 1899, in *Ber. d. Deut. Chem. Ges.* XXXII. 577)], a compound which is not itself an acid but which exists in equilibrium with, or is easily converted into, an acidic form and thus undergoes some typical reactions of acids; hence **pseudo-aci·dic** *a.*; **pseudo-aci·dity**; **pseu:do-asy·mmetry** *Chem.*, the property of an atom of being bonded to two enantiomorphic groups; hence **pseu:do-asymme·tric** *a.*; **pseu·do-base** *Chem.* [a. G. *pseudobase* (A. Hantzsch 1899, in *Ber. d. Deut. Chem. Ges.* XXXII. 595)], a compound which is not itself a base but which exists in equilibrium with, or is easily converted into, a basic form and thus undergoes some typical reactions of bases; hence **pseudo-ba·sic** *a.*; **pseu:do-basi·city**; **pseudobe·dding** *Geol.*, a structure in which an appearance of stratification has been produced by a cause other than deposition in the apparent planes of stratification; **pseudo-boléite, -boleite** (-bōᵘ·lɪ̈əit) *Min.* [a. F. *pseudoboléite* (A. Lacroix 1895, in *Bull. du Muséum d'Hist. naturelle* I. 40), f. *boléite*, similar mineral named after *Boleo*, near Santa Rosalia, Lower California, Mexico, where both were first found], a hydroxide-chloride of lead and copper occurring as translucent blue crystals; **pseudo-bulb** (later examples); **pseudo-bulbous** *a.* (later examples); **pseu:docho-line·sterase** *Biochem.*, an enzyme present in the blood and in the liver, brain, and certain other organs which acts on the same esters as cholinesterase and some others besides; † **pseudocirrhosis** *Path.* [after G. *pseudo-lebercirrhose* (F. Pick 1896, in *Zeitschr. f. klin. Med.* XXIX. 395)] = *PICK'S DISEASE 1; **pseu·docode** *Computers*, a programming language that is not a machine language and has to be translated by a computer before it can be executed; **pseu:do-compatibi·lity** *Bot.*, the fertilization of flowers by pollen which would normally be incompatible (*INCOMPATIBLE *a.* 6 b); **pseudoconglo·merate** *Geol.* (see quot. 1972); **pseudocotu·nnite** *Min.* [ad. G. *pseudo-cotunnit* (G. vom Rath 1877), alteration of It. *pseudocotunnia* (A. Scacchi 1873, in *Atti della R. Accad. delle Sci., Fis. e Matem. di Napoli* VI. IX. 38), f. *cottunia*, similar mineral named after D. *Cotungo* (1736–1822), It. anatomist], a potassium lead chloride, K_2PbCl_4, found as dull yellowish or whitish crystals on Vesuvius; **pseudocyesis** (examples); cf. *PSEUDOPREGNANCY 1; **pseudocyphe·lla** *Bot.* [CYPHELLA], a small pore in the lower surface of certain lichens; **pseudodo·minance** *Genetics*, the expression of a recessive allele as a result of the deletion of the part of the chromosome bearing the corresponding dominant allele; so **pseudodo·minant** *a.*; **pseu·do-entity, pseud-e·ntity** *Philos.*, something falsely called or regarded as an entity; **pseu·do-existence** *Philos.* (see quots.); **pseudofæ·ces** *Zool.*, a mixture of mucus and particulate matter from the water that collects in the mantle cavity of a mollusc and is expelled without passing through the digestive system; hence **pseudofæ·cal** *a.*; **pseudofo·vea** *Ophthalm.*, a point of maximum sensitivity on the retina other than the fovea, such as may develop in a squinting eye; hence **pseudofo·veal** *a.*; **pseu·dofracture** *Med.*, a defect in bone that appears on a radiograph as one of a series of narrow, well-defined lines of translucence; **pseu·dogene** *Genetics*, a section of a chromosome that is an imperfect copy of a functional gene; **pseu·dogley** *Soil Science* [a. G. *pseudogley* (W. L. Kubiëna *Bestimmungsbuch und Systematik der Böden Europas* (1953) 295)], a gley resulting from temporary or seasonal waterlogging due to poor drainage of surface water, rather than from the permanent existence of a high groundwater table; **pseudoglio·ma** *Ophthalm.*, any condition that gives rise to signs similar to those of retinoblastoma; **pseudoglo·bulin** *Biochem.* [a. G. *pseudoglobulin* (F. Hofmeister 1899: see *Zeitschr. f. physiol. Chem.* (1900) XXXI. 140, *Beiträge z. chem. Physiol.* (1901) 361)], the fraction of serum globulin that is soluble in pure water and saline solutions but precipitated by half-saturation with ammonium sulphate; **pseu·dogout** *Path.*, a joint disorder resembling gout but produced by deposits of crystals of calcium pyrophosphate rather than sodium urate and occurring most often in the knee; **pseudo·gyny** *Ent.*, pseudogynous condition; **pseu:do-hallucina·tion**, an isolated, brief, and vivid sensory experience, commonly auditory or visual, occurring in clear consciousness and in the absence of any external stimulus; so **pseu:do-hallucina·tory** *a.*; **pseu:dohomose·xual** *a.*, pertaining to or designating homosexual behaviour which acts as an outlet for the expression of fear, aggression, dependency, dominance, etc., rather than being genuinely sexual; hence **pseu:do-homosexua·lity**; **pseudo-hypertrophy** (earlier example); **pseu:dohy:poparathy·roidism** *Med.*, a familial disorder in which the features of hypoparathydroidism are accompanied by skeletal and developmental abnormalities and which is caused by a failure of tissues to respond to parathyroid hormone; so **pseu:do-hy:poparathy·roid** *a.*; **pseu·do-idea, pseu·d-idea**, a meaningless or false idea; **pseu·do-instruction** (also *pseudo instruction*) *Computers*, an instruction similar to a computer instruction in form that is not executed as an instruction by hardware but used to control a compiler or assembler; **pseu:do-isochroma·tic** *a.* *Ophthalm.*, composed of different colours that appear the same to a colour-blind person; **pseudoi·xiolite** *Min.*, an oxide of iron, manganese, tantalum, and niobium that has a highly disordered orthorhombic structure and is similar to ixiolite, differing in changing to tantalite or columbite on heating and in lacking tin; **pseu·dokarst** *Geomorphol.* [cf. It. *pseudocarsico* adj., *-carsismo* sb. (G. B. Floridia 1941, in *Boll. della Soc. di Sci. nat. ed econ. di Palermo* XXIII. 12), and see quot. 1960[1]], karst-like topography in ground other than limestone produced by subterranean erosion rather than solution; hence **pseudoka·rstic** *a.*; **pseudo-lympho·ma** *Path.*, any of various conditions involving enlargement of lymph nodes which bear some resemblance to lymphoma but are not malignant; hence **pseudolympho·matous** *a.*; **pseudomembranous** *a.*, add *Path.* and substitute for def.: applied to conditions in which mucous membranes are covered with a sheet formed of exudate; (further examples); **pseudomu·cin** *Med.* [a. G. *pseudomucin* (O. Hammarsten 1882, in *Zeitschr. f. physiol. Chem.* VI. 209)], the thick, tenacious, semi-opaque liquid present in pseudomucinous cysts; hence **pseudomu·cinous** *a.*, epithet of the commonest kind of ovarian cyst, containing mucin; **pseu:domycorrhi·za** *Biol.* [a. Sw. *pseudomykorrhiza* (E. Melin *Studier över de Norrländska Myrmarkernas Vegetation* (1917) II. v. 358)], an association of tree roots and fungi, often mildly pathogenic ones, in the absence of true mycorrhiza; so **pseu:do-mycorrhi·zal** *a.*; **pseudoneuro·tic** *a.* *Psychol.*, of or pertaining to types of mental illness in which superficial symptoms of neurosis are found in conjunction with underlying symptoms of psychosis, esp. of schizophrenia; **pseu·do-object** *Gram.*, a noun or pronoun that appears to be, but actually is not, an object; **pseu·do-operation** (also *pseudo operation*) *Computers* = *pseudo-instruction* above; **pseu·do-order** *Computers* = *pseudo-instruction* above (see also quot. 1955); **pseudo-pela·de** *Path.* [a. F. *pseudo-pelade* (L. Brocq. et al. 1905, in *Annales Dermatol. et Syph.* VI. 1): cf. PELADA], the appearance of multiple bald patches on the scalp; **pseudoperidium** (later examples); **pseu:doperithe·cium** *Biol.*, in fungi belonging to the order Laboulbeniales, a structure resembling a perithecium in which the vestigial walls have degenerated; **pseudo-pla·nkton** *Biol.*, organisms attached to drifting debris or vegetation; so **pseudoplankto·nic** *a.*; **pseudo-plasmo·dium** *Biol.*, a structureless aggregate of distinct unicellular organisms; **pseudopla·stic** *a.* and *sb.*, (a liquid) that is non-Newtonian, esp. in having a viscosity that decreases with increasing shearing stress; hence **pseu:doplasti·city**; **pseu:dopseu:dohypo-parathy·roidism** *Med.*, a familial disorder in which the skeletal and developmental abnormalities of pseudohypoparathyroidism are present without the biochemical abnormalities common to hypoparathyroidism and pseudohypoparathyroidism; **pseu·dopupil** *Ent.* [ad. G. *pseudopupille* (S. Exner *Physiol. d. Facettirten Augen v. Krebsen u. Insecten* (1891) ii. 18)] (see quot. 1977); **pseudo-quadraphony** (-ǫ·fŏni), sound reproduction in which signals from two sources are fed to four speakers in such a way as to give a partial effect of quadraphony; **pseudora·bies**, (*a*) (see quots. 1897, 1912) (?*obs.*); (*b*) *Vet. Sci.*, an infectious viral disease of the central nervous system that causes intense pruritus and usu. death in cattle and affects other domestic animals in varying ways; **pseudorace·mic** *a.* *Chem.*, applied to a racemic substance consisting of mixed or intergrown crystals of the optically active isomers; so **pseudora·cemate**; **pseu·doreaction** *Physiol.*, a spurious positive response to a test; †**pseudoredu·ction** *Cytology*, the apparent halving of the number of chromosomes through synapsis; **pseudorota·tion** *Chem.*, a change in molecular configuration involving concerted displacements of the constituent atoms, which is equivalent to a rotation of the molecule coupled with a permutation of some of the constituents, but does not involve any actual rotation of the molecule; hence **pseudorota·tional** *a.*; also **pseudorota·te** *v. intr.*, to undergo such a change; **pseudorota·ted** *ppl. a.*; **pseudoru·tile** *Min.*, an oxide of iron and titanium, $Fe_2Ti_3O_9$, that is formed as an intermediate stage in the change of ilmenite to rutile; **pseu·do-salt** *Chem.*, a compound which is normally covalent but which under certain conditions exists as or in equilibrium with an ionized, salt-like form; **pseu·dosocial** *a.*, exhibiting or designating seemingly social behaviour that arises from individual reactions to a need or external stimulus rather than from genuinely social reasons; **pseu·dospecies,** a term used for the different national or racial groups to denote the illusory nature of the belief that they have evolved genetically into different and separate species (inferior to one's own); so **pseu:do-specia·tion,** a false division into species following these lines; **pseudosphere, pseudospherical,** substitute: **pseudosphe·rical** *a. Geom.*, being or pertaining to a surface or space whose curvature is everywhere equal and negative; (further examples); hence **pseu·do-sphere,** the pseudospherical surface that is generated by rotating a tractrix about its asymptote; (examples); **pseu·do-squeeze** *Bridge*, play whereby an opponent is, or may be, misled into discarding or unguarding a potentially winning card, although he has alternative discards; cf. *SQUEEZE *sb.*; **pseu·do-statement,** an expression that formally resembles a statement but does not refer or correspond to an objective fact, being rather used for its subjective effect on the hearer or reader; **pseu·dostem,** the apparent trunk of a banana plant or a closely related species, which is made up of closely packed leaf sheaths enclosing a stem; **pseu:dostratifica·tion** *Geol.* = *pseudobedding* above; **pseudostra·tified** *a.* (*a*) *Geol.*, exhibiting or of pseudostratification; (*b*) *Histology* (see main entry below); **pseudo-ta·chylyte, -ite** *Petrogr.*, a dark glassy rock resembling tachylyte that results from vitrification by frictional heat generated during dynamic metamorphism; **pseu·dotill** *Geol.*, a deposit similar to a till but non-glacial in origin; **pseudoti·llite** *Geol.* [ad. G. *pseudotillit* (M. Schwarzbach *Das Klima der Vorzeit* (ed. 2, 1961) v. 34], a deposit similar to a tillite but non-glacial in origin; **pseudo-tra·chea** *Ent.*, a fine food-channel in the mouthparts of many flies; also, an organ found in certain woodlice which resembles an insect trachea; **pseu:do-tuberculo·sis** *Vet. Sci.* [mod.L., coined in Ger. as the specific epithet of the *Pasteurella* species causing the disease (A. Pfeiffer *Ueber die bacilläre Pseudotuberculose bei Nagethieren* (1889) 5)], any of several diseases clinically and anatomically similar to tuberculosis that occur chiefly in rodents, birds, and warm-blooded animals, esp. sheep, and are caused by species of *Pasteurella* or *Corynebacterium*; **pseudotube·rculous** *a.*, resembling (that of) tuberculosis; **pseu·dotumour** *Path.*, a swelling or other condition that gives rise to the clinical signs of a neoplasm but is not neoplastic, i.e. is not characterized by the persistent proliferation of cells having no physiological function; **pseudou·racil** *Biochem.*, the uracil residue in pseudouridine; **pseudou·ridine** *Biochem.*, a nucleoside, 5-ribosyluracil, found in transfer RNA and differing from uridine in that the sugar residue is attached to the base at a carbon rather than a nitrogen atom; **pseu·dovitamin** *Biochem.*, a compound that is not a vitamin but closely resembles some particular vitamin in molecular structure; **pseudovite·llus** *Ent.* = *MYCETOME; **pseudo-wa·vellite** *Min.* [ad. G. *pseudo-wavellit* (F. Henrich, after Laubmann, 1922, in *Ber. d. Deut. Chem. Ges.* LVB. 3016)], a hydrated basic phosphate of calcium and aluminium, $CaAl_3(PO_4)_2(OH)_5.H_2O$, found as white, grey, or yellow crystals (see quot. 1951); **pseudo-wo·llastonite** *Min.* [a. F. *pseudowollastonite* (A. Lacroix *Minéral. de la France* (1893–5) I. 624)], the high-temperature form of the calcium silicate $CaSiO_3$, which normally changes to wollastonite at ordinary temperatures; **pseudoxantho·ma (ela·sticum)** *Path.* [mod.L., coined in Ger. (J. F. Darier 1896, in *Monatschr. für prakt. Dermatol.* XXIII. 616): cf. XANTHOMA], a congenital disease in which there is widespread disturbance of connective tissue formation, leading to soft, yellowish papules and plaques in the skin, cardiovascular disorder, and ultimately death.

1928 H. M. PAULL *Literary Ethics* xvii. 189 All sorts of devices are adopted by the author, who does not wish his name to be known. He may..disguise it in various ways, using initials, asterisks, a reversed name, or one of the opposite sex,..respectively initialism, asterism, boustrophedon and pseudandry. **1961** T. LANDAU *Encycl. Librarianship* (ed. 2) 294/1 *Pseudandry*, a woman author writing under a masculine pseudonym. **1957** RICHARDS & DAVIES *Imms's Gen. Textbk. Entomol.* (ed. 9) III. 380 Pseudergates occur in *Zootermopsis* and..the so-called workers of *Mastotermes* are probably also of this form. **1969** R. F. CHAPMAN *Insects* xxxiv. 706 The pseudergate is a central form from which various others can be derived. **1979** R. M. ALEXANDER *Invertebrates* xix. 436 Pseudergates also remove the eggs as the queen lays them. **1899** *Jrnl. Chem. Soc.* LXXVI. I. 399 The author [*sc.* Hantzsch] describes as pseudo-acids those substances which do not contain a hydrogen atom directly displaceable by metals, but which are capable of changing into a salt-forming isomeride. **1910** [see *pseudo-acidity* below]. **1929** P. WALDEN *Salts, Acids, & Bases* v. 127 In the homogeneous condition pseudo-acids are associated, usually in the dimolecular form. The carboxylic acids are typical pseudo-acids. **1952** TURNER & HARRIS *Org. Chem.* ix. 135 Primary and secondary nitroparaffins are pseudo-acids, dissolving in aqueous alkali..to give the ions of the *aci*-nitroparaffin or true (nitronic) acid. **1953** C. K. INGOLD *Struct. & Mechanism in Org. Chem.* x. 576 The pseudo-basic carbinol corresponds to the pseudo-acidic phenylnitromethane. **1910** N. V. SIDGWICK *Org. Chem. Nitrogen* vii. 144 The nitroparaffins are typical instances of pseudo-acids. In fact it was in this connexion that Hantzsch developed the theory of pseudo-acidity. **1927** Pseudo-acidity [see *pseudo-basicity* below]. **1907** J. B. COHEN *Org. Chem.* ii. 93 Pseudo-asymmetry of the character of the trihydroxyglutaric acids..is afforded by cyclopropane derivatives. *Ibid.* 94 The cyclic carbon atoms 2 and 4 are asymmetrical *per se*; 3 is symmetrical though structurally identical with 2 and 4. It follows..that 1 and 3 are pseudo-asymmetric. **1962** E. L. ELIEL *Stereochem. Carbon Compounds* iii. 28 Such a pseudoasymmetric atom does not give rise to dissymmetry in the molecule as a whole. **1975** *Nature* 13 Nov. 96/3 Some of these ideas have now appeared in a very general paper..which was followed by two detailed papers on compounds showing axes and planes of pseudo-asymmetry. **1899** *Jrnl. Chem. Soc.* LXXVI. I. 400 Pseudo-bases are substances which, by isomeric change, are capable of giving a true base of the ammonium hydroxide type from which the salts are derived. **1951** C. R. NOLLER *Chem. Org. Compounds* xxx. 591 The *N*-alkyl-α-pyridones are obtained by the oxidation of the quaternary hydroxides. These strong bases appear to be in equilibrium with the α-hydroxydihydropyridines, which are called pseudo bases. **1960** K. W. BENTLEY *Natural Pigments* i. 14 The α- and γ-pyranols are, in fact, pseudo bases, forming a salt and water on treatment with acid. **1921** *Jrnl. Chem. Soc.* CXIX. 1470 One of the more characteristic reactions of pseudo-basic carbinols is the formation of ethers by simple treatment with alcohols. **1927** *Ann. Rep. Progr. Chem.* XXIV. 115 In the same way that in mobile cation tautomerism the hydrogen ion forms a more or less stable covalent link with (negative) carbon, whereas the sodium ion tends to remain in the electrovalent state (thus giving rise to the phenomena of pseudo-acidity), so..the hydroxide ion tends to co-ordinate with positive carbon, whereas very stable anions like chloride..tend to retain their ionic condition..: thus arises the phenomenon of pseudo-basicity. **1850** D. T. ANSTED *Elem. Course Geol., Mineral., & Physical Geogr.* 579/1 (Index), Pseudo-bedding. **1893** *Q. Jrnl. Geol. Soc.* XLIX. 395 Cracks, small at first, have little by little grown into deep joints, and so the pseudo-bedding has been gradually produced. **1939** *Jrnl. Geol.* XLVII. 72 The result of this nonuniformity in distribution of sand is that a type of pseudobedding is developed by concentration or combining of laminae representing the approach slopes of the ripple deposits. **1970** R. J. SMALL *Study of Landforms* xi. 365 Many of the polished surfaces observable in glaciated valleys represent pseudo-bedding planes which have been revealed by removal of overlying sheets of rock by a quite different mechanism. **1897** *Mineral. Mag.* XI. 333 Pseudo-boleite... Between boleite and cumengeite. Boleo, Lower California. **1951** C. PALACHE et al. *Dana's Syst. Mineral.* (ed. 7) II. x. 81 Pseudoboleite and boleite have been considered to be identical but the evidence favors the individual character and tetragonal symmetry of the former species. **1964** *Mineral. Abstr.* XVI. 457/2 The mineralogy of the metalliferous areas of Iran is systematically described. Rarer species include..pseudoboléite. **1890** W. WATSON *Orchids* ii. 18 Usually only one pseudo-bulb is developed at the apex or growing point of each rhizome yearly. **1934** R. STOUT *Fer-de-Lance* xvii. 292 Check..the shipment of pseudo-bulbs. **1959** T. B. MORRIS *Death among Orchids* x. 77 Fat pseudo-bulbs and leaves had been torn and bruised by the fall. **1979** B. & W. RITTERSHAUSEN *Orchids in Colour* 14 The plants [*sc.* cymbidiums] produce a number of well rounded pseudo bulbs. **1901** L. H. BAILEY *Cycl. Amer. Hort.* III. 1166/2 The pseudo-bulbous species..should be hosed over thoroughly. **1976** *Hortus Third* (L. H. Bailey Hortorium) 798/2 The rhizomes of such pseudobulbous genera, when well grown, regularly develop one or more new pseudobulbs each season. **1943** MENDEL & RUDNEY in *Biochem. Jrnl.* XXXVII. 59/1 It is the purpose of this paper to show that there exist in the animal body two esterases capable of hydrolysing acetylcholine: a true cholinesterase acting exclusively on choline esters, and a non-specific enzyme, which hydrolyses not only esters of choline but a variety of non-choline esters as well. Moreover, experiments with both enzymes at high and low concentrations of acetylcholine, have revealed a decisive difference between the two esterases, calling for a sharp distinction of the true cholinesterase from the non-specific enzyme, for which we venture to suggest the name pseudo-cholinesterase. **1974** M. C. GERALD *Pharmacol.* iii. 52 Alcohol..and the skeletal muscle relaxant succinylcholine are broken down by the enzymes alcohol dehydrogenase and pseudo-cholinesterase, respectively. **1900, 1940** Pseudocirrhosis [see *PICK'S DISEASE 1]. **1953** *Proc. IRE* XLI. 1252/1 Problems are submitted to the computer expressed in pseudo code. An 'interpretive' routine then decodes the input information and calls the subroutines into play as required. **1954, 1958** [see *INTERPRETER 5 b]. **1959** M. H. WRUBEL *Primer of Programming for Digital Computers* ii. 24 Pseudo-codes are often easier to learn than the machine language; only a single pseudo-code instruction is needed to generate frequently used functions such as square root..and log *x*. **1969** J. E. SAMMET *Programming Languages* iv. 129 The early compiling work done in the United States by Dr. Grace Hopper initially involved very artificial pseudo-codes rather than mathematical notation. **1979** *Personal Computer World* Nov. 61/2 Some [programmers] use pseudocode, a written problem definition language that looks like PL/1 or Pascal. **1943** *Nature* 16 Jan. 70/1 *N*[*icotiana*] *Forgetiana* and *N. alama* show pseudo-compatibility only in exceptional circumstances, that is, the actions of the various allelomorphs of the switch gene are always distinctive... Pseudo-compatibility marks the breakdown of the distinction between the types produced by the *S* [*sc.* sterility] allelomorphs. **1977** *Jrnl. Hort. Sci.* LII. 475 Pseudocompatibility was maximized by pollinating old flowers with large quantities of pollen. **1896** C. R. VAN HISE in *16th Ann. Rep. U.S. Geol. Survey* I. 679 The autoclastic rocks which readily show their origin may be called dynamic breccias, and those which resemble ordinary conglomerates may be called pseudo-conglomerates. **1957** F. J. PETTIJOHN *Sedimentary Rocks* (ed. 2) viii. 367 (*caption*) Brecciated siltstone... Brecciation was contemporaneous with sedimentation; a pseudoconglomerate. **1972** *Gloss. Geol.* (Amer. Geol. Inst.) 574/1 *Pseudoconglomerate*, a rock that resembles, or may easily be mistaken for, a true or normal (sedimentary) conglomerate; e.g...a sandstone packed with many rounded concretionary bodies, or an aggregate of rounded boulders produced in place by spheroidal weathering and surrounded by clayey material. **1889** J. L. LOBLEY *Mount Vesuvius* x. 313 Pseudocotunnite... Chloride of Lead with Chloride of Potassium... This mineral, which has the composition of a combination of Cotunnite and Sylvine, was obtained from the sublimations of the crater of Vesuvius following the great eruption of 1872. **1933** *Mineral. Abstr.* V. 269 New records of minerals from Vesuvius are thenardite, pseudocotunnite,.. and hieratite. **1817** J. M. GOOD *Physiol. System Nosology* v. iii. 415 Pseudocyesis. Symptoms of pregnancy without impregnation... Spurious Pregnancy. **1859** *Med. Times & Gaz.* 3 Sept. 225/1 There are two varieties of pseudo-cyesis or spurious pregnancy, a *local* and a *constitutional*. **1950** H. B. FRIEDGOOD in R. H. Williams *Textbk. Endocrinol.* x. 657 The sensation of fetal movements is reported usually during the fourth or fifth months of pseudocyesis and seems to be caused by intermittent contractions of the abdominal musculature. **1975** S. L. ROMNEY et al. *Gynecol. & Obstetr.* x. 152/2 Special forms of psychogenic amenorrhea include pseudocyesis or false pregnancy..and anorexia nervosa. **1980** *Daily Tel.* 15 Mar. 3/3 Pseudocyesis, or spurious or phantom pregnancy as it is variously known is a psychological disorder in which a woman has the false but fixed belief that she is pregnant. It is a not uncommon condition, often around the menopause. **1882** *Encycl. Brit.* XIV. 554/1 They [*sc.* cyphellæ] are generally naked, but are often also pulverulent or sorediiferous, in which latter case they are called pseudo-cyphellæ. **1964** *Oxf. Bk. Flowerless Plants* 64/1 The inner layers of the plant [sc. *Pseudocyphellaria crocata*]..show as conspicuous spots through small holes (pseudocyphellae) scattered over the lower surface. **1976** M. E. HALE in D. H. Brown et al. *Lichenology* i. 6 They [*sc.* foliose and fruticose lichens] have pores, pseudocyphellae or cyphellae, for gas exchange. **1930** *Amer. Naturalist* LXIV. 561 An actual loss or inactivation of chromatin material, leading to exaggeration and pseudo-dominance. **1938** *Yearbk. Carnegie Inst.* XXXVII. 306 The 'Minute' effect is lethal when homozygous..and gives pseudo-dominance to straw in hybrids. **1969** W. D. STANSFIELD *Schaum's Outl. Theory & Probl. Genetics* viii. 157 When an organism heterozygous for a pair of alleles, *A* and *a*, loses a small portion of the chromosome bearing the dominant allele, the recessive allele on the other chromosome will become expressed phenotypically. This is called pseudodominance, but it is a misnomer because the condition is hemizygous rather than dizygous at this locus. **1965** *Science* 26 Nov. 1123/3 This pseudodominant expression of *fa* can be understood by considering *N* as a deficiency for salivary band 3C7, wherein lies the wild-type allele of *fa*; the facet phenotype is expressed because the wild-type allele is missing. **1975** J. B. JENKINS *Genetics* iv. 165 The white-eye mutant allele was pseudodominant in deletions numbered 258-11..and 264-31. **1896** W. CALDWELL *Schopenhauer's System* iii. 149 A pseudo-entity ..like 'mere matter' or a mere Epicurean god in the interstellar spaces. **1912** *Mind* XXI. 214 'Matter' is..a pseud-entity. **1937** B. RUSSELL *Princ. Math.* (ed. 2) p. xi, I do not mean that statements apparently about points or instants or numbers, or any of the other entities which Occam's razor abolishes, are false, but only that they need interpretation which shows that their linguistic form is misleading, and that, when they are rightly analysed, the pseudo-entities in question are found to be not mentioned in them. **1944** M. BLACK in P. A. Schilpp *Philos. B. Russell* 231 Vocabulary, by promoting the hypostatization of pseudo-entities, encourages false beliefs concerning the *contents* of the world. **1956** J. HOLLOWAY in A. Pryce-Jones *New Outl. Mod. Knowl.* 31 Metaphysical jargon could be abandoned once for all, and so could all pretended references to pseudo-entities which could never conceivably be observed. **1904** B. RUSSELL in *Mind* XIII. 207 What is called the existence of an object in presentation is not really existence at all: it may be called pseudo-existence. **1934** *Mind* XLIII. 375 Confronted with Meinong's obscure and tentative utterances about immanence and pseudo-existence, Mr. Russell reasonably protested. **1953** *Phil. Trans. R. Soc.* B. CCXXXVII. 360 The pseudofaecal strings are conveyed to the end of the waste canals and so into the angle between the inner lobe of the mantle edge and the ctenidial membrane.., above which they are caught in the exhalant current and carried away. **1967** J. H. Day in G. H. Lauff *Estuaries* 401/2 It feeds at low tide levels, spooning up the surface silt with its chelae, sucking out the detritus, and discarding the silt as pseudofecal pellets. **1975** *Jrnl. Marine Biol. & Ecol.* XVII. 4 Since filtration rate and pseudofaecal production determine the amounts of material ingested they are important in studying the efficiency with which bivalves control their rates of ingestion. **1936** *Q. Jrnl. Microsc. Sci.* LXXIX. 207 It was mostly through this aperture ventral to the siphons that collections from the mantle (pseudofaeces) were expelled on sudden closure of the valves. **1976** B. L. Bayne et al. in *Marine Mussels* v. 145 All material to be removed is transferred to the rejection tracts of the mantle edge. These tracts convey the material to the posterior margin of the inhalant siphon, adjacent to the exhalant opening, where it is deposited as pseudofaeces and is carried away by the exhalant current. **1937** *Mind* XLVI. 252 A patient suffering from hemianopia developed a 'pseudo-fovea' in the sound halves of his eyes. **1967** Lyle & Wybar *Lyle & Jackson's Pract. Orthoptics in Treatm. of Squint* (ed. 5) ix. 208 The definition of the image (visual acuity) at the 'pseudo-fovea' will be less clear than at the 'suppressed' fovea. **1946** N. A. Stutterheim *Squint & Convergence* xii. 37 The technique is..to have the non-squinting eye occluded in order to encourage the true fovea and to discourage pseudo-foveal inclinations. **1930** *Amer. Jrnl. Roentgenol.* XXIV. 31/1 Fromme considers the point of involvement of those spontaneous pseudofractures to be about 1 inch below the epiphyseal line. **1950** Shank & Kerley *Textbk. X-Ray Diagnosis* (ed. 2) xi. 136 Pseudo-fractures or *umbauzonen* are always associated with systemic disease or malacic processes, such as Paget's diseases, adolescent rickets.., fibrous dysplasia and osteomalacia. **1976** Gordan & Vaughan *Clin. Managem. Osteoporoses* vii. 80 The pathognomonic x-ray finding of osteomalacia is the presence of bilateral symmetrical pseudofractures, described by Looser in 1920 and therefore often called Looser zones. **1977** C. Jacq et al. in *Cell* XII. 109/1 The 5S DNA of Xenopus laevis, coding for oocyte-type 5S RNA, consists of many copies of a tandemly repeated unit of about 700 base pairs. Each unit contains a 'pseudogene' in addition to the gene. The pseudogene has been partly sequenced and appears to be an almost perfect repeat of 101 residues of the gene. *Ibid.* 109/2 This homologous structure was nearly as long as, and almost an exact repeat of, the gene itself; hence the name —pseudogene. **1978** *Nature* 19 Jan. 205/2 The GC-rich region of 5S DNA also contains a pseudogene which is identical to the first 101 base pairs of the gene at all but 10 sites. **1953** W. L. Kubiëna *Soils of Europe* 242 The modification of 'gley-like soil' to *pseudogley* has been made here to make it conform to the rules of nomenclature, whereby the type designation should be expressed by a noun. *Ibid.* 244 In typical pseudogley the concretions are extremely numerous and are readily visible to the naked eye. **1965** B. T. Bunting *Geogr. of Soil* xiv. 163 Soils on elevated sites on clayey parent materials develop the mottling typical of gleization at some depth beneath a dark brown, granular or blocky structured surface horizon. Such soils have been termed pseudogleys. **1973** J. Mulqueen in Schlichting & Schwertmann *Pseudogley & Gley* 713 The pseudogley soils at Ballinamore are stratified into essentially two layers. **1884** H. R. Swanzy *Handbk. Dis. Eye* xvii. 307 Purulent inflammation of the vitreous humour (to which unfortunately the name pseudo-glioma is sometimes applied). **1946** Berens & Zuckerman *Diagnostic Exam. Eye* ix. 258 In children retinoblastoma (glioma) should be differentiated from an abscess of the vitreous (pseudoglioma). **1962** *New Scientist* 5 Apr. 801/1 Ophthalmologists had been used to examining babies with an abnormal mass of organized tissue behind the lens of the eye, and the non-committal and portmanteau term of 'pseudoglioma' had served as a diagnosis in many of their cases. **1905** *Jrnl. Physiol.* XXXII. 329 A portion of the globulin solution was dialysed... The euglobulin which fell out was removed... The fluid remaining after dialysis contained the pseudoglobulin. **1964** W. G. Smith *Allergy & Tissue Metabolism* vi. 69 Bradykinin is present in normal blood as an inactive precursor, bradykininogen, which is a component of the pseudoglobulin fraction of plasma. **1962** D. J. McCarty et al. in *Ann. Internal Med.* LVI. 711 (*heading*) The significance of calcium phosphate crystals in the synovial fluid of arthritic patients: the 'pseudogout syndrome'. *Ibid.* 712/1 It is suggested that these patients represent a discrete type of arthritis, labeled 'pseudogout' because in some respects it resembles classical gouty arthritis. **1972** *Daily Colonist* (Victoria, B.C.) 2 Mar. 2/2 Pseudo-gout is an attack that resembles an attack of gout, in that it strikes at a joint (usually the knee) with dramatic suddenness and with just as severe pain. **1975** *Amer. Jrnl. Roentgenol.* CXXIII. 532/1 Acute attacks of pseudogout have occurred following surgery, trauma, and injection of mercurial diuretics. **1903** *Jrnl. R. Microsc. Soc.* 172 E. Wasmann returns with fresh light to a discussion of 'pseudogyny' in *Formica sanguinea.* **1890** W. James *Princ. Psychol.* II. xix. 116 From ordinary images of memory and fancy, pseudo-hallucinations differ in being much more vivid, minute, detailed..abrupt and spontaneous, in the sense that all feeling of our own activity in producing them is lacking. **1902** A. R. Defendorf *Kraepelin's Clin. Psychiatry* 7 This group of hallucinations, which has been variously designated as psychic hallucinations.., pseudohallucinations (Hagen), and apprehension hallucinations,..involves several or all of the sensory fields, and..stands in close relation to the other contents of consciousness. **1968** P. McKellar *Experience & Behav.* iv. 120 What is sometimes called 'pseudo-hallucination'..involves a projected perceptual-like image, but one in which the person concerned recognizes the subjective nature of the occurrence. **1902** W. James *Var. Relig. Exper.* x. 251, I refer to hallucinatory or pseudo-hallucinatory luminous phenomena, *photisms*, to use the term of the psychologists. **1955** L. Ovesey in *Psychiatry* XVIII. 17 The dependency and power components..seek completely different, non-sexual goals, but make use of the genital organs to achieve them... For this reason, I have designated these two components as pseudohomosexual. *Ibid.*, This paper consists of a case study that provides clinical documentation for the concept of pseudohomosexuality. **1962** I. Bieber et al. *Homosexuality* i. 10 A neurosis divisible into true and pseudohomosexual types. **1966** I. B. Weiner *Psychodiagnosis in Schizophrenia* xiv. 309 Pseudohomosexual concerns often emerge in the course of these reflections because the thought, 'I am a failure', readily translates into ideas of being something less than an adequate man and hence a homosexual. **1878** D. F. Lincoln tr. Eulenburg in *Ziemssen's Cycl. Pract. Med.* XIV. 155 More and more stress is laid on the connection between pseudo-hypertrophy and progressive muscular atrophy. **1954** *Arch. Dis. in Childhood* XXIX. 404/1 Any effect of chronic hypocalcaemia on physique is likely to be more evident if the disease is present early, and the preponderance of dwarfism among pseudo-hypoparathyroid cases may be in part a reflection of the fact that in them the disorder is probably present from birth. **1942** F. Albright et al. in *Endocrinology* XXX. 922 (*heading*) Pseudo-hypoparathyroidism—an example of 'Seabright-Bartan Syndrome'. **1966** Wright & Symmers *Systemic Path.* II. xxxii. 1126/2 In pseudohypoparathyroidism, because hypocalcaemia is present from birth, the epiphyses and sutures close early, with the result that the patient is short and thickset in stature and has a characteristic round face. **1976** *Lancet* 20 Nov. 1106/2 Among suggested causes [of neonatal hypocalcæmia] are..decreased responsiveness of end-organs to parathyroid hormone (a form of pseudohypoparathyroidism), and vitamin-D deficiency. **1863** H. Spencer *First Princ.* ii. 36 We can entertain them [*sc.* hypotheses] only as we entertain such pseud-ideas as a square fluid and a moral substance. **1879** W. James *Coll. Ess. & Rev.* (1920) 130 Professor Bain would no doubt say that nonentity was a pseud-idea not derived from experience and therefore meaningless. **1911** —— *Some Probl. of Philos.* xii. 197 The pseudo-idea of a connection which we have, Hume then goes on to show, is nothing but the misinterpretation of a mental custom. **1957** D. D. McCracken *Digital Computer Programming* xv. 182 The very first order of business on jumping into the interpretive routine is to increase index 1 by 1 so that it contains the location of the first pseudo instruction. **1967** P. A. Stark *Digital Computer Programming* xii. 198 In addition to all the arithmetic and input-output instructions..the symbolic language has a number of pseudo-instructions to the symbolic assembler. **1975** R. M. Graham *Princ. Systems Programming* 388 Pseudo instructions are used to define symbols, define constants, reserve space in the object segment, and provide the assembler with other information. **1879** T. J. Dills tr. J. Stilling in *Arch. Ophthalm.* VIII. 182 If we intermix the different shades of both interchangeable colors in smaller or larger squares, in such manner that the squares of the one color form letters and figures, and those of the other the groundwork, so that the different intensities alternate in ground and letter..the question as to judgment of colors is rendered unnecessary, the inquiry being merely about letters, numbers, figures. This is the principle of the pseudo-isochromatic plates. **1949** H. C. Weston *Sight, Light & Efficiency* vii. 241 For distinguishing between the varieties of colour-sense deficiency,..what are called pseudo-isochromatic plates are available. **1970** R. A. Moses *Adler's Physiol. of Eye* (ed. 5) xxi. 638/1 Pseudoisochromatic color plates are patterns of colored and gray dots that reveal one pattern to the normal, another to the color deficient. **1963** E. H. Nickel et al. in *Amer. Mineralogist* XLVIII. 976 The ixiolite-like minerals that convert to columbite-tantalite on heating cannot be considered as true ixiolites. For want of a better name, it is suggested that they be referred to as disordered columbite-tantalite, or as 'pseudo-ixiolite'. **1971** *Canad. Mineralogist* X. 758 In all other pegmatites, pseudo-ixiolite forms either tabular grains in a medium-grained albite + quartz + muscovite + garnet assemblage in the internal parts of the pegmatite bodies. **1954** W. R. Halliday *Pseudokarst* (Technical Note No. 25, Nat. Speleological Soc., U.S.) 1 Because the non-solugenic processes are analogous rather than homologous, it seems preferable that they should be considered as independent phenomena, i.e. pseudokarst. *Ibid.*, Pseudokarst may be recognized in three major non-calcareous realms: basalt flows, glaciers, and certain soils. **1960** *Bull. Nat. Speleol. Soc.* XXII. ii. 109/1 About 25 years ago, European geologists began to discuss features of non-solutional origin which are analogous to those of areas of karstic geomorphology. These they termed pseudokarst... Hans Peter Kosack, noted German geomorphologist, believes that the term *pseudokarst* was first employed in print in an Italian publication in 1941... However, as Dr. Kosack has pointed out (pers. comm.),..H. Cramer employed the term in an unpublished study of the karst of the British Isles which was prepared in 1936, and believes that the term was in use in Europe as early as 1930. *Ibid.*, Areas showing pseudokarstic features are distributed quite widely throughout the Western United States. **1968** R. W. Fairbridge *Encycl. Geomorphol.* 849/2 Pseudokarsts produced by piping display disappearing streams, sinkholes,..residual hills and caves. **1971** J. N. Jennings *Karst* i. 5 More obviously pseudokarstic are larger caves..and collapse depressions. **1963** *Cancer* XVI. 928/2 A primary lymphocytic tumour of the lung will be defined as either a malignant lymphoma of the lymphocytic type or an inflammatory pseudolymphoma that originally involves only the lung, or the lung and its regional lymph nodes, and in which there is no evidence of dissemination of the tumor for at least 3 months after the diagnosis is established. **1976** *National Observer* (U.S.) 25 Sept. 14/3 'What did you find?' I asked. 'A lesion, very rare,' he exulted. 'It is called pseudolymphoma.'.. 'Is it cancer?' 'No.' **1972** *Clin. & Exper. Immunol.* X. 202 The diagnosis was localized pseudolymphomatous changes in the parotid glands and regional lymph nodes. **1976** *Chest* LXX. 358/1 Apparently these 'pseudolymphomatous' lesions have the potential to regress with appropriate therapy..or may progress to frank neoplasia. **1924** *Arch. Pediatrics* XLI. 565 (*heading*) Report of a case of pseudomembranous ileocolitis. **1952** *Gastroenterol.* XXI. 212 Acute pseudomembranous inflammation involving portions of the intestinal tract after abdominal operations has been a subject of major importance within the past decade. **1977** *Lancet* 16 Apr. 839/1 Pseudomembranous enterocolitis may arise ..as a complication of colonic obstruction. **1883** *Jrnl. Chem. Soc.* XLIV. 875 Paralbumin is only a mixture of a mucoid substance, pseudomucin, with varying proportions of albumin. **1901** J. L. Rothrock in C. A. L. Reed *Text-bk. Gynecol.* xl. 603 Pseudomucinous (Proliferating) Cysts.—To this group belong the greater proportion of ovarian cysts. **1968** J. W. Huffman *Gynecol. Childhood & Adolescence* xiv. 279/2 Pseudomucinous Cystadenomas. These tumors owe their name to their contents, a gel-like fluid, pseudomucin, secreted by the cells of the epithelium lining the locules within the cysts. **1927** M. C. Rayner *Mycorrhiza* viii. 142 These pseudomycorrhizas are usually simple and unbranched. **1934** *Forestry* VIII. 102 These pseudomycorrhizas show aberrant structure in many respects. **1952** S. A. Waksman *Soil Microbiol.* iii. 88 Pseudomycorrhiza..are endotrophic in nature. **1959** J. L. Harley *Biol. Mycorrhiza* iv. 69 The name pseudomycorrhiza must be used with some care... Those who held a pseudoreligious belief that mycorrhizas 'benefited' their hosts..would refute, by the suggestion that the state being observed was pseudomycorrhizal rather than mycorrhizal, any observation which looked contrary to their own belief. **1949** *Psychiatric Q.* XXIII. 249 In establishing the diagnosis of the pseudoneurotic form of schizophrenia, it will be necessary to demonstrate the presence of the basic mechanisms of schizophrenia. **1966** I. B. Weiner *Psychodiagnosis in Schizophrenia* xvi. 398 Borderline and pseudoneurotic are two of many nosological terms that have been proposed to identify fairly stable personality states in which schizophrenic features are implied but not overtly manifest. **1971** *Brit. Med. Bull.* XXVII. 77/1 There are schools which diagnose simple or pseudo-neurotic forms of schizophrenia. **1965** *Language* XLI. 399 Both reject the same pseudo-objects: From.. *The candidate spoke two hours*:.. (*They reported*) *the speaking of two hours by the candidate... Two hours were spoken by the candidate.* **1966** *Eng. Stud.* XLVII. 54 *It* (as a kind of pseudo-object) appears with transitive and intransitive verbs, and finally with original nouns and adjectives (to lord it, to queen it, to rough it) indicating the verbal function of these nominal parts of speech. **1956** *Jrnl. Assoc. Computing Machinery* III. 299 One of the principal objectives of the PACT I compiler has been to eliminate as much as was immediately feasible of the bookkeeping and rudimentary thinking which is involved in the preparation of a computational problem for a large-scale, high-speed digital computer. To this end, a set of PACT pseudo-operations was developed. These operations are more closely related to the computational problem than the machine operands. **1976** W. G. Rudd *Assembly Lang. Programming* v. 62 The start pseudo-operation orders the assembler to begin the assembly process. **1951** M. V. Wilkes et al. *Preparation of Programs for Electronic Digital Computer* 17 A converse of the fact that orders are represented in the machine by numbers is that numbers may be represented outside the machine by 'pseudo-orders', that is, tape entries which are punched in the same form as orders but which are merely intended to be used as constants and are never to be obeyed as orders. **1955** *Jrnl. Assoc. Computing Machinery* II. 1 It is well known that programming may be simplified by the use of pseudoorders. We define these as additional orders (like square root..) which the machine cannot perform. [*Note*] In Wilkes, Wheeler and Gill [1951: see prec. quot.]..what we call pseudoorder is denoted there by 'order', whilst the word pseudoorder is used in a different context. **1964** F. L. Westwater *Electronic Computers* ix. 143 Each subroutine was allocated a code number, and 'pseudo-orders' were written using these numbers as functions. **1909** *Brit. Jrnl. Dermatol.* XXI. 27 Dr. J. M. H. Macleod showed a case of pseudo-pelade (Brocq) or cicatricial alopecia in a man, aged 34 years, affecting chiefly the vertex of the scalp. **1975** S. L. Moschella et al. *Dermatol.* II. xxv. 1206 The etiology of pseudopelade is a mystery. **1887** H. E. F. Garnsey tr. *A. de Bary's Compar. Morphol. & Biol. Fungi* v. 275 The hymenium [of Uredineae] and the rows of spores which proceed from it are enclosed in a membranous envelope composed of a single layer of cells (the peridium, pseudo-peridium or paraphyses-envelope). **1965** Bell & Coombe tr. *Strasburger's Textbk. Bot.* 512 In some genera..all the spores of the peripheral chains and the terminal spores of the other chains lose their spore-like character before breaking through the epidermis and cohere as a firm investment (pseudoperidium). **1832** J. Lindley *Introd. Bot.* i. iii. 207 Pseudoperithecium; Pseudohymenium; Pseudoperidium; terms used by Fries to express such coverings of Sporidia as resemble in figure the parts named perithecium, hymenium, and peridium in other plants. **1895** [see *imperfect *a.* 8 b]. **1903** *Bot. Gaz.* XXXV. 154 The head, which strongly suggests the pseudoperithecium, if it may so be termed, of the more highly differentiated species of Gymnoascus, is thus a remarkable combination of two elements of independent origin. **1928** C. W. Dodge tr. *Gäumann's Compar. Morphol. Fungi* xxiv. 365 At maturity, the vestigial walls of the perithecium [of *Coreomyces*] degenerate, leaving the developing ascogonium surrounded only by the walls of the original cells of the distal region, a pseudoperithecium. **1916** B. D. Jackson *Gloss. Bot. Terms* (ed. 3) 312/1 Pseudoplankton..organisms accidentally found floating. **1935** P. S. Welch *Limnology* ix. 208 Pseudoplankton—debris mingled in plankton. **1947** R. Ruedemann *Graptolites N. Amer.* i. 19 The majority of the typical graptolites lived as pseudoplankton. **1898** *Amer. Naturalist* XXXII. 14 It is highly probable that many graptolites were indeed pseudo-planktonic. **1969** Bennison & Wright *Geol. Hist. Brit. Isles* v. 105 The graptolites were planktonic or pseudoplanktonic. **1892** R. Thaxter in *Bot. Gaz.* XVII. 392 The essential characters of a pseudo-plasmodium are common to both groups. **1966** *McGraw-Hill Encycl. Sci. & Technol.* XI. 44/1 Labyrinthulidae..are uninucleate marine organisms... An aggregate of many individuals may form a motile pseudoplasmodium. **1929** R. V. Williamson in *Industr. & Engin. Chem.* Nov. 1108/1 Certain types of dispersions do not flow in accordance with the laws of either ideal fluids or ideal plastics. The flowing properties of such dispersions are similar in many respects to the flowing properties of ideal plastics; therefore we shall refer to them as pseudoplastics. The primary difference between pseudoplastic flow and ideal plastic flow is the absence of a real yield value in pseudoplastic flow. **1958** *Ibid.* Jan. 10/2 Aqueous solutions of the poly(ethylene oxide) with intrinsic viscosity of 9 exhibit a mucous-like stringiness, and when observed in a variable shear-rate viscometer can be classed rheologically as pseudoplastic. **1962** *Lancet* 15 Dec. 1263/1 They suggest that the plastic or pseudoplastic flow of abnormally viscous bile caused by metallic ions is converted into a newtonian flow by the action of chelating agents. **1979** A. L. Lydersen *Fluid Flow & Heat Transfer* i. 2 (*caption*) Velocity gradient du/dy as a function of the shear stress $\tau = F/A$. a, dilatant fluid; b, Newtonian fluid; c, pseudo-plastic fluid; d, Bingham plastic fluid. **1938** Weiss & Louis in A. E. Dunstan et al. *Sci. of Petroleum* II. xx. 1128/2 The phenomenon of pseudo-plasticity is of importance in the physico-chemical examination of the large molecules present in petroleum. **1958** *Industr. & Engin. Chem.* Jan. 11/2 The initially high viscosity and the low shear rate pseudoplasticity are reduced. **1967** *New Scientist* 9 Feb. 334/3 Pseudoplasticity describes the fall of viscosity with increasing shear rate. **1952** F. Albright et al. in *Trans. Assoc. Amer. Physicians* LXV. 339 We wish to present today a case with all of the characteristics of pseudohypoparathyroidism except that she has no manifestations suggesting hypoparathyroidism—no hyperphosphatemia, no hypocalcemia. Thus she might be said to have..a 'pseudo-pseudo-hypoparathyroidism'. **1962** *Lancet* 19 May 1075/1 (*heading*) Chromosomal analysis in gonadal dysgenesis with pseudopseudohypoparathyroidism. **1975** *Arch. Dermatol.* CXI. 90/1 A 31-year-old woman with the characteristic features of pseudopseudohypoparathyroidism, such as shortened metacarpals and metatarsals, round facies, and normal serum calcium values, was studied. **1971** *Kybernetik* IX. 159/1 The *deep pseudopupil* of Dipterans is not to be confused with the *corneal pseudopupil*..and especially not with the *reduced corneal pseudopupil*.., in spite of the remarkable similarity of these phenomena. **1977** *Sci. Amer.* July 108/2 Looking at the eye of an insect, we frequently see a black spot in the center of the eye. As the insect rotates its head the black spot always points in the direction of the observer. The spot is known as the pseudopupil: the facets in it look black because they reflect less light in the direction of the observer than the facets in the rest of the eye. **1975** G. J. King *Audio Handbk.* 2 Pseudo-quadraphony..is designated 2–2–4, which implies that the four loudspeakers obtain their signals from the two-channel source. **1976** *Which?* May 99/3 Apart from these, there is a sort of 'fake' quad called, variously, Hafler (after its inventor), ambiophony, or pseudoquadrophony. With this system, you can derive some quadrophonic effect from ordinary stereo recordings and broadcasts. **1897** *Lippincott's Med. Dict.* 840/2 *Pseudorabies*, hysteria resembling rabies, or a condition in animals resembling rabies. **1906** *Jrnl. Nerv. & Mental Dis.* XXXIII. 741 Pseudo-Rabies.—Five cases are cited of pathological alcoholic intoxication in which the patients were wild, making murderous attacks, attempting to bite persons or even trees, bed clothes, etc. **1912** J. J. Walsh *Psychotherapy* xx. ii. 753 There seems no doubt that..pseudo-rabies occurs; that is, persons are bitten by a dog, become seriously disturbed over the possibility of rabies developing, and..there is either a neurosis simulating many symptoms of true rabies, or..even death may take place. **1931** *Jrnl. Exper. Med.* LIV. 246 Among the laboratory animals, rabbits are stated to be more susceptible to pseudorabies than guinea pigs. **1957** Smith & Jones *Veterinary Path.* ix. 258 Pseudorabies may be suspected in disease outbreaks in which animals die shortly after showing very severe prurities limited to a segment of the skin. **1926** *Jrnl. Chem. Soc.* ii. 2779 Whether he is dealing with a racemate or a pseudo-racemate. **1973** S. F. Mason in Ciardelli & Salvadori *Fund. Aspects & Rec. Devel. Optical Rotatory Dispersion & Circular Dichroism* iii. 212 A pseudoracemate of *lel* and *ob* diastereoisomers is not optically inactive. **1897** Kipping & Pope in *Jrnl. Chem. Soc.* LXXI. 991 Whilst retaining the name racemic compound for a substance belonging to class (*a*), we propose..to call those belonging to class (*b*) pseudoracemic, in order to distinguish them from mere mixtures of the two antipodes on the one hand, and from racemic compounds on the other. **1951** S. Coffey tr. *Wibaut's Org. Chem.* viii. 218 Cases are also known in which mixed crystals of the optical antipodes separate (pseudo-racemic mixed crystals). **1972** R. A. Jackson *Mechanism* v. 84 If the two compounds have opposite configurations no such solid solution will in general be possible, and either a simple eutectic mixture or a 'pseudo-racemic' compound will be formed. **1900** Dorland *Med. Dict.* 544/2 *Pseudoreaction*, a clumping or other bacterial reaction not due to the presence of the typhoid bacillus. **1928** L. E. H. Whitby *Med. Bacteriol.* xxiii. 238 A reaction occurs in both arms, that on the control being a pseudo-reaction whereas that on the test arm is a combination of a pseudo and a positive reaction. **1977** *Compar. Biochem. & Physiol.* B. LVI. 272/2 The nature and origin of the pseudo-reaction of the marine molluscan tissues remains obscure. **1899** *Jrnl. Morphol.* XV. Suppl. 71 It may be stated..in regard to the number of chromosomes, that it is plainly greater than in the first spermatocyte division, which is known to be post-synaptic, *i.e.*, after the pseudo-reduction. **1931** W. Shumway *Textbk. Gen. Biol.* vi. 149 The split..develops so that when the metaphase occurs only half the diploid number of chromosomes may be counted *but* each of these has four parts. There has been no reduction in the sense that any chromosomes have been lost; they have merely united in pairs so that the change in the number of visible chromosomes is called pseudo-reduction. **1972** Cotton & Wilkinson *Adv. Inorg. Chem.* (ed. 3) xiii. 400 A cyclic 5-coordinate intermediate is formed which then pseudorotates. **1960** *Rev. Mod. Physics* XXXII. 451/1 (*caption*) The pseudorotated figure (b) corresponds to sending (a) through a clockwise rotation of $\frac{2}{3}\pi$ and permuting nuclei $1 \rightarrow 3$, $3 \rightarrow 2$, and $2 \rightarrow 1$. **1947** *Jrnl. Amer. Chem. Soc.* LXIX. 2484/2 (*heading*) Pseudo-rotation of ring puckering. **1960** *Jrnl. Chem. Physics* XXXII. 937/1 One..attractive mechanism for the exchange process in PF_5 and PCl_5 is a purely internal pseudorotation. **1974** *Nature* 31 May 474/2 By dynamic reversal of the H_2O binding step before pseudorotation, the two oxygens in the pair of oxoniums could equilibrate with the H_2O oxygens of the medium. **1976** Emsley & Hall *Chem. of Phosphorus* ii. 60 A shorthand notation is required for the *tbp* structures and their pseudorotational transformations. **1966** Teufer & Temple in *Nature* 9 July 180/1 As a result of an investigation of several altered ilmenite concentrates by X-ray techniques hitherto not applied to this problem, a new crystalline phase has been identified as a major constituent of altered ilmenite. The new phase crystallizes in a disordered structure of hexagonal symmetry and has the theoretical composition $Fe_2O_3 \cdot 3TiO_2$. We propose the name 'pseudorutile' for this new mineral. **1975** *Amer. Mineralogist* LX. 905/2 The electrochemical corrosion model is consistent with the pseudorutile composition being a stable alteration product of ilmenite in which all the iron is in the ferric state. **1910** N. V. Sidgwick *Org. Chem. Nitrogen* vii. 152 The mercury must migrate from one position to the other, according to the solvent, just as the hydrogen atom does with a pseudo-acid, and hence mercuric nitroform should be called a pseudo-salt. **1930** *Chem. Abstr.* XXIV. 4021 In alc. soln. there can exist an equil. between the pseudo-salts and the true salts. **1953** C. K. Ingold *Struct. & Mechanism in Org. Chem.* x. 577 Pseudo-salt formation can be seen in the reactions of methylquinolinium salts with various sources of carbanions, for instance Grignard reagents, or pseudo-acidic carbonyl or nitro-compounds. **1964** M. Argyle *Psychol. & Social Probl.* v. 60 One very common type of juvenile delinquent is the 'pseudo-social' delinquent, so called because he is perfectly well behaved towards other members of his gang, but not to people outside of it. **1968** Hebb & Thompson in Lindzey & Aronson *Handbk. Social Psychol.* II. 734 It is important also to exclude pseudosocial behavior, in which grouping occurs only because of some stimulus external to the group: examples are animals running from a forest fire. **1974** *Black Panther* 16 Mar. 11/3 Without new insights, we must really fear new outbreaks of that reactionary pseudospeciation which found (we hope) its climax in Hitler. **1975** *N.Y. Times* 26 Jan. x. 1/1 Erikson calls this 'pseudospeciation'..meaning that man has falsely created divisions where there are none. **1965** E. Erikson in *Amer. Jrnl. Psychiatry* CXXII. 246/1 Sociogenetic evolution has split mankind into pseudo-species, into tribes, nations and religions..which bind their members into a pattern of individual and collective identity, but alas, reinforce that pattern by a mortal fear of and a murderous hatred for other pseudo-species. **1968** —— *Identity* i. 41 Man as a species has survived by being divided into what I have called *pseudospecies*. **1974** *Black Panther* 23 Feb. 10/2 That means we have a common faith ..that each pseudospecies and each empire in some dialectical way added new elements to a more universal sense of humanity. **1889** *Cent. Dict.*, Pseudosphere. **1909** L. P. Eisenhart *Treat. Differential Geom. Curves & Surfaces* viii. 274 The surface of revolution of a tractrix about its asymptote is called the pseudosphere, or the pseudospherical surface of the parabolic type. **1926** J. E. Campbell *Differential Geom.* ii. 28 The formulae of spherical trigonometry or of pseudospherical trigonometry will apply to any surfaces which have the same ground form as the sphere or the pseudosphere. **1947** L. P. Eisenhart *Introd. Differential Geom.* iv. 284 The length of the segment of a tangent to a meridian from the point of contact to the axis of rotation is *a*, and consequently the meridian curve is a tractrix... These pseudospherical surfaces are said to be of the parabolic type. They are called pseudospheres. **1965** J. D. North *Measure of Universe* iv. 60 In 1868 E. Beltrami..showed that Lobachevsky's plane geometry holds in Euclidean space on certain surfaces of constant negative curvature (the pseudospheres) and that these could be conformally represented on a plane. **1909, 1926** Pseudospherical [see *pseudosphere* above]. **1956** J. R. Newman *World of Math.* I. iv. 645 All we know about space, he [*sc.* von Helmholtz] said, is what we have learned from experience. If we lived in a spherical or pseudo-spherical space our sensible impressions of the world would dictate the adoption of the non-Euclidian geometries of Riemann or Lobachevsky; nothing in our intuition would require us to adopt a 'flat-space' Euclidean system. **1939** N. de V. Hart *Bridge Players' Bedside Bk.* xi. 54 The term pseudo-squeeze should be reserved for those occasions when a player by ruse or subterfuge deliberately creates in the mind of an opponent the illusion that it is safe to discard from a certain suit and fatal to discard from another, when in fact the reverse is the case. **1975** *Times* 22 July 5/1 Careful defence was needed by the British pair..to avoid being caught in a pseudo-squeeze. **1926** I. A. Richards *Sci. & Poetry* vi. 56 We must confine ourselves to the other function of words, or rather..to one form of that function, let me call it pseudo-statement. *Ibid.* 59 A pseudo-statement is a form of words which is justified entirely by its effect in releasing or organizing our impulses and attitudes..; a statement, on the other hand, is justified by..its correspondence..with the fact to which it points. **1933–5** Wittgenstein *Blue & Brown Bks.* (1958) 71 One of the reasons why we are tempted to make our pseudo-statement is its similarity with the statement 'I only see this.' **1940** *Kenyon Rev.* 271 Poetry consists essentially of pseudo-statements. **1947** D. Rynin *Johnson's Treat. Lang.* 333 Only if the expression has statement meaning shall we consider it a genuine statement; otherwise we shall call it a pseudo-statement, provided it satisfies the purely grammatical requirements. **1894** *Kew Bull.* 231 The stem (pseudo-stem) in Musas usually arises from a perennial rootstock. **1927** *Bot. Gaz.* LXXXIV. 337 If..the trunk is cut across..it is found to be a pseudostem composed of the overlapping close-fitting leaf sheaths alone. **1957** *New Biol.* XI. 71 The sappy, leafy banana trunks..are really pseudostems consisting of the overlapping leaf-bases. **1972** J. W. Purseglove *Trop. Crops: Monocotyledons* II. 357 The last leaves are produced at nodes on the flowering stem in the centre of the pseudostem. **1874** *Q. Jrnl. Geol. Soc.* XXX. 253 The great masses of gabbro in Rum often exhibit that pseudo-stratification so often observed in igneous rocks. **1941** *Amer. Jrnl. Sci.* CCXXXIX. 1 (*heading*) The development of pseudo-stratification by metamorphic differentiation in the schists of Otago, New Zealand. **1959** *Econ. Geol.* LIV. 1161 Even, regular layering is the commonest type of pseudostratification in the section. **1874** *Q. Jrnl. Geol. Soc.* XXX. 245 When the northern face of this mountain is viewed from a little distance, the whole mass presents the appearance of being made up of a number of concentrically curved beds. This pseudo-stratified appearance is..very frequently presented by masses of undoubted igneous origin. **1940** *Trans. Geol. Soc. S. Afr.* XLII. 59 The rocks in this area are very clearly pseudostratified and form hilly country. **1917** S. J. Shand in *Q. Jrnl. Geol. Soc.* LXXII. 199 The name pseudotachylyte has been adopted in recognition of the fact that these rocks have a great similarity to tachylyte. **1954** H. Williams et al. *Petrography* xi. 202 X-ray investigation and measurement of the refractive index have shown some pseudotachylytes to be cryptocrystalline products of extreme crushing of rocks such as granite, without actual melting. **1971** *Nature* 17 Sept. 189/1 More than half of the rocks consist of a very irregular pattern of small black veins embracing gneiss fragments—'pseudotachylytes'. **1977** A. Hallam *Planet Earth* 177 Very rarely temperature may rise enough for melting, and such frictionally-produced melts are called pseudotachylites. **1957** J. K. Charlesworth *Quaternary Era* I. xxvii. 569 Solifluxion..produces stony clays or pseudo-tills. **1966** *Earth-Sci. Rev.* II. 249 None of these thickness criteria, alone, can distinguish tills..from pseudo-tills. **1963** R. O. Muir tr. *Schwarbach's Climates of Past* v. 39, I would recommend that the term tillite be applied not only to undoubted moraines but to all moraine-like sediments of probable or possible glacial or glacio-marine origin. Those later shown to be..of non-glacial origin, may then, more properly, be called pseudo-tillites. **1963** D. W. & E. E. Humphries tr. *Termier's Erosion & Sedimentation* x. 205 These graywackes, which must be deposited in deep water.., consist of grains of angular sand set in an argillaceous groundmass, sometimes with boulders or fragments (pseudo-tillites) not unlike the material of glacial moraines. **1968** R. W. Fairbridge *Encycl. Geomorphol.* 473/2 Any sort of 'accidental' mixture such as is caused by a gravitational flow..can easily be taken for a glacial till, i.e., it is a pseudotillite. **1890** B. T. Lowne *Anat., Physiol., Morphol., & Devel. of Blow-Fly* I. iv. 146 The Pseudotracheæ are cylindrical channels on the oral surface of the disc. **1925** A. D. Imms *Gen. Textbk. Entomol.* iii. 595 Fine trachea-like food channels or pseudotracheæ become evident [in Diptera]. **1954** *New Biol.* XVII. 44 Those species [of woodlice] which can withstand drier conditions are also those which possess these 'pseudotracheae'. **1975** *Nature* 27 Mar. 325/1 On each half labellum of *Drosophila* there are..some 25 taste pegs between the pseudotracheae. **1896** G. M. Sternberg *Text-bk. Bacteriol.* ii. xvi. 608 Preisz (1894) has compared the bacillus of pseudo-tuberculosis described by Nocard with that of Pfeiffer, of Parietti, and of Zagari, and finds them identical. **1899** E. O. Jordan tr. *Hueppe's Princ. Bacteriol.* iv. 201 If tubercles occur in which, instead of the tubercle bacillus, other bacteria are found the affection is called pseudo-tuberculosis. **1959** R. Lovell in Stableforth & Galloway *Infectious Dis. Animals* I. vi. 250 Caseous lymphadenitis of sheep. This is a chronic disease frequently referred to as pseudo-tuberculosis and widely distributed in South America, Australia and New Zealand. **1977** Andrewes & Walton *Viral & Bacterial Zoonoses* xxviii. 145 The numerous cases of pseudotuberculosis in zoos and research establishments are most probably due to the contamination of feeding-stuffs and water by wild birds and rodents. **1907** *Jrnl. Compar. Path. & Therapeutics* XX. 53 Mainly on account of the acid-fast character of the bacilli, the disease has been referred to as a pseudo-tuberculosis, and Bang has suggested that it should be called 'chronic bovine pseudo-tuberculous enteritis'. **1957** S. L. Robbins *Textbk. Path.* xxix. 1101/1 Pseudotuberculous (giant cell) thyroiditis. This form of inflammation of unknown etiology is so named because of its histologic appearance. **1962** *Lancet* 19 May 1042/1 We describe here a further case of pseudotuberculous mesenteric adenitis,..together with evidence that 3 other children in the same family and a pet dog had also been infected with *Past. pseudotuberculosis*. **1901** A. P. Ohlmacher in Hektoen & Riesman *Text-bk. Path.* I. 288 Of the various pathogenic blastomycetic species obtained from morbid processes in man or under saprophytic conditions, all failed to produce anything else than 'pseudo-tumors'. **1938** Smith & Gault *Essent. of Path.* xxiii. 232 This resemblance [to true tumors] ceases on microscopic study when the histologic evidence of neoplastic change of the cells is found to be lacking. The cells in such pseudo-tumors will show evidence of inflammatory hyperplasia. **1944** J. F. Brailsford *Radiol. Bones & Joints* (ed. 3) xvii. 241 A pseudo-tumour of the spinal cord was recorded by W. E. Dandy—this was found to be a shell of bone surrounding the posterior half of the spinal cord. **1974** Passmore & Robson *Compan. Med. Stud.* III. xxxiv. 12/1 A pseudotumour is one of the names given to a syndrome of raised intracranial pressure unassociated with a space-occupying lesion. **1964** G. H. Haggis et al. *Introd. Molecular Biol.* ix. 218 In 5-ribosyl-uracil ('pseudo-uracil') the uracil ring is attached to the backbone ribose through the carbon at position 5 in the uracil ring, rather than through the nitrogen at position 3. **1970** Ambrose & Easty *Cell Biol.* iv. 133 It contained, like most tRNA molecules, a number of unusual bases, such as inosine.. and pseudouracil.., and certain methylated forms of normal bases. **1978** *Sci. Amer.* Jan. 62/3 In some systems the control function is associated with a particular modified nucleotide in the tRNA molecule, for example a uracil that has been converted into a pseudouracil. **1959** *Biochimica et Biophysica Acta* XXXII. 571 It is proposed (by Dr. A. Michelson) that this substance be called pseudouridine, with the symbol Ψ for the prefix 'pseudo' in abbreviations. **1964** A. White et al. *Princ. Biochem.* (ed. 3) xxx. 607 Formation of pseudouridine may also occur at the polynucleotide level, but the mode of synthesis is unknown. **1978** *Sci. Amer.* Jan. 55/1 (*caption*) Other structural modifications also occur. For example, the nucleoside pseudouridine (ψ) has its base attached to the ribose through a carbon atom instead of a nitrogen atom. **1951** *Abstr. of Papers 120th Meeting Amer. Chem. Soc.* 22c (*heading*) Crystalline pseudovitamin B_{12}. **1956** *Nature* 28 Jan. 188/1 Several substances, such as factor *A* and pseudo-vitamin B_{12}, are closely related to cobalamin. **1967** *Oceanogr. & Marine Biol.* V. 383 As in many other crustaceans, vitamin B_{12} is found in *Nephrops*... It occurs as the analogs Factor B and pseudovitamin B_{12}. **1858** T. H. Huxley in

Trans. Linn. Soc. XXII. 208 The central mass..completely simulates the vitellus of an impregnated ovum; and I will therefore term it a 'pseudovitellus'. **1899** D. Sharp in Harmer & Shipley *Cambr. Nat. Hist.* VI. viii. 588 There exists [in aphids]..a peculiar structure, the pseudovitellus, a sort of cellular, double string. **1924** *Philippine Jrnl. Sci.* XXIV. 150 Henneguy..also described the origin of the 'pseudovitellus' from the follicular epithelium. **1946** Pseudovitellus [see *MYCETOME]. **1925** *Mineral. Mag.* XX. 463 Pseudowavellite... Hydrated phosphate of aluminium with lime, ferric iron, and rare-earths; occurring as white encrustations (trigonal needles) on limonite and wavellite at Amberg, Bavaria. So named because of its resemblance to wavellite, of which it is perhaps an alteration product. **1942** [see *LEWISTONITE]. **1951** C. Palache et al. *Dana's Syst. Min.* (ed. 7) II. 837 Available evidence indicates that crandallite and pseudowavellite are best considered as a single species with some variation of composition, the name crandallite having priority. **1906** *Amer. Jrnl. Sci.* CLXXI. 105 Pseudo-wollastonite appears either in the form of small irregular grains often tabular in shape or in short prisms or fibers arranged in parallel or divergent groups. **1942** *Ibid.* CCXL. 729 It is a most remarkable fact that, if powdered glass of the composition $CaSiO_3$ is crystallized at any temperature, the product always consists almost exclusively of pseudowollastonite, but lumps of the same glass will crystallize readily to wollastonite with only a trace of pseudowollastonite present at temperatures between 800° and 1100°. **1970** R. W. Andrews *Wollastonite* 2 There are two polymorphs of calcium monosilicate: wollastonite the low temperature form, and pseudowollastonite..the high temperature form. *Ibid.* 5 Natural pseudowollastonite has been reported from only one locality, in Iran, near the head of the Persian Gulf. **1900** Dorland *Med. Dict.* 545/1 *Pseudoxanthoma*, a disease resembling xanthoma. **1901** *Brit. Jrnl. Dermatol.* XIII. 232 The author ranges himself with Darier, and considers the condition to be due to a degeneration of elastic tissue... The qualification 'pseudo'-xanthoma should be insisted upon. **1933** *Arch. Dermatol. & Syphilol.* XXVIII. 553 The histologic evidences of pseudoxanthoma elasticum are fragmentation and degeneration of the elastic tissue. **1961** *Lancet* 12 Aug. 356/2 Although the lesions attributable to pseudoxanthoma elasticum may be widely distributed through the tissues and organs of the body, it is more commonly recognised by dermatologists and ophthalmologists than by general physicians. **1977** *Proc. R. Soc. Med.* LXX. 569/1 Instead of the well ordered wavy collagen bundles of normal skin, the middle and lower dermis in pseudoxanthoma elasticum shows an irregular network of tangled, curled and branching fibres.

b. *Cytology*. **pseudodi·ploid** (**-te·traploid**, etc.) *adjs.*, having a chromosome complement which differs from the normad diploid (tetraploid, etc.) complement in constitution but not in number. So **pseudodi·ploidy**, etc.

1923 *Bot. Gaz.* LXXVI. 330 Of two plants from our cultures, each of which had a total of 48 chromosomes in their somatic cells.., one appears to have been a chromosomal mutant of the type $(4n+1-1)$ and the other a mutant of the type $(4n+1+1-1-1)$. Such forms obviously cannot properly be called $4n$ or tetraploid. They ..may be classified as modified tetraploids, or at most as 'pseudotetraploids'. **1977** *Lancet* 30 Apr. 961/1 Pseudodiploidy, 46,XX,D_9+,17q−, was observed in 14 marrow and in 10 blood-cells by the Giemsa staining method. **1978** *Nature* 16 Mar. 262/1 Stable diploid, or occasionally pseudodiploid transformed cell lines have been obtained after transformation by various tumour viruses.

pseudoallele (siūdo,æ·līl). *Genetics.* [f. Pseudo- + *allele, or a back-formation from *pseudoallelism.] Each of two or more mutations that resemble alleles of a single gene functionally, in affecting the same process or property, but differ structurally, in that crossing-over is possible between them.

1948 *Genetics* XXXIII. 113 The bithorax mutants, *bx* and bx^3 (locus, 3–58·8), are pseudo-alleles of bithoraxoid-dominant, *bxdD*. **1956** *Nature* 17 Mar. 504/2 Phenomena such as position effect and pseudoalleles make the classical corpuscular picture of the gene obsolete in modern genetics. **1962** W. R. Singleton *Elem. Genetics* xiv. 235 In any organism susceptible of precise analysis, pseudoalleles have turned out to be the rule rather than the exception. **1975** V. Grant *Genetics of Flowering Plants* iv. 75 The pseudoalleles are so close on the genetic map that crossovers between them occur only very rarely.

So **pseudoalle·lic** *a.*, behaving as or consisting of pseudoalleles; **pseudoalle·lism**, pseudoallelic state or property.

1938 *Yearbk. Carnegie Inst.* XXXVII. 305 Any dominant mutant which is lethal when homozygous and which shows pseudo-allelism to a dissimilar, non-allelomorphic but neighboring mutant is probably a deficiency. **1948** *Genetics* XXXIII. 113 Pseudo-allelism is characterized by the presence of closely linked genes, which seem to act developmentally like one. **1953** *Adv. Genetics* V. 208 The most completely investigated pseudo-allelic series is the case of 'lozenge'. **1975** J. B. Jenkins *Genetics* ix. 388 Primarily as a result of the analysis of pseudoallelic series, the gene emerged conceptually as a unit of function, or cistron. **1975** V. Grant *Genetics in Flowering Plants* iv. 74 The phenomenon of crossing-over within the limits of what had been considered a gene became known as pseudoallelism.

pseudo-American to **-book:** see *pseudo- 1a, b, 2a.

pseudobre·ccia. *Geol.* Also with hyphen. [f. Pseudo- + Breccia.] A limestone in which partial and irregular dolomitization has produced a texture similar to that of a breccia. So **pseudobre·cciated** *a.*; **pseu:dobreccia·tion**, the structure or state of a pseudobreccia.

1907 A. Strahan et al. *Geol. S. Wales Coal-Field* VIII. (Mem. Geol. Survey No. 247) 10 Mr. [R. H.] Tiddeman notes that some of the limestones of Mumbles Head..and Oxwich exhibit pitted bedding-surfaces and a pseudobrecciated structure. *Ibid.*, The structure referred to as pseudo-brecciation gives the rock the appearance of having been crushed into small angular fragments and re-cemented. *Ibid.* 12 In Callencroft Quarry a pseudobreccia..is exposed, but dolomitisation appears to have taken place along a fault also. **1913** *Jrnl. Geol.* XXI. 407 That this is actually a case of pseudobrecciation, and not a brecciated structure due to the cementation of a dolomite breccia in a calcareous matrix, is evident from a microscopical examination. **1963** D. W. & E. E. Humphries tr. *Termier's Erosion & Sedimentation* XIV. 301 This bed is a pseudo-brecciated layer of Early Malm (Late Jurassic) age. *Ibid.*, The compaction of the sediment was due to migration of 'imbibed' water... This compaction is probably associated with the pseudo-brecciation. **1969** Bennison & Wright *Geol. Hist. Brit. Isles* ix. 189 The limestones of the D Zone are oolitic or rubbly with pseudobreccias and are highly fossiliferous.

pseudo-bulb(ous, -cholinesterase: see *pseudo- 2a.

pseudocide (siū·dosəid). Also with hyphen. [f. Pseudo- + Sui)cide *sb.*[1] and *sb.*[2]] **a.** A pretended attempt at suicide, undertaken with the intention of failure. **b.** One who makes such an attempt. Hence **pseu·docidal** *a.*

1959 Lennard-Jones & Asher in *Lancet* 30 May 1138 (*heading*) Why do they do it? A study of pseudocide. *Ibid.* 1140/1 People are described who deliberately harm themselves or take an overdose of tablets without wishing to die. We have termed these actions 'pseudocide'. **1970** *Hospital Tribune* 23 Mar. 22/1 Another characteristic of the pseudocidal persons was found to be 'their understandable propensity to leave suicide notes'. *Ibid.* 22/2 The typical pseudocide is remarkably different from the usual picture associated with actual suicidal persons. **1976** *New Society* 22 Jan. 147/1 The reason this attempt is called 'pseudo-cide' is that it is invariably a gesture and is not meant to succeed—witness the fall in the number of attempts during the junior doctors' strike, when relief was not necessarily at hand.

pseudocirrhosis to **-compatibility:** see *pseudo- 1a, 2a.

pseu·do-concept. *Philos.* Also without hyphen. [f. Pseudo + Concept *sb.*] A notion which is sometimes treated as a concept though it cannot be properly conceptualized or grasped by the mind.

1866 H. L. Mansel *Philos. of Conditioned* 93 It is not to be wondered at..that our positive conception of God as a Person cannot be included under this pseudo-concept of the Infinite. **1901** A. E. Taylor *Probl. Conduct* viii. 439 The religious experience..may for all we know prove to be itself a mere illusion, and the Absolute a mere pseudo-concept. **1917** D. Ainslie tr. *Croce's Logic* ii. 37 'Conceptual fictions' is a manner of speech... For brevity's sake we shall call them pseudoconcepts. **1937** *Mind* XLVI. 228 The consequence is rigidly deduced that the 'transcendent' One cannot even without contradiction be said to be *One*; thus it is apparently a 'pseudo-concept'. **1956** J. O. Urmson *Philos. Analysis* 91 There are two objects with a certain relation between them, in spite of the fact that the concept 'object', thus used, is a metaphysical pseudo-concept. **1967** *Encycl. Philos.* II. 266/2 The work of economists, like that of all other scientists, belongs to the category of utility itself, not to that of truth. 'Economic man' is a paradigm case of a pseudo concept.

pseudoconglomerate to **-entity:** see *pseudo- 1a, b, 2a, b.

pseu·do-event. orig. *U.S.* [Pseudo- 1.] An event arranged or brought about merely for the sake of the publicity which it generates. Hence **pseudo-eve·ntful** *a.*

1962 D. J. Boorstin *Image* i. 9 A pseudo-event..is not spontaneous, but comes about because someone has planned, planted, or incited it. Typically, it is not a train wreck or an earthquake, but an interview. *Ibid.* iv. 161 A pseudo-eventful by-product of the [celebrity] star system is what *Time* magazine has accurately described as 'non-books.' These are printed matter between covers, usually put together by someone other than the ostensible autobiographer. **1962** *Spectator* 22 June 823/2 Another pseudo-event three thousand miles away. On March 17, I had stood on Fifth Avenue, barred from crossing Manhattan by a quarter of a million people..parading..in ..rosettes and badges saying 'Kiss Me, I'm Irish.' **1963** *Guardian* 21 Jan. 8/2 By enthroning the pseudo-event at the heart of an £800 million industry [*sc.* football pools], the promotors have made clear..that nothing..is what it seems. **1966** D. Jenkins *Educated Society* i. 36 The centre of the public stage will be occupied by performers, whether politicians or 'celebrities', who live out a life of highly publicised pseudo-events for the delectation of multitudes. **1969** *Daily Tel.* (Colour Suppl.) 1 Aug. 10/4 Beauty Festivals are pseudo-events of almost clinical purity. **1976** *Listener* 28 Oct. 524/3 The [US] election campaign became a perfect pseudo-event..a game played on..trains, in..planes, and in shopping precincts.

pseudo-existence to **-Freud:** see *pseudo- 1a, b, 2a.

pseudogamy (siūdǫ·gămi). *Biol.* [ad. G. *pseudogamie* (W. O. Focke *Pflanzen-Mischlinge* (1881) vii. 510): see Pseudo- and *-gamy.] **a.** In an apomictic plant, development of an embryo following pollination without fertilization.

1900 B. D. Jackson *Gloss. Bot. Terms* 213/2 *Pseudogamy*, parthenogenetic fruiting, as pollination without impregnation of ovules. **1908** *Ann. Bot.* XXII. 42 *Humaria rutilans* is..an example of the so-called apogamous development of the ascocarp, or pseudogamy. **1956** *Nature* 21 Jan. 141/2 A third group of populations [of *Culex pipiens*] is interfertile with the others in one direction only. Parthenogenesis, with pseudogamy, predetermination and multiple compatibility genes can be excluded as causative mechanisms. **1974** *New Phytol.* LXXIII. 1243 Pseudogamy is a type of agamospermic reproduction in which seed development is stimulated by pollination although the male nucleus does not fuse with the egg. **1976** Bell & Coombe tr. *Strasburger's Textbk. Bot.* (rev. ed.) 403 In many angiosperms embryos develop from diploid unfertilized egg-cells (parthenogenesis and angiospermy..), but sometimes this development requires the stimulus of pollination (pseudogamy).

b. The fusion of two vegetative nuclei.

1907 *Annales Mycologica* V. 422 Fusion of two vegetative nuclei: pseudogamy. **1928** C. W. Dodge tr. *Gäumann's Compar. Morphol. of Fungi* iv. 13 The sexual processes occurring outside in the thallus between two sexually differentiated vegetative cells..called pseudomixis (pseudogamy of Hartmann). *Ibid.*, Since the copulating cells are not morphologically distinguished from other vegetative cells and since only the release of specific developmental stimuli..marks this anastomosis of two vegetative cells as a sexual process, pseudogamy is often distinguished with difficulty from the usual pseudosexual anastomoses which are brought about by food relations.

Hence **pseudo·gamous** *a.*

1932 C. D. Darlington *Rec. Adv. Cytol.* xv. 434 Moderate or even high pollen fertility is sometimes found in the pseudogamous *Potentilla* species. **1964** W. Williams *Genetic Princ. & Plant Breeding* viii. 290 Hybrid endosperms in pseudogamous apomicts derived from crosses between unrelated parents promote stronger growth in apomictic seedlings. **1974** *New Phytol.* LXXIII. 1246 The three pseudogamous species..would set seed when pollinated by each other or intraspecifically, but not when pollinated by any of quite a large selection of different *Potentilla* species.

pseudogene to **-hallucinatory:** see *pseudo- 1a, b, 2a.

pseudoha·logen. *Chem.* Also with hyphen. [a. G. *pseudohalogen* (Birckenbach & Kellermann 1925, in *Ber. d. Deut. Chem. Ges.* LVIII. 786): see Pseudo- and Halogen.] Any of a class of compounds (in some cases hypothetical) which have small molecules built up from atoms of electronegative elements and which closely resemble the halogens in many respects.

1925 *Chem. Abstr.* XIX. 1996 (*heading*) Pseudo halogens. **1954** R. C. Brasted in M. C. Sneed et al. *Comprehensive Inorg. Chem.* III. ix. 223 The similarities between the pseudohalogens and the halogens are as follows: 1. They are in general fairly volatile. 2. They show affinity for metals, with which they combine directly to form salts. 3. The silver, lead, and mercury (I) salts are insoluble in water. [Etc.] **1962** Cotton & Wilkinson *Adv. Inorg. Chem.* xxii. 465 The most important pseudohalogens are $(CN)_2$, cyanogen; $(OCN)_2$, oxycyanogen (existence in free state uncertain); $(SCN)_2$, thiocyanogen; $Se(CN)_2$, selenocyanogen; and $(SCSN_3)_2$, azido-carbon disulfide. **1965** Phillips & Williams *Inorg. Chem.* I. xii. 467 All the pseudo-halogen anions enter into simple acid-base reactions with the proton in aqueous solution.

Hence **pseudoha·lide** [*halide], a compound, ion, or radical formed by a pseudohalogen.

1925 *Chem. Abstr.* XIX. 1996 An attempt was made to prep. $(SeCN)_2$, $(CNO)_2$ and $(TeCN)_2$ by electrolysis of K pseudo halides in alc. solns. **1965** Phillips & Williams *Inorg. Chem.* I. xii. 467 The difference between the two series of anions, halides and pseudo-halides, lies in the unsaturation of a pseudo-halide which is most marked in CN^-. The unsaturation places the pseudo-halides high relative to the halides in the spectrochemical series. **1967** *New Scientist* 28 Dec. 766/1 A novel method of making carbonyl pseudohalides by simple substitution. In this way they could obtain from potassium cyanide the pseudohalide carbonyl cyanide.

pseu:doherma·phroditism. *Med.* Also with hyphen. [f. Pseudo- + Hermaphroditism.] The condition of having the gonads and chromosomes of one sex and some anatomical and secondary characteristics of the other sex.

Contrasted with true hermaphroditism, in which there are gonads or gonadal tissue of both sexes.

1881 *Amer. Jrnl. Obstetr.* XIV. 105 The case is..an interesting and rare one, whether it be a case of double congenital ovarian hernia..or whether it proves to be that equally rare malformation, masculine pseudohermaphroditism with feminine external genitals. **1924** R. Muir *Text-bk. Path.* xix. 705 General hypoplasia of the uterus is observed in ovarian defect and may be attended by other abnormalities, e.g. pseudo-hermaphroditism. **1950** H. B. Friedgood in R. H. Williams *Textbk. Endo-*

crinol. x. 633 Another example of the importance of considering functional as well as structural changes in making a diagnosis is seen in the differentiation of intersexuality of genetic origin from female pseudohermaphroditism due to congenital adrenal hyperplasia. **1974** Passmore & Robson *Compan. Med. Stud.* III. xxiii. 70/2 In males the resulting lack of testicular androgen during intrauterine development leads to..pseudohermaphroditism, the baby being born with apparently female genitalia despite a normal male chromosome complement.

So **pseu:doherma·phrodite**, a person with this condition.

1895 *Amer. Jrnl. Obstetr.* XXXII. 528 The sexual instincts of this anomalous male being were directed toward men, not women—a fact which leads the author to remark that hermaphrodites and pseudo-hermaphrodites are *degenerates.* **1928** L. Loeb in E. V. Cowdry *Special Cytol.* II. xxxiv. 1184 In male pseudo-hermaphrodites..a development of the mammary gland may occur in certain cases. **1975** Fraser & Nora *Genetics of Man* iv. 53/1 A 46,XY male with a chromatin-negative buccal smear who is female in external appearance is a male pseudohermaphrodite.

pseudo-historic to **-literature:** see *pseudo- 1 a, b, 2 a.

‖**pseudologia fantastica** (siūdolōᵘ·dʒia fæntæ·stikă). *Psychol.* Also **pseudologia phantastica.** [mod.L., ad. Gr. ψευδολογία falsehood + Gr. fem. φανταστική or med.Lat. fem. *phantastica* imaginary.] A condition, often associated with other abnormal traits, in which a person fabricates stories about himself in order to inflate his importance but readily changes or abandons them when challenged. Also *ellipt.* as *pseudologia.*

1909 *Westm. Hospital Rep.* XVI. 68 There are some cases of moral imbecility in which this [lying] is the chief..feature, yet so pronounced that it has been looked upon by some as a distinct disease, and has been given a name all to itself: 'Pseudologia Fantastica'. **1917** C. E. Long tr. *Jung's Coll. Papers Analytical Psychol.* i. 71 Our case has another analogy with *pseudologia phantastica*: The development of the phantasies during the attacks. **1934** Owen & Zilboorg tr. *Fenichel's Outl. Clin. Psychoanal.* xi. 443 The most remarkable feature in pseudologia is that the patient really is speaking the truth..and that unwittingly the phantastic lies are distorted expressions of his repressed infantile sexual history. **1949** *Horizon* Mar. 216 A hysteric, suffering from *pseudologia phantastica.* **1960** I. Bennett *Delinquent & Neurotic Children* iii. 87 Imaginative or pathological lying (pseudologia fantastica).

pseudologic: see *pseudo- 1 a.

pseudologue (siū·dolǫg). [f. as Pseudologer: see -logue.] A compulsive liar; someone suffering from *pseudologia fantastica*; a pseudologer.

1949 *Psychiatric Q.* XXIII. 19 Pseudologues have little or no insight into real behavior or into the harm they may cause others.

pseudolymphoma to **-membranous:** see *pseudo- 1 b, 2 a.

pseudomonas (siūdomōᵘ·năs). *Biol.* [mod.L. (W. Migula 1897, in *Arbeiten aus dem Bakteriol. Inst. der Technischen Hochschule zu Karlsruhe* I. 237), f. Pseudo- + Gr. μονάς unit.] A bacterium of the genus *Pseudomonas,* which comprises aerobic Gram-negative species that occur chiefly in soil and water, are generally rod-shaped, frequently produce soluble pigments, and include many plant pathogens but few animal pathogens. Freq. *attrib.*

1917 *Jrnl. Bacteriol.* II. 174 The vibrios are..closely akin to the fluorescent (or pseudomonas) bacteria. **1950** C. J. Witton *Microbiol.* xxvi. 366 Pseudomonas intestinal infections of infants and pseudomonas bronchopneumonias have also been reported. **1961** *Lancet* 22 July 179 Recurrence of Pseudomonas infection while on i.m. polymixin after sterile culture for 16 days. **1966** *New Scientist* 21 July 150/1 Currently, research is centred on fish bacteria which cause disease, such as vibrio and pseudomonas. **1977** *Time* 24 Jan. 55/3 These have sharply reduced infection from pseudomonas bacteria, which once killed nearly a third of all burn victims.

So **pseudomo·nad,** a bacterium of the genus *Pseudomonas,* or one of the family Pseudomonadaceæ that includes it, or one of the order Pseudomonadales that includes the family.

1921 R. E. Buchanan *Agric. & Industr. Bacteriol.* xxxiv. 407 The organism is a typical yellow pseudomonad in morphology, culture and physiology. **1958** Pelczar & Reid *Microbiol.* xii. 125/1 Many *Pseudomonas* species, or 'pseudomonads', produce water-soluble pigments. **1966** *McGraw-Hill Encycl. Sci. & Technol.* XI. 63/1 Pseudomonads, as members of the genus are familiarly known. *Ibid.* 64/1 *Aeromonas* is composed of pseudomonads which physiologically resemble bacteria of the genus *Aerobacter.* **1973** J. Levy et al. *Introd. Microbiol.* xiii. 334 Order Pseudomonadales... The pseudomonads are ubiquitous in nature, are largely free-living.., and have achieved economic importance in that they are the most common cause of food spoilage. **1975** *Nature* 24 Apr. 671/1 The most striking metabolic capability of pseudomonad organisms is their versatile utilisation of organic compounds as sole sources of carbon, nitrogen and energy.

pseudomoralist, -morality: see *pseudo- 1 a.

pseudomorph. Add: Hence **pseudomo·rphically, pseudomo·rphously** *advs.* Also **pseu·domorph** *v. trans.* = Pseudomorphose *v.*; **pseu·domorphed** *ppl. a.*, **pseu·domorphing, pseudomo·rphosing** *vbl. sbs.*

1876 F. Zirkel *Microsc. Petrogr.* vi. 114 The alteration did not happen in a proper pseudomorphosing manner, since the contours of the hornblende are..no longer recognizable. **1923** *Trans. R. Soc. Edin.* LIII. 371 Olivine, pseudomorphed by brownish-green serpentine, is quite common. **1931** *Econ. Geol.* XXVI. 595 Features ..preserved pseudomorphically. **1943** *Amer. Jrnl. Sci.* CCXLIII a. 539 The early soft mineral, franckeite, was found strongly replaced, pseudomorphously, by minerals of higher-temperature significance, such as pyrrhotite. **1959** *Trans. R. Soc. Edin.* LXIII. 554 The schists exhibit distinct retrogressive characteristics, notably in the common pseudomorphing of once-idiomorphic garnet by chlorite-free assemblages. **1960** *Jrnl. Petrology* I. 211 In the aureole of the Glen Doll diorite the rocks of high oxidation ratio..have been reduced, hematite being pseudomorphed by magnetite. **1962** W. A. Deer et al. *Rock-forming Minerals* V. 50 A mineral occurring pseudomorphously after loparite..has been named metaloparite. **1971** *Canad. Jrnl. Earth Sci.* VIII. 634/1 Some of the large embayed chromites are pseudomorphically replaced and rimmed by a..garnetiferous aggregate. **1975** *Nature* 17 Jan. 183/2 The large amount of pseudomorphed olivine..suggests that the older dykes were very basic olivine basalts.

pseudomucin to **-neurotic:** see *pseudo- 1 a, b, 2 a.

pseudonym. a. (Earlier example.)

1833 J. S. Mill in *Tait's Edin. Mag.* III. 347 *Junius Redivivus* is the (somewhat inappropriate) pseudonyme of a writer who is one and indivisible.

pseudo-object to **-passivization:** see *pseudo- 1 a, 2 a.

pseu·dopatient. [f. Pseudo- + Patient *a.* and *sb.*] Someone who pretends to have the signs, symptoms, and history of a medical case in order to gain admission to a hospital as a patient. Cf. *Munchausen b.

1973 *Science* 19 Jan. 251/1 If the sanity of..pseudopatients were always detected, there would be prima facie evidence that a sane individual can be distinguished from the insane context in which he is found. **1974** *Med. Jrnl. Austral.* II. 385/2 The fact that studies using pseudopatients as a means of evaluating health services have until the present been poorly conceived should not blind us to the possible values of the technique. **1977** *Times Lit. Suppl.* 4 Feb. 125/1 Research workers and journalists are increasingly lying their way into hospitals with the intention of writing up their experiences. It is high time that the World Health Organisation added the diagnostic category of 'pseudo-patient' to its International Classification of Diseases.

pseudo-pelade to **-plasticity:** see *pseudo- 1 a, b, 2 a.

pseudopod. Add: **1.** Also *fig.*

1951 V. Nabokov *Speak, Memory* xi. 162 The undulating plump shadows of older foliage on the water..were rhythmically palpitating, extending and drawing in dark pseudopods. **1975** *N.Y. Times Bk. Rev.* 8 June 21/2 Gifts of memory and mimicry, and pseudopods of learning, extend what is only an essay into a thick 'Anatomy' of cosmic..speculation.

4. *Spiritualism.* (See quot. 1920.)

1920 E. E. Fournier d'Albe tr. *Schrenk Notzing's Phenom. Materialisation* 25 The recent investigations by W. J. Crawford have shown that white light acts destructively on the pseudopods or psychic projections from the medium's body. **1945** N. Collins *London belongs to Me* i. viii. 88 The medium was invited to materialise the ectoplasmic hand inside the wax. Then when the séance was over a cast of the pseudopod could be cast in plaster.

pseudopodium. Add: **1.** Also *fig.*

a **1902** S. Butler *Note-bks.* (1912) xii. 196 My reviewers felt no sense of need to understand me... When the time comes that they want to do so they will throw out a little mental pseudopodium without much difficulty.

pseu·dopotential. *Physics.* [f. Pseudo- + Potential *a.* and *sb.*] A potential distribution assumed for the purposes of calculation as an approximation to the actual potential.

1956 C. Herring in R. Breckenridge et al. *Proc. Conf. Photoconductivity, Atlantic City, 1954* 86 The idea of using such a repulsive pseudopotential is due to Hellman..and has been applied with some success to molecules..and metals. **1965** *Rev. Mod. Physics* XXXVII. 388/2 Since we are making the Born approximation, the best choice for *v*(r) is a pseudopotential that fits free (*p, p*) scattering. **1968** *Times* 2 Dec. 17/1 The theory, known as the 'pseudopotential method', does not allow the properties of the metal to be calculated without guessing either the shape of the wave or the force exerted by the atoms on the electrons. **1976** Coles & Caplin *Electronic Struct. Solids* iv. 93 Pseudopotential methods are now sufficiently finely developed that not only can accurate band structures be calculated for metals (and alloys) but also meaningful estimates can be made of the difference in energy of different crystallographic structures for an element.

pseudopre·gnancy. [f. Pseudo- + Pregnancy[1].] **1.** *Med.* An abnormal condition in which many of the signs and symptoms of pregnancy are present in a woman who is not pregnant; = *pseudocyesis* s.v. Pseudo- 2 a in Dict. and Suppl.

1860 T. H. Tanner *Signs & Dis. Pregnancy* i. 7 The term *pseudo-pregnancy* is also sometimes applied to diseases which simulate pregnancy. **1893** T. M. Madden *Clin. Gynæcol.* xl. 463 Symptoms of Pseudocyesis.—In cases of pseudopregnancy we frequently find all the general symptoms of pregnancy counterfeited with an exactitude that might well seem marvellous if we did not take into consideration the circumstances. **1972** M. M. Garrey et al. *Gynæcol. Illustr.* v. 92 Amenorrhœa... Causes. 1. Pregnancy and missed abortion. 2. Psychological. (a) Stress and emotional disturbance. (b) Pseudopregnancy. (c) Anorexia nervosa.

2. *Zool.* A state marked by changes in the reproductive organs and mammary glands similar to those of early pregnancy, occurring naturally in many female mammals after ovulation when fertilization has not occurred and also capable of being induced experimentally.

1913 Hill & O'Donoghue in *Q. Jrnl. Microsc. Sci.* LIX. 135 As the œstral cycle in Dasyurus differs considerably from that of the Eutherian mammal, it has been found necessary to introduce two new terms, viz. Post-œstrus, to designate the period which intervenes between œstrus and ovulation; and Pseudopregnancy, to designate the period which, in the non-pregnant animal, follows ovulation, and in which the changes in the ovary, mammary glands and uteri are essentially similar to those in the pregnant female. **1940** *Endocrinology* XXVII. 125 We produced pseudopregnancy [in mice] by three methods. (*a*) Females obtained from a low fertility group were allowed to copulate frequently but did not become pregnant. (*b*) Females were mated with vasectomised males. (*c*) Females were stimulated daily on the cervix uteri with a glass rod. **1970** W. B. Yapp *Introd. Animal Physiol.* (ed. 3) viii. 293 In those animals, such as mice, in which there is scarcely any pseudopregnancy, the corpora lutea develop very little and soon degenerate unless copulation occurs.

So **pseudopre·gnant** *a.*, of, in, or characteristic of the state of pseudopregnancy.

1913 *Q. Jrnl. Microsc. Sci.* LIX. 159 Comparison of our preparations of pseudo-pregnant uteri with those of normal post-partum uteri demonstrates..that the regressive changes in the glands are identical in the two. **1932** S. Zuckerman *Social Life Monkeys & Apes* v. 73 The pseudo-pregnant state is generally shorter than the pregnant, and varies in degree from animal to animal. **1972** *Theol. Stud.* XXXIII. 432 The resulting embryos could be transplanted to a dozen or a hundred pseudopregnant healthy but genetically nondescript surrogate mother cows.

pseudo-principle: see *pseudo- 1 a.

pseu·do-problem. [f. Pseudo- + Problem.] A problem which is unreal either because it has no possible solution or because there exists a confusion in the elements of which it is composed.

1911 W. James *Some Probl. Philos.* x. 156 There is a pseudo-problem, 'How can the finite know the infinite?' which has troubled some English heads. **1923** Ogden & Richards *Meaning of Meaning* vii. 268 When the pseudo-problems due to cross vocabularies are removed. **1933** *Mind* XLII. 339 The difficulty which, I think, led Russell to his theory of descriptions had its source in a mistake which logicians are prone to make, and which has given rise to many pseudo-problems. **1938** C. W. Morris in *Internat. Encycl. Unified Sci.* I. ii. 57 Current scientific formulations embody many pseudo problems which arise from the confusion of statements in the language of semiotic and the thing-language. **1956** F. Copleston *Contemp. Philos.* xii. 209 Some would wish to define a pseudo-problem as a question which we are unable to answer, not simply because we here and now lack the means of answering it,.. but because no way of answering it is conceivable. **1979** *Trans. Philol. Soc.* 209 The pseudo-problems introduced by prematurely formed classificatory schemes or prejudiced reactions to them.

pseudo-procedure: see *pseudo- 1 a.

pseu·do-proposition. *Philos.* [f. Pseudo- + Proposition.] An apparent proposition which is unreal because it does not have intelligible meaning.

1883 *Mind* VIII. 24 It is unnecessary here to occupy space with examples of these three familar kinds of pseudo-proposition. **1934** *Mind* XLIII. 335 A pseudo-proposition being a series of words that may seem to have the structure of a sentence but is in fact meaningless. **1966** *Philos. Rev.* LXXV. 315 In the pseudo-propositions of the *Tractatus* we see how things really are.

pseudo-proverb to **-racemic:** see *pseudo- 1 a, b, 2 a.

pseudora·ndom, *a. Math.* Also with hyphen. [f. Pseudo- + Random *a.*] Satisfying one or more statistical tests for randomness but produced by a definite mathematical procedure.

1949 *Seminar on Sci. Computation, Nov.* (Internat. Business Machines) 104/2 A random number c lying between 0 and 1 is selected from a store, or a pseudo-random number c lying between 0 and 1 is computed arithmetically. **1954** *Jrnl. Assoc. Computing Machinery* I. 88 Modern-day usage of high-speed electronic digital computing machines frequently involves the consumption of a very large quantity of random numbers. It is desirable that the machine..be able to manufacture its own random or pseudo-random numbers. **1966** A. Battersby *Math. in Managem.* vii. 170 For convenience, genuinely random numbers are replaced by 'pseudo-random' numbers; these are generated by fairly simple calculations which are known to produce strings of numbers indistinguishable in the short run from truly random ones. **1973** *Sci. Amer.* May 19/1 The recipient of a coded message can then be provided with a generator that operates exactly like the one used to add pseudorandom digits to the original message.

Hence **pseudora·ndomly** *adv.*

1963 *IBM Jrnl. Res. & Devel.* VII. 233/2 A periodic pseudorandomly generated 256-bit pattern. **1976** *New Scientist* 3 June 529 Each alarm is interrogated pseudo-randomly every 2-3 seconds and a small PDP8 computer identifies the change of state on a visual display unit.

pseudo-ra·tional, *a.* [f. Pseudo- + Rational *a.*] Assumed to be, or treated as, rational although beyond experience or proof. So **pseudo-ra·tionalism,** a theory or system based on pseudo-rational arguments or assumptions; **pseudo-ra·tionalist,** an adherent or advocate of such a theory; **pseu:do-rationa·lity,** pseudo-rational quality or nature; **pseu:do-rationaliza·tion,** unjustified or spurious rationalization.

1909 W. James *Pluralistic Universe* v. 211 Hegel was the first non-mystical writer to face the dilemma squarely and throw away the ordinary logic, saving a pseudo-rationality for the universe by inventing the higher logic of the 'dialectic process'. **1927** A. Huxley *Proper Stud.* 207 And though the earliest philosophies and religions may seem intellectually very remote from ourselves, we feel, none the less, that the emotions and intuitions to which they give rational, or pseudo-rational, expression are recognizably akin to our own. **1929** N. K. Smith tr. *Kant's Critique Pure Reason* 394 If in employing the principles of understanding we do not merely apply our reason to objects of experience, but venture to extend these principles beyond the limits of experience, there arise pseudo-rational doctrines which can neither hope for confirmation in experience nor fear refutation by it. **1936** *Mind* XLV. 268 It is the mark of a pseudo-rationalist to refer to *the* real world, or to speak of the *certainty* of any propositions, or to assume that sense-data support only one system. **1952** K. R. Popper *Open Society* (ed. 2) xxiv. 227 What I shall call 'pseudo-rationalism' is the intellectual intuitionism of Plato. **1960** Koestler *Lotus & Robot* I. i. 51 This combination of mystic assertion and pseudo-rational proof is as old as the world. *Ibid.* ii. 100 There is a tendency in the human mind never to leave a symbol alone, an itch to debase it by pseudo-rationalizations. **1976** *Contemp. Psychoanal.* XII. 93 Any dialogue of ideological infrastructures through overt discussions.. should..reflect the irretrievable ambivalence of ideas.. which..are pseudo-rational in that they unify human experience according to semiotic rules but conflict with strictly scientific statements, because they cannot be experimentally demonstrated.

pseudoreaction to **-salt:** see *pseudo- 1 a, b, 2 a.

pseu·doscalar, *sb.* and *a.* *Math.* and *Physics.* [f. Pseudo- + Scalar *a.* and *sb.*] **A.** *sb.* **a.** A quantity that transforms as a scalar under rotation but changes sign under reflection. **b.** A sub-atomic particle whose wave function is such a quantity, the particle having zero spin and odd parity.

1938 N. Kemmer in *Proc. R. Soc.* CLXVI. 137 The quantities occurring in our possible fundamental equations are one scalar (ϕ), two 4-vectors (χ_α and ϕ_α), two anti-symmetrical tensors of the second order ($\chi_{\alpha\beta}$ and $\phi_{\alpha\beta}$), two 'pseudovectors', that is, totally antisymmetrical tensors of the third order ($\chi_{\alpha\beta\gamma}$ and $\phi_{\alpha\beta\gamma}$), and finally one 'pseudoscalar' (χ_{0123}). **1950** *Physical Rev.* LXXVIII. 805/2 It then follows..that the π-meson is a pseudo-scalar. **1966** *McGraw-Hill Encycl. Sci. & Technol.* IX. 566/2 Thus **S·p** is a pseudoscalar, and so such a term cannot occur in the angular distribution of a parity conserving process.

B. *adj.* Involving or being a pseudoscalar.

1941 *Physical Rev.* LX. 151/2 Pseudo-scalar theories can give a scattering small enough to agree with that observed. **1947** *Rev. Mod. Physics* XIX. 5/1 The initial vector meson is decomposed into a pseudoscalar meson and a photon. **1949** [see *coupling constant* s.v. *coupling *vbl. sb.* 8]. **1974** *Physics Bull.* Dec. 579/2 Pions are pseudoscalar objects and cannot condense out in states of zero momentum (in infinite nuclear matter) because they do not have the quantum numbers of the vacuum.

pseu·do-science. Also **pseudoscience.** [f. Pseudo- + Science.] A pretended or spurious science; a collection of related beliefs about the world mistakenly regarded as being based on scientific method or as having the status that scientific truths now have.

1844 *Northern Jrnl. Med.* I. 387 That opposite kind of innovation which pronounces what had been before recognised as a branch of science, to have been a pseudo-science, composed merely of so-called facts, connected together by misapprehensions under the disguise of principles. **1859** [in Dict. s.v. Pseudo- 1 a]. **1911** G. B. Shaw *Doctor's Dilemma* p. xcii, The pseudo science of the commercial general practitioner, who foolishly clamors for the prosecution..of the Christian Scientists when their patients die. **1911** J. G. Frazer *Golden Bough: Magic Art* (ed. 3) I. iii. 113 Magic as a pseudo-science. **1912** J. J. Walsh *Psychotherapy* I. v. 38 Astrology, is the typical example of pseudo-science in medicine. **1928** C. Dawson *Age of Gods* vi. 134 These pseudo-sciences were held in higher honour by the Babylonians themselves than the more utilitarian branches of knowledge. **1937** *Brit. Jrnl. Psychol.* XXVII. 246 We may..consider..psychoanalytical theory as illustrative of the manner in which various influences combine to produce what we may call pseudo-science. **1957** J. S. Huxley *Relig. without Revelation* iii. 47 Theology has been, as my grandfather T. H. Huxley said, only a pseudo-science. **1960** *Guardian* 9 Dec. 5/3 The pseudo-science of the academic pollster. **1977** A. Giddens *Stud. in Social & Polit. Theory* i. 58 His [*sc.* K. Popper's] endeavour to establish clear criteria of demarcation between science and pseudo-science shares much of the same impetus as the concern of the logical positivists to free science from mystifying, empty word-play.

Hence **pseudo-scienti·fic** *a.*, **pseu·do-scientist.**

1873 *Q. Rev.* CXXXV. 192 The pseudo-scientific teachers of what has..been termed..the Agnostic Philosophy. **1898** [see *collective *a.* (*sb.*) A. 2 d]. **1902** A. Machen *Hieroglyphics* v. 126 The only people who have always a plain answer to a plain question are the pseudo-scientists..who think that one can solve the enigma of the universe with a box of chemicals. **1902** *Encycl. Brit.* XXV. 472/1 This was the pseudo-scientific note of the new anti-Semitism, the theory which differentiated it from the old religious Jew-hatred. **1914** R. A. S. Macalister *Philistines* ii. 44 The pseudo-scientific hypothesis that Samson (like Achilles, Heracles, Max Müller, Gladstone, and other demonstrated characters of mythology) was a solar myth. **1926** Fowler *Mod. Eng. Usage* 348/1 *Mentality*... Some like it because it is longer than *mind*;.. and some because it has a pseudo-scientific sound about it that may impress the reader. **1928** R. Macaulay *Keeping up Appearances* xix. 213 The pseudo-scientists..like Freud, poor old man, who's hypnotised himself with observing diseased eroto-maniacs and thinking them normal. **1960** Hanrahan & Bushnell *Space Biol.* vii. 109 Not only fiction-writers but also some pseudo-scientists have dabbled in anti-gravity. **1964** M. A. K. Halliday et al. in J. A. Fishman *Readings Sociol. of Lang.* (1968) 164 The spurious rigour of some pseudo-scientific 'measurements' of the 'efficiency' of language. **1973** C. Sagan *Cosmic Connection* (1975) viii. 59 An enormous interest is apparent in a range of pseudo-scientific or borderline-scientific topics—astrology, scientology, the study of unidentified flying objects, [etc.]. **1975** *Times* 26 Sept. 19 (*heading*) Lord Zuckerman deplores pseudo-scientists.

pseudoscopy. (Examples.)

1951 L. P. Dudley *Stereoptics* i. 21 If the two components of a stereogram be transposed so that the 'left-eye' view is seen by the right eye, and the 'right-eye' view by the left eye, the result is no longer a true stereoscopic effect, but is what is termed pseudoscopy. **1960** *New Scientist* 14 July 142/3 In 1953, when interest in 3-D had a temporary revivial, I took up experiments..on a new line. These were based on the observation that 'pseudoscopy'—that is to say, the effects of the left eye seeing what the right eye ought to have seen, and *vice versa*—were not at all as bad as one would expect.

pseu·dosex. [f. Pseudo- + Sex *sb.*] Pseudo-sexual activity; also, perverted sexual activity.

1951 E. Bergler *Neurotic Counterfeit-Sex* iii. 104 In analyzing this type of pseudo-sex, one is surprised at the seeming contradiction in the mechanical performance. **1964** *Listener* 12 Nov. 754/2 Pseudosex..takes up much of the zoo monkey's time; like violence itself, it is a symptom and a reliable index of stress in society. **1972** *Ibid.* 9 Mar. 320/2 He related the present craze for pseudo-sex to an equally current repressed hostility in society—pointing out that the kinky aim is to put us off the pleasures of real sex. **1978** M. Puzo *Fools Die* xii. 129 This was a group of publications that drowned the American public with information, pseudoinformation, sex and pseudosex: culture and hard-hat philosophy.

pseudose·xual, *a.* Also **pseudo-sexual.** [f. Pseudo- + Sexual *a.*] **1.** *Zool.* In certain crustaceans (see quots.).

1925 A. M. Banta in *Zeitschr. für Indukt. Abstammungs- und Vererbungslehre* XL. 28 (*heading*) A thelytokous race of Cladocera in which pseudo-sexual reproduction occurs. *Ibid.* 37 Since these eggs are apparently in every way like sexual eggs in other Cladocera, except that they develop without fertilization, they will be referred to as pseudo-sexual eggs and this type of reproduction will be referred to as pseudo-sexual reproduction as contrasted with the usual type of parthenogenesis and the normal sexual reproduction in Cladocera. **1957** *New Biol.* XXIII. 56 The story of reproduction in *Daphnia* is made more complex by certain races, particularly in arctic regions, which have a process of pseudo-sexual reproduction. **1967** G. E. Hutchinson *Treat. Limnol.* II. xxiv. 510 Ruttner-Kolisko (1946)..found that in *Keratella hiemalis* pseudo-sexual resting eggs are produced parthenogenetically at the height of the development of the population..in July.

2. Applied to sexual behaviour motivated by the fear of aggression, desire for dominance, etc., that frequently results from overcrowded social conditions, rather than by genuinely sexual aims.

1951 E. Bergler *Neurotic Counterfeit-Sex* iii. 141 All their sexual (one should say, rather, *pseudo-sexual*) activity is but a blind for totally unrelated baby-conflicts. **1960** *Jrnl. Nerv. & Mental Dis.* CXXXI 203/1 The difference in status shows itself very soon by a pseudo-sexual act. **1961** C. & W. Russell *Human Behav.* iii. 175 A real sexual relationship between two people lies in the fact that each is proportionately freed from pseudosexual involvement. **1969** *Sci. Jrnl.* Apr. 86/2 To the extent that such behaviour looks sexual, but in fact relates almost entirely to agonism, it can be described as pseudosexual.

Hence **pseudose·xually** *adv.*

1964 *Listener* 12 Nov. 755/1 Neglectful mothering.. produces juvenile delinquent monkeys, precociously aggressive and pseudosexually active.

pseudo-simplicity, -social: see *pseudo- 1 a, 2 a.

pseu:do-solariza·tion. *Photogr.* [f. Pseudo- + Solarization.] = *Sabatier effect* s.v. *Sabatier, *solarization 1 b.

1889 R. Meldola *Chem. of Photogr.* vi. 219 The observation of Sabatier, that a collodion wet plate becomes reversed if, towards the end of development, daylight is suddenly admitted to the room, relates to cases of what may be called pseudo-solarisation. **1969** M. J. Langford *Adv. Photogr.* xi. 228 The effect discussed here, although described by photographers as solarisation, is the Sabattier effect or 'pseudo-solarisation'. The effect is easily distinguished—the reversal of weakest densities, and the formation of a thin contour line around strong tone boundaries. **1972** *Exper. Mechanics* XII. 423 A method is described for obtaining well-defined fringes..in photoelastic stress analysis. It is based on an edge effect which occurs during the pseudo-solarization of films during development.

pseudo-sophisticated to **-stratification:** see *pseudo- 1 b, 2 a.

pseudostra·tified, *a.* [Pseudo- 2.]. **1.** (See s.v. *pseudo- 2 a.)

2. *Histology.* Applied to epithelium composed of a single layer of columnar cells each in contact with the basal lamina but whose nuclei are at varying distances from it, so that they give the appearance of several layers of cells.

1905 J. S. Ferguson *Normal Histol. & Microsc. Anat.* ii. 30 Diagram showing the manner in which all the epithelial cells of pseudo-stratified ciliated epithelium reach the basement membrane. **1974** J. G. A. Rhodin *Histology* iii. 72/1 Non-ciliated pseudo-stratified columnar epithelium occurs in parts of the male urethra, excretory ducts of many glands, the ductus epididymis.., and the ductus deferens.

pseudosuchian (siudosū·kiăn), *sb.* and *a.* *Palæont.* [f. mod.L. *Pseudosuchia* (K. A. von Zittel *Handbuch der Palæont.* (1890) Abth. I. III. 637), f. Pseudo- + Gr. σοῦχ-ος crocodile: see -ian.] **A.** *sb.* A small fossil reptile belonging to the suborder Pseudosuchia of the order Thecodontia, which includes primitive, often bipedal, carnivores, whose remains have been found in Triassic formations. **B.** *adj.* Of or pertaining to an animal of this kind.

1913 R. Broom in *Proc. Zool. Soc.* II. 624 The type of this Pseudosuchian is a fairly complete skeleton from Elgin. *Ibid.* 631 The Pterodactyl and Pseudosuchian skulls are almost exactly similar in essentials. **1926** *Glasgow Herald* 14 Aug. 4/2 The Pseudosuchians have long since passed, but they fulfilled their promise and gave us birds. **1971** *Nature* 12 Nov. 75/2 The pseudosuchians and the ornithischians would seem, in fact, to be quite irreconcilable in terms of pelvis and ankle structure. *Ibid.* 76/1 It may be deduced that the ornithischians arose from pseudosuchian reptiles which are at present unknown.

pseudotachylite to **-uridine:** see *pseudo- 1 a, b, 2 a, b.

pseudovary. (Earlier examples of **pseudo-varium, pseudovum.**)

1858 T. H. Huxley in *Trans. Linn. Soc.* XXII. 208 The number of chambers..is necessarily regulated by the.. rate at which new pseudova are detached from the pseudo-varium. *Ibid.*, The germ increases in size, and gradually becomes separated from the terminal chamber by the successive development..of new pseudova.

pseu·dovector, *sb.* and *a.* *Math.* and *Physics.* [f. Pseudo- + Vector.] **A.** *sb.* A vector whose sign is unchanged when the signs of all its components are changed.

1923 A. S. Eddington *Math. Theory of Relativity* vi. 179 R^μ is the pseudo-vector representing the displacement from the charge (ξ, η, ζ, τ) to the point (x, y, z, t) where x^μ is reckoned... We call it a pseudo-vector because it behaves as a vector for Galilean coordinates and Lorentz transformations. **1938** [see *pseudoscalar *sb.*] **1966** *McGraw-Hill Encycl. Sci. & Technol.* II. 413/1 In general, vectors associated with rotations belong to the category of pseudovectors. In particular, the angular velocity vector associated with the motion of a rigid body is a pseudo-vector. **1972** *Jrnl. Physics* B. V. 992 It is convenient to express in the standard way the (real) antisymmetric tensor $\mathbf{A}''(t)$ in terms of the pseudovector $V(t)$ which it uniquely defines.

B. *adj.* Involving or being a pseudovector.

1947 *Rev. Mod. Physics* XIX. 2/2 We are left with mesons of spin 0..or possibly spin 1 (vector or pseudo-vector fields). *Ibid.* 3/1 Little attention has been shown to the pseudovector theory. **1964** *Cambr. Rev.* 24 Oct. 51/1 The assumed conservation of the pseudovector current.

pseudovitamin to **-xanthoma:** see *PSEUDO- 1 a, 2 a.

pshent (pʃent). = PSCHENT, P-SKHENT.
1922 JOYCE *Ulysses* 500 On his head is perched an Egyptian pshent.

psi[1] (psəi, səi). [Gr. ψεῖ.] **1. a.** The name of Ψ, ψ, the 23rd letter of the Greek alphabet.
c **1400** MANDEVILLE *Trav.* (1725) iii. 25 What Lettres thei ben,..with the Names..α Alpha, β Betha,..χ Chi, ψ Psi, [etc.] **1848** [see *CHI]. **1955** W. PAULI *Niels Bohr* 30 A general agreement was reached following the substitution of abstract mathematical symbols, as for instance psi, for concrete pictures.

b. *Nuclear Physics.* A neutral, strongly interacting particle that is distinguished by an exceptionally long lifetime in relation to its mass of 3·1 MeV, has a spin of +1, zero hypercharge, zero isospin, and negative parity, and is produced by the collision either of protons or of electrons and positrons at high energies; freq. written ψ. Also (*psi prime* or ψ′), a similar particle of mass 3·7 MeV that decays into a psi and two pions.
Also designated J.
1974 *Times* 18 Nov. 1/8 American physicists yesterday announced the discovery of a new kind of elementary particle which has been given the name Psi. **1974** J.-E. AUGUSTIN et al. in *Physical Rev. Lett.* 2 Dec. 1406/2 We have observed a very sharp peak in the cross section for $e^+e^-\to$hadrons, e^+e^-, and possibly $\mu^+\mu^-$... The resonance has the parameters $E=3{\cdot}105\pm0{\cdot}003$ GeV, $\Gamma\leq1{\cdot}3$ MeV... We suggest naming this structure ψ(3105). **1974** G. S. ABRAMS et al. in *Ibid.* 9 Dec. 1453/2 The recent discovery of a very narrow resonant state coupled to leptons and hadrons has raised the obvious question of the existence of other narrow resonances also coupled to leptons and hadrons. We therefore began a systematic search..and quickly found a second narrow resonance decaying to hadrons. The parameters of this new state (which we suggest calling ψ(3695)) are $M=3{\cdot}695\pm0{\cdot}004$ GeV, $\Gamma<2{\cdot}7$ MeV. **1975** *Physics Bull.* Jan. 12/3 Discussion between the two groups soon established the authenticity of the 'J' particle, as Brookhaven called it (Stanford suggests calling it ψ). **1975** *Physical Rev. Lett.* 7 July 1/1 Although the newly discovered narrow boson resonances at $M=3{\cdot}095$ GeV (ψ or J) and at $M'=3{\cdot}684$ GeV (ψ′) have yet to be fully explored, the data so far indicate that these particles are of a hadronic nature with quantum numbers $J^P=1^-$ and $I^{G}C=0^{--}$. **1978** *Sci. Amer.* Mar. 50/2 The main significance of the discovery of the psi particle was that it provided compelling evidence for the existence of a fourth kind of quark, which had earlier been named the 'charmed' quark.

2. Paranormal phenomena or faculties collectively; the psychic force supposed to be manifested by these. Freq. *attrib.* and *Comb.*
1942 R. H. THOULESS in *Proc. Soc. Psychical Res.* XLVII. 5, I suggest that we should use a term proposed by Dr Wiesner, and call this group of effects [*sc.* extra-sensory perception] the 'psi phenomena', a term which has the important negative merit that it implies no theory as to their nature. *Ibid.* 8 Accepting the reality of *psi*, we may seek to fit it into the existing framework of scientific explanation. **1946** *Jrnl. Parapsychol.* X. 146 *Psi*, a general term to identify personal factors or processes in nature which transcend accepted laws. It approximates the popular use of the word 'psychic' and the technical one, 'parapsychical'. **1948** J. B. RHINE *Reach of Mind* ix. 112 How general psi capacities are we do not yet know. **1950** *Times Lit. Suppl.* 9 June 361/2 The whole field of 'the Unseen', survival after death, ghosts, mediums, precognition, gypsies, astrology, spiritual healing, in short, what it is now fashionable to call 'psi'. **1955** A. HUXLEY *Let.* 27 Aug (1969) 761 The effects[of amanita]..are quite alarmingly powerful, and it will obviously take a lot of very cautious experimentation to determine the right psi-enhancing dose of the mushroom. **1968** *New Scientist* 10 Oct. 77/1 He was even starting to produce scores that were significantly *below* chance (a well-known effect which parapsychologists call 'psi-missing'). **1969** J. I. M. STEWART *Cucumber Sandwiches* 31 'Are individuals any longer described as psychic, Arthur?'.. 'The jargon changes. The 'psi-factor' is all the go now.' **1976** *Jrnl. Soc. Psychical Res.* XLVIII. 267 Empirical evidence exists to the contrary; i.e. that psi can act independently of the brain without following the limiting characteristics of space, time and physical causality. **1977** *N.Y. Rev. Bks.* 13 Oct. 45/3 The very essence of sound experimental design in parapsychology is to close all cheating loopholes. Until they are closed, no experiment indicating sensational psi powers is worth publishing.

psi[2], var. *p.s.i.* s.v. *P II.

psilocin (səi·lǫsin). *Chem.* [a. G. *psilocin* (A. Hofmann et al. 1958, in *Experientia* XIV. 108): f. as next.] The alkaloid 3-(2-dimethylaminoethyl)-4-hydroxyindole, $C_{12}H_{16}N_2O$, which is the active hallucinogenic metabolite of psilocybin and is found in traces in psilocybin-containing mushrooms.
1958 A. HOFMANN et al. in *Experientia* XIV. 109/1 A second substance, closely related to *Psilocybin* but found only in traces, has been called *Psilocin.* **1963** *Listener* 7 Feb. 238/2 Psilocin, which occurs as a compound in a hallucination-causing Mexican mushroom, has also been recently synthesized by military scientists. **1974** M. C. GERALD *Pharmacol.* xvii. 324 Cross-tolerance has been demonstrated between LSD and mescaline, psilocybin, and psilocin. **1975** BRIMBLECOMBE & PINDER *Hallucinogenic Agents* iv. 108 The active principles of teonanacatl, the sacred mushroom of Central America, are the alkaloids psilocin..and psilocybin... Most species of *Psilocybe* and a number of *Stropharia* and *Conocybe* species contain these compounds.

psilocybin (səilǫsəi·bin). *Chem.* [a. G. *psilocybin* (A. Hofmann et al. 1958, in *Experientia* XIV. 108), f. mod. L. *psilocybe* (see below), f. Gr. ψιλός bare, smooth + κύβη head: see -IN[1].] An alkaloid, $C_{12}H_{15}N_2O\cdot H_2PO_3$, which is the phosphate ester of psilocin and is the hallucinogen present in several Central American species of mushroom (notably *Psilocybe mexicana*), producing effects similar to those of LSD but less strongly and for a shorter time.
1958 A. HOFMANN et al. in *Experientia* XIV. 109/1 The compound has been given the name *Psilocybin*; it possesses indole characteristics and contains phosphorus. **1962** A. HUXLEY *Let.* 18 Sept. (1969) 939 Mescalin, LSD and psilocybin all produce a state of affairs in which verbalizing and conceptualizing are in some sort bypassed. One can talk about the experience—but always with the knowledge that 'the rest is silence'. **1966** T. PYNCHON *Crying of Lot 49* i. 17 Effects of LSD-25, mescaline, psilocybin, and related drugs on a large sample of suburban housewives. **1970** K. PLATT *Push-button Butterfly* (1971) iv. 43 He would be selling grass, meth, acid..psilocybin-coated grass, peyote buttons. **1975** [see *PSILOCIN].

psionic (səi,ǫ·nik), *a.* [f. *PSI + *-onic*, as in *electronic*.] Pertaining to or involving 'psi'. So **psio·nics** *sb. pl.* [-IC 2], (the study of) the paranormal; **psio·nically** *adv.*
1952 *Astounding Sci. Fiction* XLIX. 119/2 The psionic translator in his belt would have brought him the sense of every syllable, and enabled even these psionic illiterates to understand him. **1953** T. STURGEON *More than Human* III. 207 A gravity generator, to increase and decrease..weight... Gravitics is the key to everything. It would lead to the addition of one more item to the Unified Field—what we now call psychic energy, or 'psionics'. **1960** P. ANDERSON in 'E. Crispin' *Best SF Five* (1963) 228 Research has taught us just enough about psionics to show we can't imagine its potentialities. **1966** *Analog Science Fact/Fiction* Nov. 29/1 I'm going to have to do the real end of the work—the psionics end. **1975** *Homes & Gardens* Nov. 63/3 In the years since Lakhowski first talked of fundamental, or psionic, energy in cells, radiesthesia has not come very far. **1976** *Psionic Med.* XI. 6 Dr. Wright wondered whether the case histories of patients treated psionically would throw any light on these questions. **1978** C. HUMPHREYS *Both Sides Circle* xix. 202 Dr Lawrence, at the age of ninety, founded The Psionic Medical Society... This drew together homoeopathy and radiaesthesia.

psittacine, *a.* and *sb.* Now usually pronounced (si·tăkəin). Substitute for etym.; [a. mod.L. subfamily name *Psittacinæ*, f. generic name *Psittacus* (Linnæus *Systema Naturæ* (1735)), a. L. *psittacus* parrot: see -INE[1].] (Earlier and later examples.)
1874 *Proc. Zool. Soc.* 592 Many deductions can be made as to the mutual relations of the several genera of the Psittacine suborder. **1901** *Trans. Linn. Soc: Zool.* VIII. 257 It is possible to derive the Psittacine type as a very apocentric modification of this metacentre. **1973** *Observer* 4 Nov. 5/3 Medical evidence and a growing suspicion..are adding urgency to demands..that import restrictions should be placed on the 'psittacines'. **1976** *Amer. Speech 1973* XLVIII. 265 The psittacine linguistic and cultural relativity with which the argument begins is a very dead duck at the argument's conclusion.

psittacism (si·tăsiz'm), [ad. F. *psittacisme* (Leibnitz *Nouveaux Essais sur l'entendement humain* (1765) II. 145) or G. *psittazismus*, f. Gr. ψιττακός parrot: see -ISM.] The mechanical repetition of previously received ideas or images that reflects neither true reasoning nor feeling; repetition of words or phrases parrot-fashion, without reflection, automatically. Hence **psi·ttacist**; **psittaci·stically** *adv.*
1896 A. G. LANGLEY tr. *Leibnitz' New Ess. conc. Hum. Und.* II. xxi. 196 All that they do think about it [*sc.* the future life] is but a *psittacism*, or gross and vain images after the Mahometan fashion, in which they themselves see little likelihood. **1901** J. WILSON in *N. & Q.* 9th Ser. VIII. 183/1 The words *in nomine Domini nostri J.C.* being, I fear, too often repeated psittacistically. **1902** *Amer. Jrnl. Sociol.* VII. 751 Leibnitz characterized human progress as a psittacism. **1904** *Amer. Jrnl. Religious Psychol. & Educ.* May 107 Then followed monographs on psittacism and symbolic thought, heredity, and laughter. **1923** OGDEN & RICHARDS *Meaning of Meaning* vi. 230 There will be some to whom a word is merely a stimulus to the utterance of other words without the occurrence of any reference—the psittacists, that is to say, who respond to words much as they might respond to the first notes of a tune which they proceed almost automatically to complete. *Ibid.* x. 349 Psittacism is the use of words without reference. **1936** *Amer. Speech* XI. 173/2 This procedure would reduce a science to the level of a fastidious psittacism—a blind alley leading to the dead end of a circumscribed habit. **1938** S. CHASE *Tyranny of Words* iv. 35 Speaking without knowing is called 'psittacism', but is a practice not confined to parrots. **1975** *Jrnl. Roman Stud.* LXV. 187 Military matters are also the subjects of contributions from two younger British scholars, which are remarkable not least for being unencumbered by the needlessly repetitive anthologies of modern literature, a healthy immunity from that pernicious psittacism too widespread in this volume.

psittacosis. Add: Usu. with pronunc. (s-). (Further examples.) Cf. *ORNITHOSIS.
1930 *Aberdeen Press & Jrnl.* 10 Jan. 5 Recently three persons were reported to have died from 'parrot plague' at Berlin and two at Prague. The disease is rare and is known to medical science as psittacosis. **1955** *Times* 16 Aug. 4/2 Psittacosis, or 'parrot disease', may attack or be carried by birds other than parrots. It is not yet known how the zoo budgerigars caught the disease. **1966** *Listener* 3 Nov. 652/3, I remember as a child that my father bought a pair of brightly coloured and rather handsome parakeets, almost at the same time as the great psittacosis scare started, so we got rid of our nice new parakeets. **1970** I. MURDOCH *Fairly Honourable Defeat* I. v. 52 It was called psittacosis because people thought you could only get it from parrots, but in fact you can get it from any bird. Pigeons are notorious carriers of psittacosis. **1973** *Times* 29 Oct. 15/8, I have at the moment under my care five patients with psittacosis all infected by a recently imported parrot which was ill when purchased and died a week later.
Hence **psittaco·tic** *a.*
1947 W. P. BLOUNT *Dis. Poultry* xliii. 389 Mice inoculated with psittacotic material often die about the seventh day.

psocid (sōᵘ·kid, -sid). *Ent.* [f. mod.L. family name *Psocidæ*, f. generic name *Psocus* (J. C. Fabricius *Supplementum Entomologiæ Systematicæ* (1798) 198), f. Gr. ψώχ-ειν to grind: see -ID[3].] A small winged or wingless insect with long, segmented antennæ, belonging to the family Psocidæ or the order Psocoptera, which includes book-lice and other pests feeding on fungi, algæ, cereal products, or decaying vegetable or animal matter.
1891 *Insect Life* IV. 188 The correspondence is less striking than that of a Mallophagan with a Psocid. **1922** *Entomol. Monthly Mag.* LVIII. 104 The occurrence of various species of Psocids..inside houses, has been frequently observed. **1959** [see *bark-louse*]. **1967** M. E. HALE *Biol. Lichens* xi. 159 Psocids, lice-like insects that infest larch trees, also eat lichens. **1975** R. D. HUGHES *Living Insects* ix. 226 Psocids are omnivorous, feeding on fragments of plant or animal materials.

psophometer (sofǫ·mitəɹ). *Electr.* [f. Gr. ψόφος noise + -METER.] An instrument for giving a reading approximately proportional to the subjective aural effect of the noise in a communication circuit.
1938 *Jrnl. Inst. Electr. Engineers* LXXXIII. 261/1 The circuit noise meter (or psophometer) is an instrument which has been designed for measuring the disturbing effect of power induction on telephone communication. **1953** *P.O. Electr. Engineers' Jrnl.* XLVI. 112/1 The use of the psophometer has extended in recent years from the function of power circuit noise interference measurement to the measurement of overall noise on [telephone] transmission lines and equipment. **1975** J. E. FLOOD *Telecommunication Networks* ii. 48 Noise is usually measured by a meter having a frequency-weighting network which has been standardised by the CCITT. Such instruments are called psophometers.
Hence **psophome·tric** *a.* (see quot. 1943); **psophome·trically** *adv.*
1943 *Gloss. Terms Telecommunications (B.S.I.)* 15 *Psophometric voltage*, the voltage at 800 c/s between two points in a telephone system which, if it replaced the disturbing voltage, would produce the same degree of interference with a telephone conversation as the disturbing voltage. **1951** *Electronic Engin.* XXIII. 35 Typical figures permitted are 2 mV of weighted (psophometric) ripple. **1975** J. E. FLOOD *Telecommunication Networks* ii. 48 For white noise in the band 0–4 kHz, the effect of psophometric weighting is to reduce the noise level by 3·6 dB. *Ibid.*, Noise power is..measured in units of pWp (picowatts psophometrically weighted) or dBmp (decibels relative to 1 mW psophometrically weighted).

psoralen (sōᵊ·rălen). *Chem.* and *Pharm.* Also **-ene** (-īn). [f. mod.L. *Psoral-ea* (f. Gr. ψωραλέος itchy, mangy), generic name of an Indian leguminous herb, *P. corylifolia*, from seeds of which it was first isolated + *-en* (cf. -ENE).] A crystalline tricyclic lactone, $C_{11}H_6O_3$, containing fused coumarin and furan ring systems, which occurs in certain plants and is taken orally or applied in ointments to treat certain skin disorders; any derivative of this compound.
1933 H. S. JOIS et al. in *Jrnl. Indian Chem. Soc.* X. 46 A petroleum ether extract of the seeds of *Psoralea corylifolia* gave a dark reddish-brown oil and a crystalline solid $C_{11}H_6O_3$ now named Psoralen, melting at 162°. **1959** N. CAMPBELL in E. H. Rodd *Chem. Carbon Compounds* IVB. viii. 883 Examples of the furocoumarins are found in psoralene and angelicin, which differ from each other in the points of attachment of the furan ring to the aromatic nucleus of coumarin. **1969** *Observer* 26 Jan. 5/5 Patients who are prescribed psoralens—drugs sensitive to ultra-violet light and taken to bring a healthy glow back to unnaturally white patches of skin—should resist the temptation to use them as 'sun-tan pills'. **1978** *Lancet* 11 Mar. 538/1 Psoralens form photoadducts and interstrand cross-links with D.N.A. in the presence of U.V.-A. and mounting evidence indicates that these events are mutagenic.

psoriasiform (sorəi,æ·sifǭɹm, sorəi·ăsifǭɹm). *Med.* [f. PSORIASI(S + -FORM.] = PSORIATIFORM *a.*

This is the more usual adj. of the two.

1897 *Brit. Jrnl. Dermatol.* IX. 477 Dr. Fox brought the case again to demonstrate a curious psoriasiform eruption disseminated about the wrists. **1977** *Lancet* 3 Sept. 475/2 Exfoliative dermatitis and psoriasiform, eczematous, lichenoid, erythematous, and mixed rashes were observed.

psst, *int.* An onomatopoeic sound expressing a hiss, often to attract attention.

1922 JOYCE *Ulysses* 285 What is she? Hope she. Psst! **1938** M. K. RAWLINGS *Yearling* xvi. 188 Buck hissed at him. 'Psst. You got him. Leave him lay.' **1963** V. NABOKOV *Gift* v. 302 One could already hear the energetic '*psst, psst*' of Shahmatov, who had been served the wrong order. **1972** W. M. ESTES *Streetful of People* i. 63 '*Psst!* You're going the wrong way,' hissed Calvin Turnbough. **1975** *New Yorker* 13 Jan. 28/3 So now everybody is responding. Bresson is like that. *Psst, psst, psst*—the steam gathers, then the lid blows off. **1976** *Times* 21 May 16/4 Psst! Have you heard the latest?

psy- (səi). orig. *U.S.* Abbrev. of PSYCHOLOGICAL *a.*, used esp. in *psy-war*: see *psychological warfare* s.v. *PSYCHOLOGICAL *a.* 3.

1954 *Britannica Bk. of Year* 638/1 Mental tensions were reflected in *psy-war* (psychological warfare). **1965** *Wall St. Jrnl.* 27 July 1/1 In the local bureaucratic jargon, this can come under the heading of 'civic action' or 'rural reconstruction' or 'psy war'. **1966** *New Statesman* 14 Oct. 549/1 As psy-op cadres take the field And start to reconsolidate. **1971** *Times Lit. Suppl.* 7 May 519/1 In one sense, 'psywar' is not the same as propaganda—is its opposite even: while propaganda aims to influence belief, psywar influences action, and above all persuades those it is directed at into inaction. **1974** *Jrnl. R. United Services Inst.* June 38/1 Good Psy-Ops must be addressed to the need level in force and this need level is determined by multiple factors, not simply by the efficiency of an army's logistical services or the level of combat losses. **1974** *Black Panther* 16 Mar. 13/3 Such tactics amount to nothing less than psychological warfare, or as they say in Vietnam—'psy-war'.

psych (səik), *sb. colloq.* Also **psyche.** [f. PSYCH(OLOGY, PSYCH(IATRY, etc.] **1.** Psychology or psychiatry. Freq. *attrib.*

1895 W. C. GORE in *Inlander* Nov. 64 *Psych.* n., psychology. **1910** in *Dialect Notes* (1914) IV. 129 He was feeling sadly as he thought of Psych and Chem. **1946** P. CARTER in Aldiss & Harrison *Decade 1940s* (1975) 111 Shut up or I'll have the psych corpsman go over you. **1951** *Galaxy Sci. Fiction* May 138/1 He had put the entire student body through interrogation and a psych check. **1953** 'T. STURGEON' *More than Human* III. 204 He went through medical school too, and psych. **1960** *Analog Science Fact/Fiction* Nov. 12/1, I checked with one of our own psych men... Lefferts has definite paranoid tendencies, he says. **1975** R. RIMMER *Premar Experiments* (1976) I. 78 Since I didn't feel like watching TV in the sitting room, I concentrated on my psych book. **1976** *Amer. Speech 1973* XLVIII. 297 In most large, metropolitan hospitals, there are customarily two or more units devoted to psych.

2. a. *pl.* Psychical research.

1927 *Observer* 2 Oct. 7 The story of his magic and his mysticism is good, but it is not half such satisfying spookery as is going out..from the offices of the S.P.R. Beginners in 'Psychs' may get a thrill or two from the book.

b. A psychic person.

1975 *Publishers Weekly* 7 Apr. 81/3 He has great ESP powers, so he volunteers to help his friend Ahmed of the Rescue Squad trace psyches in distress.

3. A psychologist, psychiatrist, or psychoanalyst.

1946 P. CARTER in Aldiss & Harrison *Decade 1940s* (1975) 113 The psychs probably have a spy or two planted in this room. **1947** L. MACNEICE *Dark Tower* 181 You don't mean a psycho-analyst?..We do not believe in the psych. **1962** P. MORTIMER *Pumpkin Eater* xvi. 146 It's only that the doctor, that psyche, did say that I shouldn't have another child. I'm in the middle of treatment, Jake says, for depression. **1964** R. PETRIE *Murder by Precedent* x. 156 He'd better see a psych—no, his family doctor. **1968** *Listener* 19 Dec. 810/1 'That would be very foolish, but also of some inconvenience to me,' the psych said.

4. *Bridge.* (Usu. as **psyche.**) A psychic bid.

1965 [see *PSYCH *v.* 2]. **1969** A. TRUSCOTT *Gt. Bridge Scandal* 272 His rather puerile psyche clearly indicates that he knew nothing about the hearts opposite. **1973** L. MEYNELL *Fatal Flaw* iv. 33 Vyvyan already knew Nancy's play..very dependable; no 'psyches' or fancy tricks. **1980** *Oxford Times* (City ed.) 25 Jan. 11/6 Barry Rigal reports on the two methods of dealing with psyches —the successful and the unsuccessful—against Surrey.

psych (səik), *v. colloq.* Also **psyche.** [f. *PSYCH(OANALYSE *v.*, etc.: cf. prec.] **I. 1.** *trans.* To subject to psychoanalysis.

1917 *Metropolitan Mag.* Jan. 20/1 Well, she went to this psychoanalyzer; she was 'psyched'. **1928** *Daily Express* 31 Dec. 2/5 While for some patients being 'psyched' may be a step towards being cured, to others it may amount to being infected. **1943** F. BROWN *Angels & Spaceships* (1955) 178 It isn't *fair* to psych a guy when he doesn't know what he's talking about. **1965** P. WYLIE *They both were Naked* I. i. 20 I've been psyched so much I can hardly daydream as I used to. **1973** K. GILES *File on Death* i. 10 He's been psyched to the best of our skill.

II. 2. *intr.* In *Bridge*, to make a bid that misrepresents one's hand in order to deceive one's opponents.

1952 [implied in *PSYCHING *vbl. sb.*]. **1965** *Sunday Times* (Colour Suppl.) 31 Jan. 38/2 'Obviously Jones has psyched... Don't tell me you wouldn't try five-spades.'.. You catch them out in a full-blooded psyche. **1969** A. TRUSCOTT *Gt. Bridge Scandal* 271 He had no technical reason to suppose that his partner had psyched. **1977** *Detroit Free Press* 11 Dec. 22–C/1 The psychic bid was invented by Dorothy Rice Sims in the early 1930s. It soon became the vogue to 'psyche', usually with hit and miss results.

III. 3. *trans.* To influence (someone) psychologically; to excite, stimulate; (usu. with *up*) to prepare (oneself or another) mentally for a special effort or the like; (usu. with *out*) to gain a psychological advantage over, to intimidate, to demoralize. Freq. as pa. pple. or ppl. adj. orig. and chiefly *U.S.*

1957 *Venture Sci. Fiction* Jan. 18/2 A growing moodiness had driven her..to get out alone... She couldn't understand the pull she felt... Ever since those moments in the Monster's cage... *Damn* the Monster! Had the thing psyched her? **1961** *Milwaukee Jrnl.* 8 Nov. II. 16/3 'We didn't think we could beat Maine with an orthodox offense,' Hatch said. 'We hoped this way to provoke some defensive miscues and also to "psych" our own kids into believing they had something extra going for them.' **1963** *Amer. Speech* XXXVIII. 205 *Get psyched out*, v. phr., slang term applied to losing one's nerve while skiing downhill. **1966** *Time* 29 Apr. 35 Having discovered psychology, the cops induce 'truth' by psyching the subject. **1967** J. SEVERSON *Great Surfing* Gloss., *Psyched out*, mentally incapacitated; generally referring to a surfer's reaction to the big surf. To become frightened, shook up. **1968–70** *Current Slang* (Univ. S. Dakota) III–IV. 96 *Psyched up*, adj., excited. **1968** *New Yorker* 10 Aug. 78 He's never tried to psych us, or insult us with a pep talk. **1969** *Ibid.* 14 June 72/3 It's not that I'm psyched out by him, but I'm playing great and he hits three all-time winners. **1970** N. ARMSTRONG et al. *First on Moon* xiii. 318 He always likes to get you psyched up for tragedy. **1971** E. BULLINS in W. King *Black Short Story Anthol.* (1972) 63 Dandy thought that the way she managed things and worked the love and affection from people was like a pimp who psychs out his whores. **1972** *N.Y. Times* 4 June 4/8 At tiring moments she tried to psyche herself up by muttering, 'McGovern, McGovern, I've got to win for McGovern.' **1973** P. A. WHITNEY *Snowfire* vii. 131 He was absolutely without fear. Nothing ever psyched him out before a race. **1973** *Massachusetts Daily Collegian* 26 Apr. 8/1 The states get psyched... New England..has begun to get just a little excited about the upcoming bicentennial of the American Revolution. **1974** H. L. FOSTER *Ribbin'* vi. 252 The teacher psychs himself—that is, puts himself in a certain frame of mind so that he can deal with the realities of his teaching assignment. **1974** *Canad. Mag.* 21 Sept. 27/1 It's harder for me to get myself up for practices but I still get myself up for a game. Only you have to psych yourself harder as time goes by. *a* **1976** J. QUARRY in *6,000 Words* 165 Pressure doesn't psych me. **1977** I. SHAW *Beggarman, Thief* III. viii. 313, I had no business being at the net. I was trying to psyche you into missing the shot. *Ibid.* ix. 318, I could see something was psyching him out and it worried me. **1978** *Telegraph* (Brisbane) 28 Sept. 23/4 For months we had been psyching ourselves up for this very rare entertainment delight. **1979** *Chatelaine* (Canada) Jan. 22/3 Psych yourself into ignoring your pet's emotional pleas for more food. **1979** *Tucson* (Arizona) *Citizen* 20 Sept. 6D/1 It's hard for our kids to get psyched up for a dual meet, especially this early in the season.

4. *trans.* With *out.* To analyse in psychological terms; to work out.

a **1961** D. HULBURD in *Webster* s.v., I psyched it all out by myself. **1973** *Daily Tel.* (Colour Suppl.) 30 Nov. 38/1, I would have come away from his [*sc.* Geller's] various feats as from any others I could not psych out—certain there was a simple, logical, rather ordinary explanation that escaped me. **1974** K. MILLETT *Flying* (1975) IV. 435 Mother's X-ray eyes met Celia once, had it all psyched out in three minutes. **1978** S. BRILL *Teamsters* iii. 88 Most others could never approach Hoffa's ability..to psyche out the opposition's thinking so consistently.

5. *intr.* With *out.* To break down mentally; to become confused or deranged.

1970 *Atlantic Monthly* Feb. 84, I psyched out. I'll be damned if I know how. **1971** J. MANDELKAU *Buttons* xiv. 155, I psyched out! **1972** R. BLOCH *Night-World* (1974) xiv. 90 It had been a real rip-off, and at first Tony had psyched out on the whole scene. **1973** *To our Returned Prisoners of War* (U.S. Secretary of Defense, Public Affairs) 8 *Psych out*,..to become confused or disturbed.

Hence **psy·ching** *vbl. sb.*

1952 I. MACLEOD *Bridge* vii. 95 The other main rule for intelligent psyching is to read your partner's bid as phoney before the opponents find out, and to thicken the smoke screen. **1974** *Times Lit. Suppl.* 22 Feb. 182/5 The reading and psyching of an opponent is quite as fascinating as chess. **1974** H. L. FOSTER *Ribbin'* vi. 250 The psyching function helps them overcome their middle class, nonphysical, open personality. **1975** *Time Out* 16 May 13/2 None of the heavy 'psyching' or banal superstitions that I'd expected. **1977** *Washington Post* 7 Sept. E9 In time the players realized that 'psyching' was not a dividend payer.

psychagogue. Add: Also **psychogogue. 2.** (Further example.)

1928 AUDEN *Poems* 20 Eyes Look in the glass, confess The tightening of the mouth; Know the receding face A blemished psychogogue; But symmetry will please.

Psyche. Add: **1. c.** *Psyche-knot* (earlier and later examples).

1888 A. R. DIEHL *Two Thousand Words* 170 *Psyche knot*, the style of wearing the hair in a projecting coil in the middle of the back of the head. **1968** J. UPDIKE *Couples* v. 404 Her hair was pinned up in a psyche knot.

d. *Psychol.* The conscious and unconscious mind and emotions, esp. as influencing and affecting the whole person. Also *Comb.*

1910 C. G. JUNG in *Amer. Jrnl. Psychol.* XXI. 226 Disease is an imperfect adaptation; hence in this case we are dealing with something morbid in the psyche. *Ibid.* 254 This explains a part of the conflict in the child's psyche. **1940** H. G. BAYNES *Mythol. of Soul* v. 154 Split off from the psychic hierarchy as an infantile *idée fixe*, it resisted the decisive transition from the infantile to the cultural psyche. **1949** J. STRACHEY tr. *Freud's Outl. Psycho-Anal.* i. 1 We know two things concerning what we call our psyche or mental life: firstly, its bodily organ and scene of action, the brain (or nervous system), and secondly, our acts of consciousness. **1958** *Times Lit. Suppl.* 23 May p. xii/2 The transformation and re-birth of the psyche in the individual's development towards maturity and integration. **1959** *Ibid.* 23 Jan. 44/5 If the stability of the self is threatened by too much division the psyche asserts itself by projecting an image of wholeness upon the sphere of consciousness. **1961** *Times* 4 Sept. 5/7 This democratic and psyche-conscious age. **1976** *Jrnl. Analytical Psychol.* XXI. 193 A heart ailment..need not arise from the heart only; it can also arise from the psyche of the sufferer.

2. a. (Earlier example.)

1820 M. EDGEWORTH *Let.* 19 Aug. (1979) 224 You know the prints of the Berne Costume. Pray look at the *butterfly wing* caps—Brobdignag butterflies... This picturesque Psyche costume.

psyche, var. *PSYCH.

psychedelia (səikĭdī·liă). [Back-formation from next: see -IA[2].] Psychedelic articles or phenomena collectively; the subculture associated with psychedelic drugs.

1967 *Melody Maker* 27 May 9 Apparently today's hippie must be expanded and experienced in the whys and wherefores of psychedelia but it cannot be said that the products of this society are all 'junkie'. **1967** *Listener* 10 Aug. 169/2, I am unfriendly to the whole idea of psychedelia and the very notion of a chemical paradise with all those tangerine trees and marmalade skies seems absurd and slightly tatty. **1968** *Rat* 13–16 May 17/2 Buttons, posters, trip glasses, zodiac pendants, psychedelia. **1972** D. SALE *Love Bite* xiv. 172 The crazy jumble of sights and sounds and smells... Here was psychedelia that could never be achieved artificially in a discothèque; a relaxed and happy sense of awareness without the use of pills or pot. **1976** *Maclean's Mag.* 15 Nov. 4/1 In the Sixties his [*sc.* Dr. Timothy Leary's] name was synonymous with psychedelia.

psychedelic (səikĭde·lik, -dī·lik), *a.* and *sb.* Also occas. **psychodelic.** [Irreg. f. Gr. ψυχή (see PSYCHE) + δηλ-οῦν to make manifest, reveal (f. δῆλος manifest, visible) + -IC.

Proposed by H. Osmond in a letter to Aldous Huxley early in 1956: see G. Smith *Lett. of Aldous Huxley* (1969) 795.]

A. *adj.* **1. a.** Of a drug: producing an expansion of consciousness through greater awareness of the senses and emotional feelings and the revealing of unconscious motivations (freq. symbolically); usu., = *PSYCHOTOMIMETIC *a.*

1957 H. OSMOND in *Ann. N.Y. Acad. Sci.* LXVI. 429, I have tried to find an appropriate name for the agents under discussion: a name that will include the concepts of enriching the mind and enlarging the vision... My choice, because it is clear, euphonious, and uncontaminated by other associations, is psychedelic, mind-manifesting. **1959** *Times Lit. Suppl.* 13 Nov. 665/3 He is so far from condemning the use of psychedelic drugs as to believe that, if wisely directed, they may help to open closed minds to dimensions of experience which would otherwise remain closed to them. **1965** *Jrnl. Amer. Med. Assoc.* 11 Jan. 104/1 The use of hallucinogenic (psychotomimetic, dysleptic, psychedelic) substances to produce altered states of consciousness is not new. **1965** *Brit. Jrnl. Philos. Sci.* XVI. 150 The popular issue of consciousness-expanding, or psychodelic drugs. **1967** *New Statesman* 3 Feb. 154/3 Mr. Andrews stands for many poets..who are trying to reach beyond ordinary experience, in his case through the 'mental voyages' of psychedelic drugs. 'This LSD is pure hero food.' **1970** R. C. ZAEHNER *Concordant Discord* iii. 42 If psychedelic drugs attest the existence of a timeless heaven, they none the less point to the existence of a timeless hell. **1970** H. PERRY *Human Be-In* 111 The core society's preoccupation with psychedelic drugs has been a way of avoiding their real hang-up: the attack of the young on middle-class values, particularly status and property. **1974** *Howard Jrnl.* XIV. 99 He compares religious experience to the chemical experience induced by psychedelic drugs. **1975** BRIMBLECOMBE & PINDER *Hallucinogenic Agents* i. 4 The psychedelic drug is said to enrich the mind, to enlarge the vision, and to create a mystic insight, but the term has achieved its maximum use and notoriety in the lay rather than the scientific literature.

b. Of, pertaining to, or produced by such a drug.

1963 (*title of periodical*) The psychedelic review. **1965** G. CUMMINS *Swan on Black Sea* 116 He said that yours was possibly a psychedelic condition. **1966** *New Statesman* 16 Sept. 387/1 LSD-takers, or acidheads, look upon Aldous Huxley as a sort of John the Baptist... Huxley baptised with mescalin, but now there is this larger psychedelic vision. **1967** *Punch* 22 Feb. 280/1 How.. would one set about 'integrating LSD into the fabric of American society', as one sober supporter of the psychedelic experience suggested? **1970** G. GREER *Female Eunuch* 172 The state induced by the kiss is actually self-induced, of course, for few lips are so gifted with electric and psychedelic possibilities.

c. Concerned with or characterized by the use of such drugs.

1966 *New Statesman* 4 Mar. 305/2 The work done by the 'psychedelic' specialists Timothy Leary, R. Alpert and R. Metzner in the United States has explored the possibilities of expanding awareness by the use of hallucinogenic drugs, in particular LSD-25. **1967** *Times* 3 July 7/4 Since the drug aspect of the psychedelic cult attracted a great deal of unfavourable publicity and a number of unsavoury hangers-on, Dr. Timothy Leary.. was asked to resign his appointment as Professor of Clinical Psychology at Harvard Medical School. **1967** *Los Angeles Free Press* 10 Nov. 8/3 If you want a big picture of Brando on his bike, why travel to a psychedelic shop when you can get it at the drug store. **1967** *Amer. Jrnl. Psychiatry* CXXIII. 1202/1 The rationale of psychedelic therapy with alcoholic patients is focused on the alienation-breaking potential of 'peak' or psychedelic experiences induced with the aid of LSD. **1972** M. D. DE RIOS *Visionary Vine* ii. 26 While some societies such as those in Peru have thousands of years of psychedelic tradition behind them, advanced industrial societies often find themselves in deep trouble as segments of their society are suddenly discovering the use of powerful mind-altering substances. **1976** *New Musical Express* 31 July 8/2 This obsession with the bizarrity came out of the psychedelic '60s.

2. Producing an effect or sensation held to resemble that produced by a psychedelic drug; *spec.* having vivid colours, often in bold abstract designs or in motion.

1965 *Los Angeles Free Press* 5 Nov. 4/1 (Advt.), The record stores won't sell and the radio banned..The Psychedelic Sound of 'The Trip' (original version). **1966** *Life* Sept. 61/1 The world of art is 'turning on'. It is getting hooked on psychedelic art. **1966** *Melody Maker* 12 Nov. 9/1 Bobby Darin..has come back after years of absence..right in the middle of psychedelic pop, freak-outs and happenings. **1967** *Wall St. Jrnl.* 9 Feb 1/4 Psychedelic fabrics are becoming the rage. **1967** *Daily Tel.* 24 Oct. 19 Dupont showed its spring news in the new Royal Lancaster, where a batch of whirling lights and psychedelic patterns enlivened the theatre. **1968** *Globe & Mail* (Toronto) 3 Feb. 23/4 'Topless' dancers gyrating in the glow of psychedelic slides and lights. **1968** *Southerly* XXVIII. 279 He is wearing his psychedelic union jack trousers and tee-shirt. **1969** *Observer* 12 Jan. 8/3 The very latest psychedelic colours, electric purples and greens. **1971** *Hi-Fi Sound* Feb. 71/1 A discotheque with a psychedelic lighting display making you virtually blind. **1973** C. & R. MILNER *Black Players* v. 139 He drives a secondhand Volkswagen van, which had been gaily painted in psychedelic designs by its previous owners. **1977** B. PYM *Quartet in Autumn* ii. 22 He..proceeded to check the items in his shopping-bag—a 'psychedelic' plastic carrier, patterned in vivid colours, hinting at some unexpected aspect of his character.

B. *sb.* **1.** A psychedelic drug.

1956 H. OSMOND *Let.* in G. Smith *Lett. Aldous Huxley* (1969) 795 To fathom Hell or soar angelic, Just take a pinch of psychedelic (Delos to manifest). **1957** —— in *Ann. N.Y. Acad. Sci.* LXVI. 429 The psychedelics help us to explore and fathom our own nature. **1959** R. C. JOHNSON *Watcher on Hills* x. 162 Experience under the psychedelics may have an important contribution to make to Art. **1965** A. HUXLEY *Let.* 22 July (1969) 803 As you say in your letter, we still know very little about the psychodelics. **1974** M. C. GERALD *Pharmacol.* xvii. 318 Drugs in this same category are also termed hallucinogens, psychedelics, psychotogens, psychodysleptics, and so forth. **1977** *Martindale's Extra Pharmacopoeia* (ed. 27) 880/2 The group of drugs termed variously psychodysleptics, psychotomimetics, in some cases psychodelics, or, more usually but often inappropriately, hallucinogens are substances which as their principal action provoke abnormal mental changes, particularly in cognitive and perceptual spheres. **1977** *Rolling Stone* 16 June 24/3 Ergot also contains a powerful psychedelic: lysergic acid amide, a close relative of LSD, with about ten percent of that drug's mind-altering potency.

2. A person who takes a psychedelic drug or has a psychedelic life-style.

1966 *Time* 11 Mar. 43 Such dangers do not deter the acid heads or 'psychedelics'—even though some users are willing to admit that they found no great 'show', or had a 'freak trip' (a bad one) or 'tripped out' (the worst kind). **1967** *Economist* 17 June 1240/1 The East Village has supplanted Greenwich Village as a new meeting ground for poets, beats, psychedelics and plain old-fashioned bohemians.

Hence **psychede·lically** *adv.*, in psychedelic colours; also various *nonce-words*, as **psy·chedel, psychedeliac** (-dī·liæk) = *PSYCHEDELIC *sb.* 2; **psy:chedelicate·ssen**, a shop selling psychedelic articles.

1966 *Life* 9 Sept. 68/3 True 'acid rock' goes deeper psychedelically than just lyrics. **1967** *Time* 24 Feb. 55 In Los Angeles, the leading psychedelicatessen is the Headquarters. **1967** *Listener* 24 Aug. 252/1 Those bells which announce the approach of psychedels like medieval lepers. **1970** V. CANNING *Great Affair* xvi. 300 Troops.. wearing combat helmets—some psychedelically painted. **1975** *Time Out* 9 May 55 Zig Zag badges are optional but retired psychedeliacs requesting 'Andmoreagain' are asking for disappointment and maybe even a bunch of fives. **1976** *Homes & Gardens* July 39/1 The front door of their old rectory is painted psychedelically and Shirley opens it wearing a comfortable kaftan.

psychedelicize (saikīde·lisaiz), *v. colloq.* [f. prec. + -IZE.] *trans.* To make psychedelic; to render more colourful and lively.

1966 *Life* 9 Sept. 68/4 Buttons with the slogan 'Psychedelicize Suburbia'. **1975** *Time Out* 15 Aug. 12/4 Reviewing style became a bizarre psychedelicised variant of the traditional 'Good beat. Chart chance' mode.

psychiatric, *a.* Add: (Further examples.) Also, connected with or affected by mental illness that can be treated medically; *psychiatric social work*, social work designed to support and supplement psychiatric treatment; so *psychiatric social worker*.

1919 M. C. JARRETT in *Mental Hygiene* Apr. 215 There is a misconception..that the psychiatric social worker has a different function from other social workers. *Ibid.* 219 The future social worker..will have included in her professional education some knowledge of all the different branches of social work—psychiatric social work, medical social work, family rehabilitation, child welfare, community service. **1940** HINSIE & SHATZKY *Psychiatric Dict.* 13/1 Affectation... It is perhaps more commonly observed among those who are not, strictly speaking, psychiatric, though it may..appear prominently in hysteria. **1957** *Times* 15 Oct. 14/5 Britain's first psychiatric prison, which is to be built at Grendon Underwood in Buckinghamshire, is expected to be ready for occupation in 1962. **1962** N. E. WHITTEN in A. Dundes *Mother Wit* (1973) 408/1 Cases such as the following have been given..by a white psychiatric social worker. **1965** J. POLLITT *Depression & its Treatment* i. 6 It is rarely necessary for the patient to realise that evidence for a psychiatric reaction is being sought. **1971** E. D. SMIGEL *Handbk. Study of Social Probl.* 12 Beginning in the 1920s psychiatric sociology has been a developing subdiscipline. **1976** S. B. GUZE (*title*) Criminality and psychiatric disorders. **1977** E. AMBLER *Send no more Roses* xi. 253 The book..may..be of some sociological interest to specialists, particularly in the field of psychiatric social work.

psychiatrically *adv.* (further examples).

1921 'M. B., OXON' *Cosmic Anat.* ix. 122 It is quite possible that *psychiatrically* Jung's deduction was right. **1965** J. POLLITT *Depression & its Treatment* vi. 85 Outpatient treatment and short-stay admission is now widely practised for all psychiatrically ill patients. **1975** *Times* 5 Aug. 2/8 The drugs would be administered only to people who had recovered from a period of depression and were psychiatrically well.

psychiatrist. Add: (Further examples.) Now usu. a practitioner of psychiatry.

1922 R. S. WOODWORTH *Psychology* i. 16 According to the psychiatrists, mental disturbance is primarily an affair of emotion and desire rather than of intellect. **1931** F. L. ALLEN *Only Yesterday* viii. 198 Psychiatrists were installed in business houses to hire and fire employées. **1959** *Daily Tel.* 9 Apr. 1/3 There would be psychiatrists, social psychologists, and penologists on the staff so that they could approach the problem of crime from all points of view. **1971** *Lancet* 29 May 1124/1 A radiologist to the N.H.S. is medical and a radiographer non-medical, and similarly with..psychiatrist and psychologist, ophthalmologist and optician.

psychiatrize (saikai·ătraiz), *v.* [f. PSYCHIATR(Y, -(IST + -IZE.] *trans.* To treat psychiatrically; *psychiatrize away* (nonce-use), to do away with by means of psychiatry or its concepts. Hence **psychi·atrized** *ppl.a.*; **psych-i:atriza·tion.**

1929 *Sunday Dispatch* 6 Jan. 3/5 Parents may also be psychiatrised to study their traits and home-life. **1954** E. JENKINS *Tortoise & Hare* vi. 59 He couldn't be psychiatrized against his will. **1964** P. MEADOWS in I. L. Horowitz *New Sociol.* 451 Psychiatrized conformity masked as true individuality. **1977** *Times Lit. Suppl.* 6 May 565/3 The psychiatrization of 'perverse' pleasures. **1978** *Church Times* 10 Feb. 11/1 We have psychiatrised away the Seven Deadly Sins. Pride, anger, avarice, envy, sloth, gluttony and lust have been made respectable. They have become self-fulfilment, stress, incentive, insecurity, inertia, defective metabolism and emotional tension.

psychic, *a.* (*sb.*) Add: **1. a.** (Further examples.) Also, having a psychical rather than a physical or physiological origin (cf. PSYCHICAL *a.* 1 a).

psychic blindness = *psychical blindness* s.v. PSYCHICAL *a.* 1 a; *psychic determinism* = *psychical determinism* s.v. *PSYCHICAL *a.* 1 a; *psychic energizer*, an antidepressant drug, esp. one effective against psychotic states; *psychic unity*, a supposed similarity of the mental make-up of all mankind.

1890 W. JAMES *Princ. Psychol.* I. ii. 41 Munk..was the first to distinguish in these vivisections between sensorial and *psychic* blindness... Psychic blindness is inability to recognize the *meaning* of the optical impressions, as when we see a page of Chinese print but it suggests nothing to us. **1896** *Alienist & Neurologist* XVII. 520 Hysteria is a constitutional psycho-neuropathy with morbid impulsions, caprices, delusions, hallucinations, and illusions, psychic and sensory. We see it displayed..in men with psychical impotency and in women after the menopause. **1910** *Jrnl. Abnormal Psychol.* V. 68, I have successfully treated by Freud's psychoanalytic method cases of homosexuality, psychic impotence..and many other so-called perversions. **1924** E. & C. PAUL tr. *Wittels's S. Freud* 267 By psychoanalysts the term 'sexual' is used with wide connotations, so that 'libido' becomes almost synonymous with 'psychic energy', with conation and also with what Bergson terms the 'vital impetus'. **1925** J. LAIRD *Our Minds & their Bodies* ii. 32 'Psychic' tumours or false pregnancies have deceived skilled observers. **1931** W. B. GIBSON tr. *Husserl's Ideas* I. ii. 89 Blindness to ideas is a kind of psychic blindness. **1943** *Jrnl. Nerv. & Mental Dis.* XCVIII. 184 Freud's theory of psychic determinism does not ignore human values. **1953** G. DEVEREUX *Psychoanal. & Occult* ii. 38 Due partly to the psychic unity of mankind..and partly to the limitation imposed upon the general direction of thought processes by the ethos of the culture area [etc.]. **1955** *Internat. Jrnl. Psycho-Anal.* XXXVI. 355 Although the concept of psychic determinism is generally accepted without qualification as an aspect of scientific causality, it sometimes appears difficult to reconcile it with the feeling of free will. **1957** N. S. KLINE in *Congr. Rep. 2nd World Congr. Psychiatry* I. 212 Psychic Energisers. We have found that iproniazid (Marsilid) may represent a new principle of drug action since it is capable of increasing psychic energy. **1961** Psychic energizer [see *psychostimulant* sb. and adj. s.v. *PSYCHO-]. **1963** *Listener* 7 Feb. 238/2 Such 'psychic poisons' as lysergic and diethylamide, LSD-25, which produces extreme mental confusion. **1967** J. J. HONIGMAN *Personality in Culture* iv. 97/2 The assumption of psychic unity permits an investigator to apply the same principles of psychology to many people and to use his experience in his own culture (or with other cultures he has studied) as controls. **1968** *New Scientist* 2 May 226/1 The so-called 'psychic poisons', capable of inducing temporary or even permanent insanity. **1970** AGUILERA & MESSICK *Crisis Intervention* i. 2 Psychic determinism is the theoretical foundation of psychotherapy and psychoanalysis. **1974** S. ARIETI *Amer. Handbk. Psychiatry* I. iii. 67/1 Regardless of national boundaries, great rapidity has characterized the use of these new drugs, be these 'tranquilizers'..or 'psychic energizers'. **1974** M. MENDELSON *Psychoanalytic Concepts of Depression* (ed. 2) vii. 254 Unlike the energy of science..psychic energy is directional.

d. *psychic income* (Econ.): the non-monetary or non-material satisfactions that accompany an occupation or economic activity.

1904 F. A. FELLER *Princ. Econ.* xlii. 402 It is well to recall also the distinction between wealth income, money income, and psychic income... The money expression of psychic income can be only approximately attained. **1937** GEMMILL & BLODGETT *Economics* I. iii. 56 Psychic income means the actual enjoyment or gratification which comes to a person through the consumption of commodities and services. **1948** M. H. UMBREIT et al. *Fund. Econ.* xxii. 346 The fact that individuals desire to work in..pleasant occupations has led to the concept of psychic income. **1975** *New Society* 3 July 3/2 Views of metal rooftops have been replaced by grass and flowers or attractive paving, giving office workers an inflation-proof bonus in what economists call psychic income.

3. a. (Earlier and later examples.)

psychic research = *psychical research* s.v. PSYCHICAL *a.* 3; so *psychic researcher*; *psychic surgery*, surgery that is ostensibly performed by psychic or paranormal means; so *psychic surgeon*.

1880 *Spiritualist* XVI. 18/2 (*heading*) Psychic action from a distance. **1836** *Discovery* June 185/1 A curious outbreak of what the African calls *kupagawa na pepo*, i.e., to be 'ridden by demons' has occurred recently in Mombasa..and other East African towns, almost in the form of a psychic epidemic. **1939** 'N. BLAKE' *Smiler with Knife* iii. 54 He'll write up the Yarnold Cross ghost, and that'll bring a horde of sightseers and psychic researchers up to the farm. **1968** S. HYNES *Edwardian Turn of Mind* v. 145 His spectrum of interests—biology, psychic research, and socialism—make him an Edwardian radical in spirit. *Ibid.*, The psychic researchers' arguments against scientific scepticism. **1975** MILNER & SMART *Loom of Creation* iv. 250 The greatest problem I have experienced in describing and substantiating psychic surgery is that previously most authors have reported something akin to conventional surgery in hospitals. **1975** W. & M. UPHOFF *New Psychic Frontiers* iii. 165 (*caption*) [He] witnessed eleven and filmed ten 'psychic surgeons' in the Philippines. **1977** *Time* 12 Dec. 46/2 One part reported on 'psychic surgery', in which Filipino healers supposedly diagnose tumors and other problems, and then use psychic forces—not scalpels—to make incisions and treat them.

4. *Bridge.* Of a bid, bidder, or bidding: deliberately misrepresenting the player's hand so as to deceive the opponents.

1932 D. R. SIMS *Psychic Bidding* ii. 18, I shall attempt to outline a few types of psychic bids. *Ibid.* 22 A clever psychic bidder will now employ the barricade bid of two or even three No Trumps. **1936** E. CULBERTSON *Contract Bridge Complete* I. iii. 55 How do the experts distinguish a bona fide bid from a psychic one? **1952** I. MACLEOD *Bridge* i. 13 In the years 1932–5 two notable teams were pre-eminent in duplicate Bridge in this country. One captained by Harry Ingram..devastated their opponents with their psychic bidding. **1975** *Times* 20 Dec. 10/8 A player has made a psychic opening bid and does not hold a possible trick. **1977** *Washington Post* 7 Sept. E. 9 In the early 1930s, just after the birth of psychic bidding, many players indulged in this mania of fabricating bids.

B. *sb.* **1. b.** The realm of perceptual, mental, or physical phenomena that seem to transcend known physical laws (see PSYCHICAL *a.* 3).

1909 [see *OIL *v.* 1 b]. **1960** R. F. C. HULL tr. *Jung's Nature of Psyche* in *Coll. Wks.* (1969) VIII. 181 It appears the psychic is an emancipation of function from its instinctual form and so from the compulsiveness which ..causes it to harden into a mechanism.

3. *Bridge.* A psychic bid (see sense A. 4 above); *controlled psychic*: (see quots. 1959, 1962).

1932 D. R. SIMS *Psychic Bidding* i. 15 The strategical bids which, under the name of 'psychics', are being extensively misused. **1936** *Punch* 2 Dec. 639/3 Unless

North's last bid was a pure psychic, he should certainly hold the King of Spades himself. **1959** T. Reese *Bridge Player's Dict.* 40 A controlled psychic, as opposed to an ordinary psychic, is one made in accordance with a prearranged system. **1962** *Listener* 8 Nov. 786/1 The British pair in the open room were playing what are known as 'controlled psychics'. That is to say, a player would sometimes open the bidding on very slight values without taking a great risk, for there would be a built-in mechanism to prevent the partnership going too high.

psychical, *a.* Add: **1. a.** (Further examples.) *psychical determinism*, the theory that an individual's mental responses and actions are determined by his previous mental actions or his unconscious mind; *psychical distance*, the mental distance from subjective emotions or involvement supposed necessary for the appreciation of the aesthetic qualities inherent in some kinds of experience (see quot. 1976); *psychical unity* = *psychic unity* s.v. *Psychic *a.* 1 a.

1863 J. F. Collingwood tr. *Waitz's Introd. Anthropol.* I. II. i. 273 If theology feared that an original difference of language..would involve the original unity of the human species..the science of language restores to theology the psychical unity of mankind. **1876** W. James *Coll. Ess. & Rev.* (1920) 29 We have no space to discuss the sources of the English prejudice in favor of psychical determinism. **1897** C. H. Judd tr. *Wundt's Outl. Psychol.* v. 323 The ability to produce purely qualitative effects..which we designate as psychical energy. **1902** D. G. Brinton *Basis of Social Relations* i. 19 When we have such evidence as this for the psychical unity of the human species [etc.]. **1912** E. Bullough in *Brit. Jrnl. Psychol.* V. 87 (*heading*) 'Psychical distance' as a factor in art and aesthetic principle. **1913** E. Jones *Papers on Psycho-Anal.* ii. 21 When the sublimation process is not sufficiently potent to provide an outlet for the accompanying psychical energy, other paths of discharge have to be forged. **1938** R. M. Ogden *Psychol. of Art* vii. 142 The illusion of 'psychical distance' is destroyed when the actors appear in the audience. **1960** J. Strachey *Freud's Compl. Wks.* VI. p. xiv, This is the truth which he [*sc.* Freud] insists upon..: it should be possible in theory to discover the psychical determinants of every smallest detail of the processes of the mind. **1976** Rader & Jessup *Art & Human Values* iii. 54 The phrase 'psychical distance' was employed..to denote 'the marvelling unconcern of the mere spectator' in the moment of aesthetic contemplation. Because the word 'psychical' has a misleading connotation..some recent aestheticians have preferred the term 'aesthetic distance'.

3. *psychical researcher*, one who studies or investigates psychical phenomena.

1892 W. James *Coll. Ess. & Rev.* (1920) 320 The 'psychical researchers', though kept at present somewhat out in the cold, will inevitably conquer the recognition which their labors also deserve. **1912** J. Buchan *Moon Endureth* iv. 135 The Presences might be..spirits.. behaving as psychical researchers think they do. **1931** A. Huxley *Music at Night* 102 There is the scientific Psychical Researcher, whose views on the future life ..seem to be almost indistinguishable from those held by Homer and the author of Ecclesiastes. **1965** *Jrnl. Soc. Psychical Res.* XLIII. 32 Mr Priestley..has..a number of interesting and original suggestions to offer that are well worth the serious consideration of psychical researchers.

psychics. 2. (Examples.)

1942 'M. Innes' *Daffodil Affair* III. i. 80 She represents a rare but fairly well-understood morbid condition—that of one individual split up into several personalities... I should have imagined it to be pretty well off the slate of serious psychical inquiry. Lucy is psychopathology, not psychics. **1977** *Gramophone* June 31/2 In a quite separate field, that of psychics, Percy Wilson's passing will have saddened many friends and associates.

psychism. 3. (Further examples.)

1872 Geo. Eliot *Let.* 4 Mar. (1956) V. 253 Ideas of spirit-intercourse, 'psychism' and so on, have come before me in the painful form of the lowest charlatanerie. **1895** *Folk-Lore* VI. 79 Analysed under the dry light of anthropology, its psychism [*sc.* that of psychical research] is seen to be only the 'other self' of barbaric spiritual philosophy 'writ large'. **1974** *Christian* I. 322 They want to know more about apparently unusual goings-on, and this interest is not far removed from the curiosity about psychism and the occult.

4. (Examples.)

1962 *Times* 4 May 9/6 Psychism is, of course, a function of the brain and..when psychism is disturbed the brain function is affected. **1970** G. Ordish tr. *Chauvin's World of Ants* vii. 171 *Myrmica*..is an ant relatively low on the ladder of ant psychism.

psychist. Add: **c.** A bridge-player who practises psychic bidding.

1952 I. Macleod *Bridge* vii. 95 The stupid psychist.. would perhaps bid Three No Trumps.

psycho (saɪ·ko), *sb.* and *a. colloq.* [Abbrev. of various words beginning with this element.]

A. *sb.* **1.** Psychoanalysis or psychology. Also *attrib.* or as *adj.*

1921 R. Macaulay *Dangerous Ages* v. 102 'Psycho-analysis, I mean.' 'Oh, psycho... Not that insomnia is always a case for psycho, you know.' **1938** N. Marsh *Artists in Crime* x. 148 The psycho people say one shouldn't repress things. **1939** 'J. Bell' *Death at Half-Term* vii. 133 Now don't you let loose any of your high-faluting psycho-stuff on me. **1946** J. Cary *Moonlight* xix. 138 She gave you a guilty complex... My psycho man says that's the worst kind, it's so unreasonable. **1960** *Times* 25 June 12/3 The mind was so important in this work [*sc.* radionics] that it excluded all physical considerations. They were coming down solidly on the psycho side, but not the psychic side.

2. A psychologist.

1925 A. Huxley *Let.* 5 Mar. (1969) 243 The psychos imagine that they have shed some light on art by affirming that the origin of art is an infantile coprophily.

3. A psychopath.

1942 [see *Mental *sb.*]. **1947** *Sat. Rev. Lit.* (U.S.) 18 Jan. 19/3 A large percentage of 'psychos' were exposed to unwholesome mother-influence. **1959** C. MacInnes *Absolute Beginners* 11 Wiz has for all oldies..the same kind of hatred psychos have for Jews or foreigners or coloureds. **1973** R. C. Dennis *Sweat of Fear* vii. 45 He's some kind of psycho. He gets freak vibes—you know, like pictures in the head. **1980** *Daily Tel.* 7 Nov. 15/4 He finally runs down the psycho in a morgue, of all appropriate places, where he is pursuing a girl called Amy.

B. *adj.* **1.** Psychological.

1927 *Variety* 1 June 314 Psycho drama flops... The Compagnie des Jonchets, a private club, was over its head with the psychological drama 'Le Souffle sur la Flamme'. **1976** *Denbighshire Free Press* 8 Dec. 6/2 The programme is completed by the psycho thriller 'Night Caller', AA certificate film.

2. Psychopathic.

1936 R. Chandler *Man who liked Dogs* in *Black Mask* Mar. 19/1 Since when can a cop sign as complaining witness on a psycho case? **1957** J. D. MacDonald *Executioners* ii. 22 Maybe I didn't act worried enough... I think he's psycho. **1958** A. Wilson *Middle Age of Mrs. Eliot* II. 149 Honestly I think she's a bit psycho at times. **1976** R. Barnard *Little Local Murder* ix. 109 That sort of bloke ought to be locked away. They're psycho, that's what they are.

psycho (saɪ·ko), *v. colloq.* [f. *Psychoanalyse *v.* or prec. sb.] *trans.* = *Psych *v.* 1.

1925 [see *Intense *a.* 4 b]. **1925** *Christian World* 4 June 7/2 How many of us spend twenty minutes a day in consciously 'psychoing' ourselves..? **1928** C. Mackenzie *Extraordinary Women* xviii. 343 A friend of mine took me to be psychoed last spring... It's the latest thing since the war. **1937** A. Thirkell *Before Lunch* xi. 293 He has had every inhibition psychoed and is perfectly free. **1946** J. Cary *Moonlight* xix. 138 'It's a complex,' said Kathy. 'We ought to get her psychoed.' **1960** N. Marsh *Fake Scent* ii. 66 You'd better get yourself psychoed, my poor Charles.

psycho-. Add: **psychæsthetic**, var. *psycho-æsthetic* below; **psychasthenia** (earlier and later examples); [ad. F. *psychasthénie* (P. M. F. Janet 1893, in *Rev. gén. des Sci. pures et appliquées* IV. 176)]; **psychasthenic** *a.* (earlier and later examples); also as *sb.*, a person with psychasthenia; **psychoa·ctive** *a.* = *Psychotropic *a.*; hence **psychoacti·vity**; **psycho-æsthe·tics,** the study of the psychological aspects of æsthetic perception; hence **psycho-æsthetic** (also **psychæsthetic**) *a.*; **psy·cho-babble** *colloq.* (orig. *U.S.*), jargon that is much influenced by the concepts and terminology of psychology and is used esp. by laymen in referring to their own personality or relationships; hence **psy·chobabbler,** one who uses such jargon; **psychoce·ntric** *a. Psychol.*, treating the psyche or mind, rather than the body, as the important factor in human behaviour; **psychoche·mical** *a.*, pertaining to the relationship between chemicals and the mind, esp. the way the former can be used to modify the latter; also (of a chemical), psychotropic; also as *sb.*, a psychotropic chemical; **psychoche·mistry,** the chemistry of the mind; **psychocu·ltural** *a.*, relating to the interaction of the culture in which individuals live and their psychological characteristics; **psycho-cu·rative** *a.*, of or pertaining to the healing of mental or psychological disorders; **psy:cho-diagno·sis, -diagno·stics** *Psychol.* [after Ger. (H. Rorschach *Psychodiagnostik* (1921))], the investigation of a subject's personality, esp. by means of Rorschach and other projective tests; hence **psy:chodiagno·stic** *a.*; **psycho-dysle·ptic** [Gr. δύσληπτος hard to take hold of] = *Psychotomimetic *sb.*; **psychoe·ndocrine** *a.*, relating to or involving both the endocrine glands and mood and behaviour; **psy:choendocrino·logy,** the branch of science concerned with the relationship between the secretions of the endocrine glands and a person's mood and behaviour; hence **psy:cho-endocrinolo·gic** *a.*, **-endocrinolo·gically** *adv.*, **-endocrino·logist; psychogeo·graphy,** that branch of psychological speculation or investigation which is concerned with the effects on the psyche of the geographical environment; so **psychogeogra·phic, -ical** *adjs.*; **psycholeptic** *a.*, (*b*) characterized by a sudden fall in psychic tension; (*c*) (of a drug) sedative; **psycholytic** (-li·tik) *a.* [*-lytic], applied to a drug such as LSD which can disturb or disrupt certain emotional reactions that have become fixed in the unconscious or can block normal channels of response; chiefly in *psycholytic therapy*, therapy that combines controlled use of low dosages of such drugs with psychotherapeutic instruction for the patient and subsequent discussion; **psychomime·tic** *a.* and *sb.* = *Psychotomimetic *a.* and *sb.*; **psycho-moti·lity** *Psychol.*, physical movement which reflects or is evidence of mental activity; **psychoneu·ral,** of or pertaining to the relationship or interaction between the mind and the nervous system; **psy:choneuroe·ndocrine, -neu:roe:ndocrinolo·gic, -lo·gical** *adjs.*, of or pertaining to the joint or mutual action of the nervous system, the endocrine system, and behaviour; so **psy:choneu:roendocrino·logy,** the branch of science concerned with this; **psychoneurology** (further example; cf. *Neuropsychology); hence **psy:choneuro-lo·gical** *a.*; **psychoneurosis** (delete and see as main entry below); **psycho-optic** *a.* (examples); so **psycho-o·ptical** *a.*; **psy:cho-pharmaceu·tical** *a.* and *sb.*, (a drug) that is psychotropic; **psy·cho-philosophy,** philosophical reasoning based on subjective criteria, or on subjective psychic criteria; hence **psy·cho-philosopher; psy:chophy:sicotherapeu·tics** *nonce-wd.*, remedial treatment of mind and body; **psycho-poli·tical** *a.*, characterized by the interaction of politics or political events and behaviour; so **psycho-po·litics; psycho-pri·smatism** [cf. Prismatic *a.* 2] (see quot.); **psycho-se·nsory** *a.*, pertaining to the conscious perception of sensory impulses; **psycho-sociological** *a.* (further examples); so **psycho-socio·logist, -socio·logy; psychosomatic** (delete and see as main entry below); **psy·chosphere,** the sphere or realm of consciousness; cf. *Noosphere; **psychosti·mulant** *sb.* and *a.*, (a drug that is) antidepressant; **psy·chosyn-drome,** a syndrome in which the symptoms are psychological; **psycho-sy·nthesis,** the integration of disjoint elements of the psyche or personality by means of psychoanalysis; hence (*nonce-wds.*) **psycho-sy·nthesist,** one who practises or advocates this; **psycho-synthe·tic** *a.*; **psycho-vi·sual** *a.*, pertaining to psychological factors associated with vision, such as the emotive connotations of particular colours, and to the centre in the brain associated with such processes; see also *visuo-psychic* s.v. Visuo- in Dict. and Suppl.

1900 S. B. Collins tr. *M. de Fleury's Medicine & Mind* v. 206 Psychasthenia..seemed to be modified..parallel with the oscillations of the blood pressure. **1926** [see *Extrovert *sb.* (and *a.*)]. **1968** *New Scientist* 5 Sept. 500/1 Rupp suffered from a psychasthenia which led him to ascribe fictional properties to positrons. **1901** C. R. Corson tr. *Janet's Mental State of Hystericals* vi. 520 It is very rare to meet a psychasthenic patient who is, if we may so speak, a pure type of this affection. *Ibid.* 521 Abulia is a common characteristic with hystericals and psychasthenics. **1906** W. James *Let.* 6 May (1920) II. 254 Pierre Janet discussed lately some cases of pathological impulsion or obsession in what he has called the 'psych-asthenic' type of individual. **1977** A. Sheridan tr. *J. Lacan's Écrits* ii. 16 States as diverse as phantasmatic fear, anger, active sorrow, or psychasthenic fatigue. **1961** *Perspectives in Biol. & Med.* IV. 428 Asynchrony [prevails] after application of analeptic and psychoactive drugs. **1967** *New Scientist* 19 Jan. 128/1 Glossy magazines and sombre journals of opinion alike have discovered an intense interest in psychoactive drugs, drugs which affect the way people behave and feel. **1974** M. C. Gerald *Pharmacol.* xviii. 350 These medicines are most often tranquilizers, sedatives, and other psychoactive agents. **1975** *Daily Colonist* (Victoria, B. C.) 19 Oct. 17/2 Advisers..avoided taking any position on the two most commonly used 'psychoactive or mood-altering' drugs—alcohol and tobacco. **1977** *Rolling Stone* 30 June 123/2 (Advt.), Psychoactive mushrooms... Chart, illustrations—tests for chemicals—105 alkaloid mushrooms, 42 psilocybin. **1971** *McGraw-Hill Yearbk. Sci. & Technol.* 357/2 These tribesmen, having discovered that the narcotic constituent of the mushroom is excreted with almost undiminished psychoactivity, incorporated a ritual urine-drinking ceremony. **1973** *Nature* 6 Apr. 367/3 These two amphetamine derivatives, which show profound psychoactivity in man. **1925** W. H. J. Sprott tr. *Kretschmer's Physique & Character* II. xiv. 258 An indefinite number of individual temperamental shades emerge from the psychæsthetic and diathetic proportions. **1943** [see *psychomotility* below]. **1951** *Jrnl. Aesthetics* X. 2 Our discussion will have to go in two directions: (1) What are the specific attributes of the art of the blind? (2) What psycho-aesthetic implications result from it for the world of the normal-sighted? **1973** *Screen* Spring/Summer 65 While there is perhaps no 'eternal and immutable essence' of the cinema as opposed to the theatre.., there is at least a psycho-aesthetic conditioning of each art by the technical constraints which define and constitute them. **1909** *Encycl. Relig. & Ethics* II. 448/2 *Psycho-æsthetics*,..the application of psycho-physiology to the study of æsthetic states... Helmholtz in Germany, and Grant Allen in England, tried to determine the physiological concomitants of certain phenomena of the Beautiful. **1939** *Time & Tide* 8 Apr. 454/1 Your temperament told from your taste in Old Masters. A stimulating essay in psycho-æsthetics. **1976** *National Observer* (U.S.) 8 May 15/1 For the consumer who doesn't understand psycho-babble, trying to sort out the various specialties can be downright mind-boggling: Gestalt, TA (Transactional Analysis), bio-energetics, sex therapy, behavior modification, [etc.]. **1977** R. D. ROSEN (*title*) Psychobabble. **1977** *Proc. R. Soc. Med.* LXX. 806/1 This was yet another American death book, full of psychobabble and journalistic cuttings from every other American death book. **1980** *Times Lit. Suppl.* 16 May 544/3 The book is written in colloquial American spliced with psychobabble, a language in which the highest commendation is to say of someone 'She was a person.' **1977** *N.Y. Times Mag.* 20 Nov. 124/4 The psychobabblers not only outnumber the rest of us, but..they have The Force on their side. **1978** *Guardian Weekly* 22 Jan. 19/1 She mocked the manners and morals and especially the 'mindless prattle' of the psychobabblers among whom she lives [in California]. **1936** J. O. WISDOM in *Proc. Aristotelian Soc.* XXXVI. 62, I shall try to establish my psychocentric analysis of *right.* **1949** *Mind* LVIII. 390 There is the traditional 'psychocentric' conception..: the dualistic conception, which regards the human being as a compound of two distinct but interacting entities, mind and body. **1956** J. B. RHINE in A. Pryce-Jones *New Outl. Mod. Knowl.* 205 There have been psychocentric schools of psychology ..but none of these psychocentric views has ever prevailed widely in academic psychology. **1958** Psychochemical [see *PSYCHOTOMIMETIC *a.*]. **1959** *New Scientist* 20 Aug. 222 The Committee appears to have been particularly impressed by what the US Army's chemists told it about the so-called psychochemical weapons. *Ibid.*, Whatever the intrinsic power of 'psychochemicals' may prove to be, the picture of a bloodless war painted by the Congressional committee is hard to believe. **1965** B. INGLIS *Drugs, Doctors & Disease* iii. 110 Nowhere has the evidence of the power of placebo effect been more striking than in the new market for psycho-chemicals: pep pills and tranquillisers. **1972** G. WATSON (*title*) Nutrition and your mind: the psychochemical response. **1973** 'A. HALL' *Tango Briefing* xiv. 176 Obviously psychochemicals but not related to mescaline or lysergic acid. **1977** *Rolling Stone* 21 Apr. 46/4 The Soviet Union was hard at work in psychochemical research. **1900** *Amer. Jrnl. Psychol.* XI. 600 The writer takes up..passive and then active sadness, morbid joy, their original mechanism, their psychophysiology, psycho-chemistry, [etc.]. **1931** *Chem. News* 23 Jan. 51/1 Colloidal and physiological chemistry have advanced to the extent that we should now be able to envisage a Psychochemistry, or Chemical Psychology. **1951** M. A. STRAUS in *Amer. Sociol. Rev.* June 374 One is led to what Frank has called a 'psychocultural' rather than a purely psychological explanation of the phenomena of bilingual inferiority. **1977** *Canada Jrnl. Linguistics 1976* XXI. 226 The wider implications of language as a psychocultural, evolutionary phenomenon. **1901** A. C. HALPHIDE *Psychic & Psychism* i. 21 There are many schools of Psycho-curative systems, all of which might be classified under the title Mental Medicine. **1953** *Cape Times* 14 Feb. 5/2 The doctors believe that the installation of a pigeon loft at the hospital may have a psycho-curative effect. **1940** *Proc. R. Soc. Med.* XXXIII. 173 (*heading*) Myokinetic psychodiagnosis: a new technique of exploring the conative trends of personality. **1969** J. E. EXNER *Rorschach Systems* i. 5 Rorschach might well be appalled were he to perceive how the technique is utilized in contemporary psychodiagnosis. [**1930** *Amer. Jrnl. Psychiatry* X. 50 The Rorschach 'Psychodiagnostik' test, consisting of ten symmetrical ink-blots.] **1937** *Amer. Jrnl. Orthopsychiatry* VII. 320 With this paper we want to introduce a new concept in the theory and a new tool in the practice of Rorschach's psychodiagnostic ink blot test. **1949** S. ROSENZWEIG *Psychodiagnosis* i. 1 As a psychodiagnostic art clinical psychology derives historically from two chief sources—the psychometric and the psychodynamic. **1932** *Character & Personality* I. 2 The proper aim of a quarterly for psychodiagnostics and allied studies seems to us to be to establish an organic connection among the numerous specialized branches of psychology. **1960** H. J. EYSENCK *Exper. Personality* I. p. ix, Experiments in psychogenetics, psychopharmacology, psychodiagnostics [etc.], ..all..form part of the programme of research. **1970** *Jrnl. Aesthetics* XXIX. 105 (*heading*) The ink blot test, 'psychodiagnostics' and Hermann Rorschach's aesthetic views. **1961** KALINOWSKY & HOCH *Somatic Treatments in Psychiatry* ii. 8 Psychodysleptics or psychotomimetics. This refers to a group of drugs which can produce the so-called 'model psychoses' and which have characteristically hallucinogenic and mildly stimulant properties. **1967** *WHO Chron.* XXI. 465/2 Three classes of psychotropic drugs are particularly dependence-producing: the anxiolytic sedatives, the psychodysleptics (hallucinogens), and the psychostimulants. **1974** *Nature* 27 Sept. 314/1 Some psychodysleptics (mescaline sulphate and LSD), when injected during the photosensitive larval period, suppress diapause induction as if the larvae were subjected to a long 16-h photophase. **1946** *Psychosomatic Med.* VIII. 176 (*heading*) Psychoendocrine relationships in pseudocyesis. **1958** M. REISS *Psychoendocrinol.* i. 13 The psychoendocrine concept is based on the discovery that the activity of the pituitary is related to the function of the hypothalamus. **1977** *Proc. R. Soc. Med.* LXX. 513/2 Psychoendocrine relationships in affective disorders. **1953** M. REISS in *Internat. Rec. Med.* CLXVI. 196 Psychoendocrinology will become in psychiatric research a much more recognized branch than it is at present. **1958** —— *Psychoendocrinol.* i. 20 The responsibility of the psychoendocrinologist in such a case has become very grave indeed. *Ibid.* 27 No doubt people like Tameriane..who had undescended testicles..have seemed brilliant just because they were psychoendocrinologically not completely mature, and therefore more accessible to new impressions and situations. **1961** *Psychosomatic Med.* XXIII. 449/1 (*heading*) Psycho-endocrinologic studies in a male with cyclic changes in sexuality. **1975** S. ARIETI *Amer. Handbk. Psychiatry* IV. 554/2 Psychoendocrinologists have been mainly preoccupied with the basic psychophysiological exploration of the significance of hormonal responses as reflections of intrapsychic processes. *Ibid.* 555/1 By the late 1950s, then, it was generally recognized not only that psychoendocrinology rested on a solid experimental foundation, but that psychological stimuli were, in fact, among the most potent of all natural stimuli to the pituitary-adrenal cortical system. **1953** J. L. MORENO *Who shall Survive?* III. 436 There is also in psychogeography in respect to a certain criterion either a yes or a no, whatever the motivation of this yes or no may be. *Ibid.* 440 The psychogeographic mapping of the community shows..the relationship of local geography to psychological processes. **1958** *Archit. Rev.* CXXIV. 1/1 This microclimatology of the psyche is something to which every town-dweller can testify, and in a city like Paris..it is a more than personal affair—that document of psychogeography, André Breton's *Nuit du Tournesol*, which ought on the face of it to be an entirely private exercise in erotic topography, can be read with understanding, even by those who have never visited Paris. *Ibid.*, It shows 'quartiers d'états d'âme' and 'gradients of psychogeographical drift'—factors not generally taken into account by the average planning authority. **1963** *Listener* 14 Feb. 299/1 The kind of psychogeographic studies made by the Situationists are all very well in communicating a feeling about man/environment relationships. **1974** *Times Lit. Suppl.* 14 June 630/2 The book promises to become a midwife's guide to the birth of a new discipline, which one expects will be inelegantly dubbed 'psychogeography', rather than 'geopsychology'. **1925** E. & C. PAUL tr. *Janet's Psychol. Healing* I. x. 558 Individuals in whom psychological tension is unstable, suffer from sudden relaxations of this tension, succumb to psycholeptic crises. **1940** H. G. BAYNES *Mythol. of Soul* xi. 882 We could then regard the whole drama as a psycholeptic crisis with its characteristic feeling-symptom of the end of the world. **1961** KALINOWSKY & HOCH *Somatic Treatments in Psychiatry* ii. 8 Delay has proposed the following classification of the new drugs based upon their predominant action. (A) Psycholeptics or Sedatives... (C) Psychodysleptics or psychotomimetics. **1971** ZIRKLE & KAISER in A. Burger *Med. Chem.* (ed. 3) II. lv. 1412/1 The antipsychotic agents were originally given such names as tranquilizers.., ataraxics.., psycholeptics, and psychosedatives. **1962** D. D. JACKSON in *Jrnl. Nerv. & Mental Dis.* CXXXV. 436/1 More accurately, perhaps, we should speak of psycholytic drugs given by psychosogenic therapists. **1963** R. A. SANDISON in R. Crocket et al. *Hallucinogenic Drugs* 34 This total experience of the unconscious, brought about by the power of LSD to loosen the psyche, has led to a feeling that the hallucinogenic drugs should be renamed the psycholytic drugs. This name, which is free from the many objections attached to the word 'hallucinogenic' was first suggested and adopted at Göttingen last year. **1964** D. F. DOWNING in M. Gordon *Psychopharm. Agents* I. xiii. 606 In this context they [*sc.* psychotomimetic agents] are frequently known as psycholytic drugs because of their power to loosen the psyche. **1974** ARIETI & BRODY *Amer. Handbk. Psychiatry* (ed. 2) III. 425/1 *Psycholytic therapy*, this technique consists of a series of drug sessions in which small doses of LSD..are given to a number of patients in an outpatient setting. These sessions are associated with individual or group therapy. **1964** M. MCLUHAN *Understanding Media* xxxi. 308 Our children are striving to carry over to the printed page the all-involving sensory mandate of the TV image. With perfect psycho-mimetic skill, they carry out the commands of the TV image. **1967** *WHO Chron.* XXI. 464/2 Psychodysleptics, also called 'hallucinogens', 'psychomimetics', or 'psychodelics', are compounds that produce abnormal mental phenomena, particularly in the cognitive and perceptual spheres. **1969** *Listener* 28 Aug. 295/2 *Grand Hotel, The Age of Innocence, Dr. Finlay's Casebook*..all inextricably jumbled together into a deliriously psychomimetic paradise. **1974** S. ARIETI *Amer. Handbk. Psychiatry* (ed. 2) I. 67/2 Exaggerated expectations about the uncritical use of 'psychomimetics' (mainly LSD 25) in the treatment of mental disorders and especially about the power of some drugs to enlarge the field of consciousness and provide new philosophical and religious insights are unrealistic. **1925** W. J. H. SPROTT tr. *Kretschmer's Physique & Character* ix. 134 The psychomotility of the cycloid is even and adequate to the stimulus, and motor expressions and movements are well rounded, fluid, and natural. **1934** E. B. STRAUSS tr. *Kretschmer's Text-bk. Med. Psychol.* iv. 43 In a mild degree traces of these Parkinsonian features often typify the psychomotility of advanced old age. **1943** H. READ *Educ. through Art* iv. 79 Within the main cycloid and schizoid groups, there are a considerable number of psychaesthetic variants and a considerable degree of psychomotility. **1969** H. E. KING in Zubin & Shagass *Neurobiol. Aspects of Psychopathol.* vi. 99 (*heading*) Psychomotility: a dimension of behavior disorder. **1890** W. JAMES *Princ. Psychol.* II. xx. 164 Thus we should escape the responsibility of explaining, by falling back on the everlasting inscrutability of the psycho-neural nexus. **1923** J. S. HUXLEY *Ess. Biologist* iv. 134 The mind, or shall we say the psycho-neural organization. **1949** [see *HYPNOANALYSIS]. **1969** *Word 1967* XXIII. 469 Nor can we yet identify all of the psychoneural factors which enter into the final stage of speech perception, 'understanding'. **1954** M. REISS in *Jrnl. Mental Sci.* C. 687 Such efforts are unavoidable if progress is to be made in psycho-neuro-endocrinologic problems. *Ibid.* 701 The influence of the various treatments on a psycho-neuro-endocrine cycle. **1971** —— in D. H. Ford *Influence of Hormones on Nervous System* p. xix, Our association was named Psychoneuro-endocrinological because it emphasizes not only the beginning but also the end of the most important pathophysiological vicious circle in the body. **1972** *Science* 9 June 1115/2 A group of scientists..have organized an International Society of Psychoneuroendocrinology. *Ibid.* 1115/3 The relationships of such psychoneuroendocrine studies to the clinical observations on man are dealt with in papers by Abrams. **1978** *Nature* 14 Dec. p. xii. (Advt.), Psychoneuroendocrinology is an attempt to provide the essential interdisciplinary approach to research in human reproduction. **1921** *Edin. Rev.* Jan. 61 In London the Psycho-Neurological Society has been formed..for the study and discussion of problems in psychotherapy. **1928** H. P. WELD *Psychol. as Science* viii. 156 (*heading*) Psychoneurological theories. **1943** *Amer. Jrnl. Psychiatry* C. 181/2 Apart from the therapeutic implications of the transsection of the anterior thalamic radiations, the method has important implications for experimentation in clinical neurology and in psychoneurology. **1885** LANDOIS & STIRLING *Text-bk. Human Physiol.* II. xiii. 921 The psycho-optic centre,..according to Munk, embraces the outer convex part of the occipital lobe of the dog's brain. **1937** *Arch. Neurol. & Psychiatry* XXXVII. 1173 Both kinds of movement belong to the so-called psycho-optic reflexes because, being produced by visual stimuli, they are performed more or less instinctively. **1954** S. DUKE-ELDER *Parsons' Dis. Eye* (ed. 12). xxvii. 462 The involuntary reflexes which depend on vision (fixation, fusional movements, convergence, etc.)—the psycho-optical reflexes—are centred in the visual cortex of the occipital lobe. **1964** *Dis. Nerv. System* XXV. 233/2 The effects of discontinuing psychopharmaceuticals in a large group of long-term schizophrenic patients. **1965** *New Scientist* 18 Mar. 719/1 So far medical researchers have largely had to rely on a patient's behaviour pattern to assess the effects of the so-called psychopharmaceutical drugs—those which can be used nowadays with considerable effect against certain types of nervous disorders. **1969** *Sci. News* 20 Dec. 581 One advantage of doxepin is its apparently low toxicity compared to other psychopharmaceuticals. **1966** *New Statesman* 18 Feb. 243/2 (Advt.), ESP Psycho-philosopher, having evolved new theory concerning influence on environment at a distance and through thought, seeks volunteers to co-operate in test. **1960** *IRE Trans. Electronic Computers* IX. 524/1 The pragmatic philosophy of C. S. Peirce helped save much of philosophy from the sterilizing effect of psychophilosophy. **1922** JOYCE *Ulysses* 659 Heliotherapy, psychophysicotherapeutics, osteopathic surgery. **1921** *Q. Rev.* Oct. 397 The exaggeration..would..have made its dogmatic definition sooner or later inevitable, but Manning's championship of it assisted its appearance at the psycho-political moment. **1934** H. G. WELLS *Exper. Autobiogr.* II. ix. 798 This psycho-political autobiography. **1948** J. TOWSTER *Polit. Power in U.S.S.R.* iv. 57 While the unification of nations is the goal *ne plus ultra*, there are enormous psycho-political obstacles in the way. **1971** K. MILLETT *Sexual Politics* II. iii. 73 The psycho-political tactic here is a pretence that the indolence and luxury of the upper-class woman's role..was the happy lot of all women. **1961** *Guardian* 2 Nov. 8/2 Robert Jungk..wanted to do his thesis on what he called 'psychopolitics', the interaction between mass psychology and mass psychology movements and politics. **1980** *Boston Globe* 3 Feb. B1 Kantor claims that people's current patterns of interaction, or 'psychopolitics', are based on 'critical identity images'. **1934** H. HILER *Notes Technique Painting* 332 *Psycho-prismatism*, the affective psychology of colour. The study of the reactions of human beings or animals to the various colours. **1910** W. A. TURNER *Three Lect. Epilepsy* 25 He has described the psycho-motor, psycho-sensory, psycho-visual, and psycho-auditory centre in close relation to the motor, sensory, visual, and auditory centres. **1947** H. C. ELLIOTT *Textbk. Nervous Syst.* xix. 238/1 Caudal to its upper part [*sc.* that of the sensory cortex] lies..the psychosensory region. **1959** S. DUKE-ELDER *Parsons' Dis. Eye* (ed. 13) iv. 38 The pupils participate in several reflexes, three of which are of clinical importance:.. 3. The psychosensory reflex, whereby a dilatation occurs on psychic and sensory stimuli. **1928** *Amer. Jrnl. Sociol.* Nov. 447 Knowing these [laws of suggestion], we could follow their lead into greater knowledge of phenomena of a psycho-sociological nature. **1970** TOURAINE & PÉCAUT in I. L. Horowitz *Masses in Lat. Amer.* iii. 67 The resulting normative and psychosociological changes [in the social system] are analyzed..as a function of the change in values judged necessary to attain the industrialized state. **1966** *Punch* 9 Mar. 332/3 Those big black career advertisements and their rich esoterica about openings for crystallographers, systems analysts and industrial psycho-sociologists. **1908** *Science* 10 July 54 Psycho-sociology. **1957** R. K. MERTON *Student-Physician* 53 A middle ground which has been described as social psychology (or, by some, psycho-sociology). **1973** *Screen* Spring/Summer 151 Various revelatory and therapeutic methods belonging to modern psycho-sociology. **1913** J. MURRAY *Ocean* x. 228 We may say that within the biosphere a sphere of reason and intelligence has been evolved in man, who attempts to interpret and explain the cosmos; this may be called the psycho-sphere. **1957** P. B. SEARS *Ecology of Man* 10 To these might be added *Mind*—the Psychosphere, studied by psychologists, anthropologists and other social scientists. **1975** O. L. REISER *Cosmic Humanism & World Unity* iii. 97 The Psychosphere may be regarded as a psychic-magnetic environment, an 'auric field', beyond the Van Allen Radiation Belt. **1961** MUSSER & O'NEILL *Mod. Pharmacol. & Therapeutics* (ed. 2) xix. 361 Prior to the development of these newer drugs, called psycho-stimulants or psychic energizers, apathetic and depressed patients were treated with caffeine and the amphetamines. **1963** *Wall St. Jrnl.* 21 Jan. 12/4 The three areas in which the largest number of new agents are being investigated were psycho-stimulants, broad spectrum antibiotics and cholesterol-reducing agents. **1966** J. D. P. GRAHAM *Pharmacol.* iv. 26/2 This drug [*sc.* dexamphetamine sulphate] is given to mentally depressed patients. It may therefore be termed a psychostimulant drug. **1967** [see *psychodysleptic* adj. above]. **1971** T. A. BAN in O. Vinař et al. *Advances in Neuropsychopharmacol.* 212 Conflict tolerance in humans may also increase under the influence of psychostimulants in general. **1973** *Proc. R. Soc. Med.* LXVI. 359/2 Would-be psychiatrists are taught to describe, define and treat disembodied psychosyndromes instead of learning to apply modern investigative science to finding causes. **1976** SMYTHIES & CORBETT *Psychiatry* vii. 113 Non-specific endocrine psychosyndromes occur with apathy, depression and lability of mood. **1919** C. E. LONG in M. K. Bradby *Psycho-Anal.* p. vi, We aim at a reconstruction of life which can only be conceived as a psycho-synthesis. **1924** J. RIVIERE tr. *Freud's Coll. Papers* II. xxxiv. 395 The neurotic human being brings us his mind racked and rent by resistances; whilst we are working at analysis of it and removing the resistances, this mind of his begins to grow together; that great unity which we call his ego fuses into one all the instinctual trends which before had been split off and barred away from it. The psycho-synthesis is thus achieved during analytic treatment without our intervention. **1940** H. G. Wells *Babes in Darkling Wood* 9 The mental break-down of Gemini..bring [*sic*] the methods of a leading psycho-analyst and modern psychosynthesis into the story. **1975** M. & N. Samuels *Seeing with Mind's Eye* iii. 37 Currently, visualization is being used in a number of different psychotherapeutic techniques—including..directed day-dreams, Psychosynthesis, and behaviorist desensitization. **1944** H. G. Wells *'42 to '44* 172 What a psycho-analyst calls the Unconscious, but which, according to the psycho-synthesist, is merely a multitude of reaction systems out of contact with the main directive system. **1940** —— *All Aboard for Ararat* ii. 80 The core of the new world must be (listen to these words!) Atheist, Creative, Psycho-synthetic. **1910** Psycho-visual [see *psycho-sensory* adj. above]. **1969** G. C. Dickinson *Maps & Air Photographs* iv. 63 The conventional colour sequence, which follows spectrum order from violet through shades of blue, green, yellow and orange to red (or more commonly brown), accords well with the psycho-visual properties of colours —blues for submarine areas are 'recessive', reds for hills 'stand out'—but there can be unfortunate suggestive overtones. **1971** *Nature* 19 Mar. 180/1 It is hoped that a laboratory equipped for psychovisual studies will..report on the degree to which descriptions of 'artificial' ball lightning resemble those of the natural phenomenon that are recorded in the scientific literature.

psycho-acou·stic, *a.* [f. Psycho- + Acoustic *a.*] Pertaining to the perception of sound and the production of speech or to the study of these. Also **psycho-acou·stical** *a.*, **-acou·stically** *adv.*

1885 W. Stirling tr. *Landois's Text-bk. Human Physiol.* II. xiii. 922 The psycho-acoustic centre..lies, in the dog,..in the region of the second primary convolution. **1946** *Jrnl. Aeronaut. Sci.* XIII. 255 The Psycho-Acoustic Laboratory, Harvard University. **1953** *Electronic Engin.* XXV. 24/2 Acoustic and psycho-acoustic distortion. These forms of distortion occur through imperfections in the acoustics of studios and listening rooms, the use of mon-aural (single channel) reproducing chains, [etc.]. **1953** *Language* XXIX. 85 Measurement of fidelity has to be made psycho-acoustically in terms of the whole speech signal, not just in terms of its linguistic content. **1958** *New Scientist* 30 Oct. 1165/1 A great deal of psycho-acoustical work has concerned simple sounds, like pure tones, or sharp clicks. **1971** *Computers & Humanities* V. 312 Use of the computer in investigating psycho-acoustical phenomena. **1975** G. J. King *Audio Handbk.* vii. 163 Several psycho-acoustical principles govern the subjective assimilation of quadraphony. **1976** *Gramophone* Jan. 1269/2 Now the physical and psycho-acoustic conditions for correct perception of direction of sound can be expressed by equations. **1977** *New Scientist* 1 Dec. 574/2 Ways and means of psychoacoustically handling the retrieved signals so that they produce a realistic surround of sound.

So **psycho-acou·stics,** the science of the perception of sound and the production of speech; **psy:cho-acousti·cian,** an expert or specialist in psycho-acoustics.

1948 *Mind* LVII. 388 Harvard divided psychology into two Departments—the Department of Social Relations.. and the Department of General Psychology, with three.. laboratories of General Psychology, Physiological Psychology and Psycho-Acoustics. **1958** *New Scientist* 30 Oct. 1165/3 The science of acoustics..has branched out into two fields which are essentially modern in idea and purpose... The first field is ultrasonics... The second field is psycho-acoustics, which is, essentially, the study of hearing, but more especially the whole speech-hearing process. **1963** Ervin & Miller in *Child Psychol.* (*62nd Yearbk. Nat. Soc. Study of Educ.* I) iii. 111 Information on the actual phonetic cues used by the child could be obtained by using artificially constructed vocalic stimuli. Such studies have been conducted by psychoacousticians on adults, but not on children. **1976** *Canad. Jrnl. Linguistics* XXI. I. 2 It would be pointless, e.g., to try to incorporate all of the practically infinite variations of the acoustic wave form into a descriptive system for psycho-acoustics when what is required is an adequate description of those specific properties of the sound pattern which significantly affect the perception of speech. **1977** *Rolling Stone* 30 June 41/2 Next I met David Wessel, a psychoacoustician (one who studies human perception of sound) from Michigan State University.

psychoactive, -activity, -æsthetic(s: see *psycho-.

psychoa·nalyse, *v.* Also with hyphen. [Back-formation from next, after *analysis, analyse.*] *trans.* To subject to or treat by psychoanalysis; = *analyse *v.* 3b. Also *absol.*

1911 *Amer. Jrnl. Psychol.* July 423 It is..hoped that Freud will..psychoanalyze Goethe. **1922** J. Macy in D. H. Lawrence *Sons & Lovers* p. ix, Let whoever cares to try analyze or psychoanalyze. **1924** C. Mackenzie *Heavenly Ladder* xxiii. 288, I could psycho-analyse all Bloomsbury now. They all suffer from an inferiority complex. **1969** *Listener* 14 Aug. 219/2 Professor Baker scrupulously does not diagram, hypothesise or psycho-analyse. **1973** *Amer. N. & Q.* XI. 78/1 To psychoanalyze a dramatic hero is to treat him as a human being.

Hence **psycho-a·nalysed** *ppl.a.*

1928 'R. West' *Strange Necessity* 240 A psycho-analysed person who has made the realization that all persons he dreams of are disguised versions of himself.

psychoana·lysis. Also with hyphen and (*rare*) as **psychanalysis.** [ad. F. *psycho-analyse* (S. Freud 1896, in *Rev. Neurologique* IV. 166): see Psycho- and Analysis.

Freud earlier used *psychische analyse* and *klinisch-psychologische analyse* (*Neurol. Centralbl.* (1894) XIII. 364).]

a. A therapeutic method originated by Freud for treating disorders of the personality or behaviour by bringing into a patient's consciousness his unconscious conflicts and fantasies (which are attributed chiefly to the development of the sexual instinct) through the free association of ideas, analysis and interpretation of dreams and parapraxes, etc., and allowing him to relive them by transference. **b.** A theory of personality and psychical life derived from this, based on concepts of the ego, id, and super-ego, the conscious, pre-conscious, and unconscious levels of the mind, and the repression of the sexual instinct; more widely, a branch of psychology dealing with the unconscious.

[**1898** H. Ellis in *Alienist & Neurologist* XIX. 610 The influence of fear is not denied by Breuer and Freud, but they have found that careful psychic analysis frequently reveals that the shock of a commonplace 'fear' is really rooted in a lesion of the sexual emotions.] **1906** *Jrnl. Abnormal Psychol.* I. 28 Their importance with relation to treatment (by the method of 'psycho-analysis') is made clear. **1913** *Q. Rev.* Jan. 143 'Psycho-analysis' has been strongly advocated by some men in the medical profession... It consists in carefully and systematically resuscitating the patient's past memories, thus making him aware of his buried and unconscious mental processes, when those are brought before his present consciousness. **1924** W. B. Selbie *Psychol. of Relig.* 286 Psycho-analysis is the name given to the process by which the hidden depths of the individual consciousness can be revealed. **1932** *Sun* (Baltimore) 12 Sept. 6/3 Psychanalysis for the majority of informed Marylanders is not..a new kind of gypsy dreambook. **1938** *Internat. Jrnl. Psycho-Anal.* XIX. 1 Everything of importance that we know concerning the play of instinctual forces and the course they follow in the homosexual we have derived from psycho-analysis. **1958** Thorpe & Schmuller *Personality* ix. 215 According to psychoanalysis, all of us are characterized by primitive impulses, but our parents and the culture have required us to develop standards of behavior which lead to the repression of these impulses, forcing them into the unconscious. **1964** A. Anastasi *Fields of Applied Psychol.* xiv. 383 It is apparent that active interpretation by the therapist is a major feature of psychoanalysis. **1964** M. Argyle *Psychol. & Social Probl.* ii. 26 Neither of the two major theoretical approaches in psychology—psychoanalysis or learning theory—can explain the phenomena of childhood socialization satisfactorily. **1966** *Times* 13 Jan. 11/4 Freudian and Jungian psychanalysis.. has had its day. **1974** J. Mitchell *Psychoanal. & Feminism* II. ii. 153 His theories of the nature of sexuality and the evidence of its repression..were developed in a double intellectual context, that of Marxisim and of psychoanalysis. **1975** A. Ryle *Frames & Cages* iii. 19 In psychoanalysis, the therapist will..embark on a relationship with the patient, the understanding and evolution of which is the central process of therapy... It is through this process that unconscious primitive fantasies are replaced by freer and less idiosyncratic apprehension of the self and the world.

psychoa·nalyst. Also with hyphen. [f. prec., after *analysis, analyst.*] One who practises or has training in psychoanalysis.

1911 *Amer. Jrnl. Psychol.* July 434 The business of the psychoanalyst is to provide a means by which the emotion attached to a repressed complex may find expression, by being transformed. **1918** *Jrnl. Educ.* Mar. 153/1 Dr. Pfister devotes a couple of pages to an exposition of the need for the psychoanalyst to be himself 'free from complexes'. **1921** R. Macaulay *Dangerous Ages* v. 88 The psycho-analyst doctor would really want to hear details. **1947** A. Huxley *Let.* 9 Mar. (1969) 567 Marlow is one of those classical cases, so dear to psychoanalysts, with a fixation on his mother. **1977** A. Sheridan tr. *J. Lacan's Écrits* iii. 105 Of all the undertakings that have been proposed in this century, that of the psychoanalyst is perhaps the loftiest.

psy:choanaly·tic, *a.* Also with hyphen and (*rare*) as **psychanalytic.** [f. as prec., after *analysis, analytic,* or ad. G. *psychoanalytisch.*] Of, pertaining to, or employing psychoanalysis.

1906 *Jrnl. Abnormal Psychol.* I. 31 The strict 'cathartic', psycho-analytic method advocated by Freud. **1932** *Sun* (Baltimore) 12 Sept. 6/3 In the twenties the works of Freud, Jung, Jones and others of the psychanalytic schools sold like novels. **1979** *N.Y. Rev. Bks.* 25 Oct. 23/2 *Patricide*..draws on some of the best recent psychoanalytic literature.

So **psy:choanaly·tical** *a.*, in the same sense; **psy:choanaly·tically** *adv.*, by means of, in respect of, or towards psychoanalysis.

[**1857** *Russell's Mag.* Nov. 163/2 [Poe] chose..the psycho-analytical. His heroes are monstrous reflections of his own heart in its despair, not in its peace.] **1908** *Jrnl. Abnormal Psychol.* III. 209 It would have added greatly to the interest of this question if a psycho-analytical investigation had been resorted to. **1919** *N.Y. Tribune* 22 Dec. 10/6 'Psychoanalytically speaking,' he writes, 'I think you were wrong about H. third and the carving knife.' **1927** *Observer* 12 June 12/4 The interesting question of whether medical men may treat a patient psycho-analytically was dealt with in Court the other day. **1931** R. Campbell *Georgiad* i. 13 Nor would he dogmatise his pet perversions With psycho-analytical assertions. **1959** B. Wootton *Social Sci. & Social Path.* iv. 145 Even the psychoanalytically inclined are beginning to allow a rather less rigid, and therefore less dismal attitude. **1962** *Lancet* 22 Dec. 1311/1 He begins his book with an account of Freud's philosophical theories as a background to the later development of psychoanalytical concepts by the neo-Freudians. **1971** *Times* 1 Feb. 20/4 (Advt.), Psycho-analytically Orientated Group counters inhibition, anxiety, depression. **1977** C. Storr *Tales from Psychiatrist's Couch* x. 104 The strict, psycho-analytical view that it is utterly improper for the analyst to have anything to do with the husbands, wives, parents, children.. of his patients.

psychobabble, -er: see *psycho-.

psychobio·graphy. [f. Psycho- + Biography.] **a.** A biography dealing esp. with the psychology of the subject.

1931 *Brit. Jrnl. Psychol.* XXII. 96 The majority of 'psychobiographies' and pseudo-scientific works on the psychology of character. **1969** *Daily Tel.* 20 Mar. 22/2 Frank E. Manuel, the American historian,..in this 'psycho-biography' attempts to analyse aspects of Newton's conduct. **1974** *Publishers Weekly* 13 May 56/2 To understand Mishima's death, Scott-Stokes thinks, one must understand his life. With this useful psycho-biography he would seem to have made his case. **1977** *N.Y. Rev. Bks.* 23 June 23 (Advt.), An iconoclastic psychobiography of Freud's disciple.

b. The art of writing psychobiographies; the interpretation of life histories in psychological terms, or the psychological analysis of a historical person.

1965 *Hist. & Theory* IV. 357 This is still psychobiography, but the psychopathological model has given way to a model of man in history. **1975** *Times Lit. Suppl.* 24 Jan. 90/2 The problem..is how to read the personality into the action, and it is the claim of psychobiography that this can not only be done but that it can be done systematically. The classic exercise in psychobiography is Erik Erikson's *Young Man Luther.*

Hence **psychobio·grapher,** a writer of psychobiography; **psy:chobiogra·phic, -ical** *adjs.*; **psy:chobiogra·phically** *adv.*

1972 *N.Y. Times Bk. Rev.* 10 Dec. 36 It [*sc.* a book] makes no large historiographical, mythological or psychobiographical assumptions. **1975** *Times Lit. Suppl.* 24 Jan. 90/2 A psychobiographer would naturally reply that this is to take too literal and simplistic a view of the information that is contained in the sources. **1977** *Oxf. Lit. Rev.* II. III. 8/1 This touches on processes which are not consonant either with the communal norms of cultural expectations or with the detective work of psychobiographers. **1977** *N.Y. Rev. Bks.* 15 Sept. 40/4 He is a psychobiographical critic.., interested in the poem not as artifact but as evidence. **1978** *Dædalus* Spring 229 It is ..contrary to the psychobiographic drive of most of the younger scientists. **1979** *N.Y. Times* 15 July II. 19 Leopold cuts a rather poor figure, psychobiographically, emerging as the standard narcissistic parent who sees his child only as an extension of his own ego.

psychobio·logy. Also with hyphen. [f. Psycho- + Biology.] The study of the biological basis of behaviour or mental phenomena; the interaction of mental and biological factors in an organism.

1902 *Encycl. Brit.* XXXII. 65/2 This connection of vegetal and animal functions remains one of the obscurest in all psycho-biology. **1923** A. Meyer in E. Winters *Coll. Papers* (1952) IV. 244 In connection with psychiatric work, but from an angle quite different from Freudism, there had developed during the last twenty-five years a less spectacular objective psychobiology. **1946** [see *sociobiology]. **1966** *New Scientist* 24 Feb. 464/3 Dr Allan Jacobson..reported that, by taking extracts from the brains of rats that had been taught to perform certain tasks, and injecting them into untrained rats, the latter seemed to acquire a degree of memory for these tasks... New experiments, however, undertaken by five workers from the departments of psychobiology, and of molecular and cell biology, University of California, Irvine, appear to cast considerable doubts on the validity of Dr Jacobson's conclusions. **1975** *Sci. Amer. Dec.* 7/2 (Advt.), *A Primer of Psychobiology* is a brief, informative introduction to what is known about the structure and function of the nervous system and how these relate to behavior.

So **psy:chobiolo·gic, -lo·gical** *adjs.*, of or pertaining to psychobiology; both psychological and biological; **psy:chobiolo·gically** *adv.*, in a psychobiological manner; in relation to psychobiology; **psychobio·logist,** an expert or specialist in psychobiology.

1901 *Amer. Jrnl. Psychol.* XII. 206 The experiments must conform to the psycho-biological character of an animal if sane results are to be obtained. **1934, 1935** [see *field *sb.* 17d]. **1935** Adams & Zener tr. *Lewin's Dynamic Theory of Personality* iii. 79 The environment is..to be defined not physically but *psychobiologically*, that is, according to its quasi-physical, quasi-social, and quasi-mental structure. **1941** *Amer. Speech* XVI. 216 All human behavior is a social psychobiological continuum in which there is no real dichotomy. **1946** *Nature* 24 Aug. 252/2 This is unfortunate at a time when a lot of young men are coming out of the medical services with the idea that there is something in psychosomatic medicine... It is high time we began to try to find out what this is instead of mouthing big phrases such as 'psychobiologic unit'. **1961** Webster, Psychobiologist. **1971** *Amer. Jrnl. Psychiatry* CXXVIII. 706/1 The psychobiologic changes occurring during the [menstrual] cycle do not appear to produce a specific behavioral effect since the form and severity of the symptomatology differ among the various studies. **1973** *Sci. Amer.* Sept. 25/1 We strike a balance..in graduate medical education between the preparation of technologically based specialists and psychobiologically trained generalists. **1977** *Proc. R. Soc. Med.* LXX. 690/1 The underlying pathology of anorexia nervosa may comprise one extreme of the psychobiological nutritional disturbances possibly common to many cases of 'periodic oedema'. **1977** D. M. RUMBAUGH et al. in *Language Learning by Chimpanzee* iv. 89 Yerkes was a very insightful, pioneering psychobiologist. **1979** *Time* 2 Apr. 47/2 People with titles like biochemist, psychobiologist, neurophysiologist and psychopharmacologist are..replacing traditional psychiatrists as chairmen of hospital psychiatry departments.

psychocentric, -chemical, -chemistry, -cultural, -curative: see *PSYCHO-.

psychodelic, var. *PSYCHEDELIC *a.* and *sb.*
psychodiagnosis, -diagnostic(s: see *PSYCHO-.

psy·chodrama. Also with hyphen. [f. PSYCHO- + DRAMA.] **1.** A form of psychotherapy in which a patient acts or performs extempore with or in front of fellow patients and therapists in a way that dramatizes the patient's problems or difficulties; an extempore psychotherapeutic play of this kind. Also *fig.*

1937 J. L. MORENO in *Sociometry* I. 9 The psychodrama is human society in miniature, the simplest possible setup for a methodical study of its psychological structure. **1952** W. J. H. SPROTT *Social Psychol.* xi. 241 The meetings of the various committees..became in effect..psychodramas in which the emotional undercurrents came to the surface and were duly interpreted. **1965** *New Statesman* 9 July 38/1 Conflicts came to a head last February at the Mapai convention, a psychodrama in which BG's [*sc.* Ben Gurion's] ex-colleagues acted out years of resentment against the power and personality of the old leader. **1968** *Daily Tel.* (Colour Suppl.) 20 Dec. 15 Its methods centre around group therapy, psychodrama (Stanislavsky for tired businessmen), massage and Oriental philosophy. **1977** *Time Out* 28 Jan.–3 Feb. 59/1 (Advt.), Community. A University for the Person... Using encounter, gestalt, bioenergetics, reichian massage, re-enactment psychodrama, transactional analysis, [etc.]. **1978** *Listener* 19 Oct. 500/1 Another therapy which believes the answer may lie in obtaining access to buried pains, repressed feelings and hidden desires is the treatment known as 'psychodrama'.

2. A play or film in which psychological elements are the main interest.

[**1927**: see *PSYCHO *a.* 1.] **1963** *Movie* Apr. 22/2 A kind of psycho-drama about racial relationships. **1975** C. JAMES *Fate of Felicity Fark* IX. 87 *Flick's Wedding*..was a waking dream, a psychodrama. **1977** *Time* 5 Sept. 26/2 Now comes *Equus*, Sidney Lumet's film of the long-running Broadway psychodrama.

psychodrama·tic, *a.* [f. prec., after *drama, dramatic.*] **1.** Of or by means of therapeutic psychodrama.

1937 J. L. MORENO in *Sociometry* I. 25 When we apply psychodramatic principles to art, especially in the theatre, one notes that the presentation of the role is often interrupted by foreign elements, foreign to the role, betraying the private personality of the actor. **1977** A. SHERIDAN tr. *J. Lacan's Écrits* ii. 9 Psychodramatic treatment..seeks its efficacity in the abreaction that it tries to exhaust on the level of play.

2. Pertaining to or of the nature of a psychodrama (sense *2).

1943 *Sewanee Rev.* LI. 309 It could just as easily be accidental in the psychodramatic reverie of an insane and uneducated son grieving for his dead mother. **1946** *N.Y. Times* 15 Oct. 29/1 'Frontiers of the Mind', a collection of six dramatized case histories, will be presented..under the auspices of the Denes Psychodramatic Theatre.

So **psychodrama·tics,** (*a*) the use of psychodrama as therapy; (*b*) psychological dramatics; **psychodra·matist,** (*a*) one who directs or takes part in therapeutic psychodrama; (*b*) one who writes psychodramas (sense *2).

1937 J. L. MORENO in *Sociometry* I. 10 But in interpersonal therapy, especially in one of its forms which can be called psychodramatics, the task is enormously more complicated. **1953** J. L. MORENO *Who shall Survive?* p. xvi, Therefore I became a psychodramatist and roleplayer. **1957** V. NABOKOV *Pnin* ii. 45 He went on with his Slavic studies, she with her psychodramatics. **1973** *Nation Rev.* (Melbourne) 31 Aug. 1455/2 These uncertainties..are the ruination of most politico-philosophical series produced by the modern school of psychodramatists. **1979** C. E. SCHORSKE *Fin-de-Siècle Vienna* vii. 345 The harsh psycho-dramatics of [the play] *Murderer, Hope of Women* helped the painter [*sc.* Kokoschka] to liberate himself.

psychodynamics. Add: (The study of) the activity of and interrelation between the various parts of an individual's personality or psyche. (Further examples.)

1950 *Psychosomatic Med.* XII. 113/1 Prior to the emergence of psychodynamics, interest was focused in the main on constitutional and hereditary factors in their relationship to organic disease. **1957** 'T. STURGEON' *Thunder & Roses* 175 Psychodynamics has come a long way, but it hasn't begun to alter the fact that human beings are the most feral, vicious..and self-destructive creatures God ever made. **1960** H. J. EYSENCK *Exper. in Personality* II. 105 (*heading*) Experiments in psychodynamics. The excitation-inhibition balance in neurotics and in normals. **1963** J. A. JOHNSON *Group Therapy* v. 164 The therapist will have formed an opinion of the psychodynamics of each member from previous meetings and should now use this information as a helpful guide in anticipating as well as evaluating behavior associated with separation. **1975** ROSENBAUM & BEEBE *Psychiatric Treatm.* xii. 228/1 Psychodynamics broadly refers to an understanding of the interactions of conscious, unconscious, and reality.

Hence also **psychodyna·mically** *adv.*

1961 in WEBSTER. **1972** L. J. SAUL (*title*) Psychodynamically based psychotherapy. **1973** *Pediatric Clinics N. Amer.* XX. 743 As a reflection of our Freudian legacy in medicine, the traditional approach to parents in the pediatric setting has been psychodynamically oriented.

psychodysleptic, -endocrine, -endocrinology, etc.: see *PSYCHO-.

psychogalva·nic, *a.* [ad. G. *psycho-galvanisch(er reflex)* (O. Veraguth 1907, in *Monatsschr. f. Psychiatrie und Neurol.* XXI. 387): see PSYCHO- and GALVANIC *a.*] Involving changes in the electrical conductivity of the skin associated with emotional changes; chiefly in *psychogalvanic reflex* or *response* (abbrev. PGR s.v. *P II) = **galvanic skin response.*

1907 *Brain* XXX. 191 It is of interest to ascertain whether the psycho-galvanic reflex runs a parallel course with the complex indices. **1917** C. R. PAYNE tr. *Pfister's Psycho-Anal. Method* 336 Secretion of tears, sighing, psychogalvanic phenomena, changes in the pulse, etc. **1936** *Discovery* July 201 Some remarkable results have been obtained from 'psycho-galvanic' experiments. **1949** WIMSATT & BEARDSLEY in D. Lodge *20th Cent. Lit. Crit.* (1972) 352 The affective critic is today actually able..to measure the 'psychogalvanic reflex' of persons subjected to a given moving picture. **1960** KOESTLER *Lotus & Robot* I. iii. 119 The psycho-galvanic reflex (used in lie detectors) reflects changes in the electrical properties of the body surface in response to emotional stimuli. **1973** *Times* 17 Feb. 14/5 Orme-Johnstone, in a study of the psychogalvanic response..showed that meditators had fewer responses than control subjects.

Hence **psy:chogalvano·meter,** a galvanometer used to measure the psychogalvanic response; **psy:chogalvanome·tric** *a.*

1935 H. F. DUNBAR *Emotions & Bodily Changes* iii. 87 The usefulness of the psychogalvanometer for the measurement of emotions or for research in the field of psychosomatic relationships. *Ibid.* 592 (Index), Psychogalvanometric apparatus. **1936** K. DUNLAP *Elements o Psychol.* iv. 183 For the simplest psychogalvanometric use, a d'Arsonval galvanometer is connected directly to two electrodes. **1956** *Electronic Engin.* XXVIII. 36 The earliest psycho-galvanometer consisted of a Wheatstone bridge connected to the palms of the subject's hands by means of metal electrodes. **1959** *Listener* 17 Sept. 443/1 A horrid array of forceps, scalpels, stethoscopes, electrocardiographs, and psychogalvanometers.

psychogenesis. Add: **2. b.** The psychical origin or cause to which mental illness or behavioural disturbance may be attributed.

1920 S. FREUD in *Internat. Jrnl. Psycho-Anal.* I. 125 (*heading*) The psychogenesis of a case of female homosexuality. **1939** C. G. JUNG in *Jrnl. Mental Sci.* LXXXV. 1002 Psychogenesis of schizophrenia..in the first place means the question: Can the primary symptom..be considered as an effect of the psychological conflicts and other disorders of an emotional nature or not? **1972** O. L. ZANGWILL in Cox & Dyson *20th-Cent. Mind* II. vii. 188 There was also greater tolerance for the deviants and eclectics, provided that they subscribed to the general idea of psychogenesis—i.e. the belief that neurosis has a psychological rather than a physical cause. **1979** *N.Y Rev. Bks.* 25 Oct. 25/1 Schorske's seeming demolition of Freud's Oedipal concept may in fact provide clues..for liberating Freud's heroic Complex from its imprisonment in the depths of individual psychogenesis.

Hence **psychogene·tic** *a.* = *PSYCHOGENIC *a.*

1896 *Amer. Naturalist* XXX. 443 There is a great series of adaptations secured by conscious agency, which we may throw together as 'psycho-genetic'. **1904** *Jrnl. Philos., Psychol. & Sci. Methods* I. 328 Hume..had quite unwittingly furnished what..should have been regarded as a logical deduction and justification—rather than the mere psychogenetic description, which it purported to be —of the realistic belief. **1915** M. PRINCE *Psychol. o Kaiser* viii. 67 So long as these so-called psycho-genetic thoughts are there unmodified..he [*sc.* the Kaiser] could not get rid of his fixed fear of the democracy if he would. **1975** *Times Lit. Suppl.* 24 Oct. 1253/4 If he really did regard [Queen] Anne's physical disorders as psychogenetic, eighteenth-century medicine was of precious little use to her case anyway.

psychogene·tics. [f. PSYCHO- + *GENETICS.] **1.** The branch of psychology which is concerned with the effects of breeding or inheritance on behaviour.

1951 C. S. HALL in S. S. Stevens *Handbk. Exper. Psychol.* ix. 304/1 This encouraging trend will ultimately give status and stature to an interdisciplinary science of psychogenetics. The psychogeneticist of the future will presumably be trained in the methods and techniques of both genetics and psychology. **1954** *Brit. Jrnl. Psychol.* XLV. 309 This book should be studied..by the psychogeneticists. **1960** P. L. BROADHURST in H. J. Eysenck *Exper. in Personality* I. i. 5 The use of different strains, particularly of rats and mice, has long been a favourite method of psychogenetics. Bagg was a pioneer in the application of 'the methods of genetics to the study of conduct'. **1975** *Nature* 30 Oct. 832/2 The perspectives of ethology, physiological psychology, psychogenetics, social psychology..are all represented to some degree.

2. = PSYCHOGENESIS 1.

1964 *Eng. Stud.* XLV. Suppl. 104 Locke's empiricism takes its place in the field of psychogenetics; he asks the question: where does human understanding come from?

psychogenic (-dʒe·nik), *a.* [f. PSYCHO- + *-GENIC.] Having a mental or psychological origin or cause.

1902 BALDWIN *Dict. Philos. & Psychol.* II. 382/2 The paralyses and anaesthesias of hysteria,..the pains and fears of neurasthenia, the ameliorations following appeals to faith or prayer are instances of psychogenic action. **1926** J. I. SUTTIE tr. *Ferenczi's Further Contrib. Theory & Technique Psycho-Anal.* viii. 107 A psychogenic disturbance of the voice. **1964** M. CRITCHLEY *Developmental Dyslexia* xii. 71 Only too often the backwardness in reading is deemed either an environmental, or a psychogenic problem, or both. **1973** *Sci. Amer.* Sept. 124/1 Whatever the cause of a psychotic disorder, be it biological or psychogenic, the mental content of the psychosis must reflect the input to the mind and how that input is refracted by the mind's history and functional state.

Hence **psychoge·nically** *adv.*

1933 *Jrnl. Nerv. & Mental Dis.* LXXVII. 587 (*heading*) 'Colitis'—psychogenically motivated. **1973** *Lancet* 9 June 1296/1 The psychogenically impotent subject can in fact learn to induce erection at will.

psychogeography, -geographic(al: see *PSYCHO-.

psy:chogeria·tric, *a.* and *sb.* Also with hyphen. [f. PSYCHO- + *GERIATRIC *a.*] **A.** *adj.* Of or pertaining to mental illness or disturbance in the old. Of a person: old and mentally ill or disturbed.

1961 *Guardian* 19 June 8/4 The number of psychogeriatric patients is certainly rising with increased longevity. **1965** *Lancet* 18 Sept. 583/2 A psycho-geriatric unit was established at Severalls Hospital in 1961. **1971** *Brit. Med. Jrnl.* 23 Oct. 235/1 Among psychogeriatric patients those most likely to respond appear to be those whose initial degree of memory and intellectual impairment was not of an extreme degree. **1973** *Radio Times* 1 Feb. 41/1 A 69-year-old widow, who lives with her unmarried son and regularly attends a local authority psychogeriatric Day Centre. **1975** *Daily Tel.* 1 Dec. 13/1 There was an acute shortage of psychogeriatric beds in hospitals. **1977** *Lancet* 1 Jan. 27/1 Many doctors and social workers cannot formulate a 'psychogeriatric' problem in any other terms but as the need to get it instantly off their hands.

B. *sb.* An old person who is mentally ill or disturbed.

1971 *Observer* 12 Dec. 8/4 The psycho-geriatrics form only one category of the..mentally ill. **1973** *Listener* 19 Apr. 507/1 They're all referred by the GP... They're all psychogeriatrics.

Hence **psy:chogeria·trics,** the branch of medicine concerned with mental illness and disturbance in old people.

1967 *Brit. Jrnl. Psychiatry* CXIII. 175/1 The subspeciality of geriatric psychiatry is coming to be known as 'psycho-geriatrics', an abbreviation which is not a very happy one, but which seems to be becoming generally accepted. **1972** *Lancet* 8 July 73/2 The working party are not convinced..that there is any need for the recognition of a specialty of psychogeriatrics.

psychogogue, var. PSYCHAGOGUE in Dict. and Suppl.

psychogram. Add: **2.** *Psychol.* A summary or diagram of someone's personality, esp. one based on his psychological history, responses to tests, etc. [ad. G. *psychogramm* (W. Stern *Differentielle Psychol.* (1911) III. xxii. 327).]

1918 J. WARD *Psychol. Princ.* xviii. 433 It will be possible to construct what has been called a psychogram of the concrete individual. **1924** *Jrnl. Nerv. & Mental Dis.* LX. 227 Neither was it possible to mention so much of the history of the disease as would have been necessary to prove..the correctness of the psychogram. **1935** H. READ in *Social Credit Pamphleteer* XII. 13 The æsthetic criterion is overcome by the force of the creative invention; the picture becomes a 'psychogram'. **1948** L. SPITZER *Linguistics & Lit. Hist.* 15 Linguistic deviations, of which the philologist may take stock in order to build up his 'psychogram' of the individual artist.

psychograph. Substitute for def.: A photographic image attributed to a supernatural or spiritualistic cause. (Further examples.)

1920 *London Mag.* July 443/1 Most puzzling of all forms of super-normal pictures is the psychograph—so-called because it is assumed to be psychic in its origin and production. **1939** H. PRICE *Fifty Yrs. Psychical Res.* i. 35 If a message in writing or a drawing spontaneously appears on a photographic plate, with or without it being exposed in the camera it is known as a scotograph or a psychograph. **1973** D. A. SPENCER *Focal Dict. Photogr. Technologies* 496 All available evidence suggests that these psychographs were fakes or the result of a combination of chemical fog and wishful thinking.

2. = *PSYCHOGRAM 2.

1909 *Q. Rev.* Oct. 500 This is no caricature, but almost a psychograph of the spirit which permeates many if not most of the descriptive reports of cricket matches in popular sporting papers. **1921** *Education* XLI. 513 A character psychograph of the individual is obtained. **1932** C. LANDIS in K. S. Lashley *Stud. in Dynamics of Behav.* 299 In order to visualize more clearly the results of the tests, three psychographs were drawn to represent the performance of each subject.

3. = *PSYCHOBIOGRAPHY a.

1932 *Sunday Times* 6 Mar. 8/2 It was with some anxiety I saw Dame Una Pope-Hennessy was committed to writing a psychograph of Walter Scott. **1961** *Times Lit. Suppl.* 29 Sept. 637/2 Professor Edward Wagenknecht has been driven to compose a 'psychograph', in which he competently balances opinion against opinion in the hope of discovering what Hawthorne was really like. **1967** *Amer. N. & Q.* Sept. 14/2 Forrest, first of the American tragic actors in this assemblage of 'psychographs'. **1974** *Times Lit. Suppl.* 11 Oct. 1130/3 Dickens was the principal exemplar, and Wilson's penetrating psychograph, 'The Two Scrooges', coincided with George Orwell's re-valuation in focusing upon a great novelist whose very popularity had caused him to be critically neglected.

psychographer. Add: **2.** = *PSYCHOBIOGRAPHER.

1912 G. BRADFORD *Lee the American* 269 The prince of all psychographers is incontestably Sainte-Beuve. **1930** *London Mercury* Feb. 378 He does not attempt a new 'life', but only a new character-study from the point of view of the 'psychographer'.

psychography. Add: **1.** Also, = *PSYCHOBIOGRAPHY. (Further example.)

1929 G. BRADFORD in E. C. Wagenknecht *Man C. Dickens* p. xi, Psychography discards chronology, does not concern itself in any way with the sequence of external fact, except in so far as such is absolutely necessary to make clear the background. *Ibid.* i. 13 Before proceeding definitely to the psychography of Dickens, it is interesting and amusing to speculate on just what his own attitude toward this sort of inquiry would be.

3. *Psychol.* The making of a psychogram (sense *2); the systematic experimental examination of an individual's personality. [ad. G. *psychographie* (W. Stern *Differentielle Psychol.* (1911) III. xxii. 327).]

1921 *Education* XLI. 510 Psychography may be defined as the science of making graphic records of mental traits. **1927** A. A. ROBACK *Psychol. of Character* xxiii. 426 Psychography..records a person's *total* reactions (moral, temperamental, physical and intellectual) under all sorts of conditions. **1938** G. W. ALLPORT *Personality* xv. 404 Psychography has a striking advantage to offset its limitations. It is a method particularly well suited to the *comparative* study of personality, which..demands the use of common traits.

psycho-histo·rical, *a.* Also without hyphen. [f. PSYCHO- + HISTORICAL *a.* (*sb.*).] **1.** (In Dict. s.v. PSYCHO-.)

2. Of or pertaining to the psychological analysis or interpretation of historical events and characters. Also **psycho-histo·ric** *a.*, in the same sense.

1945 I. ASIMOV in *Astounding Sci. Fiction* Apr. 10/1 It would be a psycho-historic experiment of my own. *Ibid.* 30/2, I know quite a detailed version of Hari Seldon's psycho-historical claptrap. **1964** E. ERIKSON *Insight & Responsibility* v. 206 What we may call psycho-historical actuality, that is, the sum of historical facts and forces which are of immediate relevance to the..anticipations and..apprehensions in the individuals involved. **1970** R. J. LIFTON *Hist. & Human Survival* 3 This psycho-historical approach..stems from a general uneasiness among practitioners of both psychology and history abou the capacity of their traditional methods to describe and explain man during the latter part of the twentieth century.

Hence **psycho-histo·rically** *adv.*

1957 W. ABELL *Collective Dream in Art* 5 Psycho-historically considered, art is one of the cultural symbols into which society projects existent states of underlying tension. **1968** *Partisan Rev.* 27 The principle of 'death and rebirth' is as valid psychohistorically as it is mythologically.

psycho-hi·story. Also without hyphen. [f. PSYCHO- + HISTORY *sb.*] **a.** The analysis and interpretation of historical events with the aid of psychological theory; also = *PSYCHOBIOGRAPHY b.

1934 *Reunion* I. 34 Judged by this profound philosophical test, so many of the glibly clear solutions of psycho-history are unsatisfactory. **1942** I. ASIMOV in *Astounding Sci. Fiction* June 30/2 The terms I use are at best mere approximations, but none of you are qualified to understand the true symbology of Psycho-History. **1957** W. ABELL *Collective Dream in Art* 7 The energies involved in such conflicts are neither exclusively material nor exclusively psychological... The further we penetrate into the insights of psycho-history, the more likely we are to discover the means of mastering its disruptive forces. **1972** *Sat. Rev.* (U.S.) 25 Mar. 98/2 The roots of psycho-history may go back to Sigmund Freud's *Leonardo da Vinci: A Study in Psychosexuality*, published in Vienna in 1916. **1976** *Times Lit. Suppl.* 30 Jan. 117/1 Attempts have been made to explain Hitler's personality and ideology, in part at any rate, in terms of his childhood experiences. These works of psychohistory vary in their perceptiveness.

b. A treatise on or study in psycho-history; a psychobiography.

1972 *Sat. Rev.* (U.S.) 25 Mar. 98/3 Another psycho-history to be published..next fall is a study of Hitler by Dr. Walter Langer. **1976** *New Yorker* 17 May 60/1 Erik Erikson, in 'Gandhi's Truth', a biographical exploration that he calls a 'psycho-history', attaches considerable importance to their relationship.

So **psycho-histo·rian**, an expert in or writer of psycho-history.

1934 *Reunion* I. July 34 The psycho-historians have created a new and uneasy fashion; and while we can welcome an *exposé* of some of the lies of history such as Mr. Belloc is making, there are other much-quoted verdicts of ecclesiastical historians which are more epigrammatic than true. **1949** *Astounding Sci. Fiction* Nov. 21/1 It is enough for a Psychohistorian..to know his Biostatistics and his Neurochemical Electromathematics. **1970** *Daily Tel.* 23 Feb. 9/6 A trained psycho-historian..who had witnessed the Franco-Prussian War of 1870, would have realised that the probability of a World War had been raised to higher than 70 per cent. **1975** L. DE MAUSE *Bibliogr. of Psychohist.* p. viii, What the new psycho-historians are creating is a radical empiricism.

psychoid (səi·koid), *sb.* and *a.* [f. PSYCH(E or Gr. ψυχή + -OID.] **A.** *sb.* A name variously given to vital forces that appear to direct the functions and reflex actions of the living body.

1908 H. DRIESCH *Sci. & Philos. of Organism* III. III. iii. 82, I therefore propose the very neutral name of 'Psychoid' for the elemental agent discovered in action. 'Psychoid'—that is, a something which though not a 'psyche' can only be described in terms analogous to those of psychology. **1930** E. BLEULER in *Psychiatric Q.* IV. 43 Bodily functions, too, are integrated to a high degree... Hence we have good grounds for bringing the bodily functions, too, under *one* conception. This summary, the body soul, I have called the psychoid... We cannot do otherwise than regard the psyche as a specialization of the psychoid of the organism. **1931** A. WOLF in W. Rose *Outl. Mod. Knowl.* 575 Just as the development of an animal is directed by an entelechy, so its behaviour is directed by an analogous psychoid, or an inborn intelligent urge to action. **1935** H. F. DUNBAR *Emotions & Bodily Change* i. 47 Let us therefore call the body-soul the psychoid. Now the relationship of psyche to soma becomes clear.

B. *adj.* Pertaining to these forces (see also quot. 1960).

1930 *Psychiatric Q.* IV. 43 With human beings we have a number of reactions which are half psychoid and half psychic... When we scratch ourselves..how much of this is reflex action, and how much conscious action? **1934** E. B. STRAUSS tr. *Kretschmer's Text-bk. Med. Psychol.* iv. 39 The discrete components of an intended act are associated with a minimal degree of conscious participation or are even unconscious; i.e. they are predominantly psychoid. **1944** J. S. HUXLEY *On Living in Revolution* iv. 50 All the activities of the world-stuff are accompanied by mental as well as material happenings; in most cases, however, the mental happenings are at such a low level of intensity that we cannot detect them; we may perhaps call them 'psychoid' happenings, to emphasize their difference in intensity and quality from our own psychical or mental activities. **1960** R. F. C. HULL tr. *Jung's Structure & Dynamics of Psyche* in *Coll. Wks.* VIII. iii. 177 If I make use of the term 'psychoid' I do so with three reservations: firstly, I use it as an adjective..; secondly no psychic quality in the proper sense of the word is implied, but only a 'quasi-psychic' one such as the reflex-processes possess; and thirdly, it is meant to distinguish a category of events from merely vitalistic phenomena.. and from specifically psychic processes.

psychokine·sis. Also with hyphen. [f. PSYCHO- + *KINESIS.] **1.** A psychic power by which some people are held to be able to move objects by other than physical means. Cf. *telekinesis* s.v. TELE-. Abbrev. PK., Pk. s.v. P II.

1914 H. HOLT *On Cosmic Relations* (1915) I. xiv. 216 Now assuming Telekinesis to be established, perhaps we are as nearly ready to consider what I shall call Psychokinesis as people were a generation ago to consider Telekinesis. **1943** *Jrnl. Parapsychol.* VII. 22 Psychokinesis seems better for a general term to cover both effects than telekinesis, which leaves out the psychical and emphasizes distance. **1952** *Sci. News* XXIII. 53 In particular the proponents of telepathy, clairvoyance, psychokinesis and the like have reached the conclusion that these phenomena are not affected by distance or orientation. **1957** *Times Lit. Suppl.* 13 Dec. 760/3 Mr. Rose seeks to establish the power of alleged rain-makers by testing their ability to will (by 'psychokinesis') the fall of a die. **1973** *Times* 1 Dec. 16/4 The other group of tests dealt with.. psychokinesis, and included Mr Geller's apparent ability to bend spoons, nails and other metal objects.

2. Activity or development within the psyche or spirit. *rare.*

1920 H. L. ENO *Activism* iv. 46 The collective activity of psychons, also, which we shall call 'psychokinesis' differs, with its various combinations upon its own plane, in intensity.

psychokine·tic, *a.* Also with hyphen. [f. PSYCHO- + KINETIC *a.* (*sb.*).] **1.** Of or pertaining to psychokinesis (sense *2).

1904 G. S. HALL *Adolescence* II. xviii. 724 We are now coming to study and utilize every psycho-kinetic equivalent or analogue between the higher and the lower faith. **1948** J. G. BENNETT *Crisis in Human Affairs* vii. 133 This we shall call the 'psycho-static' view, according to which the *psyche*, or essential nature of man, is unchangeable... The alternative we shall call the 'psycho-kinetic' view, which asserts the possibility of movement or transformation within man's psyche.

2. Of or pertaining to psychokinesis (sense *1).

1943 [see PK., Pk. s.v. *P II]. **1950** *Mind* LIX. 453 The random number generator will be subject to the psycho-kinetic powers of the interrogator. **1962** V. NABOKOV *Pale Fire* 165 Hazel was involved in some appalling 'psychokinetic' manifestations.

psycholeptic: see *PSYCHO-.

psycholingui·stic, *a.* and *sb.* [f. PSYCHO- + LINGUISTIC *a.* and *sb.*] **A.** *adj.* Of or pertaining to psycholinguistics (see sense B below).

1936 J. KANTOR *Objective Psychol. of Grammar* iv. 55 (*heading*) The psycholinguistic situation analyzed. **1948** *Mind* LVII. 531 The psycholinguistic point of view does not allow one to answer a question such as 'What is a number?' without having ascertained first the purpose of the question. **1953** J. B. CARROLL *Study of Lang.* iv. 120 Psycholinguistic analysis might suggest the units of selection in messages and better ways of gauging their semantic content. **1959** SCHUELL & JENKINS in L. F. Sies *Aphasia Theory & Therapy* (1974) xi. 212 Osgood (1953) has presented a psycholinguistic model for aphasia..; the model was constructed and deficits which should result from interruptions of psycholinguistic rather than neurological processes were deduced. **1967** D. G. HAYS *Introd. Computational Linguistics* xi. 187 Psycholinguistic evidence is now regarded as relevant to decisions about syntax. **1970** *Language* XLVI. 87 It was evident that the phonemes as analysed did indeed match the psycholinguistic units that the subject was manipulating in the use of his own language **1977** P. STREVENS *New Orientations Teaching of Eng.* ii. 32 Modern psycholinguistic studies of the way a small child learns his mother tongue.

B. *sb. pl.* (const. as *sing.*). The branch of linguistics which deals with the interrelation between the acquisition, use, and comprehension of language, and the processes of the mind. Cf. *linguistic psychology* s.v. *LINGUISTIC *a.* b.

1936 ALLPORT & ODBERT *Psychol. Monogr.* XLVII. i. 25 From the standpoints of the psychology of personality and psycho-linguistics the complete record is of more value. **1948** *Mind* LVII. 530 *Psycho-linguistics*.., a term which is intended to cover the spoken and written word, as well as gestures and such physical actions as are used by human being[s] to influence each other's activities. It also studies the associations which relate such acts with the mental processes which occur in the minds of the parties concerned. **1952** *Language* XXVIII. i. 115 Psycholinguistics is not linguistics plus psychology; it is a resultant of the two. **1959** *Word* XV. 192 Psycholinguistics s a relatively new discipline developing along the border between linguistics and psychology. **1967** S. SAPORTA *Psycholinguistic Theories & Generative Grammars* 7 Let us understand the central question in psycholinguistics to be the study of whatever psychological processes contribute to the acquisition, production, and comprehension of language. **1974** P. DICKINSON *Poison Oracle* ii. 36 My field is psycholinguistics... The study of the effect of language on the mind. **1978** *English Jrnl.* Dec. 63/2 The findings of social linguistics and psycholinguistics are presented in terms meaningful to the younger reader.

Hence **psycholi·nguist**, a student of or specialist in psycholinguistics; **psycholingui·stically** *adv.*; **psy:cholinguisti·cian** *rare* = *PSYCHOLINGUIST.

1953 J. B. CARROLL *Study of Lang.* iv. 121 It is also possible that the mass statistics..will provide the psycholinguist with a rewarding set of material for study. **1964** *Language* XL. 226 The problem of isolating the psycholinguistically distinctive units of sequential encoding.. has elicited some interesting experiments with pausal phenomena. **1970** *New Scientist* 24 Sept. 615/1 It is a widely held view among psycholinguists..that phonology and syntax are unique to man. **1975** M. BRADBURY *History Man* vi. 106 Do you mean am I a structuralist or a Leavisite or a psycho-linguistician or a formalist or a Christian existentialist or a phenomenologist? **1976** *Amer. Speech 1974* XLIX. 80 We can answer it psycholinguistically by claiming that two items are collocates of each other if they belong to a single remembered set. **1977** *Verbatim* Dec. 1/1 The psycholinguists working with infants by and large ignored the obvious; eye contact and touch between mother and child.

psychologese (səikǫlǒdʒī·z). *colloq.* [f. PSYCHOLOG(Y + -ESE.] Language in which technical terms in psychology are used for effect.

1961 R. HOGGART *Auden* iv. 118 On occasions..he wrote 'psychologese' in poor verse. **1974** *Publishers Weekly* 4 Nov. 70/1 The mixture of psychologese and unctuous 'poetry' goes far toward placing this among the sillier books of its sort. **1979** *N.Y. Rev. Bks.* 25 Oct. 11/3 To paraphrase Chris Edwards's psychologese, 'His new ego identity is being built up as the old one is being destroyed.'

psychologic, *a.* Add: Now freq. *poet.* (Further examples.)

1943 I. A. RICHARDS *Basic Eng. & its Uses* i. 17 No one yet knows what the fundamental factors [in changes of population] are. They may be economic, but they may equally well be psychologic. **1948** M. W. THORNER *Psychiatry in Gen. Pract.* vi. 162 For a disease so pronounced in its clinical symptoms and so apparently free of a demonstrated psychologic cause, manic-depressive disease is singularly barren of any distinguishing physical findings. **1951** R. GRAVES *Poems & Satires* 26 Their hairy bellies warming With buzz of psychologic wit And homosexual swarming. **1954** [see *GERONTOLOGY]. **1967** *Listener* 19 Jan. 91/3 You've said too much, The lot of you, of psychologic such and such, A more grotesque miscellany I've never read.

psychologics (further examples: still *rare*).

1893 M. BEERBOHM *Let.* 15 Aug. (1964) 50 *Me voici* talking self and psychologics. **1943** *Amer. Speech* XVIII. 220 General semantics, as a psychology (or 'psychologics', as Korzybski prefers to call it),..claims to put the Prince of Denmark back into *Hamlet*.

psychologic (səi·kolǫdʒik, səikǒlǫ·dʒik), *sb.* Also with hyphen. [f. PSYCHO(LOGY + LOGIC *sb.*] The practice of logical reasoning based on psychological observations and judgements rather than on abstract propositions.

1912 F. C. S. SCHILLER *Formal Logic* xxiv. 393 Provided he [*sc.* the formal logician] will let us frame a science which will concern itself with the aspects of intellectual functioning which are excluded from the Ideal of Pure Thought, let him restrict 'logic' to what *he* means thereby. We shall merely..adopt another term. Let us call this other study Psychologic... Formal Logic may be left to its own devices henceforth, and Psychologic will study real knowing without impediment. **1931** N. ISAACS in *Proc. Aristotelian Soc.* XXXI. 225 The term 'psycho-logic' has been used by Dr. Schiller in connection with his position. Before I met it in his writings, I happened to be led to the same coinage, some years ago, under the pressure, as I believe it to be, of the same facts... In my view (as in Dr. Schiller's) logic needs to be based on psychology through and through... That is the purport of 'psycho-logic': an expressly intermediate study that starts from clearly psychological facts, but examines these with logical intent, and attempts to show that a logic emerges from them, and of what kind. **1935** *Mind* XLIV. 471 The purely empirical *psychologic* which substitutes judgments for propositions as the subjects of logical discourse, frankly seeks the co-operation of psychology and is willing to be a handmaid of the sciences. **1953** MAYS & WHITEHEAD tr. *Piaget's Logic & Psychol.* iii. 25 These three difficulties force us to interpolate between psychology and axiomatic logic a *tertium quid*, a 'psycho-logic',..related to these in the same way as mathematical physics is related to pure mathematics and experimental physics. **1967** *Listener* 19 Oct. 492/2 The most likely resolution is a form of psychologic: the person gradually and unconsciously changes his values and beliefs so as to make them consistent with what he says and does. **1973** I. L. CHILD *Humanistic Psychol.* vii. 95 An account of 'psycho-logic' that he..worked out several years ago.

psychological, *a.* (*sb.*) Add: **1.** (Earlier and further examples.) Also *fig.* Also *absol.*

a **1688** R. CUDWORTH in J. H. Muirhead *Platonic Tradition in Anglo-Saxon Philos.* (1931) 64 Wherefore we have proposed another psychological hypothesis: that.. there must of necessity be in the soul one common focus or centre in which all these kinds may meet. **1802** *Monthly Mag.* XIV. 35/1 The grand drama of the Leipzig Easter-fair is certainly..very attractive and entertaining, whether one belong to the crowd of busy actors, or be only an idle looker-on—whether one have on his nose a pair of statistical, or psychological spectacles. **1951** M. MCLUHAN *Mech. Bride* (1967) 143/2 They have a more organic approach than the Germans, whose attitude is closer to the psychological. **1974** R. ASSAGIOLI *Act of Will* (1975) v. 48 This knowledge..enables us to make countless..applications of those psychological laws.

2. a. (Further examples.) Also, affecting or pertaining to the mental and emotional state of a person.

1929 *Language* V. 212 Linguistics may thus hope to become something of a guide to the understanding of the 'psychological geography' of culture in the large. **1942** E. FROMM *Fear of Freedom* iii. 49 Significant changes in the psychological atmosphere accompanied the economic development of capitalism. **1958** R. I. PERUSSE in Daugherty & Janowitz *Psychol. Warfare Casebk.* ii. 34 The expressions..'psychological operations', and 'target' should..be avoided. US observers can vouch for the discomfiture of foreign peoples at being considered by us as a fitting subject for manipulation. **1958** *Times* 15 July 11/5 Mr. Sylvester..said that to have coal stocks lying at the pithead or anywhere else had a psychological effect on the men in the industry. **1962** E. CLEAVER in A. Dundes *Mother Wit* (1973) 11/1 The destructive psychological impact of this standard of beauty. **1974** M. TAYLOR tr. *Metz's Film Lang.* viii. 190 Since the advent of the talking film, we have had the 'psychological comedy' and the 'dramatic comedy'.

c. = *MENTAL *a.*[1] 1c. *colloq.*

1952 M. ALLINGHAM *Tiger in Smoke* i. 18 If it's Elginbrodde himself, he's 'psychological'.

3. Special collocations: *psychological hedonism* (Philos.), the theory that the constitution of the human mind is such that men will always choose what is pleasurable; hence *psychological hedonist*; *psychological novel*, a type of novel in which the main interest lies in the mental and emotional aspects of the characters; hence *psychological novelist*; *psychological warfare*, the use of propaganda or other means designed to undermine the morale or allegiance of one's opponents; so *psychological war* (cf. *psy-war* s.v. *PSY-); *psychological weapon*, some particular action or reasoning designed to undermine resolution or morale in an opponent.

1884 H. SIDGWICK *Methods of Ethics* (ed. 3) I. iv. 40 There is, however, one view of the feelings which prompt to voluntary action... I mean the view that volition is always determined by pleasures or pains actual or prospective. This doctrine—which I may distinguish as Psychological Hedonism—is often connected and not seldom confounded with the method of Ethics which I have called Egoistic Hedonism. **1943** *Mind* LII. 45 Butler is, in fact, right in rejecting Psychological Hedonism. **1961** J. HOSPERS *Human Conduct* iv. 147 We must distinguish two varieties of psychological hedonism: the variety which says that all that people ever desire is pleasure or satisfaction..and the variety which says that people desire many things but these things are all desired solely for the sake of the pleasure or satisfaction they will bring to the agent. **1903** G. E. MOORE *Principia Ethica* iii. 70 It is these two different theories which I suppose the Psychological Hedonists to confuse. **1969** F. VIVIAN *Thinking Philosophically* v. 114 The psychological hedonist pushes these discoveries about our motives to what seems a logical conclusion. **1855** GEO. ELIOT in *Westm. Rev.* July 288 After courses of 'psychological' novels..where life seems made up of talking and journalizing. **1959** *Oxf. Compan. French Lit.* 676/1 He has produced..purely psychological novels, depending for plot and interest on the workings of the characters' minds and their reaction to the outside world. **1960** BECKSON & GANZ *Reader's Guide Lit. Terms* (1961) 176 This term *psychological novel* is descriptive of content rather than form or technique and is applied to work as formally conventional as the novels of C. P. Snow and as unconventional as those of James Joyce. **1915** A. D. GILLESPIE *Let.* 14 Mar. in *Lett. from Flanders* (1916) 49 He can tell a rattling good story, which many of those modern psychological novelists, with their elaborate analysis of character and of sensation, quite fail to do. **1970** G. JACKSON *Let.* 22 Mar. in *Soledad Brother* (1971) 187 The truth would aid the convict in the psychological war—con against cop. **1940** *Current Hist.* Jan. 52 (*heading*) Psychological warfare and how to wage it... Psychological warfare is the fight conducted by the state with psychological weapons to strengthen its own prestige..and to weaken that of the enemy. **1946** L. J. MARGOLIN (*title*) Paper bullets: a brief story of psychological warfare in World War II. **1949** *Sun* (Baltimore) 5 Feb. 17 Miss Gillars..is accused.. of betraying her country by aiding Hitler's psychological warfare program over a period of more than four years. **1957** G. E. WRIGHT *Bibl. Archaeol.* ix. 161/1 Tiglath-pileser..says that he 'overwhelmed' Menahem (evidently not by actual fighting but by psychological warfare!). **1974** M. BABSON *Stalking Lamb* xxi. 157 We have no objection at all to helping in what she calls her 'psychological warfare'. **1940** Psychological weapon [see *psychological warfare* above]. **1944** J. S. HUXLEY *On Living in Revolution* iv. 44 Incomplete or unsatisfactory peace aims, which will have a..lower efficiency as psychological weapons.

psycholo·gico-. *rare.* [f. by analogy with LOGICO-.] Taken as comb. form of PSYCHOLOGICAL *a.*, PSYCHOLOGY in the sense 'psychological and...'.

1869 W. JAMES *Let.* 22 May in R. B. Perry *Tht. & Char. W. James* (1935) I. 296 Charles S. Peirce has been writing some very acute and original psychologico-metaphysical articles in the St. Louis philosophic *Journal.* **1942** *Mind* LI. 178 At this stage of our ignorance we should concentrate on psychologico-mathematical patterns.

psychologism. Add: **b.** The tendency to explain in psychological terms matters which are considered to be more properly explained in other ways.

1905 *Mind* XIV. 530 Psychologism..has been universal in English philosophy from the beginning. **1937** D. KATZ in R. B. Cattell et al. *Human Affairs* iii. 36 According to this tendency logic is nothing but the psychology of thinking, mathematics nothing but the psychology of mathematical thinking... This tendency is usually called psychologism. **1945** K. R. POPPER *Open Society* II. xiv. 87 The structure..of the social environment, as opposed to the natural environment, is man-made; and therefore it must be explicable in terms of human nature, in accordance with the doctrine of psychologism. **1950** R. CARNAP *Logical Found. Probability* ii. 40 One of the important achievements in the development of modern logic has been the gradual elimination of psychologism. **1975** *Times Lit. Suppl.* 9 May 502/2 From Descartes onwards, with some notable exceptions, philosophical semantics was crippled by psychologism.

psychologist. Add: **1. b.** A person who is not an expert in psychology, yet has, or claims to have, insight into the motivation of human behaviour. *colloq.*

1896 W. CUCHER *Theatrical World of 1896* 56 In a word (though he would probably not know the meaning of the word), he must be a profound psychologist. **1951** A. P. HERBERT *Number Nine* xv. 203 Why on earth had he answered all those perilous questions?.. The 'mad Admiral'..must be a pretty subtle psychologist. **1957** P. LAFITTE *Person in Psychol.* 1 Psychology has several meanings... It may mean the person's ordinary conduct of his affairs and it does mean this when he has done something ingenious or subtle and so thinks of himself as a bit of a psychologist.

2. Phr. *psychologist's fallacy* (see quots.).

1890 W. JAMES *Princ. Psychol.* I. vii. 196 The great snare of the psychologist is the confusion of his own standpoint with that of the mental fact about which he is making his report. I shall hereafter call this the 'psychologist's fallacy' *par excellence.* **1902** BALDWIN *Dict. Philos. & Psychol.* II. 382/2 *Psychologist's fallacy*, the fallacy, to which the psychologist is peculiarly liable, of reading into the mind he is examining what is true of his own; especially of reading into lower minds what is true of higher. **1931** *Brit. Jrnl. Psychol.* XXI. 243 A danger to be avoided known as the 'psychologist's fallacy'. This arises from the fact that the experimenter is apt to suppose that the subject will respond to a stimulus or an order in the same way as he himself would respond in the circumstances.

psychologistic (səi:kǫlǒdʒi·stik), *a.* [f. PSYCHOLOG(ISM + -ISTIC.] Of, pertaining to, or characterized by psychologism.

1929 *Mind* XXXVIII. 360 His sustained and masterly demonstration of the self-ruinous character of all such 'psychologistic' theories. **1931** W. B. GIBSON tr. *Husserl's Ideas* 18 Within this view of things there grows up..a transcendental-phenomenological Idealism in opposition to every form of psychologistic Idealism. **1935** *Amer. Speech* X. 247/1 That the distinction between *langue* and *parole* does not imply any psychologistic assumptions, is shown..by the fact that it has served as a starting point to the phoneme conception of Professor Twaddell, who resolutely protests against all psychologistic definitions of the phoneme. **1957** G. RYLE in M. Black *Importance of Lang.* (1962) 165 Where Frege attacked psychologistic accounts of thinking from the outside, they attacked them from the inside. **1976** *Brit. Jrnl. Sociol.* XXVII. 304 A sociological approach is apt to imply that such groups collude in their subordinate position and then to provide psychologistic interpretations of their behaviour.

Hence **psy:chologi·stically** *adv.*

1964 I. C. JARVIE *Revolution in Anthropol.* iii. 97 The psychological problems of religion..are the only problems of religion that can be tackled psychologistically.

psychologize, *v.* Add: **1.** (Earlier and later examples.)

1830 W. JACOBSON *Let.* in J. F. Maurice *Life F. D. Maurice* (1884) I. ix. 111 Neither stay away rusticating and psychologizing, but come here and mind your books. **1967** *Listener* 19 Jan. 91/2 'Let us please psychologize In this wise,' Suggested Freud. **1974** *Sci. Amer.* Aug. 115/1 The texts still like to simplify; generally we psychologize about the local event and regard the suffused experience as secondary.

3. (Examples.)

1940 V. J. MCGILL in M. Farber *Philos. Ess.* 231 This work was a reaction against his earlier volume in which he [*sc.* Husserl] had attempted to psychologize arithmetic. **1957** *Listener* 9 May 743/2 We have been led to psychologize (to use John Dewey's rather horrid word) and to humanize learning.

4. (Earlier example.)

1877 D. D. HOME *Lights & Shadows of Spiritualism* v. 264 Dear old gullible souls who could be readily psychologized into believing that they were eating a piece of the moon in shape of 'green cheese'.

psychologizing *vbl. sb.* (further examples); also *attrib.*; also **psycho·logized** *ppl. a.*; **psychologization** (further examples).

1895 W. JAMES *Coll. Ess. & Rev.* (1920) 393, I never find myself actively taking up the soul, so to speak, and making it to do work in my psychologizing. **1922** C. E. M. JOAD *Common-Sense Theol.* v. 233 The so-called 'psychologising' tendency in modern thought. **1956** E. H. HUTTEN *Lang. Mod. Physics* vi. 224 We are once more in danger of falling victims to the psychologizing attitude of epistemology. **1961** E. NAGEL *Structure of Science* iii. 45 Various psychologized versions of the Aristotelian requirement have enjoyed wide currency. **1966** J. J. KATZ *Philos. Lang.* v. 261 This argument is a psychologization of an argument of Goodman's in some recent work of his on the concept of confirmation in science. **1970** A. TOFFLER *Future Shock* (1974) x. 221 The key to the post-service economy lies in the psychologization of all production. **1976** *Spare Rib* Oct. 38/4 A continuous stream of psychologising and explaining..leaves a reader little room to breathe or get curious about the characters.

psychologizer (səikǫ·lǒdʒəizəɹ). [f. prec. + -ER[1].] One who psychologizes, in any sense.

1895 'MARK TWAIN' in *N. Amer. Rev.* CLX. 49 The Observer of Peoples has to be a Classifier, a Grouper, a Deducer, a Generalizer, a Psychologizer. **1931** W. B. GIBSON tr. *Husserl's Ideas* III. iii. 273 The psychologizers everywhere will take offence at this; they are already disinclined to distinguish between judging as an empirical experience and judgment as 'Idea', as essence. **1966** *Listener* 4 Aug. 174/1 The 'spiritualizers' are giving way to the 'psychologizers'. Enter 'psychological man'.

psychologue. For *rare*—[1] read *rare* and add further examples.

1890 W. JAMES *Let.* 8 July (1920) II. 1 A great chance for some future psychologue to make a greater name than Newton's. **1971** K. MILLETT *Sexual Politics* (1972) III. vi. 330 It is vaguely depressing to see a literary man vending the same trash as those hundreds of psychologues and quacks.

psychology. Add: **1. a.** (Earlier and further examples of general use.) In mod. use no longer concerned with the soul.

1653 tr. *J. de Back's Discourse* in W. Harvey *Anat. Exercises* sig. H7[v], I call the generall doctrine of man *Anthropologie*, the parts of which, I do ordain to be, according to this division, *Psychologie*, *Somatologie*, and *Hæmatologie*, into the doctrine of the soul, bodie, and blood... *Psychologie* is a doctrine which searches out mans Soul, and the effects of it. *Ibid.* sig. H8[v], I do bind up the order of *Psychology* in few words. *a* **1680** R. CUDWORTH *Treat. Freewill* (1838) 19 The vulgar psychology, or the now generally received way of philosophizing concerning the soul, doth either quite baffle and betray this liberty of will, or else render it absurd, ridiculous, or monstrous. **1892** W. JAMES *Coll. Ess. & Rev.* (1920) xx. 317, I wished, by treating Psychology *like* a natural science, to help her to become one. **1897** C. H. JUDD tr. *Wundt's Outl. Psychol.* i. 3 The assignment of this problem to psychology, making it an empirical science coordinate with natural science and supplementary to it, is justified by the method of all the *mental sciences*, for which psychology furnishes the basis. **1910** *Amer. Jrnl. Psychol.* XXI. 72 Although great writers and poets have frequently made the most penetrating generalisations in practical psychology, the world has always been slow to profit by their discoveries. **1930** W. KÖHLER *Gestalt Psychol.* vi. 167 In psychology too, the influence of *gestalt* has been demonstrated..in very primitive behaviour. **1973** C. D. Kernig *Marxism, Communism & Western Society* VII. 98 Starting from the assumption that Soviet psychology is grounded on dialectical materialism, psychological historiography attempts to show how far materialist, and later dialectical and finally Marxist-Leninist thinking moulded the character of psychology.

In mod. usage, the signification of the word has broadened from the narrow concept illustrated in the Dict. to include (*a*) the scientific study of the mind as an entity and in its relationship to the physical body, based on observation of the behaviour and activity aroused by specific stimuli; and (*b*) the study of the behaviour of an individual or of a selected group of individuals when interacting with the environment or in a given social context. So *experimental psychology*, the experimental study of the responses of an individual to stimuli; *social psychology*, the study of the interaction between an individual and the social group to which he belongs.

(*a*) **1895** *Amer. Jrnl. Psychol.* VII. 78 Experimental Psychology was in its origin, and has remained for a considerable extent in its development, a German science. **1927** *Psychol. Rev.* XXXIV. 126 They adopt in regard to them [*sc.* instincts] the attitude common to the stimulus-response school of psychology, which purports to base the development of human behavior, of character and personality, upon the innately determined reactions of the organism to objective stimuli. **1940** Hilgard & Marquis *Conditioning & Learning* i. 2 The conditioned response was called the unit of habit by psychologists to whom habit was the most important concept in psychology. **1953** C. E. Osgood *Method & Theory in Exper. Psychol.* p. v, I have covered the major portion of what is called experimental psychology, including sections on sensory processes, perception, learning, and symbolic processes. **1968** *Internat. Encycl. Social Sci.* XIII. 78/2 Existential psychology is a comprehensive psychology whose aim is an integration of the observations of different psychologies into an explanatory theory about human behavior in its lived international entirety. **1976** H. Brown *Brain & Behavior* i. 5 The study of the relation between brain structure and behavior gives physiological psychology the unique mission of trying to resolve an old and basic puzzle of philosophy and science, often referred to as the 'mind-body problem'.

(*b*) **1896** G. Le Bon *Crowd* ii. 32 What we know of the psychology of crowds shows that treatises of logic need on this point to be rewritten. **1908** W. McDougall *Social Psychol.* 18 Social psychology has to show how, given the native propensities and capacities of the human mind, all the complex mental life of societies is shaped by them and in turn reacts upon the course of their development and operation in the individual. **1922** E. Glover *Roots of Crime* (1960) 4 For the first time in the history of British criminology a meeting of Justices of the Peace has invited a psycho-analyst to lecture on the psychology of crime. **1948** A. L. Kroeber *Anthropol.* (rev. ed.) viii. 323 Clinical psychology was the first recognized branch of psychology that attempted to deal with whole human beings, as distinct from..special aspects of the mind. **1963** Gough & Jenkins in M. H. Marx *Theories Contemp. Psychol.* xxix. 456 The study of verbal learning has not led to the study of verbal behavior in general, to the psychology of language. **1975** W. S. Sahakian *Hist. & Syst. Psychol.* xix. 425 The World War II years found him interested in the psychology of morale and human engineering psychology.

2. a. The attitude or outlook of an individual or a group on a particular matter or on life in general.

1899 G. Le Bon *Psychol. of Socialism* iv. 39 We find in the working classes two well-defined subdivisions, each with a different psychology. **1908** F. M. Ford *Let.* Dec. (1965) 29 Thanks for yr. letter: of course I understand yr. psychology &, God forbid that you shd. restrain yr. irritation before men of good will. **1928** *Daily Tel.* 11 Sept. 10/5 The psychology of the workaday world has infected him with its disquiet. **1931** F. L. Allen *Only Yesterday* ii. 20 War-time psychology was dominant; no halfway measure would serve. **1954** Koestler *Invisible Writing* xxiv. 264 Was not the psychology of the masses an infinitely more complex phenomenon?

b. The nature *of* an event or phenomenon considered from the point of view of psychology.

1892 C. G. Chaddock tr. *Krafft-Ebing's Psychopathia Sexualis* p. iv, It is not the intention of the author to lay the foundation of a psychology of the sexual life, though without doubt psychopathology would furnish many important sources of knowledge to psychology. **1929** B. Russell *Marriage & Morals* xvi. 182 The psychology of adultery has been falsified by conventional morals. **1932** F. C. Bartlett *Remembering* ii. 16 There is..adequate reason for beginning our detailed study of the psychology of remembering with an investigation into the character and conditions of perceiving and imagining. **1964** B. B. Gilligan tr. I. Lepp (*title*) The psychology of loving.

3. *attrib.*, as *psychology journal, student.*

1971 D. Crystal in E. Ardener *Social Anthropol. & Lang.* 194 This research, largely reported in psychology journals.., is methodologically unsatisfactory in many respects. **1890** W. James *Princ. Psychol.* II. xviii. 56, I have myself for many years collected from each and all of my psychology-students descriptions of their own visual imagination. **1972** G. W. Kisker *Disorganized Personality* (rev. ed.) xv. 494 Psychology students were employed by one investigator as 'companion counselors'.

psychomachy. Delete † *Obs. rare* and add later examples. Also (now more usually) in L. form **psychomachia.**

[**1927** H. Waddell *Wandering Scholars* i. 20 In his most famous and most considerable work, the *Psychomachia*, the Battle of the Soul, he [*sc.* Prudentius] has done more than set the stage for the struggle between the spirit and the flesh.] **1936** C. S. Lewis *Allegory of Love* ii. 55 The favourite theme of the Middle Ages—the battle of the virtues and the vices, the Psychomachia, the *bellum intestinum*, the Holy War. *Ibid.* 73 A good man, even in a panegyric, can now be good only as a result of a successful psychomachy. **1954** —— *Eng. Lit. in Sixteenth Cent.* I. i. 92 'Bewtie and the Prisoneir' is a neat but slightly frigid psychomachy. **1955** D. Davie *Brides of Reason* 22 There were minds Aware of themselves, and figuring this In psychomachia. **1972** *Times Lit. Suppl.* 10 Nov. 1353/1 Ruskin's criticism..becomes a psychomachia dramatizing his own mental state.

psychometric, *a.* Add: (Further examples.)

1879 *Brain* II. 149 (*heading*) Psychometric experiments. **1943** *Amer. Jrnl. Psychiatry* C. 181/2 The various psychometric tests can only touch the surface of this situation. **1970** *Jrnl. Gen. Psychol.* LXXXII. 101 Intelligence measures included two psychometric indices of 'general intelligence'. **1973** R. C. Dennis *Sweat of Fear* vi. 37, I had to find a way of telling her I had psychometric knowledge of her predicament.

B. *sb. pl.* (const. as *sing.*). The science of measuring mental capacities and processes; the application of methods of measurement to the various branches of psychology.

1930 *Proc. & Addr. Amer. Assoc. Stud. Feeble-Minded* XXXV. 94 To most persons who know the term at all, psychometrics is fairly synonymous with the use of intelligence tests. **1934** J. O'Connor (*title*) Psychometrics: a study of psychological measurement. *Ibid.* p. xiv, Every measuring instrument has two major aspects. In the field of psychometrics these are called reliability and validity. **1958** *Times* 27 May 2/2 (Advt.), Applications are invited for the post of Lecturer in Education with special interests in psychometrics, statistics and educational psychology. **1972** *Guardian* 24 Feb. 13/8 Psychometrics is unable to investigate the nature of intelligence. **1973** *Nature* 23 Mar. 279/2 Professor Meredith delivers a blistering attack on traditional psychometrics (i.e., the alleged 'measurement' of IQs, reading ages, and so on).

psychometrical *a.* (further example); **psychometrically** *adv.* (examples corresponding to sense 2 of Psychometry); **psychometrize** *v.* (further examples).

1903 *Nature* 3 Sept. 409/1 It appears doubtful if any other community, European or Polynesian, has been psychometrically investigated under more favourable conditions as regards both absence of disturbing factors and simplification of method. **1922** E. Wallace *Crimson Circle* ii. 14 The police might sneer at Yale's psychometrical powers. **1950** P. Tabori *Harry Price* ix. 183 He proposed..to have the box psychometrized first by the best mental mediums he could obtain. **1975** *Weekend Mag.* (Montreal) 18 Oct. 20/1 Learning of McMullen's psychic abilities, he asked him to psychometrize some artifacts. **1977** *Lancet* 1 Jan. 7/2 These children have been re-examined medically and psychometrically.

psychometrician (səɪːkomĕtri·ʃăn). [f. prec. + -ian.] An expert in or practitioner of psychometrics.

1950 in Webster Add. **1953** J. B. Carroll *Study of Lang.* i. 4. The psychometrician..tries to make tests of 'verbal intelligence' or tests of achievement in various language arts. **1965** *Language* XLI. 353 Factor analysis has been intensively cultivated by psychologists, particularly psychometricians. **1975** *Sci. Amer.* July 128/1 In seeking to devise 'culture-free' tests of intelligence psychometricians are pursuing a chimera.

psychometrist (səikǫ·mĕtrist). [f. Psychometer + -ist.] **1.** = Psychometer 1.

1864 T. L. Nichols *40 Yrs. Amer. Life* II. ii. 20 Then came psychometrists, who could tell the lives, characters, fortunes, and diseases of people they had never seen. **1879** *Spiritual Notes* May 148/1 The psychometrist enters a room and is impressed with a vision of events that in some mysterious way have left their traces on its material fabric. **1900, 1903** [in Dict. s.v. Psychometric *a.*] **1966** E. Palmer *Plains of Camdeboo* xvii. 289 Hearing of a psychometrist in Johannesburg, I took my piece of wood to her and asked her what she could tell me of its history. **1976** *Oxford Times* 6 Feb. 15/1 Guest speakers and demonstrators include..a psychometrist—for whom vibrations received from personal belongings create a mental picture of the owner.

2. = *psychometrician.

1932 *Psychol. Exchange* I. 11 The deserving psychometrists are often not discriminated from those who have just taken up mental testing. **1964** M. Critchley *Developmental Dyslexia* xiv. 82 The formal intelligence quotient was given as 65, but this was certainly a serious underestimate due to lack of cultural rapport with the psychometrist. **1974** *Maclean's Mag.* (Toronto) May 12/2 He worked as a psychometrist measuring the abilities of children.

psychometry. Add: **1.** (Later examples.)

1922 E. Wallace *Crimson Circle* vi. 38 'Nothing is absurd,' said the Commissioner quietly. 'The science of psychometry has been practised for years.' **1959** *Times Lit. Suppl.* 1 May 254/4 Such objects..enjoy a semi-consciousness drawn from the human beings who have known them. In this there is an undeniable truth, as the modern practice of 'psychometry' proves. **1966** E. Palmer *Plains of Camdeboo* xvii. 290 Most of us can on occasions sense atmosphere, and psychometry seems to be this power greatly developed. **1975** G. W. Knight *Jackson Knight* i. 44, I know now, from the witness of psychometry, that inanimate objects can indeed become impregnated by qualities gathered during their past.

2. (Earlier and later examples.) Also, psychometrics (see *psychometric *a.* B).

1879 F. Galton in *Brain* II. 149 Psychometry.. means the art of imposing measurement and number upon operations of the mind, as in the practice of determining the reaction-time of different persons. **1971** *Brit. Med. Bull.* XXVII. 35/1 Hughes and his colleagues are conducting further studies, including the use of electro-encephalography and psychometry. **1976** H. M. van Praag in *Advances in Drug Therapy of Mental Illness* (World Health Organization) 127 The third field in which psychotropic drugs have served as a pacemaker, that of psychometry... One wants to know (that is, to measure) what it [*sc.* the drug] does, and what it does not do.

psychomimetic, -motility: see *psycho-.

psycho-motor, *a.* Add: Also without hyphen. **a.** (Further examples.)

1879 *Jrnl. Mental Sci.* XXIV. 677 The 'Psychiatrischer Centralblatt' for August.., 1877, gives a *résumé* of the inaugural dissertation..of Dr. Pasternaki, who has studied the question of what he calls the Psychomotor Centres of the Brain. **1961** *Aeroplane & Astronautics* CI. 679/1 It was agreed that the animals selected for this programme should be capable of learning simple psychomotor tasks which could be performed during flight. **1976** Smythies & Corbett *Psychiatry* v. 62 In depressed patients speech tends to be slow, monotonous, and sad-sounding, in keeping with the general psychomotor slowing.

b. *Med.* Applied to a partial seizure or epileptic attack (distinct from grand mal and petit mal) characterized by a state of altered consciousness in which simple or complex automatisms may be performed for which there is subsequently at least partial amnesia.

1938 *Amer. Jrnl. Psychiatry* XXV. 268 The three main manifestations of epilepsy (grand mal, petit mal and psychomotor epilepsy) are each accompanied by a distinct pattern of disrhythmia. **1961** *Listener* 7 Dec. 967/2 An attack of psychomotor epilepsy. **1974** M. C. Gerald *Pharmacol.* xi. 212 Diphenylhydantoin..is also useful against psychomotor seizures.

Hence **psychomoto·ric, -moto·rical** *adjs.*, of or pertaining to psychomotor activity; **psychomoto·rically** *adv.*

1964 L. Kaiser in D. Abercrombie et al. *Daniel Jones* 102 Both ways of coding and decoding show a high degree of similarity, psychomotoric patterns based on language leading to neuromuscular activity, which in its turn leads to spatial coding in both cases. **1969** *Indian Mus. Jrnl.* V. 83 Music is a much directer form of expression (psychomotorically), than painting, sculpture..and ornaments. *Ibid.* 84 These psychomotorical expressions are not in the least outbursts of uncontrolled emotions. The hands of the singers accompany in refined movements the path of the voice.

psychon (səi·kǫn). [f. Psycho- + *-on[1].] A hypothetical unit of nerve impulse or energy. Hence **psycho·nic** *a.*

[**1906** H. W. Armit tr. *A. Forel's Hypnotism* i. 6 It is here that one must seek the transition from the conceived to the unconceived, and not in the strong and repeatedly conceived 'psychomes'. [*Note*] The author apologizes for this term. He has introduced it for brevity['s] sake to express each and every psychical unit.] **1920** H. L. Eno *Activism* iv. 45 Since we are already familiar with one form at any rate of this higher activity in the psychic processes, let us call these units 'psychons'. *Ibid.*, The term 'psychone' was proposed by Forel for the psychic aspect of a hypothetical unit of the nerve process. **1927** P. & W. R. Bousfield *Mind* i. 22 As the basis of the 'immaterial substance' we may postulate a second order of 'ons' which are, like protons and electrons, fashioned out of the ether. Let us call these 'ons' by the name of 'psychons'. **1931** W. M. Marston et al. *Integrative Psychol.* xiii. 314 There is no doubt whatsoever that the psychons in the sensory system differ from those in the motor system. *Ibid.*, We suggest, therefore, that from the point of view of an objective psychology, exterior to its subjects, this psychonic energy is consciousness. **1968** C. L. Burt *Psychol. & Psychical Res.* 45 As unit I would rather start with the 'pure ego', which I envisage as a sort of Leibnizian monad. This, I think, on the plane of natural science we might justifiably treat as an 'elementary particle'—a 'psychon', as I styled it.

psychoneural, -neuroendocrine, -neuroendocrinology, etc., **-neurology,** etc.: see *psycho-.

psychoneuro·sis. *Psychol.* Also with hyphen. [f. Psycho- + Neurosis.] Any of various functional nervous disorders attributed to emotional or psychological causes, often accompanied by manifestations of anxiety, and distinguished from a psychosis by the maintenance of contact with the external world; also, in psychoanalytic theory, a mental disorder attributed to repressed unconscious conflict or fantasy (as distinguished from an 'actual' neurosis, attributed to anxiety caused by present frustration of sexual drive).

1883 [in Dict. s.v. Psycho-]. **1903** W. James in *Proc. Soc. Psychical Res.* XVIII. 32 The parasitic ideas of psycho-neurosis, and the fictitious personations of planchette-writing and mediumship. **1913** E. Jones

Papers on Psycho-Anal. v. 125 Freud has pointed out that it is necessary to separate the 'actual neuroses' from the 'psychoneuroses'. *Ibid.* 129 We next come to the psychoneuroses proper... The symptoms result from the activity of certain unconscious mental processes..which the patient is unable spontaneously to recall to his memory. **1924** J. Riviere et al. tr. *Freud's Coll. Papers* II. xxi. 253 There always remains as a common feature in the ætiology both of the psychoneuroses and the psychoses the factor of frustration. **1938** *Jrnl. Aviation Med.* IX. 177/2 McFarland and Barach found that patients, on whom a diagnosis of psychoneurosis had been made, appeared to be more severely affected at an atmosphere of 10 per cent oxygen than were the normal controls. **1948** *Sci. News* VIII. 109 The conditions which benefit most from group psychotherapy are the psychoneuroses—particularly anxiety states and reactive depressions. **1959** J. Strachey *Freud's Compl. Wks.* XX. 79 In these cases—in the psychoneuroses—the reason for the accumulation of undischarged excitation was a psychological one: repression. But what followed was the same as in the 'actual' neuroses. **1972** Zax & Cowen *Abnormal Psychol.* viii. 231 The one feature common to all forms of psychoneurosis is the presence of anxiety *Ibid.* 232 In DSM-I (1952) six types of psychoneuroses were delineated: anxiety reaction; conversion reaction; dissociative reaction; phobic reaction; obsessive-compulsive; and depressive reaction. **1977** Miller & Swift *Words & Women* iv. 67 Hysteria now refers in technical use to a specific psychoneurosis that may affect anyone, male or female.

psychoneuro·tic, *sb.* and *a. Psychol.* Also with hyphen. [f. Psycho- + Neurotic *sb.* and *a.*] **A.** *sb.* A person suffering from a psychoneurosis.

1902 *Buck's Handbk. Med. Sci.* (rev. ed.) V. 28/1 In the psychoneurotic..the tendency toward imperfect mental development becomes more and more accentuated. **1924** *Proc. 7th Internat. Congr. Psychol.* 148 Though a genius is frequently a psycho-neurotic, it would be quite untrue to say that the majority of psycho-neurotics tend towards genius. **1936** *Psychoanal. Rev.* XXIII. 1 Thoughts of death and dying occur as every-day symptoms among psycho-neurotics of the anxiety, hysterical and obsessive types. **1972** Zax & Cowen *Abnormal Psychol.* viii. 231 The psychoneurotic maintains good contact with reality.

B. *adj.* Of, pertaining to, or characterized by psychoneurosis.

1909 *Jrnl. Abnormal Psychol.* June–July 144 Every psycho-neurotic symptom is to be regarded as the symbolic expression of a submerged mental complex of the nature of a wish. **1938** *Jrnl. Aviation Med.* IX. 177/2 When 50 per cent oxygen was given, the physiologic symptoms of the psychoneurotic patients were less marked. **1967** *Spectator* 1 Dec. 679/1 When one looks at the incidence of psychoneurotic disorders..it is found that these also were commoner in..flat-dwellers.

psycho-optic(al: see *psycho-.

psychopath. (Further examples; cf. *psychopathy.)

1927 *New Republic* 21 Sept. 128/2 Terms not so long ago confined to specialists are handled familiarly by the laity: moron, inferiority complex, mental age,..paranoid delusions, psychopaths. **1955** D. J. West *Homosexuality* ix. 106 Psychopaths are the last people to try to battle against their instincts; they just obey first impulses regardless of social codes. Being incapable of prolonged or deep personal attachments, they seek only an immediate outlet for their lust. **1967** *Listener* 20 Apr. 529/3 The term psychopath is bandied about in such a way as to make it cover almost any mental disorder... However the psychopath has now achieved legal status in the Mental Health Act of 1959 as having 'a persistent disorder or disability of mind..which results in abnormally aggressive or seriously irresponsible behaviour'. **1967** M. Argyle *Psychol. of Interpersonal Behaviour* i. 21 It is one of the marks of the psychopath that he will engage in social behaviour in so far as it is..profitable to do so, but he has no intrinsic attraction to other people at all. For the psychopath there is no particular difference between people and things. **1972** *Observer* 31 Dec. 23/4 If she's a psychopath I'm a fruit cake. She's just a girl who needs love.

psychopathic, *a.* (*sb.*) Add: **1. a, b.** (Further examples.) For 'mental disease' read 'mental disorder, now *spec.* psychopathy'.

1899 [see *hereditary *a.* 2 a]. **1932** *Sun* (Baltimore) 19 Sept. 2/2 The court..found that Duker is afflicted with a definite mental ailment or disorder known as psychopathic personality, which had reduced his mental and moral responsibility and control but that he is sane according to the legal standard. **1949** *Brit. Jrnl. Psychol.* XL. 12 The Psychopathic Personality (P.P.P.) is one of the major problems of the Prison Commission. **1957** R. F. C. Hull tr. *Jung's Compl. Wks.* I. 111 In many psychopathic illnesses there are persons who think unclearly and are prone to flights of ideas, who are ruthlessly egocentric..but who can hardly be said to be suffering from chronic mania. **1959** *Mental Health Act* 7 & 8 *Eliz. II* c. 72. I. § 4 In this Act 'psychopathic disorder' means a persistent disorder or disability of mind (whether or not including subnormality of intelligence) which results in abnormally aggressive or seriously irresponsible conduct on the part of the patient, and requires or is susceptible to medical treatment. **1968** [see *moral *a.* 7 a]. **1976** *Times* 4 Aug. 5/7 All we can do is protect society from them. Grossly psychopathic people cannot be befriended. **1977** P. Way *Super-Celeste* I. 53 Such men..work to please whatever passions and psychopathic urges drive them personally.

Hence **psychopa·thically** *adv.*

1961 in Webster. **1972** *Lancet* 18 Nov. 1069/2 The psychopathically aggressive, the rigidly authoritarian.

psycho-pathology. (Now usu. without hyphen.) Add: The science of the mental or psychological causation of disorders and abnormalities. (Further examples.)

1951 D. B. Klein *Abnormal Psychol.* 5 The study of mental disorder bulks large in the field of abnormal psychology, so that a good portion of this field might be regarded as coterminous with that of psychopathology. **1964** Gould & Kolb *Dict. Social Sci.* 555/1 This psychoanalytic psychopathology has..been employed to explain ..not only mental symptoms but also the physical lesions of so-called psychosomatic diseases; not only disease but also the traits and quirks of normal or deviant personalities. **1968** J. Zubin in Zubin & Shagass *Neurobiol. Aspects of Psychopathology* 289 If we define personality as the systematic aspect of a person's behavior, and psychopathology as those aspects of this systematic behavior attributable to illness, an important question arises regarding the possible connections between premorbid personality and psychopathology. **1969** T. Freeman *Psychopathology of Psychoses* i. 2 Psychopathology has a wider subject-matter than the study of 'conscious psychic events'... To be comprehensive it must take account of psychoanalysis... It must also be based on certain aspects of neurology and internal medicine.

b. A mentally or behaviourally disordered state.

1947 D. Jones in R. Hague *Dai Greatcoat* (1980) ii. 139 *Everything* one does is conditioned by one's psychopathology. **1952** Mettler & Curry in F. A. Mettler *Psychosurgical Problems* i. 16 It does not follow because a patient is discharged that his psychopathology is fundamentally altered. **1970** *Jrnl. Gen. Psychol.* LXXXIII. 61 Classifying states of psychopathology into discrete, mutually exclusive categories..does not seem to be possible. **1973** Sandler & Davidson *Psychopathology* i. 8 Tests designed to reveal the developmental history of the patient's psychopathology.

psychopathological *a.*, **-pathologist** (further examples); also **psy:chopatholo·gic** *a.*, **psy:chopatholo·gically** *adv.*

1891 *Ann. Rep. Board of Regents Smithsonian Inst. 1889–90* 636 One can thus see the links which form the psycho-pathologic chain of human life, at one end of which we may find insanity and at the other criminality. **1919** W. S. Maugham *Moon & Sixpence* i. 7 The mystic sees the ineffable and the psycho-pathologist the unspeakable. **1928** *Guy's Hosp. Rep.* LXXVIII. 458 Psychopathologically, from the content of the hypochondriacal complaints..an anal-erotic basis for some hypochondrias is strongly suggested. **1936** *Jrnl. Nerv. & Mental Dis.* LXXXIV 450 Psychopathologically, we undertake an analysis of the situation. **1971** J. J. Shapiro tr. *Habermas's Toward Rational Society* iii. 42 The use of psychopathological concepts has become necessary for the identification and explanation of a political state of affairs. **1976** *Observer* 11 Jan. 21/4 Interesting little psychopathological tour de force—or, as they say in Soho, kinks and kicks.

psychopathy. Add: **1.** In mod. use, personality disorder that lacks a physiological basis, characterized by markedly impulsive, egocentric, irresponsible, and antisocial behaviour, and an inability to form normal relationships with others, sometimes accompanied by aggressiveness or charm and manifested at all levels of intelligence; the state of such a disorder. (Further examples.)

1923 C. Mackenzie *Parson's Progress* xix. 263 Personally I have found my knowledge of psychopathy of the greatest value in the confessional. **1948** *Amer. Jrnl. Sociol.* LIII. 361/1 Caldwell indicates nomadism, inability to withstand tedium, and irresponsibility as characteristics of psychopathy. **1953** I. Skottowe *Clin. Psychiatry* ii. 32 Three qualities may be discerned biographically which are a common expression of psychopathy. The first is the lack of persistence..; the second is a curious coldness of heart..; the third is an inability to defer the immediate satisfaction of appetites and desires. **1972** G. Sereny *Case of Mary Bell* II. i. 148 The condition of psychopathy is not generally identified with mental retardation. **1972** Zax & Cowen *Abnormal Psychol.* x. 312 In trying to understand the causes of psychopathy a variety of emphases can be identified, including hereditary, neurological, environmental, and sociocultural. **1976** *Church Times* 12 Mar. 5/2 He turned loving eyes on the tormenting thugs... They, in their psychopathy, could not see him as a man like themselves.

psychopharmaceutical: see *psycho-.

psy:chopharmaco·logy. Also with hyphen. [f. Psycho- + Pharmacology.] The branch of science concerned with the way drugs affect the mind and behaviour.

1920 D. Macht in *Johns Hopkins Hosp. Bull.* XXXI. 167/1 The number of contributions to the domain of what we may be permitted to call 'psychopharmacology' is certainly very meagre. **1935** *Jrnl. Nerv. & Mental Dis.* LXXXI. 161 The psycho-pharmacology of sodium amytal. **1958** A. Huxley *Let.* 2 Feb. (1969) 845, I have been asked..to do a piece on the ethical, religious and social implications of psychopharmacology. **1969** *New Scientist* 10 Apr. 80/1 LSD..may be remembered as a herald of psychopharmacology. **1970** A. Toffler *Future Shock* (1971) viii. 160 New knowledge..in psychopharmacology, made many Freudian therapeutic measures seem quaintly archaic.

Hence **psy:chopharmacolo·gic** (chiefly *U.S.*), **-lo·gical** *adjs.*, of or pertaining to psychopharmacology; (of a drug) psychoactive; **psy:chopharmacolo·gically** *adv.*; **psy:chopharmaco·logist,** an expert or specialist in this subject.

1939 *Jrnl. Mental Sci.* LXXXV. 406 (*heading*) A psychopharmacological study of schizophrenia with particular reference to the mode of action of cardiazol, sodium amytal and alcohol in schizophrenic stupor. **1958** *Science* 10 Jan. 61/2 Depressions not accompanied by anxiety and tension are less apt to be ameliorated by a psychopharmacologic agent. **1960** *Clin. Pharmacol. & Therapeutics* I. 257/2 Studies by psychopharmacologists and comparative psychologists concerning the effects of the new psychotropic drugs on experimentally conditioned emotional responses of animals. **1964** M. Gordon *Psychopharmacol. Agents* I. i. 3 One of the new psychopharmacological agents, reserpine, had a difficult time gaining acceptance in the Western hemisphere. **1967** *Guardian* 1 July 12/3 A psycho-pharmacologist said: 'I wouldn't be dismayed if the use of marijuana were made legal.' **1970** *Nature* 5 Sept. 1008/1 Psychopharmacological experiments are beginning to yield data relevant to urban crowding as a health hazard. **1971** *Amer. Jrnl. Psychiatry* CXXVIII. 695/1 Peyote contains more than ten alkaloids, the most psychopharmacologically significant of which is mescaline. **1977** M. E. Jarvik *Psychopharmacol. in Pract. of Med.* 21 In complicated cases the individual should be referred to a psychopharmacologically oriented psychotherapist. **1979** [see *psychobiologist].

psycho-philosopher, -philosophy: see *psycho-.

psychophone·tics, *sb. pl.* (const. as *sing.*). *Linguistics.* Also with hyphen. [f. Psycho- + Phonetics *sb. pl.* Cf. Pol. *psychofonetych* (J. B. de Courtenay 1894, in *Rozprawy Akad. Umiejebności: Wydział Filol.* 2nd Ser. V. 129).] That branch of phonetics which deals with the mental correlates of speech-sound production. So **psychophone·tic** *a.*, **psychophone·tically** *adv.*

1934 *Maître Phonétique* Jan.–Mar. 3, ɔ:l ði:z difrənsiz in prənʌnsieiʃn..du: nɔt igzist saikoufənetikəli. **1934** *Ibid.* Apr.–June 44 Doctor Arend..naturally quotes from the later one [*sc.* work by J. B. de Courtenay] published in 1901, though there was a much later work on phonetics and psycho-phonetics published in 1927. **1936, 1950** [see *physiophonetics *sb. pl.*]. **1956** Jakobson & Halle *Fundamentals of Lang.* ii. 11 *The mentalist view*... In the oldest of these approaches,..the phoneme is a sound imagined or intended, opposed to the emitted sound as a 'psychophonetic' phenomenon to the 'physiophonetic' fact. **1966** M. Pei *Gloss. Linguistic Terminol.* 225 *Psychophonetics*, the treatment of a phoneme as the image aimed at in the speaker's mind (Courtenay, Entwistle). **1968** J. W. F. Mulder *Sets & Relations in Phonol.* 20 Articulatory phonetics has achieved results that are more widely accepted and provide a safer guide than the younger acoustic phonetics (let alone the still younger 'perceptive' phonetics, which could well be called 'psycho-phonetics'). **1968** Black & Singh in B. Malmberg *Man. Phonetics* v. 106 For the sake of convenience, psycho-phonetics will be treated here as (a) speech production, (b) speech acoustics, and (c) speech perception.

psycho-physic, *a.* and *sb.* **A.** *adj.* (Earlier example.)

1887 *Amer. Jrnl. Psychol.* I. 140 The conditions are as infinitely complicated as the psycho-physic constitution of man.

B. *sb.* **psycho-physics** (now usu. as one word). (Earlier and further examples.)

1878 *Rep. Brit. Assoc. Adv. Sci. 1877* II. 95 Most of you are aware of the recent progress of what has been termed Psycho-physics, or the science of subjecting mental processes to physical measurements and to physical laws. **1937** *Amer. Speech* XII. 228/1 On the psycho-physics of speech. **1944** *Jrnl. Optical Soc. Amer.* XXXIV. 66/1 Physicists..have surrendered almost the entire field of psychophysics to the psychologist. **1973** C. D. Kernig *Marxism, Communism & Western Society* VII. 91/2 A distinction is made between (a) classical psychophysics in which the physiology of the senses is studied with the help of refined..techniques..; (b) activation (arousal) research, which is concerned with..conditions for the release and course of affective and motivational states. **1976** S. George *Fatal Shadows* 37 The new scientists, men whose discoveries of gifted psychics had shot them to the top of psychophysics.

psycho-physical, *a.* Add: Also without hyphen. (Earlier and further examples.)

Psycho-physical isomorphism (see quot. 1932).

1847 H. E. Lloyd tr. *Feuchtersleben's Med. Psychol.* iii. 151 Habit, likewise, greatly modifies the psycho-physical character. **1872** *Westm. Rev.* XLII. 177 As a result of experiments according to all these three methods, Fechner arrives at what he calls a general 'psycho-physical law', and also 'Weber's law'. *Ibid.* 188 Fechner's law..embodies and illustrates the law of relativity; but it has a psycho-physical value over and above this. **1892** C. G. Chaddock tr. *Krafft-Ebing's Psychopathia Sexualis* v. 403 Large lips, idiotic expression,..and an awkward attitude complete the picture of psychophysical degeneration. **1894** Creighton & Titchener tr. *Wundt's Human & Animal Psychol.* 448 The principle of psychophysical parallelism..refers always to a parallelism of elementary physical and psychical processes. **1932** B. Petermann *Gestalt Theory* II. iii. 110 He commences with a general leading principle, that of psychophysical isomorphism. This is the assumption that a co-ordination exists between the domain of the experiences and that of the physiological processes..and that it is a co-ordination in the sense of congruence or isomorphism in regard to their systematic properties. **1941, 1956** [see *INTERACTIONISM]. **1942** W. KOEHLER *Dynamics in Psychol.* ii. 43 If an experience *A* may vary in a specific way, its correlate *a* must be capable of corresponding variations. When consistently applied, this point of view leads to the principle of psychophysical isomorphism. **1972** *Sci. Amer.* May 30/1 Young's celebrated three-color theory of color vision, published in 1802, was formulated entirely on psychophysical evidence. **1972** O. L. ZANGWILL in Cox & Dyson *20th-Cent. Mind* II. vii. 174 While still at Chicago, Watson had been much troubled by the psychophysical mould in which instruction in experimental psychology was still cast.

Hence **psychophy·sically** *adv.*, by psycho-physical means; as regards psychophysics.

1847 H. E. LLOYD tr. *Feuchtersleben's Med. Psychol.* v. 307 The so-called proximate cause of idiocy can..be no other than a psycho-physically impeded or depressed vital process. **1894** W. JAMES *Coll. Ess. & Rev.* (1920) 360 Do they mean that introspection acquaints them with a part of the emotional excitement which it is psycho-physically impossible that incoming currents should cause? **1948** L. SPITZER *Linguistics & Lit. Hist.* iv. 139 Man, this psycho-physically conditioned being. **1973** *Nature* 21 Sept. 159/2 Gibson and others have shown psychophysically that the gradient of density of visual texture is an important clue to the orientation in depth of textured surfaces.

psycho-physicist. Add: Now usu. without hyphen. (Further examples.)

1951 S. S. STEVENS *Handbk. Exper. Psychol.* i. 43/2 The psychophysicists have elaborated subtle measures that try to transcend the inconstancy of the mercurial response. **1975** *Nature* 20 Nov. 201/1 Even though psychophysicists do not necessarily share this confidence, it is worth trying to relate the neurophysiology to measurable psychophysical function.

psychophysicotherapeutics: see *PSYCHO-.

psycho-physiology and derivatives. Add: Now usu. without a hyphen. (Further examples.) Also **psy:chophysiolo·gic** *a.* (chiefly *U.S.*), **psy:chophysiolo·gically** *adv.*

1892 VAN LIEW & BEYER tr. *Ziehen's Introd. Study of Physiol. Psychol.* vii. 144 The projection and arrangement of our sensations with reference to time, the same as with reference to space, cannot be explained psychophysiologically. **1909** WEBSTER, Psychophysiologic. **1912** L. BLOOMFIELD in C. F. Hockett *Leonard Bloomfield Anthol.* (1970) 37 Sound-change and analogy..are, respectively, psycho-physiologic and psychologic processes. **1927** J. RIVIERE tr. *Freud's Ego & Id* ii. 31 Psycho-physiology has fully discussed the manner in which the body attains its special position among other objects in the world of perception. **1936** *Psychol. Rev.* XLIII. 411 The loudness scale will probably be utilized extensively by psychophysiologists and acoustical engineers. **1958** A. R. RADCLIFFE-BROWN in M. N. Srinivas *Method Social Anthropol.* I. iii. 45 The determination of what mental differences are correlated with these differences of cerebral structure is a task for the psychologist or psycho-physiologist. **1960** *Times Lit. Suppl.* 3 June 355/1 The new sciences of sociology and psychophysiology have both increasingly proposed that whether dealing with the crowd or the creative mind there are new skilled and precise ways of obtaining obedience, consent and, indeed, cooperation. **1972** *Sci. Amer.* June 91/1 The psycho-physiological basis of how contrast enables the visual system to distinguish contours. **1976** *Jrnl. Psychiatric Res.* XIII. 7 Three members of each group received a secondary or tertiary diagnosis of 'psychophysiologic gastrointestinal disorder'. **1977** *Nature* 28 Apr. 831/1 The intragroup social pressure determines the gonadal development of the subdominants. Their testes are smaller and show little or no mature testicular tissue. Low ranking males are psychophysiologically castrated.

psycho-political, -politics: see *PSYCHO-.

psychopomp. Add: Also **psy·chopompos.** Also, the spiritual guide of a (living) person's soul; a person who acts as a guide of the soul. (Further examples.)

1920 WEBSTER, Psycho-pomp.., psycho-pompos. **1941** AUDEN *New Year Let.* I. 27 For though the Janus of a joke The candid psychopompos spoke. **1946** *Antiquity* XX. 168 Hermes psychopompos, the mediator between the upper and the nether world. **1951** K. W. BASH tr. *Jacobi's Psychol. C. G. Jung* (ed. 5) III. 135 It is therefore 'an important function of the higher..super-personal animus that it guides and accompanies as a true Psychopompos the wanderings and transformations of the soul'. **1958** L. DURRELL *Balthazar* vi. 144 If I had been in your shoes and the whole damn thing wasn't just a lie to make yourself more interesting to the psychopomps—I'd..well, I'd bloody well try and sleep with him again. **1965** M. BRADBURY *Stepping Westward* vii. 336 He's a psychopomp, that's what he calls himself. You know that word? I think he gets it from Jung. A soul-saver, or something. A man who leads the spirit onward. **1971** *Southerly* XXXI. 12 The concept of the nymphet as psychopomp seems..a grotesque travesty of the Beatrice myth.

Hence **psychopo·mpically** *adv.* (*rare*).

1908 R. BROOKE *Lett.* (1968) 121, I, Hermes-like, am coming to fetch you psychopompically to Hell.

psycho-prismatism: see *PSYCHO-.

psy:choprophyla·xis. *Med.* Also with hyphen and (*rare*) anglicized as **-prophylaxy.** [f. PSYCHO- + PROPHYLAXIS.] A method intended to reduce or eliminate labour pains in which prenatal women are given an understanding of natural childbirth in order to obtain their physical co-operation with the process.

1958 I. BONSTEIN *Psychoprophylactic Preparation for Painless Childbirth* 5 It will be necessary to use them [*sc.* drugs] each time various difficulties prevent a confinement, prepared by psychoprophylaxy, from being continued until the end. **1960** D. A. MYSHNE tr. *Velvovsky's Painless Childbirth through Psychoprophylaxis* viii. 167 By psychoprophylaxis of labour pain we imply a system of measures aimed at preventing the appearance and development of labour pain and effected through influences exerted on the higher divisions of the central nervous system. **1965** *Observer* 1 Aug. 5/6 Dr. Pierre Vellay ..has made Paris a world centre of psycho-prophylaxis. **1972** J.-P. CLERC in N. Morris *Psychosomatic Med. in Obstetr. & Gynæcol.* 76 The first object of psychoprophylaxis is to eliminate the pain which is due to socio-cultural factors and may thus be regarded as psychosomatic. **1978** *Jrnl. R. Soc. Med.* LXXI. 663 Attempts have been made to measure psychological factors.., the benefits of psychoprophylaxis..and attitudinal aspects to antenatal education, but none have the precision of outcome which the obstetrician expects from tests of somatic function.

So **psy:choprophyla·ctic** *a.*, **psy:choprophyla·ctically** *adv.*

1958 I. BONSTEIN *Psychoprophylactic Preparation for Painless Childbirth* 5 The theory of the superior nervous activity, established by I. P. Pavlov.., is the basis of the psychoprophylactic preparation for painless childbirth. **1960** D. A. MYSHNE tr. *Velvovsky's Painless Childbirth through Psychoprophylaxis* viii. 199 Most of the time we consider the use of drugs for the purpose of 'enhancing' the pain prevention in psychoprophylactically well prepared women unnecessary. **1964** *New Statesman* 4 Dec. 874/3 Women in this country are most carefully taught how to cooperate with the ordinary maternity unit without abandoning their psychoprophylactic training. **1965** *Observer* 1 Aug. 5/6 The French Government is showing great interest in psycho-prophylactic obstetrics. **1972** E. D. BING in N. Morris *Psychosomatic Med. in Obstetr. & Gynæcol.* 71 Soon our first psychoprophylactically trained women gave birth, and our teachers had become the *monitrices* in order to assist the young mother in labor and delivery.

psycho-sensory: see *PSYCHO-.

psychose·xual, *a.* Also with hyphen. [f. PSYCHO- + SEXUAL *a.*] Involving the mental and emotional aspects of the sexual impulse.

1897 H. ELLIS *Stud. Psychol. Sex* I. iii. 73 (*heading*) Psychosexual inversion. *Ibid.* iv. 99 In other cases there is some degree of psycho-sexual hermaphroditism. **1913** A. A. BRILL tr. *Freud's Interpretation of Dreams* v. 200 Anxiety in dreams may be of a psychoneurotic nature, or it may originate in psychosexual excitements, in which case the anxiety corresponds to a repressed *libido.* **1946** *Mind* LV. 347 There are chapters sketching types of psycho-neurosis, psychosis, psycho-sexual disorder and other social disorders. **1963** *New Yorker* 29 June 84 The great unresolved psychosexual dilemma of modern man and woman. **1970** G. GREER *Female Eunuch* 43 Not all the massage in the world will ensure satisfaction, for it is a matter of psycho-sexual release. **1970** *Nature* 17 Oct. 203/2 Experimental studies to determine the psycho-sexual effects of pornography. **1976** S. HYNES *Auden Generation* v. 147 The [poem's] problem is set entirely in psycho-sexual terms.

Hence **psy:chosexua·lity; psychose·xually** *adv.*

1910 *Jrnl. Abnormal Psychol.* Apr.–May 67 Not only must the physician himself be able to approach the subject without prudishness and lewdness, but he must perforce know something about psychosexuality. **1912** A. A. BRILL tr. *Freud's Sel. Papers on Hysteria* (ed. 2) xi. 202 We..prefer to speak of psychosexuality, thus laying stress on the fact that the psychic factor of the sexual life should neither be overlooked nor underestimated. **1925** Psychosexuality [see *FIXATION 3 b]. **1934** WEBSTER, Psychosexually. **1956** *Nature* 14 Jan. 54/2 Through anthropological investigations, we have some idea how they develop psychosexually in other cultures. **1971** CAUTHERY & COLE *Fundamentals of Sex* v. 170 They are pathologically promiscuous but rarely obtain much pleasure from sex and are usually underdeveloped psychosexually.

psychosis. Add: **1.** (Further examples.) In mod. use, any mental illness or disorder that is accompanied by hallucinations, delusions, or mental confusion and a loss of contact with external reality, whether attributable to an organic lesion or not.

1924 J. RIVIERE tr. *Freud's Coll. Papers* I. iv. 72 The ego rejects the unbearable idea..and behaves as if the idea had never occurred to the person at all. But, as soon as this process has been successfully carried through, the person..will have developed a psychosis, and his state can only be described as one of 'hallucinatory confusion'. **1939** E. GLOVER *Psycho-Analysis* iv. 34 When deep guilt erupts, as in the depressive psychoses, we find that the self-accusations are not justified in reality. They are delusional. **1946** R. B. CATTELL *Description & Measurement of Personality* ii. 30 Psychoses are both endogenous and exogenous, organic and psychogenic... Some exogenous psychoses are..organic, in..that the provoking environmental influence—e.g., alcohol or syphilis—is organic. **1957** C. PFEIFFER in H. Abramson *Neuro-pharmacol.* (1959) 231 We have tried the Akerfeldt test in the model LSD psychosis in human volunteers. **1973** *Sci. Amer.* Sept. 117/3 The severe mental disorders we have learned to deal with more effectively are the psychoses, the most prominent of which are schizophrenia and manic-depressive psychosis. Psychoses are severe disorders characterized by profound and pervasive alterations of mood, disorganization of thought and withdrawal from social interactions into fantasy.

psycho-so·cial, *a.* Also without hyphen. [f. PSYCHO- + SOCIAL *a.*] Pertaining to the influence of social factors on an individual's mind or behaviour, and to the interrelation of behavioural and social factors; also, more widely, pertaining to the interrelation of mind and society in human development.

1899 F. W. MOORE tr. *Gumplowicz's Outl. Sociol.* II. 83 There are also psycho-social phenomena, such as language, customs, rights, religion etc., arising from the action of social elements with or upon the individual mind. **1903** *Amer. Jrnl. Sociol.* VIII. 762 In another quarter it is held that sociology is concerned only with the action of human groups on one another—social phenomena—and the influence of the group on its individual members—psycho-social phenomena. **1927** OGBURN & GOLDENWEISER *Social Sci.* xxiv. 303 Economics should also profit from such studies as the social psychologists, in the light of their knowledge of psycho-social mechanisms, see fit to make of specific institutional influences and controls. **1953** J. S. HUXLEY *Evolution in Action* i. 12 We may call these three phases [of evolution] the inorganic or, if you like, cosmological; the organic or biological; and the human or psycho-social. *Ibid.* vi. 134 Psycho-social evolution..operates by cultural transmission. **1954** [see *IDENTITY 10 c]. **1958** *Listener* 3 July 12/1 The possibility of conscious purpose arose and for the first time became a factor in man's subsequent evolution, which may be defined by Sir Julian Huxley's term as psycho-social. **1970** *Nature* 31 Oct. 422/1 The original aim of this investigation was to compare the psychosocial characteristics of a group of heroin pushers with those of a group of heroin users who did not sell drugs. **1971** I. G. GASS et al. *Understanding Earth* ix. 125/1 The nöosphere..produces idea-systems by processes of psycho-social evolution. **1977** P. B. & J. S. MEDAWAR *Life Science* vi. 53 It is because of the primacy of language as the agency which provides the link between one generation and the next that exosomatic evolution is often referred to as 'cultural' or 'psychosocial' evolution.

Hence **psycho-so·cially** *adv.*

1946 [see *PSYCHOSOMATICALLY *adv.*]. **1972** *Sci. Amer.* July 81/3 Is it in fact possible to attribute the retarded growth of psychosocially deprived children to sleep patterns that inhibit the secretion of growth hormone?

psycho-sociology, etc.: see *PSYCHO-.

psychosoma·tic, *a.* and *sb.* [f. PSYCHO- + SOMATIC *a.* and *sb.*] **A.** *adj.* **a.** Involving or depending on both the mind and the body as mutually dependent entities.

1863 C. READE *Hard Cash* II. xi. 119 The nocturnal and diurnal attendance of a Psycho-physical physician, who knows the Psychosomatic relation of body and mind. **1930** M. W. CALKINS in C. Murchison *Hist. Psychol. in Autobiogr.* I. 44 This biological form of personalistic psychology studies the psychophysical, or better the psychosomatic organism. **1933** H. DEVINE *Rec. Adv. Psychiatry* (ed. 2) i. 1 The purpose of this chapter is to discuss the modern concept of 'psychosomatic unity', or, as it is sometimes termed, the concept of 'the organism-as-a-whole'. **1956** E. L. MASCALL *Christian Theol. & Nat. Sci.* vii. 270 A human being is not just a spirit that is temporarily condemned to inhabit a material garment, but is a highly complicated psycho-somatic unity, in which the body is an essential constituent. **1976** *Verbatim* Sept. 11/2 The biblical view of personality was psychosomatic (and distinct from Platonic dualism—'the body is the prison-house of the soul'). So in both the Hebrew and Christian Scriptures, what we would call psychic or spiritual states are freely ascribed to physical organs and other parts of the human anatomy.

b. Applied to physical disorders caused or aggravated by mental, emotional, or psychological factors, and (less commonly) to mental or emotional disorders caused or aggravated by physical factors.

1938 S. BECKETT *Murphy* x. 219 Murphy..did not suffer from this—er—psychosomatic fistula. **1947** J. STEINBECK *Wayward Bus* 170 She called her mother's [headaches] psychosomatic and psychotic. **1950** A. HUXLEY *Themes & Variations* i. 67 Hypertension, neurosis, psychosis and all the varieties of psycho-somatic disorders. **1957** *New Biol.* XXII. 83 These are the so-called psychosomatic disorders. The distinctive feature of these illnesses is that, although they are of nervous origin, they come to the attention of patient and physician through some malfunctioning of an organ. **1958** H. L. & R. R. ANSBACHER *Indiv. Psychol. of Adler* II. xi. 286 The role of organ inferiority in psychosomatic disturbances proper will be discussed in the next chapter. **1964** *Ann. Reg.* *1963* 414 Mental strain..had often led to psychosomatic illness. **1975** B. WOOD *Killing Gift* v. iii. 150 We've built up a really solid case, at least statistically, for psychosomatic influence on breast-cancer incidence.

c. Applied to the branch of medicine concerned with the relations between the mind and the body.

1939 (*title of periodical*) Psychosomatic medicine. **1939** *Psychiatry* II. 465/1 Psychosomatic Medicine covers a different and broader field. Its object is to study in their interrelation the psychological and physiological aspects of all normal and abnormal bodily functions and thus to integrate somatic therapy and psychotherapy. **1946** *Jrnl. R. Aeronaut. Soc.* L. 263/2 The American Army had a separate section of the Medical Service dealing with what was called psychosomatic medicine. **1960** *20th Cent.* Mar. 267 Psychosomatic research has revealed that almost every common disease can have an emotional component. **1971** *Country Life* 9 Sept. 646/4 Psychosomatic medicine today appears to be making a full-circle exploration.

B. *sb. pl.* (const. as *sing.*). The field of study concerned with the relationship between mind and body.

1941 *Amer. Jrnl. Psychiatry* XCVII. 781 We will take up the present day research trends in the following order:..psychosomatics (psychophysiology). **1941** *Psychosomatic Med.* III. 332, I surveyed ten years' literature in the field of psychosomatics. **1946** B. MITTELMAN in P. L. Harriman *Encycl. Psychol.* 678 It is obvious..from its problems and methods that psychosomatics represents a synthesis of several streams of psychological and medical investigation. **1966** *N.Y. State Jrnl. Med.* LXVI. 3157/1 The view of the skin as a major organ of communication is not a new one; it is a basic concept of psychosomatic medicine. But if the ECM proposed here are more fully identified, some of the 'metaphors' of psychosomatics will turn out to be descriptions of real events. **1975** B. WOOD *Killing Gift* IV. i. 131 His very next paper ..was on psychosomatics... He chaired a..conference on the psychosomatics of cancer.

Hence **psychosoma·tically** *adv.*, in a psychosomatic manner; *esp.* through the (unconscious) effect of the mind on the body; **psychosoma·ticist**, an expert or specialist in psychosomatic medicine; **psychoso·matism** (*rare*), psychosomatics; **psychoso·matist** = *PSYCHOSOMATICIST.

1854 J. C. BUCKNILL *Unsoundness of Mind* 15 The psycho-somatists find in the liability of the cerebral instrument to disease, a reasonable basis for the irresponsibility of the insane. **1946** *Lancet* 10 Aug. 190/2 Epidemiology..was founded and formulated mainly upon experience gained by the study of infectious diseases, but its use as a framework of interpretation is equally applicable to many modes of morbid behaviour that are manifestations of disturbances of emotional development—i.e., of 'life' viewed psychologically, psychosomatically, and psychosocially. **1957** *Time* 4 Nov. 56/2 It was the story of a girl who went psychosomatically deaf in emotional flight from her role as the ears of a deaf father, mother and brother. **1960** *20th Cent.* Mar. 268 Psychosomatists believe..that each of us possesses a built-in homeostatic mechanism designed to keep us healthy. *Ibid.* 269 This does not mean that psychosomatists attribute all illnesses, invariably, to states of mind. *Ibid.*, Psychosomatism is not, therefore, a 'craze'. Until less than a century ago every great medical school—Hippocratean and Christian alike—subscribed to what Mr. Jelly sneers at as the 'argot' of treating 'the whole man'. **1960** *Spectator* 14 Oct. 555 The first practising psychosomatist—if the term is allowable—that I had met. **1962** N. E. WHITTEN in A. Dundes *Mother Wit* (1973) 418/1 The only reason that the effects of a spell can be removed is that they are psychosomatically caused in the first place. **1962** C. L. BUXTON *Study of Psychophysical Methods for Relief of Childbirth Pain* i. 2 The very environment thought by psychosomaticists to contribute to difficult, prolonged and painful labor is everywhere present in this episode. **1971** *Time* 7 June 96/2 The family physician bucks the case to a psychosomaticist, who flounders in jargon. **1976** *Times Lit. Suppl.* 10 Sept. 1105/2 She was psychosomatically deaf for a week.

psychosomimetic: see *PSYCHOTOMIMETIC *a.* and *sb.* **psychosphere, -stimulant:** see *PSYCHO-.

psychosu·rgery. [f. PSYCHO- + SURGERY.] Brain surgery intended to alter the behaviour of patients with certain kinds of severe mental stress or disorder.

1936 *Q. Cumul. Index Medicus* XIX. 249/1 First attempts at psychosurgery using leukotome; technic and results. **1938** *Jrnl. Nerv. & Mental Dis.* LXXXVIII. 589 (*heading*) Psychosurgery. Effect on certain mental symptoms of surgical interruption of pathways in the frontal lobe. **1952** METTLER & CANDIS in F. A. Mettler *Psychosurgical Probl.* xvi. 319 As a result of such adverse criticism practitioners of psychosurgery were forced to restrict the operative procedure to more rostral areas. **1973** *Nature* 23 Mar. 222/3 Unlike the classical lobotomy operation,..psychosurgery now rarely involves actually cutting into the brain... Psychosurgery, which is designed to alter behaviour, is usually distinguished from the treatment of epilepsy and the removal of brain tumours. **1977** M. EDELMAN *Political Lang.* iv. 58 Some psychiatrists..see political demonstrators or ghetto rioters as sick, calling for drugs or psychosurgery.

Hence **psychosu·rgical** *a.*; also **psy·chosurgeon**, a surgeon specializing in psychosurgery.

1945 WEBSTER Add., Psychosurgeon. **1946** *Canad. Med. Assoc. Jrnl.* LV. 435/1 In 1941 the research unit of the Toronto Psychiatric Hospital embarked upon the psychosurgical treatment of hopelessly mentally ill patients. **1949** M. CLARK *Medicine on March* v. 99 Summing up their ten years' work, the two psychosurgeons declared: 'The results are sufficiently good to warrant the use of prefrontal lobotomy..for the relief of the very serious and chronic forms of mental disease.' **1950** [see *LEUCOTOMY]. **1952** B. WOLFE *Limbo '90* (1953) xxii. 368 The phony rapist's phony premises become the premises of the psycho-surgeon's science. **1972** *Lancet* 8 July 70/1 The modern psychosurgeon must be versatile enough to employ different operations for different symptom complexes. **1972** M. CRICHTON *Terminal Man.* vi. 46 Computer scientists and neurobiologists had worked together for several years. From that association had come Form Q, and programs like George and Martha, and new psychosurgical techniques.

psychosyndrome, -synthesis, etc.: see *PSYCHO-.

psycho-technic (-te·knik), *sb.* and *a.* Also without hyphen. [ad. G. *psychotechnik* sb. (H. Münsterberg *Grundzüge der Psychotechnik* (1914) i. 1): see PSYCHO- and TECHNIC *a.* and *sb.*] **A.** *sb.* = *PSYCHOTECHNOLOGY. Also *pl.*

1926 *Psychol. Rev.* XXXIII. 402 In the applied division [of psychology], sometimes called psychotechnics, the aim is to make psychological facts useful in many different directions. **1927** *Daily Express* 17 June 12/3 The value of psycho-technic..is that it enables the railway company to eliminate at once the employee who will not be reliable. **1928** H. P. WELD *Psychol. as Sci.* xv. 266 Applied psychology is evidently to be classed with the technical sciences. It may be considered as psychotechnics. **1952** *Brit. Jrnl. Psychol.* XLIII. 83 He is continental in tending to leave to 'psychotechnics' areas which in England would fall within respectable occupational psychology.

B. *adj.* = *PSYCHO-TECHNICAL *a.*

1932 *Brit. Jrnl. Psychol.* XXV. 77 These results are of value in..forcing us to realize the importance of attitudes in all judgements..in the ordering of psychotechnic test results. **1957** W. ABELL *Collective Dream in Art* 4 The result has been the gradual emergence of a synthesis which we may call the..'psycho-technic' theory of culture. **1973** *Daily Tel.* 27 Nov. 12/6 Peter Riding's programme vividly simulated part of the 'psycho-technic test' to be undertaken as well as a medical check, written questions on motoring and..an examination in actual driving.

psycho-te·chnical, *a.* Also without hyphen. [f. PSYCHO- + TECHNICAL *a.*] Pertaining to or concerned with the application of psychological facts or knowledge to practical problems in industry, employment, education, etc.

1903 H. MÜNSTERBERG in *Harvard Psychol. Stud.* I. 654 The science of pedagogy is a psycho-technical discipline which makes education mechanical. **1927** *Daily Express* 17 June 12 Electrical machinery, levers, mechanical puzzles, and complete paraphernalia for psychotechnical tests. **1962** *Guardian* 20 July 5/7 To the applicants for jobs, the 'psychotechnical' examinations were at once ludicrous and frightening.

psy:chotechno·logy. [f. PSYCHO- + TECHNOLOGY.] The area of study concerned with the practical application of tested knowledge about the human mind or brain. Hence **psy:chotechno·logist**, an expert or specialist in this.

1923 F. A. KINGSBURY in *Ann. Amer. Acad. Pol. & Social Sci.* CX. 5/1 Psychotechnology, or applied psychology, is interested in acquiring facts and principles only in so far as they can be turned directly to account in the solution of practical problems, in industry, selling, teaching or other fields of human endeavour. *Ibid.* 8/2 The careful psychotechnologist submits his hypothetical solution of concrete problems to prolonged and severe experimental tests. **1928** H. P. WELD *Psychol. as Sci.* xv. 280 Psychotechnology is a product of this century, and there can be little doubt that it will, in years to come, extend its activities. **1947** *Harvard Univ. Comm. Place of Psychol. in Ideal Univ.* 11 Values of the science and of psychotechnology may be exemplified more readily than enumerated. *Ibid.* 23 Already the demand greatly exceeds the supply of trained psychologists, psychotechnologists, ..etc. **1953** J. B. CARROLL *Study of Lang.* vii. 196 In Europe applied psychology is widely identified as psychotechnology. **1973** *Sci. Amer.* Sept. 117/1 The potential power of this developing 'psychotechnology' is..creating concern about unwarranted intrusions into personal privacy and individual rights. **1973** R. L. & R. K. SCHWITZGEBEL (*title*) Psychotechnology: electronic control of mind and behavior.

psycho-therapeutic, *a.* and *sb.* Add: Now usu. without hyphen. **A.** *adj.* Also, of, pertaining to, or characterized by psychotherapy. (Further examples.)

1914 A. A. BRILL tr. *Freud's Psychopathol. Everyday Life* v. 93 The psychotherapeutic procedure which I employ in the solution and removal of neurotic symptoms. **1957** *Times Lit. Suppl.* 1 Nov. 659/4 That organized religion has been the greatest psychotherapeutic system ever invented is one of Jung's most famous dicta. **1963** A. HERON *Towards Quaker View of Sex* 51 All the large teaching hospitals have psychiatric out-patient departments of varying size and with more or less psychotherapeutic help to hand. **1970** *Jrnl. Gen. Psychol.* LXXXIII. 194 Laffal has applied this approach in studies of.. psychotherapeutic interviews. **1976** *Times Lit. Suppl.* 16 July 872/2 The spiritual healers either operate on the margin or they must be certified members or associates of a recognized psychotherapeutic fraternity.

B. *sb.* (Earlier and further examples.) Also = PSYCHO-THERAPY in Dict. and Suppl. Also (*rare*) in sing. form **psychotherapeutic.**

1872 D. H. TUKE *Illustrations of Influence of Mind on Body* p. ix, The medical reader.., I hope, may be induced to employ Psycho-therapeutics in a more methodical way than heretofore. **1903** F. W. H. MYERS *Hum. Personality* II. 515 Suggestions involving..bodily odour and chemical conditions have thus far been confined to psycho-therapeutics. *Ibid.* 527 That form of psychotherapeutic which consists in a clairvoyant diagnosis.. followed perhaps by advice avowedly based upon a recollection of earthly learning. **1906** *Boston Med. & Surg. Jrnl.* 8 Nov. 542/1 A fundamental difficulty in psychotherapeutics up to this time has been a lack of method. **1933** *Mind* XLII. 114 Abnormal psychology.. has generalised with a freedom astonishing to those who are familiar with the logical austerities of science. This may be allowed to psychotherapeutics, but not to anything that calls itself psychology.

Hence **psychotherapeu·tically** *adv.*, by means of psychotherapy, in a psychotherapeutic manner; **psychotherapeutist** (further examples).

1906 *Amer. Jrnl. Med. Sci.* Oct. 499 The neurasthenic women..rested in bed, were isolated, and treated 'psychotherapeutically' much as were the hysterical. *Ibid.* 520 The psychotherapeutist should be an honest man and an expert clinician. **1909** H. MÜNSTERBERG *Psychotherapy* p. ix, Since that time I have never ceased to work psychotherapeutically in the psychological laboratory. **1957** *Listener* 12 Sept. 401/1 The psycho-therapeutist..no longer confines his attention to the classical mental disorders, but,..has set up advisory centres to deal with problems of life or..mental hygiene, arising at almost any phase from infancy to senescence. **1962** J. MONEY *Reading Disability* i. 17 Reading tuition is individualized, scholastically and psychotherapeutically, as much as economics permit.

psycho-therapy. Add: Now usu. without hyphen. (Earlier and later examples.) In mod. use, the treatment of disorders of the mind or personality by psychological or psychophysiological methods. [Cf. van Renterghem & van Eeden *Clinique de Psycho-thérapie Suggestive* (Brussels, 1889).]

Quot. 1853, an isolated use, represents a different sense.

1853 *Jrnl. Psychol. Med. & Mental Path.* VI. 268 (*heading*) Psychotherapeia, or the remedial influence of mind. **1892** F. W. VAN EEDEN in *Med. Mag.* I. 233 As a general term for our treatment we selected in 1889, 'Suggestive Psycho-therapy'. We called psychotherapy every description of therapeutics that cures by means of the intervention of the psychical functions of the sufferer. This title is borrowed from Hack Tuke... Psycho-therapy.. has..had the misfortune to be taken in tow by hypnotism. **1897** T. H. KELLOGG *Text-bk. Mental Dis.* xi. 497 By the term psychotherapy is signified..every means and every possible agency which primarily affects the psychical rather than the physical organization of the patient in a curative direction. **1906** *Amer. Jrnl. Med. Sci.* CXXXII. 499 Prof. Dejerine was treating the psychoneuroses, especially hysteria and neurasthenia, by isolation and psychotherapy. **1947** *Nature* 4 Jan. 38/2 Psychotherapy may be useful for the criminal, but it is prolonged, and an impractical treatment with present resources. **1958** *Sunday Times* 15 June 13/3 By psychotherapy is meant the systematic application of psychological principles to the treatment of psychogenic ill-health and maladjustment. **1963** A. HERON *Towards Quaker View of Sex* 50 A number of psychotherapy clinics which give treatment for sexual difficulties. **1976** SMYTHIES & CORBETT *Psychiatry* ii. 19 Psychotherapy consists very largely in helping people to grow up, to exchange the egocentric child's role for the mature role of the adult.

Hence **psychothe·rapist**, a specialist in or practitioner of psychotherapy.

1909 A. A. BRILL tr. *Freud's Sel. Papers Hysteria* iii. 55, I was not always a psychotherapist but like other neuropathologists I was educated to the use of focal diagnosis and electrical prognosis. **1923** *Daily Mail* 19 Jan. 7 An earnest warning to nervous persons to avoid spiritualism is given by Dr. W. Stekel, the Viennese neurologist and psycho-therapist. **1930** R. S. WOODWORTH *Psychology* (ed. 8) xiii. 568 Many psychotherapists avoid the use of hypnosis because, as they say, it does not get to the root of the trouble. **1976** SMYTHIES & CORBETT *Psychiatry* xvii. 291 Most psychotherapists refuse to give specific advice as to what their patient's conduct should be in cases where ethical problems are concerned.

psychotic, *a.* Add: **a.** (Examples.)

1920 C. S. READ *Milit. Psychiatry in Peace & War* ii. 21 These figures..include pure epilepsy without any psychotic complications. **1949** *Endeavour* VIII. 37/1 The use of electric shock therapy for the treatment of certain types of psychotic patients is sometimes complicated by injuries suffered during the electrically produced convulsions. **1957** *Jrnl. Brit. Interplanetary Soc.* XVI. 8 Among psychologists, 'psychotic break' refers to the breaking loose of feeling from its previously adequate controls. **1965** J. POLLITT *Depression & its Treatment* i. 4 In advanced states the patient lacks insight and becomes psychotic. **1971** *Brit. Med. Bull.* XXVII. 77/1 An equally strong case can be made for the opposite view, that psychotic and neurotic forms of depression lie on the same continuum.

B. *absol.* as *sb.* A person with a psychosis.

1910 *Jrnl. Nervous & Mental Disease* XXXVII. 633 Thus arise the well-known 'explanation-delusions' of the psychotic. **1921** E. J. KEMPF *Psychopathology* xiv. 718 Many ask the question.., 'Why do all neurotics and psychotics have sexual difficulties?' **1939** J. DOLLARD in A. Dundes *Mother Wit* (1973) 278/2 Psychotics in American hospitals display disorders of perception. **1958** M. ARGYLE *Relig. Behaviour* ix. 109 Many psychotics believe themselves to be religious leaders, prophets or mystics. **1962** *Lancet* 8 Dec. 1212/1 It might be that because some beds had been freed from psychotics, patients with neuroses or personality disorders..could be admitted to hospital. **1975** B. MEGGS *Matter of Paradise* VII. i. 189 You're asking..whether..we might hope to identify a deteriorated psychotic *before* he enters government.

Hence **psycho·tically** *adv.*

1961 in WEBSTER. **1977** *Irish Press* 29 Sept. 6/5 The ingredients include a weak and unsuccessful father who died young and an over protective mother whose motives were selfish rather than loving, and who was almost psychotically indifferent to George's progress except to record the inconvenience it caused her.

psychoticism (səikǫ·tisiz'm). [f. PSYCHOTIC *a.* + -ISM.] The condition or state of being psychotic or of displaying psychotic tendencies; esp. as a factor showing liability to psychosis included in certain types of personality assessment.

1950 H. J. EYSENCK in *Jrnl. Personality* XIX. 129 His [*sc.* Kretschmer's] theory can best be represented in terms of two orthogonal axes, one measuring schizothymia-cyclothymia, the other normality-psychotic abnormality or 'psychoticism'. **1955** *Jrnl. Mental Sci.* CI. 876 The effect of insulin therapy is not dependent upon the initial degree of psychoticism as used in the present sense. **1957** R. B. CATTELL *Personality & Motivation* xvi. 719 At present a psychoticism measure would be considerably contaminated and distorted. **1957**, etc. [see *NEUROTICISM]. **1960** PAYNE & HEWLETT in H. Eysenck *Exper. in Personality* II. 11 It was demonstrated that only one factor was necessary to account for the differences observed between the three groups. This factor was labelled 'psychoticism'. **1964** [see *INTROVERSION 1b]. **1977** *New Society* 7 Apr. 33/3 This book aims to establish psychoticism..alongside neuroticism, extraversion and intelligence... The attribute it measures is a halfway stage to psychosis, as neuroticism is to neurosis.

psychotogenic (səikǫ:todʒe·nik), *a.* [f. as next + *-GENIC.] = *PSYCHOTOMIMETIC *a.*

1956 *Arch. Neurol. & Psychiatry* LXXV. 122/1 To the neurologist the psychotogenic agents offer a special challenge. **1962** *Lancet* 27 Jan. 200/2 There is impressive evidence of the psychotogenic effects of some adrenaline derivatives. **1971** *Nature* 19 Nov. 152/2 The differential behavioural response of subjects to *d* and *l*-amphetamine might provide clues to psychotogenic mechanisms.

Hence (as back-formations) **psycho·togen,** a psychotomimetic substance; **psycho:toge·nesis,** the production of a psychosis or psychosis-like state.

1959 *Neuropharmacology: Trans. 4th Conf., 1957* 223 Relationship between endogenous substances that are found in the brain—epinephrine, norepinephrine, and.. serotonin—and the possible relationship to the exogenous psychotogens. **1960** *Clin. Pharmacol. & Therapeutics* I. 251/2 The recovery of a chronically psychotic patient coincidentally with the administration of some drug is as dramatic as..the drug-induced psychosis. Recovery, however, is an even less satisfactory foundation for a psychopharmacologic theory than is psychotogenesis. **1971** *Nature* 19 Nov. 152/2 If noradrenergic mechanisms and behaviourally correlated motor stimulation were critical in psychotogenesis then one might expect *d*-amphetamine to have ten times the potency of the *l* form in inducing psychosis as a behavioural effect. **1974** M. C. GERALD *Pharmacol.* xvii. 318 Drugs in this same category are also termed hallucinogens, psychedelics, psychotogens, psychodysleptics, and so forth. **1976** *Nature* 8 Apr. 490/1 For many years the presence of an endogenous psychotogen in schizophrenia has been sought. **1977** *Lancet* 27 Aug. 449/2 Further study of psychotogenesis and of the relation between morphinoids and endogenous neurotransmitters and neuromodulators will probably..clarify the biochemistry both of addiction and of schizophrenia.

psychotomimetic (səikǫ:tomime·tik, -məime·tik), *a.* and *sb.* Also †**psychoso-.** [Orig. formed as *psychosomimetic*, f. PSYCHOS(IS + -O + MIMETIC *a.*, and later altered to match PSYCHOTIC *a.*] **A.** *adj.* Having an effect on the mind orig. likened to that of a psychotic state, with abnormal changes in thought, perception, and mood and a subjective feeling of an expansion of consciousness; of or pertaining to a drug with this effect.

1956 R. W. GERARD in *Neuropharmacology: Trans. 2nd Conf., 1955* 132 Let us at least agree to speak of 'so-called' psychoses when we are dealing with them in animals...Along that same line, I have liked a term which I have been using lately—'psychosomimetic'—for these agents instead of 'schizophrenogenic'. **1957** *Neuropharmacology: Trans 3rd Conf., 1956* 205 (*heading*) Effects of psychosomimetic drugs in animals and man. **1957** H. OSMOND in *Ann. N.Y. Acad. Sci.* LXVI. 417 The designation 'psychotomimetic agents' for those drugs that mimic some of the mental aberrations that occur in the psychoses had been suggested by Ralph Gerard and seemed especially appropriate. **1958** M. JARVIK in H. H. Pennes *Psychopharmacology* ix. 204 They have been called psychoso- or psychotomimetic, psychotherapeutic, tranquilizing, ataraxic,.. or, as a general class, psychochemical, neurotropic,.. and a number of other names. **1962** HENDERSON & GILLESPIE *Text-bk. Psychiatry* xi. 258 The hallucinogenic (or psychotomimetic) drugs most often employed have been mescaline and lysergic acid (LSD 25). **1964** D. F. DOWNING in M. Gordon *Psychopharmacological Agents* I. xiii. 562 Psilocybin and psilocin produce a psychotomimetic effect in man..which is similar to that produced by mescaline or LSD-25. **1967** *Sunday Mail* (Brisbane) 27 Aug. 5/1 In the field of drugs, a medical friend says that if you want another term for psychedelics you could call them..psychotomimetic. **1970** E. GOODE *Marijuana Smokers* vii. 172 The general psychotomimetic questions include: 'Is your skin sensitive?' 'Are you happy?' 'Are colors brighter?' **1970** D. H. EFRON *Psychotomimetic Drugs* 5 The use of these psychotomimetic substances in ancient times was either for religious, ceremonial or recreational purposes. **1975** BRIMBLECOMBE & PINDER *Hallucinogenic Agents* i. 3 It has been pointed out several times..that there are well-defined differences between mental states induced by the majority of pyschotomimetic drugs and those encountered in mental illness.

B. *sb.* A psychotomimetic drug.

1957 *Ann. N.Y. Acad. Sci.* LXVI. 418 We are using Gerard's term 'psychotomimetics' generally for compounds that have been called schizogens, psychotica, psychotogens, phantastica, hallucinogens and elixirs. If one believes that the importance of these compounds lies in their capacity to mimic the mental illnesses called psychoses, psychotomimetics would be the choice. **1970** A. T. SHULGIN in D. H. Efron *Psychotomimetic Drugs* 25 Ibogaine..is another example in the family of psychotomimetics, with complex structures and no resemblance to known metabolic materials. **1974** M. C. GERALD *Pharmacol.* xvi. 299 The psychotomimetics (hallucinogens) such as LSD or mescaline produce profound alterations in behavior.

Hence **psycho:tomime·tically** *adv.*

1963 *Tetrahedron* XIX. 2073 Hashish (marihuana), the psychotomimetically active resin of the female flowering tops of *Cannabis sativa L.* **1970** L. HARMON in D. H. Efron *Psychotomimetic Drugs* 349 So for Dan's N.I.M.H. hospitality (T'was psychotomimetically hip) Great thanks for new lights on mentality And a most unforgettable TRIP. **1973** R. MECHOULAM *Marijuana* p. xiii, The structure of only one [cannabinoid], the psychotomimetically inactive cannabinol, had been fully elucidated.

psychotropic (səikotrōᵘ·pik, -trǫ·pik), *a.* and *sb.* Also **-trophic** (-trōᵘ·fik). [f. PSYCHO- + *-TROPIC, *-TROPHIC.] **A.** *adj.* Affecting a person's mental state; psychoactive; *spec.* = *PSYCHOTOMIMETIC *a.*; of or pertaining to a drug of this kind.

1956 M. RINKEL in *Neuropharmacology: Trans. 2nd Conf., 1955* 240, I had considerable conversation on this subject with Dr. Goodman..and Dr. Loewi of Utah University. They made the very good proposal of calling all these drugs which affect the mind 'phrenotropic or psychotropic'. This general term would allow for a number of subdivisions: drugs that are beneficial; those which may cause psychosis; [etc.]. **1962** *Listener* 13 Dec. 1003/1 In recent years extravagant hopes have been centred on the psychotropic drugs, drugs which will relieve agitation and depression. **1968** *Sunday Mail* (Brisbane) 10 Nov. 1/2 Traffic in psychotropic drugs—ranging from LSD to sedatives—had reached 'epidemic proportions', the International Narcotics Control Board warned yesterday. **1968** A. GOLDSTEIN et al. *Princ. Drug Action* vi. 474 Despite the nearly universal exposure of the population to the 'legal' psychotropic drugs (alcohol, caffeine, and nicotine), some become habituated and some do not. **1970** *Nature* 7 Feb. 485/1 The essence of the commission's code is a catalogue of drugs of dependence—'psychotrophic drugs' as they are now called. **1972** J. I. M. Stewart *Palace of Art* vii. 66 Art, like a tomtom or a psychotropic drug, can loosen up the mind of an individual exposed to it. **1977** *It* June 2/4 If you enter a state of non-ordinary reality, as you do when you use psychotropic plants, it is only to draw from it what you need in order to see the miraculous character of ordinary reality. **1977** *Lancet* 24–31 Dec. 1326/1 None of the subjects were taking psychotrophic medication at the time of admission. **1978** *Guardian Weekly* 1 Jan. 10/1 Large numbers of prisoners are being given psychotropic drugs as a form of social control rather than medical treatment.

B. *sb.* A psychotropic drug.

1976 *Nature* 29 Apr. p. ix (Advt.), Astra Chemicals is the UK subsidiary of Scandinavia's largest pharmaceutical group which specialises in the research, manufacture and marketing of ethical drugs in the fields of local anaesthetics, bronchodilators, cardiovasculars and psychotropics. **1977** *Proc. R. Soc. Med.* LXX. 766/2 The majority are adults who have deliberately swallowed an overdose of drugs, chiefly in the category of 'psychotropics'.

Hence **psychotro·pically** *adv.*

1962 *Jrnl. Sci. & Industr. Res.* XXIA. 421/2 The psychotropically active hydrazines having a monoamine oxidase inhibiting effect are pronounced antidepressants.

psycho-visual: see *PSYCHO-.

psychro- (səikro), comb. form of Gr. ψυχρός cold (cf. PSYCHROMETER, etc.).

psychrophi·lic *a. Biol.* [*-PHILIC], (of an organism, esp. a bacterium) capable of growing at temperatures close to freezing, or having an optimum temperature that is low; so **psy·chrophil, -phile** *sb.*, a psychrophilic organism; also as *adj.*, = prec.; **psy·chrosphere,** the colder, deeper part of the oceans; hence **psychrosphe·ric** *a.*; **psychroto·lerance** *Biol.* [ad. G. *psychrotoleranz* (Horowitz-Wlassowa & Grinberg 1933, in *Zentralbl. f. Bakteriol., Parasitenkunde und Infektionskrankheiten* (Abt. 2) LXXXIX. 58)], the property of being able to grow at temperatures close to freezing; (introduced, like *psychrotrophic*, because of the ambiguity of *psychrophilic*); so **psychroto·lerant** *a.*; **psychrotro·phic** *a. Biol.* [*-TROPHIC] = *psychrotolerant* adj. above; so **psy·chrotroph,** a psychrotrophic organism.

1928 P. H. FOSTER in C. M. Hilliard *Textbk. Bacteriol.* viii. 95 Psychrophiles are organisms which develop at or very near the freezing point. **1956** *Nature* 16 June 1106 Such barophilic bacteria..are also psychrophil and very stenothermal. **1959** *New Scientist* 3 Dec. 1111/1 Psychrophils also ferment carbohydrates, decompose proteins,.. and generally go about their business like other bacteria, except that their metabolism seems to be somewhat slowed up. **1959** *Bacteriol. Rev.* XXIII. 99/1 The unique property of psychrophilic bacteria is the ability to grow well at 0 C. This was recognized from the very beginning of the study of psychrophiles...The essentially erroneous concept that psychrophiles are distinguished by their ability to grow most rapidly below 20 C did not arise until later. **1969** *Nature* 15 Mar. 1031/1 Obligate psychrophiles—organisms able to grow well at 0°C but incapable of growth at moderate temperatures—provide suitable test organisms in this respect. When the obligate psychrophile *Micrococcus cryophilus* is grown in optimal conditions at 20°C, and then transferred to 30°C—5°C above the maximum for this organism—growth halts very quickly. **1897** LEHMANN & NEUMANN *Atlas & Essentials of Bacteriol.* 98 Psychrophilic bacteria: minimum at 0°, best at 15°–20°, maximum at about 30°. These varieties usually live in water. **1958** W. C. FRAZIER *Food Microbiol.* xxiv. 304 At refrigerator temperatures, proteolysis by psychrophilic bacteria like *Pseudomonas* is most likely, and molds may follow. **1963** J. L. STOKES in N. E. Gibbons *Rec. Progress Microbiol.* 190 The maximum growth temperatures of many psychrophilic microorganisms can be quite high. **1964** [see *mesophilic* adj. s.v. *MESO-]. **1975** R. R. GILLIES *Lect. Notes Med. Bacteriol.* iii. 15 Psychrophilic bacteria, i.e. those which grow best at temperatures below 20°C, are non-pathogenic for man but exist in soil and water. **1956** A. T. BRUUN in *Nature* 16 June 1106 (*in figure*) Psychrosphere. **1957** —— in *Mem. Geol. Soc. Amer.* LXVII. 641 The division of the hydrosphere into a warm troposphere and a cold stratosphere, or the Warmwassersphäre and Kaltwassersphäre in the terms of Wüst (1950) is the most pronounced division in the oceanic water masses. In the following the terms thermosphere and psychrosphere are used for these divisions to stress this salient ecological factor. *Ibid.*, The limit of the psychrosphere may be at about 100 meters in the eastern parts of the oceans where there is upwelling, whereas in western regions it may be as deep as 700 meters. **1976** *Nature* 8 Apr. 513/2 Three major elements were involved in the evolution of oceanic circulation during the Cainozoic...The third involves the development of the present-day system of bottom waters of the world ocean, the 'psychrosphere'. **1977** *Ibid.* 2 June 399/2 Aside from benthic foraminifera, psychrospheric ostracods also occur in some Early and Middle Miocene cores, indicating water-depths in excess of 1000 m. **1977** *Sci. Amer.* June 50/3 The bacteria's only way to adapt to the environmental conditions of the deep sea appears to be the acquisition of barotolerance and psychrotolerance. **1959** *Bacteriol. Rev.* XXIII. 98/2 The recognition that low temperatures are not optimum for organisms that grow at 0 C led to the introduction of several other names as replacement for psychrophile. These included.. psychro-tolerant. **1970** *Sci. Jrnl.* May 19 Slime is caused by cold resistant, or psychrotolerant, bacteria which are not a health hazard but which produce an objectionable smell. **1979** *Nature* 21 June p. x (Advt.), An excellent survey is thus provided of the importance of psychrotrophic bacteria and of techniques involving psychrotolerant and psychtrotrophic micro-organisms. **1963** M. INGRAM in N. E. Gibbons *Rec. Progress Microbiol.* 185 To avoid such misconceptions, the term psychrotroph.. has recently been proposed for all organisms able to grow at temperatures near 0 C. **1968** *New Scientist* 18 Apr. 117/2 Farm contamination from..unclean dairy equipment, will allow psychrotrophs to proliferate if milk is stored at 5°–10°C. **1960** B. P. EDDY in *Jrnl. Appl. Bacteriol.* XXIII. 189 The writer considers that the word psychrotrophic..suggested by Dr. D. A. A. Mossel, should be used for bacteria able to grow at +5° and below, whatever their optimum temperatures. **1975** CAMPBELL & MARSHALL *Sci. of providing Milk for Man* xxiii. 499 Bulk cooling and storage..have made psychrophilic and psychrotrophic bacteria the primary organisms in raw milk.

psycter. (Examples of the form **psykter.**)

1931 *Times Lit. Suppl.* 16 July 563/1 There is a psykter signed by Duris. **1948** A. LANE *Gk. Pottery* iv. 48 Cooler (psykter) to be filled with ice or water and lowered into a wine-krater. **1973** 'D. HALLIDAY' *Dolly & Starry Bird* vi. 75 The tables were crowded with skyphoi and kylikes and psykters.

psylla (si·lă). *Ent.* Also **Psylla.** [mod. L. (E. F. Germar *Systematis Glossatorum Prodromus* (1811) 14), f. Gr. ψύλλα flea.]. Any of the jumping plant-lice belonging to the genus so called or closely related genera, which include several pests.

1852 T. W. HARRIS *Treat. Insects Injurious to Vegetation* (ed. 2) 203 The pear-tree, in Europe, is subject to the attacks of..the pear-tree Psylla. **1891** *Insect Life* IV. 127 We had occasion some time since to abstract Dr. F. Loew's remarks on the Psyllas which inhabit the pear. **1918** W. A. DAVIS *Study Indigo Soils Bihar* 8 In 1907, two diseases appeared simultaneously—the so-called 'wilt' disease and the less serious insect pest 'psylla'. **1933** *Jrnl. R. Hort. Soc.* LVIII. 283 'Eucalyptus Psylla'... Deals with a Psylla attacking Eucalypti in English greenhouses. **1972** SWAN & PAPP *Common Insects N. Amer.* xiii. 141 Pear Psylla...A major pest of pears, first introduced into the East in 1832.

psyllid (si·lid). *Ent.* Also **Psyllid.** [ad. mod.L. *Psyllidæ*, family name, f. prec.: see -ID³.] A jumping plant-louse belonging to the family Psyllidæ, which includes several species that damage plants by causing galls or spreading virus diseases. Also *attrib.*

1899 D. SHARP in *Cambr. Nat. Hist.* VI. viii. 580 Sometimes these Psyllid galls are mere changes in form of a limited part, or parts, of a leaf. **1909** H. MAXWELL-LEFROY *Indian Insect Life* 743 Kieffer describes Indian gall-making Psyllids. **1922** *Nature* 3 June 714/1, I also find a winged termite, a psyllid,..some small spiders. **1954** S. H. SKAIFE *Afr. Insect Life* xi. 111 The jumping plant lice, or psyllids.., are small insects about the size of aphids and they look something like tiny cicadas. **1962**

[see *LERP]. **1969** *New Scientist* 2 Oct. 19/1 The Australian plantsucking psyllid bug *Cardiaspina albitextura*..lives on eucalyptus leaves. **1972** SWANN & PAPP *Common Insects N. Amer.* xiii. 141 The psyllids, or jumping plantlice, are tiny insects.

psylly. Restrict *Obs. rare* to this form and add later examples of the form **psyllium**. Add to def.: Also, (a preparation of) the seeds of this plant or of *Psillium ovata* or *P. indica*, used as a laxative. Also *attrib.*

1897 W. T. FERNIE *Herbal Simples* (ed. 2) 436 In France these Psyllium seeds..are widely prescribed as a laxative. **1932** R. C. WREN *Potter's Cycl. Bot. Drugs* (ed. 4) 281 Psyllium is used successfully in dysentery in the tropics. **1959** *Times* 30 Dec. 8/6 The mailman dragged in a sack of black Psyllium seeds from France. **1977** *Martindale's Extra Pharmacopoeia* (ed. 27) 929/1 Psyllium, on account of its content of mucilage, is used as a demulcent.

psy-op, -war: see *PSY-.

pt-. In English words beginning with *pt-* the initial *p* is no longer pronounced. The Dictionary's convention of giving both (pt-) and (t-) for the pronunc. of each word of this kind has therefore been abandoned.

pteridine (te·ridīn). *Chem.* Also † **-in.** [ad. G. *pteridin* (C. Schöpf et al. 1941, in *Ann. d. Chem.* DXLVIII. 83): see *PTERIN and *-IDINE.] A synthetic yellow crystalline solid, $C_6H_4N_4$, which has a bicyclic structure formed from fused pyrazine and pyrimidine rings; any derivative of this, many examples of which occur naturally, esp. as insect pigments and vitamins of the B group.

1943 *Brit. Chem. & Physiol. Abstr.* A. II. 281 The structure of leucopterin..as 2-imino-6:8:9-trihydroxy-pteridine is confirmed. This and similar CO compounds are named as (enolic) OH-derivatives of pteridine. **1948** *Nature* 2 Oct. 524/2 Reaction of the diaminopyrimidine in aqueous solution with glyoxal bisulphite gives pteridine which crystallizes from alcohol in pale yellow plates, m.p. 140°. **1951** *Jrnl. Chem. Soc.* 474 All natural pteridines have at least one amino- and one hydroxy-substituent. **1962** [see *DROSOPHILA]. **1968** L. A. PAQUETTE *Princ. Mod. Heterocyclic Chem.* xi. 384 Another vitamin of the B group, B_2 or riboflavin.., also contains the basic pteridine ring system.

pterido-. Add: **pteridologist** (earlier and later examples); **pteridology** (earlier and later examples); **pteridomania** (later examples); **pteridophyte,** add to etym. after *Pteridophyta*: (E. Haeckel *Generelle Morphologie der Organismen* (1866) II. p. xxxix); also *attrib.*; (earlier and later examples); so **pteridophy·tic** *a.*; **pte·ridosperm** [ad. mod.L. *Pteridospermeæ* (Oliver & Scott (1904) in *Phil. Trans. R. Soc.* B. CXCVII. 239)], a fossil plant belonging to the class Pteridospermeæ or the order Pteridospermales, which include seed-bearing plants resembling ferns.

1845 E. NEWMAN in *Phytologist* I. 273, I am disposed to believe that our Pteridologists have rarely taken that comprehensive view of the characters of ferns which is requisite for their classification in accordance with nature. **1979** *N.Z. Jrnl. Bot.* XVII. 98/1 These two eminent pteridologists do not yet entirely agree on a classification for the Cyathaceae. **1855** G. B. WOLLASTON in *Phytologist* New Ser. I. 171, I venture with the greatest diffidence,.. single-handed, into the battle-field of Pteridology. **1980** *Nature* 7 Feb. 608/1 An overview of the..biochemical, physiological and genetical research which has taken place during the past 40 years in experimental pteridology. **1969** D. E. ALLEN *Victorian Fern Craze* p. xi, No one..would have thought of filling empty carboys with greenery and building up their present vogue had not Ward himself first prepared the ground... A twentieth-century 'Pteridomania'? **1970** *New Scientist* 7 May 296/1 Pteridomania had many social aspects yet it seems to have been almost forgotten outside botanical circles. **1880** C. E. BESSEY *Botany* xx. 437 The epidermis of Angiosperms does not differ in any marked way from that of the Gymnosperms and the Pteridophytes. **1910** COULTER & CHAMBERLAIN *Morphol. Gymnosperms* i. 4 (*heading*) Vascular anatomy of pteridophytes. **1938** J. C. SCHOUTE in F. Verdoorn *Man. Pteridol.* i. 3 By these discoveries the range of the Pteridophyte canon of morphology was much enlarged. **1956** B. COBB *Field Guide to Ferns* 36 Each of the four classes of the Pteridophytes has its own characteristic behavior in producing, bearing, and propagating its spores. **1978** *Fern Gaz.* XI. 349 The pteridophyte flora of Réunion Island is characterized by a high number of species. **1898** *Bot. Gaz.* XXV. 305 In pteridophytic types of embryogeny..it is always possible to distinguish the segment which is the homologue of the originally distal segment. **1977** A. HALLAM *Planet Earth* 252 This has been effected by the elimination of the free-living sexual stage (prothallus) of the pteridophytic plants. **1904** OLIVER & SCOTT in *Phil. Trans. R. Soc.* B. CXCVII. 240 The further development of our knowledge of the Pteridosperms will form one of the chief objects of palæo-botanic investigation in the near future. **1931** A. C. SEWARD *Plant Life through Ages* ix. 147 Evidence.. eventually proved that the great majority of the Carboniferous 'ferns' were seed-bearing plants—pteridosperms. **1940** J. WALTON *Introd. Study of Fossil Plants* xi. 138 The seed cupules of the Pteridosperms..were borne on fronds or leaves. **1974** G. W. BURNS *Plant Kingdom* xix. 449/1 Ovules of the Paleozoic pteridosperm *Medullosa* were probably terminally attached on the pinnae.

pterin (te·rin). *Chem.* Also **-ine.** [a.G. *pterin* (Wieland & Schöpf 1925, in *Ber. d. Deut. Chem. Ges.* LVIII. 2178), f. Gr. πτερ-όν wing, feather: see -IN[1].] Any of a class of naturally occurring pteridine derivatives found esp. as insect pigments; more generally, any pteridine.

1934 *Chem. Abstr.* XXVIII. 1353 (*heading*) Occurrence of pterins in wasps and butterflies. **1943** A. H. COOK tr. *Mayer's Chem. Natural Coloring Matters* v. 264 The pterins occur as small colored or colorless granules in association with chitin. **1950** *Thorpe's Dict. Appl. Chem.* (ed. 4) X. 264/1 The name 'pterin' denotes a group of heterocyclic compounds, of both natural and synthetic origin, the molecules of which contain..a pyrazine ring fused to a pyrimidine ring. **1954** *Sci. News* XXXIV. 91 The purines and pterines constitute a major source of colour to the wings of butterflies;..the latter as white, red, yellow, and orange pigments, which are also found in the integument of wasps. **1970** A. L. LEHNINGER *Biochem.* xxiv. 543 Folic acid..contains three characteristic building blocks (1) a substituted pterin, (2) *p*-aminobenzoic acid, and (3) glutamic acid.

ptero-. Add: **pte·robranch** [ad. mod.L. *Pterobranchia*, f. F. *ptérodibranche* (H. de Blainville 1816, in *Bull. Sci. Soc. Philomatique* XXVIII. 122)], a small marine, usually colonial, animal belonging to the class Pterobranchia of the phylum Hemichordata; also *attrib.*; **pte·romorph(a)** [*-MORPH], in certain mites, a wing-like appendage attached to the cephalothorax; **pteropleu·ron** *Ent.*, in Diptera, the section of the thorax from which the wings arise.

1949 *New Biol.* VI. 118 The construction of the tubes in which both Graptolites and Pterobranchs live gives good reason for accepting Kozlowski's thesis. **1962** D. NICHOLS *Echinoderms* xiv. 175 Grobben has shown the principal transformations necessary to convert a pterobranch hemichordate into an echinoderm. **1968** A. S. ROMER *Procession of Life* vii. 141 The pterobranchs are tiny animals, only a fraction of an inch in size, living in colonial fashion within branching tubes, with, superficially, the appearance of tiny stemmed flowers. **1978** *Nature* 23 Nov. 318/3 Examples of arborescent growth occur among sponges, hydroids, graptolites, pterobranchs. **1907** *Ibid.* 12 Dec. 142/2 The species [of mites] are to be called *Oribata bostocki*, distinguished by the pteromorphæ being attached to the anterior margin of the abdomen instead of its lateral margin. **1952** BAKER & WHARTON *Introd. Acarology* viii. 387 Within the Aptyctima we find several natural groups based on..the possession or lack of pteromorphs or wings. **1959** T. E. HUGHES *Mites* viii. 113 When big pteromorphae are present, they can usually be depressed by special muscles. **1962** *New Scientist* 20 Sept. 628/2 One group of mites is unique in possessing hinged outgrowths similar to wings, called pteromorphs. **1972** L. GOZMÁNY tr. *Balogh's Oribatid Genera of World* 22 The pteromorpha is a horizontal or inferiorly deflected chitinous lamella. **1884** C. R. OSTEN-SACKEN in *Trans. Entomol. Soc.* 503 Pteropleura, situated under the insertion of the wing, and behind the mesopleural structure. **1951** COLYER & HAMMOND *Flies Brit. Isles* 24 The wings arise from the pteropleuron. **1977** RICHARDS & DAVIES *Imms's Gen. Textbk. Entomol.* (ed. 10) II. III. 961 The pteropleuron (= dorsal part of mesepimeron) lies below the root of the wing.

pterodactyl. For **-yle** read † **-yle** and add: **2.** *Aeronaut.* Also **Pterodactyl.** An obsolete kind of tailless pusher aeroplane with swept-back wings and a very short fuselage.

1926 G. T. R. HILL in *Jrnl. R. Aeronaut. Soc.* XXX. 528 During the summer of 1925, all outstanding design questions were finally settled, and I therefore propose..to give a more detailed description of the main features of the aeroplane, which I have called the Pterodactyl, on account of its supposed resemblance to the prehistoric lizards of that breed. **1935** *Jrnl. R. Aeronaut. Soc.* XXXIX. 823 A recent proposal for a large tailless flying boat having a pterodactyl wing plus stubs. **1960** C. H. GIBBS-SMITH *Aeroplane* xiii. 103 The *Pterodactyls* contributed to a development culminating in the swept-back and delta-wing forms of today.

pteroic (te·rō,ik), *a. Biochem.* [f. *PTER(IDINE + *-OIC.] *pteroic acid*: a synthetic crystalline solid from which the pteroylglutamic acids are formally derived by peptidic linkage of glutamic acid residues to the carboxyl group; *p*-(2-amino-4-hydroxypteridin-6-ylmethyl) aminobenzoic acid, $C_{14}H_{12}N_6O_3$.

1946 [see *PTEROYLGLUTAMIC *a.* a]. **1954** A. WHITE et al. *Princ. Biochem.* xii. 263 The linkage coupling the *p*-aminobenzoic acid..and glutamic acid is a peptide bond. Hydrolysis of this bond gives pteroic acid and glutamic acid. **1963** W. SHIVE in Florkin & Stotz *Comprehensive Biochem.* XI. vii. 90 Among the synthetic derivatives, pteroic acid, because it is effective in replacing folic acid for *S*[*treptococcus*] *faecalis* R but not for *L*[*actobacillus*] *casei*, and the pteroyldiglutamate..are of biological interest. **1970** T. SHIOTA in *Ibid.* XXI. 126 The mechanism involving successive additions of L-glutamic acid residues to pteroic acid and folic acid is supported by the work of Griffin and Brown.

pteropod. Substitute for etym. and def.: [ad. mod.L. *Pteropoda*, a. F. *ptéropode* (G. Cuvier 1804, in *Ann. Mus. Hist. Nat.* IV. 232): see PTEROPODA.] **a.** A pelagic marine gastropod belonging to the class Pteropoda, which includes molluscs having a modified foot bearing lobes which act as fins; a sea butterfly. (Further examples.)

1877 T. H. HUXLEY *Man. Anat. Invertebr. Animals* viii. 505 In all Pteropods and Branchiogasteropods, the mantle secretes a cuticular shell. **1890** [see *butterfly snail*]. **1934** W. BEEBE *Half Mile Down* ix. 167 At 1825 feet coiled pteropods..appeared by the dozen. **1956** A. HARDY *Open Sea* I. xii. 228 The deep-water pteropods are dark in colour. **1976** *Sci. Amer.* July 95/1 The pteropods, wing-footed marine snails, collect phytoplankton on floating webs of sticky mucus.

b. **pteropod ooze,** a calcareous marine sediment rich in the remains of the tests of pteropods.

1891 MURRAY & RENARD in *Rep. Sci. Results Voy. H.M.S. Challenger: Deep-Sea Deposits* iii. 223 Pteropod Ooze. This name was employed by Mr. Murray during the cruise of the Challenger to designate those deep-sea deposits in which a very large part of the calcareous organisms consists of the dead shells of Pteropods and Heteropods. **1894** [in Dict.]. **1929** A. CONAN DOYLE *Maracot Deep* 17 We would bring up..a scoop of pteropod ooze. **1967** *Oceanogr. & Marine Biol.* V. 51 To the South of New Caledonia..there is a small zone of pteropod ooze.

pterosaur. Substitute for first part of etym.: [ad. mod.L. name of order *Pterosauria*, f. generic name *Pterosaurus* (L.F.J.F. Fitzinger *Systema Reptilium* (1843) 15).] (Later examples.)

1907 *Proc. Zool. Soc.* I. 226 It has been frequently assumed that the Pterosaurs enjoyed a bipedal locomotion. **1926** G. HEILMANN *Orig. Birds* IV. 140 The Pterosaurs are of interest chiefly because they are flying reptiles. **1933** A. S. ROMER *Vertebr. Paleont.* viii. 176 The brain of the pterosaurs..was exceedingly large for a reptile. **1973** J. UPDIKE *Museums & Women* 196 The iguanodon despised these pterosaurs' pretensions. **1975** *Times* 12 Apr. 12/1 The surprise created in the popular mind by Douglas Lawson's discovery of an immense pterosaur—a beast whose wings spanned about 51 feet according to the most reliable computer estimate—is only paralleled by the bewilderment experienced in scientific circles.

pterosaurian *a.* (later example).

1981 *Sci. Amer.* Feb. 95/1 The triangle was supported at the wrist by a uniquely pterosaurian innovation, the pteroid bone.

pteroylglutamic (te:rō,ailgli͞utæ·mik), *a. Biochem.* [f. *PTER(IDINE + *-OYL + GLUTAMIC *a.* in Dict. and Suppl.] **a.** *pteroylglutamic acid*: any of a series of derivatives of pteroic acid which have a side chain consisting of one or more glutamic acid residues, and include certain members of the vitamin B complex and other animal growth factors; folic acid.

1946 R. B. ANGIER et al. in *Science* 31 May 669/1 For the compounds formed from *p*-aminobenzoic acid and *p*-aminobenzoyl-*l*(+)-glutamic acid, the names pteroic acid and pteroylglutamic acid are suggested. **1949, 1955** [see *FOLACIN]. **1967** PIKE & BROWN *Nutrition* iii. 65 At one time both p-aminobenzoic acid and pteroylglutamic acid were considered to be vitamins, but it is now apparent that the species requirement is for one or the other of the two.

b. With inserted prefix indicating the number of glutamic acid residues present, as *pteroylmonoglutamic acid* (cf. *FOLIC ACID), etc. Also *pteroylpolyglutamic acid.*

1946 *Ann. N.Y. Acad. Sci.* XLVIII. 287 Whereas vitamin B_c..contains one glutamic acid residue, vitamin B_c conjugate contains seven. In the system of nomenclature suggested by the authors [*sc.* C. W. Waller et al.], vitamin B_c conjugate is therefore pteroylheptaglutamic acid. **1954** A. WHITE et al. *Princ. Biochem.* xlix. 1035 Animal tissues contain an enzyme, 'vitamin B_c conjugase', which hydrolyzes the naturally occurring pteroylpolyglutamic acid compounds to pteroylmonoglutamic acid and free glutamic acid. **1955** *Chem. & Engin. News* 6 June 2433/1 The pure substance hitherto known as folic acid, folacine, or vitamin B_c shall be named pteroylmonoglutamic acid. Compounds analogous to it but containing several glutamic acid residues united by amide linkages may be named pteroyltriglutamic acid, pteroylheptaglutamic acid, etc. **1970** PASSMORE & ROBSON *Compan. Med. Stud.* II. vii. 7/1 Folic acid in therapeutics means synthetic pteroylmonoglutamic acid but the term is sometimes used to embrace all naturally occurring substances with folic acid activity.

Hence **pte:roylglu·tamate,** (a compound or anion of) any of these acids. (Also with inserted prefix.)

1950 R. J. WILLIAMS et al. *Biochem. of B Vitamins* C. ii. 290 Both pteroic acid and formylpteroic acid are inactive for *L*[*actobacillus*] *casei* or humans, while pteroylheptaglutamate is inactive for bacteria. **1958** FRUTON & SIMMONDS *Gen. Biochem.* (ed. 2) xxxix. 999 The pteroyltriglutamate and heptaglutamate both occur in nature and are as active as folic acid in the nutrition of higher animals. **1963** [see *PTEROIC *a.*]. **1970** R. W. MCGILVERY *Biochem.* xviii. 411 (*caption*) The structure of the vitamin, pteroylglutamate, more commonly known as folate. **1970** PASSMORE & ROBSON *Compan. Med. Stud.* II. vii. 7/1 In foods, folates are found free and in conjugated forms, the latter being polyglutamates such as pteroyltriglutamate and pteroylheptaglutamate.

ptilinum. Add: [ad. F. *ptiline* (J. B. Robineau-Desvoidy *Essai sur les Myodaires* (1830) i. 10).] (Earlier and later examples.) Hence **pti·linal** *a.*

1853 F. Walker *Insecta Britannica: Diptera* II. 2 The ptilinum is a soft membrane, which in many species, and especially in the newly-hatched flies, appears between the antennæ and the front. **1925** A. D. Imms *Gen. Textbk. Entomol.* iii. 593 The Ptilinum or frontal sac is a characteristic cephalic organ of Cyclorrhapha and its presence is indicated externally by the arched frontal or ptilinal suture. **1962** Gordon & Lavoipierre *Entmol.* xxvii. 171 Having emerged from the puparium the insect pushes its way up through the soil to the surface by the alternate inflation and deflation of the ptilinum. **1969** R. F. Chapman *Insects* xxii. 441 Once the fly has hardened the ptilinum is no longer eversible and the muscles associated with it degenerate. Its position is indicated in the mature fly by the ptilinal suture.

ptosis. Add: Pl. **ptoses** (-īz). **b.** Delete *rare* and add: Also, of the breasts. (Further examples.)

1909 *Amer. Jrnl. Med. Sci.* CXXXVII. 380 Ptoses of the splenic flexure and descending colon are rare. **1934** S. Beckett *More Pricks than Kicks* 68 Man with weak bladder and tendency to ptosis of viscera. **1953** *Pageant* Aug. 68 About 4,000,000 young American women suffer in some degree from micromastia (immature breasts) and another 10,000,000 from ptosis (or collapse or sagging of the breasts). **1957** J. Lapides in J. G. Allen et al. *Surgery* xlviii. 1311/2 A number of operations have been devised and used for the fixation of the highly mobile kidney—renal ptosis. **1965** R. P. G. Sandon in R. J. V. Battle *Plastic Surg.* xiv. 319 Clothing tends to confine and flatten, rather than support correctly, such an enormous bosom, and with the years the relaxation of the skin allows an increasing element of ptosis.

ptotic *a.* (example).

1969 J. H. DeWeerd in Glenn & Boyce *Urologic Surg.* iv. 122/2 The hypermobile (ptotic) kidney.

ptygmatic (tigmæ·tik), *a.* *Geol.* [ad. Sw. *ptygmatisk* (J. J. Sederholm 1907, in *Bull. de la Commission Géol. de Finlande* xxiii. 89), f. Gr. πτύγμα, πτύγματ- folded matter: see -ic.] Applied to the highly sinuous and often discordant folding exhibited by the veins in some gneisses and migmatites, and to the veins themselves.

1907 J. J. Sederholm in *Bull. de la Commission Géol. de Finlande* xxiii. 110 [*English summary of original Sw. article.*] The primary folding caused by melting, he designates as ptygmatic...These suggestions are made with every reservation. **1926** G. W. Tyrrell *Princ. Petrol.* xxi. 333 (*caption*) Ptygmatic folding of a quartz vein in amphibolite. **1952** *Geol. Mag.* LXXXIX. 1 The term 'ptygmatic' was originally coined by Sederholm in 1907 (p. 110) to describe 'the primary folding caused by melting' in gneisses and migmatites. The word.., as defined, would embrace most of the contortions, many of which are now included in the term 'flow fold', commonly seen in migmatite zones the world over... The term was later restricted by Sederholm (1926) to those tortuous quartzo-felspathic veins, which occur in areas of granitization. **1970** K. C. Jackson *Textbk. Lithol.* vii. 420 (*caption*) Ptygmatic folding of a pegmatite dike in gneiss.

Hence **ptygma·tically** *adv.*, in a way characteristic of ptygmatic folds; also (as a back-formation) **pty·gma**, a ptygmatic fold.

1928 *Summary of Progr. Geol. Survey Gt. Brit. 1927* ii. 72 Other observers of what are certainly ptygmatically folded veins have not accepted Sederholm's explanation. **1944** *Trans. R. Soc. Edin.* LXI. 228 The foliation (gneissic structure) of the host rock appears to conform to the plications of the 'ptygma'. **1960** *Rep. 21st Internat. Geol. Congr.* XIV. 138 It is concluded that ptygmas could have been formed as the result of development in a passive host or possibly, though improbably, as the result of magmatic flowage. **1971** *Scottish Jrnl. Geol.* VII. 316 Pre-D2 quartz veins are..ptygmatically folded when at high angle to S2.

p-type (pī·təip), *a.* *Physics.* [f. *P* (repr. *positive*) + Type *sb.*[1]] Applied to (a region in) a semiconductor in which electrical conduction is due chiefly to the movement of holes (rather than electrons). Opp. *n-type *a.*

1946 [see *n-type]. **1948** Torrey & Whitman *Crystal Rectifiers* iii. 49 A semiconductor that conducts principally by holes in the nearly filled band is referred to as a '*p*-type' semiconductor. *Ibid.*, The impurities added to silicon make it *p*-type. **1970** *New Scientist* 15 Oct. (Suppl.) 6/2 In a practical integrated circuit the triangular half of the rectifier is p-type material which is diffused into the silicon chip in a pattern similar to the wall plan for a house.

pua, var. *puha.

pub, *sb.* **1.** For *low colloq.* read *colloq.* and add earlier and later examples.

1859 Hotten *Dict. Slang* 78 *Pub*, or *Public*, a public house. **1893** K. Mackay *Out Back* (ed. 2) ii. v. 188 It's Molloy's fault...He got tanked at the pub last night. **1922** Joyce *Ulysses* 70 Waiting outside pubs to bring da home. **1924** *Truth* (Sydney) 27 Apr. 6 *Pub*, hotel. **1936** M. Allis *Eng. Prelude* xxiii. 247 First comes the pub, the *Fox and Hounds*. **1946** *R.A.F. Jrnl.* May 175 There are German beer shops turned into typical English 'Pubs'. **1950** 'N. Shute' *Town like Alice* vi. 170 She was surprised at the rapidity of [the town's] growth. In 1928 it was about three houses and a pub. **1970** M. Greener *Penguin Dict. Commerce* 268 A pub offering accommodation to casual customers will probably be a hotel within the definition of the Hotel Proprietors Act 1956 and the various Innkeepers Acts. **1980** 'D. Kavanagh' *Duffy* ii. 36 They met at a drinkers' pub near Baker Street Station.

2. *attrib.* and *Comb.*, as *pub-door, food, -friend, -goer, -grub, -keeper, -landlord, manager, meal, mirror, parlour, -singer*; *pub-going, -running, -spieling* vbl. sbs.; *pub-hunting* ppl. adj.; **pub-crawl:** see *crawl *sb.*[1] b; hence as *v. intr.*; **pub-crawler**; **pub-crawling** *vbl. sb.* and *ppl. a.*; **pub-life,** the society of public houses; **pub lunch,** a lunch eaten in a pub; hence **pub-lunch** *v. intr.*, **pub-luncher**; **pub rock,** rock music of a type played in public houses; **pub-stiff** *N.Z. slang*, a look-out or sentinel acting on behalf of a licensee selling alcoholic drinks after closing-time; **pub theatre,** a public house at which theatrical performances take place; also, theatrical representation performed in a public house; **pub-time,** (*a*) the hour at which a public house opens or closes; (*b*) the time shown by a clock in a public house, with reference to the custom of advancing this slightly to bring forward closing-time.

1915 Pub-crawl [see *crawl *sb.*[1] b]. **1937** *Times Lit. Suppl.* 27 Nov. 910/1 Mr. Lyons does not 'pub-crawl' as a writer in search of copy. **1959** [see *crawl *sb.*[1] b]. **1972** J. Symons *Players & Game* xxiii. 182 He had taken a girl ..on a mild variety of pub crawl. **1974** *Canadian Mag.* (Toronto) 16 Mar. 2/3 Across Canada, kids aren't packing the discothèques; instead, they're pub-crawling. **1910** *Daily Chron.* 28 Jan. 4/4 These 'pub-crawlers' have captured the illiterate and the unthinking. **1976** J. R. L. Anderson *Redundancy Pay* ix. 145 You're turning me into quite a pub-crawler. **1919** 'W. N. P. Barbellion' *Enjoying Life* 75 Drunken Barnabee's Journal..is rhymed Latin verse..describing the author's 'pub crawlings' up and down the country. **1921** F. B. Young *Black Diamond* vii. 73, I bain't goin' to keep you in pub-crawling any longer. **1973** 'H. Carmichael' *Candles for Dead* vi. 74 A pub-crawling reporter. **1980** I. Murdoch *Nuns & Soldiers* i. 83 This sort of urban life suited Tim, pub-crawling, wandering, looking in shop-windows. **1960** T. Hughes *Lupercal* 18 The lamp above the pub-door Wept yellow when he went out. **1977** *Times* 11 June 11/7 English people care more about pub food than they used to. **1959** J. Cary *Captive & Free* xviii. 85 His father had been a steady worker, but completely devoid of ambition; a man whose only interests were football, darts, his pub-friends. **1955** T. H. Pear *Eng. Social Differences* vi. 160 Peter is primarily a pub-goer. *Ibid.* 161 The social differences which come out in pub-going. *Ibid.* 162 The new pub-going habit for girls and women is a genuine problem. **1978** *Country Life* 19 Oct. 1186/4 There are 'lounge bars' and 'singing bars' and many places advertising 'pub grub'. **1922** Joyce *Ulysses* 599 He commented adversely on the desertion of Stephen by all his pubhunting *confrères* but one. **1925** W. Deeping *Sorrell & Son* vi. 57 Our pub-keepers rarely visualize the atmosphere of a garden. **1980** D. Francis *Reflex* vi. 67 The pub-keeper from the Sussex village where he lived. **1909** *Daily Chron.* 17 July 4/7 Mr. Lewis Harcourt's reference to 'the ground and the pub-landlord seeking to hold the common fort'. **1944** Wyndham Lewis *Let.* 5 Jan. (1963) 374, I gather from Augustus that the pub-life of London is functioning as of yore. **1970** G. F. Newman *Sir, You Bastard* v. 130 When he reported, Sneed had a pub lunch with the Governor. **1971** 'F. Clifford' *Blind Side* ii. iv. 113 He pub-lunched in Richmond. **1975** *Times* 8 Mar. 10/4 Cheapness is often the only virtue of the British pub lunch. **1971** *Times* 2 June 6/1 The sound of pub-lunchers arising merrily from below. **1977** P. Cosgrave *Cheyney's Law* iv. 39 He waited, no longer the tweedy city stroller, pub luncher, book buyer. **1973** K. Giles *File on Death* v. 118, I got a letter asking if I had perhaps a vacancy for a pub manager. **1975** P. McCutchan *Very Big Bang* x. 96 He would..snatch pub meals as and when he could. **1974** *Selfridges Bk. of Xmas* 80 Victorian style pub mirrors..£18.75 each. **1977** J. Wilson *Making Hate* vii. 85 A reproduction Edwardian pub mirror. **1929** D. H. Lawrence *Pansies* 132 Little fleets ..that put to sea and boldly sink Armadas In a pub parlour, in literary London, on certain evenings. **1976** *Star* (Sheffield) 20 Nov., Pub-rock does a dying swan act at the weekend when Sheffield's most celebrated stronghold closes its doors to live entertainment. **1977** *Zigzag* Apr. 39/2 Joe was bored with singing pub rock standards. **1973** K. Giles *File on Death* v. 118, I own the local brewery...Pub-running has problems. **1975** *Radio Times* 3 Apr. 17 George Formby...His songs..have passed.. into the repertoires of every comic, impressionist and pub-singer. **1900** H. Lawson *Over Sliprails* 38 Jack Drew talked too straight in the paper, and in spite of his proprietors—about pub spieling and such things. **1946** F. Sargeson *That Summer* 63 The pub-stiff that was on the door told us to go upstairs. **1973** *Guardian* 23 Jan. 10/1 Pub theatres are in vogue for the first time since Shakespeare's day. **1976** *Alyn & Deeside Observer* 10 Dec. 11/5 As the pint is pulled downstairs, an audience is held upstairs by one of the best examples of Pub Theatre to be found in London. **1947** Dylan Thomas *Let.* 11 June (1966) 314 I'm used to working from after lunch until pub-time. **1968** L. Meynell *Death of Philanderer* x. 167 The clock behind the bar would be showing 'pub time', that is..it would be at least five minutes fast.

pub, *v.* Add: **a.** Also without *it.*

1950 *John o' London's* 24 Nov. 614/1 Pubbing through Edinburgh's Old Town and the Leith waterfront. **1960** L. Cooper *Accomplices* iii. i. 152 We went pubbing together. **1972** S. Chance *Septimus & Minster Ghost* vii. 62 'Can't have you pubbing in your canonicals,' she said, going to the door and looking out into the alley.

b. *intr.* To own or manage a public house.

1936 M. Franklin *All that Swagger* xiv. 130 The profits to be made from fools by pubbing could add to it.

pubarche (piubā·rkī). *Med.* [f. L. *pūb-ēs* pubic hair, groin + Gr. ἀρχή beginning.] The first appearance of pubic hair; chiefly in *premature pubarche*, the premature occurrence of this without other signs of sexual precocity.

1950 L. Wilkins *Diagn. & Treatm. Endocrine Disorders in Childh. & Adolescence* ix. 146/2 We would suggest for this condition the term 'premature pubarche' which does not attempt to define its etiology. **1974** N. D. Barnes et al. in M. M. Grumbach et al. *Control of Onset of Puberty* viii. 223 Premature pubarche or adrenarche, the isolated growth of sexual hair, is another form of precocious sexual development that may be neurogenically determined.

pu·bbish, *a.* [f. Pub *sb.* + -ish[1].] Of the nature or character of a public house.

1956 D. M. Davin *Sullen Bell* 56 You hardly ever use a pub, but like an old puritan you insist it must be as pubbish as possible. **1973** R. Ludlum *Matlock Paper* ii. 13 The name of the country inn was the Cheshire Cat, and..it was Englishy and pubbish.

pu·bby, *a.* [f. Pub *sb.* + -y[1].] = prec.

1959 *Good Food Guide* 361 It retains a pleasant pubby atmosphere and there's a good, mildly chaotic restaurant upstairs. **1974** *Times* 5 Oct. 12/8 Balls Brothers wine bar in the Strand had a pubby atmosphere. **1976** *Eastern Daily Press* (Norwich) 16 Dec., In the first, pubs are made to look like anything but pubs, while the 'pubbier than pub' devotees prefer a severe environment..echoing the style of the first urban public bars.

pubertal, *a.* Delete *rare* and add further examples.

1972 *Clin. Endocrinol.* (1973) (B.M.A.) 99 Pubertal development lasts on average about three years in girls and four years in boys. **1976** *Times Lit. Suppl.* 2 Jan. 2/3 A pubertal woman is always potentially taboo [among gypsies] and is actually so after menstruation, childbirth and intercourse. **1979** J. Barnett *Backfire is Hostile!* v. 49 Some rowdy youths cavorted in the rush and grope of pubertal ritual.

puberty. b. (Further examples.)

1924 A. Lipschütz (*title*) The internal secretions of the sex glands: the problem of the 'puberty gland'. **1971** *Canad. Antiques Collector* Sept.–Oct. 4 Arapaho Painted Hide Puberty Robe 67 × 46 inches. **1978** *New York* 3 Apr. 32/2 Masks and helmets used in puberty rites of Sierra Leone and Liberia.

pubic, *a.* Add: **b.** Employed to cover the pubes.

1940 A. Upfield *Bushranger of Skies* xi. 130 That Jack Johnson wore only the pubic tassel announced his non-employment by the station. **1959** S. H. Courtier *Death in Dream Time* ii. 19 The bewildering display of aboriginal weapons and implements..head-dresses and pubic bands.

public, *a.* (*sb.*) Add: **I. 1.** (Earlier and further examples.)

1484 Public administration [see Administration 1]. **1617** Public health [see Health *sb.* 2b]. **1673** J. Ray *Observations Journey Low-Countries* 163 He is entrusted with the management of public monies. **1676** in N. Brent *Sarpi's Hist. Councel of Trent* p. xiii, He was in the Publick Employment. **1721** *Mass. House of Representatives Jrnl.* (1922) III. 9 Acts have been Passed..for Striking Bills of Credit, and Issuing out the same, in order to discharge their Publick Debts. **1727** in M. M. Verney *Verney Lett.* (1930) II. xxiv. 101 The main objection against him was his making up of the publick money in the South Sea. **1781** in *Eng. Rep.* (1903) XXVIII. 1028 Treating it as a matter of public policy of the law, and similar to marriage brokage bonds, where, though the parties are private persons, the practice is publicly detrimental, [etc.]. **1785** J. Wesley *Let.* 7 Apr. (1931) VII. 266, I beseech you..to have no respect of persons.., in disposing of the Yearly Contribution and the Preacher's Fund or any other public money. **1787** M. Cutler *Jrnl.* 21 July in *Life, Jrnls, & Corr.* (1888) I. iv. 127 Congress would pay more than four millions of the public debt. **1794** Public concern [see Concern *sb.* 6]. *c* **1799** *Ess. on Political Society* i. 59 To constitute the desiderated political system, is to constitute a permanent law for regulating the public administration. **1806** in *Documentary Hist. Amer. Industr. Society* (1910) III. 67 The newspaper called the *Aurora*, has teemed with false representations ..to poison the public mind. **1827** J. Kent *Commentaries on Amer. Law* II. iv. 222 Public corporations, are such as exist for public political purposes only, such as counties, cities, towns and villages. They are founded by the government, for public purposes, and the whole interest in them belongs to the public. **1846** *Parl. Papers* I. 257 (*heading*) A bill for providing cemeteries, and promoting public health, in towns and populous districts. **1853** in *Eng. Rep.* (1901) X. 437 Public policy..is that principle of the law which holds that no subject can lawfully do that which has a tendency to be injurious to the public, or against the public good. **1868** Trollope *He knew he was Right* (1869) I. xxxviii. 300 The bias of the public mind. **1883** *Statutes at Large U.S.A.* XXII. 214 Any convict, lunatic, idiot, or any person unable to take care of himself or herself without becoming a public charge. **1887** *Polit. Sci. Q.* II. 212 Public administration is detailed and systematic execution of public law. **1889** G. B. Shaw *Fabian Ess. Socialism* 194 The Manchester

School will urge..the exemption of private enterprise from the competition of public enterprise. *Ibid.* 195 The superior prestige and permanence of public employment. **1894** Public eye [mentioned s.v. EYE *sb.*[1] 8]. **1918** *Current Hist.* Aug. 277/2 The public debt of the..United States.. At Most Recent Date [in millions of dollars] $15,008. **1919** A. M. TODD (*title*) Public ownership of railroads. **1928** *Britain's Industr. Future* (Liberal Industr. Inquiry) 63 In a modern community many services must be run by a Public Concern—meaning by this a form of organisation which..is operated or regulated in the public interest. *Ibid.* 95 We propose..a special class of Company to be designated Public Corporations...The distinction..should depend..mainly on their preponderant position in their own industry or trade. *Ibid.* 243 We stand, not for public ownership, but for popular ownership. **1928** J. BUCHAN *Runagates Club* x. 273 He had been returned to Parliament..but he wasn't much in the public eye. **1937** *Times* 12 Jan. 13/6 Three years ago it was important to use public policy to increase investment. **1943** J. B. PRIESTLEY *Daylight on Saturday* xxxi. 245 A passionate defender of private enterprise (which he was careful always to contrast with..'State ownership' and never with public enterprise). **1943** W. H. CHASE *Sourdough Pot* xix. 123 Some [gold miners] even became public charges with the passing of time. **1943** J. S. HUXLEY *TVA* ix. 69 Much curiosity has been aroused in the public mind. **1955** *Bull. Atomic Sci.* Apr. 112/3 Public employment does bring with it certain obligations beyond those required of citizens in private life. **1955** *Radio Times* 22 Apr. 15/2 It was a gramophone recording that first brought her before the public eye. **1970** E. FLORES in I. L. Horowitz *Masses in Lat. Amer.* ix. 338 It is possible to substitute a cash deposit by Public Debt bonds. **1971** D. HALLIDAY' *Dolly & Doctor Bird* i. 6 Public health is a doctor's concern. **1971** S. A. DE SMITH *Constitutional & Admin. Law* xxiv. 512 Decisions in public administration can be classified in various ways. **1971** P. WORSTHORNE *Socialist Myth* ix. 237 In a democracy..the expenditure of public money must be dependent on popular agreement. **1972** *Guardian* 24 Mar. 14/2 Ministers must..keep open minds about public investment and public enterprise in the regions. **1973** I. M. SINCLAIR *Vienna Convention on Law of Treaties* v. 110 The gradual establishment in common law jurisdictions of the principle that certain types of contract are, by their very nature, injurious to society and therefore contrary to public policy. **1973** *Listener* 26 July 111/1 Mr Maudling said: 'I don't think Michael Foot has the slightest idea what he intends to do in this field of so-called public ownership extension.' **1975** C. STUART *Reith Diaries* 66 The management of public corporations..was his particular field.

2.e. *public service*: service to the community, esp. under the direction of the government or other official agency; consideration of the common good; with *the* spec. = CIVIL SERVICE; also *attrib.*

1570–6 [in Dict., sense 1]. **1645** *Rec. Colony & Plantation New Haven* (1857) 168 The farmers that have butter and cheese were desired to keepe it in their hands, that in case the publicque service require it, they may be furnished. **1706** *House of Commons Jrnl.* 11 Dec. (1742–62) XV. 211/1 Resolved, That this House will receive no Petitions for any Sum of Money, relating to publick Service, but what is recommended from the Crown. **1709** [see SERVICE[1] 11]. **1818** *Ann. Reg. 1817: State Papers* 309/2 They are..not prepared at present to suggest to the House any alteration in *this* mode of conducting *this* important department of the public service. **1857** DICKENS *Dorrit* II. xxviii. 557 It's like a limited game of cricket. A field of outsiders are always going in to bowl at the Public Service, and we block the balls. **1908** I. N. STEVENS *Liberators* 187 The public service corporation had dictated the nomination of the entire Republican State and legislative ticket. **1921** *Daily Colonist* (Victoria, B.C.) 8 Apr. 2/3 John Mitchell, formerly of the public service, Ottawa, and now farming at Landsdowne, Ont., is mentioned as a likely Government candidate. **1921** C. W. TERRY *Pract. Motor Body Building* xxxviii. 254 (*heading*) Public service vehicles. **1926** *Daily Chron.* 13 May 2/5 The Prince of Wales has been paying strictly private visits to public service depots in the London area. **1960** *Encounter* Jan. 42/2 Those public-service advertisements which enjoin us to sneeze into a handkerchief. **1960** *Road Traffic Act* 8 & 9 *Eliz. II* c. 16 § 117 For the purposes of this Act a public service vehicle is a motor vehicle used for carrying passengers for hire or reward. **1972** *Guardian* 21 Nov. 3/2 The Civil Service ('Public Service' is the standard term here [in Canberra]). *a* **1974** R. CROSSMAN *Diaries* (1975) I. 486 The special late-night programmes on the election put on by both commercial and public-service television. **1977** *Times* 2 Sept. 4/3 An independent Public Service Commission consisting of a Chairman and four other members. **1980** *Daily Tel.* 29 Feb. 16 A much broader look ought to be taken at the whole question of public service broadcasting and the way it is financed.

f. *public menace, nuisance*, etc.: anyone or anything obnoxious or annoying to the community. See also sense 9a below.

1638 Public nuisance [see NUISANCE 2β]. **1877** TROLLOPE *Amer. Senator* I. xxvii. 288 'What a very queer bird he is.' 'He is a public nuisance,—and so is the old lady who brought him here.' **1932** KIPLING *Limits & Renewals* 293 She [*sc.* a sow] broke out again and again, till the local body..indicted Mr. Gravell once more as proprietor of a public nuisance. **1952** E. O'NEILL *Moon for Misbegotten* III. 149, I made such a public nuisance of myself that the conductor threatened if I didn't quit, he'd keep me locked in the drawing room. **1955** Public menace [see *CRICKET *sb.*[2] 1c]. **1965** *Listener* 7 Oct. 549/2 Regarded now..as Public Pest No. 1 among vertebrates.., what hell the life of wood-pigeons seems to be. **1977** *Time* 12 Dec. 41/1 Prosecutors saw Barnes as a public menace to put in prison.

g. *public interest*, the common well-being. Also *attrib.* Also, *public welfare.*

1678 BUTLER *Hudibras* III. ii. 102 Both Parties joyn'd to do their best, To Damn the Publick Interest. **1730** BOLINGBROKE *Craftsman* (1731) VII. 22 No Man, who adheres to it, hath the least pretence left him to say that he pursues the publick Interest. **1858** DISRAELI in *Hansard Commons* 27 Apr. 1822 Not..one who proposes a course which will conduce to the advantage of the public interest. **1858** M. ARNOLD *Merope* 119 Let us a union found..Bas'd on pure public welfare. **1901** *Edin. Rev.* Apr. 378 The chief trustee of public welfare is, in this country, Parliament, and with Parliament rests the responsibility of seeing that the interests of the whole community are not subordinated to those of any portions of it. **1934** G. B. SHAW *Too True to be Good* Pref. 15 They voluntarily lived holy lives and devoted themselves to the public welfare in obedience to the impulse of the Holy Ghost within them. **1955** MEYERSON & BANFIELD (*title*) Politics, planning and the public interest. **1971** *Wall St. Jrnl.* 22 July w. 1/1 To work on coal miners' rights for a Washington public-interest law firm.

h. *public law*: that part of the law pertaining to the state and its relationship with the person subject to it; (see also sense 9a).

1773 J. ERSKINE *Inst. Law Scotl.* I. I. i. 9 The public law is that which hath more immediately in view the public weal, and the preservation and good order of society. **1923** W. J. BYRNE *Dict. Eng. Law* 519/2 Public law is that part of the law which deals with the State, either by itself or in its relations with individuals. **1973** I. M. SINCLAIR *Vienna Convention on Law of Treaties* v. 110 The *jus publicum* was to be understood in a wide sense as embracing not only public law in the strict sense (that is to say, the law governing relations between individuals and the State) but also rules from which individuals were not permitted to depart by virtue of particular agreements. **1976** J. M. KELLY *Stud. Civil Judicature of Roman Republic* iii. 78 A second class obviously due for exclusion is that which can be broadly labelled 'public law'; legitimate subdivisions of this would be fiscal law, military law, and 'local government' or 'police' law.

i. *public utility*: a service or supply, such as electricity, water, or transport, considered necessary to the community, usu. controlled by a (nationalized or private) monopoly and subject to public regulation. Also (with hyphen) *attrib.*

1903 R. T. ELY *Stud. Evolution Industr. Society* 225 The principal classes of these public utilities are water, light and transportation. **1915** *Political Q.* May 106 Now coal mining is a 'public-utility' industry. **1928** *Daily Chron.* 9 Aug. 7/2 Crops have been destroyed and communications and public utilities have been crippled. **1968** P. A. S. TAYLOR *Dict. Econ. Terms* (ed. 4) 88 *Public utility*, an industry, such as gas, electricity, water and transport facilities, which requires heavy and highly specialised initial investment of capital, on which the return is slow. **1976** H. TRACY *Death in Reserve* xvii. 129 Public utilities worked with the servicemen with an impressive coherence.

j. *public sector*: that part of an economy, industry, etc., which is controlled by the state at any level of government. Usu. with *the*.

1952 [see *PRIVATE *a.* 7j]. **1969** M. ASH *Who are Progressives Now?* I. v. 122 What we in the public sector miss above all is the sense of involvement of people with progressive ideas with the State system. **1972** *Guardian* 31 Jan. 13/5 Other public sector groups. **1976** F. ZWEIG *New Acquisitive Society* I. ii. 28 The public sector seems to be the most suitable object for pressure groups' claims. **1980** *Jrnl. R. Soc. Arts* Mar. 205/1 The public sector borrowing requirement would be reduced.

3. a. (Further examples.) *public defender* (U.S.), a lawyer employed by the state who represents a defendant who is unable to pay for legal assistance, in criminal cases.

1676 in E. D. Neill *Virginia Carolorum* (1886) 361 For haveing upon specious preferences of publique works raised great unjust taxes [etc.]. **1676** Public servant [see SERVANT *sb.* 2e]. **1741** RICHARDSON *Pamela* IV. xiii. 75 Poor Housekeepers, who..are asham'd to apply for publick Relief. *c* **1810** W. HICKEY *Mem.* (1918) II. xi. 146 The parties complaining were so unreasonable as to refuse any terms, whereby the progress of the public works was impeded. **1845** Public servant [see SERVANT *sb.* 2e]. **1869** *Bradshaw's Railway Manual* XXI. 95 Public Works Loan Commissioners. **1884** B. JERROLD *At Home in Paris* II. xii. 185 That ready kindness of heart and chivalry towards the weak which pervade the 'Public Assistance' of the country. **1891** R. WALLACE *Rural Econ. Austral. & N.Z.* xxxviii. 488 No public-works undertaking can be made economically to suit any purpose whatever when that purpose has only been named without being formulated or its details settled. **1918** *Policeman's Monthly* Oct. 9/2 (*caption*) A public defender needed. **1930** *Economist* 5 Apr. 767/1 The Public Assistance Committees through which the county councils and the town councils of county boroughs are henceforward to administer what will in future be called 'public assistance'. **1931** J. S. HUXLEY *What dare I Think?* iii. 87 A..method for exerting some control over population-growth would be to link it on to public relief. **1932** *N.Y. Times* 23 Mar. 15/1 The steps advocated [at the 1st Public Housing Conference] were..the presenting of questionnaires to candidates for the Legislature seeking to commit them on the question of public housing. **1937** *Statutes at Large U.S.A.* L. I. 887 The term 'public housing authority' means any..public body..authorized to engage in the development or administration of low-rent housing or slum clearance. **1942** E. PAUL *Narrow St.* xxii. 189 She is an ideal public servant, having all the minor ailments possible, a fiendish disposition, short stature and a healthy dislike for mankind. **1961** WEBSTER s.v. Public *adj.* 1 c, Public expenditures. **1961** B. CRUMP *Hang on a Minute* 65 He was working in a Public Works road gang, clearing slips off roads and digging drains and things. **1964** MRS. L. B. JOHNSON *White House Diary* 1 Aug. (1970) 187 He spoke, disheartened, of the enormous quantity of public housing in New York City. **1965** SELDON & PENNANCE *Everyman's Dict. Econ.* 45 One central fund from which all regular public expenditures should be paid. **1965** A. J. P. TAYLOR *Eng. Hist. 1914–1945* vi. 212 Far from welcoming any increase in public spending, let alone advocating it, Labour had inherited the radical view that money spent by the state was likely to be money spent incompetently and corruptly. **1971** *Archivum Linguisticum* II. 50 A working man..on public assistance. **1974** *State* (Columbia, S. Carolina) 15 Feb. 1–B/3 Pickens County Public Defender Joseph Board represented him while Thomas M. Greene..represented the state. **1976** *Times* 21 May 1/5 The combined effects of the Government's public expenditure restraint and pay policies. **1976** *Birmingham Post* 16 Dec. 7/9 Two major hospital schemes in Dudley and Stafford, costing more than £20 million, may be delayed because of the public spending cuts. **1977** *N.Z. Herald* 8 Jan. 2–4/6 Until she breaks the seal and reads what was written in public servant scrawl 24 years ago, she cannot continue her search. **1977** *New Yorker* 27 June 85/3 Queens..has..only eighteen of the city's two hundred and forty-six public-housing projects. **1977** P. JOHNSON *Enemies of Society* v. 71 The new government public-relief system aggravated the evils it was designed to cure. **1977** G. CLARK *World Prehist.* (ed. 3) II. 75 Given the possibility of public works on an adequate scale, it was capable of producing food enough to support society at increasing levels of complexity.

4. a. (Further examples.) *public convenience*: see *CONVENIENCE *sb.* 7d.

1606 SHAKES. *Ant. & Cl.* II. ii. 234, I saw her once Hop forty Paces through the publicke streete. **1611** CORYAT *Crudities* 290 There are reported to be in Venice..twentie seven publique clocks. *Ibid.* 403 In an open court *sub dio* two publike bathes. **1613** PURCHAS *Pilgrimage* I. v. xvi. 453 They have their publike Meetings and Bankets in their Temples very often. **1699** M. LISTER *Journey to Paris* 150, I never saw in all the Markets once Sprouts.. nor in their publick Gardens any Reserves of old Stalks. **1705** *Boston News-Let.* 24 Sept. 2/1 We know not the certainty of any others besides those mentioned in the Publick Print. **1718** in *Rep. Rec. Commissioners Boston* (1883) VIII. 129 The Projection of an Act for a Publick Market in Boston..Voted disallowed. **1738** W. STEPHENS *Jrnl.* 11 Feb. in *Colonial Rec. Georgia* (1906) IV. 80 Bailiff Parker and Mr. Hugh Anderson..took a Walk first to the publick Garden. **1762** in A. EARLE *Customs & Fashions in Old New England* (1893) 247 At the Public Room of the above Inn will be delivered a series of Moral Dialogues. **1763** J. BELL *Trav. from St. Petersburg* II. 54, I was present at the representation of a kind of farce in the publick street. **1777** Public print [see PRINT *sb.* 11]. **1781** Public street [see NUISANCE 2 c]. **1785** COWPER *Tirocinium* in *Poems* II. 334 And while on public nurs'ries they rely. **1802** C. WILMOT *Let.* 16 May in *Irish Peer* (1920) 69 The most entertaining and pleasant day possible, at 'Bagatelle'... As it is a Publick garden, multitudes of people were parading about. **1804** R. SUTCLIFF *Jrnl.* 31 July in *Trav. N. Amer.* (1811) 42 This morning I was conducted..to one of the Public Baths [in New York City]. **1822** J. C. LOUDON *Encycl. Gardening* 1186 Public Parks, or Equestrian Promenades, are valuable appendages to large cities. **1825** H. WILSON *Mem.* III. 38 We wanted to go to the play..but we had..no private box. I have never in my life, frequented the public boxes. **1832** in *Whig Almanac 1844* 38/1 Within a few years.. restless men have thrown before the public their visionary plans for squandering the public domain. **1848** MRS. GASKELL *Mary Barton* I. i. 1 There are some fields near Manchester..through which runs a public footpath to a little village about two miles distant. **1850** *Eng. Jrnl. Educ.* IV. 434/2 A Public Nursery has recently been established in Nassau Street, Mary-le-Bone, for the purpose of receiving the children of the married industrious poor during the working-hours of the day. **1880** GEO. ELIOT *Let.* 6 June (1956) VII. 292 Your having learned the news of our marriage by the cable and public prints has always been a vexation to us. **1893** *McClure's Mag.* I. 394/2 There were even days when the Joneses questioned whether they were not running a public telephone, so often did the bell ring. **1898** E. HOWARD *Tomorrow* vii. 73 Their so-called 'public markets'..are by no means public in the same full sense as are our public parks, libraries, water undertakings..which are carried on upon public property, by public officials, at the public expense, and solely with a view to the public advantage. **1903** Public park [see PARK *sb.* 2 b]. **1910** *Bradshaw's Railway Guide* Apr. 1059/2 Private Hotel... Fine public rooms. **1910** W. J. LOCKE *Simon the Jester* xxii. 291, I..went in search of the nearest public telephone office. **1924** J. BUCHAN *Three Hostages* vi. 85, I went into a public telephone-booth. **1926** *Gloss. Terms Electr. Engin.* (Brit. Engin. Stand. Assoc.) 162 *Public call office* (*Pay station*, U.S.A.), a subscriber's station available for the use of the public on payment of a fee, which may be deposited in a coin box or paid to an attendant. **1927** W. B. YEATS *October Blast* 21 They hold their public meetings where Our most renownèd patriots stand. **1927** *Observer* 16 Oct. 11/4 Auto-electric advertising machines are about to be placed in 2,500 public telephone call boxes in London. **1928** D. L. SAYERS *Unpleasantness at Bellona Club* viii. 88 That phone-call..was put through..from a public call-box. *Ibid.* 90 His call came from a public box. **1930** W. S. MAUGHAM *Cakes & Ale* xi. 136 He was rather fond of going down to the Bear and Key..and having a few beers in the public bar. **1932** KIPLING *Limits & Renewals* 386 Improved sanitary appliances and gratuitous public transport. **1933** *Radio Times* 14 Apr. 75/1 The war was newly over..and public clocks had resumed their forgotten chiming. **1933** E. WAUGH *Scoop* I. iii. 50 There was a dense crowd round the public lavatory. **1933** A. G. MACDONELL *England, their England* vii. 100 He covered the twenty yards to the public telephone box. **1943** J. S. HUXLEY *TVA* vii. 50 Over a quarter of the 40,000 square miles of the Southern Highlands is or will shortly be public domain, under either Federal or State ownership. **1952** M. LASKI *Village* xiii. 181 In these public streets, love was easiest spoken of when they talked of the children. **1961** E. WAUGH *Unconditional Surrender* I. i. 23 I'll drop you back at your office. Can't have you using public transport on your birthday. *Ibid.* III. ii. 230 Guy took to walking every afternoon in the public gardens... There were winding paths, specimen trees, statuary, a bandstand. **1962** J. BRAINE *Life at Top* x. 136 The Warley Council's plan for a new public baths. **1965** *Scotsman* 14 June 8 House contains 2 public rooms, 2 bedrooms, boxroom, scullery and bathroom. **1969** A. CORNELISEN *Torregreca* iv. 139 Our meeting is not entirely private... Our mutual understanding must become public property. **1971** H. CALVIN *Poison Chasers* vii. 83 Two of the security men..came into the public bar, and the rest of the customers..went into the lounge bar. **1971** D. LEES *Rainbow Conspiracy* ix. 134 All I had to look for was a broken stile with a Public Footpath sign. **1971** R. BUSBY *Deadlock* v. 74 A public telephone stood in one corner of the discreetly lit foyer. **1972** P. CLEIFE *Slick & Dead* I. iv. 37 The job of public lavatory attendant. **1973** A. MANN *Tiara* ix. 80 Available on the terrace was a row of public toilets. **1974** M. BIRMINGHAM *You can help Me* iii. 47 There was one caller from a public call-box..and another—not from a public box. **1974** R. C. DENNIS *Conversations with Corpse* xiii. 132 Nothing appeared in the public prints about the missing money. **1975** *Country Life* 2 Jan. 38/3 In 1963 Cypress was given to the City of Charleston as a public park. **1976** P. R. WHITE *Planning for Public Transport* ii. 31 We are concerned with public transport (which is taken to mean modes available for public use rather than any distinction based on ownership). **1977** *Listener* 30 June 861/3 After years of legal wrangles and bankruptcy, Jacques Tati has managed to get his films back into the public domain. **1977** W. MCILVANNEY *Laidlaw* xxii. 94 A pub which from the outside looked as inviting as a public toilet. **1978** 'D. RUTHERFORD' *Collision Course* 121 They paid admission to the Casino and..strolled through the public rooms.

c. (Later examples.)

1869 L. M. ALCOTT *Little Women* II. xi. 162 She excited the suspicions of public librarians by asking for works on prisons. **1972** C. DRUMMOND *Death at Bar* ii. 44 Dubious books submitted to their Members of Parliament by Watch Committees, Purity Leagues and Aldermen who had power over public librarians.

† **e.** *public table* = TABLE D'HÔTE. *Obs.*

1742 M. W. MONTAGU *Let.* 23 May (1966) II. 281 Nothing is cheaper than living in an Inn in a Country Town in France..25 sous for dinner and 30 for supper and lodging of those that eat at the public table. **1842** DICKENS *Let.* 4 Apr. (1974) III. 182 The public table, at this hotel and at the hotel opposite, has just now finished dinner. **1865** TROLLOPE *Can you forgive Her?* II. xxx. 234 At Lucerne they made no acquaintances... They did not even dine at the public table.

f. *to go public*: of a privately-owned company, to seek a quotation on the stock exchange; also in trivial use (passing into sense 5) to reveal oneself, to come out into the open.

1965 H. I. ANSOFF *Corporate Strategy* (1968) iv. 62 Two major alternatives to this end [*sc.* of enhancing the liquidity of the firm's equity] are to 'go public', or to merge the firm with another large one. **1972** *Accountant* 5 Oct. 417/1 It..disregarded the probability that the company would in the near future 'go public'. **1976** 'A. HALL' *Kobra Manifesto* xv. 211 The girl's fever..had either driven or panicked Kobra into the open and in seizing the Boeing they'd gone public. **1977** *Lebende Sprachen* XII. 158/2 This will see the Arabs go public with the new second stage of their economic strategy.

5. a. (Further examples.)

1762 W. SMITH *Discourses Publ. Occasions* (ed. 2) App. 113 This attention to public speaking, which is begun here [in the College of Philadelphia] with the very rudiments of the mother-tongue, is continued down to the end. **1780** Public speaker [see SPEAKER 1b[1]]. **1825** T. MOORE *Mem. Life R. B. Sheridan* x. 322 And, in this great essential of public speaking, must be considered inferior to [etc.]. **1905** G. B. SHAW *Let.* 27 Nov. (1972) 583, I do not know yet exactly how you get your effects, except that it is not in my rather rhetorical, public-speaker kind of way. **1931** *Economist* 28 Mar. 665/2 Mr. Morrison's final conclusion that the proper authority to be set up is a 'business Board' of five members, incorporating what he defined as 'an element of public accountability'. **1940** C. MILBURN *Diary* 25 Dec. (1979) 76 We..listened to our beloved King's speech... How bravely he overcomes the difficulties of public speaking. **1950** B. PYM *Some Tame Gazelle* xxi. 232 She was a confident public speaker and this afternoon's audience of parish women.. held no terrors for her. **1959** *Observer* 18 Oct. 24/7, I am sure she disapproved of the new euphemism: public accountability. **1965** *Mod. Law Rev.* XXVIII. v. 520 Judges..had a near monopoly of the Chairmanships of Royal Commissions, indeed of public inquiries of every sort. **1965** *Times Lit. Suppl.* 25 Nov. 1059/1 The public-speaking Dr. Rosten points a neat moral. **1971** WRAITH & LAMB *Public Inquiries* i. 13 Public inquiries are constituted *ad hoc* to inquire into particular matters, and are for the most part concerned only to establish facts and to make recommendations. **1974** *Times* 17 Nov. 14/2 The important issue is that of public accountability. A body [*sc.* the BBC] which gets all its funds from the public ought to be obliged to answer any question from anyone about how the money is spent. **1975** *Oxf. Compan. Sports & Games* 1112/2 A wrestler at fault is given a warning and if he offends again he is given a public caution. *Ibid.* 1113/1 Should the same wrestler offend again he is given a second public warning. **1976** *Abingdon Herald* 9 Dec., With, it seemed, two men in the ring against him and only the whole crowd for him, Marino gave vent to justifiable retaliation and received the first public warning of the evening. **1979** *Jrnl. R. Soc. Arts* July 511/1 Mr. McWilliam knows all too well that digs at buildings in volumes so important can have a devastating effect at Public Inquiries, and can cause interesting buildings to fall victim to the destroyers.

e. *public address system*: a system comprising microphone, amplifier, and loudspeaker which enables speech or music to be projected to an assembly of people; so *public-address equipment*.

1923 *Electrical Communication* I. iv. 46 Public address systems..developed for the purpose of extending the range of the voice of a speaker addressing an audience. **1950** *Engineering* 24 Nov. 392/2 Public-address equipment using magnetic tapes for announcing and recording..has been installed. **1972** *Police Rev.* 8 Dec. 1597/3 A public address system fitted to each vehicle. **1978** R. V. JONES *Most Secret War* xxi. 176 The effect would be rather like that which occurs in public address systems where the noise from the loudspeakers impinges on the original microphone, and is therefore picked up and relayed back to the loudspeakers again.

f. *Public Lending Right*: the name given by its advocates to authors' (and publishers') entitlement to a fee for books borrowed from public libraries.

1961 *Ann. Reg. 1960* 458 Sir Alan Herbert..celebrated his seventieth birthday by opening a campaign for what came to be known as the Public Lending Right. **1970** *Guardian* 6 Apr. 8/1 His..description on the ballot paper could well be..Ardent Advocate of Public Lending Right... Of the dust-gathering plan to give authors and publishers a bit of the royalty for the books we borrow from the public libraries. **1977** *Time Out* 17–23 June 14/1 Combined with the Public Lending Right, the author would be helped twice over, more sales and more loans.

g. *public-access*: used *attrib.* to designate a form of television in which the general public can produce or contribute to programmes. *U.S.*

1972 *Listener* 6 July 1 Public-Access Television. **1976** *National Observer* (U.S.) 18 Dec. 1/1 All this appeared in recent weeks on a New York City 'public access' cable-TV channel that serves 85,000 families in Manhattan.

6. a. (Further examples.)

1611 CORYAT *Crudities* 205 The Duke sat about the publicke affaires with the other Senators. **1673** J. RAY *Observations Journey Low-Countries* 170 Those who assist the Commonwealth..have liberty granted to them to be present in this Council, and to understand the management of public affairs. **1822** *Sunday Times* 20 Oct. 1/3 (*heading*) Aspect of public affairs. **1937** *Burlington Mag.* Feb. 94/2 The management of public affairs.

7. (Further examples.) Also *transf.*

1932 H. NICOLSON (*title*) Public faces. **1961** Public image [see *IMAGE *sb.* 5 b]. **1962** *Listener* 1 Mar. 366/2 Finally, there is the question of Egypt's public face, the face which she presents to the world. **1967** M. ARGYLE *Psychol. Interpersonal Behaviour* ix. 154 There may be secondary aims [in an assessment interview], such as giving C [*sc.* the candidate] information about the job, or improving the public image of the employing organization. **1976** P. FERRIS *Detective* iii. 46 I'm not really on the board... I was only there today to report on our public image. **1977** C. STORR *Tales Psychiatrist's Couch* 8 Although she was still a difficult woman in her private relationships, she acquired a much easier public face.

II. 9. a. *public enemy* (earlier and later examples); now esp. (passing into sense 2 f above) in *public enemy number one* (orig. U.S.), the first named on a list of wanted criminals; the greatest threat to a community; also *transf.* and in extended use in similar phrases; *public law*: see also sense *2 h.

1756 G. WHITEFIELD *Short Address* 9 We may as lawfully draw our swords, in order to defend ourselves against our common and public Enemy. **1845** Public enemy [see ENEMY *sb.* 1]. **1931** *S. F. Call* (Mag.) 18 June 8 There are two people alive, at least, who love Al Capone—his wife and his kid. Public Enemy No. 1 is to them an idol. **1935** *Daily Mail* 23 Oct. 18/1 (Advt.), We all know who is Public Enemy No. 1 when it's time to get up! The 'Droops'. **1939** LD. CAMROSE in M. Gilbert *Winston S. Churchill* (1976) V. lii. 1081 Well, Winston was Public Enemy No 1 in Berlin, and Eden was the same in Italy. **1940** 'N. BLAKE' *Malice in Wonderland* II. ix. 123 The presence of a public enemy in our midst. **1958** *Listener* 17 July 75/1 Iraq..has been Public Enemy No. 1 to Egypt's propagandists. **1967** M. MURRAY *Ballad of Bonnie & Clyde* (song), 3 Bonnie and Clyde got to be public enemy number one—Running and hiding from ev'ry American lawman's gun. **1978** *Jrnl. R. Soc. Arts* CXXVI. 422/2 In some cities, the car has almost come to qualify for the title of public enemy number one. **1980** *Guardian* 19 Dec. 22/1 The fugitive Irishman..was 'a prominent member of the IRA and a public enemy'.

III. 10. *public-minded* adj. (examples).

a **1706** EVELYN *Diary* an. 1691 (1955) V. 61 This church.., being beged by Dr. Tenison Rector of St. Martines, was set up by that publique minded, charitable & pious Doctor neere my sons dwelling Dover-streete. **1976** *West Lancs. Even. Gaz.* 13 Dec. 6/5 A North Shore woman was particularly public-minded after buying some wrapping paper from a Cleveleys shop recently. She thought the paper might have been a fire hazard and took it round to Blackpool fire station for them to test it.

B. *sb.* **2. b.** With preceding possessive. The particular section of society which is sympathetic to the person or thing indicated.

1921 H. CRANE *Let.* 19 Sept. (1965) 64, I am 'sold out' and will have to rush rhymes and rhythms together to supply my enthusiastic 'public' as fast as I can. **1952** GRANVILLE *Dict. Theatrical Terms* 145 My *public* will hate me in this part.

c. *Sociol.* A collective group regarded as sharing some cultural, social, or political interest but who as individuals do not necessarily have any contact with one another.

1927 J. DEWEY *Public & its Problems* ii. 39 There are associations which are too narrow and restricted in scope to give rise to a public, just as there are associations too isolated from one another to fall within the same public. **1933** F. H. ALLPORT *Institutional Behav.* v. 87 Since the public is no specific group of individuals, but is defined wholly by the range of the common interest in a particular transaction, there may be a separate public for every issue raised. We are compelled, therefore, to think of *various* publics. **1954** G. A. LUNDBERG et al. *Sociol.* xiii. 491 A great source of difficulty has been the varied and confused image of the term 'public'. Clearly one may belong to as many publics as one has interests. **1954** GERTH & MILLS *Character & Social Structure* xv. 435 Publics are composed of people who are not in face to face relation but who nevertheless display similar interests, or are exposed to similar, although more or less distant, stimuli. **1969** G. A. & A. G. THEODORSON *Mod. Dict. Sociol.* 324 Publics are usually large, physically separated, and often quite diverse... Publics have an impact through their voting, buying, noncooperation, financial contributions, letters to the editor, etc.

4. c. Short for 'public bar'. *colloq.*

1957 N. MARSH *Off with his Head* ii. 29 The bar-parlour at the Green Man..lay at right angles to the Public. **1969** M. DUFFY *Wounds* i. 19 The pints of beer she had to pull for the pensioners in the public. **1971** L. LAMB *Worse than Death* vii. 64 They had finished doing the bars, and..were having a cup of tea in the Public.

pu·blically (-ikli), *adv.* [f. PUBLIC *a.* + -AL + -LY[2].] = PUBLICLY *adv.*

1920 E. SITWELL *Bath* i. 20 Goldsmith adds that 'the Masters, struck with such an uncommon instance of good nature, publically thanked him for his benevolence'. **1963** W. SELLARS *Sci., Perception, & Reality* 364 (Index), Publically observable. **1972** D. HOLBROOK *Pseudo-Revol.* viii. 140 Individuals leaping on to the stages of Danish sex clubs and publically copulating. **1974** GAGNON & SIMON *Sexual Conduct* ii. 56 The publically valued institution of marriage. **1977** *Grimsby Even. Tel.* 13 May 2/4 It was sometimes hard for parents to accept publically that their children had mental or physical difficulties.

publication. Add: **2. c.** *attrib.*, as *publication date, day.*

1931 H. CRANE *Let.* 13 June (1965) 373 Will you tell me something about its publication date, etc. **1976** M. HINXMAN *End of Good Woman* xiii. 168 Sometimes I think it's a plot on the part of the publishers to make sure no one can salvage the books from the packing to review them in time for the publication date. **1888** 'MARK TWAIN' *Lett. to Publishers* (1967) 250 No notice should appear before publication-day. **1979** M. RUSSELL *Touchdown* I. 6, I felt an urge to demand how many previous stacks had melted away since publication day.

publicist. Add: **3.** A press or publicity agent.

1930 *Oxford Times* 4 Apr. 7/4 This is the experience of Sir Charles Higham, the famous publicist, who celebrated his 21st anniversary as an advertising agent in Fleet-street on Wednesday. **1942** *Sun* (Baltimore) 4 Nov. 9/4 Most of the testimony..was given by Paul H. De Kruff, bacteriologist and medical publicist. **1969** R. BLYTHE *Akenfield* ii. 60 Well-printed signs of expert publicist talents being employed to disseminate the new *caritas*. **1977** *Times* 12 Feb. 12/6 Mr William Camp's appointment as publicist of the railways... He and his company..will apparently become the overlords of BR publicity.

publicitor (pʊbli·sitǫɹ). *U.S.* [f. PUBLICIT(Y + -OR.] A press or publicity agent.

1936 *Daily News* (Chicago) 24 Apr. 30/4 But in this solicitous telephonery we detected the fine Italian hand of the publicitor. **1951** *Lincoln* (Nebraska) *Jrnl.* 8 Dec. 6 O—..who rose from the job of sports publicitor..was assailed by the Judge. **1955** *Sun* (Baltimore) 15 Dec. (B ed.) 25/5 'The fancy basketball is out unless we're way on top,' Rod Hundley was saying. The publicitors call him Hot Rod. **1962** [see *COOTIE *sb.*[2]].

publicity. Add: **1.** (Further examples.) Also, public notice; the action or fact of making someone or something publicly known; the business of promotion or advertising; an action or object intended to attract public notice; material issued to publicize.

1826 J. J. AUDUBON *Jrnl.* 16 Dec. (1897) I. 186 Mrs. Rathbone, Senior, refused me the pleasure of naming a bird after her, on account of the publicity, she said. **1842** DICKENS *Let.* 30 Apr. (1974) III. 222, I found the documents of which the inclosed are copies... You will see that they are signed by the first writers in England; and that their object..is *Publicity*. **1847** A. BRONTË *Agnes Grey* xiv. 222 If you add to it by giving publicity to this unfortunate affair, or naming it *at all*, you will find that I too can speak. **1851** *Times* 28 Oct. 5/1 We have reported his proceedings..at greater length than any of the journals devoted to his cause, and we have thus secured to him all the publicity we had it in our power to bestow. **1917** *Electric Railway Jrnl.* 6 Jan. 17/1 Continuous publicity of good work would have softened a public irritation in the day of trouble. **1936** *S. P. E. Tract* XLV. 185 The prejudice that many people feel against advertising is likely to be dispelled if they can be made to believe that it is no more than *publicity*. **1946** E. O'NEILL *Iceman Cometh* I. 38 Why, even at Harvard I discovered my father was well known by reputation, although that was some time before the District Attorney gave him so much unwelcome publicity. **1953** A. HUXLEY *Let.* 21 Dec. (1969) 692 Osmond sent me a copy... I have taken the liberty of forwarding it to Cass Canfield of Harpers, who may like to quote from it in his publicity. **1981** S. RADLEY *Chief Inspector's Daughter* ii. 17 'How come she's featured in a magazine, anyway?' 'Publicity. She's a romantic novelist.'

2. *attrib.* and *Comb.*, as ***publicity agent, boy, bureau, drive, expert, film, hand-out, hound, man, manager*** (so *-manage* vb. trans.), ***-monger, officer, people, ramp, screen, section, stunt, value, woman, worker***; ***publicity-hunting, -seeking*** vbl. sbs. and ppl. adjs.; ***publicity-loving*** ppl. adj.; ***publicity-conscious, -minded, -ridden*** adjs.; ***publicity-wise*** adv.; (see also Dict.).

1911 J. C. Lincoln *Cap'n Warren's Wards* xi. 180 He and his friends needed a representative on the press—a publicity agent, so to speak. **1922** R. G. Collingwood tr. *Croce's Aesthetic* II. vi. 244 Recognizing the great gifts of Meier as publicity-agent. **1955** W. Gaddis *Recognitions* I. v. 180 The publicity agent looks it over and signs her name to it. **1929** G. Ade *Let.* 8 Dec. (1973) 142 The publicity boys seemed to think it was a great joke to float these wild-eyed stories about my pursuing Dorothy Tennant, [etc.]. **1962** 'M. Innes' *Connoisseur's Case* iii. 33 Tourists sure to come along when the publicity boys do their stuff. **1907** U. Sinclair *Industr. Republic* 142 He had an army of experts to help him..skilful lobbyists, newspapers and publicity bureaus. **1959** F. Newton *Jazz Scene* v. 74 A publicity-conscious American impresario could advertise a plan to recruit an 'international' orchestra. **1977** H. Innes *Big Footprints* III. i. 217 He had agreed to our taking a camera... Extraordinary how publicity-conscious these men were. **1935** Publicity drive [see *copy-writer]. **1915** *Truth* 4 Aug. 196/1 There are, as one publicity expert puts it, many shirkers doing remarkably well. **1969** *Morning Star* 25 Mar. 4 There has been an increase in short publicity films. **1973** *Screen* Spring/Summer 227 He [*sc.* A. Alexeieff]..made several commercials and publicity films. **1927** S. Bent *Ballyhoo* iii. 86 Washington is this country's premier city of publicity hand-outs. **1979** A. Williamson *Funeral March for Siegfried* x. 46 York..asked if they had a publicity hand-out on the singers in *The Ring*. **1928** Publicity hound [see *hound *sb.*[1] 4 e]. **1936** 'J. Tey' *Shilling for Candles* vi. 62 And they say professional people are publicity hounds! **1971** 'E. Lathen' *Longer the Thread* (1972) viii. 75 Annie was certainly no publicity hound. **1963** *Times Lit. Suppl.* 17 May 353/2 All the vices from publicity-hunting to jobbery. **1976** C. Bermant *Coming Home* II. vii. 216 Lord Longford was..regarded as a publicity-hunting fraud. **1938** *Amer. Speech* XIII. 59 A field of education that has suffered much from publicity- and money-loving quacks. **1907** J. C. Lincoln *Old Home House* 37 You two can be proprietors and treasurers if you want to. But active manager and publicity man—that's yours cheerily, Peter Theodosius Brown! **1932** *Sunday Express* 3 July 9/1 Soon Hammerstein left me with his publicity man, a human talking machine. **1957** *Times Lit. Suppl.* 25 Oct. 638/2 No one, not even a modern film star hounded by his publicity man, has ever courted popular favour more devotedly than Louis Philippe. **1978** I. B. Singer *Shosha* III. 50 What kind of publicity man will I make, anyway? **1952** L. Durrell *Let.* 14 Nov. in *Spirit of Place* (1969) 114 My boss Eden whose much advertised tour was publicity-managed by little me. **1908** *Mod. Business* Aug. 86/2 *Publicity Manager.*—Can formulate and carry through an advertising campaign. **1931** 'G. Trevor' *Murder at School* iii. 49 The rôle of 'writer-up' and general publicity manager. **1974** *Listener* 17 Jan. 66/2 Lady Glencora Palliser..settles down to become..her husband's self-appointed publicity manager and hatchet-woman. **1962** *Observer* 11 Mar. 8/5 I'm a very publicity-minded chap. **1974** *Times* 28 Nov. 17/7 The poor image of universities..[is] emanating in large part from a publicity-minded student minority. **1951** N. Mitford *Blessing* II. xi. 251 Charles-Edouard's heir was on the way to becoming a publicity-monger. **1962** *Economist* 15 Sept. 1017/1 The publicity-mongers of the various political parties. **1933** *Whitaker's Almanack* 284/2 Colonial Office... Publicity Officer, C. Becker-Platt.. £666. **1966** 'H. MacDiarmid' *Company I've Kept* viii. 186, I..spent a year in Liverpool as Publicity officer for the Liverpool Organization. **1932** *New Yorker* 14 May 44/2, I find..that all those competent publicity people in the shops around town can be counted on to call me up. **1933** Dylan Thomas *Let.* Oct. (1966) 31 Patriotism is a publicity ramp organised by holders of excess armament shares. **1961** *Times* 7 Jan. 9/7 A publicity-ridden world. **1911** R. D. Saunders *Col. Todhunter* ix. 128 This amazing projection of himself..on the publicity 'screen' of a newspaper's front page appalled Colonel Todhunter. **1927** F. L. C. Floud *Ministry of Agric.* ii. 25 There is also a small publicity section for the issue of information to the Press. **1935** Dylan Thomas *Let.* July (1966) 159, I hope to have..a little free love offstage from any publicity-seeking actresses I can find. **1939** 'N. Blake' *Smiler with Knife* v. 90 Charges of publicity-seeking. **1966** 'L. Lane' *ABZ of Scouse* Forewd., Be he a dollar-spending tourist or publicity-seeking politician. **1926** 'Sapper' *Final Count* vii. 195 It was just an advertisement—an elaborate publicity stunt. **1972** P. Dickinson *Lizard in Cup* xi. 176 The theft of the pictures..being, as Nancy had hinted, a publicity stunt. **1922** Farjeon & Horsnell *Advertising April* i. 19 The other woman. My successor. What's her name? What's her publicity value? **1978** J. Pearson *Façades* viii. 149 Beaverbrook..knew the publicity value of controversy. **1958** *Punch* 1 Jan. 50/1 Publicitywise, Sabrina and the Duke of Bedford consolidated their respective resources. **1962** *Listener* 11 Jan. 102/2 Dr. Crick, who publicity-wise appeared the king-pin, was now announced as the colleague (or perhaps subordinate) of Dr. Brenner. **1958** A. Huxley *Let.* 22 June (1969) 851 There have been endless contretemps, including, as a last straw, the collapse of the publicity woman with, of all things, chickenpox. **1926** *Amer. Speech* I. 480/1 The public is worked on by a 'publicity worker', assisted sometimes by a person who has the 'technique' of describing 'personal interest' incidents.

publicize (pʊ·blisaiz), *v.* [f. Public *a.* (*sb.*) + -ize.] *trans.* To bring to the notice of the public; to make generally known; to advertise.

1928 *Weekly Dispatch* 20 May 14/4 Nowadays the potential star has to be managed and publicised. **1938** M. Brinig *May Flavin* iv. 363 In my present position it wouldn't do any good to publicize these things. **1943** J. S. Huxley *TVA* iv. 25 One of the original aims of the TVA, and one much publicized in its earlier years. **1967** N. Freeling *Strike Out* 78 I'm not in the habit of publicising my private life. **1976** *Guardian* 21 Apr. 6/1 The board does not adequately publicise itself.

Hence **publiciza·tion**; **pu·blicized** *ppl. a.*, **pu·blicizing** *vbl. sb.*

1932 *New Yorker* 11 June 40/1, I hear that all the.. manufacturers who aren't doing business intend to spend the Summer on that publicized isle [*sc.* Majorca]. **1956** A. H. Compton *Atomic Quest* 303 These much-publicized burns have had effects that are no more tragic than those resulting from other forms of modern weapons. **1958** *Jrnl. Amer. Water Works Assoc.* L. 1057/2 Of more value ..will be accurate reporting—even publicizing—of the physical, chemical, and biological difference between the first water, the used supply, and the reclaimed water. **1966** 'H. MacDiarmid' *Company I've Kept* iv. 128 All the disgusting publicisation of our Scottish Queen Mother.

publicly, *adv.* **2.** (Further examples.)

1928 *Britain's Industr. Future* (Liberal Industr. Inquiry) II. vi. 82 We hope that neither thought nor money will be spared to furnish this country with a publicly-owned system of electrical supply. **1969** *Listener* 28 Aug. 267/1 And can capitalism..achieve the rate of growth that planning in a really publicly-owned economy has achieved? *a* **1974** R. Crossman *Diaries* (1976) II. 460 He was hoping to have a properly planned publicly-owned New Town like the others. **1980** *Daily Tel.* 16 Jan. 23/2 The first is a publicly-held corporation chartered by Congress.

public opinion: see Opinion *sb.* in Dict. and Suppl.

public relations. [Relation *sb.* 6.] **a.** (The establishment or maintenance of) relations, esp. a good relationship, between an organization, firm, etc., and the general public; (also const. *sing.*) the art or practice of establishing or maintaining such good relations; *transf.*, a department or group with responsibility for relations with the public.

1807 T. Jefferson *Writings* (1854) III. 89 Questions calling for the notice of Congress, unless indeed they shall be superseded by a change in our public relations now awaiting the determination of others. **1913** *Electric Railway Jrnl.* 16 Oct. 829/1 Effective publicity to deal with questions of public relations and to consider the molding of public opinion by the presentation of real facts. **1917** *Ibid.* 6 Jan. 17/1 This adviser in public relations—for such a man should be far more than a mere publicity agent—should constantly study the temper of the public mind. **1933** *Planning* I. xiv. 5 Public relations may be defined as covering all the contacts between an official organisation and all other bodies with which it may have to deal, directly or indirectly, otherwise than through internal administrative channels. **1943** J. D'Arcy-Dawson *Tunisian Battle* i. 21 Public Relations were now the possessors of six Simcas. **1945** *Manch. Guardian* 8 Aug. 4/6 The Central Insurance building, now headquarters of Public Relations in Italy. **1958** *Spectator* 8 Aug. 201/2 Some of our more 'enterprising' Cathedral cities have invented a new form of spiritual public relations, which is the Industrial Harvest Festival. **1961** *Observer* 19 Mar. 3/4 He..founded his own firm, first in public relations, then in advertising. *a* **1974** R. Crossman *Diaries* (1976) II. 547 Wedgy is brilliant at public relations.

b. *attrib.*

1923 E. L. Bernays *Crystallizing Public Opinion* i. 12 To some the public relations counsel is known by the term 'propagandist'. **1929** [see *hand-out 3]. **1933** *Times* 2 Sept. 15/5 The post of Public Relations Officer in the Post Office is a new one. **1937** *Rep. Proc. 14th Conf. ASLIB* 72, I asked him if he could help me in finding a nice crisp definition of the duties of a Public Relations Officer. He replied, 'His principal function is interpreting his undertaking to the public and the public to his undertaking.' **1944** A. Jacob *Traveller's War* xii. 212 Publicity which verged ever so slightly upon the personal was regarded as improper by the Public Relations department. *Ibid.*, The Public Relations people had asked war correspondents to go slow on stories about Rommel because we had made him into quite a bogey man. **1956** in W. H. Whyte *Organization Man* (1957) I. iii. 26 Every practising public-relations man is an engineer too—a *social engineer*. **1958** M. Argyle *Relig. Behaviour* v. 54 There was an elaborate public relations campaign before the meetings, by posters and other publications, by a film, and via the churches. **1961** *Times* 10 Aug. 2/4 (Advt.), Public Relations Officer..experienced in Public Relations work, both with the press and within an organization. **1967** G. F. Fiennes *I tried to run Railway* vi. 67 Before the new timetables I set out to do a public relations job. **1970** G. Greer *Female Eunuch* 151 The public relations experts seek to attract girls to nursing by calling it the most rewarding job in the world. **1976** *Church Times* 30 July 9/2 The public-relations officer improves 'image' but is reluctant to accept quantitative assessments of his own impressions of how much he has done so. **1977** *New Yorker* 19 Sept. 98/2 Mrs. Berner also hired the public-relations firm of Gurtman and Murtha to publicize the contest.

public school. Add: **1. b.** *public school accent, attitude, boy* (examples; hence *-boyish* adj.), *code, English, girl, product, spirit* (further example), *tie, type*; *public school-bred, -educated* adjs.; also appositive, as *public-school–Oxford* attrib.; also passing into *adj.*

1914 'I. Hay' *Lighter Side School Life* viii. 207 That is the Public School Attitude in a nutshell. *Ibid.* 220 We note a new factor in the composition of the Public School Type—the military factor. **1930** (*title*) The diary of a public school girl. **1930** E. Waugh *Vile Bodies* x. 174 Knowledgeable young men with..old public-school ties. **1931** D. L. Sayers *Five Red Herrings* v. 55 Waters.. spoke standard public-school English. **1933** *Granta* 26 Apr. 370/1 It is a movement for unemployed graduates and Public School boys. **1936** J. Buchan *Island of Sheep* I. ii. 21 The kind of son I had hoped for..was..the kind of public-school product you read about. *Ibid.* 22 Peter John..didn't care a rush for the public-school spirit. **1938** M. Allingham *Fashion in Shrouds* x. 162 'He's not *in* there,' said Jimmy, revealing a stammer and a public-school accent. **1943** M. Schlauch *Gift of Tongues* 264 English writers themselves have sometimes jeered at certain details of 'public school-Oxford' speech as being affected. **1943** F. Thompson *Candleford Green* ii. 29 His highly-pitched, public-schoolboyish accent. **1946** P. Bottome *Lifeline* i. 10 He was an Eton master, and the Public School code..he believed in. **1952** Koestler *Arrow in Blue* xxviii. 263 Public School-bred Foreign Office diplomats like Guy Burgess and Donald MacLean. **1962** *Times* 27 Feb. 13/2 The public-schoolboyish professional Roman soldier. **1962** R. Williams *Britain in Sixties: Communications* v. 101 In fact 'public-school English'..cannot now become a common speech-form in the country as a whole: both because of the social distinctions now associated with its use, and because of the powerful influence of American speech-forms. **1966** J. Cleary *High Commissioner* vii. 136 A veneer of public school accent had been laid over the gravel in his voice. **1967** *Listener* 30 Nov. 694/3 'The English public schoolboy', the prototype of unimaginative disciplined conformity. **1971** Halsey & Trow *Brit. Academics* xv. 421, 41 per cent of the public school educated teachers place themselves on the Left. **1973** 'D. Jordan' *Nile Green* ii. 12 It's one of the curses of the English public school girl that she never believes in making the bed first thing in the morning. *a* **1974** R. Crossman *Diaries* (1975) I. 131 While she is extremely tough in negotiation she is extremely public school when she's asked..to make a sacrifice in her departmental interests for the good of the nation or for the convenience of the Civil Service. **1975** J. I. M. Stewart *Gaudy* iii. 41 They were entirely English and very public-school. **1975** 'D. Jordan' *Black Account* xx. 108 One of those public-school ties which carry important messages between all true Englishmen. **1978** Cadogan & Craig *Women & Children First* v. 95 Eighteen-year-old Raleigh..dies still behaving in accordance with the public-school code.

3. (Examples referring to Canada and Australia.) Occas. applied to schools in other countries.

1789 *Nova Scotia Mag.* I. 80/1 This seminary is erected in consequence of a law of this Province, intitled, 'An Act for establishing a public school, in the town of Halifax'. **1872** *Canadian Monthly* June 483/1 Public Schools..are distinguished from those which until recently were entitled Grammar Schools, and were intended to afford instruction in the elements of the classical languages as well as the mother tongue. **1901** 'M. Franklin' *My Brilliant Career* iii. 14 My parents received an intimation from the teacher of the public school..to the effect that the law demanded that they should send their children to school. **1965** *Austral. Encycl.* VIII. 23/1 In Victoria (as in Tasmania) 'public school' generally carries its English meaning... In New South Wales..in 1892..'public school' then meant to most people 'State primary school'. **1968** *Globe & Mail* (Toronto) 17 Feb. 45 (Advt.), Not one street to cross to get to public school. **1972** *Mainichi Daily News* 7 Nov. 5/1 Students in Kanagawa Ken, both Japanese and foreign from public and private schools. **1976** D. Heffron *Crusty Crossed* xi. 79 In Big Point, there was nothing to fuss over. Only one school to go to until you passed grade eight. They called that kind of school a public school, which in England was the name for a private school which your parents have to pay quite a lot of money to send you to.

Hence **public-schoo·lish** *a.*, characteristic or suggestive of a public school; **public-schoo·lishness**; **public-schoo·ly** *a.* = *public-schoolish *a.*

1930 *Observer* 22 June 13 Mr Leslie Mitchell, as the simple Andy, is too public-schoolish in tone and manner. **1930** A. Huxley *Let.* 14 June (1969) 337 English literary criticism for the moment is all for being nice and gentlemanly and public-schooly. **1947** 'G. Orwell' *Eng. People* 39 Many necessary abstract words..are rejected by the working class because they sound public-schoolish, 'tony' and effeminate. *a* **1960** E. M. Forster *Maurice* (1971) I. ix. 48 During the previous term he had reached an unusual level mentally, but the vac had pulled him back towards public-schoolishness.

publish, *v.* Add: **I. 2. b.** For *obs.* read '*obs.* exc. *U.S. dial.*' and add later examples with persons as obj.

1886 P. Stapleton *Major's Christmas* 124 Then say you will marry me, and we will be published to-day. **1975** *Budget* (Sugarcreek, Ohio) 20 Mar. 8/3 Published today in above district were Sam, son of Joe J. Yoders and Mary, daughter of Eli H. Weavers. Their wedding to be Saturday, April 5.

4. a. (Examples with ref. to gramophone records.) Also *absol.* Also by metonymy, with author, etc., as obj.

1918 C. S. Lewis *Let.* 27 Oct. (1966) 45 He [*sc.* Heinemann] told me that John Galsworthy (who publishes with them) had seen my MS. **1937** J. Squire *Honeysuckle & Bee* 203 Lane..seemed to publish almost all the exciting new authors. **1941** *Sphere* 6 Dec. 361/1 If a publisher chooses to publish you, your reward is almost certain. **1952** Sackville-West & Shawe-Taylor *Record Year* 213 It looks like a re-issue of the recording published by Decca during the war and since deleted. **1961** H. M. Silver in *Webster* s.v., Pressure put on faculty members.. to publish as a condition of appointment or promotion. **1970** J. Earl *Tuners & Amplifiers* vi. 140 Test records are available for channel identification or recognition. Such a record is the excellent HFS69 published by the Haymarket Publishing Group **1971** *Black Scholar* Dec. 23/2 Dr. Ladner is frequently published in professional journals.

b. (Further examples.) *spec.* to make generally available a description or illustration of (an archæological find, a work of art, etc.).

1931 *Oxf. Mag.* 18 June 888/2 H. R. Hall publishes an Egyptian axe in the British Museum. **1968** *Listener* 31 Oct. 580/2 (*caption*) Are you from the BBC? If so it is your duty to 'publish' an open-ended political statement I intend to deliver. **1973** *Oxf. Univ. Gaz.* CIII. Suppl. v. 8 We are grateful to Professor Ashmole, who will publish the head, for kindly consenting to its illustration in this report. **1975** *Times Lit. Suppl.* 10 Oct. 1196/3 The great bronze doors of medieval Europe..are on the whole well known and fully published... Walter Cahn has now published, in *The Romanesque Wooden Doors of Auvergne*, a series of five sets of wooden doors, still extant though considerably damaged. **1976** *Nature* 1 Apr. 415/2 Unfortunately, we cannot know the V_P/V_S ratios in the decreasing stage, because of the scarcity of the data published by the Japan Meteorological Agency before 1950. **1978** *SLR Camera* Sept. 53/3, I wasn't quite sure what I was going to do with the films I shot on the way round but if I wanted to get any published I knew I had to get them back home while the race was still in progress. **1978** *Times Lit. Suppl.* 1 Dec. 1392/3 There are papyri in Greek and Latin (the Egyptian papyri are somewhere else entirely), ostraca (about 4,000 inscribed potsherds, of which only 300 have been published).

c. *intr.* in passive sense. To come into public circulation; to be published.

1928 *Public Opinion* 6 Apr. 325/1 The newspapers do not publish on Good Friday. **1972** *Evening Telegram* (St. John's, Newfoundland) 24 June 1/1 The Evening Telegram will publish Monday, June 26 which is being observed as Discovery Day in Newfoundland.

publishability (pʊbliʃăbi·lĭti). [f. PUBLISHABLE *a.*: see -ILITY.] The quality of being publishable; suitability for publication.

1870 G. H. Lewes *Let.* 8 May in *Geo. Eliot Lett.* (1956) V. 94 When you have read them and decided as to their *publishability* in the Atlantic perhaps you will make me the channel of an offer. **1969** C. Derrick *Reader's Report* 17 'Success'..means for the most part mere publishability; we are not concerned with the heights. **1974** *Jrnl. Social Psychol.* XCIV. 302 The printed form of the report was rated significantly higher..on the question of publishability than the two mimeographed forms.

publisher. Add: **2. b.** Also *spec.* a newspaper proprietor (*U.S.*).

1911 *Springfield* (Mass.) *Weekly Republican* 6 Apr. 11 Connecticut Publisher Dead. F. R. Swift, owner of the Bridgeport and Waterbury Herald, died last week. **1920** Ld. Northcliffe *Let.* May in W. F. Johnson *George Harvey* (1929) xxxvii. 383 Misunderstandings due to different meanings of the same words are among the basic difficulties of Anglo-American relations. Just now there is a discussion about the price of paper in which the use of the word 'publisher' for 'newspaper owner' confuses our people. **1949** *Manch. Guardian Weekly* 3 Nov. 2/2 Publishers and big advertising agencies in New York..are laying off salesmen, art staff, and layout men. **1974** *Lebende Sprachen* XIX. 39/1 US publisher (of a newspaper)—BE (newspaper) proprietor. Zeitungsverleger (und besitzer).

4. b. publisher's (or **publishers'**) **binding**, a uniform binding provided for an edition of a book before it is offered for sale; **publisher's** (or **publishers'**) **cloth**, a publisher's binding in which cloth is used as the covering material.

1901 D. Cockerell *Bookbinding* i. 20 For a permanent publisher's binding, something like that recommended for libraries..is suggested. **1924** M. Sadleir in *Bookman's Jrnl.* Feb. 154/1 It is obvious that no 'publisher's binding', in the accepted sense of lettered durability, was known [in the eighteenth century]. **1928** E. P. Goldschmidt *Gothic & Renaissance Bookbindings* I. 35 If the bindings with publishers' names or marks are 'original publishers' bindings'..then surely all such bindings must contain books published by the man who signed the binding. **1974** R. McLean *Victorian Publishers' Book-Bindings* 7 This is a picture book showing the richness of publishers' bindings principally in cloth or leather, produced in Britain during the nineteenth century. **1921** T. J. Wise *Bibliogr. Writings J. Conrad* (ed. 2) 1. 44 If only collectors would refrain from purchasing copies of Conrad's books unless they are in the original publishers' cloth,..their position would be perfectly safe. **1935** J. Carter (*title*) Publisher's cloth: an outline history of publisher's binding in England 1820–1900. **1972** P. Gaskell *New Introd. Bibliogr.* 246 The more fanciful styles of publishers' cloth included gilt blocking over the whole area of the covers.

publishing, *vbl. sb.* **2.** (Further *attrib.* examples.)

1862 R. H. Newell *Orpheus C. Kerr Papers* 1st Ser. 380, I'm agent for the great American publishing house of Rushem & Jinks. **1881** 'Mark Twain' *Lett. to Publishers* (1967) 143 A few days before Canadian publishing-date. **1929** H. Crane *Let.* 26 Feb. (1965) 339 A marvelous de luxe publishing establishment here. **1937** *Discovery* Mar. 80/1 A book recently published in Moscow by the Biological-Medical Publishing House. **1958** *New Statesman* 1 Feb. 136/3 Within a matter of months every single Yiddish theatre, publishing-house, magazine..etc was closed down. **1978** *Maledicta* I. II. 327 By 'year' we mean the 'publishing year' which is not identical with the 'calendar year'.

pubsy (pʊ·bzi), *a. colloq.* [f. PUB *sb.* + -SY.] Characteristic or suggestive of a public house.

1966 *New Statesman* 30 Sept. 489/1 But the most attractive numbers are in that easy, pubsy English style which suggests Bud Flanagan, Tommy Steele and Julian Slade arm-in-arm, just strolling, lazily flexing their knees and getting nowhere. **1977** *Listener* 7 Apr. 447/3 Return briefly to the pubsy, Fitzrovian atmosphere of Lord Longford's..party.

pucca, var. PUCKA, PAKKA.

Puccinian (putʃi·niăn), *a.* [-AN.] Of, pertaining to, characteristic of, or resembling the works of the Italian operatic composer Giacomo Puccini (1858–1924).

1942 *Scrutiny* XI. 74 We have an exquisitely sensitive line which, the antithesis of Puccinian or Wagnerian hysteria, is almost French and Chausson-like in its delicacy. **1958** *Listener* 20 Nov. 850/3 The cardboard figures of Puccinian melodrama. **1962** *Times* 26 Jan. 16/4 He does not allow them much..Puccinian nobility of soul. **1978** *Gramophone* Jan. 1289/2 On the Italian front, Tebaldi is dominant, giving good, cleanly sung, quite committed versions of several famous Puccinian passages.

So **Puccinie·sque** *a.*, resembling the style of Puccini's works.

1927 *Sunday Express* 19 June 10/4 Yet Tom Burke has sung only once—in 'Rigoletto', which does not give him emotional scope, for he is a tenor of the voluptuously Pucciniesque type. **1961** *Times* 6 Dec. 17/6 As to Pucciniesque lyric passages, tender feelings are unmistakably clear when set to that kind of music.

‖ **puchero** (putʃē·ro). Also **puchera.** [a. Sp. *puchero, -a.*] **1.** A glazed earthenware cooking pot. Cf. OLLA[1] 1.

1841 Borrow *Zincali* II. III. App. 125 The puchero, or pan of glazed earth, in which bacon, beef, and garbanzos are stewed. **1846** R. Ford *Gatherings from Spain* x. 113 Most classes are equally satisfied with the Oriental earthenware *ollas, pucheros*, or pipkins.

2. A composite dish of beef or lamb, ham or bacon, and vegetables, cooked as a stew.

1841 [see *GARBANZO]. **1903** Conrad & Hueffer *Romance* III. ii. 131 An old woman..cooked his food at an outside fire—his *puchero* and *tortillas*. **1923** *Glasgow Herald* 7 Nov. 6/3 The crop of garbanzo, of which is made the puchero that has superseded the olla of years ago. **1933** H. Allen *Anthony Adverse* VIII. lxi. 998 The puchero followed. Brought in separate dishes, it was finally combined into one on the diner's plate.

puck, pook, *sb.*[3] Add: **e. puckfoisted** *a.* (*dial.*), cheated by a demon, bewitched.

1932 H. J. Massingham *Wold without End* App. 294 Here are a few of the Elizabethan words that were heard at the Globe more than three hundred years ago and are heard to-day in the inns between Chipping Campden and Stow-on-the-Wold.. 'puckfoisted' for bewitched.

puck, *sb.*[3] **1.** Delete 'in Canada' and add further examples.

1930 *Times* 20 Mar. 7/2 A little later..Bencchi put the puck over his body into the net. **1951** *Sport* 7–13 Jan. 16/2 His old speciality, taking the puck at full speed and boring through to the net, is working overtime. **1971** L. Koppett *N.Y. Times Guide Spectator Sports* i. 7 The scoring objective can be stated simply: in football to advance the ball across a goal line; in basketball, hockey, soccer or lacrosse, to get the ball (or puck) into a goal. **1974** *Cleveland* (Ohio) *Plain Dealer* 13 Oct. c. 1/2 Toronto jumped to a 2–0 lead in the first period when Featherstone streaked in for an unassisted goal at 1:35 and Dillon rammed the puck home at 18:48. **1978** *N.Y. Times* 30 Mar. D. 17/6 Wayne Dillon won the draw from Mike Kaszycki but pulled the puck back to an empty spot on the circle.

2. *attrib.* and *Comb.*, as *puck-dribbling, -handling, shot*; **puck carrier**, in ice hockey the player in possession of the puck during play; **puckchaser** *colloq.*, an ice-hockey player; so **puck-chasing** *vbl. sb.*; **puck crown**, ice-hockey championship; **puck pusher** *colloq.* = **puck-chaser*; **puck sense**, natural skill in ice hockey; **puck shy**, of goalkeepers in ice hockey: afraid of being hit by a puck.

1957 *Maclean's Mag.* 28 Sept. 1/2 The top scorers in the League are the best puck carriers. **1921** *Daily Colonist* (Victoria, B.C.) 24 Mar. 11/3 Calgary puckchasers take all the honors. **1979** *Yale Alumni Mag.* Apr. CN 1 The continuing resurgence of puck-chasers and net-stuffers is to be applauded. **1950** *Sport* 24–30 Mar. 13/4 His family later moved to Fort William, in which town he did most of his puck chasing. **1955** *Penticton* (B.C.) *Herald* 17 Mar. 5/3 There is no doubt in my mind—the Vees will bring this puck crown back to Canada. **1974** *Globe & Mail* (Toronto) 28 Jan. s. 2/7 He also gave a few exhibitions of puck dribbling with his skates, the only NHL defenceman who has this unique skill. **1965** *Kingston* (Ontario) *Whig-Standard* 15 May 9/6 Flyers dominated the game with superior skating, checking, passing and puck-handling. **1897** *Medicine Hat* (Alberta) *News* 25 Feb. 1/5 We have a club which can hold its own with the puck pushers from almost anywhere. **1966** *Hockey News* (Montreal) 1 Jan. 13/2 An intangible part of Melnyk's all-round prowess is something called 'puck sense'. **1968** *Globe & Mail* (Toronto) 5 Feb. 17/3 He was lifted with three minutes to play in the second period when struck on the mask over the right eye by a puck shot at close range. **1965** *Ibid.* 29 Dec. 24/2, I think the new rule could cause a goalie to become puck shy.

puck, *sb.*[4] (Further examples.)

1922 Joyce *Ulysses* 247 One puck in the wind..would knock you into the middle of next week. **1934** J. O'Hara *Appointment in Samarra* (1935) iii. 80 What he should of done was give you a puck in the mouth when you threw the drink at him. **1961** 'F. O'Brien' *Hard Life* ii. 18 Many a good puck I had myself in the quondam days of my nonage. **1979** N. Smythe in E. Berman *Ten of Best Brit. Short Plays* 120 I'll give you a puck in the gob in short order, mate.

puck, *v.* Add: **pu·cking** *vbl. sb.* and *ppl. a.*

1922 Joyce *Ulysses* 247 Myler Keogh, Dublin's pet lamb, will meet sergeantmajor Bennett, the Portobello bruiser... God, that'd be a good pucking match to see. *Ibid.* 313 The referee twice cautioned Pucking Percy for holding.

pucka, pakka, *a.* (*sb.*) Restrict ‖ to senses a, b, d, e in Dict. and add: **c.** (Further examples.) Now usu. in form **pukka.** Also in general use outside India in various extended senses. Of things: real, not sham; of information: factually correct; of persons: authentic, not pretended; proper or correct in behaviour, socially acceptable. Freq. in *pukka sahib* (cf. *SAHIB 1 b), used with allusion to life in the former British Indian Empire.

1894 *Scribner's Mag.* XV. 548/2 The Zinal-Rothhorn or 'Moming' is, to use an Anglo-Indian phrase, a 'puckah' mountain, which means that it is the real thing and not a sham. **1917** W. Owen *Let.* 17 July (1967) 477 It was better paid than by a pukka Editor's best guineas. **1919** J. Buchan *Mr. Standfast* I. v. 113 My boy's at home, convalescing, and if he says you're *pukka*, I'll ask your pardon. **1924** E. M. Forster *Passage to India* I. iii. 26 Mrs. Turton..remarked that Mr. Fielding wasn't pukka, and had better marry Miss Quested, for she wasn't pukka. **1929** S. Aumonier in *Mercury Story Bk.* 389 McLagan and Treadway were pukka soldiers of the old army. **1932** *Daily Express* 27 June 3/3 She wants also to play pukka golf. **1934** 'G. Orwell' *Burmese Days* v. 88 The smell of pukka sahibdom. **1938** N. Marsh *Artists in Crime* xix. 280 Don't be so 'pukka sahib'. **1939** [see *POONAH]. **1942** T. Rattigan *Flare Path* I. 14 Pukka gen, sir. **1948** *Observer* 25 Apr. 2/1 Produced for the Government of Southern Rhodesia, that forty minute film..is one of many from British studios that are being specially commissioned to give straightforward information on important subjects—in fact 'pukka gen'. **1955** *Sci. Amer.* Feb. 116/3 The injunctions and other brawling seem now to have subsided, with general agreement that while Buh may not be a pukka sahib, he is a peerless climber. **1966** 'G. Black' *You want to die, Johnny?* v. 85, I just played pukka sahib greeting faithful old native servant. **1967** Singha & Massey *Indian Dances* xviii. 157 These barracks once the epitome of pukka British army tradition, for many years echoed all day to the sounds and rhythms of Indian music. **1971** *Daily Tel.* 19 Oct. 19 At one time hotels were classed with brothels in the minds of pukka brewers. **1973** C. Mullard *Black Britain* III. vii. 75 A list of the reconstituted Board in 1968 showed all the new members, with the exception of two, to be pukka members of the white Establishment. **1973** *Times Lit. Suppl.* 30 Mar. 340/2 A small but pukkah group defending the last tatty remnants of colonial gentility. **1976** *Physics Bull.* Nov. 480/1 What it does show is a pucka trade union doing a proper trade union job. **1977** *Radio Times* 12–18 Nov. 15/1 The two genuinely brown faces in *It Ain't Half Hot Mum* belong to a Pakistani and a Bangla Deshi. He is the only pukka Indian in sight.

puckarow, var. *PUCKEROW.

puckaun (pʊ·kǭn). *Anglo-Ir.* Also **puckawn.** [ad. Ir. *pocán*, a small male goat.] A billy goat.

a **1745** Swift *Irish Eloquence* in *Prose Wks.* (1957) IV. 279 His Cows..would hardly give a drop of Milk..For his herd had lost the Puckaun. **1870** P. Kennedy *Fireside Stories of Ireland* 7 Bring me the giant's puckawn with the golden bells round his neck. **1913** J. Stephens *Here are Ladies* 287 Children will dance upon the slightest provocation, so also do lambs and goats; but policemen, and puckauns, and advertisement agents, and fish do not dance at all, and this is because they have hard hearts. **1953** S. Beckett *Watt* iv. 246 Riley's puckaun again, said Mr Nolan, I can smell him from here.

pucker, *sb.*[1] **2.** (Further U.S. examples.)

1825 J. Neal *Bro. Jonathan* I. 202 Edith was in tears; Jotham, powerless with amazement;—Miriam, in a 'plaguy pucker'. **1847** J. S. Robb *Streaks of Squatter Life* i. 15 If I am delayed Gales and Seaton will be very angry, and Blair and Rives get in a pucker.

pucker, *sb.*[2] *rare.* [f. PUCK *v.*] A boxer, a fighter.

1922 Joyce *Ulysses* 247 The best pucker going for strength was Fitzsimons... But the best pucker for science was Jem Corbett before Fitzsimons knocked the stuffings out of him.

puckeroo (pʊkərū·), *a. N.Z. slang.* Also in various other phonetic spellings and with initial *b.* [ad. Maori *pakaru* broken; also vb., to break.] Useless, broken. Also as *v. trans.* (esp. in pa. pple.), to ruin.

[**1844** J. W. Barnicoat *Jrnl.* (MS.) 160 Gideon [*sc.* a Maori] foreseeing the collision..shouted out Puikero! puikero! puikero! (broken).] **1885** *Short Sk. Life T. Hancock* ii. 19 [Maoris said] 'We will *pukeru* you!' 'Very well', I said, '*pukeru* me'. **1925** Fraser & Gibbons *Soldier & Sailor Words* 220 *Pakaru*, broken; smashed. A Maori word, in use among the New Zealand Troops. **1941** Baker *N.Z. Slang* v. 42 [By the 1890's] we had begun to *pukaroo* things, when we broke something, confused an issue, or ruined some plan of action. This is derived with extraordinary simplicity from the Maori *pakaru*, broken **1943** *Amer. Speech* XVIII. 93 *Pukkaroo*, adjective.., (to make) worthless, useless—it could be used..of an engine that had broken down—..is perhaps from the Maori *pakaru*, to destroy. **1948** R. FINLAYSON *Tidal Creek* vii. 179 The surest way to buckeroo an axe. **1965** S. T. OLLIVIER *Petticoat Farm* i. 14, I come to see if you've got a spare shovel. Mine's puckerooed and I got a cow in the drain. **1970** *N.Z. Listener* 12 Oct. 12/1 Bad show, fighting. I puckerooed things properly last night.

puckerow (pʊ·kərōᵘ), *v. Army* and *Naut. slang.* Also **puckarow, puckero, puckerrow.** [ad. Hind. *pakṛo* imp. of *pakaṛnā* to seize.] *trans.* To seize, lay hold of. Also *intr.* or *absol.* (rare).

1866 G. O. TREVELYAN in *Fraser's Mag.* LXXIII. 390 Fanny, I am cutcha no longer. Surely you will allow a lover who is pucka to puckero. **1876** C. CHAPMAN *Sailor's Life at Sea* iv. 224 Now is the time; let us 'puckerow' it. **1886** YULE & BURNELL *Hobson-Jobson* p. xix, Hindustani *verbs*..are habitually adopted into the quasi-English by converting the imperative into an infinitive. Thus..to *puckarow*. **1887** *Outing* July 331/1 Charley Wheeler were the lucky man as had 'puckerowd' poor Hans' dry-goods. **1899** F. T. BULLEN *Log of Sea-Waif* xvi. 194 So mechanically did they 'puckarow' those baskets, that often one would pass from the hatch to the gang way empty. **1907** M. ROBERTS *Flying Cloud* iii. 13 What with puckerowing cases, lashing tanks, and frapping stunsail-booms on the deck-house..there was enough to do. **1919** W. H. DOWNING *Digger Dial.* 59 *Puckero*, take; seize. **1931** W. KIRK in *Cabar Feidh* Sept. 389/2 Not all the legislators, robbing poor and rich to-day, can puckarow my talisman —the Badge of Cabar Feidh!

puckery, *a.* **1.** (Earlier example.)

1830 *Massachusetts Spy* 10 Feb. 2/1, I didn't like the set of the shoulders, they were so dreadful puckery.

puckery (pʊ·kəri), *sb. rare.* [PUCK *sb.*[1] + -ERY.] = PUCKISHNESS.

1877 G. MEREDITH *Let.* 24 June (1970) I. 545, I foresee the grin up to the ear tips of exulting Puckery.

puckish, *a.* Add: Hence **pu·ckishly** *adv.*

1972 *Daily Tel.* 20 Nov. 13/5 His feet could not reach the pedals... But when his fingers remained under control..he puckishly turned grace-notes and, in the Gigue, made the music swell imposingly. **1977** *N.Y. Rev. Bks.* 13 Oct. 14/4 Vice Chairman Tower adds puckishly, 'I might say further that the matter of assassinations might be viewed in a broader context of other options that might have been available.'

puckle (pʊ·k'l), *sb.*[2] *Sc.* [Local var. PICKLE *sb.*[2]] An indefinite amount, a few.

1877 G. STEWART *Shetland Fireside Tales* x. 78 A 'puckle o' oo' when da sheep wis rued. **1917** A. S. NEILL *Dominie Dismissed* vi. 86 Aw need hardly say onything aboot the object o' this concert, but it's to get a puckle bawbees to send oot a clean pair o' socks and maybe a clean sark to oor local sojers oot in France. **1930** *Aberdeen Univ. Rev.* XVII. 103 A hinna heard o' im for a gey puckle year an' A doot 'e maun be deid. **1968** E. BUCKLER *Ox Bells & Fireflies* xii. 165 The man with a small nest egg had saved up 'quite a puckle'.

puckster (pʊ·kstəɹ). *N. Amer. colloq.* [f. PUCK *sb.*[3] + -STER.] An ice-hockey player.

1939 *Kansas City Jrnl.* 5 Feb. 23 (*heading*) Greyhounds slaughter Tulsa Pucksters. **1941** *Sun* (Baltimore) 11 Feb. 14/7 (*heading*) Georgetown pucksters schedule five games. **1955** *Toronto Daily Star* 11 Apr. 18/5 Moncton Hawks, as optimistic a band of pucksters as ever came down the Allan Cup hockey trail. **1976** *Bangor* (Maine) *Daily News* 24 Aug. 20/3 U.S. pucksters face long odds.

pud, *sb.*[1] (Further examples.)

1965 R. ERSKINE *Passion Flowers in Business* viii. 108, I saw him clutching your hot little puds. **1968** J. F. STRAKER *SIN & Johnny Inch* 165 How did they get their puds on you? More trickery?

pud (pūd), *sb.*[2] var. POOD.

1662 in M. Blundell *Cavalier* (1933) vi. 103 Twenty Russe Pud of the tooth of Sea-Horse—each Pud is 40 pound weight. Ten thousand Pud of hemp. **1814** [see POOD]. **1901** A. M. B. MEAKIN *Ribbon of Iron* xvi. 226 From mines discovered in 1866..2,500 puds of gold were extracted during a period of twenty years. **1952** E. H. CARR *Bolshevik Revolution* II. xix. 285 Kalinin estimated the total of relief supplies up to December 1921 at 1,800,000 puds of grain and 600,000 puds of other foodstuffs from home stocks.

pud (pud), *sb.*[3] Also **pudd.** Colloq. abbrev. of PUDDING *sb.* **1. a.** = PUDDING *sb.* 1, 2. Also as second element in *pock-pud* (see POKE-PUDDING). **b.** = PUDDING *sb.* 6 (now the usual sense). Also *transf.* and *fig.*

1706 in J. Watson *Choice Coll. Comic & Serious Scots Poems* I. 61, I leave my Liver, Puds and Tripes. *a* **1776, 1802,** etc. [see POKE-PUDDING 1, 2]. **1828** in P. Buchan *Anc. Ballads & Songs N. Scotl.* I. 261 Whan the puds war sodden. **1914** *Dialect Notes* IV. 164 *Pud*,..pudding. **1943** 'R. LLEWELLYN' *None but Lonely Heart* xli. 342 If you lot go to chokey, so do I, for harbouring. So we're all blackbirds in the same old pud. **1951** J. B. PRIESTLEY *Festival at Farbridge* 47 These two have finished mopping up their horrible pink puds. **1955** M. EWER *No Abiding Place* i. 13 Soup, joint, two veg, pud and cheese. **1960** T. COOPER *Winter's Day* III. i. 164, I helped make the pudd. **1976** *Southern Even. Echo* (Southampton) 15 Nov. 10/2 Nostalgic and happy memories of our traditional Christmas 'Pud'.

2. *coarse slang.* = *PUDDING 5b. *to pull one's pud*: see *PULL *v.* 19j.

1939 JOYCE *Finnegans Wake* (1964) 445 There's a lot of lecit pleasure coming bangslanging your way, Miss Pinpernelly satin. For your own good, you understand, for the man who lifts his pud to a woman is saving the way for kindness. **1944** *Publ. Amer. Dial. Soc.* II. 35 *Pud, to pull the (his)*,..to masturbate... Boys and men. Common. **1972** R. A. WILSON *Playboy's Bk. Forbidden Words* 240 *Pud*, the penis; perhaps from *pudding* in *pull the pudding*. **1977** *Amer. Speech* 1975 L. 54 *Pud*, 'penis'.

3. *fig.* = *PUDDING *sb.* 7b; *spec.* an easy college course. Also *attrib.* or as *adj. U.S.*

1938 *Amer. Speech* XIII. 6/2 *Pud*,..an easy job. **1963** *Ibid.* XXXVIII. 167 An easy college course..*pud* adj. **1967** S. B. FLEXNER in Wentworth & Flexner *Dict. Amer. Slang* Suppl. 700/1 *Pud*,..an easy course; a 'snap'... *Adj.* Easy to pass or make a good grade in, as a course or test. **1977** *Amer. Speech* 1975 L. 64 *Pud*,..soft, easy. 'Do you know any pud courses?'

pudder, var. POTHER *sb.* in Dict. and Suppl.

pudding, *sb.* Add: **I. 5. a.** (Earlier and later examples.)

1789 E. BUTLER *Diary* 7 Oct. in G. H. Bell *Hamwood Papers* (1930) 231 A great fat pudding boy brought some. **1903** [see *NON-SIGNIFICANT *a.*]. **1980** A. CORNELISEN *Flight from Torregreca* xi. 267 She is a sallow pudding of a child with a broad flat face.

b. *coarse slang.* The penis.

1719 T. D'URFEY *Wit & Mirth* III. 73, I made a request to prepare again, That I might continue in Love with the strain Of his Pudding. **1961, 1970** [see *PULL *v.* 19j]. **1972** [see *PUD *sb.*[3] 2].

c. *slang.* A fœtus; in phr. *a pudding in the oven* (and similar phrases), a child conceived but not yet born. Cf. *BUN *sb.*[2] 1.

1937 PARTRIDGE *Dict. Slang* 665/1 *With a bellyful of marrow-pudding*,..pregnant. **1965** J. PORTER *Dover Two* vi. 75 'None of us ever suspected that she'd got a pudding in the oven.' 'She was going to have a baby?' asked Dover. **1966** 'L. LANE' *ABZ of Scouse* 112 *She's got a pudden in ther uvving*, she is pregnant.

II. 6. a. (Further examples.) Now usu. in British English the course following the main course of a meal, 'afters'.

1909, etc. [see *AFTERS *sb. pl.*]. **1940** S. SPENDER *Backward Son* 12 At lunch there was fruit salad, his favourite pudding. **1954** *Good Housek. Cookery Bk.* (rev. ed.) II. 284 In this section will be found the recipes for suet and sponge puddings, and for some miscellaneous baked puddings. **1968** *New Society* 22 Aug. 266/2 Another course of a meal is called 'sweet' by the non-U... The U word for the course is pudding. **1974** E. AYRTON *Cookery of England* x. 430 Our grandfathers, even our fathers, expected a 'pudding' at least once a day, sometimes twice.

7. b. *U.S. slang.* Something easy to accomplish.

1887 G. W. WALLING *Recoll. N.Y. Chief of Police* xix. 262 It was an 'inside' job from the start... In thieves' slang it was a 'pudding';..the vault, although apparently impregnable, was easy to enter, [etc.]. **1942** BERREY & VAN DEN BARK *Amer. Thes. Slang* § 255/1 Something easy,..*pudding*. **1974** *Guidelines to Volunteer Services* (N.Y. State Dept. Correctional Services) 42 *Puddin*, light action, easy.

8. c. *slang.* A pudding-shaped bomb.

1919 *Athenæum* 25 July 664/1 *Pudding, i.e.* our 60 lb. bomb.

III. 11. a. *pudding course*; *pudding-shaped* adj.; **b.** *pudding-cloth* (examples), *fork, rice, -spoon* (examples), *-stick* (later examples).

1845 E. ACTON *Mod. Cookery* xii. 255 The bird.. wrapped in a thin pudding-cloth, closely tied at both ends. **1868** M. JEWRY *Warne's Model Cookery* 482 A pudding-cloth must be kept very clean. **1971** *Country Life* 17 June 1537/2 He tried to do it with oddments of coloured knitting wools on a pudding cloth. **1948** 'J. TEY' *Franchise Affair* iv. 40 The gentle monologue went on, all through the pudding course. **1896** *Woman's Life* 15 Aug. 368/1 If the pudding-spoon and fork are grasped from beneath instead of from above, the awkward uplifting of the elbows will be avoided. **1914** JOYCE *Dubliners* 255 Freddy Malins beat time with his pudding-fork. **1974** *Times* 10 Jan. 10/1 Long grain and short or round grain, often called 'pudding' rice. **1895** W. ROBINSON *Eng. Flower Garden* (ed. 4) v. 75 A great many delightful plants..in many cases are jammed into pudding-shaped masses void of form or grace. **1976** *S. Wales Echo* 23 Nov., A pudding-shaped mound in Energlyn near Caerphilly. **1896** Pudding-spoon [see *pudding fork* above]. **1944** A. THIRKELL *Headmistress* iv. 73 Giving a final polish to the pudding spoons with a piece of washleather. **1973** J. WAINWRIGHT *Touch of Malice* 93 Harris..handled the gear-lever like a pudding-spoon. **1852** MRS. STOWE *Uncle Tom's Cabin* I. xviii. 298 Interrupting her meditations to give..a rap on the head to some of the young operators with the pudding-stick that lay by her side. **1878** B. F. TAYLOR *Between Gates* 109 You can get an idea of it by fancying a paddle or a pudding-stick turning into a fiddle.

c. pudding-ball *Austral.* [ad. Aboriginal word], an edible marine fish resembling a mullet, perhaps the sea mullet, *Mugil cephalus*; **pudding basin**, a basin in which puddings are made; *transf.*, applied to a round hat, helmet, or hair-style; also *attrib.*; **pudding chain** *Naut.* (see quot.); **pudding class** = next; **pudding club**: see *CLUB *sb.* 14c; **pudding-face** (later examples); **pudding fender** = sense 4b; **pudding-head** (examples); **pudding-sleeve**, delete † and add later examples; **pudding way** = *pudding club* above.

1847 J. D. LANG *Cooksland* iv. 96 The species of fish that are commonest in the Bay [*sc.* Moreton Bay] are mullet, bream, puddinba (a native word corrupted by the colonists into pudding-ball)... The puddinba is like a mullet in shape, but larger, and very fat; it is esteemed a great delicacy. **1896** *Australasian* 28 Aug. 407/4 'Pudding-ball' is the name for a fish. **1945** BAKER *Austral. Lang.* xii. 214 Popular fish-names peculiar to the Australian include.. puddingball, corrupted by the law of Hobson-Jobson from the aboriginal puddinba. **1861** MRS. BEETON *Bk. Househ. Managem.* xxvi. 611 (*caption*) Pudding-basin. **1909** *Westm. Gaz.* 3 June 8/3 A grey straw hat of the inverted pudding-basin type. **1925** FRASER & GIBBONS *Soldier & Sailor Words* 231 *Pudding basin*, the British steel shrapnel helmet. (From its shape.) **1951** A. BARON *Rosie Hogarth* I. ii. 19 Each boy's hair close-cropped with a pudding-basin fringe. **1974** *Country Life* 28 Feb. 456/3 A male customer is looking for..shooting and fishing hats, saucy tweed pudding basins and tweed caps. **1977** B. PYM *Quartet in Autumn* i. 1 Now he..had adopted a medieval or pudding-basin style, rather like the American crew-cut of the forties and fifties. **1948** R. DE KERCHOVE *Internat. Maritime Dict.* 561/2 *Pudding chain*, short link chain occasionally used for running rigging. It runs well over sheaves and is easy to belay. It is used for jib halyards and sheets in small trading vessels, but has lately been generally replaced by flexible wire. **1969** E. GÉBLER *Shall I eat you Now?* 88 Girl soon comes..to announce she has a bun in the oven. I'm in the pudding class. **1890** BARRÈRE & LELAND *Dict. Slang* II. 155/1 *Pudding club* (popular), a woman in the family way is said to be in the *pudding club*. **1978** L. DAVIDSON *Chelsea Murders* v. 28 'Was she in the pudding club?'..'Probably. They aren't saying.' **1916** 'TAFFRAIL' *Pincher Martin* vii. 116 Orl right, old puddin'-face. Keep yer 'air on! **1950** G. BRENAN *Face of Spain* iv. 84 The Englishman, fresh from the dull hurry of London streets and from their sea of pudding faces. **1883** *Man. Seamanship for Boys' Training Ships R. Navy* (Admiralty) (1886) 186 Pudding fenders are used in the Navy for large boats..and sometimes on lower yards, to take the chafe on the inside part of the quarter yard. **1961** F. H. BURGESS *Dict. Sailing* 164 *Pudding fender*, a fat enclosed bundle of old strands, etc., for use over the side of boats and yachts. **1851** H. MELVILLE *Moby Dick* III. xxii. 152 Pudding-heads should never grant premises. **1893** 'MARK TWAIN' in *Century Mag.* Dec. 235/2 Perfect jackass—yes, and it ain't going too far to say he's a pudd'nhead. **1952** S. KAUFFMANN *Tightrope* xiv. 243 Why, you're not doing this at all badly, pudding head. **1978** P. G. WINSLOW *Coppergold* 153, I didn't tell Joss, no matter what that Yorkshire puddenhead thinks. **1910** 'MEMBER OF ARISTOCRACY' *Manners & Rules of Good Society* xi. 85 Archbishops, bishops, and clergy should appear in full canonicals, that is black silk full- or pudding-sleeve gowns, cassock and sash bands. **1939** M. B. PICKEN *Lang. Fashion* 136/3 *Pudding sleeve*,..full sleeve held in at wrist, or above. **1960** C. W. CUNNINGTON et al. *Dict. Eng. Costume* 172/1 *Pudding sleeve*,..a large loose sleeve, especially of a clergyman's gown. **1963** 'J. PRESCOT' *Case for Hearing* vi. 94 Getting a girl in the pudding way isn't a crime.

pudding-bag. (Earlier and further examples.)

c **1597** T. DELONEY *Jack of Newberie* (1619) iv. sig. G3, The other maide..with the perfume in the pudding-bagge, flapt him about the face. **1858** G. MEREDITH *Let.* 4 Jan. (1970) I. 32 It is a pudding-bag..a quiescent receptacle for Roast Beef, Punch, and mince Pies. **1929** F. BOWEN *Sea Slang* 107 *Pudding bag*, a stocking pennant used as a vane. **1939** F. THOMPSON *Lark Rise* 238 They..yelled: Old Hardwick skags! Come..to pick up rags To mend their mothers' pudding-bags. **1943** W. W. GILL in *N. & Q.* 9 Oct. 232/1 *Pudding-bag*, blind alley. **1961** F. H. BURGESS *Dict. Sailing* 164 *Pudding bag*, a stocking or sleeve, used as a weather vane.

pudding-grass. For *Obs.* substitute *Obs.* exc. *Hist.* Add to def.: *Mentha pulegium.* (Later examples.)

1904 G. G. NILES *Bog-trotting for Orchids* x. 132 The Wild Pennyroyal of the ancients..was known in England, during 1500, as Podding-Grasse or Pudding-Grass. **1972** Y. LOVELOCK *Veg. Bk.* III. 336 It [*sc.* pennyroyal] was especially popular as a meat-stuffing, and was thus known as pudding grass or herb.

puddle, *sb.* Add: **1. b.** Also (*colloq.*), a pool of evacuated urine; usu. in phr. *to make a puddle*, with reference to a young child or pet animal (cf. *ACCIDENT *sb.* 1d).

1968 J. LLOYD *Death at Roman Farm* i. 10 Are you sure she hasn't made a puddle? **1972** J. WILSON *Hide & Seek* vi. 107 Can I have a mop to wipe up Mary's puddle? **1977** M. UNDERWOOD *Murder with Malice* iii. 37 Why are you looking at me as if I'd just made a puddle on the floor?

c. Applied *fig.* and humorously to the sea, esp. the Atlantic Ocean; usu. in phr. *this* (etc.) *side of the puddle*. Cf. POND *sb.* 2.

1889 *Ally Sloper's Half Holiday* 6 July 214/2 There seems to be no end to the chaff which the downy dandies across the puddle have to bear. **1902** FARMER & HENLEY *Slang* V. 312 *The Puddle*,..the Atlantic Ocean... In Cornwall, the English Channel. **1978** *SLR Camera* Aug. 21/1 For many years the American company..have made fine enlarging frames (masking frames this side of the puddle) both for retail distribution and for exclusive use by Simmon-Emega.

d. *Rowing.* The circular, rippled, disturbance left in the water after the blade of an oar has been lifted from it at the end of a stroke.

1934 *Times* 17 Mar. 14/1 Holdsworth is rowing better than he has ever done before at No. 2. His puddle is worthy of a man a stone heavier. **1955** R. BANNISTER *First Four Minutes* iii. 39, I could see my oars were making some splendid 'puddles'.

e. A small pool of molten metal, esp. that

formed during welding; a piece of metal solidified from a pool.

1935 C. G. BAINBRIDGE in *Symp. Welding Iron & Steel* (Iron & Steel Inst.) II. 14 A large rod melts slowly and cools the molten puddle, causing rapid solidification. **1942** J. A. MOYER *Welding* v. 43 As the torch flame moves away, the molten metal in the puddle solidifies and joins the two plates into one solid piece. **1958** *Man* LVIII. 64/1 The first flat celts were hammered out of natural copper, and then out of rough casts or puddles of it or of poor bronze, smooth on the lower side, rough and scabbed on the open side. **1975** BRAM & DOWNS *Manuf. Technol.* ii. 47 While one hand manipulates the torch to carry a puddle across the plate, the other adds the correct amount of filler rod.

6. b. puddle-duck (examples); **puddle-jumper** *U.S. slang*, a fast, highly-manœuvrable, means of transport (see quots.), esp. a small light aeroplane; hence **puddle-jumping** *ppl. a.*

1877 *Scribner's Monthly* Nov. 6/1 Presently we heard a shrilly feeble whistle, precisely such as the young puddle-duck of the barn-yard makes in his earliest vocal efforts. **1908** B. POTTER *Tale of Jemima Puddle-duck* 9 Listen to the story of Jemima Puddle-duck, who was annoyed because the farmer's wife would not let her hatch her own eggs. **1975** J. GORES *Hammett* (1976) xix. 132 Puddle ducks..and mud hens..skittered away. **1932** *Daily Progress* (Charlottesville, Va.) 10 Oct. 9 (*caption*) Even the bicycles that these sisters use..seem to be related as they resemble each other almost as much as the owners. They are twins... They were on the way to classes on their 'puddle jumpers' when they halted for this picture. **1941** *Sun* (Baltimore) 23 Aug. 8/8 Only two power-boat tests are slated on today's program..but the 'puddle-jumpers' will take over complete control tomorrow. **1944** *Newsweek* 2 Oct. 31/2 A 'puddle jumper' observation plane with bazookas fixed on the wings dove down and knocked out two of the tanks. **1944** A. M. TAYLOR *Lang. of World War II* 161 *Puddle jumper*,..a nickname for Jeep. **1961** 'A. A. FAIR' *Stop at Red Light* (1962) viii. 127, I had to take a puddle-jumper with stops in Chicago, Denver and Salt Lake City. **1971** M. TAK *Truck Talk* 123 *Puddle jumper*, a lightweight truck. **1978** *Detroit Free Press* 16 Apr. (Parade Suppl.) 3/3 Any one..can call his plane an air ambulance even if it's just a 'puddle-jumper' without medical equipment. **1941** *Sun* (Baltimore) 2 Aug. 7/1 They are hoping to receive soon a long-promised consignment of three 'puddle-jumping' Vultee 049 planes in which they will be able to hop up and down from even the smallest corn field.

puddle, *v.* Add: **6.** (Earlier and later examples.) Also in *Opal-mining*.

1853 E. CLACY *Lady's Visit Gold Diggings Austral.* vii. 114 This soil, from being so stiff, would require 'puddling', a work of which he did not seem to relish the anticipation. **1963** *Pix* 13 July 21 Machines are used to 'puddle' (separate and sieve) opal dirt. **1967** S. LLOYD *Lightning Ridge Bk.* (1968) i. 1 Opal dirt can be brought to the surface and examined or puddled.

puddler. Add: **3. a.** Also in *Opal-mining*. (Earlier and later examples.)

1859 *Adelong Mining Jrnl.* 15 July 6/3 A rather unpleasant case occurred on Monday, at Little Bendigo, between an European, and some Chinese puddlers. **1860** *Mining Surveyor's Rep.* (Mining Dept., Victoria) Aug. 214 A valuable piece of ground which could be advantageously worked by the puddlers. **1967** S. LLOYD *Lightning Ridge Bk.* (1968) xiv. 99 Puddlers have ruined the whole Lightning Ridge Field.

b. A puddling machine.

1967 A. KALOKERINOS *In Search of Opal* ii. 19 Modern miners remove the..'pay dirt', in bulk..and spin it in a machine that sifts the dirt out and leaves the nobbies behind... These machines are called 'puddlers' and their variety is almost endless. **1971** J. S. GUNN *Opal Terminol.* 37 There are two dams..at which miners rent sites.. where they operate power-driven wet puddlers capable of handling several tons of dirt in one operation.

puddling, *vbl. sb.* Add: **4.** (Earlier and later examples.) Also in *Opal-mining*.

1851 R. TESTER *Wombat Wallaby* 61, I spurred my little mare off, and in doing so she made a plunge, and very nearly bundled me and my mutton into the puddling tub. **1853** E. CLACY *Lady's Visit Gold Diggings Austral.* vii. 117 The great thing is, not to be afraid of over-work, for the better the puddling is, so much the more easy and profitable is the cradling. **1856** *16th Gen. Rep. Emigration Comm.* (Colonial Office) 26 'Puddling machines', which are contrivances for washing the soil by horse-power, appear to be numerous and valuable. **1966** J. HACKSTON *Father clears Out* 62 He was going to do something bigger this time, something better than the tin dish and the cradle—he'd borrow a puddling machine he knew of. **1971** J. S. GUNN *Opal Terminol.* 37 *Puddling tank*, large dam at which wet puddling takes place.

puddy, *a.* (Further example.)

1912 W. DEEPING *Sincerity* ii. 9 Her round, puddy, exquisitely complacent face looked out from between clay-coloured ringlets.

pudendum. Add: **a.** esp. those of a woman. (Further examples.)

1893 T. M. MADDEN *Clin. Gynæcol.* v. 59 The value [for pruritus] of a solution of cocaine freely brushed over the pudendum..is unquestionable. **1922** A. G. MAGIAN *Sex Probl. Women* ii. 31 The Vulva, or Pudendum, includes—(1) The labia majora and minora bounding the pudendal cleft. (2) The mons veneris. (3) The vestibule, [etc.]. **1977** E. J. TRIMMER et al. *Visual Dict. Sex* (1978) v. 58 Sanskrit manuscripts show Indian women with shaved pudenda.

b. *fig.*

1938 S. BECKETT *Murphy* 47 Here are the pudenda of my psyche.

pudent (piū·dĕnt), *a. rare.* [f. L. *pudens, pudentem* pres. pple. of *pudēre* to make ashamed: cf. IMPUDENT.] Having or showing a sense of shame, esp. in regard to matters of a sexual nature; modest; delicate.

1908 G. B. SHAW in W. H. Davies *Autobiogr. Super-Tramp* p. vii, These pudent pages are unstained with the frightful language..of the fictitious proletarians of Mr. Rudyard Kipling and other genteel writers.

‖**pudeur** (‖püdör). [Fr.; see PUDOR.] A sense of shame or embarrassment, esp. in regard to matters of a sexual nature; bashfulness, modesty, constraint.

1937 WYNDHAM LEWIS *Let.* 21 Nov. (1963) 247 And why this strange *pudeur*? **1959** *Times* 22 Sept. 13/5 The choice of physical type in these figures with their sense of flaunted *pudeur*..acquires a close affinity with Italian Mannerism. **1961** *Spectator* 17 Feb. 221 There was a deep-seated *pudeur*, going back to a finely civilised upbringing in a Victorian working-class home. **1962** I. MURDOCH *Unofficial Rose* xxi. 201 She had in any case, with a sort of *pudeur*, arranged to be out of London. **1963** *Guardian* 15 June 4/7 Spencer's brother, Gilbert..could have given everyone a closer sense of the man than this editing and institutional pudeur. **1968** R. P. WARREN *Incarnations* (1970) 7 The peach has released the bough and at last Makes full confession, its *pudeur* Has departed. **1976** *Listener* 10 June 737/3 It is hard not to be goaded into guessing identities. Pudeur makes the reader bend over backwards to prevent this happening.

pudge[3], var. *PADGE.

pudge, *v.* Var. PODGE *v.*

1904 H. F. DAY *Kin o' Ktaadn* 193 Old Tay..pudges along to the tin box on the mantel. **1932** *Nat. Geogr. Mag.* July 120 Overtaken by darkness on starless nights, the swamp man crawls into a log for safety or sleep. 'We always "pudge" around first to rout out any copperheads.' **1955** E. POUND *Section: Rock-Drill* xci. 75 Farinata pudg'd still there in the cloister.

pudgily (pʊ·dʒĭli), *adv.* [f. PUDGY *a.*[1] + -LY[2].] In a pudgy manner.

1926 *Harper's Mag.* Feb. 351/1 One day she escorted the pudgily tottering six-weeks-old youngsters [*sc.* puppies] on a ramble over the lawn. **1978** R. BARNARD *Unruly Son* iii. 34 He remained pudgily sunk in the easy chair.

pudibund, *a.* Add: (Further examples.) Also ‖**pudibond.**

a **1922** T. S. ELIOT *Waste Land Drafts* (1971) 103 Pudibund, in the clinging vine. **1923** G. SAINTSBURY *Second Scrap Bk.* iii. 25 My tutor in Scholarship was the late 'Johnny' King, an expert in his subject..and a very good fellow, but rather shy and extremely pudibund. *Ibid.* xxxviii. 269, I understand that Soviet education is not at all pudibund, and that the principles of parenthood are treated and illustrated in it with a fine 'candour'. **1930** D. B. WYNDHAM LEWIS *Stuffed Owl* p. ix, The illiterate, the semi-literate, the Babu,..the hearty but ill-equipped patriot, the pudibond yet urgent Sapphos of endless *Keepsakes* and *Lady's Magazines*.

pudibundery (piū:dibʊ·ndəri). Also ‖ **pudibonderie.** [f. PUDIBUND *a.* + -ERY; cf. F. *pudibonderie*.] Bashfulness, prudery.

a **1913** F. ROLFE *Desire & Pursuit of Whole* (1934) xxii. 249 The pudibundery of Erastian peeping toms. **1915** T. BURKE *Nights in Town* 51 Everyday life is always disgusting to the funny little Bayswaterats, who are compact of timidity and pudibonderie. **1917** E. POUND *Let.* ? Jan. (1971) 107, I have only three quarrels with them: Their idiotic fuss over christianizing all poems they print, their concessions to local pudibundery, [etc.]. **1959** *Listener* 29 Oct. 744/1 This is not an isolated instance of *pudibonderie*.

pudic, *a.* **1.** Delete † *Obs.* and add later examples.

a **1913** F. ROLFE *Desire & Pursuit of Whole* (1934) 247 Water-babies (pudic, though incredibly tattered) wallow in every canal. **1974** *Times Lit. Suppl.* 22 Feb. 169/1 The instructive geographical screen fallen to reveal a pudic Lady Teazle.

pudicity. Delete 'Now *rare*' and add later examples.

1931 C. MACKENZIE *Buttercups & Daisies* xxi. 274 Dodsworth in a turmoil of alarmed pudicity at the prospect of her bedroom being used as a thoroughfare called upon Ralph and Roger to stop their goings on at once. **1958** L. DURRELL *Balthazar* vi. 132 Yet it was accompanied by a delicacy, almost a pudicity, in his dealings with them.

pudor. Delete † *Obs.* and add pronunc. (piu·dǭɹ). (Later examples.)

1922 JOYCE *Ulysses* 508 Woman undoing with sweet pudor her belt of rushrope. **1927** R. FRY *Flemish Art* i. 25 This tinge of sentimental feeling is very discreet. He never abandons himself. He has a certain shy pudor which is very attractive. **1966** *Times Lit. Suppl.* 3 Nov 1012/4 Lawrence's..first head-on collision with the forces of British pudor.

pu-é, var. *PWE.

pueblo. Add: Also with capital initial. **1.** (Earlier and later *attrib.* examples.)

1844 J. GREGG *Commerce of Prairies* I. 132 About two thousand of the insurgent mob, including the Pueblo Indians, pitched their camp in the suburbs of the capital [*sc.* Santa Fé]. **1907** Pueblo Indian [see *CREE *sb.* and *a.*]. **1923** D. H. LAWRENCE *Birds, Beasts & Flowers* 193 Across the pueblo river That dark old demon and I Thus say a few words to each other. **1949** *Nat. Geogr. Mag.* Dec. 783/2 Long-haired Pueblo Indians wrapped in cotton blankets exchange stare for stare with visiting easterners. **1957** T. VEBLEN *Theory of Leisure Class* 6 Some Pueblo communities. **1976** M. & G. GORDON *Ordeal* (1977) viii. 50 The Navajos were..quick to latch onto new ideas. From their next-door neighbours, the Pueblo people, they had borrowed sheep raising and weaving. **1979** *Arizona Daily Star* 5 Aug. (Advt. section) 21/7 This beautiful Territorial..features pueblo fireplace, exposed beams in family room.

2. (Earlier examples.)

1834 A. PIKE *Prose Sk. & Poems* 132 The Pueblos shall mount and prepare to pursue. **1844** J. GREGG *Commerce of Prairies* I. 268 Most of these Pueblos call themselves the descendants of Montezuma.

puer, var. PURE *v.* 1b in Dict. and Suppl.

puerperal, *a.* Add: *puerperal fever, sepsis*, etc., sepsis of the genital tract following parturition, or the fever associated with this.

1768 Puerperal fever [in Dict.]. **1814** J. ARMSTRONG *Facts Rel. Fever called Puerperal* p. vii, Under the common term puerperal fever are comprehended, in the following work, both the ordinary peritoneal inflammation, and the low malignant fever, of lying-in women, and these are considered as modifications of the same disease. **1876** W. S. PLAYFAIR *Sci. & Pract. Midwifery* II. v. v.302 There is no subject in the whole range of obstetrics which has caused so much discussion and difference of opinion as that to which this chapter is devoted. Under the name of 'Puerperal Fever', the disease we have to consider has given rise to endless controversy. *Ibid.*, If this view be correct, the term 'puerperal fever', conveying the idea of a fever such as typhus or typhoid, must be acknowledged to be in itself misleading, and one that should be discarded. **1935** A. C. BECK *Obstetr. Pract.* xxxvi. 583 Puerperal infection is a wound infection in the birth passages. It often is referred to as puerperal fever, childbed fever, puerperal sepsis, or puerperal septicemia. **1955** *Sci. News Let.* 11 June 373/1 Puerperal sepsis, which is better known as childbed fever. **1974** GREENHILL & FRIEDMAN *Biol. Princ. & Mod. Pract. Obstetr.* lxx. 730/1 The term puerperal infection includes all the inflammatory processes which arise from bacterial invasion of the genital organs during labour or the puerperium. Other terms for this condition are puerperal sepsis, puerperal septicemia, puerperal fever and childbed fever. **1977** J. DONNISON *Midwives & Med. Men* v. 93 The deadly 'childbed' or 'puerperal' fever..regularly closed wards and contributed to maternal death rates as high as 28 per 1,000.

puerperium (pⁱū,əɹpe·riɒ̆m, -pĭ·riɒ̆m). *Med.* L.: see PUERPERY.] The puerperal state or period; *spec.* the few weeks following delivery during which the mother's tissues return to their non-pregnant state.

1890 in BILLINGS *Med. Dict.* II. 410/1. **1894** GRANDIN & JARMAN *Obstetr. Surg.* viii. 164 Many such lacerations heal spontaneously, probably the vast majority if the course of the puerperium is aseptic. **1935** A. C. BECK *Obstetr. Pract.* xv. 232 The term puerperium is applied to the six or eight weeks following labor which are required for the involution of the maternal organism. **1977** *Lancet* Aug. 273/1 Early trials with a Lippes loop inserted in the first week of the puerperium resulted in a high and unacceptable expulsion-rate.

Puerto Rican (pwə:ɹto rī·kăn), *sb.* and *a.* Also earlier **Porto Rican** (see note below), **Porto Riquenean.** [f. the name *Puerto* (or *Porto*) *Rico* + -AN.] **A.** *sb.* A native or inhabitant of Puerto Rico, an island in the Greater Antilles group of the West Indies, now a Commonwealth in association with the U.S.A. **B.** *adj.* Of or pertaining to Puerto Rico or its inhabitants.

The name was officially changed in 1932 from *Porto Rico* to *Puerto Rico*. The Commonwealth of Puerto Rico was established on 25 July 1952.

1858 J. T. O'NEIL *Mem. Island Porto Rico* in R. S. Fisher *Spanish West Indies* 152 The Porto Riqueneans.. are generally indolent. **1898** R. T. HILL *Cuba & Porto Rico* xv. 146 The Cubans are fired with the spirit of progress and infected with American notions, while the Porto Ricans are plodding along in contentment. *Ibid.* xviii. 166 The Porto Rican Spaniards of the upper class.. are the descendants of military men. **1898** *Times* 30 July 7/2 The American troops were received by the entire population.., the piers, balconies, roofs and streets being alive with Puertoricans [*sic*] representing every class. **1899** F. A. OBER *Puerto Rico* xii. 168 Scratch a Puerto Rican and you find a Spaniard underneath, so the language and home customs of Spain prevail here. *Ibid.* 171 The Puerto Rican home life..differs in no important particular from that of Spain and Mexico. **1907** J. H. MOORE *With Speaker Cannon through Tropics* ii. 38 Bright colors are affected by the Porto Rican women. **1926** K. MIXER *Porto Rico* vi. 102 Governor Towner has come to the Island under conditions which have given him an exceptional prestige with Porto Ricans. **1952** S. KAUFFMANN *Tightrope* xvi. 263 Jerry, the building's Puerto Rican shoe-shine boy was just finishing. **1956** 'E. MCBAIN' *Cop Hater* (1958) iii. 29 Occasionally, a Puerto Rican wandered into *The Shamrock*. **1962** *Amer. Speech* XXXVII. 18 New York City.. contains 80 percent of the Puerto Ricans of the entire United States. **1969** *Listener* 13 Mar. 332/1 On this particular campus, the provocative group was the black and Puerto Rican students' commune, so-called. **1972** D. DELMAN *Sudden Death* (1973) i. 15 It's exactly what that Puerto Rican hot dog would think is funny. **1978** *Langauge* LIV. 424 An example from Romance consonantism would be the uvular *r*, which is at present very widely distributed, from Brazilian Portuguese and Puerto Rican Spanish to French, north and central Italian, and even some speakers of Rumanian. **1979** *Tucson* (Arizona) *Citizen* 20 Sept. 10A/1 They would resort to violence again in the interest of Puerto Rican independence.

puff, *sb*. Add: **1. f.** *Criminals' slang* (orig. *U.S.*). Explosive powder or dynamite used for blowing open a safe.

1904 'No. 1500' *Life in Sing Sing* 251/1 *Puff*, explosive powder. **1926** J. Black *You can't Win* ix. 107, I always crush into these powder shacks for my 'puff'.

g. *colloq*. Life, span of existence; usu. in phr. *in* (*all*) *one's puff* and varr., in all one's life.

1921 [see *cheerio *int*.]. **1922** Joyce *Ulysses* 338 You never saw the like of it in all your born puff. **1929** Wodehouse *Mr. Mulliner Speaking* ix. 301 'Did you ever see a hat like that, Stinker?' 'Never in my puff,' replied his friend. **1938** —— *Code of Woosters* vii. 156 Did you ever in your puff see such a perfect perisher? **1960** K. Martin *Matter of Time* 165 That sort of thing's never happened to me in my puff. **1967** A. L. Lloyd *Folk Song in England* iv. 226 Hannah Snell..served for years as a marine..took a public house in Wapping and wore trousers for the rest of her puff. **1972** 'A. Armstrong' *One Jump Ahead* i. 9 Here's me actually going to dial nine-nine-nine! Never in all me puff would I've thought it!

2. b. Now usu. with reference to the sleeves of a dress; = *puff sleeve*, sense 9b below.

1884 B. Potter *Jrnl*. 2 Apr. (1966) 78 Tight long sleeves with puffs to put on over them. **1908** L. M. Montgomery *Anne of Green Gables* xi. 114 They all had puffed sleeves.. it was awfully hard there among the others who had really truly puffs. **1968** J. Ironside *Fashion Alphabet* 58 *Puff*, a short sleeve, gathered into the shoulder and into a band above the elbow.

c. A low padded seat or cushion; = *pouf[1] 3.

1877 H. James *American* xii. 195 Valentin was sitting on a puff. *Ibid*. 206 Then she gave a little push to the puff that stood near her, and by a glance at Newman seemed to indicate that she had placed it in position for him.

d. *Cytology*. A short swollen region of a polytene chromosome, active in RNA synthesis. Cf. *puffed *ppl. a*. 1d; *puffing *vbl. sb*. 3c.

1937 C. B. Bridges in *Cytologia* (Fujii Jubilee Vol.) II. 751 Sections 58E and F show another characteristic peculiarity—namely, they often are converted into a much swollen light-staining 'puff' in which the banding is very hard to see. **1957** *Proc. Nat. Acad. Sci*. XLIII. 964 The correlation between the secretory activity in certain cells and the appearance and disappearance of puffs at specific loci in these cells had led many authors to the hypothesis that the genes at the locus of the puff may be actively controlling the secretory process. **1966** *Proc. R. Soc*. B. CLXIV. 284 The two different kinds of 'puff': (1).. the multi-stranded true puffs, which occur only in giant chromosomes: and (2)..the single-stranded loop 'puff' of lampbrush chromosomes. **1974** *Cold Spring Harbor Symp. Quantitative Biol*. XXXVIII. 660/2 Puffs result from the accumulation of RNA and proteins at a band which is being transcribed.

7. (Further examples.)

1774 J. Wesley *Let*. 8 Jan. (1931) VI. 66, I suppose Mr. Rivington's advertisement is only a puff, as the booksellers call it. **1822** J. Robison *Syst. Mechanical Philos*. II. 47 His encomiums..are to a great degree extravagant. resembling more the puff of an advertising tradesman than the patriotic communications of a gentleman. **1916** A. Huxley *Let*. 29 Dec. (1969) 118, I lighted in to-day's *Morning Post* on a little puff of myself, apropos of *Oxford Poetry, '16*. **1923** E. Wallace *Captains of Souls* xlvii. 258 'Ambrose Sault was executed at Wechester Jail..Billet was the executioner.' The hangman always received his puff. **1960** *Punch* 16 Mar. 383/2 Students are advised to omit fine language, puffs for the product, or any form of cosy get-togetherness. **1974** S. Chitty *Beast & Monk* III. iv. 229 In January 1864 Kingsley reviewed Volumes VII and VIII of Froude's *History of England*.., no doubt with a view to giving his brother-in-law a 'puff'.

8. d. (See also *poof *sb*.[1]) An effeminate man; a male homosexual.

1902 Farmer & Henley *Slang* V. 313/1 *Puff*... 3 (tramps'), a sodomist. **1937** Partridge *Dict. Slang* 665/2 *Puff*,..a sodomist. **1961** P. White *Riders in Chariot* xi. 414 It was that puf Mortimer would not let me alone. **1967** H. W. Sutherland *Magnie* iv. 63 He'd be a puff boy, this Magnie, and God knows what entertainment he laid on for Arthur. **1974** P. Wright *Lang. Brit. Industry* xi. 95 An infuriated spectator may shout at a plump, sleek referee, 'You nasty little ponce!' (or *puff*).

9. b. (sense 1) *puff train*; (sense 2b) *puff scarf, sleeve*; *puff-sleeved* adj.; (sense 7) *puff merchant, writer*; **puff billiards**, a game resembling billiards, in which a ball is driven about on a table by puffs of air; **puff box** (examples); **puff pipe**, (*a*) a short pipe connected to a trap or valve in a drainage system in order to ventilate it; (*b*) on a vertical take-off aircraft, a pipe out of which compressed air is blown in order to control attitude; **puff port**, on a hovercraft, a vent out of which compressed air is blown in order to control attitude; **puff-shouldered** *a*., having puffs (sense 2b) on the shoulders.

1897 Puff billiards [see *indoor, in-door *a*. 1]. **1901** *Commercial Advertiser* (N.Y.) 11 May 12/5 Mrs. Hwfa Williams is said to have invented puff-billiards. **1953** P. L. Fermor *Violins of Saint-Jacques* 74 Usually some newly arrived acquisition from Paris occupied the centre of the room—a magic lantern, a kaleidoscope or..a game of puff-billiards. **1895** *Mongomery Ward Catal*. Spring–Summer 259/1 Puff boxes, made of papier mache... $0.20. **1926–7** *Army & Navy Stores Catal*. 99 Puff Boxes. **1951** R. Chandler *Let*. 6 July (1966) 143 Puff merchants ..will go on record over practically anything including the World Almanac, provided they get their names featured. **1894** A. J. Wallis-Tayler *Sanitary Arrangement of Dwelling-Houses* ix. 58 A puff-pipe, about one inch in diameter, should be taken from the valve-box through the outer wall, and its free end be also fitted with a brass flap-valve. **1934** *Archit. Rev*. Jan. p. xliv, Puff pipes, always a doubtful practice, although admissable, under certain conditions, are..here abolished and the terminals of the vent pipes being fixed high above all openings to the building ensure a strong current of fresh air throughout the system. **1960** *Aeroplane* XCVIII. 572/1 (*diagram*) Pilot controls..attitude and yaw via 'puff-pipes'. **1965** J. L. Nayler *Aviation* xiii. 188/2 Control in hovering flight was obtained by the 'puff-pipe' system first used in the *Flying Bedstead*. **1972** J. Hastings *Plumber's Compan*. 133 In Wiltshire the ornamental end of a puff pipe is a snake's mouth. **1967** *Jane's Surface Skimmer Systems 1967–68* 37/1 Puff ports, to improve in particular low-speed yaw control, and segmented skirts will be incorporated. **1971** R. L. Trillo *Marine Hovercraft Technol*. v. 93 Puff ports used on the Parkhouse Beckingham Hovercat to assist in directional control also provided rolling moment causing the craft to roll into a turn, thereby enhancing the comfort of the turning manoeuvre. **1880** *Amer. Mail Order Fashions* in *Americana Rev*. (1961) 32 New puff-scarf, satin faced and lined. **1899** A. Conan Doyle *Duet* i. 7 A roomful of puff-shouldered young ladies. **1894** B. Potter *Jrnl*. (1966) 314, I had to take his arm in to dinner, not much encouraged by his scrutiny of my puff-sleeves. **1975** G. Howell *In Vogue* 151/2 Little-girl dresses..with..full short skirts, tucks, smocking and puff sleeves. **1883** 'Mark Twain' *Life on Mississippi* xxxviii. 404 Grandpa and grandma.. stiff, old-fashioned, high-collared, puff-sleeved. **1969** *Observer* 21 Dec. 23/4 This smocked, puff-sleeved blouse. **1896** Swinburne *Let*. 29 May (1962) VI. 100 When the 'puff-train' did 'anything particularly startling or loud'. **1870** T. A. Brown *Hist. Amer. Stage* 21/2 In September he quit the business, and soon after obtained the situation of 'puff writer' for the Bowery Amphitheatre.

puff, *v*. Add: **1. d.** Of a fungus: to discharge a cloud of spores suddenly.

1887 H. E. F. Garnsey tr. *A. de Bary's Compar. Morphol. & Biol. Fungi* iii. 89 As long as the Fungus remains shut up in the damp atmosphere no amount of shaking will cause it to puff. **1953** C. T. Ingold *Dispersal in Fungi* ii. 27 Once an apothecium has puffed it cannot, as a rule, be induced to do so again for a time.

puff-adder. Add: **1.** (Earlier and later examples.)

1789 W. Paterson *Narr. Four Journeys Country of Hottentots* 164 The Puff Adder..has its name from blowing itself up to near a foot in circumference. **1915** *Chambers's Jrnl*. July 437/1 Perhaps the most loathsome of the snakes of Natal is the dreaded puff-adder. **1969** *Times* 15 Sept. (Uganda Suppl.) p. vi/8 Puff adders were sacred at Budo, so only Europeans could kill them. **1975** H. B. Cott *Looking at Animals* viii. 160 The difficulty is met by the application of patterns, such as those exhibited by African Rock Python, Gaboon Viper, Puff Adder.

2. *U.S.* The western hog-nosed snake, *Heterodon nasicus*, which belongs to the family Colubridæ but is not dangerous to man.

1882 *Amer. Naturalist* XVI. 566 Twice afterward I noticed this strange habit of the puff adders. **1897–8** 'Mark Twain' *Autobiogr*. (1924) I. 103 Snakes..liked to lie in it [*sc*. a road] and sun themselves; when they were rattlesnakes or puff-adders, we killed them. **1966** R. C. Stebbins *Field Guide to Western Reptiles & Amphibians* x. 145 When disturbed it [*sc*. the western hog-nose snake] often spreads its head and neck and strikes with open mouth, hissing, but seldom biting. This behaviour has earned it the names 'puff adder', 'blow viper', and 'hissing adder'.

puff-ball. Add: **3.** *Naut. slang*. (See quot.)

1933 J. Masefield *Bird of Dawning* 263 Bloody Bill China had bonnets on his courses and contrivances that he called puffballs in the roaches of his topsails. *Ibid*. 307 Puff-balls *or* Save-alls. Extra sails laced to the feet of square sails.

puffed, puft, *ppl. a*. Add: The form **puft** is no longer current. **1. b.** (Examples of *puffed sleeve*.)

1802 C. Edgeworth *Let*. 30 Oct. in C. Colvin *M. Edgeworth in France & Switzerland* (1979) 21, I always repeat..that puffed slieves are *si ridicule*..just like our mantua-maker. **1932** 'E. M. Delafield' *Thank Heaven Fasting* III. iii. 278, I can remember a lovely pink evening dress you used to wear, with puffed sleeves. **1976** *National Trust* Autumn 25/1 (Advt.), *Ladies overblouses*..with V-cutaway pointed collar, cuffed and gently puffed sleeves.

c. Of cereal grain: expanded by means of high-pressure steam; used esp. in the names of breakfast foods.

1907 *Yesterday's Shopping* (1969) 11/2 *Breakfast Cereals* ..Quaker Puffed Rice—pkt. 0/5½. **1912** *Collier's* 21 Sept. 24/1 Prof. Anderson's process for Puffed Wheat and Puffed Rice requires a terrific heat. **1921** *Daily Colonist* (Victoria, B.C.) 23 Oct. 18/4 At I'Chang I saw the Chinese making puffed rice as for centuries past. **1930** B. S. Bronson *Nutrition & Food Chem*. xvi. 372 Certain grains are sometimes subjected to a very high steam pressure which is suddenly released, expanding the grains and giving the various 'puffed' cereals. **1944** M. Laski *Love on Supertax* i. 13 Would it be Puffed Rice or Shredded Wheat this morning? **1957** J. Kerr *Please don't eat Daisies* (1958) 104 They all decide to make sandwiches of boiled egg and puffed wheat. **1972** *Sci. Amer*. Jan. 50/3 Most rats limited to exclusive diets of puffed rice, wheat flakes, shredded wheat and macaroni (all 'enriched') were barely able to hold their weanling weight (about 60 grams).

d. *Cytology*. Of part of a chromosome: see *puff *sb*. 2d. Cf. *puffing *vbl. sb*. 3c.

1938 *Genetics* XXIII. 159 In the giant chromosomes of *Sciarra ocellaris* Comst. certain particular regions appear greatly expanded or 'puffed'. **1965** J. D. Ebert *Interacting Syst. in Development* vi. 110 A given section of a chromosome may appear as a sharp band in most tissues, but as a diffuse 'puff' in one tissue. Or within the same tissue, a given section may be discrete at one time and 'puffed' at another. **1970** *Cold Spring Harbor Symp. Quantitative Biol*. XXXV. 534/1 At any particular stage in development only a subset of these sites is actually puffed and the pattern of puffs changes in a very regular and highly coordinated way as development proceeds.

puffer. Add: **1. a.** Also, *spec*. (chiefly *Sc*.) a small steamboat used for carrying cargo in coastal waters. (Further examples.)

1922 *R. Cruising Club Jrnl. 1921* 98 We got under way half an hour later, having been delayed by the puffer *Anna Bhan*, which had let go almost over our anchor. **1927** [see *choo-choo]. **1946** J. Irving *Royal Navalese* 139 *Puffer*, a heavily-built fishing-boat type of vessel, usually fitted with a single cylinder Diesel engine. **1959** *Times* 12 Dec. 9/7 Para Handy and his crew of three run a 'puffer' (a small cargo boat) between the towns and villages on the Firth of Clyde. **1968** 'D. Halliday' *Dolly & Singing Bird* x. 112, I saw the anchor light of a big boat, a puffer. **1974** *Times* 7 Dec. 3/2 Mr Alan Pegler bought the majestic old LNER puffer [*sc*. the Flying Scotsman] in 1962. **1975** *Stornoway Gaz*. 5 July 1/9 A call for help was heard, stating that the puffer 'Lady Morven' had broken down and was drifting ashore in Loch Cuan.

c. Substitute for def.: In full, *puffer fish*. A carnivorous globe-fish that can swallow air to inflate itself, belonging to the family Tetraodontidæ, which includes about ninety species found in warm or temperate seas; also, a porcupine-fish belonging to the closely related tropical family Diodontidæ; cf. *puff-fish* s.v. Puff *sb*. 9b. (Earlier and later examples.)

1814 S. L. Mitchell *Fishes N.Y.* 473 Puffer... He is called in some places, toad-fish, because his back is mottled with yellow & dark. **1883** *Bull. U.S. Nat. Mus*. XXVII. 428 *Tetrodon nephelus*... Rough Swell-fish; Puffer; Blower; Swell Toad. Gulf of Mexico, abundant. **1884** G. B. Goode *Fisheries U.S.: Nat. Hist. Aquatic Animals* I. III. 170 The Porcupine Fishes—Diodontidæ. Swell Fishes and Puffers. **1930** *Times Educ. Suppl*. 18 Oct. (Home & Classroom Section) p. ii/2 Puffer fish have the habit of inflating themselves with air, which they swallow. **1941** J. Steinbeck *Sea of Cortez* x. 77 Small spine-covered puffer fish..bloat themselves when they are attacked, erecting the spines. **1947** [see *blaasop]. **1962** K. F. Lagler et al. *Ichthyology* v. 151 A remarkable modification of the stomach exists in the puffers (Tetraodontidae) and porcupinefishes (Diodontidae) which can inflate themselves with water or air to assume often an almost globular shape. **1967–8** *Bahamas Handbk. & Businessmen's Ann*. (ed. 7) 456 Here and there..the wader will find a solitary porcupine fish, also called puffers or blowfish. **1974** M. C. Gerald *Pharmacol*. i. 3 The ovaries of the pufferfish (an excellent source of tetrodotoxin, one of the most powerful poisons known to man).

d. (Earlier and later examples.)

1884 G. B. Goode *Fisheries U.S.: Nat. Hist. Aquatic Animals* I. I. 14 On the Atlantic coast occurs most abundantly the little Harbor Porpoise *Phocæna brachycion* Cope, known to the fishermen as 'Puffer', 'Snuffer', [etc.]. **1911** *Fisheries U.S. 1908* (U.S. Bur. Census Spec. Rep.) 314/1 Porpoise (*Phocæna communis*).—A cetacean found on the north Atlantic and north Pacific coasts, ascending rivers. It is known as 'harbor porpoise', 'herring-hog', 'puffer', [etc.].

e. A wheel-lock pistol.

1970 G. Boothroyd *Handgun* i. 16/2 The French makers equalled the Germans in ingenuity but..were able to combine with that ingenuity an elegance of form that is totally lacking in..the ball-butted Puffer, the German wheellock pistol. **1973** *Country Life* 29 Mar. 881 *Antique Firearms*..Saxon wheel-lock Puffer, dated 1590, length 23 inches. **1973** *Times* 22 May 18/3 A Nuremberg wheel-lock 'puffer' made £7,000.

f. A soft plastic container designed to blow powder on to the skin, etc., when squeezed; freq. *attrib*., as *puffer bottle, pack*; also *talc puffer*.

1971 *Homes & Gardens* Aug. 89/2 An insect powder in a puffer pack is convenient for this job. **1971** *Petticoat* 24 July 9/3 A must for your handbag is the..*Travel Trio* which contains a puffer talc. **1973** J. Wood *North Beat* ii. 27 It's fine powder you get in a puffer bottle—puff it on your hair to make it look right grey. **1974** *Harpers & Queen* Sept. 50/1 Talc puffer 55 p. **1978** R. Westall *Devil on Road* viii. 52 I'll take..a puffer-bottle for the [cat's] ear-mites.

puffery. Add: **1.** Now chiefly *U.S.* (Further examples.)

1929 D. G. Mackail *How Amusing!* 518 The gossip-writers had all contributed their quota of unpaid puffery. **1963** D. Ogilvy *Confessions Advertising Man* (1964) vi. 110 The reader finds it easier to believe the endorsement of a fellow consumer than the puffery of an anonymous copy-writer. **1966** *Daily Tel*. 3 Nov. 14/2 Richard Maney, Press agent to some 300 Broadway shows, and..a master of flamboyant puffery. **1970** *Observer* 1 Mar. 13/3 An

American company selling weight reducing pills was prosecuted for misleading advertising. One of its defences was puffery. **1978** J. CARROLL *Mortal Friends* I. ii. 25 If you'll not be subject to the spiritual authority of the Church even on the day of your sacrament, don't blaspheme your martyred countrymen by such puffery.

puffick (pʊ·fik), *a.* [Repr. colloq. and dial. pronunc. of PERFECT.] = PERFECT *a.* (esp. sense 5d). So **pu·fficklу** *adv.* = PERFECTLY *adv.*

1891 KIPLING *Many Inventions* (1893) 3 He knows puffickly well where he is. **1907** E. NESBIT *Enchanted Castle* iv. 105 You aint allowed to arrest a chap on suspicion, even if you know puffickly well who done the job. **1949** M. ALLINGHAM *More Work for Undertaker* xiv. 176 The chap..was a puffick stranger. **1967** 'A. GILBERT' *Visitor* viii. 139 They'll ask..why you should take a chance like that for a puffick stranger. **1972** C. DRUMMOND *Death at Bar* ii. 61 She mimicked in Cockney, 'A puffick gentlemen I'm sure, dear.'

puffily (pʊ·fili), *adv.* [f. PUFFY *a.* + -LY².] In a puffy manner.

1882 CAULFIELD & SAWARD *Dict. Needlework* 415/1 When Petticoats are to be Quilted, the Runnings should be well indented and the satin or silk set up puffily. **1904** H. G. WELLS *Food of Gods* II. ii. 197 He did the rise over by the chalk-pit crest a little puffily. **1963** A. SMITH *Throw out Two Hands* xiv. 150 We could look back at the cloud... It was brooding over us no more, but clearly and puffily to one side. **1975** S. LAUDER *Killing Time on Corvo* i. 7 He looked puffily unhealthy. **1977** C. MCCULLOUGH *Thorn Birds* ii. 21 They paused.., the five bright heads haloed against a puffily clouded sky.

puffin¹. Add: **2.** (With capital initial.) The proprietary name of a variety of children's paper-back book or series of books published by Longman Group Limited (see *PENGUIN 2c).

1947 *Trade Marks Jrnl.* 10 Sept. 535/2 Puffin 648,226. Printed publications, stationery, bookbinding materials, pens and pencils, but not including publications on puffins. Penguin Books Limited..Manufacturers and Publishers.—28th May, 1946. **1960** *Penguins Progress 1935–60* 54 Each month we publish fifteen to twenty books, varying from Penguin fiction..to Penguin Handbooks and Puffins. **1979** *Guardian* 29 Oct. 12/6 A list of leading children's writers who are not in Puffin would be a pretty short one.

3. (With capital initial.) The proprietary name of a make of duvet or continental quilt. Also *Puffin Downlet.*

1959 *Trade Marks Jrnl.* 18 Feb. 206/2 Puffin... Filled bed coverings in the nature of quilts or eiderdowns. Arthur R. Davis and Company Limited,..Croydon, Surrey; manufacturers and merchants. **1970** 'R. CRAWFORD' *Kiss Boss Goodbye* II. viii. 107 Brenda was lying on her back on top of the Puffin Downlet. **1971** *Guardian* 29 Sept. 11/2 The cleaning of feather-filled continental quilts is a problem... One reader, taking her Puffin to.. a well-known cleaners..was met with the blankest confusion.

puffing, *vbl. sb.* Add: **1. b.** The sudden discharge of a cloud of spores by a fungus.

1887 H. E. F. GARNSEY tr. *A. de Bary's Compar. Morphol. & Biol. Fungi* iii. 89 Many of the Discomycetes have the peculiar habit of 'puffing'.., of suddenly discharging a whole cloud of spores. **1953** C. T. INGOLD *Dispersal in Fungi* ii. 27 If a cup-fungus is picked and at once placed near the ear, puffing may occur and is then audible as a hissing sound. **1976** G. C. AINSWORTH *Introd. Hist. Mycol.* vii. 196 Micheli..was also the first to record and illustrate the visible 'puffing' of spores from the ascocarps of discomycetes.

3. c. *Cytology.* The occurrence or formation of puffs on a chromosome. Also *attrib.* Cf. *PUFF *sb.* 2d; *PUFFED *ppl. a.* 1d.

1938 *Genetics* XXIII. 159 Intermediate degrees of 'puffing' show the bands or discs in various stages of disruption. **1954** *Exper. Cell Res.* VI. 199 The 'lampbrushes' show a considerable degree of lateral 'puffing' as judged from the fact that the immediately neighbouring branches of the chromosome are only half as thick. **1968** H. HARRIS *Nucleus & Cytoplasm* iv. 78 It has been contended that the pattern of puffing shows organ specificity, but the evidence for this does not seem to be at all conclusive. **1970** *Cold Spring Harbor Symp. Quantitative Biol.* XXXV. 534/1 Periods of greatest puffing activity are seen as the animals molt from one instar to the next and both events, molting and the initiation of a specific sequence of puffing, are primarily controlled by the same hormone,..ecdysone.

5. puffing-hole (see quot.).

1862 J. B. JUKES *Student's Man. Geol.* (ed. 2) II. x. 220 The sea sometimes gradually forms a passage for itself in the surface above, and if that be not too lofty, forms a 'blow-hole' or 'puffing-hole', through which spouts of foam and spray are occasionally ejected high into the air.

puffing, *ppl. a.* Add: **1.** Also *Puffing Billy,* an affectionate name for a steam locomotive or train. Also *transf.* and *attrib.*

The original 'Puffing Billy' was built by William Hedley in 1813.

1934 JOYCE *Let.* 25 Apr. (1966) III. 304, I prefer Puffing Billy to Swaggering Bob. **1963** A. LUBBOCK *Austral. Roundabout* 172 A 'Puffing Billy' engine, woodfired, was dredging the silt. **1977** *Times* 19 Apr. 5/5 (*caption*) A replica of an early American 'Puffing Billy'.. at the National Railway Museum, York.

puffinry (pʊ·finri). [f. PUFFIN *sb.*¹ + -RY.] A place occupied by a breeding colony of puffins.

1954 FISHER & LOCKLEY *Sea-Birds* iii. 64 There are seven separate puffin-slopes on St. Kilda each of which is larger than..even the largest puffinry in the..Shiant Isles. **1960** WILLIAMSON & BOYD *St. Kilda Summer* xi. 113 It [*sc.* Stac Lee, St. Kilda] has large guillemot and kittiwake colonies too, and Stac an Armin many razorbills and a big puffinry. **1974** *Country Life* 14 Feb. 290/2 Much the same is true of the other puffinries on the islands.

puffy, *a.* Add: **4.** *puffy-cheeked, -eyed, -looking* adjs.

1922 H. CRANE *Let.* 27 July (1965) 94 The Man Ray photo of J...is really not a good resemblance. The face is not so puffy-looking. **1926** V. WOOLF *Writer's Diary* (1953) 89 In trotted a little puffy-cheeked cheerful old man [*sc.* Hardy]. **1929** *Sunday Dispatch* 20 Jan. 16/3 You watch the boy growing puffy-eyed and soft on his fast living. **1957** J. KEROUAC *On Road* (1958) 170 Everybody looked like a broken-down movie extra, a withered starlet; disenchanted stuntmen,..puffy-eyed motel blondes..a lemon lot.

puftaloon (pʊ·ftălūn). *Austral.* Also **puffta-loon, puftaloony, puffterlooner, puff de loon(ey),** etc. [Origin obscure; cf. PUFF *sb.* 5.] A small fried cake, spread with jam, sugar, or honey, and usu. eaten hot.

[**1853** MOSSMAN & BANISTER *Australia* 126 'Leatherjackets'—an Australian bush term for a thin cake made of dough, and put into a pan to bake with some fat... The Americans indulge in this kind of bread, giving them the name of 'Puff ballooners'.] **1871** M. CLARKE *His Natural Life* v. ii, in *Austral. Jrnl.* VI. 602/2 'Have a puffterlooner, Master Dick,' suggests Derwent Jack, 'or a bit o' sweetcake.' **1908** A. GUNN *We of Never Never* xiv. 189 The cooking lessons proceeded until the fine art of making 'puff de looneys'..had been mastered. **1935** *Bulletin* (Sydney) 27 Feb. 20/1 Camped in Tapalin Bend, River Murray, he was frying pufftaloons when a light shower caused the hot fat to jump and sting his hands and wrists. **1940** I. L. IDRIESS *Lightning Ridge* 82 Puftaloons are tasty though; fry them in fat, then smother them with treacle and swallow 'em while greasy. **1942** E. LANGLEY *Pea Pickers* 296 She was making puftaloonies all the time we talked and in next to no time had a plate of them in front of us, with a hot cup of tea. **1964** T. RONAN *Packhorses & Pearling Boat* v. 140 A camp oven full of 'puff de loons' (fried scones to the uninitiated). **1970** P. WHITE *Vivisector* i. 10 Mumma started telling all she had heard next door, with the kids stuffing on Mrs. Burt's cold puftaloons.

pufter, var. *POOFTER.

pug, *sb.*² Add: **II. 9. b.** A net or snood for tying up or holding a bun or knot of hair. Also *attrib.*

1927 *Blackw. Mag.* June 747/1 His hair tied in a knot in a little red cloth or pug, on the top of his head. **1967** E. B. NICKERSON *Kayaks to Arctic* x. 92, I had been wearing my hair in a long braid but tonight I coiled and netted it in a pug. **1967** *Boston Globe* 21 May (Confidential Chat) 17/1 The old fashioned idea of a dark, gloomy building..with an old fashioned old lady with glasses and a pug hair-do for a librarian are far out these days.

III. 13. *pug-bitch* (sense 7).

1916 E. POUND *Lustra* 111 Quite plump, with pug-bitch features.

pug, *sb.*⁴ Add: Also *Comb.*, as *pug-mark.*

1922 *Chambers's Jrnl.* Dec. 860/1, I found a good many pug-marks and from them I concluded that the man-eater was a smallish beast. **1946** J. CORBETT *Man-Eaters of Kumaon* 8 Entering the ravine.. I found the pug marks of a tiger in some fine earth..; these pug marks showed the animal to be a tigress, a little past her prime. **1974** *Country Life* 31 Oct. 1302/2 Tigers are elusive... We followed pug marks up hill and down ravine.

pug, *sb.*⁵ Add: (Further examples.) Hence **pug-glove,** a boxing-glove.

1924 J. BUCHAN *Three Hostages* v. 74 The man had been in the ring, and not so very long ago. I wondered at Medina's choice, for a pug is not the kind of servant I would choose myself. **1938** DYLAN THOMAS *Let.* 1 June (1966) 198 'Boxed' has the coffin and the pug-glove in it. **1961** *Lancet* 26 Aug. 447/2 It is well known that boxers, including fair-ground-booth pugs, can tolerate severe direct blows to the head. **1977** *Time* 19 Dec. 68/2 Hemingway had gone many rounds with pugs, and Journalist Paul Gallico once had his fillings loosened by Jack Dempsey.

pu·gginess². [f. PUGGY *a.*¹ + -NESS.] Squatness; stumpiness.

1910 H. G. WELLS *Hist. Mr. Polly* vii. 227 Mr. Hinks.. displayed a freckled fist of extraordinary size and pugginess..to Mr. Polly's close inspection.

pu·ggishness. [f. PUGGISH *a.* + -NESS.] The nature of or resemblance to a pug.

1924 W. J. LOCKE *Coming of Amos* ii. 13 There is a puggishness about her rebellious nose which would disqualify her in a competition of Classical Beauty.

puggle, var. *POGGLE *sb.* and *a.*

puggled (pʊ·g'ld), *a. Army slang* and *Sc.* Also *Sc.* **pagard, pagart.** Var. *POGGLED *a.*

1923 G. WATSON *Roxburghshire Word-bk.* 227 *Pagart, a.* Also *pagard*... Breathless: 'A was fair pagard; A couldna rin another fitlenth.' **1925** FRASER & GIBBONS *Soldier & Sailor Words* 231 *Puggled*.., Insane. Mad-drunk. **1968** *Sc. Nat. Dict.* VII. 274/2 *Puggled, -t,* at a standstill from exhaustion or frustration, done for, at the end of one's resources. **1973** 'J. PATRICK' *Glasgow Gang Observed* xii. 112 One guest in particular..was 'stoatin' aw ower the place—pure puggled she wis'.

puggly, var. *POGGLE *sb.* and *a.*

pugil³ (piū·dʒil). *U.S. Mil.* [Prob. f. L. stem *pugil-*, as in PUGILISM, etc.] In full, *pugil stick.* A short pole with padded ends used as a substitute for a rifle and bayonet in military training. Also *attrib.* and *Comb.*, as *pugil bout, training; pugil-armed* adj.

1962 *Infantry* Nov.–Dec. 26/2 *Pugil training* was first adopted by the Marine Corps... The pugil stick is an oak staff, two inches in diameter, padded on both ends with polyfoam encased in canvas. This stick represents the rifle and is the same length as a rifle with bayonet fixed. *Ibid.* 26/3 The students engage in pugil bouts, applying all the movements taught in earlier periods with the rifle. *Ibid.* 28/3 Substitute pugil-armed students for dummies. **1964** A. N. HARDIN *Amer. Bayonet 1776–1964* 188 Modern U.S. Marine Corps practice virtually eliminates fencing bayonets by substituting the 'Pugil Stick' technique. **1967** *Britannica Bk. of Year 1966* 804/1 *Pugil or Pugil stick,* a padded club with large rounded ends used in bayonet practice by the military as a substitute for rifle with fixed bayonet. **1976** *Billings* (Montana) *Gaz.* 28 June 4-B/1 The first of three sergeants..was accused of violating orders in the conduct of the..pugil stick bouts in which the recruit was pounded into a coma.

pugilant, *a.* For *rare*—¹ read *rare* and add further example.

1932 J. JOYCE in *New Statesman* 27 Feb. 260/1 A pugilant gang theirs, per Bantry!

pugilistic, *a.* (Earlier example.)

1789 *Loiterer* 27 June 4 A tolerable Proficient in pugillistic Science.

pugilistical, *a.* (Earlier example.)

a **1790** J. H. BEATTIE *Dial. of Dead* III, in J. Beattie *Minstrel* (1799) II. 195 Some learned innovator..clapping to it [*sc.* Latin *pugil*] part of a Greek termination, he made it *pugilist*; which..gave rise to the adjectives *Pugilistic* and *Pugilistical*, as in this example,..'a.. pavilion at Newmarket for *Pugilistical* exhibitions'.

Puginesque (piū:dʒine·sk), *a.* [f. the name *Pugin* (see def.) + -ESQUE.] Of, pertaining to, or characteristic of the English architect A. W. N. Pugin (1812–1852) or his style of architecture; Gothic-revivalist. So **Pu:gine·squery** [-ERY] *nonce-wd.*, matters related to Pugin or his architectural style.

1848 C. KINGSLEY *Yeast* v, in *Fraser's Mag.* XXXVIII. 286/1 When they talk Puginesquery, I stick my head on one side attentively, and 'think the more', like the lady's parrot. **1856** F. E. PAGET *Owlet of Owlstone Edge* 210 In her ambition to be Puginesque, she made her husband's chancel look as if it had been decked by a mad haberdasher. **1864** *Ecclesiologist* XXV. 345 The general idea is Puginesque, the style Middle-Pointed. **1904** A. C. BENSON *Let.* 5 Oct. in *Upton Lett.* (1905) 234 The roofs and towers of the big house—Puginesque Gothic, I must tell you—came in sight. **1907** E. GOSSE *Father & Son* xii. 339 My Father did not, indeed, forbid me to enter..the stately Puginesque cathedral which Rome had just erected. **1961** E. WAUGH *Unconditional Surrender* II. iii. 72 The Catholic parish church is..a Puginesque structure erected..in the early 1860's. **1975** V. CUNNINGHAM *Everywhere spoken Against* iii. 86 The whole set of Puginesque-Arnoldian assumptions.

pug-mill. (Further examples.)

1902 A. BENNETT *Anna of Five Towns* viii. 169 The press expelled the water, and the pug-mill expelled the air. **1930** *Industr. & Engin. Chem.* 20 Mar. 14/1 The machinery is..simple in design and operation, including, in addition to the centrifuge, a 'pug mill' in which hot water and steam are used to wash the oil-impregnated sands. **1960** [see *EXTRUDER 1]. **1980** M. FORSTER *Bride of Lowther Fell* xi. 168, I decided..to ferret out a pug-mill..together with a special plaster sink I would soon be needing.

pugnozzle (pʊ·gnǫz'l), *v. nonce-wd.* [f. PUG *sb.*² + NOZZLE *sb.* or *nozzle*, var. NUZZLE *v.*; cf. PUG NOSE.] *intr.* To move the upper lip and nostrils in the manner of a pug-dog.

1934 S. BECKETT *More Pricks than Kicks* 257 The wretched little wet rag of an upper lip, pugnozzling up and back in what you might call a kind of a duck or a cobra sneer to the nostrils.

Pugwash (pʊ·gwǫʃ). The name of a village in Nova Scotia where in 1957 the first conference was held of scientists concerned to promote international responsibility in the peaceful uses of scientific discoveries, used *attrib.* of this and subsequent conferences, and also the movement which they generated,

as *Pugwash conference, group*, etc. Also *ellipt.*
1957 *N.Y. Times* 12 July 3/6 Asked if he and his Russian colleague came to the Pugwash meeting as independent scientists, Mr. Topchiev replied [etc.]. **1957** *Science* 2 Aug. 199/3 These men all signed the 'Pugwash Statement'. **1957** *Bull. Atomic Sci.* Sept. 244/2 The Pugwash discussion showed clearly that the most important unresolved disagreement among experts concerns not the radiation exposure caused by bomb tests..but the biological consequences likely to be produced by this exposure. **1958** *Washington Post* 15 Sept. 18/2 Pugwash conferences, so named because the first one took place at Pugwash, Nova Scotia, on the estate of American multimillionaire Cyrus Eaton. **1963** *Pugwash Newslet.* July 2 Since the Pugwash Newsletter is for private circulation only, it may provide a convenient medium for testing and impromptu..ideas. **1965** *New Statesman* 16 Apr. 601/1 He [*sc.* Albert Einstein] died 10 years ago on Sunday, two days after signing the great Russell-Einstein Manifesto which launched the Pugwash Movement of scientists (the 14th meeting took place in Venice this week). **1968** *Listener* 11 July 36/1 Pugwash..has set up a study group. **1972** *Guardian* 4 Sept. 10/6 Pugwash is this week spending much of its time discussing problems of developing nations. **1976** *Chronicle-Herald* (Halifax, Nova Scotia) 19 July 21/1 The banquet meeting of the Canadian and American Pugwash groups.

puha (pu·ha). *N.Z.* Also **pua, puwha.** [Maori.] A sow-thistle belonging to the genus *Sonchus*, esp. *S. oleraceus*; the leaves of this plant used as a vegetable.
1843 E. Dieffenbach *Trav. N.Z.* II. III. 380 Pua—a sowthistle. **1868** W. Colenso in *Trans. N.Z. Inst.* I. III. 37 The fresh gum-resin from the Kauri..was commonly chewed as a masticatory..mixed with the inspissated juice of the Puwha, or Sow-thistle. **1905** W. B. *Where White Man Treads* 177 All was ready for the contents of the haangi—pork, puha, and potatoes. **1947** *Coast to Coast 1946* 2 Flora Baker gathering puha outside the Bakers' pig-sty. **1963** *N.Z. Listener* 3 May 5/4 Around in the rank growth, the puha and rariki grew, despised by the Pakeha but loved by the true Maori. **1966** J. K. Baxter *Pig Island Lett.* 6 Sea-eggs, puha, pork, and kumara. **1978** *Islands* (N.Z.) Aug. 12 Sometimes they bring food and cook it in my kitchen—mutton-bird with corn and *puha*—not my favourite dish, so greasy. **1978** P. Grace *Mutuwhenua* ix. 53 He and his flat-mate had boiled mutton quite often but there wasn't any puha near their place so they had to use cabbage.

pui, var. *poui; **puirt-a-beul:** see *port-a-beul.

puissance. Restrict *arch.* to senses in Dict. and add: **1. c.** *Show-jumping.* A competition testing a horse's ability to jump large obstacles. Also *attrib.*
1951 M. P. Ansell *Show Jumping* vi. 48 *Test* (*Puissance*). This competition is designed to test the horse's ability to jump large obstacles. **1952** R. S. Summerhays *Encycl. Horsemen* 218/2 '*Puissance*' *Jumping Competition.* In this all the straight fences in the course, with the exception of the first, are a minimum height of 4 ft. 7 in. (1 m. 40 cm.). The course usually consists of from six to eight fences, one of which is a double jump counting as one obstacle. **1954** P. Smythe *Jump for Joy* iv. 68, I lived for the week-ends, and many a lesson was passed in the haze of daydreams about jumping paddocks and over Puissance courses. **1959** *Times* 10 Aug. 5/6 It was the third triumph of the [Dublin Horse] show for Dundrum, who..shared first place in the *puissance* with Hollandia. **1974** *Country Life* 3 Jan. 9/2 Alcatraz, ridden by last year's puissance winner..attempted all three fences. **1975** *Oxf. Compan. Sports & Games* 281/1 The competition which tests jumping ability alone is known as a *Puissance*... There is no recourse to the clock, since the object is to test the horse over 'a limited number of large obstacles'.

‖ **pujari** (pūdʒā·ri). Also **poojari, pujaree.** [Hindi, f. Skr. *pūjā* worship; cf. Poojah, puja.] A Hindu priest.
1813 F. Hamilton *Jrnl. Shahabad Survey* (1926) 129 The Pujaris who are making a good thing of the ghost have lately been disturbed by a..young Brahman. **1855** H. H. Wilson *Gloss. Judicial & Revenue Terms India* 396/1 At Benares, the *Paṇḍá* officiates only on particular occasions, the duties of daily worship being performed by inferior priests or *Pujáris* in his employ. **1883** Monier Williams *Relig. Thought & Life in India* ix. 249 Then the Pūjāri, or priest, takes the Bhūta sword and bell in his hands. **1907** B. M. Croker *Company's Servant* xi. 108 Many baskets of rice were contributed..to the sacrificial pile. On this pile, a drove of buffaloes was killed by the Poojaris. **1967** Singha & Massey *Indian Dances* i. 33 Offerings of flowers and sweetmeats are placed at the base by the *pujarees* (worshippers). **1969** *Sunday Standard* (Bombay) 3 Aug. (Mag. Section) p. iv/3 Next week, Indran left the village, leaving the temple in charge of another poojari. **1969** *Enact* (Delhi) Nov. 10/3, I will not have any brahmins or *pujaris* up here, never,..any more than I will go to church for confession or have a mass said to save my soul. **1973** *Country Life* 11 Jan. 80/1 We..presented our credentials to the *pujari* (priest).

puka (pu·kă). [Maori.] An evergreen New Zealand shrub or small tree, *Griselinia littoralis*, or *G. lucida*, a related, sometimes epiphytic, species, belonging to the family Cornaceæ and bearing leathery ovate leaves and panicles of tiny, greenish flowers followed by purple or black berries.
[**1853** J. D. Hooker *Bot. Antarctic Voy.: Flora Novæ-Zelandiæ* I. 98 *Griselinia lucida*... Nat[ive] name, 'Poukater'.] **1889** T. Kirk *Forest Flora N.Z.* 67 Mr. Colenso informs me that the Native name 'puka' is correctly applied to this species [sc. *Griselinia lucida*] as well as to *Meryta Sinclairii*. **1970** M. E. Fisher et al. *Gardening with N.Z. Plants* I. 59 The puka is usually found perched high in the forks of some forest tree such as the rata.
2. A small evergreen tree, *Meryta sinclairii*, belonging to the family Araliaceæ, native to Australasia and the Pacific Islands, and bearing large glossy leaves and terminal panicles of greenish-white flowers followed by black berries. Also *attrib.*
1889 T. Kirk *Forest Flora N.Z.* 245 The Puka... This noble species is..restricted to a few individuals growing on one or two small islands near the northern extremity of the colony. **1951** *Post-Primary School Bull.* (Wellington, N.Z.) V. xii. 276 The puka (*Meryta sinclairii*)..has the largest leaves of any New Zealand tree. **1970** M. E. Fisher et al. *Gardening with N.Z. Plants* I. 78 The puka is a much branched, small tree from 12 to 20 feet in height... The leaves of this handsome tree are a beautiful glossy green, nine to 20 inches long and half as broad, usually with the broadest part near the apex. They are leathery and strongly veined and the margin is wavy.

pukaki, puka pu, varr. *pukeko, *pakapoo.

pukatea (pukăti·ă). *N.Z.* [Maori.] A tall forest tree, *Laurelia novæ-zelandiæ*, of the family Monimiaceæ, native to New Zealand, and distinguished by buttresses at the base of the trunk, pale bark, leathery, obovate leaves, and small clusters of tiny, yellowish flowers; also, the timber obtained from this tree.
1843 E. Dieffenbach *Trav. N.Z.* I. I. iii. 75 Another tree common in this part of the valley is the pukatea. **1868** W. Colenso in *Trans. N.Z. Inst.* I. III. 51 From the aromatic leaves and bark of the Pukatea..a valuable essential oil might be extracted. **1882** W. D. Hay *Brighter Britain!* II. vi. 191 The Pukatea..is a tree of the second largest class. **1949** P. Buck *Coming of Maori* III. vi. 426 Tree burial was resorted to in the thickly forested Urewera country. Natural hollow trees such as the *pukatea* were utilized when available. **1950** *N.Z. Jrnl. Agric.* June 602/3 The rata, pukatea, and titoki from which they [*sc.* the chairs] are made. **1966** *Encycl. N.Z.* II. 887/2 Pukatea grows to heights of over 120 ft.

puke, *sb.*[2] Add: **1. b.** Matter thrown up from the stomach; vomit. *coarse.*
1961 in Webster. **1972** D. Lees *Zodiac* 109, I..choked back the puke that had rushed to my throat. **1975** *New Society* 4 Dec. 526/2 At the Black Raven, by Liverpool Street station,.. there is a slight odour of puke and disinfectant.
3. b. (Earlier and later examples.)
1835 A. A. Parker *Trip to West & Texas* 87 The inhabitants..of Michigan are called *wolverines*,..of Missouri, *pukes*. **1843** 'R. Carlton' *New Purchase* II. 47 This Protestant assembly was a gathering of delegates principally from the land of Hoosiers..[with] a small chance of Pukes from beyond the father of floods. **1847** T. Ford *Hist. Illinois* (1854) ii. 68 The Illinoians..called the Missourians 'Pukes'... The lower lead mines in Missouri had sent up to the Galena country whole hoards of uncouth ruffians, from which it was inferred that Missouri had taken a 'Puke'. **1908** L. Houck *Hist. Missouri* III. xxiv. 36 'Hidalgos' the first residents of upper Louisiana and Missouri were called, until in the mouths of the vulgar the name of 'Pukes' was made current. **1944** [see *Missourian *sb.* and *a.*].

pukeko (pu·keko). *N.Z.* Also **pukaki.** [Maori.] The purple gallinule or swamp hen, *Porphyrio porphyrio* (formerly *P. melanotus*), belonging to the family Rallidæ and widely distributed in southern Europe, Africa, southern Asia, and Australasia.
1835 W. Yate *Acct. N.Z.* (ed. 2) ii. 62 *Pukeko*—A species of water-hen, the size of a well-grown capon. It..has very long red legs. **1845** E. J. Wakefield *Adv. N.Z.* I. viii. 228 The *pukeko* is of a dark blue colour, and about as large as a pheasant. **1853** W. R. Bridges *Let.* 14 Nov. in *Richmond-Atkinson Papers* (1960) I. iii. 136, I amused myself with shooting wild duck and pukeko which are very abundant. **1874** A. Bathgate *Colonial Experiences* vii. 85 In the swamps there is also the pukaki..or swamp-turkey, a bird which rises well and affords good sport. **1884** Lady Martin *Our Maoris* viii. 114 The place was populous with large black birds, called by the Maoris pu-ke-ko. They have a harsh cry like a corn-crake. **1921** H. Guthrie-Smith *Tutira* xxii. 209 The Pukeko or Swamp-hen (*Porphyrio melanotus*) has..proved able to thrive better on dry ground than wet. **1930** L. G. D. Acland *Early Canterbury Runs* 1st Ser. vii 175 There were thousands and thousands of pukaki in the swamp. **1946** *Coast to Coast 1945* 110 Poachin' flappers in the swamp... Stringy pukekoes, too, when they're winged. **1957** J. Frame *Owls do Cry* xviii. 74 Pukekos took long strides through the swamp. **1966** *Encycl. N.Z.* II. 888/1 Pukekos are not shot in any great numbers during their open season.

pukeru, var. *puckeroo *a.* and *vb.* **Pukhto:** see Pushtoo, -tu *sb.* and *a.* in Dict. and Suppl.

puking, *ppl. a.* (Later example.)
1976 'D. Halliday' *Dolly & Nanny Bird* xv. 200 Order one of your puking friends to go below.

pukka: see Pucka, pakka *a.* (*sb.*) in Dict. and Suppl.

puku[1]. Now the usual spelling of Pookoo.
1881 [see *lechwe]. **1894** [see Pookoo]. **1900** W. L. Sclater *Mammals S. Afr.* I. 193 The flesh of the puku is stated by Selous to be even more nauseous and unpalatable than that of the common water-buck. **1946, 1972** [see *lechwe]. **1973** D. Steele *Game Sanctuaries S. Afr.* 148 The puku is a medium-sized antelope, weighing up to 90 kilograms.

‖ **puku**[2] (pu·ku). *N.Z. colloq.* [Maori.] The stomach.
[**1905** W. B. *Where White Man Treads* 96 The Maori is pre-eminently gifted in the selection of suitable nomenclature... He meets a man... He looks him over... If he be massive in girth, what so delicate as reference thereto as 'Puku' (stomach)? **1918** C. H. Weston *Three Years with New Zealanders* vi. 70 The Medical Officer..injected the [anti-typhoid] serum in what the Maories call my *puku*.] **1941** Baker *N.Z. Slang.* v. 42 By the 1890's..a stomach-ache became, with excellent alliterative effect, a *pain in the puku*. **1954** *Numbers* July 5 Let's stick to matters of the *puku*. **1958** M. K. Joseph *I'll soldier no More* ii. 50 Eat, Harry boy, eat; get some of this in your puku. **1966** G. W. Turner *Eng. Lang. Austral. & N.Z.* viii. 170 The [Maori] words *potae* 'hat' and *puku* 'stomach' are still current, but North Island words mainly. **1971** *N.Z. Listener* 19 Apr. 57/1 He was too stonkered and crook in the puku to bother about it at the time. **1978** P. Grace *Mutuwhenua* xx. 140 Your puku's getting in the way.

puky, *a.* Restrict *rare* to sense in Dict. and add: Also **pukey. 2.** *fig.* Sick-making, disgusting. *colloq.*
1965 T. Capote *In Cold Blood* (1966) i. 37 It was a puky idea. What the hell would they have thought? **1969** W. Garner *Us or Them War* vi. 53 There'll be all sorts there, most of them pretty pukey and not really my thing.

pul (pŭl). Pl. **puls, pooli, puli.** [Pashto, a. Pers. *pūl*, f. Turk. *pul*; cf. Gr. φόλλις a small coin.] In Afghanistan, a monetary unit equivalent to one hundredth of an afghani; a coin of this value.
1927, 1934 [see *afghani]. **1941** *Whitaker's Almanack* 852/1 *Afghani* (of 100 *Puls*).

Pul, var. *Peulh *sb.* and *a.*

pula (pu·lă). Also †**poola.** [Tswana.] ‖ **1.** Rain. Freq. used as *int.*: in southern Africa, a traditional salute or expression of good luck.
1827 G. Thompson *Trav. & Adv. S. Afr.* I. 180 Mattebe..waved the point [of his assagai] towards the heavens, when all called out 'Poola!' i.e. rain or a blessing. **1842** R. Moffat *Missionary Labours & Scenes S. Afr.* xxi. 350 The audience shouted, 'Pùla', (rain,) on which he sat down amidst a din of applause. **1934** in C. P. Swart *Africanderisms* (M.A. thesis, Univ. S Afr.) s.v., When Prince George..uttered the traditional Basuto salute 'Pula' which means rain, a wave of enthusiasm swept the natives in the council chamber. **1974** *S. Afr. Panorama* Mar. 38/2 'Pula!' shouted the excited crowd of Bantu children.
2. The principal monetary unit of Botswana, consisting of one hundred thebe; a note of this value.
1976 *Eastern Province Herald* (S. Afr.) 23 Aug. 1 Botswana's new currency, the pula, will be introduced today. **1976** *Whitaker's Almanack 1977* 980 Botswana... Monetary unit... Pula.

Pulah, var. *Peulh *sb.* and *a.*

pulamiting (piū·lămǝi:tiŋ), *ppl. a. dial.* [Prob. f. unrecorded *pulamite* vb. + -ing[2]; cf. Pule *v.* + Mite[2] 5.] Of a child or weak person: whining, whimpering. Also **pu·lami:ter** [-er[1]], one who whines; a sniveller.
1913 D. H. Lawrence *Sons & Lovers* ii. viii. 198 'Me!' exclaimed Morel—'me a good figure! I wor niver much more n'r a skeleton.' 'Man!' cried his wife, 'don't be such a pulamiter!' *a* **1930** —— in *Virginia Q. Rev.* (1941) XVII. Suppl. 43/1 You are a base, malingering pulamiting wretch.

pulao, var. Pilau in Dict. and Suppl.

pulaski (pulæ·ski). *U.S.* Also **Pulaski.** [The name of E. C. *Pulaski* (1866–1931), Amer. forest ranger, by whom the tool was designed.] A hatchet, of which the head forms an axe blade on one side and an adze on the other. Also *attrib.*
1924 *Frontier* Nov. 20, I saw Paul, his back bowed, his Pulaski swingin' like a flail. **1940** [see *hot spot 5 b]. **1946** *Trial & Timberline* June 91/1 Planting hoes, grub hoes, and Pulaski hoes had been provided by the rangers. **1948** *Highway Traveler* Aug. 37/1 Besides technical information on fighting fire with chemicals, or with axe and pulaski, smoke-jumpers are taught to bail out from a specially-constructed tower.

pulaskite (pulæ·skǝit). *Petrogr.* [See quot. 1891 and -ite[1].] An alkali syenite containing a small proportion of nepheline.
1891 J. F. Williams in *Ann. Rep. Arkansas Geol.*

Survey 1890 II. iv. 56 Such a rock has not as yet been described and the writer suggests the name *pulaskite*—that of Pulaski county in which the city of Little Rock and Fourche Mountain are located—as a designation for this type of rock. **1962** W. T. Huang *Petrology* iv. 129 In alkalic syenites the quartz-bearing type is nordmarkite.. or simply quartz syenite... With a slight deficiency of silica, a little nepheline and sodalite may be present, leading to the formation of pulaskite... Other colored minerals found in pulaskite include aegirite-augite, barkevikite, or arfvedsonite.

pulchritudinous (pʌlkritiū·dinəs), *a.* orig. *U.S.* [f. L. *pulc(h)ritūdin-*, *pulc(h)ritūdo* beauty + -ous.] Beautiful, graceful, or fine in any way; morally excellent.

1912 L. J. Vance *Destroying Angel* xv. 217, I love my love with a P because he's Perfectly Pulchritudinous and Possesses the Power of Pleasing. **1914** 'High Jinks, Jr.' *Choice Slang* 17 *Pulchritudinous pippen*, a pretty damsel. 'A peach.' **1925** *Times* 13 Dec. 11/6 In an American paper, in which the Yarmouth councillors were described as 'pulchritudinous',..the word actually meant moral excellence. **1949** *Chicago Tribune* 21 Feb. I. 28/5 By us the hippopotamus..Is never counted pulchritudinous. **1963** *Punch* 13 Feb. 246/1 Such nice, pulchritudinous girls! **1975** *Bookseller* 20–27 Dec. 2720/1 An ageing tycoon and a pulchritudinous blonde half his years but nearly equal to him in experience.

Pulfrich (pu·lfriχʸ). The name of Carl *Pulfrich* (1858–1927), German physicist, used *attrib.* and in the possessive with reference to an optical illusion first pointed out by him (see *Naturwissensch.* (1922) X. 553), in which a pendulum that is swinging in a plane perpendicular to the line of sight appears to describe ellipses when one eye is covered with a filter and the other is uncovered.

1925 *Brit. Jrnl. Ophthalm.* IX. 65 Men, getting on in years, who have been expert in games with a moving ball, find themselves unable to judge its position with their former accuracy... Pulfrich's phenomenon seems to give a probable explanation. **1941** S. H. Bartley *Vision* vii. 170 Pulfrich's stereoscopic pendulum is another example of a set of conditions which will induce the perception of movement of a kind not corresponding with the real movement of a physical object. **1966** R. L. Gregory *Eye & Brain* vi. 78 The trading of temporal discrimination for sensitivity with dark adaptation is most elegantly, if somewhat indirectly, observed in a curious and dramatic phenomenon known as the Pulfrich Pendulum Effect. **1974** *Vision Res.* XIV. 184/2 The only thing that is important in producing a Pulfrich effect is the relative luminance of the objects which move across the retinae whether these be 'target' or 'background' or whether the subject fixates a stationary point or follows a moving object. **1980** *Sci. Amer.* May 134/2 According to most hypotheses about the Pulfrich illusion, the dark filter delays the perception of the visual signal at the retina of the covered eye.

puli (pu·li). Pl. **pulik.** [Hungarian.] A black, grey, or white sheep-dog belonging to the breed so called, characterized by a long, thick coat having a corded appearance.

1936 *Amer. Kennel Gaz.* 1 Oct. 62/1 The Puli is used primarily as a sheep herding dog in the hill sections of Hungary. In appearance he has many points of resemblance to the Old English Sheepdog, but is much smaller and more active. **1948** L. Bauvald in B. Vesey-Fitzgerald *Bk. Dog* II. 616 The Puli is probably one of the aboriginal dog races of the Magyars... Relatively few Pulik find their way to the exhibition bench. **1964** 'C. Richards' *Gentle Assassin* (1965) i. 7 A puli, a Hungarian breed of dog. **1972** *Country Life* 10 Feb. 329/1 The Hungarian pulik—puli in the singular—are increasing numerically over here. **1973** *Times* 6 Aug. 26/7 Have a Hungarian Puli puppy..small black sheepdogs with an unusual corded coat. **1978** *Times* 11 Feb. 2/4 The Hungarian puli, distinguished by its remarkable corded coat, had a class of its own [at Crufts] for the first time.

Pulitzer (piū·litsəɹ; in U.S. also pu·litsəɹ). [Name of J. *Pulitzer* (1847–1911), Amer. journalist.] Designating any of several annual awards for distinguished work in journalism, letters, and music produced or published in the U.S. Also *ellipt.*

1918 *N.Y. Times* 3 June 9/7 The annual Pulitzer Prize of $1,000 for the best play written and produced by an American playwright in 1917..awarded to Jesse Lynch Williams for his comedy, 'Why Marry?' **1934** [see *creative *a.* 1 b]. **1941** B. Schulberg *What makes Sammy Run?* i. 20 Sammy was staring..at George Opdyke, the three-time Pulitzer Prize winner. **1955** G. Greene *Quiet American* I. iii. 38 Why, that account of Road 66..that was worthy of the Pulitzer. **1962** *Publishers' Weekly* 26 Mar. 16 Pulitzer..pronounced..pullitzer"—not, as so many people say, 'pewlitzer'. **1971** R. A. Carter *Manhattan Primitive* (1972) xiii. 121 The museum's sponsors—a famous concert musician, a film actress, and a Pulitzer Prize-winning novelist. **1972** R. Ludlum *Osterman Weekend* iii. 52 You were quite successful as an investigative reporter... You were nominated for a Pulitzer, I believe. **1977** *Time* 31 Oct. 28/1 One..led last year to a Pulitzer-prizewinning photograph of a woman and a little girl plummeting from a collapsed fire escape.

pulka. Add: Also **pulkka.** (Further examples.) Also *attrib.*

1913 *Chambers's Jrnl.* Nov. 798/1 The Lapland sledge, or *pulk*, as it is called, is shaped something like a boat. **1952** *Ibid.* Jan. 33/2 In a trice he had put on her gay red-and-blue harness and fastened the traces to a pulkha, the canoe-like little sledge of north-east Lapland. **1960** G. Taylor *Mortlake* III. i. 130 A reindeer drawing a small boat-shaped sledge called a pulkka. **1964** *Punch* 25 Nov. p. xvii, This store's ski fashion wear includes the Ernst Engel collection, Canadian overboots, patterned Tyrol pullovers, Swedish pulka jackets, furry helmets. **1969** *Guardian* 31 July 3/4 All our equipment..we pull behind us on pulka sledges..made of wood. **1974** *Canad. Consumer* Feb. 11/1 A special accessory for family enjoyment is the Norwegian 'pulk' (sled) with a rigid harness for a man or dog to tow even babies along. The pulk..is boatshaped, so that it will not tip on bumpy ground.

pull, *sb.*[2] Add: **I. 1. d.** Paired with *push*: see *push *sb.*[1] 1 d.

2. a. (Earlier example in modern sense.)

1845 Dickens *Let.* 1 Nov. (1977) IV. 423 The carriage.. is to call for a pull of the first part of the *Cricket*.

f. (Earlier example.)

1865 *Lillywhite's Guide to Cricketers* 135 A fast run-getter, little too fond of a pull.

3. c. In fig. phr. *to take a pull* (*at, on oneself*), to stop or check (oneself); to pull oneself together. *colloq.* (chiefly *Austral.*).

1890 Barrère & Leland *Dict. Slang* II. 155/2 *Pull* (society): to take a *pull* means to stop, check, put an end to. **1916** C. J. Dennis *Songs Sentimental Bloke* i. 16, I tells meself some day I'll take a pull An' look eround fer some good, stiddy job. **1922** Galsworthy *Family Man* III. ii. 105 Take a pull, old man! Have a hot bath and go to bed. **1942** E. Waugh *Put out more Flags* iii. 177 Suddenly she found herself weeping in earnest. Then she took a pull at herself. This wouldn't do at all. **1946** T. E. Haughey *Railway Reminisc.* 21 Look here—, it's about time you took a pull. Just shake yourself up a bit quick. **1953** M. Scott *Breakfast at Six* xxiv. 202 She may be a wonderful friend, but she'll land you in gaol yet. For heaven's sake, take a pull. **1966** J. Hackston *Father clears Out* 110 Alf Hodgson talked so much about the Red Range Federal Capital Site Movement that people said he'd be standing for Parliament one of these days if he did not take a pull on himself.

4. b. For *U.S. slang* read *colloq.* (chiefly *U.S.*) and add further examples.

a **1911** [see *island *sb.* 1 d]. **1937** F. P. Crozier *Men I Killed* vi. 109 Having been in France for so long and lacking the very necessary 'pull' in influential circles, we were unable to oust the family favourites at the War Office. **1940** [see *bracket *sb.* 5 c]. **1978** J. Krantz *Scruples* ii. 57 His future in the giant corporation was assured in the long run through family pull, since he had, on his mother's side, as one said in slang, *du piston*.

5*. = *lay *sb.*[7] 7 d. *slang.*

1969 Fabian & Byrne *Groupie* xxx. 219 'I'm not going to sleep with you.'..'Why not?' 'Because I'm not an easy pull.' **1973** M. Amis *Rachel Papers* 33 A mental chant, *timor mortis conturbat me*, and I began on my clumsiest pull ever. *Ibid.* 37 It was so obviously me and my pull and Geoffrey and his pull getting together to plan a spotty removal to someone's house.

pull, *v.* Add: **I. 1. f.** *trans.* To extract (a tooth). *U.S.*

1880 'Mark Twain' *Tramp Abroad* xxiii. 222 A soldier was getting a tooth pulled in a tent. **1915** R. Adair *Pract. Oral Hygiene* (ed. 2) i. 8 Dr. —— used to pull teeth, but he has got to talking so much about clean mouths that he is losing some of his trade. **1927** M. R. Reidy *This Tooth Proposition* vi. 110 A long time ago, dentistry consisted mostly of pulling teeth and making plates. **1976** H. MacInnes *Agent in Place* xix. 202 It was like pulling teeth. But we did learn something important.

3. b. *trans.* To draw or to be assigned (a task or position); to carry out (a duty). *U.S.*

1894 *Lucky Bag* (U.S. Naval Acad. Yearbk.) 67 *Pull the sick list*,..to get on the sick list when not ill. **1941** Kendall & Viney *Dict. Army & Navy Slang* 11/1 *To pull guard duty*,..to do guard duty. For instance, 'I've got to pull K.P.' **1972** *Times* 13 Apr. 1/8, I feel that my life is more important than having to pull security on this place. **1976** *New Yorker* 15 Mar. 89/1 How come they got you pulling guard?

6. b. To seize (someone's belongings); to recall or rescind (a document). Also *absol.*

1967 S. Faessler in *Atlantic Monthly* Apr. 107/1 One day a month was given over to repossessing merchandise from deadbeats. 'Today I am pulling,' he would say grimly. **1972** H. Kemelman *Monday the Rabbi took Off* xlv. 263 'They [*sc.* the police] pulled his passport, didn't they?' 'No... Officially they had just mislaid it.' **1973** R. Hayes *Hungarian Game* lii. 312 He had moved easily in dip circles until the..State pulled his visa.

II. 7. b. Phr. *to pull one's coat*: (see quot. 1946). *U.S. Blacks.*

1946 Mezzrow & Wolfe *Really Blues* 377/2 *Pull somebody's coat*, enlighten, tip somebody off. **1971** B. Malamud *Tenants* 55 The black..said: 'Lesser, I have to pull your coat about a certain matter.' **1972** T. Kochman *Rappin' & Stylin' Out* 163 If someone is giving you information, he is 'pulling your coat'.

d. In imp. phr. *pull the other one*, (*it's got bells on it*) and varr., a statement of disbelief implying suspicion that 'one's leg is being pulled'.

1966 D. Francis *Flying Finish* v. 63 'They are English mares going to be mated with Italian sires,' explained Conker... 'Pull the other one, it's got bells on,' said the engineer. **1973** 'S. Woods' *Enter Corpse* 112 'Believe it or not, neither Farrell nor I has the slightest interest in the gold...' 'Pull the other one!' said Nelson derisively. **1974** M. Butterworth *Man in Sopwith Camel* viii. 84 'Pull the other leg, it's got bells on!' she said. 'A bank's a bank, and you've got yourself charge of a bank for no other reason but to dip your fingers into the till.' **1975** D. Bagley *Snow Tiger* ix. 88 'She doesn't hold the mineral rights.' 'Pull the other one,' scoffed Eric. **1977** J. Bingham *Marriage Bureau Murders* xii. 146 Pull the other one, it's got bells on it. I saw it all... So don't give me that tripe.

f. To draw or fire (a gun). Const. *on.* Also *absol. U.S.*

1854 J. F. Cooper *Deerslayer* I. iii. 54, I shall not pull upon a human mortal as steadily..as I pull upon a deer. **1883** 'Mark Twain' *Life on Mississippi* p. xxvi, When they happened to meet, they pulled and begun. **1895** *Century Mag.* June 282/1 He repeated it, and I struck him. He pulled a pistol on me. **1903** S. E. White *Forest* x. 122 The birds had proved themselves most uncultivated and rude persons by hopping promptly into the trees... I had refused to pull pistol on them. **1926** J. Black *You can't Win* (1927) xiii. 182 He would have 'pulled' on us. **1952** *Sun* (Baltimore) 4 July 42/7 Dr. Brady and the would-be bandit were in a middle room..when a second man suddenly appeared and one of them pulled an automatic pistol. **1978** S. Brill *Teamsters* ii. 70 They couldn't just pull a gun on Hoffa.

g. To stretch and draw (sugar candy, etc.) until it is ready to set. orig. *U.S.*

1842 W. T. Thompson in *Southern Miscellany* 10 Dec. 2/6 They's pullin lasses candy in the parlor. **1893** *Harper's Mag.* Feb. 442 He pulled candy with glee, but also with eager industry, covering platter after platter with his braided sticks. **1948** *Good Housek. Cookery Bk.* III. 637 Certain toffees..are pulled, which gives them a satiny, silvery look. Attractive effects are achieved by combining pulled and unpulled toffee before cutting it into cushions. The toffee should be pulled immediately it is cool enough to handle.

h. To strain (a muscle or tendon) by abnormal exertion.

1955 M. Allingham *Beckoning Lady* iii. 35, I pulled a tendon in my foot so I'm stuck at the desk. **1955** R. Bannister *First Four Minutes* 175 Until then I had never been able to understand how athletes pulled muscles. **1971** *Woman's Own* 27 Mar. 8/2, I think I pulled a muscle. **1976** P. Harcourt *Dance for Diplomats* v. 51 'You're still limping.'..'I must have pulled a muscle.'

8. b. *to pull in* or *to pieces*: in *Bookbinding*, simply, *to pull*.

1901 D. Cockerell *Bookbinding* I. ii. 34 If the book should prove to be imperfect..the owner should be communicated with, before it is pulled to pieces. This is very important, as imperfect books that have been 'pulled' are not returnable to the bookseller. **1931** A. Esdaile *Student's Man. Bibliogr.* vi. 194 The book must be 'pulled', i.e. taken to pieces, first.

9. a. (Later *fig.* example.)

1904 W. N. Harben *Georgians* 22 So you 'n the old man are still pullin' agin one another?

f. *transf.* Of the engine of a motor vehicle: to afford (adequate) propulsive force; hence, by metonymy, of the vehicle itself.

1902 C. S. Rolls in A. C. Harmsworth et al. *Motors* ix. 175 Motor will not 'pull' well or misses fire. **1933** J Buchan *Prince of Captivity* III. ii. 282 The driver stopped to examine his engine. 'She pulls badly, *mein Herr*,' he said. **1974** P. Wright *Lang. Brit. Industry* i. 24 Another transport term, *the bus* (or *car*) *won't pull*, is from the days of the horse and cart.

11. c. *intr.* To exert influence or 'root' *for* (a person, etc.); to sympathize with, favour. Chiefly *N. Amer.*

1903 C. B. Gilbert in *Forum* (N.Y.) XXXV. 311 Such committees are exposed to all kinds..of influence..all pulling for this or that applicant. **1922** G. Ade *Let.* 22 Nov. (1973) 85 Tomorrow I go up to LaFayette to pull for Purdue against Indiana and I hope we may win at least one game. **1949** *National Geogr. Mag.* Sept. 321/1 I'm usually pulling for the Indians instead of the cowboys. **1968** *Globe & Mail* (Toronto) 17 Feb. 39 It sure helps to get this evidence that so many people at home are pulling for us. **1970** G. F. Newman *Sir, You Bastard* ii. 73 The Governor was pulling for him with the Divisional D[etective] C[hief] S[uperintendent].

d. *trans.* To attract (custom); to secure (patronage). Freq. *absol.*

1905 Calkins & Holden *Mod. Advertising* xi. 264 The advertiser likes to know which particular mediums pull best. **1929** L. F. Carr *America Challenged* 96 Both Republicans and Democrats have tried to pull the farmer vote by favoring legislation which the Populists had demanded. **1938** S. V. Benét *Thirteen O'Clock* IV. 234 I'd done some advertising copy for the firm that pulled. **1962** R. Stout *Gambit* (1963) iii. 36 She attracts. She pulls. **1974** S. Marcus *Minding Store* (1975) xi. 228 The booklets pulled fairly well, both in store response and through the mails. **1976** *Record Mirror* 3 Apr. 21/1 Brook Benton..can still regularly pull standing-room-only audiences for his live gigs.

e. *N.Z.* (See quot. 1933.)

1933 L. G. D. Acland in *Press* (Christchurch, N.Z.) 18 Nov. 15/7 *Pull*, a dog *pulls* sheep when he brings them towards his masters. **1935** G. L. Meredith *Adventuring in Maoriland* v. 47 [The dog] eventually 'pulled' the mob on the slope of a hill. **1938** R. Burdon *High Country* x. 107 The heading dog is silent and is used to 'pull' or bring sheep back to the shepherd.

f. To earn (a wage or salary). See also **pull down* (sense 24 f) and **pull in* (sense 25 b). *colloq.*

1937 'M. Innes' *Hamlet, Revenge!* II. viii. 197 I'm twenty-two and pulling twelve pounds a week.

g. *coarse slang.* To pick up a partner (for sexual purposes); *spec.* to copulate with. So *to pull a train*, to copulate successively with more than one partner.

1965 C. Brown *Manchild in Promised Land* i. 15 They

thought that I was one of the guys who had pulled a train on their sister in the park the summer before. *Ibid.* iv. 112 If you gon pull a bitch, you can'[t] get excited and let her know that you pussy so bad you about to go crazy. **1965** *Sunday Express* 25 July 17/2 As a young man I could never pull (pick up) any birds of my own class. **1973** M. Amis *Rachel Papers* 23, I could easily pull the village idiotess, who in any case, one windless summer night, had wanked Geoffrey and me off through the school railings, simultaneously. **1973** Boyd & Parkes *Dark Number* vi. 69 Five years ago you did the big male-menopause bit, didn't you? Skulking off to Paris to prove you could still pull the birds. **1973** P. Cave *Speed Freaks* viii. 77 'Wanna pull a train for the movie?' Mucky asked Dodo, who was still unclothed. She shrugged resignedly. **1974** H. L. Foster *Ribbin'* iv. 148 To 'pull a train' is for a female to have consecutive sexual intercourse with numbers of males. The female pulling the train may do so voluntarily for financial remuneration, forcefully, or out of fear. *Ibid.* 149 Trains are pulled everywhere... Selby..described Tralala pulling endless trains in Brooklyn. **1976** P. Cave *High Flying Birds* iv. 47 She's certainly worth pulling... But I reckon you can forget it as long as she's got her mother with her.

12. b. Also const. *on.*

1897 T. De Leon *Novelette Trilogy* v. 44 He..strode rapidly homeward; pulling hard..on the dead cigar between his lips.

c. *trans.* To draw (beer) from a keg, etc., by means of a pump or tap.

1969 *Sydney Morning Herald* 24 May 1/10 During Thursday's strike by hotel staff, the manager..pulled 17½ 18-gallon kegs from two taps between 10 a.m. and 10 p.m. **1975** M. Kenyon *Mr Big* v. 46 The muscled barmaid pulled pints.

III. 15. b. *to pull one's weight*: also *fig.*, to perform one's share of work, to take one's share of responsibility. Also *to pull weight.*

1904 Kipling *Traffics & Discoveries* 278 They need a lot of working up before they can pull their weight in the boat. **1921** [see Weight *sb.*[1] 10 c]. **1925** E. F. Norton *Fight for Everest: 1924* 98 No members of the climbing party pulled more weight in the team than these two by their unostentatious unselfish gruelling work. **1931** *Times* 27 Feb. 16/5 Referring to people in the administrative grade who did not 'pull their weight', Sir Alfred Woodgate said that assistant principals who had been twice passed over for promotion to principals were a menace to the office and should not be allowed to remain. **1948** M. Laski *Tory Heaven* x. 138 Lord Starveleigh asked him down to address the electors... We're all expected to pull our weight, you know. **1976** J. B. Hilton *Gamekeeper's Gallows* xii. 115 How long was he going to put up with me living off the fat of the land in his kitchen, not pulling my weight with his other servants?

16. (Further examples.) Cf. also *pull in (sense 25e).

1907 J. Masefield *Tarpaulin Muster* 205 The police entered..and 'pulled the joint'—that is, they arrested and fined the proprietor. **1931** 'D. Stiff' *Milk & Honey Route* 189 He's pulled for a vag, his excuses won't do. 'Thirty days,' said the judge. **1950** Wodehouse *Nothing Serious* 244 Doom had come upon The Cedars... The joint had been pulled. **1970** G. F. Newman *Sir, You Bastard* 10 They..pulled drunks and bathed tramps, saw children across the road and directed traffic.

17. b. *Boxing.* In phr. *to pull one's punches*, to hold back or check one's blows. Also *fig.*, to use less force than one is capable of exerting, to be gentle or lenient, esp. in criticism or punishment.

1934 in Webster. **1937** H. L. Ickes *Secret Diary* (1954) II. 88 He talked about the judiciary and he didn't pull his punches at any time, although neither was he in any degree personal. **1939** L. Jacobs *Rise of Amer. Film* 459 Either because Vidor 'pulled his punches' at the revolution or because..he was confused. **1947** *People* 22 June 5/3 Two of his boys recently fought for two solid hours—and no pulled punches—to provide a minute and a half's action in the actual film. **1955** A. L. Rowse *Expansion Eliz. Eng.* 133 He charges Ormonde with..pulling his punches in pursuit of the rebels. **1957** D. J. Enright *Apothecary's Shop* 209 The fact—not a new one—that Eliot doesn't pull his punches. **1960** *Times* 4 Feb. 11/2 Lady Albemarle's committee have not pulled their punches. **1973** P. O'Donnell *Silver Mistress* xi. 191 It was a demonstration match. The kicks, chops and punches were pulled at the last instant. **1977** *Time Out* 28 Jan.–3 Feb. 33/3 The film pulls all its political punches, settling instead for sentimental narrative.

18. (Earlier *Cricket* example.) Now also used in *Baseball* (see quot. 1976).

1851 W. Clark in W. Bolland *Cricket Notes* 143 Never try to pull a straight ball across you. **1943** *Amer. Speech* XVIII. 105 If he can *pull* or *place* the ball he has a better chance of getting a hit. **1976** *Webster's Sports Dict.* 334/1 *Pull*,..[in baseball] to hit the ball to the field on the same side of the plate as the batter stands when he takes his normal position in the batter's box.

18*. *Oil Industry.* To pull up or withdraw (casing, etc.) from a well.

1916 Johnson & Huntley *Princ. Oil & Gas Production* xiv. 154 The hole in most cases gradually fills up at the bottom with cavings from the walls and sometimes from the roof of the oil sand. This makes it necessary to pull the tubing and clean the well. **1938** L. V. W. Clark in A. E. Dunstan et al. *Sci. of Petroleum* I. ix. 434/2 In this position the string may be rotated as well as pulled or lowered. **1960** C. Gatlin *Petroleum Engin.* x. 170/1 A sudden decrease in penetration rate..may mean that the inner barrel is jammed or plugged and the assembly should be pulled for inspection. **1974** P. L. Moore et al. *Drilling Practices Man.* xii. 308 If the well kicks when pulling the drill string, the formation fluid will enter the entire well bore below the drill string.

IV. 19. b. *to pull one's freight*, to depart quickly. *U.S. colloq.*

1895 F. Remington *Pony Tracks* 252 The wily old fellow..had discreetly 'pulled his freight'. **1905** 'O. Henry' in *Everybody's Mag.* XIII. 814/2 The Kid..considered it not incompatible with his indisputable gameness to perform that judicious tractional act known as 'pulling his freight'. **1913** J. London *Valley of Moon* II. xvii. 277, I guess we got a celebration comin', seein' as we're going to pull up stakes an' pull our freight from the old burg. **1926** in J. F. Dobie *Rainbow in Morning* (1965) 84 He pulled his freight in a hurry.

c. (In Supplement) *p. a boner*, 19d; *p. one's coat*, 7b, *p. one's freight*, 19b; *p. a gag*, 19e; *p. a job*, 19f; *p. leather* 19g; *p. the other one*, 7d; *p. one's pudding*, 19j; *p. one's punches*, 17b; *p. rank*, 19h; *p. a robbery*, 19f; *p. the rug*, 19k; *p. stripes*, 19h; *p. a train*, 11g; *p. a trick*, 19e; *p. one's wire*, 19j.

d. *to pull a boner* (etc.), to make a foolish mistake (*Boner[2]). *U.S. slang.*

1913 [see *boner[2]]. **1926** *Scribner's Mag.* Sept. 246/1 The Washington newspaper correspondents are the pick of the land, and their dinners are not the softest spots in the lives of the speakers. It is no place to pull a bloomer. **1929** M. Lief *Hangover* xv. 234, I pulled an awful boner when I was up in Newport last summer. *Ibid.*, That's nothing... I pulled a dumber thing than that once. **1967** *Boston Sunday Globe* 23 Apr. B 41/1 Apart from the shabby methods used by construction workers, who have been known to pull some boners, Moscovites are subjected to some truly baffling beauts from bumbling builders.

e. In various colloq. phrases denoting action or speech intended to deceive, shock, or amuse, as *to pull a fast one* (see *fast *a.* 11), *to pull a gag*, *to pull a trick*, etc.

1914 'High Jinks, Jr.' *Choice Slang* 17 *Pull a punk one* (*to*), to tell a poor joke. **1915** [see *dope *sb.* 4]. **1922** G. Ade *Let.* 11 Oct. (1973) 83 The plot of the piece was that George and Frank both loved the same girl and Frank pulled a lot of dirty stuff and deceived the girl for a while but eventually virtue triumphed. **1929** M. Lief *Hangover* xv. 235, I can tell you about the gag one of our better-known critics pulled in his review of Dillingham's new musical comedy. **1932** E. Wallace *When Gangs came to London* xxiii. 232 'Fantastical,' suggested Jiggs. 'I'm getting quite used to the word. It's the one you pull when any hard-sense suggestion is made to you.' **1937** G. Heyer *They found him Dead* xiii. 260 Not that I think anyone would pull the same trick twice. **1940** Wodehouse *Eggs, Beans & Crumpets* 238 Your aunt..has a right to early information about any rough stuff that is being pulled on the premises. **1957** H. Roosenburg *Walls came tumbling Down* ix. 208 Just be a little more careful about your company next time you pull a stunt like that. **1976** M. Machlin *Pipeline* xxviii. 333 For Christ sake, don't think about pulling any movie-type heroics. **1978** *Guardian Weekly* 2 Apr. 6/5 Many [U.S. coal] miners are now threatening to pull wildcat strikes.

f. *to pull a job, robbery* (etc.), to commit a crime, usu. theft. *colloq.* (chiefly *U.S.*).

1915 *Policeman's Monthly* Dec. 17/3 He replied that he had often noticed just before they were going to 'pull a job' his partner was happy. **1923** 'B. L. Standish' *Lego Lamb, Southpaw* viii. 58 Yet, by your own confession, you came over here to 'pull a job'. **1937** *Research Stud. State Coll. Washington* Mar. 19 Some boys think its an honor..to say..that they pulled jobs with such and such gangsters. **1967** [see *graft *v.*[4]]. **1972** J. Wambaugh *Blue Knight* (1973) i. 28 A federal fugitive who..carried a gun and pulled stickups. **1973** E. Bullins *Theme is Blackness* 160 Tootsie didn't work steady but we still ran together. Even pulled an occasional job. **1973** *Philadelphia Inquirer* (Today Suppl.) 7 Oct. 14/1, I even pulled three robberies in one night—two drugstores and a haberdashery. **1978** *Detroit Free Press* 5 Mar. B 1/1, I suggested we pull a robbery.

g. *to pull leather*, to grasp the saddle horn in order to avoid being thrown from a bucking horse (see also quot. 1933). *U.S.*

1916 *Daily Colonist* (Victoria, B.C.) 19 July 5/4 They [*sc.* bad horses] are still outlaws and..are guaranteed to send almost any rider to pulling leather. **1923** J. H. Cook *50 Yrs. Old Frontier* 16 He certainly made me 'pull leather', and I clung to his mane as well in order to keep in close touch with him. **1925** C. E. Mulford *Cottonwood Gulch* v. 60, I'm pullin' leather, but I'm stickin' to the saddle. **1933** J. V. Allen *Cowboy Lore* III. 59/2 *Pulling leather*, holding on to the saddle with the hands while riding a bucking animal, prohibited by the rules of all contests and scorned by all real cowboys.

h. *to pull (one's) rank*, to employ (one's) superior status in exacting obedience, co-operation, or privilege. Also *to pull stripes* (etc.). orig. *U.S.*

1923 *Amer. Legion Weekly* 23 Feb. 18 Don't pull your rank on him, K.P. You were only a private yourself, once. **1926** *Amer. Speech* II. 62/2 Give him..officers who do not 'pull rank', and he is well content. **1958** V. Canning *Dragon Tree* 90 He disliked pulling his rank to claim any personal privileges. **1958** M. K. Joseph *I'll soldier no More* xiii. 242 Don't you pull your stripes on me, sarge. **1959** N. Mailer *Advts. for Myself* (1961) 228 Teddy pulled seniority and they gave him his way. **1976** H. MacInnes *Agent in Place* xiv. 148 'What if he refuses to go with them?' 'They'll be senior men, they'll pull rank.'

i. *to pull a* (proper name), to imitate, to behave in the manner of (the person named). *colloq.* (orig. *U.S.*).

1927 *New Republic* 9 Mar. 72/1 The following is a partial list of words denoting drunkenness now in common use in the United States... To pull a Daniel Boone. **1931** *Technol. Rev.* Nov. 67/1 *To pull a Lindbergh* means to do something heroic, but *to go Lindbergh* means to get the flying fever in a rather callow manner. **1935** Wodehouse *Luck of Bodkins* xiii. 133 He'll be much happier in the long run if he gets it into his bean that he can't pull a James Cagney on me every time he's a mite upset.

j. *to pull one's pud(ding)* or *wire*: to masturbate. *slang.*

1944 [see *pud *sb.*[3] 2]. **1961** Partridge *Dict. Slang* Suppl. 1101/2 *Pull one's pudding*,..may have originated *pull one's wire.* **1970** J. Osborne *Right Prospectus* 30 Remember what I said about sex. Keep away from the maids and pretty boys. As for pulling your wire, that's no occupation for a gentleman. **1970** W. Smith *Gold Mine* xxvi. 61 Jesus... That was ugly. I felt like a peeping tom, watching someone, you know, pulling his pudding.

k. *to pull the rug (out) from under* (a person or thing), and varr., to weaken or unsettle (something) by an unexpected withdrawal of support or by some other action; to let down or betray (someone). *colloq.* (orig. *U.S.*).

1946 *Time* 23 Dec. 17/3 Strikes, for instance, would pull the rug out from under the best of prospects. **1948** *Sun* (Baltimore) 15 Dec. 8/3 Although both are reported to feel that United States commitments in western Europe preclude the 'bailing out' of Chiang's regime..they have chosen to say nothing that would 'pull the rug out' from under Chiang. **1952** *Manch. Guardian Weekly* 14 Aug. 3/2 What the President [*sc.* Truman] was talking about was his own part in clinching the nomination of Governor Stevenson. It entailed pulling the rug out from under Mr Harriman. **1966** 'W. Haggard' *Power House* xvi. 179 James Mott had Victor's story... At the worst it could pull the carpet out. **1967** A. Hunter *Gently Continental* ix. 132 The mat is pulled from under Shelton when he dares to assent to this point. **1973** *Physics Bull.* Feb. 75/2 Professor Jewkes..proceeds to pull the rug from under many of the assumptions and arguments used to justify government support of 'high technologies'. **1974** W. Garner *Big enough Wreath* xiii. 196 He did his last job for you... Not too successfully..which is another reason for pulling the rug from under. **1978** *Detroit Free Press* 2 Apr. C 12/2 When the rug was pulled out from under me in movies and television I went back to the theater.

V. 22. pull away. c. Of a vehicle: to draw away, as *from* the kerb on starting. Also *absol.*

1955 H. Kurnitz *Invasion of Privacy* (1956) iv. 32 The grey convertible..pulled away from the curb. **1974** *Sunday Post* (Glasgow) 14 Apr. 6/2 As it [*sc.* a bus] pulled away I was horrified to see a man..pick up the old gents shopping bag and hurry away. **1976** 'P. B. Yuill' *Hazell & Menacing Jester* iv. 44 He was pulling away from the kerb before my reggie reached the upholstery.

23. pull back. f. *Sport.* To score (a goal) restoring, or serving towards restoring, level terms between two teams.

1976 *Northumberland Gaz.* 26 Nov. 20/6 Nicholson was on hand to score from the rebound. Annitsford pulled one back but Nicholson was then again on target with a magnificent shot. **1978** *Lochaber News* 31 Mar. 20/3 In the 60th minute Donald Murchison pulled one back. Five minutes later Mike MacPherson equalised.

24. pull down. f. To earn (money, esp. as a wage or salary). *slang.*

1917 S. Lewis *Job* xiii. 192 Good job, too, assistant book-keeper, pulling down his little twenty-seven-fifty regular. **1919** Wodehouse *Damsel in Distress* xxi. 256 George pulls down in a good year, during the season—around five thousand dollars a week. **1922** [see *berry *sb.*[1] 1c]. **1933** D. L. Sayers *Murder must Advertise* v. 78 'So you have become one of the world's workers.'..'Yes; I'm pulling down four solid quid a week.' **1968** *New Yorker* 9 Nov. 56 How much does your average cornettist pull down per year? **1976** N. Thornburg *Cutter & Bone* i. 21 He..had been pulling down twenty-five thousand a year.

25. pull in. b. Delete †*Obs. rare* and add later examples. Cf. prec. sense.

1841 *Punch* 17 July 6/2 I'm a boy in a school, with a bag of apples, which..I naturally sell at a penny a-piece, and so look forward to pulling in a considerable quantity of browns. **1973** *Scotsman* 13 Feb. 8/2 The Archbishop of York..pulls in £6000 a year.

e. To arrest (a person); = sense 16.

1893 S. Crane *Maggie* x. 89 'I'll tump 'im till he can't stand.'..'What's deh use! Yeh'll git pulled in!' **1923** E. Rice *Adding Machine* vi. 101 You read in the paper all the time about guys gettin' pulled in for annoyin' women. **1933** D. L. Sayers *Murder must Advertise* ix. 162 We could pull him in any day, but he's not the real big noise. **1956** [see *heeled *ppl. a.* 2]. **1973** W. M. Duncan *Big Timer* xxiii. 159 If you hadn't come voluntarily, I'd have pulled you in.

f. *intr.* Of a locomotive train: to enter a station.

1905 D. G. Phillips *Plum Tree* 91, I didn't know you till you took out your watch with the monogram on the back, just as we were pulling in. **1929** S. Leacock *Iron Man* 143 That's your train pulling in now.

g. *absol.* or *intr.* Of a driver: to drive a vehicle to the side of a road or off a road (for some specified purpose). Also of the vehicle itself.

1938 G. Greene *Brighton Rock* III. iii. 122 Notices said: 'Pull in Here', 'Mazawattee tea', 'Genuine Antiques'. **1959** I. Jefferies *Thirteen Days* i. 13, I was forced to pull off the road on the way back... I would have pulled in thereabouts anyway. **1975** M. Russell *Murder by Mile* viii. 81 Pulling in for a truck to pass, Hamilton sat tapping the wheel.

26. pull off. c. For *slang* read *colloq.* and add further examples.

1918 *Policeman's News* 25 Feb. 3/2 Criminals can no

longer dispose of loot in Reading without the sleuths having a pretty good insight as to who pulled off the job. **1923** H. G. Wells *Men like Gods* I. i. 6 He was not really clever enough to pull such a thing off. **1968** *Times* 15 Oct. 16/8 Having succeeded in their earlier experiments, there seems no reason why they should not pull off another major 'first'. **1977** *Time* 15 Aug. 13/2 Both looked as if they had just pulled off some master stroke of détente.

d. To steal (something). Cf. sense 2 b. *slang.*

1883 [see *Leather *sb.* 2 e (*a*)].

e. Usu. *refl.* To cause (a person) to ejaculate by masturbation. *coarse slang.*

1922 Joyce *Ulysses* 745 How did we finish it off yes O yes I pulled him off into my handkerchief pretending not to be excited. **1961** Partridge *Dict. Slang* Suppl. 1236/1 *Pull oneself off*, (of the male) to masturbate: low: late C. 19–20. **1966** L. Cohen *Beautiful Losers* I. 4 Can an old scholar find love at last and stop having to pull himself off every night so he can get to sleep? **1971** 'V. X. Scott' *Surrogate Wife* 139 Spasms shook his entire body as I pulled him off.

f. *intr. Surfing.* To end a ride by bringing one's surfboard out of a wave. Cf. sense 28 g below.

1964 B. Cooper in P. L. Dixon *Men & Waves* (1966) 189, I can't really recall my first wave, but I'm sure I caught an edge and had to pull off. **1967** S. Reid in J. Severson *Great Surfing* 22/2 If someone were sliding faster than you, you had to pull off.

28. pull out. d. For 'Chiefly *U.S.*' read 'orig. *U.S.*' and add earlier and later examples. Also of a ship: to sail out of a harbour or port; of an aeroplane: to emerge from a dive; of a vehicle: to move outwards into another lane of traffic. Also of the driver, etc., or occupants of these means of transport.

1868 *Harper's Mag.* Feb. 293/1 Breakfast over we 'pulled out', for the next station. **1880** 'Mark Twain' *Tramp Abroad* xxviii. 287 We got under way..and pulled out for the summit again, with a fresh and vigorous step. **1902** C. J. C. Hyne *Mr. Horrocks, Purser* 105 We pull out from here next Tuesday. **1917** 'Contact' *Airman's Outings* 46 We swerved violently, and they pulled out of their dive well away from us. **1938** G. Greene *Brighton Rock* VII. ix. 349 A bus came upon them and pulled out just in time. **1942** T. Rattigan *Flare Path* I. 30, I put the old Wimpey into a dive and..pulled out only a few feet above his head. **1951** *Manch. Guardian Weekly* 15 Mar. 13/2 In the Far West, the San Francisco 'Chronicle' blanketed its whole page with the headline—'Wage board approved increase of 10 per cent—labour members pull out'. **1961** *Listener* 7 Dec. 962/1 Today they must choose—either to stay under an African government or to pull out..to face a new life. **1972** 'A. York' *Expurgator* I. iv. 59 The Mercedes was immediately in front of him. He pulled out, into the middle of the road,..and saw the lorry coming at him. **1977** D. Bagley *Enemy* xx. 162 We can pull out and leave Ashton to sink or swim..or we can get him out ourselves.

e. *colloq.* To extend oneself vigorously; to work hard. Cf. *to pull the stops out* s.v. *Stop *sb.*[2]

1866 Trollope *Belton Est.* III. x. 272 There's no getting people really to pull out in this country.

f. Of a drawer, etc.: to be capable of being pulled open.

1943 A. G. Hatcher in *Mod. Lang. Notes* LVIII. 12 Drawers *pull out*..easily.

g. *intr. Surfing.* (See quot. 1963.) Cf. *pull off* (sense 26 f above).

1963 *Surfing Yearbk.* 42/2 *Pull out*, ending a ride by getting your board out of a wave. There are many different ways of pulling out. **1964** J. Severson *Mod. Surfing* xvii. 157 You may also have the opportunity of pulling out before reaching the section. **1968** D. Kahanamoku *World of Surfing* xiii. 127 You can also get wiped out when the wave begins to break in front of you. It's time to pull out of it and avoid an unwanted and unscheduled swim. **1971** *Studies in English* (Univ. Cape Town) Feb. 27 This is called being locked in, because in such a condition it is virtually impossible to pull-out.

28*. pull over. a. See simple senses and Over *adv.*

b. Of a driver: to bring a vehicle to the side of a road or street, or to some other place. Cf. sense 25 g above.

1930 *Morning Post* 12 June 5, I considered that I had not time to pull over to my near side. **1932** *Sun* (Baltimore) 24 Sept. 8/6 Notify him that you are actually about to pass. In most cases he will pull over for you. **1971** *It* 2–16 June 8/1 He's signaling me to pull over! **1972** D. Delman *Sudden Death* (1973) v. 135 The rain so heavy that..the wipers..were unable to cope... 'Can't see too well,' I said. 'I better pull over.'

28. pull round. a.** See simple senses and Round *adv.*

b. *intr.* To recover from sickness or fainting; to come round.

1891 R. Buchanan *Come, live with Me* II. xx. 253 The danger's over..and the little one is pulling round. **1896** *Pall Mall Mag.* Sept. 70 He thinks he's going to pull round again; but I'll bet on his not being alive this day week.

c. *trans.* To restore (a person) to health after sickness, etc.; to put into a healthier or better condition. Also *transf.*

1900 E. Grey *Outrageous Fortune* iv. 37 The attack of meningitis..was fortunately only slight, and the excellent nursing I received..served to quickly pull me round. **1928** *Sunday Express* 29 Apr. 20/1 In the second half Cardiff made a valiant attempt to pull the game round. **1955** A. L. Rowse *Expansion Eliz. Eng.* 230 Smith had pulled the colony round at its lowest point. **1978** *Country Life* 27 July 236/3 'Twas my turn to need help. Denwood pulled me round.

29*. pull to. *trans.* To shut (a door, etc.) by drawing it towards oneself.

1898 [see To *adv.* 4]. **1910** [see *Listen *v.* 2c]. **1922** Joyce *Ulysses* 57 He pulled the halldoor to after him. **1946** W. de la Mare *Three Royal Monkeys* v. 67 He skipped out and pulled-to the door-flap behind him.

30. pull together. a. Also *transf.*

1894 W. Archer in *World* 15 Aug. 25/1 The last act wants a great deal of working-up and pulling together. **1925** J. G. Bruce in E. F. Norton *Fight for Everest: 1924* iii. 63 If the first party of porters could be pulled together again in twenty-four hours' time, they were then to be utilized to keep Camp III supplied from Camp II. **1952** *Listener* 31 Jan. 189/1 He has tried to pull together all that has been said and written about the political struggle between the western allies and Moscow. **1978** *Amer. N. & Q.* XVI. 142/1 A corpus of paintings not pulled together in any previous work.

b. Also, to restore (a person) to a normal condition.

1906 W. S. Maugham *Bishop's Apron* viii. 132 Now come and have tea... I know it'll pull you together.

31. pull up. h. Also *transf.*

1936 N. Streatfeild *Ballet Shoes* xvii. 276 The death of King George in January cut the audiences down to about a quarter..and they never really pulled up again.

pull-. Add: **1.** With advbs., forming adjs.: *pull-along, -down, -on*; *pull-away* sb. (examples); **pull-apart**, the action or result of being pulled in opposite directions so as to be ruptured; **pull-on**, a garment without fasteners that is pulled on.

1939–40 *Army & Navy Stores Catal.* 829/2 Pull-along engine for child to ride in..25/-. **1967** *Punch* 6 Dec. p. xii, Buy beautifully made wooden pull-along toys for tiny children. **1951** *Special Publ. Soc. Econ. Paleontologists & Mineralogists* No. 2. 89 (*caption*) 'Pull-apart' developed in a laminated bed of clay lying on gravel bed and covered by silts. **1954** *Sun* (Baltimore) (B ed.) 6 Feb. 2/5 As the concrete sets these wires are tightened by special jacks, thus..getting rid of the pull-apart tendency in advance. **1971** *Nature* 2 July 21/1 Fig. 3 shows the initial opening of the proto-North Atlantic Ocean and the pull-apart of North and South America. **1939** T. S. Eliot *Old Possum's Pract. Cats* 17 Abandoning their sampans, and their pullaways and junks, They battened down the hatches on the crew within their bunks. **1950** [see *last-resort* s.v. *Last *a.* C 2]. **1976** *Drive* May–June 90/2 A fuss-free pullaway from 20mph in top gear and an 11sec time from 30–50mph highlight the car's impressive flexibility. **1907** *Yesterday's Shopping* (1969) 172/1 Electric Indicator... Pull-down Replacement, consisting of 1½ yds. brass chain, pulley and ring. **1971** J. Henderson *Copperhead* (1972) vi. 76 There was a Leitz slide-projector ..and..a pull-down screen. **1978** *Daily Tel.* 24 Oct. 15/2 The pull-down compartment in the front holds six transparent pockets for credit cards. **1919** in C. W. Cunnington *Eng. Women's Clothing* (1952) v. 156 The vogue of the pull-on is still predominant. **1921** *Glasgow Herald* 25 May 4/7 The turban..does not hide all the hair as do the pull-on hat, the cloche, and other popular shapes. **1976** *Billings* (Montana) *Gaz.* 30 June 7–A/1 (Advt.), Debonair styling in delightful prints. Have yours in a V-neck pull-on with roll-up sleeves. **1978** *Detroit Free Press* 16 Apr. (*Detroit Suppl.*) 36 (Advt.), Pull-on pants in petite and average lengths, $15.

2. With sbs. *pull-engine, -toy*; **pull-bell** (later example); **pull-boat**, also *U.S.*, a motorized flat-boat which draws logs over water; also *attrib.*; **pull-bone** *U.S.* = *wish-bone* s.v. Wish *sb.*[1] 4; **pull-cord**, a cord which operates a mechanism when pulled (in quots. *attrib.*); **pull-date** *N. Amer.*, the date stamped on a container of perishable goods indicating when it must be withdrawn as no longer suitable for sale; **pull-hitter** *U.S. Baseball* (see quot. 1955); **pull-stroke**, (*a*) (earlier example); (*b*) in other technical senses, a stroke (of an oar, etc.) effected by pulling towards oneself; **pull-switch**, a switch operated by means of a pull-cord; **pull-tab**, a device, usu. comprising a ring and short tongue of metal, by means of which a tin may be opened; also *attrib.*

1919 R. Macaulay *Three Days* 52 How a pull-bell clangs when it rings! **1903** *Sci. Amer.* 17 Oct. 276/3 In the cypress swamps of Louisiana there are employed what are known as pull-boats, an evolution from the plan of placing a hoisting engine upon a scow and snaking the logs out of the swamp... The endless-rope pull-boat engines have 44-inch winding drums. **1907** 'O. Henry' *Trimmed Lamp* 136 In her mind she could hear the girls shrieking over a pullbone. **1963** *Listener* 28 Feb. 399/1 It should be..fitted with either a pull-cord switch or one outside the door. **1978** *Lancashire Life* Nov. 177/1 (Advt.), Mahogany Bracket clock—hour strike and pull-cord repeat. **1973** *Black Panther* 7 Apr. 14/2 What food manufacturer would be so foolhardy as to place his produce bearing a pack date alongside a competitor who uses a pull date. **1977** *Daily Colonist* (Victoria, B.C.) 7 Aug. 2/4 All whipped butter..bearing the pull date of Sept. 12, 1977, or before is being recalled. **1907** *Yesterday's Shopping* (1969) 1072/2 The Pull Engine. With rubber composition tyres... each 16/3. **1937** *Philadelphia Record* 2 Sept. 17/1 Medwick hits to all fields. DiMaggio is mostly a pull hitter. **1955** *Amer. Speech* XXX. 153 The term *pull hitter* denotes a hitter who pulls the ball (i.e., a right-handed hitter who hits to left field or a left-handed hitter who hits to right field). **1972** *N.Y. Times* 4 June v. 2/7 He is primarily a pull hitter to left and some teams stack defensive alignments against him. **1897** K. S. Ranjitsinhji *Jubilee Bk. Cricket* iii. 120 He..applies a marvellous pull-stroke to good-length balls just outside the off-stump. **1968** J. Arnold *Shell Bk. Country Crafts* 74 All the 'work' of a cross-cut is done on the pull-stroke [of the saw], each man alternately pulling and releasing. **1969** *Publ. Amer. Dial. Soc.* LI. 10 *Pull stroke*,..a stroke whereby the kayakist leans far forward, thrusts the paddle into the water and with extreme exertion pulls the kayak forward. **1888** D. Salomons *Managem. Accumulators* (ed. 3) II. ii. 97 The Browett pull switch is fixed near the cornice, and by pulling a cord, the light is put on; also turned off by a similar action. **1971** D. Bagley *Freedom Trap* vi. 130 The light switch in the bathroom was operated, as good building regulations insist, by a ceiling pull-switch from which a strong cord hung to a convenient hand level. **1965** *Economist* 5 June 1150/1 The successful development of pull-tab tops for beer tins, so that they can be opened by hand rather than with an opener. **1978** J. Updike *Coup* vi. 239 Take care..not to drop the pull-tab [on a can of soft drink], once removed, back into the can. **1946** *Sun* (Baltimore) 14 Dec. 14/6 Wagons and other pull-toys should have rope handles. **1958** J. G. MacGregor *North-West of 16* v. 60, I was at the pull-toy stage. I went everywhere dragging behind me a fascinating collection of tin cans, bits of roots..all tied together with string. **1978** *Neiman, Marcus Christmas Bk.* 83 A purple cow pull toy, complete with the N-M brand.

3. Forming phraseological combs. functioning either as sbs. or adjs., as **pull-and-push** *adj. phr.* = *Push-and-pull *adj. phr.* b.

1950 *Railway Mag.* XCVI. 101 (*caption*) Dolgelly to Barmouth pull-and-push train approaching Barmouth Tunnel. **1959** H. Ellis *Brit. Railway Hist.* II. II. i. 252 The Great Western and the South Western fought it [*sc.* the electric train] with steam rail motors and pull-and-push trains. **1968** *Railway Mag.* CXIV. 300/1 Pull-and-push trials on the G.N. main line..began in January.

Pullak, var. Polack *sb.* (*a.*) in Dict. and Suppl. **pull-and-push, pull-apart:** see *Pull-.

pull-back. Add: **1. b.** *spec.* An orderly withdrawal of military troops. Also *attrib.* orig. *U.S.*

1951 *Baltimore News-Post* 19 Mar. (Home Final 7th ed.) 1/2 Those who think the Red pullback is leading up to something don't put so much stock in the Red's abandonment of prepared defenses. **1953** *Sun* (Baltimore) 8 May B1/7 (*heading*) Reds continue Laos pullback. **1962** *Listener* 29 Nov. 896/2 *The New York Times* said the Chinese were now 'asking for border talks after a pull-back of troops that would still leave them in full possession of their main territorial objective'. **1971** *E. Afr. Standard* (Nairobi) 10 Apr. 2/7 He was working towards total American withdrawal and would step up the pull-back rate. **1974** *Times* 7 Jan. 4/1 (*heading*) Tel Aviv prepares pull-back offer. **1977** *Time* 10 Oct. 12/3 We had to get very deeply involved in pushing for a pullback and cease-fire.

c. *Cinematogr.* A shot in which the scene is observed to recede.

1957 Manvell & Huntley *Film Music* ii. 34 Long track, mostly in medium or medium-close shot, with one large pull-back during the market-place scene. **1959** W. S. Sharps *Dict. Cinematogr.* 121/2 *Pull back*, the backward movement of a camera from a close to a long shot. **1977** *Listener* 5 May 590/1 Will Frayn appear next time.. on the end of a zoom-in or a pull back?

d. *Tap-dancing.* (See quot. 1957.)

1957 P. Draper in *Dance Mag.* May 60/3 A pull-back is a tap made by the front part of the foot striking the floor while the body is in the air moving backwards. **1975** *New Yorker* 7 July 26/3 The last bit to be recorded..was a wonderful tap dance—a series of time steps, pullbacks, flaps..and pickups done by Michael Bennett himself.

pull-bone to **pull-date:** see *Pull-.

pull-down. Add: **1.** (Later examples.) Also *attrib.*

1938 N. Streatfeild *Circus is Coming* viii. 129 Can't we see the pull-down? Hans says it's more exciting than the build-up. **1962** *Which?* Oct. 305/2 New exercises.. were added... Pull downs (pulling down a bar attached to pulleys and weights). **1965** M. Stewart *Airs above Ground* iv. 58 If this is the last performance, they'll start the pull-down [of the big top] the minute it's over. **1975** Bram & Downs *Manuf. Technol.* vii. 204 (*heading*) Pull-down Broaching. *Ibid.* 205 An advantage of the pull-down method is that where the cutting pressure is evenly distributed around the axis of movement clamping need not be necessary.

2. b. *Cinematogr.* (See quot. 1959.)

1953 [see *ghost-image* s.v. *Ghost *sb.* 14 e]. **1959** W. S. Sharps *Dict. Cinematogr.* 121/2 *Pull down*, the intermittent mechanism used to move film in a camera, projector or printer by engaging the film perforations.

pulled, *ppl. a.* Add: **1. b.** Of wool. orig. *N. Amer.*

1904 J. M. Matthews *Textile Fibres* ii. 24 There is a certain class of wool..known in trade as *pulled wool*; this is obtained from the pelts of slaughtered sheep, and is usually removed from the skin by the action of time, the fibres being pulled out by the roots. **1921** *Daily Colonist* (Victoria, B.C.) 8 Oct. 15/2 The market for pulled wools continues dull. **1934** J. R. Hind *Woollen & Worsted Raw Materials* iii. 19 The removal of the wool is done by plucking or flipping the wool from the skins, which has given these wools the name of 'flipe' or 'slipe'. In the American wool trade, skin wool is known as 'pulled wool'. **1952** H. Haigh *Work of Woolman* vii. 60 The class called 'English Pulled' or 'Scotch Pulled' includes many varieties of wool. **1963** E. M. Pohle in W. von Bergen *Wool Handbk.* (ed. 3) I. ix. 668 The domestic production of pulled wool in 1944 reached an all time high of 74 million pounds.

3. Also, *pulled work* (see quot.).

1967 E. Short *Embroidery & Fabric Collage* ii. 48 *Pulled work.* For this holes are made without withdrawing threads from the ground fabric, but, as the name implies, by pulling and distorting the weave. *Ibid.* iii. 77 (*caption*) Detail of a tablecloth in pulled work, with a border of famous London buildings.

4. (Earlier and later examples.)

1616 W. Browne *Britannia's Pastorals* ii. i. 14 In his flesh pull'd downe As hee had liu'd in a beleaguerd towne. **1895** A. W. Pinero *Second Mrs. Tanqueray* 88 You look dreadfully pulled down. We poor women show illness so plainly in our faces.

puller. Add: **1. c.** *Cricket.* A batsman who pulls (sense 18).

1911, 1972 [see *hooker[1] 6 b].

5. One who or that which attracts custom; spec. (*N. Amer.*), a person employed to solicit passers-by into a shop. Also *puller-in.*

1894 J. L. Ford *Lit. Shop* ix. 132 The Jewish old-clothing quarter that lies close to the Five Points is near by. The 'pullers-in', as the sidewalk salesmen are termed in the vernacular of the trade, transact business with a ferocity that can be best likened to that of Siberian wolves. **1928** *Sunday Dispatch* 15 July 14/3 Next to the Prince of Wales, Shaw is the best box-office puller in the United States. **1944** *Sun* (Baltimore) 15 Jan. 6/7, I wonder whether radio announcers are descendants of the Gay street and Harrison street pullers-in and the tray men of Holliday and Baltimore streets (circa 1909)... They had to pass a law to stop the pullers-in. **1955** [see *cheese-cake 2]. **1958** N. Levine *Canada made Me* ii. 57 The cheap clothing stores—with the pullers standing in the doorways like prostitutes. **1970** J. H. Gray *Boy from Winnipeg* 199 Any country family that stopped to look at something in a window was doomed. The 'puller' would come out and sweet-talk them into the store.

pullery[2] (pu·ləri). *Tanning.* [f. Pull *v.* + -ery.] The place in which wool, hair, and bristles are removed from hides.

1903 L. A. Flemming *Pract. Tanning* 1 The relations between the soaking process and the subsequent processes of the beamhouse or pullery, and the tannery are close. **1963** E. M. Pohle in W. von Bergen *Wool Handbk.* (ed. 3) I. ix. 668 The pulling is conducted in the pulleries which..are connected with the large slaughter-houses.

pullet. Add: **1.** (Later *fig.* examples.)

1823 'J. Bee' *Slang* s.v. *Pullet*, in common life, a female barn-door fowl, which has not yet produced eggs. Young women are so denominated, occasionally. **1922** Joyce *Ulysses* 224 Blazes Boylan looked into the cut of her blouse. A young pullet. **1941** J. Smiley *Hash House Lingo* 44 *Pullet*, young woman.

2. For *Tapes pullastra* read *Venerupis pullastra.* Cf. *palourde. (Earlier and later examples.)

1803 G. Montagu *Testacea Britannica* I. 127 This species [*sc. Venus pullastra*]..is frequently eaten by the common people, and in some parts of Devonshire indiscriminately called *Pullers* or *Pullets.* **1974** S. P. Dance *Encycl. Shells* 268/1 Pullet Carpet Shell. Very similar in shape, size and ornament to *V*[*enerupis*] *rhomboides.*

3. pullet disease = *new wheat disease* s.v. *new *a.* 10 b.

1941 Jungherr & Levine in *Amer. Jrnl. Vet. Res.* II. 267/2 The majority of the cases occur between the ages of 5 and 7 months..hence the appropriateness of the term 'pullet disease'. **1945** *Vet. Jrnl.* CI. 7 The exact course of the pullet disease syndrome is unknown. **1950** [see *blue comb (disease)* s.v. *blue *a.* 13]. **1977** R. F. Gordon *Poultry Dis.* vii. 183 It is difficult to obtain an accurate estimate of the incidence of pullet disease today.

pulley, *sb.*[1] Add: **5.** *pulley-wheel* (later examples); **pulley-cone,** a cone grooved and rotating on its axis, forming a set of pulley-wheels of different sizes.

1903 *Harvard Psychol. Stud.* I. 417 A disc..about 50c. in diameter, rotating on a vertical pivot, was driven by a pulley-cone underneath mounted on the same spindle. **1956** G. Taylor *Silver* vii. 154 *Dish Rings...* The earliest type is shaped like a pulley-wheel. **1967** *Antiquaries Jrnl.* XLVII. 227 Globular flagon with moulded base-angle and pulley-wheel rim.

pulley-bone, var. *pully-bone.

pull-hitter: see *pull-.

pullicate. Delete ?*Obs.* and add: Also 8 **pullcat. b.** (Earlier and later examples.)

1792 P. Freneau *Poems* (1809) I. 31 Hum-hums are here—and muslins—what you please—Bandanas, baftas, pullcats, India teas. **1958** [see *Monteith[2}].

pu·ll-in. [f. phr. *pull in*: see Pull *v.* 25.] **1.** The action of pulling anything in or towards one. Also *attrib.* or as *adj.*

1906 [in Dict. s.v. Pull- 1]. **1976** *Offshore Engineer* July 21/1 A flowline pull-in tool has been developed..to meet this problem. **1977** *Ibid.* Apr. 27/2 The port has a step-down diameter which provides a positive stop during pipe pull-in.

2. a. A café or refreshment stand in a lay-by. Also *pull-in café.*

1938 G. Greene *Brighton Rock* iii. iii. 128 He didn't speak to her in the bus... The country unwound the other way: Mazawattee tea, antique dealers, pull-ins. *Ibid.* v. ii. 195 A window of Charlie's Pull-in Café. **1959** *Listener* 8 Oct. 593/3 At the pull-in where most of the play was enacted the café owners sometimes struck a slightly false note. **1973** J. Wainwright *Devil you Don't* 18 A blue and white sign warned five miles to the next service area... 'They'll be at the next pull-in.'

b. An entry, recess, or the like where a motor vehicle may pull in; a lay-by.

1954 E. Hyams *Stories & Cream* 163 A sprawling public-house..in front of which was a vast pull-in for motor-coaches. **1972** M. Gilbert *Body of Girl* iv. 43 The site had not been designed as a garage, and..the pull-in in front was not as deep as it should have been. **1976** *Southern Even. Echo* (Southampton) 3 Nov. (Advt.), Required. Workshop,..shop, suitable for antiques restoring. Main road. Good pull-in.

pulling, *vbl. sb.* Add: **3. b.** (Further examples.)

1866 'Mark Twain' *Lett. from Hawaii* (1967) 84 The arraigning of a ship's officers before the courts by the crew to answer for alleged cruelties practiced upon them on the high seas—such as the 'pulling' of captains and mates by the crews of the *Mercury.* **1960** G. A. Glaister *Gloss. Bk.* 333/2 *Pulling*, the removal of the cover, boards, end papers, tapes, and any lining material which, with the softening of old glue and cutting of sewing threads, are necessary stages in the preparation of a book for re-binding. **1975** J. Pidgeon *Flame* ii. 24 Jack Daniels and the D.T.s liked the Jackoranda. They didn't care much for the cramped stage..and the money was always lousy. But it was the best place they knew for pulling.

e. *N.Z.* (See quot.) Cf. *pull *v.* 11 e.

1947 P. Newton *Wayleggo* (1949) 154 The act of a heading dog bringing sheep back to his master is termed pulling.

5. *pulling boat*; **pulling-bar** = Draw-bar 1; **pulling bone** *U.S.* = *wish bone* s.v. Wish *sb.*[1] 4; **pulling power,** the ability to attract or persuade.

1892 J. G. A. Meyer *Mod. Locomotive Constr.* 528 Fig. 850 shows the wrought-iron pulling-bar which connects the tender to the engine. **1912** A. T. Quiller-Couch *Hocken & Hunken* p. xxiii, The penultimate race (randan pulling-boats) was finishing amid banging of guns and bursts of music. **1975** *Country Life* 2 Jan. 23/2 The RNLI..displays the former Whitby No. 2 lifeboat.. the last pulling boat to have been in the service of the Institution. **1877** Bartlett *Dict. Amer.* (ed. 4) 502 *Pulling-bone*, the common name in Maryland, Virginia, &c, for the yoke-like breast-bone of chickens, by pulling which till it breaks children and young ladies settle which will be the first married. **1942** H. C. Bailey *Dead Man's Shoes* i. 7 Posters..credited by the expert with much more pulling power. **1966** N. Nicolson in H. Nicolson *Diaries & Lett.* 66 Harold Nicolson's importance to Mosley, apart from the increasing pulling-power of his name, was his close connection with Beaverbrook. **1978** P. Bailey *Leisure & Class in Victorian England* vii. 147 Enterprising publicans..abolished the refreshment check ..relying on the pulling power of the entertainment.

Pullman. Add: **a.** (Earlier and later examples.)

1872 W. F. Butler *Great Lone Land* iv. 57 One takes a Pullman..as one takes a Hansom, Pullman and sleeping-car have become synonymous terms. **1951** N. Mitford *Blessing* ii. xii. 265 The Bunbury burglar was walking up the Pullman on his way..to the Trianon bar. **1972** *Daily Tel.* (Colour Suppl.) 28 Apr. 49 By the end of this decade, British Rail acknowledges,..the Manchester, the South Wales and the Bristol Pullmans..will have vanished. **1977** *Modern Railways* Dec. 476/2 The other Metro-Cammell Pullmans still mouldering away in sidings have apparently been abandoned so long that rehabilitation is now unacceptably expensive.

b. (Earlier and later examples.)

1869 *Bradshaw's Railway Man.* XXI. 419 Pullman Palace Car Company Stock $72,300. **1873** *Forest & Stream* 28 Aug. 34/1 It was a close pack..the whole scene reminding one forcibly of a 'Pullman' sleeping car. **1954** W. Tucker *Wild Talent* (1955) v. 58 Ray Palmer slept soundly in the topmost Pullman bed. **1955** D. Davie *Brides of Reason* 28 While Pullman sleepers lulled your sleeping head. **1977** *Time* 18 Apr. 22/2 The cabin can accommodate eight passengers on comfortable Pullman seats.

c. *transf.* (Usu. with small initial.) A prefabricated unit of kitchen or bathroom fixtures, compact as in a railway carriage. Usu. *attrib.* Chiefly *U.S.*

[**1932** *New Yorker* 23 July 5/2 There are many people who..would be glad to buy a Pullman section to install in their home.] **1967** 'L. Egan' *Nameless Ones* iii. 37 A chipped but spotless pullman washstand. **1968** 'R. Macdonald' *Instant Enemy* xxv. 155 It was what is called a studio apartment, consisting of one large room with a pullman kitchen. **1973** *Sunday Bull.* (Philadelphia) 7 Oct. (Parade Suppl.) F6 New double sink pullmans with bright colors are available, or, if you want to do-it-yourself, try separate wash basins. **1977** *Chicago Tribune* 2 Oct. i. 33/2 The apartments for the 16 families in the community consisted of two rooms and a Pullman kitchen.

Pullo, var. *Peulh *sb.* and *a.*

pu·ll-off, *sb.* and *a.* [Pull- 1.] **A.** *sb.* **1.** The fact or action of pulling off or of being pulled off, in various special applications.

1859, 1904 [in Dict. s.v. Pull- 1]. **1926** *Gloss. Terms Electr. Engin.* (Brit. Engin. Stand. Assoc.) 133 *Pull-off*, a metal fitting attached to an ear and used on curves for adjusting the position of a trolley-wire in a horizontal plane. **1950** *Richmond* (Va.) *News-Leader* 28 Jan. 1 Detailed on this maneuver chart are the Navy's plans for an all-out 'Operation Pull-Off' to free the U.S.S. Missouri from her Chesapeake Bay mudbank. **1953** R. Knox *St. Paul's Gospel* i. 10 You might get the printer to give you a pull-off of that childish picture all in blue, with the yellows and the reds left out.

2. *spec.* in *Parachuting* (see quot. 1947). Also *attrib.*

1933 *National Geogr. Mag.* May 614 Heels over head at the 'pull off'... The officer climbed out on the lower wing to the outer strut and, holding on with one hand, pulled his rip cord. **1940** *War Illustr.* 26 Jan. 20/2 The 'pull-off' type is used only for training novices in the 'art' [of parachuting]. **1947** M. Newnham *Prelude to Glory* iv. 14 The procedure..was for the pupil..at a signal from the pilot [to] clamber along the lower wing... The pupil let go his hold on the strut, and willy-nilly he became a parachutist. This was known as the 'pull-off' method.

3. = *lay-by *sb.* 1 c. Cf. *pull-in 2 b.

1969 V. Canning *Queen's Pawn* iv. 63 Gilpin..was waiting in a pull-off down the road with the Land-Rover. **1972** R. K. Smith *Ransom* vi. 264 Just after the city line as you come down the parkway there's a pull-off—a parking area. **1975** V. Canning *Kingsford Mark* x. 163 He..parked the car on a turfed pulloff.

B. *adj.* Designating that which may be pulled off or from which something may be pulled off.

1902 [in Dict. s.v. Pull- 1]. **1962** *Sunday Express* 7 Jan. 13/6 A pull-off calendar still showed the date. **1973** *Daily Tel.* (Colour Suppl.) 11 May 38/1 Much of it comes in supermarket-style cans with pull-off tops.

pull-on: see *pull-.

pullorum (pulōə·rəm). [mod.L., a. the specific epithet of *Bacterium pullorum* (L. F. Rettger 1909, in *Jrnl. Med. Res.* XXI. 117), f. gen. pl. of L. *pullus* young chick.] The specific epithet of *Bacterium pullorum* (now *Salmonella gallinarum*) used *attrib.* in **pullorum disease** to designate an acute, infectious, often fatal disease of young chicks, which is also known as bacillary white diarrhœa.

1929 *Bull. Mass. Agric. Exper. Station* XLVIII. 2 It was unanimously voted to accept the suggestion of Dr. Leo F. Rattger to change the name of Bacillary white diarrhea to 'pullorum disease'. **1930** M. A. Jull *Poultry Husbandry* xxvi. 411 The pullorum disease, which frequently causes such enormous losses among chicks, has been called 'bacillary white diarrhea'. **1960** *Farmer & Stockbreeder* 23 Feb. 124/1 Among these bacteria are the organisms responsible for respiratory diseases and pullorum disease. **1977** G. A. Cullen et al. in R. F. Gordon *Poultry Dis.* i. 11 Outbreaks of pullorum disease in turkeys are rare in this country.

pu·ll-out, *sb.* and *a.* [Pull- 1.] Also as one word. **A.** *sb.* **1.** The fact or action of pulling out; withdrawal from an undertaking or affair, *esp.* from military involvement or occupation.

1825 [in Dict. s.v. Pull- 1]. **1944** *Daily Progress* (Charlottesville, Va.) 2 Oct. 9/5 A correspondent reported increasing signs of a pull-out..of tens of thousands of German troops. **1968** Mrs. L. B. Johnson *White House Diary* 13 Apr. (1970) 664 Some of the headlines were easing up—'D.C. Curfew Off, Gradual Pull-Out of GI's Starts'. **1976** *Billings* (Montana) *Gaz.* 2 July 3-C/4 A weaker committee motion, specifying a one-year ban for a political pullout, was defeated by the same margin. **1976** P. Henissart *Winter Quarry* v. 60 Most people think a missile pullout is overdue. **1977** P. Theroux *Consul's File* 177, I inherited him [*sc.* a dog] in Saigon... I took him back to the States after the pull-out.

2. In various technical uses. **a.** *Aeronaut.* The transition from a dive or spin to normal flight.

1919 Pippard & Pritchard *Aeroplane Struct.* vi. 54 The combination of terminal velocity with a quick pull out is one which would break practically any aeroplane. **1932** *Discovery* Apr. 114/2 Individual records of 'pull-outs' from a dive have registered high accelerometer readings without the pilots experiencing ill effects. **1943** *Sun* (Baltimore) 20 July 3/2 All of the men were half dazed. They had been flung about the ship in its two dives and pullouts... The plane was under control, but barely so. **1962** F. I. Ordway et al. *Basic Astronautics* xii. 465 During World War II dive bomber pilots found they could minimize the effects of acceleration by.. tightening muscles, and shouting during pullouts from dives.

b. *Surfing.* (See quot. 1967.)

1967 J. Severson *Great Surfing* Gloss., *Pull-out*, steering the board over or through the back of the wave, as to end the ride. **1968** W. Warwick *Surfriding in N.Z.* 13/1 To execute a pullout, guide your board to the top of the wave, then kick it into the wave. **1971** *Studies in English* (Univ. Cape Town) Feb. 27 Like the turn, the pull-out may be forehand or backhand.

3. A self-contained detachable section of a newspaper, magazine, etc. Also, = *fold-out* sb. s.v. *fold *v.*[1] 10.

1952 *Conc. Oxf. Dict.* Add. *Pull-out*, page or plate in book that unfolds out from front edge of leaves to facilitate reference. **1955** *Sun* (Baltimore) 28 Oct. (B ed.) 26/4 TV Pull-Out... Have been meaning to write and tell you how wonderful is the new TV pull-out section of *The Sunday Sun.* **1971** S. E. Morison *European Discovery Amer.: Northern Voy.* p. viii, The reproduction of old maps in a book presents typographical problems. Nobody likes a big pull-out; but if the size is too much reduced, one cannot read the names of places. **1971** *Woman's Own* 27 Mar. 21 Next week..8-page pull-out of dairy dishes. **1977** *Listener* 17 Mar. 332/2 A potential centre-page pull-out for..*Hustler* magazine.

B. *adj.* Designating that which may be pulled out (in various senses).

1881 [in Dict. s.v. PULL- 1]. **1929** 'R. CROMPTON' *William* iv. 86 They're frightened of the big roundabout—an' the pull-out toffee makes them sick. **1950** J. D. CARR *Below Suspicion* xii. 149 Dr. Bierce lowered himself on one of the pull-out seats facing them. **1955** [see sense 3 above]. **1966** *B.B.C. Handbk.* 79 The pull-out map.. shows how..Soviet and Chinese broadcasters have exploited their geographical position. **1979** *Amat. Photographer* Feb. 62/1 The three cameras we're looking at this week..have pull-out or retracting lenses.

pull-over. Add: **4.** (Usu. as one word.) Used *attrib.* or *absol.* to designate articles of clothing that are put on by drawing them over the head; *spec.* (chiefly in *absol.* use) a knitted or woven garment for the upper part of the body; a jumper or jersey.

1907 *Yesterday's Shopping* (1969) 320c/1 The 'Pullover' Storm Coat..is especially designed without any opening when in wear, and, being made without a rubber neck, entirely obviates any discomfort in pulling the garment on or off over the head. **1921** *Daily Colonist* (Victoria, B.C.) 6 Apr. 4/5 (Advt.), Another lot of these smart Wool Pull-Over Sweaters to sell at $2.98. **1925** *Westm. Gaz.* 28 Apr. 3 The vogue of the Pullover has supplanted the waistcoat for golf. **1930** *Daily Tel.* 9 Apr. 15/1 (Advt.), Attractive three-piece suit in tweedknit..designed with.. new tuck-in pullover finely woven to tone with suit. **1940** GRAVES & HODGE *Long Week-End* iii. 42 Most women in 1919 were wearing jumpers, knitted by themselves as a relief from 'socks for soldiers'; and soon afterwards men, too, began to adopt them under the name of 'pull-over'. **1967** N. FREELING *Strike Out* 82 The young man was.. darning the worn elbow of a pullover. **1977** *New Yorker* 10 Oct. 124/3 (Advt.), Pullover Dress. A most cozy dress in thick pure cotton flannel, brushed inside and out, long known for its wearing qualities.

Hence **pu·llovered** *a.*, wearing a pullover.

1926 *Daily Chron.* 13 May 2/2 'I'll be sorry to leave the old bus tonight,' said the plus foured pull-overed youth at the wheel of the 'General' yesterday afternoon. **1977** *Film & Television Technician* Jan. 10/3 (*caption*) Making whoopee at the fun-packed Animation Social..[were] pullovered Animation Section Chairman, Barry Merritt, Joe Telford and journal editor Roy Lockett.

pull-switch, -tab: see *PULL-.

pull-up. Add: (Now usu. with stress on the first element.) **1. a.** (Earlier *fig.* and later examples.)

1837 DICKENS *Pickw.* xxxiii. 344 That's raythor a sudden pull up, ain't it, Sammy? **1842** —— *Let.* 27 Feb. (1974) III. 92, I have so much to say that I could fill quires of paper, which renders this sudden pull-up the more provoking. **1950** A. HUXLEY *Let.* 6 Aug. (1969) 628 In the plain you and the child can walk abroad without having to take the car and without being fatigued by a pull up. **1980** 'M. INNES' *Going it Alone* xvii. 153 If they did a sudden pull up like that, it wouldn't be much good just driving on.

b. A lifting-up, encouragement.

1872 GEO. ELIOT *Middlem.* IV. VIII. 360 He told Mary that his happiness was half owing to Farebrother, who gave him a strong pull-up at the right moment. **1913** G. DE H. VAIZEY *College Girl* xxi. 291 Think of all that it means..if we can keep these men from drifting, and give them a pull-up in time!

2. (Further examples.) Phr. *a good pull-up for carmen*, a roadside café; also in various *transf.* and allusive uses.

1899 [in Dict.]. **1925** H. V. MORTON *Heart of London* 50 London's tea-shops are of many kinds, from the standardized shop to the good pull-up for millionaires constructed on the Paris plan. **1928** *Sunday Express* 29 Apr. 4/4 It was known in Hollywood as 'The Legs of Carmen', but your censor doubtless attended to that. The censor's office is usually a good pull-up for Carmen. **1935** A. J. CRONIN *Stars look Down* II. xx. 442 He went into a workman's coffee-house: *Good pull up for lorrys* was on the sign outside. **1952** M. ALLINGHAM *Tiger in Smoke* ix. 153 The pull-up on the corner opens at five... I want..to get a bit o' breakfast. **1965** [see *DINER 2 b]. **1977** *Listener* 24 Mar. 382/2 Our mother..ran..a 'caff'—or what was then known as a good pull-up for car-men.

3. a. The fact or action of pulling something upwards; *spec.* in physical exercise, the action of pulling up the body by means of a bar or beam held by the hands.

1907 M. A. VON ARNIM *Fräulein Schmidt* lix. 255 'He only wants his wind,' said Vicki... 'It certainly was rather a long pull up,' said I. **1938** *Jrnl. R. Aeronaut. Soc.* XLII. 625 The manœuvres consisted of push-downs and pull-ups from level flight..and push-ups from inverted flight. **1946** J. E. Q. BARFORD *Climbing in Britain* iv. 63 The main types of holds are as follows:—A Straight Pull Up. This is a hold over which the fingers can curl as over the rung of a ladder. **1960** E. S. & W. J. HIGHAM *High Speed Rugby* 298 Pull-ups on beam, or other horizontal bar. **1971** A. A. MICHELE *You don't have to Ache* i. 21 Here are some things that you should not be doing:..Do not do push-ups or pull-ups.

b. *attrib.* or as *adj.* Designating that which may be pulled up.

1919 R. FRY *Let.* May (1972) II. 451, I live in a house which has..a real Victorian W.C. with a pull up plug. **1973** *Country Life* 26 July 260/2 The gear lever..is mounted on a floor console with the pull-up handbrake.

‖ **pullus** (pu·lŏs). Pl. pulli. [L., = young chick.] A young bird during the stage before it is fully grown or able to fly.

1774 G. WHITE *Let.* 2 Sept. in *Selborne* (1789) I. xl. 100, I had been..comparing the tails of the male and female swallow, and this ere any young broods appeared; so that there was no danger of confounding the dams with their *pulli*. **1955** R. SPENCER in *Brit. Birds* XLVIII. 468 Pull. (pullus)—nestling or chick not yet flying. **1964** A. L. THOMSON *New Dict. Birds* 904/2 The bird is technically a 'pullus'..until it is full-grown and flying. *Ibid.*, After the pullus stage a bird is described as 'juvenile' while wearing its first plumage of true feathers.

pully-bone (pu·li,bōᵘn). *U.S. dial.* Also **pulley-bone.** [f. PULL *v.* + -Y + BONE *sb.*] = *wish-bone* s.v. WISH *sb.*[1] 4. Cf. *pull-bone* s.v. *PULL- 2 and *pulling-bone* s.v. *PULLING *vbl. sb.* 5.

1939 B. K. HARRIS *Purslane* 148 The girls scrambled over the pulley-bone of the turkey. **1947** M. HENRY *Misty of Chincotiague* xvi. 152 Somethin' told me to save the pully bone from that marsh hen. **1966** *Publ. Amer. Dial. Soc.* 1964 XLII. 22 *Pully-bone*, the wish-bone or furcula, of a chicken, often pulled after a meal, to determine who is to get married first. **1976** *Amer. Speech* 1973 XLVIII. 180 If we understand that there is a connection between the Southern mountains and coastal plains, the occurrence of *you-all*, *grea/z/y*, and *pulley bone* 'wishbone' in an area as far away as the Midwest becomes readily explainable.

pulmonic, *a.* Add: **4.** *Phonetics.* Relating to the lungs as the initiator of the air stream used in the articulation of speech sounds.

1942 BLOCH & TRAGER *Outl. Linguistic Analysis* ii. 31 Stops with inner closure at the bottom of the lungs are called *pulmonic*. **1949** J. R. FIRTH in *Trans. Philol. Soc.* 1948 142 Types of sound which appear to crop up repeatedly in syllabic analysis..are..aitch or the pulmonic onset. **1959** [see *GLOTTALIC *a.*]. **1975** F. R. PALMER in W. F. Bolton *Eng. Lang.* i. 17 Almost without exception the whole of the articulation of sounds in European languages is powered by air expelled from the lungs (it is 'pulmonic egressive').

pulmotor (pɒ·lmōᵘtəɹ). [f. PULMO- + L. *mōtor* that which moves.] An apparatus for automatically forcing air or oxygen into and out of the lungs when breathing has ceased or is weak. Also *attrib.* and *fig.*

Formerly a proprietary name in the U.S.

1912 J. W. PAUL *Use & Care Mine-Rescue Breathing Apparatus* (U.S. Bureau Mines: Miners' Circular No. 4) (rev. ed.) 25 The pulmotor is intended for use in the resuscitation of persons who have partly or wholly ceased to breathe as a result of inhaling irrespirable gases, of an electric shock, or of drowning. **1913** *Official Gaz.* (U.S. Patent Office) 24 June 1052/1 Dragerwerk..Lubeck, Germany..*Pulmotor*... Mechanical respiratory apparatus and devices for administering oxygen. Claims use since February, 1909. **1928** *Daily Express* 31 Dec. 12/4, I grabbed up my bag and the pulmotor, and was over here in a jiffy. **1940** *Economist* 6 Apr. 618/2 The third view is almost..entirely mechanistic. It belongs in the pulmotor school of economics. **1951** W. KEES in *Furioso* Summer 35 Another fat woman In a dull green bathing suit Dives into the water and dies. The pulmotors glisten. **1974** S. SHELDON *Other Side of Midnight* vii. 180 She debated whether to stay in bed or call a pulmotor squad.

pulp, *sb.* Add: **4. c.** orig. *U.S.* Ephemeral literature, esp. (in derogatory use) that regarded as being of poor quality; popular or sensational writing generally. Freq. *attrib.*, as *pulp artist, fiction, novel, writer*, etc. Also *ellipt.* = **pulp magazine* (sense 5c below). Also *transf.*

1931 *Frontier* (Missoula, Montana) Nov. 82/1 Even should he fail to publish in the big magazines, and never graduate from the 'pulps', he can rise to as much as ten cents a word. **1945** [see *GLOSSY *sb.* b]. **1945** R. CHANDLER *Let.* 24 Aug. (1966) 201 Marlowe just grew out of the pulps. He was no one person. **1951** WODEHOUSE *Old Reliable* ii. 32 Half the best known writers today started on the pulps. **1952** M. STEEN *Phoenix Rising* iii. 69 [He] picked up a handful of old pulps. **1966** *New Statesman* 15 July 104/3 There's only one well-known actor... The bulk of the others' experience comes from local rep, TV pulp and Shaftesbury Avenue trivia. **1972** D. E. WESTLAKE *Bank Shot* iv. 24 He'd discovered the pulps..when he was in high school. **1976** *National Observer* (U.S.) 3 July 17/1 When I started..the pulps were gasping their last.

attrib. **1936** Pulp writer [see *ACE 2 c]. **1946** R. CHANDLER *Let.* 2 Oct. (1966) 24 We have a much better home than an out-of-work pulp writer has any right to expect. **1951** M. MCLUHAN *Mech. Bride* (1967) 151/1 Why aren't you interested in the private lives of the strippers and pulp artists who upholster our desert landscape? **1955** L. A. FIEDLER in D. Lodge *20th Cent. Lit. Crit.* (1972) 464 Wordless narrative: digests, pulp fiction, movies, picture magazines. **1958** *New Statesman* 6 Sept. 294/3 The wretched reader of pulp literature is encouraged to dream of sins and orgies he is forbidden to enact. **1959** *Listener* 30 July 176/3 The pulp novels of Mickey Spillane. **1965** *Ibid.* 27 May 788/1 Feelings should not run too high over sophisticated pulp literature. **1970** G. GREER *Female Eunuch* 164 The bored housewife..intoning the otherwise very forgettable words of some pulp lovesong. **1975** J. MCCLURE *Snake* viii. 102 Constrictors..are certainly not given to crushing anything to a bloody pulp. As pulp fiction would have it! **1976** *Listener* 29 July 122/2 Cody..met up with a pulp novelist..who proceeded to set Cody up as a regular frontier hero in a series of literary adventures. **1977** *Time Out* 17–23 June 35/3 Juicy pulp movie about the organisation's efforts to move in on the truck hi-jacking operation run by Anna and her girls.

5. a. (*a*) *pulp-maker*. **b. pulp paper,** newsprint; paper of similar texture used for books or magazines; **pulp-stone,** (*b*) a stone used like a grindstone for reducing wood to pulp; **pulpwood** (earlier and later examples). **c.** (in sense 4c) **pulp magazine,** a magazine devoted to popular or sensational literature; also (with hyphen) *attrib.*

1931 *Frontier* (Missoula, Montana) Nov. 83/1 We need some outlets for the work, with pay, of young and enthusiastic writers; something to keep them away from the 'pulp' and 'slick paper' magazines. **1934** *Sun* (Baltimore) 15 Mar. 21/1 He wrote 'Western' fiction for the 'pulp' magazines. **1937** A. HUXLEY *Ends & Means* xii. 191 Each month the pulp magazines offer to millions of readers their quota of true confessions, film fun, spicy detective stories, hot mysteries. *Ibid.* 207 Pulp-magazine stories are transcriptions of the commonest and easiest day-dreams. **1944** 'G. ORWELL' in *Horizon* Oct. 239 English imitations of the 'pulp magazine' do now exist. **1954** KOESTLER *Invisible Writing* III. xv. 186 We churned out a couple of detective stories for pulp magazines. **1968** E. A. MCCOURT *Saskatchewan* vii. 76 Farwell, as various stories attributed to him suggest, had a pulp-magazine mind. **1975** *Times Lit. Suppl.* 10 Oct. 1174/2 *The Continental Op* is the anonymous narrator of the stories which Dashiell Hammett wrote for the pulp magazine *Black Mask* during the 1920s. **1883** D. A. WELLS *Pract. Econ.* (1885) 107 Even the pulp-makers..will find difficulty in marketing their pulp in the immediate future. **1901** *Daily Colonist* (Victoria, B.C.) 31 Oct. 3/2 It is therefore just as desirable that information should be compiled for their [*sc.* fishermen's] use as for the use of miners, lumbermen, pulp-makers or farmers. **1909** Pulp-maker [see *log-lumberer* s.v. *LOG *sb.*[1] 8 b]. **1908** KIPLING *Lett. of Travel* (1920) 154 The advertising of Canadian papers,..the brittle pulp-paper, the machine-set type. **1931** *Times Lit. Suppl.* 9 July 542/3 The choice between writing for those pulp-paper magazines that pay by the word and the smooth-paper magazines that pay by the story. **1901** J. H. PRATT in *Mineral Resources of U.S.* 789 Pulpstones differ from grindstones in having a much broader face. **1957** *Encycl. Brit.* XVII. 232/2 Natural pulpstones are 27 to 36 in. wide by 54 in. or more in diameter. Artificial stones are 27 to 54 in. wide and 54 to 72 in. in diameter. **1885** *Rep. New Hampshire Forestry Comm.* 10 Telegraph-poles, pulp-wood, bark, etc. **1928** R. S. TROUP *Silvicultural Syst.* xvii. 177 Where coniferous forests are grown solely for pulpwood or mining timber, the clear-cutting system with artificial regeneration is often the only one feasible. **1960** 'N. SHUTE' *Trustee from Toolroom* x. 284 The offcuts were turned into pulpwood for newsprint. **1974** *Globe & Mail* (Toronto) 28 Nov. 45/2 The spruce, which produced its first shoot a few weeks ago, is the first pulpwood tree anywhere to be grown in this way, according to scientists involved in the project.

pulpal (pɒ·lpăl), *a. Dentistry.* [f. PULP *sb.* + -AL.] Of or pertaining to the pulp of a tooth; *spec.* applied to that surface of a cavity which overlies the pulp.

1908 G. V. BLACK *Operative Dentistry* II. 6 That wall of a cavity which is to the occlusal of the pulp, and in a plane at right angles to the long axis of the tooth, is called the pulpal wall. **1925** *Dental Rec.* XLV. 627 It has been argued that grinding the enamel in preparation for the crown renders a tooth susceptible to thermal shock, with subsequent destruction of pulpal structures. **1953** J. R. SCHWARTZ *Inlays & Abutments* xiii. 142 The pulpal and axial walls should be flat and at right angles to one another. **1967** *Brit. Dental Jrnl.* CXXIII. 420/1 Pulpal involvement may be unavoidable if preparation for a jacket is undertaken.

pulpectomy (pɒlpe·ktŏmi). *Dentistry.* [f. PULP *sb.* + *-ECTOMY.] Surgical removal of the pulp of a tooth (usu. all of it: cf. *PULPOTOMY).

1923 *Dental Items of Interest* XLV. 5 The remaining portion of a vital pulp following excision, or partial pulpectomy, will be destroyed. *Ibid.* 82 Operations upon the pulp are designated as 'Pulpotomy'. In case a portion of the pulp is excised and removed, the operation is termed 'Partial Pulpectomy'. The removal of the entire pulp is 'Pulpectomy'. **1924** F. E. HOGEBOOM *Pract. Pedodontia* v. 65 (*heading*) Pulpectomy and pulpotomy. *Ibid.*, Pulpectomy is the complete removal of the pulp. **1957** S. B. FINN *Clin. Pedodontics* xiv. 318 Pulpectomy may be complete or partial, depending on whether there is any vital tissue in the canal. **1976** ETTINGER & PINKHAM in A. J. Nowak *Dentistry for Handicapped Patient* xvi. 287/1 Pulpectomy with appropriate instrumentation and filling is a standard..treatment for pulp pathology.

‖ **pulperia** (pulperī·ă). [Sp. Amer.] In Central and South America and the south-west U.S., a grocery or tavern.

1818 A. GILLESPIE *Gleanings & Remarks Buenos Ayres* viii. 91 At the intersected corners of almost every street in that capital, pulperias, or dram, and grocery shops, are established, that vend liquors, candles, and other articles. **1840** R. H. DANA *Two Yrs. before Mast* (1841) xxviii. 192 He..came to the Pueblo de los Angelos... Here he went dead to leeward among the pulperias, gambling-rooms, &c. **1859** T. COCHRANE *Narr. Services in Liberation of Chili, Peru, & Brazil* I. x. 216 The two months' pay offered the other day could not now effect its purpose, as the whole—and more is due to the Pulperia keepers, to whose benefit, and not that of the seamen, it must have immediately accrued. **1871** H. M. & P. V. N. MYERS *Life under Tropics* iii. 21 We were forced by a sudden shower to seek shelter in a way-side pulperia. **1904** CONRAD *Nostromo* I. viii. 80 The horseman hammered with the butt of a heavy revolver at the doors of low pulperias. **1905** J. MASEFIELD

Mainsail Haul 14 When Don Alfonso was in the pulperia (that's Spanish for grog-shop), he was a bluin' down that licker. **1936** *Times Lit. Suppl.* 29 Feb. 173/1 'Charlie the Gaucho' opens outside a *pulperia* on the Pampas. **1974** D. MEIRING *President Plan* ix. 74 The single *pulperia* which he had visited to buy food.

pulping, *vbl. sb.* Add: *pulping-machine.*

1875 *Encycl. Brit.* I. 327/1 A premium was offered for machines to perform this kind of work [*sc.* pulping of turnips and mangolds for cattle], under the somewhat inappropriate designation of 'pulping-machines'. **1909** *Chambers's Jrnl.* Aug. 518/1 From this pulping machine it passes to the centrifugal pump.

pulpit, *sb.* Add: **4. b.** Also, the harpooner's standing-place on a swordfishing vessel.

1927 G. BRADFORD *Gloss. Sea Terms* 135/1 *Pulpit*, the harpooning platform on the bowsprit of a sword-fishing vessel. **1959** W. R. BIRD *These are Maritimes* v. 132 We noted the 'pulpits' constructed far forward for the use of the man who throws the spear. **1972** E. STAEBLER *Cape Breton Harbour* i. 16 A bowsprit like a diving board with a metal sort of pulpit on the end of it.

d. A small raised platform or room from which machinery can be observed and controlled.

1880 *Harper's Mag.* Dec. 62 Another shout, and the boy touches another lever in the gallery of levers, irreverently termed the 'pulpit'. **1903** *Electr. World & Engin.* 26 Dec. 1051/2 The operator of the hoisting motor stands in a pulpit above the floor. **1959** *Control* Feb. 97/3 The mill pulpit or control room..is staffed by two rollermen and a member of the metallurgical department who keeps an eye on ingot quality. **1968** 'A. HAIG' *Sign on for Tokyo* 122 They were sitting in the 'pulpit', three of them, above the bars of the rolling mill.

e. The (pilot's, etc.) cockpit of an aeroplane. *R.A.F. slang.*

1933 D. GRINNELL-MILNE *Wind in Wires* I. ii. 96 The reason for its unofficial name—'The Pulpit'—was all too obvious. A little three-ply box projected from the front of the machine... The wretched man in this box had.. an unrestricted forward view. **1941** [see *GREENHOUSE 3]. **1942** *Gen* 1 Sept. 14/1 A fighter pilot climbs into the 'pulpit' of his plane.

f. *Yachting.* (See quot. 1961). Also in other water craft.

1961 F. H. BURGESS *Dict. Sailing* 164 *Pulpit*, an elevated tubular metal guardrail set up at bow or stern. **1964** *Eng. Stud.* XLV. 23 A pulpit is a raised safety-rail in the bows of a yacht or motor cruiser. **1976** *Yachts & Yachting* 20 Aug. 382/3 (Advt.), Fast Week-ender, excellent condition..two berths, pulpit, full foam buoyancy. **1977** *Mod. Boating* (Austral.) Jan. 110/1 Deck or even pulpit-mounted lights were often hidden from view.

5. d. pulpit-cloth (later U.S. example); **pulpit-rail,** a rail on a ship's pulpit.

1872 *Atlantic Monthly* Mar. 317 Fragments of richly colored altar-pieces, fine pulpit-cloths, and pieces of old carving. **1958** S. A. GRAU *Hard Blue Sky* i. 42 Hector walked the full length of the boat and turning settled himself on the pulpit rail. **1974** G. JENKINS *Bridge of Magpies* xv. 226 A light anti-aircraft gun platform.. surrounded by a rusty metal 'pulpit rail'.

pulpitis (pʊlpəi·tis). *Dentistry.* [f. PULP *sb.* + -ITIS.] Inflammation of the dental pulp.

1882 *Dental Rec.* II. 444 The tooth became sensitive upon percussion..without signs of pulpitis. **1930** W. H. O. MCGEHEE *Text-bk. Operative Dentistry* xxvi. 776 In the later stages of acute pulpitis, tenderness of the tooth to tapping may arise, from passage of the inflammatory area to the tissues of the apical space. **1977** CURL & PRUE in Boundy & Reynolds *Current Concepts Dental Hygiene* vii. 111 Chronic partial pulpitis will tend to be associated with pain.

pulpitum (pu·lpitʊ̆m). *Archit.* [L.: see PULPIT *sb.*] A stone screen separating the choir from the nave and freq. surmounted by a loft housing the organ.

1845 R. WILLIS tr. Gervase of Canterbury in *Archit. Hist. Canterbury Cathedral* iii. 37 A screen with a loft (*pulpitum*)..separated in a manner the aforesaid tower from the nave. **1908** F. BOND *Screens & Galleries Eng. Churches* iv. 159 The pulpitum differed from the rood screen in many ways. It formed the eastern barrier of the quire, and against the eastern face of it were placed the return stalls. *Ibid.*, The pulpitum always had a spacious loft above it, and carried the organ. **1923** *Trans. Scottish Ecclesiol. Soc.* VII. 101 As originally placed the painting took the shape of a boarded tympanum, occupying the entire space upward from the back of the pulpitum, or loft, to the roof. **1937** *Burlington Mag.* Mar. 128/2 The 'Master of the Naumburg Sculptures'..was responsible.. for the sculptures on the pulpitum in Mainz Cathedral. **1966** J. FLEMING et al. *Penguin Dict. Archit.* 179/2 *Pulpitum*, a stone screen in a major church erected to shut off the choir from the nave. It could also be used as a backing for the return choir stalls.

pulpotomy (pʊlpǫ·tŏmi). *Dentistry.* [f. PULP *sb.* + -O + -TOMY.] Surgical removal of the pulp of a tooth (usu. part of it only: cf. *PULPECTOMY).

1923 [see *PULPECTOMY]. **1924** F. E. HOGEBOOM *Pract. Pedodontia* v. 66 Pulpotomy means the partial removal of the pulp. **1957** S. B. FINN *Clin. Pedodontics* xiv. 318 Pulpotomies can be performed on teeth which have been exposed for as long as 72 hours. *Ibid.* 317 There are four courses of treatment open to the dentist: (1) pulp capping, (2) pulpotomy, (3) pulpectomy with or without apicoectomy, and (4) extraction of the tooth. **1976** ETTINGER & PINKHAM in A. J. Nowak *Dentistry for Handicapped Patient* xvi. 286/1 The contraindications to pulpotomies in the chronically ill patient are the same as for direct pulp capping.

pulpwood: see PULP *sb.* 5b in Dict. and Suppl.

pulpy, *a.* Add: **1.** (Later *fig.* examples in sense *4c of the sb.)

1939 R. CHANDLER *Let.* 19 Feb. (1966) 195 *The Big Sleep* is very unequally written. There are scenes that are all right, but there are other scenes still much too pulpy. **1978** *Nature* 27 Apr. 786/1 Even the pulpiest science fiction includes this.

2. *pulpy kidney* (*disease*), a clostridial enterotoxæmia of sheep characterized by rapid post-mortem degeneration of the kidneys.

1927 *N.Z. Jrnl. Agric.* XXXIV. 217 (*heading*) 'Pulpy kidney' disease of lambs. *Ibid.* 227 Out of a mob of 290 lambs twelve died, presumably from 'pulpy kidney'. **1938** tr. *F. Hutyra's Special Path. & Therapeutics Dis. Domestic Animals* (ed. 4) III. 14 In Australia..an epizootic type of severe renal degeneration known as 'pulpy kidney disease' occurs..(the symptoms are paralysis and convulsions, and death occurs in 3 to 7 hours). **1953** *Cape Argus* 21 Mar. 7/3 Pulpy kidney disease is taking a heavy toll among sheep in the Lady Grey district. **1970** 'J. HERRIOT' *If only they could Talk* xxv. 149 The diseases which beset the lambs themselves—swayback, pulpy kidney, dysentery.

pulque. Add: **b.** *pulque alcohol, shop.*

1931 H. CRANE *Let.* 21 Sept. (1965) 382 Straight pulque alcohol in each cup. **1836** C. A. GOODRICH *Universal Traveller* 139 But, unfortunately, in the lanes near the market are found numbers of pulque-shops (pulquerias). **1910** *N.Y. Even. Post* 16 July (Sat. Suppl.) 3/2 All of the sweet savors of Araby combined could make slight headway against the reek of a pulque shop.

‖ **pulqueria** (pulkerī·ă). [Sp. Amer.] In Mexico, a shop or tavern selling pulque.

1822 J. R. POINSETT *Diary* 28 Oct. in *Notes on Mexico* (1824) v. 49 They go to the pulqueria, and there dance, carouse, and get drunk on pulque and *vino mezcal*. **1847** G. A. F. RUXTON *Adventures Mexico & Rocky Mts.* vii. 43 After leaving the pulqueria, we visited..the dens where these people congregate for the night. **1914** C. J. C. HYNE *Firemen Hot* i. 2 By the time these [dollars] had been passed across the grimy counter of a pulqueria.. they received [etc.]. **1922** *Outward Bound* Nov. 110/2 In the great pulquerias, or saloons..the gramophone is invariably to be found. **1934** S. E. WHITE *Folded Hills* 375 He can play his guitar and entertain the drunkards in the *pulquerias*.

pulsar (pʊ·lsāɹ). [f. *puls*(*ating st*)*ar*, after *QUASAR.] **1.** *Astr.* A cosmic source of radio signals that pulsates with great regularity at intervals of the order of a second or less, and is believed to be a rapidly rotating neutron star. Also *fig.*

1968 *Daily Tel.* 5 Mar. 21/3 An entirely novel kind of star..came to light on Aug. 6 last year and,..was referred to by astronomers as LGM (Little Green Men). Now..it is thought to be a novel type between a white dwarf and a neutron [*sic*]. The name Pulsar (Pulsating Star) is likely to be given to it... Dr. A. Hewish..told me yesterday: '..I am sure that today every radio telescope is looking at the Pulsars.' **1968** *Time* 26 Apr. 82 Under the careful scrutiny of increasing numbers of scientists around the world, astronomy's newest sensation —the pulsars—continued to beep away last week, confounding observers, with the breathtaking regularity of their signals. **1969** *New Yorker* 19 Apr. 55/1 A tough-looking astronomer, whose ideas stretch beyond the moon to quasars and pulsars. **1972** *Sci. Amer.* July 37/2 Although the pulsar in the Crab Nebula was first discovered at radio frequencies and was later studied visually, most of its energy is emitted in the X-ray range. **1973** L. M. BOSTON *Memory in House* xi. 132 Oscar is a pulsar, an output of concentrated energy. **1977** *Dædalus* Fall 45 Pulsars, that is, rotating neutron stars, have been detected in the Crab Nebula and in Vela X, a supernova remnant about ten times older than the Crab Nebula.

2. A kind of digital wrist-watch. (A proprietary name in the U.S.)

1970 *Daily Tel.* 14 May 13/7 Production is expected to begin next year, but at first pulsars will be sold in a limited edition at $1,500. **1971** *Official Gaz.* (U.S. Patent Office) 31 Aug. TM240/1 Hamilton Watch Co, Lancaster, Pa... *Pulsar* for watches... First use Apr. 27, 1970. **1977** R. E. HARRINGTON *Quintain* iii. 21 He flipped his wrist and the pulsar wristwatch winked on. **1979** G. SWARTHOUT *Skeletons* 69, I punched my Pulsar. Two minutes past nine p.m.

pulsatance (pʊlsēⁱ·tăns). *Physics.* [f. PULSATE *v.* + -ANCE.] The angular frequency of a periodic motion, i.e. 2π times its actual frequency.

1919 A. CAMPBELL in *Proc. Physical Soc.* XXXI. 81 In English a name has not yet been found for $2\pi n$, where n represents frequency... I would suggest that it might be called 'pulsatance'. The termination 'ance' brings it into line with words like inductance and reactance. **1946** *Electronic Engin.* XVIII. 119 The displacement (D) at any point is a periodic time function of the form: $D = \psi \sin \omega t$ ..where ω is the pulsatance and ψ is the amplitude at any point in space. **1957** *Electronic & Radio Engineer* XXXIV. 145/2 Equation (22) represents a phase vibration of natural undamped pulsatance ωn and damping factor ζ.

pulsatility. (Later examples.)

1930 *Amer. Jrnl. Physiol.* XCI. 716 The venous return to the chest must show a pulsatility which is nearly synchronous with the pulsatile outflow. **1977** *Lancet* 3 Sept. 490/2 They observed that the peak venous flow can be increased seven-fold, and its pulsatility thirty fold.

pulsating, *ppl. a.* (s.v. PULSATE *v.*). Add: *spec.* of an electric current or voltage: flowing or acting in one direction but with a periodically varying strength.

1912 THIESS & JOY *Toll Telephone Practice* ii. 20 The pulsating current is used in signaling the exchange and the alternating current for calling the various subscribers on the line by means of the usual code rings. **1960** H. W. JACKSON *Introd. Electric Circuits* ix. 202 The tendency of inductance to oppose any change in current can be used to advantage in filtering or smoothing variations in load current that would otherwise occur when the load is fed from a d-c source..which provides a pulsating emf.

pulsational, *a.* Delete *rare* and add further examples.

1969 *Nature* 19 July 279/1 Despite the trend of recent evidence..that radial pulsations may not be the source of variation in pulsars, the pulsational hypothesis has still not been disproved. **1976** *Ibid.* 15 Jan. 88/2 Periods decrease with increase of λ and of polytropic index n..for all different modes of oscillations (pulsational, transverse shear, and toroidal, modes).

Hence **pulsa·tionally** *adv.*

1969 *Nature* 19 July 280/1 Thermonuclear reactions are extremely effective in pulsationally destabilizing a degenerate star.

pulsator. Add: **4.** *Agric.* A device on a milking machine which releases the suction on the teat intermittently so as to simulate the sucking action of a calf.

1907 *Jrnl. R. Agric. Soc.* LXVIII. 133 By another flexible connection the pail communicates with a vacuum pipe, and an air exhaust, by which the pulsators are actuated. **1931** J. B. DAVIDSON *Agric. Machinery* xxxii. 339 The pulsator is an air valve so constructed as to alternate suction and release. **1950** *N.Z. Jrnl. Agric.* LXXX. 568/2 Efficient milking is not possible with leaking pulsators. **1970** R. JEFFRIES *Dead Man's Bluff* i. 12 The milk began to spurt into the glass jars... The rhythmic clicking of the pulsator, working off the vacuum line, gave him a conscious feeling of well-being.

pulse, *sb.*¹ Add: **2. c.** Phr. *on the pulse* (and variants): through one's own experience (with allusion to Keats's use).

1818 KEATS *Let.* 3 May (1931) I. 154 Axioms in philosophy are not axioms until they are proved upon our pulses. We read fine things, but never feel them to the full until we have gone the same steps as the Author. **1970** *Guardian* 23 July 10/3 As I am one of his constituents, the appointment of Sir Robert Grant-Ferris..as Deputy Speaker..has made me feel 'on the pulse'..a frustrating anomaly of our parliamentary system. **1971** R. AP ROBERTS *Trollope* ii. 42 The problem of *The Warden* is— one might say—proved on our pulses. **1973** *Listener* 6 Dec. 798/3 The committed nationalism of, say, the 19th-century Russian composers, who had felt oppression on the pulse.

4. b. In scientific use now *spec.* (*a*) a train of radio waves, sound waves, or the like, of very short duration; a short burst of radiated energy; (*b*) the more usual term for *IMPULSE *sb.* 4*.

(*a*) **1905** S. R. BOTTONE *Radium* (ed. 2) iv. 74 A third kind of emanation is also produced by radium... Röntgen rays—ether vibrations—produced as a secondary phenomena by the sudden arrest of velocity of the electrons by the solid matter, producing a series of Stokesian 'pulses' or explosive ether waves, shot into space. **1906** *Nature* 29 Nov. 105/2 The signal produced by a spark discharge consists of a series of violent pulses each consisting of a short train of strongly damped vibrations of definite frequency. **1945** H. D. SMYTH *Gen. Acct. Devel. Atomic Energy Mil. Purposes* xii. 131 In this method a neutron source is modulated, i.e., the source is made to emit neutrons in short 'bursts' or 'pulses'. **1947** CROWTHER & WHIDDINGTON *Science at War* 16 Meanwhile the pulse flies on, reaches the aircraft, and is reflected back as an echo. **1969** *Times* 8 Jan. 12/1 Working from the measured length of the successive pulses of energy, it was possible to calculate that the stars concerned would have been as massive as the sun but rather smaller than the earth in size. **1978** *Sci. Amer.* Apr. 38/2 The bats and whales were before us, but now we humans make routine use of pulses of ultrasound (or of microwave) to map the night or the depths.

(*b*) **1932** *Proc. Physical Soc.* XLIV. 77 A transformer.. translated the square-topped current pulsations into voltage pulses, alternately positive and negative, of very short duration. **1949** B. GROB *Basic Television* v. 63 The amplitude of the video signal is divided into two sections, the lower 75 per cent being devoted to the active camera signal while the upper 25 per cent is used for the synchronizing pulses. **1967** *Electronics* 6 Mar. 159/2 A simple change in d-c level cannot be used as a trigger because it locks up the flip-flop against further changes; a pulse is a must. **1975** D. G. FINK *Electronics Engineers' Handbk.* XVI. 6 In the field of radio-frequency interference..the basic response curve of the receiver is defined in terms of its response to regularly repeated pulses... The area under the pulse must be a known constant which is a function of a limited number of circuit parameters.

d. A temporary upward movement of magma through the earth's crust.

1964 *Nature* 13 June 1100/2 Difficulties with this concept have led petrologists..to postulate a pulse mechanism to explain such features as the magnetite layer near the top of the Main Norite Zone of the Bushveld Igneous Complex. **1970** *Ibid.* 25 July 365/1 A more restricted pulse (heave) of magma. **1977** A. HALLAM *Planet Earth* 68

Occasionally a new pulse of magma on its way to the surface breaks off fragments that emerge as xenoliths included in lava flows or ash falls.

4*. *Biochem.* A period during which a culture of cells is supplied with an isotopically labelled substrate or substrates. Also *attrib.* Cf. *PULSE *v.* 5.

1960 *Jrnl. Molecular Biol.* II. 308 Phage infection and the subsequent ^{32}P pulse experiment were performed at 28°C. **1961** *Nature* 13 May 580/1 The nascent protein can be labelled by a short pulse of $^{35}SO_4$. **1974** *Ibid.* 25 Jan. 243/1 If a long molecule is labelled at one end (as happens with a short pulse label) and then sheared, the labelled molecules will always appear to have lower molecular weights than the bulk material.

5. Now freq. also in sense 4b. **a.** *pulse amplitude, height, repetition* (or *recurrence*) *frequency* (or *rate*), *rate* (example of different sense), *train, width.* **b.** *pulse amplifier, analyser, compression, counter* (examples of different sense), *generator, transformer; pulse-amplifying, -counting, -forming, -generating, -shaping* adjs., *pulse-taking* (*lit.* and *fig.*). **c. pulse amplitude modulation** *Telecommunications,* pulse modulation in which variations in the signal are represented by variations in the amplitude of the pulses; **pulse code modulation** *Telecommunications,* pulse modulation in which the actual signal amplitude after each successive interval is approximated by the nearest in value of a set of permitted amplitudes, which is then represented by a short sequence of pulses in accordance with a binary code; **pulse column** = *pulsed column* s.v. *PULSED *ppl. a.* a; **pulse duration modulation** *Telecommunications* = *pulse width modulation* below; **pulse frequency modulation** *Telecommunications,* pulse modulation in which variations in the signal are represented by variations in the frequency of occurrence of the pulses; **pulse jet** *Aeronaut.,* a type of jet engine in which combustion is intermittent, the ignition and expulsion of each charge of mixture causing the intake of a fresh charge; **pulse-la·bel** *v. trans. Biochem.,* to label the metabolites of (cells) by administering a pulse (sense *4*); so **pulse-la·belled** *ppl. a.,* **pulse-la·belling** *vbl. sb.*; **pulse modulation** *Telecommunications,* modulation in which a series of initially identical, regularly recurring pulses is varied in some respect (as amplitude or timing) so as to represent the amplitude of the signal after successive short intervals of time; so **pulse-modulated** *a.,* **pulse modulator; pulse position modulation** *Telecommunications,* pulse modulation in which variations in the signal are represented by variations in the time position of the pulses, relative to their unmodulated position; **pulse pressure** *Med.,* the difference between the maximum (systolic) and the minimum (diastolic) pressure of arterial blood; **pulse radar,** radar that transmits pulses rather than a continuous beam of radio energy; **pulse radiolysis,** radiolysis by means of a very short pulse of electrons or other ionizing radiation; **pulse repeater** *Electronics* (see quot. 1971); **pulse time modulation** *Telecommunications,* pulse position or pulse width modulation; so **pulse-time-modulated** *a.*; **pulse width modulation** *Telecommunications,* pulse modulation in which variations in the signal are represented by variations in the width (duration) of the pulses; **pulse-wise** *adv.,* discontinuously; a bit at a time.

1940 *Rev. Sci. Instruments* XI. 44/1 The use of ionization chambers in conjunction with pulse amplifiers permits data to be taken much more rapidly. **1949** [see *pulse height* below]. **1962** Simpson & Richards *Physical Princ. Junction Transistors* xv. 371 (*heading*) Video pulse-amplifier equivalent circuits. *Ibid.* viii. 182 This makes the point-contact transistor inherently unstable under certain conditions and makes possible the construction of simple pulse-amplifying or trigger circuits. **1940** *Rev. Sci. Instruments* XI. 45/1 (*caption*) Wiring diagram of the pulse amplitude selector. **1947** [see *KICKSORTER]. **1947** *Bell Syst. Technical Jrnl.* XXVI. 396 When the pulses consist simply of short samples of the speech waves, their varying amplitudes directly represent the speech waves and the system is called pulse amplitude modulation or PAM. **1963** B. Fozard *Instrumentation Nuclear Reactors* iv. 42 Discrimination against gamma rays is obtained by using a pulse amplitude discriminator in conjunction with the counter. **1972** Pulse amplitude modulation [see *MODULATION 7]. **1947** Pulse analyser [see *KICKSORTER]. **1963** B. Fozard *Instrumentation Nuclear Reactors* x. 123 In some applications it is required to determine the count rate of pulses of a particular amplitude or..whose amplitudes lie in the band V and $V+\delta V$... Instruments known as pulse analysers are available which give the required result directly. **1947** Pulse code modulation [see PCM s.v. *P II]. **1967** *Times* 7 Feb. 9/3 The Post Office is to start work on the installation..of the world's first pulse code modulation exchange. This technique makes it possible for two ordinary telephone 'pairs' to carry 24 simultaneous conversations. **1976** *B.B.C. Handbk.* 71/2 Pulse Code Modulation is the system developed by BBC engineers for the distribution of high-quality stereophonic audio signals. **1954** R. Stephenson *Introd. Nuclear Engin.* ix. 333 The principal advantage of pulse columns is their greater plate efficiency which permits a column of smaller height for a given separation. **1966** *New Scientist* 15 Sept. 609/1 By employing pulse-compression radar techniques the designer can..produce a radar which has long range and yet gives good definition. **1975** D. G. Fink *Electronics Engineers' Handbk.* xxv. 74 Pulse compression is a technique in which a rectangular pulse containing phase modulation is transmitted. When the echo is received, the matched-filter output is a pulse of much shorter duration. **1963** B. Fozard *Instrumentation Nuclear Reactors* xiii. 166 Two scales..indicate approximately (*a*) the current produced in a reactor instrumentation ionisation chamber..and (*b*) the pulse rate produced by a fission-type pulse counter. *Ibid.* viii. 74 Pulse-counting systems are commonly used to measure radiation intensity in terms of count rate. **1956** S. Seely *Radio Electronics* xv. 439 In pulse-duration modulation and pulse-position modulation..the signal/noise ratio is proportional to the bandwidth. **1975** Pulse duration modulation [see *pulse position modulation* below]. **1947** Lebacqz & White in L. N. Ridenour *Radar System Engin.* x. 376 A pulse transformer can be inserted between load and pulse-forming network so that the network can be designed to use the available switching device most efficiently. **1950** Pulse frequency modulation [see *communication(s) engineer* s.v. *COMMUNICATION 12]. **1975** Pulse frequency modulation [see *pulse time modulation* below]. **1975** Pulse-generating [see *pulse transformer* below]. **1931** *Proc. IRE* XXII. 911 (*caption*) Transmitter and pulse generator with cathode ray oscillograph monitor. **1977** *Navy News* June 42 (Advt.), Ideally, applicants should be familiar with oscilloscopes, digital multimeters, pulse generators, frequency counters, etc. **1949** *Atomics* Sept. 57/1 When the gating instrument is in operation, random pulses from a Geiger counter are fed through the pulse amplifier to the pulse height selector. **1952** *Proc. Physical Soc.* B. LXV. 320 An investigation of the pulse heights produced by alpha-particles in various scintillating crystals. **1957** *Economist* 30 Nov. 779/1 Because it sorts out electrical 'kicks' or impulses according to their amplitude—more than 16,000 of them in each of 100 channels..'kick sorter' is the technicians' colloquial name for a Pulse Height Analyser. **1962** F. I. Ordway et al. *Basic Astronautics* iv. 137 The pulse height distribution of the incident particles is obtained.. by means of a sliding-channel, pulse-height analyzer. **1968** Pulse-height [see *KICKSORTER]. **1946** F. Hamann *Air Words* 43/1 *Pulse-jet,* a jet plane or motor that.. operates in short bursts of power or impulses. **1949** *Aircraft Engin.* Mar. 71/3 No analysis will decide whether ram-jet or pulse-jet is the better—such questions are decided by service experience. **1966** *McGraw-Hill Encycl. Sci. & Technol.* XI. 95/2 In addition to their use on the German V-1 buzz-bomb, pulse jets have been used to propel radio controlled target drones and experimental helicopters. **1961** *Nature* 13 May 581 (*heading*) Unstable ribonucleic acid revealed by pulse labelling of *Escherichia coli.* **1968** H. Harris *Nucleus & Cytoplasm* iii. 42 When the pulse-labelled cells were transferred to non-radioactive medium, radioactivity disappeared from the heterogeneous component and appeared in the ribosomal RNA. *Ibid.,* The pulse-labelling revealed a special class of RNA which was not ribosomal RNA or a precursor of ribosomal RNA. **1974** *Nature* 8 Nov. 168/1 Yeast protoplasts were pulse labelled for 30 min with H-adenine, then quickly cooled and lysed by osmotic shock. **1943** *Gloss. Terms Telecommunication* (*B.S.I.*) 65 *Pulse-modulated waves,* recurrent wave-trains in which the duration of the trains is, in general, short compared with the time interval between them. **1962** *Science Survey* III. 279 They also respond to pulse-modulated sounds up to pulse repetition rates of about 800 cycles per sec. **1929** *Proc. IRE* XVII. 1787 It could not be predicted with certainty that the transmitter crystal would provide a suitably constant phase reference for comparison with the echoes, particularly because of the fact that its phase..might be shifted slightly by the pulse modulation of the power amplifiers excited by the crystal circuit. **1945** *Electronics* Jan. 103/3 With pulse modulation, especially at very high carrier frequencies, problems of modulation at the transmitter are greatly simplified. **1975** D. G. Fink *Electronics Engineers' Handbk.* xiv. 28 All pulse modulation schemes require sampling analog signals, and some, such as pulse code modulation.., require the additional quantization of the analog signals. **1965** *Wireless World* July 18 (Advt.), EEV magnetrons, klystrons, pulse modulators,..offer extreme reliability in quality marine electronics. **1945** *Electronic Industries* Dec. 82 (*heading*) Pulse position modulation technic. **1975** D. G. Fink *Electronics Engineers' Handbk.* xiv. 34 In PTM the information is coded into the time parameter instead of, for instance, the amplitude... There are two basic types of PTM: pulse position modulation (PPM) and pulse width modulation (PWM), which is also known as pulse duration (PDM). **1904** J. Erlanger in *Johns Hopkins Hosp. Rep.* XII. 93 The term 'pulse-pressure' is used in place of the phrase, oscillations of the pressure in the arteries produced by the beat of the heart. It is the difference between the maximum and minimum pressures. **1966** *Lancet* 24 Dec. 1387/1 Fig. 1 shows the mean responses of pulse-rate and pulse-pressure during the insulin-tolerance tests in the six men. **1949** D. G. C. Luck *Frequency Modulated Radar* ix. 416 Pulse radar is placed at a practical disadvantage, relatively to frequency-modulated radar, by the necessity of operating transmitters at very high peak-power levels. **1966** *McGraw-Hill Encycl. Sci. & Technol.* XI. 211/2 In pulse-radar systems the transmitter and receiver generally share a single antenna. [**1960** McCarthy & MacLachlan in *Trans. Faraday Soc.* LVI. 1187 The technique of pulsed radiolysis has not heretofore been applied to the transient measurement of rapid chemical reactions.] **1961** *Nucleonics* Oct. 54/1 Pulse radiolysis has become feasible within the past few years though the availability of electron accelerators which deliver a very short pulse of high energy electrons of extremely high intensity. **1974** *Nature* 22 Nov. 323/1 On pulse radiolysis of nitrous oxide saturated solutions of either thymidine, cytidine, adenosine or guanosine..transient absorption spectra..attributable to the products of reactions of the hydroxyl radical, were observed. **1963** Pulse rate [see *pulse counter* above]. **1945** *Amer. Speech* XX. 310/1 *PRF,* Pulse Recurrence Frequency. **1953** R. Chisholm *Cover of Darkness* xvii. 187 He listened patiently to discussions on megacycles, wave-lengths and pulse-recurrence frequencies. **1949** *Jrnl. R. Aeronaut. Soc.* LIII. 447/2 The Americans now used both words, defining a transponder as a pulse repeater which received and transmitted on different wavelengths. **1971** *Gloss. Electrotechnical, Power Terms* (*B.S.I.*) iii. i. 28 *Pulse repeater,* device for receiving pulses from one circuit and transmitting corresponding pulses into another circuit. **1948** L. B. Arguimbau *Vacuum-Tube Circuits* xi. 560 Depending on the pulse height, the multivibrator will synchronize at one fifth, one fourth, or one third of the pulse repetition rate. **1962** *Gloss. Terms Automatic Data Processing* (*B.S.I.*) 57 When the pulse repetition rate is independent of the interval of time over which it is measured it may be called the pulse repetition frequency. **1978** R. V. Jones *Most Secret War* xxiii. 193 If 40 kilometres were its maximum range, its pulse repetition rate should not exceed 3750 per second. **1963** B. Fozard *Instrumentation Nuclear Reactors* ix. 105 Pulses from the counter are converted by means of an auxiliary pulse-shaping (multivibrator) circuit into rectangular positive pulses of stable amplitude. **1971** J. H. Smith *Digital Logic* v. 95 Flip flop *A* is used as a pulse shaping circuit and has no logical function to perform. **1950** *N.Y. Times* (City ed.) 20 Apr. 1/1 In the light of today's pulse-taking, it appeared unlikely that the committee would agree on such an approach. **1977** *Proc. R. Soc. Med.* LXX. 425/1 We know that pulse-taking was an important ritual, especially among doctors who did not accept Harvey's discovery of the circulation of blood. **1945** *Electronic Industries* Nov. 91/3 At the transmission end amplitude modulated speech signals are changed into pulse time modulated signals by a tube similar to the cyclophone called the Cyclo-odos. **1944** *Electr. Communication* XXII. 92/1 The merits of another method of transmission applicable to telephony were considered by the Paris Laboratories of the International Telephone and Telegraph Corporation early in 1937... At the time the method was called pulse 'time' modulation. **1975** D. G. Fink *Electronics Engineers' Handbk.* xiv. 28 The control applications [of pulse modulation] are usually confined to the use of pulse time modulation (PTM) and pulse frequency modulation (PFM), where on-off control power can be used to minimize device dissipation. **1951** A. Sheingold *Fund. Radio Communications* xx. 413 If the pulse train is applied to a low-pass filter having an appropriate cutoff value, the signal may be separated from the higher-frequency pulse components. **1975** D. G. Fink *Electronics Engineers' Handbk.* xiv. 28 By interleaving a number of single-channel, low-duty-cycle pulse trains. **1945** *Electronic Industries* Sept. 222 *Pulse transformer,* a special transformer designed to have a frequency response suitable for passing a pulse without materially altering its shape. **1955** *Times* 12 July 2/5 (Advt.), Applicants should preferably be of honours degree standard, with interest in square-loop magnetic devices, ferro-resonant circuits, magnetic amplifiers, or pulse transformers. **1975** D. G. Fink *Electronics Engineers' Handbk.* vii. 18 Lower-power pulse transformers fall into two categories: those used for coupling or impedance matching similar to the high-power pulse transformers, and blocking oscillator transformers used in pulse-generating circuits. **1947** R. Lee *Electronic Transformers & Circuits* ix. 220 Common pulse widths lie between 0·5 and 10 microseconds. **1978** *Nature* 23 Mar. 362/2 The digital nerves of the index finger were stimulated continuously at 3 times the threshold for perception (pulse width 50 μs, 50 shocks s^{-1}) through ring electrodes placed around the finger on either side of the distal interphalangeal joint. **1953** A. T. Starr *Radio & Radar Technique* i. 26 Pulse Width Modulation does not correspond to any normally emitted C. W. system, but corresponds to phase modulations of the frequencies $\omega\tilde{r}$, $2\omega\tilde{r}$,...each multiplied by the original low-frequency signal. **1978** *Gramophone* Apr. 1790/1 Sony offered the first class D (pulse width modulation) power amplifier utilizing VFETs and producing 180 watts per channel. **1909** W. James *Pluralistic Universe* vii. 285 By us it [*sc.* reality] has to be taken pulse-wise, for our span of consciousness is too short to grasp the larger collectivity of things except nominally and abstractly.

pulse, *v.* Add: **4.** (Further examples.)

1954 R. Stephenson *Introd. Nuclear Engin.* ix. 332 One of the two liquid phases present is pulsed at the rate of about 60 pulses/min, each pulse causing the liquid in the column to oscillate over a distance of about 0·9 in. **1971** C. J. King *Separation Processes* xiv. 740 The contents of either a packed column or a plate column can be pulsed by applying intermittent surges of pump pressure to the column. This pulsing promotes mass-transfer rates within the column. **1977** *Design Engin.* July 27/2 Energy in high power radar systems..is pulsed through a magnetron in discrete 'pockets' to allow the returning echo to be related in time with the initial transmission.

5. *trans. Biochem.* To subject (cells in culture) to a pulse of isotopically labelled substrate or substrates.

1960 *Jrnl. Molecular Biol.* II. 320 Uninfected cells were pulsed with ^{32}P under the same conditions and the purified soluble RNA was examined. **1975** *Nature* 14 Aug. 592/1 After various incubation periods the cells were pulsed for 1h with labelled amino acids or nucleosides, collected and macromolecular synthesis measured.

6. *trans.* To apply a pulsed signal to.

1964 *Ann. N.Y. Acad. Sci.* CXV. 665 The..16 digital output lines..can be pulsed individually by a special computer instruction. **1974** *Physics Bull.* June 257/1 The transmitter consists of a small loudspeaker pulsed by a capacitor discharge and the echoes are received by a small conventional microphone.

7. *trans.* To modulate (a wave, beam, etc.) so that it becomes a series of pulses.

1969 *Sci. Jrnl.* Dec. 42/3 Semiconductor lasers whose

output may be modulated up to 1 GHz by pulsing the pump current. **1971** *Nature* 26 Nov. 178/2 High-powered monochromatic beams of laser light..may be modulated or pulsed in times as short as 10^{-11}s. **1975** D. G. FINK *Electronics Engineers' Handbk.* xiv. 28 In usual applications [of pulse modulation], subcarriers are pulsed, time-division-multiplexed, and then used to frequency-modulate a carrier.

pulsed (pʌlst), *ppl. a.* [f. PULSE *v.* + -ED[1].]

a. Producing or involving pulses.

pulsed column: a tower for solvent extraction in which the natural countercurrent flow of the feed liquid and the solvent has mechanically superimposed on it a rapid reciprocating motion of small amplitude, in order to promote the extraction process.

1946 *Radar: Summary Rep. & Harp Project* (U.S. Nat. Defense Res. Comm., Div. 14) 143/1 Pulsed Doppler shift. **1949** *Jrnl. R. Aeronaut. Soc.* LIII. 439/1 A system employing secondary radar, i.e. a pulsed ground station working in conjunction with a responder, has been designed. **1958** *Engineering* 14 Feb. 205/3 The solvent and water solutions quickly separate after the mixing-contacting process, be this in a packed or pulsed counter-current contactor column or a mixer-settler unit. **1972** *McGraw-Hill Yearbk. Sci. & Technol.* 268/1 Progress in the development of CW devices has spurred renewed interest in pulsed chemical lasers as..sources of the very-high-energy pulses..needed for plasma heating experiments. **1978** R. V. JONES *Most Secret War* ii. 16 In 1931 W. A. S. Butement and P. E. Pollard..had devised and made a pulsed radio system on a wavelength of about 50 centimetres for detecting ships. **1978** *Nature* 23 Mar. 298/3 Because oxide fuel is highly radioactive, the process is carried out in pulsed columns (rather than mixer settlers) to minimise the contact time between the solvent and the dissolved acid fuel.

b. Consisting of pulses; in the form of pulses.

1949 *Jrnl. R. Aeronaut. Soc.* LIII. 438/1 (*heading*) Measurement of the density of the upper atmosphere by radar—pulsed violet or ultra-violet light. **1955** FRIEDMAN & WEISSKOPF in W. Pauli *Niels Bohr* 155 A pulsed initial neutron beam. **1957** F. HOYLE *Black Cloud* ix. 182 We ought to start sending pulsed messages on the one centimetre [wave-length]. **1971** *Nature* 16 Apr. 426/1 The X-rays from the hitherto unsurprising source Cygnus X-1 are pulsed at a rate of probably about 15 pulses per second.

pulser (pʌ·lsəɹ). [f. PULSE *sb.*[1] or *v.* + -ER[1].]

1. A device that generates electrical pulses.

1947 LEBACQZ & WHITE in L. N. Ridenour *Radar System Engin.* x. 373 Successful hard-tube pulsers have been made with power outputs up to 3 or 4 Mw. **1973** *Sci. Amer.* June 47/1 The resolution time, or fastest shutter time, of this type of gate is determined by the shortest duration provided by an electrical voltage pulser: about a nanosecond. **1978** *Ibid.* Mar. 58/3 The base houses..a dial pulser to signal the required numbers to the central office and a bell to signal an incoming call to the subscriber.

2. A machine for producing mechanical pulsation in a liquid.

1954 R. STEPHENSON *Introd. Nuclear Engin.* ix. 334 Until satisfactory pulsers are developed..it is doubtful that pulse columns will find any extensive use except for very special solvent extraction operations. **1963** J. H. PERRY *Chem. Engineers' Handbk.* (ed. 4) XXI. 33/1 The pipe connecting column and pulser may be of any length .., but high pressure drop in the transfer pipe contributes to cavitation difficulties.

pulsing, *vbl. sb.* (Further examples.)

1945 *Electronics* Jan. 105/1 The method of pulsing involved frequency-modulating the transmitter ±75 kc by a continuous 170-cycle tone. **1971** [see *PULSE *v.* 4].

pulsive, *a.* Add: **3.** Making a beating or throbbing sound.

1960 'W. HAGGARD' *Closed Circuit* x. 123 He knew a band, quite a small one, quiet and properly pulsive. **1969** G. MACBETH *War Quartet* 43 In wave On gathered wave of pulsive thumping, wings Grazed overhead.

pultrusion (pul-, pʌltrū·ʒən). [f. PUL(LING *vbl. sb.* + EX)TRUSION.] A process for making plastic articles reinforced with glass fibre in which long strands of the reinforcement, encased in liquid resin, are pulled through a heated die that shapes and cures the resin.

1964 OLEESKY & MOHR *Handbk. Reinforced Plastics* v. 324 (*caption*) 'Pultrusion' tank design. **1965** *Mod. Plastics Encycl. 1966* 632/2 Long lengths of reinforced plastics flat strip or sheet..can be produced economically by the pultrusion process. **1968, 1976** [see below].

Hence **pultru·de** *v. trans.*, to make by this process; **pultru·ded** *ppl. a.*

1968 *6th Internat. Reinforced Plastics Conf.* (Brit. Plastics Federation) 6/1/1 The pull-trusion process is the oldest one of the technical processes nowadays used for a continuous production of glassfibre reinforced polyester articles... The percentage of pull-truded products made from glassfibre reinforced polyester has considerably increased. **1971** *Mod. Plastics Encycl. 1970–1* 592/3 Typical volume applications for pultruded products are electrical pole line hardware, ladders, fishing rods and corrosion-resistant structural shapes. **1976** *S9* (N.Y.) May/June 116/2 Plastigage Corporation..has developed and perfected a new method to produce pultruded fiberglass rod ideal for OEM. **1976** *Reinforced Plastics* XX. 295/2 Another advantage of the pultrusion process is the ability to produce a number of similarly dimensioned products at the same time. Currently, the company are pultruding hollow section rods and solid rods at the same time. *Ibid.* 295/3 Early models of the Sky Stunter kite used aluminium tubing for the framework, but this has now been replaced with the pultruded components.

pulu. (Earlier and later examples.)

1833 W. TOLMIE *Jrnl.* 6 Apr. in *Physician & Fur Trader* (1963) 144 Met Madame Boki & retinue, her brows encircled with garlands of pulu. **1917** *Nature* 20 Sept. 58/1 These plants [*sc.* Hawaiian tree ferns] produce at the base of the stipe a great ball of brownish-yellow wool called pulu by the natives, and used by them for stuffing pillows and mattresses.

‖ **pulut** (pū·lut, pūlū). [Mal. (*padi*) *pulut* sticky (rice).] In Malaysia, glutinous rice.

1820 J. CRAWFURD *Hist. Indian Archipel.* I. IV. ii. 360 The most singular variety [of rice] is that called by the Malays *Pulut*.., the *Oryza glutinosa* of Rumphius. This is never used as bread, but commonly prepared as a sweetmeat. **1900** W. W. SKEAT *Malay Magic* 76 A special kind of glutinous rice called *pulut*..is also very generally used for sacrificial banquets. **1972** A. AMIN tr. *Ahmad's No Harvest but Thorn* ii. 10 Our children love *pulut* in the mornings before school. With *pulut* the fullness lasts a long time. *Ibid.* xiv. 148 They would also separate the *Thai* rice from the *pulut* rice.

pulverized, *ppl. a.* (Further examples.)

1926 *Jrnl. Iron & Steel Inst.* CXIII. 507 The author continues his account of practice in the use of pulverised fuel, dealing with the efficiency of the method of powdered coal-firing as compared with other methods. **1950** *Engineering* 28 July 79/1 Where a high proportion of heat recovery was required in the air heater, pulverised-fuel firing was essential. **1976** *Horse & Hound* 10 Dec. 64/2 (Advt.), The latest in animal bedding... Made from pulverised wood—cheaper than straw.

pulverizer. (Further examples.)

1956 [see *OF *prep.* 43 b]. **1967** *Punch* 6 Sept. 360/1 A small East Anglian local authority..would like to dump over 160,000 cubic yards of garbage in the four sidings... If they spend a further £30,000 on a pulveriser (which reduces all forms of household trash to a quarter of its collected volume and renders the result unattractive to flies and rodents) this novel dump should last them for sixteen years. **1971** P. GRESSWELL *Environment* 153 Giant pulverisers can shred a complete car to fist size fragments within seconds.

pulvin, pulvino (pʌ·lvin, pʌlvī·no). *Archit.* [It. *pulvino* pillow.] A cushion cap, impost-block or dosseret.

1907 *Athenæum* 30 Mar. 389/2 The use of the pulvino to enable a thick wall above to be carried on the comparatively slender diameter of the classic column. **1910** G. McN. RUSHFORTH tr. *Rivoira's Lombardic Archit.* I. i. 8 The capitals..supported pulvins ('pulvini') or impost blocks, marked with crosses. *Ibid.* 12 From Ravenna and Naples the pulvin spread over Italy and beyond. *Ibid.* II. vi. 300 The corbel pulvins with rudely curled ends..are derived from the crutch-shaped pulvins, a Lombard creation of the Xth century. **1913** T. G. JACKSON *Byzantine & Romanesque Archit.* I. iv. 52 On the capital they placed a block of stone spreading upwards from the width of the column where it rested on the abacus, to the width of the wall above, and from the top of this stone they sprang their arch, of the full thickness of the wall. This dosseret, pulvino, or impost block is an entirely novel feature. *Ibid.* xi. 171 It is difficult to follow him in claiming the invention of the pulvino for Ravenna on the strength of its use in the church of S. Giov. Evangelista in 425; for he assigns the same date to the much more important Eski Djourna at Salonica where the pulvino is thoroughly developed. **1933** J. A. HAMILTON *Byzantine Archit. & Decoration* ii. 26 Constructive reasons led to the introduction of the impost (pulvino: dosseret) above the capital... The impost was a block, approximately of trapezoidal shape, often carved with a monogram, a cross, or some other device.

pulvinule. Add: **3.** = PULVINUS.

1928 E. HUGHES-GIBB *Life-force in Plant World* vii. 153 Upon scratching or irritating the pulvinule of the terminal leaflet of either of these beans on its under-side, a downward movement very slowly begins. **1975** *Nature* 6 Mar. 69/2 We provide direct experimental evidence for cyclic changes in membrane properties in a circadian system from studies of the pulvinule cells at the base of the leaflets of clover.

pumicate, *v.* (Later example.)

1925 *Chambers's Jrnl.* Nov. 704/2 When it is thoroughly 'pumicated' the coral is rinsed and put into a second bag.

pumice, *sb.* **B. 2. a, b.** (Further examples.)

1891 R. WALLACE *Rural Econ. Austral. & N.Z.* xv. 229 Pumice-topped land..covers unfortunately about thirty per cent. of the area of the North Island. **1950** *N.Z. Jrnl. Agric.* Jan. 17/3 In the north and north-west, where annual rainfall is over 50 in., the soils are classified as yellow brown pumice soils. They are light, fluffy pumice soils formed on volcanic ash. *Ibid.* Feb. 115/2 In its natural state the open pumice country, clothed in a tangled mass of manuha and manoao..looks barren and unattractive. *Ibid.*, The pumice lands of the central plateau area of the North Island consists of soils derived from volcanic-ash showers. **1965** S. T. OLLIVIER *Petticoat Farm* i. 1 Harry stood at the roadside and watched the white pumice dust rising between the bracken at each side of the road.

pumicite (pʌ·misəit). [f. PUMIC(E *sb.* + -ITE[1].] A volcanic ash like pumice in composition but occurring as powder or granules.

1916 E. H. BARBOUR in *Nebraska Geol. Survey* IV. 358 Pumicite has been variously called geyserite, volcanic dust,..and the like... For all of these we have substituted the name pumicite, a self-explanatory term, which we have used for some years. **1949** J. A. BARR in *Industrial Minerals & Rocks* (ed. 2) xxxvi. 752 The principal use of pumicite is for concrete aggregate. **1965** G. J. WILLIAMS *Econ. Geol. N.Z.* xvi. 245/2 Other deposits at Takanini and Hurua [*read* Hunua] have been quoted as a source of diatomaceous material for fibrolite and light-weight concrete but Ritchie pointed out that this is pumicite with no diatoms. **1974** A. C. TENNISSEN *Nature of Earth Materials* vii. 394 Finely ground pumice and unground pumicite are used in general scouring powders... Other uses for unground pumicite and ground pumicite are..in insulation, as filter aids, as poultry litter, [etc.].

pummel, *v.* Add: **a.** Also *transf.* and *fig.*

1927 *New Republic* 12 Oct. 208/2 Once the greater part of the population is pummeled night and morning in underground cattle-cars,..I shall be surprised if there is any energy left. **1972** *Newsweek* 10 Jan. 1/1 For five days U.S. Phantom jets and mammoth B-52 bombers pummeled North Vietnam in the heaviest raids since the 1968 bombing halt. **1977** *Chicago Tribune* 2 Oct. III. 16/6 The Carthage Redmen..went on to pummel the North Park Vikings 34–8. **1979** *Arizona Daily Star* 19 Apr. 1/1 Typhoon Cecil headed today for Japan after pummeling the Philippines.

pump, *sb.*[1] Add: **I. 1. a.** *spec.* = *petrol pump* (*a*) s.v. *PETROL 3 b.

1925 F. SCOTT FITZGERALD *Great Gatsby* iv. 81, I had a glimpse of Mrs. Wilson straining at the garage pump. **1972** [see *petrol station* s.v. *PETROL 3 b]. **1974** A. PRICE *Other Paths to Glory* II. viii. 204 He helps with the odd jobs in the workshop and looks after the pumps.

e. *Physiol.* A mechanism in living cells by which metabolic energy is utilized to cause specific kinds of ion to pass through the cell membrane in the direction opposite to that in which they would pass under ordinary diffusion.

1947 *Arch. Biochem.* XIV. 297 (*heading*) An osmotic diffusion pump. *Ibid.* 298 The essential unit of such a pump consists of the space between two membranes, in which a coupled chemical reaction, utilizing free energy supplied from outside, permits this unit to pump either solvent or dissolved solute into itself through one membrane and out through the other membrane, at a higher chemical potential than that from which it entered. **1964** A. WHITE et al. *Princ. Biochem.* (ed. 3) xxxvii. 727 In the ascending limb of the hairpin-shaped loop of Henle an outwardly oriented sodium pump..operates while the same cells are relatively impermeable to water. **1965** *Nature* 4 Sept. 1099/1 Approximately three sodium ions are expelled for each molecule of ATP split by the pump. **1977** *Sci. Amer.* Aug. 117/3 The transfer of a phosphate group to such a protein could conceivably change the permeability of the membrane to ions,..for example by affecting the activity of an enzyme 'pump' that physically transports ions across the membrane.

III. 6. a. *pump-clip* (examples), *nail, spout.* **pump action** *attrib.* (orig. *U.S.*), designating a type of repeating firearm (see quot. 1964 and cf. *pump gun* s.v. *PUMP *v.* 14); also *absol.*; **b. pump attendant,** a garage hand who serves petrol; **pump hook** (earlier examples); **pump island,** the part of a petrol station on which the pumps stand; **pump-set, pumpset,** a complete pumping installation, comprising a pump, a source of power, and any necessary pipes, valves, filters, etc.; cf. *pumping set* s.v. *PUMPING *vbl. sb.* d; **pump-spear** (earlier example); **pump-turbine** *Engin.*, a machine designed to operate as a pump running in one direction or a turbine running in the other.

1912 *Collier's* 28 Sept. 30/1 (Advt.), The Marlin Pump Action repeating rifle. **1964** H. L. PETERSON *Encycl. Firearms* 249/2 *Pump action*, a popular term describing repeating firearms activated by a horizontally operating slide action. **1973** *Times* 1 Aug. 4/6 The Government decided..not to make self-loading rifles and pump-action shotguns prohibited weapons in its forthcoming Bill. **1977** *Field* 13 Jan. 44/1 (Advt.), A large selection of new and second-hand English weapons... Foreign side by sides, automatics, pump actions and single barrel guns. **1968** A. BINKLEY *What shall I Cry* 10 Harry was pump attendant and not in charge of mechanics. **1972** *Times* 8 Sept. 21/5 The pump attendant's life of opening and shutting filler caps. **1907** *Yesterday's Shopping* (1969) 1060/3 Cooper's patent locking pump clip. **1908** H. G. WELLS *War in Air* ii. 52 Bert stared at these over the card of pump-clips in the pane in the door. **1640** *Archives of Maryland* (1887) IV. 112 For a pump-hook. **1702** in *Essex Inst. Hist. Coll.* (1906) XLII. 161 Inventory of ship... A pumpe Hooke. **1969** *Wall St. Jrnl.* 7 Oct. 19/1 We've seen crop after crop of dolts parade to the pump island. **1974** *Petroleum Rev.* XXVIII. 706/3 Painted in BP or National livery will be the pump islands, canopies, shops, kiosks, [etc.]. **1805** *State Papers & Publick Documents of U.S.* 2 Dec. (1814) I. 455 They robbed the brig of..all her candles, pump nails, locks, and gimblets. *c* **1889** W. TATE *Princ. Mining adapted to S. Kensington Syllabus* xxi. 158 The thickness of pump sets is calculated by the following formula. **1969** *Capital* (Calcutta) 27 Feb. 354/1 In 1967–68 alone, 250,000 pumpsets, 50,000 private tubewells and 1,000 large State tubewells were installed. **1974** *Petroleum Rev.* XXVIII. 704/1 A sea water injection pumpset. **1702** in *Essex Inst. Hist. Coll.* (1906) XLII. 161 Inventory of ship..Two pump Speares. **1867** 'T. LACKLAND' *Homespun* 321 He washes his ruddy face under the pump-spout. **1888** *Harper's Bazaar* 22 Dec. 872/1 When he had filled his pail he took it carefully from the pump spout, and started back to the house. **1934** H. K. BARROWS *Water Power Engin.* (ed. 2) iii. 179 The Baldwin-Southwark Corporation..with the General Electric Company, have recently developed a combined pump-turbine operated by a two-speed motor generator for such plants, model tests of which indicate relatively high efficiencies when acting as either a turbine or a pump. **1977** *Time* 17 Jan. (Advt., verso front cover),

Bill has no idea that the six reversible pump-turbine generator-motors that now supply his area with low-cost electricity were made by Hitachi.

pump, *sb.*² Add: **a.** (Later examples.) Also occas. = *PLIMSOLL 2; in North America, freq. = *court shoe* s.v. *COURT *sb.*¹ 19.

1897 *Sears, Roebuck & Co. Catal.* 203/3 Men's gymnasium shoes.. Men's low cut canvas pumps, canvas sole, [etc.]. **1908** *Ibid.* 813/2 A dainty pump of patent coltskin, much in favour with fashionable women. **1928** *T. Eaton & Co. Catal.* Spring & Summer, These smart, attractively-trimmed Pumps can be had in either Black Patent or Honey Beige-shade of leather. **1946** *Sun* (Baltimore) 2 Nov. 3 (Advt.), Two flattering styles to choose from—black suede anklet... and classic black suede sling pump—both mounted on black faille platforms. **1967** *Oxford Mag.* 10 Feb. 205/2 Informed by a girl that she has to wear pumps (court shoes) for her Convocation (degree ceremony) [in Canada]. **1968** J. IRONSIDE *Fashion Alphabet* 132 *Dancing shoes or pumps.* Usually worn by children, they have flat soles and elastic which goes criss-cross round the ankle. Very popular among smart nannies for their charges, especially in bronze leather. **1974** P. WRIGHT *Lang. Brit. Industry* ii. 28 For rubber-soled canvas shoes we have *pumps, plimsolls, gym-shoes* and *squeakers*. **1978** J. KRANTZ *Scruples* vii. 191 Wells Cope, wearing a Dorso sweater, pale beige twill trousers, and black velvet evening pumps embroidered in gold, sat with Harriet.

pump, *v.* Add: **I. 3.** Also, to free from air or other gas by means of a pump or pumps, to evacuate; also with *down* (cf. *pump up* in sense 5) or *out* (cf. *pump out* in sense 2); also *absol.*

1923 *Phil. Mag.* XLVI. 724 The apparatus was pumped out and the residual gas removed as completely as possible. **1935** MILLER & FINK *Neon Signs* viii. 166 The average time required for pumping average lengths of tubing.. is shown. **1936** *Physical Rev.* L. 250/1 The tube was opened up for three days, then pumped down. **1952** A. L. REIMANN *Vacuum Technique* ii. 27 Seal-off constrictions are commonly made with a diameter of 6 mm. for pumping water-cooled valves. **1955** KIRK & OTHMER *Encycl. Chem. Technol.* XIV. 547 The tube is sealed onto the manifold of a vacuum system which is capable of pumping down the tube to the order of 10^{-7} mm. of mercury. **1959** N. W. ROBINSON in A. S. D. Barrett *Progress in Vacuum Sci. & Technol.* 25/1 The advocates of oil pumps consider that the ability to pump down to 10^{-6}–10^{-7} mm. Hg without a refrigerant outweighs the disadvantage..of oil contamination. **1971** *Sci. Amer.* Aug. 114/1, I do not add the slurry until the system has been pumped to 10^{-2} torr. **1977** *Ibid.* Jan. 80/2 To measure bearing balls for exoelectron emission would call for..putting the ball in a vacuum chamber, pumping the chamber down and hoping that all this would not interfere with exoelectron emission.

b. *to pump ship* (also *pumpship*), to urinate. *colloq.*

1788 GROSE *Dict. Vulgar T.* (ed. 2) s.v. *Pump*, To pump ship; to make water, and sometimes to vomit. *Sea phrase.* **1886** H. BAUMANN *Londinismen* 147/1 *To pump ship*, sein Wasser abschlagen. **1922** V. WOOLF *Let.* 22 Oct. (1976) II. 572 Its on a par with not pump shipping before your wife. **1938** J. CARY *Castle Corner* 163 The few passing guests who came now and then to smoke or to pumpship among the stacks. **1939** W. Z. FOSTER *Pages from Worker's Life* iv. 175 He excused himself from the room with the remark that he had 'to go and pump ship'. **1973** 'D. RUTHERFORD' *Kick Start* i. 12 A couple of men had come in to pump ship at the stand-up urinals.

II. 6. a. Also freq., to force, inject, or pour (something) *into* (someone or something).

1899 [in Dict.]. **1940** *War Illustr.* 12 Apr. 367/3 The other six Messerschmitts were circling round him pumping bullets into his 'plane as fast as they could work the guns. **1947** *Sun* (Baltimore) 15 Aug. 12/7 A gunman climbed on the running board of his car and pumped lead into him. **1953** *Times* 31 Oct. 2/7 The atomic energy production division..will be 'generating electrical power which would be pumped into the grid system within the next few years'. **1977** A. THWAITE *Portion for Foxes* 23 Made separate..By actions pumping fear into my blood. **1978** *Guardian Weekly* 29 Jan. 7/2 Moscow started pumping arms into Ethiopia.

b. (Later example.)

1909 *Daily Chron.* 22 Sept. 9/5 My head aches. It pumps and pumps and I can't think.

9. c. *coarse slang.* To copulate. Also *trans.*, to copulate with (a woman).

1730 in Farmer *Merry Songs & Ballads* (1897) II. 204, I work'd at her Pump till the Sucker grew dry, And then I left pumping, a good Reason why. **1937** PARTRIDGE *Dict. Slang* 667/2 *Pump*, v., to coït with (a woman): low: C. 18–20; ob[solescent]. **1971** R. K. SMITH *Ransom* v. 223 They began to pump on the soft seat... 'We never did it in no Caddy before,' he whispered. **1973** 'J. PATRICK' *Glasgow Gang Observed* xii. 108 Skidmarks had come by her name through the boys' practice of kicking her naked behind after they had 'pumped' her. **1976** G. V. HIGGINS *Judgement D. Hunter* xiv. 159 He told me Shanley's pumping Dottie Deininger... Fine-looking woman.

10. a. Also, to shake (a person's hand, or a person by the hand) vigorously.

1912 MULFORD & CLAY *Buck Peters* i. 14 'Tex!..When did you get here? Going to stay?..You look white—sick?' 'City color..,' replied the other, still pumping the hand. 'I'm goin' to stay.' **1938** M. K. RAWLINGS *Yearling* xii. 123 They pumped hands in greeting. *a* **1951** 'J. HACKSTON' in Murdoch & Drake-Brockman *Austral. Short Stories* (1951) 230 He ebbed out looking swamped, with a big man pumping him up and down in a parting, very friendly handshake. **1958** J. COURAGE in *London Mag.* Dec. 26 He pumped my hand pleasantly. **1969** [see *ETIC *a.*]. **1977** *Church Times* 14 Jan. 5/1 Clasping my hand, and pumping it up and down whilst looking intensely into my eyes.

b. (Later examples.)

1928 C. F. S. GAMBLE *Story N. Sea Air Station* xviii. 309 All submarines have a tendency to 'pump' in heavy seas, that is, they tend to move up and down in a vertical plane. **1938** M. K. RAWLINGS *Yearling* xiv. 148 The road under him was a treadmill. His legs pumped up and down, but he seemed to be passing the same trees and bushes again and again. **1976** *N.Y. Times Mag.* 12 Sept. 40/2 He [*sc.* a skateboard rider] pumped from cruise to speed, down the incline, faster until he felt almost weightless like a bird, spinning on wheels that really weren't there.

11. (Earlier examples.)

1791 F. BURNEY *Let.* 7 Nov. (1972) I. 77 She owns she found the greatest difficulty in *pumping up* decent expressions of concern. **1813** M. EDGEWORTH *Let.* 1 May (1971) 36, I could not pump up any enthusiasm for them.. I have no taste for these *hideous* old stones.

13*. *intr.* = *HUNT *v.* 7 b.

1901 L. BELL *Electric Power Transmission* (ed. 3) vi. 227 Alternators in parallel are less likely to pump if they have solid poles. **1902** [see *HUNT *v.* 7 b].

13.** *Physics.* To raise (an atom or the like) *into* or into a higher energy state by irradiation, esp. so as to produce a population inversion and make the substance work as a laser; to excite (a substance or device) in this way. Cf. *optical pumping* s.v. *OPTICAL *a.* 6.

1953 *Rev. Mod. Physics* XXV. 175/1 The vapor is illuminated with circularly polarized light..to pump atoms from the ground state *a*, in which $m = -\frac{1}{2}$, into state *b*, in which $m = +\frac{1}{2}$. **1961** *Ann. Reg. 1960* 396 The method of 'pumping' the electrons into their excited state had also to be changed for a continuous method. **1973** *Sci. Amer.* June 52/3 Most substances can be pumped with just the fundamental and second-harmonic pulses emitted by these two lasers. **1973** *Physics Bull.* July 419/3 Perhaps the most important recent development has been the successful operation of the cw rhodamine 6G dye laser, pumped by an argon-ion laser. **1975** *Nature* 28 Aug. 695/2 Laser action over the range 2·5 to 2·9 μm was achieved using the F_A(II) centre in lithium-doped potassium chloride pumped by a krypton ion laser at 647·1 nm.

III. 14. *pump jack*; **pump drill**, a primitive drill in which the shaft is rotated by sliding up and down a cross-piece to which is attached a cord that winds and unwinds about the shaft; **pump gun** orig. *N. Amer.*, a rifle having a tubular magazine and a sliding forearm; so *pump-gunner*.

1865 Pump drill [in Dict.]. **1964** W. L. GOODMAN *Hist. Woodworking Tools* 180 Another primitive method still in use by..natives of New Guinea is the pump drill,..with a flywheel made of stone. **1974** P. W. BLANDFORD *Country Craft Tools* viii. 116 Pump drills were used by many craftsmen. **1906** *Daily Colonist* (Victoria, B.C.) 16 Jan. 10/5 He was using a Winchester pump gun, and in the operation of loading, the gun was fired, the charge striking the left foot. **1970** D. DODGE *Hatchetman* vii. 101 A guard with a pumpgun across his knees sat cross-legged on the floor. **1976** *Shooting Times & Country Mag.* 18–24 Nov., The 16-bore Model 12 is a durable weapon of reasonable weight, very easy to hit with (and to the pumpgunner, at least, having positively classical lines!). **1970** J. BLACKBURN *Land of Promise* v. 74, I had not bought Unzicker's small gasoline engine and pump jack at the sale. **1973** *Times* 1 Dec. 2/3 The Kimmeridge pump jack, familiarly known in the trade as a nodding donkey, seesaws steadily on.

pumpable. Delete *rare*⁻⁰ and add examples; **pumpability** (further examples).

1935 H. MOORE *Liquid Fuels* vi. i. 193 The pour-point test..is only a rough guide in comparing the pumpability of different fuel oils at low temperatures. **1960** *Farmer & Stockbreeder* 12 Jan. 66/2 Agitators make the mass pumpable, through tractor-powered open-vane centrifugal pumps. **1970** *Sci. Jrnl.* Aug. 79/2 Traditional grouts are sand, lime or cement and sufficient water to make the mixture pumpable. **1973** *Nature* 9 Mar. 90/3 For centrifugal pumps with enclosed disk-type impellers there is likely to be a better pumpability with viscoelastic liquids. **1979** *Civil Engineering* Nov. 43/1 The bolt is installed and grouted by means of pumpable resin.

pu·mp-down. Also **pumpdown.** [f. vbl. phr. *to pump down*: see *PUMP *v.* 3.] The action or process of reducing the pressure of air or other gas inside an enclosed volume by pumping. Freq. *attrib.*

1948 *Rev. Sci. Instruments* XIX. 13/1 To obtain a conservative value for the 'pump-down' time, the pump speed ..is 0·37 liter per second. **1966** D. G. BRANDON *Mod. Techniques Metallogr.* 184 Preliminary pump-down can be performed with a liquid nitrogen-cooled sorption trap. **1971** *Sci. Amer.* Aug. 114/3 Gas will be liberated from the internal surfaces of the system during pumpdown. **1977** *Design Engin.* July 35/3 This greatly reduces pump-down time.

pumped, *ppl. a.* Add: **3.** *pumped storage*, the pumping of water to a higher level when demand for electricity is low so that its return to the lower level can be used to generate hydroelectricity when demand is high. Freq. *attrib.*

1927 F. JOHNSTONE-TAYLOR *Water-Power Pract.* x. 163 A total of 450 h.p. being required, pumped storage was resorted to. **1964** *Times Rev. Industry* Jan. 73 A pumped storage scheme..only requires the possibility of constructing two reasonably large storage basins at widely differing levels with a river or adequate rainfall to keep them filled. **1976** *National Observer* (U.S.) 12 June 5/1 In this ancient valley of the New River, American Electric Power Co... wants to build an $845 million pumped-storage project.. that would trap 42,100 acres of water behind two dams.

pumpellyite (pɒmpe·li,əit). *Min.* [f. the name of Raphael *Pumpelly* (1837–1923), U.S. geologist: see -ITE¹.] An iron- and magnesium-bearing hydrous calcium aluminosilicate, crystallographically similar to minerals of the epidote group, which occurs as colourless, greenish, or brown monoclinic crystals and is characteristic of certain low-grade metamorphic rocks.

1925 PALACHE & VASSAR in *Amer. Mineralogist* X. 412 For this mineral we propose the name of Pumpellyite for Raphael Pumpelly, the pioneer student of the detailed paragenesis of the minerals of this region. **1959** W. W. MOORHOUSE *Study of Rocks in Thin Section* vi. 170 The vesicles of basalts are filled with secondary minerals, of which the most typical are zeolites, carbonate, the silica minerals.., feldspar, epidote, pumpellyite, chlorite, and serpentinite. **1975** *Lithos* VIII. 72 The textures and crystal forms strongly suggest that the pumpellyite-quartz aggregates are reaction products which developed after equilibrium crystallization of the prehnite and chlorite. **1978** *Nature* 20 July 242/1 Prehnite and pumpellyite have been found in County Cavan, Ireland.

pumper¹. Add: **1. b.** (Examples.)

1874 *Coursing Calendar* Spring 260 All the latter part of a pumper was in favour of Mr Mill's dog. **1879** H. DALZIEL *British Dogs* I. i. 23 Without this [*sc.* a good back] the dog [*sc.* a greyhound] could not endure the exhaustive process of the 'pumpers' he is submitted to.

3. *U.S.* A fire engine that carries the hose and pumps the water.

1915 *Fire & Water Engineering* 14 July 31/3 (*heading*) New Seagrave pumpers tested at Denver. **1919** *Ibid.* 16 July 140/3 Time was, when the motor pumper was still a novelty and many of the departments were still using the horse-drawn steamer to extinguish fires. **1934** W. C. PRYOR *Fire Engine Book* 32 He showed them a big pumper engine... 'Water power alone is not strong enough to throw the water high into the air..so the pumper puts more pressure behind the water.' **1949** J. J. FLOHERTY *Fire Alarm* i. 9 Fire apparatus developed from the man-drawn hand pump to the powerful motorized pumper. **1975** *New Yorker* 10 Mar. 28/3 Pache showed us Aviation's current fire engine ('It's a 1951 Ward LaFrance pumper, and it carries five hundred and fifty gallons').

pump-handle, *sb.* Add: **b.** (Later examples.)

1892 J. E. COX *Five Years in U.S. Army* 83 Performing the 'pump-handle act' with my right arm, I hastened away to obey orders. **1909** R. E. KNOWLES *Attic Guest* xv. 204 They nearly all shook hands in the high pump-handle fashion that was almost unknown in the South.

pumping, *vbl. sb.* Add: **d. pumping set** = *pump-set* s.v. *PUMP *sb.*¹ 6 b.

c **1889** W. TATE *Princ. Mining adapted to Requirements of S. Kensington Syllabus* xlvi. 398 Pumping sets for lifting water to bank vary from 8 to 24 inches, and in extreme cases 36 inches in diameter. **1926** *Power Engineer* XXI. 333 (*heading*) A turbine pumping set. **1957** T. G. HICKS *Pump Selection & Application* vii. 199 (*caption*) Fuel-oil pumping set fitted with 5 gpm 150-psi pumps and heaters. **1962** L. B. ESCRITT *Pumping Station Equipment & Design* iii. 27 Pumping sets are classed into horizontal-spindle and vertical-spindle types.

pumpkin. Add: **2. b.** (Further examples.)

1846 *Spirit of Times* 25 Apr. 97/1 The skins, Indian relics, etc. are 'some punkins' and no mistake. **1849** [see *LAGNIAPPE]. **1859** *Harper's New Monthly Mag.* Sept. 569/2 Gin'ral! you're *some* punkins! **1903** *McClure's Mag.* XXI. 330/1 He was some pumpkin both in politics and color, and the friend of me and Jones. **1913** J. LONDON *Valley of Moon* (1916) III. vii. 380 Say, friend, you're some punkins at a hundred yards dash, ain't you? **1930** E. POUND *XXX Cantos* xii. 54 Go to hell Apovitch, Chicago aint the whole punkin. **1975** *Publishers Weekly* 21 July 67/3 New England, where the Boston radio team of Eddie Andelman, Jim McCarthy and Mark Witkin is evidently considered some punkins.

4. *pumpkin butter, -eater, patch, pudding, soup, vine* (earlier and later examples); *pumpkin orange, yellow* adjs.; **pumpkin pie** (earlier and later examples); **pumpkin pine** *U.S.*, substitute for def.: a variety of the white pine, *Pinus strobus*; also, the timber from this tree; (later examples).

1893 M. A. OWEN *Voodoo Tales* 6 The place of the vegetables was taken by..little jars of a villainous sweet compound of pumpkin stewed with watermelon-juice and known to all as 'punkin-butter'. **1918** *N. & Q.* 12th Ser. IV. 189/1 Peter, Peter, pumpkin-eater, Had a wife and couldn't keep her. Had another, didn't love her, Causing instantaneous bother. **1962** *Punch* 31 Oct. 648/1 Jake is the pumpkin eater of the title [of a novel]; he tries to put his wife in a pumpkin shell to keep her very well, as the old rhyme says, and it is this that precipitates the crisis. **1974** L. KOENIG *Little Girl* xix. 224 A waitress..wearing a pumpkin-orange uniform. **1935** Z. N. HURSTON *Mules & Men* I. iv. 99 Out dat door John come like a streak of lightning. All across de punkin patch, thru de cotton over de pasture. **1654** E. JOHNSON *Wonder-working Providence of Sions Saviour in New England* 174 This poor Wilderness hath..quince tarts instead of their former Pumpkin Pies. **1784** P. M. FRENEAU *Poems* (1786) 389 Systems they built on pumpkin pies, And prov'd that every thing went round. **1907** *St. Nicholas* May 615/2 Pumpkin pies and strawberry shortcake were also introduced to the French palate and found good. **1851** J. S. SPRINGER *Forest Life &*

Forest Trees 41 The pumpkin Pine is generally found on flat land and in ravines. **1907** *Springfield* (Mass.) *Weekly Republ.* 29 Aug. 15 The virgin white pine has practically disappeared from New England and huge 'pumpkin pines' four and five feet in diameter are now a matter of tradition. **1941** B. A. WILLIAMS *Strange Woman* vii. 576 It was an old pumpkin pine... It was better than six feet through, where I tackled it, about four feet from the ground. **1947** E. H. PAUL *Linden on Saugus Branch* 187 The solid old flooring of pumpkin pine, strewn with sawdust, rumbled and clicked beneath the tread of seamen's boots. **1951** E. M. GRAHAM *My Window looks down East* vii. 65 On the punkin pine bureau, which shines almost as golden as the heart I'd taken from the tree, were two bunches of flowers. **1805** *Indep. Chron.* 26 Dec. 3/1 Clams and oysters, succatouch and pumpkin puddings, turkies, ducks, [etc.]. **1841** A. M. MAXWELL *Run through U.S. during Autumn of 1840* I. 81 Real, genuine, Yankee, new England, pumpkin pudding. **1884** *Cottage Hearth* Apr. 189/1 *Pumpkin Soup.* Cut the inside and edible part of the pumpkin into large dice. **1955** *Caribbean Q.* IV. II. 102 After the First Communion, there is a fete for each child, with toasts in vermouth, sheepshead and pumpkin soup. **1810** M. CUTLER *Jrnl.* 9 July (1888) II. 343 Saw the cactus grandiflora, or night-flowering cereus... The plant has a long stem, resembling a pumpkin-vine, but no leaves. **1909** F. B. CALHOUN *Miss Minerva & William Green Hill* xiii. 106 How's he going to sit under a pumpkin vine when he's inside of a whale? **1962** S. WYNTER *Hills of Hebron* iii. 42 Withered pumpkin vines..littered the earth. **1912** J. WEBSTER *Daddy-Long-Legs* 173 Mr. Weaver has painted his barn..a bright pumpkin yellow.

pumpkin-head. Add: **d.** (Examples.)
1876 H. E. SCUDDER *Dwellers in Five-Sisters Court* v. 87 'Pumpkin head!' said the Doctor, more vigorously than politely. **1898** H. FREDERIC *Deserter & Other Stories* 143 You can't raise a plug of [tobacco] in a whole regiment of 'em. Regular pumpkin-heads!

pumpkin-headed, *a.* (Later example.)
1939 WODEHOUSE *Uncle Fred* xvi. 234 You know that pumpkin-headed old man's views on class distinctions.

pump log. *U.S.* A hollowed log used in the construction of a pump or as a water-pipe. Also in *Comb.* as **pump-log borer** (see quot.).
1816 *N. Amer. Rev.* III. 429 He declared also, that the mill for grinding apples, which is an overshot and is fed by a pump log..would often stop during the day. **1858** D. K. BENNETT *Chronol. N. Carolina* 108 He had some men repairing pump-logs, through which water was carried from the mountain side to his hotel. **1879** F. R. STOCKTON *Rudder Grange* xvi. 235 He looked like he'd been drawn through a pump-log. **1965** E. TUNIS *Colonial Craftsmen* iii. 40 Such a one was the pump-log borer—his trade seems to have no generic name—who made wooden pumps and wooden pipes by boring holes lengthwise through logs.

pu·mp-pri:ming, *vbl. sb.* orig. *U.S.* [f. the phr. *to prime a pump* (see PRIME *v.*[1] 4 in Dict. and Suppl.).] The stimulation of commerce or economy by means of investment; also *transf.* and *attrib.* or as *ppl. adj.*
1937 F. D. ROOSEVELT *Public Papers & Addresses* (1941) VI. 520 The things we had done, which at that time were largely a monetary and pump-priming policy.., had brought the expected result. **1938** *Sun* (Baltimore) 5 Jan. 1/7 (*heading*) Eccles urges pump-priming to end slump. *Ibid.* 18 Feb. 15/1 Farm products seemed most likely to benefit from the next 'pump-priming'. **1941** N. ALLEY *I Witness* xxxvi. 300, I spent a pump-priming week at Lisbon as the first step toward getting geared up for war coverage. **1950** *Ann. Reg. 1949* 161 Large development projects whose results would be out of all proportion to the 'pump-priming' required from U.N. **1960** *Guardian* 21 Oct. 24/6 The pump-priming period of the Welfare State. **1961** B. R. WILSON *Sects & Society* 9 The pump-priming activity of the revivalist to generate a distinctive form of religious expression. **1963** *Daily Tel.* 18 Jan. 12/2 To the financial purists, this appears as a bid for straightforward Keynesian pump-priming. Something of the sort is clearly required to stir the American economy out of its present sluggishness. **1978** M. PUZO *Fools Die* xxx. 351 He, Lieverman, would throw in the pump-priming cash, the development money.

Hence **pu·mp-pri:mer,** a financial grant or other action that stimulates economic enterprise.
1953 *Manch. Guardian Weekly* 13 Aug. 9/3 Sir Greville Maginness suggests that the grants will act as 'pump-primers' and encourage the more backward firms. **1962** *Times* 11 May 17/6 Expansion..could be effective as a pump-primer for the economy of the region. **1979** *Nature* 4 Jan. 7/3 Finance has been a constant anxiety, for the initial grants from the Wolfson Foundation and other funds were pump primers.

pumpship: see *PUMP *v.* 3b.

pun, *sb.*[1] Add: Also **pu·nkin** *rare*, a little pun.
1866 H. JAMES in *Atlantic Monthly* XVII. 197/2 Blunt and I made atrocious puns. I believe, indeed, that Miss Blunt herself made one little punkin, as I called it.

‖**punalua** (pūnălū·a). *Anthrop.* [Hawaiian.] A relationship term formerly denoting spouses who shared a wife or husband and used by L. H. Morgan in his theory of the evolution of kinship systems for a form of group marriage, assumed by him to have replaced promiscuity and preceded exogamy, in which wives' sisters and husbands' brothers were considered spouses. Hence **punalu·an** *a.*
1860 L. ANDREWS in L. H. Morgan *Anc. Society* (1877) III. iii. 427 The relationship of pūnalŭa is rather amphibious [*sic*]. It arose from the fact that two or more brothers with their wives or two or more sisters with their husbands, were inclined to possess each other in common. **1877** L. H. MORGAN *Anc. Society* III. iii. 424 The Punaluan family has existed in Europe, Asia, and America within the historical period. *Ibid.* 428 All the sisters of his wife, own as well as collateral, are also his wives. But the husband of his wife's sister he calls *pūnalŭa*, i.e., his intimate companion. **1889** C. S. WAKE *Marriage & Kinship* ii. 23 The *punaluan* group can, as will be shown hereafter, be accounted for satisfactorily without assuming the prior existence of the consanguine family. **1915** *Amer. Anthrop.* XVII. 223 He does attribute the change from the older Malayan to the later and more common Turanian form of the system to punaluan marriage as a predecessor of the institution of exogamy and to exogamy itself. **1922** B. MALINOWSKI in *Nature* 22 Apr. 502/2 Starting from promiscuity, mankind went through group marriage, then the so-called consanguineous family or Punalua, then polygamy. **1940** WEST & TORR tr. *Engels's Origin of Family* (1942) ii. 39 The American system of consanguinity ..finds, down to the smallest details, its..natural foundation in the punaluan family. *Ibid.* 42 The origin of the matriarchal gens could be derived directly from the punaluan family. **1970** K. MILLETT *Sexual Politics* II. iii. 111 A succession of sexual associations: promiscuity, group marriage, the consanguineous family, the Punalua. *Ibid.* 120 The first course of social change as Engels had charted it was from consanguine group marriage, to the Punaluan consanguine group.

punamu, var. *POUNAMU.

Punan (pū·nā·n). Also 9 **Panam.** [Native name.] A group of Dyak peoples inhabiting parts of Borneo, mostly living nomadically in interior jungles; a member of this people.
1838 J. BROOKE *Lett.* (1853) I. 25 The Panams, a race little better than monkeys, who live in trees, eat without cooking, are hunted by the other tribes, and would seem to exist in the lowest conceivable grade of humanity. **1876** *Encycl. Brit.* IV. 58/1 The fifth and lowest [branch of Dyaks] comprises the Manketans and Punans, who are still nomadic and ignorant of agriculture. **1927** *Brit. Weekly* 19 May 154/1 A Punan will never wantonly slay or attack a man of another tribe. **1960** *Spectator* 28 Oct. 662 The..elementary Punan, these..being nomadic forest hunters [of Borneo]. **1964** T. HARRISSON in Wang Gungwu *Malaysia* III. xi. 164 The nearest thing to the Malayan aborigine in Borneo is the nomadic Punan.

punch, *sb.*[1] Add: **2. c.** In mod. use, an instrument for removing a small piece of tissue from a patient.
[**1859** S. D. GROSS *Syst. Surg.* II. xi. 631 With a large, sharp saddler's punch the whole of the diseased structures ..are then removed.] **1887** *Amer. Jrnl. Med. Sci.* XCIV. 279 (*heading*) The cutaneous punch. **1915** A. MACLENNAN *Surg. Materials & their Uses* vi. 220 It is almost impossible to get punches to cut clean, and a certain amount of tearing out of the uncut tissue must be expected. **1937** C. G. DARLINGTON in S. C. Miller *Oral Diagnosis & Treatment Planning* xxix. 496 Tissue forceps,..scissors, skin or biopsy punch, may be employed, depending on the type and location of the lesion. **1957** G. L. W. BONNEY in Rob & Smith *Operative Surg.* V. 250 The impactor punch is shaped at one end so as to fit on to the convex outer surface of the femur. **1978** *Nature* 9 Mar. 171/2 Skin biopsies were taken from the upper back of 21–39-yr-old male volunteers with an electric biopsy punch 3 mm in diameter.

7. *punch operator*; **punch biopsy** *Med.*, a biopsy in which a punch is used to remove tissue; **punch card** = *punched card* s.v. *PUNCHED *ppl. a.* 2; **punch forceps** *Surg.*, a punch consisting of two hinged parts like a forceps; **punch graft,** a graft of tissue removed (usu. from the scalp) by means of a surgical punch; so **punch grafting** *vbl. sb.*; **punch-marked** *a.*, of a coin: bearing a punch-mark; **punch-press,** a press designed to drive a punch for shaping metal; **punch-ticket** *U.S.*, a railway or other ticket that has been punched.
1941 *Amer. Jrnl. Clin. Path.* XI. 519 We have..performed punch biopsies upon the livers of normal rabbits. **1955** TWISS & OPPENHEIM *Pract. Managem. Disorders of Liver, Pancreas, & Bilian, Tract* xiv. 260 Punch biopsy of the liver can be used successfully to make an etiologic distinction between the different forms of cirrhosis. **1976** *Lancet* 11 Dec. 1281/2 Some would not agree that punch biopsies should be routinely used on the face. **1945** J. VON NEUMANN in B. Randell *Origins Digital Computers* (1973) 355 These instructions must be given in some form which the device can sense: Punched into a system of punchcards [etc.]. **1971** K. GOTTSCHALK in B. de Ferranti *Living with Computer* iv. 37 The punch cards embodying the program were deemed a manner of manufacture and not patentable. **1977** *New Yorker* 29 Aug. 41/2 The production by the computer of punch-card decks representing the processed data. **1870** *Brit. Jrnl. Dental Sci.* XIII. 497 A punch forceps for punching holes in the backing for flat teeth, the peculiarity of which lay in the fact, that by a spring interposed between the jaws the plate was liberated from the punch directly the jaws of the forceps were opened. **1958** J. H. OTTY in Rob & Smith *Operative Surg.* VIII. XVIII. 93 The antrum is opened by removing a chip of bone wide enough to insert a Hajek's punch forceps, with which the opening is enlarged to the size desired. **1959** *Ann. N.Y. Acad. Sci.* LXXXIII. 465 Of a total of 284 punch grafts, only one of the punch grafts failed to take. **1968** *Plastic & Reconstruction Surg.* XLII. 446 (*heading*) Use of hair-bearing punch-grafts for partial traumatic losses of the scalp. **1976** *Daily Tel.* (Colour Suppl.) 2 July 8/4 Punch grafts require umpteen sessions and are followed by 12-week intervals of frustration before anything grows. *Ibid.* 7/3 Most bald men retain a permanent expanse of hair at the back and sides, and punch grafting has shown that this hair survives even when transplanted into bald areas of the head. **1910** HASTINGS *Encycl. Relig. & Ethics* III. 706/1 On account of this chief characteristic, the term 'punch-marked' is commonly applied to this currency. **1960** H. HAYWARD *Antique Coll.* 230/1 *Punch-marked coins*, flat, square silver coins of India of the last few centuries B.C. Surfaces covered with small punch marks of natural objects, animals and symbols, probably the marks of merchants and states guaranteeing the pieces. **1961** *Evening Standard* 17 July 16/1 (Advt.), Data Processing Department. British Wool Marketing Board—Bradford. Immediate vacancies... Punch operators. **1968** *Brit. Med. Bull.* XXIV. 191/1 The data sheets are handed to a punch operator who types out the information on a keyboard which has a punch attachment. **1911** W. J. KAUP *Machine Shop Practice* xviii. 180 Fig. 162 shows a typical modern punch press. **1935** O. W. BOSTON *Engin. Shop Practice* II. vi. 332 A punch press..is a gap or overhung type of fast, short-stroke press particularly suited for punching dies. **1976** *National Observer* (U.S.) 5 June 7/1 When Nelson Amsdill gets off work as a punch-press operator, he heads for the Veterans of Foreign Wars Post 6691. **1887** C. B. GEORGE *40 Years on Rail* xi. 227 Many cases have been reported where in punch-tickets the bits of pasteboard punched out have been saved and carefully glued in the old places. **1890** *Harper's Mag.* May 908/1 A person..who by many punch-tickets builds up the fortunes of the stockholders.

punch, *sb.*[2] Add: **1. b.** *transf.* and *fig.* Forceful, vigorous, or effective quality in an activity or in anything spoken or written; vigour, weight, effectiveness. orig. *U.S.*
1911 E. FERBER *Dawn O'Hara* xvii. 254 It lacks that peculiar and convincing quality poetically known as the punch. **1914** 'I. HAY' *Knight on Wheels* xvii. 162 The two clerks and the office-boy carried out their duties with what is known in trans-atlantic business circles as 'a punch'. **1919** H. L. WILSON *Ma Pettengill* ii. 64 A gripping drama replete with punch. *Ibid.* 75, I believe he now admits frankly that he wrote most of the play, or at least wrote the punch into it. **1921** D. W. JOHNSON *Battlefields of World War* xii. 535 The attack lost its 'punch'. **1926** *Glasgow Herald* 1 Apr. 5 They lack for the most part the quality of 'punch' which we have come to regard nowadays as one of the principal essentials in a magazine story. **1933** G. ARTHUR *Septuagenarian's Scrap Book* 307 Within a few days French, Americans and British were beginning a forward movement with the necessary 'punch' behind them of which the recent enemy assaults had been devoid. **1947** *E. African Ann. 1946–7* 98/2 (Advt.), Are you satisfied your advertisements have the necessary punch to get their message across? **1955** *Sci. News Let.* 27 Aug. 134/2 Radioiodine loses its punch within weeks. **1968** *Globe & Mail* (Toronto) 13 Jan. 41/8 Oakland Raiders' coach John Rauch said yesterday his team..has the punch to score against the defensively rugged Packers. **1976** *Oadby & Wigston* (Leics.) *Advertiser* 26 Aug. 16/3 Chances were created but there was just no punch up front.

2. Phr. *to beat* (someone) *to the punch*: of a boxer, to land a blow before his opponent can strike him; also *transf.*, to anticipate or forestall someone in speech or action. *to pull one's punches*: see *PULL *v.* 17b; *to roll with the punches*: see *ROLL *v.*[2] 21f.
1923 H. C. WITWER *Fighting Blood* vii. 226, I beat Hanley to the punch..and he went down on his haunches. **1965** *Listener* 1 July 6/1 The tracking station at Plumeur Bodou is the place that so exultantly beat Britain to the punch in getting the first pictures from America via the satellite Telstar. **1977** *Sunday Times* 3 July 28/3, I feel a batsman uses it as he thinks he will beat a fast bowler to the punch.

3. *attrib.* and *Comb.*, as *punch-packed* adj.; *punch-packing* ppl. a.; **punch-bag,** a stuffed bag suspended at a suitable height on which boxers practise punching; **punch-pull** *v. intr.*, to 'pull one's punches', to refrain from striking as hard as one can, or from expressing oneself forcefully; so **punch-pulling** *vbl. sb.*
1889 A. C. GUNTER *That Frenchman!* 8 Sling from the ceiling a punch-bag such as prize-fighters train with. **1899** *Science Siftings* 25 Mar. 329/2 A fifteen-minute controversy with an active punch-bag. **1927** *Daily Express* 20 July 9/7 His trainer..ordered Dempsey not to box, but to use the punch bag and to shadow box. **1973** D. FRANCIS *Slay-Ride* ii. 25, I..woke at seven feeling like Henry Cooper's punchbag. **1963** *Times* 25 Apr. 15/1 The year's most punch-packed novel. **1936** *Variety* 17 June 26 (Advt.), The punch-packing short short stories of the week. **1961** *New Statesman* 23 June 1010/3 The Bishop taught him how to punch-pull on all outstanding emotional issues. **1959** *Listener* 29 Jan. 224/2 There was some good photography..and a conclusion in which there was no punch-pulling.

punch, *sb.*[3] Add: **4.** *punch-pot, -room.*
1960 *Times* 16 Apr. 9/3 A punch-pot measured about 9 in. across its globular body. **1971** *Canadian Antiques Collector* Feb. 16/1 The Museum collection contains..a large and rare punch-pot, the cover with an attractive lemon knop. **1827** DRAKE & MANSFIELD *Cincinnati in 1826* iii. 30 A spacious gallery, with commodious lobbies, punch room, etc. **1841** *Southern Lit. Messenger* VII. 764/1 If you won't go home with me, you can take me down to the punch-room.

Punch, *sb.*[5] Add: **1. a.** (Earlier *attrib.* examples of *Punch and Judy.*) Also *ellipt.*, = *Punch and Judy show.*

1841 C. Fox *Jrnl.* 18 Feb. (1972) 102 He..teaches us that Punch and Judy men, beggar children and daft old men are also of our species. **1857** C. Kingsley *Two Years Ago* I. p. xviii, Those poor idolaters, and their Punch and Judy plays. **1864** [see *fair *sb.*[1] 1 a].

b. *as proud as Punch* (earlier examples).

1841 C. Brontë *Let.* 4 May in C. K. Shorter *C. Brontë & her Circle* (1896) iii. 87 Mrs. White would be as proud as Punch to show it you. **1850** Dickens *Dav. Copp.* li. 520, I am as proud as Punch to think that I once had the honor of being connected with your family. **1888** G. B. Shaw *Let.* 20 Sept. (1965) I. 200 Headlam read out all the gold and silver in the palace,..and the Bishop looked as proud as Punch of owning it all.

punch, *v.*[1] Add: **I. 2. a.** (Further examples.) Also *absol.*

1885 *Nor' Wester* (Calgary, Alta.) 12 Feb. 3/2 It would pay the stockmen to keep men out during the winter to punch the cattle out of the brush during fine weather. **1890** *Stock Grower & Farmer* (Las Vegas, New Mexico) 21 June 4/1 J. O. Phillips..will be initiated into the business of punching cattle. **1906** *McClure's Mag.* May 64/1 About ten year ago I got plumb sick of punchin' cows around my part of the country. **1910** W. M. Raine *B. O'Connor* 30 We used to punch together on the Hashknife. **1923** 'B. M. Bower' *Parowan Bonanza* xviii. 276 In that case.. you'd still be punchin' cows for your dad, most likely. **1946** F. D. Davison *Dusty* Forewd., Tailing tame old milkers into the farmyard,..punching stubborn bullocks through the mulga.

3. a. (Later examples, *esp.* in Sport.) Phr. *to punch out*: to knock out, to beat up (*U.S.*).

1920 *Isis* 5 May 9/2 He will get runs, and in the getting of them the ball will be 'punched' very hard. **1929** W. Faulkner *Sartoris* iv. 301 She put coal on it and punched it to a blaze. **1968** [see *bunt *sb.*[8] 2]. **1969** *New Yorker* 14 June 44/3 The orthodox way to hit a volley is to punch it, with a backswing so short that it begins in front of the player's body. **1971** *Current Slang* (Univ. S. Dakota) VI. 8 *Punch out*, to beat up; to fight physically. **1976** *National Observer* (U.S.) 12 June 19/2 Young blacks and Puerto Ricans..punched out Moonies who tried to restrain them. **1977** *Detroit Free Press* 11 Dec. 2-d/2 Abdul-Jabbar,..broke his own hand punching out Milwaukee's Kent Benson in the season opener. **1977** Rechin & Parker *Crock* 48 One more smart remark about my nose and I'm punching you out.

b. *to punch up*: to assault, beat up (cf. *punch-up); also *fig.* in *Cinematogr.* (see quots. 1953, 1959).

1953 Berrey & Van den Bark *Amer. Thes. Slang* (1954) §623a/8 Punch up one and fade it down, get the picture ready for fading up, as in an opening shot. **1959** W. S. Sharps *Dict. Cinemat.* 121/2 *Punch up.* In acting, this is to add emphasis to a phrase or action. In filming, the term means to increase picture brightness, and in recording, to bring in a new sound, or to increase the volume or pitch of an existing sound. **1963** *Listener* 31 Jan. 202/1 The folknicks in Washington Square when they punch up the police of a Sunday afternoon.

c. *to punch the* or *a clock*: to clock in or out; so *to punch in*.

1927 *Sunday Express* 8 May 10 Costello flatly refused to 'punch the clock', and had definite ideas about what he would and would not do in connection with his art. **1943** J. B. Priestley *Daylight on Saturday* i. 2 What happens when you have shown your pass and punched the time-clock? **1944** G. Farwell in *Coast to Coast 1943* 116 Yesterday I was late punching in. They'll be docking me. **1969** D. Clark *Nobody's Perfect* iii. 103 We're soft-hearted in the way we treat our staff. Nobody has to punch a clock. **1978** S. Brill *Teamsters* vii. 292 At the terminal Barkett punched in.

d. To press (a push-button); to operate, switch *on*, or tune *in* (a device) by doing this.

1954 W. Tucker *Wild Talent* xiv. 211 The man punched the elevator button. **1971** 'R. Macdonald' *Underground Man* x. 61, I punched on the car radio. It was tuned to a local station. **1972** M. Kaye *Lively Game of Death* (1974) vii. 40 Scott punched the intercom and asked to speak with Lasker. **1975** *Gramophone* Sept. 531/1 The user can also punch in any desired FM station frequency and scan for just stereo stations. **1977** *Guardian Weekly* 25 Sept. 19/2 The launch controller punched the destruction button and the rocket with its payload was automatically destroyed.

II. 4. a. (Further examples.) Cf. *keypunch *v.* 1 a.

1939 J. Berryman in K. Amis *Spectrum* (1961) 167 With a rattle and a whir the calculators punched and sorted the cards. **1964** F. L. Westwater *Electronic Computers* vi. 98 The cards have to be punched by hand from information on original documents. **1971** *Daily Tel.* 3 May 2/6 It lights up a wall map, serves a memory bank, punches a tape for computer use and produces a copy in type for control room operators. **1974** J. Banning *How I fooled World* ii. 13 When I..had to punch tape myself, the computer in London often rejected my copy.

c. Delete *Telegraphy* and add: = *key-punch *v.* 1 b. (Earlier and further examples.)

Quot. 1876[1] in Dict. belongs to sense 4 b.

1864 C. Babbage *Passages from Life of Philosopher* viii. 119 The Tables to be used must..be computed and punched on cards by the machine. **1890** *Jrnl. Franklin Inst.* CXXIX. 301 In order to punch the individual records upon the cards, they are placed one by one in a suitable punching machine. **1946** *N.Y. Times* 15 Feb. 16/3 When the problem is punched on the cards, they are dropped into a slot in a 'reader'. **1952** *Sci. Amer.* Sept. 112/3 The instructions..are punched in the paper tape by a special typewriter keyboard. **1968** *Brit. Med. Bull.* XXIV. 247/1 Use of the program achieves a very considerable saving in effort, which would be further enhanced if..observations of turnover diameter were punched directly on to tape at the time of measurement. **1971** H. Love in R. A. Wisbey *Computer in Lit. & Ling. Research* 51, I must not pass over his method of proofreading input, which is to have the text punched-up by two different operators and then use the computer to spot discrepancies.

d. (Later example.)

1977 *Lancet* 26 Nov. 1140/2 Two 3 mm diameter discs are punched out from the filterpaper, one for testing and the other as a control.

6. *to punch out* (Aeronaut.): see quots. *slang.*

1968–70 *Current Slang* (Univ. S. Dakota) III–IV. 98 *Punch out, v.* To eject from an aircraft. **1974** *Sunday Times* 16 June 13/2 It never occurred to me to 'punch out' (eject).

pu·nch-ball. [Punch *sb.*[2]] **1.** A stuffed or inflated ball suspended at a suitable height for practice punching by boxers. Also *fig.*

1901 *Humane Rev.* II. 218 There would be a large gymnasium with all sorts of appliances, *e.g.*, the punch-ball. **1910** *Cycling* 12 Jan. p. xxi/3 (Advt.), Punch-ball, 10s, cost double. **1927** *Daily Express* 22 June 17/5 He is developing his punch in secret, and..he has broken three punch-balls. **1932** *Pictorial Weekly* 12 Mar. 185/2 In the centre a player is using the punch-ball. **1963** *Times* 13 Mar. 12/5 The Home Office has always been something of a punchball for Mr. Sidney Silverman. **1973** M. Amis *Rachel Papers* 13 Her buttocks, when she wore stretch-slacks, would dance behind her knees like punch-balls. **1977** *Time* 3 Oct. 50/2 Among the principals: the incomparable Lizzie, a daydreamy beautiful loser, 'punchball' for many lovers, whose flaws prove even more compelling than her easy virtue.

2. *U.S.* A ball-game (see quot. 1932).

1932 *Jrnl. Health & Physical Educ.* May 48/2 *Punch Ball*... The Youngstown, Ohio, playgrounds have promoted a new game.... There are fifteen players on a side. A tightly blown rubber ball the size of a basketball is kicked, punched with the fist, or butted with the head as in soccer. **1935** C. F. Ware *Greenwich Village* v. 144 The district abounded in block teams..who played the ubiquitous game of punchball. **1976** *Washington Post* 28 July c6/3 Some of the games we played were called stickball and stoop baseball and punchball.

pu·nch board. *N. Amer.* Also with hyphen and as one word. [Punch *sb.*[2]] **a.** A board perforated with holes containing slips of paper which are 'punched' out as a form of gambling, with the object of locating a winning slip.

1912 J. P. Quinn *Gambling & Gambling Devices* 231 (*caption*) Punch board. **1935** J. Steinbeck *Tortilla Flat* xvii. 315 Tito Ralph came in with a box of cigars he had won on a punch board. **1939** *Sun* (Baltimore) 12 Sept. 7/4 The worst form of petty gambling seems to be confined to punch boards. **1949** *Democrat* 15 Dec. 4/1 We would like to amend his paragraph to include punch boards. **1951** *Manch. Guardian Weekly* 15 Mar. 10/4 The sale of punch-boards (gambling machines) was running at about $100 millions a year. **1966** *Times* 28 Feb. (Canada Suppl.) p. x/4 Any dice game, three-card monte, punch board. **1978** *Rugby World* Apr. 50 (Advt.), Now available New Lakeland (tamper proof)..Football cards & Punchboards.

b. *fig.* A promiscuous woman.

1963 *Amer. Speech* XXXVIII. 173 A female who is dated because of her lax sexual habits..*punch*... The word *punch* may well be a shortened form of *punchboard*, which was recorded twice. **1970** G. Greer *Female Eunuch* 267 Girls who pride themselves on their monogamous instincts..speak of the 'campus punchboard'. **1977** J. Wambaugh *Black Marble* (1978) iii. 23 There's one woman handler, named Wilma. A punchboard. What the hell, she's a little dumpy, but when you been looking at dogs all day.

pu·nch-drunk, *a.* and *sb.* orig. *U.S.* [f. Punch *sb.*[2] + Drunk *ppl. a.* and *sb.*[2]] **A.** *adj.* Of a boxer or one involved in physical fighting: dazed or stupefied from severe or continual punching; *spec.* exhibiting reduced muscular co-ordination, hesitant speech, slowness of thought, and other signs. Also *fig.*

1918 *Sat. Even. Post* 18 May 12/3 He was in the condition so aptly described as 'punch drunk'. **1927** *Daily Express* 29 July 1, I replied that in my opinion Moore was 'punch-drunk', that is to say that he had taken so much punishment that he could no longer feel it, and his nerves were practically gone. **1934** *Sun* (Baltimore) 2 Mar. 12/7, I am delegated to remind all who may be punch-drunk with winter that the famous Blizzard of Eighty-eight occurred on March 12. **1937** *Daily Mirror* 2 Mar. 12/4 Nowadays the Kid is punch-drunk. His limbs tremble and quiver like a man stricken with ague. His voice is so slurred that one cannot properly understand what he is saying. **1947** *Penguin New Writing* XXX. 126 A film which has been praised by critics who should certainly know better, unless they have themselves become punch-drunk with watching the hallucinated antics of the slap-happy puppets on the screen. **1952** C. Day Lewis tr. *Virgil's Aeneid* v. 105 So he called an end to the bout, saving the punch-drunk Dares From further punishment. **1954** J. Steinbeck *Sweet Thursday* 215 Doc's setting over there like he's punch-drunk. **1958** *Times Lit. Suppl.* 5 Sept. 497/3 In this punch-drunk civilization it is perverse to expect me to take seriously the horse itself, or indeed Mr. Kirkup's gracious swan, or Mr. Trypanis's seasick cock. **1959** N. Mailer *Advts. for Myself* (1961) 21, I seem to have turned into a slightly punch-drunk and ugly club fighter. **1974** 'A. Garve' *File on Lester* xxxvi. 129 The papers are terrible this morning... I'm feeling punch drunk and hardly capable of rational thought. **1974** E. Brawley *Rap* (1975) i. i. 31 You and me know he's so.. punch-drunk he'd do anything anybody told him.

B. *sb.* One who is punch-drunk (usu. in literal use).

In quot. 1928 used as the name of the condition.

1928 *Jrnl. Amer. Med. Assoc.* 13 Oct. 1103/1 The early symptoms of punch drunk usually appear in the extremities. **1943** *Gen* 16 Jan. 30/2 Your out-and-out punch-drunk is harmless rather than homicidal. **1966** 'A. Hall' *Ninth Directive* viii. 78 He spoke with the dulled tone of a punch-drunk. **1969** *Daily Tel.* 13 Nov. 18 'Punch-drunks' are completely unknown in amateur boxing.

Hence **pu·nch-drunkenness**, the condition of being punch-drunk.

1937 *Lit. Digest* 10 Apr. 40/1 The coincidence of boxers developing thickness of speech, unsteadiness of gait,..has prompted London's famed Guy's Hospital to initiate a special study of the cause and cure of punch drunkenness. **1939** J. Berryman in *Astounding Sci. Fiction* May 31 Tiny bloodclots on the lining of the brain, whose pressure on delicate centers often caused them to manifest the symptoms of punch-drunkenness. **1941** *Lancet* 14 June 759/1 There is, however, that specific problem of boxing, 'punchdrunkenness'—the permanent damage due to repeated cerebral injury. **1959** *Daily Tel.* 27 June 7/5 There was 'plenty of evidence to show that punch-drunkenness is a very real hazard to boxers'. **1977** J. Porter *Who the Heck is Sylvia?* xv. 144 A family which prided itself on never knowing when it was beaten and in which punch-drunkenness was practically an endemic disease.

punched, *ppl. a.* Add: **2.** *punched card*, a card in which a pattern of holes, punched in it in accordance with a prescribed code, represents information; similarly *punched paper*, *punched* (*paper*) *tape*. Freq. *attrib.* Cf. *paper tape* s.v. *paper *sb.* 12, *perforated tape* s.v. *perforated *ppl. a.* 1.

1876 Punched paper [in Dict.]. **1885** *Electrician* 27 Nov. 57/1 The Wheatstone fast-speed transmitter.., by which one punched tape served for twenty or thirty different wires. **1890** *Jrnl. Franklin Inst.* CXXIX. 301 These punched record cards can easily be read and verified. **1919** A. Macfarlane *Lectures on Ten British Physicists* 79 To realize the first idea..he had recourse to the device of punched cards similar to those invented by Jacquard for the weaving loom. **1940** W. J. Eckert *Punched Card Methods in Scientific Computation* 2 Tables of functions are constructed from their differences with great efficiency, either as printed tables or as a file of punched cards. **1948** *Electronics* Aug. 100/1 Approximate positions of the stars, already stored in a punched-card catalog, may be coupled to the servomechanism. **1959** *Engineering* 2 Jan. 5/3 The machine can operate from standard punched tape or can be plugged into a long distance teleprinter circuit. **1962** E. Godfrey *Retail Selling & Organ.* i. 6 Mechanized handling of goods, punched-card accounting systems and advertising direct to the consumer..involve costs which the smaller business cannot afford. **1963** *Listener* 21 Mar. 489/2 A computer..which read a quarter of a million words of Greek prose, translated into its own punched-paper language. **1968** *Brit. Med. Bull.* XXIV. 191/1 The commonest way..of inserting data and program into a computer is via punched paper tape or punched cards. **1975** T. Allbeury *Special Collection* i. 5 In Central Intelligence Records they had thousands of simple punched cards..in May 1944. **1980** D. Bloodworth *Trapdoor* v. 24 The formidable batteries of punched-card systems and data banks.

puncheon[1]. Add: Also **punchen. 5. a.** (Earlier and later examples.)

1804 in *Maryland Hist. Mag.* (1909) IV. 9 Houses or cabins..are generally made of heavy timber logs covered with split timbers called 'puncheons' which they pin to the rafters with wooden pins. **1946** C. Richter *Fields* 164 The puncheons had holes for seat legs.

b. A piece of timber used in building a railway track or a corduroy road. *N. Amer.*

1843 W. Oliver *Eight Months Illinois* 236 Trees are split up into what are called puncheons, of three or four inches in thickness, which are laid down on the sleepers. **1955** R. Hobson *Nothing too Good* xv. 165, I figure that all it will cost you is the axes, shovels, spikes for punchen, crow bars, [etc.].

6. b. For (*U.S.*) read (orig. *U.S.*). (Earlier and later examples.)

1754 J. Innes *Let.* 27 Sept. in *Lett. to Washington* (1898) I. 48, I have erected a puntion Fort. **1784** G. Washington *Diary* 20 Sept. (1925) II. 294 A Logged dwelling house with a punchion roof. **1843** 'R. Carlton' *New Purchase* xxi. 199 Adjoining the bureau was the puncheon table with its white oak legs. **1940** W. Faulkner *Hamlet* ii. i. 110 The heatless lean-to room was his desert cell, the thin pallet bed on the puncheon floor the couch of stones on which he would lie. **1963** R. Symons *Many Trails* xiv. 145 The floor was of the puncheon type—that is, poplar poles laid across stringers and smoothed with an adze, with no attempt at nailing. **1972** E. Wigginton *Foxfire Bk.* 33 Green chestnut was split into fence rails, puncheon floors, wide planking, [etc.].

pu·ncheoned, *a.* [f. Puncheon[1] + -ed[2].] Covered or laid with puncheons (Puncheon[1] 5 a in Dict. and Suppl.).

1843 'R. Carlton' *New Purchase* xv. 109 And first, the puncheoned area was separated into two grand parts.

puncher. Add: **a.** (Further examples.)

1876 *Jrnl. Soc. Telegr. Engineers* V. 492 When one clerk considers a puncher quite workable, another declares it to be useless. **1915** F. M. Hueffer *Good Soldier* i. v. 73 Ready to lend you his cigar puncher. **1951** *Sport* 30 Mar.–5 Apr. 10/2 Both have reputations as punchers. *a* **1953** Dylan Thomas *Quite Early One Morning* (1954) 33 The clip of the chair-attendant's puncher. **1973** *Irish Times* 2 Mar. 3/3 They [*sc.* a hockey team] depend enormously on John Douglas to initiate their raids and have only one recognised 'puncher' in Tom Jenkinson.

b. For *U.S.* read *N. Amer.* (Earlier and later examples.) Also *attrib.* in *puncher-boy*.
1870 *Daily Territorial Enterprise* (Virginia City, Nevada) 17 Aug. 3/1 All the time the punchers are flying from ox to ox, plying their sticks right and left. **1910** in J. Lomax *Cowboy Songs* 96 But show me a man that sleeps more profound Than the big puncher-boy who stretches himself on the ground. **1912** S. A White *Wildcatters* 137 Ben had decked him out in puncher's garb. The lariot was correctly coiled at the saddle-horn. **1972** T. A. Bulman *Kamloops Cattlemen* ii. 16 Tough as these old 'punchers' were, the years gradually took their toll.

punchery. (In Dict. s.v. Punch *sb.*^{3}) (Later examples.)
1952 *John o' London's* 1 Aug. 724/3 The eighteenth century had a forerunner of our home cocktail bar. This was the Georgian punchery, a magnificent assembly of.. bowls, spice dredgers, crystal bottles..and a..punch ladle. **1962** *Times* 20 Jan. 11/3 Well-stocked puncheries magnificently displaying colourful punch bowls.

Punchine (pʌ·nʃəin), *a. rare.* [f. Punch *sb.*^{5} 2 + -ine^{1}.] Of or pertaining to the journal *Punch*.
1846 Thackeray in *Punch* 8 Aug. 59/2 It was this braggart violence of soul that roused the Punchine wrath against Mr. O'Connell.

punching, *vbl. sb.* Add: **a.** Also, a piece of sheet metal cut out by a punch.
1903 *Electr. World & Engin.* 28 Mar. 532/2 The four-pole pieces are made of laminated steel punchings. **1947** R. Lee *Electronic Transformers & Circuits* iii. 75 There is always a certain amount of gap even with punchings stacked alternately in groups of 1. **1951** E. W. Workman in P. Kemp *Electr. Engin.* III. 633/2 In the case of electrical transformers, generators and motors, sheet-steel punchings form a large proportion of the total works cost.

b. *punching machine* (examples); **punching bag** (earlier and later examples); also *fig.*; **punching press** = *punch-press* s.v. *punch *sb.*^{1} 7.
1889 *Cent. Dict.*, Punching-bag. **1896** Ade *Artie* i. 4 Say, I like that church, and if they'll put in a punchin'-bag and a plunge they can have my game, I'll tell you those. **1911** *Boxing* IV. 456/2 Once again that old trial hope, Fred Drummond, was dragged from his stall to play the part of punching-bag. **1976** G. Sims *End of Web* x. 72 Buchanan used him like a punching-bag, hitting him with every combination he knew. **1850** *Rep. U.S. Comm. Patents 1849* I. 185 My improved punching machine. **1878** *Harper's Mag.* Apr. 645/2 The bar then goes to the punching-machine that..bites a bar through the iron. **1962** F. T. Day *Introd. Paper* viii. 87 Table mats and drip mats..are often produced on a blanking-out or punching machine. *a* **1884** E. H. Knight *Dict. Mech.* Suppl. 730/2 Punching press. **1906** C. H. Benjamin *Mod. Amer. Machine Tools* x. 282 (*caption*) 60-inch punching press.

punchless (pʌ·nʃlès), *a.*^{1} [f. Punch *sb.*^{3} + -less.] Having no punch to drink.
1903 W. Stevens *Let.* 26 July (1967) 64, I was looking forward to a cigarless, punchless weary life.

pu·nchless, *a.*^{2} [f. Punch *sb.*^{2} + -less.] Lacking a powerful punch; deficient as a boxer.
1950 J. Dempsey *Championship Fighting* ii. 11 Punchless performers who can win amateur or professional bouts on points.

pu·nch line. orig. *U.S.* Also with hyphen and as one word. [f. Punch *sb.*^{2} + Line *sb.*^{2} 23.] Words or a sentence expressing the point of a joke, play, song, etc. Hence **punch-line** *v. intr.*
1921 *Variety* 25 Nov. 8/1 All of their sure-fire punch-lines went over. **1934** S. R. Nelson *All about Jazz* vii. 158 The gentlemen who write lyrics..imagine the public hang on their doggerel—particularly the line known as the 'punch line'. **1937** *Dime Detective Mag.* Nov. 45/2 Go on..give me the punch line. **1944** S. Bellow *Dangling Man* 158 Yes, things change. *C'est la guerre. C'est la vie.* Good old punch lines. **1957** *Oxford Mail* 17 Oct. 1/2 It was Mr Dulles's punch-line and showed the Russians—and the American people—that President Eisenhower regards the Middle East crisis with great anxiety. **1959** *Time* 14 Sept. 44/2 'I'll kill myself..' said Benny. 'All right,' Truman punch-lined, 'I've got an undertaker friend.' **1961** B. Wells *Day Earth caught Fire* vii. 107 'Wonder who writes his punchlines?' remarked Reynolds. **1971** *World Archaeology* III. 226 He [*sc.* V. G. Childe] was fond of dramatic punch-lines. **1977** *New Yorker* 27 June 67/1 Reaching the punch line, he erupted in laughter.

pu·nch-up. *slang.* Also without hyphen and as one word. [f. Punch *v.*^{1} + Up *adv.*^{1}] A fight or brawl. Also *fig.*, a fierce or noisy argument.
1958 F. Norman *Bang to Rights* 28 The next morning after we had had this little punch up. **1960** H. Pinter *Caretaker* ii. 36 Bloke saved me from a punch up. **1963** K. Amis *One Fat Englishman* iii. 36 The fellow was earning a bigger and better punch-up, oral or physical, with every sentence he spoke. **1966** J. Wainwright *Evil Intent* 85 He's been responsible for more religious punch-ups than Judas himself. **1967** *New Scientist* 14 Dec. 673/1 Good old-fashioned punch-ups between the holders of rival theories, of the sort that so stimulated 19th century science, are sadly rare today. **1972** J. Wilson *Hide & Seek* viii. 151, I got six months..all because you ruzzers stuck your noses into a private little punch up. **1976** *Daily Mirror* 11 Mar. 9/6 He was fired after an alleged punch-up with another worker. **1978** *Times Lit. Suppl.* 25 Aug. 944/3 Boxing and pub punch-ups were his main amusements.

punchy, *a.*^{1} (Earlier example.)
1783 J. Woodforde *Diary* 10 Feb. (1926) II. 58 He bought..a short dark Punchy Horse with a Hog main.

punchy (pʌ·nʃi), *a.*^{3} [f. Punch *sb.*^{2} + -y^{1}.] Full of punch or vigour.
1926 Whiteman & McBride *Jazz* ii. 41, I would direct a punchy number. **1930** *Observer* 19 Oct. 19 A punchy rhetorical speech on Free Trade. **1937** *Lit. Digest* 4 Dec. 30/3 The English language may some day be as colorful and punchy as it was in Elizabethan times. **1959** *Times Lit. Suppl.* 25 Sept. 545/5 (Advt.), In over a score of punchy entertaining chapters he delights readers. **1971** *Amateur Photographer* 3 Mar. 23/2 The 10-minute playlet with a punchy plot. **1977** *Time* 30 May 55/1 More gregarious than Woodcock, a punchier speaker, a hair more liberal, Fraser signals a change in style rather than substance.

pu·nchy, *a.*^{4} *slang* (chiefly *U.S.*). [f. Punch *sb.*^{2} or *punch-drunk *a.* and *sb.* + -y^{1}.] = *punch-drunk *a.* Hence *transf.*, in a state of nervous tension or extreme fatigue. Also as *sb.* (*rare*).
1937 *Lit. Digest* 10 Apr. 39/2 'Slap-happy' or 'punchy' ex-fighters. **1937** E. Hemingway *To have & have Not* iii. xiv. 201 Shut up, slappy... You've got the old rale... You punchies make me sick. **1943** *Gen* 16 Jan. 30/1 He lives in a dream-world..he is, as the boys put it, 'punchy'. **1950** E. B. White *Let.* 12 Nov. (1976) 326 K and I are both pretty well, if a bit punchy. **1958** E. Dundy *Dud Avocado* ii. iii. 209, I am so punchy..that I don't know whether I'm coming or going. **1970** K. Platt *Pushbutton Butterfly* (1971) xiii. 149 I'm not coming at you because of what a punchy Hell's Angel tea-head told me. **1974** *Summerville* (S. Carolina) *Jrnl.* 24 Apr. 2/3 By the time the serviceman inserted a new tube,..the kids were getting punchy from sitting before a gray screen,..trying to imagine just what it was that the Roadrunner was doing to the wily Coyote. **1977** *Tennis World* Sept. 17/2 A player who breaks up on the court from nervousness is said to be 'punchy', 'gone cuckoo' or simply 'gone'.

punctiliar (pʌŋkti·liăɹ), *a.* [f. Punctilio + -ar^{1}.] Of or pertaining to a point of time; = *punctual *a.* 5e.
1906 J. H. Moulton *Gram. N.T. Greek* I. vi. 109 The Aorist has a 'punctiliar' action, that is, it regards action as a *point*. [*note*] I venture to accept from a correspondent this new-coined word to represent the German *punktuell*, the English of which is preoccupied. **1944** E. A. Nida *Morphol.* ii. ix. 130 If an action is considered as a unit, occurring so to speak, at a 'point' of time, it may be considered 'punctiliar'. In such a case an action which takes place over a considerable extent of time may nevertheless be looked upon as a unitary action of a punctiliar nature. **1964** —— *Toward Sci. Transl.* ix. 199 As a description of the kind of action involved in the verb, aspect serves to differentiate a number of contrasts, of which some of the most common are: (1) complete vs. incomplete, (2) punctiliar vs. continuous, [etc.].

punctilio. B. 5. b. (Later examples.)
1943 *R.A.F. Jrnl.* Aug. 22 All the matchless punctilio of an iron discipline coloured his daily round. **1978** J. Updike *Coup* (1979) iv. 171 These noodly motifs the French had brought, along with military science, the metric system, and punctilio.

punctual, *a.* **II. 2.** Delete † *Obs.* and add: **a.** (Later examples.)
1904 T. Hutchinson in Shelley *Wks.* p. iv, Amongst the Editor's Notes at the end of the volume the reader will find lists of the punctual variations in the longer poems. **1930** *Bookman's Jrnl.* XVIII. xiv. (Second Supplement) 15 Both books have been entirely reset for this edition, and in addition to many minor alterations, mainly punctual, there is a new preface. **1931** *Times Lit. Suppl.* 16 Apr. 305/3 A punctual variation (which is also a misprint) between the publisher's imprint in the first two and in the third volume is not recorded.

IV. 5. e. *Gram.* Of action: occurring at a point in time; of aspect or tense: relating to an action or event that occurs at a point in time. Also as *sb.*, the punctual aspect or tense of a verb.
1914 L. Bloomfield *Introd. Study Lang.* v. 145 The Slavic languages distinguish..between..durative and iterative..iterative..and..punctual and terminative action. **1924** [see *aspect *sb.* 9 b]. **1933** L. Bloomfield *Language* xvi. 272 The English categories of *aspect* distinguish between 'punctual' action (some grammarians call it perfective), envisaged as a unit, and 'durative' action.. which extends over a segment of time. **1956** J. Gonda *Character Indo-Europ. Moods* iv. 44 The pronounced preference for the aorist may be understood from the predilection for the punctual aspect in formulating prohibitions. **1962** —— *Aspectual Function of Ṛgvedic Present & Aorist* i. 19 The aorist... is considered 'punctual', whether the initial moment (δακρῦσαι 'burst into tears'), or the end (πεῖσαι 'to persuade, talk over') is indicated. **1971** *Archivum Linguisticum* II. 112 This means that the 'punctual meaning' and the other meanings traditionally thought of as the aorist's are, as far as the sigmatic aorist is concerned, simply another specialization, restricted to a limited dialectal field. *Ibid.* 113 Gonda makes some criticism of the general statement.. that VI class presents are 'punctuals', sometimes used to express punctual action, sometimes to describe actions indifferent to duration, but which sometimes can be thought of as punctual.

punctuality. Add: **I. 1. c.** *Gram.* The quality or character of being punctual (sense *5e); the punctual aspect of a verb.
1962 J. Gonda *Aspectual Function of Ṛgvedic Present & Aorist* i. 31 The basic notion of the opposition present stem : aorist stem in Greek is that of duration, the present being the marked term, the aorist which is the unmarked term sometimes being indifferent in respect to duration.. sometimes expressing punctuality. *Ibid.* 34 The fundamental idea of nondurativeness ('punctuality') in the aorist. **1971** *Archivum Linguisticum* II. 113 Both notions (non-duration and punctuality) became unified at a certain time, that is to say, their meanings became compatible, appearing alternatively according to context.

punctuate, *v.* Add: **3. b.** (*b*). (Earlier and later examples.)
c **1865** E. Dickinson *Poems* (1955) II. 731 A Flower's unobtrusive Face To punctuate the Wall. **1941** *Penguin New Writing* II. 54 They communicated with each other in a low drone.., punctuated by an occasional deep-throated 'Ah!' **1966** C. M. Bowra *Memories 1898–1939* v. 98 Roy Harrod..punctuated his speeches with such phrases as 'I dare aver' or 'if you will permit the observation'. **1971** E. Mavor *Ladies of Llangollen* ix. 159 Great delicacy had to be employed on both sides of a correspondence which was apt to be punctuated with small wounded silences, implied accusations followed by temporary reconciliations. **1977** *Times* 25 Nov. (Christmas Book Suppl.) p. xxxi/4 The novel is one of many nicely turned backward looks that have worthily punctuated the year.

punctuation. Add: **3. c.** *fig.* The repeated occurrence or distribution (*of* something); something that makes repeated or regular interruptions or divisions.
1914 *Sat. Even. Post* 4 Apr. 12/1 The endless punctuation of ties led on and on until even the marshes rose and became level with the tracks. **1933** E. O'Neill *Ah Wilderness!* i. 20 (*Stage direction*) The bang of firecrackers and torpedoes..continues at intervals..sufficiently emphatic to form a disturbing punctuation to the conversation. **1970** H. Braun *Parish Churches* ix. 125 Vertical punctuation disciplines an elevation by sorting it out into orderly compartments and replacing confusion with a pleasant rhythm... Vertical punctuation is of course achieved by the pilasters. later becoming buttresses. Horizontal punctuation is primarily concerned with maintaining a sense of stability. **1977** *Times* 16 Apr. 14/4 It requires a considerable resistance to evidence not to see the Reformation, the Enlightenment, nineteenth-century liberalism and the current decline as stages in a continuous process rather than punctuations in an otherwise stable history.

punctum. Add: **4. b.** *punctum saliens* (earlier and later examples); also *fig.*
1663 R. Boyle *Consid. Usef. Nat. Philos.* ii. i. 18 In Hen-eggs..you may observe the *Punctum saliens*, or Heart, to be ever and anon full of conspicuously red Blood. **1814** M. Birkbeck *Jrnl.* 18 Sept. in *Notes Journey through France* 83 Paris is the punctum saliens, the organ of political feeling; elsewhere political feeling is absorbed in the love of tranquillity. **1977** *Language* LIII. 56 The 'punctum saliens' is that it was the 'paradigmatic' alternation *u*~*o* which was felt to render the constituent structure opaque.

6. *punctum indifferens* (cf. Indifferent *a.*^{1} 8a), a neutral point.
1923 A. T. Quiller-Couch *Shakespeare's Much Ado about Nothing* p. xv, Such a man is the Friar in this play; its steadying sane mind, its *punctum indifferens*. **1932** J. Buchan *Sir W. Scott* xiii. 342 This *punctum indifferens* is the peaceful anchorage of good sense from which we are able to watch with a balanced mind the storm outside. **1976** 'J. Davey' *Treasury Alarm* i. 11 Things may rearrange themselves around me just because I'm there—as a *punctum indifferens*.

7. *Palæogr.* A point used as a (weak) mark of punctuation in medieval manuscripts.
1952, **1975** [see *punctus]. **1975** *Anglo-Saxon England* IV. 117 The poems in lyric metres are written across the page as prose, but each verse line is separated by at least a punctum (or greater punctuation if the syntax requires it). **1978** *N. & Q.* Oct. 396/1 Each octosyllabic couplet is written as one line, divided by a mid-line punctum.

puncture, *sb.* Add: **4. puncture mark,** a mark made by a needle point, *esp.* in the injection of drugs.
1927 D. L. Sayers *Unnatural Death* xxiii. 274 Will you go down to the mortuary again and see if you can find any puncture mark on the body. **1935** A. Christie *Death in Clouds* ii. 23 There was a minute puncture mark on the side of her throat. **1957** D. du Maurier *Scapegoat* xxi. 280 The sleeve of her black wool coat fell back, showing the puncture marks between wrist and forearm. **1974** D. Ramsay *No Cause to Kill* i. 13 She wasn't mainlining, but there's a mark on her arm that could be a puncture mark.

puncture, *v.* Add: **1. d.** (Later examples.)
1927 *Scribner's Mag.* Apr. 450b/2 There is certain value in puncturing the Washington myth which the school histories used to teach. **1974** *Economist* 7 Sept. 16 It is time to puncture the continuing Greek accusation.

e. To punctuate or intersperse.
1899 C. M. M. Sheldon *His Brother's Keeper* xi. 249 The major..made a rattling speech, punctured with frequent amens and hallelujahs from the rest of the army

3. (Later example.) Now *rare*.
1975 *Country Life* 4 Dec. 1529/2 Many cars suffered... Cowan punctured and spun.

‖ **punctus** (pʊ·ŋktʊ̈s, pu·ŋk-). *Palæogr.* [L., f. *pungere* to prick: cf. PUNCTUM.] A point, a punctuation mark. Freq. in phr. *punctus elevatus* (elĕvā·tʊ̈s), a raised point; *punctus interrogativus* (intĕrǫ:gătī·vʊ̈s), a question mark; *punctus versus* (vɜ̄·ɪsʊ̈s), a reversed point. See also quots.
1952 P. CLEMOES *Liturgical Influence on Punctuation in Late Old English & Early Middle English MSS* 4 *Punctus elevatus*, a symbol formed by combining *Punctum* and *Podatus*. It denoted the cadence with which a *Colon* ended, generally a gradual lowering of pitch followed by a return to the *Tuba* in one stage. *Ibid.* 5 *Punctus versus*, a symbol consisting of the *Punctum*. It denoted the cadence with which a *Periodus* ended. *Ibid.*, *Punctus interrogativus*, a symbol formed by combining *Punctum* and *Porrectus*. It denoted the cadence with which an interrogative sentence ended. **1954** D. WHITELOCK *Early Eng. MSS. in Facsimile* IV. 18/2 The usual mark of punctuation is the *punctus*, marking minor pauses as well as the end of sentences. *Ibid.*, A sign shaped like a semi-colon, the *punctus versus*, occurs. *Ibid.*, A mark like an inverted semi-colon, the *punctus elevatus*,..never marks the close of a period, but divides a main from a subordinate clause, or one subordinate clause from another. **1957** N. R. KER *Catal. MSS. containing Anglo-Saxon* p. xxxiv, The two marks, the dot and the ;, were reinforced at the end of the tenth century by a third mark,⁏, which had been used hitherto only in Latin texts. It was known later in the Middle Ages as *punctus elevatus* and is often called now, inaccurately, the 'reversed semicolon'. **1966** P. CLEMOES *Early Eng. MSS. in Facsimile* XIII. 24/1 Four marks are used, namely a simple point placed at about mid-height..a *punctus elevatus*..a *punctus versus*..and a *punctus interrogativus*. **1971** P. J. LUCAS in *Archivum Linguisticum* II. 5 Notably absent are the *punctus elevatus* (or so-called 'inverted semicolon') and the *punctus interrogativus*... His [*sc.* Capgrave's] failure to use both the *punctus elevatus* and the *punctus interrogativus* probably indicates a movement away from liturgical (and formal rhetorical) influence. **1975** *Anglo-Saxon England* IV. 117 This [system of punctuation] consists of a hierarc hy of punctum (.), punctus elevatus (⁏), punctus versus (;)..the punctus interrogativus (?) is also used.

pundit. Delete ‖ and add: **a.** (Later examples.)
1891 C. R. DAY *Music of S. India* v. 61 They..were probably composed by some Telegu pandit at the court of Mysore. **1901** [see *KASHMIRI *a.* and *sb.*]. **1953** *Encounter* Oct. 41/2 That this pandit (i.e. 'wise man') has become Prime Minister is one of the caprices of history. **1967** *Guardian* 26 Aug. 7/7 Having received choice jobs during the days of the Maharaja and the British Raj, the Pandits now resent the attempts to redress the balance in favour of..the Moslems. **1971** *Illustr. Weekly India* 4 Apr. 19 After the hair is cut and the *puja* is performed by the *pandit*, the turban with the sehra is placed on the head of the child by the father.
b. Delete (*colloq.* and *humorous*). (Later examples.)
1924 C. E. MONTAGUE *Right Place* xiv. 222 To say things and try to believe them, just because some aesthetic pundit or critical mandarin has said them before. **1938** R. HUGHES *In Hazard* ii. 37 First, this was developing into a true hurricane; and, second, it was not at all where it was thought by the pundits to be. **1941** C. H. WADDINGTON *Scientific Attitude* iv. 51 The architect who wished to build for a scientific and sceptical age had to..find out what was left when scepticism had done its worst. The pundits would say that nothing was left. **1957** *Listener* 5 Sept. 338/1 The British Association..is holding its 119th annual meeting... The pundits have gathered at Dublin. **1976** *Times* 30 Sept. 8/7 Though frowned upon by some pundits as out-of-date and middle-class, *Swallows and Amazons* and its many sequels remain immensely popular with children. **1977** J. I. M. STEWART *Madonna of Astrolabe* iii. 51 Here is what some pundit calls the phantom aesthetic state.

pundit (pʊ·ndit), *v. rare.* [f. prec.] *intr.* To make pronouncements like an expert. Also with quasi-obj.
1959 *Time* (Atlantic ed.) 19 Oct. 61 Huntley..is..inclined to take a panoramic view of the news, more inclined to pundit. **1967** *Punch* 4 Jan. 2/2 Take Alfie Hinds, currently punditing his head off as the BBC's escapological correspondent.

punditry (pʊ·nditri). [f. PUNDIT + -RY.] The characteristics of a pundit; opinions or actions befitting a pundit (sense b).
1926 T. M. HEALY in *Pioneer Ref. Spelling* Apr. 14, I..decry the punditry of Civil Service Commissioners in making so-called orthography a test subject. **1930** *Times Lit. Suppl.* 13 Nov. 932/2 His latest book..blends a good deal of punditry with its collectors' gossip. **1948** J. STEINBECK *Russ. Jrnl.* i. 3 News has become a matter of punditry. A man sitting at a desk in Washington or New York reads the cables and rearranges them to fit his own mental pattern and his by-line. **1958** *Oxford Mag.* 13 Feb. 278/1 All Oxford seemed to be there, with its focus in the ebullient punditry of Sir Isaiah Berlin. **1966** *Listener* 15 Sept. 397/3 It pounded and explored the whole subject of South Africa: past, present, future. Plenty of instant punditry. **1978** *Bull. Amer. Acad. Arts & Sci.* Jan. 22, I have caught him in a moment of punditry and while he was yielding to a weakness common to critics.

pundonor. (Later examples.)
1932 E. HEMINGWAY *Death in Afternoon* xviii. 210 His..body contains enough valour and pundonor to make a dozen bullfighters. **1967** MCCORMICK & MASCAREÑAS *Compl. Aficionado* ii. 45 That outcry was fascinating in its vehemence, for it had the false accents of him who protests too much; one is tempted to think that it could occur only in a land where *pundonor* is on every tongue. **1968** *Medium Ævum* XXXVII. 46 Nor do I think we have a right to assume that the sculptors followed epic pundonor so closely.

pung, *sb.*[2] For *U.S.* read *N. Amer.* and add: **a.** (Later, including Canad., examples.) Also *attrib.*
1886 [see *CLIP *v.*[2] 7]. **1908** L. M. MONTGOMERY *Anne of Green Gables* xix. 208 Her cousins are coming from Newbridge with a big pung sleigh. **1951** E. M. GRAHAM *My Window looks down East* iv. 31, I saw Carl Urlichson bringing home his fishing boat from the shore on sled runners drawn by a big Belgian horse... But I saw more than a boat on a pung. **1952** E. BUCKLER *Mountain & Valley* 171 The pung races on the lake. **1953** *N.Y. Times* 24 July 15/7 Carriages, buckboards and wagons were employed and pungs, sleds with box-like bodies, were popular.

pung (pʊŋ), *v.*[2], *sb.*[3], and *int.* *Mah Jong.* [Chinese.] **A.** *vb. intr.* To take a discarded tile in order to complete a triplet of identical tiles. Also *trans.* **B.** *sb.* A set of three identical tiles; also, the action of the verb. **C.** *int.* The call made by the player performing this action. So pu·nging *vbl. sb.*
1922 R. E. LINDSELL *Ma-Cheuk or Mah-Jongg* 12 A useless domino..is placed face upwards in the middle of the table, and can at once be claimed by any of the other three players who has already a pair or threes of that particular domino. This is called 'parking' or 'punging'. **1923** J. P. BABCOCK *Rules for Mah-Jongg* (ed. 2) ii. 15 Should a tile be discarded and any player have a pair (or three) of this same tile, even though out of his own turn, he may 'Pung', that is he says 'Pung' and takes this discarded tile, placing it with the pair (or three) from his own hand face up in front of him on the table... A Pung which completes a hand takes precedence over any other Pung. **1925** B. TRAVERS *Mischief* v. 86 Louise came in, all fatigued and heated from harbouring red dragons and punging her opponent's wind. **1934** *Neuphilologische Mitteilungen* XXXV. 132 Mah-jongg..*pung* 'set of..three identical tiles'. **1960** R. C. BELL *Board & Table Games* vi. 155 If any of the other three players holds two tiles identical with one just discarded, he may call 'Pung!' and take it out of the pool. Only the last discarded piece may be punged. **1964** E. N. WHITNEY *Mah Jong Handbk.* I. iii. 28 If you have a pair in your hand and *any* player discards an identical tile, you may declare 'pung' and claim the discarded tile instead of drawing from the wall. *Ibid.* 169 *Pung*, claiming a discard that completes a triplet. After punging, the player must meld his completed triplet.

punga, var. *PONGA.

punge, var. *PUNJI.

pungle (pʊ·ŋg'l), *v.* *U.S. colloq.* 9 **pongale, pungale.** [ad. Sp. *póngale* put it down, f. *poner* put, give.] *trans.* and *intr.* To contribute, hand over, or pay. Usu. with *down* or *up*.
1851 *Alta Californian* 19 July 2/3 A singular genius..was 'pongaling down' huge piles of gold at a monte table. **1854** *Pioneer* (San Francisco) Apr. 237 An additional slice of territory and its consequent classical influence upon our language, by the introduction of such precious words..as 'hombre',..'pungle', *et id omne genus.* **1857** *San Francisco Call* 6 Jan. 2/2 'Pungale down, gentlemen; come, pungale', as the vingt-et-un lady used to say. **1884** 'MARK TWAIN' *Huck. Finn* v. 33 'I'll ask him; and I'll make him pungle, too, or I'll know the reason why'... Next day he went to Judge Thatcher's and..tried to make him give up the money. **1910** E. S. FIELD *Sapphire Bracelet* xii. 141 I'll have him arrested, and then make him pungle up something handsome before I'll agree not to appear against him. **1959** A. K. LANG in *Alfred Hitchcock's Mystery Mag.* Feb. 71/1 The pusher couldn't pungle up Skreen's three hundred. **1975** J. GORES *Hammett* (1976) xix. 130 Hammett had coffee and pungled up the required fifty cents.

pungo, var. PUNGY in Dict. and Suppl.
1854 W. G. SIMMS *Southward Ho!* iii. 28 Their most innocent name is 'pungo'—a sort of schooner, hailing mostly from Manhattan and Massachusetts. *Ibid.*, For the better oysters..the 'pungos' pay three shillings. **1938** 'J. DIGGES' *Bowleg Bill* 24 Next morning the whole harbor is cluttered up with dories, pungoes, and anything down to harness-casks.

pungy. Add: (Earlier and further examples.) Also *attrib.*
1876 T. WESTCOTT *Centennial Portfolio* 32/2 There are models of fish-hatching houses, of fishing-rafts..and also of the oyster-catching material, vessels, pungys, canoes, drags, rafts, etc. **1884** *Forest & Stream* 24 Jan. 526/2 The model is of a round futtock with but little deadrise, with round stern, sharp, or what we call a pungy stern, but a sharp stern like that of a little canoe costs the least. **1939** *Sun* (Baltimore) 4 Apr. 12/7 The pungy was a keel boat with no centreboard. **1941** M. V. BREWINGTON *Chesapeake Bay Bugeyes* 30 Not more than a dozen square stern, or 'pungy bugeyes', seem to have been built. *Ibid.* 34 Up to about 1908 many of the bugeyes were painted 'pungy style' with dark green bends, white rail and 'flesh' colored sides. *Ibid.* 46 The ordinary pungy rig, with sharply raking masts, round mastheads, iron rod cross-trees, upper and lower cap, and with the topmast not fidded but resting in the lower cap. **1942** *Sun* (Baltimore) 28 Dec. 18/5 Several marine railways with tugs..pungies or bateaux. **1950** *Ibid.* 23 Aug. 20/5 The Old Pungy Wave, last of her type, has arrived safely in Detroit, which will be home to her for some while to come. **1967** L. S. TAWES *Coasting Captain* 4 In the fall of 1868 I left the farm and went dredging as cook on a pungy boat.

Punic, *sb.* **3.** (Earlier and later examples.)
1673 J. RAY *Observations Journey Low-Countries* 308 The language of the Natives [of Malta] is a corrupt Arabic or Moresco, introduced by the Saracens, the ancient language before their coming in probably having been Greek, with a mixture of Punick. **1971** S. E. MORISON *European Discovery Amer.: Northern Voy.* i. 11 Phoenician script is so simple that, as with the later Norse runes, it is easy for an overimaginative searcher to read Punic, like Runic, in natural grooves and scratches on rocks.

punily, *adv.* (Later examples.)
1906 BELLOC *Hills & Sea* 56 In Africa, where men build so squat and punily. **1942** W. FAULKNER *Go down, Moses* 193 That doomed wilderness whose edges were being constantly and punily gnawed at by men with plows and axes.

punish, *v.* Add: **B. 3.** (Earlier and further examples.) Also, to abuse (a musical instrument) by playing it badly.
1801 *Sporting Mag.* XIX. 62/2 This desperate contest, comprising sixteen rounds, lasted twenty-one minutes, and we never witnessed a man more *punished* than Burk. **1807** R. SOUTHEY *Lett. from England* III. lxxi. 310 When the [boxing] champion..comes off victor, after suffering much in the contest, he is said to be *much punished.* **1844** DICKENS *Martin Chuzzlewit* xxxvi. 425 Tom, taking up his knife and fork again... 'I shall punish the Boar's Head dreadfully.' **1864** *Sporting Mag.* XLV. 194 When the Eleven come to the wickets, how they punish the ball, and rapidly run-up a long score. **1891** W. G. GRACE *Cricket* xi. 312 It was a treat to watch him punish the bowling. **1930** *Morning Post* 16 July 11/5 Chapman batted remarkably well. He refused to take any risk and yet punished the loose ball. **1934** DYLAN THOMAS in *Listener* 24 Oct. 691/2 Especially when the October wind With frosty fingers punishes my hair. *Ibid.*, Especially when the October wind..With fist of turnips punishes the land. **1942** J. B. PRIESTLEY *Black-Out in Gretley* vii. 149 The bottle of brandy they'd punished was prominent on the little table. **1949** 'J. TEY' *Brat Farrar* iv. 34 Ungainly women in unseemly clothes punishing the saddles of broken-spirited horses. **1967** *Observer* 17 Dec. 1/1 An old man punishing a mandolin in Bond Street.

punishable, *a.* Add: **b.** (Later examples.)
1909 *Daily Chron.* 29 Nov. 3/1 If a punishable play is produced, the author and the lessee..should be punished. **1959** *Daily Tel.* 31 Dec. 1/7 Confiscation of the latest issue of Reichsruf, weekly newspaper of the extreme Right-wing German Reich Party, and another party journal,..was ordered by a Bielefeld court today. They were stated to have 'punishable contents'.
c. In sense 3 of the verb.
1910 *Blackw. Mag.* July 106/2 The punishable [ball] escaped scot-free.

punisher. Add: **b.** (Earlier example.) Also *Cricket.*
1812 P. EGAN *Boxiana* 113 The *Lobster* had most powerful *claws*, and was a first-rate *punisher*. **1846** W. DENISON *Cricket: Sketches of Players* 12 If the bowling be at all loose, he is a powerful punisher.

punishing, *ppl. a.* Add: **b.** (Earlier and further examples.)
1811 *Sporting Mag.* XXXVIII. 184/1 The punishing right hand of his adversary. **1846** W. DENISON *Cricket: Sketches of Players* 15 As a batsman he has a good defence, and occasionally is found to be a punishing hitter. **1900** P. F. WARNER *Cricket in Many Climes* v. i. 178 Murray Bisset..is a very sound and stylish bat with a good deal of wrist work, but is perhaps just a little short of punishing power.
c. Excessively severe and exhausting; scarcely tolerable.
1971 N. STACEY *Who Cares?* xiii. 216, I was still involved in a punishing fourteen-hours-a-day programme at Woolwich. **1973** A. ROSS *Dunfermline Affair* 180 He studied his *alter ego* almost every minute of every day for a punishing three years. **1975** *Nature* 6 Nov. 91/2 Barnes had considerable skill as a laboratory bench worker but little opportunity to exercise it in his later years because of the punishing load of advisory and administrative work that he willingly undertook. **1977** *Church Times* 14 Jan. 6/3 The OPEC countries..have been giving real aid to some of the poorer countries which has more than equalled the punishing rise in the price of oil

punishment. Add: **1. b.** *Psychol.* Pain, deprivation, or other unpleasant consequence imposed on or experienced by an organism responding incorrectly under specific conditions so that, through avoidance, the desired learning or behaviour becomes established. Cf. *REWARD *sb.*[1] 4 f.
1907 R. M. YERKES *Dancing Mouse* vi. 99 In general, the method of punishment is more satisfactory than the method of reward, because it can be controlled to a greater extent. **1912** [see *REWARD *sb.*[1] 4 f]. **1949** WOODWORTH & MARQUIS *Psychol.* xvi. 530 Punishment has

two important effects. When the child gets a burn from a hot radiator he learns to *avoid* the radiator. When any-one in following a certain lead to his goal meets with punishment..he tends to *shift to another lead.* **1953** B. F. SKINNER *Sci. & Hum. Behav.* xii. 185 In solving the problem of punishment we simply ask: What is the effect of withdrawing a positive reinforcer or presenting a negative. **1956** *Sci. Amer.* Oct 116/3 This finding contradicts the long-held theory that strong excitation in the brain means punishment. **1960** L. M. BAKER *Gen. Experim. Psychol.* xiii. 309 Punishment of undesired behavior soon led to escape activity and satisfactory conditioning in the dog. **1975** FISCHER & GOCHROS *Planned Behav. Change* iv. 54 No positive reinforcement whatsoever is provided for that behavior (as distinct from negative punishment). *Ibid.* 56 When..there is a *decrease* in the probability that the behavior will occur, that stimulus is a negative reinforcer, and the operation is called positive punishment.

2. a. (Earlier and later examples.)

1811 *Sporting Mag.* XXXVIII. 140/1 Silverthorne, with timidity, arising no doubt from punishment in the first round, kept away from his adversary. **1829** P. EGAN *Boxiana* 2nd Ser. II. 97 Burns was not reduced by the punishment he received. **1846** W. DENISON *Cricket: Sketches of Players* 24 The batsman makes up his mind that he shall administer severe punishment. **1929** *Morning Post* 13 July 11/1 Too cautious play, during which loose stuff escaped punishment. **1930** *Daily Express* 6 Oct. 11/5 He took most of the punishment in the first round. **1949** 'J. TEY' *Brat Farrar* viii. 69 Now he looked stupid, like a boxer who is taking too much punishment.

b. Of materials, machinery, etc.: excessive use or rough handling.

1930 *Engineering* 11 Apr. 473/3 Steel from which a boiler tube is manufactured should have the following qualities:—It must be capable of withstanding severe punishment during manufacture and also when being rolled into a tube plate and belled. **1955** *Times* 17 May 18/3 Only the finest film-strength oils can withstand the punishment a tractor engine receives.

3. *attrib.* (Further examples.)

1916 W. OWEN *Let.* 14 Mar. (1967) 385 Inspections, punishment parades, & more inspections. **1946** R. CAMPBELL *Talking Bronco* 16 Rather a punishment-parade For friend and enemy alike. **1958** J. TOWNSEND *Young Devils* vi. 54 In one year more than five hundred canings had been officially entered in the punishment book. **1968** L. BERG *Risinghill* 61 Risinghill, like every school, has a Punishment Book.

punitive, *a.* Add: **a.** (Later examples.) Also, in weakened sense: injurious in such a way as to have a deterrent effect.

1959 *Listener* 23 July 154/2 The double, *over* the bid, continues to be punitive. **1959** *Spectator* 14 Aug. 188/1 Punitive box-office taxation. **1973** *Black Panther* 31 Mar. 4/3 Brother Cleophus has been in punitive segregation (lock-up) since the strike. *Ibid.* 20 Oct. 6/1 Punitive damages are assessed only when the judge believes that a defendant has acted deliberately and with malice. **1978** *Lancashire Life* Mar. 107/1 A situation could now develop whereby through punitive financial strategies the independent sector could be so reduced that eventually it could be held to be of no social significance.

Punjab (pɒ·ndʒāb, -dʒǭb). Also **Punjaub.** [Hindi *Panjāb*, f. Pers. *panj* five + *āb* water (see below).] The name of an extensive region of the Indian sub-continent, so called from its five rivers, now divided between India and Pakistan, used *attrib.* of its products. **Punjab head**: see quot. 1949.

1907 *Yesterday's Shopping* (1969) 205/2 Punjab Baskets. Nest of 6 baskets, complete—3/0. **1910** *Practitioner* Jan. 18 When a man begins to worry it is time for him to go home, and that applies if he suffers from the so-called Aden or Burma or Punjaub or Madras head. **1949** PARTRIDGE *Dict. Slang* (ed. 3) (Addenda) 1145/2 *Punjab head, have a*, to be forgetful; *Punjab head*, forgetfulness.

Punjabi, Panjabi (pɒndʒā·bi, pan-, -dʒǭ·bi), *sb.* and *a.* Also **Penjabi, Punjabee, Punjaubee.** [f. prec. + *-I.] **A.** *sb.* **a.** The Indo-Aryan language spoken in the Punjab.

1801 *Asiatick Researches* VII. 230, I allude to the *Penjábí* and to the *Brij-bhákhá.* **1838** *Jrnl. Asiatic Soc. Bengal* VII. 711 The Sikhs..carried their hatred..to such an extent as to substitute a vocabulary for their native Punjábí. **1854** L. JANVIER *Dict. Panjábí Lang.* p. iv, The character here adopted, and ordinarily used in writing Panjábí, is that known as the *Gurmukhí.* **1862** R. G. LATHAM *Elem. Compar. Philol.* 219 The following.. gives a rough sketch of the grammatical character of the Punjabi. **1921** *Outward Bound* Feb. 74/1 They spoke only Punjabi, of which at that time I knew but three words. **1950** D. JONES *Phoneme* xvi. 84 Such a language as Panjabi which makes use of essential word-tones. **1964** S. K. CHATTERJI in D. Abercrombie et al. *Daniel Jones* 409 In a surrounding group of languages like Panjabi (or Eastern Panjabi), Hindki (Western Panjabi or Lahndi),..and the Himalayan dialects.., we have these new substitutes for aspirates. **1979** *Trans. Philol. Soc.* 192 The very mixed character of the language of the *Ādi Granth*..should not be allowed to obscure the fact that these scriptures provide the best available evidence for Old Panjabi.

b. A native or inhabitant of the Punjab.

1846 *Hist. Punjab* I. ii. 36 In the plains, Patans..are mixed with Jats and Cathis, who compose the bulk of the Punjabis, properly so called. **1878** G. SMITH *Life J. Wilson* xvii. 547 Nanuk, the herd-boy, was the Punjabee or Sikh. **1897** *Daily News* 21 Sept. 5/3 The brunt of the attack fell upon the portion of the camp which was held by the 5th Punjabis. **1969** *Hindu* (Weekly Mag.) 3 Aug. p. iii/1 One of the contributory factors enabling the average Punjabi to drink more milk than his counterpart in other States in the country. **1973** *Guardian* 16 Apr. 5/6 Punjabis are noted for their enterprise—and also for meanness.

B. *adj.* Of or pertaining to the Punjab.

1810 *Asiatick Researches* XI. 277 Nánac, according to *Penjábí* authors, admitted the *Hindú* doctrine of metempsychosis. **1812** W. CAREY *Gram. Punjabee Lang.* p. iv, The Punjabee language is confessedly of mixed origin. **1851** H. B. EDWARDES *Year on Punjab Frontier* I. 30 When all your fat Punjabee dogs are panting in vain after the hare. **1864** *Athenæum* 5 Nov. 597/1 To keep our regular troops..at a strength more than sufficient to render utterly harmless all the turbulent elements of Punjaubee Society. **1886** MRS. EDWARDES *Mem. Sir H. B. Edwardes* II. 315 Before landing at Calcutta, a true Punjabee welcome met him. **1921** *Outward Bound* May 27/1 Ever since I was a boy..these Punjabi lyrics have kept haunting me. **1948** A. TOYNBEE *Civilization on Trial* v. 88 The sonorous Panjabi names of stricken fields in the Anglo-Sikh wars. **1968** *Listener* 26 Dec. 844/3 Surely it's absurd to say..that a child of a..Punjabi family living in a Punjabi community, is just as much an English child as your children or mine. **1971** *Shankar's Weekly* (Delhi) 4 Apr. 4/1 It has been the vain task of the Punjabi elite of West Pakistan to hold down a section of Bengalis as their serfs.

‖**punji** (pɒ·ndʒi), *sb.* Also **panja, panji(e, punge.** [Origin unknown: prob. from a Tibeto-Burman language.] A sharpened (freq. poisoned) bamboo stake set in a camouflaged hole in the ground as a trap for enemy soldiers (or occas. for animals). Freq. *attrib.* in *punji stake, stick.* So **pu·nji** *v. trans.*, to fortify with punji stakes; **pu·njied** *ppl. a.*

1872 E. DALTON *Descriptive Ethnol. Bengal* 11 They [*sc.* the Singphos] are skilled in fortifying naturally difficult positions, using freely the 'panja', a bamboo stake of different lengths sharpened at both ends and stuck in the ground. **1876** R. G. WOODTHORPE in H. L. Thuillier *Gen. Rep. Topogr. Surveys India 1874–5* 60 Two nasty panjied ditches to be crossed. *Ibid.* 61 Steep approaches, very thickly planted with 'panjees'. **1878** G. P. SANDERSON *Thirteen Years among Wild Beasts of India* xvii. 233 Until 1870 this distant abode of the British Lion [*sc.* Tura in the Garo Hills] was defended by a stockade..whilst the neighbourhood was pleasantly *panjied.* The uninitiated may imagine that this *panjieing* is some ornamental arrangement of the grounds, so I must explain that panjies are..a device for..the discouragement, of visitors. They consist of bamboo spikes driven into the ground, almost level with the surface, the earth being scraped away round each so as to form a cup. Hundreds of these are laid in every direction; grass, falling leaves, &c., soon hide them; and if trodden upon they inflict fearful wounds. **1923** *Blackw. Mag.* May 580/2 We had warned the men against 'booby-traps'... Only one man fell into one and got a *panjie*, luckily not poison-tipped, through his leg. **1927** *Ibid.* June 819/1 Others were planting sharp-pointed panjis in the undergrowth round the village to impale the enemy as they rush to the assault. **1950** J. H. WILLIAMS *Elephant Bill* iii. 47 The only effective fence against elephants is what is called the punge... The punge fence, or trap, is made of..sharpened and lightly roasted..bamboo stakes of varying length. **1966** *Time* 4 Feb. 18 Children helped to fashion the village's huts and whittled vicious punji stakes of bamboo. **1969** I. KEMP *Brit. G.I. in Vietnam* iii. 50 Two casualties for evacuation; one had stepped on a *punji* stake, the other had stopped a sniper's bullet. **1973** R. HAYES *Hungarian Game* xxxvi. 216 A workbench directly beneath the window. The thing was loaded with tools; it would be like jumping into a punji pit. **1977** *Time* 21 Nov. 8/1 Three camps in Thailand..which have been set up for some of the thousands of refugees who have run the gauntlet of mines, snipers and *punji* stick booby traps along the frontier to reach freedom.

punk, *sb.*[1] (Further example.)

1928 A. HUXLEY *Point Counter Point* xxix. 478 It amused him to hear the cast-off locutions of duchesses in the mouth of this ageing prostitute... The poor superannuated punk was so gruesome.

punk, *sb.*[3] Add: Also 8 **Punck.**

1. a. (Earlier and further examples.)

1705 R. BEVERLEY *Hist. & Present State Virginia* III. 49 Or else they take Punck, (which is a sort of a soft Touchwood, cut out of the knots of Oak or Hiccory Trees, but the Hiccory affords the best). **1792** J. BELKNAP *Hist. New Hampshire* III. 94 They [*sc.* the Indians] raised a blister by burning punk or touchwood on the skin. **1866** LINDLEY & MOORE *Treas. Bot.* II. 941/2 Punk. Touchwood or vegetable tinder. **1923** J. H. COOK *Fifty Years on Old Frontier* 15 Each man carries a flint and steel, together with a piece of punk. **1924** *Jrnl. Polynesian Soc.* XXXIII. 155 The Maori..carried live fire. To do so he procured..dry material of slow combustion... A kind of punk that grows on trees, [was] used for this purpose. **1936** M. FRANKLIN *All that Swagger* iii. 29 Should the fire die out, a greasy rag, ignited by firing it from the gun, could be applied to punk. **1956** *Te Ao Hou* (Wellington, N.Z.) July 24/2 Little has been recorded of this bracket fungus and its importance in the generation of fire and in carrying fire... In the Thames district..it was known as 'punk' to the early settlers, who learned of its use from the Maoris. **1965** *Austral. Encycl.* VII. 313/2 Such forest pathogens as *Fomes setulosus* and *Polyporus portentosus*..are often called brown punk and white punk respectively. **1972** *Science* 27 Oct. 395/2 In moxibustion only gentle warmth is allowed by the smoldering punk applied on the flesh. **1976** *Yankee* Apr. 107/1 *Wind Bird's* hull looked like a honeycomb with the intervening wood turned to punk.

b. *transf.* Something worthless; foolish or empty talk; nonsense, rubbish. *colloq.*

1869 J. M. HOPPIN *Office & Wk. Chr. Ministry* II. ii. 315 Better have the simplest..thoughts, clearly expressed, than what Carlyle calls 'phosphorescent punk and nothingness'. **1900** ADE *More Fables in Slang* (1902) 212 Well, if they are Right, then I must be Wrong, but to me it is Punk. **1927** D. L. SAYERS *Unnatural Death* xxi. 243 We..men stuff ourselves up with the idea that they're romantic and unemotional. All punk, my son. **1938** 'J. BELL' *Port of London Murders* ix. 164, I told him a lot of punk about..a secret process, but..he knew it was all my eye. **1958** 'A. GILBERT' *Death against Clock* viii. 109 After all, except for the kids, presents seem to me punk. **1970** 'D. HALLIDAY' *Dolly & Cookie Bird* v. 73, I told him what Celeste said about Capricorn and Scorpio, and he said, 'Honestly, Sarah. You don't believe all that punk?' **1973** in *Times* 30 May 5/5, I don't like the family Stein. There is Gert, there is Ep, there is Ein. Gert's writings are punk, Ep's statues are junk, Nor can anyone understand Ein.

c. Bread. *punk and plaster*, bread and butter. *slang.*

1891 *Contemp. Rev.* Aug. 255 Bread is called 'punk' [by tramps]. **1899** 'J. FLYNT' *Tramping with Tramps* I. vi. 140 Coffee, a little meat, some potatoes, and 'punk an' plaster' (bread and butter). **1925** [see *MUD *sb.*[1] 2 e]. **1961** R. P. HOBSON *Rancher takes Wife* ii. 45 Jack Lee.. took a large slice of my bread, munched on it thoughtfully, and then pronounced it—'Good punk!' **1975** J. GORES *Hammett* (1976) i. 14 'Punk and plaster?' 'You bet.' The waiter picked up his tray... 'What's punk and plaster?' 'Bread and butter. Con talk.'

3. (Earlier and later examples.)

1870 M. S. DE VERE *Americanisms* 157 A Chinese lady of rank in San Francisco walks attended by three maids of honor, bearing lighted sticks of punk highly perfumed. **1880** *Harper's Mag.* Dec. 73 Before the ancestral tablets.. incense was consumed, punk or joss-sticks. **1953** H. MILLER *Plexus* II. viii. 12 The third night we burned Chinese punk and incense.

3*. *slang.* **a.** [This sense may be influenced by PUNK *sb.*[1]] A passive male homosexual, a catamite; a tramp's young companion or 'gunsel'.

1904 'No. 1500' *Life in Sing Sing* 251/1 *Punk*,..a pervert. **1926** J. BLACK *You can't Win* (1927) x. 129 The 'punks', young bums, were sent for 'mickies', bottles of alcohol. **1927** [see *GUNSEL 1]. **1950** [see *gay-cat* s.v. *GAY *a.* 9]. **1973** B. BROADFOOT *Ten Lost Years* x. 137 They [*sc.* hoboes]'d pick up youngsters as, well—as their playthings. These kids were called punks. **1977** *New Yorker* 24 Oct. 64/3 The involuntary homosexuals tend to be good-looking young men..forced into becoming jailhouse 'punks' by older men serving long sentences.

b. A person of no account, a worthless fellow; a young hooligan or petty criminal. Also *gen.*, as a term of contempt or abuse.

1917 [see *MUTT c]. **1928** M. C. SHARPE *Chicago May* xxxi. 287/1 *Punk*, apprentice thief. **1930** D. HAMMETT *Maltese Falcon* xviii. 216 We've absolutely got to give them a victim... Let's give them the punk... He actually did shoot both of them..didn't he? **1930** *Sat. Even. Post* 26 July 146/2 'Listen to me, you big punk!' he growled ominously. 'What do you think we are—a lot of fools?' **1933** E. HEMINGWAY *Winner take Nothing* 94 This fellow was just a punk..a nobody. **1939** C. R. COOPER *Designs in Scarlet* ii. 18 Punks like him—sixteen, seventeen, eighteen, nineteen years old. *Ibid.* iii. 37 'The punks', as youthful offenders are often called. **1940** *Sun* (Baltimore) 29 Mar. 17/4 This happens to be the Bomber's tenth defense. Most of them bums or punks? **1949** *Chicago Tribune* 10 Dec. 10 This punk must have robbed a bank or got paid off for settin' a forest fire! **1953** W. BURROUGHS *Junkie* iv. 50 Two young punks got off a train carrying a lush between them. **1959** H. NIELSEN *Fifth Caller* xiv. 207, I was a punk then... Fourteen years old and just a little punk... Then I began to fill out. I ain't a punk no more. **1963** T. PYNCHON *V.* vi. 145 There was nothing so special about the gang, punks are punks. **1964** V. S. NAIPAUL *Area of Darkness* ix. 245, I went back to the hotel. The telephone rang. 'Hallo, punk.' **1967** *Boston Sunday Herald* 30 Apr. I.16/3 Berke has no sympathy for the 'punks' who act up in school, assault teachers or destroy property. **1976** 'D. HALLIDAY' *Dolly & Nanny Bird* ix. 113 Punks give their kids a punk childhood which leads to the next generation of punks. **1978** J. UPDIKE *Coup* vi. 246 'Uh——think you've come to the wrong place. Hasn't he?'..'You bet the punk has.'

c. In show business: a youth or novice; a young circus animal. Also *transf.*

1923 *N.Y. Times* 9 Sept. VII. 2/1 *Punk*, an amateur. **1926** *Amer. Speech* I. 282 *Punk*, a baby lion or other young animal. **1926** MAINES & GRANT *Wise-Crack Dict.* 12/1 *Punk*, child in show business. **1942** *Amer. Speech* XVII. 223/2 *Punk*, a boy or any young man not yet professionally dry behind the ears. **1971** *Islander* (Victoria, B.C.) 19 Dec. 6/2 At least 71, cantankerous Lizzie's trunk had been paralyzed as the result of once having overzealously disciplined a young elephant, or 'punk'.

d. Short for (*a*) *PUNK ROCK; (*b*) *PUNK-ROCKER. (Only these senses are widely current outside the United States.)

1974 *New Yorker* 20 May 142/3, I was getting a naïve kick out of watching a woman play rock-and-roll punk. **1976** *New Musical Express* 24 Jan. 20 He's strictly for white dopes high on punks. *Ibid.* 17 Apr. 43/1 Johnny Rotten..has the makings of a good punk. **1976** *Sunday Times* 28 Nov. 37/4 Johnny Rotten and the Sex Pistols are punks. They sing 'Anarchy in the UK.' *Ibid.* 37/5 Punk will fade. Its apologists are ludicrous. **1977** *Evening News* 27 Apr. 11/1 London's growing army of punks have developed a powerful animosity for teds... For the uninitiated, punks..are the ones who match short, ragged hair with short ragged leather jackets. **1978** *Gramophone* May 1954/1 John Cale..could be branded one of the original punks as a member of Velvet Underground. **1979** *Time* 30 July 76 The music on this record ..is full of brash challenge, like the best punk.

4. a. punk-knot (examples); **punk-oak**, for *Quercus aquatica* substitute *Quercus nigra*; (examples); **punk-wood** (later example).

1920 *Bull. U.S. Dept. Agric.* No. 871. 20 The sporophores..which I find occasionally..on old punk knots from which the original sporophores have fallen and are reviving. **1934** *Forestry* VIII. 155 One of the most characteristic and interesting symptoms of *Trametes pini* rot is the so-called punk knot, a mass of brownish friable substance that develops round embedded branch stubs. **1884** C. S. SARGENT *Rep. Forests N. Amer.* 152 *Quercus aquatica*... Possum Oak. Punk Oak... Probably not used except as fuel. **1897** G. B. SUDWORTH *Nomencl. Arborescent Flora U.S.* 175 Common names [of the water oak] include..Duck Oak, Possum Oak, Punk Oak. **1903** S. E. WHITE *Forest* 180 Sometimes a faint rounded shell.. swelled above the level, to crumble to punkwood at the lightest touch of our feet.

b. (In sense 3* above), as *punk band, critic, fan, hater, kid, style*; *punk-related, -styled* adjs. **punk chic** [after *radical chic* s.v. *RADICAL *a.* 3 f], a fashionable style of design reflecting the unconventional aspects of a punk-rocker's dress or appearance; also in adj. use.

1976 *Melody Maker* 11 Sept. 37/6 Even in Britain there's a punk band called the Suburban Studs. **1977** *Whig-Standard* (Kingston, Ont.) 15 July A1/2 Wherever they go punk bands bring violence. **1977** *Time* 11 July 49/1 Of late, punk chic has even been taken up by a few high-fashion designers. **1977** *Sniffin' Glue* July 3 The sickest thing is the Zandra Rhodes 'punk chic' look. **1977** *Zigzag* Aug. 5/1, I dunno about fur coats but anyone who wears them Harpers and Queen punk chic outfits is in order for laying out. **1977** *Rolling Stone* 13 Jan. 20/3 Bangs and Meltzer usually know the difference but most of their followers and fellow punk critics do not. **1977** *Whig-Standard* (Kingston, Ont.) 15 July A1/2 The punk fans fight with other young groups. **1977** *Western Morning News* 1 Sept. 1/3 Mysterious posters..have appeared all over Plymouth in the hope that punk fans will read between the lines. **1977** *Sounds* 1 Jan., Have these Punk haters really thought about what they've heard? **1908** J. M. SULLIVAN *Criminal Slang* 17 *Punk kid*, a boy who begs and panhandles for yeggmen. **1935** *Amer. Speech* X. 19/2 *Punk kid*, an apprentice who works with any crook. **1939** C. R. COOPER *Designs in Scarlet* ii. 22 'We've got to kill 'em,' said a cop bluntly, 'or they'll kill us. Punk kids are dangerous.' **1939** R. CHANDLER *Big Sleep* xiv. 115 That punk kid?..The kid that works at the store. **1954** *Cosmopolitan* June 87/2 Small time, a punk kid, am I? **1977** *New Yorker* 23 May 32/2 When you were a nobody, a punk kid just starting out, didn't anyone ever lend you a helping hand? **1977** *Ripped & Torn* VI. 3 There's only one restriction: *Punk/Punk related* stuff only, OK? **1977** *Sounds* 1 Jan., Ten concise memorable songs, in the pop, punk style,..combine to form a dynamite package. **1977** *Ibid.*, Certain elements in what we did..created a taste for a certain kind of thing which meant that others could organise punk styled bands.

punk (pɒŋk), *a.* orig. *U.S.* [f. PUNK *sb.*[3]] **1.** Of timber: decayed; rotten, punky.

1902 S. E. WHITE *Blazed Trail* ii. 18 Supplies ran low unexpectedly; trees turned out 'punk'. **1904** —— *Blazed Trail Stories* iii. 49, I cull every log, big or little, punk or sound, that ain't sawed square.

2. *transf.* Devoid of worth or sense; poor in quality; disappointing; nonsensical; 'rotten'. *colloq.*

1896 ADE *Artie* iii. 23 And this crowd up there was purty-y-y punk. *Ibid.* xix 178 They could n't be any punker'n they are now. **1916** E. WALLACE *Let.* 13 Nov. in M. Gilbert *Winston S. Churchill* (1972) III. Compan. II. 1582 K. J. wants you to do a punk interview with.. Churchill. **1929** W. HEYLIGER *Builder of Dam* 4, I call this a punk way to spend an Easter vacation. **1943** *Amer. Speech* XVIII. 89 *Pretty punk* [in New Zealand] does some of the work performed in America by *lousy*. **1949** *Los Angeles Times* 21 May 6 This jail has about as punk, if not the punkest grub I ever packed away. **1972** *Maclean's Mag.* Mar. 48/2 When my uncle became mayor of Sherbrooke he spoke a pretty punk French.

3. *Comb.*, as **punk-ass** *a. slang* [ASS (= ARSE *sb.*)], of a person: worthless, good-for-nothing.

1972 J. WAMBAUGH *Blue Knight* (1973) vii. 102 A kid, a punk-ass kid, conned me. **1977** *Zigzag* Aug. 12/2 This period of court harassment..went on until July 25th, when I was locked up for good by punk-ass Colombo in Detroit.

punk (pɒŋk), *v. U.S. slang.* [f. *PUNK *sb.*[3] 3* a.] *intr.* To back *out*; to withdraw one's support, to quit.

1920 E. POUND *Let.* 11 Sept. (1971) 157 You lay back, you let me have the whole stinking sweat of providing the mechanical means for letting through the new movement. .. Then you punk out, cursing me for not being in two places at once, and for 'seeing no alternative to my own groove'. **1956** 'E. MCBAIN' *Cop Hater* (1958) x. 92 We never punk out, but we never go lookin' for trouble, either. **1959** H. SALISBURY *Shook-Up Generation* iv. 65 The Chimp, unfortunately, has a tendency to 'punk out' when the fighting gets tough. **1972** C. H. FULLER in W. King *Black Short Story Anthol.* 145 Where was he? She couldn't believe he *punked out* and stayed away from school. **1977** *Zigzag* Aug. 12/1 Holzman punked out, even after he told us that he wouldn't change after all.

punkah, punka. Add: **3.** *punkah-puller*; **punkah-wallah** (earlier example).

1899 CONRAD *Lord Jim* (1900) v. 39 The archway from the anteroom was crowded with punkah-pullers, sweepers, police peons, the coxswain and crew of the harbour steam-launch. **1959** *Listener* 13 Aug. 234/2 The Madras Government was still employing 714 'punkah-pullers'. **1857** A. CASE *Let.* 6 Aug. in *Day by Day at Lucknow* (1858) v. 133 Last night..a shell burst close to our door, just behind the punkah wallah.

punkie (pɒ·ŋki). *W. Country dial.* [Perh. var. of PUNKIN, itself a var. of PUMPKIN + -IE.] A lantern made by setting a candle in a hollowed-out mangel or similar vegetable. **Punkie night** (see quots. 1931, 1960).

1931 *N. & Q.* 21 Nov. 372/2 At Hinton St. George, and in the neighbouring village of Lopen, mangolds, scooped out and fitted with candle ends to form lanterns, are known as 'punkies'. During the parade of punkies, the following lines are sung: 'Tis Punkie night to-night, 'Tis Punkie night to-night. Adam and Eve, they won't believe 'Tis Punkie night to-night. This is said to be a century-old custom..based upon the fact that a party of men from Hinton and Lopen visited Chiselborough Fair..and did not return to their homes so early as promised. Their wives went in search of them, and the attractions of the fair..were so great that by the time they commenced the journey home, their lamps were innocent of oil, and improvised lanterns, made from mangold-wurzels..were utilised. 'Punkie Night' has been once more revived at Hinton St. George. *Ibid.* 26 Dec. 465/2 'Punkie night'.. might be Oct. 31, the evening before All Saints' Day, which is very generally celebrated in America as Hallowe'en. **1959** I. & P. OPIE *Lore & Lang. Schoolch.* xii. 267 To children in south Somerset a punkie is a home-made mangel-wurzel lantern of more artistic manufacture than those commonly made elsewhere for Hallowe'en. **1960** *Guardian* 10 Nov. 10/2 In Somerset 'Punkie Night', during the third week in October, is a great occasion in the little village of Long Sutton... Punkies..are made from hollowed-out mangels to resemble a face. **1972** *Folklore* LXXXIII. 240 A punkie is a general term for a mangold, turnip or similar vegetable that has been hollowed out, a face marked through the skin, and a candle placed inside. *Ibid.*, Punkie Night was in early November.

punkie, var. PUNKY *sb.* in Dict. and Suppl.

punkin: see also *PUN *sb.*[1]

punk rock (pɒnk rǫk). [f. *PUNK *a.* 2 + *ROCK *sb.*[3]] A loud, fast-moving style of rock music characterized by aggressive and deliberately outrageous lyrics and performance. Also *attrib.*

1971 D. MARSH in *Creem* May 43/3 He's [*sc.* Rudi Martinez is] doing the knee-drop, and the splits and every other James Brown move. He's the only one in punk-rock who's still got 'em and he's makin' a comeback. **1972** *Village Voice* 1 June 45/1 (*heading*) When punk rock met the Vietcong. **1973** *Fusion* Jan. 47 Punk rock top 20. **1975** *New Yorker* 26 May 6/2 On Tuesday, May 27, Manhattan Transfer returns and begins doing its thirties, forties, and fifties routines opposite Canadian punk-rock singer Lewis Furey. **1976** *New Musical Express* 21 Feb. 31/2 A quarter of spiky teenage misfits..playing 60's styled white punk rock. **1976** *Melody Maker* 14 Aug. 25/3 Now we have gone full circle. Critics groan: 'Bring back incompetent, illiterate punk-rock bands, and away with these boring old practising musicians!' **1977** *Gramophone* June 110/2 'Punk rock' groups (or 'new wave', as they are euphemistically called). **1979** *Fortune* 23 Apr. 59/2 At one extreme are hard rock, acid rock, and more recently punk rock—all characterized by the souped-up, violent sound of blaring electric guitars.

Hence **punk-ro·cker**, one who plays or admires punk rock.

1976 *Sunday Times* 28 Nov. 37/3 Punk-rockers hate Mick Jagger (also, Led Zeppelin, Yes and Genesis) as much as they hate critics. **1977** *Sounds* 9 July 36/1, I cannot accept John Peel's suggestion that punk rockers are the only truly socialist representatives we have left. **1978** *Jrnl. R. Soc. Arts* CXXVI. 197/2 What a moral price has been paid in the name of fashion—unhealthy tight corsets, leopard-killing skin coats, the broken promise of false bosoms and the pierced faces of the punk-rockers.

punkster (pɒ·ŋkstəɹ). [f. *PUNK *sb.* 3*d + -STER.] = *PUNK-ROCKER.

1976 *New Musical Express* 12 Feb. 20/1 From precocious Nazz punkster to It's-All-My-Own-Work wishful thinker and balladeer. **1977** *Oxford Times* (City ed.) 23 Sept. 6/1 An even more disturbing facet of the punksters —having the nose or cheeks pierced—does not seem to have caught on.

punky, *sb.* Add: The usual spelling now is *punkie*. (Earlier and later examples.)

1769 R. SMITH *Tour Four Great Rivers* (1906) 42 We begin to be teazed with Muscetoes and little Gnats called here [*sc.* in New York] Punkies. **1903** [see *NO-SEE-EM]. **1933** F. H. CHELEY *Camping Out* 423 The 'punkeys' and 'midgets' can outstrip them [*sc.* mosquitoes] for ferocity and the painful character of the wound which they inflict. **1957** *Biol. Abstr.* XXXI. 1535/1 Punkies of the genus *Culicoides* are an important source of annoyance to personnel engaged in outdoor occupations over much of southern and central Alaska. **1962** GORDON & LAVOIPIERRE *Entomol. for Students of Med.* xxii. 148 Those members of the family Ceratopogonidae which suck blood are known to entomologists as 'biting midges', but in some parts of the world they are given local names, such as 'punkies'.

punky, *a.* Add: **a.** (Earlier and later examples.)

1872 W. S. HUNTINGTON *Road-Master's Assistant* 117 A bridge may..have a small knot partially decayed, or 'punky', as it is termed. **1903** [see PITCHPOLL, -POLE *v.* b]. **1955** *Sun* (Baltimore) 9 Aug. 16/8 All of the punky and weak wood was removed and a glass and resin putty applied to smooth out the sleek lines. **1958** *N.Z. Timber Jrnl.* Feb. 62/2 *Punky*, applied to wood showing signs of decay, or to soft spongy heartwood. **1959** E. COLLIER *Three against Wilderness* iii. 33 She was scurrying around ..gathering punky chunks of wood for the smudge. **1968** C. HELMERICKS *Down Wild River North* II. xxiv. 386 We are seated..around a smudgy, punky fire.

b. *transf.* and *fig.* = *PUNK *a.* 2.

1886 *Harper's Mag.* Dec. 105/2 George's mother's folks did have a kind of a punky spot somewhere in their heads. **1904** *N.Y. Times* 5 May 8 Written by another man Mr Austin would doubtless find these verses as amusing as the rest of us do—would appreciate their punky pretentiousness. **1926** F. RICKABY *Ballads* 63 Were you punky, were you hollow, You had been a lucky fellow. **1979** *Maclean's Mag.* 2 July 38/2 He doesn't expect to find his punky pubescents through conventional methods.

punnet[2]. Delete *local* and add further examples. Now also a container of other materials and shapes.

1922 JOYCE *Ulysses* 289 Punnets of mushrooms. **1943** H. J. MASSINGHAM *Men of Earth* ii. 16 Some gave a pound for a punnet of strawberries, others a pound for a punnet of tomatoes. **1955** [see *CHIP *sb.*[1] 4 b]. **1971** *Morning Star* 13 July 2 Whole families prepared to descend on the regimented lines of strawberries and fill thousands of punnets. **1975** *Times* 27 Nov. 13/7 A marvellous new filler..(80p a punnet), which claims to fill everything from plaster to concrete.

punny (pɒ·ni), *a.* [f. PUN *sb.*[1] + -Y[1].] Consisting of, or characterized by, a pun or puns. Hence **pu·nnily** *adv.*

1961 WEBSTER, Punny. **1974** R. QUIRK *Linguist & Eng. Lang.* vii. 116 A confession, punnily derivative from Hannah More. **1976** *Glasgow Herald* 26 Nov. 5/7 Chris McClure..is known nowadays as Christian which provides the punny title of his impending album release, 'The First Christian'. **1977** *Time Out* 28 Jan.–3 Feb. 17/2 Risqué, funny and predictably punny. **1979** *Daily Tel.* 6 Feb. 15/6 (*caption*) 'I love ewe.' This funny punny card is one of a series of Valentine postcards done by cartoonist Haro.

punster. (Further examples.)

1965 W. S. ALLEN *Vox Latina* 107 In the sixteenth century we find punsters identifying e.g. *habitaculum* with French *habit à cul long*. **1978** *Detroit Free Press* 16 Apr. 14c/1 The latest from the most outrageous living punster, bad jokester and molester of the language.

punt, *sb.*[1] Add: **1. b.** [f. PUNT *v.*[2]] A push with a punt-pole.

1897 *Geogr. Jrnl.* IX. 12 Only practice enables one..to guide the raft by means of timely punts at the surrounding rocks with the pole with which one is armed.

3. punt-gun, -gunner (later examples).

1958 L. DURRELL *Mountolive* xvi. 302 Time for the.. tuning in of the long punt-guns. **1972** *Shooting Times & Country Mag.* 4 Mar. 21/2 A pair of fine Welney Wash punt guns. **1956** C. WILLCOCK *Death at Flight* xv. 202 'Wire cartridges,' he said. 'Punt-gunners use these to get greater range.' **1971** *Country Life* 28 Oct. 1129/2 Famous alike as punt-gunner, eel-fisher, mole-catcher and skater.

punt, *sb.*[3] Add: **1.** (Further examples.) Also in other varieties of football.

1876 *World* (N.Y.) 19 Nov. 3/4 Princeton..now played all together on the ball, the captain himself being instrumental, with a good punt, in securing the second goal. **1887** H. HALL *Tribune Bk. Open-Air Sports* 125 A goal may be won..by kicking the ball..over the cross-bar of the goal of the defence, except by a 'punt'. **1921** [see *fly-kick* s.v. *FLY *sb.*[2] 8]. **1941** *Daily Progress* (Charlottesville, Va.) 14 Jan. 11 A player can elect to run back a punt from scrimmage if the ball is caught in the end zone. **1965** *Sun-Herald* (Sydney) 4 July 51 Denis Aitken won the long-distance kicking competition with a punt of 66½ yards. **1975** *Times* 25 Aug. 9/8 A massive punt downfield from [goal-keeper] Parkes. **1979** *Arizona Daily Star* 5 Aug. 9/1 The Packers overtook the Chiefs with 12:57 remaining in the third quarter after Kansas City's Jimmy Edwards fumbled a Green Bay punt.

3. *attrib.* and *Comb.* in sense 1, as *punt return, returner*; **punt kick** = sense 1; hence **punt-kick** *v. intr.*

1876 *Sun* (N.Y.) 20 Nov. 3/1 A Harvard man redelivers the ball by a fine 'punt' kick. **1960** E. S. & W. J. HIGHAM *High Speed Rugby* ii. 27 Be sure you can punt-kick with either foot *accurately*. **1965** *Advertiser* (Adelaide) 17 July 25 Sturt back pocket player Brenton Adcock follows through with a long punt kick at training. **1961** J. S. SALAK *Dict. Amer. Sports* 345 *Punt return* (football), a planned maneuver for running back a punted ball. **1967** *Boston Sunday Herald* 14 May II. 5/5 A kickoff and punt-return man. **1970** *Globe & Mail* (Toronto) 25 Sept. 31/7 A second injury to punt returner Bryan De-Marchi.

punt, *sb.*[6] [f. PUNT *v.*[1] (perh. infl. by PUNT *sb.*[3]).] A bet, a gamble. Phr. *to take a punt* (Austral.), to take a chance or risk.

1965 J. O'GRADY *Aussie English* 71 To 'take a punt at' anything is the equivalent of to 'have a go'. **1969** *Sydney Morning Herald* 7 June 25/9 Melbourne..selectors have 'taken a punt' in naming 20-year-old Russell Collingwood as centre half-forward. **1976** *Daily Tel.* 27 Mar. 2/3 People will still have a punt on Wimbledon. **1978** O. WHITE *Silent Reach* xxiv. 253 Blackness and silence. So take a punt... He..eased the pencil torch out of his bag. **1979** *Ibid.* 29 Jan. 17/8 As a punt, or straightforward gamble with money that can be written off without hardship, there is some appeal in Carr Boyd Minerals.

punt (punt), *sb.*[7] Also **Punt.** [Ir. = 'pound'.] The Irish monetary unit, until 1979 equivalent to £1 sterling. Also *Comb.*

1975 *Irish Times* 24 May 13/2 Do we devalue below sterling? Or do we stabilise our punt? Or maybe even attempt to revalue it upwards? **1978** *Observer* 17 Dec. 2/2 The Irish Government's decision to join the European Monetary System and break the link between Ireland's pound (now the punt) and Sterling came at the end of 10 days of hectic negotiations. **1979** *Ibid.* 8 Apr. 4/6 An advertisement in last Friday's *Derry Journal*..told readers: 'Punt holders are welcome in the North.'.. But when I was there last week the small shops in the..Bogside were taking three pence off the Punt, as the Irish pound is called, when one went to buy a packet of cigarettes.

punt, *v.*[1] Add: **c.** *to punt around*, in police slang: to patrol. Also as *sb.* in phr. *to have a punt around.*

1970 P. Laurie *Scotland Yard* 293 *Punt around, to*, to patrol. **1974** G. F. Newman *Price* ii. 58 Thought I'd have a punt around, see who's about. **1977** P. Moyes *To kill a Coconut* vii. 99 To 'punt around' is to patrol.

punt, *v.*[3] Add: **1. a.** (Further examples.) Also in other varieties of football.

1905 [see *drop *v.* 24 b]. **1961** *Dallas Morning News* 10 Oct. II. 1 He..punted once for 39 yards and caught one pass for 13 yards. **1967** *Sun-Herald* (Sydney) 16 Apr. 67 Ryan coolly punted the ball straight through the middle and Geelong had won by a point. **1972** G. Green *Great Moments in Sport: Soccer* xiii. 123 Gregg immediately punted the ball far down-field, well over the half-way line. **1974** *Plain Dealer* (Cleveland, Ohio) 26 Oct. 4-D/6 On their next offensive series, the Falcons were forced to punt.

‖ **punta** (pu·nta). [It., lit. 'point'.] The narrow upper part of straw grown in Tuscany for plaiting. Also *attrib.*

1929 *Daily Express* 26 Jan. 5/2 Rough straws and picture hats are always popular... These are being shown of openwork tuscan or punta straw. **1968** J. Ironside *Fashion Alphabet* 253 *Punta*, straw made of the upper part of the grain stalk.

punt-about. (Later examples.) Also *attrib.*

1917 Kipling *Diversity of Creatures* 255 The 'tump-tump' of the puntabouts before the sides settled to games. **1924** —— *Debits & Credits* (1926) 97 An ancient, but air-tight puntabout-ball. **1963** *Times* 10 May 4/3 A puntabout at Twickenham..afforded an opportunity to bid godspeed..to England's Rugby football team.

Punt e Mes (punt *e* me·s). Also **Punt e mes.** [It. (Piedmontese dial.), lit. 'point and a half'.] An Italian aperitif, made in Piedmont.

1956 C. G. Bode *Wines of Italy* x. 100 There are two kinds, Carpano 'Vermouth'—somewhat closer to the usual line of red vermouth, and Carpano 'Punt e Mes', with the bitter tang still more emphasized. **1959** W. James *Word-bk. Wine* 152 *Punt e mes.* The Italian vermouth, of which one sees much in Italy but little elsewhere, is of the sweet type but with a pronounced bitter after-taste. **1965** *Harper's Bazaar* Jan. 45/1 A Negroni ..equal parts of Campari, gin, and Punt e Mes. **1966** R. Ardrey *Territorial Imperative* (1967) vii. 265 You.. take a table in the islet's little restaurant. You order a *Punt e Mes* or a second-rate omelet. **1974** *Times* 14 Mar. 9/6 (Advt.), *Vermouths & Aperitifs*..Pimms..Punt e Mes..Cinzano.

punter[1]. Add: **2.** Also, one who gambles on football pools.

1951 *Sport* 16–22 Mar. 22/2, I know of many punters who have decided to follow one system and then after a short losing spell switched to another system. **1976** *West Lancs. Evening Gaz.* 8 Dec. 1/7 A Great Eccleston punter has scooped £26,082 on the pools.

3. *slang.* A name for a member of various classes of criminal, esp. one who assists in the commission of a crime (see quots.).

1891 *Answers* 4 Apr. 338/1 Having filled the premises with pictures,..the auctioneer engages the assistance of what are known in the business as 'punters'. The 'punter' ..is the auctioneer's confederate, and it is his duty..to make sham bids. *Ibid.* 338/3 In addition to bidding, a 'punter' will often assist the auctioneer in cajoling the public. **1941** Baker *N.Z. Slang* vi. 52 We have also acquired [this century] some underworld slang of our own:.. *punter*, an assistant of a pickpocket who diverts the victim's attention while robbery is committed. **1973** 'J. Patrick' *Glasgow Gang Observed* iii. 28 'Punter' was 'a normal man where you live who never gets caught', to whom you took stolen goods and traded them in for guns, 'blades', or money. *Ibid.* 29 They were the people who sold bottles of wine at extortionate prices on Sundays... The word was also generalized to mean a member of a 'team' or gang, as in the much used phrase 'Ya Cumbie punter'.

4. *slang.* The victim of a swindler or confidence trickster.

1934 P. Allingham *Cheapjack* xv. 187 But when the grafter decides that it is time for him to get the punter's money, he leans casually against the stall. *Ibid.* 320 *Punter*, a grafter's customer, client or victim. **1962** [see *kite *sb.* 4 c]. **1974** G. F. Newman *Price* viii. 253 They were three card tricksters. Their patter never changed, but still punters stood for it.

5. *colloq.* A customer or client; a member of an audience or spectator; *spec.*, the client of a prostitute.

In some contexts almost synonymous with *person* (but depreciatory).

1965 *Sunday Times* (Colour Suppl.) 24 Oct. 66/3 There is plenty of irrational judgement about..but like all free-market operators, the traders have to concentrate it on people—on each other and on the 'punters' (dealer buyers). **1968** D. Braithwaite *Fairground Architecture* iii. 60 Described by veteran showmen as 'a good oncer'—that is, a ride the *punters* would normally go on once—and once only—this must have been the least successful of his inventions. **1969** *Jeremy* I. iii. 22/2 *Punter*, client. **1970** *Sunday Times* 15 Mar. 60/5, I [*sc.* a prostitute] always make the punter wear a rubber. **1975** *Ibid.* (Colour Suppl.) 23 Feb. 25/2 There's nuthin' but deid punters walkin' up and doon, wi' their beds under their airms. **1975** *Times* 20 Sept. 2/7 Their clients were known as 'punters' and the youths as 'rent boys'. Some boys, once corrupted, became male prostitutes. **1976** *Sunday Mail* (Glasgow) 28 Nov. 12 (*caption*) Ya eejit! Ah'm talkin' aboot thae punters inra Housa Lords..yir upper-crust. **1977** *Record Mirror* 7 May 17/2 The punters were well pleased. Some people even..said they preferred my sound, as far as I was concerned I played crap that night. **1977** *Drive* Sept.–Oct. 112/1 The more confused you are, the more likely you are to accept his offer. Because you are the punter. **1978** *Observer* 12 Feb. 3/5 Irene, a 19-year-old prostitute, was giving the glad eye to prospecting punters on the side streets of Chapeltown, Leeds. **1980** *Ibid.* 6 Apr. 33/3 Some of the punters [*contextually* pilgrims to Lourdes] were elderly and they were all tired.

pu·nter[3]. [f. Punt *v.*[3] + -er[1].] In various forms of football, one who punts (cf. Punt *v.*[3] 1 a).

1890 in Webster. **1910** W. Camp *Bk. of Foot-Ball* viii. 314 Accuracy should be an aim of the punter as much as distance. **1956** V. Jenkins *Lions Rampant* iv. 58 Thus .., an enormous punter as well as goal-kicker, sent them back..yards at a time. **1970** *Globe & Mail* (Toronto) 25 Sept. 31/7 Hamilton Tiger-Cats have signed University of Toronto punter and halfback Paul McKay. **1977** *New Yorker* 3 Oct. 111/1 Curry, up to now a demon punter, could not average better than twenty-nine yards a kick.

‖ **puntilla** (punti·lʸa). Also (erron.) **puntillo.** [Sp., dim. of *punto* point.] In bull-fighting, a dagger used to give the *coup de grâce* to the bull.

1838 *Q. Rev.* LXI. 419 The butchers..are able infallibly to dart the 'puntilla' into the spine. **1924** E. Hemingway *In Our Time* 23 One of the *cuadrilla* leaned out over his neck and killed him with the *puntillo.* **1932** [see *monosabio]. **1967** McCormick & Mascareñas *Compl. Aficionado* i. 21 The death of the bull at the butcher's *puntilla* was incidental to the central ritual.

Hence **puntillero** (puntilʸē·ro), an assistant at a bullring who uses the *puntilla.*

1910 *Encycl. Brit.* IV. 790/2 Should the bull need a *coup de grâce*, it is given by a *chulo*, named *puntillero*, with a dagger which pierces the spinal marrow. **1923** W. J. Locke *Moordius & Co.* x. 144 An indistinguished member of the quadrilla, dignified by the sonorous title of puntillero, knelt down and with a poignard gave him [*sc.* the bull] the *coup de grâce.* **1970** A. Fowles *Dupe Negative* xi. 152 On his faraway face had been the look a bull has the instant the *puntillero* strikes home.

punting, *vbl. sb.*[1] (In Dict. s.v. Punt *v.*[1]) Also, *spec.* in Football Pools.

1951 *Sport* 16–22 Mar. 22/2 My advice is to make sure that the system or method of punting you adopt is a good one.

punting, *vbl. sb.*[3] (In Dict. s.v. Punt *v.*[3]) (Further examples.)

1910 W. Camp *Bk. of Foot-Ball* viii. 313 In punting, the ball is kicked with the instep and not with the toe. **1974** *Liverpool Echo* (Football ed.) 31 Aug. 3/3 His timing and immaculate positioning, together with his straight-backed, stiff-legged punting are..faithfully reproduced by Alec. **1979** *Tucson* (Arizona) *Citizen* 20 Sept. 11D/8 UA's Barry Kramer is second in punting with a 42·3 average.

punto[1]. Add: **7.** *Lacework.* Used (= Point *sb.*[1] 31) in phrases to denote various kinds of Italian lace and embroidery, as *punto a maglia* (mesh stitch); *punto a rilievo* (erron. *relievo*), (stitch in relief); *punto in aria* (stitch in the air), i.e. needlepoint lace used as a border; *punto tagliato* (cut-work); *punto tirato* (drawn-work).

1865 F. B. Palliser *Hist. Lace* iv. 47 Punto tagliato. —Cut-work. *Ibid.*, Punto in aria.—Worked on a parchment pattern, the flowers connected by brides: in modern parlance, Guipure. *Ibid.*, Punto tagliato a fogliami.—The richest and most complicated of all points, executed like the former [sc. *punto in aria*], only with this difference, that all the outlines are in relief, formed by means of cottons placed inside to raise them. *Ibid.* 49 Punto a maglia quadra.—Lacis; square netting, the Modano of the Tuscans. **1865** Punto a rilievo [see *gros point* s.v. *gros *a.*]. **1881** C. C. Harrison *Woman's Handiwork* i. 81 (*caption*) Old punto tirato, or Italian drawn-work. **1881** Punto a maglia [see *darned *ppl. a.*[1] 2]. **1900** E. Jackson *Hist. Hand-Made Lace* 192 *Punto a rilievo*, the Italian name for Venice Raised Point Lace. *Ibid.* 205 *Punto a Maglia.*—Lacis, or darned netting, much used for curtains and bed furniture. **1905** L. A. Tebbs (*title*) New lace embroidery (punto tagliato). **1953** M. Powys *Lace & Lace-Making* iv. 9 *Embroidered linen*, Needlepoint, Italian, 16th century. Drawn thread work, with the pattern left in the linen. Punto Tirato e Tela Lasciato. The design typical of the period. *Ibid.* 11 *Gros point de Venise*, 17th century. Heavy raised Venetian Point. The grand effect is produced by the relief which gives the look of carved ivory and it is sometimes called 'Punto Tagliato a Fogliami', lace resembling cut or carved leaves. **1960** H. Hayward *Antique Coll.* 230/1 *Punto in aria embroidery*,..used to describe a very early form of lace, the cutwork fabric reduced to a strip supporting the needlepoint work. **1974** *Encycl. Brit. Micropædia* X. 386/3 From 1620 Venetian raised lace (in Italian *punto a relievo*, in French *gros point de Venise*) developed distinct from flat Venetian (*point plat de Venise*).

punto banco (pu·nto bæ·ŋko). [In form answers to It. *punto* point, *puntare* to bet and *banco* bank: cf. also Punt *sb.*[2] and *banco *int.*] A gambling game resembling baccarat (see also quot. 1976[1]). Also *attrib.*

1973 'R. MacLeod' *Burial in Portugal* vi. 116 The rows of tables..offering everything from roulette and boule to punto banco and blackjack. **1976** E. L. Figgis *Gamblers Handbk.* 125 Punto-Banco..is played entirely as a casino game at table with bases for 12 players, and spaces for the casino 'chips operator' between bases 6 and 7 and croupier between spaces 1 and 12. The actual banker and punter are both phantom inasmuch as all players must bet with the casino, not with each other. They may either bet 'Banco', that the phantom bank will win the coup, or 'Punto', that the phantom punter will win the coup. **1976** *Daily Record* (Glasgow) 23 Nov. 18/5 It has the biggest layout in Britain with 18 roulette, dice and punto banco tables all going under the plum-and-gold silk shades.

puny, *a.* and *sb.* Add: **A.** *adj.* **4. c.** In bad condition or health; physically weak; ailing. *U.S. dial.*

1838 K. De R. Kennedy in N.E. Eliason *Tarheel Talk* (1956) 289, I found your dear Aunt Catherine in a very puny state, not entirely confined, but obliged to rest herself on the bed more or less every day. **1866** C. H. Smith *Bill Arp* 170 Me and him like to have fit, and perhaps would, if I hadn't been puny. **1904** W. N. Harben *Georgians* xvii. 163 Little Minnie begun to fail; she got so puny she spit up ever'thing she ate. **1943** T. Pratt *Barefoot Mailman* i. 7 Don't you go making fun of sickness. Mister Dewey Durgan here has been puny the last few days and needs the best advice. **1947** *Publ. Amer. Dial. Soc.* VIII. 33/1 [S.W. Ohio] *Puny*, in poor health, thin, emaciated. **1979–80** *Verbatim* Winter 14/1 [In Missouri] *puny* was 'confined to bed', *poorly* meant 'chronically ill', and *bad sick* meant it was time to call the undertaker.

B. *sb.* **4. a.** (Later *arch.* example.)

1922 Joyce *Ulysses* 386 Thou chuff, thou puny, thou got in the peasestraw.

pup, *sb.*[1] Add: **2. a.** (Later examples.)

1856 *Porter's Spirit of Times* 15 Nov. 172/3 There were three pups..a parcel of supercilious fellows, who, with a piece of glass stuck in their eye, survey the crowd as if contamination dwelt amongst them. **1870** J. K. Medbery *Men & Myst. Wall St.* 31 Down in the cock-pit the Commodore's 'pups', as the merciless, cacophonic 'street' argot denominates the broker friends of Vanderbilt, are making an ineffective rally.

b. A youthful or inexperienced person, a beginner; a young 'blood'. *colloq.* (chiefly *U.S.*).

1890 *Punch* 7 June 270/2 You ride very nicely indeed for a 'pup'. **1903** G. H. Lorimer *Lett. Self-Made Merchant* ix. 118 Chauncey's father was the whole village, barring the railroad station and the saloon, and, of course, Chauncey thought that he was something of a pup himself. **1903** A. H. Lewis *Boss* vi. 48 'Here's a pup,' cried Big Kennedy, with his hand on my shoulder, 'I want you to look over.' **1938** *Amer. Speech* XIII. 228/1 The youngest intern..may be assigned to routine laboratory tests and called a *pup* or *junior.* **1948** F. Blake *Johnny Christmas* ii. 70 A fresh pup breezin' in, cool as you please, and takin' over Bent's? **1977** *Transatlantic Rev.* LX. 36, I can remember my Daddy brought me down once when I was a young pup.

c. Also, *Sopwith Pup.* A familiar name for the Sopwith Scout Tractor, a small, fast, aeroplane used for combative and instructional purposes in the war of 1914–18.

1917 *Jane's All World's Aircraft* 103b *Sopwith Scout Tractor.* Known as the 'Pup', and one of the fastest machines in the world... The 'Sopwith Pup' on active service has passed the 25,000 feet level with a Naval pilot. *a* **1918** J. T. B. McCudden *Five Years in R. Flying Corps* (1919) 181, I had taken charge of another machine for fighting instruction, this time a Sopwith Scout, vulgarly termed a 'Pup'. **1918** H. G. Wells *Joan & Peter* xiii. 613 They [*sc.* air force officers] made a language for themselves an atrocious slang of facetious misnomers,..the machines were "buses' and 'camels' and 'pups'. **1928** C. F. S. Gamble *Story of North Sea Air Station* xiii. 211 A single-seater machine, the Pup, which was also a product of the Sopwith Aviation Company, passed into the Service during this year [*sc.* 1916]. **1977** J. Cleary *High Road* i. 20 Pups, Camels..even some Spads and Nieuports. *Ibid.* 21 What use was a Sopwith Pup to a couple intent on adding to the postwar baby boom?

d. A four-wheeled trailer drawn by a tractor, lorry, or other road vehicle. *U.S. slang.*

1951 *Amer. Speech* XXVI. 308/2 *Pup*, a narrow four-wheel trailer. They can be 'buttoned up' in tandem and will follow the tractor, just as puppies will follow their mother. **1960** *Newsweek* 20 June 91/1 Compact, 1½-ton 'pup' semi-trailers are hitched behind regularly scheduled intercity passenger buses. **1978** *Detroit Free Press* 14 Apr. 16D/2 On two of three trials earlier, without the modifications, the second tanker or 'pup' of the same truck bounced the wheels of its safety guard sharply against the ground.

3. (Earlier and later examples.) Also, the young of the sea lion or of rats or mice.

1815 *Sydney Gaz.* 22 Apr. 1/1 The *pups* or young seal were also indiscriminately slaughtered. **1824** A. Earle *Jrnl. Residence Tristan d'Acunha* 30 Aug. in *Narr. Residence N.Z.* (1832) 354 We started off early for Elephant

Bay to procure the skin of a [seal] pup, in order to convert it into caps... The pups were nearly all black. **1937** *Discovery* May 140/2 Sea lions..resort to the island [*sc.* Lady Julia Percy Island] to breed, to raise their pups. **1944** E. C. Wood in A. N. Worden *UFAW Handbk. Care & Managem. Lab. Animals* (1947) vi. 122 The individual pups [*sc.* young rats] are of low birth-weight. **1952** L. H. Matthews *Brit. Mammals* ix. 266 The milk teeth of seal pups are shed or absorbed at a very early age. **1972** *Nature* 3 Nov. 21/2 The rats were under close observation... Mortality among offspring was very low..only 1 dead pup out of 138 born. **1975** *Storktalk* (Ches. & N. Wales Branch of Nat. Childbirth Trust) Nov. 16 The female mouse lost 54% more pups than did control mice giving birth in the normal settings for mice. **1979** *Guardian* 14 Sept. 4/4 After failing to persuade the Canadian government to stop the killing of Harp seal pups in Newfoundland, the RSPCA is to campaign for a ban on the importation of Harp seal products.

4. (Earlier and later examples.)

1898 W. B. Haskell *Two Years in Klondike* 253 Every creek has its pups, and if any of them become of considerable importance they may have pups also. **1902** *Pop. Science Monthly* July 232 The principal streams [in the Klondike region] are known as creeks; the short steep tributaries which flow into them as 'gulches'; and the streamlets which feed these as 'pups'. **1916** *Yukon Territory* (Canada Dept. Interior) I. iii. 27 On Hunker creek, below the mouth of Seventy Pup, practically all the gold occurred in a shattered porphyry bedrock. **1973** P. Berton *Drifting Home* v. 69 The little pup creeks gurgling down through the thick forests.

5. a. (Further examples.) Now usu. *fig.* and freq. *pass.*, e.g. *he was sold a pup*. Hence, *to buy a pup*.

1902 Kipling in *Collier's Weekly* 6 Dec. 8/3, I wouldn't have sold old Van Zyl a pup like that..I must hunt him up and explain. **1927** W. Deeping *Kitty* viii. 99 He was not the sort of man to advise a brother officer to buy a pup. **1930** W. S. Maugham *Cakes & Ale* xiv. 165 The public has been sold a pup too often to take unnecessary chances. **1968** *Scottish Daily Mail* 9 Aug. 5/6 The Basset is the aircraft the RAF did not want in the first place. They were sold a pup, in more ways than one. **1978** A. Ryan in Hookway & Pettit *Action & Interpretation* 75 They may insist that..we worry incessantly about what price our virtues will fetch, and about whether we shall be sold a pup by others. **1978** *SLR Camera* Aug. 36/1 Letters have arrived on my desk from petrified owners..wanting to know more, terrified that they had bought a pup.

b. *the night's* (*only*) *a pup*, the night is 'young' or not far advanced; 'it is still early'. Also, occas., *the day's* (*only*) *a pup*. *Austral. colloq.*

1915 H. Lawson *Coll. Prose* (1972) I. 913 The night was not even a pup yet—it was broad daylight, being Northern summer. **1921** K. S. Prichard *Black Opal* xii. 104 You're not taking her away yet, Michael? The night's a pup! **1928** 'Brent of Bin Bin' *Up Country* x. 167 The night is only a pup yet. **1934** T. Wood *Cobbers* xi. 138 'What's the worry?' they say; 'the day's a pup.' **1947** K. Tennant *Lost Haven* i. 28 'A man's got to get a bit of sleep.' 'Night's only a pup, hen,' Alec suggested, mildly. **1949** L. Glassop *Lucky Palmer* viii. 73 We'll get him in. The day's only a pup yet. **1968** G. Dutton *Andy* xii. 198 'Are you thinking of driving out to Hangingstone to-night?' 'It's only forty miles and the night is a pup.'

6. *pup-trained* adj.; **pupfish**, a small killifish belonging to the genus *Cyprinodon*, esp. *C. macularius*, found in fresh or saline water in desert regions of California and Nevada; **pup joint** *Oil Industry*, a piece of drill pipe of less than the standard length; **pup-tent** orig. *U.S. Mil.*, a small tent or bivouac, a dog-tent; a shelter-tent, *spec.* one comprising two shelter-halves carried separately (see Shelter *sb.* 3 in Dict. and Suppl.).

1958 *Copeia* 232/1 Ten live pupfish were captured with a fine-mesh seine. **1973** *Daily Colonist* (Victoria, B.C.) 1 Apr. 9/8 The Owens pupfish survived for eons in a changing environment—from a vast inland lake to a string of shallow desert pools. **1976** P. B. Moyle *Inland Fishes California* 251 Even the isolated and harmless pupfishes are being threatened by man's activities. **1937** *Amer. Speech* XII. 153/2 *Pup-joints*, short joint used to 'nipple out'. **1972** L. M. Harris *Introd. Deepwater Floating Drilling Operations* xii. 139 Adequate pup joints are necessary for final space out. Where 40-ft riser joints are selected, one pup joint each of 20-ft, 10-ft and 5-ft are needed. **1863** in *Ohio Archaeol. & Hist. Q.* (1929) XXXVIII. 651 About 10 a.m. we..pitched our pup-tents. **1917** *Collier's Mag.* 21 Apr. 13 When a halt is reached, each pair of men set up their tent poles, stretch the line as a ridge, tie their canvas sheets together, and peg them down as a cover. The result is familiarly called a 'pup' tent. **1929** *T. Eaton & Co. Catal.* Spring & Summer 373/3 'Pup-Tent' For Boys... Just the thing you need during your holidays... Fitted with two uprights, guy ropes and pegs. **1953** K. Tennant *Joyful Condemned* xiv. 123 They had equipped themselves for the camping holiday..: a pup-tent, blankets, a frying-pan. **1977** C. McFadden *Serial* xxv. 56/1 Carol can't pick up any signals if you're a coupla boy scouts in a pup tent. **1928** Kipling in *London Mag.* Dec. 693/2 The janitor's kitten had not been pup-trained and leaped on the table, to make sure.

pupa. Delete ‖ and add: **1.** (Earlier and later examples.)

1773 G. White *Let.* 8 July in *Nat. Hist. Selborne* (1789) II. xv. 156 The black shining cases or skins of the *pupæ* of these insects [*sc.* forest-flies]. **1898** A. S. Packard *Text-bk. Entomol.* III. 621 In some cases the obtected pupa remains within the loose envelope formed by the old larval skin. **1928** G. H. Carpenter *Biol. Insects* vii. 172 The pupa..resembles the ȧdult insect much more closely than the larva. **1932** Riley & Johannsen *Med. Entomol.* viii. 116 The pupae of mosquitoes and midges are quite active. **1964** V. Wigglesworth *Life of Insects* vi. 94 Within the pupa a most complex development proceeds.

3. (Earlier and later examples.)

1788 G. White *Let.* in *Nat. Hist. Selborne* (1789) II. xlvi. 252 All [the crickets] that I have seen at that season [*sc.* March] were in their pupa state. **1898** A. S. Packard *Text-bk. Entomol.* III. 625 (*heading*) The pupa state.

pupariate (piupēə·riˌēit), *v.* [f. Pupari(um + -ate[3].] *intr.* (See quot. 1973.)

1973 Fraenkel & Bhaskharan in *Ann. Entomol. Soc. Amer.* LXVI. 419/1 Formation of the puparium can be succinctly expressed by the term pupariation, with to pupariate as the appropriate verb. **1976** *Nature* 8 July 137/1 The posterior, which had pupariated, contained ovaries. **1978** *Ibid.* 20 Apr. 719/1 All the others were apparently full-term third instar larvae which had been produced normally and then had failed to pupariate.

pupariating (piupēə·riˌēitiŋ), *vbl. sb.* = next.

1939 Metcalf & Flint *Destructive & Useful Insects* (ed. 2) vi. 154 In the Diptera the formation of the motionless puparium may be called pupariating, to distinguish it from the shedding of the final larval skin, or true pupating.

pupariation (piupēəriˌēi·ʃən). [f. Pupari(um + -ation.] (See quot. 1973.)

1973 Fraenkel & Bhaskharan in *Ann. Entomol. Soc. Amer.* LXVI. 418/2 Formation of the puparium in cyclorrhaphous flies occurs many hours before that of the pupa and should be consistently termed pupariation to distinguish it from the process of pupation. **1977** Richards & Davies *Imms's Gen. Textbk. Entomol.* (ed. 10) I. xix. 367 The third-instar larva [of Cyclorrhaphan Diptera] eventually stops feeding and from then until the onset of puparium formation (pupariation) it may be referred to as the post-feeding larva. **1978** *Nature* 20 Apr. 720/1 In the larviparous tsetse fly, eggs hatch normally and development is not interfered with until the time of pupariation.

pupate, *v.* Add: (Later examples.) Also *fig.*

1939 Duncan & Pickwell *World of Insects* iv. 60 In its preparation to pupate, the swallowtail larva crawls to the underside of a stem. **1977** *Sci. Amer.* May 143/1 One fly larva, armed with antienzymes, feeds on the take and pupates cheerfully in the depths of the pitcher. **1979** *Times* 14 Nov. 12/7 The Parliamentary Labour Party, which has always lived on the edge of a metamorphosis into a cowardly rabble, has already begun to pupate, and will shortly complete the process.

pupation. (Later examples.)

1905 V. L. Kellogg *Amer. Insects* ii. 45 The larva, just before pupation, has spun a protecting silken cocoon about itself. **1932** Riley & Johannsen *Med. Entomol.* viii. 116 Just before pupation the larvae of many insects spin a cocoon. **1973** [see *pupariation].

pupelo. (Earlier example.)

1806 *Salem Register* 7 Apr. 1/2 Do you not deny to the poor labourer..the common refreshment of a little toddy, and stint him with a glass of *pupelo*?

pupil, *sb.*[1] Add: **3. b. pupil power**: see *power *sb.*[1] 4 f; **pupil-room**, also, † the pupils' room in a barrister's chambers; **pupil–teacher** *a.*, designating the relation between pupils and teachers; *esp.* in phr. *pupil–teacher ratio*.

1849 Thackeray *Pendennis* I. xxix. 285 In the pupil-room of Mr. Hodgeman, the special pleader,..six pupils were scribbling declarations. **1958** J. Townsend *Young Devils* vi. 47 How vitally important a good pupil–teacher, teacher–headteacher and teacher–environment relationship had been considered at my training college. **1960** *Where?* Winter 16 *Pupil–teacher ratio*, the number of pupils to a teacher in a school. **1974** *Times* 16 Jan. 13/1 The union knows that pupil teacher ratios are better in London than in some other parts of the country. **1978** C. Hookway in Hookway & Pettit *Action & Interpretation* 40 There will be a network of pupil–teacher relations connecting them.

pupillography (piūpilǫ·grăfi). [f. Pupil *sb.*[2]: see -graphy.] The recording and analysis of the movements and size of the pupils of the eyes.

1940 *Arch. Neurol. & Psychiatry* XLIV. 227 (*heading*) Pupillography: its significance in clinical neurology. **1958** *Arch. Ophthalm.* LIX. 358/2 The purpose of clinical pupillography is the detection and localization of pathological processes within the nervous centers and pathways of pupillary control. **1976** *Drive* May–June 20/1 In the late 1960s, Dr Yoss and his colleagues at the Mayo Clinic in Rochester, Minnesota, developed a technique, known as infra-red pupillography, for measuring loss of alertness.

Hence **pupillogra·phic** *a.*, **-gra·phically** *adv.*; also **pu·pillogram**, a record obtained in pupillography; **pu·pillograph**, an apparatus used for pupillography.

1940 *Arch. Neurol. & Psychiatry* XLIV. 227 Lesions.. produce characteristic modifications of the pupillary movements and reflexes which are disclosed by pupillographic examination. *Ibid.* 228 Before the Argyll Robertson stage..there can be detected, pupillographically, a long evolution of seven well defined stages [of degeneration]. *Ibid.* 229 Pupillograms dealing with intraocular conditions, such as lesions of the macula and iris. **1958** *Arch. Ophthalmol.* LIX 355/2 (*heading*) The electronic pupillograph. **1970** *Aerospace Med.* XLI. 1340/2 The pupillographic scanner measured the maximal horizontal diameter of the exposed portion of the pupils. *Ibid.* 1341/2 Three of the 32 well-rested pilots performed, pupillographically, in a less-than-perfect manner. *Ibid.* 1342/2 Data from his pupillogram are shown in Figure 5.

pupillometer. Add: Also (*rare*) pupilometer. (Examples.)

1920 *Jrnl. Optical Soc. Amer.* IV. 77 Various pupilometers have been suggested and used for determining the size of the pupil. **1975** L. S. Sasieni *Princ. & Pract. Optical Dispensing & Fitting* (ed. 3) iv. 105 The Pupillometer consists of two parallel tubes each containing a convex lens. **1975** *Sci. Amer.* Nov. 110/2 We have also been using an electronic pupillometer that scans the eye and automatically measures the diameter of the pupil while the experiment is in progress.

Hence **pu:pillome·tric** *a.*; **pu:pillome·trics**, the study of psychological influences on the size of the pupil.

1968 E. H. Hess in F. M. Bass et al. *Appl. Sci. in Marketing Managem.* 431 Pupillometrics..is an area of psychological study that is based on our finding that the pupils..dilate when we see something pleasant or positive. **1968** F. J. Van Bortel in *Ibid.* 440 A new technique of pupillometric measurement. **1977** M. P. Janisse *Pupillometry* iii. 35 The area of pupillometric research that is at once the most popular and the most controversial concerns interest and attitudes. **1980** D. Bloodworth *Trapdoor* xxv. 153 Pupillometrics—which means measuring the dilation of the pupil against ostensible emotions of the subject.

Pupin (piū·pĭ·n). *Teleph.* The name of Michael I. *Pupin* (1858–1935), U.S. physicist born in Imperial Hungary, used *attrib.* or in the possessive to designate equipment, methods, and principles introduced by him, as **Pupin cable**, a telephone cable provided with loading coils at regular intervals so as to reduce attenuation and distortion of the signal; **Pupin coil** = *loading coil* s.v. *loading *vbl. sb.* 5; **Pupin's law** (see quot. 1911). (No longer current.)

1900 *Amer. Jrnl. Sci.* CLX. 64 Pupin's interrupter may be modified to serve as an alternator in the following way. **1901** *Sci. Abstr.* IV. 1043 An intermittent direct current is produced by means of a Pupin interrupter. **1905** *Ibid.* B. VIII. 352 An adjacent insulator carries a vacuum lightning discharger contained in an ebonite case, to protect the Pupin coil from damage. **1908** *Ibid.* XI. 495 The range of transmission through a Pupin cable as compared with that through an open line having the same damping constant is smaller. **1911** J. A. Fleming *Propagation of Electr. Currents* iv. 122 Pupin reduced the solution of the problem to a verbal statement, which may be called Pupin's Law, as follows: If there be a non-uniform cable line loaded with inductance coils at equal intervals, and if we consider the total inductance and resistance to be smoothly distributed along the line, then these two lines, the non-uniform and uniform lines, having the same total resistance and inductance, will be electrically equivalent for transmission purposes as long as one half of the distance between two adjacent coils expressed as a fraction of 2π taken as the wave length, is an angle so small that its sine has practically the same numerical value as that angle in circular measure. **1934** A. L. Albert *Electr. Communication* xi. 282 It remained for Pupin successfully to solve the difficult problem of loading... His method is known as the series or Pupin system of loading. **1955** P. R. Bardell *Magnetic Materials in Electr. Industry* vii. 180 These coils are often referred to in the literature as 'Pupin' coils but are now usually known as 'Loading Coils'. **1958** [see next].

pupinized piū·pĭnəizd), *ppl. a.* *Teleph.* [f. prec. + -ize + -ed[1].] Of a telephone cable: provided with loading coils at regular intervals, so as to reduce attenuation and distortion of the signal. (No longer current.)

1910 *Electrician* 13 May 178/1 The attenuation coefficient determines the efficiency of any telephone circuit, and thus of a 'pupinised' circuit, so termed because it differs from an ordinary circuit by the introduction of inductance coils at definite points according to the formulæ of Prof. Pupin. **1913** *Sci. Abstr.* B. XVI. 152 (*heading*) Design of pupinised metallic and phantom circuits. **1933** *Jrnl. R. Aeronaut. Soc.* XXXVII. 463 Although great progress has been made in the construction of pupinised telephone cables, submarine telephony is still limited to relatively short distances, since intermediate amplifiers cannot be fitted. **1958** *New Scientist* 9 Oct. 990/3 Born.. 100 years ago on October 4, Pupin was to leave his name perpetuated in a million 'Pupin coils', used in telephone lines known as 'pupinised lines'.

puppet, *sb.* Add: **3. a.** For 'A human figure' read 'A small figure, human or animal' and add: Now also applied to a similar figure moved by rods, or to one in the form of a glove: see *glove puppet* s.v. *glove *sb.* 6, *rod puppet* s.v. *rod *sb.*[1] 12. (Later examples.)

The original sense is now sometimes distinguished as *string puppet* s.v. *string *sb.* 32.

1934 [see *puppeteer]. **1958** *Oxf. Mag.* 6 Feb. 250/2 *The Water Babies* is said to be the first full-length play to have been performed in this country by puppets. **1967** *Oxf. Compan. Theatre* (ed. 3) 776/1 There are many different types of puppets, including the Hand- or Glove-Puppet, the Rod-Puppet, the Marionette, which are all rounded figures, and the flat puppets of the Shadow Show and the toy theatre.

b. Also, a country or state which is ostensibly independent but is actually under the control of some greater power.

1933 A. J. Toynbee *Survey Internat. Affairs* 452 In the wider field of international diplomatic negotiations over the Sino-Japanese dispute, the Japanese government deliberately gave formal recognition to their puppet in Manchuria. **1945** *Evening Standard* 20 Dec. 3 The rôle she [*sc.* Siam] played as a 'puppet' of the Japs in South-East Asia, made it essential that she should give restitution to the people who were harmed. **1976** *Survey* Summer–Autumn 18, I am not depressed about the large-scale non-fulfilment by the Russians (and their puppets) of the Helsinki agreements.

9. a. *puppet administration, army, government, leader, régime, ruler, state, troops.*

1938 *Ann. Reg. 1937* 267 The threat to Chinese sovereignty constituted by..the puppet administration set up by her in East Hopei. **1968** I. Deutscher *Marxism in Our Time* (1972) 178 The support of the population permits them to make use of the jungle, while the Americans and their South Vietnamese puppet army cannot do this. **1931** *Economist* 14 Nov. 892/2 At Mukden, the puppet Chinese Government set up by the Japanese military authorities is reported to have proclaimed its independence. **1938** *Ann. Reg. 1937* 269 In December the Japanese set up two puppet Governments in North China. **1974** M. B. Brown *Economics of Imperialism* xii. 299 After the tanks came massive economic support for the Soviet puppet government. **1934** C. Lambert *Music Ho!* III. 182 The gangster film or the comic strip would seem more suitable mediums in which to treat the self-appointed puppet leaders..of the people. **1937** E. Snow *Red Star over China* 33 In 1935..the puppet régime of east Hopei was set up. **1971** *Standard* (Dar es Salaam) 7 Apr. 1/1 Those present [at the conference] were undecided about the relative merits of the Sihanouk Government and the American puppet regime. **1980** *Times* 2 Jan. 9/2 Mr Babrak Karmal, the new puppet ruler of Afghanistan, appears to have been instructed to hold out a conciliatory hand to the rebels. **1935** (*title*) The puppet state of 'Manchukuo'. **1947** *Sun* (Baltimore) 15 Aug. 12/8 We also have to ask ourselves whether strategically we can afford to let the Russians create another puppet state on the Asian mainland, just a few miles away from Japan. **1946** *News Chron.* 25 Feb. 1/1 Remnants of the Japanese forces in Manchuria, assisted by former puppet troops and Chinese reactionaries, were operating against the Red Army.

b. *puppet-like* (example); **puppet-master,** also *fig.*

1965 W. Lamb *Posture & Gesture* iii. 41 That the puppet-like pin-up girl's beauty is only skin deep is often revealed the moment she opens her mouth. **1965** M. Allingham *Mind Readers* ix. 97 Much more worrying was the question of the mind behind their experiments... Who was the puppet master? **1976** H. Wilson *Governance of Britain* 10 None of the prime ministers of my experience..has been either a puppet or a puppet-master.

puppeteer (pʌpĕtiə·ɹ). [f. Puppet *sb.* + -eer.] One who operates puppets; *spec.* one whose occupation is the creation, management, or exhibition of puppet-shows; also *fig.* (cf. Puppet *sb.* 3 b in Dict. and Suppl.).

1930 A. Gerstenberg *Comedies All* 175 (*play-title*) The puppeteer. **1934** *Church Times* 30 Nov. 614/4 Every puppeteer has his own whimsies. Mr. William Simmonds.. makes as well as manipulates his own puppets. **1947** *Sun* (Baltimore) 14 Oct. 5/4 A cartoon in the Communist party newspaper *Pravda* today pictured the United States as a puppeteer manipulating votes of delegates in the United Nations. **1958** *Times* 10 July 4/5 The Rumanian and Polish puppeteers, at least, are set on their own underivative ways towards truly creative expression. **1969** A. R. Philpot *Dict. Puppetry* 8 The compiler of the Dictionary has had around forty years as a professional puppeteer, some twenty years as an instructor and nearly as long as editor of a puppetry magazine. **1972** M. Sheppard *Taman Indera* 69 A puppeteer and a group of musicians were maintained by many northern Malay rajas in the nineteenth century. **1979** *West Lancs. Even. Gaz.* 23 Nov. 25 (Advt.), Puppeteers available—International Cabaret Puppeteers, Scarborough.

puppet-show. Add: (Further examples.) Also *transf.* and *fig.*

1774 J. Harrower *Diary* in *Amer. Hist. Rev.* (1900) VI. 87 This night finishes the Puppet shows, roape dancings &c, which has continowed every night this week in town. **1795** tr. *C. P. Moritz's Travels* 88 Electricity happens at present to be the puppet-show of the English. **1807** *Salmagundi* xi. 262, I have seen that great political puppet-show—an Election. **1836** [see *looker *sb.* 1 b]. **1914** *Amer. Rev. of Reviews* Jan. 102/1 The puppet show does not flourish in our American cities. **1951** Lambert & Marx *Eng. Popular Art* i. 6 Bunyan's contemporaries ..could see their secular prototypes..in pageants and puppet shows.

puppet showman (earlier example).

1715 R. Powel (*title*) Second tale of a tub: or the history of Robert Powel the Puppet-Show-Man.

puppet-valve. Add: The spelling *poppet-valve* is now usual. (Further examples.) Hence **poppet-valved** *a.*

1835 *Amer. Railroad Jrnl.* 25 Apr. 245/3 Let the valve be..of the kind called puppet valves. **1877** *Jrnl. Franklin Inst.* CIII. 13 These dimensions would have been reduced by the use of the poppet in place of the lantern valve. **1912** *Motor Traction* 12 Oct. 328/2 The writer has in his possession a list of some 250 poppet-valved engines, together with such data as valve diameters, [etc.]. **1919** W. H. Berry *New Motoring* xvi. 126 The poppet-valved engine, badly made and of unsuitable materials, can be an atrocious production. **1961** F. A. S. Brown *Nigel Gresley* xvii. 122 With poppet valves there is less restriction of steam flow through the ports and consequently less throttling of the steam supply to the cylinders. **1970** *Railway World* Dec. 532 The poppet valves were actuated by a semi-internal form of Walschaerts valve gear.

puppie-show, var. *poppy-show.

puppy, *sb.* Add: **2. b.** For '= Pup *sb.*[1] 2' read 'cf. Pup *sb.*[1] 3 in Dict. and Suppl.' Also, the young of a shark; so *puppy shark.*

1934 W. Beebe *Half Mile Down* iv. 85, I saw five sharks milling around the foot of the ladder. Two were yard-long puppies. *Ibid.* 310 The uppermost one, about two feet in length, was a puppy shark. **1962** *Amer. Speech* XXXVII. 194 The name *puppy shark* may be applied to any small shark.

6. puppy fat, excessive fat in a child or adolescent causing a condition of plumpness which is freq. outgrown; **puppy foot** *U.S. slang* (see quots.); **puppy-hole** *Eton slang,* a pupil-room; **puppy-love** (earlier example); **puppy-tooth,** a small dog-tooth or houndstooth check.

1937 M. Allingham *Dancers in Mourning* x. 138 A large sulky youth in a black suit..too small for his puppy-fat body. **1940** M. Dickens *Mariana* v. 152 You grew late, now you're getting your puppy-fat late. **1972** A. Christie *Elephants can Remember* xiii. 175 She was beautiful... Not when she was about thirteen or fourteen. She had a lot of puppy fat then. **1907** *Hoyle's Games* 410 *Puppy foot,* the ace of clubs. **1932** *Daily Progress* (Charlottesville, Va.) 26 Feb. 6/6 The ace of clubs is often called the puppyfoot. **1961** Webster, *Puppyfoot,* ..a card of the club suit in a pack of playing cards. **1912** G. Frankau *One of Us* i. 10 Idled in 'puppy-hole'. **1922** S. Leslie *Oppidan* vi. 75 A list of lines due was hung in his *puppy-hole.* **1940** M. Marples *Public School Slang* 144 *Puppy-hole,*..pupil-room, when boys work with their tutors. **1834** W. A. Caruthers *Kentuckian in N.Y.* I. 175 Oh! it is nothing more than puppy love! **1960** *Times* 22 Jan. 14/3 One [coat], particularly good, in black and white puppy tooth silk. **1961** *Sunday Express* 26 Feb. 7/1 A trio of dark puppytooth checks. **1968** J. Ironside *Fashion Alphabet* 218 *Hound's-tooth,* (in smaller versions —dog-tooth or puppy-tooth) is a variety of Broken check.

puppyish, *a.* Add: (Later examples.) Also in sense 2 of Puppy *sb.*

1852 F. E. Smedley *Lewis Arundel* xl. 351 His whole demeanour *blasé* and puppyish in the extreme. **1925** F. Scott Fitzgerald *Great Gatsby* (1926) iii. 61 Girls were putting their heads on men's shoulders in a puppyish, convivial way. **1931** [see *pawing *vbl. sb.* and *ppl. a.*]. **1978** P. Harcourt *Agents of Influence* ii. 45 'My daughter, Sally.'..She was round, puppyish, charming.

Hence **pu·ppyishly** *adv.*; **pu·ppyishness.**

1817 H. C. B. Campbell *Jrnl.* 10 Oct. in *Journey to Florence* (1951) 103 Mr Cornwall was puppieshly vulgar. **1941** *Scrutiny* X. 77 He becomes in short by an inevitable process Frank Churchill,..a suspicion of the original puppyishness and lack of nice feeling still attached to his character. **1949** M. Mead *Male & Female* iii. 67 There is.. much giggling puppyishness among boys.

pupton (pʌ·ptən). [Now the usu. form of Poupeton; ad. F. *poulpeton, poupeton* (Littré 1718).] (See quots. s.v. Poupeton and below.)

1723 J. Nott *Cook's & Confectioner's Dict.* sig. C 2, *To make a Pupton of Apples.* Make the Apples into a Marmalade, with Sugar and Cinnamon; then add..Eggs,.. grated Bread and some Butter; then form it as you please. .. Let it be bak'd in a slow Oven, and then turn it upside down, on a Plate, for a second Course. **1747** H. Glasse *Art of Cookery* ii. 45 A French Pupton of Pigeons. *Ibid.* ix. 83 To make a Pupton of Apples. Do them over a slow Fire... When it is quite thick..let it stand till cool. Beat ..eggs, and stir in..grated Bread, and..Butter; then form it into what shape you please, and bake it. **1944** G. Heyer *Friday's Child* viii. 84 The dinner..consisted of a broiled fowl..followed by a pupton of pears. **1975** *TV Times* 31 May–6 June 54/2 *Pupton of rabbit...* Joint the rabbit... Simmer... Make the stuffing... Add the egg yolks, mushrooms and..asparagus... Cover with.. bacon rashers... Bake.

pupunha (pupu·nyă). Also **pupuña.** [Pg., f. Tupi.] In full, *pupunha palm.* A South American palm tree, *Bactris* (or *Guilielma*) *gasipaes,* which has a spiny stem and yields edible red or yellow fruit about two inches long.

1853 A. R. Wallace *Palms of Amazon* 10 His children are eating the agreeable red and yellow fruit of the Pupunha or peach palm. **1860** [see *murumuru]. **1961** *Times* 13 May 9/7 Bananas, pupuña palms, pineapples and tobacco will grow. **1966** E. J. H. Corner *Life of Palms* vii. 171 The fruits of the American pupunha..are not eaten raw but roasted.

purau (pū·rɑu). Also **purao, puro(w).** [Tahitian.] A small evergreen tree, *Hibiscus tiliaceus,* belonging to the family Malvaceæ, native to littoral regions of the tropics, and bearing pale yellow flowers fading to deep red; also, the light wood or the fibre produced by this tree; = Mahoe[1] 1 b. Also *attrib.*

1790 W. Bligh *Narr. Mutiny on Bounty* 49 The trees that came within our knowledge were the manchineal and a species of purow. [**1865** B. Seemann *Flora Vitiensis* 18 *H*[*ibiscus*]..*tiliaceus*... Nomen vernac... Tahitiense, teste Solander, 'Purau'.] **1892** Stevenson & Osbourne *Wrecker* 2 In the whole length of the single shoreside street, with its grateful shade of palms and green jungle of puraos, no moving figure could be seen. **1894** —— *Ebb-Tide* i. 2 At the far end of the town of Papeete, three such men were seated on the beach under a *purao*-tree. **1907** J. Masefield *Tarpaulin Muster* iv. 68 Some said it was the leaf of the *puro* bush. **1933** *Jrnl. Polynesian Soc.* XLII. 306 The purau appears to be a native of most of the islands of the Pacific. **1952** R. Finlayson *Schooner came to Atia* v. 29 Where was he going there under the dark purau trees. **1959** L. M. Noble in A. H. McLintock *Descr. Atlas N.Z.* 82/2 The traditional rectangular hut with gable roof constructed of purau sticks and palm leaves is still common [in the Cook Islands].

Purcellian (pɒ̆ɹse·liăn), *a.* and *sb.* [f. the name of Henry *Purcell* (*c* 1659–95), English composer + -ian.] **A.** *adj.* Of, pertaining to, or characteristic of Purcell or his style of composition. **B.** *sb.* One who admires or imitates the style of Purcell.

1889 G. B. Shaw in *Star* 21 Feb. 4/3, I daresay many of the Bowegians thought that the unintentional quaintnesses of the amateurs in the orchestra were Purcellian antiquities. **1932** A. K. Holland *Henry Purcell* ii. i. 119 Liszt, whose songs, in their attention to immediate detail, are in the line of the Purcellian 'scena'. **1942** E. Blom *Music in England* vi. 91 Only Turner and Croft, both doctors of music and both Purcellians, counted for a good deal, and may have influenced Handel. **1949** *Scrutiny* XVI. 78 The finest passages in the third Quartet seem to be recovering a more stable rhythmic norm, without any sacrifice of Purcellian and madrigalian intensity. **1959** *Listener* 4 June 972/1 There is some danger of mistaking for Purcellian influence on Handel what is really the influence of Lully on both. **1975** *Gramophone* Jan. 1379/2, I must also especially commend..the direction of that devoted Purcellian, Sir Michael Tippett. **1978** *Early Music* Oct. 577/2 Purcellian alto-clef tenors may have to adopt that term unless they relish some neologism like Rimsky's 'tenore altino'.

purchasabi·lity. [f. Purchasable *a.*: see -ility.] Capability of being bought.

1904 F. Lynde *Grafters* vii. 91 There isn't any doubt about his purchasability.

purchasable, *a.* Add: **b.** (Later examples.) Also as *sb.*

1957 L. MacNeice *Visitations* 46 And from its branches muffled doves Drummed out the purchasable loves. **1966** *Listener* 17 Nov. 734/1 Much attention is given in this book to James Bond's exact social position and..to his use of purchasable objects. **1972** *Village Voice* (N.Y.) 1 June 13/4 Grocery stores tack on a 10-cent charge for the bag you carry your over-priced purchasables home in.

purchase, *sb.* Add: **I. 6. c.** *compulsory purchase,* the enforced purchase of privately-owned land or property usu. by a local authority under statutory powers of compulsion. Freq. *attrib.* in *compulsory purchase order.*

1869 *Bradshaw's Railway Man.* XXI. 40 Extra land, 10 acres; compulsory purchase, 2 years; completion of works, four years. **1932** *Act* 22 & 23 *Geo. V* c. 48 § 25(2) They may..be authorised to purchase that land compulsorily by means of an order (in this Act referred to as a 'compulsory purchase order'). **1962** J. Braine *Life at Top* x. 138 Hewley was the leader of the Labour group on the Council... And Hewley thought that the compulsory purchase wouldn't go through. *a* **1974** R. Crossman *Diaries* (1975) I. 67 Planning permissions and compulsory purchase orders. **1976** *S. Wales Echo* 26 Nov., Plans are in hand for compulsory purchase of 100 houses.

IV. 16. purchase tax, a tax levied (between 1940 and 1973) on goods bought at a rate that was higher on luxuries than on more essential goods.

1940 *Act* 3 & 4 *Geo. VI* c. 48 § 18 A tax, to be called purchase tax, shall be charged,..on the wholesale value of all chargeable goods bought under chargeable purchases. **1940** *Manch. Guardian Weekly* 25 Oct. 293 The purchase tax came into operation on Monday [20 Oct.], amid some confusion and protest... The tax imposes 33⅓ per cent on the wholesale value of luxury goods and 16⅔ per cent on other more essential commodities. **1944** M. Laski *Love on Supertax* iv. 50 Add on the Purchase Tax and the increased Purchase Tax and Special Tax on Luxury Goods. **1947** J. Hayward *Prose Lit. since 1939* 10 The publishers..fought successfully to prevent the imposition of a purchase-tax on books. **1959** *Daily Tel.* 9 Apr. 1/7 The Trades Union Congress yesterday welcomed the Chancellor's cuts in purchase tax. **1972** *Times* 27 Jan. 14/1 Ribena..was held not to be a drug or medicine and therefore not exempt from purchase tax.

purchase, *v.* Add: **6. c.** With money or its equivalent as the subject.

1805 M. G. Lewis *Bravo of Venice* ii. vi. 214 Will ten thousand sequins purchase your departure from the republic? **1904** L. Tracy *King of Diamonds* iii. 35 An establishment where threehalfpence would purchase a cup of coffee and a 'doorstep'. **1916** G. B. Shaw *Androcles & Lion* p. xciv, Such pleasures as money can purchase are suppressed.

d. *absol.*

1850 T. S. Arthur *Golden Grains* 50 He purchased largely and had the goods forwarded before he left the city. **1904** R. M. Williamson *Bits from Bookshop* x. 77 The great public libraries where..books are lent out for hire to those who wish to read but cannot purchase.

purchase-money. (Earlier and later examples.)

1720 *Rec. Early Hist. Boston* (1883) VIII. 146 The which purchace money to be Invested in Some Real Estate for the use of this Town. **1723** Duchess of Buckingham *Let.* 1 Aug. in *Lett. to & from Henrietta, Countess of Suffolk* (1824) I. 115 Half the purchase-money, at least, will go to build him another [house] to his mind. **1892** M. A. Jackson *Life & Lett. Gen. T. J. Jackson* viii. 114 He might be permitted to emancipate himself by a return of the purchase-money. **1961** NEW ENG. BIBLE *Acts* v. 2 He kept back part of the purchase-money. **1972** C. DRUMMOND *Death at Bar* ii. 47 Alwyn did not pay over the purchase money.

purchasing, *vbl. sb.* Add: **b.** *purchasing agent, manager, officer*; **purchasing power** (earlier and later examples); hence **purchasing power parity** (see quots. 1918, 1939).

1921 *Daily Colonist* (Victoria, B.C.) 3 Apr. 1/2 G. W. Wooster, treasurer, and G. L. McNichol, purchasing agent, two of the oldest employees of the company, have retired into private life. **1969** *Times* 2 May 34 (Advt.), *Purchasing Manager.* A large British Company in the chemical field requires a manager to establish and develop a new central section to be responsible for all research concerning materials, services and sources of supply. **1963** *B.S.I. News* Apr. 22/2 Purchasing officers should make appropriate sample tests of goods received to ensure that they complied with the contract requirements. **1824** J. S. MILL in *Westm. Rev.* II. 42 Those commodities are also the measure of its purchasing power. **1930** *Economist* 11 Jan. 78/2 Good chain-store sales this month indicate a satisfactory volume of purchasing power. **1979** *Bull. Amer. Acad. Arts & Sci.* Mar. 42 Those prices will rise, and in addition, wages and other prices will also tend to rise in order to maintain their original 'purchasing power'. **1918** G. CASSEL in *Economic Jrnl.* Dec. 413 At every moment the real parity between two countries is represented by this quotient between the purchasing power of the money in the one country and the other. I propose to call this parity *'the purchasing power parity'*. **1939** I. DE VEGH *Pound Sterling* II. 75 This point of view, known as the purchasing power parity theory, rests fundamentally on the assumption that a change in the internal purchasing power of a currency will, under certain conditions, affect the merchandise balance of the country involved. **1965** SELDON & PENNANCE *Everyman's Dict. Econ.* 350 Purchasing power parity is..only a partial explanation of exchange rates, although when other circumstances are generally stable it can give a rough guide to them.

purdah, Delete ‖ and add: **1. a.** (Later examples.) (See also quot. 1952.)

1898 C. P. STETSON *Women & Economics* iv. 66 Some air has come through the purdah's folds, some knowledge has filtered to her eager ears from the talk of men. **1927** *New Republic* 21 Sept. 127/2 Miss Mayo speaks as though the seclusion of women behind the *purdah* were universal throughout India. **1952** S. SELVON *Brighter Sun* i. 9 He didn't feel any sexual excitement... Even when he had looked at her face under the *purdah*—the white sheet thrown over them.

b. (Later examples.)

1968 *Times* 6 Apr. (Pakistan Suppl.) p. vii/5 In Pakistan today the observance of purdah is, in the broadest terms, in inverse ratio to social status. **1971** R. RUSSELL tr. *Ahmad's Shore & Wave* iv. 39 She very rarely observed purdah and on the day in question was returning from school. **1975** *Language for Life* (Dept. Educ. & Sci.) xx. 293 Mothers may be at work all day, or live in purdah, or speak no English.

c. *transf.* Seclusion; (medical) isolation or quarantine; secrecy. Usu. in phrases *in, into,* (etc.), *purdah.*

1928 J. GALSWORTHY *Swan Song* II. v. 143 The diagnosis of Kit's malady [*sc.* measles] was soon verified, and Fleur went into purdah. **1957** G. B. STERN *Seventy Times Seven* 182 He was supposed to be in purdah with Nicola and deeply occupied with those unspeakable Memoirs. **1958** *Times* 23 Oct. 15/5 The voluminous Dilke papers.. had been kept in *purdah* by the family piety of the late Miss Tuckwell. **1963** *Times* 27 Feb. 10/5 Mr. Maudling, Chancellor of the Exchequer, from now on will be in purdah whenever questions touch upon the Budget. **1977** D. BAGLEY *Enemy* xxxix. 314 When I came out of purdah, but before I was discharged, I went to see her.

3. *purdah girl*; *purdah costume, curtain, glass, party* (example).

1905 Purdah costume [see *BURKA[1]]. **1937** *Times* 13 Apr. p. xxxviii/1 In the first class compartment there are four special ventilators and purdah glass louvres above the side windows. **1955** *Times* 31 May 7/7 In Peshawar is the university and a college for women, where there are mixed debates with a *purdah* curtain dividing the sexes. **1971** R. RUSSELL tr. *Ahmad's Shore & Wave* x. 124 Let purdah girls play the men up. **1973** *New Society* 26 Apr. 198/3 A gilded door of purdah glass, which meant that Lady Jersey could see all of Lord Jersey approaching, while he could delight only in outline of her filmy silhouette. **1975** P. MASON in C. Allen *Plain Tales from Raj* 16 One formidable old lady..would fit in a purdah party for Indian ladies before her dinner party for the brigadier.

purdahed, *a.* (Later examples.)

1949 L. DURRELL *Spirit of Place* (1969) 103 All the houses in the Turkish quarter have musharabaya trellis windows for purdah-ed girls. **1959** *Encounter* Sept. 33/1 Somewhat secluded (although not purdah-ed) women.

Purdey (pɜ̄·ɹdi). The proprietary name of firearms and parts manufactured by the firm founded by James *Purdey* (1816–68).

1884 F. F. R. BURGESS *Sporting Fire-Arms for Bush & Jungle* viii. 85 For ordinary shot-guns, the Purdey bolt is a very good fastening. **1901** T. F. FREMANTLE *Bk. of Rifle* ii. 44 The Purdey was a four-grooved rifle, with an increasing twist. **1937** M. SHARP *Nutmeg Tree* ii. 17 At twelve the boy was to be given his father's old 20-bore, at eighteen the Purdey 12. **1961** C. WILLOCK *Death in Covert* ii. 31 Crumbe-Howard..was standing casually with a Purdey twelve-bore open. **1970** R. A. STEINDLER *Firearms Dict.* 185/1 *Purdey side lock*, perhaps the most famed & best of all side lock actions... The Purdey design differs in several important points from the standard side lock design... Even a well-used Purdey is considered a 'good buy'. **1974** *Trade Marks Jrnl.* 20 Mar. 468/1 *Purdey*... Guns, rifles and ammunition. James Purdey and Sons Ltd.,..London. **1976** *Shooting Times & Country Mag.* 9–15 Dec. 38/2 (Advt.), These weapons have the usual Purdey engraving with traces of original hardening colour.

pure, *a.* (*sb., adv.*) Add: **I. 1. e.** *pure tone,* a tone composed of a single frequency and represented by a sine wave.

Earlier called a *simple tone.*

1902 *Encycl. Brit.* XXXI. 751/2 Considerable difference of opinion exists as to whether beats can blend so as to give a sensation of tone; but König, by using very pure tones of high pitch, appears to have settled the question. **1929** H. FLETCHER *Speech & Hearing* iv. 167 The masking effect of one pure tone by another was determined. **1961** *Lancet* 22 July 197/2 Pure-tone audiometry is only one item in a whole range of tests that are needed to build up a complete picture of the condition of a patient who has a hearing-loss. **1976** L. H. SCHAUDINISCHKY *Sound, Man & Building* i. 30 The beat grows progressively lower and vanishes altogether when $f_1 = f_2$. This gives rise to a method of extremely accurately determining the unknown frequency of a pure tone with the aid of the calibrated output of a sine-wave generator by simply listening in.

f. *Forestry.* Of a wood or plantation; consisting of trees of only one species.

1889 W. SCHLICH *Man. Forestry* I. II. iii. 177 Such woods may be composed of one species only, or they may contain a mixture of two or more species; in the former case they are called 'pure woods', and in the latter 'mixed woods'. **1927** *Forestry* I. 11 This century saw the return in an increasing degree to pure rather than mixed coniferous stands. **1948** *Misc. Publ. Univ. Michigan Mus. Zool.* LXVIII. 16 The creosote bush, usually in pure stands, covers great expanses of the broad desert basins. **1976** H. L. EDLIN *Nat. Hist. Trees* v. 64 The plantations just described are examples of more or less even-aged stands of a single species, also called a pure even-aged forest.

II. 2. b. *pure line* [tr. G. *reine linie* (W. Johannsen *Erblichkeit in Populationen und in reinen Linien* (1903) 9)], an inbred line of descent; also *attrib.*, an individual belonging to such a line.

1906 R. H. LOCK *Rec. Progress Study Variation* iv. 110 If we were to carry on this conception to the case of bisexual inheritance, we should find that the different pure lines would become crossed and confused together. **1926** J. S. HUXLEY *Ess. Pop. Sci.* ii. 22 Beans are self-fertilising; so that if, instead of treating the sample as a whole, he kept the beans produced from each plant separate, he could be sure of dealing with a hereditarily pure stock, or as it is usually called, a pure line. **1932** *Discovery* Oct. 320/2 In the cotton industry we have the magnificent succession of 'pure lines' particularly in the Egyptian cottons. **1947** *Ann. Rev. Microbiol.* I. 27 Ritz..later showed that an apparently inexhaustible succession of immunologically distinct variants may appear in a single animal. This work..is of especial interest since the strain of *T. brucei* used was a 'pure line' derived from a single trypanosome. **1958** SRB & OWEN *Gen. Genetics* xvi. 335 Selection within pure lines..is ineffective because it is biologically meaningless. **1965** 'LAUCHMONEN' *Old Thom's Harvest* i. 5 When I get my credit-bank money to buy pure-line seeds them ricefields gwine be planted again.

d. Also, with reference to the arts (chiefly music, painting, and poetry): used of an art in its absolute, essential, or most objective form; freq. in contrast to that which is representational, didactic, or commercial in intent. Also used of an artist whose work is of this sort.

1901 A. C. BRADLEY *Poetry for Poetry's Sake* 28 Pure poetry is not the decoration of a preconceived and clearly defined matter: it springs from the creative impulse of a vague imaginative mass pressing for development and definition. **1914** [see *ORPHIC *a.* (*sb.*)]. **1924** G. MOORE *Anthol. Pure Poetry* 34 If you approve of my definition of pure poetry, something that the poet creates outside of his own personality, we three might compile a book that would be a real advancement in the study of poetry—an anthology of pure poetry. **1926** H. READ *Reason & Romanticism* iii. 59 Pure poetry, Mr. Moore holds, is born of admiration of 'the only permanent world, the world of things'. **1927** *New Criterion* V. 10 Whither would the notion of 'pure art' lead us if pushed to its farthest logical extremity? To an art completely isolated from everything but its own laws of operation and the object to be created as such. **1929** E. WILSON *I thought of Daisy* iii. 183, I thought..of those other efforts, those efforts more characteristic of our time, which aimed, also, at an absolute beauty, at an art wholly independent of the appetites and agonies of men—paintings which represented nothing, 'pure poetry' devoid of ideas. **1934** C. LAMBERT *Music Ho!* III. 174 The recent invention by certain critics of a hitherto unknown art described as 'pure music' has resulted in the criticism of music becoming more and more detached from any form of life. **1935** W. STEVENS *Let.* 31 Oct. (1967) 288 There was a time when I liked the idea of images and images alone, or images and the music of verse together. I then believed in *pure poetry*, as it was called. **1941** 'G. ORWELL' in *Listener* 29 May 768/1 James Joyce, was..about as near to being a 'pure' artist as a writer can be. **1946** A. L. BACHARACH *Brit. Music of our Time* viii. 118 The superficial æstheticians who insist on the necessity of music being 'pure', the implication being that any music that has the remotest connection with 'literature' is necessarily impure, and therefore ineligible for admission into the musical heaven. **1954** C. S. LEWIS *Eng. Lit. in Sixteenth Cent.* I. i. 92 This minuet of conventions..enables the poem to remain recognizably occasional and yet at the same time to become almost 'pure' poetry. We celebrate the royal wedding..; yet equally, we wander in a world of beautiful forms and colours. **1955** *Times* 9 May 5/1 The exhibition would attract considerable attention and must help to break down the barrier which existed between commercial and pure art. **1959** D. COOKE *Lang. Mus.* v. 231 Mozart's Fortieth Symphony and Vaughan Williams's Sixth.. would both appear to be 'pure' music, since we have no evidence that their composers ever imagined that they expressed anything at all. *Ibid.* 234 Our own age has retained the romantic period's conception of Mozart as a 'pure' composer, but adopted a different attitude. **1978** P. GRIFFITHS *Concise Hist. Mod. Music* iv. 47 His [*sc.* Debussy's] creative energies were directed..into works of pure music.

g. Philos. and Psychol. *pure ego*: the essential, transcendental 'self' distinguished from the empirical 'self', esp. in phenomenological contexts.

1890 W. JAMES *Princ. Psychol.* I. x. 292 The constituents of the Self may be divided into two classes, those which make up respectively—(a) The material Self; (*b*) The social Self; (c) The spiritual Self; and (d) The pure Ego. *Ibid.* 296 By the Spiritual Self, so far as it belongs to the Empirical Me, I mean a man's inner or subjective being, his psychic faculties or dispositions, taken concretely; not the bare principle of personal Unity, or 'pure' Ego. **1925** *Mind* XXXIV. 320 In the second edition footnotes the reader of the Logical Studies learns that Husserl has changed his views on this crucial point, and has come to accept definitely..Natorp's Pure Ego. **1931** W. R. B. GIBSON tr. *Husserl's Ideas* II. ii. 145 The thesis of my pure Ego and its personal life which is 'necessary' and plainly indubitable, thus stands opposed to the thesis of the world which is contingent. **1951** A. HUXLEY *Let.* 9 June (1969) 635 A deeper layer of 'Original Virtue', which is one of peace, illumination and insight, which seems to be on the fringes of the Pure Ego or Atman. **1961** G. W. ALLPORT *Devel. of Personality* vi. 129 Kant argued that..the knowing self is just there, a transcendental or pure ego. **1974** G. L. BRECKON tr. *de Muralt's Idea of Phenomenol.* § 52. 328 The pure ego is therefore the subject of transcendental constitution, the ego pole of intentionality, the centre and point of departure of every intentional function.

h. Biol. *pure culture*, a culture in which only one species or clone is present; also *attrib.*

1895 *Ann. Bot.* IX. 610 The method adopted by De Bary of cultivating each species separately for many generations—that of so-called 'pure cultures'—has been of inestimable value. **1930** *Forestry* IV. 66 It seemed possible..that pure culture experiments..might also yield some information..on the origin of the mycorrhizal habit in trees. **1952** *New Biol.* XIII. 110 Pure-culture technique is a 'stock-in-trade' of the micro-biologist. **1973** G. D. BOWEN in Marks & Kozlowski *Ectomycorrhizae* v. 166 Many..of 27 mycorrhizal fungi in pure culture could use nitrate as the sole source of nitrogen.

3. a. *pure and simple* (earlier and later examples).

1860 GEO. ELIOT *Let.* 7 June (1954) III. 302 But the most ignorant journalist in England would hardly think of calling me a rival of Miss Mulock—a writer who is read only by novel readers, pure and simple, never by people of high culture. **1954** C. S. LEWIS *Eng. Lit. in Sixteenth Cent.* 4 Even when hills are praised for not despising lowly plains we have still hardly reached the realm of metaphor pure and simple. **1977** *Lancs. Life* Nov. 58/3 They attract on a variety of levels: as toys or fun-things pure and simple, as tactile objects, [etc.].

IV. 8. d. *the pure quill*, the genuine article, the real thing. *N. Amer. dial.* or *colloq.*

1884 C. B. LEWIS *Sawed-off Sketches* 23 There's hairs of six different colors sticking in the splinters, and those blood stains are the pure quill. **1893** *N. & Q.* 23 Sept. 248/1 One of your correspondents..states that the expressions, 'the cheese', 'pick of the basket', &c., although now almost obsolete on this side of the Atlantic, are still to be heard in America. The expression 'the pure quill', having a similar meaning, I have often heard used in Canada and in the States. **1917** *Dialect Notes* IV. 327 That tobacco is the pure quill. **1935** H. DAVIS *Honey in Horn* xxi. 330 To prove that his product [*sc.* rattlesnake oil] was the pure quill, he also exhibited..a row of half-gallon fruit-jars, each containing one large live rattler. **1956** N. ALGREN *Walk on Wild Side* ii. 152 A pint of Bottled-in-the-Barn. They drank it down to the half-pint mark. 'That stuff is so good a feller can't hardly bite it off,' Dove told Luke. 'It's the pure quill.'

B. *sb.* **5.** Delete † and add earlier and later examples.

1845 G. DODD *Brit. Manuf.* V. ix. 189 A solution called the 'pure' or the 'pewer' is prepared in a large vessel, and into this the skins are immersed. **1946** *Thorpe's Dict. Appl. Chem.* (ed. 4) VII. 264/2 Modern artificial bates have replaced almost completely the older 'dung bate' or puer, an infusion of dog- or, less often, pigeon-dung.

6. A genuine person. *rare.*

1924 W. M. RAINE *Troubled Waters* xix. 201 You-all are losing a better man than Missie ever had. He's a pure, Mac is.

C. *adv.* **1.** (Later U.S. dial. examples.) Also, with verbs: just, simply; really, truly.

1928 J. PETERKIN *Scarlet Sister Mary* iii. 27 My jaws pure leak water just to look at em. *Ibid.* 35 What you done pure cuts my heart-strings. **1932** W. FAULKNER *Light in August* (1933) xv. 332 He was pure crazy by now, standing on the corner and yelling at whoever would pass. **1937** *Frontier & Midland* Autumn 13/2 Hit was puore accidental and it was with a shotgun he was unloadin. **1942** W. FAULKNER in *Sat. Even. Post* 28 Mar. 38/3, I would pure cut a throat if it would bring you back to stay.

D. a. *pure-blooded* (earlier, later, and *fig.* examples), *-hearted, -natured, souled, toned* adjs.; *pure-mindedness*; **pure-relational** *Linguistics* (see quots.); **pure-watered** *a.*, of unmarred brilliance (cf. WATER *sb.* 20).

1850 L. H. Garrard *Wah-To-Yah* vii. 109 The unfair horsetrader might have taken my scalp for presuming to dictate to him, a..pure-blooded Cheyenne. 1892 W. James in *Philos. Rev.* I. 149 They have quite as little [aptitude] as the pure-blooded philosophers have for discovering particular facts. 1903 *Rep. Kansas State Board Agric. 1901–02* II. 63 A quarter of a billion acres of grass, nurturing 10,000,000 head of cattle..can be doubled in value in a single decade, if only pure-blooded sires are used in all the cow herds during this time. 1832 J. G. Whittier in S. T. Pickard *Life & Lett. J. G. Whittier* (1894) I. iii. 108 Those who o'er our tarnished honor grieve..the pure-hearted and the gifted. 1891 G. Meredith *One of our Conquerors* III. vii. 135 He might have put a reluctant faith in the puremindedness of these aspirations, without reverting to her origin. 1855 Bagehot *Coll. Works* (1965) I. 319 They are emphatically pure-natured and firm-natured. Instinctively casting aside the coarse temptations and crude excitements of a vulgar earth, [etc.]. 1913 J. Masefield *Daffodil Fields* 12 Gentle she seemed, pure-natured, thoughtful, wise. 1921 E. Sapir *Language* v. 107 *Pure Relational Concepts* (purely abstract): normally expressed by affixing non-radical elements to radical elements..or by their inner modification, by independent words, or by position; serve to relate the concrete elements of the proposition to each other, thus giving it definite syntactic form. *Ibid.* vi. 145 Languages that keep the syntactic relations pure and that do not possess the power to modify the significance of their radical elements by means of affixes or internal changes. We may call these *Pure-relational non-deriving languages* or, more tersely, *Simple Pure-relational languages.* These are the languages that cut most to the bone of linguistic expression. *Ibid.*, Languages that keep the syntactic relations pure and that also possess the power to modify the significance of their radical elements by means of affixes or internal changes. These are the *Pure-relational deriving languages* or *Complex Pure-relational languages.* 1944 R. A. Hall *Hungarian Gram.* (Language Monograph No. 21) 22 There are three fundamental types of suffixes which are added to substantives: derivational (the plural suffix), concrete-relational (the personal possessive suffixes, expressing ownership of the object denoted by the noun, on the part of the person indicated by the suffix), and pure-relational (twenty suffixes, including the accusative, whose addition gives the substantive adverbial function). 1945 *Language* XXI. 255 This analysis results in three pure-relational categories in Hungarian: case suffixes, suffixed postpositions, and free postpositions. The former two classes can be grouped together as pure-relational suffixes, to preserve both Hall's (originally Sapir's) term and class. 1963 N. N. Poppe *Tatar Manual* ii. 34 Pure-relational suffixes are added to the concrete-relational (possessive) suffixes... The pure-relational suffixes serve to denote the relations between an object and other objects or between an object and an action. The system of pure-relational forms is what is commonly called 'declension'. 1910 F. M. Ford *Let.* 28 Oct. (1965) 45 When you—the unscrupulous villain and I, the pure-souled Idealist join forces how *that* dovecote will flutter! 1923 F. L. Packard *Four Stragglers* II. vii. 220 A girl, high-minded, pure-souled. 1869 J. G. Whittier *Among Hills* 36 Through her his civic service shows A purer-toned ambition; No double consciousness divides The man and politician. 1851 H. Melville *Moby Dick* III. vii. 56 In the clear air of day,..the pure-watered diamond drop will healthful glow. 1929 Blunden *English Poems* (rev. ed.) 54 Here yet its fruit-trees shield love-nooks, Its well's pure-watered diamond.

b. *pure-bred* (further examples); also *absol.* and *fig.*; *pure-breeding*, producing genetically similar progeny.

1903 *Biometrika* II. 171 Pure-bred mice usually are in-bred. 1919 'W. N. P. Barbellion' *Jrnl. Disappointed Man* 179 If only I were pure-bred science or pure-bred art. 1923 D. H. Lawrence *Birds, Beasts & Flowers* 177 Sensitive mother Kangaroo. Her sensitive, long, pure-bred face, Her full antipodal eyes. 1927 Haldane & Huxley *Animal Biol.* ii. 68 The original pure-bred rose-comb stock gives nothing but rose-combs. 1937 K. Blixen *Out of Africa* iii. 191 A stud-farm of purebreds. 1945 [see *grade *sb.* 7]. 1976 *Sci. Amer.* Sept. 186/3 The object is merely to incorporate new traits into the heterogeneous population, not to create a purebred variety. 1976 *Cumberland News* 3 Dec. 15/3 In the live cattle section the pure-breds have made a come-back with a sharp rise in entries from 294 in 1975 to 318 this year. 1927 Haldane & Huxley *Animal Biol.* ii. 69 We should get four pure-breeding types in the second generation. 1964 D. Michie in G. H. Haggis et al. *Introd. Molecular Biol.* viii. 206 Griffith injected mice with living pneumococci of a pure-breeding strain lacking the polysaccharide capsule characteristic of most members of this species.

c. pure-cone, -rod *adjs.*, having only cones, or rods, as photoreceptors; **pure food** *attrib.*, of or concerned with the maintenance and promotion of purity in food through the control of additives, avoidance of the use of chemical fertilizers, or the like; **pure-jet** *Aeronaut.*, usu. *attrib.*, denoting engines, aircraft, etc., in which all thrust is provided directly by reaction to the exhaust jet, without the assistance of fans or propellers; **pure-rod** *a.*: see *pure-cone* adj. above.

1942 G. L. Walls *Vertebrate Eye* iii. 73 Perfectly familiar to all is the increase of visual acuity with intensity... If we knew very accurately this relationship for pure-rod and pure-cone animals, we would expect to find their curves of acuity-versus-intensity to be kinkless. 1962 *Science Survey* III. 243 One of the American ground squirrels, one of the few mammalian species known to have a pure-cone retina and to be strongly diurnal. 1970 *Jrnl. Marine Biol. Assoc. U.K.* L. 454 There is no evidence of summation in early development which is to be expected in a pure-cone retina. It is, however, surprising that there is also little evidence of summation in the two pure-rod eyes (leptocephalus and macrurid). 1894 *Jrnl. Franklin Inst.* Apr. 267 Senator Paddock, of Nebraska..after years of futile struggle, succeeded in having the Senate pass what is known as the Pure Food Bill. 1913 *Collier's Weekly* 16 Aug. 24/2 The clubwomen of Idaho are banded together to have their State known as a pure-food State. 1923 Wodehouse *Inimitable Jeeves* xvi. 214, I was feeling more or less like something the Pure Food Committee had rejected. 1965 *Punch* 14 July p. xii/2 The *Four Seasons* is another of the popular pure-food centres. 1969 'I. Drummond' *Man with Tiny Head* xiv. 161 He was..a pure-food fanatic with a hatred of chemical fertilisers. 1946 *Jrnl. R. Aeronaut. Soc.* L. 360/2 The weight of a pure jet engine, as compared with that of the aeroplane in which it had to be fitted..was small. 1959 *Daily Tel.* 2 Mar. 16/4 A pure-jet plane may evade interception. 1960 C. H. Gibbs-Smith *Aeroplane* xvi. 127 Turboprop engines are ideal for commercial air-liners whose operations take them too far from the optimum conditions of altitude and speed necessary for the economic use of the pure jet. 1969 *Jane's Freight Containers 1968–69* 415/1 By..1975, Lockheed will possess unrivalled knowledge of operating large, pure-jet freighters. 1942 Pure-rod [see *pure-cone* above]. 1962 *Science Survey* III. 242 In 'pure-rod' eyes the retinal structure is always the limiting factor for visual acuity and in these eyes it is always poor. 1970 [see *pure-cone* above.]

pure, *v.* Add: **1. b.** Also **puer.** (Earlier and later examples.)

1845 G. Dodd *Brit. Manuf.* V. ix. 190 After being 'pured' for some time, the skins are taken out and scraped well. 1913 D. J. Law in G. Martin *Industr. & Manuf. Chem.: Organic* xix. 580 The goods are then 'puered', which operation consists in paddling in a weak warm infusion of fermented dog-dung.

Hence **pu·ring** *vbl. sb.*

1897 [see *graining *vbl. sb.*]. 1897 *Hide & Leather* 22 May 21/1 After puring, rinse well and work on flesh side. 1898 *Ibid.* 17 Dec. 25/2 The excrement used in puring should be as fresh as possible, hen manure being used for hides, pig manure for calfskin and dog's dung for goats. 1964 H. Hodges *Artifacts* xi. 150 This process of plumping, bating or puering, was essentially one of partial putrefaction. 1972 *Materials & Technol.* V. xii. 401 Puering and bating assist in the removal of short hairs, lime soaps, and cementing substances in the skin.

pure blood, *sb.* and *a.* [f. Pure *a.* + Blood *sb.*] **A.** *sb.* **1.** Unmixed inheritance or ancestry. Also *fig.*

1776 [see Blood *sb.* 8]. 1884 J. F. Maurice *F. D. Maurice* II. ii. 62 A number of the political economists of pure blood, who were..the fiercest in opposition to co-operation. 1945 M. F. A. Montagu *Introd. Physical Anthropol.* vii. 201 The term 'blood-relationship'..enshrines the belief that all biological relationships are reflected in, and are to a large extent, determined by the character of the blood. Such terms as..'pure blood',..and 'good blood' further reflect that meaning. 1963 [see sense B]. 1971 *Biol. Abstr.* LII. 12246/2 Investigation on the possibility of improving important properties of Sjenica sheep by breeding in pure blood and crossing with Corriedale and Precoce.

2. An animal or breed of unmixed inheritance.

1882 *Harper's Mag.* May 895/1 The half and quarter breeds..seem to have..greater powers of resistance than the pure-bloods. 1894 *Rep. Vermont Board Agric.* XIV. 166 Having bred pure bloods for almost thirty years. 1903 *Rep. Kansas State Board Agric. 1901–2* II. 63 Fifty per cent. can be added to the value if pure-bloods only are used in the northern half of this territory.

B. *adj.* Also **pure-blood.** Of unmixed inheritance or ancestry; pure-bred.

1860 *Trans. State Agric. Soc. Michigan* X. 355 The Durham cattle will keep as easy..as the pure blood, elegantly-constructed sprightly Devon. 1888 *Rep. Vermont Board Agric.* X. 49 Why don't you get some pure blood Holsteins? 1963 *English Studies* XLIV. 21 Only he and the other bears and the deer are pure-blood, and he is not so much distinguished from these other animals by his size and his age as he is representative of all pure blood, of all wildness before blood is mixed, of the wilderness itself. *Ibid.* 22 A pure-blood line Old Ben.

pure D, puredee (piūə·ɹdī), *a. U.S. dial.* [f. Pure *a.*: cf. D 3, *dee b.] Thoroughgoing, 'regular'. Also as *adv.*

1941 J. Street *In my Father's House* ix. 148 I'm pow'ful fond of Woody. He's a pure D man. *Ibid.* xvi. 346 Mama has got pure D gumption. 1941 *Sat. Even. Post* 6 Dec. 110 It takes a pure D humdinger to hunt birds... If a dog's got pure D hoss sense and a fellow's got bat brains, he can train the dog to hunt birds. 1952 B. Harwin *Home is Upriver* i. 8 Kip's lip curled at this slovenly practice, one which Pa had always called puredee shif'less. 1964 *Amer. Folk Music Occasional* I. 92 This State you can drink, this State you can't except pure-dee God-given water.

purée, *sb.*² Delete ‖ and add: Now usu. with pronunc. (piuə·rēi). (Earlier and further examples.)

1707 J. Mortimer *Whole Art of Husbandry* 593 This small Beveridge, or Cider Kin and Puree..is made for the common drinking of Servants, *&c.* supplying the place of Small-beer. 1723 J. Nott *Cook's & Confectioner's Dict.* sig. D1, *Artichokes in Puree*..take them out of the Water, and make them into Puree; then strain them through a Sieve as you do Peas. *Ibid.* sig F8ᵛ Take a Quart of clung Peas, boil them..bruise them to a Mash..and strain the clear Puree. 1929 A. Blackwood *Dudley & Gilderoy* xvi. 183 Of flight and nuts, of hot sunshine, foliage, flowers, of numerous companions, of sex, age, nests and eggs—of all these his golden dreams formed a lovely *purée.* 1951 *Good Housek. Home Encycl.* 623/1 *Purée*, fruit, vegetable, meat or fish pounded or sieved into a finely divided pulp. The thickness of the purée depends on the amount of liquid present before sieving: a purée of cooked green peas and potatoes..is very stiff and can be piped for decoration.

purée (piūə·rēi), *v.* [f. prec.] *trans.* To make into a purée. Also *fig.* Hence **pu·réed** *ppl. a.*

1934 Webster, *Purée*.., to boil to a pulp and rub through a sieve. 1948 *Good Housek. Cookery Bk.* I. 55 *To purée*, to rub (vegetables and fruit) through a sieve [etc.]. 1951 *Good Housek. Home Encycl.* 251/1 Sieves are used..for puréeing foods. 1959 J. Thurber *Years with Ross* xiv. 223 He puréed his own peas. 1961 *Listener* 31 Aug. 331/2 A combined grinder-liquidizer..purées fruit and cooked vegetables, in seconds. 1963 Hume & Downes *Penguin Cordon Bleu Cookery* ix. 357 (*heading*) Puréed and Mousseline potatoes. 1973 *Daily Tel.* (Colour Suppl.) 9 Nov. 79/1 Purée the sugar, butter, powdered almonds and most of the cointreau in a blender to obtain a light and frothy cream. 1977 *Time* 21 Feb. 47/3 There are certain plays—and this is one of them—that can be called 'blender drama': puréed bits of other, better works.

purely, *adv.* **2. b.** Delete † *Obs.* and add later U.S. regional examples.

1938 M. K. Rawlings *Yearling* xiv. 140, I purely hate to think the Forresters has trapped 'em. 1952 B. Harwin *Home is Upriver* xxi. 198 I'd purely like to see that old woman. She'd be glad. 1970 S. Ellin *Bind* lvii. 285, I purely wish you wouldn't point that thing at me..there's all kinds of accidents can happen with a gun. 1975 J. F. Burke *Death Trick* iv. 63 Managers of casbahs [i.e. hotels] like the Castlereagh purely loathe the sight of cops.

4. b. (Earlier example.)

1796 M. Edgeworth *Old Poz* in *Parent's Assistant* (ed. 2) 2nd Ser. II. 55 I'm glad to see your worship look so purely.

‖ **pur et simple** (pür e sæṅpl), *a.* [Fr.] = *pure and simple* s.v. Pure *a.* 3 a (the more usual form).

1856 *Sat. Rev.* 5 Apr. 451/1 Mr. Disraeli fights for a Blue-book, *pur et simple.* 1864 Bagehot *Coll. Works* (1965) II. 300 Inherent eccentricity, oddity *pur et simple*, is *immiscible* in the great ocean of universal thought. 1871 Lytton *Coming Race* xvi. 137 The great-grandfather was a magnificent specimen of the Batrachian genus, a Giant Frog, *pur et simple.* 1880 E. W. Hamilton *Diary* 18 Nov. (1972) I. 77 Chamberlain..says that resort to such [extraordinary] powers *pur et simple* must entail his resignation.

Purex (piūə·reks). [App. f. Pur(ification + Ex(traction.] The name of an industrial process for separating the plutonium and uranium from spent uranium fuel by using tri-*n*-butyl phosphate as a solvent.

1956 *Proc. Internat. Conf. Peaceful Uses of Atomic Energy* IX. 471/1 A schematic chemical flowsheet for the Purex process is shown. 1976 *Sci. Amer.* Dec. 33/3 When the separated uranium and plutonium streams emerge from the Purex process, they contain only about a millionth as much radioactivity due to fission products as the feed materia l did.

‖ **purga** (pūəɹgā·, pūə·ɹgă). [Russ.] A blizzard of very fine snow in the U.S.S.R.

1889 L. F. Gowing *Five Thousand Miles in Sledge* v. 75 A *purga* was raging—one of those fierce snowstorms which visit with especial violence the eastern shores of Asiatic Russia. 1977 P. E. Lydolph *Geogr. U.S.S.R.* (ed. 3) xvii. 377/2 Most of the high winds at Barnaul are associated with cyclonic storms during winter that may produce strong blizzards, the so-called *buran* or *purga.* 1978 *Soviet Geogr.* XIX. 574 A *purga* is not just any snowstorm; it is a violent storm associated with an invasion of cold air.

purgator. Delete † *Obs. rare*⁻¹ and add later example.

1933 K. Malone *Deor* 15 He conceded the possibility that 'll. 31–34 may be a later insertion, made to give the whole a religious turn', but evidently had his doubts about yielding even these lines to the purgator.

purgatory, *sb.* Add: **4. c.** A swamp, esp. one difficult to cross. Also *attrib.* local *U.S.*

1831 J. M. Peck *Guide for Emigrants* III. 308 In the low prairies near the Wabash, are swamps, called by the people *purgatories*, which are almost impassable in the wet season. 1834 —— *Gaz. Illinois* III. 172 The eastern part, towards the Wabash, contains some wet land and purgatory swamps.

5. (Earlier example.)

1841 C. H. Hartshorne *Salopia Antiqua* 537 *Purgatory*, the pit grate of a kitchen fire place; by falling through which the ashe become *purer.*

purge, *sb.* Add: **2. a.** In more recent use, the removal (from a political party, army, etc.) of persons regarded as undesirable. Also *transf.* and *attrib.*

1933 H. G. Wells *Shape of Things to Come* III. § 6. 302 The eternal espionage, censorship and 'purges' of the G.P.U. 1935 *Sun* (Baltimore) 2 Nov. 2/6 Max Schachtman..characterized the 'purge'..as a move to stifle every critical voice in the ranks of the A.F. of L. 1940 *Ann. Reg. 1939* 204 The Munich bomb..furnished a welcome pretext for a new purge on the model of June 30, 1934. 1946 A. Huxley *Let.* 27 Oct. (1969) 553 See the recent accounts of Russian purges of insufficiently patriotic and Marxist writers. 1957 R. N. C. Hunt *Guide to Communist Jargon*

xii. 47 The statements elicited at the purge trials of the middle 'thirties. **1958** *New Statesman* 15 Feb. 186/3 In this he was supported by Ernst Wollweber, the second of the three victims of the new purge, who had been Minister of Security from 1953 until last autumn, and who is now accused of 'leniency towards the class enemy' in general and the Harich group in particular. **1969** L. Hellman *Unfinished Woman* vii. 80, I did not even know I was there in the middle of the ugliest purge period. **1970** G. F. Newman *Sir, You Bastard* viii. 258 They liked nothing better than a sordid purge in an institution. **1974** *Guardian* 24 Jan. 3/1 The word 'purge', with its unhealthy overtones of Stalinism, is naturally frowned on in Yugoslavia... But..almost every party organisation has seen changes in its top leadership... As the purges have reached their climax..party members are being purged for indulging simply in 'factionalism'. **1976** *Survey* Summer–Autumn 127 The Chinese nation faces multiple crises. Deeply-rooted factionalism and a recent history of repeated purges contribute to the grave uncertainties of today. **1977** *New Yorker* 1 Aug. 50/3 To the extent that Coops politics were pro-Soviet politics, there was a falling away after every event like the purge trials or the Hitler-Stalin pact.

c. Removal of one fluid by flushing with another. Freq. *attrib.*

1958 J. B. Gardner in H. W. Cremer *Chem. Engin. Practice* VI. 254 Since traces of acetylene are present in the atmosphere..it is necessary to take steps to prevent a dangerous accumulation occurring during continuous plant operation... Essentially two techniques—purging and adsorption—or a combination of them, are generally employed. In the first, a small bleed of liquid oxygen from the main bath is maintained to keep the acetylene concentration at a suitable low figure... Withdrawal of the liquid product itself in liquid oxygen plants constitutes a large purge and little difficulty is experienced on such units. **1960** V. B. Guthrie *Petroleum Products Handbk.* III. 38 The sweet natural-gas purge is preferable. **1970** [see *headset* s.v. *head *sb.* 66]. **1976** *Offshore Platforms & Pipelining* 240/2 Oil then can be flushed from the lines by pumping through the surface manifold down the purge line.

purge, *v.*[1] Add: **1. d.** To rid of one fluid by flushing *with* another.

1960 V. B. Guthrie *Petroleum Products Handbk.* III. 37 The following precautions should be observed to prevent moisture from entering LP-Gas supplies... Purge new containers being put into service. **1962** W. Schirra in *Into Orbit* 51 In the final stages of descent, a snorkel opens automatically at about 20,000 feet, and brings in fresh, cool air from the outside which purges the hot suit and gives us our first whiff of the briny ocean. **1973** *Daily Tel.* 25 Oct. 1/5 The tank had been 'purged' 18 months ago with nitrogen to force out the remains of any gaseous contents.

2. a. (Further examples in sense 'to rid of persons regarded as politically undesirable'.)

1936 [see sense 3 a below]. **1942** [see *judenrein *a.*]. **1945** *Daily Express* 22 May 1 Tito's officials are still purging towns and villages of Italian Fascists and placing local committees in charge.

3. a. (Later examples.) In recent use, to remove (a person regarded as politically undesirable), freq. by drastic methods. Also *transf.*

1936 *Sun* (Baltimore) 11 Mar. 1/3 Reports that the AAA Administrator, who a year ago 'purged' the AAA of a number of its 'left wing' members..is himself being 'purged'. **1938** 'G. Orwell' *Homage to Catalonia* xi. 224 The Russian Consul-General..has since been 'purged'. **1939** Joyce *Finnegans Wake* 71 Purged out of Burke's. **1943** *New Statesman* 8 May 297 The sooner the more extreme elements in it are purged the better; it has throughout been a misfortune that an exiled Government here should contain members who would be more at ease collaborating against the U.S.S.R. **1958** *Spectator* 20 June 791/2 Saburov, now said to have been purged with a number of his supporters. **1974** [see *purge *sb.* 2 a]. **1976** *Survey* Winter 162 Peterson was not immediately purged in 1935, but was sent to a military position in the Ukraine.

purgee (pɒɹdʒī·). [f. Purge *v.*[1] + -ee[1].] A person who is politically 'purged', expelled from an organization, or excluded from public life.

1938 *Kiplinger Washington Let.* (Kiplinger Washington Agency) 3 Sept. 4 Reelection of purgees will strengthen non-New Dealers in next Congress. **1958** *Economist* 1 Nov. 421/2 Mr Kishi, a former 'purgee' and suspected 'war criminal', became prime minister in February last year. **1963** *Probl. of Communism* July/Aug. p. x/1 Widow of two of Stalin's purgees, Grigori Sokolnikov and L. P. Serebriakov, Serebriakova herself spent a decade in prison.

purger. Add: *spec.* One who carries out a political purge.

1938 *Sun* (Baltimore) 20 June 3/2 (*heading*) Purgers reported purged in Ukraine as Soviet foes. *Ibid.* 25 Aug. 6/5 A number of Senator Tydings' admirers have been wondering who constitute the Maryland purgers.

purging, *vbl. sb.* Add: **1. c.** Removal of political opponents.

1938 *Sun* (Baltimore) 27 Aug. 16/8 Four others marked for purging by the Washington group. **1940** E. Hemingway *For Whom Bell Tolls* xl. 398 Here it reports the purging of more of thy famous Russians. **1974** J. White tr. *Poulantzas's Fascism & Dictatorship* VII. v. 338 The judiciary..suffered least from purging after national socialism came to power.

d. = *purge *sb.* 2 c.

1950 *Sun* (Baltimore) 3 Jan. 9/5 When..natural gas is allowed to flow into the line it will 'push the inert gas or oxygen-short-air ahead of it. This will be allowed to escape until tests indicate pure natural gas has completely filled the line,' an engineer explained. 'This process is called purging.' **1958** [see *purge *sb.* 2 c]. **1973** J. G. Tweeddale *Materials Technol.* II. ii. 24 Various methods of removal can be used, such as reaction with a suitable flux, or by purging, in which an insoluble carrier-gas is bubbled through the liquid to create large surface areas at which the hydrogen can gather and be carried away. **1980** *New Scientist* 3 July 4/1 The purging of 57 000 curies of krypton from the containment building at TMI is an essential step in the $400 million clean-up operation.

‖**puri**[1] pū·ri). [Indonesian.] An Indonesian palace (the examples refer to Bali).

1937 M. Covarrubias *Island of Bali* vi. 158 Women of the aristocracy..live restricted and secluded in the palace, the *puri*, usually going out only in groups to festivals. **1961** P. Kemp *Alms for Oblivion* viii. 129, I saw ahead.. the carved gateway of the Rajah's *puri*, or palace. **1971** *Country Life* 17 June 1544/1 The puris or palaces of the nobility..are entered through elaborately sculptured split doorways.

‖**puri**[2] (pū·ri). [Hindi.] A small round cake of unleavened wheat-flour deep-fried in ghee or oil.

1952 J. Corbett *My India* v. 64 The wonderful occasion when they had been able to fill their bellies..with halwa and puris. **1960** R. P. Jhabvala *Householder* i. 79 'The puris were very good this morning,' he said sheepishly. **1971** *Shankar's Weekly* (Delhi) 11 Apr. 22/3 The Swamiji squatting before what appeared to be a veritable mountain of puris and curries. **1973** *Sat. Rev. World* (U.S.) 18 Dec. 48/2 An Indian baker..fries the bread, and it is called *puri*. **1976** *Punch* 11 Aug. 230/3 All those crowding an Indian confectionery shop and eating sweets, puris [etc.],..in typical Indian style were either Indians or Pakistanis.

purine. Now with pronunc. (piūə·rīn). Add to def.: Now known to have a bicyclic structure consisting of fused imidazole and pyrimidine rings; *spec.* adenine or guanine, two substituted purines found in nucleic acids, etc. Freq. *attrib.* (Earlier and later examples.)

1898 *Chem. News* 16 Dec. 304/1 (*heading*) Molecular transformation in the group of purines. **1921** *Spectator* 21 May 658/1 Purin bodies, precursors of uric acid, and purin-free diets have likewise had their day, although as inculcating abstemiousness the latter played a useful part. **1952** *Sci. News* XXIV. 43 The DNA isolated from different organs of the same animal species seems to be constant in composition with respect to the relative amounts of purine and pyrimidine bases but differs from samples obtained from other species. **1954** *New Biol.* XVI. 15 Nucleic acids appear to consist of alternate purine and pyrimidine nucleotides arranged in a chain. In desoxyribose nucleic acid the purine is either adenine or guanine. **1970** *Nature* 25 July 379/2 Naturally occurring cytokinins known so far have a purine nucleus as the essential moiety. **1973** R. G. Krueger et al. *Introd. Microbiol.* x. 307/2 Pairings between purines would distort the helix because of the large size of the molecules.

purinergic (piūərinɜ̄ɹ·dʒik), *a.* *Physiol.* [f. prec. + Gr. ἔργ-ον work + -ic.] Of a nerve-fibre: that liberates, and is stimulated by, a purine derivative.

1971 *Courier-Mail* (Brisbane) 16 Jan. 8/1 Professor Burnstock and colleagues..have just published a paper presenting evidence that this third type of autonomic nerve fibre acts by releasing..a purine nucleotide. Because of this they tentatively propose to call the nerves 'purinergic'. **1971** G. Burnstock in *Nature* 22 Jan. 282/3 In the early 1960s powerful nerves were found to supply that gut which were neither cholinergic nor adrenergic... Evidence has recently been presented that the transmitter substance released from these nerves may be ATP or some related purine nucleotide. It would therefore seem reasonable..to propose that the new nerves be termed 'purinergic'. **1977** *Lancet* 19 Nov. 1065/2 Work on the non-adrenergic non-cholinergic (purinergic) system will probably shed more light on and possibly lead to more rational pharmacological approaches to the deranged internal sphincter.

puriri. 1. Substitute for def.: A New Zealand forest tree, *Vitex lucens*, belonging to the family Verbenaceæ and bearing compound leaves and axillary clusters of red flowers; also, the hard, durable timber of this tree. Also *attrib.* (Earlier and further examples.)

1835 W. Yate *Acct. of N.Z.* (ed. 2) ii. 43 Puriri (*Vitex littoralis*)—This tree, from its hardness and durability has been denominated the New-Zealand Oak. **1838** J. S. Polack *N.Z.* II. 393 The Puriri..is a wood whose durability equals any of the timbers in the country. **1863** A. S. Atkinson *Jrnl.* 29 Sept. in *Richmond-Atkinson Papers* (1960) II. 64 One [ball from a rifle] pitched..in a very good line for me but stuck in a puriri log. **1910** L. Cockayne *N.Z. Plants* iii. 39 Birds also fertilise a few New Zealand plants, amongst others the puriri. **1952** *Landfall* VI. 31 The framework of this haystack cover stands on puriri uprights which though sunken into the ground are practically everlasting. **1959** *N.Z. Listener* 13 Mar. 5/4 These fascinating little owls had their nest in a clump of astelia in a puriri tree. **1973** Atkinson & Bell in G. R. Williams *Nat. Hist. N.Z.* xv. 378/1 Large numbers of kohekohe, puriri, karaka and mahoe are also present.

2. *Comb.* **puriri moth,** a large green moth, *Hepialus* (or *Charagia*) *virescens*, of the family Hepialidæ, whose larvæ bore into the wood of the puriri and certain other trees.

1966 *Encycl. N.Z.* II. 590/1 The puriri or ghost moth is the largest native moth of New Zealand. **1971** *N.Z. Listener* 6 Sept. 17/1, I hoped I might be able to get a big green puriri moth on that soft and cloudy summer night.

purism. Add: **2.** *Art.* (With capital initial.) An early twentieth-century movement in painting arising out of a rejection of cubism and characterized by a return to the representation of recognizable objects with emphasis on purity of geometric form.

1931 A. Ozenfant *Foundations Mod. Art* p. xi, I have sought to formulate those tropisms which are most clearly apprehended. On them I base the art that derives from 'constants'. I call it 'Purism'. **1959** *Archit. Rev.* CXXV. 356/2 Jeanneret's contribution to Purism was curious. It is the work of a follower, but the pictures have greater presence than those they emulate. **1961** M. Levy *Studio Dict. of Art Terms* 92 *Purism*, a movement in modern painting and sculpture, founded in 1918 by the painters, Amédée Ozenfant, Le Corbusier, and Brancusi. Purism was a reaction against the analytical spirit of Cubism and sought to remake, and thus purify, the world of objects, etc. **1973** *Times* 27 Nov. 12/5 For a time in the early twenties Servranckx worked in a style known as Purism, associated with Leger and Ozenfant, of simplified brightly coloured abstractions of machine forms.

‖**puris natura·libus.** [med.L.] = *in puris naturalibus* s.v. In *Lat. prep.* 21.

1920 Ld. F. Hamilton *Vanished Pomps of Yesterday* (rev. ed.) ix. 307 Dick and I spent hours there swimming, and basking *puris naturalibus* on the rocks. **1974** *Listener* 17 Jan. 84/2 O the joy of being idle... With a bun and towel basking *Puris naturalibus*.

purist. Add: **3.** *Art.* (With capital initial.) An adherent of Purism (see *purism 2).

1939 in Webster Add. **1959** H. Read *Conc. Hist. Mod. Painting* vi. 215 Between the years 1920 and 1925 the Purists had a decisive influence on the development of abstract art throughout Europe and America. **1974** *Encycl. Brit. Micropædia* VIII. 309/3 There were many painters..who, like the Purists, were attracted to a machine-inspired aesthetic.

4. *attrib.* or as *adj.*

1939 in Webster Add. **1945** Koestler *Yogi & Commissar* III. ii. 155 Not even the most purist critic could expect a sudden jump to total equalitarianism. **1959** H. Read *Conc. Hist. Mod. Painting* vi. 216 Nicholson began as a decorative painter of great charm, and then came under various 'purist' influences of which the most direct and powerful was that of Mondrian. **1961** R. B. Long *Sentence & its Parts* 5 The sentences of spoken English are often poorly constructed—and this is not a purist judgement. **1965** W. S. Allen *Vox Latina* ii. 55 The purist reader would therefore be justified in reading the nominative plural forms *filii, di* as *filiī, dī* respectively. **1978** *Gramophone* Jan. 1307/3 Disc and cassette reproduce about equally well, though I suspect we would like both versions a lot better if a more purist recording technique were adopted.

Puritan, *sb.* and *a.* Add: **B.** *adj.* **a.** *Puritan conscience*: a strict individual conscience requiring high standards; *Puritan ethic*: the belief in the redemptive value of work.

1901 Kipling *Let.* in C. Carrington *Rudyard Kipling* (1955) xiii. 318 Her Puritan conscience which she has inherited from her New England forbears still makes her take life too blame seriously. **1932** Q. D. Leavis *Fiction & Reading Public* II. ii. 97 (*heading*) The puritan conscience. **1972** C. Weston *Poor, Poor Ophelia* (1973) v. 28 He beamed good cheer and the puritan ethic—*work for the night is falling*. **1975** *Listener* 16 Oct. 517/2 Hale White.. did manage to write small, vigorous masterpieces of the puritan conscience trying to beat out a narrow path for itself. **1977** *Ibid.* 7 Apr. 434/1 The Puritan ethic..an ethic of discipline, work, responsibility.

c. *Puritan spoon* (see quot. 1960).

1956 G. Taylor *Silver* iv. 86 In the reign of Charles I the so-called Puritan spoon..began to appear. **1960** H. Hayward *Antique Coll.* 230/2 *Puritan spoon*, a mid-17th cent. spoon with flat stem, straight top edge and nearly oval bowl, the earliest form of English flat-stemmed spoon. **1971** *Country Life* 10 June (Suppl.) 58 (Advt.), Commonwealth 1659 Puritan Spoon.

Purkinje (s.v. Purkinjean *a.*). Add: *Purkinje('s) phenomenon* or *shift* (also *phenomenon of Purkinje*), a decrease in the apparent brightness of light of long wavelength (e.g. red) compared with light of short wavelength (e.g. blue) when the degree of illumination falls; [described by Purkinje in *Mag. für die ges. Heilkunde* (1825) XX. 225].

1900 C. Weiland tr. *M. Tscherning's Physiologic Optics* xvii. 260 A comparison of the brightness of two different colors is not easy,..and the result depends besides on the phenomenon of Purkinje. **1910** M. Greenwood *Physiol. of Special Senses* xii. 101 A particular case of adaptation which is of much interest is 'Purkinje's Phenomenon'. **1949** H. C. Weston *Sight, Light & Efficiency* i. 20 The 'Purkinje phenomenon'..is familiar to everyone who has noted..that when green leaves and red flowers are seen in twilight the green appears brighter compared with the red than is the case in full daylight. **1973** *Nature* 14 Dec. 380/1 The most familiar effect of the duality of human vision is the so-called 'Purkinje shift'.

purler. Add: **1.** (Earlier and later examples.) Also *fig.*

1867 'Ouida' *Under Two Flags* I. iii. 47 In front of that Stand was an artificial bullfinch which promised to treat most of the field to a 'purler'. **1921** H. G. Ponting *Gt. White South* 282 All went well till..on a very slippery surface I came an awful 'purler' on my shoulder. **1929** J. Masefield *Hawbucks* 209 You seemed to go a fearful purler. **1962** *Spectator* 23 Nov. 830/3 Trevelyan's Indian career ended in a magnificent purler. **1976** *Church Times* 2 July 7/3 This is not just a..catalogue of classic military purlers (the Crimea, Kut, Cambrai, Singapore, Arnhem, etc.). **1976** *Horse & Hound* 3 Dec. 6/2 Even Up went a real purler at the last fence on the far side.

2. Something of surpassing excellence. orig. *Austral.* Cf. *pearler *sb.*[2]

1941 Baker *Dict. Austral. Slang* 57 *Purl, purler*, something excellent, outstandingly good. **1966** *New Statesman* 7 Oct. 530/2 Bobby Charlton draws a couple of men and shoots that purler from 30 yards. **1973** *Listener* 8 Mar. 309/3, I hope the next goal he scores is an absolute purler. **1980** L. Mantell *A Murder or Three* iii. 45 Never thought he'd ever get round to having any [children], then they produce a purler like that..a real little darling.

‖ **puro** (pū·ro). [Sp., lit. 'pure'.] A cigar (in Spanish-speaking countries and south-west U.S.).

1841 J. L. Stephens *Incidents of Travel* I. 76, I offered for her choice a cigar and a puro. **1845** R. Ford *Hand-bk. Travellers Spain* ii. 194 Ferdinand VII.., when meditating a treacherous *coup*, would dismiss the unconscious victim with a royal *puron* [ed. 1846, *puro*]. **1963** W. McGivern *Choice of Assassins* (1964) iii. 31 To talk..with his friends over sherry and *puros*.

puro, var. *purau.

puromycin (piūᵊrəmai·sin). *Biol.* and *Pharm.* [f. Pur(ine + -o + *-mycin.] An antibiotic which is produced by the fungus *Streptomyces albo-niger* and is used esp. to treat sleeping sickness and amœbic dysentery.

1953 C. W. Waller in *Jrnl. Amer. Chem. Soc.* LXXV. 2025/1 The new antibiotic, Puromycin, isolated from the mold *Streptomyces alboniger*, has been found to be active against certain bacteria and Trypanosomes. **1960** M. E. Florey *Clinical Applications of Antibiotics* IV. vi. 162 Puromycin..had the unique advantage of not only arresting the growth of trypanosomes but also of being able to kill them. **1968** W. Hayes *Genetics of Bacteria & their Viruses* (ed. 2) xii. 288 Puromycin has a close structural resemblance to the terminal amino-acyl adenosine of t-RNA and interferes with protein synthesis, both *in vivo* and *in vitro*, by inserting itself at ribosomal slot No. 2 [etc.]. **1978** *Bio Systems* X. 194/1 Puromycin is another commercially available antibiotic which, because of its toxicity, is not used therapeutically but rather as a research tool.

purow, var. *purau.

purparty. (Later example of form **pourparty.**)

1920 *Eng. Hist. Rev.* Jan. 30 To each co-heir was allotted, as a permanent pourparty, a definite manor or castle for a chief seat.

purple, *a.* and *sb.* Add: **A.** *adj.* **3.** (Further examples with ref. to literary composition.) *purple patch* (earlier and later examples), *passage* (later examples). So *purple-patchery*.

a **1834** Coleridge in *Rev. de Litt. Comparée* (1927) VII. 253 Admirably reasoned as this Essay is, I yet regard it but as one of the rich Purple Patches of the Robe of Casuistry. **1921** *Times Lit. Suppl.* 9 June 362/1 The back-talk between the Emperor and his Empress Nourmahal, in *Aurungzebe*, is admirable purple comedy. **1926** C. Connolly *Let.* 26 June in *Romantic Friendship* (1975) 145 He realises his epic to be but a collection of purple patches. **1941** Auden *New Year Let.* ii. 37 And yet to show complete conviction, Requires the purpler kinds of diction. **1941** H. Haycraft *Murder for Pleasure* x. 216 The old, whipped-up underscoring and 'purple-patchery'. **1943** C. L. Wrenn *Word & Symbol* (1967) 139 An honoured place in English literature through Milton's 'purple passage'. **1975** V. Cunningham *Everywhere spoken Against* iii. 84 Arnold's famous purple patch about the last enchantments of the Middle Ages. **1975** *Language for Life* (Dept. Educ. & Sci.) xi. 164 Some teachers encourage children to strive for effect, to produce the purple patch, the stock response. **1975** C. N. Manlove *Mod. Fantasy* iii. 78 One [style] is 'purple' and highly emotive. **1977** *Gramophone* Sept. 507/3 One is grateful to be spared one of Wilde's purpler passages.

B. *sb.* **1. e.** *visual purple*: see *visual *a.* and *sb.*

7. a. = Blueness 4. *rare.*

1930 D. H. Lawrence *Phoenix II* (1968) 489, I should show the public that here is a fine novel, apart from all 'purple' and all 'words'.

b. *the purple*: purple passages; esp. in *to sub the purple* (Journalists' slang), to sub-edit purple passages.

1958 E. A. Robertson *Justice of Heart* iii. 33 A well-known outside contributor from whose copy he had, in his own words, 'subbed the purple'. *Ibid.* vi. 84 The 'subbing of the purple' was always a painful business for a journalist.

8. *slang.* **a.** = *purple-heart 3. **b.** = *LSD[2].

1968 C. Drummond *Death & Leaping Ladies* v. 112, I heard her on at the Doc..about some Purples to key them up but he hit the ceiling. **1971** E. E. Landy *Underground Dict.* 156 *Purple*, LSD.

C. I. 1. a. *purple-crested, -crowned, -flowered* (examples), *-hearted, -leaved* (later examples), *-lidded, -nosed* (example), *-spotted, -tinged, -zoned* adjs.

1726 Pope tr. *Homer's Odyssey* IV. xix. 263 A mantle purple-ting'd, and radiant vest. **1788** J. Woodforde *Diary* 8 July (1927) III. 36 To Mr. Aldridge for 6 Yards of purple spotted Cotton..0.12.0. **1846** D. J. Browne *Trees Amer.* 22 *Magnolia purpurea*, The Purple-flowered Magnolia. **1862** J. G. Whittier in *Atlantic Monthly* Apr. 423 Purple-zoned, Wachuset laid His head against the West. **1881** O. Wilde *Poems* 208 Pansies close their purple-lidded eyes. *Ibid.* 215 White-shielded, purple-crested rode the Mede. **1908** E. J. Banfield *Confess. Beachcomber* i. iii. 96 Purple-crowned Fruit Pigeon, *Ptilopus superbus*. **1910** *Daily Chron.* 25 Mar. 6/5 The minute purple-hearted blossoms. **1913** Conrad *Chance* i. i. 8 He envied the purple-nosed old cab-drivers on the stand. **1921** G. Bell *Let.* 25 Nov. (1927) II. xxi. 627 Grassy hollows where a tiny spring would rise cradled in purple-flowered mint. **1952** A. G. L. Hellyer *Sanders's Encycl. Gardening* (ed. 22) 130 *C[orylus]..maxima..*, var. *atropurpurea*, purple-leaved. *Ibid.* 277 *L[ilium]..daliense*, white, purple-spotted. *Ibid.* 393 *P[opulus]..tremula*, 'Aspen',..with vars. *pendula*, 'Weeping Aspen', and *purpurea*, purple-tinged foliage. **1962** R. Page *Education of Gardener* x. 281, I used..*Corylus maxima purpurea*, the purple-leaved hazel. **1971** *Country Life* 17 June 1521/3 The purple-leaved filbert, (*Corylus maxima purpurea*)..responds well to stooling.

b. *purple-black* (later example), *-blue* (examples), *-brown* (further examples), *-dark, -grey, -pink* adjs. and sbs.

1845 J. R. Lowell in *Harbinger* 2 Aug. 122/3 Far away on Katahdin thou towerest, Purple-blue with the distance. **1956** Geo. Eliot in J. W. Cross *Life Geo. Eliot* (1885) I. vii. 401 The *Corallina officinalis*..with its purple-pink fronds. **1897** Purple-brown [see *Italian earth*]. **1928** V. Woolf *Orlando* vi. 243 The wine-blue purple-dark hill. **1930** J. dos Passos *42nd Parallel* 147 Purplegray murk rose steadily. **1952** A. G. L. Hellyer *Sanders's Encycl. Gardening* (ed. 22) 93 *C[atasetum]..Rodigasianum*, flowers many, greenish, spotted purple-brown. **1957** Purple-blue [see *dracocephalum]. **1960** Purple-black [see *Carlsbad]. **1964** M. Hynes *Med. Bacteriol.* (ed. 8) 484 A colony subcultured on to the medium gives a purple-pink colour from NH_3 production in 2–8 hours.

2. a. purple airway [*airway 2], a route reserved for an aircraft on which royalty is flying; **purple death** *slang*, a cheap Italian red wine; **purple haze** *slang* = *LSD[2]; **purple lake** [Lake *sb.*[6]], a purple pigment; **purple membrane,** a membrane found within the cell membrane of the bacterium *Halobacterium halobium*; **purple zone** = *purple airway*.

1958 *Sunday Times* 30 Mar. 5/1 Now that the Duke of Edinburgh is doing a lot of flying, warnings about 'purple airway' are more frequently given to commercial pilots. Purple airway is a reserved track for a Royal flight. **1947** D. M. Davin *Gorse blooms Pale* 199 Everyone goes for the purple death. **1967** J. Hendrix in *40 Greatest Songs* (1975) 28 Purple haze is in my brain lately things don't seem the same. **1970** *Times* 24 Mar. 2/3 The American LSD..has been coming in..under such exotic names as..'purple haze', and 'blue cheer'. **1971** *Current Slang* (*Univ. S. Dakota*) VI. 9 *Purple haze*, LSD cut with methedrine. **1821** *London Mag.* Sept. 290/2 The purple-lake-coloured stuffs. **1869** *Bradshaw's Railway Man.* XXI. 460/2 (Advt.), Reds..Crimson Lake—Scarlet and Purple ditto. **1934** H. Hiler *Notes on Technique of Painting* ii. 123 *Crimson lake, Purple lake*, etc., now usually made from alizarin... Also prepared from cochineal... Should be regarded as obsolete. **1968** Stoeckenius & Kunau in *Jrnl. Cell Biol.* XXXVIII. 344/1 The purple band, henceforth called purple membranes, contains considerably less RNA and slightly less lipid than the orange-red fraction. **1975** *Nature* 25 Dec. 766/2 *Halobacterium halobium* is indigenous to warm saline pools exposed to bright sunlight. Strains of this bacterium synthesise a purple pigment in the cell membrane (the 'purple membrane'). **1970** *Daily Tel.* 1 Aug. 1/2 'A purple zone' was not in operation..because the Prince was flying only in the immediate area of Tangmere.

b. purple bacterium, [ad. G. *purpurbacterium* (T. W. Engelmann 1888, in *Bot. Zeitung* 663)], any of a group of bacteria containing a purple photo-active pigment; **purple finch,** for Latin name substitute *Carpodacus purpureus*; (later examples); **purple gallinule,** substitute for def.: (*a*) the swamp-hen, *Porphyrio porphyrio*, found in parts of Europe, southern Asia, Africa, and Australasia; cf. Porphyrio; (*b*) a similar North American bird, *Porphyrula martinica*, which is smaller than the swamp-hen and has yellow legs instead of red ones; (examples); **purple heron,** a heron with greyish-blue plumage, *Ardea purpurea*, found in central and southern Europe, Africa, and parts of Asia; (later examples); **purple martin,** a large North American swallow, *Progne subis*; (earlier and later examples); **purple sandpiper,** a small wading bird, *Calidris maritima*, found in northern parts of Europe, North America, and Asia; (earlier and later examples).

1900 A. C. Jones tr. *Fischer's Structure & Functions of Bacteria* 194/2 (Index), Purple bacteria. **1912** W. H. Lang tr. *Strasburger's Textbk. Bot.* (ed. 4) ii. i. 337 The Purple Bacteria, which develop in water with decomposing organic matter in the absence of oxygen and the presence of light, contain..a green and a red pigment. **1957** G. E. Hutchinson *Treat. Limnol.* I. xiii. 756 The second way in which hydrogen sulfide is oxidized in the hydrosphere is by the photosynthetic green and purple bacteria, of which the purple sulfur bacteria are best known. **1971** Berkeley & Campbell in Hawker & Linton *Micro-Organisms* v. 163 The phototactic behaviour of the purple bacterium Rhodospirillum rubrum..results from a response to lack of light. **1876** J. Burroughs *Winter Sunshine* i. 31 Those purple finches..are they not stealing our berries? **1884** [see Finch 1 b]. **1903** S. E. White *Forest* vii. 91 You will hear..purple finches or some of the pine sparrows warbling high and clear. **1971** *Islander* (Victoria, B.C.) 10 Oct. 13/2 Purple finches nest every year in the trees beside our house. **1813** A. Wilson *Amer. Ornithol.* IX. 71 The Purple Gallinule [was seen] in a thick swamp, a short distance from Savannah, Georgia. **1884** H. Seebohm *Hist. Brit. Birds* II. 562 The Purple Gallinule..is a resident in Algeria, Spain, and Italy. **1888** [see Gallinule]. **1909** W. Verner *My Life among Wild Birds in Spain* ii. i. 99, I have..been startled by the curious cry of the big Purple Gallinule. **1944** *Nat. Geogr. Mag.* June 694/1 There were Purple Gallinules, decked out in brilliant purple, green, sky-blue, red, and yellow. **1965** E. Richardson *Living Island* 92 [A] purple gallinule also stopped in these road-puddles after a foggy rain. **1893** Purple heron [see Heron 1 b]. **1905** Kelsall & Munn *Birds Hampshire & Isle of Wight* 198 Purple Heron. A very rare accidental visitor from Central and Southern Europe. **1971** *Country Life* 18 Feb. 356/2 The purple heron, once a common sight in the [Ebro] delta, has diminished considerably in recent years. **1743** M. Catesby *Nat. Hist. Carolina* II. p. xxvi, Land-Birds which breed and abide in Carolina in the Summer, and retire in Winter:..The yellow Titmouse. The purple Martin. The humming Bird. **1808–14** [see Martin[1] 1]. **1939** F. C. Lincoln *Migration Amer. Birds* 55 The Purple Martin is an early migrant. **1976** *National Observer* (U.S.) 29 May 12/2 We carefully watch certain species like the purple martins..and upland sandpipers, which are only now recovering from the 1972 fury of Hurricane Agnes. **1824** Purple sandpiper [see Sandpiper 1]. **1828** C. L. Bonaparte in *Ann. Lyceum Nat. Hist. N.Y.* II. 319 The Purple Sandpiper... Inhabits both continents on rocky shores only. **1860** S. F. Baird *Birds N. Amer.* I. 717 The purple sandpiper..is frequently met with on the shores of the Atlantic. **1925** [see *injury *sb.* 4]. **1940** H. F. Witherby et al. *Handbk. Brit. Birds* IV. 273 Though probably there is no wader which cannot swim well when necessary, Purple Sandpiper does so more habitually than most. **1978** C. Harrison *Field Guide Nests N. Amer. Birds* 130 Purple Sandpiper... Breeds on the tundra.

c. purple cone-flower, a perennial herb belonging to the genus *Echinacea* of the family Compositæ, native to North America, and bearing flowers with a dark central disc and purplish rays; (examples); **purple loosestrife,** a large perennial herb, *Lythrum salicaria*, belonging to the family Lythraceæ, widely distributed in temperate regions, and bearing purple flowers in clusters; (examples); **purple moor-grass,** a perennial grass with purplish panicles, *Molinia cærulea*, native to Europe and Asia; formerly called blue moor-grass; **purple osier,** a large shrub, *Salix purpurea*, belonging to the family Salicaceæ, native to Europe, North Africa, and central Asia, and distinguished by its purplish bark; **purple willow** = *purple osier*.

1848 A. Gray *Man. Bot. Northern U.S.* 223 (*heading*) Purple cone-flower. **1857** [see *cone-flower*]. **1900** L. H. Bailey *Cycl. Amer. Hort.* II. 511/2 Purple Cone-flower. Four species of North American perennial herbs. **1939** *Nat. Geogr. Mag.* Aug. 220/2 Striking contrast is provided by some of the most brilliant flowers of the prairie notably..the purple coneflower, the butterfly milkweed,..and the prickly pear. **1954** C. J. Hylander *Macmillan Wild Flower Bk.* 453 The conical receptacle which projects from the center of the Purple Coneflower bears disk-flowers which are purplish in colour. **1974** M. C. Davis *Near Woods* ii. 21 A purple cone flower..essentially is a large central disc and long ribbony rays. **1548, 1633,** etc. Purple loosestrife [see Loosestrife 1 b]. **1861** R. Bentley *Man. Bot.* ii. iii. 538 *Lythrum Salicaria*, Purple Loosestrife, is a common British plant. **1977** *New Yorker* 5 Sept. 23/2 An impenetrable marsh of..purple loosestrife and other plants clogs the length of the channel. **1859** L. H. Grindon *Manchester Flora* 439 Purple Moor-grass... Everywhere on heaths and moors. **1928** M. A. Johnstone *Plant Ecol.* viii. 93 Where water lodges even very plentifully the dominant grass is the purple moor-grass. **1979** R. Grounds *Ornamental Grasses* viii. 147/1 Purple moor grass... Deservedly one of the most popular garden grasses. **1870** J. D. Hooker *Student's Flora Brit. Islands* 342 *S[alix] purpurea...* Purple Osier. **1910** E. Step *Wayside & Woodland Trees* 71 The Purple Osier gets its name from the red or purple bark which clothes the thin but tough twigs. **1958** R. D. Meikle *Brit. Trees & Shrubs* 196 *Salix purpurea...* Purple Osier. A loose spreading shrub..with slender yellowish or purple-tinged twigs. **1776** W. Withering *Bot. Arrangement Veg. Gt. Brit.* 602 Purple Willow. Leaves serrated; smooth; spear-shaped... Banks of rivers. **1838** J. C. Loudon *Arboretum & Fruticetum Britannicum* III. 1490 *S[alix] purpurea.* The purple Willow. **1914** W. J. Bean *Trees & Shrubs Hardy in Brit. Isles* II. 487 Purple Willow. A shrub with thin, graceful branches forming a loose-habited, spreading bush, 10 to 18 ft. high. **1960** *Oxf. Bk. Wild Flowers* 186/2 Purple Willow is locally common in fens, marshes, and on river-banks.

pu·rple-heart. Also as one word or two separate words. [f. Purple *a.* + Heart *sb.*]

1. a. A large tree of the genus *Peltogyne*, belonging to the family Leguminosæ and native to areas of tropical rain forest in

Central and South America and the West Indies; also, the dark purplish-brown timber of this tree. Also *attrib.*

1796 [in Dict. s.v. PURPLE *a.* C. 2 c]. **1825** C. WATERTON *Wanderings in S. Amer.* 24 Wallaba, purple-heart,.. and mora, are met with in vast abundance, far and near, towering up in majestic grandeur. **1845** [in Dict. s.v. PURPLE *a.* C. 2 c]. **1902** G. S. BOULGER *Wood* I. v. 99 Hepplewhite and Sheraton employed Mahogany..for small articles such as tea-caddies, whilst in the inlaid work of the period it was used..with other dark woods, such as Rosewood, Laburnum, and Purple-heart. **1924** RECORD & MELL *Timbers Trop. Amer.* II. 235 There is considerable variation in the size, abundance, and arrangement of the pores in different specimens of purpleheart. **1947** J. C. RICH *Materials & Methods of Sculpture* x. 285 Amaranth wood or Purpleheart is a rich, violet-colored, tropical hardwood imported from the Guianas. **1951** J. C. FENNESSY *Sonnet in Bottle* VI. i. 200 There were no tall trees, no soaring palms or smooth-stemmed purplehearts. **1951** *Archit. Rev.* CIX. 288 Floors are in polished purpleheart hardwood. **1956** *Handbk. of Hardwoods* (Forest Prod. Res. Lab.) 193 The different species of purpleheart vary in size at maturity. **1959** P. CAPON *Amongst those Missing* 215, I haven't noticed any purpleheart trees about. **1963** *Times* 26 Jan. 4/2 A nineteenth-century kingwood commode.., its sides inlaid with chrysanthemum branches in purpleheart, made £280. **1974** *Country Life* 30 May 1338/1 A second [chest], walnut with panels and banding in purple heart, ebony and ivory.

b. An evergreen tree of the genus *Copaifera*, belonging to the family Leguminosæ and native to tropical America or the West Indies.

1866 [see PURPLE *a.* C. 2 c]. **1963** ROBERTSON & GOODING *Bot. for Caribbean* xxiii. 186 Purple-heart (*Copaifera pubiflora*).

2. *U.S.* (In form **Purple Heart.**) A decoration bestowed on a member of the armed services wounded in action. Also more fully, *Purple Heart Award*.

A decoration consisting of a heart-shaped piece of purple cloth was instituted by George Washington in 1782, but later fell into disuse. The present bronze enamelled medal was instituted in 1932.

1932 *Army & Navy Jrnl.* 27 Feb. 602/4 Awards of the Purple Heart for acts or service performed prior to Feb. 22, 1932, will be confined to the following persons. **1948** E. E. CUMMINGS *Let.* 27 Aug. (1969) 185 The hyper-scientific climax of this hero (a prominent killer, holder of Silver Stars & Clusters & Purple Hearts galore)'s experience. **1974** *Sumter* (S. Carolina) *Daily Item* 23 Apr. 4A/4 He is a recipient of the Purple Heart Award and Army Commendation Medal. **1977** J. WAMBAUGH *Black Marble* (1978) ii. 15 Mason returned to Pasadena wearing a Bronze Star and a Purple Heart.

3. Usu. *pl.* A familiar term for tablets of the stimulant Drinamyl, so named because of their shape and colour. Also *attrib.*

1961 [see *DRINAMYL]. **1962** *Daily Tel.* 31 Aug. 21/1 People involved in the investigation had already had 'purple heart' tablets prescribed for them by their own doctors. **1964** [see *DEXAMPHETAMINE]. **1968** *Times* 30 Nov. 4/7 A mixture of the stimulant amphetamine and the depressant amylobarbitone... A similar mixture of drugs was popular a few years ago in the guise of 'purple hearts'. **1971** N. STACEY *Who Cares?* xvi. 276 They became more responsible, they took more interest in life, they stopped taking purple hearts and they settled down in their homes, their schools and their jobs. **1973** H. MILLER *Open City* xvi. 179 Drugs. Purple Hearts, amphetamines. The bloke was passing the stuff to kids.

purpo·rtedly, *adv.* [f. PURPORTED *ppl. a.* + -LY².] Allegedly, ostensibly.

1949 *Scrutiny* XVI. 10 The poem..was..Frere's.. *Prospectus and Specimen of an Intended National Work* purportedly written by the brothers Whistlecraft. **1957** J. HOLLANDER in N. Frye *Sound & Poetry* 76 Orsino's appetite at the start of the play is purportedly for Olivia. **1964** D. F. GALOUYE *Counterfeit World* xii. 105 The firm I purportedly represented. **1967** R. STEIN *Great Cars* 113/1 I've never driven one. But purportedly one of these hotter types would go from 0 to 100 in 17 seconds! **1976** *Daily Tel.* 1 Mar. 2/1 Cases of purportedly sterilised women becoming pregnant had recently become more common.

purpose, *sb.* Add: **I. 3.** (Earlier and later examples in the context of novel-writing.)

1863 *Q. Rev.* Apr. 488 He never sinks so nearly to the level of the ordinary sensation-novelist as when he is writing 'with a purpose'. **1874** *Cornh. Mag.* Aug. 192 His romances are not to be confused with 'the novel with a purpose' as familiar to the English reader. **1932** *Week-end Rev.* 19 Mar. 371/1 This is a pity; for though Isabel is a 'novel with a purpose', it is also, in a high degree, a work of imagination.

III. 14. *purpose-built, -designed, -made* adjs.

1959 *Times* 9 June 11/6 Local authorities have indeed made remarkable progress in..adapted houses and small purpose-built homes. **1962** *Economist* 17 Mar. 980/2 New [bowling alley] centres will mostly be what has come to be known as 'purpose-built'. **1972** *Computers & Humanities* VII. 11 The need for a 'purpose built' command language is described in..'A Command Language for Text Processing'. **1977** *Modern Railways* Dec. 473/2 Rail movement of propylene in two weekly trainloads of purpose-built bogie tanks. **1961** *Economist* 24 June 1347/2 Special trays adapted for fitting on to the arm of the 'purpose-designed' Bingo chair. **1971** J. HOWLETT in B. de Ferranti *Living with Computer* ii. 10 Purpose-designed experiment. **1975** *Language for Life* (Dept. Educ. & Sci.) xiii. 208 It would be wrong to assume that nothing can be done unless the spaces are purpose-designed. **1930** *Times Educ. Suppl.* 11 Jan. 11/4 In some places there are 'purpose-made' bricks. **1938** *Archit. Rev.* LXXXIV. 208 (*caption*) Ketton stone has been used for the stone dressings, the facing bricks being eleven inches wide and purpose-made. **1974** *Country Life* 21 Mar. 686/1 Wearable outfits, purpose-made for women who..like inconspicuous clothes.

purpose, *v.* **6.** For † *Obs.* read 'Now *rare*' and add later example.

1924 W. J. LOCKE *Coming of Amos* v. 53 What was the use of a stick purposed to beat neither beast nor man?

purposive, *a.* Add: **2. b.** Relating to conscious or unconscious purpose as reflected in human and animal behaviour or mental activity. Hence **pu·rposivism,** the theory that all human or animal activity is purposive; **pu·rposivist** *sb.* and *a.*

1884 W. C. COUPLAND tr. *von Hartmann's Philos. of Unconscious* I. B. v. 285 For us, who have already become acquainted with the purposive activity of the Unconscious.., there is here..fresh support for our view. **1912** W. MCDOUGALL *Psychol.* i. 29 If we make our notion of purposive activity or behaviour wide enough to include these phenomena of bodily organization in the animal kingdom, it must also include the similar purposes of plant growth. **1932** E. C. TOLMAN (*title*) Purposive behavior in animals and men. *Ibid.* i. 12 Behavior as behavior, that is, as molar, *is* purposive and *is* cognitive. *Ibid.* xxv. 423 Our psychology is a purposivism; but it is an objective, behavioristic purposivism, not a mentalistic one. **1936** J. KANTOR *Objective Psychol. of Gram.* v. 69 The second group of purposivists carry speech farther away from the individual than the first group. For them, speech is primarily an instrument for achieving social purposes. **1940** R. S. WOODWORTH *Psychol.* (ed. 12) xvii. 583 The purposivist school emphasizes the importance of striving and goal-seeking. **1947** G. MURPHY *Personality* vi. 125 (*heading*) Purposivism. **1953** J. STRACHEY tr. *Freud's Interpretation of Dreams* in *Compl. Wks.* V. 528 It can be shown that all that we can ever get rid of are purposive ideas that are *known* to us; as soon as we have done this, *unknown*—or..'unconscious'—purposive ideas take charge. **1962** H. CANTRIL in J. Scher *Theories of Mind* 339 It becomes increasingly clear that we must include in our consideration the purposive behavior of the organism of which mind is an aspect.

purposively, *adv.* (In Dict. s.v. PURPOSIVE *a.*) (Further examples.)

1927 E. & C. PAUL tr. *Ludwig's Bismarck* II. vii. 192 Unless we were more intimately and purposively united with our other fellow countrymen. **1939** P. GORDON *New Archery* II. viii. 89 Never varying except purposively, to correct a mistake. **1949** WELLEK & WARREN *Theory of Lit.* xx. 298 Literary study within our universities..must become purposively literary. **1965** *New Statesman* 10 Sept. 343/1 Ministers also speak purposively (this, currently, is a vogue adverb along Whitehall) about measures on rating and leasehold reform. **1973** H. KEMELMAN *Tuesday the Rabbi Saw Red* iii. 32 Dean Hanbury walked toward them purposively.

purposiveness. (In Dict. s.v. PURPOSIVE *a.*) (Further examples.)

1932 A. H. GARDINER *Theory of Speech & Lang.* iv. 181 The characteristic feature of the sentence, as opposed to mere unintelligible words, is its purposiveness. **1965** E. E. HARRIS *Found. of Metaphys. in Sci.* viii. 163 'Purposiveness' is the word that sums up these properties, but it is a word which precipitates controversy both as to its precise meaning and as to its legitimate applicability. **1974** G. SOMMERHOFF *Logic of Living Brain* ii. 23 The peculiar purposiveness found in living nature.

‖ **purpurissum** (pɒ̆ɹpiŭri·sɒ̆m). *Obs.* exc. *Hist.* [L.: see PURPURISSE.] = PURPURISSE.

1611 CORYAT *Crudities* 266 Thou maist easily discerne the effects of those famous apothecary drugs.. *stibium, cerussa,* and *purpurissum.* For..the Cortezans.. adulterate their faces..with one of these three. **1934** *Discovery* Nov. 323/2 From the artists' materials discovered at Pompeii Professor Pozzi was able to obtain a test-tube full of the mysterious colour *purpurissum,* the actual tincture of the murex used for the Roman purple dye twenty centuries ago.

purpurite (pɒ̆·ɹpiŭrəit). *Min.* [f. L. *purpur-a* PURPLE *a.* and *sb.* + -ITE¹.] A phosphate of trivalent manganese and trivalent iron, $(Mn,Fe)PO_4$, occurring as red or purple orthorhombic crystals (sometimes altered to dark brown or black) and differing from heterosite in containing more manganese.

1905 GRATON & SCHALLER in *Amer. Jrnl. Sci.* CLXX. 146 Chemical analysis shows that the material is a new mineral, being a hydrous manganic ferric phosphate—the only manganic phosphate known. The most striking feature of this mineral is its purple or dark red color, and for this reason it has been named purpurite. **1951** [see *HETEROSITE]. **1971** *Mineral. Abstr.* XXII. 226/1 A review of phosphate minerals from Brazilian pegmatites... The minerals described are..roscherite, purpurite, saléeite, [etc.].

purpurogallin (pɒ̆:ɹpiŭrogæ·lin). *Chem.* [ad. F. *purpurogalline* (A. Girard 1869, in *Compt. Rend.* LXIX. 866), f. *purpurine* PURPURIN with inserted *-o* and *-gall* (f. *pyrogallique* PYROGALLIC *a.*): named after the unrelated purpurin by analogy with the preparation of that substance by oxidation of alizarin.] An orange-red crystalline dye, first prepared by mild oxidation of pyrogallol, which is now known to occur in some oak galls and is a tetrahydric phenol, $C_{11}H_8O_5$, consisting of fused tropolone and trihydroxybenzene rings.

1872 *Jrnl. Chem. Soc.* XXV. 703 Purpurogallin, the substance obtained by Girard..from pyrogallic acid by the action of silver nitrate, or of potassium permanganate and sulphuric acid, is the principal product of the oxidation effected by lead peroxide, hydrogen peroxide, [etc.]. **1919** *Ibid.* CXV. 1329 The investigation of the red colouring matter derived from the 'red pea gall' has..to some extent proved disappointing. It was found that dryophantin..was in no way allied either to the flavones or to the anthocyanins, but..consisted of purpurogallin and two molecules of dextrose. On the other hand, it must be mentioned that purpurogallin has not previously been found in nature. **1968** KIRK & OTHMER *Encycl. Chem. Technol.* (ed. 2) XVI. 191 Purpurogallin.., a red-brown to black mordant dye, results from electrolytic and other mild oxidations of pyrogallol.

purr, *sb.*¹ (Further examples of the sound made by a mechanical device.)

1971 G. EWART *Gavin Ewart Show* I. 12 At the lawn-mower's purr I stop for a moment. **1974** R. RENDELL *Face of Trespass* xviii. 168 The powerful purr of a Jaguar sports.

purr, *v.* Add: **2. b.** (Examples of mechanical devices.)

[**1916** G. B. SHAW *Androcles & Lion* II. 42 The lion.. purrs like a motor car.] **1922** JOYCE *Ulysses* 507 His lawn-mower begins to purr. **1962** L. DEIGHTON *Ipcress File* xxx. 190 Jay's Rolls purred along the Cromwell Road. **1974** P. WRIGHT *Lang. Brit. Industry* i. 16 Their engines *purr* or *tick over* sweetly. **1978** *Times* 3 Apr. 12/3 The white Cadillac purred to a halt.

purra, var. *PORO.

purrer. (Earlier and later examples.)

1826 *Blackw. Mag.* XX. 326/1 Invisible to every living soul..except Cyprus, our cat, a perpetual purrer. **1972** *Village Voice* (N.Y.) 1 June 92/3 (Advt.), Adopt handsome male cat: 'Purry' Japanese Harlequin,..short silky fur, great purrer, playful.

pu·rringly, *adv.* [f. PURRING *ppl. a.* + -LY².] In a purring manner; while purring.

1907 *Westm. Gaz.* 25 May 6/2 Her tail is all unfolded and she walks purringly. **1925** *Glasgow Herald* 18 Aug. 8 Zizi..would purringly allow herself to be stroked and fondled. **1939** JOYCE *Finnegans Wake* II. 234 Quite purringly excited. **1946** E. O'NEILL *Iceman Cometh* I. 56 (*Purringly*) Come now, Lieutenant, isn't it a fact that you're as guilty as hell? **1964** D. FRANCIS *Nerve* xvii. 217 Buttonhook [*sc.* a horse] was..neighing purringly in her throat when we opened her door.

Purrow, var. *PORO.

‖ **pur sang** (pür saṅ). [ad. F. *pur-sang* thoroughbred animal, f. *pur* pure, *sang* blood.] Phr. used adjectivally (freq. following a *sb.*) or adverbially to mean: of the full blood, without admixture, through-and-through, genuine.

1864 G. A. SALA *Quite Alone* I. xii. 194 The Countess was a Frenchwoman, pur sang. **1868** *Sat. Rev.* 14 Mar. 340/2 It is only the old-fashioned sort, not girls of the period *pur sang*, that marry for love. **1911** J. WARD *Realm of Ends* xi. 225 To the speculative mind *pur sang* there is nothing satisfactory about such a view. **1934** C. LAMBERT *Music Ho!* III. 192 *Pur-sang* exoticism of the fruity Oscar Wilde order is indeed extinct. **1941** *Mind* L. 52 The subjective, *pur sang*, is that which is wholly dependent upon this or the other particular subject. **1947** D. MAHON *Studies in Seicento Art & Theory* I. 16 Many of Guercino's late pictures appear far from classic *pur sang* even by comparison with some contemporary work. **1958** *Listener* 24 July 133/3 A fusion of these two traditions, bearing in mind that they are not always found *pur sang* even at the beginning. **1961** 'W. HAGGARD' *Arena* xviii. 155 He wasn't a Lohmeyer but he was Lohmeyers *pur sang.* He'd despise a Sabin Scott. **1975** *Times Lit. Suppl.* 14 Feb. 162/2 It is in fact possible to be a sociologist *pur sang* and not a black (white, yellow, piebald, Scots, Croat, Methodist, Muslim, etc, etc) sociologist.

purse, *sb.* Add: **I. 3.** (Later examples.)

1967 *Boston Globe* 5 Apr. 51/1 Race horse owners, irked at the New York state legislature for failing to approve the money necessary for increased purses, [etc.]. **1976** *Columbus* (Montana) *News* 27 May 2/5 The four-day tourney..will offer a 72-hole medal play with $25,000 purse. **1976** *Scotsman* 24 Dec. 15/2 Valsecchi refused a £25,000 purse offered by British match-makers to stage the defence in England as he preferred not to give up the advantage of fighting at home.

II. 6. e. A woman's handbag. *N. Amer.*

1955 W. GADDIS *Recognitions* I. ii. 77 A girl walking alone, swinging her purse. **1957** *New Yorker* 12 Jan. 32/2 Bernadett's purse hung over her arm. **1979** *Kingston* (Ont.) *Whig-Standard* 5 Apr. 24/3 The type of purse and the way you carry it can be enough to make purse snatchers or pickpockets think twice before choosing you as a victim.

III. 10. a. *purse-pocket*; (sense 3) *purse distribution, end, money, offer, winnings.*

1968 *Globe & Mail* (Toronto) 13 Jan. 40/4 There would have to be a reduction of approximately 20 per cent in the aggregate purse distribution. **1928** *Sunday Express* 16 Dec. 21/1 A purse end of £800 is more than Johnny need expect to receive in the States for his first fight. **1898** *Kansas City Star* 19 Dec. 3/1 Bingen's share of the purse money amounted to only $4,650. **1971** *Sunday Express*

(Johannesburg) 28 Mar. 22/2 In Britain, many boxers sell batches of tickets to their followers instead of receiving purse money. **1973** *Times* 16 Mar. 13/6 The long awaited return match between Bobby Arthur and John Stracey for the British welterweight title..is now up for purse offers. **1922** JOYCE *Ulysses* 430 Bloom pats..pursepocket. **1970** *Globe & Mail* (Toronto) 28 Sept. 20/4 In each of those starts he was carrying between 119 and 123 pounds because of his purse winnings in South America.

11. purse-bag, a handbag, often having a purse incorporated or attached; **purse-belt** = *money-belt* s.v. *MONEY *sb.* 8; **purse boat** (further examples); **purse-club** (earlier example); **purse silk** (example).

1907 *Yesterday's Shopping* (1969) 404/3 Roan leather 'Modern' Purse Bag, with inside pocket for gold. **1914** G. B. SHAW *Fanny's First Play* III. 198 Putting down.. her purse-bag. **1901** KIPLING *Kim* x. 263 A worn old purse-belt embroidered with porcupine quill-patterns. **1943** *R.A.F. Jrnl.* Aug. 25 N.A.A.F.I. are producing those useful purse belts which you may wear under your jacket. **1911** *Oysterman & Fisherman* Sept. 25/2 Conant Brothers Company, Incorporated make a specialty of the construction of Purse boats, used so widely in purse net fishing along the coast. **1950** *Richmond* (Va.) *Times-Dispatch* (Mag. Sect.) 23 July 5/1 Next 'over the side' go powered purse boats, bearing the captain, seine-setters, other crewmen and a purse net. **1790** J. WOODFORDE *Diary* 25 May (1927) III. 192 The Purse-Club..came to my House this Morning with Cockades in their Hats. **1880** L. HIGGIN *Handbk. Embroidery* i. 6 (*heading*) Purse silk is sometimes used for diapering, and..where a raised effect is required.

purse, *v.* Add: **4.** Also with *out.*

1896 O. SCHREINER *Story Afr. Farm* I. xii. 114 Pursing out his lips, and waving his hand, he solemnly addressed the boy.

pursed, *ppl. a.* Add: **1.** (Later examples with *up.*)

1937 V. WOOLF *Years* 289 Maids..with their inscrutable, pursed-up faces. **1955** P. LARKIN *Less Deceived* 34 Threading my pursed-up way across the park.

purse-net. Add: **1.** (Further examples.) Also *attrib.*

1911 [see *purse boat* s.v. *PURSE *sb.* 11]. **1931** *Sun* (Baltimore) 29 Jan. 6/2 Fish that sold for approximately $1,000 was garnered..by ten purse-net fishing boats. *Ibid.* 26 Feb. 5/6 Opponents of purse nets and buck net fishing in the Chesapeake Bay. **1971** *Stornoway Gaz.* 10 July 3/5 Over the past two weeks, a succession of large Norwegian pursers have been visiting the port, some to land purse nets for repairs. **1977** *Young's Sporting Appliances* (S. Young & Sons Ltd.) 4 Purse Net Line.. Purse Net Rings.

Hence **pu·rse-netting.**

1931 *Sun* (Baltimore) 13 Mar. 12/4 (*heading*) Mr. Denmead shows evils of purse netting. **1961** *Listener* 24 Aug. 269/1 The deadly purse-netting ships, with the aid of these depth-recorders, could pin-point the shoals at the exact depth when the fish were on spawning levels.

pursepick. For † *Sc. Obs.* read *rare* and add later example.

1977 J. WAMBAUGH *Black Marble* (1978) vi. 76 Pigeon droppers, pursepicks, muggers. Don't walk the Boulevard at night.

purse-proud, *a.* (Later examples.)

1930 L. G. D. ACLAND *Early Canterbury Runs* 1st Ser. v. 113 He was not in the least purse-proud or pompous, but always modest and unassuming. **1967** *Guardian* 27 June 8/3 One of Britain's biggest manufacturers of swimming pools..claims to have captured 40 per cent of a purse-proud market.

purser. Add: **2. b.** Also in the possessive in various combs. and phrases, as *purser's crab* (slang), a naval uniform boot; † *purser's dip* (see quot. 1867) *obs.*; *purser's name,* a false name under which, formerly, a man was entered on the books of a ship in the Royal Navy; *a purser's shirt on a handspike,* used as a type of the ill-fitting.

1810 J. MOORE *Post-Captain* v. 23 There is nothing of him left but ribs and trucks. His coat fits him like a purser's shirt upon a handspike. **1821** P. EGAN *Life in London* II. v. 308 The greatest anxiety with most individuals..is to appear what they are not; to copy some stylish *hero* for their *model,* but whose *dress* at most they merely *imitate,* and which generally fits them after the manner of a '*purser's shirt upon a handspike*'! **1828** *Night Watch* II. 82 Tom, when he was impressed into his Majesty's service, had taken the 'purser's name' literally '*un nom de guerre*' of Thomas Call, in which his warrant as boatswain was subsequently made out... Mr. Call's name, however, was in reality Thomas Whistle. **1829** MARRYAT *Naval Officer* I. viii. 231, I was down in one of the wings, reading by the light of a purser's dip—*vulgo,* a farthing candle. **1847** H. MELVILLE *Omoo* 232 Some, to be sure, had for the sake of formality, shipped under a feigned cognomen, or 'Purser's name'. **1867** SMYTH *Sailor's Word-bk.* 550 *Purser's dip,* the smallest dip-candle. **1878** *Detroit Free Press* 12 Jan. (Suppl.) 2/5 It fits him like a purser's shirt on a handspike. **1913** T. T. JEANS *John Graham Sub-Lieutenant R.N.* 18 'Now for the purser's "crabs"!' the Model gurgled, when I'd..produced a pair of service pattern boots. **1924** G. H. A. WILLIS *Royal Navy as I saw It* 83 Modern ships with wire hawsers instead of ropes, and iron decks and ladders, conduce to the wearing of shoes or 'purser's crabs'. **1927** P. RILEY *Memories* 89 Each mess being allowed a few small candles, known as 'Purser's dips', to last the week. **1970** P. O'BRIAN *Master & Commander* x. 264 'Mr Dillon, who have we aboard that speaks Italian? John Baptist is an Italian.' 'And Abram Codpiece, sir—a purser's name.'

4. a. A ship using purse-nets. **b.** A fish caught in a purse-net.

1961 *Listener* 24 Aug. 269/1 The use of these pursers was forbidden in the cod waters of Lofoten. **1971** [see *PURSE-NET 1]. **1973** *Stornoway Gaz.* 27 Jan. 1/1 The quality of the ring-net herring was mixed to very poor and soft, and the pursers very poor and soft.

purserette (pɜ̄·ɹsəre·t). [f. PURSER + -ETTE.] A female purser on a ship or other form of transport.

1959 *Times* 17 Mar. 4/4 Miss Suzette Pienaar, who has joined the Union-Castle Line to become an Afrikaans-speaking 'purserette'. **1960** *Aeroplane* XCVIII. 453/1 Inside of 707 is rather fun... The Purser (we note the big-ship touch) introduces us to the Purserette (we come ashore again rapidly). **1970** *New Scientist* 28 May 431/2 A new technique that British Rail is using to make uniforms for hovercraft purserettes—the low-flying equivalent of the air hostess. **1975** *Times* 19 Feb. 14/7 Of the 90,000 sea staff on British ships..only a thousand or two are women and..practically all are in 'female roles': nurses, stewardesses, purserettes.

purse-seine. Add: (Earlier and later examples.) **purse-seine-net** (later examples); *purse-seine boat, fisherman, fishery* (further examples), *fishing.*

1870 *Amer. Naturalist* IV. 515 Purse-seines are used to the best advantage in capturing [mackerel]. **1884** *Bull. U.S. Nat. Museum* No. 27. 697 Purse-seine boat... This model represents the class of boats exclusively used in the mackerel purse-seine fisheries of New England. **1909** Purse-seine fishing [used s.v. PURSE-SEINER]. **1935** B. R. HUBBARD *Cradle of Storms* vi. 95 Floating canneries had been allowed to invade the False Pass area, and powerful purse-seine boats had come in with them. **1960** R. KIRKBRIDE *Innocent Abroad* x. 74 These purse-seine boats moved like cats' eyes over the water, luring shoals of fish with the beams of their kerosene pressure lamps. **1971** *Stornoway Gaz.* 7 Aug. 3/7 Its provisions apply to all nets, with the exception of purse-seine nets and ring nets, constructed to take fish while being towed or hauled through the sea by or from a fishing boat. **1971** *Country Life* 9 Dec. 1642/2 It was Gardenstown men who took over the first boat built specially for purse-seine fishing. **1975** *New Yorker* 22 Dec. 54/2 When the enormous purse seine (some three hundred fathoms long by eighty fathoms deep) is cast, the boat moves in a circle round a herring shoal, pulling the net into the shape of a pocket in a pool table. **1976** *Times* 14 Feb. 2/3 Huge nets, purse seine nets, that can trap up to 200 tons of fish in a single cast. **1976** *Quoddy Tides* (Eastport, Maine) 13 Aug. 2/1 Herring purse-seine fishermen in the Bay of Fundy have organized themselves with government assistance to change the purse-seine fishery from one based on fish meal to one based on food.

Hence **purse-seiner** (further examples); **pu·rse-seining.**

1919 *Dialect Notes* V. 58 The purse-seiners are reaping a harvest here just now, lots of fish and a good price. Island Co. Times, Coupeville [Washington]. **1941** STEINBECK & RICKETTS *Sea of Cortez* i. 7 The purse-seiners of Monterey ..are dependable work-boats. **1963** *Times* 25 Feb. (Canada Suppl.) p. ix/5 Present fishing methods are gill-netting, purse-seining and trolling. **1973** *Stornoway Gaz.* 27 Jan. 1/1 Last Wednesday's total of 7,612 crans from purse-seiners and pair trawlers was a record for the port of Stornoway. **1973** *Sunday Times* 10 June (Colour Suppl.) 44/4 The third and most controversial method is purse-seining—where a net is put round a school of tuna, the base is closed and the whole lot hauled on board. **1979** P. BENCHLEY *Island* i. 13 Commercial purse-seiners telling their wives when to expect them home.

pursuant, *sb.* and *a.* **A.** *sb.* Restrict † *Obs.* to sense in Dict. and add: **2.** One who pursues; a pursuer. *rare.*

1924 W. J. LOCKE *Coming of Amos* xiii. 163 Amos..ran ..followed also at a run by Hamilton, thereby giving.. visitors..the impression of pick-pocket and pursuant. **1978** *Maledicta* 1977 I. 232 Little Bit's longtime pursuant and then casual lover.

pursuit. Add: **I. 2. c.** In track cycling, any of various kinds of competitive race (see quots. 1961 and 1975).

1938 *Encycl. Brit. Bk. of Year* 100/1, 2 miles team pursuit. **1961** F. C. AVIS *Sportsman's Gloss.* 146/2 *Australian pursuit,* a track race in which a number of riders, starting from different points on the track and equally spaced out, try to catch the rider in front, whereupon the rider caught drops out of the race. *Ibid.* 149/1 *British pursuit,* a track race between two teams starting at opposite sides of the track, the members of each team standing ready to ride a lap when the previous rider of the team has been round. *Ibid.* 162/1 *Italian pursuit,* a track race between two teams starting at opposite sides of the track, the riders being in file, and who one by one drop out of the race as the track is lapped; thus, the leader of the file rides one lap, the second two laps, and so on. **1975** *Oxf. Compan. Sports & Games* 237/1 *Individual pursuit*.. Two riders take part in each race, starting from stations on opposite sides of the track and attempting to gain on each other. Victory goes to the first rider to reach his home station on completing the distance or, less often, to the rider who overtakes his opponent. *Ibid., Team pursuit,* over 4 km., is between amateur teams of four riders. Each rider leads the team for one lap or half a lap, then swings up on the end banking and drops back to the end of the file. Thus, after another three laps or another lap and a half he finds himself leading the team once more.

III. 11. *attrib.* and *Comb.,* as *pursuit force, party, squadron;* (sense *2 c) *pursuit cyclist, race;* **pursuit aeroplane, aircraft, airplane** (*U.S.*), **biplane, plane** = *FIGHTER 3; **pursuit-flight** [repr. G. *reihen* sb. (E. Christoleit 1929, in *Beitr. Fortpflanzungsbiol. Vögel* V. 45)], a flight in which one or more male birds follow or attack a female.

1937 *Discovery* Sept. 277/2 The present type of pursuit aeroplane weighs perhaps some 4500 lb. **1940** *Jrnl. R. Aeronaut. Soc.* XLIV. 485 A Curtiss YP-36 type pursuit aeroplane. **1931** *Flight* 25 Dec. 1265/1 The contracts placed with the Detroit Corp...include five Lockheed two-seater pursuit aircraft of the type Y1P-24. **1928** CHATFIELD & TAYLOR *Airplane & its Engine* xv. 267 The pursuit airplane is..purely an offensive type. **1920** H. WOODHOUSE *Textbk. Appl. Aeronaut. Engin.* iii. 93 The D.H.5 Pursuit Biplane. **1970** *Soviet Weekly* 8 Aug. 14 In preparing for the world championship in England the Soviet pursuit cyclists did a lot of road work. **1930** J. S. HUXLEY *Bird-Watching & Bird Behaviour* iii. 54 Almost immediately he will fly at her, she will fly off, and the two will turn and twist through the air in what may be called the pursuit flight—a regular part of courtship in yellow-hammers and many other small birds. **1940** H. C. WITHERBY et al. *Handbk. Brit. Birds* III. 234 The pursuit-flights [of mallards]..have been discussed at length by German authors. **1954** D. A. BANNERMAN *Birds Brit. Isles* III. 376 Mr. Hartley describes tail-fanning by both sexes [of swallows] in pursuit flight. **1968** P. A. JOHNSGARD *Waterfowl* vi. 51 When the female is involved in incubating..these pursuit flights take a different form. **1945** *Diamond Track* (Army Board, N.Z.) 33/1 The pursuit force opened out into desert formation. **1909** *Daily Chron.* 5 July 1/6 All available attendants were mustered as a pursuit party. **1918** E. S. FARROW *Dict. Milit. Terms* 479 Pursuit plane. **1932** *Flight* 17 Nov. 1099 (*caption*) A new Boeing pursuit plane. **1962** R. B. FULLER *Epic Poem on Industrialization* 1 Zooming aloft In a pursuit plane. **1908** T. A. COOK *Olympic Games* 188 Pursuit Race Three laps (1·807 kilometres) Teams of four to start. First three to count in each heat. **1928** E. HEMINGWAY *Men without Women* 190 In a pursuit race, in bicycle racing, riders start at equal intervals to ride after one another. **1961** J. S. SALAK *Dict. Amer. Sports* 346 A pursuit race may have two or more contestants, who are started at equal distances behind and ahead of the nearest contestant or contestants so that the circuit of the track is divided equally by the starting points. A pursuit race may be run to a finish or for a specified distance. In either case the winner is he who has caught and passed all contestants or remaining contestants. **1976** 'A. HALL' *Kobra Manifesto* i. 13 He could be chased..by pursuit squadrons of the Yugoslavian air arm.

purty (pɜ̄·ɹti), *a.* and *adv.,* repr. Irish and U.S. local pronunc. of PRETTY *a.* and PRETTY *adv.* Also (before a nasal consonant) **purt', purt** (*U.S.*).

1829 G. GRIFFIN *Collegians* II. xxiii. 177 Dhrinking away! Wisha, long life to you says I, if that's the way; a purty fruit the tree bears in you, says I. **1844** 'J. SLICK' *High Life in N.Y.* I. i. 1 Purty much alone. **1860** C. M. YONGE *Hopes & Fears* viii. 312 To be shure, an' it's not such a purty young lady as yourself that need be taking the trouble. **1898** J. D. BRAYSHAW *Slum Silhouettes* 50, I can hear you purty well. *a* **1911** [see *HON[2]]. **1922** JOYCE *Ulysses* 165 Three Purty Maids from School. **1926** J. BLACK *You can't Win* (1927) vi. 67 I'd take fifty cents of it purty pronto. **1938** R. E. BASS in B. A. Botkin *Treas. S. Folklore* (1949) III. i. 461 Them things was purt' nigh as handy as the eggs from them hens. **1946** *Amer. Speech* XXI. 98 *Purt nigh,* nearly. **1977** *Time Out* 28 Jan.–3 Feb. 17/3 Lawdy lawdy Miss Linda Lewis sings real purty. **1977** *Time* 17 Oct. 54/1 The frog-voiced, razor-witted Daumier of Dogpatch for purt' near 44 years casually told an assistant: 'You can stop cutting the paper. I'm not going to draw any more.'

Purum (pu·rum). *Anthrop.* Pl. **Purum, Purums.** The name of a tribe of mongoloid peoples living near the Indo-Burmese border, whose kinship system is characterized by matrilateral cross-cousin marriage; also *attrib.* or as *adj.*

1912 J. SHAKESPEAR *Lushei Kuki Clans* II. iii. 150 It is said that 'Pu rum' means 'hide from tiger', which connects them closely with the Lamgang legend. *Ibid.* 153 Among the..Purum and Lamgang marriages must be made within the clan, but not within the family. **1945** T. DAS *Purums* 2 Terms of address used by male and female members of one sib in respect of the members of the remaining sibs also helped to form a correct idea about the ancient laws of Purum marriage. **1958** R. NEEDHAM in *Amer. Anthropologist* LX. 83 He also worked these out from Purum statements about who ought to marry whom. **1967** R. FOX *Kinship & Marriage* viii. 217 The picture of the Murngin then is of a 'Purum' type community with clans but with lineages as the operating units marrying asymmetrically. **1971** W. WILDER in R. Needham *Rethinking Kinship & Marriage* ix. 214 Some recent discussions..are about as far removed from Purum facts as it is possible to get and still call the material 'Purum'.

pus. Add: **b.** *pus-yellow* adj.

1922 JOYCE *Ulysses* 511 Virag..claps..on the wall a pusyellow flybill.

puschkinia (puʃki·niă). [mod.L. (J. M. F. Adams 1805, in *Nova Acta Acad. Petropolitanæ* XIV. 164), f. the name of Apollos Mussin-*Puschkin* (d. 1805), Russian chemist and plant collector + -IA[1].] A small spring-flowering bulbous plant of the genus so called, belonging to the family Liliaceæ, and bearing spikes of blue or white cup-shaped flowers; also called the striped squill.

1820 *Curtis's Bot. Mag.* XLVIII. 2244 *(heading)* Squil-like Puschkinia. **1914** G. JEKYLL *Colour Schemes for Flower Garden* (ed. 3) 6 The colour scheme begins with the pink of *Megasea ligulata*..and later the blue-white of *Puschkinia.* **1925** A. J. MACSELF *Bulb Gardening* xi. 197 The flowers of Puschkinia are blue and white, arranged in a short close-set spike on a stalk only a few inches long. **1959** *Times* 22 Aug. 9/4 Most of the other small bulbs—muscari, chionodoxas, puschkinias—can be grown indoors. **1974** H. G. W. FOGG *Compl. Handbk. Bulbs* vii. 122/2 As long as they are not forced, puschkinias can be grown indoors like crocuses.

Puseyite. b. (Earlier examples.)

1839 J. B. WHITE *Let.* Aug. in *Life* (1845) III. x. 131 That association, called the *Puseyite* party, from which we have those very strange productions entitled *Tracts for the Times.* **1843** J. S. MILL *Let.* 23 Oct. in *Wks.* (1963) XIII. 603 The Puseyite review the British Critic.. almost exhausts language in admiration of me & my book.

push, *sb.*[1] Add: **I. 1. b.** (Examples from *Cricket.*)

1888 R. H. LYTTELTON in A. G. Steel et al. *Cricket* ii. 72 There is..a good length ball on the legs to which this push can be usefully applied if the batsman..cannot make use of the sweep to leg. **1898** K. S. RANJITSINHJI *With Stoddart's Team* (ed. 4) xii. 233 [MacLaren].. chiefly obtained his runs by his 'push' in the slips. **1921** G. R. C. HARRIS *Few Short Runs* iii. 58 [W. G. Grace] introduced what was then a novel stroke,..viz., the push to leg with a straight bat off the straight ball. **1976** *Evening Post* (Nottingham) 14 Dec. 18/4 Both were caught by wicketkeeper Ved Raj off Lal's bowling, Fletcher playing an indeterminate defensive push.

d. Paired with *pull,* esp. to convey the concept of a force.

1878 *Proc. R. Soc. Edin.* IX. 610 The ear does distinguish, as it were, between push and pull on the tympanum. **1932** ANDRADE & HUXLEY *Introd. to Science* iii. 63 Electric and magnetic forces act across perfect emptiness, as if with invisible pulls and pushes. **1966** L. BASFORD *Sci. of Movement* xii. 33/1 We usually think of a force as the push or pull needed to move something.

e. *to give* (a person) *the push,* to eject (a person), to throw out; to dismiss, *esp.* from employment. *colloq.*

1899 C. ROOK *Hooligan Nights* ii. 23 He was employed as a chucker-out... His regular business..was 'giving mugs and other barmy sots the push out of pubs'. **1923** T. E. LAWRENCE *Let.* 23 Mar. (1938) 404 Nothing else showed up, after I got the push from the R.A.F. **1933** D. L. SAYERS *Murder must Advertise* ix. 158 He told me to string him along. And afterwards..to give him the push. **1957** W. CAMP *Prospects of Love* III. iii. 160 Mummy had her..to work here..but she was quite hopeless..and Mummy gave her the push. **1968** 'P. HOBSON' *Titty's Dead* xv. 155 His landlady's given him the push. **1976** S. BARSTOW *Right True End* III. xiv. 209 'Hedley Graham has started a month's notice.' 'You don't mean he's..?' 'Got the push? No. He gave Maurice Kendall his resignation on Friday.'

4. b. Also, *spec.,* a military advance (first widely used in the latter stages of the war of 1914–18). Also *fig.*

1916 *Punch* 7 June 407 *(caption)* The far-reaching effect of the Russian push. **1916** F. M. FORD *Let.* 7 Sept. (1965) 75 The Big Push was too overwhelming for one to notice details; it was like an immense wave full of debris. **1918** J. M. GRIDER *War Birds* (1927) 260 Henry told us that there is going to be a big push shortly. Push? What's a push to us? That's for the Poor Bloody Infantry to worry over. We push twice a day, seven days in the week. **1929** E. W. SPRINGS *Above Bright Blue Sky* 69 I've shed many a tear over you. I heard that you were killed during the push in front of Amiens. **1935** *Sun* (Baltimore) 15 July 1/8 A marked push toward early completion of the Administration's 'must' program was expected. **1942** *R.A.F. Jrnl.* 30 May 33 The only original officer of the Wing who had been in the first push. **1964** *Wall St. Jrnl.* 5 Feb. 1 We're stepping up our drive on all fronts..and that includes our whole Northern push on housing..and voter registration. **1976** S. BARSTOW *Right True End* III. xiv. 223 They joined up together in gangs in that war—Pals—and in a big push they sometimes died together. **1978** *Time* 3 July 17/1 The top-priority items are the kind of antitank and antiaircraft weapons that could be used to repulse a Soviet push across the border.

d. The act of selling drugs illicitly (cf. *PUSH *v.* 13c).

1973 J. WAINWRIGHT *High-Class Kill* 58 The push was made in one of the city's public parks. The main pusher was one of those men nobody ever really sees.

II. 8. a. (Further examples.)

1923 T. E. LAWRENCE *Let.* 21 May (1938) 422, I met your cousin once, at a push in London: had no proper talk of him. **1955** D. W. MAURER in *Publ. Amer. Dial. Soc.* XXIV. 174 A crowd is, to a pickpocket, a *tip,* a *press,* a *crush,* or a *push*... 'Three troupes is up against this push already.'

9. (Further examples.) Also *attrib.*

1903 R. BEDFORD *True Eyes & Whirlwind* xx. 127 The nightly push club assembled. **1911** [see *NIT *sb.*[2] 1]. **1914** *Sat. Even. Post* 4 Apr. 12/2 'The whole push is hungry, Kid,' he said. 'I'm hungry.' **1926** KIPLING *Debits & Credits* 307 You're from Sydney, ain't you?..I know how your push talk, well enough. **1927** [see *MOB *sb.*[1] 5 b]. **1964** C. MACKENZIE *Life & Times* III. 182 Presently there burst into the room half a dozen of the rowing 'push'. **1967** *Sunday Mail Mag.* (Brisbane) 12 Nov. 3/1 Experts on push warfare in Sydney in the early 1870's rated The Rocks Push as the No. 1 team of larrikins in the city. **1973** *Nation Rev.* (Melbourne) 31 Aug. 1436/1 He was portrayed almost as another Keynes—or, at the very least, the intellectual peer of the Friedman-Galbraith-Samuelson push.

push, *v.* Add: **I. 1. b.** *to push up daisies*: see *DAISY *sb.* 1 c.

f. *to push the bottle* (earlier example).

1788 J. WOODFORDE *Diary* 20 Aug. (1927) III. 44 Mr. Atthill being Chairman pushed the Bottle about pretty briskly.

g. Also in *Cricket.*

1893 *Cricket* 26 Oct. 442/1 Box..has a style of getting off his ground when a ball is directed to his legs, with the intention of..'pushing' it to the 'leg'. **1920** D. J. KNIGHT in P. F. Warner *Cricket* 34 If he [*sc.* the batsman] is pushing the ball away to long leg, he must face long leg. **1963** A. ROSS *Australia 63* iii. 76 He moved quick enough up the wicket to Titmus, but having got there was content to push.

h. Also, *to push away* i.e. from the shore. *push off*: also, *fig.,* to depart, go away (freq. *imp.*). Also without *off* and *to push along.*

1740 *Proc. Sessions of Peace London & Middlesex* May 164/1 He..heard somebody a cursing and swearing, and a Woman..say, *d——n it, push off,* or *go off.* **1918** K. E. HARRIMAN *Wine, Women & War* (1926) 39 Grand day to be pushing off for Bordeaux. **1923** WODEHOUSE *Inimitable Jeeves* xvii. 241 He helped himself absently to a handful of my cigars and pushed off. **1931** A. CHRISTIE *Sittaford Mystery* xxiii. 192, I shall be pushing along now. So long. **1947** WODEHOUSE *Full Moon* vii. 141 I'll be pushing along. **1949** J. B. PRIESTLEY *Delight* 231 This is my view, not yours. Push off! **1955** G. FREEMAN *Liberty Man* I. i. 21 Goodnight, Maur. I'll be pushin'. I've 'ad a day. **1964** R. JEFFRIES *Embarrassing Death* iii. 25 Bill finished his drink. 'I'd better be pushing.' **1973** E. PAGE *Fortnight by Sea* viii. 89 She must be quite certain to leave when the girl with the frizzy hair decided to push off. **1976** *National Observer* (U.S.) 26 June 16/4 A man in a small sailboat pushes away from the shore of the Atlantic and never is seen again.

k. *to push* (someone) *around,* to move or cause (someone) to be moved roughly from place to place, to manhandle. Freq. *fig.* (orig. *U.S.*), to browbeat, bully, domineer over. Also, *to push about.*

1923 H. C. WITWER in *Cosmopolitan* Aug. 45/2 Look at the pushing around he's getting because he hauled off and inherited a million. **1930** D. RUNYON in *Liberty* 8 Nov. 24/1 After..Johnny gets on the strong-arm squad, he never misses a chance to push Big Jule around. **1942** R. CHANDLER *High Window* iii. 29 If anybody tries to push Linda around, he'll have to push me around first. **1949** 'M. INNES' *Journeying Boy* i. 12 The father doted on the son, the son pushed the father around. **1963** D. BALLANTYNE in C. K. Stead *N.Z. Short Stories* (1966) 153 The Aussie..has made it bloody clear he *won't* be pushed about. **1964** M. ARGYLE *Psychol. & Social Probl.* xiv. 177 Resistance to change on the part of industrial workers is reduced if they play some part in making the decision and its augmentation. Not only is the feeling of being pushed about avoided, but those concerned are able to set up the new social system to their satisfaction. **1973** 'J. PATRICK' *Glasgow Gang Observed* xix. 170 The Glasgow gang boy feels that he is being pushed around, that he has no control over the social conditions which predetermine his future. **1974** N. FREELING *Dressing of Diamond* 93 Thought you could come and push me about. Not the first. But I'm still here. **1976** *National Observer* (U.S.) 26 June 6/2 America has pushed these people around too much, too long, and it's natural that they feel resentment and react violently.

l. Phr. *to push* (someone's) *face in,* to punch (someone) on the nose. *slang.*

1930 'R. CROMPTON' *William—The Bad* ix. 228 I'll go and find the blighter and push his face in for him. I never heard of such beastly cheek!

m. Fig. phr. *to push the boat out,* to be generous, *esp.* in paying for rounds of drinks. *slang* (orig. *Naut.*).

1937 J. CURTIS *You're in Racket, Too* iii. 39 This bloke you're meeting up the Old Jacket and Vest to-night, let him push the boat out, the bastard. Surely he can pester for a tightener if you're hungry. **1946** J. IRVING *Royal Navalese* 140 *Push the boat out, to,* a boatwork term used to imply paying for a 'round of drinks'. **1962** 'J. LE CARRÉ' *Murder of Quality* i. 10 'Fielding's giving another dinner party tonight.' 'He's pushing the boat out these days.' **1977** B. PYM *Quartet in Autumn* x. 90 'Pushing the boat out, aren't you?' said Norman, with unusual jollity, as Ken topped up his glass.

n. Phr. *when push comes to shove* and varr., when action must back up threats; when the worst comes to the worst. *colloq.* (orig. *N. Amer.*)

1958 MURTAGH & HARRIS *Cast First Stone* vii. 105 Some..judges..talk nice and polite... Then, when push comes to shove, they say 'Six months in the workhouse'. **1970** *Calgary* (Alberta) *Herald* 4 May 57/1 If push comes to shove, make good the threat. **1977** *National Observer* (U.S.) 22 Jan. 12/4 When—to use common parlance—push comes to shove, I have a great deal of faith in American youth. **1981** *Guardian* 10 Jan. 19/8 *(heading)* Push comes to shove.

7. a. Also, *to push along.*

1902 'MARK TWAIN' in *Harper's Weekly* 6 Dec. 5/1 Push along, cabby, push along—no great lot of time to spare.

II. 8. a. Delete 'Now *rare*' and add later example.

1975 *N.Y. Times* 10 Apr. 29/2 Former Governor Terry Sanford reportedly was one of the men pushing hardest for the primary repeal.

b. *trans.* To approach (a certain age). *colloq.*

1937 S. V. BENÉT in *Sat. Even. Post* 18 Sept. 42/4 I'd kind of like to beat out Ike Leavis... To hear him talk, you'd think nobody had ever pushed ninety before. **1953** R. CHANDLER *Long Good-Bye* xxiii. 148 When you're young..you can absorb a lot of punishment. When you are pushing forty you don't snap back the same way. **1959** *Housewife* Oct. 134/2 Maria's a bit old... Pushing seventy, you know. **1962** *Woman's Own* 18 Aug. 16/1 All these women, either pushing 40, or looking back at it without too much regret, have been good box-office for years. **1976** *National Observer* (U.S.) 2 Oct. 12/5 Flicka is pushing 50, but she still wears her frosted hair shoulder length.

10. a. (Further examples.) Also, with *along.*

1911 H. B. WRIGHT *Winning of Barbara Worth* xxix. 411 Give your horse a drink but don't wait to rest. You can push him from now on as hard as you like. **1962** *Which?* Oct. (Car Suppl.) 118/2 It was the back wheels which eventually broke away if the car was pushed too far. **1971** 'H. CALVIN' *Poison Chasers* vii. 90 Dai was pushing the Land Rover all out, but it was still too slow for me. **1972** 'I. DRUMMOND' *Frog in Moonflower* 18 The driver pushed the bus along... It was doing well over sixty now.

c. *Bridge.* To try to force (an opponent) into a higher and more doubtful contract by overcalling him. Also *intr.*

1927 M. WORK *Contract Bridge* 149 *Push,* to overbid for the purpose of inducing the opponents to assume a losing contract. **1934** G. F. HERVEY *Mod. Contract Bridge* xxii. 247 If you know a player is determined to play every hand, you can 'push' much more successfully against him than against the player who knows when to leave off bidding and when to double. **1959** *Listener* 24 Dec. 1118/2 When East accepted the invitation to game he was pushed beyond game. **1980** *Guardian Weekly* 21 Dec. 23/5 West cunningly bid only 5S[pades] in the hope of being allowed to play in 6S when he was pushed there.

11. a. (Further examples without advb. extension.)

1952 *Sun* (Baltimore) 22 Mar. 6/4 Even if steelworkers push their productivity, a very large share of their production goes..into war materials. **1966** A. SACHS *Jail Diary* iii. 34 He only asked one question all the time, and did not even push that one. **1970** B. MATHER *Break in Line* v. 60 'Once is funny, twice is cheeky,' he grunted. 'Don't push things, boy.'

d. *to push one's luck*: see *LUCK *sb.* 3.

e. Phr. *to push it, things,* to cause (an action) to be rushed; to hurry, cut fine. *colloq.*

1967 H. DALMAS *Fowler Formula* iii. 31 [We] could have her by Christmas... It would be pushing things a little, but they said it could be done. **1971** 'F. CLIFFORD' *Blind Side* IV. iii. 165 Fourteen twenty-five?—or is that pushing it a bit?

13. a. (Further examples.) Also (now *obs.*?) with *off.*

1873 *Punch* 26 Apr. 178/2 Why do not the managers imitate another class of persons who push off drugs by means of puffing. **1936** D. POWELL *Turn, Magic Wheel* II. 140 He saw a bad month ahead explaining to Dennis why his book was not being pushed. **1949** WODEHOUSE *Uncle Dynamite* xiv. 237 She was always complaining that her last publishers wouldn't push her books. **1977** *Jrnl. R. Soc. Arts* CXXV. 124/2, I think the improvement grants we have are fairly good. They need to be pushed more.

c. To peddle (drugs) illegally. Also *absol. slang* (orig. *U.S.*).

1938 *Amer. Speech* XIII. 190/1 *To push,* to peddle narcotics, especially as a sub-agent or small-time dealer. **1953** W. BURROUGHS *Junkie* ii. 33, I decided right then I would never push any more tea [*sc.* marijuana]. **1956** 'E. MCBAIN' *Pusher* (1959) 37 'How would I know..even if he was supplying himself and others besides?' 'Was he pushing?' **1959** J. OSBORNE *World of Paul Slickey* II. ix. 71 It will surely bug you when there is..no tea to push. **1968** B. TURNER *Sex Trap* xvi. 154 'Are you the man?..You pushing or aren't you?' **1977** 'J. FRASER' *Hearts Ease in Death* xv. 171 Was Billy Nesbitt buying amphetamines..and selling them to other kids? Was he, in fact, pushing drugs?

14. (Further examples.)

1863 TROLLOPE *Small House at Allington* in *Cornh. Mag.* XVIII. 272 'They'll be very pushed about money,' said Mr. Boyce. **1946** *R.A.F. Jrnl.* May 170 He is occasionally a little pushed by the constant stream of callers. **1967** P. MOYES *Murder Fantastical* xiv. 209 Sorry we can't invite you to lunch, Tibbett, but what with the funeral and the Fête..Vi's a bit pushed. **1972** K. BENTON *Spy in Chancery* viii. 85 We think his boss may be pushing him. **1978** G. A. SHEEHAN *Running & Being* xii. 173 You frequently read that a runner would have done better if he only had someone to push him during a race.

push-. Add: **a.** (*a*) *push-basket, -boat, -net, -nipple, -plane*; (*b*) *push-pole, -rod* (*attrib.* examples), *-stick*; (*c*) with advbs. forming sbs. and adjs., as *push-along, -in, -on, -out* (also *PUSH-DOWN *sb.* and *a.,* etc.), indicating (*sb.*) the act of pushing in the direction specified; (*adj.*) that pushes or is pushed in the direction specified. **b. push-bicycle** (earlier example); **push-bike** *colloq.,* a push-bicycle; hence as *v. intr.,* to ride a push-bicycle; also **push-biking** *vbl. sb.*; **push-car,** restrict *U.S.* to senses in Dict. and add: (*a*) (example); (*d*) a perambulator; **push-cart,** (*a*) (earlier and later examples); also *attrib.*; (*b*) a perambulator; **push-chain** *Linguistics*, a sound shift in which one phoneme approaches a second and this in turn shifts so that their differentiation is maintained; also *attrib.*; **push-chair,** a small, wheeled, usu. folding chair in which a child can be pushed along; **push-cycle** (further example); **push-cyclist,** a rider of a push-cycle; **push drive** *Cricket*, a drive (DRIVE *sb.* 1d) in which the ball is pushed instead of struck; **push fit,** a fit which enables a part to be pushed into a hole by hand but does not allow free rotation; **push-foot** = *push-pedal*; **push hold** *Mountaineering* = *pressure hold* s.v. *PRESSURE *sb.* 10; **push-in,** (*a*) *U.S. slang*, a certainty; (*b*) *Hockey*, the act or action of pushing the ball into play from the side-line; (*c*) *Austral. slang* (see quot. 1979); **push money** *U.S. slang* = SPIFF *sb.*; **push moraine** *Physical Geogr.*, an arc-shaped moraine formed by an advancing or re-advancing glacier or ice-sheet which pushes material before it into low ridges; **push-out,** (*a*) *sb.*, one who is made to leave, esp. school; *slang*; (*b*) *adj.*, that pushes out; **push pass** *Sport*, a pass effected by pushing rather than hitting or kicking the ball; **push-penny** = *push-halfpenny*; **push-pit** *Naut.* [formed humorously after *PULPIT *sb.* 4f], a raised safety rail in the stern of a boat; **push plate,** a plate attached to a door by which it may be pushed open; **push-process** *v. trans. Photogr. colloq.*, to develop (a film) in such a way as to increase or maximize its effective speed; so **push-processing** *vbl. sb.*; **push-shot** = *push-stroke*; **push-start** *v.*, to start (a motor vehicle or engine) by pushing (the vehicle), usu. after failure of normal procedures; also as *sb.* (*lit.* and *fig.*); **push-through,** (*b*) an instrument for cleaning the bore of a rifle (cf. *pull-through* s.v. PULL- 1); (*c*) used *attrib.* to designate things in which one part is pushed through another; **push-towing** *vbl. sb.*, the propulsion of a line of connected unpowered barges by a powered one at each end; also *loosely* (see quot. 1959); so **push-tow,** a line of such vessels; also *attrib.* and as *v. trans.*

1977 *Grimsby Even. Tel.* 14 May 9/2 (Advt.), Pedigree pushalong fur horse excellent condition, £4.50. **1956** *Harper's Mag.* May 20/2 She threads her pushbasket along the alleys of the super market. **1906** *Bazaar, Exch. & Mart* 16 Nov. (Suppl.) 2042/3 Exchange [motor-cycle].. for good make 25in push bicycle and cash. **1913** 'I. HAY' *Happy-go-lucky* xiv. 180 Luckily I had the old push-bike with me, and I managed to find my way down here. **1914** C. HOLME *Lonely Plough* xx. 236 Strenuous figures with bare knees and flapping overcoats push-biked past them. **1918** S. P. B. MAIS *Schoolmaster's Diary* xvi. 253, I 'push-biked' the eight miles into Lewes. **1920** *Isis* 3 Nov. 3/1 Self-advertisement, or the man who rides a push-bike with both hands in his trouser pockets. **1970** 'D. HALLIDAY' *Dolly & Cookie Bird* viii. 123 Derek..thought of a push-bike... He didn't want to be followed. **1926** *Punch* 8 Dec. 643/1 Music, Greek Plays, 'push-biking' tours—All figure in his pages. **1972** *Guardian* 22 Feb. 11/3 If you take to push-biking..you will need some pedal-pushers. **1928** P. C. CHAMBLISS in J. Schoettle *Sailing Craft* 202 The patent stern affords means of fixing davits by which bugeyes may hoist their motor yawls or push boats. **1967** *Guardian* 17 June 9/6 The pushboat picks them [*sc.* barges] up..loaded or unloaded. **1884** E. W. NYE *Baled Hay* 225 A section-crew..riding down that mountain on a push-car. **1922** JOYCE *Ulysses* 240 Edy.. was rocking the chubby baby to and fro in the pushcar. **1893** E. KING *Joseph Zalmonah* ix. 105 Some hundreds of 'push-carts' like Ben Zion's were ranged within the narrow limits of Hester Street. **1897** F. MOSS *Amer. Metropolis* III. ix. 202 The visitor may stand at one point and see without moving..sidewalk merchants and push-cart vendors. **1909** *Daily Chron.* 10 Dec. 5/4 She ran into the..street, and there found the push-cart, and saw the man hurrying away with the baby wrapped up in a travelling rug. **1921** *Daily Colonist* (Victoria, B.C.) 12 Oct. 16/3 (Advt.), Child's wicker push-cart, price $5. **1931** J. T. ADAMS *Epic of Amer.* xii. 346 Many of the other 'great' bankers..had the souls of pushcart peddlers. **1973** *Amer. Speech 1969* XLIV. 265 All the level 3 stores operated on the supermarket plan with pushcarts and terminal checkout booths. **1952** A. MARTINET in *Word* VIII. 11 It may often be difficult to tell whether we have to do with a B→A→ chain, or drag-chain, or an A→C→ chain, or push-chain. **1969** R. D. KING *Hist. Linguistics & Generative Gram.* viii. 194 If one rejects the gradualness of phonological change..and the notion that language abhors merger, push chains are deprived of their major source of plausibility. **1972** M. L. SAMUELS *Linguistic Evol.* iii. 31 If one phoneme shifts, others will also shift in such a way that the differentiation is preserved ('push-chain mechanism'), while others again will automatically increase their area of possible realisation by moving into the vacated space ('drag-chain mechanism'). **1977** *Language* LIII. 239 Graphemic change provides evidence for a push chain. **1921** *Sunday at Home* Feb. 257/2 Up the hill she struggled... She was throwing her weight against a small push-chair with a carpet seat. **1963** *Times* 25 May 9/5 As the mothers come out of the shops they pop sweets into the mouths of the two-year-olds sitting in pushchairs. **1972** J. WILSON *Hide & Seek* i. 19 She hesitated, wondering whether to pop Jamie in his pushchair and go after them. **1931** D. L. SAYERS *Five Red Herrings* ii. 32 He had the body on the floor of the tonneau and on top of it he had a push-cycle, which has left tarry marks on the cushions. **1915** W. H. L. WATSON *Adventures Despatch Rider* v. 63 We stopped and questioned a 'civvy' push-cyclist. **1927** *Daily Express* 27 Dec. 3/7 A push-cyclist..writes to protest against being forced to show a red light behind. **1920** D. J. KNIGHT in P. F. Warner et al. *Cricket* (new ed.) 28 If the ball it not struck on the half-volley, but a little later, it [*sc.* the drive] becomes what is known as the push drive, and is in fact the ordinary forward shot. **1918** D. T. HAMILTON *Gages, Gaging & Inspection* ii. 38 Push fits..are for shafts that are forced into a hole by hand and that would be free to rotate without seizing, but not free enough to rotate under anything but a very slow speed. **1960** *Practical Wireless* XXXVI. 330/1 A 2½in. length of steel knitting needle ground down to a push fit inside the nylon bearing. **1900** G. D. HISCOX *Horseless Vehicles* ii. 37 The movement..was made by a push-foot connection from a three-throw crank shaft. **1957** R. G. COLLOMB *Dict. Mountaineering* 122 *Push Hold.* (*American.*) A pressure hold. **1976** D. CLARK *Dread & Water* v. 107 Zoom lens showing handholds—push hold, jug-handle, fingers clenched on a small hold. **1948** *Daily Progress* (Charlottesville, Va.) 22 July 11/1 The statement that William and Mary [College] is a push-in for top honors in the Old Dominion is just a lot of wild talk. **1970** *Sunday Tel.* 9 Aug. 24/6 The push-in, the latest addition to the sporting glossary, makes its international debut.. today... The new rule..becomes operative for British clubs at the start of the season. **1976** READ & WALKER *Advanced Hockey for Women* v. 119 Occasionally the opportunity may arise to send the ball directly to the middle of the field from a push-in. **1976** *Sunday Mail* (Brisbane) 7 Nov. 47/11 They then walk home—and are followed by the 'push-in' merchants, the teenage savages who push their victims into their apartments from behind, slam the door and then lace into them. **1979** *Courier-Mail* (Brisbane) 20 Jan. 18/6 *Push-ins*, mugging at the door. **1939** C. MORLEY *Kitty Foyle* (1940) xxx. 296, I was getting twenty-eight a week and my push money extra. **1960** V. PACKARD *Waste Makers* (1961) xix. 231 The spiff or PM is the 'push money' offered as a reward for each item of the brand sold. **1890** T. C. CHAMBERLIN in *Bull. Geol. Soc. Amer.* I. 28. A glacier deposits material at its margin in three ways: (1) It pushes matter forward mechanically, ridging it at its edge, forming what may be termed push moraines. **1913** *Zeitsch. für Gletscherkunde* VII. 310 Part of the glacier margin was bordered by a push moraine from 5 to 8 feet high. **1960** B. W. SPARKS *Geomorphology* xiii. 292 Push moraines are a specialised form of end moraine caused by a readvance of an ice sheet thrusting till, or some similar deposit, up into low ridges. **1979** J. RABASSA et al. in C. Schlüchter *Moraines & Varves* 68/2 In March 1977, the ice front had already advanced over the proximal part of the fluvioglacial plain.., bulldozing its upper sedimentary cover into a set of push-moraines. **1920** W. T. GRENFELL *Labrador Doctor* i. 7 The shrimp fishermen..used push-nets in the channels at low tide. **1976** *Weekend Echo* (Liverpool) 4/5 Dec. 9/8 (Advt.), Shrimp push nets for sale, £12.50. **1902** *Engin. Rev.* (N.Y.) May 15/2 The sections [of the boiler] are united by malleable iron push-nipples coated with copper, and fitting accurately reamed holes in the sections. **1926–7** *Army & Navy Stores Catal.* 285/1 Massage Bath Shower and Shampoo Set complete, with large rubber push-on unions. **1974** K. CLARK *Another Part of Wood* ii. 69 The old push-on variety [of pianola]..gave the executant much more control than the later one-piece model. **1970** *Britannica Bk. of Year 1969* 798/3 *Pushout*, a student dropped from school for unsatisfactory performance. **1973** *Times* 17 Dec. 2 The growing number of girls who are becoming homeless are not 'drop-outs', as generally thought, but 'push-outs'. **1974** *Florida FL Reporter* XIII. 43/2 The 'push-out' rate of minority students is a national disgrace. **1977** *Design Engin.* July 73/2 They are easily installed by simply squeezing into punched or drilled holes in 1·5mm cold-rolled steel sheets, and resist pushout forces of 26olb. **1963** *Times* 25 Feb. 4/3 Their forwards..used the push-pass far too often on a surface which demanded hard hitting. **1977** *Time Out* 28 Jan.–3 Feb. 6 (Advt.), Push pass... There are at least 26 familiar football terms in this puzzle. **1872** B. JERROLD *London* xviii. 146 Benches where they are playing push-penny. **1975** *Country Life* 11 Dec. 1677/4, I am..looking for examples of the following regional inn sports: aunt sally (Oxfordshire)..push penny (Lincolnshire)..actually played in English pubs today. **1964** *English Studies* XLV. 23 The pulpit is in the bows; a similar device at the stern has become known..as a *push-pit.* **1976–7** *Sea Spray* (N.Z.) Dec./Jan. 90/1 (Advt.), It does not get chipped or rattle against the pushpit. **1928** V. G. CHILDE *Most Anc. East* iii. 54 A steep-ended scraper or push-plane. **1977** G. CLARK *World Prehist.* (ed. 3) v. 214 Wood-working equipment, manifested most notably in heavy bifaces and picks and in high-backed push-planes. **1907** G. A. T. MIDDLETON *Mod. Buildings* VI. xiv. 112/2 The double bolts as supplied for swing doors are the proper pattern to use... They are actuated from the inside by a small push plate. **1963** W. C. HUNTINGTON *Building Construction* (ed. 3) xv. 661 Push plates or door pulls are provided on the closing stile as required. **1906** Push-pole [in Dict.]. **1971** Push-pole [see *KILHIG]. **1977** *Sat. Rev.* 23 July 3/2 (Advt.), The 200 [*sc.* 200 A.S.A. film] can be 'push-processed' to 400 speed... Dealer can sell you a kit, including directions for 'push-processing'. **1979** *Amat. Photographer* 10 Jan. 90/1 All these fast films can be push-processed to produce even higher speeds. **1934** *Jrnl. R. Aeronaut. Soc.* XXXVIII. 191 Push rod valve mechanism for air-cooled engines..has been almost universally adopted during the last few years. **1973** *Times* 18 Oct. 35/3 The Polski 125P saloon..has the same body as the old Fiat 125 and a 1500cc push rod engine. **1909** P. A. VAILE *Modern Golf* v. 84 The push-shot is a dead straight ball, one of the straightest when well played. **1925** *Country Life* 15 Aug. 244/2 The push shots or placing shots... You can steer and guide these strokes with tolerable accuracy. **1957** S. MOSS *In Track of Speed* xiv. 182 Mechanics rushed out and push-started us. **1965** D. LODGE *Brit. Mus. is falling Down* vi. 107 He prepared to push-start his scooter. **1973** *Advocate-News* (Barbados) 29 June 3/3 (Advt.), Maybe you have an idea. And all it needs is a push-start to get if off the ground. **1977** *Daily Tel.* 12 Jan. 10/4 One of my minor objections to automatic transmissions is that they can't be push started. **1979** K. O'HARA *Searchers of Dead* viii. 80 Owen..once gave me a push-start when my battery was flat. **1922** *Woodwork Machinery Reg.* in *Statutory Rules & Orders* (1923) 276 A suitable push-stick shall be kept available for use at the bench of every circular saw which is fed by hand, to enable the work to be carried on without unnecessary risk. **1947** J. CHARLESWORTH *Law of Negligence* xviii. 388 Failure to use a 'push-stick'..may amount to contributory negligence. **1920** G. BURRARD *Notes on Sporting Rifles* 68 Greener's 'push through' is an excellent invention for all ultra small bores. **1970** *Which?* Aug. 237/2 Slip-over threading points are better than push-through points. **1979** D. FRANCIS *Whip Hand* xvi. 195 The push-through switch on a table lamp. **1955** *Bull. Soc. Naval Architects & Marine Engineers* Feb. 12/1 Single-screw tugs have been push-towing for many years. **1955** F. MARBURY *Push-Towing in Waves* (MS. thesis, Mass. Inst. Technol.) i. 1 The standard river pushtow cannot operate in waves. **1964** *Marine Engineering Log* July 59/1 The economy and flexibility of push-tow operations are gaining favor with Japanese maritime interests. **1970** *1st Internat. Tug Conf. 1969* 272/1 Petroleum barges could be push-towed. *Ibid.* 362/1 In 1957 the first real push-tow..appeared on the Rhine. **1973** *Guardian* 22 Jan. 6/5 Push-tow craft..are, basically, floating boxes which can carry 140 tons and be locked together in a procession of nine, operated by two tugs. **1974** *Encycl. Brit. Macropædia* III. 758/2 These assemblies of unpowered and individually unmanned barges are known, somewhat illogically, as push tows. **1955** F. MARBURY *Push-Towing in Waves* (MS. thesis, Mass. Inst. Technol.) vi. 22 The basic conclusion..is that as far as these tests extend pushtowing in waves is feasible. **1959** G. WALKER *Traffic & Transport in Nigeria* iii. 47 'Push-towing' has now become the accepted practice. Power craft have two barges lashed to the forequarters, a third being pushed ahead. **1972** *Daily Colonist* (Victoria, B.C.) 29 Mar. 40/5 The tugs are intended for use in..push-towing of such barges in moderate sea conditions.

pu·sh-and-go, *sb. phr.* and *adj. phr.* Also push and go. [f. PUSH-: see GO *sb.* and *v.*] **A.** *sb. phr.* The ability to develop and prosecute a scheme vigorously (see quots.); enterprise, initiative, ambition.

[**1915** D. LLOYD GEORGE in *Hansard Commons* 9 Mar. 1277 We are on the look out for a good, strong business man with some go in him who will be able to push the thing through and be at the head of a Central Committee.] **1915** *Times* 10 Mar. 14/5 The Government should..get a business man at the head of the organization. The Government were on the look-out for a good, strong business man with some push and go in him, who would be able to put the thing through. **1916** LD. FISHER *Let.* 26 Jan. in M. Gilbert *Winston S. Churchill* (1972) III. Compan. II. 1398, I said what was required was '*Push and Go*'! (NOT '*Wait and See*'!). **1959** F. M. G. WILLSON in *Polit. Stud.* VII. 224 Recruits from business, industry, and trade unions begin with Sir Eric Geddes, one of Lloyd George's men of 'push and go'..graduating to the Cabinet as the first Minister of Transport in 1919.

B. *adj. phr.* **a.** Ambitious, enterprising, pushing.

1932 KIPLING *Limits & Renewals* 80 He is one of the push-and-go type..the flower of the Higher Counter-jumpery.

b. Of a motorized toy etc.: having a mechanism that stores and releases the momentum generated by a preliminary push.

1958 *New Scientist* 9 Jan. 15 This novel type of shunting locomotive is a larger-scale version of a child's 'push-and-go' toy. **1959** *Oxf. Mail* 21 Jan. 6/3 The soft plastic trains and cars had their wheels removed very promptly and the push-and-go 'engines' soon fall out.

pu·sh-and-pull, *adj. phr.* and *sb. phr.* Also push and pull. [f. PUSH-: see PULL *sb.*[2] and *v.* and cf. *PUSH-PULL.] **A.** *adj. phr.* Involving pushes and pulls, esp. alternately. **a.** *gen.*

1914 H. CARRINGTON *Probl. Psychical Research* xii. 371 A straight push-and-pull action is easier to accomplish than the more detailed and complicated action of forming words and letters. **1949** KOESTLER *Insight & Outlook* xiii. 192 The mechanistic push-and-pull physics of the last century. **1960** *Times* 3 Oct. (Advt. Suppl.) p. ii/2 The Skid-Stac attachment..consists of a load carrying plate and push-and-pull rack.

b. Designating (the operation of) a 'reversible' train, which may journey in either direction without having its engine turned about. Also, of the locomotive engine itself. See also **pull-and-push* s.v. PULL- 3.

1939 K. G. FENELON *Brit. Railways To-day* iii. 61 The most hopeful solution would appear to be the adoption of the push-and-pull type of train, which can be driven from either end, and which can take extra vehicles if required. **1955** C. J. ALLEN *Gt. Eastern Railway* vi. 66 The Edmonton & Cheshunt line..was..reopened, on March 1st, 1915, to serve some munition factories in the neighbourhood, and was worked by a two-coach 'push-and-pull' unit with 2-4-2 tank No. 1311. **1965** K. HOOLE in *Regional Hist. Railways Gt. Brit.* IV. xii. 219 Push-and-pull units, first used between Hartlepool and West Hartlepool in 1905, became a familiar sight throughout the system. **1975** G. BYE in G. W. Knight *Jackson Knight* v. i. 367 A much planned..trip on the 'Tivvy Flyer', the push and pull train on the Tiverton and Bampton branch-line, was, alas, never made.

B. *sb. phr.* **a.** *U.S. Mil.* (See quot. 1929.) Also *attrib.*

1920 *Official Hist. 315th Infantry U.S.A.* 28 The greater part of the time was devoted to..the 'push and pull' exercise. **1921** F. T. Floyd *Company F Overseas* 37 These rides remind a soldier of that bit of army exercise popularly known as 'push and pull'. **1929** *Papers Mich. Acad. Sci., Arts & Lett.* X. 317 *Push and pull*,..sighting and aiming drill.

b. *fig.* Tug of war.

1958 *Spectator* 4 July 19/3 The dramatic centre of the book is..the push-and-pull between Yule and his devoted but mutinous daughter.

pu·sh-button, *sb.* and *a.* Also **pushbutton, push button.** [f. Push- + Button *sb.*] **A.** *sb.* A button that is pressed with the finger to effect some operation, usu. by closing or opening an electric circuit.

1878, 1901 [in Dict. s.v. Push-]. **1912** L. Weaver *House & its Equipment* 124 The multiple contact switch, which consists of a little board..on which are arranged a number of push buttons. **1920** C. Sandburg *Smoke & Steel* 218 She used to keep a houseful of girls in kimonos and three pushbuttons on the front door. **1935** *Times* 2 Feb. 9/5 Special signal lights will face pedestrians and push-buttons will be fitted to the posts. **1943** T. Horsley *Find, fix & Strike* 64 The range is point-blank... The pilot's thumb, already on the push-button on top of the throttle bar, jabs hard against the stop. **1957** *Railway Mag.* Mar. 159/2 The pantograph is raised by pressing the push-button in the driving trailer. **1976** *Gramophone* May 1835/1 Below the main controls are the following: sockets for stereo microphone and headphones, push-buttons for low filter, high filter,..and power on-off.

B. *adj.* **1. a.** Operated or effected by pressing a push-button.

1916 *Inland Printer* LVII. 830/2 (*caption*) 'Push-button control'. **1936** *Discovery* Apr. 113/1 The diesel engine is started electrically and the push-button control for this purpose is mounted in the cab adjacent to the driving positions. **1943** *Gramophone* Dec. 107/1 The radio has 3 bands with push-button tuning. **1957** *Observer* 25 Aug. 11/1 It is no doubt true that guided missiles, nuclear warheads, flame-throwers, and push-button apparatus do not in the slightest invalidate the elementary military virtues of *esprit de corps* and self-discipline. **1957** *Amer. Speech* XXXII. 313 The following list of descriptive terms that appear on the aerosol containers of..shaving creams... *push-button lather.* **1965** *Wireless World* July 8/2 (Advt.), Stereo Amplifier..push-button selection. **1978** S. Brill *Teamsters* iv. 127 He took his seat..alongside a table bearing two separate push-button phones.

b. *push-button war(fare)*, warfare conducted by means of (nuclear) missiles launched by the press of a button.

[**1945** *Life* 20 Aug. 17/1 There may be devastating 'push-button' battles.] **1945** *Richmond* (Va.) *Times-Dispatch* 9 Nov. 6/2 (*heading*) 'Pushbutton' war seen by atom men. **1946** *Ibid.* 21 Feb. 12/6 The push-button warfare forecast for the future. **1948** *New Republic* 29 Nov. 15/3 The vision of the clean, fast, economical impersonal push-button war grows dim. **1955** T. H. Pear *Eng. Social Differences* vi. 139 In what historical perspective can we see the changes which radio, television, faster-than-sound travel, push-button warfare..and social medicine are causing in our social life? **1958** *Daily Tel.* 28 June 6/3 If you are thinking in terms of push-button warfare.

2. Characterized by the use of push-buttons, *spec.* implying technological advancement; fully automated or mechanized.

1946 *Birmingham* (Alabama) *News* 3 Feb. 1/3 The Army Air Forces came forth Saturday with a real push-button plane. **1955** G. Freeman *Liberty Man* I. iii. 39 One might have thought he was a ship's boy serving on a graceful old tea clipper, rather than an efficient piece of mechanism in a modern push-button navy. **1960** *Times* 12 Jan. 13/5 The married woman of the future will live in an increasingly push-button home. **1962** *Lancet* 19 May 1081/1 The push-button type of hospital, which already exists in some countries, is not the sort of place in which one would choose to be ill. **1973** *Times* 17 Oct. 14/4 If increased mechanization should be decided on..engineering would ..offer a vastly increased number of 'push-button' jobs.

3. Easily obtainable, as at the press of a button; instant.

1947 *Sun* (Baltimore) 20 Mar. 2/1 Political rulers..have regularly resorted to manufacturing money by one process or another. This measure is the latest of these attempts at 'push-button' money. **1967** *Listener* 22 June 821/3 Some part of the price we are paying for the alleged boon of push-button entertainment..can already be discerned. **1972** [see *Jesus 3 b].

pu·sh-down, *sb.* and *a.* Also **pushdown.** [f. vbl. phr. *to push down*: see Push *v.* 1 b.] **A.** *sb. Aeronaut.* A manœuvre in which an aircraft in level flight loses altitude and resumes level flight.

1938 [see *pull-up 3 a].

B. *adj.* **1.** *Computers* and *Linguistics.* Being or pertaining to a linear store or list that receives and loses items at one end only, the first to be removed on any occasion being always the last to have been added.

1961 *12th Symp. Appl. Math.* 104 These problems seem amenable to solution by the application of techniques based on the use of what some computer people have come to call a 'pushdown' store. **1963** N. Chomsky in R. D. Luce *Handbk. Math. Psychol.* II. 343 Evidently pushdown storage is an appropriate device for accepting (generating) languages..which have..nesting of units (phrases) within other units, that is, the kind of recursive property that.. we called self-embedding. **1963** *IEEE Trans. Electronic Computers* XII. 872 A 'push-down' list is one that is manipulated in a last-in, first-out manner. **1967** D. G. Hays *Introd. Computational Linguistics* ii. 31 The importance of pushdown storage lies in the fact that it has exactly enough power to deal with context-free languages. **1972** R. Quirk et al. *Gram. Contemp. Eng.* xi. 736 The *wh*-element can be fronted from a position in a clause subordinate to the *wh*-clause (a pushdown *wh*-element); for example the informal: I don't remember *which shelf* he told me I was to fetch it from.

2. That may be or is designed to be pushed down.

1977 *Custom Car* Nov. 18/1 The Escort has sprouted chrome push-down bonnet catches.

pushed (s.v. Push *v.* in Dict.), *ppl. a.* Add: **1.** (Later example.)

1969 *Jane's Freight Containers 1968–69* 286/1 The Rhône..will be open to pushed convoys of 3,000 tons.

2. *Comb.*, as *pushed-back, -down, -up* ppl. adjs.

1922 Joyce *Ulysses* 45 They wait, their pushedback chairs..around a board of abandoned platters. **1948** P. White *Aunt's Story* iv. 80 Theodora had gone. There was only the pushed-back furniture. **1971** D. E. Westlake *I gave at the Office* (1972) 20 The pushed-down button for the line in use goes right on. **1878** *Q. Jrnl. Geol. Soc.* XXXIV. 566 Pushed-up mounds or long ridges of gravels ..are a conspicuous feature along the shores of the Polar basin. **1962** *Listener* 5 Apr. 617/2 Mr Thomas has the commanding quality of a real *Heldentenor*, not a pushed-up baritone as are many Wagnerian tenors.

pusher. Add: **1. a.** (Further examples.)

1909 *Daily Chron.* 12 Oct. 4/6 It is a very difficult matter for an agent to canvass in a legitimate manner, as these special 'pushers' have told such glowing yarns of 'increased bonuses and profits'. **1929** [see *passer 3 d]. **1946** Wodehouse *Money in Bank* xix. 159 He was not without his dark suspicions of that big-hearted pusher of oil shares. **1954** *Sun* (Baltimore) 5 June 1/8 Perry had come to this city..to act as a 'pusher' of the stolen cash. **1973** *Amer. Speech 1969* XLIV. 259 *Pusher*, locomotive that helps to start a heavy train or to push a train up a grade.

c. A girl, a young woman; *spec.* a prostitute. *slang.*

1923 J. Manchon *Le Slang* 236 *Pusher*,..girl, une typesse, une gonzesse. **1936** J. Curtis *Gilt Kid* 116 Mr. Bloody Bedbug's up here having a good time with my pusher. **1944** A. Wykes in *Penguin New Writing* XIX. 105 A pusher for me. I'm off the beer, but I could use a judy. **1971** B. W. Aldiss *Soldier Erect* 19 Nelson and his pusher took the chance to sneak away, and I managed to manoeuvre Sylvia as far as the kitchen.

d. One who peddles drugs illegally. *slang* (orig. *U.S.*).

1935 J. Hargan *Gloss. Prison Lang.* 6 *Pusher*, one who retails drugs. **1948** H. L. Mencken *Amer. Lang.* Suppl. II. 681 A marihuana smoker is a *viper*..and a peddler is a *pusher*. **1951** *N.Y. Times* 14 June 1/1 Encouraged by 'pushers' of narcotics who sometimes offered free samples to beginners. **1956** 'E. McBain' *Cop Hater* in *87th Precinct* (1959) 60 Junkies are easy to trace. Talk to a few pushers, zing, you're in. **1959** *Guardian* 3 Dec. 9/2 High-powered city detectives..looking for 'junkies' (drug-addicts) and 'pushers' (drug-peddlers). **1967** E. Wymark *As Good as Gold* ix. 140 People like Crane..were called 'pushers' and were usually addicts themselves. **1976** *Howard Jrnl.* XV. I. 46 Western loathing for temptation is vented.. upon the scapegoats of the junkie and the pusher.

2. b. *Naut.* The seventh mast of a seven-masted schooner.

1902 *Boston Even. Transcript* 23 July 20/3 The name of the masts, by the way, are in order, fore, main, mizzen, spanker, jigger, driver, and pusher. **1909** *Shipping Illustr.* 25 Dec. 327/1 As is now well known, the sixth mast was denominated the driver and the seventh the pusher.

c. *Aeronaut.* An aircraft having an airscrew behind the main wings. Freq. *attrib.*

1913 *Flight* 7 June 613/2 The 'pusher', as this machine is familiarly called to distinguish it from a tractor biplane of the same make. **1915** [see *nacelle 2 b]. **1918** Cowley & Levy *Aeronautics* i. 5 The pusher type is much less efficient as a flying machine than a tractor. **1922** *Encycl. Brit.* XXX. 20/2 The first biplanes..were of the 'propeller' type, colloquially 'pushers'; almost all monoplanes were 'tractors'. **1940** *Sun* (Baltimore) 23 Aug. 4/5 The new Nazi types are reported to be a 'pusher' fighter..and a medium bomber. **1955** *Sci. News Let.* 19 Feb. 114/1 Another small 'pusher' propeller mounted between the double tail assembly gives thrust for level flight. **1969** K. Munson *Pioneer Aircraft 1903–14* 104/2 Later in 1906 Blériot converted this machine into the Blériot IV, installing two Antoinettes driving pusher propellers. **1976** *National Observer* (U.S.) 25 Sept. 17/1 Kiceniuk's aerobike looks like some experimental light airplane. It has red wings..and a 6½-foot pusher propeller.

3. An implement, in profile resembling a rake, used by infants to push food on to a spoon or fork; also, a piece of bread used for this purpose.

1926–7 *Army & Navy Stores Catal.* 606/3 Child's silver spoon and food pusher, in case—18/–. **1937** Partridge *Dict. Slang* 671/1 *Pusher*,..a finger of bread used as a feeding-implement. **1939–40** *Army & Navy Stores Catal.* 578/1 Child's silver spoon and food pusher, in case. **1957** J. Kirkup *Only Child* v. 84 Among the cutlery were my own two personal pieces—a spoon and a 'pusher'; the latter was an inelegant little implement which I used to push food on to my spoon. **1959** *Sunday Times* 25 Oct. 20/3 The traditional pusher is..on the way out..dropped ..in favour of the spoon alone. **1963** C. Mackenzie *Life & Times* I. 155 The pusher, a small piece of crust which one was always being adjured to use more carefully to assist the cut up meat on to one's fork.

4. A push-chair. *Austral. colloq.*

1953 A. Upfield *Murder must Wait* vii. 60 Several prams and pushers parked in an alcove. **1966** G. W. Turner *Eng. Lang. Austral. & N.Z.* viii. 180 What he calls a *pushchair*..or a friend from Adelaide [calls] a *pusher*. **1970** K. Giles *Death in Church* vi. 151 With her patent folding, plasticised pusher she intended taking the twins for a walk. **1979** *Verbatim* Summer 8/1 When a headline announces that *pushers* are to be allowed on Adelaide buses, the permission extends not to 'peddlers of drugs' but to 'a child's pushchair'.

5. *attrib.* and *Comb.*, as **pusher set**, a baby's spoon and pusher; **pusher-tug** (see quot. 1970).

1939–40 *Army & Navy Stores Catal.* 543/3 Baby spoon (loop) and pusher set—Gift box 5/–. **1951** *Catal. Exhibits, South Bank Exhib., Festival of Britain* 125/1 Pusher set... Feeding set. **1970** *Guardian* 19 Sept. 18/5 A 'train' of three barges is propelled by a 300 hp twin-screw 'pusher-tug'. **1973** Hrůša & Coxon tr. *Kozák's Ships* 188/1 A new towing system..involves the pusher-tug pushing a group of closely connected barges.

pushful. (Further examples.)

1931 Wodehouse *If I were You* xiv. 163 What a pushful young devil you are. **1938** E. Waugh *Scoop* III. 272 He must be a very pushful fellow, inviting himself here like this. **1970** *Rep. Comm. on University Press* (Univ. Oxford) 71 This more 'pushful' approach. **1974** 'W. Haggard' *Kinsmen* ix. 93 The tiresomely modern bishop ..was pushful and very far to the Left.

pushfulness. Add: (Further examples.) Also *fig.*

1926 R. M. Caven *Gas & Gases* ii. 38 The great characteristic of a gas or vapour is its pushfulness: it is always pushing. *Ibid.* 39 The property of a gas which we have colloquially called its pushfulness..with more propriety we should call the expansive power. **1958** *Economist* 25 Oct. 297/2 Moscow and Peking have divided, by tacit agreement, their zones of interference: China in Asia, the Soviet Union in the Middle East and Africa. Even so, the pushfulness of the two has varied remarkably. **1968** *Listener* 29 Aug. 280/2 The Dick Whittington legend.. with its twin themes of individual pushfulness and the escape from provincial stagnation.

pushiness (pu·ʃinės). **1.** *Philos.* [f. Push *v.* + -y¹ + -ness.] A term used by A. N. Whitehead (1861–1947) for the property inherent in a material object which enables it to be apprehended and identified by touch (see quots.).

1920 A. N. Whitehead *Concept of Nature* ii. 43 We are left with spatio-temporal positions, and what I may term the 'pushiness' of the body. **1927** B. Russell *Outl. Philos.* x. 118 We must give up what Whitehead admirably calls the 'pushiness' of matter. **1944** E. Nagel in P. A. Schilpp *Philos. Bertrand Russell* 339 It seems to me grotesque to say that the 'pushiness' of matter can disappear as a consequence of a new analysis or redefinition of matter.

2. [f. *pushy *a.* + -ness.] = Pushfulness in Dict. and Suppl.

1968 *Economist* 2 Mar. 10/2 Claims in areas of particular union pushiness—say, for engineering draughtsmen—should be looked at very carefully indeed. **1976** *Times Lit. Suppl.* 23 Jan. 79/1 She had a kind of insistent pushiness in the interests of her family that brooked no contradiction.

pushing, *vbl. sb.* Add: **a.** (Further examples, in sense *13c of the vb.)

1962 'K. Orvis' *Damned & Destroyed* ix. 61 My boss don't go for guys that goof like that. So he bounced me fast. I'm through pushing. **1971** B. Malamud *Tenants* 148, I wouldn't want him to go back to numbers, or pushing, or anything like that. **1974** P. McCutchan *Call for Simon Shard* iv. 42 The body had contained no residue of heroin, so pushing was more likely to be the answer.

pushing, *ppl. a.* Add: **b.** (Further examples.)

1765 C. Brietzcke *Diary* 8 Aug. in *N. & Q.* (1964) CCIX. 13/1 Said Nothing.., for fear he should think me pushing. **1966** *Listener* 27 Oct. 613/2 Lesser men might think him pushing or selfish or out for his own ends.

pushmi-pullyu, pushme-pullyou (pu·ʃmī,-pu·lyū). [f. phrs. *push me* and *pull you*: see Push *v.* 1 a.] A fabulous creature resembling a llama, but with a head at both ends, invented by Hugh Lofting (1886–1947) in *Doctor Dolittle* (see quot. 1922); hence (with spelling rationalized), applied allusively to incoherent or ambivalent attitudes or policies.

Widely popularized by the film version of *Doctor Dolittle* (1967).

1922 H. Lofting *Doctor Dolittle* x. 92 Pushmi-pullyus are now extinct... They had no tail, but a head at each end, and sharp horns on each head... Only half of him slept at a time. The other head was always awake—and watching. **1964** *Daily Tel.* 5 May 16/2 With one hand it [*sc.* the Government] may give them incentives to get out of London. With the other, it already gives them incentives to stay where they are... The total effect of these push-me-pull-you policies must be conjectural. **1972** *Guardian* 11 Jan. 12/2 The Push-me Pull-you Bill. **1972** *Times* 28 Nov. 14/6 The [Labour] party's imitation of a Pushme-Pullyou over the European Parliament. **1974** *Economist* 21 Dec. 52/2 Wilsonologists are now trying to work out..whether his pushme-pullyou performance was due to..agnosticism on the common market..or..a shrewd eye on the polls. **1975** W. Percy *Message in Bottle* i. 19 Man's theory about himself doesn't work any more..because its parts are incoherent and go off in different directions like Dr. Doolittle's *pushmi-pullyu.* **1976** *Times Lit. Suppl.* 2 Apr. 399/3 Children likewise seem to need jabberwockies and pushmipullyous [*sic*] to help them learn the boundaries of the natural order.

pushmobile (pu·ʃmǒbīl). *U.S.* [f. Push *v.* + *-mobile.] (See quots.) Also *attrib.*

1911 A. N. Hall *Handicraft for Handy Boys* xxiv. 364 A Pushmobile is a unique form of home-made wagon that has been developed from the simple wagons which the boys used to make for coasting, and for pushing from behind, when the automobile was unknown. It is patterned as nearly as possible after an automobile, and it is pushed by the mechanician, who runs behind, while the driver rides and attends to the steering. **1952** *Milwaukee* (Wisconsin) *Jrnl.* 31 May (Green Sheet) 2/2 (*heading*) Try it! An airplane pushmobile. *Ibid.*, In this pushmobile airplane illustration I have not shown dimensions, for no two boys would work this out alike. **1974** J. Heller *Something Happened* 545 We made push-mobile scooters out of ball-bearing roller skates.

pu·sh-off, *sb.* (*a.*) [f. vbl. phr. *to push off*: see Push *v.* 1b.] **1. a.** (In Dict. s.v. Push- b.)

b. The, or an, action of pushing down with the foot so as to propel oneself into the air.

1949 Shurr & Yocom *Mod. Dance* v. 165 In the leap, the push-off from back foot onto the forward foot, gives mpetus to the leap. **1960** E. S. & W. J. Higham *High Speed Rugby* iii. 38 The take off is from the *right* foot and consists of a vigorous push-off, so that the *left* foot can take a fairly generous step diagonally to the left.

2. *attrib.* or as *adj.*, designating something that pushes off, *spec.* a powered frame or bar that pushes material from the tines of a buckrake or the like; also *absol.*

1957 C. Culpin *Farm Machinery* (ed. 5) x. 277 A hydraulically operated push-off device can be used in conjunction with a front-mounted buckrake, and this outfit is more suitable than the simpler tipping type for loading most types of vehicles. **1970** *Financial Times* 13 Apr. 8/6 A new twin-ram push off buckrake. *Ibid.*, The push-off assembly is moved forward by two hydraulic rams. **1976** *Billings*(Montana) *Gaz.* 5 July 9-c/4 (Advt.), Used F10 D loader with hay basket, steel teeth, push-off, manure fork & grapple fork.

pushover (pu·ʃōᵘvəɹ). Also **push-over, push over.** [f. vbl. phr. *to push over*: see Push *v.* 1 b.]

1. Something easily accomplished or overcome: an easy task or victory; a 'cinch'. *slang* (orig. *U.S.*).

1906 *Outing* Jan. 461/2 To me it looks like a push-over. **1926** *Amer. Mercury* Dec. 465/2 The combination is a push-over on Loew's or any other time. **1927** *Vanity Fair* (N.Y.) Nov. 67/2 Among some of Conway's more famous expressions are:..'It's a push-over' (a 'cinch'; easy to accomplish); [etc.]. **1931** E. Linklater *Juan in Amer.* ii. xiii. 147 Those Princeton guys have been boasting that this game's a pushover for them. **1943** *Amer. Speech* XVIII. 256 Americanisms which have wide currency in Australia:..pushover, [etc.]. **1951** 'J. Wyndham' *Day of Triffids* vii. 133 If Brigham Young could bring it off in the middle of the nineteenth century, this ought to be a push-over. **1973** P. Malloch *Kickback* xxi. 133 About the security van... It's going to be hard to take... Eight years ago they were a push-over.

2. Someone who is easily pushed over or overcome. *slang* (orig. *U.S.*). **a.** *Boxing.* A mediocre fighter.

1926 *Variety* 29 Dec. 7/4 A push-over, which means a fighter with round heels along cauliflower alley, was, by the same token, a dame on rockers in another circle. **1958** C. Williams *Man in Motion* (1959) iii. 27 He was a long way from being a push-over. He was a little heavier than I am, and he could really punch.

b. A woman who makes little resistance to demands for sexual intercourse; an easy 'lay'.

1926 [see sense 2 a above]. **1929** E. Wilson *I thought of Daisy* i. 16 Oh, Myra Busch is a push-over!.. She's got round heels! **1936** [see *cinch *sb.* 2]. **1949** H. Wadman *Life Sentence* ii. i. 49 Then you came along with Lawrence—the dark reasons of the blood, and so on. Naturally I was a pushover for you. **1955** D. Barton *Glorious Life* xlvi. 155 She was a pushover, hardly worth the elaborate build-up. **1978** M. Puzo *Fools Die* xlvi. 487 Why the hell shouldn't she be a pushover? Weren't men pushovers for girls who fucked everybody?

c. An easy victim.

1934 *Sun* (Baltimore) 3 May 12/7 The would-be cracksmen have come to regard a policeman as a natural pushover. **1941** W. Stevens *Let.* 13 Jan. (1967) 385, I suppose Denmark was a push-over on account of the pastry they eat there. **1959** F. Richards *Practise to Deceive* vii. 106 You tell me that I'm..such a pushover—that a good-looking man can..wrap me around his little finger? **1975** D. W. S. Hunt *On Spot* v. 83 Since then our overseas suppliers have never been quite sure that we are a pushover at any price they like to ask.

d. Const. *for*. One who is readily influenced by or susceptible to the attraction of something; a 'sucker'.

1944 H. Croome *You've gone Astray* xii. 123 Are you quite advertisement-proof yourself?.. I'm not. I'm a pushover for Vanity. **1946** 'J. Tey' *Miss Pym Disposes* xviii. 184 I'm a push-over for passing plates. It must be the gigolo in me. **1956** S. Ertz *Charmed Circle* 96 He was always trying new tooth pastes and was a 'pushover'.. for all the advertisements he saw. **1975** *New Yorker* 21 Apr. 139/1 This department, always an old pushover for a picture horse, picks Foolish Pleasure.

3. *Rugby Football.* The action whereby one side in a scrum pushes the ball over the opponents' goal line, esp. in *pushover try*.

1958 *Observer* 14 Dec. 24/2 A 'pushover' try by Blackheath..was the only score in a game in which the players could be heard ploughing their way through the mud. **1959** *Ibid.* 15 Mar. 32/8 The Welsh pack wheeled..to try a pushover. **1960** *Times* 7 Mar. 4/7 After 25 minutes came a genuine pushover. **1977** *Western Mail* (Cardiff) 5 Mar. (Rugby Suppl.) 4/3 J. J. Williams's disallowed try in that game, I felt, was only as dubious as the England push-over try, also disallowed.

push-pin. Add: **2.** Chiefly *U.S.* (See quot. 1961.)

1923 *Geyer's Stationer* 5 May 42 (Advt.), Extensive advertising has created big sales for Moore push-pins. Glass heads—steel points. **1926–7** *Army & Navy Stores Catal.* 448/2 Glass push pins... It is a steel point with a glass handle, and is surprisingly strong in wood and plaster..easily inserted, and as easily withdrawn. **1942** *Amer. Cinematographer* Apr. 188/3 A story board is a large 4 × 8 foot piece of wallboard or celotex, on which the story sketches are pinned in rows with aluminium push-pins. **1961** Webster, *Pushpin*, a steel point having a projecting glass or metal head for sticking into a wall or board and used chiefly as a picture hook or as an indicator on a map. **1974** C. C. Woodard *Cable Television* vi. 138 A pushpin is stuck in the map at that location; and that pushpin's number is written in the Work Requested section.

push-pull (puʃˌpu·l), *a.*, *sb.*, and *adv.* [f. Push- + Pull *v.* or *sb.*[2]] **A.** *adj.* **1.** Characterized by, caused by, or being a forced reciprocating motion; responding to or exerting both pushes and pulls. Also *transf.* and *fig.*

Push-pull train (see quot. 1966).

[**1894** *Phil. Mag.* XXXVIII. 301 They..show that the 'push and pull' theory is capable of giving an adequate account of the action of the telephone.] **1929** *Prof. Paper Inst. P.O. Electr. Engineers* No. 124. 34 The frequency characteristics of a Western Electric..'push-pull' carbon transmitter [*sc.* a microphone]. **1934** [see *multipole *a.*]. **1940** *Chambers's Techn. Dict.* 687/2 *Push-pull microphone*, a carbon microphone in which two carbon-granule cells are mounted on either side of a stretched diaphragm, so that amplitude distortion arising in one is largely balanced out by the opposite phase amplitude distortion in the other. **1951** *Engineering* 10 Aug. 178/3 'Push-pull' fatigue tests on welded bridge members were continued. **1959** [see *facia 2]. **1962** R. B. Fuller *Epic Poem on Industrialization* 50 Basic structural stability..by segregated satisfaction of isolated articulating push-pull forces. **1963** *Times Rev. Industry* June 117/1 Fork Truck Attachments... Drum forks, brick handling forks, push-pull device. **1966** K. Möller *Amer. & Brit. Railway English* 31 *Push-pull, reversible train*..a type of locomotive-hauled suburban train fitted with driving control apparatus connected to the engine, at the rear end. **1971** *Engineering* Apr. 110/2 (Advt.), A responsive industrial control system taking care of loads from a few ounces to over 1000 lb through push-pull cables. **1972** *Modern Railways* Sept. 364 Instances continue to occur of Glasgow–Edinburgh push-pull trains being worked by single locomotives. **1972** *Science* 20 Oct. 311/3 Cyclic AMP and cyclic GMP function in opposite directions, that is, in a push-pull fashion to exert long-term control over neuronal excitability in the sympathetic ganglion. **1978** A. Huxley *Illustr. Hist. Gardening* iv. 119 The push-pull weeder hoe—with a flat oblong blade sharpened on both edges.

2. *Electronics.* Having or involving two matched valves or transistors that operate 180 degrees out of phase on identical alternating inputs, so that they conduct for alternate half-cycles and their combined output is the sum of each acting alone, making possible increased power without reduced efficiency.

1924 *Wireless World* 4 June 277/2 With the push-pull amplifier one may employ smaller and therefore less expensive valves. **1925** *Motor* 8 Dec. 980 B/1 The Push-pull Wireless Circuit. **1932** *Oxford Times* 23 Sept. 22/5 Some manufacturers stock 'pairs' of carefully matched valves for push-pull amplification. **1945** *Electronic Engin.* XVII. 431/2 A more satisfactory way of cancelling or reducing cathode self-bias distortion is to use push-pull stages with common self-bias. **1955** *Radio Times* 22 Apr. 30/1 Table radiogram with 6-watt 'push-pull' output. **1965** *Wireless World* July 329/2 Fig. 8 shows a push-pull 55 kc/s oscillator which provides erase and bias signals. **1970** J. Shepherd et al. *Higher Electr. Engin.* (ed. 2) xxiv. 778 The fact that both *p–n–p* and *n–p–n* transistors are available enables push-pull circuits to be designed without transformers... If a *p–n–p* and an *n–p–n* transistor are fed from the same drive, a given input swing will cause one transistor to conduct more while the other conducts less, giving a push-pull operation. **1974** Harvey & Bohlman *Stereo F.M. Radio Handbk.* v. 127 The driver transistor TR_2 provides a common phase signal drive to the bases of the output pair but since they have complementary characteristics, the operation is in effect push-pull.

3. *Cinemat.* (See quot. 1973.)

1934 *Jrnl. Soc. Motion Picture Engin.* July 52 In addition to its inherent freedom from ground noise, the push-pull sound track has other advantages. **1938** *Encycl. Brit. Bk. Year* 498/1 Although not new in 1937, the use of push-pull sound recording increased considerably during the year. **1959** *B.S.I. News* Sept. 25 Sound records and scanning area of 35 mm double width push-pull sound prints (normal and offset centreline types). **1973** D. A. Spencer *Focal Dict. Photogr. Technologies* 498 *Push-pull sound track*, optical sound track on a cine film divided into two equal parts which were exposed to light modulated in opposite phase.

B. *sb.* Chiefly *Electronics.* A push-pull arrangement or state; esp. in adv. phr. *in push-pull.*

1929 *Exper. Wireless & Wireless Engineer* VI. 307/1 A pair of valves, (or banks of valves), working in opposite phase, commonly called 'Push-pull'. **1932** *Oxford Times* 23 Sept. 22/5 Push-pull gives the last stage a much greater power-handling capacity. **1943** *Electronic Engin.* XVI. 55/1 The advantages to be gained by the use of push-pull for deflection are so great that unbalanced time-bases are rarely employed in cathode-ray tube circuits. **1948** A. L. Albert *Radio Fund.* ix. 360 Radio-frequency power amplifiers often are operated in push-pull. **1962** A. Nisbett *Technique Sound Studio* 276 Movement of the stylus produces variations in the magnetic flux, which in turn generates a current in a coil (or in two coils situated on paths which are favoured alternately, and operate in push-pull). **1962** *Listener* 7 June 1006/2 One could not help speculating on the strange symbiosis or state of push-pull—call it what you like—which exists between him and his age. **1975** G. J. King *Audio Handbk.* iv. 83 The output stages of hi-fi amplifiers employ two transistors in push-pull.

C. *adv. Electronics.* In a push-pull manner.

1947 R. Lee *Electronic Transformers & Circuits* v. 109 Operation may sometimes be improved by the use of two tubes connected push-pull. **1978** *Nature* 6 Apr. p. xxxiii/2 Errors existing between the DC reference and the detected signal are amplified and applied push-pull to a transverse field electro-optic light modulator.

push-push (pʊ·ʃpʊʃ). [f. Push *v.*] (See quots.)

1907 *Westm. Gaz.* 13 Dec. 12/1 The only means of conveyance for travellers in this delightful part of India has been the 'push-push',..resembling a bathing-machine, which is impelled by relays of coolies. **1921** *United Free Church Miss. Rec.* June 187/2 All rode wherever they went, or stayed at home, if they did not care to hire the 'push-push', an unwieldy machine like a long bathing-coach on four wheels, drawn and shoved by eight or ten men.

Pushtoo, -tu, *sb.* and *a.* Add: Also **Pushto.** (Earlier and later examples.)

Pashto is now the usual form. Further examples are added here of the spellings *Pakhto, Pukhto.*

1784 H. Vansittart *Let.* 3 Mar. in *Asiatick Researches* (1790) II. 67 A book written in the Pushto language by Husain. *Ibid.* 68, I also submit a specimen of their language, which is called by them Pukhto; but this word is softened in Persian into Pushto. **1790** *Asiatick Researches* II. 76 The Pushto language, of which I have seen a dictionary, has a manifest resemblance to the Chaldaick. **1933** L. Bloomfield *Lang.* 62 *Afghan* (*Pushto*), with some 4 million speakers. **1939** L. H. Gray *Found. Lang.* 320 Besides Persian, the Modern Iranian dialects are Kurdish.., Balōčī and Afghān or Puštū, each with two principal sub-divisions, and..Ossetic. **1955** *Times* 25 May 10/3 The demand for the independence of the Pakhto- (or Pushtu-)speaking people could possibly assume some apparent validity. **1956** J. Whatmough *Language* 29 In the Pamirs dialects of Persian proper and some related dialects as Kurdish, Pashtu (in Afghanistan).., also have maintained their hold. **1962** Chavarria-Aguilar & Penzl in Householder & Saporta *Probl. Lexicogr.* 238 Pashto is taught in the elementary schools of West Pakistan's Pashto-speaking areas. **1964** H. H. Paper tr. *Shafeev's Short Gramm. Outl. Pashto* Introd., Pashto is the language of the people who inhabit Afghanistan and the northwest part of Pakistan. The Afghans themselves call their language paštó (in the east paxtó). **1965** *Language* XLI. 529 Only very rarely is there a discrepancy between the Pashto examples and the English translations. **1973** *Times* 22 Mar. (Pakistan Suppl.) p. ii/2 In Karachi, the provincial capital, Urdu-speakers probably account for about 70 per cent of the population, with Punjabis and Pashto-speakers—the latter mainly members of an itinerant Pathan labour force—making up a further 20 per cent. **1974** *Times* 30 Apr. 7/7 It should be ascertained whether the Pushto-speaking people wanted to stay with Pakistan, merge with Afghanistan or have an independent country.

Pushtun, var. *Pakhtun *sb.* and *a.*

pu·sh-up, *sb.* and *a.* Also **pushup, push up.** [f. vbl. phr. *to push up*: see Push *v.* 1 b.] **A.** *sb.* = *press-up; also, an exercise on parallel bars in which the body is supported by the bent forearms and raised by straightening the arms. Also *attrib.* Chiefly *U.S.*

1906 *Amer. Mag.* LXIII. 139/1 First they put him on the parallel bars and beseeched him to do many push-ups, prodding him gently to further exertion when he showed signs of fatigue. **1943** *Sun* (Baltimore) 16 June 8/6 Ten pushups and work details are standard punishments for other minor offences. **1952** J. Steinbeck *East of Eden* xlvi. 516 William C. Bunt died right on the armory floor in the middle of a push-up. His heart couldn't take it. **1958** *Times* 26 Feb. 8/4 Half the boys examined could not do a single push up. **1968** M. Richler *Cocksure* vii. 44 Tomasso..did push-ups on his office carpet every morning. **1973** *Black Panther* 24 Mar. 6/2 Sometimes they make you remain in a push-up position on your knuckles until your knuckles begin to bleed. **1978** S. Brill *Teamsters* iii. 107 Twenty push-ups..was all the exercise a busy union leader should have time for.

2. The act or process of picking a pocket in which the victim's arm is pushed away from his pocket by an accomplice; also *attrib.*, as *push-up man, mob. Austral. slang.*

1919 V. Marshall *World of Living Dead* 69 He acts as chief amongst his 'push-up' and 'break' men, associates skilled in their way, but unpossessed of his dexterity. **1938** F. D. Sharpe *Sharpe of Flying Squad* i. 15 Pick-pockets are known as 'Wizzers' or 'The Push Up Mob'. *Ibid.* 332 *Push Up (The)*, picking pockets.

3. A muskrat's resting-place, formed by pushing up vegetation through a hole in the ice. *N. Amer.*

1936 K. Conibear *North Land Footprints* 254 There's no danger of catching her [*sc.* a fox] either; she didn't go near the push-up. **1956** H. S. M. Kemp *Northern Trader* (1957) iv. 57 He indicated..the little 'pushup' wherein the muskrat would come to sun himself on the warmer days. **1959** E. Collier *Three against Wilderness* xxviii. 297 The ice should be sound enough for us to get onto it afoot to start staking the muskrat push-ups.

B. *adj.* **1.** That pushes or may be pushed up.

1963 *N.Y. Times* 17 Nov. 12 This slipon coverall..in deftly cut cotton with..push-up sleeves. **1966** A. E. Lindop *I start Counting* iv. 71 The big push-up windows. **1972** D. Lees *Zodiac* 145 A door that..had one of those push-up bars like the emergency door of a cinema. **1977** *Detroit Free Press* 11 Dec. 6-c/2 (Advt.), Seamless push-up bra with underwire, removable padding.

2. *Computers.* (See quots. 1966, 1977.) Cf. *PUSH-DOWN *a.* 1.

1966 C. J. Sippl *Computer Dict.* 149/2 *Push-up list*, a list of items where the first item is entered at the end of the list, and the other items maintain their same relative positions in the list. **1969** P. B. Jordain *Condensed Computer Encycl.* 406 The pushup-list concept is used whenever there is a queue of approximately equal-priority requests that are waiting to be serviced. **1977** P. Quittner *Problems, Programs* 375 *Pushup list*, a list that is constructed and maintained so that the next item to be retrieved and removed is the oldest item still in the list, that is first in, first out (FIFO).

push-wainling (pu:ʃwē̃inliŋ). *nonce-wd.* Also **pushwainling.** [f. Push- + Wain *sb.*[1] + -ling *suffix*[1] 2.] A perambulator.

1878 W. Barnes *Outl. Eng. Speech-Craft* 72 *Perambulator* (the child's carriage), push-wainling. **1908** A. C. Swinburne *Let.* 22 Jan. (1962) VI. 211, I met..a fair friend..who beamed..from the depth of her pushwainling (I hope you never use the barbaric word 'perambulator'?)... The happy term 'pushwainling' for a baby's coach of state is what makes him [*sc.* W. Barnes] immortal in my eyes. **1962** *Listener* 16 Aug. 257/1 He [*sc.* W. Barnes] was also a philologist, the kind that..advocates such coinages as 'two-horned rede-ship' (dilemma) and 'pushwainling' (perambulator).

pushy (pu·ʃi), *a. colloq.* (orig. *U.S.*). [f. Push *sb.*[1] or *v.* + -y[1].] Unpleasantly forward or self-assertive; aggressive.

1936 M. Mitchell *Gone with Wind* viii. 142 It [*sc.* Atlanta] had nothing whatever to recommend it—only its railroads and a bunch of mighty pushy people... Restless, energetic people from the older sections of Georgia. **1959** T. Griffith *Waist-High Culture* xi. 148 The more talented..can be counted on to disqualify themselves further by seeming too pushy. **1963** M. Beadle *These Ruins are Inhabited* xii. 187 A retired-colonel type.. would..turn and glare because you were being pushy. **1969** *New Yorker* 14 June 44/2 His speaking style..sounds pushy. If I'm in a bad mood, it bugs me. **1971** *Nature* 20 Aug. 510/2 Is it..that pushy polytechnics will in future be encouraged to usurp the position of the weaker universities in the academic pecking order? **1972** M. Babson *Murder on Show* vi. 71, I don't mean to be *pushy*... I just thought one had a duty as a citizen. **1979** *N.Y. Rev. Bks.* 25 Oct. 49/1 He faced the rise to autonomous power during the war of pushy new groups—generals, industrial managers, the secret police. **1980** *Times* 29 Feb. 13 The poor dancers gibber earnestly through its minimal dance content, pushy violence and unmotivated antics.

puss, *sb.*[1] Add: **3. c.** int. *puss, puss*: used to imply that the person addressed is a 'cat' (see Cat *sb.*[1] 2 a).

1926 H. Nicolson *Let.* 14 May in J. Lees-Milne *Harold Nicolson* (1980) xi. 235 The man was merely a prig..he would look very foolish..in Gordon Square (Puss, puss, puss). **1936** A. Christie *Murder in Mesopotamia* vi. 47 'We've been so very worried about dear Mrs. Leidner, haven't we, Louise?'..'Puss, puss,' I thought to myself. **1948** D. Ballantyne *Cunninghams* xviii. 95 'Stuck-up, if you ask me,' Joy said. 'Puss puss,' Ralph said. **1954** 'M. Cost' *Invitation from Minerva* 75 'Your cinema career was short-lived anyway.' 'Puss-puss,' she warned.

5. Puss in the corner: (earlier and later examples); also called **Puss, Puss.**

1709 W. King *Useful Trans. in Philos.* v. 43 The English Plays have barbarous sounding Names, as..Puss in a Corner..and the like. **1926** 'R. Crompton' *William—the Conqueror* xiii. 240 Now, what shall we play at first?.. Puss in the Corner? **1969** I. & P. Opie *Children's Games* vi. 207 The fun of 'Puss in the Corner' is that the players themselves negotiate when they are going to run; its disadvantage is that it is normally for five players, no more and no less. *Ibid.*, Names: 'Puss in the Corner' and 'Puss, Puss' (both common).

5*. = *pussy *sb.* 5*. *coarse slang.*

Quot. 1664 may not exemplify this meaning, claimed for it by Farmer and Henley.

1664 Cotton *Scarronides* 107 Æneas, here's a Health to thee, To Pusse and to good company. And he that will not do, as I do, Proclaims himself no friend to Dido. **1902** Farmer & Henley *Slang* V. 333/1 *Puss*... The female *pudendum*..also *pussy* and *pussy-cat*. **1935** in A. W. Read *Lexical Evidence from Folk Epigr. in W.N. Amer.* 71 She may (not?) be a cat trader's daughter, but she's got some puss. **1978** I. M. Gaskin *Spiritual Midwifery* (rev. ed.) 1. 32 'Vagina' is the medical term, a Latin word, but I prefer to use 'puss' because it sounds friendlier. *Ibid.* 76 A loose mouth makes for a loose puss which makes the baby come out easier.

6. *puss-house, -purr*; **puss boot, shoe** *Jamaica* (see quots. 1961 and 1970).

1942 L. Bennett *Jamaica Dialect Verses* 36 She.. Put awn wan tear-up frack Shove har foot eena wan ole puss boot An go. **1961** F. G. Cassidy *Jamaica Talk* vi. 114 Tennis shoes with rubber soles and canvas tops are widely known in Jamaica as *puss boots* or *puss shoes*. **1970** *Country Life* 26 Feb. 510/3 We [in Jamaica] say 'puss boots' for plimsolls. **1869** J. S. Mill *Let.* 16 Jan. (1910) II. 177 Among the other additions there is a puss-house. **1935** T. S. Eliot *Murder in Cathedral* i. 43 Puss-purr of leopard, footfall of padding bear.

puss (pus), *sb.*[2] *dial.* and *slang* (chiefly *Ir.* and *U.S.*). [a. Ir. *pus* lip, mouth.] A (discontented, pouting) mouth; a sour or ugly face; the mouth or face (considered as the object of a blow).

1890 D. A. Simmons *Words & Phr. Armagh & S. Donegal* in *Eng. Dial. Dict.* (1903) IV. 653/2 He has an ugly puss. **1891** J. Maitland *Amer. Dict. Slang* 213 *Puss* (P[rize] R[ing]), the mouth. **1898** G. Bartram *White-Headed Boy* 40 Say I'm the besht man, or I'll break your puss. **1910** P. W. Joyce *Eng. as we speak it in Ireland* 309 'He had a puss on him', i.e. he looked sour or displeased—with lips contracted. **1911** C. B. Chrysler *White Slavery* viii. 67 She gets 'a slam in the puss' (slugged, struck in the face). **1932** J. T. Farrell *Young Lonigan* iii. 111 He twisted his lips in sneers, screwed up his puss. **1936** 'F. O'Connor' *Bones of Contention* 210 Are you a dummy or what to be standing there with that idioty bloody smile on your puss? **1953** [see *belt *sb.*[4]]. **1961** C. McCullers *Clock without Hands* iv. 81 When you looked at the picture I didn't like the look on your puss. **1971** A. Burgess *MF* xiii. 149 You can get her to keep quiet about it, threaten her with a sock on the puss and that. **1973** 'J. Patrick' *Glasgow Gang Observed* v. 49 Ah don't fancy the look o' his puss. Go ower an' stab him fur me. **1978** *Guardian* 2 Apr. 18/3 On the air, Frost's pasty puss looked like Nixon's with the air let out of it.

puss, *v. rare.* [f. Puss *sb.*[1]] *intr.* To move or act like a cat, silently and stealthily.

a **1953** Dylan Thomas *Adventures Skin Trade* (1955) 101 They pussed and spied around the room, unaware of their dancing.

puss-cat. (Later examples.)

1915 J. Galsworthy *Bit o' Love* i. 19 Old puss-cat! **1957** [see *hep-cat].

pussens (pu·sěnz), playful elaboration of Puss *sb.*[1]

1922 Joyce *Ulysses* 55 Milk for the pussens, he said.

pusser (pʊ·səɹ), repr. naut. pronunc. of Purser (sense 2 b). Also *attrib.* and in the possessive, as issued by, or characteristic of, a naval purser (cf. *purser 2 b).

1903 [see *matlo(w)]. **1916** 'Taffrail' *Pincher Martin* ii. 13 The articles comprising Martin's kit, even down to his 'pusser's dagger' or seaman's knife. **1925** Fraser & Gibbons *Soldier & Sailor Words* 232 *Pusser's crabs*, seamen's boots. (Navy—lower-deck.) *Ibid.*, *Pusser's dip*, a candle. **1929** F. Bowen *Sea Slang* 107 *Pusser's grins*, sneers. **1943** Baker *Dict. Austral. Slang* (ed. 3) 62 *Pusser*, that which conforms to Naval regulations, e.g., 'pusser's cow', tinned milk; 'pusser's duck', a naval seaplane; 'pusser's waggon', a warship; 'pusser's rig', naval clothes. (R.A.N. slang.) **1944** J. Mallalieu *Very Ordinary Seaman* 90 All the discomfort of a small ship and the pusser routine of a big one. **1948** Partridge *Dict. Forces' Slang* 149 *Pusser's duck*, a Supermarine 'Walrus' flying-boat. *Ibid.*, *Pusser's issue*, clothing, tobacco, food, etc., provided by the Admiralty. **1964** J. Hale *Grudge Fight* iv. 69 'Hot water,' he said, 'plenty of pussers soap—and elbow grease, got it?' *Ibid.* vi. 91 A pair of pusser's long pants. **1973** *Daily Colonist* (Victoria, B.C.) 29 Aug. 2/2 Then, of course, there was Navy pusser rum—not to be confused with any other make of rum. **1977** *Navy News* June 6/3 And dancing was in pusser's shoes on planks of wood laid on the grass. **1977** *Ibid.* Aug. 18/4 Pusser's rum, obtained commercially in Gibraltar, was poured from wicker-work covered jars.

pu·ssful. *Ir. nonce-wd.* [f. *puss *sb.*[2] + -ful.] Something to fill a person's (discontented) mouth.

1922 Joyce *Ulysses* 197 The drouthy clerics do be fainting for a pussful.

pussivanting (pu·sivæ:ntiŋ), *ppl. a.* and *vbl. sb. S.W. dial.* Also **puzzivanting.** [Corruption of Pursuivant *sb.* (*a.*) or *v.*] Causing a disturbance, intruding, meddling, fussing.

1880 Courtney & Couch *Gloss. Words Cornwall* 45/2 *Pussivanting*, part., fussing; meddling. In the latter part of the seventeenth century the *Poursuivants* came into the county to search out all those entitled to bear arms. **1888** 'Q' *Troy Town* xvii. 203 'This 'ere pussivantin' may be relievin' to the mind, but I'm darned ef et can be good for shoe-leather.' (Note: in the Fifteenth Century, so high was the spirit of the Trojan sea-captains, ..that King Edward IV sent poursuivant after poursuivant to threaten his displeasure. The messengers had their ears slit for their pains; and 'poursuivanting' or 'pussivanting' survives as a term for ineffective bustle.) **1915** Galsworthy *Bit o' Love* i. 17 There's puzzivantin' folk as'll set an' gossip the feathers off an angel.

pussy, *sb.* Add: **2. a.** (Earlier example.) Also (*Austral.*), a rabbit.

1715 T. Cave *Let.* 26 Oct. in M. M. Verney *Verney Lett. of 18th Cent.* (1930) I. xvii. 342 The Dog is very young and has seen but few Pussies, but..I doubt not of his having Appear'd a profess'd enemy to your Hares by this Time. **1941** Baker *Dict. Austral. Slang* 58 *Pussy*, a rabbit.

3. a. (Further examples.) Also, a finicky, old-maidish, or effeminate boy or man; a homosexual.

1925 S. Lewis *Martin Arrowsmith* vi. 65 You ought to hear some of the docs that are the sweetest old pussies with their patients—the way they bawl out the nurses. **1932** A. Christie *Thirteen Problems* xi. 193 '*The dame de compagnie*, you described, I think, as a pussy, Mrs. Bantry?' 'I didn't mean a *cat*, you know,' said Mrs. Bantry. 'It's quite different. Just a big soft white purry person. Always very sweet.' **1941** —— *N or M?* iii. 38 Old boarding-house pussies. Nothing to do but gossip and knit. **1942** Berrey & Van den Bark *Amer. Thes. Slang* § 405/2 *Pussy*, an effeminate boy. **1952** M. Tripp *Faith is Windsock* iv. 73 'Your rear gunner is a hit with the ladies.' 'Jake knows how to make the pussies purr; it's an old Jamaican custom.' *a* **1957** J. Cary *Captive & Free* (1959) x. 50 Some of those old pussies, especially the males, are just longing to put you in a corner. **1958** L. Durrell *Mountolive* viii. 157 'I first met Henry James in a brothel in Algiers. He had a naked houri on each knee.' 'Henry James was a pussy, I think.'

4. b. *Criminals' slang.* A fur garment.

1937 'D. Hume' *Halfway to Horror* 4 Those who steal furs handle them as 'pussies'. **1960** *Observer* 25 Jan. 5/2 If it was tom or pussies (furs) it was probably one of the big buyers. **1972** J. Wainwright *Night is Time to Die* 129 The coat... Ten to one, a fur coat, and there was always somebody ready to lift a pussy. **1973** 'B. Graeme' *Two & Two make Five* vii. 66 From one house they stole every piece of Regency silver..from another..they restricted themselves to jewellery, toms and pussies.

5*. The female pudendum. Hence, sexual intercourse; women considered sexually. *to eat pussy*, of a man: to engage in sexual intercourse. *coarse slang.*

1879–80 *Pearl* (1970) 268 Her legs are wide open showing the red lips and clitoris of her pussey. **1913** L. Strachey *Ermyntrude & Esmeralda* (1969) ii. 12 I'm also sure that it's got something to do with the thing between our legs that I always call my Pussy. **1922** F. Harris *My Life & Loves* I. iii. 61 By thinking of Lucille and her soft, hot, hairy 'pussy', I grew randy again. **1940** C. McCullers *Heart is Lonely Hunter* i. iii. 37 She crossed over to the opposite wall and wrote a very bad word—*pussy*. **1959** N. Mailer *Advts. for Myself* (1961) 98 This is the magical evil of the big city, but he is wary of being taken in: 'I come to see pussy..and I ain't seen pussy yet.' **1962** J. Baldwin *Another Country* i. i. 63 You wouldn't be putting that white prick in no more black pussy. **1965** 'A. Hall' *Berlin Memorandum* xi. 105 You go to town on the tits and pussy, symbolising carnality till it moans. **1967** M. McClure *Freewheelin Frank* i. 8 When we talk about eating pussy we make it sound as dirty and vulgar as possible. **1973** A. Powell *Temporary Kings* v. 258 Louis's stuffed a charming little cushion with hair snipped from the pussies of ladies he's had. **1976** J. O'Connor *Eleventh Commandment* v. 70 He killed about five prostitutes, cut them to pieces and stuffed various objects up their pussies. **1978** J. Krantz *Scruples* ii. 21 There was nothing, he had discovered, like flying a girl away for a weekend to insure as much pussy as you could eat. **1979** *Maclean's Mag.* 12 Mar. 25/3 As one blonde in a black leather coat bluntly replied, 'I sell pussy, not opinions.'

6. a. (Earlier and later examples.) Also *fig.* Cf. also sense 3.

1842 *Amer. Pioneer* I. 182, I walked up very carelessly among the soldiers .and concluded they could never fight with us. They appeared to me to be too pussy. **1930** D. L. Sayers *Strong Poison* xvi. 197 Mrs. Pegler, a very *stout, pussy* old lady with a *long tongue* (!)

b. pussy bow = *pussy-cat bow*; **pussy four-corners** = *Puss in the corner* s.v. Puss *sb.*[1] 5; **pussy hair** *slang*, a woman's pubic hair; **pussy-hoisting** *slang*, stealing fur garments; **pussy mob** *slang*, a gang of fur thieves; **pussy palm,** = Palm *sb.*[1] 4 and *pussy-willow; **pussy posse** *U.S. slang* (see quot. 1963); **pussy power** (see quots.); **pussy-talk,** feminine gossip; **pussy-whip** *v. trans.* (slang), = Hen-peck *v.*

1972 *Times* 28 July 10/1 His satin faconne shirts tie in a neat pussy bow. **1922** Joyce *Ulysses* 477 He plays pussy fourcorners with ragged boys and girls. **1972** R. D. Abrahams in T. Kochman *Rappin' & Stylin' Out* 231 When the pepper tree begin to bear It burn off all of Jennifer' pussy hair. **1975** R. H. Rimmer *Premar Experiments* i. 68 The wild disarray of your pussy hair beneath your panties. **1962** Parker & Allerton *Courage of his Convictions* i. 82 Then I got three years for pussy-hoisting from a warehouse in the City. **1967** M. Procter *Exercise Hoodwink* xiii. 91 He became the wheel man of a 'pussy' mob... The Flying Squad caught him with a car load of stolen furs. **1936** N. Streatfeild *Ballet Shoes* ix. 134 The catkins and pussy palm showed there would not be much more winter. **1978** *Guardian Weekly* 26 Mar. 19/1 They used to start coming in April like the returning swallows and house martins. Then they arrived for the daffodils and pussy palm. **1963** R. I. McDavid *Mencken's Amer. Lang.* xi. 730 *Pussy posse*, the vice squad. **1973** *Times* 22 Mar. 8/7 The police do their best. They have special teams of detectives (known as pussy posses) who mount drives against the girls. **1970** G. Greer *Female Eunuch* 126 Women in America are reported to be manipulating their menfolk by pussy-power, which is wheedling and caressing, instead of challenging. **1970** *New York* 16 Nov. 48/1 Her specialty at political meetings was the Pussy Power speech. With it Elaine Brown originated the concept that a woman's function is to use her body to entice men into the Panther Party. **1937** Auden & MacNeice *Lett. from Iceland* xii. 161 It looks like a week of pussy-talk. **1963** *Amer. Speech* XXXVIII. 173 One informant noted that a male..is said to be *pussy whipped*, a term one of the authors recalls having heard in the Navy in 1956. **1973** C. & R. Milner *Black Players* vi. 161 White men (and square Blacks) are thought to be 'pussy-whipped' by their wives. **1978** J. Krantz *Scruples* viii. 230 Some men are pussy whipped from the day they are born, some have it happen to them later in life, some never.

pussy (pu·si), *v.* [f. the sb.] *intr.* (With advbs.) To behave or move like a cat (see also quot. 1973).

1943 K. Tennant *Ride on Stranger* xi. 134 Buzz off, Pop. You don't want to be pussying around. **1952** C. Armstrong *Black-Eyed Stranger* ii. 17 He came pussying up. **1973** 'J. Patrick' *Glasgow Gang Observed* 235 *Pussyin' aroun'*, playing about, mostly used in a sexual context.

pussy (pʊ·si), *a.*², **pussel** (pʊ·səl), *a.* Also **pussle, puzzle.** Chiefly U.S. dial. corruptions of Pursy *a.*¹ Mainly in **pussy-, pussel-gutted** *adjs.*, corpulent, obese; also **pussy-, pussel-gut,** a corpulent stomach; (*pl.*) a fat person (see also quot. 1976¹); hence **pussel-gut** *v. trans.* (nonce), to render obese.

1844 'J. Slick' *High Life in N.Y.* II. 89 As..pussy as a turkey-gobbler. *Ibid.* 92 As pussy and pompous as a prize pig jest afore killing time. **1886** F. T. Elworthy *W. Somerset Word-bk.* 598 What a *pussy* old fuller th'old Zaddler White's a-come; I can min' un when he used to go a-courtin, a slim young spark. **1892** S. Hewett *Peasant Speech Devon* 115 'Er's drefful pussy tü-day, an can't walk vast nur var. **1906** *Dialect Notes* III. 152 *Pussy-gutted*, adj., corpulent. 'He's terrible *pussy-gutted*.' **1907** *Ibid.* 197 *Pussy*.., adj., corpulent. 'He didn't use to be so *pussy*.' **1909** *Ibid.* 361 *Pussle-gutted*, adj.. same as *pussy-gutted*. *Ibid.*, *Pussy-gutted, adj.*, corpulent, having a large abdomen. Often used as a term of contempt. 'You low-lifed, *pussy-gutted* scounderl.' *Ibid.* 402 *Pussy guts, n. phr.*, a corpulent man. 'See that old *pussy guts*.' **1933** M. K. Rawlings *South Moon Under* xiii. 133 Sort o' pussle-gutted, eh? **1935** W. Faulkner *As I lay Dying* 10 You pussel-gutted bastard. *Ibid.* 35 He has pussel-gutted himself eating cold greens. **1942** Z. N. Hurston *Dust Tracks on Road* viii. 143 Goat-bellied, puzzle-gutted,..knock-kneed..so-and-so. **1946** *Amer. Speech* XXI. 99 A *body* who has gained weight enough to show signs of obesity is said to be *fleshy* or *pussy* (pursy). **1949** 'J. Nelson' *Backwoods Teacher* ix. 88 A lantern-jawed ol' varmint with a big golden watch chain acrost his ol' pussy-gut. **1959** W. Faulkner *Mansion* 55 Old pussel-gutted Hampton that could be fetched along to look at anything, even a murder, once somebody remembered he was Sheriff. **1976** C. S. Brown *Gloss. Faulkner's South* 157 In northern Florida, the pot-bellied little mosquito-fish, or gambusia, is called the pusselgut. **1976** *N.Y. Times Mag.* 10 Oct. 111/2 All watched over by a savage God, by the dead and by pussel-gutted deputies.

pussy-cat. Substitute for entry:

pu·ssy-cat. 1. A nursery word for a cat.

1805 *Songs for Nursery* 40 Pussy cat, pussy cat, where have you been I've been to London to see the queen. **1837** [in Dict.]. **1844** 'J. Slick' *High Life in N.Y.* I. 154 As affectionate as a pussy cat. **1871** E. Lear *Nonsense Songs, Stories, Bot. & Alphabets*, The Owl and the Pussy-cat went to sea In a beautiful pea-green boat. **1933** [see *baby-talk* s.v. *Baby *sb.* B. 1 d]. **1955** *Sci. News Let.* 26 Mar. 203/1 For better-fed pussycats, add to their diet a good dash of personal attention and a heaping tablespoonful of affection.

2. A willow or hazel catkin: cf. Pussy *sb.* 4.

1850 C. M. Yonge *Henrietta's Wish* xv. 216 The silver 'pussycats' on the withy. **1861** [in Dict.]. **1889** E. Peacock *Gloss. Words Manley & Corringham, Lincolnshire* (ed. 2) 421 *Pussy-cat*.., the catkins of the willow.

3. Applied to a person (cf. Puss *sb.*¹ 3, Pussy *sb.* 3 in Dict. and Suppl.); now esp. one who is attractive, amiable, or submissive.

1859 J. A. Symonds *Let.* Apr. (1967) I. 184 Dalrymple's brother is going to be married to the Lady Edith Dalhousie: I wrote a solemn letter of congratulae [*sic*] to the old pussey cat! **1864, 1881** [in Dict.]. **1955** *Amer. Speech* XXX. 119 *Pussy cat*, a pilot who is overcautious, fearful, or reluctant. **1959** *Times* 17 Aug. 12/7 Ronder, a sly pussy-cat of a man, able to scratch as well as purr. **1964** L. Nkosi *Rhythm of Violence* 25 Jimmy: (*to Mary*) Don't worry pussycat! **1973** E. Jong *Fear of Flying* 89 'Some men claim to be afraid of me.' Adrian laughed. 'You're a sweetheart,' he said, 'a pussy-cat—as you Americans say.' **1975** P. G. Winslow *Death of Angel* iv. 104 He can be a dear, but he's also one of the chief pussycats of the psychic world. **1976** C. Dexter *Last seen Wearing* v. 36 The secret sex-life of a glamorous Hollywood pussycat. **1978** G. Vidal *Kalki* i. 7, I was the one who paid the alimony... Women wrote me ugly letters. I was not apparently, a pussycat.

4. Cattiness, spitefulness. *rare.*

1911 W. J. Locke *Glory of Clementina Wing* xxiv. 361 Let us have a straight talk like sensible women, and put the pussy-cat aside.

5. *Comb.*, as *pussy-cat-like* adj.; **pussy-cat bow,** a soft, floppy bow.

1964 *Sunday Express* 2 Feb. 18/3 For dressy occasions a pussycat bow..under a high, round jacket collar. **1967** [see *Gentian 2 b]. **1977** J. Bingham *Marriage Bureau Murders* ii. 21 Her white silk blouse, with the pussy cat bow tied at the neck, lent a touch of femininity. **1881** Pussy-cat-like [in Dict.].

pu·ssyfoot, *sb.* [f. Pussy *sb.* + Foot *sb.*]

1. One who moves stealthily or warily.

1914 Jackson & Hellyer *Vocab. Criminal Slang* 68 *Pussy foot*... A detective. **1916** *Dialect Notes* IV. 279 *Pussy-foot, v.i.* To be sly, intriguing, or underhand. 'That girl goes pussy-footing around.' Also *n.* 'She's a regular pussy-foot.' **1977** 'E. Crispin' *Glimpses of Moon* xii. 257 Grateful that the creature [*sc.* a cat] was in both senses a pussyfoot, Fen drank some champagne.

2. [f. the nickname 'Pussyfoot' of an American supporter of Prohibition, W. E. Johnson (1862–1945), given to him on account of his stealthy methods when a magistrate.] An advocate or supporter of prohibition; a teetotaller. Also allusively.

1919 *Punch* 23 July 86 *Gloomy Policeman.* 'You've had enough. Better go home.' *Reveller*... 'Shurr-up—Pussyfoot!' **1920** 'Sapper' *Bull-Dog Drummond* vi. 146 We are all confirmed Pussy-foots, and have been consuming non-alcoholic beer. **1921** T. Burke *Outer Circle* 169 The tea arrived, a viscid, leathery fluid of Pussyfoot vintage. **1922** Ld. Riddell *Some Things that Matter* ii. 28 Mrs. A., a 'pussyfoot', with an ardent desire to interfere with other people's habits. **1946** G. Millar *Horned Pigeon* x. 137 There was the heavy drinker... And there was the pussyfoot who said 'poison'.

3. *attrib.* or as *adj.* **a.** Teetotal; without alcohol; non-alcoholic. **b.** Soft; easy.

1923 D. H. Lawrence *Birds, Beasts & Flowers* 15 Even the word Marsala will smack of preciosity Soon in the pussy-foot West. **1940** Dylan Thomas *Portrait of Artist as Young Dog* 217 He'd be knocking back nips without a thought that on the sands at home his friend was alone and pussyfoot at six o'clock. **1973** D. Miller *Chinese Jade Affair* xvii. 156, I was trying to deflect the inevitable course of the evening with a 'Pussy-foot' cocktail. **1974** *Country Life* 17 Oct. 1108 Covering 38 laps of the circuit.. ensured this was no genteel pussyfoot operation.

So **pussy-footed** *a.*, having a light step; elusive; evasive; **pussy-foo·tedness; pu·ssyfootism,** teetotalism, advocacy or enforcement of prohibition.

1893 Pussy-footed [see Pussy *sb.* 6]. **1919** *N.Y. Times* 7 Jan. 4/6 The Republican Party..was evidently in imminent danger of taking a 'pussy-footed' position on the war. **1923** *Daily Mail* 23 July 7 In Tudor England people sang the music they liked, and read the books they liked. They had real freedom, and there was no pussy-footism. **1924** D. S. Barry *Forty Years in Washington* v. 106 Ingalls once said of Senator William B. Allison that he was so pussy-footed he could walk from New York to San Francisco on the keys of a piano and never strike a note. **1926** 'A. Berkeley' *Wychford Poisoning Case* vii. 78 They reached the Man of Kent and ordered the night-caps to which their position as residents entitled them, in defiance of the dictates of a maternal government, pussy-footism and all the other futilities which order our lives for us in these days. **1931** *Times Lit. Suppl.* 10 Sept. 685/1 He was pussyfooted and quick to spring. **1957** *Times* 10 May 13/4 This letter may sound cautious, perhaps pussy-footed, almost priggish... We must tread softly. **1964** *Daily Tel.* 9 Mar. 14/2 There is nothing pussy-footed about this economic strategy... It is a bold mixture of more competition and more responsibility. **1966** *Economist* 30 Apr. 450/1 Politically here is confirmation..of the essential caution, not to say pussy-footedness, of the Wilson Government. **1980** *Jrnl. R. Soc. Arts* Mar. 181/2 Aesthetics is a pussy-footed way of referring to beauty.

pu·ssyfoot, *v.* [f. as prec.] **1.** *intr.* To tread softly or lightly to avoid being noticed; to proceed warily; to conceal one's opinions or plans; to behave evasively or timidly. Also with *it.*

1903 *Atlanta Constitution* 20 Mar. 3 Vice President Charles Warren Fairbanks is pussy-footing it around Washington. **1916** [see *pussyfoot *sb.* 1]. **1918** C. Sandburg *Cornhuskers* 73 Who pussyfoots from desk to desk with a speaking forefinger? **1928** *Observer* 5 Feb. 18/1 While most papers are still 'pussy-footing' on the Presidency they called their editors together and afterwards announced a unanimous decision. **1931** E. Thompson *Farewell to India* 203 Trying to coax a horse to wait while I pussy-footed up to him. **1934** D. L. Sayers *Nine Tailors* III. ii. 286 When I got out through the porch, I had to pussyfoot pretty gently over that beastly creaking gravel. **1949** *Time* 9 May 25/2 The ones who pussy-footed, side-stepped, straddled, carried water on both shoulders and compromised were left at home. **1951** E. Paul *Springtime in Paris* viii. 155, I saw you pussyfooting around the exhibition. **1973** *Times* 16 Oct. 6/6 A Labour Government should not 'pussyfoot around' with reform of the Official Secrets Act but scrap it. **1975** B. Wood *Killing Gift* (1976) IV. i. 129 Why do you pussy-foot, captain?.. Why not just say it—you think Jennifer Gilbert killed him. **1977** *Jrnl. R. Soc. Arts* CXXV. 626/1 We have 'pussy-footed' round this issue of profit for years. **1980** *Brit. Med. Jrnl.* 29 Mar. 937/1 It is time someone was honest enough to stop pussyfooting about.

2. [f. *pussyfoot *sb.* 2.] *trans.* To render teetotal; to impose prohibition on. *rare.*

1921 [implied in *pussyfooting *vbl. sb.*].

So **pu·ssyfooting** *vbl. sb.* and *ppl. a.*

1921 *Q. Rev.* Jan. 100 The tyranny that would ensue from the Pussy-footing of Canada is too horrible to contemplate. **1928** *Collier's* 29 Dec. 38/1 The wrappings which..the pussy-footing politicians impose upon a candidate. **1956** G. P. Kurath in A. Dundes *Mother Wit* (1973) 107/2 Certain qualities seem to predominate... These are whole-bodied movements,.. dynamics from pussy footing to violent acrobatics, rhythmic complexity. **1974** J. Cleary *Peter's Pence* vi. 187 Authority had been given to the pussyfooting amateur..and nothing had gone right. **1976** *Times* 16 Feb. 8/7 In the face of political dogma, 'pussy-footing' and ill-informed decision making, is Mr Laker downhearted? **1977** *Time* 8 Aug. 1/1 To hell with what timid, pussy-footing diplomats think!

pu·ssyfooter. [f. *pussyfoot *v.* and *sb.* + -er¹.] **a.** One who pussyfoots (in any sense of the verb). **b.** An advocate or supporter of prohibition.

1927 *Sat. Even. Post* 24 Dec. 9/1 A good politician is a natural-born pussy-footer. **1928** *Daily Express* 28 Dec. 8/3 The pussyfooters..have given a weary and blasé world a new game to play. **1932** *N.Y. Times* 20 May 10/4 The conditions which are attached to its operation make plain its insincerity. It is, therefore, on that very account beginning to attract the favorable attention of the trimmers and the pussyfooters. **1946** S. H. Holbrook *Lost Men Amer. Hist.* 160 The appeasers and pussyfooters of 1850 also provided that any territories that might come into the Union later could do so with or without slavery.

pussy-willow. orig. *U.S.* Substitute for def.: A popular name for several species of willow or their soft, fluffy catkins, which appear before the leaves; esp., in North America, the glaucous willow, *Salix discolor*, and, in Great Britain, the goat willow, *Salix caprea.* (Earlier and further examples.)

1869 J. G. Fuller *Flower Gatherers* 52 The aments appear before the leaves, and are covered with hairs so soft and silken that children often call them Pussy-Willows. **1878** Mrs. Stowe *Poganuc People* xvii. 182 Then the pussy-willows threw out their soft catkins. **1893** Dartnell & Goddard *Gloss. Words used in Wiltshire* 126 Pussy-willow. *Salix.* **1924** A. D. Sedgwick *Little French Girl* II. i. 103 Sometimes it [*sc.* Alix's skin] was grey, like pussy-willow. **1939** F. Thompson *Lark Rise* i. 1 There were violets under the hedges and pussy-willows out beside the brook. **1949** *Lisle* (Illinois) *Eagle* 31 Mar. 5/4 The spring motif decoration of jonquils and pussy willows.. gave a gay and festive setting. **1958** R. D. Meikle *Brit. Trees & Shrubs* 198 In recent years the childish 'Pussy Willow' has tended to replace these older names [of 'Palm' and 'Goat Willow']. **1969** *Canadian Antiques Collector* Aug. 20/1 Pussywillows are arranged in one of a collection of..sugar bowls. **1976** *Burnham-on-Sea Gaz.* 20 Apr. 12/9 All [the congregation] carried branches of pussy willow which had been cut locally for the occasion [*sc.* Palm Sunday].

puszta (pu·stă). Also **pussta, puzta.** [Hungarian = plain, steppe, waste.] The flat treeless country of Hungary; a plain in Hungary.

1842 F. W. Faber *Styrian Lake* 324 The hailstorms with white oars across the putzas [*sic*] roam. **1852** T. Ross tr. *Humboldt's Trav.* II. xvii. 86 The widely extended pastures, which reach in every direction to the horizon, are called in the country, *Puszta.* **1896** *Daily News* 9 June 7/6 Only a nation of horsemen who have the Pussta to practise upon could turn out such a number of first-class horses. **1927** *Daily Express* 14 Dec. 9/1 They are the Chicos, as the 'cowboys' are called, and the Pusztas, or prairies, are to be found only a few hours' journey from Budapest. **1947** M. R. Shackleton *Europe* v. xxvii. 334 South-east of Kecskemét the soil is impregnated with salts and there is a large area of *puszta* (= 'waste'), known as the Bugác steppe. **1972** *Guardian* 4 Nov. 14/4 The Great Hungarian Plain... Pleasant to lunch here, serenaded by Hungarian Gipsy bands as you eat your puszta steak. **1973** *Country Life* 11 Jan. 74/1 There can be few areas of Europe that are flatter..than the great plains, the *puszta*, of Hungary.

put, *sb.*¹ Add: **1.** (Later *fig.* example.)

1974 B. Brophy in *New Statesman* 28 June 929/1 The jacket, an unsuccessful but not dishonourable put at the manner of Magritte.

5. *attrib.*, as *put option.*

1881 *Guide Oper. Stocks* 15 A Put Option should be obtained when a decline in the market is expected to take place. **1961** *Daily Mail* 18 Sept. 13/4 In the past three weeks 'put' options (where a fall in the shares is expected) have been an outstanding feature of the option market. **1977** *Private Eye* 4 Mar. 17/1 One suggestion was that some of the shares had come from Jim himself as a result of a 'put' option held on him personally by former lieutenant Herbert Despard.

put, *v.*¹ Add: **I. 8. c.** (Earlier and later examples with reference to a stream.)

1773 P. V. Fithian *Jrnl.* (1900) 56 From his house we see the Potowmack, and a fine River putting from it. **1810** F. Cuming *Sk. Tour Western Country* xiii. 97 The creek..puts in from the Virginia side. **1903** A. Adams *Log of Cowboy* 347 The trail on leaving the river led up Many Berries, one of the tributaries of the Yellowstone putting in from the north side.

II. 10. f. Also const. *ellipt.*

1819 Keats *Let.* 22 Sept. in G. G. Williamson *Keats Mem. Vol.* (1921) 120 Chowder died long ago—Mrs. H. laments that the last time they *put him* (*i.e.* to breed) he didn't take.

III. 20. a. Also in colloq. phr. *to put paid to*: to deal finally or effectually with (a person); to terminate (aspirations, hopes, etc.); to eliminate or put an end to (something).

1919 *Boy's Own Ann.* XLI. 457/2 She [*sc.* a destroyer].. was about to proceed to sea on her mission of 'putting paid' to U-boats. **1931** T. R. G. Lyell *Slang* 606 You can put paid to any friendship that ever existed between him and me. **1951** J. B. Priestley *Festival at Farbridge* II. iii. 344, I thought one time Tanhead might ha' swung 'em, but Commodore put paid to him all right. **1955** 'E. C. R. Lorac' *Ask Policeman* v. 54 He and his premises..were put paid to by a land mine. **1957** J. Braine *Room at Top* xvi. 144, I wanted to put paid to Communism once and for all. **1959** *Listener* 30 July 183/3 The translator's deficiencies put paid to the book altogether. **1971** G. Household *Doom's Caravan* ii. 40 The return journey..put paid to my only pair of formal trousers. **1976** *Economist* 13 Mar. 13/2 [That choice] would also probably put paid to any hopes of fully reintegrating France into the Nato alliance.

25. a. Also in U.S. dial. phr. *to put* (someone) *in the dozen(s)*, to force (someone) to 'play the dozens' (cf. *Play *v.* 16e); *spec.* to insult (a person) by referring to his mother in a derogatory way.

1939 J. Dollard in *American Imago* Nov. 8 Herbert had been put in the Dozens by another boy in the following manner: the boy said, 'Your mama needs a bath.' **1941** W. A. Percy *Lanterns on Levee* xxiii. 301 'Some fool nigger puts you in the dozen.'..'What's putting you in the dozen?' 'That's sho nuff bad talk.' 'Like what?' 'Well,' said Ford, modest and hesitant, 'that's talking about your mommer.' **1973** A. Dundes *Mother Wit* 299 To be 'put in the dozens' is to be put in a bad or losing position. **1974** H. L. Foster *Ribbin'* v. 226 If a teacher is attempting to really stop the dozens playing, just.. holding your elbow, could be considered as putting another boy in the dozens.

26. b. Also const. *down.*

1960 R. Williams *Border Country* I. ii. 58 He was able to rent two strips of garden..and these he put down one to gooseberries and currants, the other to potatoes.

27. a. (*c*) *to put* (a person) *through it*: to impose a severe test on (a person); to subject (a person) to an ordeal or trying experience.

1872 G. P. Burnham *Mem. U.S. Secret Service* p. vii, *Put 'em through*, subjecting persons to a thorough searching ordeal. **1922** A. A. Milne *Red House Mystery* vi. 50 Everybody else is bundled off except me, and I get put through it by that inspector as if I knew all about it. **1923** Wodehouse *Inimitable Jeeves* iv. 48 Aunt Agatha ..was putting the last of the bandits through it in the voice she usually reserves for snubbing waiters in restaurants. **1935** *Discovery* Oct. 311/2 The work of the pupils whom he 'put through it'. **1940** H. G. Wells *Babes in Darkling Wood* I. ii. 59, I am afraid we have put you through it, rather. **1959** P. McCutchan *Storm South* xii. 179 Evidently she'd been put through it in the interval, for she was crying bitterly. *a* **1976** A. Christie *Autobiogr.* (1977) viii. ii. 380 Mad as a hatter... My goodness, he must have put you through it now and again!

d. Also *to put* (a person) *through* (a school, college, etc.): to pay the cost of educating (a person). Also const. *ellipt.* Chiefly *N. Amer.*

1908 L. M. Montgomery *Anne of Green Gables* xxx. 338 I'd love to be a teacher. But..Mr Andrews says it cost him one hundred and fifty dollars to put Prissy through. **1943** *Deb. House of Commons* (Canada) 4 Feb. 161/2 Voluntary committees should be set up throughout Canada to pick out..boys and girls with a view to seeing that they are put through university. **1949** *Manch. Guardian Weekly* 27 Jan. 13/2 He..put himself through Emory College.

V. 35*. put across.

a. *to put it across* (a person): (*a*) to visit with retribution or punishment; to get even with.

1915 E. Wallace *Man who bought London* iv. 39 He won't half put it across you people. **1918** 'D. Valentine' *Man with Clubfoot* xxi. 309 When you..put it across 'der Stelze'..you settled a long outstanding account we had against him. **1923** M. Arlen *These Charming People* 238 There was something—well, indecent, in talking about a man dead nine years or more as though he were alive and still wanting to 'put it across' Antony at every turn. **1928** *Daily Mail* 6 Aug. 14/6 You are a master of mob tactics, but we will put it across you yet. **1929** Wodehouse *Mr. Mulliner Speaking* iv. 129 It was his intention to..confront his erring man-servant and put it across him in no uncertain manner. **1936** —— *Laughing Gas* xvi. 179, I was glad that I had put it across him. My pride was involved. There are some remarks which one does not forgive. **1978** *Rugby World* Apr. 38/2 Meyer was a sports nut who enjoyed nothing more than seeing his pupils put it across the golden youth of Eton and Winchester.

(*b*) to impose upon; to deceive, to delude; to convince by deceit.

1919 E. P. Oppenheim *Strange Case J. Thew* ii. vi. 235 'Well,' she exclaimed, 'he does put it across you, doesn't he?' **1923** H. C. Bailey *Mr. Fortune's Practice* i. 25, I say, you have put it across us in the Dean case. **1927** *Observer* 27 Mar. 6/4 It would be difficult for a greedy, hysterical, shameless, half-insane revivalist..to 'put it across' ever-increasing audiences. **1928** *Daily Express* 26 May 13/4 How Mother Cuckoo manages to 'put it across' certain inoffensive countryside birds. **1934** D. L. Sayers *Nine Tailors* 63, I hope our friend doesn't put anything across the good Rector. **1936** A. L. Rowse *Mr. Keynes & Labour Movement* 19 They succeeded in putting it across large sections of the middle classes that Labour's economics meant financial ruin. **1959** D. Eden *Sleeping Bride* xiv. 117 Don't Let Blandina put it across you. She isn't as ill as she pretends to be.

b. To make acceptable or effective; to convey the significance of. Cf. *across *prep.* 2 b.

1922 S. Anderson in R. L. White *S. Anderson/G. Stein* (1972) 15 The author had done a thing we Americans call 'putting something across'—the meaning being that she had, by a strange freakish performance, managed to attract attention to herself. **1923** H. Crane *Let.* 13 Apr. (1965) 131 This 'new consciousness' is something that takes a long while to 'put across'. **1927** M. Diver *But Yesterday* ii. xxiii. 263 The Exchange reported, 'No answer.' She was out—naturally; very busy putting it across! **1935** [see *copy-writer* s.v. *copy *sb.* C]. **1938** E. Bowen *Death of Heart* ii. iv. 247 Supposing she had a wish to be put across, who could do this for her better than Eddie could? **1943** W. S. Churchill *Second World War* (1951) IV. 839 We must be ready with our plans in the Eastern Mediterranean, and put it hard across Turkey to come in with us. **1943** J. S. Huxley *TVA* 129 The TVA was managing to put across a good deal of its plan. **1945** Mencken *Amer. Lang.* Suppl. I. 449 He [*sc.* C. T. Onions in 1936] noted that *to put it across, to get it across*, and *to put it over* were already 'firmly domiciled' in England... They really got their vogue in the United States as baseball terms. **1959** *Times Lit. Suppl.* 9 Jan. 15/3 Many readers, however, dazzled by Mr Graves's gifts as a prose entertainer, by his ability to put across Third Programme material with a Light Programme zing, may not give the poems the attention they deserve. **1970** 'D. Halliday' *Dolly & Cookie Bird* ii. 11 If you don't put yourself across, who'll do it for you? **1977** *Wandsworth Borough News* 7 Oct. 5/1 'Help police fight crime by helping yourself'—that is the message the police are trying to put across to the public.

c. *Baseball.* To pitch (a ball) directly over home plate.

1936 Mencken *Amer. Lang.* (ed. 4) 191 The history of baseball terms also deserves to be investigated, for many of them have entered the common speech of the country, *e.g.*..*to put it* (or *one*) *across* (or *over*). **1943** *Amer. Speech* XVIII. 106 If the pitcher throws a straight ball with good control, he is said..to *put it over*, to *put it across*, or to *put it right in there*. If he has speed, he may..*put over a fast one.*

38. put away.

f. (*a*) (Further examples.)

1924 [see *buffy *a.*[2]]. **1958** *Punch* 8 Oct. 469/1 The object of a wine-tasting is not to put the stuff away but to assess the relative values of a varied assortment of bottles. **1969** G. Greene *Trav. with my Aunt* i. viii. 76 Between us we can probably put away half a bottle of vodka. **1976** R. Hill *Another Death in Venice* i. 6 You look well enough..but you don't deserve to, not the way you were putting it away.

(*b*) (Earlier and later examples.) Also, to commit to an old people's home; to confine to a mental institution.

1872 G. P. Burnham *Mem. U.S. Secret Service* p. vii, *Put away* sent to the State Prison, after conviction. **1938** N. Marsh *Death in White Tie* xvi. 179 She became hopelessly insane... He arranged to have her put away. **1952** *Sun* (Baltimore) 2 June 14/3 There is less social pressure on people to make a place for grandparents at home, less feeling that it would be disgraceful to have them put away. **1971** S. Phillips *Death in Sheep's Clothing* v. 48 The mother is nearly frantic now, she is always afraid 'they' are going to 'put him away'. **1973** W. M. Duncan *Big Timer* xxi. 138 He was an inspector then. He put me away. **1974** P. M. Hubbard *Thirsty Evil* iv. 40, I said, 'But can it go on? Won't they have to—?' 'Put him away? I suppose so, if he gets worse.'

(*c*) (Further examples.)

1909 Galsworthy *Silver Box* i. iii. 32 *Mrs. Jones.* We've not got a home, sir. Of course we've been obliged to put away most of our things. *Barthwick.* Put your things away! You mean to—to—er—to pawn them? *Mrs. Jones.* Yes, sir, to put them away. **1926** Maines & Grant *Wise-Crack Dict.* 12/1 *Putting away his ice*, pawning his diamond.

(*d*) Delete *dial.* and add earlier and later examples. Also, to kill.

1588 Greene *Pandosto* f. A4[v], Deuising with himself a long time how he might best put away Egistus without suspition of treacherous murder, hee concluded at last to poyson him. **1847** A. Brontë *Agnes Grey* p. xiv, A reward, I should have greatly valued,..were he [*sc.* a dog] not now in danger of being 'put away'. **1920** E. Wallace *Daffodil Mystery* viii. 70 If I could only put her away for it! **1932** E. Waugh *Black Mischief* viii. 311 The dogs had long been rounded up and painlessly put away. **1971** E. Lemarchand *Death on Doomsday* ix. 137 I'd like to see old Peplow put away decently. **1974** M. Butterworth *Man in Sopwith Camel* xiii. 165 What kinda guy puts a buddy away for three lousy dollars?

39. put back.

g. *trans.* With personal object: to cost. *colloq.*

1909 *Dialect Notes* III. 402 'How much did that put you back?' 'Six dollars.' **1958** B. Ruck *Third Love Lucky* iv. 31 It puts you back five shillings for a quarter of an hour.

h. To return or 'plough back' (money, etc.). Cf. *plough *v.* 9 g.

1930 *Economist* 19 July 112/2 In view of Mr. Snowden's recent refusal to consider abatement of income tax on company reserves employed for re-equipment the recent tendency to reduce the proportion of earnings 'put back' is significant. **1931** *Ibid.* 11 July 59/1 The percentage 'put back into the business' during the past twelve months, 15·7 per cent., compares unfavourably with the figure of 18·6 per cent. ascertained for the twelve months ended June 30, 1930.

40. put by.

g. (Earlier example.)

1795 J. Woodforde *Diary* 31 July (1929) IV. 216 We had it [*sc.* the pork] taken up and put by for them against another Day.

41. put down.

a. (Further examples.)

1795 J. Woodforde *Diary* 29 June (1929) IV. 210 We were put down at the White Hart in Stall Street. **1841** Dickens *Let.* 2 May (1969) III. 276 'Mind Coachman' as the old ladies say 'you take me as fur as ever you go, and don't you put me down till you come to the very end of the journey.' **1933** [see *nitwit]. **1981** R. Barnard *Mother's Boys* iv. 48 This ruddy cough. It's the climate... They shouldn't have put people down in this climate.

d. (Further examples.) Now more usually, to disparage, to criticize forcefully, to humiliate.

1923 G. M. Trevelyan *Manin & Venetian Revolution* vi. 112 The principal speaker was Avesani, an eloquent and able lawyer who at once put Palffy down when he tried to speak in a tone of authority. **1958** *Amer. Speech* XXXIII. 225 When somone *puts* you *down* he criticizes you unfavorably, he *fluffs* you. **1961** Rigney & Smith *Real Bohemia* p. xvi, *Put down, to*, to humiliate, or tell off, or part company with someone. **1969** *Down Beat* 20 Mar. 31/3 It became fashionable to put him down as too much of a showman and not enough of a jazzman. **1972** D. Delman *Week to Kill* 86 So why did you put him down that way, in front of me? **1972** W. Labov *Language in Inner City* viii. 350 Sounding is only one of the many ways of putting someone down. **1977** Miller & Swift *Words & Women* p. x, We ourselves had for years been innocently using the words and grammatical forms that put our own sex down.

g. Delete 'Now chiefly *dial.*' and add further examples.

1936 W. Holtby *South Riding* iv. v. 253 Best have him [*sc.* a dog] put down, mercifully. **1942** G. Kersh *Nine Lives Bill Nelson* vii. 41 You could of put Bill down with a Humane Killer. **1958** *Times* 20 Nov. 3/1 An unwanted husband is as easily 'put down' as any other domestic pet. **1971** *Daily Tel.* 19 Aug. 3/6 Kim was ordered to be put down last year after he had bitten two people. **1977** *Guernsey Weekly Press* 21 July 4/7 One of the Jersey police dogs which entertained the large crowd at the recent open day of the local force at Les Vauxbelets has had to be put down.

j. (Earlier example.)

1791 J. Woodforde *Diary* 14 Oct. (1927) III. 306, I dont know that I ever eat a better Hare tho' we had put it down for an old one by skinning it.

m. *Cricket.* (*a*) To hit (a wicket), dislodging a bail. (*b*) With a batsman as subject: to stop or strike (a difficult delivery) without attempting to score. (*c*) With a bowler as subject: to deliver (a ball). (*d*) With a member of the fielding side as subject: to drop a catch.

17.. [In Dict. sense 41 a]. **1816** W. Lambert *Cricketer's Guide* (ed. 6) iii. 39 If the Striker should move of his ground, with an intention to run, he [*sc.* the wicket-keeper] must then do his best endeavour to put down the Wicket, which is called *stumping out.* **1841** in *Cricket Q.* (1967) V. i. 13 *Put down,..to put down a ball* or *the bowling*... Dean putting the bowling down. **1860** *Baily's Monthly Mag.* Oct. 41 With rare patience did he stop at home and skilfully put down the slows, rarely even attempting to hit them. **1893** R. Daft *Kings of Cricket* xv. 260, I have often seen little men put down with ease a bumping ball which many taller men would let hit their fingers. **1906** A. E. Knight *Compl. Cricketer* iv. 150 When bowlers or wicket-keepers neglect this precaution [of keeping behind the wicket], it may happen that the throw forces them back upon the wicket which they are unable to legitimately put down. **1924** A. C. Maclaren *Cricket Old & New* xiv. 140 On sticky wickets I should doubt if he [*sc.* J. T. Hearne] ever put down a bad ball. **1955** I. Peebles *Ashes* vii. 67 At 26 he had another bit of luck when Hole put him down at first slip.

n. *U.S.* To preserve (food).

1843 *Knickerbocker* XXI. 436 Daniel Gilbert's property..cut up very handsomely, (to borrow the common figure upon such occasions, derived from the putting down of pork for the winter). **1881** S. O. Jewett *Country By-Ways* 40 He's put down a kag of excellent beef. **1889** R. T. Cooke *Steadfast* xxi. 229 Who'll put down my pork and beef as Almiry did?

o. *Aeronaut.* To land (an aircraft or spacecraft). Also *intr.* (with the craft or the pilot as subject).

1933 C. K. Stewart *Speech of Amer. Airman* (Univ. of Akron thesis) 85 *Put down, to*, to land. **1939** *War Pictorial* 6 Oct. 7/3 Orders are to 'put down' the machine on the two-acre landing-deck of a naval aircraft-carrier. **1946** *Sun* (Baltimore) 21 Dec. 17/1 The badly damaged C-47 landed at Phillips Field, while the Eastern Airliner put down at Washington. **1958** 'N. Shute' *Rainbow & Rose* i. 14 They put her [*sc.* a freighter] down at Launceston and taxied in. **1972** T. Lilley *K Section* xl. 183 Can you get a chopper..to bring in the District Commissioner? ..It can put down on the padang in front of the police station. **1976** 'L. Black' *Healthy Way to Die* ii. 17 The helicopter put down, the engine cut, the rotors gradually slowed. **1976** *New Scientist* 24 June 683/1 If there are no hitches the Viking lander should put him down early on 5 July.

p. *Jazz.* To establish (a rhythm or a style); to play or perform. Chiefly *U.S.*

1944 D. Burley *Orig. Handbk. Harlem Jive* 145 *Put down*, say, perform, describe, do. **1952** B. Ulanov *Hist. Jazz in Amer.* (1958) vi. 67 He put down a good walking beat. **1953** *Down Beat* 11 Feb. 16/3 Those old masters have really put something down, and it'll be a long, long time before those basic sounds change. **1968** *Ibid.* 7 Mar. 19/3 But the *tenor* saxophonists..reasoned that Coleman had been away from the source too long to know the hot licks that Harlem was putting down now.

q. *U.S. slang.* To reject or abandon.

1953 D. Wallop *Night Light* xii. 135 You really ought to put school down and play full-time. **1959** L. Lipton *Holy Barbarians* 102, I put that scene [*sc.* domesticity] down when I got divorced. **1964** *Amer. Folk Music Occasional* i. 62 My mother was the mother of all those kids and my father look like he wanted to put her down, leave her. **1966** E. Liebow *Behavior & Values of Streetcorner Negro Men* (Ph.D. thesis, Catholic Univ.) v. 111 Richard..once 'put down' a woman of thirty or so, foregoing the pleasures of her automobile as well, because 'She's too old'.

r. To replace (the receiver of a telephone), usu. abruptly, in the course of a call; to 'hang up' (the telephone) *on* someone. Freq. in phr. *to put the phone down.*

1966 A. E. Lindop *I start Counting* xxi. 263 He picked up Leonie's telephone..and got through to our flat... When he put down the phone he picked up Leonie. **1970** 'M. Carroll' *Bait* v. 67 He put the phone down on me before I could say a word. **1972** T. Lilley *K Section* xl. 187 'You know where I am now; keep in touch.' Carter put the phone down. **1975** C. Fremlin *Long Shadow* iv. 33, I was..so startled, and shocked. I..just put the phone down. **1979** K. M. Peyton *Marion's Angels* v. 77 Geoff put down the receiver and explained gloomily to Marion what was expected of them.

s. To put (a child) to bed.

1968 C. Armstrong *Balloon Man* i. 5 Johnny bounced out of his healthy three-and-a-half-year-old sleep at 6 a.m. The trouble was she had to put him down so early. **1971** D. Devine *Dead Trouble* iv. 33 Sarah Caine was putting Timmy down for his afternoon nap when the telephone rang. **1978** P. Niesewand *Underground Connection* 152 'Is the baby asleep?' 'I think so. She went off very quickly when I put her down.'

42. put forth.

g. (*b*) (Later example.)

1924 R. Macaulay *Orphan Island* xx. 262 Like some lovely fruit that puts forth, ripens, and tumbles, overmellow, to the ground.

44. put in.

b. Also *spec.* in *Cricket,* (*a*) to send (a member of one's team) in as batsman.

1823 *Lady's Mag.* July 390/2 David Willis, who, injudiciously put in first..was bowled out, without a stroke, from actual nervousness. **1833** [in Dict.]. **1888** A. G. Steel in Steel & Lyttelton *Cricket* iv. 200 It is as well not to put in two hard-hitters together if possible, as it often tends to make one hit against the other.

(*b*) To cause (a team, usu. the opposing one) to take first innings.

1836 *New Sporting Mag.* Oct. 360 Eton having won the toss, put Winchester in. **1859** *All Year Round* 23 July 305/2 The town won the toss for innings, and put their men in first. **1900** P. F. Warner *Cricket in Many Climes* 212 Lord Hawke, on winning the toss, put the other side in. **1976** J. Snow *Cricket Rebel* 78 It was to be his [*sc.* Mike Denness's] last as captain, after putting the Australians in and then losing the match.

g. Also *to put in the leather* = *to put the boot in* s.v. *boot *sb.*³ 1 b.

1943 J. Phelan *Lett. from Big House* ii. 30 Almost before he reached the ground the party piled on him. Some punched and cursed, others..'put in the leather'. **1952** M. Allingham *Tiger in Smoke* iii. 57 Someone has been 'putting in the leather'... That was done with a boot.

h. Delete ?*Obs.* and add later U.S. examples.

1855 *Harper's Mag.* Oct. 602/1 The unfortunate victim hollowed out, 'Oh, Moses, if you have any love for your brother, *put in,* and divide this fight!' **1901** W. N. Harben *Westerfelt* 290 You wus tellin' me..'at the lan'an' house wus in yore name an' her'n, an' 'at I had no right to put in.

j. (Further example.)

1972 J. Aiken *Butterfly Picnic* i. 9 The hours I have put in hanging about for her on station platforms.

l. To inform against; to 'frame'; to secure the conviction of (a person); to send to prison. Also *transf. slang.*

1922 A. Wright *Colt from Country* 153 'I might have a chance with the girl again.' 'After what you did to put her in?' laughed the detective. 'I like your hide.' **1951** S. Mackenzie *Dead Men Rising* i. 52 Nothing would give me greater pleasure than to put you in, only that's about the one thing I've never done in my life. **1958** D. Niland *Call me when Cross turns Over* vii. 174 Don't put me in. Don't try to hang anything on me. **1966** P. Cowan *Seed* iv. 106, I suppose when they make you a prefect you'll put us in.

m. To let in (the clutch of a motor vehicle).

1928 J. Galsworthy *Swan Song* iii. iv. 246 'This is where I put in my clutch,' she said, 'as they say in the 'bloods'!' **1943** A. Ransome *Picts & Martyrs* xvii. 167 He put in his clutch and drove off. **1976** 'E. McBain' *Guns* (1977) vii. 174 Colley puts in the clutch and manipulates the gear shift.

45. put off.

h. (Later example.) Also, to cause (someone) to be mistaken.

1918 A. Bennett *Pretty Lady* xxii. 146 'That's not *you*, Frankie!' said the Major with a start of recognition... 'Yes, sir,' said Molder... 'It was the red hat put me off,' the Major explained.

o. (Further examples.) Now usu., to offend, to disconcert; to cause (a person) to lose interest in or enthusiasm for something.

1909 F. Barclay *Rosary* ix. 77, I am so afraid of her putting Dal off. He is so fastidious. **1928** *Observer* 19 Feb. 6/3 The prefatory note, with its apparently exaggerated claim, rather put me off. **1932** 'E. M. Delafield' *Thank Heaven Fasting* i. ii. 34 A man is very quickly put off, if he thinks that a girl hasn't even taken the trouble to remember what he looks like. **1949** D. Smith *I capture Castle* ix. 134 He'll end by putting them off us. **1973** L. Meynell *Thirteen Trumpeters* v. 80 I'm in grave danger of becoming virtuous. To see those acres of fat Germanic flesh spread out by the pool is enough to put me off for life.

46. put on.

a. (Further theatrical examples.)

1924 A. Huxley *Let.* 29 Apr. (1969) 229 Playfair, who is producing it for the 300 club performance, seems to think that it will make a very good entertainment and has some hopes of getting it put on for a run. **1941** L. A. G. Strong *Bay* 192 A couple of new plays that some amateurs were putting on. **1977** A. Morice *Scared to Death* i. 7 Presumably, if his play is any good, this David Winter would have put it on anyway?

e. (Further examples.) Also, to impose on, to take advantage of; to puzzle or deceive intentionally. *colloq.*

1949 D. Smith *I capture Castle* xiv. 290 'We shall be ashamed of our callousness if father really is going off his head.' 'He isn't—he's putting it on or something.' **1958** *Times* 12 Nov. 3/3 Miss Mollie Sugden's wife has got into the habit of 'putting on' her husband because the husband..rather enjoys being 'put on'. **1958** *Amer. Speech* XXXIII. 225 When a hipster *puts* someone *on* he is pulling his leg (perhaps putting him on a stage to be laughed at). **1960** Willmott & Young *Family & Class in London Suburb* x. 111 'Some of the parents at the school seem to put it on a bit,' said Mr. Prior, a bank manager whose children go to a local preparatory school, 'you do get a bit of the old blue-blooded attitude among them.' **1964** H. E. F. Donohue *Conversations with Nelson Algren* xi. 272 She's putting me on and I'm putting her on, and she marvels at her good fortune in meeting me, I'll marvel at my good fortune in meeting her. **1966** T. Pynchon *Crying of Lot 49* vi. 167 Has it ever occurred to you, Oedipa, that somebody's putting you on? That this is all a hoax? **1967** 'G. Bagby' *Corpse Candle* (1968) x. 133 Greg was forever putting people on... He'd do it just for fun. The poetry was his way of putting the English faculty on. **1977** *Sci. Amer.* Dec. 17/3 Persi's brief description of the Rockwell prediction method was so outlandish that I assumed he was putting me on.

f. (*a*) Also, *to put it on.*

1933 E. Hemingway *Winner take Nothing* (1934) 35 It's terrible..the way I put it on. **1967** A. Diment *Dolly Dolly Spy* vii 98 She had put on a lot of weight... I could see her checking herself off against Veronica—who has definitely been putting it on. **1971** 'J. J. Marric' *Gideon's Art* i. 11 'You both take sugar?'..'Not for me,' Slater said, slapping his rounded belly. 'I'm putting it on again.'

(*c*) (Earlier and later examples.)

1868 *Baily's Mag.* Sept. 246 The last wicket fell for 689, six players thus putting on nearly as many hundred runs. **1921** *Glasgow Herald* 17 Oct. 13/7 In the second half P. R. Johnstone scored, and afterwards G. A. Able put on another for Stepps. **1975** [see *outfield *sb.* 3 a]. **1977** *World of Cricket Monthly* June 32/1 Haroon and Imran put on 34.

(*d*) Of a taxi-driver: to join (the end of a rank).

1930 A. Armstrong *Taxi* xii. 164 'Putting on' is the taxi man's expression for coming on at the end of the rank. A driver will say he 'put on sixth cab at the so-and-so', meaning he came on the so-and-so rank when there were only five other cabs there. **1939** H. Hodge *Cab, Sir?* 22, I decide to put on a hotel rank.

l. (*a*) (Earlier examples.)

1836 *New Sporting Mag.* XI. 360 Mr. Paterson's bowling was again very reasonably put on. **1859** *All Year Round* I. 306/1 They put on bowler after bowler,.. but they could not get us out.

(*b*) In slang phr. *to put it on* (a person), to charge to (someone else).

1895 *People* 6 Jan. 16/5 Arter all the brass..was nearly all gone, Selby says, 'I'll go round to the Mug agin, and put it on him (make him pay) for another bit.' **1944** L. Glassop *We were Rats* i. 6 I'll have a pint at the Royal tomorrer and put it on the blonde.

(*c*) *colloq.* To draw the attention of or introduce (a person) *to* a particular person or thing.

1895 *N.Y. Dramatic News* 12 Oct. 5/3 Mr. Jack is always a newspaper man's friend, and only too pleased to put one on 'to a good thing' in the shape of news. **1901** O. Wister in *Lippincott's Monthly Mag.* Aug. 199 We're awfully obliged for the way you are putting us on to this. **1902** H. G. Wells *Let.* 2 Sept. in H. Wilson *Arnold Bennett & H. G. Wells* (1960) 83 Accept I pray you my warmest thanks. And also for putting me on to that quite brilliantly done and (as Dr. Rob^{n} Nicoll would say) most unpleasant book, *Le Journal d'une Femme de Chambre.* **1924** A. Christie *Poirot Investigates* vii. 165 A friend of mine in the City put me on to a very good thing, and..I have money to burn. **1926** H. J. Laski *Let.* 21 Feb. in *Holmes-Laski Lett.* (1953) II. 833 He also put me on to a new American life of Godwin. **1949** A. Christie *Crooked House* xii. 93, I could put you on to a couple of the tame psychiatrists who do jobs for us. **1977** C. McCarry *Secret Lovers* iii. 33 He put us on to some people who turned out to be..useful.

47. put out.

b. (*b*) Also *fig.*

1937 C. Carmer *Hurricane's Children* 105 He wore waistcoats that would put your eyes out.

(*d*) (Earlier example.)

1780 J. Woodforde *Diary* 15 July (1924) I. 289 John had a fall lately..and put out his shoulder bone, being a little merry.

c. Also in *Baseball,* to cause (a batter or runner) to be 'out'; in *Boxing,* to knock out.

1845 in *Appleton's Ann. Cycl.* XXV. 77/2 A runner can not be put out in making one base, when a balk is made by the pitcher. **1910** J. Driscoll *Ringcraft* iii. 84, I have..not infrequently put opponents 'out' with a blow on the neck. **1912** C. Mathewson *Pitching in a Pinch* 107 Snodgrass was put out trying to get to third base.

d. For 'Now *rare* or Obs.' read: Now only in slang use, to kill (a person). (Perh. a *fig.* use of sense e (*b*).)

1917 W. Owen *Let.* 25 Apr. (1967) 452 For twelve days we lay in holes, where at any moment a shell might put us out. **1935** E. Wallace *Mouthpiece* xvii. 225 That's the offer the gentleman made—five hundred quid to put you out and keep me mouth shut. **1975** 'E. Lathen' *By Hook or by Crook* xii. 114 The minute his stomach started acting up, he would've been yelling for the cops. He had to be put out fast.

f. (*e*) (Earlier example.)

1861 T. Hughes *Tom Brown at Oxford* III. xvi. 290 Don't you lose heart because he won't put himself out for you.

i. Delete 'Now *rare.*' and add further examples. Also, to broadcast.

1938 H. Nicolson *Diary* 20 Feb. (1966) 323 On the late news it is put out that Eden has resigned. **1965** G. Melly *Owning Up* xi. 135 His version of 'Rock Island Line'..was put out as a single and rose to be top of the Hit Parade. **1966** *Listener* 13 Jan. 78/1 Earlier this year Midland Region and Anne Owen put out..an unusually direct and perceptive investigation of present-day standards of honesty. **1978** *Times* 26 July 4/2 The BBC says that whatever it films and tapes it is entitled to put out.

k. (*b*) *intr.* Of a river or natural formation: to extend or stretch (in relation to a specified point). *U.S.* See also sense 8 c in Dict.

1755 [in Dict., sense 8 c]. **1840** C. F. Hoffman *Greyslaer* I. 116 A ledge of bald rock to the left yonder..puts out from the ridge. **1878** J. H. Beadle *Western Wilds* 311 Commenced the ascent of the Buckskin, a low range of partially-wooded hills, putting out across the plateau nearly to the Colorado.

m. (*a*) (Earlier example of sense 'to plant out'.) Also to send out (a domestic pet) for exercise, etc.

1851 Mrs. Gaskell *Let.* 7 Apr. (1966) 149 We are sowing very few annuals this year..& relying on putting out the greenhouse things for a summer show. **1917** D. Canfield *Understood Betsy* ii. 46 'Mother, did you put Shep out?' **1925** Wodehouse *Carry On, Jeeves!* ii. 40 When he has put the cat out and locked up the office for the night, he just relapses into a state of coma. **1974** *Listener* 10 Oct. 462/1 The BBC's nightly *Campaign Report*..at an hour when most voters are putting the cat out. **1977** 'E. Crispin' *Glimpses of Moon* viii. 128, I was snug in bed... And then..I remembered..that I ought to have put Sal out... She barks rather a lot.

(*c*) (Earlier and further examples.) Also, to place (articles) for collection by tradesmen.

1653 R. Verney *Let.* in M. M. Verney *Mem.* (1894) III. iv. 112, I will keepe but one woeman kind, who must wash my small Linnen (bed & board linnen shall bee put out). **1873** A. J. Munby *Diary* 18 Feb. in D. Hudson *Munby* (1972) 322, I should like very well to clean his boots..and I said to Tarrant 'If you put 'em out I'll clean 'em with pleasure, along with mine.' **1975** 'D. Jordan' *Black Account* v. 33 It was late; Sue was in her kimono and putting out milk bottles.

n. *intr.* Of a woman: to offer oneself for sexual intercourse. Also const. *for* (a man). *slang.*

1947 *Horizon* Sept. 202 'Maybe all the whores'll be puttin' out free on New Year's!' Muggleston shouted. **1961** J. Heller *Catch-22* xiii. 131 The beautiful.. countess and her beautiful..daughter-in-law, both of whom would put out only for Nately, who was too shy to want them, and for Aarfy, who was too stuffy to take them and tried to dissuade them from ever putting out for anyone but their husbands. **1975** D. Lodge *Changing Places* vi. 232 If she won't put out the men will accuse her of being bourgeois and uptight. **1977** I. Shaw *Beggarman, Thief* iii. i. 178 Sometimes those plain-looking little dolls are powerhouses when it comes to putting out. **1978** M. Puzo *Fools Die* vi. 80 He was especially challenged if a girl had a reputation for only putting out for guys she really liked.

48. put out of.

d. *to put out of misery* (examples).

1792 J. Woodforde *Diary* 16 May (1927) III. 351 My poor old Horse, Punch..was shot by Ben this Morning to put him out of his Misery. **1855** C. Kingsley *Westward Ho!* III. xii. 353 Writhing in his great horror, he called to Cary to kill him and put him out of his misery. **1911** *Maclean's Mag.* Oct. 286/1 Get the gun, for God's sake, an' put me out of my misery. **1923** G. Atherton *Black Oxen* xxvi. 145 Tell them all about it... Put them out of their misery. **1957** D. Robins *Noble One* v. 59 Then I'll *have* to stalk him and put him out of his misery. **1975** A. Christie *Curtain* xi. 113 We were talking of euthanasia... 'Does the person most concerned ever wish to 'put himself out of his misery', as we say?'

49. put over.

b. Delete † *Obs.* and add later examples.

1871 'Mark Twain' *Lett. to Publishers* (1967) 55 If you can without fail issue the book on the 15th of May—putting the Sketch book over till another time. **1926** J. Black *You can't Win* xxii. 343 We went to court again the next day, but were put over twenty-four hours on the plea of the police that witnesses were on their way from Canada. **1978** H. Kemelman *Thursday the Rabbi walked Out* (1979) xxx. 145 The only thing to do is to put it over for a week.

i. *to put it* (*all*) *over* (*on*), to excel or surpass (in a particular enterprise); to defeat or trounce.

1898 F. P. Dunne *Mr. Dooley in Peace & War* (1899) 172 I've seen..Fitz beat Corbett; an', if I live to cillybrate me goold-watch-an'-chain jubilee, I may see some wan put it all over Fitz. **1905** J. London *Let.* 24 June (1966) 175 If Hillquit..didn't put it all over Bierce—I'll quit thinking at all. **1944** *Living off Land* viii. 155 So far as bushcraft is concerned, he [*sc.* the Aboriginal] could put it all over you. **1973** *Time Out* 2 Mar. 15/2 The teachers..only had time for the Thomas boys; we were treated like shit. So we started throwing our weight around, we put it over on them.

j. To make acceptable or effective; to convey or communicate; to present convincingly; = *to put across* (sense 35 b above).

1912 R. A. Foley in *Mag. Maker* Dec. 8 He saw his opportunity and he 'put it over'. **1914** G. Atherton *Perch of Devil* ii. 298 You don't go into any business.. and put it over without running the risk of being shot. **1928** *Daily Express* 18 Apr. 11/2 Is it true that you wanted a star name to put the play over? *Ibid.* 11 July 9/3 On the screen you..are fascinated by the extraordinary way in which he 'puts himself over'. **1929** J. B. Priestley *Good Companions* ii. i. 252 He's a find. Works hard, got personality, puts it over all the time. **1931** F. L. Allen *Only Yesterday* viii. 213 The president emeritus of Harvard had had no professional talent to put over his funeral in a big way. **1935** *Motion Picture* Nov. 6/2 Clark Gable plays one of those powerful, he-men rôles in which he glories. And he puts it over with a bang! **1958** *Times* 1 Sept. 3/6 About Mr. Presley's ability to 'put over' a song in his own particular way there can be no two opinions. **1966** *Listener* 17 Mar. 380/2, I did not know how to select what I wanted to do or really put over emotion. **1978**

D. MURPHY *Place Apart* iii. 59 They blamed 'that Paisley'... They agreed with his anti-ecumenism..but they didn't like the way he put it over.

k. To impose (something false or deceptive) *on* a person; to best or upstage (someone); to achieve by deceit.

1912 J. SANDILANDS *Western Canad. Dict.*, *Put one over on* him, catching him with the latest puzzling by-word or smart saying... A Winnipeg newspaper recently put up the heading, 'Put one over on Bernard Shaw'. **1914** 'HIGH JINKS, JR.' *Choice Slang* 17 *Put one over, to*: to beat by strategy, 'to hornswoggle'. **1916** H. L. WILSON *Somewhere in Red Gap* i. 19 Funny, the way the little man tried to put it over on us, letting on he was just puzzled—not really bothered, as he plainly was. **1923** R. D. PAINE *Comrades of Rolling Ocean* viii. 130 Who calls it a crime to put one over on the Custom House flatties? **1928** A. S. W. ROSENBACH *Books & Bidders* 117 One of the greatest hoaxes ever planned was put over by a French forger. **1945** C. WILLIAMS *All Hallows' Eve* 35 A fellow who's put it over all America and bits of England is likely to know where he is. **1958** *People* 4 May 8/3, I cannot see her letting any of the Italian or French sex-pots put one over on her. **1967** *Listener* 5 Jan. 37/1 Christmas, after all, is essentially an 'old' festival (however much Batman may seem to have put one over on Santa Claus this year). **1972** WODEHOUSE *Pearls, Girls, & Monty Bodkin* x. 150 It's low. It isn't done. You can't do the dirty on a business competitor just to stop him from putting it over on you in a business deal. **1976** *Church Times* 30 July 7/2 She may have been fleeced in Florence, robbed in Ravenna, grossly overcharged in Ostia..; but *Baedeker* at least has not tried to put one over on her. **1979** *Jrnl. R. Soc. Arts* CXXVII. 650/1 We are not appearing to put something over on the public.

l. *Baseball.* = *put across* (sense 35*c above).
1936, **1943** [see sense 35* c above].

49*. put there.

In imp. phr. *put it* (or *her*, etc.) *there*: shake hands! *colloq.* (orig. *U.S.*).

1898 R. HUGHES *Lakerim Athletic Club* i. 3 'Put her there, Punk; you're a white man!' Tug had to reconsider; and the two captains shook hands. **1915** A. CONAN DOYLE *Valley of Fear* II. i. 154 'Put it there,' he said. A hand-grip passed between the two. **1925** *New Yorker* 20 June 14/1 Well, I'll be damned. Glad ta see ya. Put it there. **1931** O. NASH *Hard Lines* 50 Put it there, Mr. Linthicum, put it there! **1947** WODEHOUSE *Full Moon* vii. 168 'I'm engaged!'... 'Well, I'm dashed,' said Freddie. 'Put it there, pardner.' So beaming was his smile, so cordial his handshake, that Tipton found his last doubts removed. **1970** *Private Eye* 13 Mar. 16 Glad to meetcha! Put it there!

50. put through.

b. Delete 'Chiefly U.S.' and add later examples.

1929 T. H. BURNHAM *Engineering Econ.* xv. 199 Rush orders are difficult to put through, even in well-organized works. **1966** 'J. HACKSTON' *Father clears Out* 54 Put through a second lot of tailings, but not from the same place.

c. (Examples.)

1891 F. C. ALLSOP *Telephones* vi. 98 In an exchange system any of the stations wishing to communicate with any other must first ring up the central station, and request to be 'put through' to the other station. **1916** 'BOYD CABLE' *Action Front* 86 Ask to be put through to the inquiry office. **1928** D. L. SAYERS *Unpleasantness at Bellona Club* viii. 59 That phone-call you asked me to trace..was put through..from a public call-box. **1949** A. CHRISTIE *Crooked House* xvii. 139 He lifted the receiver—listened and then said: 'Put her through.' **1973** J. M. WHITE *Garden Game* 182, I found the number and dialled Whitehall... I was put through to the Home Office.

d. *Econ.* (See quot. 1959.)

1959 *Economist* 21 Mar. 1099/1 Where the market is narrow, as it can be for example in rubber and tea shares, the jobbing system may not work either smoothly or perfectly. The brokers in these shares then find it convenient to 'marry' the buying and selling orders. The normal practice has been for such a deal to be 'put through' a jobber at a very small turn for him... The stock exchange council..has now proposed a change in the rules governing these 'put through' deals. **1978** *Times* 17 Nov. 21/8 The principle of the put-through deal involves the broker finding a buyer for a large line of stock which one of his clients has on offer. The jobber then puts the shares through his books at a mutually agreed price but does not necessarily make such a good turn on it as he would if he was buying them from the broker and selling them on himself.

51. put to.

f. (Earlier example.)

1791 J. WOODFORDE *Diary* 8 Aug. (1927) III. 291 We were rather put to for a Dinner in so short a time however we did our best and gave them some Beans and Bacon, mince Veal, Neck of Mutton [etc.].

52*. put under.

a. *trans.* To kill or bury (a person).

1879 R. A. STERNDALE *Afghan Knife* II. vii. 75, I wanted to see your bonny face once more, in case these blackguards put me under. **1958** C. WATSON *Coffin, scarcely Used* iii. 27 There'll be some pressure to have him put under without any unseemly inquiries.

b. To render unconscious by means of an anaesthetic or by hypnosis.

1962 L. PAYNE *Too Small for his Shoes* v. 94 Given him something to put him under. Be right as rain. **1963** E. LANHAM *Monkey on Chain* xiv. 207 He put Dora under and learned conclusively that she went down to Bleecker Street. **1971** P. O'DONNELL *Impossible Virgin* xii. 235 'Is Willie going to give the ether?' 'Yes. I'll put her under myself.'

53. put up.

a. (*c*) (Earlier and later examples.)

1848 TROLLOPE *Kellys & O'Kellys* II. ii. 46 Brien was saddled..and Pat was put up. **1953** E. COXHEAD *Midlanders* i. 32 Don't suppose you've yet been on horseback, miss? We'll put you up and see how you like it.

(*d*) (Earlier examples.)

1838 DICKENS *Let.* Nov. (1965) I. 465, I don't know what they put up at the Theatre for that night. **1852** *Punch* 11 Dec. 257/1 The entertainments this week have been of a slight and desultory character, the management being..glad to 'put up' anything they could get.

(*e*) In imp. phr. *put them* (or *'em*) *up*: (i) a challenge to raise the fists before a fight; (ii) a command to raise the hands above the head. *colloq.*

1923 E. WALLACE *Captains of Souls* xliv. 240 I'm going to give you the damnedest lacing you ever had..put 'em up! **1937** PARTRIDGE *Dict. Slang* 672/1 *Put 'em up!*, raise your arms!: from ca. 1860... Put up your fists!..late C. 19–20.

(*f*) To place (a military or other decoration) on one's uniform or other clothes.

1959 M. GILBERT *Blood & Judgement* xiv. 147 He could easily have put up a medal ribbon he wasn't entitled to. **1961** E. WAUGH *Unconditional Surrender* 5 He had been trained in the first batch of temporary officers..had twice put up captain's stars and twice removed them; their scars were plainly visible on his shoulder straps.

g. Also *to put up a fight*, to acquit oneself well in a contest. Also *fig.*

1919 H. CRANE *Let.* 7 Mar. (1965) 13 Mrs. Brooks is afflicted with consumption against which she is doubtless putting up a strenuous Scientific fight. **1928** —— *Let.* 27 Mar. (1965) 320, I put up quite a fight, but neither of us were in much condition.

i. Delete † *Obs.* and add later examples.

1912 GALSWORTHY *Justice* II, in *Plays* II. 59 *Judge.* Call the next case. *Clerk of Assize.* (To a warder) Put up John Booley. **1949** F. SARGESON *I saw in my Dream* 75 Anyhow he'd been sacked and put up for it, and he'd only got six months probation. **1960** 'M. UNDERWOOD' *Cause of Death* xii. 152 The clerk of the court..said in a loud clear voice, 'Put up David Lucas.' **1964** J. PRESCOTT *Case for Court* ix. 175 Mr. Rose asked for the Sorensens to be put up at once so that the Chief Constable might make his application... The two accused were brought up into the dock. **1976** *Howard Jrnl.* XV. I. 42 There are a number of minor errors:..On p. 20 the prisoner is sitting in the dock before he has been put up.

j. (*a*) (Further examples.) Also, to propose for an honour or award.

1840 LYTTON *Money* (ed. 4) I. 30 Shall I put you up at the clubs? **1967** N. MARSH *Death at Dolphin* vi. 154 We'll put you up for the Police Medal. **1971** J. R. L. ANDERSON *Reckoning in Ice* vii. 143 He was..a sailor, and I'd put him up for the Mariners. We met at the club occasionally.

(*c*) (Further example.)

1969 'R. GORDON' *Facts of Life* 140, I spend all my time putting up for jobs. In the last six months, I've been to Liverpool, Exeter, Oxford, and York.

m. (*b*) Delete *rare* and add further examples.

1909 P. A. VAILE *Mod. Golf* xvi. 211, I am directing my manufacturers' energies to producing the exact amount of marking required [on a golf ball]... I should not have troubled with it had it not been 'put up to me', as the American would say. **1913** F. H. BURNETT *T. Tembarom* xxiv. 306 'Oh, well, I just put it up to them.'..'You mean that you made them feel that they alone were responsible.' **1924** GALSWORTHY *White Monkey* I. viii. 58 I'll put it up to Mr. Desert; if he speaks for you, perhaps it may move Mr. Danby.

n. (*a*) (Later examples.)

1916 *Daily Colonist* (Victoria, B.C.) 2 July 4/5 Sidney women, under Mrs. Wheeler, have started putting up jam for the boys at the front. **1924** T. S. P. STRANGEWAYS *Technique of Tissue Culture* 39 To put up the cultures take the tissues or organs which have been set aside for cultivation and cut up into suitably sized fragments. *Ibid.* 73 If more cultures are desired, put them up in a similar way. **1951** [see *MID *a.*, *sb.*[1], and *adv.* 1c]. **1954** J. R. R. TOLKIEN *Fellowship of Ring* I. iv. 107 He produced a large basket from under the seat... 'Mrs. Maggot put this up for Mr. Baggins, with her compliments.' **1970** *Nature* 19 Dec. 1139/2 When either bone marrow or circulating blood cells from humans, mice or rats are put up in culture in a freshly made medium containing calf serum, few if any colonies of haematopoietic cells grow. **1971** R. THOMAS *Backup Men* v. 34 He's helping me put up some marmalade.

(*e*) (Earlier example.)

1865 'MARK TWAIN' in *N.Y. Sat. Press* 18 Nov. 249/2 And so the feller..put up his forty dollars along with Smiley's.

(*f*) In imp. phr. *put up or shut up*: defend yourself or be silent. *colloq.* (chiefly *U.S.*).

1878 F. H. HART *Sazerac Lying Club* 167 'P.U. or S.U.' means put up or shut up, doesn't it? **1884** *National Police Gaz.* (U.S.) 26 Apr. 1 (*caption*) Put up, shut up, or get! **1889** 'MARK TWAIN' *Connecticut Yankee* xl. 512 This was a plain case of 'put up, or shut up'. **1952** *Manch. Guardian Weekly* 1 May 3/4 The old alternatives will be revived: put up or shut up—get out or get on to the Yalu and beyond. **1976** *Billings* (Montana) *Gaz.* 17 June 6-c/1 It wasn't a case of put up or shut up because the money was voted as a sincere effort to clean up the mess.

q. (*c*) Sense (*b*) used without following *to* and adjunct: to annoy, to vex (a person).

1930 H. G. WELLS *Autocracy of Mr. Parham* IV. i. 266 This cheap Mussolini at Westminster is putting us up some! **1960** T. MCLEAN *Kings of Rugby* xi. 160 Hill's protest was more likely to restore the true spirit of the game than..some other method of retaliation by the Canterbury men who believed that they were being put up.

r. (Earlier example.)

1699 M. LISTER *Journey to Paris* 25 There are an infinite number of Busto's of the Grand Monarque every where put up by the Common People.

u. To judge, regard, or assess (a person, situation, etc.) in a particular way. *U.S.*

1877 'MARK TWAIN' in *Atlantic Monthly* Nov. 590/1 Would you like to have me explain that thing to you?.. Now, this is the way I put it up. **1880** —— *Tramp Abroad* xx. 192 'Didn't I put you up right?' 'Oh, yes.' 'Sho! I spotted you for *my* kind the minute I heard your clack.' **1895** *Century Mag.* Sept. 674/2 And Jack says to himself, 'Well,..I done what I could! What is to be will be.' That's about the way I put it up.

VI. 54. a. *to put the boot in*: see *BOOT *sb.*[3] 1b; *to put the fear of God into*: see *FEAR *sb.* 3e; *to put next to*: see *NEXT *a.* 13c; *not to put it past someone*: see *PAST *prep.* 3b; *to put* (a person's) *pot on*: see *POT *sb.*[1] 13k; *to put the wind up* (a person): see WIND *sb.*[1] 10b; *to put* (one) *wise* (*to*): see WISE *a.* 3b (*b*).

put, *ppl. a.* Add: **put-together** (52: in quots. 52d); **put-upon** (23f (*b*)); also *absol.* as *sb.* *to stay put*: see STAY *v.*[1] 6b.

1950 in E. C. Richards *Diary of E. R. Chudleigh* 23 Such a 'put-together' mob of wild cattle required at least six to eight experienced stockmen. **1957** J. KEROUAC *On Road* (1958) 21 Country boys in a put-together jalopy. **1970** *Times* 2 June 8/2 The essential of the put together look which stays put is a belt. **1920** *Quill* (N.Y.) Nov 12 Lulu is the ideal poor relation of fiction, the put-upon slavey. **1966** M. KELLY *Dead Corse* iv. 53 Those who follow unquestioning, docile, simple... The put-upon. **1976** *Listener* 6 May 586/2 Juliet Mills was very good as Cady's put-upon wife. **1980** G. MITCHELL *Uncoffin'd Clay* iii. 32 Having to cook..a sensitive charwoman would regard as victimisation or, in her parlance, a put-upon.

put-. Add: **put-away** *Lawn Tennis* and *Rackets* = *KILL *sb.* 2c; also *attrib.*; **put-back** (later example); **put-down,** (*a*) an act of putting (a person) down, a snub; also *attrib.*; (*b*) *attrib.*, with reference to the act of alighting from a vehicle; **put-in,** (*a*) *U.S. colloq.*, one's turn to speak, one's affair; (*b*) the act of putting the ball into a scrum in rugby football; **put-out,** (*a*) (earlier and later examples); *U.S.*, an annoyance or inconvenience (?*obs.*); **put-through,** (*a*) a measure of the number of persons or objects which have been put through a process; (*b*) *Econ.*, a financial transaction in which a broker arranges the sale and the purchase of shares simultaneously; also *attrib.* Cf. *PUT-ON *sb.*

1969 *New Yorker* 14 June 75/1 He intercepts, and sends a light and graceful putaway past Graebner, down the line. **1977** *Ibid.* 25 July 70/2 Connors..also carried off the next three games on the strength of some fine, deep approaches and remarkable put-away volleys. **1913** D. H. LAWRENCE *Love Poems* p. lviii, An' mind... Ye slip not on the slippery ridge Of the thawin' snow, or it'll be A long put-back to your gran' marridge. **1962** J. BALDWIN *Another Country* II. iv. 335 Flattery will get you nowhere, son. Or is that a subtle put-down? **1968** *Punch* 23 Oct. 593/2 Michael Denison sustains an appropriately truculent pout and Dulcie Gray delivers tart and catty put-downs with relish. **1972** G. LYALL *Blame the Dead* xiv. 100 He'd picked me up at the put-down place for Euston station... It's a one-way underground street. **1973** *N.Y. Times* 18 Feb. I. 24/1 He [*sc.* Trudeau] doesn't rise to bait—with choice epithets and that put-down Gallic shrug of his. **1974** S. ALSOP *Stay of Execution* II. 160 He [*sc.* Dean Acheson] detested silliness, and he was justly famous for his put-downs—when he put down a fool, the fool was left in no doubt that he was a fool. **1976** *National Observer* (U.S.) 20 Mar. 14/2 The woman whom former Attorney General John Mitchell immortalized with his famous putdown, 'Katie Graham's gonna get her tit caught in a big fat wringer', is hardly the 'bitch bringing down Presidents'. **1977** MILLER & SWIFT *Words & Women* vi. 100 Some speakers and writers use Ms. only as a put-down. **1853** 'MARK TWAIN' in *Hannibal* (Missouri) *Jrnl.* 25 May 3/1 Never speak when it's not your 'put-in'. **1903** W. N. HARBEN *Abner Daniel* xxxv. 301 This ain't no put-in o' mine, gracious knows. I hain't got nothin', an' I don't expect to lose or gain by what is done. **1962** *Times* 11 Jan. 4/3 The Navy came out better in the matter of put-ins against the head. **1975** *Sunday Tel.* 2 Mar. 30/1 He may have lost confidence as the game developed after being penalised four times for a crooked put-in. **1833** J. NEAL *Down-Easters* I. vi. 83, I shouldn't think twould be any put-out to you to take somebody else. **1843** A. S. STEPHENS *High Life N.Y.* ii. 32 Don't be uneasy about the trouble, it won't be no put out to Captain Doolittle. **1885** *California Athlete* 19 Dec. 5/1 He assisted yesterday in fourteen put outs. **1891** N. CRANE *Baseball* vi. 44 An 'assist' is given to every player who handles the ball in assisting a put-out or other play of the kind. **1904** R. H. BARBOUR *School & College Sports* 200 *Put-out*, a play by which a batsman or a base-runner is retired. **1972** *Evening Telegram* (St. John's, Newfoundland) 24 June 21/8 He..led the league's shortstops in fielding percentage, putouts, assists and double plays. **1958** *Punch* 8 Jan. 84/1 He..gave me the acreage, cost, cubic capacity and passenger put-through. **1959** [see *put through* s.v. *PUT *v.*[1] 50d]. **1968** *Economist* 4 May 64/1 Even in the leaders trading is often very narrow, and the resulting prices (on the basis of which an increasing amount of shunting and 'put throughs' now go on) are not struck on the total volume of trading. **1973** *Daily Tel.* 7 June 21 Trading on the Paris Bourse traditionally has consisted either of very big 'put-throughs' or of small deals for private individuals.

|| **puta** (pu·tă). *slang.* [Sp.] A whore, a slut.
1967 McCormick & Mascareñas *Compl. Aficionado* iii. 72 You must be like a young priest—do not go near the *putas*, and keep away from all women as long as you can. **1968–70** *Current Slang* (Univ. S. Dakota) III–IV. 99 *Puta*, a promiscuous girl. **1969** E. Bishop *Compl. Poems* 207 Under the false-almond tree's Leathery leaves, a childish *puta* Dances. **1971** L. Gribble *Alias the Victim* vii. 121 You tricky bitch of a *puta*.

pu:t-and-ca·ll. *Econ.* (See quot. 1905.) Also *attrib.*
1892 *Congress. Rec.* 6 June App. 448/1 Members of exchanges do not deal in '*puts and calls*'. **1893** [see Put *sb.*[1] 4.] **1905** F. Bower *Dict. Econ. Terms* 133 *Put and call*, on the Stock Exchange it is a common practice to arrange to buy or sell a certain number of shares at option at a fixed price within a specified time. The arrangement may be (1) to buy shares, known as the 'Call', (2) to sell shares, the 'Put', or (3) to buy or sell at option, called the 'Put and Call'. **1929** *Sun* (Baltimore) 26 June 1/6 She started business for herself, dealing in options, or in Wall Street slang the 'put and call' or 'put and take' brokerage business. **1962** S. Strand *Marketing Dict.* 599 Put and call contracts are written for 30, 60 or 90 days, or longer. **1973** *N.Y. Law Jrnl.* 4 Sept. 7/5 (Advt.), Lawyers, their clients and those involved in the put and call trading process.. need to have up-to-date knowledge on the nature of these investments. **1975** G. V. Higgins *City on Hill* ix. 216 He ..bought silver futures, puts and calls, I think.

pu:t-and-ta·ke. **1.** A gambling game played with a six-sided top. Also *transf.*, the top with which the game is played. Also *attrib.* and *fig.*
1922 *Daily Mail* 5 Jan. 5/4 (*heading*) Put and take in court. *Ibid.* For playing Put and Take in a recreation ground a youth was charged under the Gaming Act at Hull yesterday. **1922** *Vet. Jrnl.* XXVIII. 105 A rough-haired fox-terrier dog, 'Jazz',..was brought to me with the history that a brass 'Put and Take' top, 'put' on the hearthrug, had been 'taken' up and swallowed by him. **1940** Graves & Hodge *Long Week-End* viii. 132 In 1922 the craze was for a simple gambling device known as 'Put and Take'..a small six-sided top which players..spun in turn. **1960** R. C. Bell *Board & Table Games* v. 146 Put and Take. Each player..spins a six sided teetotum and obeys the instructions on the face falling uppermost. **1970** *Guardian* 9 Dec. 1/5 The deadly game of put-and-take brought on by the electricity generating workers' work-to-rule. **1972** *Observer* 3 Sept. 32/1 Each juror was issued with two bronze tokens with a shaft through the middle, rather like a put-and-take.
2. *Econ.* = put-and-call.
1929 [see *put-and-call].
3. The stocking of streams and lakes with fish for anglers to catch. Usu. *attrib.*
1943 *Sun* (Baltimore) 26 Jan. 6/3 (*heading*) Put-and-take fishing planned by W. Virginia. *Ibid.* The revision would take the form of stocking a much larger number of legal size trout on a 'put-and-take' basis in rivers and creeks which are not year-around trout streams. **1973** *Country Life* 21 June 1804/1 The rainbow trout is..the ideal stock fish for enclosed waters..where fishing is increasingly on a 'put and take' basis. **1974** *Ibid.* 26 Sept. 831/3 The cultivation of sizeable trout which are stocked makes Traws a sort of put-and-take fishery unlike most put-and-take places.

putanism. For † *Obs. rare*—[0] read *rare*, and add example.
1922 P. Nielsen *Black Man's Place in S. Afr.* 57 Immorality is rife amongst Natives.., but neither can putanism amongst the whites be denied.

putcheon, var. Putcher in Dict. and Suppl.

putcher. Examples of the form *putcheon*.
1898 *Birmingham Daily Post* 16 Dec. 8/6 Heavy catches of eels in 'putcheons'. **1945** J. Moore *Portrait of Elmbury* iv. 147 Jim also earned £4 by selling eel-putcheons which he'd made out of withies. **1968** J. Arnold *Shell Bk. Country Crafts* 258 Salmon traps, putchers or putcheons, are quite different in structure. *Ibid.* 260 The putcheons are arranged in a stout, permanent framework, forming a 'barrage' extending for scores of yards across the Severn grounds.

puthery: see *pothery *a.*

pu·t-on, *sb.* Chiefly *N. Amer.* [Put-: cf. Put *v.* 46e in Dict. and Suppl.]. A deception, a ruse, a hoax.
1937 Partridge *Dict. Slang* 672/2 *Put-on*, a deception, subterfuge, excuse..from ca. 1860. **1949** H. Hornsby *Lonesome Valley* xxiv. 316 He knew there was no put-on; that she was not talking just to make him feel better. **1967** *New Yorker* 24 June 34/3 What was once an occasional surprise tactic—called 'joshing' around the turn of the century and 'kidding' since the twenties—has been refined into the very basis of a new mode of communication. In all its permutations, this phenomenon is known as the 'put-on'. It occupies a fuzzy territory between simple leg-pulling and elaborate practical joke. **1968** 'E. McBain' *Fuzz* ix. 140 Meyer thought the call was a put-on, nobody had a name like Carlyle Butterford. **1970** *Globe & Mail* (Toronto) 28 Sept. 8/7 (Advt.), Wool carpet excellence is assured by the Woolmark label. Protecting you from a put-on. **1973** *Sat. Rev. Society* (U.S.) May 76/3 A wild mishmash of put-on, fantasy, and cultivated lunacy. **1975** *New Yorker* 17 Nov. 125/1 There is no hint of satire here—or, to be fair, of put-on. **1977** *Time* 4 Apr. 44/2 Much of the tone of such writing is personal, confessional, full of macho bellicosity and show-biz put-on.

|| **putonghua** (pŭtuŋhwā). Also **pu-, p'u-t'ung-hua.** [Chinese *pŭtōnghuà*, f. *pŭtōng* common + *huà* spoken language.] The standard spoken language now in general use throughout the People's Republic of China, based on the northern dialects, esp. that of Peking. Cf. *Kuo-yü.
1950 J. De Francis *Nationalism & Lang. Reform in China* v. 94 He expressed his views..in the following statement: '..China now has a *p'u-t'ung hua* (common language) which can serve as a general standard.' **1968** P. Kratochvíl *Chinese Lang. Today* v. 164 This concept of the so-called *pŭtōnghuà* 'Common Language' is largely based on the latter stage of *guóyŭ* (the two terms *guóyŭ* and *pŭtōnghuà* are now almost synonymous). **1971** R. Newnham *About Chinese* 75 The Communists took up the ['spoken language'] of the older 'literary revolutionists', renaming it *pŭtōnghuà* or 'common speech'. The inspiration became firmly social. Pŭtōnghuà is now what the West generally thinks of when it speaks of 'Mandarin'... It is adopted by all the communications media in China (the phrase 'national language' is not heard), while in print it is virtually standard. **1973** T. R. Tregear *Chinese* vi. 124 The *pai hua* has had a profound influence since today it forms the basis of *p'u t'ung hua*, 'usual words' now in universal use throughout the land. **1976** W. H. Canaway *Willow-Pattern War* xv. 156 He spoke enough *pu-t'ung hua*, the Common Chinese, for Shao to give him instructions before we left. **1978** *Nagel's Encycl.-Guide: China* 68 A common spoken language, now known as *putonghua* (Common Language) was imposed throughout China.

put-put (pʊ·tpʊt), *sb.* orig. *N. Amer.* Also **putt-putt.** [Echoic.] A muffled explosive sound characteristic of an internal-combustion engine. Also applied to objects which make such a sound, as a machine-gun, a motorized boat or bicycle, etc. Also *attrib.*
1905 *Rudder* Feb. 61/2 Already the class of small launches, of which the converted [St. Lawrence] skiffs form the majority, has achieved the distinction of a special title, of unknown origin, but of universal use; 'put-put', or more briefly, 'put'. The words themselves are now almost as common to the ear as the familiar voice of the two-cycle motor which called them into being. **1929** M. A. Gill *Underworld Slang* 9/2 *Put-put*, machine gun. **1930** J. P. Burke in *Amer. Mercury* Dec. 457/1 *Putt-putt*, an out-board motorboat used in liquor running. 'A sneaker's no good. Water's too shallow. Got to use a putt-putt.' **1959** P. Capon *Amongst Those Missing* 165 The others could hear it now, a quick-fire 'put-put-put' like a distant motor-bike. **1964** E. A. Nida *Toward Sci. Transl.* iii. 31 An onomatopoeic expression, such as *putt-putt* or *choo-choo*, is presumably an imitation of the very sound made by the object in question. **1965** S. T. Ollivier *Petticoat Farm* iv. 46 A roar of laughter drowned the put-put of the engine. **1967** *Guardian* 28 Dec. 5/3 The little put-put boat which carries passengers ashore. **1968** *Sunday Mail Mag.* (Brisbane) 15 Sept. 4/2 Anchored right in the middle was a small, old putt-putt type launch. **1974** J. Mitchell *Death & Bright Water* xii. 134 [He] listened to the putt putt of the two-stroke as he rode back to Kronis. **1977** *Time* 19 Dec. 13/2 Does he really think the new cruise missile is no better than Hitler's high-flying, inaccurate put-put? **1978** M. Z. Lewin *Silent Salesman* xv. 80 The cop..got on his putt-putt, and went away.

put-put (pʊ·tpʊt), *v.* orig. *N. Amer.* Also **putt-putt.** [Echoic.] *intr.* To make an intermittent explosive sound characteristic of an internal-combustion engine. To move, making such a noise. Also quasi-*trans.* Also *fig.* Hence **put(t)-putting** *vbl. sb.*
1905 *Outing* July 389/1 In and out between them trim little launches go *put-putting*. **1939** A. Keith *Land below Wind* vii. 113 The motor put-puts back a horrid petrol odour. **1955** 'D. Cory' *Phoenix Sings* v. 82 A peculiar *put-put-put-put*... The put-*putting* noise was increasing... I made out the shape of a great sailing-barge..its tiny donkey-engine chugging away. **1958** *Spectator* 4 July 12/2 The diesel engine put-put-puts its warm gargle. **1961** J. C. Lilly *Man & Dolphin* xi. 153 A dolphin..naturally uses other sounds to convey and receive 'meaning':.. putt-putting and whistles for exchanges with other dolphins. *Ibid.* 158 Lizzie [*sc.* a dolphin], near the hydrophone, putt-putted. **1973** 'D. Jordan' *Nile Green* xliii. 220 The helicopter..came in fast over the desert, the put-putting loud overhead. **1974** R. Jeffries *Mistakenly in Mallorca* viii. 78 Old Morley keeps boasting about how he putt-putts all his money out of England.

putrefied, *ppl. a.* Add: ¶ **2.** *U.S. dial.* A malapropism for 'petrified'.
1848 G. F. Ruxton in *Blackw. Mag.* June 714/2 'I've seen a putrefied forest.' 'La, Mister Harris, a what?' 'A putrefied forest, marm.' *Ibid.* 715/1 'I shows him the piece I chipped out of the tree, and he called it a putrefaction too; and so, marm, if that wasn't a putrefied peraira, what was it?' **1896** 'Mark Twain' in *Harper's Mag.* Sept. 536/2 Jubiter..was just fairly putrefied with astonishment.

putrid, *a.* Add: **3.** Used as a mere intensive: dreadful, awful, appalling. *colloq.*
1883 'Mark Twain' *Life on Mississippi* ii. 37 La Salle drew from these simple children of the forest acknowledgements of fealty to Louis the Putrid, over the water. **1898** *Windsor Mag.* Dec. 40/1 You're an ass—a putrid ass. **1902** S. J. Cotes *Those Delightful Americans* 104 Last night at billiards you first said your luck was 'rotten', and then you got excited and declared it was 'putrid'. **1913** 'I. Hay' *Right Stuff* p. vi, He seems to have perfectly putrid notions about some things. **1931** D. L. Sayers *Five Red Herrings* iv. 45 Some putrid fool sliced a ball..and got me slap-bang in the eye.

|| **putsch** (putʃ). [Swiss G., orig. knock, thrust, blow.]
a. A revolutionary attempt.
1920 *Times* 3 June 15/5 The possibility of a *Putsch* continues to exercise the minds of all parties. **1922** *Q. Rev.* Jan. 125 King Charles has made his second attempt to ascend the Hungarian Throne. In the circumstances outlined above it was doomed to failure. So was Louis Napoleon's second *coup d' état—Putsch* is the modern word—at Boulogne. **1930** *Economist* 4 Oct. 612/2 The officers were charged with conspiring..to secure the neutrality of the Reichwehr in the event of another 'Putsch' by the revolutionaries of the Right. **1945** A. J. P. Taylor *Course of German Hist.* xi. 192 No one who took part in the *putsch* was punished. **1950** [see *blanquism]. **1968** A. Coates *Myself a Mandarin* i. 5 Since the end of the Second World War the population [of Hong Kong] had topped the million mark, and the place was thus technically already overcrowded when the communist *putsch* began. **1975** *N.Y. Times* 29 Nov. 27/2 Allende, of course, is gone—a suicide in September 1973 when the current President, Gen. Augusto Pinochet Ugarte, seized power in a bloody putsch. **1981** *Listener* 1 Jan. 12/2 The greatest achievement had been to keep the [Ghanaian] army putsch a secret.
b. *colloq.* Any sudden vigorous effort or campaign.
1938 A. Campbell *Flying Blind* xi. 89 He grasped it firmly, and flexing his muscles prepared a putsch. **1940** C. T. Carr in *Mod. Lang. Rev.* XXXV. 71 *Putsch*, a coup d'état... The word was apparently borrowed round about 1920 and is now quite common in English newspapers.. spreading to English slang in the non-political significance of a 'push forward'. **1953** M. McCarthy *Groves of Academe* x. 215 Criticism..has been reduced to a minimum... No poet of any real merit has been excluded... You..are too impatient. You want to make a *putsch* for the sake of tighter control, more daring methods of promotion, but violence is unnecessary. **1970** *New Scientist* 30 July 221/2 The present step-by-step attack on brucellosis is much more likely to succeed than a premature *putsch*. **1973** *Observer* 14 Jan. 29/6 Apart from a much-needed putsch on our chimneys and exhaust pipes there is little more that the public health departments can do to increase the level of our good health.
Hence **pu·tsching** *vbl. sb.*; **pu·tschism,** the advocacy of a *putsch* or of the violence associated with a *putsch*; **pu·tschist,** an advocate of or participant in a *putsch*; also *attrib.* or as *adj.*
1898 A. P. Atterbury tr. *Sombart's Socialism 19th Cent.* iv. 73 Putschism..is the fanatical tendency towards street struggle, faith in the barricade. *Ibid.* v. 113 The Putschists, Clubists, and Blanquists were utopists, who through conspiracies and street riots would through all time control economic development. **1923** *Glasgow Herald* 26 Oct. 9 The Separatist 'Putschists' have succeeded in maintaining their position. **1937** E. Snow *Red Star over China* iv. v. 167 P'eng Pai..formed a Soviet, which, following a policy of putschism, was soon destroyed. **1940** K. Mannheim *Ideology & Utopia* 125 The ideology of 'putschist' groups led by intellectuals. **1954** P. Toynbee *Friends Apart* v. 65 The Communist Party.. would have regarded it as a piece of futile 'diversionism', 'putschist' and disorganised. **1966** 'Han Suyin' *Mortal Flower* i. iv. 128 The practice of shooting deserters and of inflicting corporal punishment, both of which smack of putschism. **1968** *Economist* 1 June 44/1 Mr Cecil King has gone the same way that he came in—by a boardroom putsch. Seventeen years ago it was Mr King who did the putsching. **1974** J. White tr. *Poulantzas's Fascism & Dictatorship* iv. ii. 169, 1921. A series of 'putschist' attempts in Prussia by the KPD. *Ibid.*, The Comintern, at its Third Congress, passed a severe judgement on this 'putschism'. **1975** *New Left Rev.* Nov.–Dec. 66 When the putschists struck at Nicosia in July 1974, only a few EDEK members were armed and ready to resist. **1979** *China Now* Mar./Apr. 24/2 The essentially putschist character of both Lin Biao and the Four.

putteed, *a.* (Further example.)
1929 E. Bowen *Last September* xii. 141 The last they saw of him was a putteed leg.

putter, *sb.*[1] Add: **8.** *putter down* = **putter off** (*b*); **putter up** (*b*) (later examples).
1906 *P.T.O.* 16 June 16/2 Three men as a rule take an active part in a forgery—the 'putter-up', the capitalist who finds the necessary funds; the 'blacksmith', the actual forger; and the 'putter-down', who actually presents the forged document and obtains the money. **1926** *Clues* Nov. 162/1 *Putter-down*, the party who passes forged checks for the real forger. **1929** C. Humphreys *Great Pearl Robbery* i. 12 The police knew that Grizard was the 'putter-up'. **1975** M. Crichton *Great Train Robbery* ii. 18 Edward Pierce..accumulated sufficient capital to finance large-scale criminal operations, thus becoming what was called 'a putter-up'.

putter (pʊ·təɹ), *sb.*[3] [Echoic. Cf. *put-put *sb.*] A muffled explosive sound characteristic of an internal-combustion engine, as an outboard motor, etc. Also applied to an engine or vehicle which makes such a sound.
1942 'N. Shute' *Pied Piper* 224 There was a fishing-boat..coming in from the sea; faintly they heard the putter of an engine. **1948** G. Greene *Heart of Matter* II. i. ii. 118 Across the river the tinkering in the launch went on: the sharp crack of a chisel, the clank of metal, and then again the spasmodic putter. **1964** J. Masters *Trial at Monomoy* ii. 56 The putter of the marine diesels and the slap and sigh of the sea. **1969** *Listener* 12 June 814/1 We heard the first putter of outboard motors that, by mid-morning, become the background noise of the region. **1975** *Islander* (Victoria, B.C.) 27 July 7/1 We had a small open boat with an inboard engine. This 'putter' would

provide slow but reliable transportation. **1979** R. LAIDLAW *Lion is Rampant* xiv. 111, I could hear the putter of farm machinery.

putter, *v.*[2] Delete '*dial.* and *U.S.*' and add earlier and later examples.

1878 L. M. ALCOTT *Under Lilacs* xii. 130 Ben infinitely preferred to watch ants and bugs..rather than 'putter' over plants with long names. **1878** L. C. BELL in *Wide Awake* Jan. 24/1 Every morning in the midst of his chores, Max found time for a long, hovering, puttering visit. *Ibid.*, Max likes to 'putter' with the housework, too. **1907** J. M. SYNGE *Let.* 3 June (1971) 153 Yesterday we puttered about, and today we are going for another long expedition. **1925** R. FROST *Let.* 20 June (1964) 174, I am free to putter my days out without even writing any more. **1925** J. G. MACLEOD in *Oxf. Poetry* 26 His still moving body Like a strange motor-boat propelled by nothing puttered round The headland **1931** D. L. SAYERS *Five Red Herrings* xxiv. 278 He would be the one person who might habitually see Campbell having breakfast and puttering about the house. **1952** *Arena* (N.Z.) XXXI. 5 Real man of mystery he was these days. Puttering round the whare at all hours. **1960** M. K. JOSEPH *I'll Soldier no More* 150 Tired, they putter slowly back to billets. **1977** G. DURRELL *Golden Bats & Pink Pigeons* v. 121 The Box fish puttered to and fro like some weird, orange boat.

putter (pʌ·tər), *v.*[3] [Echoic. Cf. *PUT-PUT *v.*] *intr.* To make an intermittent explosive sound characteristic of an internal-combustion engine; to move, making such a sound. Hence **pu·ttering** *vbl. sb.* and *ppl. a.*

1937 M. LANE *At Last Island* ix. 270 The boat puttered and back-fired out of the harbour. **1947** J. STEINBECK *Wayward Bus* 197 The rain had diminished so that there was only a faint puttering on the roof. **1956** J. MASTERS *Bugles & Tiger* i. 31 A groaning truck..backfired and puttered steadily down the road to the plains. **1958** *Times* 7 July 9/4 The mower must depend on human exertion and not be of the petrol-puttering kind. **1971** P. CRAMPTON tr. *Heyerdahl's Ra Expeditions* vii. 163 Our first hesitant moves were now being followed by excited journalists and experienced old salts on board the puttering vessels which circled about us. **1975** *New Yorker* 28 Apr. 98/3 They [*sc.* Hanoians] rent rowing shells or go for a ride in the motorboats that putter back and forth between its islands.

putting, *vbl. sb.*[1] Add: **9.** *putting on, out, up*: further examples.

1930 A. ARMSTRONG *Taxi* xii. 163 'Putting on' is the taxi man's expression for coming on at the end of the rank. **1968** *Listener* 31 Oct. 566/1 They acknowledged their debt to McLuhan and paraded his definition of modern myths—the putting on of an audience and its environment. **1947** S. C. ADAMS in A. Dundes *Mother Wit* (1973) 519 The younger generation are largely indifferent either as to the necessity of joining the church, or, if they are already members, as to the 'putting out' of the church. *c* **1806** D. WORDSWORTH *Jrnl.* (1941) I. 258 She did not much encourage us to go, because..it was a long way, 'and there was no putting-up for the like of us'. **1907** J. G. MILLAIS *Newfoundland* iv. 76 During the month of September the big stags keep to themselves in various 'putting up' spots..near the lakes and rivers. **1909** *Daily Chron.* 16 June 1/2 It was the biggest fight he had ever undertaken, but he was going to win it..or if he did not win he was going to give the other side a rare 'putting up'. **1914** *Chambers's Jrnl.* Aug. 536/1 Herrings cause similar bubbles, which fishermen call 'putting up'.

putting, *vbl. sb.*[2] Add: **1. b.** putting course *poet.* = *putting green*; **putting-green**: also, a miniature golf course.

1945 J. BETJEMAN *Coll. Poems* (1958) 116 Over the putting-course rashes were seen Of pink and of yellow among the burnt green. **1966** —— *High & Low* 62, I will not go to Finsbury Park The putting course to see. **1977** *Evening Post* (Nottingham) 27 Jan. 14/1 (Advt.), Local amenities bowls, tennis, putting green, paddling pool.

putting, *ppl. a.* Add: **putting-off,** disconcerting, off-putting, repellent; cf. *off-putting* ppl. adj. s.v. OFF-PUT in Dict. and Suppl.

1928 M. ARLEN *Lily Christine* vi. 86 The idea of anyone living..her life 'bravely'..is, to tell the truth, slightly embarrassing—'putting-off', the phrase is. **1932** S. GIBBONS *Cold Comfort Farm* i. 9 'Would it impress them with my efficiency?' 'No... It would be *too* putting-off.' **1945** C. WILLIAMS *All Hallows' Eve* 184 She was very putting-off, and only said: 'Pray, nurse, do not interfere.' **1959** *Sunday Times* 22 Mar. 24/5 The first act was so putting-off that I should not have been much surprised if many viewers had accepted the B.B.C.'s invitation to 'Follow The Fleet', with Fred Astaire and Ginger Rogers, on the other channel.

putto. (Examples in *sing.*)

1914 C. F. BELL *Drawings by Old Masters in Christ Church* 44 Fiammingo, François du Quesnoy, *attributed to*... A nude putto playing with a goat. **1931** B. BERENSON *Ital. Pictures of Renaissance* 109 Bramantino (*Bartolommeo Suardi*)... Milan... 16. Fresco: Putto under Vine. **1968** *Listener* 22 Aug. 247/1 The omission in Poussin's painting of anything corresponding to the *putto* in the Bordone leads to a strange placing of the left leg. **1973** *Daily Tel.* 13 Feb. 13/6 On one side are two coats of arms in Baroque mantling held together by ribbons in the hand of a flying putto.

‖ **puttony** (pu·tonʸ). Pl. **puttonys.** [Hungarian; cf. Hung. *puttonyos* holding as much as goes into one *puttony* (e.g. *öt puttonyos tokaji* five-basket Tokay).] In Hungary, a basket or dosser made of wooden staves or wickerwork used to transfer grapes from the vineyard to the wine-press.

1958 A. L. SIMON *Dict. Wines* 156/1 They [*sc.* over-ripe grapes] are gathered in wooden vessels known as *puttony*, holding about 25 quarts... When the label on the bottle records '1 puttony', it means that about 10 per cent of the grapes used were *trockenbeeren*..; if '3 puttony', the proportion was 30 per cent. **1959** W. JAMES *Word-Bk. of Wine* 190 Pickers carry a small container called a puttony, into which they put selected overripe berries..; the number of full puttonyos mixed with the ripe but not overripe grapes in the fermentation cask determines the richness of the wine, the range being from one to five (and occasionally six) puttonyos. **1967** A. LICHINE *Encycl. Wines & Spirits* 426/2 The collar label on every bottle of Tokaji Aszu will state: 3 Puttonos, 4 Puttonos, etc.—the export agency simplifies the spelling by removing the 'y'. *Ibid.* 522/2 The buckets or *puttonys* of raisin-dry, concentrated grapes added to the fermentation..are shown on each bottle of the vatting. *Ibid.* 523/1 The overripe, dried, shrivelled berries, picked separately and put into the little *puttony* pails, are worked in a trough... Alcoholic content and other characteristics of course vary with the *puttonys* content. **1972** *Guardian* 26 Jan. 9/5 In theory there can be a Tokay of 6 puttonyos; but in practice only the five turns up.

putt-putt, var. *PUT-PUT *sb.* and *v.*

putty, *sb.* Add: **3. b.** Phr. *up to putty*, worthless, useless. *Austral. colloq.*

1916 *Anzac Bk.* 32/1 A man's got a chance to hit back there, but down 'ere it's up to putty. **1953** D. STIVENS *Gambling Ghost* 24 'I don't hear anything, Cabbage-tree,' said Thunderclap. 'Your hearing's up to putty,' said Cabbage-tree. **1965** *Telegraph* (Brisbane) 5 July 8/5 *Up to putty*, no good.

c. Used *fig.* to designate one who is easily influenced or malleable. Freq. in colloq. phr. *to be (like) putty in* (someone's) *hands.*

1924 H. CRANE *Let.* 3 Feb. (1965) 173, I was quite exemplary of both sides of my family in not being made of any putty—knowing what I want to do, and sticking it out. **1946** W. S. MAUGHAM *Then & Now* ii. 3 You are infatuated with the man. You're like putty in his hands. **1979** D. KYLE *Green River High* vii. 90, I was putty in her hands... The arguments *were* very attractive.

5. c. (Earlier and later examples.)

1883 G. C. DAVIES *Norfolk Broads & Rivers* i. 5 All the other Broads have bottoms of black mud..so soft that a yacht's anchor will not hold in it, so that large blocks of iron ballast are used instead, which will not drag through the 'putty,' as the mud is locally called. **1961** P. MOYES *Sunken Sailor* ii. 33 My adorable wife has put us on the putty. On a falling tide.

d. (Further examples.)

1915 *T. Eaton & Co. Catal.* Spring & Summer Suppl. 1/2 Natty tailored Suit... In light Putty (Tan) shade only. **1926–7** *Army & Navy Stores Catal.* 698/1 *Hose*..Botany Wool, in Black, Grey, Tan, Nigger, Putty, Beige, Nude.

e. A former type of golf ball made of some material other than gutta-percha.

1891 R. FORGAN *Golfer's Handbk.* 39 The 'putty' being the popular name for the 'Eclipse'. **1900** A. E. T. WATSON *Young Sportsman* 293 Several kinds of composition balls, known generically as 'putties' in contradistinction to the 'gutties' or gutta-percha balls..have failed to take the place of those made of the raw material.

f. *Naut.* (See quots.)

1946 J. IRVING *Royal Navalese* 141 *Putty*, the ship's painter. **1961** F. H. BURGESS *Dict. Sailing* 165 *Putty*,..a ship's painter.

6. *putty beige, colour* (examples), *face, grey, shade* (example), *white*; *putty-cool* adj.; **putty-blower** (earlier example); **putty-head** *U.S.*, a stupid person; **putty-headed** *a.*, stupid, soft-hearted; **putty-hearted** *a.*, lacking in courage, cowardly; **putty medal** *jocular*, a worthless reward for insignificant service or achievement (cf. *MEDAL *sb.* 2 b); **putty-shooter** = *putty-blower*.

1969 *Sears Catal.* Spring/Summer 10 Putty beige. **1862** R. H. NEWELL *Orpheus C. Kerr Papers* 1st Ser. 156 [The muskets] are inferior to the putty-blowers of our innocent childhood. **1933** *Burlington Mag.* Sept. 122/1 The olive-grey celadon glaze has the same peculiar tint, with a slight suggestion of putty colour. **1979** 'G. BLACK' *Night Run from Java* iii. 32 Banana palms..bleached to a kind of putty colour. **1970** R. LOWELL *Notebk.* 69 Our bedroom, putty-gray and putty-cool. **1927** M. SINCLAIR *Hist. A. Waring* xvii. 88 Charlie, in spite of his putty face, was handsome in a heavy way. **1931** W. FAULKNER *Sanctuary* vii. 68 'Yes, putty-face!' the woman cried. **1969** Putty-grey [see *putty-cool* above]. **1856** M. J. HOLMES *L. Rivers* 370 He got so engaged about the darned 'liquor law', and the putty-heads that made it, that he'd no idee 'twas so late. **1873** 'MARK TWAIN' *Gilded Age* xliii. 393 In a word, the great putty-headed public loves to 'gush'. **1885** R. L. STEVENSON *Prince Otto* II. i, A springless, putty-hearted, cowering coward. **1898** R. E. F. COHEN in W. A. Morgan '*House' on Sport* 378 Not even the proverbial putty medal or a memento of any sort was awarded to the man who upheld the honour of his University by beating his rival in the water. **1958** M. KELLY *Christmas Egg* (1966) iii. 195 'You know what you'll be given for all this?'..'A putty medal. Sooner have a cheque.' **1972** *Guardian* 12 Sept. 15/7 Putty medal blues... The Americans are busy mounting a major public inquest on their showing at Munich and on the Olympic Games. **1930** *Daily Express* 6 Oct. 11/6 (Advt.), The Barry 'militaire' (in fashionable putty-shade). **1896** D. C. BEARD *Amer. Boy's Bk. of Sport* xxxiii. 395 When people depend for their dinner or personal safety upon a 'putty-shooter' you may be sure that they learn to shoot with great accuracy. **1971** *Guardian* 20 July 9/3 Caramel..and putty-white make the season's signature combination.

put-up, *ppl. a.* Add: Now usu. with stress on first syllable. **1.** (Further examples.) Also *absol.* as *sb.*

1903 *Outing* XLII. 660/2 'Why, man,' he exclaimed, 'it's a graft—a dirty put-up game. Can't you see it?' **1923** H. G. WELLS *Men like Gods* I. ii. 19 The whole of this business is, as they say nowadays, a put-up thing. **1936** J. CURTIS *Gilt Kid* xv. 148 He would believe that it was a put-up. **1941** [see *LINE *sb.*[2] 13 g]. **1974** N. FREELING *Dressing of Diamond* 213 There's going to be a lot saying it's a put-up job.

2. a. (Further examples.)

1846 DICKENS *Pictures from Italy* 124 An English lady ..who always carries..a put-up parasol. **1897** G. B. SHAW *Let.* 26 Mar. (1965) 738 He sends Felix to bid for fashionable put-up plays.

put-u-p-able-with, *a. rare.* [f. phr. *to put up with*: see PUT *v.*[1] 53 p (*b*) + -ABLE.] That may be put up with; tolerable.

1812 M. EDGEWORTH *Tales of Fashionable Life* VI. 37 The accommodations, and everything of that nature, now is vastly put-up-able with!

pu·t-you-up. Also **Put-u-up.** [f. phr. *to put up*: see PUT *v.*[1] 53 o (*a*)]. A sofa or settee which can be converted into a bed. Also *attrib.*

The form *Put-u-up* is a proprietary term.

1924 *Trade Marks Jrnl.* 20 Aug. 1898 Put-u-up... Settees convertible into bedsteads. Greaves & Thomas,.. London,..manufacturers. **1948** G. V. GALWEY *Lift & Drop* viii. 206 He did have a 'Put-u-up' in the office for firewatching. **1966** M. CRONIN *Jump Gun* iv. 45, I found some blankets, wrestled with the put-u-up and coaxed it into some semblance to a couch. **1966** A. E. LINDOP *I start Counting* i. 14 The sofa was one of those big double-bed Put-U-Ups. **1973** *Country Gentlemen's Mag.* Mar. 180/2 (*heading*) Fitted cabin trunk..ideal service cadet or world rover, £12. Or exchange settee Put-u-Up bed. **1973** *Country Life* 22 Mar. 753/1 A sofa bedstead (an early form of put-you-up). **1978** *Morecambe Guardian* 14 Mar. 9/2 Besides traditional beds, there are the convertible put-you-up types which are essential when space is short.

putz (puts, pʌts). *U.S.* [a. G. *putz* decorations, ornaments.] **1.** *dial.* In Pennsylvanian Dutch homes, a representation of the Nativity scene traditionally placed under a Christmas tree.

1902 *N.Y. Times Mag.* 14 Dec. 15/2 Only the chosen few can afford to have a really impressive 'putz' which fills half a room, and represents a landscape in miniature... This more elaborate '*putz*' requires not only money for its erection, but artistic handiwork. **1926** *Ladies' Home Jrnl.* Dec. 82/2 The putz is simply the pictured story of the Nativity, built near or at the base of the Christmas tree. **1938** A. HARK *Hex Marks Spot* 186 Everybody's curious to see what kind of putz everybody else has this year, so they go around visiting. **1970** L. M. FEINSILVER *Taste of Yiddish* i. 44 In Pennsylvania, Jews who know Yiddish are often startled during the Christmas season by ads inviting the public to some company's 'putz'... This German word for decoration means, in Pennsylvania Dutch, a Nativity scene.

2. *slang.* [Yiddish.] **a.** The penis.

1934 H. MILLER *Tropic of Cancer* (1935) 34 [She] ought to have better sense than be tripped up by every guy with a big putz who happens to come along. **1968** L. ROSTEN *Joys of Yiddish* 298 *Putz*, rhymes with 'nuts'. Literally, *putz* is vulgar slang for 'penis'... *Putz* is not to be used lightly, or when women or children are around. It is more offensive than *shmuck*;..*putz* has a pejorative ambience. **1969** P. ROTH *Portnoy's Complaint* 101 He simply cannot —*will* not—control the fires in his putz, the fevers in his brain.

b. A fool, a simpleton; an objectionable person.

1964 W. MARKFIELD *To Early Grave* (1965) vii. 127 What I think is—you're a *putz*. *P, U, T, Z!* **1966** 'E. V. CUNNINGHAM' *Helen* (1967) v. 66 'What are you telling me? That you fell for her—love at first sight?' 'Don't be a putz. I run a gambling house. I don't fall in love.' **1975** A. BERGMAN *Hollywood & Le Vine* (1976) v. 56 He understood life's mysteries and tragedies, this gold-plated putz. **1975** *Publishers Weekly* 21 July 60/1 Leaving their 'putz' of a son Harry home to nurse his ulcers. **1978** J. KRANTZ *Scruples* i. 6 'You,' she said, enunciating clearly, 'are a putz, a schmekel, a schmuck, a schlong, and a shvantz. And a WASP putz, at that.'

‖ **Putzfrau** (pu·tsfrau). [Ger.] A charwoman.

1927 J. JOYCE *Let.* 25 July (1966) III. 162 Mrs Purefoy is not a Putzfrau. **1977** *Time* 8 Aug. 22/3 Says one Greek *Putzfrau* (charwoman): 'I know the West Germans wish us to hell.'

puukko (pū·ko). Also **puuko.** Pl. **puukot.** [Finn.] A type of knife used in Finland.

1952 *Chambers's Jrnl.* Jan. 37/1 He fumbled desperately for his sharp-bladed 'puukko', expecting to be set upon forthwith by a snarling fury. **1959** A. GLYN *I can take it All* ii. 36 His knife, his puukko, a large weapon with a plain handle and a double-edge blade in an embossed leather scabbard. **1964** C. GAVIN *Fortress* xi. 188 A red braided belt from which swung..the Finnish knife, the *puuko*, in its heavy leather sheath. **1964** G. LYALL *Most Dangerous Game* iii. 24, I caught the glint of *puukot*, those nasty little hook-ended Finnish knives. *Ibid.*, The first *puukko* merchant dodged.

puwang, puwha, varr. *PAWANG, *PUHA.

puya (pū·yă). Also **puza.** [mod.L. (G. I. Molina *Saggio della Storia Naturale del Chile* (1782) 160), a. Amer. Sp., f. Sp. *puya* goad.] A herbaceous or woody plant of the genus so called, sometimes as large as a small tree, belonging to the family Bromeliaceæ, native to dry regions of the Andes, and distinguished by rosettes of spiny leaves and blue or yellow flowers borne singly or in large panicles or racemes.

1809 tr. *J. I. Molina's Geogr., Nat. & Civil Hist. Chili* I. iii. 130 The trunk of the *puya*..is used for cork throughout Chili. **1847** *Curtis's Bot. Mag.* LXXIII. 4309 (*heading*) Altenstein's Puya; gigantic variety. **1885** *Pall Mall Gaz.* 11 Mar. 11/1 We mounted over rocks and more dust for some 2,000 feet, among puzas and succulent and prickly plants. **1902** *Westm. Gaz.* 23 May 12/1 The blue Puya is known to frequenters of Kew by the beautiful picture of it painted by Miss North in Chili. **1920** *Nature* 8 Apr. 160/2 On a sandstone plateau [in Bolivia]..was growing the gigantic 'Puya'. **1963** W. Blunt *Of Flowers & Village* 240 The Chilean puyas, if it is true that they are fertilized by hummingbirds, are exceptions. **1974** T. Morrison *Land above Clouds* 149 The tallest flower spikes in the world grow from solitary stands of a giant bromeliad, the Puya.

puzzivanting, var. *PUSSIVANTING *ppl. a.* and *vbl. sb.*

puzzle, *sb.* Add: **4.** *puzzle-card, -jug* (examples), *-map, -picture, -ring* (later example), *-thing*; *puzzlewise* adj. and adv.; **puzzle-box,** a puzzle in the form of a box; *spec.* in *Psychol.*, a box with no obvious connection between its door and the opening device, designed to test the learning abilities of an animal in trying to release itself; also *attrib.*

1866 Trollope *Claverings* in *Cornh. Mag.* XIII. 396 Another girl..was engaged with a puzzle-box. **1908** M. F. Washburn *Animal Mind* x. 232 The dropping off of useless movements is further illustrated in those experiments where animals are required to work some kind of mechanism. This may be called briefly the puzzle-box method. **1921** R. S. Woodworth *Psychol.* (1922) xiii. 308 (*caption*) A puzzle box. The animal must here reach his paw out between the bars and raise the latch, *L.* **1966** H. C. Lindgren et al. *Psychol.* iv. 105/1 Guthrie and Horton.. have used the behavior of a cat trying to escape from a puzzle box as a basis for demonstrating this concept of learning. **1970** E. R. Guthrie in W. S. Sahakian *Psychol. of Learning* iii. 58 An account of the behavior of cats in a puzzle-box is here offered, with the hope that he [*sc.* the reader] will begin to see himself..in a multitude of puzzle-box situations. **1853** Puzzle-card [see **conversation card*]. **1878** Puzzle-jug [see *Caughley]. **1960** R. G. Haggar *Conc. Encycl. Continental Pott. & Porc.* 375/1 The potter, Cornelis Hendricksz (born 1566), is stated to have made surprise jugs or puzzle jugs at Haarlem. **1980** R. Rubens *Cosway Miniature* ii. 13 Bonnie's greatest love was old china..Regency-striped saucers and Swansea lustre frogs and puzzle jugs. **1870** *Food Jrnl.* Nov. 533 The arrangement of the different collections and classes reminding one of a puzzle-map well shaken in a bag. **1886** Kipling *Lispeth* in *Plain Tales from Hills* (1888) 5 There was an old puzzle-map of the World... She used to put it together. **1906** B. L. Taylor *Extra Dry* 73 (*caption*) Puzzle picture. Find the man who is paying for the drinks. **1929** W. Faulkner *Sartoris* ii. vi. 151 Pieces of a patient puzzle-picture. **1978** *Country Life* 21 Sept. 850/4 Roy Strong..treated Yeames's *And when did you last see your father?* as a puzzle picture which 'leaves us to fill in what has gone before..in a highly tantalizing way'. **1974** J. Gardner *Corner Men* v. 36 Long slim fingers and a Greek puzzle ring. **1781** J. Woodforde *Diary* 16 Mar. (1924) I. 304 To 7 pieces of wood, a Puzzle thing, pd o. o. 6. **1914** W. J. Locke *Fortunate Youth* xii. 163 Paul stood ruminating puzzlewise on the audacious behest. **1950** *Mind* LIX. 174 No doubt all this sounds stale and naive to puzzle-wise professional philosophers.

puzzledly, *adv.* (Later examples.)

1951 D. Knight *Turning On* (1967) 144 He peered at Mazurin puzzledly. 'Is that what you're for?' **1964** *Economist* 10 Oct. 114/1 They puzzledly ask what the issues..really are. **1975** J. Grady *Shadow of Condor* (1976) xvi. 251 Captain Roe looked at his executive officer puzzledly.

puzzledness. (Later example.)

1935 *Theology* XXXI. 152 The first thing which strikes a simple reader is the apparent puzzledness of the accounts in the three Gospels.

puzzlist (pʌ·zlist). *U.S.* [f. Puzzle *sb.* + -ist.] One who devises puzzles.

1961 *Times Lit. Suppl.* 24 Feb 127/1 Readers in this country are unlikely to accept 'ticktack toe' for 'noughts and crosses' or speak of their favourite composer as a 'puzzlist'. **1970** *Sci. Amer.* Feb. 112/3 This cryptarithm (or alphametic, as many puzzlists prefer to call them) is an old one of unknown origin. **1971** *Ibid.* Oct. 106/3 Let us combine the rules of the two rival puzzlists by allowing both steps and hops, as in Halma.

puzzolan, puzzuolana, etc., varr. Pozzolana in Dict. and Suppl.

‖ **pwe** (pwe). [Burmese.] Also **poi, pooay, pu-é.** A Burmese festival which includes drama, dancing, sports, or other entertainments.

1861 *Chambers's Encycl.* II. 443/1 A *pooay*, or theatrical representation, is a very favourite amusement. **1876** *Encycl. Brit.* IV. 556/1 The historical books are then read, as well as the *Pu-es* or dramatic productions. **1878** A. Fytche *Burma* II. i. 21 It is a strange and curious sight to see the large crowds of Burmese assembled for the night to witness the performance of a *pooay*, or play. **1884** T. H. Lewin *Fly on Wheel* vii. 213 The night after my arrival at Cox's Bazaar, I was invited to attend a Burmese 'poi', or dramatic representation. **1905** *Statesman* (Calcutta) 23 Aug. 5/3 What the Chief Judge had to decide was whether a foot race fell within the definition of a 'pwe'. A 'pwe' ordinarily means a puppet show or other theatrical or dramatical performance, or a native cart, pony, boat or water race held for the public entertainment. **1908** *Athenæum* 29 July 254/3 A story with a Burmese Pwe dancer for heroine. **1929** F. T. Jesse *Lacquer Lady* i. xii. 88 Each of the Princes..has his own pandal erected and has pwès acted for seven days. **1934** 'G. Orwell' *Burmese Days* viii. 128 No one with eyes in his head could resist a pwe-dance. *Ibid.* 129 They're having a pwe—that's a kind of Burmese play; a cross between a historical drama and a revue. *Ibid.* 134 The pwe girl began dancing again. **1936** F. Richards *Old-Soldier Sahib* xix. 323 The Burmese were having a *pooay*, a festival which lasted seven days and was entirely devoted to gambling and enjoyment. **1971** *Nat. Geographic* Mar. 349/1 Burmese still obey, as seen by their enthusiasm for the *pwe*, a marathon of drama, singing, dancing, and joke telling. **1974** P. Gore-Booth *With Great Truth & Respect* 205 It was one of the famous Burmese *Pwes* in the open and it went on all night.

‖ **pya** (pī·a). [Burmese.] A Burmese monetary unit, the hundredth part of a *kyat*; a coin of this value.

1952 [see *kyat]. **1962** B. Fergusson *Return to Burma* x. 201, I grudge the fare!.. I'd rather have the money! Twenty *pyas*!.. I could do with twenty *pyas*. **1971** *Whitaker's Almanac 1972* 984 Burma .. Coins... *Pyas* 50, 25, 10, 5, 1. **1975** P. Theroux *Great Railway Bazaar* xvii. 181 A Burmese with a telescope urged me to have a look. I paid my fee of 25 pyas (five cents).

Pybuthrin (pəibū·prin). Also **pybuthrin.** [Blend of *pyrethrin and *butoxide* (f. But(yl + Oxide *sb.*).] A proprietary name for an insecticide compounded of pyrethrins and piperonyl butoxide.

1951 *Trade Marks Jrnl.* 3 Jan. 5/2 *Pybuthrin*... Chemical substances used for veterinary and sanitary purposes, insecticides, fungicides and preparations for destroying vermin. Cooper, McDougall & Robertson Limited... Manufacturers and Merchants. **1958** *Times* 7 July 2/7 The simplest way of dealing with them [*sc.* red mites], and with lice at the same time, is to spray the birds while at roost.. with a fine sprayer containing pybuthrin. **1971** *Homes & Gardens* Aug. 89/1 A spray containing pybuthrin for rapid effect and chlordane for persistence will control ants in house or garden for a period of two to three months outside and up to a year indoors.

pycnic, var. *pyknic.

pycnidial, *a.* (Examples.)

1923 *Nature* 21 Apr. 553/1 The hyphomycete stage [of *Polythrincium Trifolii*] is followed by a pycnidial stage. **1971** P. H. B. Talbot *Princ. Fungal Taxon.* x. 146 Most of the pycnidial Deuteromycotina have slimy spores. **1977** *Lancet* 26 Mar. 672/2 Various pycnidial fungi related to the *Phoma* sp. isolated produce the mycotoxin responsible for lupinosis in sheep and cattle.

pycnidiospore. (Earlier example.)

1880 C. E. Bessey *Bot.* xvii. 294 The cavities are called pycnidia, and the small bodies pycnidiospores.

pycnidium. (Later examples.)

1938 G. M. Smith *Cryptogamic Bot.* I. xii. 416 If the fertile layer lies in a cup- or flask-shaped cavity that is open from the beginning, the cavity and the surrounding tissue constitute a pycnidium. **1966** K. Tubaki in Ainsworth & Sussmann *Fungi* II. iv. 127 Simple or branched sporophores may line a hollow flask-shaped fruit body, the pycnidium.

pycnium (pi·kni,ŏm). *Bot.* Pl. **pycnia.** [mod.L., f. Gr. πυκνός thick.] In rust fungi of the order Uredinales, a fruit-body resembling a pycnidium. So **py·cnial** *a.*, of or pertaining to a pycnium; **py·cniospore,** a spore from a pycnium.

1905 J. C. Arthur in *Bot. Gaz.* XXXIX. 221 For the sorus of the initial stage [of uredineal fungi], usually.. called spermogonium, pycnidium, etc., I propose pycnium..; derivatives pycnial, pycniospores, etc. **1926** *Mycologia* XVIII. 90 The inefficient sori (pycnia) are present or absent in both macrocyclic and microcyclic rusts. **1929** J. C. Arthur et al. *Plant Rusts* i. 6 The pycnia produce pycniospores. **1937** Pycnial [see *æcium]. **1937** *Nature* 8 May 800/2 Pycniospores..were present in the nectar. **1946** K. S. Chester *Nature & Prevention of Cereal Rusts* v. 49 The pycnia occur on both leaf surfaces. **1976** G. C. Ainsworth *Introd. Hist. Mycol.* v. 132 Isolated monosporidial infections gave rise to pycnia which produced pycniospores and nectar but no aecia developed as they frequently did when two or more pycnial pustules were adjacent to one another.

pycno-. Add: **pycnochlo·rite** *Min.* [ad. G. *pyknochlorit* (J. Fromme 1903, in *Min. und Petrogr. Mitt.* XXII. 70)], a chlorite, (Mg, Fe^{2+}, Al)$_6$(Si, Al)$_4$O$_{10}$(OH)$_8$, having the same silicon content as clinochlore (2·8–3·1 atoms per formula unit) but more iron (1·5–3 atoms); **py·cnocline** *Physical Geogr.*, a thin layer separating water of different densities; **py·cnogon** = *pycnogonid*; **pycnogonid,** add to etym.: [f. mod.L. class name *Pycnogonida*, f. generic name *Pycnogonum* (M. T. Brünnich *Entomologia* (1764) 84)]; also *attrib.*; (later examples); **pycnome·tric** *a.*, involving or employing a pycnometer; hence **pycnome·trically** *adv.*; † **pycnomo·rphous** *a. Cytology* [ad. G. *pyknomorph* (F. Nissl in *Neurol. Centralblatt* (1894) XIII. 683, (1895) XIV. 70), f. Gr. μορφή form, shape], characterized by much darkly staining matter; **pycnospore**: also = *pycniospore* s.v. *pycnium; (earlier and later examples).

1903 *Mineral. Mag.* XIII. 375 Pyknochlorite... A greyish-green, compact chlorite occurring in a quartz and calcite vein in the gabbro of the Radauthal, Harz. It has the same general formula..as clinochlore, but differs from this in containing much more ferrous iron and in its compact (πυκνός) texture. **1960** *Amer. Mineralogist* XLV. 797 The co-existing chlorite occurs in fairly large pale green crystals and shows the typical anomalous interference colors. Its analysis shows it to be fairly rich in Mg and Al, and following the classification of Hey (1954) it may be termed a pycnochlorite, with Fe (total):(Fe + Mg) = 0·273 and Si 2·83, on the basis of 14 oxygens (anhydrous). **1973** *Nature* 2 Mar. 28/1 Microscopic studies reveal that the metamorphic boundary involves the replacement by quartz and a chlorite mineral of fixed composition (pycnochlorite). **1978** *Ibid.* 20 July 243/1 Chlorites occurring as matrix in greywacke and amygdule fillings and groundmass replacement in spilite are either pycnochlorite or diabantite. **1957** G. E. Hutchinson *Treat. Limnol.* I. v. 282 When a wind blows over a thick layer of water lying over a second layer of greater density, not only will the surface level be raised at the lee end but the pycnocline, or plane separating the two layers of different density, will be tilted in the opposite direction. **1967** *Oceanogr. & Marine Biol.* V. 278 Changes in the sinking rate..are well substantiated... In pycnoclines a retardation of passive organisms is frequent, sometimes associated with a synthesis of pigments. **1976** *Nature* 2 Sept. 8/1 Over large areas of the present-day ocean, a permanent density discontinuity (pycnocline) arises as a consequence of the latitudinal variation in the intensity of incident radiation from the Sun. **1927** *Proc. Imper. Acad. Japan* III. 610 (*title*) Notes on some pycnogons living semi-parasitic on holothurians. **1935** T. H. Savory *Arachnida* xvi. 172 Ever since the first pycnogon was described..the problem of their affinities has been debated. **1959** A. C. Hardy *Open Sea* II. v. 100 Sea-slugs, ascidians, sea-spiders (pycnogons) and spider-crabs, starfish and brittlestars—all these, and more, may be in just one haul. **1935** T. H. Savory *Arachnida* xvi. 172 The Pycnogonid crawls about, extremely slowly. **1973** P. E. King *Pycnogonids* i. 7 The pycnogonid body is considerably reduced. *Ibid.* 8 The pycnogonids have a wide geographical and bathymetric range. **1925** *Arch. Internal Med.* XXXV. 133 Specific gravity determinations were made by the pyknometric method. **1938** *Trans. Faraday Soc.* XXXIV. 1214 (*heading*) Pyknometric studies on chemical equilibrium. **1934** *Jrnl. Chem. Soc.* 498 The samples of water obtained by combustion were carefully distilled..and their densities were measured pyknometrically. **1976** *Nature* 3 June 438/3 There is a reasonable agreement between X-ray and pycnometrically determined densities in the minerals of the oldest rocks. **1899** L. F. Barker *New Syst. Constituent Neurones* xi. 123 Nissl consequently designates the extremely darkly stained cells as pyknomorphous cells, or cells in which the stainable portions are arranged relatively most closely. **1903** *Med. Chron.* XXXIX. 19 The stained, chromophile, or tigroid substance of nerve cells is regarded as nutritional substance. When it is abundant the cell is described as being in a pyknomorphous condition. **1887** H. E. F. Garnsey tr. *Ade Bary's Compar. Morphol. & Biol. Fungi* v. 246 Pycnidia: receptacles.. producing gonidia which are known as pycnospores. **1938** G. M. Smith *Cryptogamic Bot.* I. xii. 416 In addition to forming conidia or pycnospores, a mycelium may also form large thick-walled spores.

pycnosis, var. *pyknosis.

pycnotic, *a.* Add: The form **pyk-** is now usual. **2.** *Cytology.* Displaying pyknosis.

1910 in *Lippincott's New Med. Dict.* 798/1. **1926** *Arch. Neurol. & Psychiatry* XVI. 134 This change..was characterized by pyknotic shrinking of the nuclei and an increase in cytoplasm. **1936** J. Krafka *Textbk. Histol.* i. 3 In old senescent cells a pycnotic nucleus is produced by a condensation of chromatin to the extent that no ground substance shows. **1957** C. P. Swanson *Cytol. & Cytogenetics* ii. 34 The pycnotic state..persists into interphase to form what were formerly called pro-chromosomes. **1974** *Nature* 11 Oct. 509/1 Within 3 h of furosemide administration..single cell necrosis with pyknotic hepatocytes showing eosinophilic degeneration was..occasionally present.

pye-dog, pie-dog. For '*Anglo-Ind.*' read 'orig. *Anglo-Ind.*' and add further examples.

1884 Kipling *Departmental Ditties* (1886) (ed. 2) 52 Glare down old Hecate..And bid the pie-dog yell. **1924** *Blackw. Mag.* Sept. 355/1 The men of Bokkos and their dogs—the sorriest-looking pie-dogs in all Africa..go forth to get what they can. In a poor lot these Bokkos pies are the poorest. **1940** F. Stark *Winter in Arabia* 107 The Saint who is buried in the tomb below has pye-dogs who slink in to him at night. **1954** M. K. Wilson tr. *Lorenz's Man Meets Dog* i. 14 There are lots of localities in the near East where Pie dogs and golden jackals abound, yet never intermingle. **1977** *Times* 25 June 15/5, I tied red, white and blue ribbons round the neck of my pye-dog.

pyeenock (pəi,ī·nǫk), dial. var. of Peony.

1911 D. H. Lawrence *White Peacock* ii. ix. 354 There's a fine show of pyeenocks this year.

pyelo-. Add: **py·elogram**, an X-ray photograph showing the pelvis of the kidney; †**py·elograph**, a pyelogram; hence **pyelo·graphy** [ad. G. *pyelographie* (Voelcker & Lichtenberg 1906, in *Münchener med. Wochenschr.* 16 Jan. 105)], **py·eloplasty** *Surg.*, a plastic operation on the pelvis of the kidneys.

1923 R. Knox *Radiogr. & Radio-Therapeutics* (ed. 4) I. facing p. 388 (*captions*) Pyelogram—dilated pelvis with kinking of the ureter... Pyelogram of a normal kidney. **1952** M. E. Florey *Clin. Appl. Antibiotics* xvii. 507, 25 days after the operation a pyelogram revealed no abnormalities. **1980** *Brit. Med. Jrnl.* 29 Mar. 930/1 We in Britain do not feel that intravenous pyelograms are necessary before every hysterectomy. **1913** *Jrnl. Amer. Med. Assoc.* 18 Jan. 184/2 A pyelograph is taken while the fluid is being injected and the pelvis or the ureter is kept as full as possible at the time the exposure is being made. **1914** *N.Y. Med. Jrnl.* XCIX. 1057/2 Doctor Furniss, in making pyelographs, had until recently been injecting argyrol or collargol with a syringe. **1906** *Jrnl. Amer. Med. Assoc.* 14 Apr. 1149/2 Pyelography.—Voelcker and Lichtenberg have coined this term for radiography of the kidney and ureter after these structures have been filled with a solution of a silver salt. **1975** *Daily Colonist* (Victoria, B.C.) 23 Dec. 2/1 In pyelography, a contrast medium, the 'dye', is injected intravenously. **1913** C. H. Chetwood *Practice of Urol.* xxxi. 587 (*heading*) Pyeloplasty (Fenger's operation). **1976** *Lancet* 20 Nov. 1109/2 The boy with a horseshoe kidney had a pyeloplasty and 1 of the boys with obstructed congenital megaureter had a reimplantation.

Pygmalion (pigmēⁱ·liǝn). The name of a play by George Bernard Shaw (1856–1950), used quasi-advb. in *not Pygmalion likely*, a joc. euphemism for the phrase 'not bloody likely' which occurs in Act III of the play (see *bloody *adv.* 2, quot. 1914) and was the occasion of a public sensation at the time of the first London production in 1914. Also used *attrib.* of utterances regarded as mildly shocking.

1949 Partridge *Dict. Slang* (ed. 3) Add. 1121/1 *Not Pygmalion likely!* Not at all likely; certainly not! **1960** *Guardian* 8 Mar. 7/2 (*heading*) Not Pygmalion likely. **1960** *Times* 28 Apr. 14/5 Mr. S. M. Nutley..said: 'The trouble really began when Alderman Mrs. K. Sheridan was speaking about the council fleecing tenants and used a pygmalion word.' **1964** N. Squire *Bidding at Bridge* 185 So we *pass*? Not pygmalion likely! **1967** G. Fallon *Rendezvous in Rio* xiii. 106 'Are you thinking of joining in?' 'Not Pygmalion likely,' Bland returned brusquely. **1967** A. Wilson *No Laughing Matter* II. 96 You bloody bird! No, no, Mouse, Mr Polly and I were just talking Pygmalion talk! **1976** *Times* 18 Mar. 11/5 My immediate reaction was to say, 'Not Pygmalion likely'.

Pygmalionism (pigmēⁱ·liǝniz'm). *Psychol.* Also **pygmalionism.** [f. *Pygmalion* a character in Greek mythology + -ism. According to Ovid (*Metam.* x. 243–97), Pygmalion was a King of Cyprus who made a statue of a beautiful woman and loved it so deeply that Aphrodite gave life to it.] The condition of loving a statue, image, or inanimate object; love for an object of one's own making.

1905 H. Ellis *Stud. Psychol. Sex* IV. 188 Pygmalionism, or falling in love with statues, is a rare form of erotomania founded on the sense of vision and closely related to the allurement of beauty. **1923** —— *Dance of Life* vii. 328 We find records of Pygmalionism and allied perversities in Lucian. **1940** Hinsie & Shatzky *Psychiatric Dict.* 453/1 *Pygmalionism*,..the condition of falling in love with a creation of one's own. **1946** 'M. Innes' *From London Far* III. iv. 201 'Did you ever happen to hear of something called Pygmalionism?' '..It's a fancy name for iconolagnia'. **1954** H. T. F. Rhodes *Satanic Mass* vi. 52 After the kiss, accounts agree that the priestess offered herself to the God by an act of pygmalionism. **1966** J. Cohen *Human Robots* iv. 66 We may infer that the Greeks, who had a highly developed visual sense, were inclined to *Pygmalionism. Ibid.*, We may regard *Pygmalionism* as a manifestation of a more general tendency to excitement induced by a partner's passivity.

pygmoid (pi·gmoid), *a.* [f. Pygmy *sb.* + -oid.] Resembling a pygmy; having (some of) the characteristics of a pygmy. Also as *sb.*

1933 R. G. Austin tr. O. Menghin in *Antiquity* VII. 242 Mr Clark is perfectly correct in stating (p. 12) that I connect the Mughem men with the Grimaldi and Bushman types, treating them as pygmoid (not as pygmies). **1958** *Listener* 2 Oct. 507/1 The majority of these little people whom you see outside the forests in the north-east [*sc.* of the Congo] are not pygmies. They are pygmoids, the offspring of a liaison between a pygmy and a normal-sized Negro. **1965** E. E. Evans-Pritchard *Theories Primitive Relig.* v. 102 The Pygmies and Pygmoids of Africa and Asia. **1976** Eveleth & Tanner *Worldwide Variation in Human Growth* vii. 190 In New Guinea where one encounters numerous short-statured populations there can be no clear separation of pygmoid groups. **1977** P. Johnson *Enemies of Society* xvii. 226 The Veddas, a pygmoid people of primeval hunters living in the interior of Ceylon.

pygmy, pigmy, *sb.* and *a.* Add: **C.** *pygmy-cup, -folk*; **pygmy-flint** *Archæol.*, a type of microlith.

1936 *Proc. Prehist. Soc.* II. 223 The urns comprise two food-vessels, a pigmy-cup and an encrusted urn. **1963** H. N. Savory in Foster & Alcock *Culture & Environment* iii. 43 The Breach Farm barrow, with its dry-stone wall kerb and its fine biconical Pygmy Cup. **1907** T. R. Holmes *Anc. Britain* 82 Of all stone implements the most curious are the tiny objects which are known as 'pygmy flints'. **1930** F. Elgee *Early Man in N.E. Yorkshire* v. 31 The pygmy-flint men lived by hunting and fishing. **1963** *Field Archaeol.* (Ordnance Survey) (ed. 4) 8 Various palæolithic objects like hand-axes and choppers, microliths ('pygmy' flints), arrow and lance heads. **1788** W. Collins *Ode on Pop. Superstitions Highlands of Scotl.* 18 In..small vaults a pigmy-folk is found.

pygo-. Add: **pygo·pagus** = *pygopage* [a. F. *pygopage* (I. G. St.-Hilaire 1830, in *Ann. des Sci. nat.* XX. 338)]; so **pygo·pagous** *a.*

1895 *Teratologia* II. 274 Several of the pygopagous twins of whom there are scientific records, survived birth and lived for a number of years. **1866** *Trans. Med. Soc. State of N.Y.* XXIV. 224 The symmetrical pygopagus is exceedingly rare. **1903** J. W. Williams *Obstetrics* xxxix. 680 Ischiopagi and pygopagi, as a rule, call for complicated and difficult manœuvres before delivery can be effected. **1959** *Jrnl. Chronic Dis.* X. 84 A wooden carving from the Solomon Islands suggests conjoined twins of the pygopagus type with the union of the bodies and heads and the extremities shortened by achondroplasia.

pyinkado (pyi·ŋkădo, pĭ,i·ŋk-). Also † **pingadoo, pyengadu, py(i)ngado, pynkado,** [Burmese.] The heavy timber of the tree *Xylia xylocarpa* (formerly *X. dolabriformis*), which belongs to the family Leguminosæ and is native to Burma and parts of India; also, the tree itself. Also *attrib.*

1832 W. Roxburgh et al. *Flora Indica* II. 543 It [sc. *Minosa xylocarpa*] is called Pingadoo in Pegu, where it is used for knees, crooked timbers, &c. in ship building. **1875** T. Laslett *Timber & Timber Trees* xxi. 129 The Pyengadu, or Iron-wood tree,..is a species of Acacia, of straight growth, found in the Burmese forests. **1885** W. T. Oldreave in Rattray & Mill *Forestry & Forest Products* xii. 381 Pynkado..is said to be a species of acacia. **1896** W. R. Fisher in W. Schlich *Man. Forestry* V. I. ii. 117 In London..doubtless Pyngado..and other heavy Indian woods might be used with advantage [for wooden paving]. **1902** G. S. Boulger *Wood* I. v. 92 Pynkado or Pyengadu..is the Ironwood of Pegu. **1934** 'G. Orwell' *Burmese Days* 69 At the edge of the stream there was a huge dead pyinkado tree festooned with spidery orchids. **1940** *Archit. Rev.* LXXXVII. 47 For the remainder of the building sound-proofing floors are used finished with 3 in. pyinkado strips. **1951** *Dict. Gardening* (R. Hort. Soc.) IV. 2295/1 Pyingado..is extremely hard, heavy, strong, and durable. **1956** *Handbk. of Hardwoods* (Forest Prod. Res. Lab.) 194 Pyinkado grows to a height of 100–120 ft. *Ibid.* 195 Pyinkado is unsuitable for plywood manufacture because of its weight. **1971** F. H. Titmuss *Commerc. Timbers of World* (ed. 4) 263 Pyinkado is a difficult timber to work.

pyjamas, pajamas, *sb. pl.* Add: *pyjamas*, pronounced (pădʒā·măz), is now standard in the U.K., *pajamas* in the U.S. The second part of def. is now the prevailing sense. In extended use, applied to a similar day-time or evening garment worn by women (see also *beach-pyjamas* s.v. *beach *sb.* 4, *palazzo pyjamas* s.v. *palazzo 3). Also (*occas.*) *sing.*, as *pyjama*. **a.** (Further examples.)

1878 E. S. Bridges *Diary* 6 Sept. in *Round World in Six Months* (1879) iii. 37, I relinquished my English *chemise de nuit* and took to pyjamas—bedclothes are not used at this time of year [in Japan]. **1886** *Girl's Own Paper* 23 Oct. 59/1 The pattern for this month..is a combination nightgown, or lady's 'pyjama'. **1897** [see *sleeping-suit* s.v. Sleeping *vbl. sb.* 2 b]. **1932** *Barker's Spring Catal.* This ideal pyjama is made of a very soft washing cotton. **1932** *Boston Even. Transcript* 6 Aug. 1 Clad in pajamas and admitting to police that she was returning home from a party, Mary Callahan, twenty four ..was arrested at seven o'clock this morning. **1936** A. Christie *ABC Murders* xvi. 120 Girls passed him..in summery frocks and pyjamas and shorts. **1968** J. Ironside *Fashion Alphabet* 62 *Pyjamas*, blouse or shirt and wide-legged trousers worn for lounging or for beach wear —introduced by Chanel in the late 1920s. **1976** *Washington Post* 19 Apr. A12/4 (Advt.), Pre-school boys' pajamas reduced. **1978** *Neiman-Marcus Christmas Bk.* 32 The ambient glow of soft panne velvet for party pajamas.

b. *pyjama-clothes, coat, cord, dress, jacket, leg, pants, suit* (earlier and later examples), *top, trousers* (later examples); *pyjama-clad* (later examples), *-legged, -like* adjs.; **pyjama bottom,** the bottom half of a suit of pyjamas, pyjama trousers; usu. *pl.*; **pyjama case,** a bag or other container in which pyjamas can be kept when not being worn; **pyjama party,** a party at which those present are dressed in pyjamas; also **pyjama-and-bottle-party.**

1928 *Sunday Dispatch* 5 Aug. 15/2 Mention was made of the splendid work of Mrs. X—Y—for her pyjama-and-bottle party. **1959** R. Condon *Manchurian Candidate* (1960) i. 10 The..movie actor..had opened the door of the hotel suite wearing only pyjama bottoms. **1972** J. Wainwright *Requiem for Loser* iii. 48 He..stepped out of his pyjama bottoms and began dressing himself. **1973** *Black World* Oct. 55/1 None of the kids had on a complete outfit of clothes: some were in a pajama top—or a bottom. **1925** 'R. Crompton' *Still—William* ix. 164 Thrusting his..paper fleet into his pyjama case. **1976** W. J. Burley *Wycliffe & Schoolgirls* viii. 151 Lying on it [*sc.* the bed] was a pyjama case in the shape of a dog with 'Jane' embroidered across it. **1921** R. Macaulay *Dangerous Ages* i. 2 Her slight, straight, pyjama-clad body. **1976** 'L. Black' *Healthy Way to Die* iv. 38 The pyjama-clad legs dangling inside the silken dressing-gown. **1939** Auden & Isherwood *Journey to War* 43 The Cantonese, in their light pyjama-clothes. **1916** M. Diver *Desmond's Daughter* II. v. 71 A Punjab Cavalry-man in a turban and silk pyjama coat. **1978** C. Storr *Winter's End* v. 68 She wore a blue and white striped pyjama coat. **1917** E. Fenwick *Diary* 18 Feb. in *Elsie Fenwick in Flanders* (1981) 143 He tried to hang himself with his pyjama cord. **1972** *Times* 28 July 10/1 Top coats with pyjama cord belts. **1967** *Guardian* 2 Nov. 7/6 For luscious evening attire..a pyjama dress in hot pink and orange. **1891** E. Dowson *Let.* 1 July (1967) 206, I am more elaborately vested, in a Pyjama jacket. **1976** C. Dexter *Last seen Wearing* xxxviii. 261 The top button of the pyjama jacket already undone. **1933** A. Thirkell *High Rising* ii. 48 Tony, by now in what he called his pyjama-legs, executed a dance of joy. **1977** *Transatlantic Rev.* LX. 145 The water isn't as cold as I figured, but when the bottom of my pajama-leg gets wet, I get a little nauseous. **1960** Pyjama-legged [see *culotte 2]. **1960** Koestler *Lotus & Robot* I. i. 41 Another table in the Mascot's dining-room was occupied by an Egyptian gentleman in a pyjama-like attire. **1956** 'E. McBain' *Cop Hater* (1958) iv. 38 He was wearing pajama pants and nothing else. **1980** G. Lord *Fortress* i. 7 She pulled down her pyjama pants. **1910** *Westm. Gaz.* 13 Apr. 5/3 A pyjama party held a couple of days ago at the residence of Mrs. Edwin Avon, a well-known member of Chicago society. **1928** A. Waugh *Nor Many Waters* ii. 36 They'd thought of making a dressing-gown and pyjama party of it, so you can guess what it'll be like from that. **1933** Dylan Thomas *Let.* (1966) 67 It sounds as though you'd invited me to a pyjama party. **1978** S. Sheldon *Bloodline* xii. 157 They had often invited Elizabeth to their pajama parties. **1883** C. Bell tr. *Haeckel's Visit to Ceylon* xx. 329 The rest of our attire consisted of that particularly light and airy white flannel garment, known throughout India as a pajama suit. **1973** 'G. Black' *Bitter Tea* iii. 41 She was..wearing the kind of pyjama suit some women go shopping in [in Malaysia]. **1949** N. Mitford *Love in Cold Climate* I. vi. 66 Lady Montdore..in bed..wearing what appeared to be a man's striped pyjama top under a feathered wrap. **1976** C. Dexter *Last seen Wearing* xxxiii. 225 She..fastened all but the top button of her pyjama top. **1932** D. C. Minter *Mod. Needlecraft* 146/2 For pyjama trousers cut straight down. **1975** W. J. Burley *Wycliffe & Pea-Green Boat* I. I. 10 A tall, skinny young man in pyjama trousers.

pyjamaed, *a.* Add: (Later examples.) Also **pyjama'd.**

1922 F. Hamilton *P.J. the Secret Service Boy* i. 47 Mr. Davenant sleepily extended a pyjama'd arm. **1929** D. Hammett *Dain Curse* (1930) xvi. 182, I..let in Jack Santos, pajamaed, bathrobed, and slippered. **1959** D. Campbell *Evening under Lamplight* 47 Pyjama'd figures were clambering..into the shadowy bedroom. **1959** P. McCutchan *Storm South* ix. 124 Her pyjama-ed legs. **1974** 'D. Meiring' *President Plan* xvii. 158 She knew where he slept... A light went on and..he was there, pyjamaed.

pyjams, pyjies (pǝi·-), colloq. abbrevs. of Pyjamas, pajamas *sb. pl.* Also **pygies** and (redupl.) **pyjimjams.**

1926 D. L. Sayers *Clouds of Witness* iv. 99 Why do girls wear such mimsy little pyjimjams in this damn cold climate? **1929** P. Sturges *Strictly Dishonorable* II. 139 Now go and get the pygies and things. **1937** Partridge *Dict. Slang* 674/2 *Pyjams*, abbr[eviation of] *pyjamas*. **1960** J. Betjeman *Summoned by Bells* vii. 66 House-slippers, sponge-bag, pyjams. **1962** J. Braine *Life at Top* i. 8 But Daddy has to earn pennies..for pyjies and frocks.

pyknic (pi·knik), *a.* Also **pycnic.** [f. Gr. πυκνός thick, close-packed + -ic.] In Kretschmer's theory of human physical and corresponding temperamental types, designating a stocky physique with a rounded body and head, thickset trunk, and a tendency to fat, usu. accompanied by a cycloid temperament; also *absol.*, a person belonging to this type. Cf. *asthenic *a.* b; *athletic *a.* 3; *leptosomic *a.* Phr. *pyknic practical joke* (see quot. 1964).

1925 W. J. H. Sprott tr. *Kretschmer's Physique & Character* I. ii. 29 The pyknic type..is characterised by the pronounced peripheral development of the body cavities (head, breast, and stomach), and a tendency to..fat about the trunk. *Ibid.*, The pyknics tend emphatically to a covering of fat. **1940** W. H. Sheldon *Varieties of Human Physique* (1963) iii. 32 Much of the confusion associated with Kretschmer's terminology arises from the fact that his term 'pyknic' actually applies to a physique combining endomorphy and mesomorphy. **1942** —— *Varieties of Temperament* iv. 109 The mother was a PPJ (pyknic practical joke). She was slim-waisted and active..,but after the first pregnancy she came into her full endomorphic blossom. **1958** A. R. Radcliffe-Brown *Method in Social Anthropol.* I. iv. 103 Psychiatry affords an example of a 'special psychology', as do attempts to define psychological 'types'—..pycnic, asthenic. **1960** J. Comas *Man. Physical Anthropol.* vi. 340 A well-developed thorax predominates over the shoulders in the pyknic type. **1964** L. J. Bischof *Interpreting Personality Theories* (1970) xi. 431 *Pyknic practical joke* (PPJ).., the PPJ refers to a person who has a muscular mesomorphic body in adolescence but in later life balloons out into obesity to become an endomorph. **1971** J. Z. Young *Introd. Study Man.* xxxix. 576 Kretschmer..found that his pyknics tended to be what Jung called extroverted. **1975** A. Ferraro in S. Arieti *Amer. Handbk. Psychiatry* (ed. 2) IV. 103/1 Badia found that the megalosplanchnic type of Viola, or pycnic type of Kretschmer, discloses a tendency to chronic changes in the blood vessels of the heart.

pykno-: for words beginning thus see also Pycno- in Dict. and Suppl.

pyknolepsy (pi·knolepsi). *Med.* [ad. G. *pyknolepsie* (Schröder: see *Monatsschr. für Psychiatrie und Neurol.* (1916) XL. 281), f. Gr. πυκνός thick, crowded, after *narkolepsie* Narcolepsy.] An epileptic condition in which brief attacks similar to petit mal occur many times in a day. Hence **pyknole·ptic** *a.*

1922 *Q. Cumulative Index Current Med. Lit. 1921* 533/2 (*heading*) Pyknolepsy. **1924** *Brain* XLVII. 98 Pyknolepsy, in spite of its long duration and the great frequency of the attacks, does not impede mental development nor give rise to psychical defects. *Ibid.*, Of the many that have been used the name pyknolepsy is recommended for use by English writers... It allows us to coin a handy adjective, 'pyknoleptic', by analogy with epileptic. **1952** F. A. Elliott et al. *Clin. Neurol.* vii. 133 In pyknolepsy, the attacks cease with puberty and may not recur. **1972** P. H. Hoch *Differential Diagnosis in Clin. Psychiatry* III. xiii. 395 Grand mal, petit mal, .. or other subgroup forms..such as the narcoleptic, pyknoleptic and so forth—have a special metabolic formula of their nervous system. **1975** S. Arieti *Amer. Handbk. Psychiatry* (ed. 2) IV. xiii. 320/2 The incidence of absence attacks varies from very few, often in the morning, to a great many, up to 100 or more per day ('pyknolepsy').

pyknosis (piknōᵘ·sis). *Cytology.* Also **pycnosis.** [f. Gr. πυκν-ός close, compact + -osis.] The contraction of a dying cell, or of its nuclear material, into a densely staining mass or masses.

1900 Dorland *Med. Dict.* 552/1 *Pyknosis*, a thickening; especially degeneration of a cell in which the protoplasmic substance becomes more dense and the size of the cell smaller. **1926** *Arch. Neurol. & Psychiatry* XVI. 135 In general there is a progressive shrinking and pyknosis of the nucleus. **1946** [see *hyperchromatosis 2]. **1950** A. W. Ham *Histol.* v. 60 The changes that occur in nuclei as, or after, individual cells die in the living body are of three sorts. The commonest one is called pycnosis; this consists of a shrinkage of the nuclear material into a homogeneous hyperchromatic mass. **1972** *Physics Bull.* Mar. 147/1 The biological end points that will be studied include glycogen accumulation, nerve cell pyknosis, nerve cell injury or loss and glial reaction. **1978** *Nature* 25 May 306/2 In minced muscle grafts sarcoplasmic structure was rapidly lost, and most muscle nuclei seemed to undergo pyknosis, fragmentation and lysis.

pyknotic, var. Pycnotic *a.* in Dict. and Suppl.

py korry (pəi kǫ·ri), *int. N.Z. slang.* [Maori corruption of *by golly*.] = *by golly* s.v. Golly *int.*

1938 R. D. Finlayson *Brown Man's Burden* 32 'Py korry, that right!' Wi admitted to himself. **1941** Baker *N.Z. Slang* ix. 71 There is..not much to distinguish the authenticity of an expression like *py korry!* (by God) from one like *rekureihana* (regulation) except that the former is colloquial. **1943** J. A. W. Bennett in *Amer. Speech* XVIII. 94 The Maori treatment of certain English words is conventionally indicated by such spellings as *plurry* and *py korry* for 'bloody' and 'by golly'. **1961** J. Reid *Kiwi Laughs* 12, I have steered clear in this selection of the 'Py korry, Hori' type of alleged Maori humour. **1966** G. W. Turner *Eng. Lang. Austral. & N.Z.* x. 200 Maori English interlarded with *plurry* and sentences like 'Py korry, that the nice baby, eh?' belongs to the language of journalists rather than the language of Maoris.

pykrete (pəi·krīt). Also **Pykrete.** [f. the name of G. N. *Pyke* (1894–1948), an Englishman involved in Combined Operations (where pykrete was invented) during the war of 1939–45 + Conc)rete *a.* and *sb.*] A frozen mixture of ice and wood pulp or sawdust.

1948 *Jrnl. Glaciol.* I. 96 In February 1943 the..outlook was suddenly transformed by the discovery that the inclusion of a small percentage of wood pulp improved the mechanical properties of ice in a spectacular manner. The discovery was made by Mark and Hohenstein, working at the Brooklyn Polytechnic. In view of the similarity to concrete and in honour of the originator of the bergship project, the frozen wood pulp was given the code name of pykrete (Pyke's concrete). *Ibid.* Pykrete ..was ductile and could even be machined on a lathe. *Ibid.* 104 As a protection against explosives pykrete is weight for weight as good as concrete. **1960** *New Scientist* 28 Apr. 1081/3 The aircraft carrier project showed that the engineering properties of ice are greatly improved by 'alloying' it with sawdust (to make 'pykrete'). **1966** *Ibid.* 3 Feb. 284/3 Just as the Eskimo had learned to stiffen and toughen ice by freezing moss into it, so Pykrete owed its strength to fibres of cellulose that blocked the spread of cracks.

Pylian (pī·liăn, pəi·-), *sb.* and *a.* [f. Gr. πύλος, L. *Pylos* Pylos: see -ian.] **A.** *sb.* A native or inhabitant of the Homeric town of Pylos in the southern Peloponnese, traditionally regarded as the birthplace of Nestor and the name of his dynasty, and usually identified with Messenian Pylos at the northern end of Navarino Bay. Hence, by extension, a native or inhabitant of the territory ruled by Nestor or his dynasty. **B.** *adj.* Of or pertaining to Pylos or its inhabitants.

1611 Chapman *Homer's Iliads* ii. 28 The Pylians and their townes. ? **1614** —— tr. *Homer's Odysses* iii. 32 Soone they reacht the Pylian throngs and seates, Where Nestor with his sonnes sate. *Ibid.*, When the Pylians saw These strangers come: in thrust did all men draw About their entrie. **1725** Pope in *Homer's Odyssey* I. 142 This was a very solemn sacrifice of the Pylians. **1846** G. Grote *Hist. Greece* II. i. xviii. 16 The Pylians, together with the great heroic family of Nêleus and his son Nestôr, who preside over them, give place to the Dorian establishment of Messênia, and retire to Athens, where their leader Melanthus becomes king. **1934** A. Toynbee *Study of Hist.* I. 403 In the Homeric epic, Pylos is not called 'Minyan' as Orchomenos is, nor are the Pylians called 'Minyae'. *Ibid.*, The Greek inhabitants of..the *ci-devant* Pylian domain. **1965** *Language* XLI. 315 Scribes who use different orthographies may have come from different localities within the Pylian territory.

pylon. Delete || and add: **1. a.** (Later *transf.* examples.)

1930 *Morning Post* 9 Aug. 11, 200 men have been employed excavating granite for the facing of the bridge piers and pylons. **1974** *Sci. Amer.* Nov. 145/1 The Bayonne bridge lacks the huge pylons of Sydney Harbor, which contain the thrust visually as well as in Newtonian fact.

2. *Aeronaut.* Also † **pylone** [F. *pylône*]. **a.** A tall structure used to mark out the course round which aeroplanes fly (or, formerly, in launching them); also, by extension, a structure round which cars drive on a race-track.

1909 *Flight* 13 Mar. 143/1 The machine is brought to earth conveniently close to the pylone. **1909** *Westm. Gaz.* 16 Oct. 9/3 After a successful round of the course his aeroplane came to earth near the second pylon on the south side. **1913** A. E. Berriman *Aviation* Pl. facing p. 38 (*caption*) The lower picture illustrates a similar machine banking while turning about one of the pylones at the Hendon Aerodrome. **1970** *Pop. Mechanics* Oct. 106/1, I still had the third and best run to make. A pylon was placed in the centre of the pad. Instructions were to hit the brakes as before and *steer around the pylon*, brakes full on! **1977** *Sci. Amer.* Oct. 74/3 The craft had to take off unassisted from level ground in a wind of 10 miles per hour or less, fly in a figure-eight pattern around two pylons half a mile apart and pass over a 10-foot hurdle at the start and finish.

b. A post on some early aircraft to which wires for supporting or warping the wing were attached; also, in modern aircraft, a pillar that projects from a wing or fuselage to support an engine, rotor, weapon, or the like.

1912 *Aero* Aug. 236/1 The machine bears..a resemblance to a torpedo boat on account of its squat 'funnels', which are..the..pylons carrying the wing bracing wires. **1919** Pippard & Pritchard *Aeroplane Structures* xi. 142 The pylon bracing..comes into operation (1) In high speed flight. (2) In landing. *Ibid.*, The vertical components of the loads in the pylon wires AD, CD throw an extra load in the interplane strut BE. **1955** Liptrot & Woods *Rotorcraft* iii. 20 The rear-end ring [of the fuselage] carries the pylon on which is mounted the tail rotor. **1959** *Times* 26 Feb. 10/6 On the Boeing 707-120..the engines are mounted separately on pylons beneath the wings. **1969** K. Munson *Pioneer Aircraft 1903–14* 106/1 As flown for the first time at Issy on 23 January 1909, it had a 30 h.p. R.E.P. engine.., and a small kite-shaped fin was fixed above the wing-warping pylons. **1979** *Daily Tel.* 29 May 1/4 The airline said it believes the attachments of the engine pylon to the wings of its aircraft are sound.

3. *Surg.* A temporary, unjointed, artificial leg.

1920 *Lancet* 14 Feb. 373/2, I will endeavour to illustrate the most important details in the manufacture of a thigh pylon. **1945** Thomas & Haddan *Amputation Prosthesis* ii. 49 It is the opinion of many that the most effective and rapid shrinkage and adaptation of the stump takes place with the use of a pylon or a temporary prosthesis. **1971** P. J. R. Nichols *Rehabil Severely Disabled* II. iii. 107 Many elderly patients fitted with a satisfactory pylon are reluctant to exchange it for a definitive limb, which is heavier and 'more difficult' to use.

4. A tall structure erected as a support; *spec.* a lattice-work metal tower for overhead electricity lines.

1923 E. Shanks *Richest Man* iii. 52 Half a mile up the mountain, a cable, a thin black line, traversed the crystal air, borne up on pylons. **1930** Auden *Poems* 67 Pylons fallen or subsiding, trailing dead high-tension wires. **1942** J. Lees-Milne *Ancestral Voices* (1975) 51 This unconfined, Thames estuary is rather exciting, sprinkled as it is with drifting pylons, factory chimneys and distant gasometers. **1966** J. Betjeman *High & Low* 67 Encase your legs in nylons, Bestride your hills with pylons O age without a soul. **1971** *Nature* 12 Nov. 62/3 A commercial application of the hovertrain would operate on pylons spaced up to 150 foot apart and 25 to 30 foot off the ground. **1972** R. Adams *Watership Down* xviii. 104 They had heard the unnatural humming of a pylon in the summer air. **1977** *Times* 19 Jan. 14/2 The North-Western Electricity Board were understandably forbidden to string wires on overhead pylons up the valley.

b. Used *attrib.* to designate those poets of the nineteen-thirties (chiefly Auden, Day Lewis, MacNeice, and Spender) who used industria scenes and imagery as themes of their poetry.

Spender's poem 'The Pylons' was published in 1933.

[**1935** H. A. Mason in *Scrutiny* III. 405 In *Vienna* Spender appears very clumsily dressed in the robes of Eliot (chiefly *Ash Wednesday*) the 'pylon' imagery and possible other borrowed garments.] **1951** H. Sergeant *Tradition in Making of Mod. Poetry* I. iii. 44 His [*sc.* Wilfrid Gibson's] method of recording factual details of the industrial background to many of his poems furnishes a parallel with that of the 'pylon' school of the thirties. **1957** R. Hoggart *W. H. Auden* 14 His first links were made with others who were to become writers and publicists in what has variously been called the Thirties Group, the Pylon School and the Auden Group. **1958** *Listener* 4 Dec. 924/2 The trouble with most of the 'Pylon Poets'—with the honourable exception of W. H. Auden—is that to them industry was still too much of a new thing. **1961** *Ibid.* 24 Aug. 284/1 After Eliot..there appeared Auden and Spender and the 'pylon' school of the nineteen-thirties. **1973** *Commentary* Dec. 53/2 After the withering of 30's illusions it became fashionable to laugh at 'Pylon' poetry.

5. *U.S.* A small pillar or column, used to accommodate a sign or signal.

1934 *Sun* (Baltimore) 10 Oct. 7/1 A proposal to replace the safety pylons with an overhead signal light, with pedestrians waiting on the sidewalk until ready to board a street car, was made yesterday. **1977** *Washington Post* 24 Mar. D.C. 5 Officials have recommended changes in the station that include an end to total dependence upon station names lettered sideways on upright pylons located along the station platforms, requiring passengers to crane their necks to read them.

pyloric, *a.* (*sb.*) (Examples of *pyloric stenosis.*)

1900 S. & W. S. Fenwick *Ulcer of Stomach & Duodenum* i. ii. 41 Pyloric stenosis is a frequent result of gastric ulcer. **1970** H. M. Spiro *Clin. Gastroenterol.* xvi. 272/1 The characteristic physical finding of pyloric stenosis is the succession splash. Shaking the patient's abdomen or grasping the stomach through the abdomen and shaking it will elicit a loud gurgling sound.

pyloro-. Add: **pylo·rospasm,** spasm of the pylorus.

1898 J. C. Hemmeter *Dis. Stomach* iii. ix. 643 (*heading*) Pyloric spasm (pylorospasm, cramp, convulsion, spasm of the pylorus). *Ibid.* 644 Under narcosis the pylorospasm relaxes. **1960** Jones & Gummer *Clin. Gastroenterol.* xix. 564 Pylorospasm, so frequently invoked as a cause of symptoms in peptic ulcer, gall-bladder disease, and chronic appendicitis, has been considered as a possible cause [of hypertrophic pyloric stenosis] but without any convincing evidence in its support.

pyo-. pyocyanin, delete formula and add: now known to be 5-methyl-9-oxo-5,9-dihydrophenazine, $C_{13}H_{10}N_2O$; now usu. **-ine** (-īn); (further examples); **pyode·rma,** pyodermia; **pyorrhœa** (also, *U.S.*, **-rrhea**), also, *spec.* (in full pyorrhœa alveolaris) a purulent inflammation of the tissues surrounding the teeth that results in shrinkage of the gums and loosening of the teeth; (further examples).

1947 *Sci. News* V. 90 Many bacteria in presence of certain organic substances, which they activate, reduce a molecule such as pyocyanine to its colourless leuco form. **1949** H. W. Florey et al. *Antibiotics* I. xii. 549 Pyocyanine, a substance which is now recognized to be bactericidal and to which pyocyanase probably owes some of its activity... This is the blue pigment to which 'blue pus', characteristic of infection by *Ps[eudomonas] pyocyanea*, owes its name. **1957** G. A. Swan in Swan & Felton *Phenazines* x. 176 Pyocyanine, the first phenazine compound discovered in nature. **1976** *Ann. Rev. Microbiol.* XXX. 247 The purified enzyme contains FAD, which functions when pyocyanine is the electron donor. **1930** *Arch. Dermatol. & Syphilol.* XXI. 151 The case was presented simply as pyoderma. **1930** *Ibid.* XXII. 655 The term 'pyoderma' denotes a purulent infection of the skin due to pyogenic organisms, ordinarily staphylococci. **1936** *Ibid.* XXXIII. 811 Pyodermas and ulcerations of the skin have been described under various names. **1974** Passmore & Robson *Compan. Med. Stud.* III. xix. 102/2 A rare skin lesion which is almost specific for ulcerative colitis and Crohn's disease is pyoderma gangrenosum; intra-epidermal bulla form and contain clear fluid which soon becomes milky and frankly purulent, but is sterile. **1875** *Dental Cosmos* XVII. 278 Your correspondent.. while not very definite in his descriptions, is sufficiently so to indicate the disease as 'pyorrhoea alveolaris' of the French writers. **1921** *Daily Colonist* (Victoria, B.C.) 25 Mar. 7/6 (Advt.), Be suspicious of any tenderness or bleeding of the gums. This is usually the first stage of Pyorrhea—an insidious disease of the gums that destroys the teeth. **1975** J. Symons *Three Pipe Problem* xii. 93 The brick and mortar shaking loose like teeth with pyorrhoea.

pyocyanase (pəi,osəi·ănēiz). *Med.* [a. G. *pyocyanase* (Emmerich & Löw 1899, in *Zeitschr. f. Hygiene u. Infektionskrankheiten* XXXI. 10), f. mod.L. *pyocyan-eus* (f. Gr. πύο-ν pus + κυάνεος dark blue), former specific epithet of the source bacterium + *-ase* *-ase.] An antibiotic preparation, orig. thought to be an enzyme, which was obtained from cultures of the bacterium *Pseudomonas aeruginosus* and was formerly used to treat a number of infections, esp. diphtheria.

1900 *Jrnl. Chem. Soc.* LXXVIII. II. 159 Thus pyocyanase, the enzyme of *Bacillus pyocyaneus*, destroys the deadly effect of the diphtheria toxin. **1908** *Lancet* 21 Mar. 899/1 If pyocyanase came in contact with leucocytes, their plasma was dissolved so that the granules and the nuclei only remained and these were..immobilised. **1949** H. W. FLOREY et al. *Antibiotics* I. i. 24 After 1914 the mention of pyocyanase for clinical use almost entirely disappeared from the literature. **1969** *Listener* 5 June 781/1 The experiments of Florey and Chain on pyocyanase..went to show that pyocyanase was a complicated mixture of substances, all equally poisonous to microbes and to mice.

pyramid, *sb.* Add: **1.** Also *Great Pyramid*, the pyramid of the fourth-dynasty pharaoh Cheops at Giza; freq. used (usu. *attrib.*) with reference to its supposed mystical powers. (*Great*) *Pyramid prophecy*, the prediction of events of worldwide importance, based on a belief in the occult significance of the internal measurements of the Great Pyramid; pyramidology.

1802 E. A. KENDAL tr. *Denon's Trav. in Upper & Lower Egypt* I. 102 Herodotus relates that he was informed the great pyramid was the tomb of Chæops. **1859** J. TAYLOR *Great Pyramid* p. vi, I have confined my observations to the Great Pyramid alone. **1877** [in Dict.]. **1937** E. GILL *Let.* 7 July (1947) 389, I did go and see the great Pyramid! and went up & into its middle! Nought but exclamation marks will convey to you its amazing & marvellous mad grandeur! **1948** A. CHRISTIE *Taken at Flood* I. iv. 36 Did you read the book on the Pyramid prophecies I sent you?.. Really explains everything. **1958** L. DURRELL *Balthazar* vi. 150 It gave me the respite I needed to have a go at his heart. It was silent as the Great Pyramid. **1960** M. BOUISSON *Magic* 288 The case of the Great Pyramid prophecy for the date of 20 August 1953 seems to us..inexplicable. **1961** E. WAUGH *Unconditional Surrender* II. v. 145 His objections..were..occult, being in someway based on the dimensions of the Great Pyramid. **1972** *Guardian* 5 Oct. 17/6 Innumerable errors of the Shakespeare cypher and Great Pyramid Prophecy variety. **1976** *Listener* 19 Feb. 199/1 Books on ESP, UFOs, the mystic powers of the Great Pyramid..are..strong runners in the publishing stakes.

5. b. *Finance.* A structure of financial control achieved by a small initial investment; *spec.* in *Stock Exchange*, (*a*) a series of increases in stock acquired from the increased value of stocks already held; (*b*) a system by which a controlling interest in a holding company leads to control of a series of companies and their subsidiaries. orig. *U.S.*

1911 in WEBSTER. **1932** *New Yorker* 14 May 22/1 The bankers who were setting up the biggest financial pyramids of yesterday are replaced by other steel-nerved bankers today. **1971** *Financial Mail* (Johannesburg) 26 Feb. 701/1 A further development came in 1969 when, at the height of the boom, an investment pyramid, Bivec, was floated. It had a 50 per cent interest in BBH and also controlled the properties of both Berzack and Illman. *Ibid.* 703/3 For the cautious investor seeking soundness, the yields are tempting, with the pyramid the more attractive and accessible share.

c. *U.S.* A form of lottery in which each participant recruits two or more further participants. Also *attrib.*

1949 *Washington Post* 22 Mar. 1/6 All night long people would call me up to ask how the pyramids work. *Ibid.* 11/1 He personally believes pyramid clubs are illegal and violate the State lottery laws. **1955** *Britannica Bk. of Year* 489/2 The gullibility of some members of the public gave notoriety to the *Pyramid-Party*, a new version of the old chain-letter game, in which the individual, by paying an initial subscription and by recruiting two new members for the scheme, hoped eventually to reach the top of the 'pyramid', a position which would (theoretically) involve a considerable monetary profit.

d. *attrib.* Used to designate: (*a*) a system of profit involving extensive subcontracting of work; (*b*) a sales market in which each buyer secures the participation of further buyers. See also sense 10 below.

1964 *Daily Tel.* 1 Apr. 24/5 Douglas sub-contracted the work to another firm, made only a plastic cover itself and then charged on the basis of the total cost. The Senate report..was on public hearings in 1962 into 'pyramid' profits of this type. **1970** *Toronto Daily Star* 24 Sept. 12/1 Pyramid sales is a system whereby goods are sold, often at an inflated price, but a reduction in price is offered to purchasers who supply the names of others who buy the product. **1972** *Observer* 5 Nov. 13/2 Pyramid distributors..can and may make more money by recruiting other people to sell products. **1973** *Daily Tel.* 1 Feb. 3 Scotland Yard detectives have obtained a warrant for the arrest of..an American businessman who controls Koscot Interplanetary (U.K.), a pyramid firm selling cosmetics.

8. a. (Later examples.) *spec.* Formations of men or pieces in sports and games.

1899 A. H. QUINN *Pennsylvania Stories* 25 It was Penn's ball. The pyramid started with the cheers of ten thousand back of it. **1948** C. DAY LEWIS *Otterbury Incident* iv. 39 Peter..who is super at gym.,..began a routine of tumbling, pyramids, etc. **1969** R. C. BELL *Board & Table Games* II. iii. 58 (*caption*) Initial position of pieces in 'Pyramid'. **1973** *Guardian* 28 Mar. 15/2 There was nothing new about one line [bingo] games or games such as the 'pyramid' and the 'sandwich'.

10. *pyramid-building* (also *fig.*); *pyramid-shaped* adj.; (*spec.* with ref. to the supposed mystical powers of pyramids: cf. sense 1 above) *pyramid energy, freak, power*; **pyramid-selling** *vbl. sb.*, the selling of goods by a pyramid system (see sense 5 d (*b*) above); also *pyramid-sell* vb. trans.

1961 L. MUMFORD *City in Hist.* v. 152 All this..was pyramid-building, both in the Egyptian and later Keynesian sense of the words. **1973** C. SAGAN *Cosmic Connection* ix. 67 Harold Urey has perceptively referred to the space program as a kind of contemporary pyramid-building. **1976** *National Observer* (U.S.) 30 Oct. 17/1 (Advt.), Discover pyramid energy... Send $7.50..for this 3″×5″ Pyramid Energy Generator. **1977** *Undercurrents* June–July 19/3 The Book of Revelation has remained a happy hunting ground for Jehovah's Witnesses, UFO and Pyramid freaks, and amateur apocalyptics of all denominations. **1976** *Globe & Mail* (Toronto) 24 Apr. 1/1 A book entitled Psychic Discoveries Behind the Iron Curtain says that Russia has been into pyramid power for a long time. *Ibid.* 1/2 Mrs Kelly isn't prepared to say whether it was pyramid power or whether the pyramid created a psychological effect that led to Casey's release from headaches. **1975** D. BLOODWORTH *Clients of Omega* xiv. 135 Why have you been pyramid-selling confidential information on the side to all and sundry? **1972** *Daily Tel.* 30 Mar. 3/1 A company whose cosmetic business is said to involve 'pyramid selling'—a system whereby a franchiser sells to others the right to market goods—was banned in the High Court yesterday from operating its bank account. **1973** D. FRANCIS *Slay-Ride* iv. 51 Always full of get-rich-quick schemes..I even heard him on about pyramid selling once. **1942** PARSONS & STALLARD *Dis. Eye* (ed. 10) xxxii. 657 A pyramid-shaped gauze dressing, with its apex against the wound is firmly applied. **1976** *Billings* (Montana) *Gaz.* 7 July 1-B/1 Green-uniformed troops..patrolled the pyramid-shaped twin buildings where Olympic teams are living.

py·ramid, *v.* [f. the sb.] **1.** (In Dict. s.v. PYRAMID *sb.*)

2. *trans. Finance.* **a.** To accumulate (assets); *spec.* in *Stock Exchange*, to build up (stock) from the proceeds of a series of advantageous sales. Also *absol.*

1901 G. H. LORIMER *Lett. Self-Made Merchant* (1903) v. 64 He'd invent a system for speculating in wheat and go on pyramiding his purchases till he'd made the best that Cheops did look like a five-cent plate of ice cream. **1927** P. MARKS *Lord of Himself* ii. 23 He pyramided his winnings and piled gold on gold..and finally saw himself a millionaire three times over **1961** 'E. LATHEN' *Banking on Death* (1962) xiv. 113 He started pyramiding; put up twenty dollars and got the banks to lend him eighty to a hundred dollars. **1976** *National Observer* (U.S.) 13 Mar. 3/4 (Advt.), And if you are older than 30, it is true that you do not have as long a period of time to pyramid your savings.

b. To set up (a company) as part of a pyramid (see sense *5 b (*b*) of the sb.).

1942 E. PAUL *Narrow St.* xxiv. 212 With the money Stavisky borrowed he floated several companies and sold stock, pyramiding one concern upon the other until he had a finger in practically every financial pie in France. **1955** A. S. LINK *Amer. Epoch* II. xiv. 312 The promoter might pyramid one holding company on top of another almost indefinitely.

3. To distribute (assets or costs), esp. to pass on (costs) by means of a pyramid (sense *5 d (*a*)) of subcontracted work.

1933 *Sun* (Baltimore) 19 Aug. 1/6 Cotton manufacturers are attempting to make abnormal profits by pyramiding their labor costs and the processing tax. **1973** *Time* 25 June 86/2 Southwestern pyramids its commissions to reward the chain of students and executives above the salesman for each sale.

4. *fig.* To arrange in the form of a pyramid; *gen.*, to pile up.

1945 L. MUMFORD in *Archit. Rev.* XCVII. 6/1 Centres like New York, which continue to pyramid their mistakes, will descend with Gadarene swiftness into the abyss. **1948** J. STEINBECK *Russ. Jrnl.* iii. 41 The canned goods are piled in mountains, the champagne and wine from Georgia are pyramided. **1964** GOULD & KOLB *Dict. Social Sci.* 287/1 Power may be pyramided as in the army or relatively evenly divided as in fellowships. **1976** *National Observer* (U.S.) 10 Apr. 21/1 He will pinch powdery tobacco between his thumb and forefinger, pyramid it on the back of his opposite hand, bring it to his nostrils, and sniff.

5. *intr.* To become rich; to acquire greatly increased value or wealth. Also with *up*.

1960 I. JEFFERIES *Dignity & Purity* vii. 134 There is something about the spectacle of..Gobbo pyramiding up on property—houses, flats and so on, that the ordinary person needs must have—that I don't quite like. **1962** K. ORVIS *Damned & Destroyed* ii. 21 The same ounce of heroin..has pyramided in black-market value.

Hence **py·ramided** *ppl. a.*, **py·ramiding** *vbl. sb.* and *ppl. a.*

1930 J. R. AIKEN *Eng. Present & Past* IV. xi. 226 In the words *uppermost, furthermost, innermost, hindermost*, and several others like them, we have the comparative degree combined with the doubly superlative *most*,..causing a triple pyramiding of inflections. **1933** *Sun* (Baltimore) 19 Aug. 1/1 Couzens said he 'knew of no other city in the whole world where there was such an orgy of pyramiding of corporations and the fixing of fictitious values and earnings'. **1941** *Ibid.* 25 Mar. 14/3 Because the projects are in the jurisdictions of differing metal trades unions, the unhappy welders have had to pay tribute not to just one union, not to just one local of one union, but to many metal trades unions and to many locals of metal trades unions. It is this pyramiding of initiation, membership and 'permit' fees on the welders that Mr. Hillman tried to stop. **1951** M. MCLUHAN *Mech. Bride* (1967) 128/1 Production for use? Yes. But for the briefest possible use consistent with the rigging of the market for the pyramiding of profits. **1957** D. L. BOLINGER in *Publ. Amer. Dial. Soc.* XXVIII. 18 Imputations..share the characteristic of the larger class of pyramided Qs to which they belong and may be inverted with little or no change of meaning. *Ibid.* 21 How—why Qs with *that* and their pyramiding are discussed. **1958** *Times* 22 Nov. 7/7 The pyramiding of prosperity, American style, poised more and more on the expanding leisure of a consumers' State. **1967** *Economist* 17 June 1248/4 There is strong feeling against companies..which retain control of an empire with the minimum of capital through 'pyramiding'. **1976** G. W. MCKENZIE *Econ. Euro-Currency System* vi. 78 It is possible that euro-banks may place their dollar assets with other euro-banks. This raises the possibility of a 'pyramiding' chain of inter-bank deposits being created. **1977** *Time* Feb. 33/1 Winter stress can be aggravated by the thought of pyramiding fuel bills.

pyramidal, *a.* (*sb.*). Add: **3. c.** *pyramidal orchid* or *orchis*, an orchid, *Anacamptis pyramidalis*, which is native to Europe and North Africa, and bears dense spikes of deep pink flowers. (Earlier and later examples.)

1778 W. HUDSON *Flora Anglica* (ed. 2) II. 383 Pyramidal Orchis. **1858** A. IRVINE *Illustr. Handbk. Brit. Plants* 316 Pyramidal Orchis... Flowers in a very dense, short, ovate spike, of a beautiful rose colour. **1951** V. S. SUMMERHAYES *Wild Orchids Brit.* iii. 51 The pyramidal orchid is a very beautiful example of perfect adjustment to pollination by butterflies and moths. **1977** M. ALLAN *Darwin & his Flowers* xi. 198 The Pyramidal Orchid..has its parts arranged very differently from *Orchis mascula*.

py:ramido·logy. [f. PYRAMIDO- + -LOGY.] The study of or theories about the mathematical or occult significance of the measurements of the Great Pyramid. Hence **py:ramidolo·gical; pyramido·logist.**

1924 DAVIDSON & ALDERSMITH *Great Pyramid* I. p. xi, The reader..will probably have realised that Pyramidology, for over sixty years, has consisted of intuitions, and theories based on these intuitions. **1948** 'N. SHUTE' *No Highway* i. 4 'Call yourself a scientist, and you don't know pyramidology!'.. 'Well, I don't. What is it?' 'It's all about the Great Pyramid, in Egypt. Prophecies, and all that sort of thing.' **1954** A. HUXLEY *Let.* 12 Dec. (1969) 719 What may be called the Baconian-pyramidological-cryptographic-spiritualist-theosophical syndrome afflicts a large percentage of the human race. **1964** *Listener* 23 July 117/2 Taylor..believed that he had found various mathematical truths in its [*sc.* the Great Pyramid's] measurements which showed him that the Egyptian priests knew most..of the secrets of the universe... Taylor was, therefore, the founder [1859] of the cult of pyramidology. **1972** *Guardian* 5 Oct. 17/7 Some comfort for would-be biological pyramidologists—cycles are real. **1974** *Nature* 2 Aug. 448/1 Somewhere about here one crosses the transitional zone between statistics and pyramidology. *Ibid.*, Like the pyramidologists he clearly believes that man should be very alert to the hidden meanings buried in the depths of what appear to be fairly straight forward objects or events.

Pyramidon[2] (piræ·midǫn). *Pharm.* Also **pyr-, -one** (-ōᵘn). [a. G. *pyramidon* (W. Filehne 1896, in *Berliner klin. Wochenschr.* XXXIII. 1061), f. *pyrazolon* *PYRAZOLONE with inserted *amid-* (see *AMIDO-).] A white crystalline solid used as an anti-pyretic and analgesic; 4-dimethylamino-1, 5-dimethyl-1-phenylpyrazolin-3-one, $C_{13}H_{17}N_3O$.

Formerly a proprietary term in Britain, and still registered as one in the U.S.

1898 *Jrnl. Chem. Soc.* LXXIV. II. 656 Dimethylamidophenyldimethylpyrazolone, or pyramidone, prepared by Filehne and Spiro, and recommended by them as a substitute for antipyrin..yields bluish-violet colours when oxidised by ferric chloride, nitric and nitrous acids, and the halogens. **1898** *Official Gaz.* (U.S. Patent Office) 6 Dec. 1582/2 Remedy for certain named disease. Farbwerke, vormals Meister, Lucius & Brüning, Höchst-on-the-Main, Germany... *Pyramidon*... Used since December, 1896. **1903** *Brit. Med. Jrnl. Suppl.: Weekly Epitome of Current Med. Lit.* 21 Nov. 79/3 Having heard a good account of pyramidon he proceeded to employ it in a case which he and the nurse were able to observe very closely. **1908** A. BENNETT *Jrnl.* 14 Dec. (1932) I. 300, I..saw a chemist make me a cachet of pyramidon. **1925** W. GERHARDIE *Polyglots* xlix. 358 She took pyramidon for her head, and aspirin for her cold. **1942** *R.A.F. Jrnl.* 30 May 35 A German industrialist in 1942 testified that in the Rhineland it was almost impossible to buy soothing drugs, like pyramidon, any more.

pyran (pəiᵊ·ræn). *Chem.* Also **-ane** (-ēⁱn). [f. *PYR(ONE + -AN, -ANE.] **a.** A heterocyclic compound, C_5H_6O, having a doubly unsaturated six-membered ring consisting of five carbon atoms and one oxygen atom; two isomers (differing in the positions of the double bonds) are possible, only one of which, $\underline{CH_2CH{:}CH{\cdot}CH{:}CH{\cdot}O}$ (*γ-pyran*), has been isolated, as a colourless, unstable oil. **b.** Any derivative of either isomer containing a pyran ring. Freq. *attrib.*, as **pyran ring,** a ring (which may be saturated) of five carbon atoms and one oxygen atom.

[**1901** *Jrnl. Chem. Soc.* LXXX. I. 559 7-Hydroxy-2-

phenyl-4-methylbenzopyran.] **1904** *Ibid.* LXXXVI. I. 816 (*heading*) Properties of oxygen in the pyran ring. **1927** *Ibid.* 3139 The normal sugars are thus seen to be representatives of the parent form indicated by pyran and the labile or γ-sugars have as their parent substance furan. **1952** K. Venkataraman *Chem. Synthetic Dyes* II. xxiv. 742 The γ-pyran ring..occurs in the anthocyanins, the red, violet and blue coloring matters of flowers and fruits. **1953** Fruton & Simmonds *Gen. Biochem.* xvii. 374 The ring in the cyclic form of glucose is related to the heterocyclic compound pyrane. **1962** *Jrnl. Amer. Chem. Soc.* LXXXIV. 2453/1 γ-Pyran is extremely unstable at room temperature, particularly when exposed to air. **1965** Kice & Marvell *Mod. Princ. Org. Chem.* xix. 360 The two double bonds can be conjugated or unconjugated, and two types of pyran rings are known. *Ibid.*, Like enol ethers in general these rings are unstable, and α-pyran itself is unknown.

pyranometer (pəirănǫ·mĭtəɪ). [See quot. 1916 and -METER.] An instrument for measuring the amount of radiation incident from the entire sky on a horizontal surface.

1916 Abbot & Aldrich in *Smithsonian Misc. Coll.* LXVI. No. 7. 2 The name Pyranometer, selected for the instrument we have devised, is taken from Greek words (πῦρ, fire; ἀνά, up; μέτρον, a measure) signifying that which measures heat above. The name was chosen with reference to the fact that the instrument is designed to measure the energy of radiation to or from a complete hemisphere lying above the measuring surface. **1967** *Jrnl. Appl. Meteorol.* VI. 688 (*heading*) An integrating pyranometer for climatological observer stations and mesoscale networks. **1973** *Nature* 16 Feb. 448/2 These data were obtained by subtracting the solar radiation measured by a temperature compensated Eppley pyranometer from the mean hemispherical all-wave radiation obtained from three Fritschen-type net radiometers converted to hemispherical operation.

pyranose (pəiə·r-, pi·rănōᵘz). *Chem.* [f. *PYRAN + -OSE².] A structure containing a saturated pyran ring, frequently assumed by sugars; a sugar having this structure. Freq. *attrib.*

1927 Goodyear & Haworth in *Jrnl. Chem. Soc.* 3141 On the basis of the conclusions now reached, the formula (A) must be accepted as a general representation of a normal sugar, which might be described as a pyranose. **1953** Fruton & Simmonds *Gen. Biochem.* xvii. 380 Another important hexose found in nature is..fructose... The open-chain form..is in equilibrium with the corresponding pyranose and furanose forms; in solutions of the free sugar, the pyranose form predominates. **1957, 1963** [see *FURANOSE]. **1971** *Nature* 26 Nov. 220/1 The anomers α- and β-D-mannose differ structurally only in that H and OH at the C_1 atom of the pyranose ring are interchanged.

pyranoside (pəir-, piræ·nŏsəid). *Chem.* [f. prec. + *-IDE.] Any glycoside in the pyranose form.

1932 *Jrnl. Chem. Soc.* 2254 Usually the product is also contaminated with small amounts of the corresponding pyranosides. **1934, 1966** [see *FURANOSIDE]. **1970** R. W. McGilvery *Biochem.* xxviii. 715 Furanosides and pyranosides can be distinguished by the number of moles of periodate consumed in their oxidation.

pyrazinamide (pəir-, pirăzi·năməid). *Pharm.* [f. next + AMIDE.] A white crystalline powder, pyrazine-2-carboxamide, CH:N·CH:CH·N:C·CONH₂, which is used in the treatment of tuberculosis, usu. in conjunction with other drugs.

1952 *Amer. Rev. Tuberculosis* LXV. 515 The antituberculous activity of pyrazinamide..in mice lies between that of streptomycin and that of PAS. **1961** *Lancet* 2 Sept. 533/2 With 1 g. of streptomycin daily on six days a week..and 1–1·5 g. of pyrazinamide in a single daily dose by mouth, 32..of the 57 patients..attained bacteriological quiescence by the end of the year. **1974** R. M. Kirk et al. *Surgery* ii. 29/2 Ethionamide, pyrazinamide, viomyocin and capreomycin may be used in the treatment of tuberculosis when it proves resistant to the usual combination of streptomycin, INAH, and PAS.

pyrazine (pəiə·r-, pi·răzīn). *Chem.* [ad. G. *pyrazin* (A. T. Mason 1887, at suggestion of V. Merz, in *Ber. d. Deut. Chem. Ges.* XX. 267). f. *pyridin* PYRIDINE with inserted *az-* (see Azo-).] A weakly basic white crystalline solid, CH:N·CH:CH·N:CH; any substituted derivative of this.

[**1887** *Jrnl. Chem. Soc.* LII. I. 493 Xenylenedihydropyrazine.] **1888** *Proc. Chem. Soc.* IV. 107 The author [*sc.* Mason] adopts Widman's nomenclature..: the 'Ketines'.., 'Pyrazines'.., 'Aldines'.., and all compounds containing a ring of four carbon-atoms and two nitrogen-atoms in para-position are now termed Paradiazines, or Piazines. **1926** H. G. Rule tr. *J. Schmidt's Text-bk. Org. Chem.* III. viii. 699 Pyrazine itself is produced by the condensation of amino-acetaldehyde or amino-acetal. It..has an odour of heliotrope. **1967** M. H. Palmer *Struct. & Reactions Heterocyclic Compounds* iii. 89 Pyrazines are readily prepared by the self-condensation of α-aminoketones. **1970** *Acta Crystallographica* B. XXVI. 979/1 Pyrazine..and $Cu(NO_3)_2$ form an anhydrous crystalline complex with a 1:1 pyrazine to $Cu(NO_3)_2$ ratio.

pyrazole (pəiə·r-, pi·răzōᵘl). *Chem.* [ad. G. *pyrazol* (L. Knorr 1885, in *Ber. d. Deut. Chem. Ges.* XVIII. 311). f. *pyrrol* PYRROL with inserted *az-* (see Azo-).] A weakly basic white crystalline solid, CH:CH·CH:N·NH; any substituted derivative of this.

1887 *Jrnl. Chem. Soc.* LII. II. 665 In order to examine whether the formation of pyrazoline-derivatives from phenylhydrazine and acids of the acrylic series is analogous to the formation of pyrazole-derivatives from unsaturated ketones, cinnamyl hydrazine was prepared and its products of decomposition investigated. **1926** H. G. Rule tr. *J. Schmidt's Text-bk. Org. Chem.* III. iii. 566 Pyrazole differs strongly from pyrrole in its remarkable stability and more definitely basic character. **1938** C. D. Hurd in H. Gilman *Org. Chem.* I. vii. 679 β-Diketones and β-keto esters give rise to..pyrazoles with hydrazines. **1968** [see *PYRAZOLONE]. **1970** *New Scientist* 5 Mar. 447/1 By dosing rats heavily with pyrazole, a compound that inhibits alcohol dehydrogenase, Krebs and his group have shown that quite high levels of alcohol can build up in the bloodstream if not removed.

pyrazoline (pəir-, piræ·zŏlīn). *Chem.* [ad. G. *pyrazolin* (L. Knorr 1887, in *Ann. d. Chem.* CCXXXVIII. 144): see prec. and -INE⁵.] Any of three isomeric compounds, $C_3H_6N_2$, which are dihydro derivatives of pyrazole; *spec.* CH₂·CH₂·CH:N·NH (*2-pyrazoline*), a colourless basic liquid, the only one of the three so far prepared; also, any substituted derivative of any of these compounds.

1887 [see *PYRAZOLE]. **1938** R. C. Fuson in H. Gilman *Org. Chem.* I. i. 30 Pyrazolines are unstable toward heat and decompose to give cyclopropane derivatives. **1961** G. M. Badger *Chem. Heterocyclic Compounds* v. 223 Pyrazolines are much less stable than the corresponding pyrazoles and are attacked by oxidizing agents. **1967** C. H. Jarboe in R. H. Wiley *Pyrazoles* vi. 177 Examples of each of the three tautomeric pyrazoline structures.. are well known, 2-pyrazoline being by far the most common. **1968** [see *PYRAZOLONE].

pyrazolone (pəir-, piræ·zŏlōᵘn). *Chem.* [ad. G. *pyrazolon* (L. Knorr 1887, in *Ann. d. Chem.* CCXXXVIII. 145): see *PYRAZOLE and -ONE.] Any keto derivative of a pyrazole; *spec.* NH·N:CH·CH₂·CO (*5-pyrazolone*), a weakly acidic white crystalline solid; also, any of their substituted derivatives, several of which on coupling with diazo compounds give rise to commercially important dyestuffs.

1887 *Jrnl. Chem. Soc.* LII. 601 Many of the compounds obtained by the action of ethyl acetoacetate and its derivatives on the primary aromatic hydrazines have already been described by the author as quinizines... The author [*sc.* Knorr] now regards these substances as pyrazolones. **1926** H. G. Rule tr. *J. Schmidt's Text-bk. Org. Chem.* III. iii. 566 The oxygen of pyrazolones may also be removed by heating..with phosphorus oxychloride, when chloro-derivatives are formed. **1961** G. M. Badger *Chem. Heterocyclic Compounds* v. 226 Theoretically, there are three types of..pyrazolone, but only derivatives of 3-pyrazolone and of 5-pyrazolone are known. **1968** *Kirk-Othmer Encycl. Chem. Technol.* (ed. 2) XVI. 763 Neither pyrazoles nor pyrazolines have found extensive uses, but pyrazolones have been widely utilized as fabric dyes and pigments, as food coloring agents, in color photography, as photographic developing agents, and as pharmaceuticals. **1977** *Lancet* 23 Apr. 905/1 Reversible agranulocytosis has also been described with pyrazolone derivatives (such as phenylbutazone).

Pyrenean, -aean, *a.* and *sb.* Add: The form **Pyrenean** is now standard. Also **Pyreneean.**
A. *adj.* **a.** (Further examples.)

1865 [see *hair-net* s.v. *HAIR *sb.* 10]. **1892** C. M. Yonge *Old Woman's Outlook* 50 The gorgeous Pyrenean anemone, brilliant scarlet with a black or purple centre. **1895** *Army & Navy Co-op. Soc. Price List* 1089/1 (*caption*) Dressing Jacket, Pyrenean Wool, with girdle. **1925** G. Jekyll *Colour Schemes for Flower Garden* (ed. 6) i. 2 Some groups of the pale early Pyrenean Daffodil gleam level on the ground. **1931** *Times Lit. Suppl.* 21 May 399/3 General Beatson..is already known to the reading public as the author of three monographs on Wellington's operations in the Pyreneean area. **1936** A. W. Clapham *Romanesque Archit.* vi. 132 It is curious that the XP monogram maintained its place in the Pyrenean countries well into the twelfth century. **1966** M. R. D. Foot *SOE in France* vii. 155 This donnish figure made some highly unacademic contacts with the Pyrenean smugglers.

b. Pyrenean (mountain or **† guard) dog,** a large, heavily built, white dog of the breed so called, often with grey or brown markings on the head, distinguished by a thick, shaggy, double coat; **Pyrenean sheepdog,** a small, fawn or grey, long-coated sheepdog, often with white markings, belonging to the French breed so called; also = prec.; **Pyrenean wolf-hound** = *Pyrenean mountain dog* above.

1851 H. Mayhew *London Labour* I. 358/2 The collars most in demand are brass. One man pointed out to me the merits of his stock, which he retailed from 6d each..to 3s —for collars seemingly big enough for Pyrenean sheep dogs. **1865** M. Eyre *Lady's Walks in S. France* xiv. 168 The Pyrenean sheep-dogs equal the largest Newfoundland in size. They are very sagacious and tractable, and usually snow-white. **1871** Pyrenean wolf-hound [see WOLF-HOUND]. **1885** C. M. Yonge *Two Sides of Shield* I. iv. 40 There's Basto, the big Pyrenean dog. **1894** R. B. Lee *Hist. & Descr. Mod. Dogs Gt. Brit. & Ireland* (*Non-Sporting Division*) iv. 107 The so-called Pyrenean guard dog we often see on our show benches, is a dog some one hundred and twenty pounds weight and more. **1922** R. Leighton *Compl. Bk. Dog* v. 62 The beautiful white-coated Pyrenean Dog is also essentially a Mastiff. **1927** E. C. Ash *Dogs* II. ix. ii. 589 There is..the remarkable similarity of the St. Bernard of about that time to the Pyrenean sheep-dog 'Cabbas', the property of her Majesty Queen Victoria. **1931** A. C. Smith *About our Dogs* xxiii. 364 So great was my admiration of the Pyrenean Mountain Dogs..that it is rather difficult for me to write with becoming restraint. **1945** C. L. B. Hubbard *Observer's Bk. Dogs* 184 Pyrenean Sheepdog... This is quite a distinct race from the Pyrenean Mountain Dog,.. being much smaller and seldom used for guard work. **1964** *Vogue* 15 Apr. 90 A great heap of Pyrenean mountain dog called Addo de Fontenoy. **1978** *Times* 11 Feb. 2/4 Those shaggy dogs masquerading as overcoats called Pyrenean mountain dogs.

B. *sb.* **b.** (Later example.)

1779 H. Swinburne *Trav. through Spain* viii. 58 The prospect is..grand..bounded by the mountains of Roussillon. The true Pyreneans appear only through some breaks in that chain.

c. A Pyrenean mountain dog or sheepdog.

1922 R. Leighton *Compl. Bk. Dog* v. 62 The Pyrenean has the same massive body. **1931** A. C. Smith *About our Dogs* xxiii. 364 The biggest of the Pyreneans are taller than Newfoundlands. **1950** A. C. Smith *Dogs since 1900* xii. 272 The Pyreneans..have temperaments that make them most pleasing companions. **1971** F. Hamilton *World Encycl. Dogs* 73 The Pyrenean is the smallest [French sheepdog]. **1976** *Drive* July–Aug. 31/2 Mischka ..is the Wilsons' fifth Pyrenean.

pyrethrin (pəirī·þrin). [a. G. *pyrethrin* (Staudinger & Ruzicka 1924, in *Helvetica Chimica Acta* VII. 181): see PYRETHRUM and -IN¹.] Any of a class of insecticidal terpenoid esters which are obtained from flower heads of *Chrysanthemum cinerariæfolium* and related species, or have been synthesized; *spec.* either of two such compounds (*pyrethrins* I and II) which are the major active principles of pyrethrum powder.

1924 *Chem. Abstr.* XVIII. 1819 A mixt. of the semicarbazones..of pyrethrin I..and pyrethrin II. *Ibid.* 2135 Myrcene and N_2CHCO_2Et give 31% of an acid, $C_{12}H_{18}O_2$, which yields a very slightly active pyrethrin. **1934** *Discovery* Sept. 251/2 Although the difference between pyrethrin I and II is of chemical and biological importance, their action is sufficiently similar for it to be disregarded in practical work. **1951** H. H. Shepard *Chem. & Action Insecticides* viii. 146 The pyrethrin content is higher in flowers produced in cool mountain valleys than where the mean temperature is high. *Ibid.* 150 The pyrethrins and cinerins, together referred to generally as pyrethrins, are chemically unstable. **1971** *Inside Kenya Today* Mar. 43/2 Pyrethrin-based insecticides have proved patently safe. **1971** *Nature* 15 Oct. 441/1 Six esters are found in the pyrethrum of which the most important and plentiful are known as pyrethrins I and II.

pyrethroid (pəirī·þroid). *Chem.* [f. as prec. + -OID.] Any substance possessing the terpenoid structure and insecticidal properties characteristic of the pyrethrins.

1954 *Analytical Chem.* XXVI. 604/1 In recent attempts to estimate small quantities of pyrethrins in flour which had been stored in pyrethrum-treated cotton bags..the extraction..was found to be difficult and there were apparent limitations in the accuracy of the analysis of pyrethroids. **1956** *Nature* 25 Feb. 357/2 It has now also been established that the pyrethroids undergo detoxification in the adult housefly. **1971** *Ibid.* 15 Oct. 441/2 Organochlorine and organophosphorus insecticides, many of which tend to break down less quickly than the pyrethroids. **1977** *Protecting World's Crops* (Shell Internat. Petroleum Co.) 2 Insecticides fall into four main categories: chlorinated hydrocarbons, organo-phosphorus, carbamates and synthetic pyrethroids.

pyrethrum. Add: **2.** [Adopted as a generic name in A. Haller *Enumeratio Methodica Stirpium Helvetiæ* (1742) II. 720.] Substitute for def.: A composite plant of the genus formerly so called, now included in the genus *Chrysanthemum* or the subgenus *Tanacetum.* (Later examples.)

1939 A. Cumming *Hardy Chrysanthemums* ii. 27 Efforts of the writer to cross this species with the garden chrysanthemum have been unsuccessful, which may indicate.. that it is a true pyrethrum. **1951** *Dict. Gardening* (R. Hort. Soc.) I. 469/1 The forms [of chrysanthemum] most widely grown are varieties of *C. morifolium*..and of *C. roseum*, generally known in gardens as Pyrethrums. **1964** G. B. Schaller *Year of Gorilla* (1965) iv. 86 Many Europeans have settled in the rift mountains. There they grow tea and white-flowered pyrethrum, used in making insect powder. **1976** *Hortus Third* (L. H. Bailey Hortorium) 267/1 Feverfews. These are forms of *C*[*hrysanthemum*] *Parthenium*, sometimes known as pyrethrum. *Ibid.*, Pyrethrums. These are derived from *C. coccineum*, and bloom in late spring and summer.

b. Substitute for the names of the plants listed in Dict.: *Chrysanthemum* (or *Tanacetum*) *cinerariifolium* or *C. coccineum.* (Further examples.)

1888 *Insect Life* I. 145 Pyrethrum powder was freely used. **1902** *Chambers's Jrnl.* 22 Feb. 191/1 A house where a case of fever had occurred would be fumigated with burning pyrethrum, contiguous dwellings being treated in the same manner. **1955** *Sci. News Let.* 10 Sept. 169/2 Pyrethrum is harmless to human beings and animals, but fatal to flies. **1964** *Which?* Apr. 115/1 The risk is reduced by using..short-lived insecticides, such as derris or pyrethrum. **1978** C. Jeffrey in V. H. Heywood *Flowering Plants of World* 268/3 *Tanacetum cinerariifolium* is the main commercial source of natural pyrethrum, used as an insecticide.

Pyrex (pəiᵊ·reks). Also **pyrex.** [Invented word.

Cf. the following quot.: **1957** *Amer. Speech* XXXII. 290 The assistant secretary of the [Corning Glass] company wrote me as follows: The word *pyrex* is a purely arbitrary word which was devised in 1915 as a trade-mark for products manufactured and sold by Corning Glass Works... We had a number of prior trade-marks ending in the letters *ex*. One of the first commercial products to be sold under the new mark was a pie plate and in the interests of euphonism the letter *r* was inserted between *pie* and *ex* and the whole thing condensed to *pyrex*.]

The proprietary name of a hard, heat-resistant, borosilicate glass. Freq. *attrib.*

1915 *Amer. Cookery* Aug.–Sept. 159 (Advt.), Pyrex ('fire-glass') Glass Dishes for Baking. *Ibid.*, Pyrex is a new-process glass, fire-proofed to withstand the heat of the hottest oven. **1916** *Official Gaz.* (U.S. Patent Office) 1 Aug. 245/1 Corning Glass Works, Corning, N.Y. Filed July 10, 1915 *Pyrex*... Glass. Claims use since May 20, 1915. **1917** *Trade Marks Jrnl.* 10 Jan. 30 *Pyrex*... All goods included in Class 15. Corning Glass Works..New York, U.S.A... 11th October 1916. **1927** *Glasgow Herald* 1 July 10 Housewives no longer use iron pots and pans. Their kitchenettes are bright with aluminium and pyrex ware. **1932** Auden in *Rev. Eng. Stud.* (1978) Aug. 295 Tea was served, Poured by the secretary from a pyrex teapot. **1932** *Discovery* June 199/2 The door itself is fitted with a Pyrex glass window for inspection of the flame. **1958** *Times Lit. Suppl.* 7 Feb. 70/2 Fashionable art critics' jargon which attributes organic qualities to Mr Moore's bronzes or Mr Frank Lloyd Wright's pillars of Pyrex glass. **1961** R. M. Dashwood *Provincial Daughter* 107 Odd pieces of Cornish Ware, Pyrex, Willow pattern. **1976** 'Z. Stone' *Modigliani Scandal* iv. iv. 178 Moore took out his false teeth..and dropped them in a Pyrex beaker.

Pyribenzamine (piribe·nzămīn). *Pharm.* [f. Pyri(dine + Benz(o- + Amine.] A proprietary name in the U.S. for the antihistamine tripelennamine hydrochloride.

1946 *Proc. Soc. Exper. Biol. & Med.* LXII. 65/1 B-dimethylaminoethyl benzhydryl ether (Benadryl) and pyridil-N¹-benzyl-N-dimethylethylenediamine (Pyribenzamine)..have proven effective in histamine, and anaphylactic shock and in the management of some allergic conditions in man. **1946** *Official Gaz.* (U.S. Patent Office) 27 Aug. 511/1 Ciba Pharmaceutical Products, Inc., Summit, N.J... *Pyribenzamine* for preparation indicated for use in allergic conditions. Claims use since July 12, 1945. **1962** F. J. Ferguson *Drug Therapy* xliv. 346 Recommended agents are promethazine, or Phenergan (if marked sedation is desired), tripelennamine, or Pyribenzamine (for lesser degree of sedation), and phenindamine (Thephorin). **1974** M. C. Gerald *Pharmacol.* ii. 30 Antihistamines such as tripelennamine (Pyribenzamine) do not cure allergies, but they do prevent the agonist, histamine, from initiating an allergic response.

pyridazine (piri·dăzīn). *Chem.* [f. Pyr(o- + -id⁴ + *azine.] The weakly basic colourless liquid C_4H_4N, 1,2-diazine; also, any derivative of this.

1895 *Jrnl. Chem. Soc.* LXVIII. 301 When it is heated.. with 5 per cent. hydrochloric acid at 200°, it yields pyridazine. **1926** H. G. Rule tr. *Schmidt's Text-bk. Org. Chem.* viii. i. 697 Pyridazines can often be prepared by the oxidation of their dihydro-derivatives. **1975** R. F. Brown *Org. Chem.* xxviii. 902 The three isomeric diazines are 1,2-diazabenzene (pyridazine), 1,3-diazabenzene (pyrimidine), and 1,4-diazabenzene (pyrazine).

pyridine. Add: Now with pronunc. (pi·ridīn). **b. pyridine nucleotide,** either of the two oxidizing co-enzymes di- and triphosphopyridine nucleotide (co-enzymes I and II); (sometimes with added *di-* or *triphosphate* respectively).

[**1936** *Chem. Abstr.* XXX. 8262 Cozymase is an adenine-pyridine-nucleotide, which is a H-transporter because the pyridine changes to dihydropyridine.] **1937** *Proc. R. Soc.* B. CXXII. 355 The question then arose whether or not the action of pyridine nucleotide triphosphate was specific and if it could be replaced by pyridine nucleotide diphosphate. *Ibid.* 359 The two pyridine nucleotides were active as 'V' factor, the limit of the activity of pyridine nucleotide triphosphate being about 1/600,000,000. **1951** Whitby & Hynes *Med. Bacteriol.* (ed. 5) xvi. 282 The V factor is the di- or tri-phosphate of pyridine nucleotide, coenzymes that act as intermediate hydrogen receptors in cytochrome and other respiratory mechanisms. **1966** S. P. Colowick et al. in Florkin & Stotz *Comprehensive Biochem.* XIV. i. 4 The pyridine nucleotides are thus concerned in virtually all biosynthetic and degradative processes involving oxidation-reduction steps.

pyridostigmine (pi:ridǫsti·gmīn). *Pharm.* [ad. G. *pyridostigmin*: see Pyridine and *neostigmine* s.v. *neo- 1 b.] The ion $(CH_3)_2N{\cdot}CO{\cdot}O{\cdot}C_6H_4N^+CH_3$ or its bromide derivative, a whitish crystalline powder similar in action to neostigmine but weaker and longer-acting and giving rise to fewer side-effects.

1953 *Jrnl. Amer. Med. Assoc.* 12 Sept. 175/1 Since 1948, a pyridine homologue of neostigmine (Pyridostigmine), was given a therapeutic trial in 23 patients with myasthenia gravis associated with pseudoparalysis. Results of animal experiments..showed that Pyridostigmine is five times less toxic than neostigmine. **1961** D. Dunlop et al. *Textbk. Med. Treatm.* (ed. 8) 875 Myasthenia Gravis... The drug which is most generally useful is pyridostigmine bromide, B.P.C. (Mestinon)... Pyridostigmine gives a very satisfactory smooth control with few parasympathomimetic side-effects, and the long action without sudden withdrawal effects makes it particularly suitable for treatment during the night. **1980** *Sci. Amer.* Apr. 38/2 Reversible inhibitors of acetylcholinesterase such as pyridostigmine (administered by means of pills swallowed a short time before nerve-gas exposure) may improve the prognosis.

pyridoxal (piridǫ·ksæl). *Biochem.* [f. as next + *-al².] One of the forms of vitamin B_6 (derived from pyridoxine by oxidation of the 4-hydroxymethyl group to aldehyde), which usu. occurs in mammals as the phosphate ester and is a co-enzyme in a number of metabolic processes, notably transamination. Cf. *pyridoxine.

1944 E. E. Snell in *Jrnl. Biol. Chem.* CLIV. 313 (*caption*) Pyridoxal. *Ibid.*, When pyridoxamine or pyridoxal is used as a standard of comparison with *S*[*treptococcus*] *lactis*, values for the 'B_6' content of natural materials are obtained similar to those indicated by yeast assay, instead of the absurdly high values obtained against a pyridoxine standard. **1955** *Sci. News Let.* 1 Oct. 211/1 The cancer cells..need these seven vitamins: choline, folic acid, nicotinamide, pantothenate, pyridoxal, riboflavin and thiamine. **1966** E. R. M. Kay *Biochem.* xxiii. 302 Transamination reactions appear to involve a transfer of the amino group to the pyridoxal, forming pyridoxamine and a keto acid. **1970** [see *pyridoxamine]. **1974** *Nature* 9 Aug. 502/2 Pyridoxine, the major dietary form of vitamin B_6, is rapidly converted in the body to pyridoxal phosphate.., the coenzyme form.

pyridoxamine (piridǫ·ksămīn). *Biochem.* [f. as next + Amine.] One of the active forms of vitamin B_6 (related to pyridoxine by replacement of the 4-hydroxymethyl group by an aminomethyl group), which is usu. present in mammals as the phosphate ester and is a co-enzyme in protein metabolism. Cf. *pyridoxine.

1944 E. E. Snell in *Jrnl. Biol. Chem.* CLIV. 315 (*caption*) Pyridoxamine. **1944** [see *pyridoxal]. **1950** *Thorpe's Dict. Appl. Chem.* (ed. 4) X. 316/2 Schlenk and Fisher..working with the glutamic-aspartic transaminase system from pig-heart, have suggested that the reversible interconversion of pyridoxal and pyridoxamine in the prosthetic group forms the basis of the enzyme system. **1961** [see *pyridoxine]. **1966** [see *pyridoxal]. **1968** J. Marks *Vitamins in Health & Dis.* 94/2 The B_6 group are rapidly converted in the body into the co-enzymes pyridoxal phosphate and pyridoxamine phosphate... These co-enzymes play an essential role in protein metabolism. **1970** R. W. McGilvery *Biochem.* vi. 120 The substituted pyridine ring of pyridoxal phosphate..cannot be synthesized by vertebrates, and its dietary precursors are lumped together as vitamin B_6, which includes pyridoxal, pyridoxamine, and the corresponding alcohol, pyridoxine.

pyridoxic (piridǫ·ksik), *a.* *Biochem.* [f. as next + -ic.] *pyridoxic acid* (more explicitly *4-pyridoxic acid*), an inactive oxidized derivative of pyridoxine (the 4-hydroxymethyl group having been oxidized to carboxyl), which is the form in which excess vitamin B_6 is usu. excreted.

1944 Huff & Perlzweig in *Jrnl. Biol. Chem.* CLV. 355 A fluorescent compound appearing in urine after the ingestion of pyridoxine was isolated and identified as 2-methyl-3-hydroxy-4-carboxy-5-hydroxymethylpyridine (4-pyridoxic acid). **1950** W. Shive in R. J. Williams et al. *Biochem. of B Vitamins* d. viii. 657 Pyridoxic acid is the chief metabolic product of either pyridoxine, pyridoxal or pyridoxamine. **1968** Baker & Frank *Clinical Vitaminol.* vii. 79 In subjects on a normal diet, pyridoxic acid excretion accounted for only about half the intake of vitamin B_6.

pyridoxine (piridǫ·ksīn, -in). *Biochem.* Also **-in.** [f. Pyridine with inserted Ox- 1.] One of the three common forms of vitamin B_6, a colourless, weakly basic, crystalline solid which occurs esp. in cereals, liver oils, and yeast, is also manufactured commercially, and is readily interconverted inside the body to the other forms of the vitamin, pyridoxal and pyridoxamine, with which it usu. occurs; 3-hydroxy-4,5-di(hydroxymethyl)-2-methylpyridine, $C_8H_{11}NO_3$; = *adermin.

1939 [see *adermin]. **1941** *Science* 5 Dec. 545/2 *In vitro* experiments with pyridoxine..failed to demonstrate the presence of the unknown substance. **1948** *New Biol.* IV. 24 Roots of a hybrid [tomato] are apparently able to synthesise pyridoxine and nicotinamide better than the roots of its parents. **1961** *Lancet* 16 Sept. 623/1 Pyridoxine deficiency induced by these drugs is an alternative mechanism invoked to explain the liver damage, and Coursin.. found low levels of circulating pyridoxal and pyridoxamine in a patient showing iproniazid toxicity. **1970** L. J. Harris in J. Needham *Chem. of Life* vi. 164 In 1934, a second component of the vitamin B_2 complex, at first called vitamin B_6..and now generally known as pyridoxin, was identified. **1972** *Materials & Technol.* V. xix 679 Pyridoxine hydrochloride is produced commercially by synthesis... It is used in multi-vitamin preparations and in larger quantities to counteract drug effects. **1974** M. C. Gerald *Pharmacol.* x. 182 Deficiencies of pyridoxine (vitamin B6) and niacin cause convulsions in infants and pellagra, respectively.

Now also called **pyrido·xol** [-ol].

1959 *Recueil des Travaux Chimiques des Pays-Bas* LXXVIII. 226 (*heading*) An improved synthesis of vitamin B_6 (pyridoxol). [*Note*] The name pyridoxol was proposed at the 17th IUPAC congress at Stockholm in 1953. **1966** Mahler & Cordes *Biol. Chem.* viii. 341 Numerous nutritional studies..have established that a deficiency of pyridoxol (pyridoxine)..results in many lesions in protein metabolism. **1973** Zeffren & Hall *Stud. Enzyme Mechanisms* viii. 157 The nutritional factor vitamin B_6 was known in 1934 to be involved in protein metabolism. Chemical studies showed that its structure was 3-hydroxy-4,5-di(hydroxymethyl)-2-methylpyridine.., called pyridoxol.

pyriform, *a.* Delete '(Only in scientific or technical use.)' and add further examples.

1913 *Cunningham's Text-bk. Anat.* (ed. 4) 164 The apertura piriformis [*ed.* 3 (1909): pyriformis].., which lies below and in part between the orbits, is of variable shape and size—usually piriform [*ed.* 3: pyriform], it tends to be long and narrow in Europeans. **1928** V. G. Childe *Most Anc. East* v. 117 The piriform mace has a very long history in Babylonia. **1932** *Times Lit. Suppl.* 20 Oct. 743/1 His performances on the putting green with an archaic piriform wooden putter were marked by a deadly accuracy. **1948** A. Brodal *Neurol. Anat.* x. 327 The olfactory fibres ultimately transmitting olfactory impulses to the cerebral cortex are those passing to the piriform lobe. **1948, 1962** [see *palæopallium]. **1971** *Country Life* 15 July 184/1 Shapes of fashionable cruet glass followed those of silver. Castors were at first pyriform. **1973** M. Crowell *Greener Pastures* 167 Birds like the murre..lay triangular, or pyriform, eggs that roll in tight circles. **1973** *Nature* 3 Aug. 314/2 A small snout with a small piriform aperture projected from a broad and very flat face.

pyrimethamine (pirime·þămīn). *Pharm.* [f. *pyrim(idine + eth(yl + Amine.] A white crystalline solid, 2,4-diamino-5-*p*-chlorophenyl-6-ethylpyrimidine, $C_{12}H_{13}N_4Cl_1$ which is given orally for the prophylaxis and suppression of malaria.

1953 *Brit. Med. Jrnl.* 31 Jan. 253/1 Pyrimethamine..is the latest of the new synthetic anti-malarial drugs to be tested by us... This compound is produced by Burroughs Wellcome & Co. under the trade name 'daraprim'. **1961** *New Scientist* 20 Apr. 120/1 Pyrimethamine resistance has appeared in some districts in East Africa. **1966** *Lancet* 24 Dec. 1382/1 The combination of dapsone to shorten the red-blood-cell life-span and pyrimethamine to inhibit erythropoiesis has now been used successfully on five patients with secondary polycythæmia. **1976** *Ibid.* 4 Dec. 1257/1 When a dose of 25 mg weekly is taken for malarial prophylaxis, pyrimethamine is unlikely to produce adverse hæmatological effects except in those actually or potentially folate deficient.

pyrimidine (piri·midīn, pəir-). *Chem.* Also † **-in.** [ad. G. *pyrimidin* (A. Pinner 1885, in *Ber. d. Deut. Chem. Ges.* XVIII. 760) f. *pyridin* Pyridine with inserted *-im* (f. *imid* Imide in Dict. and Suppl.).] A colourless, crystalline basic solid, CH:N·CH:N·CH:CH; any substituted derivative containing this ring structure, *spec.* cytosine, thymine, or uracil, pyrimidines found in nucleic acids, etc. Freq. *attrib.*

1885 *Jrnl. Chem. Soc.* XLVIII. ii. 751 The author substitutes the formula R·C<N·C(OH)>CH / N:CMe for that previously assigned, terming the nucleus pyrimidine. **1886** *Ibid.* L. 45 The author has tried to prepare the corresponding pyrimidines from various amidines. **1899** *Ibid.* LXXVI. i. 639 Pyrimidine..melts at 20–22°..; it has a penetrating, stupefying odour. **1924** *Nature* 12 Apr. 524/1 In these bodies [*sc.* the nucleic acids] a carbohydrate group is associated with a phosphoric acid group and also with a purin or pyrimidin base. **1947** *Sci. News* IV. 109 The I.C.I. men started on something quite different: the pyrimidine ring, an assemblage of atoms found in uric acid, in the chromosomes of the nucleus of living cells, and widely in all living things. **1952, 1954** [see *purine]. **1960** *New Biol.* XXXI. 40 The two pyrimidines, which are smaller molecules than the purines, are named thymine and cytosine. **1962** D. J. Brown *Pyrimidines* iv. 116 Until recently, pyrimidine was an exceedingly rare substance, but several good methods of preparation have now made it readily available in quantity. **1976** *Ann. Rev. Microbiol.* XXX. 92 Other auxotrophs such as those requiring amino acids, purines, and pyrimidines do not assume a colonial or semicolonial growth habit if the biochemical supplement in the medium is limiting.

pyritic, *a.* Add: *spec.* applied to a process for smelting sulphide copper ores with pyrites so that oxidation of the latter produces all the necessary heat.

1897 Huntington & McMillan *Metals* (new ed.) 331 This is the process known as pyritic smelting, and there is some prospect that it may take a prominent position in the metallurgy of copper, although at present it is mainly employed in the extraction of gold and silver from complex ores. **1926** D. M. Liddell *Handbk. Nonferrous Metallurgy* II. xxvii. 944 There are three distinct processes in blast-furnace smelting: (1) The reduction process...

The blast oxidizes the carbon of the coke and but little of the sulphur in the ore... (2) The pyritic process, in which raw massive sulphides are smelted in a highly oxidizing atmosphere without the addition of carbonaceous fuel... (3) The partial- or semipyritic process. *Ibid.* 945 The essential requirements for pyritic smelting are siliceous material which is high in free silica, and heavy pyrite ore... The pyrite ore not only furnishes the heat for the operation, but also the sulphur for the matte required. **1974** D. AVERY *Not on Queen Victoria's Birthday* xiv. 280 'Pyritic smelting', developed by Lawrence Austin and Robert Sticht at [*sic*] Montana between 1887 and 1896 and introduced at Mount Lyell in Tasmania in the latter year,..provided a means of producing much cheaper copper.

pyro-. Add: **1. pyroce·llulose,** a form of nitrocellulose containing slightly less nitrogen than gun-cotton (see quots.); **py·roclast** *Geol.*, a pyroclastic rock fragment; **pyroclastic** *a.* (earlier and later examples); also as *sb.*, a pyroclastic rock or rock fragment; **pyromagnetic** *a.*, more widely, pertaining to or exhibiting pyromagnetism; (further examples); **pyroma·gnetism;** [ad. G. *pyromagnetismus* (W. Voigt 1901, in *Nachrichten v.d. K. Ges. d. Wissensch. zu Göttingen* (*Math.-phys. Klasse*) I. 1)], magnetism that is dependent on the temperature of the material; **pyromania** (later examples); **pyromaniac** *sb.* (later examples), *a.* (example); **pyromaniacal** *a.* (example); **pyroma·nic** *a.*, of or relating to pyromania; **pyrome·tallurgy,** metallurgy in which high temperatures are employed for the extraction of metals; hence **py:rometallu·rgical** *a.*, **pyrome·tallurgist; py·rosphere** *Geol.* = *BARYSPHERE; **pyrosy·nthesis,** synthesis by the action of heat; hence **pyrosynthe·tic** *a.*

1906 E. M. WEAVER *Notes Military Explosives* iv. 123 *Pyrocellulose*, a soluble nitrocellulose of so called definite percentage of N(12·4), corresponding to the molecular formula, $C_{30}H_{38}(NO_2)_{12}O_{25}$, claimed to have been produced by Mendeléef; it possesses just sufficient content of O to burn all of the C to CO, the H to H_2O. **1920** O. W. WILLCOX in A. Rogers *Industr. Chem.* (ed. 3) xlvi. 1076 Nitrocellulose of from 12·50 to 12·70 per cent of nitrogen is called pyrocellulose, or simply pyro, and is the material from which smokeless powder for cannon is made. **1951** KIRK & OTHMER *Encycl. Chem. Technol.* VI. 36 Various types or grades of nitrocellulose are characterized by their nitrogen contents and the following names are used: pyroxylin, 8–12% nitrogen; pyrocellulose, 12·6±0·1% nitrogen; guncotton, 13·3±0·1% nitrogen. **1974** *Encycl. Brit. Macropædia* VII. 87/1 It was..the most important type of smokeless powder used by the Allies in World War I. It was made from a nitrocotton of relatively low nitrogen content, called pyrocellulose, because that type is quite soluble in ether-alcohol. **1920** A. HOLMES *Nomencl. Petrol.* 193 *Pyroclasts*, a general term for fragmental deposits of volcanic ejectamenta. **1934** *Bull. Amer. Assoc. Petroleum Geologists* XVIII. 1573 The bentonite beds in the basal McLure shale represent purer beds of originally vitric pyroclasts. **1944** A. HOLMES *Princ. Physical Geol.* xx. 443 The great clouds of gases, vapours, and pyroclasts that are the most conspicuous feature of explosive eruptions may be luminous or dark. **1972** *Nature* 21 Jan. 157/1 This eruption was extremely violent: an estimated 1·4 km^3 of pyroclast flow and fall was emitted. **1887** J. J. H. TEALL in *Geol. Mag.* Decade III. IV. 493, I venture to suggest that..we should distinguish between the three types of clastic rocks at present recognized by using the terms epiclastic, cataclastic, and pyroclastic... *Pyroclastic*—Fragmental rocks of volcanic origin. The same terms may be applied to the structures which characterize the rocks in question. **1903** *Bull. U.S. Geol. Survey* No. 213. 73 The gravels of Slate Creek contain..a certain proportion of material derived from the older quartzites, pyroclastics, and granite intrusives occurring on the south side of its lower valley. **1939** W. H. TWENHOFEL *Princ. Sedimentation* viii. 291 The coarse-grained pyroclastics fall near the places of expulsion. **1976** P. FRANCIS *Volcanoes* iv. 127 All volcanic rocks..may turn up either as lavas or pyroclastics. *Ibid.* v. 158 Pumice is the best-known of all pyroclastic..rocks. **1901** Pyromagnetic [see *piezo-magnetic* adj. s.v. *PIEZO-]. **1931** S. R. WILLIAMS *Magn. Phenomena* v. 164 A pyromagnetic crystal must show a magnetic moment at room temperature. **1975** *Jrnl. Appl. Physics* XLVI. 2250/1 The low-frequency pyromagnetic effect has been used to study the behavior of a ferromagnetic material both in the low-temperature region as well as near its Curie temperature. **1901** Pyromagnetism [see *piezomagnetism* s.v. *PIEZO-]. **1956** *Soviet Physics: JETP* III. 436/2 Recently the opinion has been expressed that pyromagnetism, piezomagnetism, etc., are impossible. **1973** *Jrnl. Appl. Physics* XLIV. 424/1 Another interesting application of pyromagnetism revealed by the present study is the possibility of verifying, or determining, the relationships between crystalline anisotropy constants and the magnetization near the critical point. **1895** Pyromania [see *ONOMATOMANIA b]. **1937** *Times* 7 Oct. 11/2 Mr. A. Lawson-Walton ..said that there was no evidence of spite.., and it seemed that the accused had a kind of pyromania and delighted in making fires. **1929** W. S. SADLER *Mind at Mischief* x. 141 We have the same condition in the case of certain types of pyromaniacs. **1967** *Listener* 6 Apr. 466/2 Jeanne Moreau lends to the role..more credibility than was apparent in her full-length portrayal of the pyromaniac school-mistress. **1972** G. W. KISKER *Disorganized Personality* (ed. 2) viii. 260/1 The defiance is usually aimed at the police in their role of father image. Pyromaniacs of this type go about setting fires indiscriminately. **1873** G. H. LEWES *Probl. Life & Mind* 1st Ser. I. 234 Phases which manifest homicidal, kleptomaniacal, and pyromaniacal instincts. **1926** J. I. SUTTIE tr. *Ferenczi's Further Contrib. Theory & Technique Psycho-Anal.* xxxi. 258 There were quite a number [of cases] in which incendiaries set fire to their *beds*, as though to indicate the..enuristic primitive source of their pyromanic character trait. **1968** G. JONES *Hist. Vikings* I. ii. 52 According to *Ynglinga Saga*, this pyromanic imbecility cost the Ynglings their realm of Uppsala. **1917** E. OBERG *Machinery's Encycl.* II. 204/2 There are three methods by means of which copper may be obtained from its ores: 1. By the pyro-metallurgical or dry method. **1971** *Daily Tel.* 29 Apr. 25 (Advt.), Applicants should have..a strong pyrometallurgical background and a minimum of 3 years' smelting or related development experience. **1960** *Times* 6 Apr. 3/1 (Advt.), Applications are invited..for appointment to the posts of Pyrometallurgist, [etc.]. **1974** *Daily Tel.* 2 May 23 (Advt.), The Pyrometallurgist will work in the Smelter, which has an annual production capacity of approximately 84,000 tonnes of copper. **1909** WEBSTER, Pyrometallurgy. **1957** *New Scientist* 26 Sept. 20/1 Pyrometallurgy, the study of metals in the molten state, may find an application in the treatment of metals which are 'hot' in the sense of being highly radioactive. **1973** R. D. PEHLKE *Unit Processes of Extractive Metallurgy* i. 5 Following the mining and concentration of minerals, their extraction is accomplished by application of chemical metallurgy in one of the three areas of extractive metallurgy: pyrometallurgy, hydrometallurgy, or electrometallurgy. **1900** *Geogr. Jrnl.* XV. 88 A coloured diagram showing an ideal section of the Earth on the hypothesis that within the solid lithosphere lies a pyrosphere of intensely high temperature. **1963** D. W. & E. E. HUMPHRIES tr. *Termier's Erosion & Sedimentation* i. 1 Glyptogenesis is the process of sculpturing of the lithosphere through the agency of the atmosphere, hydrosphere, biosphere and pyrosphere. **1947** *Bull. Geol. Soc. Amer.* LVIII. 1232 (*heading*) Pyrosyntheses of telluride minerals. **1955** *Jrnl. Amer. Chem. Soc.* LXXVII. 1048/2 (*heading*) Pyrosynthesis of aspartic acid and alanine from citric acid cycle intermediates. **1961** *Amer. Mineralogist* XLVI. 823 Differential thermal pyrosynthesis may be considered a modification of differential thermal analysis which allows investigation under closed system conditions. A record is obtained of thermal reactions which occur during synthesis by heating elemental constituents to the fusion point. **1956** *Amer. Scientist* XLIV. 357 Pyrosynthetic experiments.

2. pyrobe·lonite *Min.* [ad. G. *pyrobelonit* (G. Flink 1919, in *Geol. Föreningens i Stockholm Förhandl.* XLI. 436), f. Gr. βελόνη needle], a basic vanadate of manganese and lead, $MnPb(VO_4)(OH)$, occurring as red, transparent, needle-shaped crystals; **pyrobi·tumen,** any of a class of native hydrocarbons that differ from the bitumens proper in being relatively hard, infusible, and insoluble in organic solvents; hence **py:robitu·minous** *a.*; **pyrochlore** (further examples); also, any of a group of minerals that includes pyrochlore, microlite, betafite, and obruchevite, the members of which have the general formula $A_2B_2O_6(O,OH,F)$, where A may be sodium, potassium, calcium, cerium, or certain other elements, and B may be niobium, tantalum, titanium, or certain other elements; freq. *attrib.* in *pyrochlore group*; **py·rolite** [-LITE], † (*a*) an artificial rock (see quot. 1848) (*obs.*); (*b*) a mixture proposed as the primitive material of the earth's upper mantle (see quots. 1962, 1975); **pyrophillite,** var. *pyrophyllite*.

1920 *Chem. Abstr.* XIV. 1097 (*heading*) Pyrobelonite, a new lead-manganese vanadate from Långbanshyttan. **1969** *Canad. Mineralogist* X. 117 The specimen..was Harvard 94831 from the type locality, Långban, Sweden. It consists largely of massive to well-crystallized hausmannite in contact with, and cut by, calcite. The pyrobelonite occurs as very fine grains with a few small crystals (commonly $< 100\,\mu$ in largest dimension) primarily in the hausmannite. **1903** C. RICHARDSON in *Science* 13 Mar. 420/1 The evidence thus obtained has been carefully analyzed, and the following classification of the native bitumens deduced: Gas... Petroleum... Maltha. Solid Bitumens... Pyrobitumens: Practically insoluble in chloroform or heavy petroleum hydrocarbons. **1951** K. K. LANDES *Petroleum Geol.* iv. 127 The solid hydrocarbons may be subdivided into four main groups: petroleum bitumens, pyrobitumens, disseminated bitumens, and oxygen-bearing bitumens. **1965** Pyrobitumen [see *IMPSONITE]. **1918** H. ABRAHAM *Asphalts & Allied Substances* xi. 149 They [*sc.* pyrobitumens] are grouped into five classes, viz.: elaterite, wurtzilite, albertite, impsonite, and asphaltic pyrobituminous shales. **1937** *Bull. Amer. Assoc. Petroleum Geologists* XXI. 122 Regardless of the possible economic value of the Brazilian algal deposits and other pyrobituminous sediments, those now forming in fresh-water ponds and the related geologically young deposits have great scientific interest. **1906** J. P. IDDINGS *Rock Minerals* II. 464 Pyrochlore group. Pyrochlore, RNb_2O_6. $R(Ti,Th)O_3$.NaF. Koppite, $R_2Nb_2O_7$.⅔NaF. Microlite, $Ca_2Ta_2O_7$.pt. **1941** *Amer. Mineralogist* XXVI. 504 A study of the available analyses of pyrochlore shows that both cerium and titanium are invariably present in appreciable amounts and must therefore be regarded as essential constituents. *Ibid.* 505 Koppite... Winchell (1933) describes this mineral as 'a pyrochlore containing K' while Brandenberger (1931) states that koppite should be regarded as an iron-columbium pyrochlore. **1959** [see *PANDAITE]. **1977** *Amer. Mineralogist* LXII. 404/1 The pyrochlore group comprises those multiple cubic oxides having the following characteristics: (*a*) essential amounts of niobium, tantalum, and titanium, either individually or in combination (*b*) the space group *Fd3m*, (*c*) the pyrochlore structure as defined by Gaertner (1930) and Brandenberger (1931), and (*d*) the general formula $A_{2-m}B_2O_6(O,OH,F)_{1-n}pH_2O$... The recommended subgroups are: Pyrochlore Subgroup in which $Nb+Ta>2\,Ti$ and $Nb>Ta$. [Etc.] **1848** *Mining Jrnl.* 4 Nov. 521/1 Mr. Twining's object is to form, by chemical means, a comprehensive series of petrous substances which he proposes to designate..pyrolite or artificial lava, as..being of igneous origin. **1962** A. E. RINGWOOD in *Jrnl. Geophysical Res.* LXVII. 860/1 Immediately below the M discontinuity, the mantle consists dominantly of dunite and peridotite... This zone passes downward..into the primitive 'pyrolite'. [*Note*] Peridotite is an unsatisfactory name for the hypothetical primitive mantle material, chemically equivalent to 1 part basalt plus 4 parts of dunite. Since a rock of this composition would crystallize dominantly as a mixture of olivine and pyroxene, the name 'pyrolite' is suggested. **1975** *Sci. Amer.* Mar. 56/1 Assigning an appropriate chemistry to the residual peridotite, one arrives at the hypothetical composition of the upper mantle. Pyrolite (pyroxene-olivine rock) is the name given to one of these hypothetical peridotites. **1946** J. R. PARTINGTON *Gen. & Inorganic Chem.* xviii. 506 Montmorillonite shows the same X-ray pattern as pyrophillite, which occurs crystalline in slates. **1975** TINDALL & THORNHILL *Blandford Rock & Mineral Guide* II. 96 This structure can extend indefinitely in a two-dimensional network or 'sheet'; it is found, for example, in the mineral pyrophillite, $Al_2Si_4O_{10}(OH)_2$.

3. a. pyropho·sphate, a salt or ester, or the anion, of pyrophosphoric acid; a group or linkage formed from two condensed phosphate groups.

1836–41, 1869 [in Dict.]. **1912** E. FEILMANN tr. *Molinari's Inorg. Chem.* 348 The pyrophosphates..give a precipitate with copper salts, which is soluble in excess of pyrophosphate. **1950** N. V. SIDGWICK *Chem. Elements* I. 746 Ethyl pyrophosphate $Et_4P_2O_7$ can be made from the silver salt and ethyl iodide. **1957** G. E. HUTCHINSON *Treat. Limnol.* I. xii. 728 Though pyrophosphate plays an important role inside the organism, it is easily hydrolyzed and only orthophosphate is likely to be of importance in the environment. **1970** AMBROSE & EASTY *Cell Biol.* vii. 248 There is another type of reaction, catalysed by enzymes known as phosphorylases, in which a sugar phosphate reacts with another sugar to form a disaccharide and inorganic pyrophosphate.

b. pyroca·techol = *CATECHOL, *pyrocatechin* s.v. PYRO- 3 b.

1890 *Proc. Chem. Soc.* VI. 90 The very high price of pyrocatechol renders it desirable to discover improved methods of preparing it. **1932** I. D. GARARD *Introd. Org. Chem.* xiv. 199 Pyrocatechol is used as a photographic developer. **1956** *Nature* 28 Jan. 184/2 Copper cyanide, though it accelerates considerably the rate of autoxidation of pyrocatechol.., is not very superior to cupric ions alone as regards catalytic activity on pigment formation from pyrocatechol.

pyrobelonite to **-cellulose:** see *PYRO- 1, 2, 3 b.

Pyroceram (pəiə·roseræ:m). Also **pyroceram.** [f. PYRO- + CERAM(IC *a.* (*sb.*).] A proprietary term in the U.S. for a type of strong, heat-resistant glass which has been heat-treated so that it consists entirely of microscopic crystalline domains.

1957 *New Scientist* 23 May 27/1 The name of this fabulous stuff, which Dr. Stookey invented, is pyroceram. It is harder than flint, light as aluminium, stronger (in ratio to its weight) than stainless steel. *Ibid.* 28/2 The Corning Glass Works has at least a thousand different formulæ for pyrocerams. **1957** *Amer. Ceramic Soc. Bull.* XXXVI. 279/1 Pyroceram is melted and formed like glass, but with a formula containing one or more nucleating agents. **1958** *Official Gaz.* (U.S. Patent Office) 20 May TM 75/1 Corning Glass Works... *Pyroceram*... First use Feb. 7, 1957. **1965** *New Scientist* 4 Nov. 341/1 Housewives who can afford to pay for..coffee pots made of pyroceram are by now accustomed to being told that 'this is the material used in American rocket noses'. **1968** *McGraw-Hill Yearbk. Sci. & Technol.* 38/2 Controlled devitrification to give glass-ceramics or Pyrocerams depends upon the availability of adequate nuclei.

pyrochlore, -clast(ic: see *PYRO- 2, 1.

pyro-electric, *a.* Also **pyroelectric.** Add: Also applied to the effect exhibited by such crystals and to devices employing it. (Further examples.)

1902 H. A. MIERS *Mineralogy* 480 The pyro-electric property [of tourmaline], which was first observed at the beginning of the eighteenth century,.. can be very easily shown by means of Kundt's dusting method. **1922** GLAZEBROOK *Dict. Appl. Physics* II. 598/1 The existence of a true pyro-electric effect has been questioned by several investigators. **1973** *Physics Bull.* Mar. 161/2 The flame monitor uses two telescopes, each containing either a photoelectric or pyroelectric cell, to pinpoint and monitor a particular flame. **1979** 'R. CASSILIS' *Arrow of God* III. v. 60 Beneath a layer of Wordsworth we packed ..half a dozen pyroelectric-vidicon cameras.

pyrogen. Restrict *rare* to senses a and b and add further examples of sense c.

1955 *Times* 30 Aug. 4/3 We have now reached the stage where bacterial pyrogens in pure form can, with advantage, replace the older materials and methods for producing a general stimulation of the defence mechanisms of the body. **1957** *New Scientist* 12 Dec. 25/1 Rabbits, too, played their part..in pyrogen tests, to ensure the safety of injectable solutions. **1961** M. HYNES *Med. Bacteriol.* (ed. 7) iii. 28 Fluids for parenteral use must be pyrogen-free as well as sterile. **1973** *Nature* 16 Nov. 162/2 It is not known whether the malarial parasite produces a pyrogen, like bacteria, or whether the malarial fever results from destruction of red blood cells.

pyrogenetic, *a.* Add: **2.** *Petrol.* Of a mineral: crystallizing from a magma at a high temperature.

1920 A. HOLMES *Nomencl. Petrol.* 193 *Pyrogenetic minerals*, a term applied to the primary magmatic minerals of igneous rocks, excluding those due to pneumatolytic, hydrothermal, and thermodynamic processes. ..The solidification of a magma may constitute a continuous process beginning with indubitable pyrogenetic minerals, and yet finishing with a well-defined hydrothermal series of minerals. **1923** *Mineral. Mag.* XX. 146 In the granites, tourmaline, muscovite, and topaz.. behave as pyrogenetic minerals and commence to crystallize at an early stage but..their crystallization continued to a late stage in the consolidation of the rock. **1950** F. H. HATCH et al. *Petrol. Igneous Rocks* (ed. 10) iii. 163 The separation of these pyrogenetic minerals leaves the liquid relatively enriched in H_2O and various other components of low atomic and molecular weights. **1954** H. WILLIAMS et al. *Petrogr.* i. 9 The first minerals to form from magma are usually anhydrous... Such minerals are called pyrogenetic.

pyrogenic, *a.* Add: **1.** (Further example.)

1904 A. W. GRABAU in *Amer. Geologist* XXXIII. 230 Returning now to the..chemically deposited rocks, we may readily distinguish four groups... The first..includes the well recognized Igneous rocks, to which the term *pyrogenic* is applicable.

4. *Chem.* Caused by the application of heat.

1887 *Jrnl. Chem. Soc.* LII. I. 572 (*heading*) Pyrogenic reactions. **1912** *Ibid.* CI. II. 1453 One of the authors was engaged in examining the pyrogenic decomposition of American turpentine with the object of obtaining isoprene in quantity. **1920** *Ibid.* CXVIII. I. 589 (*heading*) Pyrogenic acetylene condensations.

pyrogenicity (pəi:rodʒi·ni·siti). [f. prec. + -ITY.] The property of producing fever; freq. *attrib.*

1956 *Nature* 17 Mar. 497/1 The procedure..to be used in toxicity, pyrogenicity and sterility tests. **1973** *Ibid.* 16 Nov. 162/2 We took advantage of this differential sensitivity to test the pyrogenicity and nature of malarial parasites. **1977** *Lancet* 2 July 47/2 Intravenous pyrogenicity tests in rabbits were negative.

pyrolite: see *PYRO- 2.

pyrolyse (pəiə·roləiz), *v.* Also **-lyze, -lize** (both chiefly *U.S.*), **-lise.** [f. *PYROLYSIS, after *hydrolysis, hydrolyse.*] **1.** *intr.* To undergo pyrolysis. Const. *to.*

1929 C. D. HURD *Pyrolysis of Carbon Compounds* ii. 12 Who would predict that the groupings $\equiv$C—CH_2OH and =N—CH_2OH pyrolyze differently? **1938** *Jrnl. Amer. Chem. Soc.* LX. 2420/1 Phenyl acetate pyrolyzed smoothly into ketone and phenol. **1970** *Sci. Jrnl.* May 68 (Advt.), The Pye range of liquid chromatographs is capable of detecting all organic compounds which vaporise or pyrolyse at temperatures up to 700°C. **1974** *Physics Bull.* Feb. 56/2 The fuel, in approaching the flame in the absence of oxygen, tends to pyrolyse to soot and other products of incomplete combustion. **1977** *Engin. Materials & Design* Aug. 26/2 On exposure to high temperatures the resin binder may undergo some further cross-linking... Thereafter, the surface layer of resin begins to pyrolise.

2. *trans.* To decompose by heating; *loosely*, to cause to undergo any chemical change by heating.

1932 *Jrnl. Amer. Chem. Soc.* LIV. 3632 Hydroanisamide was pyrolyzed and found to yield no compound which corresponded in composition to trimethoxylophine. **1959** *Times Rev. Industry* Dec. 18/1 Chlorodifluoromethane. This substance is a gas..which, on pyrolizing at about 800 deg. C., forms tetrafluoroethylene. **1973** *Nature* 23 Mar. 232/2 The results of pyrolysing 50 mg portions of the lunar samples indicated that carbon was present in the gases. **1976** *Amer. Scientist* LXIV. 625/1 The second sample was pyrolized first at 350°C to attempt to drive off most of the water and increase sensitivity to organics.

Hence **py·rolysed** *ppl. a.*; also **py·rolysable** *a.*, capable of being pyrolysed; **pyro·lysate** [after *distillate, filtrate,* etc.], a product of pyrolysis.

1934 NASH & HOWES *Princ. Motor Fuel Prep. & Appl.* x. 496 T. S. Wheeler and I.C.I. Ltd., have suggested the removal of hydrogen from pyrolyzed gas before it is passed to a second stage. **1953** D. H. R. BARTON in E. H. Rodd *Chem. Carbon Compounds* IIB. xvi. 755 The acid fraction of the pyrolysate..on dehydrogenation..gave 1:2-dimethylnaphthalene..and the anhydride. **1961** *Flight* LXXIX. 836/2 Modern finishing schemes for the internal and external surfaces of military and civil aircraft must supply protection against moisture condensation, heat, pyrolised ester lubricants, hydraulic fluids, etc. **1972** *Sci. Amer.* Oct. 83/2 The lunar samples contained less than one p.p.m. of volatile and pyrolyzable organic matter. **1976** *Ibid.* Mar. 41/3 Clusters of benzene rings, as in pyrene, benzopyrene and perylene, are..commonly found in pyrolysates. **1977** *Nature* 10 Feb. 493/3 Molecular analysis of the surface dust by pyrolysis-gas chromatography-mass spectrometry..show that it is virtually free of all pyrolysable carbon compounds.

pyrolysis (pəirǫ·lisis). [f. PYRO- + *-LYSIS.] Decomposition of a substance by the action of heat; *loosely*, any chemical change produced by heating.

1890 BILLINGS *Med. Dict.* II. 420/1 *Pyrolysis*, dry distillation, decomposing by heat. **1928** W. A. GRUSE *Petroleum & its Products* ix. 164 The growth of the petroleum industry, and of the gas-making processes using petroleum, prompted a number of interesting theoretical researches on low-temperature, and particularly on high-temperature, pyrolysis. [*Note*] The use of this word was suggested in 1918 by W. A. Hamor. **1928** *Fuel in Sci. & Pract.* VII. 539/2 Benzene has been found to be an important product of pyrolysis of methane between 875.. and 1,100 deg. Cent. **1943** *Endeavour* Jan. 27/2 In 1924–25 Kennaway succeeded in producing carcinogenic tars by the pyrolysis of petroleum, skin, hair, yeast and cholesterol. **1954** *Chem. & Industry* 13 Nov. 1418/1 It is possible that the presence of the polycyclic hydrocarbons..is due to the pyrolysis of acetylene which is known to occur in cigarette smoke. **1968** A. A. BAKER *Unsaturation in Org. Chem.* ii. 20 Modern investigations on the pyrolysis of carbon compounds have shown that when ethyl alcohol is passed through a glass tube at 610°–630°C, the yield of ethylene is only about 9 per cent. **1975** *New Scientist* 7 Aug. 315/2 Gas evolved by pyrolysis from any organic material will pass to a detector to check for the presence of carbon-14. **1977** *Nat. Westminster Bank Q. Rev.* Aug. 68 Another promising possibility is the use of Pyrolysis which involves the heating of the refuse in the absence of air in order to produce gas, liquid and char which can all be used as fuel.

pyrolytic (pəiroli·tik), *a.* Also **-litic.** [f. *PYROLYSIS: see *-LYTIC.] Of, involving, or produced by pyrolysis; *pyrolytic carbon* or *graphite*, a strong, heat-resistant, highly-ordered form of graphite deposited as a vapour from products of hydrocarbon pyrolysis and used esp. in rocket-engine nozzles and as a coating in missile nose-cones, etc.

1909 in *Cent. Dict.* Suppl. **1922** B. T. BROOKS *Chem. Non-Benzenoid Hydrocarbons* i. 36 It is..readily understood that small differences of operating temperature may cause very great difference in the character of the pyrolytic products. **1936** *Chem. Abstr.* XXX. 6176 Some general laws of pyrolytic reactions..are proved thermodynamically. **1946** *Electronic Engin.* XVIII. 66 A new component..for use in electrical communications equipment..is the pyrolytic or cracked carbon resistor. **1961** *Aeroplane* C. 70/1 The big change in the graphite situation of recent years has been the development of a new type of product deposited from the vapour and termed pyrolytic graphite. This is distinguished from the so-called conventional graphite by having a highly oriented structure, and by a higher density. **1966** *Economist* 20 Aug. 754/2 New fuels, pellets rolled and coated in pyrolytic carbon.. have overcome a good deal of the radio-active contamination problem. **1970** *Daily Tel.* 22 Jan. 18 Makers of the coloured pipes said the bowls were made of 'pyrolitic graphite', a very hard substance used in the making of nose-cones for missiles. **1972** DEPUY & CHAPMAN *Molec. Reactions & Photochem.* ii. Enol ethers are readily converted to ketones under pyrolytic conditions. **1976** *National Observer* (U.S.) 4 Sept. 3/3 Another test with the pyrolitic release experiment, which looks for evidence that carbon dioxide is being taken up by something in the soil (perhaps life), confirmed the instrument's earlier findings.

Hence **pyroly·tically** *adv.*, by pyrolysis.

1956 *Amer. Scientist* XLIV. 356 This reaction was not highly reproducible pyrolytically. **1975** *Nature* 5 June 474/1 We have studied the influence of high temperature on the tensile fracture strengths of pyrolytically deposited silicon carbide fibres.

pyromagnetic to **-metallurgy:** see *PYRO- 1.

pyrometric, *a.* (Examples of *pyrometric cone.*)

Cf. quots. 1800, 1839 in Dict.

1947 J. C. RICH *Materials & Methods of Sculpture* ii. 46 Pyrometric cones..are used to determine and thereby control the firing temperatures of the kiln. **1964** H. HODGES *Artifacts* i. 40 Today potters use small cones of clay—pyrometric cones—which melt below the maturing point of the wares being fired. **1977** *Western Living* (Vancouver) Apr. 25/3 The way you tell the temperature..is with pyrometric cones which are little triangular objects made of different combinations of ceramic materials.

pyrone (pəiə·rōun). *Chem.* [ad. G. *pyron* (Haitinger & Lieben 1885, in *Sitzungsber. d. österreichischen Akad. d. Wissensch. in Wien* XCI. (Abt. II.) 923): see *PYRO- and -ONE.] Either of two unsaturated heterocyclic compounds, $C_5H_4O_2$, which are mono-keto derivatives of the pyrans; *spec.* $\underline{\text{CH:CH·O·CH:CH·CO}}$ (γ- or 1, 4-*pyrone*), a colourless, basic, crystalline solid; also, any heterocyclic ketone or lactone containing the ring structure characteristic of either isomer. Freq. *attrib.*, as *pyrone ring.*

1891 *Jrnl. Chem. Soc.* LX. I. 458 The pyrone is almost insoluble in water or alkalis. *Ibid.* II. 939 The conversion of α-pyrone into pyridine derivatives. **1913** T. H. POPE tr. *Molinari's Org. Chem.* 626 Chelidonic acid,..which is found in celandine, loses CO_2 giving comanic acid and pyrone. **1938** G. H. RICHTER *Textbk. Org. Chem.* xxxi. 659 The pyrones are interesting also because the hetero oxygen atom is basic forming oxonium salts with strong acids. **1962** K. VENKATARAMAN in T. A. Geissman *Chem. Flavonoid Compounds* iv. 94 Isoflavones undergo hydrolysis with opening of the pyrone ring under mild conditions of alkali treatment. **1963** L. F. & M. FIESER *Topics in Org. Chem.* ii. 103 α-Pyrone has the properties expected of a doubly unsaturated δ-lactone. *Ibid.* 104 Representative natural γ-pyrones are kojic acid, formed by bacterial fermentation of carbohydrates; maltol, isolated from the bark of the larch tree; and yangonin, from the roots of the kava shrub. **1972** J. M. TEDDER et al. *Basic Org. Chem.* IV. iii. 139 The reactivity of the carbonyl group is reduced so much by the conjugation..that the α-pyrone ring is much more stable towards alkali than the unsubstituted coumarin.

pyronin (pəiə·rǒnin). *Chem.* and *Biol.* Also **-ine** (-īn), and with capital initial. [a. G. *pyronin* (trade name), prob. f. *pyro-* PYRO- + *-in* -IN[1], -INE[5] with inserted *n.*] Any of a class of synthetic red xanthene dyes employed chiefly as microscopic stains; now *esp.* either of two such dyes, called *pyronin G* or *Y* and *pyronin B.*

1895 *Jrnl. Chem. Soc.* LXVIII. I. 47 Formaldehydetetramethylamidofluorimum chloride, the zinc double salt of which is known commercially as pyronine. **1906** *Practitioner* Nov. 666 Stained with pyronin and methyl green, the nuclei were large, rounded, pale, and contained chromatin in 'lumps'. **1952** K. VENKATARAMAN *Chem. Synthetic Dyes* II. xxiv. 745 Pyronines are obtained by condensing *m*-dialkylaminophenols with formaldehyde in presence of concentrated sulfuric acid, and oxidizing the xanthene derivative. **1957** *Nature* 31 Aug. 440/1 Both the nucleolus and the puffs stain bright red with pyronin. **1960** E. GURR *Encycl. Microscopic Stains* 340 Pyronin B.. is in fairly frequent use in bacteriology and in animal and plant histology. *Ibid.* 341 Pyronin Y finds its chief application..in conjunction with methyl green for demonstrating nucleic acids. **1960** *New Biol.* XXXI. 99 Their cytoplasm is unusually strongly stained by dyes, such as pyronine, which specifically combine with ribonucleic acid. **1974** H. C. COOK *Man. Histol. Demonstration Techniques* ii. 43 For better results the pyronin should be of 'Y' or 'G' type in preference to the 'B' variety.

pyrope. 1. Delete † *Obs.* and add later *attrib.* example.

1948 R. GRAVES *Coll. Poems, 1914–1947* 237 He carved his law on tables of sapphirus, Jerusalem shines with his pyrope gates.

2. Also *pyrope garnet.* (Further examples.)

1959 *Times* 31 Oct. 9/5 Four..types of garnets interest the collector..the red varieties pyrope and almondine being the most popular... Carbuncles are the large oval red pyrope garnets which were cut *en cabochon.* **1976** *Nature* 8 Apr. 517/2 In the Elie Ness vent, high pressure pyroxenes and pyrope garnets indicate rapid elevation from depths in excess of 60 km. **1977** A. HALLAM *Planet Earth* 34/3 It is likely that the mantle consists dominantly of magnesium olivine,..together with smaller amounts of enstatite.., diopside.., pyrope garnet ($Mg_3Al_2Si_3O_{12}$) and perhaps some phlogopite mica.

pyrophoric, *a.* Add: *pyrophoric alloy*, an alloy (usu. of iron and cerium) that emits sparks when scratched or struck with a file or the like.

1906 C. A. VON WELSBACH *U.S. Patent 837,017* What I claim is—1. A pyrophoric alloy, containing cerium alloyed with iron; substantially as and for the purposes described. **1950** *Thorpe's Dict. Appl. Chem.* (ed. 4) X. 328/2 The pyrophoric alloy, in the form of a small rod, is generally pressed firmly against a hard steel wheel with a roughened surface. The shower of sparks produced on rapidly rotating the wheel is projected on to a cotton wick impregnated with..lighter fluid.

pyrophosphatase (pəirofǫ·sfătēiz, -s). *Biochem.* [f. *pyrophosphate* s.v. *PYRO- 3a + *-ASE.] Any enzyme which hydrolyses pyrophosphate esters or ions, or pyrophosphoric acid; *inorganic pyrophosphatase*, an enzyme capable of hydrolysing the free acid or its ions, liberating orthophosphate.

1928 H. D. KAY in *Biochem. Jrnl.* XXII. 1446 Both kidney extract and takadiastase..contain, therefore, a pyrophosphatase. *Ibid.* 1448 Pyrophosphatase is widely distributed in mammalian tissues. **1951** *Jrnl. Biol. Chem.* CXCII. 87 Bauer..found that autolysates of slowly dried bottom yeast were a rich source of inorganic pyrophosphatase. **1970** R. W. MCGILVERY *Biochem.* xi. 209 The inorganic pyrophosphate..is in turn hydrolyzed by the ubiquitous inorganic pyrophosphatase with an additional liberation of free energy. **1976** *Soil Biol. & Biochem.* VIII. 391/1 An assay procedure for soil pyrophosphatase activity.

pyrosphere to **-synthetic:** see *PYRO- 1.

pyrotechnic, *a.* and *sb.* Add: **A.** *adj.* **2. a.** Also more widely, capable of being ignited for technical or military purposes. (Further examples.)

1919 H. B. FABER *Military Pyrotechnics* I. I. v. 45 In the latter part of the eighteenth century and the beginning of the nineteenth, there was great activity on the part of those enthusiastic over pyrotechnic devices as war instruments. **1922** A. ST. H. BROCK *Pyrotechnics* iii. 13 Pyrotechnic compositions and gunpowder are inextricably mixed together in early European records. **1953** KIRK & OTHMER *Encycl. Chem. Technol.* XI. 324 In addition to illuminating and signal compositions there are many other types of pyrotechnic compositions such as smoke, incendiary, whistle, dark-fire, tracer, and igniter compositions. **1970** *Guardian* 18 Apr. 1/1 The astronauts fired the pyro-technic bolts that connect the command ship and the service module. **1974** *Encycl. Brit. Micropædia* VII. 186/2 Napalm is also employed in formulating a pyrotechnic gel containing gasoline.., powdered magnesium, and sodium nitrate.

B. *sb.* **2. c.** (Later examples.)

1921 F. SCOTT FITZGERALD *Let. a* 12 Dec. (1964) 150 The cruel Hebrew God, against whom such writers as even Mark Twain..have delivered violent pyrotechnics from time to time. **1970** S. SCHOENBAUM *Shakespeare's Lives* VII. x. 686 Such pyrotechnics of rationalization must be a Baconian's envy. **1977** *Rolling Stone* 7 Apr. 44/2 No emotional pyrotechnics for him, just calm, deathly calm.

3. A device or material which can be ignited to produce light, smoke, or noise, e.g. for purposes of display or illumination.

1919 H. B. FABER *Military Pyrotechnics* I. 7 The art of manufacturing military pyrotechnics. **1948** W. HAYNES *Amer. Chem. Industry* IV. ix. 130 When demand shrank to peacetime uses, chiefly in matchheads and pyrotechnics.., European manufacturers..began cutting prices. **1953** KIRK & OTHMER *Encycl. Chem. Technol.* XI. 332 Commercial pyrotechnics mainly having to do with *sound* include cannon crackers..and trick cigars. **1957** *Spaceflight* I. 51/2 A Fifth-of-November rocket or catherine wheel is a pyrotechnic, and modified forms of these have been used to ignite liquid propellant rockets. **1964** F. G. W. & M. G. JONES *Pests of Field Crops* xvi. 355 Smokes are made by combusting a mixture of pesticide and a suitable pyrotechnic. **1972** *Materials & Technol.* IV. xix. 732 The chemical reactivity of the ingredients and their particle size have very significant effects on the ignition characteristics and burning rates of pyrotechnics.

pyrotechnician. Delete † *Obs.* and add later example.

1979 F. MORTON *Nervous Splendour* (1980) xxx. 316 Pyrotechnicians labored..for Easter Sunday: a symphonic fireworks.

Pyrotenax (pəirote·næks). *Electr.* Also **pyrotenax.** A proprietary name for a make of robust, heat-resistant copper-sheathed cable with magnesia insulation.

1937 *Nature* 20 Nov. 887/2 'Pyrotenax' cable has a copper conductor, magnesia insulation, and copper sheath. **1949** *Trade Marks Jrnl.* 2 Feb. 95/2 Pyrotenax... Terminal plates and boxes for electric cables. Pyrotenax Limited, Hedgeley Road, Hebburn-on-Tyne.., Manufacturers. **1958** MOLLOY & SAY *Electr. Engineer's Ref. Bk.* (ed. 9) xxx. 84 Tailor-made lengths of Pyrotenax cables, tested at 2,000 V. after water immersion. **1958** *Oxf. Univ. Gaz.* 7 Mar. 694/1 At the same time this part of the Library was rewired with pyrotenax. **1960** *Official Gaz.* (U.S. Patent Office) 17 May TM115/2 Societe Alsacienne de Constructions Mecaniques [*sic*], Paris... *Pyrotenax.* Owner of French Reg. No. 2,373, dated June 28, 1952... For electrical conductors, [etc.].

pyroxene. Add: In mod. use, any of a group of silicates characterized by the presence of single chains of SiO_4 tetrahedra and prismatic cleavages at nearly 90 degrees, the general formula of which is approximately $XY(SiO_3)_2$. (Further examples.)

1888 J. P. IDDINGS tr. *Rosenbusch's Microsc. Physiogr. Rock-Making Minerals* 202 The orthorhombic pyroxenes become transparent in various colors, according to the position of the section and to the iron percentage. **1906** J. P. IDDINGS *Rock Minerals* II. 286 (*heading*) Pyroxene group. *Ibid.*, The triclinic pyroxenes are less closely related to the other forms, and are less frequently met with as rock-making minerals. **1959** *Dana's Man. Mineral.* (ed. 17) 434 The pyroxenes crystallize at higher temperatures than their amphibole analogues and hence are generally formed earlier in a cooling igneous magma. **1966** W. A. DEER et al. *Introd. Rock-Forming Minerals* II. 99 The pyroxene group includes both orthorhombic and monoclinic minerals. The orthorhombic sub-group consists essentially of the compositional series $MgSiO_3$-$FeSiO_3$ while the monoclinic sub-group includes members having a wide range of chemical composition. *Ibid.*, The general formula of the pyroxene group may be expressed $X_{1-p}Y_{1+p}Z_2O_6$ where X=Ca,Na; Y=Mg,Fe^{+2},Mn,Li, Ni,Al,Fe^{+3},Cr,Ti; Z=Si,Al. **1975** D. SHELLEY *Man. Optical Mineral.* vii. 143 Most pyroxenes form rather stumpy prismatic crystals, though occasionally, as in the case of aegirine, the crystals are more elongate. **1978** *Sci. Amer.* Apr. 125/2 Peridotite..is composed mainly of olivine and another silicate mineral, pyroxene.

pyroxeni·tic *a.*, of or pertaining to pyroxenite.

1933 R. A. DALY *Igneous Rocks & Depths of Earth* ix. 189 The speeds of seismic waves cannot be said to demonstrate a peridotitic or pyroxenitic layer between the 40-kilometer and 60-kilometer levels. **1979** *Nature* 5 Apr. 545/1 Gorgona is one of the rare places in the world where young pyroxenitic komatiites exhibiting typical quenched spinifex textures..occur.

pyroxenoid (pəirǫ·ksĕnoid). *Min.* [f. prec. + -OID.] Any of a small group of triclinic silicates formerly classed as pyroxenes but now differentiated from them on structural grounds.

1937 H. BERMAN in *Amer. Mineralogist* XXII. 389 The so-called 'triclinic pyroxenes' are not included here in the pyroxenes because the writer believes they are more properly considered as a separate group, with no isomorphous relations to any of the pyroxene minerals, and with physical and chemical properties clearly differing from those of the pyroxenes. To these pyroxene-like minerals we here give the name pyroxenoids. **1942** ROGERS & KERR *Optical Mineral.* (ed. 2) II. 275 Pyroxenoids include rhodonite, bustamite, pectolite, and wollastonite. **1966** J. SINKANKAS *Mineral.* II. 487 The pyroxenoids are species whose chemical compositions resemble the pyroxenes, but [whose] crystal structures differ slightly but importantly in the way the chains are linked and arranged. **1977** A. HALLAM *Planet Earth* 136 Rhodonite is closely similar in structure to the pyroxene group (for this reason it is sometimes called a pyroxenoid).

pyroxferroite (pəirǫksfe·roˌəit). *Min.* [f. FERRO- + -ITE[1], after next.] A yellow pyroxenoid, $Fe_6Ca(SiO_3)_7$, that has been found on the moon and is an iron-rich analogue of pyroxmangite.

1970 E. C. T. CHAO et al. in *Proc. Apollo 11 Lunar Sci. Conf.* I. 65 Pyroxferroite was first recognized by the LSPET (1969) as an unidentified yellow mineral that seemed to be concentrated in vuggy areas of the Type B rock. *Ibid.* 75 Lindsley (1967) recently synthesized pyroxferroite of composition $Ca_{0.15}Fe_{0.85}SiO_3$ at pressures from 10 to 17·5 kbar and temperatures from 1130 to 1250°C. **1973** SORRELL & SANDSTROM *Rocks & Minerals of World* 60 The major lunar minerals are calcic plagioclase..and pyroxene... Common are olivine..and pyroxferroite, $CaFe_6(SiO_3)_7$, a new mineral similar to the pyroxenes.

pyroxmangite (pəirǫksmæ·ŋgəit). *Min.* [f. PYROX(ENE + MANG(ANESE + -ITE[1].] A manganese- and iron-containing pyroxenoid, $(Mn,Fe)SiO_3$.

1913 FORD & BRADLEY in *Amer. Jrnl. Sci.* CLXXXVI. 169 (*heading*) Pyroxmangite, a new member of the pyroxene group and its alteration product, skemmatite. **1937** *Amer. Mineralogist* XXII. 720 The discovery of a further occurrence of pyroxmangite among the Lewisian rocks of Scotland has provided additional data on this interesting mineral. *Ibid.*, The pyroxmangite forms an important constituent of a manganiferous schist interbedded with a series of para-gneisses... Pyroxmangite in this rock occurs in pink grains of $\frac{1}{2}$–$\frac{3}{4}$ mm. average grain size. Exceptionally grains up to 5 mm. diameter may appear as porphyroblasts. **1963** W. A. DEER et al. *Rock-Forming Minerals* II. 201 Pyroxmangite is a mineral of metamorphic or metasomatic rocks, being found typically in manganese-rich assemblages in association with spessartine garnet, tephroite,.. or rhodochrosite. **1970** *New Scientist* 15 Jan. 94/2 Some 68 elements forming minerals familiar to geologists were sorted out of the lunar soil and rock, along with three new minerals. They..were identified as a titanium-chromium spinel, a ferro-pseudobrookite and a pyroxmangite.

pyrrol. The spelling **pyrrole** is now the usual form. **a.** Amend formula to read C_4H_5N and add: Also, any derivative of this containing a pyrrole ring. (Further examples.)

1902 *Jrnl. Chem. Soc.* LXXXII. I. 54 Better yields of pyrroline are obtained by reducing pyrroles with zinc and hydrochloric acid than by using zinc and acetic acid. **1926** H. G. RULE tr. *J. Schmidt's Text-bk. Org. Chem.* 521 Pyrroles are aromatic in character and possess points in common with both phenols and aromatic amines. **1954** *New Biol.* XVI. 33 The tendency of the related pyrroles to combine with metal atoms to form highly coloured reactive compounds, such as hydrogenase and cytochrome, and probably later chlorophyll and haemin, points the way to the evolution of enzyme systems and photosynthesis. **1972** J. M. TEDDER et al. *Basic Org. Chem.* IV. ix. 454 On reduction with hydriodic acid haem yields eight comparatively simple pyrroles.

b. *attrib.* and *Comb.*, as **pyrrole base,** any of a series of bases containing a pyrrole ring; **pyrrole nucleus, ring,** a doubly unsaturated ring of four carbon atoms and one nitrogen atom.

1851, 1875 Pyrrol base [in Dict.]. **1913** BLOXAM & LEWIS *Bloxam's Chem.* (ed. 10) 782 The metals are not present as bases, but as integral parts of the complex molecules, probably exercising their subsidiary valencies, and uniting a number of pyrrol nuclei. **1926** H. G. RULE tr. *J. Schmidt's Text-bk. Org. Chem.* 523 This oxidation has recently been recognised as a valuable means of determining the orientation of substituents in the pyrrole nucleus, and also for detecting the presence of a pyrrole ring in substances of unknown constitution. **1970** R. W. MCGILVERY *Biochem.* xxi. 494 The basic unit of porphyrins is the pyrrole ring, with four of these linked to form the large porphyrin ring.

Hence **pyrro·lic** *a.*

1909 in *Cent. Dict.* Suppl. **1912** *Chem. Abstr.* VI. 2749 Pyrrolic α-, β- and γ-diketones. **1955** *Endeavour* July 135/2 (*caption*) Porphobilinogen, the simplest pyrrolic substance known to be a precursor of haem and porphyrins. **1972** J. M. TEDDER et al. *Basic Org. Chem.* IV. ix. 464 The blood-red, tripyrrole microbial pigment, prodigiosin, provides an example of the biogenesis of pyrrolic compounds.

pyrrolidine (pirǫ·lidīn). *Chem.* [ad. G. *pyrrolidin* (Ciamician & Magnaghi 1885, in *Ber. d. Deut. Chem. Ges.* XVIII. 2080): see PYRROL and *-IDINE.] A saturated heterocyclic compound, $(CH_2)_4NH$, which is a colourless, pungent, strongly basic liquid obtained esp. by catalytic reduction of pyrrole; any substituted derivative of this. Freq. *attrib.*, as **pyrrolidine nucleus, ring,** a saturated ring of four carbon atoms and one nitrogen.

1885 *Jrnl. Chem. Soc.* XLVIII. II. 1243 Pyrrolidine.. C_4NH_9, is obtained with other products from hydropyrroline in the above reaction; it shows great similarity in properties to piperidine, hence the name given to it. **1926** H. G. RULE tr. *J. Schmidt's Text-bk. Org. Chem.* 532 Certain important degradation products of the *coca* and *atropa* alkaloids have been identified as carboxylic acids of pyrrolidine. **1956** I. L. FINAR *Org. Chem.* II. xiv. 531 The presence of this pyrrolidine nucleus also accounts for the formation of pyrrole when nicotine zincichloride is distilled. **1963** T. ROBINSON *Org. Constituents of Higher Plants* xii. 256 Leete..using 1, 4-labelled putrescine fed to tobacco found that it was an efficient precursor of the pyrrolidine ring in nicotine. **1976** STREITWIESER & HEATHCOCK *Introd. Org. Chem.* xxxv. 1065 Pyrrolidine and piperidine are typical secondary amines.

pyrrolidone (pirǫ·lidōᵘn). *Chem.* [ad. G. *pyrrolidon* (J. Tafel 1889, in *Ber. d. Deut. Chem. Ges.* XXII. 1861): see prec. and -ONE.] Either of two isomeric mono-keto derivatives of pyrrolidine; *esp.* $\underline{NH\cdot(CH_2)_3\cdot CO}$ (*2-pyrrolidone*), a colourless crystalline solid with weakly basic properties; any substituted derivative of either isomer.

[**1889** *Jrnl. Chem. Soc.* LVI. 961 Methylpyrrolidone.] *Ibid.* 1211 The first product..is very unstable, condensation immediately taking place, with formation of a derivative of pyrrolidone. **1926** H. G. RULE tr. *J. Schmidt's Text-bk. Org. Chem.* 517 The 2-keto-derivative of pyrrolidine is commonly known as 'pyrrolidone'. *Ibid.* 520 Since succinimides are readily prepared in quantity, this process also renders the pyrrolidones easy of access. **1951** I. L. FINAR *Org. Chem.* I. xvi. 309 When reduced with sodium and ethanol, succinimide forms pyrrolidine,.. and when reduced electrolytically, it forms pyrrolidone. *Ibid.* xxx. 617, 2-Pyrrolidone is the lactam.. of γ-aminobutyric acid. **1975** GUTSCHE & PASTO *Fund. Org. Chem.* xxvii. 817 The reaction between pyrrolidone and acetylene in the presence of potassium hydroxide to yield N-vinylpyrrolidone.

pyrroline. Now pronounced (pi·rǫlīn). Mark sense in Dict. † *Obs.* and add: **b.** formerly also **-in.** A partially reduced derivative of pyrrole having the formula C_4H_7N, of which three isomers are possible; *esp.* $\underline{HN\cdot CH_2\cdot CH{:}CH\cdot CH_2}$ (*3-pyrroline*), a colourless, basic liquid obtained by reduction of pyrrole with nascent hydrogen; also a substituted derivative of any of these compounds. [Named in Ger. as *pyrrolin* (Ciamician & Dennstedt 1883, in *Ber. d. Deut. Chem. Ges.* XVI. 1539).]

1884 ROSCOE & SCHORLEMMER *Treat. Chem.* III. II. 610 Pyrrol unites with nascent hydrogen, forming pyrrolin, $C_4H_6(NH)$, an oily liquid that boils at 90°–91°, and acts as a strong base. **1902** [see *PYRROL a]. **1926** H. G. RULE tr. *J. Schmidt's Text-bk. Org. Chem.* 517 Dihydro-pyrroles are known as pyrrolines, and the completely reduced tetrahydro-pyrroles as pyrrolidines. **1961** G. M. BADGER *Chem. Heterocyclic Compounds* ii. 17, 3-Pyrrolines have been isomerized to the corresponding 1-pyrrolines by heating with Raney nickel. *Ibid.* 18, 2-Pyrrolines have been poorly characterized. **1972** J. M. TEDDER et al. *Basic Org. Chem.* IV. ix. 463 Another group of tetrapyrrolic macrocyclic compounds found in nature are the corrins which are made up of four partially reduced pyrrole (pyrroline and pyrrolidine) rings.

pyrrolizidine (piːrǫ·li·zidīn). *Chem.* [ad. G. *pyrrolizidin* (G. Menschikoff 1936, in *Ber. d. Deut. Chem. Ges.* LXIX. 1802), f. *pyrrolidin* *PYRROLIDINE with inserted *-iz* (ult. f. *azo-* Azo-) after *chinolizin* quinolizine, an analogous compound containing six-membered rings.] A colourless basic liquid, $C_7H_{13}N$, which has a structure consisting of two fused pyrrolidine rings sharing a carbon and a nitrogen atom; any derivative of this. Freq. *attrib.*, as **pyrrolizidine alkaloid,** any of a large class of toxic alkaloids based on this structure which occur widely in plants, esp. in the genera *Senecio*, *Crotalaria*, and *Heliotropium*.

[**1936** *Chem. Abstr.* XXX. 6379 A satd. tertiary base $C_8H_{15}N$..for which is proposed the name 2-methylpyrrolizidine.] **1939** *Ibid.* XXXIII. 5850 P[relog] and H[eimbach] have found a method of preparing the hitherto unknown pyrrolizidine (I)... The free I is a water-sol. oil of basic odor, b.p. 148°. **1950** *Thorpe's Dict. Appl. Chem.* (ed. 4) X. 710/2 All Senecio and related alkaloids are esters of a cyclic amino-alcohol of pyrrolizidine type with aliphatic or alicyclic acids. **1968** *New Scientist* 20 June 619/2 Many pyrrolizidine alkaloids.. not only exert their effects as liver poisons but may also produce lung damage. **1975** K. NAKANISHI et al. *Natural Products Chem.* II. x. 299 Recent studies on the metabolism of the alkaloids have shown that it is not the pyrrolizidine alkaloids themselves, but their pyrrole derivatives, formed as metabolites, which exhibit toxicity.

pyrus. Add to etym.: Adopted by Linnæus (*Hortus Cliffortianus* (1737) 189) as a generic name. Substitute for def.: A small tree of the genus so called, belonging to the family Rosaceæ and widely cultivated for the sake of its blossom or its fruit, the pear; also, a tree or shrub once included in this genus and now in a separate one, esp. the japonica (*Chænomeles* species) or the rowan (*Sorbus* species). (Earlier and later examples.)

1849 THOREAU *Week Concord Riv.* 92 The shad make their appearance early in May, at the same time with the blossoms of the pyrus, one of the most conspicuous early flowers. **1914** W. J. BEAN *Trees & Shrubs Hardy in Brit. Isles* II. 269 All the Pyruses like a loamy soil. **1930** F. K. WARD *Plant Hunting on Edge of World* vi. 120 As for the Pyrus, its numerous clusters of reddened berries presently turned snow white.

pyruvate (pəirū·vēᵗt). *Biochem.* [f. PYRUV(IC *a.* + -ATE⁴.] **1.** A salt or ester, or the anion, of pyruvic acid; *loosely*, denoting either anions or the acid itself.

1855 H. WATTS tr. *Gmelin's Hand-bk. Chem.* IX. 419 The Pyruvates are prepared by saturating the dilute acid with the base. **1877** [in Dict. s.v. PYRUVIC *a.*]. **1905** *Jrnl. Chem. Soc.* LXXXVIII. I. 572 Butyroin..yields a pyruvate which boils at 134–138° under 12 mm. pressure. **1946** *Nature* 7 Sept. 350/1 Pyruvate accumulates in the blood of thiamin-deficient animals. **1955** *Sci. Amer.* Jan. 76/2 They [*sc.* Rickettsiæ] also proved capable of oxidizing slowly two other substances, pyruvate and succinate, which, like glutamic acid, are oxidized by most animal and plant tissues. **1970** AMBROSE & EASTY *Cell Biol.* vi. 183 Two molecules of pyruvate are finally produced. *Ibid.*, Normally, muscle respires aerobically, oxidizing pyruvate via the Krebs cycle.., but during violent exercise oxygen cannot reach the tissues fast enough. In this case muscles obtain extra energy by reduction of pyruvic acid to lactic acid. **1970** *New Scientist* 23 Apr. 168/1 Glycolysis is the process which oxidizes carbohydrates to pyruvate, ready to enter the citric acid cycle and be burnt up completely. **1976** *Ann. Rev. Microbiol.* XXX. 157 Pyruvate in polysaccharides of *R. trifolii*, *R. meliloti*, *R. radicicolum*, and Pn 27 functions as a major determinant in serological specificity.

2. Special Comb.: **pyruvate kinase**, any enzyme which catalyses the transfer of a phosphate group between adenosine triphosphate and pyruvic acid; **pyruvate oxidase** = **pyruvic oxidase*.

1951 S. P. COLOWICK in Sumner & Myrbäck *Enzymes* II. I. xlvi. 123 'Creatine kinase', 'pyruvate kinase' and '3-phosphoglycerate kinase' will refer to the respective enzymes which catalyze the reversible reaction of ATP with these substrates. **1970** *New Scientist* 23 Apr. 168/2 The enzyme pyruvate kinase..is slightly different in liver and kidney from that in other tissues. **1959** *Jrnl. Vitaminol.* V. 94 Recently, further attempts were made to elucidate whether vitamin B_{12} activates the pyruvate oxidase system in B_{12}-deficient rats. **1970** AMBROSE & EASTY *Cell Biol.* vi. 188 Pyruvate..is first converted to acetyl-coenzyme A by combination with coenzyme A. (Catalysed by pyruvate oxidase.)

pyruvic, *a.* Add to etym.: [ad. mod.L. *pyruvicus*, in *acidum pyruvicum* pyruvic acid (J. J. Berzelius 1835, in *Ann. der Physik u. Chem.* XXXVI. 5)]. *pyruvic acid*, add: The acid occurs widely in living organisms as an intermediate in many metabolic processes, notably glycolysis; (further examples); *pyruvic kinase* = **pyruvate kinase*; *pyruvic oxidase*, any enzyme or enzyme complex which catalyses the oxidation of pyruvic acid.

1927 M. BODANSKY *Introd. Physiol. Chem.* ix. 226 There is..no convincing evidence that physiologically lactic acid is converted into pyruvic acid, although the change is known to occur *in vitro* under the influence of hydrogen peroxide. **1941** *Adv. Enzymol.* I. 147 Even the pyruvic acid oxidase of *Bacterium Delbrueckii*..might be called a composite thiamin enzyme as it contains flavin adenine nucleotide besides thiamin pyrophosphate, both of which are possibly bound to the same protein. **1945** *Jrnl. Biol. Chem.* CLIX. 543 The pyruvic oxidases of *Proteus vulgaris* and *Escherichia coli* do not appear to require inorganic phosphate for activity. **1951** *Sci. News* XXII. 80 An illuminated preparation of spinach chloroplasts can reduce carbon dioxide plus pyruvic acid to malic acid. **1951** SUMNER & MYRBÄCK *Enzymes* II. II. 1433/1 (Index), Pyruvic kinase. **1962** S. G. WALEY in A. Pirie *Lens Metabolism Rel. Cataract* 357 Thiamine (as the pyrophosphate) is the coenzyme in the decarboxylation of the α-keto acids, pyruvic acid and α-ketogluric acid. **1963** CONN & STUMPF *Outl. Biochem.* xi. 201 The conversion of pyruvate to acetyl-CoA is catalyzed by the enzyme complex known as pyruvic oxidase. **1967** BATSAKIS & BRIERE *Interpretive Enzymol.* xii. 242 Pyruvic kinase deficiency leads directly to an impairment of ATP synthesis. **1970** [see *PYRUVATE 1]. **1971** C. J. GRAY *Enzyme-Catalysed Reactions* vii. 291 Porcine pyruvic oxidase catalysed the synthesis of α-acetolactate from pyruvate and the hydroxyethylthiamine pyrophosphate.

Pytchley (pəi·tʃli). The name of a village in Northamptonshire, used *attrib.* and *ellipt.* to denote a famous hunt centred there. *Pytchley (riding) coat* (see quots. 1907, 1963).

1866 J. BLACKWOOD *Let.* 26 Apr. in *Geo. Eliot Lett.* (1956) IV. 245, I enjoyed her..laughing at his French accent... It is like the House of Commons..laughing at Bright for talking of the *Pitt*chley. **1867** 'OUIDA' *Under Two Flags* I. iv. 74 It lay in the Melton country, and was equally well placed for Pytchley, Quorn, and Belvoir. **1907** *Yesterday's Shopping* (1969) 323/1 Pytchley Riding Coat. Full Skirt to cover saddle. **1919** J. BUCHAN *Mr Standfast* xiv. 257 He used to hunt with the Pytchley. **1935** *Encycl. Sports* 294/1 About 1750, the modern system of hunting was introduced in the Quorn country by Meynell and by Lord Spencer in the Pytchley Hunt. **1955** M. ALLINGHAM *Beckoning Lady* ii. 16 Two seasons with the Pytchley foxhounds. **1963** BLOODGOOD & SANTINI *Horseman's Dict.* 157 *Pytchley coat* (More usually called *Shadbelly*, *Swallow tail* or *Cutaway*), tight-fitting, Regency, double-breasted hunting coat (either scarlet or black) worn with a double-breasted buff waistcoat and named after its originators, the thrusters, or hard riding members of the Pytchley Hunt, England. **1969** A. HORSBRUGH-PORTER in A. S. C. Ross *What are U?* 51 It would be tedious to delve into the date which constituted the name of 'the shires', denoting the Pytchley, Quorn, Belvoir, Fernie and Cottesmore Hunts.

python¹. Add: **3.** *python-steak*, *-stretch*.

1953 R. CAMPBELL *Mamba's Precipice* ii. 26 He and Nyali had had python-steak for supper. **1923** D. H. LAWRENCE *Birds, Beasts & Flowers* 177 The great muscular python-stretch of her tail.

python³ (pəi·þŏn). *Mil.* [A code name.] Leave granted at the end of the 1939–45 war to members of the British forces who had served a long period overseas. Also *attrib.*, as *python leave*.

1945 L. DURRELL *Spirit of Place* (1969) 82, I took down a pomegranate..and tried to send it to her with a friend on python. **1945** *Punch* 22 Aug. 166/1 Naturally they are all either due for Python or their Age and Service Groups, and the last few days we have suffered from a constant round of farewell parties. **1949** D. E. STEVENSON *Vittoria Cottage* xiv. 95 When men come home from FARELF after doing their three years they say they are *coming home on Python*... FARELF..means Far Eastern Land Forces. **1959** I. JEFFERIES *Thirteen Days* iii. 37 Your python must be coming up soon. **1969** A. G. THOMAS in L. Durrell *Spirit of Place* 82 Under Python leave any soldier who had been in the Middle East for more than four years was granted one month at home with his family and then three months in some unit in Britain. **1976** R. LEWIN *Slim* xv. 252 *Python*, the scheme for repatriation of men who had served a minimum of three years and four months in the Far East.

pyxie (pi·ksi). *U.S.* Also **pixy.** [Abbrev. of mod.L. *Pyxidanthera* (A. Michaux *Flora Boreali-Americana* (1803) I. 152), f. Gr. *πυξίδ-ιον* box + *ἀνθηρά*, fem. of *ἀνθηρός* flowery.] In full, *pyxie moss*. A small, prostrate, evergreen shrub, *Pyxidanthera barbulata*, belonging to the family Diapensiaceæ, native to limited areas of New Jersey and the Carolinas, and bearing tiny white flowers; also called the pine-barren beauty (see PINE-BARREN b).

1882 *Harper's Mag.* June 65 Among her [*sc.* Nature's] treasures is the delicate pyxie..a little prostrate trailing evergreen. **1892** *Amer. Folk-Lore* V. 100 *Pyxidanthera barbulata*, pyxie moss. **1916** J. W. HARSHBERGER *Vegetation New Jersey Pine-Barrens* xvi. 240 The flowering-moss, or pyxie, is usually a prostrate or creeping plant. **1925** *Scribner's Mag.* July 35/1 Innumerable clusters of oval-leaved *Diapensia lapponica* in rounded clumps like red pin-cushions (closely resembling what is called pixy-moss). **1951** E. W. TEALE *North with Spring* xxviii. 276 If we had been a few weeks earlier, we would have found.. the pyxie of the pine barrens, the matted, mosslike flowering plant. *Ibid.*, One year, on the 31st of March,.. I came upon a dense mass of pyxie moss,.. across which a host of tiny waxy-white flowers were scattered. **1973** ROBICHAUD & BELL *Vegetation New Jersey* xii. 217 The most commonly known of these [pine-barren plants] include the turkey-beard, pyxie moss, goat's-rue, [etc.].

Q

Q. Add: **I. 1.** *attrib.* Used *spec.* to designate one of the two main groups of languages which developed from Common Celtic, so called because its distinctive phonological features include the retention of IE. *q^u, as *Q-Celt*, a speaker of *Q-Celtic*. Cf. *P-Celtic* s.v. *P I.1.

1891, 1913 [see *P I. 1]. **1944** J. WHATMOUGH *ΚΕΛΤΙΚΑ* 49 The possibility that traces of *q*-Keltic may lurk hidden in the magico-medical formularies of Marcellus of Bordeaux. **1962** T. C. LETHBRIDGE *Witches* vi. 72 This adds to the evidence which suggests that the Iceni were 'Q' Celts, speaking a form of Gaelic. **1972** [see *P I. 1].

2. *Q-boat, Q-ship*, an armed and camouflaged merchantman used as a decoy or to destroy submarines; also *ellipt.*; cf. *DECOY *sb.*[2] 6, *mystery ship* s.v. *MYSTERY[1] 13. Hence *Q car*, a disguised police car.

1920 *Blackw. Mag.* Mar. 325/1 They had complied with the regulations that dictated that no uniform must be shown abroad sailing 'Q's'. **1918** *Army & Navy Gaz.* 10 Aug. 501/1 Among the anti-submarine measures initiated and encouraged by Mr. Churchill and Lord Fisher were the 'Q' boats, the mystery attaching to which has now been dispelled by Sir Eric Geddes... The 'Q' boat may be briefly defined as a decoy. **1976** R. MOORE *Dubai* iv. 51 We're talking about making your dhow into a high-speed Q-boat. **1937** *Times* 13 Apr. p. xxvii/2 Among the cars used by the London police are a number to which the name 'Q' is applied... If inside a small and unimpressive body there is an engine that will develop the highest speed attainable by the most powerful vehicle the 'Q' car is complete. **1961** *Guardian* 29 Sept. 2/3 Three men jumped out of a badly-damaged car, which crashed into the side of a lorry..and in turn was rammed by a police 'Q' car. **1976** L. HENDERSON *Major Enquiry* xiv. 88 She..doubled back..to the waiting Q car. The watch was being kept by Sheehan and Milton. **1919** *Boy's Own Paper* July 458/1 One of the finest examples of coolness, discipline, and good organisation in the history of Q-ships. **1946** *Daily Tel.* 15 May 5/4 After his experience with two British 'Q' ships, the 10,000 ton Kolchak..and the motor vessel Alfred Jones,..which nearly led to his destruction in 1941, he thought U-boat captains perfectly justified in not attempting rescue work after torpedoing ships. **1972** J. BROOME *Convoy is to Scatter* I. 25 The Q-ship's lure-power lay in her half-sunken appearance appealing to the U-boat captain for his coup-de-grâce.

4. Used with reference to its shape, *spec.* in *Skating*. Also *attrib.*

1852 G. ANDERSON *Art of Skating* vi. 73 The Q Figure. Start with a curve on the outside forwards, then change the edge to inside forwards, and finish with a circle outside backwards, all on the one foot, without setting down the other. **1935** *Encycl. Sports* 559/2 A difficult but beautiful figure called the Q... The figure bears a pretty distinct resemblance to the letter.

5. Repr. clipped pronunc. of 'thank you'; = *KEW.

1925 WODEHOUSE *Sam the Sudden* ii. 13 The conductor presented himself, punch in hand. 'Fez, pliz.' 'Valley Fields,' said Kay. 'Q,' said the conductor. **1956** J. LATIMER *Sinners & Shrouds* xxiii. 181 'Son of a bitch!' 'I beg your pardon?' 'I beg yours.' 'Q.'

II. 1. c. *q.d.s.* = *quater in die sumendus* 'to be taken four times a day'; *q.i.d.* = *quater in die* 'four times a day'; *q.s.* (earlier example). **d.** Q.E.D. (earlier and later examples). Also as *sb. phr.*

a **1662** J. SYMCOTTS in *Publ. Beds. Hist. Rec. Soc.* (1951) XXXI. 101 For the shaking of the hands: Take rosemary bruised q.s. and apply it to the wrists. **1760** L. STERNE *Tr. Shandy* II. xix. 168 If..people can walk about and do their business without brains,—then certes the soul does not inhabit there. Q.E.D. **1932** *Times Lit. Suppl.* 7 Jan. 1/3 Matisse, with his frugal presentation of purely aesthetic values to a purely aesthetic appetite, appears to be the Q.E.D. of French painting as looked at in perspective. **1955** R. J. SCHWARTZ *Compl. Dict. Abbrev.* 149/1 *q i d*, four times a day (*quater in die*—Latin). **1960** LAURENCE & MOULTON *Clin. Pharmacol.* 454 q.d.s., quater in die sumendus, four times a day (q.i.d. and q.q.h are sometimes used). **1975** J. MITCHELL *Smear Job* xviii. 159 He hates himself... He drinks. Q.E.D. **1977** *Lancet* 20 Aug. 376/1 Two subjects who inhaled 400 μg salbutamol q.i.d. from the start. **1978** *Jrnl. R. Soc. Med.* LXXI. 464/2 Abbreviations such as bds and qds will not be understood by foreign readers.

2. a. Q, Quartermaster, Quartermaster-General or -Sergeant; also *attrib.* or as *adj.*, and *ellipt.* for the Quartermaster's or Quartermaster-General's Department; = QUARTO 2. **b.** Q and A, question and answer (esp. *attrib.*); Q.B.I. (*R.A.F. slang*), quite bloody impossible, (applied to flying conditions); also *ellipt.*; Q.C. (earlier examples); QCD, quantum chromodynamics; QED, quantum electrodynamics; Q.F., q.f., quick-firing; also *ellipt.*, a quick-firing gun; Q.I., quartz-iodine; Q.M. (examples); also *attrib.*; Q.M.G. (examples); Q.M.S., Quartermaster-Sergeant; QS [?f. *quadraphonic-stereophonic*: cf. SQ s.v. *S 4a], a designation (proprietary in the U.S.) of audio equipment used with reference to a system of quadraphonic recording and reproduction; QSO, quasi-stellar object (i.e. a quasar); QSS, quasi-stellar source (of radio waves); Q.T., q.t. (later examples).

1916 G. FRANKAU *Poetical Wks.*, (1923) I. 223 And the Boche shells; and 'Q.' still issues bromo. *Ibid.* 227 No more I'll turn the mordant line till 'Q' clerks blush incarnadine. **1918** *Punch* 2 Jan. 15/2 Military experts will tell you that this is a 'Q.' war, meaning thereby that the Quartermaster-General's department is the one which matters. **1919** W. S. CHURCHILL in M. Gilbert *Winston S. Churchill* (1977) IV. Compan. I. 456 Another inroad on 'Q' should it seems to me be made by transferring all discipline to the Adjutant General. **1930** H. BELLOC *Wolsey* v. 126 It was certainly he who did all the 'Q' work, to him all the letters were addressed; he gave the orders, bought provisions, organised transport, [etc.]. **1942** W. S. CHURCHILL *Second World War* (1951) IV. I. xx. 311 The arrangements for bringing off the wounded would alone open up a vista of Q problems. **1976** D. CLARK *Dread & Water* v. 119 A well-run army Q store. **1871** H. H. FURNESS in *New Variorum Ed. Shakespeare* I. p. ix, I have very seldom noted the *variæ lectiones* of the First Quarto... When referred to in the textual notes it is designated as (Q1). **1936** *Times Lit. Suppl.* 23 May 440/2 The stage directions of the stolen Q1 and of the authoritative Q2 were not contradictory. **1964** F. BOWERS *Bibliogr. & Textual Crit.* v. iv. 157 If Q is a memorially reconstructed 'bad quarto'.., its reading derives ultimately from the prompt-book. **1954** W. R. & F. K. SIMPSON *Hockshop* v. 127 We stalled until we could get the police into the Q. and A. contest. **1976** B. BOVA *Multiple Man* (1977) i. 14 McMurtie wanted..to know if I'd planned a Q and A session after the speech. **1938** *Times* 3 Mar. 7/3 Instructions..as to height and position to be kept when flying in controlled areas during 'Q.B.I.' conditions. **1942** *Tee Emm* (Air Ministry) II. 69 So now you fly in Q.B.I. *Ibid.* 143 He waited for some Q.B.I. And rushed aloft, the beam to try. **1870** A. J. MUNBY *Diary* 14 May (1972) 284 Came Vernon Lushington Q.C., and I did greet him friendly. **1887** L. GEORGE *Let.* 25 Feb. (1973) 18 A Q.C. of high standing. **1976** QCD [see *quantum chromodynamics* s.v. *QUANTUM 7a]. **1979** *Nature* 1 Feb. 349/3 The one essential difference between QED and QCD is that whereas there is but one type of electrical charge in QED, the colour charge has three independent varieties. **1969** *Physics Bull.* June 223/2 The energy splitting between the $2S_{\frac{1}{2}}$ and $2P_{\frac{1}{2}}$ states of the hydrogen atom—the Lamb shift—..arises entirely from higher order effects in QED. **1975** *McGraw-Hill Yearbk. Sci. & Technol.* 115/1 The detection of positrons from overcritical electric fields would constitute an important test of QED. **1890** G. S. CLARKE *Fortification* Pl. xxviii, Balance pillar mounting for 4·7-inch Q.F. gun. **1902** *Encycl. Brit.* XXXI. 347/2 Endeavouring..to produce a more powerful gun than the then existing Q.F. **1915** KIPLING *Fringes of Fleet* 1 They gave her Government coal to burn And a Q.F. gun at bow and stern. **1972** D. DAKIN *Unification of Greece* xi. 157 The Greek government ordered 144 7·5 mm Q.F. Schneider-Canet mountain guns. **1976** *Yorkshire Evening Press* 9 Dec. 21/1 (Advt.), Escort Mexico, 'K' reg. 60,000 miles. Q.I. headlamps, inertia belts. **1977** J. HEDGECOE *Photographer's Handbk.* 34 Q.I. lamps generate considerable heat, and must be ventilated. **1916** *Wipers Times* 12 Feb. (1918) 11/1 Obtainable from all Q.M. stores. **1933** M. LOWRY *Ultramarine* i. 49 It's good of you to ask me in, Q.M., thanks. **1907** *Field Service Pocket Bk.* viii. 160 Q.M.G. (Maj.-Gen.). **1918** in M. Gilbert *Winston S. Churchill* (1977) IV. Compan. I. 367 As regards the latter the General Staff will inform QMG of our requirements and he will take up the matter with you. **1977** 'D. MACNEIL' *Wolf in Fold* xvi. 165 I'm not leaving all those tents... Just think, the trouble there'd be with the QMG's department! **1916** *Anzac Bk.* 65, I am a Q.M.S... We have a Quartermaster, but of course, I do all the work. **1969** V. DE S. PINTO *City that Shone* ix. 207 A genial horsy character called Bob Duffield, the Q.M.S. and myself. **1971** S. HILL *Strange Meeting* ii. 157 The day I went to the village to see the Q.M.S. **1972** *Wireless World* Feb. 55/2 A way of avoiding the mislocalization..in the simple matrix technique has been adopted by Sansui in their QS system. **1975** *Official Gaz.* (U.S. Patent Office) 8 Apr. TM123/1 Sansui Electric Company Limited,.. Tokyo, Japan. Filed Dec. 13, 1972. *QS*... For disc-type music recordings... First use Oct. 23, 1970; in commerce Sept. 19, 1972. **1975** G. J. KING *Audio Handbk.* vii. 167 Image error results when a basic QS decoder is used to play an SQ record. *Ibid.* 168 SQ records also yield good stereo.., but QS records are less objectively accommodating in this respect. **1964** *New Scientist* 13 Aug. 393/3 The objects known variously as superstars, quasars, quasi-stellar objects or (for short) QSO's continue to cause intense interest among astronomers. **1973** *Nature* 23 Nov. 205/1 Although it is the majority view that QSO redshifts are cosmological in origin and related to distance by Hubble's law, several workers have proposed that QSOs may be more local objects. **1977** J. NARLIKAR *Struct. Universe* iii. 87 In looking for new QSOs, the astronomer picks upon star-like objects showing a marked ultraviolet radiation excess. **1965** SANDAGE & WYNDHAM in *Astrophysical Jrnl.* CXLI. 328 To the present time there have been positive identifications of nine quasi-stellar radio sources (hereinafter called 'QSS'). **1973** QSS [see *QUASI-STELLAR *a.*]. **1910** A. BENNETT *Clayhanger* II. xxi. 315 Mind you this is strictly q.t.! Nobody knows a word about it, nobody! **1922** JOYCE *Ulysses* 610 Sailing under false colours after having boxed the compass on the strict q.t. somewhere. **1972** *New Yorker* 17 June 24/1 (*caption*) This is strictly on the q.t., Senator.

III. As a symbol. **1.** *Q* or *q* in *Physics* represents electric charge. [f. the initial letter of *quantity*.]

1846 W. THOMSON in *Cambr. & Dublin Math. Jrnl.* I. 91 Denoting by *Q*, *Q′* the quantities of electricity constituting the charges before, and *q*, *q′* after contact, we shall have [etc.]. **1879** *Encycl. Brit.* VIII. 22/1 The law of electric force between two quantities *q* and *q′* now becomes Force = qq'/d^2. **1938** G. P. HARNWELL *Princ. Electr. & Magn.* i. 11 F is the force in dynes exerted by the charge q_1 on the charge q_2. **1973** L. J. TASSIE *Physics of Elem. Particles* xix. 40 The antiparticle of a particle of charge *Q* and baryon number *B*, has charge $-Q$ and baryon number $-B$.

2. *Theol.* [Prob. abbrev. of G. *quelle* source.] The symbol used to denote the hypothetical source of the passages shared by the gospels of Matthew and Luke, and not found in that of Mark.

1901 J. MOFFATT *Historical New Testament* 266 It is still hotly disputed..whether Matthew had access to any sources besides Q and Mark. **1920** *Jrnl. Theol. Stud.* XXI. 286 'Real Aramaism may be allowed ungrudgingly in those parts of the New Testament which are virtually translated from Aramaic oral or written sources', i.e. Mark and Q. **1935** R. H. LIGHTFOOT *Hist. & Interpretation in Gospels* ii. 27 Dr. Armitage Robinson..maintained..that he himself was the first to use the symbol... In the 'nineties of the last century, he was in the habit..of alluding to St. Mark's gospel as P (reminiscences of St. Peter), and to the presumed sayings-document as Q, simply because Q was the next letter after P in the alphabet. **1955** A. M. FARRER in D. E. Nineham *Stud. in Gospels* 56 We can conceive well enough how St. Luke could have both read St. Matthew's book as it stands, and written the gospel he has left us. Then at one stroke the question is erased to which the Q hypothesis supplied an answer. **1965** J. H. ROBERTS *Q Document* i. 33 The Q document is a hypothetical document invented by German biblical historians in the 1800s to explain a gap in our knowledge of the early Christian Era... They called this document the *quelle* or 'source' document. Later this was shortened to 'Q'. **1978** F. NEIRYNCK in *Ephemerides Theologicae Lovanienses* LIV. 123 It seems to be a fair conclusion that he [*sc.* J. Weiss] substituted Q (= *Quelle*) for Λ (= Λόγια).

3. Also *Q factor*. The ratio of the reactance of an inductor or capacitor to its electrical resistance; more widely, a parameter of any oscillatory system representing the degree to which it is undamped, equal to 2π times the ratio of the mean total energy of the system to the energy that must be supplied each cycle to sustain the oscillations. So **Q-meter,** an instrument for measuring the *Q* of a component.

1931 *Proc. IRE* XIX. 874 Let $Q = \omega_r L/R$. **1932** F. E. TERMAN *Radio Engin.* ii. 39 Tubing..has..a better current distribution..than does either flat- or edgewise-wound strip and hence has a better *Q* in proportion to the amount of conductor material employed. **1933** K. HENNEY *Radio Engin. Handbk.* VI. 109 For a coil, $Q = \omega L/R$. For a condenser, $Q = 1/\omega RC$. **1938** *Admiralty Handbk. Wireless Telegr.* II. § F19 Good coils often have a Q of the order of 100. **1943** F. E. TERMAN *Radio Engineers' Handbk.* XIII. 916 *Q* meters are frequently used to measure reactance and resistance (or conductance) of choke coils, dielectrics, etc., by the substitution method. **1943** *Electronic Engin.* XVI. 33/3 The two crystals were operated at 'Q' values of 20,000 and 5,000. **1948** P. M. MORSE *Vibration & Sound* (ed. 2) ii. 25 Another method of expressing this is in terms of the '*Q* of the system', where $Q = (\omega_0 m/R_m)$ is the number of cycles required for the amplitude of motion to reduce to $(1/e^{\pi})$ of its original value. **1965** *Wireless World* July 338/1 A technique..which had resulted in inductors with good Q factors of 50 to 80. *Ibid.* Aug. 413/1 A Q-meter can be used to establish the effective series resistance. **1971** [see *quality factor* s.v. *QUALITY *sb.* 13]. **1975** D. G. FINK *Electronics Engineers' Handbk.* XI. 13 By lowering the *Q* of the optical cavity, the laser cannot oscillate, and a large inverted population builds up. When the *Q* is restored, a single 'giant pulse'..is generated.

4. *Psychol.* Used in factor analysis to designate personality testing methods used to obtain correlations between the persons tested, by requiring each subject to rate in order those personality traits that seem most applicable to himself. Usu. as *Q-sort*, *-technique*.

1935 G. H. THOMSON in *Brit. Jrnl. Psychol.* July 75 Then we have $Y' Y = Q$..where *Q* is a *p*-square matrix of *q*-correlations, each correlation being between *two persons*, not between two tests. **1936** W. STEPHENSON in *Ibid.* Apr. 345 Following Prof. G. H. Thomson's suggestion, I shall use *Q* as the sign for correlations between persons, so distinguishing them from correlations such as r_{12} between two tests... It is convenient to designate all previous factor analysis as *r* technique, and this new inverted form as *Q* technique. **1952** R. B. CATTELL *Factor Analysis* vii. 93 He [*sc.* Stephenson] has particularly urged a method in which each subject writes down a set of traits or questionnaire-like statements about himself in order of their *significance* for his own personality (*Q-sort*). **1954** A. ANASTASI *Psychol. Testing* xx. 543 This approach..bears a certain resemblance to the procedure proposed by Stephenson in his 'Q-sort' technique. **1967** M. ARGYLE *Psychol. Interpersonal Behaviour* vii. 118 The so-called 'Q-sort' in which subjects are asked to place a series of statements on cards in order, with the cards which apply most to themselves at the top. **1972** *Jrnl. Social Psychol.* LXXXVIII. 84 The Q-sort variant known as the own-categories technique was used.

5. A unit of energy equal to 10^{18} British thermal units (very nearly 10^{21} joules).

1952 *Resources for Freedom* (President's Materials Policy Commission, U.S.) IV. xv. 213/1 In the first 18½ centuries of this era, the total input to the energy system of the world was about 6Q, equivalent to some 225 billion short tons of bituminous coal. [*Note*] $1{\cdot}0Q = 1{\cdot}0 \times 10^{18}$ B.t.u. **1971** *Nature* 29 Oct. 593/1 The present annual energy consumption rate of the world is 0·2Q. **1978** *Jrnl. R. Soc. Arts* CXXVI. 605/2 The earth and its atmosphere intercepts some 5200 Q of solar energy each year, one Q representing one million, million, million British Thermal Units.

qabab, var. *KEBAB.

‖ **qadi, qadhi, qazi,** varr. CADI.

1885 T. P. HUGHES *Dict. Islam* 255/1 It becomes a Muslim not to covet the appointment of Qāẓī. **1899** *Folk-Lore* X. 409 So strict a Musalman as one must presume a Qazi to be. **1906** F. A. KLEIN *Relig. of Islam* iv. 201 He appoints the Qádi or judge, whose office and duty is to examine law-suits. **1918** G. BELL *Let.* 6 Mar. (1927) II. xvii. 448, I sat in a row with the Qadhi, the Mudir of Church Lands.., the Judge of Appeal and so on and so on. **1955** G. E. VON GRUNEBAUM *Islam* i. 11 The canon-law judge, the qâḍî, will find himself unable to take care effectively of all contingencies. **1959** *Listener* 19 Nov. 888/1 Subsequent legislation provides for a similar *qadi*'s court at Kombo St. Mary. **1971** *Illustr. Weekly India* 4 Apr. 47/1 The imperative that the law must be enforced by a Muslim *qazi* became meaningless in British India. **1977** *Times* 21 Nov. 7/3 At the service, a *qadi* read a sermon in which he said abandoning Jerusalem was like abandoning Mecca.

‖ **qaimaqam,** var. KAIMAKAM.

1961 *Times* 17 July 11/2 The then Shaikh of Kuwait, who in the following year was invested with the rank of qaimaqam. **1970** H. TREVELYAN *Middle East in Revolution* 182 When in 1899 Mubarak as Sabah of Kuwait murdered his brothers, he sought protection with the Turkish Government which gave him the honorary title of Qaimaqam or Sub-Governor of a district.

‖ **qanat** (kanā·t), var. *KANAT.

1944 G. C. THOMPSON *Tombs & Moon Temple of Hureidha* 10 The Persian *qanat*, for instance, is seen on the coast, and in the Yemen. **1953** A. SMITH *Blind White Fish in Persia* i. 19 Shortly after the collection of facts had begun, we learnt of the qanats. It was written that there were 100,000 miles of them in Persia, that they were artificial underground water channels and that the deepest was over 1,000 feet. *Ibid.* iii. 55 As with birds before an island, the qanat wells warned you of the approach of a town. **1958** A. J. TOYNBEE *East to West* lix. 176 One sees line upon line of qanat-made molehills. **1966** P. ENGLISH *City & Village in Iran* i. 19 By the sixth century B.C.,..qanat technology was known on the Central Plateau. *Ibid.* iii. 50 The qanat-watered towns and villages on the slopes of the Kuhi Jupar. **1976** *Apollo* Apr. 302/3 Seen from the air, the ventilating shafts of these *qanats* punctuate the buff-coloured plains like perforations in paper. **1976** *Times* 17 Aug. 11/6 If the underground water resources of a semi-arid region are so immense that they can keep the 'qanats' running for the whole year then the unexploited ground-water resources of the British Isles must be incalculable.

‖ **qanon, qanun,** varr. KANOON.

1874 C. ENGEL *Descr. Catal. Musical Instruments S. Kensington Museum* 208 The *kanoon*, or *qânon*, an instrument especially appertaining to the Arabs and Persians, is, like the *santir*, a kind of dulcimer evidently of high antiquity in the East. **1931** C. S. HURGRONJE *Mekka in Latter Part of 19th Cent.* 44 Much worse is their habitual accompaniment of song with musical instruments: especially the *qabûs*, a four-stringed instrument which much resembles the *kemènjeh*, only that its strings are of gut instead of horsehair, and also the well known *qânûn* (guitar). **1957** H. G. FARMER in E. Wellesz *Anc. & Oriental Mus.* xi. 444 The psaltery was attributed to Al-Fārābi,..but the instrument is not mentioned by him under its millennium-old name of *qānūn*... As the *qānūn* it was known in Muslim Spain in the eleventh century, and in the fourteenth century it was mounted with sixty-four strings, tuned tricordally, in Persia. **1976** D. MUNROW *Instruments Middle Ages & Renaissance* 21/4 Little metal flaps fitted on the modern Arab qānūn.. enable the players to alter the pitch of a course of strings with an adroit flick of the fingers. *Ibid.* 23/2 The Arabic qānūn today is a large psaltery played with great virtuosity in Middle Eastern orchestras, and is a direct descendant of the forerunner of the European psaltery.

‖ **qasida** (kasī·da). Also 9 **kaszyde; kasida(h, quasida.** [Arab. *ḳaṣīda*.] An Arabic or Persian panegyric or elegiac poem or ode, usu. having a tripartite structure.

1819 J. L. BURCKHARDT *Trav. Nubia* 354 Like the eastern Arabs, they celebrate the praises of their warriors in the Kaszyde. **1842** McG. DE SLANE in Ibn Khallikan *Biogr. Dict.* I. p. xxxiii, The opinion held in the schools that the ancient *kasîdas* were masterpieces of art contributed also to the perversion of good taste; their plan and ideas were servilely copied, and it was by refinement of expression alone that writers could display their talent. **1885** *Encycl. Brit.* XVIII. 656/1 Those principal forms of poetry now used in common by all Mohammedan nations—the forms of the *ḳaṣîda* (the encomiastic, elegiac, or satirical poem), the *ghazal* or ode [etc.]. **1903** C. HUART *Hist. Arabic Lit.* ii. 10 According to the ancient rules..the author of a *qaṣîda* must begin by a reference to the forsaken camping-grounds. Next he must lament, and pray his comrades to halt, while he calls up the memory of the dwellers who had departed. **1907** R. A. NICHOLSON *Lit. Hist. Arabs* iii. 76 This fashion centres in the *Qaṣída*, or Ode, the only form, or rather the only finished type of poetry that existed in what..may be called the classical period of Arabic literature. **1927** F. KRENKOW in T. Houtsma et al. *Encycl. of Islam* II. 796/1 An Arabic (or Persian etc.) ḳaṣīda is a very artificial composition; the same rhyme has to run through the whole of the verses, however long the poem may be. *Ibid.* 796/2 The form of the ḳaṣīda has survived to modern times and I have specimens by poets still living where we find..a description of a desert-ride by persons who live in Cairo and travel by railway. **1934** *Times Lit. Suppl.* 27 Sept. 641/2 The four main types of Persian poetical composition are still..the *qasida*, the *ghazal*, the *masnavi* and the *ruba'iy*. **1940** F. STARK *Winter in Arabia* 45 Iuslim last night brought a singer of Qasidas. **1958** L. DURRELL *Balthazar* iv. 82 He was delighted to hear some music and listened with emotion to the wild *quasidas* that the old man sang. **1964** *Listener* 25 June 1036/1 This translation..from the Spanish of an Arabic-Andalusian *qasida* fragment from eleventh-century Toledo epitomizes one aspect of this breath of fresh air from the east which began to revivify the poetry of southern Europe. **1971** G. HOUSEHOLD *Doom's Caravan* iii. 158 My translation of Shakespeare's sonnets into kasidahs.

‖ **qat** (kat). Also **quatt.** [Arabic: var. KAT; *KHAT.] = KAT; also, the narcotic drug obtained from the leaves of this plant. Also *attrib.*

1958 *Times* 16 May 7/2 Lifting the ban on the importation into Aden Colony of qat, the narcotic leaf, was recommended by the qat commission of enquiry. **1963** *Times* 12 Mar. 12/7 Qat-chewing is not designed for the promotion of conversation. **1966** 'S. HARVESTER' *Treacherous Road* xi. 104 Ledgers and records..gave details of his exports of coffee, *qat*, fruit. **1968** *Daily Colonist* (Victoria, B.C.) 17 Dec. 5/2 A new product..is chewing gum containing..'Quatt', a mild narcotic produced from the tender leaves of a tea-like bush growing in profusion throughout the Middle East. **1971** [see *gobstopper* s.v. *GOB *sb.*[2]]. **1978** *Guardian Weekly* 17 Sept. 9/1 Normally, the day's qat session begins in the afternoon but during Ramadan it is chewed through most of the night.

Qatabanian (kæ:tăbē^i·niăn), *a.* and *sb.* Also **Catabanian, Kata-, Qatha-.** [f. *Qatabān* (see below) + -IAN.] **A.** *adj.* Of or pertaining to the kingdom of Qatabān in south Arabia, or its ancient Semitic dialect or language. **B.** *sb.* A native or inhabitant of Qatabān; the Qatabanian language. Also **Qataba·nic** *a.*

1926 A. MUSIL *Northern Ḥeǵâz* 310 It is named after the Catabanian, Esbonitan, and Scenitan Arabs. **1934, 1936** [see *MINÆAN *sb.* and *a.*]. **1939** L. H. GRAY *Foundations of Lang.* 364 *South Arabic* is known only from inscriptions (Minaean, Sabaean, Qathabānian, and Ḥaḍramautian) ranging, perhaps, from the eighth century B.C. to the sixth A.D., and by..modern dialects. **1948** D. DIRINGER *Alphabet* II. ii. 225 The Qatabanian kingdom, with its capital at Tamna'. *Ibid.* 226 The South Arabian inscriptions..are generally divided into five groups: The Minaean..the Sabaean..the Himyaritic..the Qatabanic and the Hadhramautic. **1951** W. F. ALBRIGHT in H. H. Rowley *Old Testament & Mod. Study* (1961) 9 The most archaic South-Arabic dialect, Qatabanian, shows uses of enclitic *m* more closely parallel to Proto-Sinaitic as deciphered by the writer than does any other Semitic tongue. **1959** A. F. L. BEESTON *Qahtan* I. 8 *N* is the twelfth letter of the Qatabanian alphabet. *Ibid.* 12 And when the overseer of šmr announces that he desires Qatabanians to make (trading) journeys among the tribes,..then Qatabanians may trade on their own account with the tribes. **1971** B. DOE *Southern Arabia* i. 22 It is possible to note that the languages of the Minaeans, Sabaeans, Qatabanians and Ḥaḍramant were similar but with differing dialects. *Ibid.* ii. 70 The Qatabanian kingdom was for centuries a neighbour south-west of Saba', and the capital city was Timna^e, now also known as Hajar Quḥlan (Koḥlān) in the Wadi Baihān. **1973** A. K. IRVINE in D. J. Wiseman *Peoples Old Testament Times* xii. 299 The apparent relationships of the South Arabian languages may suggest that while Minaean, Qatabanian, and Ḥaḍrami could have a north-eastern origin, Sabaean came rather from Central or North Arabia.

Qatari (kǣtā·ri, ‖ gatā·ri), *sb.* and *a.* [f. *Qatar* (see below) + *-I.] **A.** *sb.* A native or inhabitant of the state of Qatar in the Persian Gulf; also *Comb.*, as *Qatari-born* adj. **B.** *adj.* Of or pertaining to Qatar.

1959 R. HAY *Persian Gulf States* 110 The Ruler's Courts exercise jurisdiction over Qataris. **1960** *Geogr. Jrnl.* CXXVI. 447 The transcription used in this article is a conventional one, with a few exceptions which show the Qatari pronunciation of certain consonants, vowels and diphthongs. **1964** *Ann. Reg. 1963* 316 New regulations controlling foreign investment laid down that any foreign firms engaging in commerce or industry..must have Qatari partners holding at least 51 per cent of the capital. **1970** *Guardian* 10 Apr. 11/7 Qatar is regarded..as a protégé of Saudi Arabia, a point some Qataris indignantly deny. **1976** *Times* 3 Sept. (Qatar Suppl.) p. i/1 Qatari-born civil servants occupy many of the top-level posts. *Ibid.* p. i/7 Western expatriates as well as Qataris indisputably live well, usually employing a domestic servant or nanny... All educated Qataris speak English as their second language. **1978** *Financial Times* 22 Feb. 20/2 A further licence has been granted to a group of Qatari nationals to start a thirteenth bank, but it is not known when, or whether, this bank will commence business. **1979** R. S. ZAHLAN *Creation of Qatar* 118 For the next thirty years, no indication of the number of Qataris is available.

Qazaq, var. *KAZAKH.

qazi: see *QADI.

‖ **qere, Q^{e}re,** varr. KERI.

1941 R. H. PFEIFFER *Introd. Old Testament* I. v. 93 The *kethib* (written) is the consonantal text; the *qere* (read) is an accepted reading differing from the consonantal text. *Ibid.* 95 Long after the introduction of the *qere* 'Lord' for *YHWH*..vulgar expressions in the text..were removed by substituting a euphemism in the reading (*qere*). **1958** F. KENYON *Our Bible & Anc. MSS.* (ed. 5) iv. 78 Such variations were known by the name of Q^{e}re ('read') and k^{e}thib ('written'), the latter being the reading of the text, and the former that of the margin, which was to be substituted for the other when the passage was read. **1968** J. BARR *Compar. Philol. & Text of Old Testament* x. 246 Here, however, there is a rather peculiar *Qere*. *Ibid.* 247 The translation at 1 Sam. 25. 14 makes it extremely probable that the LXX is a translation not of the present *Kethibh* at 14. 32 but of the present *Qere*. **1969** R. K. HARRISON *Introd. Old Testament* (1970) IV. ii. 213 The preferred reading was known as *Q^{e}re*, meaning 'that which is to be read', as contrasted with the sacred consonantal text, the *K^{e}thibh* or 'written' Scripture. The *Q^{e}re* on occasions may have constituted a genuine variant reading.

Q fever (kiū· fī:vəɪ). [f. the initial letter of QUERY *sb.*[1] + FEVER *sb.*[1]] A disease caused by the rickettsia *Coxiella burnetii* that is variable in symptoms and often resembles influenza.

1937 E. H. DERRICK in *Med. Jrnl. Australia* 21 Aug. 282/1 The suspicion arose and gradually grew into a conviction that we were here dealing with a type of fever which had not been previously described. It became necessary to give it a name, and 'Q' fever was chosen to denote it until fuller knowledge should allow a better name. **1947** *Ann. Rev. Microbiol.* I. 342 The serological diagnosis of Q fever is at present the only satisfactory one for routine work, since the clinical picture is such that Q fever may be confused with a number of other diseases. **1964** E. H. DERRICK in *Queensland's Health* Dec. 11/2 'X' is a recognised term for an unknown quantity. But Australia already had an 'X disease', now known as Murray valley encephalitis. However, the rest of the alphabet was open. Query also signified the unknown. 'Q (for query) fever' it became. *Ibid.*, Many have wrongly assumed that the 'Q' stands for Queensland. **1978** *Jrnl. R. Soc. Med.* LXXI. 765 There appear to have been no further military outbreaks of Q fever until the Cyprus epidemic of 1974.

‖ **qi** (tʃi). Also **ch'i, Qi,** etc. [Chin. *qì* air, breath.] The physical life-force postulated by certain Chinese philosophers; the material principle.

1850 *Chinese Repository* XIX. 370 The following short expression of the doctrine of the Yih King is that in which probably all the literati would agree. It is from the 49th section of Chú-fútsz's entire works. 'All things..come only from the Great Extreme (*t'ái kih*). The Great Extreme is the primordial substance (*k'í*) which, moving along, divided and made two *k'í*; that which in itself has motion is the *Yang*, and that which had rest,.. is the *Yin*.' **1917** S. COULING *Encycl. Sinica* 436/2 The nature of man consists of this *Li*, or the Ethical Principle... In its essence it is absolutely pure and good, but seeing that it is inseparable from the material element *Ch'i*..it is from Man's birth to a greater or less extent impeded and tainted. **1958** W. WILLETTS *Chinese Art* II. vii. 586 Corresponding to this formal cause of each existence was its material cause, *ch'i*. **1964** K. K. S. CH'EN *Buddhism in China* xiv. 395 Chang Tsai (1020–1077) put forward a metaphysical system based on the theory that ch'i, ether or matter, existed at the beginning of the world. He held that ch'i consolidated itself into things at the beginning, and that things dissolved into ch'i in the end. **1971** F. MANN *Acupuncture* vi. 57 To the ancients the cornerstone of the theory of acupuncture, the concept whereby they explained its effects and action, was Qi, the energy of life. **1972** *Which?* Feb. 49/2 The energy of life (called Ch'i) flows along various 'meridians' in the body, and acupuncturists believe that if needles are inserted at..points along these meridians..the flow of energy in the body can be corrected. **1973** *Lancet* 14 July 58/1 They are not connected to internal organs, and Qi or anything else cannot flow along them. **1978** *Nature* 26 Oct 697/1 Arguably the most original Letter so far is a report of some experimental results on the physical basis of the traditional *yunqi* therapy—the curing of disorders through the passing of *qi* (pneuma) from doctor to patient without bodily contact.

Qiana (ki,ā·nă). Chiefly *U.S.* Also **qiana.** [Invented word.] A proprietary name in the U.S. for nylon.

1968 *Official Gaz.* (U.S. Patent Office) 3 Sept. TM25/1 Qiana. For Yarns of Man Made Fibers..First use May 15, 1968... E. I. du Pont de Nemours and Company. **1969** *Science Year* 274/1 Qiana is said to have color, clarity, and luster equal to or better than most luxurious silks. **1971** *New Yorker* 10 July 69 The commendable and reasonable sedate bathing suits produced by Edith Lances of sea-blue Qiana, which is a man-made silk. **1975** *Times* 13 May 12/4 Washable qiana jersey dress... Approx. £39.50. **1977** *Monitor* (McAllen, Texas) 26 June 1C/2 The mother of the bride wore a pale blue gown of

Qiana with a fitted long-sleeved jacket. **1979** *Farmington* (New Mexico) *Daily Times* 27 May 3A/5 (Advt.), Give him his favorite Qiana shirt.

qibla(h, var. KIBLAH in Dict. and Suppl.

qibli, var. *GIBLI.

‖ **qiviut** (ki·vi͵ŭt). [Eskimo.] The underwool of the arctic musk-ox; fibre made from this.

1965 *Sci. News Let.* 12 June 370/1 Many woolen manufacturers are enthusiastic about the principal product of the musk ox, its underwool, which the Eskimos call 'qiviut'. The fiber is similar to that of cashmere but about twice as long and half as thick. **1968** *Beaver* Winter 37/2 Eskimos call him [*sc.* the musk-ox] 'umingmak', the bearded one, and have long known his wonderful underwool as qiviut, a fibre far warmer than the silken down of the northern grey goose. **1972** *Guardian* 26 June 12/7 Collection of qiviut begins at the end of April. Bulls yield 6lb, and cows 5lb. **1979** R. FIENNES *Hell on Ice* viii. 125 The early explorers shot many musk-oxen. They took the soft wool that lies beneath the long brown hair. This *qiviut* was valuable to the Eskimo.

Q-spoi·ling, *vbl. sb. Physics.* [f. *Q III. 3 + SPOILING *vbl. sb.*[1]] = *Q-SWITCHING *vbl. sb.* So **Q-spoi·l** *v. trans.*, **Q-spoi·led** *ppl. a.*

1963 *New Scientist* 24 Oct. 201/2 A technique known as Q-spoiling' is used to store the laser's energy and liberate it in brief but tremendous bursts. **1966** *Appl. Physics Lett.* IX. 285 A technique involving the use of a magnetic field in '*Q*'-spoiling a ruby laser cooled to 77°K is discussed. **1970** *Physics Bull.* Mar. 116/2 By temporarily '*Q*-spoiling' the laser resonator by inserting a Kerr cell shutter between the high reflectivity mirror and the ruby laser rod, the energy storage capacity of the ruby was increased above the level at which relaxation oscillation would normally begin. *Ibid.*, By 1965 powers of 10^9 W in pulses of duration ~ 10 ns were produced by following the *Q*-spoiled oscillator with a series of ruby amplifiers. **1975** D. G. FINK *Electronics Engineers' Handbk.* XI. 13 The typical output of an optical laser consists of a series of spikes occurring during the major portion of the time that the laser is pumped... Q switching (Q spoiling) is a means of obtaining all the energy in a single spike of very high peak power.

Q-switch (kiū·͵switʃ), *sb. Physics.* Also **q-switch.** [f. *Q III. 3 + SWITCH *sb.*] A means of suddenly increasing or decreasing the *Q* of a laser by effectively unblocking or blocking the optical path to one of the mirrors.

1963 *Jrnl. Appl. Physics* XXXIV. 1000/2 (*heading*) Faraday effect as Q-switch for ruby laser. *Ibid.*, The Q-switch..was placed between the ruby and the separated end mirror. **1966** *New Scientist* 20 Oct. 93 Q-switches are employed to obtain a very powerful pulsed output from a laser by allowing the laser to store up energy; when it reaches a maximum the blockage is quickly removed, and an intense pulse of radiation is emitted. **1973** *Jrnl. Appl. Physics* XLIV. 4067/1 The oscillation of the laser with the cavity closed is sensed by a fast photodiode whose output signal opens the electro-optical *Q* switch. **1979** *Nature* 5 July p. vii/2 A compact pulsed ruby laser, that incorporates a q-switch.

So **Q-swi·tching** *vbl. sb.*, the process of pumping a laser that has a low *Q*, and so cannot oscillate, and then suddenly increasing the *Q* so that the stored energy is released in a single pulse of very high power; **Q-switch** *v. trans.*, to subject (a laser) to this process; **Q-swi·tched** *ppl. a.*

1963 *Jrnl. Appl. Physics* XXXIV. 1000/2 We wish to report the successful application of the Faraday effect (magneto-optic shutter) as a Q-switching technique for a ruby laser. *Ibid.* 3407/1 (*heading*) Q-switched $CaWO_4$: Nd^{3+} laser. *Ibid.*, A $CaWO_4$:Nd^{3+} laser was successfully Q-switched. **1965** *Wireless World* July 351/3 The ruby laser is Q-switched by a rotating prism. **1968** *McGraw-Hill Yearbk. Sci. & Technol.* 223 Saturable absorbers have recently been used very successfully to Q-switch ruby and neodymium-doped lasers. **1968** *New Scientist* 24 Oct. 205/1 Q-switching is a technique for producing giant laser pulses by preventing lasing action until a large amount of energy has been pumped into the atoms responsible. **1970** *Sci. Amer.* Mar. 41 They used the 104-inch telescope to transmit and detect pulses of 50-nanosecond duration produced by a 'Q-switched' (short-pulse) ruby laser. **1974** *Physics Bull.* Jan. 13/1 A four stage Q switched ruby laser is used to fire a pulse every three seconds, with a pulse length of a few tens of nanoseconds and an output energy of about 3 J.

qua, *adv.* Add: The pronunc. (kwā) is also common.

Qua, var. *KWA.

Quaalude (kwā·lūd). *Pharm.* A proprietary name for methaqualone; also, a tablet of this.

1966 *Official Gaz.* (U.S. Patent Office) 12 Apr. TM72/1 William H. Rorer, Inc., Fort Washington, Pa... *Quaalude.* For Sedative-hypnotic tablets. First use Aug. 5, 1965. **1967** H. BECKMAN *Dilemmas in Drug Therapy* 186/2 As 'newer' hypnotics I list the following:..methaqualone (Quaalude), 150 mg. at bedtime. **1968** *Trade Marks Jrnl.* 4 Dec. 2107/2 *Quāālude...* Sedative-hypnotic pharmaceutical preparations. William H. Rorer, Inc... Fort Washington. **1974** *Saturday Night* (Toronto) July 21/2 A quick trip to an interior bedroom, a little Quaalude to relax, a little coke to get the performing ego's motor humming and you were ready to face down King Kong. **1977** *Rolling Stone* 13 Jan. 31/1 A doctor had prescribed the chalky white Quaaludes to help her sleep at night. **1979** *Guardian* 9 Jan. 5/8 Quaalude (Mandrax in Britain) ..has a reputation as an aphrodisiac and is one of the fastest rising drugs of abuse in the US.

quack, *sb.*[1] Add: **1. b.** *slang* (orig. *Austral.* and *N.Z.*). A doctor (with no implication that he is unqualified); also in *Mil.* use, a medical officer.

1919 W. H. DOWNING *Digger Dial.* 40 *Quack*, a medical officer. *c* **1926** 'MIXER' *Transport Workers' Song Bk.* 43 And ask me if I want a 'sub'. For to take me to the 'quack'. **1943** *Coast to Coast* 1942 29 Might be he lose his leg if we don't get him across right away to the quack. **1945** C. H. WARD-JACKSON *Piece of Cake* (ed. 2) 51 *Quack*, medical officer. **1960** J. IGGULDEN *Storms of Summer* 169 I'll get the quack at the Bush Hospital to have a look at it in the morning. **1962** GRANVILLE *Dict. Sailors' Slang* 93/1 *Quack, the*, medical officer. Jocular. **1976** D. IRELAND *Glass Canoe* 136, I go along to this quack and he says Get back to the surf and get some green vegetables into you.

quack (kwæk), *sb.*[4] *U.S.* [var. of QUICK *sb.*[2]] Couch-grass, *Agropyron repens*, a European grass with creeping roots, widely naturalized elsewhere. Cf. QUICK *sb.*[2]

1833 L. C. BECK *Bot. N. & Middle States* 416 A troublesome weed. Couch Grass. Quack. **1872** *Rep. Vermont Board Agric.* I. 289 He who sets out to subdue a piece of quack must resolve on no half-way measures. **1909** *N.Y. Even. Post* (semi-weekly ed.) 11 Mar. 5 In conquering the quack he did the one thing that could have enabled him to get a crop from that unfertilized soil. **1930** *Times Educ. Suppl.* 31 May 248/1 It [*sc.* couchgrass] has a good many names: squitch, scutch, quack..are all in use. **1948** H. A. JACOBS *We chose Country* 189 The big garden across the road, where we fought quack instead of weeds, really established us.

2. *Comb.* **quack-grass** = prec.

1822 A. EATON *Man. Bot.* (ed. 3) 404 *Triticum repens*, wheat-grass, couch-grass, quack-grass... Very troublesome in fertile soil, and useful in barren sand. **1839** J. BUEL *Farmer's Compan.* xiv. 151 One of our neighbours has been enabled completely to eradicate quack-grass in his Indian corn. **1884** G. VASEY *Agric. Grasses U.S.* 108 Quack grass... There has been a good deal of discussion relative to this grass, some pronouncing it one of the vilest of weeds. **1949** *This Week Mag.* 17 Sept. 2/2 The quackgrass and the sassafras is getting the best of him. **1970** *Daily Progress* (Charlottesville, Va.) 24 May 4/2 Burning robs the topsoil of its fertility..and actually increases the growth of quackgrass, weeds, and other unwanted, troublesome, perennial plants.

quack, *v.*[1] **3.** (Later example.)

1925 *Scribner's Mag.* Oct. 385/1 Time..has not obliterated the love of being quacked.

quacker (kwæ·kəɹ). *colloq.* [f. QUACK *v.*[2] + -ER.] One that quacks; a duck. Also *fig.*

1846 *Swell's Night Guide* 75 Jest pipe her—she turns her ogles up like a croaking quacker (dying duck). **1965** *New Statesman* 18 June 980/2 The noisiest quackers have now felt a wind of deflation beginning to stir about the world and have fallen silent. **1978** *Times* 23 Feb. 16/4 Though ducks are plentiful along the Thames..two dozen quackers were brought along.

quacky, *a.*[1] (Earlier example.)

1836 *Southern Lit. Messenger* II. 327 The critical department of this work..is in our opinion decidedly quacky.

quad, *sb.*[3] Add: Also in other senses of QUADRUPLET. (Further examples.)

1951 M. ABERCROMBIE et al. *Dict. Biol.* 182 An armadillo (*Dasypodus*) always has identical quads from a single ovum. **1974** *Publishers Weekly* 26 Aug. 302/3 The good sports books seem to come in quads or pairs: four Babe Ruth books, two on [etc.]. **1975** *Nature* 3 Apr. 379/2 If the same pairs, triples, quads.., of references are observed in a number of articles, there is an implied consensus of opinion. **1978** *Daily Tel.* 4 Dec. 2/6 A five-year-old Friesian cow has given birth to quads. **1979** *Daily Tel.* 16 Nov. 3/4 Quads were born by Caesarean operation at St. Mary's Hospital, Paddington.

quad, *sb.*[5] : see *QUAD *a.*[1]

quad (kwǫd), *sb.*[6] *Teleph.* [Abbrev. of QUADRUPLEX *a.* and *sb.*] A group of four insulated conductors twisted together, the conductors usu. forming two circuits. Also *attrib.* or as *adj.*, as *quad cable.*

1922 *Bell Syst. Techn. Jrnl.* I. 72 The cable is of quadded construction, that is, the wires are first wrapped with dry paper for insulation and twisted into pairs and then two pairs are twisted into what is called a quad. **1940** *Chambers's Techn. Dict.* 691/1 *Quad* (or *star-quad*) *cable*, lead-covered cable in which the unit group is four paper-insulated conductors twisted together, opposite conductors forming the go and return circuits of a four-wire channel respectively. **1941** A. E. KNOWLTON *Stand. Handbk. Electr. Engineers* (ed. 7) xxii. 2075 A quad is formed by twisting together two individual pairs,..in the same manner that each pair is formed. **1958** J. R. G. SMITH *Elem. Telecommunications Pract.* v. 72 The quads are then made up in the number of layers required for the size of the cable.

quad (kwǫd), *sb.*[7] [Abbrev. of QUADRILATERAL *a.* and *sb.*] **1.** *Naut.* A four-sided jib used on racing yachts. Also *attrib.*

1937 *Sun* (Baltimore) 4 Aug. 14/1 Endeavour's board of strategy had ordered a new quadrilateral Genoa jib made of synthetic silk and similar to the big 'quad' which has proved so effective in Ranger's windward work. **1937** *Yachting Monthly* LXIII. 376/1 Both yachts broke out their Genoa jibs, but whereas Ranger's was a double-clewed sail, or 'quad', that aboard the challenger was somewhat smaller. *Ibid.* 378/1 Vanderbilt sprang his own choice in head rigs and set a wonderful quad Genoa. **1938** *Britannica Bk. of Year* 712/1 A feature of 'Ranger's' rig was the efficient use of quadrilateral jibs and particularly of a large 'quad' Genoa jib made of rayon.

2. *Radio.* An aerial in the form of a square or rectangle broken in the middle of one side. Freq. *attrib.*

1961 *Amateur Radio Handbk.* (ed. 3) xiii. 385/2 A quad aerial is practicable for 14 Mc/s but it is, of course, a one-band aerial; however, 21 and 28 Mc/s quads can be nested instead inside a 14 Mc/s structure without serious interference. **1962** *Flight Internat.* LXXXI. 596/1 A quad-helix aerial could be seen... It is one of 52 Cubic installations furnished for acquisition, telemetry and communications for manned orbital flights. **1976** PERKOWSKI & STRAL *Joy of CB* xi. 125 Even greater directionality is achieved with a stacked quad consisting of four elements.

quad, *sb.*[8]: see *QUAD *a.*[2]

quad (kwǫd), *sb.*[9] [Abbrev. of QUADRILLION.] A unit of energy equal to 10^{15} British thermal units (very nearly 10^{18} joules).

1974 *Newsweek* 7 Oct. 84/2 The current standard energy forecast is that U.S. demand will double in the next ten years to nearly 145 'quads' (or quadrillion BTU's). **1976** *Sci. Amer.* Jan. 21/2 Without any new initiatives the need for imported oil will rise steadily from about 12 quads at present to more than 60 in the year 2000. **1976** *National Observer* (U.S.) 17 Apr. 8/3 The nation's energy consumption in 1974 was about 73 quads. **1980** *Nature* 10 Apr. 501/2 The first assumes a level of energy consumption in the US of 71 quads, equal to estimates of consumption in 1975 when the study was started.

quad, *a.*[1] Add: Also in other contexts in the sense of QUADRUPLE *a.* (Further examples.)

1961 *Times* 30 Oct. (Brit. Posters Suppl.) p. iii/6 Posters ranging from quad-crown to crown-folio. **1967** *Electronics* 6 Mar. 158/1 One manufacturer..offers a 'quad 2-input OR gate' that actually has three 2-input AND gates and one 3-input AND gate feeding into a NOR gate. **1972** G. V. HIGGINS *Friends E. Coyle* xviii. 106 Eddie Coyle drove the old Sedan de Ville cautiously, the quad headlights on high beam. **1972** *Country Life* 10 Feb. 341/2 Asked what brought her to the forecourt apart from the imminent need for petrol, she replied unhesitatingly: 'Quad stamps and promotion offers.' **1973** D. ROBINSON *Rotten with Honour* 176 How much should I ask him for it?.. I'll try two-fifty and maybe throw in quad stamps. **1974** *Sunday Times* 16 June 29/6 Their time of 4 min 49·80 sec...was only 20 seconds slower than Eton's record in the eights, clearly indicating the potential speed of quad scullers.

B. *sb.*[5] Also **Quad.** A vehicle with four-wheel drive; *spec.* (see quot. 1948). orig. *U.S.*

1919 'I. HAY' *Last Million* xiv. 224 Smaller vehicles of American design, known as 'Quads'. These possess the unusual feature of a drive upon either axle. **1941** *Illustr. London News* 24 May 657/2 The third drawing shows 'Quads', powerfully mechanised units, which haul and guide the new guns into position and out. **1948** PARTRIDGE *Dict. Forces' Slang* 150 *Quad*, a four-wheel drive, gun-towing vehicle. **1961** W. VAUGHAN-THOMAS *Anzio* vi. 122 The Recce Regiment cars were trying to tuck themselves behind the walls as shelter for the night, a Quad, towing an anti-tank gun, was vainly trying to do the same thing.

quad (kwǫd), *a.*[2] and *sb.*[8] **A.** *adj.* Abbrev. of *QUADRAPHONIC *a.*

1970 *Sat. Rev.* (U.S.) 27 June 56/1 Their new Quadraphonic Processor is an add-on bringing true (and quite well simulated) quad sound to two-channel systems. **1972** *Observer* (Colour Suppl.) 22 Oct. 56/4 The manufacturers have been to great pains to make their quad equipment 'compatible'. **1976** *Washington Post* 19 Apr. c8/4 (Advt.), 'Jesus Christ Superstar' 7:30, 9:30. Shown in quad sound and Big Screen Projection. **1977** *Listener* 20 Oct. 507/3 With quad transmissions now a regular feature of Radio 3, the argument that the BBC cannot afford to extend stereo coverage seems a little thin. **1980** *Broadcast* 7 July 8/3 A 17-year-old 2″ quad VTR machine.

B. *sb.*[8] Abbrev. of *QUADRAPHONY.

1971 *Esquire* Nov. 228/2 The necessity of making quad compatible with mono and stereo recordings and broadcasts is probably going to necessitate the use of some system that matrixes the four channels down to one. **1974** *Radio Times* 27 June 5/1 Quad adds a depth and perspective to radio that is missing in stereo. **1975** *Time Out* 15 Aug. 49/3 They give a live electronic concert (in quad) of music by little-known younger composers.

quad, *v.*[1] Add: (Further example.) Hence **qua·dded** *ppl. a.*, **qua·dding** *vbl. sb.*

1914 H. PENDER *Amer. Handbk. Electr. Engineers* 1355 *Quadded* or *phantomed cable*,..a cable adapted for the use of phantom circuits. **1922** [see *QUAD *sb.*[6]]. **1962** *Engineering* 16 Feb. 245/1 Once insulated, the conductor wires are either twisted into pairs or 'quadded' in groups of four. *Ibid.* 245/2 After twisting or quadding each conductor wire is given a 'ring through' test with a bell and battery.

quadrangle, *sb.* Add: **1. b.** *Palmistry.* (See quot. 1883.)

1883 FRITH & HERON-ALLEN *Chiromancy* 138 The Quadrangle is that part of the human hand comprised between the line of the Head and the line of the Heart and between the line of Fate and the line of Apollo. **1895** H. Frith *Pract. Palmistry* III. i. 121 The Quadrangle is an extremely important space, for upon its width and general appearance the mind and the disposition of the man or woman may be estimated and 'reckoned up'. **1934** C. de Saint-Germain *Study of Palmistry* IV. 313/1 A cross in the Quadrangle touching the Line of Heart—Influence of the opposite sex on the subject... A cross in the Quadrangle touching the Line of Head—The subject will exert in the matters of love or friendship more influence on the other person than the said person will exert on him. **1952** J. Malcolm *Frith's Pract. Palmistry* (rev. ed.) xviii. 112 The Quadrangle should be regular and wide in the centre, and it should expand at both ends. This indicates good health, honesty and trustworthiness. **1971** *Cheiro Bk. of Fate & Fortune* xli. 122 When the quadrangle is abnormally wide in its entire length, it denotes want of order in the brain, carelessness of thought and ideas, an unconventional nature, and one imprudent in every way.

quadrangular, *a.* (Later *Comb.* example.)

1854 *Poultry Chron.* I. 431 It is a spacious, quadrangular-shaped house, built of a greyish stone.

quadrant, *sb.*[1] Add: **4. b.** *spec.* (i) *Naut.* A metal frame, shaped as the quadrant or sector of a circle, that is fixed to the rudder head or stock and to which the steering ropes or chains are attached.

1885 H. Paasch *From Keel to Truck* 32/1 *Tiller.. quadrant*, barre de gouvernail en quadrant. Quadrant als Ruderpinne. **1894** *Ibid.* (ed. 2) 223 Steering-quadrant. **1923** *Glasgow Herald* 3 Feb. 8/7 The modern helm, or its equivalent, the quadrant, is placed out-board. **1961** *Lloyd's Register of Shipping: Rules & Regs. Construction Steel Ships* 57/1 Tillers and quadrants are to be shrunk on or bolted to the rudder head. **1976** *Oxf. Compan. Ships & Sea* 731/2 It is by means of the quadrant, with the assistance of a steering engine, that force is applied to turn the rudder.

(ii) (See quot. 1940.)

1885 H. Paasch *From Keel to Truck* 80/1 *Quadrant, reversing*, secteur de changement de marche. Umsteuerungs-Quadrant. **1940** *Chambers's Techn. Dict.* 691/1 *Quadrant*, a slotted segmental guide through which an adjusting lever (e.g. a reversing lever) works. It is provided with means for locating the lever in any desired angular position. **1959** *Weekly Times* (Melbourne) 30 Sept. 1 (Advt.), At your fingertips is the 'automatic brain' of your Ferguson [tractor]—the amazingly simple control quadrant that gives you complete 4-way work control. Without moving your hand more than six inches, you can raise and lower implements or hold them rigidly in any position. **1971** 'D. Rutherford' *Clear the Fast Lane* 46 He took the sharp curve..snicking the gearbox quadrant into second. **1977** *R.A.F. News* 8–21 June 11/2 In such foggy conditions..quadrant operators would be unable to sight and pinpoint the bomb and rocket hit points.

d. (Freq. with capital initial.) A street or part of a street curved in a quarter-circle; *spec.* the eastern end of Regent Street adjoining Piccadilly Circus in London.

1822 S. Leigh *New Picture of London* (new ed.) vi. 289 Quadrant, extending from Piccadilly to Glasshouse-street, ornamented by handsome colonnades supported by about 140 cast-iron pillars. **1847** Thackeray *Van. Fair* (1848) xxxviii. 348 The bearded savages..who..scowl at you..n the Quadrant arcades. **1875** A. E. Housman *Let.* 9 Jan. (1971) 6 The Quadrant, Regent Street, and Pall Mall are the finest streets. **1885** *List of Subscribers, Brighton* (South of Eng. Telephone Co.) 3 Farringdon B.—5, North-street-quadrant. **1974** F. Selwyn *Cracksman on Velvet* II. 131 The wagon rumbled the length of Nash's elegant quadrant. **1974** J. Gardner *Return of Moriarty* 131 They were in a house near Regent Street, near the Quadrant.

6. quadrant electrometer (earlier example); **quadrant method** *Archæol.*, a method of dividing up a site to be excavated (see quot. 1954).

1777 T. Cavallo *Compl. Treat. Electr.* III. iii. 161 Fig 7th. represents Mr. Henly's quadrant electrometer. [**1930** A. E. van Giffen *Die Bauart der Einzelgräber* 7 Bei den Hügeluntersuchungen wird von mir mit Vorliebe nach der sog. Quadrantenmethode..vorgegangen. Ich verwendete sie zuerst..im Jahre 1916.] **1939** G. Clark *Archæol. & Society* iv. 97 For dealing with round barrows with internal structures of timber Dr A. E. van Giffen of Groningen has evolved what he terms the 'quadrant method'. **1954** M. Wheeler *Archaeol. from Earth* viii. 95 It is known as *quartering* or the *quadrant method*. The mound is marked out into four quarters by two strings, laid preferably to the cardinal points of the compass and over the approximate centre. Opposite quarters are then excavated in turn, a balk 1½–3 feet wide being left between each quadrant in such a fashion as to give a complete transverse section across the mound in both directions. **1967** L. de Paor *Archæol.* ii. 49 The 'quadrant method'..is much used in the excavation of circular barrows and other small mounds... It will be observed that one of the objects of the method is to preserve to the last moment two full cross-sections.

quadrantal, *a.*[1] (Examples in the sense of *quadrantic *a.*)

1914 *Trans. Ophthalm. Soc.* XXXIV. 209 Uncomplicated quadrantal unrecognised hemianopsia. **1918** *Arch. Ophthalm.* XLVII. 126 Early homonymous upper quadrantal defects in Stage I.

quadrantanopia (kwǫ:dræ̆ntănōᵘ·piă). *Ophthalm.* [mod.L., f. Quadrant *sb.*[1] + Gr. ἀν- priv. + -ωπια sight.] A quadrantic loss of perception in an eye.

1942 I. S. Tassman *Eye Manifestations of Internal Dis.* iii. 75 The quadrantanopias affecting both fields may be homonymous, bitemporal, or binasal, inferior, superior, or crossed. **1964** S. Duke-Elder *Parsons' Dis. Eye* (ed. 14) xxiv. 358 Rare cases of homonymous quadrantanopia have been reported, in which corresponding quadrants of each field—the upper or lower half of one temporal, and the upper or lower half of the other nasal—have been lost. **1979** *Internat. Rehabilit. Med.* I. 53/1 The presence of a hemianopia or quadrantanopia was assessed by a confrontation method and confirmed by peripheral perimetry.

quadrantanopsia (kwǫ:dræ̆ntănǫ·psiă). *Ophthalm.* [mod.L., f. as prec. + Gr. ὄψις sight.] = prec.

1910 *Lippincott's New Med. Dict.* 802/1 *Quadrantanopsia*, a sector defect of the eye with blindness limited to a portion of the visual field and due to cortical disease. **1947** F. H. Adler *Gifford's Textbk. Ophthalm.* (ed. 4) iv. 46 The result of a lesion in this region [*sc.* Meyer's loop] is to produce an isolated quadrantanopsia. **1964** D. O. Harrington *Visual Fields* (ed. 2) vii. 134 The quadrantanopsia [ed. 1: -opia] is truly congruous..in a patient with a cortical lesion. **1977** Tate & Lynn *Princ. Quantitative Perimetry* i. 44 Testing of both eyes assures that the pattern is not a pair of right and left homonymous quadrantanopsias.

quadrantic (kwǫdræ·ntik), *a.* *Ophthalm.* [f. Quadrant *sb.*[1] + -ic.] Involving the upper or lower part of one side of the visual field.

1914 *Trans. Ophthalm. Soc.* XXXIV. 212 Lower quadrantic right hemianopsia of four years standing. **1938** W. S. Duke-Elder *Textbk. Ophthalm.* II. xxix. 1228 If the sector defect is bounded by vertical and horizontal radii, the defect is called quadrantic anopia. **1976** *Lancet* 6 Nov. 1007/1 Neurological signs are absent—with the occasional exception of an isolated sixth-nerve palsy or an inferior-nasal quadrantic visual-field defect.

quadraphonic (kwǫdrăfǫ·nik), *a.* and *sb.* Also **quadro-, quadri-.** [f. Quadra-, Quadro-, Quadri- + Phonic *a.* (*sb.*).] **A.** *adj.* Produced by or pertaining to a system of sound recording and reproduction that employs four signal sources, two or more channels, and four loudspeakers, these being placed so that the original front-to-back sound distribution may be reproduced as well as the side-to-side one of stereophony.

1969 *High Fidelity* Sept. 63/1 The four channels might be used for double ping-pong effects—perhaps a quadriphonic version of 'Switched on Bach'. **1970** [see *quad *a.*[2]]. **1971** *Sci. Amer.* Aug. 13/3 One of my main interests ..is music—from rock to Bach—preferably in live concert or quadraphonic sound. **1972** *Sat. Rev.* (U.S.) 25 Mar. 34/2 The quadrophonic sound proves very satisfactory on stereo equipment. **1974** *Radio Times* 27 June 55/3 Raymond Raikes talks about the quadraphonic experimental broadcast which can be heard at 12.5. **1975** D. G. Fink *Electronic Engineers' Handbk.* xix. 81 Figure 19-147 summarizes the track and playback head locations for open-reel, eight-track cartridge and cassette tapes for both stereo and quadriphonic operation. **1975** *Jrnl. Audio Engin. Soc.* XXIII. 3/1 These presentations were made through each of the three basic types of quadraphonic system under test, namely, 4–4–4, 4–3–4, and 4–2–4. **1975** G. J. King *Audio Handbk.* vii. 168 All 'quadraphonic' records will play through a stereo system with varying degrees of accuracy. **1977** *Times* 13 Apr. 1/8 Quadraphonic broadcasts—radio in the round—are to be transmitted for an experimental period of 12 months by the BBC. **1977** *Time* 19 Sept. 56/2 At the starting gun in Rhode Island Sound this week, thousands of people will be watching in everything from little outboards to palatial cruisers with bars and quadraphonic sound systems. **1978** *Daily Tel.* 22 Feb. 16/6 (Advt.), BMW 528... Aluminium sports wheels. Quadrophonic radio and cassette player.

B. *sb.* = *quadraphony.

1972 *Esquire* June 55/3 (Advt.), Should you wait until quadraphonic is perfected? **1977** *Homes & Gardens* Nov. 161 Quadraphonic was boosted..when the BBC developed Matrix H, a new method of mixing and encoding quadraphonic signals.

Hence **quadrapho·nically** *adv.*, in a quadraphonic way; by means of quadraphony.

1970 *High Fidelity Mag.* Nov. 76/2 In classical music recorded quadriphonically the two front channels serve the same use as the left and right channels of conventional stereo. **1973** [see *matrix 6 e]. **1976** *Gramophone* Mar. 1441/2 The hall sound and orchestral layout were beautifully conveyed quadraphonically.

quadraphonics (kwǫdrăfǫ·niks), *sb. pl.* (usu. const. as sing.). Also **quadro-, quadri-.** [f. prec.: see -ic 2.] = *quadraphony.

1970 *High Fidelity Mag.* Nov. 76/2 (*heading*) The quadriphonics sweepstakes. **1972** *Observer* (Colour Suppl.) 22 Oct. 55/2 How could one have been taken in for so long by stereo which merely made you a member of a concert audience when quadraphonics elevate you to a member of the orchestra? **1974** H. W. Hellyer *Stereo Sound* ix. 182 Quadrophonics purports to give us back that lost illusion of reality by supplying the lost ambience. **1976** *Which?* May 99/1 One purpose of quadraphonics is to recreate this ambience properly.

quadraphony (kwǫdrǫ·fŏni). Also **quadro-, quadri-.** [f. as prec.: see -y[3].] Quadraphonic reproduction; the use of quadraphonic techniques.

1969 *High Fidelity* Sept. 3 Has quadriphony finally arrived? **1970** *Ibid.* Jan. 38/2 With musical material emanating from all four corners of the room, we found that visitors stood every which way to listen. Perhaps the most descriptive terminology for these two techniques, therefore, would be polarized and unpolarized quadriphony, respectively. **1972** *Daily Tel.* 20 Jan. 4 (Advt.), Where stereophony ends quadraphony begins. **1973** *B.B.C. Handbk.* 1974 74/1 Quadrophony involves four sound channels leading to four loudspeakers, normally placed in the four corners of a room. **1974** *Radio Times* 27 June 55/3 With your front two speakers bringing you Radio 2 on VHF Stereo.., and another Stereo Receiver driving your two back speakers and tuned to Radio 3 on VHF Stereo.., you will be able to hear this programme in Quadraphony. **1975** G. J. King *Audio Handbk.* ix. 211 For quadraphony or four-channel stereo four microphones are required. **1976** *Sci. Amer.* Sept. 144/1 (Advt.), Lowest effective stylus mass (0·39 mg) in quadriphony.

quadraplegic, var. *quadriplegic *a.* and *sb.*

quadrasonic (kwǫdrăsǫ·nik), *a.* Also **quadro-, quadri-.** [f. Quadra-, Quadro-, Quadri- + *sonic *a.*] = *quadraphonic *a.*

1970 *Time* 28 Sept. 73/2 Davis is looking forward to Columbia's further development of quadrisonic sound, a kind of double-stereo system that was introduced on tapes last year by Vanguard. **1970** *Rolling Stone* 12 Nov. 40/5 Phillips of Holland..has shown some very promising four-channel tapes and cassette machines, called a 'quadrosonic' system. **1971** *Hi-Fi Sound* Feb. 66/2 A compact system with good bookshelf speakers..can be quadrasonic if you like. **1973** *New Yorker* 24 Sept. 113/1 Be a part of New York's newest disco... Appreciate the elite atmosphere of total quadrasonic sound.

quadrat. Add: **3.** *Ecology.* Each of a set of small measured plots of land, formerly usu. one metre squares, used in studying the local distribution of plants and animals. Also *transf.* (see quot. 1960).

1905 F. E. Clements *Res. Methods Ecol.* iv. 161 Vegetation exhibits both development and structure, and is, in consequence, open to exact methods of inquiry. In the search for feasible methods, it was quickly seen that the quadrat, first used for determining the abundance of species, furnished the key to the problem. *Ibid.* 164 The unit size of quadrat is the meter, and when the term is used without qualification, it refers to the meter quadrat. **1922** *Ecology* III. 158 He does not say whether the quadrats as counted were contiguous or scattered. **1939** Clements & Shelford *Bio-Ecol.* v. 196 Cross checking rendered possible by his use of four methods, viz: trapping, censuses, hare transects, and quadrats of droppings. **1950** *Jrnl. Ecol.* XXXVIII. 108 There has thus grown up in botanical ecology a study of the distribution of species in 'quadrats' or small samples of fixed area (usually 1 sq. m. or less) in which only the presence or absence of particular species is recorded and not its numbers. **1960** *New Phytologist* LIX. 1 In the point quadrat method of vegetational analysis..thin needles are passed vertically through grassland..and the number of contacts between needles and foliage is recorded. **1974** *Nature* 25 Oct. 713/2 It is difficult to estimate the number of snails in natural populations since they move around too slowly for ordinary capture-recapture methods, and their patchy distribution makes quadrat or transect counts unreliable.

quadratic, *a.* and *sb.* Add: **A.** *adj.* **2.** Also *quadratic form* (see *form *sb.* 5 d); *quadratic programming*, a technique analogous to linear programming but dealing with a quadratic rather than a linear objective function.

1859 [see *form *sb.* 5 d]. **1896** *Bull. Amer. Math. Soc.* III. 100 The general theory of quadratic forms is not taken up. **1965** C. H. Springer et al. *Adv. Methods & Models* viii. 232 *Quadratic Programing*—a name given to a problem which looks much like a linear program, except the objective function is of second degree, i.e., contains squared terms in it. **1968** E. T. Copson *Metric Spaces* ix. 141 This space was first studied by David Hilbert in his work on quadratic forms in infinitely many variables. **1974** Adby & Dempster *Introd. Optimization Methods* v. 153 Although this is an effective strategy for quadratic programming, it can multiply unnecessary function evaluations for general *f*.

quadratically, *adv.* (Examples.)

1928 *Physical Rev.* XXXI. 74 Such an equation has no quadratically integrable solution. **1955** *Rev. Sci. Instruments* XXVI. 116/1 The mode separation varies quadratically as the limit is approached. **1974** Adby & Dempster *Introd. Optimization Methods* iv. 90 A quadratically terminating method..which makes use of conjugate gradient vectors..has been utilized in procedures for constrained optimization because of its modest memory requirements. **1979** *Sci. Amer.* May 32/3 This implies that in the past the storehouse has grown quadratically with time, as Engels said, not linearly, as Rescher argues.

quadrature. Add: **3. a.** More widely, the calculation of the area bounded by, or lying under, a curve. (Further examples.)

1911 E. B. Wilson *Adv. Calculus* xi. 313 It is therefore customary to restrict the application of the term 'area' to such simple closed curves as have $I_u = 0$, and to say that the quadrature of such curves is possible, but that the quadrature of curves for which $I_u \neq 0$ is impossible. **1942** H. M. Bacon *Differential & Integral Calculus* i. 3 The desire was to find a *square* equal in area to the area bounded by the given curve (in this case, a circle). For this reason the problem has been called the problem of quadrature. *Ibid.* xiv. 410 The definite integral, which solves the problem of quadrature mentioned in Chap. I, suggests the notation for integrals, the ∫ being a conventionalized form of 'S' for 'sum'. **1968** Fox & Mayers *Computing Methods* ix. 170 Apart from the rare possibility of being able to perform the quadrature by expressing the indefinite integral in closed form.., we have various general methods and some special methods.

4. e. *Electr.* A phase difference of 90 degrees. Usu. *attrib.* or in phr. *in quadrature (with).*

1889 T. H. Blakesley *Alternating Currents of Electr.* (ed. 2) xiii. 117 The only induction in the secondary coil is derived from the core, and is, therefore, as regards phase, in quadrature with the magnetization. **1892** S. P. Thompson *Dynamo-Electric Machinery* (ed. 4) xxii. 628 The waves of self-induced electromotive-force will lag exactly a quarter-period behind those of the current, or will be 'in quadrature' with them. **1940** *Chambers's Techn. Dict.* 691/2 *Quadrature transformer*, a transformer designed so that the secondary e.m.f. is 90° displaced from the primary e.m.f. *Ibid.* 705/1 *Reactive component*, the term now preferred for the component of the vector representing an alternating quantity which is in quadrature (at 90°) with some reference vector... Also called quadrature component. **1944** *Electronic Engin.* XVII. 58/2 The only unusual section is the reactance modulator or quadrature tube, so called because the anode circuit is back-coupled to the grid..in such a way as to cause a 90-degree phase difference between grid and anode voltages. **1967** *Electronics* 6 Mar. 120/2 The current in these resistors is in quadrature with the current in A_3's input resistor. **1974** Harvey & Bohlman *Stereo F.M. Radio Handbk.* iv. 65 The normal signal is again divided by 2 to give a 19kHz quadrature signal for feeding back along the phase-lock loop.

quadrennially, *adv.* (Later examples.)

1932 H. G. Wells *Work, Wealth & Happiness of Mankind* xii. 599 It could go to the country triennially or quadrennially for new blood and the elimination of persons who had become unpopular. **1972** *Publishers' Weekly* 24 Jan. 62/3 Campaign biographies are quadrennially the cream cheese of publishing.

quadri-. Add: **I. a. quadricentennial** (example); **quadrilingual** (later examples); **quadripa·schal**, including four passovers (cf. *bipaschal, *tripaschal* s.v. Tri- 1).

1977 *Times* 19 Apr. 14/6 The three-year quadricentennial celebrations [in California] of Sir Francis Drake's voyage round the world. **1962** Quadrilingual [see *francophone *sb.* and *a.*]. **1969** *Internat. Herald Tribune* 6 Nov. 14/2 (Advt.), Young American, excellent education U.S.A.-Europe, Ph.D. quadri-lingual, well traveled,.. seeks unparalleled + challenging position. **1883** Quadripaschal [see *tripaschal* s.v. Tri- I. 1]. **1908** J. Hastings *Dict. Christ* II. 185/1 The *long period* theory..holds that there were four Passovers in the ministry, and is hence called the *quadripaschal* theory.

b. quadrinucleate (examples); **quadrivo·ltine** [It. *volta* time, turn], (of a silkworm moth) producing four broods in a year; also as *sb.*

1956 *New Biol.* XXI. 93 At last the little quadrinucleate amoeba breaks free as a whole. **1973** *Nature* 3 Aug. 293/1 Of these multinucleate compartments 88% were binucleate, 9% were trinucleate, and 3% were quadrinucleate. **1888** Quadrivoltine [see *bivoltine *a.*]. **1969** R. F. Chapman *Insects* xxxv. 719 In *Bombyx mori*..univoltine, bivoltine and quadrivoltine strains are known.

II. a. quadricycle (later examples); also **quadracycle**; **quadripa·resis** *Med.*, paresis of both arms and both legs; hence **quadripare·tic** *a.*; **quadriva·lency** = *quadrivalence.*

1963 Bird & Hutton-Stott *Veteran Motor Car* 90 Between about 1898 and 1908 more than 100 different makes of bicycle, tricycle, quadricycle, tricar, fore-car and light car proper..were powered by De Dion Bouton engines. **1972** *Sci. Amer.* May 104/3 By the second half of 1891..the Peugeot quadricycle..had covered the 1,200 kilometers (745 miles) from Paris to Brest and back to Paris in 10 days. **1979** *Time* 8 Jan. 80/3 Accordingly, Wilson is proposing a two-seat lunar vehicle or quadracycle, made of lightweight metals. **1956** *Jrnl. Neurol., Neurosurg. & Psychiatry* XIX. 163/1 The patients remained quadriparetic and almost totally unresponsive from the time of the accident. *Ibid.* 170/2 The patient had a quadriparesis, complete in the left leg and more marked in the left arm than the right. **1977** *Lancet* 27 Aug. 461/1 By discharge on day 32 he was fully mobile with only a residual spastic quadriparesis. **1932** *Nature* 19 Nov. 756/2 The quadrivalency of carbon. **1937** A. Findlay *Hundred Yrs. of Chem.* ii. 40 The theory of molecular constitution..rested on two main postulates, the quadrivalency of carbon..and the capacity of the carbon atoms for mutual linking.

quadridentate (kwǫdride·ntēit), *a.* [f. Quadri- + L. *dentātus* (see Dentate *a.*).]

1. *Bot.* and *Zool.* (In Dict. s.v. Quadri- I. b.)

2. *Chem.* Of a ligand: forming four separate bonds. Of a complex: formed by such a ligand.

1925 Morgan & Smith in *Jrnl. Chem. Soc.* CXXVII. 2031 We have now succeeded in identifying a group capable of quadruple attachment to metallic atoms, this being the first known case of a quadridentate group in co-ordination complexes. **1937** *Chem. Rev.* XXI. 98 Probably the first synthetic quadridentate compounds.. were the copper and bivalent platinum compounds of ethylene bisthioglycolic acid. **1956** R. W. Parry in J. C. Bailar *Chem. Coordination Compounds* v. 239 The base is a quadridentate molecule in which the four nitrogen atoms can be expected to occupy the corners of a tetrahedron. **1972** M. L. Tobe *Inorg. Reaction Mechanisms* vi. 70 (*caption*) Trigonal bipyramidal complex of a 'tripod' quadridentate ligand showing how the trigonal symmetry of the ligand forces the configuration in the complex.

quadrilateral, *a.* and *sb.* Add: **B.** *sb.* **c.** *Eccl.* The four essential principles of Anglicanism, orig. enunciated in 1870 and approved by the Lambeth Conference of 1888 as a basis for the reunion of the Christian Church. Freq. *Lambeth Quadrilateral.* (Transf. use of sense b in Dict.)

1870 W. R. Huntington *Church-Idea* vii. 157 1st. The Holy Scriptures as the Word of God. 2d. The Primitive Creeds as the Rule of Faith. 3d. The two Sacraments ordained by Christ Himself. 4th. The Episcopate as the key-stone of Governmental Unity. These four points, like the four famous fortresses of Lombardy, make the 'Quadrilateral' of pure Anglicanism. **1902** [see *Lambeth 1]. **1925** J. W. Suter *Life & Lett. William Reed Huntington* vii. 162 It might, with some reason, be maintained that Dr. Huntington's chief claim to lasting fame was his invention and promulgation of the Quadrilateral... It was in a sermon preached at Worcester [Mass.], January 30, 1870, that he for the first time set forth the term. **1944** W. Temple *Church Looks Forward* ii. 14 The Lambeth Conference has repeatedly offered as a basis of negotiation the famous Quadrilateral. **1954** Rouse & Neill *Hist. Ecumenical Movement* v. 250 When Huntington had boiled Anglicanism down to its irreducible minimum, there remained his basis for a united Church—a platform later to be known as the 'Chicago-Lambeth Quadrilateral'... The House of Bishops at the General Convention of 1886 [at Chicago] finally adopted his 'Quadrilateral' and it was reaffirmed in slightly modified form by the Lambeth Conference of 1888. **1957** *Oxf. Dict. Chr. Ch.* 781/2 Lambeth Quadrilateral... The text of the Articles is as follows: A. The Holy Scriptures of the Old and New Testaments,..as being the rule and ultimate standard of faith. B. The Apostles' Creed..and the Nicene Creed... C. The two Sacraments ordained by Christ Himself—Baptism and the Supper of the Lord... D. The Historic Episcopate, locally adapted.

quadrilla, var. *cuadrilla.

1921 E. E. Cummings *Let.* 22 Apr. (1969) 75 Gentlemen in cockades..come out again heading a procession of quadrillas, bandilleros, and espadas, all of whom bow. The bull is admitted: the quadrillas—each matador has his own group—try him with cloaks. **1923** W. J. Locke *Moordius & Co.* x. 140 The proud procession of the quadrillas, matadors, banderilleros, picadores.

quadrille, *v.*² Add: (Later examples.) Also *transf.*

1903 Ld. R. Gower *Rec. & Reminisc.* 59 Teaching us how to quadrille and how to valse. **1905** W. H. Hunt *Pre-Raphaelitism* I. ii. 24, I..rejoiced with the happy birds quadrilling around the sentinel trees.

quadrillé, *a.* Add: Also **quadrille.** (Later examples.) Also *ellipt.* as *sb.*

1895 *Montgomery Ward Catal.* Spring & Summer 38/3 Red leather vest pocket memorandum... 40 leaves.. quadrille ruling. **1907** *Yesterday's Shopping* (1969) 354/2 *Manuscript and Account Books.* Ruled either with Feint lines, Cash Column, or Quadrille. **1926** *Paper Terminol.* (Spalding & Hodge, Ltd.) ii. 22 *Quadrille*, paper ruled on the surface or in watermark with a multitude of small squares. Used by draughtsmen, diary makers, and for foreign correspondence. **1960** R. G. Haggar *Conc. Encycl. Continental Pott. & Porc.* 375/1 *Quadrillé*, a diapered ground pattern with quatrefoils and squares much favoured at Chantilly, painted in blue third quarter of the eighteenth century. **1969** R. Mayer *Dict. Art Terms & Techniques* 320/1 *Quadrille paper*, paper faintly ruled with small squares. Also, paper so patterned with a watermark or a plate finish. **1978** *E & A Office Equipment Catal.* 122/1 Memo Pads... Quadrille 5 mm.

quadrillion. Add: **b.** (Further examples.)

1975 *Offshore* Sept. 246/2 Southern areas of the North Sea off the northeast coast of England produced a record 129 quadrillion BTU's last year. **1976** *Sci. Amer.* Jan. 21/1 The ERDA projections are expressed in terms of quads, or quadrillions (10^{15}) of British thermal units (B.t.u.). **1977** *Ibid.* Apr. 71/1 When *n* is 31, the total number of possible binary trees is 14,544,636,039,226,909, and each of these 14 quadrillion trees will be optimum for some set of assumed frequencies for the 31 words.

quadrillionth *sb.* (example).

1976 *New Yorker* 3 May 30/3 Further advances.. should make it possible to record even faster chemical reactions—reactions that take place in femtoseconds, or quadrillionths of a second.

quadriphonic, -phony, -plane, varr. *quadraphonic *a.*, *quadraphony, *quadruplane.

quadriplegia (kwǫdriplī·dʒiă). *Path.* [mod.L., f. Quadri- + Para)plegia.] Paralysis of both arms and both legs.

1921 *Brain* XLIV. 428 To elicit nociceptive reactions of the upper or lower limbs in our cases of hemiplegia and quadriplegia potentially painful stimuli were usually necessary. **1948** *Brit. Med. Jrnl.* 14 Feb. 289/2 A man aged 56 suffered damage to his cervical cord..following a blow. The resultant spastic quadriplegia was thought to be due to a haematomyelia. **1974** Luckmann & Sorensen *Med.-Surg. Nursing* xxxviii. 444/1 Quadriplegia is the same as paraplegia except that the level of injury to the spinal cord is cervical and thus the upper extremities are affected as well as the lower extremities.

quadriplegic (kwǫdriplī·dʒik), *a.* and *sb.* *Med.* Also **quadra-, quadru-.** [f. prec. + -ic.] **A.** *adj.* Suffering from quadriplegia. **B.** *sb.* A quadriplegic person.

1921 *Brain* XLIV. 438 Three of the quadriplegic patients ..showed extensive reflex reactions involving the trunk and limbs. **1961** Webster, Quadriplegic, *n.* **1962** *Lancet* 6 Jan. 3/1 The patient emerging from stupor was at first mute and quadriplegic. **1965** *Listener* 27 May 772/2 Young girls.. both of whom, as a result of their injuries, became quadriplegics, that is they became permanently paralysed from the neck downwards. **1969** *Age* (Melbourne) 24 May 5/6 A Geelong man who became a quadraplegic following a car accident in October 1967, was awarded damages of $100,000 yesterday. **1971** *Daily Tel.* 25 May 3/7 He was left a quadruplegic and will spend the rest of his days in a wheelchair. **1971** *Rand Daily Mail* 4 Sept. 13/4 The youth injured his spine in the accident and was totally paralysed from the neck down. Like all quadriplegics, he is tied to a wheelchair existence for life. **1974** Passmore & Robson *Compan. Med. Stud.* III. liv. 4/1 The quadriplegic patient presents greater problems than those of the paraplegic with regard to rehabilitation and resettlement. **1975** 'M. Fonteyn' *Autobiogr.* II. x. 241 It was a long time before I realized what everyone else knew perfectly well—that Tito was incapacitated and probably a quadruplegic for life. **1980** *Times* 8 Feb. 4/7 He is a quadriplegic after having sustained multiple injuries in a fall.

quadriplex, var. *quadruplex *a.* 3.

quadripole (kwǫ·dripōᵘl). [ad. F. *quadripôle* (L. J. Collet 1926, in *Ann. des Postes, Télégraphes et Téléphones* XV. 939): see Quadri- and Pole *sb.*²] **1.** *Electr.* A network or device having one pair of input terminals and one pair of output terminals; *esp.* one that is passive.

1928 *Sci. Abstr.* B. XXXI. 103 The author considers the quadripole, its..velocity of propagation, characteristic impedance and reflection properties. The amplifying valve is considered as an example of a quadripole. **1935** G. P. Harnwell *Princ. Electr. & Magn.* iv. 115 In order to effect such a transfer [of power] a device with two pairs of terminals must be used. The transfer circuit itself generally contains no source of power and hence is known as a passive quadripole. **1952** *Electronic Engin.* XXIV. 264/1 The method of dealing with the steady state analysis of passive quadripoles in terms of the matrix of the linear transformation expressed by the network equations was introduced by Strecker and Feldtkeller in 1929. **1955** [see *eigen-]. **1962** *Newnes Conc. Encycl. Electr. Engin.* 629/2 A quadripole may be designed with dissipative elements as an attenuator, or with reactive elements as a filter.

2. Var. *quadrupole.

quadrisonic, var. *quadrasonic *a.*

quadrivalent (see below), *a.* and *sb.* [f. Quadri- + L. *valēnt-em*, pres. pple. of *valēre* to be worth.] **A.** *adj.* **1.** *Chem.* (kwǫdrivēⁱ·lĕnt). Having a valency of four; capable of combining with four univalent atoms.

1865 A. W. Hofmann in *Chem. News* 13 Oct. 176/1 The nitrogen and carbon atoms, respectively trivalent and quadrivalent, are provided with three and four arms, indicating the three and four combining units respectively distinguishing these atoms. **1869, 1880** [in Dict. s.v. Quadri- I]. **1922** A. D. Udden tr. *Bohr's Theory of Spectra* III. iii. 109 While an element like titanium in the fourth period already shows a marked tendency to occur with various valencies, on the other hand an element like zirconium is still quadri-valent like carbon in the second period and silicon in the third. **1964** J. W. Linnett *Electronic Struct. Molecules* ii. 30 The carbon atom..is, of course, quadrivalent. **1978** *Sci. Amer.* Feb. 58/2 Cerium, alone among the trivalent rare earths, can be oxidized to the relatively insoluble quadrivalent state.

2. *Cytology.* (kwǫdri·vălĕnt). Applied to a meiotic structure composed of four wholly or partly homologous chromosomes joined together.

Less common than the corresp. sb. (see *B. 2).

1898 *Zool. Jahrb.* (Abt. für Anat.) XII. 44 Frequently also in the loose spirem are found quadrivalent chromosomes with a constriction about the middle. **1929** *Jrnl. Genetics* XXI. 18 The hyacinths offered an opportunity for the comparative study in the same cell of the structure and behaviour of bivalent, trivalent and quadrivalent chromosomes of distinct types.

B. *sb.* **1.** *Chem.* A quadrivalent element. *rare*⁻¹.

1880 [in Dict. s.v. Quadri- II].

2. *Cytology.* (kwǫdri·vălĕnt). A quadrivalent group of chromosomes.

1923 *Proc. Nat. Acad. Sci.* IX. 109 In one quarter and more of the pollen-mother-cells this regular distribution does not occur with regard to all of the 12 quadrivalents. **1946** [see *microsporogenesis]. **1952** [see *bivalent *a.* 2]. **1975** *Nature* 17 Apr. 595/2 A sister plant which was a monosomic ($2n$ = 41)..formed some trivalents, quadrivalents.., pentavalents and hexavalents, in addition to bivalents.

quadrivial, *a.* and *sb.* **A.** *adj.* **2.** Delete † *Obs.* and add later examples. Also *transf.*

1886 S. S. Lawrie *Rise & Constit. Universities* 61 Practically under the name of dialectic, logic was a quadrivial study. **1912** *Encycl. Relig. & Ethics* V. 172/2 The 'trivial' arts were Grammar, Rhetoric, and Dialectics... The 'quadrivial' arts were Geometry, Arithmetic, Astronomy, and Music. **1949** *Author* Winter 40/2 A quadrivial passion for theology and literature, horses and international peace. **1964** C. S. LEWIS *Discarded Image* vii. 196 The four Quadrivial Arts must here be summarily dismissed.

quadro (kwǫ·dro), *a.* and *sb.*[2] Colloq. abbrev. of *QUADRAPHONY, *QUADRAPHONIC *a.* Cf. *QUAD *a.*[2] and *sb.*[8]

1972 *Guardian* 28 July 13 The critics say that the real reason for quadro is pure commercial pressure to sell more records. **1976** *Which?* May 99/1 It's possible to use quadro to create a totally new listening experience by getting the sounds to surround you completely. **1977** *Gramophone* Aug. 357/1 This will necessitate the introduction of decks equipped with two heads to accommodate both stereo and quadro-tapes.

quadroon. Add: **2.** *quadroon ball.*

1805 J. F. WATSON in *Amer. Pioneer* (1843) II. 236 These colored women have..their weekly balls, (called quartroon balls) at which none but white gentlemen attend. **1880** G. W. CABLE *Grandissimes* iii. 19, I saw the same old man, at a quadroon ball a few years ago. **1948** *Chicago Tribune* (Grafic Mag.) 8 Feb. 18/3 Most notorious of the carnival affairs, was the Quadroon ball, given by the young men of the town for their mistresses and friends.

quadrophonic, -phony, -sonic, varr. *QUADRAPHONIC *a.*, *QUADRAPHONY, *QUADRASONIC *a.*

quadrumvirate. Delete † *Obs. rare* and add pronunc. (kwǫdrʊ·mvirĕt). (Later examples.)

1923 *Contemp. Rev.* Feb. 151 He [*sc.* Mussolini] formed a quadrumvirate..to whom he entrusted full powers. **1955** *Times* 3 May 11/3 He is the third to go of the quadrumvirate who for much of the post-war period held the leadership of the Trades Union Congress largely in their hands. **1958** P. KEMP *No Colours or Crest* viii. 155 Colonel Fiqri Dine,.. one of the original quadrumvirate of chiefs that had helped Zog in his early days of power. **1974** *Times Lit. Suppl.* 29 Mar. 315/3 Osler..one of the remarkable quadrumvirate who established the Johns Hopkins Medical School.

quadrupedal, *a.* and *sb.* Add: **A.** *adj.* **1.** (Further examples.) Also, using all four feet for walking or running; *transf.*, of a person: on hands and knees.

1854 [see *BIPEDAL *a.* 2]. **1897** *Proc. R. Soc.* LX. 412 The posture assumed suggests the taking of a forward step in quadrupedal progression. **1914** CHESTERTON *Wisdom of Father Brown* x. 249 Seeing him thus quadrupedal in the grass, the priest raised his eyebrows rather sadly. **1971** *Nature* 12 Mar. 86/1 The four gaits [of the kangaroo] identified were a slow progression, a walk, a quadrupedal bound and a bipedal hop.

2. (Later example.)

1971 *Nature* 30 Apr. 577/1 Those early or middle Miocene dryopithecines..have been dubbed 'dental apes'—primates which apparently combined a hominoid dentition with limbs which retained a more primitive quadrupedal monkey-like morphology.

Hence **quadrupe·dally** *adv.*

1847 W. J. BRODERIP *Zool. Recreations* II. 179 Ask the zoologists, and one will tell you that the jackal..is the impure source of all that is quadrupedally good and amiable. **1952** RIESEN & KINDER *Postural Devel. Infant Chimpanzees* vi. 46 (*table*) Creeps (quadrupedally for chimpanzees). **1976** *Nature* 29 Jan. 305/2 At these speeds the mice either 'trotted' with the hind legs moving independently or 'galloped' quadrupedally with the hind legs moving together.

quadruplane (kwǫ·drʊplēⁱn). Also **quadri-.** [f. QUADRU- + PLANE *sb.*[3]] An aeroplane having four sets of wings, one above another.

1909 A. BERGET *Conquest of Air* 141 Naturally we can make triplanes or quadriplanes, but one must not proceed too far in this direction. **1909** *Times* 17 Aug. 10/5 Major Baden-Powell will attempt a flight with his quadruplane. **1919** *Jane's All World's Aircraft* 60 a (*caption*) Experimental Armstrong-Whitworths.—Two of the F.K. 10 Type Quadruplanes. **1937** *Times* 5 Oct. 9/3 He [*sc.* Major Baden-Powell] made two aeroplanes, one with swivelling propellers to obtain direct lift, and the other a kind of quadruplane.

quadruple, *a.* Add: **b.** *quadruple expansion*, the use of four stages of expansion in a compound steam engine, the same steam expanding successively in four cylinders; usu. *attrib.*

1885 R. SENNETT *Marine Steam Engine* (ed. 2) i. 23 In some few cases, in which steam of 150 to 180 lbs. has been used, quadruple expansion engines have been fitted,..but there is not sufficient evidence yet to show that the additional complication thus introduced is compensated for by any marked gain in economy. **1894** J. J. ASTOR *Journey in Other Worlds* iv. 48 The electricity generated by..slow-moving quadruple-expansion steam engines, provides the power required to run our electric ships. **1919** *Jane's Fighting Ships* 260/2 Kashima..machinery: 2 sets 4 cylinder vertical quadruple expansion. **1952** FOX & MCBIRNIE *Marine Steam Engines & Turbines* vii. 137 The quadruple-expansion engine is not now so common as formerly, and modern practice appears to favour the triple-expansion engine with fairly high initial superheat.

quadruplegic, var. *QUADRIPLEGIC *a.* and *sb.*

quadrupler (kwǫdrū·plər). [f. QUADRUPLE *v.* + -ER[1].] A device that makes something four times as great.

1941 MILLMAN & SEELY *Electronics* xii. 416 The circuit.. can be extended from a doubler to a quadrupler by adding two tubes and two condensers. **1946** *Nature* 5 Oct. 477/1 During the years 1929–32 they developed together the voltage quadrupler steady potential generator of 600 kilovolts. **1947** L. B. YOUNG in C. G. Montgomery *Technique Microwave Measurem.* vi. 368 The crystal-oscillator frequency is multiplied to 5 Mc/sec by means of a push-push quadrupler.

quadruplet. Add: **2. b.** *Mus.* A group of four notes to be played in the time of three of the same value.

1873 H. C. BANISTER *Music* 13 Other irregularities.. such as four notes for three, termed a Quadruplet. **1938** *Oxf. Compan. Mus.* p. xlviii (*heading*) Irregular rhythmic groupings (duplets, triplets, quadruplets, etc.). **1946** P. HINDEMITH *Elem. Training for Musicians* ix. 117 The names of these newly established values are: duplets, triplets, quadruplets, and so forth up to decuplets... Some of these terms are so awkward (linguistically) that they are hardly ever used.

quadruplex, *a.* and *sb.* Add: **A.** *adj.* **3.** *Genetics.* Also **quadri-.** Of a tetraploid individual: having the dominant allele at some particular locus represented four times.

1923 [see *DUPLEX *a.* 1e]. **1932** SANSOME & PHILP *Rec. Adv. Plant Genetics* v. 182 There are five possible types of zygote in the tetraploid, quadruplex SSSS, triplex SSSs, duplex SSss, simplex Ssss and nulliplex ssss. **1963** [see *NULLIPLEX *a.*].

quadrupole (kwǫ·drupōᵘl), *sb.* and *a.* *Physics.* Also **quadri-.** [ad. Du. *quadrupool*: see QUADRU-, QUADRI-, and POLE *sb.*[2]] **A.** *sb.* **a.** A multipole of order $l = 2$ (cf. *MULTIPOLE *sb.*). Usu. *attrib.*

1922 *Proc. Sect. Sci. K. Akad. Wetensch. Amsterdam* XXIII. 939 Assuming the molecules to act on each other as electric quadrupoles with constant quadrupole moment ..Burgers has calculated the quadrupole moment of the hydrogen molecule. **1927** *Proc. Cambr. Philos. Soc.* XXIII. 930 A method of calculating the probability of switches due to radiation by the quadripole moment seems to be supplied by Dirac's recent theory of the interaction between matter and radiation. **1932** *Proc. R. Soc.* A. CXXXVIII. 666 Assuming for the field of the nucleus the field of a quadripole, instead of that of a dipole. **1957** [see *DIPOLE 1]. **1957** *Sci. News* XLIII. 87 There is an electrical property of nuclei..called the quadrupole moment, which is a measure of the departure of the nucleus from a spherical to an ellipoidal shape. **1970** G. K. WOODGATE *Elem. Atomic Struct.* iii. 50 Pure quadrupole radiation arises when two parts of the charge distribution are oscillating like dipoles out of phase so that the dipole contribution vanishes.

b. An arrangement of four magnetic (or electric) poles, of alternate polarity, pointing at the same volume of space (used to focus beams of sub-atomic particles).

1954 *Rev. Sci. Instruments* XXV. 289/2 The introduction of the quadrupoles Q_1 and Q_2 introduces both vertical and horizontal focusing effects for a given energy. **1961** D. LUCKEY in D. M. Ritson *Techniques High Energy Physics* ix. 429 A single quadrupole can be used to obtain vertical focusing in a broad-range uniform-field spectrometer. **1969** *IEEE Trans. Nucl. Sci.* XVI. 728/2 Work on the dipole magnetic circuits as well as on cryogenic temperature iron core quadrupoles and sextupoles has continued. **1976** *McGraw-Hill Yearbk. Sci. & Technol.* 387/2 Even when dipoles or quadrupoles are to be operated at flux densities considerably above 2 T,..addition of iron shields around the windings has important advantages.

B. *adj.* Having or pertaining to two pairs of magnetic (or electric) poles.

1955 *Rev. Sci. Instruments* XXVI. 220/1 A second possibility..is to use a succession of electric or magnetic quadrupole lenses. **1960** *Ann. Rev. Nucl. Sci.* X. 163 A single quadrupole magnet has a focusing action for motion in one plane (either horizontal or vertical) and a defocusing action in the other plane. However, two or more quadrupole magnets may be used to give a net focusing action in both planes. **1976** *McGraw-Hill Yearbk. Sci. & Technol.* 387/1 Usually, uniform or quadrupole fields are required over considerable distances along the beam path. **1979** *Sci. Amer.* May 64/3 The ZGS lacks the quadrupole and sextupole magnets that are employed for focusing in many other accelerators.

Hence **quadrupo·lar** *a.*

1950 *Physical Rev.* LXXIX. 698/1 A situation in which any quadrupolar splitting of the nuclear resonance in a magnetic field is small compared to the magnetic resonance frequency itself. **1959** G. TROUP *Masers* ii. 28 This statement can be generalized, because the dipole moment may be electric or magnetic; or the moment may be of higher order, quadrupolar, for example. **1972** *Science* 26 May 903/3 The author directly proceeds to describe the effects due to quadrupolar and hyperfine interactions between electrons and nuclei.

quæstor. Add: **2.** The chief financial officer, the Treasurer, of the University of St. Andrews and, formerly, of other universities, esp. in Scotland.

1673 J. RAY *Observations Journey Low-Countries* 85 This Senate chuses..a Quaestor, who gathers up the University Revenue and Rents [at Heidelberg]. **1754** *Session Papers* 5 Mar. 12 In effect the Quaestor of the Library, Quaestor of the University, Aerarii universitatis quaestor, falls to be deemed as one and the same Thing. **1920** H. SCOTT *Fasti Ecclesiæ Scoticanæ* III. 133/1 He was Quaestor [*sc.* collector of revenues] of the Univ. of Glasgow in 1577. **1946** R. G. CANT *Univ. St. Andrews* 109 [The Senatus] authorised the conferring of degrees, it administered the university finances, controlled the common Library, and appointed the common officers, such as the Librarian, the Quaestor, and the Archbeadle. **1966** *Times* 17 June 3/2 (Advt.), Applications are invited for the post of an additional Assistant Quaestor in the University, in the Quaestor & Factor's department, St. Andrews.

quæstorian, *a.* Delete † *Obs. rare*[−1] and add later examples.

1879 LEWIS & SHORT *Latin Dict.* 1503/1 *Quæstōrĭus*,..of or belonging to a quæstor, quæstorian. **1976** *Classical Q.* XXVI. 99 Under the Republic the *calles* of Italy were..a quaestorian *provincia*. *Ibid.* 106 At some point in the second century the occasional quaestorian *provinciae* of the *calles* and the *aquae* were devised.

quag, *sb.* Add: Also with pronunc. (kwǫg). (Earlier *fig.* example.) Also *transf.*

1842 I. TAYLOR *Anc. Christianity* II. VIII. 480 Thoughtless thousands of the people are thus beguiled into the filthiest quags of 'abominable idolatry'. **1904** *Daily Chron.* 18 May 3/4 Her clothes were a quag of blood.

quagga. Add: Now also with pronunc. (kwǫ·gă). Also **quagger.** (Further examples.)

1815 *Times* 25 July 1/4 To be Sold..Two beautiful Animals of the Zebra species, called Quaggers; they are perfectly docile..being two of the handsomest ever imported to this country. **1899** *Pall Mall Gaz.* 21 Nov. 2/1 It [*sc.* Cape Colony] was the great home of the brown quagga. ('Kwokka'..is the proper pronunciation of the name of the old friend of my childhood's natural history.) **1937** *Nature* 25 Dec. 1079/2 The blaauwbok..and the quagga have already vanished. **1966** E. PALMER *Plains of Camdeboo* viii. 141 Of all our vanished creatures we mourn these quaggas most of all. **1974** *Nature* 11 Oct. 468/2 The last quagga died in the Amsterdam Zoo in 1883, but it is thought that this one had outlived by several years the wild quagga in South Africa.

quagginess. (In Dict. s.v. QUAGGY *a.*) (Later example.)

1940 *Chambers's Techn. Dict.* 692/1 *Quagginess*, a term used to indicate the defective condition of timber having shakes at the heart of the log.

quaggy, *a.* Add: Also with pronunc. (kwǫ·gi). **1.** (Later examples.)

1956 PETERSON & FISHER *Wild Amer.* xxxiii. 356 The banks..were aproned by mud—quaggy and adhesive. **1969** P. DICKINSON *Pride of Heroes* 98 Putting his foot into a quaggy area, which sent..stinking inky ooze between shoe and sock.

2. (Later example.)

1968 G. JONES *Hist. Vikings* II. iv. 139 Alas, Einar's late-acquired nickname [*sc.* Thambarskelfir] has nothing to do with..a bowstring; it refers to his pendulous and quaggy belly.

quagmire. Add: Also with pronunc. (kwǫ·gməiᵊɹ).

quahaug, quahog. Add: (Earlier and later examples.)

1753 *Southampton* (N.Y.) *Rec.* (1878) III. 6 The Trustees shall have the care of the Fishery of Quogue. **1781** S. PETERS *Gen. Hist. Connecticut* 262 The oysters, clams, quauhogs, lobsters, crabs, and fish, are innumerable. **1815** *Topogr. & Hist. Wareham* in *Coll. Mass. Hist. Soc.* (1846) 2nd Ser. IV. 289 The quahaug clam is common. **1870** *Amer. Naturalist* III. 354 Fragments of Quahaug valves ..are quite abundant. **1934** E. REYNARD *Narrow Land* v. 249 He handed over his Old Woman's recipe for quahaug fritters. **1949** R. J. SIM *Pages from Past* 66 The quahog, or hardshell clam, is deservedly the most famous of all. **1960** S. PLATH *Colossus* 24 The gritted wave leaps The seawall and drops onto a bier Of quahog chips. **1967** *Boston Sunday Herald Mag.* 26 Mar. 11/1 Anybody who uses potatoes in quahog pie is no Cape Codder. **1977** *Time* 4 July 37/1 On the Fourth, New Englanders will be flocking to Clam Shacks for rolls stuffed with batter-fried whole quahogs or steamers.

Hence as *v. intr.*, to dig or collect quahaugs; **quahau·ging** *vbl. sb.*

1905 J. C. LINCOLN *Partners of Tide* iv. 76 How's the quahaugin' nowadays? **1949** K. KNIGHT *Bass Derby Murder* 122, I was down to the pond quahoggin', all afternoon.

quai (kēⁱ, ‖ ke). [Fr.: see QUAY *sb.*] **1.** A public way constructed on the quay or embankment of a stretch of navigable water, usu. having buildings along the land side; *spec.* such a street on either bank of the Seine in Paris.

1870 [see KIOSK 2]. **1873** BROWNING *Red Cotton Night-Cap Country* II. 89 One whose father's house upon the Quai Neighboured the very house where that Voltaire Died mad and raving. **1927** C. CONNOLLY *Let.* 11 Feb. in *Romantic Friendship* (1975) 251 The solidarity of this town [*sc.* Bordeaux] with its respectable houses and cobbled quais. **1949** E. POUND *Pisan Cantos* lxxxi. 110 And at first disappointed with shoddy The bare ram-shackle quais. **1954** I. MURDOCH *Under Net* xiv. 191 The cloudless light drew a wash of colour along the grey façades of the *quais*. **1963** V. GIELGUD *Goggle-Box Affair* xi. 103 The *quais* and the cafés of the Left Bank in spring. **1977** *Time* 28 Nov. 31/3 The canal that once passed along the quai has been replaced by a Métro station.

2. *ellipt.* for *QUAI D'ORSAY.

1960 N. MITFORD *Don't tell Alfred* iv. 47 They know absolutely everything you do..what impression Alfred makes at the Quai..and so on. **1973** H. TREVELYAN *Diplomatic Channels* i. 20 During General de Gaulle's later years, French diplomats who received their instructions from the Quai were handicapped, since the Quai often did not know what policy the General was pursuing through his inner circle.

quaich, quaigh. Add: Also in extended use: a drinking vessel or trophy of similar design.
1971 *Timber Trades Jrnl.* 14 Aug. 54/3 Play in the morning will be for the Brownlee trophy against bogey under handicap and for the Granton quaich for the best net score. **1975** *Listener* 5 June 728/2, I drink a ceremonial draught from an immense, lacquered quaich [at Koriyama, Japan]. **1976** D. MARLOWE *Nightshade* iii. 44 Lapotre had arrived accompanied by a tall negro... He was a *houngan*, a voodoo priest... Lapotre stopped before a woman..carrying a souvenir (a mahogany quaich).

Quai d'Orsay (ke dɔrse). The name of a *quai* (see *QUAI) in Paris, used by metonymy for the French Ministry of Foreign Affairs, which is situated there. Also *attrib.*
1922 W. S. MAUGHAM *On Chinese Screen* xix. 74 He represented certain important French interests in China and was said to have more power at the Quai d'Orsay than the minister himself. **1927** N. WAINWRIGHT tr. *Dekobra's Madonna of Sleeping Cars* xii. 167 The Quai d'Orsay would register a formal protest. **1933** G. ARTHUR *Septuagenarian's Scrap Bk.* 33 The Foreign Office and the Quai d'Orsay must have put their cards on the table with quite amazing confidence in one another's goodwill. **1940** H. G. WELLS *New World Order* § 11. 151 The Germans..have to get on with collectivisation..and they cannot give themselves to that if they are artificially divided up and disorganised by some old-fashioned Quai d'Orsay scheme. **1958** L. DURRELL *Mountolive* viii. 158 Your Quai d'Orsay people shock me. **1969** B. WEIL *Dossier IX* viii. 63 Asher chuckled. 'I suppose the Quai d'Orsay felt it was going to be caught with its knickers down again!' **1975** C. MOTT-RADCLYFFE *Foreign Body in Eye* vii. 138 Preliminary negotiations had taken place in Paris for several weeks between Sir Maurice Peterson from the Foreign Office, and St Quentin from the Quai d'Orsay.

quaies kateah, var. *QUAISS KITIR *int.*

quai hai, var. QUI-HY in Dict. and Suppl.

quail, *sb.* Add: **4*.** *U.S. slang.* A girl, a young woman.
1859 *Yale Lit. Mag.* XXIV. 291 (Th.), [The Freshman] heareth of 'Quails', he dresseth himself in fine linen, he seeketh to flirt with ye 'quails'. **1901** *Dialect Notes* II. 146 *Quail*, a young lady student at co-educational institution. Wesleyan Univ. **1904** *Hartford* (Connecticut) *Courant* 4 Oct. 1 Because she was hazed by the young women students at Wesleyan, one 'quail', as the boys call them, who was a freshman here last year did not return to Wesleyan this fall. **1935** J. HARGAN *Gloss. Prison Lang.* 6 *Quail*, a girl. **1935** A. J. POLLOCK *Underworld Speaks* 93/1 *Quail*, an attractive girl, not of age. **1947** *Time* 6 Oct. 68/1 A less active sport is 'piping the flock', when Cal males watch Cal 'quails' preening in the sun on the steps of Wheeler Hall. **1970** *Women Speaking* Apr. 5/1 For any woman..man has a strange conglomeration of terms:.. quail, squab, [etc.].
5. *quail-bagger, -bagging, -shot, -time, -track, -trap.*
1879 *Harper's Mag.* Oct. 703 The..advice offered by a circle of quail-baggers and other by-standers. *Ibid.*, The conclusion that a quail-bagging expedition was regarded as an event of considerable importance. **1865** 'MARK TWAIN' in *N.Y. Saturday Press* 18 Nov. 249/2 He got the frog out.. and filled him full of quail-shot. **1897** *Outing* XXX. 94/2 Ever since last quail-time I have been casting rather dubious glances at a certain old gun. **1842** *Yale Lit. Mag.* VIII. 96, I can't always decipher quail tracks. **1855** *Trans. Mich. Agric. Soc.* VI. 495 One acre of quail track corn planted on muck land. **1807** *Salmagundi* 1 Oct. 312 He was particularly adroit in making our quail-traps. **1845** Quail-trap [see *fishing-light* s.v. *FISHING *vbl. sb.*[1] 5 a].

quain (kwēⁱn), *sb.* [Prob. var. of QUOIN *sb.*] In the poetical terminology of G. M. Hopkins: an angle, a wedge-like corner; angularity. Hence **quain** *v.*[2], **quai·ning** *vbl. sb.*[2]
1868 G. M. HOPKINS *Jrnls. & Papers* (1959) 170 Swiss trees are, like English, well inscaped—in quains. *Ibid.*, Before sunrise..saw a noble scape of stars—..Cassiopeïa on end with her bright quains pointing to the right. *Ibid.* 171 The straight quains and planing of the Alps were only too clear. *Ibid.* 176 Sycomores grew on the slopes of the valley, scantily leaved, sharply quained and accidented by perhaps the valley winds. **1871** *Ibid.* 205 And if you look well at big pack-clouds overhead you will soon find a strong large quaining and squaring in them which makes each pack impressive and whole. *Ibid.* 206 Below it [*sc.* the bud]..is a half-moon-shaped sill as if once chipped from the wood and this gives the twig its quaining in the outline. *a* **1889** *Ibid.* 290 The figure may be repeated runningly, continuously, as in rhythm (ABABAB) or intermittently, as in alliteration and rhyme (ABCDABEFABGH). The former gives more tone, *candorem*, style, chasteness; the latter more brilliancy, starriness, quain, margaretting. **1953** W. H. GARDENER in G. M. Hopkins *Poetry & Prose* 114 In July the principal stars of this constellation form a sort of flattened W on end —its two base angles ('quains') pointing to the right.

quaint, *sb.*[2] [f. the adj.] An odd, unusual, or strange person.
1939 J. CARY *Mr. Johnson* 112 'He's a comic, isn't he?' 'A perfect quaint.' **1959** B. ALDISS *Canopy of Time* 164 What's it matter what a broken-down quaint like Stayker said or didn't say?

quaint, *a.* (*adv.*) **A.** *adj.* **2.** For † *Obs.* read 'Now *arch.*' and add later examples.
1742 W. SHENSTONE *Schoolmistress* xII, With quaint arts the giddy crowd she sways. **1889** 'MARK TWAIN' *Yankee* iv. 37 This quaint lie was most simply and beautifully told. **1970** C. HAMPTON *Philanthropist* i. 13 *John* puts the revolver into his mouth and presses the trigger. Loud explosion. By some quaint device, gobs of brain and bright blood appear on the whitewashed wall.
8. b. Of furniture: designed in the style of *art nouveau.*
1897 *Furnit. & Decoration* XXXIV. 197/1 That new style called 'Quaint', which seems to be carcase without the spirit of the new style promulgated by the Arts and Crafts and other societies. **1952** J. GLOAG *Short Dict. Furnit.* 377 A fashion in furniture design, corresponding with the New Art movement at the end of the 19th and the opening of the present century, was known as the quaint style. **1975** *Country Life* 2 Oct. 852/3 The spindly chairs and tables of the 'quaint' vogue.
C. *quaint-carved, -looking, -mouthed, -sounding* adjs.
1838 J. R. LOWELL *Class Poem* IX. 11 What quaint-mouthed sentences! and how profound! **1859** J. G. WHITTIER *On Prayer Bk.* in *Independent* (N.Y.) 15 Sept. 1/1 The quaint-carved, Gothic door. **1922** R. LEIGHTON *Compl. Bk. Dog* xii. 178 Most people are well acquainted with the personal appearance of this quaint-looking dog. **1957** A. N. PRIOR *Time & Modality* 55 'The True' and 'The False' are certainly quaint-sounding objects to be named by phrases like 'The conquest of Gaul by Caesar'.

‖ **quaiss kitir** (kwəis kitīə·ɪ), *int. Mil. slang.* Also **kwais ketir, quash kateer, quies kiteer,** etc. [ad. Egyptian Arab. *kway·yis*, dim. cl. Arab. *kayyis* fine + *kəṯīr*, f. cl. Arab. *kaṯīran* very.] Very good! Very well! O.K.! Also **quies, quash, quois** *a.*, good, nice, satisfactory.
1898 G. W. STEEVENS *With Kitchener to Khartoum* ii. 13 When the recruit made a bull..the white sérgeant, standing behind him with a paper, cried '*Quaiss kitir*'—'Very good'. **1919** W. H. DOWNING *Digger Dial.* 40 *Quies* (Arab.), good. *Quies-kiteer* (Arab.), very good. **1925** FRASER & GIBBONS *Soldier & Sailor Words* 233 *Quash*, good; nice. An Arabic word (khwush) in use colloquially on Eastern Fronts. *Quash kateer*, very good. **1947** D. M. DAVIN *Gorse blooms Pale* 199 Our outfit was parked in a cornfield off the track and very quois it was too. We used to go swimming in the Liri every day. **1965** BROPHY & PARTRIDGE *Long Trail* 168 *Quaies kateah*, very good. Arabic. Very common with troops in Egypt or with Regulars that had been there. **1967** W. H. CANAWAY *Mules of Borgo San Marco* ix. 101 'They'll take us off to Germany and make us have nowt but sausages and beer.' Sergeant Entwistle said, 'Sausages and beer, kwais ketir, I wish I had some now instead of this muck.' **1967** *Sunday Times* (Colour Suppl.) 10 Sept. 46/4 *Quiess*, good!, capital! 'Quiess kateer' = very well, the answer to the question 'enta quiess?', you well?

quaite (kwēⁱt), a representation of an affected pronunc. of QUITE *adv.* Also **quate.**
1929 [see *CULTURED *ppl.a.* 2]. **1933** W. S. MAUGHAM *Sheppey* I. 28, I always say I quaite understand. Noblesse oblige if you know what I mean. **1962** WODEHOUSE *Service with Smile* v. 77 'Do you mean no *beer*?' 'Quate. I shall be keeping an eye on you.' **1965** K. GILES *Some Beasts no More* i. 6 'So you're one of those funny little men who slide about big offices as if they didn't quaite belong there.' Hell, yes, she'd said *quaite*. **1979** G. PETRIE *Hand of Glory* iii. 37 She is quaite raight... Ay would not wish to seem *grotesque*.

quake, *sb.* Add: **1. a.** (Further examples of the sense 'an earthquake'.)
Now apprehended as a colloq. abbrev. of *earthquake*, and occas. written *'quake*.
1905 *Westm. Gaz.* 14 Nov. 2/1 Even the most violent quakes in the vicinity of Mount Etna are rarely felt with any force across the straits. **1956** R. ST. B. BAKER *Dance of Trees* vii. 96 It was a serious 'quake though few people lost their lives. **1973** *Express* (Trinidad & Tobago) 1 Feb. 5/1 The quake shook Mexico City and nearby provinces. **1973** 'D. SHANNON' *No Holiday for Crime* (1974) v. 83 Glasser's Ford had been demolished by the quake last August. **1976** *Nigerian Chron.* 18 Aug. 1/2 The epicentre of the quake appeared to be in the Celebes Sea, South-West of Mindanao. **1977** *Time* 3 Jan. 27 (*caption*) In May, a quake centered in the Northeastern Italian region of Friuli killed nearly 1,000.
b. *attrib.* and *Comb.*
1931 *Daily Express* 21 Sept. 2/4 (*heading*) More 'quake shocks in Baluchistan. **1937** *Discovery* Feb. 63/1 Quake-proof reservoirs of water. **1960** *Daily Tel.* 27 May 14 Apparently the depth of the Pacific Ocean makes it specially liable to serve as a vehicle for these 'quake waves'. **1973** *Daily Colonist* (Victoria, B.C.) 21 Oct. 5/5 A 36-year-old business executive built a concrete quake-proof shelter in his yard.

quake, *v.*[1] Add: **4. quake grass** = QUAKING-GRASS.
1814 O. RICH *Synopsis Genera Amer. Plants* 10 Briza.. Quake Grass. **1909** *Daily Chron.* 25 June 7/2 We used to call 'em 'quake grass', and 'cats' tail'.

Quaker. 2. a. Substitute for def.: A member of the Religious Society of Friends, founded by George Fox in 1648–50, distinguished by its stress on the 'Inner Light' and rejection of sacraments, ordained ministry and set forms of worship; noted also for pacifist principles and simplicity of life, formerly in particular for plainness of dress and speech. (Earlier and later examples.)
1651 T. HALL *Pulpit Guarded* 15 We have many Sects now abroad; Ranters, Seekers, Shakers, Quakers, and now Creepers. *Ibid.* 29 A Bastard-brood of Arrians, Arminians,.. Quakers, Ranters. **1930** G. B. SHAW *You never can Tell* in *Wks.* VIII. 208 She is too militant an Agnostic to care to be mistaken for a Quaker. She therefore dresses in as business-like a way as she can. **1924** —— *Saint Joan* p. xlvi, In war, for instance, we suppress the gospels and put Quakers in prison, muzzle the newspapers, [etc.]. **1941** A. HUXLEY *Let.* 17 Nov. (1969) 470 England and America owe an incalculable debt to the Quakers for the way in which they have educated successive generations of rulers to realize that a theocentric opposition is a thing of enormous value to the society containing it. **1972** J. G. DAVIES *Dict. Liturgy & Worship* 329/1 For Quakers the difference between cleric and layman is irrelevant. **1978** J. A. MICHENER *Chesapeake* 380 In the name of God and Jesus Christ they must be set free, and no man dare call himself a Quaker and a slave-holder, too.
b. (*d*) Substitute for def.: One of several European, grey or brown, noctuid moths belonging to the genera *Orthosia* or *Agrochola*, esp. *O. stabilis*, the common quaker, or *O. cruda*, the small quaker; (examples).
1775 M. HARRIS *Eng. Lepidoptera* 41 Quaker... Of a plain brown colour, having a small ring in the middle, and a whitish line near the edge. **1907** R. SOUTH *Moths. Brit. Isles* 1st Ser. 328 The Small Quaker... Most specimens of this species have the fore wings pale greyish ochreous. *Ibid.*, (*heading*) The Common Quaker. **1948** W. J. STOKOE *Caterpillars Brit. Moths* I. 312 The Small Quaker..appears to be common throughout England and Wales. *Ibid.* 313 The Common Quaker..is on the wing during March and April. **1968** *Oxf. Bk. Insects* 74/2 Small Quaker... Dingy, undistinguished little moths, usually with a dusky spot on each forewing. *Ibid.*, Common Quakers visit sallow blossoms. *Ibid.* 78/2 Red-line Quaker (*Agrochola lota*). All four wings of this moth are a dingy blackish-grey colour.
c. Also *ellipt.* for *quaker-colour*, etc.
1923 *Daily Mail* 21 Feb. 14 (Advt.), In Black, Nigger, Putty, Fawn, Quaker.
3. a. *quaker cap*; also designating various subdued colours, as *quaker-brown, -green, -grey*. **c. Quaker City,** Philadelphia, U.S.A.; **Quaker collar** (see quot. 1957); **quaker-ladies** (examples); **quaker-meeting** (earlier and later examples); **Quaker Oats,** a proprietary brand of oats used esp. for making porridge as a breakfast food; **Quaker state,** Pennsylvania.
1851 MRS. GASKELL *Let. c* 28 Mar. (1966) 147, I have got a new silk gown, quaker-brown coloured. **1822** M. EDGEWORTH *Let.* 16 Mar. (1971) 373 Enter Mrs. Fry in drab colored silk cloak and plain borderless quaker cap. **1851** MRS. STOWE *Uncle Tom's Cabin* (1852) I. xiii. 198 'Nicely,' said Ruth, taking off her little drab bonnet, and..displaying..a round little head, on which the Quaker cap sat with a sort of jaunty air. **1856** M. J. HOLMES *Homestead* IV. viii. 220 Grandma, in rich black silk and plain Quaker cap, was hovering near her favorite child. **1836** T. POWER *Impressions Amer.* i. 51 It was night before we gained the Quaker city. **1903** *Critic* Aug. 190 Sketches of Philadelphia life and society by a New York woman who..does not find the Quaker city so 'slow' as is generally represented. **1975** *Country Life* 2 Jan. 44/1 The First Troop, Philadelphia City Cavalry,..celebrated its 200th anniversary on November 15, 1974, the night we flew into the 'Quaker City'. **1957** M. B. PICKEN *Fashion Dict.* 267/2 *Quaker collar*, broad flat collar, similar to Puritan collar. **1974** M. HIGGINS *Changeling* ii. 8 Dark dress with wide Quaker collar. **1869** *Bradshaw's Railway Man.* 460/3 (Advt.), Greens. Brunswk. Greens, all shades. Quaker ditto. Emerald Green. **1880** *Harper's Mag.* Nov. 906/1 The powders are most deceptive in color;..black appears a purplish-gray; Vandyck brown, Quaker gray. **1922** JOYCE *Ulysses* 498 In quakergrey kneebreeches and broadbrimmed hat. **1953** 'N. BLAKE' *Dreadful Hollow* 27 The modest Quaker-grey of the house. **1871** *Scribner's Monthly* II. 102 In yonder woods, where hepatica, and May-blossoms, and Quaker-ladies twinkle into life. **1946** D. C. PEATTIE *Road of Naturalist* v. 58 There are bluets around Stonybrook in Jersey..called also 'innocence' and 'Quaker ladies'. **1954** Quaker-ladies [see *INNOCENCE 6]. **1659** in *Compact with Charter & Laws of Colony of New Plymouth* (1836) II. 125 Others thinke it meet to p[er]mitt some p[er]sons to frequent the Quaker meetings to endeavor to reduce them form [*sic*] the error of theire wayes. **1704** S. SEWALL *Diary* 23 May (1879) II. 102 Convers'd with Mr. Noyes, told him of the Quaker Meeting at Sam. Sawyers. **1848** J. F. COOPER *Oak Openings* II. i. 9 The silence resembled that of a Quaker meeting. **1974** *Encycl. Brit. Macropædia* VII. 743/2 Friends were hounded by penal laws for not swearing oaths,..for going to Quaker meetings, and for refusing tithes. **1894** *Trade Marks Jrnl.* 5 Dec. 984 Pure Quaker Oats... Rolled white oats for use as food. The American Cereal Company,..Chicago, Illinois. **1901** B. S. ROWNTREE *Poverty* viii. 285/2, 2 lbs. Quaker oats, 5½d. **1921** R. MACAULAY *Dangerous Ages* i. 11 The annoyances and disappointments..such as quaker oats because the grape-nuts had come to an end. **1980** G. GREENE *Dr. Fischer* iv. 28 Do you happen to know anything about porridge? Real porridge I mean. Not Quaker Oats. **1896** *Peterson Mag.* Mar. 309/2 It [*sc.* Pennsylvania] has been long and favorably known as 'The Quaker State', in honor of the Society of Friends. **1934** G. E. SHANKLE *State Names* ii. 142 Five nicknames are given to the State of Pennsylvania; namely, the *Coal State*, the *Keystone State*, the *Oil State*, the *Quaker State*, and the *Steel State*. **1948** MENCKEN *Amer. Lang.* Suppl. II. 598 State nicknames..of Pennsylvania... *Quaker State*.
Quakerdom (earlier example).
1824 R. SOUTHEY *Let.* 3 Apr. in *N. & Q.* (1975) Sept. 403/2 My designs upon George Fox have, as you may suppose, excited a stir throughout all Quakerdom.

Quakeress. (Earlier example.)
1721 *New-England Hist. & Geneal. Reg.* (1876) XXX. 61 [Baptism of] John Rennolds, the little child of John Rennolds, his wife a Quakeress, not consenting.

Quakerish, *a.* Add: (Earlier example.)
1743 in F. Chase *Hist. Dartmouth Coll.* (1891) i. 5 [He] made a great show of sanctity, by means whereof he was under advantage to propagate his Quakerish notions.
Hence **qua·kerishness.**

1785 G. A. BELLAMY *Apology for Life* (ed. 2) I. xiv. 80 Deceived..by the Quakerishness of my dress, (excuse the new coined word).

Quakerly, *a.* (Later examples.)
1842 DICKENS *Amer. Notes* I. vii. 235 Philadelphia,..is a handsome city, but distractingly regular. After walking about it for an hour or two,..I would have given the world for a crooked street. The collar of my coat appeared to stiffen, and the brim of my hat to expand, beneath its quakerly influence. **1879** *Church Times* 21 Mar. 187/2 The Quakerly 'simplicity' which the Persecution Company is seeking to force upon so comparatively insignificant a matter as the Worship of the King of Kings. **1958** J. SYKES *Quakers* I. ii. 49 This is the basis of Quakerly action.

quaking, *ppl.a.* Add: **1. b.** *quaking pudding* (see quot. 1971), *tart*.
1628 Quaking tart [see CUSTARD 1]. **1709** W. KING tr. J. H. van Slonenbergh in *Useful Trans. Philos.* III. 52 White Bread and Butter and Quaking-pudding. **1747** H. GLASSE *Art of Cookery* ix. 112 Quaking Pudding..Cream.. Eggs..Flour..boil it. **1971** R. HOWE *Mrs Groundes-Peace's Old Cookery Notebk.* 119 *Quaking pudding*, a pudding made of breadcrumbs, cream, eggs and spices.

quaking asp(en. *U.S.* Also **quakenasp.** The North American aspen, *Populus tremuloides*, a tall tree belonging to the family Salicaceæ; also, the soft white wood of this tree.
1822 J. FOWLER *Jrnl.* 1 June (1898) 143 The timber on the mountains Heare is Pitch Pine Spruce Pine Hemlock and quakenasp. **1825** W. H. ASHLEY in H. C. Dale *Ashley–Smith Explorations* (1918) 152 This range of mountains is.. closely timbered with pine, cedar, quaking-asp. **1845** J. PALMER *Jrnl.* 30 July in *Jrnl. Trav. Rocky Mts.* (1847) 36 Occasionally there is a grove of quaking aspen. **1848** [see ASP[1] 1]. **1878** J. H. BEADLE *Western Wilds* xi. 168 The town is in a grove of quaking asp. **1902** O. WISTER *Virginian* iv. 55 They took us..through a thicket of quaking asps. **1905** *N.Y. Even. Post* 2 Sept. (Sat. Suppl.) 1/6 Have seen quakenasp groves on the summer range. **1919** E. HOUGH *Sagebrusher* 4 A few quaking asps standing near the cabin door likewise gave motion and brightness to the scene. **1947** J. J. ROWLANDS *Cache Lake Country* 19 Up on the sandy ridge the quaking aspen grows. **1963** S. A. GRAHAM et al. *Aspens* i. 2 Two species of aspen trees are indigenous to..the so-called Lake States. These are the trembling (quaking) aspen..and the bigtooth (large-toothed) aspen.

qualification. 6. b. (Later example.)
1789 J. WOODFORDE *Diary* 26 Sept. (1927) III. 143 Ben returned by Dinner, brought..a Qualification for my sporting this year for which I am to pay 2 Guineas and 1 Shilling.

qualified, *ppl. a.* Add: **5. a.** *qualified privilege*.
1972 *Times* 16 Mar. 9/7 The defence was a denial of the words in the statement of claim, a plea of qualified privilege, a plea of absolute privilege, and also a plea of justification. **1973** *Scotsman* 21 Feb. 10/3 The occasion on which the alleged remarks were made was in his view clearly one where qualified privilege applied.
b. *euphem.* for 'bloody', 'damned', etc. *slang*.
1886 KIPLING *Plain Tales from Hills* (1888) 121 He was.. told not to make a (qualified) fool of himself. **1932** D. L. SAYERS *Have his Carcase* xxvi. 353 'I wish we'd never come up against this qualified case,' added the Superintendent bitterly. **1949** 'E. C. R. LORAC' *Still Waters* iii. 39, I..knocked my head on those qualified rocks.
B. *ellipt.* as *sb.* One who is or those who are eligible for a position, military service, etc.; one who possesses a professional qualification.
1910 *Westm. Gaz.* 22 Apr. 14/1 In 1908 of 443,385 persons fully qualified for service the [German] State took only 221,852; and it is estimated that in 1911 the State will take only about 39 per cent. of the qualified. **1972** *Accountant* 12 Oct. 12/1 (Advt.), Newly qualifieds—Birmingham.

qualifier. Add: **1.** Also, one who makes himself eligible for a tournament, or for the final rounds of a tournament, as in golf or lawn tennis. Also *transf.*, a preliminary round of a competition. Also *attrib.*
1909 *Daily Chron.* 7 May 8/4 Out in 36, he came home in a good 73, and..made certain of a place among the qualifiers. **1920** *Glasgow Herald* 15 July 8 [Rifle shooting] Along with the Prince of Wales's tie were decided the ties in the Qualifier competition. **1951** *Sport* 16–22 Mar. 20/3 Although there are still quite a few more qualifying races due between now and April 7th it looks doubtful that we shall get a better qualifier. **1976** *Tennis Today* Aug. 8/1 Representing our shores was a total of sixteen players including the sole British qualifier Corinne Molesworth. **1976** *Western Mail* (Cardiff) 22 Nov. 16/2 Irish jumping star Bannow Rambler will be sent to Chepstow for an Embassy 'Chase qualifier next Saturday week. **1977** *Daily Express* 29 Mar. 32/4 England put nine goals past Luxemburg 16 years ago in the away leg of a World Cup qualifier.
2. (Further examples.) Also, a qualifying phrase or subordinate clause.
The specialized applications of quots. 1892, 1965, and 1972 are not in general use.
1765 J. ELPHINSTON *Princ. Eng. Lang. Digested* II. viii. 183 Instead of a definition or picture, a name or *noun* was invented; instead of its specification, the qualifier or adjective. *Ibid.* 186 A sentence may also be complex and compound. Complex it becomes, when the subject or object has a qualifier joined. **1892** H. SWEET *New Eng. Gram.* I. § 34. 13 When we distinguish between *many men*, *all men*, and *some men* or *few men*, we cannot say that *many*, *all*, *some*, *few* are attribute-words; they are only *qualifiers*. **1925** GRATTAN & GURREY *Our Living Lang.* xvii. 104 A Qualifier may be a Substantive or a Case-Phrase, or even a Sentence. **1933** O. JESPERSEN *Essent. Eng. Gram.* vii. 67 *Little* is sometimes a qualifier (*a little girl*), sometimes a quantifier (*a little bread*). **1965** N. C. STAGEBERG *Introd. Eng. Gram.* xv. 226 The fourth structure-class contains the qualifiers. The qualifier position is the one just before an adjectival or an adverbial. *Ibid.*, It is evident that uninflected words like *very*, *quite*, and *rather* can be called qualifiers; and when an inflected word like *pretty* and *mighty* appears in the same position, consider it a qualifier by position. **1972** J. MUIR *Mod. Approach Eng. Gram.* i. 5 An element of structure may precede the head element: this is called the modifier; and an element of structure may follow the head element: this is called the qualifier. Thus:.. *the big boy with red hair* is a nominal group with three elements of structure, an *m* element (*the big*), an *h* element (*boy*) and a *q* element (*with red hair*) giving the structure *mhq*.

qualify, *v.* Add: **I. 1. b.** (Further examples.) Also used of attributive nouns, qualifying phrases, or subordinate clauses.
1892 H. SWEET *New Eng. Gram.* I. § 34. 14 Thus *very* in *a very strong man* qualifies the attribute-word *strong*. Qualifiers themselves may be qualified, as in *very many Englishmen*. **1924** O. JESPERSEN *Philos. Gram.* vii. 96 In any composite denomination of a thing or person.., we always find that there is one word of supreme importance to which the others are joined as subordinates. This chief word is defined (qualified, modified) by another word, which in its turn may be defined (qualified, modified) by a third word, etc. **1939** G. H. MCKNIGHT et al. *Gram. Living Eng.* x. 102 By far the largest class of adjectives is that used in qualifying nouns. **1947** A. M. CLARK *Spoken Eng.* (ed. 2) iv. 81 Frequently..noun-adjectives are joined to the nouns they qualify by hyphens:—*bird-cage*, *book-review*, etc. **1959** S. H. BURTON *Handbk. Eng. Pract.* II. 127 Add to each of the following sentences one phrase to qualify the subject word, one phrase to qualify the object word, and one phrase to modify the verb. **1972** M. L. SAMUELS *Linguistic Evol.* v. 68 *Son* is usually either modified by *my/his/her*, etc. or qualified by an *of*-group, whereas *sun* is normally preceded by the definite article. **1975** [see *QUALIFYING *ppl. a.*].
5. Also, to become eligible for an old-age pension.
1911 *Rep. Labour & Social Conditions in Germany* (Tariff Reform League) III. 92 The man cannot draw his pension until he is 70 years of age, except through invalidity; he qualifies after one year's payment. **1927** W. E. COLLINSON *Contemp. Eng.* 83 The Old Age Pensions Act (1908) supplied the language with at least one phrase: *to qualify for the pension* (to be getting on in years).
6. (Later example.)
1946 A. D. GIBB *Students' Gloss. Scottish Legal Terms* 71 *Qualify*, to make out or establish, as in the expression, *to qualify a title*.

qualifying, *ppl. a.* (Examples in *Gram.*: see QUALIFY *v.* 1 b in Dict. and Suppl.)
1892 H. SWEET *New Eng. Gram.* I. § 36. 15 When attribute-words are used in this way [*sc.* as in *give me that red book, not the blue one*], we call them *qualifying attribute-words*. **1924** O. JESPERSEN *Philos. Gram.* viii. 108 The most important of these [classes of adjuncts] undoubtedly is the one composed of what may be called *restrictive* or *qualifying adjuncts*. **1925** GRATTAN & GURREY *Our Living Lang.* xvii. 103 But it is not only variety of gender which distinguishes these qualifying nouns from Substantives. In many languages some of them have special distinguishing suffixes. *Ibid.* xli. 261 *Expansion in the Subject*:—..(*b*) Qualifying Phrases. **1939** G. H. MCKNIGHT et al. *Gram. Living Eng.* x. 102 By the use of qualifying words, the common noun *man*..might be so narrowed in meaning as to refer to one definite individual. **1975** R. A. CLOSE *Ref. Gram.* ii. 66 *Qualifying clauses*.. These qualify the main clause, in the sense of limiting its application to specific cases.

† **qualimeter** (kwǫli·mɪtəɹ). *Radiology. Obs.* [f. QUALI(TY *sb.* + -METER.] An apparatus for measuring the penetrating power of a beam of X-rays.
1911 H. BAUER in *Arch. Roentgen Ray* XV. 308 Whether this Roentgen Qualimeter, as we may call it, has all the requisites for the standard measure of hardness so much sought for by every Roentgenologist is a question which I must leave for others. **1915** R. KNOX *Radiography* 58 It is here that the qualimeter is particularly useful, since different degrees of hardness are required for the production of good pictures of various parts of the body. **1926** P. K. BOWES *X-Ray Apparatus* x. 96 This qualimeter can only be used with any degree of success with one installation, using the same X-ray tube all the time, and never altering the rate of interruptions.

qualisign (kwǫ·lisəin). *Philos.* [f. QUALI(TY + SIGN *sb.*] A term originally used by C. S. Peirce in his theory of signs (see quot. *c* 1903).
c **1903** C. S. PEIRCE *Coll. Papers* (1932) II. 142 Signs are divisible by three trichotomies; first, according as the sign itself is a mere quality, is an actual existent, or is a general law... A sign may be termed a *Qualisign*, a *Sinsign*, or a *Legisign*... A Qualisign is a quality which is a Sign. It cannot actually act as a sign until it is embodied; but the embodiment has nothing to do with its character as a sign. **1934** *Mind* XLIII. 496 The specific quality of voice by which I recognise a friend (a qualisign) must be embodied in some particular event. **1936** *Jrnl. Philos.* 17 Dec. 702 It is pretty plain that Miss Stebbing means by 'type-word' what we call a 'word' and she does not recognize our category of 'word-type' or Peirce's 'qualisign'. **1966** J. J. FITZGERALD *Peirce's Theory of Signs* iii. 65 The division into Qualisign, Sinsign, and Legisign, is based on the mode of existence of the sign vehicle, not on any relationship within the triad.

qualitated, *pa. pple.* For *Obs. rare*⁻¹ read *rare* and add later example.
1949 *Mind* LVIII. 54 The succession of somatic fields which go to constitute a single somatic sense-history may be..uniformly qualitated.

qualitative, *a.* Add: **b.** *Chem. qualitative analysis*, identification of the constituents (as elements, ions, or functional groups, etc.) present in a substance. Cf. *quantitative analysis* s.v. *QUANTITATIVE *a.* 3 b.
1842 [in Dict.]. **1923** R. M. CAVEN *Quantitative Chem. Anal.* I. 19 Often the methods of qualitative analysis are available for the quantitative separation of metals in solution. **1953** E. C. PIGOTT *Ferrous Anal.* (ed. 2) 13 The spectrograph is reliable, not merely for the rapid identification of materials, but also for a preliminary qualitative analysis, including trace elements. **1956** SIGGIA & STOLTEN *Introd. Mod. Org. Anal.* iii. 51 In the classical scheme of organic qualitative analysis, the derivatives prepared were characterized by their melting points and the identification was complete when a satisfactory mixed melting point was obtained with the derivative of a known material. **1964** CHERONIS & MA *Org. Functional Group Anal.* i. 3 Qualitative organic analysis aims to identify one or more organic compounds present in an unknown.

qualitiedness. For *rare*⁻¹ read *rare* and add later example.
1940 *Mind* XLIX. 321 My present treatment is thus concerned rather with 'qualitiedness' than with 'quality'.

quality, *sb.* Add: **I. 4. a.** (Further examples.)
1699 M. LISTER *Journey to Paris* 180 A Lady of Quality, Madam M—..askt me, What I had seen in Paris that most pleased me. **1712** [see PEOPLE *sb.* 6 b]. **1922** M. ARLEN *Piracy* II. i. 69 I'd forgotten that such a phrase was ever made by fine men for fine women—a woman of quality!
b. For 'Now *arch.* or *vulgar* and *dial.*' read 'Now *dial.* or rather *arch.*' (Further examples.)
1712 P. METCALF *Life St. Winefride* (1917) 82 He and his Son..received the Holy Sacrament of Baptism, at which the greatest Quality of that County were pleased to stand *Patrines*. **1853** MRS. GASKELL *Cranford* xiv. 270 He's dazed at being called on to speak before quality. **1894** 'MARK TWAIN' in *Century Mag.* Feb. 550 He wuz the highest quality in dis whole town—ole Virginny stock. Fust famblies, he wuz. **1904** M. CORELLI *God's Good Man* (ed. 2) xxii. 415 The quality don't seem to care for no one 'cept theirselves. **1961** *Times* 25 Apr. 20/1 In the period of his second marriage Opie..never lacked sitters among the 'quality'. **1978** M. KENYON *Deep Pocket* xiv. 184 A grouse-shoot, lad... It's a country sport for the quality.
II. 8. a. *spec.* in phr. *the quality of life*.
1943 J. B. PRIESTLEY *Daylight on Saturday* xxxi. 253 The plans already..maturing that would give all our citizens more security, better opportunities, and a nobler quality of life. **1955** E. SEVAREID *Newsmakers* (CBS Radio broadcast script) 30 Nov. (Sevareid MS. Collection, Library of Congress) 6 He [*sc.* Adlai Stevenson] seems disturbed about the *quality* of American life, when most politicians measure it only in quantity. [**1955** A. STEVENSON *Let.* 13 Dec. (Sevareid MS. Collection, Library of Congress), I have.. read Sevareid Newsmakers CBS Radio, November 30, 1955... Your summarization of my anxieties about America and its *quality* was the tonic I needed for some more utterances along that line.] **1956** A. SCHLESINGER in *N.Y. Times Mag.* 4 Mar. 60/3 The liberal's belief in working for change does..mean that he feels history can never stand still, that social change can better the quality of people's lives and happiness, and that the margin of change, however limited, is worth the effort. **1969** *Guardian* 5 Aug. 8/1 A Government which says it concerns itself with the quality of life..cannot be without a broadcasting policy. **1972** J. MANN *Mrs Knox's Profession* ii. 7 Vic was going to make a corner in housing, and the quality of life, which he had.. worked out would be closest to the hearts of his constituents. **1977** M. EDELMAN *Polit. Lang.* viii. 151 The consequence is a decline in the quality of life, springing from a lowering of real income. **1979** *Nature* 24 May 311/2 Monitoring of trace constituents of the atmosphere is becoming increasingly important because of the implications on the quality of life of growing concentrations of several compounds which, after industrial use, are released to the atmosphere.
c. *ellipt.* for *quality newspaper* (see sense 13 below).
1970 *Guardian Weekly* 25 July 11 The 'qualities'..need to earn a greater percentage of their income from advertising than the 'populars', which rely more heavily on mass sales. **1976** *Times* 18 Mar. 4/1 The 'qualities' are the *Daily* and *Sunday Telegraph*, *Financial Times*, *Guardian*, *Observer*, *The Times* and *Sunday Times*. **1977** *Vole* I. 26/2 Many of the qualities' journalists are good writers.
10. d. *Engin.* The proportion by weight of vapour in a mixture of vapour and the parent liquid.
1898 H. A. GOLDING *Theta-Phi Diagram* iv. 52 (*in figure*) Dryness fraction or quality curve. **1937** CROFT & PURDY *Steam Boilers* (ed. 2) iii. 24 The quality of steam in average practice is..from about 97 to 99 per cent. **1977** G. F. HEWITT in Butterworth & Hewitt *Two-Phase Flow & Heat Transfer* ii. 24 Data on flow patterns for a particular geometry and fluid pair can be plotted directly in terms of the velocities, flow rates, etc. of the phases. Alternatively, it is often convenient for a single-component fluid to plot the results in terms of mass flux *G* and quality *x*.
e. *Radiology.* The penetrating power of a beam of X-rays.
1903 PUSEY & CALDWELL *Pract. Applic. Röntgen Rays* II. v. 309 The quality of the rays and their intensity vary greatly. **1928** B. J. LEGGETT *Theory & Pract. Radiol.* II. vi. 162 The more or less exact measurement of the quality of X-radiation is of importance in all branches of radiotherapy. **1968** M. B. HOLLANDER *Ultrasoft X Rays* i. 3 Most articles published since about 1940 have stated quality in terms of half-value layer. **1972** BARNES & REES *Conc. Textbk. Radiotherapy* vii. 154 The choice of the radiation quality is determined by the site and the size of the lesion.

f. The degree to which reproduced sound resembles the original; fidelity.

1913 G. F. ROWELL *Hints about Gramophone* 9 He revels in the loudest records he can buy, and so long as the noise is satisfactory the musical quality does not trouble him in the least. **1938** A. E. GREENLEES *Amplification & Distribution of Sound* xvi. 230 The sales literature of manufacturers will provide much useful information as to what may be expected in the way of quality of reproduction. **1971** J. EARL *Pickups & Loudspeakers* i. 9 The tape element involved in the production of a disc record detracts very little from the overall quality these days.

IV. 13. a. (sense 4) *quality gentleman*, *-white*; (sense 8) *quality mark*; *quality-tested* adj.; (sense 9c) *quality audience*, *food*, *note*, *producer*; *spec.* = of a high cultural standard, esp. of newspapers, as *quality magazine*, *newspaper*, *paper*, *press*, *programme*, *publisher*, *Sunday*, etc.; **quality control**, the maintenance of the desired quality in a manufactured product, esp. by means of critical examination of a proportion of the output and its comparison with the specification; also *transf.*; freq. *attrib.*; hence **quality controller**, one whose responsibility this is; **quality factor** = *Q III. 3.

1938 *Time* 10 Oct. 43/1 It has a fairly large and very vociferous 'quality' audience. **1935** E. S. PEARSON (*title*) The application of statistical methods to industrial standardisation and quality control. **1943** R. E. WAREHAM in J. F. Young *Materials & Processes* xviii. 589 Quality control methods are based on the laws of probability and statistics. **1968** *Brit. Med. Bull.* XXIV. 220/1 Examination of the batch mean has proved to be one of the most valuable quality-control measures available. **1971** *Physics Bull.* July 383/3 Specialist papers were less favoured for the conference and there appeared to be a need for better 'quality control' of these. **1977** P. JOHNSON *Enemies of Society* xi. 158 This forced academic growth leads to an inevitable collapse of quality-control. **1978** *Jrnl. R. Soc. Arts* CXXVI. 670/2 The result was anarchism, disorder, inadequate production planning, cost and quality control and performance rating. **1972** M. JONES *Life on Dole* II. vii. 126 His next employer was Hoover... He became a quality controller. **1947** *Electronic Circuits & Tubes* i. 17 The ratio of the series reactance to the series resistance of a reactor is defined as *Q*, its quality factor. **1967** CONDON & ODISHAW *Handbk. Physics* (ed. 2) IV. vii. 108/1 Frequently the inverse of the loss tangent, the quality factor *Q* of the dielectric,..serves as the figure of merit, especially in waveguide problems. **1971** *Nature* 24 Dec. 461/1 Recent measurements of the quality factor, *Q*, for mechanical vibrations generated by dropping parts of the Apollo lunar module and by moonquakes indicate that the *Q* of the Moon for these vibrations is of the order of 3,000. **1961** *Wine & Food* Winter 240 Shoppers should..be well aware of the quality food that comes from their own farmers and growers. **1908** J. M. SULLIVAN *Criminal Slang* 1 *A quality gentleman*, a gentleman by birth and education. **1941** *Times* 22 May (Advt.), Issued by The National Magazine Company Limited..who publish such quality magazines as 'Good Housekeeping', 'Harper's Bazaar', 'Connoisseur', etc. **1954** W. FAULKNER *Fable* 352 The quality-mark and warrant of man's immortality: his deathless folly. **1959** *New Statesman* 14 Mar. 362/3 Independent consumer guidance—i.e., journals, quality marks, labelling, etc.—is, they say, unnecessary because advertising already provides adequate information about goods. **1971** *Gloss. Terms Materials Handling* (*B.S.I.*) v. 32 *Quality mark*, a mark which appears on some of the links of higher tensile or alloy steel chain, defining its grade. **1956** *English* Summer 48 Quality newspapers decline alarmingly, serious journals go bankrupt: **1961** *Punch* 11 Jan. 88/2 Whitbreads, for example, is the beer most favoured by forward-looking Pops [i.e. Pop People]. The advertising strikes a 'quality' note. **1962** *Listener* 11 Oct. 569/2 You can see such reporting even in the so-called quality papers. **1960** Quality press [see *quality programme* below]. **1936** *Economist* 8 Feb. 314/1 Firms in..country towns—whose recent progress has been based on lower wage scales than those paid by the 'quality' producers in the leading centres. **1960** *Guardian* 9 Dec. 12/6 Ideally..the union would like to see..'quality' programmes analogous to the 'quality' press. **1961** *Ibid.* 20 Oct. 11/4 The struggle between the commercial and the quality publisher is fierce. **1961** *Punch* 11 Jan. 86/3 When may a young man be said to have arrived?..Having his name used as a pun in a quality Sunday paper's erudite crossword puzzle. **1974** *Times* 22 May 20/6 The quality dailies have done rather better than the popular journals... Quality Sundays are up 23 per cent. **1938** *Encycl. Brit. Bk. of Year* 636/2 Guaranteed quality-tested rayon fabrics. **1974** *Times* 15 Aug. (India Suppl.) p. viii/3 (Advt.), India's cottons..are quality tested. **1966** K. L. MORGAN in A. Dundes *Mother Wit* (1973) 603/1, I never questioned the implication that..my white ancestors were 'quality' whites.

b. Passing into *adj.*

1962 R. WILLIAMS *Brit. in Sixties: Communications* iii. 29 The division of space between advertising and editorial material is not, then, governed by whether a paper is 'quality' or 'popular'. **1972** *Britain 1972* (Central Office of Information) xviii. 429 The national newspapers..fall into two categories: popular and quality.

qualming, *ppl. a.* Delete † *Obs.* and add later *poet.* example.

1952 AUDEN *Nones* 40 How will you answer when from their qualming spring The immortal nymphs fly shrieking.

qualmless (kwā·mlės, kwǭ·m-), *a.* [f. QUALM *sb.*[3] + -LESS.] Having or feeling no qualms. So **qua·lmlessness.**

1849 T. ARNOLD *Let.* 22 Nov. in *N.Z. Lett.* (1966) 158 The beautiful scenery of the Sound did not appear to advantage in this tempestuous weather, nor to tell the truth ,was I in that state of quietude and qualmlessness as to my internals, which would allow me to enjoy it. **1905** *Westm. Gaz.* 4 Mar. 5/2 Picture of Ronald absolutely qualmless facing charging rhinoceros. **1927** W. DEEPING *Kitty* xix. 244 Any qualms that she may have suffered in the beginning disappeared... By the end of January she was qualmless.

qualup (kwæ·lŭp). The name of an estate in Western Australia, used *attrib.* in **qualup bell** to designate a local shrub, *Pimelea physodes* (cf. *PIMELEA), which has greyish-green leaves and reddish-yellow bracts forming bells round the flowers.

1921 E. H. PELLOE *Wildflowers W. Austral* 50 'Qualup Bell'... An erect shrub of about 3 ft., glabrous except the flowers. **1934** *Bulletin* (Sydney) 25 July 26/2 What is the qualup bell?.. It is a native of Australia..and carries bell flowers which are tinged with yellow, green and purple. **1966** *Times* 11 Nov. (W. Austral. Suppl.) p. iv/2 The lovely qualup and mountain bells; the hoveas, the myrtles.

quandary, *v.* (Later example.)

1794 W. B. STEVENS *Let.* 19 Nov. in *Jrnl.* (1965) 206 Your Grandfather's sentiments are so far come round that he seems to be quandaryed (that's not a dictionary word I believe) and wishes for Peace.

‖ **quand même** (kaṅ mẽm). [Fr., lit. 'when the same'.] All the same, even so, nevertheless.

1825 H. WILSON *Mem.* III. 179 She was however dreadfully agitated, quand même. **1854** GEO. ELIOT *Let.* 21 Apr. (1954) II. 151, I shall always love her *quand même.* **1884** W. JAMES *Will to Believe* (1897) 162 An optimism *quand même*, a systematic and infatuated optimism like that ridiculed by Voltaire in his Candide, is one of the possible ideal ways in which a man may train himself to look on life. **1909** —— *Pluralistic Universe* ii. 71 First we hear Mr. Bradley convicting things of absurdity; next, calling on the absolute to vouch for them *quand même.* **1952** W. STEVENS *Let.* 26 June (1967) 756 We have no plans..for a holiday. We shall have a good time quand même.

quandong. 1. Substitute for def.: **a.** A small Australian tree, *Santalum acuminatum*, belonging to the family Santalaceæ, and bearing racemes of small greenish-white flowers; also, the globular red fruit of this tree. **b.** A forest tree found in northeastern Australia, *Elæocarpus grandis*, belonging to the family Elæocarpaceæ, and distinguished by grey bark and axillary racemes of bell-shaped, greenish-white flowers; also, the blue berries of this tree. Also *attrib.* (Further and later examples.)

1862 R. HENNING *Let.* 2 Nov. (1966) 114 He [*sc.* an emu] also eats quandongs, a sort of wild plum that grows in the bush. They look very like the common black plums you preserve, but they are sour and bitter and harsh to an untold degree. **1903** 'T. COLLINS' *Such is Life* ii. 74 She had watched the deepening crimson of the quandong, amidst its thick contexture of Nile-green leaves. **1908** E. J. BANFIELD *Confessions of Beachcomber* I. i. 22 The shiny blue quandong (*Elæocarpus grandis*), misleading and insipid. **1935** H. H. FINLAYSON *Red Centre* viii. 84 Of the sweet fruits, the quondong and plum are first favourites. **1936** F. CLUNE *Roaming round Darling* xvii. 162 Then there is the quondong-tree, which has a small fruit with a nut inside like a marble. **1945** *Coast to Coast 1944* 88 Give me your quandong stones and your two tortoise-shells. **1953** M. E. PATCHETT in I. Bevan *Sunburnt Country* II. iv. 117 Here are quandong trees with their thick, leathery leaves and red globes of fruit that make delicious jams and jellies. **1965** *Austral. Encycl.* III. 365/1 *E*[*læocarpus*] *grandis* (the blue, white, or silver quandong)..has large blue drupes known to children as blue figs, and sometimes, but incorrectly, as quandongs. **1967** [see *NATIVE *a.* 13 d]. **1978** *Observer* (Colour Suppl.) 1 Jan. 24/4 Yatungka..had gone east a great distance to gather the fruit of the quandong tree. *Ibid.*, Yatungka arrived at the camp about midday, carrying a dish full of quandongs.

2. *Austral. slang.* A disreputable person who lives by his wits (see also quot. 1977).

1939 K. TENNANT *Foveaux* 311 In this crowd of low heels, quandongs and ripperty men, she looked at her ease and yet not of them. **1973** F. HUELIN *Keep Moving* 178 *Quandong*, hobo who bludges or imposes on another. **1977** J. RAMSAY *Cop it Sweet* 75 *Quandong*, female who makes a practice of remaining virtuous after being wined and dined.

quango (kwæ·ŋgo). Also with capital initial and in form **QUANGO.** Pl. **quangos.** [Acronym f. the initial letters of *qu*asi *a*utonomous *n*on-*g*overnment(al) *o*rganization: see note below.] A semi-public administrative body outside the civil service but financed by the exchequer and having members appointed by the government. Also *attrib.*

The expansion given above appears in the evidence set out below from 1967. The expansion '*qua*si-autonomous *n*ational *g*overnment(al) *o*rganization' and its variants (now common) are first attested in 1976.

[**1967** A. PIFER in *Ann. Rep. Carnegie Corp. N.Y.* 3 In recent years there has appeared on the American scene a new genus of organization which represents a noteworthy experiment in the art of government... We may call it the *quasi nongovernmental organization.*] **1973** C. HOOD in *New Society* 16 Aug. 386/1 It was the Americans who first drew attention to the importance of what they have labelled the 'grants economy', the 'contract state' and the 'quasi-non-government organisation' (Quango). **1975** *Listener* 2 Oct. 433/1 What our American cousins describe as 'quangos', which..are the quasi non-governmental organisations..from the University Grants Committee to the British Tourist Authority. **1976** *Observer* 2 May 1/2 A new species of animal is multiplying in the undergrowth of Britain—the QUANGO, or Quasi Autonomous National Governmental Organisation. **1976** *Daily Tel.* 8 Sept. 8/7 While millions of workers have their pay limits rigidly fixed, their union bosses are able to increase their incomes by becoming members of 'quangos'. The word, newly-coined, stands for Quasi Autonomous National Governmental Organisations. **1977** *New Society* 17 Mar. 531/1 Now sits in the House of Lords and has an array of quango jobs. **1978** *Economist* 5 Aug. 20 A quango covers just about everything from the Price Commission to the Police Complaints Board and the British Waterways Board. **1978** *Daily Tel.* 15 Nov. 18 Baroness Young will be declaring a personal interest when she opens a timely debate in the Lords today on the growth of Quangos, Quasi-Autonomous Non-Governmental Organisations. **1979** *Daily Tel.* 8 Aug. 14 Anthony Barker of Essex University, describes the gathering as his act of atonement for having, he claims, invented the word quango..10 years ago. **1980** *Times* 1 Feb. 15/5 It seems impossible to believe that any government, however intent upon abolishing 'Quangos' (Quasi-Autonomous Non-Governmental Organizations),..would kill off the Advisory Council on the Penal System. **1980** T. SHARPE *Ancestral Vices* ix. 70 He's some sort of personal Quango... A Quasi Autonomous Non-Governmental Organization, as you very well know.

Hence **quango·cracy**, quangos regarded collectively; the power or influence attributed to quangos; **qua·ngocrat**, a member of a quango regarded (usu. unfavourably) in terms of his authority.

1979 *Daily Tel.* 17 Apr. 18/1 Mr Callaghan's quangocrats were chosen to perform socialist functions, so were most of their institutions. **1979** *Observer* 23 Sept. 5/2 The sacked quangocrats are almost all unpaid. *Ibid.* 9/6 The original attack of the Conservatives conjured up bogies..of 'union hierarchies which interlock with quangocracy'. **1980** *Times* 12 Jan. 3/2 Those great beneficiaries of quangocracy, the trade unions and the academics of the left, are beginning to fight back.

quank (kwǫŋk), *sb.* [Echoic.] A representation of sounds made by animals and birds. Hence as *v. intr.*, to utter such a sound. Also **quan·king** *vbl. sb.*

1921 *Chambers's Jrnl.* Mar. 178/1 He could even hear the nasal laugh of the zebra, the resonant 'Quank' of the gnus, the rattle of horn against horn as the bucks made play. **1965** E. RICHARDSON *Living Island* 215 Oftener we hear quanking among the tidal pools..as males beat their way to the enticing sounds—for it is the female [duck] which quanks.

quanset, var. *QUONSET, QUONSET.

quant, *sb.*[1] Add: **1.** For def. read: A pole for propelling a barge, esp. one with a cap at the top and a prong at the bottom to prevent it sinking in mud. Also *attrib.*, as *quant-pole.*

1901 *Academy* 26 Oct. 389/1 There..lay a large family-boat immovable... A quant-pole stood rigidly upright beside it. **1974** *Oxf. Jun. Encycl.* (rev. ed.) IX. 389/1 On the Norfolk Broads,..boatmen often propel their 'wherries' (sailing barges) for short distances by 'quanting' with very long, heavy poles called 'quant-poles'.

2. In a windmill: (see quots. 1936 and 1945). Also *Comb.*

1924 *Trans. Newcomen Soc.* III. 42 All the framing and gearing of these mills are of wood, the only important parts of iron being the wrought iron gudgeons upon which the shafts revolve, and perhaps the 'quants' or spindles which drove the runner stones. **1936** P. HEMMING *Windmills in Sussex* ii. 9 The drive from above is called 'quant-drive' and is the more usual drive in a windmill. *Ibid.*, This chute vibrates against the lower part of the stone-shaft, which is called the 'quant' and which is not circular, but ribbed. **1945** *Archit. Rev.* XCVIII. 78/1 When the stones are overdriven the nuts are mounted on vertical spindles or 'quants' which drive the 'runner stones' from above. **1957** S. FREESE *Windmills & Millwrighting* iii. 48 This forked shaft is called a 'crutch-pole' or 'quant', because it oscillates like a quant-pole when freed from its upper bearing (the glut-box) in order to disengage the stone-nut.

† **quant** (kwǫnt), *sb.*[2] Used for *QUANTUM 5. *Obs.*

1918 *Phil. Mag.* XXXV. 294 Sommerfeld gave a generalization of the quant-conditions which proved to be of very great importance. *Ibid.* 307 The assumption that the recombining electron comes from one other ring with a higher quant number leads to an equation of the right type. **1926** *Nature* 18 Dec. 874/1 It would seem inappropriate to speak of one of these hypothetical entities as..a corpuscle of light, a light quantum or a light quant, if we are to assume that it spends only a minute fraction of its existence as a carrier of radiant energy. **1932** STILES & WALSH tr. *Castelfranchi's Rec. Adv. Atomic Physics* II. v. 167 The light energy..always remains concentrated in the form of 'light quants', or grains, the magnitude of which depends solely on the *colour.*

quanta, pl. of QUANTUM in Dict. and Suppl.

quantal, *a.* Restrict † *Obs.* to sense in Dict. and add: **2. a.** Composed of discrete units; varying in steps, not continuously.

1917 F. H. PRATT in *Amer. Jrnl. Physiol.* XLIV. 518 Regarding the effective energy content of a biological system discharging always to full capacity as a physiological quantum, I purpose to use the derivative *quantal* to express ..the conception of structural carriers of such integers of energy in effects discontinuously graded. *Ibid.*, A series of responsive values would be quantal when composed of discontinuous steps. **1919** *Ibid.* XLIX. 38 That tetanic contractions are quantal is shown even more clearly in figure 15. **1958** *Oxf. Univ. Gaz.* 2 Oct. 84/1 Three problems arising in the analysis of quantal data. **1964** *Language* XL. 206 The most salient characteristic of these linguistic primes..is their discreteness, their discontinuity... It is obviously their quantal attributes which distinguish linguistic primes from the species units of other behavioural sciences, e.g. the 'culture trait' of anthropology.

b. *Biol.* and *Med.* Of an effect or response (see quots.).

1933 J. H. GADDUM in *Med. Res. Council Special Rep. Ser.* No. 183. 5 The term 'quantal response' is used in this paper for any 'all-or-none' biological reaction, i.e. a reaction of such a type, or observed under such conditions, that only the bare fact of its presence or absence in each animal is recorded. **1954** *Proc. R. Soc. Med.* XLVII. 203 The third kind of method used..to assay drugs depends upon quantal effects. These effects are not measured but recorded as positive or absent and the number of positive effects is counted. **1974** M. C. GERALD *Pharmacol.* iii. 58 Does the rat die at a given dose of poison or not? Let us assume that this quantal (all-or-none) response follows a normal distribution.

c. *Physics.* Of, pertaining to, or being a quantum or the quantum theory.

1936 C. G. DARWIN in *Nature* 28 Nov. 909/1 One may not infrequently see in learned journals such a phrase as 'This may be proved by quantum theoretical methods.'.. The proper English form would be ***quantum theory methods***, though even that is very clumsy, and ***quantum methods*** is quite good enough... The right procedure is to coin the adjective ***quantal***. To justify its adequacy it is only necessary to notice the impossibility of finding anything that would be ***quantally*** right, but ***quantum-mechanically*** wrong. **1951** E. M. CORSON *Perturbation Methods* iii. 36 If **q**, **p** are to be canonically conjugate in the quantal sense. **1954** *Jrnl. Physiol.* CXXIV. 571 The number of quantal units responding to a nerve impulse fluctuates in a random manner. **1975** *Physics Bull.* Dec. 545/3 Anybody who wishes to learn the mathematics of coherence, classical and quantal, of light fields and their interaction with atoms can do no better than turn to this book. **1978** *Nature* 12 Jan. 191/1 The transmitter, synthesised and packaged on the spot, is released in quantal, countable packets.

Hence **qua·ntally** *adv.*

1936 [see 2 c above]. **1957** *Psychol. Rev.* LXIV. 137/1 Such preactivation can be produced by gradual learning or quantally by instruction. **1970** *Nature* 5 Sept. 1006/2 Vesicles slotted between dense projections are thought to release transmitter quantally by exocytosis through the membrane into the cleft. **1978** *Ibid.* 13 July 136/1 The small standard error in each case shows clearly that the V_2 change is quantal and, hence, that the junctional conductance itself changes quantally.

quantasome (kwǫ·ntăsōᵘm). *Bot.* [f. *quanta*, pl. of QUANTUM + *-SOME⁴. (The quantasome was believed to be the fundamental body capable of photosynthesis.)] One of numerous small proteinaceous particles found in chloroplasts.

Quot. 1962 is only the earliest of several such seeming coinages, all in papers by Professor R. B. Park and his colleagues at the Lawrence Radiation Laboratory and Botany Department, Berkeley, California.

1962 M. CALVIN in *Science* 16 Mar. 889/1 Here we can see the lamellae on its flat side showing a granular structure, made up of fairly uniform oblate spheroids which we have called quantasomes. **1964** *Science* 22 May 1009/1 The quantasome as seen in a two-dimensional crystalline array is 185 Å long, 155 Å wide, and 100 Å thick. The surface of the quantasome appears to contain four or more subunits. The molecular weight..is 2×10^6. This..corresponds to a chlorophyll content of 230 chlorophyll molecules per quantasome. **1968** R. RIEGER et al. *Gloss Genetics & Cytogenetics* 370 According to recent evidence, the quantasomes do not participate in photoreduction reactions but show Ca^{++}-dependent ATPase activities. **1976** COOMBS & GREENWOOD in J. Barber *Intact Chloroplast* i. 12 The concept of a quantasome as the structural counterpart of a functional photosynthetic unit in the full classical sense of this term is in doubt.

quantifiable, *a.* (Later examples.)

1953 D. RIESMAN in *Amer. Scholar* XXIII. 24 The quantifiable measure of longevity. **1966** J. ELLIS in C. E. Bazell *In Memory of J. R. Firth* 80 Both phonological and formal meaning correspond to the information of information theory in being dependent on, and quantifiable in terms of, the number of oppositions in the given system. **1967** *Times Rev. Industry* July 29/1 A first-class service with quantifiable savings in the company's own accounts department s the best possible selling point. **1972** *Daily Tel.* 6 Apr. 21/4 What we wanted were not quantifiable results but actual feelings. **1974** *Sci. Amer.* May 43/1 Reconstruction, redevelopment and the redesign of approach roads and nternal streets are destroying the evidence of the city's past at a quantifiable rate.

qua·ntifiable, *sb.* *Linguistics.* [f. the adj.] = *mass noun* s.v. *MASS *sb.*² 10 d.

1957 *College English* XVIII. 351/1 These are the quantifiables, such as *furniture* and *milk* and *news*. **1961** R. B. LONG *Sentence & its Parts* ii. 39 Quantifiables such as *courage, fun, pneumonia, milk, spaghetti, machinery*, and *furniture* are not made plural, though it is true that some quantifiables have pluralizer status also.

quantification. Add: (Later examples.) Esp. in *Logic*, as *quantification theory*: theory concerned with quantifiers or with giving formal expression to the scope of variables in general propositions. Cf. *QUANTIFIER.

1918 C. I. LEWIS *Survey of Symbolic Logic* i. 24 He [*sc.* Lambert] reconstructs the whole of Aristotelian logic by the quantification of the predicate. **1940** *Brit. Jrnl. Psychol.* Jan. 233 Quantification pertains to a statistical population of persons, assessed or measured for amounts of that particular quality. **1940** W. V. QUINE *Math. Logic* p. vi, Quantification theory, like the preceding part of logic, is expounded within the medium of metamathematics; its presentation in any other medium appears disadvantageous, indeed, because of subtleties having to do with the so-called bound and free occurrences of variables. **1949** R. K. MERTON *Social Theory* iii. 109 What appears as a tendency in research for quantification (through the development of scales) can thus be seen as a special case of attempting to clarify concepts sufficiently to permit the conduct of empirical investigation. **1950** W. V. QUINE *Methods of Logic* (1952) § 28. 166 Quantification theory was founded by Frege in 1879. **1962** E. W. BETH *Formal Methods* iii. 50 If a semantic tableau for the sequent $\emptyset/Z$ is closed, then the formula Z will be called a tautology (of quantification theory). **1966** A. D. BIDERMAN in R. Bauer *Social Indicators* ii. 75 Quantification was not until fairly recently an essential element of the definition of statistics. **1969** N. I. STYAZHKIN *Hist. Math. Logic Leibniz to Peano* iii. 123 It would not be an exaggeration to say that Lambert's theory of quantification actually contains all the basic results of the studies in quantification made by W. Hamilton in the nineteenth century. **1971** *World Archaeol.* III. 122 Groups of granaries ..do not permit quantification of men by compound. **1973** J. HINTIKKA *Logic, Language-Games & Information* iii. 53 Quantification theory may be characterized from this point of view as the study of the phrases 'there is', and 'for every' over and above the study of the words 'not', and 'or', which are already studied in propositional logic plus whatever terms are required to express predication. **1974** H. WANG *From Math. to Philos.* 143 The many attractive properties of the first order or restricted predicate calculus (quantification theory) have suggested the convenient identification of it with first order logic, pure logic, or just logic. **1979** *Amer. Speech* LIV. 9 Scholars have criticized, sometimes effectively, the validity of the prescriptivists' quantifications. **1979** *Dædalus* Summer 77 A quantification of love that would be comic were it not that its effects are so awful.

quantificational (kwǫntifikēⁱ·ʃənăl), *a.* [f. QUANTIFICATION + -AL.] Of, pertaining to, or relating to quantification. Hence **quantifica·tionally** *adv.*

1940 W. V. QUINE *Math. Logic.* ii. 89 We avoid the labor of writing out specific sequences of quantificational axioms and ponentials. **1951** —— *Ibid.* (rev. ed.) ii. 81 The advent of quantification opens up a wider class of logical truths: statements which are true by virtue of their structure in terms of joint denial and quantification. These may be *quantificationally* true. **1955** *Jrnl. Philos.* LII. 753 Sententially and quantificationally valid schemata are presented. **1957** N. CHOMSKY in Saporta & Bastian *Psycholinguistics* (1961) 266/2 A 'quantificational' sentence such as 'everyone in the room knows at least two languages'. **1966** *Jrnl. Philos.* LXIII. 699 The first-order quantificational calculus with identity. **1975** *Times Lit. Suppl.* 5 Dec. 1466/3 He is equally curt with some of the most familiar arguments in favour of God's existence: Aquinas's third way is guilty of an elementary quantificational fallacy.

quantified, *ppl. a.* Add to def.: Resulting from quantification or the use of quantifiers. (Further examples.)

1951 J. ŁUKASIEWICZ *Aristotle's Syllogistic* iv. 84 Every quantified expression..consists of three parts. **1972** P. T. GEACH *Logic Matters* ii. 69 The wrong idea that a universally quantified subject-term stands for the whole class of *Ss*² *can* be put across. **1974** H. WANG *From Math. to Philos.* iii. 113 The idea that truth functions governing quantified expressions must be explained in terms of propositions in which truth functions do not govern quantified expressions.

quantifier (kwǫ·ntifəiəɹ). [f. QUANTIFY *v.* + -ER¹.] **1. a.** *Logic.* Something which quantifies, esp. an expression (such as 'all' or 'some') that indicates the scope of a term to which it is attached; *existential quantifier*, a quantifier that asserts that there exists something for which the proposition following it is true or valid. Also *attrib.*

In quot. 1876 'a person who quantifies'.

1876 *Mind* I. 213 Quantifiers of the predicate insert the word *some*, and Boole uses a special symbol V, to mark the partial character of the identity. **1885** C. S. PEIRCE *Coll. Papers* (1933) III. xiii. 232 If the quantifying part, or Quantifier, contains Σ_x, and we wish to replace the x by a new index i, not already in the Quantifier, and such that every x is an i, we can do so at once by simply multiplying every letter of the Boolian having x as an index by x_i. **1896** —— in *Monist* VII. 32 My general algebra of logic.. consists in simply attaching indices to the letters of an expression in the Boolian algebra, making what I term a Boolian, and prefixing to this a series of 'quantifiers', which are the letters Π and Σ, each with an index attached to it. **1940** W. V. QUINE *Math. Logic* ii. 106 Distribution of a universal quantifier through an alternation is not valid, nor is distribution of an existential quantifier through a conjunction. *Ibid.* 110 The last occurrence of '*y*' in (5) refers back to the last quantifier occurrence in (5). **1951** J. ŁUKASIEWICZ *Aristotle's Syllogistic* iv. 84, I denote quantifiers by Greek capitals, the universal quantifier by Π, and the particular or existential quantifier by Σ. Π may be read 'for all', and Σ 'for some' or 'there exists'. **1956** A. CHURCH *Introd. Math. Logic* iv. 288 The notion of propositional function and the use of quantifiers, originated with Frege in his Begriffsschrift of 1879... The terms 'quantifier' and 'quantification' are Peirce's. **1963** O. WOJTASIEWICZ tr. *Łukasiewicz's Elem. Math. Logic* 95 Detachment..is the same as in the quantifier-free sentential calculus. **1965** B. MATES *Elem. Logic* x. 159 A string of universal quantifiers containing *n* quantifier-occurrences. **1971** *Sci. Amer.* Aug. 96/3 Perhaps the only detail in our plan..that requires special comment is the treatment of the quantifiers $\forall$ (meaning 'for all') and $\exists$ ('there exists'). **1976** J. S. GRUBER *Lexical Struct. Syntax & Semantics* I. iii. 63 This kind of relationship with *not*, interestingly, is the same that occurs relating the universal and existential quantifiers.

b. *Linguistics.* A word or phrase indicative of quantity. Also *attrib.* and *Comb.*

1924 O. JESPERSEN *Philos. Gram.* vi. 85 All these quantifiers, as they might be called, differ from ordinary qualifying adjectives in being capable of standing alone..as when we say 'some (many, all, both, two) were absent'. **1933** —— *Essent. Eng. Gram.* vii. 67 *Little* is sometimes a qualifier (*a little girl*), sometimes a quantifier (*a little bread*). **1951** S. F. NADEL *Found. Social Anthropol.* 43 Thus I am not considering the 'formal' parts of language (conjunctions, prepositions, 'quantifiers', etc.). **1969** W. A. COOK *Introd. Tagmemic Analysis* iv. 107 *Quantifier tagmeme*, filled by numerals (num) such as: *one, two, first, second*; or quantitative adjectives. **1970** G. CARDEN in *Linguistic Inquiry* I. 287 The higher-S analysis requires an as-yet unspecified rule of Quantifier Lowering (QL) to move the quantifier from the high-S down to its surface-structure position. **1972** J. J. LAMBERTS *Short Introd. Eng. Usage* vii. 137 These are generally taken as plural unless a 'quantifier' like *a pair of* precedes the noun. **1977** *Word 1972* XXVIII. 88 If compared adjectives are to be analyzed as containing underlying quantifier-NPs in sentences such as 1 f and 1 g, then, ideally, we would expect them to be so analyzed elsewhere as well. **1978** *Language* LIV. 83 Certain quantifier constructions in Japanese were shown above to be exceptions.

2. *gen.* One who quantifies.

1963 *Economist* 9 Feb. 513/2 All that can be asked of the quantifiers is that they explore the sources thoroughly. **1970** *Computers & Humanities* V. 1 'Quantifiers' assemble in conferences, workshops and symposia to thrash out common problems and share research methods and findings.

quantify, *v.* Add: **2.** (Further examples.)

1949 *Cape Argus* 5 Nov. 5/4 It pleased them immensely.. to hear him [*sc.* Winston Churchill] fall on Sir Stafford Cripps for having recently used the word 'quantify'. **1962** *Times Lit. Suppl.* 16 Nov. 875/1 Though we can list all these factors, we cannot quantify them. **1971** I. G. GASS et al. *Understanding Earth* 40 Studies using the law of superposition and fossil faunas and floras could only produce a *relative* time scale, and efforts were made during the 19th and early 20th centuries to quantify it. **1971** *Country Life* 3 June 1350/1 What is so often missing from the survey equation is..an adequate technique for quantifying the results. **1977** *Modern Railways* Dec. 472/3 Railfreight's performance in chemicals transport is hard to quantify in terms of market share. **1979** *Dædalus* Summer 76 Lear is quantifying love, confusing it with other things that can be measured.

quantifying, *ppl. a.* (Later examples.)

1955 A. N. PRIOR *Formal Logic* 210 The presence..of..a quantifying element. **1976** *Times Lit. Suppl.* 30 Jan. 104/4 Those who would expect the author..to have little regard for received wisdoms or sacred cows (or even quantifying historians) will not be disappointed.

quantile (kwǫ·ntəil). *Statistics.* [f. L. *quant-us* how much, how great: see *-IL, -ILE 2.] Each of any set of values of a variate which divide a frequency distribution into equal groups, each containing the same fraction of the total population; also, any one of the groups so produced, e.g. a quartile, decile, or percentile.

1940 *Suppl. to Jrnl. R. Statistical Soc.* VII. 83 It is not shown that the distribution of a quantile tends to normality in large samples. **1961** KENDALL & STUART *Adv. Theory Statistics* (ed. 2) II. xxxii. 513 X_p is the p-quantile of the distribution, i.e. the value below which $100p$ per cent of the distribution lies. **1961** L. G. PARRATT *Probability & Exper. Errors in Sci.* ii. 79 If there are *M* intervals, each interval is called a quantile or an *M*-tile, or sometimes a fractile.

† **quantimeter** (kwǫnti·mĭtəɹ). *Radiology. Obs.* [f. QUANTI(TY + -METER.] An apparatus for measuring the quantity of X-rays administered. Hence **quantime·tric** *a.*

1906 R. KIENBÖCK in *Arch. Roentgen Ray* XI. 17/2 In 1905, at the Roentgen Congress at Berlin, I introduced the new method of direct dosimetry—the 'quantimetric method'. *Ibid.*, My quantimeter consists essentially of..a strip of photographic paper..and a normal scale of graduated tints, with which it is to be compared. **1915** R. KNOX *Radiography* 282 The Kienböck Quantimeter.—This method is based on the discoloration of bromide of silver under the influence of X-rays. **1926** P. K. BOWES *X-Ray Apparatus* x. 95 (*heading*) Kienböck's quantimeter.

quantitate (kwǫ·ntitēⁱt), *v.* *Med.* [f. QUANTIT(Y + -ATE³.] *trans.* To ascertain the quantity or extent of.

1960 *Anat. Rec.* CXXXVIII. 395/1 Because their appearance is sudden the time required for development can be measured and used to quantitate the rate of metabolic change produced by glucose. **1962** BURCHFIELD & STORRS *Biochem. Appl. Gas Chromatogr.* i. 117 All the components of the mixture are converted to the same substance and can be quantitated from a single curve relating detector response to amount of CO_2 or methane. **1969** *Adv. Appl. Microbiol.* XI. 51 The susceptibility of a penicillin to β-lactamases is usually quantitated by measuring its rate of hydrolysis to penicilloic acid. **1976** *Nature* 22 Jan. 236/1 Vitamin E content of the filtrate was quantitated by absorbancy at 292 nm. **1978** *Dædalus* Spring 27 If there is a danger, quantitate it.

So **quantita·tion**, the action or process of quantitating.

1959 *Jrnl. Lipid Res.* I. 76/2 The separation and quantitation of the shorter acids could have been improved by use of a lower temperature and longer column. **1964** *Analytical Biochem.* VII. 295 Quantitation of each peak was made by triangulating the peak, cutting out, and weighing on an analytical balance. **1975** *Nature* 30 Oct. 828/1 Quantitation of the spectra was aided by the use of a Nicolet 1020A signal averager.

quantitative, *a.* and *sb.* Add: **A.** *adj.* **3. b.** Chem. *quantitative analysis*, measurement of the amounts of constituents present in a substance. Cf. **qualitative analysis*.

1849 [in Dict., sense 3]. **1913** CUMMING & KAY *Quantitative Chem. Analysis* 109 One of the most difficult problems met with in quantitative analysis is the selection of good methods of separation. **1961** D. & B. A. AMBROSE *Gas Chromatogr.* x. 161 With the integral detectors described.. quantitative analysis is simple: the detector response is directly proportional to the mass of material, and the step height permits the analysis to be calculated in accordance with the property being determined (e.g. titre or volume).

4. (Later examples.)

1933 C. D. BUCK *Compar. Gram. Greek & Latin* 93 Long vowels are shortened before other vowels in various dialects. .. When the second vowel is short it may be lengthened, resulting in what is known as 'quantitative metathesis'... Homer often shows the older forms.., but also in many cases the shortening and quantitative metathesis. **1973** A. H. SOMMERSTEIN *Sound Pattern Anc. Greek* ii. 69 Quantitative Metathesis. The need for this rule arises chiefly from the vocalism and accentuation of certain third-declension genitive case forms. **1978** *Language* LIV. 441 Thus the order of the rules required by this analysis is Pre-German Accentuation followed by Quantitative Ablaut followed by Germanic Accentuation.

5. *Chem.* Of a procedure or a reaction: acting on the whole quantity of a particular substance or species; having an efficiency or a yield of 100 per cent. Hence also used of the yield or product of such a process.

1905 *Proc. R. Soc.* A. LXXVI. 116 Its [*sc.* a possible new element] quantitative extraction from thorium salts has not yet been investigated. **1907** *Chem. Abstr.* I. 1539 The yield is almost quantitative and the product very pure. **1923** [see *QUALITATIVE *a.* b]. **1930** W. T. HALL *Textbk. Quantitative Analysis* xi. 140 For practical purposes, a reaction is complete or quantitative, as we often say, when less than 0·1 mg. remains in solution. **1962** COTTON & WILKINSON *Adv. Inorg. Chem.* x. 194 Diborane..is obtained in essentially quantitative yields by reaction of metal hydrides with boron trifluoride. **1964** N. G. CLARK *Mod. Org. Chem.* xi. 204 On careful combustion there remains a quantitative residue of metallic silver.

B. *sb.* **c.** = *QUANTIFIER 1 b.

1924 H. E. PALMER *Gram. Spoken Eng.* 45 Quantitatives and Numericals (mʌtʃ), (meni), (faiv).., etc.

quantitatively, *adv.* Add: **b.** *Chem.* Completely, entirely; with a yield of 100 per cent.

1911 F. SODDY *Chem. Radio-Elements* I. 26 The radium may be precipitated quantitatively by sulphuric acid. **1950** *Thorpe's Dict. Appl. Chem.* (ed. 4) X. 447/1 An equal quantity of barium chloride is added to ensure that the radium is carried quantitatively with the insoluble residue. **1974** *Nature* 1 Feb. 291/1 Prephenate is quantitatively converted to phenylpyruvate in 10 min at acid *p*H (0·1 N HCl).

quantitativist (kwǫntitēⁱ·tivist), *sb.* and *a.* [f. QUANTITATIV(E *a.* + -IST.] **a.** *sb.* A person for whom quantity is a criterion of value. **b.** *adj.* Resulting from an evaluation of quantity.

1957 R. K. MERTON *Social Theory* (rev. ed.) x. 396 The local influential is typically concerned with knowing *as many* people as possible. He is a quantitativist in the sphere of social contacts. **1972** *Human World* Feb. 21 The.. quantitativist illusion that the level of enlightenment must correspond to the amount of time spent between the school walls. **1974** B. PEARCE tr. *Amin's Accumulation on World Scale* II. iii. 452 It is by means of concrete historical explanation that we must account for each period of price increase in the nineteenth century, and not by means of a general quantitativist explanation.

‖ **quantité négligeable** (kantite negliʒāb'l). [Fr., lit. 'negligible quantity'.] A factor of no account, something insignificant.

1886 T. P. WHITE *Ordnance Survey U.K.* vi. 98 It is certain that among the details which would not be a *quantité négligeable*, would figure the trees of any particular district or country. **1913** S. SHAW *William of Germany* viii. 151 The resolve that as Emperor he would not allow Germany to be overlooked, to be treated as a *quantité négligeable*, in the discussion or decision of international affairs. **1921** BARON VON MARGUTTI *Emp. Francis Joseph & his Times* viii. 205 The old Sovereign apparently still regarded the Slavs as a *quantité négligeable*, as they had been at the beginning of his reign. **1973** E. OSERS tr. *Waldheim's Austrian Example* 7 The geopolitical position of Austria within the contact zone or testing ground of the great ideological power-groups of our time has given this small country a meaning that is far from that of a *quantité négligeable*.

quantitive, *a.* (Later examples.)

1958 T. G. E. POWELL *Celts* 182 It cannot be argued here whether it was prestige, or quantitive representation, that won for it eventually an exclusive position. **1959** *Times* 9 Sept. 16/7 The Four No Trump bid is regarded more often than not as quantitive.

quantity. Add: **1. d.** In surveying, *bill of quantity* (or *quantities*) (see quot. 1964).

1877 B. FLETCHER *Quantities* i. 5 The operations necessary to produce the schedule, or bills of quantities, from which builders make up their tenders, are: [etc.]. **1964** J. S. SCOTT *Dict. Building* 32 *Bill of quantities*, a list of numbered items, each of which describes the work to be done in a civil engineering or building contract. Each item shows the quantity of work involved... Those contractors who wish to do the work return the bill, with an extended price opposite each item. **1972** *Guardian* 20 June 10/6 When the architect and engineer have produced drawings, the quantity surveyor can begin 'taking off' (which really means reading the drawings) and 'working up' (which means determining the total quantities of the materials and labour requirements)... He can then produce his 'Bills of Quantity'.

13. (sense 8) *quantity output, production*; **quantity surveyor**: for def. read: a surveyor who estimates the quantities of labour and materials required for building and engineering work; (later examples); **quantity theory (of money)** the hypothesis that prices correspond to changes in the monetary supply; so *quantity theorist*.

1888 M. FREWEN *Econ. Crisis* i. 5 More emphatic still is John Stuart Mill's statement of the 'quantity theory'. 'That an increase of the quantity of money', wrote Mill, 'raises prices, and a diminution lowers them, is the most elementary proposition in the theory of currency.' **1895** *Econ. Jrnl.* V. 103 So far as concerns the possible causes on the side of *money* for the fall in prices, Lex denies that the 'quantity theory' affords any ground for speaking of an appreciation of gold. **1903** J. L. LAUGHLIN *Princ. Money* vii. 225 (*heading*) History and literature of the quantity theory of money. **1908** *Westm. Gaz.* 8 May 8/3 Bills which had been through the hands of the quantity surveyor and architect. **1912** I. FISHER *Purchasing Power of Money* p. vii, The main contentions of this book are at bottom simply a restatement and complification of the old 'quantity theory' of money. **1919** *Brit. Manufacturer* Nov. 42/1 Quantity output may mean cheap production, but the manufacture of more modest quantities need not be much inferior in this aspect. *Ibid.*, An immense home market.. has encouraged him to undertake big quantity production. **1928** E. O'NEILL *Strange Interlude* v. 159 The room is a typical sitting room of the quantity-production bungalow type. **1931** *Times Lit. Suppl.* 19 Feb. 124/2 The quantity theorists have always been baffled by variations in the public's habits and other factors. **1968** *Internat. Encycl. Social Sci.* X. 433 In its most rigid and unqualified form the quantity theory asserts strict proportionality between the quantity of what is regarded as money and the level of prices. **1972** Quantity surveyor [see 1 d above]. **1979** *Jrnl. R. Soc. Arts.* CXXVII. 445/1 The quantity surveyor's functions in the construction process may be described as cost planning, cost control, and the attainment of value for money expended.

quantizable (kwǫ·ntaizăb'l), *a.* *Physics.* [f. as next + -ABLE.] Capable of being quantized.

1935 J. DOUGALL tr. *Born's Atomic Physics* v. 101 Certain quantities can only take values which are whole numbers—they are called quantisable quantities. **1946** *Nature* 31 Aug. 309/1 Our solar system is quantizable according to the equation: $n \times 137^k$ = orbital impulse/(2 × planetary spin).

quantization (kwǫntaizēⁱ·ʃən). [f. next + -ATION.] The action of quantizing; the fact or state of being quantized. **a.** *Physics.* Cf. *QUANTIZE *v.* 1.

1922 *Rep. Brit. Assoc. Adv. Sci. 1921* 473 In some cases.. the quantisation can be done in several ways and each leads to a different set of permissible orbits, but the energy of each has the same set of values and so they give the same spectrum. **1922** *Proc. Cambr. Philos. Soc.* XXI. 80 (*heading*) A general condition for the quantisation of the conditionally periodic motions with an application for the Bohr atom. **1925** *Nature* 5 Dec. 849/1 It seemed possible to formulate certain general laws, the so-called rules of 'quantisation', by means of which the stationary states were to be chosen from the continuous manifold of such motions. **1940** GLASSTONE *Text-bk. Physical Chem.* i. 63 The existence of $2j + 1$ magnetic quantum numbers for each value of j implies that the electrons can take up $2j + 1$ different orientations in a magnetic field..: in other words, there should be a quantization of electron orbits. **1975** *Physics Bull.* July 311/1 To see the departure of the specific heat of solids from the classical Dulong Petit law due to quantization of lattice vibration energies we often need to go to temperatures of the order of 100 K.

b. *Telecommunications.* Cf. *QUANTIZE *v.* 2. Usu. *attrib.*, as *quantization distortion, level, noise*.

1947 *Bell Syst. Techn. Jrnl.* XXVI. 395 PCM involves the application of two basic concepts. These concepts are..the time-division principle and the amplitude quantization principle. **1948** *Proc. IRE* XXXVI. 1324/2 Representing the signal by certain discrete allowed levels only is called quantizing. It inherently introduces an initial error in the magnitude of the samples, giving rise to quantization noise. **1951** *Ibid.* XXXIX. 44 (*heading*) Quantization distortion in pulse-count modulation with nonuniform spacing of levels. **1953** A. T. STARR *Radio & Radar Technique* i. 32 Quantization could be used with any known system of modulation, e.g. the signal wave could be quantized and then used to modulate the amplitude or frequency of a carrier. **1975** D. G. FINK *Electronics Engineers' Handbk.* IV. 44 A quantization noise..is inevitably associated with all quantized signals. This noise can be made as small as desired by choosing enough quantization levels or, equivalently, making each quantization level small enough.

quantize (kwǫ·ntaiz), *v.* [f. QUANTUM + -IZE.] **1.** *trans. Physics.* To apply quantum theory to; *esp.* to restrict the number of possible values of (a quantity) or states of (a physical entity or system) so that certain variables can assume only certain discrete magnitudes that are integral multiples of a common factor.

1922 *Rep. Brit. Assoc. Adv. Sci. 1921* 473 For the specific heats of gases..it is necessary to 'quantise' rotations instead of vibrations. **1958** *New Scientist* 27 Feb. 29/1 Yukawa had been very impressed by the success of quantum mechanics..in explaining phenomena connected with the ordinary electromagnetic field. Such a field can be 'quantised' into photons—discrete packets of light waves. **1973** *Physics Bull.* Nov. 656/2 This amplification of gravity produces a theory which cannot be quantized by standard methods, however. **1975** *Nature* 17 Apr. 560/2 The problem of quantising gravity is a pressing one if a unified theory of all the forces of nature is to be obtained.

2. *trans. Telecommunications.* To approximate (a signal varying continuously in amplitude) by one whose amplitude is restricted to a prescribed set of discrete values.

1947 *Bell Syst. Techn. Jrnl.* XXVI. 409 Over and above these effects,..the background noise which is present to a greater or lesser extent in all communication circuits, is quantized by the PCM system. **1953** *Electronic Engin.* XXV. 148/1 If the signal is sampled before being quantized, harmonics (including the first) of the pulse repetition frequency will be present. **1953** [see *QUANTIZATION b]. **1972** *Physics Bull.* Jan. 44/1 In the new technique the signals from the eddy current probes are quantized by digital means. **1977** F. G. STREMLER *Introd. Communication Syst.* vii. 356 Suppose..we wish to quantize one-half a cycle of a one-volt (peak) sinusoid using eight discrete levels.

3. *transf.* and *fig.*

1956 *Kenyon Rev.* XVIII. 412 The sounds..are then quantized into their phonemes. **1965** *Revue Internat. de la Documentation* XXXII. 21/2 To do this it is necessary to quantize the texts by dividing them into convenient units. **1969** *Language* XLIV. 14 As Hoenigswald..remarked, 'The doctrine of gradual phonetic change may turn out to be a remnant from pre-phonemic days,' when the multi-dimensional continua of speech had not yet been successfully quantized. **1974** *Sci. Amer.* Dec. 132/2 Because curves can be coded to any desired precision by numbers, a symphony, like a painting or a poem, can be quantized and expressed by a number chain.

Hence **qua·ntizing** *vbl. sb.* and *ppl. a.*

1923 E. N. DA C. ANDRADE *Structure of Atom* ix. 147 The principle laid down for the quantising of angular momentum gives $mvr = nh/2\pi$, where n is a whole number. **1948** *Bell Syst. Techn. Jrnl.* XXVII. 456 Since quantizing noise is uniformly distributed throughout the signal band, its interfering effect..is probably similar to that of thermal noise with the same mean power. **1973** *Appl. Physics Lett.* XXIII. 41/1 Because of the quantizing longitudinal magnetic field, the conduction band is split into Landau levels. **1975** D. G. FINK *Electronics Engineers' Handbk.* IV. 44 The process of quantizing is irreversible since regardless of how small the quantization level Q is taken to be, an unresolvable uncertainty of $\pm Q/2$ is associated after quantizing with each amplitude value.

quantized (kwǫ·ntaizd), *ppl. a.* [f. prec. + -ED[1].] Subject to the restrictions imposed by quantization; able to occur with certain discrete values only.

1923 H. L. BROSE tr. *Sommerfeld's Atomic Struct. & Spectral Lines* iv. 212 Both [conditions] together demand that the electron move only in certain 'quantised' circles. **1937** G. GAMOW *Struct. Atomic Nuclei* iv. 67 The atomic nucleus, being a quantized system, is in general capable of existence in any one of a number of states of different energy. **1939** V. ROJANSKY *Introd. Quantum Mech.* iv. 145 The energy of a free particle is not quantized. **1966** C. KITTEL *Introd. Solid State Physics* (ed. 3) v. 134 The lattice contribution to the heat capacity of solids..approaches zero as the temperature approaches zero; this can be explained only if the lattice vibrations are quantized. **1973** *Physics Bull.* Dec. 715/3 The flux which is trapped in a superconducting loop is quantized in units of $h/2e$.

quantizer (kwǫ·ntaizəɹ). *Electronics.* [f. as prec. + -ER[1].] A device that quantizes a signal applied to it.

1948 *Bell Syst. Techn. Jrnl.* XXVII. 450 An actual quantizer (staircase transducer) has a finite overload value which must not be exceeded and hence can have only a finite number of steps. **1953** *Electronic Engin.* XXV. 146/2 The channel modulators of a pulse-length modulated T.D.M. system feed a common quantizer and coder. **1967** *Electronics* 6 Mar. 127/2 Sierra also offers a 'quantizer' that puts thermal contours..on the scope. **1975** C. L. & J. W. S. LIU *Linear Systems Analysis* ii. 48 Consider a discrete quantizer whose output $y(n)$ at any instant n is equal to the integral part of the input $x(n)$ if the fractional part of $x(n)$ is less than 0·5.

Quantometer (kwǫntǫ·mĭtəɹ). Also **quantometer.** [f. QUANT(ITY + -OMETER.] A type of automatic spectrograph, used esp. for the analysis of alloys.

Formerly a proprietary term in the U.S.

1927 *Official Gaz.* (U.S. Patent Office) 3 May 12/1 Francis Cutler Ellis..Chicago, Ill...*Quantometer*... Instrument for diagnosis and food and remedy testing by analysis of radiant energies. Claims use since Sept. 1, 1926. **1947** *Jrnl. Iron & Steel Inst.* CLVI. 78 A commercial model, the Quantometer, consists of source, dispersing, and recording units operating as one instrument. **1958** *Engineering* 21 Feb. 61/2 (Advt.), To meet the need for still greater speed there is now in use at Corby an automatic direct-reading spectrographic analyser known as a Quantometer. **1974** J. H. Dixon tr. *Torasov's Spectroscope* i. 6 The quantometer is used for the simultaneous quantitative emission analysis of several elements in steels or alloys.

quantophrenia (kwǫntofrī·niă). [f. Quant(itative *a.* + -o + *-phrenia* as in *hebephrenia*.] A term used for an obsession with and exaggerated reliance upon mathematical methods or results, esp. in research connected with the social sciences. So **quantophre·nic** *a.*

1956 P. A. Sorokin *Fads & Foibles in Mod. Sociol.* (1958) vii. 103 When the true quantitative method is replaced by pseudomathematical imitations; when the method is misused and abused in various ways; when it is applied to phenomena which, so far, do not lend themselves to quantification..then the approach misfires. Under these conditions, use of mathematical method becomes a mere quantophrenic preoccupation having nothing in common with mathematics and giving no cognition of the psychosocial world... The tidal wave is at present so high that the contemporary stage of the psychosocial sciences can be properly called *the age of quantophrenia and numerology.* **1964** *Encounter* Sept. 72 There is quantophrenia—an obsession with statistics as the sole ground of certitude in a changing world. **1975** *Times Lit. Suppl.* 14 Feb. 162/5 Lundberg remains a sociologist honest and reflective enough to have tried to give 'quantophrenia' and testability ..a firm intellectual base.

quantum. Delete ‖. For 'Pl. **quanta** (*rare*)' read: Pl. **quanta** (*rare* except in senses 5 and 6), † **quantums** (sense 5 only). **1. a.** *spec.* in *Law*, an amount, a sum (*of* money payable in damages, etc.).

1898 in *Southern Reporter* XXIII. 718/2 The quantum of damages as fixed by the lower court is, we think, too low. **1912** *Law Rep.* (House of Lords Appeal Cases) 688 The quantum of damage is a question of fact, and the only guidance the law can give is to lay down general principles. **1945** *Tulane Law Rev.* XIX. 626 In a large majority of jurisdictions the pecuniary condition of the defendant has no bearing on the *quantum* of compensatory damages awarded the plaintiff in an action for personal injuries. **1951** *Scots Law Times* 11 Aug. 181/1 There can never be any binding precedents on quantum of damages because a sum reasonable in the circumstances of case A might be grossly unreasonable in case B. *Ibid.*, Quantum must be considered afresh in every case having regard to the particular circumstances of that case. **1970** *Internat. & Compar. Law Q.* XIX. 126 Strict liability with an unbreakable limit should confine litigation to questions of quantum. **1974** *Times* 6 Feb. 7/1 The Court of Appeal dismissed an appeal on quantum of damages by Horizon Holidays Ltd.

5. *Physics.* A minimum amount of a physical quantity which can exist and by multiples of which changes in the quantity occur.

This use of *quantum* originated in Ger. in two classic papers by Planck and by Einstein. Planck introduced the concept of a quantum in *Verh. d. Deutsch. Physik. Ges.* (1900) II. 237ff. In that paper he assumed that the energy of an oscillator is always an integral multiple of an 'energy element' (G. *energieelement*, p. 242), i.e. a quantum (sense *5 a), but he did not call it a quantum; however he did use the word in a passing reference to the electronic charge ('das Elementarquantum der Elektricität', p. 245: = sense *5 b).

Einstein, in *Ann. d. Physik* (1905) XVII. 132ff., assumed that light is radiated in the form of what he called 'energy quanta' (G. *energiequanta*, p. 133: = sense *5 a).

The affinities of the following isolated use are not clear; it seems not to be related to Planck's use, and may derive rather from the senses in Dict.

1902 Ld. Kelvin in *Phil. Mag.* III. 257 According to the well-known doctrine of Aepinus,..positive and negative electrifications consist in excess above, and deficiency below, a natural quantum of a fluid, called the electric fluid, permeating among the atoms of ponderable matter. *Ibid.* 259 The neutralizing quantum of electrons [= 'atoms of resinous electricity'] for any atom or group of atoms has exactly the same quantity of electricity of one kind as the atom or group of atoms has of electricity of the opposite kind. The quantum for any single atom may be one or two or three or any integral number, and need not be the same for all atoms... The differences of quality of the atoms of different substances may be partially due to the quantum-numbers of their electrons being different.

a. A discrete quantity of electromagnetic energy proportional in magnitude to the frequency of the radiation it represents.

1910 *Sci. Abstr.* A. XIII. 556 The absorption of the corresponding light-quantum. **1913** *Rep. Brit. Assoc. Adv. Sci. 1912* 407 Assuming that an oscillator can only emit definite, discontinuous quantums of energy, Planck showed that their magnitude is proportional to the frequency. **1913** *Phil. Mag.* XXVI. 19 These calculations strongly suggest that an electron of great velocity in passing through an atom and colliding with the electrons bound will loose energy in distinct finite quanta. **1929** D. H. Lawrence *Pansies* 28 Look then Where the father of all things swims in a mist of atoms Electrons and energies, quantums and relativities. **1934** A. J. Mee *Physical Chem.* xix. 721 We can, in a few cases, induce fluorescence of shorter wavelength than that of the absorbed light, since the energy emitted is not only that of the absorbed quantum, but also that inherent in the system before the absorption. **1965** *Physical Rev. Lett.* XV. 1013/1 He^+ ions decaying spontaneously from the $3S$ state do so via the $2P$ levels in $\sim 1 \times 10^{-8}$ seconds with the emission of a 1640Å quantum followed by a 303Å quantum. **1978** *Sci. Amer.* June 69/2 Conversely, when the atom or molecule is de-excited, it drops back one full step or more and the energy difference is either radiated away as a quantum of electromagnetic energy or transferred directly, through a collision, to another atom or molecule.

b. An analogous discrete amount of any other physical quantity (as momentum, electric charge).

1914 *Chem. Abstr.* VIII. 1050 (*heading*) Existence of quantities of electricity which are smaller than the charge of the elementary quantum or the electron. **1923** H. L. Brose tr. *Sommerfeld's Atomic Struct. & Spectral Lines* iv. 199 We see that the rotator is to be quantised not in energy quanta but in quanta of moment of momentum... The moment of momentum must be a whole multiple of $h/2\pi$. **1931** H. P. Robertson tr. *Weyl's Theory of Groups* i. 43 The constant of proportionality was equal to the quotient of the *h* obtained by Planck from black body radiation and the elementary quantum of electric charge *e*. **1958** *Nature* 31 May 1524/1 (*heading*) Detection of single quanta of circulation in rotating helium II. **1969** *Sci. Jrnl.* Jan. 87/2 There is a possibility that one day a minimum absolute quantum of length may also be found in the universe. **1973** *Sci. Amer.* Jan. 88/3 Waves of elastic crystal vibrations generate quanta of sound called phonons.

c. More fully *quantum of action.* = **Planck's constant.*

1913 *Phil. Mag.* XXVI. 2 Whatever the alteration in the laws of motion of the electrons may be, it seems necessary to introduce..a quantity foreign to the classical electrodynamics, *i.e.* Planck's constant, or as it often is called the elementary quantum of action. **1922** *Rep. Brit. Assoc. Adv. Sci. 1921* 473 The essential feature of the [quantum] theory is the existence of a universal constant, the quantum $h = 6{\cdot}55 \times 10^{-27}$ erg sec., which in some way..controls exchanges of energy. **1923** B. Russell *ABC of Atoms* vi. 80 The quantity *h*, Planck's quantum, has been found to be involved in all the very minute phenomena that can be adequately studied **1933** *Nature* 25 Mar. 422/2 A causal description in the classical sense is possible only in such cases where the action involved is large compared with the quantum of action. **1956** E. H. Hutten *Lang. Mod. Physics* v. 179 We can measure simultaneous values of both parameters only in such a way that the numerical product of their inaccuracies is, at best, equal to the quantum of action h.

d. *fig.*

1960 R. W. Marks *Dymaxion World of B. Fuller* 10/1 Fuller regards all human experiences as energy events finite in extent. All experiments performed, books written, thoughts expressed, and structures completed, are finite energy events. Together they form a totality, a cornucopia of patterned quanta. **1962** P. Strevens *Papers in Lang.* (1965) v. 67 Teaching takes place by *quanta.* Whether the teacher realizes it or not, he can teach only in steps, though these vary in size. **1969** *Daily Tel.* (Colour Suppl.) 10 Jan. 32/2 Generalisations serve a purpose, but true understanding is made up of many discrete *quanta.* I can describe the Atlantic littoral thus and so; but I *know* it—thus: [etc.]. **1977** *Times* 4 Aug. 8/6 A fine quantum of derring-do ranging from icy Sweden to a storm-threatened Scottish islet.

6. *Physiol.* Orig. a small voltage of which integral multiples go to make up the end-plate potential measured at a neuromuscular junction; hence, the unit quantity of acetylcholine corresponding to this, multiples of which are released to transmit a nerve impulse across the junction.

1952 Fatt & Katz in *Jrnl. Physiol.* CXVII. 120 The experiment throws some new light on the action of calcium at the nerve-muscle junction: lack of calcium apparently reduces the e.p.p. in definite 'quanta'. **1954** del Castillo & Katz in *Ibid.* CXXIV. 560 It has been suggested that the end-plate potential (e.p.p.) at a single nerve-muscle junction is built up statistically of small all-or-none units... A convenient picture of how hundreds of such quanta..can build up an e.p.p. of, say, 70–80 mV is provided by the hypothesis that separate parcels of acetylcholine (ACh), released from discrete spots of the nerve endings, short-circuit the muscle membrane. *Ibid.* 574 Recent evidence indicating that ACh release occurs in discrete quanta. **1970** J. W. Phillis *Pharmacol. of Synapses* ii. 17 In addition to being released by stimulation, individual quanta are released from the terminal spontaneously... At the neuromuscular junction, the number of quanta available for immediate release is probably of the order of 1000. **1978** *Nature* 9 Feb. 561/1 Acetylcholine..is released from stimulated nerve terminals in packets or quanta, each containing roughly 10,000 molecules.

7. a. *attrib.* and *Comb.* (in sense *5), as *quantum energy, hypothesis, law, physics* (hence *quantum physicist*), *property*; **quantum advance** = **quantum leap*; **quantum chemistry,** the branch of physical chemistry concerned with the explanation of chemical phenomena in terms of quantum mechanics; so **quantum chemist,** an expert or specialist in this; **quantum-chemical** *a.*; **quantum chromodynamics** [Chromo-, after **quantum electrodynamics*], a quantum field theory in which the strong interaction is described in terms of an interaction between quarks that is mediated by gluons, both kinds of particle being assigned a quantum number called 'colour'; abbrev. *QCD; **quantum condition,** a condition resulting from, or forming part of, the application of quantum theory to a system; a condition that selects from the states allowed by classical physics those that are consistent with quantum theory; **quantum defect,** a number representing the degree to which an energy level of an atom with a single valence electron is displaced from the corresponding level of the hydrogen atom, being the amount by which the true principal quantum number of the level exceeds the effective value of the number; **quantum dynamics** = *Quantum mechanics; hence **quantum-dynamical** *a.*; **quantum effect,** a physical effect attributed to the existence of quanta; **quantum efficiency,** the proportion of incident photons that are effective in causing the decomposition of a molecule, the emission of a photoelectron, or similar photo-effect; **quantum electrodynamics,** the part of quantum field theory concerned with the electromagnetic field and its interaction with electrically charged particles; so **quantum-electrodynamic, -dynamical** *adjs.*; abbrev. *QED; **quantum electronics,** the branch of physics concerned with the practical consequences of the quantization of energy states and their interaction with electromagnetic radiation; so **quantum-electronic** *a.*; **quantum field theory,** a field theory that incorporates quantum mechanics and the principles of the theory of relativity; **quantum increase,** a sudden large increase; cf. **quantum jump*; **quantum jump,** an abrupt transition between one stationary state of a quantized system and another, with the absorption or emission of a quantum; also *transf.*, a sudden large increase or advance; **quantum leap,** a sudden large advance; cf. **quantum jump*; **quantum level,** an energy level in a quantized system; **quantum liquid,** a liquid that exhibits quantum effects on the macroscopic scale; **quantum number,** a number which enters into the expression for the value of some quantized property of a system (usu. a particle, atom, or molecule) and can assume only certain integral and sometimes half-integral values; also *transf.*, the property so characterized; **quantum orbit,** an orbit (of an electron in an atom) defined by a set of quantum numbers; **quantum solid,** a solid that exhibits quantum effects on the macroscopic scale; **quantum state,** a state of a physical (esp. atomic) system that is defined by a set of quantum numbers; a quantized state; **quantum statistics,** the statistics of the energy distribution of particles when the quantization of energy is taken into account; cf. **Bose–Einstein statistics*, **Fermi–Dirac statistics*; hence **quantum-statistical** *a.*; **quantum transition** = **quantum jump* (*lit.* sense); **quantum yield** = **quantum efficiency*. Also *Quantum mechanics, *Quantum theory.

1974 *Sci. Amer.* June 105/3 When these inferences are taken together with the differences between the two material cultures..one is led to conclude that the Upper Paleolithic represents a quantum advance in human cultural evolution. **1960** *McGraw-Hill Encycl. Sci. & Technol.* XI. 145/2 The most useful of these methods, the variation method, has produced most of the important quantum-chemical concepts. *Ibid.* 146/1 The success of this method depends..on the ability of the quantum chemist to guess at trial functions which are good approximations and at the same time contain parameters in such a form that *W* can be minimized without undue labor. **1970** *Sci. Amer.* Apr. 54/1 Since the introduction of the fundamental wave equation of quantum mechanics by Erwin Schrödinger in 1926, much of the work of quantum chemists has been focused on its solution for specific chemical systems. **1944** H. Eyring et al. (*title*) Quantum chemistry. **1963** *New Scientist* 14 Mar. 582/3 After a rather long incubation period, the new subject of 'quantum chemistry' has got into its stride and is gaining rapidly in strength. [**1976** *Physical Rev. Lett.* XXXVI. 1521 In an exact color SU(3) gauge theory (chromodynamics), the dynamics of confinement may be similar to the dynamics of the string model.] **1976** *Nature* 12 Aug. 538/1 The 'gauge field theories' are underlying not only weak-electromagnetic but perhaps also strong interactions (the new jargon here being quantum chromodynamics, or QCD, analogous to quantum electrodynamics). **1979** *Sci. Amer.* Aug. 157/2 No one has yet been able to derive the confinement of quarks from the underlying theory of quantum chromodynamics. **1923** *Physical Rev.* XXII. 547 This variation principle includes formally in a single equation the results of classical dynamics and the Sommerfeld quantum conditions. **1955** O. Klein in W. Pauli *Niels Bohr* 99 The importance of transformation groups for the formulation of quantum conditions in field theories..has been strongly emphasized. **1974** G. Reece tr. *Hund's Hist. Quantum Theory* vi. 89 The 'stationary states' were selected from the possible classical motions by 'quantum conditions' $I_k = hn_k$. **1930** Ruark & Urey *Atoms, Molecules & Quanta* vii. 194 The quantum defect is a measure of the departure of the spectral term from the hydrogenic term having the same total quantum number. **1970** G. K. Woodgate *Elem. Atomic Struct.* vi. 103 We consider the sequence isoelectronic with sodium... The ionization potentials for this sequence,..together with the quantum defect $\delta(s)$ ..are given below. **1932** *Physical Rev.* XL. 406 In solving the wave mechanical perturbation problem the distance between the interacting structures has been treated as a fixed parameter. Then quantum dynamical reasoning has been abandoned, and the remainder of the problem has been solved by the method of classical statistics. **1927** *Proc. R. Soc.* A. CXIII. 621 (*heading*) The physical interpretation of the quantum dynamics. **1967** CONDON & ODISHAW *Handbk. Physics* (ed. 2) VII. i. 3/1 These laws of quantum dynamics must involve the universal Planck constant..in an essential way; and the quantum laws must go over asymptotically into the classical laws, not involving *h*, as the scale of the phenomena is increased. **1914** *Chem. Abstr.* VIII. 3141 E. detd. the at. ht. of highly compressed He at temps. from 18° to 32° abs... A small quantum effect is apparent. **1946** *Physical Rev.* LXIX. 195 (*heading*) Quantum effects in the interaction of electrons with high frequency fields and the transition to classical theory. **1975** *McGraw-Hill Yearbk. Sci. & Technol.* 114/2 The interaction between two charged particles, classically treated, is given ..by Maxwell's electrodynamic equations, if the particles are in relative motion. The inclusion of quantum effects has led to a more general theory, called quantum electrodynamics. **1926** *Trans. Faraday Soc.* XXI. 453 In the photochemical isomeric change of maleic and fumaric acid, the quantum efficiency was found to be much smaller than unity. **1940** GLASSTONE *Textbk. Physical Chem.* xiii. 1135 According to the law of the photochemical equivalent one mol of absorbing substance should decompose for every $2{\cdot}854 \times 10^8/\lambda$ kg.-cal. of radiation absorbed... This relationship..permits the law to be tested experimentally. The results are expressed in terms of the quantum efficiency. **1978** *Nature* 16 Mar. p. xiv/3 Two versions of the new EMI photomultiplier tube..are available with..typical peak quantum efficiency of about 22%. **1965** *Physical Rev. Lett.* XV. 1013 (*heading*) Measurement of the quantum-electrodynamic level shift in the $n = 3$ state of (He^4). **1956** *Physical Rev.* CI. 1410 The quantum-electrodynamical fourth-order corrections for the intervals of the triplet fine structure of helium are calculated. **1927** *Proc. R. Soc.* A. CXIV. 243 Hardly anything has been done up to the present on quantum electrodynamics. **1955** L. ROSENFELD in W. Pauli *Niels Bohr* 70 They questioned the logical consistency of quantum electrodynamics by contending that the very concept of electromagnetic field is not susceptible, in quantum theory, to any physical determination by means of measurements. The measurement of a field component requires determinations of the momentum of a charged test-body; and the reaction of the field radiated by the test-body in the course of these operations would..lead to a limitation of the accuracy of the field measurement, entirely at variance with the premises of the theory. **1971** *Sci. Amer.* June 64/3 The laws of electricity and magnetism as they are now embodied in the equations of quantum electrodynamics represent the one and only area in physics where a single quantitative description has proved valid over the entire range of experiments for which it has been tested, from cosmic dimensions down to 10^{-15} centimeter. **1976** B. BOVA *Multiple Man* (1977) i. 11 The President..was protected by an invisible laser-activated shield... Fool-proof quantum-electronic security. **1959** *Jrnl. Appl. Physics* XXX. 956/1 An international conference on Quantum Electronics—Resonance Phenomena will be held..on September 14–16, 1959. The conference will consider basic problems in physics and electronics which are important to the increasing use of molecular and atomic resonance in masers, atomic clocks, and related devices. **1965** *Wireless World* Aug. 386/2 The film..covers a wide range of applications including quantum electronics in transistors, lasers and masers. **1972** *Physics Bull.* Sept. 562/1 Quantum electronics as a field of study dates from the use of stimulated emission for microwave amplification in 1954. **1921** *Discovery* Sept. 227/2 When the quantum energy of the exciting radiation exceeds this amount the whole K series [of X-rays] is excited. **1948** *Physical Rev.* LXXIV. 224/1 (*heading*) On infinite field reactions in quantum field theory. **1956** H. UMEZAWA *Quantum Field Theory* i. 11 The present quantum field theory was formulated (Heisenberg and Pauli (1929)) by extending quantum mechanics so as to satisfy the relativity requirements and to treat the various transmutations [of particles into one another]. **1978** *Sci. Amer.* Feb. 128/1 (*caption*) The creation and annihilation of particles and antiparticles is the characteristic process that distinguishes quantum field theories from 'classical' field theories such as Maxwell's or Einstein's. **1914** *Rep. Brit. Assoc. Adv. Sci.* *1913* 378 The quite definite result is obtained that..the exchange of energy between matter and ether must take place by finite jumps of amount..$\epsilon = h\nu$. This is, of course, the hypothesis, spoken of briefly as the quantum-hypothesis, which was first suggested by Planck. **1968** F. L. PILAR *Elem. Quantum Chem.* i. 8 Planck's own feeling, which persisted for many years, was that the quantum hypothesis itself could have no basic significance but rather was an artificiality which would eventually be replaced with a more reasonable alternative. **1973** *Sci. Amer.* May 8/2 Intellectual and other exchanges with China appear to be on the verge of a quantum increase. **1974** *Daily Tel.* (Colour Suppl.) 16 Aug. 17 Throughout this enormous area..people have been dying of diseases aggravated by malnutrition, just as they have died every year since man first inhabited the Sahel, but so far there has been no *quantum* increase in human mortality as a result of the lengthy drought. **1927** N. V. SIDGWICK *Electronic Theory of Valency* ii. 18 Bohr's theory is based on two fundamental postulates... The second..is that the electron radiates energy..only when it passes in a 'quantum jump' from one of these stationary states to another of smaller energy. **1937** E. C. KEMBLE *Fund. Princ. Quantum Mech.* viii. 290 The variation in the distribution function thus defined..is commonly interpreted as due to 'quantum jumps' from one energy level to the other caused by the radiation. **1955** *Sci. News Let.* 19 Feb. 116/2 Radioactive fall-out is the 'third quantum jump' in the history of modern weapons. The first quantum jump, Dr. Lapp explained, was the A-bomb that shattered Hiroshima. **1961** *Flight* LXXX. 907/1 On the subject of launch operations, Mr Debus claimed that a 'quantum jump' was necessary to meet the challenge of the lunar programme. **1966** *Guardian* 1 Jan. 8/1 This new escalation (or 'quantum jump', to use the latest addition to the bewildering mixture of metaphors) would look better if it were preceded by another bombing pause. **1974** G. REECE tr. *Hund's Hist. Quantum Theory* x. 129 While the emission and absorption of light seemed to be connected with a quantum jump, its dispersion did not. **1975** *Chinese Econ. Stud.* VIII. iv. 52 In old China, the issue of legal tender reached astronomical figures, leading to galloping inflation and quantum jumps in prices. **1916** *Chem. Abstr.* X. 1722 (*heading*) The quantum law and the structure of the hydrogen atom. **1967** Quantum law [see **quantum dynamics*]. **1970** *New Scientist* 3 Dec. 372/1 The ability of marine technology to take 'quantum' leaps in innovation means that a laissez-faire approach to the ocean mineral resources can no longer be tolerated. **1973** *Daily Tel.* (Colour Suppl.) 2 Nov. 27/2 Hovercraft, like many inventions of modern technology, are supposed to progress in quantum leaps. **1977** *New Yorker* 13 June 108/2 The imperial Presidency did not begin with Richard Nixon although under him abuses of the office took a quantum leap. **1931** G. GAMOW *Constitution of Atomic Nuclei* iii. 63 Some elements have rather complicated γ-ray spectra, while others have only a few lines... These facts are evidently connected with the strength of the initial excitation and the relative position of the quantum-levels in the different nuclei. **1960** CHALMERS & QUARRELL *Physical Examination of Metals* (ed. 2) xvi. 751 Above the true quantum levels there are further, 'empty' levels, representing states in which nuclei may exist momentarily before disintegrating. **1950** F. LONDON *Superfluids* I. 1 The 'superfluids' or 'quantum liquids' probably exhibit the most conspicuous phenomena of macroscopic physics which have not yet been integrated into molecular theory. **1967** [see *quantum solid* below]. **1975** *Physics Bull.* July 311/3 The electrons in a metal constitute a quantum liquid in this sense at all temperatures up to the melting temperature. [**1902** Quantum-number: see sense 5 above]. **1920, 1922** [see *N I. 4 b]. **1926**, etc. [see *L 6* b]. **1939** G. HERZBERG *Molecular Spectra & Molecular Struct.* I. i. 15 The azimuthal quantum number *l* gives us therefore the orbital angular momentum of the electron in units $h/2\pi$. *Ibid.* 18 In a magnetic or electric field, a precession of the angular momentum of an atom takes place... While classically the precession could take place at any angle to the field direction, according to quantum theory, only those angles are possible for which the components of the angular momentum in the direction of the field have the discrete values $m_l(h/2\pi)$, where $m_l = l, (l-1), (l-2),.., -l...$ m_l is called the magnetic quantum number of the electron. **1967** W. R. HINDMARSH *Atomic Spectra* vi. 70 If the magnetic field is so strong that its interaction with the magnetic moment of the atom is much stronger than the spin-orbit interaction, the orbital and spin angular momenta are no longer even approximately conserved, so that *L* and *S* are not well-defined quantum numbers. **1968** J. BERNSTEIN *Elementary Particles & their Currents* xiii. 211 The strong interactions of the strange particles are characterized by a new conserved quantum number in addition to the isotopic spin. This quantum number is the 'strangeness', *S*, or, equivalently, the 'hypercharge' *Y*. **1976** *Sci. Amer.* Jan. 45/1 Some quantum numbers, such as spin angular momentum and electric charge, are invariably conserved. **1923** H. L. BROSE tr. *Sommerfeld's Atomic Struct. & Spectral Lines* ii. 67 The quantum theory asserts that all these quantum orbits are stationary states of motion, that is they are traversed without radiation being emitted. **1928** Quantum orbit [see *PACKET *sb.* 1 h]. **1946** *Mind* LV. 161 The philosopher finds support in the quantum physicist's principle of complementarity. **1964** M. MCLUHAN *Understanding Media* (1967) vii. 73 Werner Heisenberg..is an example of the new quantum physicist whose over-all awareness of forms suggests to him that we would do well to stand aside from most of them. **1931** H. JOHNSTON tr. *Planck's Universe in Light of Mod. Physics* 22 The Principle of Relativity..has proved itself a reliable and eloquent guide in the new regions of Quantum Physics. **1971** *Sci. Amer.* Mar. 75 Quantum physics normally deals with natural phenomena on a submicroscopic scale. **1978** *Ibid.* Dec. 128/3 Quantum physics predicts that captured electrons can have only discrete energies, corresponding to the atomic energy levels described above. **1927** A. S. EDDINGTON *Stars & Atoms* 68 The property here referred to (the quantum property) is the deepest mystery of light. **1978** *Nature* 16 Mar. 291/3 The quantum properties of electromagnetic radiation. **1967** *Sci. Amer.* Aug. 85/2 Solid helium..is the only known example of a 'quantum solid', just as liquid helium is the only known example of a 'quantum liquid'. **1921** *Chem. Abstr.* XV. 1843 Schottky discusses..the Nernst heat theorem from the point of view of the internal 'quantum state' of the mols. composing the system under discussion. **1946** [see *POLARON]. **1972** *Sci. Amer.* Oct. 101/1 The individual nucleons move in discrete quantum states just as the electrons in the atom exist in discrete quantum states. **1958** *Physical Rev.* CXI. 1460 (*heading*) Quantum statistical theory of electron correlation. **1932** *Jrnl. Chem. Soc.* 373 We shall.. discuss the important conclusions which can be drawn from the interpretation of molecular spectra regarding the so-called quantum statistics in their relation to the nuclei. **1935** PAULING & WILSON *Introd. Statistical Mech.* viii. 219 The quantum statistics resulting from the acceptance of only antisymmetric wave functions is considerably different. **1972** *Physics Bull.* Dec. 709/1 It is our great good fortune that the only two substances that remain liquid down to the absolute zero obey different statistics (^{3}He: Fermi–Dirac, ^{4}He: Bose–Einstein) and thus allow us to study the differing effects of quantum statistics on condensed matter. **1924** *Physical Rev.* XXIV. 330 The term to be retained is..the combination overtone asymptotically connected to the particular quantum transition under consideration. **1927** FISHER & HARTREE tr. *Born's Mech. of Atom* ii. 54 Quantum transitions can be caused by light and by molecular impacts. **1927** *Jrnl. Amer. Chem. Soc.* XLIX. 2451 These new facts make possible a better conception of the mechanism of the photochemical decomposition of ammonia... Warburg measured the quantum yield and found it to be 4 quanta per molecule for light of wave length 2025–2140 Å. **1971** *Jrnl. Appl. Physics* XLII. 567/2 The quantum yield of the Ag–O–Cs cathode for visible light is less than 5×10^{-8} electron per photon.

b. Passing into adj. (cf. *QUANTAL *a.*).

1922 *Rep. Brit. Assoc. Adv. Sci.* *1921* 474 This suggests that many phenomena which at present are thought to be satisfactorily explained by dynamics are really quantum phenomena. **1924** *Physical Rev.* XXIV. 340 This connection of the classical and quantum differential absorption we shall term the correspondence principle for absorption. **1951** *Ibid.* LXXXII. 116/2 The quantum nature of the exchange of energy between free electrons and electromagnetic fields. **1967** *Sci. Amer.* Aug. 85/2 Perhaps the most perplexing characteristic of solid helium..is the fact that in spite of its unique quantum nature solid helium behaves in so many respects as a purely classical, or nonquantum, solid. **1975** *Nature* 20 Mar. 223/3 The book is concerned mainly with electrodynamics (both classical and quantum).

quantum mecha·nics. *Physics.* [f. QUANTUM + MECHANICS.] A mathematical theory of the motion and interaction of (esp. subatomic) particles that was developed from the old quantum theory and incorporates the concept of wave–particle duality, the uncertainty principle, and the correspondence principle; cf. **matrix mechanics*, **wave mechanics*.

This is not quite the sense in quot. 1922.

1922 *Rep. Brit. Assoc. Adv. Sci.* *1921* 473 The spectrum theory is far the most important branch of the quantum theory, as it has led and is still leading to extensions of quantum mechanics. **1925** *Proc. R. Soc.* A. CIX. 642 (*heading*) The fundamental equations of quantum mechanics. **1935** B. RUSSELL *Relig. & Sci.* vi. 151 The challenge has come through the study of the atom by the new methods of quantum mechanics. **1956** E. H. HUTTEN *Lang. Mod. Physics* v. 179 The mathematical formulae of quantum mechanics permit us to predict future events only within a certain margin of error. **1956** H. UMEZAWA *Quantum Field Theory* i. 1 Quantum mechanics and relativity are respectively characterised by the constants *h* and *C* and, when *h* and (1/*C*) are taken as vanishingly small, the results of these theories are identical with those of Newtonian mechanics. **1974** G. REECE tr. *Hund's Hist. Quantum Theory* x. 132 The first strictly valid version of quantum mechanics that was both logical and capable of generalization was provided by Heisenberg's paper of July 1925. **1978** *Sci. Amer.* Feb. 126/3 There is no workable theory of gravitation that is consistent with the principles of quantum mechanics. *Ibid.* 131/1 The present understanding of the fundamental laws of nature arose from three principles: special relativity, general relativity and quantum mechanics.

Hence **quantum-mechanical** *a.*, **-mechanically** *adv.*

1927 *Proc. R. Soc.* A. CXIV. 715 One can obtain the result..by using a quantum-mechanical argument. **1936** Quantum-mechanically [see *QUANTAL *a.* 2 c]. **1949** KOESTLER *Insight & Outlook* xi. 156 Quantum-mechanical concepts slowly permeate all spheres of physics, chemistry, and..biology. **1963** G. TROUP *Masers & Lasers* (ed. 2) iv. 58 It can be shown quantum-mechanically..that there is a definite probability that A will make the transition $1 \rightarrow 2$ while B makes the transition $3 \rightarrow 1$. **1968** G. LUDWIG *Wave Mech.* I. ii. 9 These equations..are the basis even today for the construction of modern accelerators, since quantum-mechanical effects are not involved in the motion of the particles in these devices. **1971** *Nature* 15 Jan. 158/2 The existence of such a low-lying σ transition would be a surprise to theoreticians, but quantum-mechanically it is not entirely out of the question.

‖ **quantum meruit** (kwǫ·ntǝm me·rŭ,it). *Law.* [L., 'as much as he has deserved'.] A reasonable sum of money to be paid for services rendered or work done, when the amount due is not determined by any provision constituting, or forming part of, a legally enforceable contract (see also quot. 1959). Also *attrib.* and as quasi-*adv.*

1657 H. GRIMSTON tr. *G. Croke's Rep.* (Charles I) 77 It is the usual way to lay down in certainty, *viz.* That he should pay for it *tantum quantum meruit, &c.*, and then to averre what it is reasonably worth, which being the common course and alwaies allowed, Judgment was therefore affirmed. **1659** in E. Bulstrode *Rep.* III. 86 How shall a Taylor be paid upon a *quantum meruit*? **1685** J. KEBLE *Rep.* I. 422 In action by executors on *indebitatus* for wares sold to pay *quantum meruit*, not shewing what the particulars were. **1718** W. SALKELD *Rep.* II. 557 *Quantum meruit* for meat, drink, &c. **1729** G. JACOB *New Law-Dict.* sig. H h h h 2, *Quantum meruit*, i.e. how much he has deserved, is a Man's Action of the Case,.. grounded upon the Promise of another, to pay him for doing any Thing so much as he should deserve or *merit*. If a man retains any person to do work or other thing for him..without any certain agreement; in such case the law implies that he shall pay for the same, as much as they are worth, and shall be reasonably demanded; for which *Quantum meruit* may be brought. **1832** in P. Bingham *Rep.* VIII. 16, I agree that, when a special contract is in existence and open, the plaintiff cannot sue on a *quantum meruit*. **1904** *Law Rep. King's Bench Div.* II. 329 Remuneration upon the basis of a quantum meruit in respect of work and labour done for the company at its request. **1919** *Brit. Manufacturer* Nov. 36/2 The owners could, therefore, sue under the old contract (the charter party) for 23s., the agreed freight, on each of the 1208 tons of steel billets; and, in addition, could sue on the new implied contract for a *Quantum Meruit* in respect of the 987 tons of general cargo. So the only question is the rate per ton at which their *Quantum*

Meruit should be calculated. **1959** JOWITT *Dict. Eng. Law* II. 1452/2 Where the failure to complete performance of the contract is due to the fault of the other party, the party not in default has the right to sue on a *quantum meruit* for the services which he has done under it. In its early history the action for *quantum meruit* was, no doubt, a genuine action in contract... In many cases the action is now founded on what is known as 'quasi-contract'. **1962** A. TURNER *Law of Trade Secrets* IV. iv. 346 Other expressions, like 'unjust enrichment', sometimes used by the courts are recovery in *quantum meruit* and recovery under 'quasi contracts', 'constructive contracts', or, contracts 'implied-in-law'. **1964** *Mod. Law Rev.* XXVIII. 353 The carrier deserves remuneration under the *quantum meruit* rule. **1973** *N.Y. Law Jrnl.* 1 Aug. 13/3 However, since the former attorneys have the right to elect whether they will accept their compensation on the basis of a presently fixed dollar amount quantum meruit or whether, still on the basis of quantum meruit, they will accept a contingent percentage instead [etc.]. **1975** S. J. STOLJAR *Hist. Contract at Common Law* ix. 109 If, as often happened, the work was undertaken at no specified price, the plaintiff could turn to another count in assumpsit becoming known as the *quantum meruit*, a claim not for a fixed but for a reasonable amount: what the work merited or was worth.

quantum sufficit. Add: **a.** (Further examples of *quant. suff.*)

1840 BARHAM *Patty Morgan* in *Ingol. Leg.* 1st Ser. 60 One glance was enough, Completely '*Quant. suff.*' As the doctors write down when they send you their 'stuff'. **1907** G. B. SHAW *John Bull's Other Island* p. xxv, It was hardly reasonable to ask Parnell to shed blood *quant. suff.* in Egypt..and then to expect him to become a Tolstoyan or an O'Connellite in regard to his own country. **1964** C. S. LEWIS *Discarded Image* i. 9 Popular iconography.. wishing to summon up the idea of the Medieval, draws a knight errant with castles, distressed damsels, and dragons *quant. suff.* in the background.

b. (Later example of *quant. suff.*)

1863 *Fraser's Mag.* Feb. 156/2 A *quant. suff.* is beaten up with water, which is strained off after standing half an hour.

quantum theory. *Physics.* [f. QUANTUM + THEORY[1].] A theory of matter and energy based on the concept of quanta (sense *5); *spec.* the branch of physics that was developed from the ideas in Planck's paper of 1900 and Einstein's of 1905 (see *QUANTUM 5), was extended by Bohr (1913) in relation to atomic structure, and later evolved into quantum mechanics and quantum field theory; *old quantum theory*, the early form of the theory, based on classical mechanics, prior to the development of wave mechanics and matrix mechanics in the mid-1920s.

[**1911** *Sci. Abstr.* A. XIV. 1702 The quanta theory of Planck and Einstein must be modified considerably to give a quantitative interpretation of the results obtained.] **1912** *Monthly Notices R. Astron. Soc.* LXXII. 677 The constant of nature in terms of which these spectra can be expressed appears to be that of Planck in his recent quantum theory of energy. **1926** *Times Lit. Suppl.* 19 Aug. 544/3 Relativity theory and quantum theory have not yet been properly assimilated. **1927** *Proc. R. Soc.* A. CXIV. 181 This equation..was obtained originally by Sommerfeld from relativistic considerations with the old quantum theory. *Ibid.* 243 The new quantum theory, based on the assumption that the dynamical variables do not obey the commutative law of multiplication, has by now been developed sufficiently to form a fairly complete theory of dynamics. **1958** W. HEISENBERG *Physics & Philos.* vi. 106 Quantum theory does not allow a completely objective description of nature. **1970** G. K. WOODGATE *Elem. Atomic Struct.* vi. 103 For small *l* the electron orbit is highly eccentric (to use the language of the old quantum theory). **1972** *Physics Bull.* Sept. 548/1 This book consists of five short chapters, on classical mechanics and the old quantum theory, the new quantum theory, many particle systems, valence theory and quantum theory of chemical reactivity. **1978** *Sci. Amer.* Feb. 132/3 Quantum theories of the gravitational force still have serious difficulties with infinities.

Hence **quantum-theoretical** *a.*, **-theoretically** *adv.*; **quantum theorist**, an expert or specialist in quantum theory.

1920 *Chem. Abstr.* XIV. 1637 (*heading*) Quantum theoretical principles of photochemistry. **1931** *Physical Rev.* XXXVIII. 1787/1 No quantum theoretical calculations have been made for particles of very high energy. **1935** *Amer. Jrnl. Math.* LVII. 429 The algebra II is known to the quantum theorist from the process of 'superquantizing'. **1939** G. HERZBERG *Molecular Spectra & Molecular Struct.* I. iii. 84 Quantum theoretically, emission of radiation takes place as a result of a transition of the oscillator from a higher to a lower state. **1959** K. R. POPPER *Logic of Sci. Discovery* ix. 222 In his derivation of the uncertainty relations, Heisenberg follows Bohr in making use of the idea that atomic processes can be just as well represented by the 'quantum-theoretical image of a particle' as by the 'quantum-theoretical image of a wave'. **1968** G. LUDWIG *Wave Mech.* I. ii. 19 These classical results were transformed by Bohr into quantum-theoretical results. **1976** *Nature* 1 July 17/1 General Electric advertised for a quantum theorist to look into the fundamental quantum processes involved in fluorescence.

quarantinable, *a.* Delete *rare* and add earlier and later examples.

1863 *Laws N.Y. State* ccclviii. 576 With existing quarantinable disease on board,..merchandise of the first class shall be landed at the quarantine warehouse. **1906** *Daily Colonist* (Victoria, B.C.) 25 Jan. 8/1 Foreign coasting vessels touching at Victoria to the number of 947 required inspection. No quarantinable disease occurred. **1961** *Times* 25 Aug. 12/2 There are six quarantinable diseases.

quarantine, *sb.* Add: **2. a.** Also, a period of seclusion or isolation after exposure to infection from a contagious disease; *transf.*, (a period of) isolation imposed in a similar way on an animal or thing. Freq. in phr. *in quarantine.* Also *fig.*

1855 [see *ASK *v.* 4 c]. **1879** *Investigation of Diseases of Swine* (Special Rep. No. 12, U.S. Dept. Agric.) 151 All strange hogs must be kept in quarantine for fourteen days before being allowed to run with healthy herds. **1891** *Boston Jrnl.* 7 Jan. 2/3 A rigid quarantine against firearms and firewater on the reservations of the Northwest is one of the prime requirements of the Indian problem. **1913–14** *Wellcome's Nurse's Diary* 209 Isolation required after exposure to: Asiatic Cholera..12 days' quarantine. **1922** *Encycl. Brit.* XXX. 925/2 Formerly great stress was laid on the value of quarantine; all plant imports were grown in a quarantine ground under the supervision of a Government botanist until it was certain that they had no disease. **1952** *Oxf. Jun. Encycl.* X. 357/2 All dogs.. have to be isolated in quarantine for 6 months in case they may be carrying rabies. **1971** *Sci. Amer.* Oct. 49/2 To guard against the possibility..of introducing pathogenic organisms from the moon, the lunar samples were placed in quarantine for seven weeks. **1978** W. GARNER *Möbius Trip* (1979) ii. 60 Putting him in emotional quarantine.

b. *spec.* in international politics, a blockade, boycott, or severance of diplomatic relations intended to isolate a nation, or the isolation caused by such action.

This use arose from a speech by F. D. Roosevelt, President of the U.S. (see quots. 1937).

1937 *N.Y. Herald Tribune* 6 Oct. 1/5 (*heading*) President calls for 'quarantine' of aggressors. *Ibid.* 1/8 President Roosevelt today challenged the effectiveness of a policy of neutrality in keeping the United States at peace and advocated instead a collective 'quarantine' of aggressor nations. **1938** *Sun* (Baltimore) 16 Nov. 1/8 Ambassador Wilson will not return soon to his post... It may even imply a 'quarantine' or an effort to quarantine Germany. **1945** *Richmond* (Va.) *News-Leader* 4 Oct. 2/7 (*heading*) Argentina faces diplomatic 'quarantine' by Pan-America. **1962** *Daily Tel.* 23 Oct. 1/2 Mr. Kennedy announced the following actions in response to the military build-up in Cuba. The blockade against delivery of offensive weapons. The 'quarantine' would be extended, if necessary, to other types of cargo and carriers. **1975** *Ibid.* 1 Oct. 1/7 A call by the International Transport Workers' Federation..for a 48-hour quarantine of services to and from Spain.

4. *quarantine-flag* (earlier example), *-ground*, *kennel*; *quarantine-breaking* adj.

1808 *Deb. Congress U.S.* 9 Mar. (1852) 1753 The ship arrived at the quarantine ground, near the harbor of Boston. **1835** J. E. ALEXANDER *Sk. Portugal* xi. 265 After some delay before we could get our yellow quarantine-flag struck, we were allowed to land. **1852** G. COGGESHALL *Second Series of Voyages* xiii. 82 We were requested to proceed immediately to the quarantine ground. **1867** 'MARK TWAIN' in *Daily Alta California* (San Francisco) 18 Oct. 1/4 This kind of conversation did no good, further than to give a sort of dismal interest to our quarantine-breaking expedition, and so we dropped it. **1942** E. E. DALE *Cow Country* 203 Wide strips were left for trails across the Outlet and lands were also set aside for quarantine grounds. **1976** T. HEALD *Let Sleeping Dogs Die* i. 11 To prevent it [*sc.* rabies] being imported all dogs coming in to Britain had to spend six months in quarantine kennels. **1977** *Hongkong Standard* 14 Apr. 8/5 A friend visited the Government Quarantine Kennels at Shatin recently and was distressed and appalled at the neglect of the poor animals awaiting their death, particularly the puppies.

quarantine, *v.* Add: **1. a.** Also *transf.* and *fig.*; *spec.* in sense 2 b of the *sb.*

1860 *Harper's Mag.* June 137/2 Duelling had become epidemic among the midshipmen at the Gosport navy-yard. A determined effort was made..to suppress the practice. The entire body of reefers were 'quarantined', i.e. confined to the limits of the yard. **1870** W. M. BAKER *New Timothy* i. 13 The business of these [ministers] is with human nature, and from exactly that are they quarantined for years. **1937** *N.Y. Times* 6 Oct. 1/8 President Roosevelt today pledged his Administration to a 'concerted effort' with other peace-loving nations to 'quarantine' aggressor nations. **1938** [see *NOSE COUNT]. **1938** [see *QUARANTINE *sb.* 2 b]. **1945** *Sun* (Baltimore) 28 Sept. 11/2 At school, they find themselves 'quarantined' and they are the butt of jibes and social ostracism. **1953** P. C. BERG *Dict. New Words* 132/1 *Quarantine, v.t.*, to isolate (a nation). **1962** *Listener* 12 Apr. 623/2 They think that, given the Communist Powers' publicly proclaimed hostility to the West, the whole lot of them should be quarantined, as the U.S.A. quarantines China. **1976** *O.E.D. Suppl.* sv. *L* 7, LRL, Lunar Receiving Laboratory (building where astronauts and lunar samples are quarantined for a period after returning from the moon). **1980** *Early Music* Apr. 255/2 In this setting the melody is not quarantined in the tenor register.

c. To isolate (an area) by the imposition of quarantine.

1890 *Stock Grower & Farmer* 24 May 7/3 The state [*sc.* of Nebraska] is strictly quarantined against all cattle from Texas. **1955** *Sci. Amer.* June 82/2 An outbreak of disease may be localized by quarantining the infected area.

3. *intr.* To go into quarantine.

1928 *Daily News* 7 Aug. 7/3 The Mauretania..is expected to 'quarantine' at New York at 10 a.m. tomorrow.

‖ **Quarant' Ore** (kwarant ōᵊ·re). Also **Quarantore.** [It., contraction of *quaranta* forty + *ore*, pl. of *ora* hour.] = *forty hours* s.v. *FORTY *a* e.

1623 *Ven. Eng. College, Rome MS. Scritt.* 29.5.1*a.* f.4, By the church doore, which by chaunce was open by reason that the Quarante Hore were celebrated there at the same tyme. **1839** N. WISEMAN *Let.* in P. Devine *Life Fr. Ignatius of St. Paul* (1866) III. viii. 255 My idea was borrowed from my..friend, Charles Weld, and consisted in *Quarant' Ore*,..making the circuit of all England, so that by day and night the Adorable Sacrament might be worshipped through the year. **1859** A. D. HOPE *St. Philip Neri* v. 16 It was also the means of introducing into Rome, A.D. 1548, the devotion of the Quarant' Ore, which had been first practised in Milan A.D. 1534. **1890** GASQUET & BISHOP *Edward VI & Bk. Common Prayer* iv. 54 The devotions known as the benediction of the Blessed Sacrament and the *Quarantore.* **1923** C. MACKENZIE *Parson's Progress* xi. 135 If the authorities remonstrated with him for holding such a service as Creeping to the Cross on Good Friday, he remonstrated with them for allowing such vulgar innovations as the Stations of the Cross or the Devotion of the Quarant'ore. **1974** *Oxf. Dict. Chr. Ch.* (ed. 2) 524/2 *Forty hours' devotion* (also known as the *Quarant' Ore* or *Quarantore*), a modern Catholic devotion in which the Blessed Sacrament is exposed..for for a period of *c.* forty hours, and the faithful pray before it by turns throughout this time.

quare (kwēᵊɹ), *a. dial.* Also **quair.** [repr. dial. pronunc. of QUEER *a.*[1]] = QUEER *a.*[1] Also, in Ulster English, used as a general intensifier, esp. in phr. *quare and* —, very, extremely. Hence **qua·rely** *adv.*

quare fellow = *queer fellow* s.v. *QUEER *a.*[1] 1 a.

1805 E. CAVANAGH *Let.* 20 Aug. in *Russ. Jrnls. M. & C. Wilmot* (1934) II. 179 Tis *quair* things I have been seeing! **1805** —— *Let.* 4 Oct. in *Ibid.* II. 185 It was *quairly* made. **1871** E. EGGLESTON *Hoosier Schoolmaster* iii. 32 'What a quare boy Shocky is!' remarked Betsey Short, with a giggle. 'He just likes to wander 'round alone.' **1880** W. H. PATTERSON *Gloss. Words Antrim & Down* 81 Quare, Queer, *adj.* very '*quare* an' nice' = very nice. **1896** J. BARLOW *Mrs. Martin's Company* 13 Sure I know the roof's quare and bad. **1896** M. HAMILTON *Across Ulster Bog* xi. 92 You're mended quarely this last while. **1900** M. O'NEILL *Songs of Glens of Antrim* 17 Now we're quarely betther fixed. **1938** M. K. RAWLINGS *Yearling* vi. 55 Hit's mighty quare you toted a dog along wouldn't be no good to you. **1941** [see *JIST]. **1949** C. GRAVES *Ireland Revisited* i. 21 One aged groom said: '..There's a fine, mettlesome lot of gerrls here today, but they look very quare in thon harness.' **1956** B. BEHAN *Quare Fellow* I. 4 What was the commotion last night round in D. Wing? Did the quare fellow get a reprieve?.. Now which quare fellow do you mean? The fellow beat his wife to death..was reprieved. *a* **1966** 'M. NA GOPALEEN' *Best of Myles* (1977) 49 I've a quare bit of news for you. The brother's nose is out of order. **1977** G. B. ADAMS in D. Ó Muirithe *Eng. Lang. in Ireland* 67 Mine ye, A was quare an gled tae get anntae ma settle bed thaat naght.

quarenden. Add: Now usually with spelling **quarrenden.** (Further and later examples.)

1851 R. HOGG *Brit. Pomol.* 67 Devonshire Quarrenden. .. A very valuable and first-rate dessert apple. **1870** TROLLOPE *Vicar of Bullhampton* vii. 40 The quarantines are rare this year. **1905** *Westm. Gaz.* 11 Aug. 10/1 One grower in the West of England obtained 20s. a bushel for his Devonshire Quarrendens. **1907** *Ibid.* 31 Aug. 7/2 English apples..are a poor crop, except Worcesters and Quarantines—the latter an early cheap fruit. **1921** *Contemp. Rev.* Oct. 559 The Quarrendens are gone. September saw them out. **1945** H. J. MASSINGHAM *Wisdom of Fields* vii. 133 Red and sweet Quarrendons on the orchard trees. **1969** *Oxf. Bk. Food Plants* 48/1 'Devonshire Quarrendon'. Known before 1650, it was possibly originally French. It has a deep crimson fruit with white juicy flesh.

quaresimal (kware·simăl), *a. rare*—[1]. [ad. It. *quaresimale* Lenten.] Of a meal: having the qualities of Lenten fare; meagre, austere.

1923 JOYCE *Let.* 17 Dec. (1966) III. 84 Can we not have a quaresimal dinner somewhere together?

quark (kwǭɹk, kwāɹk), *sb. Physics.* [Invented word, associated with 'Three quarks for Muster Mark!' (Joyce *Finnegans Wake* (1939) II. iv).

'I employed the sound "quork" for several weeks in 1963 before noticing "quark" in "Finegans Wake", which I had perused from time to time since it appeared in 1939... The allusion to three quarks seemed perfect... I needed an excuse for retaining the pronunciation quork despite the occurrence of "Mark", "bark", "mark", and so forth in Finnegans Wake. I found that excuse by supposing that one ingredient of the line "Three quarks for Muster Mark" was a cry of "Three quarts for Mister..." heard in H. C. Earwicker's pub.'—M. Gell-Mann, private let. to Ed., 27 June 1978.]

Any of a group of sub-atomic particles (orig. three in number) conceived of as having a fractional electric charge and making up in different combinations the hadrons, but not detected in the free state.

1964 M. GELL-MANN in *Physics Lett.* VIII. 214/2 A simpler and more elegant scheme can be constructed if we allow non-integral values for the charges. We can dispense entirely with the basic baryon b if we assign to the triplet t the following properties: spin $\frac{1}{2}$, $z = -\frac{1}{3}$, and baryon number $\frac{1}{3}$. We then refer to the members $u^{\frac{2}{3}}$, $d^{-\frac{1}{3}}$, and $s^{-\frac{1}{3}}$ of the triplet as quarks q and the members of the anti-triplet as anti-quarks q̄. [*Note*] James Joyce, Finnegan's [*sic*] Wake (Viking Press, New York, 1939) p. 383. **1965** *New Scientist* 4 Mar. 575/2 Just as atoms are composed of particles (protons, neutrons and electrons) so may the heavy particles themselves be made up of combinations of simpler entities, called 'quarks'. **1967** *Observer* 23 Apr. 2/6 If quarks exist, they would represent a more fundamental building brick of matter than any yet known. **1972** *Daily Colonist* (Victoria, B.C.) 24 Feb. 5/2 The physicists hope to make the first observation of 'quarks', which many theorists believe are the fundamental building blocks,..by studying the activity of a rare and elusive sub-atomic particle called the omega-minus. **1973** L. J. TASSIE *Physics of Elementary Particles* xi. 146 Mesons have $B = 0$ and are made up of a quark and an antiquark. **1973, 1974** [see *PARTON]. **1976** *Sci. Amer.* Nov. 50/1 The *u* quark has a charge of $+2/3$, and the *d* quark and the *s* quark each have a charge of $-1/3$. **1977** *Nature* 21 July 201/1 Quarks..have not been found free in nature; and if present theories are correct they never will be: they are thought to be permanently confined to the interior of the particles they compose. *Ibid.* 204/1 Recently hadrons containing a new, heavier quark—the c-quark (for 'charmed')—have been discovered. The mass of the c-quark is thought to be roughly 1,500 MeV. The old quarks are much lighter: the u- and d-quarks may even be massless while the s-quark's mass is about 300 MeV. **1978** [see *PSI 1 b]. **1978** *Sci. Amer.* Oct. 67/1 The upsilon resonances present physics with an embarrassment of riches: an unexpected family of new particles composed of an unexpected fifth quark.

quark, var. *QUAWK *sb.*

quarrel, *v.* Add: **2.** Also with *over*.
1868 MAYNE REID *White Squaw* xxviii. 133 Ere long they [*sc.* wolves] could be seen skulking through the enclosure and quarrelling over the corpses. **1883** G. MOORE *Mod. Lover* I. xii. 244 Here a group of Cupids quarrelled over some masks and arrows. **1939** G. B. SHAW *In Good King Charles's Golden Days* 24 She has put us to shame for quarrelling over a matter of which we know nothing. **1961** *Middle East Jrnl.* XV. 3 The Istiqlal quarreled over foreign policy, labor politics and economic development.

quarrenden, var. QUARENDEN in Dict. and Suppl.

quarried, *ppl. a.*[2] Add: **b.** *Physical Geogr.* Eroded or broken off by glacial quarrying; = *PLUCKED *ppl. a.* 4.
1909 *Jrnl. & Proc. R. Soc. N. S. Wales* XLIII. 265 Moutonnées..if large..appeared to be abraded on the up slope, and heavily quarried on the downslope. **1930** *Prof. Papers U.S. Geol. Survey* No. 160. 90/2 Muir..described long trains of glacially quarried blocks which he had observed in the vicinity of Tenaya Lake.

qua·rried, *a.* [f. QUARRY *sb.*[3] + -ED[2].] Of flooring: paved with quarries. Of a window: decorated with quarries.
1842 G. FRANCIS *Dict. Arts* s.v. *Quarry*, Quarried pavements are by no means uncommon in old village churches. **1856** GEO. ELIOT in *Westm. Rev.* X. 56 In those days, the quarried parlour was innocent of a carpet. **1954** M. RICKERT *Painting in Brit.: Middle Ages* 231 *Quarried glass*, window panels divided into squares or diamonds, each containing an ornamental or heraldic motif.

quarrion (kwǫ·riən). Also quar(r)ian. [Prob. Aboriginal name.] An Australian parrot, *Leptolophus hollandicus*, which has grey plumage with white and yellow patches; = COCKATIEL. Also *attrib.*
1901 A. J. CAMPBELL *Nests & Eggs Austral. Birds* 622 The Grey and Yellow Top-knotted Parrot ('Quarrion', native name among bushmen) flies round about water-holes. **1934** *Bulletin* (Sydney) 26 Sept. 21/3 Quarians caught by broken wings on telephone-wires and emus held by the leg in fences are other casualties I've come across. **1938** N. W. CAYLEY *Austral. Parrots* 112 The Cockatiel (also called Cockatoo Parrot and Quarrian) was met with during Cook's voyage. **1943** W. HATFIELD *I find Australia* v. 87 Quarrion parrots and ring-necks, rosellas and parakeets,..and magpies and butcher-birds (singing shrikes) added their morning warbles to the screeching and trilling. **1964** *People* (Austral.) 16 Dec. 38 The quarrians, sometimes known as cockaties or cockatoo parrots, are far from home. **1966** EASTMAN & HUNT *Parrots Austral.* 176 Call-note in flight is distinctive, and is a field mark in indicating the quarrion's presence long before it is sighted.

quarromes, quarron. For † *Obs.* read *Obs.* or *arch.* and add: Also **quarroms, quarrons,** (Later examples.)
1846 *Swell's Night Guide* 128/2 *Quarroms*, a body. **1922** JOYCE *Ulysses* 48 White thy fambles, red thy gan And thy quarrons dainty is. **1932** AUDEN *Orators* III. 105 Salmon draws Its lovely quarrons through the pool.

quarry, *sb.*[1] **4.** Delete † *Obs.* and add later example.
1884 T. SPEEDY *Sport* xix. 360 We have not above half-a-dozen times seen the peregrine in the act of making a quarry.

quarry, *sb.*[2] Add: **4.** *quarry-face, -pit* (later example), *-wagon*; **quarry-water** (earlier example).
1893–4 R. O. HESLOP *Northumb. Words* II. 557 *Quarry-fyess*, the quarry face; its perpendicular side. **1936** *Discovery* Oct. 317/1 The skull..is thought to be still buried in the quarry-face. **1974** *Environmental Conservation* I. 38/1 Quarry-face risks are by no means confined to high country where population is sparse. **1911** J. MASEFIELD *Everlasting Mercy* 4 In the old quarry-pit they say Head-keeper Pike was made away. **1937** BLUNDEN *Elegy* 15 Above the square With plodding quarry-waggons filled. **1838** C. LYELL *Elements of Geol.* I. iv. 74 It is desirable to shape the stones which are to be used in architecture while they are yet soft and wet, and while they contain their 'quarry-water'.

quarry, *sb.*[3] Add: **2.** (Later examples.) Also occas. round in shape.
1913 F. S. EDEN *Anc. Glass* iv. 82 Round quarries, set close together in rows, are..formed in lieu of rectangular quarries. **1970** H. BRAUN *Parish Churches* viii. 111 The glass of medieval days was..set as a mosaic of diamond-shaped 'quarries' fixed together with a network of delicate tooled strips.
attrib.
1899 R. GLAZIER *Man. Hist. Ornament* 98 'Quarry glass', square or diamond in shape, with brown enamel details, was frequently used, where simple masses were desired. **1971** *Country Life* 20 May 1248/1, I have had an estimate made..for filling all the nave and one chancel window with quarry glass of a very pleasing though simple kind.
4. *Comb.*, as **quarry-tile** (see quot. 1940); also *attrib.*; hence **quarry-tiled** *a.*
1940 *Chambers's Techn. Dict.* 692/2 *Quarry tile*, the common unglazed, machine-made paving tile not less than ¾ in. in thickness. **1953** [see *chip-board* s.v. *CHIP *sb.*[1] 9 a]. **1966** *Listener* 28 July 128/2 Rough concrete and quarry-tile floors like a farmhouse kitchen. **1970** G. F. NEWMAN *Sir, You Bastard* 258 He rapped his knuckles against the brown quarry-tiles in frustration. **1976** *Outdoor Living* (N.Z.) I. II. 9/2 You might choose to have concrete, bricks or quarry tiles or it might suit the house more to have a timber surface for your sunny area. **1979** *Arizona Daily Star* 5 Aug. (Advt. Section) 18/9 See this family oriented 3 bedroom home with its quarry tile floors. **1960** *Farmer & Stockbreeder* 22 Mar. 66/3 The covered bullock yard at Drayton has..a flat quarry-tiled feeding floor edged with a 6 in kerb for silage.

quarry, *v.*[2] Add: **1. b.** (Later examples.)
1936 R. CAMPBELL *Mithraic Emblems* 57 The gypsies quarried from the gloom, For their carouse a silver hall. **1958** L. DURRELL *Balthazar* vi. 140 Were these words of Pursewarden's quarried from his own experience? **1975** *New Yorker* 29 Apr. 6/1 (Advt.), Dick Wellstood, a subtle and inventive pianist, reproduced the raw materials.. that the old-master pianists of the thirties and forties quarried their styles out of.
2. b. *Physical Geogr.* = PLUCK *v.* 1 b in Dict. and Suppl.
1874 *Overland Monthly* Aug. 179/1 The size of the blocks, their abundance along the line of dispersal, and the probable rate of motion of the glacier which quarried and transported them, form data by which..the rate of block denudation may be reached. *Ibid.* 180/1 They had been quarried from the base of the ridge. **1909** *Jrnl. & Proc. R. Soc. N. S. Wales* XLIII. 264 Frequently the ice impact had been of such nature that a rock block had been quarried across the dominant joint structure. **1955** LONGWELL & FLINT *Introd. Physical Geol.* xii. 191 The bottom of the glacier breaks off blocks of bedrock and quarries them out, especially from surfaces unsupported on their downstream sides. **1976** J. E. SANDERS et al. *Physical. Geogr.* x. 346 Typically, the remaining mountain rim towers high above the bottom of a cirque because centuries of frost wedging enables the glacier to quarry deeply into the rock.
quarrying *vbl. sb.* (further examples).
1904 *Jrnl. Geol.* XII. 574 The glacier will be efficient as the agent for débris removal; the result, therefore, must be quarrying and excavation, and basal sapping. **1969** D. J. EASTERBROOK *Princ. Geomorphol.* xvi. 314 Storm waves are especially effective where rocks along the shore are highly jointed or bedded, and are thus vulnerable to quarrying.

quart, *sb.*[2] (Later *attrib.* examples.)
1976 D. MUNROW *Instruments of Middle Ages & Renaissance* 44/3 Praetorius gives the following sizes of curtals: 1. Quint Bass; 2. Quart Bass. **1977** *Early Music* Oct. 570 (Advt.), [Recorders] The standard range is from Garklein to Bass, the Michael Praetorius range extends to a Quart Bass in C.

quartal (kwǭ·ɹtăl), *a. Mus.* [f. L. *quartus* fourth + -AL.] Of a harmony: based on the interval of the fourth.
1937 *Musical Q.* XXIII. 178 Once we make our choice in favour of quartal harmony, we must be ready to accept all the logical consequences. **1938** J. YASSER *Mediæval Quartal Harmony* III. 87 Unlimited freedom in unison and octave parallelism turned out to be one of the greatest obstacles to completing the rationalization of the quartal harmonic system. **1944** W. APEL *Harvard Dict. Mus.* 619/1 Quartal harmonies have been recommended to replace tertian harmonies in harmonizations of Gregorian chant. **1955** A. HUGHES in *New Oxf. Hist. Mus.* (rev. ed.) II. 329 The two-part version of Brit. Mus. Harl. 524 seems to have been written in 'quartal' harmony, i.e. harmony based on the fourth as the most important interval. **1970** W. APEL *Harvard Dict. Mus.* (ed. 2) 6/2 Attempts have been made to replace this style with..archaic idioms such as quartal harmonies or parallel organum.

quartel, var. *CUARTEL.

quarter, *sb.* Add: **I. 1. b.** (Earlier and later examples.) Cf. *MAUVAIS QUART D'HEURE.
[*a* **1851**: see MUSIC *sb.* 11.] **1875** TROLLOPE *Way we live Now* II. lxii. 70 He was prepared..to console himself when the bad quarter of an hour should come with the remembrance that he had garnered up a store. **1909** *Daily Chron.* 30 Aug. 4/7 The 'bad quarter of an hour' we all know was first given a name by the heartless Louis XIII., who, looking at his watch on the day of the execution of Cinq-Mars, supposed that the poor young fellow 'passait alors un mauvais quart d'heure'. **1922** C. MACKENZIE *Altar Steps* xxi. 233 Mark fancied that it would be the prelate who would have the unpleasant quarter of an hour. **1937** M. SHARP *Nutmeg Tree* xviii. 232 Susan was in for a bad quarter of an hour.
II. 6. a. Delete † *Obs.* and add later examples.
1959 I. & P. OPIE *Lore & Lang. Schoolch.* ix. 167 A one-man High-Street confectioner..was found to be offering..*Bassett's Liquorice Allsorts 7d.* per quarter. **1977** *Jackson's of Piccadilly Price List* 2/2 [Ox tongue] £0.48 per qtr [i.e. quarter].
7. d. *U.S.* The fourth part of a mile.
1827 J. F. COOPER *Prairie* I. iv. 56, I can make myself heard a mile in these open fields, and his camp is but a short quarter from us. **1868** H. W. WOODRUFF *Trotting Horse* vii. 84 What's the use of a horse going a quarter fast? Now, they must go a quarter fast before they can go a mile fast. **1878** J. H. BEADLE *Western Wilds* ii. 31 It was weeks before I could walk a quarter.
8. c. (Further examples.) Also without article, as *quarter of an hour*, etc. Also (*Sc.* and *N. Amer.*), 'a quarter *of* (or *till*) (a certain hour)', a quarter to (the hour specified).
1871 *Sci. Amer.* 11 Feb. 102/2 When everything was tightened..and the propellor arranged to cause elevation, it was just quarter of one o'clock. **1894** A. ROBERTSON *Nuggets* 165 His Excellency the Governor wants to see you, detective, at a quarter to eleven sharp. **1912**, etc. [see *OF *prep.* 4 c]. **1913** C. MACKENZIE *Sinister St.* I. II. i. 141 In the 'quarter' (as the break was now called) Michael would stand on..the step that led down..into the schoolground. **1920** J. S. CLOUSTON *Carrington's Cases* ix. 135, I found myself sitting in a first-class smoking carriage with nearly quarter of an hour to spare. *Ibid.* xiii. 237 It was then quarter-past eleven. **1933** P. GODFREY *Back-Stage* i. 14 Once more the call-boy appears. 'Shall I call 'the quarter', sir?' **1949** H. KURATH *Word Geogr. Eastern U.S.* ii. 30/2 In the greater part of the Midland..*quarter ti'l eleven* is current. **1952** M. LASKI *Village* vii. 119 If I'm not there by quarter to, you'll know I couldn't make it. **1963** R. I. McDAVID *Mencken's Amer. Lang.* 298 Americans may say *quarter to*, *quarter of* or *quarter till*, the last being characteristic of Pennsylvania and its dependencies, including the upland South. **1966** H. KEMELMAN *Saturday the Rabbi went Hungry* (1969) ii. 21 He said..that traffic would be heaviest between a quarter of and a quarter past seven. **1969** A. GLYN *Dragon Variation* v. 142 He checked the time on his Omega Seamaster. It would be just a quarter of three in New York.
e. *Sport.* One of four equal periods of play in a match; also *gen.*, the fourth part of the time taken to play a match.
1911 P. H. DAVIS *Football* viii. 115 The periods of the game, the halves,..were replaced by quarters. **1922** P. D. HAUGHTON *Football & how to watch It* ix. 191 In contrast to the preceding period this quarter was marked by excellent play. **1954** *New Yorker* 6 Nov. 87/1 The play of the afternoon came in the middle of the final quarter. **1963** *Times* 29 Apr. 4/6 Mellor soon recovered their balance to take a 3–0 lead in the first quarter. **1969** *Sun-Herald* (Sydney) 13 July 48/2 Footscray made a great fight of it in the final quarter. **1972** J. MOSEDALE *Football* ix. 130 Playing on an 80-yard field the teams were deadlocked near the end of the fourth quarter. **1976** *Eastern Even. News* (Norwich) 9 Dec. 19/8 In the last quarter, Reading gave UEA and their supporters a scare by scoring a well-worked try which was converted. **1979** *Tucson (Arizona) Citizen* 20 Sept. 1D/2 The young Warriors battled Sahuaro to a 7–7 draw through three quarters before falling, 16–13, in the season opener.
III. 14. a. Also *spec.*, the Latin Quarter of Paris (see *LATIN *sb.* 5).
1919 W. S. MAUGHAM *Moon & Sixpence* xxvii. 117 Lots of fellows in the Quarter share a studio. **1926** E. HEMINGWAY *Sun also Rises* I. v. 37 'What do you do nights, Jake?'.. 'Oh, I'm over in the Quarter.' *a* **1967** A. RANSOME *Autobiogr.* (1976) xii. 120 In those days the Quarter did its best for hard-up students, and I was able to furnish my studio for next to nothing.
15. c. (Earlier and later examples.)
1724 H. JONES *Present State of Virginia* iv. 36 The Negroes live in small Cottages called Quarters. **1760** G. WASHINGTON *Diary* 26 Feb. (1925) I. 131 Began Plowing the Field by the Stable and Quarter for Oats and Clover. **1799** I. WELD *Trav. N. Amer.* xi. 84 Their quarters, the name whereby their habitations are called, are usually situated one or two hundred yards from the dwelling house. **1909** 'O. HENRY' *Roads of Destiny* xvii. 282 Almost the entire population of the quarters volunteered their aid. **1916** J. B. THOBURN *Stand. Hist. Oklahoma* I. 261 'The quarters'..formed a picturesque feature of the old time plantation life. **1935** Z. N. HURSTON *Mules & Men* I. iv. 85 It sauntered on down the bark-covered road and into the quarters just as if it had really wanted to come. **1949** B. A. BOTKIN *Treas. S. Folklore* IV. i. 551 The 'South's tradition of good cooking'..belonged originally to the 'big house' rather than to the 'quarters' and the cabin.
26*. In various colloquial shortened and abbreviated forms. **a.** *U.S. Football.* = *QUARTERBACK *sb.* 2 a.
1893 W. C. CAMP *Bk. College Sports* 120 The criss-cross or double pass is another excellent example of a disguised play, the ball being passed by the quarter to one of the backs. **1907** *St. Nicholas* (N.Y.) Sept. 1013/2 A line man could..take the ball from the quarter. **1914** P. WITHINGTON *Bk. Athletics* 58 In handling the team the quarter must have absolute command.

b. (*a*) = *quartermaster-sergeant* s.v. QUARTERMASTER 2 c; (*b*) = QUARTERMASTER 1 a.

1917 A. G. EMPEY *Over Top* 304 Quartermaster-Sergeant, or 'Quarter' as he is called. A non-commissioned officer in a company who..takes charge of the company stores. **1963** M. LOWRY *Ultramarine* ii. 60 Well, it's your business to get me up, quarter.

c. *pl.* = *quarter-finals* (see sense 30 below).

1978 *Guardian Weekly* 5 Feb. 24/2 The other semi-final was disappointing. Roscoe Tanner..had upset Bjorn Borg in the quarters. **1978** *Times* 4 July 19/3, I had never won a match on grass at Wimbledon and here I am in the quarters.

V. 27. a. *quarter-bottle, century, hour, litre, truth* (after HALF-TRUTH); *quarter-armed, -hourly, -striking, -witted* (after HALF-WITTED *a.*) adjs.

1881 F. DAY *Fishes Gt. Brit. & Ireland* I. 239 *Gasterosteus gymnurus*... The quarter-armed or smooth-tailed stickleback. **1907** *Yesterday's Shopping* (1969) 99/2 *Saumur, sparkling*..In original hampers of 1 Dozen ½ bots. **1915** H. G. WELLS *Boon* ix. 333 One of those quarter-bottles of Perrier Jouet on a tray. **1977** J. R. L. ANDERSON *Death in City* v. 81, I ordered a quarter bottle of cognac. **1902** *Westm. Gaz.* 21 July 4/1 To put the result in quarter-century periods. **1920** H. G. WELLS *Outl. Hist.* xxix. 265/2 The opening quarter century of the Christian era was troubled by a usurper. **1979** *Bookseller* 23 June 2818/1 The Warsaw Bookfair continues towards its quarter century. **1883** 'MARK TWAIN' *Life on Mississippi* xxxvi. 392 My uneasy spirit kept dragging me back at quarter-hour intervals. **1977** *Detroit Free Press* 11 Dec. 24-A/1 The head of the department [should] have at least ..90 quarter hours of criminal justice courses completed. **1929** J. OWEN *Shepherd & Child* iv. 46 The church clock..had a quarter-hourly chime. **1978** J. SHERWOOD *Limericks of Lachasse* iv. 48 [He] had drunk only a quarter-litre of light carafe wine. **1959** *Times* 6 Mar. 12/5 A Breguet gold and enamelled quarter-striking, quarter-repeating clock watch. **1977** *Gay News* 7–20 Apr. 22/2 It was such dangerously oversimplified quarter-truths that led to the vilification of ——. **1979** *Daily Tel.* 12 Dec. 16 Mr Timothy Raison's article is a distressing collection of quarter truths and specious arguments. **1864** A. WALLACE *Scottish Tales* III. 38 A quarter-witted individual from Muthil. **1972** P. GREEN *Shadow of Parthenon* 128 They vaguely assume their young readers to be either quarter-witted miniature adults or innocent prelapsarian angels.

29. *quarter-knee* (KNEE *sb.* 7 a).

1941 C. O'BRIEN *Sea-Boats, Oars, & Sails* ii. 22 Breast-hook and quarter-knees..connect the gunwales with the stem and transom respectively.

30. quarter-ball *Billiards*, a ball that strikes another so that a quarter of the one overlaps a quarter of the other; **quarter-binding** (examples); now also, this style of binding using materials other than leather; **quarter-bloke** *Mil. slang*, a quartermaster(-sergeant); **quarter-blood** *U.S.*, one whose descent is only one fourth derived from the blood of a particular race (esp. Amer. Indian) or breed; also as quasi-*adj.*; **quarter-boat** *U.S.*, a boat containing living quarters for river workmen; **quarter-bound** *a.* (examples); **quarter-bred,** (*b*) *N.Z.* = *QUARTERBACK *sb.* 1; also *attrib.* or as *adj.*; **quarter-breed** *U.S.*, the offspring of a half-breed and a white; a quarter-blood; also *attrib.*; **quarter-calf** = *quarter-binding* (in calf); **quarter-caste** *Austral.* and *N.Z.*, a person of mixed breed, having one-quarter Aboriginal or Maori and three-quarters white descent; also *attrib.*; **quarter-chord** *Aeronaut.*, a quarter of the length of a chord of an aerofoil, *spec.* such a distance measured backwards from the leading edge; freq. *attrib.*, as *quarter-chord line, point*; **quarter-elliptic(al)** *adjs.*, applied to a leaf spring having the profile of a quarter of an ellipse; **quarter-finals** *pl.*, the four matches constituting the round before the semi-finals in a tournament; also *sing.*, one of these four matches; also *attrib.*; **quarter girth measure,** *HOPPUS measure; **quarter-in-the-slot** *a. U.S.*, actuated by the fall of a quarter inserted through a slot (in a machine) (cf. *penny-in-the-slot* s.v. PENNY 12 b); **quarter leather** = *quarter-binding* (in leather); **quarter-light,** (*b*) a small triangular side-window on a motor vehicle for ventilation and the admission of light; also *attrib.*; **quarter-moon** (*a*) delete † and add later examples; also *attrib.*; **quarter-note,** substitute for def.: (*a*) = *quarter-tone*; (*b*) *U.S.* a crochet; **quarter peal** *Bell-ringing*, a peal comprising one quarter of the number of changes in a full peal; **quarter pole,** add: *U.S.* (earlier and later examples); **quarter-racing** *U.S.*, the holding of quarter-races; also *attrib.*; **quarter-round** (further examples); **quarter-saw** *v. trans.*, to saw (a log) radially into quarters; to produce (a board) by quarter sawing; **quarter sawing** *vbl. sb.*, the method or action of producing boards by sawing a log radially into quarters and then sawing each quarter into boards so that the growth rings make angles of greater than 45° with the faces of the boards; **quarter-sawn** *ppl. a.*; **quarter-section** (earlier example); **quarter stretch** *U.S.*, (a part of) a racecourse that is a quarter of a mile long; **quarter-tonal** *a.*, based on quarter tones; so **quarter-tonality; quarter-tone** (further *attrib.* examples); **quarter-track,** (*b*) a track recorded on magnetic tape so that four such tracks can be accommodated side by side; usu. *attrib.*; also as *adv.*, using this width of tape; **quarter-turn,** (*b*) (example); also as *v. trans.* and *intr.*; also **quarter-turning** *vbl. sb.* (see quot. 1901); **quarter-wave** *a. Physics*, having a thickness or a length equal to a quarter of the wavelength transmitted or received; *quarter-wave plate*, a plate of a birefringent substance cut parallel to the optic axis and of such a thickness that it introduces a time difference of a quarter of a period between ordinary and extraordinary rays passing normally through it.

1873 J. BENNETT *Billiards* 34 If the half of one overlaps the half of the other, it is a half ball; and so on for a quarter ball. Anything less than a quarter ball is called a fine ball. **1912** MONK & LAWRENCE *Text Bk. of Stationery Binding* 140 Quarter binding. 55. **1932** A. F. COLLINS *Book Crafts for Schools* iii. 27 'Quarter-binding'..has the stronger material..on the back, and the weaker material ..on the sides. **1978** A. W. JOHNSON *Thames & Hudson Man. Bookbinding* 216 *Quarter binding*, an economical covering method in which the spine and part of the sides are covered in one material and a cheaper one is used on the remainder. **1919** *Athenæum* 1 Aug. 695/2 The Q.M.S. (the colour-sergeant or 'Flag' of the Old Army) is always called the 'Quarter Bloke' or 'The Bloke'. **1920** *Punch* 18 Aug. 137/2 It's great..To eat a daintier kind of grub than quarter-blokes provide. **1944** *Gen* 30 Dec. 55/2 Nickly overstepped the mark when he suggested to the quarter-bloke..that he was flogging the rations. **1950** C. MACINNES *To Victors Spoils* i. 21 I'll drop back there and talk to his quarter-bloke. **1845** *Knickerbocker* Mar. 236 Of this description was a quarter-blood [*sc.* Indian], of great beauty. **1873** J. H. BEADLE *Undevel. West* xix. 355 He had four children, only quarter-blood, but differing very much in shade. **1878** —— *Western Wilds* ii. 26 The straight black hair, and nose just aquiline enough to give piquancy to the countenance, indicated the quarter-blood. **1943** *Sun* (Baltimore) 11 Dec. 11/5 Medium shorn domestic fleeces have had a further small sale, mostly quarter-blood. **1929** *Ibid.* 23 Oct. 1/3 The President and his immediate party left Cincinnati..aboard the Greenbrier..and three other light craft—quarter boats, they are called—for the remaining members of the party. **1962** A. DAVISON *In Wake of Gemini* 228 A quarterboat is an operational center for the maintenance and repair department of the U.S. Army Corps of Engineers, Mississippi River Commission. **1888** C. T. JACOBI *Printer's Vocab.* 108 *Quarter bound*, books bound with back only in leather. **1929** A. J. VAUGHAN *Mod. Bookbinding* II. 121 (*caption*) A Quarter Bound Book. *Ibid.* IV. 217 *Quarter Bound*, where the back and some portion of the sides only of the binding consist of one material, and the remainder of the sides of another. **1960** G. A. GLAISTER *Gloss. Bk.* 338/1 Quarter-bound: a book bound with either leather spine and cloth sides, or cloth spine and paper sides. **1979** *London Rev. Bks.* 25 Oct. 11/2 (Advt.), Quarter-bound in leather. **1891** R. WALLACE *Rural Econ. Austral. & N.Z.* xviii. 259 In 1890, the better portion of the greasy quarter-bred wool fetched 1s. 2½d. *a* **1948** L. G. D. ACLAND *Early Canterbury Runs* (1951) 370 *Comeback*, a sheep three-quarters merino and one quarter long wool..but in New Zealand I think these sheep are often called quarterbreds or quarter-backs. **1826** T. L. MCKENNEY *Sk. Tour to Lakes* (1827) 387 Three were full blood, the remainder half breeds, and quarter breeds. **1880** *Harper's Mag.* Dec. 31 All four were of mixed blood their mother having been a beautiful French quarter-breed. **1909** *Lady's Realm* Feb. 465/1 El-Soo was a full-blooded Indian, yet she exceeded all the half-breed and quarter-breed girls. She was a treasure. **1956** *Library* XI. 81 The binding has no corner-pieces; and so is properly called 'quarter-calf'. **1948** D. BALLANTYNE *Cunninghams* I. i. 6 Being up the duff to a young quarter-caste..was no joke. **1952** R. FINLAYSON *Schooner came to Atia* x. 51 The crew with the exception of the quartercaste mate were all Maori. **1966** *Times* 28 Mar. (Austral. Suppl.) p. ix/4 Aboriginal people..vary from full-bloods to quarter-castes. **1976** *Times Lit. Suppl.* 9 Apr. 417/1 Prindy, an eight-year-old quarter-caste who sees himself as purely aboriginal, in spite of his fair hair and grey eyes. **1979** *Church Times* 9 Mar. 4/3 Bishop Reeves is a 'quarter-caste' Maori and a graduate of St. Peter's College, Oxford. **1946** *Jrnl. R. Aeronaut. Soc.* L. 436/2 The centre of pressure is at the half-chord instead of approximately at the quarter-chord point. **1947** C. F. TOMS *Introd. Aeronaut.* i. 26 The quarter-point of the mean chords lies very nearly on the quarter-chord line of the wing. **1957** L. L. BECKFORD *A.B.C. of Aeronaut.* 98/2 This angle, known as Sweep Back, is measured between the lateral axis and a line drawn a quarter-chord back from the leading edges. **1959** J. L. NAYLER *Dict. Aeronaut. Engin.* 207 The quarter-chord line is the line joining the quarter points of the chords across the span of the wing. **1967** *Jane's Surface Skimmer Syst. 1967–68* 12/1 Aerofoil section NACA 0009. Sweepback at quarter-chord 30°. **1926** C. T. B. DONKIN *Elem. Motor Vehicle Design* xviii. 253 The bending moment in the chassis frame set up by the reactions of a quarter-elliptic spring is very considerable, and the type is seldom used for heavy cars except in the form of a short subsidiary spring. **1963** BIRD & HUTTON-STOTT *Veteran Motor Car* 53 The characteristic reversed quarter-elliptic rear springs appear on the 5-litre model. **1909** R. W. A. BREWER *Motor Car* xiv. 140 When quarter-elliptical springs are used they may be either shackled to the side springs or pinned to them direct. **1927** *Daily Express* 28 July 1/5 Miss Helen Jacobs..scored a signal success in the quarter-finals of the Essex County Invitation Tournament. **1932** *News Chron.* 23 Sept. 2/4 The quarter-finals of the Canadian Women's Open Golf Championship. **1941** G. MARX *Let.* 23 June (1967) 27 Art plays Frank Parker in the quarterfinals of the 55th Annual Los Angeles Tournament. **1976** *Lancs. Even. Post* 7 Dec. 15/5 Morecambe's quarter final game at Runcorn is a vital one. **1977** *Whitaker's Almanack 1978* 583/2 Newcastle United were fined £4000..for fielding a weakened team in the quarter-final of the Anglo-Scottish Cup. [**1894** W. STEVENSON *Wood* 194 The Hoppus measure by string, quarter girth.. on round timber, is an overmeasure in favour of the buyer.] **1924** [see *HOPPUS]. **1954** W. E. HILEY *Woodland Managem.* ix. 127 Quarter girth or 'hoppus' measure. The volume of a felled log is determined by its length and the area of the cross section half way along it. The length is measured by a long tape,..and the middle girth by a specially marked short tape, known as a quarter-girth tape. **1903** R. L. MCCARDELL *Conversat. Chorus Girl* 80 Mama de Branscombe had a quarter-in-the slot gas meter put in. **1938** L. M. HARROD *Librarians' Gloss.* 124 Quarter leather. A term used to describe a book with a leather spine and cloth sides. **1963** B. C. MIDDLETON *Hist. Eng. Craft Bookbinding Technique* xi. 160 It was not uncommon on the Continent in the Middle Ages for books to be bound in quarter-leather. **1938** *Times* 13 Oct. 8/4 The quarter lights are taken as far aft as possible. **1972** *Police Rev.* 8 Dec. 1588/2 The campaign includes 200,000 posters, 1½ million car quarter-light stickers, and 250,000 shop-window stickers. **1976** 'Z. STONE' *Modigliani Scandal* III. i. 113 He..[was] driving with the quarter-light open and enjoying the fresh air. **1947** L. P. HARTLEY *Eustace & Hilda* v. 91. The quarter-moon was resting on the roofs. **1977** A. DESAI in P. Collenette *Winter's Tales 23* 19 He..went about dividing the melon into quarter-moon portions. **1958** Quarter note [see *EIGHTH *a.* 3]. **1959** WESTRUP & HARRISON *Collins Music Encycl.* 524/1 *Quarter-note*, American for 'crotchet'. **1888** A. P. HEYWOOD *Treat. on 'Duffield'* vii. 53 (*heading*) (1296) Quarter peal. **1931** E. MORRIS *Hist. & Art Change-Ringing* iii. 53 The above twice repeated will come round at the quarter peal end. **1980** *Times* 7 Apr. 3/1 Bellringers at the parish church rang a quarter peal. **1857** Quarter pole [see *peanut boy* s.v. *PEANUT 1 b]. **1868** H. WOODRUFF *Trotting Horse* xxxi. 259 At the quarter-pole she had recovered her stroke. **1975** *New Yorker* 3 Mar. 73/1 Susan's Girl..led past the quarter pole. **1784** J. F. D. SMYTH *Tour in U.S.* I. ii. 22 In the southern part of the colony and in North Carolina, they are much attached to *Quarter racing*, which is always a match between two horses, to run one quarter of a mile streight [*sic*] out. **1889** *Harper's Mag.* Sept. 554/1 Foot-racing for the men and quarter-racing for the horses. **1974** *New Yorker* 29 Apr. 83/2 His journey into the center of the quarter-racing world. **1963** C. R. COWELL et al. *Inlays, Crowns, & Bridges* iii. 23 A quarter-round bur for contra-angle handpieces is used to cut 2-mm. pinholes. **1975** *New Yorker* 24 Feb. 56/3 He..addressed the axe to the quarter-round log. **1898** S. B. GREEN *Forestry in Minnesota* 299 Quarter-sawing... The log is first quartered and then sawed into boards, cutting then alternately from each face of the quarter of the log. **1907** WEBSTER, Quarter-saw, *v.t.*; -sawed or -sawn. **1931** *Harper's Mag.* June 62/1 No one rived the beams for his ceiling, or quarter-sawed oak for his chairs. **1934** *Archit. Rev.* LXXVI. 64/1 When logs are riven or quarter-sawn the large rays which form the silver grain are revealed to the fullest extent. **1966** A. W. LEWIS *Gloss. Woodworking Terms* 74 Quarter-sawn boards shrink less and are less liable to warp then other boards. **1968** Quarter sawing [see *rift sawing* s.v. *RIFT *sb.*[2] 4]. **1974** *Islander* (Victoria, B.C.) 29 Dec. 15/2 When the logs have reached the proper degree of dryness staves will be quarter sawn from them. That is, the flat boards will radiate out from the centre of the log like segments of an orange. **1806** *Deb. Congress U.S.* (1852) 9th Congress 2 Sess., App. 1032 The public lands are now sold in sections, half sections, and quarter sections. **1834** *Southern Lit. Messenger* I. 182/1, I pulled and pulled till I got out of sight, and turned down the quarter stretch. **1883** H. WATTERSON *Oddities Southern Life* 439 He ran a quarter stretch down the low grounds of the base. **1934** S. R. NELSON *All about Jazz* i. 13 Maddening is that persistent beat of the tom-toms and these quarter-tonal intervals gradually rising to an overwhelming climax. **1930** *Proc. Musical Assoc.* Apr. 92 We are dogged by such words as tonality,..quartertonality, modality. **1947** *Penguin Music Mag.* Sept. 11 The romantic composers of the nineteenth century..needed a new instrument—neo-modality, atonality, polytonality, quarter-tonality. **1891** C. R. DAY *Music & Mus. Instruments S. India & Deccan* ii. 20 The quarter-tone system used in Syria. **1934** C. LAMBERT *Music Ho!* v. 311 The quarter-tone quartets of Aloys Haba..differ from the quartets of Brahms only through being written in the quarter-tone scale. **1959** WESTRUP & HARRISON *Collins Music Encycl.* 524/1 Alois Hába has written a number of compositions..for quarter-tone piano, and for quarter-tone harmonium. **1978** P. GRIFFITHS *Conc. Hist. Mod. Music* v. 53 Ives had explored atonality, free rhythm, quarter-tone harmony. **1962** R. E. B. HICKMAN *Magnetic Recording Handbk.* (ed. 3) iii. 29 Present day domestic magnetic tape recorders normally employ dual track (half-track) recording on ¼ in. tape, although four track (quarter track) recording, with alternate tracks recorded in the same direction, is also common practice. **1962** A. NISBETT *Technique Sound Studio* iv. 82 Correction can be made by..replaying only part of the full recorded track: e.g. replaying..a half-track recording quarter-track. **1967** P. SPRING *Tape Recorders* iv. 41 A correct head alignment is very much more important than in the case of a quarter-track tape recorder. **1975** G. J. KING *Audio Handbk.* x. 226 (*caption*) A mono recorder lays one track on each half of the tape, the track then having approximately the width of two quarter tracks. **1934** D. L. SAYERS *Nine Tailors* II. i. 73 Rector was saying the other day as she [*sc.* a bell] did soon ought ter be quarter-turned. **1954** W. FAULKNER *Fable* 303 It made a rigid quarter-turn. *Ibid.* 384 Some twenty men with a sergeant, who halted and quarter-turned and stood them at ease.

1964 G. C. Kunzle *Parallel Bars* ix. 403 Quarter turn into handstand on one bar, squat off with straight legs dismount. 1901 H. E. Bulwer *Gloss. Technical Terms Bells* 3 *Quarter-turning*, re-attaching a bell to its 'stock' at right angles (or less) to its former position with reference to the latter, in order that the 'clapper' may strike on a fresh segment of the 'sound-bow'. 1979 *Church Times* 5 Oct. 5/1 The bells [were] unsafe as they were. The bell-founders had recommended quarter-turning. 1882 L. Wright *Light* xiv. 298 This then is our 'quarter-wave' plate, which should be at once mounted between two glasses in balsam, and its working planes marked on the edges by scratching with a diamond, or quartz crystal. 1937 Jenkins & White *Fund. Physical Optics* xvi. 357 When a quarter-wave plate is oriented at an angle of 45° with the plane of the incident polarized light the emerging light is circularly polarized. 1943 C. L. Boltz *Basic Radio* xvii. 265 The $\frac{1}{2}\lambda$ aerial is in two halves... From the centre ends hang two wires $\frac{1}{4}\lambda$ long. The feeder is then tapped to the quarter-wave line by moving the contacts up or down until the correct impedance is found. 1970 D. W. Tenquist et al. *University Optics* II. iii. 109 Quarter-wave plates are usually made of quartz or of mica (sandwiched between glass plates). 1977 S. W. Amos *Radio, TV & Audio Techn. Ref. Bk.* xxi. 28 It is sometimes necessary to be able to change the input impedance of a $\lambda/2$ dipole from its normal value of 73Ω without inserting a separate quarter-wave transformer.

quarter, *v.* Add: **10. a.** Also, of birds of prey flying over their hunting grounds.

1919 T. A. Coward *Birds Brit. Isles* I. 309 Sharing with other Harriers the habit of closely and diligently quartering the ground with buoyant easy flight, the Hen-Harrier more frequently interrupts its progress by hovering. 1946 D. C. Peattie *Road of Naturalist* iii. 39 The hawks and the falcons quartered the dazzling playa. 1976 L. Brown *Brit. Birds of Prey* x. 121 When returning to the roost in the evening they [*sc.* Montagu's harriers] often travel straight and quarter the ground much less than they would when hunting.

d. (Earlier and later examples.)

1883 'Mark Twain' *Life on Mississippi* iii. 51, I see a black something floating on the water away off to stabboard [*sic*] and quartering behind us. 1938 M. K. Rawlings *Yearling* xx. 260 His bear was quartering from him, but he was able to draw a bead on the left cheek from the rear.

11. a. Also *fig.*

1824 C. A. Bowles *Let.* 24 Jan. in E. Dowden *Corr. Southey* (1881) 48, I keep quartering, or trying to quarter, for a yard or so, and then down goes the wheel into the old groove. I cannot keep out of blank verse.

qua·rterback, *sb.* **1.** *Austral.* and *N.Z.* (See quots.)

1891 [see *come-back *sb.*[2] 4]. 1940 E. C. Studholme *Te Waimate* 96 Using Merino rams on the cross-bred ewes, the progeny being known as Quarter Backs.

2. *U.S. Football.* **a.** (In Dict. s.v. Quarter *sb.* 30.) Add to def.: by whom the team's play is usu. co-ordinated and directed. Usu. in modern practice, a player lining up behind the centre of an offensive team, who calls the signal to initiate a play and receives the ball when it is snapped back by the centre. (Further examples.)

1947 *Sun* (Baltimore) 15 Aug. 12/6 He is a stocky man who..has the build of a quarterback. 1979 *Arizona Daily Star* 5 Aug. c. 9/1 Oakland quarterback Ken Stabler.. played the first quarter and part of the second.

b. *transf.* A supporter or critic of a football team. Also *downtown quarterback*, an interested supporter of the home team; *grand-stand quarterback* (in quot. *fig.*); *Monday morning quarterback*, one who engages in reductive 'post-mortem' criticism of a game; also *fig.*

1932 B. Wood *What Price Football* vi. 100 A kind of sportswriter known to football players and coaches as a 'Monday morning quarterback'... Not content with reporting the game..the writer must analyze it. 1947 *Collier's* 15 Nov. 17 (*heading*) Penn's downtown quarterbacks were a gloomy lot when George Munger became grid coach. 1949 *Ibid.* 19 Nov. 18/3 The quarterbacks in the stands consider Pop Warner's system..obsolete. 1976 President Ford in *Sunday Sun* (Baltimore) 10 Oct. k. 4/4 Somebody who sits in Washington D.C., 18 months after the Mayaguez incident, can be a very good grand-stand quarterback.

c. *fig.* One who directs or masterminds an operation; a leader.

1961 in Webster. 1968 *Globe & Mail* (Toronto) 10 July 27/5 Van Burkleo is an original-thinking quarter-back who can run his own show. 1971 *Sci. Amer.* Aug. 38/1 It was my privilege to be working in Colombia as 'quarterback' of a team of investigators. 1978 *Guardian Weekly* 1 Jan. 18/1 King Juan Carlos I, Franco's 39-year-old successor, and Premier Adolfo Suarez, the monarch's 44-year-old political quarterback.

3. *attrib.* and *Comb.* (sense *2), as **quarter-back club,** an association of supporters actively interested in promoting their team's success; **quarterback sack** = *sack *sb.*[1] 1 j; **quarterback sneak** (see quot. 1966).

1948 *Life* 1 Nov. 110/2 Factory workers as well as merchant princes belong to the Quarterback Club, an organization of last-ditch rooters who gather..to put questions to the Ohio State head coach..and to see movies of the team's latest games. 1951 *Sun* (Baltimore) 9 Oct. 21/1 Special funds contributed by..downtown quarterback clubs. 1974 *Plain Dealer* (Cleveland, Ohio) 26 Oct. 6-d/2 Alzado..leads the defense in quarterback sacks with four. 1923 J. Wilce *Football* viii. 105 *Quarter-back sneak*,..R. takes the ball from centre directly, pauses a moment as the line charges forward, then sneaks through any opening that may appear between the guards. 1947 *Time* 3 Nov. 74/3 The story Bob liked best was Dad's quarterback sneak. 1966 J. R. Winter *Lang. Pro Football* 132 *Quarterback sneak*, play where quarter-back moves straight ahead into line behind charge of his center and guards immediately after taking snap.

qua·rterback, *v. U.S. Football.* [f. the sb.] *trans.* **a.** To play quarterback for (a team); to direct as quarterback.

1948 *Sun* (Baltimore) 13 Jan. 13/5 McCann..has 'quarterbacked' the LaSalle team to nine consecutive victories. 1950 *Life* 9 Oct. 66/2 Bob calmly quarterbacked the team to its first victory. 1972 J. Mosedale *Football* v. 62 Detroit, coached by Buddy Parker and quarter-backed by Bobby Layne, exhibited a strange mastery. 1979 *Tucson* (Arizona) *Citizen* 20 Sept. 11 d/1 He used to..quarterback the Sun Devils from 1974 to 1977.

b. *fig.* To direct or co-ordinate (an operation).

1952 *Britannica Bk. of Year* 666/2 *Quarterback*,.. (extension of *n.* in U.S. football terminology). To direct (1945). 1971 *Daily Colonist* (Victoria, B.C.) 26 Oct. 1/7 Bush..quarterbacked what UN observers regarded as Washington's worst diplomatic defeat. 1976 *Guardian Weekly* 7 Mar. 18/3 Relations were particularly strained after the 1972 election success, which Wehner felt he had quarterbacked without credit.

So **qua·rterbacking** *vbl. sb.*, the action of playing or directing as quarterback; also *fig.*, esp. *Monday morning quarterbacking* (see *quarterback *sb.* 2 b).

1947 *Time* 17 Nov. 75/2 (*heading*) Quarterbacking by telephone. 1948 *Sat. Even. Post* 18 Sept. 24/3 There also should be less of the Western Union quarterbacking from the bench, which frequently backfired in the face of the masterminds. 1950 *Sport Life* Feb. 9/1 Royal, nominated by the coach to take over for Mitchell at the quarterbacking post. 1960 *Guardian* 9 May 6/6 The realities of sheer, hard political quarter-backing. 1966 'H. B. Taylor' *Triumvirate* iv. 30 There was the usual Thursday morning quarterbacking over what I had put in the paper and how I'd put it in. 1972 *Science* 9 June 1083/2 But Monday-morning quarterbacking is an easy sport. 1977 *N.Y. Rev. Bks.* 13 Oct. 14/3 Despite President Ford's admonition against 'Monday morning quarterbacking' about presidential responsibility for assassination plots, Rockefeller has said..that there was 'White House knowledge and/or approval of all major undertakings'.

quarter-deck. Add: **b.** (Further *attrib.* examples.) Also *transf.*

1850 H. Melville *White-Jacket* xxiii. 117 See, White Jacket, all round they have *shipped their quarter-deck faces again*... I afterward learned that this was an old man-of-war's-man's phrase, expressive of the facility with which a sea-officer falls back upon all the severity of his dignity, after a temporary suspension of it. 1893 W. C. Russell *Emigrant Ship* I. iv. 53, I saluted him with a quarter-deck flourish. 1927 H. D. Capper *Aft — from Hawsehole* p. xii, There are close upon three thousand naval officers of 'hawsehole origin'..who are, or have been, performing fine quarter-deck service for their county. 1976 *National Trust* Autumn 17/3 Still unchanged are the 'quarter-deck', a path laid so that the children could reach the river without getting muddy [etc.].

qua·rter-deck, *v.* [f. the sb.] *intr.* To walk up and down as on a quarter-deck. So **qua·rter-decking** *vbl. sb.*

1901 E. F. Benson *Luck of Vails* xviii. 207 He continued quarter-decking about the room for a few times in silence. 1913 Mrs. H. Ward *Coryston Family* viii. 164 The quarter-decking began again; and Lester waited patiently on a slowly subsiding frenzy. 1924 Kipling *Debits & Credits* 87 There was Potiphar..quarter-decking serenely below the Pebble-ridge. 1954 'M. Coles' *Not for Export* i. 20 'This it is', said Spelmann, swinging round at each turn of his quarter-decking..'to work hard and be successful.'

quarterer. Add: Also, a quartering bird (sense 10 d of Quarter *v.*).

1892 W. W. Greener *Breech-Loader* vii. 209 When the shooter facing No. 2 trap gets a quarterer to the left from No. 5.

quarter-horse. *U.S.* A small stocky horse belonging to a variety recognized as a breed in 1941 and noted for agility and speed over short distances. Also *attrib.*

1839 *Spirit of Times* 11 May 114/3 *Martha Malone*.. was evidently short of work, not fine enough drawn, and too much on the quarter-horse order for a hard race under a hot sun and over a dusty track. 1845 T. J. Green *Jrnl. Texian Exped.* x. 136 Nausea which caused me to break for the door like a quarter-horse to relieve my distress. 1887 *Outing* May 115/1 You would not think him a quarter-horse for he looks like a clumsy sleepy old plug. 1907 S. E. White *Arizona Nights* I. i. 11 A quarter-hoss couldn't have beat me to that shack. 1944 *Sun* (Baltimore) 16 May 15/3 Cross-breeding..has developed a new type of quarter horse with a thoroughbred strain. 1954 *Ibid.* 4 Jan. 16/4 An honest to goodness cowboy who runs with a football like a quarterhorse chasing a steer. 1970 *Telegraph* (Brisbane) 17 Dec. 12/3 In America.. quarter horse racing is a popular sport. 1973 'I. Drummond' *Jaws of Watchdog* xvi. 211 Holman Walker was a quarter-horse man and bred Appaloosa ponies..on his ranch. 1979 *Sunset* Apr. 6/2 The horse that helped tame the West—the quarterhorse—is still popular for its versatility and beauty.

quarter-jack. Add: **1.** (Further example.)

1971 *Country Life* 10 June 1444/3, I was fortunate in being on the spot to take this photograph when the Quarter Jack was brought down..for repairs.

3. [Jack *sb.*[1]] *Mil. slang.* = Quartermaster 2 a.

1930 G. McMunn *Behind Scenes in Many Wars* xiv. 300 Fresh caviare..annoyed our men when they got a ration of it and complained of 'that black jam, what the quarter-jack had said was fish'.

quarterly, *a.* and *sb.* Add: **A.** *adj.* **3.** Special combinations, as *quarterly-meeting*, (*a*) in the Society of Friends (Quakers): a general meeting of all the local monthly meetings of a district; (*b*) in the Methodist Church: an administrative meeting of society officials within a circuit.

(*a*) 1675 in *Extracts Minutes Yearly Meeting of Friends, London* (1783) 63 Advised that the church's testimonies and judgments against disorderly and scandalous walkers ..be recorded in the respective monthly and quarterly meetings. 1675–7 G. Fox *Jrnl.* (1911) I. 267 About this time [*sc.* 1656] I was moved to sett uppe ye mens Quarterly meetinges throughout ye nation though in ye north they was setled before. 1837 J. J. Gurney *Autobiogr.* in J. B. Braithwaite *Mem.* (1854) I. v. 85, I well remember insisting in our Quarterly Meeting, on the reading of the advice..respecting what ought to be the character of representatives. 1869 Beck & Ball *London Friends' Meetings* vii. 69 In most parts of the country, the origin of Quarterly Meetings may be traced to those periodical gatherings of Friends from different but adjoining counties, known as *General Meetings*, and held at intervals with more or less regularity in different places. 1912 W. C. Braithwaite *Beginnings of Quakerism* xiii. 336 By Quarterly Meetings we must, I think, understand General business meetings for a district. 1965 *Friend* 19 Nov. 1393/2 We welcome the proposals of the Revision Committee that..the name Quarterly Meeting be changed to General Meeting [etc.]. 1974 G. Hubbard *Quaker by Convincement* iv. i. 181 General Meetings were until recently Quarterly Meetings, but they now occur as necessary. They..offer an opportunity for Friends from a wide area to meet and discuss matters of common interest.

(*b*) 1750 J. Wesley *Jrnl.* 22 Aug. (1756) 61 We had a Quarterly Meeting, at which were present the Stewards of all the Cornish Societies. 1807 J. Nightingale *Portraiture of Methodism* xxix. 303 The *Quarterly-meetings* are composed of all the travelling-preachers in the circuit where such meetings are held; of the leaders and stewards of the society; and of such of the local-preachers and members as may be invited by any of the travelling-preachers or stewards. 1898 B. Gregory *Side Lights on Conflicts of Methodism* x. 501 Take..the essential part of our economy which, next to the Class meeting, the Conference, and the Circuit, is the oldest and most central part of our economy—the Quarterly Meeting. 1963 R. E. Davies *Methodism* App. i. 173 The Circuit consists of a group of Societies in a neighbourhood (some contain as many as fifty, others as few as five or even less); its affairs are directed by the Quarterly Meeting, consisting of the ministers, deaconesses, and local preachers of the Circuit, and the leaders and trustees of each Society. 1972 *Methodist Recorder* 6 July 16/1 A number of familiar names in the life of the churches will be changed if the proposals are accepted: circuit quarterly meeting becomes *circuit meeting*.

B. *sb.* (Earlier examples.) Also, lesson notes for Sunday schools, issued every three months.

1830 W. Sewall *Diary* 15 May (1930) 131/1 Methodist quarterly commenced. 1857 [see *Christmas number* s.v. *Christmas *sb.* 4]. 1908 L. M. Montgomery *Anne of Green Gables* xi. 110, I got a quarterly from Mr. Bell for you and you'll go to Sunday School to-morrow.

quartermaster, *sb.* Add: **2. d. quarter-master captain,** an officer in the U.S. army with the rank of captain having duties similar to those of a quartermaster.

1907 *N.Y. Even. Post* (Semi-Weekly ed.) 13 May 6 The person enjoying the title of quartermaster captain (a rank that causes our British cousins to smile).

quartermaster *v.* (example).

1936 W. James *Gangways & Corridors* i. 10 He had quarter-mastered in Cuba during the Spanish American war.

qua·rtermistress. [f. after Quarter-master.] An officer in the W.A.A.C. having the duties of a quartermaster.

1917 *Times* 13 Aug. 3/1 The W.A.A.C. will be controlled by a Chief Controller, and the following appointments are authorized:—..Quarter mistress Class I. Attached to Depôt. 2 roses.

quarter-sessions. Add: Now usu. as two words without hyphen. **1.** (Further examples.) Also, *court of quarter sessions*, a court of record held quarterly before two or more justices of the peace in counties and before a recorder in certain boroughs.

Quarter sessions were abolished on 1 Jan. 1972 by the Courts Act, 1971, and their duties largely passed to the newly-instituted Crown Court.

1889 *Act* 52 & 53 *Vict.* c. 63. sect. 13 § 14 The expression 'court of quarter sessions' shall mean the justices of any county, riding, parts, division, or liberty of a county, or of any county of a city, or county of a town, in general or quarter sessions assembled, and shall include the court of the recorder of a municipal borough having a separate court of quarter sessions. 1916 *Act* 6 & 7 *Geo. V* c. 50 § 38 A justice of the peace in England when committing for trial a person charged with burglary shall commit him for trial before a court of assize unless,..he thinks it expedient in the interest of justice to commit him for trial before a court of quarter sessions. **1967** *Act* 15 & 16 *Eliz. II* c. 58 § 8 A court of quarter sessions shall not have jurisdiction to try an indictment for any offence for which a person may be sentenced to death. **1972** *Daily Tel.* 1 Jan. 2 The ancient legal structure of assizes and quarter sessions disappears today.

3. *Comb.* **quarter-sessions rose**, var. of Quatre Saisons, the name of a variety of perpetual rose, *Rosa damascena* var. *bifera*, bearing pink or white flowers.

1892 C. M. Yonge *Old Woman's Outlook* vi. 137 The *Quatre Saisons* rose might very fairly become the Quarter Sessions rose. **1937** Partridge *Dict. Slang* 676/1 Quarter-sessions rose. A 'perpetual' rose.

quartet, quartette. Add: **1. a.** (Earlier example.)

1773 C. Burney *Present State of Music in Germany* I. 313 [Hasse] added, that..his trios, quartets and concertos for instruments, were so numerous that he should not know many of them again if he was either to see or hear them.

b. *transf.* (See quot. 1965.)

1943 T. S. Eliot (*title*) Four quartets. **1965** *New Statesman* 21 May 802/3, I asked what the four of his Quartets were four of, and he [*sc.* T. S. Eliot] answered that..'quartet' suggested Chamber Music composed for close attention by a small audience who had a fair understanding of what they were listening to.

4. *Comb.*, as **quartette table** *Obs.* exc. *Hist.*, = *quartetto table* s.v. *Quartetto 3.

1856 F. S. Cozzens *Sparrowgrass Papers* vii. 89 In one door-way stood a tray of delicate confections, upon two slender quartette tables. **1857** *Harper's Mag.* Mar. 453/1 On this quartette-table we will lay the portfolio. **1925** Penderel-Brodhurst & Layton *Gloss. Eng. Furnit.* 133 *Quartette Tables*, nests of four small tables of light make and diminishing size enclosed within each other and made to draw out. Sheraton, who may have been the first to devise them, called them 'Quartetto tables'.

quartetto. Restrict ? *Obs.* to senses in Dict. and add: **3.** *Comb.*, as **quartetto table** *Obs.* exc. *Hist.*, one of a nest of four small tables.

1802 T. Sheraton *Cabinet-Maker's & Upholsterer's Drawing-Bk.* (ed. 3) in J. M. Bell *Chippendale, Sheraton & Hepplewhite Furnit. Designs* (1900) 148 (*caption*) Cabinet and Quartetto Table. **1803** —— *Cabinet Dict.* 293 *Quartetto table*, a kind of small work table made to draw out of each other, and may be used separately. **1842** [see sense 2 in Dict.]. **1944** C. W. Drepperd *Primer Amer. Antiques* 248/2 Quartetto Tables. Sets of tables..resting in and under largest one. **1975** [see *nest *sb.* 6].

quartic, *a.* and *sb.* For **a, b** read **A, B** and add: **A.** *adj.* **1.** (Example.)

1905 R. W. H. T. Hudson (*title*) Kummer's quartic surface.

2. Applied to a steering wheel shaped like a rectangle with rounded corners.

1973 *Country Life* 17 May 1417/2 A 'quartic' steering-wheel..is a two-spoke design shaped rather like a television screen. **1974** *Daily Tel.* 17 Sept. 6/5 With two other sporting 1750cc versions also announced today, it becomes the first Allegro to abandon the controversial squared-off 'quartic' steering wheel in favour of a conventional round wheel.

‖ **quartier** (kārtye). [Fr.: cf. Quarter *sb.* 14 a.] **1.** In France: a neighbourhood, district. Also *transf.* Also *ellipt.* = *Quartier Latin* below.

1828 Lytton *Pelham* I. xxiii. 192, I love that *quartier*—if ever I went to Paris again I should reside there. **1850** Thackeray *Pendennis* II. vii. 73 I'm thinking of becoming a moral man..with a good reputation in my *quartier*. **1864** Mrs Gaskell *French Life* in *Fraser's Mag.* Apr.–June 435/1 The new Boulevard..making a clear passage..through the densely populated *quartier*. **1896** E. Dowson *Let.* 19 Mar. (1967) 346 It is a refreshing change after Paris and the Quartier. **1967** J. Porter *Chinks in Curtain* 190 The nuns have a mission in Montmartre. The Princess will work there among the—er—ladies of the quartier. **1976** *Times* 31 July 12/5 A collection of *quartiers* each expressing its own set of neighbourhood loyalties and prejudices.

2. Quartier Latin (kārtye latæ̃n), the Latin Quarter (of Paris). Also *attrib.*

1857 C. Kingsley *Two Yrs. Ago* I. i. 17 Tom Thurnall went to Paris, and became the best pistol-shot..in the Quartier Latin. **1861** in D. du Maurier *Young George du Maurier* (1951) 92 Physical prowess & muscular development—the natural antidotes to morbid Quartier-latin Romance. **1903** Chesterton *Robert Browning* v. 111 The thieves' kitchens and the studios of the Quartier Latin. **1936** C. Day Lewis *Friendly Tree* viii. 112 If everyone who comes out of the King's Head is a Bohemian, Kings Ampnett will soon rival the Quartier Latin. **1979** *Guardian* 30 Apr. 10/6 The authentic atmosphere of Paris's Quartier Latin in the late 1950s.

‖ **quartiere** (kwā:rtiē·rę). [It.; cf. prec.] In Italy: a district or area (of a city). (In quot. 1888 *transf.*)

1888 H. James *Aspern Papers* I. iii. 52 We walked together along the sala... I was afraid it would not form part of my *quartiere*. **1967** P. E. H. Durston *Mortissimo* (1968) xii. 95 Ran into them in a little antique shop. Down in your *quartiere*. **1979** 'C. Brand' *Rose in Darkness* xi. 140 This is the quartiere of the thieves.

quartile, *a.* and *sb.* Restrict *Astr.* and *Astrol.* to senses in Dict. and add: **B.** *sb.* **2.** *Statistics* (kwǭ·ɹtəil). The first and third of the three values of a variate which divide a frequency distribution into four groups, each containing one quarter of the total population (the second value of the three, the mean, is sometimes also included); also, any of the four groups so produced.

1879 D. McAlister in *Proc. R. Soc.* XXIX. 374 As these two measures, with the mean, divide the curve of facility into four equal parts, I propose to call them the 'higher quartile' and the 'lower quartile' respectively. It will be seen that they correspond to the ill-named 'probable errors' of the ordinary theory. **1931** *Biometrika* XXIII. 360 The distribution of the quartile is not so closely normal as that of the median. **1957** W. Martin in R. K. Merton *Student-Physician* III. 203 Among students in the top quartile, 28 per cent have high estimations of their ability to perform as a doctor should. **1964** Bruner & Potter in J. S. Bruner *Beyond Information Given* (1974) v. 85 For each picture, the point at which it was first recognized by any subject was obtained .., and likewise the point at which a quarter of the subjects recognized the objects (first quartile). **1977** *N.Y. Times* 4 Apr. 60 (Advt.), The top income half of the nation (those households with incomes above the national median) controls about three-fourths of total income... The top quartile always controls about 48%.

b. quartile deviation, the semi-interquartile range.

1911, etc. [see *semi-interquartile range* s.v. *semi- 5 a]. **1972** *Jrnl. Social Psychol.* LXXXII. 209 Table 1 shows the medians, quartile deviations, and composite ranks.

quart-pot. Add: **a.** Also *Austral.*, a billy-can of this measure for boiling tea-water, etc.

1838 H. Capper *South Australia* (ed. 2) 71 List of other articles provided for the passengers.—One wooden mess bowl, one ditto platter, one mess bread basket, one tin quart-pot, two three-gallon hawse buckets.—For each mess of six passengers. **1863** [see sense b below]. **1881** A. C. Grant *Bush Life in Queensland* I. v. 43 One of the quart-pots..was boiling madly. **1901** M. Franklin *My Brilliant Career* i. 4, I refilled the quart-pot in which we had boiled our tea with water from the creek. **1936** A. Russell *Gone Nomad* iii. 20 We had boiled the quartpots at a waterhole a mile or so back and were continuing on our way. **1941** *Coast to Coast* 155 He was a swaggie all right, with his roll of old blue blanket across his shoulders and his quart pot dangling from it.

b. (Earlier example.)

1863 R. Henning *Let.* 29 June (1966) 131 We..then made a fire, boiled some 'quart-pot tea', and sat down..to enjoy our dinner.

quartz. Add: **2. a.** *quartz crystal* (further simple and *attrib.* examples; cf. *quartz clock, watch* in sense *c), *dolerite*, *-fret* (poet.) [Fret *sb.*[1]], *lead* [Lead *sb.*[2] 6a], *leader* [Leader[1] 13c]; **quartz glass**, a glass consisting almost entirely of silica; = **silica glass*.

1933 K. Henney *Radio Engin. Handbk.* vii. 167 Piezo-electric quartz crystals provide standards of frequency, when permanently connected into suitable vacuum-tube circuits and allowed to oscillate continuously. **1959** R. H. Baker *Astron.* (ed. 7) iii. 77 In the quartz-crystal clock now in use in observatories, a quartz crystal controls the frequency of an electronic oscillator, imposing its natural frequency of vibration on the current. **1970** *Observer* (Colour Suppl.) 3 May 27/1 The quartz crystal clock; most accurate domestic timepiece of all. **1977** T. Allbeury *Man with President's Mind* vii. 66 It was a small quartz-crystal watch. **1911** G. W. Grabham in C. T. Clough et al. *Geol. Glasgow District* iv. 146 A very interesting feature of the quartz dolerites is their instability at temperatures slightly above the consolidation point. **1970** R. J. Small *Study of Landforms* iii. 73 Among the more important of these are..quartz-dolerite sills of the areas inland from Dippin Head. **1883** G. M. Hopkins *Poems* (1967) 96 All The thick stars round him roll Flashing like flecks of coal, Quartz-fret, or sparks of salt, In grimy vasty vault. **1903** *Amer. Jrnl. Sci.* CLXVI. 469 Quartz glass.—A very full account of the behaviour of this material has been given by H. Heraeus. **1912** J. W. Mellor *Mod. Inorg. Chem.* xl. 773 Quartz glass is used for the manufacture of elastic threads to suspend the delicate parts of electrical instruments. **1941** *Thorpe's Dict. Appl. Chem.* (ed. 4) V. 606/1 Quartz glass has an extremely small coefficient of linear thermal expansion,..and articles made from it can be heated to redness and quenched in cold water without fracture. **1965** Phillips & Williams *Inorg. Chem.* I. xiv. 553 Soda-glass is conveniently worked at a lower temperature than borosilicate glass, and the latter at a lower temperature than quartz glass. **1866** 'Mark Twain' *Lett. from Hawaii* (1967) 272 There are hundreds of men in California who are sitting on their quartz leads..and hoping for the day when they will pay. **1884** R. C. Reid *Rambles on Golden Coast N.Z.* x. 105 A slate face in which there are numerous quartz-leaders.

b. *quartz mill* (examples).

1860 H. J. Hawley *Jrnl.* 22 May in *Wisconsin Mag. of Hist.* (1936) XIX. 341 There are a Quarts Mills runing which crush the quarts that are raised from the Lodes. **1908** *Chambers's Jrnl.* Sept. 640/2 Natthey..had started a little quartz-mill on his claim.

c. Used *attrib.* to designate devices in which use is made of quartz, usu. for its optical or its piezo-electric properties; as *quartz oscillator, spectrograph, temperature sensor*; **quartz clock**, a clock in which great accuracy is achieved by employing a vibrating quartz crystal in an oscillatory electric circuit to determine the frequency of the current; **quartz-halogen** *a.*, applied to electric light bulbs which have a quartz envelope and contain the vapour of a halogen (usu. iodine) in order to prevent deposition on the envelope of tungsten from the filament; so **quartz-iodine** *a.*; **quartz lamp**, a lamp in which the envelope is of quartz rather than glass, so that ultraviolet light will pass through it; **quartz-locked** *a.*, maintained at a constant speed of rotation by means of a quartz crystal, employed as in a quartz clock; **quartz watch**, a watch in which a quartz crystal is employed as in a quartz clock.

1937 *Ann. Reg. 1936* 63 Scheibe and Adelsberger (*Phys. Zeit.*) described the comparison of three 'quartz' clocks with the mean astronomical time obtained from three observatories during the 30 months ending June, 1935. **1976** R. Condon *Whisper of Axe* I. xxii. 144 A collection was taken up to present him with a quartz clock. **1968** *Listener* 21 Mar. 391/3 Headlights..should make use of the extra brightness of the new quartz-halogen lamps. **1970** *AA Bk. of Car* 163/4 Quartz-halogen bulbs do not suffer from blackening as ordinary bulbs do. **1979** *Arizona Daily Star* 5 Aug. c5/3 (Advt.), Quartz-halogen fog light kit. Two fog lights and wiring kit. **1965** *Economist* 27 Feb. 929/2 The new quartz-iodine bulbs are being imported to Britain in growing though limited numbers... In France, quartz-iodine headlamps are now standard equipment for the Citroen Pallas. **1973** D. Kyle *Raft of Swords* (1974) xii. 122 'Lights, please.' He switched them on, pivoting the 1,000-watt quartz-iodine beams downward. **1922** *Brit. Med. Jrnl.* 4 Nov. 852/1 The recognition of the antirachitic action of sunlight..is the outcome of Huldschinsky's observations of the curative effect on rickets exerted by the ultra-violet rays emitted by the mercury-vapour quartz lamp. **1933** *Burlington Mag.* Sept. 139/1 If it [*sc.* the painting] could be closely studied with all the resources of the quartz-lamp and the microscope it seems hardly possible that it should not betray its later date. **1977** McGuinness & Stein *Building Technol.* xiv. 406/1 The quartz lamp has about three to four times the life of a normal incandescent. **1977** *Time* 14 Nov. 7 (Advt.), First they designed an all-direct-drive-motor-system. Using one motor for each reel and another quartz-locked motor for the tape capstan. **1938** *Proc. Physical Soc.* L. 413 The quartz oscillator not only is widely used for stabilizing the frequency of transmitting stations but also constitutes the most accurate means of recording the passage of time. **1905** *Astrophysical Jrnl.* XXII. 129 From negative by Professor R. W. Wood with quartz spectrograph of the Johns Hopkins University. **1966** *McGraw-Hill Encycl. Sci. & Technol.* XII. 590/1 Two types of quartz spectrographs are in common use for recording ultraviolet and visible spectra. **1978** *Sci. Amer.* Mar. 144/1 (Advt.), The HP 2804 digital thermometer achieves exceptional accuracy because HP calibrates each quartz temperature sensor. **1974** *Country Life* 5 Dec. 1763 (Advt.), Seiko sold the first quartz watch. **1976** *Times* 5 Feb. 17/5 The quartz watches now being produced fall into two groups..the traditional watch face..and digital watches.

qua:rtzofeldspa·thic, *a. Petrol.* Also **-fels-**. [f. Quartz + -o + Feldspathic, felspathic *a.*] Containing a high proportion of quartz and feldspar.

1839 H. T. de la Beche *Rep. Geol. Cornwall, Devon & W. Somerset* vi. 175 It has chiefly a quartzo-felspathic base with crystals of felspar. **1973** *Nature* 11 May 62/2 The oldest known rocks in the world are quartzofeldspathic gneisses (the Amîtsoq gneisses) from the Godthaab area of West Greenland.

quasar (kwē̆[1]·sāɹ, -zāɹ). *Astr.* [f. *quas(i-stell)ar *a.*] Any of a class of celestial objects that give a star-like (i.e. unresolved) image on a photograph and have a spectrum showing a large red shift, usu. taken to indicate great remoteness and immense power.

1964 H.-Y. Chiu in *Physics Today* May 21/2 So far, the clumsily long name 'quasi-stellar radio sources' is used to describe these objects. Because the nature of these objects is entirely unknown, it is hard to prepare a short, appropriate nomenclature for them so that their essential properties are obvious from their name. For convenience, the abbreviated form 'quasar' will be used throughout this paper. **1964** *Observer* 14 June 1/1 For the past twelve months, astronomers have been obsessed with these 'quasars' or 'quasi-stars' as they are now called. **1968** L. Durrell *Tunc* i. 18 Here was Vibart persuading poor Felix to quit quasars and debouch into memoirs. **1968** *Times* 13 Nov. 16/2 One view is that the red-shift comes about because quasars are remarkably distant at the boundaries of the known universe. The other..is that quasars are extremely massive objects, and that the light from them is reddened by gravitational effects. **1971** *Sci. Amer.* May 55/2 The term quasar..was originally applied only to the starlike counterparts of certain strong radio sources whose optical spectra exhibit red shifts much larger than those of galaxies. Before long, however, a class of quasi-stellar objects was discovered with large red shifts that have little or no emission at radio wavelengths. 'Quasar' is now commonly applied to starlike objects with large red shifts regardless of their radio emissivity. *Ibid.* 56/2 Assuming that they are at cosmological distances, one can easily show that many quasars are from 50 to 100 times brighter than entire galaxies containing hundreds of billions of stars. **1973** *Nature* 6 July 19/2 Two neutral-coloured stellar objects..have been shown to be QSOs with redshifts of 3·40 and 3·53 respectively. This has stimulated interest in other radio sources identified with stellar objects which lack the ultraviolet or blue colour excesses normally associated with quasars. **1978** *Daily Tel.* 8 June 2/5 The nearest known quasar in space, an object the size of the solar system but emitting the energy of 100 galaxies, has been discovered by an X-ray experiment aboard an American satellite. **1978** Pasachoff & Kutner *University Astron.* xxviii. 713 We now use the term quasar to include both quasi-stellar radio sources and quasi-stellar objects.

Quashee, quashie. Add: Also 8 **Quashy,** 9 **Quashi.** (Earlier and later examples.)

1778 P. Thicknesse *Year's Journey* (ed. 2) II. xlv. 104 When Quashy, found the physicians had given his master over, he stole his breeches..and went off with them... The indignant master..never recovered his *faithful* black, nor his *departed* breeches. **1825** C. Waterton *Wanderings* iv. 279 Quashi's fiddle was silent. **1960** *Tamarack Rev.* xiv. 7 'Can't catch Quashie, catch his shirt' is a West Indian proverb, so the occupiers turned to gold of another colour: brown gold, sugar.

quasi, *adv.* and *pref.* Add: Also with pronunc. (kwē̆ⁱ·zəi, kwā·zi). **I. 2.** As a prefix *quasi-* has remained a common formative element. The following is a selection from some of the more frequently occurring modern formations.

a. With sbs.: *quasi-belief, -continuum, -copula, -definition, -dereliction, -equilibrium, -existence, -implication, -jazz, -marriage, -miracle, -modal, -molecule, -monopoly, -neutrality, -object, -partner, -quotation, -quote, -religion, -science, -semi, -sensation, -statement, -substance, -totality, -universal, -verb.*

1925 C. D. Broad *Mind & its Place in Nature* iv. 217 The quasi-belief which is an essential factor in all perceptual situations. **1942** *Mind* LI. 245 When I read about Captain Costigan or about Mr. Micawber I knew perfectly well and all the time that there were no such persons. There is no temporary quasi-belief or make-believe..as there is in the case of the mirage. **1966** D. G. Brandon *Mod. Techniques Metallogr.* 179 The conduction electrons in a metal occupy a quasi-continuum of energy levels. **1979** *Sci. Amer.* May 108/1 In this region, known as the quasi-continuum, the additional rotational and translational states provide all the 'fine tuning' necessary to match the photon frequency with the quantum gap between vibrational levels. **1934** Webster, Quasi copula. **1963** F. T. Visser *Hist. Syntax Eng. Lang.* I. ii. 153 We have a similar complete change of status when verbs of this kind function as quasi-copulas, as in 'this meat eats tough'. **1966** *Eng. Stud.* XLVII. 51 An interesting..problem arises with quasi-copulas i.e. border-line cases where the verb may stand between 'copula' and 'full verb'. **1927** C. R. S. Harris *Duns Scotus* II. vi. 188 We are..able to arrive at a quasi-definition in which we can describe it [*sc.* the divine essence] more perfectly than by means of any of its other attributes. **1939** *Mind* XLVIII. 541 And this he does by discerning (between the lines) the frequent interpolations of new quasi-definitions demarcating new distinctions of meaning of the terms involved. **1978** *Dædalus* Summer 28 Let us note three elements. First, a quasidefinition of the marginal man. **1950** D. Gascoyne *Vagrant* 8, I stand still in my quasi-dereliction. **1905** *Jrnl. Geol.* XIII. 393 The surface ever wearing down, the waste..continually exported by the winds, a nearly level rock-floor,..everywhere slowly lowering at the rate of sand and dust exportation, is developed over a larger and larger area; and such is the condition of quasi-equilibrium for old age. **1964** *Amer. Jrnl. Sci.* CCLXII. 793 As the landscape slowly degrades ..rivers have a tendency to remain in quasi-equilibrium. **1978** *Dædalus* Spring 25 Most states of nature are quasiequilibria, the outcome of competing forces. **1909** W. M. Urban *Valuation* v. 127 An aspect..is given a quasi-existence. **1944** M. Black in P. A. Schilpp *Philos. B. Russell* 241 Hamlet and the Snark, the philosopher's stone and the round square, being all characterised by predicates, must all, in some versions of this position, have their being in a multiplicity of distinct limbos, realms of *Sosein, Aussersein* and *Quasisein* in which to enjoy their ambiguous status of partial or quasi-existence. **1951** *Mind* LX. 355 The truth-table for 'quasi-implication' in Professor Reichenbach's three-valued logic. **1973** J. J. Zeman *Modal Logic* ii. 21 We may refer to such formulas as 'quasi-implications'. **1947** R. de Toledano *Frontiers of Jazz* 70 Hundreds of musicians, playing in all the jazz and quasi-jazz styles. **1977** *Time Out* 28 Jan. 47 (*caption*) The already expansive Runt canvas—everything from Philly soul harmonies through wittily timeless psychedelia and inspiring quasi-jazz—has added two more excellent albums. **1926** W. J. Locke *Stories Near & Far* 166 Quasi-marriage bond. **1976** *National Observer* (U.S.) 4 Sept. 13/3 'What does it matter what we think?' says a friend of mine, three of whose sons have opted for quasi marriage. **1893** *Mind* II. 210 That seems to me but an excessively clumsy way of stating in terms of a *quasi*-miracle the very truth which Stumpf and I express by saying that likeness is an immediately experienced relation. **1971** J. Anderson in A. J. Aitken et al. *Edin. Stud. Eng. & Scots* 71 Certain 'quasi-modals', which satisfy some but not all of the criteria. **1972** W. Labov *Lang. in Inner City* ix. 376 The quasimodals produce many problems which are not fully resolved. **1968** C. G. Kuper *Introd. Theory Superconductivity* xi. 181 A pair of electrons in the immediate vicinity of the Fermi surface can form a bound quasimolecule. **1975** *McGraw-Hill Yearbk. Sci. & Technol.* 115/2 Electron ejection from an atom or a quasimolecule is due to the time-varying electric field acting on the electron as the collision partners pass each other. **1934** *Planning* II. xl. 6 Where monopoly or quasi-monopoly powers are taken there shall be an independent chairman and other independent members of the Industry Board administering the scheme. **1980** *Jrnl. R. Soc. Arts* Mar. 207/1 Once a housebuilder has bid successfully for what little land is available..a quasi-monopoly situation is created. **1934** Webster, Quasi neutrality. **1962** W. B. Thompson *Introd. Plasma Physics* ii. 9 Because of their inertia, the electrons will oscillate about the initially charged region but with a very high frequency, so that quasi-neutrality is preserved in the mean. **1963** F. T. Visser *Hist. Syntax Eng. Lang.* I. iv. 453 With verbs that do not usually take a direct object..the construction with indefinite *it* as quasi-object is also frequently met with. **1967** Quasi object [see *incomplete *a.* 2]. **1848** Bouvier *Law Dict.* (ed. 3) II. 401 *Quasi partners*, partners of lands, goods, or chattels, who are not actual partners, are sometimes so called. **1930** M. Clark *Home Trade* 3 Quasi-partners are those who have played, but no longer play, an active part. **1867** G. M. Hopkins *Let.* 15 Aug. (1956) 41 There are quotations or quasi-quotations fr. the Bible in it. **1943** *Mind* LII. 267 It may be doubted..whether the additional typographical complexity of the device of 'quasi-quotation' is worth the bother. **1937** W. V. Quine in *Jrnl. Symbolic Logic* II. 146 An expression beginning and ending in corners is to denote the expression which we obtain, from the expression between the corners, by replacing all Greek letters by the expressions which those Greek letters are intended to denote. The corners may thus be viewed as 'quasi-quotes'; but they must not be confused with ordinary quotation marks. **1949** *Mind* LVIII. 524 The quasi-quotes would not be needed if '⊃' and '∼' were being used autonymously. **1934** Webster, Quasi religion. **1952** C. P. Blacker *Eugenics* 112 Once the importance of eugenics was grasped, once its principles had 'been accepted as a quasi-religion, the result will be manifested in sundry and very effective modes of action which are as yet untried, and many of them unforeseen'. **1977** P. Johnson *Enemies of Society* xiv. 193 Pseudo-sciences, irrational quasi-religions, and phantasmagoric utopias. **1874** W. Wallace tr. *Hegel's Logic* 21 The quasi-sciences..are founded on an act of arbitrary will alone, such as Heraldry. **1924** W. B. Selbie *Psychol. Relig.* ii. 33 Frazer also regards it [*sc.* magic] as a quasi-science, in fundamental opposition to religion. **1976** *Word 1971* XXVII. 77 To me this is quasiscience, if not pseudoscience. **1974** P. Wright *Lang. Brit. Industry* xvii. 162 *Quasi-semis*, joined by their garages, certainly act as *semis*, though their Latin *quasi* sounds so foregin to English speech. **1979** *W. Lancs. Even. Gaz.* 23 Feb. 17 (Advt.), Quasi semi conveniently situated to all schools. **1922** Joyce *Ulysses* 674 What were Stephen's and Bloom's quasisimultaneous volitional quasisensations of concealed identities? **1948** *Mind* LVII. 194 Necessary statements, then, might be called 'quasi-statements', to indicate that they neither *mention* the expressions of which they are composed, nor *use* them to talk about the non-linguistic world. **1972** *Jrnl. Symbolic Logic* XXXVII. 421 A quasi-statement is a statement or a question. **1925** C. D. Broad *Mind & its Place* iii. 99 Even so extreme a dualist about Mind and Matter as Descartes occasionally suggests that a mind and its body together form a quasi-substance. **1943** *Mind* LII. 336 'Space' is the name of an entity, a quasi-substance, though according to Kant a mind-dependent one. **1941** *Mind* L. 389 A mechanism in the modern sense of the term, *viz.*, as a quasi-totality of serial and reciprocating temporal causes. **1977** *Dædalus* Fall 141 History is also connected more generally, more largely to the quasi-totality of the social sciences. **1890** W. James *Princ. Psychol.* I. xii. 475 The nominalists, on their side, admit a *quasi*-universal, something which we think *as if it were* universal, though it is not. **1957** *Publ. Amer. Dial. Soc.* xxviii. 31 The affirmative quasi-verb *better.* **1972** *Language* XLVIII. 466 Quasi-verbs.. constitute an inflectional category which is rare, or possibly unique, among Indo-European languages.

b. With adjs. (and advbs.): *quasi-æsthetic, -arithmetical, -automatic* (hence *-automatically*), *-classic, -continuous, -crystalline, -divine, -elastic, -eternal, -ethical* (hence *-ethically*), *-Fascist, -feudal, -general, -governmental, -grammatical, -hallucinatory, -historical, -horizontal, -independent, -instantaneous, -legal, -logical, -marital, -material, -mathematical, -mechanical, -mechanistic, -metallic, -metaphysical, -military, -miraculous, -molecular, -monastic, -mythical, -neutral, -normal, -official, -optical, -ossianic, -periodic, -permanent, -personal, -philosophical, -physical, -purposive, -religious, -scientific, -simultaneous* (hence *-simultaneously*), *-stationary, -technical, -thermodynamic, -totalitarian, -transitive, -universal.*

1909 W. M. Urban *Valuation* vi. 152 In certain quasi-aesthetic combinations of utilities—as in a festal meal ..—a detail..may acquire an extraordinary value. **1963** R. M. Hare *Freedom & Reason* ix. 174 The universal, quasi-aesthetic ideal of not having addicts about the place. **1944** *Mind* LIII. 242 One could of course use as M a quasi-arithmetical calculus whose integers are construed as particulars. **1965** *Language* XLI. 490 A quasi-arithmetical notation for syntactic description. **1890** W. James *Princ. Psychol.* II. xxvi. 523 The intermediary terms of an habitual series of acts leading to an end are apt to be of this *quasi*-automatic sort. **1963** F. T. Visser *Hist. Syntax* I. ii. 152 Intransitive verbs used to represent the action—as quasi-automatic, or self-originated. *Ibid.* 159 An interesting sequence of intransitive verbs and 'transitive' verbs used quasi-automatically. **1905** O. Jespersen *Growth & Struct. Eng. Lang.* vi. 123 Authors sometimes coin quasi-classic words without finding anybody to pass them on, as when Milton writes 'our *inquisiturient* Bishops' (Areop. 13). **1890** W. James *Princ. Psychol.* I. xiii. 531 The jingling of the bells on the horses of a horse-car passing the door..and the rumbling of the vehicle itself,..to our ordinary hearing merge together very readily into a *quasi*-continuous body of sound. **1973** *Jrnl. Amer. Chem. Soc.* XCV. 8301/1 The Raman spectrum of titanium tetraiodide in solution has been obtained previously..by use of 694·3 nm excitation of a quasicontinuous ruby laser. **1946** *Nature* 31 Aug. 297/2 Such scattering [of sound waves] has been ascribed either to the quasi-crystalline structure of a liquid. **1964** G. H. Haggis et al. *Introd. Molecular Biol.* ix. 220 Wilkins, Franklin and others.., by drawing out threads from concentrated DNA solutions with careful control of humidity, have been able to get the molecules into a highly-orientated quasi-crystalline form and to obtain in this way more detailed diffraction patterns. **1941** Wyndham Lewis *Let.* 21 Oct. (1963) 302 The 'Royal Academy' seems to them a quasi-divine institution. **1955** R. Graves *Crowning Privilege* 113 The living poet hero is a modernism; I think I am right in saying that Petrarch was the first poet to receive quasi-divine honours during his lifetime. **1899** *Phil. Mag.* XLVIII. 80 The destructive effects of earthquakes are..due to the propagation of quasi-elastic disturbances. **1972** *Sci. Amer.* Oct. 103/3 The observation of pairs of alpha particles with this unique signature emerging from heavy nuclei was taken to indicate the presence of essentially free alpha particles at the nuclear surface. Such scattering is called quasi-elastic because the particles are not totally free but are somewhat bound to the target nucleus. **1976** *Nature* 15 July 177/1 In these plots, the vertical lines around $A = 32$ correspond to the incident ^{32}S ions that have undergone peripheral elastic or quasielastic interactions with the loss or gain of a few nucleons. **1895** *Psychol. Rev.* II. 124 [Parts of mental contents do not] have an eternal or quasi-eternal individual existence, like the parts of objects. **1932** H. H. Price *Perception* viii. 223 We must not..think that nearness is always an 'advantage' (if we may go on using this quasi-ethical language). **1949** *Mind* LVIII. 203 The deductions which welfare economists make are quasi-ethical. **1909** W. M. Urban *Valuation* vii. 214 The feeling..is quasi-ethically qualified. **1938** *Political Q.* IX. 1. 133 The new Germany, imperialist Japan and quasi-Fascist Poland must all, at the least, be democratised. **1954** Koestler *Invis. Writing* iv. xxxv. 376 Greece, too, lived under a quasi-Fascist dictatorship. **1960** —— *Lotus & Robot* ii. x. 228 Japan was able to.. build a quasi-capitalistic state on a quasi-feudal foundation. **1977** *Dædalus* Summer 50 The straitjackets of public regulations, quasi-feudal traditions, financial dependence, and intellectual routine which have so often paralyzed the universities of postwar Europe. **1896** W. Caldwell *Schopenhauer's Syst.* ix. 47 This fact.. warrants us in calling his whole philosophy a *quasi* general overturning of the philosophy of the idea. **1948** *Mind* LVII. 50 If 'If Nero had been Seneca' means anything at all, it is a quasi-general proposition which can be analysed either as 'If Nero had had the character of Seneca' or 'If Seneca had been emperor' or in some similar fashion. **1961** *Ethical Outlook* May–June 93/2 If corporations are not to run away with us, they must become quasi-governmental institutions. **1977** P. Johnson *Enemies of Society* xii. 167 The University Grants Committee, the quasi-governmental body which distributes state cash. **1953** H. A. Hatzfeld *Crit. Bibliogr. New Stylistics* 1 A theoretical, communicable, analytical, quasi-grammatical language of the critic. **1955** J. L. Austin *How to do Things with Words* (1962) vi. 68 'I state that' seems to conform to our grammatical or quasi-grammatical requirements. **1890** W. James *Princ. Psychol.* II. xx. 220 *Optical objects not actually present*..being imagined now with a quasi-hallucinatory strength. **1979** C. E. Schorske *Fin-de-Siècle Vienna* vii. 330 A quasi-hallucinatory, erotic dream experience. **1880** A. H. Sayce *Introd. Sci. Lang.* II. vii. 98 Many of the ballads are quasi-historical. **1933** *Mind* XLII. 396 Objective Spirits..*regulate* individual personality, making personality, by participation, a quasi-historical thing, or, as I should perhaps have said, a sui-thing. **1956** *Nature* 21 Jan. 113/2 The salient place in theory taken by horizontal wind divergence..was stressed by showing its relation..with the development of circulations, cyclonic and anti-cyclonic, through the vorticity equation applied to quasi-horizontal motions on a rotating Earth. **1967** *Oceanogr. & Marine Biol.* V. 82 The analysis of the water masses of the southwest Pacific show them to be very clearly stratified,..with the different water masses lying in quasi-horizontal layers. **1933** *Mind* XLII. 385 There is..no point in '*reifying*' the system, and then treating it as something quasi-independent of its parts, because, in these cases its behaviour is inferable from a knowledge of the parts. **1966** S. Beer *Decision & Control* xv. 381 Cybernetic insights show, in particular, that the totality of the organization ought to be made up of building-blocks that will be called quasi-independent domains. **1958** *Bull. Geol. Soc. Amer.* LXIX. 111/2 In geologic writing..the standards for contemporaneity and instantaneousness are more flexible. Perhaps, H. and G. Termier's (1956) expression quasi-instantaneous (*quasi-instantané*) could be recommended as a convenient term to indicate instantaneousness in the geologic sense. **1960** C. S. Lewis *Studies in Words* 214 The words in a great poet's phrase ..strike the mind as a quasi-instantaneous chord, yet, strictly speaking, each word must be read or heard before the next. **1911** Webster, Quasi legal. **1951** E. E. Evans-Pritchard *Social Anthropol.* i. 14 The sample includes studies of..quasi-legal institutions..and of the entire social organization..of one or other people. **1965** H. Kahn *On Escalation* ix. 172 The declaration of war is just one of a series of legal and quasi-legal measures..which have a role in escalation situations. **1902** W. James *Var. Relig. Exper.* iv. 106 Philosophers usually profess to give a quasi-logical explanation of the existence of evil. **1960** *New Biol.* XXXI. 135 They form part of an entrancing quasi-logical world, but it has little in common with the pedestrian, irrational world of the empiric. **1959** G. D. Mitchell *Sociol.* 64 His wife's sisters are, therefore, in a relationship to him which Radcliffe-Brown has described as quasi-marital. **1978** *Times Lit. Suppl.* 1 Dec. 1391/4 The eighty-six men assigned to the 'dysfunctional' group also lacked any quasi-marital partnership and often expressed regret about their homosexuality, but they were sexually more active and promiscuous. **1876** *Nation* 8 June 369/1 It [*sc.* liberty] and necessity being alike indemonstrable by any quasi-material process, must be *postulated* if taken at all. **1924** W. B. Selbie *Psychol. Relig.* xiv. 269 This 'soul' was regarded as similar to the body in form and nature, and as having a quasi-material existence of its own. **1870** W. S. Jevons in *Phil. Trans. R. Soc.* CLX. 516 In Boole's system the same groups are indicated by certain quasi-mathematical symbols as follows. **1957** C. Vereker *Devel. Polit. Theory* iv. 147

Men..pursued their own happiness..by a comparison of their experienced and expected pleasures and pains in this quasi-mathematical manner. **1920** W. R. SORLEY *Hist. Eng. Philos.* xii. 265 He had started in his thinking with the quasi-mechanical view of a fixed norm of belief existing in the past. **1942** *Mind* LI. 166 The 'quasi-mechanical' reproductive and associative processes. **1923** T. P. NUNN *Education* xi. 136 Quasi-mechanistic theory, leading us to think of a man's self as built up of instincts much as a machine is built up of wheels. **1961** *Chicago Rev.* XV. I. 94 Sub-human and quasi-mechanistic powers. **1858** CARLYLE *Fredk. Gt.* I. IV. iv. 417 The voice.. was of clangorous and penetrating, quasi-metallic nature. **1968** C. G. KUPER *Introd. Theory Superconductivity* xv. 260 One electron per spine atom is in a π-state, and exhibits quasimetallic properties in one dimension. **1890** W. JAMES *Princ. Psychol.* I. v. 138 To urge the automaton-theory upon us..on purely *a priori* and *quasi*-metaphysical grounds, is an *unwarrantable impertinence in the present state of psychology*. **1959** *New Biol.* XXX. 59 So impressive is this 'organic unity' that its existence has been claimed to set living matter apart from non-living and has more than once been elevated into a quasi-metaphysical postulate. **1895** M. PEMBERTON *Impregnable City* xvii. 126 Men in quasi-military uniforms.. contributed to the impression of the scene. **1964** DENTLER & CUTRIGHT in I. L. Horowitz *New Sociol.* 425 Undemocratic leadership by a quasi-military elite. **1974** tr. *Wertheim's Evolution & Revolution* 127 It is clear that the term 'mutiny' mostly refers to an insurrection within a military or quasi-military apparatus. **1890** W. JAMES *Princ. Psychol.* I. xii. 474 They invent..as the vehicle of the knowledge of universals..an Ego, whose function is treated as quasi-miraculous. **1904** *Jrnl. Philos.* I. 541 An experience that knows another can figure as its *representative*, not in any quasi-miraculous 'epistemological' sense, but in the definite practical sense of being its *substitute* in various operations. **1968** C. G. KUPER *Introd. Theory Superconductivity* i. 2 In 1951 Onsager conjectured that conduction electrons might form quasi-molecular pairs bound by the Fröhlich interaction. **1974** *Physics. Bull.* Oct. 467/1 Fernandez..gave a review of the radiative and other properties of resonant states observed in heavy ion collisions. Usually known as quasimolecular states, these resonances represent states at approximately 30 MeV excitation in the compound system. **1979** *Sci. Amer.* Dec. 125/3 The resulting structure is called a quasi-molecular state. **1938** *Ann. Reg. 1937* 241 President Azaña emerged from his quasi-monastic retirement in a villa near Gerona to appoint a new Government. **1964** P. F. ANSON *Bishops at Large* iv. 95 The quasi-monastic character of the life. **1890** W. JAMES *Princ. Psychol.* II. xx. 211 Difficulties arise which have made psychologists appeal to new and *quasi*-mythical mental powers. **1963** M. H. ABRAMS in N. Frye *Romanticism Reconsidered* 53 Quasi-mythical agents tend to recur. **1905** *Daily Chron.* 11 May 5/1 The Admiral asserts that he is not the only one who has provisioned in neutral or quasi-neutral waters. **1962** W. B. THOMPSON *Introd. Plasma Physics* iv. 45 Also, from the extremely small value..it is clear that a conductor resembles a plasma in remaining quasi-neutral. **1909** O. LODGE *Survival of Man* i. 4 Actually more inventive sometimes of other and quasi-normal methods of explaining inexplicable facts. **1965** *Math. in Biol. & Med.* (*Med.Res. Council*) v. 228 The form of this distribution (Figure 2) is negatively exponential, high on the left and tapering away to the right quite unlike the normal and quasi-normal distributions with which we deal intuitively in most everyday situations. **1882** *Mind* VII. 186 Hegel's philosophy..must, now that it has become quasi-official, make ready to defend itself as well as to attack others. **1965** H. KAHN *On Escalation* ii. 44 A quasi-official move ordered by a government. **1940** *Chambers's Techn. Dict.* 693/2 *Quasi-optical waves* (Radio), electromagnetic waves of such short wavelength that their laws of propagation are similar to those of visible light. **1965** *B.B.C. Handbk.* 115 The signals which carry domestic broadcasting programmes are usually designed to be received by ground-wave on medium and long waves and within a quasi-optical range for television and VHF sound broadcasting. **1956** AUDEN in *Listener* 26 Jan. 137/1 The Paid Announcer..with his quasi-ossianic prose Cuts in upon the lovers, halts the band, To name a sponsor or to praise a brand. **1895** *Funk's Stand. Dict., Quasi-periodic*, noting a function in which the increase of the variable by a fixed amount is equivalent to the multiplication of the whole function by another function. **1923** *Proc. R. Soc.* A. CIII. 97 These quasi-periodic atmospherics showed considerable diversity of form, the most frequently recurring form was..similar to a uniformly damped sinusoid. **1962** W. B. THOMPSON *Introd. Plasma Physics* vii. 164 In such situations, the orbit of particles along the magnetic field lines is also quasi-periodic, and again an adiabatic invariant may be formed. **1927** B. RUSSELL *Outl. Philos.* iv. 50 The act of writing produces quasi-permanent material structures. **1967** *Oceanogr. & Marine Biol.* V. 77 The Solomon Divergence is a quasi-permanent phenomenon of the Coral Sea. **1909** W. M. URBAN *Valuation* xii. 354 Quasi-personal constructions of the group or the nation. **1934** WEBSTER, Quasi-philosophical. **1943** *Mind* LII. 100 If 'practical' means 'relevant to human happiness and misery' there is hardly anything more practically important than have been certain philosophical or quasi-philosophical ideas. **1960** *Spectator* 22 July 137 Vast quasi-philosophical works of great power. **1881** W. JAMES *Let.* 18 Dec. in R. B. Perry *Tht. & Char. W. James* (1935) I. 620 One gains an aesthetic pleasure in what you write that is of a *quasi* physical order. **1953** G. E. M. ANSCOMBE tr. *Wittgenstein's Philos. Investigations* I. 121 You interpret a grammatical movement made by yourself as a quasi-physical phenomenon which you are observing. **1964** E. PALMER tr. *Martinet's Elem. Gen. Linguistics* iv. 131 French has a class of 'adjectives' characterized by uses which are quasi-predicative. **1907** H. RASHDALL *Theory of Good & Evil* II. III. iv. 373 Biology now finds that it cannot get on without the idea of 'quasi-purposive' behaviour in accounting for the growth of the individual organisms. **1943** *Mind* LII. 346 A rationalist may be one who, admitting a hierarchy of being and value, seeks to explain the universe as exemplifying the highest degree of quasi-purposive significance, or he may be one who, like the Positivists [etc.]. **1838** J. W. SEMPLE *Kant's Relig. within Boundary of Pure Reason* p. ix, That it concerns us islanders *to know* the religious or quasi-religious opinions entertained by our next-door neighbours on the Continent, no sane man, I apprehend, can doubt. **1906** W. JAMES *Coll. Ess. & Rev.* (1920) 465 In the writings of this youthful Italian [*sc.* Papini]..I find..a tone of feeling well fitted to rally devotees and to make of pragmatism a new militant form of religious or quasi-religious philosophy. **1964** P. F. ANSON *Bishops at Large* xi. 505 A quasi-religious community known as 'The Clerks Secular of St. Basil'. **1977** P. JOHNSON *Enemies of Society* xii. 169 Marxism is a system of quasi-religious prophecy. **1979** *Dædalus* Summer 156 The Ford scheme aroused Dewey's intense and quasi-religious sense of his mission to the democracy. *a* **1873** MILL *Three Ess. Relig.* (1874) 204 It is sometimes..wrapt up in a quasi-scientific language. **1970** G. E. EVANS *Where Beards wag All* xx. 230 Many archaeologists appear purposefully to avoid the kind of folk-life material discussed here because they see in it some threat to their lately acquired quasi-scientific respectability. **1977** *Listener* 15 Dec. 782/3 Meanwhile, the mis-spelling of the quasi-scientific term *minuscule*, as *miniscule* is now so common it is close to becoming accepted English. **1922** Quasi-simultaneous [see **quasi-sensation*]. **1946** F. E. ZEUNER *Dating Past* xii. 353 Another instance of quasi-simultaneous evolution of classes and orders is provided by primitive vertebrates. **1956** *Nature* 28 Jan. 178/1 It [*sc.* the radio telescope] may be used to scan through a small angle in the meridian plane, recording five separate declinations quasi-simultaneously. **1930** *Physical Rev.* XXXV. 944 For the occurrence of raditionless transitions it is essential that the material system..be in a quasistationary state of an energy equal to the energy of some aperiodic motion of the system. **1967** *Oceanogr. & Marine Biol.* V. 38 The method first determines the wind-induced elevations of sea-level at a particular place assuming that the changing wind conditions over the North Sea and the English Channel are quasi-stationary. **1906** *Spectator* 7 Apr. 545/1 When metaphysics begin we flounder among quasi-technical platitudes. **1961** R. B. LONG *Sentence & its Parts* ix. 224 This kind of thing is commoner in quasi-technical use than in general use. **1956** *Nature* 25 Feb. 369/1 Thermodynamic, quasi-thermodynamic and non-thermodynamic methods of investigating the electrochemistry of clays. **1965** PHILLIPS & WILLIAMS *Inorg. Chem.* I. vii. 235 We shall show how by investigation of the mechanisms of chemical reactions it is possible to break them down into a series of elementary reactions, each of which may be treated by a quasi-thermodynamic approach. **1946** W. S. CHURCHILL *Victory* 80 Controls under the pretext of war or its aftermath which are in fact designed to favour the accomplishment of quasi-totalitarian systems..are a fraud which should be mercilessly exposed to the British public. **1953** M. LOWRY *Sel. Lett.* (1967) 337 B.C. at the moment has no government at all, though both of them are totalitarian... Or quasi-totalitarian. **1927** B. RUSSELL *Analysis of Matter* xii. 118 In the case of similarity, we have a relation which is capable of degrees, and may be called 'quasi-transitive'—*i.e.* if *A* is very like *B*, and *B* is very like *C*, then *A* must be rather like *C*. **1963** F. T. VISSER *Hist. Syntax* I. ii. 135 (*heading*) Quasi-transitive verbs. **1974** tr. *Wertheim's Evolution & Revolution* 177 Brinton's unsuccessful attempt to introduce a quasi-universal, cyclical model of revolution..is symptomatic of the danger of any attempt to deal with the genesis and process of revolutions in general. **1977** *Jrnl. R. Soc. Arts* CXXV. 579/1 Most significant of all is the emergence and quasi-universal adoption of the full-fledged *nagara śikhara*.

c. [through It.] With pronunc. (kwā·zi). Used in musical directions: as if, almost, as *quasi-parlando, parlato* [It., 'speaking', 'spoken'] sb. and advb.

1908 R. DUNSTAN *Cyclopaedic Dict. Music* 325/1 *Quasi parlato*, as if spoken. **1945** BRITTEN & SLATER *Peter Grimes* II. i. 183 Ellen *semplice* (*quasi parlato*) Nothing to tell me, nothing to say. **1959** *Listener* 5 Mar. 432/3 The *quasi-parlando* which Puccini uses so effectively as a stage language seems on the screen so desperately sluggish in effect..that [etc.]. **1972** V. C. CLINTON-BADDELEY *To study Long Silence* i. 45 A fine girl..twirling a malacca cane, and singing, *quasi parlando*, in a fruity baritone. **1975** *Country Life* 13 Nov. 1312/2 Singers do not *have* to be provided with tunes—in *Tristan*..they get by with almost continuous *quasi parlando*.

qua·si-co:ntract. *Law.* [QUASI *adv.* and *pref.*] (See quot. 1959^1.) Hence **qua:si-contra·ctual** *a.*

[**1618** in *Eng. Reports* (1907) LXXX. 353 For though there was no actual contract, yet there was a kind of contract in law, so it is ex quasi contractu.] **1727–41** [see QUASI *adv.* and *pref.* 2 a]. **1806** W. D. EVANS tr. *Pothier's Treat. Law of Obligations, or Contracts* I. I. i. 69 A Quasi contract is the act of a person permitted by the law which obliges him in favour of another, without any agreement intervening between them. **1847** *Louisiana Supreme Court Ann. Rep. 1846* I. 380 The act of a party in taking as security for a loan of money made to an agent for his private use, a pledge of claim against a third person, known by the lender to belong to the principal of that agent, forms a quasi-contract. **1893** W. A. KEENER *Treat. Law of Quasi-Contracts* i. 16 A statutory obligation which does not rest upon the consent of the parties, is clearly quasi-contractual in its nature. **1936** R. M. JACKSON *Hist. Quasi-Contract in Eng. Law* II. 127 The name 'quasi-contract' has become the general jurisprudential term for obligations which do not fall into the categories of contract or tort. **1959** JOWITT *Dict. Eng. Law* II. 1456/2 *Quasi-contract*, liability, not exclusively referable to any other head of law, imposed upon a particular person to pay money to another particular person on the ground that non-payment of it would confer on the former an unjust benefit. *Ibid.*, The main heads of quasi-contractual liability are: (1) money paid by the plaintiff at the request of the defendant, including payment by sureties and contribution between joint contractors; [etc.]. **1962** A. TURNER *Law of Trade Secrets* IV. iv. 348 We may consider relief under quasi-contract and relief for unjust enrichment to be for practical purposes the same.

qua·sifi:ssion. *Nuclear Physics.* [f. QUASI *adv.* and *pref.* + FISSION.] A type of interaction between heavy ions in which the reaction products have kinetic energies similar to those expected for fission of a compound nucleus but an angular distribution that is quite different.

1974 F. HANAPPE et al. in *Physical Rev. Lett.* XXXII. 738/1 A new kind of reaction was observed, which seems to occur instead of complete fusion; therefore we called it 'incomplete fusion', but the name 'quasifission' is perhaps better. **1976** *McGraw-Hill Yearbk. Sci. & Technol.* 297/1 It is now believed that for these quasifission heavy-ion projectile reactions, nuclear encounters which achieve an initial distance of approach or sufficient overlap..lead to the situation where the projectile's kinetic energy is essentially dissipated, and the nuclei remain in contact for a brief period of time, exchanging large numbers of nucleons, and then begin to separate.

‖**quasi in rem** (kwē^{i}·səi in rem), *adv. phr. U.S. Law.* [L., 'as if against a thing'.] Used of proceedings in a court with limited jurisdiction, having no power over a defendant's person (see quots.). Also *attrib.*

1887 *U.S. Reports* CXIX. 187 There is, however, a large class of cases which are not strictly actions *in rem*, but are frequently spoken of as actions *quasi in rem*, because, though brought against persons, they only seek to subject certain property of those persons to the discharge of the claims asserted. **1904** *Atlantic Reporter* LVII. 555/2 In suits quasi in rem, that is, where the suit is against the person in respect of the res—where, for example, it has for its object partition or the sale or other disposition of defendant's property within the jurisdiction to satisfy plaintiff's demand by enforcing a lien upon it—personal service within the jurisdiction or appearance is not necessary. **1910** H. C. BLACK *Law Dict.* (ed. 2) 608/1 *Quasi in rem.* A term applied to proceedings which are not strictly and purely *in rem*, but are brought against the defendant personally, though the real object is to deal with particular property or subject property to the discharge of claims asserted. **1963** C. A. WRIGHT *Handbk. Law of Federal Courts* x. 236/2 State statutes which commonly permit so-called 'quasi-in-rem' actions, which are commenced by attachment or garnishment of property within the state, with notice to the person outside the state against whom the claim is asserted. **1970** *Internat. & Compar. Law Q.* XIX. 181 One finds an interesting description..[of] the American *quasi in rem* jurisdiction. **1972** *N.Y. Law Jrnl.* 22 Aug. 12/5 The court is mindful of the quasi in rem judgment granting replevin to plaintiff by a Florida court of competent jurisdiction.

Quasimodo (kwā:zimō^{u}·do). Also (*erron.*) **Quasimoto**, and with small initial. [f. the name of the hunchback in Victor Hugo's novel *Notre-Dame de Paris.*] A surfing feat performed in a crouching position (see quots. 1962 and 1963).

1962 *Austral. Women's Weekly* 24 Oct. (Suppl.) 3/3 *Quasimodo*, trick riding, with body bent nearly double, with one hand stretched out in front and the other behind. **1963** *Surfing Yearbk.* 43/1 *Quasimoto*, riding on the nose of the board in a crouched position, with one arm forward and one arm back. **1965** J. POLLARD *Surfrider* ii. 18 If you are a 'hot dogger', you're an expert, you can perform quick turns, head dips, quasimodos. **1970** *Studies in English* (Univ. Cape Town) I. 31 Another form of crouch is the *Quasimodo*.

qua·sipa:rticle. *Physics.* [f. QUASI *adv.* and *pref.* + PARTICLE *sb.*] An excitation of a many-body system that has some of the properties of a free particle, such as momentum and position.

1957 R. T. BEYER tr. L. D. Landau in *Soviet Physics: JETP* III. 921/1 The role of the gas particles in this classification is assumed by the 'elementary excitations' (quasi-particles), each of which possesses a definite momentum. **1968** C. G. KUPER *Introd. Theory Superconductivity* xii. 193 As the idea of quasiparticles has developed, it has come to permeate the whole of solid-state theory. Thus, for example, the Debye theory of specific heat can be regarded as a quasiparticle theory in which the quasiparticles are phonons. **1968** [see *EXCITON]. **1974** D. M. ADAMS *Inorg. Solids* ix. 283 Phonons are the quasiparticles of energy associated with excitation of one of the modes of vibration of the perfect crystal.

qua:si-ste·llar, *a. Astr.* [f. QUASI *adv.* and *pref.* + STELLAR *a.*] Giving a star-like (i.e. unresolved) image on a photograph but believed not to be a star; chiefly in *quasi-stellar object* (= *QUASAR), (*radio*) *source*.

1963 *Sci. Amer.* Dec. 54/1 In recognition of their small size, and for lack of a better name, they are called quasi-stellar radio sources. **1964** *New Scientist* 28 May 532/1 The highly enigmatic 'quasi-stellar objects' whose discovery over the past year or so has been of considerable excitement to astronomers. **1964** *Listener* 20 Aug. 266/1 Radio astronomy has already revealed to us an entirely new universe... But the record for excitement and unexpectedness must surely go to the discovery within the last year of the quasi-stellar radio sources. **1973** *Nature* 23 Nov. 185/1 The physical nature of quasistellar objects is as puzzling now as it was 10 years ago when their large redshifts were discovered. **1973** SMITH & JACOBS *Introd. Astron. & Astrophysics* xix. 493 Some QSOs are strong radio sources; indeed, optical identification of such quasi-stellar sources (QSS) first drew attention to the QSOs. The majority of QSOs, however, are weak radio sources or altogether radio-quiet. **1977** J. NARLIKAR *Struct. Universe* vii. 215 When quasi-stellar objects were first discovered, some with red-shifts close to $z = 2$, it was hoped that they would settle the cosmological issue once for all... Unfortunately QSOs have made the issue more complicated than before. **1978** PASACHOFF & KUTNER *University Astron.* xxviii. 713 Sources in this new class resembled the quasi-stellar radio sources in being quasi-stellar and in having large redshifts but did not emit any detectable radio radiation. These were called quasi-stellar objects (QSO's).

quassia. Add: **3.** *quassia chips* (examples), *extract*; **quassia cup** (example).

1884 A. J. E. WILSON *Vashti* xxiv. 237, I have been forced to drink out of quassia-cups until my whole being has imbibed the bitter. **1900** G. S. SAUNDERS in E. T. Cook *Century Bk. Gardening* 508 Quassia chips should be soaked..and then boiled. *Ibid.* 509 Quassia extract may be bought... This is a very useful insecticide. **1926** *Army & Navy Stores Catal.* 479/2 Quassia Chips –lb. –/5. **1965** M. THOMAS *Grannies' Remedies* 14 A ⅞ oz. of quassia chips boiled in a pint of water and mixed with 4 oz. of treacle draws flies and kills them. **1969** E. H. PINTO *Treen* 39 Quassia chips were formerly used for washing lousy heads.

quate, var. *QUAITE.

quater-centenary. Delete *rare* and add: (kwæ:təɹsentī·nări, kwē̆ⁱ:təɹ-). (Later examples.) Also as *adj.*

1904 J. STALKER *John Knox* p. v, In 1905 not only Scotland..will be celebrating..the Quatercentenary of the birth of the greatest of Scotsmen. **1906** *Daily Chron.* 25 Sept. 4/4 That is why the Quatercentenary of the University [of Aberdeen] has created an unparalleled amount of interest in the North. **1955** *Times* 13 July 9/4 The recent quater-centenary celebrations of Queen Mary's School, Walsall. **1971** *Oxford Times* 4 July 28/5 The Jesus College quatercentenary celebrations included a concert of rarities. **1977** *Times* 31 Mar. 14/3 The Jews fled to nearby Cochin... There, in 1567, they built Jewtown and in the following year completed their Synagogue... Its quater-centenary was celebrated..in 1968.

quatercentennial (kwæ:təɹsente·niăl, kwē̆ⁱ:-təɹ-), *a.* [f. L. *quater* four times + CENTENNIAL *a.* (*sb.*).] Pertaining to a four-hundredth anniversary or celebration.

1964 *Listener* 30 Apr. 730/3 Scholars don't regard their function this quater-centennial year as involving.. scratching pocky boils.

quaternary, *a.* and *sb.* **A.** *adj.* **1. a.** Add: This sense is now *Obs.* in *Chem.*

b. *Chem.* Of ammonium and phosphonium ions and salts: in which the central atom forms four bonds to organic radicals; also applied to the central atom, and extended to analogous compounds of other elements. Of a carbon atom: bonded to four other carbon atoms.

1871 *Jrnl. Chem. Soc.* XXIV. 570 Hofmann considers that Drechsel and Finkelstein had tertiary and quaternary phosphonium salts under examination, and not a salt of the primary phosphine. **1871** *Chem. News* 9 June 275/1 Quaternary substitution. **1903** A. J. WALKER tr. *Holleman's Text-bk. Org. Chem.* I. 46 A carbon atom which is only linked to one other carbon atom is called primary. .. If it is linked..to four, quaternary. **1910** N. V. SIDGWICK *Org. Chem. Nitrogen* ii. 22 The quaternary hydroxides are strong bases. **1951** I. L. FINAR *Org. Chem.* I. xxx. 622 Pyridine forms quaternary salts when heated with alkyl halides, *e.g.*, pyridine methiodide or *N*-methylpyridinium iodide, $C_5H_5N^+{\cdot}CH_3\}I^-$. **1955** J. G. DAVIS *Dict. Dairying* (ed. 2) 879 Quaternary ammonium germicides have received considerable attention in the past 10 years in relation to their use as sterilising compounds. **1972** COTTON & WILKINSON *Adv. Inorg. Chem.* (ed. 3) xiii. 390 The stibonium compounds are the most difficult to prepare and are the least common. These quaternary salts, excepting the hydroxides,..are white crystalline compounds. **1972** *Materials & Technol.* V. x. 304 Among the more complex quaternary surfactants are some which include two quaternary nitrogen atoms. **1975** GUTSCHE & PASTO *Fund. Org. Chem.* iii. 61 If it carries no hydrogen but is attached to four carbons it is called a 'quaternary carbon'.

2. Also *absol.*

1910 *Encycl. Brit.* II. 344/2 The beginning of archaeology..may be broadly held to follow on the last of the geological periods, viz., the Quaternary. **1946** L. D. STAMP *Britain's Struct. & Scenery* ii. 16 The Quaternary is not really comparable in duration or importance with the other great eras. **1977** A. HALLAM *Understanding Earth* 234 The Pleistocene is a subdivision embracing the period from the beginning of the Quaternary until 10,000 years ago.

3. a. Of or belonging to the fourth order or rank; fourth in a series. Also *spec.* (see quot. 1961).

1874 H. W. BEECHER *Plymouth Pulpit* II. 486 The first comprehensive determination breaks itself up into subsidiary determinations, so that the primary will becomes secondary, the secondary becomes tertiary, and the tertiary quaternary. **1924** O. JESPERSEN *Philos. Gram.* vii. 96 A tertiary word may be further defined by a (quaternary) word, and this again by a (quinary) word. *Ibid.* 97 Quaternary words..may be termed *sub-subjuncts.* **1961** J. GOTTMAN *Megalopolis* xi. 576 One wonders whether a new distinction should not be introduced in all the mass of nonproduction employment: a differentiation between *tertiary* services—transportation, trade in the simpler sense of direct sales, maintenance, and personal services—and a new and distinct *quaternary* family of economic activities—services that involve transactions, analysis, research, or decision-making, and also education and government. Such quaternary types require more intellectual training and responsibility. **1973** *New Society* 15 Nov. 386/3 The 'tertiary' sector contains at least three divisions—'tertiary' proper..; 'quaternary' (information exchange and decision-making); and 'quinary' (research, development and education). **1975** J. B. GODDARD *Office Location in Urban & Regional Devel.* ii. 11 The intra-urban location of head office functions and of independent firms in the quaternary sector.

b. Biochem. *quaternary structure*, the relative configuration of polypeptide sub-units in a protein molecule, being structure of an order higher than the tertiary.

1958 J. D. BERNAL in *Discussions Faraday Soc.* XXV. 14 (*caption*) Hierarchy of polymer complexes:.. (*d*) quaternary structure (homogeneous type), linked groups of tertiary molecules, haemoglobin structure..; (*e*) quaternary structure (heterogeneous type)—linking of different types of ternary protein and primary ribonuclease, tobacco mosaic virus. **1964** G. H. HAGGIS et al. *Introd. Molecular Biol.* iv. 81 The presence of the nucleic acid chain apparently increases the cohesion between sub-units in successive turns of the helical quaternary structure. **1977** *Lancet* 26 Nov. 1116/1 The four glycoprotein hormones..possess a common quaternary structure characterised by two dissimilar polypeptide chains called the α and β subunits.

B. *sb.* **2.** *Gram.* In Jespersen's terminology: a word or phrase that belongs to the fourth order or rank.

1937 O. JESPERSEN *Analytic Syntax* 121 The possibility of having quaternaries, quinaries, and so forth. **1946** —— *Mod. Eng. Gram.* V. i. 3 In other combinations we may have quaternaries or quinaries, e.g. *a not* (5) *particularly* (4) *well* (3) *constructed* (2) plot (1).

3. *Chem.* A quaternary ammonium compound.

1947 *Ann. Rev. Microbiol.* I. 173 Jacobs and associates ..studied the relation between structure and bactericidal effects in the hexamethylene tetramine groups. This was followed in 1928 by Hartmann & Kägi's work..with other quaternaries. **1955** J. G. DAVIS *Dict. Dairying* (ed. 2) 880 The degree to which complexes of this kind will be found depends upon the particular quaternary used. **1968** KIRK & OTHMER *Encycl. Chem. Technol.* (ed. 2) XVI. 860 Some quaternaries form hydrates or other solvates.

quaternate, *a.* (Later example.)

1908 *Scott's Autumn List, Lady Beauclerc and Socialism* is the title of the last book of the Rev. H. T. Perfect's quaternate work on Lady Beauclerc's life.

quaternion. Add: **1. a.** (Further examples.) *spec.* a set of four poems.

1815 SCOTT *Guy M.* III. iii. 42 A species of florid elocution, which often became ridiculous from his misarranging the triads and quaternions with which he loaded his sentences. **1964** C. S. LEWIS *Discarded Image* iv. 68 He accepts the classical quaternion of virtues, Prudence, Temperance, Fortitude and Justice. **1967** J. HENSLEY *Wks. Anne Bradstreet* p. xxiv, The Quaternions follow the structure of Thomas Dudley's own 'On the Four Parts of the World', now lost. **1976** *Times Lit. Suppl.* 27 Aug. 1049/1 The formal elegies and quaternions she [*sc.* Anne Bradstreet] laboured over in imitation of Du Bartas.

4. c. quaternion group, the group which is generated by multiplication of the unit quaternions, *i*, *j*, and *k*.

1911 W. BURNSIDE *Theory of Groups of Finite Order* (ed. 2) viii. 132 The group defined by these relations is known as the quaternion-group. **1949** H. ZASSENHAUS *Theory of Groups* iv. 116 We wish to find non-abelian groups of order p^n which contain only one subgroup of order p. An example is the quaternion group. By the theorem of Hölder it is defined by the relations $A^4 = 1$, $BAB^{-1} = A^{-1}$, $B^2 = A^2$. **1972** F. J. BUDDEN *Fascination of Groups* xv. 245 The simplest group in this class is Q_4 of order 8 ($n = 4$), and this is usually known as the quaternion group, though in fact all the dicyclic groups may be realised as groups of quaternions.

quaternize (kwǫ·tĕɹnəiz), *v. Chem.* [f. QUATERN(ARY *a.* + -IZE.] **a.** *trans.* To convert (a tertiary compound, esp. an amine, or an atom) into a quaternary form. **b.** *intr.* To undergo this process.

1951 *Jrnl. Polymer Sci.* VI. 513 This observation suggests that some of the reluctance of 2-pyridyl ethers to quaternize may also be due to steric effects. *Ibid.*, We may consider the butyl salt to be a chain polymer with approximately every other pyridine quaternized. **1965** *Jrnl. Chem. Soc.* 6831 A specimen obtained on quaternising (−)-6-methoxytropan-3α-ol. **1969** *Encycl. Polymer Sci. & Technol.* XI. 333 By copolymerizing vinylpyridine with styrene, quaternizing the nitrogen atoms in the pyridine rings of the resulting copolymer, and..reacting with Li+TCNQ− and TCNQ a product is obtained that can be cast from solution into a film with a conductivity of 10^{-3} ohm^{-1}·cm^{-1}. **1970** J. WILLIAMSON in H. W. Mulligan *Afr. Trypanosomiases* vii. 167 The dimethylated diamino dye, Acridinium Yellow, in which the ring N atom was quaternized. **1973** *Nature* 27 Apr. 605/2 A similar reaction of nicotinamides quaternized with alkyl groups was also..investigated.

So **qua·ternized** *ppl. a.* Also **quaterniza·tion,** the process of quaternizing a compound or atom.

1949 *Jrnl. Polymer Sci.* IV. 103 An excess of butyl bromide over pyridine content was always used, so that the irreversible quaternization reaction would prevail. **1951** *Ibid.* VI. 523 Quaternized copolymers of styrene and 4-vinylpyridine. **1965** PHILLIPS & WILLIAMS *Inorg. Chem.* I. xv. 556 The quaternization reaction EtI + $Et_3N \rightarrow [Et_4N]^+I^-$ is, at 100°, 80 times faster in benzene..than in hexane. **1966** *Trans. Amer. Soc. Artific. Internal Organs* XII. 151 Simple contact of such a quaternized surface with aqueous sodium heparinate is sufficient to yield a heparinized surface. **1976** *Nature* 15 July 221/2 Quaternisation of the nitrogen atom generally caused a marked decrease in ixodicidal activity.

‖ **Quatorze Juillet** (katǫrz ʒwiyę). Also **quatorze juillet** and *ellipt.* **quatorze.** [Fr., lit. fourteenth of July.] In France, the anniversary of the fall of the Bastille (see BASTILLE *sb.* 3) on 14 July 1789, observed as a national holiday. Also *attrib.*

1934 WEBSTER, Quatorze juillet or (le) quatorze. **1951** R. SENHOUSE tr. *Colette's Last of Chéri* 196 One day, not long before the Quatorze Juillet, Charlotte Peloux was lunching with them. **1955** *Times* 18 July 6/1 *Le Quatorze Juillet*—never referred to by French people under any other name, although its official title is *fête nationale* and its most common English name, more explicitly, 'Bastille Day'—has come and gone, as in other years, in a flurry of military parades, undisciplined queues for free matinées at State theatres, firework displays, and ubiquitous *bals populaires* in the streets. **1966** H. YOXALL *Fashion of Life* xxiv. 233 A firework display..far more lavish than anything I'd seen in Paris on the *Quatorze Juillet.* **1971** *Guardian* 15 July 13/4 The 'quatorze' is.. the type of public jamboree which carries no obligations. **1977** E. AMBLER *Send no more Roses* viii. 175 It's the Quatorze today. The servants want to..go to the local fête. *Ibid.* x. 214 We had eaten simply..so that the servants could get off early to their local Quatorze juillet fête.

‖ **quatre-couleur** (katrˌkulœ̄r), *a.* [Fr., f. *quatre* four + *couleur* colour.] Of objets d'art: made of or decorated with carved gold of several (esp. four) different colours. Hence **quatrecouleurs** *sb. pl.*

1959 *Times* 19 Dec. 9/4 The one [thimble] on the left has fruit and flowers in *quatre-couleur* work round the band. **1960** H. HAYWARD *Antique Coll.* 231/2 *Quatre-couleurs*, the art of combining various colours of carved gold in a decorative scheme. The colour of gold is determined by the nature of the alloy. **1967** *Times* 7 Mar. 21/4 (Advt.), A quatre-couleur gold box..by Barrière, 1768. **1975** *Catal. Important Gold Boxes & Objects of Vertu* (Sotheby, Monaco) 66 A rectangular quatre-couleur gold and enamel snuff-box. **1978** *Times* 5 Aug. 9/1 Snuff-boxes ..in imitation of gold boxes with..'quatre-couleurs' decoration.

quatro (kwa·tro). *W. Indies.* Also **cuatro.** [ad. Sp. *cuatro*, lit. four.] A small four-stringed guitar, of a kind originating in Latin America.

1955 *Caribbean Q.* IV. II. 101 The band includes a home-made banjo, a cuatro (small 4-stringed Spanish guitar)..and shac-shacs. **1958** E. BORNEMAN in P. Gammond *Decca Bk. Jazz* xxi. 261 The instruments used were..guitar, quatro, conga drum, bongos, maraccas, cencerro. **1965** 'LAUCHMONEN' *Old Thom's Harvest* v. 59 His guitar-pickney quatro hung over his shoulder and across his back. **1968** E. LOVELACE *Schoolmaster* i. 8 There is the orchestra..with the fiddle, and the quatros and flute and tambourines. **1974** *Sunday Advocate-News* (Barbados) 3 Feb. 13/7 The programme is dedicated to the composers of the early tent brigade; men who made music with 'Cuatro, bottle and spoon'. **1975** S. MARCUSE *Dict. Mus. Instruments* 135/2 *Cuatro*.., 1. guitar of Puerto Rico, with 5 courses of strings, 4 pairs and a single chanterelle, played with a plectrum; 2. a small guitar of Venezuela, with 4 strings.

‖ **quatsch** (kvatʃ). Also **quatch.** [Ger.] Nonsense, rubbish. Freq. as *int.*

1907 M. A. VON ARNIM *Fräulein Schmidt* liv. 218 '*Quatsch*,' said Onkel Heinrich, with sudden and explosive bitterness. *Ibid.* 219 *Quatsch* is German for silly, or nonsense, and..is more rude than either. **1915** WYNDHAM LEWIS *Lett.* (1963) 72, I never did nor ever shall, as you probably divine, despite 'quatch' about malevolence. **1939** JOYCE *Finnegans Wake* (1964) 520 Quatsch! What hill ar yu fluking about, ye lameolookond fyats! **1947** D. M. DAVIN *Gorse blooms Pale* 165, I notice he commits himself to nothing about Zionism. A lot of quatsch and schmaltz, if you ask me. **1962** K. O'HARA *Double Cross Purposes* iii. 31 'I'm rusty in my law after two years...' '*Quatsch.* You're worse than rusty.' **1976** *Times Lit. Suppl.* 4 June 671/2 Fantasy masquerading as history, pure *quatsch* dressed in purple kitsch. **1979** N. FREELING *Widow* vii. 42 'Oh Quatsch,' she said. 'I..know how to look after myself.'

quattie (kwǫ·ti). *W. Indies.* [Corruption of QUARTER *sb.*] A penny halfpenny; money or a coin of the value of 1½d.

1859 TROLLOPE *West Indies & Spanish Main* ii. 20 'And now de two quatties,' he said. I knew nothing of quatties then, but I gave him the sixpence. **1873** C. J. G. RAMPINI *Lett. from Jamaica* ix. 94 'Quattie', a penny-half-penny—the 'quarter' of sixpence. **1893** R. BITHELL *Counting-House Dict.* (rev. ed.) 254 *Quattie*, a small silver coin used in the West Indies, worth about 1½d. English. **1961** F. G. CASSIDY *Jamaica Talk* ix. 209 The *tup*, of course, is an abbreviation of *twopence*, but nowadays means the same as *quattie*: 1½d. **1971** *Jamaican Weekly*

Gleaner 3 Nov. 25/2 Pound' wort' a fret nebber pay quattie wort' a debt. **1975** *New Yorker* 12 May 37/1 He put every penny, every quattie of what we had into a small herd and a prize black bull.

quattroce·ntism. [f. QUATTROCENT(O + -ISM.] The fifteenth-century style in Italian art.

1905 W. H. HUNT *Pre-Raphaelitism* II. xiii. 367 It was pointed out to them that our pictures had never attempted quattrocentism.

quattrocento. Add: Also *attrib.* or as *adj.*

1921 A. HUXLEY *Let.* 31 May (1969) 197 For my taste, at least, Florence is too tre- and quattrocento. **1955** *Times* 20 May 3/7 The settings [in a film] were purely *quattrocento*, very scholarly, and very pretty. **1965** F. RAPHAEL *Darling* xxvi. 131 The pictures started with quattrocento pieces. **1977** *N.Y. Rev. Bks.* 24 Nov. 36/4 The charming *cassone* fronts of a minor painter called Apollonio di Giovannie, which look to us like decorative charades in *quattrocento* costume. **1979** *Jrnl. R. Soc. Arts* CXXVII. 627/2 We know virtually everything we could hope to know about the decoration of a quattrocento chapel.

quaver, *sb.* Add: **1.** Also *Comb.*

1728 CHAMBERS *Cycl.* s.v. *Rest*, The Quaver-Rest of common time.

quaver, *v.* **1. a.** Delete 'Now *rare*' and add: Also, with *adv.*, to go with a tremulous or quivering movement.

1943 A. RANSOME *Picts & Martyrs* xv. 144 The three-cornered white flag..quavered up to the masthead. **1953** C. MACKENZIE *Passionate Elopement* xxx. 270 Old Tabrum would quaver in from time to time to survey the comfort of his guests, regaling them with some particularly choice floral anecdote.

3. b. *trans.* To utter with a quaver or in a quavering tone.

1872 A. C. STEELE *Broken Toys* I. vii. 102 'Oh, yes, I was the upper-housemaid,' the old woman quavered. **1897** W. W. JACOBS *Skipper's Wooing* iii. 36 'I'd rather you stayed,' he quavered. 'I would indeed.' **1912** *Red Mag.* 1 Mar. 513/2 'Gus!' she quavers. 'Oh, Gus!' **1947** *Punch* 5 Mar. 206/2 'Thank heavens you're here!' he quavered as I went up to him. **1972** 'J. HERRIOT' *It shouldn't happen to Vet* xv. 105 'Have you got a drop o' whisky handy, Jim?' he quavered.

quaverous (kwē[i]·vərəs), *a.* [f. QUAVER *v.* + -OUS.] Tremulous, quavering.

1918 J. F. BRIDGE *Westm. Pilgrim* xi. 146, I can still see two of these old gentlemen..with hardly a quaverous note to mark their years, valiantly voicing 'I saw lovely Phyllis'.

quavery, *a.* Delete *rare* and add later examples.

1965 HOUSE & STOREY *Lett. C. Dickens* I. 557 A quavery line is drawn under 'Ill! *He* ill!', and another under 'Any time while the—'. The writing of the last three lines gets progressively more shaky. **1975** *Daily Tel.* 10 Nov. 2/6 A woman's voice in the crowd soared above the others, quavery but sweet.

quawk (kwǭk), *sb. U.S.* Also **quark, quauk, quock.** [Imitative; cf. QUAWK *v.* and SQUAWK *sb.*] **1.** The black-crowned night-heron, *Nycticorax nycticorax*, which is widely distributed in temperate and tropical regions; = QUA-BIRD.

1844 J. E. DEKAY *Zool. N.Y.* II. 227 The Black-crowned Night Heron, or Quawk,..derives its popular name from the deep guttural cry. **1867** *Amer. Naturalist* I. 344 Many..were all agog to cover themselves with glory by shooting a quawk. **1877** W. WHITMAN *Specimen Days* (1882–3) 100, I find [in New Jersey].. Cheewinks, Quawks, Ground robins. **1895** F. M. CHAPMAN *Handbk. Birds Eastern N. Amer.* 136 Black-crowned Night Heron; Quawk. **1926** A. C. BENT *Life Hist. N. Amer. Marsh Birds* 197 The familiar night heron or 'quawk' is one of the best known and most widely distributed of our herons. **1962** R. S. PALMER *Handbk. N. Amer. Birds* I. 475 Characteristic *quock* of this heron has been widely used as a vernacular name: 'squawk', 'quock', etc. **1968** *Times* 28 Feb. 11/7 During a recent expedition to the Falkland Islands I was lucky enough to see and hear..the Quark. They are birds of great beauty, heron-like in appearance.

2. The cry of a duck or night-heron; = QUACK *sb.*[2]

1863 'G. HAMILTON' *Gala-Days* 73 For the heavy booming of cannon rose the 'quauk!' of ducks. **1895** F. M. CHAPMAN *Handbk. Birds Eastern N. Amer.* 137 Occasionally they [*sc.* black-crowned night herons] utter a loud, hoarse *quawk*, the origin of their common name. **1962** R. S. PALMER *Handbk. N. Amer. Birds* I. 476 The Black-crown's note can be expressed as *quock*.

quay, *sb.* Add: **b.** *quay-rail, -side* (examples), *-stone* (later example); **quay crane** = **wharf crane*; **quay-punt** (in full, **Falmouth quay-punt**), a small fore-and-aft-rigged half-decked two-masted sailing boat, orig. used on the river Fal for transporting stores between ship and shore.

1969 *Jane's Freight Containers 1968–69* 286/3 Stevedoring companies who already have modern mechanised equipment at their disposal (quay-cranes, pontoon-cranes, trucks and elevators). **1977** *Hongkong Standard* 12 Apr. (Business Suppl.) 4/5 The group has a total of seven quay cranes. **1886** D. KEMP *Man. Yacht & Boat Sailing* (ed. 5) 341 Table of offsets (Falmouth quay punt). **1925** *Yachting Monthly* XXXIX. 39/2 A quay punt before the war cost about £120 to build. **1971** *Country Life* 20 May 1224/1 They were the bum boats of the western world and ranged from such rugged deep-keel craft as the Quay Punts of Falmouth to the graceful Deal galleys. **1936** DYLAN THOMAS in *Contemp. Poetry & Prose* 53 Let the first Peter from a rainbow's quayrail Ask the tall fish. **1903** *Westm. Gaz.* 31 Dec. 5/3 He saw another man climbing up the quayside ladder. **1928** *Daily Tel.* 7 Feb. 14/1 The foundations..rested in the rock found 70 ft. under the two quaysides. **1974** *Times* 12 Nov. 3/1 Quayside fish merchants at Hull. **1979** *Jrnl. R. Soc. Arts* CXXVII. 663/1 Local fishermen..used to sell their hake, cod and herring on the quayside. **1938** DYLAN THOMAS in *20th Cent. Verse* Jan./Feb. 3, I make this in a warring absence when Each ancient, stone-necked minute of love's season Harbours my anchored tongue, slips the quaystone.

quean. Add: **1.** (Later examples.) Now *arch.*

1924 E. SITWELL *Sleeping Beauty* xiv. 47 My eyes are dim,—I yet can see You, lazy quean! Go work! **1969** *Listener* 10 Apr. 503/3 Nora (an old quean who thinks she's an old queen).

3. *slang.* A male homosexual of effeminate appearance. Cf. *QUEEN *sb.* 11*.

1935 D. LAMSON *We who are about to Die* xv. 294 We did hear startling tales..of 'family' life, of marriage ceremonies, of fights with knives for the favor of some 'quean', as the perverts are called in prison. **1937** PARTRIDGE *Dict. Slang* 676/1 *Quean*; incorrectly *queen*, a homosexual, esp. one with girlish manners and carriage; low: late C. 19–20; ob. except in Australia. **1968** J. R. ACKERLEY *My Father & Myself* xii. 127, I did not want him to think me 'queer' and himself a part of homosexuality, a term I disliked since it included prostitutes, pansies, pouffs and queans.

queasily, *adv.* (Later examples.)

1973 *Times Lit. Suppl.* 2 Feb. 118/2 We are growing somewhat queasily disillusioned with the achievements of our post-Renaissance civilization. **1976** *New Society* 4 Mar. 502/2 *Super Natural Cookery*, a typically camp title, written in the queasily flirtatious style which seems to afflict all Aquarian cookery books.

queasy, *a.* Add: (Later examples of spelling **queazy.**)

1906 C. M. DOUGHTY *Dawn in Brit.* VI. 64 Proud queazy, faltering-kneed, Men, fat of the lean people's gifts. **1912** GALSWORTHY *Inn of Tranquility* 187, I would think, Sirs, that you should rather blame the queazy state of Pranza's stomach.

6. queasy-stomached *a.* (later example).

1802 W. GIFFORD tr. *Juvenal's Satires* vi. 292 Why waste the wine and cakes The queasy-stomach'd guest, at parting, takes?

Quebec (kwĕbe·k, kĕ-). The name of the city and province in eastern Canada, used *attrib.* in *Quebec heater*, a kind of solid-fuel, domestic heating stove with a tall, cylindrical fire-box.

1918–19 *T. Eaton & Co. Catal.* Fall & Winter 461 The new Quebec heaters. Built on the popular 'Quebec Idea' pattern..burn coal, coke and any kind of wood fuel. **1927** *Toronto Daily Star* 8 Oct. 2 Dominion Circulation 'Quebec' Heater..gets the heat into every corner of the house. **1948** H. MACLENNAN *Precipice* (1949) i. 20 In the winters there had been a Quebec heater in the pavilion. **1968** E. A. MCCOURT *Saskatchewan* iii. 42 The long glorious winter evenings we spent huddled behind the old Quebec heater.

Quebecker (kwĕbe·kəɹ, kĕ-). Also **Quebecer.** [f. prec. + -ER[1].] = *QUÉBECOIS *sb.* a.

1836 *Bytown* (Ottawa) *Independent* 24 Feb. 3/2 We think the Quebecers are not such flats as to pay for measuring timber, merely because they receive it. **1837** *Montreal Transcript* 14 Jan. 2/2 The match..was played on Tuesday last, at Three Rivers, when the Quebeckers proved victorious. **1890** [see *NEW *a.* 5 d]. **1946** H. CROOME *Faithless Mirror* xiv. 153 Other Canadians go overseas..the Quebeckers stay at home. **1957** *Listener* 17 Oct. 593/1 The typical Quebecer is still a Royalist, a Conservative, even if he votes Liberal. **1963** *Times* 25 Feb. (Canada Suppl.) p. vii/3 We've got to keep control of new industries in Quebec for Quebecers. **1973** *Times Lit. Suppl.* 26 Oct. 1295/2 The backward, Church-controlled, inferiority-complex-ridden Quebecker of yesteryear. **1977** *Time* 7 Feb. 21/1 The man who wants to lead 6 million Quebeckers out of Canadian confederation. **1979** *Amer. N. & Q.* Mar. 119/2 Radwanski believes that Trudeau is the man best equipped to meet Lévesque's challenge. Most Quebecers appear to think that, too.

‖ **Québecois** (kebe̜kwa), *sb.* and *a.* Also **Québecquois.** [Fr., f. *QUEBEC.] **A.** *sb.* **a.** A native or inhabitant of the city or province of Quebec, esp. one who is a French-Canadian. **b.** The French spoken in Quebec. **B.** *adj.* Of or pertaining to Quebec or its inhabitants.

1873 J. M. LEMOINE *Maple Leaves* 171 The County and town of Joliette preserve the name of another distinguished Canadian, a Québecquois, Louis Joliette. **1954** T. H. RADDALL *Muster of Arms* 135 She was speaking in English but the mind behind the tongue was Quebecois. **1960** *Times* 21 Nov. (Canada Suppl.) p. ii/7 Mr. Dorion is the most typically Quebecois of the French-Canadian ministers. **1962** *Maclean's Mag.* 17 Nov. 4/1 Editors of French language newspapers who had wailed about the 'stupidity' of rural Québecois in the last federal election. **1963** *Ibid.* 6 Apr. 23/1 Her French sounds more Parisian than what we who don't speak French well call Quebecois. **1970** *Globe Mag.* (Toronto) 26 Sept. 17/1 The manuscripts of Pauline Archange is a first-person story of a Quebecois slum child. **1974** *Times Lit. Suppl.* 14 June 634/2 Her little book assembles..comments by prominent Québécois. *Ibid.* 634/3 M Étheir-Blais is a Franco-Ontarian, not a Québécois. **1977** H. GILES *Lang., Ethnicity & Intergroup Relations* 2 Québécois air controllers engaged in industrial action for a refusal at their not being allowed to use French as a medium of air communications. **1977** *Listener* 23 June 808/2 The beleaguered English-speaking Québécois. **1978** *Maledicta* II. 61 For the most part, Québecois imprecations flourished on the spot in response to the needs of a people living in conditions of moral and material misery.

quebracho. Add: Also **quiebrahacha.** (Further examples.) Also, the timber of these trees.

1889 G. S. BOULGER *Uses of Plants* v. 159 Red Quebracho..is a hard wood from the River Plate... Other Quebrachos..are also used in South America. **1908** W. R. FISHER *Schlich's Man. Forestry* (ed. 2) V. I. viii. 572 Experimental use is also made of pitch pine and quebracho wood [for railway sleepers]. **1913** *Chambers's Jrnl.* 28 June 480/2 Quebracho ('break-axe'), one of the hardest, heaviest, and most durable woods known. **1923** *Nature* 8 Sept. 376/2 The principal sources of this [*sc.* tannin] are oak galls and bark, mangrove bark, Myrobalans, Quebracho, and *Acacia decurrens.* **1924** RECORD & MELL *Timbers Trop. Amer.* II. 508 White quebracho is the name most commonly applied to *Aspidosperma quebracho-blanco*..of Argentina, Paraguay, and south-western Brazil. **1933** H. ALLEN *Anthony Adverse* v. xxix. 409 It was full of a thousand lush and exotic odours from ..juniper and lantana; the fragrant quiebrahacha, tamarind and rotting mastic leaves. **1955** *Times* 30 June 18/2 The production of Quebracho extract during the year amounted to 81,644 tons. **1969** T. C. THORSTENSEN *Pract. Leather Technol.* ix. 140 Quebracho extract is used in the manufacture of heavy leathers and in the vegetable re-tanning of chrome tanned upper leathers. **1974** D. MEIRING *President Plan* ix. 74 A big fire of *quebracho* glowed and flickered.

‖ **quebrada** (kebrā·dă). [Sp., fem. of *quebrado*, pa. pple. of *quebrar* to break.] **1.** A mountain stream in S. America.

1833 *Blackw. Mag.* Aug. 144/2 Next morning I rode out on my mule, to take my last dip in the *Quebrada* of the *Loseria*, which was a rapid in a beautiful little rivulet, distant from Panama about three miles. **1920** *Chambers's Jrnl.* Dec. 979 The many quebradas which flow down the mountain ravines. **1973** K. BENTON *Craig & Jaguar* v. 45 The Chasco [river] was fed by the *quebradas* that brought down meltwater from the high ranges.

2. A ravine in S. America.

1845 *Encycl. Metrop.* XIV. 565/1 Abrupt precipices.. occur in every part of the parent chain of the Andes near the equator, and diversify its appearance with the most horrid chasms, or rents, here called Quebradas, varying from 100 feet to 4 or 5,000 feet in depth. **1860** MAYNE REID *Odd People* 456 The stupendous ravines termed 'barrancas' & 'quebradas', which intersect the Cordilleras of the Andes in other parts of South America. **1927** *Blackw. Mag.* Aug. 229/2 We will build another house in the quebrada at Palalle Grande. **1949** *Américas* Sept. 17 The men wore rags and undoubtedly lived in one-room shanties in the quebradas. **1974** *Encycl. Brit. Macropædia* I. 1135/1 To the west are the Salto-Jujeña, cut by canyons called *quebradas* through which run small rivers.

Quechua (ke·tʃwă), *sb.* and *a.* Also **Quichua, Kechua,** and other varr. [Sp., ad. Quechua *k'echua, k'eshua*, plunderer, despoiler.] **A.** *sb.* **a.** An Indian people of Peru and neighbouring parts of Bolivia, Chile, Colombia, and Ecuador; a member of this people. **b.** The language (actually a group of related languages) spoken by this people. **B.** *adj.* Of or pertaining to this people or their language.

1840 *Penny Cycl.* XVIII. 6/2 They [*sc.* the Peruvian Indians] speak the Quichua language, which is generally called the language of the Incas, and which is used by all the natives of South America, from Quito near the equator, to Tucuman in La Plata, 27° S. lat. *Ibid.* 9/2 As the aborigines who inhabit this extensive country speak one language, the Quichua, it must be supposed that they belong to one race. **1843** J. C. PRICHARD *Nat. Hist. Man* xlv. 431 Among the Peruvian nations, the dominant race were the Quichuas, or Incas, distinguished by their language, which is the Quichuan. **1860** [see *AYMARA]. **1877** [see *CHIBCHA]. **1891** D. G. BRINTON *Amer. Race* II. i. 203 The Kechua..was spoken by an unbroken chain of tribes for nearly two thousand miles from north to south. **1908** [see *CHOLO, CHOLO]. **1921** [see *AYMARA]. **1926** *South Amer.* Sept. 71/2 We take with us a native helper who can speak Quechua. **1937** R. H. LOWIE *Hist. Ethnol. Theory* xiv. 258 The absence of hoes from all of South America would be of real interest were it not that their undoubted use among the Quichua, past and present, eliminates the problems otherwise raised. **1948** A. L. KROEBER *Anthropol.* (ed. 2) x. 431 The Aztec, Otomí, Maya, Quechua, or Aymará Indians were economically oppressed by their conquest. **1950** J. A. MASON in J. H. Steward *Handbk. S. Amer. Indians* VI. 197 Quechua (Kechua, Quichua, Keshwa, etc.) is the South American analogue of Aztec. *Ibid.*, Today probably several millions of Indians in Perú, southwestern Ecuador, western Bolivia, and northwestern Argentina speak Quechua, and most of them nothing else. **1952** *Language* XXVIII. 366 (*title*) Semantic components in Kechua person morphemes. **1966** *Chambers's Encycl.* VIII. 366/2 Quechumaran comprises two branches..the Quechuan branch, spoken from Colombia to Chile, has as its main member Quechua, of Peru, Ecuador and Bolivia. This is by far the most important native language of South America. **1973** [see *PICK *v.*[1] 20 f]. **1974** *Times* 6 Dec. 15/7 The Quechua Indian women of Southern Peru. *Ibid.* 15/8 The Quechua hitherto have lived in inconveniently scattered farmholdings. **1977** C. F. & F. M. Voegelin *Classification & Index of World's Languages* 21 Quechua and Aymara were said to be genetically related as early as Steinthal (1890).

Quechuan (ke·tʃwăn), *a.* [f. prec. + -an.] Also **Quichuan, Kechuan.** = prec. B. Also as *sb.*

1843 [see prec.]. **1853** F. L. Hawks tr. *Rivero & Tschudi's Peruvian Antiquities* v. 93 We here present a short review..of the character of the Quichuan or Peruvian tongue. **1862** R. G. Latham *Compar. Philol.* 482 The capital Cuzco, Quichuan as it is in many respects, is a town upon Aymara ground. **1901** A. H. Keane *Central & S. Amer.* 207 The Incas were originally a tribe of Quichuan stock. **1931** W. A. Read *Louisiana-French* 142 A French adaptation of Spanish *ñapa*, which is taken in turn from Kechuan *yapa*, 'a present made to a customer'. **1933** L. Bloomfield *Language* iv. 73 *Kechuan*, the language of the Inca civilization. **1966** [see prec.]. **1972** W. B. Lockwood *Panorama Indo-Europ. Lang.* iii. 35 A large majority of Aymarans and Quechuans are monoglots. **1973** K. Benton *Craig & Jaguar* xii. 190 The men, under Huaman's directions, spiced with obscene Quechuan oaths, lowered it.

Queckenstedt (kwe·kĕnstet). *Med.* The name of Hans Heinrich *Queckenstedt* (1876–1918), German physician, used *attrib.* and in the possessive to denote the procedure proposed by him (*Deutsch. Zeitschr. f. Nervenheilk.* (1916) LV. 326) of compressing a patient's jugular veins while observing the pressure of the cerebrospinal fluid (the absence of a marked increase in this indicating obstruction of the subarachnoid space).

1928 R. J. E. Scott *Gould's Med. Dict.* (ed. 2) 1175/2 *Queckenstedt's test*, in healthy persons pressure on the veins of the neck causes a prompt rise in the pressure of the cerebrospinal fluid, which disappears on release of the pressure on the veins. **1934** D. Munro in *Practitioners Library of Med. & Surg.* V. xi. 803 If..the Queckenstedt test is positive, that is, if flow of cerebrospinal fluid is partly or completely interfered with by a block in the subarachnoid space, the rise on jugular compression will be totally absent if the block is complete, or greatly slowed and diminished in height if the block is incomplete. **1968** Passmore & Robson *Compan. Med. Stud.* I. xxiv. 76/2 In performing Queckenstedt's test, it is as well not to squeeze or even seem to squeeze the trachea. **1970** R. G. Feldman in Keefer & Wilkins *Medicine* xliii. 957 Compression of the jugular vein (Queckenstedt maneuver) has been used to observe the response of intracranial pressure to a change in venous pressure.

queen, *sb.* Add: **2. c. Queen Mum,** colloq. alteration of Queen-mother, used with affectionate reference to Queen Elizabeth, the Queen Mother (b. 1900).

1960 L. R. Banks *L-Shaped Room* ix. 135, I kept it a treat. I could've had the Queen Mum to tea there and not been ashamed. **1965** J. Potter *Death in Office* x. 101 Mrs Barber..extending a gloved hand from the sitting position: her imitation of the Queen Mum no doubt. **1974** J. Gardner *Corner Men* xiii. 185 What do you think I do all day..? Play canasta with the Queen Mum and help feed the royal corgis? **1980** *Times* 4 Aug. 4/1 The dear old Queen Mum is..'the best loved lady in the land'.

d. *Queen and country*: the objects of allegiance for a patriot whose head of state is a queen.

1706 Farquhar *Recruiting Officer* v. 72, I endeavour by the Example of this worthy Gentleman to serve my Queen and Country at home. **1861** C. M. Yonge *Young Step-Mother* xxix. 443 His son got his death fighting for his queen and his country. **1900** *Times* 2 Apr. 7/1 It was a keen joy..to be allowed to fight for his Queen and country. **1906** W. S. Churchill *Lord Randolph Churchill* (1907) xxi. 792 Night after night he had risen in his place to discharge..his duty—as he would have phrased it—to 'Queen and country'. **1948** F. Thompson *Still glides Stream* ii. 41 Thank God he died for his Queen and country! **1966** J. Gardner *Amber Nine* i. 28 Anyway, got to go. Queen-and-Country as my lovable boss would say. **1977** *Sounds* 9 July 20/6 Step up the beaches and annihilate somebody for Queen and country, get a medal pinned on your chest.

e. *ellipt.* as *the Queen*: the national anthem 'God save the Queen'.

1898 J. D. Brayshaw *Slum Silhouettes* 37 The curtain fell at last, and the band struck up the 'Queen'. **1916** M. Diver *Desmond's Daughter* iv. iv. 341 They're playing 'The Queen'. I *must* be on the spot to say good-bye to people. **1965** 'W. Haggard' *Powder Barrel* ix. 86 The police band..crashed into The Queen in time in a formal way. **1970** *Daily Tel.* 18 Aug. 13/7 Wherever the Prince was present at a function organised by the association three anthems were played—the Queen, 'Land of My Fathers' and 'God Bless the Prince of Wales'.

3. b. *Queen Mary.* (*a*) Used *attrib.* in *Queen Mary hat*, a variety of toque popularized by Queen Mary (1867–1953), wife of King George V, who favoured it because it enabled the public to have a clear view of her face; so *Queen Mary toque.* (*b*) A type of long low-loading road trailer (in allusion to the Cunard passenger liner: see below).

(*a*) **1938** L. Bemelmans *Life Class* ii. iii. 140 She is dressed in a trotteur, and wears a hat with a thousand cloth violets, a Queen Mary toque. **1947** *New Yorker* 22 Nov. 38/1 A Queen Mary hat protected her from the autumnal sunlight. **1950** J. D. MacDonald *Brass Cupcake* (1955) xv. 157 She sold power shovels, sang baritone and wore Queen Mary hats. **1967** L. J. Braun *Cat who ate Danish Modern* ix. 76 There was enough blue blood to float a ship... You never saw so many pince-nez and Queen Mary hats. **1977** G. Markstein *Chance Awakening* x. 25 Golly sat down in the deck chair..with the grey-haired gentleman..and the old ladies with Queen Mary toques.

(*b*) **1943** C. H. Ward-Jackson *It's a Piece of Cake* 50 *Queen Mary*, a type of long, low-loading, articulated vehicle specially designed for the road transportation of airframes. **1949** *Jrnl. R. Aeronaut. Soc.* LIII. 822 The Council wish to acknowledge their appreciation of the 'Queen Mary' which was kindly provided by Hawker Aircraft Ltd. for the transport of some of the aircraft of the Shuttleworth Collection. **1960** *Picture Show Ann.* *1961* (Austral.) 151/2 *Queen Mary*, a 60ft. trailer used for moving scenery. **1968** I. Lambot *Queen dies First* v. 34 There's a signal in, from the salvage boys. They'll be sending a Queen Mary on Monday to shift it.

c. *the Queens*: the Cunard passenger liners, 'Queen Mary' and 'Queen Elizabeth'.

1949 P. Duff *Brit. Ships & Shipping* i. 28 The two *Queens* of the North Atlantic did invaluable service in every theatre of war. **1956** H. Grattidge *Captain of Queens* 291 Both *Queens* had the same 118 foot breadth, but at 1,031 feet the *Elizabeth* eclipsed the *Mary*'s length by ten clear feet. **1959** *Daily Tel.* 9 Apr. 1/4 Plans to replace the 'Queens' must be modern and far-reaching. **1968** O. Wynd *Sumatra Seven Zero* vi. 85 The first clang of metal sounded like a mid-Atlantic collision between the two Queens. **1970** W. G. Roberts *Quest for Oil* xi. 116 This may seem slow compared with the 30 knots of the 'Queens' or even with the 20 to 25 knots of the majority of other passenger liners.

4. *Queen of Spain fritillary*, an orange butterfly with black markings, *Argynnis lathonia*, belonging to the family Nymphalidæ and widely distributed in Europe, N. Africa, and parts of Asia.

1775 M. Harris *Eng. Lepidoptera* 3 Fritillaria, Queen of Spain... Orange brown spotted with black. **1866** [see Fritillary 2]. **1906** R. South *Butterflies Brit. Isles* 91 The Queen of Spain Fritillary... This butterfly is not unlike a small example of the Silver-washed Fritillary. **1976** *Country Life* 18 Mar. 680/2 The remaining nine fritillaries include three occasional migrants, the Queen of Spain fritillary, the cardinal and the weaver's fritillary.

5. d. (Further examples.) Also, a woman who has pre-eminence in an unspecified sphere. See also *beauty queen* s.v. *beauty *sb.* III b, etc.

1847 C. Brontë *Jane Eyre* II. i. 14 Most of them.. looked handsome; but Miss Ingram was certainly the queen. **1958** *Spectator* 22 Aug. 247/1 A robust, jolly-looking person, more like a hockey queen than a film star. **1962** E. Lucia *Klondike Kate* 9 Rare instances of chivalry and devotion were exhibited by the miners toward this frontier queen. **1979** C. MacLeod *Family Vault* (1980) xxiv. 213 She decided to become a society queen and married a man who had the cash but not the inclination.

e. *slang.* An attractive woman; a girl-friend, female partner.

1900 *Dialect Notes* II. 53 *Queen*,..an attractive girl. **1914** 'High Jinks, Jr.' *Choice Slang* 17 *Queen*, a pretty girl. 'A Beauty'. **1937** J. T. Farrell *Fellow Countrymen* 181 Wouldn't it be luck if a ritzy queen fell for him! **1944** C. Himes *Black on Black* (1973) 196 My queen 'gan bouncin' out her twelve-dollar dress. **1952** S. Selvon *Brighter Sun* x. 207 Same ting happen wen my old queen was sick. **1955** P. Sillitoe *Cloak without Dagger* xiv. 128 Both gangs used hatchets, swords, and sharpened bicycle chains..and these were conveyed to the scenes of their battles by their 'queens'. **1975** *Globe & Mail* (Toronto) 11 June 3/7 Since some of the members have no respect for the law, they refuse to enter into a legal marriage. They view it as an unnecessary burden and responsibility. Instead, some Rastafarians have many 'Queens'.

6. b. *queen of puddings*, a pudding made of breadcrumbs, milk, and other ingredients, freq. with a layer of meringue on top; *queen-of-the-meadow(s*, (*a*) substitute for def.: the meadow-sweet, *Filipendula ulmaria*, native to Europe and Asia and naturalized in eastern North America; (further examples); (*b*) *U.S.* = *joe-pye weed; *queen-of-the-night*, a variety of night-blooming cereus (see *night *sb.* 14), esp. *Selenicereus grandiflorus*, which is native to the West Indies and bears fragrant white flowers; *queen-of-the-prairie*, substitute for def.: a perennial North American herb, *Filipendula rubra*, found in meadows and prairies and bearing clusters of small pink flowers; (examples); *Queen of the West*: Cincinnati, Ohio (cf. **Queen city* in sense 13). Similarly with an *of* phrase to designate other cities.

1784 *Mem. Amer. Acad.* I. 451 Queen of the Meadows. Blossoms red or purple. In moist pastures. **1835** C. F. Hoffman *Winter in West* I. 130 It is in vain for thriving Pittsburg or flourishing Louisville..to dispute with Cincinnati her title of 'Queen of the West'. **1838** H. Martineau *Retrospect* II. 254, I should prefer Cincinnati as a residence... The 'Queen of the West' is enthroned in a region of wonderful and inexhaustible beauty. **1840** *Knickerbocker* XVI. 157 In this way we glided in our broad-horn past Cincinnati, the 'Queen of the West' as she is now called. **1851** *San Francisco Picayune* 19 Sept. 2/4 Some person, gifted with a sufficient amount of patience, may undertake to compile the history of San Francisco..the Queen of the Pacific. **1852** H. R. Noll *Bot. Class Bk. & Flora Pennsylvania* 100 S[piræa] lobata, Murr. Queen of the Prairie. **1892** *Amer. Folk-Lore* V. 98 *Eupatorium purpureum*, Queen of the meadow. **1898** C. A. Creevey *Flowers of Field, Hill & Swamp* 146 Queen-of-the-prairie... A stately, beautiful plant adorning the meadows and prairies south and west of Pennsylvania. *Ibid.* 484 Meadow-sweet. Queen-of-the-meadows... A slender, reddish-stemmed shrub, 2 to 6 feet high. **1911** Queen-of-the-meadow [see *Indian turnip* s.v. *Indian *a.* 4 b]. **1917** M. Byron *Pudding Book* iii. 72 Queen of Puddings... Soak a pint of breadcrumbs in boiling milk, and the yolks of four eggs well beaten. **1920** Britton & Millspaugh *Bahama Flora* 294 *Selenicereus grandiflorus*... Queen-of-the-Night. Often cultivated. **1949** H. Hornsby *Lonesome Valley* xxii. 291 The wind was working among the alder bushes and the willows and queen of the meadow. **1963** M. Patten *Puddings & Desserts* (recipe no. 389) Queen of puddings. **1968** Peterson & McKenny *Field Guide to Wildflowers N. Amer.* 284 Queen-of-the-prairie... Flowers deep pink. **1971** *Fashion Panorama* (Ceylon) Apr.-June 21 The Queen of the night was in full bloom outside and its heavy and overpowering scent reached her from the garden. **1972** E. Wigginton *Foxfire Bk.* 242 Take one root from a queen-of-the-meadow plant. **1977** H. Fast *Immigrants* i. 30 For almost nine weeks, the shattered city [*sc.* San Francisco], known not only as the 'Queen of the Pacific' but as the 'queen of larceny' as well, entered into a period of benign brotherhood.

10. a. Substitute for def.: A small scallop, *Chlamys opercularis*, found off several parts of the coast of north-western Europe; = Quin; (later examples).

1901 E. Step *Shell Life* 84 The Quin or Queen..is more nearly circular in shape, thin and smooth. **1928** Russell & Yonge *Seas* iii. 74 Another animal which can move about is the scallop, especially the smaller 'queen'. **1959** A. C. Hardy *Open Sea* II. vi. 143 The smaller and delicious 'queens'..may occasionally be brought in by trawlers..in sufficient quantities to be marketed. **1971** *Country Life* 21 Oct. 1040/1 Last year nearly 5,000 tons of queens..were brought into Scottish ports.

11. (Later examples.)

1934 P. Wade *Siamese Cat* iv. 45 Not only should the queen herself be excellent, but her pedigree must be above suspicion. **1954** D. Hartley *Food in England* 660 You cannot keep a cat on milk only... Nursing queens should be given water to drink and solid food. **1960** *Amer. Speech* XXXV. 300 Cat fanciers use the name queen in speaking of their litter-bearing female cats. **1977** *Proc. R. Soc. Med.* LXX. 3/1 This calcium deficient diet produced..fractures of vertebrae and limb bones in growing kittens and young zoo felids. Calcium deficiency also occurred in lactating queens and their young litters.

11*. A male homosexual, esp. the effeminate partner in a homosexual relationship. *slang.* Cf. *quean 3.

1924 *Truth* (Sydney) 27 Apr. 6 *Queen*, effeminate person. **1929** M. Lief *Hangover* vi. 100 'What's those?' 'You know—all those queens.' **1930** E. Waugh *Vile Bodies* 61 'Now what may *you* want, my Italian queen?' said Lottie as the waiter came in with a tray. **1938** N. Marsh *Artists in Crime* ix. 127 We met the chap that runs the place. One of those die-away queens. **1952** A. Wilson *Hemlock & After* i. v. 88 Anyone would think he was just another routine, harmless old queen. **1962** [see *faggot, fagot 6 b]. **1971** F. Forsyth *Day of Jackal* xx. 333 He must be..how marvellous! A handsome young butch looking for an old queen to take him home. **1977** *New Yorker* 24 Oct. 64/2 There are only a handful of 'queens' at Green Haven at any one time—men with feminine characteristics they do their best to enhance. The queens are usually given women's nicknames.

12. a. *queen-woman.*

1904 W. B. Yeats *Stories of Red Hanrahan* 20, I heard under a ragged hollow wood, A queen-woman dressed out in silver, cry.

13. Queen At, A.T. *Mil. slang* (see quot. 1943); **queen bee,** for 'also *transf.*' read 'also *transf.* and *fig.*' and add earlier and later examples; *spec.* (*Mil.*) an automatically-controlled aeroplane used as a target in firing practice; **queen-cake** (later examples); **queen cat** (later examples); **Queen City** *N. Amer.*, an epithet applied to the chief or pre-eminent city (*of* a region) (cf. sense *6 b); **queen conch** (later examples); **queen-excluder** (examples); **queen-fish,** (*a*) *U.S.* (examples); (*b*) a large Australian marine fish, *Scomberoides sancti-petri*, of the family Carangidæ; **queen olive,** the particularly large fruit of certain varieties of olive; **queen-pin** *colloq.*, a woman who controls the (successful) organization of a specified institution or event; (see King-Pin in Dict. and Suppl.); **queen pudding** = **queen's pudding*; **queen scallop** = *queen *sb.* 10 a; **queen-side** *a. Chess*, of or pertaining to the side of the board in which both queens start the game; **queen-size** *a.*, of an extra large size, though occas. in a series (as of beds), smaller than **king-size*; also *queen-sized* adj.; **Queen staysail,** a triangular main topmast staysail in a schooner yacht (see quot. 1948); **queen-stitch** (earlier examples); **queen substance,** a pheromone produced by a queen bee and given to the colony's workers to prevent the production of more queens; **queen trigger-fish,** a deep-bodied, blue and yellow marine fish, *Balistes vetula*, found in the Indian and Atlantic

Oceans; **queenwood,** substitute for def.: an Australian evergreen tree, *Daviesia arborea*, of the family Leguminosæ, or its wood; (examples).

1943 Hunt & Pringle *Service Slang* 54 *Queen At*, a Chief Commander of the A[uxiliary] T[erritorial] S[ervice]. **1947** N. Streatfeild *Grass in Piccadilly* 33 That queen A.T. of yours must have been a holy terror. **1807** R. Southey *Lett. from England* II. xxx. 41 Wherever one of the queen bees of fashion alights, a whole swarm follows her. **1935** *Sun* (Baltimore) 18 July 2/6 King George today saw the British fleet repel an attack by robot planes. The feature of the war game was the fight between the new aircraft guns on the battleship and the radio-controlled 'queen bee' flying machines. **1938** *Times* 26 Aug. 11/1 'Queen Bees'—pilotless, wireless controlled target machines—were only available at two of the..camps. **1943** C. H. Ward-Jackson *It's a Piece of Cake* 50 *The Queen Bee*, the Director of the Women's Auxiliary Air Force; or the senior W.A.A.F. officer on a station. **1951** A. Christie *They came to Baghdad* xv. 139, I thought it was just some female who was coming out to boss things. A kind of Queen Bee. **1956** N. Streatfeild *Judith* i. 44 Beatrice became a queen bee in London's civil defence force. **1960** P. Stanton *Village of Stars* 63 She walked into the W.R.A.F. sitting-room... There was a little radio in the corner... The Queen Bee had no doubt been wangling the Comforts Fund. **1973** G. Bromley *Chance to Poison* v. 79 She's a very dominating character..Queen Bee of the Women's Institute—without her it would collapse. **1978** R. V. Jones *Most Secret War* xxxix. 356 We had in fact evolved our own 'Queen Bee' remote controlled aeroplane for use as an anti-aircraft target in the years before the war. **1894** W. B. Yeats *Land of Heart's Desire* 32, I will have queen cakes when you come to me! **1977** *Radio Times* 12–18 Mar. 16/4 They added a domestic touch by selling their own home produce, little queen cakes and jam. **1893** J. Jennings *Domestic or Fancy Cats* iv. 31 At what age should the queen cat breed? **1960** *Amer. Speech* XXXV. 300 Has this name [*sc.* queen] arisen from the often-observed imperious bearing of queen cats? **1838** B. Drake (*title*) Tales and sketches from the Queen City [= Cincinnati]. **1844** in C. Cist *Cincinnati Misc.* (1845) I. 9/1 [Cincinnati] is now familiarly called the Queen City of the West. **1870** *Colorado Gazetteer* 40 Denver, the principal city and capital of Colorado—the Queen City of the Plains—is the county seat of Arapahoe county. **1879** Whitman *Specimen Days* (1882) 147 So much for my feeling toward the Queen City of the plains and peaks [= Denver]. **1880** *Harper's Mag.* Dec. 70 Local prejudice..and proverbial procrastination..unite to keep 'Chinatown' practically a sealed book to the better-class denizens of the Queen City of the Pacific [= San Francisco]. **1943** *Colorado Mag.* Jan. 15 The Queen City of the Plains [= Denver] started in 1878. **1949** *Bull. Hist. & Philos. Soc. Ohio* Apr. 99 That enthusiastic booster for the 'Queen City' [= Cincinnati], Dr. Daniel Drake. **1979** M. G. Eberhart *Bayou Road* v. 47 How *could* the Yankees have injured..New Orleans, the Queen City, so completely. **1918** *Chambers's Jrnl.* Aug. 541/2 It is the Queen conch my friend has come to buy. **1975** M. Humfrey *Sea Shells W. Indies* i. 29 The powerful Queen Conch..may weigh more than five pounds. **1881** T. W. Cowan *Brit. Bee-keeper's Guide Bk.* [vii. 33 One of the features of this hive is the possibility of preventing swarming, by confining the queen..by placing a zinc excluder..near the front of the hive.] *Ibid.* 134/1 Queen-excluder. **1887** F. R. Cheshire *Bees & Bee-keeping* II. iii. 74 This [*sc.* the restriction of the queen] is now accomplished by what is called 'excluder-zinc', or 'queen-excluder'. **1930** W. Herrod-Hempsall *Bee-keeping* I. ix. 447 The first queen excluder, made from wood, was invented and used in Scotland in 1849. **1976** T. Hooper *Guide to Bees & Honey* iv. 76 A queen-excluder will be necessary for each [hive]. **1883** J. J. Lalor *Cycl. Political Sci.* II. 217/2 The queen-fish, the bagre and the roncador are..well known in California. **1905** D. S. Jordan *Guide to Study of Fishes* II. xx. 354 The queenfish, *Seriphus politus*, of the California coast, is much like the others of this series... It is a very choice fish. **1937** Z. Grey *Amer. Angler in Austral.* x. 111 The queen fish, a beautiful silvery dolphin-like leaper, is one of the greatest fish I have caught. **1951** T. C. Roughley *Fish & Fisheries Austral.* i. 60 The queenfish has a wide distribution from northern New South Wales to the north-west coast of Western Australia, and..is considered to be one of the fastest and most spectacular game-fish. **1965** A. J. McClane *Stand. Fishing Encycl.* 223/1 The queenfish, *Seriphus politus*, is elongate... Its body is bluish and the fins are yellowish. Growing to about a foot, it occurs from central California to Baja California in shallow water. **1969** *Northern Territory News* (Darwin) *Focus '69* 63/1 The next biggest catch is the threadfin..followed by the mackerel..and queenfish. **1911** *Daily Colonist* (Victoria, B.C.) 15 Apr. 10/1 (Advt.), Spanish Queen Olives, bottle, 50c or $1.00..Rowat's Selected Queen Olives, bottle 50c. **1974** Queen olive [see *manzanilla 2]. **1961** *Guardian* 16 Jan. 4/2 A break for the 'queen-pin'..is utterly essential if you are to keep going. **1972** *Daily Tel.* 21 Jan. 13/1 Welcome to Elaine May..not just as a voice but as the queen-pin—director, author and actress. **1891** T. F. Garrett *Encycl. Pract. Cookery* II. 267/2 Queen pudding. **1971** *Jean Bowring Cookbook* 227 Queen pudding. [Recipe follows]. **1959** A. C. Hardy *Open Sea* II. vi. 143 (*caption*) The queen scallop..showing the swimming action. **1972** *Aquaculture* I. 280 The fish were fed a mixed diet of fresh or frozen chopped herring and queen scallop (*Chlamys opercularis*) meat, at a rate of 750 g twice weekly. **1941** F. Reinfeld *Keres' Best Games of Chess* 70/1 Richter prefers to retain the Queen-side Pawns, even at the cost of exchanging Rooks. **1966** J. R. Capablanca *Last Chess Lectures* (1967) i. 37 His Queen-side majority of Pawns could be converted into a passed Pawn. **1959** *Punch* 28 Oct. 371/1 A motel in Los Angeles advertises Queen-size beds. **1967** *Boston Sunday Herald* 30 Apr. (Bedding Suppl.) 1/5 Queen size is the answer if a king-size bed doesn't fit your plans... Its 60-by-80-inch innerspring mattress is six inches wider and five inches longer than the old double size. **1973** *Publishers Weekly* 23 July 66/3 An appealing and handsomely produced queen-size book. **1976** *Washington Post* 19 Apr. A9/4 (Advt.), Traditionally styled Queen Size Sleep Sofa and matching love-seat combination. **1979** *Arizona Daily Star* 5 Aug. (Advt. Section) 8/8 It is beautifully designed, complete with queen-size bed. **1955** *Sun* (Baltimore) 19 Mar. 9/4 Mrs Daniel J. Flood, wife of a Democratic Congressman from Pennsylvania, is introducing a new fad here—'queen-sized' colored cigarettes to match her costume. **1975** A. Bergman *Hollywood & Le Vine* (1976) ix. 123 A queen-sized mattress. **1978** *New York* 3 Apr. 74 (Advt.), And for just $50 more, we'll transform the Sofa into a queen-sized sleeper convertible! **1944** H. A. Callahan *Rigging* 130 The late J. Rogers Maxwell introduced a funny little staysail on his famous schooner *Queen* and it has always been known as the queen staysail. **1948** L. F. Herreshoff in *Rudder* Aug. 58 Because previous staysails had to be lowered away in tacking, when my father designed the schooner Queen he did away with the triatic stay and in its place ran a stay called a 'fresh water stay' between the topmast heads. This staysail with which a schooner can tack is called a 'Queen staysail', as it was first used on the schooner Queen. **1631** J. Taylor *Needles Excellency* (1634) sig. A2, col. 2, Bred-stitch, Fisher-stitch, Irish-stitch, and Queen-stitch. **1841** Lady Wilton *Art of Needle-work* (ed. 3) xx. 317 There are..ferne- and queen-stitches. **1954** C. G. Butler in *Trans. R. Entomol. Soc.* CV. 14 It is necessary for the bees to have physical contact with their queen in order to obtain this 'queen substance'. **1972** *Sci. Amer.* Sept. 56/3 The 'queen substances' are outstanding in the complexity and pervasiveness of their role in social organization. **1924** J. T. Nichols in J. O. La Gorce *Bk. Fishes* 166/2 The gaudy colors of the Queen Trigger-fish..are an exception among such forms. **1971** 'D. Halliday' *Dolly & Doctor Bird* xii. 166 Bahamian waters are full of extraordinary fish, from Striped Grunts to Queen Triggerfish. **1889** J. H. Maiden *Useful Native Plants Austral.* 415 *Daviesia arborea*..'Queen-wood'. This wood is hard, close-grained, with beautiful pink streaked lines. **1902** G. S. Boulger *Wood* ii. 300 Queen-wood.. North-eastern Australia... Streaked with pink, hard, close-grained, susceptible of a fine polish.

14. a. *Queen's speech*: see *speech *sb.*[1] 8 d.

b. queen's chair, a makeshift seat (cf. *queen's cushion*); **queen's cloth** (later example); **queen's conch** = *queen conch* (sense 13 in Dict. and Suppl.); **queen's cushion,** for 'Jamieson, 1808' in Dict. read 'Jamieson, 1825'; (examples); **Queen's English,** the English language regarded as under the guardianship of the Queen; hence, standard or correct English; **Queen's Guide,** a holder of the highest award in Guiding, *spec.* during the reign of a queen; **queen's head** (earlier and later examples); **queen's pattern** (see quots. 1910 and 1957); **queen's pudding,** a steamed suet pudding (occas. used for *queen of puddings*, sense 6 b above); **Queen's Scout,** a holder of the highest award in Scouting, *spec.* during the reign of a queen; **Queen's shilling:** also *transf.* and fig.; (earlier and later examples); **Queen's staysail** = **Queen staysail*; **queen's stuff** (later example); **queen's taste:** in phr. *to the* or *a queen's taste*, to perfection; **queen's ware,** (*a*) (earlier and later examples); (*b*) (earlier and later examples); **queen's weather** (earlier and later examples); **queen's woman** *slang* (now *Hist.*), a prostitute who received medical attention under the terms of the Contagious Diseases Acts of the 1860s.

1965 S. T. Ollivier *Petticoat Farm* vi. 77 Henry's buggy reins, tied to a cream-can lid, had formed a queen's chair for Harry. **1818** M. Edgeworth *Let.* 29 Oct. (1971) 130 Tell me which you prefer the Merino or the Queens cloth... The queens cloth comes to a guinea the dress cheaper. **1812** E. Weeton *Let.* June in *Jrnl. of Governess* (1969) II. 93, I have inquired the price of shells... Yours are conch shells; these are called Queen's conches. **1963** *Times* 27 Apr. 11/2 The pink queen's conch shell from the Caribbean. **1825** J. Jamieson *Suppl. to Etym. Dict. of Scottish Lang.* II. 253/1 *Queen's*, also *king's cushion*, a mode of carriage, whether in sport, or from necessity... Two persons, each of whom grasps his right wrist with his left hand, with the other lays hold of his neighbour's wrist, so as to form a seat of four hands and wrists conjoined. On these the person, who is to be carried, seats himself, or is seated by others, putting both his arms, for greater security, round the necks of the bearers. **1873** C. M. Yonge *Pillars of House* IV. xl. 161 The hands were clasped, queen's-cushion fashion, beneath her, the necks were bent for the arms to be thrown round them. **1592** T. Nashe *Strange Newes* sig. B1ᵛ, He must be running on the letter, and abusing the Queenes English without pittie or mercie. **1848** [see *on *prep.* 6 a]. **1864** H. Alford *Plea for Queen's Eng.* (ed. 2) 2 The *Queen's English* is not an unmeaning phrase, but one which may serve to teach us some profitable lessons with regard to our language. **1867** F. S. Cozzens *Sayings of Dr. Bushwhacker* 82 In fact, that arbitrary style of speaking which is commonly known as the Queen's English. **1885** *Punch* 4 July 5/2 (*heading*) The Premier's Primer; or Queen's English as she is wrote. **1902** F. Hume *Fever of Life* 146, I! Oh, how can you? I speak the Queen's English. **1975** *Verbatim* Dec. 15/2 One irate caller said, according to the network [NKH], 'How dare you deprive us of our one chance to hear the Queen's English?' **1968** M. E. Brimelow *Guide Handbk.* iv. 70 If a Guide has..taken a full and active part including earning badges, in all the Eight Points of the Programme..she can qualify as a Queen's Guide. **1976** *Milton Keynes Express* 9 July 5/7 Three North Bucks girls received Queen's Guides awards at Milton Keynes College of Education, Wolverton, on Tuesday evening. **1840** *Chambers's Edin. Jrnl.* 11 July 193/2 The perplexed purchaser immediately devotes a queen's head, as he most irreverently calls it, to the purpose of asking the editors what he is to do. **1879** Trollope *John Caldigate* III. x. 132 That stamp, that effigy, that two-penny queen's-head. **1915** *Chambers's Jrnl.* Sept. 599/1 When the new stamp was introduced it was invariably called the 'queen's head'. **1769** *Catal. Worcester Porcelaine* in J. E. Nightingale *Contrib. towards Hist. of Eng. Porcelain* (1881) 95 Twelve fluted handle cups and saucers, 6 coffee cups, and two tea pots plain Queen's pattern 2*l.* **1910** R. L. Hobson *Worcester Porcelain* vii. 58 The catalogue of a sale of Worcester porcelain at Christie's, in 1769, includes several references to a 'Queen's pattern', which was no doubt the same as the traditional 'Queen Charlotte's pattern' of today. **1928** W. B. Honey *Old Eng. Porcelain* viii. 167 A design in Oriental style long popular at Worcester..consists of vertical or spirally curved panels alternately red on white and white on blue, with gilding... It was variously known as the 'whorl', 'spiral', 'catherine-wheel' and 'Queen's pattern'. **1957** Mankowitz & Haggar *Encycl. Eng. Pottery & Porcelain* 186/1 *Queen's pattern*, a counter-changed pattern consisting of alternate radiating whirling bands of red-on-white and white-on-blue ornament with gilded embellishments used at Worcester from c. 1770 onwards. **1974** K. Royce *Trap Spider* i. 12 The cutlery was mid-Georgian Queen's pattern. **1884** *Cassell's Dict. Cookery* 675/2 *Queen's Pudding.* [Recipe follows.] **1917** N. Soyer *Standard Cookery* 271 Queen's Pudding. Ingredients.—Eight ounces of finely-chopped suet [etc.]. **1935** G. Greene *Basement Room* 9 It was a pudding he liked, Queen's pudding with a perfect meringue. **1955** *Radio Times* 22 Apr. 14 St. George's Parade of Queen's Scouts. **1962** L. Deighton *Ipcress File* iii. 24 He picked the limp Raven off the..table like a Queen's scout with a rucksack. **1975** *Scout Handbk.* xxix. 274 Beyond the Membership Badge you'll aim for the Venture Award and the Queen's Scout Award. **1877** G. W. Godfrey (*title*) The Queen's Shilling. **1975** N. Luard *Travelling Horseman* vi. 161 If you've had enough of the Queen's shilling, try Pat Foley. **1976** *Listener* 1 Apr. 403/2 He took the Queen's shilling and joined the Royal West Kents..as a private soldier. **1926** *Yachting Monthly* XLI. 244/1 Above the mainstaysail was another triangular sail, commonly known as a 'Queen's' staysail. **1845** S. Judd *Margaret* ii. xi. 358 Rose had on..a queens-stuff habit of the same colour. **1902** W. N. Harben *Abner Daniel* xxxiii. 279 You worked 'im to a queen's taste—as fine as split milk. **1911** R. D. Saunders *Col. Todhunter* ix. 126 It's the best and truest thing I ever saw in my life! They've got you finished off to the Queen's taste. **1767** J. Wedgwood *Sel. Lett.* (1965) 58 The demand for this said *Creamcolour*, Alias *Queens Ware*, Alias *Ivory* still increases. **1863** W. Chaffers *Marks & Monograms on Pott. & Porc.* 120 The principal inventions of Wedgwood were, 1, the cream-coloured table ware, afterwards called *Queen's ware*; [etc.]. **1872** 'Mark Twain' *Roughing It* lix. 432 By-and-by he went home to his lodgings—an empty queensware hogshead—and employed himself till night trying to make up his mind what to buy with it. **1897** [see *merchant *sb.* 1 d]. **1900** F. Litchfield *Pottery & Porcelain* iii. 32 [Thomas Whieldon's] celebrated cream ware, called 'Queen's ware'. **1906** *Dialect Notes* III. 152 *Queensware*.., ordinary crockery. 'You can get queensware at Hansard's grocery or the ten-cent store.' **1961** *Connoisseur New Guide to Antique Eng. Pottery, Porcelain & Glass* 54 [Wedgwood's] Queensware was copied by most of the potters of his time. **1851** *Illustr. London News* 7 June 512/2 The 'Queen's weather', as it has been styled, did not hold good to-day, for..the rain began to come down. **1893** S. Grand *Heavenly Twins* I. ii. iv. 234 'Queen's weather!' he remarked. 'Yes,' she answered, looking out at the sparkling water. **1937** M. V. Hughes *London Home in Nineties* x. 167 The 'Queen's weather' of glorious sunshine began to work in the early part of the year [1897]. **1979** G. St. Aubyn *Edward VII* v. 251 There could hardly have been a more convincing demonstration of 'Queen's Weather' than on..the day of the Diamond Jubilee... The sun burst through the clouds. **1871** *Rep. R. Comm. Admin. Contag. Dis. Acts* I. 14 in *Parl. Papers* (C. 408) XIX. 1 Some of them are called 'Queen's women'; some exhibit the printed order to attend the periodical examination as a certificate of health. **1981** F. K. Prochaska *Women & Philanthropy* vi. 205 One effect of the [Contagious Diseases] Acts was the creation of an outcast and more professional class of prostitute, 'Queen's women' as they were sometimes called.

c. queen's lace *U.S.*, the wild carrot or Queen Anne's lace, *Daucus carota*.

1906 M. E. W. Freeman *By Light of Soul* 52 The fields ..were white and gold with queen's lace and golden rod. **1947** L. M. Beebe *Mixed Train Daily* 88 This freight train, carrying its passengers in the caboose and wading pleasantly through springtime Arkansas meadows brave with daisies and queen's lace, is the Graysonia, Nashville and Ashdown's morning redball.

queen, *v.* Add: **4. b.** (Earlier example.)

1842 *Chess Exemplified* 78 If the pawn have the move—it will queen.

Queen Anne. Add: **b.** (Earlier and later examples.)

1863 A. J. Munby *Diary* 12 May (1972) 160 The house.. is noble, having a fine Queen Anne front and elaborate scrollwork gates. **1878** C. L. Eastlake *Hints on Househ. Taste* (ed. 4) i. 25 The recently revived taste for the so-called 'Queen Anne' style..for that domestic type of brick architecture which prevailed..from the Caroline to the Georgian period. **1879** M. E. Braddon *Vixen* I. xiii. 253 The Queen Anne kettle was hissing merrily over its spirit-lamp. **1913** W. J. Locke *Stella Maris* ii. 13 A Queen Anne gem of a tiny house in Kensington. **1936** *Archit. Rev.* LXXIX. 213 (*caption*) This house claims to be the first brick-built house of the 'Queen Anne' Revival; No. 1 Palace Green, Kensington, by Philip Webb. **1964** S. Nowell Smith *Edwardian England* iv. 152 Tudor, Jacobean, Queen Anne, and Chippendale pieces..often jostled each other in the same room. **1977** *Times* 28 May 22/7 The audio and radiogram..designs are in Jacobean, Regency, Queen Anne and Scandinavian contemporary.

c. In the possessive in the names of plants: **Queen Anne's (double) daffodil,** a daffodil, *Narcissus capax plenus,* with pale yellow double flowers; **Queen Anne's (double) jonquil,** a small variety of *Narcissus jonquilla* with clusters of double, yellow, fragrant flowers; **Queen Anne's lace,** a popular name for various umbelliferous plants bearing clusters of small white flowers, esp., in North America, the wild carrot, *Daucus carota,* and in Britain, cow parsley, *Anthriscus sylvestris.*

1806 *Curtis's Bot. Mag.* XXIV. 934 Varies with very double flowers, and is then called by some Gardeners 'Queen Anne's Jonquil'. **1886** G. NICHOLSON *Illustr. Dict. Gardening* II. 413/1 A double form of this species [sc. *Narcissus jonquilla*] is known as Queen Anne's Jonquil. **1889** *Jrnl. R. Hort. Soc.* XI. 90 Its name of 'Queen Anne's Daffodil' was no doubt originally given in honour of Queen Anne of Austria. **1894** *Amer. Folk-Lore* VII. 89 *Daucus Carota,* Queen Anne's lace, somewhat general. **1913** W. P. EATON *Barn Doors & Byways* 273 Wild carrot bears a dainty, flat-topped white bloom sometimes as large as a saucer, and a long bed of them will often appear like a strip of delicate embroidery along the wayside, making their more aristocratic title of Queen Anne's lace entirely applicable. **1926** W. DE LA MARE *Connoisseur* 318 Only the rotting sleepers remained, matted with weeds and bordered with Queen Ann's [*sic*] lace, golden rod and Michaelmas daisy. **1930** F. A. POTTLE *Stretchers* 204 The fields..are rioting with the delicate blooms of Queen Anne's lace. **1934** E. A. BOWLES *Handbk. Narcissus* viii. 89 *N*[*arcissus*] *eystettensis,*.. otherwise known as capax plenus or Queen Anne's Double Daffodil, is another plant of mysterious origin. *Ibid.* 90 Queen Anne's Daffodil may be a garden hybrid of the sixteenth century. *Ibid.* xiv. 137 Its double form is known as 'Queen Anne's Jonquil'. **1946** D. C. PEATTIE *Road of Naturalist* i. 21 In Maryland the Queen Anne's lace was dancing under the apple trees that made wide pools of shadow. **1951** M. JEFFERSON-BROWN *Daffodil* x. 117 Queen Anne's Double Daffodil is another flower with which this monarch's name is associated. *Ibid.,* Queen Anne's Double Jonquil..is but six inches high. **1955** W. GADDIS *Recognitions* III. ii. 760, I remember..tall weeds including Queen Anne's laces. **1961** M. FISH *Cottage Garden Flowers* iii. 29 *N*[*arcissus*] *capax plenus* (Syn. *N. eystettensis*) is the flower that was known as 'Queen Anne's Double Daffodil'. **1961** P. SYNGE *Collins Guide to Bulbs* 236 *N*[*arcissus*] *jonquilla flore pleno* is the double form often known as Queen Anne's Double Jonquil. **1971** P. LARKIN in *Listener* 29 July 144/1 Young-leafed June,.. With hedges snowlike strewn,.. Lost lanes of Queen Anne's lace. **1974** M. INGATE *Sound of Weir* xix. 164 A dragonfly..settled for a moment among the litter scent of Queen Anne's lace. **1978** *Church Times* 23 June 14/5, I waded into waist-high cow-parsley (or, if you prefer it, Queen Anne's lace, hemlock or bogy's gruel).

Hence also **Queen A·nn(e)ish** *a.,* suggestive of, or designed in, a Queen Anne style; **Queen A·nnery,** a style (of utterance, etc.) characteristic or reminiscent of the reign of Queen Anne.

1881 G. M. HOPKINS *Let.* 29 Oct. in Hopkins & Dixon *Corr.* (1955) 83 The language is a quaint medley of Middle-Ages and 'QueenAnnery'. **1926** *Spectator* 24 July 154/2 Gradually Queen-Annish cornices began to creep in. **1943** J. LEES-MILNE *Ancestral Voices* (1975) 269 It is a low, rambling, attractive house, Queen Anne-ish but not of architectural distinction. **1975** *Country Life* 9 Oct. 909/1 The Queen Anne-ish windows fill the room with light.

queenie (kwī·ni). Also **queeny.** [f. QUEEN *sb.* + -IE, -Y[6].] **1. a.** An effeminate male, a homosexual; used esp. as a term of address. **b.** *Comb.,* as *queenie-fashion* advb.

[*c* **1736** POPE *Poems* (1954) VI. 367 The Motley Race of Hervey queenies [*var. reading* Harvequini's] And Courtly Vices, Beastly Venyes.] **1933** N. ERSINE *Underworld & Prison Slang* 60 *Queenie*.., a homosexual man. **1936** J. CURTIS *Gilt Kid* viii. 79 'You're not a man. You're a pouf.'.. 'I'll show you who's a pouf.' 'Call yourself a man do you this morning, Queenie? Well you wasn't one last night, see. You gets into bed and goes straight off to kip.' **1948** D. BALLANTYNE *Cunninghams* xx. 261 The dark, good-looking kid..who always had his shirt collar turned up queeny-fashion. **1966** 'L. LANE' *ABZ of Scouse* II. 87 *Queenie,* an effeminate male. **1974** R. BLY tr. *Hamsun's Hunger* I. 41, I felt a hand on my shoulder, and turned: 'Queeny' was saying good morning... The sight of this aimless, painted-up creature somehow enraged me.

2. (With capital initial.) An affectionate informal term for Queen Elizabeth II.

1976 C. STORR *Unnatural Fathers* xiii. 131 'The Queen absolutely refuses.'.. 'So Queenie's turned up trumps, has she? Good for her!' **1979** *Time* 13 Aug. 6/1 When Britain's Queen Elizabeth II arrived in Lusaka,..she was cheered by Zambians everywhere she went as 'Queenie! Queenie!'.

queening, *vbl. sb.* (In Dict. s.v. QUEEN *v.*) Add: Also *attrib.* in *queening square,* the square on a chess board on which a particular pawn may be queened.

1922 A. EMERY *Elements of Chess* iv. 32 Under no circumstances whatever can a solitary pawn on either rook's file be advanced to the queening square, if it is possible for the adverse king to take up a position in front of it on the same file. **1937** M. EUWE *Strategy & Tactics in Chess* viii. 168 In choosing the queening square Black takes care that, at all cost, the White Rook is standing on the adjacent file. **1966** *New Statesman* 9 Sept. 371/3 The draw is secured either by stalemate or by perpetuating the Black Bishop's command of the queening square. **1969** A. GLYN *Dragon Variation* ii. 58 If he takes your Knight now, you play Pawn on and then Queen it, and his own Pawn protects the queening square from his Bishop.

queenly, *a.* Add: **3.** Characteristic or reminiscent of a male homosexual (see *QUEEN *sb.* II*).

1968 *Listener* 11 July 59/3 Paul Scofield..is using his queenliest *Staircase* manner to play a bisexual script-writer. **1976** *Times* 5 Apr. 6/8 A..rumour went around that the play was really about homosexuals. Certainly some of the dialogue does have a queenly tinge.

queenright (kwī·nrəit), *a.* [f. QUEEN *sb.* + RIGHT *a.*] Of a colony of social insects, esp. bees: provided with a queen. (In quot. 1932, 'relating to the presence of a queen'.)

1932 E. B. WEDMORE *Man. Beekeeping* ii. 38 In the writer's opinion the bees in the portion of the hive in question conclude that the queen is failing, and he calls the impulse [to rear a second queen] 'queenright supersedure'. **1966** LAIDLAW & ECKERT *Queen Rearing* ii. 33 A strong queenright colony can care for 45 grafted cells a day. **1971** E. O. WILSON *Insect Societies* xvii. 333/2 Marchal..also reported the presence of laying workers in queenright wasp colonies. **1974** *Country Life* 2 May 1041/1 The owner of the colony who hasn't an ear for the contented hum of what apiarists call a 'queenright-hive' waits until his slow wits tell him that tragedy has struck.

Queensberry (kwī·nzbəri). Also (*erron.*) **-bury.** The name of Sir John Sholto Douglas (1844–1900), eighth Marquis of Queensberry, used *attrib.* in *Queensberry rules,* a code of rules drawn up in 1867 under his supervision to govern the sport of boxing in Great Britain; also, the name by which the present rules of boxing are known; also *transf.*

1895 G. B. SHAW in *Sat. Rev.* 28 Sept. 410/1 There the contest was in the presence of a court, with measured ground and due formality—under Queensberry rules, so to speak. **1899** A. CONAN DOYLE in *Strand Mag.* XVIII. 368/1 It's twenty rounds, two-ounce gloves, Queensberry rules. **1931** *Times Lit. Suppl.* 11 June 472/3 Ever since 1866, when the Queensberry rules were introduced, pugilism has lost much of its romantic interest. **1960** *Observer* 24 Jan. 7/2 You would have thought that the average citizen would be only too anxious to see property being protected and would not worry so much about the Queensberry Rules being observed. **1975** *Oxf. Compan. Sports* 110 Broughton's rules were so sensible that they formed the basis of the London Prize-ring Rules drawn up in 1838..and even of the Queensberry Rules introduced towards the end of the nineteenth century in London. **1977** *New Yorker* 13 June 121/1 An at last complete love affair with a married woman..was in the Queensberry rules; she could not object.

Queensland (kwī·nzlănd). [The name of a state in north-eastern Australia.] **a.** In the names of local trees or their woods, esp. **Queensland kauri,** a tall evergreen tree, *Agathis robusta,* of the family Pinaceæ; **Queensland maple,** either of two evergreen trees, *Flindersia brayleyana* or *F. pimenteliana,* of the family Rutaceæ; **Queensland nut** = *MACADAMIA; also, the fruit of this tree; **Queensland walnut,** an evergreen tree, *Endiandra palmerstonii,* of the family Lauraceæ. **b. Queensland blue** = **blue heeler* s.v. *BLUE *a.* 12a; **Queensland sore,** a sore which does not heal readily because of scurvy.

1956 G. CASEY in *Coast to Coast 1955–56* 80 It was a noble animal, a true Queensland-blue, with jaws like an alligator, sagacity in its eye, and limbs like a well-muscled leopard. **1977** C. MCCULLOUGH *Thorn Birds* iv. 80 The big Queensland blue fawning and cringing at Father Ralph's feet. **1889** J. H. MAIDEN *Useful Native Plants Austral.* 414 'Queensland Kauri', or 'Dundathu Pine'. Wood of a light yellow colour..largely used by joiners and cabinet-makers. **1932** R. S. TROUP *Exotic Forest Trees in Brit. Empire* 32 *Agathis robusta*..Queensland kauri. A very large tree attaining 160 ft. in height. **1919** R. T. BAKER *Hardwoods Austral.* II. 33 The soft woods are those most generally found on the market, such as Red Cedar, Red Bean, Queensland Maple, Beech, and Pines. **1928** E. H. F. SWAIN *Timber & Forest Products Queensland* 147 Placed on the Southern markets later under the name of Queensland Maple, the wood has risen to fame under this unsuitable trade appellation. **1967** A. RULE *Forests Austral.* xii. 140 Australia's cabinet timbers—Queensland walnut, Queensland maple, red cedar, silky oak, black bean and so forth—were found to make fine sliced veneers. **1881** *Official Rec. Sydney Internat. Exhib. 1879* 750 Queensland Nut... A small-sized tree with a very dense foliage. **1928** E. H. F. SWAIN *Timbers & Forest Products Queensland* 472 The Queensland Nut is one of the finest edible nuts. **1929** [see *MACADAMIA]. **1950** *N.Z. Jrnl. Agric.* Dec. 527/1 A number of Queensland nut trees growing in Northland are producing good crops annually. **1963** A. LUBBOCK *Austral. Roundabout* 93 A great, dark tree, rather like an ilex,..bears the Queensland nut. **1892** G. L. JAMES *Shall I try Australia?* xxiv. 242 'Queensland Sores'..are, I believe, generally attributed to excessive thinness and poverty of the blood, caused by the great heat and an absence of vegetable diet. **1945** BAKER *Austral. Lang.* iii. 62 *Barcoo rot, Kennedy rot* or *Queensland sore,* a festering sore difficult to cure under inland conditions—it rapidly disappears when the sufferer eats plenty of fruit or green vegetables. **1919** R. T. BAKER *Hardwoods Austral.* II. 339 'Queensland Walnut'..is a good commercial timber. **1967** Queensland walnut [see *Queensland maple* above].

Quee·nslander. [f. prec. + -ER[1].] A native or inhabitant of the state of Queensland in Australia.

1861 J. D. LANG *Queensland, Australia* viii. 238 A letter addressed to the editor of the 'Moreton Bay Courier',..is signed 'A Queenslander'. **1883** G. W. RUSDEN *Hist. Australia* III. xvii. 235 The gallant conduct of the 'Queenslander', a well-managed newspaper in Brisbane, enables me to use the words of witnesses or neighbours. **1899** E. W. HORNUNG *Amateur Cracksman* 176 The Queenslander handed it to me. **1924** KIPLING *Debits & Credits* (1926) 316 'An' what about your Queenslander?' the Australian asked. **1963** *Times* 12 Mar. p. vi/3 The wise detective could deduce from such a sign that Queenslanders are easy-going to an incredible degree, that they have a loathing for formality and they live in a warm climate. **1978** R. V. JONES *Most Secret War* xvi. 130 A buccaneering Queenslander, Sidney Cotton, who had been a pilot in the Royal Naval Air Service.

queeny (kwī·ni), *a.* Also **queenie.** [f. *QUEEN *sb.* II* + -Y[1].] Effeminate; also as *adv.,* in an effeminate manner.

1936 N. MARSH *Death in Ecstasy* xxiv. 299 Alleyn may talk queeny, but he's doped that out. **1937** —— *Vintage Murder* vii. 72 He talks with a corker sort of voice. Not queeny, but just corker. **1952** *Arena* (N.Z.) xxxI. 2 Up in front would be Slick, the leader [*sc.* a sheepdog], stepping along in a queenie way. **1965** G. MCINNES *Road to Gundagai* xv. 265 Thereafter he said he'd rather play football with the other fellows: reading aloud was a bit 'queeny'. **1977** 'J. LE CARRÉ' *Honourable Schoolboy* i. 19 'So what's happened, Lukie?' whined the dwarf, in his queeny Greenwich Village drawl.

queer, *a.*[1] Add: **1. a.** *queer fellow,* an eccentric person. Also used, esp. in Ireland and in nautical contexts, with varying contextual connotations (see quots.) Cf. *QUARE *a.*

Possibly some examples illustrate QUEER *a.*[2]

1712 [in Dict.]. **1883** J. F. KEANE *On Blue Water* 212 Remembering that incident, the 'queer-fellow's' disappearance didn't alarm me very much. **1910** D. W. BONE *Brassbounder* 64 D'ye think th' queer-fella' is goin' t' pay them prices for 'is kit? **1922** [see *middle leg* s.v. *MIDDLE *a.* 6]. **1932** J. W. HARRIS *Days of Endeavour* 17 No matter what ship you serves your time in, you'll find there'll be a queer-feller. **1936** J. CURTIS *Gilt Kid* vi. 60 He'd a good mind to tear over and spoil her lark with the queer fellow. **1939** J. BROPHY *Queer Fellow* 10 When I am 'making up' a story,..I am never my normal self, the man that other people know. Nor dare my normal self return for a moment in the hope of catching the other one, The Queer Fellow, as they say in Ireland, at work. **1958** M. PROCTER *Man in Ambush* xii. 134 Mobsters, queer fellows, bar flies and layabouts. **1961** PARTRIDGE *Dict. Slang* Suppl. 1240/2 *The queer fella,* the person that happens to be in command: Regular Army: late c. 19–20. **1962** GRANVILLE *Dict. Sailors' Slang* 93/2 *Queer fella,* any merchant seaman who does not conform to the average type. A nautical eccentric. **1966** 'L. LANE' *ABZ of Scouse* II. 87 *Whur's ther queer feller?* Where is the boss or foreman whose name I don't know?

b. Of a person (usu. a man): homosexual. Also in phr. *as queer as a coot* (cf. COOT *sb.*[1] 2b). Hence, of things: pertaining to homosexuals or homosexuality. orig. *U.S.*

1922 *Pract. Value of Scientific Study of Juvenile Delinquents* (Children's Bureau, U.S. Dept. of Labor) 8 A young man, easily ascertainable to be unusually fine in other characteristics, is probably 'queer' in sex tendency. **1931** G. IRWIN *Amer. Tramp & Underworld Slang* 153 *Queer,* crooked; criminal. Also applied to effeminate or degenerate men or boys. **1936** J. G. COZZENS *Men & Brethren* i. 24 'He's not queer, or something, is he?' 'Lord, no! Worse than that. He's a convert.' **1937** *Listener* 10 Mar. (Suppl.) p. vii/2 'Queer', in a specifically sexual sense—a word imported from America. **1939** C. ISHERWOOD *Goodbye to Berlin* 296 Men dressed as *women*?.. Do you mean they're *queer*? **1952** [see *CAMP *a.* (and *sb.*[5])]. **1958** P. MORTIMER *Daddy's gone a-Hunting* xxx. 169, I suppose they're queer as coots. **1960** [see *BENT *ppl. a.* 5 c]. **1963** [see *GAY *a.* 2 c]. **1974** *Amer. Speech 1971* XLVI. 81 *Female homosexual,* lesbian, screwball, queer, lady-lover, minty. **1975** *Times* 9 July 14/2 *Bombus fragrans*..sprinkles himself..with attar of roses, and..is as queer as a coot. **1976** A. WHITE *Long Silence* I. 10 'I say, Peter, you're not turning *queer* by any chance, are you?' The thought that I might be queer had haunted me.

c. In U.S. colloq. phr. *to be queer for* (someone or something): to be fond of or 'keen on'; to be in love with.

1953 W. BURROUGHS *Junkie* ii. 28 She began talking about Jack. 'I'm queer for Jack,' she said. 'He works at being a thief just like any job.' **1956** J. BALDWIN *Giovanni's Room* I. ii. 45 Actually, I'm sort of queer for girls myself. **1957** M. SHULMAN *Rally round Flag, Boys!* iv. 51 When..the cellars were finally snug and dry, Waldo promptly persuaded the homesteaders to fill them with.. a huge, gleaming variety of tools. This took no great persuasion, for..the average commuter was queer for tools. **1977** *Time* 28 Mar. 54/2 The sister (Carol Potter) is crazy about him and Francis is queer for her brother (Reed Birney), or so he fears.

2. (Earlier and further examples.)

1781 S. CRISP *Let.* 1 Mar. in W. H. Hutton *Burford Papers* (1905) 60, I have been very queer for some time, sleepless and indigestion. **1837** [see *EARTHQUAKY *a.*]. **1889** J. K. JEROME *Three Men in Boat* i. 14 So I set my face against the sea trip. Not, as I explained, upon my own account. I was never queer. But I was afraid for

George. **1922, 1938** [see *COME *v.* 66 f]. **1952** A. CHRISTIE *Mrs McGinty's Dead* iv. 28 Either the husband's taken queer, or the old mother... With old McGinty, at least it was only she herself who came over queer. **1978** 'F. PARRISH' *Sting of Honeybee* iv. 43 Jake's off queer, wi' a rumblin' stummick.

3. (Earlier and later examples.)

1811 *Lex. Balatron.*, *Queer Street*, wrong, improper, contrary to one's wish. It is queer street, a cant phrase, to signify that it is wrong or different to our wish. **1821** P. EGAN *Real Life in London* I. xi. 186 Limping Billy was also evidently in *queer-street*. **1829** —— *Boxiana* 2nd Ser. II. 503 Gas let fly right and left, give Pope a tremendous blow over his left *ogle*, putting him a little into Queer-street. **1952** A. WILSON *Hemlock & After* III. i. 208 He enjoys a little flutter..and if he finds himself in Queer Street now and again, I'm sure no one would grudge him his bit of fun. **1963** *Times* 8 May 9/2 He felt that the levy should not be applied so rigidly as to force companies into Queer Street if their costs rose faster than their incomes. **1980** J. WAINWRIGHT *Man of Law* xlvii. 222 If Patsold talks, Webb's in queer street.

4. *queer-shaped* (earlier example).

1876 H. SIDGWICK in A. & E. M. Sidgwick *Henry Sidgwick* (1906) v. 323 Stone hovels that a generation ago were the ordinary houses here: things with a hole in the roof, low, queer-shaped.

queer, *a.*[2] and *sb.*[1] For **a, b.** read **A, B.** and add: **A.** *adj.* **b.** Of coins or banknotes: counterfeit, forged.

1740 *Ordinary of Newgate, his Account* III. 15/1 Instead of returning the good Guinea again, they used to give a *Queer One*. **1812**, etc. [see SCREEN *sb.* 2]. **1848** *Ladies' Repository* Oct. 316/2 *Queer*, counterfeit. *Queer screen*, counterfeit paper money. *Queer wedge*, counterfeited silver money. *Queer ridge*, counterfeited *gold money*. **1877** J. HABBERTON *Jericho Road* xvi. 151 'Let's give him fifty [dollars] to send her.' 'Fifty queer?' asked Mr. Lodge. 'No, fifty straight,' said the little man. **1890** *Buckskin Mose* ii. 34 At the same time he pulled out of his pocket a lot of 'queer' or counterfeit bills. **1941** R. CHANDLER in *Detective Story Mag.* Sept. 52 If it was discovered to be queer money, as you say, it would be very difficult to trace the source of it.

B. *sb.*[1] **a.** (Later examples.) Also (*U.S.*), forged paper currency or bonds. Phr. *to shove (the) queer:* see SHOVE *v.* 10a.

1821 P. EGAN *Life in London* II. i. 154 That admired sort of Life in London, all jostling against each other in the Park... The Duke and the 'Dealer in Queer'—the Lady and her Scullion [etc.]. **1847** *National Police Gaz.* (U.S.) 9 Jan. 137/1 'Bogus' is base coin, 'queer' is counterfeit paper. **1859** [see SHOVE *v.* 10]. **1889** G. GISSING *Nether World* II. xi. 233 'Got any *queer* to put round?'..'You know what he meant, Bob?' Bob nodded and became reflective. *Ibid.* III. ii. 38 He opened it, and showed about a dozen pieces of money—in appearance half-crowns and florins... 'The snyde' or the 'queer' is the technical name by which such products are known. **1898** A. M. BINSTEAD *Pink 'Un & Pelican* xi. 240 He hardly ever uttered the spurious coins himself..and, consequently, seldom had any 'queer' about his person. **1926** *Flynn's* 16 Jan. 640/2 After I coughed up an' promised to quit the queer he give me th' gate. **1949** E. L. IREY *Tax Dodgers* v. 112 An alcoholic engraver..turned out the best 'queer' that ever competed with the Bureau of Engraving's product and Lustig took over the distribution of the counterfeit money. **1954** W. R. & F. K. SIMPSON *Hockshop* ix. 232 Eagle-eyed concessionaires..always on the lookout for shovers of the queer. **1981** 'E. LATHEN' *Going for Gold* iii. 37 Nobody's laying off any queer on the Sloan [Bank].

b. *on the queer*: living dishonestly; *spec.* engaged in the forging of currency.

1905 C. H. DAY *Actress & Clerk* ii. 22 Only just feeling of you to see if you was on the queer. **1909** R. A. WASON *Happy Hawkins* 277 Dick may have been on the queer all right, but he was smooth enough to hide it. **1910** C. E. B. RUSSELL *Young Gaol-birds* x. 150 Convinced that he could get along as well 'on the queer', *i.e.*, by thieving, as he could by keeping straight. **1935** *Amer. Speech* X. 11/1 Boys who are *on the queer* are handsomely equipped to print anything from twenty dollar bills to fake government bonds. **1942** BERREY & VAN DEN BARK *Amer. Thes. Slang* § 494/2 Counterfeit; forge,..*be on the green goods,—the queer* or *the spud(s)*.

queer (kwīəɹ), *sb.*[2] *slang.* [f. *QUEER *a.*[1] 1b.] A (usu. male) homosexual. Also in *Comb.*, as *queer-bashing* vbl. sb., the attacking of homosexuals; hence *queer-basher*.

[**1932** AUDEN in *Rev. Eng. Stud.* (1978) Aug. 294 An underground cottage frequented by the queer.] **1935** *Amer. Speech* X. 19/2 *Queer*... A male homosexual. **1936** L. DUNCAN *Over Wall* xx. 277 There was even a little room..where the 'fairies', 'pansies', and 'queers' conducted their lewd practices. **1946** E. WAUGH *Jrnl.* 21 Nov. (1976) VI. 663 The headmaster, an old queer. **1952** A. WILSON *Hemlock & After* I. iii. 58, I quite like queers if it comes to that, so long as they're not on the make. **1959** ANON. *Streetwalker* I. i. 18 Jackie, one of the commercial queers..is a tall, gangling boy with long hair..combed into carefully casual curls. **1965** *Spectator* 19 Feb. 239/1 Smith pursues Lulu in Valletta only to discover that she is a queer. **1966** [see *FAGGOT, FAGOT *sb.* 6 b]. **1970** *Times* 5 Feb. 2/3 Four of 12 youths said to have taken part in a 'queer bashing' expedition on Wimbledon Common on September 25 were found Guilty of murder. *Ibid.* 25 Nov. 9/5 (*heading*) 'Queer-bashers' lose appeal. **1975** [see *PANSY 3 a]. **1977** *New Wave Mag.* No. 7. 6 To fight the National Front, the queer-bashers and any other diseases.

Hence **quee·rdom.**

1965 *New Statesman* 9 July 58/1 Its climactic evocation of high Hapsburg queerdom at its annual drag ball. **1977** *Daily Express* 29 Jan. 7/2 This is a groin-directed compound of mime, ballet and freak show which, as a mere heterosexual, I take to be a celebration of the erotic imagery of queerdom.

queer, *v.* Add: **1.** (Later example.)

1854 W. HARCOURT *Let.* in A. G. Gardiner *Life W. Harcourt* (1923) I. iv. 76 The American Minister..spat on the floor all dinner-time. I hear he does this to queer the Britishers, and does not practise those manners at home.

2. a. (Later examples.) Also, with a person as object: to spoil the reputation of, to put (a person) in bad odour (with someone); to spoil (a person's) undertaking, chances, etc.

1895 J. L. FORD *Bohemia Invaded* 91 Without having you come in and queer me right in the middle of it [*sc.* a story]. **1895** E. W. TOWNSEND *Chimmie Fadden* 38 De Duchess gives me de orders, an' I wasn't goin' to queer meself wid 'er any more. **1904** *N.Y. Tribune* 12 Jan. 2/1 Van Wyck will queer the whole thing. His appearance before the National Committee will recall..things that knocked Tammany out in 1901. **1913** *Dialect Notes* IV. 11 *Queer, v.* To spoil the reputation (or good impression) a person has made or is trying to make. 'That *queered* me with the teacher.' **1919** E. O'NEILL *Moon of Caribbees* 17 *Bella*... Don't talk so loud... Think I wants the ole captain to put me off the ship, do you? *Yank*. Yes, nix on hollerin', you! D'yuh wanta queer all of us? **1927** [see *HORN *v.* 3 c]. **1941** *Sun* (Baltimore) 25 Aug. 10/1 (*heading*) Queering the oil conservation drive.

b. *to queer the pitch*: to interfere with or spoil the business (of a tradesman or showman) (cf. PITCH *sb.*[2] 11a); now freq. *to queer one's pitch* (in more general use). Hence in similar phrases, as *to queer the game, the job*, etc.

1846 *Swell's Night Guide* 47 Rule iv... Nanty coming it on a pall, or wid cracking to queer a pitch. **1866** M. MACKINTOSH *Stage Reminisc.* vii. 93 The smoke and fumes of 'blue fire' which had been used to illuminate the fight came up through the chinks of the stage, fit to choke a dozen Macbeths, and—pardon the little bit of professional slang—poor Jamie's 'pitch' was 'queered' with a vengeance. **1875** T. FROST *Circus Life* xvi. 278 The spot they select for their performance is their 'pitch', and any interruption of their feats, such as an accident, or the interference of a policeman, is said to 'queer the pitch'. **1889** E. SAMPSON *Tales of Fancy* 38 They could not understand it when their pitch was queered, and one or two of the gang arrested. **1890** *Punch* 16 Aug. 74/3 Wy, they'd queer the best pitches in life, if they kiboshed the Power of the Quid! **1901** *Windsor Mag.* Dec. 204/1, I think you and I between us have queered the game. **1911** L. MERRICK *Position of Peggy Harper* III. i. 287 'You leave the contract to me...' 'I can do all that's wanted... You'd go asking too much and queering the job for me.' **1919** H. JENKINS *John Dene of Toronto* (1920) i. 17 'Suppose the Germans were able to sink a ship without even showing their periscopes?'.. 'Oh, shucks!' cried John Dene in disgust. It would queer the whole outfit... It would mighty soon finish the war.' **1927** *Observer* 4 Dec. 19/4 It may conceivably queer the pitch of Mr. de Valera, who..is about to approach the American public for a substantial sum. **1934** J. E. NEALE *Queen Eliz. I* xix. 334 Elizabeth..tried to break off... He went on, determined to queer the pitch for Coke and his supporter Burghley. **1973** E. LEMARCHAND *Let or Hindrance* iv. 31 He's a decent lad... He would never have risked queering Wendy's pitch with Eddy. **1977** *Rolling Stone* 5 May 50/1 Since trying to crash a closed Stones party the first night would likely queer the whole deal, I decided to check out El Mocambo with a local reporter.

queerie (kwīə·ri). *slang.* [f. *QUEER *a.*[1] 1b + -IE.] One who is queer; esp. one who is soft, effeminate, or homosexual.

1938 *Amer. Mercury* Oct. 181/1 Any boy showing interest in [classes] is correctly considered a 'queerie'. **1940** L. L. STANLEY *Men at their Worst* xx. 201 In every prison are many sex perverts. We know them the minute they step through the front gates on their way into prison. They are known as the 'Queens', the 'Fairies', the 'Queeries', and by other names. **1942** BERREY & VAN DEN BARK *Amer. Thes. Slang* § 405/1 Effeminate man or masculine woman; homosexual,..*queerie*. **1951** *N.Y. Jrnl.–American* 14 Aug. 3/1 Why then does he want to get his hands on these millions? To pay the wages of a lot of queeries in the State Department? **1972** B. RODGERS *Queen's Vernacular* 165 *Queer*,..*queerie* ('that little "queerie" is the only one I know who shoots Sal Hepatica').

quee·ringness. *rare*$^{-1}$. [f. QUEER *v.* + -ING[1] + -NESS.] Aptness to distort or to falsify.

1955 E. BOWEN *World of Love* ii. 49 She mistrusted the past's activity and its queeringness..who did not speak of it either with falsifying piety or with bitterness.

queerness. Add: **2.** Homosexuality. Cf. *QUEER *a.*[1] 1 b.

1956 L. MCINTOSH *Oxford Folly* 104 Some of the most brilliant Oxford figures are queers, and the others simply ape their mannerisms without having the courage to imitate their queerness. **1958** *Observer* 4 May 15/5 A play which says more about the simple, non-tragic aspects of queerness than anything our theatre has so far permitted. **1965** *New Statesman* 9 July 58/1 Osborne has taken queerness as his subject precisely as Nabokov took the love of pubescent girls.

quelea (kwī·liă). [mod.L., the specific name of *Emberiza quelea* (Linnæus *Systema Naturæ* (ed. 10, 1758) I. 177), perh. f. med.L. *qualea* QUAIL *sb.*; adopted as a generic name by H. G. L. Reichenbach (*Avium Systema Naturale* (1850) pl. lxxvi).] An African weaver-bird of the genus so called, belonging to the family Ploceidæ, esp. the red-billed dioch, *Quelea quelea*, which is an important pest of grain crops; = *DIOCH. Also *attrib.*

1930 C. F. BELCHER *Birds Nyasaland* 316 (*heading*) Black-fronted Quelea. **1936** E. L. GILL *First Guide S. Afr. Birds* 26 Southern Pink-billed Weaver, Quelea Finch... The adult male in breeding plumage, with his black face surrounded by a halo of pink, is readily recognizable. **1957** BENSON & WHITE *Check List Birds N. Rhodesia* 123 Red-billed Quelea... Only numerous in drier, more open areas. **1964** [see *DIOCH]. **1969** N. W. PIRIE *Food Resources* ii. 67 The weaver bird, or quelea, infests 2m square miles of Africa. **1969** *Sci. Jrnl.* Apr. 15/1 Quelea birds..raid cereal crops in swarms numbered in millions. **1973** *Bokmakierie* XXV. 46/2 Colleagues in Kenya handed Mr. Skead over to the Quelea Control officers. **1975** *Times* 19 Feb. 14/6 Other exhibits [at the Centre for Overseas Pest Research] relate to army-worms, quelea birds, and termites.

‖ **Quellenforschung** (kve·lənfoːrʃuŋ). [Ger., f. *quelle* source + *forschung* research.] The study of the sources of, or influences upon, a literary work.

1958 C. S. LEWIS in *Times Lit. Suppl.* 28 Nov. 689/3, I wonder how much *Quellenforschung* in our studies of older literature seems solid only because those who knew the facts are dead and cannot contradict it? **1966** J. WAIN in *Punch* 27 Apr. 616/2, I hadn't read the book when I wrote *Hurry On Down*, but I had read Orwell's literary and social criticism... Conclusion of *Quellenforschung*. **1975** *Times Lit. Suppl.* 29 Aug. 974/4 Intertextuality would appear to be so universally applicable to medieval literature as to imply, at best a statement of the obvious, at worst *Quellenforschung* in sheep's clothing.

‖ **quemadero** (kemaðe·ro). [Sp., f. *quemar* to burn.] In Spain and former Spanish territories, a place where convicted heretics were executed by burning. Also *transf.*

1855 W. H. PRESCOTT *Hist. Reign Philip II* I. II. iii. 353 The place of execution—the *quemadero*, the burning-place, as it was called—was a spot selected for the purpose without the walls of the city. **1874** W. H. RULE *Hist. Inquisition* I. xiv. 208 Outside the city..was a hearth, or place of burning. As our own language is too poor to provide a name for such a thing, we consent to borrow from Spanish its peculiar and exclusive designation, and call it the *quemadero*. The quemadero was a piece of pavement devoted to the single use of burning human bodies. **1908** H. C. LEA *Inquisition in Spanish Dependencies* vi. 206 It was not until 1596 that the municipality [*sc.* Mexico], at a cost of four hundred pesos, constructed a *quemadero* or burning place, where concremation could be performed decently and in order. **1932** C. ROTH *Hist. Marranos* ii. 43 A *quemadero*, or burning place, was constructed in the Campo de Tablada. **1934** A. HUXLEY *Beyond Mexique Bay* 189 On each mound were..hearths of broken potsherds, blackened with smoke—the *quemaderos*, or burning places of the Indians. **1960** S. BECKER tr. *Schwarz-Bart's Last of Just* (1961) I. 11 He died very old..on the vast white slab of the *Quemadero* in Seville. Around him, scattered among the fagots, was the daily ovenful of three hundred Jews.

quench, *sb.* Delete *rare* and add: **1.** (Further example.)

1972 A. D. FRANKLIN in Crawford & Slifkin *Point Defects in Solids* I. i. 33 The special property of ductility possessed by many metals allows thin wires to be drawn, which may be very rapidly quenched, at maximum cooling rates of 10^5 deg/sec or higher. With such rapid quenches, one may hope to retain the equilibrium defects present at the high quench temperature.

2. *Electronics.* The process of stopping an oscillation, esp. in a superregenerative receiver; a signal used for this. Freq. *attrib.*, as **quench frequency,** the frequency with which oscillations are stopped.

1938 *Proc. IRE* XXVI. 94 The use of a rectangular wave quench voltage would not be practicable in most applications of superregenerative receivers. *Ibid.* 96 In a given design of a separately quenched superregenerative receiver there is a particular quench frequency which gives maximum sensitivity. **1948** *Electronics* Sept. 98/3 This action..is eliminated by restricting the frequency content of the quench. **1950** J. R. WHITEHEAD *Super-Regenerative Receivers* vii. 125 A super-regenerative receiver with grid quench and a.g.s. controlling the oscillator grid bias. **1959** G. TROUP *Masers* vii. 118 A 600 c/s quench frequency was used. **1965** *Wireless World* July 336/2 Quench oscillators in super-regenerative receivers..have..set their own problems. **1975** D. G. FINK *Electronics Engineers' Handbk.* IX. 56 Electron current flow is initiated by an rf input signal and is terminated at the end of the rf input signal either by a voltage pulse or a dc bias voltage applied to a quench electrode.

quench, *v.* Add: **I. 1. a.** (Further example with *out.*)

1863 E. WETHERELL *Old Helmet* (1864) I. xi. 230 In Africa they sit in the darkness of centuries, till almost the spark of humanity is quenched out.

d. *Radio.* To cause (the spark in a spark transmitter) to cease by mechanical means, so that the secondary (aerial) circuit is no longer coupled to the primary; hence, to stop (oscillation).

1910 G. W. Pierce *Princ. Wireless Telegr.* xxiii. 267 The spark is quenched when the energy in the primary attains its first minimum. **1913** *Chambers's Jrnl.* Mar. 232/2 The oscillatory current in the aerial, and therefore the wave-train radiated, continue long after the spark has been quenched. **1927** O. F. Brown *Elements of Radio Communication* iv. 53 The spark is produced between projecting studs on a rapidly revolving metal disc and two fixed electrodes... The rotation of the disc will rapidly increase the distance between the studs and the electrodes, so that the spark is quenched and the oscillation in the primary circuit ceases. **1938** *Proc. IRE* XXVI. 76 In a typical superregenerative receiver the regenerative coupling between the plate and grid circuits of the detector tube is great enough so that self-sustained oscillations are produced, and these oscillations are periodically quenched, by applying..an alternating voltage having a frequency much lower than that of the oscillations. **1959** G. Troup *Masers* vii. 117 These authors measured the noise figure of an ammonia maser amplifier operated superregeneratively: that is, oscillations were allowed to build up and then quenched. **1966** *McGraw-Hill Encycl. Sci. & Technol.* I. 362/1 A regenerative detector in which the oscillations are periodically stopped or quenched is called a superregenerative detector.

3. d. *Physics.* To suppress (luminescence); hence, to de-excite (an atom that would otherwise give rise to this effect).

1928 *Proc. Nat. Acad. Sci.* XIV. 851 The results show that hydrogen quenches the resonance radiation of cadmium as effectively as it does that of mercury. **1932** *Jrnl. Amer. Chem. Soc.* LIV. 572 The apparent decrease in quenching at high pressures or temperatures does not at all preclude the possibility that some fraction of the mercury atoms are being quenched to the normal state. **1954** C. Zwikker *Physical Properties of Solid Materials* xiii. 230 Fluorescence may be quenched by radiation, *e.g.* infra-red of too long a wavelength to excite fluorescence. The quenching photons raise electrons from the crystal lattice..to the copper ions..and thus inhibit the recombination effect. **1976** *Sci. Amer.* June 47/2 (Advt.), While the list of molecules which will react with $^1O_2$ is growing rapidly, the list of molecules which will quench $^1O_2$ back to O_2 is much smaller.

e. *Physics* and *Chem.* To suppress (the orbital angular momentum of an electron and the associated magnetic moment).

1932 J. H. Van Vleck *Theory of Electric & Magn. Susceptibilities* xi. 282 Solids or solutions in which interatomic forces quench the orbital angular momentum but leave the spin free. **1955** Townes & Schawlow *Microwave Spectrosc.* vii. 175 In nonlinear molecules, the orbital motion of electrons is almost completely 'quenched' or suppressed, and a spin momentum is the only angular momentum in the molecule of distinctly electronic origin. **1962** Cotton & Wilkinson *Adv. Inorg. Chem.* xxiv. 508 The electric fields of other atoms, ions, and molecules surrounding the metal ion in its compounds interfere with the orbital motion of the electrons so that the orbital angular momentum and hence the orbital moment are wholly or partially 'quenched'. **1971** J. D. Patterson *Introd. Theory of Solid State Physics* iv. 240 The cubic field acts to 'quench' the orbital angular momentum.

f. To prevent (the discharge in a Geiger counter) from continuing too long and reducing the possible counting rate; also with the counter as obj.

1940 *Physical Rev.* LVII. 1036/1 If we merely assure ourselves that the counter wire is falling somewhat below the starting potential with each discharge, then we can be sure that the discharge is quenched after the first stage and we will have a clean, fast pulse. **1942** Pollard & Davidson *Applied Nucl. Physics* iii. 30 A very common device to quench a counter is to employ a vacuum tube. **1958** O. R. Frisch *Nucl. Handbk.* xv. 14 The discriminator circuit used with Geiger counters..should provide facilities for quenching the counter for a period of several hundred microseconds after each pulse. **1963** W. E. Burcham *Nuclear Physics* vi. 218 It is the function of the alcohol in the gas filling to 'quench' the discharge. **1975** K. H. Goulding in Williams & Wilson *Biologist's Guide to Princ. & Techniques Pract. Biochem.* vi. 178 To overcome this, the tube is quenched by the addition of a suitable gas, which reduces the energy of the ions.

II. 7. *Physics.* To change from the superconducting state to the non-superconducting state.

1969 *Sci. Jrnl.* Apr. 42/2 Increasing current is passed through the superconductor until the material 'quenches' (goes normal). **1975** *Physics Bull.* May 214/1 The normal metal (copper or combinations of copper and cupronickel) is still required to protect the conductor when it reaches the limit of its current carrying capacity and 'quenches' (ie undergoes a transition to the normal state).

III. 8. Combs. (from sense 2b): **quench-ageing,** changes in the properties of steel, notably hardening, which occur after the metal has been quenched from a high temperature (see quot. 1968); **quench-cracking,** fracture of a metal caused by thermal stresses during rapid cooling; **quench-hardening,** hardening of steel by heating it above a critical temperature for some time, quenching rapidly, and then allowing further slow cooling; also = *quench-ageing* above; so **quench-harden** *v. trans.*

1935 *Trans. Amer. Soc. Metals* XXIII. 1049 To one of the three most important examples of aging, found in practically all soft steels, the designation 'Carbonizing' has been given for purposes of this discussion. It has also been called 'sub-critical quench-aging'. **1938** *Jrnl. Iron & Steel Inst.* CXXXVIII. 247P The usual theory put forward to explain the process of quench-ageing, whether in steel or in any other age-hardening alloy, is that it is caused by the precipitation from super-saturated solid solution of particles of the solute in a highly dispersed form on the lattice of the solvent,..preliminary to precipitation. **1961** G. E. Dieter *Mech. Metallurgy* v. 137 Quench aging is a type of true precipitation hardening that occurs on quenching from the temperature of maximum solubility of carbon and nitrogen in ferrite. **1968** E. R. Petty *Physical Metall. of Engin. Materials* v. 92 These changes involve an increase in hardness, elastic limit and tensile strength, accompanied by a fall in ductility and impact resistance, and may occur in low carbon steels finished by rapid cooling from a softening temperature above 600°C or by cold working. In the former case the phenomenon is referred to as quench ageing while the latter is known as strain ageing. **1971** *Engineering* Apr. 20/1 The absence of the defects of material or liquation on the surface of the pins and journals is of particular importance..where these areas are to be hardened by flame or induction, as the risk of quench cracking is almost entirely eliminated. **1973** J. G. Tweeddale *Materials Technol.* I. vi. 172 There is usually a limiting rate of cooling from the outside for any given steel, beyond which it is impractical to go because too-rapid contraction from the outside may cause quench-cracking. **1934** H. O'Neill *Hardness of Metals & its Measurement* vi. 201 Mehl..has reported that quench-hardening a pearlitic steel does not alter its compressibility. *Ibid.* 202 Ordinary quench-hardening practice by continuous rapid cooling to room temperatures will produce martensite if the rate is sufficient to preserve austenite down to Ar″. **1961** G. E. Dieter *Mech. Metallurgy* v. 146 Quench hardening results in an increase in yield stress and a decrease in the rate of strain hardening. **1969** D. K. Allen *Metallurgy Theory & Pract.* vii. 194/2 Most all carbon steels can be quench-hardened but the hardness does not become appreciable until the carbon content..reaches about 0·35 percent. *Ibid.* 196/2 The second requirement for quench hardening is that the steel be heated to the recommended hardening temperature and held for a sufficient length of time to allow the steel to become fully austenitized.

quenched, *ppl. a.* (s.v. Quench *v.*). Add: **a.** Also with *out* and in other senses of the vb. (Further examples.)

1881 O. Wilde *Poems* 211 The quenched-out torch, the lonely cypress-gloom. **1938** [see *quench *sb.* 2]. **1946** [see *quenching rate* s.v. *quenching *vbl. sb.* 2]. **1958** [see *aggregate *sb.* 6]. **1963** B. Fozard *Instrumentation & Control Nucl. Reactors* v. 50 Organically quenched counters are characterised by high starting and operating voltages.

b. Radio. *quenched spark*, a spark in a spark transmitter that is extinguished mechanically soon after it begins (see *quench *v.* 1d); so *quenched gap*, a spark-gap designed to bring this about.

1910 G. W. Pierce *Princ. Wireless Telegr.* xxiii. 269 The quenched spark is..economical in transmitting energy, and is favorable to sharp tuning. **1927** O. F. Brown *Elements of Radio Communication* iv. 53 The two methods most frequently employed for quenching are either the use of a rotating spark gap or a specially designed spark gap known as the 'quenched gap'. **1962** J. H. & P. J. Reyner *Radio Communication* vii. 294 Owing to the rapid cooling a very high spark frequency may be used, and quenched spark sets operated with a spark frequency of 1,500 per second or more.

quencher. a. (Further examples.)

1950 H. W. Leverenz *Introd. Luminescence of Solids* iv. 132 A phosphor center may function as..a poison (or killer, or quencher), by having the excited-state equilibrium level sufficiently near or above *f* so that radiationless transitions predominate. **1961** G. R. Choppin *Exper. Nuclear Chem.* v. 61 The effect of multiple discharges due to failure of the quencher is included..but will be negligible for a good tube operating at the proper plateau voltage. **1971** *Nature* 13 Aug. 444/3 It is well known that paramagnetic ions are efficient quenchers of electronically excited states. **1976** *Sci. Amer.* June 47/2 (Advt.), This is because the excitation energy of $^1O_2$ is unusually low; a quencher molecule to relieve $^1O_2$ of this energy must have an even lower excited state.

quenching, *vbl. sb.* Add: **1.** (Further examples.)

1908 J. A. Fleming *Elem. Man. Radiotelegr. & Radioteleph.* 338 (Index), Quenching noise of an electric spark. **1928** *Proc. Nat. Acad. Sci.* XIV. 849 (*heading*) The quenching of cadmium resonance radiation. **1943** B. F. Weller *Radio-Technol.* iv. 114 Quenching may be effected by a separate valve,..or the reacting detector valve may be arranged to oscillate at the quenching frequency, as well as the radio-frequency. **1963** B. Fozard *Instrumentation Nucl. Reactors* ii. 25 Because of the need for 'quenching' in a Geiger–Mueller counter for example, its detailed design may be quite different from that of an ionisation chamber. **1972** De Puy & Chapman *Molec. Reactions & Photochem.* iii. 37 Sensitization and quenching are important methods for determining the spin multiplicity of excited states responsible for photochemical reactions.

2. *quenching crack, medium, rate, trough.*

1926 A. Sauveur *Metallogr. & Heat Treatment of Iron & Steel* (ed. 3) xv. 220 Water quenching is to be preferred to oil quenching if it can be performed without producing quenching cracks. **1966** C. R. Tottle *Sci. Engin. Materials* x. 224 The strain in the transformed martensite is tensile, in the circumferential direction, and so radial cracks form in the martensite to relieve the stress; these are known as quenching cracks. **1932** E. Gregory *Metallurgy* iv. 112 Water is obviously the cheapest quenching medium, and is invaluable for tools and purposes where an extremely hard surface is desired. **1946** *Nature* 31 Aug. 308/1 Experiments with various iron-carbon alloys quenched in various ways tend to show that the amounts of ferrite, martensite and retained austenite obtained in the quenched specimen are independent of the quenching-rate so long as a certain critical rate..is not exceeded. **1896** F. S. Meyer *Handbk. Art Smithing* ii. 19 In the front part of the forge are found, as a rule, a quenching trough, hollows and receivers for fuel and slack. **1973** *Canad. Antiques Collector* May–June 7 (*caption*) The stone quenching trough from the oldest smithy in eastern Ontario.

quenching *ppl. a.* (later examples).

1954 [see *quench *v.* 3 d]. **1958** W. K. Mansfield *Elem. Nucl. Physics* vi. 50 Positive ions arriving at the cathode are sometimes able to eject an electron. If this were to occur..a continuous series of pulses might be observed. This is prevented in a Geiger counter by the inclusion of a quenching agent. **1966** D. G. Brandon *Mod. Techniques Metallogr.* iii. 154 The addition of a small amount of a second, 'quenching', gas..serves to prevent secondary electron emission by the positive ion bombardment of the cathode.

quenchless, *a.* (Further examples.)

1838 W. Howitt *Rural Life Eng.* II. i. ii. 35 The Romances of Scott..have..piled quenchless fuel on this social flame. **1895** Yeats *Poems* 12 And with quenchless eyes and fluttering hair A beautiful young man followed behind. **1952** C. Day Lewis tr. *Virgil's Aeneid* iv. 78 And consecrated their quenchless flames. **1976** *New Yorker* 15 Nov. 59/1 Vaccaro and Jack Smith, the underground filmmaker, shared a quenchless passion for 'Siren of Atlantis', 'White Savage', 'Cobra Woman', and other nineteen-forties epics starring Miss Montez.

quenelle. (Earlier and later examples.) Also **quenelle de volaille,** a ball made with chicken or other fowl meat.

1845 E. Acton *Mod. Cookery* vi. 180 *French Forcemeat called Quenelles.* This is a peculiarly light and delicate kind of forcemeat. **1846** [see *croûton]. **1861** Mrs. Beeton *Bk. Househ. Managem.* 202 *Veal Quenelles...* If the quenelles are not firm enough, add the yolk of another egg. **1889** J. Whitehead *Steward's Handbk.* iv. 420/1 *Richelieu garnish*, quenelles of chicken, cockscombs and slices of fat livers in brown onion sauce. **1936** Lucas & Hume *Au Petit Cordon Bleu* 53 Decorate the tops of each *paupiette* with small fillets of anchovy and the *quenelles* with strips of anchovy. **1976** *Punch* 27 Oct. 737/1 Is it also prejudice..to prefer *quenelles* to fish cakes, to hate Coca-Cola and adore wine? **1977** C. McFadden *Serial* (1978) vi. 18/1 She could really dig *quenelles* about now.

quenselite (kwe·nsĕləit). *Min.* [ad. G. *quenselit* (G. Flink 1925, in *Geol. Föreningens i Stockholm Förhandl.* XLVII. 377), f. the name of P. D. *Quensel* (b. 1881), Swedish mineralogist: see -ite[1].] An oxide of lead and manganese, $PbMnO_2(OH)$, found as black, tabular, monoclinic crystals.

1926 *Mineral. Abstr.* III. 110 Quenselite, another new mineral from Långban, Sweden, occurs as small (1 mm.) pitch-black crystals with calcite and baryte in crevices of the granular haematite ore. **1958** *Proc. Nat. Inst. Sci. India* A. XXIV. 95 This is probably the first reported occurrence of quenselite in manganese ores of metamorphic origin. **1971** *Zeitschr. für Kryst.* CXXXIV. 331 The significance of the quenselite structure lies in its role as a connecting link between certain of the Pb oxides and the lithiophorite-chalcophanite group... In addition to red and yellow PbO, quenselite has structural similarities to Pb_2O_3.

quercetin. Add to def.: 3,3′,4′,5,7-Pentahydroxyflavone, $C_{15}H_{10}O_7$. (Further examples.)

1949 *Thorpe's Dict. Appl. Chem.* (ed. 4) IX. 300/2 Quercetin gives red-brown, brown-orange, bright orange and olive-black shades on wool mordanted with chromium, aluminium, tin, and iron, respectively. **1962** T. R. Seshadri in T. A. Geissman *Chem. Flavonoid Compounds* ii. 9 Quercetin and its glycosides can be conveniently extracted by borax and can be liberated by acidification.

quercitron. Add: **2.** Special Combs. **quercitron lake, yellow,** the yellow pigment obtained from quercitron bark, yielding quercetin and rhamnose on hydrolysis; quercetrin.

1886 H. C. Standage *Artists' Man. Pigments* iv. 43 Yellow Lakes (Madder Yellow,..Quercitron Yellow or Lake). **1918** Perkin & Everest *Natural Org. Colouring Matters* xix. 628 Quercitron-yellow lake, Flavin-lake, or Dutch pink can be made..by precipitating a decoction of quercitron bark containing alum with chalk. **1934** Quercitron lake [see **Italian pink*]. **1947** L. S. Pratt *Chem. & Physics Org. Pigments* vii. 65 Quercitron lake is a yellow coloring matter made from the inner bark of a species of oak, *Quercus tinctoria*, that is indigenous to North America.

‖ **querencia** (kere·nþia). [a. Sp. *querencia* lair, haunt, home ground, f. *querer* to seek, desire, f. L. *quærere* to seek.] **1.** *Bullfighting.* The part of the arena where the bull takes his stand; stamping ground.

1932 E. Hemingway *Death in Afternoon* xiii. 150 A querencia is a place the bull naturally wants to go to in the ring; a preferred locality. That is a natural querencia and such are well known and fixed, but an accidental querencia is more than that. It is a place which develops in the course of the fight where the bull makes his home. **1957** R. Campbell *Portugal* vi. 115 He [*sc.* the bull] may choose his *querencia* for some strategical advantage—near the body of a dead horse, for instance. **1964** *Listener* 27 Aug. 317/1 It is when the bull leaves his *querencia*—the place where he feels safe—that he falls a victim to delusion. **1974** F. Nolan *Oshawa Project* i. 3 Some taunted fighting bull seeking its *querencia*.

2. *fig.* A (person's) favourite place; home ground, refuge.

1952 R. CAMPBELL *Lorca* i. 8 Andalusia is Lorca's *querencia*. **1977** A. SCHOLEFIELD *Venom* III. 98 Returning always to the centre of the gold carpet for there, like a bull in a ring, he had instinctively made his *querencia*, his territory.

Queres, var. *KERES.

‖ **Querflöte** (kvē·ɹflötə). *Mus.* [a. G. *querflöte* cross-flute, f. *quer* transverse + *flöte* flute.] **1.** A transverse flute, blown through an opening at the side; = *cross-flute* s.v. *CROSS B.

1876 STAINER & BARRETT *Dict. Mus. Terms* 373/1 *Querflöte* (*Ger.*),..The flute played sideways, as opposed to the flute which was blown at one end, and held straight in front of the performer. **1914** H. M. FITZGIBBON *Story of Flute* iii. 30 (*caption*) Prætorius' Bass Querflote, 1620. **1959** WESTRUP & HARRISON *Collins Mus. Encycl.* 525/1 *Querflöte*,..'Cross' or 'transverse flute', i.e. the modern flute as distinct from the recorder or *Blockflöte*. **1976** D. MUNROW *Instruments Middle Ages & Renaissance* 53/3 Back in medieval times the different playing positions of the two instruments had provided a means of distinction..: hence the use of..*Querflöte*, or *Querpfeife* (German, cross flute) for the transverse flute.

2. An organ stop that emits a sound resembling that of a flute.

1921 G. A. AUDSLEY *Organ-Stops* 217 *Querflöte*...The name..has been frequently used by German organ-builders to designate the stop which, in its voice, imitates, as closely as practicable in organ-pipes, the tone of the Flute of the orchestra. **1966** P. WILLIAMS *European Organ 1450–1850* 286 *Querflöte* (Ger. 'cross flute'), properly, an open cylindrical metal or wood flue stop (usually 4'), over-blowing to the first or second overtone due to the pipe's narrow scale, large foot-holes and fairly low cut-up.

‖ **querida** (keri·ðɑ). [Sp. *querida*, pa. pple. *querer* to seek, desire, f. L. *quærĕre* to seek.] A sweetheart, darling: freq. used as a term of address. Also **querido** (-ðo), the male equivalent.

1846 R. FORD *Gatherings from Spain* xx. 274 His short-petticoated *querida*. **1926** W. N. BURNS *Saga of Billy the Kid* xiv. 185 In every *placeta* in the Pecos some little señorita was proud to be known as his *querida*. **1963** E. LININGTON *Death of Busybody* i. 9 Be careful now, *querida*. Lock both doors on your way home. **1970** KOENIG & DIXON *Children are Watching* iii. 23 Did her *querido* have to go back to work at the restaurant? **1976** 'S. WOODS' *My Life is Done* 40 Everything will be well, *querido*.

querl, *sb.* (Earlier and later examples in form *quirl*.)

1854 B. F. TAYLOR *Jan. & June* 23 [The grape vine's] aspirations were manifested in the display of divers mermaidish-looking ringlets, with two or three dainty 'quirls' therein. **1871** L. M. ALCOTT *Little Men* v. 78 Sally, loading her pie with quirls and flourishes. **1889** R. T. COOKE *Steadfast* xv. 162 A hundred resolute little quirls above the low forehead. **1950** *Publ. Amer. Dial. Soc.* XIV. 55 *Quirl*, a *curl*, as on a watermelon vine. A melon is supposed to be nice when the quirl is dead.

querl, *v.* Add: Also **quirl.** (Examples.) So **querled** *ppl. a.*, **que·rling** *vbl. sb.* and *ppl. a.*

1787 *Amer. Museum* II. 571/1 She thought there was something alive in her side, for, to use her own expression, she plainly perceived a tickling and quirling in it. *Ibid.* 574/1 She next complained of a quirling pain, that would last three or four hours with the utmost violence. **1830** *Northern Watchman* (Troy, N.Y.) 30 Nov. 3/5 We..come out of the plagid lock, wrong end foremost, all quirled up in a h—l of a twist. **1840** J. F. COOPER *Pathfinder* I. xiii. 206 One of his hands coiled a rope against the Sun, and he called it *querling* a rope, too, when I asked him what he was about. **1890** *Dialect Notes* I. 75 'Quirled way up'... 'Quirl, both noun and verb, is familiar to me.' **1893** H. A. SHANDS *Some Peculiarities of Speech in Mississippi* 52 *Quirl*,..this word is largely used by negroes, and to some extent by white people, for *curl*. It is also thus used in New England. In Mississippi a snake is nearly always said to be *quirled* or *quoiled up*, instead of *curled* or *coiled up*. **1944** *Publ. Amer. Dial. Soc.* II. 30 *Quirl*, to curl. 'Does hit *quirl* like a pig's tail?'... Common.

querulist. (Later example.)

1922 C. E. MONTAGUE *Disenchantment* iv. 52 The querulist of the book took it hard..that more kind words did not come to the men.

query, *sb.*[1] Add: **2. b.** *spec.* in the Society of Friends, an item in a formal list of questions issued for the guidance of Friends; now freq. in phr. *Advices and Queries* (see quot. 1954).

1654 BURROUGH & HOWGILL (*title*) Answers to severall queries put forth to the despised people called Quakers. **1701** G. KEITH *Answer to 17 Queries Quarterly Meeting Quakers, Oxford* 3 Those seventeen Queries ye sent me being only Queries, contain little or nothing Affirmatively or Negatively, by way of position. **1768** in *Extracts Minutes Yearly Meeting Friends, London* (1783) 269 This meeting directs, that the 11th query remain as it now stands. **1797** *Encycl. Brit.* XV. 737/2 At the quarterly-meeting are produced written answers from the monthly-meetings, to certain queries respecting the conduct of their members, and the meeting's care over them. **1898** *Friends' Q. Examiner* 483 For about a century it was uncertain whether the interrogations addressed to the meetings of Friends should be termed 'questions' or 'queries'. The former term was chiefly employed up to 1762, but 'queries' has held the field since 1783. **1921** R. M. JONES *Later Periods of Quakerism* I. iv. 134 At first the Queries were formal questions asked for the sake of securing information in reference to the number of members suffering under persecution. *Ibid.* 135 As fresh moral issues arose,..the list of Queries enlarged. They grew in number and in importance until they embodied almost all the essential aspects of the Quaker moral ideal, and they furnished a kind of silent confessional for each individual member, as well as a moral measuring rule to guide the Overseers in their work of looking after the flock. **1928** *Advices & Queries* (Society of Friends) 5 The Queries being directed in recent years to arouse the thought and conscience..rather than to obtain specific information. **1954** H. LOUKES *Friends face Reality* viii. 107 Quakers have performed this process of moral illumination of each other, while at the same time guarding against the danger of setting up an external moral code, by a system of 'Advices and Queries', moral and spiritual reflections couched in the form most calculated to set the individual searching his own heart.

3. Also written out as a quasi-*adj.* or *-adv.*, preceding the word(s) to which it refers.

1942 *Jrnl. R. Naval Med. Service* XXVIII. 21 Admitted with a diagnosis of 'query' septicæmia. **1953** R. LEHMANN *Echoing Grove* 61 'You reminded me of someone I once knew...' (Query her sister?) **1967** G. F. FIENNES *I tried to run Railway* iii. 21 It would have had to be an unwary Hun that let me get near him with my pike—design Circa 1500; origin query Birmingham Small Arms Company. **1977** J. MCCLURE *Sunday Hangman* x. 109 '*Murders*..,' snapped Colonel Muller. 'Query murders,' corrected Kramer, recognising an urgent need ..to treat the situation as routinely as possible.

query, *v.* Add: **1. b.** (Later examples with direct speech as obj.)

1905 *Smart Set* Sept. 119/2 'Been here long?' I queried. **1976** B. FREEMANTLE *November Man* iii. 38 'The elections?' queried Hollis.

2. For *rare* read 'Now chiefly *U.S.*' and add further examples.

1943 *Sun* (Baltimore) 30 Nov. 10/7 He queries me concerning the passage. **1952** *Time* 14 Apr. 17/1 Before an issue of *Time* goes to press..a twin-bed position may be dummied, a stringer queried for a checking point. **1974** *Spartanburg* (S. Carolina) *Herald* 18 Apr. A6/2 College Students..who were queried at Iowa State University, have some curious ideas about what 'academic freedom' means. **1977** *Daily Times* (Lagos) 11 Jan. 20/2 When these officers were queried, they felt unhappy.

3. a. (Later example.)

1961 [see *EAR *sb.*[1] 5].

‖ **quesadilla** (kesadī·lʸa). [Sp.] A variety of turnover, usu. with a cheese filling.

1944 E. ZELAYETA *Elena's Famous Mexican & Sp. Recipes* iv. 35 Quesadilla. Tortilla Stuffed with Cheese. Take fresh tortillas..place generous piece of Monterey cream cheese..in the center, and fold it over as you would a turnover... Cook lightly, turning often until cheese is melted. **1957** *House Beautiful* Sept. 176/4 Quesadillas. Small-size tortillas made into turnovers and filled with cheese or squash flowers or sometimes chicken *molé*. They are baked or deep-fat fried. **1963** *Sunset* Jan. 70/1 Quesadillas (Fruit and Cheese Turnovers). **1965** *House & Garden* Sept. 223/3 Quesadillas. These turnovers are made with unbaked tortillas stuffed with a variety of fillings. **1978** *Chicago* June 249/1 Start with nachos..and quesadillas (miniature tortillas filled with guacamole or thick white cheese and onions—60c).

quest, *v.*[1] **1. a.** (Later examples.)

1954 J. I. LLOYD *Beagling* 142 *Quest*, draw for a hare. **1969** M. PUGH *Last Place Left* x. 60 We heard the shot then saw the spaniel questing. **1976** *Shooting Times & Country Mag.* 16–22 Dec. 25/2 Two short toots on the horn..had hounds questing among the tufts of coarse grass and gorse bushes.

questing, *vbl. sb.* (Later example.)

1923 M. SADLEIR *Desolate Splendour* iv. 72 From externals only need the weary questing of a stranger mind seek teaching or enlightenment.

que·stingly, *adv.* [-LY[2].] In a questing manner.

1926 R. CLEMENTS *Stately Southerner* 89, I..looked questingly right and left.

question, *sb.* Add: **II. 3. b.** (Earlier and further examples.) From the 18th cent., *spec.* a question put in Parliament by a Member to the Government or to a Minister.

1549 *House of Commons Jrnl.* 28 Mar. 21/1 In the Question, it is agreed, That the Number, which said No to the Bill, be the greater Number by One Person. **1559** *Ibid.* 17 Apr. 60/1 Carnesew declared to the House, that Thrower, Servant to the Master of the Rolls, did say against the State of the House, that if a Bill were brought in for Womens Wyers in their Pastes, they would dispute it, and go to the Question. **1614** *Ibid.* 13 Apr. 464/1 Mr. Hackwill:—That nothing to pass, by Order of the House, without a Question; and that no Order, without a Question Affirmative and Negative: And that ordered to be, upon the Question. **1778** *Parl. Reg.* 16 Dec. 181 Lord Newhaven put a variety of questions to the gentlemen belonging to the board of ordnance. **1844** T. E. MAY *Treat. Law, Privileges, Proceedings & Usage of Parl.* viii. 166 Any member may propose a question, which is called 'moving the house', or, more commonly, 'making a motion'. *Ibid.* 171 In the commons, when the motion has been seconded, it merges in the question, which is then proposed by the speaker to the house, and read by him. **1908** A. E. STEINTHAL tr. *Redlich's Procedures House of Commons* II. VII. vi. 241 Requests for information, 'Questions' are regularly addressed by members of the House to the Government, and at times to the Speaker or to private members. **1929** G. F. M. CAMPION *Introd. Procedures House of Commons* iv. 124 Oral Questions are by far the most numerous. To them is allotted the whole of 'Question time' proper, *i.e.* from not later than three o'clock to not later than a quarter to four. **1956** P. HOWARTH *Questions in House* i. 17 Apart from the procedural reasons, there were also reasons of a political or a constitutional nature why the custom of asking parliamentary questions developed slowly. **1958** S. HYLAND *Who goes Hang?* xvi. 72 As the only office-holder present, he knew about the Colonial Secretary's statement due at the end of Questions. **1971** P. D. G. THOMAS *House of Commons in 18th Cent.* ii. 30 The eighteenth century saw the evolution of the Parliamentary question. *Ibid.* 32 Questions in the House proper may well have been established practice long before the first instance found of a question put to and answered by a minister. **1976** *Ann. Rep., Howard League for Penal Reform 1975/76* 6 On the Bail Bill..the two organizations suggested a number of amendments... We are grateful to several MP's..who asked Questions, some at our suggestion.

d. (Later examples.)

1930 G. B. SHAW *Apple Cart* I. 17 You cant. You mustnt. Of course not. Out of the question. **1977** A. ECCLESTONE *Staircase for Silence* iv. 76 Anything like an attempt to impose a parochial structure, new or old, was out of the question.

5. c. *no questions asked*: with no need to give an account of oneself or one's conduct.

1948 M. LASKI *Tory Heaven* ix. 121 Under the old system, I could have had the pair of them and no questions asked. **1962** WODEHOUSE *Service with Smile* x. 160 Give him a skipper and a little daughter..and he could have made straight for the reef of Norman's Woe, and no questions asked. **1968** *Listener* 4 July 30/2 They can.. sign a contract with a sports or tobacco firm and will then be..able to play lawn tennis for profit 365 days in the year—and no questions asked.

6. a. *a good question*: see *GOOD *a.* 14c.

d. In various proverbial phrases and expressions, as *ask me no questions and I'll tell you no lies* and varr.; *a civil question deserves a civil answer* and varr. Also *ask a silly question and you get a silly answer*: see *SILLY *a.*

1773 GOLDSMITH *She stoops to Conq.* III. 51 Ask me no questions and I'll tell you no fibs. **1818** SCOTT *Ht. Midl.* I. ix. 247 If ye'll ask nae questions, I'll tell ye nae lees. **1844** T. C. HALIBURTON *Attaché* 2nd Ser. II. iv. 62 Let me give you a piece of advice;—Ax me no questions, and I'll tell you no lies. **1853** —— *Sam Slick's Wise Saws* II. ii. 48 Give a civil answer to a civil question. **1858** S. A. HAMMETT *Piney Woods Tavern* xxvii. 285 The Squire there asked me a civil question, and that desarves a civil answer,—at least that's manners where I come from. **1900** H. LAWSON *Over Sliprails* 135 'Where did you buy the steer, father?' she asked. 'Ask no questions and hear no lies.' **1955** W. C. MACDONALD *Destination Danger* xii. 140 Quist smiled. 'Ask me no questions, I'll tell you no lies.' **1970** V. CANNING *Great Affair* xii. 221 'What has happened to Sarah?'..'Ask no questions hear no lies.'

III. 7. b. *question-answerer*, *-answering* (examples), *-asking* (further examples), *-beggar*, *-begging* (earlier and later examples), *-putting* (example), *raising*. **d. question-master**, the chairman of a discussion panel (*PANEL *sb.*[1] 5b), by whom the questions are put; **question pitch**, the rising intonation of an interrogative sentence; **question time** (earlier example); *spec.* a time set apart in Parliament for Members to question Ministers; **question word**, an interrogative pronoun, etc., used to introduce a question.

1900 *Westm. Gaz.* 20 Jan. 9/2 (Advt.), It is also a great question-answerer, or work of reference. **1972** *Computers & Humanities* VII. 9 Simmons is particularly good in describing the extensive progress made in second-generation question-answering systems. **1977** *Dædalus* Fall 123 The various attempts to process natural language by machine—analysis and synthesis of speech, automatic translation, question-answering,..and the like. **1938** *Ann. Reg. 1937* CLXXIX. 303 To the same medley of generations in England belong Mr. Richard Aldington's *The Crystal World*..and Mr. W. H. Auden's question-asking *Spain*. **1972** *Jrnl. Social Psychol.* LXXXVII. 9 English praise delivered to small groups of these children by a familiar Anglo adult exerted some degree of reinforcing effects on their question-asking behavior. **1935** A. P. HERBERT *What a Word!* viii. 229 The chief kind is the Question-beggar, the epithet or phrase which assumes or imputes that the question under discussion has been conclusively answered already. **1824** J. BENTHAM *Book of Fallacies* IV. i. 213 (*heading*) Fallacies of Confusion, the object of which is, to perplex, when Discussion can no longer be avoided... Question-begging appellatives. **1863** GEO. ELIOT *Romola* III. xiii. 130 There was no argument more widely convincing than question-begging phrases in large type. **1910** A. SIDGWICK *Application of Logic* vii. 217 Question-begging in the extended sense..occurs just so far as any attempt is made on the part of either disputant to prevent question-*raising*. **1911** H. G. WELLS *New Machiavelli* I. iv. 113, I scoffed at that pompous question-begging word 'Evolution'. **1957** *Times Lit. Suppl.* 27 Dec. 782/2 He is not above question-begging in the most ingenious way. **1979** C. MOULE in M. Goulder *Incarnation & Myth* v. 138 Evidence of this kind in no way depends.. upon question-begging theories of scriptural authority. **1946** L. MACNEICE *Dark Tower* (1947) 165 Listeners will have the privilege of hearing a number of experts on Truth, all of them equally infallible; our question-master is the March Hare. **1952** *Gloucestershire Echo* 3 Oct. 6/2

It has become traditional for the Festival to end..with a Brains Trust. With Gilbert Harding as question-master and..a varied team. **1977** 'E. Crispin' *Glimpses of Moon* ii. 36 The bright, uncommitted fashion of a television question-master..in a quiz. **1933** L. Bloomfield in Saporta & Bastian *Psycholinguistics* (1961) 244/2 *Yeah?* and *Is that so?* with a peculiar modification of the question-pitch, have been used as facetious vulgarisms expressing disbelief. **1964** C. C. Fries in D. Abercrombie et al. *Daniel Jones* 244 Formal yes-or-no questions, along with question-pitch. **1884** E. W. Hamilton *Diary* 30 July (1972) II. 663 My main points are:.. 2. Confinement of question-putting to Private Members' nights [etc.]. **1910** Question-raising [see *question-begging* above]. **1959** *Times* 25 Sept. 8/4 Curious and question-raising as they are, the megapodes are worth a more serious..programme of research. **1852** Mrs. Gaskell *Let.* 4 Sept. (1966) 197 (*heading*) Saty schoolroom, Question-time. **1891** W. Fraser *Disraeli & his Day* 381 Colonel Makins, the.. Member for Essex..said, 'They have got it hot this afternoon about a Dissolution.' I replied, 'Oh, nonsense!' This was during 'Question-time'. **1936** H. Nicolson *Diary* 3 Dec. (1966) 281 Members crowd in as question-time draws to its end. **1976** H. Wilson *Governance of Britain* vii. 132 Harold Macmillan, a highly successful performer at Question time. **1924** H. E. Palmer *Gram. Spoken Eng.* 263 In Direct Questions, the question-words are said to be interrogative; in Indirect Questions, they are said to be conjunctive. **1964** E. Uldall in D. Abercrombie et al. *Daniel Jones* 274 Question-word question: 'What did he think they were doing?' **1978** *Language* LIV. 86 In English, questions are typically initiated by question words or verbs, so as to distinguish them from declarative sentences.

question, *v.* **5. b.** Delete † *Obs.* and add later example.

1879 G. Meredith *Egoist* III. xiv. 291 At the game of Chess it is the dishonour of our adversary when we are stale-mated: but in life..such a winning of the game questions our sentiments.

questionability. (Later examples.)

1966 *Listener* 1 Sept. 317/3 It is in the fact that only *one* of this grossly neglected composer's works has appeared that the questionability lies. **1969** R. Harper *World of Thriller* ii. 51 Only occasionally for most men is life reduced to total questionability by any particular situation.

question and answer. A dialogue consisting of alternate question and answer. Also (with hyphens) *attrib.*; occas. also **question-answer.**

1817 Keats *Let.* 10 Sept. (1931) 39 My dear Fanny, Let us now begin a regular question and answer — a little pro and con. **1839** [see Question *sb.* 7 c]. **1908** Mrs. H. Ward *Diana Mallory* ii. xii. 237 The trivial question-and-answer of the tea-making. **1940** N. Marsh *Surfeit of Lampreys* (1941) xiii. 187 She maintained a question-and-answer attitude, replying in the most meagre phrases. **1941** L. MacNeice *Poetry of W. B. Yeats* i. 14 He may be answering quite different questions from mine but the question-answers which he evolves are the same kind of organism, and result from the same kind of activity as my own question-answers. **1945** C. S. Lewis *Great Divorce* 41 That question-and-answer conception of thought only applies to matter of fact. **1957** E. Bott *Family & Social Network* ii. 42 The question-and-answer pattern of fact-collecting. **1960** *Guardian* 9 June 9/1 Police interrogators ..now hold a daily..question-and-answer session with the former Nazi. **1965** *Language* XLI. 387 The question-answer pair *What does he do? He draws cartoons* can be analyzed in the same way. **1977** *Oxford Diocesan Mag.* Oct. 20/2 It was decided to organise..a question-and-answer programme on an electronic screen. **1980** *English World-Wide* I. i. 28 It is not easy to elicit syntactic information by using the short direct question-answer technique.

questionary, *sb.*² Delete *rare* and add later examples. Also *attrib.*

Now largely superseded by *questionnaire, exc. in *Med.* use.

1951 *Lancet* 7 July 23/1 The questionary method used in this particular study has certain limitations. **1957** *Brit. Med. Jrnl.* 7 Sept. 550/2 The clinical concept of the disappointed undergraduate is therefore given some support by the answers to a general questionary. **1959** *Times* 5 Sept. 10/2 The proposed Welsh dialect atlas, information for which was gathered by means of a questionary of about 1,000 items. **1970** *Jrnl. Gen. Psychol.* Jan. 97 How did you answer when the item was difficult? And why did you answer in such a manner? (verbalization questionary). **1977** *Lancet* 27 Aug. 417/2 After 21 days, the patient was interviewed by one of us..using a standard questionary.

questionee. Delete *rare*⁻¹ and add earlier and later examples.

1838 Carlyle *Lett. to Mill &c.* (1923) lix. 164 Your answer is according to your question, and your questionee,—'as the fool thinks the bell clinks'. **1905** *Grand Mag.* Feb. 131 The..questionee does not overlook the fact that [etc.]. **1953** *Rep. Sel. Comm. Delegated Legislation* 27/2 in *Parl. Papers* 1952–3 IV. 115, I am not sure that the questioner could not answer that rather better than the questionee. **1971** J. Wainwright *Last Buccaneer* ii. 183 He..murmured his questions in a very low voice. This forced the questionee consciously to *listen.*

question mark. (In Dict. s.v. Question *sb.* 7 d.) **1.** *Gram.* A mark of interrogation, represented by the sign ?

1905 T. F. & M. F. A. Husband *Punctuation* ii. vi. 74 A question-mark is sometimes placed in the middle of a sentence. In such a position it concentrates attention on certain elements of the thought. **1930** M. A. Pink *Dict. Correct Eng.* 147 To complete the list of stops we may mention here that the Question Mark (?) is used at the end of direct questions. **1960** Kierzek & Gibson *Macmillan Handbk. Eng.* ii. 278 A question mark is used after a direct question but not after an indirect question. **1971** N. Stacey *Who Cares?* xii. 207 We agreed that the article should be called 'A Mission's Failure'. But I thought it ought to have a question mark after it.

2. *fig.* A point about which there is uncertainty or doubt; an unresolved problem, an enigma. Also, a person whose character is unknown or unfathomable (usu. in some particular respect). Freq. in phr. *a question mark hangs* (etc.) *over* (something), there is doubt about (that thing).

1869 [see *question-mark* s.v. Question *sb.* 7 d]. **1924** R. Macaulay *Orphan Island* xxv. 322 Across the future of Orphan Island..is scrawled a question mark. **1945** A. Huxley *Time must have Stop* xxx. 286 Contemporary science..is engaged in destroying, not only things and lives, but entire patterns of civilization. So we find ourselves faced with yet another set of question marks. **1952** M. Allingham *Tiger in Smoke* xv. 215 Luke was destined to become one of the great policemen... The man was a living question-mark. **1957** J. S. Huxley *Relig. without Revelation* (rev. ed.) iii. 62 The great question-mark of our continuance after death. **1958** *Daily Express* 23 July 4/3 It is a question mark which has been ringing in my mind. **1960** *Economist* 15 Oct. 215/2 Question marks now loom hugely over the future of the white-dominated states of southern Africa. **1963** *Listener* 24 Jan. 152/1 His death will take its place as one of the great question marks in English political history. **1971** A. Price *Alamut Ambush* viii. 95 Razzak, the unknown quantity,..wasn't quite such a question mark since he'd turned up at the Ryle reception. **1973** *Times* 15 Oct. 22/1 The project..is near to completion of its first stage. But a question mark hangs over the second stage. **1974** *Plain Dealer* (Cleveland, Ohio) 19 Oct. 6-D/2 Caffery..could become a question mark if his knee does not respond to a couple of operations. **1978** G. Greene *Human Factor* ii. iii. 85 A question mark kept him awake for a long while: had there always been a taxi rank so close to Davis's flat? **1979** *Nature* 15 Feb. 506/1 The question mark hanging over the whole meeting was precisely what principle was at stake.

3. (With hyphens.) *attrib.*

1962 *Listener* 15 Nov. 835/2 The effect of changing Byron's tragic question-mark ending to a kind of 'redemption'..is quite unconvincing. **1966** J. S. Cox *Illustr. Dict. Hairdressing* 124/1 *Question-mark curl*, a stand up curl with a very long stem, like a quaver in music. **1973** M. Amis *Rachel Papers* 130 Shaving-cream bubbled inside the nearer of his question-mark ears.

Hence **que·stion-marked** *a.*, accompanied by a question mark.

1950 G. Barker *True Confession* vi. 33, I will not care who Or what you are, save palliation Of the question marked heart. **1975** C. Weston *Susannah Screaming* (1976) x. 52 The guff was already sorted, checked where possible, question-marked where not.

questionnaire (kwestyənēᵊ·ɹ, ‖ke-). [a. F. *questionnaire*, f. *questionner* to ask questions.]

a. A list of questions by which information is sought from a selected group, usu. for statistical analysis; a questionary.

The word was resisted by purists (see Fowler *Mod. Eng. Usage* (1926) 479/1) for many years after its first use in English. Some retained a Fr. pronunc. (kestionę̄r), whilst others preferred the Eng. word Questionary *sb.*² The anglicized pronunc. is now dominant.

1901 E. B. Titchener *Exper. Psychol.* I. i. xii. 197 The questionary or 'questionnaire' is a series of questions bearing upon the matter to be investigated, and submitted to a large number of persons for introspective answer. **1920** *Glasgow Herald* 20 Aug. 7/1 Valuable information, never previously collected, is being obtained through a questionnaire by the Federation of British Industries concerning the fuel requirements of the great industrial centres. **1924** W. B. Selbie *Psychol. Relig.* i. 4 A careful study of the phenomena of religious experience derived mainly from biographies, introspection, and a systematic use of the questionnaire. **1931** *Times Lit. Suppl.* 19 Feb. 126/2 There was issued recently the report of a study (by *questionnaire*) of two hundred marriages. **1952** *Shell Aviation News* June 9/2 The moment for the distribution of a printed questionnaire is obviously in flight, when passengers are frequently bored and glad of any distraction. **1975** *New Yorker* 21 Apr. 45/2 The reports involve the verification of routine information that has already been supplied by citizens in response to questionnaires included in application forms for insurance, for employment, for mortgages or apartment leases. **1978** S. Brill *Teamsters* viii. 312 Drivers..responded to questionnaires placed as advertisements in trucking magazines.

b. *attrib.*

1924 R. M. Ogden tr. *Koffka's Growth of Mind* ii. 45 With the aid of Hall's questionnaire-method, one of his students has collected a large mass of material concerning children's play. **1941** J. S. Huxley *Uniqueness of Man* xi. 231 The questionnaire method is widely used. **1949** M. Mead *Male & Female* 457, I have had access to enormous varieties of..original questionnaire blanks. **1964** I. L. Horowitz *New Sociology* 6 Specialized techniques of questionnaire design [etc.]..make the interviewing process into the end of research rather than merely its instrument. **1978** *Regional Lang. Stud.—Newfoundland* viii. 31 The purpose of the project was..to give experience in questionnaire design and administration.

questionous (kwe·styənəs), *a. rare.* [f. Question *sb.* + -ous.] Given to asking questions; inquisitive.

1893 R. Bridges *Humours of Court* ii. i. 914 Of late you are grown questionous and prying.

questor. 3. (Further example.)

1977 *Times Lit. Suppl.* 23 Dec. 1498/5 The prosing of that coruscating bore Dr Emily Brightman, a notator and questor of the first water.

‖ **Questore** (kwestō·re). [It. *questore*, f. L. *quæstor*, contraction of *quæsitor* investigator, f. *quærere* to seek, enquire.] = Questor 2 b.

1943 I. Origo *Diary* 10 Dec. in *War in Val d'Orcia* (1947) 120 His family succeeded in speaking to the Questore, and inquired what charge there was against him. **1969** G. Greene *Travels with my Aunt* ii. vii. 296 If the *Questore* had described me as a rat, I would have had no objection. **1972** K. Benton *Spy in Chancery* v. 36 The Questore of Rome had done his polished best to make the luncheon for the Interpol delegates a success.

‖ **Questura** (kwestū·rǎ). [It. *questura*, f. L. *quæstura* the office of a quæstor: see prec.] In Italy: the police station or headquarters; the police.

1907 *Daily Chron.* 22 Aug. 4/4 He had been kicked out of the Central Questura, whither he had gone to give information, because the Neapolitan city police were in the pay of Camorrist assassins. **1950** E. Hemingway *Across River & into Trees* viii. 65, I fill out a slip there for the Questura. **1965** 'W. Haggard' *Hard Sell* ii. 15 Charles Russell took a taxi from the *questura* back to his hotel. **1975** 'D. Rutherford' *Mystery Tour* vii. 149 No one leaves before the inspector from the Questura in Varese gets here.

‖ **quête** (kę̄t). [Fr., quest.] The traditional act of begging for food or alms to the accompaniment of folk-song; *spec.* as part of a folk-play. Also *attrib.*, as *quête song.* Cf. Quest *sb.*¹ 7.

1903 E. K. Chambers *Mediaeval Stage* I. vi. 119 Hardly a rural merry-making..is without its procession; if it is only in the simple form of the *quête* which the children consider themselves entitled to make. *Ibid.* viii. 168 The rest..have either become..mere *quête* songs, or..have taken on a Christian colouring. **1933** —— *Eng. Folk-Play* 13 Structurally, the piece falls into three parts: the Presentation.., the Drama.., the *Quête. Ibid.* 21 To his normal lines Father Christmas may add others which.. are also found as independent *quête*-songs of the Christmas season. **1967** A. L. Lloyd *Folk Song in England* ii. 102 Here is another set of wassailing verses... The begging motive..is important... We call such pieces *quête* songs. **1979** R. Palmer *Eng. Country Songs* 15 A number of such songs..provided the opportunity for a *quête.*

quetsch (kvetʃ, kwetʃ), *sb.* Also **quetsche,** † **quitch.** [a. G. *quetsche*, dial. form of *zwetsche* plum.] A variety of plum with oval, dark-skinned fruit; also, the liqueur made from plums of this kind. Also *attrib.*

1839 C. McIntosh *Orchard & Fruit Garden* 327 The German Quitch Plum is dried and preserved in immense quantities. **1842** J. C. Loudon *Suburban Horticulturist* iii. iv. 559 Quetsche... A good bearer, and well adapted for drying. **1860** R. Hogg *Fruit Man.* 251 Quetsche... Fruit medium sized, oval... Skin dark purple... A culinary plum. **1936** Bentley & Allen *Trent's Last Case* xi. 130 His wife was a Lorrainer and responsible for the Quetsch, the liqueur made from her father's plums. **1940** [see *mirabelle]. **1961** *Sunday Times* 16 July 36/6 Of plums and damsons there will not be a single one, and worst of all there will be no quetsch for jam making. Quetsch jam is one of the very best. **1966** P. V. Price *France: Food & Wine Guide* 51 Two [plums] that may be met with in open tarts are *mirabelles*..and *quetsches.* **1969** *Listener* 2 Jan. 31/1 The [Romanian] national drink..is a plum brandy like quetsch or slivovitch. **1975** Wood & Crosby *Grow it & cook It* vi. 234 Quetsche... October. Long oval, black. When stewed has the flavour of Carlsbad plums. **1977** M. Jancath *Seatag* ii. v. 99 A heavy lunch of Quenelles with sauerkraut and..a Quetsch tart.

quetzal. 1. For Latin name substitute the spelling *Pharomachrus mocino.* (Later examples.)

1930 R. Macaulay *Staying with Relations* ii. 26 Above their heads a quetzal, bright emblem of his country, his lovely tail caught in a liquorice vine. **1950** *Caribbean Q.* II. ii. 24 The gorgeous plumage of the Macaw, the Quetzal and the Wild Turkey were sewn or gummed, feather by feather, onto cotton cloth to form resplendent cloaks. **1961** *Guardian* 22 May 5/4 The quetzal is a bird of rainbow plumage which symbolises Central America. **1978** *Washington Post* 7 July B2/3 The normal heart rejoices to think of wolves and quetzals flourishing in the great world.

2. (Pl. **quetzales.**) The name of a silver Guatemalan coin, initially equivalent to one U.S. dollar, and comprising 100 centavos.

1928 *Whitaker's Almanack* 778 Revenue (Budget, 1927–28) *Quetzals* 11,031,102. **1962** R. A. G. Carson *Coins* 433 The coinage reform [in Guatemala] of 1924 created a new unit the quetzal in silver with subdivisions and with multiples in gold..on obverse the quetzal, a Central American bird of the parrot family. **1974** *Nat. Geographic* Nov. 673 For five quetzals (five dollars, U.S.) I savored a grilled filet mignon, [etc.]. **1977** *Westworld* (Vancouver, B.C.) May–June 20/2 The average income of a [Guatemalan peasant] family ranges from 200 to 300 quetzales a year (a quetzal equals one American dollar).

Quetzalcoatl (ketsa:lko,ā·t'l). Forms: 6 **Quecalcouatl,** 7 **Quetzaalcoalt, Quezalcouatl,** 8 **Quatzalcoatl, Quezalcoatl,** 8- **Quetzalcoatl.** [a. Nahuatl *quetzalli* (see Quetzal) + *coatl* snake.] The Plumed Serpent of the Toltec and Aztec civilizations, traditionally known as the god of the morning and evening star, later as the patron of priests, inventor of books and of the calendar, and as the symbol of death and resurrection. Hence **Que:tzal-coa·tlian** *a.* and **Que:tzalcoa·tlism.**

1578 T. NICHOLAS tr. *L. de Gomara's Pleasant Hist. Conqu. Weast India* 203 There was one rounde temple dedicated to the God of the ayre called Quecalcouatl. **1604** E. GRIMSTONE tr. *Acosta's Naturall & Morall Hist. E. & W. Indies* v. ix. 354 In *Cholula* which is a commonwealth of *Mexico*, they worship a famous idoll which was the god of marchandise, being to this day greatly given to trafficke. They called it *Quetzaalcoalt.* **1613** PURCHAS *Pilgrimage* I. VIII. ix. 656 They had sacrificed ten children ..to *Quezalcouatl* their god. *Ibid.* 657 Their chiefe god was *Quezalcoualt*, god of the Aire. **1725** J. STEVENS tr. *de Herrera's Gen. Hist. Amer.* II. II. vi. 375 There were forty or more great or small, and other lesser Temples.. which being all of different Sizes, and each of them dedicated to a several God, there was one among them round, consecrated to the God of the Air, call'd Quezalcoatl. **1726** —— *Ibid.* III. II. x. iii. 206 At Chulula, a City near Mexico, they ador'd a famous Idol that was the God of Commerce... His Name was Quatzalcoatl, he stood in a very lofty Temple, in a spacious Square, with Gold, Silver, Feathers, and costly Cloaths about him, bearing the Figure of a Man, his Face like a Bird... His name signify'd Snake of rich Feathers. **1787** C. CULLEN tr. *Clavigero's Hist. Mexico* I. II. 88 The Toltecas..built in honour of their beloved god Quetzalcoatl, the highest pyramid of Cholula. **1843** W. H. PRESCOTT *Hist. Conqu. Mexico* I. I. iii. 53 A far more interesting personage in their mythology was Quetzalcoatl, god of the air, a divinity who, during his residence on earth, instructed the natives in the use of metals, in agriculture, and in the arts of government. **1907** L. SPENCE *Mythol. Anc. Mexico & Peru* ii. 20 The worship of Quetzalcoatl was antipathetic if not directly opposed to that of the other deities of Anahuac. **1924** D. H. LAWRENCE *Let.* 15 Nov. (1962) 820 Well, I shall try and finish my *Quetzalcoatl* novel [sc. *The Plumed Serpent*] this winter. **1926** —— *Plumed Serpent* xxvii. 459 If you want to be so—so abstract and Quetzalcoatlian, then bury your head sometimes, like an ostrich in the sand, and forget. **1934** A. HUXLEY *Beyond Mexique Bay* 300 The Indians..can..practise whatever queer blend of catholicism and Quetzalcoatlism pleases them best. **1955** W. GADDIS *Recognitions* I. i. 56 True, many stirred with indignant discomfort..to find they had been attending, not Christ, but..Balder, Attis, Amphion, or Quetzalcoatl. **1973** *Guardian* 23 Mar. 12/4 Quetzalcoatl, the ancient god of the Toltecs.

queue, *sb.* Add: **2.** (Further examples.)

1904 L. HEARN *Japan: an Attempt at Interpretation* xii. 257 All classes excepting the nobility, samurai, Shinto priests, and doctors, shaved the greater part of the head, and wore queues. **1947** R. BENEDICT *Chrysanthemum & Sword* iv. 77 Insignia and distinctive dress of caste were outlawed—even queues had to be cut. **1959** E. TUNIS *Indians* 117/1 The Hopi had brown skins and straight black hair. Men wore it either in a queue bound up in the back or in the long bob they inherited from the Basket-makers. **1976** 'D. FLETCHER' *Don't whistle 'Macbeth'* 22 One of her habitual wigs..that..ended in a pert *queue* at the back.

3. (Further examples.) Also *transf.* and *fig.* *to jump the queue*: see *JUMP *v.* 10c.

1903 E. CHILDERS *Riddle of Sands* xxvi. 298, I joined a *queue* of three or four persons who were waiting their turn, flattened myself between them and the partition till I heard him walk out. **1943** E. M. ALMEDINGEN *Frossia* ii. 64 Paulina had a mind above bread queues and unlit streets. **1951** *Jrnl. R. Statistical Soc.* B. XIII. 152 My own interest in the subject arose from a correspondence.. about queues of taxis in station yards and of customers in retail shops. **1953** *Times* 5 Nov. 4/2 It would be for the Commons to discuss whether the claim of the judges on salaries in the queue of claims should be met before others. **1956** *Newsweek* 9 Jan. 43/1 In Leningrad, Gershwin's music and Heyward's 'Porgy' were anticipated by a two-day queue for tickets priced up to $15 apiece in rubles. **1958** *Listener* 20 Nov. 839/3 After the war the railways had to take their place in the queue after housing and housing repairs. **1966** *Rep. Comm. Inquiry Univ. Oxf.* II. 279 In arts and social studies, most of those with a college post before a university post were tutorial fellows in the 'queue' for a CUF lectureship. **1968** *Sci. Amer.* Aug. 96/1 Airplanes stacked over an airport, shoppers,.. freight cars lined up for unloading at a railroad terminal and messages seeking a free path through a telegraph network all have one thing in common: they are members of a queue, or a line waiting for a service. **1969** *Listener* 28 Aug. 267/3 Are we going to wait until Marxism and socialism have conquered the world, and then stand there last in the queue, waiting for its return to us? **1977** *Spare Rib* May 19/4 Women in poor areas are always at the end of the queue for anything.

6. (Perh. a different word.) A barrel or cask capable of holding approximately one and a half hogsheads of liquid, usu. wine.

1777 P. THICKNESSE *Year's Journey* I. vi. 47 The carriage of a queue of wine from Dijon to Dunkirk..costs an hundred livres..but if sent in the bottle, the carriage will be just double. **1851** C. REDDING *Hist. & Descr. Mod. Wines* v. 91 The names applied in various wine districts of France to the casks which they use, differ without reference to the measure; in the department of the Marne, the *tonneau* is called the *queue.* **1931** W. E. MEAD *Eng. Medieval Feast* iii. 81 In 1385–6 Jean de Neele declared that his household used in one year between six and seven 'queues' of verjuice or between 2,346 and 2,737 litres. **1956** *Atlantic Monthly* June 94/2 In Burgundy the barrel is called *pièce* and contains from 226 to 228 liters, in the Mâconnais 215 liters, in the Beaujolais 216 liters, in Alsace 114 liters. In the Champagne it's called a *queue* and contains 216 liters.

7. *attrib.* and *Comb.*, as *queue day, discipline, driving, form, number, system, theory* (hence *queue-theoretic* adj.); **queue-barging** *vbl. sb.*, = *QUEUE-JUMPING.

1977 *Time Out* 30 Sept.–6 Oct. 15/1 The elaborate queue system is an attempt to eliminate queue barging. **1908** *Daily Chron.* 4 Aug. 3/4 It was queue day at the Franco-British Exhibition yesterday. At 6 o'clock..a line of people a quarter of a mile long extended on either side of the Flip Flap. **1951** *Jrnl. R. Statistical Soc.* B. XIII. 152 The queue-discipline is the rule or moral code determining the manner in which the customers form up into a queue and the manner in which they behave while waiting. **1972** *Guardian* 29 Aug. 2/1 The high standard of British queue discipline. **1970** *Sunday Tel.* 20 Dec. 7/5 Yet another factor contributing to fast 'queue' driving in fog on motorways..is that drivers with their families as passengers tend to drive quickly for fear that a car behind might ram them. **1902** *Westm. Gaz.* 14 Nov. 10/1 From the pens to the steps of the car the intending passengers will go in queue form, as now adopted with so much success at most of the theatres. **1956** R. BRADDON *Nancy Wake* I. i. 9 Each day they received queue numbers so that they could take up their correct positions next morning. **1941** *New Statesman* 27 Dec. 523/2 The argument that the queue system is fair to everybody. **1966** S. BEER *Decision & Control* ix. 176 This thoroughly basic situation is so important in operational research as applied to dynamic systems that a whole branch of mathematical statistics, known as queue theory, has been developed round it. *Ibid.* 178 Some of the earliest queue-theoretic notions were developed around the problem of the doctor's waiting room.

queue, *v.* Add: **2. b.** *trans.* To cause to form a queue; to arrange (persons or things) in or as in a queue or queues.

1928 *Daily Express* 8 Oct. 1/1 The foot and mounted police..had queued the concourse into twisting lines of people. **1973** P. C. SANDERSON *Interactive Computing in BASIC* ii. 23 Multiplexors..checking for transmission errors, and storing and queuing the messages received.

c. *intr.* To stand in a queue; to form *up* in a queue; to take one's place at the end of a queue; also *fig.*

1933 *Observer* 5 Mar. 23/4 There were stuffs at the White City which made French buyers queue up. **1938** E. BOWEN *Death of Heart* I. iv. 71 They hung their hats and coats in the annexe cloakroom, and queued up for the mirror. **1945** 'TACKLINE' *Holiday Sailor* i. 9 Whilst we queued-up before him to have our cap-tallies—*not* capribbons, we now discovered—secured. **1949** E. TAYLOR *Wreath of Roses* i. 11 They have to do all the wretched jobs not even a paid servant will do—queue for tomatoes, etc. **1955** *Times* 1 Aug. 8/7 Everywhere people are queueing—even at the bureau de change and of course at the cafeteria. **1964** L. DEIGHTON *Funeral in Berlin* xxiii. 128 Do you think that the whole of Germany was queueing up to fight Bolshevism? **1976** C. DEXTER *Last seen Wearing* xx. 155 The suspects are beginning to queue up, aren't they, Lewis? **1978** D. FRANCIS *Trial Run* i. 17 We are damned lucky to have been given the few weeks' option. They've got other buyers practically queueing for it.

3. *trans.* To follow or track (a person's steps, etc.).

1906 HARDY *Dynasts* II. v. i. 254 Perhaps within this very house and hour, Under an innocent mask of Love or Hope, Some enemy queues my ways to coffin me.

Hence **queue·ing** *ppl. a.*

1949 N. MITFORD *Love in Cold Climate* I. ix. 91 The large crowd in Park Lane was rewarded by good long stares into the queuing motor cars. **1976** M. RUSSELL *Double Deal* xi. 88, I don't happen to be the queueing type.

queueing, queuing (kiū·iŋ), *vbl. sb.* [f. prec.] **a.** The action of waiting in a queue. Also const. *up*.

1927 *Brit. Weekly* 21 Apr. 55/3 When the public-houses opened their doors in the evening there was no queuing-up. **1946** G. MIKES *How to be an Alien* I. 44 Queueing is the national pastime of an otherwise dispassionate race. The English are rather shy about it, and deny that they adore it. **1948** M. LASKI *Tory Heaven* ii. 28 James was delighted to see a row of taxis... There was none of that queuing he had been led to expect. **1951** *Jrnl. R. Statist. Soc.* B. XIII. 180, I assumed that a newly arriving vehicle could always find somewhere in the station yard to unload, so that the problem was in effect not one of queueing. **1956** L. H. C. TIPPETT *Statistics* (ed. 2) vii. 125 This is typical of a number of congestion problems that arise in telephony, in road and rail traffic, in the queuing of patients at a hospital, and so on. **1958** *Manch. Guardian Weekly* 22 May 15/4 Even with a Ponselle a day or two of queueing was all you needed. **1967** *Times Rev. Industry* Aug. 28/2 These techniques include stock control, linear programming and queueing. **1979** *Bookseller* 23 June 2816/3 To avoid queueing..we did not ask visitors to register attendance.

b. *attrib.*, as **queueing theory,** the mathematical study of the structure and behaviour of queues of people or articles.

1951 *Jrnl. R. Statist. Soc.* B. XIII. 168 The different people associated with a queueing system will assess its merits and demerits in different ways. *Ibid.* 181 The congestion should be measured at the peak, but this would need the non-steady solution of a complex queueing problem with non-steady traffic conditions. **1954** *Science News* XXXIV. 112 One particular application [of operational research] is that of queueing theory. This was employed during the design of London Airport and has also been used for such diverse subjects as omnibus routing, toll gate staffing, and determining the number of grinding wheels required by a toolroom. **1966** *Listener* 3 Feb. 162/2 Queueing theory has in fact been used in this calculation in an attempt to relate the time on the waiting list to the number of beds made available, and the demand for these beds. **1974** GROSS & HARRIS *Fundamentals Queueing Theory* i. 1 'How long must a customer wait?' and 'How many people will form in the line?' Queueing theory attempts (and in many cases succeeds) to answer these questions through detailed mathematical analysis.

queue·-jumping. [f. QUEUE *sb.* + JUMPING *vbl. sb.*] Pushing forward out of one's turn in a queue; also *fig.* Cf. *JUMP *v.* 10c. Hence (as a back-formation) **queue·-jump** *v.*; also **queue·-jumper.** one who jumps a queue.

1959 *Guardian* 22 Oct. 1/1 Mrs. Braddock..complained of Tory queue-jumping. **1960** *Ibid.* 17 June 2/3 There are three types [of private patients]—the snobs..the queue-jumpers..and the business executive. **1965** M. DRABBLE *Millstone* 67 Afraid that I would be accused of queue-jumping, I rose to my feet and went in search of authority. **1968** *Daily Tel.* 13 Nov. 14/7 A major hindrance to smooth traffic-flow is the queue-jumper, who invariably gets stuck. **1972** *Ibid.* 30 Mar. 16 Private patients in National Health hospitals..are widely regarded as rich queue-jumpers. **1973** *Listener* 6 Sept. 298/3 News reports of Asians who were trying to 'queue-jump' into Britain. **1975** J. PIDGEON *Flame* i. 7 Daniels, having queue-jumped up the crowded stairs..gazed out above the lowered, pebbled window. **1976** *Daily Tel.* 20 Dec. 3/8 The row started when shop stewards complained that the women had queue jumped a union waiting list of people wanting to become ferry drivers.

queuer (kiū·əɪ). [f. QUEUE *v.* + -ER[1].] One who waits in a queue.

1948 'J. TEY' *Franchise Affair* xxii. 260 This was fare that not even the most optimistic queuer outside the court had anticipated. **1952** *Time* 6 Oct. 64/1 The queuers were hoping for standing room. Reserved seats had been gone since July. **1958** *Times Lit. Suppl.* 21 Nov. 669/4 They become refugees somewhere across the border, queuers for charitable soup, squatters on alien school-room floors. **1960** V. JENKINS *Lions down Under* xv. 230 Some queuers who had been waiting from 3.30 a.m. **1976** *Times* 10 June 10/3 He watched a senior army officer walk straight to the head of a long taxi queue. The tired queuers grumbled curses.

Queuetopia (kiutoᵘ·piă). [Blend of QUEUE *sb.* + UTOPIA; cf. *SUBTOPIA.] A humorous designation of Great Britain under Labour or Socialist rule, supposedly characterized by universal queueing. Also *transf.*

Said to have been coined by Winston Churchill.

1950 *Manch. Guardian Weekly* 2 Mar. 9/1 (*heading*) 'Queuetopia'. Few of our national disorders have made better campaign material than..the continual queues, the swelling bureaucracy.., and the general mechanisation of the British Way of Life. **1975** S. POTTER *Changing Eng.* 82 London..has far too many *queuetopias* at its bus stops and supermarket checkouts.

‖ **que voulez-vous** (kᵊ vule vu). [Fr., lit. 'what do you want?'] An expression denoting mild exasperation or resignation; 'what do you expect?', 'what can one expect?'.

[**1830** C. CLAIRMONT *Let.* 28 Mar. in J. Marshall *Life & Lett. Mary Shelley* (1889) II. xxi. 202 He [*sc.* Trelawny] receives all his impressions through his heart, I through my head. *Que voulez vous? Le moyen de se recontrer* when one is bound for the North Pole and the other for the South?] **1841** W. M. THACKERAY in *Britannia* 5 June 363/2 No doubt she was dancing away last night..and finished the morning at the Courtille. *Que voulez vous?* it is her nature. **1878** H. JAMES *Europeans* I. vi. 239 The Baroness gave a little philosophic shrug. 'Que voulez-vous? They are princes.' **1880** G. GISSING *Let.* 21 Dec. in J. Korg *George Gissing* (1965) iii. 90, I fear they put me down for a prig, an upstart, an abominable aristocrat, but *que voulez-vous*? **1923** W. J. LOCKE *Moordius & Co.* xxi. 288 *Que voulez-vous*, mademoiselle? A train-omnibus stopping at every station is bound to be late. **1935** LADY FORTESCUE *Perfume from Provence* 35 Are there not floods..all over the world? *Que voulez-vous?* **1945** 'O. MALET' *My Bird Sings* I. v. 37 The poor Comte is hopelessly in love..but *que voulez-vous?* She will not have him.

‖ **queyu** (kwē̆·u). Also **keweyu, kuyu, kway, queyou,** etc. [Guyana Creole, app. from a Cariban language.] In Guyana and neighbouring regions, a small apron-like garment worn by the women of certain Amerindian tribes, consisting of a panel of coloured beads set in intricate geometrical patterns and surrounded by a fringe of cotton.

1796 J. G. STEDMAN *Narr. Five Years' Exped.* I. xv. 386 The women wear an apron of cotton, with party-coloured glass beads strung upon it, which they call *queiou.* This covering is no great size, being only one foot in breadth by eight inches in length..but being heavy..it answers all the purposes for which it was intended. **1806** G. PINCKARD *Notes on West Indies* II. 444 Sometimes, instead of the band, the women use a small apron about three or four inches square, which being tied around the waste [*sic*], and left to hang loose before, serves by way of a fig-leaf. These aprons they call *kways.* **1866** R. DUFF *Brit. Guiana* xi. 261 The only covering which the females wore was the quieyoo, an article of dress, worked out of seeds of trees, about ten inches long, and six or eight broad, hung in front of the person by a string fastened round the loins. **1867** W. T. VENESS *El Dorado* 141 *'Cuyus'*, or *'Queyus'*, the entire dress of Indian women, of the Accawai tribe. **1895** *Timehri* June 144 The queyus too were remarkable owing to their small bead surface, the greater extent being taken up by wide cotton fringes. **1904** W. H. HUDSON *Green Mansions* v. 71 Oalava herself would be ready to bestow her person—queyou, worn fig-leaf-wise, necklace of accouri teeth, and all—on so worthy a suitor as myself. **1912** J. RODWAY *Guiana* 216 Geometrical patterns of most intricate lines are found on basket-work, old pottery, *queyus* or aprons, and on their [*sc.* the Indians'] painted faces. **1923** W. E. ROTH tr. *R. Schomburgk's Trav. Brit. Guiana, 1840–1844* II. xii. 379 The queyu of the woman was made out of seed pips. **1924** *38th Ann. Rep. U.S. Bureau Amer. Ethnol.* xxi. 446 The Creole terms kway.., queyu, kuyu, etc., applied to the glass-bead apron, is [*sic*] apparently identical with that of the original cotton loin-cloth guayuco of the Orinoco Indians. **1964** V. G. C. NORWOOD *Jungle Life in Guiana* v. 99 The commonest form of covering adopted by Indian women generally is a small apron made from..coloured glass beads strung on cotton strands, this latter form originally Acawoian, called a 'quayo'. **1965** J. YDE *Material Culture of Waiwái* 199 The bead apron, *keweyu*.., is as indispensable a garment to the women as is the *kamisa* to the men.

‖ **quia timet** (kwī·ă ti·met). *Law.* [L., lit. 'because he fears'.] An action brought to prevent a possible future injury. Also as *attrib.* or *advb. phr.*

1628 E. COKE *First Part of Institutes of Lawes of Eng.* II. vi. 100 There be 6. Writs in Law that may be maintained quia timet, before any molestation, distresse, or impleading. **1697** *Cases Argued & Decreed in High Court of Chancery* 223 It was objected, that the Daughter is not of Age, and so this Bill is *quia timet* only;..and the Court would be vexed with vain Suits if any one might be admitted to sue only *quia timet*, to prevent a remote Possibility. But the Court answered, that Suits *quia timet* only were proper in Law and Equity. **1815** H. MADDOCK *Treat. on Princ. & Pract. High Court of Chancery* I. ii. 178 The denomination of Bills *Quia Timet* was borrowed, probably, from the Title of some ancient Writs at the Common Law. **1860** J. J. S. WHARTON *Law-Lexicon* (ed. 2) 619/1 *Quia Timet Bill*, it is filed for the purpose of quieting a present apprehension of a probable or possible future injury to property. **1927** P. G. OSBORN *Conc. Law Dict.* 41 *Bill Quia Timet*, a proceeding in the old Court of Chancery for providing against an apprehended injury. Now replaced by the injunction. **1961** *Times* 14 Feb. 5/1 Dismissing with costs their *quia timet* claim for an injunction. **1971** [see *LIE *v.*[1] 12].

quibblingly, *adv.* (Later example.)

1901 W. J. CRAIG *King Lear* 117 *note*, Perhaps 'roarer' in *Tempest* I. i. 18, quibblingly applied to the raging waters.

quiche (kīʃ). [Fr., ad. Alsatian *küchen* (G. *kuchen*).] An open flan or tart with a savoury filling. Also *attrib.* *quiche Lorraine*: properly, a quiche containing a savoury custard with bacon or ham; also used of other types of quiche.

1949 A. L. SIMON *Dict. Gastron.* 199/1 *Quiche*, a savoury custard in an open tart, a Lorraine *spécialité*. **1951** E. DAVID *French Country Cookery* 92 *Quiche Lorraine*.. Make a pastry... Onto the pastry spread the bacon ..beat the 2 eggs into the cream..pour on to the pastry.. bake for about 30 minutes. **1960** —— *French Provincial Cooking* 206 There have been various evolutions in the composition of a *quiche*... A *quiche* is a flat open tart... The fillings, of course, vary enormously. **1966** *Daily Tel.* 18 Oct. 13/5 After a soup..we had a smoked salmon *quiche*. **1967** *Woman's Day* (Austral.) 5 June 55 Most widely known is Quiche Lorraine, which traditionally contains only eggs, cream or milk, and bacon or ham. **1969** S. BURNFORD *Without Reserve* v. 180 So we sat in the sun on the dock, eating the quiche Lorraine that Mary had providently packed for just such an occasion. **1970** *Islander* (Victoria, B.C.) 16 Aug. 8/1 Some writers tell us this savory custard tart belongs to German cookery... Designed as a main dish, the quiche originally was baked in a pie pan..and was basically a custard, sometimes flavored with bacon. **1972** K. STEWART *Times Cookery Bk.* viii. 107 Roll the pastry out..slightly larger all round than an 8-inch flan or quiche tin. **1979** P. SIMMONDS *Mrs Weber's Diary* 27 Quiches are marvellous! They're all out of my freezer. Now, the vegetarian ones are at the front.

Quiché (kītʃē·), *sb.* and *a.* [Native name.] **A.** *sb.* **a.** Name of a people inhabiting the western highlands of Guatemala; a member of this people. **b.** One of the principal languages of the Mayan family, spoken by this people. **B.** *adj.* Of or pertaining to this people.

1823 J. BAILY tr. *Juarros' Statistical & Commercial Hist. Guatemala* II. ii. 168 In all these places the Quiché language is spoken. *Ibid.*, It may be inferred..that the greater part of the province of Sapatitlan,..was a colony of the Quichées. **1823** [see *KEKCHI *sb.* and *a.*]. **1883** *Encycl. Brit.* XVI. 208/1 The *Popol-Vuh* or national book of the Quiché kingdom of Guatemala. *Ibid.*, After this comes the creation of the four men and their wives who are the ancestors of the Quichés. **1933** A. HUXLEY *Let.* 24 Mar. (1969) 368 From there to Chichicastenango, which is the centre of the native life of the Quiché Indians, who thickly inhabit the plateaus. **1934** [see *LADINO[1] 2]. **1948** A. L. KROEBER *Anthropol.* (rev. ed.) xviii. 794 Highland Maya, of upland Guatemala, speaking languages like Quiché, Cakchiquel, and Mam. **1950** I. VELIKOVSKY *Worlds in Collision* vi. 131 In the years of this gloom, when the world was covered with clouds and shrouded in mist, the Quiché tribe migrated to Mexico. **1963** *Times* 7 May 14/6 Judas is dressed in the costume of a Solola tribe—it is told that they were jealous of the Quiche and appealed for help to the Spaniards, who sent de Alvarado to liquidate them. **1968** *Language* XLIV. 191 It is in Quiché that the fascinating legends and history of the *Popol vuh*, 'the sacred book of the ancient Quichés', were recorded. It is also in Quiché and its near relatives of the 'Quichean' group that we have the largest accumulation of other written documents. **1974** *Encycl. Brit. Micropædia* VIII. 353/1 The Quiché Maya had an advanced civilization in pre-Columbian times. *Ibid.*, Written records of Quiché history and mythology are preserved in the *Popol Vuh*, written down in the Quiché language.. shortly after conquest by the Spaniards in 1524. **1977** *Language* LIII. 261/2 In a final appendix, a 100-word vocabulary list is given in..Quiché (also Mayan), and in Proto-Mayan as reconstructed by Kaufman.

Hence **Quiche·an** *a.*, applied to the subgroup of the Mayan family of languages to which Quiché belongs.

1956 N. A. MCQUOWN in *Internat. Jrnl. Amer. Linguistics* XXII. 195/2 It differs from Kroeber..in suggesting a closer link between Quichean and Kekchian than between Quichean and Mamean. **1968** [see above]. **1978** *Language* LIV. 496 Kaufman's paper, 'New Mayan languages in Guatemala', summarizes identifications of 'new languages' made since 1969: Sacapultec and Sipacapa in the Quichean subgroup; [etc.].

Quichua, Quichuan: see *QUECHUA *sb.* and *a.*, *QUECHUAN *a.*

quick, *a.*, *sb.*[1], and *adv.* **A.** *adj.* **I. 2. c.** Delete † *Obs.* and add later examples of *quick flesh*; now also *quickflesh.*

1926 T. E. LAWRENCE *Seven Pillars* (1935) xliii. 251 If such animals [*sc.* camels] were taken suddenly inland for long marches over flints or other heat-retaining ground, their soles would burn, and at last crack in a blister; leaving quick flesh..in the centre of the pad. **1928** H. A. MANHOOD *Nightseed* 56 Men worn away to quickflesh, their eyes staring, reddened at the rims, men who coughed and coughed with a dry, torn-paper sound, mud to the waist. **1956** D. LESSING in *New Statesman* 30 June 768/3 With quickflesh contest if you need: There is no argument with bone.

II. 9. *quick water* (further N. Amer. examples). Also *transf.*

1857 THOREAU *Jrnl.* 30 July in *Maine Woods* (1864) 276 The Indian navigator naturally distinguishes by a name those parts of a stream where he has encountered quick water and forks. **1894** *Harper's Mag.* Apr. 782/1 That quick water's the Mahkin Rapids. **1905** L. MOTT *Jules of Great Heart* xxi. 260 Nearer and nearer sounded the quick water of the thoroughfare between Lac des Rochers and the dead-water of Rivière du Renard. **1951** H. E. GILES *Harbin's Ridge* xxiii. 201, I couldn't say a word for the knot in my throat, and my eyes stung with quick water. **1958** *Montreal Star* 22 Oct. 14/3 On the subject of water also there is the definition of quickwater. .. It used to be used in the Maritimes, a term designating water running rapidly but not broken by rapids.

10. Delete 'Now *rare*'. (Further examples.) Cf. *quick-clay* in sense *D.

1895 *Trans. Australasian Inst. Mining Engin.* III. 141 *Quick.* Veins are said to be quick when productive, and dead when non-productive. *Quick-ground*, ground in a loose incoherent state; soft watery strata, e.g., running sand. **1901** *Norges Geol. Undersøgelse* No. 32. 221 All kinds of soft clay are often called 'quick' clay; in a more restricted sense it means clay which has the property of being comparatively stiff when it lies in its original bed, but becomes fluid when it is set in motion. **1963** MEANS & PARCHER *Physical Prop. Soils* xi. 333 The velocity of the upward flowing water required to cause the soil to become quick. **1967** A. R. JUMIKIS *Introd. Soil. Mech.* iv. 32 Quicksand is not a special type of soil, but a condition. Any granular material through which an upward flow of water takes place may become 'quick' under proper hydraulic conditions. **1978** *Sci. Amer.* Nov. 143/2 Sand does not become quick without an influx of water, because any extra water separates out on top of a bed of closely packed sand, creating a situation similar to the ones encountered on the beach and in the demonstration with a bottle.

III. 19. d. *Cricket.* Of a bowler.

1967 [private letter from Mr. R. Bowen]. **1976** J. SNOW *Cricket Rebel* 36, I was not fast enough to be classed as a genuine quick bowler.

25. b. *quick one*: an alcoholic drink intended to be taken rapidly. *colloq.*

1928 D. L. SAYERS *Unpleasantness at Bellona Club* ix. 105 They had a quick one together. **1936** A. HUXLEY *Eyeless in Gaza* xlii. 503 After the second 'quick one' in the bar of the theatre. **1948** R. A. KNOX *Mass in Slow Motion* viii. 80 The conductor slipping in to the Corner house to have a quick one. **1959** B. COBB *Don't lie to Police* (1960) xii. 194 We go in a bunch at half-past eleven and have a quick one, or rather one or two quick ones. **1968** *Listener* 19 Dec. 811/3 We've time for a quick one and then we'll go and do our bit of business. **1976** G. MOFFAT *Over Sea to Death* vii. 79 Ken Maynard came into the cocktail lounge... 'Just in time for a quick one... Two lagers, please.'

28. c. with *about.*

1937 W. H. SAUMAREZ SMITH *Let.* 29 July in *Young Man's Country* (1977) ii. 85, I shall have to be very quick about writing this letter as the Air Mail goes from the Club in half an hour.

IV. 29. *quick-eared* (later example), *-footed*, *-worded* adjs.

1920 D. H. LAWRENCE *Lost Girl* viii. 182 He turned like a quick-eared animal. **1839** W. C. BRYANT in *U.S. Democratic Rev.* Apr. 406 Here the quick-footed wolf.. crushed the flower Of Sanguinaria. **1938** *Times Lit. Suppl.* 5 Mar. 158/1 A very quick-footed batsman. **1954** J. R. R. TOLKIEN *Two Towers* III. iv. 81 It [*sc.* a song] is..quick-worded, and soon over.

B. (*sb.*[1]) **4.** Also, the sensitive part of a horse's foot, above the hoof. Also *attrib.* (Later U.S. examples.)

1925 W. G. L. TAYLOR *Saddle Horse* i. 81 The hoof is pared down to the quick in streaks, leaving only enough for the animal to stand on. **1940** W. FAULKNER *Hamlet* iii. 60 The newcomer darting between Houston and the raised hoof and clapping the shoe onto it and touching the animal's quick with the second blow of the hammer. **1949** D. F. MONTGOMERY *Essentials of Horsemanship* iv. 37 The sensitive sole or 'quick' inside the foot follows the shape of the hoof. **1954** W. FAULKNER *Fable* 196 They was trying..to pull the quick shoe. **1963** M. C. SELF *Compl. Bk. Horses & Ponies* iii. 56 As with your finger nail, we must be careful not to trim too close to the 'quick', or sensitive part of the horse's foot.

8. *Cricket.* A fast bowler.

1960 I. PEEBLES *Bowler's Turn* 63 He was a fine player of every type of bowling, fast of foot against spin, and strong and resolute against the quicks. **1977** *World of Cricket Monthly* June 66/3 He..still considers Lindwall the greatest of quicks he faced.

C. *adv.* **1. a.** (Later examples.)

This use is now usually avoided in educated speech and writing, though found in some standard colloq. constructions.

1901 M. FRANKLIN *My Brilliant Career* xxxii. 272 Lizer, shut the winder quick. **1922** JOYCE *Ulysses* 47 He [*sc.* a dog]..pissed quick short at an unsmelt rock. **1936** C. SANDBURG *People, Yes* 83 Some men dress quick, others take as much time as a woman. **1968** *Listener* 11 July 38/3 I've never known a journey go so quick. **1979** *Times* 23 Nov. 5/4 The brash and selfish values of a 'get rich quick' society.

3. a. *quick-acting* (later examples), *-drying*, *-firing* (later examples), *-growing* (later examples), *-loading*, *-seeing*, *-setting* (later examples), *-speeding*, *-springing*, *-surprising*, *-talking* adjs.

1931 A. HUXLEY *Music at Night* I. 12 Chemically pure pornography..is a quick-acting emotional drug. **1960** *Farmer & Stockbreeder* 8 Mar. 88 'Nitro-Chalk' 21, a granular fertilizer containing 21%N, is free-flowing, quick-acting. **1869** *Bradshaw's Railway Man.* XXI. 460/3 (Advt.), Varnishes..Qck. Dryg. Copal..Qck. Drying Oak. **1913** V. B. LEWES *Oil Fuel* 91 Explosions..from leakages of volatile spirit used in making up anti-fouling and quick-drying paint..led to extended investigations being made. **1969** *R. & E. Coordinator* Apr. 8/1 A meter and a modified IGT Printability Tester are used to measure the drying time and penetration of quick drying inks into paper. **1890** G. S. CLARKE *Fortification* xiv. 207 Quick-firing guns require only two or three men..to work them. **1940** *Chambers's Techn. Dict.* 691/1 *Q.F. guns*, quick-firing guns. These may be guns, or howitzers, that are loaded with ammunition having brass cartridge cases, either attached to the shell or separate. **1979** A. FOX *Threat Warning Red* i. 3 That twin 4.5" turret-radar-controlled, quick-firing automatic. **1941** J. S. HUXLEY *Uniqueness of Man* III. vi. 100 The quick-growing beast..suffers. **1968** *Trees* Spring 15 The algaroba..is a quick-growing tree. **1874** J. W. LONG *Wild-Fowl Shooting* 37 A quick-loading [powder] flask, i.e., one having a large feed-hole to the charger, should also be used. **1925** J. GREGORY *Maid of Mountain* xxxvi. 327 Very keen, quick-seeing eyes withal. **1962** H. C. WESTON *Sight, Light & Work* (ed. 2) viii. 229 It is desirable to select workers who are quick-seeing for objects of the apparent size with which they will have to deal. **1887** J. NEWMAN *Notes on Concrete* iv. 25 The hardening of slow-setting cements is generally considered more trustworthy than that of quick setting cements. **1963** C. R. COWELL et al. *Inlays, Crowns, & Bridges* ii. 7 Very deep parts of a cavity..should have a sedative sub-lining of quick-setting zinc oxide and eugenol. **1973** J. WAINRIGHT *Touch of Malice* 188 She stiffened—as if quick-setting concrete was suddenly working in her veins. **1919** V. WOOLF *Night & Day* xxviii. 416 The quick-speeding silver moon. **1663** R. HEAD *Hic et Ubique* sig. A2v, Your sublime dignity, quick-springing wit. **1911** E. M. CLOWES *On Wallaby* xi. 308 To grapple with all the quick-springing mass of undergrowth which leaps to life, almost in a night. **1937** BLUNDEN *Elegy* 42 And though you marked my last arising, My next shall be as quick-surprising. **1963** *Punch* 4 Sept. 358/2 Gerry is a show-off, a quick-talking egotist. **1980** P. LIVELY *Judgement Day* v. 51 Those long-haired quick-talking women.

b. *quick-spread* adj.

1895 KIPLING *Second Jungle Book* 8 The quick-spread ears of the deer caught the last sentence.

D. Special combs.: **quick-action,** *attrib.* of apparatus having a quick action; **quick bread,** a bread or cake that can be prepared quickly, usu. one made with a leavening agent that permits immediate baking; **quick-break** *a.* *Electr. Engin.*, applied to (the action of) a switch designed to break a circuit and stop a current quickly regardless of the speed with which it is operated; **quick buck** chiefly *U.S.* [*BUCK *sb.*[8]] = *fast buck* s.v. *FAST *a.* 11; **quick-cake,** a cake that can be prepared and baked in a short time; **quick-change** *attrib.* (later examples); also *transf.* and *ellipt.*; **quick-change** *v. intr.*, to perform a 'quick change'; *trans.*, to change (clothes) quickly; **quick-clay** [tr. Norw. *kvikkleire*, formerly *kvikler*], clay that is quick (sense 10); **quick death** *U.S.* = *sudden death* s.v. SUDDEN *a.* 3b in Dict. and Suppl.; **Quick Dick** *Mil. slang*, a quick-firing gun; **quick-disconnect,** *attrib.* of couplings and the like that can be quickly disconnected; **quick-fire**: also *fig.*; **quick-firer** (earlier and later examples); also *fig.*; **quick-fix** *a.*, that can be quickly fixed into place; also *fig.*; **quickgold** *fig.* [prob. modelled on QUICKSILVER *sb.*], living or liquid gold; **quick-heel** *v. intr.*, in Rugby Football, to heel rapidly from a scrum; **quick kill,** a sudden or rapid victory (cf. KILL *sb.*[1] 2 in Dict. and Suppl.); also *attrib.*; **quick-knit** *a.*, used (*a*) of very thick wool with which a garment can be knitted in a short time; (*b*) of a garment made with such wool; also *ellipt.*; **quick-look** *Astronautics*, used *attrib.* with reference to the rapid provision of information; **quick-lunch(eon**, *attrib.* of a person or establishment selling lunches that can be served and eaten quickly; also *fig.*; **quick-minded** *a.*, having a quick or ready mind; quick-witted; **quick reference** *attrib.*, giving quick and easy access to information; **quick-release,** *attrib.* of any device designed for rapid release; also *ellipt.*; **quick-return** (examples); more widely, applied to any reciprocating motion or mechanism in which the speed in one direction is greater than the speed in the other; also *ellipt.*; **quick-seller,** an article, esp. a book, that sells quickly; **quick-service** *attrib.*, that is characterized by quick service; **quick-spot** (see quot.); **quick-start** *a.*, pertaining to or characterized by rapid starting; **quick-stick(s)** (earlier and later examples); also as *v. intr.* (see quot. 1935); **quick succession,** a change in ownership of property twice within a limited period; used *attrib.* of remission of part of capital transfer tax (formerly estate duty) in such an eventuality; **quickthorn,** delete † and add: esp. a hawthorn; (earlier and later examples); **quick trick,** in Bridge, a card or combination of cards which should furnish a trick in the first or second round of the suit; a trick won 'on top'; *attrib.*, of a system valuing the hand according to the holding of such cards; **quick turnover,** *attrib.* of a person concerned with selling goods as rapidly as possible after they have been bought or produced; **quick worker** *colloq.*, one who rapidly achieves intimacy with persons of the opposite sex.

1909 *Cent. Dict.* Suppl., Quick-action *a.* **1960** *Farmer & Stockbreeder* 1 Mar. 72/1 Four quick-action jacks adjust the tilt to vary the throughput. **1920** M. WILSON *Cook Book* 36 Quick breads include griddle cakes, waffles, muffins, Sally Lunn's, shortcakes and biscuits. **1940** *Quantity Food Service Recipes* 20 (*heading*) Quick breads. Baking powder biscuits...muffins...griddle cakes. **1960** A. E. BENDER *Dict. Nutrition* 106/1 *Quick breads* include biscuits, muffins, popovers, waffles and griddle cakes. **1970** *Islander* (Victoria, B.C.) 29 Nov. 8/2 Use it [*sc.* cranberry sauce] as an ingredient in pies, quick bread and basting sauce. **1891** J. B. VERITY *Electr. up to Date* v. 62 (*caption*) 'Quick-make and quick-break' switch. **1900** *Electrician* 21 Dec. 325/2 Mr. Duddell..pointed out a danger with concentric cables and metal break, quick-break switches. **1930** MOYER & WOSTREL *Industr. Electr. & Wiring* xvii. 382 Circuits carrying large currents.. should be provided with either a quick-break switch or a circuit breaker. **1962** *Newnes Conc. Encycl. Electr. Engin.* 728/1 Shunt limit switches range from the very simple, in which speed of break is entirely dependent on the speed of operation, to considerably more elaborate designs in which some form of quick-break action is incorporated. **1960** *Christian Herald* July 12/2 This is most discouraging to those who stoop to make a 'quick buck' through propagating immorality. **1972** *National Observer* (U.S.) 27 May 20/2 Richard Chamberlain is no dripping-behind-the-ears graduate of the school of 'charm acting' (his phrase) out for a quick buck at the expense of the classics. **1980** R. BARNARD *Death in Cold Climate* xvii. 193 Dreaming of luxury, of the quick buck dubiously acquired. **1925** J. GREGORY *Maid of Mountain* ii. 15 I'll stir up a quick-cake for him. **1896** Quick change [see *trick-change* s.v. TRICK *sb.* 13]. **1905** *Daily Chron.* 13 Mar. 5/7 Mr. Balfour's first..Ministry may reasonably be dubbed the 'Quick-change Ministry'. **1906** *Ibid.* 12 Nov. 6/4 He quick-changed with the deftness and speed of a Fregoli. **1928** *Collier's* 18 Aug. 18/3 We had to quick-change our hats, put on badges [etc.]. **1939** T. S. ELIOT *Old Possum's Bk. Pract. Cats* 22 As knockabout clowns, quick-change Comedians..They had an extensive reputation. **1973** C. EGLETON *Seven Days to Killing* i. 14 They stripped off their uniforms and changed into civilian clothes..in a time which would have been a credit to a troupe of quick-change artists. **1901** Quick clay [see sense A. 10 above]. **1950** *Géotechnique* II. 58 A very soft and extremely sensitive clay, known in Norway as *kvikkleire* (quick-clay). **1968** R. W. FAIRBRIDGE *Encycl. Geomorphol.* 640/2 A special class of mudflows are those developing in quick clays which spontaneously liquefy and may flow readily on very gentle slopes, rafting houses, roads and trees appreciable distances. **1972** Quickclay [see *ILLITE]. **1942** Z. N. HURSTON in A. Dundes *Mother Wit* (1973) 225/1 I'm quick death and easy judgment. **1958** *Washington Post* 20 June A 16/4 Miss McKeever advanced to the final..by beating medalist Mrs. Thomas Konopa.. on the 19th green with a birdie in a quick death playoff. **1918** *Sat. Even. Post* 31 Aug. 34 A fifty-millimeter gun which they dubbed Quick Dick played on them with direct fire. **1936** J. G. HARBORD *Amer. Army in France 1917–1919* xvii. 283 The time of warning usually varied from practically nothing with the 'Quick Dicks' as the boys called the Austrian 88's..to as many as five seconds with the heavier calibers. **1962** F. I. ORDWAY et al. *Basic Astronautics* xii. 468 Quick-disconnect pins allow the astronaut to detach himself from a conventional aircraft type seat..once the period of acceleration is over. **1969** *Jane's Freight Containers 1968–69* 577/3 Two hydraulic pressure lines to trailer, with quick-disconnect couplings. **1954** *Encounter* Mar. 70/2 Such chiefly subjective variables are difficult to elicit in fairly short, single, quick-fire interviews. **1960** I. PEEBLES *Bowler's Turn* 44 He was an even timer with a beautiful economical action, and a sure quick-fire return. **1977** *Cleethorpes News* 27 May 5/5 They have a polished act which includes skilful harmony, impressions and quickfire jokes. **1891** MARQUIS OF SALISBURY *Let.* 20 Sept. in G. Cecil *Life Salisbury* (1932) IV. 314 They must carry Maxims and quickfirers. **1933** F. RICHARDS *Old Soldiers never Die* xii. 162 When we had no time to write letters we sent field-service post cards which we called 'quick-firers'. We simply wrote the address on them and signed our names and dates of sending on the backs. **1956** Quick-firer [see *MORALE 3]. **1959** *Archit. Rev.* CXXV. p. xcv (Advt.), Quick-fix reflectors and diffusers, heavy duty bi-pin lampholders. **1972** *Times* 30 Nov. 18/5 Quick-fix, switch-operated adaptor fittings. **1976** *National Observer* (U.S.) 25 Dec. 5/4 On the one hand, he is urged to make quick-fix tax cuts and get the economy moving. **1877** G. M. HOPKINS *Poems* (1967) 66 The grey lawns cold where gold, where quickgold lies! **1954** I. MURDOCH *Under Net* xx. 276, I took two gulps of the whiskey; it ran through me like quickgold. **1936** *Times* 30 Nov. 5/4 A pack who shoved to the last man and quick-heeled from the tight and loose. **1969** *Listener* 14 Aug. 221/3 Wilson..lost interest in the 'quick kill' approach and tried to make a deal with Smith. *a* **1974** R. CROSSMAN *Diaries* (1975) I. 382 James Callaghan, for example, said he thought that..we should try to get a quick kill... In that case the preparations for the quick kill should have taken place *before* U.D.I. **1935** *Home Notes 2nd Knitting Bk.* p. iii (Advt.), W. B. Kwiknit The original quick-to-knit wool. *Ibid.*, W. B. Kwiknit is a thick 2 ply, ideal for outdoor sportswear. **1957** *Vogue Knitting Bk.* 16 (Advt.), Two such outstanding wools as Patons Quickerknit Botany and Quickerknit Baby Wool. **1960** *Ibid.* 9 Lister Lavenda quick-knits are the.. chunkiest, quickest-to-knit-with wools in knitting today! **1962** J. WADE *Running Sand* vi. 64 Some Tyrolean quick-knit jumper. **1966** G. N. LEECH *Eng. in Advertising* xv. 141 More or less common types of compound structure: 'quick-knits'; 'speedy-knit'; 'flip-tops'. **1972** C. FREMLIN *Appointment with Yesterday* xi. 84 Milly turned down the third remnant of tattered quick-knit cardigan. **1964** *Proc. Joint Computer Conf.* (*Spring*) 125/1 The requirement of the programming system for OGO was to provide quick-look analysis and control of the status of the spacecraft and selective experiments on board the satellite. **1966** *Electronics* 3 Oct. 134 Displaying quick-look performance data for evaluation by the astronaut. **1975** *Geos* (Dept. Energy, Mines, & Resources, Canada) Spring 8/1 A 'Quick Look' facility attached to the satellite station at Prince Albert, Sask., provides black and white photography of Arctic sea-ice within 20 minutes of the satellites pass over Canada. **1979** *Nature* 3 May 47/1 We concluded that to within the accuracy of the SAS 3 quick-look data timing (± 1 s), the onset of the optical burst was coincident with that in X rays. **1903** *Everybody's Mag.* Aug. 191/1 He figured them out with the stub of a blue pencil..sometimes on the slippery edge of reeking quick-lunch counters. **1903** *N.Y. Even. Post* 24 Sept. 8 The quick lunch man a few blocks away from the grocery store. **1909** CHESTERTON *Tremendous Trifles* 242 One of those quick-lunch restaurants in the City. **1911** E. M. CLOWES *On Wallaby* iii. 51 The haste of the Fisher Government to do things lately moved Alfred Deakin to describe its proceedings as 'quick-lunch legislation'. **1930** [see *DRIVE-IN]. **1975** *New Yorker* 22 Sept. 96/3 Men whose money derives from, and whose deepest loyalties adhere to, insurance companies,..quick-lunch chains, and the like. **1928** J. BUCHAN *Runagates Club* viii. 220 At a quick-luncheon counter he got into talk with a man. **1852** W. BAGEHOT *Coll. Works* (1965) I. 346 But he was a quick-minded..man of the world. **1908** *Daily Chron.* 24 Aug. 1/3 They say they never met such a quick-minded man. **1938** L. M. HARROD *Librarian's Gloss.* 124 Quick-reference books, Books which are essentially of a reference character, such as directories, dictionaries, and gazetteers. **1978** *Early Music* Oct. 599/2 Part II is a quick-reference chart summarizing the advice given on French in Part I. **1905** *Internat. Libr. Technol.* LXII. XLI. 48 Instead of moving the valve handle to this [slow-release] position..it is moved to the extreme left to quick-release positition... The brake-cylinder air rushes out, allowing the release springs to release the brakes suddenly. **1916** G. FRANKAU *Guns* 11 Now the foul clay cakes on britching strap and clogs the quick-release. **1933** *Gloss. Aeronaut. Terms* (*B.S.I.*) 73 *Quick release*, a device enabling the user to clear himself from the parachute and/or the harness. **1942** *Tee Emm* (Air Ministry) Sept. 135/2 Immediately you are grounded, turn on your back and unlock the quick release mechanism. **1961** *AWA Techn. Rev.* XI. Fig. 8 (*caption*) The sub-chassis can be removed by means of quick-release fasteners. **1972** [see *HARNESS *sb.* 4 c]. **1976** J. WAINWRIGHT *Walther P.38* 58, I saw him bend to work the quick-release mechanism. The car gave a gentle heave as the weight of the caravan left its rear bumper. **1864** Quick return [see *RAM *sb.*[1] 5 e]. **1894** W. J. LINEHAM *Text-Bk. Mech. Engin.* v. 169 The tool cuts in one direction only, and the back stroke is wasted. To minimise this loss, and at the same time reverse the stroke without changing the continuous rotation of main shaft, ingenious motions called quick returns have been devised. **1915** [see *KINEMATICALLY *adv.*]. **1930** *Engineering* 14 Mar. 341/3 Starting, stopping and the quick-return motion are all effected through a plate clutch. **1964** S. CRAWFORD *Basic Engin. Processes* viii. 218 Shaping machines are fitted with a quick-return mechanism. **1926** *Ironmonger* Suppl. 16 Jan. 50 (Advt.), Dealers who stocked early are now enjoying the profits from this quick-seller. **1934** *Archit. Rev.* LXXV. 11 True, academicians like Herkomer ..deigned to use photographic labour-saving devices for quick-service portraiture. **1976** H. MACINNES *Agent in Place* vii. 63 A hamburger at a Madison Avenue quick-service counter. **1873–4** G. M. HOPKINS *Note-Books & Papers* (1937) 223 Every visible palpable body has..a centre of illumination or *highspot* or *quickspot*. **1950** *Archit. Rev.* CVIII. 424 Quickstart or starter switch control gear can be supplied and the four-lamp fittings can be arranged for two-circuit control. **1962** A. NISBETT *Technique Sound Studio* viii. 147 Quick-start techniques fall into two categories, depending on the type of drive employed by the turntable. **1977** *Gramophone* Oct. 716/2 Technics have applied the quartz control direct-drive principle of their high-torque (quick-start) SP10 Mk. 2 turntable..to a lower priced deck. **1835** *Dublin Univ. Mag.* Apr. 391/2 'All's right,' said Denis, putting the musket to his shoulder; 'I see them. Now stand clear, boy, and hand along fresh cartridges cleverly. I'll give them a blaze in quick sticks—nothing like a long range; stand clear!' **1860** HOTTEN *Dict. Slang* (ed. 2) 196 *Quick sticks*, in a hurry, rapidly; 'to cut *quick sticks*', to be in a great hurry. **1935** A. J. POLLOCK *Underworld Speaks* 94/1 *Quicksticks*, to escape from the law. **1936** J. B. PRIESTLEY *They walk in City* xvi. 483 She can pop into that kitchen an' dish yer up something nice in quicksticks. **1966** *Listener* 29 Sept. 461/1 Then, with Mr Buchanan safely making up, it was quick-sticks for the Hippodrome and a performance of *Mercenary Mary*. **1914** *Act* 4 & 5 *Geo. V.* c. 10 § 15 Relief in respect of quick succession where property consists of land or a business. **1936** G. M. GREEN *Death Duties* v. 123 If any such other allowance is available on the second death, the 'quick succession' allowance is computed first and the other allowance is made against the reduced duty. **1967** E. RUDINGER *Wills & Probate* 14 Estate duty might have to be paid twice on the same property... There is a reduction in duty, known as quick succession relief, which helps a bit in this situation. **1973** *Times* 6 Oct. 19/2 Quick succession relief will reduce the double burden to some extent. **1611** A. STANDISH *Commons Complaint* 44 Have a good ditch double or treble set with quicke Thornes,..which hedge will last well three yeares. **1838** J. C. LOUDON *Arboretum et Fruticetum Britannicum* II. 836 Three rows of quickthorns shall be set in each ridge. **1971** *Country Life* 21 Oct. 1066/1 A variety of hedge plants—elm, ash, quickthorn, dogwood—..show the boundary hedge line is of great age. **1927** M. C. WORK *Contract Bridge* iii. 58 Two quick tricks..is the minimum strength with which a Contract denial should be made. **1955** I. FLEMING *Moonraker* viii. 81 It's a famous Culbertson hand... He used it to spoof his own quick-trick conventions. **1958** *Listener* 23 Oct. 669/2 East's King might fill West's club suit to produce nine quick tricks at No Trumps. **1977** *Homes & Gardens* Feb. 17 Your five quick tricks ought to be enough to see him [*sc.* your partner] home in Five Diamonds. **1951** M. MCLUHAN *Mech. Bride* (1967) 129/2 If there's anything this type of quick-turnover gent can't see..it's cold facts. **1956** Quick-turnover [see *EASY *a.* 13]. **1938** E. WAUGH *Scoop* II. ii. 157, I will say you're a quick worker. Sorry to barge in on the tender scene. **1969** O. HESKY *Sequin Syndicate* v. 48 'But there's something going on.' 'Well,' the old man said cheerfully, 'that's all right, isn't it? I didn't think Tarni was such a quick worker, though.'

quick, *v.*[2] Add: **2.** *trans.* To coat with mercury by immersion. Cf. QUICKEN *v.* 4 b, *QUICKING *vbl. sb.*[2] 2.

1873 E. SPON *Workshop Receipts* I. 308/1 A little of this solution is poured into a basin, and with a brush dipped therein they stroke over the surface of the metal to be gilt, which immediately becomes quicked. **1891** G. E. BONNEY *Electro-Platers' Handbk.* v. 112 Brass and silver are best quicked in a solution of the double cyanide of mercury and potassium. **1923** W. R. COOPER *W. G. McMillan's Treat. Electro-Metallurgy* (ed. 4) vi. 116 Many articles are 'quicked' before being subjected to the operation of depositing other metals, especially silver and gold, upon their surfaces.

quicken, *v.* Add: **5. b.** Also, to make (a slope) steeper.

1838 *Civil Engin. & Archit. Jrnl.* I. 376/2 Retaining walls, or quickening the slopes, might perhaps get over the difficulty.

quickening, *vbl. sb.* (Later examples in sense 6 b of the verb.)

1890 BILLINGS *Med. Dict.* II. 424/2 *Quickening*.., first sensation of movement of the foetus in a pregnant woman, occurring generally in the first or second week of the fifth month. **1922** JOYCE *Ulysses* 377 Send us, bright one, light one, Horhorn, quickening and wombfruit. **1975** *Church Times* 27 June 20/5 A foetus that had not reached the time of quickening (twelve to fourteen weeks old).

quick-freeze (kwi·kˌfrīz), *v.* Also written as one word. [f. QUICK *adv.* + FREEZE *v.*] *trans.* To freeze (perishable material) rapidly so that it can be stored at a low temperature for a long time. Also *absol.*

1930 *Popular Science* Sept. 27/2 Obviously, it would take longer to quick-freeze a six-pound cut of beef than a half-pound fillet. **1940** *Daily Progress* (Charlottesville, Va.) 20 Mar. 1/5 The range of food which can be quick-frozen has..brought a variety of business combinations into the field. **1957** *Daily Mail* 5 Sept. 11/5 In Florida.. they are quick-freezing water-melon concentrate..and making it available to any hospital anywhere in the country. **1959** *Times* 4 Nov. 23/11 (*heading*) Crosse & Blackwell to quick-freeze. **1967** *Heretaunga Plains* (School Publications Branch, N.Z.) 48/1 Fifteen tons of raspberries were quickfrozen and two more tons processed.

Hence **qui·ck-freeze** *attrib.*, that consists of or is used for quick-freezing; also *absol.*; **qui·ck-freezing** *vbl. sb.* and *ppl. a.*; **qui·ck-frozen** *ppl. a.*

1930 *Popular Science* Sept. 26/1 Clarence B. Birdseye.. succeeded in placing quick-frozen fish on the market. *Ibid.* (*caption*) Oysters, sealed in a package, are turned solid by quick-freeze process. **1932** *Sun* (Baltimore) 26 May 29/2 The comparatively new process known as quick-freezing. **1940** *Daily Progress* (Charlottesville, Va.) 20 Mar. 1/5 Quick-frozen foods..are rapidly becoming an important part of the American food production and distribution scene. **1943** J. S. Huxley *TVA* 103 TVA research has also led to the marketing of new types of quick-freezing machinery. **1945** Nelson & Wright *Tomorrow's House* vi. 74/2 A kitchen..will almost inevitably have a quick-freeze unit. **1950** *Times* 27 Feb. 4/5 No points are now needed for canned pork and some other imported ready-cooked and quick-frozen meats. **1951** *Good Housek. Home Encycl.* 514/2 Set the dial at 'maximum' or 'quick freeze' about an hour before the mixture is ready. **1959** *Times* 4 Nov. 23/11 The plant.. would provide some quick freezing facilities..to enable the company to enter the quick freezing field on a limited scale. **1965** *Supermarket & Self-Service* (Johannesburg) June/July 13/3 Quick-frozen polywrapped broilers. **1973** *Press & Jrnl.* (Aberdeen) 3 Aug. 3/2 The processing and quick-freezing of prawns. **1976** *Woman's Day* (U.S.) Nov. 95/1 Another argument against performing a biopsy..is that it depends on quick-frozen sections of the suspicious tissue.

quick-grass (in Dict. s.v. Quick *sb.*²). Add: **1.** (Later example.)

1878 *Golden Hours* X. 200/2 She tripped lightly past a knot of Quick Grasses.

2. *S. Afr.* = *kweek.

1931 E. P. Phillips *Introd. Study S. Afr. Grasses* vi. 79 Quick grass. *Cynodon Dactylon*; *C. incompletus*; *Stenotaphrum secundatum.* **1972** *Stand. Encycl. S. Afr.* V. 320/2 The quick-grasses (*Cynodon* spp.)..are amongst those grasses that are commonly planted as lawns.

quickie (kwi·ki). *colloq.* Also **quickey, quicky.** [f. Quick *a.* + -y⁶, -ie.] **1. a.** A cinematographic film that is made quickly and cheaply. See also *quota quickie* s.v. *quota *sb.* 4.

1926 *Amer. Mercury* Dec. 465/1 Motion pictures which are ground out wholesale by the studios at the rate of one a week are called *quickies.* **1937** *Times* 13 Nov. 8/1 It is not handicapped, as the quickie is, by the expenditure of £1 a foot. **1946** *Sun* (Baltimore) 4 Oct. 12/1 The possibilities of the subject are barely touched on in 'Down Missouri Way', for this is a quickie, made..on a limited budget. **1958** *Observer* 16 Mar. 15/2 Those early wartime quickies. **1961** *John o' London's* 14 Sept. 307/4 An equally pleasant semi-amateur quicky, *One More River.* **1977** *Time* 22 Aug. 43/3 Producer Charles Band plans to return by Christmas with another quickie titled *Laser Blast.*

b. In various extended and *transf.* senses: anything produced or carried out quickly.

1940 *Washington Post* 6 July 5/7 The publishers have their firecrackers, too. They call them 'quickies'. They are books pushed through the presses to meet the headlines of the day, to go off with a bang, even if they are but rubbish in the grass when the holiday is over. **1941** B. Schulberg *What makes Sammy Run?* x. 187, I may not have time to see you again. This trip is one of those quickies. **1942** *Gen* 1 Sept. 14/1 Then he [*sc.* a fighter pilot] 'screams downhill' and sends the German into the 'drink' with a 'quickie'. **1943** *Newsweek* 8 Feb. 56/1 Some observers interpreted the growing trend toward 'quickies'—undeclared strikes in the form of work stoppages for a few hours or a day or two—as the rank and file's way of spurring their leaders to a crackdown on the WLB for more money. **1944** *Sun* (Baltimore) 19 July 22/8 It [*sc.* a meeting] looked like 'one of those quickies which the Mayor held in his office'. **1948** *Variety* 25 Aug. 54/1 Deitz, due back by air from a quickie to Paris last week. **1950** W. Hammond *Cricketers' School* xvi. 151 Close was bowling right-arm off-spinners, and 'quickies' with the new ball. **1952** *Word Study* Feb. 8/1 In a publicity release Alfred A. Knopf, Inc., describes one of its Fall books, Richard G. Baumhoff's *That Dammed Missouri*, as follows: 'Though the appearance of this book could not be better timed, it is not what in publishing circles is called a 'quicky' (or, 'quickie')—that is, a book written and rolled off the presses hot on the heels of a national news event.' **1957** *Spectator* 15 Mar. 341/1, I think we've just got time for a quickie, and it's a real tickler from Mr. Bumple, of Bedford. **1958** [see *library¹ 2*]. **1969** A. Glyn *Dragon Variation* v. 142 Debbie had been keen on a Mexican divorce, a quickie in Mexico City followed by a honeymoon in Acapulco. **1970** *Times* 13 Jan. 8/3 The usual mishmash of buzzers, bonus points and quickies to confuse the looker-on. **1971** *Petticoat* 17 July 38/3 Here's a quicky for you when you get a blank spot about what to make for that summertime snack or light supper. **1975** R. H. Rimmer *Premar Experiments* ii. 210 Yesterday they were asking some of the girls if they were hookers or 'hos'. Kathy told Mohammed that a tough Irish kid offered her ten dollars for a 'quickie'.

c. A rapidly-taken alcoholic drink; a short drink.

1941 Baker *Dict. Austral. Slang* 58 *Quickie*, a drink taken quickly. **1942** Berry & Van den Bark *Amer. Thes. Slang* § 101/4 Cocktail names of slang and facetious origin..quickie. **1943** S. Lewis *Gideon Planish* xv. 143, I guess that calls for a drink. Let's make it a quickie, because I got to go out shopping with George. **1947** B. Marshall *Red Danube* iii. 25 'I could do with a quicky'.. Lined along the bar the other high ups..were having quickies too. **1959** H. Hobson *Mission Ho. Murder* iii. 21 Have you finished with the bottle?.. Give it to the musicians, there's just about three quickies. **1970** H. McLeave *Question of Negligence* xxiv. 220 'Drink?' Conway-Smith asked. 'Just a quickie,' she replied. **1974** P. Haines *Tea at Gunter's* xv. 156 Are you in the bar, dear?.. Ronald and I just dropped in for a quickie—we're on our way back from a party.

2. *Cricket.* A fast bowler.

1934 *Evening News* 21 June 1/1 Whatever chance England may or may not have, it will be a better one if there are two or three 'quickeys' in the side in any of the remaining Tests. **1963** R. Gilchrist *Hit me for Six* i. 15 It just happened that the first team wanted a 'quickie'. **1966** B. Johnston *Armchair Cricket 1966* 108 *Quickie*, a slang term for a fast bowler. **1977** *News of World* 17 Apr. 20/8 Their other unknown quickie, Len Pascoe.., isn't as fast as Lillee or Thomson.

3. *attrib.* or as *adj.*

1927 *Daily Express* 12 Dec. 13 The most eminent 'quickie' producer is Phil Goldstone, who can make a full-length film..in eight days. **1936** *Sun* (Baltimore) 21 Dec. 8/2 In recent months there have been scores of 'sit-down' or 'quickie' strikes in the automobile factories. **1940** *Common Sense* Mar. 20/1 [Cordell Hull] found his way to a quicky law school in the county. **1944** *Sun* (Baltimore) 15 Nov. 11/2 Another quickie bridge and the town was ours. **1959** M. Dolinsky *There is no Silence* iv. 57 Virtually every model in the country lived on these quickie love affairs. **1960** *Guardian* 27 Oct. 9/6 He made as many as eight 'quickie' Westerns..a year. **1969** A. Glyn *Dragon Variation* v. 142 Joann's rumour that there now were quickie divorces in Nevada too was apparently unfounded. **1976** H. Nielsen *Brink of Murder* ii. 19 He's kept a packed travel-bag in his office for these quickie trips. **1979** *Yale Alumni Mag.* Apr. (Suppl.) cn14/3 The deadline conflicts with a planned quickie vacation in Puerto Rico.

quicking, *vbl. sb.*² Restrict *rare* to senses in Dict. and add: **2.** Coating with mercury by immersion; also *concr.*

1863 *Brit. Patent 1512* 1 This Invention consists in preserving the silvering or quicking applied on glass and objects made of silvered or quicked glass. **1873** E. Spon *Workshop Receipts* (Ser. 1) 307/2 When a sufficient quantity of mercury is dissolved, the articles to be gilt are put into the solution, and stirred about with a brush till they become white. This is called quicking. **1923** W. R. Cooper *W. G. McMillan's Treat. Electrometallurgy* (ed. 4) vi. 116 Quicking is..often resorted to in order to increase the adhesiveness of deposited metals on objects which would have no action on the bath; for the mercury..retains a bright surface when exposed to the air for a period which would suffice to provide a film of oxide upon an unquicked surface. *Ibid.* 117 The quicking-solutions more commonly used are: the per-nitrate or proto-nitrate of mercury..or the cyanide of mercury. **1930** Field & Weill *Electro-Plating* 104 A thin, bright film of mercury is applied by simple immersion in a suitable solution. This process is called quicking. **1952** H. Silman *Chem. & Electro-Plated Finishes* (ed. 2) 478/2 (Index), 'Quicking' solutions.

qui·ckish, *a.* [f. Quick *a.* + -ish¹.] Somewhat quick; in *Cricket*, of a bowler, fast-medium.

1900 O. Agnus *Jan Oxber* iii. 194 Be quickish downstairs, mind 'ee. **1955** *Times* 9 July 4/7 Neame and Parker, for Harrow, made steady progress against Sinclair and Douglas Pennant, a quickish left-hander. **1963** *Times* 4 June 3/6 He is tall, well built, and quickish, and Hampshire think that they may have a real find in him. **1977** *Sunday Times* 3 July 28/6 Nottinghamshire's quick and quickish bowlers had two wickets..in the first four overs. **1978** *Gramophone* Apr. 1713/1 The quickish pulse, less accommodatingly shaped than Karajan's.., does occasionally suggest a nature ramble being hastened along by a warden who senses rain in the offing.

quicklike, *adv.* Chiefly *U.S.* [f. Quick *a.* + -like.] In a quick manner; quickly.

1913 G. Stratton-Porter *Laddie* viii. 235 He.. looked down the hole I showed him and he cried out quicklike. **1951** H. E. Giles *Harbin's Ridge* xxi. 186 He slewed his eyes at me quick-like. **1978** A. Price *'44 Vintage* vi. 70 We've to nip in quick-like.

quickness. Add: **6.** Mobility or plasticity (of soil).

1969 *Engin. Geol.* III. 135 A series of experiments.. was carried out with the purpose to investigate if quickness could be produced by leaching of a clay deposited in salt water. **1972** *Nature* 28 Jan. 220/2 It may be the hitherto neglected non-clay mineral fraction which is responsible for quickness.

quickset, *sb.*¹ and *a.* Add: **A.** *sb.* **1. b.** (Later example.)

1938 M. Hadfield *Everyman's Wild Flowers & Trees* 63 Common Hawthorn... A valuable hedge plant, as such, called quick-set.

2. (Later example.)

1973 R. Adams *Watership Down* xlv. 375 Hazel halted among the quickset on top of the nearer bank.

B. *adj.* **b.** Also *fig.*

1938 L. MacNeice *Earth Compels* 56 Columns of ads, the quickset road to riches. **1948** [see *hair-trigger b].

quick-set (kw·ikset), *a.*² [f. Quick *adv.* + Set *v.*] **1.** Also **Quickset.** Applied to a type of surveyor's level in which the foot-screws in the levelling head are replaced by a ball and socket joint to facilitate quick setting.

1930 S. W. Perrott *Surveying for Schools* xiv. 114 In the case of the Quickset level, there are no foot-screws, the telescope and bubble being set approximately level by a ball and socket joint. **1948** B. G. Manton *Highway Surveying & Setting Out* iii. 58 Many instruments of the 'quick-set' type are fitted with a prismatic device which enables the bubble position to be seen from the eye-piece end of the telescope. **1971** R. J. P. Wilson *Land Surveying* x. 215 The essential difference between the quickset level and other types is that it is a tilting level without footscrews in the levelling head.

2. That hardens or dries quickly.

1967 Karch & Buber *Offset Processes* vii. 266 Quickset inks are also used when printing on coated paper stock. **1970** R. Johnston *Black Camels of Qashran* xi. 178 The quickset cement was dry and hard.

quick step, quickstep. Add: **1.** (Earlier U.S. example of quasi-*adv.* use.)

1864 *Sunset Stories No. 1* 10 Stir round, can't you, Jem? take your fingers out of your mouth, and get some kindlins, quick step.

3. A quick dance; *spec.* a fast modern ballroom dance in 4/4 time.

1880 [see *lassu]. **1927** V. Silvester *Mod. Ballroom Dancing* 25 For Charleston, Quickstep, and Tango the right hand should be held further round. *Ibid.* 64 Owing to the speed at which foxtrots are played, it is not possible to do the slow foxtrot unless the orchestra plays slowly, hence the evolution of the Quickstep. This dance is now done mixed in with the Charleston. **1937** E. Porter *Music through Dance* viii. 142 The dances of the post-war period were still the Quickstep, and the Foxtrot in its quick and slow variations. **1955** *Radio Times* 22 Apr. 7/2 The Gold Star Trophy..will be awarded for the best all-round performance in the four basic ballroom dances—the waltz, foxtrot, tango, and quickstep. **1976** *Times* 11 June 14/6 The bandleader..changed the tempo to what the programme said was a foxtrot but which..was more of a quickstep.

qui·ck-step, *v.* [f. the sb.] **1.** *intr.* To march in quick time; also quasi-*trans.* and *fig.*

1906 *Daily Chron.* 27 Aug. 4/4 They quick-step it up and down the asphalted front at Hythe. **1961** *Time* 28 Apr. 22/2 The G.O.P. majority quick-stepped behind his program. **1964** G. McDonald *Running Scared* vi. 78 The streets were filled with people..all slim and quick-stepping. **1975** *New Yorker* 17 Feb. 101/1 Lightning Mandate, who won a division of the recent Malibu, was right behind him, and these two probably quickstepped themselves out of the money.

2. To dance the quick-step.

1935 C. Day Lewis *Time to Dance* 32 For no silver posh plane was their pigeon, no dandy dancer quick-stepping through heaven.

Hence **qui·ck-stepping** *ppl. a.*

1908 *Daily Chron.* 1 Oct. 7/3 The quick-stepping figure in white flannels glanced around at the click of the latch. **1936** C. Day Lewis *Friendly Tree* i. 14 Her gait was delicate, quick-stepping.

quick time. b. (Later Jamaican examples.)

1956 in Cassidy & Le Page *Dict. Jamaican Eng.* (1967) 372/1 You better come here quick time!.. Him run quick-time an' tell him mumma. **1971** *Jamaican Weekly Gleaner* 3 Nov. 5/1 The real tourist types..did not miss the chance to dress quick time in tee-shirt and so forth emblazoned with 'Miami, Florida'.

‖ **Quicunque vult** (kwīku·ŋkwe vult). Also **Quicumque vult.** [L.] The Athanasian Creed, so called from its opening words *quicumque vult* (*salvus esse*) 'whosoever will (be saved)'. Also *ellipt.*, as *Quicunque*, and *fig.*

c **1400** *Mandeville's Travels* (1967) xvi. 106 Seynt Athanasie, that was bisshopp of Alisandre, that made the psalm *Quicumque vult.* *a* **1530** *Myroure of oure Ladye* (1873) ii. 139 This psalme *Quicumque vult*, enformeth vs fyrste in faythe of the godhed and after in faythe of the manhode of cryste. *Ibid.* iii. 312 And the thyrde crede that ys. *Quicunque vult*, was made by a holy bysshop. called Athanasius. **1567** J. Jewel *Def. Apol. Ch. Eng.* ii. 83 The Creede called, *Quicunque vult*, written, as some thinke, by Athanasius. **1724** D. Waterland *Crit. Hist. Athanasian Creed* ii. 25 Robertus Paululus, Presbyter of Amiens, in the Diocess of Rheims, speaking of the Offices recited at the Prime, observes that the Piety of good Christians had thereunto added the *Quicunque vult*, that the Articles necessary to salvation might never be forgotten any hour of the Day. **1855** F. Procter *Hist. Book Common Prayer* ii. i. 214 Another title of this Creed was 'Psalmus *Quicunque vult*': hence the custom of reciting it antiphonally. **1877** *Encycl. Brit.* VI. 562/2 Nothing definite as to the authorship of the Quicunque can be rested on such resemblances. **1910** *Jrnl. Theol. Studies* XI. 401 (*heading*) A critical text of the *Quicumque Vult. Ibid.* 402 The first three are the earliest known MSS of the *Quicumque.* **1921** G. Sampson *English for the English* ii. 32 Let *Quicunque vult* and threatened excommunications of all kinds remain in the realm of theology and outside the realm of education. **1963** Auden *Dyer's Hand* 54 Herewith, then, what I might describe as..a kind of private *Quicunque vult.* **1964** J. Kelly *Athanasian Creed* vii. 126 For these reasons the Quicunque deserves to retain its place among the normative formularies of Christendom. **1967** H. Chadwick *Early Church* xv. 235 It was a theologian living in Southern Gaul, or perhaps in Spain, who produced the catechetical compendium.. *Quicunque Vult*, which soon (if not from the start) passed under the august title of the Creed of St. Athanasius. **1980** *Times* 20 Nov. 17/7 The very bases of belief..the Catechism, the Quicunque Vult, the Thirty-nine Articles.

quid, *sb.*² Add: **1. a.** (Further examples.) Also, one pound sterling. *slang.*

1907 G. B. Shaw *Major Barbara* ii. 241, I ad two quid saved agen the frost; an Ive a pahnd of it left. **1917** A. G. Empey *Over Top* 304 *Quid*, Tommy's term for a pound or twenty shillings... He is not on very good terms with this amount as you never see the two together. **1929** W. P. Ridge *Affectionate Regards* 71 Milton received only ten quid for the first edition of 'Paradise Lost'. **1951** *People* 3 June 2/2 It took less than a couple of quid on the down trip. **1959** I. Jefferies *Thirteen Days* xi. 183 You buy a car, it costs you a thousand quid; but you get a gir like that free. **1968** K. WEATHERLY *Roo Shooter* 74, I was thinking of moving on a bit but there are still enough here to make a few quid. **1971** *Venerabile* XXV. III. 191 It is surprising what difficulties the good old English quid can cause. **1977** C. McCULLOUGH *Thorn Birds* vii. 160 Do you want to go after Auntie Mary's thirteen million quid?

b. Phr. *quids in*: in luck or profit; well off for money. *slang.*

1919 *Athenæum* 1 Aug. 695/2 *Quid's in*, for a stroke of good fortune. **1939** W. ALLEN *Blind Man's Ditch* 236 We'll be quids in to-morrow. **1960** O. MANNING *Great Fortune* xix. 226 Anyone who financed the trip would be quids in. **1969** J. N. CHANCE *Abel Coincidence* x. 187 If you know about people and they know nothing about you, you're quids in at the starting grid. **1976** *News of World* 14 Mar. 19/4 And to make sure you are quids in anyway, we'll give you as well the starting price odds to £10 each way on whichever horse does win.

c. Phr. *the full quid*: (see quot. 1959). *Austral.* and *N.Z. slang.*

1946 *Coast to Coast 1945* 106 'There's some say Lizzie's not the full quid either,' he said. **1959** BAKER *Drum* II. 111 *Full quid*, in full possession of one's faculties. A person who is said to be *ten bob in the quid* or any smaller sum down to *tuppence in the quid*, is held to be stupid. **1960** N. HILLIARD *Maori Girl* III. vi. 213 Not that she was simple in the sense that she was short of the full quid. **1972** I. MOFFITT *U-Jack Society* xiv. 227 We avoid individuality as firmly as we suspect joy ('You're not the full quid!'). **1975** *Sydney Morning Herald* 5 July 9 It's perfectly clear that not all members of our community are the full quid.

quid, *sb.*³ Add: **2.** = CAST *sb.* 19 and *PELLET *sb.*¹ 2 c.

1834 [see *PELLET *sb.*¹ 2 c]. **1879–81** G. F. JACKSON *Shropshire Word-bk.* 315 Them owls..sin a mouze..an' ketchen 'im..an' chawen 'im..'an crushen 'im, an' sooken 'im till theer inna nuthin' left on 'im, an' then they droppen the quid.

quid, *v.*² **1.** (Further example.)

1902 J. MASEFIELD *Salt-Water Ballads* 66 Quiddin' bonded Jacky out a-lee.

‖ **quidditas** (kwi·ditɑs). [L.: see QUIDDITY.] = QUIDDITY I.

1878 *Encycl. Brit.* VIII. 758/1 This matter is differentiated into particular things..through the addition of an individualizing principle (*hæcceitas*) to the universal (*quidditas*). **1911** *Ibid.* XXIV. 354/2 The additional determinations are as truly 'form' as the universal essence. If the latter be spoken of as *quidditas*, the former may be called *haecceitas*. **1934** 'H. MACDIARMID' *Stony Limits* 16 Lyin' in wait in vain for a single grey drop To quicken into a perfect quidditas. **1976** 'M. INNES' *Gay Phoenix* iii. 41 A man's identity—his *quidditas*, as the learned might say.

quidlet (kwi·dlėt). *slang.* [f. QUID *sb.*² + -LET.] A sovereign; one pound sterling; (see also quot. 1912).

1911 L. TRACY *Sylvia's Chauffeur* v. 96 [He] handed Dale a fiver—five golden quidlets, if you please! **1912** J. W. HORSLEY *I Remember* xi. 254 'Quidlet', for half a sovereign, has recently been coined from the older 'quid'. **1940** A. W. UPFIELD *Bushranger of Skies* xvi. 183 It cost four thousand quidlets—Australian.

quid pro quo, *sb.* Add: **2.** *attrib.* (Earlier example.)

1838 J. S. MILL in *Westm. Rev.* Aug. 489 We did not expect that the *petite morale* almost alone would have been treated, and that with the most pedantic minuteness, and upon the *quid pro quo* principles which regulate *trade*.

3. With substantial elements considered discretely.

1939 S. DE MADARIAGA *Christopher Columbus* xii. 136 The contractual sense, that attitude which sees every event of life as a transaction and expects and demands a definite *quid* for every *quo*. **1961** *Daily Tel.* 1 Sept. 12 She could well take all and give nothing in return, pocket the quos as well as the quids. **1979** M. McCARTHY *Cannibals & Missionaries* xi. 304 Conditions for the committee's release..had never been 'aired'... Not a *quid* or a *quo* vouchsafed.

quidsworth (kwi·dzwɒɹþ). *slang.* [f. QUID *sb.*² + WORTH *sb.*¹] The amount of anything which may be bought for one pound.

1966 P. O'DONNELL *Sabre-Tooth* v. 83 Modesty was after that ten million quidsworth of diamonds. **1968** 'O. MILLS' *Sundry Fell Designs* xix. 192 There's thousands of quidsworth of equipment in there. **1977** F. BRANSTON *Up & Coming Man* v. 51, I went to a Chinese takeaway and bought a couple of quidsworth of indigestion.

‖ **quien sabe** (kie·n sa·be). [Sp.] 'Who knows?', 'who can tell?' Also *attrib.*

1836 in *Papers of M. Buonaparte Lamar* (1921) I. 436 Austin..will be elected and will do well provided he selects a *good* Cabinet—and an honest one—quen Sabe—. **1846** J. W. ABERT *Jrnl.* 17 Oct. in *Rep. Exam. of New Mexico* (1848) 51 To all our other questions with regard to this ancient town, we received the usual Mexican reply of 'quien sabe'. **1849** T. ARNOLD *Let.* 7 July (1966) 124, I wonder what you are doing now. Whether the 'daily possibility of falling in love'..has ripened into a certainty ..? Quien sabe? as Matt used to say. **1864** *Weekly New Mexican* 23 Dec. 2/4 We cannot trust an answer in the common vernacular to which we are accustomed, and must reply in all the Spanish we are master of, *quien sabe.* **1925** D. H. LAWRENCE *Reflections on Death of Porcupine* 110 What makes the difference? *Quien sabe!* **1933** A. HUXLEY *Let.* 13 Aug. (1969) 372 Do you think I am kind and unpossessive? Quien sabe? **1947** M. LOWRY *Under Volcano* i. 38 But why had all this happened? he asked himself now. Quién sabe? **1949** *Southwestern Rev.* Summer 235/1 One yarn thrown in as a sort of *quien sabe?* item suggests an even more unpalatable morsel. **1965** L. MEYNELL *Double Fault* I. i. 14 'Does this mean that he is..too wealthy to work, or what?' '*Quien sabe?* Maybe he's just on holiday.' **1976** A. WHITE *Long Silence* iii. 28 It's one thing for us all to make our decision here..but there—quien sabe?

quiescence. Add: Also, the action of making quiet or calm.

1859 TROLLOPE *Bertrams* viii. 71 He had been useful as a great oil-jar, from whence oil for the quiescence of troubled waters might ever and anon be forthcoming.

quiescent, *a.* and *sb.* Add: **A.** *adj.* **3.** *Electronics.* Corresponding to or characterized by an absence of an input to a device ready to receive one.

1923 E. W. MARCHANT *Radio Telegr. & Teleph.* vi. 84 Attempts have been made to arrange the transmitter in such a way that the speech-current will act as a switch for starting up the continuous waves at the transmitting end. This arrangement of circuit has been called the 'Quiescent aerial' system. **1952** E. ARMITAGE *Wireless Fund.* ix. 167 The advantage of Class B amplification is that the steady anode current flowing through the circuit when the valve is quiescent is very much smaller than under Class A conditions. **1965** *Wireless World* July 325/2 This imposes a problem on the restricted signal handling capacity of TR1 due to its very low quiescent current. **1975** D. G. FINK *Electronics Engineer's Handbk.* IX. 56 In the absence of an rf input signal, these amplifiers remain quiescent even with full operational voltage applied.

quies kiteer, quiess kateer, varr. *QUAISS KITIR *int.*

quiet, *a.* Add: **I. 1. b.** Also phr. *quiet American*: freq. used ironically, as of an undercover agent or spy.

1955 G. GREENE (*title*) The quiet American. **1963** *Listener* 10 Jan. 96/3 She has much data on these delightful grasshopper people, though a certain 'Quiet American' ingenuousness is difficult to digest. **1963** *Times* 23 Feb. 4/5 Mr. H. F. Johnson..is a model quiet American. **1973** *Times* 11 Jan 10/6 There never was much 'reality' about Washington's presence in Vietnam from the moment when the first quiet Americans moved in. **1980** J. McNEIL *Spy Game* ix. 99 I've heard of you.. The Quiet American, no less.

2. b. (Further examples.)

1853 C. BRONTË *Villette* I. xiv. 257 Her dress was almost as quiet as mine. **1895** G. B. SHAW in *Sat. Rev.* 28 Sept. 409/1 He associates low tones ('quiet colors' they call them in Marshall & Snellgrove's) with dignity and decency. **1957** *Observer* 28 July 5/6 Both Hardy Amies and Victor Stiebel are masters of the art of inserting contrasting lines which define the figure in the quietest way. **1977** *Spare Rib* May 15/1 Quiet shades of blue, brown and grey were almost *de rigueur*.

d. Of the sun: marked by an absence of all transient and localized emission of radio waves such as accompanies sunspots. Of other celestial objects: = *radio-quiet* adj. s.v. *RADIO *sb.* 7. Also, in *Geophysics*, marked by no local fluctuations of magnetism.

1946 *Nature* 2 Nov. 632/2 Edlén's recent work..shows that the coronal matter is normally at a temperature approaching 10^6 degrees. We should therefore expect to find black-body radiation of about 1 metre wave-length having a normal (quiet sun) intensity corresponding nearly to $T = 10^6$. **1961** *I.U.G.G. Chron.* No. 34. 6 To December 1963 (i.e. approximately up to the commencement of the proposed International Year of the Quiet Sun). **1962** *Nature* 24 Mar. 1145/1 During magnetically quiet days. **1963** *Daily Tel.* 18 Mar. 19 (*heading*) 60 nations will seek 'quiet sun' secrets. **1966** *Sci. Amer.* Nov. 54/1 At the beginning of each [sunspot] cycle the surface of the sun is quiet, disturbed only by the 'granulation' effect. **1974** *Nature* 13 Sept. 129/1 The seamount possesses a strong magnetic signature..in marked contrast to the main part of the Rockall Trough which is magnetically quiet. **1977** *Sci. Amer.* Aug. 32/1 A number of giant elliptical galaxies radiate prodigiously at radio wavelengths, where stars and normal galaxies are quiet.

II. 3. a. Phr. *anything for a quiet life*: see *LIFE *sb.* 3 c.

d. *quiet number*, an easy job (cf. *NUMBER *sb.* 6 f (iii)). *Naut. slang.*

1948 PARTRIDGE *Dict. Forces' Slang 1939–1945* 129 *Number, quiet*, an easy job at sea or ashore. **1977** *Navy News* July 18 (*caption*) 'Got a nice quiet number for you after the Review,' he says... 'Just scoop up any odd little bit of gash,' he says.

4. a. *quiet-room*, (*a*) a room set aside for quiet activities; (*b*) a room especially designed so as not to transmit any noise made within it, usu. in a mental institution.

1938 [see *PAD *sb.*³ 1 c]. **1968** M. TORRIE *Your Secret Friend* i. 15 The Sixth have the boudoir as their 'quiet' room and the bedroom is now the staff common-room. **1976** [see *PADDED *ppl. a.*²]. **1977** C. H. JAQUES *Dragon Century 1877–1977* xxi. 241 A complete re-organisation.. with..the Doctor's surgery and consulting room taking over the Quiet Room, while the old Dining area is divided up into new Quiet Room, Headmaster's study and Secretary's office. **1977** *Spare Rib* Jan. 15/2 The second half of the day passes so quickly and imperceptibly that at first I don't grasp why it's suddenly got so noisy in our 'quiet' room.

c. (Further examples.)

1891 [see THINK *sb.* 1]. **1905** CHESTERTON *Heretics* xiv. 181 A place where a man can have what is somewhat fantastically called a quiet chop. **1953** R. USBORNE *Clubland Heroes* II. 99 An off-day for a good Buchan type was: a cold bath or plunge, a big breakfast, a quiet pipe, and then off to the hills in filthy tweeds. **1963** E. SUMMERS *Where No Roads Go* v. 72 I'll go out on the verandah for a quiet smoke. **1977** *Private Eye* 1 Apr. 23/3 (Advt.), A quiet word about hair transplants. **1977** *Zigzag* Apr. 28/1, I can just see the nice young couples out for a quiet Sunday drink.

d. Of a period of time: spent in seclusion for the purposes of prayer, meditation, etc.; *quiet time*: a daily session of private Bible study or prayer.

1884 *Lichfield Diocesan Mag.* Jan. 10 A *Quiet* day, to which all the clergy and lay readers of the archdeaconry were invited, was held at Stoke, on Tuesday Dec. 18th. **1896** C. T. STUDD *Let.* in N. P. Grubb *C. T. Studd* (1933) xi. 106, I have had such a good day to-day, early up and a quiet time for most of the day and the Lord has been opening up the Word. **1934** R. MACAULAY *Going Abroad* xxx. 263 That must have been about the same time I was having *my* quiet time. **1935** *Methodist Recorder* 1 Aug. 5/4 A large number of ministers assembled..for the 'Quiet Day'. **1945** [see *SHARING *vbl. sb.*² 2]. **1957** J. R. W. STOTT *Being a Christian* 23 What many people call the daily 'quiet times', first thing in the morning and last thing at night. **1960** I. KUHN *In Arena* iii. 35 Some students were trying to let classwork reading [of the Bible] do for personal quiet time. *Ibid.* 36 Letting the day's business occupy the central place and trying to fix a quiet time with the Lord somewhere shoved into the odd corner. **1967** M. GRIFFITHS *Take my Life* iii. 61 Maintaining a regular 'Quiet Time' unhurriedly in the Lord's presence, reading the Bible, hearing His word and responding in prayer from the heart, becomes harder. **1973** *Franciscan* XV. 169 A quiet afternoon during the Pentecost season was conducted by the Dean of Worcester.

III. 8. For **1873** *Slang Dict.* read **1863** HOTTEN *Dict. Slang* (ed. 2) and add further examples.

1862 *Otago: Goldfields & Resources* 35 Unless men can work [the gold] on 'the quiet', they are not likely to make 'piles' so rapidly as Messrs. Hartley and Riley. **1873** 'MARK TWAIN' *Gilded Age* xi. 112 The other day he let me into a little secret, strictly on the quiet. **1903** A. H. LEWIS *Boss* 59 They've put out a lot of money on the quiet among my own people. **1967** N. FREELING *Strike out where not Applicable* 36 She has a good act of letting Francis rule the roost, but on the quiet I think she makes the decisions.

9. *quiet-eyed* (examples), *-footed*, *-tinted*, *-toned*, *-voiced*, *-walled*; *quiet-smiling* adjs.

1895 W. B. YEATS *Poems* 197 The Druid, gray, wood-nurtured, quiet-eyed. **1956** R. FINLAYSON in *Landfall* (N.Z.) X. 12 A handsome..Jersey, sleek and quiet eyed. **1954** J. R. R. TOLKIEN *Fellowship of Ring* I. ii. 62 Long after, but still very long ago, there lived by the banks of the Great River on the edge of Wilderland a clever-handed and quiet-footed little people. **1952** R. CAMPBELL tr. *Baudelaire's Poems* 84 An huntress born, sure-eyed, and quiet-smiling. **1909** *Westm. Gaz.* 14 Sept. 1/2 It included the following: Shirts, 72;..socks of quiet-tinted silk, 2 dozen; hats, evening suits, smoking coats. **1965** *Times Lit. Suppl.* 25 Nov. 1049/4 A quiet-toned, carefully tender book. **1940** T. S. ELIOT *East Coker* ii. 9 Had they deceived us Or deceived themselves, the quiet-voiced elders. **1974** P. GORE-BOOTH *With Great Truth & Respect* 394 What disturbed me immensely was their quiet-voiced extremism. **1865** G. M. HOPKINS *Poems* (1967) 34 Those charms accepted of my inmost thought The towers musical, quiet-walled grove.

quiet, *v.* Add: **2. d.** *Electronics.* To reduce automatically the gain of (a radio receiver) in the absence of a usable signal; = *SQUELCH *v.*

1950 J. K. HENNEY *Radio Engin. Handbk.* (ed. 4) xvii. 821 The purpose of these circuits is to squelch or quiet the receiver when sufficient signal for satisfactory reception is not present. **1960** COOKE & MARKUS *Electronics & Nucleonics Dict.* 453/2 *Squelch*, to quiet a receiver automatically by reducing its gain in response to a specified characteristic of the input.

4. (Further examples of *to quiet down.*) Now chiefly *N. Amer.*

1897 A. BEARDSLEY *Let.* 17 Mar. (1970) 279 There has been no return of haemorrhage. The lung too is quieting down. **1914** G. B. SHAW *Misalliance* 85 You would then be charged and imprisoned until things quieted down. *Ibid.* 93 Let us postpone the discussion. Wait until Monday: we shall have Sunday to quiet down in. **1916** *Daily Colonist* (Victoria, B.C.) 30 July 7/4 The trade had quieted down somewhat lately and some mills have lacked an adequate supply of logs. **1944** *New Yorker* 25 Mar. 84/2 Moved back into London when things quieted down. **1974** *Sci. Amer.* July 47/2 The effect of the drugs is often dramatic, with the children quieting down, paying attention to their schoolwork and in some cases doing better in school.

‖ **quieta non movere** (kwiē·tă nōᵘn movēᵊ·ri). [L., lit. 'not to move settled things'.] A maxim expressing preference for the *status quo*; 'let sleeping dogs lie'.

1771 H. WALPOLE *Let.* 26 Mar. in *Corr.* (1937) VII. 289 My father's maxim, *Quieta non movere*, was very well in those ignorant days. **1854** W. BAGEHOT in *Prospective Review* X. 526 It lived on the fat of the land; *quieta non movere*, was its motto. **1887** *Athenæum* 27 Aug. 276/2 But was the book quite worth publishing? 'Quieta non movere' holds good even of dormant articles. **1905** D. M. WALLACE *Russia* I. xix. 373 *Quieta non movere* is her [*sc.* the Russian Church's] fundamental principle of conduct. **1960** *Encounter* XIV. III. 88 *Quieta non movere* is the motto of many once aggressive..radicals.

quieten, *v.* Add: **1.** Also const. *down.*
1902 C. HYNE *Mr. Horrocks, Purser* 37 Mr Horrocks had given the wink to the chief steward to go and quieten down the Second-Class passengers. **1908** G. A. BIRMINGHAM *Spanish Gold* xxi. 296 We got them quietened down after a bit.
2. (Further example.)
1897 *Daily Tel.* 28 Aug. 6/4 It [*sc.* Afghanistan] is beginning to quieten down now, in my opinion.

quietener. Add: Also 9 **quietner.** (Earlier example.)
1856 *Punch* 19 July 22/1 The conjugal powders are called in the town of Bolton 'Quietners'... These quietners are sold at one penny each.

qui·etening, *ppl. a.* [-ING².] That quietens or becomes quiet.
1905 *Daily Chron.* 25 Mar. 7/3 The presence of a large addition of police has had a quietening effect on the.. operatives on strike. **1907** *Smart Set* Mar. 26/1 She lay there on her pillow, grateful..for the sheltering, homely realities, that enmuffled her and gave tangibility to her quietening thoughts.

quieting, *vbl. sb.* Add: **2.** *Radio.* **a.** The automatic reduction of the gain and therefore the noise of a receiver when there is no usable signal.
1937 F. E. TERMAN *Radio Engin.* (ed. 2) xiii. 561 In tuning a sensitive receiver provided with automatic volume control, the noise output between stations is high because, when no signal is being received, the A.V.C. system increases the sensitivity of the receiver to the maximum possible value. Arrangements for eliminating this interstation noise are variously known as *Q* circuits, quieting systems, squelch circuits, etc. **1959** R. L. SHRADER *Electronic Communication* xvii. 554 (*caption*) A squelch interstation quieting, or Q, circuit.
b. The reduction of the noise level in a receiver caused by the presence of an input at the frequency to which it is tuned.
1949 *Proc. IRE* XXXVII. 1373/2 The quieting-signal-sensitivity test input is the least unmodulated signal input which, when applied to the receiver through the standard dummy antenna, reduces the receiver noise by a factor of 20 decibels. **1960** *IRE Trans. Vehicular Communications* Dec. 32/2 Two methods of measuring sensitivity are recognized... The oldest and probably the most used is the quieting method. This procedure measures the on-frequency signal level required to reduce the noise output of a receiver by 20 db. **1974** HARVEY & BOHLMAN *Stereo F.M. Radio Handbk.* iii. 41 Receiver sensitivity must be quoted together with the corresponding noise figure; a typical figure for a good circuit is 2μV for 30 dB quieting.

quietish (kwəi·ĕtiʃ), *a.* [f. QUIET *a.* + -ISH¹.] Somewhat quiet.
1913 R. BROOKE *Let.* May (1968) 464, I wasn't *sick*: just quietish, and I had a bleedin' headache. **1925** G. S. GORDON *Let.* 13 May (1943) 177 The house seems quietish without you! **1939** N. MARSH *Overture to Death* xiii. 125 Though lately it's been quietish—hasn't it, Mr. Alleyn? **1977** *Hot Car* Oct. 49/1 It's obviously got to be neat, safe and quiet-ish.

quietism. 2. (Later example.)
1976 *Gramophone* Aug. 266/1 In its place there is.. almost a sense of quietism.

quietist. Add: **1.** (Further examples.) Also *fig.*
1923 W. DEEPING *Secret Sanctuary* xxiii. 241 In love he had become a Quietist. **1924** —— *Three Rooms* xxix. 268 She sat like a quietist, hands folded, her brown eyes benignly equivocal.

quietistic, *a.* Add: (Later examples.) Also *transf.*
1909 *Quarterly Rev.* July 117 Altogether, quietistic analysis breaks down while leaving the reality and value of the experience untouched. **1973** B. R. WILSON *Magic & Millennium* xii. 387 Among less-developed peoples the autonomous introversionist movement would appear to rely on the quietistic prophet. **1978** *Gramophone* July 231/1 He does not overpoint the ostinato of No. 4, which remains essentially quietistic.

quietlike, *a.* and *adv.* For *Sc.* read 'orig. *Sc.*' and add later examples of advb.
In some or all of these examples the formation may have been influenced by the parenthetic use of *like* (see LIKE *adv.* 7 in Dict. and Suppl.).
1909 J. MASEFIELD *Tragedy of Nan* II. 31 He was fiddlin' quiet-like, all the time 'e were a-singing. **1913** W. DE LA MARE *Peacock Pie* 98 Calling me, 'Sam!'—quietlike. **1976** *New Yorker* 8 Mar. 102/2 Someone said, 'It wasn't no mortar round,' real quietlike. **1977** I. SHAW *Beggarman, Thief* I. iv. 49 Wesley turned to him and said, quiet-like, 'Shut your big trap about Americans, limey.'

quietly, *adv.* Add: **a.** Also, surreptitiously, without attracting public notice.
1961 *Minnesota Rev.* I. III. 349 In the prison camp's Black Market civilian clothes were quietly bought..for him. **1976** *N.Y. Rev. Bks.* 15 Apr. 22/4 When the recent coal rush got underway, companies would quietly obtain mineral leases for as little as twenty-five cents an acre from the Interior Department.
b. *just quietly* advb. phr., confidentially, between ourselves. *Austral.* and *N.Z. colloq.*
1937 PARTRIDGE *Dict. Slang* 448/2 *Just quietly* was, in the G[reat] W[ar], a tag-c[atch] p[hrase] among New Zealanders. It had virtually no meaning. **1941** BAKER *Dict. Austral. Slang* 40 *Just quietly*, between you and I. **1952** E. LAMBERT *Twenty Thousand Thieves* II. 123 'That Chips Prentice is a soldier and a half. Just quietly, he's up for a decoration.' Dick found no cause for surprise at this. Chips with a decoration seemed natural. **1966** G. W. TURNER *Eng. Lang. in Austral. & N.Z.* viii. 177 Much New Zealand colloquialism is shared with Australia, e.g. *just quietly* 'between you and me', [etc.].

quiff (kwif), *sb.*¹ *U.S.* and *dial.* [Var. of WHIFF *sb.*¹] Also **quift. 1.** A puff or whiff of tobacco smoke. Also *fig.*
1831 J. M. GALLOWAY *Poems* 27 Thou'st warm'd my nose at mony a speil; Ae quiff o' thee [*sc.* a pipe] Has made me play wi' care and skill. **1840** *Southern Lit. Messenger* VI. 447/2 A quiff would now and again ascend and hang like a tropical cloud over the hemisphere of his cranium. **1866** J. E. BROGDEN *Provincial Words* 159 *Quiff*, a puff. *Ex.* Should you like a quiff? **1876** F. K. ROBINSON *Gloss. Whitby* 149/2 *Quiff*, a whiff, a puff of smoke, an exhalation. 'I got a *quiff* on 't,' caught the scent. **1889** *Brighouse News* 14 Sept. 3/7 Hah nivver heeard a quift on't.
2. A puff or blast of wind.
1912 J. MASEFIELD *Dauber* v. 268 She came within two shakes of turning top, Or stripping all her shroud-screws, that first quiff.

quiff, *sb.*² *dial.* and *slang* (esp. *naut.*). [Origin unknown.] A clever trick or dodge; a hint.
1881 *Advertiser Notes & Queries* I. 77/2 *Quiff.* What is the origin of this word, so often used in the sentence, 'I'll teach thee a quiff', meaning something clever. It is often heard in Cheshire. **1890** BARRÈRE & LELAND *Dict. Slang* II. 164 *Quiff*..(Tailors), a word used in expressing an idea that a satisfactory result may be obtained by other than strictly recognised rules or principles. **1925** FRASER & GIBBONS *Soldier & Sailor Words* 223 *Quiff, a*, any specially ingenious smart, tricky, or novel or improvised way of doing anything. (Navy). In the Army used of any drill method peculiar to a battalion, and not usually done in others. Where the wording of the Drill Book is vague, units often read different meanings into the phraseology and invent their own 'Quiffs'. **1925** N. LUCAS *Autobiogr. of Crook* v. 72 I'll give you one quiff, right now, because I like your face and your nerve. Never touch the dope, it's hell—and worse than that. **1928** *Weekly Dispatch* 13 May 10/4 Suddenly a faint grey blur on the horizon in the expected direction. The seaman blinks his eyes—an old quiff which prevents many a false alarm—and then makes his report. **1933** J. MASEFIELD *Bird of Dawning* 107 It was young Mr. Abbott worked that quiff on you, sir. **1961** F. H. BURGESS *Dict. Sailing* 166 *Quiff*, a trick or artifice that makes a job easier.

quiff, *sb.*³ Also **quif.** [Origin obscure: cf. *QUIFF *sb.*¹] A curl or lock of hair plastered down on the forehead, worn orig. by soldiers; more recently, a tuft of hair brushed upwards over the forehead. Also *attrib.*
1890 BARRÈRE & LELAND *Dict. Slang* II. 164 *Quiff* (military), the small curl on a soldier's temple just showing under his glengarry or forage cap. **1908** *Daily Chron.* 19 Mar. 4/4 He wears a quif of hair soaped down on his forehead in a slimy arc that nearly touches his eyebrows. **1919** H. G. JENKINS *John Dene of Toronto* XVI. 255 He's quite a nice youth, with black hair greased into what I think he would call a 'quiff'. **1925** H. G. WELLS *Christina Alberta's Father* II. iii. 224 He had..highly oiled and entirely subjugated sandy hair with an army 'quif' on the forehead. **1929** P. GIBBS *Hidden City* xlii. 206 Revealing his well-plastered hair curled into a quiff over his forehead. **1953** N. JACOB *Morning will Come* iv. 72 A man with a short clipped beard and his hair parted in what was called a 'militiaman's quiff'. **1965** M. BRADBURY *Stepping Westward* ii. 108 He could see the quiffs of his three cabinmates as they moved round getting dressed. **1968** J. IRONSIDE *Fashion Alphabet* 197 *Quiff*, where the hair falls forward over the forehead before being brushed back. Made fashionable by Elvis Presley and Cliff Richard, so adapted for girls. **1969** H. E. BATES *Vanished World* iii. 38 There were..plenty of men who were great dandies in that generation [his grandfather's]—the moustache-waxers, the quiff-plasterers, [etc.]. **1976** *Times* 8 Mar. 6/3 Mr Reagan..is certainly the best turned out candidate. The 1950s quiff is immaculate.

quiff, *sb.*⁴ *dial.* and *slang.* [Origin obscure: cf. *QUIFF *v.*¹] A young woman; *spec.* a prostitute, a 'tart'.
1923 G. WATSON *Roxburghshire Word-bk.* 244 *Queef*,.. an engaging girl. **1931** *Amer. Speech* VI. 440 *Quiff*, a cheap prostitute. **1966** R. H. RIMMER *Harrad Experiment* 107 'This looks like a rich quiff,' King Arthur said. 'I think we'll look into her suitcase.' **1973** L. SNELLING *Heresy* I. i. 6 If only there was some other quiff about I might be able to deal with her indifference.

† **quiff,** *v.*¹ *Obs. coarse slang.* [Origin obscure.] *intr.* To copulate *with.* As **qui·ffing** *vbl. sb.* in quots.
1719 T. DURFEY *Wit & Mirth* V. 243 By quiffing with Cullies three Pound she had got. **1796** GROSE *Dict. Vulgar T.* (rev. ed.), *Quiffing*, rogering.

quiff, *v.*² [f. *QUIFF *sb.*³] *trans.* To arrange hair into a quiff. Also with *up.*
1940 R. LEHMANN in *Folios of New Writing* Spring 101 There was one [sailor] in particular, large, with a genial, knobby raw-beef face and a flaxen curl quiffed up in the forefront of his sailor cap. **1972** *Daily Tel.* 24 Jan. 11/5 Fringes can be quiffed up too. **1977** *West Briton* 25 Aug. 5/8 They turned up in three-quarter length jackets, drain-pipe trousers and shoelace ties. Their hair was quiffed and oiled.

qui-hy. Add: Also 9 **qui-hye; quoi hai, quai hai,** etc. (Further examples.) See also *KOI HAI.
1848 J. H. STOCQUELER *Oriental Interpreter* 195/1 *Qui-hye! qui-hi!* or *koee-hye!* 'Who is there?' or 'Who waits?' In domestic establishments in Bengal..a servant..is summoned to the presence by the foregoing exclamations. Hence, the Europeans who reside in Bengal are called *Qui-hyes*, to distinguish them from the residents of Bombay, Madras, or Ceylon. **1858** G. F. ATKINSON *Curry & Rice* Pref., The 'Qui Hye' of Bengal, the 'Mull' of Madras, and the 'Duck' of Bombay. **1939** 'E. BELL' *Memory be Good* i. 15, I must have been a bit of a nuisance to the old *quoi hais* who wanted to read quietly in their deck-chairs [on an India-bound Anchor Line boat]. **1965** B. SWEET-ESCOTT *Baker Street Irregular* viii. 240 Most of Gavin's principal assistants were drawn from British business houses operating in the Far East... There was an inevitable tendency for some of them to regard themselves as old qua'hais. **1977** *Times* 25 June 15/4 An Old Quai Hai, as the diminishing band of servants of the Raj still living in this country [*sc.* India] are affectionately known.

quill, *sb.*¹ Add: **1. c.** pl. *spec.* = PAN-PIPE. *U.S.*
1883 J. C. HARRIS *Nights with Uncle Remus* xiii. 69 Uncle Remus declared that Brother Rabbit could perform upon the quills, an accomplishment to which none of the other animals could lay claim. **1886** *Century Mag.* Feb. 521/2 But to show how far the art of playing the 'quills' could be carried..see this 'quill tune'..from a gentleman who heard it in Alabama. **1952** B. ULANOV *Hist. Jazz in Amer.* (1958) iii. 20 The homemade instruments of the Negro are described in some detail, the tambo, bones, quills, fife, triangle. **1970** *Western Folklore* XXIX. 231 Blues singer Big Joe Williams..recalls..a two-stringed cigar box guitar, a cane fife, a set of pan pipes or 'quills', and an upturned bucket, which served as a drum.
e. The whistle of a steam locomotive. *U.S.*
1945 F. H. HUBBARD *Railroad Avenue* ii. 9 With its interpretive tone the ballast scorcher could make that quill say its prayers or scream like a banshee. **1961** *Listener* 24 Aug. 270/2 The fabled Casey Jones..was a 'quill artist' of note, who always carried with him his own quill (that is what they used to call a chime in the deep South).
f. An improvised straw or channel through which narcotics may be sniffed or smoked; the narcotic itself. *U.S.*
1935 A. J. POLLOCK *Underworld Speaks* 94/2 *Quill*, choicest grade opium. **1970** C. MAJOR *Dict. Afro-Amer. Slang* 95 *Quill*, folded matchbook cover in which a narcotic is held and smoked or sniffed. **1971** *Black Scholar* Sept. 36/1 He..rolled a ten dollar bill up into a quill and gave the coke and quill to Christine, who snorted up half of the line on the card.
2. d. A hollow sleeve rotating in bearings which is used to transmit the drive from a motor to a concentrically-mounted axle.
1910 *Engineering* 12 Aug. 246/3 A gearless concentric motor for each driving-axle is mounted on a quill flexibly connected to the driving-wheels. **1930** *Ibid.* 6 June 722/1 Two new types of drive had been developed... The first consisted of a geared quill surrounding the driving axle and carrying two crankpins, the latter being connected by a flexible linkage to two crankpins on the driving wheels. **1968** D. W. & M. HINDE *Electr. Traction Systems & Equipment* ii. 32/2 A certain amount of experimental work has been carried out with the motor armature shaft of the hollow or quill pattern. **1975** BRAM & DOWNS *Manuf. Technol.* vii. 208 The spindle rotates in the quill to provide the rotary motion for cutting tools.
3. g. Phr. *the pure quill*: see *PURE *a.* 8d.
8. a. (sense 1b) *quill-machine*; (sense 3b) *quill-case, -cleaner.*
1795 J. WOODFORDE *Diary* 28 Mar. (1929) IV. 186 Mr. Thorne..applied a Caustic to it just touching the part with it with a small kind of very fine hair pencil in a Quill-Case. **1968** *Canadian Antiques Collector* Nov. 25/2 It would seem that the ink bottle was usually on the right of the inkstand, the pounce on the left, with the quill standing in the central bottle, which was the quill cleaner. **1971** *Country Life* 1 July 23/1 This shelf carried writing equipment: inkpot, quill cleaner and sand box. **1846** G. DODD *Textile Manuf. Gt. Brit.* VI. 182 Sail-making. The quill machines..have a considerable number of quills arranged in a row, and made to rotate rapidly.
b. quill drive, (the apparatus for) the transmission of power from a motor by means of a quill (sense *2d); **quill shaft** = sense 2d above; **quillwork,** a type of embroidery, using the quills of a porcupine, done by North American Indians; hence **quillworker.**
1912 SHELDON & HAUSMANN *Electr. Traction* 306/1 (Index), Quill drive. **1927** R. E. DICKINSON *Electr. Trains* vi. 111 There are several other forms of suspension; e.g. the quill drive in which the motor-armature is on a hollow 'quill' inside which is the axle of the wheel. **1970** LIGHTBAND & BICKNELL *Direct Current Traction Motor* iii. 47 The great majority of direct-current traction motors in service are either axle-suspended or fitted with some form of quill drive. **1934** *Jrnl. R. Aeronaut. Soc.* XXXVIII. 738 The turbine itself is mounted on a quill shaft which telescopes the pinion shaft, the latter being attached to the quill shaft at the low pressure end of the turbine. **1949** *Ibid.* LIII. 143/1 As originally designed the gear was a compound epicyclic gear, the sun gear of which was driven by a quill shaft from the front end of the com-

pressor. **1843** *Knickerbocker* XXII. 164 The Indians prepare it in bark, curiously ornamented with quill work and beads. **1908** *Encycl. Relig. & Ethics* I. 827/2 Closely akin to beadwork is quillwork, especially among the Plains Indians (now done in its purity by few except the Eskimos, the tribes of the north-west coast, and the northern Athapascans). **1966** L. Cohen *Beautiful Losers* I. 97 With a bowed head she received the compliments which the quillwork on her deerskin gown evoked. **1976** *San Antonio* (Texas) *Express* 8 Dec. 5-B/2 Quillworkers' tools have not changed. Today they still consist of some awls, strands of sinew and a knife.

quill, *v.* Add: **5.** *trans.* To write (with a quill), to pen.

1890 J. Coghill *Poems, Songs, & Sonnets* 67 This screed whilk he's juist new dune quillin'. **1945** J. Dickson in *Sc. Nat. Dict.* (1968) VII. 309/3 For each and a' the cheque's been quilled Wi' nae successors. **1977** *Even. Standard* 18 July 13/2 In 1677..Henry Vaughan quilled the immortal lines [etc.].

quill-driving, *ppl. a.* (*pres. pple.*). (Further example.)

1877 O. Wilde *Let.* Aug. (1962) 47, I had two jolly letters yesterday, one from Bouncer who is quill-driving or going to.

quiller (kwi·ləɹ), *sb.*[2] [f. Quill *v.* + -er[1].] One who quills material, esp. into the form of a ruff.

1853 Mrs. Gaskell *Ruth* II. vii. 172, I shall quill up a ruff for you. You know I am a famous quiller of net.

quillet, *sb.*[3] (Earlier example.)

1872 C. M. Yonge *P's & Q's* ix. 95 Rolling up her papers into little quillets.

quilling, *vbl. sb.* Add: **2.** (Earlier example.)

1790 A. M. Woodforde *Let.* 3 Sept. in *Parson Woodforde Soc. Jrnl.* (1972) V. iii. 56 Lady Bacon was dress'd in a striped muslin Gown and Coat..and a quilling of Black Lace at the edge.

3. *U.S.* The art of blowing distinctive sounds on the whistle of a steam locomotive. Cf. *quill *sb.*[1] 1e.

1945 F. H. Hubbard *Railroad Avenue* ii. 8 The engineman put on a whistle of his own with a tone that suited him and then practised a technique of blowing it that would be distinctive. This was called 'quilling' and was a highly developed art. **1947** *Richmond* (Va.) *News Leader* 13 May 13/5 But the art of '*quilling*', or 'making her talk', went out with electric and diesel locomotives, with their shrill horns and pneumatic whistles. **1966** *Listener* 14 Apr. 542/1 The variety of weird sounds he was able to extract from the six-tone engine whistle of his own property—an art known in railroad vernacular as 'quilling'.

quillon. Add: **1.** (Earlier and later examples.)

1884 R. F. Burton *Book of Sword* 125 The quillons may be either straight—that is disposed at right angles—or curved. **1978** N. K. Sandars *Sea Peoples* 158 The sword has a tapered blade, flanged tang and quillons.

2. *Comb.*, as **quillon-dagger** (see quot. 1960).

1950 *Proc. Prehist. Soc.* XVI. 24 The 'short iron sword' from Woodcuts, Dorset,..is actually a quillon-dagger of the 13th or 14th century A.D. **1960** H. Hayward *Antique Coll.* 232/1 *Quillon dagger*, a type of dagger with a simple cross-guard.

quilly, *a.* Delete *rare* and add: **2.** Consisting of or covered by quills.

1935 E. R. Eddison *Mistress of Mistresses* xviii. 355 A porcupine's quilly rump. **1938** T. H. White *Sword in Stone* xx. 294 Archimedes [*sc.* a hedgehog] got married, and brought up several handsome families of quilly youngsters.

quilt, *sb.*[1] Add: **1. d.** A layer of warm, thick material placed over the frames of a bee-hive to prevent draughts and contain the bees.

1870 *Amer. Bee Jrnl.* June 258/2 We finally had some little quilts (or whatever you choose to call them) made, and they answer admirably. **1873** *Brit. Bee Jrnl.* Nov. 100/1 His quilts, for so they are called by him, are laid close to the tops of the frames; they are not sufficiently heavy to crush the bees, even if laid directly on them, and they mould themselves to any possible condition. **1904** J. R. G. Digges *Irish Bee Guide* 50 Sheets and Quilts are required upon the frames or supers to preserve heat; to prevent draught; and to keep the bees from ascending into the roof... The quilts should be of felt, carpet, or other warm material. **1927** *Chambers's Jrnl.* XVII. 91/2 Place between the tops of the frames containing the combs and the bottom 'quilt' or cover two strips of wood an inch or two apart. **1952** H. Mace *Bee-Keeper's Handbk.* i. 15 Although many bee-keepers still use quilts, an increasing number have returned to an improved form of Crown board. **1962** A. S. C. Deans *Bees & Beekeeping* x. 66 November. Carry out a periodic inspection of all hives to make sure that mice have not settled under the roofs and on top of the quilts if crown boards are not in use.

3*. The interior of a cricket ball (see quot. 1921).

1882 *Baily's Mag.* Nov. 391, I took up the inside of a [cricket] ball just newly finished..and laid it on a bench, and hammered it with a wooden mallet, which rebounded without making the slightest impression on the substance which is called 'the quilt'. **1921** *Dict. Occup. Terms* (1927) §688 *Quilter*.., wraps worsted thread, by hand, round a cork to make quilt, or core, of cricket ball.

quilt, *v.*[1] Add: **1. a.** *transf.* and *fig.* (Further examples, in sense 'to cover as with a quilt'.)

1924 R. Campbell *Flaming Terrapin* v. 75 The lilies..quilted the land with snow. **1930** —— *Adamastor* 79 The gorgeous Ram..whose great pelt is rolled To quilt a thousand hills with fire.

b. *spec.* with a ball as object.

1886 W. H. Long *Dict. Isle of Wight Dial.* 53 *Quilt*,..to cover a ball with a network of twine.

quilt, *v.*[3] Add: **a.** Also *Austral.*

1945 Baker *Austral. Lang.* 120 One of the inevitable consequences..has been the development of an extensive vocabulary of fighting terms. Here are some of the best..*roll into, vacuum, quilt* and *stoush* a person. **1973** D. Stuart *Morning Star Evening Star* 111 More than one bloke I've seen Joe quilt good and proper for trying to make a joke of it.

b. *Cricket.* To hit (the ball, bowling, etc.) about the field with great force, usu. for a sustained period of time.

1866 *Baily's Mag.* Feb. 92 Mr Lyttleton had an early taste of the lobs; these he quilted awfully. **1867** *J. Lillywhite's Cricketers' Compan.* 69 That punishing bats-man, Mr. Lucas, 'quilted' the Colts' bowling tremendously. **1897** K. S. Ranjitsinhji *Jubilee Bk. Cricket* ii. 56 A batsman may get bowled first ball, a bowler may be quilted all over the field without getting a wicket, but both can redeem themselves by good fielding.

quilted, *ppl. a.* **2.** Delete † and add later examples.

1925 E. Sitwell *Troy Park* 50 One candle spills out thick gold coins Where quilted dark with tree shade joins. **1968** *National Observer* (U.S.) 3 June 15/1 This quilted personality has regenerated a sorrowful team. **1971** A. Sampson *New Anat. Brit.* xxxi. 561 The English pattern of hedgerows and quilted landscape.

quilter. Add: (Examples in sense of an apparatus.)

1895 *Montgomery Ward Catal.* Spring & Summer 264 Each..Sewing Machine will be supplied..with..1 braider, 1 binder, 1 quilter, 4 hemmers. **1908** *Sears, Roebuck Catal.* 41/2 We furnish with every [sewing] machine a complete set of accessories, consisting of one quilter, six bobbins..and one instruction book. **1964** *McCall's Sewing* v. 74/2 The quilter has a short open foot and an adjustable or removable space guide that may be used to the right or left of the needle.

quilting, *vbl. sb.*[1] Add: **3.** (Earlier and further N. Amer. examples.)

1768 in *Essex Inst. Hist. Coll.* (1879) XVI. 260 Quilting at my house. **1770** J. Parker *Diary* 22 Feb. in *New-England Hist. & Geneal. Reg.* (1915) LXIX. 10 Naby went to Mr Wildes to Quilting. **1825** J. Neal *Bro. Jonathan* I. 58 She returned however to the quilting and Peters..to the study of Mr. Harwood. **1913** *Atlantic Monthly* Dec. 826/2 Zobbie often met Pauline at the quiltings and other gatherings at the homes of non-partisans. **1939** L. M. Montgomery *Anne of Ingleside* xxxii. 228 The Ladies' Aid is going to have their quilting at Ingleside. **1975** *Budget* (Sugarcreek, Ohio) 20 Mar. 15/6 Mrs. Eli Y. Byler had 2 quiltings last week and will have another one this week.

4. quilting-bee (earlier and later examples); also *Canad.*; **quilting day** *N. Amer.*, a day devoted to a quilting-party; **quilting-feast** (example); **quilting frame** (examples); **quilting match** *U.S.* = *quilting-party*; **quilting-party** (earlier and later examples); also outside the U.S.

1832 S. G. Goodrich *System of Univ. Geogr.* vii. 167 The females also have similar meetings called 'quilting bees', when many assemble to work for one, in padding or *quilting* bed coverings or *comforters*. **1921** *Daily Colonist* (Victoria, B.C.) 5 Oct. 6/5 It was decided to hold a quilting bee at the home of Mrs. Scott. **1976** 'D. Halliday' *Dolly & Nanny Bird* x. 126 He looked..like a lush from a quilting bee. **1939** L. M. Montgomery *Anne of Ingleside* xxxii. 230 The quilting day was more like June than October. **1968** Quilting feast [see *quilting-party* below]. **1739** *Pennsylvania Gaz.* 15 Nov. 4/1 Just imported and to be sold by John Brientnall, in Chestnut-street Tenter-hooks of several sizes, fit for Butchers, Skinners, Fullers, and for Quilting-Frames. **1854** M. J. Holmes *Tempest & Sunshine* xx. 274 Said she, 'Mighty good opinion Mr. Quilting-frames has of me (alluding to Mr. Miller's height); glad I know his mind.' **1908** L. M. Montgomery *Anne of Green Gables* xxi. 235 If Marilla..was actuated by any motive save her avowed one of returning the quilting-frames. **1813** M. L. Weems *Drunkard's Looking Glass* (ed. 2) 5 He does not trouble his head about asking the Fool where he has been, whether at a Funeral or a Wedding..or a Quilting-match. **1881** A. B. Alcott *New Connecticut* 108 The Wolcott Dialect..Quilting match. **1833** S. Smith *Life & Writings J. Downing* 139 A few others..wouldn't invite poor Mrs. No-tea to their husking and quilting parties. **1835** *Knickerbocker* VI. 180 It so happened that there was a great quilting-party invited to Tecumseh-Place, which assembled all the principal young people of the county. **1907** *St. Nicholas* (N.Y.) 1044/2 She has gone, with her grandmother whom she was visiting, to a quilting-party. **1948** *Minneapolis Star* 17 Sept. 31/1 Nobody sees Nellie home when the women of Halvarson Bowers post 187, VFW auxiliary, have a quilting party. **1968** J. Arnold *Shell Bk. Country Crafts* xxix. 310 It was..possible for as many as six people..to be sewing at the same time. Such gatherings became known as quilting parties or feasts.

quilting, *vbl. sb.*[2] (Earlier example.)

1829 P. Egan *Boxiana* 2nd Ser. II. 242 The *quilting* Bob had previously received, rendered him in a great measure incapable of taking advantage of his adversary's distress.

quim (kwim). *coarse slang.* [Origin obscure: perh. rel. to Queme *a.* or *v.*; cf. Quaint *sb.*]

1. The female external genital organs; the vagina.

An example of 1613 cited in Farmer & Henley's *Dict. Slang* has not been traced.

c **1735** *Harlot Un-mask'd* (Ballad), Tho' her Hands they are red, and her Bubbies are coarse, Her Quim, for all that, may be never the worse. **1796** Grose *Dict. Vulgar Tongue* (rev. ed.), *Quim*, the private parts of a woman: perhaps from the Spanish *quemar*, to burn. **1846** *Swell's Night Guide* (rev. ed.) 57 Vell, rattle my dice box for a musty quim, but that Sall is a splitter! *c* **1863** 'Philo Cunnus' *Festival of Passions* II. 7 Gently pulling up my shift his hand touched my thigh, and instantly I sighed as it was laid on my quim. **1882** in 'P. Fraxi' *Catena Librorum Tacendorum* (1885) 267 My imagination fills the empty galligaskins with cosy bottoms and hirsute quims. **1922** Joyce *Ulysses* 550 Were you brushing the cobwebs off a few quims? **1936** H. Miller *Black Spring* 253 'Now,' he says, 'I'm going to pay you as usual,' and taking a bill out of his pocket he crumples it and then shoves it up her quim. **1951** N. Coghill tr. *Chaucer's Cant. Tales* 113 He made a grab and caught her by the quim And said, 'O God, I love you!' **1966** P. Willmott *Adolescent Boys* iii. 50, I got my hand on her tit and I thought well, that's all right. So I thought I'd try for her quim. **1974** H. R. F. Keating *Underside* ii. 25 Is it worse to have it on me belly than to have it in me quim?

2. A woman; women collectively. *N. Amer. slang.*

1935 A. J. Pollock *Underworld Speaks* 94/2 *Quim*, a female. **1974** *Saturday Night* (Toronto) Jan. 35/2 The key to success in this contest is a flashy car; and if the car is both expensive and impressive 'you have to beat the quim off with a hockey stick'.

quin, *sb.*[2] [Shortened f. Quintuplet.] One of five children born at one birth; such a child in later life. Also *attrib.*

1935 *Dionne Quintuplets growing Up* (*caption*), My, what big girls the 'Quins' are getting to be. **1936** W. Thornton *Country Doctor* 127 In Portugal in 1866, one quin baby attained an age of 50 days. **1937** R. Macaulay *I would be Private* I. i. 16 Another little boy! Win's got quins! Can you beat it?... It took me and her poor father ten years to get five, and here's you and Win done it in a year. **1951** L. Barker *Truth about Dionne Quins* i. 11 Dr. Dafoe..held Press conferences..in addition to his quin column, a newspaper feature, written by various ghost writers. *Ibid.* xxiii. 178 Emilie, the happy-go-lucky tomboyish quin,..was not inclined to worry. **1968** *Economist* 15 June 49/1 Despite the title [of the book], Dr Scheinfeld is less good on supertwins, on triplets, quads and quins. **1976** *Liverpool Echo* 6 Dec. 1/1 The condition of Fiona, the fourth quin, has deteriorated and she has had difficulty in breathing since birth.

quinacridone (kwinæ·kridōᵘn). *Chem.* [f. Quin(oline + Acrid(ine + -one.] Any of four synthetic isomeric compounds, $C_{20}H_{12}N_2O_2$, or their substituted derivatives, which have a heteroaromatic structure consisting of a string of five fused rings (three benzene and two 4-pyridone arranged alternately) and which include a class of usu. red or violet pigments. Also *attrib.* and in *Comb.*, as *quinacridone red, violet*, etc.

[**1896** *Jrnl. Chem. Soc.* LXX. i. 261 Hydroxyquinacridone.] **1906** *Ibid.* XC. i. 459 Quinacridone,..crystallises in yellow needles..and dissolves in concentrated sulphuric acid to a yellow solution with a greenish-blue fluorescence. **1958** *Chem. Abstr.* LII. 10215 Dihydroquinacridones..can be oxidized to quinacridones, pigments of good light fastness. **1963** *Jrnl. Oil & Colour Chemists' Assoc.* XLVI. 29 Quinacridone red yellowish, quinacridone red bluish and quinacridone violet which were issued by Du Pont in 1958,..were the first of the quinacridones. Chemically, all three pigments are one and the same unsubstituted linear *trans*-quinacridone. **1969** R. Mayer *Dict. Art Terms & Techniques* 321/2 Besides this relatively yellowish or scarlet shade, bluish, magenta, and violet shades are also made from the same dyestuff (linear quinacridone) that yields quinacridone red. **1972** *Materials & Technol.* V. xi. 358 Quinacridone reds, maroons and violets are a comparatively recent introduction. These very expensive pigments have excellent light-fastness in full colours and in pastel shades. **1973** Tilak & Ayyangar in R. M. Acheson *Acridines* (ed. 2) viii. 603 Diketoquinolinoacridines are designated by the trivial name 'quinacridones'. They can be linear *trans* (71) and *cis*..or angular. .. The compound 71, which is usually referred to as quinacridone, and its derivatives are..valuable as high quality pigments.

quinacrine (kwi·năkrīn). *Pharm.* [f. Quin(ine + Acr(id)ine.] A name for mepacrine (hydrochloride). Also *attrib.* and in *Comb.*, esp. with reference to the use of quinacrine or quinacrine mustard to stain chromosomes.

Formerly a proprietary term in the U.S.

1934 *Official Gaz.* (U.S. Patent Office) 23 Oct. 771/1 Société des Usines Chimiques Rhone-Poulenc, Paris... *Quinacrine*... Pharmaceutical product to be used in the treatment of malaria. Claims use since Feb. 20, 1933. **1934** *Chem. Abstr.* XXVIII. 3792 Quinacrine is chloro-2-diethylaminopentylamino-5-methoxy-7-acridine dihydrochloride. **1936** *Trade Marks Jrnl.* 4 Mar. 267/1 *Quinacrine*... Chemical substances used in medicine and pharmacy. Société des Usines Chimiques Rhone-Poulenc, ..Paris..; manufacturers. **1960** C. Achebe *No Longer at Ease* xi. 105 He said the poor man must be suffering from malaria, and the next day he bought him a tube of quinacrine. **1970** *Nature* 6 June 897/1 The quinacrine staining test shows up the number of *Y* chromosomes in a human interphase (non-dividing) cell. *Ibid.* 961/2 (*caption*) A group of quinacrine-stained spermatozoa showing fluorescence. **1971** *Oxford Times* 26 Mar. 2/5 Samples of fluid surrounding the foetus were treated with quinacrine dihydrochloride, an anti-malaria drug. The effect was to make the 'Y' chromosomes..take on a fluorescent glow when viewed through an ultra-violet microscope. **1975** FRASER & NORA *Genetics of Man* ii. 10/1 Quinacrine binds preferentially to certain regions of metaphase chromosomes to produce characteristic banding patterns ('Q-bands').

2. Special Comb.: **quinacrine mustard,** a nitrogen mustard derived from quinacrine and used as a fluorescent stain for chromosomes.

1957 R. JONES et al. in *Jrnl. Org. Chem.* XXII. 783/2 We here wish to report on the conversion..of 2-methoxy-6,9-dichloroacridine to 2-methoxy-6-chloro-9-[4-bis(β-chloroethyl)-amino-1-methylbutylamino]acridine (quinacrine mustard). **1970** [see *MUSTARD *sb.* 2* b]. **1970** *Nature* 4 July 101/1 The trivial name 'quinacrine mustard' has been used..to describe at least two chemical species. *Ibid.* 101/2 May I..suggest that if authors wish to continue to use the expression 'quinacrine mustard' this be restricted to the true quinacrine derivative [*sc.* 2-methoxy - 6 - chloro - 9 - [4 - *bis*(2 - chloroethyl)amino - 1 - methyl-butylamino] acridine]. **1971** *New Scientist* 18 Mar. 606/1 When hamster and bean chromosomes were stained with..quinacrine mustard, and viewed with long wavelength ultraviolet light, the chromosomes fluoresced differently along their length.

quinalbarbitone (kwinæ̆lbā·ɹbitōᵘn). *Pharm.* [f. L. *quin-que* five + AL(LYL + *BARBITONE.] The compound 5-allyl-5-(1-methylbutyl)-barbituric acid, which is used as a sedative-hypnotic, esp. for pre-operative sedation, usu. in the form of its sodium salt, $C_{12}H_{17}N_2O_3Na$, a white powder often known by the proprietary name *SECONAL. Cf. *SECOBARBITAL.

1951 *Addendum to Brit. Pharmacopœia 1948* 46 Quinalbarbitone Sodium should be kept in a well-closed container. **1960** *Brit. Med. Jrnl.* 19 Mar. 872/2 For older children quinalbarbitone ('seconal') may be given. **1971** 'D. HALLIDAY' *Dolly & Doctor Bird* xiv. 199, I..stayed behind to administer a mild dose of quinalbarbitone. **1977** *Proc. R. Soc. Med.* LXX. 773/2 Barbiturates took pride of place as the commonest lethal drug, and quinalbarbitone sodium (Tuinal) headed the list.

quinarius (kwinā·riɒ̆s). Pl. **quinarii** (-i,ī). [L.: see QUINARY *a.* and *sb.*] = QUINARY *sb.* 2 a.

1601 P. HOLLAND tr. *Pliny's Nat. Hist.* II. XXXIII. iii. 463 At what time ordained it was, that the Denarius or Denier should go for tenne Asses or pounds of brasse money; the halfe Denier, Quinarius, should be currant for five; and the Sesterce reckoned worth two and a halfe. *a* **1666** EVELYN *Diary* an. 1645 (1955) II. 398 Now other observations I made in Rome are these amongst other, As to Coynes & Medails, that 10 Asses make the Roman Denarius, 5 the quinarius. **1708** KERSEY *Dict. Anglo-Britannicum, Quinarius*.., a Roman Coin of the Value of Five Asses, equal to 3 Pence 3 Farthings English. **1771** [see SESTERCE]. **1840** [see DENARIUS 1]. **1962** R. A. G. CARSON *Coins* 110 The new system comprised three denominations in silver—the denarius worth ten asses, the quinarius of five asses and the sestertius of two and a half.

quinary, *a.* and *sb.* Add: **A.** *adj.* **2.** Of or belonging to the fifth order or rank; fifth in a series.

1924 [see *QUATERNARY *a.* 3]. **1953** *Amer. Econ. Rev.* May *Papers & Proceedings* 365 Logically and empirically, quinary industries as we shall define them are not once more a residual category. These industries comprise medical care, education, research, and recreation... The principle that guides this grouping is that they all have to do with the refinement and extension of human capacities. **1973** *New Society* 15 Nov. 386/3 The 'tertiary' sector contains at least three divisions—'tertiary' proper (pure service provision..); 'quarternary' [*sic*] (information exchange and decision-making); and 'quinary' (research, development and education).

B. *sb.* **3.** Something that belongs to the fifth order or rank.

1937, 1946 [see *QUATERNARY *sb.* 2].

quinazoline (kwinæ·zǒlīn). *Chem.* [ad. G. *chinazolin* (A. Weddige 1887, in *Jrnl. f. prakt. Chem.* XXXVI. 142), f. *chinolin* QUINOLINE with inserted *az-* (see AZO-).] A yellow, basic, crystalline solid, $C_8H_6N_2$, which has a bicyclic structure formed from fused benzene and pyrimidine rings; any substituted derivative of this.

1887 *Jrnl. Chem. Soc.* LII. II. 1044 Anhydroacetyl-orthamidobenzamide is regarded as a derivative of a hypothetical base, quinazoline,..isomeric with cinnoline and quinoxaline. **1903** *Ibid.* LXXXIV. I. 446 By oxidising this base with potassium ferricyanide, quinazoline..was at last successfully prepared; it..crystallises from light petroleum in glistening flakes resembling naphthalene, has a bitter, burning taste, and..is odourless at the ordinary temperature. **1926** H. G. RULE tr. *J. Schmidt's Text-bk. Org. Chem.* 700 Quinazolines..are strong bases, which are readily reduced to their dihydro-compounds. **1950** *Thorpe's Dict. Appl. Chem.* (ed. 4) X. 346/2 A variety of substituted quinazolines have been prepared recently as part of the search for effective antimalarials. **1968** L. A. PAQUETTE *Princ. Mod. Heterocyclic Chem.* ix. 326 Quinazoline 3-oxide..shows the same reactivity as quinazoline toward nucleophilic reagents, but the addition products frequently eliminate water with the net effect that 4-substituted quinazoline results.

‖ **quincaillerie** (kæ̃kāyəri). [Fr.] **a.** (See quot. 1883). **b.** A hardware or ironmonger's shop. Also *attrib.*

1883 J. W. MOLLETT *Illustr. Dict. Art & Archæol.* 272 *Quincaillerie*, a general term for all kinds of metallurgical work in copper, brass, iron, etc. **1951** W. SANSOM *Face of Innocence* xi. 164 Past the paper shop... Past the dark leathern hole of the shoe-menders, past the sharp quincaillerie. **1966** P. V. PRICE *France: Food & Wine Guide* 83 Spend an hour in the hardware department of a good store or a *quincaillerie*. **1968** *Guardian* 3 May 9/1 Red-faced *quincaillerie* reps sit in the dark brown bar totting up their accounts over a Ricard.

quince. Add: **1. b.** Phr. *to get on* (*a person's*) *quince*, to irritate or exasperate. *Austral. slang.*

1941 BAKER *Dict. Austral. Slang* 58 *Get on one's quince*, to annoy or aggravate deeply. **1948** *Sydney Morning Herald* 3 July 9/1 Aw, can it boss! You're gettin' on me quince. **1963** A. E. FARRELL *Vengeance* ii. 19 These bloody trees are getting on me quince! **1974** D. O'GRADY *Deschooling Kevin Carew* 95 In an unguarded moment, he told Bill Moynihan 'This joint is getting on my quince.'

3. *quince cream* (examples), *jam, jelly, marmalade* (earlier and later examples), *pudding*; *quince-coloured, -flavoured* adjs.

1907 Quince-coloured [see *low-sized* s.v. *LOW *a.* 21]. **1723** J. NOTT *Cook's & Confectioner's Dict.* sig. Ee 4 (*heading*) To make quince cream. **1974** J. GRIGSON *Eng. Food* 216 (*heading*) Gooseberry, pear, apple or quince cream. **1950** D. GASCOYNE *Vagrant* 55 And whilom most becomingly strums On his poignantly Quince-flavoured lute! **1936** *Farmhouse Fare* 113 Quince jam... Put the pulp through a sieve, or mash very finely with wooden spoon. **1978** R. V. JONES *Most Secret War* xxxvii. 330 My moment came when I asked him one day whether he had ever made quince jam. **1861** MRS. BEETON *Bk. Househ. Managem.* 795 *Quince jelly*... To every pint of juice allow 1 lb. of loaf sugar. **1971** M. MCCARTHY *Birds Amer.* 35 They stole quinces..and she put up quince jelly. **1636** P. MASSINGER *Great Duke of Florence* IV. ii. sig. H3, This Quince-Marmalade Was of my owne making. **1728** E. SMITH *Compleat Housewife* (ed. 2) 190 (*heading*) To make white Quince Marmalade. **1832** L. M. CHILD *Amer. Frugal Housewife* 118 Quince Marmalade.—To two pounds of quince put three quarters of a pound of nice sugar. **1963** A. L. SIMON *Guide Good Food & Wines* (rev. ed.) IV. 292/1 Its name in Portuguese—*Marmelo*—is the origin of the name *Marmalade*, which was at first applied to no other but *Quince Marmalade*. **1723** J. NOTT *Cook's & Confectioner's Dict.* sig. Ee 6 (*heading*) To make a quince pudding.

Quincke (kvi·ŋkə). *Med.* The name of Heinrich I. *Quincke* (1842–1922), German physician, used in the possessive and with *of* to designate an acute form of urticaria, described by him in 1882 (*Monatshefte für prakt. Dermatol.* I. 129–31).

1894 *Jrnl. Nerv. & Mental Dis.* XXI. 627 The recognition of angioneurotic œdema as a special form of disease is generally credited to Quincke who described it..as acute circumscribed œdema, and it has by some authors been designated as Quincke's disease. **1933** E. A. COCKAYNE *Inherited Abnormalities of Skin* xiv. 370 (*heading*) Angioneurotic oedema. Acute circumscribed oedema. Quincke's oedema. **1934** DORE & FRANKLIN *Dis. of Skin* iv. 46 Giant urticaria sometimes called acute circumscribed œdema of Quincke.., is characterized by the rapid development on the cutaneous or mucous surfaces of large patches of localized œdema, varying in size from a hazel-nut to an ordinary orange. **1974** WARIN & CHAMPION *Urticaria* i. 5 Bannister..protested at the use of the term Quincke's disease.

qui·ncunx, *v. rare.* [f. the sb.] *trans.* To put in quincunx arrangement.

1847 *Simmonds' Colonial Mag.* June 165 Some [say] that the bushes are not near enough together, and that I ought to quincunx them.

Quinean (kwəi·niăn), *a.* [f. the name of the U.S. logician Willard Van Orman *Quine* (b. 1908) + -AN.] Of, pertaining to, or characteristic of Quine or his theories.

1966 S. BEER *Decision & Control* viii. 170 For the record, this is what the three propositions look like in formal Quinean terms. **1972** J. J. KATZ *Semantic Theory* vi. 243 Quinean arguments do not apply to the analytic-synthetic distinction..such as the one developed here. **1978** C. HOOKWAY in Hookway & Pettit *Action & Interpretation* 31 Once we recognise that relativism of this kind is at least an option in translation theory, we can see how to construct a Quinean response to the charge that the argument involves arbitrary discrimination in favour of the theory of nature and against translation theory.

quinella (kwine·lă). orig. *U.S.* Also **quinela, quiniela.** [ad. Amer. Sp. *quiniela* in same sense.] A form of (usu. totalizator) betting in which the punter is required to select the first two place-getters in a race or other contest, not necessarily in the correct order.

1942 BERREY & VAN DEN BARK *Amer. Thes. Slang* § 734/6 *Quinella*, a separate betting pool in which the bettor attempts to pick the first and second horses of a given race. **1944** *Amer. Speech* XIX. 231/2 *Quinella*, Saturday and Sunday off together. The term is used in dog races where the better must pick two winners on a single ticket. **1949** *Rocky Mountain News* 2 July 9/1 A parlay or quiniela is a combination wager coupling the first two animals to finish in one race... Odds on parlay and quiniela are heavy and, when hit, the return is great. **1956** *Sun* (Baltimore) 6 Oct. (B. ed.) 9/1 A petition for quinella wagering at Maryland thoroughbred tracks. **1964** A. WYKES *Gambling* viii. 193 Or there is the 'quiniela', in which the bettor tries to pick the first and second horse of a race. **1967** *Punch* 5 July 20/2 Incomprehensible to the non-punter are notices which attest the management's determination to accept, or not to accept, Castellas, Couplets, Duellas, Eliminators, Jackpots, Plums, Quinellas and Yankees. **1969** *Australian* 7 June 36/1 She picked..first and second in two races—including the final quinella which paid $7.60. **1971** [see *NAP *sb.*⁶ 2 c]. **1974** *Dominion* (Wellington, N.Z.) 11 July 9/9 Two relative outsiders..returned a quinella of $473.60 when they were first and second in the Seatoun Handicap. **1977** *Listener* 30 June 847/3 Didn't put number five in the Quinela.

quingenary (kwindʒī·nări), *sb.* and *a.* [ad. L. *quingēnārius*, f. *quingēnī*, distrib. of *quingentī* five hundred.] **A.** *sb.* A five-hundredth anniversary or the celebration of this; = QUINCENTENARY *sb.*

1926 FOWLER *Mod. Eng. Usage* 72/2 Quingē'nary, sescē'nary, septingē'nary. **1965** E. GOWERS *Fowler's Mod. Eng. Usage* (ed. 2) 83/1 *Quatercentenary* and *quincentenary*..are unlikely to be ousted by *quadringenary* and *quingenary*.

B. *adj.* Of an ancient Roman military unit: consisting of five hundred men.

1969 G. WEBSTER *Roman Imperial Army* iii. 148 There are examples of the six barrack blocks of a quingenary fort at the Welsh fort of Gellygaer. *Ibid.* 149 According to Hyginus, the quingenary unit was composed of 380 infantry and 120 cavalry. **1976** E. N. LUTTWAK *Grand Strategy of Roman Empire* ii. 122 The new formations were clearly useful in bridging the gap between the legions and the quingenary *auxilia*.

quinhydrone. For 'green crystalline substance' read 'brown crystalline substance with a green lustre' and add: Also, any analogous molecular compound formed by a quinone and another aromatic compound. (Earlier and later examples.)

1857 H. WATTS tr. *Gmelin's Hand-bk. Chem.* XI. 164 Quinhydrone. [*Ibid.*, When kinhydrone is heated, it sublimes partly undecomposed, partly converted into yellow kinone.] **1908** *Chem. Abstr.* II. 104 In the reaction of α-hydronaphthoquinone with quinone, the former is oxidized to α-naphthoquinone and the latter reduced to hydroquinone, and these react to give the mixed quinhydrone. **1963** I. L. FINAR *Org. Chem.* (ed. 4) I. xxvii. 670 Quinhydrones are a group of coloured substances formed from quinones and other aromatic compounds. Some are believed to be charge-transfer complexes. *Ibid.* 671 Another type of quinhydrone is the one formed between one molecule of benzoquinone and one molecule of quinol... It is believed that the rings of the two molecules are parallel and held together by hydrogen bonds at both ends.

2. *attrib.* **quinhydrone electrode,** an electrode (usu. of platinum) immersed in a test solution to which quinhydrone has been added, which has a potential dependent upon the pH of the solution and can thus be used to measure the pH potentiometrically.

1921 E. BIILMANN in *Jrnl. Soc. Leather Trades' Chemists* V. 27 In the quinhydrone electrode two hydrions disappear, and at the same time a mol. of quinone is hydrogenated to one of hydroquinone. **1930** G. D. ELSDON in C. A. Mitchell *Recent Advances in Analytical Chem.* I. vii. 250 Certain difficulties are encountered in the determination of the *p*H value of milk. These have been overcome to a considerable extent..by the use of the quinhydrone electrode. **1969** H. ROSSOTTI *Chem. Applications Potentiometry* viii. 92 The quinhydrone electrode can..be used as a probe for hydrogen ions in the acidity range $1 \leqslant pH \leqslant 8$.

qui·nine, *v.* [f. the sb.] *trans.* To dose or treat with quinine.

1927 *Bulletin* (Glasgow) 18 Mar. 5/5 The 'choleric colonel from India'..is apparently more sinned against than sinning. His medical man has 'quinined' him.

quinion (kwi·niǒn), abbrev. of QUINTERNION.

1897 R. GARNETT in *Bibliographica* III. 37 Their [*sc.* Sweynheym and Pannartz's] spacious premises are choked with unbound sheets in quinions. **1927** E. K. RAND in W. M. Lindsay *Palaeographia Latina* v. 53 A quinion may consist of a quaternion ruled four leaves at a time plus an extra leaf. **1959** P. H. BLAIR in *Moore Bede* 11/2 It contains thirteen gatherings of which II, IV, V and VIII–XII inclusive are regular quinions, that is, each of five bifolia making ten leaves after folding.

quinnat. For the specific epithet of the Latin name substitute *tschawytscha*; also *attrib.* (Later examples.)

1874 J. S. HITTELL *Resources Calif.* 407 The most important fish of California is the quinnat salmon. **1881** [see *king salmon* s.v. *KING *sb.* 13 a]. **1907** T. W. LAMBERT *Fishing in Brit. Columbia* 73 They are the king salmon or quinnat, a large fish running up to over 80 lb. **1925** J. T. JENKINS *Fishes Brit. Isles* 216 The Chinook, Quinnat or King Salmon.., the most valuable species [of Pacific salmon], attaining a length of 4 to 5 feet. **1948** *Pacific Discovery* July 26/2 When referring to 'salmon' we will mean the true salmon (also known as quinnat, chinook or king) which invariably dies after spawning. **1962** L. WEDLICK *Fishing in Austral.* III. 87 It is unfortunate that the king or chinook salmon—known as quinnat salmon in Australia—has never been successfully acclimatized in our streams, for this fish is the largest of all the Pacific salmon.

quino, var. KENO in Dict. and Suppl.

quinoid (kwi·noid), *a.* and *sb. Chem.* [f. QUIN(ONE + -OID.] **A.** *adj.* = *QUINONOID *a.* **B.** *sb.* A quinonoid compound.

1900 E. F. SMITH tr. *V. von Richter's Org. Chem.* (ed. 3) II. 364 The colored alkali salts are quinoid derivatives of phenolphthaleïn. **1907** *Chem. Abstr.* I. 300 (*heading*) Oxidation of benzidine. (VIII Communication on quinoids.) **1908** *Ibid.* II. 827 The quinoid theory of colour. **1938** G. H. RICHTER *Textbk. Org. Chem.* xxx. 627 The *ortho* and *para* quinoid structures show strong chromophoric properties. **1949** ENGLISH & CASSIDY *Princ. Org. Chem.* xx. 396 It is thought that some metabolic processes involve a reduction-oxidation system involving quinoid and hydroquinoid molecules. **1961** B. J. STOKES *Org. Chem.* xxiv. 437 Addition of alkali to phenolphthalein causes a change in structure and a molecule containing a quinoid ring is made. **1975** LEWIS & PETERS *Facts & Theories Aromaticity* v. 76 The quinones and quinoids generally are usually thought to be non-aromatic yet they apparently contain the magic 6π-electrons in a ring, an electron arrangement which is often regarded as characteristic of aromaticity.

Hence **quinoi·dal** *a.*

1907 *Chem. Abstr.* I. 302 The presence of methylene destroys the ability of the two phenyl groups to assume the quinoidal state. **1975** *Nature* 20 Feb. 625/1 Its infrared spectrum in $CHCl_3$ further substantiates a quinoidal structure, showing a strong carbonyl absorption at 1,654 cm^{-1} and an olefinic absorption at 1,584 cm^{-1}.

quinol. (Earlier and later examples.)

1879 *Jrnl. Chem. Soc.* XXXVI. 464 (*heading*) Derivatives of quinol (hydroquinone). **1964** [see *CATECHOL]. **1976** *Nature* 17 June 621/3 The central biological roles of quinones, quinols and chromanols had become as acceptable as they were surprising.

quinonoid (kwi·nonoid), *a. Chem.* [f. QUINON(E + -OID.] Being, resembling, or characteristic of a quinone; being or exhibiting a molecular structure typified by that of quinone, viz. a doubly unsaturated ring with double bonds to two substituents (usu. in *para* positions).

1878 *Chem. News* 5 July 9/1 (*heading*) Quinonoid body found in a species of agaric. **1892** *Proc. Chem. Soc.* VIII. 101 It was maintained that in the case of azo-dyes, the rosanilines, methylene-blue, &c., colour was conditioned by a quinonoid structure. **1908** *Jrnl. Chem. Soc.* XCIV. I. 806 The meaning of the term quinonoid must be widened to include substances..in which the quinonoid oxygen atom is displaced by a bivalent imine or hydrocarbon group. **1951** I. L. FINAR *Org. Chem.* I. xxvii. 545 The yellow colour of *p*-benzoquinone is due to the presence of the quinonoid structure =⟨=⟩=. **1956** *Nature* 14 Jan. 79/2 The quinonoid product of the catecholase reaction.. is an active oxidase in the cresolase reaction. **1974** *Ibid.* 20 Dec. 710/2 The sclerotisation and tanning of insect cuticles is generally thought to result from a crosslinking of the cuticular proteins by quinonoid derivatives of tyrosine.

quinoxaline (kwinǫ·ksālīn). *Chem.* [ad. G. *chinoxalin* (O. Hinsberg 1884, in *Ber. d. Deut. Chem. Ges.* XVII. 319), f. *chin-olin* QUINOLINE + *-oxal* (f. *glyoxal* GLYOXAL) + *-in* -INE⁵. So named on account of its structural similarity to quinoline and its preparation from glyoxal.] A weakly basic colourless crystalline solid, $C_8H_6N_2$, which was first prepared by reaction of glyoxal and *o*-phenylenediamine, and has a bicyclic structure formed from fused benzene and pyrazine rings; any substituted derivative of this compound.

1884 *Jrnl. Chem. Soc.* XLVI. 1052 He [*sc.* Hinsberg].. proposes to call this series of compounds quinoxalines. The formula of quinoxaline (the lowest homologue) is undoubtedly $C_6H_4<^{N:CH}_{N:CH}>$. **1887** [see *AZINE]. **1926** H. G. RULE tr. *J. Schmidt's Text-bk. Org. Chem.* 700 Quinoxalines..are weakly basic compounds, which may be reduced to hydro-quinoxalines, but are stable towards oxidising agents. **1951** I. L. FINAR *Org. Chem.* x. 189 It [*sc.* glyoxal]..combines with *o*-phenylenediamines to form quinoxalines..; *e.g.*, with *o*-phenylenediamine it forms quinoxaline itself. **1974** *Nature* 20 Dec. 654/1 The quinoxaline chromophores of echinomycin are similar in size to the quinoline chromophore of chloroquine, which is known to bind to DNA by intercalation.

quinquagint (kwi·nkwădʒint). *nonce-wd.* [ad. L. *quinquāgintā* fifty.] A set of fifty persons or things.

1843 THACKERAY *Irish Sk.-Bk.* II. xiv. 264 There are 220 voters, it appears;..but as parties are pretty equally balanced, the votes of the quinquagint..carry an immense weight.

quinquennial, *a.* and *sb.* Add: **A.** *adj.* **1. b.** (Earlier example.)

1847 J. S. MILL *Let.* 19 Nov. in *Wks.* (1963) XIII. 725 The number of deaths..is *less* in each quinquennial period.

2. (Later examples.)

1903 *Westm. Gaz.* 14 Jan. 5/2 The Board of the London Hospital..has been impelled to issue its quinquennial appeal two or three weeks in advance of the appointed time. **1955** *Times* 3 May 15/2 A quinquennial valuation of the 'Royal' life and annuity business was made at December 31.

B. *sb.* **3.** A fifth anniversary.

1903 *Westm. Gaz.* 14 Jan. 5/2 The hospital only begs widely every five years, and this year is our quinquennial.

quinquennially, *adv.* (Later examples.)

1972 *Nature* 4 Feb. 246/3 Is this fraction to be reviewed annually or quinquennially, and, if so, by whom? **1979** *Daily Tel.* 3 Jan. 2/1 There is no excuse for the use of phrases like reversionary bonus compounded quinquennially, when what is meant is a five-yearly pay-out with interest added.

quinta. Add to def.: Also, a country estate; in Portugal, a wine-growing estate; in S. America, a house or estate on the outskirts of a town. Also *attrib.* (Earlier and further examples.)

1754 FIELDING *Let.* Aug.–Sept. in A. Dobson *At Prior Park* (1912) 143 He hath a little Kintor..or Villa at a Place called Jonkera. *a* **1770** A. HERVEY *Jrnl.* an. 1748 (1953) 75, I used, too, to go out to my friend Mr. Mayne and Barn's quinta, where I was very much at ease. **1818** C. A. RODNEY *Let.* in *Amer. State Papers: Foreign Relations* (1834) IV. 219 The small farms, or quintas, in the neighborhood of cities, are in fine order. Those around Buenos Ayres..are, by irrigation, in the highest state of culture. **1870** *Weekly Standard* (Buenos Aires) 7 Sept. 2/5 The people in the quintas and suburbs were all flocking into Montevideo. **1878** E. CLARK *Visit S. Amer.* x. 128 The elegant quintas and country houses that surround the city. **1931** *Discovery* Oct. 310/2 The dipleidoscope and the gravity escapement are both due to a gifted inventor who worked at my Quinta [in Madeira]. **1960** *Spectator* 15 Jan. 91/3 'Noval' is the name of the *quinta*, or estate, from which the port comes. **1969** J. MANDER *Static Soc.* v. 132 Bolivar's *quinta*, a modest eighteenth-century lodge on the slopes overlooking the city, may still be inspected. **1976** F. GREENLAND *Misericordia Drop* I. i. 14 The property..belonged to..the venerable hospital that employed him... Periodic inspection of this *quinta* was one..of Dr Sá's duties. **1976** *Times* 6 Nov. 13/2 Quinta wines—ports from one particular vineyard.

quintal, kintal, kentle. a. (Further eastern N. Amer. and later examples.)

1645 in *Deeds Suffolk Co., Mass.* (1880) I. 65 One thousand Kintall of dry Cod fish. **1712** N. TREVANION in D. W. Prowse *Hist. Newfoundland* (1895) x. 272/2 And planters very backward in paying, he got only one hundred quintals of fish this season. **1897** KIPLING *Captains Courageous* vii. 144 Then pray back my son to me! Pray back a nine-thousand-dollar boat an' a thousand quintal of fish. **1912** N. DUNCAN *Best of Bad Job* xxv. 169 A quintal here an' a quintal there. **1918** A. HUXLEY *Let.* 12 Aug. (1969) 160 He drains..twelve hogsheads of rich milk, to say nothing of the nineteen Imperial Kilderkins of cream and the thirty two quintals of sugar. **1964** *Newfoundland Q.* Spring 27/1 A prior pre-quintal charge is reserved from the entire voyage's value for this labour called 'fish-making'. **1967** *Times* 23 Nov. 5/7 An agreement for the sale of 200 tons of Sudan cotton c.i.f. Bombay, at a price of Rs. 393.68 per quintal. **1974** D. AVERY *Not on Queen Victoria's Birthday* vi. 102 By February 1815 the price of imported south American copper had risen to 20 dollars a *quintal* (£8 per 100 lb).

quinte·ssenced, *ppl. a. rare.* [f. QUINTESSENCE *v.* + -ED¹.] Reduced to its quintessence; quintessential.

1898 G. E. B. SAINTSBURY *Short Hist. Eng. Lit.* VII. vii. 467 Its charms..consist in extreme strangeness, in quintessenced or preternatural art.

quintessential, *a.* Add: **B.** *sb.* The most essential part of a thing; a quintessential element.

1899 'MARK TWAIN' in *Harper's Mag.* Sept. 529/1 These are the very quintessentials of good citizenship. **1916** J. G. HUNEKER *Ivory, Apes, & Peacocks* 37 He, too, dreamed of quintessentials, of the sheer power of golden vocables and the secret alchemy of art.

quintessentially. (Later examples.)

1936 *Delineator* CXXIX. 49/2 All of those early musicians in New Orleans were quintessentially swing players. **1958** [see *BALDING *a.*]. **1971** *Country Life* 24 June 1584/3 Montgeoffroy is everything that is quintessentially French. **1978** *Language* LIV. 275 That master negotiator and persuader, the quintessentially pragmatic Odysseus.

quintile, *a.* and *sb.*¹ Restrict *Astrol.* to sense in Dict. and add: **2.** *Statistics.* Any of the four values of a variate which divide a frequency distribution into five groups, each containing one fifth of the total population; also, any of the five groups so produced.

1951 *Brit. Jrnl. Nutrition* V. 199 For the purposes of classification of the subjects into categories of fatness, we have used the twentieth, fortieth, sixtieth and eightieth percentile. These limit values are sometimes called 'quintiles'. **1973** *Jrnl. Genetic Psychol.* CXXIII. 79 Each class's ranked students were divided into quintiles: high, medium-high, middle, medium-low, and low status. **1974** *Nature* 22 Nov. 294/2 These are quintiles for temperature and terciles for rainfall. **1976** *Lancet* 6 Nov. 979/2 Apart from smoking, where no such division into quintiles is practicable, the five measures used are systolic and diastolic blood-pressure, overweight, [etc.].

‖ **quinton** (kæ̃ntoṅ). [Fr.] A musical instrument of the viol or violin families, having five strings (see also quots. 1941, 1954).

[**1870** C. ENGEL *Descr. Catal. Mus. Instr. in S. Kensington Mus.* 77 Five-stringed viol. Called by the French *Quinton*.] **1889** [see *PARDESSUS 2]. **1916** STANFORD & FORSYTH *Hist. Mus.* ix. 195 True viols have no fewer than six strings apiece... But the makers are beginning to see the necessity of reducing the number... They are just introducing a modified type of instrument with five strings. They call these the *quintons*. **1941** [see *PARDESSUS 2]. **1954** *Grove's Dict. Mus.* (ed. 5) VI. 1037/1 The rather ugly word quinton seems to have originated as a 19th-century dealers' name to describe a curious hybrid sort of viol-violin... The instruments appear to belong to the late 18th century... The name drifted into reference books where it was misapplied to the perfectly normal treble and *par-dessus* French viols of the mid-16th century, which often have only five strings. **1961** T. DART in A. Baines *Mus. Instr. through Ages* 189 During the eighteenth century certain hybrids between the two families of viols and violins made a brief appearance on the musical scene—for instance, the quinton, the baryton, and the arpeggione—but few musicians regretted their equally abrupt departure. **1976** *Early Music* July 361/2 The quinton is built basically like a violin, with arched back, shallow ribs and pointed bouts, but with sloping viol shoulders.

quintuple, *sb.* (Later example.)

1975 N. CHOMSKY *Logical Struct. Linguistic Theory* ix. 327 A set of ordered quintuples $\{(Z, K, Z^1, Pr^{(1)}, Pr^{(2)})\}$.

quintuplicate, *sb.* Add: **a.** Also, *in quintuplicate*.

1941 F. SCOTT FITZGERALD *Last Tycoon* iii. 41 Miss Doolan's notes would be typed in quintuplicate. **1968** H. EDWARDS *Thirty Years Spiritual Healer* v. 51 In Holland, no one can be admitted to a healing meeting unless he becomes a member of the society, and even then records in quintuplicate have to be made for each person attending. **1978** B. NORMAN *To nick a Good Body* vii. 55 Statements..typed out in quintuplicate.

quintu·pling, *vbl. sb.* [f. QUINTUPL(E *v.* + -ING¹.] Fivefold increase, multiplication by five.

1975 *N.Y. Times* 25 Sept. 65/7 The quintupling of oil prices in the last two years, most economists agree, has accelerated world inflation and intensified the recent slump in world business. **1976** *Times Lit. Suppl.* 20 Feb. 193/3 The burden on the British balance of payments of a quintupling of the price of oil.

‖ **quintus.** *Mus.* [a. L. *quintus* fifth.] (See quot. 1883.)

1883 GROVE *Dict. Mus.* III. 61/1 *Quintus*.., the Fifth Part in a composition for five Voices: called also Pars quinta and Quincuplum. **1954** *Ibid.* (ed. 5) VI. 570/1 When a *quintus* is needed half of it is written on the left-hand page below the *tenor* and the remainder (*reliquium*) below the *bassus*, on the right-hand page. **1977** *Early Music* July 419/3 Those intending to sing through the motet volume should note that the quintus is not in the same vocal range throughout and six voices are needed.

quinze. Add: *Comb.* Also, *quinze table*.

1782 J. HARE *Let.* 11 Feb. in *15th Rep. R. Comm. Hist. Manuscripts* App. VI. 576 in *Parl. Papers 1897* (C. 8551) LI. I. 1 A deep Quinze Table has taken away from Richard and Charles almost the whole profits of the Bank. **1803** *Lett. Miss Riversdale* II. 190 'I never before knew Mrs. Blandford guilty of affectation,' said Lord Lessingham, from the quinz-table.

quip, *v.* Delete 'Now *rare*' and add: **1. b.** With speech as direct object: to say or reply as a quip.

1950 *New Yorker* 25 Mar. 26/3 'Looks like somebody lost their head!' quipped Detective Garnet P. Quail. **1965** D. LODGE *Brit. Mus. is falling Down* viii. 132 'Someone taking my name in vain?'.. 'In bane,' Adam quipped, and laughed immoderately. **1974** *Times* 11 Oct. 10/1 'I became a tremendous bargain. I went from a million to nothing,' she quipped to reporters. **1978** *Woman's Own* 16 Sept. 12/1 My daughter was rather amused and quipped: 'Most parents have problem teenagers but we have a problem mother.'

2. (Later examples.) Also, const. *with*.

1908 *Smart Set* June 50 Audrey in her blithesome way Would quip and jest with roguish glee. **1942** Z. N. HURSTON *Dust Tracks on Road* xii. 225 The educated Negro..is fighting entirely out of his class when he tries to quip with the underprivileged.

quipper. (Later examples.)

1951 O. NASH *Family Reunion* 36 She'll nogg his eggs and she'll toast his kippers, And disparage the quips of the current quippers. **1960** *Guardian* 19 Nov. 3/6 His intervention has at least provided the quippers with a not very good quip.

quippery (kwi·pəri). *rare.* [f. QUIP *sb.* or *v.* + -ERY.] The uttering or bandying of quips; quips collectively.

1960 *Guardian* 22 July 10/6 This is campaign quippery, and we shall have a bellyful of it before the winter.

quippish, *a.* (In Dict. s.v. QUIP *sb.*) Add: (Example.) Hence **qui·ppishly** *adv.*, **qui·ppishness.**

a **1834** S. T. COLERIDGE in *N. & Q.* (1888) 7th Ser. VI. 501/2, I prefer Fuller's [version] as more quippish and adagy. **1909** A. Bennett *Literary Taste* vi. 31 Charles Lamb's essay on *Dream Children*..enlivened by a certain quippishness concerning the children. **1976** *New Scientist* 22 July 190/3 Another speaker quippishly suggested that we should treat them [*sc.* 'core' journals] like apples.

quipster. (In Dict. s.v. Quip *sb.*) (Later examples.)

1962 *Punch* 15 Aug. 224/2 The one who provides the old Russian sayings is his nearest equivalent to [Bob] Hope's tarmac quipster. **1976** *National Observer* (U.S.) 14 Aug. 16/2 He doesn't mind being called Gooey Lombardo or Guy Lumbago; he smiles when quipsters dub him the Pied Piper of the geriatric set. **1977** *Time* 6 June 39/2 A quipster with no audience for his one-liners?

quire, *sb.*[1] Add: **3.** *quire signature* [Signature *sb.* 6a]; *quire-folded* adj.; **quire-wise** *adv.* (examples).

1882 J. Southward *Pract. Printing* xiii. 117 Folio sheets are sometimes required to be..folded within each other, or *quirewise.* **1888** C. T. Jacobi *Printers' Vocab.* 108 *Quire folded*.., folded in quires—not sent in 'flat'. *Ibid.* 109 *Quirewise*, jobs of single leaves printed on both sides of the paper. **1922** Joyce *Ulysses* 120 The nethermost deck of the first machine jogged forward its flyboard with sllt [*sic*] the first batch of quirefolded papers. **1957** N. R. Ker *Catal. MSS. containing Anglo-Saxon* p. xl (*heading*) Quire-Signatures and Leaf-Numbers. **1978** *Anglo-Saxon England* VII. 232 It may have its own series of quire signatures.

Quirinal (kwi·rināl). [ad. It. *Quirinale* (also used), f. L. *collis Quirīnālis*.] The name of the royal (now presidential) palace on the Quirinal hill in Rome, and hence used to designate the Italian monarchy or government, *esp.* as distinct from the Vatican. Also *attrib.*

1851 W. E. Gladstone tr. *Farini's Roman State* II. i. 3 The Civic Guards and the commonalty gave the wonted expression of their thanks in the Piazza of the Quirinal. **1881** E. W. Hamilton *Diary* 7 Dec. (1972) I. 195 Errington..whom suspicious people regard as a probable diplomatic agent at the Quirinal, seems..to be going rather too fast ahead. **1905** J. Webster *Wheat Princess* vii. 78 Being interested in the domestic arrangements of kings, she was insistent that they visit the Quirinal. **1917** N. Douglas *South Wind* xxxiv. 408 A feeling of joyous elation at the prospect..of a battle between the Vatican and the Quirinal. **1922** *Contemp. Rev.* Nov. 583 The complete accord which exists in practice between the Vatican and the Quirinal. **1927** E. M. Forster *Aspects of Novel* viii. 193 He..sets him out to explore [Roman] society..café, studio, Vatican and Quirinal purlieus are all reached. **1949** N. Mitford *Love in Cold Climate* i. x. 107 Friendship with royal personages only ever began for her when their days of glory were finished. Tsarkoe-Selo, Schönbrunn, the Quirinal,..and the island of Corfu had never known her, unless among an enormous crowd in the state apartments. **1979** N. Slater *Falcon* v. 91 He looked more like a country squire than Her Majesty's Ambassador to the Quirinale.

quiring (kwəiᵊ·riŋ), *vbl. sb.* [f. Quire *v.*[1] + -ing[1].] **a.** A series of signatures indicating the order of quires. **b.** The arrangement of a series of quires.

1922 *J. & J. Leighton's Catal. Old & Interesting Bks.* N.S. iii. 209 Without printed quiring, &c., but original MS. signatures remain. **1957** N. R. Ker *Catal. MSS. containing Anglo-Saxon* p. xxv, A book in which the sheets are arranged like this shows two hair sides where one quire ends and the next begins... The collation of such books is simple and the original quiring can be made out even if the leaves have been mounted separately. **1968** G. Pollard in *Bodl. Libr. Rec.* VIII. 82 Having thus established the arrangement of the first twenty-eight leaves, we must now consider the quiring at the opposite end of the book. **1975** N. Barker in R. W. Hunt et al. *Studies in Bk. Trade in Honour of G. Pollard* 11 The quiring may have been put in and later trimmed away.

quiring: see Choiring *vbl. sb.* and *ppl. a.*

quirk, *sb.*[1] Add: **4. b.** A peculiar feature or result (*of* an event); a peculiarity, an anomaly, a freak.

1961 *Yale Rev.* LI. 190 It is one of the ironic quirks of history that the viability and usefulness of nationalism and the territorial state are rapidly dissipating at precisely the time that the nation-state attained its highest number. **1973** A. H. Sommerstein *Sound Pattern Anc. Gr.* ii. 74 The other two rules..are mere quirks, survivals that play no active role in the system of the language, but merely go on existing. **1976** *Scotsman* 20 Nov. (Weekend Suppl.), In the San Blas Islands, off the coast of Panama, they found that through a quirk of history they had come a step closer to home. **1976** *Star* (Sheffield) 29 Nov. 12/7 Perhaps..it was something of an unfortunate quirk of the draw that they had to meet in the first round of the Roebuck Cup.

5. Delete † '*Obs. rare*—[1]' and add later example.

1928 Galsworthy *Swan Song* ii. x. 188 That indefinable look of a damned soul..awakened within Soames..the queerest little quirk of sympathy.

7. e. (Earlier and further examples.) Also *attrib.* or as *adj.*

1799 A. Young *View Agric. Lincoln* 29 Window shutters quirk, ogee and astragal with ½ and 2 heights and 4 panels, at 12 d. **1842** Gwilt *Encycl. Archit.* § 2367 A two-panel door, square on one side, with quirk ovolo and bead upon the other. **1882** Nodal & Milner *Gloss. Lancs. Dial.* 220 *Querk, sb.*, a moulding in joinery. **1966** J. Fleming et al. *Penguin Dict. Archit.* 181/2 *Quirk*, a sharp v-shaped incision in a moulding and between mouldings.

8. quirk-moulding (example); hence *quirk-moulded* ppl. adj.

1833 Loudon *Encycl. Archit.* 1129/2 *Quirk moulding*, a quirk in a moulding signifies a sharp turn. **1842** Gwilt *Encycl. Archit.* § 2368 Shutters... Add ·016 to the rate for every extra panel, and ·012 for any extra height, and ·008 if they are quirk moulded.

† **quirk** (kwɜ̄ɪk), *sb.*[2] *R.A.F. slang. Obs.* [Perh. f. prec.: cf. *erk.] **a.** An inexperienced airman.

1916 *Daily Chron.* 13 Oct. 4/5 The quirk becomes used to the handling of the craft..until..the instructor allows him to fly the machine himself. **1917** *Sunday Times* 20 May 8/4 'Quirks', it may be explained, are young enemy aviators in an embryonic stage. **1918** E. C. Middleton *Glorious Exploits Air* ii. 33 Once he has his air-legs there is little the 'hun' or 'quirk'—Service terms for beginners—does not feel himself capable of tackling. **1919** *Glasgow Herald* 19 Dec. 14/2 The..airman..uses the word 'quirk' in two senses, first to denote the learner's aeroplane, the clanging, clattering 'rumpty' of his youth, or, secondly to denote the learner himself. **1928** C. F. S. Gamble *Story N. Sea Air Station* ix. 133 The pilot, a very harmless, innocent 'quirk', hardly fledged, straight from Chingford. **1931** [see *kiwi 3].

b. (See quot. 1925.)

1917 'Contact' *Airman's Outings* 128 The ferry-pilot who had brought me left for Rafborough almost immediately on a much-flown 'quirk'. **1917** *Let.* Apr. in A. J. L. Scott *60 Squad* (1920) iii. 49 One place was pointed out to us where there was an old 'quirk'. [*Note*] A pet name used for artillery machines of the B.E. type. **1919** [see prec. sense]. **1925** Fraser & Gibbons *Soldier & Sailor Words* 234 *Quirk*,.. a name for a 'B.E.' type of aeroplane; very stable, but very slow. Also any freak type, or unusually designed aeroplane.

quirk, *sb.*[3] var. Quirt *sb.* in Dict. and Suppl.

1870 De. B. R. Keim *Sheridan's Troopers* xx. 139 While belaboring the poor brute with the heavy end of a quirk. **1929** *Amer. Speech* V. 62 When the 'rider' is saddled' on the 'pony', he may hold in one hand a 'quirk' ('quirt') or 'lasher', a short whip, having a small lead-filled handle and rawhide lashes two feet or more long.

quirk, *v.*[1] Add: **3. a.** (Further examples.)

1948 G. H. Johnston *Death takes Small Bites* i. 8 Her mouth quirked with tiny crinkles of amusement. **1958** S. Ellin *Eighth Circle* ii. xx. 159 'I really am better. Just a little weak in the knees, that's all.' Her lips quirked in a pale smile. 'You must think I'm pretty much of a mess, don't you?' **1975** L. Gillen *Return to Deepwater* ii. 28 His wide mouth quirked briefly into an answering smile.

b. *trans.* To move (something) jerkily.

1978 J. Krantz *Scruples* viii. 222 He quirked one eyebrow at Billy.

quirked, *ppl. a.* Add: **2.** Of the mouth, eyebrow, etc.: set in an attitude by quirking. Also with *down.*

1951 H. Giles *Harbin's Ridge* iv. 28 Lucibel's mouth was quirked down at the corners. **1955** W. Gaddis *Recognitions* ii. vii. 619 Her eyes searched his face, to find no betrayal but a quirked eyebrow which started to rise, and did not.

quirkily (kwɜ̄·ɹkili), *adv.* [f. Quirky *a.* + -ly[2].] In a manner which displays a randomness or quaintness of choice or performance.

1957 *New Yorker* 2 Nov. 166/3 All the way from the primarily non-objective..to the quirkily archaic. **1965** *Times Lit. Suppl.* 25 Nov. 1068/3 In a much more quirkily disorganized way, a poem like John Berryman's *Homage to Mistress Bradstreet* (1959) makes a similar effort of disenchanted excavation. **1969** *Daily Tel.* (Colour Suppl.) 1 Aug. 8/3 Miss Norway likes to read poetry. Miss Ireland likes the Moderns. Miss Sweden, quirkily, likes Science Fiction. **1975** J. Butcher *Copy-Editing* xiii. 221 Scientists and mathematicians often use terms which have not yet become absorbed into general scientific language and may be quirkily hyphenated and capitalized.

quirkiness. (Later examples.)

1971 *Record* (Oxford Univ. Press) Dec. 1/2 He enjoyed anecdotes of human quirkiness and folly. **1977** *Times Lit. Suppl.* 15 July 846/1 It is an example of the 'quirkiness' which makes Powell such a difficult colleague.

quirking, *ppl. a.*[2] (Later example.)

1946 J. W. Day *Harvest Adventure* vii. 94 Mallard and querking teal.

quirkish, *a.* Add: **2.** Eccentric, idiosyncratic; erratic, random; = *quirky *a.* 1 b.

1969 A. Stevenson *Reversals* 23 The wall's approach, the quirkish ambivalence of photographs, today in daylight, were pieces of balance. **1972** *Daily Tel.* 16 Nov. 14/7 Is this because their leader..succumbed less frequently to his quirkish approach to notes by deviously subtle routes that so often misfire? **1975** *Ibid.* 24 June 11 Quirkish and baffling to the last, *Churchill's People* (BBC 1) ended last night with a protracted scene showing five men..being hanged after failing to assassinate the Cabinet. **1977** *Times* 31 Oct. 5/4 The selection of Caribbean territories visited has been a trifle quirkish. **1978** *Gramophone* Feb. 1439/2 There are other small details of phrasing in this performance more quirkish than gracious, though certainly the music flows with a will.

Hence **qui·rkishly** *adv.*

1963 *Times* 15 Jan. 11/4 Two of L. S. Lowry's quirkishly lively figure-subjects catch the eye.

quirky, *a.* Add: **1. b.** Characterized by certain unexpected and often unspecified traits; idiosyncratic; peculiar. Also as *sb.*, an eccentric or peculiar person.

1960 *Guardian* 8 July 4/2 There is..quirky colloquialism, idiomatic punning, play with unusual words. **1966** *New Statesman* 8 July 62/3 It was perhaps unduly testing to place two substantial new works in the same programme; it was certainly quirky to preface them with Poulenc's Organ Concerto. **1972** *Times Lit. Suppl.* 5 May 520/2 The best of it is individual, quirky, and moving. **1975** *Publishers Weekly* 21 July 62/1 Capricorn of Scotland Yard..investigates Smoky's suspect connections. He encounters quirkies aplenty. **1976** *National Observer* (U.S.) 31 July 6/4 (Advt.), We're fascinated by strange, quirky questions that can lead us into corners of reality most people never even think about. **1978** *Amer. Poetry Rev.* July/Aug. 36/3 Schwartz was also a fine (if uneven) writer of fiction whose best prose is characterized by a cynical urban realism that foreshadows Bellow's quirky, densely textured work.

quirl, *sb.* and *v.*: see *querl *sb.* and *v.*

quirley (kwɜ̄·ɹli). *U.S.* and *Austral. slang.* Also **quirly.** [f. *quirl*, var. Querl *v.* in Dict. and Suppl. + -y[6].] A (usu. hand-rolled) cigarette.

1932 'Spindrift' *Yankee Slang* 30 *Quirly, quirley*,.. cigarette. **1940** *Amer. Speech* XV. 335/2 A cigarette is a.. *lung-duster*, or a *quirley* (or *spill-quirley*). (*Note*) Dr. R. D. Scott reports the use of *quirley*..among the cowpunchers of Arizona and New Mexico. **1945** R. F. Adams *Western Words* 122/1 *Quirly*, the cowboy's name for his cigarette. **1953** Baker *Austral. Speaks* iv. 106 To return to the field of popular Australianisms, here are some more items worthy of record..*quirley*, a cigarette; [etc.]. **1955** W. Foster-Harris *Look of Old West* iv. 113 The cowboy's hand-built smoke was, as he called it, a quirly.

quirt, *sb.* Substitute for etym.: [ad. Mexican Sp. *cuarta* whip.] Add earlier and later examples.

1845 *Amer. Rev.* Feb. 127/2 The 'quirt', with its long heavy lash of knotted raw-hide. **1910** C. E. Mulford *Hopalong Cassidy* v. 61 Hopalong cut him short by hitting him across the face with his quirt. **1934** *Amer. Ballads & Folk Songs* 377 My quirt in my hand, my slicker on my saddle. **1955** W. Foster-Harris *Look of Old West* vii. 218 The cowboy's quirt was ordinarily about 2 or 3 feet long, of plaited leather, though sometimes of stitched buckskin or woven horsehair. **1972** K. Bonfiglioli *Don't point that Thing at Me* xiii. 101 She..flicked the thong of her quirt under the stallion's belly and was away. **1980** *Daily Tel.* 18 July 1/3 Police in South Africa have unveiled their latest riot control weapon, which they call a quirt, a whip made of flexible plastic about three to four feet long.

quirt, *v.*[2] Add: (Further examples.) Hence **qui·rting** *vbl. sb.*

1910 C. E. Mulford *Hopalong Cassidy* vii. 76 He says you did—an' somebody quirted him. **1918** W. M. Raine in *Popular Mag.* 20 June 23/1 Quirt him on the shoulders and rake him down the hip. **1932** H. W. Bentley *Dict. Spanish Terms in Eng.* 131 From the noun has come the verb to *quirt* and the Anglicized *quirting* used in such a phrase as 'He gave the animal a sound quirting'. **1973** R. D. Symons *Where Wagon Led.* i. iv. 49 So I quirted that pony a couple of times.

quis (kwis, kwiz), *pron. School slang.* [L. interrog. pron., = who.] 'Who (wants this)?', asked by the possessor of a specified object which he no longer requires, to a group of his fellows.

The first person to reply 'ego' (*ego 2) receives the object.

1913 [see *ego 2]. **1916** E. F. Benson *David Blaize* vi. 111 '*Quis* for a catapult?' he said heroically, and a chorus of 'Ego' answered him. **1927** W. E. Collinson *Contemp. Eng.* 22 While at the Prep. I fell into the way of using pater for *father* and came to know the schoolboy question quis for *who wants?* with the answer ego. **1945** E. Waugh *Brideshead Revisited* ii. v. 281 Who wants it? Quis? Would you like it, Cara? No, of course you would not. Cordelia? **1959** [see *ego 2]. *a* **1966** 'M. na Gopaleen' *Best of Myles* (1968) 217 'Quis?' 'Ego.' 'See, man, you meant him.'

quisby, *a.* Add: Also **quizby.** (Earlier and later examples.)

1807 H. Tufts *Narrative* iii. iv. 316 *Quisby cove*, a mean fellow. **1846** *Swell's Night Guide* 129/1 *Quizby*, bad. **1848** *Ladies' Repository* (U.S.) Oct. 316/2 *Quisby*, ragged; dirty; suspicious. **1897** A. St. J. Adcock *East End Idylls* iv. 69 'Ow's the missus?.. An' the kid? Bin quisby, ain't 'e?

Quisling (kwi·zliŋ). Also with small initial. [The name of Major Vidkun *Quisling* (1887–1945), Norwegian officer and diplomatist, who collaborated with the Germans during their occupation of Norway from 1940 to 1945.] **1.** A traitor to one's country, a collaborationist, esp. during the war of 1939–45. Also *transf.* and *fig.*

1940 *Times* 15 Apr. 5/3 Comment in the Press urges that there should be unremitting vigilance also against possible 'Quislings' inside the country [*sc.* Sweden]. **1940** H. Nicolson *Diary* 10 May (1967) II. 81 He is hurrying back to Holland to fight. He says..they will fight to the last man, but that they are worried about their Quislings. **1941** *Sun* (Baltimore) 7 Mar. 1/6 No report of the size of the attacking fleet..was given, but small craft actually allowed British and Norwegian troops to take 215 Germans and ten 'Quislings' as prisoners. **1943** C. S. Lewis *Christian Behaviour* i. 9 The results of bad morality ..press on us every day: war and poverty and graft and quislings and shoddy work. **1946** *Downside Rev.* 51 In our striving after this way of love, we are confronted by a threefold enemy, the devil, the world, both external to us, and the quisling within us, called 'Self', the most dangerous of all the foes. **1950** *N.Y. Times* 1 July 16/5 The attempts that the Communist-dominated governments are making to create 'national' Catholic Churches through the appointment of religious 'Quislings'. **1958** P. Kemp *No Colours or Crest* vii. 125 Isa Toska, a notorious Albanian quisling..was a brigand who with Italian help had equipped a strong band of mercenaries. **1961** B. Fergusson *Watery Maze* iii. 78 They brought back 225 prisoners (including a dozen quislings), 314 Norwegian volunteers, [etc.]. **1966** 'H. MacDiarmid' *Company I've Kept* xiii. 260 A Scot far more typical in his attitude than the English care to recognise, or Anglo-Scottish quislings dare admit. **1974** *Globe & Mail* (Toronto) 22 Apr. 3/2 But a spokesman..denounced the appointment, dismissing Mr. Marouf as a 'quisling' who did not represent the Kurdish liberation movement. **1976** *Economist* 16 Oct. 74/2 But for years the government has used them [*sc.* moderate leaders of South African blacks] only to put on a front of 'consultation', while paying scant regard to their views. It is this which has left them feeling like quislings whose only purpose is to give the system a look of respectability.

2. a. *Comb.*, as *Quisling-hearted*, *-minded* adjs.

1946 P. Bottome *Lifeline* xxi. 176 The boastful triumph of the quisling-hearted. **1940** *Times* 4 Oct. 9/6 Its organizers had assembled..sympathizers and other potentially Quisling-minded adults from neutral countries.

b. *attrib.* passing into *adj.*

1941 *Times* 11 Mar. 4/7 The quisling newspapers not only endorse this but accuse the British of plundering Lofoten shops. **1942** 'G. Orwell' in *Partisan Rev.* Mar.–Apr. 159 The quisling intellectual is a phenomenon of the last two years. **1943** S. G. Evans *Christians in World Struggle* 2 The normal service of the cathedral.. had been replaced by a pagan 'Quisling' ceremony. **1945** H. G. Wells *Happy Turning* v. 13 He [*sc.* Jesus] began his career as a good illiterate patriotic Jew in indignant revolt against the Roman rule and the Quisling priests who cringed to it. **1947** *Times* 28 Apr. 8/3 Certainly the story itself shows no lingering trace of quisling quality: it is conventional to the very last joint. **1959** *Listener* 30 Apr. 765/1 *Brand* was written in anger against Ibsen's smug, quisling and bourgeois Norway of the nineteenth century. **1973** *Ibid.* 16 Aug. 226/3 Television..cast a regretful backward glance at Czechoslovakia under the heel of its wretched Quisling government.

Hence (as a back-formation) **qui·sle** *v.* (*joc.*), to betray one's country, in the manner of a Quisling; **qui·sler**, one who 'quisles'; **qui·slingism**, a political doctrine based on the collaborationist principles of Quisling; **qui·slingist**, a Quisling; also *attrib.*; **qui·slingite**, a Quisling; **qui·slingize** *v.*, to cause to act as a Quisling; **qui·slingized** *ppl. a.*; also *transf.*

1940 *Times* 22 Apr. 8/2 There seem to have been no Quislings, partly because it was unnecessary to 'quisle' in a country which, as the Nazis have always said 'could be taken by telephone'. *Ibid.* 4 Oct. 5/2 The Quislingists have begun Jew-baiting in Norway. *Ibid.* 15 Oct. 3/5 Lunde, the Quislingist Minister of Propaganda—the Norwegian Goebbels—has announced his intention to 'Quislingize' all newspapers. **1940** *Amer. Speech* XV. 261/1 '*Quislings* everywhere', 'Nazi sympathisers who might *quisle*', 'Other potential *quislers* are now at large'. **1940** *Manch. Guardian* 19 Oct. 6/3 So far the most significant and valuable addition in this war is 'Quisling'. Will there be a verb, 'to quisle'? **1941** *Times* 6 Feb. 3/5 The new secret police..have arrested many hundreds of persons who were known to be hostile to Quislingism. **1942** *Ann. Reg. 1941* 239 But for the protection of the German troops..the Quislingites would..undoubtedly have been wiped out. *Ibid.* 240 After the British raid.. the Reichs-kommissar..ordered them to pay the maintenance of the Germans and Quislingites taken to England. **1942** *Times* 28 Feb. 3/5 Over 1,000 teachers stuck to their resignations from the quislingized teachers' association even after the Church Department had decreed that such resignations were tantamount to resignation of office. **1944** 'G. Orwell' in *Horizon* X. 244 The modern political scene, in which..bribery and quislingism are normal. **1945** *Sun* (Baltimore) 28 Sept. 11/2 They bear the label of Quislingism, but they also carry the cross of illegitimacy. **1946** 'G. Orwell' in *Tribune* 26 Apr. 7/2 All that is left of him [*sc.* the Vicar of Bray] is a comic song and a beautiful tree, which..must surely have outweighed any bad effects which he produced by his political quislingism.

quisquose, -quous, *a.* Add: also **quisquis.** (Later examples.)

1856 J. Strang *Glasgow & its Clubs* 61 Mr. G. M——, a very unpopular and *quis-quis* character. **1899** J. B. Montgomerie-Fleming *Desultory Notes on Jamieson's Scott. Dict.* 122 Strangers arriving in a place and being considered of doubtful character are spoken of as 'Very quisquis sort of people'.

quit, *sb.*[2] Restrict *rare* to sense in Dict. and add: **2. a.** *U.S.* The act or an instance of quitting; one who quits.

1923 J. D. Hackett *Labor Terms* in *Managem. Engineering* May, *Quit*, a voluntary separation from work by an individual worker, usually without notice of intention. **1976** *Billings* (Montana) *Gaz.* 6 July 8-A/4 The scope of the 'voluntary quits', persons who leave their jobs for any reason is not precisely tabulated. *Ibid.* 8-A/5 Barrett was reluctant to estimate the impact of voluntary quits on the state.

b. *attrib.* and *Comb.*, as *quit-form*, *notice*; **quit rate**, the proportion of people in a section of society who voluntarily leave their jobs.

1966 'A. Hall' *9th Directive* xxii. 209 The hospital superintendent..didn't want to release me..but I forced a personal responsibility quit-form out of him and signed it and left. **1976** K. Thackeray *Crownbird* vi. 111 If..he got a quit notice from the Kenyans, he'd wind up being stateless. **1970** *Women Speaking* Apr. 10/2 For both men and women workers, the lowest quit rates occur among skilled workers and professional and managerial workers. **1973** *N.Y. Law Jrnl.* 26 July 5/3, 41 per cent of married mothers do work; women's 'quit-rate' is lower than men's, making them most dependable workers. **1975** *Sci. Amer.* Jan. 21/1 Let us consider the indicator called the quit rate, which measures the number of people in manufacturing industries (per 100 employed) who voluntarily leave their jobs.

quit, *v.* Add: **I. 6. a.** For 'Now *U.S.*' read 'Now chiefly *U.S.*' and add further examples.

1892 A. C. Gunter *Miss Dividends* ii. xiv. 208 Quit calling him bishop. He has repented and become a Christian like us! **1917** R. L. Alsaker *Eating for Health* iii. xvii. 237 Quit lunching. Quit taking eggs and milk and olive oil between meals. **1931** T. H. Rynning *Gun Notches* xviii. 130 So the Judge opened court with the usual formalities, throwing out a couple of drunks who wouldn't quit snoring during the proceedings. **1948** M. Laski *Tory Heaven* xii. 162 For God's sake, quit arguing politics. **1958** 'A. Bridge' *Portuguese Escape* xv. 256 In her anger the Countess's voice took on the rasping accents of the Middle West, and she reverted to her native idiom. 'Quit stalling, Monsignor, and tell me where my daughter *is*?' **1967** *N.Y. Times* (Internat. Ed.) 11 Feb. 4/8 Dr. Higginson quit smoking cigarettes some time ago for, he says, 'the obvious reasons'.

b. (Further examples.) Also *esp.*, to give up, renounce, or cease to be engaged in one's employment, or other specified activity. Chiefly *N. Amer.*

1773 P. V. Fithian *Jrnl.* 27 Nov. (1900) I. 54, I was introduced to one Mr Walker..lately a School-master but has quit. **1807** *Deb. Congress U.S.* (1852) 10th Congress 1 Sess., App. 478 [Robert A. New] inquired of them whether they would stand by Colonel Burr and go on, or quit. **1843, 1889** [see *day *sb.* 20 b]. **1932** *Atlantic Monthly* Mar. 316/2 The..farmer..let the place run down to almost a raw land value before he quit. **1961** *New Yorker* 12 Aug. 34/3, I came over to tell you I was quitting, Mr Sherman. **1968** *Globe & Mail* (Toronto) 3 Feb. B4/1 It's fine by me; I quit a couple of years ago. **1976** H. Nielsen *Brink of Murder* xii. 105 Reardon dug out a package of cigarettes..and offered them to Simon. 'I'm quitting,' Simon said... 'I've quit seventeen times this year... Right now I need a smoke.' **1977** *News of World* 17 Apr. 2/3 He has already quit as chairman of the firm.

7. c. (Later example.)

1977 I. Shaw *Beggarman, Thief* i. v. 59 'Has it ever occurred to you to just pull out?' 'What do you mean?' 'I mean quit... Just pick up and leave.'

quite, *adv.* Add: **I. 3. a.** (Further examples.)

1838 J. Kemper in *Wisconsin Mag. Hist.* (1925) VIII. 429 It was quite one when we arrived at Lathrop's tavern at Mineral Point. **1927** M. de la Roche *Jalna* xix. 223 There were quite eight books in the packet.

d. *colloq.* Expressing appreciation of or agreement with a statement. Freq. *quite so.*

1892 A. Conan Doyle *Adv. Sherlock Holmes* x. 246 'This maid Alice, as I understand, deposes that she..put on a bonnet, and went out.' 'Quite so. And she was afterwards seen walking into Hyde-park.' **1896** [see So *adv.* 5 b]. **1924** Galsworthy *White Monkey* ii. ii. 131 'I don't hold with it, myself.' 'No, quite!' **1931** Wodehouse *If I were You* xxii. 243 'Our likes and dislikes are not the point,' she said. 'The thing's impossible.' 'Quite,' agreed Sir Herbert. **1953** E. Simon *Past Masters* i. 26 'I didn't know there was a settlement..only a cemetery.' 'The burial ground: quite so.' **1962** D. Lessing *Golden Notebook* i. 131 'I've been supporting policies that should put an end to the whole bloody business.' 'Quite. And quite right.' **1976** K. Bonfiglioli *Something Nasty in Woodshed* x. 123 'No takers,' I said. 'Quite. By the way, I'm sorry to say 'quite' all the time but..my work lies amongst Americans and they *expect* Englishmen to say it.'

II. 4. b. *quite a few*: see Few *a.* 2d.

c. (Further examples.)

1890 Barrère & Leland *Dict. Slang* II. 164/2 *Quite too nice* (society), expression much used by the aesthetic female portion of society, meaning much the same as 'awfully jolly'. **1897** A. Beardsley *Let.* 26 Apr. (1970) 308 It is quite too nice to be here... Yesterday we had a charming lunch party at Lapérouse. **1909** J. R. Ware *Passing Eng.* p. v, It may be hoped that there are errors on every page, and also that no entry is 'quite too dull'. **1977** P. Scupham *Hinterland* 15 Paquerelle, we fall back on the language of the Aesthetics: Your composition is quite too utterly too too.

d. (Earlier and later examples.)

1863 F. Locker-Lampson *London Lyrics* (1870) 106 And all that sort of thing, of which Dear Hawthorne's 'quite' the best describer. **1911** G. B. Shaw *Getting Married* 218 Don't you think her letters are quite the best love-letters I get? **1934** W. B. Yeats *Words upon Window-Pane* 36 Exactly: quite the best kind of mediumship if you want to establish the identity of a spirit. **1981** *Country Life* 12 Feb. 409/1 The high degree of accuracy ..quite the highest, surely, that *can* be attained.

5. a. (Further examples.) Also in mod. usage, implying emphatic, and occas. ironic, commendation.

1816 Jane Austen *Emma* iii. vi. 86 You are an odd creature!.. You are a humourist... Quite a humourist. **1859** C. M. Tuttle *Diary* 30 May in *Wisconsin Mag. Hist.* (1931) XV. 78 Council Bluffs is quite a place containing about 3 thousand inhabitants. **1917** *Dialect Notes* IV. 398 An extension of the adverbial use as in 'He is *quite* a lad'. **1938** E. Hemingway *Fifth Column* i. iii. 28 Comrade's quite a word. I suppose I oughtn't to chuck it around. **1950** 'D. Divine' *King of Fassarai* xx. 166 We had us a party last night—quite a party. **1962** 'A. Garve' *Prisoner's Friend* ii. 97 Sheila was in a much happier frame of mind... As he was beginning to think she was quite a girl. *a* **1974** R. Crossman *Diaries* (1975) I. 219 It had been quite a week and I wanted a day of relaxation.

c. With sbs. preceded by *some.* Chiefly *U.S.*

1894 *Dialect Notes* I. 333 *Quite*..common in C[entral] J[ersey] in such expressions as 'quite some'. **1896** *Ibid.* I. 422 You'll have *quite some* potatoes on the patch. **1931** *Amer. Speech* Oct. 20 It was quite some excitement we had for a while. **1977** *Lancs. Life* Nov. 58/2 A wooden toy..for £125. It was, as you will have gathered, quite some toy.

d. Phr. *quite something*, a remarkable thing; a good deal. *colloq.*

1958 'N. Blake' *Penknife in Heart* iv. 60 Well now, that's quite something. Thank you. **1968** *Guardian* 10 Oct. 7/2 She found out that I was sleeping with someone else and she had to accept the situation which was quite something because it wasn't even a woman. **1971** 'L. Black' *Death has Green Fingers* iii. 25 Your village seems to be quite something with the lid off. **1973** *Where* Jan. 27/2 Ideally, of course, all readers should have been included—but the work involved in analysing such a mass of information would have been quite something. **1977** *Lancs. Life* Nov. 74/3 The Women's Institute itself is quite something.

III. 8. In a weakened sense: rather, to a moderate degree, fairly.

This sense has developed out of sense II, and is often difficult to distinguish from it. As a result, sense I is usually felt to be old-fashioned or stilted, and has become less common, except where *quite* is in collocation with certain types of adjective (and their derived adverbs) such as *different, separate, right, wrong, sure, definite*, etc.

1854 Thoreau *Walden* 226 Perhaps I have owed to this employment and to hunting, when quite young, my closest acquaintance with Nature. **1886** *Science* 30 Apr. 403/1 The lithographer has done his work quite, though hardly very, well. **1889** J. K. Jerome *Three Men in Boat* ix. 144 If so, who was the real one that was dreaming, and who was the one that was only a dream: it got quite interesting. **1919** G. B. Shaw *Heartbreak House* ii. 54 Theyve been proud of my poverty. Theyve even joked about it quite often. **1931** E. O'Neill *Homecoming* i, in *Mourning becomes Electra* (1932) 16 Borne on the light puffs of wind this music is at times quite loud. **1952** A. Wilson *Hemlock & After* iii. 58, I quite like queers if it comes to that, so long as they're not on the make like Evelyn's boys. **1958** 'A. Bridge' *Portuguese Escape* xvi. 265 You shall..when you have answered one quite small question: where is now Dr. Antal Horvath? **1970** G. F. Newman *Sir, you Bastard* ii. 43 Sneed quite liked DI Johnny Doleman, and the man treated him like an intelligent equal. **1976** C. Sarfas *Space & Space Travel* 19 But the astronauts were wearing their heavy spacesuits and equipment, so even on the moon it was quite hard to move. **1980** J. McClure *Blood of Englishman* xvi. 144, I only said a 'quite' brilliant idea, sir—not a 'very'.

IV. 9. Quasi-*adj.* *ellipt.* for 'quite a gentleman (lady, etc.)'; socially acceptable. Usu. in neg. Also *quite-quite.*

1867 Trollope *Last Chron. Barset* I. xlii. 371 Still he wasn't quite,—not quite, you know—'not quite so much of a gentleman as I am'—Mr Walker would have said, had he spoken out freely that which he insinuated. But he contented himself with the emphasis he put upon the 'not quite', which expressed his meaning fully. **1878** —— *Is he Popenjoy?* I. xiv. 195 'I have always liked the Dean personally,' said Lady Sarah... 'But he isn't—he isn't quite—' 'No; he isn't quite—,' said Lord George, also hesitating to pronounce the word which was understood by both of them. **1907** M. E. Braddon *Dead Love has Chains* vi. 124 Oh, she is quite quite, don't you know... Her father is Sir Michael Thelliston. **1915** V. Woolf *Voyage Out* xi. 159 Mr. Perrott..knew he was not 'quite', as Susan stated..not quite a gentleman she meant. **1926** *Whispering Gallery* viii. 114 He's not 'quite quite', you know, but he's so clever. **1930** C. Williams *Poetry at Present* 165 That awful moment when..one feels that one is 'not quite'. **1945** A. Huxley *Time must have Stop* xxi. 200 'You'll find him a bit..well, you know, not quite...' The deprecating gesture sufficiently indicated what he quite wasn't. **1956** J. Masters *Bugles & Tiger* xv. 182 This was supposed to be not quite quite, and British officers took no part in it. **1960** M. Cecil *Something in Common* 7 'She's a Lady' (acceptable), or 'He's not Quite' (rejected).

‖ **quite** (ki·te), *sb.* *Bullfighting.* [Sp.] The action of distracting the bull from a man or a horse by means of elaborate capework.

1926 E. Hemingway *Sun also Rises* xviii. 225 His first 'quite' was directly below us. The three matadors take the bull in turn. **1932** —— *Death in Afternoon* xvii. 184 The spectator..will be liable to..watch the horse and miss the quite that the matador has made. **1957** A. MacNab *Bulls of Iberia* v. 52 As the picador falls on the sand, the first matador rushes in with his cape, to distract the bull... This rescue job is called making a *quite.* **1967** McCormick & Mascareñas *Compl. Aficionado* ii. 36 We are told that the glory of the early corrida was the emphasis upon cape work in the *quites* necessitated by the large number of pics to the toro. **1975** *Oxf. Compan. Sports & Games* 140/1 The measures take the form of keeping the bull under control at all times..making certain that the animal is not excessively enfeebled during the *suerte de varas* due to tardy *quites.*

quits, *a.* Add: **2. d.** *to call* (*it*) *quits* = *to cry quits*; hence, to give up or call off a venture, occas. with suggestion of cutting one's losses.

1898 J. London *Let.* 30 Nov. (1966) 5 Tomorrow I would cut my throat and call quits with the whole cursed business. **1950** *Manch. Guardian Weekly* 16 Mar. 2/2 The old isolationists want to 'call quits' on the whole business. **1963** J. Joesten *They call it Intelligence* II. viii. 75 Vic smelled a rat and decided to call it quits. **1972** *Islander* (Victoria, B.C.) 13 Feb. 2/4 Nearly bitten alive with mosquitoes.. I called it quits and joined the gang in the [boat].

quitter, quittor, *sb.*[1] **1.** For *Obs.* read '*Obs.* except *Jamaican*' and add later examples.

1943, 1952 in Cassidy & Le Page *Dict. Jamaican Eng.* **1961** F. G. Cassidy *Jamaica Talk* i. 4 The ginger-grower in Christiana who spoke of the *quitter* (pus) in a wound.. which the OED traces no later than 1689 in this sense.

2. (Later examples.)

1900 *Times* 2 Oct. 13/4 He examined the mare and found it suffering from a bad quitter which was discharging matter. **1917** W. Owen *Let.* 21 Feb. (1967) 437 Certain cases of Thrush, Quitter, and such suppurations go one worse than the battlefield-exhalations.

quitter, *sb.*[2] **2.** For *U.S.* read orig. *U.S.* and add further examples.

1908 'O. Henry' in *American Mag.* LXVII. 69/2, I can stand the fabulous monster that..blows hot birds and cold bottles with the same breath. But I can't stand a quitter. **1923** *Auckland Weekly News* 11 Oct. 16/6 He dropped in on me one evening and started to upbraid me for being a quitter. **1931** *Sun* (Baltimore) 12 Jan. 8/6 George Muehlebach..who..became a quitter in the draft fight via the secret mail-vote route is still filled with fight. **1937** G. Frankau *More of Us* viii. 94 Stout lad was Jack, and last to play the quitter From lady's side for any casual stares. **1949** *Sat. Even. Post* 15 Oct. 141/3 It's been worn by great battlers in every sport, but never by a quitter or dirty player. **1976** *Billings* (Montana) *Gaz.* 6 July 8-A/5 Records show about 14 per cent of the benefits paid in 1975 were to voluntary quitters.

quitter, *v.*[2] For *Sc. obs.* read 'orig. *Sc. arch.*' and add: **a.** (Later examples.)

1872 Mrs. Stowe *Oldtown Fireside Stories* 64 There was the old tom-turkey a struttin' and a sidlin' and a quitterin', and a floutin' his tail-feathers in the sun. *Ibid.* 156 An old tom-turkey, that'll strut and gobble and quitter, and drag his wings on the ground. **1935** E. R. Eddison *Mistress* ix. 171 Shall then these ram-cats of Meszria reap all the honour, whiles we of the Queen's true party sit quittering here? *Ibid.* xix. 394 Then strike. Not to stand quittering like quails when the event walketh on razors' edges.

qui·tting-time. Chiefly *U.S.* Also *Sc.* **quating-time.** [f. Quitting *vbl. sb.* + Time *sb.*] The time at which work is ended for the day.

1835 D. Webster *Orig. Scot. Rhymes* 165 Should he come when crowdie time, Or quating time draws on, Our bairns maun todlin meet wi' him. **1850** H. C. Watson *Camp Fires Revol.* 111 Every day, he'd come into the workshop, about quitting time, and follow me up to the house. **1888** J. Kirkland *McVeys* 203 Once more Strafford sought Phil at the shop at 'quitting-time', after the latter had got in and cleaned his engine. **1906** *Dialect Notes* III. 122 *Quittin time*, regular expression for the time to cease work. **1958** P. Oliver in P. Gammond *Decca Bk. of Jazz* i. 21 There were, and still are, hollers that told the time of day, that announced 'quitting-time' or summoned the water-boy. **1977** *Rolling Stone* 19 May 18/2 A sign near the kitchen reads: if you don't believe the dead come back to life, you should be here at quitting time.

quiver, *sb.*[2] Add: **2.** *Comb.* **quiver-grass,** = Quaking-grass.

1860 C. M. Yonge *Hopes & Fears* II. vi. 105 Blue harebells and pale bents of quiver-grass edged the path. **1869** —— *Let.* 6 Aug. in C. Coleridge *C. M. Yonge* (1903) ix. 242 The Norman name for quiver-grass is *Langue de femme*.

quivery, *a.* Delete (*rare*) and add later examples.

1889 'Mark Twain' *Connecticut Yankee* xxvi. 339 The headlines sent a quivery little cold wave through me. **1925** T. Dreiser *Amer. Tragedy* I. I. xv. 116 She..hinted of a mood which made Clyde a little quivery and erratic. **1927** *Chambers's Jrnl.* May 315/1 You and he have made my face quite quivery with excitement. **1975** L. Gillen *Return to Deepwater* viii. 152 'If you kiss me I'll—I'll scream for help,' she said in a small and strangely quivery voice.

Quixotish (kwiksǫ·tiʃ), *a. rare.* [f. Quixote *sb.* + -ish[1].] = Quixotic *a.* 2a.

1810 Shelley *Let.* 20 May (1964) I. 11, I act unlike every other mortal enough in all conscience, without seeking for more Quixotish adventures.

quiz, *sb.*[2] For *U.S.* read orig. *U.S.* and add: **1. a.** (Earlier and later examples.) Also in written form upon a specified topic. Also, more generally: a set of questions to be answered as an entertainment, etc.; an informal questionnaire.

1867 W. James *Let.* 26 Dec. in R. B. Perry *Thought & Char. W. James* (1935) I. xiv. 254 Occasional review articles, etc., perhaps giving 'quizzes' in anatomy and physiology..may help along. **1907** *Springfield* (Mass.) *Weekly Republican* 7 Feb. 16 For the food chemists the quiz included a study of both French and German. **1931** H. F. Pringle *Theodore Roosevelt* I. xvi. 228 This distinguished jurist agreed to lend books and give him a quiz each Saturday. **1941** L. MacNeice *Poetry of W. B. Yeats* i. 114 We must..in literary criticism be careful not to write as if we were solving a popular Quiz—as if there were a stock set of answers. **1957** *Economist* 19 Oct. 202 To what kind of searching test should an advertiser subject a prospective agent? A friendly personal quiz? **1973** *Houston Chron. Mag.* 14 Oct. 16/4 The teacher erased the board, wrote up new multiplication problems, distributed paper and drilled for the next day's quiz.

b. A form of competitive entertainment, esp. on radio and television, in which questions are put to individuals or to a team.

1941 *Scribner's Commentator* Feb. 86 (*heading*) Quiz by the Quiz kids. **1951** *Ann. Reg. 1950* 415 The quiz mania showed no signs of abatement during the year. **1956** *B.B.C. Handbk. 1957* 70 Archaeology triumphantly holds its special place with its somewhat unexpected quiz presentation of 'Animal, Vegetable, Mineral?' **1958** *Times* 1 Aug. 11/1 In these days of brains trusts, musical quizzes, and increased attention to musical appreciation as a subject for schools and evening classes. **1976** *Loughborough Monitor* 26 Nov., On November 17, Nanpantan [W.I.] were hostesses to Thorpe Acre and Mountfields in a three-cornered friendly quiz, with Mr. Peter Lewis as question master. **1977** *Evening Post* (Nottingham) 24 Jan. 7/9 Tuxford Young Farmers A team defeated their B team in the third round of the county Inter-Club Quiz to reach the semi-finals.

2. *attrib.* and *Comb.* **a.** Simple *attrib.*, as *quiz compère, game, -paper, party, programme, show, team, -viewer*; *quiz-type* adj.

1959 Quiz compère [see *hand *sb.* 15]. **1945** *East Jefferson Sentinel* (Edgewater, Colorado) 26 July 5/4 Mrs Critchfield, chairman and hostess, then conducted three quiz games. **1959** G. Freeman *Jack would be Gentleman* i. 7 It was wonderful what you learned from the tee-vee.. quiz games, politicians having arguments. **1967** *Listener* 10 Aug. 170/3 The latter sit in the hotel night after night, sipping German beer and watching the quiz games on Indonesian TV. **1914** D. R. Campbell *Proving Virginia* xiii. 226 The black-robed Seniors assembled..to perform the last holy rites over their antique manuscripts, quiz papers, precious testimonials of mid-night toil. **1936** L. C. Douglas *White Banners* viii. 163 It was not easy to concentrate on classroom lectures, student interviews, quiz-papers, and seminars. **1949** 'J. Tey' *Brat Farrar* vi. 47 He..had always come to an examination paper with the same faint pleasure that an addict brings to a quiz party. **1942** D. Powell *Time to be Born* (1943) ii. 41 Five hundred rags and tags that..were nothing more than cues in a quiz program. **1947** Auden *Age of Anxiety* (1948) i. 28 And now Captain Kidd in his Quiz Programme How Alert Are You. **1952** W. R. Burnett *Vanity Row* (1953) xiv. 97 'What time did Ilona Vance call you last night?'.. 'I don't like the quiz programme type of conversation.' **1960** *Guardian* 18 Oct. 10/4 Big-money winners on American television quiz programmes. **1972** *Language* XLVIII. 341 Elicitory question intonation..presupposes that there is information being withheld, and hence is easily associated with teachers or quiz-program M.C.'s. **1946** F. Wakeman *Hucksters* ii. 17 Vic had heard a story of how he went to a sponsor all primed to sell a quiz show. **1954** G. Marx *Let.* 16 Aug. (1967) 93 The gibbering idiots on panel shows, quiz shows, and other half hours of tripe. **1961** A. Miller *Misfits* ii. 18 Just say it: it doesn't have to be true. It's not a quiz show, it's only a court. **1974** P. De Vries *Glory of Hummingbird* (1975) xi. 149 Like all of us watching quiz shows I would call out answers I knew. **1957** R. Hoggart *Uses of Literacy* vi. 155 The typically outspoken member in a radio quiz-team represents both the old-style 'card' and this modern allegorical figure, the 'idiosyncratic hero'. **1976** *Lancs. Evening Post* 7 Dec. 2/4 Preston's BBC Radio 2 quiz team to meet Blackpool's in a broadcast competition. **1963** *Times* 19 Jan. 4/6 It was Sound, after all, which invented several other quiz, or quiz-type, programmes. **1959** *New Statesman* 24 Jan. 107/2 Its audience was almost certainly enlarged this week by the unconscious sadism, latent in all quiz-viewers, which such entertainments harmlessly release and satisfy.

b. Special Combs.: **quiz kid** orig. *U.S.* [after *whizz-kid], a child, usu. one of a team, chosen on account of his or her intelligence to answer extempore questions submitted by the audience of a quiz; also *transf.*, an ostentatiously intelligent person; **quiz-master,** (*a*) (see quot. 1889); (*b*) one who presides over a quiz-game, esp. on radio or television; = *question-master* s.v. *question *sb.* 7d.

1941 Quiz kid [see sense 1 b above]. **1941** F. Brown in *Unknown Worlds* Aug. 120/1 If the episode had become known..Herbie would..get more acclaim even than a quiz kid. **1959** *Encounter* July 38/2 He [*sc.* Northcliffe] was a true child of the age—the first and greatest of all quiz-kids. **1972** *Times* 19 Oct. 10/3 He suppresses his taste for swanky, quiz-kids words (telangiectatic, ichor, fastigiate). **1889** *Cent. Dict.*, *Quiz-master*, the teacher or leader of a quiz-class. **1949** *Radio Times* 15 July 15/1 Round Britain Quiz... Quiz-Master, Gilbert Harding. **1952** *News Chron.* 15 Jan. 1/4 In 'What's My Line' on TV last night..Elizabeth Allan introduced Harding as 'the Ace of Quizz-masters'. **1964** C. Barber *Ling. Change in Present-Day Eng.* ii. 20 B.B.C. announcers may be less influential than comedians, quizmasters, compères, and 'personalities'. **1976** J. van de Wetering *Corpse on Dike* ii. 19 The voices of the comics..the quiz masters and the newscasters.

quiz, *v.*[2] For '*dial.* and *U.S.*' read 'orig. *dial.* and *U.S.*' and add: Also **quizz,** *dial.* **quies. 1. a.** (Earlier and later examples.)

1847 Southey *Doctor* VII. 85 She com back an' *quiesed* us. **1922** *History* Apr. 72 Only 43·4 per cent. of the teachers quiz in class. **1928** J. Sykes *M. A. Disraeli* viii. 79 So far forgot his good manners as to quiz Mrs. Disraeli at the dinner-table. **1958** *Daily Mail* 24 Feb. 12/1 To find him I had to drive to the sleepy Sussex town of Pulborough, quiz the locals, [etc.]. **1978** J. Irving *World according to Garp* xiii. 248 He quizzed him about emergency phone numbers.

2. *trans.* and *intr.* To watch or examine closely, to peer (at).

1906 Hardy *Dynasts* II. II. vi. 199 Better quiz evils with too strained an eye Than have them leap from disregarded lairs. **1909** —— *Time's Laughingstocks* 77 The stars..Quiz downward curiously. **1911** C. Mackenzie *Passionate Elopement* 26 But somehow it was no longer amusing to quizz the young woman..through his ivory rimmed perspective.

quizzee[2] (kwizī·). [f. Quiz *v.*[2] + -ee[1].] A panellist on a radio or television quiz programme.

1940 *Words* VI. 107/1 *Quizzee*, one who undergoes questioning. **1947** *N.Y. Times* 7 Dec. X13/1 Asking questions of eager quizzees. **1966** *New Statesman* 23 Dec. 947/3 Sheer ignorance about reality (had Mr Livings.. ever actually watched a TV quiz?), and an ideology dependent on sentimentality (children being led past 'surgical booths'..indicated the quizzee's deficient life).

qui·zzery, *sb.*[2] *joc.* [f. Quiz *sb.*[2] + -ery.] A collection of quizzes; quizzes collectively.

1957 *Daily Tel.* 24 Dec. 6/6 (*heading*) Quizzery for all. This starts with the easy ones, and gets more specialised as you go on. **1963** *Ibid.* 9 Feb. 8/7 Their answers would therefore belong to the inferior realm of quizzery, in which knowledge of facts is valued for its own sake and not as a passport to wisdom.

quizzy (kwi·zi), *a.*[2] [f. Quiz *v.*[2] + -y[1].] Inquisitive.

1933 M. Lowry *Ultramarine* iii. 158 'You're either one way or the other!' 'A quizzy little bitch, anyhow!' '—that's unfair.' **1955** D'A. Niland *Shiralee* 86, I don't want to be quizzy, Mac, but, if it's a fair question what's the drum? **1959** I. & P. Opie *Lore & Lang. Schoolch.* x. 183 Quizzy flies never grow wise. **1968** 'J. Le Carré' *Small Town in Germany* vi. 99 Still quizzy:..he had to know exactly what each of us was up to. **1978** O. White *Silent Reach* xii. 127 Don't be so quizzy, David..Mr. Sinclair needs a drink, not a cross-examination.

Qum (kum). Also **Quoom.** Name of a city in N.W. Iran, used *attrib.* and *ellipt.* to designate a type of rug produced there.

1953 A. C. Edwards *Persian Carpet* xvi. 340/1 The charm of the Qūm carpet lies primarily in its designs, rather than in its quality or colour. **1962** C. W. Jacobsen *Oriental Rugs* 273 (*heading*) *Qum rugs* (*Also spelled Qom, Gum, Goum, Ghum*). *Ibid.*, Qums are made in the sizeable town of Qum, which is some 90 miles South of Ispahan... When rug weaving began in Qum some 20 years ago, their designers preferred the all over designs. **1973** *Guardian* 1 Mar. 21/1 Afghan Carpet.. Silk Quoom.. Pakistan Bokhara.. Itamadan Carpet. **1974** *Evening Standard* 12 Feb. 48/5 (Advt.), Superb oriental carpets & rugs. Including:.. Silk Quoom rugs exceptionally finely knotted in precious Caspian silk. **1975** 'E. Lathen' *By Hook or by Crook* ix. 87 They joined Barney in genial contempt for a job lot of Hamadans, outdid him in admiring two spectacular Qums.

Qumran (kumrā·n). The name of a region on the western shore of the Dead Sea, used *attrib.* to designate (*a*) a collection of ancient Jewish scrolls (the 'Dead Sea Scrolls'), discovered in caves there in 1947, or the contents of these scrolls; and (*b*) a religious community which inhabited a site (Khirbet Qumran) in this region, and to which the scrolls belonged. Hence **Qumra·nite** *sb.*, a member of the religious community of Qumran; also as *adj.*

1954 *Biblical Archaeologist* XVII. 8 Represented..is a fragment of the 'Zadokite work'. This document, long an enigma to scholars, had been recognized as related to the Qumran sectarian works as soon as the finds of 1947 became known. **1955** H. H. Rowley *Dead Sea Scrolls & their Significance* i. 8 The type of Biblical text which was used by the Qumran community. *Ibid.* 11 Palaeographically these appear to be later than the Qumran texts. **1961** T. F. Glasson *Gk. Influence in Jewish Eschatology* viii. 55 Dupont-Sommer thinks that the Essenes (whose identity with the Qumranites he accepts) were originally influenced by Zoroastrianism. *Ibid.* 53 The Qumranite community connected with the Dead Sea Scrolls..is thought to have been either Essene or a very closely related movement. *Ibid.* 55 The Qumranite library evidently welcomed a number of the apocalyptic and other non-biblical writings. **1963** *Times Lit. Suppl.* 22 Feb. 138/3 Influence of the sect on the church is recognized, though without making the church into a daughter of the Qumran sect. **1967** H. Chadwick *Early Church* i. 15 The New Testament writings and the Qumran Scrolls mutually illuminate one another. **1971** R. T. France *Jesus & Old Testament* v. 173 The Qumran sect was not a major influence in first century AD Palestine. *Ibid.* 194 Neither the Pseudepigrapha nor the Qumran literature show any use of this passage. **1976** *Jrnl. Theol. Stud.* Oct. 533 For them [*sc.* the Christian Jews], as for the Qumran community, the communal meal replaced the animal sacrifices of the Temple and was endowed with spiritual meaning.

quock, var. *quawk *sb.*

quod, *sb.*[1] Add: (Later examples.) Also, *spec.* in phr. *in quod.*

1872 G. P. Burnham *Mem. U.S. Secret Service* p. vi, *In quod*, in prison; committed, permanently. **1884** [see *fiddling *vbl. sb.* 3]. **1917** Kipling *Holy War* 2 A tinker out of Bedford, A vagrant oft in quod. **1933** *Sun* (Baltimore) 11 July 1/5 According to the representations of the other four Mr. Fullerton was in no way responsible for the incident which put them in quod. **1968** *Listener* 18 July 72/3 Now, one of this chap's maternal uncles.. has got to pay a 50 quid debt or go to quod.

quod, *v.* (Later examples.)
1888 J. Runciman *Chequers* 80 A woman answered, 'You've struck me, you swine; and if I've got a black eye I'll quod you, sure as I'm yere. Ain't I lushed you, and fed you, and found your clobber long enough?' **1923** D. L. Sayers *Whose Body?* iii. 60 That's her story. Sugg's delighted,..and quodded Thipps on the strength of it. **1930** R. H. Mottram *Europa's Beast* v. 136 In England the police would have 'quodded' her.

quodlibetal, *a.* (Later example.)
1975 Alluntis & Wolter tr. Duns Scotus (*title*) God and creatures: the quodlibetal questions.

quodlibetarian. b. (Later examples.)
1943 Beerbohm *Lytton Strachey* 22 That agile and mellifluous quodlibetarian, Dr. Joad. **1966** *Duckett's Reg.* Feb. 14/2 The clever quodlibetarians called it an obvious strategic move.

quoi hai, var. Qui-hy in Dict. and Suppl.

quoin, *sb.* Add: **4. quoin-wedge** = sense 2.
1923 D. H. Lawrence tr. *Verga's Mastro-don Gesualdo* I. iv. 71 We want more man-power—a crane!—or tie a pulley-wheel up there to the beam of the roof—then a quoin-wedge underneath.

quoit, *sb.* Add: **3. c.** The backside, the buttocks. Phr. *to go for one's quoit,* to hurry. *Austral. slang.*
1941 Baker *Dict. Austral. Slang* 58 *Quoit,* the buttocks. *Ibid., Go for one's quoits,* to travel quickly, go for one's life. **1951** E. Lambert *Twenty Thousand Thieves* x. 165 See those jokers sitting on their quoits over there? **1952** J. Cleary *Sundowners* i. 42 Going for the lick of his coit up the street. **1954** T. A. G. Hungerford *Sowers of Wind* xiv. 176 Gawd, he blew the tripes outa me for nothing at all, and then he kicks a Nip in the coit. **1972** J. Bailey *Wire Classroom* x. 82 'I think he needs a good kick up the coit,' says Cromwell.

quoit, *v.* **1.** (Later example.)
1871 L. W. M. Lockhart *Fair to See* II. xi. 15 The quoiters quoited.

quoiter. Add: **b.** A curler.
1833 J. Cairnie *Essay on Curling & Artificial Pond Making* 93 He was a grand quoiter, he never missed a shot. **1899** J. Kennedy *Compl. Sc. & Amer. Poems* (ed. 3) 128 May quoiters' joys be mair an' mair.

quoiting, *vbl. sb.* Add: Also, = Curling *vbl. sb.*[1] 2. (Further examples.)
1811 J. Ramsay *Acct. Game Curling* 20 From one end of Scotland to the other, it was always named *kuting,* to curl, meaning nothing more than to slide upon the ice. In some parts of Ayrshire..it is pronounced *coiting.* **1884** J. Taylor *Curling* 74 He had seen Bryan o' the Sun Inn and the deil *quitin'* (curling) on the Auld Water.
Comb. **1853** W. Watson *Poems* 71 The lee-side was cheer'd by the quoitin'-stane roar. **1969** R. Welsh *Beginner's Guide Curling* ii. 15 Kuting stones, channel stanes or loofies are the oldest curling implements known to us.

quokka (kwǫ·kă). [Aboriginal name.] A small short-tailed wallaby, *Setonix brachyurus,* found in restricted coastal areas of south-western Australia.
1863 J. Gould *Mammals Austral.* II. 38 At Augusta.. its [the short-tailed wallaby's] native name, Quāk-a, is the same as at King George's Sound. **1943** C. Barrett *Austral. Animal Bk.* xi. 96 The quokka or short-tailed pademelon..inhabits the coastal districts of South-western Australia. **1963** *Spectator* 25 Jan. 102/2 The quokka, indigenous to Western Australia, is a 'species of rat', albeit rather friendly. **1968** *New Scientist* 29 Feb. 455/2 At night the place [*sc.* Rottnest Island] quivers with wallabies about the size of hares. They are what the Aborigines call quokkas. **1976** *Nature* 1 Jan. 42/1 Female quokkas mate soon after giving birth.

quoll. (Later examples.)
1924 *Truth* (Sydney) 27 Apr. 6 *Quoll,* aboriginal name of native cat. **1970** *Courier-Mail* (Brisbane) 15 June 12/5 In 1955, during intensive searches for taipans in scrubs and huge lantana thickets at Chatsworth near Gympie, I was astonished when I captured a savage little quoll (native cat) almost a thousand miles south of what I thought was its home country. **1978** *Ibid.* 18 Feb. 18/8 And talking of this native cat or Quoll, it is a marsupial and a carnivore and it is a clever and persistent hunter.

quondam, *adv. sb.,* and *a.* **B.** *sb.* Delete † *Obs.* and add later examples in *spec.* sense (see quot. 1962).
1888 A. Blomfield *Let.* in H. H. Henson *Retrospect* (1942) I. ii. 30 My dear Henson (If I may as a quondam thus familiarly address you). **1962** A. Sampson *Anatomy of Britain* xiii. 214 The most worldly college has been All Souls... The fellows and ex-fellows (called Quondams) are supposed to be the cream of Oxford intellectuals... Lord Curzon, the Viceroy of India, 'an enthusiastic quondam'.

Quonset, quonset (kwǫ·nsėt). orig. and chiefly *U.S.* Also (erron.) **quanset.** [f. the name of *Quonset* Point, Rhode Island, where the article was first made.] Used *attrib.* and *ellipt.,* esp. in *Quonset hut,* of a kind of prefabricated building consisting of a semi-cylindrical corrugated metal roof on a bolted steel foundation.
A proprietary name in the U.S.
1942 *Collier's* 19 Sept. 21/1 The boys practiced erecting on deck their 'Quonsett huts', queer little igloos, the roofs of which are designed to catch rainwater to be saved for a sunny day. **1943** *Pop. Mechanics* Apr. 61/1 'Quonset Huts', those portable barracks, begin replacing the tent city. **1946** *New Yorker* 16 Mar. 22/1 The first American-made Nissens, or Quonsets, were sent to England under lend-lease in June, 1941. **1946** *Official Gaz.* (U.S. Patent Office) 19 Nov. 287/2 Great Lakes Steel Corporation, Wilmington, Del... Filed Mar. 15, 1946. *Quonset.* For readily erectable buildings, knock-down buildings, portable buildings, and prefabricated buildings. Claims use since September 1941. **1949** 'P. Michaels' *This Perverse Generation* viii. 67 From sturdy, roomy architectural loveliness to quonset hut—civilization marches on! **1957** J. Kerouac *On Road* xiii. 90 A tremendous aluminum Quonset warehouse. **1959** E. Tunis *Indians* 32/2 There seems to have been a quonset-shaped house, too, in Virginia and North Carolina. **1966** T. Pynchon *Crying of Lot 49* iv. 82 She parked in an enormous lot next to a quonset building painted pink and about a hundred yards long. **1972** E. Staebler *Cape Breton Harbour* ii. 24 A long scalloped row of traps made of raw wood slats, shaped like a quanset hut. **1973** 'B. Mather' *Snowline* iii. 30 Nissen and Quanset huts hastily erected in World War II. **1974** *Spartanburg* (S. Carolina) *Herald-Jrnl.* 21 Apr. A6/5 The family's quonset hut home on Oahu Island's north shore was washed away by a swollen river. **1977** *Time* 27 June 48/2 The final dozen hippies..last week evacuated their grimy quonset hut on the edge of town.

Quoom, var. *Qum.

quorate (kwō^ə·rĕt), *a.* [f. Quor(um + -ate[2].] Of a meeting: attended by a quorum (and thereby constitutional). Hence **inquo·rate** *a.,* not attended by a quorum.
1969 *PI* (University College London, Students' Union) 20 Oct. 3/2 Even barely quorate General Meetings could be dominated by an organised minority. **1971** J. Henderson *Copperhead* xv. 192 This meeting is now closed. We're quorate without you. **1973** *Times Higher Educ. Suppl.* 11 May 14/1 In a tiny department of three, what happens if the head is wed to one of the other two? The department meeting becomes quorate during intercourse. **1974** *Times* 13 May 17/6 The meeting..was an inquorate one and therefore had no validity and was entirely unofficial. **1976** *Cherwell* 30 Jan. 2/3 A barely quorate JCR passed a motion..that freshmen at the college should 'fag' for second and third year men. **1978** *Evening News* 22 Apr. 4/3 The motion was passed but there were several people who were in strong disagreement and walked out making the meeting in-quorate.

Quorn (kwǭɹn). The name of a village in Leicestershire (now Quorndon), used *attrib.* and *ellipt.* to denote a famous hunt centred there.
1867 'Ouida' *Under Two Flags* I. iv. 74 It lay in the Melton country, and was equally well placed for Pytchley, Quorn, and Belvoir. **1904** A. E. W. Mason *Truants* ii. 16 He hunted with the Quorn that winter. **1933** Kipling in *Strand* Feb. 126, I..was a Gentleman in Red When all the Quorn wore woad, Sir. **1966** J. Betjeman *High & Low* 23 The rumble of the railway drowned The thunder of the Quorn. **1971** *Guardian* 30 Sept. 16/8 Melton was frequented by many of the nobility and gentry who came for the Quorn hunting season. **1972** *Country Life* (Suppl.) 26 Oct. 11/1 *Hotel*..in the heart of the Quorn countryside.

quota, *sb.* Add: **1.** Also *Eccl.,* the proportion of the funds of a parish that is contributed to the finances of the diocese; in full *diocesan* (formerly *parochial*) *quota.* (Later examples.)
1911 *Archbishops' Committee on Church Finance Rep.* iv. 45 We recommend... That a system of parochial assessment..should be adopted... That the amount of this apportionment or contribution (which may conveniently be called the Parochial Quota) should from time to time be fixed by the Diocesan Board of Finance. **1919** W. B. Incledon *Vicar Reconstructs* vi. 27 So the Diocesan Finance Committee has been worrying you about the diocesan quota. My advice is to let them worry until you have your parochial finance scheme in proper working order. **1936** W. K. L. Clarke *Almsgiving* ii. i. 82 The diocesan income in its turn is raised by assessing the parishes, each of which is expected to pay its 'quota'. *Ibid.* vi. 115 In many parishes the diocesan quota is paid reluctantly. **1976** *Church Times* 2 July 12/1 Any extra money raised by a parish for some specific occasion..is engulfed by the diocese by an increase in quota. **1978** *Ibid.* 29 Sept. 12/5 Parishes are already struggling to meet vastly increased quotas.

2. b. In a system of proportional representation, the minimum number of votes required to elect a candidate.
1857 T. Hare *Machinery of Representation* 17 No person shall be returned as a member to serve in parliament for whom there shall not be recorded the full quota or number of votes specified. **1930** C. F. Strong *Mod. Polit. Constitutions* viii. 177 Instead of having to gain an absolute majority, the candidate needs only to reach the *quota,* i.e. the number of votes cast divided by the number of seats to be filled. **1943** J. F. S. Ross *Parliamentary Representation* xxiii. 219 The *quota* has next to be determined: this is done by dividing the grand total of votes by a number which is one more than the number of members to be elected. The quota is the whole number next above the result of this division. **1955** Lakeman & Lambert *Voting in Democracies* v. 91 If the number of envelopes containing..the Socialist list amounts to one d'Hondt quota, the Socialist candidate whose name appears first on the list is declared elected. **1973** *Irish Times* 2 Mar. 8/1 Carlow-Kilkenny. Seats, 5... Valid vote, 46,717;.. Quota, 7,787. **1975** H. Berrington in S. E. Finer *Adversary Politics & Electoral Reform* 281 Neither Labour nor the Conservatives would have 'wasted' many votes—the Tories would have polled two quotas, with little to spare, and Labour would have accumulated three.

3. The maximum number (of immigrants or imports) allowed to enter a country within a set period; a regulation that imposes such a restriction on entry to a country. Also *transf.*
1921 *Washington Post* 21 May 4/5 North European countries may not furnish the full 20 per cent of their entire quotas each month. **1921** *U.S. Congr. House Report* No. 169. 1 The law provides that not in excess of 20 per cent of the yearly quota allotted to any country may come in one month. **1930** W. K. Hancock *Australia* xii. 239 In recent years we have extended its operation by instituting 'quotas', which limit the immigration from Southern Europe. **1931** *Foreign Affairs* Apr. 401 On the score of its domestic economic consequences alone, the wisdom of an embargo or fixed import quota is disputable. **1931** *Contemporary Review* Aug. 221 It has not yet been realised, even by some Free Traders, how insidious and dangerous a form of protection is that latest expedient of the tariff-mongers, known as the 'Quota'. **1932** E. Bowen *To North* xxi. 224 'I have decided to go to America.'.. 'You couldn't stay more than six months, though, because of the quota.' **1949** [see *immigration]. **1973** *Nation Rev.* (Melbourne) 31 Aug. 1448/2 The board doesn't call for quotas on imports. **1976** *Survey* Winter 128 Quotas upon Jews in higher education had, to be sure, been a staple of the Soviet scene since the postwar period.

4. *attrib.* and *Comb.,* as *quota act, film, immigrant, immigration, law, limit, period, plan, restriction*; **quota method,** the statistical method of using quota samples (usu. for opinion polls); **quota quickie** [*quickie 1 a], a cheap cinematographic film, rapidly made outside the United States to offset American films shown in other countries; **quota sample,** a sample that is chosen so that various categories of individual (when classified by age, sex, social class, and the like) are represented in the same proportions as in the general population; **quota sampler,** one who devises or uses quota samples; **quota sampling,** the use of the quota method; **quota system,** a law or custom restricting the number or proportion of persons or goods that may be admitted to a country or an institution; also, one prescribing the minimum number of persons to be admitted.
1938 *Times* 22 Feb. 19/3 British film production has made considerable progress during the past ten years as a result of the first Quota Act. **1939** 'N. Blake' *Smiler with Knife* ii. 29 Those extras, dressed up to look like rustic ancients for a British quota film. **1974** R. Harrison *Rex* ii. 29 The British film industry had only just begun to stir [in 1927], with Gaumont Films, and then with American quota films—'quota quickies' made over here by American companies, on a budget of £1 per foot of film and never mind the quality, so that they could then unload their Hollywood products on England. **1924** *U.S. Laws & Statutes* (1925) XLIII. 155 When used in this Act the term 'quota immigrant' means any immigrant who is not a non-quota immigrant. **1965** *Listener* 2 Sept. 340/2 Some [Australian] commentators advocate quota immigration for Asians. **1922** *Proc. Conf. Social Work* xlix. 460 Just what effect the quota law has had on immigration.. cannot be accurately determined. *Ibid.* 465 Under the quota law..we have exclusion for the first time on the basis of numbers alone. **1975** J. Cleary *Safe House* 10 Every country..had a quota limit when..asked to extend its sympathy into acceptance of the Jews as immigrants. **1946** Hauser & Leonard *Govt. Statistics for Business Use* xii. 356 A commonly used type of sample design is that usually referred to as the 'quota' or 'in-ratio' method of sampling. **1953** W. G. Cochran *Sampling Techniques* v. 105 Sampling theory cannot be applied to quota methods which contain no element of probability sampling. **1971** *Guardian* 9 June 13/4 Teams of interviewers were sent out to a random sample of areas to find certain numbers of consumers determined by sex, age, and social class. This is known as the quota method of sampling. Random sampling—where lists are drawn from an 'unbiased' source such as the electoral register—is more rigorous, but much more expensive and is rarely used for commercial work. **1958** *Economist* 18 Oct. 280/1 For the first two quota periods (6 months) of the current year, the permitted output averaged 118 tons per month. **1977** *Grimsby Even. Tel.* 13 May 1/5 It showed we have no confidence in him and his quota plans. **1936** *Economist* 5 Dec. 456/2 The primary objective of the Board of Trade..was the complete extirpation of the 'quota quickie'. **1948** H. Wilson in *Hansard Commons* 21 Jan. 226 To protect this section of the industry against the so-called 'quota quicky' shorts. **1976** *Oxf. Compan. Film* 574/1 'Quota quickies'—cheap programme-fillers made with local personnel and technical resources but financed from the US—kept standards down while fulfilling legal requirements. **1924** J. S. Huxley in *Spectator* 20 Dec. 981/1 The 1924 Immigration Law takes the quota idea as its basis... The quota restrictions do not apply to Canadians. **1938** *Ann. Reg. 1937* 17 In Great Britain there were no exchange controls and no quota restrictions save in the case of iron and steel imports. **1944** *Jrnl. Marketing* July 26/2 The current method, perhaps most-widely employed in the selection of respondents in market surveys and in polls of opinion, is that of 'in ratio' or 'quota sampling'... The essentials of this method consist in:..(3) the fixing of quotas for each enumerator in such a way that the re-

spondents..will include the specified proportion of each class of the population agreed upon. **1952** *Economist* 20 Sept. 689 (Advt.), Checking the quota sample against a random sample. **1966** *Guardian* 25 Apr. 8/5 Under the quota method..people are interviewed in the street... The random sample, which involves contacting named individuals..is much more expensive than the quota system. **1974** *Times* 15 Feb. 5/7 The Gallop Poll..plans to do a mixture of random and quota samples. **1952** *Jrnl. R. Statistical Soc.* A. CXV. 412 Quota samplers invariably attempt, as one of their controls, an economic or social breakdown of the sample. **1958** C. A. MOSER *Survey Methods Social Investigation* vi. 105 Quota samplers generally claim that instructions to, and constraints on, interviewers are sufficient to guard against the main dangers of selection bias. **1944** *Jrnl. Marketing* July 29/1 One of the most important advantages of area sampling over..quota sampling is that which reduces the dependence of the investigator on knowledge of the characteristics of the population. **1950** M. PARTEN *Surveys, Polls, & Samples* i. 31 Up to 1946, the nationwide tabulations were usually based on about 3,000 cases selected according to a stratified quota sampling procedure. **1973** *Guardian* 27 Oct. 13/5 Quota sampling sets the interviewer the..task of finding people who are socially representative... Random means what it says, and should..be based on the picking of names at random from the electoral register. **1924** *N.Y. Times* 8 Dec. 17/1 A bill amending the immigration law and abolishing the quota system is being drafted for presentation to Congress. **1934** A. G. MACDONELL *How like an Angel* II. v. 86 It was the business of the All-British Company to produce seventeen exceptionally bad and cheap films every year in England in order to allow two hundred and forty-six exceptionally bad and expensive films to be imported every year into England from Hollywood. This is called the Quota System. **1936** *Discovery* Dec. 374/1 Under the quota system..2,894 Japanese were entitled to admission [to Brazil] during 1935. **1969** *Listener* 14 Aug. 201/1 *The quota system.* Thirty per cent of first features shown in this country have to be made here. **1976** *National Observer* (U.S.) 14 Feb. 11/5 Demanding what amounts to a quota system for college and university faculty hiring.

quotation. Add: **3. c.** A short passage or tune taken from one piece of music to another or quoted elsewhere.

1906 E. NEWMAN *Elgar* v. 147 The clarinet softly gives out a quotation..from Mendelssohn's 'Calm Sea and Prosperous Voyage' overture. **1942** G. ABRAHAM *Beethoven's Second-Period Quartets* 42 A note-for-note quotation of a figure much used in the first movement of Mozart's great Quartet in C major, K.465. **1960** *New Oxf. Hist. Music* III. v. 156 The following quotation will..serve to show the extent to which the late Gothic composers intentionally subordinated the natural verbal rhythm to the rhythmic compulsion of the music. **1972** *Jazz & Blues* Oct. 26/3 Flashes of humour in the form of oblique quotations.

quotatious (kwotēⁱ·ʃəs), *a.* [f. QUOTATI(ON + -OUS.] Fond of using quotations; inclined to quote.

1903 *Daily Chron.* 10 Apr. 3/2 The myriad quotations of that most 'quotatious' of authors are identified every one—no easy task with such a perverter of phrases as Hazlitt. **1910** *Ibid.* 29 Jan. 6/1 A certain person endeavoured to quench my flaming optimism by a stream of frigid quotation... I sought knowledge from the quotatious person.

quotative, *a.* Add: **2.** Of a construction or expression: indicating that the speaker is quoting a word, phrase, etc., attributed to another person.

1927 L. BLOOMFIELD in *Amer. Speech* II. 438/2 Whatever is hearsay and not the speaker's own experience has the predicate verb or particle in a special *quotative* form. **1957** D. L. BOLINGER in *Publ. Amer. Dial. Soc.* XXVIII. 26 A reflex..may be re-worded to make it less quotative. **1975** *Language* LI. 804 Normally a sentence containing the quotative clitic translates with 'one says'.

quotative (kwōᵘ·tătiv), *sb.* [f. the adj.] A quotative word or expression (see prec.).

1902 *Amer. Anthropol.* IV. 401 The quotative *wAnsū'ga*, 'they say', is used extensively in the Skidegate dialect. **1957** D. L. BOLINGER in *Publ. Amer. Dial. Soc.* XXVIII. 95 With other verbs, notably the outright quotatives that concord the adoption or assertion of a view..concord gives a different meaning. **1965** *Language* XLI. 68 A few further elements—pseudo-constitutes.., multiple constitutes.., and quotatives. **1975** *Ibid.* LI. 804 The first example is provided by quotatives in Luiseño.

quo·tativeness. [f. QUOTATIVE *a.* + -NESS.] **a.** Fondness for the use of quotations. **b.** The quality of being quotative (sense *2).

1886 G. B. SHAW in *Pall Mall Gazette* 26 July 5/1 A certain facetiousness and quotativeness. **1957** D. L. BOLINGER in *Publ. Amer. Dial. Soc.* XXVIII. 27 The quotativeness of the echo suggests that it be classed as a frag Q.

quote, *sb.*² Add: **2.** (Later examples.)

1922 T. S. ELIOT *Let.* ? Jan. in E. Pound *Lett.* (1951) 236 Do you mean not use the Conrad quote or simply not put Conrad's name to it? **1950** G. B. STERN *Ten Days of Christmas* i. 27 The title must be a quote. **1959** *Times Lit. Suppl.* 23 Jan. 45/4 The blurb..and 'quotes' selected from the American Press inaccurately suggest brashness. **1968** *Listener* 25 July 108/2 Don't ask me questions, since I have no wish to figure as the father of all the quotes in your stories. **1978** *Guardian Weekly* 15 Oct. 7/3 A quote from Dayan is painted on one of the twisted gun doors: 'The Bar-Lev line looks like a piece of cheese with a hole in it.'

b. (Later examples.)

1920 WODEHOUSE *Coming of Bill* I. ii. 24 Below the signature, in what printers call 'quotes', a line..'Bear the torch and do not falter.' **1937** *Daily Express* 4 Feb. 6/3 New use for 'quotes' ('inverted commas') came to light at the Scottish Literary luncheon in London yesterday. **1955** T. H. PEAR *Eng. Social Differences* iii. 90 The upper class fashion of speaking in 'quotes'—'I don't mind if I do' (in a pronounced Cockney accent). **1969** 'J. MORRIS' *Fever Grass* ii. 24 He'd have witnesses if I put him in the dock. Witnesses in quotes, I mean. **1976** *New Yorker* 16 Feb. 37/1 Freezes over close quote, paragraph.

3. = QUOTATION 6.

1959 *Daily Mail* 8 June 2/3 'Quotes' for readers. The following list of prices is a selection from readers' requests for quotation of some of their shares which do not fluctuate sufficiently to be quoted daily. **1965** E. GUNDREY *Foot in Door* xii. 91 She was shown a long list of things that needed doing..and was given a quote for 'about £28'. **1970** *Globe & Mail* (Toronto) 25 Sept. 4/4 The Duke price was consistently lower than other quotes. **1976** J. DRUMMOND *Funeral Urn* iv. 14 Do the work, will I?.. I'll give you a quote before I get stuck in. **1980** *Daily Tel.* 3 Jan. 15/6 Yesterday..he was appointed chairman of construction company Tebbitt, which has a market value of £1·3 million. 'It is a small start, but I needed a vehicle with a quote and Tebbitt is exactly right.'

quote, *v.* Add: **3. b.** Also, to repeat a statement by (someone); to give (a person's name) as the authority for a statement. Freq. in phr. *don't quote me.*

1953 A. CHRISTIE *Pocket Full of Rye* ii. 12 Of course, I *may* be wrong—don't quote me, for Heaven's sake. **1965** *Word Study* Apr. 6/2 We might happen to have such a quotation from Public Enemy No. 1, and we wouldn't hesitate to quote him. **1973** *Times* 15 Feb. 18/5 They won't be here at all in three years time. And you can quote me on that too. **1976** 'R. MACDONALD' *Blue Hammer* xviii. 150 'Who had reason to kill him?' 'I don't know. His wife, perhaps... Don't quote me, but I wouldn't put it past her.'

4. a. Also *transf.*, of a composer or musical composition: to reproduce or repeat (a passage or tune that forms part of another piece of music).

1946 E. BLOM *Everyman's Dict. Mus.* 138/1 Dies irae. The 2nd section of the Requiem Mass, orig[inally] associ[ated] with a distinct plainsong theme which has been frequently used or quoted by var[ious] comp[oser]s. **1954** *Grove's Dict. Mus.* (ed. 5) II. 955/1 Var. XIII [of the 'Enigma Variations'] quotes from Mendelssohn's 'Calm Sea and Prosperous Voyage' Overture. **1975** R. S. GOLD *Jazz Talk* 213 *Quote*,..of a vocalist or soloing instrumentalist to insert a phrase from another tune into the one being played.

c. *quote..unquote*: a formula used in dictation to introduce and terminate a quotation. Freq. *transf.*, in speech or writing, introducing and terminating words quoted (or ironically imagined to be quoted) from the speech or writing of another.

1935 E. E. CUMMINGS *Let.* 3 Oct. (1969) 145 The Isful ubiquitous wasless&-shallbeless quote scrotumtightening unquote omnivorously eternal thalassa pelagas or Ocean. **1950** 'S. RANSOME' *Deadly Miss Ashley* xvii. 198 She says, quote, 'What girl wouldn't?' unquote. **1956** *Times* 5 Dec. 1/5 (Advt.), Today, America, you sure are quote in the Big Time unquote. **1958** B. HAMILTON *Too Much of Water* xi. 245 But he did have, quote, a jolly good reason for bumping off one special person, unquote. **1961** P. USTINOV *Loser* viii. 140 He expressed the personal opinion that the picture was quote great for America unquote. **1973** D. ROBINSON *Rotten with Honour* 8 The British... see too many people like you in London... East Germans, Bulgarians, and Rumanians, all of them quote diplomats unquote.

7. Also, to name a racehorse *at* specified odds; *absol.* or with a person as *obj.*, to give (someone) a quotation for goods or services. (Earlier and later examples.)

1865 *Atlantic Monthly* May 575/1 The artist is like the stock which is to be quoted at the board and thrown upon the market. **1888** *Economist* (Chicago) 3 Nov. 4/3 The effect of quoting Gas Trust upon the ticker..has been to stimulate trade in this stock here. **1934** *Collier's* 11 Aug. 48/2 Black Gold was quoted at 200 to 1 for the Coffroth event. **1938** *Times* 29 Sept. 19/1 War Loan..was being quoted 95 middle in inter-office dealings. **1971** *Timber Trades Jrnl.* 14 Aug. 71 (Advt.), Your machines..reconditioned, re-installed... Let us quote you.

quotee. (In Dict. s.v. QUOTE *v.*) (Earlier and later examples.)

1813 W. S. WALKER *Let. to Sir Walter Scott* in *N. & Q.* (1961) Jan. 19/2 You see I am addicted to comparisons, like your quotee Fluellen. **1926** *Eng. Jrnl.* May 395 The quotee protests. Professor Baker has asked that attention be called to a quotation by Professor Campbell..which he feels does not present his meaning fairly. **1973** *Publishers' Weekly* 7 May 19/2 Ruland was not a manufactured quotee.

quotha, *interj.* (Later examples.)

1917 W. OWEN *Let.* 4 Feb. (1967) 432 Distaste? Distaste, Quotha? **1958** L. DURRELL *Mountolive* v. 111 A fellow-romantic quotha!

‖ **quot homines tot sententiae** (kwǫt hǫ·minēⁱz tǫt sente·nti,əi). [L.] An observation on the diversity of opinions, deriving from Terence *Phormio* II. iv. 14 *quot homines tot sententiae*: *suus cuique mos* 'there are as many opinions as there are men: to each his own way'.

1539 R. TAVERNER tr. *Erasmus's Proverbes or Adagies* f. xiii, Quot homines, tot sentenciæ. So many heades, so many iudgementes. **1575** G. GASCOIGNE *Certayne Notes of Instruction concerning Making of Verse or Ryme in English*, And therwithall I pray you consider that *Quot homines, tot Sententiæ*, especially in Poetrie. **1602** W. WATSON *Quodlibeticall Questions concerning Relig. & State* 343 They follow each one of them their owne priuate foule spirits of deceit and error, & so *quot homines tot sententiæ*, So many men so many minds. **1869** *Fraser's Mag.* LXXX. 68/1 Here all is to be pleasure. The opinions as to what is pleasure vary as a matter of course. *Quot homines tot sententiæ.* **1969** *Listener* 13 Nov. 680/2 A visitor from another planet might well have marvelled at the fertility of the human race in generating opinion—*quot homines tot sententiae* with a vengeance. **1975** *Times* 13 Nov. 17/6 No one has ever agreed entirely about Kipling; *Quot homines, tot sententiae.*

quotidian, *a.* and *sb.* Add: **A.** *adj.* **3.** (Later example.)

1978 *Studies in Eng. Lit.: Eng. Number* (Tokyo) 121 Malory..omits many of the 'quotidian' actions of chivalric life.

Hence **quoti·dianism.**

1920 A. HUXLEY *Limbo* 261 'It is our cheap press. The ephemeral overwhelms the permanent, the classical.' 'This journalism,' I agreed, 'or call it rather this piddling quotidianism, is the curse of our age.'

quotient. Add: **1. b.** *quotient ring*; **quotient group** = *factor group* s.v. *FACTOR *sb.* 9.

1893 *Bull. N.Y. Math. Soc.* III. 74 The quotient-group of any two consecutive groups in the series of composition of any group is a simple group. **1911** W. BURNSIDE *Theory of Groups of Finite Order* (ed. 2) iii. 39 Herr Hölder has introduced the symbol *G/H* to represent this group; he calls it the quotient of *G* by *H*, and a factor-group of *G*. **1958** R. V. ANDREE *Mod. Abstract Algebra* iv. 101 The order of the quotient group is the order of *G* divided by the order of *H*, providing *G* is finite. *Ibid.* viii. 188 The term *quotient ring* is also used because of the similarity to the concept of quotient groups. **1965** PATTERSON & RUTHERFORD *Elem. Abstract Algebra* iii. 101 If *S* is an ideal in the ring *R*... The set of all cosets of *S* in *R* is a ring:..this is called the..quotient ring of *R* by *S*. **1972** F. J. BUDDEN *Fascination of Groups* xxi. 409 A group which resolves into a succession of *cyclic* quotient groups in this way is called a 'soluble' group.

Quran, Qur'an, Qur(')anic, varr. KORAN¹, KORANIC *a.*

1876 T. P. HUGHES in A. Qádir *Qurán, Transl. into Urdu Language* p. iii, There is no ***authorized*** translation of the Qurán in any language. **1885** —— *Dict. Islam* 483/2 *Qur'ān*.., the sacred book of the Muhammadans. **1905** W. ST. CLAIR TISDALL *Orig. Sources of Qur'ân* iii. 63 The *Source* of the rest of the Qur'ânic account of the murder is the legend in the *Pirqêy Rabbî Eli'ezer.* **1919** H. U. W. STANTON *Teaching of Qur'ān* 5 The best studies on quranic theology in English are the pamphlets by Rev. W. R. W. Gardner. **1931** *Times Lit. Suppl.* 11 June 459/2 The tales ..vary from Qur'anic legends to popular stories of the most ribald and grotesque description. **1932** *Ibid.* 17 Mar. 185/1 He had forgotten the Quran and could not recite one of the suras. **1939** L. H. GRAY *Foundations of Lang.* 363 *Arabic*, famous as the language of the Qur'ān. **1954** *Scott. Jrnl. Theol.* VII. 334 The non-expert will find this an eminently readable and absorbing book, and one that might well stimulate to a lasting interest in the Qur'an and the Islamic world. *Ibid.*, Again, the book is the fruit of a lifetime's devotion to Qur'anic studies. **1971** *Nigerian Jrnl. Islam* II. 45 Thus, the emphasis in the Quranic School is on the moral development of the child. **1972** *Computers & Humanities* VI. 195 Arabic, the native language of 100 million people, is also used by many more millions as the language of the Quran and Islamic Law. **1976** *Daily Tel.* 6 Apr. 11/3 Their loans have been supplemented by Qur'ans from the British Library's own collection. **1980** *Oxf. Diocesan Mag.* Feb. 9/1 The total restriction of women to their homes..has been a matter of social custom, not Quranic law.

QWERT, QWERTY, qwerty (kwɜ̄ɹt, kwɜ̄ɹti). Part of the series of letters that label the first row of letter keys on typewriters in English-speaking countries; also **qwert yuiop,** the full series in that row. Also (in form *qwerty*) used *attrib.* or as *adj.* to designate a keyboard or machine that incorporates this type of non-alphabetical lay-out.

1929 *Times Lit. Suppl.* 11 July 552/2 The 'qwerty' keyboard appears first on the Yost in 1887. **1961** *Courier-Mail* (Brisbane) 5 June (*heading*) 'QWERTS' girls are in demand. **1962** *Which?* Dec. 356/2 The keyboards of all the machines were laid out in the traditional—and irrational—pattern, sometimes called 'qwert yuiop', which gives the left hand a lot of work to do, and its little finger too big a share of that. **1967** *Crescendo* Dec. 15/1 As soon as I had the virgin sheet of paper threaded into my type-writer I discovered that I was at peace with the world. Not a single hostile thought came to mind. I wrote QWERT a couple of times and gazed at my brain-child. **1975** *Nature* 16 Oct. 556/1 Input is usually by Qwerty keyboard, either direct entry or off-line, using punched tape. **1976** *Times* 9 Nov. 16/7 Mutterings..are to be heard among non-French secretaries employed by the European Commission in Brussels over plans to introduce a standardized typewriter based on the French AZERTY keyboard... The Commission..points out that if English QWERTY machines had been chosen..this decision would have been just as open to accusations of discrimination. Germans..operate QWERTZ machines, while Italians..prefer QZERTY.

Qy. (Earlier example.)

1819 M. EDGEWORTH *Let.* 17 Apr. (1971) 195 We had been presented to the (Qy.) Duchess of Sussex.

R

R. Add: **I. 1. c.** Phonetics. *r-less* adj.; *r-colour*, the modification of a vowel sound caused by a following *r*, as in the U.S. pronunciation of *bird*, etc.; hence *r-coloured* adj., *r-colouring*. Also *intrusive r* (see introductory note in Dict.); *linking r*: see *LINKING *ppl. a.* d.

1887 *Trans. Philol. Soc. 1885–6* 3 The intrusive *r* has actually produced an additional syllable in modern English. 1902 H. L. Wilson *Spenders* xxiv. 277 Her speech bore just a hint of the soft r-less drawl of the South. 1909 O. Jespersen *Mod. Eng. Gram.* I. 372 In literature the intrusive *r* is frequently indicated as a characteristic mark of vulgarity; the oldest example, perhaps, is in Smollett. 1928 I. C. Ward *Phonetics of Eng.* xiii. 130 There is no doubt that the intrusive r is spreading; even in districts where it has not been known, the younger generation is using it. 1935 J. S. Kenyon *Amer. Pronunc.* (ed. 6) 158 In Southern American speech, instead of accented 3, an '*r*-colored' vowel varying to ɝ is often heard. *Ibid.* 191 The retroflexion is slight, or replaced by raising and retraction of the tongue, but..the vowel is still '*r*-colored', giving the impression of an *r* sound. *Ibid.* 193 In South England..the '*r* color' itself disappeared, leaving the sound 3. 1940 *Maître Phonétique* Oct.–Dec. 63 ðə nouteiʃnz..witʃ dinout prisaisli vauəlz wið r-kʌlariŋ. 1941 *Language* XVII. 240 This occurs frequently in the mixed dialect of those who have both '*r*-pronouncing' and '*r*-less' forms in their speech. 1950 D. Jones *Phoneme* xvi. 82, r-colouring, when vowels are said with simultaneous lowering of the soft palate. *Ibid.*, r-coloured vowels are found with significant function in various types of American and British English. 1965 *Canad. Jrnl. Linguistics* XI. I. 65 Nine free vowels occur under stress in all dialects..; a tenth occurs only in *r*-less dialects. 1977 P. Strevens *New Orientations Teaching of English* xii. 151 In American English, in all words spelled with *r* there is an *r* sound which occurs simultaneously with the vowel before it. (..The vowels in such cases are said to be *r*-coloured.)

II. 1. b. (Examples.) Also (occas.) as *v. intr.*

1816 *Catholicon* II. 264 Obituary..On the 24th inst. Mr. Cornelius Peter Murphy..possessed of a heart glowing with the most generous sentiments, he contracted his illness by the devotedness of his friendship to a deserving youth, from whom, during the course of his long and fatal malady, he could not be separated. R.I.P. 1917 A. G. Empey *Over Top* 306 'R.I.P.' In monk's highbrow, 'Requiescat in pace', put on little wooden crosses over soldier's graves... Tommy says like as not it means 'Rest in pieces', especially if the man under the cross has been sent West by a bomb. 1962 *Punch* 5 Sept. 334/1 We had a field mouse RIP-ing under the cupboard. 1976 *Liverpool Echo* 22 Nov. 4/1 Fortified by rites of Holy Church (R.I.P.). Requiem Mass Thursday, November 25.

2. a. R = *RAND *sb.*^{2} 2; ®, registered (of a trademark: incorporated in *Statutes at Large U.S.A. 1946* (1947) LX. I. 436); R, restricted (rating) (*U.S.*); R, reverse (as on the selector mechanism in a vehicle with automatic transmission); R, r, right; also *spec.* of a stage (examples); R (*Bacteriol.*) = *ROUGH *a.* 1 e; R, rupee (examples); R.A., Royal Academy or Academician (further examples); R.A., Royal Artillery; R.A.A.F., Royal Australian Air Force; R.A.C., Royal Armoured Corps; R.A.C., Royal Automobile Club; R.A.E., Royal Aircraft Establishment; R.A.F., Royal Air Force (see as main entry in Suppl.); R.A.F. [G. *Rote Armee Fraktion*], Red Army Faction (in West Germany); R.A.F.V.R., Royal Air Force Volunteer Reserve; RAM (*Computers*), random-access memory; R.A.M., Royal Academy of Music; R.A.M.C., Royal Army Medical Corps; R and B, R & B, R'n B, r'n'b = **rhythm and blues*; R and D, R & D, research and development (chiefly *U.S.*); R and R, R & R, rest and recreation (leave) (orig. *U.S.*); R. and R., R.'n' R., r'n'r = *ROCK AND ROLL; R.A.O.C., Royal Army Ordnance Corps; R.A.P., Regimental Aid Post; R.A.S.C., Royal Army Service Corps; R. Aux. A.F., Royal Auxiliary Air Force; R.B.C., red blood cell or corpuscle; red blood (cell) count; R.B.E., relative biological effectiveness (of radiation); R.B.I. (*Baseball*), run batted in; RC (*Electronics*), resistance/capacitance (or resistor/capacitor); R.C., r.c., reinforced concrete; R.C., Roman Catholic (examples); R.C.A., Radio Corporation of America; R.C.A.F., Royal Canadian Air Force; R.C.M., radio (or radar) counter-measures; R.C.M.P., Royal Canadian Mounted Police; R.D., refer (also loosely understood as return) to drawer (of cheque); R.D.C., Rural District Council; R.D.F., radio direction-finding, -finder (in quots., referring to radar); also as *v. trans.*, to employ R.D.F. against; RDV, rdv = RENDEZVOUS *sb.* (orig. *U.S.*); R.E., religious education; R.E., Royal Engineers; r.f., R.F., radio-frequency; R.F., representative fraction; usu. *attrib.*; R.F.A., Royal Field Artillery; R.F.A., Royal Fleet Auxiliary; R.F.C., Royal Flying Corps; R.F.D., rural free delivery (of letters) (*U.S.*); R.G.A., Royal Garrison Artillery; R.G.N., Registered General Nurse; Rh, rhesus (blood group); usu. *attrib.*; R.H.A., Royal Horse Artillery; R.I., religious instruction; RIAA, Record (since 1970, Recording) Industry Association of America; R.I.A.F., Royal Indian Air Force; R.I.B.A., Royal Institute of British Architects; R.I.C., Royal Irish Constabulary; R.I.N., Royal Indian Navy; R.K., religious knowledge; R.M., Reichsmark; R.M., Resident Magistrate (examples); R.M., Royal Marines; R.M.A., Royal Marine Artillery; R.M.C., Royal Military College (at Sandhurst); R.M.L.I., Royal Marine Light Infantry; r.m.s., R.M.S. (chiefly *Electr.*), root mean square; usu. *attrib.*; R.M.S., Royal Mail Steamer (also Ship); R.N., Registered Nurse; R.N., Royal Navy (examples); R.N.A.S., Royal Naval Air Service; R.N.D., Royal Naval Division; R.N.L.I., Royal National Life-boat Institution; R.N.R., Royal Naval Reserve; R.N.V.R., Royal Naval Volunteer Reserve; R.N.Z.A.F., Royal New Zealand Air Force; ROA [Russ. *Rússkaya osvobodítel'naya ármiya*], the Russian Liberation Army; R.O.C., Royal Observer Corps; R.O.K., Rok (rǫk), Republic (also Relief) of Korea; also *pl.*, soldiers of the Republic of Korea; ROM (*Computers*), read-only memory; R.O.P., rop, run of paper (as of advertisements not booked for a specific position in a newspaper); also *fig.*; also in colour printing (see quot. 1967); ROSLA (also with pronunc. rǫ·zlă), raising of the school-leaving age; RoSPA (rǫ·spă), Royal Society for the Prevention of Accidents; RP, rp = *received pronunciation* s.v. *RECEIVED *ppl. a.* 1 b; R.P.M., r.p.m., resale price maintenance; r.p.m., R.P.M., revolution(s) per minute; RPV, remotely piloted vehicle (orig. *U.S.*); R.Q. (*Med.*), respiratory quotient; rRNA, ribosomal RNA; R.S., rs, received standard; formerly, received speech; R.S.A., Royal Society of Arts; also *pl.*, R.S.A. examinations; R.S.F.S.R. [Russ. *Rossíĭskaya Sovétskaya Federatívnaya Sotsialistícheskaya Respúblika*], the Russian Soviet Federative Socialist Republic; RSJ, rolled steel joist; RSLA = *ROSLA* above; R.S.M., Regimental Sergeant Major; R.S.P.B., Royal Society for the Protection of Birds; R.S.P.C.A., Royal Society for the Prevention of Cruelty to Animals; R.S.V., Revised Standard Version (of the Bible); RSV (*Biol.* and *Med.*), Rous sarcoma virus; R/T, R.T., radio-telegraph or -telephone; usu. *attrib.*; RTE, Radio Telefis Eireann, the official broadcasting authority of the Republic of Ireland; R.T.O., Railway Transport(ation) Officer, Railroad Transportation Officer; R.T.U. (*Mil.*), returned to unit; R.U.C., Royal Ulster Constabulary; RV, rateable value; RV (earlier RecV), recreational vehicle, as a motorized caravan (*U.S.*); hence *RVer*; *RVing* ppl. a.; R.V., r.v. = RENDEZVOUS *sb.* and *v. intr.*

See also *R.A.D.A., *RDX, *REM *sb.*^{2}, *R.E.M.E., *RNA, *R.O.T.C. (as main entries).

1961 *Times* 27 Jan. 19/4 Offers of 'one-ninetyfour' and 'one-ninetyfive'..were chalked up as 'R1.94' and 'R1.95'. 1961 *Africana Notes & News* Mar. (recto rear cover), Subscription R2 per annum..Holt, B. Place-Names of the Transkeian Territories, 1959, R0·75. 1971 J. McClure *Steam Pig* iv. 40 She kept her money in the post office, just over R200. 1925 *Registration of Trade-Marks* (U.S. Congress Senate, Comm. on Patents) 20–1 Jan. 8 It shall be the duty of the registrant to accompany a registered trade-mark with the words 'Registered in U.S. Patent Office',..or by letter 'R' in a circle, thus ®. 1977 *Gloss. Terms Unfair Competition* (U.S. Trademark Assoc.), ®, one of several notices prescribed by law to indicate that a mark is registered in the U.S. Patent and Trademark Office. 1965 *Acronyms & Initialisms Dict.* (Gale Research Co.) 589 R... Restricted (Military document classification). 1972 *Daily Colonist* (Victoria, B.C.) 6 Feb. 2/3 The Strawberry Statement, the MGM version of a campus rebellion..was rated R (no one under 17 admitted without parent or guardian). 1976 *New Yorker* 12 Jan. 70/2 Peckinpah was forced to trim 'The Killer Elite' to change its R rating to a PG. *Ibid.*, Many of these theatres wouldn't have taken it if it had an R and the kids couldn't go by themselves. 1951 R = reverse [see L = low s.v. *L 7]. 1846 J. R. Planché *Bee & Orange Tree* ii. 7 On (R.) a Cavern. Tempest. A Vessel is seen in distress. When it is out of sight, enter (R.) from Cavern, Princess Amy. 1893 G. B. Shaw *Let.* 27 Apr. (1965) I. 392 The old style—the Princess & the audience grouped R, and Adrienne beginning L in profile. 1976 M. S. Hoque *Hunger* I. i. 1, Moina and Latif appear—R. They are just visible by the door. 1977 *Rolling Stone* 24 Mar., (*caption*) (Opposite, l to r): John, Mick, Christine McVie, Lindsey Buckingham and Stevie Nicks. 1920 J. A. Arkwright in *Jrnl. Path. & Bacteriol.* XXIII. 359 The R form grows in colonies which have a more or less jagged outline, are flatter and often have an irregular, rough, or dull surface and are slightly opaque. 1973 Klainer & Geis *Agents of Bacterial Dis.* i. 23 Rough (R) colonies have a dry, flat, irregular, wrinkled appearance and are generally formed by cells that lack a capsule. 1885 Kipling *Let.* 30 July in C. Carrington *Rudyard Kipling* (1955) iv. 67 One Proprietor offered My Mother Rs 1,000 for an Anglo-Indian story. 1971 *Shankar's Weekly* (Delhi) 4 Apr. 9/3 'It won't cost much.' 'No, about Rs. 10,000.' 1829 J. Constable *Let.* 5 Apr. (1965) III. 21, I beg my best regards to Mrs Leslie—I am always dear Leslie. / your obliged friend / John Constable R.A. 1890 Lloyd George *Let.* 10 June (1973) 28 He had numerous R.A.'s & in fact I should fancy his picture gallery alone must have aggregated £10,000 in value. 1970 *Oxf. Compan. Art* 547/2 He was trained as a chorister in the Chapel Royal, and later received an allowance..to study at the R.A. Schools. 1815 J. Kane *List Officers R. Regiment Artillery* 65 List of Subaltern Officers of the Corps of R.A. Drivers. 1955 *Times* 16 June 4/3 Both achieved a creditable rate of bangs per minute, the R.E. with various demolitions and a set piece assault by flail tanks, the R.A. with gunfire. 1936 *Age* (Melbourne) 5 May 13 (*caption*) Aircraftsmen making adjustments to fuselage and bomb racks on the R.A.A.F. Hawker Demon at the Exhibition. 1955 *Times* 21 June 9/5 Melbourne, June 20... Four hundred soldiers, police and bushwalkers, helped by R.A.A.F. Dakota aircraft are searching 5,000ft. Mount Baw Baw for Mihran Haig. 1973 *Parade* (Melbourne) Sept. 22/1 The RAAF Lockheed Hudson, carrying a VIP load, was about to land at Canberra from Melbourne. 1942 Partridge *Dict. Abbrev.* 81/1 *R.A.C.*, Royal Armoured Corps; armoured fighting vehicles and tanks. 1950 *Jrnl. R. United Service Inst.* XCV. 289 The Royal Armoured Corps, as such, did not come into being until April 1939 (A.O. 58/1939)... In the same Army Order it was also stated that on transfer to the R.A.C. the R.T.C. would be re-designated Royal Tank Regiment. 1908 *Autocar Handbk.* (ed. 2) xxvi. 201 Members of most of the best clubs require only one proposer when joining the R.A.C. 1934 *Glasgow Herald* 11 Apr. 13/3 The R.A.C. will continue to press for a regulation that all pedal cyclists should be compelled to carry red rear lamps. 1977 J. Bingham *Marriage Bureau Murders* v. 61 A large, respectable hotel, mentioned in the A.A. and R.A.C. handbooks. 1926 *Encycl. Brit.* I. 20/2 (*heading*) The R.A.E. Bubble Sextant. 1977 *R.A.F. News* 11–24 May 11/2 Over at the R.A.E.'s Air Transport Flight. *Ibid.* 11/3 The Experimental Flying Squadron..is widely referred to as the sharp end of RAE flying. 1977 *Time* 19 Sept. 8/3 It was signed 'Kommando Siegfried Hausner, R.A.F.'—referring to a terrorist who died after a 1975 attack on the West German embassy in Stockholm. 1980 C. Moorehead *Fortune's Hostages* viii. 155 The freeing of six jailed 'RAF' prisoners. 1938 *Times* 2 Feb. 18/6 (*heading*) New branch of R.A.F.V.R. 1951 *Sunday Pictorial* 21 Jan. 13/6 (Advt.), They must undertake to fly with the R.Aux. A.F. or R.A.F.V.R. during their subsequent reserve service. 1957 R. K. Richards *Digital Computer Components & Circuits* vii. 347 'Random access storage' (or RAM, for 'random access memory'). 1977 *Design Engin.* July 15/2 The MM5799..contains 1,536 8-bit instructions in its ROM, and its RAM can store 96 BCD digits of 4 bits each. 1891 G. B. Shaw in *World* 23 Dec. 15/2, I am not in the habit of advising novices to lay the foundations of their vocal methods in the R.A.M. 1954 *Grove's Dict. Mus.* (ed. 5) 271/1 The R.A.M. continues its own separate examination in London..of music teachers and performers. 1900 *Morning Post* 25 July 5/6 Surgeon-Captain Rupert Fawssett, R.A.M.C. *a* 1944 K. Douglas *Alamein to Zem Zem* (1946) 128 Presently an R.A.M.C. warrant officer came. 1971 S. Hill *Strange Meeting* i. 67 Dick's in the R.A.M.C. but he's gone out to Egypt. [1949 *Billboard* 12 Nov. 110/2 Could score in pop as well as b & r mart.] *Ibid.* 31 Dec. 83, I Ain't Fattening Frogs for Snakes..with its catchy tag, could have a pop as well as r and b future. 1955 L. Feather *Encycl. Jazz* (1956) 70 Today's top R & B artists, contemporary equivalents of the Bessie Smiths and other 'race record' favourites of the 1920s. 1967 L. Deighton *London Dossier* i. 30 Deafening foreground music is provided by a giant jukebox. This is where the working City mod goes for his mid-day transfusion of R'n B. 1973 *Publishers Weekly* 14 May 48/3 Devoted to r'n'b groups, blues and r'n'b vocalists. 1977 *Rolling Stone* 13 Jan. 55/1 'Autobiography'..and 'Shakey Ground' have no doubt been formulated by producer David Rubinson to bring Snow into an R and B-flavored pop mainstream. 1952 Pohl & Kornbluth in *Galaxy* Aug. 129/1 'How's Research and Development doing on the Venus question?'..'R. and D. is in there punching.' 1966 *Inland* (Inland Steel Co., Chicago) Autumn 5/1 The American iron and steel industry alone will spend $200 million on R & D this year. 1978 Nature 2 Mar. 2/2 A reprocessing plant for throughput of about 1,000 tons per annum will cost in excess of £500 million, including radioactive waste storage, some R & D expenditure (say 5% of the total) and a decade of operating costs (perhaps 25% of the total). 1953 Britannica Bk. of Year 639/2 A similar idea is contained in the expression R. and R., the initials standing for 'Rest and Recreation'. 1966 New Statesman 14 Oct. 549/2 R & R = Rest and Recreation. Local leave for American troops, mostly in Hong Kong, Bangkok and Singapore. 1968 Telegraph (Brisbane) 3 May 1/7 American troops visiting Australia on R and R leave are to be briefed on the exploits of Diggers in Vietnam. 1977 J. Gardner Werewolf Trace xv. 129 Tonight was for R & R, tomorrow he would have another go at her to get the facts straight. 1955 Life 18 Apr. 168 On a list of 10 top juke box best-selling records last week, six were r'n r. 1958 Listener 9 Oct. 572/1 The musical basis of R.'n' R.. is the blues. 1973 Publishers Weekly 10 Dec. 39/1 This fat collection is devoted solely to writing about music (though not restricted to r'n'r). 1977 Sounds 1 Jan. 4/3 From head-bashing r&r, through Sixties pop..to an exquisite kick-in-the-teeth for Definitive Punk Rock. 1918 Times 28 Nov. 9/3 (heading) R.A.S.C., R.A.V.C., and R.A.O.C. 1930 War Office Regulations for Equipment of Army (Provisional) II. i. 3 Scabbards, bayonet, No. 1... R.A.O.C. on mobilization if especially ordered. 1971 S. Milligan Adolf Hitler III. 75 Thirty Signallers drove to the R.A.O.C. Depot at Reigate in a three-ton truck. 1942 E. Waugh Put out More Flags ii. 154 'I don't think you mentioned the R.A.P., did you, Smallwood?' 'R.A.P. sir. No, sir, I'm afraid I don't know where it is.' 1948 E. H. Smith Guns against Tanks 29 The 26th Battalion's Medical Officer..who earned the admiration of the gunners by bringing his RAP truck to within fifty yards of the forward positions. 1954 J. Masters Bhowani Junction xix. 174, I came to the R.A.P., swallowed, and went down to report to Captain Chaney. 1918 R.A.S.C. [see R.A.O.C. above]. 1955 Times 12 Aug. 4/7 In the permanent hutment camp by the wartime airfield..the Army Emergency Reserve transport columns of the R.A.S.C. are carrying out in succession their annual 15 days' training. 1976 Daily Mail (Hull) 16 Dec., Kenneth William Tully Bodfield, T.D., Major late R.A.S.C. 1948 R.A.F. Rev. Jan. 19/1 The short title of the Royal Auxiliary [Air Force] will be R. Aux. A.F. 1972 L. Hunt Twenty-One Squadrons 12 It was on 16th December 1947 that King George VI gave permission for the 'Royal' prefix and from that date until the squadrons disbanded in March 1957 they were R Aux AF units. 1922 Indian Med. Gaz. LVII. 126/2 The results of blood examination before treatment of soamin was R.B.C. 3,000,000, W.B.C. 3,500. 1968 Passmore & Robson Compan. Med. Stud. I. xxvi. 2/2 The red cell count (RBC) ranges from 4·5–6·5 million/mm³ in men and 3·9–5·6 million/mm³ in women. 1978 Nature 16 Feb. 674/2 Ageing of circulating RBC. 1954 P. E. Smith in A. J. Fleming et al. Mod. Occupational Med. xiii. 179 When irradiation with two different types of radiation requires different doses to achieve the same biological effect, the radiations are said to have a relative biological effectiveness (R.B.E.) different from one. The R.B.E. is the inverse of the dosage ratio required for equal effect. 1961 G. R. Choppin Exper. Nuclear Chem. ii. 10 The RBE (relative biological effectiveness) is defined as the ratio of the absorbed dose in rads of gamma radiation to the absorbed dose of the given radiation which is required to give the same biological effect. 1975 S. C. Bushong Radiologic Sci. for Technologists xvi. 286 Diagnostic x-rays have an RBE of approximately 1·0. 1951 Sun (Baltimore) 6 Oct. B-1/7 (heading) Yankee hurler says own R.B.I. gave him biggest thrill. 1976 Billings (Montana) Gaz. 1 July 4-E/1 Rusty Staub..had three RBI's, including a two-run homer on Monday. 1979 Honolulu Advertiser 8 Jan. C-2/5 Ahu got his six R.B.I.s on three hits, including two doubles and a grand-slam homer. 1932 C. L. Boltz Everyman's Wireless x. 190 The stage gain from an R.C. stage is E/e, where E is the voltage (A.C.) developed across the anode resistance and e is the voltage (A.C.) applied between grid and filament. Ibid., A 2-valve circuit incorporating detector and one stage of L.F. amplification with R.C. coupling. 1965 Wireless World July 326/1 RC coupling has been employed throughout, in preference to direct coupling, to minimize drift and facilitate the setting up procedure while still preserving the lower audio frequencies. 1932 Civil Engin. Sept. 17 Each column is supported by two vibro piles capped with a small R.C. slab. The whole area between the pile caps is covered with a 4 in. R.C. slab. 1953 Archit. Rev. CXIV. 305/1 Floors are of r.c. slab with a lightweight screed containing embedded heating coils. a 1762 Lady M. W. Montagu in Lett. (1967) III. 92 If the S[cripture] is true the R.C. Religion is false because contrary. 1820 J. Milner Suppl. Mem. Eng. Catholics II. 176 If it be true, that the Lords Grenville and Grey had any arrangements..inconsistent with the integrity and safety of the R.C. Religion, we declare, that we consider such arrangements as foreign to the obvious meaning of the Resolution we have signed. 1860 Queen Victoria Let. 7 Jan. in R. Fulford Dearest Child (1964) 227 Dear good Leopold Hohenzollern arrived... Oh! if only he were not a R.C.!! 1977 Belfast Telegraph 24 Jan. 10/1 (Advt.), R.C. Gent, of good family background, with means, wishes to meet teacher, nurse, or respectable farmer's daughter. 1922 Radio enters Home (Radio Corp. of Amer.) 7/1 The distributors of R.C.A. sets and apparatus have been selected carefully. 1938 Rev. Sci. Instruments IX. 219/1 (caption) The tube is an RCA 32. 1967 Cox & Grose Organization & Handling Bibl. Rec. by Computer II. 48 Both Linotron and RCA Digiset have this facility for checking enlarged characters. 1924 Pay & Allowance Regulations R. Canad. Air Force IV. 14 Officers..not carried on the General List, R.C.A.F., but..attached to the Royal Canadian Air Force for flying duty. 1943 Times 13 Dec. 2/2 A Royal Canadian Air Force Sunderland of Coastal Command with a mixed R.C.A.F. and R.A.F. crew. 1958 'Castle' & 'Hailey' Flight into Danger ii. 27 'I know it looks a bit like RCAF,' Dun was saying, fingering his great bush of a moustache. 1945 Electronic Industries Sept. 222 RCM, radar counter measures. 1947 Jrnl. R. Aeronaut. Soc. LI. 432/2 The job of the R.C.M. aircraft of the new Group was to impair these systems... Consequently we developed a jamming screen for the purpose of blinding the enemy's early warning system. 1978 R. V. Jones Most Secret War xxxiii. 289, I was amazed to sit through meetings of the Radio Counter Measures Board right up to the end of 1942 discussing whether it was advisable for us to start an 'R.C.M. War'. 1920 Globe (Toronto) 9 Feb. 3/4 The great increase in the membership of the force consequent of the extensions of its duties to Eastern Canada and the absorption of the Dominion Police within the organization of the R.C.M.P. 1967 Canad. Ann. Rev. 1966 21 Prime Minister Pearson had asked for any information in the RCMP files which indicated impropriety or wrongdoing. 1977 Financial Times 11 Nov. 5/5 Prime Minister Pierre Trudeau ordered a Royal Commission to investigate the RCMP's activities. 1913 W. T. Rogers Dict. Abbrev. 163/2 R.D. (bank.), refer to drawer (of cheque). 1938 N. Marsh Death in White Tie iii. 41 One of my cheques has been returned R.D. 1974 M. Butterworth Man in Sopwith Camel ii. 24 No..girl was going to rest a wet RD stamp on one of Stryvers' cheques by accident! 1904 Local Govt. Jrnl. 2 Jan. 3/1 (heading) Contracts open. 3/2 Granite.—The Clerk, R.D.C., Midhurst. a 1974 R. Crossman Diaries (1975) I. 114 At the time, I wasn't too alarmed when Alderman Reeves, the chairman of the R.D.C., called the decision the worst he had ever seen. 1938 F. A. Lindemann 8 Mar. in R. V. Jones Most Secret War (1978) iv. 40 Lest too much reliance be placed upon the R.D.F. methods, it is perhaps worth pointing out that certain difficulties may easily be encountered in actual use. 1942 E. Waugh Put out More Flags i. 28 We've got a most valuable invention called R.D.F. Ibid., The German air-bases are too far away for them to be able to attack us. If they do, we'll R.D.F. them out of the skies. 1963 L. Deighton Horse under Water xxiii. 101 Just behind me on the bridge Singleton was admiring the R.F.D. and the electronic depth-gauge. 1975 S. Johnson Urbane Guerilla III. 147 We didn't RDF him... The trouble is RDF-ing, radar direction finding, requires a cross-bearing. 1976 Oxf. Compan. Ships & Sea 685/2 In its earliest days, radar in Britain was known as RDF, the initial letters of radio direction finding, but the name was changed early in the Second World War to avoid confusion with H/F D/F, high frequency direction finding. 1955 R. J. Schwartz Compl. Dict. Abbrev. 152/3 RDV, rendezvous (US Army). 1973 'A. Hall' Tango Briefing iv. 45 I'm speaking from base. We shall need a little more time to set up the radio, so the next rdv is for 15.00 hours tomorrow. 1963 R. Acland We teach them Wrong 9, I told the deputy head master that I was a Lay Reader in the Church of England and could perhaps help with R.E. lessons. 1972 Guardian 29 Aug. 13/7 RE has been crippled by dogmatism and an arid biblicism. 1978 Times 3 Oct. 15/7 Some LEA's have been bold enough to recast their RE curriculum. .. The RE Council keeps a monitoring eye on emerging methodologies for RE. 1848 Brit. Army Despatch 24 Nov. 307/3 Captain Chapman, R.E., has returned to Zante from Cephalonia. 1877 Army Circular Dec. App. 18 Each Officer of R.E. below the rank of Major..is allowed 2 public horses. 1921 V. E. Inglefield Hist. 20th (Light) Div. iii. 37 Rations, R.E. material, etc., had to be brought up a long way from the dumps under very difficult conditions. 1959 I. Jefferies Thirteen Days xi. 175 If that's all you have to say you can get out. This is the R.E. office. 1918 W. H. Eccles Wireless Telegr. & Teleph. (ed. 2) 471 The r.f. generator 1 and microphone 2 induce currents in circuit 5. 1930 Proc. IRE XVIII. 1339 A relatively simple outfit is used comprising an r-f oscillator of variable frequency. 1931 Electronics July 17/1 A new impregnation compound for r.f. transformers affords better protection in humid atmosphere. 1956 Proc. CERN Symposium I. 64/2 Synchrotron oscillations (if an rf is present) are damped. 1967 Electronics 6 Mar. 2 (Advt.), Sweep Oscillators with RF and marker plug-ins meet virtually all of your swept frequency testing requirements. 1886 H. D. Hutchinson Military Sketching made Easy i. 12 A French map may show a scale of mètres, but to be generally useful to Englishmen it would be necessary to add to it a scale of yards with the same R.F. 1969 G. C. Dickinson Maps & Air Photographs vii. 102 In countries using the metric system scales of so many centimetres to a kilometre usually also give R.F.s with convenient round numbers. 1900 W. S. Churchill in Morning Post 27 Mar. 7/7, 1 battery Corps artillery (R.F.A.). 1974 A. Price Other Paths to Glory vi. 71 See how those casualties in the first two years [of the First World War] came from the..8th Hussars and the RFA—I'll bet they were all regulars. 1911 Shipping World 15 Mar. 276/1 (caption) The R.F.A. 'Burma'. 1931 Jane's Fighting Ships 84/2 Oilers (R.F.A.). 1913 Flight 12 Apr. 404/1 (heading) Motto for the R.F.C. 1933 V. Brittain Testament of Youth II. vii. 293 As we left the harbour a transport of the R.F.C. cheered us. 1977 R.A.F. News 27 Apr.–10 May 2/2 The final meeting of the North West Royal Flying Corps Association..was attended by Mr. Walter Sumner, a member who is now the sole RFC veteran to be a pensioner at the Royal Hospital, Chelsea. 1903 (title) R.F.D. news; devoted to the interests of the Rural Free Delivery Carriers of the U.S. 1903 R.F.D. News Feb. 21/2 Pa doesn't go to town for mail; we've got the R.F.D. 1974 M. Hoyt Thirty Miles for Ice Cream xv. 187 Our mail used to be delivered by an R.F.D. mailman riding behind a horse in a sort of outhouse on wheels, painted red, white and blue, and lettered U.S. Mail. 1907 Field Service Pocket Bk vi. 120 R.G.A. 1909 Army & Navy Gaz. 6 Feb. 140/1 Sir F. D. Blake, Bt., late Northumberland R.G.A. (Mil.). 1924 Nursing Mirror Pocket Encycl. & Diary 1924 85 R.G.N., Registered General Nurse (Scotland). 1975 Irish Independent 27 May 16/5 (Advt.), Resident R.G.N., or S.E.N., required for day duty in nursing home in Dublin south east. 1940 Landsteiner & Wiener in Proc. Soc. Exper. Biol. & Med. XLIII. 223 The capacity possessed by some rabbit immune sera produced with blood of Rhesus monkeys, of reacting with human bloods that contain the agglutinogen M has been reported previously. Subsequently it has been found that another individual property of human blood (which may be designated as Rh) can be detected by certain of these sera. 1954 A. E. Mourant Distribution Human Blood Groups iii. 12 The Rh blood groups depend upon three very closely adjacent loci on each of a pair of chromosomes, which may be called the C, D and E loci. 1958 L. P. Strean Birth of Normal Babies iv. 60 If the fetus is Rh-positive and the mother is Rh-negative, then the mother is actually immunized by the developing child's blood and she develops antibodies against the Rh-positive factor. 1968 Passmore & Robson Compan. Med. Stud. I. xxvi. 19/2 Only the ABO and Rh blood group systems contribute significantly to isoantibody incompatibility in the giving of blood transfusions. 1854 Times 20 Oct. 7/1 Captain Maude's Battery, R.H.A., was most useful. 1916 Ld. E. Hamilton First Seven Divisions 27 The 119th Battery R.F.A. was at this time just south-west of Eloges, and L Battery R.H.A. just north-east of Andregnies. 1962 M. Carver El Alamein iv. 51 While F Battery R.H.A. put down a 'stonk' the carriers counter-attacked and drove the enemy infantry back. 1961 Where? III. 16/2 Religious instruction (RI): The only subject which state schools are obliged to teach by law: in county and voluntary controlled schools. 1976 Evening Post (Nottingham) 15 Dec. 13/3 (Advt.), A teacher required in January and April for Independent School.. (3) R.I. with an interest in general counselling for girls 11 and over. 1952 Billboard 16 Feb. 18/1 Selection of an executive secretary for RIAA..was put off until early next week. 1971 J. Earl How to choose & use Pickups & Loudspeakers iii. 90 It is often necessary to attenuate the signal from a piezo cartridge before applying it to the RIAA amplifier input. 1975 Gramophone Jan. 1421/3 Also the RIAA correction curve for discs shows only the slightest deviation from the ideal playback curve. 1946 Civil & Milit. Gaz. 2 June 11/3 Disciplinary standards in the R.A.F. and R.I.A.F. 1971 R. Russell tr. A. Ahmad's Shore & Wave xv. 161 On one side stood Hasan, looking very smart in his R.I.A.F. uniform. 1913 W. T. Rogers Dict. Abbrev. 167/1 R.I.B.A. (Soc.), Royal Institute of British Architects. 1938 Times 7 Feb. 9/2 The article consists of a memorandum by the Public Relations Committee of the R.I.B.A. and correspondence therein between the Minister of Health and the R.I.B.A. Council. a 1974 R. Crossman Diaries (1975) I. 86, I had a difficult task when I had to go to the R.I.B.A. and give the certificates and prizes for the best-designed houses of the year. 1903 Somerville & 'Ross' All on Irish Shore 196 Two tall constables of the R.I.C. stood at the door of the cottage. 1972 A. Hezlet 'B' Specials i. 4 The I.R.A. issued a proclamation referring to the R.I.C. as spies and traitors. 1978 J. Carroll Mortal Friends I. iv. 47 He saw a private soldier, not an RIC Auxiliary, but an honest to God Tommy. 1946 Civil & Milit. Gaz. 2 June 11/3 R.I.N. ratings. 1959 R. K. [see physical torture s.v. *physical a. 7]. 1968 G. Mitchell Three Quick & Five Dead i. 24 'Edward teaches history and something he calls R. K.' 'Religious Knowledge,' said Laura. 'They used to call it Scripture in my young day.' 1875 Anglo-Brazilian Times 23 July 6/1 On Hamburg the rates for Bank paper at 90 days have been 442 Reis per R.M. 1963 L. Deighton Horse under Water 251 Peterson had a Reise-pass..and 200 RM. 1888 V. Martin Diary 24 June in M. Collis Somerville & Ross (1968) iv. 56 Jostled as to our seat by Brady R. M. 1899 Somerville & 'Ross' (title) Some experiences of an Irish R.M. 1947 Daily Gleaner (Kingston, Jamaica) 3 Nov. 12/5 Some cases before the R.M. Court... His Hon. Mr. S. T. B Sanguinetti, R.M. observed that he had left over the case from last week. 1827 J. Wright Let. 13 Nov. in P. H. Nicolas Hist. Record of Royal Marine Forces (1845) II. viii. 313 (heading) Deputy Adjutant-general's office, R.M. 1923 Admiralty Fleet Order No. 1643 22 June The R.M. Artillery at Eastney, and the R.M.L.I. at Forton will be combined into the Portsmouth Division, R. M. Ibid., Shoulder Letters.—Letters 'R.M.' to be worn by all ranks. 1962 S. Bassett Royal Marine iii. 69 If I got high marks, I'd be appointed Superintendent RM Signals, a Corps appointment. 1883 A. Cooper Key Let. in L. Conway-Gordon Case of Lt. Lewis Conway-Gordon (1884) 17, I might be able to give you a final answer to your request as to the removal of the names of the two Officers from..the list of Lieutenants, R.M.A. 1931 Times Lit. Suppl. 26 Mar. 246/3 After 1894 the R.M.A. were no longer sent to sea in small craft, but assigned only to first-class ships and flagships. 1893 W. S. Churchill Let. 10 Sept. in R. S. Churchill W. S. Churchill (1967) I. Compan. I. vii. 412 Tonight I go back to RMC. 1956 J. Masters Bugles & Tiger ii. 36 Bert King..led me up the steps and into the low grey pile before me—the Royal Military College, Sandhurst. From that moment..I was Gentleman Cadet John Masters, of No. 5 Company of the R.M.C., as I soon learned to call it. 1968 A. Powell Military Philosophers i. 55 Chu enjoyed the RMC so much he wants to go to Eton. 1889 W. Richards Her Majesty's Army II. 195 Lieutenant H. Earle, R.M.L.I., was sent as an envoy to the King of Dekra. 1916 'Taffrail' Pincher Martin ix. 166 He..hastily told the marine corporal of the watch to turn out twenty marines..and then to inform Captain Hannibal Chance, R.M.L.I., that a Zeppelin was in sight. 1930 Times Lit. Suppl. 3 July 542/3 It is the evacuation of the Y Beach at Gallipoli, in which the 1st Battalion was concerned, with one company of the 2nd South Wales Borderers and the Plymouth Battalion R.M.L.I. (consisting entirely of men specially enlisted for the War). 1980 Globe & Laurel July/Aug. 241/1 The original Forton RMLI Cadet Band was disbanded on amalgamation of the RMLI and RMA. 1897 A. Hay Princ. Alternate-Current Working vii. 93 When we speak of so many volts of an alternating P.D., or so many amperes of an alternating current, we thereby mean their R.M.S. values. 1940 Jrnl. Acoustical Soc. Amer. XI. 278/1 Peak and r.m.s. pressures in one-eighth-second intervals..from the voices of six men and five women. 1945 Electronic Engin. XVII. 737/3 The oscillator output voltage was 20V R.M.S. 1977 S. A. Book Statistics ii. 40 The standard deviation is the square root of the mean of the squared deviations. (In some applied contexts, it is referred to as the 'root-mean-square deviation' or the 'rms deviation'.) [1852 Nautical Mag. XXI. 91 To the Secretary R.M.S.P. Company.] 1870 Weekly Standard (Buenos Aires) 12 Jan. 1/3 The R.M.S. La Plata arrived in port..with the following passengers. 1936 Discovery June 181/2 R.M.S. 'Queen Mary', the greatest achievement of British shipbuilding. 1976 Oxf. Compan. Ships & Sea 684/1 R.M.S., the prefix, short for Royal Mail Ship, placed before the name of a British merchant ship with a licence to carry the Royal Mails. 1938 Amer. Speech XIII. 228/2 She is an 'R.N.', which means registered nurse—one who has graduated from an accredited school of nursing. 1974 Publishers Weekly 11 Feb. 62/2 Irish Katie, R.N. in a nursing home. 1846 H. D. Chads Let. in Madras Artillery Record VI. 323 [signed] H. D. Chads, Captain R.N. 1946 'Tackline' You met such Nice Girls in Wrens xiii. 144 It is very strange..why R.N. officers are so much meaner with their clothing-coupons than R.N.V.R. officers. 1975 'J. Bell' Victim iv. 52 Wing-Commander Redfern, Late R.A.F., his wife, Amanda, and Commander Pilcher, R.N., retired. 1918 W. S. Churchill Let. 10 Sept. in M. Gilbert W. S. Churchill (1975) IV. vii. 144 How much flying, for instance, is done by the RNAS for the 45,000 first-rate fighting men and skilled men they employ? 1977 Air Mail Spring 21/1

So this RAF phrase, like 'port' and 'starboard', came with the RNAS when the flying sailors merged with the RFC in 1918 to become the Royal Air Force. **1914** R. BROOKE *Let.* 24 Sept. (1968) 619 The nucleus of the R.N.D. is marines, Naval Reserve, etc.—more or less trained men. **1916** W. S. CHURCHILL *Let.* 29 Nov. in M. Gilbert *W. S. Churchill* (1977) IV. Compan. I. 34, I rejoiced to read of the glorious achievements of the RND. **1924** *Life-Boat: Centenary Number* 33 Small wonder that its sister-organization in little Holland has kept its eye upon the largest and oldest organization, the R.N.L.I. **1948** *Life-Boat* Mar. 157 The R.N.L.I. Roadless Tractor..can take the boat over all types of beach. **1977** *Navy News* June 1/2 The Merchant Navy and fishing fleets 'will be represented, as well as organizations like the R.N.L.I., Trinity House and H.M. Coastguard. **1868** *Times* 1 July 2/2 (Advt.), John Gray, R.N.R., Commander. **1902** C. J. C. HYNE *Mr. Horrocks, Purser* 85 What's the use of being R.N.R. if you don't let people know it? **1977** *Stornoway Gaz.* 27 Aug. 3/1 As were many other Lewismen, Alick was a member of the R.N.R. **1905** *Text Book for Royal Naval Volunteer Reserve* 3 The smartness, efficiency, and the credit of the R.N.V.R. depend upon the following principles. **1934** *Brassey's Naval & Shipping Ann.* 25 New rules were notified in Fleet Orders dated April 6, 1933, respecting the rank of Commodore in the R.N.R. and R.N.V.R. **1977** *Listener* 25 Aug. 241/2 Lambert was given a commission in the RNVR. *c* **1944** *Mod. Jun. Dict.* (Whitcombe & Tombs) 454/1 R.N.Z.A.F., Royal New Zealand Air Force. **1947** *Air Force News* (Cairo) 14 Jan. 1/2 The first two senior RNZAF officers nominated for participation in the exchange scheme with the RAF. **1959** *Listener* 23 July 146/2 We follow the fortunes of Vlasov's Army of Liberation, the ROA, during the last months of the war. **1974** T. P. WHITNEY tr. *Solzhenitsyn's Gulag Archipelago* I. I. vi. 253 As for the leaflets reporting the creation of the ROA, the 'Russian Liberation Army', not only were they written in bad Russian, but they were imbued with an alien spirit that was clearly German. **1942** PARTRIDGE *Dict. Abbrev.* 84/2 *R.O.C.*, Royal Observer Corps..A civilian body that scans the skies. Modest and selfless. **1947** *R.A.F. Rev.* Sept. 20/2 We hope to live up to its claim, as did the R.O.C. **1950** *N.Y. Times* 2 July IV. 1/6 The man who took over direction of operation ROK—Relief of Korea—in these dire circumstances was General MacArthur. **1950** *Life* 11 Sept. 51/2 (*heading*) The Durable Roks. *Ibid.*, But the Rok (for Republic of Korea) army was more durable than anybody thought. **1972** P. M. BARTZ *South Korea* 2/2 South Korea's correct title is the Republic of Korea, usually abbreviated R.O.K. **1966** *IEEE Trans. Electronic Computers* XV. 502/1 Transformer memories are read-only memories (ROM) which make use of magnetic coupling..between a set of interrogation lines and a set of sense lines. **1975** *Sci. Amer.* May 37/3 ROM's are non-volatile: their contents cannot be altered during the operation of the computer, and the retention of stored data does not depend on a supply of power. **1979** *Personal Computer World* Nov. 82/1 Monitors are held in ROM so that they are available and running as soon as the computer is started. **1947** K. M. WELLS *Owl Pen Reader* (1969) I. 97 Our goats..were neither registered, accredited, pure-bred, or R.O.P. **1955** R. J. SCHWARTZ *Compl. Dict. Abbrev.* 155/3 *rop*, run of paper (advertising). **1961** *Penrose Ann.* LV. 110 Only in recent years was the reproduction of colour transparencies taken up by means of ROP printing, where the full range of colours is produced by superimposing the three basic colours. **1967** E. CHAMBERS *Photolitho-Offset* 276 *R.O.P.*, an American term (run of paper) applying when colour half-tones are printed at the same time as the type matter. **1972** J. R. BRIDGE in *Mathematics in School* Sept. 8 (*title*) ROSLA and after. *Ibid.* 9/2, I believe ROSLA will be rewarding for groups 2 and 3. **1977** *Jrnl. R. Soc. Arts* CXXV. 300/1 When the additional ROSLA year operated, the prospect of a further year of standard education seems to have been unpalatable to some of the potential beneficiaries. **1948** *Fire Protection & Accident Prevention Year Book 1948–49* III. 139 The Royal Society for the Prevention of Accidents (RoSPA)... The aim of the Society is the prevention of accidents of all kinds. **1955** *Proc. National Industrial Safety Conf.* 7 Attract new members to your local groups, encourage them to become members of RoSPA. **1965** *Autocar* 24 Sept. 609/1 The leaflet recently published by RoSPA in conjunction with the Ministry of Transport. **1889** A. J. ELLIS *Early Eng. Pronunc.* v. 6 Other Abbreviations in Frequent Use... rp., received pronunciation, or that of pronouncing dictionaries and educated people. **1964** R. H. ROBINS *Gen. Linguistics* ii. 57 The pronunciation characteristic of this type of English has been called 'received pronunciation' or 'R.P.'. **1964** *English Studies* XLV. 26 There is no Standard Accent of English, and almost the only people who think there *is* are a small number of RP speakers who feel that their accent is..in some way superior. **1977** P. STREVENS *New Orientations Teaching of English* xi. 138 In Britain, the non-regional accent is RP. **1960** *Times Rev. Industry* Mar. 3/2 In the absence of price competition, distributors may compete by offering extra services. R.p.m. does not guarantee that they do. **1964** *Financial Times* 31 Jan. 6/4 However, the pending abolition of R.P.M. has confused some M.P.s in deciding their attitudes. **1966** J. F. PICKERING *Resale Price Maintenance* i. 15 In a number of trades r.p.m. was enforced privately through the mechanism of the relevant trade association. **1978** *Bookseller* 17 June 3183/1 In Australia and in Sweden the abolition of r.p.m. has had these very effects. **1906** *Trans. Inst. Engineers & Shipbuilders in Scotland* XLIX. 30 Especially should this be done in cases where..the weight increases more rapidly in inverse proportion to the R.P.M. and the diameter than it does with other types. **1931** *Discovery* Nov. 344/2 Running the engine at a higher r.p.m. **1950** *Down Beat* 5 May 16 (*heading*) Here's LP, 45 RPM jazz list. **1966** R. THOMAS *Spy in Vodka* (1967) xix. 218 The engine was responding nicely..and I was estimating the rpm's needed for the next bend. **1970** *Air Force Mag.* Oct. 40/2 This study of the Remotely Piloted Vehicle (RPV) potential consisted of detailed examinations of presently available technologies. **1972** *Observer* 13 Aug. 1/6 Remotely Piloted Vehicles (RPVs) that promise a bizarre kind of 'bloodless' warfare. **1977** *Time* 23 May 33/3 That will make being a pilot a cushy job: he sits at a TV console 200 miles away and gets the RPV to provide surveillance or relay radio messages or pinpoint targets for precision bombing. **1905** W. H. HOWELL *Textbk. Physiol.* xxxviii. 632 In connection with other data,..the R.Q. may be used to throw light upon the character of the nutrition. **1968** PASSMORE & ROBSON *Compan. Med. Stud.* I. xlii. 4/2 Ingestion of glucose within minutes restores the blood glucose concentration and the working ability, without changes in the RQ. **1967** *Jrnl. Molecular Biol.* XXIII. 149 Abbreviations used: rRNA, ribosomal RNA. **1977** *Nature* 8 Dec. 473/3 It is probable that no rRNA gene is integrated into the chromosomal DNA of the macronucleus [of *Tetrahymena*]. **1889** A. J. ELLIS *Early Eng. Pronunc.* v. 3 They all spoke 'received speech' (abbreviated to rs.) in 'received pronunciation' (abbreviated to rp.) **1934** H. C. WYLD *S.P.E. Tract* xxxix. 605 With this type [of spoken English]..I contrast what, for want of a better name, I call *Received Standard* (henceforward referred to in this paper by the initials R.S.). **1964** C. BARBER *Ling. Change Present-Day Eng.* ii. 22, I shall use the expression Received Standard (R.S.) to refer to all aspects of the language. **1920** *R. Soc. Arts Syllabus Examinations, 1921* p. xviii (Advt.), A selection from many books suitable for R.S.A. examinations. **1973** M. AMIS *Rachel Papers* 64 Not that age was a helpful grouping criterion, the elder lot ranging as they did from fifteen (a delinquent ghoul studying for RSAs) to nineteen (myself). **1980** *Jrnl. R. Soc. Arts* Feb. 145/1 Nor is the RSA alone. **1923** *Nation* 31 Jan. 130/1 The Russian Socialist Federated Soviet Republic (RSFSR)..and the Transcaucasian Socialist Federated Soviet Republic (Georgia, Azerbaijan, and Armenia) are concluding the present treaty on their consolidation into one united state. **1975** *Whitaker's Almanac 1976* 956/1, By the 1947 Peace Treaty with Finland, the district of *Petsamo*..was added to the territory of the R.S.F.S.R. **1940** *Chambers's Techn. Dict.* 733/1 *R.S.J.*, rolled steel joist. **1954** *Archit. Rev.* CXV. 334 The extension has a reinforced concrete frame with the exception of the top floor of the main block, which has a RSJ portal frame and a flat roof of asbestos cement decking. **1978** *Private Eye* 17 Mar. 15 We had..three RSJs put across the ceiling to stop the upstairs coming downstairs. **1971** *Circular* (Dept. Educ. & Sci.) No. 8. 1 The effect of raising the school leaving age (RSLA) is to substitute 16 for 15 in all the provisions of the Education Acts which deal with the upper limits of compulsory school age. **1979** *Rep. on Educ.* (Dept. Educ. & Sci.) No. 95. 1/1 The raising of the school leaving age to 16 (RSLA)—on 1 September 1972 with effect from 1 September 1973—marked the achievement of a long held objective. **1913** W. T. ROGERS *Dict. Abbrev.* 170 *R.S.M.* (tit.), Regimental Sergeant-Major. **1955** E. WAUGH *Officers & Gentlemen* I. ix. 107 The RSM sent up the rocket which announced the start of the exercise. **1978** R. V. JONES *Most Secret War* x. 90 The Grenadiers had sent an R.S.M. to Dover to pick up any Grenadiers and drill them. **1907** *Bird Notes & News* II. 52/2 In our parish nearly all belong to the R.S.P.B. **1937** *Discovery* Jan. 21/2 We are not planning to have our own bird sanctuaries with watchers to protect them, as this work is already being carried out with great success by the R.S.P.B. **1979** *Birds* Summer 34/1 The RSPB has seven reserves with major reedbeds. **1870** *Animal World* (Suppl.) 1 July 177/1 (*heading*) Annual report of the R.S.P.C.A. **1924** FAIRHOLME & PAIN *Century of Work for Animals* iii. 53 At the present time the R.S.P.C.A., working in England and Wales, alone employs two hundred and three full-time inspectors. **1978** *Daily Tel.* 18 July 1/8 The RSPCA is to launch an investigation today after about 2,800 of a cargo of 4,000 mink were found dead at Manchester airport. **1961** F. F. BRUCE *English Bible* xiv. 186 The R.S.V. dispenses with one of the most distinctive features of what English-speaking people have come to regard as 'Bible language'. **1974** *Oxf. Dict. Chr. Ch.* (ed. 2) 171/2 The RSV is widely used not only in America but also in Britain..and other English-speaking countries. **1956** *Jrnl. Nat. Cancer Inst.* XVI. 365 Lesions of the central nervous system produced by a duck variant of the Rous sarcoma virus (RSV). **1974** J. D. ACTON et al. *Fund. Med. Virol.* xxiii. 301 Some strains of RSV will induce transformation of mammalian (mouse, rat, hamster, primate, human) fibroblast cells. **1942** *Tee Emm* (Air Ministry) II. 64 If the R/T transmission is a bit distorted, 'Say again' is a set expression. **1971** 'D. HALLIDAY' *Dolly & Doctor Bird* xiii. 180 The R/T isn't functioning, and neither are the radar or echo sounder. **1975** J. WYLLIE *Butterfly Flood* (1977) xxxii. 156 Keep within R.T. range of us. **1969** W. B. EMERY *Nat. & Internat. Syst. Broadcasting* vi. 117 RTE now has a repertory company of twenty-eight actors. **1979** J. J. LEE *Ireland 1945–70* 173 Over 50 per cent of RTE television broadcasting featured imported programmes at the end of the 1960s. **1917** *B.E.F. Times* 8 Sept. (1918) 4/2 There is also a rumour that the R.T.O. of Bath has not got a decoration in the new list. **1919** G. S. GORDON *Let.* 20 June (1943) 95 We then drove over to the Gare de Lyon, where we hung about the R.T.O.'s office till 11, getting tickets made out, and our luggage registered. **1930** *Amer. Speech* V. 385 *R.T.O.*, Railroad transportation officer. **1955** E. WAUGH *Officers & Gentlemen* I. v. 45 Guy sought aid of the RTO and was rebuffed. **1978** LD. LOVAT *March Past* I. viii. 132 His last appointment was that of Railway Transport Officer (RTO) at Euston Station. **1917** KIPLING *Book of Words* (1928) 147 I'm not defending ragging—I've known cases where everyone who took part in it ought to have been R.T.U. **1976** K. BONFIGLIOLI *Something Nasty in Woodshed* ix. 103 Mortdecai [*sic*] would never wear the coveted red tabs on his khaki. 'RTU' (Returned to Unit) would follow his name for ever. **1922** M. GILBERT *Winston S. Churchill* (1977) IV. Compan. III. 1948 The Secretary of State for the Colonies..stated that the RUC were not up to strength. **1941** T. J. CAMPBELL *Fifty Years of Ulster* xxii. 322 The R.U.C. are an armed force, provided with revolvers and rifles. **1977** *Irish Times* 8 June 11/8 Last night the injured RUC man was stated to be seriously ill in hospital. **1975** *Ibid.* 9 May 24/1 (Advt.), Long Lease. G.R. £12·50. R.V. £25. **1976** *Dumfries & Galloway Standard* 25 Dec. 17/7 (Advt.), Modernised ground floor flat... R.V. to be reassessed. **1967** *Wheels Afield* June 42 (*heading*) Handling your RV in traffic. **1968** *Trailer Life* June 52/2 For early Rec V construction the terms cracker box or bullets served as type designation. **1973** *Ibid.* Apr. 134/2, I sure wish there was some way to allow RVers to utilize those great areas. *Ibid.* 194/2 An RVing woman's luck in being able to take along a wardrobe for every occasion. **1978** *Sunday Sun-Times* (Chicago) 1 Jan. 120/2 The RV industry..has regained its feet. **1942** PARTRIDGE *Dict. Abbrev.* 86/1 *r.v.* or *R.V.*, (place of) rendezvous. (Common to all three services.) **1973** C. EGLETON *Seven Days to Killing* xiv. 163 He had no way of knowing whether Tarrant would have set up a fail-safe RV or not. **1975** N. LUARD *Travelling Horseman* vi. 162 We'll r.v...in the boozer, and I'll take him over to the garage.

b. Substitute 1825 for date of first example in Dict. and add further examples.

1828 *New Jersey Eagle* (Newark, N.J.) 23 May 3/3 The three R's—honest 'Rithmetic, Reading & 'Riting I think I can say, I'm no fool in. **1976** *Times* 26 Mar. 6/3 In some primary and secondary schools the three Rs have been neglected or devalued. **1979** *Jrnl. R. Soc. Arts* CXXVII. 483/1 Writing is, after all, one of the three R's on which education is based.

3. Also as *v. intr.*

1969 R. V. BESTE *Next Time I'll pay my Own Fare* viii. 111 The Duchess de Santine Miorna requests the pleasure of Detective-Inspector John Gage's company to dinner tonight... R.S.V.P... Gage R.S.V.Ped in Spanish. **1978** *Observer* 19 Feb. 7/1 The printed invitations to 27 journalists were delivered... We all RSVP'd.

4. R or r (*Physics*): abbrev. of *roentgen* (*unit*) s.v. *ROENTGEN 2. Also *r-unit*.

1922 *Physics Abstr.* A. XXV. 508 The instrument is calibrated in terms of a unit R (the Röntgen), i.e. the ionisation produced in 1 sec. by 1 gm. of Ra at a distance of 20 mm. after filtration by 0·5 mm. of Pt. **1938** R. W. LAWSON tr. *Hevesy & Paneth's Man. Radioactivity* (ed. 2) iv. 58 The γ-radiation from 1 mg. Ra..supplies 8·6 *r* per hour at a distance of 1 cm. *Ibid.* xxiv. 260 The maximum permissible daily dosage of neutrons is estimated to be one-tenth that for γ- or X-rays, or 0·01 *r* unit. **1962** *Newnes' Conc. Encycl. Nuclear Energy* 205/1 Thus for X- and γ-radiation of energy between 0·3 and 3 MeV, 1 *r* is nearly equivalent to 1 rad in water or soft tissue. **1973** KAYE & LABY *Tables of Physical & Chem. Constants* (ed. 14) iii. 285 The unit of exposure is the roentgen (R) which is equal to $2{\cdot}58 \times 10^{-4}$ coulomb per kilogram of air.

III. As a symbol. **1.** *Chem.* [Initial letter of *radical*.] R is used in chemical formulæ to represent an unspecified radical or group of radicals (usu. organic).

1866 WATTS *Dict. Chem.* IV. 219 In these formulæ, R+ represents a positive organic radicle, and R− a negative radicle: no negative organic radicle as such, has yet been introduced into these compounds. *Ibid.* 227 Stannic compounds of the form $Sn^{iv}R^4+$ are colourless mobile liquids. **1872** [see *POLYMERIZATION]. **1909** C. A. KEANE *Mod. Org. Chem.* viii. 130 In the formula for ketones, the radicals R and R′ may be either like or unlike. **1932** I. D. GARARD *Introd. Org. Chem.* vi. 74 The aldehydes have one of these valences attached to carbon and one to hydrogen, so that for any hydrocarbon radical, R the aldehyde is R—C=O (with H attached below the C). **1950** N. V. SIDGWICK *Chem. Elements* I. 30 It can be shown that the cyanamides $H_2N{\cdot}CN$ and HRN·CN are highly associated in benzene, while $R_2N{\cdot}CN$ is monomeric. **1966** WILLIAMS & FLEMING *Spectrosc. Methods in Org. Chem.* ii. 38 The absorption maximum of the nitroaniline XXXVI (R=Me) is at 385 mμ..showing a red shift and marked reduction in intensity from that of the parent compound XXXVI (R=H) at 375 mμ.

2. Physical Chem. *R* is used to denote the *gas constant*, i.e. the constant of proportionality in the equation of state for an ideal gas, $PV = nRT$, where P = pressure, V = volume, n = the number of moles of gas, and T = absolute temperature; now usu. taken to be 8·314 joule kelvin^{-1} mole^{-1}. [Arbitrary: first used by J. D. Van der Waals 1873, *Over de Continuitet van den Gas- en Vloiestoestand* (Leiden) 58.]

1880 *Phil. Mag.* IX. 393 In relation to pressure, volume, and temperature, gases follow..with a certain degree of approximation, the laws of Mariotte and Gay-Lussac, which can in common be expressed by the following equation—pv = RT..wherein..R is a constant dependent on the nature of the gas. **1895** C. S. PALMER tr. *W. Nernst's Theoret. Chem.* I. i. 31 The factor R is only conditioned by the unit of measure chosen, but is independent of the chemical composition of the gases in question. **1940** GLASSTONE *Textbk. Physical Chem.* ix. 654 The value of *R* for solutions is thus very close to that of *R* usually accepted for a gas, namely 0·0821 liter-atm.., so that it is possible to write $\Pi V = RT$, where *R* may be taken as the gas constant [and Π = osmotic pressure]. **1978** P. W. ATKINS *Physical Chem.* 13 In this expression *R*, the gas constant, is another fundamental constant with the value 8·3 J K^{-1} mol^{-1}.

3. Biol. **a.** *r* is used in formulæ and elsewhere to denote the rate of increase of a population, usually representing the factor by which its size is multiplied in each generation; or the value which this factor would have if resources (food etc.) were unlimited.

1918 *Q. Publ. Amer. Statistical Assoc.* XVI. 123 Where b = birth rate per head per annum, r = natural rate of increase per head per annum... The formulae thus obtained give the relationship between *b* and *r*. **1954** ANDREWARTHA & BIRCH *Distribution & Abundance of Animals* iii. 33 In nature, one or several components may predominate to determine the *actual* rate of increase, which we shall call *r*. **1967** MACARTHUR & WILSON *Theory of Island Biogeogr.* vii. 150 Clearly..*r* will be increased by a habitat or food shift which increases the density of available food. **1971** A. S. BOUGHEY *Fundamental Ecology* iii. 97 The biotic potential is usually expressed by a factor representing the intrinsic rate of natural increase *r*. **1977** J. L. HARPER *Population Biol. of Plants* i. 3 There is a growing tendency to talk and write about *r*-phases in the life of a population—phases when it explodes with near-exponential growth after a disaster or after a new colonization into an unexploited environment.

b. *r selection*, the form of natural selection which acts on populations having ample resources and little or no competition.

1967 MacArthur & Wilson *Theory of Island Biogeogr.* vii. 149 In an environment with no crowding (*r* selection), genotypes which harvest the most food (even if wastefully) will rear the largest families and be most fit. **1973** P. A. Colinvaux *Introd. Ecology* 618/2 *r-Selection*, selection for an opportunist strategy leading to an opportunist species. Traits are preserved which use energy to obtain a high natural rate of increase 'r'. **1976** *Nature* 12 Feb. 478/2 MacArthur and Wilson coined the terms *r* selection and *K* selection to describe two general kinds of selection they believed could be functioning in nature (*K* refers to carrying capacity and *r* to maximal intrinsic rate of natural increase, r_m). **1979** *Sci. Amer.* Jan. 26/3 The poles of evolutionary adaptation, *r* selection increasing the number of offspring (the prodigal mackerel roe with half a million eggs) and *K* selection ensuring survival (the proverbial royal litter, only one cub born at a time, but that one a lion).

4. Spectroscopy. *R* is used to denote the *Rydberg constant* s.v. *RYDBERG I.

1920 *Phil. Mag.* XXXIX. 47 If the nucleus be a simple point-charge, the negatived total energy *W* belonging to any one of the stationary orbits is given by $W/ch = \kappa^2 R/n^2$,.. where *n* is an integer, *c* the light velocity in vacuo, *h* Planck's constant, and *R* the Bohr expression of Rydberg's constant. **1926** G. Birtwistle *Quantum Theory of Atom* ii. 21 In 1913, Niels Bohr. . gave a theory of the hydrogen spectrum which . .led. .to an expression for the Rydberg constant *R* in terms of known physical constants. **1965** R. N. Dixon *Spectroscopy & Struct.* ii. 31 Since the lowest energy level has $n = 1$, and the highest $n = \infty$, the Rydberg constant R_H corresponds to the minimum energy required for the removal of the electron. **1978** P. W. Watkins *Physical Chem.* xiv. 427 Balmer. .pointed out that the wavelength of the light in the visible region. .fitted the expression $1/\lambda = R(\frac{1}{4} - 1/n^2)$, $n = 3, 4$. .where *R* is a constant now called the Rydberg constant, and having the value 109 677 cm^{-1}, or $3{\cdot}289\,8 \times 10^{15}$ Hz.

5. Psychol. *R*, or *r*, is used in some methods of factor analysis in which traits or abilities are the variables (see quots.); also *attrib.*, as *R, r technique*. Cf. *Q III. 4.

1925 *Brit. Jrnl. Psychol.* July 75 Where *R* is the matrix of the *r*-correlation coefficients. **1927** C. Spearman *Abilities of Man* vi. 73 The form recently preferred is given below. In it, as usual, the letter *r* stands for any correlation, whilst its two subscripts indicate the two abilities (tests, school marks, etc.) that are correlated. **1936** *Brit. Jrnl. Psychol.* Apr. 345 It is convenient to designate all previous factor analysis as *r* technique, and this new inverted form as *Q* technique. **1950** R. B. Cattell *Personality* ii. 30 In *R* technique one would point to a particular trait-indicator test and say, 'This is the test measure of the surface trait or factor in question'. **1974** W. B. Arndt *Theories of Personality* viii. 99 In an actual application of the procedure just described, fifty or more measurements would be made on one hundred or more subjects. This technique, based on normative data, is called the *R-technique*.

6. *Chem.* [Abbrev. of L. *rectus* right.] *R* is used to designate (compounds having) a configuration about an asymmetric carbon atom in which the substituents, placed in order according to certain rules, form a clockwise sequence when viewed from a particular direction. Opp. *S (see S 13).

1956 R. S. Cahn et al. in *Experientia* XII. 83/2 The suggested indications for asymmetry leading, under the sequence and conversion rules, to a right- and left-handed pattern, are capital italic *R* and *S* respectively, where *R* derives from the Latin *rectus*, meaning 'right', and *S* from *sinister*... For the description of pseudo-asymmetric atoms, it is proposed to employ the corresponding lower-case italic symbols, *r* and *s*. *Ibid.* 85/2 The simplest case may be exemplified by bromochloroacetic acid (XV). Priority of the groups (a, b, c, d) is here determined simply by the atomic numbers as Br, Cl, C (of CO_2H), H. Hence, by the conversion rule. .formula (XV) represents an (*R*)-form. **1966** Rakoff & Rose *Org. Chem.* xiv. 477 Going from OH to CHO to CH_2OH traces a clockwise path, so the configuration about the asymmetric center in D-glyceraldehyde is rectus, and the compound would be designated (R)-glyceraldehyde. **1971** *Sci. Amer.* Aug. 46/3 One enantiomeric form of carvone, *R*-carvone, has a strong odor of spearmint; the other form, *S*-carvone (which is geometrically a mirror image. .) has the odor of caraway. **1973** *Times* 20 Jan. 16/6 Most of the tests were therefore carried out using the R analogue which seemed to be free from side effects.

7. *Astr.* [Initial letter of *rapid*.] *r-process*: a process believed to occur in stars in circumstances of high neutron flux (e.g. in supernova explosions), in which heavy atomic nuclei are formed from lighter ones by a combination of rapid neutron captures and slower beta decays.

1956 F. Hoyle et al. in *Science* 5 Oct. 612/2 We have distinguished two conditions under which the Neutron capture can take place, a slow (*s*) process and a rapid (*r*) process. *Ibid.*, The *r*-process we associate with the explosion of supernovae, the time scale being as small as 10 to 100 seconds. **1975** *Nature* 2 Oct. 362/1 The measured charge distribution in the vicinity of the Earth at ~0·5 GeV per nucleon strongly favours synthesis of these cosmic rays by the r-process (rapid neutron capture) within the last 10^7 yr. **1977** J. Narlikar *Struct. Universe* ii. 49 Whereas the s-process produces proton-rich nuclei, the r-process produces neutron-rich nuclei.

8. *Microbiology.* [Initial letter of *resistance*.] *R* is used to denote certain plasmids which confer drug-resistance on bacteria and can be transferred to other bacteria by conjugation.

1961 *Gunma Jrnl. Med. Sci.* X. 59 It is strongly suggested that there is a transmissible drug-resistance factor (R) which makes R^- cells drug resistant when infected with R^+ cells following cell-to-cell contact. **1962** *Jrnl. Bacteriol.* LXXXIV. 902/2 *R* or *R factor* is a general term for the infectious drug-resistance factors (Mitsuhashi, 1960; at the Meeting of Microbial Genetics at Mishima, Japan, it was agreed by investigators in this field to use the term 'R' for the multiple drug-resistance factor). **1967** *Jrnl. Gen. Microbiol.* XLIX. 97 Genetic alterations resulting in the loss or acquisition of F or R pili are strictly correlated with loss or gain of ability to transfer the chromosome by conjugation. **1969** A. M. Campbell *Episomes* iii. 41 Cells harboring R can transfer it to other cells. **1975** *Sci. Amer.* July 28/3 Antibiotic-resistant *E[scherichia] coli* isolated in many parts of the world. .were found to contain plasmids, designated *R* factors. .carrying the genetic information for products that in one way or another could interfere with the action of specific antibiotics.

‖ **ra²** (rā). *Physical Geogr.* Pl. **ras,** ‖ **raer.** [Norw.] One of the terminal moraines near the coast in southern Norway and Sweden that are in the form of long ridges of gravel and clay with a covering of large stones.

1902 *Geol. Mag.* Decade IV. IX. 319 Outside the terminal ra, that is, between the moraine and the coastline,. .there is a widely spread deposit of clay. **1957** J. K. Charlesworth *Quaternary Era* II. xxx. 627 The radially dispersed erratics and diverging striae transverse to the morainic *Raer*. .finally overcame both prejudice and honest conviction. *Ibid.* xlii. 1172 The *Ras*, traceable as far as Stavanger, have been correlated with the double moraines observed in many fjords and fjord-valleys.

‖ **raad** (rāt), *sb.*¹ *S. Afr.* [Du., = council; freq. as shortening of *HEEMRAD, *VOLKSRAAD, etc.] A council, an assembly; *spec.* (usu. with capital initial) the legislative assembly of one of the former Boer republics (*Hist.*).

1850 R. Gray *Jrnl.* 8 May in *Jrnl. Bishop's Visitation Tour in 1850* (1851) 25 These men have formed themselves into a Republic, and have their 'Raad' (Council). **1856** C. J. Andersson *Lake Ngami* v. 57 He laid his complaint before the chief of the tribe; and a 'raad', or counsel, was held. **1873** F. Boyle *To Cape for Diamonds* xii. 153 The gentlemen. .obtained their grant under solemn seal and bond of the Transvaal Parliament, or *raad*. **1930** *Times Lit. Suppl.* 7 Aug. 635/2 The tribal council has become a 'raad' consisting of the chief, ex-officio, and of members elected at the mass meeting. **1940** F. B. Young *City of Gold* 261 So the Raad sat. .voting Burgers down. **1963** S. Cloete *Rags of Glory* vi. 53 Field Kornet Adriaan de la Rey, the member of the Raad who had been against the war. **1973** *Hansard S. Afr.* 8 Feb. 297 The Minister of Labour. .says that in no circumstances will he sit in the same 'raad' as a non-white.

raad (raˌad), *sb.*² [Arabic.] The electric cat-fish, *Malapterurus electricus*, belonging to the family Malapteruridæ, found in the Nile and other rivers of central and western tropical Africa, and distinguished by electric cells in the fatty tissue just beneath the skin.

In quot. 1878 = TORPEDO *sb.* 1 a.

1869 A. Günther in J. & B. H. Petherick *Trav. Cent. Afr.* II. 240 (*Raad* or *Raasch*.) The electric Silurus is spread over the whole of tropical Africa. **1878** *Encycl. Brit.* VIII. 8/2 The Arabians had long before given this fish [*sc.* the torpedo] the name of *raad* or lightning. **1931** J. R. Norman *Hist. Fishes* viii. 149 This species is used by the Arabs for food, and they refer to it as the Raad or Thunder-fish. **1957** E. Le Danois *Fishes of World* iv. 130 The electric cat-fish. ., the raad or thunder-fish, lives in African rivers.

rab³. Chiefly *Cornish* (orig. *dial.*). [Shortened f. Cornish *rabman, -men* in the same sense. Ultimate origin obscure. Also recorded from Wales (quot. 1910).

There is no apparent connection with Scottish and Northumberland dial. *raab, rab* (the fall of a cliff, a mass of broken rock, etc.), which is of Scandinavian origin (see e.g. S.N.D.).]

Rough or stony subsoil; rubble, gravel.

[**1769** W. Borlase *Antiquities Cornwall* 452/1 *Rabman*, rubble; that mixture of clay and stone which has not been moved since the flood, and generally lies over the karn. **1868** *Proc. Soc. Antiquaries London* IV. 164 The floor. .is composed of the hard subsoil of the country, called by the Cornish 'rabman'.] **1880** Courtney & Couch *Gloss. Words Cornwall* 46/1 *Rab*, decomposed granite used for mending roads. **1910** W. M. Morris *Gloss. Demetian Dial.*, *Rab*, rough, stony soil; sub-soil. **1928** *Jrnl. Brit. Archaeol. Assoc.* XXXIV. 153 The paving stones had been laid on the rab or subsoil. **1912** *Antiquity* XXVI. 90 The site of the hut was cleared and levelled by cutting back into the hillside and spreading the excavated rab over the lower part of the floor. **1961** E. Clark *Cornish Fogous* ix. 68 A drain passes from the fogou to the outer wall, the floor of which is composed of the natural rab... The floor of the main structure is of stoneless rab. **1962** *Punch* 30 May 836/3 Clutching for dear life at the poor rab (the local name for the pink subsoil) this tree has grown.

rabab, rababa, varr. *REBAB.

rababoo, var. *RUBBABOO.

rabanna (răbæ·nă). [Malagasy.] A fabric woven from raffia.

1883 *Encycl. Brit.* XV. 172/2 The chief articles of export being. .ròfia palm cloths (*rabànnas*) and fibre. **1969** R. T. Wilcox *Dict. Costume* (1970) 281/1 *Rabanna*, a textile imported from Madagascar. Used for hats and bags.

rabap, var. *REBAB.

rabat². Delete *Sc.*, for † *Obs.* read '*Obs.* exc. *Hist.*', and add: **a.** (Later examples).

1865 F. B. Palliser *Hist. Lace* viii. 126 Suddenly, at the court of Henry [III of France], the fraise gave way to the rabat, or turn-down collar. **1953** M. Powys *Lace & Lace-Making* vii. 77 With the coming of the wig or natural long curled hair the ruff was given up and men wore their lace in front falling under the chin in the form first of a cravat or Rabat and later in ruffles.

b. A type of turned-down clerical collar. Also, = STOCK *sb.*¹ 44 b. Also, a similar garment worn by a layman.

1889 in *Cent. Dict.* **1931** D. Attwater *Catholic Encycl. Dict.* 441/1 *Rabat*... Part of the dress of the French secular clergy. A white *rabat* is worn by the Brothers of Christian Doctrine, university professors, magistrates, barristers and attorneys. **1936** J. G. Cozzens *Men & Brethren* 122 You can go courting, if you like; but you have to go in a rabat, so to say. **1966** H. Kemelman *Saturday the Rabbi went Hungry* (1967) ii. 18 In spite of the clerical collar and black silk rabat, he looked more like a football player than an Anglican minister. **1975** *New Yorker* 3 Feb. 23/1 He is dressed in an ultra-attractive robin's-egg-blue rabat and brown velvet suit.

rabat (răbæ·t), *v.* *Geom.* Also **rebat(e.** [ad. F. *rabattre* to lower, fold back, rabat.] *trans.* To rotate (a plane) about its line of intersection with another plane, *spec.* the horizontal plane, until the two coincide. Hence **raba·tted** *ppl. a.*, **raba·tting** *vbl. sb.* Also **raba·tment,** the process of rabatting.

1885 *Encycl. Brit.* XIX. 801/1 In rabatting the plane π_3 its trace OB with the plane π_2 will come to the position OD. **1908** L. N. G. Filon *Introd. Projective Geom.* i. 7 For practical purposes. .it is convenient to rotate one of the two planes about *x* until it coincides with the other plane. A figure in the former plane rotates with it, but is fixed in it. Such a process is termed rabatting. *Ibid.*, If. .we rabat the figure 2 upon the plane a_1 we obtain a new figure 3 in the plane a_1. *Ibid.* 10 Locus of vertex of projection during rabatment. **1931** A. H. Jameson *Contour Geom.* i. 13 A. .way to find the true angle between two lines or the true shape of any figure drawn on a plane, is to 'rebate' the plane in which the two lines or the figure lies, i.e. to rotate the plane into a horizontal position about one of the contour lines as axis. Draw a vertical section across the plane at right angles to the contours and draw circular arcs. ., giving the rebated contours. *Ibid.* (*heading*) Rebatement. **1949** N. L. Reece *Newnes Building Geom.* 206 A rebattement is the name given to the construction when a figure lying in an inclined plane is turned or 'rebatted' so as to lie in the horizontal plane. **1950** G. A. Hanby *Geometry* viii. 92 Find the true shape of the surface *abcdef* by rabatment. *Ibid.* 93 The true shape of the section is rabatted to the left to keep it clear of the plan, so with *T* as centre, rabat *b'c'* to B'C'.

rabbi, *sb.*¹ **2. b.** Delete † *Obs.* and add later examples.

1855 Macaulay *Hist. Eng.* III. xi. 98 One of the great Presbyterian Rabbies. .might well doubt whether. .he should be benefited by a comprehension. *a* **1894** Stevenson *Weir of Hermiston* (1896) i. 24 'I can't see it,' said the little Rabbi... 'No, I cannae see it.' **1932** *Amer. Speech* VII. 278 [New York Post Office] *Rabbi*, one who aids in the securing of a special privilege or favor. **1969** *New Yorker* 3 May 64/2, I asked him if he had done any thinking lately about. . violence... 'Mitch Ginsberg has been my rabbi in that,' the Mayor answered. **1972** B. F. Conners *Don't embarrass Bureau* (1973) ii. 192 You're damn lucky. You came out of the thing pretty clean. You got a rabbi down at the Bureau?

rabbi (ræ·bi, ræ·bəi), *sb.*² [Corruption of RABAT².] = STOCK *sb.*¹ 44 b. Cf. *RABAT² b.

1909 J. A. Nainfa *Costume of Prelates* iii. 50 Our Roman Collar. .consists of two parts, a starched circle of white linen—the collar, and a piece of cloth or silk to which the collar itself is fastened by means of buttons, hooks, etc., and has been given the. .name of 'rabbi'. **1948** H. J. McCloud *Clerical Dress & Insignia of R. C. Ch.* viii. 74 The rabbi is a loose breast piece of silk or woolen material. **1978** J. Carroll *Mortal Friends* iv. ii. 386 Father McShane. .was carefully decked out, too, but clerically and with such fastidiousness as to seem almost the dandy. He wore his black suit and rabbi, of course, with the spotless high collar which was too tight.

rabbinic, *sb.* Add: **2.** *pl.* The study of the writings or doctrines of the rabbins.

1905 *Jewish Encycl.* XI. 93/2 In 1892 Schechter was elected reader in rabbinics [at Cambridge]. **1973** *Jewish Chron.* 2 Feb. 16/5 Dr Nicholas de Lange, lecturer in rabbinics at Cambridge University. **1976** *N.Y. Times* 30 Dec. 26 A Russian-born professor of rabbinics.

rabbit, *sb.*¹ **1. a.** For *Lepus* substitute *Oryctolagus*. Add: Also, one of several North American animals of the same family, esp. the varying hare, *Lepus americanus*. (N. Amer. examples.)

1634 W. Wood *New Englands Prospect* vi. 22 The Rabbets be much like ours in England. **1743** M. Catesby *Nat. Hist. Carolina* II. p. xxviii, The Monax. This animal is about the bigness of a wild rabbet. **1831** J. J. Audubon *Ornithol. Biogr.* I. 268 Small hares, or, as we usually call them, Rabbits, are also frequently caught. **1842** [see *ORKNEYMAN]. **1872** R. L. Dashwood *Chiploquorgan* 88 There is a species of hare. .mis-called a rabbit, which is numerous but hardly eatable. *c* **1897** 'Mark Twain' *Autobiogr.* (1924) I. 97 The sumptuous meals—well, it makes me cry to think of them. Fried chicken,. .squirrels, rabbits, pheasants. **1907**

St. Nicholas July 835/1 Sometimes rabbits and prairie-dogs scampered among the bushes. **1958** J. G. MacGregor *North-West of 16* v. 69 Many an Alberta farmer and business man is alive today because of rabbits. **1969** M. M. Firestone in Halpert & Story *Christmas Mumming in Newfoundland* 64 Many 'rabbits' (varying hares) are caught in snares.

b. *to buy the rabbit* (slang), to conclude a transaction unfavourably, to fare badly.

1825 J. Neal *Bro. Jonathan* II. xviii. 156 If that air invoice aint ready soon, thee'll buy the rabbit, I guess! **1935** A. J. Pollock *Underworld Speaks* 52/2 *He bought the rabbit*, a criminal case in court poorly handled by attorney; got the worst of it in a business deal.

c. Used (freq. *fig.* or allusively) with reference to the conjuring trick of producing a rabbit from a hat (cf. *hat *sb.* 5 c).

1877 E. Sachs *Sleight of Hand* xviii. 183 The production of..rabbits from a hat is always very startling. **1906** Kipling *Puck of Pook's Hill* 99 I've seen a man take rabbits out of a hat, and he told us we could see how he did it, if we watched hard. **1932** L. Golding *Magnolia Street* II. iv. 322 His wife..gave the impression of having emerged like a rabbit from the Conjurer's top-hat. **1938** M. Allingham *Fashion in Shrouds* vii. 108 There you are... Once more the veteran conjuror staggers out with the rabbit. **1940** A. Christie *Sad Cypress* II. ii. 121 You want me..to be the conjuror. To take out of the empty hat rabbit after rabbit. **1965** 'D. Shannon' *Death by Inches* (1967) xx. 245 Well, you pulled the rabbit out of the hat. **1967** *Guardian* 21 Sept. 7/1 Will man..control or stop the ever increasing flow of white rabbits..out of our technological top hats? **1975** *Times* 20 Sept. 6/5 Almost any of the Poirots of the 1930s..produce the authentic rabbit-from-the-hat shock that is the whole aim of their sort of book.

d. *pl.* Also *white rabbits*. Repeated as a good-luck charm, esp. on the first day of a month (see quots.).

1920 'D. Yates' *Courts of Idleness* II. ii. 195 On the first day of the month you have to say 'Rabbits'. If you say it to me first, I have to give you a present, and if I say it to you first, you have to give me a present. **1949** H. Nicolson *Diary* 31 Dec. (1968) 178, I hear the clock strike midnight and say 'rabbits'... That is the end of 1949. **1959** I. & P. Opie *Lore & Lang. Schoolch.* xiii. 299 'On the first morning of the month,' notes a typical informant, 'before speaking to anyone else, one must say 'White rabbits, white rabbits, white rabbits' for luck.' Subject to minor modifications the utterance of this spell appears to be the accepted routine throughout Britain. Some children feel it is enough just to cry 'Rabbits'. **1972** Evans & Thomson *Leaping Hare* xvi. 233 A Claydon (Suffolk) woman told us she used to say *Hares, Hares* before going to bed on the last day of the month, and *Rabbits, Rabbits*, when she got up in the morning. **1977** *Times* 20 Aug. 12/2, I took the opportunity of asking them what was the magic word which they..should have said, first thing that morning... They replied 'Rabbits' except for a few..who said 'White Rabbits'.

2. a. (Later examples.) *spec.* (slang) a poor performer at any game; a novice; also *attrib.*

1904 *Daily Mail* 29 Jun. 4/6 Terms now used in describing the game of cricket... 'Googlies, rabbits'. **1906** *Westm. Gaz.* 8 May 1/3 Nearly every eleven has a 'rabbit' or two at the end. **1908** A. W. Myers *Compl. Lawn Tennis Player* 184 There was no draw at all, the manager..merely selecting the four semi-finalists and filling in the gaps with the other players, most of them 'rabbits'. **1924** *Punch* 4 June 620 (*caption*) *Nervous beginner (to caddy)*. 'I-er-suppose you get an occasional 'rabbit' here?' **1927** *Observer* 17 Apr. 17/2 Fencing is no more considered to be a feeble pastime for 'Rabbits', for those boys who cannot play the more vigorous games of youth. **1930** A. E. M. Foster *Contract Bridge for All* 7 Many people of the 'rabbit' class, and even average Auction players, are deterred from giving it a trial at all. **1932** A. J. Worrall *Eng. Idioms* 12 That girl is a rabbit. She's afraid to say 'Boo' to a goose. **1932** *Sun* (Baltimore) 24 Sept. 20/2 He found the appearance of the young women improved by abandonment of 'rabbit rules'... Freshman girls were required..to refrain from using cosmetics... But now the 'rabbits' can appear in all their glory of pink lips and powdered noses. **1947** *People* 22 June 7/4 Engines roar and the four 'rabbits' get away as best they can, but definitely not in the style of champions. **1952** E. O'Neill *Moon for Misbegotten* I. 10 I'll bet you're a mile away by now, you rabbit! **1957** *Sun* (Baltimore) 9 Apr. 20-B/3 'I think we owe it to the sponsors,' Ford explained after his remarkable closing 66... 'They help us when we're rabbits (a term for novices) and we should help them when we become winners.' **1974** J. I. M. Stewart *Gaudy* v. 95, I must have been accustomed to think of wee Dreichie as what we called a rabbit, meaning a timid boy wholly without aptitude either for games or for ragging around. **1976** *0–10 Cricket Scene* (Austral.) 41/2 Dennis Amiss..will have a special desire to prove to the Australian public that he is no longer Dennis Lillee's 'rabbit'. *a* **1976** A. Christie *Autobiogr.* (1977) VI. iv. 320 He could get no fun out of playing [golf] with a rabbit like me. **1979** *Daily Tel.* 14 Apr. 13/2 In '*Rabbits Review*' B. P. Floyd aims..to cater with a light touch for the poorer player.

d. Also in *gen.* use of a horse. *slang.*

1900 F. P. Dunne *Mr. Dooley's Philos.* 170 'Well,' says th' horse rayporther, 'they's a couple iv rabbits goin' to sprint around th' thrack at th' fair groun's,' he says. **1940** W. Faulkner *Hamlet* ii. 47 He lifted his own reins. 'Come up, rabbits,' he said. 'Let's hit for town.'

e. Liquor; a bottle of beer. *to run the rabbit*: see quots. 1916, 1941. *Austral. slang.*

1895 E. Gibb *Thrilling Incidents Convict System in Australasia* 46 'Ikeing the rabbit for a fake for his Bingy, and making a coil of a conkey myrnionger'... Convict slang ..it may be freely translated as having surreptitiously concealed some liquor under the excuse that one was ill and it was required for medicine, and ('making a coil') complaining loudly of some fancied grievance on the part of a ('conkey myrnionger') contemptible or ignorant newly-arrived convict. **1916** C. J. Dennis *Songs of Sentimental Bloke* Gloss. 124 *Rabbit, to run the*, to convey liquor from a public-house. **1941** Baker *Dict. Austral. Slang* 58 *Rabbit*, a bottle of beer. *Ibid.* 62 *Run the rabbit*, to secure liquor, often illegally, e.g. after hours.

f. A smuggled or stolen article (see also quot. 1945). *Naut.* and *Austral. slang.*

1929 F. Bowen *Sea Slang* 109 *Rabbit*, property stolen from the Royal Dockyards, most frequently used in Devonport. **1945** Baker *Austral. Lang.* viii. 163 *Rabbit*, an article made by a sailor at sea as a gift to a friend or girl. As verb, to scrounge. **1955** G. Freeman *Liberty Man* I. i. 11 All at once he remembered his presents for them. 'Rabbits' they called them in the navy. **1958** *Times* 10 Feb. 11/6 'Making rabbits' is a collective term for seamen's 'hobbies'. **1961** F. H. Burgess *Dict. Sailing* 167 *Rabbit*, an article unlawfully obtained and smuggled ashore.

g. [Shortening of **rabbit-and-pork*.] A conversation, a talk. Also, a lingo. *slang.*

1941 [see *rabbit-and-pork* below]. **1950** P. Tempest *Lag's Lexicon* 173 To have a 'rabbit' = to have a pow-wow. **1958** F. Norman *Bang to Rights* III. 155 We still had quite a heated rabbit about it. **1962** R. Cook *Crust on its Uppers* i. 20 Moody rabbits in Spanish bars. **1976** E. Ward *Hanged Man* xxvii. 171 Touchy old place, Glasgow...you can't understand that Scotch rabbit they talk.

h. = *pig *sb.*[1] 8*.

1949 *Amer. Speech* XXIV. 33 The piece of steel or iron dropped or pushed through racked pipe to remove obstructions is known as a rabbit. **1975** G. Anderson *Coring* v. 95 The core is not completely out of the barrel until a metal slug, called 'the rabbit', appears.

i. A pneumatically or hydraulically propelled container used to convey material into a nuclear reactor or other place where it is to be irradiated.

1950 S. Glasstone *Sourcebk. Atomic Energy* xiii. 356/2 The study of the delayed-neutron emitters of short life is facilitated by the use of a device referred to colloquially as a 'rabbit'; by this means a sample of fissionable material, after exposure to a high density of neutrons,..is rapidly transferred to a counter where the emission of the delayed neutrons is registered automatically. **1954** R. Stephenson *Introd. Nuclear Engin.* x. 367 The rabbit (holder for the material to be irradiated) is rapidly shot into and out of the reactor by about 100 lb pressure of filtered air or carbon dioxide. **1967** J. G. Wills *Nuclear Power Plant Technol.* 318 'Rabbits' often consist of small cylinders of aluminium or plastic, moved by air pressure through a long pipe.

3. a. *rabbit-blood, farm, fence, fur, -hutch* (earlier and later *lit.* and *fig.* examples), *netting, snare, soup, trap, -warren* (earlier and later *lit.* and *fig.* examples), *wire*.

1923 D. H. Lawrence *Birds, Beasts & Flowers* 207 Eagle of the Rockies..Lifting the rabbit-blood of the myriads up into something splendid. **1964** M. Hynes *Med. Bacteriol.* (ed. 8) xxviii. 438 Culture is effected on Novy and McNeal's medium or in the water of condensation at the bottom of a rabbit-blood agar slope. **1900** J. K. Jerome *Three Men on Bummel* v. 106 A man starting a rabbit farm with twelve selected rabbits..must, at the end of three years, be in receipt of an income of two thousand a year. **1939–40** *Army & Navy Stores Catal.* 982/1 1¼″ Mesh for Rabbit fences, proof against the smallest Rabbits. **1944** F. Clune *Red Heart* 53 Colson travelled on to Birdsville, crossing the old rabbit fence (built in 1886) to keep vermin out of Queensland. **1873** *Practical Mag.* I. 282 (*heading*) Rabbit fur as a substitute for wool and cotton. **1973** 'D. Halliday' *Dolly & Starry Bird* iii. 37 A long coat of gray glacé snakeskin, edged..with lime green rabbit fur. **1743** W. Ellis *Mod. Husb.* June xviii. 141 An old Rabbit hutch, that had several Rooms in it. **1859** [see *penny plain* adj. s.v. *penny 12 c]. **1905** *Pall Mall Mag.* July 28/2 The *concierge* in his 'rabbit hutch' down below smiles and even sometimes whistles in tune. **1965** G. McInnes *Road to Gundagai* ix. 134 Hurstbridge station was a low gravel platform with a small rabbit hutch of a booking office. **1977** P. G. Winslow *Witch Hill Murder* II. 135 The collection of rabbit hutches that was now the Manor. **1907** *Yesterday's Shopping* (1969) 664/2 Rabbit and Hare Nettings..4 ft. wide, for half grown rabbits. **1915** Kipling *Let.* 22 Aug. in C. Carrington *Rudyard Kipling* (1955) xvii. 436 Don't forget the beauty of rabbit netting overhead against hand-grenades. **1973** *Country Life* 1 Mar. 511/1 The only solution is a deer fence..using large mesh, light-gauge wire above the ordinary rabbit netting. **1907** *Yesterday's Shopping* (1969) 664/3 Rabbit snares..A few made up ready for use generally in stock. **1978** P. O'Donnell *Dragon's Claw* viii. 159 There was a noose of wire round his neck which..tightened like a rabbit snare. **1845** E. Acton *Mod. Cookery* i. 37 (*heading*) Rabbit soup à la reine. *Ibid.* 38 (*heading*) Brown rabbit soup. **1960** *Good Housek. Cookery Bk.* (rev. ed.) 65/2 (*heading*) Rabbit soup. **1824** *Cobbett's Weekly Register* 27 Mar. col. 797 It is the invariable practice of the farmers to have a number of rabbit-traps constantly set on the farms. **1856** C. Patmore *Angel in Ho.* II. Prol. 3 But she turn'd pale, for now the beast Found stock-still in the rabbit-trap,..Unglobed himself. **1976** J. B. Hilton *Gamekeeper's Gallows* vii. 61 Brunt ..came upon a rabbit trap. **1766** Smollett *Trav.* I. 32 Open downs, where there is a rabbit warren. **1821** M. Wilmot *Let.* 10 Apr. (1935) 104 This Rabbit Warren in the air. **1905** *Birmingham Institute Mag.* Oct. 187 The Institute has been graphically..described as a rabbit-warren. **1973** 'S. Harvester' *Corner of Playground* III. vii. 219 Their dull dusty sunless offices in the chaotic rabbit-warren of officialdom. **1906** Kipling *Puck of Pook's Hill* 259 A quick movement of the hand as though he were pegging down a rabbit-wire. **1945** N. Collins *London belongs to Me* III. xxxix. 301 The special visitors' room where they saw their loved ones through a screen of rabbit-wire. **1973** 'M. Campbell' *Halfbreed* iv. 30 We took Daddy's rabbit wire and strung it across two small green trees on either side of the footpath.

b. *rabbit-catcher* (earlier example; also *transf.*), *-courser, farmer, -farming, -hunting, -inspector, -shooting* (later example), *-trapping*; *rabbit-hunt* vb.

1724 Swift *Wks.* (1941) X. 146 Rabbet Catcher. I'll Ferret him. **1955** *Sun* (Baltimore) 23 Feb. 5-B/2 Engineers ..have stretched a nylon tennis net across a miniature landing field and are 'serving' Model F86 Sabre Jets into it. The purpose of the experiment is to test a new device, called a 'rabbit catcher'. **1875** Rabbit-courser [see *dog-racer* s.v. *dog *sb.* 17 a]. **1900** J. K. Jerome *Three Men on Bummel* v. 106, I have never met a rabbit farmer myself worth two thousand a year. **1889** G. F. Morant (*title*) Hutch rabbit-farming in the open [in K. W. Knight *The book of the rabbit*]. **1943** J. Stuart *Taps for Private Tussie* xvii. 172 Uncle Mott cut wood for the fireplace in the mornins and rabbit-hunted in the afternoons. **1873** *Trans. Illinois Dept. Agric.* X. 65 They prevailed on him to suspend his rabbit-hunting, and 'show them 'round'. **1953** N. Tinbergen *Herring Gull's World* iv. 27 Rabbit-hunting is a regular feature in the Dutch North Sea sand dunes. **1936** F. Clune *Roaming round Darling* xiii. 114 They were collected by the rabbit-inspector a number of years ago. **1978** H. Wouk *War & Remembrance* xxxix. 400 The slaughter that ensued was mere rabbit-shooting by our aircraft and submarines. **1880** W. Carnegie *Practical Trapping* 20 The same sort of gins, the use of which I advocated for rabbit-trapping, will do. **1935** *Discovery* June 168/1 Gamekeepers in winter in Ross-shire often come across wild-cat tracks in the snow when rabbit-trapping.

c. *rabbit-coloured, -eared* (later examples), *-faced, -hearted, -mouthed, -scared, -toothed* adjs.

1953 R. Graves *Poems* 18 Such gross-headed, rabbit-coloured litters As soon they shall be happy to desert. **1939** *Times Lit. Suppl.* 30 Dec. 756/1 Once there was a hasty glimpse of the rabbit-eared bandicoot. **1977** *Jersey Even. Post* 26 July 4/1 And the rabbit-eared bandicoots, small marsupials, only come out to feed at night. **1905** E. F. Benson *Image in Sand* i. 12 He was a rabbit-faced little man. **1920** *Chambers's Jrnl.* Dec. 812/1 'Rabbit-hearted' is an expression commonly used not only by white races, but also by red and brown people. **1909** *Cent. Dict.* Suppl., Rabbit-mouthed,..having a rabbit-mouth; harelipped. **1956** H. Gold *Man who was not with It* (1965) xxix. 272 His soft and rabbit-mouthed touchiness. **1936** *Partisan Rev.* III. 21/1 Standing there, his big gun smoking, Rabbit-scared, alone. **1971** *Maclean's Mag.* Oct. 3/2 We've never seemed so rabbit-scared as a nation as we did in August. **1800** D. Wordsworth *Jrnl.* 14 May (1941) I. 37 The grassy-leaved rabbit-toothed white flower. **1963** D. Lessing *Golden Notebk.* II. 246 His mouth is a rabbit-toothed hole, and his eyes are sunk in scar tissue. **1980** 'T. Hinde' *Sir Henry & Sons* iv. 33, I am round-faced and stocky... I became rabbit-toothed.

d. instrumental, as *rabbit-browsed, -haunted, -nibbled* adjs.

1923 Kipling *Land & Sea Tales* 81 A little rabbit-browsed clearing of turf. **1921** F. B. Young *Black Diamond* iv. 38 Evening visits to rabbit-haunted banks. **1947** W. de la Mare *Coll. Stories for Children* 30 The rabbit-nibbled turf.

4. rabbit-and-pork *Rhyming slang* = Talk *sb.*, *v.* (usu. *ellipt.*: see sense 2 g above and *rabbit *v.* 6); **rabbit ball** *U.S.*, a baseball that is springy in construction and lively in action; also *fig.*; **rabbit-bandicoot**, substitute for def.: a small Australian marsupial belonging to the genus *Macrotis* of the family Peramelidæ, living in a burrow and having rabbit-like ears; cf. *rabbit-eared* in sense 3 c above; (later examples); **rabbit-beagle**, a beagle used for the hunting of rabbits; so **rabbit-beagling** *vbl. sb.*; **rabbit berry**, substitute for def.: a deciduous North American shrub, *Shepherdia argentea*, of the family Elæagnaceæ, or its red berries; (earlier and later examples); **rabbit brush, bush**, substitute for def.: a western North American shrub of the genus *Chrysothamnus*, esp. *C. nauseosus*, belonging to the family Compositæ and bearing clusters of yellow flowers; (earlier and later examples); **rabbit drive** *U.S.*, a driving together of jack rabbits for slaughtering; **rabbit fever**, a vernacular name for tularæmia; **rabbit-fish**, (*a*) (earlier and later examples); (*b*) substitute for def.: *U.S.*, the smooth puffer, *Lagocephalus lævigatus*, or the spotted balloon fish, *Cyclichthys schoepfi*; (earlier and later examples); (*c*) a small herbivorous fish belonging to the family Siganidæ, found in tropical Indo-Pacific seas and bearing venom glands on the fins; **rabbit flea**, one of several fleas which infest rabbits, esp. the European rabbit flea, *Spilopsyllus cuniculi*, or the North American rabbit flea, *Cediopsylla simplex*; **rabbit food** (also **rabbit's food**), food such as is eaten by rabbits; hence (*slang*), lettuce; green salad; **rabbit-foot**: see also *rabbit's foot; **rabbit-foot (clover)** (earlier and later examples); **rabbitfoot grass**, an annual grass, *Polypogon monspeliensis*, distinguished by soft hairs on its flower-head, native to Europe and widely naturalized elsewhere; **rabbit-hawk** *U.S.*, the red-tailed hawk, *Buteo jamaicensis*, or the hen harrier, *Circus cyaneus*; **rabbit('s) pea** *U.S.*, a perennial herb, *Tephrosia virginiana*, belonging to the family Leguminosæ and bearing white, pink, or yellow flowers; also called goat's rue and wild sweet pea; **rabbit-proof** *a.*, proof against rabbits; esp. of a fence, that excludes rabbits (in Austral. *spec.* such a fence marking a border between States); *ellipt.*, such a fence; **rabbit-rat,** substitute for def.: an Australian rodent belonging to either of the genera *Mesembriomys* and *Conilurus*, distinguished by long ears and a bushy tail, esp. the white-footed tree rat, *C. albipes*, the only one not restricted to northern parts of the country; (examples); **rabbit test,** a pregnancy test in which rabbits are used; **rabbit tobacco** *U.S.*, the sweet everlasting, *Gnaphalium obtusifolium*, belonging to the family Compositæ, and bearing clusters of fragrant white flowers; also, the dried flowers of this plant, used as a substitute for tobacco; **rabbit tooth** *slang* = BUCK-TOOTH (usu. *pl.*).

1941 G. KERSH *They die with their Boots Clean* I. 27 He uses slang... Talk is Rabbit, or Rabbit-an'-Pork. **1960** *Spectator* 4 Mar. 326 We only allow ourselves a second to remember that rabbit-and-pork is talk. **1971** *National Times* (Austral.) 13 Dec. 20/1 (*heading*) Cockneys lay claim to their rabbit and pork. **1922** *N.Y. Times* 5 June 10/3 The officials who control the destiny of the big leagues let it be known at the opening of the current season that the 'rabbit' ball had seen its day. **1937** *Sun* (Baltimore) 18 Aug. 8/3 There does not seem to be any question of the changes that have been worked in baseball by the lively rabbit ball. **1973** *Times* 15 Aug. 7/3 The rabbit-ball..jumps like a rabbit. **1977** *Time* 11 Apr. 17/1 Rawlings Co. now makes the official major league baseball.., and the scuttlebutt is that Rawlings is turning out a rabbit ball. **1923** F. W. JONES *Mammals S. Austral.* I. 154 The animal..is usually termed the Common Rabbit-Bandicoot, but it would be most misleading to apply the term 'common' to it to-day. **1941** E. TROUGHTON *Furred Animals Austral.* 69 The very descriptive name of rabbit-bandicoot was provided by the early colonists who regarded them with a certain amount of tolerance because of their extremely useful share in the destruction of mice and insects. **1970** W. D. L. RIDE *Guide Native Mammals Austral.* vii. 104 There are generally thought to be only two species, the Common Rabbit Bandicoot and the small Central Australian Yallara or Lesser Rabbit Bandicoot. **1824** *Sporting Mag.* XIV. 312/2 There is no prettier sport for youth than rabbit beagling... Rabbit beagles should never be permitted to run hare. **1888** H. DALZIEL *Brit. Dogs* (ed. 2) I. xvi. 226 Beagles may be fairly classed as Hare-Beagles and Rabbit-Beagles, other distinction than size being minor. **1804** J. WHITEHOUSE *Jrnl.* 24 Aug. in *Orig. Jrnls. Lewis & Clark Exped.* (1905) VII. ii. 52 We found some red berreys which they call Rabbit berrys. **1891** [see *mountain tea* s.v. *MOUNTAIN 9d]. **1952** A. G. L. HELLYER *Sanders' Encycl. Gardening* (ed. 22) 454 *S[heperdia] argentea*, 'Rabbit Berry', 'Buffalo Berry',..scarlet fruits. **1914** E. STEWART *Lett. Woman Homesteader* 18 Our horse was midside deep in rabbit brush, a shrub just covered with flowers that look and smell like goldenrod. **1927** W. CATHER *Death comes for Archbishop* 95 The sandy soil of the plain.. was splotched with masses of blooming rabbit brush. **1946** D. C. PEATTIE *Road of Naturalist* i. 17 The burro bush and rabbit brush are the natural sons of the desert. **1955** *Daily Progress* (Charlottesville, Va.) 2 Nov. 11/5 That's rabbit-brush, a hearty range perennial that moves in quickly when other vegetation is killed. **1980** *Blair & Ketchum's Country Jrnl.* Oct. 46/3 The first mule I ever owned was rescued from a prairie dog town in southern Colorado, where she had lived for who knows how long on fresh air and rabbit-brush. **1852** H. STANSBURY *Expl. & Survey Valley of Gt. Salt Lake* 235 The only vegetation today has been a little dwarf artemisia, grease-bush, rabbit-bush. **1972** R. & R. WRIGHT *Cariboo Mileposts* 16 Grass and trees are scarce, with only sage and rabbit bush covering the ground. **1979** *Tucson* (Arizona) *Citizen* 28 Apr. 3A/9 Pollen count (yesterday)..Rabbit bush 4. **1887** *Lisbon* (N. Dakota) *Star* 23 Dec. 7/1 Several hundred people..assembled to engage in the rabbit drive. **1963** R. SYMONS *Many Trails* xii. 119 A hunt in the manner of the California rabbit drives. **1977** *New Yorker* 11 July 43/3 We have rabbit drives there. Drive the rabbits from one end of the island to the other and kill them. **1925** *Jrnl. Amer. Med. Assoc.* 25 Apr. 1244/1 A man..working in the Washington, D.C., market went to his physician..in 1921, for treatment for what he informed the physician was 'rabbit fever', adding that 'rabbit fever' was well known among market men... This was the first case of tularemia to be reported for the eastern United States. **1955** *Sci. News Let.* 16 July 43/1 Some species of ticks are occasional spreaders of Rocky Mountain spotted fever and tularemia (rabbit fever). **1973** *Daily Colonist* (Victoria, B.C.) 29 July 2/2 Then he mentioned that he had been doing some squirrel hunting and the doctor immediately ordered a blood test which showed he had tularemia, or 'rabbit fever'. **1828** J. FLEMING *Hist. Brit. Animals* 173 The specimen [of *Chimæra*], from which the preceding description was taken, was sent from Unst, where it is termed the Rabbit-fish. **1842** J. E. DEKAY *Zool. N.Y.* IV. 330 The Lineated Puffer..is called Rabbit-fish, according to Schoepfi, on account of the whiteness of its flesh. **1884** *Bull. U.S. Nat. Museum* No. 27. 428 Spiny Box-fish; Rabbit-fish; Swell Toad. East coast of the United States. **1897** *Rep. N.Y. Forest, Fish, & Game Comm.* II. 224 Rabbit-fish; Smooth Puffer.—Occasionally taken in the fall in Gravesend Bay. **1905** D. S. JORDAN *Guide to Study of Fishes* II. xxiv. 423 In the [American] rabbit-fishes..the body is box-shaped. **1925** J. T. JENKINS *Fishes Brit. Isles* 349 From its great cutting teeth it [sc. *Chimæra monstrosa*] is known to the Shetlanders as the Rabbit-fish. **1941** R. FAHERTY *Big Old Sun* xi. 255 'I'm a blow-puffing rabbitfish,' he sputtered. **1953** J. L. B. SMITH *Sea Fishes S. Afr.* 328 Rabbitfishes. Compressed ovate body with slippery skin and minute concealed scales. .. Curious small herbivorous fishes of reefs and weeds of the tropical Indo-Pacific. **1962** K. F. LAGLER et al. *Ichthyol.* iv. 32 Non-fatal but nevertheless painful to man..are stings of the venomous sharks,..rabbitfishes, and dragonets. **1973** *Aquaculture* I. 361 Rabbitfish are widely spread throughout the Indian and the western and central Pacific oceans. **1975** *Times* 5 Dec. 12/3 The deep-sea species..can be portrayed as menacing horrors. The specific name for one of them, rabbitfish, is Chimaera Monstrosa. **1904** *Proc. U.S. Nat. Museum* XXVII. 368 In the United States the cat, dog, and rabbit fleas..will readily attack the human being. **1925** A. D. IMMS *Gen. Textbk. Ent.* III. 663 The rabbit flea.. commonly affects the ears of hares and rabbits. **1963** O. BRELAND *Animal Life & Lore* i. 26 In some regions, it [sc. myxomatosis] is transmitted by rabbit fleas. **1967** J. M. BROWNJOHN tr. *Grzimek's Four-Legged Australians* xii. 250 For some years, European rabbit-fleas refused to propagate themselves in Australian research centres. **1975** *Times* 23 June 4/2 The rabbit flea..spreads myxomatosis. **1907** *Yesterday's Shopping* (1969) 58/1 Rabbit Food..Pigeon Food..Foal Food. **1936** *Amer. Speech* XI. 44/2 *Rabbit's food*, lettuce. **1941** J. SMILEY *Hash House Lingo* 45 *Rabbit food*, lettuce. **1959** I. & P. OPIE *Lore & Lang. Schoolch.* ix. 163 Tomatoes are generally 'squashers', and 'rabbit's food' is any green salad. **1972** A. PRICE *Colonel Butler's Wolf* ix. 98 You can both come back with me and eat pounds of rabbit food. **1817** A. EATON *Man. Bot.* 84 *Trifolium..arvense* (field clover, or rabbit-foot) heads cylindric. **1850** S. F. COOPER *Rural Hours* 125 The downy 'rabbit-foot', or 'stone-clover', the common red variety..[is] introduced. **1889** *Cent. Dict.* s.v. Clover. Other species, mostly weeds of little value, are the yellow or hop clover,..the stone, hare's-foot, or rabbit-foot clover. **1954** *Amer. Speech* XXIX. 15 *Trifolium arvense*, a cosmopolitan woolly-headed clover,..is known in America both as the rabbitfoot (clover) and hare's-foot (clover)... Rabbitfoot clover is the commonest designation in the United States, whereas hare's-foot is the usual British term. **1935** A. S. HITCHCOCK *Man. Grasses U.S.* 350 *Polypogon monspeliensis*..Rabbitfoot Grass. **1954** C. E. HUBBARD *Grasses* 285 Annual Beard-grass. *Polypogon monspeliensis*... Known in N. America as 'Rabbitfoot Grass'. **1968** F. W. GOULD *Grass Systematics* v. 172 Most common and widespread is..rabbitfoot grass, present in moist areas along streams. **1851** *De Bow's Rev.* XI. 54 1st, Rabbit hawk. **1880** G. W. CABLE *Grandissimes* vii. 43 A great rabbit-hawk sat alone in the top of a lofty pecan-tree. **1904** 'O. HENRY' *Heart of West* 64 The other eye noticed a rabbit-hawk sitting on a dead limb in a water-elm. **1964** *Publ. Amer. Dial. Soc.* XLII. 22 Rabbit-hawk. The marsh hawk (*Circus cyaneus*), so called because of its flying low over the pastures in search of rodents. **1938** M. K. RAWLINGS *Yearling* xvii. 199 A rabbit-pea vine was in blossom. **1976** *Hortus Third* (L. H. Bailey Hortorium) 1101/1 *Tephrosia..virginiana*..Goat's rue, catgut, rabbit's pea. **1832** *Useful & Ornamental in Brit. Husbandry* (1840) III. III. 26 The fence of a forest-tree nursery requires to be rabbit-proof. **1894** W. ROBINSON *Wild Garden* (ed. 4) xv. 209 Periwinkle, which is named amongst rabbit-proof plants, is generally eaten to the ground in severe weather. *a* **1902** H. MORANT in *Penguin Bk. Austral. Ballads* (1964) 212 But once we're through the rabbit-proof..it's 'West-by-North' again. **1957** R. STOW *Bystander* 29 That's the coldest little bitch this side of the rabbit-proof fence. **1961** *Times* 19 Apr. 14/7 Her rabbit-proof fence is not high enough. **1976** D. HEWETT *Bonbons & Roses for Dolly* 28 Best little ticket takers this side of the rabbit-proof. **1837** G. BENNETT *Catal. Specimens Nat. Hist. Austral. Mus.* 6 The Rabbit Rat of the Colonists. Habitat, Interior of Australia. **1863** J. GOULD *Mammals Austral.* III. 1 White-footed Hapalotis... The Rabbit Rat of the Colonists. **1879** A. R. WALLACE *Australasia* iii. 55 Bandicoots and rabbit-rats, are small animals with sharp nose and long claws, allied to the kangaroos. **1941** E. TROUGHTON *Furred Animals Austral.* 305 The various species..are sometimes called 'rabbit-rats' in reference to the rather large ears. **1970** W. D. L. RIDE *Guide Native Mammals Austral.* ix. 142 Little is known of the White-footed Tree-rat of eastern Australia; early settlers called this the Rabbit Rat because of its rounded form and long ears. It has not been seen alive in this century. **1949** S. T. DE LEE *Safeguarding Motherhood* 133 (Index), Rabbit test. **1958** H. SPEERT *Obstetr. & Gynecol. Milestones* xxviii. 244 The urine of pregnant women contains a gonadotrophic substance simulating the secretion of the anterior pituitary in its effect on the mouse ovary. Applying this observation to the rabbit, Friedman proceeded to develop the pregnancy test known by his name, popularly as the 'rabbit test'. **1977** E. LEONARD *Unknown Man No. 89* i. 7 The guy was a gynecologist. So he went in with Rita for her rabbit test, the concerned hubby. **1880** J. C. HARRIS *Uncle Remus* xiii. 66 'Den he drawd de rockin'-cheer in front er de fier, he did, en tuck a big chaw terbarker.' 'Tobacco, Uncle Remus?' asked the little boy, incredulously. 'Rabbit terbarker, honey.' **1909** 'O. HENRY' *Options* 200, I don't give a pipeful of rabbit tobacco whether Queen Sophia Christina or Charlie Culberson rules these fairy isles. **1936** M. MITCHELL *Gone with Wind* xxix. 488 'You all got any chewing tobacco, Scarlett?' 'Nothing but rabbit tobacco. Pa smokes it in a corn cob.' **1937** *Amer. Speech* XII. 235/1 On all the poor land in the middle and far West there is a weed known as..rabbit tobacco. **1964** *Publ. Amer. Dial. Soc.* XLII. 22 Rabbit tobacco. Life everlasting.., used in many folk remedies for catarrh; also chewed and smoked by boys. **1980** Rabbit tooth [implied in *rabbit-toothed* above]. **1915** W. OWEN *Let.* 4 Apr. (1967) 330 Will he be 13 or 14 next birthday?.. Are his rabbit-teeth humanising? **1980** E. LEATHER *Duveen Let.* viii. 98 He was tall, thin, with large rabbit teeth.

rabbit, *v.*[1] Add: **3.** *intr.* To go; to move quickly; to run away. *dial.* and *colloq.*

1887 *Rep. & Trans. Devonshire Assoc.* XIX. 77 Miss — du rabbut 'bout en awl wethurz. **1937** D. JONES *In Parenthesis* IV. 71 You can't find the lane—the one way—you rabbit to and fro. **1960** WENTWORTH & FLEXNER *Dict. Amer. Slang* 416/1 *Rabbit..v.i.*, to move quickly, to run; specif., to flee, to escape. **1962** J. F. STRAKER *Coil of Rope* iii. 22 Susan.. kept skipping from one side of David to the other... David said irritably, 'For heaven's sake stop rabbiting around!' **1972** J. WAMBAUGH *Blue Knight* (1973) ii. 33, I noticed another junkie watching me. He was trying to decide whether to rabbit or freeze.

4. To copulate. *rare.*

1919 J. MASEFIELD *Reynard the Fox* 16 I'll learn 'ee rabbit in my shed.

5. *trans.* To borrow or steal. *Austral. Naut. slang.* Cf. *RABBIT *sb.*[1] 2 f.

1943 BAKER *Dict. Austral. Slang* (ed. 3) 63 *To rabbit*, to borrow, 'scrounge'. (R.A.N. slang.) **1953** K. TENNANT *Joyful Condemned* xxi. 198 Why were Australian Navy men better at 'rabbiting' little valuable articles than Americans?

6. [See *rabbit-and-pork* s.v. *RABBIT *sb.*[1] 4.] *intr.* To talk, to discourse volubly; to gabble. Freq. const. *on*. *colloq.*

1950 P. TEMPEST *Lag's Lexicon* 173 One who 'rabbits' all the time is one who never stops talking. **1959** *Encounter* Mar. 63/1 The next thing I knew, I was rabbiting away to a geezer. **1960** *News Chron.* 16 Feb. 6/6 She don't want to stand rabbiting away about colourful denizens. **1963** 'A. GARVE' *Sea Monks* iii. 108 Then stop rabbitin' an' get that wall cleaned. **1967** A. DIMENT *Dolly Dolly Spy* iv. 39, I let him rabbit on about the twilight hours of the Third Reich. **1976** J. BINGHAM *God's Defector* vii. 99 You go into a pub with a short-back-and-sides and people stop rabbiting and stare at you. **1977** *Guardian Weekly* 9 Oct. 20/3 A girl reporter from Rolling Stone rabbits on idiotically about the Maharishi.

rabbitish, *a.* Delete *rare* and add later examples.

1941 E. R. EDDISON *Fish Dinner* xiii. 225 Young man a bit rabbitish by the look of him: doesn't seem to know quite what to do. **1978** J. SYMONS *Blackheath Poisonings* I. 24 Bertie, who was fair and pale, with pinkish eyes, had a slightly rabbitish appearance.

ra·bbit-o. *Austral. slang.* Also **Rabbit-O, rabbit-oh.** [f. RABBIT *sb.*[1] + *-O[2].] An itinerant seller of rabbits as food. Also *attrib.*

[**1908** T. E. SPENCER *Budgeree Ballads* 84 When I ought to think of bizness, I can only think of you, And instead of 'Rabbit-oh!' I sings out 'Liza!'] **1911** A. WRIGHT *Gambler's Gold* 75 Engaged in the hopeless task of trying to win the Rabbit-O man's money. **1945** K. TENNANT *Time enough Later* x. 150 Mrs. Drew knew all about her neighbours from the butcher and the grocer and the rabbit-o. **1975** *Sydney Morning Herald* 9 Apr. 1 Now 65, he is probably the last rabbit-oh in Sydney.

ra·bbit punch. Also **rabbit's punch.** [f. RABBIT *sb.*[1] + PUNCH *sb.*[2]] A sharp, chopping blow to the back of the neck delivered with the side of the hand. Also *fig.*

1915 E. CORRI *30 Years Boxing Referee* 175 The occipital punch is well described by its other name, the 'rabbit-punch', derived from the way in which a gamekeeper puts a rabbit out of pain. **1936** *Daily Tel.* 30 Jan. 20/7 The only incident to which any exception could be taken was Petersen's habit of using the 'rabbit punch'—a cuff downwards on the back of the neck. **1958** *Daily Mail* 7 June 5/7 Simpson admitted to the police that he had killed the dog. He said he..gave it a 'rabbit punch'. **1959** I. & P. OPIE *Lore & Lang. Schoolch.* x. 202 A 'Rabbit's Punch' is delivered by pulling a child's head forward, usually by his hair, and slicing the back of his neck with the side of the hand. **1968** A. DIMENT *Bang Bang Birds* iii. 27 Another gust of warm wind caught me in a rabbit punch. **1973** G. SIMS *Hunters Point* xiii. 123 As he toppled forward Buchanan delivered a murderous rabbit punch.

So **ra·bbit-punch** *v. trans.*; **ra·bbit-punching** *ppl. a.* and *vbl. sb.*

1936 R. CHANDLER in *Black Mask* Jan. 18/2 Somebody rabbit-punched him from behind. **1940** DYLAN THOMAS *Portrait of Artist as Young Dog* 72 The strange boy rabbit-punched me twice. **1968** T. STOPPARD *Real Inspector Hound* (1970) 11, I dream of champions chopped down by rabbit-punching sparring partners. **1971** *Times* 16 Feb. 8/5 A controversial disqualification for rabbit punching. **1972** T. COE *Don't lie to Me* (1974) xx. 161 He rabbit-punched me in the back of the neck.

rabbitry. Add: **1.** Also, rabbit-breeding.

1968 *Punch* 12 June 858/3 Anyone with distressful childhood memories of pet does unconcernedly making away with their blind and naked young may like to know that commercial rabbitry has just about eradicated such uneconomic vice.

2. *slang.* In sport, poor performers (*collect.*). Also, poor play or performance in any game. Cf. *RABBIT *sb.*[1] 2 a.

1930 *Observer* 25 May 16 The rabbitry..is faithful to the definition of the game [*sc.* golf] as 'pedestrianism round the margin of the links'. **1932** A. MARSHALL *Mrs. Jim* v. 44 Her two younger girls..were made welcome at these [tennis] parties, so that Mrs. Gurdon's rabbitry should not be put to shame.

rabbit's ear. Also **rabbit ear.** [f. RABBIT *sb.*[1] + EAR *sb.*[1]] **1.** A perennial herb, *Stachys olympica* (formerly *S. lanata*), belonging to the family Labiatæ, distinguished by greyish foliage and dense white tomentum covering the whole plant; usually called lamb's ears.

1928 V. WOOLF *Let.* 15 Oct. (1977) III. 545 Might I beg some Saviour's flannel or rabbit ear? *Ibid.* 22 Oct. 547 A thousand thanks for the rabbits ears. **1949** H. NICOLSON *Let.* 15 June (1968) 171, I think of it [*sc.* a garden] as *cineraria* in masses, Rabbit's Ears in masses,..predominantly grey.

2. An indoor television aerial consisting of a base supporting two stiff wires that form a V. *U.S.*

1967 *Boston Sunday Herald Mag.* 16 Apr. 32/2 (Advt.), Top back lifts for rabbit ears—doors fold flat against sides for televiewing. **1972** T. KENRICK *Tough One to Lose* ii. 30 There wasn't much... A TV set in the corner that needed rabbit's ears. **1978** *Tucson Mag.* Dec. 37/1, I use rabbit ears with my set and get a perfect picture.

ra·bbit's foot. [RABBIT *sb.*[1] 4.] **1.** Also **rabbit-foot.** The foot of a rabbit carried to bring luck; also *transf.* Phr. *to work the rabbit('s)-foot* (U.S.), to cheat, to trick.

1879 L. HEARN *Amer. Miscell.* (1924) I. 185 After the girl told that [ghost] story, Banjo Jim seldom passed along the row at night without a rabbit's foot in the breast pocket of his woolen shirt. **1902** W. N. HARBEN *Abner Daniel* 309 Pole worked the rabbit-foot on them back there. **1922** *Sunset* Dec. 10/2 Presently the word went round that I was a 'rabbit's foot'—a bringer of good luck—and the gamblers began to give me money to place for them. **1948** *Salt Lake Tribune* 17 Dec. 34/6 A dimestore rabbit's foot paid off with one of 1948's biggest football surprises and landed his team in the Delta bowl. **1972** C. WESTON *Poor, Poor Ophelia* (1973) viii. 45 Don't you know a charm when you see one? This is my rabbit's foot.

2. Special combs.: **rabbit's foot (clover)** = *rabbit-foot clover* s.v. RABBIT *sb.*[1] 4 in Dict. and Suppl.; **rabbit's foot (fern)** *U.S.*, an epiphytic fern, *Polypodium aureum*, native to tropical America and cultivated elsewhere as a house plant; **rabbit's foot grass** = *rabbitfoot grass* s.v. *RABBIT *sb.*[1] 4.

1878 H. M. JACKSON *Bits of Travel at Home* 186 [There grows] Rabbit's foot, May-weed, shepherd's purse. **1968** PETERSON & MCKENNY *Field Guide to Wildflowers N. Amer.* 246 Rabbit's-foot Clover... The soft silky foliage and the fuzzy, grayish-pink heads of bloom are unmistakable. **1972** G. BEINE *Land of Coyote* 90 These are rattle boxes, and there, some rabbitsfoot clover. **1951** E. GRAHAM *My Window looks down East* vii. 63 The rabbit's foot fern and all the other green things looked so radiant and fresh. **1964** F. G. FOSTER *Gardener's Fern Bk.* 182 Golden Polypody... Commonly called 'rabbit's-foot' fern. Actually, the 'rabbit's foot' is a colorful orange-brown or white, scaly rhizome. **1973** J. L. FAUST *N.Y. Times Bk. House Plants* 107 Ferns..best for indoors are..coarse-leaved polypody..and rabbit's-foot. **1973** *Times* 20 Oct. 16/7 Upright 'rabbits' [*sic*] foot', cock-spur or barnyard grasses have been common.

rabbity, *a.* Add: (Further examples.) Also, suggestive or characteristic of a rabbit. Also *Comb.*, as *rabbity-faced, -looking* adjs.

a **1930** D. H. LAWRENCE *Last Poems* (1932) 98 There are too many people on earth Insipid, unsalted, rabbity, endlessly hopping. **1931** D. L. SAYERS *Five Red Herrings* xvi. 177 The rabbity-faced fellow in the train. **1937** C. DAY LEWIS *Starting Point* III. iv. 284 Darling, you're not going to turn me into a rabbity little wage-earner, are you? **1963** AUDEN *Dyer's Hand* 120 A leporello who, in real life, is a rabbity-looking..professor. **1965** M. SHADBOLT *Among Cinders* xi. 96 I'd been starving on rabbity salads. **1974** T. P. WHITNEY tr. *Solzhenitsyn's Gulag Archipelago* I. II. ii. 544 But somehow this is hard for our rabbity brains to grasp. **1976** *Gramophone* Nov. 878/3 My own family's verdict on the book [sc. *Watership Down*] was that it was 'extraordinarily rabbitty'. **1978** G. GREENE *Human Factor* III. v. 144 He thought he recognised all the faces except for one woman in a shabby rabbity fur.

rabble, *sb.*[1] (and *a.*). **2. e.** Delete entry.

The word printed 'rabble' in the 1766 ed. of *Swift's Lett.* is 'babble' in the author's MS.

rabble, *sb.*[2] Add: **4.** *Comb.*, as **rabble-arm** = sense 3.

1905 *Electrochem. & Metall. Industry* May 194/1 The upper four hearths are provided with two rabble-arms each, the sixth and seventh with three rabble-arms, in order to increase the stirring and discharge rather on one side of the furnace.

rabble, *v.*[2] Add: **2.** Also, to behave as a rabble; to go *off* as a rabble.

a **1861** T. WINTHROP *John Brent* (1883) ix. 76 He dismissed his audience with an..injunction to keep closer to the train..and not be 'rabbling off to catch grasshoppers'. **1970** O. CHADWICK *Victorian Church* II. vi. 355 The agitators began to disturb and rabble at services.

rabble, *v.*[3] Add: (Earlier example.) Cf. *RAVEL *v.*[4]

1860 C. TOMLINSON *Useful Arts & Manuf.* 2nd Ser. II. 17 The door of the furnace is removed, and the liquid mass well *rabbled* or stirred.

rabble-rouser (ræ·b'l,rauzəɹ). [f. RABBLE *sb.*[1] + ROUSER.] **a.** One who practises rabble-rousing; a demagogue.

1843 'R. CARLTON' *New Purchase* I. xxii. 211 Nothing surpasses the munificent promises..of a genuine rabble rouser, just before an election. **1926** *Even. Standard* 12 July 3/2 You need not be a Tammany politician to know the meaning of boodle, gerrymander, carpet-bagger, wirepuller, rabble-rouser. **1959** 'M. M. KAYE' *House of Shade* xiv. 190 The murder of a rabble-rouser would probably be considered as of little account. **1972** *Listener* 28 Dec. 899/1 Thomas Paine..was never a rabble-rouser. **1978** J. A. MICHENER *Chesapeake* 543 Paul..astounded the more conservative Steeds by prevailing upon an itinerant Methodist rabble-rouser to spend five days at Devon.

b. Something, esp. music, that excites an audience.

1958 *New Statesman* 1 Feb. 133/3 The symphony ends with a noisy finale which seemed no more than an unusually prolonged rabble-rouser. **1965** G. MELLY *Owning Up* iv. 38 They chose their fastest, loudest numbers, 'rabble rousers' was the trade name, in the hope of making some impact on the audience.

rabble-rousing (ræ·b'l,rauziŋ), *a.* and *sb.* [f. RABBLE *sb.*[1] + ROUSING *ppl. a.* and *vbl. sb.*[1]]

A. *adj.* Tending to arouse the emotions of a rabble or disorderly crowd, esp. for political ends; demagogic, inflammatory, excitatory.

1802 [in Dict. s.v. RABBLE *sb.*[1] 5]. **1933** *Sun* (Baltimore) 8 Aug. 8/2 They are as old as rabble-rousing nationalism itself. **1951** T. STERLING *House without Door* xi. 126 Mouthing the rabble-rousing opinions of Communist filth. **1969** *N.Y. Rev. Bks.* 30 Jan. 12/4 Convinced that this was a rabble-rousing exaggeration, Booth set out to compile his own statistics. **1976** *Eastern Even. News* (Norwich) 9 Dec. 2/1 Mussolini made a rabble-rousing appearance in Milan after the Allies had landed in the south.

B. *sb.* The act or process of arousing the emotions of a crowd; demagoguery, trouble-stirring.

1933 *Sun* (Baltimore) 18 Sept. 8/2 It is not necessary to pay a great deal of attention to this form of economic rabble rousing. **1962** D. H. LAURENCE in G. B. Shaw *Platform & Pulpit* p. xii, He was not concerned with rabble-rousing or spell-binding. **1974** A. ROSS *Bradford Business* 9 Heated rabble-rousing in our seats of learning.

Hence (as a back-formation) **ra·bble-rouse** *v. intr.*, to arouse the emotions of a crowd by a demagogical harangue.

1959 *Time* 15 June 36/3 He rabble-rouses more fluently in English than in Chinese. **1971** *Guardian* 1 July 11/6 Did he [*sc.* Oswald Mosley] make speeches in such a way as to rabble-rouse?

Rabelaisian, *a.* (and *sb.*) Add: **A.** *adj.* (Earlier example.)

1817 LADY MORGAN *France* II. viii. 167 He talked of recovery,..and still emitted some of those sparks of Rabelaisian humour, attributed to him by contemporary wits.

B. *sb.* (Earlier example.)

1882 HARDY *Let.* 17 May (1978) I. 106 We Rabelaisians have not as yet reached the state of enlightenment which distinguishes you Noviomagians, & do not include ladies in our company.

Rabelaisianism. Add: (Further example.) Also, a Rabelaisian feature or characteristic.

1908 A. BENNETT *Old Wives' Tale* II. ii. 166 The robust Rabelaisianism of his more private conversation. **1922** *Times Lit. Suppl.* 5 Jan. 9/1 His [*sc.* Balzac's] mere Rabelaisianisms sometimes bring a later accent into what should be a very simple atmosphere.

‖**Rabfak** (ræ·bfæk). Also **rabfac.** [a. Russ. *rabfák*, f. *rab(óchiĭ) fak(ul'tét)* workers' school.] A workers' school, established after the Russian Revolution, to prepare workers and peasants for higher education. Also *attrib.*

1928 *Observer* 19 Feb. 12 Among the candidates for admission to the local 'rabfac', or workers' high school, appeared a young woman..who announced herself as 'Sheem Sheem', daughter of Sun-Yat-sen. **1943** E. M. ALMEDINGEN *Frossia* ix. 316 'Rabfaks?' she asked. 'Oh yes, I have heard of them. Workers' Faculties, are they not?' *Ibid.* 337 A few [teachers] deplored the Rabfak system—always in cautious undertones. **1960** *Twentieth Cent.* June 573 In 1922 he [*sc.* Kruschschev] was sent by the Party for a three-year adult education course at a 'Rabfak' school.

rabies. Now usu. with pronunc. (rē̆ⁱ·bīz, -iz). Add to def.: A contagious virus disease of dogs and other warm-blooded animals, which produces paralysis or a vicious excitability and in man causes a fatal encephalitis with throat spasm upon swallowing and convulsions. (Earlier and later examples.)

1598 J. FLORIO *Worlde of Wordes* 307/2 *Rabbino, Rabi, Rabis*, the Rabbies. **1967** SWAIN & DODDS *Clinical Virol.* xiii. 184 Eradication of rabies can be achieved only when the total elimination of the reservoir of animal infection is possible. It has been achieved in Great Britain by rigid quarantine laws which govern the importation of all livestock. **1976** *Daily Tel.* 20 July 3/3 A 32-year-old teacher, fined £300 at Uxbridge for contravening the rabies regulations had the penalty reduced on appeal to £100 yesterday. **1976** T. HEALD *Let Sleeping Dogs Die* ii. 30 'But surely he got an injection?' 'Not even anti-tetanus. Let alone a rabies jab. It was only a little bite.' **1977** D. A. WARRELL in C. Kaplan *Rabies: the Facts* iii. 32 In man the disease called rabies is a severe inflammation of the brain and spinal cord ..associated with invasion of these tissues by rabies virus. **1980** *Sci. Amer.* Jan. 109/1 Fox rabies is particularly serious in Europe, where the disease has spread steadily at the rate of about 30 kilometers per year from east to west since World War II.

‖**Rabkrin** (ræ·bkrin). [a. Russ. *rabkrín* f. *rab(óche)-kr(est'yánskaya) in(spéktsiya)* worker–peasant inspectorate.] An organization established in 1920 by Lenin to examine the conformity of state organizations to official policy.

1928 *Observer* 18 Mar. 19/5 The Rabkrin (the Russian abbreviation for the Commissariat of Workers' and Peasants' Inspection) is a supreme controlling and auditing department, which is supposed to expose deficiencies in the work of State and industrial institutions. **1949** I. DEUTSCHER *Stalin* vii. 230 The Rabkrin, as the Commissariat was called, was set up to control every branch of the administration.

Racah (ra·kā). *Physics* and *Chem.* The name of Giulio *Racah* (1909–65), Italian-born Israeli physicist, used *attrib.* with reference to his work in quantum mechanics, as *Racah coefficient* or *parameter*, either of two coefficients representing electrostatic interactions within a system of equivalent charged particles, esp. electrons within an atom.

1952 *Physical Rev.* LXXXVIII. 581/2 The coefficients of the transformation have been given by Racah..in terms of his *W* function and are called the Racah coefficients. **1959** *Astrophysical Jrnl.* CXXIX. 441 By means of a few simple formulae, all multiplet strengths..can be expressed in terms of only two basic quantities, viz., the Racah coefficients and the coefficients of fractional parentage. **1962** COTTON & WILKINSON *Adv. Inorg. Chem.* xxvi. 595 The Racah parameters are measures of the energy separations of the various Russell-Saunders states of an atom. **1966** PHILLIPS & WILLIAMS *Inorg. Chem.* II. xxiii. 162 The total electron-electron repulsion energy of each *LS* state arising from a d^n configuration can be calculated and expressed in terms of so-called Racah parameters. **1968** A. B. P. LEVER *Inorg. Electronic Spectroscopy* vii. 207 The Racah interelectronic parameter *B* (and to a lesser extent *C*) is a function of ligand, central ion and stereochemistry. **1975** *Physics Bull.* Apr. 169/3 The classification of particle and nuclear properties uses techniques such as spinors and Racah algebra which are not for the first degree student.

race, *sb.*[1] **III. 8. c.** Delete 'Now chiefly *U.S.*' and add further examples.

1901 M. FRANKLIN *My Brilliant Career* xiv. 117 They have cut races between the two creeks. **1912** B. E. BAUGHAN *Brown Bread* 99 Little runnels and 'races' of water led through the plain from the mountain rivers. **1941** I. L. IDRIESS *Great Boomerang* xxxi. 243 We would take the water from a creek on one side of a mountain and by means of a race (channel) take it completely around the mountain. **1976** *Jrnl. Lakeland Dial. Soc.* 35 Ah thowt Ah wud ga up t' race an' then cross t' beck on t' steppin steans.

e. (Earlier example.)

1833 J. C. LOUDON *Encycl. Archit.* 470 The back wall of the barn is to be sunk sufficiently deep for the wheel of the threshing-mill and the race (horse-course) from it.

f. (Earlier and later examples.) Also *Austral.*

1865 M. A. BARKER *Station Life in N.Z.* (1870) v. 34 The newly-shorn [sheep]..have passed thro' a narrow passage, called a 'race'. **1878** E. S. ELWELL *Boy Colonists* 214 They made a 'lead' in the stockyard for branding the cattle. This was something like a 'race' for drafting sheep, with a swing gate. **1934** T. WOOD *Cobbers* iv. 41 'Bullicks come aboard along a *race*. This is a race,' and he pointed to narrow gangways, railed in on both sides, which sloped from the main deck down to the cattle deck. **1950** *N.Z. Jrnl. Agric.* Apr. 373/3 The units [of the pig house] are usually placed side by side under one continuous roof, a service race being provided along the front. **1963** A. LUBBOCK *Austral. Roundabout* 180 The cattle were in the yards and the drovers and dogs were putting them through a 'race'—two rows of wooden fencing with a swing gate at the end. **1977** *N.Z. Herald* 8 Jan. 4–7/9 (Advt.), At present dairy and beef. Good race and fencing, tidal boundary, ample hay storage.

g. (Example.)

1825 J. NICHOLSON *Oper. Mech.* 104 The stones of the race are hewn to a mould, and laid in their places with great care.

h. Each of the two grooved rings of a ball or roller bearing.

1903 *Sci. Amer. Suppl.* 2, Feb. 22689/1 The rollers are made to fit the inner and outer treads of the roller race. **1907, 1908** [see *ball-race* s.v. *BALL *sb.*[1] 22]. **1930** *Engineering* 4 Apr. 462/1 There are two rings of rollers running side by side between hardened and ground inner and outer races. **1960** [see *COIN *v.*[1] 3 b]. **1968** *Autocar* 25 Jan. 49/2, I drove the 2-litre car at Monte Carlo and we had transmission trouble there which was bad luck because it was a ball race that broke. **1971** B. SCHARF *Engin. & its Language* xii. 135 Ball bearings..consist of..an inner race, which is a grooved ring firmly attached to the shaft, and an outer race in the stationary housing. The balls which are free to rotate between the races are kept apart by means of a cage. **1980** *Dirt Bike* Oct. 33/1 You may even need to replace the balls and races if they're dented or worn.

IV. 10. c. *fig.* An electoral contest for public office. Phr. *to make the race*, to run for public office (see also quot. 1881). *U.S.*

1855 I. C. PRAY *Mem. J. G. Bennett* 288 He had been the first to start many of them upon the ground for a successful political race. **1881** H. W. PIERSON *In Brush* 132 To 'make the race' was to secure an election. *Ibid.* 133 This pursuit of office was always spoken of as a 'race'. **1903** *N.Y. Even. Post* 17 Sept. 1 Mr. Cutting ran up stairs to tell Dr. Gould.. that Mr. Gront would make the race. **1949** *Dallas Morning News* 1 May 1/7 He might perhaps consider making the Senate race. **1976** *National Observer* (U.S.) 6 Nov. 24/3 New totals for..U.S. Senate races and gubernatorial races will churn out every five minutes.

d. As the second element in Comb. with a defining sb., as *armament race, arms race, moon race, space race*, etc.: see the sbs. in Suppl.

e. In colloq. phr. *to be in the race*, to have a chance. Usu. in neg. contexts. *Austral.*

1945 M. TRIST *Now that we're Laughing* x. 73 With you and Daffy dressed up, none of us others will be in the race. **1953** T. A. G. HUNGERFORD *Riverslake* x. 227 'See that bloke?' He pointed down the road after the vanished car. 'A few years ago he wouldn't have been in the race to own a car like that.' **1956** J. T. LANG *I Remember* vi. 34 The trade unions realised that if the Chinese could get away with long hours and low pay they would not be in the race to get better conditions.

f. *Electronics.* In a switching circuit, a condition in which the time a component secondary circuit or device takes to operate has to be taken into account (as when two are required to operate simultaneously, though in practice one will operate before the other). Freq. *attrib.*

1954 *Jrnl. Franklin Inst.* CCLVII. 170 In a composite transition matrix the presence of two or more of the digits '1' indicates that at least two of the secondary relays are simultaneously unstable, and that a race condition exists. **1958** S. H. CALDWELL *Switching Circuits* xii. 469 The race condition in this instance can lead to false operation and we designate this as a critical race. **1969** J. J. SPARKES *Transistor Switching* vii. 161 It is customary to arrange the logic so that all races are removed or rendered non-critical. **1975** J. C. BOYCE *Digital Logic* ix. 267 Races are characterized by arrows that skip rows on flowtables, since more than one gate must change at the same time to allow the operating point to follow the arrow.

V. 11. a. (sense 10) *race-boat* (earlier and later examples), *-colt, driver, -ground* (earlier examples), *mare, record, report, -rider* (later examples), *-time*; (sense 8 f) *race gate, shed.* **b. race-ball** (later example); **race card** (later examples); **racecaster** orig. *U.S.*, a radio or television broadcaster who reports on horse-racing; **race game,** a board game simulating a horse-race in which rival counters proceed at the throw of a dice; also *transf.*; **race gang,** a group of petty criminals who frequent race-meetings; **race-glass:** now usu. in *pl.* (examples); **race-goer,** a frequenter of race-meetings; also **race-going** *a.* and *sb.*; **race-mark,** a mark attached to pigeons before a particular race; hence **race-mark** *v. trans.*, to supply (pigeons) with race-marks; **race-path,** (*a*) a race-track; (*b*) the channel along which water flows to a mill-wheel; **race-reader,** (*a*) one who forecasts the performance of horses in a given race; (*b*) (see quot. 1953); also, a race commentator; hence **race-reading**; **race stand** (earlier example); **race-track** orig. *U.S.* = RACE-COURSE 1 a; also *transf.* and *attrib.*; **race train,** a special train which runs to and from a race-meeting; **race-trough,** a plank with raised edges along which goods are passed in loading or unloading ships or wagons; **race walking,** the act or practice of competing in a walking race; hence **race walker**; **race walk** *v. intr.*

c **1838** W. H. MURRAY in M. R. Booth *Eng. Plays of 19th Cent.* (1973) IV. 162, I saw Charlotte at the race-ball, and fell over head and ears in love with her. **1839** *Spirit of Times* 15 June 177/1 It is most probable we would still have continued to get our race boats from Philadelphia. **1972** C. MUDIE *Motor Boats & Boating* 144 The race boat hull form is not of great value for cruising boats. **1967** *Listener* 14 Sept. 325/3, I got hold of a race-card and I said to him: 'This one's got a marvellous chance.' **1979** D. FRANCIS *Whip Hand* ii. 23 It took a course in the country to..run out of racecards. **1938** *Amer. Speech* XIII. 239/2 *Newscaster* and *sportscaster* are now common terms in *Variety*. *Racecaster* is also found. **1969** *Australian* 24 May 35/1 The caller will be 3DB's race-caster, Bill Collins. **1850** 'M. TENSAS' *Odd Leaves Life Louisiana 'Swamp Doctor'* 47 She couldn't 'tend races, and have a race-colt of her own to comfort her 'clinin' years. **1935** A. G. KENNEDY *Current Eng.* xiv. 613 In a recent issue of a widely read city paper..the following headings appeared..'*Race* Driver Pinned under Flaming Car.' **1972** *N.Y. Times* 3 Nov. 45/2 Look at that guy jumping lanes... You have race drivers the same way, but they never amount to nothin'. **1895** *Montgomery Ward Catal.* 235/2 The Grand Race Game, consists of a substantially cloth bound, folding board..printed in colors to represent a race track... Has six colored cardboard horses and riders..two wooden dice cups and two dice. **1903** J. M. FALKNER *Nebuly Coat* xiii. 187 A 'race-game' where the little leaden horse is moved steadily forward. **1930** A. P. HERBERT *Water Gipsies* xiv. 196 In that light the hare seemed tinier and the greyhounds toys... The place might have been some monstrous nursery 'race-game'. **1973** *Daily Tel.* (Colour Suppl.) 29 June 40/2 Backgammon is a race game..and the precursor of every modern board-pieces-and-dice game. **1931** M. ALLINGHAM *Look to Lady* xxiv. 250 Gipsies and race gangs always hate each other. **1937** E. RICKMAN *On & off Racecourse* xii. 271 The term 'race gang' is still a very favoured one by newspaper sub-editors. **1930** L. G. D. ACLAND *Early Canterbury Runs* 1st Ser. x. 251 He once asked Moore why he didn't put race gates into his yards. **1865** *Let.* 11 June in Ld. W. Lennox *My Recoll.* (1874) II. 153 General Fleury almost forced a race-glass into the hands of the Emperor. **1938** F. D. SHARPE *Sharpe of Flying Squad* xix. 204 From the coach descended a number of the boys one of whom was carrying a pair of race-glasses. **1974** D. FRANCIS *Knock Down* (1976) xii. 137 The runners went down the far side and we lifted race-glasses to watch. **1880** *Baily's Monthly Mag.* Feb. 71 Race-goers are not, as a rule, early drinkers. **1948** *Sunday Pictorial* 18 July 13/4 It has now been in operation for some time, and many race-goers are fed up with it. **1975** D. FRANCIS *High Stakes* i. 9 Racegoers were hurrying towards the stands to watch the imminent steeplechase. **1848** *Sporting Life* 2 Sept. 324/2 A great favourite with the race-going public. **1929** S. ERTZ *Galaxy* xv. 332 He had always been so busy with his..shooting, his race-going, and latterly his horses. **1963** *Times* 23 Jan. 3/5 Waiting for any crumbs that may be going are the racecourses, the owners and the racegoing public. **1977** D. FRANCIS *Risk* ii. 12 Near the course the crawling racegoing jams would mean half an hour for the last mile. **1698** J. COLLIER tr. Tertullian in *Profaneness & Immorality Eng. Stage* vi. 253 We have nothing to do with the Frensies of the Race-Ground..or the Barbarities of the Bear-Garden. **1727** in *Maryland Hist. Mag.* (1912) VII. 400 This Vestry Resolve to meet on Thursday..at the race Ground near Mr Bensons. **1853** *Southern Lit. Messenger* XIX. 70/1 He brought with him a small race mare which excited the acquisitiveness of his father. **1976** *Times Lit. Suppl.* 15 Oct. 1296/2 Park Top..began to emerge as the outstanding race-mare of her decade. **1890** *Homing News* 3 Jan. 14/3 (Advt.), He is not certain about the race marks. **1928** *Sunday Dispatch* 8 July 22/3 Birds competing in the..race from Marennes,..will be racemarked at No. 5 platform. **1837** *Knickerbocker* X. 413 The only race-path known in this new settlement was that on which the husband and wife contended for the prize of domestic comfort. **1853** F. W. THOMAS *J. Randolph* 84 Along the devious narrow race-path to the mill-dam. **1951** E. RICKMAN *Come racing with Me* iii. 23 Some practised race-readers tend to become ridiculously self-opinionated. **1953** P. G. BERG *Dict. New Words* 133/1 *Race reader*,..an expert attached to a radio commentator who helps in giving a broadcast of a horse-race. **1955** *Radio Times* 22 Apr. 29/3 Racing at Newmarket... Commentary by Raymond Glendenning, assisted by Tom E. Webster as race-reader. **1968** 'J. WELCOME' *Hell is where you find It* ii. 33 'Mountpatrick still well clear,' came the race-reader's voice. 'Then Blue Soldier, Mark Twain, Kitchener..all in a group together.' **1963** 'J. PRESCOT' *Case for Hearing* iv. 60, I think you can rule out..the gift of race-reading in advance by looking into a crystal ball. **1976** *Horse & Hound* 10 Dec. 6/3 Michael O'Hehir, whose Telefis Eireann race-reading they [*sc.* the BBC] have taken in previously. **1893** *Outing* XXII. 101/1 Goldsmith Maid left the turf with a race record never equalled. **1977** *N.Z. Herald* 5 Jan. 1–11/1 He set a race record for the track when he went 1 m 58·5 s. **1934** T. S. ELIOT *Rock* i. 29 Many read nothing but the race reports. **1827** J. F. COOPER *Prairie* p. xxiii, She is no great race-rider. **1973** *Country Life* 22 Feb. 457/2 Lester Piggott came from a family of race-riders and trainers. **1950** *N.Z. Jrnl. Agric.* Apr. 375/2 The race shed was..popular many years ago. **1829** P. EGAN *Boxiana* 2nd Ser. II. 30 The Race-stand, at ten *bob* per *nob*, was opened for their reception. **1702** LADY VERNEY *Let.* 25 Aug. in M. M. Verney *Verney Lett.* (1930) I. vii. 113 We shall have Company at Claydon, it being our Race-time. **1893** W. B. YEATS *Celtic Twilight* The race-time came round. **1862** *N.Y. Tribune* 6 Mar. 6/6 We don't think that Tennessee is likely to be much of a battle-ground hereafter. There's more probability of her being a race-track. **1927** *New Republic* 21 Sept. 120/2 No American town is more completely absorbed in race-track gambling. **1945** *Transit News* (Capital Transit Co., Washington, D.C.) 15 June, I picked an early straight on the race track... Translated into plain English, the operator said: 'I signed up for a day's work on 16th street.' **1958** *New Scientist* 30 Jan. 18/3 We.. began the construction of an aluminium torus of 12-in. bore diameter,..and in it were two straight sections—making the torus into a race-track. **1963** *Times* 24 May 16/6 The problem is best presented in terms of the dimensions of the race-tracks round which nuclear particles..are caused to circle repeatedly while gaining energy at each circuit. **1973** D. MACKENZIE *Postscript to Dead Letter* 15 A set of Dufy racetrack prints on the walls. **1938** F. D. SHARPE *Sharpe of Flying Squad* xx. 223 The gymer gets out of the race train and boards the Underground railway. **1977** *Times* 18 June 12/8 The race train from Waterloo to Sandown Park. **1842** CARLYLE in *Cornh. Mag.* (1922) Oct. 496 A huge high pier of wood..lowered down upon us a long race-trough of wood, by the side of which at due distances some four men stationing themselves [etc.]. **1973** F. WAKEFIELD et al. *Track & Field Fundamentals for Girls & Women* (ed. 3) 253 Because some people do not want to race walk, the field of competition is small. **1962** *Sport of Race Walking* (Race Walking Assoc.) 34 Race-Walking can only be as strong as its Judges. .. To this end they have striven..to select men of integrity, mainly former race-walkers themselves. **1972** PICKERING & HARRIS *Olympics* 74/2 The difference between the fast, fair race walker and the ordinary person at $3\frac{1}{2}$ miles per hour is the straight leg action. **1954** *Times* 20 Sept. 3/3 Delegates [to the annual meeting of the Road Walking Assoc.] decided to change the name to Race Walking Association following the Amateur Athletic Association's authority to develop track walking. **1976** *Cumberland News* 26 Nov., The Olympic Games authorities seem hell bent on pushing race walking into the distant background.

race, *sb.*[2] Add: **I. 2. d.** (Further examples.) The term is often used imprecisely; even among anthropologists there is no generally accepted classification or terminology.

1936 *Nature* 18 Apr. 636/2 The races or types into which the anthropologist groups the varieties of *Homo sapiens* are ideal types. **1959** *New Biol.* XXIX. 69 From the U.N.E.S.C.O. statement we can define 'race' as 'a division of man, the members of which, though individually varying, are characterized as a group by certain inherited physical features as having a common origin'. **1971** R. M. & F. M. KEESING *New Perspectives in Cultural Anthropol.* 51 It is at this point that the term 'race' becomes relevant. Though in popular usage it is emotionally charged and imprecise, it has a straightforward and important meaning in evolutionary biology. A race is a geographically separated, hence genetically somewhat distinctive, population within a species.

II. 11. a. Now found in almost unlimited *attrib.* and *Comb.* uses: caused by, based on, of or pertaining to race, as *race-aversion, -blood, -conflict, culture, discrimination, division, equality, -experience, -feeling, -hatred* (further examples), *-heritage, -history, -improvement, -inheritance, instinct, law, line, -mixture, -name, prejudice, pride, problem, quarrel, -question, relationship, solidarity, superiority, -survival, tension, -type, war*; *race-conscious, -hating, -perpetuating, -proud* adjs.

1897 'MARK TWAIN' *Following Equat.* xxi. 207 It must have been race-aversion that put upon them a good deal of the low-rate intellectual reputation which they bear. **1906** W. H. FLEMING *Slavery* 37 The one is based on a supposed duty to God; the other on a supposed duty to one's race-blood. **1880** A. W. TOURGÉE *Invis. Empire* xii. 513 Any one who asked the support of colored men as against a Democratic nominee was precipitating a race-conflict. **1949** *Caribbean Q.* I. II. 28 Countless little stories..about..present life, in country and town..in race-conflict, and class-conflict. **1927** *Observer* 5 June 5/3 Frenchmen are not so race-conscious as either Englishmen or Americans. **1977** P. JOHNSON *Enemies of Society* viii. 106 Nigger..is now frequently employed by the more race-conscious blacks, but only among themselves. **1909** C. W. SALEEBY (*title*) Parenthood and race culture. An outline of eugenics. **1917** *Cases Argued U.S. Supreme Court: Lawyers' Ed.* (1918) 155/2 Plaintiff is not in a position to raise the issue of race discrimination, not being himself a negro. **1906** *Westm. Gaz.* 21 Feb. 2/3 That simple principle [of One Vote One Value]..at once supplies a strong motive for those who once had everything to gain from the race-division to talk about 'bringing both races together'. **1974** *Race* XV. 462 The present race divisions are projected into the past as though they were always a feature of South African society. **1911** G. SPILLER *Papers on Inter-Racial Problems* I. 31 It becomes a vital matter to grapple with the problem of race equality. **1890** O. WILDE in *19th Cent.* Sept. 443 The imagination is the result of heredity. It is simply concentrated race-experience. **1888** KIPLING *City of Dreadful Night* (1891) 18 A casual reference to Hindus and Mahometans... There is race-feeling, to be explained away. **1944** J. S. HUXLEY *On Living in Revolution* 169 The actual physical kinship, which is frequently claimed as 'race feeling', must be fictitious. **1941** AUDEN *New Year Let.* III. 68 Self-respect drives negroes from The one-crop and race-hating delta. **1901** *Times* 5 Aug. 7/2 The object of these documents has usually been..to fan the race-hatred of the Dutch in South Africa. **1935** *Economist* 27 July 175/2 The new excesses are confined to the special domains of class hatred, race hatred and hatred of religion. **1976** *Birmingham Post* 16 Dec. 5/2 Intent to stir up race hatred. **1911** W. JAMES *Some Probl. Philos.* i. 4 Philosophy, thus become a race-heritage, forms in its totality a monstrously unwieldy mass of learning. **1894** *Psychol. Rev.* Nov. 651 The one criticism which I would venture to make upon this paper..is that it neglects the phylogenetic point of view, the considerations from race-history. **1907** W. JAMES *Pragmatism* v. 169 The most primitive ways of thinking.. may remain as indelible tokens of events in our race-history. **1903** *Daily Chron.* 29 July 4/5 We have a great deal yet to learn on matters bearing upon race-improvement. **1909** W. JAMES *Meaning of Truth* viii. 214 Dr. Schiller has shown that all our truths, even the most elemental, are affected by race-inheritance with a human co-efficient. **1901** —— *Let.* 3 Mar. (1920) II. 141 Empire anyhow is half crime by necessity of Nature, and to see a country like the United States..perversely rushing to wallow in the mire of it, shows how strong these ancient race instincts be. **1942** 'G. ORWELL' *War-time Diary* 22 Mar. in *Coll. Ess.* (1968) II. 412 German propaganda is..offering..emancipation to the Kaffirs and stricter race laws to the Boers. **1960** *Twentieth Century* Nov. 407 Race-laws make camps almost impossible within the Union. **1978** G. GREENE *Human Factor* II. i. 62 'I fell in love.' 'Yes. So I see. With an African girl... You broke their race laws.' **1883** G. W. WILLIAMS *Hist. Negro Race* II. xxviii. 543 Race lines must be obliterated. **1891** *Congress Rec.* App. 17 Jan. 101/1 At Marion, Ind.,..when the Democrats were attempting to have a rally,..they were attacked by the colored people, the race line being distinctly drawn by that race. **1905** O. JESPERSEN *Growth & Structure Eng. Lang.* iii. 47 There we had a real race-mixture, where people speaking two different languages were living in actual contact in the same country. **1935** HUXLEY & HADDON *We Europeans* ix. 278 From what has been said, it will be clear that 'race-mixture' has in the past been beneficial. **1924** Race-name [see *ATESTINE *a.* and *sb.*]. **1950** PARTRIDGE *Here, There & Everywhere* 17 The other self-confident Asiatic race-names are fully qualified. **1915** R. LANKESTER *Diversions of Naturalist* xxi. 194 Natural automatically-growing mechanisms of life-saving or race-perpetuating importance. **1890** O. WILDE in *19th Cent.* Sept. 457 Criticism will annihilate race-prejudices, by insisting upon the unity of the human mind in the variety of its forms. **1913** J. LONDON *Let.* 25 Aug. (1966) 395 First of all..by stopping the stupid newspaper from fomenting race prejudice. **1920** H. CRANE *Let.* 6 Mar. (1965) 35, I am as anti-Semitic as they make 'em, but Frank's comments cannot afford to be ignored merely because of race prejudice. **1942** E. PAUL *Narrow St.* xii. 91 Guy delivered a concise impassioned talk against race prejudice. **1956** L. KUPER *Passive Resistance in S. Afr.* 18 Then Dr. Naicker commented on..the United Party's pandering to race-prejudice to catch votes. **1905** W. BAUCKE *Where White Man Treads* 276 On our side race prejudice, race pride, preaching honesty, yet unblushingly swindling him and each other. **1973** A. DUNDES *Mother Wit* 2/1 The relationship between folklore and race pride..corresponds to the relationship between folklore and nationalism in the nineteenth century. **1890** A. W. TOURGÉE *Pactolus Prime* xi. 141 If every one could do as much, the race-problem would soon be solved. **1923** O. SCHREINER *Thoughts on S. Afr.* vii. 296 To..attempt to comprehend or deal rationally with race-problems. **1980** *Bananas* Aug. 7/1 Talking about Korea, Chicago, war, the race problem. **1937** E. MUIR *Coll. Poems* (1960) 72 Now I am shackled to a Grecian dolt, Pragmatic, race-proud as a pampered colt. **1931** F. L. ALLEN *Only Yesterday* iii. 68 If a white man stood up for a Negro in a race quarrel, he might be kidnapped and beaten up. **1889** *Boston Jrnl.* 26 Dec. 2/4 Time only can solve the race-question in the South. **1920** L. STODDARD *Rising Tide of Color* xi. 293 She [*sc.* Japan] should not allow her immigration to be treated as a race-question. **1908** R. S. BAKER *Following Colour Line* x. 217, I have found a sharper feeling and a bitterer discussion of race relationships among the Negroes of the North than among those of the South. **1942** Z. N. HURSTON in A. Dundes *Mother Wit* (1973) 25/1 'Race Solidarity' looked like something solid in my childhood, but like all other mirages, it faded as I came close enough to look. As soon as I could think, I saw that there is no such thing as Race Solidarity in America with any group. **1901** E. A. ROSS in *Ann. Amer. Acad. Pol. Sci.* XVIII. 67 (*title*) The causes of race superiority. **1951** J. MASTERS *Nightrunners of Bengal* v. 58 She was goading herself to wipe out a sense of race superiority she presumed him to have... She wanted..him to acknowledge beauty in an Indian woman. **1933** A. N. WHITEHEAD

Adventures of Ideas vi. 97 We can observe insects performing elaborate routine actions..which yet are essential either for their own individual survival or for race-survival. **1954** P. MASON *Ess. Racial Tension* iii. 45 One would expect race tensions to be most acute..in the country where there is a temperate climate. **1974** *Allendale* (S. Carolina) *County Citizen* 24 Apr. 6/3 We found ourselves discussion-slanted toward race tension and struggles. **1864** W. D. WHITNEY in *Ann. Rep. Board of Regents Smithsonian Inst. 1863* 113 The kind and amount of modification which external circumstances can introduce into a race-type is as yet undetermined. **1892** KIPLING *Lett. of Travel* (1920) 30 Seven million negroes..their race-type unevolved. **1927** PEAKE & FLEURE *Priests & Kings* 181 'Race-type' in a general sense is a very difficult matter to define. **1897** *Chicago Tribune* 28 July 3/7 This gave the negroes an excellent chance to start a 'race' war. **1977** P. JOHNSON *Enemies of Society* xix. 247 He realized he was taking part in a race-war, as well as a class-war.

b. Of, pertaining to, or designating a style of music, originating among Blacks of the Southern U.S. (cf. RACE *sb.*² 6 b), freq. in a twelve-bar sequence (see also quot. 1938).

1926 H. NILES in W. C. Handy *Blues* 31 Listen to the 'race records', for this craft is *sui generis*. **1927** *Jrnl. Abnormal & Social Psychol.* Apr.–June 12 'Race blues'..are not always what they seem. **1935** *Vanity Fair* (N.Y.) Nov. 71/3 Negro bands play 'race music' (a curious euphemism spread by phonograph companies). **1938** *Collier's* 30 Apr. 24/4 We were afraid to advertise Negro records. So I listed them in the catalogue as 'race' records and they are still known as that. **1942** PARTRIDGE *Usage & Abusage* 208/2 'Race (phonograph) *recordings*' for recordings made by Negroes. **1946** R. BLESH *Shining Trumpets* (1949) vi. 145 It was considered authentic enough for the uncritical Victor Company to issue in its race catalogue. **1946** MEZZROW & WOLFE *Really Blues* (1957) ix. 161 Preaching blues was strictly race music. **1952** B. ULANOV *Hist. Jazz in Amer.* (1958) iv. 32 Their masterpieces appeared on the so-called 'race' labels of the record companies. **1968** P. OLIVER *Screening Blues* 5 In the ensuing months more stores carried Race records, specially pressed for the Negro market... Race records from jazz to vaudeville to rural blues reached the remotest districts. **1976** A. MURRAY *Stomping Blues* iv. 50 The period of the race catalogs was also the decade of the so-called revolution in race consciousness known as the Harlem Renaissance. **1977** *Times* 17 Aug. 14/4 Negro styles traditionally stigmatized as 'race' music.

c. Special combs., as **race consciousness,** emotionally based awareness of those differences between people or social groups that can be ascribed to racial factors; the supposed intuitive awareness of a common heritage shared by members of a race or culture; **race-gap,** a difference between racial groups; **race man** *U.S. colloq.*, a Black, esp. one who advocates the rights of Blacks; **race memory,** (a) subconscious memory of events in the history of one's race or of the human race which, it is suggested, is transmitted genetically; **race relations,** a term for such social contacts between racial groups living within a particular area as arise from or are affected by differences in cultural origin or skin colour; freq. *attrib.* or as *adj.*; **race riot,** a riot that results from racial hostility; hence **race rioting; race suicide,** the self-extinction of a racial group through failure to reproduce itself sufficiently, esp. of one with high cultural standards and a low birth-rate in competition with a racial group having lower standards and a high birth-rate; the self-destruction of a race; also *attrib.*; **race theory,** a hypothetical assertion that some racial groups are endowed with specific 'superior' qualities; hence **race theorist,** an advocate of a race theory; **race-thinking** (see quot. 1937); also **race-thinker.**

1905 Race consciousness [see *AMALGAMATION 2]. **1926** G. CALLAWAY *Native Probl. in S. Afr.* 2 It is conceivable that the Native people of South Africa might have lived alongside of the Europeans without developing a strong race consciousness. **1968** *Internat. Encycl. Social Sci.* XIII. 269 Relationships which are capable of producing race conflict and race consciousness. **1890** W. JAMES *Will to Believe* (1897) 260 We here..catch the only glimpse it is allotted to us to attain of the working units themselves, of whose differentiating action the race-gaps form but the stagnant sum. **1936** R. L. ABBOT in *Chicago Defender* 13 June 16/5 One Race man, finding out this outrage, fired on the officers. **1942** Z. N. HURSTON in A. Dundes *Mother Wit* (1973) 25/1 A 'Race Man' was somebody who always kept the glory and honor of his race before him... It was a mark of shame if somebody accused: 'Why, you are not a Race Man (or woman).' People made whole careers of being 'Race' men and women. They were champions of the race. **1969** *Publ. Amer. Dial. Soc.* LI. 29 Names used..by both Negroes and Whites [for Negroes who demand equal status with whites]..civil rights man, mau mau, race man. **1974** YI-FU TUAN *Topophilia* xiii. 209 The upper shadies can identify emotionally with the ghetto poor; they are recognized by the poor as Race Men, that is, supporters of black causes. **1904** *Folk-Lore* XV. 349, I have heard this belief referred to a 'race-memory' of antediluvian reptiles. **1912** A. CONAN DOYLE *Lost World* i. 10 That race-memory which we call instinct. **1934** R. KNOX *Still Dead* xi. 138 A cave has, for all of us, an atmosphere of..terrifying mystery. The anthropologists would tell us..that it is due to race-memory. **1950** [see *OLDEST *a.* 3]. **1972** C. FREMLIN *Appointment with Yesterday* xiv. 110 A race-memory of the days when servants weren't quite real, and so it didn't matter what they heard. **1911** *Pol. Sci. Q.* XXVI. 193 (*title*) Race relations in the Eastern Piedmont region of Georgia. **1925** *Scribner's Mag.* July 12/2 On two occasions great intercollegiate conventions of students have dealt with race-relations,..and war itself. **1934** *Race Relations* I. 32/1 We have to deal in this country not only with relations between English and Dutch but also between Jews and Gentiles, and between Whites and Coloured, Whites and Indians, as well as between Whites and Bantu... Hence, we decided to invite certain men..to give us their views on how race relations problems strike them. **1965** *Act* 13 & 14 *Eliz. II* c. 73 (*heading*) Race Relations Act 1965... An Act to prohibit discrimination on racial grounds in places of public resort; to prevent the enforcement or imposition on racial grounds of restrictions on the transfer of tenancies; to penalize incitement to racial hatred. *Ibid.* § 2 For the purposes of securing compliance with the provisions of..this Act..there shall be constituted a board to be known as the Race Relations Board, consisting of a chairman and two other members appointed by the Secretary of State. **1970** *Oxf. Univ. Gaz.* 30 Apr. Suppl. 14 During the course of the year two visiting Fellows in Race Relations were appointed in collaboration with St. Antony's College. **1977** *Whitaker's Almanack 1978* 348/2 A Lords amendment to the Race Relations Bill..was reversed in the Commons on Oct. 27. **1890** *Our Day* May 406 Race Riots in the South. **1921** *Palestine Weekly* 2 Dec. 779/2 With regard to the actual question as to which side initiated the race riot, the Commission speaks with definiteness and precision. **1928** F. HURST *President is Born* xxiv. 250 Race-riots out in Chicago. **1958** *Daily Mail* 3 Sept. 6/6 After three nights of race-riots in their streets the people who live in Notting Hill have been asked to put themselves under a voluntary curfew. **1979** *Dædalus* Spring 103 Race riots broke out in Marseilles in 1973 that left six Algerians dead. **1968** *Economist* 20 July 43/1 The second problem is the emergence of race rioting as a regular, not to say an annual, occurrence. **1901** E. A. ROSS in *Ann. Amer. Acad. Pol. & Social Sci.* July 88 The American farm hand, mechanic and operative might wither away before the heavy influx of a prolific race from the Orient... For a case like this I can find no words so apt as 'race suicide'. **1904** *Daily Chron.* 9 June 3/2 I'm with the President on this race-suicide question. **1936** M. PLOWMAN *Faith called Pacifism* 14 If war has become race suicide by a perfectly natural process of evolution, why should we continue to call it 'war'? **1945** C. F. MCCLEARY (*title*) Race suicide. **1921** *Times Lit. Suppl.* 25 Aug. 543/1 In defiance of the German race-theorists, and similar superficial or prejudiced observers, Dr. Curtius insists that French culture..cannot be dismissed with the formulae 'esprit' and 'décadence'. **1949** KOESTLER *Promise & Fulfilment* 334 With the exception of the 'race-theorists' nearly all modern authorities hold that Jewish characteristics are a product of sustained environmental pressure. **1895** W. D. BABINGTON (*title*) Fallacies of race theories. **1945** KOESTLER *Yogi & Commissar* II. ii. 192 Within a century or two..race-theory and Jew-baiting would have shrunk to episodes of the past. **1937** J. BARZUN *Race: Study in Mod. Superstition* x. 263 Then came the 'biological revolution' and race-thinkers pinned their hopes on anatomy. *Ibid.* i. 17 We must..see what men who have thought and written about race think it is. Their ideas form, not a definition of race, for they all disagree among themselves, but a type of thinking, which I shall call race-thinking. **1965** *Listener* 11 Nov. 740/2 This kind of thinking involves what are, in fact, vague figures. It has been described as 'race thinking'. People who think this way..are becoming racists.

race, *v.*¹ Add: **2. c.** Also of an electric motor, car engine, etc. (Further examples.)

1893 S. R. BOTTONE *How to manage Dynamo* ii. 29 The dynamo..if shunt-wound..will race and go much faster than usual. **1907** C. W. BROWN *Petrol Engine* i. 3 Neglect of this matter will cause the engine to develop a knocking sound, especially..when 'racing' with the governor out of action. **1980** *Sci. Amer.* Jan. 118/3 If the load on the turbine was suddenly removed, then unless the turbine was shut down promptly it would pick up speed and race, conceivably until it flew to pieces.

3. a. Also *refl.*

1963 *Daily Tel.* 17 July 1/4 He said he got the impression that America was 'racing herself' in this quest [to the Moon].

4. a. (Further examples.)

1906 E. DYSON *Fact'ry 'Ands* ii. 17 She raced her work. **1945** *ABC of Cookery* (Ministry of Food) vii. 22 Take care not to race the boiling or the eggs may crack.

d. To cause (an engine) to race; to 'rev'.

1932 *New Yorker* 23 July 14/3 The cop got on his machine, raced his engine,..and throttled down. **1973** W. MCCARTHY *Detail* ii. 117 He started the car and raced the engine noisily.

e. *to race off,* to seduce (a woman); to hurry (a woman) away in order to seduce her. *Austral. slang.*

1965 W. DICK *Bunch of Ratbags* xii. 185 Three of Knuckles's boys had raced Sharon off to the park to see if they could do any good for themselves. **1967** M. WILDING in *Coast to Coast 1965–6* 250 Perhaps Peter thought he would try to race her..off. He relished the phrase, race off. He had not heard it in England. **1969** W. MOXHAM *Apprentice* vii. 87 'That's one bird you won't race off,' Rufe said. 'I know her and the bloke she's with.' **1978** *TV Week* (Austral.) 24 June 46/4 Luckinbill blabs to his wife Cannon that he raced off most of her best friends.

raceable (rēⁱ·săb'l), *a.* [f. RACE *v.*¹ + -ABLE.]

a. Of a racehorse: capable of being raced.

1965 D. FRANCIS *For Kicks* iii. 40, I might well be given a raceable horse to look after.

b. Of a racecourse: fit for horse-racing.

1976 *Daily Record* (Glasgow) 4 Dec. 27/7 It is raceable at present. **1976** *Horse & Hound* 10 Dec. 6/1 He got to Chepstow [racecourse] only to find..that although the ground there was raceable thick local fog meant that proceedings could never get off the ground.

ra·ceabout. *U.S. Naut.* [f. RACE *v.*¹ + ABOUT *adv.*] A sloop-rigged racing yacht with a smaller keel and larger sailyards than those of a knockabout (see *KNOCK-ABOUT, KNOCKABOUT *a.* 3 b). Also *attrib.*

1897 *Forest & Stream* 6 Mar. 194/2 The next size, the 'raceabout', or the *fin de siècle* perversion of the knockabout, promises to be more popular and numerous. **1899** *Ibid.* 25 Feb. 157/1 The yacht will have two rigs, knockabout and raceabout, which can be shifted one for the other in half an hour. **1905** *St. Nicholas* Aug. 865 There were other prizes, of course: the much-coveted silver cup,..pennants for the raceabouts and halfraters, and a first money prize of twenty-five dollars for the fishermen's sloops. **1907** *Forest & Stream* 30 Nov. 863/1 The old jib and mainsail sand-bag rig has been replaced by the modern raceabout. **1927** E. P. MORRIS *Fore & Aft Rig in Amer.* 75 It [*sc.* the knockabout rig] has been somewhat diverted from its original purpose by being used on small racing boats, which are not knockabouts in the strict sense and have been ironically called 'race-abouts'.

race-horse. Add: Now usu. without hyphen.

1. a. (Earlier and later *attrib.* examples.)

1839 DICKENS *Let.* 25 Nov. (1965) I. 605 Barnaby moves—not at racehorse speed. **1868** H. WOODRUFF *Trotting Horse* ii. 47, I do not undertake to disparage the method pursued by the race-horse men. **1962** D. FRANCIS *Dead Cert* iii. 27 Pete Gregory, racehorse trainer. **1973** *N.Y. Law Jrnl.* 1 Aug. 11/6 An arrest of other persons..who were involved in 'racehorse policy' gambling activities.

3. *transf.* and *fig.* Anything racy, sleek, or speedy. Also *attrib.*

1845 W. G. SIMMS *Wigwam & Cabin* 1st Ser. 32 He had the sanguine, the race-horse temperament. **1903** [see *monthly ship* s.v. *MONTHLY *a.* 4]. **1953** K. TENNANT *Joyful Condemned* xviii. 164 He sat rolling a very thin cigarette, known as a 'racehorse'. **1974** *State* (Columbia, S. Carolina) 15 Feb. 5-B/2 Freshman flash Adrian Dantley triggered a racehorse offense for Notre Dame with 27 points. **1978** *English Jrnl.* Dec. 72/1 What Charles Cooper refers to as 'race-horse studies'..often compared tactics for forcing students through the hoops handed down from the textbook writers.

4. racehorse lizard, a small Australian lizard, *Amphibolurus caudicinctus*, the ring-tailed dragon.

1937 *Discovery* May 137/1 The Racehorse or Cycling Lizard..runs at an incredible speed. *Ibid.*, Place a Racehorse Lizard on a pink handkerchief and it will quickly assume that colour. **1978** O. WHITE *Silent Reach* iv. 50 The little racehorse lizards skittering away through the spinifex with their tails up.

race-knife. Add: (Examples.) Also *ellipt.*

1923 G. STURT *Wheelwright's Shop* vi. 30 The various points for cross-cutting the tree were scratched with a 'race'—a sort of knife with point turned back and sharpened at the bend for this especial purpose. **1964** H. HODGES *Artifacts* vii. 109 A row of wedge-pits or triangular slots was cut with an axe-shaped tool (race, gad or jad). **1969** E. H. PINTO *Treen* 401 The saddler's race or race knife,..used for marking leather, is the same tool that is also used by coopers, lumbermen, and carpenters to mark or scribe logs or timber sections, or to register tallies.

racemate. Add: **a.** (Earlier example.)

1835 *Rec. Gen. Sci.* II. 101, 3.20 grs. of neutral racemate of lead.

b. A racemic (sense *b) form of a compound.

1907 *Jrnl. Chem. Soc.* XCI. I. 906 In the case of substances known only in the liquid state, no general method has as yet been obtained to establish in a sufficiently convincing manner the existence of liquid racemates. **1936** *Discovery* Nov. 341/2 A solution of the racemic form (or racemate as it is sometimes called) is treated with the active form of a Base..obtained from Nature. **1953** *Jrnl. Amer. Chem. Soc.* LXXV. 4587/2 The possibility of strong *intra*molecular hydrogen bonding in the case of α-phenethyl phthalate would offer an alternative explanation for the similarity in the spectra of the enantiomorphs and racemate. **1973** C. H. SNYDER *Introd. Mod. Org. Chem.* viii. 129 Since attack by bromide ion is equally likely at either carbon, the product is a racemate. **1973** D. WHITTAKER *Stereochem. & Mechanism* i. 8 Racemates..often have different melting points from the optical isomers.

racemic, *a.* Add: **a.** (Earlier example.) [ad. F. (*acide*) *racémique* (printed *racenique*) (J. L. Gay-Lussac *Cours de Chimie* (1828) XXIV. 23).]

1835 *Rec. Gen. Sci.* II. 97 The term racemic acid given by the French is preferable.

b. Composed of dextro- and lævorotatory isomers of a compound in equal molecular proportions, and therefore optically inactive.

1892 *Jrnl. Chem. Soc.* LXII. II. 822 The fact that the racemic modification of gulolactone cannot be obtained by crystallisation from water is of general interest, but not without analogy. **1894** G. M'GOWAN tr. *Bernthsen's Text-bk. Org. Chem.* (ed. 2) 39 Optically inactive modifications, which result like racemic acid from the conjunction of two active components, are termed 'racemic' modifications. **1926** H. G. RULE tr. *J. Schmidt's Text-bk. Org. Chem.* 37 In a few instances it is possible, by allowing a solution of the racemic mixture to crystallise under certain conditions, to obtain the two enantiomorphs depositing individually. **1947** *Endeavour* VI. 97/2 Pasteur not only showed that the effect on polarized light was due to asymmetry of molecular architecture, but devised methods of resolving racemic mixtures. **1964** N. G. CLARK *Mod. Org. Chem.* iii. 34 The racemic modification of a substance is sometimes said to be 'externally compensated' because its optical inactivity is due to the balancing of two equal and opposite rotations which do not occur within the same molecule. **1971** *Sci. Amer.* May 6/1 L-Leucine has a bitter taste, D-leucine has a sweet taste and the racemic mixture (both) is tasteless.

Hence † **ra·cemism,** the state of existing in a racemic form; † **ra·cemoid** *a.* = RACEMIC *a.* b.

1896 *Proc. Chem. Soc.* 23 Apr. 97 The ethereal salts..were examined for racemoid compounds, but the quantity found was not sufficient to account for the low activity. **1897** *Jrnl. Chem. Soc.* LXXI. 990 Notwithstanding these marked differences, which may be accepted as conclusive evidence of racemism, this modification of the inactive acid has the same melting point as the active compound. **1902** *Proc. Chem. Soc.* XVIII. 198 Amygdalic acid is racemoid with respect to its asymmetric carbon atom. **1904** *Science* 5 Aug. 178/2 In the cases of some double nuclei (as the camphor group) racemism appears to be impossible, owing to the peculiar molecular structure.

racemization (ræːsĕməizēⁱ·ʃən). *Chem.* [f. prec. + -IZATION.] Conversion of an optically active substance into a racemic form.

1895 A. EILOART in *Sci. Progress* III. 503 If the temperature of racemisation[1] lies below the ordinary temperature, the difficulty of separating the active isomers is accounted for. [*Note*] [1] This term is used to indicate the formation of the inactive aggregate from two isomers of opposite activity. **1927** ARNALL & HODGES *Theoret. Org. Chem.* II. vi. 59 Pinene and limonene undergo racemisation on simple heating. **1950** R. C. FUSON *Adv. Org. Chem.* vi. 111 When L-2 iodoöctane is treated with sodium iodide in acetone solution..racemization occurs. **1966** PHILLIPS & WILLIAMS *Inorg. Chem.* II. xxix. 455 The complexes $[Cr(C_2O_4)_3]^{3-}$ and $[Co(C_2O_4)_3]^{3-}$ will not exchange oxalate with radioactive oxalate in aqueous solution under conditions in which complete racemization takes place. **1975** *Kingston* (Ontario) *Whig-Standard* 5 Sept. 7/5 The ages were obtained by the so-called racemization method. This records the extent to which molecules of aspartic acid in a specimen have altered their configuration from the form that occurs in living bones to its mirror image.

racemize (ræ·sĕməiz), *v. Chem.* [f. as prec. + IZE.] **a.** *trans.* To convert (an optically active substance) into a racemic form. **b.** *intr.* To undergo conversion to a racemic form.

1896 [implied in *RACEMIZED *ppl. a.* below]. **1902** *Proc. Chem. Soc.* XVIII. 198 The author concludes that in alkaline solution the glucoside is racemised by the catalytic action of the hydroxyl ions. **1913** *Jrnl. Chem. Soc.* CIII. 607 The hydrogen *d.* camphorate..racemises within twenty hours of making up the aqueous solution. **1938** G. H. RICHTER *Textbk. Org. Chem.* xvii. 335 Many natural products which occur only as one optical antipode may be racemized and resolved into both optical antipodes. **1965** G. HALLAS *Org. Stereochem.* ii. 35 Several compounds are known to racemize via non-ionic planar intermediates. **1971** *Nature* 12 Mar. 107/1 In fossil material..the free or bound amino-acids slowly racemize. **1976** LOWRY & RICHARDSON *Mechanism & Theory Org. Chem.* v. 218 The excess of rate of loss of optical activity..over rate of product formation..means that some process racemizes the substrate more rapidly than the substrate can form products.

Hence **ra·cemized** *ppl. a.*, **ra·cemizing** *vbl. sb.*

1896 *Proc. Chem. Soc.* 23 Apr. 97 Examining..for the presence of racemised salt by converting it into zinc lactate. **1904** *Jrnl. Chem. Soc.* LXXXV. 1253 The racemising effect of the alkali during hydrolysis of the esters. **1940** *Biochem. Jrnl.* XXXIV. 300 Small amounts of partially racemized aspartic acid, as well as of glutamic acid, can be isolated from both normal and malignant tissue protein material. **1951** C. R. NOLLER *Textbk. Org. Chem.* xvii. 273 The racemizing action of halide ion was known to Kekulé in 1864. **1972** S. J. WEININGER *Contemp. Org. Chem.* vii. 158, 2-Octyl bromide in aqueous ethanol forms, among other products, 2-octanol that is partly racemized.

racemous, *a.* (Later example.)

1821 W. P. C. BARTON *Flora N. Amer.* I. 79 In this case, the floriferous ramuli must be considered as racemous branches.

racer¹. **2. b.** For 'the name of several species of American snake' substitute: a North American snake belonging to the genera *Coluber* or *Masticophis*, esp. a variety of *C. constrictor*. (Earlier and later examples.)

1823 E. JAMES *Acct. Exploring Exped. Pittsburgh to Rocky Mts.* I. 267 *Coluber constrictor*—Racer. **1866** J. C. GREGG *Life in Army* 18 This species, were called racers on account of their great speed. **1900** *Ann. Rep. Bd. Regents Smithsonian Inst. 1898* 794 The *Zamenis constrictor* is the 'black snake' of the East and the 'blue' and 'green racer' of the West. **1926** J. K. STRECKER in J. F. Dobie *Rainbow in Morning* 76 W. S. Blatchley..speaker of many 'lies' about the blue racer, or blacksnake. **1946** J. STUART *Tales from Plum Grove Hills* 85 They slid to the foot of the mountain like racer snakes before a new-ground fire. **1954** R. C. STEBBINS *Amphibians & Reptiles Western N. Amer.* 373/2 When foraging, like most racers, the head and neck are held well above the ground. **1969** A. BELLAIRS *Life of Reptiles* I. iii. 103 Even the fastest snakes such as the North American racers and whip-snakes..cannot exceed more than about four miles an hour.

3. a. (Further examples.)

1903 *Sci. Amer.* 8 Aug. 96/1 Barney Oldfield, on the Ford-Cooper racer..has been steadily lowering track records. **1923** [see *CHIRPILY *adv.*]. **1935** A. J. CRONIN *Stars look Down* III. viii. 553 They swooped and soared and dived from giddy heights on the Giant Racer until the whole glittering Fun Fair spun around them in one glorious daze. **1974** D. RAMSAY *No Cause to Kill* II. 158, I wanted a bicycle, and she ran right out and bought me an English racer. **1978** *Dumfries Courier* 20 Oct. 11/1 The newcomers range from fairly basic family saloons to the exotic Mazda RX7 and BMW's M1 sports racer.

5. An article of clothing designed in a racing style; *spec.* (*pl.*) a pair of swimming trunks (*Austral.* and *N.Z.*).

1969 *New Yorker* 20 Sept. 149/2 (Advt.), Baby him with our soft, zip-front creepers... Racer in medium blue. **1971** *Telegraph* (Brisbane) 21 Sept. 18/1 (Advt.), Ash boys racers in bright florals..and plain colours. **1977** *N.Z. Herald* 8 Jan. 2–4/8 (Advt.), Speedo togs in quick-drying Bri-nylon. Racers, boys..$4.75.

raceway. For *U.S.* in Dict. read 'Chiefly *U.S.*' and add: **1. a.** (Earlier examples.)

1828 in S. Jenkins *Story of Bronx* (1912) ix. 199 Fourteen mill sites, each fifty by one hundred feet, were mapped out along the raceways. **1837** *Knickerbocker* IX. 254, I was jerked out with great spite, and, with an imprecation, thrown into the raceway.

b. An artificial channel of running water for the rearing of fish.

1897 *Man. Fish Culture* (U.S. Comm. Fish & Fisheries) 74 The object of these boards is to form four avenues leading to the raceway, so that one or two pugnacious fish can not command the approach and keep back spawning fish inclined to enter. **1913** W. E. MEEHAN *Fish Culture* vii. 104 There has been a tendency in recent years for fish-culturists to abandon raceways. **1953** H. S. DAVIS *Culture & Dis. Game Fish* ii. 21 Raceways for holding small fingerlings are usually constructed of concrete. **1972** *Aquaculture* I. 229 Water requirements for 'raceway' production of turbot would be very low compared with the requirements in current trout farming practice. **1976** *San Antonio* (Texas) *Express* 23 Sept. 8-G/1 The facility includes a laboratory, office building, 20 ponds, eight concrete raceways and two wells.

2. Also, a groove in a type-setting machine along which types are moved; also, a groove in which ball-bearings run.

1898 *Inland Printer* Nov. 178/1 This machine will select the type, place them in a raceway and move them along until a line is set up. **1946** *Richmond* (Va.) *Times-Dispatch* 8 Dec. IV. 6-D/1 The balls are held in place by two concentric steel rings. They run in grooves or 'raceways' cut in the rings. A retainer or separator is usually inserted to keep them from rubbing against each other.

3. A metal pipe or plastic tube enclosing electrical wires; piping or tubing so used.

1897 F. C. MOORE *How to Build* iv. 58 Conduits or raceways for carrying wires through the house should be of iron or other metal. **1964** R. F. FICCHI *Electrical Interference* ix. 168 Metal boxes, cabinets and fittings, or noncurrent-carrying metal parts of other fixed equipment, if metallically connected to grounded cable armor or metal raceway, are considered grounded by such connections. **1976** LIEBERMAN & RHODES *Compl. CB Handbk.* v. 105 Stick the snake through the 'raceway' (the space in which the tail-light wires run through the trunk).

4. A track or circuit on which harness races, etc., take place; a racecourse. Also *attrib.*

1936 *Sun* (Baltimore) 19 Oct. 12/6 Topping ..had purchased the Maserati car which Philippe Etancelin, of France, drove in the Roosevelt raceway test. **1942** *Ibid.* 24 Aug. 11/4 Saratoga Raceway's new harness racing venture. **1958** *Washington Post* 30 Aug. A12/5 Raceway officials told the commission the plant would be ready for night racing by next March 1. **1968** *Globe & Mail* (Toronto) 17 Feb. 43 (*heading*) Greenwood Raceway. Saturday, Feb. 17. **1979** *Beautiful Brit. Columbia* Winter 33 The fans..turning to the racing form for the next race in to-night's harness racing card at Cloverdale Raceway.

rachel (rāʃe·l). Also **Rachel.** [f. *Rachel*, the stage-name of Elisa Félix (1820–58), French actress.] A light, tannish colour (used orig. and chiefly of face-powder). Also *attrib.* or as *adj.*

1887 *Illustr. London News* 6 Aug. 163/1 (Advt.), Toilet powder... In three tints: Blanche, for fair skins; Naturelle, for darker complexions; and Rachel, for use by artificial light. **1907** [see *PAPIER]. **1907, 1927–8** [see *NATURELLE *a.*]. **1936** M. KENNEDY *Together & Apart* IV. 320 'If you must use powder at your age, do at least find a more becoming shade.' .. 'It's not dead white,' muttered Elisa furiously. 'It's Rachel.' **1970** 'D. HALLIDAY' *Dolly & Cookie Bird* xii. 195 She has facial plates like a rachel armadillo.

rachi-, rachio-. Add: **rachi·schisis** (-skisis) [Gr. σχίσις cleavage] = *MYELOCELE 1 b; **rachitome,** (*b*) *Palæont.*, a labyrinthodont belonging to the suborder Rhachitomi; usu. written *rh-*; **rachitomous** *a.* (earlier and further examples); usu. written *rh-*.

1890 BILLINGS *Med. Dict.* 427/2 *Rachischisis*, congenital posterior fissure of spinal column, a form of spina bifida. **1900** *Boston Med. & Surg. Jrnl.* CXLIII. 458/2 (*heading*) A case of rhachischisis. **1901** T. M. ROTCH *Pediatrics* (ed. 3) v. 301 Rhachischisis is one of the principal forms of congenital defects of the spine. It is characterized by a deficiency of the vertebral arches either complete or partial. **1963** K. M. LAURENCE in A. P. Norman *Congenital Abnormalities in Infancy* ii. 26 Myelomeningocoeles, myelocytocoeles, hydromyelocoeles, and syringomyelocoeles, localized rachischisis and myelocoeles are all essentially the same lesion, and best regarded as myelocoeles. **1966** WRIGHT & SYMMERS *Systemic Path.* II. xxxiv. 1234/2 Spina Bifida... The severest and rarest form is rachischisis, in which the spinal canal is open to the exterior, either for a short distance or over its whole length. **1947** *Bull. Museum Compar. Zoöl. Harvard Coll.* XCIX. 103 In the skull roof [of *Edops*], a primitive character is the presence of a distinct intertemporal element, lost in characteristic rhachitomes. **1964** *Jrnl. Animal Morphol. & Physiol.* XI. 7 The temnospondyls, forming the 'main line' of labyrinthodont evolution, began with Carboniferous types of primitive structure but with rhachitomous vertebrae, evolved in the later Carboniferous and Permian into typical rhachitomes, and eventually gave rise to stereospondylous forms. **1971** E. C. OLSON *Vertebr. Paleozool.* IV. iv. 591 In the Lower Carboniferous limestone of Scotland..is the Gilmerton ironstone from which a number of labyrinthodonts have come:..*Loxomma*, a rhachitome; and..an anthracosaur, *Crassigyrinus*. **1882** E. D. COPE in *Amer. Naturalist* XVI. 334 (*heading*) The rhachitomous Stegocephali. **1884** —— in *Ibid.* XVIII. 30 Rachitomous vertebræ from the same locality are of larger size and resemble those of Eryops. **1947** *Bull. Museum Compar. Zoöl. Harvard Coll.* XCIX. 102 The skull pattern is typically rhachitomous in key features, such as the firm fusion of cheeks and table. **1964** [see *rachitome* above]. **1971** E. C. OLSON *Vertebr. Paleozool.* IV. iv. 591 Although rhachitomous amphibians occur early, in the upper Mississippian, the limbs from this age have not been worked out.

rachill, var. RATCHEL in Dict. and Suppl.

rachitogenic (rækitodʒe·nik), *a.* [f. RACHIT(IS + -O + *-GENIC.] Tending to cause rickets.

1932 *Biochem. Jrnl.* XXVI. 202 The rachitogenic property of Steenbock's diet is due to its high value for Ca/P together with its lack of vitamin D. **1976** *Lancet* 20 Nov. 1132/2 The rachitogenic activity of oatmeal.

Rachmanism (ræ·kmăniz'm). [f. the name of Peter *Rachman* (1919–62), a London landlord + -ISM.] Exploitation of slum tenants by unscrupulous landlords. Hence **Ra·chman,** any such unscrupulous landlord. Also **Ra·chmanite** *a.*, of or resembling a Rachman, and other nonce-ish derivatives.

1963 H. WILSON in *Guardian* 23 July 2/3 The disease of Rachmanism is to buy controlled properties at low prices, and to use every means..to bring about evictions which.. have the effect of decontrolling the property. **1963** *Daily Tel.* 23 July 10/2 (*Editorial*) Emotion appeared to get the better of precision in Mr. Harold Wilson's opening contribution to the Rachman debate yesterday... More powers..will not remove the basic conditions in which the Rachmans of this world can thrive. That can only be done by increasing the supply of housing space and bringing down rents. **1963** *Guardian* 7 Aug. 8/3 (*heading*) Rachmanship lives on. *Ibid.* 8/5 The sprawling, sordid acres of what has become known as Rachmanland. **1963** *Daily Tel.* 30 Aug. 19/3 Bringing Rachman-type racketeers to heel. *Ibid.* 22 Nov. 28/4 'Rachman-like' landlords illegally withheld deposits totalling more than £1,400. **1965** *Economist* 6 Mar. 976/2 The poorer tenants who have suffered most from Rachmanite and neo-Rachmanite intimidation. **1968** *Guardian* 13 Sept. 3/3 Rachmanism—harassment of unwanted tenants—has simply grown more subtle since the 1965 Rent Act. **1969** D. WIDGERY in Cockburn & Blackburn *Student Power* 137 The same crisis which forces council rents up and allows the domination of the Rachmans of Islington, Moss Side and Liverpool 9. **1973** C. MULLARD *Black Britain* II. iv. 46 Rachman-type landlords offered as little as they could for as much as they could get. **1973** *Times* 29 Dec. 11/4 Rachmanite landlords..make millions out of office blocks and luxury flats. **1975** *Times* 8 Jan. 15/3 On a fair rents basis..the transaction..would not be attractive to the speculative builder or the Rachman. **1977** *Jrnl. R. Soc. Arts* CXXV. 116/2 Recently, we have added to the problem by extending the area of control to include furnished tenancies. Mr. Tilbe of *Shelter* will no doubt tell you in two weeks time that this was necessary to prevent Rachmanism. **1981** *Times* 9 Feb. 17/5 The long-term tenant's legitimate need for protection against the Rachmanite landlord.

Rachmaninovian (ræːχmæninōᵘ·viăn), *a.* and *sb.* [f. the name of Sergei Vasilyevich *Rachmaninov* (1873–1943), Russian pianist and composer.] **A.** *adj.* Of or resembling the style or the works of Rachmaninov. **B.** *sb.* An admirer of Rachmaninov.

1958 *Times* 3 Nov. 14/4 In their recital..there was only one original composition, a Toccata by Murgatroyd Farrar, which made suitably Rachmaninovian noises. **1962** *Times* 5 July 15/1 A verbose Rachmaninovian Scherzo by John White. **1973** *Times* 27 July 15/4 Mr Previn drew the right pliable phrasing from the LSO without overdoing the succulence (like some older Rachmaninovians one could name). **1976** *Gramophone* May 1816/3 The Rachmaninovian flavour of 'Whitechapel'..making a delightful treasure of sound. **1977** *Ibid.* Nov. 874/1 What Rachmaninovians ought to be shouting for now, however, is a recording of the *Liturgy*, Op. 31.

racial, *a.* **a.** (Further examples.)

A word of considerable frequency in the 20th century. The examples that follow illustrate some of the more usual modern collocations.

1889 [see *NURTURAL *a.*]. **1892** F. W. GAGE *Negro Problem* iii. 56 If it be demonstrated that individual members of the race under favourable circumstances are capable of mature mental development, then the question of racial development is settled. **1899** A. NUTT in *Folk-Lore* June 146 In determining the relative importance of either element for racial discrimination in folklore, I was guided by observation of man in the civilized stage. **1899** C. WALDSTEIN *Expansion of Western Ideals* 141 An historical basis for German unity was not enough; an ethnological, racial unity had to be established. **1914** G. K. CHESTERTON *Wisdom of Father Brown* ix. 266 An attitude we must always remember when we talk of racial prejudices. **1929** H. MILES tr. *P. Morand's Black Magic* I. 63 He supported..racial equality. **1935** HUXLEY & HADDON *We Europeans* ix. 286 Ethnic intercrossing and culture-contacts have proceeded so far that 'racial purity', like complete isolationism or self-sufficiency, is impossible of attainment. **1942** H. A. WALLACE *Century of Common Man* (1944) vi. 32 In June of 1941 he [*sc.* Roosevelt] issued an executive order prohibiting racial discrimination in the employing of workers by national defence industries. **1942** Z. N. HURSTON in A. Dundes *Mother Wit* (1973) 32/2, I did not have to consider any racial group as a whole. **1943** E. H. BROOKS *Bantu in S. Afr. Life* ii. 3 When I say 'a similar point of view', I mean the doctrine of racial domination: there are Africans who still think that the Europeans can be driven into the sea. **1947** 'G. ORWELL' in *Tribune* 7 Feb. 12/2, I should like to think that the position of the racial minorities could be safeguarded. **1954** H. GIBBS *Background to Bitterness* 7 Racial conflict between the groups has not been witnessed on a major scale for many years. **1954** *Harvard Law Rev.* XXIV. 80 Judge Edgerton wrote that as the Supreme Court had..recognized that enforced racial segregation in housing was unconstitutional, it followed that enforced racial segregation in schooling was even more so. **1955** B. SCHWARTZ *Amer. Constitutional Law* ix. 224 There has been a profound change in recent years in the attitude of that tribunal [*sc.* the Supreme Court] toward racial discrimination. **1958** *Spectator* 22 Aug. 239/1 The Little Rock High School must resume racial integration when the new term began. **1960** J. RAE *Custard Boys* II. xix. 210 You think this is a case of racial prejudice and you're probably right. **1960** 'I. ROSS' *Murder out of School* i. 7 There's none of what the papers like to call 'racial tension' at Mark Hopkins [School]. **1967** *Boston Sunday Herald* 7 May III. 4/1 'Racial imbalance in Parochial Schools' is the topic for a panel discussion. **1971** R. BENDIX in A. Bullock *Twentieth Cent.* xv. 357/1 Racial minorities..constitute a lower class as women obviously do not. **1971** *Publishers' Weekly* 2 Aug. 46 Mr. Fuller finds that the anthology's one story by a black author—an Eldridge Cleaver story first published in *Playboy*—is racial tokenism. **1976** *CRC Jrnl.* July 3/1 All of the recent immigration debates..have connected the general anxiety about immigration with the current racial tension. **1977** *Whitaker's Almanack 1978* 595 South African Government declared that where feasible there should be an end to racial segregation on buses. **1979** MILES & PHIZACKLEA *Racism* i. 17 A reaction by blacks in Britain to racial discrimination and violence.

racialism (rē^{i}·ʃăliz'm). [f. RACIAL *a.* + -ISM.] Belief in the superiority of a particular race leading to prejudice and antagonism towards people of other races, esp. those in close proximity who may be felt as a threat to one's cultural and racial integrity or economic well-being.

1907 *Daily Chron.* 2 Jan. 6/5 The two principal planks in the party platform are opposition to all racialism and co-operation with the Government. **1910** *Westm. Gaz.* 11 Apr. 10/3 What appears to me to be the greatest results of the Botha–Smuts Government is the abolition of Racialism and the construction of roads. **1925** E. S. JONES *Christ of Indian Road* ii. 67 Amid the racial clash and bitterness there stands one who is the Son of man. Racialism withers at his touch. **1934** R. MACAULAY *Going Abroad* xv. 127 A Cape Afrikander ..had renounced Dutch racialism and the detestation of the English. **1938** *Sun* (Baltimore) 2 Sept. 10/1 The Italian Jews are thus to be added to the victims of Hitler's imbecile 'racialism', now adopted by Mussolini as a sop to superior force. **1940** R. BENEDICT *Race: Science & Politics* vii. 215 Racialism has become involved in scientific absurdities under the Third Reich. **1955** *Times* 20 Aug. 5/5 The Prime Minister spoke on race relations, commenting that in the last session of Parliament there had been less racialism in debate and more moderation. **1960** *Spectator* 6 May 650/1 The two main convictions of racialism are, firstly..'The highest aim of human existence is the conservation of the race..the maintenance of the racial stock unmixed'..and secondly, that once a man's mind is made up about this, he can never think of changing it. **1971** S. ABBOTT *Prevention of Racial Discrimination* i. 16 Britain's long history of colonialism overseas does not sufficiently explain the present racialism in this country. **1975** *Daily Tel.* 13 Nov. 16/3 Racism, or racialism, or racial discrimination,..covers everything from a vile form of monomania to the innocent preference of human beings for association with their own kind. **1977** P. JOHNSON *Enemies of Soc.* ii. 25 Racialism was linked to wishful-thinking, and almost deliberate self-deception.

racialist (rē^{i}·ʃălist), *sb.* and *a.* [f. RACIAL *a.* + -IST.] **A.** *sb.* A partisan of racialism; an advocate of a racial theory.

1917 *Deb. House of Commons Canada* 5870/2 We all become nationalists in the true sense of the word, as distinguished from provincialists and racialists. **1930** *Observer* 22 June 13/4 Some of its characters said things that were calculated to make the blood of headstrong racialists boil. **1937** *Discovery* July 224/2 Curiously enough.., the 'nigger' is much more likely to be treated with contempt by the half-educated in England than among the politically-organised racialists of Germany. **1939** A. TOYNBEE *Study Hist.* IV. 19 We can even drive the racialists out of their one remaining Italian stronghold by finding an alternative explanation for the rise of the Roman Republic. **1940** R. BENEDICT *Race: Science & Politics* i. 6 The racialists have rewritten history to provide the scion of such a race with a long and glamorous group ancestry. **1958** *Times Lit. Suppl.* 28 Mar. 164/3 It is easy today for Britain to see Hertzog as a bitter, anti-British racialist, who deprived the remaining Cape Africans of their vote. **1960** *Spectator* 6 May 650/1 A racialist..lives according to what most people think is a fantasy. **1977** M. WALKER *National Front* iv. 85 He [*sc.* A. K. Chesterton] went on to warn of the perils of racialist extremism, while wholeheartedly agreeing with the racialists' arguments about '..mongrelization'.

B. *adj.* Of, pertaining to, or characterized by racialism.

1946 W. S. KNICKERBOCKER *20th Cent. Eng.* 81 It would be, however, an error to consider this Nazi literary history simply as racialist. **1952** B. DAVIDSON *Rep. S. Afr.* I. vii. 75 Members even of the highly racialist Electors' Union of Kenya..have expressed to me their horror at the explosive possibilities induced by white policy in South Africa. **1960** [see *Africanistic* s.v. *AFRICANIST *sb.* (and *a.*)]. **1971** E. POWELL *Let.* in *Observer* 14 Mar. 8/6 The adjective 'racialist' has gained a strange sort of currency in recent years and seems to wear all sorts of meanings. I have even once or twice heard it applied to myself.

Hence **raciali·stic** *a.*

1960 *Guardian* 14 Dec. 16/2 The extreme racialistic African leaders. **1969** *Daily Tel.* 18 Jan. 18/4 Coomaraswamy was more than a little influenced by the sort of racialistic sentiment applied to art that has become one of the curses of the 20th century. **1977** P. JOHNSON *Enemies of Society* xix. 248 The statement is purely racialistic.

racialization (rē^{i}:ʃăləizē^{i}·ʃən). [f. RACIAL *a.* + -IZATION.] The process of making or becoming racialist in outlook or sympathies. Hence **ra·cialize** *v. trans.*

1918 *Encycl. Relig. & Ethics* X. 557/2 Why should the most progressive Muslim populations be affected most powerfully by 'racialization', which is clearly a retrogressive tendency? **1930** *Month* Dec. 485 A Catholic, following St. Paul, will repudiate this attempt to racialize the universal genius of Christianity. **1977** M. BANTON *Idea of Race* 18 There was a social process, which can be called racialization, whereby a mode of categorization was developed.

racially, *adv.* Add: (Further examples.) Freq. linked with a ppl. adj. to form adjs., as *racially-blended, -integrated, -selected.*

1914 'SAKI' *When William Came* x. 170 The record of your racially-blended supper-party. **1921** J. BRYCE *Mod. Democracies* I. xiv. 163 Where a racially distinct body of unwilling subjects is included within a State..are they to be reckoned as part of the people? **1962** Racially-integrated [see *COLOUR-BLINDNESS b]. **1976** *Drum* (E. Afr. ed.) Sept. 13/2 The team pulled out of the Olympics..in protest against New Zealand sending a rugby team to play in South Africa against racially-selected sides. **1976** E. K. FRANCIS *Interethnic Relations* xxii. 280 Particular populations that are racially distinct from their social environment occasionally show typical mental and cultural differences.

raciation (rē^{i}si,ē^{i}·ʃən). [f. RACE *sb.*^{2} + -ATION; cf. *SPECIATION.] The evolutionary development of distinct biological races.

1952 *Sat. Rev.* (U.S.) 5 July 16/3 The methods he [*sc.* Edgar Anderson] describes are very like those used by the anthropologist interested in tracing the wanderings of peoples, their mixture, and 'raciation'. **1971** *Nature* 28 May 250/1 This approach to microsystematics has been of particular value in the study of raciation..in commercially important marine fishes.

racing, *vbl. sb.*^{1} Add: **1.** (Further examples.)

1901 *Chambers's Jrnl.* Apr. 221/2 The *Turbinia* has been run..in almost all states of the sea, and on no occasion has the slightest symptom of racing occurred. **1912** G. GREENHILL *Dynamics of Mech. Flight* v. 106 Racing of the screw is due chiefly to variation of axial flow. **1980** G. M. FRASER *Mr American* xviii. 336 Pip's method of travel was..constant racing of the engine.

2. (Some functionally indistinguishable from *racing* used as ppl. adj.) *racing bicycle, canoe, car, change* (*CHANGE *sb.* 1 g), *correspondent, cycle, cyclist, driver, establishment* (earlier example), *guide, motor-car, motorist, page, result, rig, stable* (later example), *stud* (earlier example), *-track*; **racing colours,** the colours (COLOUR, COLOR *sb.* 6 a) by which an owner's racehorses are identified; **racing demon** (see *DEMON 2 f) (examples); **racing dope** *U.S.*, information about races contained in a *dope-sheet* (see *DOPE *sb.* 5); **racing flag** *Naut.* (see quot. 1961); **racing game** = *race-game* s.v. *RACE *sb.*^{1} 11 b; **racing pigeon,** a homing pigeon taking part in competitions to complete a specific journey as quickly as possible; **racing-plate** (see quot.).

1910 *Encycl. Brit.* III. 915/1 Wood rims are used on racing bicycles. **1959** I. & P. OPIE *Lore & Lang. of Schoolchildren* x. 191 Who's teacher's pet boy and was given a racing bicycle? **1876** Racing-canoe [see *long-spooned* s.v. *LONG *a.*^{1} 16]. **1932** *Man* May 106 The coffin is placed in a large racing canoe. **1909** Racing car [see *power producer* s.v. *POWER *sb.*^{1} 18]. **1977** M. KENYON *Rapist* iv. 44 He said he..had been an important racing car driver. **1959** I. FLEMING *Goldfinger* vii. 86 James Bond flung the DB III through the last mile of straight and did a racing change down into third. **1907** *Yesterday's Shopping* (1969) 302/2 About seven days required to execute orders for Racing Colours. **1955** W. GADDIS *Recognitions* I. v. 196 She handed a folded twenty-dollar bill to a boy wearing her racing colors. **1961** A. CLARKE *Later Poems* 87 At Maynooth, instead of skulls, His racing colours were displayed. **1961** E. WAUGH *Unconditional Surrender* III. ii. 240 His brief experience as a racing correspondent seemed irrelevant to the zeitgeist. **1976** 'J. WELCOME' *Grand National* i. 11 That is Andrew Mostyn, our chief racing correspondent. **1976** *Eastern Even. News* (Norwich) 22 Dec. 11/3 (Advt.), Racing cycles at discount prices. **1974** *Times* 29 Oct. 17/4 Scores of club racing cyclists. **1945** N. MITFORD *Pursuit of Love* ix. 74 The Kroesigs obviously longed for bridge, and did not seem to care so much for racing demon when it was offered as a substitute. **1977** *Times* 24 Dec. 10/2 Try racing demon for the party card game if you have a large table and fast-playing, shouting screaming players. **1931** F. L. ALLEN *Only Yesterday* iv. 81 Workmen forgot to be class-conscious as they..studied the racing dope about Morvich. **1961** *Daily Tel.* 21 May 10, I used to be a racing driver. **1977** 'D. CORY' *Bennett* iii. 88 Shop girls identify themselves with film stars, bank clerks with racing drivers. **1811** J. STEELE *Let.* 29 Jan. in *Papers* (1924) II. 649 There is nothing..which wd. afford me greater pleasure than to see a respectable racing establishment at this place. **1860** 'VANDERDECKEN' *Yarns* 135 Cut the racing flag clear, and send a hand aloft to lash it to the stump as a signal that you'll fight to the last. **1961** F. H. BURGESS *Dict. Sailing* 167 *Racing flag*, a private flag hoisted when racing, instead of the burgee; it is hauled down only on retiring, or when a race is completed. **1860** C. M. YONGE *Hopes & Fears* I. I. v. 123 She beheld his sister..at the racing game.. Honor waited, however, till the little white horseman had reached the goal. **1890** —— *More Bywords* 154 The 'racing game',..which was now spread on the dining-table, with all the young people playing in high glee. **1909** A. L. BRUCE *Bridge-Fiend* 12 A peppery, red-faced old gentleman, who was reading a racing-guide..was then appealed to. **1909** *Westm. Gaz.* 21 Oct. 5/1 Fewer accidents have happened to aviators in proportion to their numbers than to racing-motor-car drivers in the same period. **1906** *Chambers's Jrnl.* Apr. 347/1 The trophy which is the prize for which racing-motorists compete. **1948** 'J. TEY' *Franchise Affair* xiv. 156, I went to rest every afternoon with.. the racing page of the daily paper. **1978** *Islands* (N.Z.) Aug. 78, I got the paper of course. For the racing page really. **1910** A. H. OSMAN *Pigeon Bk.* xiii. 148 It is impossible to say what breeds have and have not been used to 'make' the racing pigeon. **1933** *Discovery* Nov. 344/1 Racing and homing pigeons are often captured. **1960** *Farmer & Stockbreeder* 26 Jan. 4/2 Demand is expected to broaden as the racing-pigeon season approaches. **1977** *Wandsworth Borough News* 16 Sept. 15/5 Literally rescued from the teeth of a predatory cat, a blue racing pigeon now awaits a claimant at the home of Mr. I. A. McWilliam.' **1958** J. HISLOP *From Start to Finish* 174 *Racing-plate*, a light shoe (usually made of some form of aluminium) with which horses are shod when they race. **1926** Racing result [see *bedtime story* s.v. *BEDTIME]. **1976** 'J. WELCOME' *Grand National* ii. 27 He turned on the radio to get the racing results. **1906** CONRAD *Mirror of Sea* viii. 39 Of those three varieties of fore-and-aft rig, the cutter—the racing rig *par excellence*—is of an appearance the most imposing. **1981** E. WARD *Baltic Emerald* xxiv. 189 A racing stable with high pasturelands for gallops. **1828** T. CREEVEY *Let.* in *Creevey Papers* (1963) xii. 241 We started about 3 for Petworth..Sefton's object being to see Lord Egremont's Racing Stud before dinner. **1913** *O.E.D.* s.v. *Track* sb. 6 b, Racing-track. **1917** [see *MORNING *sb.* 7 ¶]. **1929** W. E. COLLINSON *Spoken Eng.* 72 They've built a greyhound racing-track just near the house.

Racinian (rasī·niăn), *a.* and *sb.* Also **Racinean.** [f. the name of Jean *Racine* (1639–99), French dramatic poet.] **A.** *adj.* Of, pertaining to, characteristic of, or resembling Racine or his writings. **B.** *sb.* An admirer or imitator of Racine.

1927 *Sunday Times* 13 Mar. 8/3 He [*sc.* Otway] still remains the most Racinian of all our poets. **1931** *Times Lit. Suppl.* 1 Jan. 1/3 Shakespearian, Racinian or Sheridanesque convention. **1946** *Month* May–June 229 His brilliant and enthusiastic appreciation of the great cycle of tragedies, above all *Athalie*, will please the most ardent Racinian. **1950** M. MCCARTHY in *Reporter* 18 July 37/2 This Racinean world, where stepmother Phèdre and grandmother Athalie queened it. **1948** L. SPITZER *Linguistics & Lit. Hist.* 178 The Racinian, the Vergilian power of poetic alchemy whereby brute reality is transmuted. **1962** *Listener* 30 Aug. 315/2 This Racinian reading of modern life which is dramatized in terms of passion versus reason, will versus duty. **1974** *Ibid.* 8 Aug. 185/2 *A Month in the Country*..harks back to Racine. There is the Racinian web of emotional incompatibilities.

raciology (rē^{i}siǫ·lŏdʒi). [f. RACE *sb.*^{2} + -OLOGY; cf. F. *raciologie.*] The study of the races of man. Hence **raciolo·gical** *a.*; **racio·logist,** a student of raciology.

1924 *Glasgow Herald* 7 Feb 6/5 Societies were formed for the study of their language and raciology, just when the authentic gipsies themselves had begun to disappear. **1926** *Ibid.* 27 Jan. 10/4 A new and searching process of selection.. will result in a revisal of our preconceived notions of African raciology. **1939** C. S. COON *Races of Europe* viii. 286 Von Eickstedt, the most articulate of the modern German raciologists. **1950** E. W. COUNT *This is Race* 703 For a commentary on Buffon's raciology, see Scheidt. *Ibid.* 734 The Russian raciologists were very actively engaged..in combating..'bourgeois' racism in general. *Ibid.* 735 Some other works of Fleure have a raciological bearing.

racism (rē^{i}·siz'm). [f. RACE *sb.*^{2} + -ISM; cf. F. *racisme* (Robert 1935).] **a.** The theory that distinctive human characteristics and abilities are determined by race. **b.** = *RACIALISM.

1936 L. DENNIS *Coming Amer. Fascism* 109 If..it be assumed that one of our values should be a type of racism which excludes certain races from citizenship, then the plan of execution should provide for the annihilation, deportation, or sterilization of the excluded races. **1938** E. & C. PAUL tr. *Hirschfeld's Racism* xx. 260 The apostles and energumens of racism can in all good faith give free rein to impulses of which they would be ashamed did they realise their true nature. **1940** R. BENEDICT *Race: Science & Politics* i. 7 Racism is an *ism* to which everyone in the world today is exposed. **1952** M. BERGER *Equality by Statute* 236 Racism, tension in industrial, urban areas. **1952** *Theology* LV. 283 The idolatry of our time—its setting up of nationalism, racism, vulgar materialism. **1960** *New Left Rev.* Jan./Feb. 21/2 George Rogers saw fit to kow-tow to the incipient racism of his electorate by including a line about getting rid of 'undesirable elements'. **1964** GOULD & KOLB *Dict. Social Sci.* 571/2 *Racism* is a newer term for the word *racialism*... There is virtual agreement that it refers to a doctrine of racial supremacy. **1971** *Ceylon Daily News* (Colombo) 18 Sept. 8/5 Mr. Seneviratne is welcome to his ideal of inter-racial marriages as panacea for Racism. **1972** J. L. DILLARD *Black English* iii. 90 In the British sailors' reactions to the slaves.., the very early existence of racism is as well documented as the difference in language. **1974** M. FIDO *R. Kipling* 50/2 In *The Story of Muhammad Din* he wrote one of the most economical and bitter attacks on British racism ever penned. **1976** *Plain Dealer* (Cleveland, Ohio) 4 Mar. A2/4 The Vatican radio said..'Racism might have different faces but it will always be reprehensible.' **1977** M. WALKER *National Front* vi. 155 A strike of the Asian workers against racism in the factory.

racist (rēⁱ·sist), *sb.* and *a.* [f. RACE *sb.*² + -IST.] **A.** *sb.* = *RACIALIST *sb.*

1932 M. EASTMAN tr. *Trotsky's Hist. Russ. Revol.* i. 27 This brief comment completely finishes off not only the old philosophy of the Slavophiles, but also the latest revelations of the 'Racists'. **1934** H. G. WELLS *Exper. Autobiogr.* I. iii. 107 So much for the Hitlerite stage of my development, when I was a sentimentalist, a moralist, a patriot, a racist. **1940** R. BENEDICT *Race: Science & Politics* vii. 214 Classic German racists..ascribed all achievements beyond the Alps to infiltrations of northern blood. **1959** *New Statesman* 30 May 754/2 They see nothing to be gained..if they are dismissed and replaced by fanatical racists. **1965** *San Francisco Examiner* 15 Apr. 34/5, I recently heard a man denounced as a racist for having observed that the rate of illegitimacy in New York is 14 times as high among the Negro population as among the white. **1973** A. DUNDES *Mother Wit* p. xii, Folklore has been used as the tool of racists.

B. *adj.* = *RACIALIST *a.*

1938 E. & C. PAUL tr. *Hirschfeld's Racism* xv. 201 Elective affinity laughs at the maxims and prohibitions of racist wiseacres. **1938** *Mag. Digest* Aug. 22 The racist revue, *Archiv für Biologie und Rassengesellschaft*, one of the organs of the National Socialist Party, published an article..on 'The utility of aerial bombardments from the point of view of racial selection and social hygiene'. **1938** *Sun* (Baltimore) 14 Nov. 6/2 On Thursday..Rome approved new decrees increasing the severity of Italian Fascism's new 'racist' principles. **1940** R. BENEDICT *Race: Science & Politics* vii. 188 The racist traditions..of the fair, blue-eyed narrow-heads. **1957** P. WORSLEY *Trumpet shall Sound* App. 268 Racist doctrines and rule by force 'worked' to a degree in the short run of Nazidom, they failed in the (not very) long run. **1960** *Guardian* 23 Mar. 8/2 The President is trying to knock out the racist props from under the present immigration law. **1970** E. BULLINS *Theme is Blackness* (1973) 167 I'm too mature and sophisticated to get sucked in by racist arguments. **1979** *Globe & Mail* (Toronto) 28 Nov. 8/4 [Mr. Levesque] can't bear any suggestion that he or his party could be racist, could treat non-francophones as second-class citizens.

Hence raci·stic *a.* (*rare*).

1950 E. W. COUNT *This is Race* 734 Combating racistic theories. **1963** *Observer* 7 Apr. 22/2 This society is dedicated to pleasure and not over-concerned with the big racistic abstractions.

rack, *sb.*¹ Add: **4. a.** (Later examples.)

1899 H. T. TIMMINS *Nooks & Corners of Shropshire* 65 We go down a rough footpath, or 'rack', as they call it hereabouts. **1904** G. A. B. DEWAR *Glamour of Earth* v. 81, I came down the rack—the narrow path which is cut through ripe underwood fifteen years old, and marks the end of one lot and the beginning of another. **1919** T. WRIGHT *Romance of Lace Pillow* xii. 110 What a relief..to be absolutely free for a few hours; to be able to..roam the ridings, racks, and glades of Yardley Chase. **1957** *Brit. Commonw. Forest Terminol.* II. 149 *Rack*, (*a*) A narrow woodland track maintained for inspection and communication and for extraction of poles, etc. by hand or animal haulage.

e. (Earlier and later U.S. examples.)

1832 J. F. WATSON *Historic Tales of Olden Time N.-Y. City* 27 The 'Racks' so called, along the [Hudson] river, were Dutch names for Reaches. **1930** *Amer. Speech.* V. 164 The Dutch navigators divided the Hudson into *racks* or *reaches*. The former word remains in Claverack.

rack, *sb.*² Add: **3. e.** *to stand* (or *come*) *up to the rack*: to face or bear the consequences of what one has undertaken; to take one's share of hard work or responsibility. *U.S.*

1834 D. CROCKETT *Narrative of Life* iv. 61, I was determined to stand up to my rack, fodder or no fodder. **1835** —— *Col. Crockett's Tour* 69 It was a hard row to hoe; but I stood up to the rack. **1837** R. M. BIRD *Nick of Woods* II. xiv. 183 But, you see, captain, there's a bargain first to be struck between us, afore I comes up to the rack. **1848** J. F COOPER *Oak Open.* II. iii. 43 The English used to boast that the Americans wouldn't 'stand up to the rack', if the baggonet was set to work. **1890** *Stock Grower & Farmer* 12 July 4/2 For several years cattlemen have been severe losers but most of them have stood pluckily to the rack.

4. b. *spec.* One on which items of clothing are transported and displayed for sale. Phr. *off the* (or *a*) *rack* = *off the peg* adv. phr. s.v. *PEG *sb.*¹ 1 e.

1948 H. MCCLENNAN *Precipice* (1949) ii. 189 Shipping clerks pushing racks of women's dresses. **1962** W. SCHIRRA in *Into Orbit* 47, I acted as a kind of consultant tailor on the pressure suit. It is not possible just to walk in and buy one off the rack. **1976** 'R. BOYLE' *Cry Rape* xx. 91, I chose a simple navy shirtmaker dress from the $20-and-under rack. **1976** *Times* 2 Nov. 12/2 In the women's outfitting department, there was..a scramble around the racks of camel coats. **1978** R. LUDLUM *Holcroft Covenant* xxxiii. 385 His suit was off a rack.

5. b. A large, vertical, metal framework, usu. of standardized dimensions, for supporting items of telephonic or electronic equipment and allowing ready access to them.

1893 PREECE & STUBBS *Man. Telephony* xix. 311 An even more effective contrivance for cable racks..is shown in fig. 240. **1906** J. POOLE *Pract. Telephone Handbk.* (ed. 3) xxi. 299 Condenser Rack.—This frame is for the accommodation of the 2½-microfarad condensers used in connection with the incoming junction lines... The frame is 7 feet 3½ inches wide and 7 feet 10 inches high. **1930** *Proc. IRE* XVIII. 1320 The amplifiers are mounted on relay racks and connected by twin lead wire pulled in rigid conduit. **1951** *Short Wave Mag.* May 179/1 The left-hand rack, No. 1, starting at the bottom, contains the filament supplies for all transmitters; the 1000 v. HT supply for the 430 and 144 mc exciters; [etc.]. **1977** *Gramophone* June 118/2 In the professional world it is common practice for tuners, preamplifiers, power amplifiers, equalizers, etc. to be mounted on slotted panels, which are mounted vertically into racks. Now several domestic manufacturers are also mounting their units in neat vertical racks, but usually they are less than the professional 48cm (19-inch) width.

h. *U.S.* (See quots.)

1903 *Nation* (N.Y.) 6 Aug. 115/2 Another Americanism we miss under Racks, the technical name for the side plankings or buffers of our ferry slips. **1905** *N.Y. Even. Post* 20 Dec. 1 Three of the Lackawanna 'racks', as the arrangement of piles to fit the ferryboats are called, were left intact.

i. *N. Amer.* A set of antlers. Also *attrib.*

1945 *Richmond* (Va.) *Times-Dispatch* 27 July 14/1 There is no real means of comparing a rack of antlers killed in Bath County and one in New Kent, unless they are placed side by side. **1958** *Outdoor Life* Sept. 34/1 I'd shot moose in British Columbia but never a really big one. This trip I was determined to get a trophy rack. **1971** D. C. BROWN *Yukon Trophy Trails* i. 22 'Wow, he's sure got a big rack,' someone else yelled. **1976** *Listener* 15 Apr. 466/2 The moose ..had a rack of five points, which meant that it was five years old and almost fully grown. **1978** L. L. RUE *Deer N. Amer.* iv. 66 A deer with more than four points is called a rack buck... Some racks are large but have few points, some are small but have more points.

j. *U.S. Naut. slang.* (See quot. 1962.)

1955 C. KENTFIELD *Alchemist's Voyage* I. iii. 68 'Where's D'Alessio?' 'In his rack.' **1962** *Amer. Speech* XXXVII. 288 A Marine's bed is not a *sack*, but a *rack*. He *hits the rack* or *puts in rack time*. **1963** *Ibid.* XXXVIII. 78 The term *rack* was borrowed by the Marines from the Navy, and it began to supersede *sack* as the popular term in Marine speech during the early 1950s.

6. b. (Later example.)

1965 G. MCINNES *Road to Gundagai* ix. 134 Up again, straining on the rack-and-pinion of the Rigi.

c. (Further examples.)

1903 *Baedeker's Northern Italy* 13 From Capolago to the Monte Generoso, rack-and-pinion railway in 56 minutes. **1958** R. LIDDELL *Morea* II. ii. 55, I took the rack and pinion railway up to Calávryta. **1969** *Observer* (Colour Suppl.) 23 Mar. 29 Rack-and-pinion steering 'can be twirled from lock to lock with the flat palm of one hand'. **1972** *Modern Railways* Sept. 334 This was overcome on the BOB [*sc.* Berner Oberland Bahn] by the use of rack-and-pinion operation with gradients as steep as 1 in 8. **1973** *Country Life* 18 Oct. 1172/1 The Haflinger, a forward-control platform truck..seems to wind on inexorably, rather like a rack and pinion train climbing a mountain. **1978** *Daily Tel.* 16 Aug. 10/6 The ride is on the firm side with the handling being safe and predictable from the rack and pinion steering.

8. b. = *rack-rail* in sense 9.

1909 *Westm. Gaz.* 7 Aug. 7/2 The greater part of the line would traverse exceedingly difficult country, necessitating.. possibly a few short lengths of rack.

9. rack car, (*b*) *U.S. Logging*: see quot.; **rack chain** (later examples); **rack chase** *Printing*, a chase having racked sides into which fit two adjustable bars; **rack-meat,** fodder placed in racks for horses; **rack mounting** *vbl. sb.*, the use of standardized racks for supporting telephonic or electronic equipment; so **rack mount** *sb.* and *v. trans.*; **rack-rail, railway** (later examples); **rack saw,** (*b*) see quot.; **rack-way,** (*b*) a path through a wood, *esp.* one used for timber extraction.

1958 W. F. MCCULLOCH *Woods Words* 145 *Rack car*, a railroad car specially equipped with stakes or racks to handle pulpwood. **1958** J. HISLOP *From Start to Finish* iv. 20 Do not leave your horse tied up by the rack-chain, in your hurry to get away. **1963** E. H. EDWARDS *Saddlery* xxii. 167 Usually a rope..to the rear of a head collar is best for tying up unless one has rack chains. **1882** J. SOUTHWARD *Practical Printing* vi. 72 Rack chases for fixing small formes on presses are made the size of a press table, and obviate the use of furniture. **1898** —— *Mod. Printing* I. ix. 66 Rack chases..are made to fit the carriage of a press and the bed of a machine. **1743** W. ELLIS *Mod. Husbandman* Dec. vii. 46 To..further their Fattening, by enough of dry, hearty Trough and Rack-meat in Time. **1849** G. A. DEAN *Essays on Construction of Farm Buildings & Labourers' Cottages* 23 Many persons consider that the racks are best placed by the sides of the mangers..others, that horses who work hard should have no rack-meat given to them, considering that they satisfy their hunger much quicker. from the manger. **1965** *Wireless World* July 2 (Advt.), Series 'Y' instruments are housed in strong metal cases and, in some instances, can be rack-mounted. **1976** *Physics Bull.* Jan. 9 Available in either a rack-mount or a cabinet configuration, it is designed to be used by persons with little or no previous experience with signal averagers. **1978** *Chicago* June 106/1 Rack mounts, for instance, are 'in'... These racks will hold pre-amps, amps, equalizers, tuners and tape decks. Some can even accommodate a turntable. **1940** *Chambers's Techn. Dict.* 697/1 *Rack mounting*, the use of standard racks..for mounting panels carrying apparatus..with a uniform scheme of wiring. **1977** *Gramophone* June 118/1 A Sony rack mounting amplifier using pulse width modulation. **1979** *Sci. Amer.* June 8/2 (Advt.), The 5315B is essentially the same instrument housed in a metal case for rack mounting or stacking. **1918** *Chambers's Jrnl.* Jan. 13/1 See hazardous bridges being built, and the rack-rail employed to surmount steep gradients. **1931** *Times Educ. Suppl.* 21 Feb. p. iii, An engraving showing a Blenkinsop rack-rail engine and train. **1913** *Chambers's Jrnl.* Jan. 128/2 This railway introduces a cheaper means of ascending rugged mountains than the rack-railway laid upon the ground. **1931** *Times Educ. Suppl.* 21 Feb. p. iii, John Blenkinsop, the inventor of the rack railway, died 100 years ago. **1973** C. BONINGTON *Next Horizon* xii. 183, I..plunged through the deep powder snow..down to the rack-railway track that led up to Kleine Scheidegg. **1971** F. C. FORD-ROBERTSON *Terminol. Forest Science* 209/2 *Rack saw*, a head saw (circular or band) with a travelling table operated by rack-and-pinion. **1727** D. EATON *Let.* 16 May (1971) 120 The rack ways in Priors Haw are all brush'd up regularly... I was yesterday in Priors Haw whilst Mr. Goods servant was tything the brush-wood that was cut out of the rack ways. **1969** *Gloss. for Landscape Work* (*B.S.I.*) v. 40 *Rackway*, a narrow unpaved pathway left or cut through a tree crop to give access and to facilitate the extraction of timber to a wider ride or road.

rack, *sb.*⁴ **1. a.** Delete 'Now only *dial.*' and add later examples.

1964 J. MASTERS *Trial at Monomoy* iii. 101 Mary Tolley began to serve the main course, a rack of lamb. **1972** *New York* 12 June 63 Purée of cold carrot soup, rack of lamb, cauliflower provençale. **1974** *Observer* (Colour Suppl.) 22 Sept. 60/3 (Advt.), Fresh river trout followed by rack of highland lamb. **1977** *Time* 21 Nov. 44/3 Recently he ordered a hotel restaurant billboard repainted after noticing that the rack-of-lamb dinner on it 'looked raw'.

3. c. *U.S. colloq.* **rack of bones,** a skeleton; an emaciated person or animal. Also *rackabone, rackerbone, rack-o'-bones.*

1804 J. ORDWAY in Lewis & Ordway *Jrnls. Western Explor.* (1916) 128 We saw the rack of Bones of a verry large fish. **1854** M. J. HOLMES *Tempest & Sunshine* iv. 58 Turn that old rackerbone of yourn straight round, and turn down that ar street. **1856** G. D. BREWERTON *War in Kansas* xxxi. 314 Indeed she was to all appearances but a mere rack of bones, over whose unpicturesque outline nature had condescended to draw an angular wrinkling of skin. **1877** J. HABBERTON *Jericho Road* xvi. 146 Ain't it bad enough to be a good-for-nothin' rack of bones that's no comfort to myself? **1900** *Congress. Rec.* XXXIII. App. 6 Mar. 117/2 A Western farmer had a college-bred son who went off preaching... He came back with an old rackabone. **1911** J. C. LINCOLN *Cap'n Warren's Wards* ix. 140 If she fell on that poor rack-o'-bones,..'twould be a final smash. **1949** *Sat. Even. Post* 2 Apr. 97/2 Mount that rack o' bones you call a horse and ride in front o' me..

rack, *sb.*⁵ Add: **2. c.** *U.S.* **rack-heap,** (*a*) a heap of wreckage; (*b*) (see quot. 1958).

1883 'MARK TWAIN' *Life on Miss.* xxiii. 258 There was only one boat advertised..a Grand Tower packet... She was a venerable rack-heap, and a fraud to boot. **1889** P. BUTLER *Personal Recollections* vii. 72 There were in the river heaps of drift-wood, called 'rack-heaps', dangerous places into which the water rushed with great violence. **1892** 'MARK TWAIN' in *Sun* (N.Y.) 13 Mar. 18/2 Fridolin entered..with a tall skeleton stalking in his rear... The testimony of this wandering rackheap of unidentified bones. **1909** —— *Is Shakes. Dead?* i. 18 When the *Pennsylvania* blew up and became a drifting rack-heap freighted with wounded and dying. **1958** W. F. MCCULLOCH *Woods Words* 145 *Rackheap*. *a.* A piled-up drift or heap of logs and trees in a river. *b.* Sometimes applied to a heap of logs piled up ready to be splashed down a river.

rack, *v.*² Add: **3. b.** (Earlier and later examples.)

1743 W. ELLIS *Mod. Husbandman* Dec. iv. 29 When the Landlord came to rack up the Horse for all Night. **1960** G. E. EVANS *Horse in Furrow* ii. 43 The baiters' mates.. were expected..to *rack the horses up* for the night—that is, to fill their racks with fodder.

c. (Earlier example.)

1856 'STONEHENGE' *Brit. Rural Sports* 330/2 The lad first racks up his horse, so that he cannot lie down, but can reach his manger.

d. *fig.* To chalk up, to notch up; to achieve, to score. *N. Amer.*

1961 in WEBSTER. **1970** *Globe & Mail* (Toronto) 28 Sept. 18/3 The winners won the statistical battle by a wide margin, racking up 22 first downs to 16 for the losers. **1974** E. MCGIRR *Murderous Journey* 82 I've got some leave of absence piled up... I would have racked up close on a month. **1976** *Billings* (Montana) *Gaz.* 16 June 3-c/1 Billings began racking up runs in the fourth and fifth innings, while Missoula managed only one more run. **1977** *Time* 14 Nov. 25/1 Over the short run the U.N. vote may even have played into the hands of South African Prime Minister John Vorster, who is anxious to rack up a big majority in the country's Nov. 30 elections. **1978** G. VIDAL *Kalki* vi. 139 CBS had racked up a Nielsen rating of 36.3, the highest ever in that particular time slot. **1979** *Sci. Amer.* Dec. 30/3 She professionally ferries light aircraft (very often Beeches), the number of engines your choice, out of the U.S. to anywhere at all, having racked up almost 350 ocean crossings in 17 years of action.

4. a. (Later examples.) *spec.* in the *Oil Industry*, to place (lengths of drill pipe) in a pipe rack or derrick.

1949 *Our Industry* (Anglo-Iranian Oil Co. Ltd.) (ed. 2) ii. 39 When the drill pipe is being withdrawn, it is uncoupled in 'stands' of three 30-ft. lengths, these 90-ft. 'stands' being racked upright in the derrick. **1970** W. A. SMITH *Gold Mine* xxix. 81 Big King..wiped down his glossy shoes and racked them. **1971** C. BONINGTON *Annapurna South Face* xiii. 163 Mick got ready for the next pitch,..racking his pitons on karabiners slung to one side so that he could free them easily. **1973** J. W. JENNER in Hobson & Pohl *Mod. Petroleum Technol.* (ed. 4) iv. 120 The floormen..swing the bottom end of the stand away from the table and it is lowered on to the rig floor, at which time the derrickman..pulls the top of the stand over and racks it against the side of the derrick. **1974** *BP Shield Internat.* Oct. 18/2 The second noise was..the drilling pipe being racked in the derrick.

5. a. (Later example.)

1906 *Westm. Gaz.* 18 Aug. 14/2 If the image is too big, rack out the camera a little and bring the board nearer. If too small, rack in and push the board away.

rack, *v.*⁴ Add: **a.** (Later examples.) Also *trans.* with a distance as object.

1887 E. CUSTER *Tenting on Plains* vi. 187 He [*sc.* a horse] is very affectionate, and he racks a mile inside of three minutes. **1935** H. DAVIS *Honey in Horn* xi. 175 He saddled and bridled the mare..and racked out on the road. *Ibid.* xv. 254 When the wagon went out of sight..he spurred up and racked after it.

b. Used *transf.* of vehicles or of persons. *to rack off* (Austral.), to go missing, 'get lost'.

1935 Z. N. Hurston *Mules & Men* i. iv. 95 Pretty soon the log-train came racking along. **1975** *Sun-Herald* (Sydney) 29 June, [*title of record*] Rak Off Normie. **1980** *Courier-Mail* (Brisbane) 10 Apr. 36 (*caption*) 'Gimme ya money mate or I'll shoot ya!' 'No... Now rack off!'

rack (ræk), *v.*[7] *Building.* [var. Rake *v.*[3]] *trans.* To build (a brick wall) by stopping each course a little short of the one below, so that the end slopes (usu. temporarily until the work is completed). Usu. with *back.* Cf. Raking *vbl. sb.*[3] in Dict. and Suppl.

1873 F. Robertson *Engin. Notes* ii. 35 In repairing masonry where there is a crack or junction, or where new work is to be connected with old, the adjoining ends should be racked back from each other, as it were in ascending steps, and the resulting wedge-shaped void subsequently built in. **1904** C. F. & G. A. Mitchell *Brickwork & Masonry* ii. 77 (*caption*) Angles of walls racked preparatory to building. *Ibid.* 78 The base of the corner is extended along the wall, and is racked back as the work is carried up. **1945** E. L. Braley *Brickwork* iii. 58 Usually five or seven courses are built at each corner, the work being racked back, e.g. first of all three stretchers, then four headers and one closer, then two stretchers, two headers and a closer, one stretcher, and finally the heading face of the top brick. **1972** S. Smith *Brickwork* iv. 17 When building a wall, it is usual to raise the 'quoins' (corners) first, 'racking back' the work as necessary.

rackan hook. Also **reckon hook** (the usual form). [f. Rackan + Hook *sb.*] = Rackan-crook.

1645 *Essex County* (Mass.) *Probate Rec.* (1916) I. 50 Estate of William Goog of Lynn... One gridiron & recke hookes [etc.]. **1647** *Ibid.* 99 Estate of John Jarrat of Rowley ..Reckon hooks & some small things, 4s. **1867** B. Brierley *Marlocks of Meriton* 41 His eyes still intent upon the 'rack-an'-hook' hanging in the kitchen. **1961** M. W. Barley *Eng. Farmhouse & Cottage* iii. v. 175 In such houses as these, cooking was usually done in the house body. There, along with the iron range and the reckon hook, were the bakestone and the wooden boards..with which oatcakes were made.

rack-bone. (Later example.)

1831 W. Youatt *Horse* ix. 153 The other neck, or *rack-bones*, as they are denominated by the farrier,..are of a strangely irregular shape.

rackensak (ræ·kənsæk). [Prob. altered form of *Arkansan.*] *U.S. colloq.* A native of Arkansas. ? *Obs.*

1845 [see *corn-cracker 1]. **1854** *Putnam's Mag.* III. 665/2 Artillerists and dragoons, suckers and rackensacks, were all mixed up in confusion.

racker[2]. (Later examples.)

1891 *Harper's Mag.* Aug. 366/1, I have seen more than one racker of true Norman blood. **1903** A. D. McFaul *Ike Glidden* xiv. 108 Lickety got ter puffin' up his ole hoss, soze you'd a thought it was the Millbridge Racker.

racket, *sb.*[2] Add: **3. b.** (Earlier example.)

1846 P. J. de Smet *Oregon Missions* (1847) xiv. 193 The savages travel over these marshy places in *Rackets.*

racket, *sb.*[3] Add: **2. c.** A dance: see quots.

1882 L. O. Carpenter *J. W. Pepper's Universal Dancing Master* 33 *Racquette.*.Make three galop steps or slides to the left, throwing the foot out in second position... Slide to right [etc.]. **1882** P. V. Cartier *Practical Illustrated Waltz Instructor* 45 *The Racquet.*.Take two long galop slides with left foot on accent, and as right foot is brought up to left foot for second time, rest, and hold left foot in air. Repeat by sliding with right foot, etc. **1885** A. Dodworth *Dancing* vii. 51 Racket Waltz (One-Slide Racket in Waltz Time). *Ibid.* 52 Changes are made..by alternating the one-slide racket with the three-slide. **1935** D. N. Cropper *Dance Dict.* 54 *Racket*, popular 6/8 number of the 'nineties'. Basic step: a waltz form with leap (1) slide (&) change-cut (2).

3. a. Now usually, any scheme or procedure which aims at obtaining money or effecting other objects by unusual, illegal, and often violent means; a distinctive form of organized crime.

1928 *Daily Express* 14 Sept. 1/1 The 'racket' has for years been distinctively a Chicago institution; and it has been found to be such a profitable form of crime there that it is spreading to the other large cities of the Middle West. **1931** *Sun* (Baltimore) 4 Apr. 1/4 One racket in New York State alone—that of fake securities—is known to total approximately $100,000,000 a year. **1940** E. Gill *Autobiogr.* vii. 259 It [*sc.* politics] is all a confused business of ramps and rackets—pretended quarrels and dishonest commercial schemings, having no relation to the real interests of peoples, neither to their spiritual nor their material welfare. **1944** M. Laski *Love on Supertax* xii. 117 You organised all this Black Market racket, didn't you? **1950** G. Brenan *Face of Spain* ii. 54 Of all the rackets recorded in history, the Spanish Inquisition, during the first hundred years of its career, was perhaps the most mean and repulsive. **1956** 'C. Blackstock' *Dewey Death* iv. 83 Mr. Wilson is now telling everybody that I.L.D.A. is the secret headquarters of the drug racket. **1974** J. Gardner *Return of Moriarty* 31 All our family is affected if we start to lose in any racket, any lay. **1977** *Times* 29 Nov. 14/2 Ulster by the middle of 1974 was suffering from rackets and violent crime on a scale equal to some of Europe's most notorious cities.

b. In more weakened senses: an activity, a way of life; a line of business.

1891 [in Dict.]. **1907** R. Dunn *Shameless Diary of Explorer* xviii. 251 The Professor is working his faith-in-God-and-self, and line-of-least resistance racket, a mite too strong. **1916** J. Buchan *Greenmantle* i. 4, I thrive on the racket and eat and sleep like a schoolboy. **1927** *Vanity Fair* (N.Y.) XXIX. 132/3 'What's your racket?' meaning 'What do you do for a living?' **1930** *Sun* (Baltimore) 12 Feb. 10/7 My satisfaction would be complete if there were a 100 per cent rush for the doors that would entirely eliminate the encore racket. **1931** F. L. Allen *Only Yesterday* vii. 172 At the beginning of the decade advertising had been considered a business..by the end of the decade many of its practitioners..were beginning to refer to it—among themselves—as a racket. **1936** *Amer. Speech* XI. 274/2 Nowadays a *racket* may be a legitimate business... A man may say..'I rather like the racket I'm in', referring to his business. **1938** *Downside Review* LVI. 100 It is true that the phrase 'muscling in on the culture racket' reflects a development of English word-usage from which the present reviewer had perhaps been preserved by monastic seclusion. **1942** *R.A.F. Jrnl.* 3 Oct. 11, I sold insurance, and..that's the racket to develop your wits. **1944** J. S. Huxley *On living in Revol.* 23 What with football, racing, the cinema, the theatre, popular literature, and holiday resorts, recreation is today one of the most profitable commercial rackets. **1978** J. Updike *Coup* (1979) vi. 239, I am in the insurance racket. I am a claims adjuster.

4. *to stand the racket* (further examples). Also, (*c*) to pay.

1846 *Swell's Night Guide* 132/2 *Stand the racket*, treat, pay for all. **1904** G. K. Chesterton *Napoleon of N.H.* iii. iii. 168 'Can we do fifteen hundred pounds?' 'I'll stand the racket.' **1905** *Pall Mall Mag.* Dec. 678/2 If there is trouble, it will be for Great Britain to stand the racket. **1930** *Punch* 19 Feb. 204/3 If her..friend had been a sportsman he'd have stood the racket himself.

6. *attrib.* and *Comb.*, as *racket-buster*, *-busting* (sb. and adj.), *-ridden* (adj.), *ring.*

1940 *Sun* (Baltimore) 21 Nov. 1/2 Sol Gelb..had been assigned by the New York 'racket-buster' to watch the hearing. **1959** *Times Lit. Suppl.* 30 Jan. 55/4 Mr Danforth was senior investigator..from 1935–1951, when former Governor Thomas E. Dewey was the courageous D.A...and his famous racket-busting took place. **1972** 'H. Howard' *Nice Day for Funeral* iv. 58 Until the motive is established beyond doubt this case remains part of the DA's racket-busting programme. **1978** *Time* 3 July 55/2 Died. Luther W. Youngdahl, 82, unflappable federal judge who..was appointed to the bench in 1951 after five years as a racket-busting Republican Governor of Minnesota. **1931** F. D. Pasley *Muscling In* v. 138 New York stood revealed as the most racket-ridden city in the country. **1973** *Black Panther* 5 May 2/2 It is widely known that Inman is himself a king pin in the city's organized crime and racket rings.

racket, var. *rackett.

racket, *v.*[1] **1. b.** (Later *transf.* example.)

1861 F. W. Robinson *No Church* I. iv. 95 An improvident young man, who..would racket away all the money he might be able to leave her.

racket, *v.*[2] Add: **2. a.** (Later examples.) Also const. *about, along, around.*

1885 B. Potter *Jrnl.* 6 May (1966) 141 How is it these high-heeled ladies who dine out..can racket about all day long, while I..am so tired toward the end of the afternoon that I can scarcely keep my feet? **1914** W. Owen *Let.* 21 Dec. (1967) 309, I racketed about all Saturday making luggage out of lumber. **1916** 'Boyd Cable' *Action Front* 197 A dozen paces away two of the battalion machine-guns were clattering and racketing in rapid gusts of fire. **1929** M. de la Roche *Whiteoaks* xiv. 188 Aha..that's what I like to hear! Young lads racketing about! **1936** A. Ransome *Pigeon Post* vi. 69 But do you think we'll hear it?' said Mrs. Blackett, 'when we're racketing about and busy with other things.' **1967** J. C. Holmes *Nothing More to Declare* i. 20 We read it in an empty subway car racketing along under the deserted streets. **1970** G. Greer *Female Eunuch* 331 The first significant discovery we shall make as we racket along our female road to freedom is that men are not free. **1977** 'L. Egan' *Blind Search* i. 12 That girl racketing around heaven knows where or with what sort of characters. **1977** W. M. Spackman *Armful of Warm Girl* 34 Guests..racketing up into the bedroom.

racketeer (rækėtīə·ɹ), *sb.* orig. *U.S.* [f. Racket *sb.*[3] + -eer.] A member of a gang or association of criminals practising extortion, intimidation, violence, and other illegal acts on a large scale; any person making easy money by such means. Also *transf.*, one who achieves an easy result by illegitimate means.

1928 *Time* 9 July 14 In the old days it was a mark of distinction to be seen at gangster funerals, but during the Loesch prosecutions, probably not even U.S. Senator Deneen of Illinois would care to be seen near the bier of a 'racketeer'. **1928** *Daily Express* 14 Sept. 1/4 'Racketeers'..now control 150 lines of business in Chicago, and collect an enormous tribute for immunity from their violence. **1929** *Sun* (Baltimore) 15 Nov. 1/6 'Spike' along with six police captains and a dozen politicians and racketeers, is accused of participation in the profits of gambling machines placed in speakeasies. **1931** *Times* 24 Sept. 11/2 The campaign against gangsters and 'racketeers' in New York City has resulted today in the arrest of..one of the most powerful 'labour racketeers' in the city. **1935** J. T. Farrell *Judgment Day* iv. 76 We got to get a strong man in the White House..to kick out the bankers and grafting politicians and racketeers. **1939** *Scrutiny* VII. 439 The older generation of middlebrow propagandists, whom *Scrutiny* used to refer to as literary racketeers. **1948** *Sunday Pictorial* 18 July 7/1 The public are completely at the mercy of these racketeers. **1956** 'C. Blackstock' *Dewey Death* iii. 52 You romantic writers are as much a menace to the community as drug racketeers. **1967** *Wall Street Jrnl.* 24 Apr. 32/2 Rosenberg, according to Illinois authorities, was secretly associated with..an important Chicago racketeer. **1978** *Cornish Guardian* 27 Apr. 3/1 Metrication will be an open invitation for every spiv and racketeer to cheat the British public.

racketeer (rækėtīə·ɹ), *v.* *U.S.* [f. the sb.] **a.** *trans.* To subject to racketeering. **b.** *intr.* To engage in fraudulent business.

1928 *Time* 30 Jan. 11/2 In 36 years in Chicago I have never been held up, robbed, or racketeered. **1933** G. B. Shaw *Polit. Madhouse in Amer.* 56 What is the use of paying you money to racketeer with? **1934** *Words* Nov. 5/2 *To press-agent*,..*to service*,..*to gesture, to racketeer*..are new, and most of them are obviously American.

racketee·ring, *vbl. sb.* *U.S.* [f. *racketeer *sb.* + -ing[1].] The business of racketeers; a system of organized crime directed chiefly to extorting money from business firms by intimidation, violence, or other illegal methods. Also *attrib.*

1928 *N.Y. Times* 18 Aug. 15 Two gang murders within the last week prompted Judge Edwin O. Lewis..to order the August Grand Jury to delve to the bottom of 'racketeering' in Philadelphia. **1928** *Daily Express* 14 Sept. 1/4 'Racketeering' is the new word that has been coined in America to describe the big business of organised crime. **1929** *Sun* (Baltimore) 10 Jan. 1/6 The defendants are charged with compelling..manufacturers to pay tribute to them by threatening to call strikes. The indictment was one of the first to be returned here in connection with a Federal investigation of racketeering. **1930** *Observer* 19 Oct. 17 He had hoped..perhaps to introduce and organise 'racketeering' processes. *Ibid.*, The only new detail is the paid protection of blackmail which now exists in many cities, described by the term 'racketeering'. **1931** *Sun* (Baltimore) 29 Jan. 1/6 Another effort is to be made to prohibit congressional nepotism now commonly recognized as 'pay-roll racketeering' on the part of members of both the House and Senate. **1941** L. B. Namier *Conflicts* (1942) 163 Look at this Jew! What did he do in the war? Some racketeering? **1959** *Ann. Reg. 1958* 187 Only on three major Bills was the President defeated..the attempt to regulate the affairs of trade unions to cut out racketeering [etc.]. **1978** S. Brill *Teamsters* ii. 41 It was at the time when he was being charged with racketeering that Bufalino joined Hoffa's legal team.

racketee·ring, *ppl. a.* [f. *racketeer *v.* + -ing[2].] Characterized by or engaging in rackets.

1931 *Times* 30 July 11/3 Sometimes employers trying to operate an 'open shop' hire strike breakers... In other cases 'racketeering' gangs take the initiative in intimidating employers with 'open shops'. **1967** *Sunday Times* 8 Oct. 24/8 Kim, at this period, 'gave the impression of being a complaisant passenger in a racketeering upper-class world'.

racketiness (ræ·kėtinės). [f. Rackety + -ness.] The quality of being rackety; fondness for noise, excitement, etc.

1939 C. Day Lewis *Child of Misfortune* iii. ii. 270 No doubt racketiness was just part of the fashionable sexual lure then. **1979** *Listener* 1 Nov. 508/2 Her racketiness and smart friends arouse less appreciation.

rackett (ræ·kėt). Also **racket, ranket(t.** [a. G. *rackett, rankett.*] **1.** A Renaissance musical instrument of the oboe family, consisting of a squat cylinder containing nine parallel channels joined alternately at top and bottom to form a continuous tube nine times the length of the cylinder.

1876 Stainer & Barrett *Dict. Mus. Terms* 374/1 *Rackett, Rankett*, (1) an obsolete wind-instrument of the double bassoon kind. **1891** C. R. Day *Catal. Mus. Instr. R. Milit. Exhib. 1890* 100 Racket. This beautiful instrument is constructed in the form of an ivory cylinder, and it is played by means of a rather large double reed. **1910** F. W. Galpin *Old English Instr. of Music* ix. 167 A yet shorter instrument of bass pitch with a cylindrical-shaped tube.. was called the Racket. **1939** A. Carse *Musical Wind Instr.* xiv. 206 In the racket or sausage-bassoon the air-passage is doubled and redoubled to such an extent that the sounding-length of the tube is quite nine times as long as the body of the instrument. **1961** A. Baines *Mus. Instr. through Ages* ix. 232 The deep soft buzz of one racket among recorders, cornetts, etc., made a better effect than a whole consort of them [*sc.* mixed instruments]. **1966** —— *Europ. & Amer. Mus. Instr.* 98 The *racket* contains a number of short parallel bores connected in series to make up a total windway of a metre or more. **1968** *Radio Times* 26 Sept. 48 A unique collection of medieval instruments—including rackett, rebec, crumhorn. **1970** *Daily Colonist* (Victoria, B.C.) 26 Feb. 28/1 They have chosen to play medieval music on a number of rare and little-used instruments, including the krummhorn, rauschfeiffer, ranket, and baroque oboes. **1976** D. Munrow *Instr. Middle Ages & Renaissance* 46/1 The rackett's narrow cylindrical bore consists of no less than nine parallel channels drilled in a wooden or ivory cylinder and connected alternately top and bottom.

† **2.** An organ stop. *Obs.* exc. *Hist.*

1876 Stainer & Barrett *Dict. Mus. Terms* 374/1 *Rackett, Rankett*..(2) An organ stop of 16 ft. or 8 ft. pitch now obsolete. **1897** H. Riemann *Dict. Mus.* 629/1 *Rackett* (Ranket),..in the organ an obsolete reed-stop almost entirely covered, of quiet tone (16 and 8 feet). **1962** S. Irwin *Dict. Pipe Organ Stops* 160 *Rankett*, a very old form of short-resonatored Reed stop, at 16′ or 8′ on both manual and pedals.

rackety. Add: **1.** (Later examples.)

This and sense 2 are tending to merge.

1975 I. Murdoch *Word Child* 257 It was raining, and a rackety wind was sweeping the rain in little wild gusts across the windows. **1976** A. Powell *Infants of Spring* v. 80 In the middle age-group of most houses there inclined to occur a cluster of fairly rackety boys, from whom the house-tutor might expect trouble. **1977** *Daily Tel.* 20 Jan. 12/1 Crosby did not much like Harvard, but he seems to have been a fairly conventional undergraduate there, even if wilful and rackety.

2. (Later examples.)

1927 C. Connolly *Let.* 11 Feb. in *Romantic Friendship* (1975) 250 One misses the thrilling rackety journey to the wagon restaurant. **1961** A. Ritner *Seize Nettle* 158 The big basket of clothes to be coaxed through the rackety old washer. **1974** C. Milne *Enchanted Places* xix. 129 A room designed—as a nursery should be—for doing things in, messy things, racketty things, rough-and-tumble things. **1975** J. Symons *Three Pipe Problem* xviii. 201 He unlocked the door, switched on the engine, and listened to its rackety coughing.

Rackhamesque (rækăme·sk), *a.* [See -esque.] Characteristic of or resembling the drawings of Arthur Rackham (1867–1939), book illustrator.

1935 *Forestry* IX. 15 There was also strong feeling about the way in which Rackhamesque trees of the forest were rapidly being replaced by pines. **1936** 'G. Orwell' *Keep Aspidistra Flying* iv. 88 The trees..twisted themselves into whimsy Rackhamesque attitudes. **1961** S. Gilruth *Drown her Remembrance* iii. 30 A few isolated olive trees, gnarled and twisted into weird Rackhamesque shapes.

racking, *vbl. sb.*[2] Add: **2.** Shelving designed to be functional and inexpensive rather than decorative.

1937 G. Frankau *More of Us* viii. 91 While Art Department hummed like dynamo As frenzied hands tore pictures from their racking. **1976** *Gloss. Documentation Terms (B.S.I.)* 52 *Racking*, shelving, usually of a cheaper quality, used for storage purposes in non-public stacks and areas of a library.

racking, *vbl. sb.*[3] Add: **2.** *spec.* Distortion of a structure under shear. (Further examples.)

1957 *Brit. Commonw. Forest Terminol.* II. 149 *Racking*, in timber testing, the application of loads to an assembly, tending to deform it in shear. **1976** W. J. Patton *Construction Materials* 386 *Racking*, tendency of a rectangular frame to distort from its rectangular shape due to lack of stiffness against shear forces. **1977** *Engin. Materials & Design* Aug. 17/1 A batch of fifty radiators made in this way have been subjected to tests against thermal shock cycling, pulsating pressure, vibration and racking.

racking, *vbl. sb.*[4] (Later example.) Also *attrib.*, as *racking event, horse.*

1974 *Marlboro Herald-Advocate* (Bennettsville, S. Carolina) 18 Apr. 10/3 In ladies racking, Sherry Jean Nolan..rode King to a first-place win. *Ibid.*, Larry Griggs rode King to a first place victory in the junior racking event. **1974** *Greenville* (S. Carolina) *News* 23 Apr. 11/2 Friday performances, beginning at 1 p.m. and 7 p.m., have the pleasure horse classes,..along with three racking horse classes.

racking, var. Raking *vbl. sb.*[3] in Dict. and Suppl.

ra·ck-jobbing, *vbl. sb.* [f. Rack *sb.*[2] + Jobbing *vbl. sb.*[2] 2.] The supplying of goods to a retailer for display on racks on condition that the supplier undertakes to accept unsold stock after an agreed period. Hence (as a back-formation) **ra·ck-job** *v. intr.* and *sb.* (used *attrib.*). Also **ra·ck-jobber.**

1959 *Economist* 12 Dec. 1090/1 A complete 'rack jobbing' service. Here the supplier takes responsibility for the stock and display from week to week; the retailer simply provides the space, and accepts a lower margin on the goods that are sold. **1964** *Credit Trends* Sept. 5 Some supermarket operators are new to these lines, and the profession of rack-jobbing has grown up. The retailer leases out shelf space to these specialist concessionaires in return for an agreed profit margin related to normal earning for the space used. **1967** *Economist* 15 July 238/3 Smith and other wholesalers can help by teaching them [*sc.* newsagents] and stocking for them—as some paperback publishers already rack-job for the small newsagent or supermarkets. **1968** *Times* 29 Nov. p. iv/5 E.M.I., Decca and Pye have recently set up a joint company called Record Merchandisers to exploit what is referred to in the trade as rack jobbing. This is a system where the servicing company supplies the records for display on racks in non-conventional outlets (such as stationers and supermarkets) taking full responsibility for what is put on display and taking back unsold stock. **1969** *JEMF Quarterly* V. iii. 101 In recent years, the introduction of rack-job merchandising of LPs in supermarket and other retail outlets has obviated the need for printed graphics to complement record distributions. **1977** *Rolling Stone* 19 May 14/4 It further states that Klein instructed 'another person' to sell the records at a profit to wholesalers, rack jobbers and distributors.

ra·ckman. *U.S.* [f. Rack *sb.*[2] + Man *sb.*[1]] A man who distributes newspapers from the publishing office to local newspaper racks.

1943 *Sun* (Baltimore) 17 Sept. 20/2 The..Court of Appeals upheld today a lower court decision that rackmen distributing papers..for the publishing company of the Baltimore Sun were not engaging in interstate commerce within the meaning of the Fair Labor Standards Act. **1944** *Ibid.* 18 Jan. 17/7 (*heading*) Rackmen decision refused review.

rack-out, *a.* [f. Rack *v.*[2] 5.] Designed to rack out.

1893 *Photogr. Ann.* 333 This camera is well known. It has double extension leather bellows... The extension is rack-out, but by an ingenious arrangement instantly extended as required.

rack-pin. 1. (Earlier example.)

1832 *Blackw. Magazine* XXXII. 471 Friend, if thou be'st not nautical, thou knowest what a *rack-pin*, something of the stoutest, is.

rack-renting, *vbl. sb.* (s.v. Rack-rent *v.* in Dict.) (Earlier and later examples.)

1663 E. Butterfield *Let.* 1 Feb. in M. M. Verney *Memoirs of Verney Family* (1899) IV. ii. 43, I hate this rack-renting 'tis worse than usury. **1840** J. S. Mill in *Edin. Rev.* LXXII. 46 Much alteration may be requisite in the system of rack-renting and tenancy at will. **1963** *Economist* 3 Aug. 421/1 The rack-renting of London's tenantry. **1969** *Listener* 12 June 815/3 Communism appeals to hundreds of thousands of peasants who hate corruption, rack-renting and foreign intervention.

racks (ræks). *Television slang.* (See quots.)

1960 O. Skilbeck *ABC of Film & TV* 104 *Racks*, colloquial term for the vision control department (T.V.) between cameras and vision mixer. **1974** *Some Technical Terms & Slang* (Granada Television), *Racks*, the television control area between studio camera and control box.

‖ **raclette** (raklet). [Fr., = scraper.] **1.** *Archæol.* [A. Cheynier 1930, in *Bull. Soc. Préhist. Française* XXVII. 488] An end-, or side-scraper, of a type discovered in the valley of the Vézère, dating from the Early Magdalenian age. Also *attrib.*

1931 *Proc. Prehist. Soc. E. Anglia* VI. 322 Dr. André Cheynier,..working at Badegoule, has obtained from a special layer several hundreds of..tools, to which he has given the name of Raclettes. **1936** *Nature* 11 July 79/2 (*heading*) An Early Magdalenian 'raclette' industry in the Lower Thames valley.

2. A fondue-like dish consisting of cheese melted before an open fire, scraped on to the plate, and served with potatoes. Also *attrib.*

1949 A. L. Simon *Dict. Gastron.* 200/2 *Raclette*, the name given in the Valais Canton of Switzerland to the local *Fondue*. **1958** *Times* 15 Nov. 11/6 There is dried meat of the Valais..and there are *raclettes* and *fondues*. **1961** *Times* 23 Mar. 16/7 The Seiler family arranged an enormous *raclette* party on the slopes of the Riffelalp. **1971** *Vogue* 15 Sept. 118/1 *Raclette*..is..a speciality of the Valais... A whole side of cheese is grilled in front of a brazier..the sizzling bits scraped on to your plate..served with potatoes boiled in their skins and gherkins. **1974** *Times* 4 Feb. 17/5 Six helpings of raclette cheese with potatoes.

racloir (raklwā·ɹ). Chiefly *Archæol.* [Fr., = scraper.] A scraper, esp. of a type discovered amongst the remains of the Mousterian period of the Middle Palæolithic period.

1892 P. L. Simmonds *Commercial Dict. Trade Products* 311/2 *Racloir*, a scraper; a grater; an instrument to strike off the heaped corn in a measure. **1923** *Nature* CXII. 118/2 The latest group which is found upon the Stoke Newington 'floor' is a clearly-defined Mousterian industry, with fine examples of both racloirs and of the equally characteristic trimmed-flake points. **1935** *Antiquity* IX. 118 [Flint] blades of Upper Palaeolithic facies, racloirs, tranchets, and carinated fragments. **1956** A. L. Armstrong in D. L. Linton *Sheffield* vi. 94 Zones II and III yielded quartzite hand-axes, racloirs, and scrapers displaying great skill and a refined technique.

racon (rēⁱ·kǫn). orig. *U.S.* [f. *Ra(dar + Bea)con *sb.*] = *radar beacon* s.v. *Radar[2].

1945 *Army & Navy Jrnl.* 18 Aug. 1534/4 *Racon*, radar beacons. Stations which serve as the radar equivalents of lighthouses. **1947** L. A. Turner in L. N. Ridenour *Radar System Engin.* viii. 246 Beacons of the synchronous sort just described have been variously called 'radar beacons', 'responder beacons', 'racons', and 'transponders'. **1958** *Proc. Inst. Electr. Engineers* CV. b. Suppl. No. 8. 351/1 A racon has recently been developed at the Admiralty Signals and Radar Establishment for use on lightvessels, the intention..being that a number of such racons shall be fitted around the shores of Great Britain on both lightvessels and lighthouses. **1967** B. Knox *Blacklight* vii. 142 'The screen was registerin' one o' those blacklight beacons.'.. 'The deep-water racon,' nodded Carrick. **1977** *Globe & Mail* (Toronto) 24 Feb. b16 Lakes shipping..can also obtain guidance from racons (shore-based radar reflectors).

raconteur. (Earlier and later examples.)

1828 J. C. Young *Jrnl.* 3 July in *Memoir Charles Mayne Young* (1871) I. v. 169 Sir Charles is a handsome, thoroughbred gentleman, and a capital *raconteur*. **1922** Joyce *Ulysses* 604 A gifted man, Mr Bloom said of Mr Dedalus senior, in more respects than one and a born *raconteur* if ever there was one. **1937** *Discovery* Oct. 326/1 Mrs. Johnson says little about herself, indulges in no purple passages, and without the conscious effort of the *raconteur* she manages to introduce many good stories and telling anecdotes. **1958** L. Durrell *Mountolive* xv. 296 The inevitable anecdote of a famous *raconteur* to round off the letter. **1972** J. Mosedale *Football* iii. 35 (*caption*) Jimmy Conzelman functioned as quarterback, coach, raconteur, songwriter..and promoter.

racoon, raccoon, *sb.* Add: **a*.** The skin or fur of the racoon.

1815 C. Wilt *Let.* in J. C. Luttig *Jrnl. Expedition Upper Missouri* (1920) 130 Raccoon from your country will not bring 62½c in Kentucky. **1901–2** *T. Eaton & Co. Catal.* Fall & Winter 42/1 Alaska Sable... Black Persian Lamb... Raccoon. **1976** 'D. Halliday' *Dolly & Nanny Bird* ii. 28 Hefty young men clad in Timberwolf, Raccoon, Scimmia, Tibetan Yak and Natural Unplucked Nutria.

b. racoon-cap *U.S.*, a cap made from the dressed skin of the racoon; **racoon dog,** a mammal about the size of a fox, *Nyctereutes procyonoides*, belonging to the family Canidæ, native to eastern Asia, and distinguished by thick greyish-brown fur and black, racoon-like markings on its head; so **racoon-like dog** (in same sense); **racoon oyster,** substitute for def.: a small, brown-shelled oyster, *Ostrea frons*, found in clusters off the shores of south-eastern North America; (earlier and later examples).

1840 *Knickerbocker* XVI. 163 He then made me a rakish raccoon-cap, with a flaunting tail to it. **1848** in H. Howe *Hist. Coll. Ohio* 151 For..several years after the war, raccoon-caps, with fur outside..were almost universally worn. [**1833** J. E. Gray *Illustr. Indian Zool.* II. plate 1 (*caption*) Racoon-faced Dog.] **1868** *Proc. Zool. Soc.* 522 Raccoon Dog. Tail short, bushy. **1876** A. R. Wallace *Geogr. Distrib. Anim.* I. x. 226 The quadruped figured is the curious racoon dog. **1959** *Times* 23 Feb. 10/5 Two of the strangest members of the dog family arrived recently at the Regent's Park Zoo. They are the maned wolf..and the raccoon-dog from Siberia. **1974** L. E. Bueler *Wild Dogs of World* 217 In Japan..the raccoon dog was once common to all the principal islands. **1890** St. G. Mivart *Dogs, Jackals, Wolves, & Foxes: Monogr. Canidæ* 135 The Raccoon-like Dog is an inhabitant of Japan, the valley of the Amoor, and China. **1931** *Proc. Zool. Soc.* 174 A female Raccoon-like Dog..lived..5 years. **1964** L. S. Crandall *Managem. Wild Mammals in Captivity* 280 The raccoon-like dog..is a small grayish animal,..with a black facial mask which is the basis for its name. **1834** J. J. Audubon *Ornith. Biogr.* II. 504 Shrimps..have been detained at low water on the banks of racoon oysters, a kind of shell-fish so named under the idea that they are eaten by that quadruped. **1854** W. G. Simms *Southward Ho!* iii. 28 They procure the ordinary 'racoon oyster'—the meanest of the tribe. **1885** *Harper's Mag.* Jan. 219/1 When the mangrove grows on the outer edge of the water-line, and drops its aerial roots,..the spat of the raccoon oyster finds a lodgement.

racquetball (ræ·kĕtbǭl). orig. *U.S.* Also **racquet ball.** [f. Racquet + Ball *sb.*[1]] A game resembling paddle ball played with a light ball and a racket in a four-walled hand-ball court. Also *attrib.* Hence **ra·cquetba:ller,** one who plays racquetball.

1972 Wickstrom & Larson (*title*) Racquetball-paddle-ball fundamentals. **1974** *Wall Street Jrnl.* 12 June 1 Mr. Kendler split with the International Racquetball Association last year to form a rival organization, the National Racquetball Club, which sponsors a professional tour for 16 top-ranked racquetballers. **1976** *Milton Keynes Express* 23 July 17/4 Over the five week period they will include trampoline, squash, volley-ball, racquet ball, gymnastics, football, table tennis, five a side football,..chess and draughts. **1978** *Monitor* (McAllen, Texas) 29 May 3b/7 The newest indoor sports craze for physical fitness nuts is racquetball. The game is a cross between tennis and hand-ball. **1979** *Tucson Mag.* Apr. 55/1 Racquetball courts and numerous other recreation centers are spotted throughout the city.

racy, *a.* **3.** (Further examples.)

1901 'P. Bee' *Vagaries of Men* 107 Women who tell racy stories..can rouse a great deal of enthusiasm in a room full of men. **1955** *Times* 19 Aug. 8/2 Lieutenant-Colonel R. J. T. Hills..contributes to the summer number of the *Household Brigade Magazine* some racy memories of Combermere, the Household Cavalry barracks at Windsor. **1971** D. Potter *Brit. Eliz. Stamps* xv. 179 Every new Great Britain stamp appears on the front cover in full colour, and there is hardly a week without a racy, but informative piece, on some aspect of Great Britain collecting. **1973** *Nature* 27 July 241/2 The introductory passages are autobiographical in content and colourful, frank and uninhibited in style—racy is the only word.

rad, *sb.*[1] Add: Also **Rad.** (Earlier and later examples.)

1820 Lady J. Campbell *Let.* 18 Nov. in Duke of Argyll *Intimate Society Lett.* (1910) II. 654 We shut all our shutters for fear our lights shd seem *Rads* too. **1898** H. N. Page *Red Rock* xxxiv. 411 He..was abusing Leech and Still and pretty much all the Rads. **1912** J. Galsworthy *Eldest Son* I. ii. 27 Plenty of time to work up the constituency before we kick out these infernal Rads. **1973** R. Hayes *Hungarian Game* viii. 61 A clumsy bribe and a gambit about student rads.

rad (ræd), *sb.*[3] Abbrev. of Radian.

1913 Godfrey & Siddons *Four-Figure Tables* 38 Radians and degrees... Rad. **1960** C. L. McClure *Theory of Inertial Guidance* i. 11 The total inertial angular velocity of the terrestrial geoid: $\omega_{EI} = 7{\cdot}2921 \,.\, 10^{-5}$ rad/sec...measured in radians per mean solar second. **1973** *Nature* 6 Apr. 372/3 The Mars 2 and 3 experiments were intended to give a continuous scan of the planet's surface using a field of vision of 0·01 rad (15 km from a distance of 1,500 km).

† **rad** (ræd), *sb.*[4] *Obs.* [f. Rad(iation.] A unit of X-ray dose (see quots.).

1918 S. Russ in *Arch. Radiol. & Electrotherapy* XXIII. 226 [I venture to put forward a suggestion for a new unit, by which the dose of X rays administered to a patient may be measured; the new unit is primarily intended for use in what is known as 'deep therapy'.] *Ibid.* 231 The radium capsule, when applied to malignant cells, causes complete inhibition of their proliferation after an exposure thereto for one hour; this latter quantity is the suggested unit, viz., the Rad. **1922** S. Russ et al. in *Lancet* 4 Feb. 213/1 As yet there is no international unit by which X rays are measured, and during the course of this work we have employed the 'rad' as our working unit—i.e., the minimum dose of X rays which..is needed to prevent the growth of Jensen's rat sarcoma when inoculated into normal rats.

rad (ræd), *sb.*[5] Abbrev. of RADIATOR. Also *attrib.*

1935 F. BRETT YOUNG *White Ladies* v. vi. 558 The rads are stone-cold. **1967** L. DEIGHTON *Expensive Place* xxvii. 169 He..opened up the rad cap. **1975** J. SYMONS *Three Pipe Problem* iii. 28 It was an air bubble, we've bled the rads. **1977** *Hot Car* Oct. 19/2 The fan should be left off and an electric one fitted in front of the rad.

rad (ræd), *sb.*[6] Pl. **rad, rads.** [f. initial letters of *radiation absorbed dose.*] A unit of absorbed dose of ionizing radiation, corresponding to the absorption of 100 ergs of energy per gramme of absorbing material (0·01 joule per kilogramme).

In the International System of Units replaced by the gray, equal to 100 rads.

1954 *Brit. Jrnl. Radiol.* XXVII. 243/1 The rad is the unit of absorbed dose and is 100 ergs per gramme. **1957** *Financial Times Ann. Rev. Brit. Industry* 87/2 For example, a 1,000 curie cobalt source has a total power output of 15 watts and gives a radiation intensity of the order of 100 rads per second of high penetration at a convenient operating distance. **1968** *Times* 16 Dec. 7/4 During the flight the three astronauts are expected to receive radiation doses of less than one rad a man, less than from chest X-ray series. **1971** J. Z. YOUNG *Introd. Study Man* xxviii. 393 The minimum dose of radiation that will produce a doubling of the spontaneous mutation rate is likely to be in the region of 10 rad per 30 years. **1972** 'J. LANGE' *Binary* 64 Two rad cartridges... Bars of plutonium-238 oxide. That's a radioactive isotope. **1976** *Lancet* 6 Nov. 993/1 The intended tumour dose was 4000 rads in four weeks. **1976** *Path. Ann.* XI. 368 (*caption*) Follicular thyroid carcinoma excised 26 years after approximately 700 rad were applied for enlarged tonsils and adenoids.

rad, *a.*[2] Add: Also **radd.** (Further examples.)

1861 R. QUINN *Heather Lintie* 56 We'd na be rad o' scath frae wather, Though snow was wreathin'. *a* **1870** H. S. RIDDELL *Poet Wks.* (1871) II. 250 That ye might saints and angels meet And no be rad. **1930** in *Sc. Nat. Dict.* (1968) VII. 319/3 I'm radd ye ken mair aboot youres and sick like than yer buiks.

R.A.D.A., RADA (rā·dă). Also **Rada.** [Acronym f. the initials of *R*oyal *A*cademy of *D*ramatic *A*rt, founded in 1904 and granted a royal charter in 1920.] One of the leading acting schools in Britain, at present situated in Gower Street, London. Also *attrib.*

1921 *Times* 19 July 8 (*heading*) R.A.D.A. Ex-Students First Production... The author of the play was Mr. Kenneth Barnes, Director of R.A.D.A., and his maiden effort was a worthy one. **1937** W. S. MAUGHAM *Theatre* xx. 191, I always say you're the greatest actress on the stage. I've learnt more from you than I did all the years I was at the R.A.D.A. **1949** *Listener* 21 Apr. 676/1 They were, in fact, R.A.D.A. students at play. **1962** J. BRAINE *Life at Top* iv. 68 A different voice, the voice of the red-haired girl from RADA whom now I dimly remember talking to earlier. **1965** *Observer* 19 Sept. 1/5 The new man for Rada? **1968** *Listener* 26 Dec. 873/3 The melodies are dim, the lyrics wanly snobbish, the costumes are rainwear ads and the Cockney accents (except Breeze's) RADA-provincial. **1977** L. MEYNELL *Hooky gets Wooden Spoon* xiv. 179 Sergeant Fitt could certainly have won a medal at RADA for..complete impassiveness.

Rada (rā·dă). [App. ad. *Allada*, the name of a former principality of Dahomey (now Benin).] The name of a group of deities of West African derivation venerated in Haiti; the worship of these deities. Also *attrib.*

1929 W. B. SEABROOK *Magic Island* I. i. 11, I knelt at last before the great *Rada* drums. *Ibid.* iii. 43 Some..danced, not the mad *Rada* of the night, but boisterous, gay Congo dances. **1937** M. J. HERSKOVITS *Life in Haitian Valley* viii. 149 When *vodun* deities are discussed in Mirebalais, most often two 'companies' of them are mentioned, the Rada and the Pétro 'squads'. **1941** J. G. LEYBURN *Haitian People* vii. 145 To the spirits..not drawn from Christianity the name 'loa' is applied. There seem in general to be two classes of these: those who have an African origin, and those with a Haitian background only. The former group is called 'Rada', the latter 'Petro'. **1957** *Amer. Anthropologist* LIX. 821 Members of two African-derived religions, Yoruba 'Shango'..and Dahomean 'Rada'..consider themselves also to be Roman Catholics.

radappertization (rædæ:pəɹtəizēɪ·ʃən). [f. L. *rad-iāre* to furnish with rays, shine + F. *appertization* kind of heat treatment of food (f. the name of Nicolas-François *Appert* (d. 1841), French inventor: see -IZATION).] The treatment of food with ionizing radiation so as to reduce the number of micro-organisms sufficiently to prevent future spoilage in the absence of recontamination (see quot. 1964). Cf. *RADICIDATION, *RADURIZATION.

1964 H. E. GORESLINE et al. in *Nature* 17 Oct. 237/2 Type I is the application to food of doses of ionizing radiation sufficient to reduce the number and/or activity of viable organisms to such an extent that very few, if any, are detectable in the treated food by any recognized method (viruses being excepted) while no spoilage or toxicity of microbial origin is detectable no matter how long or under what conditions the food is stored in the absence of recontamination... The following are names we suggest... Type I, radappertization. **1966** *Proc. Internat. Symp. Food Irradiation* 352 Salmonellae could be said to be moderately radiation-sensitive when bacteria are generally considered.. and therefore the dose requirement for their inactivation in food will be very much lower than that needed for radappertization (4·5–5·0 Mrad). **1975** *Appl. Microbiol.* XXX. 811 (*heading*) Low-temperature irradiation of beef and methods for evaluation of a radappertization process.

Hence **rada·ppertize** *v. trans.*, **rada·ppertized** *ppl. a.*

1974 *Jrnl. Food Sci.* XXXIX. 806 The accepted procedure for estimating the 12D dose of radappertized food has shortcomings that ought not to be ignored. **1975** *Appl. Microbiol.* XXX. 811/1 The wholesomeness of beef radappertized..with ^{60}Co gamma rays and with 10 MV electrons. **1977** *Jrnl. Food Sci.* XLII. 338 (*heading*) Variables affecting the acceptability of radappertized ground beef products.

radar (rēɪ·dāɹ). orig. *U.S.* [f. *ra*dio *d*etection *a*nd *r*anging.] **1. a.** A system for detecting the presence of objects at a distance, or ascertaining their position or motion, by transmitting short radio waves and detecting or measuring their return after being reflected; also (*secondary radar*), a similar system in which the return signal consists of radio waves that a suitably equipped target automatically transmits when it receives the outgoing waves. Cf. *RADIOLOCATION.

1941 *N.Y. Times* 18 Nov. 8/4 The Navy undertook a special enlistment campaign today to recruit men for training in maintenance of the radio device known as 'Radar', which is used to locate ships and aircraft that are hidden by fog or darkness. **1943** *News Chron.* 9 Feb. 4/6 He described Radar as 'probably the most dramatic new weapon to come out of this war'. **1943** *Times* 24 June 4/6 It is expected also to improve 'radar', the device for detecting enemy aircraft and ships. **1946** *Electronics* Apr. 130/3 Frequency-modulation radar determines the distance to a reflecting surface..by measuring the frequency shift between transmitted and reflected waves. **1957** *Economist* 7 Sept. 831 (Advt.), The performance of modern aircraft must be matched by the radio, radar and Doppler navigational aids necessary for their safe and efficient operation. **1959** K. HENNEY *Radio Engin. Handbk.* (ed. 5) xxv. 34 Secondary radar, or the ATC radar-beacon system, solves the problem of identification of the individual aircraft in air-traffic control. **1960** J. D. HAIGH *Radiolocation Techniques* xiv. 213 Another advantage of secondary radar is that if the 'responding' transmitter is made to radiate on a frequency different from that of the 'interrogating' transmitter, the received picture will be completely free from all permanent echoes and no targets other than those with responding transmitters will be seen. **1962** R. M. PAGE *Origin of Radar* i. 15 The name 'radar' was coined from the words Radio Detection *A*nd *R*anging by two U.S. Naval officers, F. R. Furth and S. M. Tucker. **1971** D. W. SCIAMA *Mod. Cosmol.* i. 2 The distance of the Sun is determined most accurately by radar. **1977** C. MCCULLOUGH *Thorn Birds* xvii. 451 The field which had fascinated him since he first got acquainted with radar: electronics.

b. (An) apparatus or an installation used for this system.

1945 *Electronics* Apr. 92/1 The free-space radar equation relates the power radiated from the radar..to the power delivered to the terminals of the receiver. **1945** *Proc. IRE* XXXIII. 740/2 An army radar, the SCR-270, gave warning of the impending attack on Pearl Harbor. **1959** K. HENNEY *Radio Engin. Handbk.* (ed. 5) xxv. 34 Present-day precision approach radars look only 20 deg in azimuth and 6 deg in elevation. **1967** *Listener* 9 Feb. 185/3 A 'thin area defence' for the whole United States, consisting of a dozen Spartan batteries and the relevant radars, would cost about $4,000 million. **1971** *Sci. Amer.* Oct. 73 (Advt.), APQ-140 is a digitally controlled phased array radar system that does the job formerly requiring several radars. **1977** *Navy News* Aug. 34 (Advt.), We're working on a wide variety of radars for applications throughout the world.

c. *fig.* An intuitive perception or sense of awareness attributed to or regarded as a characteristic of a person.

1950 'D. DIVINE' *King of Fassarai* xxix. 262 Thirty-kid power radar. Nothing ever gets by 'em. **1959** *Listener* 1 Jan. 31/3 With that political radar with which all good Levantine rulers are endowed, he succeeded for years. **1975** D. M. DAVIN *Closing Times* vi. 142 With that radar sense of quality that governed his taste in poetry and other people's clothes, he chose her own favourite scarf. **1976** P. ALEXANDER *Death of Thin-Skinned Animal* xviii. 183 That's what Joan thinks..intuition, female radar, or maybe she read it in the tea-leaves.

d. *transf.*

1963 [see *LIDAR]. **1974** *Physics Bull.* Jan. 11/2 Like ordinary radar, laser radar is based on the detection of a signal scattered from some object. If a laser beam is emitted into the atmosphere, some of the radiation will be absorbed by atmospheric molecules, some will be scattered by them.. and some will be scattered by aerosols. **1974** *Sci. Amer.* Mar. 83/2 One of the more promising instruments is an acoustic-radar detector, in which a noise signal is transmitted from the ground and is deflected by interaction with the vortex.

2. *attrib.* and *Comb.* *radar altimeter, astronomy, beam, dish* [*DISH *sb.* 4 b], *echo, equation, equipment, eye, operator, reconnaissance, set, signal, station, system*; *radar-controlled, -directed* ppl. adjs.; *radar-ranging* vbl. sb.; **Radar Alley** (see quot. 1971); **radar beacon,** a radio transmitter that automatically transmits a return signal when it receives a signal from a radar transmitter; *esp.* one that transmits a coded signal enabling it to be identified; **radar fence,** a line of radar stations for giving warning of intrusions into the air space behind it; **radar man, radarman,** a man trained to operate radar equipment; **radar map,** a map compiled from radar observations; hence **radar-map** *v. trans.*, **-mapping** *vbl. sb.*; **radar net,** a network of radar stations, esp. a radar fence; **radar picket,** a picket-ship specially equipped with radar; **radar plotter,** one who plots the direction and course of objects from radar observations; **radar scanner,** a rotatable aerial for transmitting and receiving radar signals; **radar screen,** the screen of a radarscope; also *fig.*; **radar-sonde,** a sonde which can be tracked by radar so that information on the wind may be obtained as well as the usual meteorological information; **radar speed detector, trap,** etc. = **radar trap*; **radar-track** *v. trans.*, to track by radar; also *fig.*; **radar trap,** a speed trap in which speed is measured using radar and the Doppler effect.

1971 M. TAK *Truck Talk* 127 *Radar Alley*, Interstate 90, between Cleveland and the New York line; so named because of the numerous radar traps set on the road. **1976** PERKÖWSKI & STRAL *Joy of CB* 174 The name of Radar Alley..aptly applies to the Ohio Turnpike..that is heavily patrolled by bears. **1946** *Electronics* Apr. 130/2 A detailed description of an f-m radar altimeter may now be given, following the declassification of the model AN/APN-1 altimeter. **1951** *Jrnl. Brit. Interplanetary Soc.* X. 101 This means a vertical descent using reverse rocket braking in conjunction with a radar-altimeter and landing legs. **1978** *Nature* 10 Aug. 540/1 Balloon-borne radar altimeters have also been used to map surface topography in Antarctica. **1959** DAVIES & PALMER *Radio Studies of Universe* i. 3 This discovery laid the foundation for the second branch of the science of radio astronomy, that of radar astronomy which probes the nearest inhabitants in space—the meteors, moon and planets—using the radio-echo technique. **1969** *Sci. News Yearbk.* 83 Radar astronomy had done particularly well with its studies of nearer planets, especially Venus. **1945** *Electronic Engin.* XVII. 685/2 By this means our airborne forces were enabled to direct themselves to any given point in hostile country where an advance party had already installed a 'Radar beacon'. **1958** *Listener* 13 Nov. 779/1 Navigational aids, such as radio stations and radar beacons, are few. **1959** [see sense 1 a above]. **1965** D. K. BARTON in R. S. Berkowitz *Mod. Radar* ii. 12 A modern radar beacon weighing a few pounds can receive signals 100 db below 1 watt and retransmit them as 100-watt pulses, providing tremendous range extension. **1958** *Times* 9 Oct. 10/2 When the rockets burn out,..the missile coasts to the target, riding along the centre of a radar beam which is directed by the pilot of the launching aircraft. **1959** N. MAILER *Advts. for Myself* (1961) 183 The other-directed man is flexible... His movement is 'radar-controlled',..his 'taste' rather than his work the primary concern... He obeys 'the process of paying close attention to the signals from others'. **1978** R. V. JONES *Most Secret War* xxxi. 265 He also concluded that some of the lights were radar-controlled. **1947** CROWTHER & WHIDDINGTON *Science at War* 75 H.M.S. *Warspite* fired her first radar-directed broadside. **1952** *Electronic Engin.* XXIV. 126/1 A 3 centimetre radar installation with a V.H.F., D.F. receiver, the radar dish being mounted on a common rotatable shaft with the D.F. aerial. **1969** *New Yorker* 11 Oct. 51/1 In the gaunt shade of oil rigs and radar dishes. **1946** *Electronic Engin.* XVIII. 149/2 The technique of setting the calibration pip against the radar echo is one which gives surprisingly accurate results. **1962** F. I. ORDWAY et al. *Basic Astronautics* iii. 65 The first radar echoes were returned from the Moon in 1946. **1945** D. G. FINK in *Electronics* Apr. 92/1 The basic factors concerned are the formation and propagation of radio beams, and the reflection of radio waves when they encounter a sudden change in the electrical properties of the transmission medium... The equation which links these factors may be termed appropriately the radar equation. **1966** *McGraw-Hill Encycl. Sci. & Technol.* XI. 200/2 The strength of echo signals is related to the parameters of the radar system by the radar equation. **1944** *Jrnl. R. Aeronaut. Soc.* XLVIII. 103 Tests of various wireless and Radar equipment. **1976** *Daily Mirror* 16 July 2/2 The cases are believed to contain aircraft parts and radar equipment. **1957** R. WATSON-WATT *Three Steps to Victory* xliii. 249 British fighters could entrust themselves to the..far-seeing radar-eye. **1977** *R.A.F. News* 5–18 Jan. 9/1 The Shackleton airborne early warning aircraft of Lossiemouth's 8 Squadron..act as airborne radar eyes searching for low-flying aircraft. **1948** *Sat. Even. Post* 21 Aug. 27/1 There are wide gaps in the Soviet radar fence. Russia is too huge to be rimmed completely with twirling antennas. **1957** R. WATSON-WATT *Three Steps to Victory* (*caption to plate facing p.* 320) The 350 ft. steel lattice masts on 'T' site. Combined with ultra-short-wave-radiation these ensured that the outer edge of the radar fence could be set far enough from the British coasts. **1942** *Radio-Craft* Jan.–Feb. 332/1 'Radar' men will operate the newly perfected radio device which locates planes in flight. **1946** P. CARTER in Aldiss & Harrison *Decade 1940's* (1975) 109 He was at once geologist, radarman, vibration expert and navigator. **1966** M. WOODHOUSE *Tree Frog* x. 75 Pzenica, the radar man from Poland, was standing over me. **1977** *R.A.F. News* 5–18 Jan. 8/2 The Buchan radarmen help to look after the safety of these fliers. **1960** *Sci. Amer.* Aug. 59/1 The radar mapping experiment marks the first trial of this technique. *Ibid.* 59/2 (*caption*) Radar map of the moon. **1962** F. I. ORDWAY et al. *Basic Astronautics* iii. 65 In January, 1960, a preliminary radar map of the Moon was made from 440 mc observations performed with the 84-ft antenna at Millstone Hill, in Massachusetts. **1970** *New Scientist* 19 Feb. 361/1 Each Victor can radar-map the entire Mediterranean in one seven-hour sortie. **1948** *Sun* (Baltimore) 3 June 2/3 Representative Vinson (D., Ga.) introduced a bill to authorize construction of a radar net along the coasts of the United States and Alaska. **1964** G. LYALL *Most Dangerous Game* vi. 48 The border could be flown all right... The Finns didn't have a complete radar net along it, and most pilots knew just where the Finnish radar stations were. **1945** *Yank* 5 Oct. 16/3 Radar operators and observers were known as 'radio operators'. **1967** L. B. ARCHER in Wills & Yearsley *Handbk. Management Technol.* vii. 129 Some of the early experiments [in ergonomics] were to determine the best spacing of markings on instrument dials so that the pilot or gunner or radar operator could read them rapidly and accurately. **1952** *Jane's Fighting Ships 1952–53* p. vii, Among the recent U.S. photographs added to this issue are those of the..radar picket *William T. Powell*. **1966** *McGraw-Hill Encycl. Sci. & Technol.* XII. 264/2 Some U.S. Navy destroyers are specially fitted as radar pickets, and some British ones as aircraft fighter directors. **1957** *Technology* Dec. 358/3 This new principle of design may be contrasted with the old by considering the radar plotter tracking targets on his radar tube. **1978** R. V. JONES *Most Secret War* xxiii. 196 She..had been taken on with two other girls at Bawdsey by Watson-Watt to see whether girls would make good radar-plotters. **1976** *Sci. Amer.* Feb. 51/1 The second astronomical experiment consists of precise radar-ranging measurements of the distance between the earth and the inner planets Mercury and Venus. **1959** *Daily Tel.* 7 Mar. 7/3 An area equal to the whole of the Mediterranean could be covered in a single radar reconnaissance by one aircraft. **1946** *Electronics* Oct. 35 (Advt.), Aircraft radar scanner. **1947** *Daily Progress* (Charlottesville, Va.) 15 Dec. 2/3 New radar scanner to watch the skies for airplanes approaching New York airport is now in experimental operation. **1976** 'A. YORK' *Dark Passage* xiii. 164 Her radio aerial and the radar scanner on her wheelhouse roof remained visible. **1945** *Instruments* XVIII. 745/1 Its beam-splitter..allows operator to view radar reflection in normal manner while image on radar screen is reflected up into camera. **1958** *New Statesman* 18 Jan. 64/1 What is needed is 'patience': the West is to sit behind the radar screens and rocket bases waiting for a change of heart, and perhaps a change of regime, in Russia. **1977** J. BINGHAM *Marriage Bureau Murders* v. 58 He was reluctant to switch from thinking about her... He kept her within the radar screen of his mind. **1946** *Electronic Engin.* XVIII. 2 The operation of a Radar set as a position finder. **1947** *Daily Mail* 22 May 3/6 Radar sets which will 'see' through fog are to be fitted in long-distance passenger trains as soon as materials are available. **1969** *Times* 25 Mar. 12/6 By bouncing radar signals off Venus, scientists from the United States have counted the numbers of electrons in the space between the planets. **1949** *Jrnl. R. Aeronaut. Soc.* LIII. 441/1 At T.R.E. the wind-finding responder is being adapted for use as a 'radarsonde', meteorological instruments to measure pressure, temperature and humidity being mounted towards the top of the responder. **1956** *Nature* 17 Mar. 520/1 Progress was made in the measurement of solar radiation and in the development of the new radar-sonde. **1957** *Times* 4 Oct. 6/4 A London electronics engineer described to Leyland magistrates to-day the effects of laboratory and outside tests he had carried out on a radar speed detector to assess the effects of extraneous sources on the accuracy of the instrument. **1962** *Daily Tel.* 22 May 24/6 [He] complained through his solicitor that police radar speed traps were 'un-British' when he was fined £10..for speeding... Police said Cadbury went through a radar speed check at 58 mph. **1971** *Observer* 26 Sept. 9/5 Radar speed traps are being planned for a 60-mile stretch of the River Nene..to stop boats from exceeding the seven m.p.h. limit. **1945** *Times* 15 Aug. 5/6 By December 1935, the experimental work was sufficiently advanced for the Air Ministry to decide on establishing a chain of five radar stations on the east coast of England... This was the first operational radar system installed anywhere in the world. **1958** *New Statesman* 22 Feb. 223/2 Radar stations at sea picked up 'blips' suggesting that an air armada was flying at 2,000 mph towards the interior of the United States. **1978** R. V. JONES *Most Secret War* xxiii. 196 It happened that this sortie was also plotted by a German radar station north-west of Brest. **1945** Radar system [see *radar station* above]. **1956** *Tuscaloosa* (Alabama) *News* 31 July 11/6 The Italian Line said the Doria radar-tracked the oncoming Stockholm before the fatal crash. **1973** M. AMIS *Rachel Papers* 24, I felt a hand traverse the lower areas of my back. In seconds—radar-tracked by my whisker-sensitive pubic hairs—it was treading air above my groin. **1962** *Punch* 18 July 74/3 A motorist has been acquitted of a speeding charge because the radar trap that provided the evidence against him could not be put on oath. **1975** *Globe & Mail* (Toronto) 4 June 1/6 A check with the radar trap involved showed the limousine was doing a mere 71 miles an hour in a 70-mile-an-hour zone.

radarscope (rēⁱ·dɑːskōᵘp). Also **radar scope.** [f. *RADAR + -SCOPE.] A cathode-ray oscilloscope on the screen of which radar echoes are represented for observation; also, the screen itself.

1948 *Nat. Geographic Mag.* Feb. 255/1 Then an operator 'talks them down', watching each plane on the radarscope. **1958** *Observer* 22 June 12/6 The future of mankind might lie at the mercy of an officer reading a radarscope in the Canadian Arctic, who might conceivably mistake an electronic storm..for the trajectory of a Soviet I.C.B.M. **1959** K. HENNEY *Radio Engin. Handbk.* (ed. 5) xxv. 34 Precision Approach Radar... Distance, bearing, and elevation above ground are presented continuously on the face of the radar scope. **1966** M. WOODHOUSE *Tree Frog* xxi. 154, I can never stand by a radarscope..without recalling the Rubaiyat; the moving Finger writes. **1972** *Sci. Amer.* Jan. 52/3 The image..is a direct representation of the scene ahead of the driver rather than the usual maplike plan view of the radarscope.

Radcliffian (rædkli·fiăn), *a.* Also **Radcliffean.** [f. the name of (Mrs.) Ann *Radcliffe* (1764–1823), English 'Gothic' novelist.] Of or characteristic of Mrs. Radcliffe or her works.

1801 M. EDGEWORTH *Belinda* II. xx. 265 Here is a Radcliffean tour along the picturesque coasts of Dorset and Devonshire. **1884** *Spectator* 19 Jan. 91/1 There is, too, a Radcliffian eeriness about his castle, with its mysterious noises, secret passages, and buried rooms. **1931** *Times Lit. Suppl.* 26 Feb. 151/3 The 'Radcliffian' novel, or *roman noir*, as the French call it. **1966** *English Studies* XLVII. 287 But symbol, action, and the perceiving sensibility. add to the Radcliffean question, 'what is the mystery of the veil?'

raddle, *v.*² (Later example.)

1966 J. F. H. THOMAS *Sheep Farming Today* v. 57 Recently there has been introduced a breast harness device which holds a colour marking crayon on rams in lieu of raddling their breast wool with colour.

raddled, *ppl. a.*² Add: (Further examples.) Also *fig.*, worn, worn out.

1901 W. BARRY *Wizard's Knot* vii. 74 Raddled like scabby sheep with red paint. **1922** GALSWORTHY *In Chancery* II. vii. 621 An 'old Johnny' in a gown and long wig, looking awfully like a funny raddled woman, came through a door. **1922** JOYCE *Ulysses* 96 Outside them and through them ran raddled sheep bleating their fear. **1969** *Listener* 30 Jan. 156/2 Ruth Gordon's Minnie might be a typical New York eccentric, a raddled Carmen Miranda. **1975** *Nature* 28 Aug. 738/2 They were all kept in identical conditions of housing and management, and oestrus was detected by raddled vasectomised rams at 0900 daily. **1978** *Time* 3 July 10/3 By day she rests, and her face, without makeup, softens but still retains the raddled quality of hard living.

raddling (ræ·dliŋ), *vbl. sb.* [f. RADDLE *v.*² + -ING¹.] The action of marking sheep with raddle, or some other red substance.

c **1873** J. ALBERY *Fortune* III, in *Dramatic Wks.* (1939) I. 574 Mark 'em [*sc.* sheep] all with two red letters, Johnny; they always do that;—raddling they call it, I think.

radiæsthesia, etc., varr. *RADIESTHESIA, etc.

radial, *a.* and *sb.* Add: **A.** *adj.* **2. d.** *Bot.* and *Timber.* Applied to a longitudinal section or cut along a radius or diameter, and to the surface so exposed. Also as *adv.*, as *radial-sawn* adj.

1881 J. S. GAMBLE *Man. Indian Timbers* 175 Medullary rays fine, equidistant, prominent on a radial section. **1924** HOLMAN & ROBBINS *Textbk. Gen. Bot.* iv. 104 The annual rings appear in radial section as more or less parallel bands which impart to the wood its characteristic grain. **1938** H. E. DESCH *Timber* ii. 19 The rays are usually just visible to the naked eye on radial surfaces, where they appear as narrow, horizontal ribbons. **1958** *N.Z. Timber Jrnl.* Apr. 61/2 Radial sawn. **1969** H. L. EDLIN *What Wood is That?* i. 20 (*caption*) The radial cut through a birch-log, which splits it into two, becomes convex after seasoning. **1972** H. J. DITTMER *Mod. Plant Biol.* viii. 151 Radial or quarter-sawed wood is taken through the radius of the log.

e. Of a road, route, etc.: running directly from the centre of a town or city to an outlying district (usu. as part of a system of such roads). Hence also used of transport services using such routes.

[**1909** H. I. TRIGGS *Town Planning* ii. 88 In cities laid out upon the radial system, the radiating streets form as it were the skeleton of the system.] **1937** [see *parkway* s.v. *PARK *sb.* 7]. **1942** *Policy on Rotary Intersections* (Amer. Assoc. State Highway Officials) 1 Each road approaching a rotary hereafter is called 'radial road'. **1948** T. SHARP *Oxford Replanned* 7 *Radials.* Oxford has a highly developed pattern of radial roads which all centre on Carfax. **1957** *Encycl. Brit.* XXII. 335 Wren suggested the use of radial streets integrated with the rectangular plotting of intervening areas, broad streets and location of industry outside the city limits. **1976** P. R. WHITE *Planning for Public Transport* v. 93 The major growth during the twentieth century was in improvement of principal radial roads beyond the limit of the then built-up areas, and construction of bypasses or ring roads. *Ibid.* 106 Even on the radial Green Line Services, the heaviest loads are often between inner and outer suburban centres.

3. c. *radial engine*, a type of internal-combustion engine (used chiefly in aircraft) having its cylinders fixed radially around a rotating crankshaft. Hence *radial-engined* adj.

1909 R. KENNEDY *Flying Machines* vii. 115 Miesse aeromotor: 8-cylinder radial engine, having the cylinders arranged in pairs and in an horizontal position. **1934** *Discovery* Dec. 353/1 The tendency in Great Britain is to develop both types, the large in-line engine being composed of four banks of cylinders forming an H, and the corresponding radial engines with two circles of cylinders one immediately behind the other. **1942** *R.A.F. Jrnl.* 16 May 14/1 Single-seat, low-wing, radial-engined monoplane fighters..are standardised by the Army. **1963** BIRD & HUTTON-STOTT *Veteran Motor Car* 21 The interesting radial-engined Enfield–Allday. **1971** L. J. K. SETRIGHT *Power to Fly* vi. 162 Each of the 9 cylinder banks had its own overhead camshaft, a most uncommon luxury in radial engines.

d. Also *radial-ply*. Denoting a tyre in which the layers of fabric are laid with the cords running at right angles to the circumference of the tyre, and the tread is strengthened by further layers of fabric running round the circumference. Also *ellipt.* as *sb.*

1964 *Economist* 26 Sept. 1191/2 British manufacturers have shied away..from buying components at more than minimal cost. They are changing their attitudes..with the advent of the radial-ply tyre, whose greater expense is.. compensated for by better wear. *Ibid.* 1254/1 Firestone has been experimenting with fibreglass cords for radials. **1966** *Ibid.* 22 Oct. 388/2 Michelin, pioneers of radial-plies, have yet another new tyre. **1967** *Autocar* 5 Oct. 19/2 Radial tyres..add appreciably to the car's safety margin, especially in the wet. **1971** *Guardian* 23 Mar. 18/4 Patents for radial-ply tyre design were first registered in about 1912. It was not until 36 years later that Michelin..introduced the first radial for commercial sale. **1972** *Practical Motorist* Oct. 82/1 Since July 1 it has been illegal to fit a cross-ply tyre and a radial on the same axle. **1972** C. WESTON *Poor, Poor Ophelia* (1973) viii. 42 His car whirled up, radial tires singing on the glossy pavement. **1976** *Field* 18 Nov. 1021 (Advt.), The..radial ply tyres produce a very peaceful ride.

4. c. *radial-flow* adj.: being or employing a turbine, pump, or the like in which fluid is forced to move at right angles to an axis of rotation.

1881 *Encycl. Brit.* XII. 527/1 For radial flow turbines the wheel may have the form A or B, fig. 191, A being most usual with inward, and B with outward flow turbines. **1914** W. M. WALLACE *Hydraulics* vii. 101 It is usual to designate turbines as radial flow or parallel flow according as the water flows in a radial or axial direction through the wheel. **1958** *Technology* Mar. 29/3 The basic principles of the Derwent, radial-flow, jet engine are described. **1972** J. M. K. DAKE *Essentials of Engin. Hydraulics* vi. 160 The centrifugal pump and the Francis turbine are examples of radial flow reaction machines.

d. *Astr. radial velocity*, the velocity of a star or other body along the line of sight of an observer.

1895 *Nature* 13 June 155/2 (*heading*) Measurement of radial velocities. **1930** R. H. BAKER *Astron.* viii. 315 Radial velocities of the stars up to 30 km./sec.. are usual. **1966** J. D. KRAUS *Radio Astron.* viii. 353 The wisps of nebulosity show a large radial velocity of over 5,000 km sec⁻¹, indicating a rapid expansion. **1977** F. N. BASH *Astron.* iii. 67 The Doppler effect..gives astronomers a way of measuring radial velocity.

e. *Physical Geogr.* Of (a pattern of) drainage: being or involving a pattern of streams flowing outwards from a central dome or other elevated region.

[**1910** LAKE & RASTALL *Text-bk. Geol.* iv. 86 The arrangement of the principal valleys, in most of which are considerable lakes, is distinctly radial.] **1932** W. H. EMMONS et al. *Geol.* vi. 106 (*caption*) A radial stream pattern developed on the surface of the dome-like uplift of the Black Hills in South Dakota. **1939** A. K. LOBECK *Geomorphol.* xv. 513 A radial drainage pattern is characteristic of very young and undissected domes. **1954** W. D. THORNBURY *Princ. Geomorphol.* v. 126 In radial patterns,..the individual stream patterns may well be dendritic or pinnate, and radial designates more their arrangement with respect to each other than it does the stream pattern. **1969** *Geography* LIV. 199 The almost perfect radial drainage developed on the andesite volcano of Mount Egmont.

6. *radial energy*: in the writings of Teilhard de Chardin, a form of energy postulated to be independent of the conventional laws of thermodynamics and to tend to produce increasing organization and complexity in both the physical and spiritual worlds; it was held to be manifest, for example, in the evolution of living organisms and in the development of ideas. Cf. **tangential energy*. [Introduced in Fr. *c* 1938 in *Le Phénomène Humain* (1956) 62.]

1959 B. WALL et al. tr. *Teilhard de Chardin's Phenomenon of Man* I. ii. 65 In each particular element this fundamental energy is divided into two distinct components: a tangential energy which links the element with all others of the same order (that is to say, of the same complexity and the same centricity) as itself in the universe; and a radial energy which draws it towards ever greater complexity and centricity—in other words forwards. *Ibid.* iii. 72 Spiritual energy, by its very nature, increases in 'radial' value, positively, absolutely, and without determinable limits, in step with the increasing chemical complexity of the elements of which it represents the inner lining. **1965** *Listener* 15 Apr. 558/2 We really need different kinds of language to deal with the concepts proper to biology and those proper to thermodynamics. One thinks at once of Teilhard's brilliant pioneering neologisms, such as 'radial' and 'tangential' energy, phrases devised precisely to meet some at least of the difficulties. **1969** A. RICHARDSON *Dict. Christian Theol.* 333/1 It is through increase in radial energy that decisive 'critical points' are reached, whether, for example, at the molecular level or at the leap from instinct to thought.

B. *sb.* Restrict subject-label *Anat.* to senses in Dict. and add: **4.** *Aeronaut.* A radial engine.

1920 G. C. BAILEY *Complete Airman* xii. 93 The rotary is very similar in appearance to the radial. **1944** P. H. WILKINSON *Aircraft Engines of World* 44 The M-11 engine is a 100 h.p. 5-cylinder air-cooled radial which is used in secondary training planes. **1960** C. H. GIBBS-SMITH *Aeroplane* xiv. 110 The 247..was powered by two 550-h.p. Pratt and Whitney *Wasp* radials.

5. a. A radial road or route. **b.** *Canad.* A train or tram running on a radial route.

1948 [see sense A. 2 e above]. **1966** *Globe & Mail* (Toronto) 12 Sept. 16 (*caption*) The radials: commuter dream of the auto killed. **1972** J. MOSHER *Adultery* III. xiv. 134 Father had already gone off on the half-past six radial.

6. (See quot. 1956.)

1956 W. A. HEFLIN *U.S.A.F. Dict.* 417/2 *Radial*, any one of a number of lines of position radiating from an azimuthal radio-navigation facility,..identified in terms of the bearing of all points along that line from the facility. **1971** *Flying*

Apr. 42/2 Then via the Coyle 270 radial until intersecting the 113 radial of Modena. **1972** R. L. TAYLOR *Instrument Flying* viii. 114 The number that now appears under the OBS index is your course to the station (inbound it will always be the reciprocal of the radial you are on).

7. A radial-ply tyre (see sense A. 3 d above).

radiance. Add: **3.** The radiant flux emitted by unit area of a source into unit solid angle.

1917 H. E. IVES in *Astrophysical Jrnl.* XLV. 43 If now we divide this radiant intensity in any direction by the projected area of the opening in that direction.., we obtain the specific radiant intensity or radiance in that direction. *Ibid.* 48 'Radiance', as a time-saving word for 'specific radiant intensity', is frankly taken from the dictionary, as the appropriate synonym for 'brightness'. **1944** *Jrnl. Optical Soc. Amer.* XXXIV. 253/2 The luminance of any surface is the product of the radiance of that surface by the absolute luminosity *K* of the energy radiated by the surface. **1951** [see *luminosity curve]. **1972** *Science* 22 Sept. 1100/1 Radiance gradients determined from data gathered by the infrared spectrometers aboard the Nimbus III and Nimbus IV satellites.

radiant, *a.* and *sb.* Add: **A.** *adj.* **1. d.** Designed to send out radiant heat.

1936 FABER & KELLS *Heating & Air-Conditioning* iv. 81 The warming effect of convectors is slower than with the radiant type of heater. **1936** *Economist* 28 Mar. 738/1 Our High Beam fires have proved to be the most efficient radiant gas fires in the world. **1951** *Good Housek. Home Encycl.* 35/2 More recently the use of 'radiant radiators'..has become more common. **1957** *Heating, Ventilating, Air Conditioning Guide* XXXV. 399 Radiant heaters..have a refractory directly above the burners which is heated to incandescence. **1962** *Listener* 13 Sept. 411/3 It [*sc.* an electric cooker] has two radiant plates. **1964** J. J. BARTON *Heating & Ventilating* xii. 318 The principal heat requirements are provided by convection, with a small radiant unit providing sufficient beamed heat for topping-up. **1977** *Direct Electric Heating* (Electricity Council) v. 21/1 Direct electric heating appliances and equipment... They may be divided into four basic groups, namely—(i) Low intensity radiant systems incorporated in the building fabric. (ii) Individual radiant-convector units. (iii) Forced warm air systems. (iv) Hot water radiator systems.

3. Also *radiant heating*; *radiant-heated* adj.

1912 *Cassier's Mag.* XLI. 569/1 (*heading*) Radiant heating. *Ibid.* 570/1 The demonstrations were continued..at the experimental works of the Radiant Heating Syndicate. **1962** *Punch* 24 Jan. 178/2 The 'tropical radiant-heated indoor pool'. **1966** *McGraw-Hill Encycl. Sci. & Technol.* XI. 213/1 Any radiant-heating system using a fluid heat conveyor may be employed as a cooling system by substituting cold water or other cold fluid.

b. *radiant efficiency*, the ratio of the radiant flux emitted to the power consumed; *radiant energy*, energy in the form of (usu. electromagnetic) radiation; *radiant flux*, the rate of flow of radiant energy; *radiant power* = *radiant flux* above.

1914 *Rep. Brit. Assoc. Adv. Sci. 1913* 435 The true remedy must be sought for in increasing the 'radiant efficiency' of the [gas] fire. *Ibid.* 436 Part of the radiant energy is directly determined..by using a radiation calorimeter. **1917** *Astrophysical Jrnl.* XLV. 44 Through this space radiant energy is passing at a certain rate. This rate constitutes the radiant flux through the space. **1923** *Sci. Papers U.S. Bureau of Standards* No. 475. 132 The ratio of luminosity to radiant power—the luminous efficiency. **1932** HARDY & PERRIN *Princ. Optics* i. 19 If the human eye were uniformly sensitive to radiation of all wave lengths, the radiant power expressed in watts would provide an adequate method of evaluating the flux. **1936** FABER & KELL *Heating & Air-Conditioning of Buildings* iv. 74 Their [*sc.* gas fires'] radiant efficiency is about 50 per cent. (with an additional 10 per cent. convection). **1944** *Jrnl. Optical Soc. Amer.* XXXIV. 252/2 When radiant flux is evaluated with respect to its capacity to evoke the brightness attribute of visual sensation it is called luminous flux. **1970** M. V. KLEIN *Optics* iv. 121 The radiant energy density..is the radiant energy contained in a unit volume of space. Radiant power or radiant flux..is the time rate of change, or rate of transfer, of radiant energy.

B. *sb.* **1. b.** Each of the units in a radiant fire that are designed to radiate heat.

1914 *Rep. Brit. Assoc. Adv. Sci. 1913* 436 A little later a more marked step in the evolution of the new radiating fire consisted in joining the two or three fireclay pieces into one, and thus making the firefront consist of a series of hollow fireclay columns (now known as radiants). **1936** *Economist* 28 Mar. 738/1 Our 'Thermo-XX Beam' radiant..was the first radiant designed to emit an increased proportion of short infra-red rays, and its introduction marked a new stage in the development of the gas fire. **1953** 'N. SHUTE' *In Wet* 173 They sat down in arm chairs before the radiants of the electric fire. **1958** *Woman's Journal* Mar. 20/2, I..sat down by my hissing gas fire. One of the radiants was missing.

radiantly, *adv.* Add: **3.** By means of radiant energy.

1948 R. W. SHOEMAKER *Radiant Heating* i. 11 A radiantly heated room.

radiata. Add: **2.** [a. the specific epithet of *Pinus radiata* (D. Don 1837, in *Trans. Linn. Soc.* XVII. 442).] In full, *radiata pine*: = *INSIGNIS, *Monterey pine* s.v. MONTEREY in Dict. and Suppl.

1953 *N.Z. Jrnl. Forestry* V. 374 The development of major industries, dependent wholly or substantially on radiata pine as a basic raw material, is well advanced. **1959** A. MCLINTOCK *Descr. Atlas N.Z.* p. xiii, Plantation and shelter belts of introduced (exotic) trees, mainly radiata pine and macrocarpa, break up the farmlands. **1963** *Times* 11 Feb. 9/1 At Kaingaroa..273,000 acres of radiata pines were planted during the depression. **1972** *Daily Colonist* (Victoria, B.C.) 24 May 5/4 It was found, however, that the radiata pine (Monterey pine) would flourish in this otherwise 'dead' [volcanic] soil. **1973** T. E. SIMPSON *Kauri to Radiata* vii. 310 By 1959 radiata would have achieved prominence in sawn output over that of our indigenous timbers.

radiate, *sb.* Add: **3.** A classical coin with rays issuing from the device.

1939 *Oxoniensia* IV. 61 The coins discovered during the exploration of the Cemetery are listed below... 1 Radiate *Antoninianus.* **1974** *Sci. Amer.* Dec. 122/3 The radiate was by then [*sc.* A.D. 301] reckoned to be equal to two of the seldom-seen *denarii.*

radiate, *v.* Add: **1. b.** More widely, to emit energy of any kind in the form of rays or waves.

1927 I. B. CRANDALL *Theory of Vibrating Systems & Sound* ii. 55 Dissipation due to radiation is usually of much greater importance than dissipation due to friction in the neck of the resonator, provided the resonator is so situated that it can radiate. **1960** *Practical Wireless* XXXVI. 414/2 The VHF transmitter also radiates during daylight but continues throughout the hours of darkness. **1962** A. NISBETT *Technique Sound Studio* iii. 64 Remembering that it is the soundboard that is radiating, an alternative is to move the piano well away from the wall and stand the microphone on a chair at the back. **1978** *Nature* 2 Mar. 37/1 The ability of degenerate dwarfs..to radiate at X-ray wavelengths has created much theoretical interest.

3. d. *Biol.* Of an animal or plant group, to spread from its area of greatest concentration into new habitats.

1923 F. W. JONES *Mammals S. Austral.* I. 24 A stock will become progressively altered by adaptation to its environment as it radiates from its centre of domicile. **1949** W. C. ALLEE et al. *Princ. Animal Ecol.* xxxiv. 661/1 The Australian marsupials..radiated into a great variety of habitats. **1957** P. J. DARLINGTON *Zoogeogr.* ii. 58 Over a longer period of time, the whole of the Ostariophysi may have radiated from the Old World tropics. **1978** *Sci. Amer.* Sept. 111/1 Many of the early amphibian lineages developed rather large body sizes and radiated into the available habitats, becoming herbivores and predators on many food items in aquatic, semiaquatic and terrestrial settings.

4. a. More widely, to emit (energy of any kind) in the form of rays or waves. Also with *away*.

1937 *Discovery* Nov. 331/1 It is possible that the Baird video transmitter..will be removed to Birmingham, since only small alterations would be required to make it radiate the signals generated by Marconi-E.M.I. cameras. **1971** *Nature* 29 Jan. 304/1 The compactness of the hot plasma cloud suggests that it is probably gravitationally confined and, as the thermal energy is radiated away in a fraction of a second, continuously replenished in some way. **1978** *Ibid.* 27 Apr. 784/2 Stars radiate their heat away, and must burn nuclear fuel to keep going.

c. To transmit (radio waves); to broadcast.

1923 *Radio Times* 28 Sept. 12/3 A ninety-minute excerpt ..will be simultaneously radiated from all other stations. **1951** *Times* 4 Jan. 7/6 Items, mainly music, are selected from one of the three home services. They are radiated simultaneously by a 25-kw. frequency modulated (f.m.) transmitter..and a standard amplitude modulated transmitter. **1956** *B.B.C. Handbk. 1957* 59 Thirty-nine high-power, short-wave transmitters..radiate the BBC's External Services programmes. **1967** *Listener* 30 Mar. 423/3 All three programmes in the United Kingdom will eventually be radiated in colour on 625 lines. **1972** *Radio Times* 28 Sept. 42/1 World News is also radiated on medium waves.

radiation. Add: **1. b.** In mod. use (usu. in *sing.*), energy transmitted in the form of rays, waves, or sub-atomic particles; in non-*techn.* use *spec.* ionizing radiation. (Further examples.)

1896 *Strand Mag.* July 108/1 If a solid object is placed in the path of this [negative] stream..it may become the seat of the production of that..which is variously known as Röntgen radiation or X-radiation. At the solid object the new radiation springs into being, and then travels away from it in all directions, in very much the same way that ordinary light would do. **1899** *Phil. Mag.* XLVII. 109 The remarkable radiation emitted by uranium and its compounds has been studied by its discoverer, Becquerel. **1934** H. M. VERNON *Princ. Heating & Ventilation* iii. 50 The intensity of the radiation from a coal fire varies enormously. **1958** *New Statesman* 25 Oct. 545/3 This week's inquest on the second serviceman to die after the Christmas Island tests reveals once more the astonishing medical and scientific ignorance of the effects of radiation. **1962** A. NISBETT *Technique Sound Studio* iii. 52 With stringed instruments, very little of the sound we hear is directly from the strings; what we are actually listening to is the radiation from a sounding board to which the strings are coupled. **1966** *McGraw-Hill Encycl. Sci. & Technol.* XIV. 265/2 The trapped radiation consists of protons and electrons constrained to bound orbits by the geomagnetic field. **1972** *Daily Tel.* (Colour Suppl.) 3 Mar. 17 Our planet is constantly being bombarded by all kinds of radiation—from natural radio waves to infra-red, visible light, ultraviolet, X-rays and gamma radiation. **1978** *Sci. Amer.* July 82/1 Although bees are most sensitive to ultraviolet radiation, it is not the color that they learn best. To the bee ultraviolet radiation is sky radiation, and it seems not to be expected as a pure color at food sources.

2. In mod. use, the emission of energy of any kind in the form of rays or waves, esp. electromagnetic waves. (Further examples.)

1908 C. C. F. MONCKTON *Radio-Telegr.* iv. 69 There will be a certain amount of radiation possibly from the tree back towards the radiator, and a consequent distortion of the field. **1934** *Discovery* Dec. 347/2 The noise in aeroplanes can be reduced..; little can be done for reducing the external radiation of noise. **1956** *B.B.C. Handbk. 1957* 9 The radiation of signals from the transmitting aerial.

3. c. *Biol.* The spread of an animal or plant group from an area in which its greatest concentration is or was found. Cf. *adaptive radiation* s.v. *ADAPTIVE *a.*

1949 W. C. ALLEE et al. *Princ. Animal Ecol.* xxxiv. 662/2 The early radiation of the orders of insects is even more remarkable than that of the orders of mammals. **1957** P. J. DARLINGTON *Zoogeography* vii. 414 The most profound patterns of geographical radiation, reflecting spread of great, dominant groups from definite centers, are found among the animals which disperse most slowly over land. **1977** *Sci. Amer.* May 28/3 In the course of their wide and long-lasting radiation these apes seem to have encountered increasingly cooler environments. **1978** *Nature* 17 Aug. 662/1 The *Dicroidium* complex, a diverse group of seed ferns characteristic of the Triassic, became nearly entirely extinct and was replaced by a Jurassic radiation of conifers.

4. In mod. use freq. *attrib.* with the sense 'ionizing radiation', as *radiation dosage, dose, dosimetry, level, meter, monitor*; *radiation, induced, -proof* adjs.; in the names of bodily disorders caused by ionizing radiation, as *radiation cachexia, carcinogenesis, dermatitis, osteitis, ulcer*; **radiation accident,** an accident involving potentially hazardous exposure to ionizing radiation; **radiation badge,** a badge that changes its appearance when a prescribed dose of ionizing radiation has been received; cf. *film badge* s.v. *FILM *sb.* 7 b; **radiation belt** *Astr.*, a region surrounding a planet where charged particles accumulate under the influence of the planet's magnetic field; **radiation burn,** a burn caused by over-exposure to ionizing radiation; **radiation chemistry,** the study of chemical changes arising from the impact of ionizing radiation; (cf. *RADIOCHEMISTRY); hence *radiation-chemical* adj.; *radiation chemist*; **radiation counter** = *COUNTER *sb.*[2] 3 b; **radiation damage,** damage caused by ionizing radiation; **radiation efficiency** *Telecommunications* (see quot. 1977); **radiation field,** an extent of space in which there is radiation; *spec.* the space around an aerial in which there is a continuous outward flow of energy, separated from the aerial by the induction field; **radiation fog,** substitute for def.: fog formed when the ground loses heat by radiation and cools overlying moist air; (further examples); **radiation frost,** frost which occurs when the ground loses heat by radiation; **radiation genetics,** the branch of biology concerned with the genetic effects of ionizing radiation; **radiation hazard,** a risk to health owing to the presence of ionizing radiation; **radiation injury,** an injury caused by over-exposure to ionizing radiation; **radiation pattern,** the way in which the intensity of the radiation from an aerial or other source varies in different directions from it; **radiation pressure,** mechanical pressure exerted by electromagnetic radiation or by sound waves; **radiation pyrometer,** a pyrometer which functions by measuring radiant energy; hence *radiation pyrometry*; **radiation resistance,** the part of the electrical resistance of an aerial that is due to its radiating properties, being the ratio of the radiated power to the mean square current in the aerial; an analogous property of a sound radiator; **radiation sickness,** disease caused by exposure of the body to ionizing radiation; **radiation therapy, treatment,** medical treatment by means of radiation, such as X-rays or ultraviolet light.

1954 A. HOLLAENDER *Radiation Biology* I. 1255/2 (Index), Radiation accidents. **1970** PASSMORE & ROBSON *Compan. Med. Stud.* II. xxxiii. 1/1 Further knowledge of the acute effects of high doses of radiation in man has been provided by the outcome of radiation accidents. **1964** C. HODDER-WILLIAMS *Main Experiment* I. i. 18 Some of you are not wearing radiation badges. **1959** *Times* 14 Feb. 8/4 By a 'radiation belt' is meant a region in which incoming charged particles are trapped and held captive by the magnetic field of the earth. **1959** *Sci. Amer.* Mar. 47/2 The radiation belts obviously present an obstacle to space flight. **1962** *Daily Tel.* 2 May 1/8 American scientists have said it may take 10 or even 100 years before the radiation belts return to their present conditions [after the explosion of a hydrogen bomb]. **1977** F. N. BASH *Astron.* xiii. 398 Jupiter's radiation belts are not only more intense, but also much larger than the similar Van Allen belts that girdle the earth. **1949** *Surg., Gynecol., & Obstetr.* LXXXVIII. 609 (*heading*) Surgical treatment of radiation burns. **1960** *Gloss. Atomic Terms* (Atomic Energy Authority) 42 Patients subject to intense irradiation, e.g. in cancer therapy by X or gamma rays sometimes get surface or skin radiation burns. **1961** R. D. BAKER *Essent. Path.* vii. 127 Heavy dosages of x-ray, especially to the upper abdomen, may lead to radiation sickness, nausea and vomiting shortly after the radiation; radiation cachexia, weakness, anemia, and leukopenia several weeks after exposures. **1947** *Radiology* XLIX. 359/2 The question of radiation carcinogenesis in the lungs cannot be fully dismissed. **1951** *Jrnl. Chem. Educ.* XXVIII. 407/2 Not all instruments shown in Table 1 are equally useful for the radiation chemist. *Ibid.* 419/2 From the more theoretical point of view radiation chemical reactions should be studied to determine how internal conversion and energy transfer affect yields. **1940** *Chem. Abstr.* XXXVI. 229 (*heading*) The significance of radiation chemistry and its procedures for the science and technology of glass. **1951** *Jrnl. Chem. Educ.* XXVIII. 416/2 We may note finally in the radiation chemistry of water the anisotropic distribution of H_3O^+ and OH^- ions, particularly in cases of heavy particle bombardment. **1961** G. R. CHOPPIN *Exper. Nuclear Chem.* xii. 192 Most of the early research in radiation chemistry used natural nuclear emissions. **1974** J. E. WILSON *Radiation Chem. of Monomers, Polymers, & Plastics* iv. 185 A study of the radiation chemistry of small molecules is helpful in understanding the radiation chemistry of polymers. **1979** *Nature* 15 Feb. 583/3 Work was soon under way in the β and γ-ray spectrometry of (mainly) naturally radioactive species, and in radiation chemistry. **1947** *Nucleonics* Sept. 23/1 (*heading*) Crystal and Cerenkov radiation counters. **1941** *Jrnl. Appl. Physics* XII. 293/1 Cases of severe radiation damage to the hands of radiologists and technicians. **1957** BENEDICT & PIGFORD *Nuclear Chem. Engin.* iii. 66 The extent to which fuel elements of a power reactor can be irradiated may be limited..by physical changes in the fuel caused by radiation damage. **1970** PASSMORE & ROBSON *Compan. Med. Stud.* II. xxxiii. 7/2 That harmful mutations may result from radiation seems almost certain... The demonstration of microscopic radiation damage to human chromosomes makes the occurrence of finer damage almost beyond question. **1961** R. D. BAKER *Essent. Path.* xx. 542 Radiation dermatitis, usually from overexposure to X-rays and less commonly to radium, results in similar atrophic changes in the skin..which, after a number of years, become squamous cell carcinoma. **1934** *Radiology* XXIII. 738 (*heading*) Some mathematical aspects of radiation dosage. **1922** tr. Friedrich & Glasser in Kroenig & Friedrich *Princ. Physics & Biol. of Radiation Therapy* 241 (*heading*) The distribution of the radiation dose in intra-corporeal radium and mesothorium therapy. **1970** PASSMORE & ROBSON *Compan. Med. Stud.* II. xxxiii. 1/2 Other important aspects of radiation dose are the rate of delivery, whether it is fractionated in time and the duration of the radiation-free periods between doses. **1937** *Brit. Jrnl. Radiol.* X. 600 (*heading*) Radiation dosimetry. **1968** *Courier-Mail* (Brisbane) 16 Nov. 15 (Advt.), The Australian Atomic Energy Commission is in the process of establishing a programme of research and development in the field of radiation dosimetry and radiation standards. **1913** J. ERSKINE-MURRAY *Handbk. Wireless Telegr.* (ed. 4) xix. 367 (*heading*) A direct experimental method for the determination of the radiation efficiency, earth resistance and other constants of a transmitter. **1977** S. W. AMOS *Radio, TV & Audio Technical Ref. Bk.* xxi. 5 Antenna radiation efficiency = power radiated by antenna/input power to antenna. **1924** *Physical Rev.* XXIV. 339 The energy which is removed from a radiation field..by the positive absorption of quanta by *N* oscillators all in $(n-1)$ quantum states. **1928** STERLING & KRUSE *Radio Man.* 663/1 (Index), Radiation field of antenna. **1948** A. L. ALBERT *Radio Fund.* xiii. 494 At a distance greater than, say, a few wavelengths from the antenna, the induction field approaches zero, and the radiation field exists... The energy in the radiation field does not return to the antenna when the antenna voltage and current die out. **1971** *Nature* 20 Aug. 572/1 The ultrasonic field was monitored by a small, sensitized, thermistor probe which could be positioned at any point in the radiation field by means of a micromanipulator attached to the irradiation chamber. **1937** G. T. TREWARTHA *Introd. Weather & Climate* iii. 109 Radiation fog is at its worst in the vicinity of large cities where the air is rich in hygroscopic smoke particles. **1971** W. HILLEN *Blackwater River* xiii. 121 Morning radiation fog shrouded the lake..and filled the lower valley. **1889** *Q. Jrnl. R. Meteorol. Soc.* XV. 23 It was not an ordinary radiation frost, but one in which the entire valley was filled with an almost uniformly cold atmosphere. **1906** *Daily Chron.* 8 Mar. 7/4 It will surprise many people.. to know that a slight radiation frost actually occurred on the grass early yesterday morning. **1945** R. BUSH *Frost & Fruitgrower* iii. 13 Cloud coming up when a radiation frost is beginning sends the temperature up surprisingly quickly. **1959** *Chambers's Encycl.* VI. 93/2 The occurrence of radiation frost at night is associated with the growth of an inversion in the surface layers of air. **1934** *Lancet* 28 July 214/1 A new subject to many members is 'radiation genetics'. **1956** C. AUERBACH *Genetics in Atomic Age* viii. 69 In the twenty-eight years since its beginning, radiation genetics has developed into a large and flourishing branch of research. **1945** H. D. SMYTH *Gen. Acct. Devel. Atomic Energy Mil. Purposes* vii. 73 Two types of radiation hazard were anticipated—neutrons generated by the pile, and alpha-particles, beta-particles, and gamma rays emitted by products of the pile. **1964** C. HODDER-WILLIAMS *Main Experiment* I. iii. 34 She's batty on the subject of radiation hazards. She used to flirt with the CND. **1946** U.S. Atomic Energy Comm. Rep. MDDC-700 (*title*) Radiation-induced changes in ultraviolet absorption spectra of urine. **1962** *Times* 12 July 3/1 The effects of radiation-induced mutations on mouse populations. **1971** *Brit. Med. Bull.* XXVII. 66/1 The Survey is occasionally referred to as a source of information about mongols and leukaemia, but never in connexion with radiation-induced cancers. **1942** *Radiology* XXXIX. 663 (*heading*) Influence of the medium on radiation injury of sperm. **1970** PASSMORE & ROBSON *Compan. Med. Stud.* II. xxxiii. 7/2 In other respects the histological appearance of the tissue are those of a nonspecific inflammatory response although some features suggest a radiation injury. **1955** Radiation level [see *RADIOBIOLOGY]. **1947** *Nucleonics* Sept. 61/1 (*heading*) Beta and gamma radiation meter. **1961** *Economist* 23 Dec. 1220/2 'Survival biscuits'.., water, first-aid kits and radiation meters. **1951** GRAY & MARTENS *Radiation Monitoring in Atomic Defense* xii. 91 Emergency workers, particularly radiation monitors, should be equipped with dose meters for their own protection. **1955** [see *film badge* s.v. *FILM *sb.* 7b]. **1964** C. HODDER-WILLIAMS *Main Experiment* I. iii. 29 Recessed radiation monitors placed at fifty-foot intervals. **1926** *Acta Radiol.* VI. 399 (*heading*) Radiation osteitis. **1948** A. L. ALBERT *Radio Fund.* xiii. 496 (*caption*) The radiation patterns of a half-wave antenna. **1978** *Nature* 5 Jan. 48/2 The radiation pattern of the antenna is similar to that of a half-wave dipole. **1978** *Sci. Amer.* Aug. 120 (*caption*) Flask arrangement for measuring the radiation pattern from a conventional grate. **1901** *Physical Rev.* XIII. 308 Radiation pressure, from its nature, must reach its maximum value instantly. **1905** [see *RADIOMETER 2]. **1926** H. C. MACPHERSON *Mod. Astron.* vi. 96 It is now generally admitted that the chief factor in producing comets' tails is the radiation pressure. **1966** *McGraw-Hill Encycl. Sci. & Technol.* XI. 317/1 Since the radiation pressure is $p = 2E$, where *E* is the energy of the acoustic wave per unit area, a direct measurement of this pressure will determine the energy of a plane wave. **1976** *Nature* 2 Sept. 15/2 Theoreticians.. remained frustrated in their attempts to explain motions in the great straight tails [of comets] by means of solar radiation pressure alone. **1952** B. WOLFE *Limbo '90* (1953) IV. xiv. 220 Heat-proof and radiation-proof name plates. **1904** *Physical Rev.* XIX. 422 The best types of radiation pyrometers that are at present available to the experimentalist. **1959** *Techn. Survey Dorman Long (Steel) Ltd.* (Iron & Coal Trades Rev.) 59/2 Each furnace also has two radiation pyrometers focussed on the crown of the roof ten feet on either side of the tap-hole. **1972** G. F. WARNKE in H. H. Plumb *Temperature* IV. I. ii. 503/2 The instrument engineer seeking to employ infrared radiation pyrometers for process temperature measurement and control. **1904** *Physical Rev.* XIX. 422 Under the term radiation pyrometry may be grouped all those methods in which the temperature of bodies is estimated from the radiant energy emitted, either in the form of visible light radiation or of the longer infra red waves. **1922** GLAZEBROOK *Dict. Appl. Physics* I. 643/1 In radiation pyrometry generally the term 'full radiator' or 'black body' denotes one that will absorb all the radiation it receives. **1913** J. ERSKINE-MURRAY *Handbk. Wireless Telegr.* (ed. 4) xiv. 223 The fourth numeric of the antenna, namely *r*, the radiation coefficient or 'radiation resistance', is that on which transmission actually depends. **1938** F. E. TERMAN *Fund. of Radio* xiv. 389 The magnitude of the radiation resistance depends..upon the point in the antenna system at which the resistance is considered as being inserted. *Ibid.* xvii. 435 The presence of the air in contact with the vibrating diaphragm produces a mechanical radiation resistance..which varies with frequency. **1975** D. G. FINK *Electronics Engineers' Handbk.* XIX. 55 A loudspeaker designed to resonate at a low frequency combines decreasing velocity with increasing radiation resistance to yield a uniform response within the frequency range where the assumptions hold. **1924** *Lancet* 23 Aug. 365/1 Dodds and Webster have recently summarised the literature of radiation sickness in *The Lancet*. **1948** *Sci. News* VII. 8 Radiation sickness, its prevention, its treatment, is..a problem for the medical services. **1961** R. D. BAKER *Essent. Path.* vii. 127 Heavy dosages of x-ray, especially to the upper abdomen, may lead to radiation sickness, nausea and vomiting shortly after the radiation. **1978** *Sci. Amer.* May 49/3, 10 percent of the people exposed to 150 rads will die from radiation sickness. **1922** tr. Krönig & Friedrich (*title*) The principles of physics and biology of radiation therapy. **1961** R. D. BAKER *Essent. Path.* vii. 127 Radiation therapy of the cervix under abnormal circumstances may result in damage to the mucosa of the rectum or of the urinary bladder. **1980** *Daily Tel.* 4 Dec. 6/8 It can implant radioactive seeds by needle when..patients can no longer sustain external radiation therapy. **1924** *Lancet* 4 Oct. 725/1 (*heading*) Chloride metabolism in radiation treatment. **1968** *Brit. Med. Bull.* XXIV. 190/1 Someone without training using the computer procedure can produce a competent radiation-treatment plan. **1970** PASSMORE & ROBSON *Compan. Med. Stud.* II. xxxiii. 7/2 A radiation ulcer of the skin often fails to heal.

radiational (rēⁱdiˌēⁱ·ʃənăl), *a.* [f. prec. + -AL.] Of, pertaining to, or involving radiation.

1902 *Encycl. Brit.* XXXIII. 213/1 This wider theory [of the electric telegraph] is founded upon Maxwell's theory of electromagnetic radiation, and may be accordingly termed the radiational theory. **1949** KOESTLER *Insight & Outlook* xi. 156 The 'particles' in the atom..are capable of persisting as functional wholes in the teeth of mechanical, thermal and radiational disturbances. **1964** M. MCLUHAN *Understanding Media* (1967) xix. 198 The wheel and the road expressed and advanced this explosion by a radiational or center-margin pattern. **1969** *Sci. Jrnl.* Jan. 64/2 Analysis of the tides at other localities suggests that the ratio of radiational: gravitational tide of O-2 is fairly typical.

Hence **radia·tionally** *adv.*

1969 R. BUCKMINSTER FULLER *Operating Man. Spaceship Earth* vi. 76, I would like to inventory rapidly the system variables which I find to be by far the most powerful in the consideration of our present life-regenerating evolution aboard our spaceship as it is continually refueled radiationally by the Sun and other cosmic radiation.

radiationless (rēⁱdiˌēⁱ·ʃənlės), *a. Physics* and *Chem.* [f. RADIATION + -LESS.] Not involving the emission of electromagnetic radiation.

1919 *Proc. Nat. Acad. Sci.* V. 590 For any real motion, where the velocity is less than that of light,..radiationless orbits, other than straight lines uniformly described, are impossible. **1931** *Proc. R. Soc.* A. CXXXII. 668 It is uncertain whether these γ-rays are actually emitted or whether the β-ray lines from which their existence is inferred are due to a radiationless transition. **1939** *Trans. Faraday Soc.* XXXV. 142 The radiationless transfer of energy from A to A' is caused by the close electrical coupling (resonance) between the electrons in atoms close together as in crystals. **1974** *Nature* 15 Mar. 196/1 The excited molecule loses its energy, first, by radiationless conversion to the lower excited singlet state and finally by fluorescence from this state at 28,600 cm^{-1}.

Hence **radia·tionlessly** *adv.*

1974 GILL & WILLIS *Pericyclic Reactions* v. 137 However, the BO 'hole' provides a mechanism for the system to relax radiationlessly into the ground state.

radiative, *a.* **a.** Add to def.: Occurring by means of radiation; involving or accompanied by the emission of radiation. (Further examples.)

1894 *Mem. R. Astron. Soc.* LI. 145 There are two causes affecting the distribution of density, which respectively cease at different known points, namely, convection at a uniform distribution, and unequal radiative cooling at the distribution given on p. 144. **1930** *Proc. R. Soc.* A. CXXIX. 2 Radiative transitions in the nucleus resulting in the emission of a γ-ray. **1934** *Nature* 10 Feb. 211/1 The energy of these rays corresponds roughly to that which would be emitted in the radiative combination of a neutron and a proton. **1958** *New Scientist* 16 Jan. 14/1 A radiative heat loss due to this process (technically known as *bremsstrahlung* radiation) is thus an unavoidable feature of a thermonuclear reactor. **1973** W. K. ROSE *Astrophysics* ii. 63 The transport of energy in the interior of a star can be caused by radiative transport, convection, or electron conduction. **1977** J. NARLIKAR *Struct. Universe* ii. 29 The star therefore is no longer completely convective, and it develops a 'radiative core'. That is, the energy transport in the core takes place by radiation rather than convection.

b. *radiative capture*, capture of a particle by an atomic nucleus with accompanying emission of one or more gamma rays; *radiative equilibrium*, a state of equilibrium in which the total energy flux emitted is equal to that absorbed; a state of equilibrium in which radiation is the predominant energy transport mechanism.

1926 A. S. EDDINGTON *Internal Constitution of Stars* v. 99 Radiative equilibrium has a natural precedence over convective equilibrium, since in radiative equilibrium convection ceases, whereas in convective equilibrium radiation remains and tends to destroy it. **1934** D. BRUNT *Physical & Dynamical Meteorol.* vii. 138 It is impossible for the upper region of the atmosphere to be kept in an isothermal condition by radiative equilibrium when it is only irradiated from below by long-wave radiation. **1935** *Physical Rev.* XLVII. 508/1 (*heading*) Radiative capture of protons by carbon. **1953** B. STRÖMGREN in G. P. Kuiper *Sun* ii. 40 In regions in radiative equilibrium, i.e., where the transport of energy..is entirely by radiation, the transport by convection and conduction being negligible by comparison, the temperature gradient is given by equation (4*a*). **1962** *Newnes Conc. Encycl. Nuclear Energy* 287/1 In radiative capture the compound nucleus de-excites through intermediate states to the ground state, each step yielding a γ-ray.

Hence **ra·diatively** *adv.*, by means of (esp. electromagnetic) radiation; with emission of radiation.

1957 F. HOYLE *Black Cloud* ix. 177 The volume of information that can be transmitted radiatively is enormously greater than the amount that we can communicate by ordinary sound. **1969** *Nature* 16 Aug. 727/1 The permitted lines are probably radiatively excited from the lowest levels. **1973** *Physics Bull.* Apr. 243/1 The introduction of thallium into the crystal allows the exciton to decay radiatively by luminescence.

radiator. Add: Also, anything that emits sound waves.

1927 *Physics Abstr.* A. XXX. 415 (*heading*) Performance and design of sound radiator consisting of an acoustic transformer and horn. **1936** P. M. MORSE *Vibration & Sound* vii. 240 Few radiators of sound are so much longer than they are wide that they behave like long cylinders, but many radiators behave like spherical sources. **1962** A. NISBETT *Technique Sound Studio* iii. 60 'Cellos and basses differ from violins and violas in that they are much more efficient as radiators in the lower register. **1977** G. PORGES *Appl. Acoustics* xii. 140 A dipole is a less efficient radiator of sound than a monopole, and a quadrupole is even less efficient.

b. Add to def.: Now usu. a tank or compact array of pipes, having a large surface area, which is heated usu. by circulating hot water and gives off warmth also by convection. Also applied to various kinds of electric space heater. (Earlier and additional examples.)

1851 C. CIST *Cincinnati* 213 The introduction of evaporatory radiators and registers. **1891** W. P. BUCHAN *Ventilation* xv. 166 The so-called steam or hot-water 'radiators' heat principally by conduction, as may be easily proved by suspending one thermometer, say, a foot high right above the 'radiator' and another right in front of it and six inches from it. *a* **1910** 'MARK TWAIN' *Europe & Elsewhere* (1923) 178 The German stove..is lovely,..compared with any 'radiator' that has yet been intruded upon the world. **1959** N. MAILER *Advts. for Myself* (1961) 153 She has shut the window and neglected to turn off the radiator. The room is stifling. **1966** N. CHAPMAN *Heating* 37 A storage radiator..provides the most comfortable conditions in a room early in the morning because the air is warmer from the heat given off during the charging period. **1975** R. H. WARING *All about Home Heating* ii. 14 Modern radiators are usually either of panel type or radiant panel, of relatively slim construction and with inlet and outlet connection at the bottom on each end. Panel radiators have a ribbed surface. Radiant panel radiators consist of a radiator tube attached to the back of a metal sheet..or sandwiched between two metal sheets for complete enclosure.

c. Part of the cooling system of a liquid-cooled internal-combustion engine, consisting of a large bank of thin tubes in which the circulating fluid (freq. water) is cooled by the surrounding air after passing round the engine.

1900 *Sci. Amer. Suppl.* 25 Aug. 20617/3 The present water circulating plan..has..the defect of complicating the mechanism by the addition of tanks, radiators and pumps, causing multiplied trouble. **1905** *Daily Chron.* 6 July 5/2 Lancia had negotiated half of the round when his radiator suddenly burst, and left him stranded. **1932** Kipling *Limits & Renewals* 80 Private Gillock..was stage-whispering me for leave to 'put a shot into his radiator'. **1935** C. G. Burge *Compl. Bk. Aviation* 271/2 In a single-engined aircraft the radiator may be mounted below the fuselage. **1970** K. Ball *Fiat 600, 600D Autobook* iv. 40/2 Maintenance of the cooling system is confined to periodical flushing of the radiator, refilling with antifreeze solutions for cold weather or clean water for warm, [etc.].

d. An aerial for transmitting (and often also receiving) radio waves.

1903 *Sci. Amer. Suppl.* 4 July 23000/3 The 'aerial', or radiator; that was, the tall wire which..sent electric waves off into the ether. **1947** D. G. Fink *Radar Engin.* v. 303 The radiator forms the radiated beam and presents the absorption area for reception of the echoes. **1952** E. A. Laport *Radio Antenna Engin.* ii. 94 The type of radiator that is generally used for medium-frequency broadcasting is the straight uniform vertical with its lower end near ground. **1973** W. E. Kock *Radar, Sonar, & Holography* ii. 42 In radars and sonars, this ability to steer the beam electrically, that is, without moving the radiator, permits much larger arrays to be used.

2. *attrib.* and *Comb.*, (chiefly sense *1 c), as *radiator cap, fluid, grill(e*.

1913 *Collier's* 11 Jan. II. 9/1 If it has a new radiator cap or a new form of rear spring suspension..it is immediately surrounded by a crowd of motor sharps. **1948** M. Laski *Tory Heaven* ix. 130 James managed to undo the radiator cap and poured the water in. **1979** *Arizona Daily Star* 5 Aug. c 5/3 (Advt.), Includes pressure-checks of radiator cap, hoses and fittings for leaks. **1972** D. E. Westlake *Bank Shot* ii. 16 Glass was broken, chrome was bent, and.. radiator fluid was making a green puddle on the blacktop. **1938** *Decorative Art* 53/2 The floral designs over the bookcases and the radiator grille are hand-painted on wood. **1959** *Motor* 4 Mar. 168/1 Wider than hitherto, the radiator grille is flanked by combined sidelamps and turn-signal flashers. **1973** D. Miller *Chinese Jade Affair* xxi. 212 Potter was still in the Mini... I kicked the radiator grill in passing.

radical, *a.* and *sb.* Add: **A.** *adj.* **1. c.** Philos. *radical empiricism*: a name given by W. James (1842–1910) to a philosophical position according to which even underlying postulates are regarded as hypotheses to be verified (see quot. 1897); more generally, a rigorous or sceptical empiricism; hence *radical empiricist*, one who adopts this position. Similarly *radical pluralism, pluralist*.

1897 W. James *Will to Believe* p. vii, Were I obliged to give a short name to the attitude in question, I should call it that of *radical empiricism*... I say 'empiricism', because it is contented to regard its most assured conclusions concerning matters of fact as hypotheses liable to modification in the course of future experience; and I say 'radical', because it treats the doctrine of monism itself as an hypothesis. *Ibid.* p. ix, This is pluralism, somewhat rhapsodically expressed. He who takes for his hypothesis the notion that it is the permanent form of the world is what I call a radical empiricist. **1904** —— *Ess. Radical Empiricism* (1912) ii. 90 These are the main features of a philosophy of pure experience... In my own mind such a philosophy harmonizes best with a radical pluralism. **1911** —— *Some Prob. Philos.* x. 164 He concluded that such realities as present beings, past events and causes, steps of change and parts of matter, must needs exist in limited amount. This made of him a radical pluralist. **1949** *Mind* LVIII. 369, I remember well the dismay in an undergraduate philosophical society when one of the members..announced that he had adopted the 'radical pluralism' of this author [*sc.* Russell]. **1965** P. A. Bertocci in B. B. Wolman *Scientific Psychol.* xvi. 295 Radical empiricism, synoptic examination as well as analysis—this is the methodology that alone can provide hypotheses which.. will not lose their anchorage in what is phenomenally given. **1973** K. B. Madsen in D. Berlyne *Pleasure, Reward, Preference* xi. 286 We expect a radical empiricist to be a materialist rather than a dualist.

3. c. Also *radical reformation*.

1781 C. Wyvill *Polit. Papers* (1794) I. vi. viii. 341 While independent men, supported by large bodies of their fellow citizens, have the virtue thus to resist corruption..the hope of a radical reformation cannot be ill-founded.

d. *Politics.* Advocating 'radical reform' (see sense 3 b in Dict.) or any thorough political and social change; representing or supporting the extreme section of a political party; hence, in more recent use (orig. *U.S.*) left-wing, revolutionary. Also in *Comb.* with sense 'radical and —'.

This sense overlaps and merges with sense B. 5 c in Dict. Because of political changes the examples given are of course not restricted to those of 'the extreme section of the Liberal party' in Britain as stated in the Dict.; on the continent of Europe in the present century, parties bearing the title of 'Radical' have in fact freq. tended towards the centre or even a conservative standpoint.

1832 J. S. Mill *Let.* 17 Sept. in *Wks.* (1963) XII. 117 Several friends of mine, radical-utilitarians of a better than the ordinary sort. **1835** *Knickerbocker* VI. 92 The tendency of Americans, instead of being aristocratic, is decidedly radical. **1844** C. M. Yonge *Abbeychurch* xiv. 303 The window ..was adorned with all the worst caricatures which had found their way to Abbeychurch, the portraits of sundry radical leaders. **1847** *Semi-Weekly News* (Fredericksburgh, Va.) 21 Oct. 2/2 The Barnburners with their 'Radical democracy' can never long govern this great State. **1865** *Atlanta Daily Intelligencer* 1 Oct. 3/1 The radical Republicans are now proposing a compromise on the negro-suffrage question. **1884** E. W. Hamilton *Diary* 6 Oct. (1972) II. 699 He is sure the Opposition will insist on our strengthening our Navy and he believes that even the 'Radical Economists' will advocate this. **1905** *Daily Chron.* 30 June 6/2 It is reported that. a Radical-Protectionist Government will take office. **1908** *Ibid.* 6 Apr. 7/4 Under Mr. Asquith, the balance of power in the Government shifts from the Radical-Socialist to the more moderate Radical side. **1912** W. E. Walling *Socialism as it Is* iii. 166 While one element is growing more radical another is growing more conservative and the breach between the Independents and the other Labourites is widening. **1927** W. Irwin *How Red is America?* ii. 47 The half-century when the radical parties were getting their foothold in Europe and America. **1940** B. Miall tr. *Salvatorelli's Conc. Hist. Italy* xx. 616 Since there was an anti-ministerial movement even in the Radical party, Giolitti resigned. **1950** Theimer & Campbell *Encycl. World Politics* 171/2 The radicals..are associated with..the *Union démocratique socialiste et radicale*, in the *Rassemblement des Gauches*..; they still use the old name of radical-socialists, but are not socialist. **1953** *Manch. Guardian Weekly* 1 Jan. 2 He deplored the 'pinks', 'radical cliques' and other victims of the 'Communist line'. **1965** E. Nolte in Rogger & Weber *European Right* 297 The antigovernmental Right..often attacked Hitler for being a Catholic or insufficiently radical. **1968** *Ann. Reg. 1967* 5 Mr Thorpe represented the radical wing [of the Liberal Party], while Mr Lubbock epitomized the suburban vote. **1969** *Ann. Reg. 1968* 491 British students (with the exception of a radical handful at the London School of Economics in 1967) had been quiet and conservative. **1969** [see *Marxist *a.*[1]]. **1969** G. S. Jones in Cockburn & Blackburn *Student Power* 38 A country [*sc.* the U.S.] where the hysteria of the Cold War had previously smothered all radical politics. **1974** A. J. Gregor *Fascist Persuasion in Radical Politics* 16 The Fascist emphasis..on the 'primacy of politics', on a 'collectivistic' rather than a 'liberal' social order..are all emphases that have become more and more characteristic of *all* radical political ideologies.

e. Characterized by independence of, or departure from, what is usual or traditional; progressive, unorthodox, or revolutionary (in outlook, conception, design, etc.).

1921 *Daily Colonist* (Victoria) 20 Mar. 24/1 In appearance the Coats car is attractive, but not at all radical in design. **1928** E. O'Neill *Strange Interlude* I. 15 A natural tendency toward a prim provincialism where practical present-day considerations are concerned (though he is most liberal—even radical—in his tolerant understanding of the manners and morals of Greece and Imperial Rome!). **1938** H. A. Murray *Explor. in Personality* iii. 148 Radical sentiments: the origination, promulgation or defence of sentiments, theories or ideologies that are novel, questionable or opposed to tradition. **1958** *Listener* 23 Oct. 648/1, I would describe as radical paintings that make a difference to our ideas about art. The American contribution to radical art in this sense is particularly to be seen in the big picture. **1962** *New Statesman* 25 May 768/2 A true modernist, a radical functionist, would have rejected this basic proposition. **1971** C. Hampden-Turner *Radical Man* i. 17 While Conservative Man is caused to behave, Radical Man imagines and reasons autonomously. **1977** *Western Mail* (Cardiff) 5 Mar. (Rugby Suppl.) 2/7 The 'radical rugby thinker' Jika Travers from Australia and Oxford University, capped as a war veteran at 27.

f. Special collocations in senses 3 d and e, as *radical chic*, the fashionable affectation of radical left-wing views or of dress, style of life, etc., associated with such views; also *transf.*, those who embody such an affectation; *radical feminism*, advocacy of radical left-wing views designed to counter the traditional dominance of men over women; hence *radical feminist* adj. and sb.; *radical left* = *New Left; *radical right*, extremist conservative or fascist views favouring group action to protect or re-instate certain social traditions.

1970 T. Wolfe in *New York* 8 June 40/2 Radical Chic invariably favors radicals who seem primitive, exotic, and romantic, such as the grape workers..the Panthers..and the Red Indians. *Ibid.* 56/1 Radical Chic..is only radical in style; in its heart it is part of Society and its traditions. Politics, like Rock, Pop, and Camp, has its uses; but [etc.]. **1973** *Guardian* 5 Mar. 20/4 (*heading*) For a taste of radical chic—try a plum jam buttie. **1977** *Rolling Stone* 24 Mar., Right now bisexuality is the big radical chic on campuses. **1977** *Daily Tel.* 16 July 12 The environmental lobby, a cause largely invented by the Manhattan radical chic. **1980** *Church Observer* Apr. 18/2 By translating the actions of ancient Judea into modern radical chic, the whole story [sc. *Monty Python's Life of Brian*] comes dangerously close to life today and threatens to upset the safe, neat and tidy arrangement we favour in Sunday morning religion. **1923** A. R. Wadia *Ethics of Feminism* i. 19 These would also have to be studied so as to enable us to judge how far they afford a stable basis for the advocates of radical feminism. **1971** S. Firestone *Dialectic of Sex* ii. 16 In the radical feminist view, the new feminism is not just the revival of a serious political movement for social equality. **1976** *Papers on Patriarchy Conference London 76* 3 Radical feminists/separatists place importance on the subjective, personal perceptions of oppression to provide the guidelines for 'political' action. **1977** *Rolling Stone* 24 Mar., I've read some radical feminist reviews of your book which gripe about your excessive closeness to men. **1969** *N.Y. Times Mag.* 9 Feb. 34/1 They are members of a newly assertive radical left group called Women's Liberation. **1970** *New Yorker* 26 Sept. 136 The Wallace voters and the radical right—often ideologically distinct, though not always—and the radical left. **1977** *Times* 21 Sept. 1/6 Although the 'radical left' are still only a minority in the institutes of higher education, they deserved serious.. rebuttal. **1954** T. Taylor *Grand Inquest* (1955) p. xvi, The Communist *Weltanschauung* and conception of the individual's relation to the State have much more in common with the nationalism of the radical right than with the liberal internationalism of the left. **1965** E. Weber in Rogger & Weber *European Right* 20 The violence and brutality of the radical Right became acceptable to conservatives who viewed them as defenders against the threat of a radical Left. **1970** C. Hampden-Turner *Radical Man* (1971) ix. 267 This explains the relative efficiency and speed of organized groups on the Radical Right and the Communist Left. **1977** M. Walker *National Front* v. 117 The [Monday] Club accepts. the name 'Radical Right'.

5. *radical word* (earlier and later examples).

1605 Bacon *Adv. Learn.* II. f. 59ᵛ, They [*sc.* the Chinese] haue a vast multitude of Characters, as many (I suppose), as Radicall words. **1921** E. Sapir *Language* ii. 29 Radical-words may and do occur in languages of all varieties.

B. *sb.* **1. c.** One of the set of basic Chinese characters (usu. reckoned to number 214) which, occas. in modified form, constitute elements, freq. with semantic significance, in the composition of other characters and are a means by which characters can be classified and arranged in dictionaries. Cf. *phonetic *sb.*

[**1736** R. Brookes tr. *Du Halde's Hist. China* II. 393 As in Hebrew there are radical letters.. so likewise the Chinese have their radical characters; for instance the characters of mountains, of trees,..under which must be sought all that belongs to mountains, trees.] **1824** J. Johnson *Typographia* xii. 368 (*heading*) Table of the Chinese Radicals. *Ibid.* 369 Each Radical is placed at the head of a new family of characters. **1834** *Chinese Repository* May 31 The most conspicuous portions of characters were adopted as 'heads of tribes', which in Europe have been called keys and radicals... The radicals..rarely have any relation to the sounds of the characters of which they form component parts. **1874** [see *phonetic *sb.*]. **1907** W. Hillier *Chinese Lang.* i. 4 We..divide Chinese characters into two parts—one, the *sound* indicator, to which the name 'phonetic' is generally given; the other, the *idea* indicator, which is commonly called the 'radical'... The radicals are limited in number, there being only 214 of them altogether. **1921** *New China Review* III. 390 The sign..does not figure.. as a phonetic but rather as the genuine hieroglyph, to which a classifying radical has been added. **1948** R. A. D. Forrest *Chinese Lang.* ii. 38 After we have deducted the 'sheep' device from each of the three examples, the part remaining in each case is known as the 'radical', or better, as the 'signific'. **1973** *Sci. Amer.* Feb. 54/1 A dictionary published in 1971..has merged some radicals, reducing the number to 189. **1978** *Nagel's Encycl.-Guide: China* 88 Character 14 was described as consisting of a phonetic and a radical; the phonetic showed the reader that the word was pronounced in much the same way as 'door', and the radical showed that the meaning was linked with 'ear'.

5. a. Also *gen.*, an advocate of any thorough political or social change; one who belongs to the extreme section of a political party; a member or supporter of a radical movement (cf. sense *A. 3 d), a left-winger or revolutionary. Also *transf.*

1822 J. Q. Adams *Diary* 16 June in *Memoirs J. Q. Adams* (1875) VI. iii. 22 General Scott..said Archer was a Radical and inclined to be Jacobinical. **1829** *Western Monthly Rev.* II. 593 The schism in the Methodist Church..exists between the sticklers for the ancient structure of episcopalianism.. and the *radicals*, who seem to be contending for a more democratic form of church government. **1847** *Semi-Weekly News* (Fredericksburgh, Va.) 21 Oct. 2/1 The Barnburners are the progressives, the radicals. **1862** O. W. Norton *Army Lett.* (1903) 129, I suppose the radicals have got enough of Burnside now. **1876** *San Francisco Daily Examiner* 10 Oct. 2/1 The real issue with the Radicals is to divert public attention from the unexemplified corruption of the Radical party during the past eight years. **1888** W. H. Dawson *German Socialism* i. 22 The association was joined by South German Radicals, North German students... All that came of it was an outbreak..at Frankfort on April 3rd, 1833. **1912** W. E. Walling *Socialism as it Is* iii. 35 Whether the radical of to-day, the 'State Socialist' favors political democracy or not, depends on whether these 'passive beneficiaries' of the new 'altruistic' system are in a majority. **1921** *N. Amer. Rev.* Aug. 316 Liberals are merely terror-stricken Radicals. **1938** N. M. Butler *Family of Nations* vi. 86 There are very few radicals who are liberals; radicals are almost without exception advocates of compulsion in some one of its forms. **1942** E. Paul *Narrow St.* iv. 35 Some radical that year [*sc.* 1923] (they called them anarchists, not communists, then) had taken a pot shot at Léon Daudet. **1946** E. O'Neill *Iceman Cometh* (1947) i. 10 There is a foreign atmosphere about him, the stamp of an alien radical, a strong resemblance to the type Anarchist as portrayed, bomb in hand, in newspaper cartoons. **1950** [see sense A. 3 d above]. **1962** S. E. Finer *Man on Horseback* iv. 59 The Egyptian army officers were..right-wing radicals..with motivations much more akin to the Nazi storm-troopers. **1976** *Guardian* 8 Nov. 2/6 Hundreds of police sealed off the red brick social club where the Right-wing radicals gathered. **1977** *New Yorker* 1 Aug. 49/1 A radical—someone who continued to defend the Soviet revolution after other Socialists had turned against it.

c. *radical-minded* adj.

1890 W. James *Princ. Psychol.* I. 24 The more radical-minded reader can always read 'ideational process' for 'idea'.

ra·dicalish, *a.* [f. Radical *a.* and *sb.* + -ish[1].] Characterized by, or suggestive of, political radicalism.

1837 R. H. Barham *Let.* 29 Apr. (1870) II. 24 There is a sort of Radicalish tone about *Oliver Twist* which I don't altogether like.

radicalism. Add: **1. c.** Views or principles favouring radical social or political change and reform (see *Radical *a.* 3 d).

1899 C. B. R. Kent *Eng. Radicals* i. 4 When contentment reigns, and there is satisfaction with the present, then radicalism languishes. **1925** tr. *Trotsky's Lenin* 45 What a contrast Vera Ivanovna, with her indefinite radicalism, her subjectivity, and her confusion presented to Vladimir Ilyich. *Ibid.* 85 The shell of intellectual radicalism. **1938** H. A. Murray *Explor. in Personality* iii. 226 The S [*sc.* subject] favours modern art, the rejection of sex taboos, socialism,..progressive schools, the humane treatment of criminals, etc. Radicalism is usually opposed to authority, to any force that restrains liberty. **1960** A. B. Ulam *Unfinished Revol.* iii. 78 The element of ethnic hostility..may become subdued..if that radicalism is assimilated into socialism. Or it may become expanded if the radicalism is absorbed into a revolutionary movement with nationalistic or fascist characteristics. **1968** *Internat. Encycl. Social Sci.* XIII. 299/1 Radicalism is a part of the general theme of the growth of rationalistic ethics. **1974** J. White tr. *Poulantzas's Fascism & Dictatorship* vi. ii. 282 Like the urban petty bourgeoisie, the small-holders are at once drawn towards 'democratic' radicalism, *and*..especially likely..to give massive support to Bonapartist forms of State.

d. Psychol. *radicalism–conservatism*: an axis of attitude measurement sometimes used for personality testing.

[**1930** T. F. Lentz in *Jrnl. Social Psychol.* I. 537 Since the original purpose was to measure radicalism and conservatism, statements were chosen which would involve this characteristic. The statements used are drawn from various fields of interest: ethics, education, feminism,. sex and marriage, politics, race relations.] **1944** G. Myrdal *Amer. Dilemma* II. App. ii. 1038 The place of the individual scientist in the scale of radicalism-conservatism has always had strong influences upon both the selection of research problems and the conclusions drawn from research. In a sense it is the master scale of biases in the social sciences. **1953** H. J. Eysenck *Structure of Human Personality* vii. 224 His [*sc.* Carlson's] second factor, radicalism-conservatism, opposed belief in God to an attitude favourable to pacifism and communism. **1965** R. Brown *Social Psychol.* x. 535 Our problem..is that communism and fascism are opposite extremes on a left to right or radicalism-conservatism dimension.

radicality. 1. (Later example.)

1979 *Dædalus* Winter 30 The radicality of these changes.. had lent credence to the set of beliefs described above.

radicalization. (In Dict. s.v. Radicalize *v.*) (Later examples in sense *3 d of the adj.)

1935 *Communist* XIV. 884 (*heading*) The radicalization of the masses. *Ibid.* 885 The bourgeoisie..are alarmed at the rapid radicalization of the workers. **1953** R. Bendix in Bendix & Lipsett *Class, Status & Power* 605 The radicalization of people who had not participated actively in party politics..gave a major impetus to the rise of fascism. **1960** *New Left Rev.* Nov.–Dec. 7/2 This is a question of the radicalisation of Labour politics. **1969** G. S. Jones in Cockburn & Blackburn *Student Power* 53 British students..are for the first time showing a certain radicalization. **1971** *Nature* 19 Feb. 513/1 What might have been a valuable public discussion on the ethical problems of modern biology..seems to have tailed off into discussion of the process of radicalization of science and even some of the familiar problems of Vietnam. **1977** *Time* 27 June 21/1 As in so many other places, the suppression of legitimate, moderate opposition leads to radicalization.

radicalize, *v.* Add: **1.** (Later examples in sense *3 d of the adj.) Hence **ra·dicalized** *ppl. a.*

1966 *New Statesman* 11 Feb. 185/2 Volunteers returning from two years living with poor people..find that their notions about the world have been radicalised. **1969** *N.Y. Rev. Books* 30 Jan. 17/2 The strongest force for 'radicalizing the campus' may not, after all, be the Cossacks' whips, as many radical tacticians—including those at Columbia—have thought. **1972** *Maclean's Mag.* Sept. 6/2 Being in prison for eight days..helped to radicalize me, as it did so many others. **1976** *National Observer* (U.S.) 24 Apr. 17/1 After all, isn't economic freedom one very important kind of human freedom? Obviously it is, and yet many college students, most particularly the radicalized students of the late 1960s, have been unable to make the connection. **1979** *Dædalus* Summer 19 It disrupts the delicate balance of pluralistic societies and radicalizes everyone.

radicalizing, *ppl. a.* (Later examples.)

1905 *Daily Chron.* 1 May 4/5 The united French Socialist party from now henceforward..will draw to itself..all the radicalising elements in the country. **1973** *Bulletin* (Sydney) 25 Aug. 26/2 It was an amazing revelation and a radicalising one. **1978** *New York* 3 Apr. 34/3 Those themes also spoke to a significant section of the radicalizing, college-educated young, the members of Students for a Democratic Society.

radically, *adv.* Add: **3.** *Comb. radically-minded* adj.

1978 J. Anderson *Angel of Death* x. 112 He's..radically-minded, and doesn't go much for that old-fashioned religion.

radicel. (Earlier and later examples.)

1819 J. Lindley tr. *Richard's Observ. Fruits & Seeds* 68 A slight rim round the base of the radicel. **1944** S. Putnam tr. *da Cunha's Rebellion in Backlands* i. 31 Their principal roots are atrophied..and in their place is a wide expanse of secondary radicels, clustered in sap-swollen tubercles.

radicidation (ræ:disəidēɪ·ʃən). [f. L. *radi-āre* to furnish with rays, shine + *oc-cid-ere* to strike down, kill + -ation.] The treatment of food with ionizing radiation so as to reduce the number of micro-organisms in it to an undetectable level (see quot. 1964). Cf. *radappertization, *radurization.

1964 H. E. Goresline et al. in *Nature* 17 Oct. 237/2 Type II is the application to foods of doses of ionizing radiation sufficient to reduce the number of viable specific non-spore-forming pathogenic micro-organisms (other than viruses) so that none is detectable in the treated food by any standard method... The following are the names we suggest for these types of treatment:.. Type II, radicidation. **1972** *Poultry Sci.* LI. 277 (*heading*) Poultry feed radicidation. **1973** N. F. Lewis et al. in *Radiation Preservation of Food* (Internat. Atomic Energy Agency, Vienna) 203 'Radicidation' is synonymous with a 'bactericidal' effect of radiation where a specific pathogenic species is eliminated. Thus, when the process is used solely for destroying enteropathogenic and enterotoxinogenic organisms belonging to the genus *Salmonella*, it is referred to as '*Salmonella* radicidation'.

radiculitis (rædikiŭləi·tis). *Path.* [ad. F. *radiculite*, f. *radicule* radicle (f. L. *rādicula*, dim. of *rādix* root): see -itis.] Inflammation of the root of a spinal nerve.

1907 *Jrnl. Amer. Med. Assoc.* 5 Oct. 1227/2 (*heading*) Radiculitis. **1940** S. A. K. Wilson *Neurol.* xiii. 260 For self-evident anatomical reasons, radiculitis can scarcely occur by itself. *Ibid.* 261 Radiculitis and 'spinal neuritis' will not here be distinguished. **1973** *N.Y. Law Jrnl.* 19 July 12/2 Her physicians testified that she had suffered from severe cervical sprain and cervical radiculitis since the accident.

radiesthesia (rēɪ:di,isþi·ziă). Also **radiæsthesia.** [ad. F. *radiesthésie*: see Radio- and *Æsthesia.] The detection of radiation by, or by means of, the body: a process believed by some to be responsible for the operation of dowsing rods, pendulums, and the like as means of locating buried substances, diagnosing illness, etc.

1935 *Jrnl. Brit. Soc. Dowsers* II. 337 The field of radiesthesia is beset with many pitfalls for the unwary. **1950** V. D. Wethered *Radiesthetic Approach to Health & Homeopathy* iv. 30 The term radiesthesia has been given to the detection by human reactions of ultra-fine radiations or influences such as are given off by the body. **1958** B. Nichols *Sweet & Twenties* xi. 146 A few doctors who are making the first, hesitant steps into the uncharted science of radiaesthesia. **1960** *Times* 19 July 18/4 Radiaesthesia and radionics were studied and believed in by many persons. **1960** *Spectator* 28 Oct. 653/2 Radiesthesia may be described as the utilising of psychic powers for the diagnosis of disease, with the help of some mechanical apparatus. **1962** M. Ash *Health, Radiation & Healing* iv. 81 The practice of radiesthesia is based on two fundamental facts: first the muscular response of human beings to fields of radiating energy, and secondly the radiating energy emitted by the human body itself. **1975** *Homes & Gardens* Nov. 63/1 More than 20 doctors in this country practise radiesthesia and some belong to the Medical Society for the Study of Radiesthesia.

So **radiesthe·sic** *a.*, radiesthetic; **radie·sthesist**, a radiesthetist; **radiesthe·tic** *a.*, of or pertaining to radiesthesia; **radiesthe·tically** *adv.*; **radie·sthetist**, one skilled in the techniques of radiesthesia.

1934 *Jrnl. Brit. Soc. Dowsers* I. 142 *Study of radiesthetic fields*, by Maurice Alby, describes in rather complicated detail the nature and position of fields surrounding underground water. **1936** *Discovery* Dec. 395/2 Radiesthesists have not hesitated to borrow, often irrationally and incautiously, from the terminology of physics. **1939** Maby & Franklin *Physics of Divining Rod* 436 Many investigators have thought that dowsers work radiesthetically. **1950** F. A. Archdale *Elem. Radiesthesia & Use of Pendulum* i. 9 Radiesthesists have different methods, although they achieve the same results or at least hope to, that is to develop and intercept the reflexes resulting from their sensitiveness to radiations emanating from other bodies, either animal, vegetable or mineral. **1957** V. D. Wethered *Introd. Med. Radiesthesia & Radionics* xiii. 130 A foreign radiesthetist travelling in a train on the Continent was able to diagnose accurately what a fellow traveller was suffering from. **1959** B. Copen *What Radiesthesia is & What it can Do* 15 All Radiesthesic research, diagnosis or therapy does not involve vivisection or cruelty to animals in any way. **1959** M. Clement tr. *A. Mermet's Princ. & Pract. Radiesthesia* iii. 36 No insulating substance is known which can affect radiesthetic radiations. *Ibid.* 37 Some reveal themselves to be radiesthetists at the first attempt, sometimes while undertaking an experiment for fun. **1962** M. Ash *Health, Radiation & Healing* iv. 88 He showed me how he took a radiesthetic reading by allowing a pendulum held in his hand to swing radially away from a patient's body and moving the pendulum gradually outwards until it began to swing in a different direction. **1977** D. V. Tansley *Dimensions of Radionics* p. xvii, Out of the investigation we made, there developed in due course his remarkable discovery that it was possible, radiesthetically, to find the archetypal pattern of any substance. **1978** Copen & Kowa *Pendulum* 7 There are radiesthesists in every country of the world, many who use it [*sc.* radiesthesia] as a hobby, others as a full-time profession.

† **radiferous** (rădi·fĕrəs), *a. Obs.* [f. *Radi(um + -ferous.] Containing or yielding radium.

1903 W. J. Hammer *Radium* 18 They used two small bulbs.., one containing one gramme of radiferous barium chloride. **1913** J. Cox *Beyond Atom* vi. 89 Several investigators made a thorough search of all the known radiferous minerals.

radio (rēɪ·dio), *sb.* orig. *U.S.* [Independent use of the initial element of *radio-telegram, *radio-telegraphy, etc.] † **I. 1.** A message sent by wireless telegraphy or telephony; a radio-telegram. *Obs.*

[**1906** *Internat. Radiotelegraphic Convention: Regulations* (Internat. Radiotelegr. Conf., Berlin) 34 Radiotelegrams bear the service instruction 'Radio' in the preamble.] **1915** R. H. Davis *With Allies* 2 For any exhibition they gave of excitement or concern, the news the radio brought them might have been the result of a by-election. **1920** *Glasgow Herald* 10 Aug. 7 In reply the Polish Government sent the following radio. **1923** R. D. Paine *Comrades of Rolling Ocean* xiv. 245, I shall have to get a radio off to my wife to come on from Ohio and meet me. **1924** R. Keable *Recompence* (1926) i. 18 There's a radio in. The *Balmoral* sailed a fortnight after we did.

II. 2. a. The transmission and reception of radio-frequency electromagnetic waves, esp. as a means of communication that does not need a connecting wire; wireless telephony or telegraphy.

Orig. in *attrib.* use only. *Radio-receiver* in quot. 1903 is prob. f. *radio- 4 and not necessarily to be taken as evidence of a word *radio*.

1903 Radio-receiver [see sense *5 a]. **1907** L. de Forest in *Electr. World* 22 June 1270/1 This factor, damping, is of far more vital import than any regulation of wave-lengths... Radio chaos will certainly be the result until..regulation is enforced. **1911** Radio-communication [see sense *5 a]. **1912** Radio station [see sense *7]. **1913** Radio operator [see sense *5 a]. **1914** Radio transmitter [see sense *5 a]. **1917** *Electr. Experimenter* Jan. 650 (*heading*) Election returns flashed by radio to 7,000 amateurs. **1919** *Pop. Sci. Monthly* Mar. 116/3 Instead of taking bearings by known landmarks, the bearings are determined from known wireless stations by means of radio. **1921** *Sci. Amer.* 2 July 5/1 Armstrong became interested in radio and erected a radio station at his home. **1922** C. W. Taussig (*title*) The book of radio: a complete, simple explanation of radio reception and transmission. **1924** *Glasgow Herald* 26 Jan. 11/5 At the time when radio is in its infancy, experimentalists midway in the United States summoned their friends to hear the Atlantic waves and Pacific surf simultaneously. **1948** A. L. Albert *Radio Fund.* x. 380 In radio, the feed-back coil of an oscillator is sometimes called a tickler. **1960** C. H. Gibbs-Smith *Aeroplane* xi. 76 In August [1910], radio was used for the first time between the ground and an aeroplane in flight. **1964** R. H. Baker *Astron.* (ed. 8) xvii. 505 (*heading*) Tracing of spiral arms by radio. **1975** Fink & McKenzie *Electronics Engineers' Handbk.* xviii. 62 In radio, polarization usually refers to the electric vector. **1976** Perkowski & Stral *Joy of CB* i. 6 It's the initial onslaught that is difficult to take, and that is somewhat the condition that we find ourselves in today with CB radio.

b. Organized wireless broadcasting in sound; the sound broadcasting network or service as a whole; sound broadcasting considered as a medium of communication or as an art form.

1922 *Sci. Amer.* June 376/2 Radio today is a continuous performance. You purchase your ticket in the form of a receiving set..and then listen in..to the music of today.. the news of the minute, stock quotations, and so on. **1944** W. C. Greet *World Words* p. v, For effective radio.. pronunciation is not an opportunity to be elegant but an everyday problem of what to do with..words. **1946** *B.B.C. Year Bk.* 29 Plays were a popular form of radio before the beginning of the war. **1951** *Ann. Reg. 1950* 415 Not only did these forums..make good radio, but they were also excellent publicity for the B.B.C. **1958** *Listener* 25 Sept. 482/1 It [*sc.* a play] was also made into some very good radio by the adaptation of the prologue spoken by Luxury and her daughter Poverty. **1960** *B.B.C. Handbk.* 33 In addition to the series of Party Political Broadcasts, the Budget broadcasts, and the Ministerial broadcasts (on sound radio and television), there were reports on Parliamentary topics..in the Home Service. **1966** *Listener* 2 June 816/3 Going back over reviews of the past three months I cannot find a dozen productions which were unequivocally radio and nothing else. **1967** *Ibid.* 18 May 653/1 In the evening they will have radio to listen to, television to watch, and darts and billiards as well in a light and attractive recreation room. **1972** G. Green *Great Moments in Sport: Soccer* xxii. 186 They invited me..to examine the organisational set-up they were planning—for spectators, press, radio, television and the rest. **1977** *Daily Tel.* 9 Feb. 11/2 The programme itself was not an outstanding piece of radio. **1978** *Times* 12 June 3/2 Mainly because of economies, radio had become very run down... Some equipment had not been replaced, studios were becoming less suitable. *Ibid.* 3/3 He welcomed the competition of commercial radio.

c. (Preceded by a proper name, esp. of a place.) A particular radio station or network.

1943 C. J. Rolo *Radio goes to War* xxii. 207 The Berlin radio continued to rely most heavily on divisive propaganda. **1958** *Whitaker's Almanack 1959* 582/1 Moscow radio announced that Russia had launched an earth satellite. **1967** *Listener* 12 Jan. 58/1, I do recall that Cairo radio—as well as many Western sources—had interpreted the Soviet warning to Britain and France requiring them to cease operations as implying a threat to bomb London and Paris by missiles. **1968** *Ibid.* 27 June 824/1 Ask Goose Bay Radio if they have any other traffic in this area. **1975** *Whitaker's Almanack* 593/1 The Ethiopian army took control of the national radio station in Addis Ababa and of the independent Voice of the Gospel Radio owned by the World Lutheran Federation. **1978** *Oxford Mail* 20 Feb. 1, Twelve Egyptian soldiers died and 19 were injured in the commando raid at Larnaca airport, Cyprus radio said today.

d. (With capital initial.) Forming the first part of the proper names of particular radio stations or services (the second part freq. being a place-name); *Radio 1, 2, 3, 4,* (also *Radio One*, etc.), the four national radio networks of the BBC (inaugurated on 30 Sept. 1967 in place of the programme services that had existed previously).

1920 *Wireless World* Jan. 587/2 A new Dutch wireless company, called the Nederlandsche Telegraaf Maatchappij 'Radio-Holland' has been formed... 'Radio-Holland' has been formed... 'Radio-Holland' acquires the rights of wireless installations on Dutch mercantile vessels..and the contracts relating thereto. **1926** *Encycl. Brit.* I. 455/1 In 1924–25 the Cie. Française de Radiophonie set up 'Radio Paris'..and provincial stations at Toulouse and Lyons. **1938** *Ann. Reg. 1937* 161 On New Year's Eve, a message from General Smuts, one of the founders of the League, was transmitted from 'Radio-Nations', the League wireless station at Geneva. **1958** *Economist* 25 Oct. 331/1 Radio Free Europe..concentrates on Poland, Czechoslovakia, Hungary, Rumania and Bulgaria, while Radio Liberation broadcasts to the Soviet Union, in no less than seventeen languages. **1964** *Daily Tel.* 13 May 1/8 Radio Atlanta, Britain's second floating commercial 'pirate' radio station, went on the air with programmes for the first time yesterday. **1967** *Listener* 17 Aug. 194/1 The new 247 metres network will be known as Radio 1. The 1500 metres and VHF network will be Radio 2, and..the present Third Network will become Radio 3 and the Home-Service network Radio 4. **1968** *B.B.C. Handbk.* 29 Our first local station, Radio Leicester, began broadcasting on 8 November 1967, followed shortly afterwards by Radio Sheffield and Radio Merseyside. **1973** P. Dickinson *Gift* ix. 139 Penny was listening to Radio One. **1976** *Daily Tel.* 30 June 1/4 Radio Uganda, monitored in Nairobi, gave no immediate indication of the 'penalties' involved. **1976** *Times* 29 Sept. 16/6 That all this may be entering the field of immodesty is redeemed by a quick smile and the admission that perhaps Radio 3 takes itself too seriously. **1978** *Bookseller* 1 July 54/1 Mike Stevenson, author of Ward Lock's biography of cricketer *Ray Illingworth*..has been interviewed on Radios Leicester, Leeds, Cleveland, Pennine, Piccadilly, Hallam and City.

3. Radio equipment; *spec.* a receiving set.

[**1913**: cf. *radio operator* in sense *5 a]. **1917** *Electr. Experimenter* May 3/1 When the German spies..found that it was not very healthy to operate their outfits in attics or in house chimneys..they simply put their radios in touring cars, cleverly concealing the aerial wires inside of the car bodies. **1925** H. L. Foster *Trop. Tramp with Tourists* 97 It fairly shrieked with the blare of jazz—of jazz from radios, jazz from mechanical pianos. **1936** King Edward VIII in *Manch. Guardian Weekly* 6 Mar. 185/1 Science has made it possible for me..to speak to you all over the radio. **1941** Auden *New Year Let.* II. 36 He moves on tiptoe round the room, Turns on the radio to mark Isolde's Sehnsucht for the dark. **1968** *New Society* 22 Aug. 265/2 Non-U *radio*/U *wireless* is no longer true; the U call it a radio too. **1973** J. Pattinson *Search Warrant* ii. 28 There was a load of noise... It sounded like a radio going full belt on a pop-music channel.

4. = *radio spectrum* in sense 7 below; radio wavelengths.

1968 *Physical Rev. Lett.* XXI. 1540/1 NGC1275 and 3C120..are a hundred times more luminous in the radio than most of the Seyferts. **1975** *Nature* 3 Jan. 7/1 It [*sc.* the Crab nebula] is unique in that it has been detected over the entire electromagnetic spectrum from radio through infrared and the visual to X rays and γ rays.

5. *attrib.* **a.** In general uses, as *radio aerial, antenna, apparatus, beacon* (= *beacon *sb.* 6 d), *beam, bearing, black-out, cabinet, communication, countermeasure, detector, fade-out, fix, intercept, link* (= *link *sb.*[2] 3 f), *marker, mast, message, operator, receiver* (in quot. 1903 prob. f. *radio- 4), *relay, room, set, shop, traffic, transmission, transmitter, valve.*

1949 E. B. Moullin (*title*) Radio aerials. **1968** *Times* 16 Oct. 8/8 It also seems to have a large radio aerial more suitable for a trip to the planets. **1927** B. F. Dashiell *Popular Guide to Radio* v. 71 (*heading*) The use of radio antennas and grounds. **1972** K. Bonfiglioli *Don't point that Thing at Me* xi. 89 It was the same car..but overnight it had..acquired a suit of whitewall tyres and another radio antenna. **1912** *Statutes U.S.A.* XXXVII. I. 303 The President..may cause the closing of any station for radio communication and the removal therefrom of all radio apparatus. **1916** *Lit. Digest* (N.Y.) 1 Jan 13/1 It is conceivable that this small body of men might have neither sending or receiving radio-apparatus. **1919**, etc. Radio beacon [see *beacon *sb.* 6 d]. **1966** D. Francis *Flying Finish* ii. 27, I flew contentedly along..checking my direction by the radio beacons over which I passed. **1923** E. W. Marchant *Radio Telegr.* i. 12 A ship coming into harbour will pick up the radio beam at the instant at which its direction is towards the ship. **1966** *McGraw-Hill Encycl. Sci. & Technol.* IX. 20/1 Radio beams that are transmitted from moving aircraft to the ground will have an apparent change of frequency. **1977** Radio beam [see *radio detector* below]. **1978** R. V. Jones *Most Secret War* xvii. 139 Milch, the Head of the Luftwaffe, was advising Goering that the current policy of night attacks was useless without special radio-beam devices, like the new X-Gerät. **1935** Radio bearing [see *fix *sb.* 3]. **1957** *Encycl. Brit.* XVI. 174/1 The accuracy of radio bearings ..[is] dependent upon properly functioning equipment and skilful operation. **1958** *New Scientist* 6 Mar. 8/3 The storm and its associated radio blackout. **1925** *Scribner's Mag.* Sept. 19/1 Have you seen a radio cabinet which..actually does not look like one? **1911** *Statutes U.S.A.* XXXVI. I. 629 (*heading*) An act to require apparatus and operators for radio-communication on certain ocean steamers. **1912** *Ibid.* XXXVII. I. 308 The expression 'radio communication' as used in this Act means any system of electrical communication by telegraphy or telephony without the aid of any wire connecting the points from and at which the radiograms, signals, or other communications are sent or received. **1942** *Electronic Engin.* XV. 116/1 Planck's constant *h*, is a universal one which is applicable to all radiations, including.. the wavelengths used in radio-communication. **1947** *Jrnl. R. Aeronaut. Soc.* LI. 425/2 The use of radio countermeasures, introduced for the first time with such telling effect in the last war, will be a prominent feature in all future large-scale conflicts. **1978** R. V. Jones *Most Secret War* xxii. 180 With our nightfighters and guns powerless, radio countermeasures were our only means of defence. **1936** *Discovery* Mar. 70/1 Each of these observatories is equipped..with..a radio detector, which enables the specialist to learn at once which station is transmitting. **1977** C. Forbes *Avalanche Express* x. 106 It takes two radio-detector vans..five minutes to take a fix on a secret transmitter—to plot from two locations the cross-point of the radio beams indicating where the transmission is coming from. **1937** Radio fade-out [see *fade-out 3]. **1942** Radio fix [see *fix *sb.* 3]. **1977** C. Forbes *Avalanche Express* xxi. 218 The operator in the radio-detector van..reached for the radio-telephone.. 'We have a radio fix, sir... Positive.' **1974** G. Markstein *Cooler* liv. 192 It was a radio intercept by security monitoring. The message, decoded, read: 'Stand by 24-hourly.' **1928**, etc. Radio link [see *link *sb.*[2] 3 f]. **1971** A. Diment *Think Inc.* xii. 208 'I love you,' I said and cut the radio link. **1978** *Dumfries Courier* 20 Oct. 10/2 A special Police control room on site at the NEC will have radio links with Police helicopter, car, motor cycle and foot patrols. **1933** *Nat. Geogr. Mag.* May 618/2 Radio-range and radio-marker beacons. **1942** B. A. Shields *Air Pilot Training* xxx. 515 Low-powered radio stations, called radio markers, ..are placed along the airways to serve as radio fixes. **1950** 'D. Divine' *King of Fassarai* v. 38 The metereological station was completed... The radio masts went up. **1976** *Cumberland & Westmorland Herald* 27 Nov., The committee approved the Corporation's application to build a radio mast almost 50 ft. high and a modular equipment building. **1916** *Lit. Digest* (N.Y.) 1 Jan 13/2 The radio-message containing this intelligence is flashed over the hills. **1974** M. Hastings *Dragon Island* xiii. 112, I have to..send a radio message to Djakarta. **1913** *Year-bk. Wireless Telegr.* 96 The radio operator..must furnish to the inspector evidence that he is 'skilled in the use of the apparatus'. **1925** *Scribner's Mag.* July 44/2 Hank Quiller was rated as chief radio operator on board the S.S. *Omega*. **1974** G. Markstein *Cooler* lxii. 218 If we find your killer we find your mysterious radio operator. **1903** C. H. Sewall *Wireless Telegr.* iv. 154 The first radio-receiver in which cause and effect were observed and recognized was devised by Hertz in 1886. **1929** J. H. Morecroft *Elem. Radio Communication* vii. 220 With coils having a power factor of about 1 per cent, as is the case with the average radio receiver, one tuned circuit will not give sufficient selectivity to eliminate interference. **1976** B. Jackson *Flameout* (1977) i. 22 They all wore Bellboy radio receivers in their shirt pockets, in case they could not be reached by telephone. **1926** *Wireless World* 1 Sept. 307/1 The wireless signals received in this Radio Relay Office are relayed to the Central Radio Office in the same building. **1927** B. F. Dashiell *Popular Guide to Radio* xi. 195 The radio relay scheme, whereby a program from a central station is broadcast, received and rebroadcast by other stations, has been successfully tried out. **1966** *McGraw-Hill Encycl. Sci. & Technol.* V. 520/2 Radio relays are used for simultaneous transmission of up to hundreds of telephone conversations over a trunk route. **1921** R. D. Paine *Comrades of Rolling Ocean* xiv. 244 A message from the radio-room, sir. **1976** 'J. Fraser' *Who steals my Name?* ii. 15 Later..the radio room springs into life, dispatching police cars..over the face of the city. **1913** *Proc. IRE* I. 43 The purpose of this paper is to describe some recent radio sets designed for the Marconi Wireless Telegraph Company of America to meet the new specifications of the United States Navy. **1926** S. Lewis *Mantrap* ii. 22 How necessary for hardy camp-life are the portable radio set, the pneumatic cushion. **1971** *Daily Tel.* 13 Sept. 1/8 The radio ham..heard two men planning the raid over short-wave radio sets. **1974** E. Jones *Barlow comes to Judgement* 127 He works in a radio shop in Bayswater. **1927** *Jrnl. Franklin Inst.* CCIV. 240 Beam stations are carrying regular radio traffic between England and Canada. **1973** D. Kyle *Raft of Swords* (1974) i. ix. 88 There had been remarkably little radio traffic. So he would sit in the radio room. **1935** C. G. Burge *Compl. Bk. Aviation* 506/1 The number of channels available for radio transmission is limited. **1974** G. Markstein *Cooler* li. 181 The interception stations..noted every illicit radio transmission. **1914** R. Stanley *Text Bk. Wireless Telegr.* xix. 300 The range of a given size of radio transmitter has been greatly increased since the time when coherer detectors were used in conjunction with a Morse tape machine or siphon recorder. **1970** V. Canning *Great Affair* x. 167 He probably had a secret radio transmitter and receiver somewhere. **1929** *Radio Times* 8 Nov. 434/2 (Advt.), The Radio Valves—with the only filament that has stood the test of time. **1970** P. Dickinson *Seals* ix. 178 It provided a short-cut in the mass-production of radio valves.

b. Connected with, participating in, or transmitted as part of organized sound broadcasting, as *radio acting, actor, actress, adaptation, announcer, audience, ballad, broadcast, broadcasting, bulletin, celebrity, comedian, commentator, commercial, company, critic, criticism, drama, dramatist, interview, journalism, journalist, listener, news, organization, personality, play, producer, production, programme, reporter, revue, script, serial, series, spot, star, talk, writer.*

1940 *Radio Times* 23 Aug. 6/4 Frederick Allen..had also done a considerable amount of radio acting and singing before becoming a BBC announcer. **1968** *Daily Tel.* (Colour Suppl.) 15 Nov. 32/3 He returned to a contract with Mr Beaumont, radio-acting, poetry recitals, bit parts in films. **1938** *Encycl. Brit. Bk. of Year* 123/1 The widespread unionization of radio actors. **1975** *Times* 20 Sept. 8/4 That uncommon breed, the exceptional radio actor. **1972** P. Black *Biggest Aspidistra in World* i. iv. 39 Jenny was played by Lilian Harrison, the leading radio actress of her day. **1931** T. H. Pear *Voice & Personality* viii. 94 Holt Marvell's radio-adaptation of..*Carnival*. **1927** *Scribner's Mag.* Apr. 437/2 We must listen to radio announcers who insist that the instant programme is most colorful. **1970** 'T. Coe' *Wax Apple* (1973) iv. 29 His voice was deep and resonant, like that of a radio announcer. **1932** *Radio Times* 29 July 251/3 Christopher Stone keeps the radio audience amused with a selection from the new discs. **1972** P. Black *Biggest Aspidistra in World* i. vii. 56 Mabel Constanduros, who in 1925 introduced the Buggins family..aiming..at the entire radio audience listening in its own family groups. **1960** *Times* 16 Aug. 5/2 Singing the Fishing; radio ballad by Ewan MacColl and Charles Parker. **1956** H. Kurnitz *Invasion of Privacy* xviii. 117 The late radio broadcasts..had given the Morley case a big spread. *a* **1974** R. Crossman *Diaries* (1976) II. 549 A B.B.C. experiment for live radio broadcasts of extracts from the House of Commons debate. **1922** Radio broadcasting [see *radiography 2]. **1975** *Listener* 25 Dec. 853/3 The poem, with its five voices, is suited to radio broadcasting. **1965** *B.B.C. Handbk.* 65 During the day well over twenty million people listen to at least one radio bulletin. **1948** E. E. Cummings *Let.* 20 Aug. (1969) 184 A charming & handsome & tall & sweet youth named Billy; think he later became a radio-celebrity. **1930** H. Nicolson *Diary* 18 Oct. (1966) 57, I have become 'famous' as a radio comedian, and shall never be able to live down the impression thus acquired. **1980** S. Brett *Dead Side of Mike* vi. 60 The programme was merely a showcase for the talents of a once-loved radio comedian. **1938** Radio commentator [see *commentator 2 c]. **1953** *Manch. Guardian* 21 May 1/4 Raymond Gram Swing was the most powerful and admired radio commentator working between the two major allies during the war. **1978** *Listener* 27 July 111/3 The skilled radio commentator..was there to tell you what is happening. **1951** M. McLuhan *Mech. Bride* (1967) 117/2 The big hefty heartiness of this is very familiar in the radio commercials. **1980** *Broadcast* 7 July 17/2 (Advt.), Production of radio commercials, voice-overs, stereo programmes. **1920** *Sci. Amer.* 24 July 79/1 A leading radio company is about to begin construction of a super-powered radio station. **1938** Joyce *Let.* 6 June (1966) III. 424 His (my son's) experience of broadcasting in the U.S.A...is that these Radio Companies are all in watertight compartments and that the director who has charge of the singing almost resents even a friendly introduction from the director, say, who controls the sports programme. **1974** *IBA Evidence to Annan Comm.* 46 The local radio companies should retain their creative initiative. **1929** *Vox* 9 Nov. 3/1 Heaven forbid that I should try to emulate the new Radio critics of the *Daily Express* who have apparently been told..to sit down immediately after tea and listen right through the evening, after which they are expected to discuss their indigestion attractively next morning. **1966** *B.B.C. Handbk.* 14 Every critic (and who is not his own television and radio critic?) would do well to temper his occasional rage with the thought that there is much to admire about the BBC. **1976** *Listener* 15 Jan. 42/1, I stopped being radio critic of the *Guardian*. **1940** R. S. Lambert *Ariel & all his Quality* vii. 173 It seemed desirable for the BBC to try and build up a..solid school of radio criticism. **1978** *Listener* 27 July 111/2, I was writing radio criticisms for *The Listener*. **1925** *Glasgow Herald* 1 Sept. 8 One of the many limitations of radio-drama will be the impossibility of introducing any but audible actions of a simple kind. **1951** M. McLuhan *Mech. Bride* (1967) 157/2 Soap operas are written and acted quite as well as the ordinary evening radio drama. **1929** *Radio Times* 8 Nov. 388/2 Conrad has, curiously, attracted the radio-dramatist. **1944** Radio dramatist [see *actuality 4 b]. **1926** G. Frankau *My Unsentimental Journey* ii. 37 A new form of torment, the 'radio interview'. **1974** *Guardian* 21 Mar. 1/3 Mr Edward Short, Leader of the House, said in a radio interview. **1968** *Listener* 21 Mar. 380/2 When the war was over Ed Murrow went back home, the 'first authentic original' of radio journalism. **1977** *Times* 14 May 10/5 Mary Goldring is a radio journalist... She has now concluded three reports on contemporary India. **1926** *Public Opinion* 2 July 17/2, 27,000,000 persons are now radio listeners in the United States. **1974** *Listener* 24 Jan. 123/3 Faithful radio listeners were entitled to their regular programmes. **1940** J. Flanner in *New Yorker* 7 Dec. 60/2 To Parisians, the most trusted radio news is what they get from the American short-wave broadcasts. **1973** A. Price *October Men* iii. 46 Not a word in the morning paper..or on the radio news. **1962** A. Nisbett *Technique Sound Studio* x. 168 At a radio organization such as the BBC it is easy to feel spoilt for choice. **1941** J. W. Welch in *Listener* (1978) 18 May 626/1 The BBC is now building up Joad as a radio personality. **1972** P. Black *Biggest Aspidistra in World* i. vii. 56 Tommy Handley..in 1929..was already a radio personality. **1924** *Variety* 24 Dec. 35/4 Gene Rouse, announcer for WOAW, has written a 'radio play'. **1973** M. Amis *Rachel Papers* 75, I slammed the door, so that the sounds of the radio-play on the kitchen wireless were reduced to an underground rumble. **1955** T. H. Pear *Eng. Social Differences* ix. 195 'Living by the clock' is a virtue in a radio-producer. **1974** *Listener* 14 Feb. 219/2 The radio producer hears the play over and over again. The lives and all the action become crystal-clear to him. **1959** D. Cooke *Lang. Mus.* iv. 200 A private tape-recording of a radio-production of *King Lear*. **1978** *Listener* 2 Feb. 152/1 *The Beggar's Opera*..is a splendid new radio production. **1922** *Variety* 10 Mar. 7/2 Among the theatres which will provide acts exclusively for the 'Star's' radio programs are the Shubert, Orpheum,..Royal and 12th streets. **1925** A. H. Morse *Radio* v. 78 There need be no limitation of the public enjoyment of the radio programme. **1972** *Sat. Rev.* (U.S.) 27 May 18/2 In Israel I was invited to go on a radio program to discuss the problem. **1926** *Wireless World* 18 Aug. 231/1 The radio reporters are kept busy all the summer, carrying their microphones to the important sporting events, [etc.]. **1975** *Times* 6 Jan. 12/8 Why did Sir Keith tell a radio reporter..that it [*sc.* a speech] was meant to be 'light-hearted'? **1929** *Radio Times* 8 Nov. 395/3 The brilliant little skit..which enlivened a recent radio revue. **1941** B. Schulberg *What makes Sammy Run?* ii. 30 He had written a radio script. **1962** A. Nisbett *Technique Sound Studio* ix. 156 Such a 'radio script' will probably have to be reinterpreted. **1958** M. Kennedy *Outlaws on Parnassus* ii. 28 A Dickens novel had to end sometime, whereas a radio serial can go on for ever. **1977** S. Brett *Star Trap* iv. 40, I can't do Friday... Doing a pilot of a radio series. **1973** *Black Panther* 28 Apr. 11/2 Bobby has layed out his program..in countless radio spots, interviews and discussions. **1932** *Radio Times* 29 July 279/3 (Advt.), A permanent..record of your favourite radio stars. **1980** P. Ableman *Shoestring's Finest Hour* i. 11 Lonely women who ring up famous radio stars..in the hope of getting to sleep with them. **1940** R. S. Lambert *Ariel & all his Quality* vii. 173 Experts are able..to express themselves freely..about current radio drama, music, talks, and television programmes. **1943** D. Powell *Time to be Born* i. 8 My days are filled with my war committees and my refugee children and my radio talks. **1977** *Listener* 16 June 800/3 BBC Television now appears to be giving radio talks. **1944** L. MacNeice

Christopher Columbus 8 The radio writer has to think of words in the mouths of actors.

c. Designating devices controlled or operated by radio, as *radio bomb*; vehicles equipped with radio for receiving information, directions, etc., as *radio cab, car, taxi, van.*

1974 D. SEAMAN *Bomb that could Lip-Read* xxiv. 243 Once they discover it was a radio bomb, they will take this hamlet apart. **1977** *Times* 18 July 1/4 (*heading*) Provisional IRA widen use of radio bombs. **1955** J. B. PRIESTLEY in Priestley & Hawkes *Journey down Rainbow* xii. 173 Most of the taxis down here are like our radio cabs in London, but the voice of the distant operator, calling cabs and giving addresses, is always left turned on. **1977** F. WELDON in *Winter's Tales 23* 190 Maureen's on the phone, calling radio cabs. **1925** *Sci. Amer.* Nov. 308/1 The Yard has seven radio-equipped motor cars attached to the Criminal Investigation flying squad... These radio cars not only aid in detecting crime but also perform a helpful service in regulating heavy traffic along the highways. **1967** *Listener* 19 Jan. 95/2 WINS reporters were there with their radio cars and tape recorders inching the story along every few minutes or so with eye-witness reports, [etc.]. **1973** 'E. MCBAIN' *Hail to Chief* i. 3 Two radio-car cops, on routine patrol. **1962** *Spectator* 13 Apr. 486 Lots of tourist information, though we do have radio-taxis here too. **1977** E. AMBLER *Send no more Roses* x. 215, I had used the time..to check out the local radio-taxi services. **1950** J. FLANNER in *New Yorker* 8 Apr. 79/1 On the street, crowds had collected and a radio van had arrived. **1974** N. FREELING *Dressing of Diamond* 10 They [*sc.* the police] say they've two radio vans.

d. Chiefly *Astr.* Connected with the natural emission of radio waves (freq. denoting objects or entities which emit radio waves in unusually large quantities or are being considered as sources of radio waves), as *radio brightness, emission, emitter, flux, galaxy, noise, observatory, sky, source, sun, universe.*

1960 RODMAN & VARSAVSKY tr. *I. S. Shklovsky's Cosmic Radio Waves* iii. 174 The radio brightness of the hypothetical objects, averaged over time, would thus exceed that of the sun by some ten orders of magnitude. **1974** *Sci. Amer.* Aug. 26/3 In the direction of this cloud of ionized gas, designated 30 Doradus, there is a decrease in the radio brightness of the sky. **1949** *Nature* 12 Nov. 816/1 Only a proportion of the flares have associated radio bursts, the bigger flares being the more likely to produce strong radio emissions. **1958** *Listener* 27 Nov. 870/1 One of the earliest of the post-war surprises was the discovery by Appleton and Hey that the sun spots and flares which occasionally appear on the solar surface are associated with large and irregular increases in the solar radio emissions. **1978** *Nature* 14 Sept. 111/1 One of the most important features of the jovian decametric radioemission comes from the geometry of the observed radiation. **1954** *Ann. Reg. 1953* 373 Future accurate measurements of the positions of cosmic radio emitters. **1951** *Monthly Notices R. Astron. Soc.* CXI. 366 The intensity of the radio flux from M31 observed on the Earth at a wavelength of 1·89 metres is 10^{-24} watts/square metre/c.p.s. **1960** RODMAN & VARSAVSKY tr. *I. S. Shklovsky's Cosmic Radio Waves* vi. 356 The relative radio emitting power of radio galaxies is 10^3 and even 10^5 times as great as for normal galaxies. **1973** *Sci. Amer.* Sept. 72/3 Many 'classic' radio galaxies consist of an optically bright galaxy situated halfway between two radio-emitting regions. **1979** *Jrnl. R. Soc. Arts* CXXVII. 582/1 The so-called 'radio galaxies', whose power output in radio waves exceeds the total galactic luminosity of all the stars. **1933** *Gen. Electr. Rev.* XXXVI. 201/1 The radio-noise meter..detects radio noise, measures its intensity, and locates its source. **1946** *Nature* 17 Aug. 234/1 The solar radio noise from sunspots is also characterized by strong fluctuations. **1977** *New Yorker* 19 Sept. 137/1 In 1964, two radio astronomers..made the unexpected discovery that there was cosmic radio noise entering their system which they could do nothing to get rid of. **1958** *Ann. Reg. 1957* 472 The principal radio-observatories developed during the previous few years. **1969** *Times* 18 Apr. 12/6 The Parkes radio observatory in New South Wales. **1959** DAVIES & PALMER *Radio Studies of Universe* iv. 46 The early maps of the radio sky were made with small aerials which could not readily distinguish radio sources from the background of radio emission. **1950** *Monthly Notices R. Astron. Soc.* CX. 519 The five major extra-galactic nebulae in the selected area are listed.. together with the radio sources which appear to be associated with them. **1961** *New Scientist* 5 Jan. 50/1 About 30 per cent of the accurately measured and suitably placed radio sources can be identified with visible galaxies. **1971** *Sci. Amer.* May 56/3 Before 1960 radio astronomers had identified and catalogued hundreds of radio sources. **1961** WEBSTER, Radio sun. **1965** M. R. KUNDU *Solar Radio Astron.* i. 1 Decimeter-wave observations of the radio sun during a solar eclipse. **1974** G. L. VERSCHUUR *Invisible Universe* iii. 32 (*heading*) The radio sun and planets. **1960** RODMAN & VARSAVSKY tr. *I. S. Shklovsky's Cosmic Radio Waves* vi. 355 Further investigations of the variations in the cosmic radio-wave background at high galactic latitudes will undoubtedly reveal new peculiarities of the 'radio universe'.

6. *Comb.* (cf. *RADIO- 4): *radio-controlled* (so *radio-control* vb. trans.), *-emitting, -equipped, -linked, -minded, -receiving, -steered, -transmitting* adjs.

1959 K. VONNEGUT *Sirens of Titan* vii. 121 Without Boaz, their real commander, to radio-control them, they fought bitterly. **1979** *Amat. Photographer* 30 May 162/3 The Post Office refusing him a license to radio-control a camera. **1936** *Punch* 4 Mar. 273/1 Then possibly another sequel in which the generations are estranged over the question of small rubber electric radio-controlled fish. **1958** I. ASIMOV *Naked Sun* i. 9 The radio-controlled flight would be smooth; there would scarcely be any sensation of motion once the plane was airborne. **1976** L. ST. CLAIR *Fortune in Death* xi. 109 The gates swung wide—radio-controlled. **1960** Radio-emitting [see *radio galaxy* in sense 5 d above]. **1971** *Sci. Amer.* May 56/3 Object 3C 48 was thought to be a unique kind of radio-emitting star in our own galaxy until 1963. **1935** C. G. BURGE *Compl. Bk. Aviation* 499/1 By means of radio and land-line the pilot of a radio-equipped 'plane is to-day in closer touch with the ground than the driver of a normal road vehicle. **1963** A. LUBBOCK *Austral. Roundabout* 36, I wouldn't like to say what my radio-equipped bikes and plane save me in time and labour. **1974** H. R. F. KEATING *Bats fly up for Inspector Ghote* iii. 33 Ghote, in yet a third radio-linked car, would be a useful addition to the team. **1930** *Wireless World* 10 Dec. 655/3 To the housewife anxious to please her radio-minded family I would say fill the Christmas pudding this year with a fair sprinkling of miniature fuse lamps instead of with sixpences. **1922** *Glasgow Herald* 21 Apr. 10 Already the number of radio receiving outfits installed in private houses runs into seven figures. **1936** *Discovery* Mar. 69/2 Some 70 radio-receiving observatories all round the earth. **1917** *Nature* 2 Aug. 442/2 Attempts to develop a radio-steered torpedo. **1935** C. G. BURGE *Compl. Bk. Aviation* 511/1 The purpose of the radio compass is to determine whether or not one is flying directly towards a radio-transmitting station. **1959** *Observer* 3 May 17/5 The Authority has now developed radiotransmitting tide gauges which will continuously relay to Gravesend the height of the water at all points of navigational importance. **1978** R. V. JONES *Most Secret War* xliv. 422 We had not known beforehand of these radio-transmitting samples.

7. Special Combs. (cf. *RADIO- 4): **radio altimeter,** an altimeter which functions by emitting a radio signal and measuring the time it takes to be reflected back from the ground; **radio amateur,** one who makes a hobby of picking up, and often also transmitting, radio messages; **radio compass,** a radio direction-finder used for the purpose of navigation; **radio contact,** the state or an instance of being in communication by radio; **radio dial** = *DIAL *sb.*[1] 6 e; **radio direction-finder** = **direction-finder*; so **radio direction-finding; radio dish** = *DISH *sb.* 4 b; **radio echo** = *ECHO *sb.* 1 d; **radio energy,** energy transmitted in the form of radio waves; **radio engineering,** the branch of engineering concerned with the design, construction, and operation of radio equipment; so **radio engineer; radio ham** *colloq.* [*HAM *sb.*[1] 6], = *radio amateur* above; **radio industry,** the radio engineering or sound broadcasting industries; **radio licence,** a licence certificate that owners of radios are required to have; (such licences for radio only were abolished in the U.K. in 1971); **radio-loud** *a. Astr.*, emitting significant quantities of radio waves; **radio man,** (*a*) a man who operates, repairs, or otherwise deals with radios; (*b*) a man employed in sound broadcasting; **radio map** *Astr.*, a diagram showing the strength of the radio emission from different parts of the sky; **radio microphone** (see quot. 1962); also (*colloq.*) **radio mike; radio navigation,** navigation by means of radio signals; so **ra:dio-naviga·tional** *a.*; **radio net,** a system of intercommunicating radio sets, operated esp. by a police force or similar body; **radio network,** a system of radio stations for navigation, communication, or broadcasting; a sound broadcasting organization or channel; **radio pager** = *PAGER *sb.*[3]; so **radio paging** *vbl. sb.*; **radio-pho·nograph** *U.S.* = *RADIO-GRAMOPHONE; **radio pill** *colloq.* = *endoradiosonde* s.v. *ENDO-; **radio pirate** = *PIRATE *sb.* 4 b; **radio-qui·et** *a.*, emitting a negligible amount of radio waves; hence **radio-qui·etness; radio-radar,** used *attrib.* of devices, systems, etc., combining radio and radar; **radio range,** (*a*) = *radio spectrum* below; (*b*) a radio beacon transmitting directional radio signals which can be used by aircraft possessing appropriate receiving apparatus to determine the bearing of the transmitter; **radio shack,** a small building housing radio equipment; (esp. *Naut.*) a radio room; **radio show,** (*a*) an exhibition of radio equipment, etc.; (*b*) a radio programme, usu. featuring light entertainment; **radio signal,** a radio message; a group of radio waves transmitted or emitted by any source; **radio silence,** deliberate abstention from radio transmission; failure to communicate by radio; **radio-silent** *a.*, (*a*) maintaining radio silence; (*b*) = *radio-quiet* adj. above; **radio sounding,** the use of radiosondes or radar techniques for investigating the atmosphere, sea bed, or the like; so **radio sounder; radio spectrum,** the radio-frequency part of the spectrum of electromagnetic radiation; also, the spectrum of any particular source at these frequencies; **radio star,** any discrete source of radio waves outside the solar system (rarely a star in the usual sense); **radio station,** a radio-transmitting installation or establishment; a sound broadcasting establishment or organization; **radio telescope** *Astr.*, an apparatus or installation for detecting and recording radio waves from the sky with great sensitivity and a high degree of resolution, consisting essentially of a large sensitive directional aerial together with a receiver and recording equipment; (in quot. 1929, a fictitious apparatus in which a 'radio contrivance' is attached to an optical telescope); **radio wave,** an electromagnetic wave having a frequency within the range used for telecommunication; (cf. *RADIO-FREQUENCY); usu. *pl.*; so **radio wavelength.**

1940 *Chambers's Techn. Dict.* 698/2 Radio altimeter. **1953** R. CHISHOLM *Cover of Darkness* I. xii. 123 My Mosquito had a radio altimeter, a device which gave absolute readings of height. **1968** *Times* 15 Nov. 8/6 The radio-altimeter, which made only one measurement of the probe's altitude, must have been wrong. **1916** *Lit. Digest* (N.Y.) 1 Jan. 13/1 But there will be a lone radio amateur on the alert who has seen the approaching fleet. **1977** *N.Z. Herald* 5 Jan. 1. 1/8 Mr Kilpatrick said radio amateurs—there are almost 4000 in New Zealand—were anxious to have aerial installation defined because of the growing public interest in town planning and the environment. **1918** *Flying* 14 Aug. 150/3 The radio-compass and wireless log signals will doubtless be pressed into service in the age of commercial aviation. **1946** *Happy Landings* July 9/1 A severe thunderstorm can be detected by intelligent use of the Radio Compass. **1966** *McGraw-Hill Encycl. Sci. & Technol.* III. 332/2 The modern radio compass uses a nondirectional antenna in combination with a bidirectional loop antenna to provide a unidirectional bearing indication. **1958** *Times* 18 Jan. 8/7 It will enable the masters or pilots of vessels coming in and out of Southampton to coordinate their movements with other shipping by direct radio contact with the radio information centre. **1962** V. GRISSOM in *Into Orbit* 130, I was in radio contact with..the helicopters which were on their way to pick me up. **1975** T. ALLBEURY *Special Collection* v. 34 He had a long radio contact with London and..gave full details. **1976** H. MACINNES *Agent in Place* xvii. 185 'Emil is sleeping on board.' 'You've radio contact with him?' 'Of course.' **1934** WEBSTER, Radio dial. **1974** *Listener* 7 Nov. 593/3 Twiddling his radio dial to hear what is top of the pops. **1922** *Sci. & Invention* May 10/1 (*caption*) The radio direction finder aboard this vessel can locate the transmitting station within one half a degree accuracy. **1966** *McGraw-Hill Encycl. Sci. & Technol.* IV. 232/2 This ground-based radio direction finder, operating at frequencies of 2 to 20 megacycles, is used mainly for navigational assistance in the long-distance en-route zone. **1920** *Radio Rev.* Oct. 644 Radio direction finding..has become a practical possibility owing to the use of powerful amplifiers. **1974** *Encycl. Brit. Macropædia* XII. 903/2 Radio direction finding..developed in two ways. First, radio transmitters, or 'beacons', were sited..to enable ships or aircraft to fix their positions. Second, ground DF stations that could pick up radio signals sent out by a ship or an aircraft were built. **1960** *Aeroplane* XCVIII. 366/2 The largest steerable radio 'dish' in the World, at Jodrell Bank in England. **1977** *Nature* 9 June 478/1 Australia leapt into the big league of astronomical nations with the building of the giant 64-metre radio dish at Parkes, New South Wales. **1928** Radio echo [see *ECHO *sb.* 1 d]. **1947** *Sci. News* V. 36 Radio echoes do not come from the meteors themselves but from the lengthy filament of highly conducting gas which forms their trail or streak. **1975** *Nature* 30 Oct. 780/2 A radio-echo technique gave the surface velocity relative to a layer that reflected electromagnetic waves—evidently from a level close to the base of the ice. **1946** *Proc. IRE* XXXIV. 558/2 Presumably, radio energy could..be focused by means of lenses made of a material such as plastic or glass which is transparent at the transmitter frequency. **1955** *Sci. Amer.* Mar. 36/1 The radio energy given forth by..Cygnus A, startles even astronomers. **1974** F. W. COLE *Fund. Astron. Solar Syst. & Beyond* xiv. 379/1 Certain peculiar galaxies emit thousands of times more radio energy than does an average galaxy. **1912** *Electrician & Mechanic* Aug. 140/1 The Institute of Radio-Engineers comprises the bodies formerly known as the Society of Wireless Telegraph Engineers and the Institute of Wireless Engineers. **1937** *Discovery* Apr. 111/1 Radio engineers have recorded an increasing number of sudden and complete fadings affecting reception on short-wave wireless transmission. **1974** *Encycl. Brit. Macropædia* XV. 429/2 Marconi's faith in the successful commercial operation of the system was more than justified, and radio engineers elsewhere were quick to change from skepticism to enthusiasm. **1917** *Wireless World* Apr. 10 The name 'wireless system' in radio engineering seems now to have no scientific meaning. **1942** P. C. SANDRETTO *Princ. Aeronaut. Radio Engin.* p. v, It is necessary to explain how I determined the point where ordinary radio engineering ends and aeronautical radio engineering begins. **1975** D. G. FINK *Electronics Engineers' Handbk.* p. xiii, This new Handbook is the first to be devoted to the field of electronics engineering at large. Earlier important handbooks..treated the field primarily from the point of view of the first important application in the field—radio engineering. **1928** Radio ham [see *HAM *sb.*[1] 6]. **1951** H. M. WATSON et al. *Understanding Radio* (ed. 2) xxvi. 642 The exploits of the radio hams in times of disaster..are well known. **1971** *Daily Tel.* 13 Sept. 1/8 The radio ham..heard two men planning the raid over short-wave radio sets. **1926** *Wireless World* 18 Aug. 229/1 American business men engaged in the radio industry. **1933** *Radio Times* 14 Apr. 94 (Advt.), Mullard valves have always taken the radio industry ahead. **1951** M. MCLUHAN *Mech. Bride* (1967) 22/2 This is not a situation peculiar, for example, to the radio, movie or book industries. **1928–9** *T. Eaton & Co. Catal.* Fall & Winter 245/3 Radio License... The law requires that every radio set be licensed. **1969** *Morning Star* 9 Aug. 5 Heavier fines for TV and radio licence dodgers have been called for by the Postmaster General. **1975** *Times* 26 Sept. 15/4 His father was one of the original radio licence holders. **1978** *Nature* 14 Sept. 91/3 Less than 10% of these [QSOs] are turning out to be 'radio-loud'. 1921 R. D. Paine *Comrades of Rolling Ocean* iv. 73 The radio man reports storm signals hoisted all the way from Key West to Norfolk. 1928–9 *T. Eaton & Co. Catal.* Fall & Winter 245/3 Our radio goods..are purchased and inspected by qualified radio men. 1945 M. Lowry *Let.* 6 June (1967) 46 A great friend of mine who was at college with me—a well-known radioman in Canada. 1977 *Time* 3 Jan. 35/2 He lied about his age to get into the Navy and served as a radioman in the Pacific during World War II. 1977 *New Statesman* 2 Sept. 298/1 This is not because Bush has a particularly high quota of veteran radio men. 1978 Pasachoff & Kutner *University Astron.* viii. 221 (*caption*) A radio map of the sun made at a wave-length of 2·8 cm with the 100-meter dish of the Max Planck Institute for Radio Astronomy. 1962 A. Nisbett *Technique Sound Studio* 267 *Radio microphone*, microphone and small transmitter sending a signal which can be picked up at a distance of up to perhaps several hundred yards. 1978 *Broadcast* 6 Feb. 12/3 Licences which authorize..mobile radiotelephone, radiomicrophones, radiopaging devices. 1980 J. Ball *Then came Violence* (1981) xvi. 144 He picked up the radio microphone. 1974 *Listener* 14 Mar. 330/3 Rix..had me fitted with a radio mike, which is..a small and highly sensitive transmitter, enabling me to record impressions unobtrusively. 1931 B. Jones *Avigation* xv. 274 (*heading*) Radio navigation. 1951 *Sci. News* XXII. 110 Positions were fixed by radio navigation. 1974 *Encycl. Brit. Macropædia* XII. 908/2 Loran..is a radio-navigation system that permits a ship to locate its position accurately by timing the arrival of pulses from synchronized shore transmitters. 1921 *Brit. Pat. 161,448* (*title*) Improvements in or relating to radio-navigational systems. 1958 *Times* 18 Aug. 8/3 The Nantucket field had no instrument landing system, no high intensity approach lights, and only a minimum of radio navigational aids. 1978 R. V. Jones *Most Secret War* xxiv. 210 The drive at last started for us to emulate the Germans in their radio navigational techniques. 1941 *Sun* (Baltimore) 15 Oct. 5/5 The Twenty-ninth Division has its full complement of radio nets, and is maintaining its communications of this nature with considerable success. 1976 C. Egleton *State Visit* ix. 84 A re-broadcast system had been installed which allowed them to monitor the police radio net. 1935 C. G. Burge *Compl. Bk. Aviation* 503/1 Air transport is essentially international in character, and the organization and control of the radio networks, if they are to benefit air transport, must also be applied on an international basis. 1966 N. Wymer *From Marconi to Telstar* viii. 85 Since the war all the great nations have steadily expanded their overseas services until today the radio network covers the entire world. 1972 J. Mosedale *Football* iv. 52 New York..is the communications capital of the world—home to national magazines and the television and radio networks. 1968 Radio pager [see *pager *sb.*[3]]. 1960 Radio paging [see *page *v.*[1] c]. 1978 *Times* 3 Nov. 27/4 The Post Office itself has listed the main telecommunications services ..envisaged for the years 1985 and 2000... By 1985 there will be..radiopaging, confravision (conference television), viewphone. 1925 *Scribner's Mag.* Sept. 80 (Advt.), Model 50 Radio-Phonograph Combination. Price $325. 1952 Auden *Nones* 18 According to the gospel Of the radio-phonograph. 1979 T. Gifford *Hollywood Gothic* (1980) xxi. 216 An ancient Philco radio-phonograph. 1957 *Nature* 4 May 898/1 This 'radio pill', as it is termed, was designed by Dr. V. K. Zworykin and developed by engineers of the Radio Corporation of America at Camden, New Jersey. 1962 *New Scientist* 10 May 288/3 A radio pill contains an electronic circuit that generates a radio frequency signal. 1970 *Sci. Jrnl.* June 84/1 Pressure changes within the vagina and uterus have also been measured, by using a tiny device known as the radio-pill. 1933 Radio pirate [see *pirate *sb.* 4 b]. 1964 *Daily Tel.* 11 May 20 (*heading*) Radio 'pirates' problem for Cabinet. 1965 *Astrophysical Jrnl.* CXLI 1560 Members of the class called here quasi-stellar galaxies..resemble the quasi-stellar radio sources..in many optical properties, but they are radio-quiet. 1977 *Sci. Amer.* Aug. 38/3 Many quasars have no detectable radio emissions. In fact, the great majority of quasars may be radio quiet. 1971 D. W. Sciama *Mod. Cosmol.* v. 73 It must be emphasised that the radio-quietness of ethse new objects is only relative. 1949 *Sun* (Baltimore) 26 July 18/3 The wing tip 'radomes', as the compact radio-radar installation is called, were developed for the Air Force. 1966 M. Woodhouse *Tree Frog* viii. 62 A radio-radar control system with a range of seven hundred miles. 1976 G. H. Morrison in L.-H. Lee *Characterization of Metal & Polymer Surfaces* I. 362 Our laboratory has been involved in an examination of steel strands in the cables suspending a 525-ton feed platform in the world's largest radio-radar telescope at Arecibo, Puerto Rico. 1926 *Physical Rev.* XXVII. 202 The ionic term will be negligibly small compared to the electronic term, except for very long waves outside of the usual radio range. 1929 *Proc. IRE* XVII. 2147 The so-called 'aural' type of directive radiobeacon, or 'radio range' as it is now called, was finally considered to be most applicable to the Airways Service. 1942 P. C. Sandretto *Princ. Aeronaut. Radio Engin.* i. 7 By the late fall of 1929, there was installed in the United States a line of radio ranges extending from New Jersey to Iowa. 1949 *Nature* 12 Nov. 816/2 The radio range from about 1 cm. to 20 m. 1951 *Oxf. Jun. Encycl.* IV. 291/1 The Radio Range, a long-range navigational aid..transmits the letters A..and N..in Morse code simultaneously in different directions. If the pilot is flying directly on his proper course, he will be midway between the paths of the two signals. 1960 Rodman & Varsavsky tr. *I. S. Shklovsky's Cosmic Radio Waves* ii. 84 Thus if the sun appears to be the dominating source of radiation at optical frequencies, in the radio range it plays a much more modest role. 1966 *McGraw-Hill Encycl. Sci. & Technol.* XI. 255/2 *Consol*... This radio range navigation aid provides a number of characteristic signal zones that rotate in a time sequence. 1946 R. E. Higginbotham *Wine for my Brothers* v. 97 He paused a moment before the door of the radio shack. 1973 D. Kyle *Raft of Swords* (1974) xiv. 152 Bill Harrison was sitting in his radio shack at Bella Bella. 1976 'M. Nelson' *Crusoe Test* iii. 42 He had veered off into the captain's room..taken the radio shack key... He had only needed seconds in the radio room. 1922 *Moving Picture Stories* 4 Aug. 22/2 When the Women's Radio League of America some months ago asked me to join them and appear at their exhibition at a radio show, I thought it a unique invitation. 1932 *Radio Times* 29 July 239/2 Peter Creswell will produce *Ball and Dance*, a German radio show built up from scenes at famous balls of history. 1940 G. Marx *Let.* 10 Oct. (1967) 26 I'm..discussing a radio show that I might do... A kind of human interest story with a slightly wacky father, who, of course, would be me. 1971 D. Nathan *Laughtermakers* ii. 50 When the series was over Milligan went to Australia, where he did thirteen radio shows similar to the Goons. 1976 B. Took *Laughter in Air* i. 11 Theatre magnates still held the whip hand, making offers they couldn't refuse to Arthur Askey and Jack Warner for stage versions of their hit radio shows. 1923 E. W. Marchant *Radio Telegr.* ix. 100 The problem of finding the direction from which a radio signal is coming has been referred to already, and its practical importance..is obvious. 1937 *Discovery* Jan. 3/2 Radio signals can travel round the world and not be lost in space as would be the case if the ionosphere did not exist. 1962 F. I. Ordway et al. *Basic Astronautics* iii. 46 The planet [*sc.* Mercury] emits natural radio signals. 1969 *Times* 16 Jan. 4/7 Measurements of the radio signals from sulphur hydride may be a valuable check of estimates of the amount of sulphur in interstellar space. 1974 L. Deighton *Spy Story* xix. 208 That radio signal obliges us to continue with the pick-up. 1946 Radio silence [see *radiolocator]. 1959 R. Collier *City that wouldn't Die* vii. 106 [He] exultantly broke radio-silence: 'I've got two dirty great Huns in my sights!' 1970 A. Dekker *Divers Diamonds* ii. 15 *Toledo* [*sc.* a submarine] has subsequently maintained total radio silence and has gone without trace. 1977 *Observer* 3 Apr. 1/6 The control tower said sharply, 'Radio silence please, I will continue to call up KLM.' 1978 *Peace News* 25 Aug. 8/2 This 'strike' lasted some three days, and rumour had it that GCHQ feared that the Russians were maintaining 'radio silence', the traditional prelude to offensive action! 1976 B. Lecomber *Dead Weight* xiii. 154 Filing incomplete flight plans and going radio-silent for long periods is bloody silly. 1977 *Sci. Amer.* Aug. 38/3 Only later, when the sky was searched at optical wavelengths for bright blue and ultraviolet objects, were the radio-silent quasars discovered. 1931 *Flight* XXIII. 278/1 The trials proceeding in America with a radio-sounder have been successful and appear to promise good results. 1969 *Times* 20 Jan. 8/1 Alouette 1, the first of a series of satellites built in Canada..is equipped with a radio sounder which probes the atmosphere beneath the satellite. 1929 *Bull. Amer. Meteorol. Soc.* X. 220 The radio sounding balloons to be released from the *Graf Zeppelin* will employ a radio sending device developed under the direction of P. A. Moltchanoff. 1936 *Meteorol. Mag.* LXXI. 5 (*heading*) Radio-sounding of the atmosphere. 1958 Miller & Parry *Everyday Meteorol.* i. 29 The radio-sounding balloon..has the advantage that it need not be visible. 1963 *Times* 31 May 16/2 A form of radio sounding, similar to radar, may provide a new means of charting the depth of rock surfaces covered by snow and ice, as in Greenland and Antarctica. 1929 *Bell System Techn. Jrnl.* VIII. 313 Fortunately this frequency was so located in the radio spectrum that a band of the desired width..could be obtained. 1932 *Proc. IRE* XX. 96 Ultra-short waves in point-to-point propagation resemble light waves rather than the longer and more conventional waves of the radio spectrum. 1964 R. H. Baker *Astron.* (ed. 8) iv. 116 The only known emission line in the radio spectrum was first observed..in 1951. 1978 *Nature* 8 June 431/2 Samples of QSOs with flat radio spectra were chosen. 1949 *Sci. Amer.* Sept. 38/1 The small spots are tiny enough to be considered 'radio stars'. 1957 *New Scientist* 27 June 32/1 Ryle concludes that his weak radio stars are evidence of more crowded days when the universe was young. 1963 *Times* 20 Apr. 8/4 The first true radio stars—stars (in the ordinary sense) that emit radio waves at sufficient intensity to be detected and identified by radio telescopes—have been discovered by Sir Bernard Lovell. 1969 *Times* 18 Apr. 12/5 Pulsars, the radio stars whose clock-like regularity has so far eluded explanation. 1912 *Statutes U.S.A.* XXXVII. 1. 303 Every Government station on land or sea shall have special call letters designated and published in the list of radio stations of the United States. 1934 Joyce *Let.* 20 Nov. (1966) III. 328 You don't say what those radio stations pay. 1968 A. Diment *Bang Bang Birds* iii. 41 One of the local radio stations gave me the news. 1977 C. McCullough *Thorn Birds* xv. 340 Progress had finally come to Gillanbone in the shape of an Australian Broadcasting Commission radio station. 1929 *Amazing Stories* June 202/1 Well, what do you think of it?.. How do you like my radio-telescope? 1948 *Newsweek* 18 Nov. 98/2 The newer radio telescope..is designed to gather radio static in the microwave region. 1953 *N.Y. Times* 19 Apr. E9/5 The foundations of Britain's million-dollar radio telescope.. are now being built at Jodrell Bank, Cheshire. 1969 *Times* 25 Mar. 12/6 The experiment was carried out with the giant radio telescope carved out of a natural bowl in the hills of Puerto Rico. 1976 L. Deighton *Twinkle, twinkle, Little Spy* xxiii. 229 Two huge radio telescopes, the dishes about sixty feet across. 1916 *Electr. Experimenter* IV. 486/3 If the radio waves were powerful enough to travel from Mars to the moon, they..could travel from the moon to Mars. 1946 *Nature* 3 Aug. 150/1 As radio-waves are reflected by obstacles of any kind, they can be used in darkness as well as daylight, in thick fog or other obscuring atmospheric conditions, as light to show whether the way is open or not. 1969 G. Lyall *Venus with Pistol* xxxiii. 212 The dark air between us slowly started to hum like radio waves. 1977 *Times* 20 June 5/2 Through vibrations, the radio wave can transmit conversation and noise back from the room it is aimed at. 1937 *Proc. Nat. Acad. Sci.* XXIII. 178 The low opacity in the radio wavelengths, arising from the small relative size of the particles, will selectively permit the escape of these longer wavelengths. 1972 *Sci. Amer.* Aug. 51/3 Neutral atomic hydrogen emits and absorbs radiation at the radio wavelength of 21 centimeters and can be readily observed by radio telescopes.

radio (rē[1]·dio), *v.* [f. the sb.] **a.** *trans.* To transmit or send (a message or information) by radio. **b.** *intr.* To send a message, etc., by radio; to give information or make a request by radio (with dependent clause). (In both senses freq. with advbs.)

1919 *Pop. Sci. Monthly* Sept. 116/2 He radios the information to the ship. 1926 H. T. Wilkins *Marvels Mod. Mech.* 213 As soon as the observer spots a shoal of fish, he marks a square on the chart,..and at once radios to the port. 1926 *Glasgow Herald* 20 Dec. 9 The British ship Defender has radioed that it has saved two members of the crew of the schooner Lincoln. 1937 G. Frankau *More of Us* xiii. 136 Let Pink flay Anti-Pink, or vice versa, 'Delicious weather', radio'd still our purser. 1958 *Industr. & Engin. Chem.* Mar. 22A/2 Explorer has radioed back information that the temperature inside is between 20° and 50 °C., tolerable enough for a human passenger. 1958 'Castle' & 'Hailey' *Flight into Danger* ii. 29 Let me know if she gets any worse and I'll radio ahead. 1969 *New Yorker* 12 Apr. 68/2 A satellite..radioed information about the fields of low-energy particles far above the earth. 1970 *Daily Tel.* 14 Oct. 1/3 The lifeboat later radioed back that the dead man and the others were being taken by the trawler to Boulogne. 1972 *Oxford Times* 25 Feb. 1/8 Our beat policemen radio through if congestion is building up anywhere. 1973 J. Rossiter *Manipulators* xxvi. 244 He had to get away before Jackson found Bradley's body and radio'd back. 1977 *Daily Tel.* 18 Mar. 1/7 The police radioed for assistance and a detachment of Irish troops arrived. 1978 J. Irving *World according to Garp* xv. 313 Go radio our position.

Hence **ra·dioed** *ppl. a.*, transmitted or reported by radio.

1943 J. Flanner in *New Yorker* 29 May 42/3 A radioed appeal from General de Gaulle in London. 1953 A. Huxley *Let.* 9 Aug. (1969) 682 Robots responsive to the radioed will of their masters. 1973 'A. Hall' *Tango Briefing* xii. 149 London wanted photographs and a full radioed report of the freighter's cargo. 1977 'W. Wingate' *Fireplay* i. 12 *Doneska* could have foundered anywhere from her last radioed position off Los Angeles to close by Valparaiso.

radio-. Add: **2.** [Now apprehended as a comb. form of Radiate *v.* or Radiation.] Esp. connected with ionizing radiation. **radiode·nsity,** the degree to which a material will absorb ionizing radiation; radio-opacity; **ra:diodermati·tis,** dermatitis caused by X-rays or other ionizing radiation; **ra:diodiagno·sis,** the diagnosis of disease by means of X-rays or other ionizing radiation; hence **ra:diodiagno·stic** *a.*; **radio-eco·logy,** the study of the ecological effects of radioactive materials and ionizing radiation; hence **ra:dio-ecolo·gical** *a.*; **radio-eco·logist**; **radiogene·tics,** the study of the genetic effects of ionizing radiation; hence **radiogene·tic, -ical** *adjs.*; **ra:diolumine·scence,** luminescence caused by ionizing radiation; hence **ra:diolumine·scent** *a.*; **ra:dio-micro·meter,** an instrument for measuring minute degrees of infra-red or microwave radiation; **radiomime·tic** *a.*, of (the action or properties of) a substance: producing effects upon living cells resembling those produced by ionizing radiation; **ra:dionecro·sis** *Med.*, necrosis caused by excessive exposure to ionizing radiation; **ra:dio-pasteuriza·tion,** pasteurization of food by exposure to ionizing radiation; so **radio-pa·steurized** *a.*; **ra:diopharmaceu·tical** *a.* and *sb.*, (being or pertaining to) any radioactive compound or preparation which is administered to a patient for the purpose of radiotherapy or diagnosis; **ra:diopharmaco·logy,** the use of drugs in radiology; also, the study of physiology and the metabolism of drugs by means of radiopharmaceuticals; so **ra:diopharmacolo·gical** *a.*, **-pharmaco·logist**; **radiopha·rmacy,** the preparation and use of radiopharmaceuticals; a laboratory for this work; so **radiopha·rmacist**; **ra:dio-prote·ction,** the prevention or countering by chemical means of the harmful effects produced in living tissues by ionizing radiation; so **ra:dio-prote·ctive** *a.*, being or possessing this property; **ra:dio-prote·ctor,** a substance possessing this property; **radio-resi·stant** *a.*, resistant to the action of ionizing radiation; so **radio-resi·stance**; **radiose·nsitive** *a.*, sensitive to the action of ionizing radiation; so †**radiose·nsitiveness, radiosensiti·vity**; **radiose·nsitize** *v. trans.*, to make (more) radiosensitive; so **radiose·nsitizing** *vbl. sb.*; also **ra:diosensitiza·tion**; **radiose·nsitizer,** a substance which is used to increase the sensitivity of particular organisms or tissues to ionizing radiation; **ra:diosteriliza·tion,** (*a*) the process of rendering sterile by means of ionizing radiation; (*b*) the process of rendering free from micro-organisms by means of ionizing radiation; also (in either sense) **radio-ste·rilized** *a.*; **radiosu·rgery,** the use of beams of ionizing radiation in surgery; so **radio-su·rgical** *a.*; **ra:diotranslu·cent** *a.* = *Radiolucent *a.*; hence **ra:diotranslu·cency.**

1936 B. J. M. Harrison *Textbk. Roentgenol.* iii. 62 Of the media of greater radiodensity than the tissues the most commonly used is sulphate of barium. 1977 *Proc. R. Soc. Med.* LXX. 518/2 If the stone is still *in situ* then the chemical composition may be assessed by the radiodensity. **1903** *Progressive Med.* III. 161 Heidingsfeld's case was a bullous radiodermatitis. **1930** *Times Educ. Suppl.* 2 Aug. p. iv/3 The Cross of the Legion of Honour has been conferred on Dr. Jean Chabry, whose experimental work in radiology has resulted in an attack of radiodermatitis, necessitating amputation of his right arm. **1968** A. ROOK et al. *Textbk. Dermatol.* xv. 359/2 Chronic radiodermatitis is not an inflammatory process and should strictly be termed roentgen atrophy or perhaps roentgen poikiloderma. **1904** F. P. FOSTER *Appleton's Med. Dict.* 1676/2 *Radiodiagnosis*, diagnosis by means of Röntgen ray examination. **1910** A. ABRAMS *Diagnostic Therapeutics* iv. 627 Radio-diagnosis is more accurate than percussion in defining the dimensions of the organ. **1978** *Lancet* 25 Feb. 434/1 The current practice of treating radiodiagnosis as cost-free, risk-free, and done in a flash has seriously affected medical standards over the past three decades. **1907** *Jrnl. Amer. Med. Assoc.* 17 Nov. 1392/2 (*heading*) The correlation of clinical and radio-diagnostic findings. **1961** *Lancet* 29 July 257/1 Dr. C. Pickard..was..critical of past and future planning for radiodiagnostic departments. **1956** E. P. ODUM in *Conf. Radioactive Isotopes in Agric.* (U.S. Atomic Energy Comm.) 102/2 Radio-ecological research at AEC installations..has been handicapped by (1) lack of prior knowledge of the environment, and (2) uncontrolled experimental conditions. **1975** *Nature* 3 Jan. p. xiii (Advt.), The successful candidate should have knowledge and some experience in marine radioecological research and related techniques. **1959** E. P. & H. T. ODUM *Fund. Ecol.* (ed. 2) xiv. 477 This rather surprising finding, repeatedly documented by radioecologists working at the Nevada Test Site.., is apparently to be explained by the fact that the smaller particles which fall at a distance stick to the leaves of plants and dissolve more readily. **1956** E. P. ODUM in *Conf. Radioactive Isotopes in Agric.* (U.S. Atomic Energy Comm.) 100/1 Only now that we have some familiarity with the functional aspects of our ecosystem are we ready to begin controlled experiments in radio-ecology. **1964** *Oceanogr. & Marine Biol.* II. 256 Radioecology or radiation ecology is the branch of ecology which concerns itself with the dispersion and interaction of radionuclides in and with the physical, chemical, and biological environment. **1974** *Nature* 13 Dec. 618/2 The two fundamental problems in radioecology are to determine how radionuclides migrate within biogeological systems and how ionising radiations affect microorganisms, plants and animals. **1971** *Radiation Bot.* XI. 119 (*heading*) Radiogenetic effects of gamma- and fast neutron irradiation on different ontogenetic stages of the tomato. *Ibid.*, Pollen, which has advantages for radiogenetical studies, seems to hold little promise for mutation breeding purposes. **1950** *Genetics* XXXV. 56 (*heading*) On the interpretation of the dose-frequency in radiogenetics. **1955** [see *RADIOBIOLOGY]. **1963** *Biol. Abstr.* XLI. 642/2 Valuable data have been obtained in the field of radiogenetics. **1911** *Chem. Abstr.* V. 3059 The intensity of the radioluminescence is proportional to the distance in mm. **1946** *Thorpe's Dict. Appl. Chem.* (ed. 4) VII. 405/2 Radioluminescence of solids induced by *X*-rays finds considerable technical application in industrial and medical fields. **1966** G. F. J. GARLICK in P. Goldberg *Luminescence of Inorg. Solids* xii. 689 It was the existence of the particle-excited radioluminescence of uranyl salts that led Becquerel to the discovery of radioactivity in 1896. **1919** *Chem. Abstr.* XIII. 2806 A long discourse on the underlying principles and the preparation of radioluminescent paints. **1887, 1888** Radio-micrometer [in Dict. s.v. RADIOMETER]. **1908** *Rep. Brit. Assoc. Adv. Sci.* 1907 621 The first thing is to tune up the receiver accurately. This can be done by a Duddell radio-micrometer, which measures the received [radio] energy satisfactorily although it is very small. **1966** *McGraw-Hill Encycl. Sci. & Technol.* XI. 319/1 The radiomicrometer was invented by C. V. Boys in 1887 to avoid the limitations of a separate thermocouple and galvanometer. However, because it is delicate and inconvenient, it has virtually gone out of use. **1947** P. DUSTIN in *Nature* 14 June 796/2 These effects are remarkably similar to those of ionizing radiations: the mitotic poisons of the trypaflavine type are radiomimetic. **1965** *New Scientist* 25 Nov. 586/2 The still unidentified agent causing the haemorrhage is a radiomimetic compound—that is, it poisons the bone-marrow very much as radiation does. **1974** R. M. KIRK et al. *Surgery* ii. 9/2 Irradiation and radiomimetic drugs..administered in the treatment of neoplasms, cause delay in wound healing by their damaging effects on dividing cells. **1933** WARD & SMITH *Rec. Adv. Radium* viii. 85 In this way radio-necrosis may result in the more radio-resistant tumours without destruction of the tumour. **1963** *New Scientist* 9 May 334/3 Early treatment of certain irradiation accident cases with 'vasodilators' may prevent radionecrosis altogether. **1977** *Lancet* 27 Aug. 460/1 Radionecrosis of the brain may follow therapeutic irradiation of the pituitary. **1959** *Internat. Jrnl. Appl. Radiation & Isotopes* VI. 128/1 Extensive investigations..will be necessary before radio-pasteurization without refrigeration can be recommended for meats. **1968** *Biol. Abstr.* XLIX. 2446/2 Freshly killed pre-rigor fish respond better toward the radio-pasteurization process than do post-rigor fish. **1966** E. R. KILLAM et al. in *Proc. Interant. Symposium Food Irradiation* 839 A petition was submitted to the FDA on April 29, 1966 for the approval of radio-pasteurized strawberries for public consumption. **1971** *Jrnl. Food Technol.* VI. 82 Blackening in radio-pasteurized shrimps can be effectively controlled by pre-blanching treatment. **1960** *Jrnl. Amer. Med. Assoc.* 10 Sept. 162/1 The production of radiopharmaceutical compounds that concentrate in organs, such as colloidal gold in the liver and chlormerodrin..in the kidneys. **1963** P. F. BELCASTRO in H. M. Burlage et al. *Physical & Technical Pharmacy* xvii. 701 Radiopharmaceuticals can be used as therapeutic agents for treating specific diseases more efficiently than by traditional methods. **1966** G. V. LEROY in G. A. Andrews et al. *Radioactive Pharmaceuticals* xxxvii. 669 There is a continuing disagreement about the appropriate dose of almost all the radiopharmaceutical agents currently in use. **1977** *Lancet* 23 Apr. 907/2 Adverse reactions to radiopharmaceuticals are rare, and are generally due to the carrier portion rather than to the isotope itself. **1973** Radiopharmacist [see *RADIOCHEMIST]. **1963** *Biol. Abstr.* XLIV. 479/2 (*heading*) Radio-pharmacological investigations of the mechanism of action of sympathetic alpha and beta receptors in the region of the cardia of the rabbit. **1960** *Jrnl. Amer. Med. Assoc.* 10 Sept. 165/2 The clinician, biochemist, physiologist, or radiopharmacologist will eventually discover substances that will concentrate in the pancreas and adrenal and parathyroid glands. **1968** *Australasian Radiol.* XII. 239/1 Pancoast, in 1914, appears to have initiated radiopharmacology when he used morphine to stimulate gastric peristalsis. **1976** M. TUBIS in Tubis & Wolf *Radiopharmacy* xv. 406 Radiopharmacology..is concerned with the use of labeled compounds, the 'radiophores' carriers of radioactivity, to demonstrate the distribution, deposition, kinetics of metabolism, turnover, and the excretion. *Ibid.*, Radiopharmacy..is the science and art of preparing and dispensing the labeled compounds of pharmaceutical quality that are used in nuclear medicine for diagnosis and therapy. **1977** K. KRISTENSEN et al. *Quality Control in Nuclear Med.* xxxiii. 271/1 The radiopharmacy should be designed so that dispensing and radioactive waste handling do not interfere with or contaminate each other. **1957** *Brit. Jrnl. Radiol.* XXX. 97/1 This..underlines the importance of the liver in radio-protection. **1975** *Internat. Jrnl. Radiation Biol.* XXVIII. 41 It appears that cystamine may be limiting the availability of reducing equivalents and thus providing radioprotection to lipogenesis. **1956** *Brit. Jrnl. Radiol.* XXIX. 623/1 Scientists..have studied the radio-protective activity of cysteamine and cystamine. **1958** *Ibid.* XXXI. 339/2 All the radio-protective substances effective in mice have the common action of lowering body temperature. **1975** *Biochem. & Biophys. Res. Communications* LXVII. 1170 The increase..in the amount of exogenous superoxide dismutase associated with the eluted bone marrow stem cells was also accompanied by an enhancement in the radioprotective effect of the enzyme on the proliferative capacity of the cells. **1960** *Internat. Jrnl. Radiation Biol.* II. 231 (*heading*) Sub[s]trates as radioprotectors of hexokinase. **1977** *Nature* 3 Nov. 15/3 A significant contribution to radiobiology was the demonstration that SOD is an effective radioprotector exerting a protective role even when administered after radiation doses have been delivered. **1927** *Cancer Rev.* II. 397 The degree of radio-resistance seems to be more marked in proportion as the treatment has been unwisely prolonged. **1957** *Brit. Jrnl. Radiol.* XXX. 97/1 A higher concentration of cysteamine in the liver increases radio-resistance. **1929** *Radiology* XIII. 316/2 Squamous carcinoma, malignancy of varying grades, radioresistant. **1959** *Internat. Jrnl. Appl. Radiation & Isotopes* VI. 157/1 The alkaline phosphatase of milk is extremely radio-resistant. **1977** *Lancet* 27 Aug. 460/1 The endocrine-active adenomas are characteristically more radio-resistant than the endocrine-inactive variety. **1920** *Amer. Jrnl. Roentgenol.* VII. 53/1 Remarkable examples of radio-sensitive tumors are ectodermal and basal-celled epitheliomata derived from the basal-celled layers of the epidermis. **1956** C. AUERBACH *Genetics in Atomic Age* viii. 80 Tissues in which division is going on are so much more radiosensitive than tissues in which cell division has ceased. **1976** *Nature* 17 June 588/1 If these cells are less radiosensitive, ionising radiation could favour their overgrowth. **1921** *Arch. Radiol. & Electrotherapy* XXV. 348 A further factor in tissues is the blood or lymph content; the more this is, the more is the radio-sensitiveness. **1924** *Brit. Jrnl. Radiol.* XXIX. 270 The radio-sensitivity was found to vary greatly according to the stage of cellular division. **1971** G. G. LUCE *Body Time* v. 167 Perhaps the rhythm of radiosensitivity may be traced to cycles of activity in the bone marrow and spleen where blood is formed. **1951** *Jrnl. Chem. Educ.* XXVIII. 414/2 Radiosensitization may be significant in radiation chemistry. **1976** *Radiology* CXIX. 221 This..would ostensibly lead to some degree of tumor reoxygenation ('radiosensitization') as well as direct chemotherapeutic effects. *Ibid.* 725/1 Cetylpyridinium chloride did not radiosensitize bacteria suspended in nutrient broth. **1953** *Brit. Jrnl. Cancer* VII. 316 This compound (Synkavit) has a small but useful effect as a clinical radiosensitiser. **1972** *Lancet* 22 Sept. 638/2 A true radiosensitiser is a chemical which increases the cell-killing effect of a given dose of radiation. **1936** *Biol. Abstr.* X. 1905/1 His researches concern the radio-sensitizing effect of metabolic exchanges and the degree to which substances modifying the metabolism also modify the radiosensitivity. **1953** *Brit. Jrnl. Cancer* VII. 314 A radiosensitising chemical agent..in combination with radiotherapy should produce a mean survival time after treatment double that after radiotherapy only. **1978** *Jrnl. R. Soc. Med.* LXXI. 672 The radiosensitizing properties of the group of nitroimidazoles. **1964** *Jrnl. Econ. Entomol.* LVII. 756/1 For mosquito sterilization..the desired goal of highly competitive, yet permanently sterile, males is more readily attainable with chemosterilization than radiosterilization. **1966** E. R. KILLAM et al. in *Proc. Internat. Symposium Food Irradiation* VIII. 842 The radiosterilization of certain cuts of beef may require irradiation at this temperature [*sc.* −80 °C]. *Ibid.*, Future developments in cryogenics should lower the..cost of radiosterilized meat products. **1967** *Jrnl. Econ. Entomol.* LX. 696 (*heading*) Mating competitiveness in radiosterilized males. **1975** *Ibid.* LXVIII. 595/2, 300 radiosterilized ♀ and 4200 radiosterilized ♂ were released each evening. **1933** *O.E.D.* Suppl. s.v. *Radio-* 2, Radio-surgery. **1963** *New England Jrnl. Med.* 19 Sept. 597/2 In 1954 we set out upon a study in clinical medicine in which these high-energy protons and alpha particles have been used in various forms of so-called 'bloodless' surgery, or radiosurgery. **1973** *Internat. Jrnl. Radiation Biol.* XXIV. 229 (*heading*) Split-brain cats prepared for radiosurgery. **1929** *Daily Express* 16 Jan. 9/6 Even if the growth should have extended to the glands, radio-surgical methods would offer a good prospect of eradication. **1959** *Probl. Oncol.* V. 98 (*heading*) Radio-surgical treatment of skin cancer involving a free skin graft. **1973** *Internat. Jrnl. Radiation Biol.* XXIV. 239 A 3 mm beam of protons is too wide for safe radiosurgical use in the rat brain. **1974** A. HENRY in R. M. Kirk et al. *Surgery* xv. 295/2 X-rays show an area of radiotranslucency in the metaphysis, which may cross the growth plate to involve the epiphysis. **1959** *New Biol.* XXX. 25 If the process is observed radiologically, the solid lungs become radio-translucent rapidly, as if a light has been turned on. **1964** L. MARTIN *Clin. Endocrinol.* (ed. 4) iv. 149 Destructive bone lesions..cause sharply demarcated radiotranslucent areas in affected bones.

3. a. Connected with radioactivity, as **ra:dioallergoso·rbent** *a.* [*ALLERG(Y + -O + *SORBENT *sb.* (*a.*)], in *radioallergosorbent test*, a form of radioimmunoassay for measuring antibodies to an allergen (see quot. 1967); **radioa·ssay** *sb.*, an assay performed by measuring radioactivity from a radioisotope; also as *v. trans.*; **ra·dio-atom**, an atom of a radioactive substance; **radioau·tograph** = *AUTORADIOGRAPH; also **ra:dioautogra·phic** *a.*; **radioauto·graphy**; **ra:diochroma·togram**, a chromatogram of a radioactively labelled preparation which is recorded or measured by means of a radiological technique; **radioco·lloid**, a radioactive substance in colloidal form; hence **radiocolloi·dal** *a.*; **radio-da·ting** *vbl. sb.*, isotopic dating; **ra·dio-element**, a radioactive element; **radioha·lo** = **pleochroic halo*; **radio-i·odinate** *v. trans.*, to label (a substance) with radio-iodine; so **radio-i·odinated** *ppl. a.*; **ra:dio-iodina·tion**; **ra·dioligand**, a radio-labelled compound that has a strong chemical affinity for a particular receptor; **radio-nu·clide**, a radioactive nuclide; **radiopu·rity** = **radiochemical purity*; **ra·dioscan**, a determination of the distribution of radioactive material (esp. a tracer) in a sample, an organ, etc.; **ra:dioste:reoa·ssay**, any biological assay technique in which the test substance is determined by allowing it to bind to a suitable protein or antibody in competition with a known quantity of radioactively labelled material, the extent of reaction being measured radiologically; (usu. applied to non-immunological methods: cf. *radioimmunoassay* s.v. *RADIOIMMUNO-); **radiotoxi·city**, the property of a radioactive substance of being injurious to a living organism when present in its tissue; hence **radioto·xic** *a.*; **radiotra·cer**, a radioactive tracer.

1967 L. WIDE et al. in *Lancet* 25 Nov. 1105/2 An in-vitro method, called the radioallergosorbent test, has been developed for the detection of allergen-specific antibodies of a new immunoglobulin class, provisionally called IgND. *Ibid.* 1106/1 The principle of the method, the radioallergosorbent test (R.A.S.T.) is as follows: an allergen coupled to an insoluble polymer is added to the serum to be investigated, if antibodies to the allergen are present they should react with the conjugate; after the removal of all unbound serum components ^{125}I-labelled anti-IgND antibodies are then added, they will bind to the antibodies of the IgND class which have reacted with the polymer-coupled allergen; the uptake of labelled antibodies, measured in terms of radioactivity, on the particles is essentially proportional to the IgND allergen antibodies. **1971** *Internat. Arch. Allergy & Appl. Immunol.* XLI. 443 The radioallergosorbent test (RAST) was applied for quantitative estimation of IgE antibodies to various common allergens. **1977** *Lancet* 22 Oct. 847/2 Radioallergosorbent tests..for specific IgE antibody were also positive. **1951** *Nucleonics* Nov. 60 (*heading*) A simple inexpensive sample changer for the radioassay of..simple samples. **1963** *Analytical Biochem.* V. 89 The radioassay of cholesterol-C^{14} digitonide by gas flow technique..using methanol as the solvent for solution and plating. **1970** *Steroids* XV. 470 The method..requires only a simple extraction and an alumina thin layer chromatographic separation prior to radioassay. **1972** *Nature* 22 Dec. 463/2 Out of a series of a hundred [silver] bars, we have radio-assayed seven bars picked at random. **1905** *Phil. Trans. R. Soc.* A. CCIV. 209 It may..be supposed that occasionally one of the outlying revolving electrons, comprising the radio-atom, lapses into a position which results in a slow loss of energy from the atom in the form of radiation. **1947** *Instruments* XX. 712/1 The qualities which make radio-atoms ('hot' atoms) useful to science and industry make them hazardous to handle. **1941** *Jrnl. Appl. Physics* XII. 328 Slides of radio-autographs showing the distribution of phosphorus in various plant tissues will be shown. **1956** *Sci. Amer.* Nov. 144/2 (*caption*) Radioautographs indicate how Isoniazid is concentrated in brain tissue. **1974** K. N. PRASAD *Human Radiation Biol.* xxi. 426 For the radioautographs of soluble materials, the tissue sections must be cut in a frozen state and then dried in a vacuum. **1947** *Radiology* XLIX. 327/2 Extensive radioautographic studies were made of these organs in which a high degree of selective localization took place. **1967** F. O. SCHMITT in G. C. Quarton et al. *Neurosciences* 211/2 The radioautographic method using tritiated precursors lends itself well to the determination of the fate of axoplasm moving cellulofugally, both down the axon and possibly out along the dendrites. **1978** *Bull. Amer. Acad. Arts & Sci.* Feb. 17 These radioautographic experiments have revealed that in normal female somatic cells, one member of each pair of X chromosomes always replicates much later than all the other chromosomes including the second X chromosome. **1941** *Jrnl. Appl. Physics* XII. 446/1 Stout and his co-workers have followed the metabolism of inorganic phosphate in the leaves and fruit of the tomato plant by..the technique of radio-autography. **1973** *Nature* 20 Apr. 523/2 Whole-body radioautography is a useful method for studying the distribution of radio-labelled compounds among all the organs and tissues of an experimental animal. **1952** F. P. W. WINTERINGHAM et al. in *Nucleonics* Mar. 56/1 When the radiochromatogram is plotted as net rate of count against distance along the strip, *w* [*sc.* the total weight of labelled component] is proportional to the area enclosed by the relevant part of the curve. **1972** *Physics Bull.* May 298/1 At the 1971 Physics Exhibition Panax showed a unique rapid imaging system which promised to shorten the time to locate the radioactive regions on thin layer radiochromatograms. **1930** *Chem. Abstr.* XXIV. 1279 Recent expts. on solns. of the 'radiocolloid' Th C (Bi). **1956** *Nature* 28 Jan. 184/1 It is more likely..that the high concentration of chromate ions in the resin promotes the formation of a radio-colloid, which is then adsorbed on the resin. **1977** *Proc. R. Soc. Med.* LXX. 522/2 In the normal subject the radio-colloid is taken up avidly by the mononuclear phagocytes of the liver and only a small amount is taken up by other organs. **1936** O. HAHN *Appl. Radiochem.* 275/1 (Index), Radiocolloidal particles, size of... Radiocolloidal thorium X. **1950** *Thorpe's Dict. Appl. Chem.* (ed. 4) X. 433/1 Some portion..of the radiocolloidal phenomena is due to adsorption of the radioactive ions on particles of dust and solid impurities fortuitously present in the solutions. **1969** *New Scientist* 25 Sept. 632/1 Radiodating has revealed..that the lunar samples are at least 3100 million years old. **1975** K. H. GOULDING in Williams & Wilson *Biologist's Guide to Princ. & Techniques Pract. Biochem.* vi. 196 The assumptions made in radiodating are sweeping and hence palaeontologists and anthropologists who use this technique can only give very approximate dates to their samples. **1903** *Contemp. Rev.* May 709 In the Periodic table of elements arranged in the ascending order of their atomic weights the three radio-elements are therefore at the extreme end. **1937** *Discovery* Mar. 65/2 A search for new radio elements of very short life whose existence is suspected. **1967** *New Scientist* 15 June 675/1 The main problem here is to ensure that dangerous long-lived radio-elements are not inadvertently produced. **1971** *Science* 20 Aug. 728/1 A new type of composite radiohalo has been found with rings attributable both to the ^{218}Po decay sequence and to ^{212}Po and possibly ^{212}Bi. **1974** *Nature* 13 Dec. 564/1 Polonium radiohaloes occur widely and not infrequently (total about 10^{15}–10^{20}) in Precambrian rocks. **1971** *Ibid.* 4 June 322/1 This protein was radio-iodinated to a specific activity of 0·6 μCi/μg with ^{125}I-iodide. **1955** *Ibid.* 26 Mar. 536/1 (*heading*) Radioiodinated human serum albumin. **1970** *Ibid.* 3 Oct. 58/1 Radioiodinated polypeptide hormones are widely used as tracers for both radioimmunoassay and *in vivo* metabolic studies. **1977** *Lancet* 13 Aug. 355/1 Dr Chait and his colleagues have studied the metabolism of very-low-density lipoprotein (V.L.D.L.) in a patient with type III hyperlipoproteinæmia..by injection of radioiodinated V.L.D.L. from a donor with endogenous hypertriglyceridæmia (type IV). **1957** *Jrnl. Laboratory & Clin. Med.* XLIX. 128 (*heading*) A method for radioiodination of antibody protein. **1974** *Nature* 25 Jan. 175/2 Several groups of investigators have subjected lymphocytes to enzymatic radioiodination of their cell surface proteins. **1972** *Jrnl. Clin. Endocrinol. & Metabolism* XXXIV. 130/1 Radioligand assays enable the biological activity of hormones at the target cell to be evaluated without the additional and variable effect of metabolism *in vivo*. **1978** *Nature* 8 June 472/1 This radioligand, which has been used in identifying and quantifying β-adrenoreceptors in a variety of intact and disrupted cell preparations, has enabled us to study cellular cyclic AMP accumulation and binding to β-adrenoreceptors in similar experimental conditions. **1947** T. P. KOHMAN in *Amer. Jrnl. Physics* XV. 356/2 *Radionuclide* should replace *radioelement* and *radioisotope* in most applications. **1963** *Engineering* 20 Sept. 378/3 The use of short-lived radionuclides makes it imperative to transfer the sample from the irradiation area to the activity-measuring location as speedily as possible. **1976** J. FOLLETT *Doomsday Ultimatum* 73 What is the exact nature of the radionuclides stored.. and what will happen if they are released? **1977** I. M. CAMPBELL *Energy & Atmosphere* vii. 187 The radionuclide ^{14}C is produced naturally in the atmosphere by cosmic radiation but the level was almost doubled by the atmospheric nuclear-weapon testing of the 1960's. **1956** *Internat. Jrnl. Appl. Radiation & Isotopes* I. 227/2 The only disadvantage of the method of measurement is its extreme sensitivity to gamma-emitting impurities, although this can be turned into an asset in the determination of radiopurity. **1973** *Weed Res.* XIII. 340 The radiopurity of the isolated metabolites was checked by thin-layer chromatography..and autoradiography. **1965** *Amer. Rev. Respiratory Dis.* XCII. 959/2 (*caption*) The per cent of total pulmonary blood flow calculated from the radioscan for the diseased lung. **1966** *Amer. Jrnl. Cardiol.* XVIII. 819/2 The radioscan accurately reflected the pattern of arteriolar-capillary blood flow. **1974** *Nature* 1 Nov. 68/1 The radiopurity of these compounds was determined by radioscan of thin layer chromatograms. **1967** B. E. P. MURPHY in *Jrnl. Clin. Endocrinol.* XXVII. 973/2 Such methods have been termed by the author 'competitive protein binding (CPB) analysis' and by R. P. Ekins 'saturation analysis', but because of their basic similarity to radioimmunoassays..the name 'radiostereoassay' has also been suggested [by the writer] as an analogous term which could be applied to both types of assay. **1974** *Nature* 22 Feb. 563/2 Before it can act, vitamin D must first be converted to its 25-hydroxy derivative..in the liver, and this chief circulating metabolite can be measured by radio-stereo-assay, thus providing a precise index of vitamin D nutritional status. **1950** *Nuclear Sci. Abstr.* IV. 398/1 Rat erythrocytes were irradiated with 6,030r and then injected subcutaneously..in order to determine the severity and nature of radiotoxic effects. **1975** *Nature* 27 Mar. 278/3 The dose limit for bone is based on uniformly deposited ^{226}Ra: but Pu, collecting at the bone surface, is considered ~5 times as radiotoxic. **1946** D. ANTONY et al. *Radiotoxicity of Injected Sr^{89} for Rats, Mice & Rabbits* (U.S. Atomic Energy Comm. Rep. MDDC 1540) 6 Radium, hitherto the only substance of which the radiotoxicity had been extensively studied. **1961** G. R. CHOPPIN *Exper. Nuclear Chem.* ii. 12 Some of the commonly used nuclides are listed..according to their relative radiotoxicities. **1977** S. L. BARKER in B. A. Rhodes *Quality Control in Nuclear Med.* xxviii. 243/1 Prepared formulations of long-lived nuclides present no special problems with the exception of possible radiotoxicity. **1950** *Mining Engin.* Mar. 364/2 Radiotracers were demonstrated to be of considerable value in the study of a typical mineral-collector system, dithiophosphate-galena. **1977** *Lancet* 19 Nov. 1072/2 No abnormal localisation of the radiotracer was observed in muscles of any of the controls.

b. Prefixed to the names of chemical elements and compounds: (i) Designating a radioactive isotope (usu. one prepared artificially) of the named element († occas. of an element other than that named), as *radio-caesium, -chlorine, -cobalt, -gold, -iron, -potassium, -silver, -sodium*, etc.; † **radio-acti·nium,** a thorium isotope (mass number 227) which is produced by beta decay of actinium and is an alpha emitter of half-life 18·2 days; **radio-i·odine,** esp. iodine 131, an artificial isotope with a half-life for beta decay of about 8 days, which is widely used as a tracer (esp. in investigating thyroid function), and for radiotherapy of the thyroid gland; **radio-lea·d,** a mixture of isotopes of lead, together with some bismuth and polonium, which constitutes the longer-lived product of the decay of radon; sometimes *spec.* lead 210, the major radioactive component of this mixture, which has a half-life for beta decay of 21 years; **radio-pho·sphorus,** *spec.* phosphorus 32, an artificial isotope which is widely used as a tracer and decays by beta emission with a half-life of 14·3 days; **radio-stro·ntium,** *spec.* strontium 90, a beta emitter with a half-life of roughly 28 years which occurs among uranium fission products; (in quot. 1941 referring to strontium 85); † **radio-tellu·rium,** a former name for a polonium isotope of mass number 210 (originally thought to be tellurium), which occurs in the radium decay series and decays by alpha emission with a half-life of 138 days; † **radio-tho·rium,** thorium 228, an alpha emitter of half-life 1·91 years which occurs in small amounts in natural thorium and is formed by the beta decay of mesothorium II; (see also quot. 1950). Also *RADIO-CARBON.

1906 O. HAHN in *Nature* 12 Apr. 560/1, I have found that a new product is present in actinium which is intermediate between actinium and actinium X, and..will be called.. 'radio-actinium'. **1926** R. W. LAWSON tr. *Hevesy & Paneth's Man. Radioactivity* xxiii. 164 The β-radiation of actinium, the existence of which it is necessary to assume in order to explain its transformation into radioactinium, is too weak to be detected. **1955** *Bull. Atomic Scientists* Oct. 287/3 The long-lived useful products radiocaesium and radiostrontium will be separated from the rest of the fission products and concentrated into radioactive sources. **1935** *Physical Rev.* XLVIII. 571/1 During a study of the beta-radiation from a sample of silver radiochloride, it was found possible to follow the decay of the radiochlorine. **1949** *Atomics* Oct. 75/2 Radio-cobalt and radio-strontium have been used to dissipate charge from textile machinery. **1959** *Listener* 22 Oct. 675/2 The new knowledge does not only apply to atomic bombs and radio-cobalt but to the mechanisms of biology as well. **1955** *Sci. News Let.* 19 Mar. 184/3 A gram of radiogold, costing about $25, can irradiate tissues with the power that would be obtained from a $20,000 chunk of radium. **1938** R. W. LAWSON tr. *Hevesy & Paneth's Man. Radioactivity* (ed. 2) 303/1 (Index), Radio-iodine. **1940** *Amer. Jrnl. Physiol.* CXXXI. 135 The radio-iodine was prepared by the Berkeley cyclotron and converted to sodium iodide. **1961** *Lancet* 2 Sept. 551/1, 8 mC of radioiodine was administered..to achieve a permanent remission of the hyperthyroidism. **1970** PASSMORE & ROBSON *Compan. Med. Stud.* II. vi. 8/2 The rapidity of uptake and the speed with which the plasma is cleared of radioiodine provide measures of the activity of the thyroid gland. **1960** *Proc. Soc. Exper. Biol. & Med.* CIV. 442/2 This calculation is based on the assumption that loss of radioiron from liver between 0–3 hrs is negligible. **1903** *Phil. Mag.* V. 585 Thus the radio-lead described by Hoffmann and Strauss and by Giesel cannot be regarded as a new element until it is shown that it has permanent activity of a distinctive character. **1910** *Nature* 24 Feb. 492/1 The most natural source of polonium is radium D (radio-lead), which grows polonium and has a period of half-transformation of about twenty years. **1910** A. T. CAMERON *Radiochem.* v. 52 The lead obtained from pitchblende was strongly and permanently radioactive—hence the name radio-lead. **1926** R. W. LAWSON tr. *Hevesy & Paneth's Man. Radioactivity* xiv. 118 Polonium..can be prepared..from solutions of the salts of radio-lead, which.. contains an isotope of bismuth (RaE) and three isotopes of lead (RaD, RaG, Pb). **1941** *Jrnl. Appl. Physics* XII. 440/2 The detection of radio-lead by its radioactivity is more than a million times more sensitive than the ordinary chemical and physical methods. **1938** R. W. LAWSON tr. *Hevesy & Paneth's Man. Radioactivity* (ed. 2) x. 122 For every 10^7 α-particles of high energy value..only 6 are effective in the activation of aluminium, i.e. in the production of radiophosphorus. **1951** *New Biol.* X. 36 Mosquito larvae grown in water containing phosphorus-32 (radiophosphorus) produce radioactive adults whose presence in a swarm can be picked out immediately. **1963** BALL & HOOPER in Schultz & Klement *Radioecology* 227/1 The movement of radiophosphorus through the ecosystem of a cold water stream was studied by adding spikes of approximately 23 millicuries of phosphorus-32 to the water during the summers of 1958, 1959, and 1960. **1973** P. A. COLINVAUX *Introd. Ecol.* xiv. 207 Radiophosphorus has a half-life of 14 days. **1948** *Sci. News* VII. 38 The release of heat from radio-potassium must have been 200 times greater than from uranium and thorium combined. **1938** R. W. LAWSON tr. *Hevesy & Paneth's Man. Radioactivity* (ed. 2) v. 118 A 40-fold yield in the preparation of radio-silver. **1971** *Nature* 10 Dec. 347/1 The reaction ^{109}Ag (*n*, 2*n*)^{108m}Ag does seem to be important in thermonuclear bomb production of radiosilver. **1935** *Physical Rev.* XLVII. 17 Doubtless radio-sodium will find many uses in the physical and biological sciences. **1951** *New Biol.* X. 39 In animals, it has also been shown that radiosodium is actively transferred inwards across a frogskin membrane into a solution of higher sodium concentration than that of the external medium. **1941** *Jrnl. Appl. Physics* XII. 456/2 Radio-strontium has a half-life of 55 days, can be readily prepared in relatively large amounts, and emits very energetic beta-particles. **1946** *Chemistry* Jan. 20/1 The use of radio-strontium in the treatment of metastatic carcinoma in bone and for other diseases can now be tried in a much larger field than was ever possible before. **1957** *New Scientist* 9 May 30/1 He..argues that..the level of radio-strontium in human bones will eventually rise to between 5 and 20 'sunshine units' if test firings of bombs continue indefinitely at their present rate. **1958** *Times* 12 Nov. 4/2 A further report will be published shortly by the Atomic Energy Research Establishment, Harwell, giving the 1957 figures for radiostrontium in soil, herbage, animal bone, and milk samples from the United Kingdom. **1972** GOLDMAN & BUSTAD (*title*) Biomedical implications of radiostrontium exposure. **1904** *Technics* II. 173/1 There is at present a good deal of evidence that the radio-active substance, separated from pitchblende by Marckwald, and called by him radio-tellurium, is in reality the fifth product of the disintegration of the radium atom. **1906** *Phil. Mag.* XII. 361 A bismuth rod coated with radiotellurium was used as a source of α rays. **1962** O. HAHN in *Coll. Papers Ld. Rutherford* I. 168 Eventually it turned out that polonium and radiotellurium were identical, and the latter name had to be dropped, although polonium is in fact a higher homologue of tellurium. **1905** *Jrnl. Chem. Soc.* LXXXVIII. II. 789 The author [*sc.* Ramsay] hence considers it very probable that the radioactive power of thorium is to be attributed to small quantities of this element, radiothorium. **1921** *Phil. Mag.* XLI. 572 A much weaker source of α rays was obtained by dipping a nickel plate for a few seconds in a more dilute solution of radiothorium. **1950** *Thorpe's Dict. Appl. Chem.* (ed. 4) X. 435/1 The term radiothorium is loosely applied to the mixture of isotopes that can be separated from natural thorium and which contain the bulk of its activity. Such radiothorium consists of a mixture of meso-ThI, meso-ThII, radium, and actinium isotopes, respectively, Th-*X*, a radium isotope, and their decay products, including true radiothorium or ^{228}Th.

(ii) Designating a compound containing a radioactive label.

1935 Radiochloride [see *radiochlorine* in (i) above]. **1951** *New Biol.* X. 40 A sample of blood is withdrawn and mixed with radiophosphate, in the form of sodium or chromium phosphate. **1952** *Ibid.* XIII. 64 The addition of anti-thyroid substances to the incubating fluid resulting in a diminished formation of radiothyroxine and radiodiiodotyrosine. **1963** *Amer. Jrnl. Obstetr. & Gynecol.* LXXXVII. 208/1 One hundred microcuries of sodium radiochromate is added and the mixture allowed to incubate at room temperature for 25 minutes. **1977** *Lancet* 5 Feb. 303/2 We infer that the clots were formed after radio-fibrinogen had been administered.

4. Connected with radio (cf. *RADIO *sb.* 6, 7), as † **ra:dio-condu·ctor,** a former term for a coherer; **radiohe·liograph** *Astr.*, an interferometric radio telescope system designed to record instantaneous high-resolution pictures of the sun as observed at radio wavelengths; **radiome·teorograph** [METEOROGRAPH] = *RADIOSONDE; so **ra:diometeoro·graphy**; **radiophy·sics,** the branch of physics concerned with the properties and applications of radio waves; hence **radiophy·sical** *a.*; **radiophy·sicist; ra:dio-teleme·tering** *vbl. sb.*, **ra:dio-tele·metry,** telemetry by means of radio; hence **ra:dio-teleme·tric** *a.*; **radio-te·letype,** a teletype which transmits and receives information by radio.

1898 Radio-conductor [in Dict. s.v. RADIO- 2]. **1906** S. R. BOTTONE tr. *Mazzotto's Wireless Telegr. & Telephony* vii. 166 Branly gave the name of 'radio-conductors' to the tubes with filings, a name which some prefer, as it only points to the fact, leaving the true nature of the phenomenon unexplained. **1962** *Nature* 18 Aug. 649/1 The Ford Foundation has announced the grant of 550,000 dollars to the Radiophysics Division of the Australian Commonwealth Scientific and Industrial Research Organization for the construction of a radioheliograph for photographing the sun in its natural radio emission. **1966** *New Scientist* 7 Apr. 27/1 The main circle of the radioheliograph will observe events in the Sun's atmosphere with all the detail and definition to be expected from a dish aerial of the same diameter. **1973** *Sci. Amer.* Oct. 72/3 Spatial structure in the corona is studied on a second-by-second basis by a radioheliograph composed of 96 linked antennas each 45 feet in diameter at Culgoora in Australia. **1932** *Nature* 31 Dec. 1006/1 What is believed to be the first kind of such radio-meteorograph was devised a few years ago by Prof. Moltchanoff, of Leningrad, records of temperature and pressure being obtained in several test ascents in January, 1930. **1944** C. P. LENT *Rocket Res.* 74/2 Improved balloons and radiometeorographs..are now being developed by meteorologists. **1934** *Monthly Weather Rev.* LXII. 221 (*heading*) Radiometeorography as applied to unmanned balloons. **1974** R. RODMAN tr. *Al'pert's Radio Wave Propagation & Ionosphere* (ed. 2) II. p. ix, Various radiophysical and radio-engineering problems. **1961** *Flight* LXXX. 531/1 From the point of view of Soviet radiophysicists and astronomers the West Ford project, if carried out, may have consequences dangerous to artificial satellites, and especially to those with a man on board. **1929** *Compt. Rend. des Séances des Commissions* (Union Radio Scientifique Internationale) II. 29/2 The Commission of Radiophysics held in Brussels in 1928. **1947** *Nature* 18 Jan. 103/1 The Division of Radiophysics [of the Australian Council for Scientific and Industrial Research] was formed early in the War. **1960** RODMAN & VARSAVSKY tr. *I. S. Shklovsky's Cosmic Radio Waves* i. 11 It is shown in radiophysics that if a receiving antenna is used as a transmitting antenna the power radiated by it in each direction will have the same angular dependence $A(\theta,\phi)$. **1976** *Nature* 24 June 663/1 *The Australian Journal of Physics* has had a reputation..for specialising in radiophysics and high energy physics. **1946** *Trans. Amer. Inst. Electr. Engineers* LXV. 865/1 The accuracy and stability of the airborne radio telemetering equipment depend upon a high degree of stability of the plate supply. **1949** *Electronic Engin.* XXI. 209/1 The data.. is transmitted to the ground by radio telemetering methods.

1974 *Physics Bull.* Oct. 443/2 Launch and subsequent collection of data by radiotelemetric methods demand access to major ground facilities. **1976** L. Brown *Birds of Prey* 60 Advanced radiotelemetric techniques may be the only method of learning much detail about many forest raptors. **1951** *Rev. Sci. Instruments* XXII. 2/1 Almost every application of radio telemetry involves some form of multiplexing—i.e., the transmission of several channels of information by the same radio carrier. **1967** E. L. Gruenberg *Handbk. Telemetry & Remote Control* iv. 2 The development of radio telemetry has been principally centered around the drone and missile programs of the armed forces. **1974** *Country Life* 13 June 1572/2 Roding behaviour and its purpose are still not fully understood, and until radiotelemetry or a similar technique is used to discover what different individuals are doing, we have to watch and guess. **1939** H. K. Morgan *Aircraft Radio & Electr. Equipment* xii. 325 It may be that by 1945 it will be considered profitable to equip transports with a tape or page radio teletype. **1949** Koestler *Promise & Fulfilment* ii. iii. 236 Communications..are rather precarious, depending as they do on the vagaries of the American consul's radio teletype. **1976** *S9* (N.Y.) May/June 137 (*caption*) Bart also monitors RTTY (radioteletype) and amateur radio SST (slow-scan television) signals.

radio-actinium: see *radio- 3 b (i).

radioa·ctivate, *v.* Also with hyphen. [f. as next + -ate[3].] *trans.* To make radioactive. Also *fig.* So **radioa·ctivated** *ppl. a.*; **radioa·ctivating** *vbl. sb.*

1903 *Electr. World & Engin.* 28 Mar. 529/2 An account of the investigation of the radio-activating process at the foot of waterfalls. **1949** M. Muggeridge *Affairs of Heart* iii. 47 Even the atomic bomb..may prove a great deception, only serving to radio-activate yet another attempt to re-define human rights. **1971** P. Kruger *Princ. Activation Analysis* vi. 223 The energies of most gamma-ray transitions from radioactivated nuclides are less than 2 MeV. **1978** *N.Y. Times* 30 Mar. c 19/2 Both Russia and America are looking for an excuse to try out on each other a new variation of the neutron bomb that will radioactivate the earth for 1,000 years.

ra:dioactiva·tion. *Chem.* [f. next + -ation.] The process of making radioactive; freq. *attrib.*; **radioactivation analysis,** chemical analysis in which a sample is made radioactive by exposure to radiation and its components are then identified, and their concentrations measured, by radiochemical methods; also called *activation analysis*.

1938 *Brit. Chem. Abstr.* A. i. 112/2 (*heading*) Artificial disintegration and radioactivation. *a* **1947** Clark & Overman in *Determination Trace Elem. by Radioactivation Anal.* (U.S. Atomic Energy Comm. Rep. MDDC–1329) (1947) 1 The potential uses of radioactivation analysis for the determination of trace amounts of substances have been recognized for some time. **1950** *Ann. Rep. Progr. Chem.* XLVI. 285 Although radioactivation analysis was first used in 1936, it is still in the early stages of development. **1960** *Times* 19 July (Royal Society Suppl.) p. xv/1 The geochemist is particularly trying..new techniques of analysis such as the isotope dilution and radioactivation methods. **1971** P. Kruger *Princ. Activation Analysis* iii. 62 The most copious and controllable sources of neutrons for radioactivation are found in nuclear reactors. **1971** *Nature* 15 Oct. 506/2 Radioactivation analysis..is now well established in its own right as an important tool in science and technology.

radioactive (rēidioˌæ·ktiv), *a.* Also with hyphen. [f. Radio- 2 + Active *a.*] **1.** Of an atomic nucleus, a substance, etc.: (capable of) undergoing spontaneous nuclear decay involving emission of ionizing radiation in the form of particles or gamma rays; *spec.* of an element: consisting of a radioactive isotope.

1898 *Nature* 28 July 312/1 On a new radio-active substance contained in pitchblende. **1904** E. Rutherford *Radio-Activity* v. 161 This increase of activity is due to the continuous production by the radium of the radio-active emanation or gas, which is occluded in the radium compound. **1913** *Q. Rev.* July 117 The disintegration of atom after atom of the radio-active element. **1926** R. W. Lawson tr. *Hevesy & Paneth's Man. Radioactivity* i. 4 We now define a substance as being radioactive when the atoms of which it is composed disintegrate spontaneously, and regardless of whether or not the emission of rays can readily be detected in the process. **1935** *Nature* 9 Nov. 754/1 The radio-active phosphorus in the urine..was then investigated. **1952** *New Biol.* XIII. 63 The introduction of radio-active iodine (I^{131}) has provided a tool..of the greatest value..to the comparative physiologist. **1955** *Times* 18 Aug. 8/6 Radioactive caesium recovered from waste fission products has been made available to the Royal Marsden Hospital..for treatment of deep-seated cancer. **1957** *Times Lit. Suppl.* 15 Nov. p. iv/3 Death waits for us on the zebra crossing; and tomorrow morning's milk may be radio-active. **1959** *Daily Tel.* 10 Mar. 16/3 He also asked the secretary..to advise us of the possibility of any appreciable rise in radioactive content in the river which may result. *Ibid.* 23 Mar. 18/3 The rate of descent from the stratosphere of radio-active debris, including strontium 90, from nuclear explosions. **1961** G. R. Choppin *Exper. Nuclear Chem.* vi. 77 The average time of existence τ of a radioactive atom before decay is the reciprocal of the decay constant. **1966** C. R. Tottle *Sci. Engin. Materials* i. 23 Almost all elements of atomic number greater than $Z = 83$ (bismuth) are naturally radioactive. **1969** N. W. Pirie *Food Resources* v. 127 Marine organisms concentrate several of the radioactive isotopes enormously. **1977** *Nature* 14 Apr. 585/1 Any radioactive chemical which enters one organism may be transported a considerable distance as it travels through the food chain.

2. Of a process, phenomenon, etc.: of, pertaining to, involving, or produced by radioactivity.

1903 *Phil. Mag.* V. 580 These rays have not yet been sufficiently examined to make any discussion possible of the part they play in radioactive processes. **1906** *Nature* 25 Oct. 634/1 The escape of the emanation causes a radio-active contamination of the laboratory which renders delicate experiments on radio-activity or ionisation very difficult. **1919** *Phil. Mag.* XXXVII. 537 Results showed..that..the H atoms from a glass α-ray tube were a product of radio-active disintegration. **1926** R. W. Lawson tr. *Hevesy & Paneth's Man. Radioactivity* vii. 78 Ions are produced along the tracks of the radioactive rays. **1938** *Ibid.* (ed. 2) iv. 55 (*heading*) Absorption measurements with γ-rays as applied to radioactive analysis. **1956** A. H. Compton *Atomic Quest* v. 303 At the instant of the flash there is a burst of radio-active rays of enormous magnitude. **1961** G. R. Choppin *Exper. Nuclear Chem.* i. 3 The formation of a more stable nucleus as a result of radioactive decay is accompanied by a release of energy. **1969** Bennison & Wright *Geol. Hist. Brit. Isles* i. 6 Only the limitations of radioactive dating..are here dealt with. **1971** *Nature* 6 Aug. 367/2 The dating of the earlier part of the Pleistocene period still presents considerable problems, but further exploitation of the various 'radioactive clocks' should eventually overcome these difficulties. **1977** *Ibid.* 10 Mar. 106/1 Even the most resolute proclaimers of radioactive doom seem to have convinced themselves that fusion power will be gentle and on a homely scale, and that radioactive pollution will be a thing of the past when dirty fission gives way to clean fusion.

3. *fig.* (Possibly also influenced by *radio- 4.)

1905 S. Macnaughtan *Lame Dog's Diary* x. 128 Eliza has found that London is radio-active, hence enjoyable. And Eliza had only been once to the Royal Institution when she said it! **1909** A. Bennett *Glimpse* x. 71 She did not begin to live, socially, till her body was at rest... Then her individuality would be radioactive whereas the individuality of Inez spent itself mildly without ceasing in a persuasive appeal to the sight. **1919** D. H. Lawrence in *Eng. Rev.* June 477 Our plasmic psyche is radio-active, connecting with all things, and having first-knowledge of all things. **1923** L. P. Smith *S.P.E. Tract* xii. 57 This radio-active quality of popular idiom, this power to give out life and never lose it. **1934** *Punch* 5 Sept. 280/2 The invalid son, who ultimately comes out at least all even in the contest with the radio-active Audrey. **1955** Koestler *Trail of Dinosaur* 12 The logic of expediency leads to the atomic disintegration of morality, a kind of radioactive decay of all values. **1974** *Times* 27 May 6/1 His [*sc.* Byron's] was a radio-active personality that had shattering effects on all who came in contact with him.

4. Special collocations: **radioactive constant,** the average proportion of nuclei of a given radioactive nuclide which will decay in a given time; now usu. called *decay constant*; = **disintegration constant*; **radioactive equilibrium,** a condition in which the quantities of radioactive daughter nuclides in a material remain constant because each is decaying at the same rate as that at which it is being formed; **radioactive indicator** = *indicator 2 b (ii); **radioactive series,** a series of radioactive nuclides each member of which decays into the next, together with a non-radioactive end-product; the series of transformations relating such a set of nuclides; (four such series exist among the nuclides heavier than lead: see quot. 1974); **radioactive tracer** (see *tracer[1]); **radioactive waste,** waste material that is radioactive, esp. spent nuclear fuel.

1903 Rutherford & Soddy in *Phil. Mag.* V. 581 The law of radioactive change may therefore be expressed in the one statement—the proportional amount of radioactive matter that changes in unit time is a constant... λ may therefore be suitably called the 'radioactive constant'. **1923** Glazebrook *Dict. Appl. Physics* IV. 574/2 λ, the radioactive constant, represents the average fraction of the number of atoms which break up per unit time. **1942** J. D. Stranathan *'Particles' of Mod. Physics* viii. 325 (*heading*) Relationships among the several radioactive constants. **1904** E. Rutherford *Radio-Activity* vii. 189 In uranium and thorium compounds there is a continuous production of active matter which keeps the compound in radio-active equilibrium. **1923** Glazebrook *Dict. Appl. Physics* IV. 576/1 If a radioactive mineral is sealed up so that the products of transformation are allowed to accumulate, a stage is ultimately reached in which the amount of each product formed is equal to the amount transformed per unit time throughout the series... Material which has reached this state is said to be in radioactive equilibrium. **1946** *Physical Rev.* LXIX. 672/2 Since the age of the earth is much greater than the life of C^{14} a radioactive equilibrium must exist in which the rate of disintegration of C^{14} is equal to the rate of production. **1968** Musset & Lloret *Conc. Encycl. Atom* 95/2 Radioactive equilibrium is also referred to when a radioactive body is produced by nuclear reaction, such as bombarding a target with a beam of particles having a constant intensity. After a certain time, the body formed in the nuclear reaction also acquires a constant radioactivity through the balance of its rates of formation and decay. **1923** *Biochem. Jrnl.* XVII. 439 (*heading*) A contribution to the application of the method of radioactive indicators in the investigation of the change of substance in plants. **1943** Radioactive indicator [see *indicator 2 b (ii)]. **1923** *Phil. Mag.* XLVI. 647 There are only four complete radio-active series of the type that is known. **1926** R. W. Lawson tr. *Hevesy & Paneth's Man. Radioactivity* xxiv. 184 The element thorium is the parent element of a radioactive series. **1956** I. Asimov *Inside Atom* v. 85 The entire set of changes is an example of a radioactive series. This particular one we have been talking about is the uranium-238 series. **1974** *Encycl. Brit. Micropædia* VIII. 378/2 *Radioactive series*, any of four independent sets of unstable atomic nuclei that decay through a sequence of nuclear transformations until a stable nucleus is achieved... Three of the sets, the thorium series, uranium series, and actinium series..are headed by naturally occurring species of unstable nuclei whose half-lives are comparable to the age of the Earth... The fourth set, neptunium series.., came to light after the discovery of induced radioactivity (1934). **1947** C. D. Coryell in C. Goodman *Sci. & Engin. of Nucl. Power* I. vii. 249 In general, radioactive wastes from separation processes must be stored indefinitely in systems free from leaks. **1958** *Engineering* 21 Feb. 236/2 The problem of radioactive waste disposal is finally solved only by the complete natural decay of the constituent fission product activity—a process which may take hundreds of years. **1969** N. W. Pirie *Food Resources* v. 127 Nuclear power stations discharge slightly radioactive waste into the sea near the shore. **1977** *Nature* 10 Mar. 109/2 One of the major obstacles to have arisen to the expanded use of nuclear power has focused on the re-processing and storage of radioactive waste.

Hence **radioa·ctively** *adv.*, by radioactive decay; with radioactive material; by means of a technique dependent upon radioactivity.

1925 J. Joly *Surface-Hist. of Earth* ix. 147 This method would not be reliable..if the lead was in either case unstable—i.e. ultimately changed radioactively into something else. **1936** O. Hahn *Appl. Radiochem.* vi. 171 In the Kjeldahl determination of nitrogen, the ammonia formed is led into a solution of lead nitrate that has been radio-actively activated. **1948** *Physical Rev.* LXXIV. 279/1 Individual atoms of this isotope transform radioactively. **1959** *Oxf. Univ. Gaz.* 16 Mar. 795/2 In the event of nuclear warfare, farm products, particularly milk, obtained from a radio-actively contaminated soil might be positively harmful. **1968** R. A. Lyttleton *Mysteries Solar Syst.* ii. 65 The release of radioactively produced energy means that the internal temperatures of the planets will have risen from their initial values. **1976** *Nuclear Sci. Internat.* Nov. 36/2 Direct measurements of bronchial clearance rates (by inhalation of radioactively labelled dust followed by measurements of radiation from the chest) show little difference between smokers and non-smokers.

ra:dioacti·vity. Also with hyphen. [f. Radio- 2 + Activity.] **1. a.** The property or condition of being radioactive; (the field of study concerned with) the phenomena displayed by radioactive materials. Hence, the radiation emitted by a radioactive material, or such material itself in a dispersed form.

1899 *Nature* Nov. 71/1 On the radio-activity induced by the Becquerel rays. **1900** [see Radio- 2]. **1902** *Harper's Mag.* Aug. 364/1 For days Professor Curie was unable to approach his electrometers..owing to his acquired radio-activity. **1920** *Discovery* Apr. 122/1 This was the first discovery in the science which later became known as radio-activity. **1947** *Sci. News* V. 55 Between them, these three series of radioactive elements include the whole of the known natural sources of radioactivity. **1955** *Sci. Amer.* Aug. 35/1 Radioactivity is measured in curies: one curie is equal to the radioactivity from one gram of radium (37 billion atoms disintegrating per second). **1955** *Bull. Atomic Scientists* Sept. 253/1 Radioactivity can travel in the air over large distances, and its very nature and action are unknown and unfamiliar to most people. **1962** S. G. Waley in A. Pirie *Lens Metabolism Rel. Cataract* 359 When the enzyme is treated with isotopically labelled iodoacetate..and the enzyme is boiled, no radio-activity is released. **1969** *Daily Tel.* 23 Jan. 1/4 A small Swiss nuclear research and training reactor at Lucens was closed yesterday after developing a leak of radio-activity. **1978** L. Deighton *SS-GB* xvi. 135 Do you know what radio-activity is?.. It's the emission of radiation from unstable atomic nuclei—alpha particles, nucleons, gamma rays, electrons and so on.

b. *fig.*

1922 C. E. Montague *Disenchantment* (1924) xv. 210 In men and women of high mental vitality, in places where any of the radio-activity of gifted teaching breaks out for a while..the mind is easily delighted. **1928** *Manch. Guardian Weekly* 27 July 74/1 That radio-activity and that consummate technique shine out from poem after poem.

2. The property of emitting radio waves.

1959 *Sci. Amer.* Feb. 66/1 (Advt.), This is Messier 87—one of many galaxies and nebulae radiating radio energy throughout time and space. What primeval force motivates this celestial radioactivity? **1972** *Nature* 20 Oct. 440/2 It seems unlikely that Cygnus X-3 is unique with respect to its radioactivity and it may therefore represent only one member of a large number of objects that exhibit highly variable radio emission, and which may have been overlooked in classical radio surveys. **1978** *Ibid.* 11 May 131/1 We show here that these non-Io-related..decametric radio activities are affected by solar wind conditions around Jupiter.

radioallergosorbent, -assay: see *radio- 3 a.

radio astronomy. Also with hyphen and as **radioastronomy.** [f. *radio *sb.* + Astronomy.] The branch of astronomy concerned with the study and interpretation of radio waves reaching the earth from space, and with the astronomical use of radio-echo techniques.

1948 *Sci. News Let.* 1 May 279/1 Radioastronomy is a new branch of astronomy only recently announced, Dr. Shapley stated. By use of high-frequency radio waves meteors are tracked in their flight. **1951** *Sci. News* XXI. 40 There are two basic methods of observing in radio astronomy. In the first, we use the familiar processes of radar to explore space around us... The second method is the one in general use. Radiation of radio wavelengths, emitted..by extra-terrestrial bodies, is collected. **1951** *Nature* 7 July 17/1 Dr. Alfred Charles Bernard Lovell has been appointed to a newly created chair of radio-astronomy in the University of Manchester. **1958** *Listener* 27 Nov. 869/2 Out of the cataclysm of a world war have emerged two technical developments which are creating a revolution in astronomical observations—radio astronomy and the earth satellite. **1966** *McGraw-Hill Encycl. Sci. & Technol.* XI. 247/1 Large radio antennas designed for radio astronomy are now used for radar, radio communications, and satellite telemetering. **1973** 'D. HALLIDAY' *Dolly & Starry Bird* xiii. 188 Innes is a Steady-State man, having done a sabbatical on radio astronomy at Cambridge. **1977** J. NARLIKAR *Struct. Universe* iii. 66 Radio-astronomy has played an important part in galactic explorations. For example, 21-cm radio wavelength observations are useful for detecting neutral hydrogen. **1978** R. V. JONES *Most Secret War* xlix. 486 We supplied German radar components..to both Bernard Lovell and Martin Ryle, to help them in their start on radio-astronomy.

Hence **radio astronomer**, a person engaged in radio astronomy; **ra:dio-astrono·mical** *a.*, of or pertaining to radio astronomy; obtained by means of radio telescopes.

1949 *Nature* 12 Nov. 815/2 Three British research organizations which have played a major part in radio-astronomical research. **1952** *Ibid.* 1 Mar. 350/1 It appears likely that..experimental radio astronomers will concentrate their attention on devices for achieving increased angular accuracy. **1959** *Listener* 31 Dec. 1152/2 Interest in peculiar galaxies has been stimulated recently by radio-astronomical observations. **1962** *New Scientist* 5 Apr. 827/3 The primary gamma-ray picture of the Universe might resemble the radioastronomical one. **1968** *Times* 26 Oct. 4/4 A new pulsar has been discovered by radio astronomers at Jodrell Bank. **1973** C. SAGAN *Cosmic Connection* vi. 47 We see..in radio-astronomical studies of the interstellar medium, a profusion of simple and complex organic molecules. **1976** *Time* 27 Dec. 37/2 Radioastronomers..have beamed coded signals toward the stars to let any other civilization know that intelligent life exists on earth.

radio-atom, -autograph (etc.): see *RADIO- 3 a.

† **radiobe** (rēⁱ·di,ōᵘb). *Obs.* [f. *RADI(O- 3 + *-obe*, after MICROBE.] A cell-like body observed to form in large numbers in gelatin solutions in the presence of radium salts, which was formerly claimed to be a living organism owing its existence to radioactivity.

1905 J. B. BURKE in *Nature* 25 May 79/2 As these bodies cannot be identified with microbes, on the one hand, nor with crystals on the other, I have ventured..to give them a new name, *Radiobes*, which might..be more appropriate as indicating their resemblance to microbes, as well as their distinct nature and origin. **1905** *Daily Chron.* 20 June 4/4 Tubes of bouillon containing radium and tubes without radium were stopped up with cotton-wool, subjected to a temperature far above the boiling point of water, under pressure, for half an hour. The control tubes which contained no radium were then watched, and 'nothing happened'... But the surface of the beef-gelatine in the other tubes began to show a peculiar 'growth'. This 'growth'..was examined by a very high power of a microscope and found to consist of minute rounded objects which looked like bacteria... Like living cells they contain nuclei and these have been photographed through the microscope... They exhibited a property possessed by no crystals; a property possessed by living things alone... When they reach the maximum size already named, they subdivide... Mr. Burke calls them radiobes. **1908** *Encycl. Relig. & Ethics* I. 26/1 Mr. Butler Burke inclines to the conclusion that they are organisms on the border lines between microbes and crystals, and, provisionally, he names them 'radiobes'. **1920** *Punch* 7 Jan. 7/2 Let scientists on various fronts Indulge in their atomic stunts, Or harness to our prams and punts The puissant radiobe.

radiobio·logy. Also with hyphen. [f. RADIO- 2, *3 + BIOLOGY.] The branch of biology concerned with the effects on living organisms of radiation and radioactivity, and with the application in biology of radiological techniques.

1919 *Med. Sci. Abstr. & Rev.* I. 358 In radio-biology, when we wish to show the selective action of X-rays we usually choose, as an example, one of the glands of external secretion. **1935** *Discovery* Aug. 225/1 A Congress of Radiobiology was held..last year in Venice. **1955** *Times* 18 Aug. 6/1 The organization that he thought necessary would consist of experts in radiophysics and radiobiology, including radiogenetics, and would be empowered to promote essential research in its field and to organize continuous general supervision of the radiation level of the world. **1962** *Lancet* 26 May 1106/2 The subjects cover almost every aspect of radiobiology, from radiation chemistry to straightforward radiotherapy. **1972** *Physics Bull.* Mar. 147/1 Typical of the radiobiology experiments is one carried out by a team at the Ames Laboratory of NASA in which some 56 pocket mice..were irradiated by the 250 MeV/nucleon nitrogen ion beam.

Hence **ra:diobiolo·gic** (chiefly *U.S.*), **-lo·gical** *adjs.*, of or pertaining to radiobiology; **ra:diobiolo·gically** *adv.*; **radiobio·logist.**

1929 *Radiology* XII. 454/2 (*heading*) Radio-biologic investigations on eggs of Ascaris. **1931** *Gen. Electr. Rev.* XXXIV. 98 (*heading*) Instruments for radiometric and radio-biological investigations at the Desert Sanatorium and Institute of Research, Tucson, Arizona. **1945** C. W. WILSON *Radium Therapy* iii. 81 Innumerable radio-biological experiments and clinical studies have shown that..a number of purely physical factors influence the biological effects produced by high-voltage radiation. **1946** *Nature* 2 Nov. 601/2 Radiobiologists should be grateful for accurate data such as these. **1955** *Times* 18 Aug. 6/1 The problem of extending the present international standards of radiobiological protection from the occupational workers..was discussed. **1956** *Proc. Internat. Conf. Peaceful Uses Atomic Energy* XI. 3/1 It is our belief that, if we take sufficient care radiobiologically to look after mankind..the rest of nature will take care of itself. **1961** *Ann. N.Y. Acad. Sci.* XCV. 828 (*heading*) Radiobiologic observations on human hemic cells *in vivo* and *in vitro*. **1971** *New Scientist* 8 Apr. 108/2 Even if radiobiologists could quantify the deaths and deformations caused by radiation, planners and government consultants feel that these numbers then need to be translated into economic terms. **1976** *Nature* 22 Jan. 209/1 Among the many important radiobiological findings recently summarised are the following: the mutation rate depends on sex, on the type of germ cell irradiated, on radiation quality (X rays, neutrons), [etc.]. **1977** *Lancet* 20 Aug. 411/1 Complete recovery of thyroid function after prolonged ^{125}I-induced hypothyroidism can be explained radiobiologically.

radio-cæsium: see *RADIO- 3 b (i).

radio-ca·rbon. Also **radiocarbon.** [f. *RADIO- 3 b + CARBON.] **1.** A radioactive isotope of carbon; *spec.* = **carbon 14*, which is formed in trace amounts by the effect of cosmic rays on atmospheric nitrogen. Also *ellipt.* for *radio-carbon dating*.

1940 *Physical Rev.* LVII. 549/2 Large quantities of nitrogenous material have been exposed to neutrons for several months and will be shortly worked up for radio-carbon. **1946** *Ibid.* LXIX. 672/1 The purpose of this letter is to..suggest that radiocarbon might be found in living matter especially in connection with the concentration of C^{13} for tracer uses. **1956** W. F. ALBRIGHT *Archaeol. of Palestine* (rev. ed.) i. 22 Radiocarbon has a 'half life' of some 5,600 years, and the count loses any significance beyond 25,000–30,000 years ago. **1957** *Times* 11 Sept. 6/2 Recent studies using radiocarbon indicated that the yield of photosynthesis by the plankton of the oceans was at least equal to that of the land flora, and might be several times greater. **1963** G. M. B. DOBSON *Exploring Atmosphere* i. 12 The radiocarbon formed in the upper atmosphere becomes radiocarbon dioxide and is gradually mixed throughout the whole atmosphere. **1970** *Nature* 4 Apr. 45/1 The chronology of several glacial stages has been recognized in the microfossils and dated by radiocarbon. **1976** P. L. BROWN *Planet Earth* iii. 77 Radiocarbon then combines with oxygen to form $C^{14}O_2$ which is diffused through the atmosphere and then is absorbed by plants via photosynthesis and ultimately by all living things.

2. *attrib.* and *Comb.* (usu. with reference to radio-carbon dating), as *radio-carbon age, content, method, year*, etc.; **radio-carbon dating**, a method of isotopic dating which is applicable to dead organic matter and in which the proportion of carbon 14 (which has decreased at a known rate since the death of the sample material), is measured and compared with the known natural abundance of the isotope; hence *radio-carbon date; radio-carbon-dated* ppl. adj.

1949 *Antiquity* XXIII. 113 A method of dating dead pieces of formerly living substances (such as wood and bone) by means of their radiocarbon content. **1949** *Science* 23 Dec. 679/2 These results indicate that the two basic assumptions of the radiocarbon age determination method—namely, the constancy of the cosmic radiation intensity and the possibility of obtaining unaltered samples—are probably justified for wood up to 4600 years. **1950** ARNOLD & LIBBY (*title*) Radiocarbon dates. **1951** *Amer. Jrnl. Sci.* CCXLIX. 257 (*heading*) Radiocarbon dating of Late-Pleistocene events. *Ibid.*, All of the dates are of the right order of magnitude, with a few exceptions where it seems likely that the stratigraphic position of the sample, and not the radiocarbon age, has been incorrectly given. *Ibid.* 268 The radiocarbon date, 12,148 ± 700 years. **1956** M. WHEELER in A. Pryce-Jones *New Outl. Mod. Knowl.* 399 A radio-carbon dating gives 7538 B.C. (with a possible error ± of 350 years) for the settlement. **1957** G. E. HUTCHINSON *Treat. Limnol.* I. i. 8 The dating of the events, based primarily on the varve chronology, is in fair accord with the radio-carbon chronology. **1963** D. W. & E. E. HUMPHRIES tr. *Termier's Erosion & Sedimentation* iii. 55 (*caption*) Old peat deposits (radio-carbon-dated to the Early Holocene) dot the area 'drowned' by the Flandrian transgression. **1966** *Radiocarbon* VIII. 534 The result of a radiocarbon determination is commonly expressed as an age given in radiocarbon years. *Ibid.*, The conversion of a radiocarbon age..to a true calendar year makes necessary certain assumptions with respect to: (1) the half-life of C^{14}, (2) the production rate of C^{14} by cosmic rays, (3) the size of reservoirs into which C^{14} is distributed and the exchange rate of this distribution. **1973** *Nature* 1 June 266/1 Three radiocarbon laboratories, at La Jolla, Philadelphia and Tucson, have obtained radiocarbon dates over the past decade for specimens of bristlecone pine already dated dendrochronologically, thereby allowing the 'correction' of the radiocarbon scale. **1973** *Nation Rev.* (Melbourne) 31 Aug. (Suppl.) 2/3 Until 1972 only two radiocarbon-dated remains of Chinese origin were known. **1978** *New Scientist* 2 Mar. 599/2 The dating of carbon in glacier varves would extend the calibration of the radiocarbon dating curve.

radiocast (rēⁱ·diokɑst), *sb.* and *v.* *U.S.* [f. *RADIO *sb.* + *-cast*, after BROADCAST.] **A.** *sb.* A radio broadcast.

1931 *Daily Progress* (Charlottesville, Va.) 10 Feb. 5/3 J. B. Priestley..is going to Tahiti, via New York, to write his next novel. He said in a radiocast he'd need a small island to recover from the fright he expects to receive on the gigantic island of Manhattan.

B. *v.* To broadcast by radio; so **ra·diocasting** *vbl. sb.*

1931 *Amer. Speech* VI. 253 Where the writer wishes to leave no doubt that he means *to radio-broadcast*, he is taking now to *to radiocast*. **1940** *Christian Sci. Monitor* 16 Mar. (Mag. section) 3/3 (*caption*) From this radiocasting structure, 400 feet high, music without static is being sent to listeners. **1947** PARTRIDGE *Usage & Abusage* 260/1 Both 'to *radio*' and 'to *broadcast*' are infinitely preferable to either *radiocast* or *radio-broadcast*.

radioche·mical, *a.* (*sb.*) Also with hyphen. [f. *RADIO- 3 + CHEMICAL *a.*] **1.** Of, pertaining to, or considered in terms of radiochemistry; *radio-chemical purity*, the state of being free from radioactive impurities. Also as *sb.*, a radioactive chemical.

1915 F. SODDY *Chem. Radio-Elements* (ed. 2) I. 46 In a condition of complete radio-chemical purity. **1946** *Chem. & Engin. News* 10 Dec. 3168/1 Laboratory facilities for radio-chemical research are classified according to the level of radioactivity involved in the operations. **1961** G. R. CHOPPIN *Exper. Nucl. Chem.* ix. 129 Radiochemical purity is frequently of greater importance than chemical purity; it may be better to have a milligram of inert impurity in the final sample than 10^{-9} gm of radioactive contaminant. **1971** *New Scientist* 1 Apr. 26/2 The US market is estimated to be worth over $80 million a year with some $25 million spent on radiochemicals, $40 on radiopharmaceuticals, and about $20 million on basic radioisotopes and sealed sources. **1973** D. L. HORROCKS in Moghissi & Carter *Tritium* i. 34 The total fissions are determined by radiochemical assay of a fission product (i.e., ^{140}Ba) of known yield. **1978** *Nature* 11 May p. xii/1 (Advt.), Our supply of radiochemicals of the highest quality and technical specifications.

2. (With hyphen.) Of or pertaining to chemical changes caused by radiant energy. *rare.*

1921 D. H. LAWRENCE *Let.* 2 Mar. (1962) II. 512 The sun is dangerous these months—it has a radio-chemical action on the blood which simply does for me. **1935** *Mind* XLIV. 545 In general, chemical reactions are coming to be conceived in the light of the 'radio-chemical' hypothesis, *viz.* that no structural modification can take place except as the result of quantities of radiant energy imparted in rhythmic pulses.

Hence (sense 1) **radioche·mically** *adv.*, by a radiochemical method or process; in terms of radiochemistry.

1915 F. SODDY *Chem. Radio-Elements* (ed. 2) I. 44 Another and very important sense [of the term 'pure'], which may conveniently be termed 'radio-chemically' pure. **1923** GLAZEBROOK *Dict. Appl. Physics* IV. 590/1 A product may be prepared 'radio-chemically' pure, in which the radio-element may be mixed with a certain amount of inactive matter, but is free from substances chemically analogous to itself. **1957** *Jrnl. Biol. Chem.* CCXXIX. 443 A substance subsequently shown to be radiochemically pure was treated in a similar manner. **1975** *Nature* 1 May 77/1 The plutonium in each right testis was measured radiochemically.

radioche·mistry. Also with hyphen. [f. *RADIO- 3 + CHEMISTRY.] The chemistry of radioactive substances; sometimes held to include also *radiation chemistry* s.v. *RADIATION 4. Hence **radioche·mist.**

In quot. 1904 perh. = **radiation chemistry*.

1904 *Jrnl. Physical Chem.* VIII. 506 Under chemical energetics we find the mass law relations for equilibrium and reaction velocity,..electrochemistry, photochemistry and radiochemistry. **1910** A. T. CAMERON (*title*) Radiochemistry. **1911** F. SODDY *Chem. Radio-Elements* 11 A special branch of chemistry, which may be appropriately termed 'Radio-Chemistry' has come into existence. **1938** R. W. LAWSON tr. *Hevesy & Paneth's Man. Radioactivity* (ed. 2) xxiv. 247 The study of the chemical effects of the rays from radium is sometimes called 'radio-chemistry' in the narrower sense... However, we shall confine the use of the term 'radio-chemistry' to the chemistry of the radio-elements, or the study of their chemical properties and reactions. **1952** F. E. ZEUNER *Dating Past* (ed. 3) IV. x. 346 One can confidently expect the radio-chemist to be aware of the difficulties. **1953** E. SIMON *Past Masters* III. 141 A radiochemist [should] be called in to carry out tests on the stone fabric of this and the other huts in order to determine age. **1971** I. G. GASS et al. *Understanding Earth* ii. 42/1 Direct measurements of long half-lives..have been carried out in many physics and radiochemistry laboratories. **1973** *Nature* 3 Aug. p. xiii. (Advt.), South African Atomic Energy Board. Radiochemist or Radiopharmacist. Applications are invited.

radio-chlorine to **-element:** see *RADIO- 2, 3, 4.

ra·dio-frequency. Also **radio frequency, radiofrequency.** [f. *RADIO *sb.* + FREQUENCY.]

1. A frequency in the range used for telecommunication; greater than that of the highest audio-frequency and less than that of the shortest infra-red waves (i.e. between about 10^4 and 10^{11} or 10^{12} Hz).

1915 *Electrician* 2 July 463/1 Mercury arc rectifiers can be operated at a good efficiency even at radio frequencies. **1937** *Discovery* Mar. p. xxiii/1 Loud Speaker output at radio frequencies. **1976** A. WHITE *Long Silence* xi. 95 You can often get close enough..without them being aware of it, especially if they're listening to a radio frequency.

2. *attrib.* Pertaining to (electromagnetic radiation having) such a frequency; operating at or having such a frequency; employing alternating current having such a frequency.

1915 *Engin. Mag.* XLIX. 253/2 The usual radio frequency transformers. **1919** *Wireless World* May 75/1 The arc transforms..the 1,500-volt direct current power into radio frequency energy. **1922** *Nature* 20 May 650/2 A six-tube amplifier having three stages of radio-frequency amplification. **1943** *Electronic Engin.* XV. 344/2 When the bridge goes off balance a radio-frequency current flows through the meter. **1946** *Nature* 10 Aug. 194/1 Radio-frequency heating is not an economic proposition for heating stable liquids, but may prevent serious losses of activity in heat-sensitive ones. **1955** J. G. Davis *Dict. Dairying* (ed. 2) 828 The use of radio-frequency heating for the pasteurization of milk. **1957** *Endeavour* XVI. 187/1 Electronic equipment to generate the radio-frequency radiation and to measure its absorption by the sample. **1965** *B.B.C. Handbk.* 116 For best results on short waves, a receiver should incorporate a tuned radio-frequency amplifier preceding the frequency-changer stage. **1967** M. Chandler *Ceramics in Mod. World* ii. 76. Other methods of drying, of more limited and special application, include infrared and radio-frequency drying. **1970** G. K. Woodgate *Elem. Atomic Struct.* viii. 148 Many precise measurements of *gJ*..have now been made by the methods of radio-frequency spectroscopy.

radiogenetic(al, -ics: see *radio- 2.

radiogenic (rēɪdiodʒe·nik), *a.* [f. *radio- 3, 4 + *-genic (in sense 1 after *photogenic*).] **1.** Well suited for broadcasting by radio; providing an attractive subject for a radio broadcast.

1928 *Radio Times* 24 Aug. 342/2 Their object is to discover..a form (or forms) of drama which shall be truly 'radiogenic'. **1931** T. H. Pear *Voice & Personality* xii. 149 England has greater artistic variety of 'radiogenic' material. **1943** S. Lewis *Gideon Planish* xxxii. 418 The..Great Leaders: Governor Blizzard and..the dazzle-sounding, radiogenic Winifred Marduc Homeward. **1946** *Electronic Engin.* XVIII. 207/3 Transatlantic Quiz, even if radiogenic, is not pictorial and there seems no good reason for transplanting it into television. **1959** *Listener* 27 Aug. 332/2 Radiogenic in the extreme, Miss Jacob led her interlocutors more of a dance than anyone else in this series since Thurber. **1975** *Encounter* Sept. 43 This short play..has appeared in book form; but so totally radiogenic is its very nature that the printed page cannot represent it.

2. Produced by or resulting from radioactive decay or ionizing radiation.

1935 *Jrnl. Amer. Chem. Soc.* LVII. 470/2 There seems to be no definite trend in the relation of the atomic weight of uranium lead to the period during which the radiogenic lead has been forming. **1947** *Endeavour* VI. 104/1 The present rates of production of radiogenic lead are known with a remarkable degree of accuracy. **1960** *New Scientist* 5 May 1114/3 No evidence of radiogenic mutations has been discovered so far. **1970** *Nature* 5 Dec. 906/1 It could be..that the Moon is expanding slowly as a result of radiogenic heating. **1971** *Brit. Med. Bull.* XXVII. 68/1 There were about 15 times as many spontaneous cases as radiogenic cases.

Hence **radioge·nically** *adv.*, by means of radioactive decay.

1956 *Sci. News* XXXIX. 14 Any helium nuclei produced radiogenically would all be of mass 4. **1970** *Nature* 23 May 692/1 These dykes have been radiogenically aged at 2,420 million years.

radio-gold: see *radio- 3 b (i).

ra:diogonio·meter. Also with hyphen. [f. *radio- 4 + Goniometer.] = *goniometer 2. Hence **ra:diogoniome·tric, -me·trical** *adjs.*, of, pertaining to, or by means of a radiogoniometer; **ra:diogonio·metry**, direction-finding by means of a radiogoniometer.

1908 L. H. Walter tr. Bellini & Tosi in *Electr. Engin.* 5 Mar. 348/1 In the present article it is proposed to treat in a more detailed manner the theory and construction of the instruments above referred to, and to which the name of radio-goniometers has been given by the authors. **1913** *Year-bk. Wireless Telegr.* 310 The radiogoniometer..consists of two coils wound over and at right angles to each other, each coil being connected to one of the directive aerials. **1921** *Nature* 23 June 542/2 Radiogoniometry and atmospheric influences. **1927** *Daily Express* 13 Oct. 11/5 A radiogoniometric aerial, an ingenious piece of wireless apparatus which enables the exact position of an air liner in flight to be located. **1932** *Times Lit. Suppl.* 9 June 429/4 He had several narrow escapes..before a cleverly-hidden radiogoniometer ran the Whisperer to earth. **1935** C. G. Burge *Compl. Bk. Aviation* 480/1 Visual radio-goniometry, or the actual wireless compass, will no doubt come into being when a solution is found to a number of the present wireless problems. **1936** *Discovery* Apr. 125/2 Radiogoniometrical control of such a projectile..is quite beyond accomplishment at present. **1961** *Engineering* 16 June 825/1 A new radiotelephone transmitter-receiver..may be used with a radiogoniometer unit. **1971** Watson & Wright *Radio Direction Finding* iv. 46 The radiogoniometer is designed to give maximum accuracy and sensitivity..to the direction finding equipment. **1978** D. Bloodworth *Crosstalk* xvi. 136 Interception and radiogoniometrical checks show irregular traffic on one high-frequency waveband.

radiogram[1]. Add: **1.** (Further examples.) Cf. *radiograph *sb.* 2.

1921 A. V. Knox in A. V. & R. Knox *Gen. Pract. & X-Rays* I. i. 21 A radiogram may be defined as a shadow-picture of structures lying in different planes reproduced on a flat surface. **1962** G. Cremer-Bartels in A. Pirie *Lens Metabolism Rel. Cataract* 444 (*caption*) Radiogram after digestion with phosphatase. **1975** B. Wood *Killing Gift* (1976) I. 13 She could be crippled if that hip is broken and I don't set it. And if I have to set it without a radiogram, I can't be sure of doing it properly.

2. = *radio-telegram.

1904 *Prelim. Conf. Wireless Telegr. Berlin 1903* 10 It seems to us inadvisable..to insist on the interchange of radiograms between ships on the high sea. **1925** H. L. Foster *Trop. Tramp Tourists* 172 Radiogram just came in. The railway can only furnish us with six cars. **1929** *Star* 21 Aug. 12/4 The wireless message was in reply to the following radiogram. **1938** E. Waugh *Scoop* I. v. 90 William hastened to consult him about a radiogram which had arrived that morning. **1949** *Radio Times* 15 July 6/1 I'm from the radio room. Here's a radiogram for you. **1966** *McGraw-Hill Encycl. Sci. & Technol.* XIII. 423/2 In overseas communication, telegraph messages usually are referred to as cablegrams or radiograms, depending on the overseas transmission medium. **1980** L. St. Clair *Obsessions* ii. 58 Helen had replied with her own radiogram: 'What's wrong? No shipboard romance?'

radiogram[2] (rēɪ·diogræm). Abbrev. of next.

1932 G. Wilson *Gramophones* viii. 43 If you have no electricity in your house you should avoid the radio-gram. **1933** *Sunday Referee* 2 July 16/2 In the living-room..is a ply-wood built-in book-case, at one end of which is..a built-in electric radiogram and loud-speaker. **1935** M. Egan *Dominant Sex* III i. 86 She switches on the radiogram and dances gaily for her own amusement. **1938** Auden & Isherwood *On Frontier* II. ii. 77 Valerian and Stahl..are listening to the Leader's speech on the radiogram. **1945** J. Betjeman *New Bats in Old Belfries* 31 Softly croons the radiogram, loudly hoot the owls. **1970** J. Earl *Tuners & Amplifiers* i. 21 The old-style radiogram with inbuilt speakers..rarely yields good stereo reproduction. **1977** *Gramophone* Jan. 1217/1 The widespread development of the music centre as successor to the radiogram.

radio-gra·mophone. [*radio *sb.* + Gramophone in Dict. and Suppl.] A radio and gramophone combined in a single cabinet (with a speaker).

1927 *Wireless World* 19 Oct. 539/1 (*heading*) A combined radio-gramophone installation. **1930** *Times Educ. Suppl.* 15 Feb. p. iv/4 We may reasonably expect a radio-gramophone to work without an outside aerial. **1935** *Economist* 23 Nov. 1042/1 Radio receiving sets and radio-gramophones had formed the largest part of the sales in the home markets. **1976** *Broadcast* 29 Nov. 19/1 Granny and her pre-war radiogramophone.

radiograph, *sb.* Add: **1.** (Earlier example.)

1880 D. Winstanley in *Chem. News* 30 Apr. 205/1, I will now ask your attention to the description of another and much more perfect apparatus, one which continuously records the intensity of thermal radiation in which it is exposed. This instrument I have called the 'Radiograph'.

2. Add to def.: Now also made using other forms of ionizing radiation. (Further examples.)

1923 Glazebrook *Dict. Appl. Physics* IV. 618/1 Tool-marks and fine mould-marks often show up in a radiograph. **1948** *Sci. News* VII. 104 A new type X-ray tube permits radiographs to be made with exposures of 1/500,000th second. **1966** *McGraw-Hill Encycl. Sci. & Technol.* XI. 304a/1 Radiographs made with γ-rays have high resolving power because of the absence of scattering. **1971** *Sci. Amer.* Oct. 16/3 Radiographs of the chest in persons on a starvation diet have indicated that the heart shrinks in size. **1972** *Nature* 15 Sept. 157/2 It has been the practice among nuclear physicists to take 'radiographs' with beams of accelerated light nuclei to determine the location of detector targets..relative to the position of the beam.

† **3.** = *radio-telegraph. *Obs.*

1904 *Prelim. Conf. Wireless Telegr. Berlin 1903* 5 It is to him [*sc.* Popoff] that we owe the first radiograph apparatus.

radiograph (rēɪ·diogrɑf), *v.* [f. the sb.] *trans.* To make a radiograph of; to study by radiography. Also *fig.* Hence **ra·diographing** *vbl. sb.*

1896 [in Dict. s.v. Radiograph *sb.*]. **1897** *Treatment* I. 43/2 It is almost routine practice..to radiograph fractures. **1908** *Sci. Abstr.* A. XI. 105, 1M of No. 5 rays will suffice for the radiographing of a hand. **1924** *Observer* 6 Apr. 12/3 He [*sc.* Byron] has been radiographed to the bone. **1940** J. A. Ross *Handbk. Radiography* xii. 112 Various methods of examination have been devised in an attempt to radiograph movement. **1951** L. P. Dudley *Stereoptics* vi. 106 The tube-film distance adopted in radiographing the subject must be the same as that adopted in radiographing the wire model. **1977** *Lancet* 19 Nov. 1059/2 Each section was photographed in colour, radiographed, drawn in black-and-white and compared with the scanner image at the corresponding level.

radiographer (rēɪdiǫ·grăfəɹ). [f. prec. + -er[1].] One who practises radiography; a person qualified to operate radiographic equipment.

1896 [in Dict. s.v. Radiograph *sb.*] **1907** *Oxf. Univ. Gaz.* 19 Feb. 395/2 The Committee for appointment of Honorary Medical Officers will shortly proceed to the Election of a Radiographer. **1917** *Med. Jrnl. Australia* 5 May 386/1 The radiographer, who had made a screen examination, reported the presence of a large aneurysm of the aortic arch. **1958** *Times* 4 Aug. 9/3 Recent figures have revealed a serious shortage of more than 500 radiographers in the National Health Service. **1971** [see *radiologist]. **1975** E. Lawson *Seeing through You* i. 16 The radiographer was turned towards her patient, one hand outstretched to guide him safely against the cassette containing the X-ray film.

radiographic (rēɪdiogræ·fik), *a.* [f. as prec. + -ic.] **1.** Of, pertaining to, or carried out by means of radiography.

1896 [in Dict. s.v. Radiograph *sb.*]. **1921** *Lancet* 22 Jan. 175/2 (*heading*) Radiographic appearances of pyorrhœa. **1933** *Jrnl. Franklin Inst.* CCXXVI. 183 The radiographic method is useless..in detecting cracks in which the two conjugate surfaces are pressed closely together, leaving no open space. **1976** *Offshore Platforms & Pipelining* 167/1 The most effective way to determine weld quality is by radiographic inspection.

† **2.** = *radio-telegraphic *a. Obs.*

1904 *Prelim. Conf. Wireless Telegr. Berlin 1903* 5 It was Hughes..who laid, in 1877, the first stone of radiographic practice by his detailed experiments. **1907** *Liverpool Post* 10 Sept. 7 On Wednesday night..the Lusitania will..get into radiographic touch with the American coast.

Also **radiogra·phical** *a.* (*rare*) = sense 1; also *fig.*; **radiogra·phically** *adv.*, by means of radiography; as regards radiography.

1898 Radiographic, -ically [in Dict. s.v. Radiograph *sb.*]. **1925** *Jrnl. Anat.* LIX. 149 Dubreuil employed lead pellets, periodically measuring the intervals between the pellets, radiographically. **1931** S. Beckett *Proust* 63 He describes the radiographical quality of his observation. The copiable he does not see. **1977** *Lancet* 14 May 1053/1 Although similar clinically and radiographically, the two syndromes show marked differences when pulmonary surfactant is examined.

radiography (rēɪdiǫ·grăfi). [f. Radio- 2 + -graphy.] **1.** The science or process of making radiographs.

1896, 1898 [in Dict. s.v. Radiograph *sb.*]. **1922** G. W. C. Kaye *Pract. Application of X-Rays* vi. 85 When the art of radiography had sufficiently advanced in medicine, it extended its scope to industry. **1948** *Sci. News* VII. 104 Radiography of rapidly-moving enclosed machine parts, such as pistons or the impeller blades of turbines, has become practical. **1948**, etc. [see *neutron radiography* s.v. *neutron 2]. **1966** C. R. Tottle *Sci. Engin. Materials* vi. 147 With γ-rays, down to 10^{-2}Å, the penetration through metals is even greater; hence the use of X- and γ-rays for radiography. **1971** *World Archaeol.* III. 240 My colleague, Miss Theya Molleson, assisted in the radiography of the skeleton.

† **2.** = *radio-telegraphy. *Obs.*

1904 *Prelim. Conf. Wireless Telegr. Berlin 1903* 5 It is due to radiography that communication has been created between parts of the globe which had previously been deprived of it. **1922** *Hotel World* 15 Apr. 6/2 Mr. Eastman, in charge of the radio broad-casting station in Chicago,..said: 'When I took charge of this work I knew very little about radiography.'

radiohalo, -heliograph: see *radio- 3 a, 4.

radioimmuno- (rēɪ:dio͵i:miuno, -imiū:no). [f. Radio- 2 + *immuno-.] Formative element in terms pertaining to analytical techniques combining immunological and radioisotopic methods. (In the following words secondary stresses vary as indicated above, and are not in general marked in each word.)

radioimmunoa·ssay, an immunological assay in which the test sample is determined by allowing it to react with a prepared antiserum in competition with a known quantity of radioisotopically labelled antigen, the extent of reaction being measured from the amount of radiation emitted (see quot. 1974); hence **radioimmunoa·ssayable** *a.*, capable of determination by radioimmunoassay; **radioimmunoche·mical** *a.*, deriving both from immunology and from radiochemistry; employing radioisotopically labelled antigens and antibodies as reagents for chemical analysis; hence **radioimmunoche·mically** *adv.*; **radioimmunoe:lectrophore·sis,** immuno-electrophoresis carried out using radioisotopically labelled samples, usu. as a means of studying the formation or binding of proteins; so **radioimmunoele:ctrophore·tic** *a.*; **radioimmunoprecipita·tion,** the use of radioisotopically labelled antigen or antibody in a precipitin test, the radioactivity in any precipitated complex being measured.

1961 *Jrnl. Clin. Investigation* XL. 1086/1 A specific radioimmunoassay of human growth hormone..has been devised. **1966** *Lancet* 24 Dec. 1389/2 Glucose was measured by the potassium-ferricyanide method..and insulin by radio-immunoassay. **1974** R. M. Kirk et al. *Surgery* ii. 36 To carry out radioimmunoassay, an antiserum is first raised by injecting the substance repeatedly into laboratory animals, and later withdrawing serum containing antibody. A known concentration of antigen, labelled with a radioactive marker, is placed in competition with the test serum for combination with the antibody. **1977** *Time* 24 Oct. 52/1 Yalow and her late collaborator, Dr Solomon Berson, devised a sensitive new biological analytic technique called the radioimmunoassay (RIA). **1973** *Nature* 27 July 230/1 The serum level of radioimmunoassayable (RIA) growth hormone. **1978** *Ibid.* 12 Jan. 178/2 The radioimmunoassayable enkephalin content of the basal ganglia does not change after cortical ablation. **1968** *Gastroenterology* LV. 317/2 The supernatant solutions were analyzed in triplicate for gastrin by a radioimmunochemical technique *Ibid.* 326/2 The gastrin contents..were measured radioimmunochemically. **1977** *Lancet* 26 Mar. 666/2 Blood obtained by antecubital-vein puncture was assayed radioimmunochemically for insulin, glucagon, gastrin, and pancreatic polypeptide. **1962** Morse & Heremans in *Jrnl. Laboratory & Clin. Med.* LIX. 893 This method of immunoelectrophoresis, followed by autography, will be referred to as radioimmunoelectrophoresis. **1970** *Nature* 12 Dec. 1086/2 Radioimmunoelectrophoresis was also performed on dialysed supernatant from cell cultures incubated with either amino-acids labelled with ^{14}C or with reconstituted protein hydrolysate similarly labelled. **1975** *Ibid.* 11 Dec. 547/2 Radioimmunoelectrophoresis of serum from snakes injected with HEA revealed that the gamma precipitin line specifically bound HEA^{131}I. **1962** *Jrnl. Immunol.* LXXXIX. 744/2 Similar radio immunoelectrophoretic technique was applied in insulin-binding antibodies from human patients. **1962** *Jrnl. Clin. Investigation* XLI 260/1 Our observations with radioimmunoprecipitation confirm the information obtained with more orthodox immunologic procedures. **1971** *Jrnl. Immunol.* CVI. 1167/1 The radioimmunoprecipitation test (RIP) was performed by the microtiter method as modified by Sever..using V-bottom thin plastic plates. **1974** *Nature* 25 Jan. 176/3 In addition the antigen was detected by radioimmunoprecipitation in the supernatant fluid of a few cultures which had been serially passaged.

radioimmunology (rēⁱ:dioˌimiunǫ·lŏdʒi). [f. Radio- 2 + *immunology.] The application of radiological techniques in immunology.

1971 *Biol. Abstr.* LI. Ann. Cum. Index 4200/1 (*heading*) Radio immunology. **1976** *Scand. Jrnl. Immunol.* V. 609 (*heading*) Unified mass-action theory for virus neutralization and radioimmunology.

So **ra:dioimmunolo·gic** (chiefly *U.S.*), **-lo·gical** *adjs.*, combining radiological and immunological methods; of or pertaining to radioimmunology; **ra:dioimmunolo·gically** *adv.*

1965 *Jrnl. Clin. Endocrinol.* XXV. 1043 (*heading*) A radioimmunological assay method for insulin using insulin-^{125}I and gel filtration. *Ibid.* 1457 (*heading*) Radioimmunologic measurement of human placental lactogen in plasma by a double antibody method. **1970** *Ibid.* XXXI. 679/2 HGH antibodies were determined radioimmunologically. **1976** *Science* 24 Dec. 1428/3 Radioimmunologic techniques have markedly increased the sensitivity with which viruses can be detected. **1977** *Lancet* 7 May 1006/2, 194 rural men, aged 55–74 and leading the same agricultural life, were screened for milk antibodies by a radioimmunological method.

radio-iodinate(d, -iodination: see *radio- 3 a. **radio-iodine, -iron:** *radio- 3 b (i).

radioisotope (rēⁱdioˌəi·sǫtōᵘp). Also with hyphen. [f. *radio- 3 + *isotope.] A radioactive isotope.

1946 *Chem. & Engin. News* 10 Dec. 3168/1 The availability of radioisotopes of nearly all elements in quantities hitherto unachievable. **1950** *Times* 8 May 4/4 Also being shown are the machines and methods used for the extraction and synthesis of C-14, a radio-isotope of carbon, which has many uses in industrial, medical, and biological research work. **1958** *Economist* 8 Feb. 496/2 Radio-isotope departments are being set up in the Royal Hospital in Baghdad and the University of Shiraz for the diagnosis and treatment of disease. **1976** *Daily Colonist* (Victoria, B.C.) 15 Apr. 5/5 A freshly fallen meteorite..contains radioisotopes which decay in a matter of days or weeks. **1980** *Brit. Med. Jrnl.* 29 Mar. 931/1 The clinical use of radioisotopes has developed over the last 30 years from a technical science into a recognisable clinical specialty.

Hence **ra:dioisoto·pic** *a.*, **-isoto·pically** *adv.*

1956 *Nature* 7 Apr. 639/1 The kinetics of biological systems as studied by radioisotopic methods. **1970** *Ibid.* 13 June 1025/1 Detection of regulatory proteins present in such small amounts would probably require radioisotopically labelled proteins of very high specific activity. *Ibid.* 24 Oct. 383/1 Radioisotopic tracer experiments have established that carbonate from seawater is incorporated into the skeleton by many corals. **1978** *Ibid.* 19 Oct. 667/2 We used a radioisotopically labelled complementary DNA probe.. generated from an *in vitro* reverse transcriptase reaction.

radioize (rēⁱ·dioˌəiz), *v.* *U.S.* [f. *radio *sb.* + -ize.] *trans:* To equip with radio.

1922 *Sci. & Invention* May (Advt., rear cover), Radioize your phonograph with a guaranteed adapter. **1950** *Sun* (Baltimore) 19 July 13/1 Russia is in the middle of an all-out campaign to 'radioize' the entire population of its sprawling Soviet Socialist Republics.

ra·dio-label, *v.* and *sb.* *Biol.* and *Chem.* Also **radiolabel.** [f. *radio- 3 + Label *v.* in Dict. and Suppl.] **A.** *v. trans.* To label with a radioactive isotope (see *label *v.* 2). So **ra·dio-labelled** *ppl. a.*, **radio-la·belling** *vbl. sb.*

1953 *Adv. Biol. & Med. Physics* III. 149 It may be possible to demonstrate the existence of such autoantibodies by the use of radio-labeled sera. **1962** *Jrnl. Immunol.* LXXXIX. 559/1 In the present study with poliovirus, this hindrance was overcome by radiolabeling the virus. **1970** *Nature* 16 May 649/1 In radiolabelling experiments, synchronized cultures were incubated with radioactive amino-acids for the required time and radiolabelled γG_{2a} was assayed. **1972** *Science* 16 June 1226/3 The tube is then washed, radiolabeled HBAb is added, and the new mix incubated. **1976** *Chem. in Brit.* XII. 375 (*heading*) Radiolabelling water's courses. *Ibid.* 379/1 Radiolabelling has become the preferred method for studying the metabolic fate of foreign compounds in biological systems.

B. *sb.* A radioactive label (*label *sb.*[1] 7 d).

1972 *Science* 16 June 1226/3 The use of a radiolabel makes the technique expensive. **1978** *Nature* 12 Jan. 111/3 That these phenomena are not due to breakdown and reincorporation of the radiolabel is shown by the negligible label in juice if the radiolabelled protein presented is albumin.

radiolarian, *a.* and *sb.* Add: Also *Geol.* **A.** *adj. radiolarian chert*, a cryptocrystalline type of radiolarite; *loosely* = *radiolarite; *radiolarian earth*, unconsolidated siliceous rock formed from the remains of radiolaria; *radiolarian ooze*, a siliceous marine sediment rich in the remains of the tests of radiolarians.

1876 [see *ooze *sb.*[2] 2 b]. **1890** *Geol. Mag.* VII. 144 (*heading*) Radiolarian chert in the Ballantrae series. **1911** [see *ophiolitic *a.*]. **1913** Hatch & Rastall *Petrology of Sedimentary Rocks* I. iv. 143 One of the most notable instances of the abundant presence of this division of the Protozoa is afforded by the so-called Radiolarian earths of Barbados. *Ibid.* II. iii. 233 An interesting example of the metamorphism of a nearly pure siliceous rock is found in the Galloway district, where certain radiolarian cherts of Arenig age are altered by the Loch Doon granite. **1926** W. H. Twenhofel *Treat. Sedimentation* v. 377 Radiolarian ooze is confined to the Pacific and Indian oceans. **1944** A. Holmes *Princ. Physical Geol.* xv. 317 The siliceous remains persist to greater depths, some of them down to 5,000 fathoms, the average for radiolarian ooze being about 3,000. **1953** *Caribbean Q.* III. III. 179 Barbados..has a foundation of rocks...On top of this is a layer of deep sea deposit (radiolarian earth) and on top of this a slab of white limestone. **1971** B. W. Sparks *Rocks & Relief* ix. 306 Certain beds of radiolarian chert..are sufficiently resistant to form series of hog-back ridges across both outcrops. **1971** [see *ooze *sb.*[2] 2 b]. **1975** Fox & Heezen in Nairn & Stehli *Ocean Basins & Margins* III. x. 430 Piston cores obtained from the base of one escarpment recovered Early Eocene radiolarian ooze.

radiolarite (rēⁱdiolēᵊ·rəit). *Geol.* [a. F. *radiolarite* (F. Jaccard 1904, in *Bull. des Laboratoires de Géol.*, etc. (Univ. of Lausanne) II. viii. 79): see Radiolaria *sb. pl.* and -ite[1].] A type of homogeneous fine-grained siliceous sedimentary rock formed mainly from skeletal remains of radiolarians; also applied loosely to other sedimentary rocks similarly formed.

1910 *Proc. Sect. Sci. K. Akad. Wetensch. te Amsterdam* XII. 141 In the year 1894 I [*sc.* G. A. F. Molengraaff] discovered in the basin of the Upper Kapoewas in Western Borneo cherts and hornstones, consisting almost entirely of tests of Radiolaria, which I described as deep-sea deposits. Such rocks are also known as Radiolarite. **1924** J. G. A. Skerl tr. *Wegener's Orig. Continents & Oceans* ii. 20 The practically non-calcareous 'radiolarites' of the Alps. **1938** Hatch & Rastall *Petrol. of Sedimentary Rocks* (ed. 3) x. 203 In Great Britain, two principal types of radiolarite may be distinguished, one represented by the jaspers and jasper-like cherts, and the other by the culm type of chert. **1945** M. F. Glaessner *Princ. Micropalaeont.* ii. 11 Radiolarite- and serpentine-zones in close association form important structural elements in many folded zones of different age. **1972** *Gloss. Geol.* (Amer. Geol. Inst.) 587/1 *Radiolarite*,..(a) the comparatively hard, very fine-grained, chert-like, homogeneous, consolidated equivalent of radiolarian earth. (b) Indurated radiolarian ooze. (c) A term that is often applied as a syn. of radiolarian earth. **1977** A. Hallam *Planet Earth* 254/1 Ancient radiolarian-rich sediments are known as radiolarites, and many of these are believed to be deep-water deposits.

radiole (rēⁱ·diōᵘl). *Zool.* [f. L. *radiolus*, dim. of *radius* Radius.] One of the spines or prickles of a sea-urchin. Also *radiole spine*.

1929 *Encycl. Brit.* VII. 900/2 Primarily radioles serve for protection, but the larger radioles may be used like stilts for locomotion or for digging. **1979** *Nature* 8 Nov. 135/3 Differing feeding processes in echinoids were correlated with differing fine structure of their radiole spines.

radio-lead: see *radio- 3 b (i).

radioless (rēⁱ·diolės), *a.* [f. *radio *sb.* + -less.] Without radio broadcasting or radio equipment.

1937 *Daily Express* 3 Mar. 8/3 'Wilky' was an R.A.F. war pilot, and after the armistice was one of the heroes to work the radioless, single-engined air-mail service for the Rhineland Army. **1938** *Times Lit. Suppl.* 29 Jan. 69/1 Sir John [Reith] would have liked to impose a radioless Sabbath on the listening public. **1973** H. Gruppe *Truxton Cipher* xviii. 189 Cutter had been radioless, his ship last reported as destroyed.

radioligand: see *radio- 3 a.

ra:dioloca·tion. Also with hyphen. [f. *radio- 4 + Location.] The term orig. used in Britain for *radar; the determination of the position and course of ships, aircraft, etc., by means of radar.

1941 *Flight* 26 June 430/1 In the Battle of Britain the advantages of radiolocation were even more apparent. **1941** *Hutchinson's Pict. Hist. War* 14 May–8 July 180 Radiolocation has been described by Air Chief Marshall Sir Philip Joubert as Britain's secret weapon against the German bomber. Rays are sent out and any aircraft or ship in their path immediately reflects a signal. **1942** *R.A.F. Jrnl.* 30 May 30 By what, then, is the R.A.F. kept in the air?.. Its radio-location girls,..its operations staff? **1947** J. Hayward *Prose Literature since 1939* vi. 43 The public should be disabused of the notion that science..is merely another word for technology; and that its purpose is..to develop and supply 'modern conveniences'.. in the form of..radiolocation for the General Staff. **1976** M. Gilbert *Winston S. Churchill* V. xxxiii. 659 The existence of 'radar' was not publicly acknowledged until 1941, when it was referred to as 'Radiolocation'.

Hence **ra:dioloca·te** *v. trans.*, to locate (an aircraft, etc.) by means of radar; **ra:dioloca·ted** *ppl. a.*; **ra:dioloca·tor,** an apparatus for radiolocation.

1941 *Flight* 26 June 430/1 They could rely on the vast radiolocator system to tell them in plenty of time when the enemy were coming and from what direction. **1942** *Times* 20 Jan. 2/2 Members of the A.T.S. have taken over the working of the radiolocators, predictors, and height-finders. **1943** *Times* 25 Oct. 3/4 Many experts are convinced that the attack was..ordered from a German patrol boat that had radio-located the aircraft. **1945** *Electronic Engin.* XVII. 679/3 It is no exaggeration.. to say that the first object to be radiolocated was the Heaviside layer. **1945** *Jrnl. Inst. Electr. Engineers* XCII. I. 342/1 In this method of determining the distance of a radiolocated object, short radio-frequency pulses are sent out at regular intervals. **1946** P. Carter in Aldiss & Harrison *Decade the 1940s* (1975) 108 He passed by the radio locator and the radioman. Their jobs would come later, meantime radio silence was enforced. **1947** Crowther & Whiddington *Science at War* 18 The radiolocator requires as strong an echo as possible.

radiologic (rēⁱdiolǫ·dʒik), *a.* Chiefly *U.S.* [f. as next + -ic.] = next.

1909 in *Cent. Dict.* Suppl. **1914** *Jrnl. Amer. Med. Assoc.* 28 Mar. 980/2 Increased gastric peristalsis has been commonly listed among the radiologic signs of duodenal ulcer. **1945** *Radiology* XLIV. 82/2 His interest in radiology has made him an energetic participant in local and national radiologic organizations. **1975** S. C. Bushong (*title*) Radiologic science for technologists. **1978** *Detroit Free Press* 5 Mar. 9/1 Career training offered at Madonna for deaf students includes..radiologic technology, business administration, [etc.].

radiological (rēⁱdiolǫ·dʒikăl), *a.* [f. next + -ical.] **a.** Of, pertaining to, or concerned with radiology.

1909 *Proc. R. Soc. Med.* II. I. (Electro-Therapeutical Section) 5 Two most interesting papers were those by Béclère, of Paris, and Alban Köhler, of Wiesbaden, on the 'Radiological Exploration of the Liver'. **1923** *Daily Mail* 7 Aug. 5/6 In the radiological department of the hospital there he was shown his hand with the X rays. **1947** *Radiology* XLIX. 345/2 One of the old ideas running through the entire radiological literature is that small doses of X-rays exert a stimulating effect. **1955** *Bull. Atomic Scientists* May 171/1 The composition and possible radiological effects of the super-bomb tested in the Pacific last spring. **1969** P. Jacobs in D. Sutton *Textbk. Radiol.* I. ii. 31/2 Since the surgeon is likely to explore the lesion as soon as it is suspected clinically, one will seldom nowadays observe the radiological phases corresponding to the pathological changes mentioned above. **1976** *Globe Democrat* (St. Louis, Missouri) 18 Sept. 8F/3 Six sections of radiological shield manufactured here..are being shipped by rail to..a nuclear power plant.

b. Of warfare, weapons, etc.: involving the deliberate release of ionizing radiation or radioactive material in harmful quantities.

1951 *Britannica Bk. of Year* 686/2 *Radiological warfare*, warfare with radioactive material. **1952** B. Wolfe *Limbo '90* (1953) vii. 79 H-bombs..supplemented with radiological-warfare dust. **1958** *Ann. Reg. 1957* 478 Radiological warfare was now a distinct possibility through the use of low altitude explosions of high fission energy yield which could contaminate large areas beyond the range of physical damage. **1963** *New Scientist* 28 Mar. 679 (*heading*) A radiological arms race in the Middle East? *Ibid.* 679/3 The radiological bomb would, presumably, come into the same military category as a persistent gas.

Hence **radiolo·gically** *adv.*

1924 *Brit. Jrnl. Dermatol.* XXXVI. 516 When studying radiologically the osseous lesions..I had been struck by the clear delimitation of the pathological loci. **1955** *Sci. News* XXXV. 87 It was shown radiologically that the sphincter is capable of shutting off the venous return. **1979** *Guardian* 1 May 3/3 The Windscale site is known to be radiologically 'dirty'.

radiology (rēⁱdiǫ·lŏdʒi). [f. Radio- 2 + -logy.] **a.** The medical use of X-rays, esp. in diagnosis; also extended to include the diagnostic use of other forms of radiation. † **b.** (See quot. 1905.) Cf. *roentgenology* s.v. *roentgen-, roentgeno-.

1900 *Pop. Sci. Monthly* May 110/1 An International Congress of Medical Electrology and Radiology has been connected with the International Congress system of the Paris Exposition, 1900. **1905** A. M. Clerke *Syst. Stars* (ed. 2) vi. 80 The many suggestions of 'radiology' (as the new science of radioactivity might be designated) cannot be inconsiderately set aside. **1928** *Daily Express* 6 Dec. 7/4 A specialist in radiology and electrical treatment. **1938** S. C. Shanks et al. *Text-bk. X-Ray Diagnosis* I. p. vii, Diagnostic radiology is becoming an increasingly complex specialty, and it is difficult for one person to be equally expert in all its branches. **1959** W. T. Moss *Therapeutic Radiol.* i. 23 The selective destruction of tissues forms the basis of therapeutic radiology. **1979** Bartrum & Crow *Case Stud. in Ultrasound* p. v, Even more than in conventional radiology, the satisfactory application of ultrasound requires that the practitioner know the clinical history. **1980** D. Sutton *Textbk. Radiol. & Imaging* p. vii/1 When the last edition of this book was published in 1975 Radio-isotope Scanning was well established and Ultrasound had already made a major impact on radiology... Nuclear Medicine has also steadily progressed. Imaging, as these new disciplines are usually called, is now a major force which has profoundly influenced the practice of radiology.

Hence **radio·logist,** a person employing ionizing radiation or radioactive material in any field, esp. a medically qualified practitioner of the diagnostic use of X-rays.

1906 *Arch. Roentgen Ray* XI. 20/1 Hitherto the majority of radiologists have been accustomed to work without any measurement of the Roentgen light. **1926** *Encycl. Brit.* XXXII. 284 This region of the intestinal tract is becoming an open book to the radiologist. **1955** *Sci. News Let.* 11 June 372/2 Because the field of radiation itself is so well-defined, City of Hope radiologists and physicists found it possible to dispense with the customary heavy, lead-lined door. **1958** *Times Lit. Suppl.* 2 May 233/3 The radiologists in their helmets of lead, the scientists tracking down the atom, cast their strange shadows on the Pyramids. **1971** *Lancet* 29 May 1124/1 A radiologist to the N.H.S. is medical and a radiographer non-medical.

radiolucent (rēⁱdiolⁱū·sěnt), *a.* [f. RADIO- 2 + TRANS)LUCENT *a.*] Transparent to X-rays. So **radiolu·cency,** the state or property of being radiolucent.

1917 K. THOMA *Oral Roentgenol.* IV. iv. 197 The Roentgen evidence of alveoloclasia is due to the dissolution of bone and replacement by radiolucent pathological tissue. **1936** B. J. M. HARRISON *Textbk. Roentgenol.* iii. 62 Of the relatively radiolucent substances those used are air, carbon dioxide, and oxygen. **1940** *Bull. Johns Hopkins Hosp.* LXVI. 91 The cutaneous region of the foetus is usually represented by a dark line, due to radiolucency. **1961** *Dental Progr.* I. 177/2 Most of the difficulty in diagnosis was caused by general graininess of the film combined with poor contrast between areas of varying radiolucency. **1973** *Daily Tel.* 22 Oct. 13/6 The plastics used in the modern motor car..are radiolucent and do not reveal themselves on an X-ray film.

radioluminescence, -ent: see *RADIO- 2.

radiolysis (rēⁱdiǫ·lisis). *Chem.* [f. RADIO- 2 + *-LYSIS.] Decomposition of a compound by the action of ionizing radiation. Hence **radioly·tic** *a.*, of, pertaining to, or formed as a result of, radiolysis.

1948 *Jrnl. Physical & Colloid Chem.* LII. 516 The kinetics of the radiolysis of pure water and of indirect action on solutes are discussed. **1950** *Ann. Rev. Physical Chem.* I. 120 Negative ions make important contributions to the general radiolytic process only in special cases. **1951** *Jrnl. Amer. Chem. Soc.* LXXIII. 532/2 H_2O_2 produced in the radiolysis may affect the pH. **1963** DAWSON & SOWDEN *Chem. Aspects of Nuclear Reactors* II. iii. 96 The discovery..that cupric ion would act as an effective homogeneous catalyst to promote the recombination of radiolytic gas within the reactor core.. was of the highest importance to homogeneous aqueous reactor technology. **1977** J. WEISMAN *Elem. Nuclear Reactor Design* ii. 35 Ions which participate in electron-transfer reactions can combine with H or OH ions thus preventing recombination and leading to an increased radiolysis.

Ra·diometal. Also **radiometal.** An alloy consisting largely of nickel and iron in approximately equal proportions and having a high magnetic permeability.

1940 *Chambers's Techn. Dict.* 699/1 *Radiometal*, an alloy of permalloy type. Contains iron 50%, nickel 45%, and copper 5%. **1941** *Jrnl. Brit. Inst. Radio Engineers* II. 101 A group of metallurgists and electrical technicians concentrated on the problem of high permeability materials and carried out intensive research on alloys with 80%, 50% and about 36% nickel content. The outcome of the work was the commercial introduction of the well known alloys Mumetal (78% Ni), Radiometal (48% Ni) and Rhometal (36% Ni). **1946** *Nature* 13 July 54/2 The stator core consists of radiometal laminations 0·010 in. thick. **1951** *Electronic Engin.* XXIII. 330/1 The smoothing choke is wound on a radiometal core. **1957** W. J. JOHN *Mod. Electr. Engin.* I. iv. 116/2 Radiometal, or Permalloy B, has a saturation of 16,000 gauss and a maximum permeability of 10,000 to 30,000 at H = 0·3 to 0·4 oersted... Composition: nickel 50 per cent, iron 50 per cent.

radiometeorograph(y: see *RADIO- 4.

radiometer. Add: **2.** Also, more generally, any device used to detect, or measure the intensity of, electromagnetic radiation (freq. *spec.* infra-red). Also extended to instruments (in the first cases adapted from Crookes's device) used to measure the intensity of sound by means of its radiation pressure. (Further examples.)

1905 R. W. WOOD in *Physical Rev.* XX. 113 It occurred to me that a mill-wheel or radiometer driven by these [sound] waves would be useful for purposes of demonstration in treating of radiation pressure. **1920** *Q. Jrnl. R. Meteorol. Soc.* XLVI. 399 (*heading*) The ether differential radiometer. **1927** I. B. CRANDALL *Theory Vibrating Syst. & Sound* iv. 180 The radiometer is a simple torsion balance; a thin hollow metal box filled with air, on being submerged serves as a very good totally reflecting vane. **1930** R. H. BAKER *Astron.* x. 396 Abbot,..working with the 100-inch reflector, made use of delicate radiometers, having vanes of blackened bits of fly-wings, to measure the energy in different parts of the spectrum. **1963** G. L. PICKARD *Descriptive Physical Oceanogr.* vi. 92 The downward directed component of the long-wave radiation term..is determined by means of a radiometer. **1966** *McGraw-Hill Encycl. Sci. & Technol.* XI. 317/1 Other radiometers use the pressure of sound waves to deflect a spherical body. *Ibid.* 317/2 The Crookes radiometer survives in jewelers' windows as a 'perpetual motion' device. **1969** *Times* 19 Feb. 13/6 An infra-red radiometer will map the temperature across the surface of Mars. **1973** *Nature* 20 Apr. 506/2 The radiometer was a load-switched superheterodyne microwave receiver. **1977** *R.A.F. News* 11–24 May 11/1 Radiometers to measure infra-red and solar radiation.

3. An instrument for determining the amount of X-radiation administered to a patient.

[**1904** *Sci. Abstr.* A. VII. 362 A 'chromo-radiometer' has been invented by Holzknecht, which consists of two parts—a measurer and a comparative scale.] **1912** *Med. Ann.* 73 The..method of using Holzknecht's new radiometer for the more exact measurement of the *x*-ray dose. **1918** R. KNOX *Radiogr.* (ed. 2) II. 437 The radiometer is so sensitive that it is possible to measure with accuracy the pastille tint when it has not become nearly such a dark colour as in the case of the Sabouraud method. **1934** H. DAVIES *Pract. X-Ray Therapy* iii. 31 (*caption*) Holzknecht radiometer, showing both halves of the pastille in position.

radiometric (rēⁱdiome·trik), *a.* [f. RADIO- 2 + *-METRIC.] **1.** Of or pertaining to the radiometer (sense 2) or its use.

1877 *Chem. News* 12 Jan. 21/2 (*heading*) New radiometric experiments. **1883** [in Dict. s.v. RADIOMETER]. **1904** *Electrician* 28 Oct. 58/2 Prof. Nichols also suggests a new radiometric receiver, whose action is based on the electrostatic and electrodynamic action between equal resonators **1927** H. N. RUSSELL et al. *Astron.* II. xxi. 735 With a suitable thermoelectric device the heat radiation of the stars may now easily be measured and the results expressed as 'radiometric magnitudes'. **1964** *Yearbk. Astron. 1965* 111 For Mars, information about ground temperatures may be obtained from radiometric observations, and the amount of insolation is easily calculable. **1977** A. HALLAM *Planet Earth* 111 Magnetic, electromagnetic and radiometric techniques are commonly adapted to airborne surveys.

2. Of, pertaining to, or involving the measurement of radioactivity or ionizing radiation; *radiometric dating*, isotopic dating.

1906 *Sci. Abstr.* A. IX. 50 Sabouraud and Noiré..point out that their radiometric value is not in any way diminished. **1938** R. W. LAWSON tr. *Hevesy & Paneth's Man. Radioactivity* (ed. 2) xviii. 169 This method of 'Radiometric Microanalysis' has rendered it possible..to carry out a determination of the nitrogen content of organic substances to the order of magnitude of some ten-thousandths of a milligram. **1951** *Engineering* 2 Feb. 148/1 Radiometric methods are frequently used in the investigation of uranium-bearing minerals. **1962** F. I. ORDWAY et al. *Basic Astronautics* v. 191 Gamma ray scintillation spectrometers make radiometric assays. **1968** *Sci. Jrnl.* Oct. 122/3 *Geologic Time* is concerned with how the present knowledge of the Earth's history has been built up;..palaeomagnetism and continental drift; biostratigraphy and radiometric dating. **1969** *Beaver* Summer 34/2 The coal deposits there are overlaid by volcanic ash determined as 72–73 million years old by radiometric dating processes. **1972** *Science* 2 June 977/1 Radiometric ages obtained for the Apollo 14 examples.. cluster around a value of $3{\cdot}9 \times 10^9$ years.

Hence (in either sense) **radiome·trically** *adv.*, by a radiometric method.

1920 *Jrnl. Franklin Inst.* CLXXXIX. 27 The energy was determined in the spectrophotometric laboratory, visually on a König-Martens Spectrophotometer, by a substitution method of comparison with a radiometrically calibrated Mazda lamp. **1962** F. P. W. WINTERINGHAM in *Radioisotopes & Radiation in Entomol.* (Internat. Atomic Energy Agency) 117 P^{32} and S^{35} are readily differentiated radiometrically. **1968** *Palaeogeogr., Palaeoclimatol., Palaeoecol.* V. 69 The paleobotanical event has been radiometrically dated at about 12,000,000 years B.P. **1972** *Science* 2 June 978/1 The times of formation of lunar craters have been determined radiometrically. **1973** *Physics Bull.* Apr. 239/3 The centre is equipped with radiometrically and photometrically calibrated sources and a range of calibrated detectors for continuous wave and pulsed radiation.

radiometry (rēⁱdiǫ·mėtri). [f. RADIO- 2 + -METRY.] The use of a radiometer; *spec.* the detection and measurement of infra-red radiation.

c **1890** [in Dict. s.v. RADIOMETER]. **1906** *Sci. Abstr.* A. IX. 50 They have used this method of radiometry in 5,000 cases of tinea tonsurous without accident. **1923** GLAZEBROOK *Dict. Appl. Physics* III. 718/2 The second method of attack is by means of thermal radiometry with non-selective receivers. **1934** *Discovery* Oct. 282/2 The combination of visual observation at the telescope with the employment at some of the great observatories of the resources of photography, spectroscopy, radiometry, and polarimetry. **1977** I. M. CAMPBELL *Energy & Atmosphere* iii. 44 One of the methods which has been used to measure the temperature profile of the atmosphere as a function of altitude, namely infrared radiometry from satellites.

radio-micrometer, -mimetic, -necrosis: see *RADIO- 2.

radionic (rēⁱdiǫ·nik), *sb.* and *a.* [f. RADI(O- 2 + *-onic*, after *ELECTRONIC *a.*] **A.** *sb. pl.* (const. as *sing.*) † **1.** *U.S.* Electronics, esp. those aspects of electronics connected with radio. *Obs.*

1943 *Radio News* May 4/2 In its simplest form, radionics would be understood by we Americans as being an all-inclusive term of any equipment or science where the use of vacuum tubes is employed [*sic*]. **1943** *Proc. IRE* XXXI. 192 He [*sc.* Hitler] was stopped because the RAF had gone him one better on the new weapon which had paced his early victories, the only new weapon this war has produced: Radionics.

2. The study and interpretation of radiation believed by some to be emitted by and to characterize living and other substances, and to be detectable by skilled use of various complicated electrical instruments.

1954 *Brit. Jrnl. Radiesthesia* I. 111. 18 Radiesthesia.. applied to the use of the pendulum, Radionics..applied to instrumental detection and use, and Dowsing, the use of the Divining Rod. **1960** *Times* 21 June 5/4 The plaintiff alleged that the defendant is an exponent of and practitioner in the pseudo-science of radionics, and that..he fraudulently represented that there were associated with substances distinctive waves, vibrations or radiations capable of affecting a device..called a Delawarr Diagnostic Instrument. **1960** *Spectator* 28 Oct. 653 The founder of what today is known as radionics was Dr. Albert Abrams (1863–1924), a..physician who came to believe that the basis of disease was atomic or electronic..and that disease could therefore be treated by giving healthy radiations to neutralise the unhealthy ones. **1969** B. COPEN *Radionic Computer Handbk.* 8 Radionics is the science of radiation detection which uses the extra sensory perception of the operator..and automatic instruments, of which this computer is but one. Modern Radionics is a combination of the older Radiesthesia (detection with pendulum) and the more modern semi-automatic instruments (Radionics). **1976** T. GRAVES *Dowsing* xii. 124 *Radionics*, the specific form of medical dowsing which uses as its instrument a 'box' containing a number of dials in a particular sequence or pattern, seems to be a compound-word formed from 'radiesthetic electronics'—so the word is another product of the tangle over the assumed physical basis of dowsing.

B. *adj.* **1.** Of or pertaining to radionics (sense 1); electronic. orig. *U.S.*

Quot. 1963 represents an independent use not connected with the orig. use of radionics (sense A. 1 above).

1943 *Radio News* May 75/1 Radio News will use 'radionic' in preference to 'electronic' wherever it is more descriptive. **1943** *Proc. IRE* XXXI. 193 This one [*sc.* war], at the front, is run by radio and radionic devices. **1963** *Spectator* 15 Nov. 616/3 Even in this radionic age, a Prime Minister cannot hope to make his way in the country without establishing his mastery over the House of Commons.

2. Of, pertaining to, or practising radionics (sense 2).

1947 *Radiesthesia* III. 58 The development of a new technique in Radionic Diagnosis. **1969** B. COPEN *Radionic Computer Handbk.* 54 Any potency of the lower order may be chemically analysed, but the higher potencies are non-analytic in nature, by the orthodox system, but are by the Radionic system. **1972** D. V. TANSLEY *Radionics & Subtle Anat. of Man* 7 Today, most if not all radionic practitioners would agree that it is their belief that man does have what is referred to as an etheric body. **1975** *Homes & Gardens* Nov. 63/2 Sometimes a diagnostic box helps to make the diagnoses and may also broadcast the treatment. The instrument is not electrically powered but gains its energy from the patient's witness which is put into the box... The radiesthetist determines the diagnosis and then uses the radionic box to broadcast the selected rate of the remedy.

radionuclide: see *RADIO- 3 a.

ra:dio-opa·que, *a.* Also **radiopaque.** [f. RADIO- 2 + OPAQUE *a.*] Impervious to X-rays. So **ra:dio-opa·city, radiopa·city,** the state or property of being radio-opaque.

1917 K. THOMA *Oral Roentgenol.* IV. iv. 197 Unsanitary concretions, such as salivary..calculi, can be seen on account of their radiopacity. **1926** *Jrnl. Amer. Med. Assoc.* 19 June 1883/1 In the stenotic larynx, the extent of the destruction may be visualized by the introduction of radiopaque substances. **1940** *Brit. Jrnl. Radiol.* XIII. 261/2 To determine the depth of the foreign body, the observer places a radio-opaque guide-mark on the skin..; then he moves the X-ray tube horizontally. **1961** *Dental Progr.* I. 178/2 Radio-opacity of the palatal vault blotted out the apices of the maxillary teeth. **1970** H. MCLEAVE *Question of Negligence* xxvii. 228 They had trundled in a portable X-ray machine.. injected a radio-opaque substance into a neck artery. They ran off six plates. **1971** G. H. BOURNE *Ape People* vii. 186 A series of cinemagraphs were taken with radiopaque material being injected into different chambers of the heart. **1971** *Brit. Dental Jrnl.* CXXX. 430/1 The localised radiopacity caused by the superimposition of shadows can be very misleading, therefore patients should be instructed to remove their ear-rings before the picture is taken.

radio-pasteurization, -ized: see *RADIO- 2.

radiophare (rēⁱ·diofēᵊɹ). [f. *RADIO- 4 + PHARE.] A navigational radio beacon.

1915 W. H. ECCLES *Wireless Telegr. & Telephony* 362 The French Government is installing wireless lighthouses or radiophares round the French coast. **1922** *Nature* 20 May 650/1 Until two or three years ago the radiophares—or radio-beacons as they are called in America—were purely stations for giving ships their positions. **1966** *McGraw-Hill Encycl. Sci. & Technol.* IV. 231/2 Radio stations erected specifically for use with the ADF are known as NDB (non-directional beacons or radiophares).

radiopharmaceutical, -pharmacist, -pharmacology (etc.), **-pharmacy:** see *RADIO- 2.

radiophone. Add: **2.** Also **radio-phone, radio phone.** = *RADIO-TELEPHONE.

1919 *Wireless World* May 105/2 (*heading*) Radiophones over London. **1922** *Sci. Amer.* Sept. 160/1 The receiver can be worked on very short waves, well below 200 meters, thus opening up a new field of wave lengths for radio-phone broadcasting. **1926** *Popular Radio* IX. 91 (*caption*) The first radiophone booth on an ocean liner. **1940** N. MONKS *Squadrons Up!* ii. 39 The boys [*sc.* pilots] wisecracked to each other into their radio-'phones. **1971** J. BRUNNER *Honky in Woodpile* xii. 90 A luxuriously-equipped Mercedes convertible—it even boasted a radiophone. **1978** R. LUDLUM *Holcroft Covenant* xxviii. 322 We use a radiophone off Cap Camarat.

radiophonic, *a.* Add: **2.** Pertaining to or designating synthetic sound produced by electronic means and the use of tape recorders, usually for use in broadcasting in conjunction with conventional material.

1958 *Times* 24 May 10/2 B.B.C.'s Radiophonic Workshop. A 'workshop' for producing synthetic sounds, partly by electronic oscillators and partly by trickery with conventional sounds recorded on tape has been set up by the

B.B.C. at their Maida Vale studios. **1958** *Observer* 22 June 14/3 He [*sc.* Patrick Magee] must be the only actor who can sound as if he's talking through a radiophonic filter. *Ibid.* 6 July 14/2 Those radiophonic plays where an old woman's memories or a young man's nightmares are made the slender excuse for the latest in ghost-train noises. **1960** *BBC Handbk.* 67 Special effects..created..for the occasion by 'radiophonic' devices. **1961** *Listener* 16 Nov. 834/1 Michael Bakewell employed radiophonic effects to communicate the variant senses of time experienced by the normal and the mentally ill characters in this double bill. **1972** *Ibid.* 21 Dec. 872/3 Not a *Goon Show* script, but..one of Michael Mason's radiophonic workshop larks.

Hence **radiopho·nicist**, an exponent of radiophonic sound; **radiopho·nics** *sb. pl.*, the production and use of radiophonic sound; the sounds themselves; **radio·phonist** = *radiophonicist* above.

1958 *Listener* 28 Aug. 319/3 Our local radiophonicists and 'concrete' music men have too often seized upon noise in the higher octaves to drive home dramatic nails that would have seemed excruciating even to Jael. **1962** A. Nisbett *Technique Sound Studio* xii. 203 Radiophonics does not in general attempt to assert itself as an art form in its own right; it is always an element in a larger picture. **1963** F. C. Brooker (*title*) Radiophonics in the B.B.C. **1976** *Listener* 21 Oct. 511/3 The tinkling celeste tune—now, alas, abandoned in favour of radiophonics—that used to introduce *Listen with Mother.* **1977** *Listener* 18 Aug. 217/2 What was crushing to the fond memory was the way the poverty had affected the radiophonics, too. **1977** *Times* 3 Sept. 10/3 Isaac Asimov's *Foundation Trilogy*..on Radio 4 certainly provided a field day for the radiophonists.

radio-phosphorus: see *radio- 3 b (i).

radiophoto (rēⁱ·diofoto). [f. *radio- 4 + Photo.] A photograph transmitted by means of radio.

1942 *Wireless World* Sept 217/2 The first..radiophoto service between America and Egypt was recently opened. **1961** *New Scientist* 13 July 91/2 If the radiophotos show recognizable evidence of hurricane breeding in the clouds, hurricane-hunting planes will be sent out. **1971** *Encycl. Americana* XXIII. 121n/1 The channel capacity of an HF system is limited to four voice or radiophoto channels.

radiophoto·graphy. Also with hyphen. [f. *radio- 2 + Photography.] **1.** = *radiography 1 (see also quot. 1939).

1897 *Chem. News* 26 Feb. 102/2 (*heading*) Radiophotography of the soft parts of man and the lower animals. **1934** *Jrnl. R. Anthrop. Inst.* LXIV. 70 It may be demonstrated by radiophotography that bronze, on exposure to the atmosphere, immediately begins to oxidize. **1939** *Jrnl. Amer. Med. Assoc.* 6 May 1844/1 Radiophotography, or indirect radiography, consists in simultaneously photographing the thoracopulmonary images as they are observed at radioscopic examination.

2. The transmission of photographs by means of radio.

1915 *Wireless World* Apr. 60/1 The number of interruptions per second required is very high, as in radiophotography. *Ibid.* 60/2 A system of radio-photography.. would be of great military use.

Hence **radiopho·tograph** = *radiograph *sb.* 2; (in either sense) **ra:diophotogra·phic** *a.*

1897 *Chem. News* 26 Feb. 102/2 We have been able to place the muscles, the ligaments, and the tendons in such a state that they have yielded radio-photographic images. **1915** *Wireless World* Apr. 60/2 Even were they possessed of radio-photographic apparatus, the received message would be unintelligible unless they knew the exact speed. **1924** *Times* 13 Sept. 12/5 In this section are some radiophotographs showing considerable advance on any hitherto.

radiophysics (etc.): see *radio- 4. **radio-potassium:** *radio- 3 b (i). **radio-protection, -protective, -protector:** *radio- 2. **radio-purity:** *radio- 3 a.

ra·dioreceptor. *Physiol.* [f. Radio- 2 + Receptor.] †**1.** Written **radio-receptor.** A sensory receptor which responds to electromagnetic radiation of any kind. *Obs.*

1927 [see *mechanoreceptor]. **1935** *Brit. Jrnl. Psychol.* XXV. 266 As Parsons describes, the receptors differentiated along three main lines, chemo-, radio-, and mechanoreceptors.

2. *radioreceptor assay*, a radiological assay for hormones in which the test sample, together with a known quantity of radioactively labelled hormone, is allowed to bind to a standard preparation containing receptor sites.

1973 *Science* 1 June 968 A radioreceptor assay with a sensitivity of 5 nanograms per milliliter has been developed for mammalian and avian pituitary prolactin, placental lactogenic hormones, and human growth hormones, using a membrane receptor preparation isolated from rabbit mammary glands. **1974** *Nature* 29 Mar. 436/2 At this time the PL concentrations measured by radioreceptor assay were almost entirely due to the cross reaction of pituitary prolactin in the receptor assay. **1978** *Ibid.* 20 Apr. 730/2 The fact that affinity to rat opiate receptors was demonstrated in the plasma using a radioreceptor assay..indicates that a loss of the postulated biological activity by metabolic or other processes can be excluded.

radio-resistance, -ant: see *radio- 2. **radioscan:** *radio- 3 a.

radioscopy. Add: *spec.* = *fluoroscopy (earlier and later examples); **radioscopic** *a.* (earlier and later examples); also †**ra·dioscope** = *fluoroscope.

1897 [see *radiotherapeutic *sb. pl.* and *a.*]. **1897** *Treatment* I. 43/2 It makes his own heart beat faster as the observer sees for the first time thrown upon the radioscopic screen a living heart in action. **1898** *Amer. Jrnl. Med. Sci.* CXV. 464 The capsules are readily seen (in thin persons) with the radioscope. **1908** *Chem. Abstr.* II. 229 (*heading*) The radioscope and the radiograph applied to the inspection of tubercular meats. **1915** R. Knox *Radiogr.* 188 Radioscopy, or the examination of a patient with the fluorescent screen, is a method of great value, as a diagnosis can often be made from it alone, to be subsequently confirmed by radiographic exposures. **1928** B. J. Leggett *Theory & Pract. Radiol.* III. x. 459 (*heading*) Radiographic and radioscopic rooms. **1937** M. Campbell in *Brit. Encycl. Med. Pract.* VI. 352 Radioscopy is of great help; the presence of a large left ventricle or of a dilated left auricle in mitral stenosis,..may clinch a doubtful diagnosis. **1946** *Surg. Clinics N. Amer.* Oct. 1286 Such long radioscopic exposures are only possible without danger of dermatitis when a very small radioscopic field is used. **1979** *SLR Camera* Sept. 5/1 Now the holiday season is on us perhaps a word, or two, about the precautions needed to safeguard films from damage by radioscopic screening is pertinent.

radiosensitive(ness, etc.: see *radio- 2. **radio-silver, -sodium:** *radio- 3 b (i).

radiosonde (rēⁱ·diosǫnd). *Meteorol.* Also **radio-sonde, radio sonde.** [a. G. *radiosonde* (P. Moltchanoff 1931, in *Beiträge z. Geophysik* XXXIV. 36), f. *radio-* Radio- + *sonde* probe, sounding-line.] A small package of meteorological instruments which is carried through the atmosphere by balloon or other means and automatically transmits measurements of conditions at various heights by radio. Freq. *attrib.* So **radiosondage** (-sǫ·ndēdʒ), sounding of the atmosphere by radiosonde.

1937 *Geogr. Jrnl.* XC. 381 The use of the radio-sonde, from which automatically transmitted W/T signals can be transformed into data of temperature and pressure. **1939** *Meteorol. Gloss.* (Meteorol. Office) (ed. 3) 153 Radio-sondages (Radio-soundings). **1940** *Manch. Guardian* 30 Jan. 6/6 The staff of our Meteorological Office..receives great help from an instrument called the radio sonde, which is sent up attached to a small balloon and automatically reports by wireless the air conditions up to a great height. **1946** *Electronics* May 123/3 Several methods of radiosonde tracking have been used in order to determine the speed and direction of the wind at various altitudes. **1948** *Times* 23 Feb. 6/7 The radio-sonde equipment..was insufficiently sensitive to detect the rapid temperature changes within the first few hundred feet of the sea surface. **1951** T. F. Malone *Compendium Meteorol.* 1215/2 The parachute radiosonde was designed to be launched from a weather-reconnaissance plane. **1955** W. Girvan *Flying Saucers & Common Sense* ix. 110 The weather-balloon..crossed the coast near Eastbourne and then burst, the radio-sonde falling into the Channel at approximately 3.30 p.m. after descending slowly by parachute. **1959** H. R. Byers *Gen. Meteorol.* (ed. 3) vi. 101 Several types of rawinsonde systems, combining radiosondage with tracking of the radiosonde to get wind drift of the balloon, have been developed. **1960** *Times* 19 July (Royal Society suppl.) p. x. 6 Preparations are being made to launch a hydrogen-filled balloon carrying a radiosonde transmitter. **1976** B. Jackson *Flameout* (1977) xii. 205 The radiosonde balloons from the unnamed Air Force base in Nevada.

radiostereoassay: see *radio- 3 a. **radio-sterilization, -ized:** *radio- 2.

Radiostol (rēⁱ·diostǫl). Also **radiostol.** [f. Radio- 2 + *-stol.* (f. *ergosterol from which calciferol can be prepared by irradiation with light).] A proprietary name for a preparation of calciferol (vitamin D_2).

1927 *Trade Marks Jrnl.* 27 Apr. 737/1 *Radiostol*... Chemical substances prepared for use in medicine and pharmacy. The British Drug Houses, Limited. **1928** *Daily Express* 27 Jan. 3/3 It is possible to give margarine the rich food value of the best butter by treating it with radiostol. **1934** *Nature* 2 June 821/2 Modifications [in the diet]..were additions of oatmeal, olive oil, cod liver oil or radiostol (irradiated ergosterol), and milk, [etc.]. **1967** *Martindale's Extra Pharmacopoeia* (ed. 25) 258/2 Radiostol (*British Drug Houses*). Calciferol, available as Capsules..; as a Solution [etc.].

radio-strontium: see *radio- 3 b (i). **radio-surgery, -surgical:** *radio- 2.

radio-te·legram. [f. *radio- 4 + Telegram.] A telegraphic message sent by radio.

1902 *Sci. Amer. Suppl.* 15 Nov. 22474/1 The radio-telegrams arrived from Poldhu constantly and surely at the receiver on board the 'Carlo Alberto'. **1904** *Prelim. Conf. Wireless Telegr. Berlin 1903* 16 We desire to grant to existing systems a fair share of the charge to be collected for radio-telegrams. **1913** *Wireless World* Aug. p. xxx (Advt.), Hand your message in at any Telegraph Office, where full particulars concerning radio-telegrams can be obtained. **1920** *Glasgow Herald* 2 Apr. 5/7 The charge for such radio-telegrams is 10½d. per word.

radio-te·legraph. Also **radiotelegraph.** [f. *radio- 4 + Telegraph *sb.*] A means of sending telegraphic messages by radio rather than along a wire. Usu. *attrib.* So **ra:dio-telegra·phic** *a.*, **-telegra·phically** *adv.*, **-tele·graphist** (all *rare*); **radio-tele·graphy,** wireless telegraphy.

1898 J. Munro in *Electrician* 21 Jan. 428/2 'Wireless telegraphy' is not a bad technical term; but if a more scientific name be desirable would not Radiotelegraphy or Ray Telegraphy be preferable to 'Space Telegraphy'? which Dr. Lodge employs. **1902** *Nature* 25 Sept. 538/2 The creation of a radio-telegraphic station communicating with the stations established..by the Marconi companies in London and in America. **1903** *Ibid.* 23 Apr. 590/1 The establishment on the coast and on the islands off the Italian coast of a system of twelve Marconi radio-telegraph stations of an average range of 300 kilometres. **1906** *Westm. Gaz.* 19 Dec. 2/2 Wireless telegraphy, or 'radio-telegraphy', as it is more technically called. **1907** *Athenæum* 14 Sept. 308/1 The Report and Evidence of the Radiotelegraphic Convention Committee. **1907** *Daily Chron.* 11 Nov. 6/6 The Amalgamated Radio-Telegraph Company, Limited. **1908** J. A. Fleming *Radiotelegr. & Radiotelephony* p. vi, Expositions of electrical phenomena which are..unnecessary to the practical radiotelegraphist. **1918** *Wireless World* June 192 (*heading*) Senatore Marconi radiotelegraphically expresses the national sentiment of Italy. **1921** *Jrnl. R. Soc. Arts* 9 Dec. 68/2 Marconi..was able to dispatch wireless messages across the Atlantic which made long-distance radio-telegraphy a demonstrated achievement. **1945** *Sun* (Baltimore) 23 Oct. 1/3 (*heading*) Radio telegraph plan announced. **1955** *Times* 12 Aug. 5/3 A feature of the year has been the development in leased channel operations, that is, in the provision of direct customer-to-customer private radio-telegraph circuits. **1966** *McGraw-Hill Encycl. Sci. & Technol.* I. 364/2 Much of the radiotelegraph traffic of the world uses AM telegraphy, although there had been extensive conversion to frequency-shift (frequency-modulation) telegraphy since 1944. *Ibid.*, Most aviation and marine radiotelegraphy uses AM manual methods.

radio-telemetering, -telemetric, -y: see *radio- 4.

radio-te·lephone. Also **radiotelephone, radio telephone.** [f. *radio- 4 + Telephone *sb.*] A transmitting and receiving set for radio-telephony.

1909 *Daily Chron.* 15 Feb. 1/2 Mr. Lee De Forest,..whose radio-telephone system has been adopted by the American navy. **1922** *Encycl. Brit.* XXXII. 1027/2 Compact lightweight sets of radio-telephone transmitters and receivers. **1935** H. G. Wells *Shape of Things to Come* 15 There will be a radio telephone arrangement on his chest no more obtrusive than a modern breast pocket. **1957** *Practical Wireless* XXXIII. 517/1 Cable and Wireless Ltd. announce that a radiotelephone service has been opened between Saudi Arabia and Bahrein. **1966** P. O'Donnell *Sabre-Tooth* xiv. 187, I will arrange for you to speak to her briefly over the radio-telephone. **1973** *Sat. Rev. Society* (U.S.) Mar. 52/2 An immaculately uncluttered teakwood desk, flanked by..two telephones, a radio-telephone and an intercom.

So **ra:dio-telepho·nic** *a.*; **ra:dio-telepho·nically** *adv.* (*rare*); **radio-tele·phony,** telephony in which the signal is transmitted by radio over part of the route; wireless telephony.

1908 J. A. Fleming (*title*) Radiotelegraphy and radio-telephony. *Ibid.* 325 We have..in the combined radio-telephonic transmitter and receiver, a wonderful transformation of energy. *Ibid.* 329 Transmitting speech radio-telephonically from Paris..to Dieppe. **1923** *Radio Times* 28 Sept. 12/1 We are most enthusiastic admirers of this remarkable radio-telephonic invention. **1930** *Daily Express* 8 Sept. 3/7 The principal means of communication; both in the brigade and battalions, will be radio-telephony. **1935** *Times* 12 Nov. 20/5 It is a strange thing that in radio-telephony across the Atlantic..some wave-length, which has been behaving admirably, will rather swiftly fade and fail. **1966** *McGraw-Hill Encycl. Sci. & Technol.* I. 364/1 Since radio is the only way to communicate with ships and aircraft, hf AM radiotelephony has remained essential to these operations. **1974** *Guardian* 22 Mar. 13/7 Will you see to it that the cars used by public figures are fitted with..radio-telephonic methods of communication?

radio-teletype, -tellurium: see *radio- 4, 3 b (i).

ra:diotherapeu·tic, *sb. pl.* and *a.* Also with hyphen. [f. Radio- 2 + Therapeutic *a.*] **A.** *sb. pl.* = *radiotherapy. **B.** *adj.* Of, pertaining to, or employing radiotherapy. Hence **ra:diotherapeu·tically** *adv.*; †**ra:diotherapeu·tist** = *radiotherapist.

1897 *Treatment* I. 43/1 (*heading*) Radiography, radioscopy, and radiotherapeutics. **1904** *Bristol Medico-Chirurg. Jrnl.* XXII. 43 What this variation is is a question for the radio-therapeutists to solve. **1906** *Arch. Roentgen Ray* XI. 20/1 It is to be hoped that in radiotherapeutic practice the use of the dosimeter may become universal. *Ibid.* 20/2 Radio-therapeutists are divided into..those who believe in the large (so-called) measured dose, and those who administer small unmeasured doses at intervals. **1932** *Discovery* Aug. 255/2 The report urges the establishment of radio-therapeutic centres associated with large general hospitals. **1937** *Amer. Jrnl. Obstetr. & Gynecol.* XXXIV. 50 In the surgically or radiotherapeutically induced menopause, much can be done by prophylactic psychotherapy. **1975** *Nature* 13 Mar. 97/1 The Medical Research Council is to set up a new unit for research in clinical oncology and radio-therapeutics at Cambridge. **1977** *Proc. R. Soc. Med.* LXX. 591/2 This is a very comprehensive review of the present state of knowledge of the investigation and treatment, medical, surgical and radiotherapeutic, of these lesions.

radiothe·rapy. [f. RADIO- 2 + THERAPY.] The treatment of disease by means of X-rays or other forms of ionizing radiation.

1903 *Boston Med. & Surg. Jrnl.* CXLIX. 325/1 He had been interested in comparing the effects of phototherapy and radiotherapy. **1904** *Westm. Gaz.* 29 Dec. 2/1 A working knowledge of the technique of radio-therapy. **1955** *Bull. Atomic Sci.* Oct. 287/3 These will become available in source strength varying from kilocurie sources of radio-caesium for use in radiotherapy to megacurie sources for industrial applications. **1970** *Sci. Jrnl.* Mar. 62/3 Where a cancer has become disseminated to other areas, treatment with drugs or radiotherapy is used. **1974** 'H. CARMICHAEL' *Motive* iv. 47 Dr. Egan will see you. He's in the Radio-Therapy department.

Hence **radiothe·rapist**, one who practises radiotherapy.

1918 R. KNOX *Radiogr.* (ed. 2) II. 388 It is easy..to understand the complexity of the problem which confronts the radiotherapist in dealing with morbid growths. **1934** *Lancet* 29 Sept. 697/1 The patient should..be examined in consultation with an expert radiotherapist before any operation on the primary tumour or glands. **1976** *Ibid.* 6 Nov. 992/1 The introduction of improved techniques has enabled radiotherapists to treat relatively large volumes of the body with comparative safety.

radiothon (rē¹·diopɒn). *U.S.* [f. *RADIO *sb.* + *-A)THON.] A prolonged radio broadcast by a person or group, usu. as a fund-raising event.

1964 *Richmond* (Va.) *Times-Dispatch* 26 Jan. 6B/1 With only an hour to run, the radiothon had netted the March of Dimes here more than $1,200. **1974** *State* (Columbia, S. Carolina) 15 Feb. 20-A/3 A 15-day try for a world record radiothon is being made by WCOS-AM disc jockeys to benefit the Heart Fund. **1976** *Long Island Traveler-Watchman* 8 July 1/3 (*caption*), The radiothon, to raise funds for Kiwanis youth programs, will be broadcast WRIV.

radiothorium: see *RADIO- 3 b (i). **radio-toxic(ity, -tracer:** *RADIO- 3 a. **radiotrans-lucency, -ent:** *RADIO- 2.

ra·diovision. Also with hyphen. [f. *RADIO- 4 + VISION *sb.*] **1.** The combination of a radio programme with a specially prepared film strip or series of slides, esp. as an educational aid. Freq. *attrib.*

1964 *Guardian* 14 Feb. 7/2 The technique..is to issue film strips to accompany selected broadcasts; it is becoming known as 'radiovision'. **1965** *B.B.C. Handbk.* 70 The use of radio-vision in the teaching of languages was the subject of an experiment in fifty schools in the autumn of 1963. **1966** *Listener* 24 Sept. 786/2 In a radiovision talk of great virtuosity..Mr Morris explained the nature of an atmospheric depression. **1971** *Daily Tel.* 4 May 2/2 The radio-vision programmes were more easily taped and film-strips could be stored for parent evenings.

2. Radio broadcasting accompanied by the simultaneous showing of the broadcasters on television.

1980 *Daily Tel.* 6 Nov. 19/4 Miss Monica Sims, controller of Radio 4 and a former head of children's television, has been asked to chair an immediate feasibility study on the possibilities of 'radiovision' and report by next spring to Sir Ian Trethowan, B B C director-general.

radish. Add: **2. radish communist**, one who professes communism but is not sincerely devoted to it. Also *ellipt.*

1920 *Times* 31 Oct. 11/1 A 'radish' is a man who fervently professes devotion to the Communist cause while harbouring a secret longing for its overthrow. Red outside, but white.. inside. The epithet was invented by Trotsky. **1966** *Listener* 29 Sept. 445/1 Stalin would speak disparagingly of Mao's men as being 'not real communists', mere 'margarine communists', 'radish communists'—red on the outside and white on the inside.

radishy (ræ·diʃi), *a.* [f. RADISH + -Y¹.] Resembling or suggestive of a radish.

1861 H. MAYHEW *London Labour* III. 64/2 The matches were tied..to his [*sc.* the guy's] radishy and gouty fingers.

radium (rē¹·diŭm). [f. L. *radius* ray, RADIUS: see -IUM.] **1.** *Chem.* **a.** [a. F. *radium* (P. Curie et al. 1898, in *Compt. Rend.* CXXVII. 1217).] A radioactive element, chemically a member of the alkaline earth metals, which occurs in small amounts in uranium ores, notably pitchblende; atomic number 88, symbol Ra.

1899 *Chem. News* 6 Jan. 1/2 These different reasons lead us to believe that the new radio-active substance contains a new element, to which we propose to give the name of radium. **1903** *Daily Mail* 11 Sept. 3/1 All the speakers recognised that the discovery of radium, with its apparent power of emitting heat for ever without diminution, has opened the door to something like a new world of science. **1904** *Daily Chron.* 7 Jan. 5/1 It is quite as good as any other assertion to say that an ounce of radium is worth the British Empire; no more having yet been obtained than about the weight of a lump of sugar. **1909** 'O. HENRY' *Roads of Destiny* xxi. 358 'Change the treatment,' says I... 'Call a consultation or use radium or smuggle me in some saws or something.' **1933** BOWING & FRICKE in O. Glasser *Sci. of Radiol.* xv. 281 The paramount advantage of the use of radium in medicine..consists in the proved fact that the rays of radium have a selective action on cancer cells. **1950** *Thorpe's Dict. Appl. Chem.* (ed. 4) X. 446/1 The history of radium refining during the 50 years, 1898–1948,..covers the rise of radium from a scientific curiosity to a commodity of almost fabulous value and wide importance, and its subsequent relegation to a minor role following the development of the atomic pile. **1958** *Daily Express* 11 Mar. 7/1 An escape of radium at a hospital led to the dumping of tons of material down a disused pit shaft. **1974** *Encycl. Brit. Micropædia* VIII. 382/1 Metallic radium has high chemical reactivity. It dissolves in water with vigorous evolution of hydrogen.

b. (Followed by capital letter.) Designating substances (mostly radioactive) subsequently identified as isotopes of other elements, which are formed successively in the radioactive series of radium: *radium A*, polonium 218; *radium B*, lead 214; *radium C*, bismuth 214 together with some polonium 214 (*radium* C_1 or *C′*) and thallium 210 (*radium* C_2 or *C″*); *radium D*, lead 210; *radium E*, bismuth 210; *radium F*, polonium 210; *radium G*, lead 206, the non-radioactive end-product of the series.

The substances now designated *radium E* and *F* were in the first instances named *radium* D_1 and *E* respectively.

1904 E. RUTHERFORD in *Phil. Mag.* VIII. 636 For convenience, the products in the active deposit will be termed Radium A, Radium B and Radium C, respectively. *Ibid.* 641 Following the nomenclature suggested, radium C gives rise to the β ray product, which will be called Radium D, while radium D changes into the α ray product, which will be called Radium E. **1905** —— in *Nature* 9 Feb. 342 In order to avoid confusion, I have called the new radium product 'radium D_1'. If no further intermediate products of radium are brought to light, it would be simpler to call it radium E and to call the α ray product (polonium) radium F. **1905** —— in *Phil. Mag.* X. 293 This rayless product will be called radium D. The β ray product which arises from it will be called radium E. The α ray product (previously termed radium E) will be called Radium F. **1910** *Westm. Gaz.* 16 Feb. 4/1 Sir William Ransay's description..of 'Radium D', one of the mysterious products of radium, as 'rather dull-looking, like lead'. **1911** *Phil. Mag.* XXII. 628 Fajans has suggested that the name radium C_2 should be given to the new product of period 1·4 minutes. **1913** *Nature* 28 Aug. 659/2 That radium-G and lead are identical is supported by much indirect evidence, though no direct proof has been advanced. **1933** FAILLA & QUIMBY in O. Glasser *Sci. of Radiol.* xiii. 249 In about a month the equilibrium amounts of radon and radium A, B, and C will have accumulated, and the preparation has a maximum beta and gamma ray activity. **1936** *Discovery* July 218/2 The radium E was produced..through the bombardment of bismuth, with deuterons at an energy of 5,500,000 electron volts. **1966** R. OLIVER *Radiation Physics in Radiol.* vi. 71 Radium then disintegrates to form radon which is a gas at normal temperature and pressure. There follows a long series of disintegrations through nuclides referred to as radium A (RaA), B, C, C′, C″, D, E, F and G. The last nuclide (radium G) is a stable isotope of lead. **1974** *Encycl. Brit. Micropædia* VIII. 382/1 A sample of radium, sealed to prevent the escape of gaseous radon, reaches radioactive equilibrium in about a month and becomes a powerful source of gamma radiation, due especially to radium C (bismuth-214).

2. A smooth, plain fabric with the sheen of silk (see quots.).

1904 *Daily Chron.* 12 Mar. 8/5 The newest ribbon is radium, and what a future lies before it! **1930** *Daily Express* 6 Oct. 5/2 (Advt.), Radium velvet. Rich quality panne velvet giving a fashionable brilliance for afternoon and evening wear. **1957** M. B. PICKEN *Fashion Dict.* 269/1 *Radium*, smooth, pliable lingerie fabric of synthetic yarn in plain weave, with dull finish and natural sheen of silk. **1970** R. T. WILCOX *Dict. Costume* 281/2 *Radium*, a lustrous, plain, smooth silk or rayon, which has crispness, yet supple, draping quality.

3. a. *attrib.* and *Comb.*, as (sense *1) *radium atom, bromide, chloride, salt, sulphate, treatment*; (sense *2) *radium poplin, silk, velvet*; *radium-bearing, -coloured* adjs.

1903 *Daily Mail* 11 Sept. 3/1 Illustrating the amazing properties of a radium atom. **1926** R. W. LAWSON tr. *Hevesy & Paneth's Man. Radioactivity* xxiii. 161 St. Joachimstal in the Erzgebirge is the most important source of radium-bearing ores in Europe. **1904** *Chem. News* 24 June 301/1 As radium bromide yields electrolytic gas, containing an excess of hydrogen, the pressure gradually rose. **1913** *Med. Ann.* 647 Each capsule contains ·0002 mgram radium bromide. **1966** P. ASTBURY tr. *G. Amaldi's Nature of Matter* iv. 125 Pierre and Marie Curie..had to examine about seven tons of pitch-blende..in order to prepare a single gram of radium bromide. **1902** *Harper's Mag.* Aug. 360/2 M. Curie possesses about two to three hundredths of a gram of chemically pure radium chloride. **1904** *Daily Chron.* 2 Sept. 8/3 A magnificent mantle fully trained and made of radium-coloured taffetas mousseline, the blue, pink, and moonlight shades of which mingle with one another. **1952** C. W. CUNNINGTON *Eng. Women's Clothing* 296 *Radium poplin*, a silk and wool textile looking like a silk poplin. **1905** KIPLING *Actions & Reactions* (1909) 121 An expense of one hundred and seventy-odd pounds..for radium salts and such trifles. **1956** J. K. ROBERTSON *Radiology Physics* xii. 228 When radium needles are used, the dose delivered to the region treated depends on..the amount of absorption by the materials enclosing the radium salt. **1972** BARNES & REES *Conc. Textbk. Radiotherapy* viii. 178 Radium is prepared as the salt, radium sulphate, and mixed with a suitable filler, it is sealed into thin-walled metal capsules. **1936** *Discovery* Nov. 351/2 Apparatus for radium treatment recently installed at the Hampstead annexe of Westminster Hospital. **1930** Radium velvet [see sense 2 above].

b. Special Combs.: **radium beam**, a beam of gamma radiation from a radium source, used in radiotherapy; **radium bomb**, a container holding a large quantity of radium and used in radiotherapy as a source of a gamma ray beam; **radium burn**, a burn caused by over-exposure to radiation from radium; **radium clock**, a device utilizing the β-rays of radium to charge two electroscopic leaves, which discharge at regular intervals when they diverge sufficiently to touch two earthed metal plates; **radium emanation**, the radon isotope of atomic weight 222, which is the first product of the radioactive decay of radium; cf. *EMANATION 2 c; **radium needle**, a needle containing radium which can be inserted into tissue for radiotherapy; **radium plaque** = *PLAQUE 3; **radium therapy**, radiotherapy using radiation from radium.

1933 *Jrnl. Amer. Med. Assoc.* 12 Aug. 533/2 The work before the radium beam therapy research will be to..discover how far the present limited field of operation for a mass radium unit..may be extended. **1940** *Ibid.* 16 Mar. 999/1 Treatment of carcinoma of the mouth and throat by the radium beam is at least as satisfactory as by surgery or interstitial radium. **1956** J. K. ROBERTSON *Radiology Physics* xii. 227 In radium beam therapy, the source contains several grams of this radioactive element. **1930** *Brit. Med. Jrnl.* 19 July 98/1 An attempt to measure accurately the gamma radiation field, in air, of the radium 'bomb' in use at Westminster Hospital annexe. **1952** W. M. LEVITT *Handbk. Radiotherapy* iii. 42 It is probable that the radium bomb can do nothing that super-voltage x-ray therapy cannot do at least as well and little that deep x-ray therapy cannot do. **1908** *Jrnl. Amer. Med. Assoc.* 30 May 1871/1 (*heading*) Radium burns of the skin. **1926** R. W. LAWSON tr. *Hevesy & Paneth's Man. Radioactivity* xxv. 211 Radium burns are especially troublesome, because. even if they mend there remains a supersensitiveness of the skin. **1940** S. CADE *Malignant Dis. & Treatm. by Radium* 246 Radium burns of the skin or mucous membrane may take 8 to 10 months to heal. **1905** W. HAMPSON *Radium Explained* 69 We are now able to understand the action of the radium clock. **1905** E. RUTHERFORD *Radio-Activity* (ed. 2) iv. 123 This 'radium clock' should work at a sensibly uniform rate for many years, but..the number of β particles emitted would decrease exponentially with the time, falling to half value in about 1200 years. **1926** R. W. LAWSON tr. *Hevesy & Paneth's Man. Radioactivity* xxv. 211 The so-called 'radium clock'..illustrates how the rays from radium may be utilized indirectly to give rise to motion. **1901** *Nature* 13 June 157/2 The radium emanation..preserved its radiating power for several weeks. **1910** *Daily Chron.* 17 Feb. 3/3 Take the next product, the gas which it is continually giving off, and which is called radium emanation. That can be worked with because it is only half gone in four days. **1946** F. E. ZEUNER *Dating Past* x. 318. As radium decays, a gas called radium-emanation is formed which, in turn, emits another atom of helium and thereupon changes into a solid substance, called radium A. **1921** *Pennsylvania Med. Jrnl.* XXIV. 218/1 Radium needles should be inserted directly into the glands. **1959** C. L. & J. A. MARTIN *Low Intensity Radium Therapy* iii. 33 Low intensity radium needles still seem to provide the best available medium for interstitial therapy. **1960** A. HUXLEY *Let.* 20 May (1969) 890 For cases like mine, radium needles are now standard procedure at the University of California. **1919** *Amer. Jrnl. Roentgenology* VI. 134/1 It is..a very simple matter to treat a small lesion with a radium plaque. **1962** J. THEWLIS *Encycl. Dict. Physics* VI. 171/1 Formerly, radium plaques were used as β-emitters, but these have now been almost completely replaced by applicators containing strontium-90. **1904** *Med. Electrol. & Radiol.* V. 336 (*heading*) Radiumtherapy. **1905** *N. Amer. Jrnl. Homœopathy* LIII. 720 It would seem wise to postpone judgment as to the worth of radium therapy in dermatology. **1931** G. B. SHAW *Doctors' Delusions* 28 Nobody would dream of excluding radium therapy from the medical curriculum merely because more nonsense has been written about radium than about the philosopher's stone. **1964** L. DEIGHTON *Funeral in Berlin* xxix. 152 Began work as a representative [for] radium therapy machinery 1948. Assigned to Northern Spain as radium therapy equipment salesman 1949.

radiumize (rē¹·diŭməiz), *v.* [f. *RADIUM + -IZE.] *trans.* To subject to the action of radium. Hence **ra·diumized** *ppl. a.*

1906 *Jrnl. Amer. Med. Assoc.* 21 July 184/2 Two fine examples of spindle-celled sarcoma..have been thoroughly radiumized. **1914** *Chambers's Jrnl.* Oct. 688/2 The process of radiumising the soil. **1920** *Amer. Jrnl. Roentgenology* VII. 54/1 Such radiumized tissue will not grow when inoculated in mice. **1928** *Daily Tel.* 10 July 9/5 Work..is being pursued upon the immunity conferred upon rats and mice by X-rayed or radiumised tumour tissues. **1939** *Jrnl. Amer. Med. Assoc.* 1 Apr. 1280/1 (*heading*) Radiumized health pad.

radius. Add: **3. d.** *radius of action*: in *Aeronautics*, the distance that an aircraft can cover so as to leave sufficient fuel for its return to base.

1908 *Aeronaut. Jrnl.* Apr. 44/2 In a 10 hours' run a distance of 300 kilm. (186 miles) might be traversed, the radius [of] action being 150 kilm. **1918** *Flying* 20 Mar. 188/3 The problem of any extension of the radius of action is almost entirely one of increased efficiency..of modern aircraft.

5. radius rod (further examples).

1907 [see *chain case* s.v. *CHAIN *sb.* 19]. **1946** *Happy Landings* July 2/1 The inner radius rod of the starboard undercarriage was pulled away from the undercarriage. **1970** K. BALL *Fiat 600, 600D Autobk.* 165/1 *Radius rod*, pivoted arm confining movement of a part to an arc of fixed radius.

radius (rē¹·divs), *v.* [f. the sb.] *trans.* To round off, make (a corner or end) curved.

1938 J. Healey *Metal Aircraft* ii. 14 Tubular rivets are a reamer fit, so having reamered the hole to size, radius the edge of the metal slightly. **1954** *Electronic Engin.* XXVI. 538/1 All corners and bends should be 'radiused', i.e. finished with as large a radius as possible. **1962** *Engineering* 6 July 10/1 The effect of radiusing the corners is also discussed. **1972** Greer & Howell *Mech. Engin. Craft Stud.* II. III. 157 (*table*) Millsaw. For sharpening circular saws, radiusing slots etc.

Hence **ra·diused** *ppl. a.*

1954 *Archit. Rev.* CXV. 144/1 Radiused blocks are made for use at corners. **1959** *New Scientist* 31 Dec. 1339/2 Sharply radiused members are more expensive than straight members. **1975** *Mariner's Mirror* LXI. 406 A slightly more radiused stem rabbet where it meets the keel.

radix. For 7–9 read 7– and add: Also with pronunc. (ræ·diks). **1. b.** (Further *attrib.* examples.)

1950 W. W. Stifler *High-Speed Computing Devices* vi. 80 For any radix arithmetic the basic tables corresponding to the addition and the multiplication tables of decimal arithmetic can be written. *Ibid.* 87 Corresponding representations of the same numbers for radices 2, 3, 4, 5, 8, and 10 are tabulated. **1960** N. R. Scott *Analog & Digital Computer Technol.* vii. 224 To represent the *r* digits in a radix *r* system by *r* binary digits is highly inefficient, and this figure of merit unduly penalizes radices not close to *ε*. *Ibid.* 227 If numbers can have *n* digits to the left of the radix point, the radix complement of a negative number is formed by adding the radix raised to the *n*th power to the negative number. **1969** P. B. Jourdain *Condensed Computer Encycl.* 412 If a number is added to its radix complement, the result is a 1 followed by a 0 for every position in the original number. Radix complement is used in some computers.. and desk calculators for representing negative numbers. **1970** O. Dopping *Computers & Data Processing* xvii. 280 In radix sort, the records usually pass through the sorting device—a computer or a card sorter, as many times as there are digits in the sorting key.

radome (rē¹·dōᵘm). [Blend of *Radar and Dome *sb.*] A dome or other structure, transparent to radio waves, protecting a radar aerial.

1945 in *Amer. Speech* XX. 310/2 *Radome*, housing enclosing a radar scanner. **1949** *Sun* (Baltimore) 29 Dec. 5/1 Supported by air pressure.., the balloon-like buildings, called radomes, are ideal for the housing of large radar antennae. **1951** *Electronics* Aug. 89/2 The radar antenna is enclosed in a streamlined radome aft of the big bomb bay. **1962** *Guardian* 3 Oct. 3/7 The Air Ministry should..mitigate the 'nuisance' of a station in the National Park by keeping buildings..away from the main road..and by making the radomes a pale blue to tone with the sky. **1968** *New Scientist* 21 Mar. 631/2 The *Vladimir Komarov* is distinguished by two massive radomes of some 50ft diameter and a smaller radome amidships. **1973** C. Mason *Hostage* x. 136 Radar picket aircraft..with grotesque radomes projecting above and below the fuselages. **1977** *Time* 4 Apr. 13/1 A mushroom-shaped 'radome' 30 ft. in diameter and 6 ft. thick sprouts from the rear of the grey fuselage on two large struts.

radon (rē¹·dǫn). *Chem.* [a. G. *radon* (C. Schmidt 1918, in *Zeitschr. f. Anorg. Chem.* CIII. 114): see *Rad(ium and *-on².] **1.** A short-lived radioactive element which belongs to the group of noble gases and occurs naturally in trace amounts as a result of the decay of radium and other radioactive elements; orig. *spec.* the longest-lived isotope, radon 222, having a half-life of 3·82 days. Atomic number 86, symbol Rn (orig. Ro). Cf. *radium emanation* s.v. *Radium 3 b.

1918 *Jrnl. Chem. Soc.* CXIV. II. 306 Radium emanation is given the name Radon, Ro, which at once indicates its origin and its relationship to the argon group. **1927** *Observer* 3 Apr. 20/2 The Radium Institute sends radium, or rather radon, its active principle, to hospitals all over the country. **1938** R. W. Lawson tr. *Hevesy & Paneth's Man. Radioactivity* (ed. 2) xxiii. 227 The first five disintegration products of the gas radon are isotopes of the metals polonium, lead, bismuth, or thallium. **1942** S. Tolansky *Introd. Atomic Physics* xiii. 218 A body exposed for a short time to radon coats with an active deposit which emits α-, β-, and γ-radiation and exhibits a regular decay. **1974** *Environmental Conservation* I. 24/1 Uranium miners are known to suffer from an increased risk of lung cancer from inhaled radon. **1977** *Time* 22 Aug. 8/2 The radon in these waters is supposed to be good for everything from paralysis to curvature of the spine.

2. Special comb.: **radon seed**, a short tube containing radon that is used in radiotherapy as a source of alpha radiation.

1925 A. E. H. Pinch *Clin. Index Radium Therapy* 61 Treatment by the burying..of numerous unscreened radon 'seeds'..will often prove effective. **1930** *Sunday Times* 12 Oct. 24/2 Medical evidence showed that the child was placed under an anæsthetic and radon seeds..were placed in the growths. **1966** Henschke & Hilaris in G. H. Fletcher *Textbk. Radiotherapy* i. 43/1 Ninety radon seeds each 0·75 cm. were permanently implanted through 17 needles and the uterus was sutured over the implant.

radula. 2. (Later examples.)

1901 E. Step *Shell Life* iii. 42 The number of these teeth to one tongue or radula varies to a remarkable extent. **1928** Russell & Yonge *Seas* ix. 202 In common with many other members of the snail family they [*sc.* limpets] possess a very characteristic feeding apparatus consisting of a long horny ribbon, made up of many rows of fine teeth, and known as the 'radula'. **1959** A. C. Hardy *Open Sea* II. vi. 128 A radula is a remarkable structure found in the mouths of all typical gastropods; it is a long ribbon, bearing a vast number of transverse rows of sharp horny teeth. **1975** *Sci. Amer.* Feb. 106/3 The snail combines the functions of teeth and tongue in a single organ: the radula, a toothed, filelike muscle inside the mouth.

radurization (rædiū°rəizē¹·ʃən). [f. L. *radiāre* to furnish with rays, shine + *dūr-āre* to make hard, preserve + -ization.] The treatment of food with ionizing radiation so as to enhance its keeping qualities by killing many of the micro-organisms in it (see quot. 1964). Cf. *Radappertization, *Radicidation.

1964 H. E. Goresline in *Nature* 17 Oct. 237/2 Type III is the application to foods of doses of ionizing radiation sufficient to enhance keeping quality by causing substantial reduction in the numbers of viable specific spoilage micro-organisms... The following are the names we suggest for these types of treatment... Type III, radurization. **1973** N. F. Lewis et al. *Radiation Preservation of Food* (Internat. Atomic Energy Agency) 201 'Radurization' is essentially a pasteurization treatment that results in prolonging shelf-life of foods by a selective control of spoilage microflora. **1977** *Biol. Abstr.* LXIII. 5003/1 Irradiation preservation of Korean fish: I. Radurization of croaker, yellow corvenia and roundnose flounder.

radwaste (ræ·dwē¹st). orig. *U.S.* Also **rad-waste.** [Short for *rad*ioactive *waste*.] = *radioactive waste* s.v. *Radioactive *a.* 4.

1973 *Trans. Amer. Nucl. Soc.* XVI. 176/1 (*heading*) A cyrogenic approach to fuel reprocessing gaseous radwaste treatment. **1975** *Proc. Symp. on Reliability of Nuclear Power Plants* (Internat. Atomic Energy Agency) 373 A computerized reliability-risk model has been developed to simulate the rad-waste system. **1978** *Times* 28 July 1 Principal components of typical radwaste calcin[ation]. **1979** *Nature* 15 Mar. 219/1 The most popular procedure advocated by the nuclear power establishment during the past 25 yr has been to incorporate the radwaste into a borosilicate glass.

Rætian, Rætic: see *Rhætian, *Rhætic.

R.A.F. Also (*colloq.*) **raf, raff** (ræf). [f. initial letters of *R*oyal *A*ir *F*orce, founded in 1918 on the amalgamation of the Royal Flying Corps with the Royal Naval Air Service.] The British Air Force or (*collect.*) members of this organization.

1920 M. Baring *R.F.C., H.Q.* xxi. 276 On the 20th of May we started on a long expedition to the R.A.F. Headquarters. **1924** G. Bell *Let.* 2 July (1927) II. xxiv. 701 The most interesting thing which happened during this week was a performance by the R.A.F., a bombing demonstration. **1941** W. S. Churchill *Into Battle* 310 Operating from new Greek bases, the R.A.F. attack Bari and Brindisi, and bomb military objectives in Naples. **1946** 'Tackline' *You met such Nice Girls* vii. 73 And it is a peculiar thing, but the Raff and the Wavy Navy do not mix at parties, and in fact the only place the Wavy Navy like the Raff to be is in the air. **1950** C. MacInnes *To Victors the Spoils* ii. 227 They're Raf bods, escaped prisoners. **1954** 'E. C. R. Lorac' *Shroud of Darkness* xvi. 173 I'd fly the plane for you if the Raf'd let me. **1957** M. Swan *Brit. Guiana* iv. 76 He was a big man, in his late twenties, with an R.A.F. moustache, wearing a bush-hat and a bush-shirt whose breast pockets bulged with papers. **1965** J. Porter *Dover Two* v. 60 'A decent lad like our Rex..in the Raf.' 'R.A.F., Dad... I've told you before not to call it Raf!' **1974** S. Milligan *Rommel* 186, I never dreamed, one day he, I, and a lone RAF erk called Sellers.. would make a sort of comic history. **1980** J. Ditton *Copley's Hunch* I. i. 11 For a Raff bloke, that's good going. You're not trained to make full use of ground cover, are you?

Hence as *v. trans.* (see quot. 1940) and *intr.* (*rare*).

1930 T. E. Lawrence *Let.* 8 Jan. (1938) v. 675, I spend innocent days R.A.F.ing. **1940** *Daily Mail* 28 Aug. 3/1 Yesterday I heard: 'He'll get R.A.F.'d if he doesn't mind.' There's surely a rousing neologism in this—to 'raff' the Nazis instead of the old 'strafing Fritz'. Why not say 'Berlin has been raffed to blazes?'

‖**rafale** (rafal). [Fr., lit. a gust of wind.] A series of bursts of gun-fire; a roll of drums. Also *fig.*

1903 P. de B. Radcliffe tr. *G. Rouquerol's Tactical Employment Quick-Firing Field Artillery* II. i. 33 To obtain the instantaneous effect, to produce that which he [*sc.* Gen. Langlois] vividly termed the *rafale*, or shell-storm, he conceived a special device which he called '*échelon* fire'. **1914** *Sphere* 3 Oct. 8/1 The second diagram shows a 'rafale', or 'shell-storm'. This is the method practised by batteries of French artillery to prevent the advance of infantry. **1916** *Chambers's Jrnl.* Sept. 604/2 The ·75, by rafale and curtain tactics, is able to isolate an attacking force by keeping the supports at bay. **1922** *Public Opinion* 28 July 85/1 If I had a few private batteries I should fire a private rafale in honour of the best book of the year. **1928** *Blackw. Mag.* Jan. 69/1 This was delivered with a slobbering roll of 'r's' like a rafale of water-logged kettle-drums. **1931** E. Linklater *Juan in Amer.* II. xii. 137 Now the staccato ear-splitting *rafale* of cheering rowels them afresh.

raff, *sb.*¹ Add: **3. b.** *spec.* Ore which requires re-crushing; *raff-wheel*, a wheel for lifting such ore.

1867 *Ure's Dict. Arts* (ed. 6) II. 72 The hopper is continuously charged, and that portion which is not reduced sufficiently fine is returned by the raff wheel to be recrushed. **1902** *Trans. Inst. Mining & Metall.* X. 459 The stuff rejected by..[a cylindrical trommel] is brought back by means of a Raff wheel and re-crushed.

raffe. Substitute for entry:

raffee (ræfī·). Also **raffeé.** [Of obscure origin.] (See quots. 1880 and 1891.) Also *attrib.*

1880 D. Kemp *Man. Yacht & Boat Sailing* (ed. 2) 547 *Raffee*, the square topsail set flying on the foretopmast of schooners, and formerly often set on cutters and ketches above the squaresail. Sometimes this topsail is triangular in shape, like a scraper. **1891** H. Patterson *Illustr. Naut. Dict.* 144 *Raffeé Rail*, a sail in the shape of an equilateral triangle △ which is sometimes set over the highest yard... This sail is common to English schooner yachts rigged to carry a squaresail, as the *raffeé* is set over the yard. **1922** *Field* 8 July 59/1 A square sail and a raffee, or the topsail set over it, are such old-fashioned sails that many modern yachtsmen have never seen them. **1942** C. Crockett *House in Rain Forest* i. 18 The southeast trades filling our squaresail and raffee. **1976** *Oxf. Compan. Ships & Sea* 687/1 *Raffee*, another name for the sail in a square-rigged ship known as a moonraker, set only in light weather.

Rafferty (ræ·fəɹti). *Austral.* and *N.Z. slang.* [Eng. dial. corruption of *refractory* (Eng. Dial. Dict.).] Used *attrib.* or in the possessive, as *Rafferty('s) rules*, no rules at all, esp. in boxing.

The customary initial capital suggests that the word is felt by many to be the Irish surname *Rafferty*.

1928 *Bulletin* (Sydney) 5 Jan. 37/4 M.Q. (and Rafferty) Rules. **1935** *Sydney Morning Herald* 28 Dec. 11 Rafferty rules may suit Mr Keenan and the Communist party, but they are repugnant to the trade union movement. **1941** Baker *Dict. Austral. Slang* 58 *Rafferty rules*, no rules at all, applied to any system, organisation or contest run in slip-shod fashion. **1958** A. Wall *Queen's English* xxxii. 112, I do not know that the Queensberry Rules ever acquired any figurative usage; but the 'Rafferty Rules' certainly did. This term means no rules at all; in Australian, and hence New Zealand slang, it means any free and easy way of running things; 'Rafferty' here is thought to be an English dialect corruption of 'refractory'. **1964** H. P. Tritton *Time means Tucker* (ed. 2) 34 The Show adjourned at noon for the races. They seemed to be run on the 'Rafferty Rules' principle, but I heard no complaints. **1974** *Bulletin* (Sydney) 18 May 63 Rafferty's rules predominate. **1977** *Financial Times* 17 May 37/8 Because of the nature of the town and its 'Rafferty's rules' violence is a way of life and it is a well known haunt for criminals and tribal outcasts.

raffia. Add: **1.** (Further examples.)

1906 *Westm. Gaz.* 26 Sept. 8/1 Mr. William H. Hunt.. announced the discovery, in the leaves of the rafia palm, of a product which..may be classed between wax and gum. **1958** C. Achebe *Things fall Apart* I. viii. 57 Obierika was sitting outside under the shade of an orange tree making thatches from leaves of the raffia-palm.

2. Also, extensively employed in the making of baskets, lamp-shades, mats, and similar articles. (Further examples.)

1901 M. White *How to make Baskets* ii. 11 It is a rare thing to find a material at once so soft and so strong as raffia. **1912** *Educ. Handwork* Nov. 201/1 The materials most suitable for weaving are, wool, bast or raffia, and cane. **1937** A. H. Crampton *Raffia Work & Basketry* 7 Raffia work although allied to the ancient craft of Basket Making, may be termed a modern craft. **1951** 'R. Brinley' *Raffia Work* i. 11 One of the chief advantages of working with raffia is the very low cost of the material. **1978** P. Van Greenaway *Man called Scavener* vi. 84 He noticed a confusion of raffia, macramé and pieces of knitting.

3. *attrib.* and *Comb.*, as (sense 2) *raffia bag, basket, cloth, fibre, grass, lace, mat, needle, tape, work, workbag*; *raffia-embroidered* adj.

1932 S. Gibbons *Cold Comfort Farm* viii. 121 Raffia bags and linen bags embroidered with hollyhocks. **1960** G. Durrell *Zoo in my Luggage* iii. 77, I bent down, picked up a raffia bag and held it aloft. **1914** S. G. Fitzgerald *Priscilla Juniors' Basketry Bk.* 19 (*heading*) Handle for raffia basket. **1977** G. Scott *Hot Pursuit* iii. 25 Dried fish, piled in raffia baskets, on the pavement. **1932** D. C. Minter *Mod. Needlecraft* 59/1 Raffia work is really another form of embroidery... The materials for working on are.. hessian, raffia cloth, and woven straw. **1967** E. Short *Embroidery & Fabric Collage* iii. 84 Fabrics with unusual textures, raffia cloth, for instance, can be decorated with simple embroidery such as bands of drawn threads. **1904** *Daily Chron.* 3 May 8/3 A pretty and attractive novelty..is the raffia embroidered cushion. **1906** *Westm. Gaz.* 26 Sept. 8/1 The natives gather the rafia fibre. **1910** M. T. Priestman *Handicrafts in Home* 207 Delicate strands of raffia fibre should be secured for this purpose. **1904** *Daily Chron.* 3 May 8/3 The embroidery is worked with raffia grass dyed in various colours. **1906** *Queen* 5 May 757/1 Raffia lace hats are the choicest things in headgear that ingenuity has ever devised out of vegetable fibre. **1914** S. G. Fitzgerald *Priscilla Juniors' Basketry Bk.* 6 (*heading*) Woven raffia mat. **1953** E. Simon *Past Masters* iv. 263 Raffia mats, cutlery and glasses defined the full number of places. **1976** *Daily Times* (Lagos) 22 Sept. 16/4 To build a crib to store maize harvested from a one-hectare plot requires only six 12-ft (360-cm)-long bamboo poles; another six of such poles of 180 cm length each; 45 raffia mats; [etc.]. **1914** H. C. Walker *Rafia Work* 7 The reasons for urging the claims of rafia work are many... It requires no tools beyond rafia needles, wool needles..and knitting needles. **1932** D. C. Minter *Mod. Needlecraft* 226/2 Use a small packing needle, or a raffia needle, and a backing of Helvellyn canvas with Persian, or Straight, or Shetland rug wool. **1979** *Dryad Catal.* 89/3 Raffia needles..For coiled raffia basketry. **1907** *Daily Chron.* 5 Jan. 9/1 Sometimes the flowers require staking, and this should be done..with stiff, straight wires or sticks, to which the stems should be fastened with West's Raffia Tape. **1939–40** *Army & Navy Stores Catal.* 956/1 Raffia Tape..balls in coloured string nets. **1908** M. E. Morgan *How to dress Doll* vii. 65 Little girls who know how to do raffia work can easily make such a hat. **1974**

C. Fremlin *By Horror Haunted* 88 He attended his own classes in Braille and raffia-work. **1928** *Chambers's Jrnl.* 24 Mar. 261/1 From a corner of one of the baskets she unpacked her raffia workbag.

raffinate (ræ·fineᶦt). [ad. G. or F. *raffinat*, f. G. *raffinieren* (F. *raffiner*) to refine + *-at* -ATE[1] (as in *distillate*, *filtrate*, etc.).] The refined fraction which results after removal of impurities by solvent extraction, *spec.* in oil refining. Also *attrib.*

The term was first used in oil refining, in connection with the solvent extraction process invented by the Romanian chemical engineer L. Edeleanu and introduced on a commercial scale at Rouen *c* 1911.

1928 L. Edeleanu *U.S. Pat. 1,661,565* 2/1 The finished hot raffinate is taken from the last evaporator 21 by the pump 23 and passed..to the storage tank. **1932** *Jrnl. Inst. Petroleum Technologists* XVIII. 919 Dr. Edeleanu could lay claim to a further distinction, in having added two words to the English language—the words 'edeleanize' and 'raffinate'—words which, if not already in the dictionary, soon would be. **1941** W. L. Nelson *Petroleum Refinery Engin.* (ed. 2) xxvii. 617 Elaborate equipment is required to distill the solvent (or oil) from the extract and raffinate solutions. **1950** *Jrnl. Amer. Chem. Soc.* LXXII. 12/2 Now the flask in the 'R' position contained penicillin which was emptied into a larger container as raffinate pool. **1958** *Engineering* 14 Feb. 205/2 The presence of this dissolved salt in the fission-product raffinate stream limits the degree of concentration which may be achieved by evaporation while still keeping all the material in solution. **1970** W. G. Roberts *Quest for Oil* ix. 95 The raffinate is given a final sweetening and is ready for use as premium kerosene.

‖**raffiné** (rafine), *a.* (*sb.*) [Fr.] Of manners or judgement: refined. Also as *sb.*, a person distinguished by the possession of refinement in manners, action, or feeling.

1876 [see *méfiance]. **1883** *Atlantic Monthly* Aug. 179/1 The ingenious Catherine—she was a *raffinée*. **1920** D. H. Lawrence *Lost Girl* i. 10 No French marquis..could have been more elegant and *raffiné*. **1943** *Scrutiny* XI. 317 He is an older and wiser Tonio Kröger who has broken away from the precious and the *raffiné*. **1966** *Punch* 2 Feb. 173/1 The waiter, the actor, the communist, the painter all have their says [in a play] but it is through the analyst and the raffiné aristocrat..that we learn of hate-objects. **1970** *New Yorker* 23 May 126/3 He has a tendency..to favor his vigorous vulgarians at the expense of his effete *raffinés*.

raffinose. Substitute for entry:

raffinose (ræ·finōᵘz, -s). *Chem.* [a. F. *raffinose* (D. Loiseau 1876, in *Compt. Rend.* LXXXII. 1058), f. *raffiner* to refine: see -OSE[2].] A non-reducing trisaccharide sugar found in sugar-beet, cotton seed, and many cereals.

1876 *Jrnl. Chem. Soc.* XXX. 398 At 20° water dissolves one-seventh of its weight of raffinose. **1881, 1894** [in Dict.]. **1934** *Industr. & Engin. Chem.* Apr. 462/1 The cottonseed meal has been the raw material from which most of the small supply of pure raffinose has been obtained. **1950** *Thorpe's Dict. Appl. Chem.* (ed. 4) X. 468/1 The arrangement of the hexoses in raffinose is galactose–glucose–fructose. **1970** A. L. Lehninger *Biochem.* xi. 227 Raffinose (fructose, glucose, galactose) is found in abundance in sugar beets and many other higher plants.

raffle, *sb.*[1] Add: **3.** *attrib.*, as *raffle prize*, *ticket*.

1976 *Milton Keynes Express* 16 July 9 The raffle prize of a 10 foot canoe went to Mr Sheldrick of Tandra, Bean Hill. **1976** *Jrnl.* (Newcastle) 26 Nov., Mr. Large produced a bundle of official raffle tickets offering Michael's models, which include a gypsy caravan, as prizes.

raffle, *sb.*[2] **1. a.** Delete † and add later example.

1921 G. C. Shedd *Lady of Mystery House* xix. 171 Probably the drunken raffle were seeking far and near to take me.

2. a. (Further examples.)

1895 Kipling *Day's Work* (1898) 343 He..was pushed and prodded through the slack back-waters of the Lower Fourth, where the raffle of a school generally accumulates. **1906** *Macmillan's Mag.* Aug. 755 A heavy cattle-boat limping past us..with its raffle of pens and its sour sweet reek. **1977** A. Hunter *Gently Instrumental* iv. 50 It was a pleasant-enough spot up there, in spite of the raffle of the yard below.

raffle, *v.*[1] Add: **2.** Also const. *off*.

1889 'Mark Twain' *Connecticut Yankee* xv. 175, I shan't know what to do with them: unless I raffle them off. **1976** *Washington Post* 7 Nov. K2/3 We'll raffle off a 'possum and award a prize to the wearer of the biggest beehive hairdo.

Raffles (ræ·f'lz). The name of A. J. *Raffles*, hero of *The Amateur Cracksman* (1899) and other books by E. W. Hornung (1866–1921), used allusively of a gentleman who engages in crime, esp. burglary. Also *attrib.*

1908 'O. Henry' *Gentle Grafter* 142 It's part of my business..to play up to the ruffles when I want to make a riffle as Raffles. **1930** G. Smithson *Raffles in Real Life* i. 16 What an ignominious ending to the ambitious ideas that had filled my mind when I set out on the perilous career of a modern Raffles! *Ibid.* 18 By steady, if somewhat painful, steps, I had graduated from a middle-class cracksman to a Raffles of the gentleman type. **1953** J. Trench *Docken Dead* viii. 113 It [is] a good thing to look to one's way of retreat. Have you thought of that, my good Raffles? **1960** *John o' London's* 31 Mar. 384/3 An educated renegade..in the classic *Raffles* tradition. **1974** *Listener* 21 Feb. 242/3 Damiaen van Doorninck, a Dutch Naval officer, made a reputation..as a cracksman—'the Raffles of Colditz'.

rafflesia. Substitute for def.: A stemless, leafless, parasitic plant of the genus so called, of the family Rafflesiaceæ, native to Java and Sumatra, and remarkable for the size of its flowers. (Later examples.)

Quot. 1820 in Dict. should be dated 1821.

1933 L. Ainsworth *Confessions Planter in Malaya* 111 This plant..is known as the 'Rafflesia', and is one of the largest parasites in the world. **1954** R. E. Holttum *Plant Life in Malaya* xiv. 192 Rafflesia plants are only found in deeply shaded forest.

‖**rafik** (rafī·k). Also **raffik, rafiq.** [ad. Arab. *rafīḳ*.] In Arabia: a companion or escort (see quot. 1920).

1856 R. F. Burton *Pers. Narr. Pilgrimage to El-Medinah* III. 84 The payment of a small sum secures..a 'Rafik', and this 'friend', after once engaging in the task, will be faithful. **1888** C. M. Doughty *Trav. Arabia Deserta* I. viii. 235 The Arabian rafik, often an enemy, is a paid brother-of-the-road, that for a modest fee takes upon him to quit the convoy from all hostile question and encounter of his own tribesmen. **1911** T. E. Lawrence *Let.* 18 June (1954) 170 'Am I not your friend, your raffik?' said the zaptieh. **1913** G. Bell *Let.* 20 Dec. (1927) I. xiii. 314 We have a Rafiq, a comrade of the Ghiyatah with us—we fetched him from Dumeir to stand surety for us if we met his tribe. **1920** *Handbk. of Arabia* (Admiralty) I. 21 The one thing needful is a *rafiq*, i.e. a companion derived from the tribe through whose range one must pass, or from some tribe allied with it or authorized to share its range.

raft, *sb.*[1] Add: **4.** esp. ducks; also, a group of other aquatic animals. (Further examples.)

1848 W. E. Burton *Waggeries & Vagaries* 70 We've shoals of shad, hull rafts of canvass-back ducks, and no eeend of terrapins. **1872** *Fur, Fin & Feather* 26 The great collections [of ducks] are termed rafts. **1949** Sprunt & Chamberlain *S. Carolina Bird Life* 135 The Greater Scaup ..congregates there in large flocks or 'rafts', as they are called. **1952** *Chambers's Jrnl.* Jan. 19/2 That black mass far away to starboard, what is it—brent geese? And the bigger one over there? It looks like a good raft of wigeon. **1959** E. Collier *Three against Wilderness* xxi. 210 A raft of newly hatched geese had been perched on the beaver house. **1961** *Guardian* 4 Mar. 4/1 Rafts of widgeon cry *wee-too* from the steamer lines. **1972** S. Burnford *One Woman's Arctic* ii. 48 There were long rafts of murres out in the middle. **1975** *Country Life* 16 Jan. 132/3 A tiny band of sea otters.. had grown to a raft of 130. **1975** P. A. Johnsgard *Waterfowl N. Amer.* II. 347 Scaup in such rafts do not all forage at the same time.

4*. *Building.* A layer of reinforced concrete forming the foundation of a building.

1903 *Engineering* 17 Apr. 517/1 Finally, the Co-operative Wholesale Society resolved to adopt their architect's recommendation to have recourse to a raft of Hennebique ferro-concrete over the whole area of the ground. **1936** *Concrete & Constructional Engin.* XXXI. 423 There are a great many districts where rafts are the best and often the only solution to foundation problems. **1970** R. Jeffries *Dead Man's Bluff* iii. 21 A concrete raft on which was a feeding trough and about fifty Kow Kennels. **1978** *Daily Tel.* 12 May 19/3 All the floors in the houses are dropping out because they were built on a concrete raft. The raft is now sinking into the peat below.

5. *raft-man* (further examples), *-voyage*; *raftwise* adv.; **raft-deck,** an under-water protecting deck formerly used to cover the unarmoured parts of some warships; **raft-duck,** add after 'scaup or blackhead duck': (*Athya marila*); (later examples); **raft foundation** = sense 4* above; **raft-fowl** (for 1718 read 1709 in def. and quot.).

1886 *Encycl. Brit.* XXI. 822/2 But the sailors of 1854–1860 did not take the view that buoyancy and stability.. were the vital parts, needing defence by armour or by a raft-deck. **1872** E. Coues *Key to N. Amer. Birds* 289 Greater Scaup Duck... Raft Duck. Flocking Fowl. **1975** P. A. Johnsgard *Waterfowl N. Amer.* II. 347 The 'rafting' behaviour of migrant and wintering scaup is well known and indicated by their vernacular names—'raft duck', 'flock duck', and 'troop duck'. **1904** C. F. Marsh *Reinforced Concrete* 541/1 (Index), Raft foundations. **1910** F. Rings *Reinforced Concrete* iv. 61 For ordinary level or raft foundations wire meshing or expanded metal are extremely useful. **1974** *Encycl. Brit. Macropædia* III. 458/1 Of mat, or raft, foundation, there are two types—the beam-and-slab type and the flat-slab type. **1828** A. Sherburne *Mem.* vi. 234 The raft men had the privilenge [*sic*] of cooking, and sleeping under cover, in the boat. **1847** C. Lanman *Summer in Wilderness* xviii. 111 The principal anglers for this fish are steamboat hands and raftmen. **1903** *Blackw. Mag.* Feb. 228/1 The figures of the raftmen seem to walk magically on the water. **1963** A. Smith *Throw out Two Hands* xv. 153 We wished..to be a raft in the air, and to pay as little attention to our conveyance as raft-men do. **1891** 'Mark Twain' *Let.* 1 Oct. (1917) II. 558 A pedestrian tour in Europe doesn't begin with a raft-voyage for hilarity and mild adventure. **1905** 'Q' *Shining Ferry* I. vi. 61 A hatch opened in her bows, through which the long balks of timber were thrust..to be laid raftwise and lashed together with chains.

raft, *sb.*[2] Delete '*dial.* and *U.S.*', and '(Used disparagingly)' and substitute 'orig. *dial.* and *U.S.*' (Earlier and later examples.) Freq. in phr. *a whole raft of* (persons or things).

1830 W. A. Ferris *Life in Rocky Mts.* (1940) vi. 29 We.. would have fought a whole raft of them. **1922** S. Lewis *Babbitt* viii. 116 They say there's a whole raft of stuff being smuggled across at Detroit. **1936** P. Bottome *Level Crossing* xxiv. 298 You've got to stand on what results there are, and not take on a whole raft of things that have nothing to do with it. **1947** 'N. Shute' *Chequer Board* x. 298 There's a whole raft o' things here that I never seen before. **1959** *Sunday Times* 7 June 21/5 Only very rich companies with a raft of employees build them. **1972** *Guardian* 19 Oct. 14/4 A year or two of keeping house, loving and looking after a raft of kids. **1977** *Time* 3 Jan. 36/1 There were a whole raft of programs in the '60s followed by eight years when there was no attempt to work with any degree of compassion. **1977** *Guardian Weekly* 16 Oct. 20/2 It has a raft of actors with the energy and skill to bring humour, depth and resonance to even the smallest parts. **1978** P. Theroux *Picture Palace* ix. 71 There was a whole raft of photographers in New York at the time. **1979** *Amer. Speech* LIV. 44 He reserved what he called 'a great raft' of *Beowulf* materials for a more leisurely time.

raft, *v.*[1] Add: **1. a.** (Further examples.) Also *transf.*

1896 Kipling *Seven Seas* 26 With cedars out of Lebanon Which Hiram rafted down. **1921** *Discovery* Feb. 48/1 The water hyacinth..causes an annual loss of one-fourth of the value of the logs rafted down the river. **1961** *Nature* 3 June 856/2 Sial blocks..being rafted to down-welling sites. **1972** *Sci. Amer.* May 62 (*caption*) In this schematic view the lithosphere is thicker under the continent it is rafting toward a subduction zone.

b. (Earlier and later examples.)

1689 H. Kelsey *Jrnl.* 22 July in *Kelsey Papers* (1929) 30 This morning tryed to gett over yᵉ mouth of it but could not so..went up yᵉ river to Raft our selves over. **1847** *Knickerbocker* XXIX. 314 We crossed it on the following day, rafting over our horses and equipage with much difficulty. **1972** *Nat. Geographic* Oct. 469/2 Wielding huge sweeps, Peruvians raft bananas down the Ucayali River.

2. (Further examples.) Also with *up*, and in sense 4 of Raft *sb.*[1]

1883 J. Fraser *Shanty, Forest & River Life* xxix. 340 The timber is floated in single pieces down all the numerous tributaries of the Ottawa, and then 'rafted-up' at 'the mouth' of each. **1924** R. Campbell *Flaming Terrapin* ii. 38 Stacked with flaming spears Old Ocean shone, as swaying through the Night He rafted up his monstrous chandeliers. **1950** E. Hemingway *Across River* xli. 242 They [*sc.* ducks] must really be rafted up out there, the Colonel thought. **1976** *Yachts & Yachting* 20 Aug. 353/1 In St. Peter Port I have seen yachts rafted-up almost wall-to-wall on the buoys, like the trots used to be at Cowes. **1978** J. A. Michener *Chesapeake* 665 There must have been three thousand ducks rafted there beneath a frozen late-rising moon.

3. (Later examples.)

1844 J. C. Frémont *Rep. Exploring Expedition* (1845) 251 We had expected to raft the river. **1955** E. Pound *Classic Anthol.* I. 17 Ready to raft the deep, Wade shallow or dive for gain. **1974** *Marlboro Herald-Advocate* (Bennettsville, S. Carolina) 22 Apr. 6/2 During the four day exercise, members of the 541st engineer company rafted the Rhine river and secured tactical positions.

5. *intr.* Of an ice floe: to be driven on top of or underneath another floe. Also *trans.*, to drive (ice) in this way.

1883 Hatton & Harvey *Newfoundland* III. iii. 301 Or, under pressure of the storm, it frequently happens that the ice is 'rafted', as the sealers call it; that is, the fragments are piled in layers one over the other to the height of thirty or forty feet, being lifted by the swell and hurled forward as if from huge catapults. **1919** E. Shackleton *South* i. 11 In obedience to renewed pressure this young ice 'rafts', so forming double thicknesses of a toffee-like consistency. **1939** *Beaver* Mar. 13/2 On the sea and large lakes ice seldom forms smoothly. Early storms break it and pack it in confusion, and pressure causes it to 'raft'.

raft (ræft), *v.*[3] *Southern dial.* [Origin unknown.] *trans.* To rouse; to disturb, disquiet, or unsettle. Hence **ra·fted** *ppl. a.*[2], **ra·fting** *ppl. a.*[2]

1851 *Gloss. Provincial Words Dorset* 6 *Raft*, to irritate. **1895** Hardy *Jude* IV. iv. 290 'I think you are rafted, and not yourself,' he continued. 'Do go back and make up your mind to put up with a few whims.' **1896** —— *Under Greenwood Tree* (rev. ed.) I. iv. 32 They should ha' stuck to strings. Your brass-man is a rafting dog—well and good; your reed-man is a dab at stirring ye—well and good; your drum-man is a rare bowel-shaker—good again. **1904** in *Eng. Dial. Dict.* V. 11/1 When a sick person is at the point of death, old nurses think it wrong to disturb the spirit of the dying by speaking to him, lest by doing so his spirit may be 'rafted', i.e. disturbed by earthly thoughts, and so bereft of the consolation of religion [Hants.]. **1920** Hardy *Coll. Poems* 377 My rafted spirit would not rest.

rafted (rɑ·fted), *ppl. a.*[1] [f. Raft *v.*[1] + -ED[1].]

1. Of floating ice: piled up as a result of one floe having been driven on top of another.

1897 J. W. Tyrrell *Across Sub-Arctics of Canada* vii. 92 Toward the north end of the lake we passed great piles of rafted ice on the shore. **1924** R. J. Flaherty *My Eskimo Friends* III. ii. 93 On the tenth of April we came face to face with a gigantic pile of rafted ice. **1960** G. Blanchet *Search in North* viii. 109 Sunlight created strange effects from rafted ice. **1974** L. Deighton *Spy Story* xix. 203 We'll go south until we find the end of the rafted ice.

2. Of swimming birds: gathered into a dense flock.

1962 R. Haig-Brown *Whale People* x. 89 They covered the canoe with brush and allowed it to drift in on the rafted ducks. **1978** J. A. Michener *Chesapeake* 844 With a gentle ..push he launched the skiff toward the rafted geese.

rafter, *sb.*[2] Add: **1.** (Further examples.)
1891 C. ROBERTS *Adrift in Amer.* 206 The rafters were engaged in making the rafts up. **1905** 'Q' *Shining Ferry* vi. 70 In fifty strokes he brought her alongside the barque where the rafters—twenty-five or thirty—were at work. **1936** [see *CROSS-CUTTER]. **1954** A. M. BEZANSON *Sodbusters invade Peace* xxii. 160 Rafters kept coming quite a while. They all finally got tired waiting for God to freeze the rivers again, and came down on rafts.

2. One who travels on a raft.
1978 *TV Bk.* (Detroit Free Press) 16–22 Apr. 21/2 Adventures of a group of white water rafters on the Chatooga River in South Carolina. **1979** *Sunset* Apr. 38 (*caption*) Jagged, glacier-dotted Mount Moran hobnobs with the clouds as rafters laze along Jackson Lake towards shore for Teton camping.

rafter, *v.* Add: **1.** Also *fig.*
1935 C. DAY LEWIS *Time to Dance* 64 A hungry soul Urged them to try new air-routes, and their skill Raftered the sky with steel.

4. *N. Amer.* Of ice: = *RAFT *v.*[1] 5.
1792 G. CARTWRIGHT *Jrnl.* II. p. vii, Raftering of ice. Ice is said to rafter, when, by being stopped in its passage, one piece is forced under another, until the uppermost ones rise to a great height. **1861** L. DE BOILIEU *Recoll. Labrador Life* viii. 100 It is a sad sight to see a ship on the weather edge of ice not enabled to work off; for when the ice begins to rafter she is thrown up, falls over, and becomes like corn between two millstones, and is literally ground up. **1908** N. DUNCAN *Every Man for Himself* ii. 60 The ice begun t' drive an' grind an' rafter. **1924** R. J. FLAHERTY *My Eskimo Friends* III. iii. 99 Miles and miles of ice, raftering and rearing and overriding us it fought its way to the sea. **1964** *Newfoundland Q.* Spring 16/3 Evidently, just like frozen masses of ice raftered, one layer rising above the other by pressure, the crust of the earth broke and travelled southward.

raftered, *ppl. a.* Add: Also *transf.*, and in sense 4 of *RAFTER *v.*
1916 N. DUNCAN *Billy Topsail, M.D.* xvii. 130 It was six miles from the edge of the raftered ice to the first island. **1924** R. CAMPBELL *Flaming Terrapin* ii. 32 She skimmed along—Till, raftered by the forest,..She saw the monsters that the jungle breeds.

rafterless (rɑ·ftəɹlės), *a.* [f. RAFTER *sb.*[1] + -LESS.] Having no rafters.
1854 'G. GREENWOOD' *Haps & Mishaps* vii. 128 This is a picturesque, roofless, rafterless edifice, in a good state of preservation. **1943** L. B. LYON *Evening in Stepney* 20 Who tremble, yet dare not call On the crushed bones to bear witness And rafterless heaven to fall.

rafting, *vbl. sb.* Add: **a.** (Earlier and later examples.)
1697 H. KELSEY *Jrnl.* 16 Aug. in *Kelsey Papers* (1929) 95 Our 3 boats went to ten shilling creek to rafting. **1905** 'Q' *Shining Ferry* I. vi. 69 'Have they begun the rafting?' 'Bless your life, they've been working all night. There's one raft finished.' **1920** W. T. GRENFELL *Labrador Doctor* ix. 180 On then swept the floe, crashed into the fixed ice, shattered its edge, rose up out of water over it, which is called 'rafting', forced itself on the unfortunate ship. **1967** *Vogue* Jan. 76/1 Jamaica has..skin-diving, rafting, cheap rum. **1975** B. L. FAIRBANK *Cruising Guide to Lake Ontario* 19 Rafting alongside is accepted practice on crowded weekends, although it is good manners to ask permission of the boat you are coming alongside.

b. rafting chain, a chain used to bind logs together into a raft; **rafting distance,** the distance that can be traversed in a raft; **rafting works** (see quot. 1969).
1842 A. LANGTON *Jrnl.* 4 Nov. in *Langton Records* (1904) 319 His errand..was to get a rafting chain. **1904** *Daily Chron.* 29 Jan. 3/3 Unlike Crusoe he has no ship within rafting distance filled with everything he might want. **1931** *Sun* (Baltimore) 20 Mar. 10/6 The Mississippi Logging Company..maintained a boarding house..on the way to the rafting works at West Newton. **1969** L. G. SORDEN *Lumberjack Lingo* 94 *Rafting works,* booming grounds. A place where logs are held.

rafting (rɑ·ftiŋ), *ppl. a.* [f. RAFT *v.*[1] + -ING[2].] Of ice: that rafts (see *RAFT *v.*[1] 5).
1883 HATTON & HARVEY *Newfoundland* III. iv. 311 When they are in danger from 'rafting' ice, or fragments of floes.. the self-sacrificing affection of the mothers leads them to brave all dangers. **1935** *Discovery* Mar. 77/1 A suitable block-and-tackle is essential in order that the boat may be hauled far enough up the shore to be safe from 'rafting' ice. **1966** *Weekend Mag.* (Montreal) 19 Mar. 34/1 Each year.. seals congregate on the rafting ice pressing in around the shores of Canada's Magdalen Islands.

rafwire (ræ·fwəiəɹ). *Aeronaut.* Also **Rafwire, RAFwire, raf-wire.** [f. the initial letters of the *R*oyal *A*ircraft *F*actory + WIRE *sb.*] A kind of wire having a flattened, semi-streamlined cross-section formerly used as bracing wire on aircraft.
1918 W. E. DOMMETT *Dict. Aircraft* 38 *Rafwire,* wires of flattened section, approaching to streamline shape, designed originally at R.A.F. **1920** *Techn. Rep. Advisory Comm. Aeronaut. 1915–16* 15 Recent Laboratory tests have shown that raf-wires of the type developed at the Factory show little or no aerodynamic disadvantage as compared with wires of stream-line section. **1922** *Encycl. Brit.* XXX. 34/2 The elliptical-section wires were called 'Rafwires', to distinguish them when they were standardized. **1933** *Flight* 4 May 412/2 External bracing is by RAFwire. **1933** *Jrnl. R. Aeronaut. Soc.* XXXVII. 788 The 'singing' of a rafwire when yawed in the wind at an angle greater than the stalling angle is an example of this type of oscillation.

rag, *sb.*[1] Add: **I. 1. f.** *pl.* Personal clothing or garments of any kind. Also in *sing.*, a garment, esp. a dress or coat. Cf. *glad rags* s.v. *GLAD *a.* 4 f. *colloq.* (orig. *U.S.*).
1855 *Knickerbocker* XLV. 502 Oh! the robe was of *moire antique*, (a very expensive 'rag'). **1883** 'MARK TWAIN' *Life on Mississippi* iii. 43, I stood up and shook my rags off and jumped into the river. **1903** *N. & Q.* Dec. 513/1 'Raggie' is of course diminutive or fond for 'rag', *i.e.* coat, tunic. I remember my uncle, writing to congratulate me on passing into the R.M. Academy, Woolwich, many years ago, asking me if I was 'going to sport the blue rag or the red one'—R.A. or R.E. **1906** E. DYSON *Fact'ry 'Ands* x. 126 In their secon' best baggin', they're sort iv subdood... Look at ther difference when they get inter ther rags. **1966** 'L. LANE' *ABZ of Scouse* II. 88 *Rags,* any form of clothing. **1974** H. L. FOSTER *Ribbin'* iv. 171 *Rags,* clothing.

g. (*from*) *rags to riches*: used variously to describe a 'fairy-tale' rise from poverty to wealth; esp. as *attrib. phr.*
1947 R. DE TOLEDANO *Frontiers of Jazz* 148 Goodman was the first real rags-to-riches success in the swing-jazz field. **1953** *Gramophone* Dec. 256/2 The Irish flavour is readily apparent in *Begorrah* as sung by Ray Burns... This is great fun, and infinitely preferable to the more commonplace *Rags to Riches* verso. **1954** M. EWER *Heart Untouched* ix. 156 Isn't this a Cinderella story—a rags to riches? **1959** *Times Lit. Suppl.* 13 Nov. 658/2 The story he has to tell is..a classic American rags-to-riches story with nothing lacking. **1965** 'H. CARMICHAEL' *Post Mortem* x. 120 One of those spectacular companies that came up from nowhere. You've heard of them—from rags to riches in five years. **1972** D. LEES *Zodiac* 34 It stands up as a rags to riches yarn. **1977** *Cornish Times* 19 Aug. 9/2 Last week's *Cornish Times* spelt out a success story with the rare theme of rags to riches by sheer hard labour.

2. b. (Further examples.)
1922 E. SITWELL *Façade* 14 Limp in bright crackling rags of laughter. **1924** R. CAMPBELL *Flaming Terrapin* iii. 45 Their spirits shed their gross Rags of despair. **1963** S. CLOETE (*title*) Rags of glory.

c. (Later examples.)
1811 *Lexicon Balatronicum,* s.v. *Rag,* ..Money in general. The cove has no rag; the fellow has no money. **1846** *Swell's Night Guide* 14 The pleasure-seeker may gain admission, if his appearance proclaim that he is in possession of the *rag*—the *tin* to defray the unavoidable demands upon his purse.

d. A familiar name applied to the Army and Navy Club in London. In full *the Rag and Famish* (see quot. 1908[1]). *slang.*
1858 TROLLOPE *Three Clerks* II. i. 5 He delighted in the Rag and Famish, and there spent the most of his time. **1908** NEVILL & JERNINGHAM *Piccadilly to Pall Mall* vi. 235 The familiar name of the 'Rag', by which it is generally known, was invented by Captain William Duff, of the 23rd Fusiliers. .. Coming in to supper late one night, the refreshment obtainable appeared so meagre that he nicknamed the club the 'Rag and Famish'. **1908** 'ONE OF OLD BRIGADE' *London in Sixties* xvii. 224 These touts and store-keepers and bonnet-shop keepers will make the Rag a den of thieves, by Gad. **1941** E. NASH *I liked Life I Lived* iv. 33 Cairnes, who was a most hospitable man, invited me to dine with him once a week at the Rag, while the sales of the book were in full swing... No member of the Army and Navy Club was aware that Cairnes had written the book. **1974** R. McDOUALL *Clubland Cooking* 12 Unlike the clubs on the south side of Pall Mall..the Junior Carlton and the Rag owned their freeholds.

e. Phr. *to knock all to rags*: to knock senseless. *U.S.*
1889 'MARK TWAIN' *Connecticut Yankee* xxxiii. 432 The blow came crashing down and knocked him all to rags.

3. a. (Further examples.) Also, a napkin worn during menstruation, a sanitary towel; esp. in phr. *to have the rag(s) on.*
1782 J. TRUMBULL *M'Fingal* IV. 97 O'er heaps of rags, he waves his wand, All turn to gold at his command. **1811** *Lexicon Balatronicum,* s.v. *Rag,* bank notes. **1816** *Deb. Congress U.S.* 29 Jan. (1854) 775, I say cash, sir, for we, there, have nothing of that circulating medium which the gentleman from Virginia..denominates rags. **1846** *Swell's Night Guide* 129/1, *Rag,* money—I've no rag; meaning, I've no notes. **1859** J. W. COLE *Life & Times C. Kean* I. i. 8 Our old friends of the Dublin gallery, who, in days of yore, never failed to cry, 'Up with the rag!' even before the act-drop, so classically designated, had time to reach the ground. **1906** E. DYSON *Fact'ry 'Ands* xvii. 233 Ther revolvin' arm [of a machine] was bent out, 'n' it got home a left lead 'n' er right cross, 'n' ther rag went in from ther Pelican's corner. **1920** J. FERGUSON *Northern Numbers* 101 The lights are lowered and the 'rag' divides. **1929** A. CONAN DOYLE *Maracot Deep* 200 Has your rag commissioned you to obtain an interview? **1948** *Amer. Speech* XXIII. 249/2 *Riding the rag,* menstruating. **1955** D. W. MAURER in *Publ. Amer. Dial. Soc.* XXIV. 115 That working stiff had over two C's in rag on him. **1961** PARTRIDGE *Dict. Slang* Suppl. 1242/2 *Rags (on), have the,* to be having one's period. **1970** G. GREER *Female Eunuch* 51 Male disgust [for menstruation] expressed in terms like *having the rags on.* **1974** *National Skat & Sheepshead Q.* Mar./Apr. 7 The bills [*sc.* paper money] wear out down here very fast due to the humidity. They all become 'rags' in a short period. **1977** J. I. M. STEWART *Madonna of Astrolabe* i. 27 A fugitive rag put out by one of our junior members. **1978** *Maledicta* II. 50 There were several references to menstruous conditions or activities, found equally commonly in both male and female rest rooms ('Sue Ellen's on the rag' [etc.]).

c. Colloq. phrases. (*a*) Miscellaneous, as *to drop the rag* (U.S.): to give the signal, to give notice; *to take the rag off* (*the bush* or *hedge*) (chiefly U.S.): to excel, to surpass everything or everyone; to take the palm. Also *to chew the rag*: see *CHEW *v.* 3 g. (*b*) Expressing anger, as *to get one's rag out* and varr.: to become or make angry; *to lose one's rag*: to lose one's temper; *on the rag* (U.S.): angry, irritable.
1810 *Norfolk* (Va.) *Gaz.* 19 Sept. 2/3 This 'takes the rag off the bush' so completely, that we suppose we shall hear no more..about the Chesapeake business. **1837** *Davy Crockett's Almanack Wild Sports of West* I. iii. 40, I can take the rag off—frighten the old folks—astonish the natives—and beat the Dutch all to smash. **1868** *Accrington Times* 16 May 5/3 These three elegant flags ull teck th' rag off th' edge, un ull be mich admir'd bi all them ut's i' th' love o' fine arts. **1880** 'MARK TWAIN' *Tramp Abroad* xx. 194 I've got to stay here, till the old man drops the rag and gives the word,——yes, *sir,* right here in this——country I've got to linger till the old man says *Come!* **1897** *Halifax Courier* 12 June, He's getten his rag drawn. **1901** W. N. HARBEN *Westerfelt* 3 That gal certainly takes the rag off'n the bush. **1902** —— *Abner Daniel* 264 You are a jim-dandy, young man... That's all there is about it. You take the rag off the bush. **1914** D. H. LAWRENCE *Prussian Officer* 185 An' that got your rag out, did it? **1927** W. E. COLLINSON *Contemp. Eng.* 116 Anger is expressed by such phrases as.. he got shirty or hairy, he got his rag out, [etc.]. **1938** G. GREENE *Brighton Rock* VII. vii. 329 'I've told you before how I won't stand..' 'You needn't get your rag out,' the Boy said. **1959** I. & P. OPIE *Lore & Lang. Schoolch.* x. 178 They taunt the person [who is easily provoked]:..'Don't lose your bait' ('rag', 'rise', or 'wool'). **1960** L. COOPER *Accomplices* I. vi. 60 Roger was definitely shirty about that. .. He really got his rag out. **1969** *Current Slang* (Univ. S. Dakota) I–II. 65 *On the rag,* in a bad mood.—College males, Arizona. **1975** HILL & THOMAS *Give Little Whistle* x. 95 Allison lost his rag with me over two goals by Leicester's Mike Stringefellow, both of which he considered were offside. **1977** *Rolling Stone* 16 June 31/1 *Time* has Joan Baez on the rag.

6. b. The fibrous pithy part of an orange, lemon, or other citrus fruit.
1895 *U.S. Dept. Agric. Yearbk. 1894* 196 The fruit resulting is usually of poor quality, inclined to be large and rough, with a thick rind and abundant rag.

II. 8. a. *rag-baby* (examples), *-carpet* (examples), *-carpeting, doll* (earlier and later examples), *-rug, -torch, -wick*; *rag-carpeted* adj.
1809 *Deb. Congress U.S.* 20 Jan. (1853) 1165 If they insist upon dressing up, in their own ways, their rag-babies,..it is not for me to interfere. **1900** J. DE F. SHELTON *Salt-Box House* xvii. 143 Dolls were almost as mythical as fairies, but a 'rag-baby' was loved. **1837** *Southern Lit. Messenger* III. 333 There was a snug little bed room..and a comfortable good-sized one for Charlotte, with a neat rag carpet on it. **1904** M. E. WALLER *Wood-Carver of 'Lympus* 72, I have begged Aunt Lize to take up the rag-carpet. **1845** C. M. KIRKLAND *Western Clearings* 185, I led the young gentleman through the shop into the rag-carpeted sitting-room. **1813** *Niles' Weekly Reg.* III. 329/1, 24 yards rag carpeting. **1853** J. RUSKIN *Let.* 17 Nov. in *Wks.* (1904) XII. p. xxxiv, She thought me so wise that anybody might make an idol of me ..but when she got to talk to me, I turned out only a *rag doll* after all. **1972** M. WOODHOUSE *Mama Doll* xiii. 194 She slumped like a rag doll. **1923** E. SITWELL *Bucolic Comedies* 42 The witch's rag-rug takes its flight. **1937** [see *KEWPIE]. **1969** M. HARRIS *Kind of Magic* 30 By the fire stretched a lovely rag rug. **1973** J. THOMSON *Death Cap* xiii. 177 Finch was reminded of his grandmother's bedroom... There had been the same kind of rag rug on the floor; the same marble-topped wash-hand stand. **1894** KIPLING in *To-day* 6 Jan. 5/1 And the doolie-bearers lit the noisome, dripping rag-torches. *a* **1918** G. STUART *40 Yrs. on Frontier* (1925) I. 31 A tin lamp holding about a quart of lard with a rag wick in its spout which, when lighted, would cast a strong light for several yards.

b. *rag-gatherer* (earlier example), *-picking.*
1704 *Visits from Shades* iii. 21 Rag-gatherers, Cynderwomen, and Oyster Wenches wou'd disclaim her Acquaintance. **1931** 'D. STIFF' *Milk & Honey Route* ix. 101 It is not surprising to find the moper turning to rag-picking if the notion comes to him to earn a living. **1966** *National Observer* (U.S.) 5 Dec. 15/3 There are ways to hold rag-picking down. One can, for example, specialize in $1 bills.

c. *rag-and-bone gatherer, man* (examples), *merchant, shop, warehouse*; *rag-and-bottle man, merchant, warehouse.*
1901 B. S. ROWNTREE *Poverty* iii. 35 Rag and bone gatherer. Married. One room. One child. **1904** E. NESBIT *Phoenix & Carpet* xii. 236 An insane millionaire who amused himself by playing at being a rag-and-bone man. **1960** 'H. CARMICHAEL' *Seeds of Hate* xix. 157 Someone had sold them to a rag-and-bone man. **1963** *Times* 6 Mar. 9/3 Four Soviet rag and bone merchants have been sentenced to death in Azerbaijan for heading a gang which robbed the state of hundreds of thousands of roubles. **1895** C. M. YONGE *Long Vacation* xix. 188 Transforming the draperies from the aspect of a rag-and-bone shop to a wonderful quaint and pretty fairy bower. **1939** W. B. YEATS *Last Poems* 31 In the foul rag and bone shop of the heart. **1848** MRS. GASKELL *Mary Barton* I. v. 74 Public-houses, pawnbrokers' shops, rag and bone warehouses, and dirty provision shops. **1904** E. NESBIT *Phœnix & Carpet* xii. 229 It's the rag-and-bottle man's day to-morrow... He will take it away. *a* **1902** S. BUTLER *Way of All Flesh* (1903) lv. 254 A rag and bottle merchant in..the last stage of dropsy. **1852** DICKENS *Bleak Ho.* (1853) v. 35 A shop, over which was written, *Krook, Rag and Bottle Warehouse.*

9. rag-book, a book for children of which the pages are made of untearable cloth; **rag-box,** (*a*) a box in which rags are contained; (*b*) *slang,* the mouth; **rag-chawing, -chewing** *vbl. sbs.*, protracted discussion or argument (cf. *to chew the rag* s.v. *CHEW *v.* 3 g); also *attrib.*; **rag content,** the proportion of rag in paper; freq. *attrib.*; **rag end,** the extreme and untidy end of something; cf. FAG-END 2; **rag frame** *Mining* (see quot. 1964); **rag-front**, in a carnival or circus: a façade or banner made of painted canvas; **rag-head** *N. Amer. slang*, one who wears a turban or cloth about the hair; **rag-lamp** *U.S.*, a lamp in which a rag serves as a wick; **rag running**, whippet-racing; **ragsack-man** *nonce-wd.*, a ragman bearing a sack; **rag-shop** (earlier example); also *fig.*; **rag-store** *U.S.* = *rag-shop*; **ragtop** *U.S. slang*, a convertible car with a soft hood (see also quot. 1971); also *attrib.*; **rag trade** (further examples); now usu. applied to the manufacture and sale of women's garments; freq. in humorous or ironical use; also *attrib.*

1905 *Athenæum* 16 Dec. 833/1 The improvements recently made in the productions called rag-books are strikingly exemplified in *Dog Toby*. **1974** P. DICKINSON *Poison Oracle* iv. 111 He had packed..rag books, fruit, favourite toys. **1801** D. WORDSWORTH *Jrnl.* 12 Nov. (1941) I. 79, I put the rag-boxes into order. **1890** KIPLING in *Scots Observer* 28 June 149/1 Now all you recruities what's drafted to-day, You shut up your rag-box an' 'ark to my lay. **1885** *Santa Fé Weekly New Mexican* 1 Oct. 1/3 After a few minutes rag-chawing a verdict of 'came to his death from unknown causes', is promptly rendered. **1904** 'H. MCHUGH' *I'm from Missouri* v. 66 The news of the proposed joint debate spread like wildfire, and it soon became patent that whoever won the rag-chewing contest would also win the election. **1937** G. FRANKAU *More of Us* xii. 130 Great work Lord Bubbles put in presently Over their teas and pastries and rag-chewing. **1976** PERKOWSKI & STRAL *Joy of CB* viii. 86 In the evening you can set up your rig at home for extended rag-chewing sessions. **1930** *Official Gaz.* (U.S. Patent Office) 7 Oct. 25/1 Rag Content Paper Manufacturers. **1957** J. B. CALKIN *Witham's Mod. Pulp & Paper Making* (ed. 3) ii. 20 Rag papers cover a considerable spread of products from 100 per cent rag to the so-called 'rag content' papers which are made from various percentages of wood and rag fibers. **1967** KARCH & BUBER *Offset Processes* xi. 479 The finer, longer-lasting paper, made from cotton and cloth clippings, is called 'rag content', or lately, 'cotton content' paper... Rag content is usually 25 percent, 50 percent, 75 percent, or 100 percent. **1976** *Cincinnati Enquirer* 16 Sept. A-19/3 The documents and letters are as legible as the handwriting of their authors. The high rag content of the paper has preserved them. **1917** E. POUND *Lustra* 192 And the booths Were scattered align, the rag ends of the fair. **1904** *Eng. Dial. Dict.*, Rag frame. **1920** *Conquest* Nov. 17/1 The stream is dammed and the sludge or slime settles, and is allowed to flow through launders which feed automatically-tilting tables of the most ingenious structure... These tables are called rag frames. **1964** A. NELSON *Dict. Mining* 358 *Rag frame*, a broad, slightly inclined wooden frame for the rough concentration of slimes. **1926** *Variety* 29 Dec. 7/4 The outdoor show game with its 'rag front', 'silver men', [etc.]. **1927** K. NICHOLSON *Barker* 150 *Rag front*, painted canvas banners. **1921** *Dialect Notes* V. 111 *Raghead*, a Hindu; any Asiatic. From the turbanned Asiatics who are common on the campus [of the University of California]. **1970** C. MAJOR *Dict. Afro-Amer. Slang* 96 *Raghead*, black male who wears a scarf tied around his head to protect an expensive hairdo. **1975** *Canadian Mag.* 8 Mar. 6/1 East Indians are called 'rag-heads' if they continue to wear the traditional turban of the Sikh religion. **1889** 'MARK TWAIN' *Connecticut Yankee* xlii. 531 He had re-instituted the ancient rag-lamp. **1893** —— in *Cosmopolitan* Nov. 59/2 The house was shut up tight and the rag lamps lighted. **1927** *Daily Express* 25 May 12 A little more foresight and push..might have made 'rag running' a very popular entertainment. **1922** JOYCE *Ulysses* 429 A sackshouldered ragman bars his path. He steps left, rag-sackman left. **1829** P. EGAN *Boxiana* 2nd Ser. II. 643 'It's the Bank of Ireland,' said an Irish swell, 'to a rag shop.' **1894** G. B. SHAW *Let.* 23 Apr. (1965) I. 427 You have a perfect rag shop of old ideas in your head. **1903** —— *Man & Superman* p. xiii, His profligacy and his dare-devil airs have gone the way of his sword and mandoline into the rag shop of anachronisms and superstitions. **1869** 'MARK TWAIN' *Innoc. Abroad* xvi. 157 Filthy dens on first floors, with rag stores in them (the heaviest business in the Faubourg is the chiffonier's). **1882** Rag store [see *junk store* s.v. *JUNK *sb.*[2] 5]. **1955** *Sun* (Baltimore) 27 Aug. B11/1 Every American manufacturer with a 'ragtop' in his line will be represented. **1971** M. TAK *Truck Talk* 127 *Rag top*, 1. a low-sided trailer with metal bows over the top to support a tarpaulin... 2. an open top van with a tarpaulin covering over the top. **1974** D. WESTHEIMER *Olmec Head* xvii. 235 Get a ragtop trailer. That's one with a fabric cover instead of a solid top. **1976** *Springfield* (Mass.) *Daily News* 22 Apr. 4/3 (*caption*) The last U.S. built convertible, a Cadillac Eldorado, rolls along the assembly at the General Motors' plant in Detroit Wednesday. It ended an era for ragtops that began 74 years ago. **1979** T. GIFFORD *Hollywood Gothic* (1980) ix. 100 Eddie's ragtop had a small tear that let the rain draw a bead on the back of the seat. **1907** *Daily Chron.* 31 Dec. 8/4 They do an enormous business with the 'rag trade'—that is to say, the wholesale drapers, silk mercers, hosiers, and so on. **1938** *Times Lit. Suppl.* 11 June 405/2 The few years which she spent as fashion-goods buyer in what is known to its members as 'the rag trade'. **1957** J. COATES *Ship of Glass* 241, I know that line. It's going to be fashionable... Forgive the digression but I'm in the rag trade. **1967** *Listener* 2 Feb. 168/3 These delicate and puzzling effects..were seized upon with glee by rag-trade designers and window dressers. **1975** R. BUTLER *Where All Girls are Sweeter* i. 2 I'd sold her to a man in the rag-trade.

rag, *sb.*[3] Add: (Earlier and later examples.) Now usu. a programme of satirical revues, frivolous stunts, etc., organized by students to raise money for charities. Also *attrib.*

1864 H. SIDGWICK in A. & E. M. Sidgwick *Henry Sidgwick* (1906) ii. 111 They enjoy beer, tobacco and students' 'rags'. **1885** *Punch* 5 Dec. 273/1 We had a good rag when he was away. **1905** *Westm. Gaz.* 25 Apr. 3/3 It [*sc.* Sheridan's 'Critic'] has been left alone of late except for an occasional 'rag' performance at a charity matinée. **1924** *Glasgow Herald* 26 Feb. 9/7 Liberals played up skilfully in their interrogative zest, and the P.M.G...found the 'rag' more embarrassing than any miners' indiscipline. **1930** J. BUCHAN *Castle Gay* iv. 60, I do not wish to have my name associated with an undergraduate—'rag', I think is the word. **1946** L. P. HARTLEY *Sixth Heaven* iii. 76 He organised one or two rags..of the more painful kind. **1958** *Oxford Mail* 15 Feb. 1/1 A 1902 James and Browne vintage car removed from the Imperial College, South Kensington, London, by students of Southampton University for their 'rag' day. **1974** *Times* 4 Nov. 14/6 The university's Rag Week..[with] the 24-hour piano-playing marathon..and the joke kidnapping of the president of the athletic union.

rag (ræg), *sb.*[5] orig. *U.S.* [Of obscure origin: perh. f. RAGGED *a.*[1] 3; see *RAGTIME.] **1.** A dance or ball; esp. a variety of dance performed to ragtime music. ? *Obs.*

1896 *Dialect Notes* I. 423 *Rag*, dance, ball. 'We can go to *rags*.' **1899** *Musical Rec.* (Boston) 1 Apr. 158/1 The negroes call their clog-dancing, 'ragging', and the dance, a 'rag'. **1914** 'HIGH JINKS, JR.' *Choice Slang* 17 *Rag*, one of the newer gyrations now included under the category of dancing. **1923** *Dialect Notes* V. 218 *Rag*,..dance.

2. A musical composition written in ragtime, a ragtime tune.

1897 W. H. KRELL (*song-title*) The Mississippi rag two-step: the first rag-time two-step ever written. **1897** T. TURPIN (*song-title*) Harlem rag: two step. **1916** *Variety* 25 Aug. 8 Ash..is seen daily on the streets playing rag dance numbers. **1922** T. S. ELIOT *Waste Land* ii. 21 But O O O O that Shakespeherian Rag—It's so elegant So intelligent. **1947** G. SKLAR *Two Worlds J. Truro* iii. 24 They listened to rags and stomps, to fox trots and marches. **1957** G. LASCELLES in S. Traill *Concerning Jazz* 77 Few of the original rags were written, and those which were, had often no bass part added beyond the conventional harmonies. **1977** *New Yorker* 19 Sept. 96/2 She would play some Menotti, Barber, and Gershwin, a piece by Paul Tufts, a Seattle composer, and some Scott Joplin rags.

3. *attrib.* and *Comb.* in sense 'ragtime', as *rag music*, *musician*, *rhythm*; *rag-flavoured* adj.

1959 'F. NEWTON' *Jazz Scene* vi. 103 Rag-flavoured numbers also became part of the staple repertoire of New Orleans jazz. **1934** C. LAMBERT *Music Ho!* II. 95 The *Rag-time*, like the piano *Rag Music*, is an abstract pattern created out of the raw material of certain syncopated devices. **1955** R. DAVIES in J. McCarthy *Jazzbk. 1955* 37 They left the Crescent City..intending to disseminate through the dance halls of Chicago the rag music they had created. **1976** R. SANDERS in D. Villiers *Next Year in Jerusalem* 198 One of the great Negro rag musicians, Ben Horney, a composer and singer. **1923** R. H. MYERS *Mod. Music* 65 Darius Milhaud has sought, by the use of rag-rhythms, to evoke the exotic yet intensely human atmosphere of the Bar and its inhabitants.

rag, var. *RAGA.

rag, *v.*[2] Add: **1. a.** (Earlier example.) Also, to examine or question.

1739 *Proc. Sessions of Peace* June 107/2 On Monday Night Bird and Clark came to their House to ragg (scold) her Grandfather for what he had talk'd of, concerning them. **1908** A. S. M. HUTCHINSON *Once aboard Lugger* I. iv. 47 Not one had ever worked. Each had been 'ragged' on a subject of which he knew absolutely nothing.

b. (Further examples.)

1891 *Spectator* 3 Jan. 3/2 The revellers went round and 'ragged' several men in their rooms. **1956** 'C. BLACKSTOCK' *Dewey Death* vii. 156 You're always ragging me, and I know you think I'm an ass. **1975** *Times* 30 Dec. 4/2 The President is now ragged mercilessly on national television, by talk show hosts, by comics, and in cartoons.

rag (ræg), *v.*[5] orig. *U.S.* [f. *RAG *sb.*[5]] **1.** *intr.* To play, sing, or dance in ragtime. Also const. *it.*

1905 *Dialect Notes* III. 152 *Rag*,..to dance. 'Everybody *rag* as pooty (puti) as you can.' **1923** R. D. PAINE *Comrades of Rolling Ocean* viii. 137 They were dancing on the pavement of the public market or ragging it on the smooth white streets. **1928** F. SCOTT FITZGERALD in *Sat. Even. Post* 29 Sept. 118/3 Oh, listen!.. Do you know how to rag? **1946** B. TREADWELL *Big Bk. Swing* 125/1 *Rag*, to play the blues and jazz. **1971** C. C. ADAMS *Boontling* 237 *Rag*, to dance in 'ragtime' form, considered indecent in valley dance halls in the Boontling era.

2. *trans.* To convert (a melody, etc.) into ragtime; to play ragtime music on (an instrument).

1917 *Lit. Digest* 25 Aug. 28/2 The jazz bands take popular tunes and rag them to death to make jazz. **1922** H. L. FOSTER *Adventures Trop. Tramp* v. 47 The camp victrola was broken and..I was the only man in camp that could rag the piano. **1949** R. BLESH *Shining Trumpets* viii. 181 The violin played the melody straight while Bolden ragged it. **1956** G. P. KURATH in A. Dundes *Mother Wit* (1973) 108/1 The slaves ragged and syncopated their clog dances. **1960** [see *ANTI-[1] 2 c].

raga (rā·gă). Also **raag, rag** (rāg). [a. Skr. *rāga*, colour, passion, melody; Hindi *rāg*, a mode in music, music.] **1.** In Indian music, a melodic type which provides a framework for improvised melodies; such an improvised melody. Also *fig.*

1788 W. JONES in *Asiatick Researches* I. 264 The beautiful allegories of the Hindus in their system of musical modes, which they call Rágás, or Passions, and suppose to be Genii or Demigods. **1807** *Asiatick Researches* IX. 447 The Indian Rágas and Ráginís are fixed respectively to particular seasons of the year and times of the night or day. **1891** C. R. DAY *Music & Mus. Instr. S. India & Deccan* ii. 23 Mode and râga are..perfectly distinct from each other. *Ibid.* 24 In almost all these works a somewhat similar classification of the râgs and râginis has been adopted. **1924** E. M. FORSTER *Passage to India* vii. 80 The song is composed in a raga appropriate to the present hour, which is the evening. **1934** C. LAMBERT *Music Ho!* v. 289 Although the scales of folk music may vary from the simple pentatonic scales of the Hebridean to the complicated ragas of the Hindu, the same outlook on tonality is implied. **1944** W. APEL *Harvard Dict. Mus.* 332/2 The ragas fall under the classification of melody-types... A raga is a much more specialized tonal frame than a mode; it prescribes..not only a scale and a center-tone (*amsa*), but also the avoidance of certain tones. **1958** *Times* 30 May 16/5 The Indian *raga* provides the structure for an improvisatory kind of music which..approaches the articulation of speech. **1962** I. HOLST *Tune* iv. 53 It is impossible to memorize fragments of a raga during a performance. **1967** 'LA MERI' *Spanish Dancing* (ed. 2) v. 67 The *Rag* (roughly, melody) has a definite mood throughout. **1969** *Sunday Standard* (Bombay) 3 Aug. (Magazine Section) p. iv/6 Instead of outlining the form of his 'raag' in sinuous, unbroken contours he seems to have preferred segment sketching. **1970** W. BURROUGHS *Speed* vii. 151 On stage, a couple of young guys played a mediocre raga. **1971** J. MANDELKAU *Buttons* vii. 81 'The Truth is the Only Law!' It's sewn on the inside shoulder of William's jacket and has become my daily prayer. My holy raga. **1972** P. HOLROYDE *Indian Music* 277 *Ragas* developed as an arrangement of intervals so that seven notes are in a certain relationship with each other and thus define a melody. **1975** *Guardian Weekly* 25 Jan. 21/3 The score by Alan Lloyd can best be described as Schubertian raga, a non-stop prelude (vamp till ready) to the verbal fugues on the stage. **1977** Y. MENUHIN *Unfinished Journey* xii. 258 A *raga* is a scale-cum-melody, a given sequence of notes whose interrelationships are already determined.

2. *attrib.* and *Comb.*, as *raga form*, *quality*, *system*; **raga rock**, rock music characterized by improvisation, etc., in the style of a raga.

1968 *Jrnl. Mus. Acad. Madras* XXXIX. 7 The classical music of India has thus for its aim the delineation of the Raga-forms. **1972** *Last Whole Earth Catalog* (Portola Inst.) 3/1 Fuller's lectures have a raga quality of rich nonlinear endless improvisation full of convergent surprises. **1960** *Melody Maker* 30 Apr. 12/1 America's..Byrds come up with a new formula! Raga-rock, based on Eastern musical forms. **1967** P. WELLES *Babyhip* (1968) xv. 108 'Leave me alone,' she said, 'you're some kind of sex fiend. And anyway, I'm looking for raga rock.' She turned the station to another. **1957** A. BAKE in *New Oxf. Hist. Mus.* I. iv. 213 In the classical *râga* system such a new creation usually bears the name of its parents, as, for instance, *Megh-Malhâr*.

‖**ragazzo** (raga·tso). Pl. **ragazzi**; fem. **ragazza.** [a. It. *ragazzo* boy, *ragazza* girl.] In Italy: a youngster; a lad or a young girl.

1862 BORROW *Wild Wales* I. xxiv. 283 When I was a ragazzo I knew many from the Lake of Como, who dressed much like yourself. **1897** A. T. RITCHIE *Let.* Mar. (1924) xi. 239 Two nice little ragazzi showed us the way. **1906** W. DE MORGAN *Joseph Vance* xliv. 404 In a day or two Beppino was bored, and..I noticed that he was keeping at a respectful distance from every ragazza. **1957** 'N. CULOTTA' *They're Weird Mob* (1958) ii. 24 'What please is a sheila?' 'A sheila? A bint. A ragazza.' **1975** *Publishers Weekly* 27 Jan. 230/1 A novel concerning a *ragazza* of the streets grown to movie star.

rag-bag, *sb.* Add: **a.** (Earlier and later examples.)

1820 M. WILMOT *Let.* 7 Aug. (1935) 76 Well, and well and well, what have I got to say in my *ragbag* of a brain? I have a hundred odds and ends. **1850** DICKENS *Dav. Copp.* xlviii. 490 Sheets in the rag-bag. **1853** C. BRONTË *Villette* I. ix. 174 Your mind..seems..chaotic as a rag-bag. **1917** E. POUND *Lustra* 181 And that the 'modern world' Needs such a rag-bag to stuff all its thought in. **1964** A. SEXTON *Sel. Poems* 57, I hid in the kitchen under the ragbag.

b. (Further examples.) Also *spec.* a sloppily-dressed woman, a slattern. *slang.*

1888 KIPLING *Under Deodars* 70 If I were a man I would perish sooner than be seen with that rag-bag. **1937** PARTRIDGE *Dict. Slang* 683/2 *Rag-bag*,..a slattern. **1973** 'W. HAGGARD' *Old Masters* vi. 75 Lord Tokenhouse was no sort of economist, indeed he despised the whole ragbag wholeheartedly. **1976** P. CAVE *High Flying Birds* iii. 31 She was neither attractive nor plain; not a raver or a ragbag. **1980** *Jrnl. R. Soc. Arts* Feb. 149/2 The design courses are in danger by their very existence of joining Art, Music and Technical Drawing in the ragbag of the system.

2. *attrib.*

1907 *Daily Chron.* 13 Mar. 8/4 The association of wealth and rag-bag poverty in London is one of her most remarkable features. **1948** *Life* 13 Sept. 152/2 In the old days..some of them little 'rag-bags' shows used to carry a lot of grift. **1953** S. KAUFFMANN *Philanderer* vi. 104 The living-room, with its rag-bag summer cottage furnishings. **1968** *Listener* 31 Oct. 583/2 There is certain to be some inherent weakness in the direction of generalisation and 'rag-bag' proliferation of studies that I deplore. **1980** *Jrnl. R. Soc. Arts* Feb. 154/1 That is what I call the ragbag attitude.

rage, *sb.* Add: **7. a.** Also const. *after.*

1790 *Loiterer* 2 Jan. 4 This prevailing rage after knowledge.

b. (Further examples.)

1802 *Monthly Mag.* 1 Oct. 253/1 The *rage* for the dotting style of engraving..is on the decline. **1811** BYRON *Let.* 15 Dec. (1973) II. 149 Tomorrow, I dine with Rogers & am to hear Colridge, who is a kind of rage at present. **1834** LYTTON *Last Days of Pompeii* I. I. 173 Sylla is said to have transported to Italy the worship of the Egyptian Isis. It soon became 'the rage'—and was peculiarly in vogue with the Roman ladies. **1861** K. STONE *Jrnl.* 28 Aug. in *Brokenburn* (1955) 48 Plaiting palmetto for baskets has been the rage for several days. **1881** [see COLLOQUIALISM 2]. **1940** GRAVES & HODGE *Long Week-End* iii. 38 After the war the new fantastic development of Jazz music and the steps that went with it, became, in the contemporary phrase, 'all the rage'. **1951** [see *DEAD *a.* 30].

rageless, *a.* For *Obs. rare*—[1] read *rare* and add later example.

1948 R. GRAVES *Coll. Poems* 218 My self reversed, my rage-less part, a slimy yellowish cone.

Hence **ra·gelessness,** absence of rage or rages.

1904 E. F. BENSON *Challoners* v. 101 London, tired with its spinster ragelessness, rose at them as trout rise in the days of May fly.

rager. a. (Later example.)

1925 G. MURRAY tr. *Aeschylus' Eumenides* 4 The ragers sleep: the Virgins without love.

ragesome (rēi·dʒsəm), *a. U.S. rare.* [f. RAGE *sb.* + -SOME.] Rageful, angry.

1913 G. STRATTON-PORTER *Laddie* xvii. 580 He can be awful ragesome when he's excited.

‖ **raggare** (ra·garə). Pl. **-(s).** [Sw., f. *ragga* to pick up (girls).] In Sweden: a member of a gang of youths who cruise about in cars; a street-tough, a teddy-boy.

1964 *Pix* 25 Jan. 45/3 By midnight even most of the 'raggare'—Sweden's beatniks—have disappeared from the streets. **1971** *Daily Tel.* 2 Aug. 4/8 About 300 'raggares'—Sweden's motorised teddy boys—clashed with 90 police in..Stockholm yesterday. **1977** *Time* 25 July 10/1 To their bitterest enemies, a group of restless young toughs known as the Raggare, the Assyrians are despised 'black-skulls', to be attacked with chains and clubs.

ragged, *a.*[1] Add: **II. 6.** Also of mood or condition: tired, run-down. Colloq. phr. *to run* (one) *ragged* (orig. *U.S.*): to exhaust or debilitate (a person).

1925 *New Yorker* 5 Sept. 10/3 This eighteen-year-old youngster ran Bill Johnston, the Californian, ragged. **1951** W. STEVENS *Let.* 26 Mar. (1967) 712 This is simply typical of the sort of thing that runs one ragged. **1969** M. PUGH *Last Place Left* xxix. 213 Sorry, sir, I'm pretty ragged. Is Miss Drummond okay? **1970** A. DRAPER *Swansong for Rare Bird* v. 35 We really ran the teachers ragged. **1977** P. HILL *Liars* (1978) iii. 36 All four of them were now feeling mentally ragged.

7. *ragged-edged, -looking* (earlier example) adjs.; **ragged edge** *U.S. slang*: in phr. *on* (also *in*) *the ragged edge*, on the extreme edge or verge; also *transf.*, in a state of distress or resourcelessness; **ragged r** (see quots.).

1885 *N.Y. Mercury* 10 Jan. 4/7 It seems fair to assume that father, daughter and her child sailed yesterday for Paris, leaving poor Tom on the ragged edge. **1889** 'MARK TWAIN' *Connecticut Yankee* xvi. 196 He was always on the ragged edge of apprehension. **1892**—— *Amer. Claimant* ii. 28 It was away out in the ragged edge of Washington and had once been somebody's country place. **1935** A. J. POLLOCK *Underworld Speaks* 84/1 *On the ragged edge*, slight chance to make good; down and out. **1916** 'BOYD CABLE' *Action Front* 164 The face of one house was marked by a huge splash, with solid centre and a ragged-edged outline of radiating jerky rays. **1833** F. WITTS *Diary* 8 Apr. (1978) 91 One tract of common over which we passed is called Coalpitheath, a ragged-looking spot. **1755** J. SMITH *Printer's Gram.* iv. 117 Black letter..has two different r's, one of which is called the ragged r [ꝛ], and is particularly used after letters that round off behind. **1969** H. CARTER *View of Early Typogr.* iii. 62 The ragged r—the r that followed letters that had once been round.

ragged (rægd), *ppl. a.*[2] [f. RAG *v.*[2]] That has suffered ragging, teasing, or annoyance.

1903 *Westm. Gaz.* 11 May 6/2 The 'ragged' officer was allowed leave of absence and has not yet returned to duty.

ragged (rægd), *ppl. a.*[3] [f. *RAG *v.*[5]] Of music: that has been converted to ragtime.

1956 G. P. KURATH in A. F. C. Wallace *Men & Cultures* (1960) 155 They represent the following steps:..Two-step (ragged). **1958** C. WILFORD in P. Gammond *Decca Bk. Jazz* ii. 40 Ragtime lives on in jazz, for all jazz is based on ragtime, though it is true some parts are more ragged than others.

raggedy, *a.* Substitute for entry (s.v. RAGGED *a.*[1]):

raggedy (ræ·gėdi), *a.* Chiefly *U.S.* and *dial.* Also 9– **raggety; raggity.** [f. RAGGED *a.*[1] + -Y[1].] **1.** Of a ragged form or appearance.

a. Of persons. Cf. RAGGED *a.*[1] 6.

1890 J. W. RILEY in *Century Mag.* Dec. 318/2 Oh, the Raggedy Man! He works fer Pa; An' he's the goodest man ever you saw! **1894** [in Dict.]. **1939** J. STEINBECK *Grapes of Wrath* xxiv. 462 A raggedy kid with no shoes. **1959** *Encounter* Dec. 17/2 The covey of raggety small boys. **1960** C. DAY LEWIS *Buried Day* iii 38 The bridge..was lined..with raggedy men. **1975** *New Yorker* 1 Dec. 48/2 A lady's..raggedy kids lined up by the track where they'd put pennies.

b. Of clothing. Cf. RAGGED *a.*[1] 5 a.

1893 *Trans. Devonshire Assoc.Adv. Sci., Lit., & Art* XXV. 201 My smock's a-got cruel raggety, I sim. **1929** D. RUNYON in *Hearst's Internat.* Oct. 62/2 Mostly she is wearing raggedy clothes and busted shoes. **1967** H. PORTER in *Coast to Coast 1965–6* 171 Underwear got more raggedy. **1978** J. CARROLL *Mortal Friends* III. v. 322 It serves me right for asking what raggedy clothing you'd flung off.

2. Of a rough, irregular, or straggling form. Cf. RAGGED *a.*[1] 2. **a.** *gen.*

1896 'MARK TWAIN' in *Harper's Mag.* Aug. 358/1 Raggedy white patch between the shoulders..looked like somebody had hit him with a snow-ball. **1899** [in Dict.]. **1938** L. MUMFORD *Whither Honolulu?* v. 16 Cities throughout America have been..over-extending themselves in raggedy fragments. **1955** J. MASTERS *Coromandel!* i. 23 Voy sucked his raggedy moustache.

b. Of branches, plants, etc.

1912 J. STEPHENS *Crock of Gold* v. 40 There was a raggedy blackberry hedge all round the field. **1927** D. H. LAWRENCE *Mornings in Mexico* 12 Like rather raggedy green buds climbing to the sun.

3. Of music or rhythm: irregular, uneven, broken. Cf. RAGGED *a.*[1] 3 b.

1949 R. BLESH *Shining Trumpets* viii. 186 The tempo is buoyant, the beat is alive, and the rhythm is very *raggedy.* **1975** *New Yorker* 19 May 113/2 A casual encounter between a boy and a girl who compete to the piled-up, off-center rhythms of many raggedy dances.

4. *Comb.*, as **Raggedy Andy** *U.S.*, a rag-doll, the male counterpart of Raggedy Ann (see next); **Raggedy Ann** orig. *U.S.*, a rag-doll with short, mop-like, red hair; also *attrib.*; **raggedy-ass(ed)** *a. U.S. slang* (orig. *Mil.*) [cf. Ass, vulgar and dial. var. ARSE in Dict. and Suppl.], of persons: inexperienced, raw; also *transf.*

1920 J. GRUELLE *Raggedy Andy Stories* 2 Gran'ma had told Daddy..that at the time Raggedy Ann was made, a neighbor lady had made a boy doll, Raggedy Andy. **1974** *News & Reporter* (Chester, S. Carolina) 22 Apr. 5-A/1 He was honored with a family party at his home with guests enjoying Raggedy Andy Cake. **1918** J. GRUELLE *Raggedy Ann Stories* Pref., To the millions of children and grown-ups who have loved a Rag Doll, I dedicate these stories of Raggedy Ann. **1957** M. B. PICKEN *Fashion Dict.* 124/2 *Raggedy Ann costume*, costume taken from child's story book about a stuffed doll. Consists of bright colored patched skirt, patched apron, simple white blouse, white socks and black shoes. Usually worn with ragged woolen wig. **1966** J. S. COX *Illustr. Dict. Hairdressing* 124/2 *Raggedy Ann Bob*, a short hair style for women similar to the wind-blown bob. **1967** *Southerly* XXVII. 209 Katrina..brushed the short, raggedy-ann hair until it shone. **1970** *New Yorker* 14 Nov. 50/3 She removed the clothes from a Raggedy Ann doll and stuck a pin..into the center. **1976** *Times* 8 July 12/1 (*caption*) Raggity Ann patched up trousers. **1977** *Redbook* Mar. 81/2 Kim wanted a Raggedy Ann cake. **1930** T. FREDENBURGH *Soldiers March* vii. 50 The Raggedy Ass Cadets are out today. **1956** B. HOLIDAY *Lady sings Blues* (1973) vi. 57 I'd have to travel five hundred to six hundred miles on a hot or cold raggedy-ass Blue Goose bus. **1967** E. LIEBOW in T. Kochman *Rappin' & Stylin' Out* (1972) 406 A nice woman does not dress in 'raggedy-ass clothes'. **1969** J. A. MCPHERSON *Hue & Cry* 58 Who taught you the moves when you were just a raggedy-ass waiter? **1929** in J. J. Niles et al. *Songs My Mother never taught Me* 182 The raggedy assed cadets are on parade. **1971** R. FLANAGAN *Maggot* 252 Respect what man, you raggedy-assed little fuck?

ragger[2]. [f. RAG *v.*[2] + -ER[1].] One who rags or teases; *spec.* a participant in a student rag.

1903 *Speaker* 7 Feb. 451/1 There is much to be said in favour of the 'raggers'. Mere 'ragging' as distinguished from ..persistent and brutal bullying..never yet did a youngster any harm. **1905** *Westm. Gaz.* 15 May 7/3 One of the raggers received a bullet in the mouth, and is seriously injured. **1909** H. G. WELLS *Ann Veronica* xi. 220 Ann Veronica decided that 'hoydenish ragger' was the only phrase to express her. She was always breaking rules. **1930** *Daily Express* 6 Nov. 1/2 Guys were then thrown on the blazing piles amid the wild shrieks of the 'raggers'.

raggie (ræ·gi). *Mil.* Also **raggy.** [f. RAG *sb.*[1] + -IE.] † **1.** A mess jacket. *Obs.*

1843 F. J. BELLEW *Mem. Griffin* I. ix. 126 As for myself, in my scarlet raggie, brimstone facings,..and regulation sword, in my own opinion, I looked quite the god of war. **1903** *N. & Q.* 26 Dec. 512/2 In India, in the early part of last century,..the scarlet 'shell' jacket, or mess jacket—almost the only uniform then worn in that country—was invariably called a 'raggie', and this not jocularly or as slang, but seriously and as a matter of course.

2. *Naval slang.* (See quot. 1912.)

1912 'AURORA' *Jock Scott* xiv. 170 A 'raggy' is a friend whom you know so intimately that you feel you could with confidence keep your brass-rags in the same bag as his. **1914** 'BARTIMEUS' *Naval Occasions* xiv. 111 'If I don't get no letter this mail—so 'elp me I stops me 'arf pay,' he confided grimly to a 'Raggie'. **1916** 'TAFFRAIL' *Carry On!* 27 Men who are friendly with each other are 'raggies', because they have the free run of each others' polishing paste and rags; but if their friendship terminates they are said to have 'parted brass-rags'. **1946** J. IRVING *Royal Navalese* 143 *Raggie*, a very close friend.

ragging, *vbl. sb.*[2] (Further examples.) Also *attrib.*

1888 E. DOWSON *Let.* Nov. (1967) 19 After a good deal of ragging with Chitty J. two days ago, the affair was settled. **1920** *Chambers's Jrnl.* 1 May 337/1 An ugly ragging mood was astir. **1932** *Daily Tel.* 8 Oct. 12/4 Ragging in the army, such as we have at home (this was said just after one of the so-called 'ragging scandals' in the Guards) would be impossible here. **1942** *R.A.F. Jrnl.* 2 May 31, I miss the comradeship, the ragging, the talks in Mess.

ragging, *vbl. sb.*[3] Add: **2.** (Earlier example.)

1860 C. TOMLINSON *Useful Arts & Manuf.* 2nd Ser. *Dressing ores* 10 That portion [of a dredging] occupying the bottom of the sieve, called ragging, which is also in a marketable state.

3. = STRAGGLING *vbl. sb.*[2]

1850 [see STRAGGLING *vbl. sb.*[2]].

ra·gging, *vbl. sb.*[4] orig. *U.S.* [f. *RAG *v.*[5]] The act or practice of playing, singing, or dancing in ragtime.

1899 [see *RAG *sb.*[5] 1]. **1913** *Collier's Mag.* 15 Feb. 6/2 The worst of these dance halls..are habitually frequented by people of the fashionable and so-called decent class, who go..for the purpose of joining in the 'ragging'. **1914** 'HIGH JINKS JR.' *Choice Slang* 17 *Ragging*, the act of doing the 'Rag'. **1936** *Harper's Mag.* 3 Apr. 570/2 'Jamming', 'cat-time', 'swing', 'riffing', 'getting off', 'going to town', 'ragging', 'gut-bucketing',..are names for the *hot* performance, which is the heart and soul of jazz. **1958** *Life* (Internat. ed.) 13 Oct. 96/2 The rhythm was called ragtime (after a Negro clog dance sometimes called 'ragging').

raggle, *sb.*[1] (Earlier and later examples.)

1835 in *Sc. Nat. Dict.* (1968) s.v. *Raggle* v.[1], n.[1] **1956** *Scotsman* 22 Sept. 9/1, I am..taken aback by the nonchalance with which these..men stroll about among the chimney pots..uttering deep thoughts about raggles and sarking, flashing and skews and Raffit verges.

raggle-taggle (ræ·g'l,tæ:g'l), *a.* and *sb.* Also **wraggle-taggle.** [App. fanciful var. RAG-TAG.]

A. *adj.* Of a group of persons: ragged, rambling, straggling; disreputable, unorganized (freq. used in allusion to the song referred to in quot. 1904). Hence of a person and in extended use of appearance, etc.

1904 in Sharp & Marson *Folk Songs from Somerset* 1st Ser. 19 What care I for my house and my land? What care I for my money, O? What care I for my new wedded lord? I'm off with the wraggle taggle gipsies, O! **1913** C. MACKENZIE *Sinister St.* I. i. ii. 29 He made up his mind..that it was better to be a raggle-taggle wanderer than anything else. **1923** J. BUCHAN *Midwinter* i. 34 My companions are the moor-men and..the raggle-taggle gypsies. **1933** W. STARKIE *Raggle-Taggle* ii. 7 It was no easy task to convince my family of my sanity in wishing to follow the raggle-taggle Gypsies. **1936** C. DAY LEWIS *Friendly Tree* 132 Like the lady who ran away with the wraggle-taggle gipsies. **1942** C. BARRETT *On Wallaby* vi. 122 It was a Paddy's market day and a raggle-taggle crowd had gathered to bargain shrewdly and noisily. **1970** N. BAWDEN *Birds on Trees* v. 83 It's not easy for someone of my generation to accept this raggle-taggle look, we had a bit more self-respect. **1977** O. JACKS *Autumn Heroes* viii. 118 How would you rate your raggle-taggle band of poorly armed warriors?

B. *sb.* **a.** A wanderer, a rover. **b.** A straggling, unorganized, or disreputable collection of persons.

1933 W. STARKIE (*title*) Raggle-taggle. **1958** *Times* 19 Mar. 7/4 President Nasser's permanent Afro-Asian guests—that Cairo raggle-taggle ranging from the permanent representatives of the Algerian National Liberation Front on the one hand to the office of the Deputy Imam of Oman on the other. **1972** 'H. CALVIN' *Take Two Popes* ii. 18 The Curia..considered *all* non-Italians as an unfortunate raggle-taggle.

raggling. Add: Also 5 **raggalyne,** 7– **raglin(e, ragling. a.** *Build.* Substitute for def. = RAGGLE *sb.*[1]

1500 in *Sc. Nat. Dict.* (1968) s.v. *Raggle* v.[1], n.[1] **1683** [in Dict. s.v. RAGGLE *v.*]. **1704–1898** in *Sc. Nat. Dict.* (1968) s.v. *Raggle* v.[1], n.[1] **1929** H. MARWICK *Orkney Norn* 137/1 *Raglins*, the top of the side walls of a house, the space between top of wall and the slates. **1964** J. S. SCOTT *Dict. Building* 255 *Raglet* or *raggle* or *raglin*, a thin groove, in stone often dovetailed, cut in stone or in a mortar joint of brickwork to receive the end of a lead flashing, which is fixed by burning in or wedging.

b. *Mining.* (See quot. 1886.)

1839 URE *Dict. Arts* 985 There is a simple mode of conducting air from the pit bottom to the forehead of the mine, by cutting a ragglin, or trumpeting, as it is termed, in the side of the gallery. **1886** J. BARROWMAN *Gloss. Scotch Mining Terms* 53 *Raggling*, a channel cut in the side of a mine and covered with boarding to serve as an airway.

raggy (ræ·gi), *a.*[2] *slang.* [f. RAG *v.*[2] + -Y[1].] Annoyed; irritated.

1900 G. SWIFT *Somerley* 21 He was jolly raggy about us taking his old gee.

raggy (ræ·gi), *a.*[3] orig. *U.S.* [f. *RAG *sb.*[5] + -Y[1].] Of music: pertaining to or resembling ragtime; characterized by ragtime.

1933 *Fortune* Aug. 92/1 At sixteen he began to play raggy music for Washington society with Louis Thomas' orchestra. **1944** W. RUSSELL in M. T. Williams *Art of Jazz* (1960) iv. 36 His feeling for a joyful, raggy, and stompy rhythm. **1952** B. ULANOV *Hist. Jazz in Amer.* (1958) xv. 181 Duke wove tricky, raggy, endlessly inventive variations around the Miley theme. **1958** in P. Gammond *Decca Bk. Jazz* xv. 185 Arthur Schutt, whose raggy piano sounded on many a Mole or Nichols session. **1972** *Jazz & Blues* Dec. 30/2 Billie's very raggy piano.

raggy, var. *RAGGIE.

raging, *ppl. a.* Add: **1. d.** Highly successful, tremendous; also as a mere intensifier. *raging favourite*, 'hot' favourite. *colloq.*

1886 H. BAUMANN *Londinismen* 151/2 A raging favourite. **1889** 'MARK TWAIN' *Connecticut Yankee* xxxi. 398 He..was doing a raging business. **1894** —— in *St. Nicholas* Mar. 400/2 A raging lot of sand. **1977** *Hongkong Standard* 12 Apr. 12/2 Raging favourite Orange Peel was pushed to the limit by Glynn Parry.

‖ **ragini** (rā·ginī). [a. Skr. *rāgiṇī*, lit. coloured, impassioned.] In Indian music, a modification of a raga.

1788 W. JONES in *Asiatick Res.* I. 264 The Nymphs of Musick are the thirty Ráginís or Female Passions. **1807, 1891** [see *RAGA]. **1944** W. APEL *Harvard Dict. Mus.* 333/1 The theoretical system..knows 6 (main) ragas and 30 *raginis*, each of which are duplicated according to the sa-grama or the ma-grama scheme (perfect or augmented fourths). **1948** B. BOSE *Acre of Green Grass* 41 In classical Indian music..words are no more than pleasing containers of the *ragini*, or the melodic pattern. **1954** *Grove's Dict. Mus.* (ed. 5) IV. 457/1 Seven were chosen in the end..to serve as basic modes or pure *jâtis*. From these seven *jâtis* the whole elaborate structure of *râgas* and *râginis* was eventually developed. **1968** *Indian Mus. Jrnl.* V. 33 He minutely studied the nature of various *rāga-s* and *rāginī-s*, to find out their suitability for expressing different emotions.

Raglan. Add: Now usu. with small initial. **a.** (Earlier and later examples.)

1863 'G. HAMILTON' *Gala-Days* 27 A thousand considerations, in the shape of raglans..induce you to modify your view. **1926** *Daily Colonist* (Victoria, B.C.) 5 Jan. 2/6 (Advt.), Overcoats... Some with half belts, full belters and raglan-back styles. **1948** M. LASKI *Tory Heaven* xii. 166 A thick raglan overcoat over his dinner jacket. **1976** 'J. Ross' *I know what it's like to Die* ii. 11 His thick raglan overcoat.

b. *attrib.* Applied to the shoulder or sleeve of any (esp. knitted) garment designed after the style of a raglan. Also *absol.*, a garment with such sleeves.

1906 *Daily Chron.* 4 Oct. 3/4 As for the Raglan shoulders they are only to be worn with sporting clothes. **1930** M. STORY *Individuality & Clothes* II. ii. 204 Raglan and kimono sleeves tend to increase the breadth of the figure. **1957** M. B. PICKEN *Fashion Dict.* 269/2 *Raglan sleeve*, sleeve with long armhole line extending to neckline. **1966** *Illustr. London News* 26 Feb. 5 (Advt.), The knitwear is made of Shetland wool and is fully fashioned with raglan sleeves. **1969** *Sears Catal.* Spring/Summer 26 *Cardigan sweater* interlock knit of Orlon acrylic... Rib knit cuffs on the long sleeves, raglan shoulders. **1978** *Detroit Free Press* 2 Apr. 5D/1 One reason for the great popularity of 'knit-from-the-neck-down' raglans is the fact that there are no sleeves to set in. **1980** *Times* 11 Nov. 10/5, I liked..the reversible coats with raglan shoulders.

c. *Comb.*, as *raglan-coated*, *-sleeved* adjs.

1975 J. SYMONS *Three Pipe Problem* xviii. 207 Twenty yards ahead..stalked the raglan-coated figure of Sheridan Haynes. **1974** S. MARCUS *Minding Store* (1975) iv. 81 The first raglan-sleeved fur coat.

ragman[1]. Add: **3. a.** (Later examples.)

1966 F. SHAW et al. *Lern Yerself Scouse* 24 *De ragman*, the old-clothes man. **1976** *New Yorker* 23 Feb. 39/2 The street down which will sometimes come, on his rattling wagon, a ragman.

4. [See *RAG *sb.*[5]] A musician who plays ragtime music.

1938 J. R. MORTON in *Downbeat* Sept. 4/1 Blues players who could play nothing else... What we call 'ragmen' in New Orleans. **1950** BLESH & JANIS *They all played Ragtime* (1958) vi. 108 Following 1907–8 there comes a second generation of ragmen. **1970** C. MAJOR *Dict. Afro-Amer. Slang* 96 *Ragmen*, jazzmen who play that type of music.

Ragnarök (ræ·gnărök). Also 8 **Ragnarockur; Ragnarok, Ragnarökr.** [ON. *ragna rök*, f. *ragna* gen. of *regin* the gods + *rök* destined end (a conventional usage in this phrase of *rök* the course of events from origin to end, their causes and consequences); properly as above, but the form *Ragna rökr* (*rökr* twilight, a more readily comprehensible substitute for the archaic *rök*) occurs in the prose Edda, and the mod. sense is freq. founded upon this (see Cleasby-Vigfusson ed. 2).] In Scandinavian mythology, the destruction of the gods or the twilight of the gods; *spec.* the last battle of this world, in which gods and men will be defeated by monsters and the sun will grow dark. Also *fig.*

1770 T. PERCY tr. *Mallet's Northern Antiquities* I. vi. 119 The end of the world, that is,..the time of that universal desolation of nature which was to be followed by a new creation, and what they called *Ragnarockur*, or the Twilight of the Gods. **1866** *Chambers's Encycl.* 525/2 This terrible age of destruction, the Ragnarök, or twilight of the gods, will be marked by a three years' winter of hard frost. **1887** A. LANG in *Contemp. Rev.* Nov. 693 If the battle between the crocodile of Realism and the catawampus of Romance is to be fought out to the bitter end—why, in that Ragnarôk, I am on the side of the catawampus. **1899** A. H. YAPP *Cuckoo* III. 178 The ragnarok of the cuckoos—the last band of the migrating males. **1933** A. THIRKELL *Hign Rising* xi. 199 Zeus dethrones Chronos..Ragnarok swallows up the Gods. **1953** G. TURVILLE-PETRE *Origins Icelandic Lit.* i. 15 The giant..predicts the *Ragnarǫk* (Fall of the Gods) and the manner of Óðinn's death. *Ibid.* ii. 57 The treacherous Loki was bound in chains, but he will break them when the gods' Doomsday (*Ragnarǫk*) draws near. **1965** H. M. SMYSER in Bessinger & Creed *Medieval & Linguistic Stud.* 110 It is not the place where Odin's *einherjar* fight daily as they await Ragnarøkr. **1978** *Islands* (N.Z.) Aug. 86 Ragnarök and Loki's frames Lie curing in the dust.

rag-tag. Add: **B.** Passing into *adj.* Of form or appearance: ragged, raggle-taggle; disreputable; disorderly, unorganized, straggling. **a.** Of persons, etc.

1883, 1884 [see sense 1 a in Dict.]. **1969** *Telegraph* (Brisbane) 19 Aug. 19/4 In unison a ragtag band of motorcyclists drank a toast. **1978** S. BRILL *Teamsters* ix. 322 These were by and large a ragtag group of overaged ne'er-do-wells.

b. Of things.

1922 BLUNDEN *Shepherd* (ed. 2) 30 When on the green the rag-tag game had stopd. **1969** *Jrnl. Amer. Chem. Soc.* XCI. facing p. 4946 (Advt.), Such rag-tag, sometimes illegible copies probably stay in your files..permanently. **1977** *Rolling Stone* 5 May 11/1 The audience was evenly divided between under-18s in ragtag street wear and those first-generation rock fans now moving into Sisley jeans affluence.

rag-time. Substitute for entry:

ragtime (ræ·gtaim). orig. *U.S.* Also **rag-time.** [Prob. f. *RAG *sb.*[5] + TIME *sb.*] **1. a.** A musical rhythm characterized by a syncopated melodic line and regularly-accented accompaniment, evolved among American Negro musicians in the 1890s; hence, music (esp. for the banjo and piano) of this character, the immediate precursor of jazz.

1897 W. H. KRELL *Mississippi Rag* (title-page of sheet-music), The first rag-time two-step ever written. **1898** *Étude* Oct. 285/3 'Rag time' is a term applied to the peculiar, broken, rhythmic features of the popular 'coon song'... Unfortunately, the words to which it is allied are usually decidedly vulgar, so that its present great favor is somewhat to be deplored. **1899** *Musical Rec.* (Boston) 158/1, I feel safe in predicting that rag-time has come to stay. **1900** *Musical Courier* 23 May 20/2 'Rag-time' is a rhythm which is the most characteristic feature of what may be called American negro music. **1906** 'O. HENRY' *Four Million* 238 They sing 'Home Sweet Home' in rag-time. **1916** A. HUXLEY *Let.* 7 Aug. (1969) 109, I have been sleeping out on the roof..spending most of the night in conversation or in singing folk-songs and rag-time to the stars. **1934** C. LAMBERT *Music Ho!* III. 206 Jazz, or to be pedantically accurate, 'ragtime',..has suddenly achieved the status of a 'school'. **1938** *Sun* (Baltimore) 6 Sept. 8/7 Under their ministrations, the simplest ragtime becomes jazz. **1956** B. EDWARDS in S. Traill *Play that Music* 59 Ragtime, to give it its contemporary title [in 1920], was absolute anathema to both my parents. **1957** G. LASCELLES in S. Traill *Concerning Jazz* 76 In the late nineteenth century there started a music which was a rather modern development of the old dance rhythms such as the schottische and polka... This development was later to be known as 'ragtime', and was essentially piano music. **1968** *Blues Unlimited* Nov. 23 Ragtime one probably loves or loathes. **1976** *New Yorker* 8 Mar. 32/3 He started to play, and before long he was lost in some wildly effervescent ragtime.

† **b.** A piece of music in rag-time; = *RAG *sb.*[5] 2. *Obs.*

1914 G. B. SHAW *Misalliance* p. cviii, If they [*sc.* our young people] had learnt what can be done with syncopation from Beethoven's third Leonora overture, they would enjoy the ragtimes all the more. **1916** *Oxford Song Bk.* p. iii, An authority has just informed me that 'rag-times are "back numbers" now'.

2. a. *attrib.* and *Comb.*, as *ragtime accompaniment, band, melody, music, party, rage, record, saloon, singer, song, sound, tune, wedding.*

1901 Ragtime accompaniment [in Dict.]. **1911** I. BERLIN (*song-title*) Alexander's Ragtime Band. **1949** R. BLESH *Shining Trumpets* vii. 156 Buddy Bolden's Ragtime Band of 1893, generally considered the first jazz band. **1906** *Westm. Gaz.* 23 Apr. 7/2 He is amusing the crowd with ragtime melodies. **1921** R. D. PAINE *Comrades of Rolling Ocean* v. 75 Through an open hatch rose the rag-time melodies of a piano. **1897** ADE *Pink Marsh* 159 He told of his belief that the angels in heaven played 'rag-time' music. **1977** *Monitor* (McAllen, Texas) 9 Jan. 5C/3 Tichenor..says *ragtime music* peaked in the 1920s and died in the Depression. **1960** *Times* 29 Sept. 16/6 She pushes him downstairs during a ragtime-party. **1900** *Musical Courier* 23 May 20/1 (*heading*) The rag-time rage. **1906** TAYLOR & GIBSON *Extra Dry* 71 Putting a ragtime record in the graphophone he pulls the throttle wide open. **1903** *Outing* Aug. 552/1 He has as many eyes for the ragtime saloon. **1917** E. WALLACE *Kate plus Ten* (1930) v. 74 A peer of the realm and a ragtime singer. **1914** Ragtime song [see *high kick* s.v. *HIGH *a.* 21]. **1927** *Jrnl. Abnormal & Social Psychol.* XXII. 19 The earliest ragtime songs, like Topsy, 'jes' grew'. **1974** *Times* 27 Apr. 9/8 We've ended up with a ragtime sound you might even have heard from the piano accompanying the silent movies. **1913** KIPLING *Diversity of Creatures* (1917) 282 The boys and girls at the piano played the rag-time tunes of their own land. **1922** F. SCOTT FITZGERALD *Beautiful & Damned* II. i. 131 Kept telling me she wished this was a ragtime wedding.

b. *attrib.*, passing into *adj.* Ragged; irregular, inferior, disorderly; disreputable, mean. *slang.*

1919 H. CRANE *Let.* 17 June (1965) 20 Your remarks 'about the ladies' really hurt me with a kind of ragtime vulgarity. **1926** F. M. FORD *Man could stand Up* ii. 119 A Hun up against a Tommie looked like a Holbein *lansknecht* fighting a music-hall turn. It made you feel that you were indeed a rag-time army. *c* **1926** 'MIXER' *Transport Workers' Song Bk.* 47 Note the constant drop in wages..Endorsed by every rag-time press That the master-class command. **1929** *Papers Mich. Acad. Sci., Arts & Lett.* X. 317/2 *Ragtime Army*, the Australasian forces. **1940** GRAVES & HODGE *Long Week-End* ii. 26 The topic of 'this rag-time f—g peace' succeeded that of 'this bloody f—g war'. *Ibid.* iii. 38 The more extravagant 'rag-time' dances had not been socially approved. 'Rag-time' was an adjective of reproach; a rag-time regiment was a disorderly and untrustworthy one. **1948** V. PALMER *Golconda* ii. 14 But what if some really big concern swallowed up the three ragtime companies and planned to open up the whole mountain? **1974** P. WRIGHT *Lang. Brit. Industry* xiv. 142 Hated shifts in that [electrical engineering] industry are the *rag-time* or *spare-shift*, one necessary to make up the required number of hours for the week.

Hence **ra·gtimer,** one who plays ragtime; **ra·gtim(e)y** *a.*, suggestive of ragtime; **ra·gtiming** *a.*

1912 G. FRANKAU *One of Us* x. 92 Where the Rat Mort's rag-timing Ethiope Dins in one's ears. **1915** D. O. BARNETT *Let.* 7 Jan. 37 Been making out forms of times. Feel rather ragtimy. **1927** *Daily Tel.* 1 Nov. 9/3 Most nimble of rag-timers at the piano. **1950** BLESH & JANIS *They all played Ragtime* (1958) i. 26 Under Joplin he quickly became an adept ragtimer and was soon playing at dances in and around Sedalia. **1952** B. ULANOV *Hist. Jazz in Amer.* (1958) xxii. 306 They played their ragtimey work..with a finish and polish. **1974** *Country Life* 7 Nov. 1360/1 The ragtime music chosen..was the least..heard of Scott Joplin, supplemented by less well-known ragtimers such as..Joseph Lamb.

Ragusan (răgū·zăn), *sb.* and *a.* Also † **Ragusian. A.** *sb.* **a.** An inhabitant of Ragusa, now Dubrovnik, on the Adriatic coast of Yugoslavia. **b.** An extinct dialect of Dalmatian, spoken formerly by inhabitants of Ragusa.

1652 HEYLIN *Cosmogr.* II. 197 Languste, environed about with very high Mountains, in which are the Ragusians Farms. **1905** *Westm. Gaz.* 29 Apr. 4/1 The advent of Napoleon I. early in the nineteenth century deprived Ragusans for ever of their freedom. **1933** [see *DALMATIAN *a.* and *sb.* 2]. **1967** D. S. PARLETT *Short Dict. Lang.* 38 Ragusan extinct since beginning C17.

B. *adj.* Of or pertaining to Ragusa.

1788 GIBBON *Decl. & F.* V. vi. 613 The Apulian and Ragusian vessels fled to the shore. **1799** R. SMELT *Let.* 6 Dec. in B. Ward *Dawn Catholic Revival* (1909) II. xxxi. 220 We sailed from Palermo on Saturday night, November ye 2nd: altogether seventeen sail, Imperial, Sicilian, Ragusian and American. **1932** *Times Lit. Suppl.* 14 Jan. 27/1 If all the Ragusan men knew Italian, most of the ladies to whom their love poems were dedicated spoke only Slovinski. **1971** *Textile Hist.* II. 10 In 1420 the Ragusan government arranged for a colony of traders from the Italian textile town of Prato to live in Ragusa.

rag-wheel. 1. (Earlier and later examples.)

1812 *Niles' Reg.* II. 393/2 A rag wheel [of a mill machine] of three feet diameter is kept in complete motion. **1848** *Rep. Comm. Patents 1847* (U.S.) 79 The feeding is usually effected by a band taking into a ratchet, or rag wheel. **1873** J. M. BAILEY *Life in Danbury* 9 He employed a carpenter from a place twenty miles distant to make a new rag-wheel.

ragworm. Substitute for def.: a polychæte worm belonging to the family Nereidæ, esp. *Nereis diversicolor*, found in sand or under stones and often used as bait for fish. (Earlier and later examples.)

1865 J. C. WILCOCKS *Sea-Fisherman* 99 The larger Rag Worms, are found by digging in stoney ground. **1906** *Daily Chron.* 6 Jan. 8/6 An enormous specimen of the king ragworm has been found by a bait-digger at Southend-on-Sea. **1928** RUSSELL & YONGE *Seas* 34 It [*sc. Nereis diversicolor*] is frequently used as a bait, being known as 'rag-worm' in many parts. **1967** *Daily Tel.* 21 Oct. 14/6 There were other ways of catching bass than with ragworm or sandeels. **1978** B. GLEDHILL *Cod Fishing* ii. 58 The ragworm likes hard ground usually.

rah, *int.* and *sb.* Add: Also **ra.** (Earlier and later examples.)

1870 D. J. KIRWAN *Palace & Hovel* xxiv. 372 The 'Rah, 'Rah, 'Rah, of Harvard pierces the air...'Oxford has just got into her careless, easy swing. **1887** *Harper's Mag.* Feb. 395/1 The junior class filed into the green enclosure amidst the 'rahs of their friends. **1889** 'MARK TWAIN' *Connecticut Yankee* xxxiii. 421 'Rah for protection—to Sheol with free-trade! **1905** *N.Y. Even. Post* 29 June, Harvard almost immediately increased her stroke, and the way their cut-water slid along called forth the nine long 'rahs again and again. **1917** R. FROST *Let.* 3 Dec. (1972) 20 Rah rah rah for some other college than Wellesley. **1924** H. T. LOWE-PORTER tr. *Mann's Buddenbrooks* II. VII. iv. 24 A voice..shouts suddenly: 'Heine Seehas is 'lected—'rah for Heine Seehas!' **1942** ADE *Let.* 1 Feb. (1973) 227 We didnt play basket-ball or foot ball [at school in the 'seventies and eighties'] and we never learned to stand up on our hind legs and let out a rah-rah. **1972** 'E. LATHEN' *Murder without Icing* (1973) iv. 41 'Way to go, Billy!' 'Rah! Rah! Billy Siragusa!' **1977** *Lancashire Life* Mar. 56/1 Ra-ra-ra! Give a cheer from the sidelines for Accrington, the town that is instilling new life into American baseball.

‖ **rahat lokum** (rāhat lǫku·m). Also **rahat lakoum, lahkoum, lakuhm,** etc. [a. Turk. *rahat lokum*, ad. Arab. *rāḥat al-ḥulqūm* throat's ease.] Turkish delight. Also (occas.) *ellipt.* as *rahat*. Cf. *LOCOUM.

1856 R. F. BURTON *Personal Narr. Pilgrimage to El-Medinah* III. 362 Squares of Rahah, a comfiture highly prized in these regions, because it comes from Constantinople. **1861** *Punch* 12 Jan. 12/1 Rahat lahkoum, or lumps of delight! **1894** [see *DELIGHT *sb.* 4]. **1900** *Confectioners'*

Union Handbk. 167 Butter-Scotch, nougat, rahat lakuhm. *Ibid.* 169 Hawes, J., & Son... Rahat Lakoum and water mould fancies. **1907** *Yesterdays' Shopping* (1969) 32/1 Rahat La Koum or Turkish Delight. **1931** A. J. Cronin *Hatter's Castle* I. vii. 126 They come off to the ship in boats at Port Said and sell very good rahat-lakoum which is an excellent sweet. **1931** *Discovery* Nov. 359/2 Today the Turks here [on the island of Ada Kaleh] live by some gardening and fruit cultivation, a little cigar manufacture, the preparation of rahat ('Turkish Delight') and mild catering for the few individuals who visit the island. **1935** M. Morphy *Recipes of All Nations* 767 The Turks are extremely fond of sweetmeats..and among the most popular is *rahat el halkum*. Make a thick syrup..adding.. lemon juice..starch..almonds, pistachio nuts..hazel nuts ..cut into squares. **1945** C. S. Forester *Commodore* xviii. 198 He had eaten Westphalian ham and Italian beccaficoes and Turkish rahat lakoum. **1960** *Times* 24 Oct. (Financial Rev.) p. xiv/6 The sweetmeat was called Rahatlokum, but today it is better known as Turkish delight. **1963** *Punch* 20 Nov. 748/2, I..went for coffee and rahat lakoum. **1968** C. Roden *Bk. Middle Eastern Food* xv. 295 *Rahat Lokum*, Turkish Delight. This little sweet epitomizes luxury, pleasure and leisure. **1970** [see *locoum].

rah·ing, *vbl. sb.* = Hurrahing *vbl. sb.*

1904 *Daily Chron.* 25 July 7/7 There was not nearly so much 'rahing' and flag-waving as in 1899.

rah rah (rā rā), *sb.* and *a. slang* (orig. *U.S.*). Also **rah rah rah, ra ra.** [Reduplication of Rah *int.*] **A.** *sb.* A shout of support or encouragement, as for a college team: see Rah *int.* and *sb.* in Dict. and Suppl. **B.** *adj.* with hyphens. Of or pertaining to college, collegiate; (of behaviour, etc.) characteristic of college students; marked by the generation of enthusiasm or excitement, as in cheer-leading, etc. *U.S.*

1911 [see *cut-up *sb.* 1 b]. **1914** S. Lewis *Our Mr. Wrenn* iii. 41 Bunches of rah-rah boys wanting to cross..to England. **1924** *Public Opinion* 15 Feb. 152/1 When father was a rah-rah boy and wore those comedy clothes. **1945** L. Shelly *Jive Talk Dict.* 31/2 *Rah rah drapes*, collegiate clothing. **1948** *Landfall* II. 312 Of course, it was all eyewash —rah-rah publicity if you like. **1959** *Economist* 27 June 1151/1 If there is an October election there will be time only for a two-day ra-ra conference before going into battle. **1960** I. Cross *Backward Sex* iii. 72 The team and three busloads of their ra-ra supporters arrived about midday. **1970** *People* (Austral.) 25 Mar. 24/3 The possible solution to the growing world-wide problem of football game disorder comes clad in a delightfully brief skirt and twirls a baton. In America she is known as a 'Rah-Rah girl', in Australia as a Drum Majorette. **1972** *Sat. Rev.* (U.S.) 24 June 18/2 People..are real rah-rah, knocking on doors and asking you to come to parties. **1974** *Sunday Sun* (Brisbane) 18 Aug. 5/4 The rah-rah teams, Brothers, University and GPS have won 28 of the past 30 grand finals. **1976** *National Observer* (U.S.) 3 July 8/2 'In spite of all the rah-rah rhetoric about recycling's merits, a large market share eludes recycling,' says M. J. Mighdoll, executive vice president.

Hence **rah-rah·ing** *ppl. a.*, **rah-rah·ism.**

1892 *Outing* Oct. 37/1 He no longer felt stage-fright surrounded by the 'rah-'rahing mob'. **1930** *Chicago Daily Maroon* 9 Dec. 4/1 Students engage in rah-rahism because it gives them a certain simple amount of enjoyment.

Rai (rai), *sb.* and *a.* [Native name.] **A.** *sb.* **a.** A member of a tribe of eastern Nepal; this people collectively. **b.** The language of the Rai people. **B.** *adj.* Of or pertaining to the people or their language.

1906 E. Vansittart *Gurkhās* xi. 128 In the history of Nēpāl it is stated that the Rāis conquered the Nēpāl Valley. *Ibid.* 129 It would be merely a repetition..to enter into details regarding Rāi customs. **1928** Northey & Morris *Gurkhas* xv. 216 Khambus and Yakhas..are now both regarded as Rais. They both speak the Rai language. **1957** F. Tuker *Gorkha* v. 37 For every Rai a different language, the Gurkhas say. **1962** D. Forbes *Heart of Nepal* xi. 119 Beyond..lies the territory of the tribes..the Magars and Gurungs to the west, Rais and Limbus to the east. **1970** L. Caplan *Land & Social Change in E. Nepal* v. 96 The land was repossessed..and re-pledged to a Rai landholder. **1974** *Encycl. Brit. Macropædia* XII. 954/1 The languages of the north and east belong predominantly to the Tibeto-Burman family. These include Magar, Gurung, Rai, [etc.]. **1975** C. von Fürer-Haimendorf *Himalayan Traders* iii. 63 Grain which the Sherpas brought from the Rai country.

raid, *sb.* Add: **I. 1. c.** = *air-raid. Also *attrib.* and *Comb.*

1908 H. G. Wells *War in Air* xi. 354 The Asiatics endeavoured to establish..fortified centres from which flying-machine raids could be made. **1916** Mrs. Belloc Lowndes *Let.* 2 Nov. (1971) 77 The Raid night was *horrid*... Every moment we expected to hear the bombs drop close by or *on* us, for the machines sounded overhead. **1917** R. Fry *Let.* 6 Oct. (1972) II. 417 There was a scare of a raid on Monday while I was hanging at Heal's. We were all shepherded down into the basement. **1939** H. Nicolson *Diary* 3 Sept. (1966) 422 We learn afterwards that the whole raid-warning was a mistake. **1940** [see *auxiliary *a.* 1 b]. **1942** 'N. Shute' *Pied Piper* i. 9, I thought of ringing her up, but it's not a very good thing to clutter up the lines during a raid. **1953** C. Day Lewis *Italian Visit* ii. 31 Recall how flyers from a raid returning, Lightened of one death, were elected for another. **1974** *Listener* 7 Feb. 176/3 My father..had the idea that we were being shelled from the river—no one thought anything about a raid from above. *Ibid.* 177/1 By the autumn of 1915, there had been 19 zeppelin raids... They were raids intended to bring Britain to her knees.

2. c. Also, = *police raid* s.v. *police *sb.* 6.

1892 A. W. Pinero *Magistrate* III. 109 *Lugg*..(*Reading*) 'Raid on a West End Hotel. At an early hour this morning —' *Wormington*. Yes..a case of assault upon the police. *a* **1922** T. S. Eliot *Waste Land Drafts* (1971) 5 We've only had a raid last week, I've been warned twice. **1924** J. Buchan *Three Hostages* xv. 215 It would never do for him to be caught in a raid on a dance-club. **1973** W. McCarthy *Detail* iii. 264 We're making a raid and will need your help. Can you have your cars and sheriffs' cars block all the roads from Palm Springs?

d. A forceful or insistent attempt at making a person or group provide something. Const. *on, upon.*

1931 *Economist* 10 Jan. 58/1 Although he is willing to ask for a further $100,000,000 to $150,000,000 for constructional and other public works, he is averse to spectacular raids on the Treasury for relief purposes. **1940** T. S. Eliot *East Coker* v. 14 Each venture Is a new beginning, a raid on the inarticulate With shabby equipment always deteriorating In the general mess of imprecision of feeling. **1967** *Listener* 23 Mar. 404/2 Here..we have..one who has..devoted long years..to a series of attempts, raids upon the articulate, at making available to the English tradition this least accessible of German poets.

e. *dawn raid* (Stock Exchange slang), a swift operation effected early in trading whereby a stockbroker obtains for his client a markedly increased shareholding in a company (freq. preparatory to a take-over) by clandestine buying from other substantial shareholders.

1980 *Times* 28 May 17/6 'Dawn raids', in which a stock-market raider suddenly buys a substantial stake in a company and possibly denies non-professional shareholders the opportunity to sell at a price above that in the market, were causing a 'great deal of anxiety'. *Ibid.* 22 July 17 De Beers went into the market on the morning of February 12 and bought another 11·6 per cent in a 'dawn raid'. **1981** *Bookseller* 21 Feb. 568/3 Following his 'dawn raid' last July, which gained him 29·4 per cent of BPC, Robert Maxwell.. clearly plans to secure and consolidate his control of the group.

raid, *v.* **2.** (Further examples.)

1894 [see *raider a]. **1902** R. Machray *Night Side of London* xi. 173 Such dens have been raided by the police out of existence. **1908** H. G. Wells *War in Air* xi. 351 The Germans were..already raiding London and Paris when the advance fleets from the Asiatic air-parks..were reported. **1930** L. G. D. Acland *Early Canterbury Runs* 1st Ser. vi. 138 A cowboy of his brought a disastrous career to an end by raiding the pantry. **1940** C. Milburn *Diary* 1 July (1979) 49 It is a few days since the Channel Islands were raided. **1953** K. Tennant *Joyful Condemned* ii. 12 This place..is.. never raided... The Vice Squad are always in and out of the place two doors down—but us—we never seem to have them. **1970** *Daily Tel.* 2 June 1/7 The Israeli Air Force yesterday raided Egyptian military positions near Port Said, killing five soldiers and wounding eight.

raider. Add: **a.** (Later examples.) Also *transf.*

1894 'Mark Twain' in *Century Mag.* XLVII. 776/2 It's perfectly plain that the thief took advantage of the reception ..to raid the vacant houses... It's the same old raider. **1976** *Daily Record* (Glasgow) 4 Dec. 26/1 Seldom do we find Irish raiders at the Market Rasen track, but trainer Moore has sent two over in a bid for a winning double. **1979** *Austral. Financial Rev.* 7 Aug. 1/1 (*caption*) Raider [*sc.* a stock-exchange speculator] hits Ansett.

b. An aircraft on a bombing operation. Hence phr. *raiders passed* (or *past*), the 'all clear' signal given by sirens, etc., after an air-raid.

1908 H. G. Wells *War in Air* viii. 248 He is now in the act of bombarding the chief manufacturing city..by means of three raider airships. **1917** 'Contact' *Airman's Outings* II. iii. 258 Certainly they do not include speculation about the men who man the raiders. **1940** *New Statesman* 19 Oct. 372/1 The 'Raiders Passed' went and the tens of thousands of East Londoners poured out of the shelters. **1941** *Ann. Reg.* *1940* 69 The damage inflicted by the raiders was little less serious. **1942** *R.A.F. Jrnl.* 13 June 27 When the 'raiders past' had sounded..we emerged, coughing, from our subterranean dens. **1943** G. Greene *Ministry of Fear* I. i. 22 Three flares came sailing..down... Yet another raider came up from the south-east. **1966** A. Powell *Soldier's Art* ii. 158 'That one didn't take long.'..'Another tip-and-run raider,' said Pilgrim.

raiding, *ppl. a.* (s.v. Raid *v.* in Dict.). Add: *raiding party*, a small military group taking part in an organized foray into enemy territory, esp. in order to seize prisoners or supplies.

1865 R. H. Kellogg *Life & Death in Rebel Prisons* iii. 97 All communications were interrupted by our '*raiding parties*'. **1885** *Harper's Mag.* Mar. 611/1 Washington detailed soldiers to guard them from British raiding parties. **1892** M. A. Jackson *Life & Lett. Gen. Jackson* xxiii. 462 The raiding-parties of the enemy were operating all through the intervening country. **1914** G. Bell *Let.* 21 Jan. (1927) I. xiii. 327 They had spied us as we passed under the Thlaithuwât and, taking us for a raiding party, had followed us to see where we were going. **1918** E. A. Mackintosh *War* iv. 126 The raiding party dispersed each to a dug-out to feed at other people's expense. **1923** Kipling *Irish Guards in Gt. War* I. 220 Raiding-parties dove in and out of the front lines. **1931** *Times Lit. Suppl.* 16 Apr. 300/2 When he saw a German raiding-party approaching he forgot in his excitement to take off his safety-catch. **1977** B. Lucas tr. *C. De Foucauld's Lett. from Desert* vii. 140 He was killed on 13 December..by a raiding party of thirty horsemen who then disappeared.

‖**raie ultime** (rę ültīm). *Spectroscopy.* [Fr. (A. de Gramont 1907, in *Compt. Rend.* CXLIV. 1101), f. *raie* line + *ultime* ultimate, last.] An emission line in the spectrum of an element which is the last (or one of the last) to remain detectable as the concentration of that element is decreased.

1922 W. F. Meggers et al. in *Sci. Papers U.S. Bureau of Standards* XVIII. 239 The raies ultimes are the most sensitive spectral lines of an element. **1923** F. Twyman *Wave-length Tables for Spectrum Anal.* 79 It is in the ultra-violet that the 'Raies Ultimes' almost always lie. **1937** C. Candler *Atomic Spectra* II. xvii. 120 As the proportion of calcium in the powder is diminished step by step, the weaker lines successively disappear until finally only one is left; this is known as the *raie ultime*. **1948** G. R. Harrison et al. *Pract. Spectroscopy* xv. 429 The *raie ultime* is the last line of an element to disappear as the quantity of the element burned in a sample is decreased to the vanishing point. **1962** Walker & Straw *Spectroscopy* I. i. 94 The identification of the persistent (the *raies ultimes*) lines proves without doubt the presence of the corresponding element.

rail, *sb.*[2] Add: **1. e.** In various (mainly *U.S.*) phrases: *to split a rail*, to split timber for rails; *to ride a rail* (see quot. 1836); *to ride* (someone) *on a rail*, to punish someone by carrying him about astride a rail to be mocked; *as thin* (or *lean*) *as a rail*.

1714 J. Hempstead *Diary* in *Coll. New London Hist. Soc.* (1901) I. 38, I was at home al day spliting Railes & holing Posts. **1820** *Niles' Reg.* XVIII. 256/1 At 97 he went into the woods and split 100 chesnut rails in less than a day. **1907** *St. Nicholas* Oct. 1078/1 You never split a rail in your life.

1834 *New England Mag.* VII. 455 The mill-men resolved to bestow public honors on Dominicus Pike, only hesitating whether to tar and feather him, ride him on a rail, or refresh him with an ablution at the town-pump. **1836** T. Power *Impressions of Amer.* I. 180 Here I enjoyed my first lesson in..riding a rail;.. The term is derived from a fence-rail being occasionally used to supply the place of a broken thoroughbrace, by which all these stages are hung. **1853** 'Mark Twain' in *Hannibal* (Missouri) *Jrnl.* 23 May 3/1 The gentleman ought to be ducked, ridden on a rail, tarred and feathered. **1900** *Congress. Rec.* 5 Feb. 1521/2 Up in Maine.. they mobbed two preachers, tarred and feathered them, and rode them on a rail because they preached the doctrine of Jesus Christ.

1872 'Mark Twain' *Roughing It* xv. 125 You'll marry a combination of calico and consumption that's as thin as a rail. **1927** W. E. Collinson *Contemp. Eng.* 117 Here I will insert a few current comparisons which are in frequent colloquial use:. as thin as a lath or rake or rail. **1934** 'J. S. Strange' *For Hangman* xvi. 183 He was a bright looking boy of about sixteen..and thin as a rail. **1939** *Amer. Speech* XIV. 261 A skinny person [in Indiana] is 'thin as a rail'. **1946** W. S. Maugham *Then & Now* viii. 39 Machiavelli, himself as lean as a rail, did not like fat men. **1967** G. Jackson *Let.* 30 Sept. in *Soledad Brother* (1971) 131, I am getting thin as a rail, feel all right, however.

2. f. The fence or railings forming the boundary of a racecourse. Hence phr. *on the rails*, beside the rails, on the track nearest the rails. Also *fig.*

1928 Galsworthy *Swan Song* II. iii. 122 On the rails they were almost opposite the winning post. **1930** *Times* 24 Mar. 4/2 Rubicon II and War Mist were running side by side with Porthaon, the last-named being on the rails. **1931** *Daily Express* 21 Sept. 15/4 Smirke followed the Wootton tradition and secured the rails. **1931** T. H. Dey *Leaves from Bookmaker's Bk.* ii. 34 He achieved a great success amongst the 'swells', who formed the bulk of his clientèle 'on the rails' at the principal race meetings. **1951** 'J. Tey' *Daughter of Time* vii. 89 It's as reliable as a bookie's tips would be. He's on the wrong side of the rails. **1962** D. Francis *Dead Cert* xiii. 144 The bookmakers on the rails—those..who stand along the railing between Tattersall's and the Club enclosures,..send out weekly accounts. **1975** H. Carvic *Odds on Miss Seeton* (1976) vii. 87 Stay here till the jockeys are up, then..get close up to the rails so you can see properly. **1977** *Irish Press* 29 Sept. 13/4 She is drawn on the rails, and on her immediate right is Sprightly Peg.

g. *Surfing.* (See quot. 1962.) Also **rail turn** (see quot. 1969).

1962 T. Masters *Surfing made Easy* 65 *Rails*, the edge of the surfboard. **1965** *N.Z. Listener* 17 Dec. 5/2 You crouch down, grab a rail (side of board) and get shot like a catapult. **1968** W. Warwick *Surfriding in N.Z.* 3/2 He also screwed beading around the outside rail to prevent him sliding off the board. **1969** *Observer* 3 Aug. 35/1 He may execute the spectacular 'rail turn', during which the whole of one edge or rail is buried in the face of the wave.

4. a. (Later examples.) Usu. *pl.*

1932 G. Greene *Stamboul Train* I. i. 3 A wilderness of rails and points. **1954** J. Masters *Bhowani Junction* I. i. 17 The coal train..ran off the rails. **1976** *Illustr. London News* Nov. 53/4 One gets a much greater thrill from speeding on rails at 300 kmh than from flying in Concorde.

b. (Earlier and further examples.) Also opp., *on the rails.*

1848 G. E. Jewsbury *Let.* Mar. (1892) 242, I was very worried, and I felt as if the least thing would throw me off the rails. **1883** E. W. Hamilton *Diary* 1 Aug. (1972) II. 467 'To be on the rails', as Mr. G. said this morning, 'and to be off the rails are two different things'. **1916** J. Buchan *Greenmantle* i. 5 He told me just how and why and when Turkey had left the rails. **1935** B. Malinowski *Coral Gardens* II. vi. v. 235 Where Durkheim 'goes off the rails', so to speak, is in reducing his sound conception to a very narrow formula of the direct emotional experience of the crowd and of the influences of crowd phenomena on the individual. **1938** E. M. Forster in *Nation* 16 July 68/1 They [*sc.* citizens] are obliged to be born separately and to die separately and, owing to these unavoidable termini, will always be running off the totalitarian rails. **1953** K. AMIS *Lucky Jim* xxii. 228 He resolved not to run off the rails again. He cleared his throat, found his place, and went on in a clipped tone. **1954** T. S. ELIOT *Confidential Clerk* II. 63, I make decisions on the spur of the moment, But you'd never take a leap in the dark; You'd keep me on the rails. **1955** G. GREENE *Quiet American* II. ii. 132 All my conversations with Pyle seemed to take grotesque directions. Was it because of his sincerity that they so ran off the customary rails? **1971** *Daily Tel.* 20 Oct. 12/7 They are proud, stubborn and steady—even if dad appears to have gone off the rails. **1975** M. BABSON *There must be Some Mistake* xvi. 128 Would John have gone off the rails like this if she had been paying enough attention?

c. *N. Amer.* A railwayman.

1938 L. M. BEEBE *High Iron* 223/2 *Rail*, railroad man. **1960** [see *biscuit-toss* s.v. *BISCUIT 3 b]. **1974** *Maclean's Mag.* Jan. 16/2 She spent too much time..listening to a bunch of young 'rails' repeat lies handed down over the years.

d. *Electronics.* A conductor which is maintained at a fixed potential and to which other parts of a circuit are connected.

1960 in H. CARTER *Dict. Electronics* 255. **1965** *Wireless World* Aug. 399 The common rail for input signals is the positive line, while the common connection to the thyristor is the negative line. **1977** *Gramophone* Feb. 1344/1 Gramophone inputs are to feedback pairs on a 25-volt rail giving a reasonable overload margin. **1979** *Personal Computer World* Nov. 3 (Advt.), 30 Amp, 8v power supply, 5 Amps on ±16v rails (all rails are separately fused).

5. a. (Further examples.) *spec.* **British Rail**, the name of the national railway of Britain.

1843 *Ainsworth's Mag.* III. 361 My lord and lady start, per rail, To London for the Season. **1848** J. J. RUSKIN *Let.* 17 Mar. in M. Lutyens *Ruskins & Grays* (1972) xi. 98 For Godsake be done with Rails and Shares—or you will not have a Business, for who will confide in Railway people I am not clear. **1858** QUEEN VICTORIA *Let.* 8 May in R. Fulford *Dearest Child* (1964) 103 We went by rail, nice, quick! **1867** in 'Mark Twain' *Innoc. Abr.* (1869) i. 21 They can by rail go on to Florence. **1884** E. W. HAMILTON *Diary* 5 Aug. (1972) II. 666 His solution of the financial difficulty is that we should guarantee 'the Rails', the slang phrase for the Preference Debt to which the Railroads are assigned. **1892** B. POTTER *Jrnl.* 30 July (1966) 243 The Volunteers broke up and several companies went off by rail. **1926** *Daily Colonist* (Victoria, B.C.) 15 July 17/1 The advance in rails has slowed up temporarily, although a strong investment demand is reported for several of the high grade issues. **1935** *Economist* 27 July 191/1 Rails and utilities..have hardly participated at all in this week's upward movement. **1965** *Evening Standard* 4 Jan. 9/3 (*heading*) Now it's British Rail —Beeching's last new look for trains, stations, men. *Ibid.*, A new image for British Railways—'British Rail'—is being launched tonight when Dr. Beeching opens an exhibition showing the new symbols, train liveries and uniforms at the Design Centre in the Haymarket. 'There's been a lot of criticism about the new name,..' Mr. George Williams, the railways Director of Industrial Design, said at a preview of the exhibition today. 'Personally I think that passengers..will soon find themselves saying British Rail.' **1965** *Observer* 31 Jan. 12/8 British Rail officials admit there appears to be an injustice. **1976** *Illustr. London News* Nov. 52/4 Fruit and vegetables now tend to go increasingly by road..where a few years ago they travelled by rail. *Ibid.* 53/3 The productivity a head has more than quadrupled since 1945, whereas..for British Rail [it has] only doubled. **1981** *Daily Tel.* 3 Mar. 18/2 Lucky evening travellers tonight..will each be presented with a miniature of British Rail sherry.

c. Usu. *pl.* A railway station.

1854 *Poultry Chron.* I. 117/2 The middle and humble classes..are oft times virtually prohibited from attending if bad weather; sets in more especially if out of the way of rails. **1939** H. HODGE *Cab, Sir?* xv. 222 The 'Rails' are railway stations, as distinct from the Underground.

6. a. *rail-under* (poet. adv.); **rail-bird** *U.S.*, (*b*) one who watches from the rails or sidelines (*lit.* and *fig.*); **rail-cut**, a length of timber cut off for a rail; **rail-fence**: see as main entry in Suppl.

1931 *Daily Progress* (Charlottesville, Va.) 26 Mar. 13/7 Louisville's railbirds are..watching and clocking the workouts of Derby eligibles. **1947** *Sun* (Baltimore) 4 Nov. 16/1 With the grandstand crowded when regular railbirds pushed their way into the shelters, betting dropped away. **1957** [see *COOKIE 4]. **1959** *Washington Post* 8 Oct. A21 Political railbirds out here suspect that Brown is beginning to think of himself as something more than a favorite son. **1971** *Daily Colonist* (Victoria, B.C.) 27 May 54/3 He gave them a three-week course of instruction in lacrosse fundamentals, banned railbirds who might make the boys feel self-conscious then turned them loose in lacrosse games. **1836** D. B. EDWARD *Hist. Texas* IV. 69 The farmers often get it measuring three rail cuts in length. **1881** *Scribner's Monthly* Feb. 503/2 The pole fence was laid after the same fashion of a rail fence only the poles were longer than rail-cuts. **1930** J. MASEFIELD *Wanderer of Liverpool* 23 The ship..Beaten rail-under by tempest and deluged by billows.

b. *rail-bed*; **rail bond**, an electrical connection between consecutive lengths of rail in a railway or tramway.

1880 'MARK TWAIN' *Tramp Abroad* xxix. 306 There was no level ground at the Kaltbad station; the railbed was as steep as a roof. **1969** E. W. MORSE *Fur Trade Canoe Routes* II. vi. 78 The portage is rough, and at its western end leads into an abandoned rail-bed once used for logging. **1893** in K. Hedges *Amer. Electr. Street Railways* (1894) iii. 22 Each joint of the rails is supplied with two rail bonds of No. 0000 copper wire, each only 12 inches long. **1907** WILSON & LYDALL *Electr. Traction* I. vi. 107 The 'Protected' rail bond is made by fusing terminals of solid copper upon a loop of flattened copper wire.

c. *rail-bridge, -end, -fare, -service, -side, tanker*; *rail-borne, -minded, -mounted* adjs.; **rail-bus**, (*a*) a vehicle resembling a bus but running on a railway track; (*b*) in Denmark, etc.: a tramcar running on tram-lines set in the road; **rail-car**, (*a*) = CAR *sb.* 2 (earlier and later examples); (*b*) (see quot. 1949); **railcard**, a pass entitling the holder to reduced fares on the railway; **rail-cutting**, the destruction of railway communications; **rail-head**, (*a*) the furthest point reached by a railway; (*b*) the point on a railway from which branch-line or road transport of supplies begins; hence *railhead facilities*; also *fig.*; **rail-line**, a railway line; **rail link**, a railway service joining two established transport systems; **rail-motor**, a passenger train which consists of a single coach attached to a small locomotive or having its own engine; a rail-car; also *attrib.*; **railplane** (see quots.); **railsickness**, sickness caused in a passenger by the motion of a train.

1928 *Britain's Industr. Future* (Liberal Industr. Inquiry) IV. xxiii. 313 In Germany the tonnage of canal and river traffic is equivalent to one-fifth or one-sixth of rail-borne traffic. **1976** *Illustr. London News* Nov. 52/4 The trend has been for rail-borne freight to lose ground to passenger traffic and to road transport. **1963** *Times* 8 June 14/3 Two-day talks between English and French Government officials on whether there should be a Channel rail bridge or road rail tunnel ended in London yesterday. **1978** H. R. F. KEATING *Long Walk to Wimbledon* IV. 59 The massive yellow-brick rail-bridge. **1933** *Morning Post* 30 Aug. 10/4 The London and North-Eastern Railway Company will put the new..stream-lined Diesel-electric 'railbus' into regular service on the suburban and outlying railway systems round Newcastle, within the next two weeks. **1956** *Railway Mag.* Mar. 195/1 The 'railbus' advocated for branch-line use by a correspondent in your January issue may have disadvantages. **1968** *Drive* Spring 37/2 British Rail could save many of their rural routes by introducing rail buses—a sort of single-decker diesel tramcar, operated by a driver-conductor not as a train but as if the vehicle were on the open road. **1976** J. TATE tr. *Bodelsen's Operation Cobra* viii. 42 The access road..is to be blocked..where the rail-bus cuts across it. *Ibid.* x. 54 The empty road along which the rail-bus ran. *Ibid.* xi. 56 Frederik cycled across the rail-bus tracks. **1977** *Modern Railways* Dec. 485/3 An early example was the German MAN railbus built in 1932, which remained in service for 30 years. **1834** *Knickerbocker* III. 112 After two hours past in this fair presence on rail-cars, I returned with my head running most uncomfortably upon this new acquaintance. **1860** J. S. C. ABBOTT *South & North* ix. 206 Thence, in rail-cars..through the heart of Alabama. **1934** *Discovery* Nov. 314/1 The term railcar is a convenient one to apply to the fast self-contained passenger units now running on many of the world's railways. **1949** *Richmond* (Virginia) *Times-Dispatch* 27 Oct. 4/2 This new-fangled transport is called a 'rail-car'.., principally for the reason that it is built compactly into a single unit... It operates much on the same principle as a streetcar, with controls at each end so that it can travel in either direction. The car, with a seating capacity of 90 persons, is especially designed for local passenger traffic. **1959** A. MCLINTOCK *Descr. Atlas N.Z.* 63 New Zealand Railways: Some Facts..Wagons 18,650..Railcars 23. **1963** *Times* 27 Feb. 5/1 Fiat was the first to start mass production of railcars. Its products are used by the railways not only of Italy but of a number of other countries. Fiat railcars are in service in Spain, Portugal, Egypt, Greece, Yugoslavia, Argentina, Brazil, Mexico, Venezuela, India and elsewhere. **1971** *Railway World* Mar. 116 There are also several diesel locomotives and a couple of railcars. **1976** *Sci. Amer.* Jan. 27/2 After the cooling period the fuel will in the future be shipped in specially protected trucks or railcars to a chemical-reprocessing plant. **1977** *Times* 16 Mar. 6/4 The senior citizens' Railcards will become available from April 1 for a full year regardless of the date of purchase. **1978** *Oxford Consumer* Mar. 18/1 Railcards for the 14–17 yr olds will be able to be purchased at most local stations from the above mentioned date. **1899** *Westm. Gaz.* 9 Dec. 5/3 We shall hear a good deal more of rail-cutting operations on the part of the enemy. **1944** Rail-cutting [see *INTERDICTION 4]. **1869** W. BARNES *Early England* 106 When the railway was taken into the hands of more learned men, we had..the *terminus* instead of the rail-end. **1955** R. W. & M. L. SETTLE *Saddles & Spurs* xii. 205 The first rail was laid in Sacramento October 26, 1863. Two years later rail-end had reached Colfax, fifty-five miles away. **1976** S. HYNES *Auden Generation* vii. 229 Details of landscape—the mountains, the pass, the rail-end—take on symbolic meanings. **1974** *Times* 22 Oct. 14/4 I'll pay rail fares, of course. Second class. **1976** B. WILLIAMS *Making of Manchester Jewry* vi. 157 If the synagogue was prepared to pay the rail fare of a Jewish pauper as far as Hull, the society undertook to see him across the North Sea. **1905** *Daily Chron.* 14 June 4/2 The political rail-head..has not got beyond Balfour Junction, and there are no definite lines of policy laid down beyond that point. **1905** *Athenæum* 24 June 781/2 When Lord Kitchener, during the operations of the Soudanese war, sternly relegated the war correspondents to the railhead, he earned the hostility of those who regard the distribution of news as of more importance. **1915** A. D. GILLESPIE *Lett. from Flanders* (1916) 243 There are some hills not far away, beyond the rail-head from which I marched in February. **1941** I. L. IDRIESS *Great Boomerang* xvii. 119 Now mineral wealth comes in—copper at the Duchess, with a railhead at Dajarra. **1955** *Times* 22 July 9/7 The Indian Government pays for the long, expensive haul from Pathankot, the railhead on the plains. **1961** *Times* 30 June 9/4 Railwaymen have come to talk of such goods stations as 'railheads'. **1972** *Oxford Times* 5 May 4/1 Culham, Clifton Hampden, Stadhampton and Little Milton are all on the route from the Didcot railhead—and lorries are due to start rolling in three weeks' time... No-one..expected Didcot to be the railhead for the materials. **1973** *Times* 29 Nov. 16/7 Every factory and warehouse and all the rest—is provided with railhead facilities. **1974** *Times* 8 Jan. 2/5 We have said we would go ahead provided all those who wanted a railhead were prepared to make good the financial shortfall. **1979** *Jrnl. R. Soc. Arts* CXXVII. 412/2 This was in general only temporary until the pipeline, gathering stations and railhead installations..had all been fully run in. **1961** E. F. MCKINNEY *Educ. in Violence* 365 Garrard's Covington raid and Rousseau's Opelika raid cut two-thirds of the rail lines he had to break. **1976** *Jrnl.* (Newcastle) 26 Nov., Holly Avenue, a quiet street sandwiched endways between Osborne Road and the rail-line. **1978** *Amer. Poetry Rev.* Nov./Dec. 6/3 The linear travel of the rail-line has become three-dimensional. **1975** *Guardian* 21 Jan. 12/1 The rail link from Folkestone to London. **1976** *Illustr. London News* Nov. 52/1 The first rail link with Britain by train and boat had been opened with the Calais Docks station in 1849. **1963** *Times* 23 May 13/7 Switzerland is the most rail-minded country in the world. **1906** *Westm. Gaz.* 5 June 5/3 An excursion train on the Great Western line colliding..with an empty rail-motor coach. **1927** *Observer* 13 Nov. 13/3 'Rail motors' or 'motor trains', may either take the form of self-contained vehicles having a steam or petrol engine built into the coach, or of trains hauled by very small engines and arranged to be driven from either end. **1962** *Coast to Coast 1961–62* 202 Rattling along on a rail-motor somewhere south-west of Bundaberg, recollection nagged busily and painfully. **1967** G. F. FIENNES *I tried to run a Railway* iii. 24 They allocated a railmounted gun..to Norfolk. **1969** *Jane's Freight Containers 1968–69* 241/3 All these cranes are rail-mounted, pneumatic tyred cranes will not be used. **1933** *Sun* (Baltimore) 25 Sept. 6/8 A railplane car, built along the lines of airplane architecture and designed to carry passengers over railroad tracks at ninety miles an hour, was announced today by the Pullman Car and Manufacturing Corporation. **1968** S. E. ELLACOTT *Everyday Things in Eng. 1914–68* xii. 185 A gallant pioneer effort..to revolutionize rail travel by suspending a carriage on an overhead rail..was the invention of a Scot, George Bennie, who built his first railplane in 1929... Ironically, a monorail service was running with apparent success in Tokyo in 1957. **1976** *Illustr. London News* Nov. 29/2 The most effective way of providing a 'rapid transit' is to improve the rail service. **1892** SWINBURNE *Lett.* (1962) VI. 30, I have got over the unnerving effects of railsickness. **1928** *Daily Tel.* 17 July 4/5 Freehold railside factory. **1959** *Listener* 8 Jan. 50/1 Iron ore is brought down to rail-side by country carts from the nearby mountains. **1958** *Times Rev. Industry* Feb. 74/1 Railtankers standing in readiness then loaded up and took the crude oil the remaining 250 miles to the sea at Philippeville for storage. **1979** *Jrnl. R. Soc. Arts* CXXVII. 406/1 The oil would be transmitted by pipeline to a rail terminal for transmission by rail tanker.

rail (rē^i^l), *sb.*[6] [Origin uncertain: cf. prec.] A hot-rod or dragster.

1962 *Punch* 17 Oct. 560/2 A dragster, or rail, is the most skeletal vehicle of all. **1965** *Daily Mail* 2 Oct. 5/5 There is no lonelier place on earth than the cockpit of a rail... A rail? That is race-jargon for a dragster. **1977** *Hot Car* Oct. 42/2 A reasonable crowd showed to watch rails, gassers, comp altered, and street saloons race together.

rail, *v.*[2] **5.** (Later examples.)

1916 E. W. HAMILTON *First Seven Divisions* 142 Four Army Corps were railed up from the eastern frontier. **1936** R. C. K. ENSOR *England, 1870–1914* ix. 299 It cost as much at that time to rail coal from the Rhondda to North Dorset as to ship it 3,000 miles to Alexandria. **1973** *Sunday Times* 7 Oct. 46 Forty-four-thousand gallons of sterile milk are daily railed from Anand to Bombay. **1975** *Times* 27 Dec. 9/7 Next year's Motorail brochure has just come... For many years I railed my car to Scotland. Not again, at £100 a time.

rail, *v.*[4] Add: **1. b.** (Later examples with *on.*)

1611 BIBLE *Mark* xv. 29 And they that passed by, railed on him. *Ibid. Luke* xxiii. 39 And one of the malefactors.. railed on him, saying, If thou be Christ, save thy selfe and us. **1855** MACAULAY *Hist. Eng.* III. xii. 213 His very soldiers railed on him in the streets of Dublin.

railage (s.v. RAIL *sb.*[2] in Dict.). Add: (Later examples.) Also *attrib.*

1903 *Daily Chron.* 19 June 5/2 Food and forage..are continually coming forward from the coast at high cost for railage. **1907** *Westm. Gaz.* 19 Jan. 7/1 Welsh smokeless coal is now 19s. per ton at the pit's mouth, and to that has to be added 8s. 4d. per ton for railage to London. **1955** *Times* 3 June 10/6 Further increases in the cost of commodities and stores, the latter resulting largely from the higher railage rates introduced in recent years. **1972** P. NEWTON *Sheep Thief* i. 14, I would require two horses.. and I would like to take my own. This would involve the cost of railage.

railed, *ppl. a.* Add: **1.** (Later examples with *off.*)

1930 *Times Educ. Suppl.* 23 Aug. 364/4 A railed-off enclosure. **1973** 'D. HALLIDAY' *Dolly & Starry Bird* ix. 119 The man we were following..gazed..at the railed-off pieces of terrazzo on the pavement.

railer[2]. Add: **2.** One who travels by rail.

1874 J. ALBERY *Two Roses* I. 12 Wherever you go there's Stone before you... Stone's a railer. **1889** F. E. GRETTON *Memory's Harkback* 103 Your constant 'railers' are blindly ignorant of the localities they scud over.

3. *Racing.* A runner that stays close to the rail.

1958 *Times* 29 Nov. 7/7 A 'railer' will always stick to the rails and a slow starter will always be such.

rail-fence. orig. *U.S.* [f. RAIL *sb.*[2] + FENCE *sb.*] **1.** A fence made of wooden posts and rails. Hence *rail fencing.*

1649 *Charlestown* (Mass.) *Land Rec.* (1878) 110, I doe sell..five Akers of planting Land,..Bounded on the..

North by the ould raile fence. **1725** *Manchester* (Mass.) *Town Rec.* (1889) 166 For making a rail fence from ye s[ai]d pound. **1807** *Salmagundi* 15 Oct. 331 Some..enjoy the varied and romantick scenery of..rail fences..potatoe patches, and log huts. **1848–70** [see RAIL *sb.*^{2} 6 a]. **1902** S. E. WHITE *Blazed Trail* xxxix. 355 It was near the 'pole-trail', which was less like a trail than a rail-fence. **1924** LAWRENCE & SKINNER *Boy in Bush* i. 7 Her easy indifference to English rail-fences. **1945** J. HORN in B. A. Botkin *Lay my Burden Down* 181 He was so fat he couldn't git through the fence. You know what sort of fence, a rail fence it was. **1968** J. ARNOLD *Shell Bk. Country Crafts* v. 101 Rail fencing usually consists of cleft or sawn oak posts set at 9 ft intervals, each mortised to take three rows of rails. **1973** L. RUSSELL *Everyday Life Colonial Canada* ii. 32 Easiest to construct was the rail fence... Rails were about six inches in thickness and something like 12 feet long. **1979** *Yale Alumni Mag.* Apr. 24/3 The rail fence, the center of campus life for many years, was originally erected in the 1830s.

2. *Cryptology.* A cipher or code obtained by splitting the plaintext between two or more lines in a zig-zag pattern (see quot. 1963). Also *rail-fence cipher*.

1939 H. F. GAINES *Elementary Cryptanalysis* iii. 12 Passing on to irregular types [of cryptogram], we find these in all degrees of difficulty, from the very simple 'rail fence' to the formidable 'U.S. Army' double transposition. **1943** J. M. WOLFE *First Course in Cryptanalysis* (rev. ed.) II. x. 1 During the Civil War the *rail fence* transposition was one of the cryptographic systems used as a field cypher. **1963** D. KAHN *Plaintext* 16 *The rail-fence cipher* can extend the number of lines in which the plaintext is distributed beyond two... If the key is 3, the cipher is still a rail-fence as in the encipherment m e s
a v l u = mesavluro.
r o

railinged, *a.* (s.v. RAILING *vbl. sb.*^{1} in Dict.). Add: (Later examples.) Also *railinged off*.

1938 *Archit. Rev.* LXXXIV. 104 The plain railinged balcony outside the first floor windows was replaced, for obvious aesthetic as well as structural reasons, by balconettes related in style to many which adorn the Adelphi. **1974** K. ROYCE *Trap Spider* ii. 37 The houses were railinged off, with sub-basements. *Ibid.* vii. 120 The squares were big..with a railinged green in their middle.

railless, *a.* (Later examples.)

1905 *Westm. Gaz.* 11 Mar. 7/2 Considerable amusement was created among the crowded audience by the pictures of bygone 'railless engines'. **1981** *Daily Tel.* 6 June 11/3 It will be sad..to see the rail-less cutting and the crumbling station.

railman (rē^i·lmæ̆n). [f. RAIL *sb.*^{2} 6 c.] A person employed on a railway; a railwayman.

1923 *Weekly Dispatch* 11 Feb. 3 (*heading*) Lord Lascelles and the Railmen. *Ibid.* 25 Mar. 1 (*heading*) Railmen forbidden to obey the French. **1927** *Sunday Times* 6 Mar. 15/6 (*heading*) Duke and the railmen. **1967** *Guardian* 11 Dec. 1/1 Management proposes to replace the many dozens of [railway] job classifications..by four broad and flexible grades. They would be called Railmen..Leading Railmen..Senior Railmen..and Chargemen. **1976** *Milton Keynes Express* 11 June 5/4 Wolverton Works this week scotched rumours that psychological tactics were being used in an attempt to squeeze out any of the local railmen involved in the closed shop row. **1977** *Listener* 2 June 703/1 Our industry is always associated with rattling a begging bowl. Some railmen are even embarrassed about going into the pub.

† **railodok** (rē^i·lǒdǫk). *Obs.* Also **-doc, -dock, R-.** The name given to an observation car, running on rails and conveying visitors round the British Empire Exhibition at Wembley in 1924. Also *attrib.*

1924 *Glasgow Herald* 31 May 8 (*heading*) Railodok Tour of the Exhibition. *Ibid.*, Her Majesty..toured the Exhibition in a railodok car. **1924** *Times* 29 July (Brit. Empire Suppl.) p. xxi/6 The Railodok cars..travel from point to point and make circular tours. *Ibid.*, It is possible for goods to be taken right up to the stalls..inside the bigger halls by Railodok trolley. **1924** *British Weekly* 21 Aug. 446/3, I made the complete tour in the railodoc. **1925** *Ibid.* 9 July 331/3 Boats on the lake were well patronised, and the railodok cars were partly full. **1927** W. E. COLLINSON *Contemp. Eng.* 16 The terms for the various vehicles to take visitors round like the railodocks are probably doomed to extinction.

† **railophone** (rē^i·lǒfō^{u}n). *Obs.* Also with capital initial. [f. RAIL *sb.*^{2} + -O + PHONE *sb.*^{2}] A telephone in a train. Also *attrib.* Hence as *v. trans.*, to telephone by means of such a phone.

1911 *Times* 8 Feb. 25/2 Any train fitted with the Railophone can be instantly spoken to. **1911** *Chambers's Jrnl.* Apr. 268/1 (*heading*) The Railophone system of wireless telephony on trains. **1912** *Morning Post* 29 June 10/7 Last year the first public installation of the railophone..was made on the Stratford-on-Avon and Midland Junction Railway, and the process of telephoning to and from moving trains and the sending of messages from stations to trains and *vice versa* was then clearly demonstrated. *Ibid.*, These instruments are electrically connected with two large insulated copper coils mounted in a wooden casing called the railophone frames. *Ibid.*, Messages to and from passengers can be railophoned with ease.

railroad, *sb.* Add: **1. a.** (Earlier and later examples.)

1757 in *Trans. Hon. Soc. Cymmrodorion 1897–98* (1899) Laying rails or making a railroad to the pits from the main or great road. **1771** T. PENNANT *Tour in Scotl. 1769* 29 The collieries lie at different distances..and the coal is brought down in waggons along rail roads. **1855** 'Q. K. P. DOESTICKS' *Doesticks what he Says* xvi. 138 Every stitch was as long as a railroad. **1873** 'MARK TWAIN' *Gilded Age* xvii. 163 Yes, this is the railroad, all but the rails and the iron-horse. **1888** RUSKIN *Praeterita* III. iv. 174 You enterprised a railroad.. you blasted its rocks away... And now, every fool in Buxton can be at Bakewell in half-an-hour, and every fool in Bakewell at Buxton. **1949** *Sun* (Baltimore) 28 Sept. 14/5, I came along the old railroad to town this morning.

2. a. (Earlier and later examples.)

1825 T. TREDGOLD *Rail-Roads & Carriages* i. 15 The Surrey rail-road commences on the south bank of the Thames, near Wandsworth..and proceeds..to Croydon, and from thence..to Merstham, making a total distance of about 18 miles. **1830** M. EDGEWORTH *Let.* 18 Oct. (1971) 419 A regular communication goes on now by trains of cars on this railroad backwards and forwards to Liverpool and Manchester. **1969** *New Statesman* 4 July 23/3 I'd also like to know whether the late Peter Arno coined, or merely repeated, three of his cartoon captions..'What a way to run a railroad'. **1976** *New Yorker* 16 Feb. 75/1 Here, at last, is an explanation of why the railroads in the United States have been decaying.

b. *pl.* Railway shares.

1848 J. J. RUSKIN *Let.* 17 Mar. in M. Lutyens *Ruskins & Grays* (1972) xi. 98 If you do not..deceive yourself or are led to plunge farther into Railroads—your situation is much better than I expected. **1916** C. SANDBURG *Chicago* in *Poetry* Mar. 191 Hog Butcher for the World, Tool Maker, Stacker of Wheat, Player with Railroads and the Nation's Freight Handler. **1957** [see *DOW-JONES]. **1964** *Financial Times* 12 Mar. 3/1 All the Dow Jones Indices made headway, with new all-time closing peaks again recorded by Industrials and Railroads.

3. a. *railroad agent, bookstand, box-car, brakeman, camp, car, carriage* (later examples), *charge, coach* (earlier example), *company* (earlier and later examples), *conductor, crew, cut, depot, detective, engineer, equipment, fare, hat, hotel, land, line, man, map, omnibus, pace* (earlier example), *pass, police, president, security, speed* (later example), *spur, station* (later examples), *town, track* (earlier and later examples) (also as *v. trans.*), *train* (later example), *whistle*.

1859 REDPATH & HINTON *Handbk. Kansas Territory* ii. 24 Select your route before buying your ticket, without consulting any railroad agent. **1847** F. A. KEMBLE *Rec. Later Life* (1882) III. 289 One of those pale green volumes headed, 'Reading for Travellers', to be found on all the railroad bookstands. **1976** *Billings* (Montana) *Gaz.* 4 July 1-c/3 'Beet shacks' vary in luxury. But few are as primitive as the old railroad boxcars that once housed migrants and still dot the area. **1898** *Kansas City Star* 18 Dec. 2/3 Grant Meade became a railroad brakeman. **1976** *Washington Post* 19 Apr. C1/2 When Mack was born in 1902 in Greeley, Colo., his father, a railroad brakeman, named him William Edward Maguiness. *a* **1927** F. M. CANTON *Frontier Trails* (1930) ii. 33 Stolen cattle were driven into railroad camps and sold to contractors at half their value. **1977** H. FAST *Immigrants* 11 He was nursed in railroad camps while his father drove spikes and handled steel rails. **1830** *Mechanics' Press* (Utica, N.Y.) 17 Apr. 183/3 Prizes..are offered on the following subjects: Iron castings,..Steam Carriages, Rail Road Car, [etc.]. **1863** B. TAYLOR *H. Thurston* v. 71 We ask that his boasted chivalry be put into practice, not merely in..giving us his seat in a railroad-car. **1923** C. R. COOPER *Under Big Top* i. 4 A circus..has its own railroad cars. **1967** *N.Y. Times* (Internat. Ed.) 11–12 Feb. 4/6 The snow, loaded in 14 railroad cars, arrived here yesterday as Chicago officials sought to clear out some of the nearly 40 inches that has fallen there since Jan. 26. **1865** RUSKIN *Sesame & Lilies* I. 85 Your *one* conception of pleasure is to drive in railroad carriages round their aisles. **1979** A. HOLLAR tr. *W. Schivelbusch's Railway Journey* (1980) vi. 92 The entirely different development of the railroad and the railroad carriage in the United States. **1848** *Amer. Railroad Jrnl.* 29 July 481/1 We wish to call attention to the subject of *railroad charges*, for *passengers* and *freight*. **1833** *Niles's Reg.* XLIV. 98/2 Comfortable naps may be taken in the rail-road coaches, if desired. **1815** *New Jersey Acts* 69 The New-Jersey Rail Road Company. Said president and directors so to be chosen shall be called The New-Jersey Rail Road Company. **1903** E. JOHNSON *Railway Transportation* 73 The railroad company derives its powers from a charter granted to it by the State. **1979** A. HOLLAR tr. *W. Schivelbusch's Railway Journey* (1980) ii. 35 The railroad companies' *monopoly* on transportation. **1842** *Liberator* (Boston) 21 Jan. 10/1 The kingly power of a rail-road conductor. **1942** E. PAUL *Narrow St.* vii. 61 The time came for Mariette to marry the railroad conductor of her choice. **1967** Railroad conductor [see *BRAKESMAN 2]. **1976** *Times* 23 July 11/6 Buffalo Bill..had been..buffalo hunter for a contractor supplying food to the Kansas Pacific railroad crews. **1862** *Rebellion Rec.* V. II. 403 On Friday morning we held the ridge, in front of which runs an incomplete railroad-cut. **1940** *Quiz on Railroads & Railroading* (Assoc. Amer. Railroads) Quest. 13 What is a railroad cut? When the right-of-way of a railroad is cut through a hill, knoll or slope to provide a roadway, the excavation is called a cut. **1836** *Southern Lit. Messenger* II. 735 Away we whirled with great rapidity to the railroad depot, where the cars were ready to receive us. **1980** L. ST. CLAIR *Obsessions* i. 36 Companies of Red troops..were marching toward the railroad depot. **1903** R. L. MCCARDELL *Conversations Chorus Girl* 78 Aunt Em says the railroad detectives seen him in a saloon. **1942** Z. N. HURSTON *Dust Tracks on Road* xii. 229 De white man..he was a railroad engineer. **1976** A. WHITE *Long Silence* vi. 44 The signals office contained the latest railroad equipment. **1910** *N.Y. Even. Post* 17 Dec. 7 The round-trip railroad fare will be $6.80. **1957** J. KEROUAC *On Road* I. iii. 15 All the men were..wearing railroad hats, baseball hats. **1869** *Bradshaw's Railway Manual* XXI. 427 *Expended*..Railroad hotel—$6,082. **1872** F. F. VICTOR *All over Oregon & Washington* xvi. 188 The railroad lands will be mostly taken in the foot-hills. **1872** *Newton Kansan* 17 Oct. 3/3 Mr. Wm. B. Blake..having purchased railroad land east of town, is about building a fine residence thereon. **1908** *Pacific Monthly* Jan. 6/1 The people on the railroad lands began to want deeds. **1841** *Punch* 16 Oct. 165/2 The infernal smashes that have recently taken place on several railroad lines. **1979** A. HOLLAR tr. *W. Schivelbusch's Railway Journey* (1980) vi. 98 American railroad lines proceed by curves. **1845** THOREAU *Jrnl.* 14 July in *Writings* (1906) VII. 366 Railroad men who take care of the road. **1980** L. ST. CLAIR *Obsessions* i. 21 The yard superintendent tells us you are a good railroad man. **1976** J. LEE *Ninth Man* 70 He would need railroad maps and timetables. **1858** C. M. YONGE *Christmas Mummers* i. 9 They had actually hopes of being able to hire the railroad omnibus. **1838** DICKENS *Let.* 20 May (1965) I. 400, I hope to make a great dash tomorrow, however, to proceed at railroad pace. **1895** W. H. CHAMBLISS *Diary* 48, I did not come out on one of those railroad passes especially designed for the accommodation of senators. **1976** *New Yorker* 15 Nov. 41/3 They also included bookplates, letterheads, railroad passes, commercial paperweights and music sheets. **1913** J. LONDON *Valley of Moon* in *Cosmopolitan* July 241/1 Up Pine Street..was coming a rush of railroad police..firing as they ran. **1914** *Sat. Even. Post* 4 Apr. 52/3 The train slowed down. The Kid swung off. He feared the railroad police in the terminal yards. **1892** 'MARK TWAIN' *Amer. Claimant* xiv. 134 There isn't a lawyer, doctor, editor, author, tinker, loafer, railroad president, saint..in the United States that wouldn't jump at the chance. **1949** *Chicago Daily News* 9 Aug. 10/5 His chance of becoming an American railroad president is probably about one in ten million. **1912** Railroad security [see *KILLING *vbl. sb.* 2]. **1859** C. E. DELONG *in Calif. Hist. Soc. Q.* (1931) X. 45 Committee convened.. hurried through at rail road speed. **1976** *National Observer* (U.S.) 12 June 4/2 It includes..construction of a railroad spur into the plant. **1978** S. SHELDON *Bloodline* xvi. 191 A nest of research buildings, manufacturing plants, experimental laboratories, planning divisions, and railroad spurs. **1923** R. HERRICK *Homely Lilla* xi. 172 She passed the county building on her way from the railroad station. **1976** *National Observer* (U.S.) 22 May 19/3 Sadly, a beautiful stone railroad station in the hamlet of Slingerlands is gone, replaced by a fire station. **1872** F. F. VICTOR *All over Oregon & Washington* xvi. 188 Some parcels, lying along the lines of the roads, or near railroad towns, will increase considerably in value during the current year. **1834** *Knickerbocker* V. 53 Rail-road tracks are projecting in all directions. **1947** *Southern Folklore Q.* Dec. 265 One of the most vivid of these images is one which describes a person's squirming 'like a country mule hitched beside the railroad track'. **1973** M. R. CROWELL *Greener Pastures* 54 Apple maggots have railroad-tracked the flesh of others [*sc.* apples]. **1922** C. SANDBURG in *Bookman* (U.S.) LV. 151 The little flivs of women, ready to throw themselves in front of railroad trains for men they love. **1854** A. M. MURRAY *Lett. from U.S.* (1856) 149 It does seem an extraordinary recklessness which causes these dreadful occurrences, when railroad whistles would guard against them.

b. *railroad director, manager; railroad-building* vbl. sb.

1873 'MARK TWAIN' *Gilded Age* xxiii. 216 Philip devoted himself day and night..to the science of railroad-building. **1849** J. J. RUSKIN *Let.* 4 June in M. Lutyens *Ruskins & Grays* (1972) xxiii. 211 We have not heard a word from Scotland..of John's Book... If Railroad Directors ever trouble themselves with such work, I should like to hear their notion of it. **1848** *Amer. Railroad Jrnl.* 29 July 482/3 In a short time, the railroad managers found that it would be convenient to grant to this company the use of their canal.

c. railroad bull, a policeman or detective on a railroad; **railroad bunk-car,** an old sleeping-car used as quarters for railway workers; **railroad commission,** a committee appointed to guard the public interest in relation to railroads; so **railroad commissioner; railroad euchre**: see EUCHRE *sb.* 1; **railroad fever,** (*a*) enthusiasm for the construction of railroads; (*b*) a passion for riding on trains; **railroad flat** *U.S.*, a flat consisting of a series of long, narrow rooms; **railroad guide,** a railway timetable; **railroad king,** a leading business man in the railroad industry; **railroad service,** in real tennis, an overhead service (see quot. 1961^1); **railroad tie,** a railway sleeper; **railroad worm,** the larva or the adult female of the South American beetle, *Phrixothrix tiemanni*, of the family Phengodidæ, which bears luminous red and green patches on its body.

1941 S. LONGSTREET *Last Man around World* xxxiii. 357 Hobo and railroad bull..and people who once shook hands with Warren G. Harding..fill the land. **1945** Railroad bull [see *MESQUITE, MESQUIT^2 1 b]. **1961** H. GARNER *Ten for Wednesday Night* 131 It had probably been some native-born jerk in a railroad bunk-car or construction boarding-house.. who had named him. **1887** *Statutes at Large U.S.A.* XXIV. 384 Investigate any complaint forwarded by the railroad commissioner or railroad commission of any State or Territory. **1913** R. M. LA FOLLETTE *Autobiogr.* vi. 238 He was now making a dogged fight for a railroad commission to regulate rates. **1914** *Cycl. Amer. Govt.* III. 109/1 At the beginning of the twentieth century, nearly every state in the United States had a railroad commission. **1845** *Massachusetts Acts & Resolves* 582 The Governor..shall appoint.. five persons, who shall, together, constitute 'the Board of Rail-road Commissioners'. **1946** S. H. HOLBROOK *Lost Men of Amer. Hist.* xii. 262 He was made railroad commissioner of Iowa. **1852** *Oregon Statesman* 20 Jan. 1/6 The people up country are likewise agitated with the railroad fever. **1880** *Bradstreet's* 15 Sept. 8/1 A railroad fever is pervading various portions of the state. **1899** 'J. FLYNT' *Tramping with Tramps* I. ii. 53 The tramp's theory of them [*sc.* runaway boys], is that they are possessed of the 'railroad fever'. **1956**

B. Malamud in *New Yorker* 22 Sept. 149/1 A five-room railroad flat above a butcher store. **1962** S. J. Perelman *Rising Gorge* 283 His apartment, a railroad flat.. Halfway down its central corridor, Barber flung open a door. **1859** L. D. Tierney *Hist. Gold Discoveries on South Platte River* 25 Persons starting from points east of Chicago, by obtaining a railroad guide, can easily estimate the distance and cost of travel for themselves to that point. **1868** *Commercial & Financial Chron.* VI. 295/1 Two railroad kings..have entered the lists. **1871** Mrs. Stowe *My Wife & I* xvi. 176 He is a railroad king—a prince of stocks—a man going with a forty thousand steam power through New York waters. **1890** W. James *Princ. Psychol.* I. xiv. 579 Such new attributes as make up the notions of a 'railroad king'. **1903** T. M. Tarbell in *McClure's Mag.* Jan. 254/2 The acquiescence of the 'railroad kings'..was followed by an unwilling promise to break the contracts with the company. **1898** Kennedy & Cohen in W. A. Morgan *'House' on Sport* I. 421 His railroad service did not have nearly the effect he expected. **1959** *Times* 6 May 4/3 Hampel who set up a promising attack based on a railroad service. **1961** J. S. Salak *Dict. Amer. Sports* 352 *Railroad service* (court tennis)—an overhead service delivered by the server standing near the wall between the last gallery and the dedans wall. **1961** *Times* 13 Jan. 16/2 Each showed skill in handling the other's railroad service. **1856** Railroad tie [see *Douglas^1]. **1877** [see **fencing post*]. **1927** [see *bohunk]. **1935** Z. N. Hurston *Mules & Men* i. iv. 86 They were accustomed to strange women dropping into the quarters, but not in shiny gray Chevrolets. They usually came plodding down the big road or counting railroad ties. **1977** R. E. Harrington *Quintain* viii. 78 The railroad-tie steps that led down to the terrace. **1979** *Arizona Daily Star* 5 Aug. (Advt. Section) 9/5 Railroad ties, $9 ea. **1944** E. N. Harvey in *Jrnl. Cellular & Compar. Physiol.* XXIII. 31 (*heading*) The nature of the red and green luminescence of the South American 'railroad worm'. **1973** C. A. Villee et al. *Gen. Zool.* (ed. 4) iv. 79/2 One of the more spectacular luminescent creatures is the 'railroad worm' of Uruguay, the larva of a beetle, which has a row of green lights on each side of its body and a pair of red lights on its head.

railroad, *v.* Add: **2. b.** (Later examples.) (Now common outside the U.S.) Also const. without prep., to hustle, to coerce. Occas. const. *from*.

1917 E. H. Hadlock *Journalism & Authorship* 23 'Railroad' means to rush matter through without the usual precautions against typographical errors. **1924** P. C. MacFarlane *Tongues of Flame* xxv. 222 They railroaded it [*sc.* the bill] through the senate before I was awake. **1934** J. M. Cain *Postman always rings Twice* xi. 123 If all cases were railroaded through that quick, it would do more to prevent crime than passing a hundred laws. **1952** *Manch. Guardian Weekly* 12 June 3 The most ruthless block railroads its man into the nomination. **1958** M. Dickens *Man Overboard* x. 151 How had he let himself be railroaded into this? **1961** A. Huxley *Let.* 5 May (1969) 911 I'm very thankful I didn't let myself be railroaded..into having half my tongue and a quarter of my neck cut out. **1963** J. N. Harris *Weird World Wes Beattie* vii. 83 Paget..had been primarily responsible for railroading the case through the magistrate's court. **1967** *Boston Sunday Herald* 7 May (Show Guide) 17/2 It is..unbelievable that he would railroad his alcoholic daughter..into a mental hospital. *a* **1974** R. Crossman *Diaries* (1976) II. 223 The timetable was fixed and it was railroaded through the Cabinet. **1974** *News & Courier* (Charleston, S. Carolina) 21 Apr. A-1/1 Nixon's accusers then would be vulnerable to the charge they were trying to railroad him from office. **1975** B. Garfield *Death Sentence* xi. 59 Take all the time you want. Nobody wants to railroad him.

c. To send (someone) to a place of punishment with summary speed or by means of false evidence.

1877 *N.Y. Herald* 9 Mar. 8/4 'Railroaded!' Joe Coburn takes the cars for his ten years' home [*i.e.* Sing Sing]. **1900** [see *fair *sb.*^{2} 1 c]. **1930** *Sat. Even. Post* 26 July 26/2 He broke up the best gang of counterfeiters the country ever saw... He went into the post-office department and railroaded six of the smartest mail workers that ever hit a prison. **1935** A. J. Pollock *Underworld Speaks* 94/1 *Railroaded*, sentenced to prison when innocent. **1942** E. Paul *Narrow St.* xv. 108 It was no new thing to the French to have undesirables railroaded and executed on one flimsy pretext or another. **1964** C. Chaplin *Autobiogr.* xxvii. 464 In spite of the absurdity of the charges there lurked in the back of my mind the possibility that I might be railroaded. **1974** *Black Panther* 27 Apr. 9/1 Concrete evidence smashed American military intelligence attempts to illegally railroad eleven Black sailors in U.S. military court here.

4. (Earlier example.)

1887 C. B. George *40 Yrs. on Rail* iv. 69 A couple of fast runs that were made while I was railroading in Vermont.

railroader. (Earlier and later examples.)

1856 *Iroquois Republican* (Middleport, Illinois) 8 May 3/2 A scuffle between young Walker, a railroader, and Cochran, a rail ripper. **1907** *Daily Chron.* 20 Sept. 3/2 Here are particulars of some of the new novels which Messrs. Cassell will publish in October:-.. 'Caleb Conover, Railroader', by Mr. A P. Terhune. **1973** *Sunday Bull.* (Philadelphia) 14 Oct. (Parade Suppl.) 20 (Advt.), *The Old West*..shows you the people who met its most extraordinary challenges, people who became *The Forty-Niners, The Trailblazers, The Railroaders.* **1977** *Modern Railways* Dec. 461/1 On the one hand he rages that the railroad's proposal to pay by the hour instead of by the mile would lower the American railroader to the social and economic level of his Soviet counterpart.

railroading, *vbl. sb.* Add: **1.** (Earlier and later examples.)

1842 F. A. Kemble *Let.* 16 June in *Rec. Later Life* (1882) II. 258 An hour's railroading from London has brought me into a lovely country. **1905** *Daily Chron.* 9 Feb. 33 Automobilism has been taken too much as a matter of course, though its position is obviously midway between cycling and rail-roading.

2. (Later examples.)

1907 *Daily Chron.* 20 Feb. 4/7 [Bad management] has brought American railroading into the position of being the most slovenly of all our great business enterprises. **1915** *Lit. Digest* 4 Sept. 458/1 The New Haven was wrecked by excessive capital issues either alien to the business of railroading or for properties and purposes without equivalent value. **1945** H. Hubbard *Railroad Avenue* ii. 7 The prevalence of Joneses in railroading, as elsewhere, is shown by the fact that in 1944 there were 1,078 Joneses on the Canadian National pay roll. **1977** *Modern Railways* Dec. 460/3 Precious little has been heard of how they order things in the land of—still largely—free enterprise railroading. **1979** *Tucson Mag.* Apr. 47/3 His re-creation of early British railroading will warm the cockles of every train buff's heart.

rail-splitter *U.S.* [f. Rail *sb.*^{2} + Splitter *sb.*^{2}] One who splits wood for rails; used *transf.* of Abraham Lincoln. Hence *fig.*, a Republican. Also *attrib.* in apposition.

1860 *Congress Globe* 36th Congress 1 Sess. App. 462/2 They call him 'Uncle Abe', 'Old Abe', 'Honest old Abe', 'The old rail splitter', 'The flat-boatman', &c. **1864** A. Gurowski *Diary* 17 Sept. (1866) III. 350, I rejoice that Lincoln's mind is not befogged by that limited scholarship; and..I prefer the railsplitter to any narrow, classical hairsplitter. **1865** *Harper's Mag.* July 227/2 His [*sc.* Lincoln's] national reputation as a rail-splitter. **1885** *Mag. Amer. Hist.* Mar. 298/1 Clubs of 'Rail-Splitters' were formed during the campaign. **1887** J. D. Billings *Hardtack & Coffee* i. 19, I had taken an active part in the torchlight parades of the 'Wide-awakes' and 'Rail-splitters', as the political clubs of the Republicans were called. **1901** W. Churchill *Crisis* i. v. 150 What they seemed proudest of was that he had been a rail-splitter. **1903** J. G. Nicolay in *Cambr. Mod. Hist.* VII. xvi. 548 Both classes very naturally doubted whether a rail-splitter candidate..possessed the wisdom and the strength of will to conquer a formidable rebellion. **1925** *Scribner's Mag.* Oct. 361/1 Did Lincoln say that to America? He was only a rail-splitter. He had reason to think that he might not count. **1952** *Manch. Guardian Weekly* 17 July 3 The patron saint of the Republicans is an uncouth rail-splitter. **1960** B. Keaton *My Wonderful World of Slapstick* i. 11 James Agee described my face as ranking 'almost with Lincoln's'. I can't imagine what the great rail splitter's reaction would have been to this.

† **rail timber.** *U.S. Obs.* [f. Rail *sb.*^{2} + Timber *sb.*^{1}] Timber suitable for making rails.

1662 *Portsmouth* (New Hampsh.) *Rec.* (1901) 396 He is to preserve all the Rayle timber. **1681** *Town Rec. Topsfield, Mass.* (1917) I. 36/2 There shall be noe raile timber feled. **1786** G. Washington *Diary* 30 Oct. (1925) III. 131 The Wood part, of wch. there is a good deal, is tolerably full of rail timber and wood. **1816** U. Brown *Jrnl.* in *Maryland Hist. Mag.* (1915) X. 281 A poor stony rocky Country..with an abundance of good Chestnut rail Timber. **1843** N. Boone *Jrnl.* 23 July in L. Pelzer *Marches of Dragoons* (1917) 233 There being a great scarcity of water and no building or rail timber. **1860** H. Greeley *Overland Journey* v. 65 The squatter can give you a hundred good excuses for his miserable condition:..he has no good rail-timber [etc.].

railway, *sb.* Add: **1. b.** (Later examples.)

1945 G. Millar *Maquis* ii. 30 On the side of the aircraft near the hole there were several little metal railways for holding the fixed end of the static lines. **1979** W. Golding *Darkness Visible* iii. 39 The place [*sc.* a shop] grew a spider's web of wires along which money trundled in small, wooden jars..the overhead railway.

2. a. (Earlier and later examples.) Also *British Railways*: formerly, the name of the national railway system of Great Britain. Cf. *British Rail* s.v. *rail *sb.*^{2} 5 a.

1812 (*heading*) Map of the railways in the Newcastle on Tyne Coal Field in 1812 [reproduced in A. Hollar tr. *W. Schivelbusch's Railway Journey* (1980) i. 6]. **1830** M. Edgeworth *Let.* 18 Oct. (1971) 418 We were invited..to go on the Liverpool railway in the very carriage in which the Duke of Wellington went...4 of these cars similar in size and shape..were linked together on the rail way. **1892** B. Potter *Jrnl.* 13 Sept. (1966) 260 To Perth with Papa, the first time I have been on the railway since we have been here. **1955** *Times* 9 May 4/5 The start of a new era for the railways. **1964** *Ann. Reg. 1963* 12 British Railways, a weary and over-extended system, had been slithering ever deeper into deficits since 1953. **1965** *Ann. Reg. 1964* 486 British Railways signed an agreement in January with the Central Electricity Generating Board for the delivery of coal by continuously moving merry-go-round trains to selected power stations. **1976** *Illustr. London News* Nov. 51/3 The first iron railway in France was designed, as in Britain, for the transport of coal from the mines to the water... But it used horse traction as often as steam.

3. a. *railway accident* (later examples), *age, arch, bank, book, bookstall, bus, cab, car, cat, company* (later example), *cottage, cutting* (later examples), *director* (later example), *economics, enthusiast, excursion, fare, garden, horse, interest, junction, labourer, line* (later example), *man* (later examples), *manual, map, marshalling yard, office, platform, police, policeman, porter, poster, sandwich, share* (later example), *siding, stall, station* (later examples), *stock* (earlier example), *switch, system* (later examples), *tea, terminus, ticket, timetable, town, track* (later example), *traveller, truck, viaduct, wagon* (later example), *worker, works*.

1850 J. H. Newman *Christ upon Waters* 23 You know what a sensation railway accidents occasion. **1939** T. S. Eliot *Family Reunion* i. i. 43 We know about the railway accident. **1877** E. Blanchard in E. Farjeon *Nursery in Nineties* (1935) iv. i. 162 In this railway Age..Fresh lines are still appearing. **1976** A. Price *War Game* i. v. 99 The railway age was..part of bygone history. **1892** B. Potter *Jrnl.* 9 Sept. (1966) 257 A charming game of 'bolting the pony' under the railway arch. **1976** A. Powell *Infants of Spring* v. 79 We were making for the open country beyond the railway arches that link Windsor with the main line. **1894** B. Potter *Jrnl.* 25 Sept. (1966) 346 Our nerves were rather startled by the sight of some cattle up the railway bank between Sprouston and Kelso. **1854** C. M. Yonge *Heartsease* I. ii. ii. 142 It was a green railway book. Theodora made me read it. **1893** Railway bookstall [see *big *a.* 3 e]. **1974** in A. Briggs *Ess. Hist. of Publishing* 289 The first railway bookstall was opened at Euston by W. H. Smith in 1848. **1892** B. Potter *Jrnl.* 26 July (1966) 239 He [*sc.* a dog] used to be very much in evidence..until safely hoisted on to the top of the railway bus in front of the luggage. **1893** Yonge & Coleridge *Strolling Players* xxviii. 254 A railway cab dashing up to the door. **1828** *Deb. Congress U.S.* 9 Apr. 2249 The rail way car at Charleston, South Carolina..weighs upwards of one ton. **1830** M. Edgeworth *Let.* 18 Oct. (1971) 418 Francis was prevented from going in the common train of *railway cars* from Liverpool to Manchester. **1894** *Harper's Mag.* July 316/1 Railway cars for transporting the army were appropriated at Omaha. **1939** T. S. Eliot *Old Possum's Bk. Pract. Cats* 40 (*heading*) Skimbleshanks: the Railway Cat. *Ibid.* 41 You can leave all that to the Railway Cat, The Cat of the Railway Train! **1976** A. White *Long Silence* vi. 43 Five shunting engines were..presented to the railway company. **1962** M. Duffy *That's how it Was* ii. 22 The warren of railway cottages run up at the end of the nineteenth century. **1976** *Milton Keynes Express* 23 July 2/6 Time is running out for the Bradwell residents who have petitioned against the preservation of the town's railway cottages. **1878** *Q. Jrnl. Geol. Soc.* XXXIV. 496 Railway-cuttings and other workings made since the date of the survey have exposed masses of rock not then known to exist. **1976** A. White *Long Silence* xviii. 147 The road that led to the railway cutting. **1845** *Punch* VIII. 101 The old maxim that civility costs nothing, seems to be utterly repudiated by Railway Directors. **1976** *Illustr. London News* Nov. 53/3 One aspect of railway economics in which the SNCF has made remarkable progress in recent years is productivity. **1950** *Oxf. Jun. Encycl.* IX. 399/2 Ian Allan..brought into being the first club for young railway enthusiasts who wished to collect the numbers of locomotives. **1976** *Scotsman* 20 Nov. (Weekend Suppl.) 5/8 Information and photographs are wanted from railway enthusiasts about historic rail buildings, either extant, demolished or adapted. **1853** *Punch* XXIV. 92/2 Railway Maxims,.. After a Railway excursion, the Doctor. **1885** *List of Subscribers, Classified* (United Telephone Co.) (ed. 6) 181 Railway Excursion Agents..Cook Thomas & Son. **1891** Kipling *Life's Handicap* 30 Ye might give me my railway fare. **1980** A. Morice *Death in Round* xxi. 169 The idea of thumbing a lift was reasonable... The railway fare is quite steep. **1892** B. Potter *Jrnl.* 26 July (1966) 239 It [*sc.* a hedgehog] was gobbling up little spring cabbages in a promising little Railway Garden. **1976** *Field* 18 Nov. 994/1 (*caption*) Nationalization came that year [*sc.* 1947] and this was almost the end of a long railway-horse tradition. **1869** *Bradshaw's Railway Manual* XXI. p. xi, The railway interest in parliament, etc. **1845** A. H. Clough *Sic itur* in *Poems* (1862) 24 As, at a railway junction, men Who came together, taking then One the train up, one down, again Meet never! **1977** V. S. Pritchett *Gentle Barbarian* iii. 45 When Dickens stayed there with the Viardots he complained that..the place..was like a railway junction where people were changing trains. **1845** Wordsworth *At Furness Abbey* in *Poetical Wks.* (1954) III. 63 Well have you Railway Labourers to *this* ground Withdrawn for noontide rest. **1976** *Illustr. London News* Nov. 29/2 London is adequately served with railway lines..either by London Transport or British Rail. **1906** *Daily Chron.* 30 Apr. 3/1 Near the junction of the northern and western railway lines,..two stones and a piece of iron had been placed on the rails. They were removed by a railwayman. **1938** F. D. Sharpe *Sharpe of Flying Squad* xxiv. 251, I could see by their 'railwaymen's' trousers that they were country splits. **1976** W. Greatorex *Crossover* 194 They found a pub..packed with railway porters and shunters... A couple of railwaymen moved out to make room. **1863** (*title*) Bradshaw's railway manual. **1845** *Punch* IX. 163 (*heading*) A railway map of England. **1853** J. E. Millais *Let.* Sept. in M. Lutyens *Millais & Ruskins* (1967) 90 My face..would be lined like a Bradshaw railway map. **1907** *Yesterday's Shopping* (1969) 1106/2 District Railway Map.. 0/9. **1976** A. White *Long Silence* vii. 53 The railway marshalling yards we were to disable were crescent-shaped. **1831** W. Dalton *Let.* 16 Oct. in *N. & Q.* (1920) 11 Dec. 461/2 We drove to the railway office at Warrington. **1976** A. White *Long Silence* vi. 44 She had no other thought than to seek employment in the railway office. **1922** C. Mackenzie *Altar Steps* xix. 218 While Father Rowley was speaking the Bishop of Silchester had been looking like a man on a railway platform who has been ambushed by a whistling engine. **1846** *Punch* XI. 11/1 The corps of Railway police was next put through its exercise. **1972** J. Wainwright *Requiem for Loser* viii. 165 The man..in charge of the goods yard police activity was a uniformed Railway Police inspector. **1838** *Penny Mag.* 31 Aug. 331/2 The railway policeman, holding up at intervals red or white flags. **1972** M. Gilbert *Body of Girl* i. 9 A very big consignment of used notes..was coming up for pulping... There were two railway policemen to meet it. **1890** P. Geddes in *Scots Mag.* Aug. 192 The student..needs a better greeting than the railway porter's when he arrives at his destination. **1978** Ld. Drogheda *Double Harness* xiii. 132 His father..obliged him to take a job as a railway porter. **1926** *Scribner's Mag.* Aug. 221/2 Byron was too grandiose to travel well. He founded the railway-poster style of description. **1931** D. L. Sayers *Five Red Herrings* xiv. 153 A board which displayed time-tables and railway posters. **1948** M. Laski *Tory Heaven* xii. 159 There were some benches round the walls.. and a lot of gaudy railway posters. **1847** Dickens *Dombey* (1848) xv. 155 There were railway plans, maps, views, wrappers, bottles, sandwich-boxes, and time tables. **1868**

TROLLOPE *He knew he was Right* (1869) I. xxxvii. 292 The real disgrace of England is the railway sandwich. **1915** J. BUCHAN *Thirty-Nine Steps* vii. 177, I never ate a meal with greater relish, for I had had nothing all day but railway sandwiches. **1972** Railway sandwich [see *railway tea* below]. **1876** 'L. CARROLL' *Hunting of Snark* III. 30 You may seek it with thimbles—and seek it with care; You may hunt it with forks and hope; You may threaten its life with a railway-share; You may charm it with smiles and soap. **1942** C. MILBURN *Diary* 26 Feb. (1979) 130 The King and Queen slept in *our* railway siding on Tuesday night. **1976** A. WHITE *Long Silence* vi. 43 The railway sidings became one of the principal marshalling yards. **1866** GEO. ELIOT *Let.* 11 Sept. (1956) IV. 309 My 6/- editions are never on the railway stalls. **1849** DE QUINCEY in *Blackw. Mag.* Oct. 492/1 Interesting personal communications,..revelations of impressive faces..could not have offered themselves amongst the hurried and fluctuating groups of a railway station. **1892** B. POTTER *Jrnl.* 25 Aug. (1966) 252 A large proportion of the seven thousand spectators poking away through the small Railway Station. **1964** G. L. COHEN *What's Wrong with Hospitals?* vi. 115 Their baronial board-room..dignified by a staircase for consultants only, in Railway Station Gothic. **1852** *Jewish Chron.* 10 Dec. 78/2 The poor..are induced to go..from town to town; each congregation..assisting to pay a portion of the dividends on railway-stock, under the name of..charity. **1838** *Civil Engin. & Archit. Jrnl.* Oct. 358 Railway Switch Signal. **1872** GEO. ELIOT *Middlem.* III. lvi. 227 The infant struggles of the railway system. **1981** *Times* 10 Feb. 6/6 The railway system and the port of Mombasa have.. benefited from the growing volume of tea exports. **1972** 'G. NORTH' *Sgt. Cluff rings True* iv. 31 Travellers..reviving themselves with railway tea and railway sandwiches. **1845** *Punch* VIII. 101 An applicant for information at a Railway Terminus. **1942** E. WAUGH *Put out More Flags* iii. 228 They reached the classic columns of the railway terminus. **1976** G. SEYMOUR *Glory Boys* iv. 42 The big railway termini of North London. **1839** F. WITTS *Diary* 4 May (1978) 158 Meantime the passengers receive a railway ticket to London which purports to be worth 5s 6d. **1895** E. LEAR in *Nonsense Songs & Stories* 87 On his nose there was a Cricket,—In his hat a Railway-Ticket. **1912** W. OWEN *Let.* 4 June (1967) 140 Does the Railway Ticket Problem assume a different aspect now? **1977** *Lancashire Life* Dec. 60/2 In those wartime days, holiday-period railway tickets were at a premium. **1847** Railway timetable [see *railway sandwich* above]. **1932** D. L. SAYERS *Have his Carcase* xxvi. 352 Do you happen to have a railway time-table on you? **1980** *Times* 12 Aug. 10/1 He wants the centre of the British railway system moved from London to Birmingham..to rewrite the entire railway timetable around Birmingham. **1881** A. BEGG *Gt. Canadian N.W.* 106 The railway is constructed to a point on the eastern side of the river opposite Selkirk, so that there is every chance of its becoming a railway town. **1888** *Lippincott's Monthly Mag.* XLII. 783 There stood close to the opposite wall a large piano of the class known as the 'grand', rare enough among the railway towns west of the Mississippi States. **1943** *Sun* (Baltimore) 13 Dec. 5/2 The Peiping Hankow railway town of Sinyang. **1976** A. WHITE *Long Silence* vi. 44 She propelled the creaking vehicle..up and down the railway tracks. **1891** *Murray's Handbk. India & Ceylon* p. xv, In Bombay, the Indian *A.B.C. Guide* and the *Indian Railway Travellers' Guide*.. give..the railway routes for all India. **1980** G. M. FRASER *Mr American* xxvi. 552 The vaguely hostile silence of the British railway traveller. **1838** *Civil Engineer* I. 390/1 A new Railway Truck, the invention of Mr. Robert Grant, of Maine. **1839** F. WITTS *Diary* 4 May (1978) 158 There the carriages are placed each on a railway truck. **1841** DICKENS *Let.* 13 June (1969) II. 302 One is hoisted bodily, carriage and all, on a Railway Truck. **1867** QUEEN VICTORIA *Jrnl.* 22 Aug. in D. Duff *Victoria in Highlands* (1968) 223 We went by the side of Eildon Hills, past an immense railway viaduct. **1976** C. DEXTER *Last seen Wearing* xxi. 162 He..slept beneath a railway viaduct. **1976** A. WHITE *Long Silence* xiv. 121 They might hide themselves in a railway wagon. **1943** J. FLANNER in *New Yorker* 29 May 45/1 The Nazis..had decided to kill the French railroad men's resistance movement..by inviting twelve thousand French railway workers to go to Germany. **1979** P. ALEXANDER *Show me Hero* xv. 161 Crumbling terraced cottages, once occupied by railway workers. **1869** *Bradshaw's Railway Manual* XXI. 371, 17,500,000 *thalers* were to be applied to railway works. **1976** *Milton Keynes Express* 16 July 7/7 The part time station at the Wolverton is still dependent on men from the railway works.

4. railway beetle = *railroad worm* s.v. *RAILROAD *sb.* 3 c; **railway bull** = *railroad bull* s.v. *RAILROAD *sb.* 3 c; **railway crossing** = *level crossing* s.v. LEVEL *a.* 3 b; **railway edition,** a cheap edition of a book suitable for reading on a railway journey; **railway guide,** a train timetable; **railway hotel,** an hotel sited near to a railway station for the convenience of travellers; **Railway Institute,** a (social) club building for railway workers, esp. in India; **railway label,** an address or destination label stuck on a passenger's luggage; **railway letter** (see quot. 1933); **railway novel** (earlier and later examples); **railway pass,** a ticket authorizing the holder to travel by rail; **railway rug** (earlier example); **railway sickness** = *railsickness* s.v. *RAIL *sb.*[2] 6 c; **railway spine** (later examples); **railway time:** see as main entry; **railway volume** = **railway edition*; **railway warrant** = **railway pass*; **railway whistle,** a whistle blown by the guard as a signal to the driver to start the train; **railway wrapper,** a travelling-cloak.

1915 E. R. LANKESTER *Diversions of Naturalist* 234 A peculiar grub-like female glow-worm, three inches long, is found in South America, which produces a red light at each end of the body and numerous points of green light on each side of it. It is called the 'railway-beetle' in Paraguay. **1973** B. BROADFOOT *Ten Lost Years* ii. 17 [To] the town cop or the railway bull..you automatically became a criminal. **1907** *Yesterday's Shopping* (1969) 1040/2 Railway Crossing, finely japanned, to be opened and shut..8 in. long. **1937** *Discovery* May 144/2 A railway crossing west of Scarborough. **1859** G. H. LEWES in *Blackw. Edin. Mag.* July 101/1 Twice or thrice have the railway editions been out of print. *c* **1838** W. H. MURRAY in M. R. Booth *Eng. Plays of 19th Cent.* (1973) IV. 161 That woman..[is] as difficult to understand as an Act of Parliament, or a Railway Guide, or a Weather Almanack. **1855** MRS. GASKELL *North & South* II. vii. 87 One of the very common mistakes in the 'Railway Guide' as to the times when trains arrive at the smaller stations. **1932** D. H. LAWRENCE *Etruscan Places* i. 13 The inestimable big Italian railway-guide says the station is Palo. **1847** F. A. KEMBLE *Rec. Later Life* (1882) III. 265 To this Hull Railway Hotel is attached a magnificent Railway Station (or rather *vice versâ*). **1871** GEO. ELIOT *Let.* 20 Aug. (1956) V. 179 There is a palatial bedroom here, but if you reject that, there is a Railway Hotel, just opposite the station. **1911** BEERBOHM *Zuleika Dobson* ii. 13 She took a night's sanctuary in some railway-hotel. **1972** *Country Life* 5 Oct. 799/1 The Great Northern, designed by Lewis Cubbitt..was far more restrained than any of the railway hotels of the next decade. **1937** K. BLIXEN *Out of Afr.* iv. 299 The High Court was set in Nakuru, in the Railway Institute. **1954** J. MASTERS *Bhowani Junction* I. v. 42 There were two Railway Institutes..one for Europeans and Anglo-Indians, and one for Indians.. Ours was a fine big building with a dance floor and card rooms and a bar. **1979** *Times* 26 Nov. 14/7 Giving song recitals at the Railway Institute at Lahore. **1909** BEERBOHM *Yet Again* 125 Railway-labels are..crudely coloured, crudely printed. **1917** *Science Progr.* XI. 685 The railway labels jealously preserved on travellers' portmanteaux. **1933** *Post Office Guide* Jan. 42 The following Railway Companies..under agreement with the Postmaster-General, accept and convey letters, both on week-days and on Sundays, by the next available train or ship, either to be called for at the Station of address or to be transferred there to the nearest Post Office letter box. Such letters are called Railway Letters. **1971** D. POTTER *Brit. Eliz. Stamps* xii. 132 In 1969 two other railway lines decided to avail themselves of the privilege of accepting and carrying railway letters. **1857** C. M. YONGE *Dynevor Terrace* I. ii. 12 'Reading... See here', as he held up maliciously a railway novel. **1896** B. MATTHEWS *Bookbindings* IV. i. 239 In England the railway novel is incased in boards sheathed in paper. **1981** V. POWELL *Flora Annie Steel* i. 6 The yellow-backed novels.. known as 'railway novels' and bought to beguile the long haul from Harrow to the West of Argyll. **1901** KIPLING *Kim* vii. 178 Colonel Creighton's railway pass lay in his hand, and Kim..was still lord of two rupees seven annas. **1915** W. B. YEATS *Reveries* 5 An uncle called me out of bed one night, to ride..to Rosses Point to borrow a railway-pass from a cousin. **1853** *Illustr. London News* 12 Nov. 409/2 Blankets and railway rugs have formed the chief protection against the low temperature. **1895** SWINBURNE *Lett.* (1962) VI. 85, I am now sufficiently recovered from railwaysickness. **1895** G. B. SHAW in *Liberty* 27 July 6/2 The connection between degeneration and 'railway spine'. **1954** W. MAYER-GROSS et al. *Clin. Psychiatry* iv. 135 The days of neurasthenia and railway-spine at the time of Beard. **1869** D. G. ROSSETTI *Let.* Aug. (1965) II. 710 In the above year [1862] Messrs. Routledge reprinted it as a shilling railway volume. **1919** J. BUCHAN *Mr. Standfast* ix. 183, I..emerged in the uniform of a British private... I had a railway warrant made out in my name for London. **1978** T. ALLBEURY *Lantern Network* ii. 30 He had been released..with a railway warrant to Southampton. **1854** DICKENS *Seven Poor Travellers* in *Househ. Words* VIII. Extra Christmas No. 4/1 A..young man connected with the Fly department, and well accustomed to the sound of a railway whistle which Ben always carries in his pocket. **1847** Railway wrapper [see *railway sandwich*, sense *3 a]. **1860** DICKENS *Uncomm. Trav.* (1861) i. 1 No hotel-room tapestried with great-coats and railway wrappers is set apart for me. **1866** G. M. HOPKINS *Let.* 14 Dec. (1956) 34 Tell Anne to pack my railway-wrapper (which will help to keep the books fr. jolting).

railway, *v.* Add: **3.** To provide with railways.

1917 H. MACFALL *Germany at Bay* xii. 243 When Russia was gunned and munitioned and well railwayed, she was more than a match for the Germans.

railwayana (rēⁱ:lwēⁱ,ā·nă). [f. RAILWAY *sb.* + ANA *suffix.*] Material pertaining to railways; railway relics.

1970 *Sunday Mail Mag.* (Brisbane) 7 June 9/3 In the wake of steam's demise, the collection of railway relics has become almost a national obsession. Enthusiasts have invented a new word—Railwayana... On May 21, Sotheby's held its 'first sale of Railwayana'. **1970** *Railway Mag.* Oct. 541/2, I discovered, in one of the many stalls selling 'railwayana', a line-drawing of Highland Railway No. 103. **1972** *Times* 30 Dec. 14/1 When it proved possible to buy a section, preservationists realized there was more to 'railwayana' than static museums. **1975** *Times* 15 Jan. 15/5 British Rail might do better to invest their pension funds in their own surplus railwayana. Steam locomotive nameplates.. now change hands at £200–300 each.

railwaydom (rēⁱ·lwēⁱdəm). [f. RAILWAY *sb.* + -DOM.] Railways considered collectively; the railway world.

1881 *Punch* 17 Sept. 132/1 The public ought to devise some means of putting the screw on railwaydom. **1885** *Ibid.* 10 Oct. 170/2 For one of the ways By which Railwaydom pays Is to keep us at work day & night, my dear!

railway time. [RAILWAY *sb.*] A standard time adopted throughout a railway system to supersede local time for railway operations (in Great Britain, London time before the adoption of Greenwich Mean Time).

1847 DICKENS *Dombey* (1848) xv. 155 There was even railway time observed in clocks, as if the sun itself had given in. **1851** *London at Table* 1. 19 A private note,..has been sent out, naming eight, railway time, and at that hour to a minute the guests are seated. **1898** *Murray's Handbk. India* (ed. 3) p. xvi, Railway time throughout India is Madras time.. Karachi time is 52 min. behind railway time... Allahabad [time is] 7 min. before railway time. **1959** *Chambers's Encycl.* XIII. 641/1 Till the end of the first half of the 19th century local time was largely used in Great Britain, but the development of railways caused a need for a common system of time-keeping throughout Great Britain, thus the use of 'railway' i.e. Greenwich time became fairly general. **1968** *Guardian* 17 Feb. 8/4 A 24-hour electric clock was built into a wall at Greenwich, and this master clock controlled, by 'galvanism', another clock at London Bridge station, and all the other stations followed London Bridge. Greenwich Mean Time, or Railway Time, as it was called, prevailed. **1975** *Times* 21 June 12/2 From 1840 Greenwich or 'London' time began to be used as 'railway time' throughout Great Britain.

rain, *sb.*[1] Add: **1. b.** Also in fig. phr. *to know enough to come in out of the rain,* and varr., to be sensible enough to act prudently in a given situation. Cf. *RAIN *v.* 1.

1848 F. A. DURIVAGE *Stray Subjects* 95 *Ham* was one of 'em—*he* was! He 'knew sufficient to get out of the rain'. **1884** 'MARK TWAIN' *Huck. Finn* xiv. 122 De man dat think he kin settle a 'spute 'bout a whole chile wid a half a chile doan' know enough to come in out'n de rain. **1894** STEVENSON & OSBOURNE *Ebb-Tide* I. vi. 102 You seem to think underwriters haven't got enough sense to come in out of the rain. **1920** 'SAPPER' *Bull-Dog Drummond* ii. 47 Either, James, I am a congenital idiot, and don't know enough to come in out of the rain; or we've hit the goods. **1932** 'A. GILBERT' *Body on Beam* i. 23 A girl who's lived..in Menzies Street knows when to come in out of the rain. **1941** B. SCHULBERG *What makes Sammy Run?* i. 9 He didn't know enough to come in out of the rain and he died of..dumbness. **1973** J. WAINWRIGHT *Devil you Don't* 47 Come on in, out of the rain, Sugden—your brain is growing moss.

c. *rain or shine*: see *SHINE *sb.*[1] 3 b.

3. b. (Further example.)

1963 C. D. SIMAK *They walked like Men* xxiv. 142 It was raining. Not much of a rain, just the beginning of a rain, cold and miserable.

4. a. (Further examples.)

1935 T. S. ELIOT *Murder in Cathedral* ii. 75 A rain of blood has blinded my eyes. **1942** *R.A.F. Jrnl.* 2 May 4 The continuous rain of pamphlets in all languages told of the enemy's defeats. **1975** J. G. EVANS *Environment Early Man Brit. Isles* iv. 81 It is difficult to work out vegetational structure from the pollen record due to the wide area from which the pollen 'rain' derives.

5. a. *rain-blast, -blur, -cult, -curtain, -dew, -ditch, -drift, -dust, -gem, -land, -light, -mist, -pearl, -pipe* (further examples), *-shine, -song, -spout, -squall, -stain, -storm* (further examples), *-tear, -vapour, -washing, -world.*

1863 G. M. HOPKINS *Poems* (1967) 12 But if the rain-blasts be unbound And from dank feathers wring the drops. **1930** E. POUND *XXX Cantos* vii. 27 Passion to breed a form in shimmer of rain-blur. **1923** L. SPENCE *Gods of Mexico* i. 11 We shall..attempt to descry..an incipient rain-cult. **1926** M. LEINSTER *Dew on Leaf* II. iii. 159 The rain-curtain that swayed like a grey chiffon veil before Rhona's window. **1954** J. R. R. TOLKIEN *Fellowship of Ring* I. viii. 146 Frodo heard a sweet singing running in his mind: a song that seemed to come like a pale light behind a grey rain-curtain. **1922** JOYCE *Ulysses* 416 The air is impregnated with raindew moisture. **1949** E. POUND *Pisan Cantos* lxxiv. 12 Tovarish blessed without aim wept in the rainditch at evening. **1910** W. DE MORGAN *Affair of Dishonour* xiii. 207 The rain-drift..strengthened ever from the seaward. **1912** GALSWORTHY *Inn of Tranquility* 48 The mist had thickened to a white, infinitesimal rain-dust. **1931** BLUNDEN *To Themis* 27 The impulses of April, the rain-gems, the rose-cloud. **1930** T. S. ELIOT *Ash-Wednesday* 18 Not On the mainland, in the desert or the rain land. **1957** LD. HAILEY *Afr. Survey* xiv. 1011 Subject to a fixed annual payment to the former 'rainland landholders'. **1904** W. H. HUDSON *Green Mansions* x. 143 This subdued rain-light did not last long. **1893** KIPLING *Seven Seas* (1896) 76 Then softly as a rain-mist on the sward, Came to the Rose the Answer of the Lord. **1936** *Discovery* Aug. 242/2 A leaf which is slightly damp with dew or rain-mist. **1968** 'HAN SUYIN' *Birdless Summer* vi. 136 The peaks were shrouded in rain-mist. **1879** O. WILDE in *Time* Apr. 30 Brush the rain-pearls from the eucharis. **1926** M. LEINSTER *Dew on Leaf* II. iv. 191 Eastern music..was to him..as soft as whispered words of love, delicate as tumbling rain-pearls. **1913** J. MASEFIELD *Daffodil Fields* 92 The water..gurgled through the rain-pipe to the butt. **1969** *Sears, Roebuck & Co. Catal.* Spring/Summer 924/2 All guttering and rainpipes have double-locked seams and rolled edges for added strength. **1960** C. DAY LEWIS *Buried Day* i. 15, I am still haunted by the rainshine of orchards in the vale of Evesham. **1907** N. CURTIS *Indians' Bk.* 365 The Rain-Youth made the rain-songs and gave them to the Navajos. **1954** J. R. R. TOLKIEN *Fellowship of Ring* I. vii. 140 It seemed plain to them that the song was a rain-song, as sweet as showers on dry hills, that told the tale of a river from the spring in the highlands to the Sea far below. **1922** JOYCE *Ulysses* 470 Boys from high school are perched on the..rainspouts, whistling and cheering. **1962** *Publ. Amer. Dial. Soc.* XXXVIII. 38 *Rain spouts* and *water spouting* predominate in Midland territory. **1978** J. A. MICHENER *Chesapeake* 488 The two Steeds, tumbling from their widow's walk, had caught momentarily on rainspouts edging the roof, and then fallen heavily into flowerbeds. **1849** N. KINGSLEY *Diary* (1914) 80 A few rain squalls headed off this forenoon to the NE. **1902** CONRAD *Youth* 40 Before sunset a thick rain-squall passed over the two boats..and that was the last I saw of them for a time. **1930** *Times Educ. Suppl.* 24 May 4/2 Dense rain-squalls forced her to deviate from her course. **1923** W. DE LA MARE *Riddle* 183 The mosses and rain-stains and frost-flowerings of centuries of autumns and winters. **1952** DYLAN THOMAS *Let.* 6 Nov. (1966) 381 This tumbling house whose every rain-stain..I know in my sleep. **1905** *Macmillan's Mag.* Nov. 42 Everything European was washed off, as is paint off a woman's face in a rain-storm. **1979** 'A. BLAISDELL' *No Villain need Be* ix. 147 Sunday morning broke bright and clear..which was normal for Southern California after a rainstorm. **1909** E. POUND *Personae* 13 Cloud and rain-tears pass they fleet! **1922** JOYCE *Ulysses* 416 Those burgeoning stars overhead, rutilant in thin rainvapour. **1886** HARDY *Mayor Casterbr.* II. xxii. 306 The walls..had been worn by years of rain-washings to a lumpy crumbling surface. **1970** T. HUGHES *Crow* 43, I am the uncrowned Of the rainworld.

b. *rain-affected, -beaten* (later examples), *-bedraggled, -blown, -blurred, -born, -bruised, -burdened, -cold, -darkened, -dishevelled, -drenched* (further examples), *-fed, -filled, -flawed, -fragrant, -gorged, -heavy, -laden, -laid, -logged, -loud, -molested, -murmured, -pitted, -pocked, -rusted, -shimmery, -sleeked, -slicked, -soaked* (further examples), *-sodden, -stained, -starred, -streaked, -sunken, -sweet, -swept, -varnished, -washed* (further example), *-weathered, -wet, -worn* adjs.

1905 *Daily Chron.* 26 July 1/7 A brilliant innings by Darling was the redeeming feature of Australia's batting on a rain-affected wicket at Manchester. **1962** *Times* 30 Aug. 3/3 Essex won the toss, decided to bat on a rain-affected wicket. **1976** J. SNOW *Cricket Rebel* 26 The rain affected wicket was a little suspect all through. **1914** W. B. YEATS in *Poetry* (Chicago) May 60 The pale unsatisfied ones Appear and disappear..With all their ancient faces like rain-beaten stones. **1932** D. GASCOYNE *Roman Balcony* 7 From the rain-beaten roses under the balcony. **1909** *Daily Chron.* 21 Aug. 1/2 (*heading*) Rain-bedraggled Suffragettes removed by Police. **1922** JOYCE *Ulysses* 434 Her dark den furtive, rainbedraggled. **1917** R. GRAVES *Fairies & Fusiliers* 24 I'm away to the rain-blown hill. **1901** 'L. MALET' *Hist. Sir R. Calmady* v. i. 384 Actuality of rain-blurred, wind-scourged town without, and anger-begetting memories of Brockhurst within. **1965** M. MORRIS in *Overland* XXXI. III. 11 A gateway that still bore, rain-blurred and tattered, the printed notices. **1862** G. M. HOPKINS *Poems* (1967) 114 Then while the rain-born arc glows higher Westward on his sinking sire. **1916** D. H. LAWRENCE *Amores* 130 The rain-bruised leaves are suddenly shaken. **1932** D. GASCOYNE *Roman Balcony* 15 Clouds rear, Dark and ominous, rain-burdened. **1916** E. POUND *Lustra* 22 Grey olive leaves beneath a rain-cold sky. **1928** V. WOOLF *Orlando* v. 224 Her eyes slowly lowered themselves down and down till they came to the rain-darkened earth. **1962** I. MURDOCH *Unofficial Rose* i. 13 Her bright hair..hidden now except where a few rain-darkened ends clung to her neck. **1917** D. H. LAWRENCE *Look! We have come Through!* 56, I listen For the sluicing of their rain-dishevelled petals. **1901** *Contemp. Rev.* Mar. 437 This process of disafforesting is ruinous in a rain-drenched country. **1932** D. GASCOYNE *Roman Balcony* 75 To wait in the weary, rain-drenched queues. **1979** *Arizona Daily Star* 5 Aug. C1/4 The drive found the rain-drenched fairway. **1892** KIPLING *Barrack-Room Ballads* 192 Till he heard as the roar of a rain-fed ford the roar of the Milky Way. **1979** *Nature* 27 Sept. 251/3 Some good progress has certainly been made in research on dry-land farming, largely aimed at reducing risks in cultivation in rainfed areas. **1942** W. FAULKNER *Go down, Moses* 356 The tent-flap falling on the same out-waft of faint and rain-filled light. **1963** A. LUBBOCK *Austral. Roundabout* 4 Across the paddock the sheen of water glittered from the rain-filled dams. *a* **1918** W. OWEN *Poems* (1963) 95 Or be you in the gutter where you stand, Pale rain-flawed phantom of the place. **1916** JOYCE *Portrait of Artist* (1969) 228 The brother's face was bent upon her fair rainfragrant hair. **1917** KIPLING *Diversity of Creatures* 404 Rain on rain-gorged channels raised the water-levels round them. **1943** D. GASCOYNE *Poems 1937–1942* 59 Beside the stolid opaque flow Of rain-gorged Thames. **1942** W. FAULKNER *Go down, Moses* 240 Now the woods ahead of them and the rain-heavy air were one uproar. **1916** JOYCE *Portrait of Artist* (1969) v. 176 The rainladen trees of the avenue evoked in him, as always, memories of the girls and women in the plays of Gerhart Hauptmann. **1921** W. DE LA MARE *Mem. Midget* viii. 47 We..mounted into a four-wheeled cab, and once more were in motion in the rain-laid dust. **1970** G. E. EVANS *Where Beards wag All* viii. 90 On some Suffolk farms it was used in the 'fifties, though admittedly for special jobs like..the saving of wind- or rain-laid crops. **1960** T. HUGHES *Lupercal* 27 Rain-logged, wind-unroofed, The manor farm hulked its last use As landmark. **1926** A. HUXLEY *Two or Three Graces* 173 Peddley broke the rain-loud silence. **1845** LONGFELLOW *To Old Danish Songbook* in *Poems* (1846) 377 Yellow are thy time-worn pages, As the russet, rain-molested Leaves of autumn. **1942** W. FAULKNER in *Story Mag.* May–June 51/2 The tent, the rain-murmured canvas globe, was filled with it once more. **1916** H. G. WELLS *Mr. Britling* II. iii. 285 Men shouted and women sobbed and cowered, and flares played upon the rain-pitted black waves. **1931** V. WOOLF *Waves* 227 One bone lay rain-pocked and sun-bleached. **1947** AUDEN *Age of Anxiety* (1948) ii. 49 O the drains are clogged, Rain-rusted, the roofs of the privies Have fallen in. **1905** *Academy* 21 Oct. 1103/1 The rabbit that scuttled before us, the league-footing hare That shot from her form with tawny and rain-sleeked coat. **1964** *Listener* 9 Jan. 67/1 In darkness outside Foxes and rain-sleeked stones and the dead. **1970** *Globe & Mail* (Toronto) 28 Sept. 12/4 She braked and skidded on rain-slicked pavement but had no real chance to stop. **1890** KIPLING *Departmental Ditties* (ed. 4) 94 The rotten, rain-soaked *khud*. **1975** N. LUARD *Robespierre Serial* iii. 11 They'd gathered in his suite at the Vendôme as soon as they got back from the Loti, without even pausing to change their rain-soaked clothes. **1904** *Westm. Gaz.* 10 May 2/1 The Cossacks were drawn up on a large, rain-sodden, muddy field. **1978** *Cornish Guardian* 27 Apr. 4/8 In the second half it was the clay club who played the game to suit the rain-sodden conditions. **1895** M. PEMBERTON *Impregnable City* II. xiii. 270, I..watched for a while the sleeping island through the rain-stained glass. **1958** L. DURRELL *Balthazar* iii. 62 The gonfalons bellied like sails in the rain-starred afternoon. **1956** H. GOLD *Man who was not with It* (1965) xii. 100 The carnival smelled the same, and The rain-streaked sign swung there. **1980** *Jrnl. R. Soc. Arts* July 530/1 She made an artificial stone, but this was nothing like the dismal, rain-streaked concrete of today. **1916** BLUNDEN *Harbingers* 20 Rainsunken roof, grown green and thin For sparrows' nests and starlings' nests. **1913** W. DE LA MARE *Peacock Pie* 127 Feathered birds in the rain-sweet sky. **1932** BLUNDEN *Face of England* 177 Those blackening rain-swept fields. **1978** R. LUDLUM *Holcroft Covenant* xxxi. 366 His last assignment had been at Kennedy Airport during a rainswept night when a cordon of police surrounded the glistening fuselage of a British Airways 747. **1867** J. R. LOWELL in *Atlantic Monthly* July 99 The candle she held in the door, From rain-varnished tree-trunk Flashed fainter. **1965** *New Statesman* 19 Nov. 803/1 We shared a rainwashed picnic with some shy, boyish chaps. **1940** J. BETJEMAN *Old Lights for New Chancels* 39 The rain-weathered streets of adjacent Rumsaa. **1916** D. H. LAWRENCE *Amores* 49 All round the yard it is cluck, my brown hen, Cluck, and the rain-wet wings. **1928** E. SITWELL *Five Poems* 16 The airs like rain-wet shrinking petals curl. **1904** W. DE LA MARE *Henry Brocken* vi. 51 She trod with cautious foot and peering eye the green, rainworn paths. **1968** T. KINSELLA *Nightwalker* 11 A rain-worn, delicate Stone shape.

c. *rain-giver, -maker* (see as main entry in Suppl.); *rain-bringing, -repellant, -repelling, -resistant, -resisting* adjs.

1922 W. G. KENDREW *Climates of Continents* v. 25 But in the south, south-west winds begin to make their appearance and the southern limit of the [Sahara] desert is found about 18° N. lat. where these rain-bringing winds become predominant in summer. **1946** F. E. ZEUNER *Dating Past* vii. 203 The secondary effects of the glaciation..affected the Mediterranean, through the deviation of many rain-bringing depressions. **1922** W. G. KENDREW *Climates of Continents* xx. 110 The south-west monsoon is essentially the rain-giver of India. **1927** P. M. LARKENS in *Sudan Notes & Rec.* IX. 46 But in spite of this it is Liwa's spirit, and not *Mbali*, that is supposed to be the rain-giver here. **1968** *Daily Tel.* 4 Nov. 11/5 Best outfits..included a gleaming parchment kid coat, rain-repellant. **1892** C. M. YONGE *Old Woman's Outlook* 178 Sheaves..built up in the rain-repelling arrangements. **1958** *Times* 6 Oct. 13/1 And all the tweeds are mothproofed as well as rain-resistant. **1963** *Economist* 20 July 256/2 Novelties (such as 'rain-resistant' petunias..from Japan). **1952** R. LEIGHTON *Compl. Bk. Dog* (rev. ed.) viii. 126 The outer-coat [of the Alsatian] is also close,..so that it is rain-resisting.

6. rain-belt, a stretch of land much subject to rain; also *fig.*; **rain bonnet** chiefly *U.S.*, a plastic fold-up bonnet worn as a protection against the rain; **rain boot** *U.S.* (see quot. 1975); **rain-cape,** a waterproof cape (CAPE *sb.*[2] 3) furnishing protection from rain; hence **rai·ncaped** *a.*, wearing a rain-cape; **rain-charm,** an object, action, or incantation used by a rainmaker to summon rain; **rain check, cheque** chiefly *U.S.*, (*a*) a ticket given to a spectator at an outdoor event providing for a refund of his entrance money or admission at a later date, should the event be interrupted by rain; *transf.*, a ticket allowing one to order an article before it is available, and to collect it when it becomes so; (*b*) *fig.* (see quot. 1930); also, esp. in phr. *to take a rain check on*, to reserve the right not to take up a specified offer until such time as it should prove convenient; **raincoat** (examples); used *attrib.* of someone or something thought to be lewd or unseemly, esp. in phr. *raincoat brigade*, disreputable, raincoat-clad, frequenters of cinemas that show pornographic films (also in extended use); hence **rai·ncoated** *a.*, wearing a raincoat; **rain crow** *U.S.*, the yellow-billed or black-billed cuckoo, *Coccyzus americanus* or *C. erythrophthalmus*; cf. RAINBIRD 2; **rain dance,** a dance performed by a tribal group in the hope of summoning rain; **rain date** *U.S.*, an alternative date upon which an outdoor activity can be held if rain should cause the intended date to be unsuitable; **rain-day** *Meteorol.*, a day, commencing for statistical purposes at 9 a.m. G.M.T., on which the recorded rainfall is not less than 0·01 inch or 0·2 mm.; **rain dog** (see DOG *sb.* 10 a and quot.); **rain-fly,** a blood-sucking, greyish fly, *Hæmatopota pluvialis*, of the family Tabanidæ; **rain frog,** a name used in North and Central America for a small tree frog or spring peeper belonging to the genus *Hyla*; **rain-god** (earlier and later examples); also **rain-goddess**; **rain-hat, hood,** a head-covering designed spec. to afford protection against the rain; **rain jacket,** a short raincoat designed in the shape of a jacket; also, a small protective covering worn by a dog; **rain-jungle** = *RAIN FOREST; **rain load,** the weight of rain on an airship; **rain-pitting** (example); **rain-shadow,** an area of small annual rainfall, brought about because it is sheltered from prevailing rain-bearing winds by a range of hills (see also quot. 1955); hence **rain-shadowing,** the action of producing a rain-shadow; **rain-stone,** a stone believed to possess certain qualities and used in primitive rain-making rituals; **rainsuit,** a jacket and leggings designed to protect one against the rain; **rain-temple,** a temple in which supposedly rain-provoking rituals are enacted; **rain-tree,** substitute for def.: (*a*) an evergreen shrub, *Brunfelsia undulata*, of the family Solanaceæ, native to Jamaica and bearing white, bell-shaped flowers; (later example); (*b*) = *GUANGO, *SAMAN[2]; **rain-wash** (further examples); **rainwear** (see quot. 1953). See also *RAIN FOREST.

1878 R. J. HINTON *Handbk. Arizona* vii. 201 The Santa Cruz [Valley], up to Tubac, marks the western limit of a notable rain-belt. **1948** E. WAUGH *Loved One* 69 Water played everywhere from a buried network of pipes, making a glittering rain-belt waist-high. **1968** *Punch* 19 June 892/3 Weinsoff can have his name on his key tag..hatband and sponge (and Mrs. Weinsoff on her pot holder, thimble and rain bonnet). **1975** S. LAUDER *Killing Time on Corvo* vi. 53 She grinned chummily, tucking strands beneath the rain bonnet. **1951** *Sun* (Baltimore) (B ed.) 23 May 7/6 (Advt.), The only rainboot made of Norlon, the wonder plastic!.. Folds neatly and compactly in a fit-in-your-purse plastic pouch. **1975** *Listener* 25 Dec. 845/1 American rain boots.. are a kind of mid-calf galoshes which pull over your shoes. **1921** *Daily Colonist* (Victoria, B.C.) 1 Oct. 3/5 (Advt.), Children's good quality tan colored raincapes to fit girls 4 to 12 years; made with lined hood. **1922** D. H. LAWRENCE in *Dial* Jan. 54 Fat cab-men, whose rubber rain-capes flapped like wings in the wind. **1976** *Southern Even. Echo* (Southampton) 1 Nov. (Advt. section) 8/6 Cindico Pushchair Raincape, royal blue, new, unwanted gift. **1977** *Observer* (Colour Suppl.) 7 Aug. 41/2 Dress properly for riding a bike... Avoid rain capes that flap about the wheels. **1922** JOYCE *Ulysses* 406 They hear the heavy tread of the watch as two raincaped shadows pass the new royal university. **1973** A. PRICE *October Men* iii. 41 The rain-caped policeman materialised out of a gap in the hedge to stop the car. **1890** J. G. FRAZER *Golden Bough* I. iii. 403 The story that the body of Osiris enclosed in a coffer was thrown by Typhon into the Nile perhaps points to a custom of throwing the body of the victim, or at least a portion of it, into the Nile as a rain-charm. **1936** E. E. EVANS-PRITCHARD in *Essays Soc. Anthrop.* (1962) viii. 188 On one occasion, at Tambura, a rainmaker buried his rain charm with the body of his son, in revenge for the latter's death, which he suspected to have been caused by magic. **1884** *St. Louis* (Missouri) *Post-Dispatch* 26 May 8/2 The heavy rain yesterday threw a damper over local operations. At each of the parks the audience had to be content with three innings and rain checks. **1919** *Nat. Geogr. Mag.* Aug. 103 Even the sport-loving Britons are said to have admired and wondered at the American dough-boy..issuing occasional rain-checks in mid-inning when the downpour of bursting shells became too distracting. **1930** J. LAIT *Big House* 6 A parole is a 'rain check'. **1939** R. CHANDLER *Big Sleep* xi. 83 The Sternwoods have money. All it has bought them is a rain cheque. **1959** P. H. JOHNSON *Humbler Creation* xviii. 120 Westlake said, 'I'll take a rain-check. Be back.' Maurice, not certain of this idiom which he vaguely knew to be American, watched him go. 'Has he had enough?' he asked Kate... 'I should make a guess that he has to have a drink.' **1970** *Washington Post* 30 Sept. D3/5 (Advt.), If our stores cannot perform this work within the time indicated we will give you a raincheck enabling you to have work done within 30 days at the advertised price. **1976** L. DEIGHTON *Twinkle, Twinkle Little Spy* xiv. 141 'Let me take a rain-check.' 'On a love affair?' I said. **1976** *New Yorker* 26 Apr. 31/1 Levin's project is to array miniature open-air versions of a hundred New York restaurants side by side along the Central Park Mall on Saturday, May 22nd (rain check for Sunday). **1977** *Time* 14 Nov. 41/3 Unless he can cash his rain check by early 1978, the President will run smack into France's March elections. **1830** J. F. WATSON *Ann. Philadelphia* App. 52 As a defence from rain, the men wore 'rain coats', and the women 'camblets'. **1871** A. B. MITFORD *Tales Old Japan* II. 3 The farmers, dressed in their grass rain-coats. **1897** *Sears, Roebuck Catal.* 187/1 Men's Double Texture Mackintosh Rain Coats..Made from good quality diagonal cloth..suitable to wear in place of an overcoat. **1925** *Scribner's Mag.* Sept. 238/2 His raincoat was split up the back, under his belt. **1976** *Vogue* Jan. 22/4 Raincoats in rust, khaki and navy blue..£74. **1976** *Times Lit. Suppl.* 9 July 842/2 The serious press in England is still being penalized for having so long tolerated less high-minded efforts at disclosure by the raincoat press. **1976** *Observer* 12 Dec. 24/4 Mindful of its duty to the raincoat brigade, however, the film abandons investigation at regular intervals to provide the expected, and inordinately protracted, bouts of titillation. **1977** *New Yorker* 23 May 33/2 O.K. for the raincoat brigade, but rather bland for the longhairs. **1930** W. FAULKNER *As I lay Dying* 74 Slowly he strokes his hands on his raincoated thighs. **1974** D. FRANCIS *Knock Down* i. 10 The rain-coated assembly looked.. miserable. **1806** M. LEWIS *Jrnl.* 16 July in *Orig. Jrnls. Lewis & Clark Exped.* (1905) V. 205, I saw both yesterday and today the Cookkoo or as it is sometimes called the *rain craw.* **1831** J. J. AUDUBON *Ornith. Biogr.* I. 19 The Dutch farmers of Pennsylvania know it [*sc.* the yellow-billed cuckoo] better by the name of Rain Crow. **1872** E. COUES *Key to N. Amer. Birds* 190 American cuckoos..are..noted for their loud jerky cries, which they are supposed to utter most frequently in falling weather, whence their popular name, 'rain crow'. **1880** G. W. CABLE *Grandissimes* xxviii. 237 The dismal ventriloquous note of the rain-crow. **1899** B. TARKINGTON *Gentleman from Indiana* viii. 118 The rain-crow that sat on the fence. **1917** T. G. PEARSON *Birds Amer.* II. 130/1 Both species are known as the 'Rain Crow' because of the belief—especially among farmers—that their guttural cry predicts rain. **1935** H. DAVIS *Honey in Horn* xv. 237 A rain-crow..sang like clanking a little copper bell. **1946** G. STIMPSON *Bk. about Thousand Things* 55 The

American cuckoo is known to country people as the rain or storm crow because its plaintive note..is regarded as a sign of rain or storm. **1930** J. M. Buttree *Rhythm of Redman* 89 It is the privilege of all to improvise the new song for each rain dance. **1968** E. McCourt *Saskatchewan* 6 Old Chief Sheepskin, nominally a Christian, summoned his braves to perform a rain dance. **1977** *Time* 18 Apr. 25/1 When the wet season in Northern California turned up bone dry, about 2,000 San Franciscans staged a modern rain dance in the Hyatt Regency Hotel. **1972** *Village Voice* (N.Y.) 1 June 34/5 The Blue Mountain Paper Parade will present choreographer Barbara Roan's latest work, 'Waystation/Truckers Only,' on Saturday, June 3, at 3 p.m. on the Brooklyn Heights Promenade... The rain date is June 4. **1975** *New Yorker* 7 July 11/3 Wednesday, July 2, at 8:30 (rain date, July 3), 'La Traviata'. **1978** *Chicago* June 201/2 It's open house at the Durant's on June third..Stop in between ten a.m. and five p.m. $1.50 admission. Rain date is June fourth. **1906** *Brit. Rainfall 1905* 123 This improvement may be traced by the steady increase in the number of rain days reported. **1928** *Nature* 14 Apr. 591/2 The variations of the number of rain-days over the British Isles are much less than the corresponding variations of rainfall. **1976** *Southern Even. Echo* (Southampton) 2 Nov. 13/6 According to meteorological office statistics, rainfall in the city was more than double the average and the number of 'rain-days' ranked as the highest in 50 years. **1866** 'Mark Twain' in *Sacramento Union* 24 Aug. 3/2 What the sailors call 'rain dogs'—little patches of rainbow—are often seen drifting about the heavens in these latitudes. **1921** E. Step *Brit. Insect Life* 231 This is the Clegg or Rain-fly.., the grey, dusty-looking Fly that you have no suspicion is sitting on your hand or neck until its sharp lancet is thrust into your flesh. **1952** E. F. Daglish *Name this Insect* 277 Rain-fly or Clegg... Common in fields, meadows, woods, and about hedgerows. **1958** J. Carew *Black Midas* v. 79 A money-spider was struggling with a rain fly. **1971** *Country Life* 21 Oct. 1035/1, I am not partial to the bite of the rainfly. **1827** T. L. McKenney *Sk. Tour to Lakes* 158 We found the few people who live near its mouth..[with] rain frogs on the logs of their huts to sing them to repose. **1938** M. K. Rawlings *Yearling* i. 6 A rain frog sang a moment and then was still. **1958** J. Carew *Wild Coast* iv. 59 Outside, rain frogs were complaining to the stars. **1962** S. Wynter *Hills of Hebron* v. 70 From the dark hollows rain-frogs cracked sharp sad notes. **1864** Rain-god [see *mganga]. **1968** *New Larousse Encycl. Mythol.* 438 (*caption*) Tlaloc, the Aztec rain god enjoyed a similar popularity and was also one of the chief gods of the pantheon. **1904** Rain-goddess [see *Earth-Mother* s.v. *earth *sb.*[1] II.]. **1967** J. R. Crawford *Witchcraft & Sorcery in Rhodesia* xii. 188 We go to *Hosana*, that is the rain goddess, and appeal to *Hosana* for rain. **1921** *Daily Colonist* (Victoria, B.C.) 28 Oct. 7/1 (Advt.), Women's and children's rain hats at $1.50 each. **1955** E. Pound *Classic Anthol.* IV. 208 With a crowd of rain-hats And clicking hoes Out goes the weed To mulch and rot. **1967** *Punch* 21 June 907/1 Prizes for the best set of answers include restrung celebrity-used rackets, foldaway rain hats and transistor radios for getting the cricket commentaries. **1977** *Chicago Tribune* 2 Oct. XIII. 4/1 Besides, you have only a mile and a half to go, and you have boots, raincoat, and rain hat. **1964** 'E. Peters' *Flight of Witch* ii. 34 Did she go off wearing her rain-hood, and her heavy shoes, a night like this? **1977** P. Kemp in P. Collenette *Winter's Tales 23* 49 She was busy.. untying a transparent plastic rain-hood that she was wearing over a rayon head-square. **1975** *Country Life* 29 May 1424/2 The newest thing in rainwear is the suit... Next to the suit, the rain jacket is very much around. **1976** *Evening Times* (Glasgow) 1 Dec. 26/6 Rain jackets, royal, sky, red and yellow, all sizes from £8·99. **1960** *Spectator* 30 Sept. 493/2 The Brookes..stayed a hundred years as landgraves of an impoverished swatch of rain-jungle. **1964** R. Perry *World of Tiger* i. 3 There are..less than four thousand scattered over India,..from Goa to the rain-jungles of Assam. **1928** C. F. S. Gamble *Story N. Sea Air Station* xv. 249 Rain load also had to be reckoned with, which may go as far as 3,000 kg. **1879** *Encycl. Brit.* X. 294/1 *Sun-cracks, Rain-pittings*, &c.—Proofs may not infrequently be found that during deposition aqueous strata have been laid bare to air and sun. **1902** H. J. Mackinder *Britain & Brit. Seas* 165 This dryness to leeward of the heights has been termed their rain-shadow. **1955** *Sci. News Let.* 2 Apr. 212/1 Prevailing winds..smack against the mountains, and are then forced down the eastern slopes. These winds are so strong they keep warm, moist air from the Gulf of Mexico from penetrating deep inland. The air is sinking rather than rising. Result: no moisture falls. Weathermen call this effect the rain shadow. **1974** M. Peissel *Great Himalayan Passage* vi. 112 This entire area is within what is known as the 'rain-shadow' of the Himalayas, a sheltered spot where clouds never break. **1936** *Geogr. Jrnl.* LXXXVII. 11 Valley routes have certain advantages as well as disadvantages for air travel. Among their advantages I would put..the finer weather, owing to local rain-shadowing. **1897** W. E. Roth *Ethnol. Stud. N.-W.-Central Queensland Aborigines* xii. 167 The rain-stick, *koo-roo-mun-do*, is formed of a thin piece of a species of 'white' wood, about 20 inches long, on to the top of which is fixed a mass of the ordinary cementing-substance: into this the three 'rain-stones', pieces of white quartz-crystal, are stuck. **1932** *Times Lit. Suppl.* 1 Dec. 915/2 Such rain-stones may be of quartz, of which the transparency is suggestive of water. **1975** *Islander* (Victoria, B.C.) 2 Feb. 3/1 When the medicine man..wishes to produce rain he plunges his rain-stone in water, takes a split-top peeled cane in hand and beckons with it to the clouds. **1965** *Harper's Bazaar* Feb. 39 *News now, the rainsuit*, newer still if it's trousers. **1966** *Daily Tel.* 14 Nov. 10/7 Not certain of the weather? Then for town or country a rainsuit could be the answer. **1974** M. Hoyt *30 Miles for Ice Cream* x. 114 So I, for one, wear the rubber pants of a rain suit when I'm shanty-fishing. **1977** *New Yorker* 27 June 74/2 Six miles downstream, I had added..a rain suit, hood to heel. **1907** R. S. Rattray *Some Folklore Stories & Songs in Chinyanja* II. ix. 118 Next morning at dawn everyone comes together and they go to the rain temple. **1911** J. G. Frazer *Golden Bough: Magic Art* (ed. 3) I. v. 250 When the rains do not come..the people of Central Angoniland repair to what is called the rain-temple. **1911** *Chambers's Jrnl.* Feb. 206/1 The rain-tree..can withstand extreme climatic fluctuations, needs but little care in its cultivation, and grows rapidly. **1924** Record & Mell *Timbers Trop Amer.* 204 The 'samán' or rain tree..belongs to this genus. **1939** R. C. Marshall *Silviculture Trinidad & Tobago* 119 Rain Tree..is a short-boled tree with an enormous wide spreading crown. **1961** *20th Cent.* Jan. 64 Rain-trees, whose leaves close up at night, enfolding moisture which in the morning the unfurling foliage discharges. **1963** [see *guango]. **1969** [see *monkey-pod (tree)* s.v. *monkey *sb.* 17 b]. **1975** *Bangladesh Observer* 25 July 5/6 Rain-tree..is found in abundance all over Bangladesh. **1976** *Hortus Third* (L. H. Bailey Hortorium) 185/2 *Brunfelsia..undulata*..Rain tree. Slender, evergreen shrub. **1942** Rain-wash [see *bad lands]. **1965** G. J. Williams *Econ. Geol. N.Z.* vii. 80/1 In his view all the components of the schist except the quartz and gold and such resistant heavy minerals as zircon were reduced to clay and generally removed by rain-wash. **1977** A. Hallam *Planet Earth* 81/1 Because of the dominance of rainwash over other erosional forces, these features are most common in warmer climates. **1953** P. C. Berg *Dict. New Words* 134/1 *Rainwear*, garments suited for wearing in rain; e.g. 'Britain's Best Rainwear'. **1958** *People* 4 May 15/7 (Advt.), Have your suit for £1 down and add whatever else you need—rainwear, shoes, shirts, sportswear, etc. to your account. **1975** *Country Life* 6 Feb. 347/3 Ismat also sell..T-shirts and rainwear. **1977** J. Aiken *Last Movement* i. 33 It was still pouring, so..Gina..put herself back into her red plastic rainwear.

rain, *v.* Add: **I. 1.** Phr. *to go* (or *come*) *in when it rains*: to take measures for one's own safety; to exercise ordinary prudence; to shift for oneself. *U.S.* Cf. *rain *sb.*[1] 1 b.

a **1852** F. M. Whitcher *Widow Bedott Papers* (1856) iii. 36 He was a *saftly* feller—dident scarcely know enough to go in when it rained. **1866** 'Mark Twain' *Lett. from Sandwich Islands* (1937) 84 A..majority..that knew just about enough to come in when it rained. **1873** —— *Choice Humorous Wks.* III. 524, I perceive that thou art none of them that know not to come in when it doth rain. **1906** *Springfield* (Mass.) *Weekly Republ.* 12 July 2 Every citizen of Vermont who is capable of going in when it rains ought to understand [etc.]. **1923** E. F. Wyatt *Invis. Gods* I. ii. 19 Hetherington Marshfield, who doesn't know enough to go in when it rains!

b. Also const. *on*.

1925 R. Torrence *Hesperides* 60, I was weak as a rained-on bee. **1937** *Burlington Mag.* June 262/1 Rained-on, as it were, by Nature. **1972** J. Gores *Dead Skip* xvi. 113 Two big recently rained-on cardboard boxes of trash.

II. 6. a. (Further example.)

1871 W. D. Howells in *Atlantic Monthly* Dec. 722/2 It was raining one of those cold rains.

b. Phr. *if it should rain porridge, he would want his dish* and varr., denoting a person's recurrent bad luck or management.

1670 J. Ray *Coll. Eng. Proverbs* 191 If it should *rain* pottage, he would want his dish. **1732** T. Fuller *Gnomologia* 112 If it should rain Porridge, he'd want a Dish. **1889** C. H. Spurgeon *Salt-Cellars* 257 If it rained porridge, the lazy man would have no basin. **1950** K. S. Prichard *Winged Seeds* ii. 29 Unluckiest man ever I knew. If it was raining pea soup, he'd only have a fork. **1970** R. Beilby *No Medals for Aphrodite* (1971) v. 169 Gawd, we're an unlucky battalion, we are. If it was rainin' virgins we'd be washed away with a poofta, dinkum!

7. a. (Further examples.)

1939 *Ann. Reg. 1938* 260 Air-raids rained bombs on Barcelona, Tarragona, and a number of peaceful seaside towns where there was no trace of any military objective. **1977** *Time* 14 Mar. 53/1 Fans rained bottles and cans on to the ground.

8. b. *pass.* and *intr.* Of particulate matter: to be removed from the atmosphere as a result of being incorporated into raindrops as they form. Cf. *rain-out.

1975 *Nature* 13 Nov. 134/2 The importance of this observation is that it makes nonsense of the assumption..that practically everything that can..be rained out as air ascends into the stratosphere, actually is rained out and thus removed. **1979** *McGraw-Hill Yearbk. Sci. & Technol.* 153/1 The ^{3}H generated was largely injected into the upper atmosphere, from which it 'rained out' into the oceanic-hydrologic system.

9. a. (Later examples.)

1924 C. Mackenzie *Old Men of Sea* ii. 17 The sky had rained itself out. **1944** T. D. Clark *Pills, Petticoats & Plows* 88 Behind him at home was a cotton crop which had been rained out. **1976** G. Moffat *Short Time to Live* ix. 85 She was a walker rained off the hill.

b. *to be rained out* (U.S.) or *off*, of an outdoor event (esp. a match), an airline flight, etc.: to be terminated or cancelled because of rain. So **rained-off** *a.*

1928 *Chicago Tribune* 18 June 27/7 (*heading*) Sox, Boston series final is rained out. **1937** *Sun* (Baltimore) 18 May 17/8 Today's [baseball] game was rained out. **1955** *Times* 24 May 10/2 An open-air meeting was rained off, but pickets patrolled the dock entrances carrying sandwich boards. **1960** C. Day Lewis *Buried Day* i. 20 Their tiny tragedies—a rained-off picnic, a broken toy. **1964** *Observer* 12 Jan. 32/1 Rain check..is the receipt or counterfoil of a ticket taken for a baseball game which entitles you to see another match if the one you wanted to see is 'rained off'. **1969** 'E. Lathen' *When in Greece* ix. 98 Unfortunately the planes are rained out, but the train should get her here before midnight. **1974** *Union* (S. Carolina) *Daily Times* 19 Apr. 6/1 In the American League..Minnesota clipped California 3–2 and Baltimore's game at Detroit was rained out. **1977** 'J. Le Carré' *Hon. Schoolboy* xvi. 399 Watching a rained-off cricket match where the contestants wanted only to go back to the pavilion. *Ibid.* xxii. 525 The match was rained off... Another date would be fixed. Stand by, they said.

rain-bird. 1. For *Gecinus* substitute *Picus*. (Later examples.)

1913 H. K. Swann *Dict. Eng. & Folk-Names Brit. Birds* 187 Rain-bird, Rain-fowl, or Rain-pye: The Green Woodpecker... It is still a country belief that when the cry of this bird is much heard rain will follow. **1979** *Country Life* 20 Sept. 829/3 Now I hardly ever hear the rainbird, as the green woodpecker is called.

rainbow. Add: **1. a.** Phr. *the end of the rainbow, the rainbow's end*: with allusion to the proverbial belief in the existence of a crock of gold (or something else of great value) at the end of a rainbow. Cf. *rainbow-chase* at sense 4 d below.

1836 W. D. Cooper *Gloss. Provincialisms Sussex* 16 Go to the end of the rainbow, and you'll find a crock of money. **1916** R. E. Beach (*title*) Rainbow's end. **1971** A. Diment *Think Inc.* ii. 21 Every wornout hack of an agent retires there... It's the end of the rainbow for every British spy. **1973** R. Lewis *Blood Money* i. 12 He'd found the jackpot again, the end of the rainbow. **1976** *Times* 9 Aug. 10/5 Until recently West Germany has [been]..relegating reunification to the dream world at the rainbow's end. **1977** *Times* 27 Apr. 11/1 Holyhead could do with some oil at the end of the rainbow... It has seen a substantial decline in trade.

3. b. (Earlier and later examples.)

1779 P. Freneau in *U.S. Mag.* Feb. 85 The rainbow cuts the deep of varied green. **1909** *Westm. Gaz.* 13 Feb. 16/2 If there is a river in which rainbows should grow large and wax fat it is the Thames. **1940** R. Pertwee *Master of None* v. 27, I caught a sizeable rainbow with it [*sc.* a rod] last season. **1963** *Times* 8 June 13/2 The rainbow is a fish of American origin. **1977** F. Parrish *Fire in Barley* iii. 33 The Mullett family had eaten a good many of his fat rainbows. **1979** *Fisherman's Weekly* 21 June 5/4 Top fish was a rainbow of 7lb. 7oz. taken by Eddy Ouslie of Exeter.

3*. A capsule containing the barbiturates Amytal and Seconal, one end of which is red and the other blue. *slang* (orig. *U.S.*).

1968–70 *Current Slang* (Univ. S. Dakota) III–IV, 100 *Rainbows*, n. A type of barbiturate in red and blue capsules. (Drug users' jargon.) **1972** *Sunday Sun* (Brisbane) 2 July 14/3 The barbiturate addict takes red devils..rainbows.. all 1972 junkie names for various drugs. **1972** J. Wambaugh *Blue Knight* (1973) xvi. 303 One lousy time I dropped a red devil and a rainbow with some guys at school, and that's all the dope I ever took. **1976** M. Millar *Ask for me Tomorrow* xiv. 115 Getting their kicks by mixing drinks and drugs, like..the high school kid carrying a flask of vodka to wash down the rainbows.

4. a. *rainbow flower* (later example), *light* (later examples), *-space*.

1928 Blunden *Retreat* 67 What angel dropped her rainbow-flowers In that horizon blue of ours? **1854** Thoreau *Walden* 218 It was a lake of rainbow light, in which, for a short while, I lived like a dolphin. **1924** R. Graves *Mock Beggar Hall* 78 Then since laws move in rainbow-light Let faith be therefore strong. **1918** E. Sitwell *Clowns' Houses* 14 A glassy ball that clowns have hurled Through the rainbow-space of laughter.

c. *rainbow-gay, -happy, -sweet, -tailed, -tinted* (earlier and later examples) adjs.

1893 Kipling *Seven Seas* (1896) 69 O rainbow-gay the red pools lay that swilled and spilled and spread. **1940** Blunden *Poems 1930–1940* 190 How comes the rainbow-happy shower! **1942** L. Hughes *Shakespeare in Harlem* 20 So if you want to know beauty's Rainbow-sweet thrill, Stroll down luscious, Delicious, *fine* Sugar Hill. **1929** *Oxf. Poetry* 32 Conjure..rich waterlilies lightly to be embraced by rainbowtailed delirious dragonflies. **1827** Disraeli *Viv. Grey* IV. VI. vi. 196 The sun..lent additional brilliancy to the rainbow-tinted birds of paradise. **1897** E. L. Voynich *Gadfly* viii. 352 The surplices of the choristers gleamed, rainbow-tinted, beneath the coloured windows.

d. rainbow-bird *Austral.*, the bee-eater, *Merops ornatus*, a small, brightly coloured bird belonging to the family Meropidæ and native to northern Australia; **rainbow boa**, a large iridescent snake, *Epicrates cenchris*, of the family Boidæ, found in forest areas of northern South America; **rainbow cactus**, a small, cylindrical cactus, *Echinocereus pectinatus*, native to southwestern North America and bearing red flowers and spines in bands of various colours; **rainbow-chase** *fig.*, a quest which is rendered pointless by the illusory nature of its object; hence **rainbow-chaser, -chasing**; **rainbow-fish**, for New Zealand substitute Australia; also, a brightly coloured wrasse belonging to the family Labridæ; (examples); **rainbow-serpent**, in Australian aboriginal mythology, a large snake associated with water; **rainbow wrasse** (earlier and later examples).

1911 J. A. Leach *Austral. Bird Bk.* 107 Rainbow-bird, Aust. Bee-eater,..Spinetail, Pintail, *Merops ornatus.* **1933** *Bulletin* (Sydney) 11 Oct. 21/3 One of the loveliest birds of N. Australia..is the rainbow-bird, which, with its green coat, black tail, and bright orange throat, well deserves its name. **1944** A. Russell *Bush Ways* v. 28 The mutton-birds make underground nesting burrows, and so, too, do the rainbow-bird..and the white-backed swallow. **1963** A. Lubbock *Austral. Roundabout* 167 A rainbow-bird darted across the road, a brilliant flash of emerald, blue and orange. **1975** I. Rowley *Bird Life* 253 Hole-nesting birds such as pardalotes, kingfishers, rainbow-birds, parrots, mutton-birds and penguins can all be captured while they are visiting the nest. **1910** R. L. Ditmars *Reptiles of World* IV. 231 The Rainbow Boa..derives its name from a gorgeous iridescence playing over the scales of a healthy example. **1937** A. H. Verrill *Strange Reptiles* ix. 120 We found two of the lovely iridescent rainbow boas, one barely five feet in length, the other a trifle over six feet. **1958** J. Carew *Black Midas* vi. 119 On our way back I saw a rainbow boa coiled around a branch. **1965** R. & D. Morris *Men & Snakes* viii. 198 But what *is* the true life span of a snake?.. An anaconda managed 28 years, a rainbow boa 27. **1972** M. Richardson *Fascination of Reptiles* vii. 79 A relation [of the Cuban boa] is the rainbow boa..found between the south of Mexico and northern Argentina. **1892** J. G. Lemmon in G. W. James *In & Around Grand Canyon* (1900) xxxi. 325 Rainbow cactus, with bright-coloured zones. **1930** J. M. Breazeale *Color Schemes of Cacti* 14 (*caption*) A flower of the rainbow cactus..about three-fourths natural size. **1976** *Express-News* (San Antonio, Texas) 27 Nov. 10-c/1 We..saw a spiny little cactus growing upright out of the ground like a fat ear of corn. Its bands of colors were the colors of the rainbow—and that's its name—the rainbow cactus. **1886** *St. James's Gaz.* 2 June 10 A fact which had led Mr. Rylands off a rainbow-chase after a visionary Chancellorship. **1892** *Courier-Jrnl.* (Louisville, Kentucky) 1 Oct. 1/8 The rainbow chasers of the Administration are not idle these days. **1925** D. Senior *Rainbow Chasers* iii. 33 'We are all Rainbow-Chasers in youth,' I retorted. 'And even in old age the hope of finding the Crock of Gold is hard to kill.' **1904** *N.Y. Even. Post* 1 Sept. 7 Early in the campaign he had told his associates that it was of no use to go rainbow chasing after Massachusetts, Wisconsin, or Illinois. **1908** *Hampton's Broadway Mag.* Nov. 599/1 We had no business whatever to go rainbow chasing. **1888** G. B. Goode *Amer. Fishes* 205 In this limpid pool were many gorgeously-colored species, the angel-fish, the parrot-fish, the rainbow-fish. **1908** E. J. Banfield *Confessions of Beachcomber* I. iv. 156 In the rainbow and parrot fishes they [*sc.* pharyngeal teeth] are highly specialised. **1927** [see *GUPPY[1]]. **1955** I. S. R. Munro *Marine & Fresh Water Fishes Ceylon* 183 Rainbow Fish, Wrasses... Mostly brilliant coloured species. **1962** D. W. Tucker tr. *Sterba's Freshwater Fishes of World* 807 Dwarf Rainbowfish, Black-lined Rainbowfish. Northern Australia. **1973** *Stand. Encycl. S. Afr.* IX. 237/2 Rainbow-fishes... Tropical fishes, known also as wrasses, mostly living about coral reefs in warm seas. **1977** J. M. Thomson *Field Guide Sea & Estuary Fishes Austral.* 92 The female Rainbow Fish is less colourful than her mate. **1926** A. R. Radcliffe-Brown in *Jrnl. R. Anthrop. Inst.* XXIX. 19 There is found in widely separated parts of Australia a belief in a huge serpent which lives in certain pools or water-holes. This serpent is associated, and sometimes identified, with the rainbow... Hence the rainbow-serpent may come to occupy an important place in the beliefs and customs relating to medicine-men and the practice of magic. **1930** *Oceania* I. 270 It [*sc.* the snake represented] is both the rainbow-serpent who brings spirit babies into water-holes, and also a 'quiet' python which is eaten. **1950** Elkin & Berndt *Art in Arnhem Land* i. 17 A diffusion from the south of Rainbow Serpent mythology. **1965** R. & D. Morris *Men & Snakes* i. 19 By far the most spectacular snakes in Australian aboriginal art are the mythical rainbow serpents. These usually live deep in waterholes during the dry season, but take to the thunder clouds when the rains come, sometimes appearing in the sky as rainbows. **1977** *Bulletin* (Sydney) 22 Jan. 65/1 At the foot of the monolith is an extensive Aboriginal art gallery including an ochre rock painting of the sacred rainbow serpent. **1836** W. Yarrell *Hist. Brit. Fishes* I. 291 (*heading*) The Rainbow Wrasse. **1972** *Oxf. Bk. Vertebrates* 62/1 *Coris julis* (Rainbow Wrasse), common in the Mediterranean and adjacent Atlantic, appears only rarely in British waters.

rain forest. Also with hyphen. [tr. G. *regenwald* (A. F. W. Schimper *Pflanzengeographie* (1898) III. iii. 281): see Rain *sb.*[1] and Forest *sb.*] A dense forest in an area of high rainfall with little seasonal variation, esp. a tropical forest characterized by a rich variety of plant species. Also *attrib.*

1903 W. R. Fisher tr. *Schimper's Plant-Geogr.* I. iii. 260 The Rain-forest is evergreen, hygrophilous in character, at least thirty meters high, but usually much taller, rich in thick-stemmed lianes, and in woody as well as herbaceous epiphytes. **1922** W. G. Kendrew *Climates of Continents* 327 The air is always moist, and the forests are very luxuriant. Dense rain-forest, with rubber, vanilla, and cacao, flourishes up to about 4,000 feet. **1926** T. F. Chipp in Tansley & Chipp *Aims & Methods in Study of Vegetation* x. 207 The tropical rain forest is a type developed under abundant water supply, with high temperature of little variation, and but a short, if any, dry season. **1937** Allee & Schmidt *Hesse's Ecol. Animal Geogr.* xxi. 428 This rain-forest reaches its largest continuous extent in South America. **1952** P. W. Richards *Tropical Rain Forest* i. 1 The name 'Rain forest' is commonly given, not only to the evergreen forest of moist tropical lowlands..but also to the somewhat less luxuriant evergreen forest found at low and moderate altitudes on tropical mountains, and to the evergreen forests of oceanic subtropical climates. **1956** *Nature* 25 Feb. 367/2 A detailed entomological survey..has been commenced in and around Ilobi, a typical rain-forest belt village fifty miles from Lagos. **1960** N. Polunin *Introd. Plant Geogr.* xiv. 430 In lowland rain forest any luxuriant herbaceous ground-vegetation is found chiefly in clearings..where illumination is above the average. **1973** *Sci. Amer.* Dec. 59/1 Sizable areas of rain forest still stand in Amazonia, Africa, Borneo and New Guinea, but..the rain forest is retreating. **1974** *Country Life* 9 Oct. 894/3 Apes, monkeys, rhinoceroses, okapis, bongoes, tapirs and antelopes are just some of the other rain forest animals dependent on this habitat for their survival. **1978** *Vole* Dec. 25/1 Tropical rain forests are one of the world's most remaining wild places.

rai·nmaker, rain-maker. [f. Rain *sb.*[1] + Maker.] **a.** A member of a tribal community believed or claiming to be able to procure rain by the use of magic. **b.** One who attempts to cause rainfall by a technique such as seeding. Hence **rai·n-making** *sb.* and *a.*

1775 [see Rain *sb.*[1] 5 c]. **1775** J. Adair *Hist. Amer. Indians* 87 Rain-making, in the Cheerake mountains, is not so dangerous an office, as in the rich level lands of the Chikkasah country, near the Mississippi. **1856, 1889** [see Rain *sb.*[1] 5 c]. **1890** J. Frazer *Golden Bough* I. i. 13 The third, who was called 'the rain-maker', had a bunch of twigs with which he sprinkled water from a vessel. **1903** *Folk-lore* Sept. 252 The sorcerers..are capable of rain-making, sun-making, and wind-making. **1930** E. R. B. Gribble *40 Yrs. with Aborigines* ix. 87 One old fellow was a noted rain-maker. **1934** V. G. Childe *New Light Most Anc. East* i. 10 These are ruled by rain-maker magicians or by divine kings who were until recently ritually slain. **1960** *Times* 22 Apr. 9/2 The rainmaker must try to induce artificially the formation of ice crystals. **1971** *Islander* (Victoria, B.C.) 18 July 12/3 Here in Canada, where lawmakers are now eyeing rainmakers suspiciously, I might not have been able to try at all. **1976** G. A. Browne *Slide* (1977) 14 The Air Force had been conducting rain-making manoeuvres above the Mojave and Death Valley. **1978** D. Bates in C. Allen *Tales from Dark Continent* vi. 88 They took chickens or pots of beer to a rain-maker in order to pray for rain.

rai·n-out. Also rainout. [f. Rain *v.* + Out *adv.*] **1.** *U.S.* The termination or cancellation of an outdoor event because of rain. Cf. *RAIN *v.* 9 b.

1947 *Richmond* (Va.) *Times-Dispatch* 1 June 12-c/3 Barring professional uncertainties such as rainouts, wrecks, engine trouble, etc., a racer has a chance for good money. **1967** *Boston Sunday Herald* 14 May II. 3/5 National League figures show the senior circuit was hit hardest with 20 rainouts compared with 11 for the same period last year. **1977** *New Yorker* 15 Aug. 24/3 The day after the rainout, the sun emerged, and that evening Jimmy Buffett and his band, the Coral Reefers, finally made it to Wollman Memorial Rink, in Central Park.

2. [After *FALL-OUT.] Incorporation into raindrops of radioactive debris from a nuclear explosion and its localized deposition on the Earth's surface (see quot. 1974).

1954 *Science* 7 May 619/1 The extent of the rainout was much greater than that detected in the area from any previous nuclear detonation. *Ibid.* 620/1 Although there were several days of rain immediately after the rainout, the activity was firmly adsorbed on the pavement and disappeared at a rate about equal to that for decay alone. **1955** *Sci. News Let.* 25 June 406/3 'Rain-out' might take place instead of fallout, Dr. Lapp suggested, thus producing localized areas of contamination 'hotter' than the surrounding region by a factor of ten or more. **1974** *Population Dose Evaluation* 492 Several mechanisms have been conceived for deposition from the atmosphere to the earth's surface. In addition to dry deposition, there is washout by rain falling through a cloud of activity in the atmosphere, or rainout in which the activity is incorporated into rain drops at the time of their formation.

rai·nproof, rain-proof, *a.* (and *sb.*). [f. Rain *sb.*[1] + Proof *sb.*] Impervious to rain. Hence as *sb.*, a rainproof garment, esp. a raincoat. Also **rai·n-proofed** (*a*) rendered impervious to rain; (*b*) wearing a rainproof; **rai·nproofer,** a manufacturer of rain-proof fabrics.

1831, 1870 [in Dict., s.v. Rain *sb.*[1] 5 c]. **1902** *Daily Chron.* 7 Jan. 6/3 The greatcoat is to be made of rain-proofed drab-mixture cloth. **1908** *Ladies' Field* 25 July p. iii/3 (Advt.), J. W. Elvery & Co., waterproofers and rain-proofers,..London, W. **1923** W. Deeping *Secret Sanct.* xiii. 136, I was a wiser virgin than you. I did take a rainproof with me. **1960** *News Chron.* 6 May 8/4 His identically rainproofed escorts prepare to shoot him. **1965** D. Francis *For Kicks* ii. 29 Everything from under-clothes to washing things, jodhpur boots to rainproof, jeans to pyjamas. **1967** N. Freeling *Strike Out* 34 The figure wears a black track-suit now gone greenish, with khaki rainproof trousers and an English suède windcheater. **1977** M. Kenyon *Rapist* xii. 165 George in rainproof hat.

rain-shower. (Later examples.)

1910 W. Owen *Let.* 29 Dec. (1967) 66 We have been prevented from going this morning by the first rain-shower of the week. **1981** L. Deighton *XPD* xxvi. 214 London..The chilly climate with frequent rain showers.

rain-water. Add: **b. rain-water goods,** exterior pipework, guttering, etc., designed to conduct rain-water from a building; **rain-water head,** a collecting piece, freq. ornamental in design, at the top of a drainpipe.

1949 J. F. L. D'Esté in A. C. Martin *Mod. Pract. Plumber* (ed. 3) III. xiv. 321 (*caption*) Surveyor's dimensions for quantities of rainwater goods. **1955** *Times* 8 July 3/3 The Government would have to look at the restrictive practices and rings in the building industry, particularly in the rain-water goods section. **1981** *London* (*North*) *Telephone Directory: Yellow Pages* Jan. 401/1 Bond & White Ltd. Suppliers—sanitary ware—plumbing—rainwater goods. **1876** W. P. Buchan *Plumbing* xiii. 86 Fig. 149 shows conductor with rain-water head, carrying off water from gutter. **1936** P. E. Thomas *Mod. Building Pract.* IV. 225 The lower end of a gutter..can be formed so as to discharge direct into a rain-water head. **1963** *Times* 8 May 6/2 Mr. Lipton (Brixton, Lab.) asked if the Minister would give a list of the persons whose initials were inscribed on the rainwater heads in the new buildings in Downing Street.

rainy, *a.* Add: **2. c.** *rainy season*: in certain, esp. tropical, regions, an annually recurring season of heavy rain (in *Meteorol.*, of at least one month's duration).

1720 Defoe *Capt. Singleton* 135 We could not expect to reach it till an other rainy Season would be upon us. **1817** S. R. Brown *Western Gazetteer* 13 The rainy season.. commences after midsummer. **1872** R. G. McClellan *Golden State* xxii. 294 December..and the succeeding months until May are termed winter, or the 'rainy season', in California. **1910, 1922** [see *BAI-U]. **1977** 'J. Le Carré' *Hon. Schoolboy* xvii. 410 'This [tarmac road is] where he lands?' 'Only in the rainy season.'

5. *rainy-shimmery, -sounding, -wet* adjs.

1930 J. Dos Passos *42nd Parallel* 27 Through the rail of the bridge we can look way down into the cold rainy shimmery water. **1896** A. E. Housman *Shropshire Lad* xxvi. 37 Overhead the aspen heaves Its rainy-sounding silver leaves. **1952** R. Campbell tr. *Baudelaire's Poems* 70 There the suns, rainy-wet, Through clouds rise and set.

raion, var. *RAYON[2].

raise, *sb.*[1] Add: **3.** *spec.* in *Mining*, a sloping shaft excavated from the lower end. Cf. Rise *sb.* 10 b. (Further examples.)

1877 [in Dict.] **1898** S. J. Truscott *Witwatersrand Goldfields* xiii. 293 It being usual in that mine for the man who is driving the levels with machines to come back and put up the raises. **1930** *Economist* 26 Apr. 951/2 The work done by means of drives, winzes, raises and incline shafts to open up new ground. **1973** L. J. Thomas *Introd. Mining* vi. 167 Most raises are in the orebody and follow the footwall in grade in narrower stopes.

4. (Further examples.)

1845 J. J. Hooper *Some Adventures Simon Suggs* iv. 48 The chances were altogether favourable for making a 'raise'. **1878** J. H. Beadle *Western Wilds* II. 41 At last I made a little raise..and concluded to come home. **1900** S. Handsaker *Pioneer Life* (1908) 35 The two brothers 'made quite a raise' in the California mines soon after their discovery. **1914** 'High Jinks, Jr.' *Choice Slang* 15 Make a raise, to secure a loan.

5. a. (Earlier examples.) Also, an increase in the price, rate, or value of a thing. Cf. Rise *sb.* 16 a.

1728 *Maryland Hist. Mag.* (1923) XVIII. 335 You wil certainly find Crops short this year..which I hope may contribute to the Raise of that on hand. **1883** 'Mark Twain' *Life on Mississippi* xxxix. 366 France and Italy.. cracked on such a rattling impost that cotton-seed olive-oil couldn't stand the raise. **1904** [see *JACK *v.*[1] 1 b]. **1931** W. G. McAdoo *Crowded Yrs.* xxx. 469 A gigantic raise in [freight] rates would have added materially to the inflation.

b. An increase of a stake or bet at poker; in Bridge, a higher bid in the same denomination as a previous bid by one's partner.

1821 *Hoyle's Games Improved* 164 The player who last goes the double, raise, or brag, has the right, in his turn, of increasing either. **1887** 'S. Cumberland' *Queen's Highway* vi. 277 You feel certain that every 'raise' he makes will be his last. **1887** J. W. Keller *Draw Poker* 11 Limit, a condition made at the beginning of the game limiting the amount of any single bet or raise. **1921** C. E. Mulford *Bar-20 Three* vii. 86 He had a reputation to maintain, and he saw the raise and returned it. **1923** [see *PRE-EMPTIVE *a.* 2]. **1929** [see *GOOD *a.* 22 j]. **1959** [see *LIMIT *sb.* 2 g (*b*)]. **1964** *Official Encycl. Bridge* 192/2 A raise to two spades would be appropriate when one spade has been overcalled by two hearts. **1976** Scott & Koski *Walk-In* (1977) xxxii. 236 They were making another raise in that poker game, they were threatening to break off diplomatic relations.

c. An increase in wages or salary. Cf. Rise *sb.* 15 b. Chiefly *U.S.*

1898 *Scribner's Mag.* Oct. 489/1 A. J. Packer..had begun to ponder doubts of his wisdom in agreeing to the second 'raise'. **1902** G. H. Lorimer *Lett. Merchant* xiii. 187, I ear-marked Charlie for a raise and a better job right there. **1921** H. L. Mencken *Amer. Lang.* (1922) iv. 131 When her wages are increased she does not get a *raise*, but a *rise*. **1934** T. Wilder *Heaven's my Destination* 28, I keep getting raises all the time. **1956** S. Ertz *Charmed Circle* xiii. 217 She could go on working. She had lately had a raise. **1968** *Globe & Mail* (Toronto) 3 Feb. 37/1 'Stay in shape and I'll give you a raise next season,' advised coach George Imlach. **1971** C. Fick *Danziger Transcript* (1973) 25 My bureau.. were delighted that I got to Cambodia... I got a raise.. when I went back to Cuba. **1977** *Time* 10 Jan. 46/2 Workers strike like clockwork to protest high prices, and nearly always win raises from management.

raise, *v.*[1] Add: **I. 4. b.** (Later examples.)

1874 J. W. Long *Amer. Wild-Fowl Shooting* ix. 157 Watch this old fool of a duck coming, and see me 'raise her'. **1976** *Globe & Mail* (Toronto) 21 Jan. 36/1 A jack rabbit was loping his way. It was only 250 yards from where he first raised it.

II. 8. a. (Earlier and later Amer. examples.)

1657 in *Essex Inst. Hist. Coll.* (1865) VII. 40/1 The said John norman is..to be paid in corne & cattell the one halfe att or before the house be raised. **1712** S. Sewall *Diary* 15 July (1879) II. 355, I, and Mr. Gerrish went to Hog-Island and saw the Barn Rais'd. **1846** *Knickerbocker* XXVIII. 338 After the usual amount of eating, drinking, swearing, and joking, the house..was raised and covered in. **1879** *Harper's Mag.* June 142/1 If a man raised a house or barn, the rum flowed freely. **1943** W. Faulkner in *Sat. Even. Post* 13 Feb. 70/3, I told you we would meet here tomorrow to roof a church...We'll meet here in the morning to raise one.

10. a. (Further examples.)

1824 A. Hodgson *Lett. from N. Amer.* II. 208 One of my young Canadian female companions..was *raised*, as they say here, in Portsmouth. **1846** J. Hall *Wilderness & War Path* 160 'I can't back out,' said he, 'I never was raised to it, no how.' **1882** G. C. Eggleston *Wreck of Red Bird* 3 Maum Sally was born and 'raised', as she would have said, in 'Ole Firginny'. **1929** D. Runyon in *Hearst's International* Oct. 63/1 She slips this baby off to her sister in a little town in Spain to raise up. **1953** *Manch. Guardian Weekly* 15 Jan. 13/3 It [*sc.* Wenatchee, Wash.] is a pleasant town of sixteen thousand home-loving people, mostly engaged in raising nice children and very good eating apples. **1977** 'J. Le Carré' *Hon. Schoolboy* xv. 354 The American wife asked Jerry where he was *raised* and..where his ***home*** was.

11. c. To establish contact with (a person, etc.) by radio or telephone.

1929 *Amer. Speech* V. 49 *Raise*, to secure [radio] communication with. **1969** 'J. Morris' *Fever Grass* xxii. 208 Raise McKay on that [radio] set of yours. **1974** 'M. Hebden' *Pride of Dolphins* III. i. 210 She's gone off the air... We can't raise her. **1976** G. Seymour *Glory Boys* vii. 87 She raised Jimmy, still waiting beside the receiver. **1979** *Daily Tel.* 3 Jan. 1/1 A British Airways plane which tried to get into Teheran had to turn back to Kuwait when it could not raise air traffic control.

14. e. (Further examples.)

1890 Kipling *Barrack-Room Ballads* (1892) 53 Ship me somewheres east of Suez, where the best is like the worst, Where there aren't no Ten Commandments an' a man can raise a thirst. **1930** 'Sapper' *Finger of Fate* 79 He grinned and said, 'We're not all savages, Mrs. Dankerton. Even though there aren't no Ten Commandments, and a man can raise a thirst.'

III. 17. e. Fig. phr., *to raise its (ugly) head*, to make an (unwelcome) appearance; to present itself as a (troublesome) subject for attention. Cf. *rear *v.*^{1} 10 b.

1822 Scott *Peveril* II. i. 27 The ancient superstition.. is raising its head. **1930** Wodehouse *Very Good, Jeeves!* ix. 230, I am starving on my feet. Well, when I tell you that it's weeks since a beefsteak pudding raised its head in the house, you'll understand what I mean. **1966** *Listener* 28 July 141/3 The subject of money for the arts raised its head again when *New Release*..investigated the facts behind the Authors' Society recent publication about the stipends of professional writers. **1971** Wodehouse *Much Obliged, Jeeves* xiii. 133 The snag which had raised its ugly head was one of formidable—you might say king-size—dimensions.

f. Other phrases. *to raise one's eyebrow(s)*: see *eyebrow 1 c; *to raise the roof*: see *roof *sb.* 1 e (*a*).

19. d. *spec.* in relation to consciousness: to heighten (sensitivity or awareness).

1970 K. Millett *Sexual Politics* (1971) I. ii. 38 The hope of seeking liberating radical solutions of their own seems too remote for the majority to dare contemplate and remains so until consciousness on the subject is raised. **1976** *Spare Rib* Dec. 22/2 We're raising consciousness, affecting some concrete issues like age discrimination, putting lousy pay on the agenda too. **1977** *Rolling Stone* 7 Apr. 53/3 My efforts to raise the consciousness of whites who are so against Indians in the States were bound to be stopped by the FBI sooner or later.

19*. *Phonetics.* To articulate (a vowel) with the tongue closer to the roof of the mouth. Cf. *raising *vbl. sb.* 1 d.

1874 H. Sweet *Hist. Eng. Sounds* in *Trans. Philol. Soc.* *1874* 506 To assume that the low-narrow [ê] was first widened, and then raised to the mid position, would be to ignore the fundamental laws of short vowel change. **1914** H. C. Wyld *Short Hist. Eng.* vii. 136 Old tense ē was raised to [ī] at least by the end of the first third of the sixteenth century. **1934** C. Davies *Eng. Pronunc.* 5 ME ā. Was early fronted and raised to [ē]. **1957** E. J. Dobson *Eng. Pronunc. 1500–1700* II. 612 The view that ME ę̄ tended to be raised to ME ē is strongly supported by the parallel case of ME ǭ, which is shown by seventeenth-century evidence and by that of the modern dialects to have been raised to ME ō, ModE [u:]. **1959** A. Campbell *Old Eng. Gram.* 122 By the tenth century ǣ of whatever origin had been raised to ē in Kt. [*sc.* Kentish]. **1968** Chomsky & Halle *Sound Pattern Eng.* III. 255 The environments where /ī/ and /ū/ are lowered to [ē] and [ō] are distinct from those where /ē/ and /ō/ are raised to [ī] and [ū].

20. b. Also, *to raise Ned* (U.S. slang). *to raise Cain*: see also *Cain^{2} 1 b; *to raise hell*: see *hell *sb.* 10 n, q; *to raise hob*: see *hob *sb.*^{1} 2 b.

1848 J. R. Lowell *Biglow Papers* 1st Ser. 69 Your fact'ry gals..'ll go to work raisin' promiscoous Ned. **1904** J. C. Lincoln *Cap'n Eri* ii. 28 The boy sort of run loose, as yer might say. Went to school when he had to, and raised Ned when he didn't, near's I can find out.

21. Also *fig.*

1921 H. Crane *Let.* 1 Oct. (1965) 65 It will be time for me to raise my voice in praise of Anderson soon, as his new book..is on the market.

22. See also *sand *sb.*^{2} 7 e.

23. a. (Further examples.)

1851 H. Melville *Moby Dick* I. xxxv. 259 Whosoever of ye raises me a white-headed whale..he shall have this gold ounce. **1928** Belloc *Chanty of Nona* 1 Before it was morning he raised Lundy Light.

24*. To reach the crest or summit of (a hill, ridge, etc.). *U.S.*

1804 J. Ordway in Lewis & Ordway *Jrnls. Western Explor.* (1916) 168 We raised a Steep bank back of this bottom. **1866** 'Mark Twain' *Lett. from Hawaii* (1967) 291 We 'raised' the summit of the mountain and began to canter along the edge of the crater. **1872** —— *Roughing It* xli. 287, I 'raised the hill' overlooking the town. **1934** J. R. Barrows *Ubet* 280 Every time I would raise a ridge, I expected to see him; for the signs were fresh.

25. a. (Earlier and later examples in *gen.* sense.)

1838 J. W. Carlyle *Let.* 28 Nov. (1903) I. 71 We have.. *raised* (as dear Mary used to say) a capital easy chair. **1948** 'N. Shute' *No Highway* vi. 171, I..told Miss Learoyd to see if she could raise two cups of tea. **1973** M. Woodhouse *Blue Bone* xv. 162 Would you please see if you can raise us all a drink? **1976** *Daily Mirror* 16 July 3/4 He..was living on what his wife Susan could raise by selling her furniture and jewellery.

29. (Later N. Amer. examples.)

1824 P. Ogden *Jrnl.* 20 Dec. in *Publ. Hudson's Bay Rec. Soc.* (1950) XIII. 5 The Kootonnies & Flat Heads are likewise here waiting our arrival intending to raise Camp together. **1837** W. Irving *Rocky Mts.* I. vi. 78 On the following morning, just as they were raising their camp, they observed a long line of people pouring down a defile of the mountains. **1855** A. Ross *Fur Hunters of Far West* II. xi. 61 The next morning on raising camp, I ordered Martin's horses to be loaded and we set off.

IV. 32. a. Also *Cards* (orig. *U.S.*), to lay a higher stake than (one's opponent); to increase (a stake or bid); freq. *absol.* and with partner as obj. *to raise out* (earlier example). Also *fig.* Cf. *raise *sb.*^{1} 5 b.

1821 *Hoyle's Games Improved* 163 After the first three cards are dealt, but before taking in, the eldest hand after seeing his cards, may raise the ante. **1864** W. B. Dick *Amer. Hoyle* 165 When *any* player makes a bet, it is the privilege of the *next player to the left* to *raise him*, or..to deposit in the pool the amount already bet by his adversary, and make a still higher bet. **1872** 'Mark Twain' *Roughing It* 332 'I have to pass, I judge.' 'How?' 'You've raised me out, pard.' **1890** Champlin & Bostwick *Young Folks' Cycl. Games & Sports* 269/1 The third player may stay out, see, or raise the second player. **1901** R. F. Foster *Poker* 40 Twice the amount of the blind is the amount of the ante, unless some player has raised it. **1951** E. Culbertson *Bidding & Play in Duplicate Contract Bridge* v. 55 In rubber bridge he might take a chance and raise partner to three of the minor suit. **1959** T. Reese *Bridge Player's Dict.* 142 North opens one spade and South..raises to two spades. **1965** *Listener* 4 Nov. 735/2 The only course open to him therefore is to raise to Four Clubs. **1981** P. Van Greenaway *'Cassandra' Bell* xv. 183 I'll raise you. Any odds you care to name I walk out of here a free man.

33. Also *absol.*

1869 'Mark Twain' *Lett. to Publishers* (1967) 25, I had a bargain about concluded for the purchase of an interest in a daily paper and when everything seemed to be going smoothly, the owner raised on me.

V. 35. For † *Obs.* read *'Obs.* exc. *U.S.'* and add further examples.

1770 C. Carroll *Let.* 5 Sept. in *Maryland Hist. Mag.* (1918) XIII. 61, I am quite indifferent whether Stephenson takes or Refuses the tob[acc]o, as I think the Price will raise again. **1785** G. Washington *Diary* 22 Sept. (1925) II. 415 The Water having raised,..I could form no accurate judgment of the progress. **1808** in J. H. Beadle *Undevel. West* (1873) xxi. 410 Should the accused person or persons raise up with arms in his or their hands. **1819** T. Forsyth in *Minnesota Hist. Coll.* (1880) III. 143 As the Mississippi was raising, the current was very strong. **1861** *Trans. Illinois Agric. Soc.* IV. 102 The milk sours before the cream all raises. **1911** H. P. Fairchild *Greek Immigration to U.S.* 70 About 1,000 houses are vacant in Athens, and yet the prices of rent have raised 15 to 20 per cent.

37. *intr. Mining.* To drive a raise (Raise *sb.*^{1} 3 in Dict. and Suppl.).

1898 S. J. Truscott *Witwatersrand Goldfields* xiii. 294 With machine drills it costs slightly more to sink a winze than to raise. **1973** L. J. Thomas *Introd. Mining* i. 9 The connections may be made by driving upwards, known as rising or raising, or working downwards, known as winzing.

raised, *ppl. a.*^{1} Add: **3. a.** Also *raised eyebrows*, eyebrows raised in censure or query (see *eyebrow 1 c).

1968 P. Durst *Badge of Infamy* v. 39 'I'll bet that causes some raised eyebrows,' Gina said. **1974** E. Ambler *Dr. Frigo* II. 82, I expected another violent reaction. None came. He merely glanced with raised eyebrows at Delvert, who nodded.

b. *raised beach* (earlier and later examples); *raised bed*, a flower-bed, at a higher level than the adjacent garden; *raised bog*, an area of acid, peaty soil, esp. that developed from moss, in which growth is most rapid at the centre, giving rise to a domed shape.

1834 *Proc. Geol. Soc.* II. 102 These are the only instances which the author could discover of a raised beach on this part of the coast. **1959** J. D. Clark *Prehist. S. Afr.* vi. 164 The earliest Middle Stone Age is probably that associated with the 20-foot raised beach at Blind River, East London. **1969** Bennison & Wright *Geol. Hist. Brit. Isles* xvi. 366 The evidence of uplift is found in the form of marine-cut erosion platforms, or raised beaches where these erosion surfaces have a cover of beach material. **1910** L. B. Meredith *Rock Gardens* ii. 25 The best and most usual form [of small rock garden] is a raised bed. **1959** C. Spry *Favourite Flowers* xxiii. 166, I wanted a raised bed of well-drained agreeable soil. **1974** *Country Life* 21 Mar. 650/1 Raised beds housing all manner of plants became characteristic features. **1938** *New Phytol.* XXXVII. 425 Since the primary lakes are frequently of glacial origin, raised bogs have generally proved to be extremely satisfactory sources of long continuous profiles illustrative of post-glacial forest and climatic history. **1946** *Proc. Prehist. Soc.* XII. 4 Raised-bogs very commonly occur in peri-glacial regions, often upon the sites of lakes created by the laying down of terminal moraines across glaciated valleys. **1966** F. H. Brightman *Oxf. Bk. Flowerless Plants* 88 Sometimes fen becomes choked with vegetation, and acid conditions develop at the top, so that species of Sphagnum can grow on the surface, forming 'raised bog'. **1976** *Nature* 23 Sept. 281/1 Raised bogs represent a special type of peat bog... They..have their own water regime, with all of the moisture supplied from the atmosphere.

4. a. (Further examples.)

1873 *Young Englishwoman* Aug. 406/2 The medallions are worked on brown American cloth..in raised embroidery. **1900** E. Jackson *Hist. Hand-made Lace* 216 *Raised work*, in bobbin lace this term denotes the raised edge worked down one side of leaves and flowers. Honiton and Duchess each have occasionally raised work, which heightens the effect of the lace considerably. **1960** B. Snook *Eng. Hist. Embroidery* 86 Stump work originally was known as 'raised work', its present name probably not being used before 1894.

c. *raised bands* (see quots.).

1835 J. Arnett *Bibliopegia* I. 23 The old mode of sewing on raised bands combined many advantages. **1846** G. Dodd *Brit. Manuf.* 6th Ser. iv. 96 'Raised bands'..are sometimes used for ornament in the better kinds of books; they consist of little strips of leather or cord pasted across the back of the book before it is covered. **1875** [see Panel *sb.*^{1} 8 c]. **1901** D. Cockerell *Bookbinding* i. 26 The public having become accustomed to raised bands on the backs of books, and the real bands being sunk in the back, the binders put false ones over the 'hollow'. **1952** J. Carter *ABC for Bk.-Collectors* 147 When a book is bound..the gathered sections are sewn on to horizontal cords or bands... When the boards are covered, these cords (unless sunk in grooves to make a flat spine) will stand out in the form of ridges. These are known as raised bands. **1972** P. Gaskell *New Introd. Bibliogr.* 148 The cords themselves could be placed either outside the backs of the folded sheets, where they would show as raised bands across the spine of the book, or in slots sawn into the folds.

d. Of a cake, biscuit (see U.S. sense s.v. Biscuit 1), etc.: made with baking-powder or other raising agent. *U.S.*

1889 R. T. Cooke *Steadfast* xvii. 189 Then it [*sc.* the election cake] wore only the style of 'raised cake'. **1890** *Harper's Mag.* Oct. 707/1 I've got raised biscuit for supper. **1907** *N.Y. Even. Post* (semi-weekly ed.) 18 July 5 The everlasting repetition of salt meats, potatoes, and raised biscuit in their bill of fare. **1914** G. Atherton *Perch of Devil* i. 28 I've got fried chicken..and raised biscuit. **1937** E. K. Haines *Cook Bk.* xii. 360 *Raised muffins*..A good old-fashioned change from the modern quick muffin.

6. *Phonetics.* Articulated with the tongue in a higher position.

[**1888** H. Sweet *Hist. Eng. Sounds* 2 Intermediate positions are: ***retracted***..and ***advanced***, ***raised***..and ***lowered***.] **1942** J. S. Hall *Phonetics Gt. Smoky Mountain Speech* (Amer. Speech Repr. & Monogr. No. 4) 15 There is a tendency in some speakers to use a tense, slightly raised [ɪ̝]. **1957** E. J. Dobson *Eng. Pronunc., 1500–1700* II. 614 The struggle of the raised ME ę̄ to replace the normal ME ę̄ was in StE [*sc.* Standard English] a long-drawn-out process. *Ibid.* 642 The raised pronunciation was not accepted in any but careless speech in the seventeenth century. **1972** M. L. Samuels *Linguistic Evol.* iii. 44 There is often a process of systemic regulation..by the selection of raised variants.

raiser. Add: **1. a.** Also, a nurseryman who breeds or cultivates new varieties of plants.

1707 J. Mortimer *Whole Art of Husbandry* xvi. 315 A planter or raiser of trees ought to consider the under soil, as well as the superficies of the earth. **1845** *Florist's Jrnl.* VI. 198 For the beginner, whose chance of competing with the more established raiser is so remote, this suggestion holds forth the most flattering hopes. **1921** *Sat. Westm. Gaz.* 10 Sept. 16/2 We owe this new race [of freesias] largely to Continental raisers. **1970** *Daily Tel.* 17 Oct. 9/1 New roses from the same raiser..are Golden Times and Rosy Mantle.

2. (Further example.)

1908 *Animal Managem.* 121 The utility of boiled foods in the service is limited to their occasional use as condition raisers for horses which require fattening.

4. *Bridge.* **a.** A player who increases his partner's bid. **b.** A card or combination of cards which justifies the increase by a player of his partner's bid. Cf. *raise *v.*^{1} 32 a.

1912 F. Irwin *Fine Pts. Auction Bridge* 89 No guarded queens nor guarded jacks in side-suits, may be counted as raisers. **1929** M. C. Work *Compl. Contract Bridge* iv. 34 In the latter case the raiser must have Hearts stopped at least once. *Ibid.* v. 100 It is impossible to translate each individual element directly into raisers. **1964** *Official Encycl. Bridge* 447/1 *Raiser*, the player who bids for a greater number of tricks in a suit first bid by his partner.

raisin. Add: **2. d.** The dark purplish-brown colour of raisins.

1909 *Westm. Gaz.* 4 Sept. 3/2 The long-suffering mole is to find serious rivals in coal-dust grey, elephant's breath, and a purplish black called raisin. **1927** *Daily Express* 7 Mar. 6 (Advt.), Light mulberry, new blue, raisin, rosewood. **1971** *Guardian* 7 Sept. 9/1 A choice of colours: greengage,.. fig, raisin, grape, black.

3. *raisin bread, brew, cake, pudding, -wine* (earlier and later examples); *raisin-coloured* adj.

1902 A. Bennett *Anna of Five Towns* xii. 316 The delicacies which differentiate high tea from tea..hot toast, sardines with tomatoes, raisin-bread, currant bread [etc.]. **1965** W. R. Harding *Days of Henry Thoreau* x. 183 Thoreau experimented frequently with his bread making and soon learned that an unleavened variety was the simplest. When he added raisins to the dough, it was said that he became the inventor of raisin bread. **1980** A. Auswaks *Trick of Diamonds* iii. 80 Toasted raisin bread and butter. **1919** H. Crane *Let.* 27 Dec. (1965) 28, I got dreadfully drunk on dreadful raisin brew. *Ibid.* 29 This fellow of the raisin brew is another poor soul like myself, in Akron exile from N.Y. **1907** *Yesterday's Shopping* (1969) p. iii/1 Raisin cakes. **1973** M. Amis *Rachel Papers* 83 Two kinds of sandwiches, raisin cake, sliced ham, unlimited tea. **1939** Spender & Gili tr. *Lorca's Poems* 47 Raisin-coloured shoes. **1767** J. Woodforde *Diary* 24 July (1924) I. 64, I gave them a fine ham..and a good rich raisin pudding. **1861** Mrs. Beeton *Bk. Househ. Managem.* 671 (*heading*) Baked raisin pudding (plain and economical). **1723** J. Nott *Cook's & Confectioner's Dict.* sig. Ff1^{v} (*heading*) To make raisin wine. **1976** 'Trevanian' *Main* (1977) viii. 165 The proprietor of the Greek restaurant..keeps refilling her glass with raisin wine.

raising, *vbl. sb.* Add: **1. a.** (Further examples.)

1842 Dickens *Amer. Notes* II. ii. 58 Down Easters, and men of Boston raising. **1929** M. C. Work *Compl. Contract*

Bridge p. xv, Any advice given for bidding, raising, etc., applies when the score is 'love-all'. **1967** *Gloss. Mining Terms* (*B.S.I.*) IX. 11 *Raising*, the process of excavating a shaft from the bottom upwards. **1978** *Sci. Amer.* July 112/3 Raising (making a new bet by putting more money into the pot than is required for calling).

b. (Examples in sense 10 a of vb.)

1929 D. RUNYON in *Hearst's International* Oct. 63/1 Madame La Gimp figures a baby is not apt to get much raising-up off of her as long as she is on Broadway. **1972** J. S. HALL *Sayings from Old Smoky* 113 In my raisin' up two or three besides your own would set up with sick people.

c. (Earlier Amer. examples.)

1651 *Rec. Waterhouse, Mass.* (1894) I. I. 29 [For] raising of the howse. **1711** J. GREEN *Jrnl.* 6 June in *Essex Inst. Hist. Coll.* (1869) X. I. 91, I went to ye raising ye New Meeting House at Col. Gardner's.

d. *Phonetics.* Articulation (of a vowel) with the tongue closer to the roof of the mouth; an instance of this. Cf. *RAISE v.[1] 19*.

1874 H. SWEET *Hist. Eng. Sounds* in *Trans. Philol. Soc. 1874* 533 The short vowels do not seem to have changed much in the last few generations. The most noticeable fact is the loss of *æ* among the vulgar. It is modified by raising the tongue into the mid-front-wide, resulting in the familiar *ceb* for *cæb*. This anomalous raising of a short vowel is gradually spreading among the upper classes. **1909** O. JESPERSEN *Mod. Eng. Gram.* I. viii. 231 The great vowel-shift consists in a general raising of all long vowels with the exception of the two high vowels. **1934** C. DAVIES *Eng. Pronunc.* 7 From the fourteenth century on this vowel [*sc.* ME. ǭ] underwent a gradual raising and rounding. **1957** E. J. DOBSON *Eng. Pronunc. 1500–1700* II. 635 There are parallels enough for isolative raisings occurring in spite of, but hardly any for a combinative raising because of, a following *r*. **1959** A. CAMPBELL *Old Eng. Gram.* 71 Just as all back vowels are subject to fronting by *i*-umlaut, so certain front vowels are subject to raising. **1972** M. L. SAMUELS *Linguistic Evol.* iii. 44 In ME..we find widespread new raisings to /ɪ/. **1975** *Language* LI. 307 The asymmetry between front and back vowels is due to the raising of /ǣ/.

3. a. (Earlier example.)

1857 *Hunt's Merchants' Mag.* XXXVI. 755 Mr. Pease claimed it [*sc.* the tobacco] as his own raising and pointed to his mark to corroborate his statement.

4. raising-gig (example).

1952 *Chambers's Jrnl.* Aug. 455/2 For really fine-quality face cloths..nothing has yet been found to equal the slower and less rigorous action of the traditional west of England teazle raising-gig.

raisiny (rēⁱ·zĭni), *a.* [f. RAISIN + -Y[1].] Like or suggestive of (the taste of) raisins. Also *Comb.*

1864 J. A. GRANT *Walk across Afr.* 157 Plantain-wine..is a sweet raisiny-tasting wine; if aerated, nearly equal to sparkling hock in richness of flavour. **1975** *Times* 5 Apr. 11/5 Fortified dessert wines—rather more raisiny than port.

‖**raison d'état** (rẹzoṅ deta). [Fr.] = *reason of state* s.v. REASON *sb.*[1] 5 b.

1869 MILL *Subj. Women* iii. 92 The *raison d'état*, meaning the convenience of the government,..was deemed a sufficient explanation and excuse for the most flagitious crimes. **1939** A. TOYNBEE *Study of Hist.* VI. 38 The god who was worshipped by the Imperial Dynasty was not..a product of *raison d'état*. **1958** E. H. CARR *Socialism in One Country* I. i. 6 *Raison d'état* is tough enough to emerge unscathed from the revolutionary turmoil. **1965** *New Statesman* 23 Apr. 648/2 The Third Reich, whose ideologists preferred the declamatory pathos of Fichte to Hegel's dispassionate concern with *raison d'état*. **1976** *Times Lit. Suppl.* 26 Nov. 1483/2 Hanged, on very dubious law, for raisons d'état by a post-war Labour Lord Chancellor. **1977** *Times* 14 Jan. 17/4 The Elysée's short-sighted conception of *raison d'état*.

raison d'être. (Earlier and later examples.)

1864 J. S. MILL *Let.* 18 Mar. (1910) II. 3 Modes of speech which have a real *raison d'être*. **1889** A. JAMES *Diary* 14 Dec. (1964) 67 The French ladies of the 18th century..whose whole *raison d'être* was the graceful, and the light. **1927** C. CONNOLLY *Let.* 5 May in *Romantic Friendship* (1975) 301 With Desmond gone I have no *raison d'être*. **1959** J. BRAINE *Vodi* vii. 102 There were a few trees and fields, and even a small colony of expensive privately-built houses, which was rare for a place for which the raison d'être now was Rimelby Main [colliery]. **1975** J. G. EVANS *Environment Early Man Brit. Isles* v. 104 A possible *raison d'être* for these sites was the chert, a desirable raw material.

‖**raisonneur** (rẹzonȫr). [Fr., lit. 'one who reasons or argues'.] A character in a play, etc., who gives expression to the author's message, standpoint, or philosophy. Also *transf.* and (*nonce-wd.*) as *v. intr.*

1903 M. BEERBOHM in *Sat. Rev.* 5 Dec. 700/2 There is an old man [in Gorki's *Lower Depths*]..in whom we dimly descry a 'raisonneur'. **1913** G. B. SHAW *Quintessence of Ibsenism* 177 Poins, who was originally meant to be the *raisonneur* of the piece, and the chief figure among the prince's dissolute associates. **1950** E. H. CARR *Bolshevik Revol.* I. ii. 38 The Mensheviks..were primarily men of theory; in Bolshevik terminology they were *raisonneurs*, 'dry-as-dust archivists', the 'party intelligentsia'. **1955** *Times* 24 May 3/3 The *raisonneur*, for example, the family friend who announces the thesis of the play, draws the moral, and preaches his little sermons to the parties concerned, is bound to strike us as something of a nuisance. **1959** *Listener* 29 Oct. 749/1 He is clearly introduced as the play's *raisonneur*, the doughty exponent of a radical viewpoint. **1963** WODEHOUSE *Stiff Upper Lip, Jeeves* xii. 97, I saw that the time had come to be a *raisonneur*... 'Are you sure,' I said, raisonneuring like nobody's business, 'that you were altogether wise in confining him to spinach and what not?' **1969** M. R. BOOTH *Eng. Plays of 19th Cent.* II. 345 It seems rather unfair that..the worldly *raisonneurs*..are responsible for breaking up love affairs between young people and..forcing unhappy wives to stay with unpleasant and incompatible husbands, yet are themselves blessed with the hands in marriage of comely widows of means. **1980** *Times Lit. Suppl.* 23 May 581/1 Dottie..is a scatterbrained raisonneur, on stage throughout, directing her two lovers..to their respective concealment in kitchen or spare bedroom.

raj. Add: **b.** *spec.* the British dominion or rule in the Indian sub-continent (before 1947). In full, *British raj*. Also *transf.*

1859 M. THOMSON *Story of Cawnpore* xvi. 229 But Delhi had fallen when these gentlemen threw their strength into the tide of revolt, and they were too late for a decisive superiority over the British *râj*. **1876** *Hansard Commons* 16 Mar. 141 Without upsetting the British Raj. **1890** [in Dict.]. **1908** *Daily Chron.* 21 June 4/4 The Indian agitators who represent the British raj as the author of the plague. **1955** *Times* 25 Aug. 9/7 It was effective against the British raj in India, and the conclusion drawn here is that the British knew that they were wrong. **1969** R. MILLAR *Kut* xv. 288 Sir Stanley Maude had taken command in Mesopotamia, displacing the raj of antique Indian Army commanders. **1971** *Illustr. Weekly India* 18 Apr. 4/2 Though it appears paradoxical, in the last days of the Raj, the British were the only people who wished to keep India united. **1975** H. R. ISAACS in H. M. Patel et al. *Say not the Struggle Nought Availeth* 251 The post-independence régime in all its incarnations since the passing of the British Raj.

Rajasthani (rādʒästā·ni), *sb.* and *a.* [f. the name *Rajasthan* (see below) + *-I.] **A.** *sb.* A collective term for the dialects spoken in Rajasthan, a state in north-west India; also, a member of the people of Rajasthan. **B.** *adj.* Of or pertaining to this language or people; *spec.* used of a style of dancing.

1901 [see *JAIPUR]. **1933** L. BLOOMFIELD *Lang.* iv. 63 A number of dialect areas..cover the larger part of India and include such great languages as..Panjabi (16 millions), Rajasthani (13 millions),..Bihari (36 millions). **1957** [see *JAIPUR]. **1958** [see *MEWATI *sb.* and *a.*]. **1967** D. C. COOKE *C/o Amer. Embassy* (1968) v. 40 The Rajasthani women labourers. **1969** [see *KATHAK]. **1972** W. B. LOCKWOOD *Panorama Indo-Europ. Lang.* xii. 198 The language Rajasthani..is essentially a linguist's term to denote a theoretical concept. *Ibid.* 203 Rajasthanis normally practice literacy through Hindi/Urdu. **1975** A. B. SHAH in H. M. Patel et al. *Say not the Struggle Nought Availeth* 105 Rajasthanis have settled down in all parts of the country without coming into conflict with the local people. **1976** H. R. F. KEATING *Filmi, Filmi, Inspector Ghote* vi. 50 Some simple Rajasthani peasant girl in *ghagra* and *choli*. *Ibid.* vii. 64 Tiny mosaic fragments of purple and gold Rajasthani enamel work.

raja yoga (rā·dʒă yōᵘ·gă). Also with capital initials. [Skr., f. *rājan* king + *yoga* YOGA.] A form of Yoga by which the practitioner attains control over his mind and emotions. Also *attrib.* Hence ‖**raja-yogin**, one who practises raja yoga.

1885 M. N. DVIVEDI *Rája Yoga* I. 44 The Vedántic process ..of attaining to this state of Brahma generally described as *Rájayoga* is purely mental, and deals entirely with rules for restraining the mind. **1911** [see *HATHA-YOGA]. **1913** E. F. BENSON *Thorley Weir* v. 167 For those three years he..lived a life of meditation that would have done credit to a student of Râja Yoga attaining Samâdhi. **1956** E. WOOD *Yoga Dict.* 127/2 *Rāja-yoga*, the system of yoga in which the man within asserts himself as the king (*rāja*) of all his mental and bodily possessions and powers. **1960** J. HEWITT *Yoga* 14 Others of the Raja Yoga school consider only a little Hatha necessary. *Ibid.* 15 Raja Yoga is designed to..put our mental house in order and concentrate our scattered energies. **1960** R. ROLLAND in *Ibid.* 95 It [is] astonishing that Western reason has taken so little into account the experimental research of Indian Raja-yogins. **1962** [see *KARMA-YOGA]. **1977** C. MCFADDEN *Serial* (1978) xviii. 42/1 She had like *mutated* over the years through..hatha and raja yoga.

Rajmahali (rā·dʒmăhāli), *sb.* and *a.* Also **Rajmahal.** [f. the name of the *Rajmahal* hills of northern India + *-I.] = *MALER *sb.* and *a.*

1848 *Jrnl. Asiatic Soc. Bengal* XVII. II. 553 Comparative Vocabulary of the Aboriginal languages of Central India... 5. Múndala. 6. Rájmahali. 7. Góndi. **1853** J. R. LOGAN in *Jrnl. Indian Archipelago* VII. 49, I now proceed to the south Gangetic or Vindyan tribes, the Male or Rajmahali, the Kol, the Khond and the Gond. **1856** R. CALDWELL *Compar. Gram. Dravidian Lang.* 21 There are two uncultivated idioms of Central India, the Ûrâon and the Râjmahal, which contain..many Drâvidian roots of primary importance. **1872** E. T. DALTON *Descr. Ethnol. Bengal* VIII. ii. 272 The Rájmaháli version of the Oráon ceremony called the 'rog-pelowa', expulsion of an evil spirit. **1873, 1885** [see *MALER *sb.* and *a.*]. **1906** G. A. GRIERSON *Linguistic Survey of India* IV. 446 The Maler also call themselves Sauriā, and their language is also known under the name of Rājmahālī, *i.e.*, the language of the Rajmahal Hills.

Rajpoot, rajput. Add: **Rajput** is now the accepted form. (Earlier examples of *Rajpoot* and later example of *Rajput*.)

1829 J. TOD *Rajast'han* I. 137 The poorest Rajpoot of this day retains all the pride of ancestry, often his sole inheritance. **1836** N. WISEMAN *Lect. Doctr. Cath. Ch.* I. vi. 174, I consider the soul of the meanest and poorest in the lowest caste, equal, in the estimation of God, to that of the Rajpoot. **1971** *Illustr. Weekly India* 4 Apr. 8/3 The non-Vedic and non-Aryan Kshatriyas..had been admitted to the military class by Shankaracharya. These (along with certain other families who claimed descent from Raja Ram Chandra) became the masters of Rajputana. Their royal families acquired the title of Rajputra or *Rajanya*, which ultimately became 'Rajput'.

attrib. (later examples.)

1931 *Times Lit. Suppl.* 18 June 482/3 They [*sc.* hill paintings] differ not only from the metropolitan art of the Mughal Court, but from the Rajput paintings of other parts of India. **1937** [see *candy pink]. **1974** *Encycl. Brit. Micropædia* VIII. 396/3 *Rajput painting*, the art of the independent Hindu feudal states in India, as distinguished from the court art of the Mughal emperors.

‖**rajpramukh** (rā·dʒprămuk). [Hindi, f. *rājya* state + *pramukh* chief.] In the Republic of India between 1948 and 1956, a governor of a state which was formerly a princely state or which resulted from the unification of several princely states.

1949 *Britannica Bk. of Year* 339/1 The remainder [of the Indian states] were grouped under the aegis of a *Rajpramukh* or presiding prince into 30 homogeneous groups, the rulers retaining their titles, dignities, and personal estates [in 1948]. **1950** G. N. JOSHI *Constitution of India* VII. 232 The head of a Part B State is called the Rajpramukh. *Ibid.* XIX. 342 As the executive heads of the Union and the State, the President and the Governor or Rajpramukh are given immunity from proceedings in court. **1957** *Listener* 5 Dec. 925/1 The Ruler..has since become..Rajpramukh of Rajasthan. **1958** G. MIKES *East is East* 171 He [*sc.* the Nizam of Hydèrabad] became *rajpramukh*—appointed democratic governor—of his own state and all has gone well ever since. **1962** *Times* 26 Jan. (India Suppl.) p. xx/4 The office of *Rajpramukh* was abolished.

‖**Rajya Sabha** (rā·dʒyă sā·bă). Also **Raj Sabha.** [Hindi, f. *rājya* state + *sabhā* assembly, council.] The upper house of the central Indian parliament.

1948 *Whitaker's Almanack* 772/1 The Union Constitution Committee of the Constituent Assembly recommended the bicameral union of the legislature on the British model with two Houses to be called 'Lok Sabha'..and 'Raj Sabha' or the House of States. **1954** BINANI & RAMA RAO *India at Glance* (rev. ed.), (Index), Rajya Sabha (Council of States). **1955** M. P. SHARMA *Govt. Indian Republic* (ed. 2) vii. 144 The Parliament..consists of the President and the two Houses—the Council of States and the House of the People now formally styled as Rajya Sabha and Lok Sabha respectively. **1969** *National Herald* (New Delhi) 29 July 4/3 The two Rajya Sabha seats from UP for which by-elections are due on August 13. **1972** *Times of India* 28 Nov. 8/2 (*heading*) Rajya Sabha to debate world situation. **1979** *Ibid.* 17 Aug. 1/5 Those in the alignment were willing to accommodate Mr. Mahadev Prasad Varma of the Charan Singh faction as deputy leader of the party in the Rajya Sabha, but not Mr. Amin.

Rakah (rā·kă, ‖ra·kaχ). [mod. Heb., acronym f. *Reshimah Komunistit Ḥadashah*, New Communist List (of candidates).] One of the two communist parties in Israel, formed in 1965.

1969 W. LAQUEUR *Struggle for Middle East* ix. 166 From July 1967 RAKAH was recognized as the official Israeli Communist party by the Soviet bloc. *Ibid.* 167 RAKAH demanded the unconditional surrender of all the Israeli-occupied territories. **1970** A. DERSHOWITZ in *Commentary* Dec. 76/2 They [*sc.* some Israeli Arab citizens] may..belong to the Maoist-oriented Rakah party which has eight members in the Knesset. *Ibid.* Sharing office space with an older Arab lawyer active in Rakah. **1974** N. CHOMSKY *Peace in Middle East?* v. 176 One of the communist parties (Rakah) is 'pro-Arab', a testimonial to Israeli democracy. *Ibid.*, Sabri Jiryis..describes Rakah as 'the Communist sector of the Israeli establishment'. **1977** *Hongkong Standard* 14 Apr. 9/4 Until now, discontent has been expressed through voting for Rakah, the pro-Moscow Israeli Communist Party whose membership is overwhelmingly Arab.

rake, *sb.*[1] Add: **2. a.** *spec.* (*a*) an implement with a blade instead of teeth for gathering money or chips staked in a game of chance; (*b*) (see quot. 1966).

1865 TROLLOPE *Can you forgive Her?* II. xxv. 280 The money..was all drawn back by the croupier's unimpassioned rake. **1884** [see CROUPIER 2]. **1907** *Yesterday's Shopping* (1969) 109/3 Aluminium Combs—Dressing or Rakes.. each 1/6... Rakes, Vulcanite..1/3. **1937** [see *PASSE]. **1966** J. S. COX *Illustr. Dict. Hairdressing & Wigmaking* 125/1 *Rake*, a strong comb with large even-sized teeth. Used for removing tangles in long hair. **1972** D. LEES *Zodiac* 47 If you don't want Françoise to blue in all her winnings..you'd better get her away from the table. The way she's going the croupier's going to have to send out for a bigger rake. **1973** 'R. MACLEOD' *Burial in Portugal* vi. 117 A blonde..was the only player to avoid the croupier's rake on the first couple of spins of the wheel.

3*. An act of raking.

1869 'MARK TWAIN' *Innoc. Abr.* xii. 114 The first rake of his razor loosened the very hide from my face. **1961** Y. OLSSON *Syntax Eng. Verb* vii. 207 (From garden talk:) Let me have a rake!

4. *rake-head* (earlier example), *-stem*; **rake-comb** = *RAKE *sb.*[1] 2 a (*b*); **rake-up,** something concocted; a fabrication.

1790 Rake-comb [see *dressing-comb* s.v. *DRESSING *vbl. sb.* 5 a]. **1969** E. H. PINTO *Treen* 364 The boxwood H comb is an 18th-century type barber's comb, used on wigs after the coarse or 'rake' comb. **1644** *Essex County, Mass. Probate Rec.* (1916) I. 39 Rakes and rake hedds, 7s. 8d. **1880** HARDY *Trumpet-Major* II. xxiii. 160 For use at home as rake-stems, benefit-club staves, and pick-handles. **1957** M. Spark *Comforters* v. 95 On the front of the [cigarette] case was a tiny raised crest... 'It's the Hogarth crest. Only a Victorian rake-up, I imagine.'

rake, *sb.*[3] Add: **4.** (Earlier and later examples.) Also, the amount carried in a single journey by a railway train.

a **1779** D. Graham *Writings* (1883) II. 59 I'll gar haf-a-crown and haf-a-mutchkin or a rake o' coals do it a'. **1930** *Times Educ. Suppl.* 20 Sept. 397/3 When the boys of the Clachan had finished dinner, their customary task was to fetch the day's 'rake' of water to their homes. **1934** T. Wood *Cobbers* v. 69 Before we could board, however, they said we must see the Rake for the Day go by: all the trees we had seen felled. **1976** *Indian Express* 23 Jan. 5/4 The first rake of 1000 tonnes for Iran was despatched from the Bhilai Steel Plant yesterday. **1979** *Times of India* 17 Aug. 10/2 Actual daily arrivals, according to food department sources, has recently been two rakes or one and half rakes less than what it should be.

8. *spec.* a series of wagons or carriages on a railway or of wagons or trucks in a mine or a factory (in this sense, no longer restricted to *Sc.* and *north. dial.*).

1901 [in Dict.]. **1909** *Daily Chron.* 11 Dec. 4/5 In reaching the shaft some of the men got on to the top of a loaded rake of hutches. **1921** H. Foston *At Front* viii. 60 The ballast engine, with her 'rake' of empty trucks. **1940** L. A. G. Strong *Sun on Water* 224 The train I join is made up locally. The rake of carriages does be waiting at the station, and a tank engine comes in. **1949** D. M. Davin *Roads from Home* II. vii. 175 Geordie Smith on his shunter had just given a rake of meat waggons a bit of a nudge. **1961** *Trains Illustrated* Dec. 762/2 A special seven-car rake of B.R. standard stock provided the final services, hauled alternatively by Class E1 4-4-0 No. 31739 and Class Q1 0-6-0 No. 33029. **1962** *Times* 26 Oct. (Spencer Steelworks Suppl.) p. xviii/3 The operator uses a Beetle to bring forward the first rake of 15 wagons. **1969** *Sunday Standard* (Bombay) 6 July 1/7 Only 27 rakes were available out of the normal complement of 31 rakes for running the scheduled number of trains. **1973** C. D. Garratt *Masterpieces in Steam* 108 The engine was bringing its last rake of wagons through the colliery yard. **1977** *Modern Railways* Dec. 492/1 Positioning two cars at one end of the train would lead to excessive buckling forces when propelling, hence the central position which was also claimed to provide two relatively-short virtually-identical rakes of trailer cars for operational flexibility.

rake, *sb.*[4] Add: **2. a.** (Later examples.)

1932 *Pictorial Weekly* 19 Mar. 223/2 Most stages have to rise in floor level towards the back in order to make the action visible to the audience... This is known as the 'rake'. **1939** Joyce *Finnegans Wake* (1964) 560 Spotlight working wall cloths. Spill playing rake and bridges. **1951** [see *Cossack 2 e]. **1955** *Times* 10 May 7/7 The front seat is immediately adjustable over a range of 5 in., and further adjustments for rake and height are provided. **1967** *Oxf. Compan. Theatre* (ed. 3) 40/2 The Chicago Opera House.. was a tamed Bayreuth, with a flattened rake and a wedge auditorium. **1973** *Country Life* 22 Feb. 468/3 Front seats have ample adjustment for reach and rake. **1974** B. Forbes *Notes for Life* xii. 92 The rake on the stage of the Theatre Royal, Brighton, is a violent one.

b. The inclination of an edge or face of a cutting tool (or other tool) with respect to some line or plane (freq. to a line perpendicular to the surface of the work). Also *angle of rake, rake angle*.

1888 *Lockwood's Dict. Terms Mech. Engin.* 276 *Rake.* (1) A term usually applied to signify the angles of metal turning tools, as side rake, front rake, &c. (2) The amount of forward angle, or pitch of saw teeth. **1901** *Shop & Foundry Practice* (Colliery Engineer Co., Scranton, Pa.) I. v. 8 This tendency to spring is greatly increased when the tool has insufficient side rake or clearance. **1903** W. H. Van Dervoort *Mod. Machine Shop Tools* xv. 198 The cutting edge of the lathe tool..has what we term an angle of clearance A and an angle of rake B. *Ibid.*, A tool may have front rake..or side rake... A tool without rake requires greater force to drive it through the cut as it tears rather than cuts the metal. *Ibid.* 550/1 (Index), Rake angles. **1923** T. R. Shaw *Mechanisms of Machine Tools* i. 71/1 With a flat top face either so much metal has to be removed that the tool is weakened or the rake angle must be so slight that there would be no proper cutting action. **1938** R. T. Kent *Kent's Mech. Engineers' Handbk.* (ed. 11) III. xxi. 41 Rake angle of a milling cutter..is defined as the angle by which the face of the tooth is displaced back of the radial line drawn from the center of rotation to the cutting edge. **1964** S. Crawford *Basic Engin. Processes* v. 119 Rake angles influence chip formation, tool wear, cutting force, surface finish, and permissible cutting speed. **1975** *Drilling Technol. & Collet Chuck* (Bristol Erickson Ltd.) 3 Figures 1 & 2 illustrate the variation in normal rake angle across the cutting edge of a standard ½" diameter drill. *Ibid.* 11 Helic angle is the angle between the outer edge of the drill land and the drill axis, and is equivalent to the top rake of a flat cutting tool.

rake, *sb.*[5] Add: **c.** Phr. *rake's progress* [the title of a series of engravings (1735) by William Hogarth: see Hogarthian *a.*]: a course of dissipation; a progressive degeneration or decline.

1849 Thackeray *Pendennis* I. xx. 183 (*heading*) Rake's progress. **1925** T. E. Lawrence *Let.* 13 June (1938) 476 If you want to trouble yourself still with the rake's progress of this deplorable work. **1937** H. G. Wells *Brynhild* x. 202 I'd have been ashamed not to have been her lover. Another score in the rake's progress. **1950** A. Huxley *Themes & Variations* 250 If the Western Powers had a positive instead of a mainly negative international policy, they would come forward with a plan to check this rake's progress towards human and planetary bankruptcy. **1959** *Listener* 17 Sept. 451/3 The later rake's progress toward corruption, aggression, humiliating subjection to Hitler, pathological megalomania and final catastrophe. **1961** *Times* 9 Feb. 15/2 A literary rake's progress from false materialist to fake romantic. **1976** *Times* 20 Feb. 19/4 Mr Healey has described the course of Britain's recent financial history as a 'rake's progress'.

rake, *v.*[1] Add: **I. 3. b.** (Further examples.)

1865 Trollope *Can you forgive Her?* II. xxviii. 224 The croupier raked it [*sc.* money] all up, and carried it all away. **1913** W. Owen *Let.* 9 Apr. (1967) 182 Unless I raked up matter from the past,..I have had nothing to deliver myself of. **1939** 'N. Blake' *Smiler with Knife* ii. 33 Had tea? No? Good, I'll see what Mrs. Raikes can rake up.

c. (Further examples with *in.*) *To rake in the shekels*: see *shekel 2.

1851 *Oquawka* (Illinois) *Spectator* 22 Oct. 1/4 Then, of course, they 'dropped the gate' upon them and 'raked in the pile'. **1893** 'Mark Twain' *Lett. to Publishers* (1967) 343 We are at a heavy expense, now, in breaking up housekeeping and raking-in old bills. **1926** *Punch* 22 Dec. 682/2 His having been raked in to complete the officers' team at the last minute in place of an absentee. **1959** *Economist* 11 Apr. 153/2 The Bank of France has 'raked in' part of the working balances of foreign currency held by the French commercial banks. **1969** *Observer* 21 Dec. 28/3 He's raking it in already. Writes 'think pieces' for *Honey* magazine.

d. *to rake down*: (esp.) to win (money) at cards, etc. *U.S. slang.*

1839 *Spirit of Times* 13 July 223/3 If he has anything like as good a horse as the balance, he is certain to *rake down the corn.* **1843** *Ibid.* 18 Nov. 431 She [*sc.* a horse] is a perfect wax figure and all believed that she would rake down the socks. **1846** S. F. Smith *Theatr. Apprenticeship* 151 With one hand he gracefully turned over *four Kings* and a Jack, and with the other tremblingly 'raked down' the pile of bank notes, gold and silver. **1853** J. G. Baldwin *Flush Times Alabama* 8 What lots of 'Ethiopian captives' and other plunder he *raked down* vexed Arithmetic to count. **1882** B. Harte *Flip & Found at Blazing Star* 164 You kin rake down the pile now.

III. 9. a. (Further examples.)

1939 Joyce *Finnegans Wake* (1964) 349 Spraygun rakes and splits them from a double focus: grenadite, damnymite, alextronite, nichilite. **1959** 'B. Mather' *Achilles Affair* I. ii. 22 The Nazi patrol..could have raked us with their Schmeissers. **1967** *Boston Sunday Globe* 23 Apr. 17/2 Artillery and air strikes raked the Communist positions in the battle. **1973** *Times* 13 Feb. 7/1 Mr Rashad al-Shawa, the former mayor of Gaza town, narrowly escaped today when his car was raked by automatic weapon fire.

d. (Earlier and later examples.)

1763 J. Bell *Travels from St. Petersburg* II. 78 The hawks generally raked in the pheasants while flying. **1896** A. Austin *England's Darling* II. iii. 42 Until the unseamed falcon learned to wing its way..And, binding, rake its quarry to the ground.

rake, *v.*[3] **2.** (Earlier and later examples.)

1842 J. Gwilt *Encycl. Archit.* II. iii. 635 If dwarf wainscoting be framed with two panels in height, add ·016 to the rate... When raked to stairs, ·023 extra. **1930** W. Faulkner *As I lay Dying* 100 The broken hat raked at a swaggering angle. **1964** *Listener* 23 Apr. 664/2 Two of the best modern theatres, merely for the fact that the auditorium is steeply raked. **1977** *Transatlantic Rev.* LX. 83 He spoke with the microphone..his TWA captain's hat raked across one eyebrow.

raked (rē̆ikt), *ppl. a.*[2] [f. Rake *v.*[3] + -ed[1].] Inclined from the perpendicular or from the horizontal; also, swept-*back*. (For earlier examples of pa. pple. see Rake *v.*[3] 2 in Dict. and Suppl.)

1948 H. Innes *Blue Ice* iv. 96 A single raked-back funnel. **1955** *Times* 5 July 5/6 The well-raked steering wheel gives a sense of precise control at speed without being heavy in manoeuvring. **1972** *Soviet Weekly* 22 Apr. 13 Lecturers use portable TV cameras, and students have screens over their heavily raked desks. **1976** B. Jackson *Flameout* xi. 185 The clean aerodynamic form of the airliner:..the raked-back wings..supporting streamlined engine pods. **1977** *Time* 21 Feb. 41/2 The action is carried out on a raked stage.

ra·ke-off. *slang* (orig. *U.S.*). Also **rakeoff, rake off.** [Cf. *rake *sb.*[1] 2 a (*a*).] A share (of the winnings in gambling, of profits, etc.), a 'cut'; commission. (Freq. with derogatory overtones.)

1888 *Texas Siftings* 28 Jan. 16/1 We always give him a rake-off, so he makes a good enough thing of it. **1890** J. P. Quinn *Fools of Fortune* 188 This percentage is technically known as the 'rake-off', and insures the proprietors of the establishment a handsome royalty on all winnings. **1899** B. Tarkington *Gentleman from Indiana* vii. 95 In oil it's the farmer that gets the rake-off. **1903** *Sun* (N.Y.) 2 Nov. 3 This is a day of rake-offs. The boss..gets his rake-off from every service he renders to his party. The laborer gets his rake-off for selling his vote. **1905** D. G. Phillips *Plum Tree* 61 It means a big rake-off for Dunkirk. Politics is on a money basis nowadays. **1914** 'J. H. Keate' *Destruction of Mephisto's Greatest Web* ii. 60 The slot that receives the 'rake off', or percentage. *Ibid.* iii. 91, I would do my best to prepare him a meal. This I was willing to do, as my 'rake off' for the night had only been ten cents. **1926** E. Wallace *Yellow Snake* xxvii. 224 This was something more profitable than the smuggling of cocaine,..a quicker way to fortune than the rake-off of coppers from a forbidden game of fantan. **1929** M. A. Gill *Underworld Slang* 10/1 *Rake-off man*, nickel taker at dice game. **1934** J. T. Farrell *Young Manhood* viii. 121 'Hey, Hugo, what undertaker's giving you a rakeoff?' interrupted Arnold Sheehan. **1934** *Punch* 26 Dec. 722/2 Why don't you make the cost of The Club Dinner inclusive of wines and spirits? I suppose it is because the hotel where you are having the meal won't give you a rake-off on all liquor served? **1936** [see **football pool*]. **1951** *Proc. Prehistoric Soc.* XVII. 174 The Burmese ones are reputed better, and always fetch a bigger price—in fact they must do so or they would never reach the western villages, as the rake-off from passing them on would be inadequate. **1959** J. Cary *Captive & Free* lxix. 315, I didn't say fifty to you. Sorry. But the agency would give me a rake off on reprints. **1968** *Globe & Mail* (Toronto) 3 Feb. 11/1 Police and politicians in Vancouver may be getting a rake-off from the ring. **1973** 'D. Rutherford' *Kick Start* viii. 174 The vendors were waiting... Obviously the courier would receive a handsome rake-off. **1977** *Time* 31 Oct. 23/3 The President again assailed the big oil companies, charging that deregulation of natural gas prices would produce 'big profit rake-offs and huge cost increases to the American consumers'.

raker[1]. Add: **5.** = *raking-coal* s.v. Raking *vbl. sb.*[1] 3. *dial.* Cf. Rake *v.*[1] 5.

1858 Geo. Eliot *Scenes Clerical Life* II. 250 The kitchen fire..was kept in under a huge 'raker'—a possibility by which the coal of the midland counties atones for all its slowness and white ashes. *c* **1909** D. H. Lawrence *Collier's Friday Night* (1934) iii. 87 Ernest has come from the cellar with a large lump of coal, which he pushes down in the fireplace so that it shall not lodge and go out... He puts the candle on the table, and puts some coal on the fire, round the 'raker'.

6. An inclined beam or strut.

1882 C. H. Stock *Treat. Shoring & Underpinning* ii. 5 The outer shore is called the top raker, the middle shore the middle raker, and the lowest is called the bottom shore. **1887** G. H. Blagrove *Shoring* ii. 32 The foot of the middle raker thrusts against a cleat bolted to the foot of the bottom shore. **1956** *Archit. Rev.* CXX. 327/2 The existing balcony rakers, the main roof and the back stage parts were retained, but the stalls floor..was rebuilt. **1963** M. J. Tomlinson *Foundation Design & Construction* vii. 404 A large pile cap is provided to counteract the uplift on the backward raker.

raker[2]. Add: **1. a.** (Earlier example.)

1876 *Coursing Calendar* 38 Poacher, going a raker from Cannobie lea, never let the latter next the hare in a well-run course of good length.

b. A good stroke at golf.

1899 *Golf Illustr.* 15 Sept. 393/2 Vardon drove a 'raker' from the first tee, nearly hole high.

raki. Add: Now also used of a liquor made from other ingredients (see quot. 1959) in various countries of eastern Europe and the Middle East. Also, a drink or glass of this. (Further examples.)

1775 R. Chandler *Trav. Asia Minor* lxxv. 255 Not far from us were booths of the Turcomans... Some of them joined us, and one or two wanted rakí or brandy. **1845** E. Warburton *Crescent & Cross* I. xxvi. 295 Their dram is distilled from rice, and called *Raki.* **1919** E. H. Jones *Road to En-Dor* iii. 34, I..poured myself out a tot of Raki from Alec's bottle. **1933** 'G. Orwell' *Down & out in London & Paris* xvi. 122 Raki, the Arab drink, was very cheap. **1941** 'R. West' *Black Lamb* (1942) I. 410 Raki, the colourless brandy loved by Slavs. **1956** R. Macaulay *Towers of Trebizond* xii. 125 We had supper at the khan, and sat on there smoking and sipping raki..while Turks played trictrac at little tables beneath the trees. **1959** W. James *Word-bk. Wine* 154 *Raki*, a fairly general name for spirits in Balkan countries; it may be made from wine, grain, molasses, potatoes, plums, and so on; in Turkey it is a spirit resembling Pernod, which goes milky when diluted. **1969** J. Mavor *Voyage to Atlantis* ix. 206 The old woman with two eye-teeth brought us raki or tsipuro, a 40-proof sort of grappa. **1980** M. Bar-Zohar *Deadly Document* ix. 158 He sat down and ordered a *raki.*

rakia (rā·kia, rakī·ya). Also **rakija.** [a. Bulg. *rakia*, Serbo-Croat *rakija*: cf. Raki.] In the Balkan countries: brandy, liquor; = prec.

1845 *Encycl. Metrop.* XXV. 1290/2 *Rakia* is a Dalmatian spirit, drawn from the murk of the wine-press, mingled with aromatics. **1926** *Blackw. Mag.* Apr. 526/1 It was a large scent-bottle filled with *rakija.* **1932** G. Greene *Stamboul Train* IV. i. 179 Ninitch sipped his glass of *rakia*; the heavy plum wine brought tears to his eyes. **1950** V. Canning *Forest of Eyes* iii. 62 He took the *rakia* bottle from his desk drawer and set two glasses. **1959** F. Maclean *Back to Bokhara* ii. 103 Rakia, the plum brandy of Bosnia. **1966** *New Statesman* 11 Nov. 705/2 A Montenegrin town, in 1943, is garrisoned by a tattered Venetian legion... The garrison stifles in rock heat, bloats on rakija. **1980** J. Hone *Flowers of Forest* I. 21 Playing chess over a bottle of rakia somewhere in Yugoslavia.

rakily (rēi·kili), *adv. rare.* [f. (**rakey* f.) Rake *sb.*[5] + -ly[2].] In a rakish manner; rakishly.

1904 C. Hamilton *Passing of Arthur* xx. 167 His newly-ironed tall hat was rakily cut, and he wore an immaculate light grey frock coat and waistcoat.

raking, *vbl. sb.*[1] Add: **1. a.** (Further example.)

1942 *R.A.F. Jrnl.* 18 Apr. 8 There should be full scale raking down of land and sowing.

c. (Later examples.) Also *fig.*

1868 in *Trans. Illinois State Agric. Soc.* (1870) VII. 434 The supply of hogs..appeared to be made up of the rakings and sweepings of the country. **1977** *Times* 24 Dec. 14/5 A series of ovens had been cut into the back of the rampart, their rakings being deposited in the abandoned ditch of the superseded marching camp.

d. A rebuke or scolding. Also with *down*, = a 'dressing down'. Chiefly *U.S.*

1854 *La Crosse* (Wisconsin) *Democrat* 17 Jan. 2/4 Mr. Wright..gave Smith a small raking down. **1883** J. D. Shields *Life & Times S. S. Prentiss* 125 He cheerfully paid it, vowing that the 'raking down' which Prentiss had given his prosecutor was worth that. **1897** G. Bartram *People of Clopton* iii. 80 He got such a terrific raking-down from Aunt that his long black shadow never darkened our doors again. **1907** *Black Cat* Jan. 7 I'll bet somebody has got a raking for losing it.

raking, *vbl. sb.*[3] Add: *spec.* in *Building*, the action of *rack *v.*[7]; also, the resulting arrangement of bricks or stones. Usu. written **racking,** in phr. *racking back.* (Further examples.)

1873 A. M. Lang *J. G. Medley's Roorkee Treat. Civil Engin. in India* (ed. 3) I. xvii. 345 (*heading*) Racking back. **1894** C. F. Mitchell *Building Construction* iii. 132 Racking is the term applied to the method of arranging the edge of a brick wall, part of which is unavoidably delayed while the remainder is carried up. **1902** *Encycl. Brit.* XXVI. 437/1 The foundations must be spread below the column bases... This is accomplished by rackings of stone or brickwork. **1945** E. L. Braley *Brickwork* iii. 60 Racking back is the best method of executing this particular job, as by this means the bonding bricks can be perfectly bedded. **1946** Holgate & McDougall *Bricklaying* vi. 88 Corbling and raking are also largely used in the building of chimney flues. Since a chimney flue always runs upwards at an angle, raking is necessary on one side and corbling on the other. **1964** J. S. Scott *Dict. Building* 254 The normal way of building a *brick* wall consists of first building the corners or ends..in steps rising one course at a time from the middle part of the wall. The gradual increases of height to the corner are called racking back.

raking, *ppl. a.*[3] Add: **b.** *raking bond* (see quot. 1876); also, *raking stretcher bond*; *raking-piece* (*b*) (earlier example).

1876 P. G. L. Smith *Notes Building Construction* II. xiii. 221 Raking Bond is of two kinds, *Diagonal* and *Herring-bone.* In both the bricks in the interior of the wall are placed in directions oblique to the face. A course or two of raking bond is sometimes introduced at intervals in thick walls built in English bond. The proportion of stretchers in a brick wall diminishes according to its thickness... The raking courses are therefore useful in giving longitudinal strength to thick walls which are deficient in stretchers. In both kinds of raking bond alternate courses rake in opposite directions. **1937** P. E. Thomas *Mod. Building Pract.* III. 294 The direction of the diagonal or raking bond is changed in each course to further strengthen the bond of the wall. **1884** Raking-piece [see *cut cloth* s.v. *cut *ppl. a.* 12]. **1974** *Bricks: Their Prop. & Use* (Brick Devel. Assoc.) I. 29 (*caption*) *Raking Stretcher bond.* Economical and more interesting than normal Stretcher Bond. Joints tend to become very prominent unless mortar colour is chosen with care.

rakish, *a.*[2] **1.** (Earlier *Comb.* example.)

1838 Poe *Narr. A. G. Pym of Nantucket* in *Wks.* (1902) III. 146 She was a long, low, and rakish-looking schooner.

‖ **rakshasa** (rā·kʃăsă). Also **raksasa, rakshas;** fem. **rakshasi.** [a. Skr. *rākshasa* demon, f. *rakshas* something to be guarded against or warded off.] In Hindu mythology, a malignant demon, esp. one of a band at war with Rama and Hanuman. Also, an artistic representation of such a demon.

1866 *Chambers's Encycl.* VIII. 101/1 Rakshas, or râkshasa, is, in Hindu Mythology, the name of a class of evil spirits or demons,..imagined..more frequently as mischievous, cruel, and hideous monsters, haunting cemeteries, [etc.]. **1899** F. H. Groome *Gypsy Folk-Tales* p. lxxiv, In the folk-tales of India..a *rakshasi* makes nothing of polishing off the entire population of a city. **1917**, etc. [see *pishachi]. **1937** M. Covarrubias *Island of Bali* vii. 178 The most complete statue is that of a wild *raksasa* crowned with skulls. *Ibid.* viii. 239 The giant Rawana, the *raksasa* king, a monster of wickedness and lechery. **1967** Singha & Massey *Indian Dances* x. 106 A pair of enormous discs are often held by an unseen helper on either side of the face of a rakshasa or demonic character [in Kathakali dancing]. **1972** *Daily Tel.* (Colour Suppl.) 12 May 58/3 The most feared Indian vampire, the Rakshasa, was all powerful; it animated dead bodies, snatched babies,..could change into any form and lengthen its arms to 80 miles.

‖ **rakshi** (rā·kʃi). Also **raksi.** [a. Nepali *raksi*; cf. Tibetan *rag-śi.*] In Nepal and Tibet, a liquor distilled from rice or grain.

1877 D. Wright *Hist. Nepal* ii. 30 The Newārs, and most of the lower castes consume a considerable quantity of a coarse spirit called Rakshī, which is distilled from rice and wheat. **1954** W. Noyce *South Col.* v. 72 Hospitably entertained with tea..and a not very good *rakshi* or rice spirit. **1959** *Times* 23 May 7/7 We spent half a day at the famous monastery of Thyangboche, where we were entertained to dinner by the head lama and sampled his excellent *rakshi*, the local distillation. **1966** C. Bonington *I chose to Climb* x. 124 The Sherpas had settled down to a celebratory binge, consuming huge quantities of rakshi, a potent spirit distilled from barley or rice. **1971** —— *Annapurna South Face* iv. 50 And then supper—chicken and rice washed down by *raksi*, the local spirit made from distilled millet. *Ibid.* vii. 81 Meanwhile, Pasang had taken the unwise step of making a *raksi* issue to some of them.

‖ **raku** (ra·ku). Also **Raku.** [Jap., lit. ease, relaxed state, enjoyment: see quot. 1882.] A kind of lead-glazed Japanese pottery, often used as tea-bowls and similar utensils. Also *attrib.*

1875 Audsley & Bowes *Keramic Art Japan* I. 52 Raku is occasionally covered with lacquer, and it is made in other places than in Kioto. **1882** C. Dresser *Japan* II. iv. 371 Shōgun Taikosama..honoured this particular manufacture with a golden seal, on which the character 'raku' (meaning enjoyment) was engraved... The competition for objects specially valued (as some of these black raku cups) was such that wars were often waged between Daimios with the sole view of possessing certain coveted goods. **1890** B. H. Chamberlain *Things Japanese* 278 The *Raku-yaki* of Kyōto is the parent of all the rest... The *Raku* faience owed much of its popularity to the patronage of the 'tea clubs'. **1960** B. Leach *Potter in Japan* ii. 51 One bowl was old Corean and the other, used alternately, was a 'Doniu' black raku. **1970** *Oxf. Compan. Art* 610 The famous *Raku* is a very soft glazed ware widely used for deliberately mis-shapen vessels. **1979** C. McCarry *Better Angels* II. i. 105 The elegant old man pouring tea into Raku bowls.

râle. Add: Also **rale.** (Earlier and later examples.)

1828 *Glasgow Med. Jrnl.* I. 72 The respiratory murmur is often rendered fainter, and it is accompanied and obscured by certain *râles*, or unnatural sounds. **1963** *Lancet* 12 Jan. 76/1 There were a few dry rales at the right lung base. **1977** *Ibid.* 17 Dec. 1265/2 At this stage there are usually rales in the chest but no definite signs of lung consolidation.

rale (rēⁱl), *a. U.S.* and *dial.* var. of Real *a.*[2]

1835 D. Crockett *Acct. Col. Crockett's Tour* 60 Folks need not go out of Boston to find rale hospitality. **1873** C. M. Yonge *Pillars of House* II. xvi. 108 A fellow that..makes verses—rale, superior, iligant articles. **1901** M. Franklin *My Brilliant Career* xxviii. 237 'Wot's she like?' 'Oh, a rale little bit of a thing.' **1922** E. O'Neill in *Hearst's Internat.* Mar. 47/1 It was..aisy for a rale man with guts to him, the like of me. **1940** *Amer. Speech* XV. 46 Characteristic of those encountered in the Cumberlands and Ozarks are.. *rale*, real.

rall (ræl). *Mus.* Abbrev. of Rallentando.

1876 Stainer & Barrett *Dict. Mus. Terms* 374/1 *Rall.*, abb. for rallentando. **1886** [see *a tempo]. **1959** *Collins Music Encycl.* 530/1 *Rallentando*,..often abbreviated *rall.*

rallentando. Add: (rælĕntæ·ndo). (Examples.) Also *transf.*

1861 Geo. Eliot *Let.* 6 Oct. (1954) III. 456 Our violoncello..is..a man who is all assent and perpetual rallentando. **1926** *Brit. Weekly* 27 May 161/2 The beauty of the theme was heightened by a perfect rallentando. **1946** A. Christie *Come, tell me how you Live* i. 24 Its [*sc.* the Orient Express's] tempo..gradually slows down in a *rallantando* [*sic*] as it proceeds eastwards. **1965** A. T. Hatto *Nibelungenlied* 349 The strophe of the *Nibelungenlied* is normally a balanced and self-contained unit with a marked *rallentando* in the last half-line owing to its extra filled bar. **1978** R. Donington in J. M. Thomson *Future of Early Music in Britain* 13 What sort of rallentandos and how many of them.

ralliance. (Earlier example.)

1826 T. Jefferson *Writings* (1854) IX. xlviii. 510 The good Old Dominion..will then..become a centre of ralliance to the States whose youth she has instructed.

ra·llied, *ppl. a.*[2] *rare.* [f. Rally *v.*[2] + -ed[1].] Subjected to raillery or banter.

a **1704** Locke *Educ.* (1705) 255 The rallied Person also finds his account, and takes part in the diversion.

rallier, *sb.*[1] (Later example.)

1904 F. Lynde *Grafters* i. 11 They..presently found themselves in the thick of the crowd of debarking ralliers.

rally, *sb.*[1] Add: **1. a.** (Further example.)

1928 *Observer* 19 Feb. 27/1 In a belated rally Ivor Jones scored and converted his own try for Llanelly.

2. b. *spec.* a rapid rise in share prices after a fall.

1930 *Economist* 22 Nov. 965/1 Despite all the bad news, a rally in prices made some headway after the liquidation of Monday. **1979** *Daily Tel.* 6 Oct. 23/1 The Index fell..to be 478.8 (down 2.6 at 1 p.m.), but some new account demand after the official close of the market brought an encouraging rally to 480.4.

3. b. For *U.S. colloq.* read 'orig. *U.S.*'. (Earlier and later examples.) Also, a mass-meeting of the supporters of any specified cause.

1840 *Niles' Reg.* 12 Sept. 20/3 Rally of the democracy of Niagara. **1921** *Proc. 3rd Nat. Country Life Conf.* 48 Funds for the school are obtained through rallies held in the churches on the fifth Sunday. **1930** A. P. Herbert *Water Gipsies* iii. 27 At an annual rally of the Boy Scouts..the band was playing the National Anthem. **1960** M. Laurence in *Tamarack Rev.* Autumn 8 'Hey, you Sabina!' Mammi Ama shouted. 'Were you at the rally?' **1973** D. Aarons *Unwritten War* III. viii. 129 His passions were literary, not political. He disliked speeches, rallies, meetings.

c. *dial.* A crowd of persons, a large group.

1837 M. Palmer *Dialogue in Devonshire Dialect* II. 16 There was a whole rally of us at the Pigeons. **1892** S. Hewett *Peasant Speech Devon* 116 There's a turrabul rally aw'm down there. **1908** *Daily Chron.* 16 Jan. 8/5 There's a whole rally of us driving over in Peter's wagonette.

d. Also **rallye** [Fr.]. A competitive event for motor vehicles, usu. over a long distance on public roads.

1932 *Radio Times* 29 July 267/1 Some of the big motoring events of the year—the Ulster Motor Rally, [etc.]. **1949** C. A. N. May *'Wheelspin' Abroad* v. 79 There can be no guarantee of a 1949 Rallye actually taking place. **1963** P. Drackett *Motor Rallying* i. 9 The true progenitor of the rally was the reliability trial. **1973** E. Lemarchand *Let or Hindrance* viii. 90 He seemed more interested in cars than in girls. Went to rallies, and so on.

4. a. Also, a sustained flurry of blows in a boxing match.

1829 P. Egan *Boxiana* 2nd Ser. II. 20 A terrible rally was the finishing stroke of the round. **1885** G. B. Shaw in *Mag. of Music* Nov. 178/3 Exciting pantomime music to what is called by stage managers and prize-fighters a rally.

b. Also used in similar games.

1955 *Times* 9 May 15/3 Kershaw was now increasing his own pace of stroke which led to many long rallies [Real Tennis]. **1977** 'S. Woods' *Law's Delay* III. 125 [The bell] chimes in the hall... We might not have heard it if we were in the middle of a rally [Table Tennis].

5. *attrib.* and *Comb.*, as (sense 3 b) *rally-goer*; (sense *3 d) *rally atmosphere, car, coat, driver, -driving, motorist, plate, seat, wheel, winner*; *rally-bred, -prepared, -proved, -sickened, -toughened* adjs.

1952 W. Leonard *Rallies & Races* i. 19 We touched the real Rally atmosphere. **1977** *Belfast Telegraph* 17 Jan. 10 (Advt.), Safe rally-bred handling, failsafe disc braking all round, safety cage construction. **1976** *Morecambe Guardian* 7 Dec. 18/7 A young Morecambe man had been drinking and was well over the limit for driving when his high-powered rally car smashed into a tree, an inquest at Preston was told on Tuesday. **1973** *Perthshire Advertiser* 17 Feb. 10/1 (Advt.), Gent's rally coats. Concealed hood. 2 inside pockets. **1952** W. Leonard *Rallies & Races* 14 They are rather nice chaps, these Rally-drivers. **1976** *Cumberland News* 3 Dec. 21/3 Even the hardened rally drivers..said it was the worst spectator behaviour they had ever seen. **1954** C. Meisl tr. *J. A. Grégoire's Best Wheel Forward* 121 The future racing driver passes through three well-defined phases: rally driving, hill climbs and endurance tests. **1973** *Guardian* 26 Jan. 13/1 Monte Carlo Rally drivers..should have been able to check in..on time without having to resort to full-blooded rally driving techniques. **1960** *Ibid.* 11 July 6/7 There were few of the familiar, regular rally-goers. **1955** *Times* 9 Aug. 7/7 In making their cars comfortable living places for several days on end, rally motorists have 'invented' several ideas which could add to the comfort and convenience of the ordinary motorist. **1949** C. A. N. May *'Wheelspin' Abroad* iii. 40 One car.. carrying the official Rallye plates. **1968** *Autocar* 25 Jan. 30/1 Like all the rally-prepared cars we have tried, the Triumph handled beautifully. **1961** *Times* 5 Oct. 11/6 You get the rally-proved, highly-praised Anglia engine. **1976** *Liverpool Echo* 22 Nov. 15/4 (Advt.), Mini 1000, blue, Rostyle wheels, rally seats etc. **1961** *Times* 4 Aug. 11/6 To visit any of Britain's several hundred rally-sickened villages during the sport's 'close' season is an edification that regular rally teams should not miss. **1963** P. Drackett *Motor Rallying* iv. 52 From a rag-bag of memories one recalls the blush brought to the rally-toughened countenance of Gregor Grant. **1966** *Motor Trends* Dec. 52/1 (*caption*) Our great Rally II wheels... Wider white-walls are available. **1951** S. C. H. Davis *Rallies & Trials* viii. 108 The Rally winner is rarely decided by the acceleration and brake test.

rally, *v.*[1] Add: **I. 2*.** To drive (a vehicle) in a motor rally. *colloq.*

1969 *Guardian* 18 Aug. 10/2 He drove it around, occasionally attending vintage meetings, but never rallying the car. **1976** L. Deighton *Twinkle, Twinkle Little Spy* xxii. 220 You want to buy a car?.. One owner. Never raced or rallied. **1977** *Drive* Sept.–Oct. 113/1 The punter-hunter fills his advert with euphemisms. Such as: *1974 model* made in 1973;..*never raced nor rallied.*

II. 6. a. (Further examples.)

1866 Geo. Eliot *Felix Holt* I. iii. 87 People were told they must 'rally' at the coming election. **1905** R. Fry *Let.* 21 Jan. (1972) I. 233, I find that these people will rally and do all they can. **1915** J. Webster *Dear Enemy* 201 His friends rallied about the babies, sold..the studio fittings..paid off the debts. **1940** 'N. Blake' *Malice in Wonderland* II. ix. 123 Those who were loudest..are now..the first to rally round. **1963** P. Willmott *Evolution of Community* vii. 75 When one of the neighbour's children married a little while ago we all rallied round. **1978** J. Barnett *Head of Force* iii. 19 The demonstrators marched..to Trafalgar Square where they planned to rally, sing the National Anthem and dismiss.

c. *to rally round the flag*: of a group, to demonstrate loyalty to a cause, as at a moment of impending danger. Also as *attrib. phr. U.S.* (orig. in Civil War use).

1862 G. F. Root *Battle Cry of Freedom* (song) 3 Yes we'll rally round the flag, boys, we'll rally once again, Shouting the battle-cry of Freedom. **1957** M. Shulman (*title*) Rally round the flag, boys! **1964** *New Yorker* 4 Jan. 77 Much of the book is written in a tough, choppy, emotional style, but this approach disguises a spurious rally-round-the-flag vision. **1968** *Listener* 8 Feb. 164/2 The immediate reaction of the American people is to rally round the flag and demand that its honour be upheld.

7. a. (Earlier examples.)

1744 Ellis *Mod. Husbandman* Jan. vi. 60 After the first Mowing..they do not *rally*, as we call it, *i.e.* they do not grow again to much Profit. **1792** H. Newdigate *Let.* Feb. in A. E. Newdigate-Newdegate *Cheverels* (1898) viii. 111 Sally Rally'd last night and sang Charmingly.

rally, *v.*[3] Add: Also 8 **ralley.** (Earlier example.)

1728 *Calendar Virginia State Papers* (1875) I. 215 We were like a sow that had lost her pigs, would ralley for a little time and then have done.

rallycross (ræ·likrǫs). [f. *rally *sb.*[1] 3 d + *auto)cross.] A form of motor racing combining elements of rallying and autocross. Also *attrib.*

1967 *Daily Mirror* 26 Aug. 9/5 What is the sport that scales down motor rallying to a seven-minutes sensation?.. Rallycross, which combines the thrills of autocross where old 'bangers' tackle mud-covered hills—with the ordeals of the Monte Carlo rally. **1968** *Observer* 21 Apr. 7/4 (Advt.), 'It's got these ingredients that cut the corrosion cars suffer from when they're left hanging about.' Roger Clark, leading Ford rally driver and rallycross man. **1978** *Morecambe Guardian* 14 Mar. 11/1 Motor sport is having trouble finding suitable space for short track speedway racing and rallycross.

rallying, *vbl. sb.*[1] Add: **a.** Also, the action or practice of participating in a rally (in senses of *sb.*[1]).

1960 S. Turner *Rallying* i. 12 There are four levels of rallying: Closed, Restricted, National and International. **1971** 'D. Rutherford' *Clear Fast Lane* 39 The usual changes needed before a production car is ready for rallying. **1978** *Times* 4 July 19/2 He [*sc.* Nastase] mixed the pace and pattern of his rallying with..nonchalant grace.

b. *rallying-round* (later example).

1930 Wodehouse *Very Good, Jeeves!* iii. 69 Cold and haughty. No symp. None of the rallying-round spirit which one likes to see.

rallyist (ræ·li,ist). [f. Rally *sb.*[1] + -ist.] One who competes in a motor rally or rallies.

1961 *Times* 4 Aug. 11/7 With some common sense.. rallyists could avoid strangling their own lusty child. **1963** P. Drackett *Motor Rallying* ii. 28 Another outstanding rallyist, John Sprinzel, writes a regular column for the monthly *Motor Racing*. **1972** *Sci. Amer.* Jan. 11/1 Since becoming involved in this task I've met a fascinating variety of nonacademic types—automobile wreckers, automobile racers, rallyists, manufacturers of technical equipment.

ram, *sb.*[1] Add: **1. c.** *transf.* A sexually aggressive man; a lecher. *colloq.*

1935 *N. & Q.* 23 Nov. 366/2 *Ram*, a male, sexual enthusiast. **1946** *Penguin New Writing* XXVIII. 185 'Yes, it's the Chalk all right,' Willie said. 'The old ram!' he added, happily. **1977** J. Wainwright *Do Nothin' till You hear from Me* viii. 128 One day, May will wise up on the ram she has for a husband and pan him in the chops.

3. c. (Further U.S. example.)

1898 C. A. Dana *Recoll. Civil War* iii. 37 First came seven ironclad turtles and one heavy armed ram.

e. *U.S. Naut.* (See quot. 1961.)

1909 *Sun* (Baltimore) 1 Aug. 14/2 Capt Andrew Hubbard, who later, with all hands, was lost at sea, saw the queer craft coming down stream. He shouted at Captain Insley 'That's certainly a Nanticoke ram.' **1953** *Sun Mag.* (Baltimore) 25 Oct. 30/5 Rams which once hauled lumber are now summer cruise ships. **1961** J. E. Marvil *Sailing Rams* 9 *Ram*, 3 masted bald headed schooner, flat bottom, straight sides without jib boom built and sailed mainly on Chesapeake Bay.

f. *Eton slang.* (See quot. 1977.)

1922 S. Leslie *Oppidan* xvii. 200 A strange procession... There was no variation in the *ram*, as it was called by a football metaphor. **1930** *Daily Tel.* 1 Dec. 21/2 On the last occasion Lori-Phillip touched a rouge, but the ram failed. **1942** J. Lees-Milne *Ancestral Voices* (1975) 30 Then to evensong in [Eton] College Chapel where the traditional ceremonial is invariable. The 'ram' marches in the same deliberate, self-conscious manner. **1977** A. J. Ayer *Part of My Life* ii. 44 After scoring a rouge the attackers could gain an extra point by charging in column and bundling their opponents and the ball into the goal. The column was known as a ram, which was also the name given to the twin columns of Colleger and Oppidan sixth-formers, as they processed into Chapel.

g. An underwater projection from an iceberg or other body of ice.

1952 *Functional Gloss. Ice Terminol.* (U.S. Navy Hydrogr. Office) 22 More rapid melting at the water line than above and below causes a notch to be formed at the water line below which is the ram. **1974** *Encycl. Brit. Macropædia* IX. 160/2 In the Labrador current, sailing at one or two knots toward the North Atlantic shipping routes, this iceberg had a ram (underwater projection), as most icebergs do by the time they enter the warmer waters near the Gulf Stream. **1976** *Jrnl. R. Soc. Arts* CXXIV. 644/1 Ice headlands are elevated because the underwater 'ram' at the seaward side gives more buoyancy.

5. e. The reciprocating arm on which the tool is mounted in a shaping or slotting machine.

1864 D. K. Clark *Exhibited Machinery of 1862* iii. §1. ii. 133 Machines..for shaping levers, cranks, connecting rods... The ram is moved by means of a peculiar crank-motion, with a quick return. **1935** *Buck & Hickman Ltd. Gen. Catal. Tools & Supplies* 126 Hand shaping machine... There are nine different working positions of handle, the ram having three holes and the handle three holes. **1964** S. Crawford *Basic Engin. Processes* viii. 216 Most shaping machines are of the crank type... The ram is located in the top slideway of the body and is reciprocated by the crank mechanism. **1977** *Buck & Hickman Catal. 1977–1979* High speed shaping machine... The ram, carriage and table are all mounted in dovetail guides.

6. a. (sense 1) *ram-faced* adj.

1921 R. Graves *Pier-Glass* 49 Ram-faced lecher, the blood on his own beast head!

b. (sense *3 e) *ram schooner*; *ram type* adj.

1904 *Naut. Gaz.* 14 Apr. 211/2 Geo. K. Phillips & Co., Bethel, Del., have on the stocks a three-masted ram schooner 140 ft. long. **1956** *Sun* (Baltimore) 19 Apr. 38/8 Mr. Katz said he would prove the captain of the ill-fated 'ram type' schooner ran for shelter when hurricane winds were predicted.

7. ram-coupler, a form of coupler used between closely-set organ manuals.

1881 W. E. Dickson *Pract. Organ-Building* xii. 156 The ram-coupler can be used between manuals arranged too closely to admit of tumblers.

ram, *sb.*[3] Add: Also, the centre plank of a coble. Also *attrib.*

1933 *Yachting Monthly* LVI. 108/1 The centre plank [of a coble] is called the 'ram'. **1970** E. J. March *Inshore Craft Gt. Brit.* I. iv. 137 The true coble is built up on a 'ram plank' not a keel. **1973** W. Elmer *Terminol. Fishing* iv. 113 The *ram* denotes the broad central bottom plank in the cobles, which have no keel.

ram, *sb.*[4] Add: **2. a.** The compressive effect experienced by air which is constrained to enter a moving aperture or restricted space (*spec.* the intake of a jet engine); (cf. *ramjet). orig. and freq. *attrib.*, as *ram compression, effect, pressure.*

1944 *Jrnl. R. Aeronaut. Soc.* XLVIII. 445 Air is led from the intake A, under full ram due to the forward speed of the aircraft, to the compressor B. **1945** P. H. Wilkinson *Aircraft Engines of World* 343 Ram effect in flight compresses air to more than atmospheric pressure. **1948** C. E. Chapel *Aircraft Power Plants* iii. 30/2 Ram pressure is that developed in the carburetor air scoop by the forward speed of the airplane. **1953** J. Liston *Power Plants for Aircraft* ii. 65 Compression is obtained by utilizing the forward motion of the aircraft to produce a dynamic pressure or 'ram' in the diverging inlet section of the engine. **1960** D. G. Shepherd *Introd. Gas Turbine* (ed. 2) iii. 84 This increase of temperature and pressure due to aircraft speed is called the ram effect, or simply ram. **1969** W. Thomson *Thrust for Flight* 43 At the high forward speeds made possible by jet propulsion the pressure in the turbine compressor intake can be raised by ram effects to such an extent that the turbines of fast aircraft become very efficient. *Ibid.* 53 Increase of pressure by ram is not a free gift. **1971** P. J. McMahon *Aircraft Propulsion* iii. 111 All the compression needed for it [*sc.* the ramjet] to operate as a heat engine comes from ram compression in the intake due to forward motion.

b. Special Combs.: **ram air,** air which is constrained to enter a moving aperture; freq. *attrib.*; **ram-wing,** a wing-like structure on an air-cushion vehicle which generates lift by means of a ram effect, compressing air between itself and the ground or water surface as it moves.

1953 Jennings & Rogers *Gas Turbine Analysis & Practice* i. 9 Ram air slightly compressed by the forward progress of the airplane enters the impeller, where the pressure of this air is increased by some 10 to 20 in. Hg. **1962** *Engineering* 31 Aug. 258/2 If..all the engines were out, two ram-air turbines provide electric and hydraulic power for essential flying control and aircraft services. **1978** A. Welch *Bk. of Airsports* vi. 92/2 The Para-Foil, or ram-air 'chute, was developed in the late 1960s by Domina Jalbert. **1962** *Air-Cushion Vehicles* Oct. 70/2 Of particular interest.. is a Kawasaki ram-wing craft now being built. **1968** Elsley & Devereux *Hovercraft Design & Construction* i. 13 The ram wing is another type of aerodynamic craft... This is essentially a low-aspect-ratio wing with its trailing edge virtually touching the surface and with endplates sealing the tips to the surface. Suction pressures are developed on the upper surface together with ram or dynamic pressure underneath.

ram, *v.*[1] Add: **6. b.** Of a ship: to force *a way* by ramming.

1914 *Times* (Weekly ed.) 10 Apr. 293/1 The Bellaventure was nine hours yesterday in ramming her way through four miles of ice.

-rama: see *-orama.

ramada (rămā·dă). *U.S.* [Sp.] In the Western U.S.: an (orig. temporary) arbor or similar structure; a porch.

1869 B. I. Hayes *Pioneer Notes from Diaries* (1929) viii. 289, I paid them a dollar for my bath, at the rustic bathing establishment they have constructed, consisting of two goods' boxes sunk in the ground, sheltered by a *ramada*. **1911** H. B. Wright *Winning of Barbara Worth* 201 Every evening under the ramada Barbara sat with her father, often alone. **1949** *Desert Mag.* Apr. 24/1 In a brush ramada the Navajo women weave their blankets while the older children tend the sheep. **1957** G. Shirreffs *Rio Bravo* (1972) i. 8 Someone walked across the boardwalk beneath the *ramada* in front of the building. **1976** *Arizona Republic* (Phoenix, Arizona) 27 May b–15/3 Desert Foothills Scenic Drive..a 17-mile desert drive with ramadas and rest rooms. **1979** *Arizona Daily Star* 5 Aug. (Advt. Section) 17/1 Common areas with playgrounds and ramada.

Ramadan, ramazan. Add: The form **Ramadan** is now usual. (Later examples.)

1927 C. Connolly *Let.* Mar. in *Romantic Friendship* (1975) 279 It is Ramadan at present and nobody eats till the evening. **1935** H. Edib *Clown & his Daughter* xli. 67 He has been back for some time, and is getting ready to open his shop for Ramazan. **1971** *Sun* (Colombo) 17 Sept. 3 November 8... Ramazan Festival Day. **1976** *Hanna* (Alberta) *Herald* 16 June 10/5 During one month each year the Muslims observe Ramadan.

ramage, *sb.*[2] Restrict *arch.* to senses in Dict. and add: **1. b.** *Anthrop.* A corporate descent group which includes members of both maternal and paternal lineages.

1936 R. Firth *We, the Tikopia* x. 371 One term that might be employed to characterize such kinship groups is 'ramage', for which there is literary authority, though it has fallen out of use. *Ibid.* xvi. 586 The patrilineal principle of descent in the ramage ('joint family' is the translation given of the native term *hoa*) is modified. **1957** —— in *Man* LVII. 6/1 In former publications I have used *ramage* to include the Tikopia unilineal descent group. This, I think, is better described functionally as a lineage. *Ibid.* 6/2 Ramage would then be defined as a corporate descent group of a non-unilinear (ambilineal) character, membership being obtained ambilaterally..according to circumstances. **1963** *Brit. Jrnl. Sociol.* XIV. 24 The word *ramage* has been used to mean a corporate group in which membership may be acquired through either parent. **1976** Hunter & Whitten *Encycl. Anthropol.* 330/1 *Ramage*, nonunilineal descent group composed of individuals who are descended from one ancestor through any combination of male and female links.

Ramage (ræ·mėdʒ), *sb.*[3] The name of Adam *Ramage* (1770–1850), a printer of Philadelphia, used *attrib.* to denote a (usu. wooden) printing-press, or part of one, designed by him.

1827 *Hallowell* (Maine) *Gaz.* 20 June 4/3 For Sale, a small font of Brevier, nearly new; also a Printing Press with a new Ramage Screw. **1874** B. F. Taylor *World on Wheels* i. iii. 24 The cargoes of those boats..was something wonderful,..plows, axes and Bibles, teachers, preachers and Ramage presses. **1923** L. E. Young *Founding of Utah* xxxiii. 349 The old Ramage press had a lever which the printer pulled in the printing of each page. **1949** *Mississippi Valley Hist. Rev.* Mar. 634 It was..printed on a small wrought-iron Ramage press.

Raman (rā·măn). *Chem.* and *Physics.* Also (*rare*) **raman.** The name of Sir Chandrasekhara Venkata *Raman* (1888–1970), Indian physicist, used *attrib.* and in *Comb.* with reference to the Raman effect he discovered, as *Raman band, line, shift* (so *Raman-shifted* adj.), *spectrometer, spectroscopy*, etc.; **Raman-active** *a.*, capable of giving rise to Raman scattering; **Raman effect, scattering,** the scattering of light by a substance with a change in the frequency of the light by an amount which is characteristic of the scattering substance and represents a change in the vibrational, rotational, or electronic energy of the substance; occas. with ellipsis of *effect*; **Raman spectrum,** a spectrum of scattered light showing additional bands produced by the Raman effect.

1928 *Nature* 29 Sept. 477/2 (*heading*) The Raman effect in crystals. **1929** *Ibid.* 24 Aug. 301/1 The Raman spectra for various liquids. **1937** *Jrnl. Amer. Chem. Soc.* LIX. 1139/1 It is generally admitted that the 3654 cm^{-1} Raman band of water vapor corresponds to the symmetric..vibration. **1945** G. Herzberg *Infrared & Raman Spectra of Polyatomic Molecules* iii. 243 All three vibrations of non-linear symmetric..XY_2 are Raman active as well as infrared active. **1947** *Nature* 11 Jan. 60/2 The principal feature noticeable in the spectra is the appearance of a whole series of sharply defined Raman lines. **1947** *Thorpe's Dict. Appl. Chem.* (ed. 4) VIII. 190/1 Fundamental frequencies will be active in Raman scattering only when the mode of vibration of the molecule associated with that fundamental frequency causes an equiperiodic variation in the polarisibility of the molecule. **1950** W. J. Moore *Physical Chem.* xi. 332 Since the Raman spectra are studied with light sources in the visible or ultraviolet, they provide a convenient means of obtaining the same sort of information about molecular structure as is given by the infrared spectra. In many cases, the two methods supplement each other, since vibrations and rotations that are not observable in the infrared..may be active in the Raman. **1958** *Oxf. Univ. Gaz.* 23 Apr. 881 Application of raman spectra to chemical problems. **1962** *Times* 9 Mar. 2/6 (Advt.), The successful applicant will work in one of the following fields:..ultra-violet, infra-red and Raman spectroscopy of aromatic, *N*-heterocyclic and tautomerizable substances. **1966** D. H. Whiffen *Spectroscopy* ix. 110 The Raman lines are always extremely weak with respect to the incident light intensity. **1967** L. A. Woodward in H. A. Szymanski *Raman Spectroscopy* I. i. 16 In practice, the pure rotational Raman shifts are small.. and it is necessary to use a spectrograph of high dispersion and resolving power. **1970** Gilson & Hendra *Laser Raman Spectroscopy* ii. 21 In the basic Raman spectrometer, the sample under examination is subjected to irradiation from a suitable monochromatic source, and the Raman spectrum is observed by use of a system comprising a monochromator, detector, and recorder. **1974** *Nature* 8 Mar. 124/1 Raman-shifted backscatter of laser radar radiation from atmospheric constituents in the troposphere has been reported. **1976** *Jrnl. Chem. Soc. Dalton Trans.* 1148/2 Five of the six Raman-active vibrations of the two octahedral anions.. were clearly observed. **1978** P. W. Atkins *Physical Chem.* xvii. 563 The molecule is active in the Raman because the end-over-end rotation modulates its polarizability as viewed by a stationary observer.

ramanas (ræ·mănăs). [perh. f. Jap. *ranman* full bloom.] *ramanas rose* = *rugosa.

1876 *Garden* 3 May 452/2 (*heading*) The Ramanas Rose of Japan. **1955** N. D. G. James *Forester's Compan.* xxii. 246 Shrubs of value for food and cover..Ramanas rose (*Rosa rugosa*). **1956** [see *Japanese rose* s.v. *Japanese *a.* b].

Ramapithecus (rāmăpi·þikŏs). [mod.L. (G. E. Lewis 1934, in *Amer. Jrnl. Sci.* CCXXVII. 162), f. *Rāma*, the name of an Indian prince of Ayodhyā + Gr. πίθηκος ape.] A fossil anthropoid ape, sometimes considered a hominid, belonging to the genus so called and known from remains found in northern India and East Africa. So **ramapi·thecine** *sb.* and *a.*, a fossil anthropoid closely related to *Ramapithecus*; pertaining to or resembling an anthropoid ape of this kind.

1934 *Discovery* July 197/2 The other [ape], *Ramapithecus*, is represented by an upper jaw in which the teeth are set in a rounded V, approaching the human form, instead of the U-shape characteristic of the anthropoids. **1965** *Folia Primatologica* III. 90 No finds of *Ramapithecus* or any other dryopithecine or hominid have ever been made in the Tatrot or Pinjor zones. **1968** D. Pilbeam in *Nature* 28 Sept. 1337/1, I would argue..that *Ramapithecus* is probably a hominid,..even if fossil evidence were produced which showed that it was not yet a habitual biped. **1969** J. E. Pfeiffer *Emergence of Man* ii. 47 Imagine an adventurous hominid or prehominid, a primitive *Ramapithecus* perhaps, looking for food in the savanna. **1971** [see *Kenyapithecus]. **1973** *Listener* 10 May 604/3 Some anthropologists would boldly put *Ramapithecus* among the hominids. **1976** R. Ardrey *Hunting Hypothesis* 35 Were the ramapithecines close to the common ancestor of chimp and man? **1977** *Sci. Amer.* May 31/1 Kretzoi now recognizes his fossils as being 'ramapithecine' even if they are not generically *Ramapithecus*. **1978** *Nature* 5 Jan. 12/1 It is of interest and of uncertain significance that not all ramapithecines have been found in woodland deposits.

ramarama (ra·măra:mă). Also **ramiram, rummyrum.** [Maori.] An evergreen New Zealand shrub or small tree, *Myrtus* (or *Lophomyrtus*) *bullata*, belonging to the family Myrtaceæ and bearing small white flowers followed by dark red berries.

1843 E. Dieffenbach *Travels in N.Z.* II. iii. 382 Rama rama—name of a tree (*Myrtus bullata*). **1851** H. W. Richmond *Let.* 15 June in *Richmond–Atkinson Papers* (1960) I. ii. 97 A letter might be written about the tapitap so useful for hammer handles..and the ramiram for ramming in the posts in fencing. **1882** W. D. Hay *Brighter Britain!* II. vi. 196 The Rama-rama..has a good hard wood. **1889** T. Kirk *Forest Flora N.Z.* 273 The ramarama is the largest and most attractive of the New Zealand myrtles. *Ibid.*, The wood of the ramarama is red, straight, and compact. **1928** H. H. Allan *N.Z. Trees & Shrubs* 131 Ramarama..Bushy shrub up to 15 ft; branchlets tomentose. **1946** *Jrnl. Polynesian Soc.* LV. 157 Ramarama, a tree.., often corrupted to rummyrum. **1970** M. E. Fisher et al. *Gardening with N.Z. Plants* i. 75 The ramarama is easily distinguished from all other native plants by its reddish-brown leaves, the spaces between the veins of which are inflated.

Ramayana (rā·māyană). Also † **Ramayuna, -unu.** [a. Skr. *Rāmāyaṇa*, f. *Rāmā* Rama, the seventh incarnation of Vishnu + *ayana* a going.] An ancient Hindu epic, ascribed to the poet Valmiki. Also *attrib.*

1788 *Asiatick Researches* I. 351 The first Indian Poet was Válmíci, author of the Rámáyana, a complete Epick Poem on one continued, interesting, and heroick, action. **1806** Carey & Marshman tr. *Ramayuna* I. p. ii, The Committee.. have made choice of the Ramayuna of Valmeeki to be the first in the series of translations from the Sungskrit. **1811** W. Ward *Acct. Hindoos* I. p. viii, Next follow Translations of the Contents of the Mŭhabharŭtŭ, the Ramayŭnŭ, and the Shrēē-Bhagŭvŭtŭ. **1841** *Penny Cycl.* XX. 401/1 There are three pieces of his, one in which a domestic subject is treated..and two others taken from the cycle of traditions of the Rāmāyana. **1870** F. Richardson *Iliad of East* p. vii, The Rāmāyana comprises in all some twenty-four thousand verses, or *slokas*. **1937** M. Covarrubias *Island of Bali* viii. 235 The great epics of the Hindus, the famous *Ramayana* and *Mahabharata*..came by way of Java as propaganda for the ancient Hindus and as part of their religious teachings. **1974** *Times* 5 Nov. 11/4 The play is a stirring episode from the Hindu *Ramayana* epic: Rama's courtship of the lustrous Siti Dewi.

rambai (ra·mbai). Also † **rambé, rambeh.** [Malay.] An evergreen tree, *Baccaurea motleyana*, or a closely related species, belonging to the family Euphorbiaceæ, native to Malaysia, and bearing large dark green leaves and racemes of tiny yellowish-green flowers; also, the fruit of this tree, which is an oval about two inches long with white flesh and pale brown seeds in a smooth brownish-yellow skin. Also *attrib.*

1811 W. Marsden *Hist. Sumatra* (ed. 3) 101 The *chupak*, *ayer-ayer*, and *rambé* are species or varieties of the same fruit [*sc.* lanseh]. **1820** J. Crawfurd *Hist. Indian Archipelago* I. iv. 432 The *Langseh*, *Rambeh*, and *Dukuh* are indigenous fruits. **1839** T. J. Newbold *Straits of Malacca* I. ii. 53 In the valley grow various fruit-trees, such as..the rambai. **1911** [see *Langsat]. **1924** H. N. Ridley *Flora of Malay Peninsula* III. 250 *B*[*accaurea*] *Motleyana*... The Rambeh, cultivated all over the peninsula. **1940** E. J. H. Corner *Wayside Trees of Malaya* I. 241 In habit, trunk, bark and strings of buff-coloured fruits with green seeds and white pulp, the *Rambai* and *Langsat*..are very much alike. **1975** B. M. Allen *Common Malaysian Fruits* 11 Rambai is native to Malaysia and is commonly cultivated in the lowlands. *Ibid.*, Rambai fruits are easily confused with Duku and Langsat.

‖ **rambla** (ra·mblă). [Sp., ad. Arab. *ramla*, lit. 'sandy ground'.] **1.** A Spanish ravine, usu. waterless; the dry bed of an ephemeral stream.

1829 W. Irving *Conq. Granada* I. xii. 97 Sometimes their road was a mere rambla, or dry bed of a torrent. **1845** R. Ford *Hand-bk. Spain* I. 398/2 Three long L[eagues], by a *rambla* of red rocks, lead to Berja. **1923** *Blackw. Mag.* Oct. 509/2 Before we reached this *rambla*, coming around a series of sharp bends down a hillside to a lower level, we were tempted by a combination of sun, dust, and the fortuitous appearance of a wayside venta to halt the Colonel. **1960** *Geogr. Rev.* L. 60 Long stretches of drainage channels have been filled up..with erosion debris of rock fragments, gravel, and sand. Such debris-choked channels are called *ramblas*. **1977** *New Yorker* 16 May 34/3 On the perimeter of the terrace were a four-foot-high chain-link fence, then a narrow *rambla*, and then another..fence.

2. A broad street in a city of eastern Spain, built on a shallow watercourse; *spec.* (now usu. in *pl.*) a broad avenue in Barcelona.

1829 A. S. Mackenzie *Year in Spain* i. 37 Our fonda was situated..upon the Rambla, an immense highway through the city, the chief thoroughfare and promenade of Barcelona. **1873** *Amer. Cycl.* II. 304/1 Foremost among its numerous promenades is the Rambla (so called from the Arabic *raml*, sand, applied to a dry river bed, used as a road). **1893** *Johnson's Universal Cycl.* I. 497/1 The city is divided into the old and the new town by a beautiful promenade called La Rambla. **1923** *Blackw. Mag.* Aug. 197/1 The rambla turned into a narrow valley. **1968** *Encycl. Brit.* III. 154/2 Cutting through the old city to the west is the street called the Ramblas leading from the Puerta de la Paz to the Plaza de Cataluña, the centre of the modern Barcelona where are numerous banking houses. **1975** D. Beaty *Electric Train* 34 She had seen the boys and girls promenading up and down in the evening on the *ramblas*.

ramblage (ræ·mblėdʒ). *Manx law.* [f. Ramble *v.* + -age.] Chiefly in phr. *right of ramblage*, the right to ramble over land in addition to passing across it.

1887 *Peel City Guardian* 17 Sept. 5/2 The public will not only be able to claim right of way but also right of ramblage over the whole of the headlands down to the shores. **1898** *Ibid.* 19 Feb. 3/5 The defendant claimed right of ramblage for the people of Rushen. *Ibid.* 3/6 His Honour said that was ramblage. **1930** *Times* 11 Nov. 10/5 Surely the word 'ramblage' is as worthy of preservation as 'the right of ramblage' itself.—The Rev. T. G. Phillips, Wesley Manse, Peel, Isle of Man.

ramble, *v.* Add: **3.** (Earlier and later examples.)

1810 E. Weeton *Let.* 4 June (1969) I. 265 If my time were my own, [I] would ramble the country over. **1930** V. Woolf in *Death of Moth* (1942) 19 The greatest pleasure of town life in winter—rambling the streets of London.

rambler. Add: **a.** In later use, one who walks through the countryside on a specified route, freq. in company with others.

1888 C. F. Wardley (*title*) The rambler's guide to Buxton and neighbourhood, specially compiled for pedestrians. **1932** *Ramblers' Federation Handbk.* III. 15 Many ramblers have made acquaintance with the Batham Gate on visits to the Peak Forest district. **1955** *Times* 11 July 7/1 Such acts of vandalism, said an official of the Peak Park Board, turned the farmers and villagers against genuine ramblers. **1977** *Times* 5 Oct. 14/5 The animal is..in a very unsuitable field and frightening the wits out of innocent ramblers.

c. A type of house, usu. a single-storey suburban building; a ranch house. *U.S.*

1958 *Washington Post* 16 Aug. b1/4 These 3-bedroom, full-basement ramblers and split-foyer ramblers will be sold on terms of no money down to qualifying G.I. buyers. **1967** T. Baird *Finding Out* x. 88 The houses in lots..Cape Cod cottages, ramblers, colonial split-levels, random provincials. **1975** P. Moyes *Black Widower* ii. 20 She would not have traded their tiny frame house..for a modern split-level rambler in any smart suburban development. **1976** *Washington Post* 19 Apr. c17/2 (Advt.), Forestville—Rambler, 3-br. $325.

rambling, *vbl. sb.* Add: Also *Comb.*, as *rambling club.*

1902 *Encycl. Brit.* XXXII. 682/2 Sketching clubs and rambling clubs are formed among young people. **1974** *Country Life* 7 Mar. 471/3 Many rambling clubs..[are] printing on their club programmes that dogs must be kept on a lead on farm land.

rambling, *ppl. a.* **4.** (Earlier examples.)

c **1702** C. Fiennes *Journeys* (1947) 152 There are no good houses but what are old rambling ones [in Bury St. Edmunds]. **1790** *Loiterer* 2 Jan. 10 C—— Castle is a wretched, irregular, heavy, and rambling pile of building. **1816** Jane Austen *Emma* III. vi. 93 The house was..rambling and irregular. **1836** F. Witts *Diary* 12 July (1978) 115 A large rambling mansion first built in the close of the 17th century.

rambo (ræ·mbo). *U.S.* [See Rambure.] A variety of eating or cooking apple which ripens late in autumn and has yellowish, red-streaked skin. Also *attrib.*

1804 J. Mease in A. F. M. Willich *Domestic Encycl.* (Amer. ed.) III. 113/1 Rambo. From Delaware; a fine fall apple. **1817** W. Coxe *View of Cultivation of Fruit Trees* 116 Rambo, or Romanite. This apple is much cultivated in Delaware, Pennsylvania, and New Jersey. **1867** *Hours at Home* V. 318/1 There, too, was the 'rambo-row'—alas! how it is thinned out. **1880** *Harper's Mag.* Aug. 355/1 Outside there were great orchards..with old fashioned Baldwins and Rambos. **1898** M. Deland *Old Chester Tales* 178 Its apples ..were poor enough—hard, gnarly russets, or small, bitter rambos. **1906** *N.Y. Even. Post* (Saturday Suppl.) 5 May 3/2 There were still the meetings of an evening..beneath the rambo apple tree. **1913** G. Stratton-Porter *Laddie* xi. 329 There was a teasing fragrance in the spiced vinegar for pickles, a reminder of winesap and rambo in the boiling cider. **1942** C. Weygandt *Plenty of Pennsylvania* 64 The Rambo apple is not generally raised nowadays.

rambunctious (ræmbʌ·ŋkʃəs, ræ·mbʌ:ŋkʃəs), *a. colloq.* (orig. and chiefly *U.S.*). Also **rambunkshus, rumbunctious,** etc. [Origin unknown: cf. Rumbustious *a.*] Of a person: rumbustious, exuberant; boisterous, unruly; flamboyant; of an animal: wild, high-spirited. Also *transf.* Hence **rambu·nctiously** *adv.*, **rambu·nctiousness.**

1830 *Boston Transcript* 1 Sept. 3/1 If they are 'rumbunctious' at the prospect, they will be 'riprorious' when they get a taste, for a 'copious acquaintance' with Vinegar. **1859** 'Dow, Jr.' *New Patent Sermons* 120 Some [men] are mild and peaceable as lambs, while others are as uproarious and rambunctious as tigers. **1866** C. H. Smith *Bill Arp* 54 A plan was set on foot to procure a fierce and rambunkshus animal from the mountains of Hepsidam. **1886** *Galaxy* 1 Oct. 275 'Rampunctious' is belligerent. **1899** *Century Mag.* Aug. 623/1 Och, Misther McGeever, now..I niver heerd no man accuse you of bein' anyway rambunkshus about yer nabor's house. **1902** Kipling *Traffics & Discoveries* (1904) 181 'The petrol will light up and the boiler may blow up.' 'How rambunkshus!' **1904** E. Robins *Magnetic North* I. 123 And it hasn't thought of sleetin'..or anything else rambunksious. **1914** *Blackw. Mag.* July 123/1 Our western bronco retains much of his primitive rambunctiousness. **1922** Joyce *Ulysses* 146 Those slightly rambunctious females. **1926** 'J. J. Connington' *Death at Swaythling Court* xvi. 284, I was a bit worried and not feeling particularly rambunctious. **1928** W. A. White *Masks in Pageant* 442 Outside of Vermont, in these expansive, more rambunctious United States, economy is a low virtue ordinarily. **1962** J. E. Hartshorn *Politics & World Oil Econ.* xiii. 193 In the United States these companies, and a host of smaller, even more rambunctiously 'free enterprisers' in the domestic oil business there, get on very comfortably thank you with state agencies. **1962** *Guardian* 4 May 16/5 It then seemed that Mr Fulbright's opponent would be..Dale Alford, a weak but rambunctious man who had promising connections with the Walkerites, the Indignationists, the Birchites. **1971** G. H. Bourne *Ape People* xi. 247 This animal was a rough, tough, rambunctious creature. **1976** *Time* 27 Dec. 13/2 Brezhnev inherited many problems from his rambunctious, buccaneering predecessor, Nikita Khrushchev **1977** *New Yorker* 8 Aug. 47/3 The club that initiated the championship was Prestwick, which occupies a rambunctious stretch of duneland on the east shore of the Firth of Clyde. **1980** *Daily Tel.* 19 Feb. 17/4 J. Edgar Hoover, the then-director of the FBI and the man in charge of all counter-intelligence operations in the United States, personally ordered the probe into Flynn's off-screen activities after the rambunctious star was accused in California of sexually assaulting two under-age girls.

rambutan, -bootan. Add: Also **rambotan.** Also, the tree bearing this fruit, which belongs to the family Sapindaceæ. Also *attrib.* (Further examples.)

1795 tr. *C. P. Thunberg's Travels* (ed. 2) II. 277 The Rambutan (*Nephelium lappaceum*) grows in large clusters and is very generally eaten. **1839** T. J. Newbold *Straits of Malacca* I. ii. 53 In the valley grow various fruit-trees, such as the mangostin,..the rambotan, etc. **1895** *Natural Sci.* VI. 25 He came upon a brisk fight between a large number of Kras and about half a dozen Lotongs (*Semnopithecus*) for the possession of a Rambutan tree..in fruit. **1920** W. Popenoe *Man. Tropical Fruits* x. 328 The rambutan is eaten fresh. **1940** E. J. H. Corner *Wayside Trees of Malaya* I. 592 Mangosteen, Durian and Rambutan generally flower together. **1962** B. Harrisson *Orang-Utan* iii. 106 The only alternatives were some rambutan trees in the back of the garden... We were little surprised that the new trees, though they had only a small supply of ripe rambutan, stimulated a bout of nest-building. **1966** [see *Jack *sb.*[4] b]. **1969** *Oxf. Bk. Food Plants* 100/2 The rambutan is limited to tropical lowlands and requires a high rainfall. **1976** 'G. Black' *Moon for Killers* ix. 125, I had two helpings and followed them with a couple of rambutans. **1977** *Borneo Bull.* 7 May 2/2 The corn potential is shown in the centre's annual report for 1976, which also underlines pepper and rambutans as two other valuable income-earning crops.

ramdohrite (ræ·mdōᵊrəit). *Min.* [ad. G. *ramdohrit* (F. Ahlfeld 1930, in *Centralbl. f. Min.*, etc. A. 367), f. the name of Paul *Ramdohr* (b. 1890), Ger. mineralogist: see -ite[1].] A sulphide of lead, silver, and antimony found as long, grey-black prisms.

1931 *Chem. Abstr.* XXV. 2940 Ramdohrite is found as bluish, grey-black prisms in quartz with accompanying pyrite, stannite, sphalerite, jamesonite and pyrargyrite at the Chocaya la Vieja mine, Potosi [Bolivia]. **1954** *Amer. Mineralogist* XXXIX. 161 Most specimens of andorite are syntaxic intergrowths of two distinct species, which have also been observed separately... We propose to call them andorite IV and andorite VI... Ramdohrite = andorite VI. **1972** *Mineral. Abstr.* XXIII. 128/2 The dark phase is thus andorite whereas the light-coloured phase gives a new formula; the formula previously assumed for ramdohrite ($Ag_2Pb_3Sb_6S_{13}$) occupies an exactly intermediate position... The name 'ramdohrite' must be transferred to the Pb-rich phase with formula $AgPb_2SbS_7$. **1975** *Amer. Mineralogist* LX. 621 Another solid solution includes the compositions of andorite ($PbAgSb_3S_6$), ramdohrite ($Pb_3Ag_2Sb_6S_{13}$), and fizelyite ($Pb_5Ag_2Sb_8S_{18}$).

ramekin, ramequin. Add: (The latter form is now *Obs.*) **b.** A dish in which ramekins or other portions of food are baked and served.

1895 in *Funk's Stand. Dict.* **1946** *Farmhouse Fare* 19 Flake fish... Mix well and pile into buttered ramekins. **1957** *Housewife* Sept. 89/2 Scandinavian saucepan in oven-proof pottery. There is a ramekin..in the same design. **1974** M. Babson *Stalking Lamb* xviii. 129 Sybilla was standing beside the oven, having just transferred the ramekins into it.

1976 *Field* 18 Nov. 1028 (Advt.), These superb oven proof ramekins each depict a different game bird of Great Britain.

ramenas (ramənaˑs). *S. Afr.* Also **ramnas.** [Afrikaans, f. Du. *ram(m)enas* black radish.] The wild radish, *Raphanus raphanistrum*, belonging to the family Cruciferæ; also, formerly, the wild mustard, *Sinapis arvensis*, a similar plant also belonging to the family Cruciferæ.

[**1896** R. WALLACE *Farming Industries of Cape Colony* vi. 117 Charlock, wild mustard, or 'rọminas', *Sinapis arvensis*, L., is a widely prevalent weed of the corn-fields of Cape Colony.] **1913** C. PETTMAN *Africanderisms* 391 Ramenas..*Raphanus raphanistrum*—Wild mustard is known by this name in the Western Province. **1932** WATT & BREYER-BRANDWIJK *Medicinal & Poisonous Plants S. Afr.* 56 *Raphanus raphanistrum* L., an introduced species known as Charlock (jointed), Ramenas, Ramnas, and Knopherik, is used by Europeans in the treatment for gravel. **1950** *Cape Times* 8 Aug. 9/6 Weeds such as 'wilde ertjies', ramenas and sorrel,..are regarded by farmers as their biggest enemies. **1953** *Ibid.* 20 May 8 The ramnas, the wild radish of the Cape..is a weed of cultivation also introduced from Europe.

ramet (rēᶦˑmĕt). [f. L. *rāmus* branch + -ET.] An individual plant belonging to a clone.

1929 A. B. STOUT in *Jrnl. N.Y. Bot. Garden* XXX. 33 It is here suggested that the word 'ramet'..be used for a member of the clon. **1938** *Jrnl. Ecology* XXVI. 379 *Silene maritima* was remarkable for the quick completion of first flowering by all ramets on sand and chalky clay as contrasted with the slow completion by ramets on calcareous sand and Potterne soil. **1963** DAVIS & HEYWOOD *Princ. Angiosperm Taxonomy* x. 345 Cloning has obvious advantages in that the vegetative divisions or ramets are genetically identical. **1977** J. L. HARPER *Population Biol. Plants* i. 24 The 'ramet' is the unit of clonal growth.

ramie. Add: Also **rami** (rami). **a.** and **b.** (Further examples.)

1832 W. ROXBURGH et al. *Flora Indica* III. 590 Rami, the Malay name in the Island of Pulo Pinang. A native of the Island of Sumatra, where it is cultivated for its bark, which abounds in fibres of very great strength and fineness. **1839** T. J. NEWBOLD *Straits of Malacca* I. vii. 444 The Rámi Rámi.., the fibres of which the Malays twist into fishing lines, cordage, etc., flourishes on the peninsula. **1868** A. GRAY *Field, Forest & Garden Bot.* 299 Ramie, or the Grass-Cloth Plant of China,..is recently planted S.W. for its very valuable textile fibres. **1874** *Rep. Comm. Agric. 1873* (U.S. Dept. Agric.) 262 A treatise has been prepared by Emile Lefranc, of the 'Southern Ramie-Planting Association'. **1895** [see *FILASSE]. **1906** *Westm. Gaz.* 21 July 5/3 The ramie plant —a tall, bushy member of the nettle family. *Ibid.*, The ramie undergarments are so light and..occupy so little space that they make one covetous on a hot July day. **1909** *Chambers's Jrnl.* Nov. 699/2 The future of the mantle lies in the discovery of some material which can take the place of cotton or ramie. **1909** *Public Ledger* (Philadelphia) 24 June 5/6 (Advt.), Ramie-cloth and natural linen. **1949** *Sun* (Baltimore) 11 Mar. 7/2 The pioneer ramie producers and manufacturers. **1955** *Sci. News Let.* 2 Apr. 213/2 Ramie.. produces a strong silky fiber used to make upholstery material. **1963** R. R. A. HIGHAM *Handbk. Papermaking* xiii. 264 Ramie..and hemp..were used prior to the third century AD. **1965** 'HAN SUYIN' *Crippled Tree* ii. 22 The weavers of ramie cloth along the water courses are Hakkas ('guest people'). **1976** *Times* 29 Apr. 8/8 A wall hanging made in..herdwick, swaledale, Welsh kemp, raw and treated ramie, flax, alpaca, mohair. **1978** *Nagel's Encycl.-Guide: China* 277 China produces tobacco (400,000 tons in 1956) and fibre-bearing plants—jute, ramie, hemp.

c. A garment woven of ramie fibre.

1922 *Chambers's Jrnl.* Mar. 145/1 Mrs. Godfrey, insufficiently but comfortably clothed in a *rami*, sat under the shade of her veranda. **1928** *Funk's Stand. Dict.*, *Ramie*,..3. (Papua.) A skirt, waist-cloth, or kilt of ramie.

ramin (ramiˑn). [Malay.] A tree of the genus *Gonystylus*, esp. *G. bancanus*, belonging to the family Thymelæaceæ and native to fresh-water swamps of Malaysia, Sarawak, and the Philippines; also, the light-coloured hardwood obtained from this tree.

1955 *World Timbers* (Timber Development Assoc.) III. 94 There are very large stands of ramin in Sarawak. The timber is comparatively new to the European market, the first shipment being in 1949. **1955** F. G. BROWNE *Forest Trees of Sarawak & Brunei* II. 340 *Ramin* can be sawn without difficulty. **1959** *Archit. Rev.* CXXVI. 13 The wall is pale yellow ramin, the floor maple. **1970** *Timber Trades Jrnl.* 21 Mar. 54/1 Ramin, too, is becoming more expensive and shipments increasingly extended. **1977** *Ibid.* 17 Dec. 30/1 The slight improvement in demand has helped prices in the Far East. Ramin remains rather weak, but kerning has started to firm up.

ramisection (ræmiseˑkʃən). *Surg.* [f. L. *rami-*, comb. form of *rāmus* (see RAMUS) + *sectio*, *section-* cutting.] Section of some of the *rami communicantes* so as to prevent sympathetic nervous impulses from reaching some region of the body.

1924 *Med. Jrnl. Australia* 14 June 589/1 After ramisection of the second, third and fourth ganglia has been effected, the cord is divided below the fourth ganglion and the operation completed. **1930** *Lancet* 19 July 127/2 The operation of ramisection, or division of the sympathetic rami to the limbs, was devised by J. I. Hunter and N. D. Royle in the course of some experimental observations upon muscle tone in animals. **1954** E. L. FARQUHARSON *Textbk. Operative Surgery* iv. 104 The operation of pre-ganglionic rami-section came to be recommended in place of ganglionectomy for denervation of the upper limb.

ramisectomy (ræmiseˑktŏmi). *Surg.* [f. as prec., blended with *-ECTOMY.] = prec.

1924 N. D. ROYLE in *Med. Jrnl. Australia* 26 Jan. 85/2 Sympathetic ramisectomy is a procedure which deals with efferent nerve fibres and prevents discharge from the central nervous system into the affected muscles. **1935** H. P. JENKINS *Terminol. of Operations* vi. 35 Section of nerve roots includes..Ramisectomy.

Ramist, *sb.* (and *a.*) Add: **A.** *sb.* (Further examples.)

1837 K. H. DIGBY *Mores Catholici* VIII. vi. 194 Petrus Ramus, to whom adhered Francis Fabricius, the poet Milton, and others, who obtained the title of Ramists, applied himself [etc.]. **1976** *Times Lit. Suppl.* 2 July 812/4 The same idea had already been popularized on the Continent long before Bacon wrote. As McRae has pointed out, for example, the Ramists had already stressed that knowledge ought to be 'for use'.

B. *attrib.* or as *adj.* (Earlier and later examples.)

1852 H. L. MANSEL *Artis Logicæ Rudimenta* (ed. 2) p. xl, The mixed school represented by Keckermann, Aristotelian in matter, Ramist in method. **1955** D. DAVIE *Brides of Reason* 38 But Wesley's sermons could be methodized According to a Ramist paradigm.

Ramiˑstic, *a.* = RAMISTICAL *a.*

1962 *Listener* 5 July 19/1 Behind Bacon stands not only the Ramistic Cambridge of his youth, but also the body of London craftsmen and scientists. **1965** K. CHARLTON *Educ. in Renaissance Eng.* v. 153 Ramistic texts..poured from the presses.

ramjet (ræˑmdʒet). Also **ram-jet, ram jet.** [f. RAM *v.*^{1} + JET *sb.*^{3}; see also *RAM *sb.*^{4} 2.] A simple form of jet engine in which the air used for combustion is compressed solely by the forward motion of the engine. Also *attrib.* and *Comb.*

1942 in *29th Ann. Rep. U.S. Nat. Advisory Comm. Aeronaut. 1943* (1948) 407/2 An experimental investigation of an idealized ram-jet propulsion system was conducted in the.. wind tunnel at the Langley Memorial Aeronautical Laboratory in March 1941. **1945** *Sci. News Let.* 17 Nov. 317/3 A ramjet motor of new and unusual design. **1947** *Sun* (Baltimore) 3 Sept. 20/7 He had been working on the development of the supersonic ram jet engine. **1948** *Times* 2 Feb. 3/2 An aerial missile driven by a 'ram-jet' engine is reported, on its first flight over the desert at Inyokern, California, to have 'far exceeded' the speed of sound. **1955** *Sci. Amer.* Jan. 38/2 Probably the simplest helicopter built so far is the Hiller Hornet. It is powered by ramjets, mounted in the tips of the rotor blades. **1957** *Jane's Fighting Ships 1957–58* 439/3 The ramjet-propelled 'Talos' is capable of engaging both supersonic and subsonic targets. **1967** M. CHANDLER *Ceramics in Mod. World* vi. 177 The ramjet engine..is little more than a plain tube with a very high-temperature fire inside it. **1974** *Encycl. Brit. Micropædia* VIII. 407/2 Ramjets work best at speeds of Mach 2..and higher. **1977** *Times* 5 Nov. 4/5 (*caption*) Five turbojet engines would power it from take-off until it reached 600 mph when five ramjet engines using liquid hydrogen fuel would take over.

‖ **ramkie** (raˑmki). *S. Afr.* Also **raamakie, ramkee,** etc. [Afrikaans, ad. Nama *ramgi-b*, prob. ad. Pg. *rabequinha* dim. of *rabeca* fiddle.] A stringed instrument, roughly resembling a guitar, played by the Hottentots and Bushmen of Southern Africa.

[**1790** E. HELME tr. *Le Vaillant's Trav. Afr.* II. vii. 128 The *rabouquin*..is, indeed, a kind of guittar [*sic*].] **1805** *Gleanings in Afr.* xxvii. 232 Others were busily employed in dancing to the music of the ramky, (as they call it,) and seemed highly delighted with their exertions. **1827** G. THOMPSON *Trav. & Adv. Southern Afr.* I. 391 In the evening we were entertained by a Bushwoman..playing on the *Raamakie*—an instrument about forty inches long by five broad, and having the half of a calabash affixed to one end, with strings somewhat resembling those of a violin. **1835** J. W. D. MOODIE *Ten Yrs. S. Afr.* I. 224, I have often listened with great pleasure to the wild and melancholy notes of the 'gorah' and 'ramkee'. *Ibid.* 226 The 'ramkee' is constructed on the same principle as a guitar, by stretching six strings along a flat piece of thin board, with the half of a gourd or 'calabash' at one end, over which a piece of dried skin is strained, on which the bridge is placed. It is played after the manner of a guitar; and in the hands of a skilful performer, makes no contemptible music. **1934** P. R. KIRBY *Mus. Instr. of Native Races of S. Afr.* x. 249 Another stringed instrument, the name of which is familiar to most South Africans, is the *ramkie*. **1969** J. M. WHITE *Land God made in Anger* 41 There is everything here..from the two-note whining of the Bushman *ramkie* to Schönberg. **1970** P. OLIVER *Savannah Syncopators* 109 *Ramkie*, *remkie*, three- or four-stringed guitar related to the Portuguese *rabequinha* brought from Malabar to South Africa and developed by the Cape Hottentots. Also *rabekin*, *ramakienjo*, *raamakie*, *ramki*. **1972** *Stand. Encycl. S. Afr.* V. 609/1 Besides stringed instruments, such as the *!goura* (gorah), the *!guba* and the *ramgyb* (ramkie), they [*sc.* the Hottentots] used a set of reed-pipes.

Ramlila, Ram Lila (rā·mˌlīˑlă). *India.* [Hindi, f. *Rām* the god Rama (cf. *RAMAYANA) + *līlā* sport, deeds.] A drama, representing episodes from the *Ramayana* and commemorating the victory of Rama over Ravana, performed during the festival of Dusserah. Also *attrib.*

1880 *Encycl. Brit.* XI. 474/2 The principal religious fairs are the following:— At Bilgrám, in September, on the occasion of the *Rám Lila* festival, lasting ten days and attended by about 40,000 persons. **1894** J. C. OMAN *Great Indian Epics* I. iii. 71 A large space for the performance of the Ram Lila was kept clear by sepoys. **1935** L. S. S. O'MALLEY *Popular Hinduism* ii. 59 In North India the *Ramlila* thrills multitudes of villagers every year with the moving story of Rama and Sita. **1953** L. IREMONGER in *Caribbean Anthol. Short Stories* 20 There was a *Ram Lila*, and they went. They did not often leave their fields. But one must go to a *Ram Lila*. Dharam and Dharup dressed up..in European shirts and Indian *dhotis*. **1968** *Indian Mus. Jrnl.* V. 32 Omkar..also performed as an actor..in a Rāmlīla party. **1969** *Cultural News from India* Nov. 28 Both shows were largely attended and are now as much a part of the Delhi scene as the yearly 'Ramlila'.

rammelsbergite (ræˑmĕlzbɜːɡəit). *Min.* [ad. G. *rammelsbergit* (W. Haidinger *Handb. der bestimmenden Mineral.* (1845) 560), f. the name of K. F. *Rammelsberg* (1813–99), German mineralogist: see -ITE^{1}.] An arsenide of nickel, $NiAs_2$, that occurs as white granular or fibrous masses.

1854 J. D. DANA *Syst. Min.* (ed. 4) II. 61 Rammelsbergite... Trimetric... Slightly ductile. **1913** [see *MAUCHERITE]. **1939** [see *pararammelsbergite* s.v. *PARA-^{1} 2 c]. **1963** [see *MAUCHERITE]. **1973** SORREL & SANDSTROM *Rocks & Minerals of World* 106 Rammelsbergite..is found with loellingite, skutterudite minerals, sulfides, and other arsenides in medium-temperature veins.

rammies (ræˑmiz), *sb. pl.* *Austral.* and *S. Afr. slang.* [Origin unknown: cf. *RAMIE c.] Trousers.

1919 W. H. DOWNING *Digger Dial.* 41 *Rammies*, breeches. **1933** *Bulletin* (Sydney) 26 Apr. 20/1 Old Bill watched the youngest jackeroo disrobing... 'If I was you, young feller,' he said, 'I'd leave them rammies on.' **1953** T. A. G. HUNGERFORD *Riverslake* ii. 42 Elastic for the old girl's rammies. **1961** *Personality* 16 May 27 Narrow trousers have ceased to be 'drain-pipes' and are now identified..as 'rammies'.

rammy (ræˑmi), *sb.* *Sc. slang.* [? f. Sc. *rammle* row, uproar, var. RAMBLE *sb.*^{1}: see *S.N.D.* s.v. *rammle*.] A brawl, a fight (esp. between gangs); a quarrel.

1935 MCARTHUR & LONG *No Mean City* iv. 45 Evidence about a 'rammy' is always conflicting, never reliable and frequently perjured. **1938** *Evening Standard* (Glasgow) 1 Apr. 17 Gallaher had the body, he was Irish, he laid out two slops in the last rammy. **1944** *Scots Mag.* Oct. 46 Not so long ago, in a dance hall rammy, a fella had laid hands on Hardy. **1967** 'H. CALVIN' *DNA Business* iv. 49, I enjoy a good rammy... I think I must have an adrenalin hunger. **1973** J. WOOD *North Beat* vi. 82 He'd had a rammy with his missus. **1977** *Time Out* 28 Jan.–3 Feb. 10/3 Still, the Villiers at Charing Cross plans a rammy where the only authentic ingredients missing will be the blood and hair on the walls.

ramnas, var. *RAMENAS.

‖ **Ramon Allones** (ramoˑn alʸoˑnes). The proprietary name of a brand of cigar. Also *attrib.*

1907 *Yesterday's Shopping* (1969) 65/2 *Havana cigars*.. 'Ramon Allones.' ('Flor fina.') **1913** *Trade Marks Jrnl.* 22 Jan. 122 Ramon Allones... Havana cigars and Havana cigarettes. Allones, Limited,..London,..cigar manufacturers. **1965** V. CANNING *Whip Hand* xv. 173 He pulled out a cigar... It was certainly Havana, and probably Ramon Allones. **1973** 'M. INNES' *Appleby's Answer* i. 11 His droopy moustache held the particular tinge of brown..known to proceed only from the smoking of *Ramon Allones* (or would it be *Romeo y Julieta*?) cigars.

ramonda (rămǫˑndă). Also **ra(y)mondia.** [mod.L. (A. Richard in C. H. Persoon *Synopsis Plantarum* (1805) I. 216), f. the name of L. F. *Ramond* (d. 1827), French botanist and traveller + -A or -IA^{1}.] A small perennial herb of the genus so called, belonging to the family Gesneriaceæ, native to mountainous regions of Europe, and having hairy leaves in a basal rosette and single stems of white, pink, or violet flowers.

c **1828** B. MAUND *Bot. Garden* I. 83 (*heading*) Borage-leaved Ramonda. **1865** M. EYRE *Lady's Walks in South of France* xxiv. 267 Mrs. Nash took a small *terrine* with a *Raymondia* in it with her to Switzerland. **1907** R. FARRER *My Rock-Garden* xv. 243 Much more beautiful..to my mind, is the Queen of all Ramondias, Queen Natalie's Ramondia. **1931** *Discovery* Nov. 354/1 We stopped..at the gorge of the Treska river to collect ramondia. **1942** T. G. MANSFIELD *Alpines* i. 80 Ramonda... The name is frequently mis-spelt Ramondia. **1955** L. D. HILLS *Alpine Gardening* vii. 248 All the Ramondas like a soil that is both leafy and limy. **1971** D. BARTRUM *Rock Gardens* iii. 113 Grow Ramondas in low crevices of a rock wall.

ramp, *sb.*^{2} Add: **3. b.** *U.S.* A small, wild onion, *Allium tricoccum*. Cf. *RAMPS 2.

1923 A. PRICE *Dreams* 102 A gorge of trout and hot corn pone, Mountain dew that would float a stone, All topped off by a mess of ramps. **1939** *Sun* (Baltimore) 11 Feb. 5/6 Ramps are tiny, green, onion-like bulbs that dot West Virginia's slopes each spring, taste like the food of the gods and smell..a dozen times worse than limburger cheese and burning rubber. **1952** R. BISSELL *Monongahela* iii. 40 We boys would go out on what we called the Hogback near the fort to hunt ramps. **1967** *National Observer* (U.S.) 10 Apr. 6/3 Back in the hills of West Virginia it's ramp season again. **1976** *Daily Colonist* (Victoria, B.C.) 9 Mar. 3/7 The ramps are sprouting and requests are coming in from ramp lovers in many states.

ramp, *sb.*[4] Add: **I. 1. a.** (Further examples.) Also, *spec.* a movable slope or passageway which may be positioned to admit access to another level, as on to a boat or aeroplane.

1893 KIPLING *Day's Work* (1898) 2 At either end rose towers of red brick, loopholed for musketry and pierced for big guns, and the ramp of the road was being pushed forward to their haunches. **1901** 'LINESMAN' *Words by Eyewitness* xii. 230 They [*sc.* animals] are then led out..down the slippery ramp, stepping gingerly, much afraid of man's extraordinary devices. **1908** *Animal Managem.* 267 The only difficulty which occurs is from the nervousness of some horses to step across or up the ramp. **1909** *Cent. Dict.* Suppl., *Ramp*, an inclined traveling platform or carrier for transferring freight from a boat to a dock or warehouse. **1938** *New Yorker* 24 Sept. 29/2 Meek-eyed parents hasten down the ramps To greet their offspring, terrible from camps. **1961** WEBSTER, *Ramp*,..the stairway by which passengers enter the main door of an airplane. **1976** *Lancs. Evening Post* 7 Dec. 1/7 They..were driving off the ramp of the landing craft type vessel when the accident happened.

b. *Railways.* (*a*) The tapering end of a conductor rail, provided to guide the collector shoe on to or off the rail. (*b*) An apparatus used to replace derailed rolling stock on the track.

1922 F. W. CARTER *Railway Electr. Traction* v. 218 Ramps are provided at the ends of each length of conductor rail, in order that the shoes may be brought to the contact surface without shock. **1926** *Chambers's Jrnl.* Aug. 539/1 The turned up edge of the ramp guides the wheels of the vehicle back to the rail... Four ramps are used, one for each wheel. **1927** R. E. DICKINSON *Electr. Trains* vii. 161 Sudden re-application of motor current occurring at ramps caused pressure surges. **1956** R. A. HAMNETT *Brit. Rail Track* iv. 191 At the ends of sections of conductor rail, ramps are provided to pick up the shoe. **1960** *Chemins de Fer* (Bureau Internat. de Documentation des Chemins de Fer) 212/3 Rerailing ramp.

c. An inclined slip road leading on to or off a main highway. Cf. *OFF-RAMP. *N. Amer.*

1952 [see *EXPRESSWAY]. **1965** *Tamarack Rev.* Winter 10 The town must be five or six miles off the highway and one of the county roads connects. One of these days I'll take the ramp, turn off north. **1979** *Upper Valley Progress* (Mission, Texas) 9 Aug. 1/4 Frontage road traffic shall yield the right of way to traffic..leaving an off-ramp on controlled access highways.

d. (See quots.)

1940 *Highway Engin. Terms* (*B.S.I.*) 12 *Ramp*, a short slope formed to overcome differences in level or for some other special purpose. **1961** WEBSTER, *Ramp*,..a contrivance (as of blocks or wedges of wood) laid parallel in a roadway for passing traffic over lines of hose.

e. A low platform from which competitors leave successively at timed intervals at the start of a motor rally.

1963 P. DRACKETT *Motor Rallying* iv. 57 The start was in Blackpool, from a Mille Miglia type ramp. **1971** *E. Afr. Standard* (Nairobi) 13 Apr. 1/3 There were 107 starters from the ramp outside City Hall, Nairobi, on Thursday.

4. orig. *U.S.* The point or area at an airport where unloading and loading of aircraft takes place; the 'apron'. Freq. *attrib.*

1947 M. B. BAKER *Airline Traffic & Operations* viii. 205 We're not too bothered with other aircraft parked on the ramp. **1961** *New Scientist* 13 Apr. 15/2 On stages up to 1,000 miles in length the turboprop is equal to the jet in ramp to ramp speeds. **1971** *Daily Colonist* (Victoria, B.C.) 24 Aug. 7/1 We are flying at 33,000 feet, the outside temperature is 24 degrees and our expected ramp time in Los Angeles is..oh..about 3.30. **1974** P. S. SMITH *Air Freight* x. 399 Ramp handling is the operation of loading and unloading freight on and off an aircraft and moving it across the apron.

II. 5. *Electronics.* An electrical waveform in which the voltage increases linearly with time. Freq. *attrib.*, as **ramp function,** a mathematical expression of the shape of a ramp.

1957 J. D. RYDER *Engin. Electronics* xviii. 618 The response of the first-order system to a so-called ramp input θ_i..is also of interest. **1959** J. MARKUS *Handbk. Electronic Control Circuits* 281/1 An output pulse begins when the ramp voltage starts increasing and terminates when the ramp and signal voltages are equal. *Ibid.* 281/2 The flip-flop opens a transistor switch, allowing the ramp generator to begin generating a linearly rising voltage. **1962** HUSKEY & KORN *Computer Handbk.* xviii. 31 The stability is a function of..the stability of the ramp function itself. **1965** *Wireless World* Aug. 399 By the introduction of an integral of the ramp voltage as a feedback term it should be possible to generate an ultra-linear ramp. **1976** *Austral. Jrnl. Physics* XXIX. 187 A second phase-sensitive detector yielding a ramp-function output is used to indicate, by the positive or negative gradient of the ramp, the sense of the Doppler frequency shift, i.e. decreasing or increasing. **1980** *Sci. Amer.* Mar. 73/1 To compensate for echo decay over longer distances, receiver sensitivity is enhanced by ramp gain and a Q filter.

III. 6. *Comb.*, as **rampway** *N. Amer.*, a sloping passageway formed by a ramp between different levels.

1970 I. PETITE *Meander to Alaska* II. xi. 105 Then we walked up the long, cleated rampway to the sidewalk above. **1976** B. BOVA *Multiple Man* (1977) vi. 68 We stepped through one of these rampways into a different building.

ramp, *sb.*[5] Add: **a.** (Further examples.) Also, † (see quot. 1812); *spec.* the act or practice of obtaining profit or benefit fraudulently, as by the unwarranted increase of the price of a commodity.

1812 J. H. VAUX *Vocab. Flash Lang.* in *Mem.* (1964) 261 *Ramp*, to rob any person or place by open violence or suddenly snatching at something and running off with it... A man convicted of this offence, is said to have been done for a *ramp*. This audacious *game*, is called by *prigs, the ramp.* **1895** J. CAMINADA *Twenty-Five Years of Detective Life* 161 Watching them perform the 'ramp'—a sudden rush and bustle in which robberies are committed. **1915** *Truth* 2 June 890/2 The ramp in connection with the shares of the East Rand Amalgamated Gold Estates. **1922** *Daily Mail* 20 Nov. 8 (Advt.), Is there a coal 'ramp'? Miners, middlemen and merchants in the coal trade all blame one another for the high price of coal. **1934** R. MACAULAY *Going Abroad* xxiii. 195 If I had my way, you would sign a paper..confessing that your whole business is a ramp and a fraud. **1956** *People* 13 May 8/3 From Manchester, Glasgow and Bristol, examples of this growing ramp have reached 'The People'. *a* **1966** 'M. NA GOPALEEN' *Best of Myles* (1968) 228 You know the limited edition ramp. **1976** W. G. KERR *Scottish Capital on Amer. Credit Frontier* iii. 77 On their arrival in Dallas, Wellesley and Renshaw discovered that some serious 'ramps', or swindles, had been going on there.

b. bankers' ramp (see quot. 1932). Also *transf.*

1931 J. R. MACDONALD in *Times* 26 Aug. 12/3 We are told that this is a bankers' 'ramp', or a conspiracy, or something of the kind, against a Labour Government. **1932** *Ann. Reg. 1931* 68 Mr. Hayday..elaborated the theory of what was known in Labour circles as 'the bankers' ramp'—a financial crisis deliberately engineered for the purpose of forcing Britain to curtail its expenditure on social services, and so remove one of the chief barriers to a reduction of the wage level. **1958** *Times* 10 July 13/2 The orthodox Labour version is that the second Labour Government was broken by a 'bankers' ramp'. **1976** LD. ROBBINS *Against Inflation* (1979) xx. 98 What I hope your Lordships will agree is a pure fallacy; namely, the suggestion that what has happened recently is all a pure conspiracy, a banker's ramp and so on.

ramp, *v.*[1] Add: **2. c.** Delete 'Now *dial.*' and add later examples.

1921 [see *FLETCHERIAN *a.*]. **1959** *Listener* 29 Oct. 754/3 The schizanthus..is ramping away and will need potting.

3. a. (Further examples.)

1922 E. R. EDDISON *Worm* xiv. 203 It stamped with its silver hoofs, flapping its wings, ramping like a lioness. **1924** R. CAMPBELL *Flaming Terrapin* v. 79 Panthers..And tigers..And lions..They ramped in the morning light. **1974** R. ADAMS *Shardik* xv. 100 Kelderek..remained constantly near the bear, observing all that it did, attentive to its moods and ways—its frightening habit of ramping from side to side in excitement or anger; [etc.].

5. b. (Later example.)

1951 DYLAN THOMAS *Poems* (1971) 206 Wherever I ramped in the clover quilts.

6. b. Also with *along.* (Further examples.) Also *transf.*

1933 P. A. EADDY *Hull Down* 283 *Ramp along*, sailing with all sails drawing to the wind. **1941** J. CARY *House of Children* xxxv. 153 It won't waste your time because you'll learn more too—it's a place for teaching stupid young men how to pass into the army, so you'll simply ramp along.

ramp, *v.*[2] Add: **2. b.** To search (a prisoner) in jail. Also of a prison cell. *Austral.*

1950 *Austral. Police Jrnl.* Apr. 117 *Ramp*, search a prisoner in gaol, as distinct from a search anywhere else. **1979** *Courier-Mail* (Brisbane) 2 Aug. 9/3 He heard noises from Gage's cell, but presumed the cell was being 'ramped' (searched).

rampa·ciously, *adv. rare.* [f. RAMPACIOUS *a.* + -LY[2].] In a rampacious or unruly manner.

1915 V. O'CONNOR *Mary's Meadow Papers* x. 127 During such a wet summer the grass had grown rampaciously.

rampage, *sb.* Add: (Further examples.) Also in U.S. colloq. phr. *to ride* (*a*) *rampage.* Also *fig.*

1906 'MARK TWAIN' in *Harper's Mag.* Aug. 335 The raven ..sets on her shoulder often when she rides her breakneck rampages. **1927** H. CRANE *Let.* 19 Dec. (1965) 313 Her drunken and exclamatory rampage through *Edificios Blancos* [*sc.* H. Crane's *White Buildings*]. **1955** *Times* 29 Aug. 10/5 Mr. Jack Warner, representing Scotland Yard, is indeed a comfort to have at hand when Things are on the rampage. **1967** *Boston Sunday Herald* 2 Apr. (T.V. Mag.) 57/1 A gang on a rampage through Matt Dillon's territory.

rampage, *v.* Add: **3.** *trans.* To rampage about or over (a place).

1905 E. M. ALBANESI *Brown Eyes of Mary* i. 7 Where is the beast now? Is she rampaging the premises?

rampart, *sb.* Add: **1*.** *Canad.* A steep bank of a river or gorge. Usu. *pl.*

a **1853** R. CAMPBELL *Two Journals* (retyped from MS, Vancouver Publ. Libr.) 112 Yesterday and today we have been passing through what they call the ramparts—rocks and steep banks along the river. **1921** W. A. FRASER *Red Meekins* I. iii. 32 Cast high on a rampart by a thrust of the waters lay the stern half of their canoe. **1940** *Beaver* June 29/1 After forty miles more came to the ramparts, a large canyon or gorge where for seven miles the river flows between perpendicular cliffs of limestone from one hundred to two hundred feet high. The channel is very deep here—three hundred feet in places. **1973** D. ANDERSEN *Ways Harsh & Wild* i. 48 Here in the upper ramparts there were steep cliffs and mountains rising on each side of the river.

2. *rampart-base, -walk.*

1915 G. FRANKAU *Tid'apa* v. 25 Green-dark to the rampart-bases, save where, like a wild beast's eye One red light glowered and glimmered in the shadow-tracery, stretched jungle. **1923** R. G. COLLINGWOOD *Roman Britain* ii. 30 Along the top [of Hadrian's wall] was a rampart-walk, patrolled by the sentries, and reached by stairs either at a fort, a milecastle, or a turret.

rampike. For '*dial.* and *U.S.*' read '*dial.* and *N. Amer.*' and add: (Earlier and later examples.) Also *attrib.*

1853 S. STRICKLAND *Twenty-Seven Years in Canada West* II. 198 The recently burnt fallow, with its blackened stumps and rampikes did not contribute much to improve the landscape. **1908** C. MAIR *Through Mackenzie Basin* 146 The 'rampike' country would be..converted from a burnt-wood region to a bare one. **1936** J. MASEFIELD *Letter from Pontus* 19 With blackened rampikes from old forest fires. **1955** *Jrnl. Canad. Ling. Assoc.* Oct. 6 Apparent survivals from various Scottish and English dialects, such as *bultow, drake, glitter, knap, rampike.* **1961** R. M. PATTERSON *Buffalo Head* vi. 220 There they stood—three gaunt, upstanding rampikes of charcoal with the humus burnt away from their roots.

ramping, *vbl. sb.*[2] (Earlier example.)

1830 LYTTON *Paul Clifford* I. viii. 150 Before this initiatory process, technically termed 'ramping'..had reduced the bones of Paul..to the state of magnesia, [etc.].

ramps. Add: **2.** *U.S.* = *RAMP *sb.*[2] 3 b.

1939 *Jrnl. Tennessee Acad. Sci.* XIV. 280 One kind [of wild onion] is much sought after by mountain folk, who call it 'ramps', and gather and eat its bulb with great relish. **1960** *Washington Post* 29 Apr. 12/1 It [*sc.* a smell] will emanate from the cooking of ramps—a wild plant somewhat like an onion. **1976** *Amer. Speech 1974* XLIX. 21 'There's a wild onion, smells like ramps, you know.'

rampsman (ræ·mpsmæ̆n). *slang.* [f. RAMP *sb.*[5] + MAN *sb.*[1]: cf. *cracksman*, etc.] One who commits robbery with violence.

1859 HOTTEN *Dict. Slang* 80 *Rampsman*, a highway robber who uses violence when necessary. **1862** H. MAYHEW *Lond. Lab.* Extra vol. 31/2 The '*Rampsman*' or '*Cracksman*' plunders by force; as the burglar, footpad, etc. **1882** *Sydney Slang Dict.* 7/2 *Rampsmen*, burglars, highway robbers. **1932** H. WALPOLE *Fortress* III. iv. 467 The perils of London—the cracksmen, the rampsmen, the snorrers and thimble-screwers. **1975** M. CRICHTON *Great Train Robbery* xiii. 72 Barlow was a reformed buzzer turned rampsman—a pickpocket who had degenerated to plain mugging.

ramrod. Add: **2.** *transf.* † **a.** *Cricket.* (See quots.) *Obs.*

1870 R. B. MANSFIELD *School-Life at Winchester College* 228 *Ramrod, Raymonder*, names given to a ball bowled all along the ground. **1880** *Baily's Monthly Mag.* Feb. 93 It [*sc.* a quick underhand ball] must be very straight so as to ensure a L.B.W., and provided it pitches half-way—for 'ramrods' are *not* cricket proper—the more irregular the pitch the better.

b. A foreman or manager. *N. Amer.*

1881 E. W. NYE *Bill Nye & Boomerang* 60 John Humpfner, the ram-rod of the New York House, feared that the explosion might break the large French plate glass windows of his palatial hotel. **1905** *Dialect Notes* III. 92 *Ramrod*, mainstay, manager, superintendent. **1942** *Amer. Speech* XVII. 75/1 The man in charge of a herd on the trail [in Nebraska] is the *trailboss* or *ramrod.* **1973** R. SYMONS *Where Wagon Led* I. i. 10 Jake..acted in between times as a sort of foreman, or in western parlance, 'ramrod' of the outfit.

c. With sexual connotations.

1951 DYLAN THOMAS *Poems* (1971) 206 Sighed the old ram rod, dying of women. **1974** H. S. KAPLAN *New Sex Therapy* i. 17 The glans also becomes enlarged. It does not become hard, however, thus guarding against the possibility that the female will be hurt by the ramrod of the phallus.

3. a. *attrib.* and *Comb.*, as *ramrod-maker, spring*; *ramrod-backed, -like, -rigid, -stiff, -straight* adjs.; **ramrod roll** *U.S.* (see quot.).

1939 'N. BLAKE' *Smiler with Knife* ii. 33 The major or his ramrod-backed housekeeper. **1861** Ramrod-like [in Dict.]. **1860** Ramrod maker [in Dict.]. **1961** *Countryman* LVIII. 515 We lay ramrod rigid. **1936** M. MITCHELL *Gone with Wind* xxviii. 477 The men added as dessert some 'ramrod rolls'..and this was the first time Scarlett had ever seen this Confederate article of diet... The soldiers mixed their ration of corn meal with water, and salt too when they could get it, wrapped the thick paste about their ramrods and roasted the mess over camp fires. **1841** *Ordnance Man. for Use of Officers of U.S. Army* (U.S. Ordnance Dept.) 120 In the musket of the model of 1840, the trigger screw and trigger are taken off after the guard, then the pin for the ramrod spring and the ramrod spring. **1961** *Times* 6 Dec. 17/3 A ramrod-stiff naval officer. **1979** G. HAMMOND *Dead Game* xii. 150 A slim man, ramrod-straight.

b. *attrib.*, passing into adj. Rigid, inflexible; solemn, formal.

1905 *Pall Mall Gaz.* 18 Dec. 2 Under the pretence that, apart from such ramrod rule, the nation would tumble to pieces. **1920** D. H. LAWRENCE *Lost Girl* vii. 137 He was a tall Swiss with..a flattish face and a rather stiff, ramrod figure. **1932** *Times Lit. Suppl.* 19 May 366/3 Mrs. Stainlit, an elderly lady of the ramrod breed. **1978** J. A. MICHENER *Chesapeake* 74 He saw him as..a man of petty foibles and ramrod rectitude.

Hence **ra·mrod** *v. trans.*; to force or drive (something), as with a ramrod; *spec.* (*U.S.*), to manage, direct (a ranch, event, etc.); also, to beat or thrust in the form of a ramrod.

1948 *Popular Western* June 15/2 This is Tex Grant, the star-toter who ramrods this burg. **1955** R. HOBSON *Nothing too Good* vi. 50 You're Rich Hobson, ramrodding the Batnuni end of Frontier Company. **1966** S. HEANEY *Death of Naturalist* 39 A volley of cold blood ramrodding the current. **1973** R. SYMONS *Where Wagon Led* I. vii. 118, I ramrodded the Circle Diamond for quite a few years after that. **1976** *Publishers Weekly* 1 Mar. 84/1 The skittish livestock Kingman must ramrod to a distant army post. *Ibid.* 8 Mar. 57/1 Railroad builders par excellence who ramrod tracks across the virgin countryside. **1979** *Tucson* (Arizona) *Citizen* 20 Sept. 11A/3 Scores of volunteers rallied around this charitable event which was ramrodded by the city of Tucson.

ram-sammy (ræ:msæ·mi). *slang* (orig. *dial.*). [Origin unknown.] **a.** A family quarrel; a noisy gathering. **b.** A fight; a scrap.

1891 *N. & Q.* 12 Sept. 206/1 'A ram sammy' = [in the W. country] a family quarrel or, in variation, a noisy gathering. **1902** *Western Morning News* 22 Apr. 5/5 A 'ram sammy' was a family quarrel. **1967** H. W. SUTHERLAND *Magnie* v. 70 She'd sent for Big Hughie in case there was a ram sammy. Magnie was no match for Big Hughie. **1976** J. WAINWRIGHT *Walther P. 38* 98, I was there, at this jazz club..in a cramped basement... Some people might have called it a 'jam session'. Some people might have called it a 'ram-sammy'.

Ramsauer (ræ·mzɑuəɹ). *Physics.* The name of Carl Wilhelm *Ramsauer* (1879–1955), Ger. physicist, used *attrib.* with reference to the Ramsauer effect, as *Ramsauer cross-section, free path*; **Ramsauer effect,** the sharp decrease, almost to zero, of the scattering cross-section of atoms of inert gases for electrons with energies below a critical value (first described by Ramsauer in 1921 and independently by Townsend in 1922; now usu. called the Ramsauer–Townsend effect: see next); **Ramsauer minimum,** the minimum in the scattering cross-section for electrons exhibiting the Ramsauer effect.

1930 *Chem. Abstr.* XXIV. 5218 An historical and critical review of the Ramsauer effect. **1938** L. B. LOEB *Atomic Structure* xix. 338 The Ramsauer cross sections..vary in some cases over wide ranges with electron energy. *Ibid.*, Ramsauer's pioneer measurements and the later ones of Ramsauer and Kollath have been carried to such perfection that we today speak of the electron free paths as Ramsauer free paths. **1960** *Physical Rev.* CXVII. 1416/2 For argon, krypton, and xenon $\sigma_t(\epsilon)$ is approximately proportional to ϵ except below the Ramsauer minimum. **1963** *Ibid.* CXXX. 1021/1 This method of analysis might be characterized as a short circuiting of the procedure used by Holtzmark in his remarkable analysis of the Ramsauer cross sections for argon and krypton. **1972** A. GILARDINI *Low Energy Electron Collisions in Gases* iv. 338 Argon has a large Ramsauer minimum at ~0·3 eV, so that electrons experience far fewer collisions with molecules at these energies than at lower and higher energies. **1974** G. REECE tr. *Hund's Hist. Quantum Theory* xi. 146 It was possible to explain the Ramsauer effect qualitatively in terms of the diffraction of long waves by small spheres.

Ramsauer–Townsend (ræ·mzɑuəɹ tɑu·nzend). *Physics.* The names of C. W. *Ramsauer* (see prec.) and John Sealy Edward *Townsend* (1868–1957), Irish physicist, used *attrib.* with reference to the Ramsauer effect (see prec.).

1952 MASSEY & BURHOP *Electronic & Ionic Impact Phenomena* i. 9 The remarkable transparency of the heavier rare gases atoms towards electrons of energy 1 eV or so.. will be referred to as the Ramsauer–Townsend effect. *Ibid.* iii. 115 It is now of interest to consider the contribution from higher-order cross-sections. These are very small at the Ramsauer–Townsend minimum. **1963** *Physical Rev.* CXXX. 1022/2 It might be guessed that the Ramsauer–Townsend minimum should occur at approximately the same place in both scattering and momentum transfer cross sections. **1977** P. G. BURKE *Potential Scattering in Atomic Physics* vii. 73 The balance of this repulsion with the long range r^{-4} attraction caused by the polarization of the atom in the field of the incident electron is the cause of the Ramsauer–Townsend effect.

ramsayite (ræ·mze͵əit). *Min.* [ad. Russ. *ramzait* (E. E. Kostyleva 1923, in *Compt. Rend. de l'Acad. des Sci. de Russie* A. 55), f. the name of Wilhelm *Ramsay* (1865–1928), Finnish geologist: see -ITE[1].] A silicate of sodium and titanium, $Na_2Ti_2Si_2O_9$, occurring as orthorhombic crystals.

1924 *Mineral. Abstr.* II. 250 (*heading*) On a new mineral—ramsayite from the Khibinsky and Lovozersky tundras. **1967** *Norsk Geol. Tidsskr.* XLVII. 249 Ramsayite is an important constituent of the mosandrite pseudomorphs... The crystals range in length from about 0·1 mm to 1·5 mm. They are colourless to greyish.

ramsdellite (ræ·mzdĕləit). *Min.* [f. the name of Lewis S. *Ramsdell* (1895–1975), U.S. mineralogist + -ITE[1].] An oxide of manganese, MnO_2, similar to pyrolusite, occurring as orthorhombic crystals and platy masses of a grey to black colour.

1943 FLEISCHER & RICHMOND in *Econ. Geol.* XXXVIII. 278 Ramsdellite. [*Note*] This is the first use of this name in print. The mineral was described in 1932 by Ramsdell.. as a possible dimorph of pyrolusite. **1965** G. J. WILLIAMS *Econ. Geol. N.Z.* xiii. 190/2 Coombs (in Reed, 1959) mentioned the existence of ramsdellite (a polymorph of pyrolusite) at Taieri Mouth in ore which consists of pyrolusite with minor manganite. **1969** *Econ. Geol.* LXIV. 221/2 Ramsdellite can very easily be mistaken for pyrolusite. **1972** *Mineral. Rec.* III. 210 Ramsdellite, a relatively common mineral in the Chihuahua geodes, is found as fibrous dendritic masses on quartz but is more commonly found growing as well developed crystals on goethite blades in two different habits.

Ramsden (ræ·mzdĕn). The name of Jesse *Ramsden* (1735–1800), English instrument-maker, used *attrib.* and in the possessive to designate an eyepiece commonly used in astronomical telescopes (see quot. 1847) which he described in 1783 (*Phil. Trans. R. Soc.* LXXIII. 94).

1787 *Phil. Trans. R. Soc.* LXXVII. 55 The telescope.. was an achromatic object-glass of Dollond, of 16 inches focal length, and 2 inches aperture; with a Ramsden's eye-glass, magnifying about 25 times. **1847** R. POTTER *Elem. Treat. Optics* I. vii. 117 Ramsden's eyepiece is formed of a plano-convex and a convexo-plane lens of equal focal lengths, set at a distance of about two-thirds of the focal length of either. **1900** R. A. HERMAN *Treat Geom. Optics* vi. 137 Both Huyghens' and Ramsden's eye-pieces have convergent powers, and the image appears inverted. **1923** GLAZEBROOK *Dict. Appl. Physics* IV. 77/1 When a Ramsden eyepiece is employed even pronounced apparent distortion is of no importance for exact measurements. **1971** SMITH & THOMSON *Optics* viii. 133 The focal plane of eyepieces of the Ramsden type is close to the first lens.

ramshack (ræ·mʃæk), U.S. Black English var. RANSACK *v.*

1901 W. CHURCHILL *Crisis* III. vi. 413 Supper, Miss Jinny. Lawsy, if I ain't ramshacked de premises fo' you bof. **1935** in Z. N. Hurston *Mules & Men* (1970) 323 Me and my buddy and two three more, Going to ramshack Georgy everywhere we go. **1962** W. FAULKNER *Reivers* i. 13 Now you got to ramshack the country to locate another back window you can crawl in.

ramshackledom (ræ·mʃæk'ldəm). [f. RAMSHACKLE *a.* + -DOM.] = next.

1962 L. G. PINE (*title*) Ramshackledom: a critical appraisement of the Establishment. **1962** *Listener* 15 Nov. 835/2 Originality he [*sc.* Berlioz] possessed..but it does not consist in hopeful random ramshackledom (almost a principle of composition nowadays). **1963** *Guardian* 1 Feb. 9/1 The condition of British ramshackledom exceeds anything hitherto known.

ramshackleness (ræ·mʃæk'lnės). [f. RAMSHACKLE *a.* + -NESS.] Ramshackle character or state.

1922 'R. WEST' in *Public Opinion* 17 Nov. 486/2 These Houses of Parliament are the symbol of a real miracle, a real mixture of ramshackleness and nobility.

ramshackling, *a.* (Further example.)

1951 DYLAN THOMAS *Poems* (1971) 211 And the tusked, ramshackling sea exults.

ramshackly, *a.* Add: **1.** Substitute for def.: = RAMSHACKLE *a.* 1. (Further examples.)

1897 E. A. BARTLETT *Battlefields of Thessaly* xii. 262 There was also the araba with our baggage, a very ramshackly weather-beaten old carriage. **1924** E. M. FORSTER *Passage to India* xxiv. 217 The chuprassies..filed into the ramshackly room with a condescending air, as if it was a booth at a fair. **1939** in B. A. Botkin *Treas. S. Folklore* (1949) I. iii. 59 The cabin was ramshackly.

2. = RAMSHACKLE *a.* 2

1910 E. M. FORSTER *Howards End* v. 38 Helen, you must not be so ramshackly. You took this gentleman's umbrella away from Queen's Hall, and he has had the trouble of coming round for it. **1927** —— *Aspects of Novel* i. 28 In the rather ramshackly course that lies ahead of us, we cannot consider fiction by periods. **1976** *Daily Tel.* 8 July 16 The accelerating shift to the Left which has rendered that great ramshackly confederation [*sc.* the Labour party] increasingly vulnerable to the subversive activities of Marxists.

ramshandry (ræmʃæ·ndri), *a. nonce-wd.* [Fanciful combination of RAM-STAM *a.* and SHANDY *a.*] Thoughtless; light-headed; precipitate.

1907 W. DE MORGAN *Alice-for-Short* xxviii. 280 Don't you go making a runaway match with a ramshandry sort o' half-French girl.

ram's head. Add: **2. b.** (See quots.)

1944 L. T. C. ROLT *Narrow Boat* 206 *Ram's head*, the boatman's name for the wooden rudder post of a narrow boat; usually it is bound with pipe-clayed Turk's-head knots, and occasionally decorated with a horse's tail. **1947** S. WOOLFITT *Idle Women* ii. 26 The tiller is called the 'ram's head' and is curved like a swan's neck towards the steerer. It is metal, on the motor, and is painted in sections with.. red, white and blue. *Ibid.* Gloss. 222 *Ram's Head*, in the butty, the post at the top of the rudder, usually highly decorated with Turk's heads and/or horse-hair; in the motor, the steering column. **1976** A. HILL *Summer's End* i. 12 The ram's head was part of the tiller, and by putting our hands to it we got the 'feel' of boat-steering.

ram's horn. Add: **1. a.** Also, in proverbial phr. *as † right* (*straight, crooked,* etc.) *as a ram's horn*. (Earlier and later examples). Also *transf.* and *fig.*

c **1320** in Wright & Halliwell *Reliquæ Antiquæ* (1843) II. 19 As ryt as ramis orn. **1658** MENNIS & SMITH *Wit Restor'd* 102 Straight as a rams horne is thy nose. **1834** C. A. DAVIS *Lett. J. Downing* xxxvi. 324 As crooked as a ram's horn. **1842** [see SHEEP'S EYE(S 2]. **1878** HARDY *Return of Native* II. III. iii. 107 I'm as stiff as a ram's horn, stooping so long. **1914** C. MACKENZIE *Sinister Street* II. III. v. 588 A ramshorn of snuff and glasses of mead waiting for casual callers. **1947** *S. Folklore Q.* Dec. 263 More conventionally..a seasoned reprobate is characterized as 'old as the hills and crooked as a ram's horn'.

attrib. and *Comb.*

1897 *Sears, Roebuck Catal.* 612/2 *Handle bars*,..up or down or ram's horn as desired. Our ram's horn bar is the neatest and most comfortable made. **1909** *Daily Chron.* 17 Aug. 7/4 A great silver-mounted ram's-horn snuffbox. **1934** *Archit. Rev.* LXXVI. 64/3 Material [*sc.* timber] possessing 'ram's horn' figure, is also met with, and 'stripe' or 'ribbon-grain' is relatively common. **1964** J. S. SCOTT *Dict. Building* 256 *Ram's horn figure*.., a ripple like *fiddleback*.

6. In full, *ram's-horn* (*pond*) *snail*. A herbivorous aquatic snail belonging to the family Planorbidæ, esp. *Planorbis planorbis* or *P. corneus*.

1901, 1926 [see *flat-coil* s.v. *FLAT *adj.* 15]. **1950** *Sci. News* XV. 101 These absorption bands have not got precisely the same wave-lengths in the blood of man and in that of the ramshorn pond snail. **1952** J. CLEGG *Freshwater Life Brit. Isles* xvi. 254 The larger species of Ram's Horn Snails..live at least two or three years. **1960** *Times* 4 Aug. 1/3 (Advt.), Pond Naturalist would gratefully acknowledge information where to collect Ramshorn Snails. **1971** *Oxf. Bk. Invertebrates* 68 The ramshorns can possibly live in more stagnant conditions than other water-snails.

ram-stam, *a.*, *sb.*, and *adv.* Add: **A.** *adj.* (Later examples.)

1934 M. WATT *Visitors at Birkenbrae* 12 John's that ramstam..he wad be sure tae come oot wi' something. **1976** *Scottish Rev.* Spring 19 In 'The Steeple Bar, Perth'..his [*sc.* Sydney Goodsir Smith's] ram-stam bacchanalian voice is heard, as naturally as if he had been attuned to spoken Scots from childhood. **1976** *Ibid.* Summer 32 This is a rather ramstam, happy-go-lucky, whimsical procedure.

C. *adv.* (Further examples.)

1910 *Blackw. Mag.* Jan. 31/1 He proposed, ramstam, by telegraph; was accepted, and the lady came home..that he might marry her. **1922** T. S. CAIRNCROSS *Scot at Hame* 54, I left my gless a meenit, ran ram-stam. **1967** 'H. CALVIN' *Nice Friendly Town* ix. 136 The way young folk nowadays go ram-stam at things without a by-your-leave.

ramus. Add: **1. b.** A major branch of a nerve; *ramus communicans* (pl. *rami communicantes*), a branch of one nerve that joins another; *esp.* one of those joining a sympathetic ganglion with a spinal nerve.

1811 J. BELL *Anat. Human Body* (ed. 3) II. 515 Whilst it [*sc.* the tibial nerve] is yet in the hollow behind the joint formed by the hamstring tendons, it gives off a nerve which comes out from the ham, and descends superficially on the back of the leg. This has been called ramus communicans tibialis. *Ibid.* 517 When it [*sc.* the fibular nerve] arrives at the anular ligament, it is much diminished. Here it divides into the ramus dorsalis pedis profundus, and superficialis. **1893** H. ST. J. BROOKS in H. Morris *Treat. Human Anat.* v. 864 Each of the thoracic ganglia is connected to the corresponding spinal nerve by two rami communicantes, a white and a grey. The white ramus communicans consists of medullated fibres... The grey ramus communicans or revehent nerve is formed of non-medullated fibres. *Ibid.* 865 Occasionally the number of rami is increased to five or six. **1927** W. KEILLER *Nerve Tracts* I. 147 The spinal nerves distal to the root ganglia divide almost immediately into anterior and posterior rami. **1946** *Gray's Anat.* (ed. 29) 1078 The sensory root [of the ciliary ganglion] is formed by a ramus communicans from the nasociliary nerve. **1964** A. J. BERGER *Elem. Human Anat.* v. 84 The definitive spinal nerve is very short because it splits into two main branches (or rami) almost as soon as it is formed. The smaller dorsal primary ramus innervates the deep back muscles. **1967** G. M. WYBURN et al. *Conc. Anat.* iii. 93/1 Incise one or two intercostal spaces to expose the intercostal nerves and find their slender connections with the sympathetic trunk, i.e. the grey and white rami communicantes. **1972** C. R. & T. S. LEESON *Human Structure* iii. 11/1 Immediately after emerging from an intervertebral foramen, the spinal nerve divides into a posterior primary ramus and an anterior primary ramus.

3. *Zool.* In the mastax of rotifers, each of the two articulated parts of the incus that are attached to the fulcrum.

1856 *Phil. Trans. R. Soc.* CXLVI. 426 The incus..consists of distinct articulated portions. The principal are two stout rami..resting on what appears to be a slender pedicel (fulcrum, *h*). **1886**, etc. [see *FULCRUM 2 c]. **1972** M. S. GARDINER *Biol. Invertebrates* vii. 236/2 The wall [of the mastax]..is extended into seven firm, sclerotized pieces, the trophi, moved by small individual muscles. These pieces are a single median fulcrum and three pairs of lateral ones, two rami, two unci, and two manubria.

Rana (rā·nă). [Nepali and Hindi *rānā* prince, f. Skr. *rājana* royal: cf. RAJA, RAJAH.] The title used by members of the family which virtually ruled Nepal from 1846 to 1951. Also *attrib.*

1951 *Britannica Bk. of Year* 462/2 Although the relations between the exiled members of the ruling Rana family with the hereditary prime minister..had been unfriendly [etc.]. **1959** *Manch. Guardian* 18 Aug. 5/1 The Ranas married their daughters to Rajput princes. **1971** C. Bonington *Annapurna South Face* iii. 32, I could pick out Rana palaces with spacious courtyards and rusty, corrugated-iron roofs. *Ibid.* 37 The Ranas have lost their power but many of them still hold high office, particularly in the armed forces. However, most of the old Rana palaces..have now been turned into offices or hotels. **1971** K. Kent in *Ibid.* 311 In early 1951 a democratic form of government [in Nepal] was established by proclamation. It kept the existing Rana, Sir Mohan Chamsher, as Prime Minister, but in November 1951 a revision replaced this last Prime Minister with Mr M. P. Koirala of the Congress Party. **1977** *Times* 15 Nov. 15/1 The overthrow of the Rana regime in 1951.

ranai, var. *lanai.

Ranal (rē¹·năl), *a.* and *sb. Bot.* [f. mod.L. name of order *Ranales* (J. Lindley *Nixus Plantarum* (1833) 9), f. Ran(unculus + L. *-āles*, pl. of *-ālis* -al.] **A.** *adj.* = *ranalian *a.* **B.** *sb.* A ranalian plant.

1839 T. Baskerville *Affinities of Plants* 73 We shall find there a collection of orders constituting the Ranal and Anonal alliances. **1846** J. Lindley *Veget. Kingdom* 416 In appearance Ranals are singularly different in the same Order.

ranalian (rănē¹·liăn), *a. Bot.* Also **Ran-, -ean.** [f. as prec. + -ian.] Of or pertaining to a plant of the order Ranales or the group as a whole.

1915 C. E. Bessey in *Ann. Missouri Bot. Garden* II. 116 The opposite-leaved class..is the first to emerge from the cycadean phylum, appearing as the ranalean complex. *Ibid.* 127 Ranalean evolution has..been one of more and more simplification of flower structure. **1926** *Jrnl. Bot.* LXIV. 83 In following the lead of those who assume a common Ranalian origin for Angiosperms, Mr. Hutchinson has burnt his boats. **1931** A. M. Johnson *Taxonomy of Flowering Plants* i. 11 We have thus a phylogenetic tree of three main branches radiating from the polycarpellate, apocarpous, hypogynous, Ranalian base. **1959** Foster & Gifford *Compar. Morphol. Vascular Plants* xviii. 458 It is clear that these ranalian plants are primitively vesselless. *Ibid.* 480 It is only by such laborious procedures that we shall be able to test the importance of recent investigations on ranalean families. **1972** *Nature* 14 Apr. 353/2 The Magnoliidae association corresponds with the 'Ranalian' and the Hamamelidae-Dilleniidae associations with the 'Rosalian' cluster as conceived above.

ranch, *sb.*[2] For '*U.S.*' read 'orig. *U.S.*'. Add: **1. b.** A single-storey or split-level house.

1960 'E. McBain' *Killer's Payoff* xi. 111 Some real estate agent had decided to give the title 'ranch' to any house that had all of its living space on one floor. **1965** H. Hood in *Tamarack Review* Winter 12 Our house was the first California-redwood ranch in the town of Mount Royal. **1965** 'L. Egan' *Detective's Due* (1966) 10 Big newish expensive homes. The one they wanted turned out to be a split-level ranch with a lot of synthetic stone on its front. **1974** R. B. Parker *God save Child* (1975) x. 73 A one-story house..a low ranch built on a slab.

2. a. (Earlier and later examples.) Also *transf.* Phr. *meanwhile, back at the ranch*: orig. used in Western cowboy stories and films, introducing a subsidiary plot. Also *attrib.*

Quot. 1831 may belong to sense 1.

1831 J. O. Pattie *Personal Narr.* 221 [At] a ranch..I procured a horse for three dollars. **1847** B. Lundy *Life* x. 58 We set off at day-break, and went twenty-one miles to a *ranche*. **1870** J. C. Duval *Adventures Big-Foot Wallace* xl. 247 When I have got through with..my 'inheritance', I shall come back to my ranch here, put on my old buckskins, and run after stock and fight Indians for a livelihood the balance of my life. **1888** R. W. Buchanan *Heir of Linne* II. xx. 121 I've got a cattle ranche in the wild west. **1933** J. D. Higinbotham *When West was Young* 201 A ranch frequently takes the name of the horse or cattle brand of its owner... Other ranches took the name of a locality. **1950** *Sun* (Baltimore) 2 Mar. 8/5 A New Zealander has swopped his cow pastures for a 'whale ranch'... The 'ranch' has been set up in a bay of Arapawa Island off Wellington by Gill Perano, who carries out his 'round-ups' by motor boat. **1958** L. van der Post *Lost World of Kalahari* iv. 72 He went out to East Africa to one of its remote frontier areas and started a ranch of his own. **1963** J. Crist in *N.Y. Herald Trib. Sunday Mag.* 24 Nov. 40/2 Kramer keeps any number of old 'meanwhile, back at the ranch' side adventures going. **1972** *Buenos Aires Herald* 2 Feb. 7/6 He..seduced several women after promising he would marry them later in Venezuela where he said he owned several ranches. **1978** *Observer* (Colour Suppl.) 29 Jan. front cover (*caption*) Meanwhile, back at the ranch...

b. A farm (arable, fruit-growing, etc.); spec., one on which foxes or mink are bred and raised for their fur.

1865 'Mark Twain' in *Californian* 28 Oct. 5/3, I have a ranch of quite unknown extent, Its turnips great, its oats without compare. **1890** *Stock Grower & Farmer* 12 July 5/1 They are pasturing on the Alfalfa ranches. **1900** *Sci. Amer.* 21 Apr. 242/3 There are..no less than thirty-five [Alaskan] islands occupied by proprietors of fox ranches. **1948** [see *mink ranch* s.v. *mink 4]. **1953** A. R. M. Lower *Unconventional Voy.* 146 The Okanagan with its pleasant little towns and its fruit ranches—everything is a ranch in B[ritish] C[olumbia]. **1958** H. B. Allen in *Publ. Amer. Dialect Soc.* xxx. 6 *Ranch*, denoting an establishment for cattle-raising..although the somewhat prestigious nature of the word has spread it eastward through its adoption by farmers who have large wheat-farms. **1976** *Billings* (Montana) *Gaz.* 4 July 8-D/2 (Advt.), Experienced worker..for dryland grain & livestock ranch South of Billings.

3. a. *ranch-boarding, -building, country* (earlier example), *dog, experience, girl, guitar, hand, hide, -house* (earlier and later examples), *-hut, job, -land, -life, -mark, -overseer; ranch-owning* adj.; **ranch egg,** a fresh egg; **ranch mink,** mink bred on a ranch, or its fur; also *ellipt.*, a coat made of ranch mink fur; **ranch wagon,** (*a*) a horse-drawn wagon used on a ranch; (*b*) = *estate car* s.v. *estate *sb.* 14.

1976 *Rhyl Jrnl. & Advertiser* 9 Dec. 22/3 (Advt.), Reclaimed and new timber for sale..Perspex corrugated sheets, Target board, plywoods, ranch boarding, chipboard, melamine etc. **1926** D. H. Lawrence *Plumed Serpent* vi. 109 The telephone was in the old ranch-building. **1885** *Weekly New Mexican Rev.* 22 Jan. 2/5 Texas..is still as good, if not a better ranch country, than New Mexico. **1897** E. Hough *Story of Cowboy* 227 In the Indian Nations the writer has been out with a pack of greyhounds, which included a good pack of ranch dogs. **1923** D. H. Lawrence *Birds, Beasts & Flowers* 156 Now you've come sex-alive, and the great ranch dogs are all after you. **1908** *Sunset* Dec. 792/2 If you were working with ranch eggs, store eggs or yard eggs, it might be different. **1966** 'L. Holton' *Out of Depths* xv. 149 Two ranch eggs with ham. **1976** *Billings* (Montana) *Gaz.* 4 July 8-D/2 (Advt.), Must have Animal Science or Animal Husbandry degree. Previous sales, ranch or feed lot experience preferred. *c* **1894** C. Hoyt *Texas Steer* 1, in M. J. Moses *Representative Amer. Dramas* (1925) 17 Oh, I do so want to be something besides a Texas ranch girl. **1951** M. McLuhan *Mech. Bride* (1967) 148/1 There is a story about a little ranch girl. **1947** R. Taylor *Bar Nothing Ranch* xvi. 190 She'd cuddle the ranch guitar and croon heartbreakingly. **1951** Gillis & Myles *North Pole Boarding House* 6 A minister to the spiritual needs of the husky ranch-hands in Alberta's godless foothills. **1977** *Herald* (Melbourne) 17 Jan. 18/7 (Advt.), Sheepskin car seat covers and rugs, ranch hides, kangaroo and calf skin. **1978** *Lancashire Life* Mar. 70 (Advt.), The seating area is in hard wearing ranch hide. **1862** *Harper's Mag.* June 14/1 Having awakened my mule I rode on about five miles further, where I reached a small ranch-house. **1933** J. Steinbeck in *North Amer. Rev.* Nov. 423/2 At the ranch house, he found his mother sitting on the porch. **1930** R. Macaulay *Staying with Relations* xix. 273 At El Refugio,..there's a tiny ranch-hut where I tried for a drink of Mexicali. **1976** *Billings* (Montana) *Gaz.* 4 July 7-D/7 (Advt.), Competent college girl for summer ranch job. **1933** *Times Lit. Suppl.* 9 Feb. 94/2 The arrival of a stranger on the ranchlands of Clinton Prescott coincided with a fierce snowstorm. **1979** *Time* 8 Jan. 40/2 In Texas, Prince Franz Joseph..bought 16,000 acres of ranch land. **1899** 'Mark Twain' in *Harper's Monthly Mag.* (1914) Dec. 4/2 It told me where to begin to talk ranch-life in Carson Valley. **1903** A. M. Binstead *Pitcher in Paradise* iv. 110 Sleep, someone, whose name and ranchmarks I have forgotten, once observed, is much overrated. **1952** S. Ellin *Key to Nicholas Street* 1. i. 10 A ranch mink that is worth laying your life down for. **1960** *Bull. Retail Trading-Standards Assoc.* Nov. 2 Ranch Mink should..be so described unless it is a mutation mink. **1964** *Harper's Bazaar* Nov. 83 Ranch mink hat. **1976** *Daily Record* (Glasgow) 23 Nov. 18/2 Ranch mink brushes expensive mohair and the whole atmosphere is narcotic and totally unreal. **1926** D. H. Lawrence *Plumed Serpent* vi. 112 He was not really an hotel manager, but a ranch-overseer. **1977** *New Yorker* 29 Aug. 46/3 Harlow comes from a ranch-owning family whose roots were established in northern California over several generations. **1886** T. Roosevelt in *Outing* July 387, I took along the ranch wagon, drawn by four shaggy horses. **1970** *Globe & Mail* (Toronto) 26 Sept. 48/1 (Advt.), 69 Ford 6-passenger ranch wagon, finished in a rich dark blue. **1975** *Country Life* 2 Jan. 32/1 One feature of these New World ranch wagons..is the tailgate.

b. Of a modern building: built in the style associated with a ranch; single-storey; as *ranch bungalow, dormitory, home, house*; also *ranch-style, -type* adjs.

1966 *Globe & Mail* (Toronto) 30 June 30/5 (Advt.), Rustic 7 room ranch bungalow on ½ acre lot, trees galore! **1973** *Irish Times* 2 Mar. 22/6 (Advt.), Delightful American ranch bungalow..in exceptional position and close to all amenities. **1974** *Country Life* 21 Feb. Suppl. 36/1 American Ranch Bungalow in Surrey..£60,000. **1976** *Columbus* (Montana) *News* (Joliet Suppl.) 27 May 2/3 Housing [malefactors] in ranch and dairy dormitories. **1973** *N.Y. Law Jrnl.* 26 July 16/8 (Advt.), Mini-farm, 19 acres, neat 5 room ranch home, almost borders Summit Lake. **1978** *Detroit Free Press* 16 Apr. F9/1 (Advt.), Bar with 2 bdrm ranch home & soft ice cream business. **1952** H. Innes *Campbell's Kingdom* 1. ii. 33 The Fergus home was a low, sprawling ranch-house building. **1959** N. Mailer *Advts. for Myself* (1961) 378 Eitel's rented ranch-house in the desert. **1975** *Woman's Jrnl.* Sept. 62/1 Today..she lives in style in a palatial ranch-house in Beverly Hills. **1961** J. Mitford in *Life* 4 Aug. 8/2 Motels..may be Tudor, Queen Anne, Colonial, Knotty Pine, Ranch Style, or Futuristic in décor. **1962** E. Snow *Other Side of River: Red China Today* lx. 461 To people who live in American ranch-style bungalows, all the new multiple dwellings in China would seem primitive. **1970** *Cape Times* 28 Oct. 19/9 (Advt.), Outstanding architect designed, owner built ranch style house on high foundation. **1978** *Detroit Free Press* 16 Apr. (Parade) 20/2 Just before Christmas, Dan Scarborough, the senior state senator from northeast Florida, was entertaining some friends in his family's sprawling ranch-style home. **1956** W. H. Whyte *Organization Man* 11 It is difficult to see the three-button suit as more of a strait-jacket than overalls, or the ranch-type house than old law tenements. **1976** J. Philips *Backlash* (1977) iii. 118 [She] lived in a modern ranch-type house about a mile out of town.

ranch, *v.*[1] Add: **1. a.** (Earlier and later examples.)

1866 B. Harte in *Californian* 26 May 1/1 Ranchin' out this way? **1872** 'Mark Twain' *Roughing It* xxxiv. 242 He had been farming (or ranching as the more customary term is) in the Washoe District. **1976** *Billings* (Montana) *Gaz.* 28 June 5-A/2 The bridegroom graduated..with a degree in agriculture. The newlyweds will ranch near Boyes. **1976** *Laurel* (Montana) *Outlook* 30 June 14/1 He farmed and ranched at Acton until 1974.

b. To let land for grazing.

1910 *Blackw. Mag.* July 126/2 He is 'ranching', that is, letting grazing on the eleven months' system.

2. *trans.* **a.** To put (an animal) on a ranch.

1873 J. H. Beadle *Undevel. West* xxx. 663 Six hundred miles..had worn out my horse, and on the 16th instant I 'ranched him' twenty miles south of Beaver. **1916** *Yukon Territory* (Canada Dept. Interior) x. 177 Foxes should be ranched in woodland areas. **1935** *Discovery* Feb. 50/2 Animals so purchased will be ranched and tended by the vendor. **1980** *Times* 18 Mar. 14/8 Mink being ranched, humanely killed and kept in a life of luxury.

b. To use (land) as a ranch.

1901 B. Harte *Under Redwoods* 74 It caused her to remove to Santa Ana, where her old father had feebly ranched a 'quarter section' in the valley. **1927** *Daily Tel.* 23 Aug. 11/6 The large arable farms..must..be grassed down, and ranched at a nominal rent. **1965** F. Symington *Tuktu* 13 If the central Arctic were being systematically 'ranched' with caribou herds.

Hence **ranched** *ppl. a.*, of an animal: confined to or bred on a ranch. Also *transf.*, of the fur of a ranched animal.

1954 *Economist* 20 Feb. 567/1 Ranched Russian mink. *Ibid.*, Wild furs and ranched furs. **1970** *Daily Tel.* 10 Oct. 14 Tourists who visit emergent countries do so to see the animals in their natural environment—not confined and 'ranched'. **1977** *Harpers & Queen* Sept. 65 Very dark natural ranched mink coats from £2,750.

rancher. (In Dict. s.v. Ranch *v.*[1]) Add: **1.** (Earlier and later examples.)

1836 *Papers of M. Buonaparte Lamar* (1921) I. 337 Capt King went..to Lopes..for the purpose of chastising some ranchers. **1866** *Rep. Indian Affairs* (U.S.) 189 Teamsters, packers, herders, ranchers and miners all over the country have become exasperated. **1953** *Manch. Guardian Weekly* 18 June 3 The surviving farmers and ranchers have bought up the land from the men who went away. **1958** *Publ. Amer. Dialect Soc.* xxx. 6 A man with such a dual [*sc.* wheat and cattle] establishment in central Nebraska..is more likely to identify himself as a rancher rather than as a farmer. **1961** L. van der Post *Heart of Hunter* 1. vii. 112 One of the foremost ranchers near Gemsbok Pan was in the Union and coming back by truck across the desert. **1973** *Sunday Advocate-News* (Barbados) 21 Jan. 14/1 There are a few ranchers..on the Brazilian border, a few miners, a few lumberjacks. **1976** *Billings* (Montana) *Gaz.* 4 July 1-A/5 Z— C— was born into a family of ranchers who had come to Montana from Canada a few years before the first Yegen arrived.

2. A modern single-storey house.

1965 *Sun* (Vancouver) 8 Aug. 47/7 (Advt.), Rancher..close to Burnaby Park and swimming pool. **1968** H. Waugh *Con Game* ii. 23 The Demarest home was a rancher in the $25,000 class. **1970** *Globe & Mail* (Toronto) 28 Sept. 24/3 (Advt.), Lovely buff brick rancher on wide 80 ft. lot. **1978** *N.Y. Times* 29 Mar. B8/6 (Advt.), Beautiful rambling Rancher. 2 yrs old, 7 spac rms, [etc.].

rancheral (rɑnʃē³·răl), *a. rare.* [f. Ranchero + -al.] Of or pertaining to rancheros.

1847 G. F. A. Ruxton *Adventures in Mexico* xiii. 94 Of these eight mozos, he who bore away the palm of rancheral superiority..was the third son.

rancheria. Add: (Further examples.) Also **rancheree, rancherie** (rɑ·nʃĕrī).

1854 C. E. De Long in *Calif. Hist. Soc. Q.* (1929) VIII. 200 Anderson & I fell in with an Indian Rancheria. **1872** R. B. Johnson *Very Far West Indeed* 197 I'd take a dozen Injuns straight out of the rancherie, an' make a better government out of 'em than they've got up thar. **1901** *Canad. Mag.* XVIII. 179/1 Jim is the policeman at the Indian rancheree. **1901** *Daily Colonist* (Victoria, B.C.) 15 Oct. 3/2 A heavy cargo, including everything from shipments of lumber for Bella Coola and Kitimaat, to new gravestones for various Indians at Northern rancheries. **1914** A. H. Fitch *Junipero Serra* iii. 222 There were many rancherias on the banks of the Colorado. **1955** *Sci. News Let.* 16 Apr. 245/3 These [South American] Indians..live in very small communities called 'rancherias', consisting of from two to 15 individuals. **1963** R. Symons *Many Trails* vii. 71 Although they own small reserves—which they call rancheries—most of them prefer a nomadic life. **1976** *Islander* (Victoria, B.C.) 27 June 2/3 Sent their logs downstream to a booming ground near the Indian rancherie.

ranchero. Add: (Earlier and later examples.) Also *attrib.*

1826 J. E. B. Austin *Let.* 31 Oct. in C. Barker *Austin Papers* (1924) I. ii. 1482 The old Ranchero was much surprised, but overjoyed to see me. **1836** C. J. Latrobe *Rambler in Mexico* ii. 27 You have here..every degree from the substantial *Ranchero*, or proprietor, bespurred,..embroidered vest, and gaudy *serape*,..or the trusty *arriero*, with his long string of mules. **1927** W. Cather *Death comes for Archbishop* iii. 78 He and the *rancheros* had run their church to suit themselves, making a very gay affair of it. **1947** M. Lowry *Under Volcano* iii. 90 The orange juice and ranchero eggs. **1963** *Punch* 20 Feb. 285/2 Women have gone overboard for their ranchero hats. **1968** *Esquire* July 99/3 John Weitz..designed this yellow-and-black-striped blazer suit. With it, Ranchero tie over a neckband shirt. **1973** *Country Life* 6 Dec. 1970/1 The Mexican heavy knit woollen jacket..worn by *rancheros*... The coat looks good on either sex. **1977** *Times Lit. Suppl.* 21 Jan. 88/5 In the ranks of the Cristeros [in Mexico 1926–29] there figure small landowners, rancheros, Indians.

ranchette (rɑnʃe·t). *U.S.* [See -ette.] A

small, modern, single-storey or split-level house.

1956 R. A. HEINLEIN in *Mag. of Fantasy & Sci. Fict.* Oct. 23/2, I wanted a ranchette near the plant; she favored a flat in Town. **1966** *Punch* 9 Nov. 692/2 Their split-level Graeco-Moorish ranchette, set on teetering stilts above the green Los Angeles smog. **1979** *Tucson* (Arizona) *Citizen* 3 Oct. 18c/3 (Advt.), 1½ to 2 commercial acre Ranchettes overlooking the city.

ranching, *vbl. sb.* (In Dict. s.v. RANCH *v.*[1]) Add: (Earlier and later examples.) Also, the raising of game and other animals. Also *attrib.*

1863 E. R. MEREDITH *Let.* May in *Frontier & Midland* (1937) XVII. 288/1 A ranch is properly a grazing farm and the term 'ranching' sometimes means farming but is generally applied in this country [*sc.* Idaho] to taking care of stock. **1870** J. C. DUVAL *Adventures Big-Foot Wallace* xlvi. 302 We would try our hands at 'ranching'. **1873** J. H. BEADLE *Undevel. West* xv. 267 'Ranching' came next, and all this industry is not lost. **1916** [see *mink ranching* s.v. *MINK 4]. **1950** *Manch. Guardian Weekly* 5 Jan. 10 Teamsters carried it through the ranching country. **1971** *Inside Kenya Today* Mar. 52/2 Arrangements have also been finalized for the establishment of a ranching scheme at Jaldesa. **1974** *Listener* 2 May 572/3 [The land] is all earmarked for ranching development. **1975** *Nature* 5 June 449/2 Interest in game ranching of natural animal populations as a food source goes back a long way. **1980** *Daily Tel.* 30 Dec. 7/2 Salmon ranching, inshore fishing and tourism are the immediate projects for economic development.

ranchito (rɑntʃī·to). Also **ranchita.** [Sp., dim. of RANCHO.] In the Western U.S., a small ranch or farm.

1850 L. H. GARRARD *Wah-to-Yah* xvii. 231 To the Ranchita is something less than a mile. **1906** A. ADAMS *Cattle Brands* 92 He had sent to a nearby ranchito for a man who had at least the reputation of being quite a hunter. **1976** *New Yorker* 26 Apr. 122/2 Many descendants of the *pobladores* still live in villages that seem dominated by cracked adobe or on tiny *ranchitos* with a garden patch and a few head of cattle.

ranchman. (In Dict. s.v. RANCH *sb.*[2]) (Earlier and later examples.)

1856 *Spirit of Times* 4 Oct. 75/1 The dusty, rusty, rough-clad, huge-pawed creatures, known as ranch-men. **1926** J. F. DOBIE *Rainbow in Morning* (1965) 97 A barbecue required the coöperation of the substantial citizens of the country, for they furnished the beef to barbecue. A ranchman might contribute a calf, a yearling, or steer; or he might contribute money. **1949** *Daily Ardmoreite* (Ardmore, Oklahoma) 4 Dec. 10/1 The ranchmen are piling up hay in strategic places to feed stock if the severe cold comes again. **1959** T. D. CLARK *Frontier America* xxvii. 640 A ranchman could homestead 160 acres in his own name... A ranchman could purchase public lands outright.

rancho. Add: **1. a.** (Later example.)

1931 *Times Lit. Suppl.* 19 Mar. 214/2 To live in a mud 'rancho', eat frugally..was no hardship for this class of immigrant.

b. (Further examples.) Hence, in extended use, a roadhouse or inn.

1849 J. T. BROOKS *Four Months Among Gold-Finders in Alta California* ii. 8 Bradley urged us to proceed a few miles farther, where we could take up our quarters at a rancho belonging to a friend of his. **1854** C. E. DE LONG in *Calif. Hist. Soc. Q.* (1929) VIII. 199 Took Dinner at the Empire Rancho.

c. (See quots.)

1957 P. KEMP *Mine were of Trouble* iii. 45 *Rancho*, usually some form of stew, was at half past twelve... And, at six-thirty, the evening *rancho*. **1976** *National Observer* (U.S.) 17 July 10/1 A 23-inch TV is in the dining room, and most of the population are able to eat the *rancho*—the Mexican native meals—because it is very good.

ranchy (rɑ·nʃi), *a. U.S. slang.* [Perh. var. *RAUNCHY *a.*] Dirty, disgusting, indecent.

1903 A. M. BINSTEAD *Pitcher in Paradise* xii. 283 Then they brought the monkey in—the sad-faced, bare-based, flea-ranchy old monk. **1959** LD. KINROSS *Innocents at Home* xxii. 196 The bridegroom, an Englishman, declared his intention of having the English as opposed to the American marriage service. This included..the worshipping of her with his body. There was an embarrassed pause at this; and then one of the bridesmaids remarked, 'A bit ranchy, that.'

rancid, *a.* Add: **2.** (Earlier and later examples.) Also as *sb.*

1833 J. CONSTABLE *Let.* 3 Apr. (1965) III. 98 He is too fond, of *rancid old art.* **1892** 'MARK TWAIN' *Amer. Claimant* xv. 156 He couldn't get his breath at first. When he did get it, it came rancid with sarcasm. **1912** B. PAIN *Locris of Tower* in *Stories in Grey* 195 Black kid gloves, the most rancid form of gloves. **1924** E. F. BENSON *David of King's* v. 79 'When Milton talked of a pansy, he called it "freaked with jet".' 'O Lord, did he really?' said David. 'How frightfully rancid!' *a* **1930** D. H. LAWRENCE *Old Men* in *Last Poems* 251 The rancid old men that don't die because the gods don't want them..Old people fixed in a rancid resistance to life, fixed to the letter of the law. **1941** E. P. O'DONNELL *Great Big Doorstep* ix. 125 If she ain't a rancid! She's sweet as sugar to Evvie jiss to get Evvie in a good humor, then she turn around and talk sarcastic. **1973** *Times Lit. Suppl.* 16 Mar. 304/3 The movement was sufficiently vague for any rancid provincial mediocrity to come to believe that he was himself at the centre.

rancieite (rænsi͵ēi·əit). *Min.* Also **rancieite,** † **rancierite.** [ad. F. *rancierite* (A. Leymerie *Cours de la Minéralogie* (1857) II. 329), f. Rancié (formerly also Rancier), name of the mountain near Vicdessos, Ariège, France, where it was first found: see -ITE[1].] A hydrated oxide of calcium and manganese, $(Ca,Mn^{II})\ Mn^{IV}{}_4O_9 \cdot 3H_2O$, occurring as soft flakes and as compact or friable masses.

1861 H. W. BRISTOW *Gloss. Mineral.* 313/1 *Rancierite*... Occurs in earthy masses of a deep brown colour. Soils the fingers. **1907** *Mineral. Mag.* XIV. 408 *Rancieite.* (Collection de Minéralogie du Muséum d'Histoire Naturelle, Paris, Guide du Visiteur, 2nd edit., 1900, p. 29 (Rancieite).) The correct spelling of rancierite (A. Leymerie), a variety of wad. **1923** *Mineral. Abstr.* II. 144 A mineral found by G. Friedel in the haematite of Villerouge, Aude, was identified as rancieite of Lacroix. **1943** *Econ. Geol.* XXXVIII. 594 The manganese is in the form of rancieite, a finely flaky, soft, brownish-black, hydrous calcium-manganese oxide, mixed with calcium carbonate in the form of calcareous tuffs. **1969** *Mineral. Abstr.* XX. 225/2 Rancieite, from old workings at Rancié, forms soft brown scales with metallic lustre;.. pleochroic yellow to deep brown. **1979** *Nature* 12 July 137/1 That rancieite belongs to the birnessite group (family) has been established by Bardossy and Brindley.

rand, *sb.*[1] Add: **1.** (Further example.)

1958 *New Biol.* XXVI. 92 The underlying fen peat acts as a reservoir of wetness while the margins of the peat-filled basin insulate the raised centre from the soil water which is draining into the basin... Such a bog is called a raised bog, the sloping slides being called the rand, and the insulating zone round the edge the lagg.

3. c. *Basketry.* (See quots. 1910 and 1912.)

1903 R. M. JACOT *Useful Cane Work* I. p. ix/2 *Trade or workshop terms*,..randing, or a 'rand'. **1910** *Encycl. Brit.* III. 482/2 The chief strokes used in constructing an ordinary basket are:— the 'slew'—two or more rods woven together; the 'rand', rods woven in singly. **1912** T. OKEY *Introd. Art of Basket-Making* v. 20 The next section is formed by a *Rand*—one single rod worked alternately in front of and behind each Stake. **1959** D. WRIGHT *Baskets & Basketry* vi. 136 *Rand*: a single rod worked in front of one stake and behind the next.

rand (rænd, ‖ rɑnt), *sb.*[2] *S. Afr.* Also **randt, rant.** Pl. **rands,** ‖ **rande.** [Afrikaans, a. Du. *rand(t)* edge, margin: rel. to RAND *sb.*] **1. a.** In South Africa: a rocky ridge or area of high sloping ground, esp. overlooking a river-valley. **b.** *spec. The Rand,* the Witwatersrand, a notable gold-mining area of the Transvaal.

1839 J. COLLETT *Diary* 27 May in *Voorloper* (1976) 663 Finished making New Kralls to day on Willow fountain rant. **1856** F. FLEMING *Southern Africa* v. 109 The country, lying between the Rand and the Fish River, is thickly populated with Fingoes. **1890** *Digger's Doggerel* 28 The best Crushing Spec..on the Rand. **1891** B. MITFORD *Romance of Cape Frontier* iv. 23 He stood on the top of the *randt* for a brief blow after his exertions. **1899** G. B. SHAW *Let.* c 26–30 Dec. (1972) II. 124 The conflict that was inevitable from the moment that gold was discovered in the Rand..had to come. **1900** A. H. KEANE *Boer States* iii. 22 We can here speak of 'rands', that is, ridges of moderate elevation, which, however, are sometimes high enough to form water-partings. **1928** E. WALKER *Hist. S. Afr.* xii. 413 Mining areas were proclaimed on the Rand. **1947** H. C. BOSMAN *Mafeking Road* 3 'I don't think they [*sc.* the stars] would be good for growing mealies on, though,' I answered, 'they look too high up, like the rante of the Sneeuberge, in the Cape.' **1953** D. LESSING *Five* iii. 129 He thought of the old prospectors..panning gold.., washing the grit for those tiny grains that might proclaim a new Rand. **1972** D. FRANCIS *Smokescreen* ix. 123 Most of Johannesburg sank about three feet..after all the reef was out... The Rand gold fields are shallower.

2. (freq. with capital initial.) Pl. *rand* or *rands.* [f. with ref. to sense 1 b.] A unit of decimal currency, orig. equivalent to ten shillings sterling, and containing 100 cents, adopted by the Republic of South Africa in 1961, and subsequently by certain other southern African countries. Also *attrib.*

1961 *Times* 27 Jan. 19/4 There was a boom on the Johannesburg Stock Exchange last night... The occasion was the second dress rehearsal for trading in rand and cents when decimalization overtakes South Africa on the second Tuesday of next month. **1961** *Guardian* 26 May 3/3 A two-rand (formerly one pound) postal order bought in a Cape-town post office. **1970** *Daily Nation* (Nairobi) 16 Jan. 14/5 Lesotho's currency is the South African Rand. **1972** P. DRISCOLL *Wilby Conspiracy* ii. 37 You want wine? It'll cost you two rands a bottle. **1978** J. PAXTON *Dict. European Econ. Community* (rev. ed.) 21 In March 1976 the E.E.C. agreed to provide Botswana with about 90m. Rand in aid over four years.

rand, *v.*[1] Add: **2. c.** *trans.* and *intr.* To weave by randing (sense *1 b).

1959 D. WRIGHT *Baskets & Basketry* ii. 45 After the initial pairing the base may be randed. **1962** *Punch* 1 Aug. 170/3 The basket workers..still keep their rhymed boast: I can rand At your command..Wale all right And keep my stakes in order.

ran-dan, var. *RAN-TAN *v.*

randed, *a. Basketry.* [f. RAND *sb.*] Woven by randing (sense *1 b).

1907 *Yesterday's Shopping* (1969) 153/1 Basket, fine randed buff wicker. **1912** T. OKEY *Introd. Art of Basket-Making* ix. 91 The chief difference to be noted in the methods of Randed work are: that fine White or Buff is normally used. **1959** D. WRIGHT *Baskets & Basketry* ii. 42 For a Randed base..an extra short stick will be needed to make an odd number.

randing, *sb.* Add: **1. b.** *Basketry.* The action or process of weaving rands (sense *3 c); randed work.

1903 R. M. JACOT *Useful Cane Work* I. p. x/2 The basket maker..would speak of driving down the stakes..into the 'randing' or 'pairing' of a bottom. **1912** T. OKEY *Introd. Art of Basket-Making* ix. 91 Randing is sub-divided into Coarse, Slight, Light, Fine and Close. **1946** N. WYMER *Eng. Country Crafts* vii. 73 He now fills in the sides by weaving single willows..a stage known as 'randing'. **1964** H. HODGES *Artifacts* x. 146 The simplest weave, *randing*, was done with a single rod passed behind one stake and in front of the next.

‖ **randjie** (rɑ·ntʸi). *S. Afr.* Also **randje, rantjie.** [Afrikaans, ad. Du. *rand(t)je, rantje,* dim. of *rand(t)* *RAND *sb.*[2]] A narrow ridge of rocky ground, not as high as a kopje.

1889 *'Argus' Ann. & S. Afr. Directory* 849/1 Stony hills and knolls—known locally as *randjes* and *spitskops.* **1914** L. H. BRINKMAN *Breath of Karroo* i. 17 Here and there a few kopjes relieved the monotony of the view, and every few miles, randjes, or low stony hills, stretched across the plains. **1939** S. CLOETE *Watch for Dawn* 31 The small path that runs along the randjie. **1944** V. POHL *Adventures Boer Family* i. 11 There were roebuck in the *rantjies.* **1949** M. LEIGH *Cross of Fire* v. 99 The track climbed the randjie on which we stood and petered down again into the darkness and the gloom towards Matzana's kraal.

‖ **randkluft** (ra·ntkluft). [Ger., lit. 'edge crevice'.] A crevasse between the head of a glacier and a surrounding rock wall.

1934 C. F. MEADE in S. Spencer *Mountaineering* vi. 122 Another sort of chasm closely related to the bergschrund is the *randkluft.* This is the name given to the gap between the glacier and the bare rock-wall of a peak. **1958** *Polar Record* IX. 91 *Bergschrund*, the crevasse which occurs at the head of a cirque or valley glacier and which separates the moving glacier ice from the rock wall and the ice apron attached to it. When the ice apron is absent the gap is known as a Randkluft. **1970** R. J. SMALL *Study of Landforms* xi. 380 Temperature changes such as these seem insufficient to cause powerful shattering of the rock, and in any case they are presumably still less pronounced in the crack ('randkluft') between the névé and the headwall.

Randlord (ræ·ndlǭɹd). *slang.* Also with small initial. [f. *RAND *sb.*[2] + LORD *sb.*, after LANDLORD *sb.*] The owner or manager of a gold-field on the Rand in South Africa.

1904 *Daily Chron.* 21 Mar. 5/5 The Randlords' proposal really drives the British workman out of the Transvaal. *Ibid.* 14 May 4/7 Recent newspaper writers, in coining the word Randlords—have they not all done what they could to popularise a wrong pronunciation of Rand? **1936** R. J. M. GOOLD-ADAMS *S. Afr. To-day & To-morrow* ii. 54 The black man may..die a premature death, but that—so the Rand-lords say—is not the fault of the mines in which he worked. **1938** J. CARY *Castle Corner* v. 255 There's no religion any more—no honesty either—it's all money—these randlords, as they call 'em. **1955** L. HOTZ in Saron & Hotz *Jews in S.Afr.* xix. 357 Among the leading figures from Kimberley who quickly assumed a commanding position on the gold-fields, the so-called Randlords, were Barnato, the Joels, Alfred Beit, Albu, and Lionel Phillips.

random, *sb., a.,* and *adv.* Add: **A.** *sb.* **I. 1. a.** (Later U.S. example.)

1889 'MARK TWAIN' *Conn. Yankee* xv. 180 Two knights came together with great random.

3. a. (Further examples. Cf. sense *B. 1 b.)

1898 W. A. WHITWORTH *Expectation of Parts* 7 If a magnitude *s* be divided at random into *n* parts, the expectation of each part is *s*/*n*. **1921** *Biometrika* XIII. 309 An event happens at random once in a period *m*, therefore its chance of occurring in an interval of time or space δ*t* is δ*t*/*m*. **1931** H. JEFFREYS *Scientific Inference* iii. 24 We select at random *m* of the objects... We need a definition of what we mean by *at random*. We mean that every possible selection of *m* objects from the original *n* is equally probable. **1951** *Jrnl. Ecol.* XXXIX. 172 The principle of contagion..is that the groups are distributed at random and that the number of individuals in each group is also random.

4. Also, that which is random; random state, randomness.

1929 R. BRIDGES *Testament of Beauty* II. 44 As when a high moon thru' the rifted wrack gleameth upon the random of the windswept night. **1969** *Listener* 13 Nov. 678/3 'There's a lot of random in our songs,' says Paul [McCartney].

8. *Printing.* (see quots.)

1888 C. T. JACOBI *Printers' Vocab.* 110 Random, a special frame used by compositors in making-up. **1898** J. SOUTHWARD *Mod. Printing* I. iv. 29 Making-up Frames.. consist of an ordinary whole frame, fitted with a 'random'—that is, a sloping board, corresponding to a case, with ledges running along it transversely. **1910** A. BENNETT *Clayhanger* I. xii. 101 Under the furniture rack was the 'random', full of galleys. **1922** W. H. SCLATER *What Compositor should Know* I. 82 Randoms, on which new composition is placed for the purpose of being 'made up' into column form or page form. **1960** G. A. GLAISTER *Gloss. Bk.* 341/2 *Random*, the sloping work-top of a composing frame.

B. *adj.* **1. b.** *Statistics.* Governed by or involving equal chances for each of the actual or hypothetical members of a population; also, produced or obtained by a random process (and therefore completely unpredictable in detail); *random distribution,* a probability distribution, esp. the Poisson distribution; *random error*: see *ERROR 4 d; *random noise* (see quot. 1954); *random number*, a number selected from a given set of numbers in such a way that all the numbers in the set have the same chance of selection; also, a pseudo-random number; *random process*, (a process characterized by) a sequence of random variables (see also quot. 1937); *random sample*, a sample drawn at random from a population, each member of it having an equal or other specified chance of inclusion (sometimes contrasted with *quota sample* s.v. *QUOTA *sb.* 4); so *random sampling*; *random selection*, a random sample; random sampling; *random variable, variate*, a variable whose values are distributed in accordance with a probability distribution; *random walk*, the movement of something in successive steps, the direction, length, or other property of each step being governed by chance independently of preceding steps.

1898 *Phil. Trans. R. Soc.* CXCI. 230 Every artificial or even random selection of a group out of a community changes not only the amount of variation, but the amount of correlation of the organs of its members as compared with those of the primitive group. **1900** *Phil. Mag.* L. 157 (*heading*) On the criterion that a given system of deviations from the probable in the case of a correlated system of variables is such that it can be reasonably supposed to have arisen from random sampling. *Ibid.* 164 The question we wish to determine is whether the sample may be reasonably considered to represent a random system of deviations from the theoretical frequency distribution of the general population. **1905** K. PEARSON in *Nature* 27 July 294/2 (*heading*) The problem of the random walk. **1924** *Bell Syst. Technical Jrnl.* III. 88 (*heading*) Deviation of random samples from average conditions. **1925** F. C. MILLS *Statistical Meth.* xvi. 552 Great care is generally needed in securing a purely random selection. The obvious procedure of picking the most readily available cases would by no means meet the condition of random selection. **1927** *Tracts for Computers* xv. p. iii, In order to form this table of random numbers 40,000 digits were taken at random from census reports and combined by fours to give 10,000 numbers. *Ibid.*, These numbers, if truly random, could be used in a very great variety of ways for artificial sampling. **1933** *Forestry* VII. 149 As far as possible a random arrangement of replicated treatments and controls was adopted. **1936** *Jrnl. Ecol.* XXIV. 232 The simplest assumption, and the one most frequently made, concerning the distribution of the individuals of a plant species, is that it is random, i.e. that the chance that an individual shall occur in a given spot is the same for all spots... The chances that 0, 1, 2, 3,..individuals shall occur in a sample area large enough to contain very many individuals, are given by the terms of the Poisson series. *Ibid.* 240 Fig. 5 illustrates the divergence from random distribution. **1937** H. CRAMÉR (*title*) Random variables and probability distributions. *Ibid.* viii. 90 The set of variables Z_τ will be said to define a homogeneous random process if, for $\tau_1 \geqslant 0$, $\tau_2 > 0$, the difference $U_{\tau_1\tau_2} = Z_{\tau_1+\tau_2} - Z_{\tau_1}$ is a random variable which is independent of the variable Z_{τ_1} and has a d[istribution] f[unction] which is independent of τ_1. **1938** *Jrnl. R. Statist. Soc.* CI. 147 In colloquial speech the word 'random' is applied to any method of choice which lacks aim or purpose; and this usage is also found in certain sciences. In statistics, however, the word has a somewhat different and more definite significance, closely related to probability. **1939** *Jrnl. Franklin Inst.* CCVII. 747 Corresponding to the constrictions in the vocal passages from which are made the unvoiced sounds the Voder contains an electrical 'random noise' source which by itself produces a continuous hissing sound. **1946** C. E. WEATHERBURN *First Course in Math. Statistics* ii. 21 The method thus uses the similarity of the marbles to ensure that the selection is random. **1948** *Tracts for Computers* xxv. (*title*) Random normal deviates. *Ibid.* p. iii, They may be regarded as fair random samples from a normal universe having a zero mean and a unit standard deviation. **1949**, etc. [see *PSEUDORANDOM *a.*]. **1951** *Jrnl. Ecol.* XXXIX. 172 In a random distribution the variance is equal to the mean, and the variance divided by the mean..can be used to test departures from a random distribution. **1952**, etc. [see **quota sample*]. **1953** J. B. CARROLL *Study of Language* vii. 204 Communication theory is forced to regard messages as random processes. *Ibid.* 245 We use the term *random process* in the statistical sense: a random process is the sampling at random from a population of *potential* events. **1954** T. W. ANDERSON in P. F. Lazarsfeld *Math. Thinking in Social Sci.* i. 35 Since each individual's sequence of opinions is a random variable (i.e., there is a probability attached to each possible sequence), the total number of individuals holding a given sequence is a random variable. **1954** L. L. BERANEK *Acoustics* xiii. 393 Random noise is an acoustical quantity (*e.g.*, sound pressure) or an electrical quantity (*e.g.*, voltage) whose instantaneous amplitudes occur, as a function of time, according to a normal (Gaussian) distribution curve. A common random noise is that resulting from the random motion of molecules of the air... Random noise need not have a flat (uniform) frequency spectrum. *Ibid.*, White noise need not be random. **1959** *Oxf. Univ. Gaz.* 5 Mar. 678/1 Random variates, probability, and likelihood. **1963** B. FOZARD *Instrumentation & Control of Nuclear Reactors* vii. 71 Radioactive disintegrations are truly random, *i.e.* the probability of a disintegration is independent of the occurrence of other events. **1967** C. BERNERS-LEE in Wills & Yearsley *Handbk. Managem. Technol.* 5 In an agricultural experiment to determine the effect of two different fertilizers, *N* and *P* for instance, the classical approach would be to compare unfertilized plots with suitably chosen random selections of plots fertilized with *N*; also to compare with the unfertilized plots a number of plots fertilized only with *P*. **1967** G. WILLS in *Ibid.* 186 Random samples..ensure that if we are drawing a sample from the 27,000 paint retailers in the United Kingdom each retailer would have an equal chance of being selected. This is *not* what is generally meant in common parlance by 'random', but it is what the statistician means. **1968** P. A. P. MORAN *Introd. Probability Theory* i. 6 A random variable is also sometimes called a 'variate'. *Ibid.* x. 459 The study of random walks is the study of the sums of random variables, these variables varying in complexity from simple independent distributions in one dimension to random variables of a much more complicated character. **1970** W. B. DAVENPORT *Random Processes* ix. 299 Such an infinite family of random variables is commonly called a random sequence or random process (or stochastic sequence or stochastic process). **1971** [see **quota method*]. **1973** LORD & ROBINSON tr. *Kuttruff's Room Acoustics* viii. 211 The room under investigation..is excited by stationary random noise..with a large frequency bandwidth. **1973** F. E. FISCHER *Fund. Statistical Concepts* vii. 139 We can think of most discrete random variables as counts (how many heads, children, spades, or accidents?) and most continuous random variables as measures (how tall, long, heavy, or intelligent?). **1975** R. B. ELLIS *Statistical Inference* ii. 17 What counts is making sure that the sample really is random, that at any time any item in the population has as much chance of being chosen as any other item in the population. **1975** *Sci. Amer.* May 48/3 A series of numbers is random if the smallest algorithm capable of specifying it to a computer has about the same number of bits of information as the series itself. **1977** *Private Eye* 1 Apr. 5/2 The naive random walk theory..rules out the application of any device based upon the movement of past prices in the market. **1978** *Sci. Amer.* Apr. 71/2 One way to test for the role of chance in such a situation is to devise a Monte Carlo computer program, which generates random numbers to determine the distances and angles between consecutive directional changes of simulated tracks.

c. *Psychol.* Of activity, movements, etc.: seeming to be without purpose or direct relationship to a stimulus, sometimes thought of as an organism's initial reaction to unfamiliar stimuli, and giving way to directed action as learning takes place.

1905 *Psychol. Bull.* II. 251 Fuhrmann noted prevalence of predicative association and of the egocentric factors; moreover, especially in the beginning of tests, random association. **1911** E. L. THORNDIKE *Animal Intelligence* vi. 242 If the movements are really random, they occur by virtue of some force that works at random. **1927** J. ADAMS *Errors in School* x. 304 The knowledge the psycho-analyst acquires by random-answering is knowledge-by-the-way so far as the instructor is concerned. **1927** M. K. THOMSON *Springs of Human Action* v. 74 *Undifferentiated activity* (random movement), among the native tendencies none is more primitive and fundamental than activity. **1934** CROZIER & HOAGLAND in C. Murchison *Handbk. Gen. Exper. Psychol.* 20 It is to be noted that there is obtainable in this way a *measure* of 'random' movements and a key to their interpretation. **1935** K. KOFFKA *Princ. Gestalt Psychol.* xiii. 629 Trial and error may then mean that he gets a 'hunch' from the data... This would no longer be random activity, but activity determined by the nature of the task. **1935** E. L. THORNDIKE *Psychol. of Wants, Interests & Attitudes* ii. 13 The fact of multiple response or varied reaction..has led to the error of assuming that man at least had a tendency to make responses that were random. *Ibid.*, There doubtless is a residuum of behavior that may be called random. **1948** E. R. HILGARD *Theories of Learning* v. 116 Although it was often convenient to talk about 'random' or 'spontaneous' responses, it was not doubted that stimuli were present to elicit them.

5. *random access* (Computers): used to designate a memory or file all parts of which are directly accessible, so that it need not be read sequentially; esp. one in which the access time for any item is effectively independent of the location and the access time of the item last accessed.

1953 *Proc. IRE* XLI. 1264/2 The random-access property also makes it easier to operate input, output, and external storage devices out of synchronism with the central computer. **1967** *New Scientist* 5 Oct. 13/1 This type of memory, in which all addresses are directly accessible, is known as random-access, to distinguish it from the slower but cheaper type which is scanned sequentially, used for backing stores. **1969** P. B. JORDAIN *Condensed Computer Encycl.* 414 The true random-access devices are static memories: core, thin film, electrostatic cathode-ray tubes, electronic. Most of the so-called random-access devices—drum, disk, tape loop, magnetic card file..—are really cyclic access devices. **1971** *Publishers' Weekly* 9 Aug. 24/3 The advantage of random access disc storage is that all required files for a specific application will be on-line to the computer when that application is being processed. **1975** T. W. PRATT *Programming Languages* iii. 87 A random access file is organized as a set of unordered records. Access is through an address that indicates the position of the record on the external device.

C. *adv.* **2. a.** *random-blown, -fashioned, -rubbed* adjs.

1871 TENNYSON in *Contemp. Rev.* XIX. 12 Tristram.. sank Down on a drift of foliage random-blown. **1906** HARDY *Dynasts* II. v. viii. 287 Ephemeral at! the best all honours be,..So random-fashioned, swift, perturbable! **1862** *Illustr. Catal. Internat. Exhib., Industr. Dept., Brit. Div.* II. No. 2253 Castellated circular turret, random rubbed; white quartz.

randomly *adv.* (further examples); **randomness** (earlier and further examples); also **randomi·city** = prec.

1866 J. VENN *Logic of Chance* ii. 30 We must also idealize the 'randomness' of the throwing of the penny. **1921** J. M. KEYNES *Treat. Probability* xxiv. 281 Many important differences of opinion in the treatment of probability have been due to confusion or vagueness as to what is meant by Randomness. **1936** *Rev. Sci. Instruments* VII. 459/2 Fluctuations to be expected due to the randomicity of the counting. **1938** *Nature* 14 May 881/2 Four tests for randomness..were applied to these numbers, with satisfactory results in each case. **1957** P. GREIG-SMITH *Quantitative Plant Ecol.* iii. 51 Departure from randomness of distribution of a species indicates that one or few factors are determining the performance or survival of the species. **1959** *New Scientist* Dec. 1144/3 An interesting point of this arrangement is that the lengths of the delays can be chosen randomly. **1963** H. M. MORRIS *Twilight of Evolution* ii. 44 The natural tendency of all change is to create a greater degree of disorder and randomness. **1963** T. & P. MORRIS *Pentonville* iv. 75 Half the men in each group were randomly selected on the basis of throwing dice. **1972** *Science* 27 Oct. 392/3 Environmental randomicity of various kinds may have important implications in triggering evolutionary sequences that would be impossible or unlikely in non-stochastic environments. **1980** *Jrnl. R. Soc. Arts* Feb. 138/1 The cosmos will end in heat death with all matter randomly diffused.

random (ræ·ndəm), *v. rare.* [f. the sb.] *intr.* To do something at random, to occur at random.

1889 'MARK TWAIN' *Conn. Yankee* xxvii. 349 A thought came randoming overthwart this majestic dream. **1921** R. FROST *Let.* 15 Apr. (1964) 127 She wasn't experimenting, poor thing. She was randoming, as Alisande hath it.

randomization (ræːndəməizē^i^·ʃən). [f. next + -ATION.] The action, process, or result of randomizing.

1926 *Jrnl. Min. Agric.* XXXIII. 510 A process of randomization by which one is selected at random out of the total number of Latin Squares possible. **1934** *Math. Gaz.* XVIII. 294 The process of randomisation has in recent years come to play such a central part in experimental design that it is of some interest to find that it affords a means of resolving one of the oldest paradoxes which arose in discussions of gaming. **1946** G. W. SNEDECOR *Statistical Methods* (ed. 4) 253 The degree of randomization is no longer evident, but the weekly heights and the block differences are brought into prominence. **1960** *Daily Tel.* 23 Aug. 16/5 Because the experiments were made over five years, using a 'randomisation' method, the Australian results were considered by other experts at the conference to be the first to be absolutely conclusive. 'Randomisation' means that clouds are selected in a completely random manner. **1966** *Lancet* 24 Dec. 1371/2 We tested the randomness of these four groups; except for age-distribution, randomisation was satisfactory. **1980** *Times Lit. Suppl.* 15 Feb. 160 A 'genuinely open society' is, presumably, one in which relative mobility chances have been equalized. But how?.. By the randomization of access to the labour market?

randomize (ræ·ndəməiz), *v.* [f. RANDOM *sb.*, *a.*, and *adv.* + -IZE.] *trans.* To render unpredictable, unsystematic, or random in order or arrangement; to employ random selection or sampling in (an experiment or procedure).

1926 *Jrnl. Min. Agric.* XXXIII. 509 The distinction between errors eliminated in the field, and the errors which are to be carefully randomized in order to provide a valid estimate of the errors which cannot be eliminated, may be made most clear by one of the most useful and flexible types of arrangement, namely, the arrangement in 'randomized blocks'. **1939** H. JEFFREYS *Theory of Probability* iv. 192 Most physicists, of course, will envy workers in subjects where uninteresting systematic effects can be randomized. **1958** *New Scientist* 21 Aug. 659/3 Having produced a beam of the required energy, the Oak Ridge group then try to randomise it by firing it into a magnetic bottle produced by two mirror coils. **1959** *Test House Rep.* No. OTL/M1/5/59 (Inspectorate of Fighting Vehicles & Mech. Equipm. Test House. Oil Test Lab.) 4 A programme of two tests on each of the seven oils was arranged and the tests randomised to eliminate bias. **1967** *Listener* 26 Jan. 134/2 A number of years ago Sir Ronald Fisher made a statistical analysis of the problem and came to the unexpected conclusion that the best rule in each case was not to have any fixed rule at all, but to randomize one's actions by an appeal to chance. **1971** *Jrnl. Gen. Psychol.* LXXXV. 172 The order of these pronouns was randomized. **1977** *Sci. Amer.* Sept. 42/2 Assume that the deck of cards is finite, so that an umpire can indeed randomize them.

Hence **ra·ndomized** *ppl. a.*, chosen at random; deliberately made random or unpredictable; **randomizing** *ppl. a.*, generating random output; **randomizing** *vbl. sb.*, the act of rendering random.

1926 Randomized [see *RANDOMIZE *v.*] **1936** *Nature* 15 Feb. 253/1 It is with applications of the principle of testing null hypotheses by means of randomised and replicated experiments that the first nine chapters of this book deal. **1936** *Jrnl. R. Statist. Soc.* Suppl. No. 3. 118 The tendency of deliberate randomizing is to increase the error. **1938** *Nature* 14 May 881/1 M. G. Kendall and B. B. Smith have designed a randomizing machine. **1955** *Sci. Amer.* Feb. 81/2 The idea is to let chance play a role in the choice of strategy, that is, to use a randomized or 'mixed' strategy. **1962** *Times Lit. Suppl.* 2 Feb. 73/3 To randomized numbers where no fancy boggles The Great Boondogglers go. **1968** P. A. P. MORAN *Introd. Probability Theory* i. 44 Decimal digits which were obtained by a 'randomizing machine'. **1970** *Nature* 12 Dec. 1113/1 Each block of twenty trials contained all possible combinations of test stimuli presented in randomized sequence. **1978** *Lancet* 14 Jan. 72/2 The claim that an upright maternal posture during labour improves the efficiency of the uterus to the benefit of both mother and fetus has been investigated in a randomised prospective study.

randomizer (ræ·ndəməizəɹ). [f. prec. + -ER[1].] A device which generates random output.

1974 *Sci. Amer.* Apr. 112/2 It is very easy to use a penny as a randomizer for deciding between two alternatives with probabilities expressed by rational fractions. **1976** *Times*

Lit. Suppl. 13 Feb. 172/4 Chickens..which appear capable of influencing mentally an electronic randomizer controlling the switching mechanism of a lamp.

‖ **randori** (randō·ri). [Jap., lit. 'informal practice'.] A (session of) informal practice in Judo.

1913 E. J. HARRISON *Fighting Spirit of Japan* iv. 65 The non-esoteric branches of *judo* are called *randori*, in which the pupil freely applies his knowledge in open practice.. with others. **1932** —— *Art of Ju-Jitsu* iii. 30 It is not absolutely necessary for the pupil to master all these details ..before beginning '*randori*' practice. **1954** E. DOMINY *Teach Yourself Judo* vi. 63 In 'randori' which is free practice you never find an opponent who is willing to lie passively on his back. **1972** *Oxf. Mail* 1 Aug. 10/3 This initial practice very soon develops into 'randori', the form of training in which most players spend most of their judo time. This involves moving about with a partner.

randy, *a.* and *sb.*[1] Add: **A.** *adj.* **2. b.** Delete *dial.* and add further examples.

c **1888–94** *My Secret Life* III. 280 She'll be randy directly her belly is filled. **1922** [see *PUSSY *sb.* 5*]. **1939** J. STEINBECK *Grapes of Wrath* vi. 69 Fust time I ever laid with a girl..snortin' like a buck deer, randy as a billygoat. **1957** W. CAMP *Prospects of Love* II. v. 62 Suffers from too much sex, if anything—he's a randy old man. **1965** F. SARGESON *Mem. Peon* iv. 87, I was randy myself at your age. But be careful. These native girls can put you right into hospital if you don't take care. **1978** K. J. DOVER *Greek Homosexuality* ii. 38 The gangs or clubs of randy and combative young men.

3. *Comb.*, as (sense 2 b) *randy-arsed* adj.; also with sbs. forming attrib. compounds, as *randy-dog*.

1968 Randy-arsed [see *LENGTH *sb.* 11 c]. **1963** *Times Lit. Suppl.* 18 Jan. 37/4 Harold Barlow is an Amis character ..with that special randy-dog flavour. **1973** M. AMIS *Rachel Papers* 173 Tom, Geoffrey's analogue of my own Sebastian: sixteen, wealthy in pustules, randy-dog smells, sebum-moist hairline, and other adolescentiana.

Hence as *v. trans*, to render (a person) lascivious (*nonce-use*); **ra·ndiness,** the quality or condition of being randy (sense 2 b); lustfulness.

1911 *Conc. Oxf. Dict.*, Randiness. **1953** W. COOPER *Ever-Interesting Topic* 145 Attending Dr Foy's series of lectures on sex was inducing in the boys a distinctly higher-than-usual state of—there is no other word for it—randiness. **1967** A. WILSON *No Laughing Matter* III. 305 This bloody randiness always threatened to suck him down into the vast, empty emotional gulf of Ted's shapeless life. **1976** W. GREATOREX *Crossover* 103 He didn't like randy old sods. He thought randiness should be forbidden after the age of, say, forty. **1961** A. WILSON *Old Men at Zoo* v. 278 You've randied him into the looney bin now..the highest-minded little whore that ever almost gave herself out of charity.

randy, *sb.*[2] Add: (Further example.) Also *on the* (or *a*) *randy*, 'on the spree'.

1877 E. PEACOCK *Gloss. Words Manley & Corringham, Lincolnshire* 202/1 Bill's on the *randy* to-day. **1934** L. MACNEICE *Poems* (1935) 18 Over the randy of the theatre and cinema I hear songs. **1940** DYLAN THOMAS *Portrait of Artist as Young Dog* 67 'Hush! hush! your mother'll be waiting. You must come home.' 'No she won't. She's gone on a randy with Mr Robert.'

ra·ndy-da·ndy. Redupl. form of RANDY *sb.*[2]

1917 J. M. BARRIE *Old Lady shows her Medals* 34, I have a theatre tonight, followed by a randy-dandy.

Raney (rēi·ni). *Chem.* The name of Murray *Raney* (1885–1966), U.S. engineer, used *attrib.* in **Raney nickel,** a form of nickel catalyst first prepared by him (see quot. 1932) which has a high surface area and is used in organic hydrogenation reactions.

First described by Raney in U.S. Patent 1,628,190 (1927).

1932 *Jrnl. Amer. Chem. Soc.* LIV. 4116 The Raney catalyst is prepared by alloying equal parts of nickel and aluminum and dissolving out the latter with aqueous sodium hydroxide. **1940** *Ibid.* LXII. 1687/1 The catalytic hydrogenation of azo compounds at normal temperature and pressure over Raney nickel is not only of scientific interest, but also of considerable practical value. **1964** G. H. HAGGIS et al. *Introd. Molecular Biol.* xii. 325 The cysteine was then converted to alanine with the aid of a catalyst called Raney nickel. **1977** L. F. & M. FIESER *Reagents for Org. Synthesis* VI. 54 The corresponding 1,4-diketones can be obtained by hydrolysis catalyzed by mercuric chloride or by treatment with Raney nickel.

‖ **rangatira** (raŋătī·ră). *N.Z.* Also *erron.* **rangitira.** [Maori.] A Maori chief (male or female), a noble.

1820 *Gram. & Vocab. Lang. N.Z.* (Church Missionary Soc.) 200 *Ránga tíra*, a gentleman or lady. **1824** H. WILLIAMS *Let.* 27 Jan. in H. Carleton *Life of Henry Williams* (1874) I. 35 We told him that *rangatiras* [gentlemen] do not steal. **1843** E. DIEFFENBACH *Travels in N.Z.* II. I. vii. 112 The principal person in a tribe is the Ariki; but as he is *per se* a Rangatira, he is rarely called by the former name. **1855** V. LUSH *Jrnl.* 23 Sept. (1971) 165 This addition to the Native Ministry is a fine, tall and highly intelligent man, and being by birth a Rangatira (a Chief) he has far, far more influence among his countrymen than Rota has, who formerly was but a slave. **1863** F. E. MANING *Old N.Z.* i. 6 The chief..having made some inquiries..such as, whether I was a *rangatira*. **1882** W. D. HAY *Brighter Britain!* I. 253 The caste styled tana, or chieftains, a degree above that of rangatira, or simple gentlemen-warriors. **1903** *Daily Chron.* 21 Sept. 5/1 This lad, Victor Huia, was born in New Zealand thirteen years ago, and by the Maoris was formally created a native chief, or rangatira, being duly decorated with the sacred feather of the huia. **1936** R. HYDE *Check to your King* 146 Maori *rangatira*..promise that in future jury trial shall be observed. **1937** N. MARSH *Vintage Murder* xxii. 242 My grandfather was a deeply-instructed rangitira. **1943** —— *Colour Scheme* ii. 37, I am a *rangitira*. My father attended an ancient school of learning. He was a *tohunga*. **1962** M. K. JOSEPH *Pound of Saffron* iv. 65 I'd like to see old Blennerhassett in a flax mat—some rangatira he'd make. **1967** A. & D. REID *Paddle Wheels on Wanganui* 69 According to local history a rangatira had in decades past been buried in a certain upriver area. **1978** B. MASON in *Islands* Aug. 18 In the past of our people, he would have been a splendid *rangatira*, a glory to his *taua*.

range, *sb.*[1] Add: **I. 2. c.** (*Austral.* examples in *sing.* and *pl.* of sense 'hill' or 'mountain'.)

1839 J. MORPHETT in J. Stephens *Land of Promise* ii. 17 We passed the range at the point where the shingle-splitters have their settlement. **1846** F. DUTTON *S. Australia & its Mines* xi. 297 The Ranges, immediately at the back of Adelaide, are at present the principal locality where this ore has been met with in great abundance. **1864** J. ROGERS *New Rush* 31 How merrily passes the digger's life..To live in the ranges free from strife. **1901** M. FRANKLIN *My Brilliant Career* v. 31 The furnace-breath wind which roared among the trees on the low ranges at our back. *Ibid.* viii. 60 Those trees are Five-Bob Downs—see, away over against the range. **1946** K. TENNANT *Lost Haven* (1947) 6 Alec's father..set up a farm for himself far enough off in the ranges to be out of reach of his father's interference. **1966** 'J. HACKSTON' *Father clears Out* 11 There's a big fire burning left of the ranges. *Ibid.*, It's over the range now.

d. For *U.S.* read *N. Amer.* (Earlier and further examples.)

Ranges were established by the U.S. Congress on 20 May 1785.

1785 *Jrnls. Continental Congress U.S.* (1933) XXVIII. 376 The geographer shall designate the townships..by numbers progressively from south to north; always beginning each range with number one. **1790** *Deb. Congress U.S.* 27 Dec. (1834) 1832 Mr. Clymer wished to know how much land these seven ranges included. **1811** R. SUTCLIFF *Jrnl.* 28 Nov. in *Trav. N. Amer.* (1811) ix. 148 They meted out the tract into divisions and ranges, which are numbered. **1837** J. M. PECK *Gazetteer Illinois* (ed. 2) I. 76 In numbering the townships east or west from a principal meridian they are called ranges, meaning a range of townships. **1960** DAVIES & VAUGHAN *Beyond Old Bone Trail* iii. 23 The land had been split up into townships, ranges, sections, and quarter-sections. Townships and ranges were six miles square. **1977** *Chicago Tribune* 2 Oct. II. 14/6 (Advt.), Section 23 in Chapel Hills Garden South of the North West quarter of Section 21, Township 37 North, Range 13, East of the Third Principal Meridian.

II. 6. a. For '*U.S.*' read 'orig. *U.S.*'. (Further examples.)

1640 *Essex Inst. Hist. Coll.* (1863) V. 170/1 The range of the cattle at the fforest river head. **1851** S. STEPHENS *Jrnl.* 18 Apr. (typescript) II. 507 There is plenty of grass for [stock] there [*sc.* Wairau, N.Z.] and an extensive range, more suited for growing young stock..than the more limited boundary of the farm. **1911** *Daily Colonist* (Victoria, B.C.) 6 Apr. 8/3 Here they were able to learn something about a country where the sheep growers are able to raise their herds on expansive ranges. **1946** *Richmond* (Va.) *Times-Dispatch* 24 Nov. II. 1/4 Turkeys in the Valley of Virginia generally are raised 'on the range', which means that after they're nine weeks..old, in the Summer they're put out in fenced fields with a few shelters or roosts and plenty of room to wander about. **1949** J. NELSON *Backwoods Teacher* iii. 29 He..steals hogs off the range for winter meat. **1963** R. SYMONS *Many Trails* v. 52 When a rancher spoke of his 'range', he meant the natural grazing area around his holdings.

b. For '*U.S.*' read 'orig. *U.S.*' (Earlier and later examples.)

1626 in *Virginia Mag. Hist. & Biogr.* (1894) II. 52, 300,000 acres of land, which will feed such nombers of people, with plentifull range for Cattle. **1959** *Times* 18 May 10/4 There are plenty of range rearers who annually take their pullets off range into straw yards without trouble. **1961** *Guardian* 17 May 3/5 There was insufficient land in Britain to keep sufficient birds on range. **1977** in *Fremdsprachen* (1979) XXIII. 131/1 After a maximum of two years in lay birds on range continue to lay for a further two or three years.

7. (Further examples.)

1866 A. MURRAY *Geogr. Distrib. Animals* ii. 19 Even birds are subject to the same law, although it cannot be expected that rivers should often limit their ranges. **1900** B. D. JACKSON *Gloss. Bot. Terms* 221/1 *Range*, the region over which a given form grows spontaneously. **1951** *Jrnl. Ecol.* XXXIX. 205 By 'range' is intended the geographical area within which, at a given time, a taxon or a plant community is to be found. **1963** DAVIS & HEYWOOD *Princ. Angiosperm Taxonomy* xiii. 425 Species tend to occur in more restricted, and often more extreme, habitats at the edge of their range than in the centre of it. **1975** P. A. JOHNSGARD *Waterfowl N. Amer.* II. 346 No specific information on home ranges of the greater scaup is available. **1980** *Nature* 3 Jan. 15/2 The recurring theme was the problem of identifying the stresses and stratagems of animals exposed in different parts of their range to widely differing environmental conditions.

8. a. (Further examples.)

1942 [see *LEVEL *sb.* 4 c]. **1966** *Oxf. Univ. Gaz.* 23 Dec. 430/1 Important general questions of constitutional arrangements..down to those individual points with which you are familiar... That is the range we have at present.

10. b. (Further examples.)

1892 *Photogr. Ann.* II. 549 Three sets..of apparatus which will prove..to give a range for demonstrating purposes that will embrace most experiments that are required. **1921** *Glasgow Herald* 7 Nov. 11 Manufacturers were called upon to make far too many patterns. In preparing their ranges for the particular season, manufacturers are guided largely by the experience of the seasons which have just gone. **1967** E. SHORT *Embroidery & Fabric Collage* ii. 45 Today there is a wide range of beads and sequins on the market.

c. *Statistics.* The difference observed in any sample between the largest and the smallest values of a given variate.

1911 G. U. YULE *Introd. Theory Statistics* viii. 133 The simplest possible measure of the dispersion of a series of values of a variable is the actual range, *i.e.* the difference between the greatest and least values observed... The range is..subject to meaningless fluctuations. **1948** G. HERDAN *Quality Control* ii. 22 The range is the difference between the greatest and smallest dimensions in one sample of *n* specimens. **1975** A. K. S. JARDINE et al. *Statistical Methods for Quality Control* ii. 15, 1. Range = class mark of highest class – class mark of lowest class; *or* 2. Range = upper class limit of highest class – lower class limit of lowest class... It can be seen that range is not uniquely defined in such cases. **1978** *Nature* 3 Aug. 490/2 Seven normal volunteers (four males, three females; mean age 25 yr, range 21–30) were studied.

d. *Math.* The set of values that the dependent variable of a function can take; the set comprising all the second elements of the ordered pairs constituting some given set.

1914 [see *DOMAIN *sb.* 4 e]. **1959** J. G. KEMENY et al. *Finite Math. Structures* ii. 70 Let $f(x)$ be the age of x, expressed to the nearest year. The range of f consists of a set of whole numbers, starting with 0, presumably including all integers up to 100, and even having a few integers above 100 in the set. **1968** E. T. COPSON *Metric Spaces* i. 19 The set of all points..which are images of points of E is called the range of the mapping. **1977** C. B. ALLENDOERFER et al. *Elem. Functions* iii. 49 The values of the dependent variable constitute a subset of the reals called the range of the function. *Ibid.* 50 It is often difficult to determine the range.

11. a. More widely, the distance anythinh can travel, as (*a*) *Nucl. Physics*, the maximum distance which an ionizing particle of a given energy can travel in a given medium; (*b*) the maximum distance at which a radio tranrmission may reliably be received; (*c*) the distance which an aircraft can travel without refuelling, normally under stated assumptions regarding factors such as speed, air speed, and altitude; (*d*) the distance on the earth's surface which a rocket or missile can traverse from launch to landing.

1904 *Phil. Mag.* VIII. 725 The first breakdown of the radium atom is responsible for the α particle of..the least range. **1906** G. EICHHORN *Wireless Telegr.* vi. 37 Bearing in mind..the enfeebling influence of obstructions and the curvature of the earth, the range of normal installations is reduced to about 300 miles. **1924** *Harmsworth's Wireless Encycl.* 1635/2 It is a common experience for ship sets of only one and a half kilowatts to transmit over a range of 1,000 miles. **1926** R. W. LAWSON tr. *Hevesy's Man. Radioactivity* vii. 78 Fig. 25..shows the tracks of individual α-particles. Almost without exception they are rectilinear, and the ionization produced by the rays ceases quite suddenly, which indicates that they have a definite range. **1928** V. W. PAGÉ *Mod. Aircraft* xix. 818 *Range at economic speed*, the maximum distance a given aircraft can cover while cruising at the most economical speed and altitude at all stages of the flight. *Range at full speed*, the maximum distance a given aircraft can cover at full speed at sea level. **1947** C. F. TOMS *Introd. Aeronautics* iii. 141 The range.. depends on the air-speed, on the initial all-up weight.., and ..on the bomb-load. **1947** *Jrnl. Inst. Electr. Engineers* XCIV. I. 176/1 On the Plan Position Indicator these objects will appear in their correct relative position provided we correct for the fact that radar measures slant range and not plan range. **1949** G. P. SUTTON *Rocket Propulsion Elements* viii. 246 Altitudes above 250 miles and ranges over 300 miles can generally be attained only with single-step missiles having small payloads or multiple-step missiles. **1965** [see sense 11 c below]. **1965** STUHLINGER & MESMER *Space Sci. & Engin.* xvi. 191 The range of a particle can be obtained directly by integrating the reciprocal of the stopping power over the appropriate energy range. **1967** KETCHAM & MARTIN *Propulsion* ix. 197 It is possible to make an approximation for the maximum range of a ballistic missile from the geometry of the elliptical flight path and the intersections with the spherical earth surface. **1968** SANDS & TELLET *VHF-FM Marine Radio* i. 21 The range of VHF transmissions is limited to a little more than line-of-sight distance. **1970** M. SMITH *Aviation Fuels* xxxvii. 256 When boiling occurs, the loss of fuel can be serious both from the viewpoint of lost range and from danger to the aircraft structure from excessive tank pressures.

c. (Earlier and later examples.) Also, a strip of land or sea used for testing rockets or missiles in flight between their launch and return to earth.

1862 *St. Andrews Gaz.* 3 Oct. 3/4 At the rifle range, the corps was divided into two squads, the one party firing against the other. **1900** KIPLING *Let.* 24 July in C. Carrington *R. Kipling* (1955) xiii. 315 We've started a rifle-club in the village... We've got a 1,000 yards range among the downs. **1947** *Jrnl. Brit. Interplanetary Soc.* VI. 191 Some details have appeared of an American rocket-testing range comparable to the projected Anglo-Australian one. **1955** *Times* 19 Aug. 4/6 The crofters last night unanimously agreed to a six-point resolution protesting that the range, which is expected to absorb crofting land in Benbecula and North and South Uist, represented a threat to the Hebridean way of life. **1965** L. E. FOSTER *Telemetry Systems* vii. 283 The range of these vehicles requires an accurate real-time 'picture' of the vehicle position to assure that it does not go beyond the safety corridor of the range and impact on some populated territory. **1971** GREEN & LOMASK *Vanguard* viii. 133 In the fall of 1955 the 15,000-acre missile firing range on the snake-infested and palmetto-covered sand dunes of the

Florida flatlands was completing its sixth year as the..Proving Ground for American guided-missile development.

III. 12. a. Also, a gas or electric cooker, typically with a grill, ring burners or plates, and one or more ovens. Now chiefly *U.S.*

1895 *Montgomery Ward Catal.* Spring & Summer 423/2 Gas range... This range..has four top burners..and is fitted with movable ovens. **1908** *Sears, Roebuck Catal.* 529/2 Ranges,..gas..oil. **1929** *T. Eaton & Co. Catal.* Spring & Summer 416/2 Acme Electric Range... One of the most efficient cooking devices of its kind. **1935** *Words* Jan. 31/2 (Advt.), Entirely automatic gas ranges..with..aluminum cooking burners;..fuel saving oven; sanitary high burner tray (porcelain); choice of closed or open top cooking surface; Astogril broiler in rollout drawer. **1959** *Sears, Roebuck Catal.* Spring & Summer 932/2 Our best Kenmore kerosene-burning range. **1970** *Washington Post* 30 Sept. B13/4 (Advt.), We have everything you'll need to transform your kitchen, including the fantastic Modern Maid flameless electric range with all the newest, most wanted features. **1973** *Sunday Express* (Trinidad) (Suppl.) 1 Apr. 2/5 Today's squared off ranges are designed for a close fit. **1977** *Sci. Amer.* Dec. 51/2 Between them, in ascending order, are a washing machine, a dishwasher, a color television set, a free-standing electric range, a gas clothes dryer, a freestanding gas range, an electric clothes dryer and a refrigerator.

14. e. (Earlier example.)

1726 *Maryland Hist. Mag.* (1923) XVIII. 216, 20 tables Crown glass cutt into Ranges 7 inches high.

h. (See quot.)

1923 *Daily Mail* 28 Apr. 8 Eighty ranges, the young wood of ten acres—a range consists of all but the grown timber of twenty rods—had passed under the hammer.

IV. 16. a. *range boss, -land, management, rider*; **range egg**, an egg laid by a hen which has ranged outdoors for its food; **range war** *U.S.*, a struggle for the control and use of a cattle or sheep range.

1893 W. L. Chittenden *Ranch Verses* 94 The range boss's outfit rides in through the herd. **1922** *Short Stories* Feb. (early issue) 70/2 He dominates everybody but Ben Whitman and.. dad's range-boss. **1963** *Punch* 19 June 891/1 We..keep hens and if they pack up buy 'range' eggs. **1931** *Sun* (Baltimore) 23 Dec. 15/1 Ranchers in the district are unable to care for them [*sc.* starving horses] and the rangeland is covered with snow. **1949** *Daily Progress* (Charlottesville, Va.) 26 Jan. 1/3 The winter snows have..laid the foundation for a good growth of rangeland grasses next summer. **1958** *Yearbk. Agric. 1957* (U.S. Dept. Agric.) 765/2 *Range* (or *rangeland*), land that produces primarily native forage plants suitable for grazing by livestock, including land that has some forest trees. **1961** *Times* 7 Feb. 3/1, 40 million acres of rangeland north of Brisbane. **1969** *Science & Technology* Jan. 49/2 Rangelands is an American term now used throughout the world to describe areas where rainfall is too low or too unreliable for crops or sown pastures. **1976** *Billings* (Montana) *Gaz.* 11 July 1-D/5 The fires apparently were started by lightning and began on the rangeland two miles south of Interstate 90 on the Big Horn-Yellowstone County line. **1979** *Arizona Daily Star* 5 Aug. A4/4 Four fires..destroyed more than 3,100 acres of timber and range land in western and central Oregon. **1972** *Agric. Handbk.* (U.S. Dept. Agric.) No. 435. 1/1 Values for each of the range management practices were determined from published sources and from experience of USDA Forest Service experts in this field. **1979** *Arizona Daily Star* 1 Apr. (Advt. Section) 3/9 Natural resource manager..2 years experience, preferably in range management. **1890** *Stock Grower & Farmer* 28 June 3/4 A few years more will see all the last of the range rider. **1909** 'O. Henry' *Roads of Destiny* xxii. 368, I slapped that old captive range-rider half across his little garden. **1955** *Radio Times* 22 Apr. 44/2 A programme of films.. 'The Range Rider' with Jack Mahoney and Dick West. **1908** Murray & Miller *Round-Up* xiv. 288 We don't want no range-war. **1939** C. W. Towne *Her Majesty Montana* 89 In the days of the big ranges there never was any trouble between the cattlemen and the sheepmen, and there never was a 'range war' between them in Montana. Many of the cattlemen also had bands of sheep. **1976** A. Price *War Game* I. 67 It was a typical feud situation—like a range war in the Wild West.

b. *range-indicator*; *spec.* in radar, as *range (-amplitude) display, gate, mark, -marker, measurement, resolution, ring, step.*

1946 *Jrnl. Inst. Electr. Engin.* XCIII. IIIA. 1559/1 The Range or Type A display is one of the basic forms of presentation of radar information. **1948** K. Ullyett *How Radar Works* vii. 101 Range-amplitude, or type A, display on the CRT of a radar receiver would be of very little use with many modern systems, as the information it gives is not sufficiently accurate, nor can it be deciphered sufficiently speedily. **1967** G. J. Wheeler *Radar Fund.* v. 55 A range gate..is a switch which opens at a time coinciding with a prescribed range and closes at a set time later. **1973** Meyer & Mayer *Radar Target Detection* ii. 29/2 The majority of operational radar detection devices have some collapsing loss. The loss can be caused by..improper range gate width. **1977** *Electronics Lett.* XIII. 416/1 The range gate first resets the tunnel diode D, and any subsequent transition of D which is within the range gate produces a 1 output at the AND gate. **1916** 'Boyd Cable' *Action Front* 131 When the range-indicator told that it was within reach of their shells the first gun opened with a trial beltful. **1948** J. L. Hornung *Radar Primer* iii. 69 A simple kind of range-indicator consists of a cathode-ray tube with a time-base voltage applied to the left and right deflection plates and echo-pulse voltages connected to the top and bottom plates. **1945** *Electronic Industries* Sept. 222/3 *Range mark*, a mark on the CRT screen which indicates distances from the radar set of the various echoes appearing on the screen of the CRT. **1949** H. E. Penrose *Princ. & Pract. Radar* xv. 281 In the simplest calibrating system a generator (range mark generator)..produces at equal intervals of time, short sharp signals or pips.., and these are imposed upon the trace just as though they were incoming signals. **1944** *Princ. Radar* (Mass. Inst. Technol. Radar School) ii. 3 A very common method [of range determination] for search-type sets is the use of range markers generated in the timer. **1977** J. French *Small Craft Radar* ii. 69 Two types of range markers are in common use, the variable range marker giving only one ring which can be set by the operator, and fixed rings which appear at fixed distances usually preset by the Range switch. **1949** H. E. Penrose *Princ. & Pract. Radar* i. 1 When velocity is a known constant and time can be measured, distance can be calculated = velocity × time. This is the basis of range measurement. **1978** R. V. Jones *Most Secret War* xxi. 177 Only later did I find that there was no foundation to our original reasoning that the Y system would involve a beam and a range measurement. **1959** R. L. Shrader *Electronic Communication* xxix. 833 Range resolution is the ability to distinguish two or more targets in the same direction but at different distances. **1970** G. Kennedy *Electronic Communication Systems* xv. 625 Another argument in favor of short pulses is that they improve the range resolution, which is the ability to separate targets whose distance from the transmitter differs only slightly. **1956** D. G. Lang *Marine Radar* vii. 80 Range pulses are applied to the P.P.I. [*sc.* plan position indicator], but as the P.P.I. is intensity modulated and the trace rotates around the screen's centre, the pulses appear as rings encircling the centre of the screen... Fixed rings are known as calibration or range rings, and a variable ring is known as a variable-range marker. **1977** J. French *Small Craft Radar* ii. 71 The output from this circuit is added to the video amplifier, often via a Brightness control or on/off switch so that the operator can check for the possible presence of echoes under the range rings. **1946** *Princ. Radar* (Mass. Inst. Technol. Radar School) (ed. 2) i. 23 Higher precision with a Type A indicator may be attained by the addition of a range step. The horizontal sweep is displaced vertically, producing the effect of a step in the sweep.

d. range beacon = *radio range* (*b*) s.v. *RADIO *sb.* 7; **range-finder**, a device used for the estimation of the distance separating the observer from an object; *spec.* (*a*) *Mil.*, usu. attached to a weapon, to estimate the range of a target; (*b*) *Photogr.*, as an aid to focusing a camera, freq. coupled to the lens (see quot. 1958); so **range-finding** *vbl. sb.* (also *transf.*); **range-plate**, a ring-burner inset on the surface of a gas or electric range; **range-proof** *a.* (*U.S.*), unbreakable by heat from a ring burner on a gas or electric range; **range safety crew**, a team of persons responsible for ensuring the safety of people and structures should a rocket deviate from its intended path after launching by destroying it in flight if necessary; **range safety officer**, the principal member of a range safety crew; **range work**, (*c*) practice in shooting at a range; **range-zone** *Palæont.* (see quots.).

1931 P. V. H. Weems *Air Navigation* xiv. 271 Range beacons may be of the aural type, which operate an ordinary aural receiving set with head phones, or of the visual type which operate vibrating reeds in a special visual indicator. **1935** C. G. Burge *Compl. Bk. Aviation* 503/1 The system.. employs a number of beacons whereby the pilot approaching the aerodrome along the route marked by range beacons is advised of the locality of the 'drome by first an approach marker beacon and secondly by a boundary marker beacon. **1940** A. Black *Story of Flying* xvii. 183 Each range-beacon signal is interrupted every 30 seconds by an identification characteristic. **1872, 1876** Range-finder [in Dict., sense 16 b]. **1916** 'Boyd Cable' *Action Front* 38 He..was..followed by his trumpeter and a man with the six-foot tube of a range-finder strapped to the saddle. **1930** *Pop. Sci. Monthly* Dec. 33/3 A new 'gravity range finder' that clips to the camera bed eliminates guesswork in judging the distance. **1934, 1935** [see *COUPLE *v.* 2 e]. **1958** *Oxf. Mail* 19 May 7/2 *Coupled rangefinder.* This means a rangefinder which you work usually by making two images coincide. It is coupled to the lens, so that when you have focussed the image on the rangefinder the lens is automatically focussed. **1973** *Times* 1 Oct. 16/5 Exactly what the cost of the new tank will be is anyone's guess. One estimate is that it might cost as much as £200,000 by the time one has installed the £50,000 fire control system with its laser range-finder and computer. **1977** J. Hedgecoe *Photographer's Handbk.* 13/1 The range-finder focusing system uses two windows,..one the actual viewfinder and another placed further along the camera body. *Ibid.* 13/2 The Leica CL..is a sophisticated direct vision 35 mm camera with coupled rangefinder. **1890** Range-finding [in Dict., sense 16 b]. **1946** *Jrnl. Inst. Electr. Engineers* XCIII. I. 378/2 A corresponding advance in precision of range-finding was achieved by Pollard in work..on the radiolocation equipment for the laying of heavy anti-aircraft artillery. **1971** *Nature* 16 Apr. 460/2 Range-finding experiments have shown that the maximal tolerated doses of propylene imine and propane sultone, in distilled water,..were 20 mg/kg and 56 mg/kg, respectively. **1954** *Archit. Rev.* CXVI. 270 72B 'Main' gas rangeplate in cast iron and pressed steel, finished in cream vitreous enamel. **1969** *New Yorker* 29 Nov. 109/1 The ware is ovenproof but not rangeproof. **1966** *Electronics* 17 Oct. 37/1 Range safety crews must monitor the handling and launch of a rocket on the ground, and then watch such flight parameters as critical velocity, position and impact prediction for signs of danger. **1965** L. E. Foster *Telemetry Systems* vii. 284 During the transition from aerodynamic to ballistic missiles, the range safety officer found he had need of an impact predictor. **1971** Green & Lomask *Vanguard* ix. 162 The displays in the Central Control room gave the range safety officer a second-by-second picture of the path the vehicle was following. **1908** *Daily Chron.* 16 Apr. 4/6 Some 200 of the London Scottish will be quartered at Aldershot for range work and field exercises, their sergeants sharing the mess of the Gordon Highlanders. **1957** E. D. McKee et al. in *Bull. Amer. Assoc. Petroleum Geologists* XLI. 1880 Vertical and horizontal limitations in the absolute three dimensional distribution of individual taxonomic entities in the rocks of the earth's crust provide the basis for biostratigraphic subdivision of strata into range-zones or zones comprising the total body of strata through which specimens of a particular taxonomic entity..range or occur. **1976** H. D. Hedberg *Internat. Stratigr. Guide* vi. 53 A biostratigraphic range-zone may represent the stratigraphic range of some one taxonomic unit.., or of a grouping of taxons, or of a lineage or segment of a lineage, or of any particular paleontological feature whatsoever.

range, *v.*[1] Add: **I. 4.** (Further example.)

1903 M. Beerbohm in *Sat. Rev.* 16 May 615/2 Suppose that, when he disembarked at S. Helena, Napoleon so 'ranged himself' as to become a gentle, agreeable,..old gentleman.

II. 6. a. (Further example.)

1877 G. H. Lewes *Let.* 27 Feb. in *Geo. Eliot Lett.* (1956) VI. 345 When do you think we ought to issue the 7/6 edition? It would of course be made to range with the edition I speak of.

b. Also *trans.*

1841 R. H. Dana *Seaman's Man.* 79 She [*sc.* a ship] may be ranged a little ahead, or deadened, by filling or backing the cross-jack yards.

IV. 11. c. To cast (one's eyes) over a series of objects.

1862 Mrs. H. Wood *Channings* I. i. 11 The master ranged his eyes round the circle.

rangé, *a.* Add: **1.** (later example.)

1894 Gough & Parker *Gloss. Heraldry* 489 *Rangé*, (fr.): arranged in a line.

2. Domesticated, orderly, regular, settled. Also in fem. form **rangée.**

1893 A. Atkinson *Let.* 6 Feb. in F. Stark *Traveller's Prelude* (1950) ii. 29 He is stolider than ever and getting fat—looked terribly rangé and bourgeois. **1906** W. De Morgan *Joseph Vance* xviii. 149 It [*sc.* a public house] is still the George the Fourth, but the gas-jets no longer sow wild oats of lamp-black—they are *rangés*. **1927** *Observer* 17 July 14/3 Beckmesser (Bruce Anderson) displayed a fine voice,..and was amazingly quick on his legs for a tolerably *rangé* mastersinger. **1931** *Times Lit. Suppl.* 29 Oct. 838/2 Experiences that left her mature, to enter, possibly, on the next stage of her life definitely *rangée*. **1934** 'A. Bridge' *Ginger Griffin* iv. 46 It's possible for girls to be too *rangées*. **1935** *Essays & Studies* XX. 117 The best printers, whose spelling was far more *rangé* than that of even the most scholarly and learned writers. **1941** 'R. West' *Black Lamb & Grey Falcon* (1942) I. 195 That bias would make it very difficult for Slavs ever to settle down under a government, and lead a *rangé* political life. **1951** R. F. Harrod *Life of J. M. Keynes* iii. 131 By comparison with Strachey he was *rangé*. **1952** 'J. Tey' *Singing Sands* v. 78 He listened..to the talk of the two fellow sheep-farmers... Nothing hounded these large *rangé* creatures. **1977** A. Wilson *Strange Ride* vii. 334 Kipling was a..respected writer in France, particularly in *rangé* circles.

ranged, *ppl. a.*[1] Add: **2.** *transf.* Systematically arranged; ordered.

1869 Tennyson *Pelleas & Ettarre* 152 in *Idylls of King* 313 Whose lightest whisper moved him more Than all the ranged reasons of the world.

3. = *RANGÉ *a.* 2.

1899 G. Kegan Paul *Memories* v. 142, I have loved less many more ranged and orderly men.

ranger, *sb.*[1] Add: **1. a.** Also *spec.* = Bush-ranger.

1840 *Sydney Herald* 9 Sept. 2/3 It seems as though the constabulary there, are either too weak-handed or hearted! —for the rangers are still there, and at large. **1862** *Mudgee* (N.S.W.) *Liberal* 28 Nov. 2/6 Down on his knees pops our repentant ranger, and earnestly pleads for mercy for the sake of his wife and babes. **1918** C. Featherstonhaugh *After Many Days* 364 The rangers then went on to the store... 'We have come to bail you up, young man.'

2. a. (Further examples.) Now esp., a warden of a park or resort. Also *attrib.*

1938 R. D. Finlayson *Brown Man's Burden* 40 The rangers had spotted them spearing the trout. **1943** *Amer. Speech* XVIII. 242 As the years went on, the rangers and other forest officers began to help with the good work [of map revision]... One name..was 'Pomas Creek', submitted by Ranger Jim McKenzie. **1966** *Weekly News* (N.Z.) 3 Aug. 7/4 Fiordland's chief ranger..emphasises that the authority's huts are 'spartan'. **1970** *Cape Times* 28 Oct. 3/2 (*heading*) Rangers wanted. *Ibid.*, the Simonstown Town Council is inviting applications from people to act as beach rangers during the summer season at R20 a week. **1973** *Sun-Herald* (Sydney) 26 Aug. 85/3 It is no easy job being a national park ranger. **1976** J. van de Wetering *Tumbleweed* xiii. 132 He became a ranger on a nature reserve. **1978** *Nature* 26 Jan. 343/1 According to accounts of the rangers at Volcan Poas National Park, bushes at the high plateau level, 300–500 m, above the lake, were set on fire.

b. orig. *U.S.* An officer who rounds up straying domestic animals or livestock.

1744 *Pennsylvania Gaz.* 15 Nov. 3/3 Any Person or Persons, who have lost one or more of the following Strays, by applying to William Hartley, of Charles Town, Chief-Ranger for Chester County,..may be informed where to find them. **1796** in G. Imlay *Topogr. Descr. W. Territory N. Amer.* (1797) 535 [The county court] shall also have power to appoint one register and ranger for the county, who shall hold their offices during good behaviour. **1828** *Cherokee Phoenix* (New Echota, Georgia) 27 Mar. 1/2 The ranger shall be entitled to one dollar for every horse so posted. **1886** *Buck's Handbk. Med. Sci.* II. 304/1 In Mississippi the coroner is also the county ranger, and performs the duties of that office. **1886** [see Pound-keeper]. **1926** A. Webb *Miss Peters' Special* 50 The ranger's got the cow.

3. a. (Earlier and further examples.) Also in *sing.*

1670 *Massachusetts Hist. Soc. Coll.* (1800) VI. 211, [I] saw one of captain Willet's rangers coming on post on horseback. **1692** *Calendar Virginia State Papers* (1875) I. 38 [Petition of Lef^{t} David Straughan and] 'eight Rangers' [for pay for services]. **1713** *Colonial Rec. Carolina* (1886) II. 32, I have ordered all our Rangers..to march that way. **1733** *Colonial Rec. Georgia* (1905) III. 90 Captain Macpherson with fifteen of the Rangers..cover'd and protected the new Settlers. **1789** in O. Browning *Despatches from Paris* (1910) II. 169 The strongest proof is given of His disinterestedness by His proposing to resign the Office of Ranger (Capitainerie) of different Districts. **1906** *Westm. Gaz.* 2 June 8/3 Governor Ysabel, of the Mexican province of Senora [*sic*],..will be met there by a force of American rangers from Bisbee... It is thought that the arrival of the Rangers from Bisbee will restore order. **1909** 'O. Henry' *Roads of Destiny* xvi. 257 Standifer himself had served the commonwealth as Indian figther, soldier, ranger, and legislator.

b. Chiefly *U.S.* A member of an élite American military unit established in 1941 for close combat and raiding; = *commando 3 a. Also *attrib.*

1942 *N.Y. Times* 20 Aug. 1/5 The first American troops to receive a baptism of fire in Europe in this war were the men of the United States Ranger Battalion who fought in the Dieppe raid today. It was the first time the name Rangers had appeared in a war communiqué anywhere. **1942** *Newsweek* 31 Aug. 21/3 Mention in last week's communiqués of a detachment of a 'United States Ranger battalion' that had taken part in the Dieppe raid was the first disclosure of the existence of these Commando-type American troops... All Rangers are volunteers, they reported. *Ibid.* 22/1 The Rangers were named after Rogers's Rangers, the rough and crafty Indian fighters of colonial days who battled near the Canadian border. **1961** B. Fergusson *Watery Maze* vii. 180 The Commandos had a number of Rangers, their American counterparts, attached to them for experience. **1976** R. Moore *Dubai* ii. 22 A newly organized unit.., the U.S. Army Special Forces..made up of soldiers who were paratroopers, rangers, and combat men from World War II.

5. In full now *Ranger Guide.* A member of the Girl Guides Association who is in the section for older girls, aged between 14 and (usually) 18. *Ranger Guider,* a leader of a unit of Ranger Guides. Cf. *guide *sb.* 2 d.

1921 G. I. J. Potts *Girl Guide Badges* 2 The Service Star for Guiders and Rangers is worn on a red cloth ground. **1929** *Second Bk. of Ranger Games* 72 This is a favourite game with Rangers. **1944, 1969** [see *Guider* s.v. *guide *sb.* 2 d]. **1969** [see *guide *sb.* 2 d]. **1976** *Ulverston* (Cumbria) *News* 3 Dec. 1/4 She has kept up her membership of the Ranger Guides and still finds time for some needlework. **1977** *National Trust* Spring 21/3 The Ranger Guides of S.E. England were invited to steward, usher and sell programmes. *Ibid.* 21/4 The smartness, efficiency and good humour of the Rangers.. evoked most favourable comment. **1977** *Daily Tel.* 2 June 18 Early photographs showing the Queen, Princess Margaret and other members of the Royal family as Brownies, Guides or Rangers will be among the exhibits. *Ibid.*, The exhibition..also marks the diamond jubilee of the Ranger Guide section. **1977** *Guider* July 319/2 An enthusiastic Ranger Guider will invite older Guides to some of the interesting Ranger activities as 'tasters'.

‖ **ranger** (raŋʒe), *v.*[1] [a. F. *se ranger* (also used) to settle down.] *refl.* To settle down. Cf. *rangé *a.* 2.

Used only in the infinitive form.

1854 Thackeray *Newcomes* I. xxxii. 320 It is high time that Kew should *ranger* himself... I am sure he will make the best husband..in England. **1883** W. James *Let.* 2 May in R. B. Perry *Tht. & Char. W. James* (1935) I. 753 The time had come that I should *ranger* myself. **1924** J. Buchan *Three Hostages* xiii. 182, I heard somewhere you were goin' to be married... What do you call it—*ranger* yourself? **1979** A. Buchan *Scrap Screen* iii. 40 He desired to *se ranger* himself, having sown his wild oats.

ranger (rē^{i}·ndʒəɹ), *v.*[2] [f. Ranger *sb.*[1]] *intr.* To be a ranger.

1909 'O. Henry' *Roads of Destiny* xvi. 263 We fought Kiowas, drove cattle, and rangered side by side nearly all over Texas. **1979** P. L. Sandberg *Stubb's Run* ii. 9 He had rangered in the Sawcut for seventeen years.

rangette (rē^{i}ndʒe·t). *N. Amer.* and *N.Z.* [f. Range *sb.*[1] 12 a + -ette.] A small gas or electric cooker.

1959 *Sears, Roebuck Catal.* Spring & Summer 934/1 Kenmore 20-inch Gas Rangettes. **1968** *Globe & Mail* (Toronto) 5 Feb. 25/9 (Advt.), Wanted to buy. Household furniture, fridge, stove, washer, rangette, urgent. **1977** *N.Z. Herald* 5 Jan. 1–20/4 She cooks on an electric rangette.

rangey, rangily: see *rangy *a.*

ranginess (rē^{i}·ndʒinės). [f. Rangy *a.* + -ness.] **1.** Capacity for ranging.

1872 *Rep. Vermont Board Agric.* I. 213 A 1100 or 1200 lb horse, with bone, ranginess and endurance.

2. The state of being tall and slender.

1965 G. McInnes *Road to Gundagai* xiv. 257 He was..of a Gary Cooper ranginess.

ranging, *vbl. sb.* Add: **1. a.** *spec.* The action of measuring the distance to an object by radar or other means.

1919 *Sci. Amer.* 17 May 511/3 Sound-ranging is a vast improvement [for]..locating hostile points of fire. **1946** *Jrnl. Inst. Electr. Engineers* XCIII. i. 378/2 The foundation for precision radar ranging in fire control was firmly laid in 1938. **1965** Filipowsky & Muehldorf *Space Communications Techniques* ii. 136 The reference frequency of 29⅝ or 32 Mc is transmitted..over the microwave link to the receiver where the ranging equipment is situated. **1970** *Nature* 12 Dec. 1024/2 The Smithsonian Astrophysical Observatory has..smaller instruments for satellite ranging.

rangiora (raŋiō^{ə}·ră). [Maori.] An evergreen New Zealand shrub or small tree, *Brachyglottis repanda,* belonging to the family Compositæ, and bearing large ovate leaves with white tomentum on the under side and terminal panicles of small greenish-white flowers. Also *attrib.*

1868 W. Colenso in *Trans. N.Z. Inst.* I. iii. 38 For wounds..they used the large leaves of the Pukapuka, or Rangiora. **1882** *Trans. N.Z. Inst.* XIV. 357 The Maoris also distinguish the two plants by different names, the present plant being known as Rangiora. **1921** H. Guthrie-Smith *Tutira* vii. 51 Later, appeared slender matapo [*sic*]..and rangiora. **1933** *Bulletin* (Sydney) 9 Aug. 21/2 The large leaves of the rangiora bushes growing near tracks. **1966** *Encycl. N.Z.* II. 785/2 Gums and resins..were obtained from kauri,..rangiora..and wharangi.

ra·ngled, var. Wrangled *ppl. a.*[1]

1924 A. J. Small *Frozen Gold* x. 220 The trail led through four miles of rugged, rangled bushland to the Yukon water edge. **1929** R. Bridges *Testament of Beauty* iii. 84 Nor the rangled shroud that she wove for his sire.

Rangoon (ræŋgū·n). The name of the capital of Burma, used *attrib.* in **Rangoon bean,** the Lima bean, *Phaseolus lunatus* var. *limensis* (see Lima in Dict. and Suppl.); **Rangoon creeper,** a tropical climbing shrub, *Quisqualis indica,* belonging to the family Combretaceæ, native to south-east Asia, and bearing spikes of white, pink, or red flowers having an elongated calyx tube.

1877 G. M. Woodrow *Hints on Gardening in India* (ed. 2) 110 *Quisqualis Indica* (Rangoon Creeper). A straggling shrub, which may be trained to cover a wall..; flowers vary in colour, from white to rose. **1901** L. H. Bailey *Cycl. Amer. Horticulture* III. 1486/2 This [genus] includes the Rangoon Creeper, a tender woody plant with 5-petaled red flowers. **1922** Joyce *Ulysses* 289 The extremely large wains bring foison of the fields, flaskets of cauliflowers, floats of spinach, pineapple chunks, Rangoon beans, strikes of tomatoes. **1928** K. Gough *Garden Bk. for Malaya* viii. 111 Kopsia and Rangoon creeper are respectively a shrub and a creeper with flowers that shade from pale-pink to deep red-pink. **1971** C. Flieger in E. L. Wardman *Bermuda Jubilee Garden* viii. 163/2 Rangoon creeper. A deciduous clambering shrub with very attractive drooping spikes of elongated pink and red flowers, and a perfume that suggests a mixture of ripe fruits. **1972** Y. Lovelock *Veg. Bk.* i. 55 A variety known as Lima bean.., also Tonga, Burma, Rangoon, Java and Madagascar bean, bears large white seeds which are dried, canned and marketed under the names wax or butter beans.

Rangri (rā·ŋgrī). Also **Rangree.** A form of the Malvi dialect of Rajasthani.

1823 J. Malcolm *Mem. Central India* II. xiv. 166 In Central India they learn the Rangree or Hindui dialect, in which business is commonly transacted. **1878** R. N. Cust *Mod. Languages of E. Indies* ii. 49 Sir J. Malcolm..alludes to Rangri as the Dialect of Hindi taught in the schools of Central India... By Rangri he meant at that time Dialects of Hindi, spoken all over Central India, and now resolved into separate Tribal and Political subdivisions. **1908** G. A. Grierson *Ling. Survey of India* IX. ii. 52 The form of Mālvī spoken by Rajputs of Malwa proper is called Rāṅgṛī. It is distinguished by its preference for Mārwāṛī forms. *Ibid.* 53 As stated above, Mālvī, in the Malwa country, has two forms, *viz.*:— Rāṅgṛī..or Rāj-wāṛī, spoken by Rajputs, and Mālvī.., spoken by the rest of the population. **1920** —— *Index of Language-Names* 172 Rāngrī... A form of the Mālvī Dialect.

rangy, *a.* Delete 'Chiefly *U.S.*' and add: Also **rangey. 1.** Also of persons. **a.** (Earlier and further examples.)

1868 H. Woodruff *Trotting Horse* xlvii. 381 The latter was a fine, rangy gelding. **1885** T. Roosevelt *Hunting Trips of Ranchman* 21 The ponies..used for the circle riding in the morning have need rather to be strong and rangey. **1936** F. Clune *Roaming round Darling* xxiv. 252, I counted over four score of rangy mangy looking racehounds all capable of running a kangaroo to earth. **1955** *Times* 20 May 10/5 Some bulls—black and white beasts of the Holmogorky breed, somewhat like British Friesians, but rather bigger and rangier. **1977** J. Bingham *Marriage Bureau Murders* iii. 30 She had been out cubbing one autumn on a great rangy beast. **1977** *Time* 19 Sept. 61/1 The royal government provided no housing materials and no food beyond a few rangy cattle.

b. (Earlier and further examples.)

1876 *Rep. Vermont Board Agric.* III. 215 They were.. light colored, rather rangy sheep. **1899** G. Ade *Doc' Horne* 42 He was considerably over six feet tall, raw boned and rangy. **1910** *Daily Chron.* 18 Apr. 8/3 Truxton King is a tall, raw-boned, 'rangy' American—notice particularly the 'rangy', as it seems to be his chief characteristic—though we don't quite know what it means. **1932** L. C. Douglas *Forgive us our Trespasses* (1937) x. 197 You're rangy enough. Tall as Craig, himself. **1956** C. Willock *Death at Flight* iv. 51 The Americans..would describe such a man as 'rangy'. **1968** J. Lock *Lady Policeman* viii. 76 He's tall, rangy, with skin-tight pants, long dark hair and plum-coloured lipstick. **1971** *Guardian* 28 Aug. 9/1 A rangy 26-year old Australian who walks and talks with equal stamina. **1977** *Time* 3 Jan. 36/3 A freewheeling, gregarious politician, the rangy (6ft. 2in.) Bergland is married to a farmer's daughter and is the father of six children. **1977** J. F. Fixx *Compl. Bk. Running* i. 4 Carver is tall, rangy and sturdily built, but at thirty-three he was out of shape.

Hence **ra·ngily** *adv.*, in a rangy fashion.

1976 'S. Woods' *My Life is Done* 62 He was..very tall.. and rangily built.

ranid (rē^{i}·nid), *sb.* and *a.* [ad. mod.L. family name *Ranidæ*, f. L. *rāna* frog + -id[3].] **A.** *sb.* A frog of the family Ranidæ, which includes typical amphibious frogs. **B.** *adj.* Of, pertaining to, or designating a frog of this family.

1888 *Proc. Zool. Soc.* 509 Our attention was early arrested by the general similarity between the proximal syndesmoses in the Hylids and Ranids and the knee-joint in the higher Vertebrata. **1901** *Ibid.* I. 58 (*heading*) On abnormal ranid larvae from North-Eastern India. **1946** *Nature* 23 Nov. 749/2 In *L[eptodactylus] pentadactylus*..both the uteri and the Wolffian ducts run separately throughout their course as in ranid frogs. **1957** P. J. Darlington *Zoogeogr.* iii. 170 Ranids have evolved in the main part of the Old World tropics. **1974** H. R. Heusser in B. Grzimek *Animal Life Encycl.* V. vi. 397 In true frogs or ranids..the presacral vertebrae are typically amphicoelous.

ranikaboo: see *rannygazoo.

‖ **ranjau** (ra·ndʒau). Also 8–9 **ranjow.** [Malay.] A stake or caltrop of bamboo or iron placed in the ground to pierce the feet or body of an enemy.

1783 W. Marsden *Hist. Sumatra* 278 *Ranjows* are sharp pointed stakes of *bamboo*, of different lengths, stuck into the ground, in order to penetrate the naked feet, or body, of an enemy. **1839** T. J. Newbold *Straits of Malacca* II. xii. 210 A Malay considers himself completely armed with..the tombak (spear), and a quiver of ranjows, or caltrops, at his back. **1936** G. B. Gardner *Keris* x. 118 While the chiefs might have used horses for purposes of display, on account of the *ranjau* or pointed stakes planted in the passes they could not have been employed effectively.

rank, *sb.*[1] Add: **1. a.** (Examples in *Teleph.*)

1924 *Brit. Stand. List Terms Telegraphs & Telephones* 13 *Rank of switches*,..the switches which provide for any one stage of call selection. **1929** *P. O. Engin. Dept. Techn. Instr.* XXV. ii. 6 The number of ranks of selectors is one less than the required number of digits to call a number on the exchange. **1969** S. F. Smith *Telephony & Telegraphy A* v. 119 If more than 1000 numbers are required, another rank of group selectors can be used.

c. A row of public vehicles waiting to be hired, or the place where these stand; a taxi-rank.

c **1843** J. R. Planché *Extravaganzas* (1879) II. 240 My Minstrel Boy for a cab is gone, In the ranks no doubt he'll find one. **1851** [see sense 1 a in Dict.]. **1903** *Daily Chron.* 29 Sept. 3/1 These proposals include the use of such large ranks as that in Berkeley-square as feeders for smaller ones in the vicinity. **1922** *Daily Mail Year Bk. 1923* 74/2 One London firm having an air-garage with machines waiting for hire always on its 'rank'. **1930** D. L. Sayers *Strong Poison* i. 21 The taxi-driver Burke, who was standing on the rank in Guilford Street, was approached by Philip Boyes. **1962** S. Beckett in *Evergreen Rev.* Jan.–Feb. 16, I learnt there were still some cabmen who spent their day snug and warm inside their cabs on the rank. **1974** 'J. Ross' *Burning of Billy Toober* ix. 88 She returned..by taxi... The driver..picked her up at the rank in the town square. **1978** *Taxi* 16 Feb. 2/2 On Alf's return to the forecourt the dozen cabmen who had gathered decided that a protest boycott was necessary and they began picketing the rank.

3. a. *to close ranks*: see Close *v.* 10 b. Also *fig.*

1796–7, 1873 [see Close *v.* 10 b]. **1941** 'G. Orwell' *Lion & Unicorn* i. iii. 35 England..is a family... It has its private language and its common memories, and at the approach of an enemy it closes its ranks. **1948** W. Churchill *Gathering Storm* i. xxi. 382 The tide of events brought with it a closing of the ranks between England and France, and also at home. **1974** G. Hubbard *Quaker by Convincement* ii. i. 68 Some Friends occasionally suggest that a creed might help to clarify our thoughts... At this suggestion the majority close their ranks, and hold firm to their beliefs, which are not to be contained in the strait-jacket of a creed. **1977** *Oxford Mission Quarterly Paper* Jan.–Mar. 16 When surrounded by astronomical numbers of non-Christians, Christians tend to show their solidarity by closing their ranks.

b. (Earlier *transf.* example.) *to rise from the ranks*, of a private or non-commissioned officer: to receive a commission, to become a commissioned officer; freq. *transf.*, to rise from a lowly social, etc., position. Cf. *other *a.* 5 f.

1845 *Punch* VIII. 127 I've flattered Peel; he smiles back thanks... But still he keeps me in 'the ranks'. **1853** Ruskin *Let.* 6 Nov. in M. Lutyens *Millais & Ruskins* (1967) 106 Mr. Beveridge [has]..been effecting singular cures..and rose from the ranks—as Jephson did. **1936** B. Kellermann *Tunnel* ii. iii. 84 There was no doubt about the fact that Woolf had risen from the ranks. **1958** J. Wain *Contenders* ii. 27 Baxter, a harmless bore of about thirty-five, had risen from the ranks, so to speak. **1977** *Times* 2 June 15/7 St. George..is acclaimed as a soldier who rose from the ranks to become a tribune.

5. b. (Further *transf.* examples.) Now freq. hyphened. Cf. *rank-and-file *a.*

1927 *New Republic* 12 Oct. 205/2 The rank and file have grown tired of the persistent effort of the Communists to subvert trade-union discipline. **1939** H. Nicolson *Diary* 14 Mar. (1966) 392 The ignorance of the Tory rank-and-file in regard to foreign policy is as terrifying as the prospect of a gardener suddenly driving a Rolls Royce. **1972** *History Workshop Pamphlet No. 6* 37 In the depression of the later 1870s the demand from the rank-and-file for a policy of restriction became very strong. **1976** E. MACLAREN *Nature of Belief* ix. 91 Professional theologians might refine beyond recognition the bald credal outlines demanded of the rank-and-file. **1976** tr. Wang Chin-fu et al. in *Yenan Seeds & other Stories* 113 You'd better go to the rank-and-file to find out what they think.

8. b. Also in professional, military, and other walks of life. Phr. *to pull rank*: see *PULL *v.* 19 h.

1964 M. BANTON *Policeman in Community* iv. 116 One Carolina City officer had served in a United States army unit which was stationed alongside the Black Watch..and he commented: 'Why, a man with one stripe in that outfit had more rank than a master-sergeant in ours.' **1968** J. LOCK *Lady Policeman* xv. 129 Most days we wouldn't see any rank. **1972** J. R. T. POLLARD in G. W. Knight *Jackson Knight* 10 One who stood above rank,..and took just as much interest in the problems and activities of the..College domestic staff as he did in those of the students and his fellow academics. **1977** *Transatlantic Rev.* LX. 21 Why doesn't he wear his rank on his coat, he had once asked his mother.

9. a. *spec.* in *Statistics*, position in a numerically ordered series; the number specifying the position. Cf. *RANK *v.*[1] 3 b.

1883 F. GALTON *Inquiries into Human Faculty* 53 We are often called upon to define the position of an individual in his own series... In reckoning this, a confusion ought to be avoided between 'graduation' and 'rank', though it leads to no sensible error in practice. *Ibid.* 54 All..ranks stand half a degree short of the graduation bearing the same number. *Ibid.*, His rank of No. 5 will correspond to the graduation 4°.5. **1904** *Amer. Jrnl. Psychol.* XV. 81 Rank has..the useful property of allowing any two series to be easily and fairly combined into a third composite one. **1907** *Drapers' Company Res. Mem.* (Biometric Ser.) IV. 10, I term rank the actual position in order of an individual with regard to any variate in a given series obtained by measurement or observation. If v_1 be the 'rank' of an individual for a given character this signifies that in the observed population there are $v_1 - \frac{1}{2}$ individuals with character greater than x. **1936** *Ann. Math. Statistics* VII. 32 Continuous variates expressing these qualities are likely not to be normally distributed... We may therefore resort to the ranks, ignoring any exact values that have been assigned. **1943** M. G. KENDALL *Adv. Theory Statistics* xvi. 390 The ranks are ordinal numbers and cannot without justification be operated on by the laws of cardinal arithmetic. **1976** T. D. V. SWINSCOW *Statistics at Square One* x. 60 The ranks for the two samples are..added separately and the smaller total is used. *Ibid.* xii. 74 Boys K, L, and M are tied at rank 12.

b. *Linguistics.* The position of a unit in a grammatical or phonological hierarchy.

1961 *Word* XVII. 251 The units of grammar form a hierarchy... The relation among the units, then, is that.. each 'consists of' one, or of more than one, of the unit next below... The scale on which the units are in fact ranged.. may be called 'rank'. **1964** M. A. K. HALLIDAY et al. *Linguistic Sci.* 27 The term used to name the hierarchical relation among the units is *rank*; they can be arranged on a scale, and this is known as the 'rank scale'. **1965** J. C. CATFORD *Linguistic Theory of Translation* i. 6 The units of grammar or of phonology operate in hierarchies—'larger' or more inclusive units being made up of 'smaller' or less inclusive units. They form a scale of units at different ranks... The sentence is a unit of higher rank than the clause. *Ibid.* 9 The concept of rank..is an important one both in theoretical linguistics and..translation-theory. **1971** R. A. HUDSON *Eng. Complex Sentences* ii. 70 What a grammar will contain..is not a number of different system-networks, each for a different 'rank' (clause, phrase, etc.) or a different environment (subject, main verb, etc.), but a single network which includes all the grammatical systems needed for the language. **1977** *Language* LIII. 192 Although admitting that a sentence could be regarded as a special type of clause, she in fact treats them as distinct ranks.

9*. *Math.* Used variously, at the discretion of the author, to denote some integer that characterizes the entity being discussed.

1835 *Rep. Brit. Assoc. Adv. Sci. 1834* 528 *i* in the denominator..names, according to the author's nomenclature, the 'order' of the logarithm, and *i*, in the numerator, its 'rank' in that order. **1913** C. E. CULLIS *Matrices & Determinoids* ix. 265 The rank of the matrix *A* is the greatest order which a non-vanishing derived determinant can have. **1914** H. HILTON *Homogeneous Linear Substitutions* ii. 50 Suppose that..the determinant itself and all the 1st, 2nd,.., $(m-r-1)$-th minors vanish, but that not all the $(m-r)$-th minors vanish. Then the determinant is said to be of rank *r*. If the determinant does not vanish, it is of rank *m*; if the determinant vanishes but not every first minor vanishes, the determinant is of rank $m-1$', and so on. **1941** [see *NULLITY 6]. **1953** N. JACOBSON *Lect. Abstr. Algebra* II. i. 22 Any two maximal linearly independent subsets of a set *S* have the same cardinal number. We call this number the rank of the set *S*. **1965** J. J. ROTMAN *Theory of Groups* xi. 241 If *F* is a free group, the rank of *F*, $r(F)$, is the number of elements in a free set of generators. **1972** R. J. WILSON *Introd. Graph Theory* viii. 121 The rank $\rho(A)$ of a subset *A* of *E* is defined as the number of elements in the largest partial transversal of $\mathscr{S}$ contained in *A*. **1979** *Proc. London Math. Soc.* XXXVIII. 532 Let *G* be a reduced torsion-free abelian group of finite rank.

9.** *Petrol.* The degree of metamorphic maturity or hardness, esp. of coal.

1914 *Bull. U.S. Bureau of Mines* No. 38. 4 The higher rank ('grade') of coal differs from the respective lower rank of the same genetic type by the effects of the greater metamorphism and devolatilization to which the higher rank of coal has been subjected. **1928** *Jrnl. Chem. Soc.* 2971 What we have termed the 'degree of coalification' of a coal is sometimes..termed its 'rank', a coal of lowest rank being one in which the processes of coalification..have had least result. **1948** *Mem. Geol. Soc. Amer.* No. 30. 55 Metamorphic rank and grade are synonymous terms denoting the stage of metamorphism reached. **1964** A. NELSON *Dict. Mining* 360 Lignite is a low-rank coal whilst anthracite is a high-rank coal. *Ibid.* 89 Coal rank indicates the stage of coalification which any particular coal deposit has reached between peat at one end of the scale and anthracite at the other. *Ibid.* 218 Hitt..came to the conclusion that in a vertical succession at any point in the coalfield the rank of the coals increased with the depth. **1976** *Nature* 1 July 48/1 Coals of various ranks have been treated in electrical arcs. **1979** *Sci. Amer.* Jan. 29/3 When adjustments are made for the inferior heating value of the lower ranks, the recoverable tonnage comes to about 600 billion tons of hard-coal equivalent, enough for more than 200 years' consumption at current rates.

10. (sense 3) *rank-closing*; (sense 8) *rank badge, -class, -holder, -mark, tab*; (sense *9 b) *rank-scale, -unit*; *rank-based, -bound* adjs.; **rank correlation** *Statistics*, the correlation between two ways of assigning ranks to the members of a set; **rank difference** *Statistics*, the difference between two ranks assigned to the same thing; freq. *attrib.* Also *RANK ORDER.

1961 *Men Only* June 37/2 His eyes flicked contemptuously to the rank badges on his right sleeve. **1975** T. ALLBEURY *Special Collection* v. 32 Wehrmacht men..with their insignia and rank badges torn off. **1966** G. N. LEECH *Eng. in Advertising* ii. 11 A rank-based description avoids these confusions, because of the insistence that each sentence should be fully described at all ranks. **1965** J. C. CATFORD *Linguistic Theory of Translation* ii. 25 The cruder attempts at Machine Translation are rank-bound in this sense..; that is, they set up word-to-word or morpheme-to-morpheme equivalences, but not equivalences between high-rank units such as the group, clause or sentence. **1968** *Meta* XIII. 7 *Replacement*..may be *rank-bound* (as when only word-to-word equivalences are sought) or unbounded (as when equivalences occur between higher rank units such as sentences). **1930** C. G. SELIGMAN *Races of Africa* ix. 221 The Akamba have age-grades, and within them rank-classes. **1966** *New Society* 12 May 5/3 Rank-closing had generally made the seamen as solid as a filled-in ditch... But there was more to the solidarity than just the rank-closing. **1907** *Drapers' Company Res. Mem.* (Biometric Ser.) IV. 25 No two rank correlations are in the least reliable or comparable unless we assume that the frequency distributions are of the same general character..provided by the hypothesis of normal distribution. *Ibid.* 3 Dr. Spearman has suggested that rank in a series should be the character correlated, but he has not taken this rank correlation as merely the stepping stone..to reach the true correlation. **1943** M. G. KENDALL *Adv. Theory of Statistics* xvi. 391 A second coefficient of rank correlation which has certain advantages may be obtained as follows. *Ibid.* 408 Up to this point we have considered the problem of rank correlation without reference to any variate system which might underlie the rankings. **1977** S. A. BOOK *Statistics* xi. 427 The technique, called the Spearman test of 'rank correlation', requires us to rank each set of data and then compute the correlation coefficient of the ranks. **1904** *Amer. Jrnl. Psychol.* XV. 86 (*heading*) Method of rank differences. **1907** *Drapers' Company Res. Mem.* (Biometric Ser.) IV. 39 Mean square of rank differences will be more accurate than mean positive rank difference. **1972** KAGAN & HAVEMANN *Psychol.* xiii. 485 In some cases it is convenient to use the rank-difference method, which produces a different coefficient of correlation called ρ. **1951** S. F. NADEL *Found. Social Anthropol.* i. 18 As a rank-holder..features of social life on lower levels may be closed to you. **1928** C. F. S. GAMBLE *Story N. Sea Air Station* iv. 76 They were entitled to wear the 'curl' on their gold lace rank-marks. **1964** Rank scale [see sense 9 b above]. **1970** G. C. LEPSCHY *Survey of Structural Linguistics* vii. 124 Along the rank scale five grammatical units (sentence, clause, phrase, word, morpheme) and four phonological units (tone group, foot, syllable, phoneme) are used in English. **1974** 'G. BLACK' *Golden Cockatrice* xii. 212 Janey, in her neat uniform without rank tabs. **1968** Rank unit [see *rank-bound* above].

rank, *a.*, (*sb.*[3]), and *adv.* Add: **D.** *Comb.* **c.** *rank-smelling, -tasting.* **d.** *rank-old* adj.

a **1889** G. M. HOPKINS *Poems* (1967) 179 What being in rank-old nature should earlier have that breath been. **1904** W. DE LA MARE *Henry Brocken* vii. 71 Near by me grew some rank-smelling waterside plant. **1919** 'K. MANSFIELD' *Let.* 21 Nov. in *Lett. to J. M. Murry* (1951) 401, I remember standing in a rank-smelling field. **1921** D. H. LAWRENCE *Sea & Sardinia* ii. 63 A massive yellow omelette..cooked in the usual rank-tasting olive oil.

rank, *v.*[1] Add: **3. b.** *Statistics.* To assign a rank to (*RANK *sb.*[1] 9 a).

1907 *Drapers' Company Res. Mem.* (Biometric Ser.) IV. 25 It is easier to rank individuals than to measure their attributes accurately. **1944** *Jrnl. Anat.* LXXVIII. 185/1 The severity of the inflammation can easily be ranked, i.e. given an ordinal number. **1951** BROOKES & DICK *Introd. Statistical Meth.* ix. 221 It is possible to rank depths of colour without requiring some form of graduated scale, and to rank dimensions of objects..by comparing one with another and arranging them in sequence. **1977** [see *rank correlation* s.v. *RANK *sb.*[1] 10].

5. a. (Earlier and later examples.)

1841 *Southern Lit. Messenger* VII. 766/1, I have Mr. Sanford under my command—I *rank* him,..and then I have charge of the *whole* ship. **1860** *Congress. Globe* 10 Dec. 27/3, I shall..submit a few reasons for this opinion..but not until other Senators are heard who rank me in age, experience, and wisdom. **1904** *Delineator* Dec. 933 The Secretary of State ranks all the other members of the Cabinet. **1907** [see *IMPORTANCE 2 b]. **1976** J. WAINWRIGHT *Who goes Next?* 177 Bear..ranked Sullivan, neck-and-neck—they were both deputy chief constables.

b. *U.S. Mil.* To deprive or turn (someone) *out* of quarters, etc., by virtue of superior rank.

1872 F. M. A. ROE *Army Lett.* (1909) 66 Faye has been turned out of quarters—'ranked out', as it is spoken of in the Army. **1891** C. KING *Trials of Staff Officer* 184 We were 'ranked' out of those quarters presently. **1932** L. H. NASON *Among Trumpets* 13 What's the good of havin' three stripes if you can't rank somebody out of a bunk or horse or something?

c. *U.S. Blacks.* (See quots.) Cf. *RANKING *vbl. sb.*[1] c.

1971 C. MITCHELL-KERNAN in A. Dundes *Mother Wit* (1973) 316/2 'Barbara was trying to *rank* Mary', to put her down by typing her. **1974** H. L. FOSTER *Ribbin', Jivin', & Playin' Dozens* iv. 171 *Rank*, to insult someone. **1978** *English Jrnl.* Dec. 56/1 'We're ranking people out.'..'What does that mean?' I asked... 'We're saying things about other people to put them down,' answered one helpful student.

6. b. (Further examples.) Also in phr. *to rank high.*

1824 MACAULAY in *Knight's Q. Mag.* II. 357 Ovid, Catullus, Tibullus, Horace, and Propertius, in spite of all their faults must be allowed to rank high in this department of the art. **1828** CARLYLE *Crit. & Misc. Ess.* (1840) I. 157 This play should rank high among that class of works. **1885** *Nature* 8 Jan. 223/2 The man who ranks 5th from the bottom of a class of 100 males would rank 10th from the top in a class of 100 females. **1932** *N.Y. Times Book Rev.* 3 Jan. 9/5 Nevertheless, as an imaginative humorist he ranks very high, and his omnibus can be warmly recommended to those who have hitherto been unfamiliar with his work. **1973** *Daily Tel.* (Colour Suppl.) 13 July 9/1 Diplomats caught have ranked up to ambassador.

c. (Further examples.) Also, to qualify *for.*

1899 I. PITMAN *Commercial Corresp.* xix. 197 Statement of Affairs: Cross Liabilities; Liabilities as Estimated by Debtor; Expected to Rank; [etc.]. **1928** *Daily Mail* 3 Aug. 18/2 The new shares did not rank for the interim dividend. **1930** *Daily Express* 22 May 7/4 Mr. Bottomley's amended statement of affairs showed gross liabilities £116,769, ranking at £115,899. **1976** *Milton Keynes Express* 11 June 13/1 There may well be very considerable sums to be spent on essential repairs which will not rank for subsidy aid.

8. *trans. U.S. slang.* **a.** To betray (a person), to give away (in quot. *refl.*). Also, to apprehend in the act of committing a crime.

1929 [see *FUZZ *sb.*[3]]. **1955** D. W. MAURER in *Publ. Amer. Dial. Soc.* XXIV. 175 *Whiz dicks* are on the lookout..to *rank* a pickpocket.

b. To spoil or thwart (an action), esp. in phr. *to rank the play.*

1937 C. HIMES *Nigger* in *Black on Black* (1973) 125 The landlady..had sent Mr. Shelton on up to catch him there in the hopes of ranking Fay's play. **1968–70** *Current Slang* (Univ. S. Dakota) III–IV. 101 *Rank*, to spoil.

ranking *ppl. a.* (earlier and later examples, chiefly in sense 5 of vb.).

1863 *Yale Lit. Mag.* XXIX. 80 His two ranking officers both gone. **1885** E. CUSTER *Boots & Saddles* xiii. 137 The ranking lady had a sabre which her chief had received as a present, and this she waved over the others in command. **1906** *Westm. Gaz.* 4 Apr. 7/2 It was estimated that his [*sc.* the bankrupt's] ranking indebtedness would be about £2,280. **1925** T. DREISER *Amer. Tragedy* (1926) II. II. xlvii. 73 These tall, close, ranking pines. **1931** *Publishers' Weekly* 20 June 2849/1 The publishing industry of this country..now takes a ranking place in the economic structure. **1962** PLANO & GREENBERG *Amer. Polit. Dict.* vii. 141 *Ranking member*, that member of the majority party on a legislative committee who ranks first after the chairman in number of years of continuous service (seniority) on the committee. **1970** E. R. JOHNSON *God Keepers* xii. 132 There was a lot of merit in having the ranking man right where the heat was going to be. **1974** P. GORE-BOOTH *With Great Truth & Respect* 315, I learned it on the afternoon of a Sunday on which we had arranged for a dinner in honour of Sir James Cassels, the new British Chief of the General Staff. The ranking guest was to be General Muchu Chaudhuri, the Indian Commander-in-Chief. **1976** *Washington Post* 19 Apr. B6/5 Six ranking generals carried the coffin to the simple military grave. **1976** H. WILSON *Governance of Britain* vii. 150, I approached Sir John Arbuthnot, then, as the Americans would have put it, 'ranking' Conservative Member on the Committee. **1978** R. LUDLUM *Holcroft Covenant* xv. 175 The offspring of a ranking member of the Third Reich's High Command.

ra·nk-and-file, *a.* [f. *rank and file*: RANK *sb.*[1] 5 b.] **a.** *Mil.* Of or belonging to the rank and file; private; ordinary.

1885 [see *CHEW *v.* 3 g]. **1904** *Westm. Gaz.* 27 Feb. 2/3 Those who know the rank-and-file men of the Russian army will agree. **1907** *Daily Chron.* 19 Dec. 3/3 The memoirs of a rank-and-file man like this are very touching and painful reading. **1966** *Times* 9 July 9/7 Command Orders say.. Rank and File Mess is altered to 'soldiers' mess'.

b. *transf.* Of, pertaining to, or designating an ordinary member of a group (as a political party, union, etc.) as opp. to a leader or principal.

1887 [see RANK *sb.*[1] 5 a]. **1931** *Times Lit. Suppl.* 4 June 437/2 He always assumed that the rank-and-file politician was actuated by his own high motives. **1945** KOESTLER *Yogi & Commissar* III. i. 131 The absence of any rank-and-file influence on the party-line. **1955** *Times* 2 May 17/4 He came in for much criticism for not being in touch with the rank-and-file members of his union. **1974** *Times* 19 Sept. 1/1 No party leader or rank-and-file MP can exclude..the possibility..that..the electorate may once again create a parliamentary deadlock. **1976** *Church Times* 15 Oct. 13/1 More than twenty years ago a refreshing, highly competent and, for rank-and-file Christians in the parishes, most stimulating and encouraging publishing event took place. **1977** *Times* 7 Sept. 4/3 That might be because many rank-and-file union members are unenthusiastic about the so-called war on Grunwick.

ra:nk-and-fi·ler. orig. *U.S.* [f. as prec. + -ER[1].] A member of the rank and file; an ordinary member (of a group, society, etc.).

1940 *Sat. Even. Post* 27 Jan. 82/1 Others assert he never in his life toiled as an active rank-and-filer. **1943** *Sun* (Baltimore) 1 June 10/2 Many of the AFL transit rank and filers—perhaps even many of their union leaders—agree at heart with Messrs. Green and Katz. **1950** E. H. CARR *Bolshevik Rev.* I. ii. 33 Lenin's followers were rank-and-filers with scarcely a known name among them. **1959** *Encounter* Aug. 74/2 No 'ordinary people', no John Doe, Tommy Atkins, rank-and-filer, man-in-the-street. **1966** *New Statesman* 13 May 680/1 Some 30 members of the union's executive are sea-going ex-rank-and-filers. *a* **1974** R. CROSSMAN *Diaries* (1976) II. 63 Three of the rank-and-filers were ultra-left-wingers and my part of the programme developed into a futile shouting match. **1978** S. BRILL *Teamsters* i. 25 Barkett was more involved in the union than most rank-and-filers.

ranked, *ppl. a.*[1] Add: **2.** *Statistics.* Assigned a position in a series.

1907 *Drapers' Company Res. Mem.* (Biometric Ser.) IV. 36 The actual size of organ corresponding to a bracket rank may differ widely from the size really belonging to the ranked organ. **1931** *Biometrika* XXIII. 396 The mean interval between any two individuals in a ranked series. **1937** YULE & KENDALL *Introd. Theory Statistics* (ed. 11) xiii. 247 We arrange the students *in order* of their ability... We then allot to each student a number which indicates his position... The students are then said to be *ranked*, and the number of a particular individual is his rank.

ranker. 3. (Further examples.)

1905 *Daily Chron.* 11 May 4/7 The 'ranker' officer..has been explaining how his bankruptcy was due to expenses connected with his promotion. **1926** A. BENNETT *Lord Raingo* I. xxxi. 143 He regretted his humorous remarks to her about the war..for they took no account of the daily torture of millions of young men, including Delphine's own promoted ranker. **1943** J. W. DAY *Farming Adventure* (1949) xviii. 210 The village and the Army discussed ranker-officers with great candour. There had been two of them at the Hall with a previous unit—an ex-farmer and an ex-sergeant-major.

rankest (ræ·ŋkest), *a. colloq.* (chiefly *U.S.*). Now *rare.* [Irreg. f. RANK *sb.*[1] + -EST, as adj. of superlative degree; cf. RANK *v.*[1] 5 and RANKING *ppl. a.*] Of the highest rank; most senior, 'rankingest'.

1907 B. M. CROKER *Company's Servant* xxiv. 257 All the 'Rankest' or senior ladies, had received their due meed of attention. **1926** *Sat. Even. Post* 6 Mar. 154 As he's the rankest man he'll have to take charge while I'm gone. **1930** T. FREDENBURGH *Soldiers March!* 86 It's very hard on a self-respecting Corporal to be seen publicly with the rankest soldier in the outfit.

ranket(t, var. *RACKETT.

Rankine (ræ·ŋkin). [The name of William John Macquorn *Rankine* (1820–72), Scottish physicist and engineer.] **1.** Used *attrib.* or in the possessive to designate concepts propounded by Rankine or arising out of his work, as **Rankine cycle,** a thermodynamic cycle which describes the operation of an ideal composite engine worked by steam or another condensable vapour, and is used as a standard of efficiency; **Rankine efficiency,** the efficiency of an engine relative to that of an ideal engine following the Rankine cycle; **Rankine's** (occas. **Rankine) formula,** any of a number of formulæ derived by Rankine in his work in various fields; *spec.* (see quot. 1940).

1868 J. BOURNE *Treat. Steam-Engine* (ed. 8) i. 86/1 (*heading*) Rankine's formula. **1891** S. ANGLIN *Design of Structures* xi. 209 Apply Rankine's formula to determine the breaking weight of a wrought-iron hollow cylindrical column, its length being 10 feet, [etc.]. **1896** R. H. THURSTON in *Jrnl. Franklin Inst.* CXLII. 444 Comparing the efficiency of the best modern steam-engine employing saturated steam, about 0·20, with the Rankine cycle, which is that ideal cycle which constitutes the closest approximation to its method of steam distribution, the ideal case giving an absolute efficiency, 0·25, it is found to have, measured by this latter standard, a relative efficiency of 80 per cent. **1897** J. A. EWING *Steam-Engine* (ed. 2) iv. 120 Rankine's formula ought to be applicable when the amount of superheating is very great. **1907** W. H. P. CREIGHTON *Steam Engine* viii. 196 This engine is one which follows the Rankine cycle, where steam at a constant pressure is admitted into the cylinder with no clearance, and after the point of cut-off is expanded adiabatically to the back pressure. **1913** J. DUNCAN *Appl. Mech. for Engineers* x. 237 At present, most designers rely on the Rankine formula coupled with a liberal factor of safety. **1930** *Engineering* 6 June 739/3 The new Barton turbine is 8½ per cent. more efficient relative to the Rankine cycle than the older units. **1933** T. H. TAFT *Elem. Engin. Thermodynamics* ix. 130 (*heading*) Effect on the Rankine efficiency of changing conditions. **1940** *Chambers's Techn. Dict.* 702/2 *Rankine's formula*, an empirical formula giving the collapsing load for a given column. **1954** L. PILBOROUGH *Appl. Heat & Heat Engines* xviii. 313 The Rankine efficiency may be used when determining the efficiency ratio of a steam plant. **1967** *Trans. Inst. Engineers & Shipbuilders in Scotland* CX. 21 As turbine efficiency increases with superheat and decreases with pressure the Rankine efficiency gains are modified accordingly. **1976** T. J. REYNOLDS et al. *Struct. Steelwork* (ed. 14) xi. 237 Using Rankine's formula, find the safe axial load for a 308 × 305 × 97 kg universal column 3·3 m high —to be regarded as having ends fixed—using the usual constraints for mild steel and adopting a factor of safety of 4. **1978** *Jrnl. R. Soc. Arts* CXXVI. 608/2 We have not, however, been complacent about more advanced thermodynamic cycles. We have studied a number of possibilities of achieving higher thermal efficiency than the Rankine cycle used in most of our existing plant.

2. Used *attrib.* to designate a temperature scale in which the zero is identified with absolute zero and the degrees are equal in size to those on the Fahrenheit scale. Also *degree Rankine* (or *Rankine degree*), a degree of this scale; *Rankine temperature*, a temperature expressed in terms of this scale.

1941 H. T. WENSEL in *Temperature* (Amer. Inst. Physics) i. 10 The Rankine Scale is essentially the same scale [as the Kelvin]. Temperatures on the Rankine Scale are simply 9/5 of temperatures on the Kelvin Scale. **1941** L. S. MARKS *Mech. Engineers' Handbk.* (ed. 4) 295 Degrees Rankine (R) = degrees Fahrenheit + 459·69. **1962** J. THEWLIS *Encycl. Dict. Physics* VII. 207/1 On the Rankine scale, absolute zero is zero degree Rankine, the freezing point of water is 491·7° and the boiling point of water 671·7°. **1963** EASTOP & MCCONKEY *Appl. Thermodynamics* i. 8 Note that 1 Kelvin degree is equivalent to 1·8 Rankine degree. **1974** P. L. MOORE et al. *Drilling Practices Manual* v. 131 T_s = Temperature at surface, degrees Rankine.

ranking, *vbl. sb.*[1] Add: **a.** (Later examples.) Also, the outcome of such action; ordering, classification. Also *attrib.*

1903 *Daily Chron.* 29 Sept. 3/1 The provision of additional ranking accommodation [for cabs] in suitable places. **1909** *N.Y. Even. Post* 31 Dec. 4/5 William A. Larned..and Hackett and Alexander..lead the tennis players, according to the official ranking. **1926** W. S. BRUCE *Salt & Sense* viii. 64 The men of money are supposed to be above the men of mind. That ranking is entirely wrong. **1939** A. E. TRELOAR *Elem. Statistical Reasoning* iii. 38 Arrangement of a series of values in order of magnitude is known as ranking. **1948** *Sporting Mirror* 21 May 14/1 According to American world ranking he places one higher than our own Alan Paterson. **1962** C. L. BARBER in F. Behre *Contrib. Eng. Syntax* 28 The complete ranking-order of the ten tenses in my material is as follows: 1. Present Simple Active (64%). 2. Present Simple Passive (25%) [etc.]. **1969** C. DAVIDSON in Cockburn & Blackburn *Student Power* 345 The question of ranking and university complicity with the Selective Service System needs to be tied to a general anti-draft and 'No Draft for Vietnam' movement. **1978** *Taxi* 16 Feb. 17/2 All the Airport hotels refused..to allow ranking facilities on their premises.

c. *U.S. Blacks.* (See quot. 1958.) Cf. *RANK *v.* 5 c.

1958 W. B. MILLER in *Jrnl. Social Issues* XIV. III. 16 The term 'ranking', used to refer to the pattern of intra-group repartee, indicates awareness of the fact that this is one device for establishing the intra-group hierarchy. **1974** H. L. FOSTER *Ribbin', Jivin', & Playin' Dozens* v. 183 In a Brooklyn, New York, secondary school the terms ranking and sounding are still used.

rankinite (ræ·ŋkinəit). *Min.* [f. the name of G. A. *Rankin* (1884–1963), U.S. physical chemist + -ITE[1].] A white, monoclinic polymorph of a calcium silicate, $Ca_3Si_2O_7$, of which kilchoanite is another polymorph.

1942 C. E. TILLEY in *Mineral. Mag.* XXVI. 194 For the new mineral the name rankinite is now proposed in honour of Mr. G. A. Rankin, who has contributed so much to our knowledge of the binary and ternary systems in which it was first discovered as a constituent phase. **1961** [see *KILCHOANITE]. **1966** W. A. DEER et al. *Introd. Rock-forming Minerals* I. 77 Rankinite occurs at contacts between limestone and basic igneous rocks, as at Scawt Hill, Northern Ireland, and Ardnamurchan. **1974** *Mineral. Abstr.* XXV. 322/1 Rankinite occurs in the metasomatic formations of the Anakitsk trap massif, in the Lower Tunguska area [of the U.S.S.R.], where it is associated with other high-temperature phases.

rankle, *sb.*[2] Delete *rare*—[1] and add later examples. Also without article, rankling, bitterness.

1913 H. SUTCLIFFE *Open Road* xviii. 275 She won't get the rankle out of her mind. **1922** *Blackw. Mag.* June 710/2, I had come prepared to find they loved us as much as we loved the Germans—or perhaps the rankle might be unkinder, for we did not lose the war. **1941** B. WEBB *Why does God permit Evil?* 117 Suffering ill borne causes rankle in the soul.

rankle, *v.* Add: **II. 5. b.** (Later *N. Amer.* examples.)

1962 E. LUCIA *Klondike Kate* vii. 142 It probably rankled a great many of them just to patronize his theatres. **1971** *Daily Colonist* (Victoria, B.C.) 31 Oct. 4/1 The demonstrations of glee..which understandably rankled President Nixon. **1976** *National Observer* (U.S.) 19 June 7/2 Rome's unbending attitude towards mixed marriages of Roman Catholics and non-Catholics rankled Anglicans. **1978** *National Geographic* Nov. 627/1 The low sum [of money] rankles many Yakimas, who complain of poor management.

rank order, *sb. Statistics.* Also **rank-order.** [f. RANK *sb.*[1] + ORDER *sb.*] An arrangement of the members of a set in order, with consecutive integers assigned to them. Also *attrib.*

1920 *Amer. Jrnl. Psychol.* XXXI. 32 We are left..with the rank-orders of our psychological quantities, given by reference to a fixed but arbitrary extra-psychological scale. **1959** SCHUELL & JENKINS in Saporta & Bastian *Psycholinguistics* (1961) 441/1 Table 3 presents the rank-order correlation coefficients between the order of difficulty of the tests for the entire group, and for each of the subgroups. *Ibid.*, Table 4 presents the tests on which rank-orders of the three subgroups differed by three or more ranks. **1973** *Jrnl. Genetic Psychol.* CXXIII. 79 Rank-order correlations were obtained by correlating the rank of each student on the original test with his rank on the retest. **1975** Z. GOVINDARAJULU *Sequential Statistical Procedures* iii. 259 One can derive an explicit expression for the probability of a rank order.

Hence **rank-order** *v. trans.*, to arrange in such a way.

1972 *Jrnl. Social Psychol.* LXXXVIII. 169 The concepts are rank-ordered in terms of the pre-GSRI attitude change correlations.

ra·nkshift, *sb. Linguistics.* [f. RANK *sb.*[1] + SHIFT *sb.*] A downward shift in the rank of a grammatical unit (see quot. 1966).

1961 M. A. K. HALLIDAY in *Word* XVII. 251 The theory allows for downward 'rank shift': the transfer of a (formal realization of a) given unit to a lower rank... It does not allow for upward rank shift. **1966** G. N. LEECH *Eng. in Advertising* ii. 20 *Embedding* is a shift in rank, whereby a group acts as a word, or a word acts as a morpheme, etc... The nominal genitive is another case of double rank shift: (((Mary)'s aged grandmother)'s faithful servant). The nominal groups 'Mary' and 'Mary's aged grandmother' act as morphemes. **1969** —— *Towards Semantic Descr. Eng.* iii. 52 Rank-shift or downgrading, as forms of subordination, introduce an extra factor of order into semantic structure, so that by reversing the relation of dependence between two predications, one may account for a difference of meaning. **1972** M. L. SAMUELS *Linguistic Evolution* iv. 59 Many later additions to the inventory of English prepositions resulted from a similar process of historical rankshift, e.g. *concerning, regarding, according to, owing to*, and (more recently) *due to.* **1977** *Language* LIII. 192 Although *the men's halls and the women's halls* is a group consisting of two smaller groups, B does not regard this as an instance of 'rankshift': this is restricted to cases where an element of a multivariate structure is filled by an expression of higher or equal rank.

Hence as *v. trans.*, to assign an inferior rank or function to a unit in a grammatical structure. Also **ra·nkshifted** *ppl. a.*; **ra·nkshifting** *vbl. sb.*

1964 M. A. K. HALLIDAY et al. *Linguistic Sci.* 27 In English some clauses are rankshifted and work inside the pattern of a group. If I say 'where I live it always rains', this sentence consists of two clauses, which together make up the structure of the sentence. But if I say 'the house where I live is very damp', the sentence consists, *in its structure*, of only one clause; the clause 'where I live' is rankshifted and operates in the structure of the *group* 'the house where I live'. **1969** *Eng. Studies* L. 36 We shall not go into the question of whether examples here quoted under the heading of headlines with FB structure do not really belong in the section rankshifted clauses. **1969** G. N. LEECH *Towards Semantic Descr. Eng.* ii. 26 There is no defined limit of tolerance to the depth of constituent structure produced by rank-shifting one predication inside another. **1972** *Language* XLVIII. 451 Limitations of space permit both L [*sc.* G. N. Leech] and myself only to raise, but not to answer, the question whether one can express within the notation of logic the operations of rank-shifting and downgrading. **1973** G. W. TURNER *Stylistics* iii. 82 'If you expect to get something good, for nothing, you are likely to get something good for nothing'..in the second clause 'good for nothing' is rank-shifted to behave as one word and become a single qualifier. **1977** *Language* LIII. 192 It follows that *from Glasgow* is rankshifted in *the man from Glasgow*, where it functions as qualifier in a multivariate nominal group.

ra·nnel-balk. *north. dial.* = RANNEL-TREE.

1790 GROSE *Provincial Gloss.* (ed. 2) sig. K4, *Rannel-tree*, cross-beam in a chimney, on which the crook hangs; sometimes called *Rannebauk*; North. **1817** *Edin. Monthly Mag.* June 241 The rusticity of their benisons amused me.— One wished them, 'thumpin luck and fat weans'; another, 'a bien rannle-bauks, and tight thack and rape o'er their heads'. **1859** A. WHITEHEAD *Legends of Westmorland* (1896) 11 Fair shack'd the rannel bawk et swang The keayle pot ower the grate. **1906** H. D. RAWNSLEY *Months at Lakes* 236 A great cauldron of spiced ale..hung on the 'rannel bowk', and was ladled out from time to time into basins and presented to the guests. **1910** W. G. COLLINGWOOD *Dutch Agnes* 47 In the chimney at this time of the year mutton-hams hanging from the rannelbalk. **1931** H. S. WALPOLE *Judith Paris* II. i. 218 He was aware of..sides of bacon hanging, the oak settle screened by the 'heck', the 'rannel-balk' or great wooden beam across the chimney.

rannygazoo (ræ:nigǎzū·). Chiefly *U.S. dial.* or *slang.* Also **ranikaboo, reinikaboo, renicky-boo.** [Origin unknown.] A prank, trick; horseplay, 'nonsense'. (See also quots. 1901, 1940.)

1901 *Dial. Notes* II. 146 *Reinikaboo*.., a newspaper story which is midway between a fake and a statement of fact; a statement of news out of all proportion and almost out of relation to the facts, yet having a certain origin and shadowy foundation. **1907** S. E. WHITE *Arizona Nights* iii. 255 'You —bluffer!' shouted a voice, 'don't you think you can run any such ranikaboo here!' **1917** *Dial. Notes* IV. 328 *Renicky*..or *renicky-boo.* 'He wants to run some sort of bluff or *renicky* on us.' **1924** WODEHOUSE *Bill the Conqueror* xi. 204 I'll hang around for a while just in case friend Pilbeam starts any rannygazoo. **1940** *Time* 14 Oct. 28 Wilkie went to N.Y.C. to tour Democratic Brooklyn... Still he refused to make a..speech, still turned down..pleas ..to let loose with a ring-tailed, rabble-rousing rannygazoo.

1947 *Sun* (Baltimore) 20 Jan. 1/2 A ranikaboo in Arizona would be known as a prank in other states. **1974** WODEHOUSE *Aunts aren't Gentlemen* vii. 59 Her lips were tightly glued together, her chin protruding, her whole lay-out that of a girl who intended to stand no rannygazoo.

ransacking, *vbl. sb.* (Later example.)

1955 H. ROTH *Sleeper* i. 10 What..happened before the ransacking?

ransom, *sb.* Add: **2. d.** (Earlier and later examples.)

1816 SCOTT *Antiquary* I. iii. 59 Could a copy [of Caxton's 'Game of Chess'] now occur..Lord only knows what would be its ransom. **1875** W. ALEXANDER *Sk. Life among my Ain Folk* viii. 133 Some said Sandy Mutch had taken the farm 'at a ransom'. **1932** A. J. CRONIN *Three Loves* II. xviii. 352 But the price of things... It's shameful. Everything a ransom now.

5. a. *ransom demand, money* (later examples), *package.*

1976 R. L. BOYER *Giant Rat of Sumatra* (1977) x. 150 None of the staff..were aware of the ransom demand. **1969** B. MALAMUD *Pictures of Fidelman* iii. 69 The insurance company..would at once kick in with the ransom money. **1976** T. HEALD *Let Sleeping Dogs Die* vii. 130 These particular villains were interested in ransom money, not selling. **1974** *Aiken* (S. Carolina) *Standard* 24 Apr. 5-A/3 Police said a dummy ransom package with a note asking the alleged abductors for more time was delivered according to the instructions Dantzler said his kidnapers had given him.

b. ransom note, a letter sent by a kidnapper or kidnappers to interested parties demanding ransom money or other satisfaction, and specifying the consequences should this not be forthcoming.

1935 M. M. ATWATER *Murder in Midsummer* xiv. 135 Maybe it's a kidnapping, but there's no ransom notes. **1975** D. PITTS *This City is Ours* viii. 28 That ship might explode if it's tampered with. That's what the ransom note says, and I believe it.

ransomite (ræ·nsəməit). *Min.* [f. the name of F. L. *Ransome* (1868–1935), U.S. mining geologist + -ITE[1].] A hydrated sulphate of copper, ferric iron, and aluminium, $Cu(Fe,Al)_2(SO_4)_4 \cdot 7H_2O$, formed as blue monoclinic crystals in a mine fire.

1928 C. LAUSEN in *Amer. Mineralogist* XIII. 221 Ransomite occurs as crusts lining cavities in the crushed rocks and also as small tufts of radiating crystals. **1970** *Ibid.* LV. 729 Ransomite..occurs only in the United Verde mine at Jerome, Arizona where it formed as the result of a mine fire.

rant, var. *RAND *sb.*[2]

ran-tan, *sb.* **2.** (Further examples.)

1936 I. L. IDRIESS *Cattle King* v. 43 When sober, he worked miracles with his limited materials. When 'on the ran-tan', which was every three months, Charlie did the cooking. **1959** G. SLATTER *Gun in my Hand* iv. 42, I remember you on that trip to Nelson for the footie. You really got on the rantan. I bet you never been back to that pub! **1963** A. PRIOR *Z Cars Again* (1964) ii. 22 Wilson had been out on the ran-tan, came home late.

ran-tan (ræn,tæn), *v. north. dial.* Now *rare.* Also **ran-dan.** [f. the sb.] *intr.* To make a noise with unruly singing, and the beating of pots and kettles, at the house of a man who has beaten his wife. Also *trans.*, with husband as obj. Hence **ra·nta·nning** *vbl. sb.*

1866 J. E. BROGDEN *Provincial Words & Expressions Lincs.* 163 *Ran-dan*, to ride the stang (or pole) connected with agricultural lynch-law, usually applied to husbands who have beaten their wives. **1886** *Folk-Lore Jrnl.* IV. 262 He'd ought to be *ran-dan'd* out o' the town. **1891** *Lincolnshire N. & Q.* II. vi. 186 As the news spreads, 'So-and-so threshed his wife yisterday mornin',' it is accompanied by the comment, 'We must 'ran-tan' him to-night.' **1928** *Observer* 26 Feb. 17/2 Seventeen villagers of Lincolnshire have been fined for 'rantanning'... Rantanning is the 'rough music' of kettle and pan, in which the rustic moralist conveys his sense of outraged propriety.

ranter, *v.* Add: **2.** To join (two edges of cloth) with fine stitching (see also quot. 1902).

1902 M. PRINCE BROWNE *Pract. Work of Dressmaking & Tailoring* II. iii. 87 *Rantering.*—This is a stitch used for joining cloth, and the two edges to be joined are put together—level..with the right side of each piece facing; they must then be neatly 'back-stitched' together by hand, as *near* to the edge of the cloth as possible... A cloth which is too thin to join by 'fine drawing', can be 'rantered' together. **1933** J. E. LIBERTY *Pract. Tailoring* iii. 24 (*caption*) Seaming and rantering. An alternative to stoting for use on loose materials (tweeds, etc.).

ranterpike (ræ·ntəɹpəik). Now *Hist.* Also **rantipike.** [Origin unknown.] (See quot. 1948.) Also *attrib.*

1892 L. ANDERSON *Among Typhoons & Pirate Craft* 38 Like the *Ranterpikes*, that used to ply between Liverpool and Glasgow, before the day of steamers, there was no taking in sail here as long as she would stand up to it. **1929** *Mariner's Mirror* XV. 316/1 They were two of the famous Ranterpikes employed carrying pig-iron and heavy castings to Liverpool. *Ibid.*, The correct name is Ranterpike, not Rantipike. **1948** R. DE KERCHOVE *Internat. Maritime Dict.* 579/2 *Ranterpike*, three-masted topsail schooner or brigantine of the River Clyde of about 250 tons... These vessels were generally engaged in the transportation of pig iron from Glasgow to Liverpool. The type is now extinct. Also called *rantipike.* **1973** D. R. MACGREGOR *Fast Sailing Ships* iii. 91/3 The ranterpike rig is rarely referred to but apparently necessitated that one of the upper masts on the fore mast was stepped abaft the other.

ranting, *vbl. sb.* Add: **2.** *attrib.*, as *ranting ground.*

1814 JANE AUSTEN *Mansfield Park* I. xiv. 276 There was some very good ranting ground in [the part of] Frederick.

ranting, *ppl. a.* **2.** (Further examples.)

1894 'MARK TWAIN' *Pudd'nhead Wilson* 333 'Bob Riley' is a common rackety slam-bang secular song, one of the rippingest and rantingest and noisiest there is. **1929** *Oxford Poetry* 40 The ranting numbers do not pierce your ear.

rantipike, var. *RANTERPIKE.

rantipole, *sb.* (and *a.*) **2.** (Later examples.)

1866 *Hansard Commons* 27 Apr. 91 But, notwithstanding all the statements that are made—notwithstanding this rantipole rhetoric—it is not true that the North of England is superior in population or property to the South. **1970** *Times* 7 Jan. 9/7 Four rantipole businessmen lament the problems faced by the wolfish married man. **1976** *Times Lit. Suppl.* 12 Mar. 297/4 [Marlborough's] letters to the duchess are intact and ample but allowances have to be made for anyone writing to that rantipole lady.

ranty (ræ·nti), *a. Sc.* and *north. dial.* [f. RANT *sb.* or *v.* + -Y[1].] Wildly excited; riotous, boisterous, lively; inclined to rant.

1783 in *Eng. Dial. Dict.* **1790** J. FISHER *Poems on Various Subjects* 115, I us'd to be right ranty, An' mak the youngsters spring like bucks. **1867** 'H. LEE' *Mr. Wynyard's Ward* I. I. iii. 94 Master'll be ranty again. We once afore got as much gowld as was worth a pound or two, and you'd have thought we'd found a Californy to hear him talk. **1913** D. H. LAWRENCE *Let.* 10 Feb. in F. Lawrence *Not I but the Wind* (1934) 81 Well, do write about what you think—say Dehmel is ranty and tawdry.

Ranvier (rañvie). *Anat.* [The name of Louis Antoine *Ranvier* (1835–1922), French histologist.] *node of Ranvier* (also *Ranvier('s) node*): each of the interruptions of the myelin which occur regularly along the sheaths of myelinated nerves; (described by Ranvier in *Leçons sur l'Histologie du Système Nerveux* (1878) vii. 110–12).

1881 T. E. SATTERTHWAITE *Man. Histol.* ix. 110 Each fibre has a double contour and is divided at tolerably regular intervals by transverse divisions, which are now known as Ranvier's nodes. **1885** [see *NODE 3 c]. **1912** J. D. LICKLEY *Nervous Syst.* ii. 11 On the outside of the medullary sheath..is a thin structureless membrane known as the neurilemma... It is a continuous sheath and is not interrupted at the nodes of Ranvier. **1966** *McGraw-Hill Encycl. Sci. & Technol.* VIII. 198/2 The all-or-nothing nerve impulse ..was shown to arise at the first Ranvier node adjacent to the ending. **1968** PASSMORE & ROBSON *Compan. Med. Stud.* I. xiv. 4/1 Generally, the greater the diameter of the fibre the less frequent are the nodes of Ranvier, so that the internodal length of a nerve fibre 5 μm in diameter is about 0·5 mm while that of a 10 μm fibre is about 2 mm.

ranz-des-vaches. Add: Also † **rens de vache.** (Earlier example.) Also *transf.*

1773 C. BURNEY *Present State of Music in Germany* II. 125 His lordship next confirmed to me, the account of the *Maladie du Païs* or home-sickness, being brought on by the tune called the *Rens de Vache*, if heard by any of the Swiss troops in foreign service. **1841** C. LEVER *Charles O'Malley* I. xxxvi. 201 Your wild countrymen [*sc.* Irish troops] have heard their *Ranz des vaches*, it seems.

Rao (rɑu). Also **Raw, Row.** [Hindi *rāo* chief, prince, f. Skr. *rājan* king: see RAJA, RAJAH.] In W. and N.W. India: a title given to a chief or prince, and affixed to the names of other distinguished persons.

1799 *Asiatick Researches* VI. 67 The Raw or Rajah is of the tribe Nirooka, and a feudatory of the Rajah of Jynagur. **1801** *Ibid.* VII. 129 The districts adjoining to the eastern parts of the Mahratta territory, were at this term under Inkut Row, a Goand chief. **1845** *Encycl. Metrop.* XIII. 468/2 Mohammed Ali had also allured into his service the famous Morari Rao, chief of the Mahrattas. **1887** QUEEN VICTORIA *Let.* 27 Aug. in D. Duff *Victoria in Highlands* (1968) 362 Fritz..kindly helped me in receiving the Rao of Kutch... The Rao is most amiable, gentle, and unaffected. **1927** *Blackw. Mag.* Sept. 395/1 At the head of each valley squats the domed and generally crumbling fortress of the local 'Rao'. **1978** 'M. M. KAYE' *Far Pavilions* xiv. 224 The Rao Sahib, a brother of the late Maharajah.

Raoult (ra,ul, ra,ult). *Physical Chem.* [The name of François-Marie *Raoult* (1830–1901), French physical chemist.] *Raoult's law*: (*a*) the freezing point and boiling point of an ideal solution are respectively depressed and elevated relative to that of the pure solvent by an amount proportional to the mole fraction of solute; (*b*) the vapour pressure of an ideal solution is proportional to the mole fraction of solvent.

The two statements are closely related. In recent use *Raoult's law* usu. refers to (*b*).

1892 BEDSON & WILLIAMS tr. *L. Meyer's Outl. Theoret. Chem.* 137 The molecular weights of other bodies..can be determined by aid of Raoult's Law in the following manner. **1899** R. A. LEHFELDT *Text-bk. Physical Chem.* vi. 269 This result is included in Raoult's law of the lowering of vapour pressure. **1950** W. J. MOORE *Physical Chem.* vi. 133 An example exhibiting a positive deviation from Raoult's Law is the system carbon bisulphide-methylal, whose vapor-pressure–composition diagram is shown. **1966** GUCKER & SEIFERT *Physical Chem.* xvii. 465 In the last two diagrams dotted lines represent partial pressures calculated from Raoult's law. **1977** MONCRIEFF & JONES *Elem. Physical Chem.* xvii. 379 An ideal binary solution is defined as one in which both components obey Raoult's law over the entire concentration range.

rap, *sb.*[1] Add: **I. 1. b.** (Earlier example in Spiritualism.)

1853 *Spirit Rappings* 4 'Hush!' she exclaims, 'I think I hear a rap.' The spirit-seeker stretches his neck and intently listens, and a sound like the dripping of water is distinctly heard.

II. *transf.* **4. a.** A rebuke; an adverse criticism.

1777 in *Amer. Pioneer* (Cincinnati) (1843) Jan. 17 The post master general..has lately had a rap, which I hope will have a good effect. **1803** P. CANVAS (*title*) A rap for the P.R.A., or three words to Mr. West on his late attempt to pass off an old lady of 76 for a beauty of eighteen hundred and three. **1932** 'A. ROLLS' *Lobelia Grove* x. 227 It's up to us to keep a damn sharp look-out, my boy... We've had a bit of a rap over it, between you and me. **1976** *Cumberland News* 3 Dec. 16/9 A top Carlisle haulage firm got a council room rap yesterday for jumping the gun over planning. **1977** *National Observer* (U.S.) 22 Jan. 16/7 'Mr Fixit' is coming to town, and that is no rap on Jimmy Carter. More than anything else, the American people want government to work.

b. A criminal accusation, charge. Freq. in phr. *bum rap*, a false charge, an undeserved punishment (cf. *BUM *a.*); also *fig. slang* (chiefly *U.S.*).

1903 H. HAPGOOD *Autobiogr. of Thief* (1904) xii. 265 'What makes you look so glum?'..'Turned out of police court this morning.' 'What was the rap, Mike?' 'I'm looking too respectable. They asked me where I got the clothes.' **1910** *New England Mag.* July 587 A complaint or charge of crime is a 'rap' and the complainant is the 'rapper'. **1926** J. BLACK *You can't Win* (1927) xii. 165 We've got two tough raps... In the first place a hypo ain't supposed to be found within a block of police headquarters... In the second place, a hypo ain't allowed to leave Chinatown. **1927** CLARK & EUBANK *Lockstep & Corridor* vii. 45 Edgar is now..in prison for what I honestly believe is a bum rap. **1930** *Sat. Even. Post* 26 July 145/1 We ran into a funny rap out there, kid. On some fool income-tax trick, they locked up seven of my best men. **1936** J. CURTIS *Gilt Kid* 229 There was no burglary rap because the offices had not been inhabited. **1946** 'P. QUENTIN' *Puzzle for Fiends* xxv. 239, I couldn't.. leave them to face the rap for three murders they hadn't committed. **1970** R. D. ABRAHAMS *Positively Black* iii. 79, I was standing on the corner, wasn't even shooting crap, When a policeman came by, picked me up on a lame rap. **1978** S. BRILL *Teamsters* i. 21 The 1961 kidnap-murder rap would move toward trial. **1980** *Outdoor Life* (U.S.) (North-east ed.) Oct. 138/1 Two years ago a local chapter of the National Rifle Association hung a bum rap on Udall as 'likely to vote for gun registration'.

c. An identification (see quot. 1926). *Criminals' slang.*

1914 JACKSON & HELLYER *Vocab. Criminal Slang* 68 *Rap*, ..an identification; a charge of guilt. **1926** *N.Y. Times* 30 May 2/3 In order to understand the news of the day the innocent must..familiarize themselves with new words from the bright lexicon of crime. The newest is 'rap', meaning identification. When one is singled out from a line of suspects as the dip who slid the ticktick, one is the victim of a 'rap'.

d. A prison sentence. *slang* (chiefly *U.S.*).

1927 *Amer. Speech* II. 281/1 *Rap*, sentence imposed by law. **1935** 'E. QUEEN' *Spanish Cape Mystery* xiv. 300 You're in a tough spot. Do you know what the rap for blackmail is in this State? **1956** B. HOLIDAY *Lady sings Blues* (1973) xii. 108, I might explain the first rap was a freak accident. But the second was tougher.

e. Phrases: *to beat the rap* (chiefly *U.S.*), to escape punishment, esp. a prison sentence; *to get the rap*, to suffer a rebuke or scolding; to receive the blame; *to hang* (*pin, tie*) *the rap on*, to charge (a suspect), showing (occas. dishonestly) that circumstantial evidence is incontrovertible; *to take the rap*, to accept responsibility and the consequent punishment (orig. for a crime).

1865 *Atlantic Monthly* Mar. 297/2 He who has the bad taste to meddle with the caprices of believers..gets the rap and the orders of dismissal. **1927** CLARK & EUBANK *Lockstep & Corridor* vii. 42, I told him that the only way for his brother to beat the 'rap' was to..furnish bond and beat it. **1930** E. H. LARINE *Third Degree* ii. 17 Good, honest cops will often take a 'rap' or complaint,..rather than..testify against a fellow cop. **1932** 'SPINDRIFT' *Yankee Slang* 58 Pin the rap on him and make it 'stick'. **1936** J. CURTIS *Gilt Kid* xxvi. 265 You're not going to hang a bum rap on me. **1943** P. CHEYNEY *You can always Duck* iv. 75 You can't hang any murder rap on me. **1952** *Chambers's Jrnl.* May 309/1 Groteman was quite calm. 'Arresting me? Nonsense! In any case, what about you? Do you think I would leave you here to take the rap? I wouldn't do that, Rudolf.' **1953** W. BURROUGHS *Junkie* viii. 78 At the time, he was out on bail, but expected to beat the rap on the grounds of illegal seizure. **1962** WODEHOUSE *Service with Smile* vi. 88 Keep saying 'Is zat so?'..confident that she can never pin the rap on you. **1965** H. GOLD *Man who was not with It* xxvi. 245 How do I know the fuzz aren't waiting back here to tie on a rap for Aiding and Abetting? **1969** J. MCPHERSON

Hue & Cry 56 Damn if I'm takin' the rap for you niggers. **1970** N. FLEMING *Czech Point* ii. 39 He could have pinned that rap on the Australian girl in the PVC outfit any day he cared. **1972** 'H. HOWARD' *Nice Day for Funeral* iii. 51 Suppose somebody gets the rap for killing Frankie? What good will that do her? **1978** S. BRILL *Teamsters* iv. 143 He thought Sammy Provenzano had made a deal with Briguglio to get him to take the rap. **1978** M. PUZO *Fools Die* xx. 226, I even felt that Frank might beat the rap.

5. a. Conversation, talk, chat. *dial.*

1898 R. BLAKEBOROUGH *Wit N. Riding Yorks.* 433 Lets 'ev a pipe an' a bit o' rap.

b. Among American Blacks, a special style of verbal display, repartee, etc. (see quot. 1967). More generally, impromptu dialogue, talk, or discussion. *colloq.* Cf. *RAP *v.*[1] 3 d.

1967 J. HORTON in *Trans-Action* Apr. 6/1 Sometimes used synonymously with street conversation, 'rap' is really a special way of talking—repartee... For example, one needs to throw a lively rap when he is 'putting the make on a broad'. **1970** D. LEE *We walk Way of New World* 52 The national rap deliberately continues, 'wipe them niggers out'. **1970** *New Yorker* 8 Aug. 36/1 Around Jane Fonda you may call it a rap, but here it's still called a powwow. **1971** *Black Scholar* Jan. 17/2 The indigenous, enduring black folk rap, then, is populated with witches, tyrants, befrienders of young children, the strong, the stoic, the quick-witted. **1972** *Last Whole Earth Catalog* (Portola Inst.) 183/3 Ordinarily the talk about their Uncle Emmit would have led D.R. and Marcella on into a general rap about other relatives. **1973** S. HENDERSON *Understanding New Black Poetry* p. xi, An extension of this is the emergence over the past few years of the 'rap' as an authentic Black literary form. **1974** *Black World* Sept. 55/2 The percussion group introduces Roach's rap, whose text is ministerial on 'the power of love'. **1974** H. L. FOSTER *Ribbin'* ii. 51 George is sitting on the steps in the school running a strong rap with a number of girls. **1975** *Time Out* 7 Feb. 43/2 Although their rap between songs seems more suited to a family variety show it can at least be excused as 'professionalism'. **1976** *New Musical Express* 31 July 6/4 Five minutes into the rap and the singer who replaced Ian Gillan three years ago seems prepared to reveal a damn sight more than one of the original members. **1977** *Zigzag* Apr. 46/1 'Dum Dum Boys' opens with a 'whatever happened to me mates' rap. **1978** *Amer. Poetry Rev.* July/Aug. 44/3 Each section of the book ..is an interlude, a rap, a seeming improvisation on some aspect of the blues. **1978** *Verbatim* Feb. 10/1 Each sees Black English as richly metaphoric and imagistic, its speakers adept at creative compounds and the double entendre, frequently extraordinarily skilled in traditional verbal battles and games which are integral to their world, a world in which the baddest dude is often the one with the best rap. (A word..whose meaning in Black English differs from the meaning it took on when assimilated into White English.)

6. A commendation, 'boost'. *Austral. colloq.*

1939 K. TENNANT *Foveaux* II. iv. 176 Everyone wants to be seen with a high-up feller. When I pass the time of day to a cove he feels that's a rap for him, see? **1973** K. DUNSTAN *Sports* 229 And if someone does something good, takes a good mark, give him a rap. Tell him.

7. *attrib.* and *Comb.* (chiefly *U.S. colloq.*), as (sense *4 d) *rap partner*; **rap centre**, the meeting-place of a rap group; **rap club**, a club that ostensibly provides companionship and conversation but is really a brothel; **rap group**, a group that meets to discuss problems; **rap parlour** = **rap club*; **rap session**, a group discussion; **rap sheet**, a police record.

1973 *Tucson* (Arizona) *Daily Citizen* 22 Aug. 28/1 Those turned off by rap centers, afraid of encounter groups and frightened to death by pillows-on-the-floor revelations may be seeking someone to listen to them. **1976** *National Observer* (U.S.) 16 Oct., The committee decided we needed a sort of rap center for teenagers with the exhibit, and we wanted to do something that would be appealing to them. **1973** *N.Y. Post* 22 June 7 In the face of a crackdown on street prostitution many of the girls..are taking shelter in 'rap clubs'—which have replaced massage parlors in the sex-for-sale world. **1970** *Time* 30 Aug. 18 The heart of the [women's liberation] movement is made up of hundreds of 'rap groups', usually formed on an *ad hoc* basis. **1971** *N.Y. Times* 12 June 28 The New York chapter of the Vietnam Veterans Against the War instituted weekly 'rap groups' where men meet and talk about their experiences and feelings. **1972** *Listener* 31 Aug. 270/1 We created..a kind of anti-war community consisting of veterans and professionals. To avoid clinical terminology, we called the programme we established 'rap groups' rather than 'therapy groups'. **1978** *Chicago* June 82/3 Women's center—for lesbians and other women... Rap-group organizing, info on pregnancy testing, birth control etc. **1975** *N.Y. Times* 4 Oct. 1/8 'Rap' parlors, 'sensitivity training' centers and other establishments that use imaginative covers for illicit sex other than the pretense of being a massage parlor would not be affected by the measure. **1971** *Black Scholar* Sept. 37/1 He thought about..the four rap partners he had on his last beef. **1970** *Time* 24 Aug. 12 In every major city, women, most of them young, gather for 'consciousness-raising' rap sessions, the awareness rituals of The Sisterhood. **1973** *Publishers Weekly* 18 June 9 (Advt.), Secret tapings of rap sessions where seven suburban wives tell with startling candor of their search for personal identity. **1974** *Greenville* (S. Carolina) *News* 23 Apr. 16/1 Special-interest rap sessions will be conducted by Campus Scouts from Furman University. **1976** *Sunday Times* (Lagos) 3 Oct. 13/2, I drive straight to the NBC studios for a recording of my rap session on the weekly programme for youths. **1977** *Times Lit. Suppl.* 18 Feb. 179/2 For years Americans have been participating in rap sessions and consciousness-raising groups. **1980** *Underground Grammarian* Mar., The ensuing rap session will be quite long enough to provide yet another day's respite from the tedious and dehumanizing study of language and thought. **1960** *Washington Post* 3 Dec. A3 You will not find violence on his rap sheet. **1976** G. V. HIGGINS *Judgement D. Hunter* xvi. 179 He was convicted... Two charges..were dismissed, but remained on his rap sheet as having been brought.

rap, *sb.*[2] Add: **3.** *transf.* A worthless person, rascal, good-for-nothing.

1771 R. CUMBERLAND *Let.* 4 July in D. Garrick *Private Corr.* (1831) I. 426 Assisted by a jury of printers, compilers, devils, hawkers, and raps of all sorts. **1842** S. LOVER *Handy Andy* xix. 168 What do you mean, you rap?—do you intend to say I'm drunk? **1949** M. MOLLOY *King & Friday's Men* in *Plays of Year 1949* (1950) 400 (Murty drags her violently across the room and flings her on to the sofa.) *Murty* (savage and scared): Biddy, watch over this rap.

rap, *v.*[1] Add: **1. c.** To charge, prosecute; to apprehend with a view to prosecution. *slang.*

1904 'No. 1500' *Life in Sing Sing* 252/1 *Rap*,..to prosecute. **1960** 'M. CRONIN' *Begin with Gun* viii. 93 If I [*sc.* a policeman] hear that Kehely has been getting in our way ..I'll have to rap him.

d. To criticize adversely; to rebuke; to mention unfavourably. orig. *U.S.*

1906 *N.Y. Even. Post* 23 Nov. 5 Football was sharply rapped and rowing was highly praised by President Eliot in his address. **1926** J. KERNEY *Political Educ. Woodrow Wilson* 105 In screamer headlines the conference was rapped as a secret and reprehensible thing. **1967** *Boston Globe* 20 May 2/2 (*heading*) Teachers rapped for failure to understand their pupils. **1973** *Trinidad & Tobago Overseas Express* 28 May 21/3 (*heading*) Bar body raps Sir Hugh for attack. **1976** *Abingdon Herald* 9 Dec. 5/2 (*heading*) Parties unite to rap county.

2. a. (Later example with *in*.)

1968 *Globe & Mail* (Toronto) 15 Jan. 19/6 Keon rapped in Mahovlich's rebound to make it 5-0 and Oliver tipped in Hillman's slap shot during a power play to complete the scoring.

3. b. (Further examples.) Also in weakened sense: to say, talk.

1879 *Macm. Mag.* Oct. 501 A reeler came up to me and rapped (said), 'Now—you had better guy,..or else I shall give you a drag (three months in prison).' **1887** J. W. HORSLEY *Jottings from Jail* I. 7 So I said, 'All right,' but he rapped, 'It is not all right.' **1929** *Sat. Even. Post* 12 Jan. 72/3 'Remember now, don't rap anything to Swinnerton.'.. 'I'm not goin' to talk,' Barr answered. **1951** M. MCLUHAN *Mech. Bride* (1967) 60/2 An indignant girl who raps out, 'You've *had* it!' **1975** *High Times* Dec. 22/3 All those veteran comedians..used to rap about the drunk. **1976** K. ROYCE *Bustillo* xv. 215 'Bustillo still has to get out,' rapped Susumu mildly. **1977** C. MCCULLOUGH *Thorn Birds* ii. 31 That dry old voice rapped a curt question at her.

d. *intr.* In more informal contexts than sense 3 b: to talk or chat in an easy or discursive manner. Freq. const. *with*. *colloq.* (chiefly *U.S.*). Cf. *RAP *sb.*[1] 5 b.

1929 D. RUNYON in *Hearst's Internat.* Oct. 65/2, I wish Moosh a hello, and he never raps to me but only bows, and takes my hat. **1965** E. CLEAVER *Let.* 19 Sept. in *Soul on Ice* (1968) I. 46 In point of fact he is funny and very glib, and I dig rapping (talking) with him. **1967** *Time* 7 July 17/1 Hirsute, shoeless hippies huddled in doorways, smoking pot, 'rapping' (achieving rapport with random talk), or banging beer cans. **1968** *Negro Digest* Jan. 4/2 Karenga is a spokesman..with the power to rap in a manner thoroughly black. **1971** P. KAVANAGH *Triumph of Evil* iv. 35 It really helped me to talk to you, Miles. You're the only older person I know that I can rap with. **1973** S. HENDERSON *Understanding New Black Poetry* 26 The younger poet will usually rap or declaim or sing, but if he wants to create a Black character..he usually turns to drama or the short story. **1975** *Times Lit. Suppl.* 13 June 675/2 Eavesdropping on.. Ishmael Reed when he raps along quite disingenuously about a press dominated by white reviewers. **1978** *Detroit Free Press* 16 Apr. F6/4 Can you rap with students? **1979** *Tucson* (Arizona) *Citizen* 20 Sept. 7A/1 Obviously relishing the opportunity to rap with what Jordan called the 'press biggies from out of town'. **1979** *Quarto* Oct. 3/3 Like a good investigative journalist, Wolfe has raided official sources and rapped with those in the know. **1980** *Oxford Times* 4 Jan. 15/2 She 'raps' (i.e. talks) in the intimate style of Millie Jackson.

4. a. (Further examples.)

1950 [see *crystal-gaze* vb. s.v. *CRYSTAL *sb.* and *a.* B. 2 c]. **1972** S. CHANCE *Septimus & Minster Ghost* (1974) vii. 72 He went into a trance and rapped away like mad.

rapable (rēɪ·păb'l), *a.* Also **rape-able.** [f. RAPE *v.*[2] + -ABLE.] Of a person: regarded as a suitable object for sexual pursuit or assault.

1972 J. ROSSITER *Rope for General Dietz* xiii. 183 He looked so eminently rape-able with his spaniel's brown eyes. **1976** K. BONFIGLIOLI *Something Nasty in Woodshed* vii. 75 I've no intention of distributing cantrips and costly crucifixes to every rapable woman in the Parish. **1977** J. I. M. STEWART *Madonna of Astrolabe* xi. 155 The virgin bloom remained, Duncan. You were very rapable still.

rapadura. (Later example.)

1933 P. FLEMING *Brazilian Adventure* I. xvii. 146 *Rapadura*..is a product of sugar-cane, and is manufactured in rectangular blocks six inches long. It looks exactly like a huge slab of home-made toffee.

rapakivi (ræpăkī·vi, ræ·păkīvi). *Petrol.* Also † **Rapa-, -kiwi.** [a. Finn. *rapakivi* crumbly stone, f. *rapa* mud + *kivi* stone.] A form of granite characterized by plagioclase mantles surrounding large crystals of potash feldspar; orig. *spec.* that occurring in southern Finland. Usu. *attrib.*

[**1784** R. KIRWAN *Elem. Mineral.* I. viii. 149 A stone of this sort which moulders by exposures to the air, is found in Finland, and is said to contain sometimes saltpetre, and sometimes common salt, it is there called Rapakivi.] **1795** *Ibid.* (ed. 2) I. 345 The aggregate of felspar and mica is called Rapakivi. **1906** J. P. IDDINGS *Rock Minerals* II. 487 Quartz..may often be the darkest mineral visible megascopically, as in some varieties of rapakiwi from Finland. **1933** R. A. DALY *Igneous Rocks* viii. 141 Sederholm concluded that the Rapakivi granite in southern Finland is a thick flow, poured out on the surface of a fault trough or graben, the liquid rising along one or more of the faults concerned. **1944** *Proc. Geologists' Assoc.* LV. 74 The typical rock, the rapakivi granite proper, is characterised by abundant large ovoids..of potash-felspar which lie in a matrix of quartz, potash-felspar, plagioclase and dark mica, and, sometimes, hornblende; often the potash-felspar ovoids are mantled by a ring made up of small oligoclases, and it is this striking phenomenon which is usually in mind when the rapakivi granites are considered. **1976** *Nature* 10 June 482/2 The granites locally display the well developed rapakivi texture characteristic of anorogenic granites throughout the world.

rape, *sb.*[2] Add: **3. a.** Also, in mod. usage, sexual assault upon a man.

1976 *Listener* 27 May 683/1 The brutal assault with flagellation and homosexual rape. **1977** *New Yorker* 24 Oct. 64/3 Hardly a year goes by without a gang rape at Green Haven. On New Year's Eve, 1976,..a..man was forcibly assaulted and sodomized. **1981** *Times* 9 Mar. 4/8 The president of the National Viewers' and Listeners' Association ..is bringing a summons against the director of the play.. over the scene of homosexual rape.

c. (Later example.)

1975 *Times Lit. Suppl.* 10 Oct. 1217/5 It is his job to save Juli from the hangman and, in the final court scene, he does it by the public rape of the boy's secret personality and the destruction of his genius.

5. *attrib.* and *Comb.*, as *rape fiend, hound, -novel, -scene*; *rape-happy* adj.; **rape artist**, one who successfully plans and executes a rape or rapes.

1974 *News & Courier* (Charleston, S. Carolina) 28 Apr. E-2/1 The majority result from spur-of-the-moment urges, although 'rape artists' who plan their assaults ahead of time and attack on a regular basis, do exist. **1935** N. ERSINE *Underworld & Prison Slang* 61 *Rape fiend, rape hound*, a person serving time on a rape *rap*. He is held in contempt by all *cons* on other charges. **1973** C. HIMES *Black on Black* 40 You dirty, lying rape fiend, I hope they beat you up. **1953** 'M. SPILLANE' *Kiss Me, Deadly* i. 7 Damn rape-happy dame. You think all guys are the same? **1961** R. WILLIAMS *Long Revolution* 336 The horror-film, the rape-novel. **1961** *John o' London's* 3 Aug. 163/2 A truly Moravian rape-scene in a ruined church. **1981** *Times* 11 Mar. 14/8 The rape scene is handled with a casual certainty that robs it of all offence.

rape, *sb.*[5] **2. b, c.** Substitute for defs.: An annual or biennial yellow-flowered herb, a variety of *Brassica napus* or a closely related species, belonging to the family Cruciferæ, widely cultivated in Europe, North America, and Japan and used as cattle fodder or the source of a seed yielding an edible oil; also known as cole or coleseed. (Later examples.)

1889 G. S. BOULGER *Uses of Plants* III. 133 Rape..yields from its seeds an oil still largely used for lamps and lubricating. **1937** A. F. HILL *Econ. Bot.* ix. 218 The rape..is extensively cultivated in Europe. **1958** GILL & VEAR *Agric. Bot.* ix. 119 Rapes are forms with..rather small leaves. **1970** J. G. VAUGHAN *Structure & Utilization of Oil Seeds* 49 The rapes and mustards are crops adapted to temperate regions and also to certain subtropical areas. **1976** *Western Producer* (Saskatoon) 24 June C7/2 On the other hand a field of rape shining glowing and bright—as yellow as any field of mustard.

rape, *sb.*[6] Add: **I. 3.** *rape-shed.*

1845 G. DODD *Brit. Manuf.* 5th Ser. iv. 76 In a building called the 'rape-shed' are some enormous wooden vessels called 'rapes'.

rape, *v.*[2] Add: **1. a.** (Further examples.) Also *transf.* and *fig.* (in some examples, also influenced by sense 3).

1927 *Blackw. Mag.* Apr. 494/2 The stone walls on either side pressed close, threatening to rape from us our faithful caravan. **1949** WYNDHAM LEWIS *Let.* 6 Aug. (1963) 502 Their women *rape* 'culture' (clubs, 'circles' for weekly absorption of potted literature etc). **1950** D. GASCOYNE *Vagrant* 27 Rockets released tonight rush up to rape the grapebloom sky. **1976** *Bookseller* 14 Feb. 811 (Advt.), Browning, whose life he saved in 1944, is now his rival, raping the Great Land with oil-wells and pipelines. **1977** *Undercurrents* June–July 41/2 We are not going to 'subsistence production' because the capitalists have raped our land and resources. **1978** G. VIDAL *Kalki* ii. 30 Dr Ashok's eyes had a tendency to pop whenever he wanted to rape your attention.

d. Delete *rare*. Also used with a group of people as object.

1972 *Business Week* 18 Mar. 70/1 'Our underwriter raped us,' reports the president of a small New York company that sold $250,000 in stock in 1968. **1973** *Black Panther* 21 July p. B, The Reading administration will continue to rape the poor.

3. Also, with a man as the sexual object and a man or woman as the subject.

1928 D. H. LAWRENCE *Let.* ?28 Oct. (1962) II. 1096 Why do men only thrill to a woman who'll rape them? **1971** *Southerly* XXXI. 6 The first of the series of sexually voracious women who seek virtually to rape him. **1972** *Times* 31 Oct. 2/4 The girls had taken their clothes off and intended to rape him. **1977** *New Society* 1 Sept. 449/2 These women have been confined for a variety of offences, chief among which are soliciting and manslaughter. When a man finds his way into their midst, he is promptly raped. **1977** *New Yorker* 24 Oct. 64/3 A man..claimed he had been assaulted and raped by four other prisoners.

raped, *ppl. a.*^{1} (In Dict. s.v. RAPE *v.*^{2}) (Later examples.)

1960 O. MANNING *Great Fortune* xiv. 180 The raped boys who, once corrupted, sold themselves for a few *lei.* **1977** *Sunday Times* 30 Jan. 38/1 Squads of sexologists, whole studios full of raped girls, etc., etc.

rape-oil. (Further examples.)

1723 J. NOTT *Cook's & Confectioner's Dict.* sig. Kk3^v Fry it [*sc.* a sturgeon] in four Gallons of Rape-oil clarified. **1839** H. T. DE LA BECHE *Rep. Geol. Cornwall* xv. 601 The undermentioned articles are included under the head of Materials and Water-cost..Coals..Rape-oil..Books and Stationery. **1913** V. B. LEWES *Oil Fuel* vi. 177 The number of seconds taken by the oil to flow up to the 50 c.c. mark on the flask is noted, and the results brought into comparison with the viscosity of rape oil, that being the oil with which the apparatus is standardised. **1926** [see *HYDROXAMIC *a.*]. **1937** A. F. HILL *Econ. Bot.* ix. 218 Cold-pressed rape oil is also edible.

raper (rēⁱ·pəɹ). [f. RAPE *v.*^{2} + -ER^1.] One who rapes. Also *fig.*

1927 *Contemp. Rev.* July 85 In woman's eyes this magic creature was phallic man, 'old Adam', the raper, who started life. **1930** L. W. MEYNELL *Camouflage* vii. 102 Notorious in the countryside as the attempted raper of women. **1951** M. MCLUHAN *Mech. Bride* (1967) 129/2 It is the savage dream of Místah Kurtz..the raper and rifler of nations and continents. **1959** M. BRADBURY *Eating People is Wrong* iv. 114 He's sexually unpleasant, Stuart. I call him The Solitary Raper. He's like a walking phallic symbol. **1971** L. P. HARTLEY *Mrs Carteret Receives* 178 Some women locked theirs [*sc.* bedroom doors] even when there was no threat of a nightly visitant, burglar, marauder, raper, or such-like.

Raphaelite. Add: Also **Raf-.** [Back-formation f. PRE-RAPHAELITE *sb.* and *a.*] (Example.) So **Ra·phaelitism** = RAPHAELISM.

1851 RUSKIN *Pre-Raphaelitism* 59 And thus Pre-Raphaelitism and Raphaelitism, and Turnerism, are all one and the same, so far as education can influence them. **1905** W. HOLMAN HUNT *Pre-Raphaelitism* I. 137 The artists who thus servilely travestied this prince of painters at his prime were Raphaelites. **1928** GALSWORTHY *Swan Song* I. xii. 89 Harold is the only Rafaelite... He'll be the last, too.

raphe^2. Add: Also **raphé.** **1.** (Further examples.) Also, a median plane between two halves of a part of the brain, esp. that of the medulla oblongata and that of the tegmentum of the mid-brain.

1811 J. BELL *Anat. Human Body* (ed. 3) II. 410 Betwixt these salient lines there is..a kind of rut, called sometimes the rapha, or suture,..which..forms the accurate division of the two sides of the whole brain. **1858** GRAY *Anat.* 462 Along the middle line [of the corpus callosum] is a linear depression, the raphe. **1882** *Quain's Elements Anat.* (ed. 9) II. 297 Traced backwards into the raphe, the deep arcuate fibres appear to cross obliquely to the other side of the medulla. **1890** A. HILL tr. *Obersteiner's Anat. Central Nervous Organs* 215 All the way up to the third ventricle the median plane of the brain-stem is occupied by fibres which cross one another at an acute angle, but the area in which this decussation occurs is reduced to a vertical plate, termed the raphe. **1939** O. LARSELL *Textbk. Neuro-Anat.* xvi. 191 Some of these masses of cells in the tegmentum are sufficiently distinct to have individual names, but little is known of their individual functions. The most important are the..tegmental nuclei, the reticulotegmental nucleus, the superior central nucleus and the dorsal nucleus of the raphé. **1971** *Nature* 23 Apr. 532/2 Adult rats of both sexes..were anaesthetized..and a bipolar steel stimulating electrode was placed stereotaxically in the caudal mid-brain raphé. **1976** SMYTHIES & CORBETT *Psychiatry* xiv. 266 Lesions of the raphe nuclei of the lower brain stem cause a profound disturbance of sleep.

rapid, *a.*, (*adv.*), and *sb.* Add: **A.** *adj.* **2. a.** *rapid eye movement*, a type of jerky, binocular movement of the eyes of a sleeping person that is associated with a distinctive kind of sleep (REM sleep: see *REM *sb.*^{2}).

1916 [see *SACCADIC *a.* 1]. **1953** ASERINSKY & KLEITMAN in *Federation Proc.* XII. 6/2 Rapid eye movements..were observed to appear from 2 to 5 hr...after the onset of sleep in 10 subjects. **1955** —— in *Jrnl. Appl. Physiol.* VIII. 3/1 As a nomenclature..is lacking, the first type of movement will be referred to as slow eye movement and the second type as rapid eye movement. **1968** *Brit. Med. Bull.* XXIV. 257/1 There is a reduction in the amplitude of the evoked response during rapid eye-movement sleep as compared with slow wave sleep. **1971** J. Z. YOUNG *Introd. Study Man* x. 134 In man phases of sleep somewhat similar to the paradoxical ones of the cat are accompanied by rapid eye movements. **1977** *Listener* 16 June 787/2 What he calls 'active sleep' (which used to be called 'rapid eye movement' sleep). **1980** *Brit. Med. Jrnl.* 29 Mar. 896/1 Only one of the..patients had an episode of sleep apnoea during stage II sleep as opposed to rapid eye movement sleep.

6. *rapid-breeding, -closing, -firing* (further example), *-growing, -hardening, -selling, -travelling* adjs.; *rapid-fire* (further examples); **rapid-transit** (usu. *attrib.*) orig. *U.S.*, (a system of) carriage of persons by fast public transport, esp. within a heavily built-up area.

1922 T. S. ELIOT in *Dial* (Chicago) Dec. 662 The encouragement of the cheap and rapid-breeding cinema. **1969** *Jane's Freight Containers 1968–69* 238/3 An interior rapid-closing floor valve NW 32. **1900** F. P. DUNNE *Mr. Dooley's Philos.* 61 Th' paapers says th' rapid fire gun'll make war in th' future impossible. *Ibid.* 185 In him th' counthry loses a valu'ble an' acc'rate citizen, th' state a lile an' rapid firin' son. **1925** C. CONNOLLY *Let.* 27 June in *Romantic Friendship* (1975) 94 Will you start a rapid fire of postcards etc. if I do, just for a bit? **1969** *Times* 25 Mar. 9/1 The new play relies for its theatrical effect on rapid-fire repartee. **1976** *All about Games* (Com. Org. des Jeux Olympiques) 76 The competition now includes..small-bore rifle shooting, rapid-fire pistol shooting. **1976** *New Yorker* 15 Nov. 120/2 The classic symptoms of stuttering..include rapid-fire repetitions of consonant or vowel sounds. **1907** *Westm. Gaz.* 22 Mar. 2/3 These creatures..are chickens fed so generously that they are marketable..three weeks before the most rapid-growing Aylesbury duckling is saleable. **1964** A. BATTERSBY *Network Analysis* v. 58 For example, even if expensive rapid-hardening cement is used for laying foundations, they must have at least a day to harden. **1967** *Gloss. Highway Engin. Terms* (*B.S.I.*), *Rapid-hardening Portland cement*, a Portland cement which has the property of attaining a high early strength. **1962** E. GODFREY *Retail Selling & Organization* ii. 20 Generally speaking, rapid-selling stock is placed on open fixtures. **1873** *Daily Graphic* (N.Y.) 26 Mar. 3/3 In addition to the accommodations which are afforded the citizen of New York in the way of rapid transit ..our elevated road will be the great 'accommodator'. **1904** *N.Y. World Mag.* 21 Aug. 5/1 But the cars buzz on, heedless, as they do at the beck of a private citizen, and the great General must feel, unless his nerves are iron, that rapid transit gloria mundi. **1961** L. MUMFORD *City in Hist.* xiv. 425 Señor Soria y Mata..boldly proposed to make the new city a function of a spinal rapid-transit system. **1968** *Economist* 2 Nov. 50/3 There will also be 75 per cent grants available for big new passenger projects (e.g. new rapid transit system, such as the one investigated at Manchester). **1976** *Illustr. London News* Nov. 29/2 A rapid transit system is essentially one with an exclusive right of way. **1977** *Chicago Tribune* 2 Oct. II. 30/1 Closed by the strike were two Pullman-Standard plants in Hammond, which manufacture railroad freight and passenger cars, and the plant at 720 E. 111th St., which manufactures rapid-transit cars. **1932** *World Today* Feb. 213/2 By ten o'clock the narrow strip of timber some three miles long and an eighth of a mile wide was well aflame and had arrived at the rapid-travelling stage.

B. *sb.* **1.** (Earlier and later examples.) Also *fig.*

1765 G. CROGHAN *Jrnl.* 2 June in R. G. Thwaites *Early Western Trav.* (1904) I. 136 What is called the Fall here, is no more than rapids. **1900** G. B. SHAW *Let.* 11 Apr. (1972) II. 157 We steered the Society safely through a rapid in which it might have been wrecked. **1911** CHESTERTON *Innocence of Father Brown* x. 265 She was already in the rapids of an ethical tirade about the 'sickly medical notions'. **1979** P. L. SANDBERG *Stubb's Run* xxvii. 174 They were in the middle of the rapid, picking up speed.

2. Usu. *pl.* Rapid-fire shooting.

1913 A. G. FULTON *Notes on Rifle Shooting* 20 A man who is a good deliberate shot can, with very little practice, become good at 'rapids'. **1923** KIPLING *Irish Guards in Gt. War* II. 142 They indulged the enemy..with five minutes' 'rapid' of Lewis-guns or rifles. **1932** J. A. BARLOW *Elements of Rifle Shooting* v. 62 It is this conflict between the desire to have the aim correct before firing, and the desire to let the round off before too much time is wasted, which is the most usual cause of bad rapids.

‖ **rapide** (rapid). [Fr.] A French express train.

1904 A. E. W. MASON *Truants* i. 14 No 'Rapide' passed from France on its way to Italy during his leisure hours. **1923** W. J. LOCKE *Moordius & Co.* xxi. 288 She had lost the *rapide* from Cannes, the only train she knew of. **1946** G. MILLAR *Horned Pigeon* xix. 306 They only appeared to be stopping passengers who were catching the *rapide* for Marseilles. **1979** *Business Traveller* Mar.–Apr. 60/1 The landing..took us within 50 yards of the connecting 'rapide'.

‖ **rapido** (ra·pido), *adv.*, (*a.*), and *sb.* [It.] **A.** *adv. Mus.* With rapidity. Also quasi-*adj.*

1876 STAINER & BARRETT *Dict. Mus. Terms* 374/2 *Rapido* (*It.*), with rapidity. **1955** *Times* 6 June 9/2 The veiled purity of his pianissimo singing touch, and the unruffled evenness of his *rapido* flourishes in Chopin.

B. *sb.* An Italian express train.

1957 *Punch* 7 Aug. 163/1 In the restaurant car of the *Rapido* from Rome to Florence next day there was one of his private clients. **1964** P. JONES *Month of Pearl* vii. 65 An early evening train, a Rapido scheduled to stop only at Latina on its way to Rome. **1980** *Cook's Internat. Timetable* Nov. 209 Excess fare is charged for Rapido trains.

rapier. For '*Sc.* 6–7 **rapper**' in Dict. read '*Sc.* and *north. dial.* 6– **rapper**' and add: **1. a.** (Examples of var. form.)

1911 C. J. SHARP *Sword Dances Northern Eng.* 9 The long-sword Yorkshire dances differ very considerably from those gathered in the more northern counties, where the short-sword or 'rapper' is used. **1933** E. K. CHAMBERS *Eng. Folk-Play* 126 A long sword, found in Yorkshire, and a short sword or 'rapper', found in Durham. **1956** N. MARSH *Off with his Head* (1957) iii. 62 Hand over thik rapper... Us'll take the edge off of it.

c. *rapier-girdled, -like, -snouted, -thin* adjs.; **rapier dance** (later example); also **rapier-sword dance**; hence **rapier-sword dancer.**

1960 *Times* 16 Jan. 12/5 A Tyneside rapper dance. **1908** C. W. WALLACE *Children of Chapel* xiv. 177 The local and personal drives have caused my rapier-girdled courtier and fine gentleman to avoid the public theatres. **1975** R. BARCLAY *Ernest Bevin & Foreign Office* ii. 42 Quite untrue, of course, and not exactly rapier-like diplomacy, but it effectively crushed the Ambassador. **1906** *Daily Chron.* 11 Oct. 3/6 This rapier-snouted fish [*sc. Belone vulgaris*] consorts with the mackerel. **1937** *Times Lit. Suppl.* 20 Feb. 155/3 Long-sword dances, Rapper-sword dances. **1977** *Sunday Mail* (Brisbane) 6 Feb. 10/4 An ancient English dance came to Brisbane yesterday as Moreton Bay rapper sword dancers rehearsed for the Folk Music Festival. **1961** *Times* 7 Apr. 18/3 The acting, though it may broaden some of the rapier-thin parts, is as good as can be demanded.

Hence as *v. trans.*, with direct speech: to comment or query pointedly (*nonce-use*).

1957 O. NASH *You can't get there from Here* 151 Has the moment come, rapiered Mr. Webster, to abjectly surrender to journalese?

rapilli. Add: (Later examples.) Cf. LAPILLI.

1871 C. KINGSLEY *At Last* I. ii. 46 Soils of still unexhausted fertility, save when—as must needs be in a volcanic region—patches of mere rapilli and scoriæ occur. **1882** A. GEIKIE *Text-bk. Geol.* 162 Lapilli (rapilli).—Ejected fragments of lava.

‖ **rapin** (rapæ̃). [Fr.] In France: an apprentice in an artist's studio; an (unruly) art student.

1891 M. S. VAN DE VELDE tr. *H. Lavedan's Mamzelle Vertu* in *French Fiction of To-day* I. iv. 88 Nothing disturbed her, neither the stifled laughter of a group of *rapins* in front of a Hercules, or the 'shocking' bleated by a herd of female English visitors. **1894** G. DU MAURIER *Trilby* I. 11. 94 From the kind of laughter with which the points were received by the 'rapins' in Carrel's studio he guessed these little songs were vile.

rapine, *sb.* Add: Now freq. with pronunc. (ræ·pəin).

ra·ping, *vbl. sb.* [f. RAPE *v.*^{2}] The action of the vb.; rape, ravishment.

1961 *Life* 15 Dec. 33 Presently the well-armed members of the *Force Publique*..erupted in mutiny, rioting, raping and looting. **1972** *Daily Tel.* 3 Nov. 19/8 The raping of a 14-year-old Girl Guide at Totton, Hants, last May..led to jail sentences being imposed on three Hells Angels.

rapist. For *U.S.* read 'orig. *U.S.*' and add earlier and later examples. Also *fig.*

1883 *National Police Gaz.* (U.S.) 5 May 6/4 (*heading*) The stalwart resistance a married woman offered a would-be 'nigger' rapist. **1901** *Nation* (N.Y.) 18 Apr. 313/1 A bill having been passed by the State legislators, March 20, 1901 'providing for the public execution of convicted rapists'. **1937** *Sun* (Baltimore) 16 July 1/4 The State demanded the chair for Norris as 'a warning to other rapists and a protection for the womanhood of the State'. **1938** I. KUHN *Assigned to Adventure* vi. 54 Men had lived with death so long that they seized upon life with a rapist's lust. **1949** *Time* 19 Dec. 23/3 We follow a system which amounts to rape of the land. We are no careful husbandmen—not husbands but rapists. **1953** R. CHANDLER *Long Good-Bye* xxiv. 153 Take your hands off me, you goddamned rapist. **1959** *Guardian* 20 Oct. 9/1 A convicted kidnapper and rapist. **1975** *Daily Mirror* 14 Apr. 5/2 Hooded rapist claims victim no 6... The rapist who is terrorising a city's bed-sitter girls struck again yesterday.

ra·p-jacket. *Southern U.S.* [f. RAP *v.*^{1}] (See quot. 1893.) Also *transf.* Now *rare* or *Obs.*

1893 H. A. SHANDS *Some Peculiarities of Speech in Mississippi* 52 *Rap-jacket*,..a term used by all classes to mean a game of whipping, in which two boys are given switches, and whip each other with all of their might until one says 'enough'. They both thus have their jackets thoroughly rapped, if they happen to have on those garments. Two boys who have been fighting at school are very frequently punished by the teacher's making them play *rap-jacket* until he tells them to stop. **1904** *Westm. Gaz.* 12 Feb. 2/1 He up en say dat he be dad blame ef he ain't gwineter play at rap-jacket wid de whole-hoggers ef he kotch um.

raploch, *a.* (Later examples.)

1894 R. REID *Poems, Songs & Sonnets* 134 Rough and raploch mountain cheer. **1927** *Scots Observer* 21 May 16/1 Thistle and lily are alike admirable though one be raploch and the other circumspect.

rapped, *ppl. a.* (In Dict. s.v. RAP *v.*^{1}) Add: Also *rapped-out.*

1906 *Daily Chron.* 7 June 6/1 There was certainly nothing theatrical about the sound, stately, straight-backed, rapped-out rowing of those Eton eights.

rappee·^{2}. *nonce-wd.* [f. RAP *v.*^{1} + -EE^1.] One who raps or knocks; a rapper. (In quot., with punning allusion to RAPPEE.)

1819 KEATS *Let.* 27 Sept. (1958) II. 216, I heard a rap at the door... There came a louder rap... A little girl in the house was the Rappee—I assure you she has nearly made me sneeze.

rappel, *sb.* Restrict ‖ to sense in Dict. and add: **2.** (ræpe·l). *Mountaineering.* (The technique of) descending a steep face by means of a doubled rope fixed above the climber; = *ABSEIL. Also *attrib.*

1931 *Times Lit. Suppl.* 19 Feb. 129/3 On it [*sc.* Mont Blanc], climbing guideless, they practise every modern refinement, the use of crampons, scarpetti and the rappel. **1943** E. SHIPTON *Upon that Mountain* iv. 84 We could only proceed by a series of *rappels*. This is a method of 'roping down'. **1950** Rappel sling [see *LINE *sb.*^{2} 1]. **1952** MORIN & SMITH tr. *Herzog's Annapurna* viii. 119 We..fixed our spare rope for a rappel... Terray went down first on the doubled rope. **1959** S. CLARK *Puma's Claw* xii. 143 In 1956 the two of us had used the technique of 'abseil' or 'rappel' for seven hours continuously on a descent in the Alps. **1965** A. BLACKSHAW *Mountaineering* viii. 240 Roping down.. This involves:..pulling the rope round the anchor and down (the '*rappel*' from which the manœuvre takes its name). **1971** D. HASTON in C. Bonington *Annapurna South Face* xvii. 209 The descent took only twenty minutes as I was so enraged with myself. I caught Nick up on the last rappel. *Ibid.* 218 Don was already fixing a rappel peg.

rappel, *v.* Restrict † *Obs. rare* to sense in Dict. and add: **2.** (ræpe·l). *intr. Mountaineering.* To make a steep descent on a doubled rope; to rope down. Hence **rappe·lling** *vbl. sb.*

1957 P. MANSFIELD *Final Exposure* xvi. 239 He *rappelled* downwards, with the feel of good rock beneath his feet and the bite of the rope at his back. **1969** *Time* 22 Aug. 8/2 It is a stirring demonstration ranging from scuba diving..to archery and rappelling (descending a cliff on a double rope). **1974** *Telegraph* (Brisbane) 7 Aug. 23/3 There goes Harry Garner Haskell Jr. rappelling down the side of Abercrombie and Fitch.

‖ **rappen** (rɑ·pən). Also (anglicized) rap(p). [Ger., pl. as sing. f. *rappe* raven.] In the German-speaking cantons of Switzerland: the Swiss centime.

1838 *Murray's Hand-bk. Travellers Switzerland* p. viii, 1 batz contains 10 rappen, and = 1½*d.* (nearly) English. The Swiss coins most frequently met with are pieces of 5 batzen, or ½ a Swiss franc; 1 batz, ½ batz, and rappen. *Ibid.* p. ix, 1 French franc = (commonly) 7 batzen or exactly 6 batzen 8 rapps. **1864** *Baedeker's Switzerland* ii. p. xix, The Swiss monetary system has since 1854 been assimilated to that of France. Coins of 5, 2, 1 and ½ fr. in silver; 20, 10 and 5 Rappen (centimes) in plated copper; 2 and 1 Rappen in copper. 1 fr. = 100 Rappen = ..9¾d. **1911** *Encycl. Brit.* XIX. 907/2 Like Belgium, Switzerland had before her adhesion to the Latin Monetary Union adopted the French system, with the franc of 100 centimes or rappen as the unit of value. **1938** *Baedeker's Switzerland* iii. p. xvii, The monetary unit is the *Swiss franc* (fr.) of 100 *Centimes* (c.) or *Rappen* (in the German-speaking cantons). **1960** H. HAYWARD *Antique Coll.* 233/2 *Rappen*, small Swiss copper coin of late 18th and early 19th cent. with types of shield in wreath and value and date. **1962** R. A. G. CARSON *Coins* 326 In 1798 Switzerland was invaded by the revolutionary armies of France and a Helvetic republic was established and a new unified and decimal coinage was instituted with the franc as the unit, divided into 10 batzen, the batz divided in turn into 10 rappen. The system included pieces of 32 and 16 francs in gold; 40, 20, 10 and 5 batzen in silver and in billon the batz, its half and the rap. **1973** *Daily Tel.* 4 Aug. 15/2 In Zurich..the dollar lost 1 rappen to 2·84½.

rapper. Add: **1. a.** (Later example.)

1857 P. CARTWRIGHT *Autobiogr.* xix. 276 There is a dark, motley crowd of..spiritual rappers, so called.

† **b.** *slang.* One who tells a downright lie; a professional perjurer. Cf. sense 3 a and RAPPING *vbl. sb.*[1] 2 b. *Obs.*

1840 in Fielding *Jonathan Wild* (new ed.) p. lxii, The rapper, I think (as the cant phrase has it), is the most necessary man for your purpose.

c. *U.S. slang.* A complainant, plaintiff; a prosecutor. Cf. *RAP *v.*[1] 1 c.

1904 'No. 1500' *Life in Sing Sing* 252/1 *Rapper*, prosecutor; complainant. **1910** *New England Mag.* July 587 A complaint or charge of crime is a 'rap' and the complainant is the 'rapper'. **1926** *Clues* Nov. 158/2 *Lam* up to the *pagey* and see the *rapper*. **1935** *Jrnl. Abnormal Psychol.* XXX. 364 *Rapper*, the complainant in the case. **1955** D. W. MAURER in *Publ. Amer. Dial. Soc.* xxiv. 108 A *rapper* is a mark who prefers charges against a pickpocket; sometimes he can be bought off with a return of his money. 'If the law won't take, the next thing is to try the rapper.'

d. An itinerant purchaser of antiques; esp. one who buys valuable objects cheaply from credulous householders. Cf. *KNOCKER 2 e.

1914 H. A. VACHELL *Quinneys'* x. 146 Gossip had it that he had begun life as a 'rapper'. **1928** *Daily Express* 29 Feb. 14 The rapper frequently adopts the Aladdin method of offering new lamps for old, undertaking, for example, to give the innocent owner of a little old Queen Anne bureau a brand-new chest of drawers and a cash sum in exchange.

e. *U.S. slang.* A talker; a chatterer. Cf. *RAP *v.*[1] 3 d.

1971 *Time* 22 Feb. 38 Boulez clearly hopes there will be as many rappers as listeners. **1973** C. MILNER *Black Players* i. 8 He is recognized as among the best talkers or 'rappers' in the hustling world. **1972** C. WESTON *Poor, Poor Ophelia* iii. 18 Let's you and me talk like crazy. You look like a rapper, and I feel like rapping.

rapper: for 'obs. Sc.' in Dict. read 'dial.'

rapping, *vbl. sb.*[1] Add: **1.** Also, = SPIRIT-RAPPING (earlier and later examples). Also *transf.*

1848 M. FOX in A. Conan Doyle *Hist. Spiritualism* (1926) I. iv. 62 The children, who slept in the other bed in the room, heard the rapping, and tried to make similar sounds by snapping their fingers. **1894** A. LANG *Cock Lane* 29 The facts of rappings, ghosts, clairvoyance..are very doubtful facts after all. **1923** *Times Lit. Suppl.* 6 Dec. 853/3 He writes in short snappy sentences, the persistent rapping of which makes it very difficult for the reader to keep up his attention for long. **1954** J. F. RINN *Searchlight on Psychical Res.* vi. 56 'What are the points of your coming exposé?' asked Creelman. 'First the rappings,' Mrs. Kane smiled. **1974** *Encycl. Brit. Macropædia* XVII. 513/1 The spirits,..it is alleged, use different methods [of communication].., such as rappings, table tippings, [etc.].

2. c. *colloq.* (orig. *U.S.*). The action or practice of talking or chatting; conversation, gossip. spec. *U.S. Blacks*, repartee, banter. Cf. *RAP *v.*[1] 3 d.

1969 *Observer* 16 Feb. 40/6 Pendennis boogaloos, falls by cats into numbers, and lays down heavy outasight rapping. Translation: Pendennis arranges events, calls on people in the money, and produces a lot of fantastic gossip. **1969** T. KOCHMAN in *Trans-Action* Feb. 27/1 While often used to mean ordinary conversation, rapping is distinctively a fluent and lively way of talking, always characterized by a high degree of personal style. *Ibid.* 27/2 Rapping between men and women often is competitive and leads to a lively repartee. **1972** M. J. BOSSE *Incident at Naha* i. 60 After this failure of communication, our rapping dragged on like that of two old ladies. **1973** *Black World* Mar. 85 Jiving, bopping, rapping, signifying, sounding—all modes of Afro-American expression—seek to affirm the vitality of the Black American experience. **1977** *Rolling Stone* 13 Jan. 60/2 (Advt.), Multiracial magazine features workable self-help articles, rapping, fiction.

3. *attrib.*, as **rapping bar**, a pointed iron bar used in founding for loosening patterns from moulds; **rapping iron**, an implement used in basketry to tap the rows of weaving into the desired position; **rapping plate** *Founding*, a metal plate attached to a pattern in order to prevent damage to the pattern when it is loosened from the mould.

1888 *Lockwood's Dict. Mech. Engin.* 277 Rapping bar. **1948** H. W. BAKER *Mod. Workshop Technol.* I. iii. 60 For a wood pattern the rapping bar may be pointed and driven into the wood itself; or special rapping plates with suitable holes may be fixed to it. **1960** R. LISTER *Decorative Cast Ironwork in Gt. Brit.* ii. 31 The rapping bar is tapped with a mallet to loosen the pattern. **1924** C. CRAMPTON *Cane Work* 12 Rapping iron to tap the rows of weaving to make the work quite level. **1979** *Dryad Catal.* 87/1 Canework tools..Rapping iron for levelling (or regulating) cane weaving. **1885** *Pattern Making* xxii. 158 (*heading*) Rapping plates. **1894** W. J. LINEHAM *Textbk. Mech. Engin.* ii. 67 Rapping plates have become necessary in order to prevent injury to the pattern by the moulder. **1948** Rapping plate [see *rapping bar* above]. **1960** R. LISTER *Decorative Cast Ironwork in Gt. Brit.* ii. 25 To further facilitate the withdrawal, metal rapping and lifting plates are available.., ready drilled and countersunk for screwing to the pattern, and tapped to receive the lifting screw.

rapping, *ppl. a.* **1.** (Further example.)

1933 N. FODOR *Encycl. Psychic Sci.* 321/2 *Rudolf of Fulda*, a chronicle dating from 858 A.D. speaks of communications with a rapping intelligence.

rapport, *sb.* Add: Now usu. with pronunc. (rɑpō·ɪ, ræ-). **2. a.** (Further examples.) Also, harmonious accord, co-ordination. Now freq. used of relations between persons.

1915 'W. N. P. BARBELLION' *Jrnl.* Apr. in *Enjoying Life* (1919) 67 It wounds my self-esteem not to be..in direct telepathic rapport with the universe and its beauty. **1919** *Lancet* 8 Feb. 206/2 A lack of complete *rapport* between the muscles and the brain nerve centres. **1934** C. LAMBERT *Music Ho!* III. 175 This lack of rapport between the tune and harmony is particularly noticeable in some of the later works of Bartók. **1941** A. WHITE *Let.* 7 Feb. in *Hound & Falcon* (1969) 114 It was one of our good 'rapports' that I should have hit on Huvelin's admirable sayings just as you had written to me quoting some of them. **1957** J. KEROUAC *On Road* (1958) III. xi. 247 Dean's second baby, the result of a few nights' rapport. **1969** *Morning Star* 18 Nov. 2 The animal kingdom is in rapport with its environment, but man is not, unless he makes it so by taming his planet and remaking it to suit his needs. **1976** J. I. M. STEWART *Memorial Service* vii. 104 Jiffy temperately signalled the gratification proper to be felt on establishing this sort of *rapport* with a stranger.

b. (Earlier and later examples.) Also, a feeling of sympathy and co-operation between therapist and patient or tester and subject that is considered necessary for successful therapy or psychological testing. Also *attrib.* and *Comb.*

1845 POE in *Amer. Rev.* Dec. 564/2, I endeavored to place each member of the company in mesmeric *rapport* with him. **1894** CREIGHTON & TITCHENER tr. *Wundt's Lect. Human & Animal Psychol.* xxii. 331 There then arises what the animal-magnetism school term the *rapport* of the medium with the magnetiser. **1923** J. T. MACCURDY *Probl. Dynamic Psychol.* xi. 121 Manipulation of *rapport* is thus made the core of psychoanalytic treatment. **1924** J. RIVIERE tr. *Freud's Coll. Papers* I. 293 In his treatment of her case Brewer could make use of a very intense suggestible rapport on the part of the patient. **1954** A. ANASTASI *Psychol. Testing* iii. 50 It is apparent that the establishment of rapport, prior to the administration of the test, is generally an important part of the testing procedure. **1965** F. M. LOPEZ *Personnel Interviewing* i. 12 Then there are the *rapport* behaviors that help the interviewer to establish a bond of communication with the interviewee. **1970** A. MAGONET *Psychotherapy by Hypnosis* i. 3 Mesmer discovered that it was important that there should exist between physician and patient a close interest in and sympathy for each other. He described this as rapport. **1971** D. B. PESKIN *Human Behavior & Employment Interviewing* vii. 170 If the response seems neutral, the interviewer applies more of the same rapport-producing small talk and humor. **1976** A. ANASTASI *Psychol. Testing* (ed. 4) ii. 34 The training of examiners covers techniques for the establishment of rapport.

3. Substitute for def.: in a state of rapport or close and harmonious relation; in sympathy, in harmony. Usu. of persons. (Further examples.)

1846 GEO. ELIOT *Let.* Apr. in J. W. Cross *George Eliot's Life* (1885) I. ii. 116 See what it is to have a person *en rapport* with you, that knows all your thoughts. **1884** *Proc. Soc. Psychical Res.* II. 127 A mesmerised 'subject' who is sufficiently *en rapport* with his mesmeriser. **1933** WODEHOUSE *Mulliner Nights* v. 151 'I fear we were not exactly *en rapport*,' sighed Sacheverell.

‖ **rapportage** (rapɔ̄rtāʒ). [Fr., 'tale-telling': Eng. usage is influenced by REPORTAGE.] The reporting or describing of events in writing; mere description, uncreative accounting. Also *transf.*

1903 *Independent* 22 Jan. 210/2 It has nearly disabled prose fiction..by making of it a trade or handicraft, an affair of *rapportage*. **1935** S. SPENDER *Destructive Element* i. 26 James's earlier books are much fuller of descriptive writing and *rapportage* than the later books. **1957** *Times Lit. Suppl.* 8 Nov. 667/2 In describing his visits to the three North African territories in 1956 he has produced the modern counterpart to those brilliant pieces of pre-war *rapportage*. **1960** K. CLARK *Looking at Pictures* 145 The *Snowstorm* is very far from rapportage. It is the essence of all that Turner had discovered about himself and his art during forty years of practice. **1966** C. MACKENZIE *My Life & Times* V. 141, I decided it was too soon to write a novel about the war. Experience which had not been 'cooled a long age' might produce *rapportage* instead of genuine creative work.

rapporteur. Restrict † *Obs. rare*—[1] to sense in Dict. and add: ‖ **2.** A person who prepares an account of the proceedings of a committee, etc., for a higher body. Cf. REPORTER 1 c.

1791 LD. PALMERSTON *Diary* 13 July in O. Browning *Despatches Earl Gower* (1885) 290 The Rapporteur said that the Committees did not consider the king's flight as a constitutional crime in him. **1927** *Daily Tel.* 8 Mar. 11/5 The representative of Holland, as the rapporteur, submitted a report of the Permanent Mandates Commission which was adopted by the Council. **1937** *Nature* 17 Apr. 683/1 Two *rapporteurs* were appointed to summarize the papers. **1949** I. DEUTSCHER *Stalin* v. 143 At the conference he was the *rapporteur* on the problem of nationalities. **1955** *Times* 1 July 8/5 The congress..has appointed five *rapporteurs* on economic and financial policy, agriculture, foreign affairs, and the French oversea territories. **1964** *Ann. Reg. 1963* 175 The recommendation submitted by the Defence Committee's rapporteur..urged full nuclear co-operation between Britain and France. **1977** *Daily Tel.* 24 May 16 Normanton is to be the rapporteur of a study into the industrial and economic aspects of buying arms through a Common Market agency.

rapprochement. (Further examples.)

1905 *Daily Chron.* 19 Jan. 4/3 The retiring Premier is fully justified in claiming as a distinctive mark of his Government that it aimed at a 'rapprochement between peoples'. **1934** C. LAMBERT *Music Ho!* III. 207 The same rapprochement between highbrow and lowbrow..can be seen in literature. **1940** [see *ARTIFY *v.*]. **1955** *Times* 17 May 9/5 They should not assume that a Soviet–Yugoslav *rapprochement* was outside the framework of current conciliatory developments. **1958** L. DURRELL *Mountolive* xii. 228 With some half-formulated idea of offering the silent figure another chance to open up a discussion with him or seek a *rapprochement*, he rode his horse into the courtyard. **1974** J. WHITE tr. *Poulantzas's Fascism & Dictatorship* IV. iii. 211 It was only with the split in the Socialist Party, in October 1922, that rapprochement with the Maximalists was attempted. **1979** *Dædalus* Winter 78 The Community's structures were designed..to accommodate the Franco-German rapprochement.

rapsca·llionism. *rare.* [f. RAPSCALLION + -ISM.] Rapscallions collectively; the conduct or condition of rapscallions.

1920 GALSWORTHY *In Chancery* III. ix. 288 Soho seemed more than ever the disenchanted home of rapscallionism.

rapscallionly, *a.* (Further example.)

1899 G. B. SHAW *Let.* 29 Sept. (1972) II. 106. There being between Maggie [*sc.* Margaret Hobhouse] & myself a sort of rapscallionly freemasonry.

rapt, *pa. pple.* (and *pa. t.*). Add: **I. 3.** Also const. *away*.

1924 A. D. SEDGWICK *Little French Girl* II. xii. 194 The heir..stood with his little shoulders screwed up, his elbows in his hands, rapt away from shyness and self-consciousness by his sincere delight.

raptly, *adv.* Add: **c.** Intently, concentratedly, absorbedly.

1924 E. POWER *Medieval People* ii. 52 The crowd of Venetian prisoners and Genoese gentlemen, raptly drinking in all the wonders of Kublai Khan. **1971** *Daily Tel.* 13 Feb. 7/1 There was a delightful sequence of a 7 year-old girl 'cellist playing raptly and well for her judges.

raptor. **1.** For † *Obs.* in Dict. read *rare* and add: (Later example.) Also, an abductor.

1884 ADDIS & ARNOLD *Cath. Dict.* 436/1 The councils..prohibit subsequent marriage between the raptor and his victim. **1975** *Daily Tel.* 12 Aug. 12 What I had in mind was the ruling that there was no rape provided the raptor believed..that the woman consented.

3. (Later examples.) Also *attrib.* and *fig.*

1933 *Condor* XXXV. 19 (*heading*) Food habits of Southern Wisconsin raptors. *Ibid.*, The ex post facto recording of raptor kills encountered in the field should not be regarded as a proper source of quantitative data. **1963** D. P. MANNIX *All Creatures Great & Small* vi. 86 Raptors (birds of prey) do not have the nervous, active minds of the Corvidæ. **1974** *Sci. Amer.* Dec. 156/3 A cruel human raptor..boasted of killing golden eagles with a sawed-off shotgun as he flew beside them. **1976** *Nature* 23 Sept. 321/1 Other relevant predators such as large raptors or felids do not occur on these islands. **1980** *Observer* (Colour Suppl.) 6 Jan. 57/1 Hundreds of thousands of raptors—birds of prey such as stork, buzzard, kite and eagle—commute across this corner of north-western Turkey.

raptorial, *a.* (and *sb.*) Add: **1. a.** *raptorial bird* (further examples).

1919 T. A. COWARD *Birds Brit. Isles* I. 330 Most raptorial birds are variable in plumage. **1931** —— *Life of Birds* vi. 46 The flesh-eating or raptorial birds kill birds which we call useful as well as those which are troublesome. **1968** *Nature* 14 Dec. 1098/1 Declining populations of raptorial and fish-eating birds. **1976** *Field* 30 Dec. 1281/1 Goats shot this year have helped to nourish a foundation stock of ten white-tailed eagles, brought over from Norway by special arrangement with the government of that country in an attempt to reintroduce a raptorial bird once native to Britain.

2. (Later examples.) Also *fig.*

1916 *Sci. Progress* XI. 245 'Canto di cigno'..—a droll metaphor having regard to Spallanzani's raptorial countenance. **1933** *Condor* XXXV. 19 Erroneous impressions obscure the true proportions of one prey species to another in raptorial diets. **1955** W. GADDIS *Recognitions* II. vii. 620 At that instant the room was pierced by a raptorial cry like that of the bird descending. **1973** *Nature* 20 July 179/2 Planktonic crustacea exhibit selective feeding behaviour ranging from passive size selection in *Daphnia* to raptorial feeding in cyclopoid copepods.

rapture, *sb.* Add: **5. e.** *rapture(s) of the deep* or *depths*, nitrogen narcosis.

1953 J. Y. COUSTEAU *Silent World* ii. 14 (*heading*) Rapture of the deep. *Ibid.* 21 We called the seizure *l'ivresse des grandes profondeurs* (rapture, or 'intoxication', of the great depths). **1955** R. & B. CARRIER *Dive* iii. 77 This nitrogen narcosis or 'rapture of the depths'..seems to have varying effects on different types of people. **1955** J. SWEENEY *Skin Diving & Exploring Underwater* vii. 89 It has not been established with absolute certainty how nitrogen causes a narcotic effect ('raptures of the deep') when breathed under high pressure. **1962** [see **nitrogen narcosis*]. **1971** J. F. BERNARD tr. *Cousteau's Life & Death in Coral Sea* 261 The diver's threshold of susceptibility to rapture of the depths can be pushed back..by replacing the nitrogen in one's breathing mixture by a lighter gas, such as helium. **1974** *Petroleum Rev.* XXVIII. 672/1 Nitrogen narcosis, popularly called 'raptures of the deep' but perhaps more accurately described as 'the uglies', is the malady caused by nitrogen under pressure, interfering with the normal function of the nervous system.

rapture, *v.* Add: **b.** *intr.* To express oneself in raptures; to take rhapsodic delight *in* or display ecstatic excitement *over* something.

1908 A. LIPDEGRAFF in *Smart Set* June 133, I rapture in some lonely night-bird's cries. **1965** E. O'BRIEN *August is Wicked Month* i. 12 She went out and raptured over the tent and said what a genius he was.

raptus. Add: **2.** (Further examples.) Also, an instance of this.

1902 W. JAMES *Var. Relig. Exper.* xvi. 412 In the condition called *raptus* or ravishment by theologians, breathing and circulation are so depressed that it is a question among the doctors whether the soul be or be not temporarily dissevered from the body. **1964** L. WOOLF *Beginning Again* I. 32 Beethoven, every now and again, used to have what his faithful disciple called 'a raptus', a kind of volcanic creative outburst... The raptus or inspiration is clearly only a rare and wonderful form of a well-known everyday mental process. **1977** A. SHERIDAN tr. *J. Lacan's Écrits* vi. 207 The subject had his first attack of anxious confusion with suicidal raptus.

raquette. (Earlier and later examples in sense 3 a of RACKET *sb.*[2])

c **1665** P. E. RADISSON *Voyages* (1885) 66 We found snowes in few places, saving where the trees made a shaddow, wch hindred the snow to thaw, wch made us carry the raquetts. **1760** T. JEFFERYS *Nat. & Civil Hist. French Dominions* I. 57 The texture of the raquette or snow-shoe, consists of straps of leather about two lines in breadth, bordered with some light wood hardened in the fire. **1849** J. E. ALEXANDER *L'Acadie* II. 19 It was ludicrous to witness the mishaps of those who figured on the broad racquettes for the first time. **1965** *Canad. Geogr. Jrnl.* Feb. 62/2 The 'raquettes' of today are strung, usually, with especially prepared cowhide, rather than the original deerhide.

ra-ra, var. *RAH-RAH *a.*

‖ **rara avis** (rēᵊ·rǎ ēⁱ·vis, rā·ra a·vis). Pl. **rara avises,** ‖ **rarae aves.** [L., 'rare bird' (Juvenal *Sat.* vi. 165; cf. also Persius *Sat.* i. 46).] **1.** A person of a type seldom encountered; an exceptional person, a paragon. Occas. without article.

1607 G. WILKINS *Miseries Inforst Mariage* sig. A3ᵛ, And by that, thou hast beene married but three weekes, tho thou shouldst wed a *Cynthia rara avis*, thou wouldest be a man monstrous: A cuckold, a cuckold. [**1654** E. GAYTON *Pleasant Notes Don Quixot* IV. xv. 251 But all to Donna Clara The judges daughter yield, shee's *Avis rara*.] **1748** SMOLLETT *R. Random* II. li. 166 Calling my Lord Strutwell by the appellations of Jewel, Phœnix, *Rara avis*. **1749** FIELDING *Tom Jones* III. VIII. i. 150 A single instance..is not sufficient to justify us, while we are writing to thousands who never heard of the person, nor of any thing like him. Such Raræ Aves should be remitted to the epitaph-writer. **1813** SOUTHEY *Let.* 30 Nov. (1856) II. 338, I sent them, thinking that a char in London must be like a tortoise-shell Tom cat, a *rara avis*. **1825** MILL in *Jrnl. Adult Educ.* (1929) IV. 54 A good doubter may as yet be truly pronounced to be *rara avis*, etc. **1852** 'G. GREENWOOD' *Haps & Mishaps* (1854) iv. 91 A pretty Irish peasant girl we found the rarest of *rara avises*. **1892** D. H. TUKE *Dict. Psychol. Med.* 854 A good nurse for neurotic patients is a *rara avis* indeed. **1919** V. WOOLF *Night & Day* xii. 154 'But I do read De Quincey.., more than Belloc and Chesterton, anyhow.' 'Indeed!' exclaimed Mrs Cosham...'You are, then, a *rara avis* in your generation.' **1931** 'G. TREVOR' *Murder at School* i. 13 That *rara avis*, the headmaster who was also a man of the world. **1955** *Times* 23 May 3/3 The harpist is a *rara avis* among recitalists. **1975** *Listener* 31 July 140/1 Peter Jay is the *rara avis* of broadcasting. He is the high-flyer who descends from the thunderous crags of the *Times* to perch, with no hint of condescension, on the television aerials of the nation.

2. That which is seldom found; an unusual occurrence, etc.; something very remarkable.

1884 J. J. HISSEY *Old-Fashioned Journey* vii. 99 A perfect day with us is somewhat of a *rara avis*. **1906** [see *REDOUBLE *sb.*[2]]. **1942** *Burlington Mag.* Feb. 50/2 Truly a *rara avis* among books of memoirs! **1979** *Guardian* 15 Mar. 11/1 It is a moving document, not to say a *rara avis*.

3. *lit.* A rare bird.

1891 H. M. SMITH in *Proc. U.S. Nat. Museum* XIII. 171 The Dick Cissel [*sc.* a bird]..is now a veritable *rara avis*.

rare, *a.*[1] (*adv.*[1] and *sb.*) Add: **5. c.** *rare earth* (Chem.), any naturally occurring oxide of an element of the lanthanide series (usu. including lanthanum and freq. also scandium and yttrium); also (*loosely*), any of these elements themselves; a lanthanide. Hence *rare-earth element, metal.*

In earliest examples used in a less restricted sense, including oxides of other metals.

1875 *Jrnl. Chem. Soc.* XXVIII. 1001 (*heading*) The quantivalence of the metals of the rarer [*sic*] earths [= tr. G. seltenen Erdmetalle]. **1877** *Ibid.* XXXI. 49 (*heading*) The quantivalence of the rare earth-metals. **1878** *Chem. News* 13 Sept. 136/2, I found nearly one-half of the known elements represented, and separated a group of oxides belonging to the rare earths. **1902** *Encycl. Brit.* XXVI. 710/1 Helium has since been extracted from a variety of minerals consisting of salts of uranium, yttrium, thorium and other rare earths. *Ibid.* 710/2 In the case of the rare-earth metals, the elements from air and the radio-active elements, the discovery of new elements has frequently been consequent on the introduction of novel methods. **1933** *Discovery* Jan. 1/1 Samarium has an atomic number 62 and a mass of about 150. Chemically it is a 'rare earth'. **1937**, etc. [see *LANTHANIDE]. **1958** *Optima* Mar. 22b/2 Thorium occurs chiefly in association with the rare-earth elements in monazite ore. **1959** *Nomencl. Inorg. Chem.* (I.U.P.A.C.) 6 The name rare-earth metals may be used for the elements Sc, Y, and La to Lu inclusive. **1965** D. ABBOTT *Inorg. Chem.* i. 36 The third transition series is interrupted after lanthanum by a set of elements known as the Rare Earths or Lanthanons. **1968** *Times* 18 Oct. 16/8 Gadolinium belongs to the little known family of minerals called the rare earths... The name rare earth is something of a misnomer, since many of the minerals in the family are widely distributed throughout the earth's crust. **1972** *Nature* 31 Mar. 197/1 Also concentrated in this liquid are a group of trace elements, including barium, yttrium, rare earths, zirconium, hafnium, phosphorus and niobium, about which are centred many of the geochemical arguments concerning the differences between terrestrial and lunar rocks.

d. *rare bird* = *RARA AVIS 1, 2.

1890 G. B. SHAW in *Star* 21 Feb. 2/5 She [*sc.* the perfect dancer] is the rarest of rare birds. **1912** R. LYND *Rambles in Ireland* i. 45 In Ireland..one drunk man is as conspicuous as a thousand sober ones... But he is, comparatively speaking, a rare bird and an exception for all the show he makes. **1934** C. DAY LEWIS *Hope for Poetry* x. 66 The true lyric poet is a very rare bird indeed. **1950** W. SAROYAN *Assyrian* 21 The writer who is only a writer is a rare bird these days, most writers having taken posts at universities, [etc.]. **1962** *Which? Car Suppl.* Oct. 141/1 The foreign cars are still somewhat rare birds. **1977** *Times* 20 Oct. 16/3 That rare bird, a historian who was also a history-maker.

e. *rare book*, a book which is in demand and made valuable by its actual or prospective rarity. Also *attrib.*

[**1862** J. H. BURTON *Book-Hunter* II. 210 David Clement..lays it down with authority, that 'a book which is difficult to find in the country where it is sought ought to be called simply rare'.] **1895** W. ROBERTS *Rare Bks.* 7 This is a very unusual contingency even in the history of rare books. **1910** A. W. POLLARD in *Encycl. Brit.* IV. 223/1 The Boccaccio ..went to Earl Spencer (d. 1834) for £750, to pass with the rest of his rare books to Mrs Rylands in 1892. **1930** R. CURIE *Collecting Amer. First Editions* vi. 168 (*heading*) Rare books still obtainable. **1941** B. SCHULBERG *What makes Sammy Run?* v. 97 One of the finest collections of rare books in the country. **1948** J. CARTER *Taste & Technique in Book-Collecting* p. ix, I am the first member of the rare book trade to have been appointed Sandars Reader. **1952** —— *ABC for Book-Collectors* 148 The First Folio Shakespeare and the Gutenberg Bible are certainly 'rare books' as the term is generally understood. **1967** E. GRIERSON *Crime of one's Own* I. 12 The 'rare book' trade, which he was trying to build up. **1976** 'O. BLEECK' *No Questions Asked* ii. 22 The Library of Congress is an interesting place... The reading room of the Rare Book Division turned out to be a peaceful place. **1980** *Times* 29 Jan. 14/6 It was a characteristic out-of-season sale, containing faulty copies of rare books.

f. *rare gas* (Chem.) = *inert gas* (*b*) s.v. *INERT *a.* 1 c. (Cf. sense 1 a in Dict.)

1901 M. W. TRAVERS *Exper. Study Gases* xi. 116 Mercury, which somewhat resembles the rare gases with regard to its low boiling-point and monatomic character, would be chemically inactive at 1000° C. **1937** *Discovery* Aug. 227/2 The separation of the 'rare gases' from the atmosphere. **1963** J. H. POMEROY in H. H. HYMAN *Noble-Gas Compounds* III. 125, I..suspect that the discovery of the rare-gas compounds has been greeted with particular enthusiasm by the producers of textbooks in chemistry, since it gives them..a sort of windfall of unplanned obsolescence. **1972** *Nature* 8 Dec. 345/2 Radon (^{222}Rn)—a radioactive rare gas emanating essentially from large continental land areas.

9. Also used advb. (mainly *poet.*) with adjs. or ppl. adjs. *rare-bred, -coming, -composed, -dear, -feathered, -felt, -grown, -seen, -spoken, -veined.*

1877 *Coursing Calendar Autumn 1876* 327 Westeria..was put out in a bad trial. She is a rare-bred one, being by Contango out of Joan-of-Arc. **1937** BLUNDEN *Elegy* 90 Where the dogs..regard The rare-coming stranger in the yard An excitement not to be missed. **1601** MARSTON *Jack Drums Entertainment* sig. A2ᵛ, If he could..distill the quintessence of heauen In rare composed Sceanes. **1876** G. M. HOPKINS *Wreck of Deutschland* xxxv, in *Poems* (1967) 63 Let him [*sc.* our King]..be a crimson-cresseted east, More brightening her, rare-dear Britain, as his reign rolls. **1904** *Westm. Gaz.* 19 Nov. 9/2 The class for pied, albino, or rare-feathered British birds contains a pure yellow, pink-eyed, yellow-hammer. **1785** T. DWIGHT *Conquest of Canäan* IV. 97 A rare-felt joy inspir'd the friendless band. **1922** BLUNDEN *Shepherd* 85 And rare-grown daisy in the meadow. **1794** T. DWIGHT *Greenfield Hill* I. 18 The rare-seen felon startles every mind And fills each mouth with news. **1915** D. H. LAWRENCE *Rainbow* i. 8 A rare-spoken, almost surly man. **1879** G. M. HOPKINS *Duns Scotus's Oxford* in *Poems* (1967) 79 Of realty the rarest-veinèd unraveller.

rare, *a.*[2] Add: **a.** (Later U.S. examples.)

1836 *Public Ledger* (Philadelphia) 19 Apr. 1/3 [Certain persons] in calling for boiled eggs, instead of ordering them to be done rare, order them to be '*boiled soft*'. **1856** *Knickerbocker* XLVII. 249 'Do you like your eggs done rare?' asked the good landlady.

b. Now usu. of grilled beef-steak. (Now also quite customary outside American English.)

1904 *N.Y. Sun* 6 Aug. 5 The waiter took his order for a sirloin rare. **1911** E. FERBER *Dawn O'Hara* ii. 20 I've devoured rare porterhouse and roast beef day after day for weeks. **1940** R. CHANDLER *Farewell, my Lovely* xxv. 186 Would you like your steak rare or medium, sir? **1977** *Times* 24 Aug. 14/8 A reader ordered a steak, rare, at a Yorkshire roadside café.

rare, *v.* orig. *U.S.* and *dial.* [Var. of REAR *v.*[1]] **1. a.** *intr.* = REAR *v.*[1] 15.

1833 *Sketches & Eccentricities D. Crockett* vii. 92 He just *rared* up upon his hind legs. **1898** H. S. CANFIELD *Maid of Frontier* 100 Break 'em with a curb an' they rare an' fall back on you. **1938** [see *JES, JES'].

b. colloq. *to be raring to* (*go*, etc.), to be extremely eager or fully ready to (do something). Also *transf.*

1909 E. BANKS *Mystery F. Farrington* iv. 13/2 They make me raring, tearing mad to look at 'em. **1927** F. N. HART *Bellamy Trial* i. 10 Both sides are rarin' to go, and they are not liable to touch their peremptory challenges [of jurymen]. **1935** WODEHOUSE *Luck of Bodkins* xv. 167 Keep it crisp, because I'm raring to go. **1957** A. MACNAB *Bulls of Iberia* viii. 79 The bull was a *toro de bandera*, the bravest of the brave,..and was 'rarin' to fight'. **1971** J. TYNDALL *Death in Lebanon* vii. 114 He's laid it on that the preacher makes some inflammatory remarks..so that the congregation..will be rarin' to go. **1979** *Church Times* 9 Feb. 9/1 We were at the starting-gate and raring to go.

2. *trans.* = REAR *v.*[1] 9.

1901 M. FRANKLIN *My Brilliant Career* v. 24 It was my duty to 'rare the poddies'. **1961** 'F. O'BRIEN' *Hard Life* ix. 67 Well, there's no doubt about it, we rare up strange characters in this country.

raree-show. Add: **2. a.** (Further examples.)

1931 BLUNDEN *To Themis* 22 Colours flying, drums drubbing, boys run miles for the raree-show. **1955** W. GADDIS *Recognitions* II. vii. 634 He'll show you... He'll put up a real maudlin raree-show for you. **1971** *Daily Tel.* 8 Nov. 9/1 Religious people today protest against 'Jesus Christ Superstar' as a vulgar raree-show cashing in on an adolescent fad.

3. *raree-show box* (earlier example), *-performance.*

1737 *London Mag.* June 324/2, I presume that he [*sc.* Punch] will not be tolerated, either upon the Stage, or even in a Raree-shew Box. **1812** S. JONES *Baker's Biographia Dramatica* (rev. ed.) III. 306 A frivolous raree-show performance.

rarefactional (rēᵊrĭfæ·kʃənăl), *a.* [f. RAREFACTION + -AL.] Characterized by rarefaction.

1909 in *Cent. Dict.* Suppl. **1971** I. G. GASS et al. *Understanding Earth* xix. 272/1 On either side of the fault, the first waves to leave the source are compressions in the direction of motion and rarefactions away from it. This gives the symmetrical distribution of compressional and rarefactional first motions shown. **1972** *Sci. Amer.* May 58/3 After an earthquake one finds that the seismological stations that have received the first waves can be assigned to one of four geographic quadrants. In two of the quadrants, lying opposite each other, the first waves are compressional; in the other two quadrants the first waves are rarefactional.

rarefied, *ppl. a.* Add: Also *transf.* and *fig.*

1961 *Blackw. Mag.* Oct. 290/1 From the light of common day into the rarified atmosphere of the late eighteenth century. **1977** G. MICHANOWSKY *Once & Future Star* iv. 33

In the rarefied world of cuneiform scholarship, it is known as BM—86378. **1978** N. Moss *What's the Difference?* (ed. 2) 93 *Professor, n*—a less rarefied post than at a British university, since there are usually several professors to a department.

rarefy, *v.* Add: **2. d.** *intr.* To discourse exaltedly. *nonce-use.*

1928 Blunden *Undertones of War* iv. 44, I remember how Limbery-Buse and myself chirped and rarefied over some crayfish and a great cake.

Rarey (rēᵊ·ri). The name of the horse-breaker J. S. *Rarey*, used *attrib.* and in the possessive to denote methods or equipment employed by him for the taming of horses. Hence **Ra·reying**, the action or fact of breaking in a horse by Rarey's methods. Cf. Rareyfy *v.*

[**1856** J. S. Rarey (*title*) The modern art of taming wild horses.] **1875** S. Sidney *Bk. of Horse* xxvi. 562 The Rarey principle consists in teaching the colt as much as possible without putting him in any pain, and without frightening him by any strange sight or sound. *Ibid.* 565 (*caption*) Horse, with Rarey fittings. *Ibid.* 567 The application of the Rarey straps in the following manner affords a better chance of success than the ordinary exhausting plans of old-fashioned colt-breakers and of circus-riders. **1896** M. H. Hayes *Illustr. Horse-Breaking* (ed. 2) iv. 124 Having 'picked up' the foot, we may secure it..by Rarey's leg-strap, which is about 3 ft. long, and is furnished at one end with a buckle, below which a leather 'keeper' is placed on both sides. *Ibid.* 175 Mr. Norton Smith adopted..a modification of Rarey's system. **1905** S. Galvayne *20th Century Bk. on Horse* 100 (*heading*) The Rarey system. *Ibid.*, It may not be uninteresting to the reader to briefly explain the method of 'Rareying' a horse. **1911** *Encycl. Brit.* XIII. 725/1 The method of subduing a colt by 'galvayning' is as good as any. It is a more humane system than 'rareying', which overcame by exhaustion under circumstances which were not fruitful of permanent results. **1942** Rareying [see *Galvayne]. **1979** *Jrnl. R. Soc. Arts* Oct. 724/2 The 'Rarey' method of throwing a horse is explained.

raring: see *rare *v.* 1 b.

‖**rariora** (rēᵊriōᵊ·ră, rari-), *sb. pl.* [L., neut. pl. comparative of *rārus* rare.] Rare books. Cf. *rare *a.*[1] 5 e.

1863 *Macm. Mag.* VIII. 36 (*heading*) *Rariora* of old poetry. **1908** *Daily Report* 26 Aug. 8/3 Such books fetch far better prices in London and Paris than in New York, where the demand for such *rariora* is small. **1932** J. Buchan *Gap in Curtain* iv. 189 There was a fine set of Donne, two of the Shakespeare folios,..besides a quantity of devotional and political *rariora*. **1964** D. Cox in D. Daiches *Idea of New University* ix. 162 Where sufficient copies of not only European but of American *rariora* have been unavailable, microfacsimile has been called in.

rarish, *a.* Add: Also **rare-ish.** (Further examples.)

1875 Browning *Inn Album* iii. 92 Would..I winged were..And so could straightway soar..Back to my nest where broods whom I love best—The parson o'er his parish —garish—rarish—. **1959** N. Marsh *False Scent* (1960) i. 19 It's rare-ish. The frame's contemporary. I'm afraid it's twelve guineas.

‖**rarissima** (rēᵊri·simă, rari·-), *sb. pl.* [L., neut. pl. superlative of *rārus* rare.] Extremely rare books. Also **rari·ssime** *a.* [lit. 'very rarely (*sc.* found)'], extremely rare.

1903 A. Bennett *Truth about Author* iv. 56, I possessed a *rarissime* illustrated copy of *Manon Lescaut.* **1952** *Times Lit. Suppl.* 14 Nov. 752/3 The..books..of which Mr. Wing has been able to locate only a single copy..are not as *rarissime* as one would infer. **1972** *Ibid.* 29 Sept. 1173/3 A few of the important *rarissima*, like Fust and Schoeffer's *Canon Missae* of 1458.

rarity. Add: **6.** *Comb.*, as *rarity value.*

1962 *Listener* 30 Aug. 329/1 Shots..came across with a breezy freshness that is only partly explained by their rarity value on television. **1978** P. McCutchan *Blackmail North* xiii. 138 The cave is *under* a layer of schist... Because of the rarity value the geologists play it down and hope to keep the tourists away.

Rarotongan (rærŏtǫ·ŋăn), *sb.* and *a.* [f. *Rarotonga*, the name of the largest of the Cook Islands in the South Pacific + -an.] **A.** *sb.* **a.** A native or inhabitant of Rarotonga. **b.** The language of Rarotonga: Cook Islands Maori, a member of the Polynesian group. **B.** *adj.* Of or pertaining to Rarotonga or its language.

1842 M. Russell *Polynesia* vi. 226 The Rarotongans were a most ferocious class of men. **1851** G. Browne *Let.* 8 July in A. Buzacott *Mission Life Islands of Pacific* (1866) xiii. 188 It was resolved to request Miss Buzacott to accept ..a copy of the Bible in Rarotongan and English. **1854** A. Buzacott *Rarotongan & Eng. Gram.* 2/2 The Rarotongan alphabet has five soft letters. **1866** —— *Mission Life Islands of Pacific* xiv. 198 It is scarcely credible how strange it was to Mr. Buzacott to preach..in the English language..his mind being prone to think according to the habits and ideas of the Rarotongans. **1897** *Jrnl. Polynesian Soc.* VI. 10 The word *akono*..appears from its use in the Rarotongan scriptures, to be..akin to 'appointed'. **1910** F. W. Christian *Eastern Pacific Lands* 193 The history of the Christianizing..and progress of these Rarotongan Maori is the brightest chapter in the history of the South Seas. **1947** *Jrnl. Polynesian Soc.* LVI. 197, I wish to acknowledge assistance given to me by..other Rarotongans. *Ibid.* 215 The manuscript..requires translation into modern Rarotongan. **1966** J. E. Buse in C. E. Bazell *In Memory of J. R. Firth* 52 Rarotongan Maori is spoken on the island of Rarotonga in the Southern Cooks. **1977** *Times* 2 Dec. 19/2 Rarotongans are almost wholly dependent on inflation-prone imported tinned goods.

‖**ras** (rās). [a. Amharic *rās* head, chief, from Arab.: cf. Reis[2], rais.] **1.** The title of a leading citizen. **a.** An Ethiopian king, prince, or feudal lord.

1682 tr. *H. Ludolf's New Hist. Ethiopia* ii. xii. 213 To these succeeded another Chief Officer whom the Ethiopians call Ras, from the Arabic word which signifies a Head. **1710** B. Tellez *Trav. Jesuits in Ethiopia* x. 54 They constituted another call'd Raz, which signifies Head; because he who has that Employment is next the Emperor, Head of all the great Men in the Empire. **1735** Johnson tr. *Lobo & Le Grand's Voy. to Abyssinia* 262 There is now a Generalissimo established under the title of Ras, or Chief. [**1759** —— *Rasselas* i. 2 Rasselas was the fourth son of the mighty emperour, in whose dominions the Father of waters begins his course.] **1833** *Penny Cycl.* I. 58/1 Mr. Salt saw..the Ras's wife. **1904** S. Walpole *Hist. Twenty-Five Yrs.* II. xi. 269 Practically, the power was in the hands of several ras, or chiefs—of whom Ras Ali was the foremost—who carried on a turbulent warfare among themselves. **1921** *Glasgow Herald* 14 Sept. 6/3 Most of the power lies in the hands of the important 'Rases', who correspond with the Dukes of mediæval Europe, and although nominally members of a vague State Council, are to a large extent independent rulers, with governors and chiefs in practically feudal subordination to them. **1926** *Ibid.* 27 Apr. 7 Mr Rey said that when he arrived in the capital of Abyssinia, Adis Ababa,.. he was most kindly received by the Empress and by the Regent, Ras Tafari, who was much interested in the expedition. The Ras not only gave the necessary permits, without which no one could move in Abyssinia, but supplied also some rifles for Mr Rey's men. *Ibid.*, He had an extraordinary welcome from the Governor, Ras Hailu, who was the last of the hereditary Provincial Governors in Abyssinia. The Ras exercised a feudal despotism in his government, and he maintained the old time hospitality. **1936** E. Waugh *Waugh in Abyssinia* i. 38 The rases and officials copied the Emperor.

b. = Reis[2], rais 2.

1935 *Words* May 7/1 Legionaire Aurelius Philinus of ancient Palmyra set up in 251 A.D. an honorary statue to Septimius Hairan, illustrious senator and head man (*ras*) of Tadmor (Palmyra) accompanied by a bilingual inscription in Semitic and Greek.

2. *transf.* An Italian Fascist leader; a petty despot.

1923 *Glasgow Herald* 16 Oct. 6/4 The strength of the materialist group is to be found in the 'rases' or 'bosses' who have found in the revolution an excellent opportunity to establish themselves as the petty tyrants of their town or district. **1924** *Ibid.* 27 June 8/4 It [*sc.* a declaration] will compel the 'rases' and the physical force party generally to abandon their methods or to resist Mussolini's authority in the open. **1967** C. Seton-Watson *Italy from Liberalism to Fascism* xiii. 594 The local fascist bosses were commonly known as *ras*, a title borrowed from the feudal nobility of Ethiopia. *Ibid.*, Mussolini hit back.., condemning the parochialism of the *ras* and the degeneration of Emilian fascism into the defence of sordid private interests. **1973** P. A. Allum *Politics & Society in Post-War Naples* ix. 301 The leadership of the party has been taken over by a solid conservative block..that has as solid supporters that poor class of bosses (*ras*) of the various provincial centres. **1975** *Times Lit. Suppl.* 11 July 783/3 A biography of Roberto Farinacci, arguably the toughest and unquestionably the most uncouth of the Fascist 'ras'.

ras, var. *rasa[1,2].

‖**rasa**[1] (ra·sa). Also **ras.** [a. Skr. *rasa* juice; essence, character; sentiment.] Essence, character, sentiment.

1799 F. Wilford in *Asiatick Researches* VI. 503 The Greeks supposed that mount Parnassus was the favorite abode of the Muses. The Hindus have not limited their residence to any particular spot... They are called Rasa in Sanscrit, in which language this word signifies juice in general, but is more particularly understood as the honied juice of flowers: it implies also any thing which we particularly delight in. *Ibid.* 505 The nine Rasas are represented as beautiful damsels. **1828** H. H. Wilson in *Ibid.* XVI. 118 The Bhakti of the followers of this division of the Hindu faith is supposed to comprehend five Rasas or Ratis, tastes or passions. **1926** in P. Hartog *On Relation of Poetry to Verse* 6 With them [*sc.* Sanskrit authors] what is essential in poetry is something incomprehensible, something which cannot be directly expressed, but only suggested—the aesthetic delectableness which they call *rasa*, a subjective condition of the reader's mind. **1967** [see *nritya]. **1968** *Indian Music Jrnl.* V. 34 His life became lonely. Perhaps this accounts to some extent for his successful evocation of *Karuṇā* rasa. **1968** *Jrnl. Musical Acad. Madras* XXXIX. 8 In one sense there is only one Rasa, *Bhakti*, that runs through the songs of Tyagaraja... Thus *Bhakti Rasa* can wear different complexions... In these songs the melody is itself suggestive of the Rasa of the song. **1977** S. Pandit *Approach to Indian Theory of Art & Aesthetics* ii. 32 An object which does not contain *rasa* cannot be classified in the category of an art work, and no experience without it can be called aesthetic.

‖**rasa**[2] (rā·sa). Also **ras.** [a. Skr. *rāsa* dance, sport.] A rustic Indian dance (commemorating that) performed by Krishna and the Gopis; a festival celebrating this.

1828 H. H. Wilson in *Asiatick Researches* XVI. 92 Another [festival] is the *Rás Yátra*, or annual commemoration of the dance of the frolicksome deity. *Ibid.* 93 The *Rás Yátra* is celebrated at the village of Sivapur. **1887** W. J. Wilkins *Mod. Hinduism* iv. iii. 233 *Rāsa Jātra.* This festival is held to commemorate the sports of Krishna with the milkmaids of Vrindāvana. **1912** *Encycl. Relig. & Ethics* V. 889/2 The *rāsa*, or sportive dance, performed by Kṛṣṇa's cowherds and cowherdesses. **1921** *Glasgow Herald* 29 Dec. 7 Graceful dancing women from Manipur..went through their most famous diversion, the 'Ras' dance, in which 'Krishna', here played by a boy, is teased by his feminine playmates. **1933** S. Sitwell *Canons of Giant Art* 122 And now he pipes for them the pastoral rasa, The dance, the shepherds' dance, the Indian cordax. **1951** L. R. Dayal *Manipuri Dances* p. ix, The main forms of dance are the Ras, which is performed in the months of Vaishak (May), Kartik (November), and Phalgoon (February). **1953** F. Bowers *Dance in India* 130 Manipur's two most celebrated distinctions are polo and Ras Lila... Ras Lila is played according to season, and usually on mountain sides or in far-off temples. **1969** *Femina* (Bombay) 26 Dec. 27/1 Of all the seasonal delights of Winter that I've known, those of Gujarat remain the most clearly defined in my memory, especially the beautiful garba and ras dances, with their unforgettable rhythm and sheer vitality. **1972** N. Hein *Miracle Plays of Mathurā* vi. 129 We have seen that the deeds of Vishnu are *līlās*, 'sports'. Ras is the name of a particular one of these deeds, which was done by Vishnu in his Krishṇa incarnation. *Ibid.*, Krishṇa favored the gopis by dancing with them a circular dance, which the Vishṇu Purāṇa calls the rasa. *Ibid.* 130 The rāslīlā is a drama of which Braj claims the sole guardianship.

rasagoola, rasagulla, varr. *rasgulla.

rasant, *a.* (Later example.)

1944 S. Putnam tr. *E. da Cunha's Rebellion in Backlands* v. 256 Eight hundred rifles blazing, eight hundred rifles aimed in a rasant line down the drop of the hill.

‖**rascasse** (raskas). [Fr.] A small Mediterranean scorpion-fish, *Scorpæna scrofa*, which has reddish skin and spiny fins which can cause painful wounds, and which is used esp. as an ingredient of bouillabaisse.

1921 W. J. Locke *Mountebank* xvi. 206 The wondrous dish [*sc.* bouillabaisse] was set before them..*Rascasse, loup de mer*, mostelle, *langouste*—a studied helping of each. **1940** A. Simon *Conc. Encycl. Gastron.* ii. 81/1 Rascasse..is caught in the Mediterranean only. **1950** E. David *Bk. Mediterranean Food* 54 *Rascasse*..is a red spiny fish. **1957** R. Campbell *Portugal* iv. 67 The *rascasse*..is the chief component of..bouillabaisse. **1961** E. McLeod tr. *Colette's Break of Day* 36 A southern luncheon..salads, stuffed *rascasse* and aubergine fritters. **1975** *Sat. Rev.* (U.S.) 29 Nov. 55/1 The ugly rascasse, without which, they say in Marseilles, a proper bouillabaisse cannot be made.

raschel (ræ·ʃĕl). Also **Raschel.** [ad. G. *Raschelmaschine*, f. the name of the French actress *Rachel* (1820–58): cf. *rachel.] **a.** A kind of knitting-machine (see quots. 1940, 1968). **b.** The coarse warp knitting produced by such a machine. Also *attrib.* Hence **ra·schel** *v. trans.*, to knit with a raschel machine (in quot. pa. pple.).

1940 *Chambers's Techn. Dict.* 703/1 *Raschel* (Hosiery), the name for the two-bar warp loom, fitted with latch needles. **1957** M. B. Picken *Fashion Dict.* 195/1 *Raschel knitting*,.. type of warp knitting resembling tricot, but coarser. Done by machine in plain and Jacquard patterns, often with lacy effect. Used for underwear. **1968** J. Ironside *Fashion Alphabet* 246 *Raschel*, a type of knitting-machine producing ribbed fabric. **1970** *Times* 12 May 11/6 The designer demonstrated the uses..of the acrylic yarn in all its many shapes, in fabrics blended, bonded, Neospun, raschelled, knitted, woven, [etc.]. **1972** *Daily Tel.* 30 Oct. 12/6 Frank Usher will have this look, appropriately braid-edged, in a beautiful raschel knit of shaded brown and beige scallops on cream. **1974** *Ibid.* 7 Jan. 9/5 Acrylics, cotton bouclés and raschels, cotton mixed with linen or Vincel: all these give a crisper look to the stripes in your spring sweater than we've had for some time now. **1974** *Encycl. Brit. Macropædia* XVIII. 182/2 The two types of warp knitting are raschel, made with latch needles, and tricot, using bearded needles. *Ibid.*, In the Raschel machine, the needles move in a ground steel plate, called the trick plate.

Raschig (ra·ʃig). Also (*rare*) **raschig.** *Chem. Engin.* The name of Friedrich *Raschig* (1863–1928), German chemist, used *attrib.* († or in the possessive), as **Raschig process**, a process developed by workers in Raschig's chemicals company in which phenol is produced by heating benzene vapour with hydrogen chloride and air over a copper-containing catalyst to yield chlorobenzene, which is then hydrolysed to form phenol; **Raschig ring**, a small cylindrical ring, introduced by Raschig, made of ceramic or other suitable material and used in bulk as a packing material in towers and columns for fractionation, solvent extraction, etc.

1920 *Chem. Abstr.* XIV. 2054 Attention is directed to the advantages attained by the use of Raschig's rings as a filling material for absorption towers in the manuf. of H_2SO_4, HNO_3, HCl, etc. **1926** *Ibid.* XX. 2214 Raschig rings have been used advantageously for clearing of liquids, the turbid liquor being run in at the bottom of a 80-cm. layer of rings, 15 × 15 mm. **1937** *Discovery* Sept. 282/2 Another form of acetifier contains raschig rings. **1940** *Chem. & Engin. News* 10 Nov. 921/1 The unit, which has been in continuous operation for four months.., employs the Raschig process, a catalytic vapor-phase system for the chlorination of benzene and the hydrolysis of the chlorobenzene produced. The process, invented by Prahl and Mathes of the Raschig organization, Ludwigshafen, Germany, produces a phenol purer than U.S.P. and does so with less than 0·1 per cent of by-product. **1947** KIRK & OTHMER *Encycl. Chem. Technol.* I. 16 Raschig rings have the greatest number of applications because they provide a large effective surface of contact between the gas and the liquid phases and they have a large free volume. They are available in sizes from ¼ to 6 in., and the usual design has a height equal to the diameter. **1959** R. J. HENGSTEBECK *Petroleum Processing* xi. 265 Modern furfural extraction columns contain about 40 to 50 ft of Raschig rings, with redistribution equipment at about 5-ft intervals. **1963** *Economist* 14 Dec. 1193/3 The ICI plant uses the Raschig process. **1972** *Materials & Technol.* IV. viii. 309 A modification of the Dow process is the Raschig process, in which benzene is chlorinated by Cl_2 generated by the catalytic oxidation of HCl with oxygen at 230° C, and HCl is recovered in the hydrolysis at 425° C, promoted by Cu catalyst without alkali.

raser[1]. Add: (Later examples.) Also **razer.**

1684 LD. STRATHMORE *Jrnl.* 6 Aug. in *Publ. Scottish Hist. Soc.* (1890) IX. 65, 19 Razers wheat sold at 8 lib 15 sh. s. **1915** C. A. MERCIER *Leper Houses* 40 During Lent each had a razer of wheat..and two razers of beans.

‖**rasgado, rasgueado** (rasgā·do, rasgeā·do). *Mus.* [a. Sp. *rasgado, rasgueado*, pa. ppl. of *rasgar, rasguear* to strum, to make a flourish.] The act of sweeping the strings of a guitar with the fingertips. Also, an arpeggio so produced.

1876 STAINER & BARRETT *Dict. Mus. Terms* 374/2 *Rasgado*.., to sweep the strings of a guitar with the thumb, for the purpose of producing a full chord, *arpeggio*. **1944** W. APEL *Harvard Dict. Music* 628/1 *Rasgado*,..in guitar playing, sweeping the strings with the thumb to produce an arpeggio. **1974** *Early Music* July 185/2 Guitar arrangements in the popular *rasgado* or strumming style. **1979** *Guardian* 29 Oct. 13/2 What he [*sc.* Segovia] didn't like was the *rasgeado*..—the boastful chatter, the flourishes of strokes with the tips of the fingers.

‖**rasgulla** (rasgū·la). Also **rasgoola, rasgula,** etc. [Hindi, f. *ras* juice + *gullā* ball.] An Indian sweet; balls of soft milk cheese soaked in syrup.

1936 E. P. VEERASAWMY *Indian Cookery* 207 Rasgollah... Drop these into a rose-flavoured syrup. **1944** M. R. ANAND *Barber's Trade Union* 72 A sweetmeat seller hawked: 'Gulab-jaman, rasgula, burfi, jalebi.' **1954** S. CHOWDHARY *Indian Cooking* 150 Rasgullas are served warm or cold. **1960** *Harper's Bazaar* July 76/2 Tables laden with curries, chutneys and rasgolas. **1961** B. SINGH *Indian Cookery* VII. 149 Rasgulla is a delicious Bengali sweet. The land of Bengal has long been famous for the preparation of exquisite sweets and in making rasgullas they have excelled themselves. **1962** HOSAIN & PASRICHA *Cooking Indian Way* 225 Rasagulla... They should be double their original size and floating on the surface of the syrup. **1968** P. LAL *Indian Recipes* 218 Rasogoolas... Drop the rasogoolas in the clean boiling syrup. **1969** *Femina* (Bombay) 26 Dec. 27/2 Our dinner however, in the midst of all this rusticity, was certainly no rustic fare;..and to top it all, delicious ice-cream and *rasagoolas!* **1975** R. H. CHRISTIE *Twenty-Two Authentic Banquets from India* xviii. 123 *Rasgullah*, (Milk Croquettes), six tumblers of milk, lemons sufficient in number. **1976** *Times* 18 Aug. 12/7 Try rasgoulas—balls of curd in syrup at 7p each.

rash, *sb.*[3] Add: **2.** *transf.* and *fig.* A proliferation or spate; a sudden outbreak *of* something.

1820 J. HOGG *Winter Evening Tales* I. 312, I was workin' at the loom, wi' my leather apron on, an' a rash o' loom needles in my cuff. **1907** W. DE MORGAN *Alice-for-Short* xl. 427 There too appear more bells than Poe ever wrote about ..a rash of bells that makes you think before you ring. **1930** R. CAMPBELL *Adamastor* 67 A rash of stars upon the sky, A pox of flowers on the earth. **1933** *Times Lit. Suppl.* 16 Mar. 186/1 Her prose is marked by a rash of exclamation marks. **1956** J. M. MOGEY *Family & Neighbourhood* i. 8 By 1870 the pleasant meadow land..had disappeared beneath a rash of bricks and pavements. **1968** B. HINES *Kestrel for Knave* 30 Great rashes of buttercups spread across the fields. **1980** J. MCNEIL *Spy Game* xix. 189 A piece of open ground which has miraculously escaped the rash of building covering the rest of the site.

rash (ræʃ), *sb.*[5] *Coal Mining.* orig. *dial.* (esp. *S. Wales*) and *U.S.* [Prob. f. RASH *a.*] Usu. *pl.* = *RASHING *vbl. sb.*[2]

1903 A. STRAHAN *Geol. S. Wales Coal-Field* IV. iii. 26 Black rashes, fireclay, and clift. *Ibid.* 27 Clift, rashes and rock. **1912** *Federal Reporter* (U.S.) CXCIII. 125 The appearance of rash in the eighth and ninth west entries and at the face of the slope justified the belief that the coal in that vicinity of the mine was inferior and unmerchantable. **1917** GIBSON & CANTRILL *Geol. S. Wales Coalfield* (ed. 2) IV. v. 70 Rashes and clod 1 ft. 3 in. **1964** [see *RASHING *vbl. sb.*[2]]. **1964** WOODLAND & EVANS *Geol. S. Wales Coalfield* (ed. 3) IV. v. 126 At Western the section (from top): coal 7 in, rashes 2½ ft, coal 7 in, fireclay and rashes 5 ft.

rash, *a.* **2. b.** Delete † *Obs.* and add later example.

1876 G. M. HOPKINS *Wreck of Deutschland* xix, in *Poems* (1967) 57 The rash smart sloggering brine Blinds her.

rashing (ræ·ʃiŋ), *vbl. sb.*[2] *Coal Mining.* orig. *dial.* (esp. *S. Wales*) and *U.S.* [Prob. f. RASH *a.* + -ING[1].] Usu. *pl.* A loose brittle deposit of shale or poor coal (see quot. 1964). Cf. *RASH *sb.*[5]

1883 W. S. GRESLEY *Gloss. Terms Coal Mining* 200 *Rashings* (S[outh] W[ales]), loose dirt or shaley beds of rock. **1903** A. STRAHAN *Geol. S. Wales Coal-Field* IV. iii. 10 Rashings 0 ft. 9 in. **1905** *Maryland Geol. Survey* V. 534 Immediately overlying the 'Big Vein' is a brittle slate interstratified with thin seams of coal known as the 'Wild Coal' or 'Rashings'. Upon exposure to the air the wild coal crumbles and falls. **1917** GIBSON & CANTRILL *Geol. S. Wales Coalfield* (ed. 2) IV. iv. 47 The Wet-and-Dry Coal is said to lie 14 yds. below the Lantern, and to consist of top coal, 2 ft. 8 ins. thick, bottom coal, 1 ft. 4 ins. to 1 ft. 6 ins. thick, with 6 ins. of soft rashings between. **1954** A. TRUEMAN *Coalfields Gt. Brit.* ii. 23 Black carbonaceous shales, containing abundant plant remains (the 'rashings' of some coalfields). **1964** WOODLAND & EVANS *Geol. S. Wales Coalfield* (ed. 3) IV. iv. 75 *Rashes* or *rashings, either* soft carbonaceous shale with streaks of coal *or* highly disturbed, slickensided, comminated shale or mudstone formed by movement parallel to the bedding and usually associated with the roof or dirt bands in coal seams. Normally 'rashes' should be retained for the former definition and 'rashings' for the latter. **1967** I. A. WILLIAMSON *Coal Mining Geol.* vii. 55 Batt and rashings are approximately synonymous for shale containing thin coal streaks.

rashleighite (ræ·ʃli̯ əit). *Min.* [See quot. 1948 and -ITE[1].] A hydrated basic phosphate of copper, aluminium, and iron, $Cu(Al,Fe)_6(PO_4)_4(OH)_8 \cdot 5H_2O$, found as crusts and friable masses of triclinic crystals.

1948 A. RUSSELL in *Mineral. Mag.* XXVIII. 353 The name rashleighite commemorates Philip Rashleigh, F.R.S., F.G.S., F.S.A., 1729–1811,..one of the earliest Cornish mineralogists and famous for having amassed the finest collection of Cornish minerals ever made. **1971** *Country Life* 3 June 1382/2 Turquoise in the form of rashleighite occurs on St. Austell Moor, in Cornwall. **1972** *Amer. Mineralogist* LVII. 1681 Rashleighite..can be described as a substitutional solid solution of turquois and chalcosiderite.

rashling. For '† *Obs. rare*—[1]' read '*rare*' and add later example.

1922 BARONESS ORCZY *Triumph of Scarlet Pimpernel* v. 57 The young Hotspur and his crowd of rashlings would ere now have been torn from their seats.

‖**raskol** (ræskǫ·l). Also **rascol.** [Russ.: see RASKOLNIK.] **1. a.** The schism in the Russian Church which resulted from the reforms of Patriarch Nikon, who excommunicated dissenters in 1667.

1887 A. F. HEARD *Russ. Church & Russ. Dissent* ix. 179 Both German Protestantism and Russian Raskol preserve the stamp of their similar religious origin, as issuing each from an established State Church. **1900** 'ODYSSEUS' *Turkey in Europe* vi. 288 This energetic and ambitious prelate [*sc.* Nikon]..provoked by his reforms the great schism (or *raskol*) from which spring the various sects of Old Believers. **1908** W. F. ADENEY *Greek & Eastern Churches* II. III. vii. 444 The Raskol obtained new vigour from another source—popular resistance to Peter the Great's Western innovations. **1963** N. V. RIASANOVSKY *Hist. Russia* xix. 221 The raskol constituted the only major schism in the history of the Orthodox Church in Russia. **1969** K. MINOGUE in Ionescu & Gellner *Populism* 203 The Russian *raskol* after 1654, although a religious phenomenon, has been taken as a peasant reaction to urban culture.

b. Dissent from an established orthodoxy.

1947 *Partisan Rev.* XIV. 396 Russian revisionism was a heterodoxy, a fanatic schism, a *raskol*.

2. *collect.* A body of dissenters under the raskol (sense *1 a).

1888 'STEPNIAK' *Russ. Peasantry* II. 441 The *Rascol* proper, the 'Old Believers'.

Raskolnik. (Earlier example.)

1723 in tr. *F. C. Weber's Present State of Russia* I. 82 He was reported to be of the Sect of the Raskolniks, who have entirely separated from the Russian Church, a few Ceremonies excepted.

rasogoola, var. *RASGULLA.

rasophore (ra·zofōɹ). Also **rasophor, rhasophore.** [ad. med. Gr. *ρασοφόρος*, f. *ράσον* cassock + *-φορος* bearer.] The lowest grade of monk in the Greek Orthodox Church. Also ‖ **rhasophoria,** the grade of a rasophore.

1887 A. RILEY *Athos* v. 68 The monks are divided into two classes, the *dokimos*.., or novice and the *caloyer*.., or professed monk. The caloyers, again, are divided into three grades—*rhasophoria*.., *the little habit*..and *the great habit.* **1934** WEBSTER, *Rhasophore*. **1960** P. SHERRARD *Athos* 63 The monk of the lowest grade is called a Rasophore, after the *rason* or tunic which he wears as part of his habit... He is..more than a novice in the western sense. **1964** P. F. ANSON *Bishops at Large* i. 37 Almost any alien, provided that he..calls himself an abuna,..pappas, rasophor, starets, synkellos,..vartapet..invariably finds a warm welcome in England.

rasour: see also *RÉSEAU.

rasp, *sb.*[1] Add: **2. c.** A ribbed band or organ in some insects.

1826 KIRBY & SPENCE *Introd. Entomol.* III. xxx. 143 This animal..has on it a double series of rasps. **1871** DARWIN *Descent of Man* I. x. 378 The rasp generally consists of a narrow, slightly-raised surface, crossed by very fine, parallel ribs.

4. (Further examples.)

1976 *National Observer* (U.S.) 25 Dec. 4/1 'Christ, can you believe that?' he cries in his staccato, Brooklyn-accented rasp that has been honed just enough so that his 'thats' don't come out 'dats'. **1977** *Rolling Stone* 30 June 113/1 Like many such groups, Detective centers around a guitarist (Michael Monarch, whose aggressive rasp distinguished the earliest Steppenwolf sides).

rasp, *v.*[1] Add: **2. c.** Also with *on.*

1898 F. P. DUNNE *Mr. Dooley in Peace & War* 232 But wan day it happened that that whole fam'ly begun to rasp on wan another. **1905** *Pall Mall Mag.* Dec. 674/2 Any reference to the Philippine campaign rasped on his nerves.

d. To grate (the hard crust) off (a roll); also *intr.* for *pass.*

1889 R. WELLS *Pastrycook & Confectioner's Guide* ii. 11 French rolls must always be rasped. **1892** —— *Mod. Pract. Bread Baker* 57 They must be well baked, or they will not rasp as all French rolls should. **1908** J. KIRKLAND *Mod. Baker* II. xxvi. 162 These rolls are occasionally baked with a very hard crust, which is afterwards rasped off.

4. Delete *rare*—[1] and add further examples. Also *absol.* and *transf.* Also with *out.*

1877 *Harper's Mag.* Oct. 664/1 A somewhat harsh clock rasped out the seconds. **1905** *Pall Mall Mag.* Sept. 276/1 Commander McTurk stiffened. 'Ah,' he rasped, 'that's news to me.' *Ibid.* Nov. 543/1 'Really, Bridget!' her brother rasped out, 'I wish you wouldn't interfere.' **1922** JOYCE *Ulysses* 442 A bunch of loiterers listen to a tale which their broken snouted gaffer rasps out. **1937** C. S. FORESTER *Happy Return* x. 124 'Hard-a-starboard,' he rasped at the quartermaster. **1962** [see *HELL *sb.* 10 h]. **1976** W. GREATOREX *Crossover* 142 'I'm not thirsty,' Calder said. 'I've had enough for one night.' 'You're telling *me*,' the inspector rasped. **1977** *Time* 28 Nov. 50/3 Rasped an Agriculture official: 'That was a technically accurate statement. But it also was a god-damn lie.'

5. a. (Earlier example.)

1808 S. W. RYLEY *Itinerant* I. iv. 91 A blind fiddler, mounted on a three footed stool, rasped away very *seriously* the black *Joke*.

raspberry. Add: **3*. a.** [App. an ellipt. use of *raspberry tart* (*b*) below.] A derisive sound; = *Bronx cheer* s.v. *BRONX 2.

1890 in BARRÈRE & LELAND *Dict. Slang* (1890) II. 171/1 The tongue is inserted in the left cheek and forced through the lips, producing a peculiarly squashy noise that is extremely irritating. It is termed, I believe, a *raspberry*, and when not employed for the purpose of testing horseflesh, is regarded rather as an expression of contempt than of admiration. **1899** A. M. BINSTEAD *Gal's Gossip* 144 A loud and offensive noise, like the rending of glazed calico, made by obtruding the wet tongue between the closed lips, and by low cabmen and persons of that class, called a 'raspberry', came from the gallery. **1912** *Confessions of Dancing Girl* iv. 69 The custom of 'guying' a performer and giving him what is called a 'raspberry'. Not a few artistes have had 'raspberries' from the audiences in the Glasgow variety halls. **1932** A. J. WORRALL *Eng. Idioms* v. 33 As soon as the speaker rose the crowd gave him the raspberry. **1940** R. CHANDLER *Farewell, my Lovely* xxix. 211 The kind of bossy knock that makes you want to..emit the succulent raspberry. **1955** [see *BRONX 2]. **1960** G. DURRELL *Zoo in my Luggage* vi. 157 To my complete astonishment Minnie responded by..giving a prolonged raspberry of the juiciest variety. **1975** *South Wales Echo* 30 Oct. 8/4 The only answer to that kind of nonsense is a long-drawn-out vintage raspberry.

b. *fig.* A refusal; a reprimand, disapproval; dismissal.

1920 WODEHOUSE *Damsel in Distress* vi. 71 Convict son totters up the steps of the old home and punches the bell! What awaits him beyond? Forgiveness? Or the raspberry? **1923** —— *Inimitable Jeeves* ix. 89 He was given the respectful raspberry by Jeeves, and told to try again about three hours later. **1927** *Punch* 14 Dec. 649/2, I have embodied the above suggestions in a memo, and they are now on their way to the Army Council... They may even be on their way back, with a raspberry from Somebody Very Senior written across the top left-hand corner. **1942** *New Statesman* 1 Aug. 75/1 An ordinary reprimand is a *raspberry* (often referred to by other ranks as a *razzer*), which has been adopted from that form of civilian disapproval which one hears in the gallery of a theatre. **1947** [see *ALL *adv.* 2 c]. **1960** O. MANNING *Great Fortune* I. 67 Miller made it! Nice scoop for Miller! And a raspberry for the rest of us. **1973** M. SPARK *Hothouse by East River* iv. 69 The security officer mutters all the way to the compound about what a raspberry the police are going to get because of this, a raspberry in these days being already an outdated expression meaning a reprimand. A man less set in his limited ways.. would call it a rocket in this English spring of 1944. **1977** *Western Morning News* 1 Sept. 1/2 Controversial punk rock band Sex Pistols blew a raucous raspberry at the Establishment by sneaking into Plymouth to play an unannounced concert at Woods.

3.** The colour of a raspberry, varying from pink to scarlet. Also *attrib.* or as *adj.*

1923 *Daily Mail* 19 Feb. 15 New tailor-mades of black or navy serge have shawl collars of mattelassé silk in a contrasting colour—raspberry, green, or kingfisher blue. **1935** *Times* 2 Oct. 17/4 A raspberry cellophane wrap has been shown over a white and gold lamé gown. **1941** [see *HACKMANITE]. **1951** E. PAUL *Springtime in Paris* ii. 17 Two neon signs,..one..in a faint raspberry shade, and another..in a luminous tone of white. **1969** 'H. PENTECOST' *Girl Watcher's Funeral* (1970), II. i. 88 The raspberry dress that clung to her lush figure. **1972** [see *LIME *sb.*[2] 1 c]. **1978** J. KRANTZ *Scruples* ii. 24 The floor of the air-conditioned room was covered from one wall to another in thick raspberry carpet.

4. *raspberry bitters, drop, jam* (earlier and later examples), *jelly, noyau, pie, roll, seed, syrup, tart* (earlier examples), *vinegar* (later example); **raspberry beetle,** a beetle of the genus *Byturus*, esp. *B. tomentosus* (formerly *B. urbanus*), the larva of which attacks the fruit of raspberries and related plants;

raspberry fruitworm = prec.; **raspberry jam (tree)** (later examples); also, the wood itself; **raspberry tart** *rhyming slang*, (*a*) the heart; (*b*) a breaking of wind or 'fart'.

1884 E. A. ORMEROD *Observations Injurious Insects 1883* 65 A small brown Beetle..proved to be the 'Raspberry Beetle',..which was causing fearful havoc and entirely devouring the Raspberries. **1909** F. V. THEOBALD *Insects & Other Pests of Orchard, Bush & Hothouse Fruits* 420 There is no insect enemy so serious to raspberries as the Raspberry Beetle. **1959** E. F. LINSSEN *Beetles Brit. Isles* II. 23 This genus [sc. *Byturus*] includes a well-known pest of raspberries, loganberries and blackberries, commonly referred to as the Raspberry Beetle. **1849** THACKERAY *Pendennis* I. xv. 131 He..drank a glass of raspberry bitters at the Clavering Arms. **1897** 'S. GRAND' *Beth Book* iii. 19 Give me a ha'porth ..of raspberry-drops. **1939–40** *Army & Navy Stores Catal.* 52/2 *Boiled sweets*..Raspberry drops. **1924** *Ann. Rep. Connecticut Agric. Exper. Station* 91 The Raspberry Fruit Worm or Raspberry Beetle has long been known as a pest of red raspberries in the United States. **1945** L. PYENSON *Pest Control in Home Garden* vii. 122 The formula used in these two sprays controls the raspberry fruit worm. **1972** SWAN & PAPP *Common Insects N. Amer.* 396 The Western Raspberry Fruitworm..is a serious pest of raspberries and loganberries. **1747** Raspberry jam [see JAM *sb.*[2] a]. **1846** [see *gooseberry jam* s.v. *GOOSEBERRY 7 a]. **1865** J. E. TENISON-WOODS *Hist. Discovery & Exploration Austral.* II. 68 The other trees beside the palm were known to the men by colonial appellations, such as the bloodwood and the raspberry-jam. **1896** *Australasian* 15 Feb. 313 The raspberry-jam-tree is so called on account of the strong aroma of raspberries given out when a portion is broken. **1948** F. H. TITMUSS *Conc. Encycl. World Timbers* 113 Raspberry Jam is rather a difficult timber to work. **1965** *Austral. Encyl.* VII. 389/1 Raspberry-jam, a popular name standardized in the timber trade for *Acacia acuminata* of Western Australia; the dark reddish-brown, durable, close-grained wood of this wattle has a distinct raspberry-like scent. **1861** MRS. BEETON *Bk. Househ. Managem.* 797 Raspberry Jelly... To each pint of juice allow ¾ lb. of loaf sugar. **1913**, **1963** Raspberry noyau [see *NOYAU 1 b]. **1828** E. LESLIE *Seventy-Five Receipts* 25 Raspberry and apple-pies are much improved by..pouring in a little cream. **1864** *Harper's Mag.* Nov. 735/1 A green cheese, a dish of cucumbers, and two raspberry pies supplied a finish to the entertainment. **1974** J. GRIGSON *Eng. Food* 206 Raspberry Pie..Filling 1 lb raspberries About 4 oz sugar [etc.]. **1868** A. D. WHITNEY *Patience Strong's Outings* (1869) xii. 138, I..made her give up..the special raspberry-roll for dinner. **1841** M. EDGEWORTH *Let.* 23 Mar. (1971) 590 Dr. Lindley..saw that they were raspberry seeds and he put them in ground and they..have grown to real raspberry bushes. **1728** E. SMITH *Compl. Housewife* (ed. 2) 192 Two Ounces of Syrup of red Poppies, and as much of Raspberry Syrup. **1965** *Savoy Cocktail Bk.* (ed. 3) 177 *Raspberry Lemonade Cocktail.* Put into tumbler juice of 1 Lemon..sugar.. Raspberry Syrup..ice..water. **1723** J. NOTT *Cook's & Confectioner's Dict.* sig. Ff3 (*heading*) To make a Raspberry Tart. **1848** [see HARD-BAKE]. **1892** *Sporting Times* 29 Oct. 1/2 Then I sallied forth with a careless air, And contented raspberry tart. **1959** I. & P. OPIE *Lore & Lang. Schoolch.* i. 9 Breaking wind was, at one time, by the process of rhyming slang, known as a 'raspberry tart'. **1960** J. J. ROWLANDS *Spindrift* 55 That was the era of raspberry vinegar, lemonade, and homemade root beer.

rasper. Add: **2.** (Later example.)

1929 H. A. VACHELL *Virgin* iii. 53 In front was a big solid fence, a rasper.

3. (Earlier and later examples in sense 'anything remarkable or extraordinary in its own way'.)

1844 *Spirit of Times* 19 Oct. 403/2 She promises to be a perfect 'rasper', and will have some 'tall' chronicling in the 'Spirit' before all of her yarn is spun. **1977** SCOLLINS & TITFORD *Ey up, mi Duck!* II. 52 *Rasper*, another expression of excellence; often describes a good goal in football.

rasping, *vbl. sb.* Add: **2. a.** (Further examples.) In mod. usage, *spec.* breadcrumbs made from baked or stale bread.

1846 *Jewish Manual Cookery* 47 Butter a mold, sprinkle it with raspings. **1945** *ABC of Cookery* (Ministry of Food) iii. 14 *Raspings*, very fine crumbs obtained by grating the crust of stale bread on a fine grater. Browned breadcrumbs are sometimes called raspings. **1951** *Good Housek. Home Encycl.* 629/1 Sprinkle raspings over the fat of cooked ham. **1976** M. PATTEN *Barbecue* 31/2 Cut the crusts from the loaf; these need not be wasted, but can be turned into crumbs (raspings) as described below.

raspite (ræ·spəit). *Min.* [ad. G. *raspit* (C. Hlawatsch 1897, in *Ann. des K. K. Naturhist. Hofmuseums* XII. 33), f. the name of Mr. *Rasp*, discoverer of the Broken Hill mines, New South Wales, where the first specimen was found: see -ITE[1].] A lead tungstate, $PbWO_4$, that is dimorphous with stolzite and occurs as brownish, yellow, or grey prismatic monoclinic crystals.

1898 *Mineral Mag.* XII. 47 Raspite, a new dimorphous form of lead tungstate, is found on some of the stolzite specimens as brownish or yellow monoclinic crystals with a strong adamantine lustre. **1931** J. W. MELLOR *Compreh. Treat. Inorg. & Theoret. Chem.* XI. lxii. 793 Stolzite occurs in tetragonal crystals, raspite in monoclinic crystals. **1956** *Mineral Abstr.* XIII. 30 Natural raspite transforms irreversibly to stolzite at about 400° C. **1968** I. KOSTOV *Mineralogy* II. viii. 486 Stolzite is uniaxial negative..; raspite biaxial positive.

Rasputin (ræspiū·tin, ræ·spiutin). The acquired name (lit. 'debauchee') of Grigory Yefimovich Novykh (*c* 1872–1916), mystic and favourite at the court of the Russian Emperor Nicholas II, used allusively of one who resembles Rasputin in exercising an insidious or corrupting influence over another or (esp.) over members of the governing class. Also *attrib.*

1937 H. G. WELLS *Star Begotten* viii. 152 My professional gifts give me a kind of Rasputin hold on one or two exalted families. **1975** *Economist* 8 Feb. 35/2 Referred to in private ..as a Rasputin or a Svengali, her private secretary, Sr José López Rega, has enlarged his power. **1975** *Times* 23 May 2/2 Mr Wilson..drove home the policy divisions on the Tory front bench by noting that Sir Keith Joseph—'Mrs Thatcher's..mentor and Svengali'..the right hon lady's Rasputin—had been kennelled up for the debate. **1978** G. MITCHELL *Wraiths & Changelings* xv. 149 He was becoming a sort of Rasputin where Mrs Crieff-Tweedle was concerned... I'm sure she was coming under..a sinister influence.

So **Raspu·tinism,** the principles and practices held to be characteristic of Rasputin, chiefly with reference to his libertinism and his corrupting influence over government.

1918 *Pall Mall Gaz.* 26 Jan. 3/1 Some exceedingly fine shades of difference were explained, and some striking affinities pointed out. For instance, Bolshevism, in Mr. Wilton's opinion, is nothing but Rasputinism under another name. **1919** W. LE QUEUX *Rasputinism in London* xii. 160 London is surely vicious enough without the evil practices of Rasputinism! **1933** H. G. WELLS *Shape of Things to Come* II. iv. 169 It had a touch of Rasputinism, this revival of the ancient heresy that one must sin *thoroughly* before one can be saved. **1975** *Economist* 8 Feb. 35/3 But a new decree, signed by Sra Perón herself, has made it clear that he [*sc.* her private secretary] will have the last word about whom she sees and what she is told. This latest step towards the legitimisation of rasputinism (the latest word to be coined here [*sc.* in Argentina]) has aroused the armed forces.

raspy, *a.*[1] Add: **2.** (Earlier example.)

1869 L. M. ALCOTT *Little Women* II. i. 20, I don't wish to get raspy, so let's change the subject.

3. *Comb.*, as *raspy-gaspy*.

1903 KIPLING in *Windsor Mag.* Sept. 363/2 She said it in a raspy-gaspy whisper that would have frightened a steam-cow.

rass (rās), *sb.* (*a.*) and *v.* *Jamaica. coarse slang.* [f. ARSE *sb.* by metathesis and perh. partly also by metanalysis (of *your arse*).] **A.** *sb.* The buttocks, the arse. Also *transf.* as a term of contempt, and *attrib.* or as *adj.* **B.** *vb. trans.* = *BUGGER *v.* 2; also *ellipt.* for 'shove it up your arse' used as an insult.

1790 J. B. MORETON *Manners & Customs in W. India Islands* 154 Then missess fum me wid long switch, And say him da for massa; My massa curse her, 'lying bitch!' And tell her 'buss my rassa!' *c* **1918** in CASSIDY & LE PAGE *Dict. Jamaican Eng.* (1967) 372/2 /raas/ as in 'Raas to you!'—common among schoolboys. **1952** *Caribbean Q.* II. iv. 27 Fred dropped his hoe and hit him hard. Big Joe was up roaring:— 'Rass yah today!' **1959** A. SALKEY *Quality of Violence* vii. 101 You rass clothes going rip off... You, class-war rass hole, you! *Ibid.*, They believe they is superior and all that rass! **1965** I. FLEMING *Man with Golden Gun* xiii. 173 'Rass, man! Ah doan talk wid buckra.' The expression 'rass' is Jamaican for 'shove it'. **1976** BOOT & THOMAS *Jamaica* 88 If he gave them any *rass* they'd hit from all sides with a gale of maniacal rhetoric that would reduce the poor man to blubber.

rasse[1]. Substitute *Viverricula indica* for *V. malaccensis* in def. (Later examples.)

1896 R. LYDEKKER *Handbk. Carnivora* 216 While all the other civets are non-arboreal animals, the Rasse is said to be an expert climber. **1971** L. H. MATTHEWS *Life of Mammals* II. ix. 273 The rasse, *Viverricula indica*, widespread in India and southeast Asia, is smaller but similar [to the African civet] in diet and habits.

‖ **rassenschander** (ra·sənʃa:ndəɹ). *rare.* [erron. f. G. *rassenschande*, f. *rasse* race + *schande* violation.] The violation of the purity of the ('Aryan') race by marriage to one of a different race.

1937 AUDEN in Auden & MacNeice *Lett. from Iceland* xiii. 201, I ought to be the prize, the living wonder, The really pure from any Rassenschander... The Nordic type, the too too truly Aryan.

‖ **rasta** (rasta), *sb.*[1] [Fr., abbrev. of *RASTAQUOUÈRE.] = *RASTAQUOUÈRE.

1905 *Truth* 18 May 1267/2 The *rasta*—for the word undergoes contraction—was twenty years ago apt to be unpleasant on account of his airs. **1929** J. BUCHAN *Courts of Morning* 25 One of his South American colleagues had taken him to dine at a restaurant much in vogue among the *rastas*. **1937** G. FRANKAU *More of Us* vii. 77 Doyen de Bouche, that celebrated rasta, Inventor of the coup de limonade.

Rasta (ræ·stā), *sb.*[2] Also **rasta.** [Shortened form of *RASTAFARI or *RASTAFARIAN(ISM).] **a.** = *RASTAFARIAN *sb.* **b.** = *RASTAFARIANISM. Freq. *attrib.* and *Comb.* Hence **Ra·staman,** a (male) Rastafarian.

1955 G. E. SIMPSON in *Social Forces* XXXIV. II. 167/1 The 'Rasta' people consider Marcus Garvey..as the forerunner of their movement. **1960** M. G. SMITH et al. *Ras Tafari Movement in Kingston, Jamaica* 11 Those people who worshipped the Emperor and were locally known as 'Ras Tafaris' or 'Rastamen' came to describe themselves as 'Niyamen'. **1962** *Listener* 1 Feb. 209/1 There are other Rastas, fanatic and militant, whose ideology is a blend of myth, religion, anarchistic politics, and black nationalism. **1965** I. FLEMING *Man with Golden Gun* vi. 84 'You carry a gun?' 'Of course. You don't go after the Rastas without one.' **1966** [see *LOCKSMAN[2]]. **1976** BOOT & THOMAS *Jamaica* 79/1 Rasta is not just some half-witted heretic sect selling space in the hereafter. *Ibid.* 93/1 Why should a Rastaman lift a finger to participate in a society that thinks he's just some poor dope-fiend with fried spinach for brains? **1976** *New Musical Express* 27 Mar. 19/6 Doris Day's son Terry Melcher and ex-Beach Boy Bruce Johnston scraping the bottom of the barrel with this well known primary school rasta chant. **1977** MCKNIGHT & TOBLER *Bob Marley* ii. 31 Remember the words of the song *Jah Live*, a Rasta-minded admonishment to all those who suggest that Selassie's physical and merely temporal death might represent the death of the living God. **1977** *Westindian World* 3–9 June 13/3 They are also reflections of Tosh's world view; a combination of Pan African nationalism and rasta mysticism.

Rastafari, Ras Tafari (ræ:stăfā·ri; *locally also* ra:stafarəi·). Also **Rastafaria.** [f. the name *Ras Tafari* (cf. *RAS), by which Emperor Haile Selassie of Ethiopia (1892–1975) was known from 1916 until his accession in 1930.] A Jamaican sect which believes that Blacks are the chosen people, that the late Emperor Haile Selassie is God Incarnate, and that he will secure their repatriation to their homeland in Africa. Also *pl.*, the members of this sect, and *attrib.* So **Rastafa·rinism, Rastafa·rism, Ras Tafa·rism; Rastafa·rite,** a member of this sect.

1953 F. HENRIQUES *Family & Colour in Jamaica* iii. 62 The current expositors of black consciousness in Jamaica are a group of people who call themselves Ras Tafarites. **1955** G. E. SIMPSON in *Social & Econ. Stud.* (Kingston, Jamaica) IV. II. 133 The Ras Tafari movement began to take shape about 1930. *Ibid.* 137 Among the favourite chapters of the Ras Tafaris are: Isaiah 43. *Ibid.* 146 Ras Tafarism provides explanations of their plight to economically disadvantaged people. **1960** *Guardian* 12 Apr. 9/3 The 'Rastafari' cult, who have long, matted hair and beards and believe that the drug marihuana..is ordained by the Bible for man's use. **1962** *Listener* 22 Feb. 345/1 The 'uppressors' ..go off into weirdness such as Rastafarinism. **1962** *Times Lit. Suppl.* 10 Aug. 578/4 The surcharge of an equally false nationalistic fantasy, at its most absurd and dangerous in the 'Rastafarism' of Jamaica with its worship of Haile Selassie and its slogan 'Death to the Whites'. **1965** I. FLEMING *Man with Golden Gun* iii. 41 He has groups of admirers (e.g. the Rastafari in Jamaica). **1973** *Caribbean Contact* Feb. 15/1 The Rastafaria brethren, too, who venerate Haile Selassie I and who keenly look forward to repatriation to their lost homeland of Africa, remain today faithful Garveyites. **1977** *Times Lit. Suppl.* 7 Jan. 9/5 Inadequate housing and insufficient jobs [in Kingston, Jamaica]..also contributed to the rise of the Ras Tafari with their dreams of escape to Africa.

Rastafarian (ræ:stăfā·riăn, -fē·riăn), *a.* and *sb.* Also **Ras Tafarian.** [f. prec. + -AN.] **A.** *adj.* Of or pertaining to the Rastafari sect. **B.** *sb.* A member of this sect. Hence **Ra:sta-fa·rianism.**

1955 G. E. SIMPSON in *Social & Econ. Stud.* (Kingston, Jamaica) IV. II. 134 Emphasis..is placed on love and kindliness to fellow Ras Tafarians. **1960** *Guardian* 28 June 9/4 The bearded Marijuana-smoking Rastafarian sect. *Ibid.*, The Rastafarians run a campaign to get Jamaican negroes to return to Africa. **1963** *Times* 19 Apr. 9/1 Eight people were killed and others injured after members of the ganja-smoking Rastafarian cult went wild with guns and machetes. **1968** F. HENRIQUES *Family & Colour in Jamaica* (ed. 2) xiv. 181 The response of the University was to send a team of experts to investigate and report on Rastafarianism. **1976** *Peace News* 25 June 3/1 A group of Rastafarian West Indians wearing brightly-coloured woolly hats walking along the pavements alongside us, shaking their maracas. **1976** G. SIMS *End of Web* x. 69 A couple of Rastafarians whose thick matted tassels of hair hung down over their shoulders. **1977** *Vole* No. 4. 41/2 The cult of Rastafarianism, involving the deification of Haile Selassie, the promise of Ethiopia as their spiritual home, and above all, the rejection of..white society.

Rastaman: see *RASTA *sb.*[2]

‖ **rastaquouère** (rastakwḗr). Also **rasta-couaire, rastaquoère,** etc. [F. *rastaquouère, rastaquère*, ad. S. Amer. Sp. *rastacuero* upstart.] A social intruder or upstart of exaggerated manners or dress, esp. from a Mediterranean or S. Amer. country; a dashing but untrustworthy foreigner. Also *attrib.*

1883 M. E. BRADDON *Phantom Fortune* III. v. 110 He was the typical *rastaquouere*, a man of finished manners, and unknown antecedents. **1904** J. T. GREIN *Dramatic Crit.* *1902–1903* 56 Even *rastaquoères*..do not err in this direction. **1913** M. LARISCH *My Past* ix. 104, I rather liked the Baroness, although Count Larisch rudely termed the whole family *rastaquouères*. **1924** J. BUCHAN *Three Hostages* xiii. 199 The usual *rastaquouère* crowd of men and women drinking liqueurs and champagne. **1930** BELLOC *New Cautionary Tales* 28 Ambassadors and Papal Counts, And Rastaquouères from Palamerez. **1930** A. HUXLEY *Vulgarity in Literature* vi. 34 The *rastacouaire* might display the twin cabochon emeralds at his shirt cuffs and the platinum wrist watch.

1940 J. BUCHAN *Memory Hold-the-Door* vi. 128 There was a vulgar display of wealth, and a *rastaquouère* craze for luxury. **1975** *Times Lit. Suppl.* 19 Dec. 1511/2 The worst book ever written by an Old Etonian, even by a rather *rastaquouère* Old Etonian.

raster (ræ·stəɹ), *sb.*[2] [a. G. *raster* screen, frame, f. L. *rastrum* rake, f. *rāsum*, supine of *rādĕre* to scrape.] **a.** A usu. rectangular pattern of parallel scanning lines forming or corresponding to the display on a cathode-ray tube; also more widely, with reference to other instruments and techniques involving systematic scanning movements or patterns without the use of a cathode-ray tube. Also *raster pattern, scan*; *raster-scan* vb. trans., *raster-scanning* vbl. sb. and ppl. adj.

1934 BEDFORD & PUCKLE in *Jrnl. Inst. Electr. Engineers* LXXV. 64 The path of the spot must, so to speak, be mapped out beforehand into a suitable line *raster*, which is of such a size and shape as to allow the real image of the spot to explore the whole of one picture. [*Note*] This word, imported from the German, is used to mean a scanning field or grating. **1939** *Television & Short-Wave World Pract. Handbk.* No. 1. vi. 54/1 The production of the series of lines, or 'raster' as it is generally termed, is..purely a local function of the receiver and quite independent of any reception of signals. **1940** *Jrnl. R. Aeronaut. Soc.* XLIV. 103 It is claimed that the electron Raster microscope overcomes these difficulties. The principle of the microscope is as follows:— A thin electron beam is made to scan the object in a 'Raster' as in television. **1946** *Jrnl. Inst. Electr. Engineers* XCIII. IIIA. 1560/2 A raster approximately an inch square was then substituted for the noise pattern, obtained by applying the output from two saw-tooth oscillators, one of 50 c/s and the other of 10 kc/s, to the two pairs of plates of the tube. **1952** *Electronic Engin.* XXIV. 166/1 If a raster composed of horizontal scanning lines is further divided into the appropriate number of vertical lines, each line will become broken up into dots. **1966** [see *INTERLACE *v.* 6]. **1968** P. R. THORNTON *Scanning Electron Microscopy* i. 8 Three years later [in 1938] v. Ardenne..built the first scanning electron microscope which used two magnetic lenses to provide a small electron spot at the specimen. Two sets of magnetic coils were used to scan the beam across the specimen in a television-like raster. **1969** BARTON & WARD *Handbk. Radar Measurement* viii. 227 Raster-scanning pencil beams. These radars can be analyzed as search radars or sequential-processing trackers in both angular coordinates. **1970** *New Scientist* 4 June (Suppl.) 7/2 The screen can be 'raster-scanned' as on a TV screen (i.e. the light is deflected across the screen in a series of lines gradually moving to the bottom). **1973** *Sci. Amer.* Oct. 73/1 The spectroheliograms were made by holding the diffraction grating at one angle, so that only a single wavelength fell on the photomultiplier. The solar image was then scanned in a raster pattern to build up a picture of the sun in that one wavelength. **1973** *Physics Bull.* May 275/1 A flying spot performs a raster scan of the whole picture and with the help of a photodetector transforms the entire optical information—spots and all—into the memory of a large online computer. **1977** *Sci. Amer.* Oct. 84/2 In a circular-scan radar system the raster of the cathode-ray tube rotates synchronously with the antenna.

b. *Cinemat.* and *Photogr.* A fine grid, comprising wires, slits, or lenticular elements, placed in front of the projection screen in some stereoscopic cinematography systems, notably that invented by F. Savoye in 1942. Also *raster screen*.

1952 E. F. LINSSEN *Stereo-Photogr. in Practice* xxi. 291 In 1945 B. T. Ivanov wrote on 'raster-stereoscopy in the cinema'. *Ibid.* 292 Savoye's Cyclostereoscopic system... The cone allows the two beams to pass through many slits.. with which it is provided, and these same slits (constituting a revolving grid or raster) also act as selectors for the spectators. **1957** K. C. M. SYMONS *Stereo Photogr.* 205 Another method depends on the provision of a grid or raster screen in front of the projection screen. This method, which has a certain affinity with the parallax stereogram..forms the basis of two methods of projection, one Russian, the other French. *Ibid.* 213 *Raster*, a term used to describe certain autostereoscopic methods which depend on the use of a screen for multiplying and selecting the images. **1958** *Newnes Compl. Amat. Photogr.* 235 An alternative method of projection is the Cyclosterscopic system... This system consists of a metal cone of fine grids or rasters which revolves around the screen and is not noticeable in motion. **1965** *Focal Encycl. Photogr.* (rev. ed.) II. 1207/1 Raster screens consist of an arrangement of vertical wires interposed between the screen surface and the audience... There are also patented screens in which the projection surface is composed of vertical lenticular prisms, or of spherical lenticular elements graduated in size.

Hence as *v. trans.*, to scan (an area) with a beam that goes over it in a raster pattern; **ra·stered** *ppl. a.*, (of a beam) made to scan an area thus.

1975 *Nature* 9 Oct. 521/1 Methods by which the properties of inorganic materials may be measured quantitatively using the interaction of a rastered kilovolt electron beam with a solid. **1978** *Ibid.* 3 Aug. 457/2 Fig. 1 shows..two X-ray maps obtained (using electron microprobe X-ray fluorescence) by rastering the same region with a 30-kV electron beam and collecting in sequence the K Kα and Ca Kα rays.

Rastus (ræ·stŭs). *U.S.* [Prob. shortened form of the personal name *Erastus*.] A name applied joc. in a number of songs and moving picture films to a 'typical' Negro, subsequently used as an offensive term for a Black person.

1895 K. MILLS *Rastus on Parade* (song) 5 No use in talking he's hot stuff, Is Rastus when on Parade. **1909** C. W. HAYES in *Lippincott's Mag.* May 636 (*title*) Rastus's baby. **1910** *Moving Picture World* 7 May 749/2 Rastus in Zululand.—Rastus is an odd-jobs man, that is he does odd jobs when he has to. **1932** F. DUBOSE *Episodes in Black & White* 1 Two little pickaninnies were sitting by the fire when in came Uncle Rastus with a pumpkin pie. **1932** E. V. WHITE *Chocolate Drops from South* 13 Mandy: 'Rastus, yo' makes me think yo' got the equator on yo'.' Rastus: 'How cum, Mandy?' Mandy: 'Yo' got sech a hot line!' **1944** H. L. MENCKEN in *Amer. Speech* XIX. 172 In my boyhood *Cuffy* had disappeared and *Sambo* was being supplanted by *Rastus*. **1955** W. MOORE *Bring Jubilee* vi. 59, I call him Sambo because it sounds nicer than Rastus. **1965** W. MCCORD *Mississippi: Long Hot Summer* vi. 163 Leaders like Medgar Evers..discovered in the armed forces a new sense of personal dignity... They returned to their state determined to play roles other than 'Sambo' and 'Rastus'. **1965** 'MALCOLM X' *Autobiogr.* (1966) ii. 104 Wherever I showed my face.. the audiences 'niggered' and 'cooned' me to death. Or called me 'Rastus'. **1978** J. BLACKBURN *Dead Man's Handle* vi. 73 On your way, Rastus. Me and Massa's buddies.

rat, *sb.*[1] Add: **1. a.** For *Mus* substitute *Rattus*. (Later *fig.* examples.)

1888 KIPLING *Letters of Marque* (1891) xv. 111 Ram Baksh..headed his two thirteen-hand rats straight towards the morning sun. **1900** R. BARR *Unchanging East* 258 The Turkish Government has a little rat of a boat..which dare not venture out in a storm. **1907** J. MASEFIELD *Tarpaulin Muster* 186 'I've been looking for truth,' he says; 'looking for truth in all these books... There's not a rat of truth in one of them. Not a solid rat, there isn't.' **1977** *Best of Austral. Angler* 12/2 Earlier, Col Noakes and myself had landed some 10 kg kings—comparative 'rats' that chased bait past all day.

b. esp. the North American musk-rat, *Ondatra zibethica*, of the family Cricetidæ, an aquatic rodent hunted for its thick brown fur; also, the pelt of this animal or its flesh used as food. (Examples.)

1584 R. HAKLUYT *Discourse concerning Westerne Planting* in *Maine Hist. Soc. Coll.* (1877) II. 27 There is greate store of..bevers, squirrells, badgers, and ratts excedinge greate. **1800** A. N. MCLEOD *Jrnl.* 18 Nov. in C. M. Gates *Five Fur Traders* (1933) 130 The first paid his Debt, the next gave 40 Ratts en present. **1824** S. BLACK *Jrnl. Voy. from Rocky Mountain Portage* (1955) 153 Saw no appearance of the Otter, Rat or Mink. **1882** *Edmonton Bull.* 18 Feb. 3/2 They are living principally on rats and jackfish from Buffalo Lake. **1944** J. MARTIN *Canad. Wilderness Trapping* 48 It is the food which makes the pelt..and in the northwest we get the best rats. **1946** *Sun* (Baltimore) 15 Nov. 18/3 The 'rats' referred to are, of course, the musk-rats of the rich Dorchester marshes. **1953** *Jessen's Weekly* 19 Feb. 5/2. The trapping of Beaver and muskrat in the Huslia area does not show much promise as the ice is from three to six feet thick in the rivers and lakes... Many of the rats have been frozen in.

2. e. (Earlier and later examples.) Also as a general expression of disgust, annoyance, etc.

1886 *Lantern* (New Orleans) 20 Oct. 5/2 What a rotten game. Rats! **1888** *Texas Siftings* 7 Jan. 5/2 Smaller Boy—'Let me shine 'em up, Sir; for I have to support a poor little sick brother at home who is lame and can't see.' Bigger Boy—'Rats! I'm that poor little sick brother myself.' **1901** S. R. CROCKETT *Cinderella* xxvii. 188 'My cousin has lessons along with the younger children.' 'Rats!' declared Vic, smiling broadly; 'she sees that they do theirs—that's more like it.' **1914** G. B. SHAW *Misalliance* 23 *Mrs Tarleton*. Dont boast, John. Dont tempt Providence. *Tarleton*. Rats! You dont understand Providence. Providence likes to be tempted. **1951** J. CORNISH *Provincials* I. ii. 21 'I don't kiss girls,' I said hurriedly. 'I never kiss girls. Never.' 'Oh, rats!' **1976** *National Observer* (U.S.) 21 Feb. 9/2 About a day later another letter from the company turned up in my mailbox. Rats, I thought, they have discovered their mistake and are going to take all the fun out of my life. **1977** *New Yorker* 27 June 30/3 Rats, you sound like a sorority pledge at Sophie Newcomb College.

f. *to give* (a person) *rats*: to give (him) a hard time; to berate, rebuke. orig. *U.S.*

1863 *Sunday Herald* (Boston) 15 Feb. 4/1 Hooker is doing something in the way of giving the rebels 'rats'. **1869** 'MARK TWAIN' *Sk. New & Old* (1875) 48 You may write a blistering article on the police—give the Chief Inspector rats. **1940** F. D. DAVISON *Woman at Mill* III. 245 She was now going to give me rats, treat me as if I were personally responsible for the short-comings of the land of my birth.

g. *to get* (or *have*) *a rat* (or *rats*): to be eccentric or insane. *Austral.* and *N.Z. slang*.

[**1890** BARRÈRE & LELAND *Dict. Slang* II. 171/2 (American), 'to have *rats*', to have wild or eccentric fancies.] **1906** E. DYSON *Fact'ry 'Ands* vii. 84 The factory flat loudly asserted that Spats had 'got a rat'. **1908** H. FLETCHER *Dads & Dan* 65 In a town a whole population gets rats together, an' though they's all clean daft at times, yet, 'cause they all thinks alike, they don't doubt they's sane. *c* **1926** 'MIXER' *Transport Workers' Song Bk.* 12 'Lend us a quid!' 'Lend you a what! Blime, have you got a rat?'

h. *rats and mice*: rhyming slang for 'dice'; a game of dice.

1932 P. P. *Rhyming Slang* 23 *Rats and mice*, dice. **1938** F. D. SHARPE *Sharpe of Flying Squad* xv. 170 We used to play dice with them... Rats and Mice the game was called.

3. a. (Later examples.)

1901 G. B. SHAW *Caesar & Cleopatra* IV. 188 Now, by great Jove, you filthy little Egyptian rat, that is the very word to make him walk out alone into the city. **1927, 1928** [see *double-crosser* s.v. *DOUBLE-CROSS, DOUBLE CROSS 1]. **1929** [see *FINK *sb.*[2]]. **1945** S. LEWIS *Cass Timberlane* xliii. 324 The sort of male once described with relish as 'an agreeable scoundrel'..could now be referred to..as..a louse, a stinker, a rat, a twirp, a crumb, or a goon. **1959** [see *FINK *sb.*[2]]. **1976** *Western Mail* (Cardiff) 27 Nov., He turned to a group of policemen and said, 'I hope you are satisfied, you rats.' **1977** *Rolling Stone* 16 June 43/3 This is the terrible part of me, it's awful and I'm really a rat.

b. Preceded by a specifying sb., applied to one who is associated with or frequents the place specified (originally esp. a dock or riverside: in this context occas. without defining word); see also *rink-rat* (*RINK *sb.*[2] 5), *river rat* (RIVER *sb.*[1] 4 e), *wharf-rat* (*b*) (WHARF *sb.*[1] 3). Chiefly *U.S.*

1864 *Harper's Mag.* Feb. 341/1 At our swimming-place we were often much molested by the river-border citizens of the town, variously known as 'dock-rats' and 'townies'. **1870** *Scribner's Monthly* I. 41 Many of the inmates.., as 'dock-rats', house-thieves, peace-breakers, and horse-stealers, have grown preternaturally quick-witted. **1872** *Harper's Mag.* Oct. 673/2 Our business is with those smaller, but terribly annoying vermin, the 'dock rats', with the river thieves, and with the junk-shops. **1883** J. GREENWOOD *Tag, Rag, & Co.* 33 Then, again, there's the regler 'rats'. How many of them, sneaking about craft at anchor,.. make a slip and get drowned? *Ibid.* 35 He was drowned, and carried away with the tide, and it wasn't till a week after that the 'rats'..fell in with the body and robbed it. **1890** [see *EXTRA C. *sb.* b]. **1928** H. ASBURY *Gangs of New York* xi. 240 The police found him in company with a gang of notorious little dock rats. **1962** N. MAXWELL *Witch-Doctor's Apprentice* iii. 25, I..gathered a lot of information on jungle medicine. I spent hours in bars buying *aguardiente* (local rum) for old jungle rats. **1967** *Boston Sunday Herald* 14 May (This Week Mag.) 2/2 As a kid, I was an airport rat. I rode my bike to the airport, 15 miles each way, and I would hang around and help. **1978** K. BONFIGLIOLI *All Tea in China* III. vi. 80 A gaggle of waterfront rats, wasters, the scum of the sea.

4. d. (Earlier and later U.S. examples.)

1824 [see *rat-printer*, sense 7 e below]. **1836** *Proc. Nat. Typogr. Convention, Washington* 4 Martin H. Andrews..has been recognised as being one of the individuals published on the *Rat List* of the Columbia Typographical Society. *Ibid.* 11 Men pronounced *Rats* by one society, shall be considered such by all others. **1851** *Proc. 1st Nat. Convention Journeymen Printers U.S., 1850* 11 The present system is prolific of 'rats'. Our trade should be purged of this vermin. **1868** *Oregon State Jrnl.* 17 Oct. 1/6 The President of the National Typographical Union has pronounced a general amnesty, by virtue of which all expelled members, 'rats', etc., will be admitted to the Unions. **1896** *Typographical Jrnl.* IX. 100 A force of rats were doubled up from the Evening Ledger to get out the paper. **1902** *Encycl. Brit.* XXXIII. 411/1 A strike occurred in Mr Weed's office in 1821 on account of the employment of a non-union man, who was then designated a 'rat'.

e. *U.S.* A new student or freshman, esp. a newly-recruited cadet.

1850 'M. TENSAS' *Odd Leaves Life Louisiana 'Swamp Doctor'* 113 There were four or five brother 'Rats' besides myself residing in the hospital, all candidates for graduation, and..all desirous of obtaining sufficient medical lore. **1896** *Bomb* (Virginia Military Institution) 109 An unfortunate 'Rat' whose face was glum, As he often to himself did hum—Guard Duty. **1900** *Dialect Notes* I. 54 *Rat*, a new student. **1930** *Amer. Speech* VI. 129 The freshman class at this institution [*sc.* Alabama Polytechnic Institute] is known as 'The Rats', and any given member is a 'rat'. **1937** W. COUPER in J. E. Johnston *Echoes of V.M.I.* 43 One of the recollections of every Rat is the comforter who goes through the barracks purring—'Mister, do you see that tree? Well, all the leaves have got to go, and all the leaves have got to come back, before you..' and you know the rest. **1939** W. FAULKNER *Wild Palms* 35 'This is Rat,' she said. 'He is the senior living ex-freshman of the University of Alabama. That's why we still call him Rat.' **1951** *Time* 28 May 50/2 Of all the cadets, the 'rats' of the entering class have the roughest time.

f. A police informer; an informer in a prison. *slang*.

1902 FARMER & HENLEY *Slang* V. 376/1 *Rat*... 6. (thieves').—A police spy. **1917** *New Republic* 13 Jan. 294/1 In most cases they were 'rats', and the best tools the keepers had. **1929** [see *HEEL *sb.*[3]]. **1970** G. JACKSON *Let.* 22 Mar. in *Soledad Brother* (1971) 186 You see every time a rat does get put away, the prison authorities always release a different reason for the attack, never that he was an informer. **1977** *New Yorker* 24 Oct. 72/3 Like all prisons, Green Haven is run with the help of informers—'rats'... One way..of rewarding rats is with jobs.

7. a. *rat-cage, -fur, -horde, -land, -plague, -run, -season*; (sense *4 e) *rat rule*.

1936 J. STEINBECK *In Dubious Battle* ii. 21, I did hate being in the rat-cage. **1977** P. DICKINSON *Walking Dead* I. i. 17 The neat rank of rat-cages in the animal room. **1907** *Daily Chron.* 24 Aug. 4/7 The hair was gathered up, chignon-fashion, and tied behind with strings made of rat-fur. *a* **1930** D. H. LAWRENCE *Last Poems* (1932) 189 In the moment of choice, the soul..utterly fails to recognize any more the grey rat-hordes of classes and masses. **1955** J. R. R. TOLKIEN *Return of King* v. x. 166 Dwarf-coat, elf-cloak, blade of the downfallen West, and spy from the little rat-land of the Shire. **1936** I. L. IDRIESS *Cattle King* (*caption facing p.* 50) These birds, in immense numbers, harry the 'rat plagues' which occur occasionally in portions of the interior. **1933** *Sun* (Baltimore) 8 Nov. 20/3 The sophomore victory..meant that the freshmen would continue to wear little red caps and obey 'rat' rules. **1939** *Amer. Speech* XIV. 29 *Rat*, new cadet, recruit... *Rat rules*,..see recruit regulations. **1893** *Baily's Mag.* Oct. 253/1 The rat-runs had been stopped up, and he killed nearly..a hundred rats before he paused. **1980** I. MURDOCH *Nuns & Soldiers* iii. 195 There were rat-runs of thought here into which Gertrude did not want to enter. **1921** *Beaver* May 14 The rat season closes today. All the hunters are now in.

b. *rat-hunting* (earlier and later examples).

1810 E. WEETON *Let.* 18 Jan. in *Jrnl. of Governess* (1969) I. 223, I set out on my rat-hunting expedition. *a* **1817** JANE

AUSTEN *Persuasion* (1818) IV. x. 229 We had a famous set-to at rat-hunting all the morning. **1966** *Beaver* Winter 54/1 All the different Indians started back to their own countries for rat [*sc.* muskrat] hunting.

c. *rat-borne, -eaten, -infested* (later examples) adjs.

1928 *Moderna Språk* Sept. 187 Terms like..*mother-craft, rat-borne* diseases, *wholemeal* bread. **1938** *Sun* (Baltimore) 1 Nov. 22/2 To protect the public health and to prevent the spread of rat-borne disease. **1901** 'L. MALET' *Hist. R. Calmady* I. viii. 69 The fusty atmosphere of a cottage garret, right up under the rat-eaten thatch. **1951** P. ABRAHAMS *Wild Conquest* 49 He had a funny, rat-eaten beard. **1916** E. & O. SITWELL *20th Cent. Harlequinade* 23 On to that rat-infested maze. **1974** *Country Life* 14 Mar. 588/1 The pond was a rat-infested rubbish tip.

d. *rat-brained, -fat, -grey, -poor, -shrewd, -souled, -swift, -toothed* adjs.

1971 B. MALAMUD *Tenants* 75 Those rat-brained Jews. **1930** E. SITWELL *Coll. Poems* 256 To show the shame Of the rat-fat soul to the grinning day. **1937** E. MUIR *Coll. Poems* (1960) 71 The light was rat-grey. **1952** J. STEINBECK *East of Eden* ii. 9 A man who might have been well-to-do on ten acres in Europe was rat-poor on two thousand in California. **1960** S. PLATH *Colossus* (1967) 63 Rat-shrewd go her squint eyes. **1921** R. GRAVES *Pier-Glass* 49 Was Sisera then more ripe for the knife or nail Than rat-soul'd Becker? **1969** G. MACBETH *War Quartet* 61 Air gushed in..Rat-swift. **1930** S. SPENDER *Twenty Poems* 14 And older whores Skuttle rat-toothed into the dark outdoors.

e. rat-bat *W. Indies* = BAT *sb.*[1]; **rat-bite fever,** either of two similar fevers of which the bacteria causing it are carried by rodents; **rat cheese** *U.S. colloq.* = *MOUSETRAP *sb.* 2; **rat-fish,** substitute for def.: a fish of the family Chimæridæ, characterized by a long tail, esp. *Hydrolagus colliei,* which is found off the Pacific coast of North America; (later examples); **rat flea,** a flea infesting rats, esp. *Nosopsyllus fasciatus* or the tropical *Xenopsylla cheopis,* which are vectors of the bacillus causing plague; **rat-fucker** *coarse slang,* a base, despicable person (see also quot. 1967[1]); **rat-house,** (*b*) *Austral.* and *N.Z. slang,* a lunatic asylum; **rat-hunt,** a hunt for rats; also *fig.*; **rat-kangaroo,** add to def.: a very small kangaroo belonging to the subfamily Potoroinæ; (earlier and later examples); **rat pack** *slang* (orig. *U.S.*), a gang of disorderly young people; **rat-printer** = sense 4 d; **rat-proof** *a.,* able to keep out rats; hence **rat-proofing** *vbl. sb.*; **rat-run,** (one of) a maze-like series of small passages by which rats move about their territory; freq. *transf.* and *fig.* (usu. in derogatory sense); **rat-snake,** substitute for second part of def.: esp. a colubrid snake of the South Asian genus *Ptyas,* esp. the Indian *P. mucosus*; = *DHAMAN 1; (later examples); **rat-tight** *a.* = **rat-proof* adj.

1851 P. H. GOSSE *Naturalist's Sojourn in Jamaica* 163 All Bats are called by the negroes Rat-bats, probably to distinguish them from Butterflies, to which they give the name of Bats. **1956** J. HEARNE *Stranger at Gate* xviii. 142 A cave full of rat-bat droppings. **1910** *Q. Jrnl. Med.* III. 125 To the pathogeny of rat-bite fever I am at present unable to offer any clue. **1910** *Lancet* 11 June 1618/1 The January issue of the Quarterly Journal of Medicine contains an interesting paper by Dr. T. J. Horder on three cases of irregularly periodic fever associated with the bite of a rat, and so alike in their other features as to cause him to group them together under the name of 'rat-bite fever'. **1917** *Jrnl. Exper. Med.* XXV. 42 The clinical symptoms of rat-bite fever are inflammation of the bitten parts, paroxysms of fever of the relapsing type, swelling of the lymph glands, and eruption of the skin. **1924** *Ann. Trop. Med. & Parasitol.* XVIII. 171 The correct name for the causal organism of rat-bite fever is *Spirillum minus,* Carter 1887. **1949** H. W. FLOREY et al. *Antibiotics* II. xxxi. 1030 In man the results of treating rat-bite fever due to Actino. muris [*sc. Streptobacillus moniliformis*] were from the first exceedingly good on very moderate doses of penicillin. **1970** *New Scientist* 27 Aug. 407/2 The mouse has been incriminated in the transmission of rat-bite fever (or soduku). **1939** *Sun* (Baltimore) 4 May 8/5 Guilty of saying, in regard to macaroni, that 'it is merely associated with a dish whose other component part is rat cheese'. **1952** J. STEINBECK *East of Eden* xvii. 159 Their lunch of..bread and rat cheese. **1976** *Washington Post* 7 Nov. K1/5 We will try to recreate the atmosphere of a country store. Sardines, pickled pig's feet..rat cheese. **1905** D. S. JORDAN *Guide to Study of Fishes* I. xxxi. 564 The existing Chimæras are known also as spookfishes, ratfishes, and elephant-fishes. **1936** P. S. BARNHART *Marine Fishes California* 14 *Hydrolagus colliei*..Ratfish..San Diego to Alaska, in cold bottom waters. **1955** *Sci. News Let.* 19 Feb. 121/3 Liver oil from ratfish is the richest source of batyl alcohol. **1965** [see *holocephalian* sb. s.v. *HOLO-]. **1974** *Daily Colonist* (Victoria, B.C.) 28 July 17/2 Kevin's prizes..were awarded for a two pound, 15 ounce ratfish, the heaviest landed. **1871** *Hardwicke's Science Gossip* May 99/2 The rat has two kinds of fleas, that is, the banded Rat Flea..and the common Rat Flea. **1907** *Daily Mail* 19 Aug. 7/1 The Plague Commission has decided..that the vehicle of contagion is the rat-flea. **1929** H. E. EWING *Man. External Parasites* v. 170 The Common Rat Flea, *Ceratophyllus fasciatus* Bosc., is the flea most commonly found on rats in Europe and North America. **1953** L. F. HIRST *Conquest of Plague* xii. 335 Hygiene improvements must have greatly reduced the rat and rat-flea population of the old-fashioned cities. **1953** *New Biol.* XIV. 111 The species from which we have gained most of our knowledge are the tropical rat flea, *Xenopsylla cheopis,* and..the rat flea of temperate countries, *Nosopsyllus fasciatus.* **1977** RICHARDS & DAVIES *Imms's Gen. Textbk. Entomol.* (ed. 10) II. 111. 941 In India the species mostly implicated [in the transmission of plague] is the rat flea. **1967** *Amer. Speech* XLII. 229 *Rat-fucker,* a tool, usually made from a straight piece of metal coat hanger, approximately six to ten inches long, with a ninety degree bend two inches from each end, in such a manner that it ultimately has the shape of an old car crank handle. **1967** P. WELLES *Babyhip* vi. 61 'Scum,' John mumbled... 'Rat-fucker, prick,' George said. **1913** A. J. REES *Merry Marauders* ii. 24 It was a rat-house—an asylum, to be perlite. **1922** A. WRIGHT *Colt from Country* 83 He'll be the long lost boy, instead of the guy that's missed and landed in the rat-house. **1946** F. SARGESON *That Summer* 108 Maybe they'd have to take me away to the rat-house. **1948** V. PALMER *Golconda* xxxiii. 278 Hadn't it been plain all along that there was a streak of madness in the old boy?.. He had done a spell in the rat-house and was only out on sufferance. **1957** I. CROSS *God Boy* (1958) ii. 17 You're heading for the rat house, the way you talk. Imagining things. **1825** G. SIMPSON *Jrnl.* 2 May in F. Merk *Fur Trade & Empire* (1931) 150 The Rat hunts have likewise failed in consequence of the lowness of the Waters, but the returns in Beaver are very fair about 3,000. **1843** *Ainsworth's Mag.* III. 78 If my father's keepers invited me to a private rat-hunt, Tickle was sure to smell a rat. **1961** *Guardian* 1 Dec. 13/1 It is also to be doubted whether the OAS leaders, for all their deliberate use of murder and plastic bombs, want the 'rat hunts'. **1841** Rat-kangaroo [see KANGAROO *sb.* 2]. **1926** LE SOUEF & BURRELL *Wild Animals of Australasia* 232 The rat-kangaroos for the most part live on the surface of the ground. **1944** F. CLUNE *Red Heart* 21 The two aboriginal guides ran tirelessly.., supplementing the larder by killing lizards, rat-kangaroos, and other small creatures. **1965** D. MORRIS *Mammals* 66 Rat-kangaroos differ from other members of the family in having well-developed canine teeth. **1978** D. OVINGTON *Austral. Endangered Species* 76/1 Also known as ..the burrowing rat kangaroo, the boodie is the only burrowing member of the kangaroo family. **1951** R. S. PRATHER *Bodies in Bedlam* ix. 65 It looked like three or four of L.A.'s juvenile moron gangs, sometimes called rat packs, had taken turns going over the place. **1973** *Observer* 8 Apr. 48/4 Constance throws aside worldly success..and the ratpack to immerse herself in her first love—history. **1974** H. L. FOSTER *Ribbin'* iii. 91 More recently, gangs, fraternities, cliques, organizations, and 'rat packs' have again begun to be reported. **1977** *Time* 25 July 10/1 This summer Sweden has been hit by a small but ugly wave of racial incidents, three of which have been violent encounters between a rat pack of young Swedish ruffians and a community of Assyrian immigrants from the Middle East. **1824** *Microscope* (Albany, N.Y.) 6 Mar. 191/2 Loren..Webster, chief ink-dauber in a rat-printing office at the west. Ralph Walby, nothing at all but a rat-printer. **1931** T. S. STRIBLING *Forge* xviii. 159 The Lacefield barns were rat proof. **1960** *Farmer & Stockbreeder* 26 Jan. 51/3 The virus is handled inside areas surrounded with a rat-proof fence. **1929** *Times* 2 Nov. 9/5 Surely it would be an economy to employ a man permanently for rat proofing and rat catching at £150 per annum. **1870** *Gentl. Mag.* Sept. 497 The barracks are a mouldy rat-run now. **1893** *Baily's Mag.* Oct. 253/1 The rat-runs had been stopped up, and he killed nearly..a hundred rats before he paused. **1924** GALSWORTHY *White Monkey* III. i. 223 Hurrying along the rat-runs of the Tube, she slipped her hand into his pocket. **1940** BLUNDEN *Poems 1930–1940* 202 In roofless barns, in rat-run saps. **1953** *Spectator* 13 Feb. 194/2 She will be able, through her own will and capacity, to escape from the rat-run of her environment. **1974** *Country Life* 24 Jan. 148/4 During weekday rush hours..a normally peaceful residential street can become a rat run. **1882** C. C. HOPLEY *Snakes* iv. 85 The rat snake..and the *Clothonia* of India are 'said' to suck the teats of cows. **1907** *Country Life* July 328/3 The yellow rat snake or chicken snake is one of the most useful and is entirely harmless. **1927,** etc. [see *DHAMAN 1]. **1958** R. CONANT *Field Guide Reptiles & Amphibians U.S.* 154 (*heading*) Rat Snakes: Genus *Elaphe. Ibid.* 155 All the Rat Snakes vibrate their tails rapidly when alarmed. **1969** A. BELLAIRS *Life Reptiles* I. vi. 242 In some genera such as the rat snakes (*Ptyas*), the viper *Echis* and most sea snakes it [*sc.* the right lung] stretches almost back to the cloaca. **1893** *Jrnl. Soc. Arts* 5 May 623/1 What is wanted is a mode of running the wires..that shall not only be electric-tight, but shall also be water-tight, air-tight, oil-tight, fire-tight, and rat-tight. **1908** *Installation News* II. 33/1 The union between two screw threads does not make a perfectly 'watertight, airtight, gastight, and rat-tight' joint, as the saying is.

rat, *v.*[1] Add: **2. a.** (Earlier and later examples.) Also, to turn traitor; in *Criminals' slang,* to inform.

1812 SOUTHEY *Let.* 18 May in *Life & Corr.* (1850) III. 341 W— and C—, I doubt not, ratted upon the Catholic question because they expected the Prince upon that ground would eject Perceval. **1814** LD. BROUGHAM *Let.* 29 June in *Creevey Papers* (1903) I. ix. 195 The Whigs have just discovered old Sherry to be 'an old and valued friend and an ancient adherent of Fox'. They therefore support him. To be sure, he has ratted and left them—he kept them out of office twice—and he now openly stands on Yarmouth's influence and C[arlton] House. **1910** *Blackw. Mag.* Aug. 256/2 Those who, in the slang of politics, are said to 'rat'. **1934** *Sun* (Baltimore) 20 Aug. 5/1 Misunas..has 'turned State's evidence'—'ratted' in gangland parlance. **1938** [see *HOOLIGAN]. **1938** E. BOWEN *Death of Heart* III. iii. 371 The girl at the switchboard must have ratted. **1969** *Listener* 24 July 102/2 One's feeling for the Chamberlain government was one of such utter contempt that one felt they might very well rat once again. **1974** S. E. MORISON *European Discovery of Amer.: Southern Voyages* xx. 480 The captain of *San Gabriel* ratted..and sailed for Spain.

c. With *on.* To default on; to let (someone) down; to behave disloyally towards; (orig. *Criminals' slang*), to inform on.

1932 A. J. WORRALL *Eng. Idioms* 12 Of course I won't do that. Do you think I'd rat on a pal. **1938** E. AMBLER *Cause for Alarm* xviii. 311 The Italians may rat on that contract. **1938** E. BOWEN *Death of Heart* III. ii. 351 In a small way I have just ratted on Anna. **1938** *Sun* (Baltimore) 1 Sept. 4/2 This pair..have admitted the fatal attack on another prisoner for 'ratting on us'. **1948** *Richmond* (Va.) *Times-Dispatch* 13 Feb. 30/1 But of all persons to rat on the set up McKeever, the planner and perpetrator..should have been the last. **1957** C. MACINNES *City of Spades* II. xiv. 199 Why isn't Muriel here, anyway? She's ratted on him. **1973** *Times* 1 Dec. 9/6 If they were to rat on these policies he would become one of their strongest opponents and critics. **1974** *Socialist Worker* 2 Nov. 1/2 The Labour government has ratted on these men. **1977** *New Yorker* 24 Oct. 128/2 Finando and the two men he had ratted on..were all transferred to the same prison.

4. *trans.* To search (a person, his belongings, etc.) for things to steal; to pilfer. Chiefly *Austral.* and *N.Z.*

1919 DOWNING *Digger Dial.* 41 *Rat* (vb.), (1) Search a prisoner or dead body. (2) Pick a pocket. **1925** FRASER & GIBBONS *Soldier & Sailor Words* 236 *To rat,* to steal. To search a dead body. **1931** V. PALMER *Separate Lives* 267 'Look here, you slinking cur!' he began. 'You've been ratting other people's property for months.' **1937** J. A. LEE *Civilian into Soldier* 194 There must be a lot of dead Huns to rat. **1941** K. TENNANT *Battlers* i. 9 Some thieving (*adjective*) robber was 'ratting' his tucker-box. **1971** J. S. GUNN *Opal Terminol.* 38 *Rat,* to pilfer opal from a miner's hiding place or enter someone's mine and take out opal rock.

rata. Also 8 **ratta(h).** Substitute for def.: An evergreen tree or woody climber belonging to one of several species of *Metrosideros,* of the family Myrtaceae, esp. a New Zealand species, the small *M. lucida* or the much larger *M. robusta,* both bearing terminal clusters of red flowers with long stamens; also, the fruit or the heavy reddish timber of a tree of this kind. (Earlier and further examples.)

[*a* **1771** S. PARKINSON *Jrnl. Voy. to South Seas* (1773) 40 E ratta, or e pooratta... This tree, or shrub, grows upon the Tooaroa, or Lower-hills... The flowers are full of beautiful scarlet stamina.] **1792** W. BLIGH *Voy. to South Sea* xi. 139 The *rattah,* not much unlike a chestnut,..grows on a large tree. **1829** W. ELLIS *Polynesian Researches* I. xiii. 376 The wood of the rata has a fine straight grain. **1847** [see *NIKAU]. **1853** A. S. ATKINSON *Jrnl.* 7 Sept. in *Richmond-Atkinson Papers* (1960) I. 130 We found a beautiful little scorpion spider—it was under a rata log. **1896** [see *PAKIHI]. **1935** [see *NIKAU]. **1949** F. SARGESON *I saw in my Dream* 127 Mr Anderson and Dave sat with their backs against the twisted barrel of a fallen rata. **1968** [see *INANGA 2]. **1974** *Nat. Geographic* Aug. 195 The nightmare tree called rata, which begins as an innocent-seeming vine, and, in the end, strangles the tree to which it attaches itself.

ratafia. Add: **1.** (Later examples.) Now applied esp. to a type of aperitif made from grape-juice and brandy.

1907 *Yesterday's Shopping* (1969) 18/1 Essences, for flavouring..ratafia. **1946** A. L. SIMON *Conc. Encycl. Gastron.* VIII. 139/2 *Ratafia,* a generic name for a number of Cordials, usually home-made, always sweet and often of very highly alcoholic strength. Ratafia may be made with new wine or grape juice and sufficient spirit to stop its fermentation; being further flavoured with various fruits, herbs and spices; or else by the infusion of the same ingredients in brandy. **1959** W. JAMES *Word-bk. Wine* 155 *Ratafias* were infusions of fruit or herbs in brandy, made by housewives in happier days when brandy was cheap... In the champagne country, ratafia is an aperitif, somewhat stronger than sherry or vermouth, made by mixing some unfermented champagne grape juice with brandy. **1964** *Harper's Bazaar* Nov. 146/2 *Ratafia*..bears no resemblance to our ratafia, which is a home-made liqueur, usually made with almonds. *Ratafia* is an aperitif made with local white wine and brandy. **1973** *Daily Tel.* 12 July 16, I was interested to learn..that Ratafia is an aperitif made in Champagne by mixing brandy with unfermented champagne grape juice. I have 'essence of Ratafia'..which..is made from bitter almonds.

attrib. (Earlier examples.)

a **1711** in E. Hamilton *Mordaunts* (1965) vi. 134 Rattefea biscakes, sugar puffs, chips. **1728** E. SMITH *Compl. House-wife* (ed. 2) 100 *A Ratafia Pudding*..Cream..Naples-bisket ..Butter, some Sack, Nutmeg, and Salt..Almonds..Eggs ..bake... Scrape Sugar on it. *Ibid.* 142 (*heading*) To make Ratafia Cream. **1755** H. GLASSE *Art of Cookery* (ed. 5) xvi. 285 To make a Trifle. Cover the Bottom of your Dish..with ..Ratafia Cakes.

ratama, var. *RETAMA.

rat-a-tat. Add: (Further examples.) Also *attrib.* in **rat-a-tat ginger** (see quot. 1959).

1916 N. DOUGLAS *London Street Games* 64 Rat a tat tat, who is that? Only grandma's pussy-cat. What do you want? A pint of milk. **1959** I. & P. OPIE *Lore & Lang. Schoolch.* xviii. 381 Illegally knocking at doors... *Rat Tat Tat.* Abertillery and Newbridge in Monmouthshire, Barry in Glamorgan, Coventry. A variant in Lydney is *Rat-a-Tat Ginger. Rat-a-Tat-Tat.* Solihull, near Birmingham, and Grenoside, near Sheffield. **1961** *Times* 17 June 3/2 Any passing rat-a-tat of close volleying.

‖ **ratatouille** (ratatūi^y). [Fr.: the final element is app. f. *touiller* to stir up.] † **a.** A ragout. **b.** In full, *ratatouille niçoise*: a dish, originating in Nice, consisting of aubergines, tomatoes, onions, peppers, and other ingredients stewed in olive oil.

1877 *Cassell's Dict. Cookery* 717/2 *Ratatouville* [*sic*]. This is a popular French method of making a savoury dish out of the remains of cold meat. **1946** F. M. FARMER *Boston*

Cooking-School Cook Bk. (ed. 8) 472 Ratatouille Niçoise... Place in shallow baking dish, sprinkle with cheese and brown under the broiler. **1950** E. DAVID *Bk. Mediterranean Food* 125 Ratatouille is a Provençal ragoût of vegetables, usually pimentos, onions, tomatoes and aubergines, stewed very slowly in oil. **1956** L. MCINTOSH *Oxford Folly* 36 She prepared a *ratatouille* of aubergines, peppers, tomatoes, onions, and, of course, garlic. It was the only foreign dish she knew. **1960** E. DAVID *French Provincial Cooking* 242 Ratatouille Niçoise. Aubergines, tomatoes, onions and peppers stewed in oil. **1969** *Times Lit. Suppl.* 25 Dec. 1465/3 On the Riviera, the liberator's cause is seen as a distant grey dream, so easily dulled by ratatouille and red wine. **1973** R. LITTELL *Defection A. J. Lewinter* iv. 26, I have some cold *ratatouille* in the fridge.

ratbag (ræ·tbæg). *Austral.* and *N.Z. slang.* Also **rat-bag.** [f. RAT *sb.*[1] + BAG *sb.*] A stupid or eccentric person, a fool; an unpleasant person, a trouble-maker. Also *attrib.*, stupid, idiotic, uncouth.

1937 'W. HATFIELD' *I find Australia* 138 'You brought one rat-bag *in*,' said Evans to me, 'so now do me a favour by taking one off my hands.' **1948** V. PALMER *Golconda* xiv. 107 Why the hell, Donovan, are you backing that old ratbag, Christy Bangham? **1954** *Coast to Coast 1953–1954* 172 Or a ratbag watchman who'd run amuck if you breathed on a window. **1955** D. NILAND *Shiralee* 24 And what a ratbag situation, what a story. **1956** D. M. DAVIN *Sullen Bell* I. iii. 19 How did you ratbags get here, a highbrow joint like this? **1961** B. CRUMP *Hang on a Minute, Mate* 164 This'd be the best scrapper among you bunch of ratbags, wouldn't it? **1963** *Australasian Post* 14 Mar. 51/2 'He's not one of your ratbag mob, though, he—.' That cough again... 'He's a gentleman, you see.' **1965** W. DICK (*title*) A bunch of ratbags. **1967** H. HUNTER *Case for Punishment* ii. 37 Reading all about our little ratbags?.. A lot of kids from this school are involved. **1970** *N.Z. Listener* 12 Oct. 13/2 A bit late to find that out, you snobbish ratbag wowser. **1973** [see *LEAD *sb.*[2] 1 f]. **1976** I. MURDOCH *Henry & Cato* I. 42 Well, it's just a game, you know me, scare a few ratbags, does no harm.

rat-catcher. Add: **2.** Unconventional hunting dress. Also *transf.* and *attrib.*

1910 KIPLING *Diversity of Creatures* (1917) 310 He came back to the bar, after he'd changed into those rat-catcher clothes. **1928** J. B. THOMAS *Hounds & Hunting* 254 *Rat-catcher*—referring to one informally dressed when hunting. **1930** *Field* 29 Nov. 764/1 The self-respecting beginner will want to be turned out properly, in the right 'rat-catcher style'. **1933** A. POWELL *From View to Death* viii. 200 Both sons were in ratcatcher and Torquil wore a canary-coloured waistcoat. **1963** M. MALIM *Pagoda Tree* xvi. 101 While one could exhibit oneself and did to the Cricket Club in rat-catcher, so to speak, one had to dress for presentation on the Thursday committee night at the Tulyar. **1976** *Horse & Hound* 3 Dec. 32/2 (Advt.), Moleskin ratcatcher trousers. Warm, tough, supple. Shirt-grip self-supporting waist... Slim leg style. **1977** 'E. CRISPIN' *Glimpses of Moon* xi. 205 Nor were they a very distinguished Hunt: the men mostly turned up in ratcatcher (Fen had that morning noted one.. who was wearing a hoicked-up caftan and prayer beads above his shining riding boots).

ratch, *v.*[1] **3.** (Later example.)

1904 HARDY *Dynasts* I. I. iii. 31 The thousands called.. will ratch the lines Of English regiments..To glorious length.

ratch (rætʃ), *v.*[3] *north. dial.* and *Sc.* [f. RACHE, RATCH *sb.*[1]] **a.** *intr.* To forage for food, to ferret *around*; to ramble or wander *about*. **b.** *trans.* To search thoroughly, ransack. Hence **ra·tching** *vbl. sb.*

1801 'BERWICKSHIRE SANDIE' *Poems* 73 Hens ratch'd through the house wi' greed. **1859** W. DICKINSON *Gloss. Words & Phrases Cumberland* (foreword), Yan wad ratch ivry neukk ov oald Cummerlan. *Ibid.* 91 *Ratch*, to ramble, to search vigorously. 'Ratchan about like a hungry hound.' **1869** A. C. GIBSON *Folk-Speech Cumberland* 96 Cook's house was ratch't through an' through. **1971** *Country Life* 9 Sept. 630/1 There's oalas an odd yan or two that'll leave their lambs an' ratch aboot. *Ibid.* 7 Oct. 900/1 Hill sheep can be very active, and when they feel like ratching it takes a very formidable fence to prevent them. **1973** *Guardian* 26 Feb. 10/2 The grass is poor, as yet, so some of the fell-sheep go foraging in and out of the woods..and into any fell-side garden with an open gate... 'Ratching' is part of their nature. **1976** *Jrnl. Lakeland Dial. Soc.* 21 Yan day t' auld Friesian bull gat oot, a' caved an' ratched aroond, Neabody durst gan near him as he rwoared an' scratted t' groond.

ratchell. 1. (Later example of form **rachill.**)

1884 R. HUNT *Brit. Mining* 912 *Rachill*, small loose stones that are usually found on the top of the rock forming as the depth increased into the nature of beds.

ratchet, *sb.* Add: **3*.** = **ratchet-knife.*

1975 *Globe & Mail* (Toronto) 11 June 3/1 Walking with the road with a ratchet (knife) in your waist, Johnny you're too bad. **1976** *Daily Mirror* 2 Apr. 20/2 *Ratchet*, knife.

4. *ratchet screwdriver*; **ratchet effect** (see quots. 1977); **ratchet knife,** a type of knife popular in Jamaica.

1970 *Times* 13 Apr. 20/7 It appears that there has been a ratchet effect in employment in the service industries. **1977** *New Society* 31 Mar. 643/2 One of the curiosities of political life is what you might call the 'ratchet effect'. This is the process by which one party makes the running over an issue, and gradually winds the other (or others) along after it. **1977** *Listener* 31 Mar. 397/2 It was Sir Keith Joseph who drew attention to the 'ratchet effect' in politics, whereby the right seems to have acquiesced in the changes the left brings about. Curiously, in broadcasting matters, the ratchet effect has worked the other way: the Conservatives broke the BBC's monopoly in the Fifties.., and it has been the left that has acquiesced. **1979** *Dædalus* Spring 122 These efforts are illustrated by the rediscovery of the 'ratchet effect' theory, which simply begins with the common wisdom that prices go up more freely than they go down. **1971** *Jrnl. Commonwealth Lit.* Dec. 140 The DJE..passed by such terms as..*ratchet-knife, trouble.* **1976** BOOT & THOMAS *Jamaica* 40/1 Just the sort of deft digital flourish you need to whip out the blade of a ratchet knife—which is a particular kind of nicely curved blade in a tapered handle, made in Germany for gutting fish. **1897** *Sears, Roebuck Catal.* 80/1 The old and well-known Gay's Double-Action Ratchet Screw Driver. **1979** S. BRETT in *Winter's Crimes 11* 12 A ratchet screwdriver... Just the job for putting up shelves.

ratchet, *v.* Add: **a.** Also *transf.* and *fig.*

1977 *Time* 3 Jan. 44/3 The signal, according to some radio operators who have heard it ratcheting over their headsets, sounds like a 'buzzsaw' or 'the whirring of helicopter blades'. **1977** *Rolling Stone* 16 June 36/1 The movie director, age 34, spirals, ratchets, thrusts his chin like Mussolini.

b. *trans.* To move (something) *up* as by a ratchet. Cf. *ratchet effect* s.v. *RATCHET *sb.* 4.

1977 R. JENKINS *Europe's Present Challenge & Future Opportunity* (Jean Monnet Lect.) 8 Floating exchange rates transmit violent and sudden inflationary impulses... Each new impulse ratchets up the inflationary process. **1979** *Daily Tel.* 9 Aug. 2/7 We are quite clear that the union movement has not been responsible for ratcheting up inflation.

rate, *sb.*[1] Add: **II. 7. a.** Also in phr. *at the rate of knots*: see *KNOT *sb.*[1] 3 c.

b. (Further examples.)

1912 in C. B. SMITH *Testing Time* (1961) ii. 32 The rate of rising loaded as above has been tested up to 600 feet & found to be at the rate of 155 feet per minute. **1930** C. DIXON *Parachuting* ii. 21 Hampton descended very slowly.. landing after a most pleasant experience, such as the modern parachute gives, in thirteen minutes. This rate of descent worked out at 8 feet per second. The modern rate is about 21 feet per second. **1943** T. HORSLEY *Find, fire & Strike* 21 Both pilots throttled back..and used just sufficient engine to give them a rate of sink of 250 feet a minute. **1946** *Happy Landings* July 9/1 Your rate of climb indicator may show as much as 3,500 feet per minute up. **1963** B. FOZARD *Instrumentation Nuclear Reactors* xiii. 163 Reactivity must be released slowly by withdrawal of the control rods at a rate which is known to keep the rate of divergence within safe bounds.

8. c. Of a spring: a quantity relating the applied load to the compression or extension produced (see quots. 1959, 1961).

1957 E. B. JONES *Instrument Technol.* III. I. 6 For each value of the measured variable there will be a definite position of the feed-back bellows, and as the spring rate of the bellows and spring is fixed, this must mean a definite value of the transmitted pressure. **1959** *Motor Manual* (ed. 36) v. 123 This ratio can be expressed in terms of pounds weight required to produce a deflection of one inch..and this figure is known as the spring rate. **1961** W. R. BERRY *Spring Design* i. 12 The rate *S* of the spring is equal to the load per unit of deflection. **1964** H. A. ROTHBART *Mech. Design & Systems Handbk.* xxxiii. 12 Some springs are such that their rate is constant over the entire usable range of deflection.

III. 9. c. (Later examples.) Also, = RATING *vbl. sb.*[1] 2 b.

1963 *Amer. Speech* XXXVIII. 76 *Crow* (the embroidered eagle on the rating badge) was used to designate the insignia of rate for the petty officers of the Navy. **1977** *Navy News* Feb. 18/3 H.M.S. Tartar has no fewer than eight 'stripeys' among the junior rates on board. **1978** *Ibid.* Oct. 4/3 These numbers are calculated from the requirement, which is the number of ratings needed in each rate and branch to fill all sea and shore billets.

IV. 16. (Later examples.)

1921 G. B. SHAW *Back to Methuselah* p. lx, But how, at this rate, did Darwin succeed with the capitalists too? **1930** —— *Apple Cart* I. 20 Oh for Heaven's sake dont contradict her, Joe. We shall never get anywhere at this rate.

17. a. *rate-determining, -limiting* adjs., *-making, -payer* (later examples), *rebate, -setting* adj., *-support, -supported* adj.; **rate-buster** *slang*, a piece-worker whose high productivity causes or threatens to cause a reduction in piece-work rates; hence **rate-busting** *vbl. sb.*; **rate-card,** a list of charges for advertising; **rate constant** *Physical Chem.*, a coefficient of proportionality relating the rate of a chemical reaction at a given temperature to the concentration of reactant (in a unimolecular reaction), or to the product of the concentrations of reactants (in a reaction of higher order); **rate-cutting,** a lowering of charges or of rates of pay; † **rate factor** *Biol.*, a biological factor which influences or determines the speed of a developmental process, and so may affect the phenotype of the mature organism; **rate-fixer,** one who fixes the rates at which piece-workers are paid; so **rate-fixing** *vbl. sb.*; † **rate gene** *Biol.*, a gene which acts as a rate factor; **ratemeter,** an instrument which displays or records the counting rate, usu. averaged over a time interval, of pulses in an electronic counter, esp. those resulting from incidence of ionizing radiation.

1939 ROETHLISBERGER & DICKSON *Managem. & Worker* xxii. 522 You should not turn out too much work. If you do, you are a 'rate-buster'. **1948** *Appl. Anthropol.* VII. 5/1 In every work group there is nearly always a very small minority of individuals who refuse to be held back and insist on making as much bonus as they like... In current American industrial literature such workers are referred to as 'rate-busters'. **1972** M. ARGYLE *Social Psychol. of Work* vi. 113 A rate-buster may be given a raised eyebrow, a look of disapproval, a blow on the arm, or may simply be avoided. **1967** C. MARGERISON in Wills & Yearsley *Handbk. Managem. Technol.* 31 However, such practices as the prevention of rate-busting are extremely logical and rational from the workers' point of view. **1905** CALKINS & HOLDEN *Art of Mod. Advertising* 352 A rate-card is a card or printed sheet giving the advertising rates in a given publication. **1962** *Rep. Comm. Broadcasting 1960* 69 in *Parl. Papers 1961–2* (Cmnd. 1753) IX. 259 These figures represent the cost, as shown in the programme companies' rate-cards, of booking the time taken for advertisements during the year. **1977** *Listener* 31 Mar. 399/2 The NBC and CBS affiliate stations.. are getting worried. Can they hold their advertising rate-cards when audiences are falling? **1927** *Jrnl. Amer. Chem. Soc.* XLIX. 1620 Let K_∞ be the fraction decomposed per second at high pressures, or the unimolecular rate constant. **1950** W. J. MOORE *Physical Chem.* xvii. 516 The units of the rate constant depend on the order of the reaction. **1956** *Nature* 21 Jan. 127/1 The results allowed determination of the approximate values of the pseudo first-order hydrolytic rate-constants of the amide groups in these substances. **1972** R. A. JACKSON *Mechanism* iii. 28 If the equilibrium constant is known.., and the kinetic order and reaction rate constant is determined for the reverse reaction, the order and rate constant for the forward reaction can be calculated. **1888** *Scribner's Mag.* Oct. 485/2 Its percentage being fixed there is no motive for rate-cutting. **1956** J. A. C. BROWN *Social Psychol. Industry* v. 145 The most frequent reasons given by the unorganized worker for such practices were rate-cutting, fear of unemployment, [etc.]. **1978** *Detroit Free Press* 16 Apr. 2A/1 Capitol Cartage and its owners deny that they have used shakedowns, payoffs, bribery, rate-cutting, intimidation and terror to eliminate competition. **1935** *Jrnl. Chem. Physics* III. 113 When the rate determining step shifts to the collision process..we again use well-known statistical methods. **1968** R. O. C. NORMAN *Princ. Org. Synthesis* xiv. 436 The rate-determining step in the reaction of neopentyl bromide is the formation of the high-energy primary carbonium ion. **1927** *Brit. Jrnl. Exper. Biol.* V. 121 (*heading*) Summary of families carrying accessory rate-factors. **1931** E. B. FORD *Mendelism & Evolution* II. ii. 29 It is probable that such rate-factors controlling the speed and time of onset of processes in the body, are of very general occurrence. **1932** J. S. HUXLEY *Prob. Relative Growth* i. 4 Any genes controlling relative size of parts will have to exert their action by influencing the rates of processes, and so fall in line with the numerous other rate-factors whose importance has been summarized by Goldschmidt (1927) and by Ford and Huxley (1929). **1930** *Engineering* 30 May 696/2 In this office, the operations are made out on a master card and forwarded to the rate fixers. The latter carefully estimate the cost of the work, and add the workmen's allowance of 33⅓ per cent. **1907** *Daily Chron.* 19 Mar. 2/6 The operations of a specially-constituted rate-fixing branch as regards piece work in the Royal Carriage Department. **1959** *Times* 14 Jan. 2/5 They [*sc.* candidates] must also be experienced in the running and organising of process planning, ratefixing. **1932** J. S. HUXLEY *Probl. Relative Growth* v. 230 (*caption*) Diagram to show effects of rate-genes on eye pigmentation. **1938** R. GOLDSCHMIDT *Physiol. Genetics* II. iii. 52 Goldschmidt..first drew attention to rate genes and their importance for an understanding of gene action. **1946** *Nature* 28 Sept. 448/2 A slow heterolysis of nitric acid cannot depend only on proton transfers, and therefore the rate-limiting fission.. must occur in an NO-bond. **1974** M. C. GERALD *Pharmacol.* xii. 219 The rate at which this reaction occurs determines the speed at which alcohol is removed from the body, and hence this reaction is termed 'the rate-limiting step'. **1969** *Jane's Freight Containers 1968–69* 126/1 The formation of a Market Research Department to develop new methods of rate-making. **1949** *Nucleonics* Feb. 74/1 After the charge in the tank circuit of the rate meter has reached equilibrium, the rate meter indicates the counting rate at a glance. **1962** G. A. T. BURDETT *Automatic Control Handbk.* ix. 33 The electronic system usually associated with nucleonic switches and gauges incorporating Geiger counters is known as a 'ratemeter'. This unit provides an indication of the rate at which the counter is detecting incident radiation and is usually provided with a variable integrating time control. **1974** *Physics Bull.* Aug. 349/1 The intensity of the x ray reflection is indicated by the frequency of clicks in a loud speaker, by the flashes of a GaP lamp and by the reading of a ratemeter. **1898** G. B. SHAW *Let.* 12 Mar. (1972) II. 15 Ratepayers' Association in the evening. **1955** *Times* 27 June 9/3 No ratepayer can properly gauge the effect of revaluation until he knows what rate his local authority intends to levy in the new dispensation. **1976** *Daily Tel.* 30 June 2/6 Honest citizens and rate-payers alike. **1965** *Economist* 4 Dec. 1050/1 (*heading*) Rate rebates. Helping the needy. *a* **1974** R. CROSSMAN *Diaries* (1975) I. 303 The main issue was whether I should be allowed a special short Bill introducing rate rebates *before* the long-term reform of rating. **1963** *Economist* 7 Sept. 828/1 The foreign shipowners who dominate the rate-setting consortiums. **1966** *Times* 21 Dec. 12/6 Mr. Greenwood, Minister of Housing and Local Government.., moved that the Rate Support Grant Order, 1966, be approved. **1976** *Scotsman* 25 Nov. 9/4 They condemned the reduction in rate support for Scotland as mere transfer of existing expenditure from central government to the ratepayer. **1905** *Daily Chron.* 1 Feb. 6/1 A remission in rates should be made to companies which were the chief ratepayers in districts in which rate-supported tramways run. **1922** JOYCE *Ulysses* 710 Ratesupported moribund lunatic pauper. **1961** T. LANDAU *Encycl. Librarianship* (ed. 2) 296/1 There is only one local authority area in the whole of the U.K. which has not a rate-supported public library.

b. *pl.* used *attrib.* in sense 6 d, as ***rates aid, man, rebate, reduction, tribunal.***

1966 *Times* 11 May 1/4 (*heading*) Rates aid to start next April. **1953** DYLAN THOMAS *Let.* 17 Mar. (1966) 397 Friendly Brown's can wait. These tradesmen and rates-men can't. **1966** *Times* 17 Aug. 8/6 Rates rebates in the first six months' operation of the Rating Act, 1966, are expected to total £6,850,000. **1971** *Reader's Digest Family Guide to Law* 90 (*heading*), How to apply for a rates reduction. **1935** *Economist* 23 Feb. 429/1 The task of the Railway Rates Tribunal will be unenviable when, next November, they are due to fix the rebates for the year 1935–36.

rate, *sb.*[2] (Later example.)

1976 *Shooting Times & Country Mag.* 18–24 Nov., Never fail to give a severe rate and a flick of your whip if any young hound gives a challenging voice to a bullock, cow, or a strange dog.

rate, *v.*[1] Add: **3. a.** Also, to set a high value on, to think much of.

1973 *Times* 10 Feb. 7/7 You can never be sure of Brazil, of course, but I don't rate the South Americans next time. I believe 1974 will be dominated by the Europeans. **1973** *New Society* 12 Apr. 64/2 He would like to play cricket for Surrey, but he doesn't rate his chances. **1976** E. DUNPHY *Only a Game?* iv. 104 He's a good honest pro, but somehow Benny doesn't rate him. **1977** *World of Cricket Monthly* June 85/1, I must say we rated our chances going up to Headingley.

4. (Later examples.)

1932 *Sun* (Baltimore) 27 Apr. 15/2 Major General, avoiding interference going to the first turn, was rated in front until reaching the homestretch. **1950** *Amer. Jrnl. Psychol.* LXIII. 521 The *Ss*..rated each pair on a scale of similarity. **1956** C. WILLOCK *Death at Flight* vi. 76, I still rate your type of scatter-gun old-fashioned. **1962** *Observer* 25 Feb. 21/4, I still rate him the tops. **1976** *Billings* (Montana) *Gaz.* 27 June 4-A/2 Gen. Antonio Ramalho Eanes, a dour disciplinarian pledged to restore law and order, was rated an overwhelming favorite Saturday to win the Portuguese presidency.

6. b. (Later examples.) Also, to be accorded a certain position; to be considered *as*, to count *as*.

1949 *Sun* (Baltimore) 23 May 16/6 She will rate near the top of her class, which means that in racing she will have to give time to most of her competitors. **1959** A. FULLERTON *Yellow Ford* xiv. 186 I'm important to him, too, but I don't rate that high. **1961** *Observer* 12 Mar. 29 (Advt.), You can be an important person all the same. You'll certainly rate as one if you own a 'Retinette', the Kodak precision camera. **1965** *Listener* 16 Sept. 425/2 Although Madame de Beauvoir rates as an 'intellectual', her book is a narrative of doings and feelings rather than of ideas and reflections. **1966** J. PORTER *Sour Cream* viii. 104 The disappearance of Melkin didn't even rate as a nine-days' wonder. **1976** *National Observer* (U.S.) 18 Dec. 17/1 A show may rate as expected, may languish or may exceed expectations. **1977** *Ibid.* 1 Jan. 1/4 Toy poodles rate dumbest in a test you can give your dog too.

c. *trans.* To merit, to deserve; to be worthy to attain or obtain; to be treated as worthy of, be accorded.

1921 *Collier's* 3 July 22/1 Where does he rate that stuff?.. Where does he fit to grab off that Jane? **1928** *Amer. Speech* III. 220 *Rate, v.*, to obtain, or to be entitled to. 'Did you rate a bid to the Kappa party?' **1940** A. W. FEARN *My Days of Strength* xiv. 153 Fond as the Chinese are of weddings and funerals, only virgins in China rate weddings with all the trimmings. **1957** E. HYAMS *Into Dream* II. i. 93 His power of command barely rated his two stripes. **1959** *Listener* 4 June 992/3 Nor is one certain..whether C. W. Brodribb or Harold Child, nice men though they both were, really rate the *Dictionary of National Biography*. **1962** *New Statesman* 28 Dec. 935/1 Christmas cards don't even rate a mention in the *Encyclopaedia Britannica*. **1974** 'A. GILBERT' *Nice Little Killing* vi. 82 He got out his old second-hand car—the village bobby didn't rate a panda. **1974** *Howard Jrnl.* XIV. 95 Mannheim, Radzinowicz [etc.]..rate between them nine titles in the bibliography. **1976** *Times Lit. Suppl.* 16 Apr. 460/5 The work of A. Z. Steinberg, for instance, whose contribution to Dostoevsky studies is sadly undervalued, rates no more than a mention in a half-page summary. **1978** G. GREENE *Human Factor* v. i. 236, I rate a lifetime in jail. **1979** 'A. HAILEY' *Overload* III. xii. 257 The statement by the Governor of California in support of the project rated a brief paragraph near the end of the..report.

d. *intr.* To have some standing, to be of importance; to matter, 'count'; to be highly esteemed.

1928 *Amer. Speech* III. 220 Sometimes the word is used in another sense; 'Price is rating pretty high with Betty these days' means that he stands very high in her estimation. **1938** *Chatelaine* Feb. 44/1 Nowadays to really 'rate' you must have more than an attractive face and figure. **1951** M. MCLUHAN *Mech. Bride* (1967) 112/1 The eye is anxiously turned on the neighbor or friend with a 'How do I measure up?' 'Do I rate?' **1967** *Listener* 14 Sept. 350/3 As a rock group, then, the Kinks don't rate musically.

7. d. To cause to proceed at a moderate pace, to regulate the pace of; *spec.* in horse-racing, to ride (a horse) at a moderate pace, conserving his energy for the finish. Also *intr.* for passive, of a horse: to be ridden in this way. orig. *U.S.*

1920 H. C. WITWER in *Collier's* 3 July 9/2 Ring generalship, that's what you're minus, and the only way you can get it is by experience. You gotta be rated along, not rushed... Many a promisin' kid has been ruined at the start by bein' overmatched. **1946** *Sun* (Baltimore) 28 June 9/2 Villa Nova, escaping the jam at the half-mile pole, was rated to head of stretch, then closed well through last eighth of a mile. **1961** J. S. SALAK *Dict. Amer. Sports* 354 *Rating* (harness racing), maintaining an even rate of speed and timing finishing rush. Harness horses are rated to a fraction of a second in miles. **1977** *N.Z. Herald* 5 Jan. 1–12/5 He rated Red Vesta perfectly in front, kicked clear in the straight and won comfortably. **1977** *Time* 20 June 51/2 But Turner's gentle methods have made Slew, a natural front runner, into a sound horse who 'rates kindly', or can tolerate another horse in front of him—at least for a while.

8. To assign a rating (sense *3) to (a piece of equipment, etc.). Const. *at* the value concerned. Usu. in *pass.*

1893 *Trans. Amer. Inst. Electr. Engineers* X. 255 Manufacturers cannot accurately rate their fuse-wire unless the length of the specimen to be used is specified. **1905** *Jrnl. Inst. Electr. Engineers* XXXV. 388 Fuses rated to blow with an excess current of 50 per cent of their normal carrying capacity get far too hot. **1940** *Amat. Radio Handbk.* (ed. 2) ii. 39/1 This valve..is rated at 25 watts dissipation at 500 volts. **1953** J. LISTON *Power Plants for Aircraft* i. 7 Nearly all aircraft power plants are capable of developing much more power than that at which they are rated. *Ibid.* iii. 104 By definition, iso-octane was given an octane number of 100 and normal heptane was rated at zero octane number. **1975** D. G. FINK *Electronics Engineers' Handbk.* VII. 6 Such resistors are rated from 5 to 20 kV, have a resistance range of 2,000 Ω to 1,000 MΩ, and are rated from 5 up to 20 W. **1977** *Offshore Engineer* Apr. 75/2 Average life of the new type thallium iodide bulb is rated by UMEL at approximately 500 hours.

rate, *v.*[2] **2.** (Later example.)

1872 A. C. STEELE *Broken Toys* II. xxv. 151 Ben Alymer..took up the butt-end of his gun and rated the pointer back.

‖ **raté** (rate), *a.* and *sb.* [Fr.] **A.** *adj.* Ineffective, miscarried; of a person, consistently unsuccessful. **B.** *sb.* A person who has failed in his vocation.

1905 R. FRY *Let.* 21 Jan. (1972) I. 233 His scheme being *raté* is a blow to his prestige. **1910** B. W. WELLS *Mod. French Lit.* xiii. 477 The mean spirit of D'Argenton, the poet, who, with his attendant group of *ratés*, the failures of literature and art, forms a sort of mutual admiration club. **1949** E. HYAMS *Not in our Stars* v. 47 A raté sensualist, he would willingly have enjoyed an 'affair' with Miriam. **1966** *New Statesman* 9 Sept. 369/1 Yves Montand..is too plump and groomed to make a creditable *raté*. *a* **1970** E. STARKIE in J. Richardson *Enid Starkie* (1973) iii. 58 The *raté*, the typical Paris figure. **1977** *Times* 7 Sept. 10/7 They are failures... They will all be *ratés* and hopeless when they are 30.

rateable, *a.* Add: **2.** *rateable value*, the value ascribed to a property for the purpose of assessing the rates to be levied on it.

1836 *Act* 6 & 7 *Will. IV* c. 96 Gross estimated Rental. Rateable Value. Rate at 6*d.* in the Pound. **1874** *Act* 37 & 38 *Vict.* c. 54 §4 The gross and rateable value of any land used for a plantation or a wood..shall be estimated as follows. **1909** *Daily Chron.* 13 Aug. 4/3 Mr. Lloyd George is understood..to have promised favourable consideration to the plea of the London Members for some alteration in the 'rateable-value' basis. **1925** *Act* 15 & 16 *Geo. V* c. 90 §2 Every general rate shall be a rate at a uniform amount per pound on the rateable value of each hereditament. **1962** L. GOLDING *Dict. Local Govt.* 408 The net annual value is in most cases the rateable value. **1971** *Reader's Digest Family Guide to Law* 88/1 Ratepayers do not pay an amount equal to the full rateable value of their property each year. They pay a proportion of it—the rate in the £. **1976** *Evening Post* (Nottingham) 14 Dec. 4/7 The rateable values did not take into account the disadvantages of living in the city centre.

rateably, *adv.* (Later U.S. example of spelling *ratably*.)

1973 *N.Y. Law Jrnl.* 4 Sept. 17/1 The widow's elective share must be paid ratably by all beneficiaries under the will.

rated, *ppl. a.*[1] Add: **2.** Of a numerical characteristic or property: having the value that a device, apparatus, etc., is designed to operate at or attain under normal conditions, or at which other characteristics are evaluated.

1893 *Trans. Amer. Inst. Electr. Engineers* X. 260 Promptness of action requires that the temperature of fusion should not be too far removed from that attained when the wire is being worked at its rated capacity. **1916** [see *RATING *vbl. sb.* 3]. **1931** R. N. LIPTROT in *Handbk. Aeronautics* (R. Aeronaut. Soc.) ii. 121 From ground level to the rated height the r.p.m. and horse-power progressively increase until at the rated height normal r.p.m. and horse-power are reached. **1942** I. GLEED *Arise to Conquer* ii. 16 One of my jobs was to test them [*sc.* Spitfires] at rated altitude, about 18,000 feet. **1945** G. V. WELBOURNE *Flight & Engines* xi. 135 The use of two separate jets is but one way of ensuring a sufficiently rich mixture at full rated power and take-off. **1975** D. G. FINK *Electronics Engineers' Handbk.* VII. 9 The surge voltage applicable to electrolytic capacitors is a voltage in excess of the rated voltage which the capacitor will withstand for a specified limited period at any temperature. **1978** *Nature* 6 Apr. 520/1 The wind speed data.. were fed into simulated wind generators having the following characteristics: rotor diameter, 60 m; rated wind speed, 14 $m\ s^{-1}$; furling wind speed, 27 $m\ s^{-1}$.

ratel[1]**.** Substitute for def.: The honey badger, *Mellivora capensis*, belonging to the family Mustelidæ, native to Africa and southern Asia, and distinguished by a coat that is light grey on the back and black elsewhere, powerful claws on the front feet, and a diet that includes honey, insects, reptiles, birds, and small mammals. (Later examples.)

1902 *Chambers's Jrnl.* Oct. 667/2 The camel and llama, the badger and ratel, all of which may be seen and compared at the Zoo. **1947** J. STEVENSON-HAMILTON *Wild Life S. Afr.* xxix. 242 The ratel does not hesitate to attack the most venomous species of snakes. **1961** L. VAN DER POST *Heart of Hunter* iv. 73 He gave me such a vivid picture of the ratel eating snakes that I saw it gobbling up tangles of serpents like spaghetti. **1969** B. SESHADRI *Twilight of India's Wild Life* v. 139 The ratel, or honey badger..has lived its life adapting it to many types of forest and plain. **1975** H. B. COTT *Looking at Animals* iii. 73 Ratels are said to trot unhurriedly with a long, swinging stride.

ratelier. Restrict † *Obs. rare*—1 to sense in Dict. and add: **2.** A set of teeth; a set of false teeth.

1839 THACKERAY in *Fraser's Mag.* June 746/1 In the large picture, everybody grins, and shows his whole *ratelier*. **1863** CROWN PRINCESS OF PRUSSIA *Let.* 1 Sept. in R. Fulford *Dearest Mama* (1968) 261 We are left to the care of a very funny old gentleman of the bedchamber who wears a 'ratelier' and is very tiresome besides. **1916** R. FRY *Let.* 8 Sept. (1972) II. 402, I dread the flashing *râtelier* of that Chicago girl. **1923** R. NEVILL *World of Fashion 1837–1922* iii. 62 When alone in his study he [*sc.* Labouchère] would take out his *ratelier* and lay it on the ground.

‖ **ratemahatmaya** (ra:temaha·tmayā). *Sri Lanka.* [Sinhalese, f. *rate* of the district + *mahatmaya* gentleman.] A chief headman of a Kandyan district.

1821 J. DAVY *Acct. Interior of Ceylon* v. 147 The duties of Rate-mahatmeyas were similar to those of Dissaves; but their official rank was inferior. **1841** J. FORBES *Eleven Years in Ceylon* iv. 67 The authorities under the Kandian dynasty were thus arranged... The Rate Mahatmeás, chiefs of inferior districts. **1913** L. WOOLF *Village in Jungle* ii. 37 Disa Mahatmaya is the title used by villagers in referring to chief headmen or Ratemahatmayas. **1956** R. PIERIS *Sinhalese Social Organization* I. iv. 24 The *ratēmahatmayās*, as they were colloquially styled, bore the title *ratērāla* at court.

rater[1]**. 1.** Delete 'Now *rare*' and add later examples.

1957 D. T. HERMAN et al. in Saporta & Bastian *Psycholinguistics* (1961) 540/1 Two raters independently rated each of the reproductions. **1967** M. ARGYLE *Psychol. Interpersonal Behaviour* x. 182 The use of 'blind' ratings, where the raters do not know which of the individuals they are rating are being trained or belong to a control group. **1973** *Jrnl. Genetic Psychol.* Mar. 40 Raters had no knowledge of whether a given interview protocol was from the psychopathic or nonpsychopathic sample. **1977** RYAN & CARRANZA in H. Giles *Lang., Ethnicity & Intergroup Relations* ii. 70 Ethnicity of rater did not affect evaluation of the standard speakers. **1979** *Nature* 22 Mar. 357/2 The assessment on HRS was made by two independent raters who showed a satisfactory concordance.

rat fink. *slang* (chiefly *U.S.*). Also **rat-fink, ratfink.** [f. RAT *sb.*[1] + *FINK *sb.*[2]] One who is obnoxious or contemptible, esp. (*a*) an odiously pretentious person; (*b*) an informer, a traitor. Also *attrib.* or as *adj.* Hence as *v. trans.*, to inform *on*.

1964 *Guardian* 8 July 7/6 That's the hitcheroo, baby,.. this time when Cliff and Shirley dance on top of Everest it's a send up. That keeps the intellectual rat-finks happy, see. *Ibid.*, This is going to bring them all in: the dads and mums, the squares, the rat-fink intellectuals, and the teenagers. **1965** D. BOROFF *State of Nation* 212 In fitting American youth for its destiny in the free world of tomorrow, our schools may be virtually compelling them to become a bunch of ratfinks. **1965** P. DE VRIES *Let me count Ways* xx. 273 So cool and rat fink. What college did you go to? That made you so cultured and rat fink. **1966** *Listener* 9 June 838/1 The cool cats and the rat finks and the camp hips [in America]. **1969** C. BURKE *God is Beautiful, Man* 88 His name was Judas and he was a rat fink. So this dirty rat fink he says to the pres of the gang, Caiaphas, 'What's in it for me if I put the finger on him?' **1973** M. & G. GORDON *Informant* x. 46, I may be a rat fink but I'm not going to be a paid rat fink. **1973** *Houston Chron.* 21 Oct. 10/2 As for informing on an honor violator, the colonel said you didn't exactly rat fink on such a man, you usually confront that man with his conduct and expect him to do the honorable thing. **1975** A. PRICE *Our Man in Camelot* iii. 52 Gildas.. was..denouncing the rulers of Britain as a bunch of rat-finks who were letting the country go to the dogs. **1976** L. DEIGHTON *Twinkle, twinkle, Little Spy* v. 30 It was Tony Nowak's rat-fink cousin Stefan who put the spaghetti in the piano. **1976** *Courier-Mail* (Brisbane) 19 Feb. 5/2, I still think you were a rat fink. **1977** *New Yorker* 26 Sept. 127 The hairy little hipster Go Go, a ratfink wearing a cross and a yarmulke.

rath (rɑþ), *sb.*[2] A factitious word introduced by 'Lewis Carroll' (see quot. 1855[2]).

Quot. 1855[1] also occurs in the first verse of 'Jabberwocky' in *Through the Looking-Glass* (1871) i. 21.

1855 'L. CARROLL' *Rectory Umbrella & Mischmasch* (1932) 139 All mimsy were the borogoves; And the mome raths outgrabe. *Ibid.* 140 *Rath*, a species of land turtle. Head erect: mouth like a shark: the fore legs curved out so that the animal walked on its knees: smooth green body: lived on swallows and oysters.

‖ **Rathaus** (rā·thaus). Also **Rath-haus, Rathhaus.** [Ger., lit. council-house.] A German town hall.

1611 CORYAT *Crudities* 619, I..will make mention of their *Prætorium* or Senate house, which they commonly call the Rathausz [in Cologne]. **1855** GEO. ELIOT in *Fraser's Mag.* June 703/2 The Markt, a cheerful square [in Weimar], made smart by a new Rath-haus. **1864** C. M. Yonge *Bk. Golden Deeds* 208 The grim effigy..grins over the door of the Rathhaus [in Freiburg]. **1962** K. O'Hara *Double Cross Purposes* vii. 95, I did see two cars parked outside..the local Rathaus. **1975** *Times* 26 Apr. 10/5 The [Hamburg] Rathaus..has a cellar restaurant of quite Gothic splendour.

rathe, *sb.*² **2.** (Further example.)
1875 *Ure's Dict. Arts* (ed. 7) III. 1111 A comb or raithe ..guides the threads with precision on to any length of beam.

rathe, rath, *a.*¹ Add: **1.** (Later example.)
1949 E. Pound *Pisan Cantos* lxxxi. 113 Pull down thy vanity, Rathe to destroy, niggard in charity.
3. (Later example.)
1914 C. Mackenzie *Sinister Street* II. III. xiv. 787 Spring on these rathe mornings of wind and scudded blue sky was forward with her traceries.

rather, *adv.* **II. 7.** For (*vulgar*) read (orig. *vulgar*) and add: freq. with emphatic pronunc. (rāːðəˑɹ). Now, or until recently, common also in upper-class or affected speech. (Later examples.)
1885 A. Edwardes *Girton Girl* I. xiv. 280 Rather proud of my own accent... But Arbuthnot puts me in the shade, ra-*ther*. **1905** H. Vachell *Hill* i. 2 'You'll enjoy it—as I did —amazingly.' 'Ra-ther,' said John. **1928** C. A. Nicholson *Hell & Duchess* II. vi. 286 'May I give Audrey your blessing?' 'Ra-ther and my love.' **1933** J. Buchan *Prince of Captivity* II. i. 153 'You've heard Kenneth speak of him.' 'Rather. I want to meet him.' **1975** *Listener* 10 Apr. 472/2 The producer had..prevented the willing son in the parable from saying 'Yes, ra-*ther*, Dad,' when asked to get on with the 'allotment'.
9. f. Ellipt. phr. *rather you than me* (or *I*): I would rather that you did or underwent something than I (used to convey admiration, commiseration, etc.).
1968 'C. Aird' *Henrietta Who?* xv. 192 A proper mix-up, isn't it?.. Rather you than me. **1969** V. Gielgud *Necessary End* xiii. 104 'You're a brave fellow. Rather you than I. Good luck.

rather (ræˑðəɹ), *sb. U.S. dial.* [f. the adv.] A choice, preference. Cf. *druther, *ruther.
1903 *Dialect Notes* II. 326 'I would stay at home if I *had my rather*.' Also pronounced *ruther*. **1913** H. Kephart *Our Southern Highlanders* xiii. 283 'It matters not, so I've been told, Where the body goes when the heart grows cold; But,' she concluded, 'a person has a rather about where he'd be put.' **1930** W. Faulkner *As I lay Dying* 106 And if I had my rathers, you wouldn't be here at all. **1961** C. Himes *Black on Black* (1973) 46 If I had my rathers I'd make up my own band.

rathest, *adv.* Restrict † *Obs.* to senses 1 and 2 in Dict. and add: **3.** (Later example.)
1884 B. Potter *Jrnl.* 27 Oct. (1966) 107, I would rathest of all copy the raised plaques of Wedgwood.

rathite (rāˑtəit, raˑþəit). *Min.* [ad. G. *rathit* (H. Baumhauer 1896, in Zeitschr. f. Kryst. und Min. XXVI. 594), f. the name of G. vom *Rath* (1830–88), German mineralogist: see -ite¹.] Any of a group of sulpharsenites of lead found in the Binnental in southern Switzerland.
1897 *Mineral. Mag.* XI. 225 Characteristic of rathite, but not invariably present, are parallel systems of very fine striæ..on the crystal faces and on the fractured faces. **1905** [see *hutchinsonite]. **1953** *Amer. Mineralogist* XXXVIII. 330 Weissenberg and precession camera studies on baumhauerite, dufrenoysite and rathite, lead to the following new structural data... Rathite-II is monoclinic... The unit cell dimensions do not agree with previous structural or morphological data on rathite, although they were obtained on a fragment of the original material. **1965** *Zeitschr. für Kristallogr.* CXXII. 434 Rathite-I, $(Pb,Tl)_3As_4(As,Ag)S_{10}$, is a mineral of a sulfosalt group, to which rathite-II, rathite-III, rathite-IV, dufrenoysite, baumhauerite and scleroclase belong. *Ibid.*, Rathite-I and -III form two modifications of a single species and should perhaps have a name different from rathite-II... In the Lengenbach quarry rathite-II is frequently found, whereas rathite-I occurs rarely, and then usually polysynthetically twinned. **1974** *Neues Jahrb. für Mineral.: Monatshefte* 530 Several kinds of minerals which belong to a group of lead sulfarsenites called 'rathite group' have been found in Lengenbach quarry (Ct. Wallis, Switzerland) and crystallographically investigated. The existence of two common periods of about 7·9 Å and 8·4 Å is a marked characteristic of them.

Rathke (rāˑtkə). *Anat.* [The name of Martin Heinrich *Rathke* (1793–1860), German anatomist, who described the structure in 1838 (*Arch. für Anat., Physiol. und Wissenschaftl. Med.* 482).] *Rathke's pouch* or *pocket* (also *pouch of Rathke*): a diverticulum of the oral cavity, which in developing vertebrates forms the anterior lobe of the pituitary body.
1889 A. Macalister *Textbk. Human Anat.* 620 The stomodæum joined the oral end of the mesenteron at about the fourteenth day and from its upper part is projected the hypophysial pouch of Rathke. **1892** E. L. Mark tr. *O. Hertwig's Textbk. Embryol.* xiv. 285 Even after the rupture of the pharyngeal membrane there is retained, in front of its attachment, a small pit, which constitutes Rathke's pocket. **1906, 1915** [see *hypophysis 3]. **1945** W. J. Hamilton et al. *Human Embryol.* x. 153 An ectodermal diverticulum, Rathke's pouch, arises from the stomatodaeal roof. *Ibid.* xii. 253 Rathke's pouch loses its attachment to the pharyngeal roof..and develops into the various subdivisions of the anterior lobe of the definitive hypophysis. **1962** [see *pars intermedia]. **1973** F. Beck et al. *Human Embryol. & Genetics* xvii. 188 The thickening in the anterior wall of Rathke's pouch becomes the *pars anterior* of the adult pituitary gland.

raˑt-hole, *sb.* [Rat *sb.*¹ 7.] **1.** A hole used by a rat for passage or abode. Also *fig.*, a cramped or squalid building, room, or the like; a refuge or hiding-place. Also *attrib.*
1812, 1879 [see Rat *sb.*¹ 7 a]. **1879** [see *junk-shop* s.v. *junk *sb.*² 5]. **1912** *Dialect Notes* III. 581 He wouldn't know enough to pound sand in a rat-hole; so don't get him. **1922** D. H. Lawrence *Let.* 30 Apr. (1962) II. 701 Yet I don't believe in Buddha—hate him in fact—his rat-hole temples and his rat-hole religion. **1941** M. U. Schappes *Let.* 21 July in *Lett. from Tombs* (1941) 85 The rat-hole: a hotel where state's-witnesses are kept! *a* **1944** K. Douglas *Alamein to Zem Zem* (1946) 133 We stayed in our positions, like a terrier at a rat-hole. **1976** 'B. Shelby' *Great Pebble Affair* 164 The warehouse is..a dummy warehouse designed to mask our rathole. **1976** N. Thornburg *Cutter & Bone* iii. 80 Mo was not just frigid,..she was dead, a cadaver with a welded womb and a cunt like a rathole, full of dust and bits of straw and feathers from old nests.
2. *Oil industry.* **a.** A shallow hole drilled near a well hole to accommodate the kelly or a pipe joint when it is not in use. **b.** A hole of smaller diameter drilled at the bottom of a larger hole.
1921 W. H. Jeffery *Deep Well Drilling* v. 209 Some rotary drillers drill a shallow well at a point midway and in front of the slush pumps, in which they rest the drill stem when not in use or when waiting to set in another joint of drill pipe. This is termed the 'rat hole'. **1939** D. Hager *Fund. Petroleum Industry* ix. 210 When the kelly is deep enough for a joint of drill stem, the kelly and bit are pulled out. The kelly is set to one side, fitting in a hole (the 'rat-hole') cut in the floor of the derrick. **1972** L. M. Harris *Introd. Deepwater Floating Drilling Operations* xvi. 164 During and immediately following the unloading of the water cushion and the rathole mud, the surface pressure is determined by the amount of fluid to be unloaded. **1975** G. Anderson *Coring* v. 89 Most diamond coring is now done in the full diameter of the borehole. Whether coring is done this way or in a rat hole depends on the full gauge-keeping ability of the rock bits used prior to initiating the coring operation.
3. *N. Amer.* A seemingly bottomless hole; used *fig.* or allusively of something that demands excessive expenditure.
1961 in Webster. **1975** D. Lambro *Federal Rathole* vi. 43 The contractor was refused..additional loan money because..it would be 'pouring money down a rathole'. **1976** *Globe & Mail* (Toronto) 21 Dec. 7/1 The committee will examine..Minaki Lodge, the rathole in northwestern Ontario down which increasing quantities of public money seem to be disappearing. **1977** *Time* 19 Dec. 13/2 Since the B-1 bomber will not be part of our military inventory, to build two more airplanes would simply amount to pouring half a billion dollars down a rathole.

raˑt-hole, *v.* [f. prec.] **1.** *intr.* and *trans. Oil Industry.* To drill a hole of smaller diameter at the bottom of (one of larger diameter).
1922 L. C. Sands in D. T. Day *Handbk. Petroleum Industry* 268 If the oil stratum should inadvertently be penetrated before the casing has been set and all water excluded from overlying formations, it will be expensive, if not impossible, to make a successful producer of the well. To forestall this danger it is common practice to 'rat-hole' ahead at intervals. **1939** D. Hager *Fund. Petroleum Industry* ix. 228 If the sand is expected, the hole can be reduced and 'ratholed' ahead, a smaller hole being drilled.
2. To hide or store; not to invest or spend (money).
1948 *Amer. Speech* XXII. 220 Stashing was overt and frequently a co-operative enterprise, whereas to *rat-hole* implied that an individual was storing something of possibly public property for his own use. **1971** *Wall St. Jrnl.* 17 June 1/5 Everyone ratholed their money last year. Then they saw the (economic) situation hasn't changed so they decided if they're going to buy, now's the time to do it. **1977** *New Yorker* 4 July 55/1 Speaker said he was 'ratholing' the Jif jar. He was not ready to pay the Internal Revenue Service any portion of the gold's value (his privilege until it is sold).

Rathskeller, rathskeller (rāˑtskeləɹ). Also **ratskeller.** [ad. G. *ratskeller* (formerly *rathskeller*), f. *rat* council as in *Rathaus + -*s* gen. ending + *keller* cellar.
The form *rathskeller* was preferred to avoid the phonetic association with Rat *sb.*¹ + Cellar *sb.*]
a. A cellar in a German town hall in which beer or wine is sold. **b.** An underground beer-hall or restaurant. Also *transf.*
1900 Ade *More Fables* 159 Mr. Byrd..happened to be in a Rathskeller not far away. **1903** *Current Lit.* Apr. 495/2 The first rathskeller was established in New York in 1863 by Fred. Hollander. **1916** *Harper's Mag.* Dec. 18 He likes the religious cool of the rathskeller... He takes his ease in his inn. **1929** *Papers Mich. Acad. Sci., Arts & Lett.* X. 318/1 *Rathskeller*, a dugout. **1934** S. R. Nelson *All about Jazz* vi. 121 They used to work the *Rathskellers* or night-clubs of the lower grades. **1946** E. O'Neill *Iceman Cometh* (1947) I. 27 It's the No Chance Saloon. It's Bedrock Bar, The End of the Line Café, The Bottom of the Sea Rathskeller! **1969** *Courier-Mail* (Brisbane) 30 June 3/4 The ratskeller will be a 'cellar, with barrels of wine and beer, where people will dine at leisure'. **1975** *Country Life* 11 Dec. 1676/1 The *Rathaus* or town hall..stands in the cobbled market square with the usual *Ratskeller* for refreshments.

raticide (ræˑtisəid). Also **ratticide.** [f. Rat *sb.*¹ + -i- + -cide.] **a.** One who, or that which, kills rats, esp. a chemical substance used as a rat poison. **b.** *rare.* The killing of rats.
1847 W. J. Broderip *Zool. Recreations* 319 The celebrated ratticide Billy has long since gone to that bourne whence neither rats, dogs, nor travellers ever return. **1908** W. R. Boelter *Rat Problem* iv. 146 Raticide. This preparation.. is manufactured in the United States, where it is sold under the name of Azra. **1922** *Jrnl. R. Sanitary Inst.* XLII. 316 Practical experience..supports the view that the safety margin for Squills is greater than for any other practical raticide at present in use. **1936** *Times* 21 Aug. 11/5 The end of real research into effective raticides. **1941** *Nature* 1 Mar. 263/1 Guidance in production, research and application as relating to insecticides, fungicides, raticides and repellents for all purposes. **1976** *New Scientist* 26 Aug. 454/2 William Kotzwinkle's *Doctor Rat* is a comic triumph. About half is narrated by a mad laboratory rat, whose perceptions into the relationship between mass ratticide and grantsmanship do make delightful satire.

ratification. (Earlier and later examples of *ratification meeting*.)
1848 *Campaign* (Washington, D.C.) 21 June 64/2 A great democratic ratification meeting was held at New Orleans on the night of the 8th June. **1904** *N.Y. Even. Post* 23 June 2/6 The first Roosevelt ratification meeting..will be held this evening..when the Republican Club of the Thirty-first Assembly District will endorse the nominees of the Chicago convention.

ratificaˑtionist. [f. Ratification + -ist.] One who favours ratification (of a treaty, etc.).
1921 *Glasgow Herald* 23 Dec. 7/3 On the ratificationists' side it had been suggested that there should be a time limit to speeches.

ratine (rătīˑn). Also ‖ **ratiné** (ratine). [Fr., pa. pple. of *ratiner* to frieze.] A clothing fabric of rough open texture.
1913–14 *T. Eaton & Co. Catal.* Fall & Winter 17 The materials for Suits are very beautiful..Whipcords, Corduroys, Boucle Tweeds, Ratines. **1922** *Daily Mail* 15 Nov. 1 (Advt.), All-silk ratine. For frocks, children's wear, furnishings. **1923** *Westm. Gaz.* 22 Mar. 9/2 Mrs. Almond's blue ratine looked as if it had just descended on her and had been made in heaven. **1934** Webster, *Ratiné*... Also *ratine*. **1966** *Vogue* Dec. 71 White ratine tunic dress. **1967** *Times* 21 Feb. 9/1 Ratiné..was launched, or rather relaunched, at the French prêt-à-porter fair last year. **1969** N. W. Parsons *Upon Sagebrush Harp* xi. 57 We noticed a long cobweb floating over our heads... Long silvery strands moving through the motionless air from west to east. Each was like a white ratiné string, fine as silk except for knots at irregular intervals.

rating, *vbl. sb.*¹ Add: **2. b.** (Later examples.)
1906 *Westm. Gaz.* 6 June 6/2 The cruiser..landed fourteen officers, 290 ratings, and eighty-five marines. **1925** *Nation* 26 Sept. 756/2 Numerous ground ratings are needed to handle airships in and out of the hangars in addition to a very considerable repair staff of specially skilled ratings. **1932** *Daily Express* 27 Jan. 1/2 Many of the ratings belong to Portsmouth, and some are married and have families. **1955** *Times* 12 May 7/5 Two naval ratings, both aged 19, were arrested on board H.M.S. Ark Royal. **1979** *Jrnl. R. Soc. Arts* CXXVII. 545/2 Six scholarships for deck ratings were awarded.
3. The value of a property which is claimed to be standard or limiting for a piece of equipment or a material, or to be necessary for its optimal or standard use; a rated value (*rated *ppl. a.*¹ 2).
Quot. 1893 repr. the action of *rate *v.*¹ 8 rather than the result.
1893 *Trans. Amer. Inst. Electr. Engineers* X. 260 This wire was quite uniform in diameter, and gave evidence of careful rating. The curve of rating should be of the same general equation as that of fusion, since both represent isothermal conditions. **1905** *Jrnl. Inst. Electr. Engineers* XXXV. 367 The 'normal carrying capacity' or 'rating' of a fuse wire may be defined as: The maximum current which the fuse is capable of carrying continuously without deterioration or undue heating. **1916** *Standardization Rules Amer. Inst. Electr. Engineers* 25 A transformer of given kv-a rating must be capable of delivering the rated output at rated secondary voltage. **1941** E. Molloy *Aero-Engine Pract.* 57 The rating of an aero-engine is prepared not with the mere hope that it may be suitable for some aircraft or other, but with the intention of fulfilling a definite specification, whether civil or military. **1967** G. Arnold *Re-Wiring House* 19 Cables used in house wiring usually operate at below their maximum current rating. **1967** M. Chandler *Ceramics in Mod. World* iv. 123 This enables the insulator to be operated at higher ratings than would otherwise be possible. **1968** Miller & Sawers *Techn. Devel. Mod. Aviation* iii. 94 The fuel used in the 1920's was no better than that sold for cars, with an octane rating of about 50. **1969** *Jane's Freight Containers 1968–69* 12/1 *Rating*, means the maximum gross weight and is the maximum permissible combined weight of the freight container and of its contents. **1974** *Homes & Gardens* Apr. 150/2 The fuse rating is given in the accompanying instruction book as well as being clearly marked on the appliance rating plate. **1978** *Amateur Photographer* 2 Aug. 131/1 It is important that the total current drawn from all sockets should not exceed the rating of the supply socket—13 or 15-amp.

4. a. An assessment or measure (of a person's achievement, behaviour, skill, status, etc.); a grade, category or standing.

1921 A. W. PROCTER *Princ. Public Personnel Admin.* viii. 162 A rating of individual efficiency is intended to be a measurement of the value of the services rendered throughout a given period of time by an individual employee. **1939** [see *DATING *vbl. sb* c]. **1948** B. G. M. GUNDKLER *Bantu Prophets S. Afr.* iv. 88 The farmer has certain definite rules for social rating. **1951** M. MCLUHAN *Mech. Bride* (1967) 58/2 Culture ratings à la Emily Post are not often made in accordance with the consumer mentality. *Ibid.* 59/2 Woe to the indigent intellectual who accidentally acquires a 'high' rating without the economic appendages. **1964** M. ARGYLE *Psychol. & Social Probl.* xi. 138 Suppose a firm selects personnel by interviewing applicants. We can find out how effective this is by comparing ratings (or the rank-order) of candidates made by the interviewer with their subsequent success at the job. **1968** *Listener* 6 June 748/2 There is to be a ballot during the interval to determine which of three works..should be repeated after the interval. One doesn't have to think very long to discover how invidious this could turn out to be. First performances are quite bad enough for the composers concerned without their having to worry about Instant Popularity Ratings as well. **1974** *Plain Dealer* (Cleveland, Ohio) 26 Oct. 4-D/4 Many sports publications may have underestimated the Cavaliers in the pre-season ratings.

b. *Broadcasting.* Usu. *pl.* orig. **Crossley rating** [from Archibald M. *Crossley* who in 1930 began the regular reports of the Co-operative Analysis of Broadcasting]: an estimate, based on statistical sampling, of the size of the audience of any particular radio or television programme; its popularity so assessed.

1939 *Business Week* 25 Feb. 36/2 You've heard some radio comedian crack, after getting off a poor gag, 'There goes my Crossley'. He is referring to his popularity rating with one of the services that measure..the size of radio listening audiences. **1940** *Time* 29 Jan. 50/2 In the radio business, 'Crossley ratings' are the official box-office count. Crossley's boss is the Cooperative Analysis of Broadcasting, instituted eleven years ago..and now subscribed to by 635 sponsors. **1941** G. MARX *Groucho Lett.* (1967) 47 The Tommy Riggs show, which I spurned, now has a Crosley rating of seventeen... This will give you an idea of how little I know about audiences and what they want. **1947** *Billboard* 1 Nov. 3 The majority of new shows on the air—so far at least—are failing to show evidence of any particular rating strength. This is especially true when ratings are related to talent budgets. **1952** H. V. GROHMANN *Advertising Terminol.* 64 *Rating*, the popularity test for a specific show. **1959** *Daily Mail* 11 Aug. 8/8 According to the ratings, the only court of public opinion that counts in these circles, Hylton shows are successful. **1962** *Times* 19 May 4/3 Public-service broadcasting, free from 'the tyranny of the ratings'. **1971** *Daily Tel.* 2 Aug. 7/4 Though the two BBC channels between them still share the ratings with ITV on a 50–50 basis, the trend is sufficiently strong to alarm the major companies. **1977** *Time* 7 Feb. 40/3 The hokiness of Hollywood fame got to him too. He would say, 'Even my friendships are related to ratings.'

5. *attrib.* and *Comb.*, as (sense 1) *rating area, authority*; (sense 2) *rating badge*; (sense *3) *rating point, scale*; (sense *4 b) *ratings battle, issue, terms, war.*

1928 *Britain's Industr. Future* (Liberal Industr. Inquiry) v. 408 Rating areas should be drastically revised with a view to a more equal distribution of the burden of rates. **1962** L. GOLDING *Dict. Local Govt.* 328 Rating authorities, i.e., the local authorities responsible for levying and collection of rates, are the councils of county boroughs and county districts. **1910** *Our Navy* (U.S.) Apr. 19/1 A following the sea Is plenty good enough for me, Since I've got a ratin' badge tacked on my arm. **1921** *Sea Bag* (U.S.S.S. Oklahoma) 22 June 2/1 How many men suddenly wake up to the fact that they haven't watch-marks on their jumpers or rating-badges on their sleeves? **1976** *Sun* (Baltimore) 16 May A12/4 Since it [*sc.* Washington] is a bigger TV market than Baltimore, it costs more for a political advertisement. The price in Washington is $90 a rating point. In Baltimore it is $50 a rating point. In Baltimore, a rating point represents about 7,500 homes. **1974** *Times* 15 Oct. 16/6 The silly ratings battle..claims about the number of viewers watching each channel. **1927** *Scribner's Mag.* Apr. 418/2 One institution, in its confidential rating scale to be filled out by the school principal,..and others.., asks..as to 'moral earnestness, loyalty,..modesty'. **1967** M. ARGYLE *Psychol. Interpersonal Behaviour* v. 102 Another method [of measuring competence] is to use ratings: a number of rating scales are devised covering various aspects of a task, and are filled in by special observers. **1958** *Wall St. Jrnl.* 28 Nov. 1/6 Behind the ratings issue is the bigger question of whether the big TV networks, including the Columbia Broadcasting system, National Broadcasting Co. and American Broadcasting Co., should come under Federal regulation. **1977** *TV Times* (Brisbane) 13 Aug. 11/1 Australian ratings terms have been revised to incorporate the introduction of colour TV and consequent multi-set use in many homes. **1980** *Times* 25 Jan. 19/6 The ratings war—the battle to win as many viewers as possible for a programme.

ratio. 1. a. Delete † *Obs. rare* and add: spec. *Law.* Reason or rationale upon which a juridical decision is based; = *ratio decidendi* (see sense *1 b).

1964 G. ABRAHAMS *Police Questioning & Judges' Rules* i. 20 Therein, it is submitted, is the *ratio* of that decision against the admissibility of statements. **1971** *Mod. Law Rev.* XXXIV. VI. 691 The judge considered..that *Torquay Hotel Co.* v. *Cousins* was authority, 'that this tort of interference with contracts applies not only where there is interference with contracts already made but where there is interference with contracts to be made in accordance with a regular course of dealing.' Is this the *ratio* of the *Torquay* case? **1976** J. M. KELLY *Stud. Civil Judicature of Roman Republic* v. 112, I have, by negative implication, foreshadowed certain characteristics of the *unus iudex* inasmuch as the factors which form the *ratio* of the *centumviri* or *recuperatores* will not be present in his case. **1977** *Times* 23 Dec. 18/5 That restricted definition was unnecessary for the ratio of that decision.

b. In Lat. phrases, esp. *Philos.* and *Law*: **ratio cognoscendi,** that in virtue of which knowledge of something is possible; that in virtue of which something is known to exist; **ratio decidendi** (pl. **rationes decidendi**), rationale of judgment; a principle underlying and determining a judicial decision; **ratio essendi, existendi,** that in virtue of which something exists.

1830 W. HAMILTON in *Edin. Rev.* LII. 178 The existence of external things, which is given only *through* their intuition, it admits; the intuition itself, though the *ratio cognoscendi*, and *to us* therefore the *ratio essendi* of their reality, it rejects. **1862** in C. CLARK *House of Lords Cases* VIII. 392 The observations made by Members of the House, whether law Members or lay Members beyond the *ratio decidendi* which is propounded and acted upon in giving judgment, although they may be entitled to respect, are only to be followed in as far as they may be considered agreeable to sound reason and to prior authorities. **1865** S. H. HODGSON *Times & Space* vii. 488 Now both the cause, or ratio existendi, and the reason, or ratio cognoscendi, in every particular case must be given by actual experience. **1877** *Law Rep. Exchequer Division* II. 233 The ratio decidendi in these cases does not appear in the reports. **1890** W. JAMES *Princ. Psychol.* I. x. 337 But if the brand is the *ratio cognoscendi* of the belonging, the belonging, in the case of the herd, is in turn the *ratio existendi* of the brand. **1902** J. W. SALMOND *Jurisprudence* viii. 176 A precedent, therefore, is a judicial decision which contains in itself a principle. The underlying principle which thus forms its authoritative element is often termed the *ratio decidendi*. **1903** G. E. MOORE *Principia Ethica* iv. 127 Kant..admits that Freedom is the *ratio essendi* of the Moral Law, whereas the latter is only *ratio cognoscendi* of Freedom. **1923** C. D. BROAD *Sci. Thought* viii. 267 Sensa are..in some way the *ratio cognoscendi* of the physical world, whilst the physical world is.. the *ratio essendi* of sensa. **1948** *Law Q. Rev.* LXIV. 463 The court is always at liberty to propound alternative rules of law, each of which it may elevate to the status of a ratio decidendi. **1970** *Internat. & Compar. Law Q.* XIX. I. 37 Which of these *rationes decidendi* possesses binding force? **1972** *Evangelical Q.* XLIV. 241 These activities compose the *ratio cognoscendi* of the pardoning grace of God; they make us aware of God's activity which is the *ratio essendi* that calls forth man's response. **1977** *Law Q. Rev.* XCIII. 378 The importance of the *ratio decidendi* is that it is the rule of law for which a case is authority.

5. Special Comb.: **ratio detector** *Electronics*, an F.M. detector whose two output voltages are such that their sum is constant and their ratio, rather than their difference, is proportional to the ratio of the two applied frequency-dependent voltages, so that its insensitivity to changes in amplitude is not confined to the carrier frequency. Also *RATIOMETER.

1947 *RCA Rev.* VIII. 201 A new circuit for f-m detection known as the ratio detector is coming into wide use. **1965** *Wireless World* July 8 (Advt.), Printed circuit for I.F. amplifiers and ratio detector. **1974** HARVEY & BOHLMAN *Stereo F.M. Radio Handbk.* v. 99 Normally, in a ratio detector of the balanced type, the centre-point of the load is earthed and the output signal is taken from the tertiary winding.

ratio (rēⁱ·ʃio, rēⁱ·ʃⁱo), *v.* [f. the sb.] *trans.* To enlarge, amplify, or reduce by a certain ratio. So **ra·tioed** *ppl. a.*, **ra·tioing** *vbl. sb.*

1943 H. T. U. SMITH *Aerial Photographs* viii. 196 Each print which departs from the average scale or shows any apparent tilt is rectified and 'ratioed', or corrected for scale, by means of a projection printer. *Ibid.* 352 *Ratioed print*, a print prepared at a predetermined scale by photographic enlargement or reduction. **1970** J. A. HOWARD *Aerial Photo-Ecol.* ix. 105 Aerial photographs..sometimes.. are enlarged or reduced in size for a special purpose. These photographs are then known as ratioed prints or ratioed photographs. **1978** *Nature* 9 Mar. 142/2 This ratioing operation reduces the effective amplitude fluctuations of the laser by more than 100-fold.

ratiocinable (ræʃi-, rætiǫ·sinăb'l), *a. nonce-wd.* [f. RATIOCINATE *v.* + -ABLE.] Arrived at or deducible by reasoning.

1916 G. B. SHAW *Androcles & Lion* Pref. p. lxxxvii, An inveterate Roman Rationalist, always discarding the irrational real thing for the unreal but ratiocinable postulate.

ratiocinate, *v.* Add: Also with pronunc. (rætiǫ·sinēⁱt). Also (*rare*) *trans.* and *refl.* So **ratio·cinated** *ppl. a.*

1900 G. B. SHAW *Let.* 30 Dec. (1972) II. 214 The conventional, factitious, ratiocinated motives & conclusions of his characters. **1926** FOWLER *Mod. Eng. Usage* 483/2 *Ratiocinate* & its derivatives..may fairly be pronounced rătĭ- rather than răshĭ-;..the OED, however, gives only răshĭ-. **1934** C. P. SNOW *Search* II. iv. 180 Ratiocinating myself into honesty about my posturings.

ratiocinatively (ræʃi-, rætiǫ·sinĕtivli), *adv.* [f. RATIOCINATIVE *a.* + -LY².] By the process of reasoning; by ratiocination.

1965 J. LAWLOR in J. Gibb *Light on C. S. Lewis* 68 Some of the inconsistencies we were after could be approached ratiocinatively, and examined for logical contradiction; but the deeper kinds of awareness were to be reached intuitively rather than through rationalizations.

ratiocinator. (Later example.)

1971 HEATH & PRENDERGAST tr. J. Kristeva in *Signs of Times* 4 His [*sc.* Leibniz's] attempt to construct a 'calculus ratiocinator'.

ratiometer (rēⁱʃiǫ·mĭtəɹ). [f. RATIO + -METER.] A device for measuring the ratio of two electrical quantities.

1925 R. O. KAPP *G. Kapp's Transformers* (ed. 3) ix. 220 The ratio of a transformer is tested by an apparatus known as a ratiometer. This is really an autotransformer of which the windings are so subdivided that any ratio within very fine limits is obtainable. **1942** *Jrnl. Sci. Instruments* XIX. 23/2 A suitable current ratiometer has been constructed.. consisting of two coils on the same spindle maintained in a non-uniform field by a torsionless suspension. **1976** *Physics Bull.* Nov. 509/1 It has two amplifiers, phase sensitive detection or 'lock-in' and a ratiometer in one unit.

ratiomorphic (ræʃiomǭ·ɹfik), *a. Psychol.* [f. RATIO + Gr. μορφ-ή + -IC.] (See quots. 1954 and 1966.) Hence **ratiomo·rphous** *a.*

1954 E. BRUNSWIK in *Acta Psychologica* XI. 109 Perception and thinking thus emerge as different forms of imperfect inferences regarding the environment, subsumable to a common behavior model patterned upon reasoning ('ratiomorphic' reduction, if this Latin–Greek hybrid be permitted). **1966** K. R. HAMMOND *Psychol. E. Brunswik* i. 38 By 1955, however, he [*sc.* Brunswik] had coined the term 'ratiomorphic' to represent the organism's process of coordinating uncertain data in order to make an inductive inference from them. Perception is a '..ratiomorphic subsystem of cognition..'. The process is, in other words, 'reasoning-like'. **1971** R. MARTIN tr. *Lorenz's Stud. Animal & Human Behaviour* II. 302 All kinds of constancy apparatus are—in principle—'ratiomorphic' in the most rigorous sense of the term, since all incorporate processes analogous to those of both induction and deduction. **1977** R. TAYLOR tr. *Lorenz's Behind Mirror* vii. 119 Egon Brunswik coined the term 'ratiomorphous' to describe..all these sensory and nervous processes [which] take place in areas of our nervous system which are completely inaccessible to our consciousness and our self-observation. *Ibid.* 162 These unconscious processes are what Egon Brunswik called 'ratiomorphous' computing mechanisms.

ration. Now with pronunc. almost always (ræ·ʃən). Add: **3. a.** (Further *pl.* examples.)

1862 R. HENNING *Let.* 19 Oct. (1966) 110 Biddulph or Mr Hedgeland goes to the out-stations with provisions, or rations, as they call them. **1917** A. G. EMPEY *Over Top* 305 *Rations*, various kinds of tasteless food issued by the Government to Tommy, to kid him into the fact that he is living in luxury, while the Germans are starving. **1919** W. H. DOWNING *Digger Dial.* 41 'Wet rations':..Cooked foods etc..'Dry rations':..Uncooked food..'Iron rations': ..Emergency rations. **1922** C. E. MONTAGUE *Disenchantment* ii. 15 A little famished London cab-tout, a recruit, still rectilinear as a starved cat even after a month of army rations.

c. *esp.* an officially limited allowance for civilians in time of war or shortage. Hence phr. *off* (*the*) *ration*, in addition to the allowance; unrestricted.

1917 *Times* 28 Feb. 10/3 Captain Bathurst, replying to Mr. Faber, said the Food Controller, since the issue of voluntary rations, had been in communication with the War Office, and an Army Council instruction was issued last week limiting the sugar ration for civilian and combatant prisoners of war to 7 oz per week. **1919** E. H. STARLING *Feeding of Nations* vi. 127 Each individual can buy of it according to his desire and satisfy his Calorie needs above those supplied in the rations. **1922** H. W. CLEMESHA *Food Control in North-West Division* ii. 34 There must have been many families who were unable to afford the additional rations of meat which the cards of children would have enabled them to obtain. **1928** W. H. BEVERIDGE *Brit. Food Control* x. 230 The wealthy classes in particular suffered from the reduction of the meat ration. **1944** *Ourselves in Wartime* vii. 154/2 More often than not, they forfeited their personal sweet ration, which amounted to 3 ozs. of sweets or chocolate a week in 1943, for the sake of the children. **1948** *Ann. Reg. 1947* 246 Food shops were compelled to limit strictly the amount of 'off ration' foods which customers could buy at one time. **1950** N. STREATFEILD *Mothering Sunday* 31 She was the last person to look for extras off the ration. **1959** in I. & P. Opie *Lore & Lang. Schoolch.* vii. 105 We are three spivs of Trafalgar Square Flogging nylons tuppence a pair, All fully fashioned, all off the ration, Sold in Trafalgar Square. **1960** J. RAE *Custard Boys* I. iv. 41 A little shop..where the old lady would sell us sweets and chocolate off the ration. **1975** S. BRIGGS *Keep Smiling Through* 150 Some articles off the ration could add an exotic touch to the menu. There was turbot in 1940 and whalemeat in 1942. *Ibid.* 161 'Off the ration' foods..like salt cod were publicized as 'grand for children as well as grown-ups and what a bargain!'

d. *transf.*

1850 BROWNING *Christmas Eve* ii. 7 Still, as I say, though you've found salvation, If I should choose to cry—as now—'Shares!'—See if the best of you bars me my ration!

e. Mil. slang phr.: *come up* (or *be given*) *with the rations*, to be awarded automatically (used deprecatingly, of military medals and decorations, to imply that they have not been earned).

1925 *N. & Q.* 25 July 71/2 Came up with the rations. **1928** H. WILLIAMSON *Pathway* xvii. 378 'Did *you* get the Military Cross?' asked Mrs. Ogilvie. 'Yes, it came up with the rations.' 'Oh!' 'A soldier's joke, Mrs. Ogilvie.' **1937** J. A. Lee *Civilian into Soldier* 204 'Bit of decoration. Congratulations.' 'Came up with the rations.' He took the ribbon. But if he joked he was pleased in his soul. **1957** J. Braine *Room at Top* xviii. 162 Lampton has no decorations apart from those which all servicemen who served his length of time are given, as they say, with the rations. **1973** A. Price *October Men* xv. 210 The British Military Cross.. didn't come up with the rations.

4. a. *ration bag, -beef* (earlier example), *boot, party, rum, -sugar, -tea*; **ration book,** a book entitling its holder to a ration; **ration card, coupon,** a card or coupon entitling its holder to a ration; **ration sheep** *Austral.*, the sheep to be killed for food for the workers on a station; also *ration-sheep paddock, ration paddock*; **ration strength,** the number of men in an armed force, estimated by the rations supplied to them; **ration ticket** = **ration card*.

1862 R. Henning *Let.* 5 Sept. (1966) 103 The 'ration bags' contained flour, sugar, tea, sardines, bacon, cheese, salt beef and salmon and jam. **1917** A. G. Empey *Over Top* 305 *Ration bag*, a small, very small bag for carrying rations. **1835** J. E. Alexander *Sketches in Portugal* iv. 101 Into an upper room marched two troopers, with a camp-kettle between them containing water, followed by two others with another kettle, containing a savoury mess of ration-beef, boiled with bread and onions. **1918** *Times* 1 Nov. 3/2 The Ministry of Food wish to remind the public that persons registered with retailers for tea must renew their registration as soon as possible by depositing with the retailer the 'spare counterfoil 2' on leaf 7 of their new ration books. **1939** *New Statesman* 18 Nov. 700/1 The ration books ..have now been distributed. **1973** *Country Life* 20 Dec. 2120/1 As these notes are written, ration books are being issued and motorists seem anxious to use them. **1902** 'Coldstreamer' *Ballads of Boer War* vii. 70 If you find a time to suit, Just cop 'im with a ration boot. **1882** H. Vizetelly *Paris in Peril* II. vii. 35 At some establishments strangers were politely informed that dinners were only served to the regular clientèle, who had handed over their ration-cards to the proprietor. **1922** H. W. Clemesha *Food Control in North-West Division* ii. 39 When the ration cards and the vouchers had all been distributed they were lodged either with retailers or wholesalers. **1940** *Economist* 9 Mar. 415/1 A general census is to be taken preparatory to the issue of ration-cards [in France]. **1975** T. Allbeury *Special Collection* v. 32 The ration cards were no longer honoured. The food wasn't there any more. **1944** *Sun* (Baltimore) 12 Dec. 12/8 A 'red market' in meat—collection of ration coupons for point free cuts. **1935** G. L. Meredith *Adventuring in Maoriland* v. 41, I sometimes have to do the slaughtering. There is no 'ration paddock'. **1917** A. G. Empey *Over Top* 305 *Ration party*, men detailed to carry rations to the front line. **1928** Blunden *Undertones of War* xiii. 145 At the ration-party's rendezvous.., our hearty Quartermaster Swain..was guarding..our issue of rum. **1918** E. A. Mackintosh *War* 94 Punch concocted out of ration rum. **1911** C. E. W. Bean *'Dreadnought' of Darling* xxxiv. 293 In some of the Western towns they find a convenient substitute even for ration sheep. **1914** H. B. Smith *Sheep & Wool Industry Australasia* vi. 34 On a station the first sheep that are usually shorn are the ration sheep. These are the sheep that are to be killed for household and shearers' use. **1946** F. Davison *Dusty* viii. 81 From then on he took him [the pup] out whenever he had to bring in the ration sheep for a killing. The ration sheep grazed in a small paddock near the homestead. *Ibid.* x. 105 The fence bounding the ration-sheep paddock. **1931** W. S. Churchill *World Crisis* VI. xxi. 323 Out of 425,000 men comprising the entire manhood of the country, borne on the ration-strength of the Serbian army at the beginning of October, over 100,000 had been killed or wounded. **1965** B. Sweet-Escott *Baker St. Irregular* vii. 201 The ration strength of A.F.H.Q. at this time was..something like that of a fighting division. **1892** *Missing Friends* iii. 54 The most inferior goods in the market are called *ration-tea* and *ration-sugar*. **1938** N. MacOwan *Glorious Morning* II. ii. 59 There's food to get. Our ration tickets are only available today.

rational, *a.* (*adv.*) and *sb.*[1] Add: **A.** *adj.* **1. a.** (Later examples.)

1908 *Jrnl. Abnormal Psychol.* III. 166 Everyone feels that as a rational creature he must be able to give a connected.. account of himself. **1975** J. Plamenatz *K. Marx's Philos. Man* i. 17 He always speaks of man as a self-conscious, rational, active being who can make choices and can initiate change deliberately.

c. *rational psychology, psychological science*: psychology, or the science of mind, as studied by deduction from general principles, and distinguished from an empirical approach. Now *Obs.*

1817 Coleridge *Biog. Lit.* I. ix. 139 These delusions were such, as might be anticipated..from his ignorance of rational psychology. **1849** L. P. Hickok *Rational Psychol.* 21 Those a priori conditions which give the necessary and universal laws to experience, and by which intelligence itself is alone made intelligible, are the elements for a higher Psychological Science which we term *Rational*. **1861** J. S. Mill *Let.* in A. Bain *John Stuart Mill* (1882) iv. 118 It will enable me..to do the kind of service which I am capable of to rational psychology. **1892** W. James *Coll. Ess. & Rev.* (1920) xx. 321 We certainly need something more radical than the old division into 'rational' and 'empirical' psychology, both to be treated by the same writer between the covers of the same book.

3. c. *rational mechanics*: mechanics as deduced logically from first principles.

[**1687** Newton *Philosophiæ Naturalis Principia Mathematica* p. v, *Mechanicam* vero duplicem Veteres constituerunt: *Rationalem* quæ per Demonstrationes accurate procedit, & *Practicam*. *Ibid.*, Quo sensu *Mechanica rationalis* erit Scientia Motuum qui ex viribus quibuscunq; resultant, & virium quæ ad motus quoscunq; requiruntur, accurate proposita ac demonstrata. **1729** A. Motte tr. *Ibid.* I. p. vii, The ancients considered Mechanics in a twofold respect; as rational, which proceeds accurately by demonstration, and practical.] *Ibid.* p. ix, In this sense Rational Mechanics will be the science of motions resulting from any forces whatsoever and of the forces required to produce any motions, accurately proposed and demonstrated. **1902** J. W. Gibbs *Elem. Princ. Statistical Mech.* p. ix, Nothing will more conduce to the clear apprehension of the relation of thermodynamics to rational mechanics..than the study of the fundamental notions and principles of that department of mechanics to which thermodynamics is especially related. **1928** R. De Villamil *Rational Mech.* p. vi, I have been asked: Why I call this a book on 'Rational Mechanics'? and Do I not consider all Mechanics as being 'Rational'? **1952** *Jrnl. Rational Mech. & Anal.* I. p. ii, The *Journal of Rational Mechanics & Analysis* nourishes mathematics with physical applications, aiming especially to close the rift between 'pure' and 'applied' mathematics and to foster the discipline of mechanics as a deductive, mathematical science in the classical tradition. **1958** *Science* 4 Apr. 729/1 In the United States..rational mechanics is not a recognized science. Indeed, there are some who disbelieve in its existence. **1977** C. Truesdell *First Course Rational Continuum Mech.* i. 4 Rational Mechanics is the part of mathematics that provides and develops logical models for the enforced changes of position and shape which we see everyday things suffer.

5. a. (Further examples.)

1901 H. B. Fine *College Algebra* II. i. 86 An expression is called rational if it does not involve an indicated root of an expression in which a variable letter occurs. **1917** T. M. MacRobert *Functions of Complex Variable* v. 89 The ratio of two polynomials is called a Rational Function. **1940** C. C. MacDuffee *Introd. Abstract Algebra* iii. 82 A quadratic equation with rational coefficients which does not have a rational root. **1946** A. A. Albert *College Algebra* iv. 111 A rational function of several symbols is any algebraic expression obtainable by formally applying a finite number of the rational operations of addition, subtraction, multiplication, and division to the symbols and numbers. **1966** R. E. Johnson *University Algebra* i. 20 There exist consecutive integers n and $n+1$, but there do not exist consecutive rational numbers.

c. (With admixture of sense 4.) *Physics.* The epithet given by O. Heaviside to electrical units and equations now described as *rationalized.

1882 O. Heaviside in *Nature* 24 Aug. 391/1 If..electricity stands foremost amongst the exact sciences, it follows that its unit measures should be determined with the utmost accuracy. Yet, twenty years ago very little advance had been made toward the adoption of a rational system. **1892** *Ibid.* 28 July 293/1 If we let the rational practical units be the same multiples of the 'absolute' rational units as the present practical units are of *their* absolute progenitors, then [etc.]. **1905** *Proc. R. Soc.* A. LXXVI. 551 The calculations would have been the same if e had been measured in 'rational' electric units instead of those in common use, but we should then have had an experimental value equal to 4π times that mentioned above. **1905** [see *Giorgi]. **1911** *Encycl. Brit.* XXVII. 744/2 If the filament is an endless or poleless iron filament magnetized uniformly by a resultant external magnetic force H, the flux density will be expressed in rational units by the equation $B = I + H$. **1925** W. H. Timbie *Elements of Electricity* (ed. 2) vi. 171 In order to have Ohm's Law hold with these units, the rational oersted must be equal to 1·26 C.G.S. units. **1942** *Phil. Mag.* XXXIII. 487 All the above formulæ, whether those of the rational system or of the ordinary system, are entirely independent of any choice of units.

7. Descriptive of methods of analysis and planning that make use of calculation to bring about a projected result, esp. in economic or social organization.

1915 M. Epstein tr. *Sombart's Quintessence of Capitalism* xii. 182 He is ever ready to adopt a newer method if it is more rational, whether in the sphere of organization, of production, or of calculation. **1926** E. Grossmann *Methods Econ. Rapprochement* 30 The most important economies will follow not from the simplification of the machinery of distribution but from a rational organization of production itself. **1930** T. Parsons tr. *Weber's Protestant Ethic* 21 But in modern times the Occident has developed..a very different form of capitalism which has appeared nowhere else: the rational capitalistic organization of (formally) free labour. *Ibid.*, Rational industrial organization, attuned to a regular market..is not, however, the only peculiarity of Western capitalism. **1943** J. A. Schumpeter *Capitalism, Socialism & Democracy* xi. 122 The rational attitude presumably forced itself on the human mind primarily from economic necessity. *Ibid.*, When the habit of rational analysis of.. the daily tasks of life has gone far enough, it turns back upon the mass of collective ideas and criticizes..them by way of such questions as why there should be kings..or tithes or property. *Ibid.* 123 Capitalist practice turns the unit of money into a tool of rational cost-profit calculations, of which the towering monument is double-entry bookkeeping. **1969** Simon & Stedry in Lindzey & Aronson *Handbk. Social Psychol.* (ed. 2) V. xl. 272 The classical economic theory of markets with rational agents and perfect competition is a deductive theory that requires almost no contact with empirical data..to establish its propositions. **1977** A. Giddens *Stud. in Social & Polit. Theory* v. 206 Weber's characterization of modern capitalism as involving above all the 'rational' organization of resources geared to the accumulation of profit is unsatisfactory.

C. *sb.*[1] **3.** Delete † *Obs. rare.* and add later examples.

1958 D. E. Littlewood *University Algebra* (ed. 2) ix. 150 The set of integers K can be embedded in a field of quotients. This field of quotients is defined as the rationals. **1971** D. G. H. B. Lloyd *Mod. Syllabus Algebra* vi. 110 Between any two rationals a third rational can be inserted. In this respect the set of rationals differs completely from the set of naturals or the set of integers.

rationalism. 2. Restrict *Theol.* to a, b in Dict. and add: **c.** The view that reason is the only guide leading to the improvement and progress of the human race and that adherence to religious or other 'non-rational' beliefs is out-dated.

1876 (*title*) Constructive rationalism. **1897** *Agnostic Ann.* I. 18 In my progress from Rome to Rationalism many other considerations have influenced me. **1923** J. S. Huxley *Ess. Biologist* 231 It is the task of Rationalism to see that religion, this fundamental and important activity of man, shall neither be allowed to continue in false or inadequate forms, nor be stifled or starved, but be made to help humanity in a vigorous growth that is based on truth and in constant contact with reality. **1968** A. J. Ayer *Humanist Outlook* 3 A broader movement of Rationalism or Free Thought, which was not merely anti-clerical but hostile to any form of religious belief. **1973** C. Campbell in *Rationalism in 1970s* 81 If the aim of rationalism is merely to attack and demolish the myths that we and others hold then there is more than enough work to keep us busy for a very long time. **1973** C. Macy (*title*) Rationalism and humanism in the new Europe.

3. (Earlier and later examples.)

1831 *Edin. Rev.* Sept. 247 The fundamental principles of Rationalism we take to be these:—That human reason, or the reasoning faculty, is the sole arbiter as to what is to be received as truth, and what is to be regarded as error, by the human mind; that facts recognized by sense or consciousness form the materials on which the reasoning faculty is to be exercised. **1967** *Encycl. Philos.* VII. 69/1 The philosophical outlook..which stresses the power of a priori reason to grasp substantial truths about the world and correspondingly tends to regard natural science as a basically a priori exercise... The spirit of rationalism in this sense is particularly associated with..Descartes, Spinoza, and Leibnitz.

5. The principle or practice of effecting assessment, planning, or organization in the economic or social sphere by rational (sense *7) methods.

1915 M. Epstein tr. *Sombart's Quintessence of Capitalism* xii. 182 Absolute rationalism is the first [principle]. Economic activities are ruled by cold reason, by thought. *Ibid.* xxv. 325 Economic rationalism owes much of its growth to technical rationalism. **1930** R. H. Tawney in T. Parsons tr. *Weber's Protestant Ethic* 1 (e) The word 'rationalism' is used by Weber..to describe an economic system based..on the deliberate and systematic adjustment of economic means to the attainment of the objective of pecuniary profit. **1935** *Encycl. Social Sci.* XIII. 114/1 In social and historical life the power of rationalism derives from the confidence which individuals and societies place in reason. **1958** G. Myrdal *Value in Social Theory* vii. 135 Basic to the eagerness in trying to drive valuations underground is the rationalism of our Western culture.

rationalist, *sb.* and *a.* Add: **1. b.** One who applies scientific methods of reasoning or calculation to social and economic life.

1958 G. Myrdal *Value in Social Theory* iii. 57 The American has..started to measure, not only human intelligence,..and personality traits, but moral leanings and the 'goodness' of communities. He is a rationalist. **1969** A. Etzioni in Lindzey & Aronson *Handbk. Social Psychol.* (ed. 2) V. 547 In effect, the rationalists advocate an approach that maximises conflict and makes nuclear war more likely. **1977** T. Parsons *Social Syst. & Evol. of Action Theory* i. 71 Phrasing it as 'the problem' I hope makes clear that I have not been a naïve rationalist.

2. a. Also, one who believes that reliance upon human reason does away with the need for religion. Cf. *rationalism 2 c.

1876 *Constructive Rationalism* 5 The destruction of orthodox Christianity being accomplished, there remains for the Rationalist much more to do. He has to frame a code which shall rule in the place of the code of Moses and of Jesus. **1897** *Agnostic Ann.* I. 42 Why do eminent Rationalists, Freethinkers, and Agnostics stand aloof. **1908** [see *ethicist]. **1942** E. T. Kerr in *Why I am a Rationalist* 33 Few Rationalists..owed to their schools..any kind of.. approach to independent thinking. **1954** *Rationalist Ann.* 73, I cannot possibly make my probabilities into certainties, and this is what some Rationalists appear..to do. **1973** C. Campbell in *Rationalism in 1970s* 81 It is an important part of a rationalist's duty to clear himself of myths..as well as to expose the myths of others.

b. (Further examples, esp. in sense of *rationalism 2 c and 5.)

1921 G. B. Shaw *Back to Methuselah* p. lxxiii, They banish the Bible from their houses, and sometimes put into the hands of their unfortunate children Ethical and Rationalist tracts of the deadliest dullness, compelling these wretched infants to sit out the discourses of Secularist lecturers. **1942** J. A. Schumpeter *Capitalism, Socialism & Democracy* (1943) xi. 122 There is however one more point about the concept of rationalist civilizations that I will mention here. *Ibid.*, The rationalist attitude may go to work with information and technique so inadequate that [etc.]. **1955** P. Edwards *Logic of Moral Discourse* ii. 52 The Rationalist view of causation. **1973** F. A. Hayek *Law, Legislation & Liberty* i. 33 The desire to remodel society after the image of individual man..since Hobbes has governed rationalist political theory. **1974** *New Humanist* May 16/1 Clerical pressure continued to be applied to booksellers, discouraging them from displaying Rationalist books. **1977** A. Giddens *Stud. Social & Pol. Theory* vii. 239 Durkheim replied by asserting the existence of a radical distinction between 'egoism' and 'rationalist individualism'.

rationalistically, *adv.* (Earlier and later examples.)

1854 Geo. Eliot tr. *Feuerbach's Essence Christianity* xxv. 245 Zwinglius only expressed..rationalistically..

what the others declared mystically. **1910** W. Temple *Faith & Mod. Thought* iii. 79 Why rationalistically minded folk should suppose that in a moment of almost intolerable joy people are going to have an exact memory for dates and places I cannot conceive. **1934** A. C. Ewing *Idealism* v. 258 The more rationalistically inclined philosophers have.. erred in putting forward extravagant claims to certainty.

rationality. Add: **2. b.** (Further examples.) Also *attrib.*

1908 *Jrnl. Abnormal Psychol.* III. 166 Any act..is immediately justified by distorting the mental processes concerned and providing a false explanation that has a plausible ring of rationality. **1933** J. L. Gillin *Social Path.* xxvi. 452 Capitalism is characterized by rationality. By that we mean a tendency to long range planning, careful consideration of the adaptation of means to ends, and cold and careful calculation of what measures will bring the greatest gain. **1961** H. M. Johnson *Sociol.* ix. 204 The expression 'economic rationality'..is perhaps confusing, since purely technical rationality in production is also 'economic', although not necessarily economical. **1969** Simon & Stedry in Lindzey & Aronson *Handbk. Social Psychol.* (ed. 2) V. xl. 272 The first [principle] is the assumption of objective rationality, which permits strong predictions to be made about human behavior without the painful necessity of observing people. **1975** T. McCarthy tr. *Habermas's Legitimation Crisis* (1976) II. iii. 46 Output crises have the form of a rationality crisis in which the administrative system does not succeed in reconciling and fulfilling the imperatives received from the economic system. *Ibid.* v. 62 A rationality deficit can arise because contradictory steering imperatives..are then operative within the administrative system. **1976** H. Leibenstein *Beyond Economic Man* v. 73 Suppose, but only for a moment, that rationality is interpreted as 'calculatedness'.

rationalizable, *a.* Add: Hence **ra:tionaliz-abi·lity.**

1936 Wirth & Shils tr. *Mannheim's Ideology & Utopia* iii. 124 The intuitional approach..conceives of knowledge and rationalizability as somewhat uncertain.

rationalization. Add: **1. b.** *Psychol.* The justification of behaviour to make it appear rational or socially acceptable by (subconsciously) ignoring, concealing, or glossing its real motive; an act of making such a justification.

1908 *Jrnl. Abnormal Psychol.* III. 166 Two different groups of false explanations can be distinguished..according as they are formed mainly for private or mainly for public consumption. The former of these I would term 'evasions', the latter 'rationalisations'. **1924** J. Riviere tr. *Freud's Coll. Papers* I. 341 His [*sc.* Adler's] theory does what all patients do and what our waking thought in general does—namely, makes use of a rationalization, as Jones has called it, in order to conceal unconscious motives. **1947** E. F. Frazier in *Amer. Sociol. Rev.* XII. 271 A dynamic sociological theory of race relations which will discard all the rationalizations of race prejudice. **1953** R. F. C. Hull tr. *Jung's Coll. Wks.* VII. 214 My patient clung to his intellectual world and defended himself with rationalizations against what he regarded as his illness. **1961** H. Bonner *Psychol. of Personality* ix. 281 The term 'rationalization' has become a household word. It is essentially a method of self-justification. It is motivated by the fear of criticism and disapproval by others. **1977** F. J. Bruno *Human Adjustment* ii. 67 The defense mechanism called rationalization is used when the real motive for one's behavior is unacceptable to the ego.

2. b. *Physics.* The reformulation of the equations and definitions of electromagnetism so that the factor 4π is removed from those relating to systems without spherical symmetry.

1891 O. Heaviside in *Electrician* 16 Oct. 656/2 When.. the real advantages of the rational system become widely recognized and thoroughly assimilated, then will come a demand for the rationalisation of the practical units. **1942** *Phil. Mag.* XXXIII. 486 The simplification of formulæ due to rationalization can be illustrated by considering a parallel plate condenser. **1951** *Electr. Engin.* LXX. 332/2 Note that, in effect, a 4π was inserted in the denominator of the classical expression for force between parallel wires to accomplish rationalization, and that the elimination of 4π from the magnetomotive force relation followed without any additional arbitrary insertion of 4π. **1969** L. Young *Systems of Units Electr. & Magn.* 197 The appearance or disappearance of 4π's in the equations of electromagnetism upon rationalization can be interpreted in two ways... Just as our point of view has been described as 'rationalization of units', so the other point of view has been called 'rationalization of quantities'.

c. *Econ.* and *Sociol.* The process of applying rational (sense *7) methods, esp. of standardization and simplification, to the planning and organization of economic enterprises or the administration of social groups in order to achieve a particular result such as maximum profit or efficiency; an example of this.

[**1905** M. Weber in *Archiv f. Sozialwissenschaft u. Sozialpolitik* XX. 29 Alsdann nun wiederholte sich, was immer und überall die Folge eines solchen „Rationalisierungs"-Prozesses ist.] **1921** E. & C. Paul tr. *Rathenau's In Days to Come* iii. i. 125 The general wellbeing of the country is doubled or trebled by the setting of idle hands to work and by the rationalisation of production. **1926** D. Houston *Memorandum on Rationalisation in U.S.* 3 The term rationalisation as used in Europe today includes, I take it, the three elements of stabilisation, standardisation and simplification of industry or of individual enterprises. **1934** P. & I. Petroff *Secret of Hitler's Victory* iii. 38 The soullessness of modern labour, which had reached its climax in consequence of the rationalization, became the outstanding feature of the whole period. **1936** H. A. Phelps *Princ. & Laws of Sociol.* xx. 424 A compensating general trend is the increasing rationalization of social life. **1939** H. Hodge *Cab, Sir?* 259 The would-be Napoleon..puts his rationalisation schemes into the waste-paper basket. **1947** Henderson & Parsons tr. *Weber's Theory Social & Econ. Organization* i. 112 One of the most important aspects of the process of 'rationalization' of action is the substitution for the unthinking acceptance of ancient custom, of deliberate adaptation to situations in terms of self-interest. **1959** *Listener* 31 Dec. 1147/2 A rationalization proposal [in the U.S.S.R.] is a technical improvement using known means which lacks the degree of originality demanded of a patentable invention. **1971** J. J. Shapiro tr. *Habermas's Toward Rational Society* vi. 99 Until then [*sc.* the 19th century] modern science did not contribute to the acceleration of technical development nor, consequently, to the pressure toward rationalization from below. **1972** W. J. Mommsen *Age of Bureaucracy* iv. 80 Another secular force of social change is found, namely rationalization..by which tradition-bound or value-oriented forms of political and social organization are gradually replaced by purely instrumentally rational institutions. **1976** *Star* (Sheffield) 20 Nov., The company had announced 'rationalisation' plans meaning the closure of the Dronfield works.

rationalize, *v.* Add: **1. a.** (Earlier and later examples.)

1803 *Lett. Miss Riversdale* II. 79 This interesting sentiment [*sc.* friendship]..secures the permanence of happiness, by rationalizing (if I may use such a word) its origin. **1935** *Encycl. Social Sci.* XIII. 116/1 The problem was to rationalize human social life on the basis of self-evident and universal principles. **1965** W. J. Harvey in Geo. Eliot *Middlemarch* 11 Bulstrode..who rationalizes his worldly success as an example of divine providence.

c. *Psychol.* To give plausible reasons for (one's behaviour) that ignore, conceal, or gloss its real motive. Also *absol.* or *intr.*

1922 H. Somerville *Pract. Psycho-Anal.* i. 14 It is clear that patient is rationalising, and that as a matter of fact he is eaten up with jealousy. **1925** J. Riviere tr. *Freud's Coll. Papers* III. 330 The patient's consciousness naturally misunderstands them and puts forward a set of secondary motives to account for them—rationalizes them, in short. **1932** H. G. Wells *Work, Wealth & Happiness of Mankind* vii. 279 To rationalize has one meaning in psychology, another meaning in the sociological writings of Max Weber, and quite another in the loose discussions of modern politicians and business men. **1966** *Word Study* Dec. 3/2, I think we all rationalize with the thought that the free democratic society which produced us..had a right to be presented (*sic*) in such a fashion.

2. b. *Physics.* To subject (the units or equations of electromagnetism) to rationalization (sense *2 b).

1892 *Nature* 28 July 292/2 It is..very desirable that the practical units themselves should be rationalized. **1899** *Electrician* 29 Dec. 325/2 If we take the permeability of ether to be 4π units instead of unity, we rationalize at one stroke all our present units except the units of magnetic force and magnetic pole strength. **1973** J. Yarwood *Electricity & Magnetism* ii. 32 In rationalising electrical units the object..is to avoid the occurrence of 4π in systems without spherical symmetry and of 2π where cylindrical symmetry is absent.

c. To organize (economic production or the like) according to rational or scientific principles so as to achieve a desired or predictable result; esp. to reduce the number of (personnel, industrial plants, etc.) in such a way that the remainder are more efficiently deployed.

1926 E. Grossmann *Methods Econ. Rapprochement* 30 International cartels will be able to rationalise production in a way impossible in the present state of affairs. **1931** *Ann. Reg. 1930* ii. 26 The Lancashire cotton industry. The steps taken to 'rationalise' the industry. **1953** J. B. Carroll *Study of Lang.* iv. 127 A recent attempt to rationalize an artificial language by making maximal use of elements common to the most widely used natural languages is Interlingua. **1962** *Listener* 22 Mar. 509/2 Their numbers go down: they are 'rationalized'. In 1920 there were nine evening newspapers in London; now there are two. **1977** *R.A.F. News* 11–24 May 7/2, I am..aware..of the need to rationalise reporting systems to reduce paperwork.

rationalized, *ppl. a.* Add: *spec.* in *Physics*, applied to units, equations, and definitions in electromagnetism that are formulated so that the factor 4π appears only when a system with spherical symmetry is involved. Cf. *Rational *a.* 5 c.

1933 [see *Giorgi]. **1951** *Electr. Engin.* LXX. 332/1 The MKS Rationalized system seems now to be replacing the others rapidly and may well come to be the accepted system for all theoretical work in electricity. **1969** L. Young *Systems of Units Electr. & Magn.* vi. 78 The rationalized form of the CGS practical system is theoretically possible but is never used. **1973** J. Yarwood *Electricity & Magnetism* xvi. 608 The rationalised mksA units in electricity form a part of the wider SI system of units.

rationalizing, *vbl. sb.* (Earlier and later examples.)

1865 J. S. Mill *Auguste Comte* 54 The way to a complete rationalizing of those sciences..has been shown nowhere so successfully as there. **1927** A. Huxley *Let.* 25 Feb. (1969) 284, I can't see that there's anything to distinguish his rationalizings of religious emotions from those of anyone else. **1971** P. Gresswell *Environment* 105 Footpaths in some parishes need reorganising and rationalising for today's needs.

rationative, *a.* Delete † *Obs.* and add later example.

a **1966** 'M. na Gopaleen' *Best of Myles* (1968) 195 An issue too imponderable for rationative evaluation.

rationing, *vbl. sb.* (In Dict. s.v. Ration *v.*) (Later examples.) *rationing by the purse*, raising the price of a commodity so as to restrict the number of people who can afford to buy it. Similarly *rationing by price.*

1917 *Times* 1 May 7/6 The German Government now knows all about rationing, but while it has been learning the German people has eaten up its supplies. **1924** E. M. H. Lloyd *Experiments in State Control* xxiii. 290 As for the argument that rationing increases consumption, this was not true of the articles most severely rationed in Great Britain. **1930** *Economist* 22 Mar. 637/1 In the last resort, a rationing of credit was the only expedient left to central banks. **1940** *Times* (Weekly ed.) 10 Jan. 9/3 Rationing may have to be used to a much greater extent than in the last war. **1947** *People* 22 June 2, I find school lunches a great help with the rationing problems. *Ibid.*, It is the end of the rationing period. **1950** *Hansard Commons* 24 Apr. 617 Is this not a case of rationing by the purse? **1975** S. Briggs *Keep Smiling Through* 149 The great wartime invention, borrowed from the Germans, was points rationing. This widened choice as much as it could be widened within a rationing system. You could even..choose where to shop without being tied to the grocer where you were registered for basic rations. **1979** W. Safire in *N.Y. Times Mag.* 9 Sept. 16/1 *Rationing by price*, a system in which economic goods go to the people who are most willing to pay for them. This is the normal way of distributing goods in capitalist countries, and is increasingly used in Communist countries. Economists generally consider it an efficient system, but some politicians consider it immoral and prefer a system of rationing by political pull.

‖ **ratissage** (ratisāʒ). *Econ.* [Fr., lit. 'scraping, raking in of stakes'.] A device whereby the Bank of France calls in a portion of its country's commercial banks' foreign currency balances, and so temporarily improves its reserves of foreign exchange.

1957 *Economist* 28 Dec. 1144/1 The technique of *ratissage* dates from March of this year even though it is only now that it has been broadened to include dollars as well as EPU currencies. **1959** *Ibid.* 10 Jan. 155/2 A substantial part of the EPU deficit is ascribed to further *ratissage* by the Bank of France. **1959** *Times* 7 Apr. 17/1 The French recovery has now gone far enough for the French authorities to hope that their so-called 'ratissage' operations may be liquidated this month.

ratite, *a.* Add: (Later examples.) Also as *sb.*, a bird belonging to this group.

1911 J. A. Leach *Austral. Bird Bk.* 52 'Discontinuous distribution' as applied to land animals, e.g...ratite birds in South America..implies a land connexion. **1939** J. Fisher *Birds as Animals* iii. 32 Sometimes..it [*sc.* the hallux] is altogether absent, as it is in auks, bustards and ratite birds. *Ibid.* vi. 73 Ostriches flock, so do the other ratites. **1978** *Sci. Amer.* July 102/2 Among the other ratites are the ostrich, the emu and the extinct giant moa of New Zealand. **1979** *Nature* 14 June 633/2 The supposed presence of a ratite bird, a member of a group otherwise restricted to the Southern Hemisphere, in the Upper Cretaceous of Mongolia is very doubtful.

ratlin(e, ratling. **1.** *ratline stuff* (earlier and later examples).

1833 Poe *MS. found in Bottle* in *Gift 1836* (1835) 80 A pile of ratlin-stuff and old sails. **1883** *Man. Seamanship for Boys' Training Ships R. Navy* (Admiralty) (1886) 312 Hitch your rattling stuff round the third shroud from aft. **1954** Bradford & Quill *Gloss. Sea Terms* 154/1 *Ratline stuff*, twelve- or fifteen-thread but usually eighteen-thread right-handed, tarred rope, used for ratlines, heavy lashings and heavy lines.

Rato (rēⁱ·to). *Aeronaut.* Also **rato.** [f. the initial letters of *r*ocket-*a*ssisted *t*ake-*o*ff.] A jato in which the engine is a rocket engine.

1953 P. C. Berg *Dict. New Words* 134/2 *R.A.T.O., Rato*, rocket-assisted take-off. **1962** *Aeroplane* CIII. 26/1 Designed to carry outsize cargo, the Stratocruiser is to have an increased payload of 60,000 lb and rato units will be used.

ratomorphic (ræ:tomǭ·ɹfik), *a. rare.* [f. Rat *sb.*¹ + *-omorphic*, after Anthropomorphic *a.*] (See quot. 1964.) Also **ra·tomorph**, one who holds a ratomorphic view of human behaviour.

1964 Koestler in *Listener* 14 May 786/2 It refuses to attribute to man any mental processes which cannot be shown to occur in lower animals. In other words, for the anthropomorphic view of the rat, Behaviourism has substituted a ratomorphic view of man. **1967** *Economist* 21 Oct. 295/3 The author [*sc.* Koestler] presents a trenchant.. criticism of behaviourism and experimental 'ratomorphic' views of men. **1977** H. G. Burger in B. Bernardi *Concept & Dynamics of Culture* 460 In trying to overlook symboling, those who oversimplify subhuman abilities are 'ratomorphs', and have overlooked two and a half million years of hominid evolution.

ratoon, *v.* Add: **b.** *trans.* To cut down (plants) to induce them to send up new shoots. So **ratoo·ned** *ppl. a.*

1925 *Glasgow Herald* 23 Apr. 14/2 Reports indicate that ratooned cotton has suffered. Ratooned plants produce a much earlier crop than new plants and..Zululand had ratooned a considerable quantity this year.

ratooner (rătū·nəɹ). [f. prec.+-ER.] A plant that ratoons.

1922 *Chambers's Jrnl.* Dec. 800/2 A second crop can be obtained from the dwarfed stumps of the trees after the first crop has been picked, but the ochro is a bad ratooner.

rat race. Also **rat-race.** [f. RAT *sb.*[1]] † **1.** A dance. *U.S. slang. Obs.*

1937 *Amer. Speech* XII. 74/2 C.C.C. speech... Terms for recreations: *rat-race*, dance of low-grade nature. **1948** MENCKEN *Amer. Lang.* Suppl. II. 707 The vocabulary of the jazz addict... A dance is a *rat-race* or *cement-mixer*.

2. A fiercely competitive struggle or contest; a struggle to maintain one's position in work or life. orig. *U.S.*

1939 C. MORLEY *Kitty Foyle* xxvi. 261 Their own private life gets to be a rat-race. **1940** *Time* 16 Dec. 26/3 Veteran fliers blanched when they saw the hourly, crowded 'rat race' at Randolph—the close-packed stream of trainers, gliding in to land and take on fresh cadets and instructors. **1946** *War Report* (B.B.C.) 350 Our armour is now 'swanning' as they say in the British Army, or in American parlance, 'the rat race is on'. **1947** J. STEINBECK *Wayward Bus* 214 He was afraid of his friends and his friends were afraid of him. A rat race, she thought. **1954** WODEHOUSE & BOLTON *Bring on Girls* 219 'Is anything the matter with you?' 'Just the rat-race. I don't quite know why I've been doing it.' **1956** R. FULLER *Image of Society* iii. 70 A boy's got to have guts to make his way in this rat race of a modern world. **1958** *Spectator* 19 Sept. 381/2 Modern economic life is more like a rat-race than a rational way of life. **1959** *Observer* 8 Mar. 17/7, I don't like this rat-race for promotion. **1959** *Spectator* 2 Oct. 435/2 A realism that encourages in its popular press a rat-race morality in the guise of room at the top. **1960** *Daily Tel.* 18 May 17/7 A spirited criticism of 'the daily rat race' to get to work in London. **1967** G. F. FIENNES *I tried to run Railway* iv. 31 It became a rat race to see who could get teams in first so as to improve recruitment. **1973** C. BONINGTON *Next Horizon* iv. 68 Another artist, who had abandoned the rat-race and settled in Coniston. **1976** F. ZWEIG *New Acquisitive Society* I. v. 52 The shedding of middle-class values and style of life in the younger generation..is an outright negation of middle-class existence, defined in such derogatory terms as 'rat race'. **1978** D. A. J. SEARGENT *UFO's* v. 111 A motor car—the prime symbol of our motorised, machine-orientated, rat-race society.

Hence as *v. trans.* and *intr.*, to take part in a 'rat race'; **ra·t-racer, ra·t-racing** *vbl. sb.* and *ppl. a.*

1937 *Clarionette* (Univ. of Denver) (St. Patrick ed.) 18 Mar. 1/3 If you're off for a little body-swaying to music, you are..'rat-racing'. **1960** *Listener* 7 Jan. 41/2 A scarifying glimpse of rat racing in local government. **1962** *Guardian* 15 Oct. 7/2 A new modern figure—the new kind of ambitious rat-racer, the Snopes in the grey flannel suit. **1968** *Ibid.* 5 Oct. 6/5 Literary people in this country seem to have been..rat-racing each other to the nearest vacant editor's chair. **1968** *New Scientist* 21 Nov. 418/3 Looking into an aquarium..is just the medicine for a chap who has spent all day rat-racing against a computer. **1969** E. LEMARCHAND *Alibi for Corpse* ix. 116 I'm a damn sight saner than people who spend their lives rat-racing and jabbering their heads off. **1971** *New Scientist* 1 July 5/1 The belief among rat-racers that the physical exercise delays thrombosis. **1971** *Guardian* 3 July 8/6 Middle aged Frank who wants to be a drop-out from rat-racing society. **1977** D. MORRIS *Manwatching* 124 Eccentricity of dress and behaviour is commonplace for them and they enjoy social freedoms unknown to other rat-racing citizens.

ratsbane. Add: **1.** (Further example.)

1877 'MARK TWAIN' in *Atlantic Monthly* Dec. 723/1 What was that cat's name that eat a keg of ratsbane by mistake over at Hooper's?

Hence **ra·tsbany** *a.*

1937 BLUNDEN *Elegy* 24 And sets pot to mouth And once again moistens his ratsbany drouth.

rat's-tail. Add: **2. d.** (Earlier example.)

1810 J. LAMBERT *Trav. Lower Canada* I. ix. 162 The dress of the Habitant is simple, and homely;..His hair is tied in a thick long queue behind, with an eelskin; and on each side of his face a few strait locks hang down like, what are vulgarly called, 'rats' tails'.

f. = *rat's-tail fescue* (see 3 below).

1950 *N.Z. Jrnl. Agric.* Sept. 219/3 In a way the rapid ingress of ratstail into pastures during the 1930's was a good thing.

3. rat's tail cactus = *rat-tail cactus* s.v. *RAT-TAIL 5; **rat's-tail fescue**, an annual grass, *Vulpia myuros*.

1957 *Dict. Gardening* (R. Hort. Soc.) I. 146/2 Rat's Tail Cactus. Stems weak, pendent, slender. **1958** S. H. SCOTT *Observer's Bk. Cacti* 61 *Aporocactus flagelliformis*. Usually referred to as the 'rat's tail cactus' because of its pendent method of growth. **1858** G. BENTHAM *Handbk. Brit. Flora* 602 Rat's-tail Fescue... A tufted annual, usually about a foot high. **1917** S. F. ARMSTRONG *Brit. Grasses* vii. 100 Rat's-tail Fescue... An annual, occurring chiefly in waste places. **1944** W. J. STOKOE *Caterpillars Brit. Butterflies* 224 Rat's-tail Fescue Grass... This small tufted grass grows mostly in dry pastures. **1954** C. E. HUBBARD *Grasses* 137 (*heading*) Rat's-tail Fescue.

rat-tail. Add: **3. b.** A rat-tailed spoon (see RAT-TAILED *a.* 2). **c.** = RAT'S-TAIL 2 d.

1974 *Country Life* 14 Nov. 1447/1 Spoons ranging from 1661 to 1718..include..split-ended rat-tails or treffid spoons. **1977** J. WAINWRIGHT *Day of Peppercorn Kill* 121 The woman's hair was in sodden rat-tails... Her shoes squelched water.

4. Substitute for def.: A deep-water marine fish belonging to the family Coryphænoididæ, esp. one of the genus *Macrurus*, characterized by a long, tapering tail. Also *attrib.* (Later examples.)

1905 D. S. JORDAN *Guide to Study of Fishes* I. xii. 209 In the deep-sea allies of the codfishes, the grenadiers or rat-tails (*Macrouridæ*), the numbers [of vertebrae] range from 65 to 80. **1928** RUSSELL & YONGE *Seas* iv. 91 That curious fish of the cod family known as the Macrurus or rat-tail.. spends the greater part of its life in the cold dark depths over the abyssal plain. **1936** P. S. BARNHART *Marine Fishes California* 24 Rat-tails. The fishes of this family are deep-water fishes, and are seldom seen or taken. **1956** J. L. B. SMITH *Old Fourlegs* ix. 92 In this they [*sc.* seals] are like humans, who will not eat those perfectly wholesome but.. unfortunately named 'Rat Tails'. **1975** *New Yorker* 19 May 32/1 There might be a few rattails (bottom feeders related to the shark family) near the ocean floor. **1975** *Sci. Amer.* Oct. 86/3 The bait was visited by only a few eelpouts, brotulids and rattail fish (grenadiers).

5. (Further examples in sense 2 of RAT-TAILED *a.*) **rat-tail cactus**, a pendent or creeping cactus, *Aporocactus flagelliformis*, native to central America and having spiny stems bearing scarlet flowers; **rat-tail comb**, a comb with a long tapering handle at one end; **rat-tail file** (earlier and later examples); **rat-tail radish** (example); cf. *RAT-TAILED *a.* 1 d.

1744 in *Maryland Hist. Mag.* (1926) XXI. 251, 6 Ratt Tale Files. **1867** *Gardeners' Chron.* 3 Aug. 807/1 (*heading*) Raphanus caudatus, or Rat-tail Radish. **1895** *Army & Navy Co-op. Soc. Price List* 754 (*caption*) Queen Anne or Rat-tail [spoons]. **1900** L. H. BAILEY *Cycl. Amer. Hort.* I. 283/2 Rat-tail Cactus. Creeping or pendent, slender and very branching. **1904** *Daily Chron.* 20 July 5/6 The bride's father presented her with a superb tiara of diamonds and pearls, and a canteen of rat-tail silver. **1925** S. T. WARNER *Espalier* 77 The rat-tail spoons, The china dishes. **1945** *Sun* (Baltimore) 30 Jan. 6-0/3 It was made in 1898 from a rat-tail file which had been used in a bicycle factory. **1946** M. FREE *All about House Plants* xvii. 203 Rat-tail Cactus..has long flexible stems about ½ inch in diameter covered with bristly hairs. **1972** F. PERRY *Flowers of World* 60/1 *Aporocactus flagelliformis*, the Rat-tail Cactus, is well named for the long flexible stems..hang down all round the plant. They are covered with bristly hairs and carry masses of crimson flowers. **1978** *Chatelaine* (Canada) Dec. 67/1 Tuck ends in with a rat-tail comb.

rat-tailed, *a.* **1. b.** For 'tail' substitute 'flexible respiratory organ resembling a tail'. In full, *rat-tailed maggot*. (Later examples.)

1895 L. C. MIALL *Nat. Hist. Aquatic Insects* ii. 198 The Rat-tailed Maggot, a common inhabitant of stagnant pools. **1935** *Discovery* July 212/1 The problem [of breathing under water] had been solved long before by the rat-tailed maggot, with its telescopic tube reaching to the surface. **1952** J. CLEGG *Freshwater Life Brit. Isles* ii. 27 The larvae of one or two insects, such as the Rat-tailed Maggot,..are well adapted for living in the black mud at the bottom of these unwholesome waters. **1968** *Oxf. Bk. Insects* 130/2 They swim freely, breathing through their long tails, which can be extended to 6 inches to reach the water surface—hence their name Rat-tailed Maggots.

d. In the names of certain plants, esp. *rat-tailed radish*, an Asian radish, *Raphanus caudatus*, cultivated for its edible fruit. Cf. RAT-TAIL 5 in Dict. and Suppl.

1867 *Gardeners' Chron.* 3 Aug. 807/1, I shall continue to grow the Rat-tailed Radish. **1885** W. ROBINSON tr. *Vilmorin-Andrieux's Veg. Garden* 499 Rat-tailed Radish... The edible part of this Radish is not the root, but the silique or seed-vessel, which is gathered before it is fully grown. **1949** *Nat. Geogr. Mag.* Aug. 213/2 In India the rat-tailed radish..is grown for its fleshy, edible seed pods. **1969** *Oxf. Bk. Food Plants* 170/2 The Rat-tailed Radish..is grown in southern Asia. The part eaten is not the root but the fruit, which reaches a length of 8 to 10 inches.

2. b. Of a comb: having a long, tapering, handle at one end. Cf. *rat-tail comb* s.v. *RAT-TAIL 5.

1973 *Daily Colonist* (Victoria, B.C.) 15 July 1/3 It turned out to be an ordinary, black rat-tailed comb.

rattan, ratan, *sb.*[1] Add: **4.** *rattan chair, furniture, mat, rocker, rope, screen, ware.*

1879 *Harper's Mag.* July 211 In the large parlor..with rattan chairs galore..presided Karl Whitaker. **1925** W. S. MAUGHAM *The Letter* I. 9 The room is..quite simply furnished with rattan chairs, in which are cushions. **1972** D. BLOODWORTH *Any Number can Play* xv. 140 Comfortable rattan chairs. **1895** *Montgomery Ward & Co. Catal.* Spring & Summer 617/3 (*heading*) Rattan and reed furniture. **1966** D. FORBES *Heart of Malaya* ii. 31 The old kind, built on stilts like a Malay house, with wide verandahs and rattan furniture, is still the best. **1925** W. S. MAUGHAM *The Letter* I. 9 Rattan mats on the floor. **1895** *Montgomery Ward & Co. Catal.* Spring & Summer 617/3 We show a larger assortment of rattan rockers in our special Furniture Catalogue. **1900** W. W. SKEAT *Malay Magic* 172 Six or eight coils of rattan rope..are placed on a triangle formed with three rice-pounders. **1902** CONRAD *Youth* 205 The straggling building of bricks,..resounded with the incessant flapping of rattan screens. **1971** K. HOPKINS *Hong Kong* 247 Industries in which collective agreements have been signed include.. rattan ware.

Hence **ratta·nning**, chastisement with rattan sticks.

1847 H. MELVILLE *Omoo* xxix. 110 The ratanning of the young culprits..may also be considered as in some measure characteristic of the [French] nation.

rat-tat, *sb.* Add: **c.** *Comb.*, as **rat-tat ginger** = *rat-a-tat ginger* s.v. *RAT-A-TAT.

1962 M. DUFFY *That's how it Was* ii. 26 Rat-tat ginger, two door-knockers tied together and a piece of black cotton leading round the corner so I could knock on two doors at once.

rat-tat-tat, etc.: (further examples); also freq. used to represent the noise of reports from fire-arms.

1793 S. E. PHILLIPS *Let.* 6 May in F. Burney *Jrnls. & Lett.* (1972) II. 109 The dear Postman is just arrived... A loud *rattat tattoo* was heard at the door. **1907** G. MANINGTON *Soldier of Legion* iii. 127 The sombre background was punctuated again and again..by lightning like red flashes. Rat! tat! tat! tat!... These were Winchesters. **1957** L. MACNEICE *Visitations* 42 Rat-tat-tat-tash of shields upon Ida. **1972** *Angling Times* 6 Apr. 14/5 It is only a matter of time before I get that tiny rat-tat-tat on the rod tip. **1974** M. BUTTERWORTH *Man in Sopwith Camel* i. 12 Rat-tat-tat-tat, his rear gunner was spraying a libation back on to Braithwaite's riddled body.

Hence **rat-ta·t(-tat,** etc.) *v. intr.* (and *trans.*), to (cause to) make a sharp rapping sound, to knock.

1910 *Daily Chron.* 14 Apr. 9/5 The lady rat-tat-tatted for half an hour. Then the housekeeper..sternly asked the visitor to be so good as to go away. **1916** H. S. WALPOLE *Dark Forest* I. vii. 188 A machine gun 'rat-tat-tat-tated' close to us. **1953** 'N. BLAKE' *Dreadful Hollow* 106 Nigel rat-tat-tatted an imaginary tommy-gun at them. **1966** A. CAVANAUGH *Children are Gone* II. vi. 49 'Well, g'night.' Her heels rat-tatted down the hall.

ratten-, ratting-crook. (Later examples.)

1866 E. L. LINTON *Lizzie Lorton of Greyrigg* I. xii. 268 Two large iron 'ratten-crooks' and several smaller ones, for cauldrons and kettles, hung from the 'rannel balk'. **1974** *Country Life* 17 Oct. 1149/2 A *ratten-crook* is a pot crane hanging from the *rannel-balk* which is the wooden beam across and above an open hearth.

ratter. 1. For 'a dog' in Dict., read 'a dog, cat, or other animal', and add earlier and later examples.

1857 S. H. HAMMOND *Wild Northern Scenes* xi. 121 There was an assemblage of all the cats in that part of the town... Off at the right was an old spotted ratter. **1946** E. O'NEILL *Iceman Cometh* IV. 233 With that..line of bull, you ought to be able to sell skunks for good ratters! **1972** R. ADAMS *Watership Down* xxv. 190 The farm cat was bewildered by the speed and fury of Bigwig's charge. It was no weakling and a good ratter.

3. *Austral.* One who steals opal from another's mine.

1931 I. L. IDRIESS *Prospecting for Gold* xxvi. 239 Ratters are men, a gang as a rule, who work your opal out for you while you sleep. **1964** W. C. EYLES *Bk. of Opals* vii. 83 When the miners..went down the shaft, they found the ratters had cleaned the place out entirely. **1976** *Nat. Geographic* Oct. 564/2 The mine ratters (thieves) are here, but that's been going on since King Solomon's mines.

ratticide, var. *RATICIDE.

rattinet. For **1832** read **1838** and add earlier and later examples.

Appears to be *Obs.*

1811 *Weekly Reg.* 21 Sept. 46/1 Rattinets..can only be made of wool long enough to be combed. **1836** H. MANWARING *Tailor's New Guide* 15 Velveteen Jacket, body and skirt, may be lined with rattinet.

ratting, *vbl. sb.* **1.** (Later examples.)

1946 *Sun* (Baltimore) 17 June 18/3 His turning long-distance state's evidence, his ratting, so to speak, to the cops..strikes at the very core of the latest design to maintain 'power' in the hands of a people's government. **1948** *Richmond* (Va.) *Times-Dispatch* 13 Feb. 30/1 McKeever.. performed the most odious job of 'ratting' college football has known.

3. *Comb.*, as **ratting canoe** *Canad.*, a small native boat designed for hunting muskrats in swamps and marshes.

1962 R. SLOBODIN *Band Organization of Peel River Kutchin* 14 A child armed with a .22 rifle, paddling or portaging the light, narrow ten-foot ratting canoe. **1968** R. M. PATTERSON *Finlay's River* 74 A— gave an initial display of his dexterity by upsetting a small ratting canoe with Butler and himself in it.

rattle, *sb.*[1] Add: **II. 4. a.** Also **rattle-rattle.** (Further examples.) *fig.* phr. *with a rattle*: with sudden or unexpected rapidity (orig. *Horse-racing*).

1888 *Daily Chron.* 10 Dec. 6/2 Bachelor came on with a rattle and won by a length and a half. **1909** in J. R. WARE *Passing Eng.* 206/2 The only approach to a sensation was caused by Warrington and Kettleholder, the former coming 'with a rattle' in the morning to the price taken about him in the excitement caused by his forward running in the Cesarewitch. **1926** E. BOWEN *Ann Lee's* 251 Only the rattle-rattle of my bicycle. **1928** D. H. LAWRENCE *Lady Chatterley's Lover* ii. 11 She heard the rattle-rattle of the screens at the pit. **1977** *Evening Gaz.* (Middlesbrough) 11 Jan. 13/5 The Merryweather crew came with a rattle to level at the penultimate end 15–15 [in Bowls].

e. *N. Amer.* A succession of small, noisy waterfalls forming rapids; a fast-moving stream.

1776 G. CARTWRIGHT *Jrnl.* 14 Aug. (1779) 200 We fished in the stream below the rattle, and also in the lower pool, and killed seventy-eight fish. **1861** L. DE BOILIEU *Recoll.*

Labrador Life xiii. 166 In the different bays are brooks, and in these brooks are 'rattles', as they are termed, or, more properly speaking, 'falls', though none are of any great magnitude. **1907** J. G. MILLAIS *Newfoundland* iii. 70 We had only to unload twice in passing 'rattles', as they called the strong rapids. **1925** *Dialect Notes* V. 339 *Rattle*,..a swift brook. **1975** *Canad. Antiques Collector* Mar.–Apr. 23/1 From the sealhunt we have:..rattle, river rapids, and so on.

f. The rustling quality of a sheet of finished paper when handled, indicative of its hardness and density.

1900 CROSS & BEVAN *Paper-Making* (ed. 2) v. 137 As a consequence, it adds the quality of 'wetness' to the pulp, which again confers the quality of hardness and 'rattle' upon the finished paper. **1962** F. T. DAY *Introd. to Paper* ii. 24 Starch is added to paper furnishes and serves either as a sizing agent or to give the paper more substance and better handle for its use imparts stiffness and 'rattle' to the finished sheet.

g. *Hunting*. A particular note on the horn.

1908 L. C. F. CAMERON *Otters & Otter Hunting* 203 *Rattle*, the note sounded on the horn at the 'worry'. **1954** J. I. LLOYD *Beagling* 143 *Rattle*, an exciting, vibrant sounding of the horn. **1976** *Shooting Times & Country Mag.* 16–22 Dec. 25/2 A rattle on the horn had hounds racing to the spot.

5. b. (Later example.)

1842 C. RIDLEY *Let.* in *Cecilia* (1958) ix. 111 Wells..is tiresome again... I wish I had courage to give her a good rattle, but if I did I think she would not bear it.

6. b. (Earlier example.)

1748 RICHARDSON *Clarissa* III. 127 Sir, said I, I see what a man I am with. Your rattle warns me of the snake.

7. (Earlier and later examples.)

1716 D. RYDER *Diary* 17 May (1939) 235, I was vexed to see her so long entertained with such a rattle as he. **1969** *N.Y. Rev. Bks.* 2 Jan. 3/4 Editor of a biographical history of philosophy yet welcomed as a rattle and raconteur..Lewes stands in these pages like a wax effigy. **1971** E. MAVOR *Ladies of Llangollen* i. 33 Great confidante, greater rattle, she was ever recording..what she was pleased to call 'boosey' whist parties beneath the Woodstock oaks.

9*. *Naut.* phr. *in the rattle*: on the commander's report of defaulters; in confinement; in trouble.

1914 'BARTIMEUS' *Naval Occasions* ii. 10 'In the bloomin' rattle, I am,' explained the disturber of traffic. **1919** W. LANG *Sea-Lawyer's Log* xii. 152 Ordinary Seaman Oldroyd spent the first dog-watch last night..washing his undergarments, but, having done so, he hung the same up to dry in the fore ammunition lobby, where they were subsequently discovered by the Gunner, who promptly placed Oldroyd 'in the rattle', hence his appearance as a defaulter. **1942** *Penguin New Writing* XV. 13 He was taken off, bawled out, put in the rattle. **1951** H. HASTINGS in *Plays of Year 1950* IV. 72 You ain't gonna put him in the rattle on account of a bit of leg-pull? **1964** J. HALE *Grudge Fight* vi. 91 The Andrew, that had taken him round the world a few times, given him his good conduct stripes and removed them when he'd been in the rattle. **1973** 'B. MATHER' *Snowline* xviii. 212 The Old Man..let the others out, but..your bloke is back in the rattle.

10. rattle-box, (*c*) (earlier and later examples); (*d*) *transf.*, applied to a conveyance or machine; **rattle-free** *a.*, devoid of rattles; **rattleproof** *a.*, capable of preventing rattling; hence **rattleproofing** *vbl. sb.*; **rattle-weed,** (*a*) substitute for def.: the bugbane, *Cimicifuga racemosa*; (*c*) = LOCO[1]; (*d*) = *rattle-box* (*c*) in Dict. and Suppl.; (earlier and later examples).

1817 A. EATON *Man. Bot.* 80 *Crotalaria..sagittalis*, (rattle-box) leaves lance-oblong. **1835** J. E. ALEXANDER *Sk. in Portugal* viii. 179 In May, the fleet of her Most Faithful Majesty consisted of the following ships:—..18, Audax,.. Fine, stout brig, but very ugly. 16. Providenza, .. Ditto, a perfect rattle-box. **1884** [see *LOCO *sb.*[1] a]. **1929** M. A. GILL *Underworld Slang*, *Rattle box*, machine gun. **1943** R. HOLT *George Washington Carver* 199 He would caution stockmen against the rattlebox (*Crotalaria*). **1972** G. BEINE *Land of Coyote* 90 These are rattleboxes, and there, some rabbitsfoot clover. **1973** 'H. HOWARD' *Highway to Murder* vii. 87 He was crowding ninety and so was his rattlebox. **1962** *Times* 3 May 19/4 It [*sc.* a car] is impressively quiet throughout..completely rattle-free and draughtproof. **1924** *Motor* 21 Oct. 626/1 Table utensils held in rattleproof devices. **1976** *Norwich Mercury* 19 Nov. 8/5 (Advt.), But Ziebart is rustproofing and soundproofing..and squeak-proofing and rattleproofing. **1791** *Trans. Amer. Philos. Soc.* III. 114 American Bane-berry, Black Snake-root, Rattle-weed. **1851** R. GLISAN *Jrnl. Army Life* (1874) vi. 70 The rattle-weed..derives its name from the fact that its pod is full of loose seed, and makes a rattling noise when dry. **1864** *Rep. Maine Board Agric.* 45 Last year nothing grew on the field where it had been applied but rattle-weed. **1931** W. N. CLUTE *Common Names Plants* 110 *Crotalaria sagittalis*..is frequently known as rattle-box or rattle-weed.

rattle, *v.*[1] Add: **I. 4. a.** Also with *about*, *around*, esp. *transf.* and *fig.*, implying the occupation of an area or space larger than that which is comfortable, necessary, or desirable.

1869 L. M. ALCOTT *Little Women* II. iii. 43, I saw you two girls rattling about in the what-you-call-it [*sc.* charabanc], like two little kernels in a very big nutshell. **1926** M. J. ATKINSON in J. F. Dobie *Rainbow in Morning* (1965) 81 He rattles around in his office like one pea in a pod. **1967** T. STOPPARD *Rosencrantz & Guildenstern are Dead* III. 95 We can move,..change direction, rattle about, but our movement is contained within a larger one that carries us along. **1973** *Washington Post* 13 Jan. A23/6, I don't want that kind of power rattling around inside the bureaucracy.

II. 5. d. *Cricket*. To bowl *down* the opposing team's wickets speedily and cheaply; to skittle *out* batsmen in a similar manner.

a **1842** B. AISLABIE in P. Norman *Scores & Ann. W. Kent Cricket Club* (1897) 370 M was a Morgan, who rattled them down. **1862** *Baily's Mag.* Apr. 259 Caffyn and Bennett rattled down their wickets..for 20 runs. **1873** *Ibid.*, July 409 In the second innings the two fast bowlers..rattled out the Marylebone men in grand style. **1898** G. GIFFEN *With Bat & Ball* vii. 94 On the sticky wicket..Hearne and Poughet 'rattled' us out. **1926** H. S. ALTHAM *Hist. Cricket* xviii. 207 He..saw Kent rattled out by Painter and Roberts for 76.

6. d. To fire (bullets) rapidly; to carry off (a person) by firing.

1890 KIPLING in *Scots Observer* 12 July 200/2 If a beggar can't march, why, we [*sc.* machine-guns] kills 'im an' rattles 'im into 'is grave. **1916** 'BOYD CABLE' *Action Front* 198 He rattled off burst after burst of fire.

7. a. Delete † *Obs.* and add earlier and later examples.

1542 N. UDALL *Erasmus's Apophthegmes* sig. K5, How Diogenes ratleed & shooke vp couetous persones. **1931** S. W. RYDER *Blue Water Ventures* xvi. 217 He should have rattled his officer-of-the-watch for slackness.

9. *to rattle off* (further examples); also spec. *Cricket*: to score or 'knock off' with ease (the runs necessary for victory); *to rattle up* (chiefly *Cricket*): to score rapidly, within a certain time, or before enforced retirement.

1860 *Baily's Mag.* Sept. 427 Captain Bathurst, in the fine old family style, rattled up 10 and 21. **1875** *Ibid.* June 108 Ultimately the South were left with about 40 to get to win, and Mr. W. G. Grace and Jupp rattled off these without difficulty. **1896** G. B. SHAW *Let.* 15 Feb. (1965) I. 597, I do not make a third of the income expected by men who rattle off their copy at anything from 20/- to 40/- a thousand. **1926** H. S. ALTHAM *Hist. Cricket* xviii. 208 Jackson and Sellars rattled up 24 in a quarter of an hour. **1973** *Advocate-News* (Barbados) 20 Feb. 14/5 Such an 'uncertainty' would take the form of a dramatic batting collapse, giving the Australians enough time to rattle up a good second innings score. **1976** *0–10 Cricket Scene* (Austral.) 30/2 And to show he has lost none of his zest for runs, he rattled off scores of 171 not out, 12, 114 not out and 36 in the World Cup series in England.

10. (Further examples.)

1977 J. LAKER *One-Day Cricket* 66 The Sri Lankans rattled the score along. **1977** *Sunday Times* 9 Jan. 28/6 They rattled their reply of 240 for four to the Bangladesh score of 266 for nine declared, at more than four runs an over.

11. For *U.S.* read 'orig. *U.S.*' and add earlier and later examples. Also, to irritate, to 'nettle'.

1869 J. R. BROWNE *Adventures Apache Country* xxviii. 282, I think he was slightly rattled by the formidable appearance of our escort. **1904** F. LYNDE *Grafters* xxviii. 360 For once in a way the ex-district attorney was too nearly rattled to be fully alert to his surroundings. **1905** *Pall Mall Mag.* Nov. 546/1, I don't see you need be rattled. **1927** M. DE LA ROCHE *Jalna* xxii. 276 Don't be a duffer... The more Piers sees he can rattle you the more he'll do it. **1928** E. WALLACE *Double* iv. 52 Why the devil are they bothering me? There's something about this business that is rattling me. **1936** P. FLEMING *News from Tartary* 65 But I had the empty satisfaction of seeing that I had (slightly) rattled Pai. **1959** E. H. CLEMENTS *High Tension* v. 82 Trust a woman to put her oar in! That's got Alister nicely rattled! **1977** J. F. FIXX *Compl. Bk. Running* p. xviii, I was less easily rattled by unexpected frustrations.

rattled (ræ·t'ld), *ppl. a.* [f. RATTLE *v.*[1] + -ED[1].] Agitated, confused, frightened. Also *Comb.*

1910 *N.Y. Even. Post* 10 Feb. 8/1 The plight of Ohio's rattled Republicans is enough to win grimy tears from the stony basilisk. *a* **1974** R. CROSSMAN *Diaries* (1976) II. 413 'Oh God!' I thought, 'Harold's in such a rattled state, with Wigg on one side and poor Marcia and Gerald on the other.' **1977** W. M. SPACKMAN *Armful of Warm Girl* 62 It had seemed to her that he, rather, had been rattled-sounding.

rattle-mouse. 1. (Later example.)

1960 M. BURTON *Wild Animals Brit. Isles* 48 In the Isle of Wight it [*sc.* the serotine bat] is known as rattle-mouse.

rattler. Add: **1. c.** (Earlier and later examples.)

1709 W. KING *Useful Trans. Philos.* II. sig. A 2v, Nothing could be more useful than a full..Inspection of Human Tongues... It is hop'd that if any Persons know themselves to be..Tongue-Padds, Spokesmen, Rattlers, Bouncers, &c. they would..bequeath their Tongues to be dissected. **1959** *She* May 21/3 *Rattler*, great talker.

2. b. (*a*) (Further example); (*b*) *gen.*, any (rattling) form of transport, esp. a train.

1829 P. EGAN *Boxiana* 2nd Ser. II. 674 Boscoe made his appearance in a rattler, with four prime prads. **1871** *Lakeside Monthly* Oct. 323/1, I am going on the rattlers tomorrow to nick a lot of flats and molls. **1903** A. M. BINSTEAD *Pitcher in Paradise* viii. 193 On the followin' Saturday afternoon I took the rattler down to Aldershot. **1904** 'No. 1500' *Life in Sing Sing* 252/1 *Rattler*, a car. **1922** R. PARRISH *Case & Girl* 333 We caught another rattler two hours later, and got off at Patacne. **1924** D. H. LAWRENCE *England, my England* 102 Miss Stokes had a puncture. 'Let me wheel the rattler,' said Albert. **1936** I. L. IDRIESS *Cattle King* xli. 348 'Well, sir, for last year you certainly paid your fare on the railways.' 'I've never jumped the 'rattler' in my life.' **1951** *Collier's* 17 Nov. 8/2 We're rolling across the country in a very luxurious rattler. **1966** 'L. LANE' *ABZ of Scouse* II. 88 *Rattler*, a tram or street-car. **1977** 'J. FRASER' *Hearts Ease* v. 38 'Where's the ambulance?' 'We sent it away... The first one was an old rattler. We've sent for the Daimler which has better springing.'

c. For *U.S.* read 'orig. *U.S.*' (Later examples.)

1909 *Chambers's Jrnl.* July 431/2 Many of the little snakes of the tropics are as poisonous as the dreaded rattler. **1918** W. CATHER *My Antonia* I. ii. 17 She had killed a good many rattlers. **1949** G. B. SHAW *Buoyant Billions* IV. 48 You cannot charm the rattlers and gaters as I can. **1956** L. M. KLAUBER *Rattlesnakes* I. i. 11 Some believe any snake that vibrates its tail when angry or alarmed to be a rattler. **1963** D. P. MANNIX *All Creatures Great & Small* xi. 190 A friend sent me a very fine Mexican green rattler nearly six feet long. **1978** P. THEROUX *Picture Palace* ii. 8, I was moving round the room, hunched like a cowboy that hears a rattler.

3. a. (Earlier example in sense of 'storm'.)

1835 T. POWER *Jrnl.* 25 Mar. in *Impressions Amer.* (1836) ii. 266 Our breeze freshened gradually all the evening, until by midnight it blew a rattler.

b. Also *gen.*, anyone or anything remarkably good or able, esp. with regard to speed.

1853 F. GALE *Public School Matches* 13 The first ball is well pitched and comes in a rattler to the middle stump. **1883** 'MARK TWAIN' *Life on Mississippi* xxiv. 271 That 'Cyclone' was a rattler to go, and the sweetest thing to steer that ever walked the waters. **1886** M. THOMPSON *Banker of Bankersville* ix. 134 Your partner is a whole team, hain't he? He's a rattler! **1894** 'MARK TWAIN' in *St. Nicholas* Mar. 395 It was a rattler, that caravan, and a mighty fine sight to look at. **1917** H. GARLAND *Son of Middle Border* xxiv. 290 You may consider yourself hired for as long as you please to stay. You're a rattler.

d. A long, resounding word.

1865 'MARK TWAIN' in *Californian* 18 Mar. 8/1 One of them rattlers with a clatter of syllables as long as a string of sluice boxes.

5. *attrib.* and *Comb.*, as (sense 2 c) *rattler hatband*; **rattler-jumper,** one who jumps (JUMP *v.* 6 b) a train; so **rattler-jumping** *vbl. sb.*

1978 *Detroit Free Press* 5 Mar. 23/1 'One day when we were in a local shop, the owner remarked that he would pay $10 for a rattler hatband.' That casual remark launched the couple into a business. **1934** *Bulletin* (Sydney) 7 Mar. 33/2 It looks as though the Queensland Government will have to run special trains to cope with 'rattler'-jumpers, who nowadays travel in packs. **1933** *Ibid.* 3 May 20/1 Of all vocations rattler-jumping is the least easy.

rattlesnake, *sb.* Substitute for first part of def.: A venomous American pit viper belonging to the genus *Sistrurus* or *Crotalus* of the family Crotalidæ. (Later examples.)

1910 *Encycl. Relig. & Ethics* III. 143/1 The rattlesnake-doctor, who cured or prevented the bite of the rattlesnake, was usually distinct from other medicine-men. **1932** W. FAULKNER *Light in August* ii. 29 He carried with him his own inescapable warning, like a flower its scent or a rattlesnake its rattle. **1956** L. M. KLAUBER *Rattlesnakes* I. i. 13 All rattlesnakes have rattles, and no other kind of snake has them. **1975** R. L. BEALS *Peasant Marketing System of Oaxaca, Mexico* iii. 31 The rattlesnake was associated with the rain cult.

b. rattlesnake fern (earlier and later examples); **rattlesnake grass** (examples); **rattlesnake herb** (earlier examples); **rattlesnake leaf** (see quots.); **rattlesnake('s) master** (examples); **rattlesnake orchid,** an epiphytic orchid of the genus *Pholidota*, esp. *P. imbricata*, which is native to parts of south-east Asia and bears pendant racemes of light brown flowers; **rattlesnake plantain** (earlier and later examples); **rattlesnake root,** (*c*) one of several other plants believed to help cure the effect of rattlesnake bites; (later examples); **rattlesnake weed** (*c*) = **rattlesnake root* (*c*); (later examples).

1814 F. PURSH *Flora Amer.* II. 656 *Botrychium virginianum*..is known by the name of Rattle Snake Fern. **1931** W. N. CLUTE *Common Names Plants* 109 The spore-cases of one of our ferns are borne in spikes that so strongly suggest the rattles of the rattlesnake that it is commonly known as the rattlesnake fern. **1814** J. BIGELOW *Florula Bostoniensis* 25 Rattlesnake grass... A large grass found in meadows and readily recognized by its swelling spikelets. **1878** J. B. KILLEBREW *Grasses of Tennessee* 232 Rattlesnake Grass..resembles quaking grass very much. **1736** B. FRANKLIN *Poor Richard 1737* 3 (*caption*) Rattle-Snake Herb. **1763** tr. *L. du Pratz's Hist. Louisiana* II. 43 The Rattle-snake-herb has a bulbous root like that of a tuberose, but twice as large. **1822** A. EATON *Man. Bot.* (ed. 3) 294 *Goodyera pubescens*, rattle-snake leaf, scrophula-weed. **1829** A. H. LINCOLN *Familiar Lect. Bot.* 288 *Goodyera pubescens*, rattle-snake leaf. **1806** *Farmer's Calendar* sig. D4, Notwithstanding a free use of sweet oil, plantane, hoarhound, *prenanthet alba*, called here rattlesnake's master, &c. the swelling and pain progressed. **1836** M. HOLLEY *Texas* v. 103 A root called rattlesnake's master grows abundantly in the pine woods and is said to be an efficient remedy. **1843** F. MARRYAT *Narr. Trav. & Adv. M. Violet* II. vi. 134 Close to my feet I beheld five or six stems of the rattlesnake master weed. **1899** H. B. CUSHING *Hist. Choctaw Indians* 229 They [*sc.* the Choctaws] possessed an antidote for the bite and sting of snakes and insects, in the root of a plant called rattle snake's master. **1943** D. C. PEATTIE *Great Smokies* 189 Thus a little orchid, the rattlesnake plantain, with net-veined leaves, looks enough like a snakeskin to suggest that it may be a 'rattlesnake master' or cure for snake bites. **1887** G. NICHOLSON *Illustr. Dict. Gardening* III. 105/1 *Pholidota*..Rattlesnake Orchid. **1903** H. J. CHAPMAN *Watson's Orchids* (ed. 2) 430 It [sc. *Pholidota*] is commonly known as the Rattlesnake Orchid. **1965** A. D. HAWKES *Encycl. Cultivated Orchids* 369/1 The persistent or deciduous, large, concave bracts which occur in most species—often almost hiding the blossoms—give the common name of 'Rattlesnake Orchid' to at least some of the cultivated Pholidotas. **1778** J. CARVER *Trav. Interior Parts N. Amer.* 482 The Rattle Snake Plantain, an approved antidote to the poison of this creature. **1943** [see **rattlesnake master*]. **1972** *Islander* (Victoria, B.C.) 16 Apr. 16/3 Rattlesnake plantain ..is a denizen of the woods. **1889** *Cent. Dict.* 786/3 Cancer-weed, the rattlesnake root, *Prenanthes alba*, of the United States, a milky-juiced composite having an intensely bitter root. **1941** R. S. WALKER *Lookout* 48 Among the wild plants once employed as antidotes for the bites of poisonous reptiles are..Virginia snakeroot, button snakeroot, and rattlesnake-root. **1885** *Outing* Nov. 180/1 A pretty thing sends a creeping feeling down our backs, because it is rattlesnake weed. **1936** G. A. REICHARD *Navajo Shepherd & Weaver* 45 A yellow-green commonly seen is made by brewing the leaves and stems of one of the goldenrods (Bigelovia) called by some Whites 'tall rattlesnake weed'.

II. *transf.* **2.** In full, *rattlesnake cocktail, whisk(e)y.* A potent alcoholic drink or cocktail.

1862 [see *COBBLER 3]. **1867** T. C. BAKER *Hist. U.S. Secret Service* xix. 246 It is hardly worth the while to present to the Government a bill for a few decanters and rattlesnake whisky. **1903** A. M. BINSTEAD *Pitcher in Paradise* iv. 110 He went from bar to bar drinking 'rattlesnake cocktails'. **1930** *Savoy Cocktail Bk.* 132 Rattlesnake Cocktail... So called because it will either cure Rattlesnake bite, or kill Rattlesnakes, or make you see them. **1947** *Daily Progress* (Charlottesville, Va.) 3 Sept. 8/5 A bottle of 'rattlesnake whiskey' was seized in a recent Chinatown raid by the Federal Bureau of Narcotics, which offers this recipe for the concoction: Place a live rattlesnake in a large jar; add rice wine, dried toads, soy beans, sliced deer antlers and a handful of dried sea horses. Age six months. **1953** T. SHANE *Bar Guide* ii. 31 Rattlesnake. 2 dashes Pernod. 1 tsp. Lemon Juice. ½ tsp. Powdered Sugar. ½ Egg White. 1 oz. Rye. Shake with cracked ice and strain.

rattlesnake (ræ·t'lˌsnēⁱk), *v. rare.* [f. prec.] **1.** *trans.* To deceive or trick, as with the cunning of a serpent.

1818 KEATS *Let.* 3 Feb. (1958) I. 223 We must cut this, and not be rattlesnaked into any more of the like.

2. *trans.* and *intr.* To snake (see SNAKE *v.*¹ 4) with a rattling sound; to travel like a rattlesnake.

1961 M. SPARK *Prime of Miss Jean Brodie* ii. 23 The evening paper rattle-snaked its way through the letter box. **1981** J. BARNETT *Firing Squad* II. 155 Messerschmitts came in at low level, rattlesnaking along the beaches.

rattling, *ppl. a.* Add: **4. c.** (Later examples.)

1885 *Punch* 4 July 4/1 You do see some rattling pretty, fresh faces. **1930** A. G. HAYS in W. E. Weeks *All in Racket* 13 This is a rattling good story. **1978** *Jrnl. R. Soc. Arts* CXXVI. 636/1 Herkomer's *The Last Muster* is a rattling good picture.

6. *Comb.*, as *rattling-boned* adj.

1933 E. SITWELL *Eng. Eccentrics* ii. 42, I am afraid the ancient and rattling-boned gallant rather gloried in this fall from grace.

rat-trap. Add: **1. a.** Also *attrib.* in sense 'resembling a rat-trap'.

1904 *Westm. Gaz.* 3 Mar. 1/3 A gaunt man with a rat-trap face. **1907** *Ibid.* 20 Sept. 4/2 His [*sc.* a pike's] rat-trap jaws. **1978** R. WESTALL *Devil on Road* xxiii. 217 He had a rat-trap jaw and little deep-set eyes.

b. *transf.* A shabby or ramshackle building or dwelling. *colloq.*

1838 DE QUINCEY in *Blackw. Mag.* XLIII. 21/2 Ay; but mind you,—put case that he or that she should die in this rat trap before sentence is passed. **1876** H. T. WILLIAMS *Pacific Tourist* 205 The following are among the..oddities which have, through miners' freaks and fancies, been used to denote settlements and camps and diggings, small or large:..Rat-Trap Slide. **1892** 'MARK TWAIN' *Amer. Claimant* iv. 56 It wouldn't have occurred to anybody else to name this poor old rat-trap Rossmore Towers. **1974** *Amer. Speech 1971* XLVI. 77 *Shabby hotel*,..flop joint, joint, rat trap.

2. (Further examples.)

1931 H. W. BARTLEET *Bartleet's Bicycle Bk.* 33 Every practical cyclist who saw my pedals praised the scheme of rattrap and rubber in combination. **1974** *Sumter* (S. Carolina) *Daily Item* 24 Apr. (Western Auto Advts. Suppl.) 4 Chromed rat trap racing pedals! **1976** *Billings* (Montana) *Gaz.* 28 June 2-c (Advt.), Rat trap pedals... Big 'knobby' tread tires.

3. *Building.* Applied *attrib.* to a form of Flemish bond (BOND *sb.*¹ 13 a) in which the bricks are laid on edge and the 'headers' span the whole thickness of wall, dividing the wall cavity into square spaces.

1932 E. GUNN *Economy in House Design* ix. 31 Brickwork beneath the tile hanging should be built in rat trap bond. **1939** —— *Building Technique* 39/1 Rat-trap or box-bond... This form of walling, which may be briefly described as Flemish-bond with all bricks laid on edge, is well-recognised in Sussex and adjoining counties where tile-hung walls are common. **1974** *Bricks* (Brick Development Assoc.) I. 33 (*heading*) Rat-trap bond.

ratty, *a.* Add: **2. a.** (Earlier and later examples.)

1867 'MARK TWAIN' *Notebk.* (1935) viii. 99 Village of Bethany... It is fearfully ratty—some houses—mud. **1884** —— *Huck. Finn* ix. 78 We got..a ratty old bed-quilt off the bed. **1962** J. D. MACDONALD *Girl* xii. 185 Pooty-Tat sat on a ratty couch. **1969** E. B. WHITE *Let.* 2 Nov. (1976) 586 When he received me, in a ratty apartment in the West Seventies or thereabouts, he was wearing toga and sandals. **1970** 'D. HALLIDAY' *Dolly & Cookie Bird* iv. 51 A ratty half-dozen people had spilled out of the bar-café... A lot of money changed hands rather quickly. **1974** R. M. PIRSIG *Zen & Art of Motorcycle Maintenance* III. xxvi. 317 John always kept his BMW spic and span. It really did look nice, while mine's always a little ratty, it seems.

b. *colloq.* Ill-tempered, irritated, angry.

1909 M. B. SAUNDERS *Litany Lane* xvi. 215 Shut up. She's ratty. **1913** H. S. WALPOLE *Fortitude* I. iv. 53 All right, you needn't be ratty about it! **1929** W. P. RIDGE *Affect. Regards* 226 Have I ever got ratty with you, Elsie? **1976** T. HEALD *Let Sleeping Dogs Die* vi. 122 I'd simply have asked her what the hell she was so ratty about.

3. *Austral.* and *N.Z. colloq.* Mad, eccentric, silly. Phr. *to be ratty over*: to be infatuated with.

1900 H. LAWSON *On Track* 75 Trav'lers and strangers failed to see anything uncommonly ratty about him. **1906** E. DYSON *Fact'ry 'Ands* xiv. 184 Already the Beauties had decided that Connie was 'as ratty as rabbits'. **1922** A. WRIGHT *Colt from Country* 86 There was a rough-up in a pub; he got a knock, had a fit, and went real ratty, and that was the end of him. **1941** BAKER *Dict. Austral. Slang* 59 *Ratty*, stupid, silly. *Ratty over* (a person), infatuated with.

4. *Comb.*, as *ratty-looking* adj.

1884 'MARK TWAIN' *Huck. Finn* xix. 182 Both of them had big, fat, ratty-looking carpet-bags.

Hence **ra·ttily** *adv.*, ill-temperedly, irritably.

1977 T. HEALD *Just Desserts* vii. 169 'We're supposed to be buddies,' said Bognor, rattily. **1980** *Times Lit. Suppl.* 4 July 754/2 Compliments fly and are quoted in abundance in this symposium. One reads on, rattily, in the hope of meeting some unusual personal habit,..some outstanding trait of character or behaviour.

‖ **ratu** (ratu·). Also **ratoo.** [Indonesian.] The title of a petty monarch or native regional ruler in parts of Indonesia and in Fiji.

1798 S. H. WILCOCKE tr. *Stavorinus's Voy. E. Indies* I. II. i. 214, I..appoint the said *pangorang*, to be *pangorang ratoo*, or hereditary prince, and heir to the crown and the whole empire of Bantam. **1820** J. CRAWFURD *Hist. Indian Archipelago* III. VIII. i. 22 The genuine native term for king in Javanese is *Ratu*, which is the same word that is written *Datu* in some other languages. **1821** J. LEYDEN tr. *Malay Annals* 157 The toddy-man's son became ratu of Majapahit. **1880** *Encycl. Brit.* XIII. 607/2 Ratu Loro Kidul is princess of the southern sea, and has her seat among the caves and fiords of the southern coast. **1907** *Daily Chron.* 30 Nov. 4/6 They are captained by Ratu Kadavu Levu, the grandson of the last native monarch of Fiji, Thakombau. Ratu is Fijian for Prince. **1937** M. COVARRUBIAS *Island of Bali* (1972) viii. 250 Finally it is time for the prince, the *ratú*, to appear; the *patih* recites his praises and..begs him to enter. **1966** *Economist* 16 Apr. 232/1 General Suharto, Indonesia's strong man, has found a way of remaining loyal both to his guru..and to his ratu (king). **1977** *South China Morning Post* (Hong Kong) 14 Apr. (Business Suppl.) 11/3 Ratu Sir Kamisese Mara of Fiji, representing the developing countries, said in reply [etc.].

‖ **rature** (ratūr). *rare.* [Fr.] A scribal erasure or deletion.

1931 T. S. ELIOT *Charles Whibley* 5 He..composed rapidly..and made very few *ratures* or corrections.

Raudive (rǭdi·v). The name of Konstantin *Raudive* (1909–74), Latvian psychologist, used *attrib.* in connection with a phenomenon involving tape recordings of sounds said to represent voices of paranormal origin.

1971 *Psychic News* 20 Mar. 8/6 The Raudive story appears to have started when a Swede, Frederick Jurgenson wrote a book in 1969 describing how when he was in the woods recording birdsong, faint voices appeared on his tape. Some years later, Dr. Raudive contacted Jurgenson and discussed the phenomena. **1972** P. BANDER *Carry on Talking* vii. 85 It would require a fevered imagination to convert it to Raudive-type voices. **1973** *Times* 4 Dec. 17/7 There is nothing new in PK (psychokinesis) and telepathy, or even the seemingly incredible Raudive voices. **1974** C. F. PANATI *Supersenses* iv. 109 Professor..Dean..feels that the Raudive phenomenon is real enough and that the explanation is simple and straightforward. **1975** C. WILSON *Mysterious Powers* vi. 94 As a result of the publicity surrounding Dr. Raudive's work, voice phenomena have been dubbed 'Raudive voices'.

Raudixin (raudi·ksin). *Pharm.* [f. *RAU(-WOLFIA + -*dixin*.] A proprietary name for a hypotensive preparation containing the dried root of *Rauvolfia serpentina* (*RAUWOLFIA).

1953 *Trade Marks Jrnl.* 9 Sept. 811/1 *Raudixin*... Anti-hypertensive agents... E. R. Squibb and Sons Limited. **1953** *Official Gaz.* (U.S. Patent Office) 10 Nov. 317/1 Mathieson Chemical Corporation, New York..*Raudixin*... Claims use since May 4, 1953. **1954** *Jrnl. Amer. Med. Assoc.* 16 Oct. 736/1 About two months prior to the incident ..he had received Raudixin (a whole rauwolfia root), 50 mg. twice a day. **1956** N. M. FERGUSON *Textbk. Pharmacognosy* viii. 207 There are several proprietaries on the market which contain rauwolfia or its constituents. Chief among these are Raudixin, Rauwiloid and Serpasil. **1967** [see *RAUWILOID].

rauli (rau·li). [Amer. Sp., f. Mapuche *ruili*.] A deciduous tree resembling a beech, *Nothofagus procera*, belonging to the family Fagaceæ and native to temperate regions of Chile and Argentina; also, the reddish hardwood timber of this tree.

1908 ELWES & HENRY *Trees Gt. Brit. & Ireland* III. 555 *Nothofagus procera*, known as *Rauli*, is less common than *N. obliqua*. **1943** RECORD & HESS *Timbers of New World* 168/1 Rauli..has about the same range as Roble, but its timber is much more highly esteemed. **1955** *World Timbers* (Timber Devel. Assoc.) III. 97 Rauli works easily with both hand and machine tools. **1979** *Timbers of World* (Timber Res. & Devel. Assoc.) 214 Rauli occurs in pure stands on rich soil. *Ibid.*, There is also a tendency for rauli to show a pore ring on the tangential face.

raunch (rǭnʃ). *colloq.* (orig. *U.S.*). [Back-formation from next.] **a.** Shabbiness, grubbiness, dirtiness. **b.** Crudeness, vulgarity, licentiousness; boisterousness, earthiness.

1964 *Time* 21 Feb. 46/2 Presley made his pelvis central to his act, and the screams of his admirers were straight from the raunch. **1967** *Time* 18 Aug. 63 Calvin Coolidge High is an actual Manhattan school building, its rust and raunch unretouched for the camera. **1975** *Manch. Guardian Weekly* 2 Aug. 20 Bette Midler is..no Streisand, her material is blue and her songs are old. Yet she's been camped out at one of Broadway's biggest theatres for several months now, making raunch respectable in a sellout review called Clams on the Half Shell. **1976** *N.Y. Times* 9 July C19 There are bars that are all elegance, and bars that are all raunch, and bars that breathe both elegance and raunch and therefore are considered chic. **1978** *Maclean's Mag.* 4 Dec. 65/1 The result is a 200,000-word flop, in which raunch doesn't work and the highfalutin philosophy sinks without a trace. **1979** *Guardian* 14 Mar. 13/6 Her co-producer wanted to raise the raunch-quotient by having her perform in a garter belt.

raunchy (rǭ·nʃi), *a. colloq.* (orig. *U.S.*) [Origin unknown: cf. *RANCHY *a.*] **1.** Inept, incompetent, sloppy; unpleasant, contemptible, mean, disreputable; dirty, grubby.

1939 *Forum & Century* July 45/1 Depending on how good or how 'raunchy' we [*sc.* Air Force cadets] were, we drilled from one to three hours in the torrid heat. **1949** *Cavalier Daily* (Univ. of Va.) 22 Oct. 4/1 This situation could become embarrassing—if the writer in question happened to be well-known as a somewhat raunchy character in reality. **1953** BERREY & VAN DEN BARK *Amer. Thes. Slang* (1954) § 759/2 *Raunchy flying*, clumsy flying technique. **1965** D. E. WESTLAKE *Fugitive Pigeon* 170, I suddenly felt raunchy. Still in the same slacks I'd been wearing when this thing started. **1968** *Amer. Speech 1967* XLII. 229 *Raunchy*,..a pejorative adjective used to modify anything which the speaker wishes to denigrate, with the general connotation of 'stinky, grubby, scabby, dirty, or cheap'. **1971** *Daily Colonist* (Victoria, B.C.) 30 Nov. 18/7 I'll bet..the girls would boycott guys with dirty, tangled hair, filthy jeans, raunchy sweat shirts and bare feet. **1979** *Now!* 14 Sept. 87/3 Millgarth police station, down the rough, raunchy end of Leeds's city centre.

2. Of persons, their actions, etc.: boisterous, earthy, sexually provocative, aggressively licentious, suggestive. Also in extended uses, esp. of language, humour, songs, etc.: bawdy, salacious, smutty; tending to excite sexual feeling.

1967 'E. QUEEN' *Face to Face* iv. 17, I fell in love with him. In a raunchy sort of way he's beautiful. **1969** *Sat. Rev.* (U.S.) 31 May 44/2 A blend of raunchy humor, unpleasant perversity, and..sickening brutality. **1970** *Melody Maker* 12 Sept. 7 Most of the songs were too twee, and the rest seemed to be too raunchy. **1971** *Sunday Australian* 7 Nov. 27/6 Russell now has two albums of his own on which to disport his raunchy rock compositions. **1973** *Daily Colonist* (Victoria, B.C.) 23 Nov. 23/1 A drunk at the next table was singing some raunchy songs. The songs kept getting dirtier and dirtier. **1974** T. P. WHITNEY tr. *Solzhenitsyn's Gulag Archipelago* I. I. i. 21 They had noticed two raunchy broads going to bathe. **1976** *Times* 4 Feb. 14/4 Jurors are asked to pronounce judgment on a particularly raunchy book, while lawyers make suggestive jokes. **1977** *Gay News* 7–20 Apr. 38/3 (Advt.), Interested in meeting guys in tight raunchy levis to show me around. **1977** D. ANTHONY *Stud Game* xxiii. 145 If you mean *Couplings*, I liked it... I happen to like raunchy films.

Hence **rau·nchily** *adv.*, in a raunchy manner; **rau·nchiness.**

1972 *Time* 17 Apr. 66/3 They are a raunchily genteel exercise. **1975** *New Yorker* 20 Jan. 62/3 A shaggy-dog tale of a raunchiness Tolstoyan in scale, if not in tone, is related with single-minded, uninterruptible passion by one of the male guests. **1977** D. O'SULLIVAN in D. Marcus *Best Irish Short Stories* II. 96 No..customs and excise officer ever streaked from his intimations of mortality as raunchily as Emily Brontë from the stool. **1980** *Observer* 13 Jan. 36/2 The language is nearly devoid of metaphor, but doesn't shirk a beguiling raunchiness.

raupo. Add: (Further examples.) Also *ellipt.*, a hut built of raupo.

1851 V. LUSH *Jrnl.* 25 Apr. (1971) 75 Reached the Lusks' *raupo* about 9. **1863** 'PAKEHA MAORI' *Old N.Z.* vi. 79 My house was a good commodious *raupo* building. **1897** [see *KORUPE]. **1905** W. BAUCKE *Where White Man Treads* 145 Here and there a patch of stunted raupo standing listless in its sour and stagnant ooze. **1920** J. MANDER *Story N.Z. River* xxvi. 317 There was suddenly a ghostly movement in the rapoo and the reeds. **1933** *Bulletin* (Sydney) 9 Aug. 21/2 The pollen and roots of the raupo..were..regularly eaten. **1944** *Coast to Coast 1943* 96 They [*sc.* fleas] came from the dust under the raupo mats. **1960** *Guardian* 9 Dec. 6/3 It was five months on voyage and a tent or a raupo (rush) hut at the end of it. **1975** *Turangi* (N.Z.) *Chron.* 2 Apr. 1/1 Prior to the tailrace being established the area had been raupo swamp.

raurekau (raure·kau). Also **raureka.** [Maori.] A small evergreen tree, *Coprosma australis*, belonging to the family Rubiaceæ, native to New Zealand, and bearing small white flowers and red berries. Also *attrib.*

1905 W. BAUCKE *Where White Man Treads* 254 Pork.. alternated with stacks of eels enclosed in wrappings of 'raurekau' leaves. **1928** Cockayne & Turner *Trees N.Z.* 36 Raurekau. A low, bushy tree..or tall shrub, with dark-coloured bark. **1949** *Landfall* III. 31 He stumbled through a jungle of raureka and gorse. **1963** Poole & Adams *Trees & Shrubs N.Z.* 173 Raurekau. Small tree reaching 7 m... Flowers in fascicles.

rauriki (rau·riki, ra·riki). Also **rariki.** [Maori.] = *puha.

1944 *Mod. Jun. Dict.* (Whitcombe & Tombs) 331 Rauriki, raddiky..The Maori word for sowthistle. **1949** E. de Mauny *Huntsman in his Career* ii. 122 Weeds grew in profusion, rariki and nettle. **1958** A. Wall *Queen's English* ix. 48 Sowthistle..is actually edible and much used by the Maoris as *rauriki*, corruptly 'raddiky'. **1966** *N.Z. Encycl.* II. 785/2 The juice of rauriki.., a latex, was also used.

‖ **rauschpfeife** (rau·ʃpfəifə). *Mus.* Pl. **-n.** [Ger., = reed-pipe.] **1.** (See quot. 1964.)

1876 Stainer & Barrett *Dict. Mus. Terms* 374/2 *Rauschpfeif* [*sic*],..a stop in old organs of two ranks of pipes, consisting of a twelfth and fifteenth, or a fifteenth and octave twelfth. **1964** S. Marcuse *Mus. Instruments* 436/1 *Rauschpfeife*,..2..organ stop first mentioned by Arnold Schlick in 1511. It seems to have consisted originally of reed pipes with conical resonators; it became transformed in the course of the c. to a 2-rank stop of flue pipes. Since the mid-17th c. the stop was treated as a mixture, often 3-rank... In the 18th c. it was enlarged further... The original meaning of the word had long been forgotten: to Praetorius already it was a 'rustling' pipe (from [G.] *rauschen*, to rustle). **1976** D. Munrow *Instruments Middle Ages & Renaissance* vii. 60/1 The 'manual', the main part of the instrument [*sc.* a Renaissance organ], with eleven registers, was composed of reeds and flue stops, including a *Zink*, *Regall*, and *Rauspfeiffen*.

2. A reed-cap shawm of the Renaissance period.

1939 A. Carse *Mus. Wind Instruments* xi. 128 Two instruments of the shawm type figure in one of Burgkmair's famous series of woodcuts 'Kayser Maximilians I Triumph' (c. 1516) and are there named *rauschpfeiffen*. **1964** S. Marcuse *Mus. Instruments* 436/1 *Rauschpfeife* (? MHGer. *Rusch*, rush), 1. family of Ger. Renaissance reed-cap shawms, with wide conical bore.., terminating in a bell, the double reed concealed in a wooden cap. **1968** *Observer* 19 May 40 David Munrow..has a collection of more than 100 historic woodwind instruments with engaging names like..the rauschpfeife. **1976** D. Munrow *Instruments Middle Ages & Renaissance* vi. 50/4 *Rauschpfeifen* and *schreierpfeifen*.. are reed-cap shawms... Of the two, rauschpfeifen seem to have been more common. **1978** *Early Music* Apr. 253/1 No rauschpfeifen..are preserved, and yet no one denies they existed.

Rauwiloid (rau·wiloid). *Pharm.* [f. *rau-w(olfia + -*iloid*.] A proprietary name for a hypotensive preparation containing a number of alkaloids extracted from *Rauvolfia serpentina* (*rauwolfia).

1953 *Trade Marks Jrnl.* 15 July 616/2 *Rauwiloid*... Medicinal tablets for the treatment of hypertension. Riker Laboratories Inc... City of Los Angeles. **1953** *Official Gaz.* (U.S. Patent Office) 13 Oct. 295/1 *Rauwiloid*... Claims use since Oct. 28, 1952. **1954** *Jrnl. Amer. Med. Assoc.* 17 July 1027/1 The treatment of hypertension of varying degrees of severity with alseroxylon (Rauwiloid). **1956** [see *raudixin]. **1967** H. Beckman *Dilemmas in Drug Therapy* 175/1 Usual doses of the Rauwolfia preparations employed in treating hypertension are..alseroxylon (Rauwiloid), 2–4 mg. daily; ..rauwolfia (Raudixin, Rauserpa, Rauval), 200–400 mg. daily in divided doses.

rauwolfia (rauwǫ·lfiă, -vǫlfiă). Also **rauvolfia** and with capital initial. [mod.L. (P. C. Plumier *Nova Plantarum Americanarum Genera* (1703) 19), f. the name of Leonhard *Rauwolf* (d. 1596), German physician, botanist, and traveller + -ia[1].] **1.** A tropical shrub or small tree of the genus so called, belonging to the family Apocynaceæ and bearing clusters of small white flowers and red or black berries; *esp.* a shrub of one of the several species cultivated for the medicinal drugs obtained from their roots.

1752 P. Miller *Gardeners Dict.* (ed. 6) s.v. *Rauvolfia*, Four-leaved Rauvolfia, with narrow Leaves. **1823** *Curtis's Bot. Mag.* L. 2440 (*heading*) Three-leaved Rauwolfia. **1902** L. H. Bailey *Cycl. Amer. Hort.* IV. 1503/2 The Rauwolfia flourishes with great luxuriance in the shade of other shrubs. **1955** *Sci. Amer.* Oct. 81/1 Reserpine is an alkaloid extract from the snakeroot plant (named Rauwolfia for a 16th-century German physician). **1962** N. Maxwell *Witch-Doctor's Apprentice* i. 1 Many types of rauwolfia were employed by jungle shamans centuries before our medical men thought of tranquillizers. **1976** *Hortus Third* (L. H. Bailey Hortorium) 942/1 Rauvolfias are cultivated as ornamentals and for curiosity. **1976** W. A. R. Thompson *Herbs that Heal* ix. 148 This unleashed the flood-gates of the pharmaceutical industry, whose scouts started scouring the earth for rauwolfia.

2. *Pharm.* Also **Rauwolfia Serpentina.** The dried roots of *Rauvolfia serpentina* or related species, or an extract therefrom, containing a number of alkaloids (notably reserpine) and used medicinally, esp. to treat hypertension.

[**1949** *Brit. Heart Jrnl.* XI. 350/2 This overwhelming body of support in favour of regarding *R. Serpentina* as the remedy of choice. *Ibid.* 354/1 The hypotensive action of *R. Serpentina*.] **1952** *Ann. Internal Med.* XXXVII. 1149 In our clinic we have relied chiefly upon various combinations of hydrazinophthalazine, Rauwolfia and veratrum, principally because these drugs appear to be the safest..of any medicinal regimen we have tried. **1954** *Brit. Pharmaceutical Codex* 649 Rauwolfia has a depressant action on the central nervous system. **1957** H. W. Youngken in R. E. Woodson et al. *Rauwolfia* ii. 32 The drug Rauwolfia or Rauwolfia Serpentina consists of the dried root of *Rauwolfia serpentina*. .. The commercial sources of the drug..have been India, Pakistan, Ceylon, Burma, and Siam. **1966** *New Scientist* 27 Jan. 236/2 Physicians and pharmacists..are inclined to think that only a few vegetable drugs such as..digitalis, penicillin and rauwolfia are important in the present day *materia medica*. **1977** Lewis & Elvin-Lewis *Med. Bot.* vii. 187/1 *Rauwolfia* acts synergistically with other hypotensive drugs, and in the more severe cases of hypertension it is used in combination with *Veratrum viride* or protoveratrines A and B.

3. *attrib.*, as *rauwolfia alkaloid, berry.*

1942 *Biol. Abstr.* XVII. 117/2 The various effects suggest that the *Rauwolfia* alkaloids probably act on the vasomotor system and also directly on plain muscles of the blood vessels and intestines. **1977** S. Loebl et al. *Nurse's Drug Handbk.* 252 The rauwolfia alkaloids decrease blood pressure and have a sedative effect accompanied by bradycardia. **1932** *Discovery* July 231/1 Three kinds of starlings come with the great blue pigeons to the Rauwolfia berries.

rav (rǫv). Also **rov.** [Yiddish.] A rabbi; freq. prefixed to personal names.

1892 I. Zangwill *Childr. Ghetto* I. i. xiv. 314 'Ah, you will become a Rav!'.. 'What's that about a Rav?.. Does he want me to become a Rabbi?' **1893** —— *Ghetto Tragedies* 4 The great Rav Rotchinsky from Brody was to deliver a sermon. **1962** 'E. McBain' *Empty Hours* iii. 115 'I know who killed the *rov*.'.. 'She says she knows who killed the rabbi.' **1967** C. Potok *Chosen* xiv. 238 From one to three we would have the actual Talmud session itself, the shiur, with Rav Gershenson. **1973** *Jewish Chron.* 19 Jan. 34/2 The daughters and family of the late Mrs B—. C—...wish to thank the Rav, rabbonim..and friends for their visits..and numerous letters of sympathy.

ravanastron (rā·vănā·strǫn). Also **ravanastra.** [Origin unknown: freq. associated with the legendary King Ravana (see quots.); cf. Skr. *rāvaṇahasra* a kind of stringed instrument.] An ancient Hindu stringed instrument played with a bow.

1864 C. Engel *Music of Most Anc. Nations* ii. 81 The Hindoos maintain that the *ravanastron*, one of their old instruments played with the bow, was invented about five thousand years ago by Ravanen, a mighty king in Ceylon. **1876** Stainer & Barrett *Dict. Mus. Terms* 374/2 Ravanastron, a stringed instrument played with a bow in use among the Buddhists. **1896** H. Saint-George *Bow* ii. 7 Of existing bowed instruments the Ravanastron..most certainly seems to be the oldest. **1903** R. Hughes *Mus. Guide* I. 249/1 *Ravanastron*, a primitive violin with one or two strings... It is still used by the Buddhists. **1953** S. Beckett *Watt* 71 A ravanastron hung, on the wall, from a nail, like a plover. **1965** S. Krishnaswami *Mus. Instruments of India* 16 One of the earliest stringed instruments played with a bow was called the *ravanastra*. This instrument was associated with Ravana. **1969** N. Deane tr. *Bachmann's Origins of Bowing* i. 8 The quest for rudimentary types of bowed instruments led to the Welsh crwth and the Indian *ravanastron*, both regarded as the ancestor of our violin.

rave, *sb.*[2] **1. b.** (Examples.)

1847 *Rep. Comm. Patents 1846* (U.S.) 81 The raves are carried in front in such a form as to furnish a frame for the dash-board. **1851** J. S. Springer *Forest Life* v. 106 It was astonishing to see how he [*sc.* a teamster] had gnawed the rave of the sled. **1895** *Montgomery Ward Catal.* Spring & Summer 594/1 Bob Sleigh Gearing..Bob Knees..Bob Raves ..Bob Rollers.

rave, *sb.*[3] Add: **2.** *slang.* **a.** A passionate (and usu. transitory) liking for or infatuation with a person or thing; a sudden display of extreme enthusiasm or popularity, a 'craze'. Also, one who or that which excites feelings of this kind.

1902 Farmer & Henley *Slang* V. 380/2 *Rave*,..a strong liking; a craze: as 'X has a *rave* on Miss Z.' **1924** G. B. Stern *Tents of Israel* xvi. 240 Even if Jeanne-Marie had a rave on me, I'm not responsible. **1927** L. Mayer *Just between us Girls* xv. 91 He said I was simply a rave in these pajamas. **1941** L. Eyles *For my Enemy Daughter* vii. 161 That, too, is a bit schoolgirlish, isn't it? Getting a 'rave' on a woman I admire. **1949** N. Marsh *Swing, Brother, Swing* iii. 38 Carlisle remembered the confidences that Félicité had poured out in her convent days, concerning what she called her 'raves'. **1958** *People* 4 May 14/7 Kitza Kazacos, Greek singer, who became a rave on B.B.C. but was allowed to languish without follow-up dates, now tells me from New York that she is on three TV programmes. **1959** C. MacInnes *Absolute Beginners* 70 The newest of the teenage singing raves. **1962** L. Davidson *Rose of Tibet* 8 T.L. had been having at the time one of his not uncommon raves; on this occasion for the mental-disciplinary benefits of a classical language.

b. A highly enthusiastic or laudatory review or notice of a book, play, film, etc. Also in extended use, a favourable opinion; a strong recommendation. Freq. *attrib.* (passing into *adj.*). orig. *U.S.*

No earlier definite example of this use has been traced in *Variety* (see quot. 1926).

1926 *Amer. Mercury* Dec. 464/2 One of the paper's [*sc.* *Variety's*] coinages should be officially embraced by the dictionary and bred into the language. It refers to a flattering, enthusiastic review by a sycophantic critic as a *rave*. **1935** E. E. Cummings *Let.* 31 Jan. (1969) 135 Have been epistling with Pound, whom yessed in Paris for a full ½ hour under lurid misapprehension that his 'Douglas' rave intended 'South Wind'. **1936** *Amer. Speech* XI. 221 The producer waits for the early editions of the morning papers. He scans them avidly for the notices. They may be raves, in which case the critics have reviewed the show in glowing superlatives. **1942** *Melody Maker* 4 July 5/4 Raves coming thick and fast for George Auld's new powerhouse band now at the Arcadia Ballroom, N.Y. **1943** D. Powell *Time to be Born* i. 6 The critical raves and the big sale. **1951** Wodehouse *Old Reliable* ix. 114 Of course he can open the safe. He's an expert. You should have read what the papers said of him at the time of the trial. He got rave notices. **1958** *Listener* 27 Nov. 898/1, I yield to none in my admiration for this pianist, whose first London notice I had the honour to write long before the war (a 'rave' in case you think I am always wrong). **1961** *John o' London's* 12 Oct. 423/1, I don't suppose *The Young Doctors*..will collect rave tributes. **1969** Gish & Pinchot *Lillian Gish* xv. 222 Richard Barthelmess also received raves for his sensitive portrayal of Cheng. **1972** [see *pan *sb.*[1] 10*]. **1974** *Publishers Weekly* 26 Aug. 299/2 The later work is distinctly finer than the earlier (though that was good enough to draw a rave foreword, here reprinted, from Ford Madox Ford). **1977** M. Kenyon *Rapist* v. 50 His music..had opened to raves in New York. **1979** *Tucson Mag.* Apr. 68/3 These three-day bus tours..have received rave notices from all who have gone along. **1980** *Times Lit. Suppl.* 10 Oct. 1131/1 Enzensberger's rave review of the novel is reprinted.

c. A lively party; a rowdy gathering.

1960 *News Chron.* 16 Feb. 6, I wandered around to a rave I knew was going on in Covent Garden. **1963** *Sunday Times* 8 Sept. 29/3 A rave, blast or orgy—all synonyms for party. **1964** C. Dale *Other People* iv. 96 A man who..thought that parties—'raves'—ended at ten-thirty. **1965** G. Melly *Owning-Up* vii. 75 We..organized all-night raves. **1968** *Listener* 7 Nov. 606/1 Have you heard, the Touch-Paceys are economising this year by combining their children's bonfire party with their annual fancy dress rave?

Hence **rave-in** (see *-in[3]), **rave-up** = sense 2 c above.

1967 *Melody Maker* 21 Jan 10 Pop enthusiasts have been treated to rave-ups featuring such world-class stars as the Four Tops. **1967** *New Statesman* 17 Mar. 356/3 Last week police arrested scores of teenagers at a rave-in, and left-wing Catholics staged a pray-in. **1972** 'Miss Read' *Tyler's Row* vii. 88 'Well, let's have this rave-up of a meal now,' suggested Peter. **1973** H. Miller *Open City* ix. 89 Phyllis McBain is invited to an old-style rave-up, knickers and husbands optional. **1974** R. Rendell *Face of Trespass* ii. 29 Some Victorian pretence that a simple Westbourne Grove rave-up was really a conference. **1977** *Rolling Stone* 7 Apr. 20/1 (Advt.), When Argent, that legendary British band of so many hit songs and rave-up performances, began to wane, these three musicians stepped out of its shadow and into the fierce light of their own creative genius.

rave, *v.*[1] Add: **3. a.** (Earlier and later examples with *about.*)

1816 Jane Austen *Emma* II. xv. 282, I quite rave about Jane Fairfax. **1921** *Collier's* 16 Apr. 20/2 He began to 'rave', about the place he had built on Long Island for him and Delores. **1978** J. Updike *Coup* iv. 150 So you're the young man my daughter has been raving about.

b. *slang.* To give oneself over to enjoyment; to 'live it up'; to depart rowdily or with the intention of having a good time. Cf. *rave *sb.*[3] 2 c.

1961 *New Statesman* 26 May 830/2 When we got there, most of the art-student element had raved off to some shindig. **1965** G. Melly *Owning-Up* vii. 75 The word 'rave', meaning to live it up, was as far as I know a Mulligan–Godbolt invention. **1965** *Sunday Times* (Colour Suppl.) 19 Sept. 13/3 He started out by raving at weekends to Bridlington.

ravel, *sb.*[1] Add: **1.** Also, a cluster.

1913 D. H. Lawrence *Sons & Lovers* xiii. 380 There was a lovely yellow ravel of sunflowers in the garden.

ravel, *sb.*[3] (Earlier example.)

1805 J. Austin in *Trans. Soc. Arts* XXIII. 242 An universal ravel or sniffle, useful at the beaming of all kinds of webs.

ravel, *v.*[1] **2.** (Later *fig.* examples.)

1956 *Essays in Crit.* III. 320 The discussion then ravels out into a note on such secondary Virgilian sources as the Saturnian prophecy. **1963** Oglesby & Hewes *Highway Engin.* (ed. 2) xvii. 544 The roads raveled rapidly and in the worst instances became during a single season merely a pile of loose stones.

ravel (ræ·v'l), *v.*[4] Var. Rabble *v.*[3] in Dict. and Suppl.

1923 *Discovery* Nov. 291/2 The other furnace..in which the flames actually play over the surface of the mundic which is 'ravelled' from the side by a pole some eight or nine feet long.

Ravelian (rave·liăn), *a.* Also **Ravellian.** [f. the name of Maurice *Ravel* (1875–1937), French composer.] Of, pertaining to, or characteristic of the works of Ravel. Also as *sb.*, an exponent of Ravel's music.

1933 M. D. Calvocoressi in *Listener* 22 Feb. 305/1 There is no mistaking the thoroughly 'Ravel-ian'—and therefore French—quality of the mind and imagination which is at work. **1937** *Times* 29 Dec. 12/3 The charm of the early quartet and septet will keep them fresh when some of the more purely Ravellian works have been discarded as too dry. **1946** *Penguin Music Mag.* Dec. 32 The progress of Walton from his early and somewhat Ravelian *Facade* to the Violin Concerto. **1952** B. Ulanov *Hist. Jazz in Amer.* (1958) xxii. 310 Johnny Richards' excursions into Debussyan and Ravelian pasture. **1965** *Listener* 28 Oct. 680/2 The two syllables '*Ma-man*', pronounced as a falling fourth (a characteristic Ravelian fingerprint), strike an almost sentimental note. **1970** L. Davies *Ravel Orchestral Music* 46 It culminates in a more virtuoso episode which leans too obviously on skimming Ravelian scales. **1981** *Times* 26 Feb. 13/6 Manuel Rosenthal, a Ravelian to his fingertips.

ravelling, *vbl. sb.* **2.** (Later *fig.* example.)
1903 B. POTTER *Tailor of Gloucester* 22, I am worn to a ravelling.

raven, *sb.*[1] Add: **4. a.** Similative, as *raven-shadowing* adj.; instrumental, as *raven-covered* adj.
1895 W. B. YEATS *Wanderings of Usheen* in *Poems* 7 We think on Oscar's pencilled urn, And on the heroes lying lain, On Gabhra's raven-covered plain. **1950** C. DAY LEWIS in *Penguin New Writing* XXXIX. 22 A driven heart, a raven-shadowing mind Loom above all my pastorals.
b. raven-tree, a tree in which ravens build their nests.
1904 *Westm. Gaz.* 23 July 13/1 The 'raven tree' is all that remains..to remind one of the former existence of these birds in those localities. **1908** *Chambers's Jrnl.* Apr. 284/1 Nearly every parish had its 'raven-tree'.
c. raven's duck (examples).
1761 *Newport* (Rhode Island) *Mercury* 28 Apr. 4/3 Just imported..Russia and ravens duck. **1775** in *New Hampsh. Hist. Soc. Coll.* (1863) VII. 4, 120 Tents, to be made of Raven's duck. **1868** G. G. CHANNING *Recoll. Newport* 200 A miller called one day at the store to purchase a piece of ravensduck, with which to make or to repair sails for his windmill. **1931** *Sun* (Baltimore) 12 Jan. 6/6 Hemp sails, known as raven's duck, were used, the cotton duck being unknown at that time.

Raven (rēⁱ·v'n). The name of J. C. *Raven*, 20th-cent. psychologist, used *attrib.* and in the possessive with reference to non-verbal intelligence tests devised by him to measure Spearman's *g* factor in the ability to understand abstract relationships, solve problems, etc., and designed to be especially useful where language disadvantages exist; esp. *Raven('s) Progressive Matrices (Test)*.
1948 *Psychometrika* XIII. 28 The results obtained by means of the Raven tests are indicative of the fact that these ..fulfill most of the requirements needed for testing normal and handicapped subjects. *Ibid.* 34 Apart from Raven B.. the remaining tests..are not loaded in factor *L.* **1954** A. ANASTASI *Psychol. Testing* x. 270 The..Raven Progressive Matrices Test provides a promising tool for this purpose. **1964** M. CRITCHLEY *Developmental Dyslexia* xiv. 82 On Raven's progressive matrices he scored 32 out of 60: his I.Q. was estimated to be 93. **1972** *Jrnl. Social Psychol.* LXXXVII. 69 Intelligence scores were available only for the controls, who had been administered the Raven's Progressive Matrices Test. **1973** B. B. WOLMAN *Introd. Gen. Psychol.* xxxii. 666/1 One of the most widely used nonverbal tests is the Raven Progressive Matrices Test. *Ibid.*, A vocabulary test is also available to accompany the Raven Matrices. **1976** H. M. PROSHANSKY et al. *Environmental Psychol.* (ed. 2) ix. 129/2 The..tests of spatial skills were..a short form (six items) of the Embedded Figures Test..and the Ravens Matrices.

Ravenna (rave·nă). The name of a town in northern Italy, used *absol.* or *attrib.* in *Ravenna grass* to designate *Erianthus ravennæ*, a large ornamental grass native to southern Europe and distinguished by greyish leaves and spikes of purplish-grey flowers.
1900 L. H. BAILEY *Cycl. Amer. Hort.* II. 540/1 Ravenna Grass. A tall, hardy grass, 4–7 ft. high, very ornamental. **1929** J. W. BEWS *World's Grasses* vi. 243 'Ravenna' is a Mediterranean species, extending as far north as upper Italy. **1976** G. S. THOMAS *Perennial Garden Plants* x. 308 Ravenna Grass. In hot summers this grass is a striking addition to the garden.

ravenously, *adv.* (Later examples.)
1907 G. B. SHAW *Major Barbara* II. 217 Shirley (looking at it ravenously but not touching it..). *Ibid.*, (He turns to the table and attacks the meal ravenously). **1915** W. S. MAUGHAM *Of Human Bondage* xliv. 211 She could not have eaten more ravenously if she were starving. **1951** C. S. LEWIS *Prince Caspian* iii. 37 He would have made much more fuss about this if he had not by now been so ravenously hungry.

Ravenscroft (rēⁱ·vĕnzkrǫft). [The name of George *Ravenscroft* (1618–81), English glassmaker.] An article made of the flint-glass or lead-glass devised by George Ravenscroft. Also *attrib.* or as *adj.*
1929 W. A. THORPE *Hist. Eng. & Irish Glass* I. iv. 128 Threads of trailed glass applied on the surface..are evident in several marked Ravenscroft glasses. **1948** E. B. HAYNES *Glass through Ages* I. ix. 127 This..piece must be a Ravenscroft glass, perhaps the first example to be found with the plain seal. **1961** E. M. ELVILLE *Collector's Dict. Glass* 87/1 (*caption*) Ravenscroft roemer bearing the seal of the raven's head..circa 1677. **1970** G. SAVAGE *Dict. Antiques* 348/1 (*caption*) A rare Ravenscroft showing signs of criselling... Lead glass. 17th century. **1975** *Country Life* 2 Jan. 11/3 (*heading*) A Syllabub Jug in Ravenscroft Glass. *Ibid.*, This jug..is typical Ravenscroft of, I suppose, the late 1680s. **1976** *Times* 4 May 14/6 A documentary item of the beginning of English glass, a Ravenscroft silver-mounted and engraved decanter jug,..sold for £2,420.

raver. Add: **b.** A passionate enthusiast for a particular thing, idea, or cause; a fanatic. Also, one who likes to 'live it up' or have a wild time esp. in sexual relationships (cf. *RAVE *v.*[1] 3 b). *slang.*
1959 C. MACINNES *Absolute Beginners* 63, I did actually begin to be a raver for those weekly meetings. **1960** [see *MOD *sb.*[3] and *a.*]. **1961** *Guardian* 6 Mar. 3/4 The bearded ravers usually associated with the more esoteric ranges of HiFi. **1968** BUSBY & HOLTHAM *Main Line Kill* v. 44 There's a bloke I know makes his own LSD. Some of the ravers are giving it a try. **1971** *Cape Herald* 15 May 7/4 She looks like a raver But I could never please her. **1976** P. CAVE *High Flying Birds* iii. 31 She was neither attractive nor plain; not a raver or a ragbag. **1976** *Listener* 22 Jan. 84/2 Things hot up when a raver and his girl swoop in by motor-bike. **1978** *Sunday Mail* (Brisbane) 24 Sept. 34/4, I have never analysed why, but many pop musicians are ravers—people who like to live it up—with a strong self-destructive streak.

ravers (rēⁱ·vəɪz), *pred. a. slang.* [f. RAV(ING *ppl. a.*[1]; cf. *CRACKERS *pred. a.*] Raving mad, delirious. Also, in weakened sense, furious, angry.
1938 N. MARSH *Death in White Tie* xxii. 242 Bart has driven me stark ravers, he's been so awful. **1939** —— *Overture to Death* xvii. 189 In Henry's..opinion Miss Prentice is practically ravers. **1951** E. HYAMS *Sylvester* xxviii. 150 'You said you wanted to meet Sylvester Green. Well, here I am.'.. 'Stark ravers. I served for two years with Green. This man isn't even much like him.' **1967** N. MARSH *Death at Dolphin* iv. 100 Jeremy..will probably go stark ravers if they're sold out of the country.

‖ **ravigote** (ravigǫ·t). Also **ravigotte.** [Fr., f. *ravigoter* to invigorate.] (See quot. 1877.)
1830 R. DOLBY *Cook's Dict.* 435/2 *Ravigote*, shred.. chervil, chives, pimpernel, and tarragon; this latter ought to predominate; (the mixture of these articles constitutes the *ravigote*); take some *velouté*,..add..butter and the *ravigote*; stir.., and serve. **1861** MRS. BEETON *Bk. Househ. Management.* 240 Ravigotte, a French Salad Sauce. **1877** E. S. DALLAS *Kettner's Bk. of Table* 373 *Ravigote*, pick-me-up.. from the French verb *ravigoter*, to cheer or strengthen... The French give the name of Ravigote to an assemblage of four herbs—tarragon, chervil, chives, burnet—minced small or used as a faggot, and supposed..to have a rare faculty of resuscitation. *Ibid.*, *Ravigote sauce* is simply the English butter sauce to which a ravigote is added. **1943** D. POWELL *Time to be Born* x. 255 A dish of crab meat ravigote. **1951** *Good Housek. Home Encycl.* 594/1 Serve with a ravigote sauce flavoured with chopped chives, chervil and tarragon. **1964** A. LAUNAY *Caviare & After* 142 *Ravigotte*, a highly-seasoned white sauce which is served either hot or cold. **1975** *Amer. Speech 1969* XLIV. 94 There is one instance of *ravigote*, but with two *t*'s, in *crabmeat ravigotte*..; it is 'a sauce or dressing coloured green with spinach purée and seasoned with vinegar and a mixture of herbs'.

ravin[1], **raven**[2]. **2. a.** (Example in spelling *raven.*)
1935 W. EMPSON *Poems* 4 Nor heeds if the core be brown with maggots' raven.

ravine, *sb.* Add: **3.** (Earlier and later examples.) Also *fig.*
1781 G. WASHINGTON *Diary* 30 Sept. (1925) II. 263 We also began two inclosed works on the right of Pidgeon Hill—between that and the Ravine above Moves Hill. **1926** [see *PEAK *sb.*[2] 5 c]. **1930** R. CAMPBELL *Adamastor* 51 The phosphorescent whales..Bore through the gloom their long ravines of gold.
4. *ravine-gully*; *ravine-wrinkled* adj.
a **1930** D. H. LAWRENCE *Etruscan Places* (1932) 22 A modest, Italian sort of ravine-gully. **1950** C. DAY LEWIS in *Penguin New Writing* XXXIX. 20 Earth's face grew rapidly older, ravine-wrinkled.

ravinement (rǎvī·nmĕnt). *Geol.* [a. F. *ravinement* gullying.] An unconformity in river or shallow marine sediments caused by interruption of deposition by erosion.
1921 L. D. STAMP in *Geol. Mag.* LVIII. 109 A 'ravinement' may be defined as an irregular junction which marks a break in sedimentation... Although one of the commonest of geological phenomena, there is no English word which expresses quite so aptly the relationship. *Ibid.*, The period between two successive 'ravinements' constitutes a 'cycle of sedimentation'. **1923** —— *Introd. Stratigr.* i. 17 When such an unconformity is traced laterally into a continuous series of marine deposits it is frequently found that, although the bedding of the upper series is parallel to that of the lower, there are signs that the sea, in depositing the upper series, has slightly eroded the top of the lower series. Such an erosion line is termed a 'ravinement'. **1969** BENNISON & WRIGHT *Geol. Hist. Brit. Isles* i. 8 In the field an unconformity can..be proved because the erosion surface or ravinement is conspicuous.

ravioli (rævi͵ōᵘ·li), *sb. pl.* [It., pl. of *raviolo* in the same sense: see RAVIOL.] Small square pasta cases filled with meat or vegetables.
1841 THACKERAY in *Fraser's Mag.* June 721/2 For the same money, I might have had..a heap of macaroni, or ravioli. **1846** DICKENS *Pictures from Italy* 47 Real Genoese dishes, such as Tagliarini; Ravioli..with fresh green figs. **1898** L. MERRICK *Actor Manager* 66 Oliphant was duly introduced to ravioli. **1947** H. INNES *Lonely Skier* i. 23 'No need to try and catch their eyes,' Joe Wesson said through a mouthful of *ravioli.* **1956** A. WILSON *Anglo-Saxon Att.* II. iii. 363 *Ravioli* was in preparation for dinner. **1969** B. MALAMUD *Pictures Fidelman* 160 The deaf woman was up and down to supply the glass blower with ravioli, cheese, bread. **1972** H. C. RAE *Shooting Gallery* IV. 247 She cooked up a tin of Ravioli, spiced it with Parmesan and mixed herbs. **1975** J. GORES *Hammett* xvi. 110 Soup to start. Ravioli. Salad after.

ravish, *v.* **2. b.** (Later examples.) Also *absol.*
1939 G. B. SHAW *Geneva* III. 70 Am I to allow him to kil me and ravish my wife and daughters? **1981** *Sunday Time* (Colour Suppl.) 8 Mar. 104 He ravished and pillaged..lef sons to hate him, women to fight over his wealth.

ravished, *ppl. a.* **2.** (Later examples.)
1901 G. B. SHAW *Caesar & Cleopatra* I. 102 A man come from the south with stealing steps, ravished by the myster of the night. **1953** R. LEHMANN *Echoing Grove* 22 Ravished startled, they watched the apparition wave up and down,. with rapid wing beats, low above the terraces.

raw, *a.* (*sb.*) Add: **A.** *adj.* **1. a.** Also, *rau milk.*
[**1743** W. ELLIS *Mod. Husbandman* July x. 48 If we mak raw Milk Cheese.] **1871** *N. & Q.* 4th Ser. VIII. 415, I thin that 'rammilk' is *rahm* milk—*i.e. cream* milk and not rav milk. **1950** *N.Z. Jrnl. Agric.* Mar. 221/2 Some doctors sa raw milk is better for health than pasteurised milk, so wh is to be believed? **1979** A. PARKER *Country Recipe Notebk* viii. 103 Raw milk ('farm milk') is at present officiall described as untreated milk.
f. Applied to the taste of tea: harsh, no mellow.
1881 *Tea Cycl.* III. 220/1 To obtain a raw, rasping an pungent flavor I am compelled to underferment, the indica tion of which is that the colour of infused leaves are of greenish brown tint. **1892** J. M. WALSH *Tea, its Hist. & Myst.* vii. 170 Ceylon and Javas are either 'raw', 'uncooked' .. or sour in flavour. **1933** C. R. HARLER *Culture & Mar keting of Tea* xiv. 278 The infused leaf of tea made fron under-withered leaf is generally *greenish.* The infusions fron such leaf are usually *raw* and *rasping.* **1958** T. EDEN *Te* xiv. 176 *Tea-Tasting Terms..Harsh, Raw, Rasping.* Bitter due to the presence of unfermented polyphenols; a commo defect of non-wither teas.
g. *raw humus*, vegetable matter not ye fully decomposed; incompletely formed humus.
1891 W. SCHLICH *Man. Forestry* II. i. 32 (*heading* Accumulation of raw humus. **1926** TANSLEY & CHIPP *Stud of Vegetation* vii. 117 In cold, moist soils poor in minera salts and acid in reaction..the leaf litter and other plan debris remain on the surface very little changed and ofte form a thick layer which is called raw humus. *Ibid.* 132 Th soil is covered with a thick layer of raw humus. **193** *Forestry* IX. 43 Raw humus is characterized by its excessiv accumulation (slow decomposition), expandibility, an frequently by the presence of some structural remains o plants... [It is] characterized also by an extremely low bas content. **1952** S. A. WAKSMAN *Soil Microbiol.* v. 136 I evergreen forests, the largely organic surface layers ar usually not mixed with the inorganic soil layers; the forme are referred to as the 'raw humus' or 'duff'. *Ibid.* 144 Th surface layer of the raw humus soil may undergo considerabl leaching. **1975** *Soil Sci.* XX. 25/1 The raw humus..ha been extracted successively with hexane, ether, an ethanol.
h. *to come the raw prawn*: see *PRAWN *sb.* 3 c.
2. a. *raw silk*, also, a fabric of spun silk; also *attrib.*
1866 A. D. WHITNEY in *Our Young Folks* Feb. 104 Two pairs of bright brown raw silk stockings..completed the mountain outfit. **1953** M. MCCARTHY in *Harper's Mag.* Mar 42/1, I was wearing a bright apple-green raw silk blouse. **1965** D. MACKENZIE *Lonely Side of River* i. 18 Raw-silk summer curtains rustled in the drawing room. **1978** *Observer* 29 Jan. 25/4 There are lots of clothes around made in what is loosely termed 'raw silk'. This is a misnomer as raw silk is actually the silk before it has been woven into fabric and what we call raw silk is actually a slub silk.
c. *rawhide* (earlier and later examples). Hence *rawhiding*, a whipping; also *fig.*; *rawhide* vb. trans., to whip; also *fig.*
1829 *Massachusetts Spy* 16 Sept. 2/4 She..took down a raw hide..and..kept the whip moving. **1848** *Knickerbocker* XVIII. 519 The editor, it was predicted, would catch a raw-hiding before sun-set. **1858** *Spirit of Times* 6 Feb. 356/3 One of our citizens was rawhided in the street.. by a Mr. Huntington. **1935** W. FAULKNER *As I lay Dying* 109 Like as not you got to take a rawhiding for thinking they meant it. **1935** H. L. DAVIS *Honey in Horn* viii. 100 He had been rawhided into a hunt that showed up his lack of endurance. **1944** H. EVATT *Snow Owl's Secret* 85 The huskies do like the sound of the singing rawhide. **1949** *Sat. Even. Post* 7 May 103/1 Joe went along as packer, rawhiding a string of bony horses up into the brownie country. **1979** *Tucson Mag.* Apr. 28/2 Sometimes the whole door was of rawhide.
attrib. (Earlier and later examples.) Also *fig.*
1841 G. CATLIN *Lett. on N. Amer. Indians* I. x. 71 The raw-hide thong, with which it was tied to a stake. **1883** SWEET & KNOX *On Mexican Mustang through Texas* i. 18 I'm just pining away for a fight. I'm a rawhide Texan, *I* am. **1897** *Slocan* (B.C.) *Pioneer* 8 May 1/2 A rawhide and pack trail has been constructed from the town of Brandon to the Two Friends mine. **1940** *Chambers's Techn. Dict.* 704/1 *Rawhide hammer*, a hammer the head of which consists of a close roll of hide projecting from a short steel tube; used by fitters to avoid injuring a finished surface. **1957** J. KEROUAC *On Road* (1958) iii. 21 Here came this rawhide old-timer Nebraska farmer. **1973** J. WAINWRIGHT *Devil you Don't* 14 The expensive, rawhide shirt. **1976** A. MURRAY *Stomping Blues* iv. 51 Down from the cloudlike realms of abstraction and fantasy to the bluesteel and rawhide textures of..the everyday struggle for existence.
d. Undistilled (water): delete † and add later examples; also, not filtered or otherwise treated; unrefined or partly refined (sugar),

undeveloped (land), (*N. Amer.*), untreated (sewage).

1797 Raw sugar [see SUGAR *sb.* 1 b]. **1868** *Chem. News* 20 Nov. 248/2 Several accidents happened; one..by which no less than 150,000 gallons of raw sewage were pumped into a tank holding 430,000 gallons of purified sewage. **1882** C. G. W. LOCK et al. *Sugar Growing & Refining* p. vii, Sugar-cane..is extensively cultivated, and the manufactured product, under the name of 'raw sugar', forms the staple produce of many of our colonies. **1883** SWEET & KNOX *On Mexican Mustang through Texas* xxi. 282 [He] came to Atascoso County, Texas, and bought a piece of raw land. **1925** G. FAIRRIE *Sugar* vii. 151 At the commencement of the nineteenth century the methods of converting the juice of the cane into raw sugar and the process of refining the raw sugar were very different from what they are to-day. **1930** *Engineering* 25 July 121/1 The net quantity of raw water distilled and passed into the feed line as make-up amounts to 1,138 tonnes per day. **1939** *Sun* (Baltimore) 11 Apr. 3/2 His agency is not interested in the price paid for the 'raw land' on which such developments were built. *Ibid.* 28 Sept. 12/1 The work might be done in part by carrying raw sewage lines to Colgate creek. **1956** *Jrnl. Amer. Water Works Assoc.* XLVIII. 1281 (*heading*) Relation of treatment methods to limits for coliform organisms in raw waters. **1958** Raw sewage [see *RECIRCULATE *v.*]. **1972** *Works Engineer* Nov./Dec. 32/1 Raw feed may contain domestic detergents, in which case, antifoaming agents must be added to the treated water. **1973** *Daily Colonist* (Victoria, B.C.) 7 July 3/1 Speculation in raw land is a major contributor to high housing costs..according to Mayor Art Phillips. **1976** *Chem. in Brit.* XII. 375/3 A recent exercise which nicely illustrates the applications of radiotracers in large systems was carried out, in a raw-water reservoir of capacity 3.10^6 m^3. **1978** *Daily Tel.* 7 July 19/1 The slide in the daily price of raw sugar on the London futures market continued yesterday. **1978** *Oxford Times* 15 Dec. 4/6 Raw sewage has been bubbling up through manhole covers.

e. *raw material* (further examples).

1864 J. H. NEWMAN *Apologia* VII. 392 The raw material of human nature. **1930** R. CAMPBELL *Poems* 12 Taking as raw material for his lays The good old English beer he loves to praise. **1971** I. G. GASS et al. *Understanding Earth* i. 26/2 The processes of erosion, which provide the raw materials of the sedimentary rocks.

f. Of measurements, data, or the like: not yet subjected to a process giving them significance; unadjusted; naïvely calculated.

1904 *Amer. Jrnl. Psychol.* XV. 263 Weight..has a raw correlation of 0.34, after correction we eventually get 0.43. **1920** YOAKUM & YERKES *Mental Tests* iii. 78 The result of examination alpha is expressed in a total score which is the sum of the raw scores of the several tests. **1945** *Jrnl. Exper. Psychol.* XXXV. 46 Only the general problems involved in the evaluation of the raw data will be treated in this paper. **1950** *Sun* (Baltimore) 11 May 4/3 McCarthy's frequent statements that the proof of his charges of Communist infestation in the State Department lies..in the 'raw files, of the FBI. **1954** A. ANASTASI *Psychol. Testing* ii. 24 The 'raw score' on the test..may be expressed as number of correct items, time required to complete a task, number of errors, or some other objective measure appropriate to the content of the test. Such a raw score is meaningless until evaluated in terms of a suitable set of norms. **1971** *World Archaeol.* III. 120 Naroll's formula..shows too much variation in raw numbers of population and square meters. **1974** *Nature* 1 Nov. 27/1 A raw spectrum was obtained by averaging the values for a given grating position weighted according to the reciprocal of their variances. **1975** *Ibid.* 31 Jan. 327/2 The raw magnetic field data are translated to a Jupiter centred spherical coordinate system. **1977** *Time* 4 Apr. 13/2 The console operators do not see a raw radar picture. The information is translated into digital bits and then filtered through complicated computer programming. **1978** *Daily Tel.* 16 Jan. 2/1 Sir Charles..said he had been given warnings as far back as April about the deteriorating situation but had not been prepared to release what he felt were 'raw' forecasts about losses.

g. Of manufactured material: unused.

1917 BENNETT & HERON *Guide to Kinematogr.* i. 12 Raw stock is divided broadly into two classes, Ordinary and Non Flam. **1934** *Tit-Bits* 31 Mar. 12/2 Exposed film is 'stuff'; unexposed film is 'raw stock'. **1968** *Globe & Mail* (Toronto) 3 Feb. 27/3 She paints on the floor of her..studio, beginning with raw canvas. **1971** W. G. SALM *Stereo in your Home* xii. 168 Prerecorded open-reel tape production line in Ampex plant records all four tracks simultaneously, taking raw tape from large blank pancake. **1973** *Center City Office Weekly* (Philadelphia) 9 Oct. 5 We could not shoot today. No money to buy the raw stock film. **1979** *N. & Q.* Aug. 348/2 Print-outs from the raw text tapes.

h. Of a glaze: (see quot. 1934).

1934 WEBSTER, *Raw glaze*, a glaze made from materials which need no preparation, but can be bought ready for use. **1964** H. HODGES *Artifacts* ii. 46 Any glaze in which the raw materials are simply ground up and applied in this way is called a raw glaze.

3. a. *raw sienna, umber*, sienna and umber which have not been calcined; also, the colours of these pigments; *raw deal*: see *DEAL *sb.*[2] 4 c; *raw edge*, the unfinished edge of a cut piece of fabric; also *fig.*; (cf. *raw-edged*, sense 9 in Dict. and Suppl.).

1869 *Bradshaw's Railway Man.* XXI. 460/1 (Advt.), Raw Turk. Umb. **1886** H. C. STANDAGE *Artists' Man. Pigments* iv. 43 *Yellow ochres* (these include Jaune de Mars, Sienna, or Raw Sienna). *c* **1890** tr. *T. de Dillmont's Encycl. Needlework* 6 Rounded seam.—Back-stitch your two edges together.. then..roll the outer one in, with the left thumb, till the raw edge is quite hidden, hemming as you roll. **1895** *Montgomery Ward Catal.* Spring & Summer 252/3 Artists tube oil colors... Prussian blue. Raw sienna. Raw umber. Roman ochre. **1906** R. FRY *Let.* 17 Apr. (1972) I. 263, I did the wood-work in one coat, pure raw umber and white over a burnt sienna stain. **1908** M. MORGAN *How to dress Doll* ii. 20 Overcasting is only used to keep raw edges on a seam.. from fraying. **1948** F. A. STAPLES *Watercolour Paintings* (1951) iv. 49 *Raw sienna.* Bright yellow with slight reddish tone. Transparent. **1951** R. MAYER *Artist's Handbk.* ii. 59 *Raw umber...* Its composition is similar to that of sienna but it contains no manganese. A dark brown, its tones vary from greenish or yellowish to violet-brown. **1978** *Detroit Free Press* 5 Mar. D9/1 Stitch a one-inch hem on each side, turning under raw edge. **1979** A. V. BADGLEY *Rembrandt Decisions* (1980) viii. 108 Hot cups of coffee..slowly salved the raw edges of Duncan Forbes' departure.

c. *Psychol. raw feel*, a term for the immediate impression evoked by a stimulus, prior to conscious evaluation.

1932 E. C. TOLMAN *Purposive Behavior in Animals & Men* 250 The dyed-in-the-wool mentalist will again protest. Such discrimination-box experiments..will not and cannot convey what may be called the 'raw feel' of these discriminanda. *Ibid.* 452 *Raw feel*, a name for the peculiar *quale* of experience. **1950** *Mind* LIX. 174 What a psychology of discriminations leaves out..he calls 'raw feels'. **1956** MEEHL & SELLARS in Feigl & Scriven *Minnesota Stud. Philos. Sci.* I. 249 To suppose that 'raw feels' as we shall call them, will be found to be emergent..is to suppose that raw feels..are the *a*'s and *b*'s in the *generalized* function. **1969** H. D. LEWIS *Elusive Mind* ix. 181 There seems, in short, to be some 'immediate data of first person experience..(e.g. directly experienced sensations, thoughts, feelings..etc.)'. These are also described in many places as 'raw feels', a somewhat inelegant but suggestive term made popular, I believe, by Professor R. W. Sellars.

6. e. Of a person: naked (esp. when sleeping). *colloq.*

1931 D. RUNYON in *Hearst's International* May 64/2 He puts her in the 'Vanities' and lets her walk around raw. **1952** M. R. RINEHART *Swimming Pool* xx. 185 Or maybe she sleeps raw. **1962** J. F. STRAKER *Coil of Rope* vii. 69 Did I shock you? I always sleep raw. **1974** H. WAUGH *Parrish for Defence* (1975) lxvii. 309 She didn't own any night-gowns. She slept raw.

9. *raw-edged* (earlier and later examples), *-jawed, -ribbed* (later example), *-seamed, -skinned, -smelling* adjs.

1828 W. CARR *Dial. Craven* (ed. 2) II. 75 *Raw-edg'd*, not hemmed, without a selfedge. **1920** E. SITWELL *Wooden Pegasus* 105 Where raw-edged shadows sting forlorn As dank dark nettles. **1972** *Ulster* (Sunday Times Insight Team) ix. 151 How raw-edged the relationship was..was demonstrated by..the first Army 'victory' in Ulster. **1932** *Flynn's* 24 Dec. 136/1 They..resort to what they call a 'cold-turkey' heel or a 'raw-jawed clout'... They refer to the act of going into a store and carrying out several articles without using any finesse at all. **1967** R. LOWELL *Near Ocean* 13 The chinook Salmon..Raw-jawed, weak-fleshed. **1922** BLUNDEN *Shepherd* 81 The young black heifer and the raw-ribbed mare. **1957** T. HUGHES *Hawk in Rain* 51 Suddenly he awoke and was running-raw In raw-seamed hot khaki. **1922** JOYCE *Ulysses* 233 A rawskinned crown, scantily haired. **1906** *Macmillan's Mag.* Apr. 476 Next morning I woke in the raw-smelling dawn, feeling like a corpse.

B. *sb.* **2. a.** *on the raw* (further *fig.* examples). *in the raw* (see quot. 1934); also, naked.

1915 W. S. MAUGHAM *Of Human Bondage* 71 He had a knack of saying bitter things, which caught people on the raw. **1926** A. BENNETT *Lord Raingo* II. lxxiv. 341 What got 'im on the raw was Tommy Hogarth going against 'im in that business. **1934** WEBSTER s.v. Raw n., *In the raw*, in one's natural or crude state; hence, in one's or its true nature or character; in naked truth; as, to present life in the raw. **1941** B. SCHULBERG *What makes Sammy Run?* viii. 188 To go swimming in the raw. **1942** *R.A.F. Jrnl.* 27 June 24 There is a long tale of other victims of nature in the raw. **1944** E. WAUGH *Diary* 16 Apr. (1976) 561 Auberon surprised her in her bath and is thus one of the very few men who can claim to have seen his great-great-grandmother in the raw. **1959** *Times* 9 Nov. 6/7 That is an argument which gets me very much on the raw. **1961** NEW ENG. BIBLE *Acts* v. 33 This touched them on the raw, and they wanted to put them to death. **1970** V. CANNING *Great Affair* iv. 68 As Xavier's pyjamas were much too small for me I slept in the raw. **1972** L. P. DAVIES *What did I do Tomorrow?* vii. 93 My, my. Village life in the raw.

c. *the raws*, the bare fists. *slang.*

1899 C. ROOK *Hooligan Nights* ii. 27 The average Hooligan ..has usually done a bit of fighting with the gloves... But he is better with the raws.

3. Also *transf.*

1928 *Daily Mail* 16 Aug. 19/3, I am not at all sure that here is not a star in the raw.

4. a. Also *Comb.* in **raw bar** *U.S.*, a bar selling raw oysters.

1943 *Sun* (Baltimore) 5 Oct. 16/6 The boys at the raw bar in the end of Bill's place last night said the way oysters are this season a feller'll have to eat shells and all to get a mess. **1973** *Washington D.C. Yellow Pages* 1314 Chuck O'Brien's Riverboat. Featuring fine seafood and steaks. Informal raw bar. Cocktail lounge.

Rawang (răwæ·ŋ). [Native name.] A Tibeto-Burman language.

1934 J. T. O. BARNARD *Handbk. of Răwang Dial. of Nung Lang.* p. v, This is the first book on the Nung language, which has many dialects, of which, however, Răwang may be taken as the one most commonly spoken. **1954** E. R. LEACH *Polit. Syst. Highland Burma* iii. 45 *Nung*—several distinct dialects. Rawang and Daru dialects said to be mutually unintelligible. **1964** E. A. NIDA *Toward Sci. Transl.* ix. 202 In Rawang, a language of Burma, a somewhat similar distinction between dead and alive is employed, but with special restrictions. **1976** *Sci. Amer.* Oct. 140/1 A translator has had to restate most of them, from the Japanese or the Xhosa or the Rawang ('just one of hundreds of Tibeto-Burman languages spoken').

raw-boned, *a.* Add: Also *transf.*

1802 C. WILMOT *Let.* 19 Oct. in T. V. Sadleir *Irish Peer* (1920) 102 A cold wild desolate country bare and rawboned. **1886** W. MORRIS *Let.* 23 June in Mackail *Life Morris* (1899) II. xvi. 161 Stirling..a very raw-boned town.

raw-head[1]. (Earlier and later *attrib.* examples.)

1823 SCOTT *St. Ronan's Well* II. vi. 110 Tell a raw-head-and-bloody-bone story about a footpad. **1918** [see *FUNK-HOLE].

rawin (rē^{i}·win). *Meteorol.* [f. *RA(DAR + WIN(D *sb.*[1]] A determination of the atmospheric wind speed and direction made by tracking a balloon-borne target with radar; also *transf.*, the instrument itself.

1946 *Bull. Amer. Meteorol. Soc.* XXVII. 371/1 A system of obtaining winds-aloft reports by electronic means known as rawins is now gaining great favor. **1948** T. A. BLAIR *Weather Elements* (ed. 3) iii. 70 By the use of radar methods developed during World War II, a balloon carrying a radar target (reflector) can be followed through and above the clouds, making possible the determination of upper-air wind direction and force in all kinds of weather... Such soundings are known as rawins. **1951** *Jrnl. Meteorol.* VIII. 126/1 Monthly resultant rawins for 24 United States stations were obtained for the layer surface to 10,000 ft and for the 10,000-ft level. **1967** R. W. FAIRBRIDGE *Encycl. Atmospheric Sci.* 581/1 It [*sc.* a radiosonde] consists of a small radio transmitter sent aloft by a helium or hydrogen-filled balloon which transmits the values of the meteorological elements in code to ground stations. If the instrument is tracked by radar to determine wind speed and direction aloft, it is called a rawin. If the two are combined in one, it is called a rawinsonde. **1979** C. KILIAN *Icequake* vi. 103 A few tractors and a collapsed rawin tower were all that was left of the station.

rawinsonde (rē^{i}·winsǫnd). *Meteorol.* [f. prec. + *SONDE.] A balloon-borne device comprising a radiosonde and a radar target which both transmits meteorological data to ground stations and permits rawin observations to be made, freq. applied to the balloon and instrument package combined.

1946 *Bull. Amer. Meteorol. Soc.* XXVII. 371/1 The recent trend in practice is to combine radiosonde observations and winds-aloft observations in one operation, a Rawinsonde. **1955** *Sci. News Let.* 24 Sept. 197/1 Equipment the Weather Bureau plans to purchase includes:..sixty-five new rawinsondes, to measure winds aloft, including the 200-mile-per-hour river of air known as the jet stream. **1959** *Jrnl. Geophysical Res.* LXIV. 1835 Because of the great altitude of the core of the 'polar-night' jet stream, only isolated rawinsonde observations have penetrated the core. **1970** *Jrnl. Atmospheric Sci.* XXVII. 420/1 Sufficient information content exists within the operational U.S. rawinsonde network to resolve the three-dimensional structure of frontal zones. **1975** *Q. Jrnl. R. Meteorol. Soc.* CI. 336 The rainfall patterns are interpreted within a framework provided by routine upper air data supplemented by long sequences of nominally 1-hourly rawinsondes.

rawky, *a.*[2] (later examples.)

1935 E. R. EDDISON *Mistress of Mistresses* x. 194 The air between the cliffs, ruffled in mists and rawky vapours. **1936** J. G. HORNE *Flooer o' Ling* 22 Or rawky day creeps up the sky.

Rawlplug (rǭ·lplɒg), *sb.* and *v.* Also **Rawl-plug,** and with small initial. [f. the name of J. J. and W. R. *Rawl*ings, English electrical engineers, who introduced it + PLUG *sb.*] **A.** *sb.* A proprietary name for a kind of thin cylindrical plug, made of fibre or plastic, which can be inserted into a hole in masonry, etc., in order to hold a screw or nail. Also applied *loosely* to any plug of this type.

1912 *Trade Marks Jrnl.* 30 Oct. 1648 *Rawlplug...* A wall plug for electric wiring made of fibre. Rawlings Bros., Limited, 82, Gloucester Rd., London, S.W.; Electrical engineers. **1923** *Radio Times* 28 Sept. 35/1 For any job connected with Wireless where you use a screw..always use Rawlplugs. **1941** M. TREADGOLD *We couldn't leave Dinah* vii. 124 The shelf for brushes that Nick Lindsay had fixed up with rawl-plugs. **1947** 'G. ORWELL' in *Tribune* 7 Feb. 12/1 The amateur handyman, with his tack hammer and his pocketful of rawlplugs. **1960** WILLMOTT & YOUNG *Family & Class in London Suburb* ii. 24 Her role is..to stand at the bottom of a ladder handing up his power-tool..or a box of Rawlplugs. **1962** H. THURSTON *Where is thy Sting?* iv. 55 A long panel of looking-glass which Philippa had fixed with rawlplugs on one side of the fireplace. **1972** D. HASTON *In High Places* i. 9 The climber drills a hole in the rock, hammers in an expansion bolt (something like the domestic Rawlplug), attaches a carabiner and proceeds in normal fashion.

Also **Rawl**, a proprietary term used *attrib.* or as a prefix in names of tools, screws, bolts, and related accessories.

1937 *Trade Marks Jrnl.* 29 Sept. 1151 *Rawl...* Cutlery and edge tools. The Rawlplug Company Limited. **1958** *Engineering* 14 Feb. 54 (Advt.), The holes are drilled with a Rawltool to the exact size, the Rawlbolts dropped in and after the machine has been positioned the bolts are tightened. **1971** C. BONINGTON *Annapurna South Face* 246 American rawl stud bolts for hard rock. **1976** *Shooting Mag.* Dec. 9/1 (Advt.), The cabinet has been designed for fixing to the wall by means of three Rawlbolts through strengthening bars.

B. *v. trans.* To attach by means of a Rawlplug or the like; to drill a hole in (a wall, etc.) and insert a Rawlplug. Hence **ra·wlplugging** *vbl. sb.*

1960 'A. BURGESS' *Right to Answer* i. 5 He'd rawlplugged his pictures..deep into the walls. **1964** E. & M. A. RADFORD *Hungry Killer* xiv. 133 The bookcase, Rawlplugged to the wall. **1971** *Ideal Home* Apr. 52/1 Brass hooks rawlplugged to the wall hold it in place. **1972** R. QUILTY *Tenth Session* 92 You should have Rawl-plugged the wall. You're cracking the plaster. **1974** M. BUTTERWORTH *Man in Sopwith Camel* i. 17 Plastering, paperhanging, rawlplugging, joinering.

rawly, *adv.* Add: **4.** (Later examples.)

1955 E. BLISHEN *Roaring Boys* II. 99 For..two years I had been rawly warring with my classes. **1979** *Chatelaine* Jan. 64/3 The secret realm in which their love flowered—so rawly, with such unanticipated greed!

5. So as to be bare or exposed.

1924 'L. MALET' *Dogs of Want* ix. 270 Every nerve of his body seeming rawly outside his skin instead of normally and decently covered by it.

raxed, *ppl. a.* (Later example.)

1898 N. MUNRO *John Splendid* xv. 147 A raxed shoulder he had met with at Dumbarton.

raxing, *vbl. sb.* and *ppl. a.* (Later examples.)

1876 C. C. ROBINSON *Gloss. Mid-Yorks.* 110/2 A person will tell of 'a nasty raxin' pain' he is subject to. **1893** R. L. STEVENSON *Catriona* I. xiii. 143 My craig'll have to thole a raxing. **1935** A. J. CRONIN *Stars look Down* I. ix. 67 What he did mind was the bother when a tub ran off; it nearly killed him, the raxing and straining to lift it back upon the line.

ray, *sb.*[1] Add: **I. 1. a.** Fig. phr. (*little*) *ray of sunshine*, a person (freq. a young woman) who enlivens or cheers another; a happy or vivacious person. Cf. SUNSHINE *sb.* 2 a.

1915 A. BENNETT *These Twain* (1916) xx. 485 You're a little ray of sunshine, and all that, and I'm the first to say so. **1929** J. B. PRIESTLEY *Good Companions* II. iv. 364 Why are you now our little ray of sunshine? **1959** M. SCOTT *White Elephant* v. 56 Are you two in this to make money or just to be little rays of sunshine? **1972** C. FREMLIN *Appointment with Yesterday* iv. 31 Milly rather fancied herself in the rôle of little ray of sunshine to brighten his declining years. **1978** 'M. M. KAYE' *Far Pavilions* xxxvii. 540 He hasn't exactly been a ray of sunshine up to now.

5. c. Chiefly *Science Fiction*. A supposed destructive beam of energy emitted by a ray-gun or similar device. Cf. *death-ray* s.v. *DEATH *sb.* 19.

1898 H. G. WELLS *War of Worlds* vi. 39 Only the fact that a hummock of heathery sand intercepted the lower part of the Heat-Ray saved them. **1919** G. B. SHAW *Heartbreak House* 39, I will discover a ray mightier than any X-ray: a mind ray that will explode the ammunition in the belt of my adversary before he can point his gun at me. **1926** G. HUNTING *Vicarion* xiii. 215 I'm glad they never perfected that ray they used to talk about for disposing of an enemy at a distance without betraying the disposer. **1940** GRAVES & HODGE *Long Week-End* vi. 93 An inventor..claimed to have produced a ray that would set fire to anything inflammable. **1969** E. VON DANIKEN *Chariots of Gods?* ii. 25 They will hammer and chisel in the rock pictures of what they had once seen: Shapeless giants,..staves from which rays are shot out as if from a sun.

8. c. (Later examples.)

1925 EAMES & MACDANIELS *Introd. Plant Anat.* vii. 176 The ray is more or less like a brick wall, the individual cells representing the bricks. **1953** K. ESAU *Plant Anat.* xi. 252 The dicotyledons typically contain only parenchyma cells in the rays.

9*. *Astr.* Any of the long bright lines of pale material that can be seen to radiate from some lunar craters.

1838 J. P. NICHOL *Phenomena & Order Solar Syst.* II. vi. 171 The most remarkable circumstance connected with this variety in the Moon's shining power is those rays issuing chiefly from craters and extending over a large space. **1873** R. A. PROCTOR *Moon* iv. 253 The telescope..has discovered numerous small craters of varying depth in the midst of many of the rays, and it reveals the fact, that these small craters..do not penetrate through the matter we are examining, inasmuch as there comes from their bases always the same kind of light that characterizes the ray. **1895** T. G. ELGER *Moon* 27 The rays emanating from Tycho surpass in extent and interest any of the others. **1922** H. S. JONES *Gen. Astron.* iv. 102 From some of the craters, under favourable conditions of illumination, bright rays or streaks can be seen radiating radially in all directions. **1962** *Listener* 1 Feb. 223/2 The mysterious lunar rays issuing from Tycho, Copernicus, and other craters also fit better into an igneous theory. The rays cross mountains, walled formations, ridges, and seas without marked deviation.

10. a. *ray-shorn* adj.

1872 GEO. ELIOT *Middlem.* II. xxxvii. 265 The other great dread—of himself becoming dimmed and for ever ray-shorn in her eyes.

b. In sense 8 c, as *ray cell, initial, tracheid.*

1907 D. P. PENHALLOW *Man. N. Amer. Gymnosperms* v. 83 Pits on the lateral walls of the ray cells are an invariable feature of all investigated species of..Coniferales. **1933** *Forestry* VII. 93 It is essential to study..the development of the ray cells in the wood. **1953** K. ESAU *Plant Anat.* vi. 126 The ray initials give origin to the ray cells. **1975** *Sci. Amer.* July 102/2 Among the components of the cambium are what are called ray initials; the continuation of a ray initial down into the sapwood of a stem, a branch or a trunk is known as a wood ray. **1907** D. P. PENHALLOW *Man. N. Amer. Gymnosperms* vi. 88 In the higher Coniferæ the medullary ray is distinguished by the presence of an element which differs materially in its structure from the associated parenchyma cells. These elements have been designated as ray tracheids. **1940** BROWN & PANSHIN *Comm. Timbers U.S.* vii. 128 Ray tracheids attain their best development in the genus *Pinus*. **1956** F. W. JANE *Structure of Wood* v. 91 Ray tracheids often form the marginal cells of the rays.

c. In sense 9 a, *ray-finned* adj.

1933 A. S. ROMER *Vertebr. Paleontol.* iv. 85 That [*sc.* the history] of the later ray-finned fishes has no such interest. **1968** [see *lung-fish* s.v. *LUNG *sb.* 7]. **1970** R. M. BLACK *Elements Palaeont.* xvii. 249 The ray-finned fish have had an expansionist evolution.

d. ray blight, a fungus disease of chrysanthemums caused by *Ascochyta chrysanthemi*, which attacks the flowers, causing discoloration and shrivelling of the petals; **ray diagram**, a diagram showing the paths of light rays through an optical system; **ray-fin**, a fish belonging to the subclass Actinopterygii, to which most living bony fish belong and which includes those having thin fan-like fins with dermal rays; **ray fleck**, the marking caused by the exposure of a ray in sawn timber; **ray gun**, a hand-held device that can be made to emit rays, esp. (in *Science Fiction*) destructive or harmful ones; **ray therapy treatment**, the treatment of disease with radiation; radiotherapy; **ray-tracing**, the calculation of the path taken by a ray of light through an optical system.

1907 F. S. STEVENS in *Bot. Gaz.* XLIV. 241 The Chrysanthemum Ray Blight... The common name chosen for the disease..is taken from the most conspicuous symptom of the malady, a blighting of the corolla. **1961** *Amat. Gardening* 21 Oct. 6/2 Ray blight is much less common than the other two bloom diseases. **1965** NAKAJIMA & YOUNG *Art of Chrysanthemum* vii. 81 If the ray blight is not checked, it may continue on to destroy all blooms in the immediate area. **1980** J. W. HILL *Intermediate Physics* xii. 123 Draw two ray diagrams to show how a real and virtual image may be obtained of an object placed the same distance away from two different mirrors. **1945** A. S. ROMER *Vertebr. Paleontol.* (ed. 2) v. 89 Most of the more characteristic Paleozoic ray-fins were once assigned to *Palaeoniscus*. **1963** P. H. GREENWOOD *Norman's Hist. Fishes* (ed. 2) xvii. 306 The Bony Fishes can be divided into three main groups or subclasses: Actinopterygii (ray-fins), Crossopterygii (fringe-fins) and Dipneusti (lung-fishes). **1934** BROWN & PANSHIN *Identification Comm. Timbers U.S.* 211 Ray fleck: a portion of a ray as it appears on the quarter surface. **1940** —— *Comm. Timbers U.S.* viii. 201 Some woods possess low, closely spaced, but relatively conspicuous ray flecks. **1968** *Canad. Antiques Collector* July 26/1 Quarter sawed figure is characterised by the annual growth rings appearing as parallel stripes and by the appearance of rays on the surface. In such woods as oak and chestnut these rays are called ray fleck or flake. **1931** *Amazing Stories* Dec. 804/1 The rayguns of the battlecraft, being of superior range, melted down the mortars of the fort at the magazine. **1951** A. C. CLARKE *Sands of Mars* iv. 40 It was a modified air pistol... 'If you say it's like a ray-gun I'll certify you.' **1957** [see *BUG-EYED *a.*]. **1958** *Spectator* 19 Sept. 379/1 But as a space-veteran who once triggered a ray-gun with Flash Gordon, let me advise you to read on. **1967** *Autocar* 28 Dec. 29/3 As the car nears each set of lamps a patrolman..points the ray gun at the cell situated between the two lamps. A beamed radio signal from the gun activates the fog warning lamp switch. **1977** W. MCILVANNEY *Laidlaw* xxvi. 116 It was a beautiful smile... It hit Harkness like a ray-gun and he felt his concentration atomise. **1928** *Daily Express* 20 Dec. 8/3 When the phrase 'ray-therapy' crept into one of the royal bulletins, I heard educated persons explaining that it meant treatment by wireless! **1943** *Gloss. Terms Electr. Engin.* (*B.S.I.*) 144 *Radio-therapy*, [deprecated synonym] *ray therapy*, the treatment of diseases by radiation. **1918** L. SILBERSTEIN *Simplified Method of tracing Rays* p. v, Our purpose is not to treat the whole subject of geometrical optics, but..that part of it which is called by the short name of 'ray tracing'... Given the ray incident upon any system of lenses..find the emergent ray. **1943** D. H. JACOBS *Fund. Optical Engin.* xxiv. 381 Ray-tracing equations are all derived from one *exact* law: Snell's law. **1974** W. T. WELFORD *Aberrations of Symmetrical Optical Syst.* iii. 41 This process of finding a ray path in terms of the numerical values of the incidence heights and convergence angles at each surface in turn is called raytracing. **1904** *Science Siftings* 12 Mar. 320/2 The Finsen light concentrates as much violet rays as can be found in a hundred square feet of sunlight. The same principle enters into all ray treatment. **1905** *Westm. Gaz.* 4 May 12/2 Six patients suffering from skin diseases..died after the ray-treatment.

Ray (rēⁱ). The name of the English naturalist, John *Ray* (1627–1705), used in the possessive to designate **Ray's bream,** a deep-bodied, dark brown and silver, European, marine fish, *Brama brama* (formerly *B. raii*), of the family Bramidæ, which was named in his honour by M. E. Bloch (*Ichtyologie* (1797) VII. 75).

1836 W. YARRELL *Hist. Brit. Fishes* I. 117 Ray's Bream.. appears to have been less perfectly known to the older writers than might have been expected. **1925** J. T. JENKINS *Fishes Brit. Isles* 74 Ray's Bream is a fish of characteristic appearance, with a body elevated and compressed, and a very long dorsal fin. **1959** A. C. HARDY *Open Sea* II. x. 208 This species should not be confused with Ray's bream.. which has also been called the black sea-bream. **1969** A. WHEELER *Fishes Brit. Isles & N.-W. Europe* 339/2 Ray's bream has little commercial value in northern waters though its flesh is very palatable.

ray, *v.*[1] Add: **4. a.** (Later examples.)

1899 P. H. WICKSTEED tr. *Dante's Paradiso* 341 A point I saw which rayed forth light. **1922** E. R. EDDISON *Worm Ouroboros* xxx. 372 Yellow flames of candles..on either side of the mirror rayed forth tresses of tinselling brightness.

6. *trans.* To treat with, or examine by means of, X-rays or other invisible radiation.

1921 *Science* 23 Sept. 278/1 The total number of offspring by the pairs in which the females were rayed..was 2460. **1933** *Discovery* Feb. 46/2 Tissues taken from an animal which had been rayed [with doses of Gamma rays]. **1955** *Proc. Nat. Acad. Sci.* XLI. 155 The *Tradescantia* microspore chromosomes react..as double threads when rayed at prophase.

raying *vbl. sb.*[1] (further examples, without *out*).

1921 *Science* 23 Sept. 278/1 Eggs which were laid during the first six days after raying and mating. **1933** *Discovery* Feb. 46/2 The dose of gamma rays needed to kill a culture at once..is enormous, and as the dose decreases the interval between the raying and the death of the culture becomes larger. **1955** *Proc. Nat. Acad. Sci.* XLI. 150 Accurate analysis of chromosomal aberrations could not be made until about 6 hours after raying.

rayed, *ppl. a.*[1] Add: **2.** = *IRRADIATED *ppl. a.* 1 c.

1921 *Science* 23 Sept. 277/2 Wild type (red-eyed) females ..were X-rayed... Sisters of the rayed females were used as controls. **1938** HEVESY & PANETH *Man. Radioactivity* xxiv. 245 The rayed rock-salt assumes a blue-violet colour.

rayed, *ppl. a.*[3] (Later *arch.* or *poet.* examples.)

1905 W. H. HUNT *Pre-Raphaelitism* I. 163 From the depth of this rayed region we ascended to the further margin of the mist lake into the crystal air. **1918** W. STEVENS in *Others* Dec. 11 We hang like warty squashes, streaked and rayed.

ray·ing, *ppl. a.* [f. RAY *v.*[1] + -ING[2].] **a.** Moving in rays. **b.** Emitting rays; radiating.

1891 G. MEREDITH *One of our Conq.* III. vii. 131 Popular artists..have figured in scenes of battle the raying fragments of a man from impact of a cannon-ball on his person. **1905** *Westm. Gaz.* 25 Apr. 2/3 The day That crowns us royal with the raying sun.

rayl (rēⁱl). *Acoustics.* [f. *RAYL(EIGH.] A unit of specific acoustic impedance equal to one dyne-second/cm.^{3} (in the C.G.S. system) or one newton-second/m.^{3} (in the S.I.).

1954 L. L. BERANEK *Acoustics* i. 11 The specific acoustic impedance is the complex ratio of the effective sound pressure at a point of an acoustic medium or mechanical device to the effective particle velocity at that point. The unit is newton-sec/m^3, or the mks rayl. (In the cgs system the unit is dyne-sec/cm^3, or the rayl.) **1971** W. W. SETO *Schaum's Outl. Theory & Probl. Acoustics* ii. 40 At standard atmospheric pressure and 20 °C..the characteristic impedance of air is..415 rayls.

Rayleigh (rēⁱ·li). *Physics.* [The title of J. W. Strutt, 3rd Lord *Rayleigh* (1842–1919), English physicist.] **1.** Used, usu. *attrib.*, to designate various concepts, devices, and phenomena he invented or investigated, as **Rayleigh('s) criterion,** the criterion by which adjacent lines or rings of equal intensity in a diffraction pattern are regarded as resolved when the central maximum of one coincides with the first minimum of the other; **Rayleigh disc,** a lightweight disc suspended by a fine thread so that when it is placed at an angle to incident sound waves their intensity can be calculated from the measured torque on the disc; **Rayleigh instability** (see quot. 1977); also called *Rayleigh–Taylor instability* [Sir Geoffrey *Taylor* (1886–1975), English mathematician]; **Rayleigh limit,** the upper limit of a quarter of a wavelength placed on the difference between the optical paths of the longest and shortest rays of those going to form an image in order that the definition shall be close to the ideal (which corresponds to no path difference); **Rayleigh number,** a dimensionless parameter that is a measure of the instability of a layer of fluid due to differences of temperature and density at the top and bottom (see quot. 1950); **Rayleigh scattering,** the scattering of light by particles small compared with its wavelength, the intensity of the scattered light being inversely proportional to the fourth power of the wavelength (and therefore much greater for blue light than for red); so **Rayleigh-scattered** *a.*; **Rayleigh wave,** a type of wave that travels over the surface of a solid with a speed independent of its wavelength, the motion of the particles being in ellipses so that the surface undulates.

1937 JENKINS & WHITE *Fund. Physical Optics* v. 123 Extending Rayleigh's criterion for the resolution of diffraction patterns..to the circular aperture, two patterns are said to be resolved when the central maximum of one falls on the first dark ring of the other. *Ibid.* vii. 159 The Rayleigh criterion for resolving of images. **1970** D. W. Tenquist et al. *University Optics* II. v. 197 The chromatic resolving power of a prism, defined as $\lambda/\delta\lambda$ where $\delta\lambda$ is the smallest change of wavelength discernable [*sic*] in accordance with the Rayleigh criterion at a mean wavelength λ, is given by [etc.]. **1913** *Physical Rev.* I. 309 (*heading*) A method of producing known relative sound intensities and a test of the Rayleigh disk. **1972** J. M. Taylor tr. *Meyer & Neumann's Physical & Appl. Acoustics* vi. 209 The Rayleigh disk..is practically never used any more to determine particle velocity, which can be derived much more quickly and conveniently from electroacoustic sound pressure measuring devices. **1961** S. Chandrasekher *Hydrodynamic & Hydromagnetic Stability* x. 428 An important special case ..is that of two fluids of different densities superposed one over the other (or accelerated towards each other); the instability of the plane interface between the two fluids, when it occurs (particularly in the second context), is called Rayleigh–Taylor instability. **1971** I. G. Gass et al. *Understanding Earth* xix. 277/1 A Rayleigh instability..does not necessarily depend upon the existence of a density inversion. .. Where the depth of the fluid is very large, the fluid at the bottom is compressed by the overlying fluid and, in many cases, an instability develops before the temperature is high enough to produce a density inversion. **1977** *Sci. Amer.* Oct. 144/2 The instability at the interface between a denser fluid overlying a lighter fluid, when the interface is otherwise in hydrostatic equilibrium, is called a Rayleigh instability (or sometimes a Rayleigh–Taylor instability). **1923** Glazebrook *Dict. Appl. Physics* IV. 216/1 The adoption of the Rayleigh limit thus makes it possible considerably to increase the aperture of a lens system of any given type and to come close to the full theoretical resolving power with systems which, judged geometrically, would appear hopelessly over- or under-corrected. **1976** *Sci. Amer.* Aug. 77/2 Ideally a lens should be at the Rayleigh limit for light of all wavelengths. **1950** O. G. Sutton in *Proc. R. Soc.* A. CCIV. 298 The existence of a sustained convective regime depends upon the value of the non-dimensional quantity $Ra = -\beta g\alpha h^4/\kappa v$, which we shall call the Rayleigh number. **1980** *Sci. Amer.* July 82/2 Convection begins when the Rayleigh number exceeds a critical value. **1971** *Physics Bull.* July 387/1 More detailed studies of the linewidths of Rayleigh scattered lines can provide hitherto inaccessible information on the behaviour of fluids near their critical point or in the neighbourhood of phase transitions. **1937** Jenkins & White *Fund. Physical Optics* xii. 280 The first quantitative study of the laws of scattering by small particles was made in 1871 by Lord Rayleigh, and such scattering is frequently called Rayleigh scattering. **1973** C. Sagan *Cosmic Connection* (1975) xiii. 90 The beauty of the sunset, the sky, and distant landscapes are all due to Rayleigh scattering. **1920** A. E. H. Love *Treat. Math. Theory Elasticity* (ed. 3) xiii. 313 The waves travel over the surface with a velocity, which is independent of the wave-length $2\pi/f$, and slightly less than the velocity of equivoluminal waves propagated through the body. Waves of this kind are often called 'Rayleigh-waves'. **1956** J. C. Jaeger *Elasticity, Fracture & Flow* iii. 135 Rayleigh waves are not the only simple type of surface wave which can be predicted and identified. **1971** I. G. Gass et al. *Understanding Earth* xxiv. 336/1 (*caption*) A Rayleigh wave from an earthquake in Columbia recorded in Montana.

2. *Astr.* Also **rayleigh.** A unit of luminous intensity equal to one million photons per square centimetre per second.

1956 D. M. Hunter et al. in *Jrnl. Atmospheric & Terrestrial Physics* VIII. 345 We suggest that $4\pi B$ be given the unit of 'rayleigh' (symbol *R*), where *B* is in units of 10^6 quanta/cm² sec sterad. Hence $1R = 10^6$ quanta/cm² (column) sec. (The word 'column' is often inserted into these units to convey the concept of an emission-rate from a column of unspecified length). **1970** *Nature* 2 May 435/2 In the direction of maximum intensity the Lyman-α flux is 160 Rayleighs, which can be regarded as typical for the direction of the solar apex. **1974** *Science* 25 Jan. 317 A two-channel ultraviolet photometer aboard Pioneer 10 has made several observations of the ultraviolet glow in the wavelength range from 170 to 1400 angstroms in the vicinity of Jupiter. Preliminary results indicate a Jovian (1216 angstrom) glow with a brightness of about 1000 rayleighs and a helium (584 angstrom) glow with a brightness of about 10 to 20 rayleighs.

Rayleigh–Jeans (rēⁱ·lidʒī·ns). *Physics.* The name *Rayleigh and that of Sir James *Jeans* (1877–1946), English physicist and astronomer, used *attrib.* with reference to an approximation to Planck's law (see *Planck) that is valid at long wavelengths, according to which the flux of radiant energy from a perfect radiator, at any particular wavelength, is proportional to its temperature divided by the fourth power of the wavelength.

1930 Ruark & Urey *Atoms, Molecules & Quanta* iii. 57 We obtain the radiation density, $\rho_\lambda d\lambda = 8\pi kT\lambda^{-4}d\lambda$. This is called the Rayleigh–Jeans distribution law. *Ibid.* 59 Planck's law approaches the Rayleigh–Jeans law if *h* approaches zero. **1948** Worthing & Halliday *Heat* xiii. 445 Rayleigh erroneously included a factor of 8 in his evaluation of c_1. The error was pointed out by the English physicist James Jeans (1877–). For that reason, the law is often referred to as the Rayleigh–Jeans law. Just the reverse of what occurred in connection with the Wien law, the Rayleigh law predicts correct values in the long-wavelength region but fails elsewhere. **1970** G. K. Woodgate *Elem. Atomic Struct.* iii. 36 The approximation corresponds, for thermal radiation, to..$\bar{n} \approx kT/h\nu \gg 1$, which in eq. (3.16) or (3.13) leads at once to the Rayleigh–Jeans approximation for the energy density per unit frequency range.

rayless, *a.* Add: † **2. c.** *Physics.* Not accompanied by or emitting alpha, beta, or gamma rays. *Obs.*

1904 *Proc. R. Soc.* LXXIII. 493 The first change is a 'rayless' one, *i.e.*, the transformation is not accompanied by the appearance of α, β, or γ rays. **1906** [see *actinium 2]. **1907** N. R. Campbell *Mod. Electr. Theory* ix. 210 It appears that many changes which are usually classed as 'rayless' are accompanied by the emission of β rays without α rays, but the liberation of energy in such changes is so small compared to those in which α rays are emitted that it seems desirable to make the distinction implied by the term.

raymonder (rēⁱ·mǫ̆ndəɹ). *Cricket.* = *ramrod 2 a.

1870 [see *ramrod 2 a]. **1878** H. C. Adams *Wykehamica* xxiii. 431 *Raymonder*, a ball bowled underhand, in a series of hops along the ground, (traditionally said to be derived from one Raymond, who bowled after this fashion). Sometimes it was pronounced 'ramroder'.

Raynaud (rēⁱ·nōᵘ). *Med.* [The name of Maurice *Raynaud* (1834–81), French physician, who described various cases displaying Raynaud's phenomenon in 1862 (*De l'Asphyxie Locale et de la Gangrène Symétrique des Extrémités*).] *Raynaud's disease* or *syndrome*: an ill-defined disease or syndrome characterized by *Raynaud's phenomenon*, in which spasm of the arteries of the digits (often due to low temperature or vibration) leads to pallor, pain, and numbness, and in severe cases to gangrene.

1883 *Trans. Clin. Soc.* XVI. 179, I have watched three cases which came within the category of Raynaud's disease. **1901** J. Hutchinson in *Med. Press & Circular* CXXIII. 403/1 The expression 'Raynaud's disease' would imply that there is some one malady complete in itself, and having all the symptoms the same in all cases which is suitably denominated by that name. That is not the case. *Ibid.*, I would rather speak of Raynaud's phenomena than of Raynaud's disease, for the former are things which we understand and are the same in all cases... What do we mean by Raynaud's phenomena?.. Local syncope, local asphyxia, symmetrical gangrene of the extremities are synonymous terms. **1925** Raynaud's disease [see *ganglionectomy]. **1932** *Amer. Jrnl. Med. Sci.* CLXXXIII. 188 The increasing amount of literature attests to the tendency to utilize the terms 'Raynaud's disease' or 'Raynaud's syndrome' as a general depository for a heterogeneous group of cases far removed from the condition originally described by Raynaud. **1936** *Q. Jrnl. Med.* XXIX. 399 For more than sixty years the term 'Raynaud's disease' was used as a convenient label for case after case of obscure aetiology in which pallor, cyanosis, pain, or gangrene of hands, feet, nose, or ears, happened to be symptoms, prominent or otherwise. *Ibid.* 401 'Raynaud's Phenomenon' may, therefore, be defined as 'Intermittent pallor or cyanosis of the extremities, precipitated by exposure to cold, without clinical evidence of blockage of the large peripheral vessels and with nutritional lesions, if present at all, limited to the skin'. **1937** Raynaud's syndrome [see *ganglionectomy]. **1946** E. V. Allen et al. *Peripheral Vascular Dis.* vii. 185 The predilection of Raynaud's disease for the female is one of the outstanding etiological factors. *Ibid.* viii. 206 Raynaud's phenomenon may occur primarily as in Raynaud's disease or it can occur secondarily in association with a number of conditions and diseases. **1973** *Times* 26 May 3/3 The name for the unusual affliction was Raynaud's Phenomenon, Mr Alan Lipfriend, Mr Lambert's counsel, told Mr Justice Mocatta. It was also known as vibratory white finger. The fingers went white, numb and stiff. **1975** *Daily Colonist* (Victoria, B.C.) 18 Nov. 2/1 My doctor says I have Raynaud's disease... It is just like I am allergic to cold... My hands and feet are affected and hurt.

rayograph (rēⁱ·ogrɑf). Also with capital initial. [f. the name of Man *Ray* (1890–1976), U.S. artist and photographer + -o + -graph.] A type of photograph made without a camera by arranging objects on light-sensitive paper which is then exposed and developed. Cf. *photogram 3. Also **ray·ogram.**

1932 *N.Y. Times* 17 Apr. viii. 11/5 Julien Levy Gallery—Photographs by Man Ray. A fine retrospective, including a group of 'rayograms'. **1937** *Photography 1839–1937* (Museum of Mod. Art, N.Y.) 68 Man Ray refers to his shadowgraphs as 'rayographs' or 'rayogrammes'. **1942** P. Guggenheim *Art of This Century* 106 Man Ray..took up photography in 1917. Invented Rayograph technique, 1921, and explored other possibilities of photography, especially in making Dada and Surrealist compositions. **1951** J. I. H. Bauer *Revolution & Tradition Mod. Amer. Art* iii. 28 Dada attracted only one distinguished American follower, the painter and photographer Man Ray, much of whose life was spent in Paris where he produced without the use of a camera his extraordinary 'rayographs'. **1956** *Focal Encycl. Photogr.* 836/2 Further developments came about 1921 when Man Ray and L. Moholy-Nagy..made their 'rayographs' and photograms, using not merely opaque flat objects but also three-dimensional and translucent ones. **1972** C. W. E. Bigsby *Dada & Surrealism* ii. 19 The photomontage consisted of a collage of photographs. Like the Rayogram (a photographic process devised by Man Ray) it was a joke at the expense of realism. **1974** *Encycl. Brit. Macropædia* XIV. 320/2 Man Ray was supporting himself by making fashion photographs in 1922 when he accidentally set a glass funnel, a graduate, and a thermometer on a piece of photographic paper, thus producing 'Rayographs'. **1975** *New Yorker* 19 May 13/1 (Advt.), The prices are more out of the ordinary: $7,500 is asked for Ray's rayograph 'Egg-beater and Abstracted Segment of Living Space'.

rayon¹. Add: **3. a.** Any of the class of fibres and filaments composed of or made from regenerated cellulose; also, fabric or cloth made from these. Formerly known as *artificial silk*.

1924 *Drapers' Record* 14 June 685/2 'Glos' having been killed by ridicule, the National Retail Dry Goods Association of America has made another effort to produce a suitable name for artificial silk. This time their choice has fallen on 'rayon'. **1925** *Glasgow Herald* 26 Mar. 15/1 The Viscose Company states that it will discontinue the use of wood pulp as a base for rayon when its wood pulp contracts expire. **1927** T. Woodhouse *Artificial Silk* 1 The sight of almost any article made from artificial silk (or Rayon, as it is also called) is sufficient to arouse admiration. **1951** *Good Housek. Home Encycl.* 230/2 Rayons are classified according to the highly technical processes by which they are manufactured. **1966** [see *man-made *a.*]. **1969** *Encycl. Polymer Sci. & Technol.* XI. 844 High-tenacity rayons are consumed by industry as reinforcing cords for manufacturing all types of rubber tires, drive belts, high-pressure hoses, and straps and tapes. **1973** H. McCloy *Change of Heart* ii. 18 Her stockings were real silk, not flimsy nylon..or coarse rayon.

b. *attrib.* and *Comb.*, as *rayon damask, gabardine, jersey, satin, stocking, taffeta, yarn*; *rayon-containing, -corded* adjs.

1930 *Daily News Rec.* 17 Feb. 19/2 The manufacture of rayon-containing fabrics normally is a highly competitive business. **1964** *Economist* 26 Sept. 1254/1 The rayon-corded SP tyres. **1952** M. Laski *Village* iv. 66 The rayon-damask couch of the three-piece suite. **1930** *Silk & Rayon Directory & Buyer's Guide of Gt. Brit.* 296/2 (*heading*) Gabardine, Rayon. **1947** *Sun* (Baltimore) 31 Oct. 3/7 (Advt.), Confident of its own good looks, this rayon gabardine wins your heart at once. **1965** *Which?* Mar. 94/2 *Rayon garberdine*, a fabric with a diagonal rib effect. *Ibid.* 94/3 *Rayon jersey*, a soft stretch, knitted fabric. Drapes well. **1973** *Guardian* 19 June 15/1 Matte viscose rayon jersey, long evening dress. **1977** B. Pym *Quartet in Autumn* v. 51 The dressing gown was a jazzy rayon satin. **1929** *Rayon Record* III. 587/1 The lower temperature up to about 110° is utilized for silk or rayon stockings. **1948** 'J. Tey' *Franchise Affair* xi. 119 Fawn-grey rayon stockings. **1974** M. Kelly *That Girl in Alley* iv. 70 She was wearing.. beige rayon stockings. **1952** M. Laski *Village* viii. 137 A counterpane of rayon taffeta machine-embroidered with flowers. **1929** *Rayon Record* III. 411/2 A few samples of yarns and fabrics illustrating the decorative value of rayon yarns..have been received. **1947** *British Rayon Man.* x. 168 Much attention was given to the question of the best kind of package for rayon yarns.

‖ **rayon²** (rayǫ·n). Also **raion.** [a. Russ. *raĭón*.] In the U.S.S.R., a small territorial division for administrative purposes.

1936 [see *oblast]. **1948** J. Towster *Polit. Power in U.S.S.R.* iv. 66 All the units are divided into districts (*raions*). **1959** *Economist* 14 Mar. 946/1 In at least two of Moscow's fifteen raions, the chaps at the local Agitpunkts seem to have been lying down on the job. **1964** S. P. Dunn tr. *Levin & Potapov's Peoples of Siberia* 9 The creation in 1931–1932 of nomadic and rural soviets, rayons and national okrugs on a territorial basis finally undermined the importance in the social structure of the peoples of the North, of their former clan and tribal organizations and of the social elements which headed them. **1976** [see *okrug].

Rayonism, Rayonnism (rēⁱ·ǫ̆niz'm). Also **rayon(n)ism,** ‖ **rayonnisme.** [ad. F. *Rayonnisme*, f. *rayon* Rayon¹ + *-isme* -ism; cf. Russ. *luchizm*, f. *luch* ray.] A style of abstract painting developed *c* 1911 in Russia by M. Larionov (1881–1964) and N. Goncharova (1881–1962), in which projecting rays of colour are used to give the impression that the painting floats outside time and space. Hence **Ray·on(n)ist** *a.*, of or pertaining to Rayonism; also as *sb.*; **Rayoni·stic** *a.*

1922 *Encycl. Brit.* XXXII. 9/1 Gontcharova's setting for the 1914 production of the 'Coq d'Or' and Larionov's 'Les Contes Russes' of 1915 mark the invasion of the theatre by cubist ideas. The colour scheme was still that of Russian peasant art; but the design was based on abstract forms, and aimed at a rhythm in harmony with the music and the dances. To this development the name of *rayonnisme* has been given. **1956** B. S. Myers *Encycl. Painting* 295 *Larionov, Michel* (1881–), Russian abstract painter who in 1909 developed a type of painting known as Rayonnism, a dynamic form of space penetration consisting of rays of light and suggesting in some ways the work of the Futurists. **1956** Lake & Maillard *Dict. Mod. Painting* 241/1 *Rayonism*,..launched by Michael Larionov in 1911–12... A Rayonist canvas must give the impression of gliding out of time. **1968** D. Barran tr. *Veronesi's Into Twenties* iii. 76 Larionov founded the rayonnist movement, loosely based on the concepts of the futurist movement. **1969** Denis & de Vries *World's Art* II. xi. 224 Rayonism in Russia was of the same nature, (*Rayonistic Manifesto*, 1912, by Larionov). **1972** C. W. E. Bigsby *Dada & Surrealism* ii. 10 In some ways it [*sc.* Dada] was a part of that artistic re-examination which spawned such schools as impressionism, cubism, futurism and, more exotically, suprematism, rayonism, plasticism, vorticism and synchronism. **1975** *Physics Bull.* Feb. 60/3 The art world was no less fertile with the cubists, the futurists, vorticists, rayonnists and the Blauer Reiter group all active. *Ibid.* 61/1 Rayonnism was a style of painting invented by Mikhail Larionov and used by him and Natalia Goncharova around 1912–14. **1977** *New Yorker* 2 May 31/3 What makes it unique is the inclusion of some dazzling experimental pictures from the early twentieth century—Cubist, Futurist, Rayonist, and Suprematist.

‖ **rayonnant** (rẹyonaṅ), *a.* Also fem. **rayonnante** (-aṅt); pl. **rayonnants.** [Fr.] Beaming, radiant. Also **rayonnant de joie**, radiant with joy.

The form with *-te* in quot. 1825 is erron.

1821 M. W. Shelley *Let.* 2 Apr. in P. B. Shelley *Lett.* (1964) II. 278 Yesterday he came *rayonnant de joie*—he had been ill for some days, but he forgot all his pains. **1825** H. Wilson *Mem.* II. 79 The next evening found us all quite rayonnante, waiting for our dinner. **1831** C. C. F. Greville *Mem.* (1874) II. xiii. 111 The Ministers were *rayonnants*. **1965** Lady Birkenhead *Illustrious Friends* ix. 92 Her ladyship was rayonnante... She sallied forth in a blue silk ball-dress and lively spirits.

‖ **rayonné**, *a.* Add: **3.** Of a person: radiant, effulgent.

1860 Queen Victoria *Let.* 20 June in R. Fulford *Dearest Child* (1964) 260 She is so embellié and rayonné as to look like a young girl.

‖ **rayonnement** (rɛyɔnmaṅ). [Fr.] Radiance, effulgence; influence (of culture, etc.).

1910 Wyndham Lewis *Lett.* (1963) 45 The benevolence and rayonnement that is the sign and beauty of a fine nature shines on faults without hiding them. **1966** *Economist* 23 Apr. 340/2 Nor are the producers allowed to show the film outside France, because it might damage the reputation of 'communities' which contribute to the 'cultural and humanitarian *rayonnement* of France'.

Rayonnism, Rayonnist: see *Rayonism, Rayonnism.

‖ **Raza** (rā·sa). [Mexican Sp., a. Sp. *raza* race.] Usu. in phr. *La Raza*, the race, designating the strong sense of racial and cultural identity held by Mexican-Americans.

1964 W. Madsen *Mexican-Americans of S. Texas* iii. 15 The Mexican-American thinks of himself as both a citizen of the United States and a member of *La Raza* (The Race). **1968** *Economist* 8 June 54/1 The preservation of *La Raza* within the dominant American culture means that Mexican-American families observe the Roman Catholic faith, speak Spanish and yield to the male the authority associated with Mediterranean custom. **1969** *Time* 4 July 14/2 *La Raza*, the race, meaning all Mexicans and Mexican Americans, and derived from the mystical theory of the 19th century philosopher, José Vasconcelos, that people of mixed race will inherit the earth. At best, it is a rallying cry betokening a mild form of cultural nationalism; at worst, it connotes outright racism. **1973** *Black Panther* 7 Apr. 4/3 The Oakland Mexican-American 'Raza' community continues its boycott of public schools.

‖ **Razakar** (razākā·ɹ). Also **Razakhar.** [Urdu *razākār*.] A Muslim who voluntarily pledges to fight in defence of his religion; hence, a member of a fanatical semi-military faction with this end. Also *attrib.*

1948 *Keesing's Contemp. Archives* 31 July–7 Aug. 9421 Hyderabad's Moslems formed the Razakar (volunteer) movement which, in recent months, has in effect become the private army of the Moslem party in Hyderabad. **1957** P. Griffiths *Mod. India* xii. 107 The Ittehad-ul-Muslimeen, with its semi-military organisation known as the Razakars, took a bitterly communal line. Each Razakar vowed to 'fight to the last to maintain the supremacy of the Muslim power in the Deccan'. **1968** H. Gray in M. Weiner *State Politics in India* viii. 402 Kasim Razvi organized a voluntary group of fighters named 'Razakars', who provided protection to landowners and the government administration during a Communist-led uprising. **1970** R. Wingate *Ismay* viii. 180 Attlee replied in a long personal letter [*c.* Sept.–Oct. 1948] pointing out that in fact the Nizam had not been a free agent, but in the hands of the 'Razakars' (the extreme Muslim party). **1971** *Guardian* 29 Oct. 13/1 They [*sc.* Pakistani army units] have left in the countryside a patchwork of police and Razakhar regimes. **1971** *Peace News* 29 Oct. 5/1 The mukti fouj attacked a radio station occupied by the Pakistani army and their civilian hirelings, the *razakars*. **1972** M. Shakir *Muslims in Free India* iv. 56 The emergence of the Razakars was a logical corollary of the Ittehad's political doctrine of collective Muslim sovereignty... It is the biggest exclusive Muslim Party in Hyderabad. **1974** *Encycl. Brit. Macropædia* IX. 76/1 Immediately after Indian independence a fanatical Muslim faction, the Razākārs, fomented tensions in the state and the city [*sc.* Hyderabad].

razamataz(z, varr. *razzmatazz, razzamatazz.

razee, *sb.* Add: Also † 8 **raze.** (Earlier example.)

1794 R. F. Greville *Diary* 14 Sept. (1930) 335 Two large Ships razes which are line of Battle Ships cut down & mounted with very heavy guns 24 Pdrs.

razee, *v.* Add: **2.** (Earlier example.)

1820 *Deb. Congress U.S.* 28 Jan. (1855) 1008 It would not follow that they should have power to *razee* a State..by depriving the admitted State of equal rights.

razeed *ppl. a.* (earlier U.S. examples).

1847 *Knickerbocker* June 496 The 'Chicken Mauma' was persecuting the Cherokee advocate with her *razeed* (i.e., reduced,) offers in reference to the sale of the 'funny chickens'. **1867** *Harper's Mag.* Oct. 679/2 This 'mittimus' of the Squire's was a razeed, square-topped old chaise.

razer, var. Raser¹ in Dict. and Suppl.

‖ **razet** (raze). *Bullfighting.* [Provençal *raset.*] In southern France: a contest in which teams of combatants compete to snatch a rosette from between the bull's horns.

1932 R. Campbell *Taurine Provence* ii. 43 The finest thing in the French arena..is the razet, or the course of the cocarde-bearing bulls. **1967** McCormick & Mascareñas *Compl. Aficionado* vi. 210 Confusion with Spanish toreo arises in the sport which the French call the *course de cocardes* (or *razet*), in which the athlete, unarmed with cape or muleta, attempts to snatch from between the bull's horns the rosette (*cocarde*), or divisa, of the owner.

‖ **razeteur** (razetœ̄ɹ). [Provençal, f. prec.] A member of a bullfighting team which engages in a *razet*.

1932 R. Campbell *Taurine Provence* ii. 43 They [*sc.* the bulls] know every habitual razeteur by sight. **1961** *Times* 8 July 10/6 There are two classes, a *tourneur* or decoy, whose function is to turn the bull in order to favour the chances of his partner, the *razateur* (sometimes *crocheteur*). **1963** E. & A. Heimann tr. *Droit's Camargue* iii. 28 The razéteurs... Called thus because they pass so close to the bull that they literally graze, or shave, by him. **1976** N. Roberts *Face of France* ix. 106 The *razeteurs*, the young men who get their name from the *razet*, or running half circle, which they describe in their efforts to snatch the [bull's] *cocarde*.

razmataz(z, varr. *razzmatazz, razzamatazz.

razoo¹ (rǎzū·). *N. Amer. slang.* Also **razzoo, razzooh.** [Prob. alteration of *raspberry 3* (cf. *razzberry, *razz *sb.*) with arbitrary suffix *-oo*, perh. after Kazoo.] Ridicule; the arousing of indignation or the like, provocation; a sound of contempt, a 'raspberry'. Also in phr. *to give the razoo*: to ridicule. So as *v. trans.*, to arouse or provoke; to manhandle.

1890 *Grip* (Toronto) 18 Jan. 40/1 Shall I razoo old Mowat on the Separate School business? *Ibid.* 19 Apr. 265/1 What is all this racket about the Independence of Parliament?.. It is dependent on the presence of Members..on the whips razoo round. **1908** H. Green *Maison de Shine* 208 Can't a man take a flat o' beer wit' out gittin' the razoo? **1926** *Flynn's* 16 Jan. 639/2 The ginny with th' poke gave th' fly th' razoo an' we split a bunch of nifty kale. **1939** R. Chandler *Big Sleep* xxvi. 235 My information is Apartment 301, but all I get there is the big razzoo. **1942** Berrey & Van den Bark *Amer. Thes. Slang* § 297/1 Ridicule; banter, ..*razoo*. *Ibid.* § 297/4 (*Ripe*) *raspberry* or *razzberry*, *razoo*, a sound of contempt by vibrating the tongue between the lips, loosely any expression of derision or ridicule, hence ridicule. *Ibid.* § 297/5 Ridicule; banter,..*give the razz* or *the razoo*. **1944** H. Wentworth *Amer. Dial. Dict.* 496/1 *Razoo*, to manhandle, use roughly. **1959** *Washington Post* 22 Dec. c-18/5 Yesterday's hero, Fidel Castro, now gets the lustiest Bronx razzoohs since Adolf Hitler was flipping his wig for the cameras.

razoo² (rā·zū). *Austral.* and *N.Z. slang.* Also **rahzoo, razhoo.** [Origin uncertain.] A (non-existent) coin of trivial value, a 'farthing'. Also in phr. *brass razoo*. Used in neg. contexts only.

1930 *Bulletin* (Sydney) 5 Nov. 21/1 The useless graft on patch and flat! They never think a bloke has earned a darned razoo for that. **1931** W. Hatfield *Sheepmates* xxx. 268 Richards never has a rahzoo. **1940** F. D. Davison *Woman at Mill* ii. 151, I found myself on the streets again, without a brass razoo. **1943** *Coast to Coast 1942* 118 Up till the present he hadn't a brass razoo towards the seven and sixpence. **1947** J. Morrison *Sailors belong Ships* 187, I wouldn't give you a razhoo for anything between there and Charmian Road. **1964** J. Cleary *Flight of Chariots* viii. 361, I wouldn't give a brass razoo for his chances out there. **1968** R. Clapperton *No News on Monday* vii. 80 He isn't rolling in the stuff—he hasn't got two brass razoos to rub together. **1976** *Sunday Mail* (Brisbane) 25 Apr. 16/7 Last week he signed a contract for the new $356,000 building and then cheerfully announced: 'I haven't a razoo.'

razor, *sb.* Add: **1. b.** (Further examples.) Also *Ockham's razor*.

1901 T. C. Allbutt *Science & Medieval Thought* 57 Now this scientific economy, perhaps first formulated, or effectively used, by William Ockham, in the phrase 'entia non sunt multiplicanda'—known as 'Ockham's rasor'—is what is called now-a-days 'materialism'. **1907** Ld. Curzon *Frontiers* 7 Frontiers are indeed the razor's edge on which hang suspended the modern issues of war or peace, of life or death to nations. **1936** J. Buchan *Island of Sheep* xii. 235 In the Norlands life had always been on a razor's edge. **1944** W. S. Maugham (*title*) The razor's edge. **1960** A. Huxley *Let.* 17 July (1969) 894 Perhaps Ockham's razor isn't a valid scientific principle. Perhaps entities sometimes ought to be multiplied beyond the point of the simplest possible explanation. For the world is doubtless far odder and more complex than we ordinarily think. **1976** A. White *Long Silence* vi. 49 He was living on a razor's edge. Sooner or later, the Germans were going to begin to suspect. **1977** M. Goulder in J. Hick *Myth of God Incarnate* iii. 60 Natural explanations, where they are at all plausible, are surely to be preferred on the basis of Occam's razor.

3. a. *razor blade* (further examples), *strop* (earlier and later examples).

1936 *Discovery* Aug. 255/1 Glass razor blades can be ground to powder under foot when used. **1945** 'G. Orwell' *Animal Farm* viii. 64 Making cocks fight with splinters of razor-blade tied to their spurs. **1977** *Jersey Even. Post* 26 July 18/3 Also reported stolen is a silver razor-blade-shaped pendant. **1759** *Newport* (Rhode Island) *Mercury* 26 June 4/3 Hones, Razor-strops &c. **1866** *Harper's Mag.* Nov. 788/2 Packwood, some fifty years ago, led the way in England of..systematic advertising, by impressing his razor-strop indelibly on the mind of every bearded member of the kingdom. **1946** G. Millar *Horned Pigeon* i. 1, I only heard the noise of a man's razor strop.

b. *razor-edged* (later example), *-shaped* (earlier example); *razor-keen, -sharp, -thin; razor-like.*

1972 K. Bonfiglioli *Don't point that Thing at Me* xiii. 98 Even the shadows, razor-edged, purple and green, were painful to look at. **1955** *Times* 11 May 14/6 Political interest is razor keen. **1978** *Detroit Free Press* 5 Mar. (Parade Suppl.) 14D/1 (Advt.), With special Holder hands never come near razor-keen stainless steel blades. **1842** Poe in *Gift* 148 The razor-like crescent. **1977** *Rolling Stone* 19 May 93/2 The sultry title cut, with its razorlike clarion guitar lead. **1829** P. Egan *Boxiana* 2nd Ser. II. 299 He had now not the slightest chance with Curtis, who..drew streams of blood from his razor-shaped nose, and knocked him down. **1921** R. Hichens *Spirit of Time* v. 80 Something of it he must have seen—but what?.. The suggestion of a razor-sharp silhouette? **1975** J. Grady *Shadow of Condor* viii. 132 She carried..a flat, thinly sheathed razor-sharp knife taped to her stomach. **1979** *N.Y. Rev. Bks.* 25 Oct. 48/1 (Advt.), A witty, razor-sharp satire on monogamy. **1971** C. Bonington *Annapurna South Face* viii. 95, I..peered over the top, to see that the ridge was now razor-thin and looked even more difficult beyond the point I had reached. **1973** P. Evans *Bodyguard Man* viii. 64 He cut razor-thin slices through the most congested areas of traffic.

c. razor clam (later examples); **razor-cut** *v. trans.*, to cut (hair, etc.) with a razor; also *fig.*; hence as *sb.*, a haircut effected with a razor instead of scissors; also as *ppl. a.*; **razor-cutting** *vbl. sb.*; **razor-edge,** also *attrib.*; (further *fig.* examples); **razor gang,** (*a*) a gang of thugs armed with razors; (*b*) *Railway slang* (see quots. 1966 and 1970); **razor-grass,** substitute for def.: a West Indian sedge belonging to the genus *Scleria*, esp. *S. pterota*, which has sharp-edged leaves; (earlier and later examples); **razor-man,** a thug armed with a razor; **razor plug, point,** a power-point for plugging in an electric razor; **razor-slasher,** one who slashes another (usu. across the face) with a razor; a member of a razor gang; hence **razor-slash** *v. trans.* [back-formation], to slash with a razor; also as *sb.*, the action of lacerating thus; a wound so made; **razor-slashing** *vbl. sb.*; **razor strop fungus,** the birch polypore, *Piptoporus betulinus*; **razor toe,** a pointed toe on a shoe; an (outmoded style of) shoe with a razor toe.

1935 J. C. Lincoln *Cape Cod Yesterdays* 48 The dictionary ..even mentions the 'razor clam' among them. **1960** M. Sharcott *Place of Many Winds* ix. 162 Commercial crab fishermen often use clams, particularly razor clams, as bait. **1964** F. Warner *Early Poems* 77 Cruelty razor-cut my arteries. **1965** *Family Circle* Oct. 60 Hair as dark as this ideally goes into a sleek and sophisticated styling of the very short tapered razor cut. **1969** J. N. Smith *Is he dead, Miss ffinch?* vi. 27 I'd had time for a hair-do..a razor-cut, tapered down to the neck. **1971** R. Falkirk *Chill Factor* vi. 57 His hair was razor-cut. **1974** R. B. Parker *God save Child* (1975) iv. 33 He was dark-skinned with longish black hair carefully layered with a razor cut. **1976** Scott & Koski *Walk-In* (1977) xii. 66 Their hair was razor cut to just above the collar line. **1968** J. Ironside *Fashion Alphabet* 197 Razor cutting became popular in the 1950s, first in men's barber shops and later in women's hairdressers. The use of a razor means that the hair can be layered and thinned when wet and shaped more effectively. **1977** *Oxford Consumer* June 6/1 Razor cutting is now a rarity,..and only 7 people had had a perm recently. **1927** D. H. Lawrence *Mornings in Mexico* 61 The instant moment is forever keen with a razor-edge of oblivion. **1941** B. Schulberg *What makes Sammy Run?* iii. 49 With one razor-edge phrase he had cut me down to his level. **1962** H. O. Beecheno *Introd. Business Stud.* i. 7 Ours is a razor-edge economy and maintaining our balance of payments.. becomes a matter of overriding importance. **1976** 'A. York' *Dark Passage* xiii. 152 His finances..were in a razor edge state... He lived like a millionaire,..but there was no cash around. **1957** *Essays in Criticism* VII. 311, I suppose that Mr. Conquest would not consider deliverance from the caprice of motorists, or even of wide boys and razor gangs, altogether undesirable for the free mind. **1966** H. Sheppard *Dict. Railway Slang* (ed. 2) 10 *Razor gang*, economy men from Headquarters. **1970** F. McKenna *Gloss. Railwaymen's Talk* 38 *Razor gang*, an investigating committee, searching rosters and rotas for 'unproductive time'. **1977** *Times* 4 May 10/6 There were razor gangs on our race-courses. **1864** A. H. R. Grisebach *Flora Brit. W. Indian Islands* 787 Razor-grass: *Scleria scindens.* **1922** *Blackw. Mag.* July 11/1 The great sweep of razor-grass rustled golden. **1954** *Farmer's Guide* (Jamaica Agric. Soc.) 587 Razor-grass... At least nine different kinds of Scleria occur in Jamaica, and all of them can be unpleasant weeds due to the cutting edges of the leaves. **1969** S. M. Sadeek *Windswept & Other Stories* 29 The cart rolled on..into the savannah of..beezie-beezie reeds and razor-grass. **1958** *New Statesman* 5 Apr. 436/3 The razor-men arrive at his door. **1977** E. W. Hildick *Loop* vii. 36 Noah..was..a 'painter' or razorman with some northern racetrack gang. **1961** *Times* 26 May 9/6 Putting razor plugs in the bathrooms. **1969** C. Hodder-Williams *98.4* i. 7 There was a razor point so I went out to the car and fetched my shaver. **1978** *Cornish Guardian* 27 Apr. 15/1 (Advt.), 21 letting bedrooms (basins, razor points). **1958** M. Procter *Man in Ambush* xiv. 162 This girl had reason to be afraid. She had been razor-slashed once. **1959** N. Mailer *Advts. for Myself* (1961) 292 In the worst of perversion, promiscuity, pimpery,..rape, razor-slash, bottle-break.., the Negro discovered a morality of the bottom. **1963** T. Tullett *Inside Interpol.* xi. 160 A razor-slash across the face. **1976** R. HILL *Another Death in Venice* I. iii. 55 Dunkerley the pimp, razor-slashing young prostitutes who wouldn't pay. **1980** P. ABLEMAN *Shoestring's Finest Hour* ii. 30 The pimp..is called..Ted the Slash because he's got a razor slash on his cheek. **1951** S. SPENDER *World within World* iv. 213 Some of the recruits turned out to be a gang of Glasgow razor-slashers. **1961** *John o'London's* 6 July 24/2 Greene's slum *Faust* was articulate in a way unlikely in the most intelligent razor-slasher. **1938** F. D. SHARPE *Sharpe of Flying Squad* xix. 204 Warfare between the gangs was confined to individual beatings-up and razor-slashings. **1979** W. J. FISHMAN *Streets of E. London* 106/2 His face.. resembling the cross lines of a railway complex as a result of razor slashing. **1923** J. RAMSBOTTOM *Handbk. Larger Brit. Fungi* 129 The name 'razor-strop fungus' is often given to *P[olyporus] betulinus*, as up till the early part of last century it was used for making strops. **1966** F. H. BRIGHTMAN *Oxf. Bk. Flowerless Plants* 116/2 *Piptoporus betulinus*..has also been recommended for stropping razors, and is sometimes referred to in books as the 'Razor Strop Fungus'. **1895** *Montgomery Ward Catal.* Spring & Summer 509/1 The Razor Toe... This style shoe is becoming very popular on account of the long narrow toe, and patent tip. **1897** C. T. DAVIS *Manuf. Leather* (ed. 2) xxii. 303 The pedestrian or runner avoids 'razor toes'.

razor, *v.* Add: **a.** Also, to cut *out* (with a razor blade); to shave *away, off.*

1974 *Globe & Mail* (Toronto) 24 July 5/1 Articles taken out of magazines in the libraries..'I'll just say they were razored out. Definitely.' **1975** M. KENYON *Mr Big* xviii. 175 He..had razored off the moustache. **1977** D. SEAMAN *Committee* 42 A roughness on the chin each morning that had to be razored away.

b. To slash or assault with a razor.

1937 E. AMBLER *Uncommon Danger* viii. 110 By the time I'd finished with the beggar he would have..razored his own father and mother if I'd told him to. **1954** 'N. BLAKE' *Whisper in Gloom* vii. 91 They might..terrorise a suspected informer—beat him up or razor him.

Hence **ra·zoring** *vbl. sb.*

1950 W. SANSOM in *Penguin New Writing* XL. 44 It was not the kind of shop one would have expected of Sally—and perhaps this proved a key to the outcome of that night's razoring. **1963** *Times* 5 June 16/1 Mr. C. Lindsay, for the defence, said Osborne had been afraid of possible razoring by the barons over a debt of £1 and four or five ounces of tobacco.

razor-back, *sb.* and *a.* Add: **A.** *sb.* **1.** (Earlier example.)

1823 W. SCORESBY *Jrnl. Voy. Northern Whale-Fishery* 143 Several razor-backs (Balaena physalis) had been seen, but no whales.

2. (Earlier and later examples.)

1849 J. BARROW *Facts Texas* iii. 57 Hogs are a very numerous family, but they are of very indifferent breed, and receive the appellation of 'razor backs', which is significant enough of their appearance. **1878** C. HALLOCK *Amer. Club List & Sportsman's Gloss.* p. ix, *Razorback*, a domestic hog which runs wild in the woods of the Southern States. **1941** *Arkansas: Guide to State* 99 Outside the imagination, a true razorback probably does not exist. **1976** N. THORNBURG *Cutter & Bone* xiii. 302 It has come to him now, what it was about the razorback.

3. A narrow ridge-like back in cattle and horses.

1844 H. STEPHENS *Bk. of Farm* II. 164 A high narrow shoulder is frequently attended with a rigid back bone, and low-set narrow hooks, a form which gets the appropriate name of razor-back. **1908** *Animal Managem.* 25 The 'razor' back may..be due only to want of muscle which judicious rest, food, and work will produce. **1941** I. L. IDRIESS *Great Boomerang* vii. 51 Fine upstanding beasts... No 'razor-backs' going away with nothing behind. These were 'table-tops'; you could throw your blanket on any beast and camp on his back.

4. Chiefly *Austral.* and *N.Z.* A steep-sided, narrow ridge of land.

1874 W. M. BAINES *Narr. E. Crewe* xi. 247 From a high 'razor-back', I had a magnificent view. **1889** *Trans. N.Z. Inst.* 110 Supposing the traveller to be standing on a narrow spur, or razorback, leading to the mountain-top. **1902** [see *cow-track* s.v. *COW *sb.*[1] 7]. **1911** *Chambers's Jrnl.* Dec. 30/1 Twice the way led along a real 'razor-back'. On both sides the mountain sloped precipitously. **1957** P. WHITE *Voss* vi. 153 Presently the path, which had reached a razorback..wound suddenly..and plunged down.

5. *U.S. Circus slang.* A circus hand; *spec.* one who loads and unloads the wagons.

1904 *Everybody's Mag.* X. 658/1 That night it took the Old Man 'n Early Jim both to keep a razorback from carvin' up Ibree. **1909** *Youth's Compan.* LXXXIII. 289/4 There was too much worth seeing outside. The loaders—'razor-backs', in circus language—were putting the great gleaming parade wagons on the flat cars. **1926** R. E. SHERWOOD *Here we are Again* 162 Canvasmen or 'razorbacks', as they are known in the slang of the circus, are rarely in funds. **1975** *New Yorker* 13 Oct. 38 Some people..were watching the roller coaster... I went up to the razorback who ran the controls.

B. *adj.* (Further examples.)

1851 G. S. COOPER *Jrnl. Expedition Overland* 110 Gullies.. ran down from each side of the razor-back ridge. **1896** [see *HUMP-BACKED *a.*]. **1899** B. TARKINGTON *Gentleman from Indiana* iv. 44 A squad of thin, 'razor-back' hogs. **1924** J. MASEFIELD *Sard Harker* III. 126 It was one of the half-wild razor-back hogs which the negroes allowed to stray in the woods there. **1976** N. THORNBURG *Cutter & Bone* xiii. 302 As it fell open Bone was able to see his T-shirt underneath, and the emblem on it: a red Arkansas razorback hog, name and symbol of the state university's sports teams.

razor-backed *a.* (further example).

1904 *Daily Chron.* 12 May 5/3 A fierce struggle ensued for the possession of two razor-backed ridges above which runs the main Peking road.

razor-grinder. 1. (Earlier examples.)

1789 *Boston Directory* 184 Fillis William, razor-grinder. **1798** D. WORDSWORTH *Jrnl.* 22 Feb. (1941) I. 9 Met a razor-grinder with..a boy to drag his wheel.

razor-shell. Add: (Further examples.) Also *attrib.*

1792 J. BELKNAP *Hist. New Hampshire* III. 183 The Razor-shell clam '*Solen ensis*'. **1901** E. STEP *Shell Life* ix. 155 We now reach the Razor-shell family, characterised by having the valves of the shell of equal length. **1928** RUSSELL & YONGE *Seas* ii. 38 The long razor-shells (*Solen*) may occasionally be dug at low tide. **1971** *Oxf. Bk. Invertebrates* 80 The razor shells, looking like the old-fashioned cut-throat razors, are among the most specialized of the burrowing bivalves.

razz (ræz), *sb. slang* (orig. *U.S.*). [Short for *RAZZBERRY.] = *RASPBERRY 3*.

a **1919** C. BRIGGS *Oh Man!*, She'll prob'ly give me the razz for being out late last night! **1920** S. LEWIS *Main Street* xxiii. 282 The Red Swede got the grand razz handed to him. **1921** *Collier's* 15 Jan. 20/1 The mob gave him the razz. **1926** N. V. LINDSAY *Going-to-the-Stars* 52 Let us think of the Irish flute in the morn,..And forget our jazzes and our razzes and our hates. **1935** *Punch* 27 Feb. 248/2, I wasn't asked parties; I got no rise..; the girls gave me the razz—and all for the reason I'd no badge to show. **1960** E. W. HILDICK *Jim Starling & Colonel* viii. 62 That band chap blew him the razz! **1961** *Punch* 18 Jan. 129 What say, honey?—let's give this communal living the razz and just go off somewhere, the two of us. **1961** *Spectator* 9 June 835/1 He selects one of them for punishment.., delivers a sonorous 'razz' and pretends to cane him. **1967** J. D. R. MCCONNELL *Eton* 61 Offenders may be summoned to the Library for a 'razz'. **1977** *Times Lit. Suppl.* 29 Apr. 534/5 Even the peppiest, most two-fisted and up-and-coming borough librarian would get the razz for buying it.

razz (ræz), *v. slang* (orig. *U.S.*). [f. the sb.] *trans.* To hiss or deride; to make fun of (a person). Hence **ra·zzing** *vbl. sb.*

1921 *Collier's* 19 Feb. 5/3 It [*sc.* a crowd]..will razz its local favorite with as much enthusiasm as it will the visitin' boxer at the first sign of foul fightin'. **1921** *Sat. Even. Post* 18 June 65/2 I'd of rather took fifty socks on the jaw than the razzing the crowd give Bat. **1924** P. MARKS *Plastic Age* 52 The fellows razzed the life out of me. *Ibid.* 60, I don't mind the razzing myself,..but I don't like the things they said to poor little Wilkins. **1932** J. LAWSON *Man's Life* xvi. 161 The person who never could appreciate institutional life..is always with us... His chief hobby when at home has been razzing the wife, or his mother, because the bacon is too fat or too lean..and anyhow he doesn't like bacon at all. **1939** L. JACOBS *Rise Amer. Film* 378 He turned out a series of domestic comedies that caused him to be hailed for his 'razzing' of American foibles. **1941** J. MCCORMACK in L. A. G. Strong *John McCormack* x. 168, I have seen a great deal of baseball in America, but I have never been able to reconcile myself to the continuous razzing of the pitcher. **1956** B. HOLIDAY *Lady sings Blues* (1973) iii. 33 When I came to work the other girls used to razz me, call me 'Duchess' and say, 'Look at her, she thinks she's a lady.' **1968** *Punch* 24 July 129/2 Ilya Ilf, pooh-poohing purges, Razzed Red Russians with wry stories. **1975** A. BERGMAN *Hollywood & Le Vine* ii. 29, I continued on down the street... I anticipated the razzing of the Dead End Kids. **1977** *TV Times* (Austral.) 20 Aug. 29/1 My kids will get razzed about it at school the next day. No one knows more about my mistakes than I do.

razzamatazz, var. *RAZZMATAZZ.

razzberry (ræ·zbĕri). *N. Amer. slang.* Also **razbery.** [Var. of RASPBERRY.] = *RASPBERRY 3*.

1922 *Collier's* 15 July 4/3 No matter if all the rest of the crowd gives me the razzberry, why they'll be at least two guys pulling for me. **1927** [see *BIRD *sb.* 5 b]. **1928** C. SANDBURG in *Woman's Home Compan.* Aug. 112/3 Hand 'em the razzberries. **1948** *Daily Ardmoreite* (Ardmore, Okla.) 27 May 8/3 Here in the home of the Bronx jeer it usually is rewarded with a noisy razberry. **1975** E. IGLAUER *Denison's Ice Road* ii. 35, I sure got the razzberries from the boys.

razzia. Add: **b.** (Earlier and later examples.)

1855 *Poultry Chron.* 4 Apr. 98/1 The owners of manors.. carried out a 'razzia' on the enemy's territory of Leadenhall market. **1965** C. D. EBY *Siege of Alcázar* (1966) v. 100 Small bands had been stealing out of the fortress at night to scavenge in the houses near by. The purpose of these *razzias* was to bring back food for the infirmary.

So **ra·zzia** *v. intr.*, to maraud.

1846 R. FORD *Gatherings from Spain* iv. 34 The object of these border *guerrilla*-warfares was..to 'harry', to 'razzia'.

razzle (ræz'l), *sb. slang.* [Short for RAZZLE-DAZZLE.] **a.** A 'good time', a spree; usu. in phr. *on the razzle.*

1908 A. BENNETT *Old Wives' Tale* IV. i. 435 'What puzzles me most is what the devil you were doing in a place like that. According to your description, it must be a ——.' 'I went there because I was broke,' said Matthew. 'Razzle?' Matthew nodded. **1915** W. S. MAUGHAM *Of Human Bondage* 249 We won't 'alf go on the razzle. **1927** *Daily Express* 2 June 6/4 Its heroine..is a Frenchman's idea of a great English lady out on the razzle. **1930** J. B. PRIESTLEY *Angel Pavement* v. 213 And now we're going on the razzle. **1943** —— *Daylight on Saturday* xxvi. 201 I've got three [absentees]... One's off on a razzle. **1968** 'J. LE CARRÉ' *Small Town in Germany* 210 Your wife was in England, and you went on the razzle with Leo. **1978** 'L. BLACK' *Foursome* vii. 56 He loved making new friends, joining up with them for a razzle in the nightspots.

b. = RAZZLE-DAZZLE *sb.* b in Dict. and Suppl.

1969 *Wall St. Jrnl.* 30 Sept. 1/1 His specialty is 'Razzle', a game that in one form or another has entranced fair-goers since ancient times.

ra·zzle, *v. slang.* [f. the sb.] *intr.* To live a life of pleasure, to enjoy oneself; to go 'on the razzle'.

1908 G. B. SHAW *Lett. to Granville Barker* (1956) 120 He will probably put it to you whether, as a gentleman, you can ask for a salary when you have been doing nothing but razzling in America. **1951** E. BAGNOLD *Loved & Envied* iii. 39 We ought to be fairly flush... It's not an expensive island. We ought to be able to razzle a bit, if there's anywhere to razzle.

razzle-dazzle, *sb.* Add: **a.** (Earlier and further examples.) Also, deception, fraud; extravagant publicity.

1889 *Gallup* (New Mexico) *Gleaner* 18 Mar. 4/2 A Kansas paper..recently told of a 'regular old razooper, who, having got a skate on, indulged in a glorious razzle-dazzle'. **1898** G. B. SHAW *Mrs. Warren's Profession* I. 175, I don't bet much and I never go regularly on the razzle-dazzle as you did when you were my age. **1928** *New Yorker* 15 Dec. 24/1 Suspecting some sort of razzle-dazzle, the wiser of the two men said he would buy the seats at their box-office value. **1938** *Sun* (Baltimore) 20 Jan. 3/2 With such razzle-dazzle financing the general practice, it is not surprising to find oil derricks sprouting up on the grounds of the State capitol. **1962** 'K. ORVIS' *Damned & Destroyed* vii. 51 The razzle-dazzle I had handed the two drug-ring musclemen. **1969** *New Yorker* 29 Nov. 47/1, I want models, I want a private plane, I want this, I want that, I want some razzle-dazzle. **1977** *Time* 19 Sept. 25/1 Lance ran for the Democratic gubernatorial nomination, using the financial razzle-dazzle that later was to become such a liability. **1978** *New York* 3 Apr. 17/3 It [*sc.* a musical] has pizzazz and razzle-dazzle, bursts of energy and invention, music and laughter.

b. (Later examples.) (See also quot. 1935).

1896 [see SWITCHBACK *a.*]. **1935** *Amer. Mercury* June 230/2 *Razzle-dazzle*, kelsy [i.e., a prostitute]; also used by the public in reference to carnival rides, although not so used by carnies themselves. **1968** D. BRAITHWAITE *Fair. ground Archit.* iii. 34 The steam swing and 'Razzle Dazzle' drew inspiration from mechanisms in the spinning frame, [etc.]. *Ibid.* 60 Four years before his death in 1897, Savage patented the 'Razzle Dazzle', otherwise known as 'Whirligig' or 'Aerial Novelty'.

c. *attrib.* or as *adj.* Of, pertaining to, or characterized by, razzle-dazzle; dazzling, spectacular.

1889 *Road* (Denver, Colorado) 28 Dec. 5/1 Clint Butterfield incloses us a razzle-dazzle card of some kind that has a very neat little design of a nightmare etched in blood red and India ink. **1946** *N.Y. Times Bk. Rev.* 4 Aug. 5/1 A great many people are reading Mr. Wakeman's razzle-dazzle novel these days. **1951** M. MCLUHAN *Mech. Bride* (1967) 10/2 The newsreel is provided with a razzle-dazzle accompaniment. **1965** *Economist* 22 May p. xxiv/1 A front page [of a newspaper] full of short items and a Gallic profusion of typefaces, alike in text and headlines—..what the Americans call 'circus' or 'razzledazzle' make-up. **1971** *Daily Tel.* 19 Oct. 19 Mr Thorley's chairmanship is, or was, intended to be an interregnum between the razzle-dazzle rule of Sir Derek Pritchard and the accession of the Showering dynasty. **1974** *Plain Dealer* (Cleveland) 13 Oct. c. 12/6 Freshman halfback Pat Healy scored three touchdowns, the last on a razzle-dazzle 32-yard pass from quarterback Bruce Basile. **1977** *Time* 13 June 39/1 Erdman comes to his subject with the sure hand of one who knows, from the inside, what lurks in the hearts of financial razzle-dazzle artists.

razzle-dazzle, *v.* (Later example.)

1976 *Houston* (Texas) *Chron.* 22 Sept. 7–4/4 Lady Bird eats it in an orange print pants suit and that Texas smile that razzle-dazzles 'em.

razzmatazz, razzamatazz (ræ:zmătæ·z, ræ:zămătæ·z). *colloq.* (orig. *U.S.*). Also **razamataz(z, razmataz(z, razz-ma-tazz,** etc. [Origin unknown; perh. alteration of RAZZLE-DAZZLE.] **a.** A type of rag-time or early jazz music; old-fashioned 'straight' jazz; sentimental, 'corny' jazz; hence anything old-fashioned; stuff, rubbish. **b.** Noisy, showy publicity; meretricious or extravagant display; an event surrounded by such publicity or display; fuss, commotion, garishness. Also *attrib.* or as *adj.*

In quot. 1899 the sense is uncertain but may be 'up-to-date, stylish' or 'cultured, superior'.

1899 G. ADE *Fables in Slang* 37 It would be a Big Help to the Poor and Uncultured to see what a Real Razmataz Lady was like. **1901** T. D. COLLINS (*title of piano music*) Raz-a-ma-taz. **1901** W. H. SMITH (*title of piano music*) Raz-ma-taz. **1936** *Amer. Mercury* XXXVIII. p. x/2 *Rooty-toot*,—unadulterated corn; razz-ma-tazz. **1937** *Amer. Speech* XII. 48/1 *Razmataz band*, a band which plays in an outmoded style. **1938** *Brit. Empire Mod. Eng. Illustr. Dict.* 1257/1 Razz-ma-tazz (*Am.*), old-fashioned jazz. **1942** BERREY & VAN DEN BARK *Amer. Thes. Slang* § 579/2 'Straight Jazz.' (Old-fashioned jazz, which reproduces the score faithfully, as distinguished from 'swing'.)..*razzmatazz.* **1947** *Sat. Rev. Lit.* (U.S.) 25 Oct. 65/2 Expert horsing of the old razzmatazz style by an expert horsewoman. **1950** C. COBEN *Old Piano Roll Blues* (*song*), And while we kiss, kiss, kiss away all our cares, The player piano's playin' razzmatazz, I wanna hear it again. **1953** BERRY & VAN DEN BARK *Amer. Thes. Slang* (1954) (ed. 2) § 233/5 Something old-fashioned, ..*razzmatazz.* **1958** *People* 4 May 8/2 She will, from next

Friday when she flies to Cannes, be getting the full razza-ma-tazz, big-star build-up. **1958** *Spectator* 1 Aug. 174/3 Don't you remember *anything* about the Twenties but crime, booze, flappers, religious razzmatazz? **1959** J. WAIN *Travelling Woman* x. 148 The enormous selling bonanza that was going on about him, in its astonishing flood of genuine goodwill, even a grain here and there of genuine piety, with unscrupulous salesman's razzmatazz, heightened his sense of living in a dream. **1961** *Sunday Times* 26 Nov. 48/3 Barbara Murray, a girl who is entirely wasted on rats, retorts and all that razzmatazz. **1963** *The Beatles* 9 Though some of our material is a bit out of the way for a razzamatazz chap like him. **1965** G. MCINNES *Road to Gundagai* iv. 59 The great wide streets have an air of grandeur which even the razz-ma-tazz of neon cannot wholly mar. **1969** *Listener* 17 Apr. 544/1 *Oh! What a lovely war* (Paramount) is a razz-ma-tazz spectacular. **1970** *Times* 9 Mar. 13/1 He turned, as might have been expected, a fairly serious event into a razamataz. **1971** *Morning Star* 8 Mar. 4/7 Some of the hotels and centres can be a bit razzamataz and noisy, especially at night. **1972** *Daily Colonist* (Victoria, B.C.) 16 Feb. 32/1 There was no need to go through 'all this razz-matazz'. The replacing of white centre lines with yellow ones wasn't all that difficult to comprehend. **1973** *Daily Tel.* 8 Nov. 5 (Advt.), We thought the car good enough not to need any launch gimmicks or razmataz. **1973** *Daily Colonist* (Victoria, B.C.) 23 Nov. 22/3 Opening day Thursday had all the razzmatazz of a revival meeting. **1974** *Time Out* 27 Sept. 23/1 There is the host, resplendent in white satin, razmatazz shirt. **1977** *Listener* 20 Oct. 508/3 This programme included a razzmatazz of presentational devices which seemed better suited to a giveaway quiz show. **1979** *Guardian* 1 May 30/1 In keeping with the showbiz, razz-matazz side of the election, the most glamorous transport belongs to the media.

razzo (ræ·zo). *slang.* [Prob. alteration of RASPBERRY.] The nose.

1899 [see *LOWER *v.* 1 e]. **1936** [see *ACID *sb.* 3].

razzoo(h, varr. *RAZOO[1].

R-boat. [Partial tr. G. *R-boot*, abbrev. of *räumboot* minesweeper.] In the war of 1939–45, a German minesweeper.

1942 *Times* 10 June 4/3 An R-boat is stated to be an armed motor minesweeper. **1945** P. SCOTT *Battle of Narrow Seas* ii. 5 Besides E boats there were flotillas of R boats (corresponding roughly to our M.Ls.), used for minesweeping and defensive patrolling along the occupied coasts. **1961** GRANVILLE & KELLY *Inshore Heroes* vii. 71 The Raumboot (R-boat) was a patrol vessel of between 85 and 115 feet, with a speed of about 20 knots. **1978** F. MACLEAN *Take Nine Spies* v. 183 A whole group of German R-boats was sent from Sicily to the Aegean.

RDX (ā.ɪ,dī,e·ks). [f. *R*esearch *D*epartment (Woolwich, England) E*x*plosive.] = *CYCLONITE.

1941 *Newsweek* 8 Dec. 43/2 One [explosive], developed in cooperation with the British and identified with the stuff used in Britain's 'superbombs', is known as RDX and credited with 40 per cent more bursting power than TNT. **1947** *Times* 9 July 5/7 RDX, the main high explosive development of the war, was yet another chemical contribution to victory—opening up, incidentally, a new field of organic chemistry. **1974** *Encycl. Brit. Macropædia* VII. 89/1 The torpedo warhead torpex..is a cast mixture of RDX, TNT, and aluminum.

re, *sb.*[2] Add: (Later examples.) Now freq. apprehended as a preposition, and used in weakened senses to mean 'about, concerning'.

The use as a preposition has freq. been condemned: see Fowler *Mod. Eng. Usage* (1926) s.v. *illiteracies* and A. P. Herbert (examples below).

1926 in H. W. Fowler *Mod. Eng. Usage* 484/1 Dear Sir,—I am glad to see that you have taken a strong line re the Irish railway situation. *Ibid.* 484/2 Reference had been made in a former issue to some alleged statements of mine re the use of the military during the recent railway dispute. **1935** A. P. HERBERT *What a Word!* iii. 80 We herewith enclose receipt for your cheque £4 on a/c *re* return of commission *re* Mr. Brown's cancelled agreement *re* No 50 Box Street top flat. **1939** [see *INCLUSIVITY]. **1976** *Time* 27 Dec. 2/2 Re your article on legitimized gambling..and specifically state lotteries: the inefficiency of revenue collection is horrendous and the odds for winning are unconscionable. **1977** *Time* 7 Feb. 1/3 Re my archaeological explorations in Syria: it is not true that '..the Italian archaeologists have been slow to publicise their discoveries'. **1979** *Verbatim* Summer 5/2 G. Bocca's observations re public signs.

re, abbrev. of RUPEE.

1913 W. T. ROGERS *Dict. Abbrev.* 164/1 *Re.* (money), rupee. **1962** *Housewife* (Ceylon) Apr. 10 These courses are practical, economical (Re. 1/- for 3 lessons). **1971** *Hindustan Times Weekly* (New Delhi) 4 Apr. 11/2 Gramdal was better by Re 1 on good offtake.

re-, *prefix.* Add: **4. b.** (Later examples.)

1885 G. B. SHAW *Let.* 14 Dec. (1965) I. 146, I re-return the cheque, and if you re-re-return it I will re-re-re-return it again. **1922** JOYCE *Ulysses* 526, I rererepugnosed in rererepugnant. **1954** *New Biol.* XVI. 43 Under the title 'Vital Blarney'..I reviewed, or to be pedantic I re-re-reviewed, Bernal's book *The Physical Basis of Life.*

5. a. *re-abolish* vb., *-alliance*, *-apportion* vb. (further examples), *-apportionment* (further examples), *-bandage* vb., *-beam* vb., *-biff* vb., *-break* vb. (earlier and later examples), *-cable* vb., *-calibrate* vb., *-calibration*, *-canalization*, *-canalize* vb., *-canvass* vb., *-carve* vb., *-centrifuge* vb., *-certification*, *-certify* vb., *-chromatograph* vb., *chromatography*, *-clean* vb., *-clone* vb. (hence *-cloning* vbl. sb.), *-codify* vb., *-conceptualization*, *-conceptualize* vb., *-configure* vb., *-conscript* vb., *-contamination*, *-contrast* vb., *-cool* vb., (hence *-cooling* vbl. sb.), *-debit* vb., *-decontaminate* vb., *-decontamination*, *-demarcation*, *-differentiate* vb. (further examples), *-differentiation*, *-enrich* vb., *-enrichment*, *-equilibrate* vb., *-equilibration* (further examples), *-estimate* vb. and sb., *-evocation*, *-exploration*, *-explore* vb., *-expose* vb., *-fabricate* vb., *-feature* vb., *-fecundate* vb., *-flush* vb., *-foliate* vb., *-foliation*, *-format* vb., *-forward* vb. (hence *-forwarding* vbl. sb.), *-incubate* vb., *-infarction*, *-initialize* vb., *-input* vb., *-intensify* vb., *-isolate* vb., *-license* vb., *-list* vb., *-lubricate* vb., *-mapping* vbl. sb., *-nucleation*, *-orchestrate* vb. (further examples), *-orchestration*, *-origination*, *-originator*, *-pattern* vb. (hence *-patterning* vbl. sb.), *-peg* vb. (hence *-pegging* vbl. sb.), *-phosphorylate* vb., *-pile* vb., *-postpone* vb., *-proportion* vb. (further examples), *-punch* vb., *-punctuation*, *-rat* vb. (later example), *-recovery*, *-remember* vb., *-remembrance*, *-riddle* vb., *-scrutinize* vb., *-scrutiny*, *-sex* vb. (further example), *-shade* vb., *-show* vb. (hence *-showing* vbl. sb.), *-stack* vb., *-stage* vb., *-structuration*, *-suspend* vb., *-suspension*, *-suture* vb. and sb., *-synthesis*, *-synthesize* vb., *-tailor* vb., *-target* vb., *-tightening* vbl. sb., *-time* vb., *-triangulate*, vb., *-triangulation*, *-uptake*, *-walk* vb., *-winded* ppl. a., *-zip* vb.

1963 AUDEN *Dyer's Hand* 461 The distinction between the things of God and the things of Caesar is reabolished. **1847** WEBSTER, Realliance. **1973** *Jrnl. Genetic Psychol.* Mar. 137 Their [*sc.* neo-Freudians'] realliance will contribute something to the explanation of the latter theory. **1967** M. E. JEWELL *Legislative Representation in Contemp. South* v. 124 The Kentucky legislature was one of the first to reapportion both houses substantially on a population basis. **1971** C. A. AUERBACH in N. W. Polsby *Reapportionment in 1970s* ii. 90 All state legislatures will be reapportioned according to the principle of one vote, one value. **1931** *Times Lit. Suppl.* 18 June 476/4 There should be a reapportionment of seats. **1974** *Anderson* (S. Carolina) *Independent* 19 Apr. 1B/1 Members of the House-Senate conference committee asked ..for free conference power that would allow them to re-write district lines in the House reapportionment bill. **1920** C. H. STAGG *High Speed* x. 180 Dan helped him rebandage his hands. **1979** *Sunday Express* 28 Jan. 3/8 Within an hour of starting that wound had been stitched and rebandaged. **1919** E. POUND *Quia pauper Amavi* 16 The infant beams at the parent, The parent re-beams at its offspring. **1934** BLUNDEN *Choice or Chance* 53 Ye men of England, hear the clarion. If Inferior nations biff you, them rebiff. **1805** R. W. DICKSON *Pract. Agric.* II. 943 And when the weather is bad these cocks are never re-broken out, being only lightened up to let the air pass through them more freely. **1905** *Daily Chron.* 31 July 4/7 The leg was badly set, and had to be re-broken. **1943** V. SACKVILLE-WEST *Eagle & Dove* I. xv. 89 Her left arm..had had to be re-broken and re-set most painfully several times. **1908** *Daily Chron.* 7 Apr. 1/7 Chicago, Monday... This afternoon..an alleged interview with Hackenschmidt is re-cabled from a London newspaper. **1909** *Cent. Dict.* Suppl., Recalibrate. **1971** *Nature* 6 Aug. 391/2 We are currently recalibrating our Dobson ozone spectrophotometers. **1978** *Sci. Amer.* Feb. 34/3 In the 1980's shuttle-recoverable instruments that can be recalibrated and still better instruments in high orbit may answer the questions. **1911** WEBSTER, Recalibration. **1977** *Nature* 6 Jan. 18/1 Node markers..can thus easily be reset by 93 yr periodic recalibration observations of maximum northerly midwinter full moonrise azimuth. **1961** R. D. BAKER *Essent. Path.* v. 82 New blood vessels form in the lumen (recanalization). **1943** *Amer. Speech* XVIII. 222 General semantics..is offered as a means of recanalizing those responses..that cause morbid over-excitation of the nervous system. **1962** *Punch* 12 Sept. 366/2 Water conservation..to the extent of recanalising the water. **1925** T. DREISER *Amer. Trag.* II. III. xxvi. 329 The twelve men..re-canvassing for their own mental satisfaction the fine points made by Mason. **1924** J. MASEFIELD *Sard Harker* 4 Men remembered this rhyme, and pled that it should be recarven. **1956** *Nature* 7 Jan. 45/2 The homogeneous supernatant was recentrifuged once or twice. **1976** *Ibid.* 15 Jan. 114/2 The supernatant was recentrifuged at 20,000g for 10 min. **1976** P. R. WHITE *Planning for Public Transport* i. 20 Maintenance facilities may be very limited, problems of major overhaul and recertification being handled by sale of a vehicle to a dealer who provides a reconditioned vehicle in part exchange. **1978** *Jrnl. R. Soc. Med.* LXXI. 13 Such developments..could be more effective and acceptable than some form of periodic recertification in maintaining standards in practice. **1934** WEBSTER, Recertify. **1976** *National Observer* (U.S.) 17 July 11/3 The Israelis were recertifying their credentials as a people of almost unbelievable resourcefulness and courage. **1977** *Proc. R. Soc. Medicine* LXX. 58/2 Only the American Board of Family Practice is putting the idea into practice by an MCQ recertifying exam from October 1976. **1945** Rechromatograph [see **re-chromatography*]. **1948** *Amer. Scientist* XXXVI. 511 If either of these two zones is cut out, eluted, and rechromatographed on a fresh column, it will form a single zone. **1971** *Nature* 16 Apr. 456/2 After 24 h dialysis against 0·01 M phosphate buffer..the residual fibre was rechromatographed, the peak fractions were pooled and reduced to a final volume of 1 ml. **1945** *Jrnl. Biol. Chem.* CLVII. 327 Rechromatography was usual, especially when two zones were bordering upon one another. In such instances they were cut out as one and rechromatographed. **1950** L. ZECHMEISTER *Progress in Chromatogr.* xii. 162 The peptides were characterized by the ratio, total nitrogen/amino nitrogen. Such ratios observed were not altered by rechromatography. **1978** *Nature* 14 Dec. 735/2 Rechromatography on Sephadex G-50 gave only a single peak. **1921** *Daily Colonist* (Victoria, B.C.) 29 Oct. 8/1 (Advt.), Fine re-cleaned currants. **1960** *Farmer & Stockbreeder* 29 Mar. 5/1 The following are wholesale prices for recleaned seed per cwt ex-store unless otherwise stated. **1971** *Nature* 30 July 313/2 Six clones were mixed (*GdH*/*GdD*), two of these were recloned, and 106 out of 107 of these sub-clones showed either *GdH* or *GdD* while one was again mixed. **1962** *Cold Spring Harbor Symp. Quantitative Biol.* XXVII. 410 Recloning of these clones gives rise to all converted clones. **1973** *Listener* 20 Dec. 846/3 We shall not avoid increasing dislocation..unless we can re-codify large areas of international behaviour. **1961** WEBSTER, Reconceptualization. **1973** *Sci. Amer.* Sept. 120/2 With a reconceptualization of the hospital as a therapeutic community.., many of the chronic inpatients were able to be returned to the community. **1977** FONTANA & VAN DE WATER in Douglas & Johnson *Existential Sociol.* iii. 126 Understanding the world in this manner demands a thoroughgoing reconceptualization of our usual notions of truth and progress in knowledge. **1961** WEBSTER, Reconceptualize. **1977** A. GIDDENS *Stud. in Social & Polit. Theory* ii. 118 Let us at this juncture reconceptualize 'structure' as referring to *generative rules and resources* that are both applied in and constituted out of action. **1964** M. MCLUHAN *Understanding Media* II. xxxi. 313 The viewer of the TV mosaic, with technical control of the image, unconsciously reconfigures the dots into an abstract work of art. **1946** L. B. LYON *Rough Walk Home* 17 Only his singular, re-conscripted breath Could fan to a purpose all that pyre his death. **1961** WEBSTER, Recontamination. **1962** *Economist* 19 May 706/2 The gas must be protected against re-contamination through leaks. **1966** D. G. BRANDON *Mod. Techniques Metallogr.* 187 The gas used must be extremely pure if immediate recontamination of the surface is to be avoided. **1957** R. N. C. HUNT *Guide to Communist Jargon* xlviii. 160 In connection with the Brest-Litovsk treaty [Lenin] recontrasted those who were 'revolutionaries out of sentiment' with 'real revolutionaries'. **1934** WEBSTER, Recool. **1969** *Gloss. Terms Water Cooling Towers* (*B.S.I.*) 5 *Recooled water temperature*, average temperature of the circulating water entering the basin. **1968** C. G. KUPER *Introd. Theory Superconductivity* v. 93 These nucleation centres are remarkably stable—they often survive the heating of the specimen to room temperature and subsequent recooling. **1934** S. W. ROWLAND *Hughes-Onslow's Lawyer's Man. Book-keeping* (ed. 3) i. 9 The bank, for its part and from its point of view, credited when the cheque was paid in. Consequently when the cheque is found to be worthless, it redebits. **1968** *Lebende Sprachen* XIII. 87/2 The bank may redebit the account. **1935** A. P. HERBERT *What a Word!* vi. 187, I do not think that she [*sc.* the Ship of State] was ever..'re-decontaminated'. *Ibid.* i. 21 The answer from high places was: 'A process of redecontamination would be advisable.' **1969** *P.E.N.* IX. 48 He recalled that at the beginning of the 1939 War the use of the word 'contaminate' for a gas attack had seemed comic, particularly when it involved 'decontamination' and 'redecontamination' stations. **1938** *Times* 17 Jan. 11/5 The chief violations [of the Soviet constitution] have been the redemarcation of internal frontiers and the formation of new territorial and administrative units. **1960** *Observer* 20 Mar. 1/4 The Ghana Government claimed that 14 people arrested last week..had conspired to conduct a campaign of violence and civil disturbance there to provoke 'foreign intervention' and the redemarcation of frontiers. **1911** *Cornh. Mag.* Apr. 497 It is as if John Brown on his death-bed were to have his tissues pass into a state of flux, and then get simpler and simpler, until you would have to say, This is no longer a man, but merely a mass of man's protoplasm, and as if finally this mass were to redifferentiate up again. **1960** *New Biol.* XXXI. 90 A second possibility is that tissue cells undergo an apparent de-differentiation to form the young regenerate or the bud but, like cells in tissue culture, retain their tissue specificity and later re-differentiate into tissues of the same kind as those from which they came. **1970** *Jrnl. Gen. Psychol.* LXXXII. 182 He must again re-differentiate these boundaries. **1889** *Cent. Dict.*, Redifferentiation. **1921** *Discovery* Feb. 28/2 Such a process, which we may style dedifferentiation followed by redifferentiation, is clear evidence of the possibility of reversing development. **1960** *New Biol.* XXXI. 89 Some cells..normally change their shapes and functions in the fulfilment of their proper roles in the organism's economy. Such reversible changes have been called 'modulations' by Weiss, and the distinction between them and more profound re-differentiations may seem rather arbitrary. **1951** *Sci. Amer.* Nov. 18/2 The gas is..cycled back into the reservoir several times to be re-enriched. **1976** *Ibid.* Dec. 33/3 If the uranium is to be returned to the gaseous-diffusion plants for reenrichment, it is converted into uranium hexafluoride. **1971** I. G. GASS et al. *Understanding Earth* i. 27/1 Once an igneous rock has completely solidified, however, the absence of a fluid phase and the reduction of temperature make it very difficult for the minerals to re-equilibrate to new assemblages which would be stable at lower temperatures. **1970** G. GERMANI in I. L. Horowitz *Masses in Lat. Amer.* xvi. 591 It satisfied their need for re-equilibration through the emphasis on 'order, discipline, hierarchy', and through the demobilization of the lower classes. **1971** I. G. GASS et al. *Understanding Earth* i. 33/1 The process of re-equilibration..is materially aided by the introduction of water in the environment of weathering. **1934** WEBSTER, Re-estimate, *v.t.* **1952** S. SPENDER *Shelley* 44 Not so much a re-estimate, as a restoring of some sort of balance. **1964** K. G. LOCKYER *Introd. Critical Path Analysis* ix. 89 An alternative is to insert the actual (or re-estimated) times. **1924** S. JOYCE in J. Joyce *Lett.* (1966) III. 104 This re-evocation and exaggeration of detail by detail and the spiritual dejection which accompanies them are purely in the spirit of the confessional. **1952** C. P. BLACKER *Eugenics* 138 The re-evocation of the repressed memory, though painful like an incision, cured the sufferer. **1977** *Proc. R. Soc. Med.* LXX. 385/2 One re-exploration was done over the same period as 36 cholecystectomies overall. **1933** *Proc. R. Soc.* A. CXLII. 350 For this reason we have not re-explored this region, since we could not hope to detect the presence of groups of such weak intensity. **1977** *Proc. R. Soc. Med.* LXX. 385/2 Over the same period another 22 patients were reexplored after operation elsewhere. **1946** *Nature* 28 Dec. 946/1 The slides are located in their former position and re-exposed. **1950** F. E. Zeuner *Dating Past* (ed. 2) 264 A Final wet phase, of a very minor character re-exposes by stream erosion the levels containing Middle Stone Age. *a* **1942** B. Malinowski *Sci. Theory of Culture* (1944) 164 In a small farcical form, such a charter has been refabricated in the *Blut und Boden* doctrine of modern Naziism. **1976** *Dumfries & Galloway Standard* 25 Dec. 12/2 The policy favoured at present is to re-process all nuclear fuel in a few politically-stable countries, return the re-fabricated fuel to the country of origin, and retain the wastes for 'safe' storage. **1922** Joyce *Ulysses* 554 The face of Martin Cunningham, bearded, refeatures Shakespeare's beardless face. **1957** L. Durrell *Justine* III. 199 The resonance of this one phrase refecundated his powers of feeling. **1880** 'Mark Twain' *Tramp Abroad* xlvii. 495 The tints remained during several minutes..paling almost away for a moment, then re-flushing,—a shifting, restless, unstable succession of soft opaline gleams. **1937** *Discovery* Aug. 246/2 Wintering, refoliating, flowering, and seeding. **1963** *Times Lit. Suppl.* 22 Feb. 143/1 The Book of Durrow..was taken to pieces,..rearranged, refoliated, repaired, reconditioned and..superbly rebound. **1956** *Nature* 31 Mar. 619/2 *Oidium heveae* is most prominent in Malaya at the time of refoliation after 'wintering' of the trees. **1977** J. L. Harper *Population Biol. Plants* xii. 398 Defoliation is often complete and is followed by refoliation. **1967** E. R. Lannon in Cox & Grose *Organiz. Bibliogr. Rec. by Computer* IV. 88 The user may initially employ his own Preprocessor to edit and reformat his data. **1973** *Computers & Humanities* VII. 214 The cards were built onto a disk file by a program that reformatted the material into fixed-length records. **1911** Mrs. H. Ward *Case of Richard Meynell* xxiii. 484 Hester's telegram, sent originally to Upcote and reforwarded, had reached Meynell in Paris. **1957** M. Lowry *Let.* 29 Apr. (1967) 407 Your letter of March 12..Cape sent it back to Canada again, so that it had to get reforwarded again from B.C. before I received it. **1947** J. Hilton *So well Remembered* IV. 265 George's last two letters had never reached Charles... (They did arrive, eventually, after a series of fantastic re-forwardings.) **1962** H. L. Kern et al. in A. Pirie *Lens Metabolism Rel. Cataract* 386 The lenses were subsequently removed, dipped in saline containing antibiotics, and reincubated at 37 °C. **1961** *Lancet* 22 July 213/2 Absence of reinfarction. **1972** *Computers & Humanities* VI. 282 As before, the user must establish output procedures and appropriate tests for upper and lower limits and reinitialize counters. **1973** C. W. Gear *Introd. Computer Sci.* vi. 246 It is very easy to make the mistake of transferring back to the start of the loop, forgetting to re-initialize variables when it is required. **1964** C. Dent *Quantity Surveying by Computer* vi. 88 The items are queried and re-input, except for zero items, which will not be required to appear in the bill in any case. **1967** J. D. Dews in Cox & Grose *Organiz. Bibliogr. Rec. by Computer* II. 24 The tape..can then be corrected and re-input to correct the file. **1963** *Daily Tel.* 1 Nov. 14/2 To these torments must be added that of reintensified bombing. **1967** E. Chambers *Photolitho-Offset* ix. 133 Reintensify if added contrast is required. **1946** *Nature* 14 Sept. 379/1 Leaf infection of onion seedlings was obtained by ascospore inoculation, and the fungus was re-isolated from the lesions. **1977** J. L. Harper *Population Biol. of Plants* xi. 348 The bacterial agent must be re-isolated from the experimentally infected plant. *Ibid.*, The re-isolated micro-organism and that originally inoculated must be tested for identity. **1934** Webster, Relicense. *a* **1974** R. Crossman *Diaries* (1977) III. 870, I then said that we must break this relicensing operation into two stages. **1977** *Times* 11 Oct. 4/3 Dr Lemon..did not favour relicensing all pilots who had suffered heart attacks. **1963** *Times* 29 May 7/2 The practice of 'stop-listing', 'delisting', and then 'relisting' areas can be a powerful deterrent to industrialists. **1976** *Times* 25 Oct. 14/7 Save in cases of nullity, the jurisdiction to relist depended on the likelihood of an injustice having been done. **1967** Karch & Buber *Offset Processes* x. 474 Old grease should be removed and the gears re-lubricated every one million impressions. **1965** G. J. Williams *Econ. Geol. N.Z.* viii. 99/1 A detailed remapping of the area will reveal the importance of deep pre-Second Period weathering. **1933** H. G. Wells *Shape of Things to Come* III. 261 The need for a planned 'renucleation' in the social magma that arose out of this dissolution. **1934** —— *Exper. Autobiogr.* II. vii. 481 Socialism, if it is anything more than a petty tinkering with economic relationships is a renucleation of society. **1901** *Westm. Gaz.* 13 May 4/3 The 'Marseillaise' has just been reorchestrated by order of the Minister of War. **1975** *New Yorker* 19 May 85/1 It seems to me that the actual personalities and events of the Nez Perce war were possibly even more interesting..than were the respectfully created counterparts..reorchestrated for us today. **1940** L. MacNeice *Poems* 251 Smuggling over the frontier Of fact a sense of value, Metabolism of death, Re-orchestration of world. **1975** *New Yorker* 16 June 97/1 In the late sixties, the opera was quite often given..but always in an edition by Claudio Abbado marred by many cuts, by some reorchestration, and, most gravely, by the recasting of Romeo as a tenor. **1854** Thoreau *Walden* 163, I occasionally observed that he was thinking for himself and expressing his own opinion, a phenomenon so rare that I would any day walk ten miles to observe it, and it amounted to the re-origination of many of the institutions of society. **1832** J. S. Mill *Let.* 22 Oct. in *Coll. Wks.* (1963) XII. 128 They were the reoriginators of *any* belief among us. **1935** L. MacNeice *Poems* 32 The basic facts repatterned without pause. **1952** C. P. Blacker *Eugenics* x. 246 The gene-complex has a holistic or integrative action of its own, a capacity to undergo changes, to adjust itself to a re-patterning of its constituent elements. **1972** *Guardian* 28 Oct. 24 It is open to Mr Barber..to repeg the pound at an exchange rate far above the level to which it has now fallen. **1978** *N. Y. Times* 30 Mar. D1/6 The yen..has actually been revalued upward by 38.43 percent since it was repegged at the Smithsonian rate of 308 to the dollar in December 1971. **1938** *Sun* (Baltimore) 12 July 14/5 Accompanied by rumors..of a possible 'repegging' at its old ratio of between $4.86 and $4.87, the British pound sterling declined today..to its lowest point in more than a year. **1964** G. H. Haggis et al. *Introd. Molecular Biol.* vi. 182 (*caption*) An enzyme at the inner boundary rephosphorylates the diglyceride to phosphatidic acid, in interaction with ATP. **1965** Phillips & Williams *Inorg. Chem.* I. xvii. 638 The ADP is then rephosphorylated via various sugar-phosphates and the oxidation of glycogen. **1877** *Nature* 27 Sept. 468/2 In repiling and reheating this iron several times this defective appearance is gradually removed. **1947** *Penguin New Writing* XXX. 104 The lame boy stayed behind and helped me re-pile the tins. **1956** D. Gascoyne *Night Thoughts* 37 To swell the roar that rises with each climax repostponed. **1967** Karch & Buber *Offset Processes* iv. 125 Modification is possible to condense, expand,..reproportion height and width. **1969** P. L. Berger *Rumor of Angels* v. 121 The openness and the re-proportioning this attitude entails have a moral significance, even a political significance, of no mean degree. **1963** *Rep. Comm. Inquiry Decimal Currency* xiv. 138 Ancillary machine costs:..re-punching card and tape records. **1965** *Math. in Biol. & Med.* (Med. Res. Council) II. 48 A start has now been made on re-punching the British Columbia marriage records for 1946–55 in a form suitable for testing such a system. **1887** G. B. Shaw *Let.* 7 Feb. (1965) I. 162 The American printer..has taken upon himself the re-punctuation of 'Cashel Byron'. **1966** *Mod. Lang. Q.* Sept. 256, I was, I believe, responsible for most of the detailed examination of poems in *A Survey of Modernist Poetry*—for example showing the complex implications of Sonnet 129 before its eighteenth-century repunctuations. **1975** D. W. S. Hunt *On Spot* iv. 54 As I heard him say over the lunch table once, 'to rat is difficult; to re-rat..' and he broke off as though to show that to find a description of a second change of party was beyond even his eloquence. **1938** *Times* 22 Jan. 5/1 The prospects of a re-recovery in the United States. **1922** Joyce *Ulysses* 671 With greater difficulty remembered, forgot with ease, with misgiving reremembered. **1923** D. H. Lawrence *Birds, Beasts & Flowers* 24 For we are on the brink of re-remembrance. **1922** Joyce *Ulysses* 133 But my riddle! he said. What opera is like a railway?—Opera? Mr. O'Madden Burke's sphinx face reriddled. **1973** *Nature* 6 Apr. 377/1 The role of postgraduate students may well be rescrutinized. **1963** *Punch* 6 Feb. 182/3 The whole business ..deserved re-scrutiny. **1955** Auden *Shield of Achilles* ii. 45 Re-sex the pronouns, add a few details. **1951** L. MacNeice tr. *Goethe's Faust* I. 14 The little god of the world, one can't reshape, reshade him. **1961** Webster, Reshow. **1976** *Times Lit. Suppl.* 21 May 620/5 Pabst's maligned film, which is still frequently reshown. **1977** *Listener* 24 Mar. 385/2 Most programmes are not re-shown. **1976** K. Benton *Single Monstrous Act* iii. 17 Let's go and see that film at the local. It's a re-showing of *The Godfather*. **1841** *Civil Engin. & Arch. Jrnl.* IV. 341/2 Scintling (removing and restacking the bricks in the hacks). **1892** *Daily News* 26 Feb. 5/7 A patch of brickwork, six feet by three feet, had been taken out of the chimney to be re-stacked. **1923** *Daily Mail* 30 May 7 The combat will be restaged at the forthcoming pageant. **1929** *Daily Express* 16 Jan. 6 A famous comedian ..suddenly decided to alter his programme and not restage his old, worn-out material. **1962** M. Cook tr. *Dia's Afr. Nations & World Solidarity* ix. 97 It will be vain to hope for a profound change toward a progressive economy..without a bold restructuration incompatible with an exaggerated desire to spare the former capitalist structures. **1970** B. Brewster tr. *Althusser & Balibar's Reading Capital* (1975) III. iii. 259 Reproduction appears to be the general form of permanence of the general conditions of production, which in the last analysis englobe the whole social structure, and therefore it is indeed essential that it should be the form of their change and restructuration, too. **1972** *Times* 26 June 12/4 The restructuration of a basic sector of European economy. **1900** *Daily News* 27 Sept. 7 The Count..is hard at work directing the repairs to the airship, which has already been resuspended. **1946** *Nature* 5 Oct. 486/2 The mixture is..re-suspended in saline to give a concentration of 2–5 per cent. **1976** *Nucl. Engin. Internat.* Nov. 37/2 Eventually the Pu settles to the ground and may be resuspended by being blown up by winds. **1884** *Pall Mall Gaz.* 16 Oct. 5/2 The Exchequer, however, is still in want of funds, and the resuspension is expected before long. **1978** *Nature* 27 Apr. 754/2 The lack of response to fire in the pollen input could be due to..the resuspension and resedimentation which occurs in the lakes. **1884** *Practitioner* XXXIII. 289 (*heading*) Resuturing of granulating wounds. **1901** *Brit. Med. Jrnl.* 2 Feb. 263/1 Should any difficulty be met with in replacing the bowel, the opening can be enlarged and then resutured without causing any weakening in the lower part of the abdominal wall. **1961** *Lancet* 19 Aug. 402/2 After resuture of the wound the patient's general condition gradually improved. **1977** *Ibid.* 1 Jan. 28/1 One of these is abdominal wound disruption—a complication fatal at worst and a serious nuisance at best, for, should all go well directly after resuture, there is both a prolonged hospital stay and a much increased risk of incisional hernia. **1927** Haldane & Huxley *Animal Biol.* v. 120 The actual process of contraction may have an efficiency of 90 to 100 per cent., but an amount of energy greater than the work done in contraction is wasted as heat during the re-synthesis of the lactic and phosphoric acids, so that the whole process has an efficiency of only about 40 per cent. **1956** *Nature* 7 Jan. 22/2 There is little to support the notion that phospholipids act as intermediates in the resynthesis of triglycerides during fat absorption. **1978** *Ibid.* 12 Oct. p. ix/1 (Advt.), Components of cells in all living organisms undergo continual breakdown and resynthesis. **1928** A. B. Callow *Food & Health* 21 The fats are split up into their component parts, fatty acids and glycerol. These substances are absorbed by certain body-cells and again resynthesized into fats. **1964** G. H. Haggis et al. *Introd. Molecular Biol.* v. 137 All cells require new proteins during growth and division, and are subsequently constantly resynthesizing their enzymes and other proteins. **1928** *Daily Express* 9 Aug. 14/1 (Advt.), O'coats turned and retailored. **1949** M. Mead *Male & Female* xii. 260 The reactionary and the cynic make common cause in suggesting that..laws and ideals should be re-tailored to recognize the deviations and discrepancies between ideal and practice. **1977** *Times* 27 Apr. 23/8 On the bonus side value-added tax machinery is retailored to harmonize with EEC directives. **1966** *Aviation Week & Space Technol.* 18 Apr. 31 This was the retargeted date after the March 30 attempt. **1893** *Pall Mall Gaz.* 25 Jan. 7/1 The wedding of the Princess Sophie to the Crown Prince of Greece implied a further re-tightening of the bonds of friendship between Copenhagen and Berlin. **1960** *Times* 1 June 18/7 But the production as a whole needs re-timing. **1967** Karch & Buber *Offset Processes* x. 468 The sheets should be ½ inch away from the guides at this point. If not, the feeder must be retimed to the press. **1977** *Dædalus* Summer 109 He persuaded the Survey of India to retriangulate part of the region. **1927** *Blackw. Mag.* Feb. 256/1 It would mean the retriangulation of the whole area, and endless delays and doubts as to the fixing of the position of soundings already taken off the coast. **1975** J. B. Harley *U.S. Maps* i. 7 Supplementary work on the re-triangulation continues. **1974** M. C. Gerald *Pharmacol.* v. 101 Norepinephrine is taken back into the presynaptic neurons (re-uptake process), thus removing it from the receptor area. **1977** *Lancet* 21 May 1081/1 The amount of catecholamine entering the blood is dependent upon a complex process of neuronal release and reuptake into nerve terminals. *c* **1864** E. Dickinson *Bolts of Melody* (1945) 246 One rewalks a precipice. **1969** J. T. Burtchaell *Catholic Theories of Biblical Inspiration since 1810* vii. 303 The individual Christian can and certainly should rewalk the route from paganism to Christ. **1877** G. M. Hopkins *Poems* (1967) 68, I hear the lark ascend, His rash-fresh re-winded new-skeinèd score In crisps of curl. **1970** 'D. Halliday' *Dolly & Cookie Bird* xi. 168 He..pulled back a zipper..re-zipped it. **1974** 'M. Underwood' *Pinch of Snuff* xi. 97 Brian watched him re-zip the bag.

b. *re-brighten* vb., *-catholicization*, *-centralization*, *-civilianization*, *-civilianize* vb., *-institutionalization*, *-institutionalize* vb., *-modernize* vb., *-phonemicization*, *-phonologization*, *-phonologize* vb., *popularize* vb., *-solemnize* vb., *-stabilization*, *-Stalinization*, *-Stalinize* vb., *-standardization*, *-sterilization*, *-sweeten* vb., *-vascularization*, *-vascularize* vb., *-volatilization.*

1925 E. Sitwell *Poetry & Crit.* 23 Miss Stein..breaks down the predestined groups of words..; then she re-brightens them,..and builds them into new and vital shapes. **1949** *Scottish Jrnl. Theol.* II. 241 The pressure for visible unity, for a recatholicisation of the Churches, has ..[come] from the 'evangelical' movements burdened with fulfilling the mission of the Gospel to the whole world. **1925** *Glasgow Herald* 5 Oct. 11 Only Scotland and the Northern (Newcastle) [administration] will continue to function, but the official policy is definitely recentralisation because of the enormous fall in the volume of the work. **1957** C. P. McVicker *Titoism* p. x, Decentralization as Re-centralization. **1967** *Economist* 14 Oct. 149/2 There is not necessarily a contradiction between the drive for reform and the temporary re-centralisation of investment policy, plus a restrictive incomes policy. **1947** *Manch. Guardian* 18 July, Certain foreigners are eligible for 'recivilianisation'. **1962** S. E. Finer *Man on Horseback* xi. 190 How far it is possible for a military régime, starting with quasi-civilian institutions,..ultimately to re-civilianize itself. *Ibid.* 197 Could the régime not pass..from a quasi-civilianized military régime..to a re-civilianized one? What would be the criteria of such re-civilianization? *Ibid.* 198 In both these cases it has taken a long time for the 're-civilianization' to take root. **1978** *Sci. Amer.* Feb. 50/2 Most patients are placed in nursing homes.., a process the Department of Health, Education, and Welfare has labeled 'reinstitutionalization', since most homes have more than 100 beds (and yet offer only custodial care). **1976** *Guardian Weekly* 14 Nov. 7/2 The first task of the Carter administration must be to reinstitutionalise American foreign policy. **1973** *Courier & Advertiser* (Dundee) 7 Aug. 1/3 (Advt.), Remodernised 4-apartment house. **1976** *S. Wales Echo* 27 Nov. 9/4 (Advt.), Remodernised fur coats. **1951** Z. S. Harris *Methods in Structural Linguistics* ix. 93 The following not infrequent situation is also a special case of resegmentation of a segment for purposes of rephonemicization. **1972** R. Jakobson in A. R. Keiler *Reader in Hist. & Compar. Linguistics* 135 Within the framework of an isolated functional dialect, one cannot speak either of an increase or a reduction of a phonological system, but only of a restructuring, that is, of its rephonologization. **1975** *Amer. Speech 1971* XLVI. 266 Change cannot be incorporated within Saussurian idealized homogeneity of structure; that does not change, it is merely rephonologized. **1906** *Westm. Gaz.* 11 Aug. 12/2, I do not intend to repopularize the stereoscope. **1959** I. & P. Opie *Lore & Lang. Schoolch.* ii. 38 The following favourite accumulates on the principle of 'The House that Jack built'. It was repopularized by the American folk-singer Burl Ives in 1953, but had been current in Britain for anyway forty years before his visit. **1949** 'J. Nelson' *Backwoods Teacher* xvi. 173 There before an assemblage they wrote their names in the Bible and took each other for better or worse—the same to be re-solemnized later when the preacher should come through. **1953** P. L. Fermor *Violins of Saint-Jacques* 28 A phoenix's funeral that was resolemnised each evening. **1921** *Nineteenth Cent.* Feb. 231 A disastrous blow to the restabilization of Europe. **1958** A. J. Toynbee *East to West* xxv. 75 The population started to increase at an accelerating rate (it is still increasing today, though re-stabilization is now in sight). **1956** *Washington Post* 19 Nov. A21/1 Even today, after the unspeakable horror of the blood bath in Hungary, the betting is still somewhat against a 're-Stalinization'. **1974** R. J. Osborn *Evolution Soviet Politics* v. 195 Just as with Khruschev's anti-Stalin campaign, Brezhnev's cautious but firm 're-Stalinization' has been a weapon for dealing with current problems. **1968** *Russian Rev.* XXVII. 309 All this evidence might appear to be leading to the conclusion that the party leadership is trying to re-Stalinize, but is forced to proceed very gradually in the face of opposition. **1911** Webster, Restandardization. **1938** *Mind* XLVII. 103 It is to be urgently hoped that a similar restandardization will be attempted for the present scale. **1952** C. P. Blacker *Eugenics* 204 The Pintner-Patterson scale (1917) and the Arthur Performance scale, the latter a restandardization of ten of the tests used in the former, are now in common use. **1900** A. H. Buck *Ref. Handbk. Med. Sci.* (ed. 2) I. 567/2 The best silk sponges are expensive so that resterilization would be necessary. **1966** Auden *About House* 29 Shrines.. Rose again Resweetened the hirsute West. **1924** *Jrnl. Path. & Bacteriol.* XXVII. 205 Revascularisation of the lobule takes place. **1954** Martin & Hynes *Clin. Endocrinol.* (ed. 2) i. 4 If the grafts were placed at a distance away from the portal trunks revascularization from other vessels was not followed by active function. **1963** *Lancet* 12 Jan. 89/2 Given sufficient time..dead bone can become revascularized, and a case that starts off as a non-union with no callus can ultimately unite. **1971** *Nature* 23 July 279/2 The question of how skin grafts are revascularized is still not resolved. **1866** *Q. Jrnl. Geol. Soc.* XXII. 441 The volatile matters removed by distillation..have found a reception where no revolatilization could occur. **1938** R. W. LAWSON tr. *Hevesy & Paneth's Man. Radioactivity* (ed. 2) xviii. 170 The condensation and revolatilization of bismuth hydride.

c. *re-cane, -fenestrate, -lampshade, -litter, -mine, -neck, -pew* (earlier example), *-staff, -washer* vbs.

1971 *Islander* (Victoria, B.C.) 16 May 5/4 There was also a small chair that went with the set but he was having the seat re-caned. **1970** H. BRAUN *Parish Churches* xvii. 214 Few early churches escaped being at least in part re-fenestrated during the High Gothic era. **1971** *Country Life* 3 June 1366/3 He did not make great changes..other than to refenestrate the east and south sides. **1918** A. BENNETT *Roll-Call* I. ii. 24 The lampshade craze increasing in virulence, they had between them re-lampshaded the entire house. **1775** W. H. MARSHALL *Minutes Agric.* (1778) sig. D3, Shovelling the gangways, and re-littering them with long dung. **1960** *Farmer & Stockbreeder* 16 Feb. 145/3 The whole place is then thoroughly cleaned,..and rested a week before being re-littered. **1917** J. MASEFIELD *Old Front Line* iii. 38 It was all mined, countermined, and re-mined. **1967** *Guardian* 2 Mar. 6/6 A genuine theorbo, built as a lute in 1584 and renecked in 1730. **1978** *Early Music* Oct. 531/2 It seems to have been cut down all round and re-necked in the 18th century to make a seven-string viol. **1839** F. WITTS *Diary* 20 May (1978) 160 The church has been recently repewed with deal. **1898** *Westm. Gaz.* 4 Apr. 7/2 The hospital committee accepted the resignation, and a special meeting has been called to consider the subject of restaffing the institution. **1898** *Daily News* 16 Apr. 9/5 The Management Committee..decided to close the Institution..and restaff the place with as little delay as possible. **1960** *Times* 16 Sept. 13/5 Recently a tap over a wash hand basin in my office..required re-washering. *Ibid.*, The local water company re-washer water taps free of charge in order to save water. **1974** J. WAINWRIGHT *Evidence I shall Give* xx. 92 The handyman who re-washers a tap.

're (-əɪ, -ɪ), contraction of ARE, pl. pres. ind. of BE, as *you're, they're.* Freq. used in the representation of speech (and for metrical reasons in verse). Cf. YARE, Y'ARE.

1591 SHAKES. *Two Gent.* v. iv. 44 O, 'tis the curse in love, and still approv'd, When women cannot love where they're belov'd. **1676** G. ETHEREGE *Man of Mode* IV. i. 56 The women indeed are little beholding to the young men of this age; they're generally only dull admirers of themselves. **1738** SWIFT *Polite Conv.* 2, I hope, you're never the worse. But where's your manners? **1836** DICKENS *Pickw.* (1837) ii. 12 'They're beginning up stairs,' said the stranger—'hear the..fiddles tuning.' **1978** J. UPDIKE *Coup* (1979) i. 39 Whoever the hell you are, you're the best thing I've seen today.

reable, *v.* Restrict †*Sc. Obs.* to sense in Dict. and add: **2.** (riˌēɪ·b'l) *trans. Med.* To rehabilitate (a patient).

1945 *Lancet* 24 Mar. 387/2 For some year or two I have suggested to friends who write or teach that we should say 'reable' instead of 'rehabilitate'. It therefore gives me pleasure..to read of 'reabling' and 'reablement' in your last three issues. **1947** E. SPRIGGS in I. Brown *Say Word* 101, I am glad to see that the words Reable and Reablement are now being frequently used in the *Lancet* and other journals.

Hence **rea·blement**, rehabilitation.

1945 *Lancet* 3 Mar. 275/2 The committee believe that a revised programme of reablement should be administered by a senior tuberculosis officer. **1945, 1947** [see above]. **1955** *Brit. Jrnl. Physical Med.* XVIII. 119/1 Reablement is seen as an intricate problem which has to be considered from very various aspects. **1968** *Lancet* 2 Nov. 985/2 To be comprehensive and successful any reablement programme must be built on well-organised services for health, education, social work, and vocational training.

reabsorb, *v.* Add: **b.** *intr.* for *pass.* To be reabsorbed.

1916 GALSWORTHY in *Scribner's Mag.* Jan. 17/1 In one's heart rose an ecstasy of love for this..earth which breeds us all, and into which we reabsorb.

reabso·rptive, *a.* [RE- 5 a.] Having the quality of reabsorbing.

1946 *Nature* 23 Nov. 730/1 The concept of competition for secretory and reabsorptive mechanisms in the renal tubules has proved very fruitful. **1975** *Ibid.* 27 Feb. 747/1 Mammalian bladder possesses, in addition to an exceptionally high electrical resistance, an aldosterone-stimulated Na^+ reabsorptive mechanism.

reaccommodate, *v.* (Later example.)

1920 *Nineteenth Cent.* Oct. 629 It will take time before the Jews can again reaccommodate themselves to the local conditions.

reach, *sb.*[1] Add: **I. 4. b.** (Later examples.) Also, a course that is approximately at right angles to the wind.

1949 *Sun* (Baltimore) 20 June 16/1 From the start to Sandy Point, the skippers had to face a headwind, the next leg..was a reach, while the trip to Poole's Island Light resulted in another beat. **1976** *Oxf. Compan. Ships & Sea* 695/1 *Reach*, the point of sailing of a vessel which can point her course with the wind reasonably free and her sails full throughout. A broad reach is the same but with the wind abeam or from slightly abaft the beam. **1977** *Modern Boating* (Austral.) Jan. 14/1 Destiny II will go like a rocket on a reach or a run.

II. 5. *spec.* in *Cricket*, the extent to which a batsman can play forward without moving his back foot; in *Boxing* (see quot. 1958).

1851 *F. Lillywhite's Guide to Cricketers* 18 A good length ball depends entirely upon the size and reach of a batsman. **1897** K. S. RANJITSINHJI *Jubilee Bk. Cricket* iii. 67 Batsmen vary greatly as to their 'reach'—that is, the distance they can safely play forward or advance the bat in making a drive. **1951** *Sport* 30 Mar.–5 Apr. 11/3 He quickly found that O'Hara, his opponent, was longer in the reach. **1958** F. C. AVIS *Boxing Ref. Dict.* s.v. *Reach*: the distance from the extremity of one hand to that of the other when the arms are fully held out sideways.

III. 12. c. (Later examples.)

1955 *Times* 9 May 3/3 The action therefore slows almost to a standstill in the middle reaches of the play. **1971** J. B. CARROLL et al. *Word Frequency Bk.* p. xxxvi, *Hapax legomena*..come from almost anywhere in the lower reaches of the theoretical type distribution.

IV. 16. *attrib.* and *Comb.*, as (sense 13 a) *reach land*; **reach rod**, a connecting rod for transmitting manual motion to a remote part of a mechanism.

1795 T. CHAPMAN *Jrnl.* 4 Nov. in *Hist. Mag. Amer.* (1869) V. 359 They appear contented and Happy, having Plenty of fine reach Land. **1909** *Cent Dict.* Suppl., *Reach-rod*, in a locomotive, a rod which connects the reverse-lever in the cab to the bell-crank on the reverse-shaft of the valve-gear. **1972** L. M. HARRIS *Introd. Deepwater Floating Drilling Operations* 238 Some compartments will have reach rods to bilge drainage valves.

17. Used *attrib.* to designate a fork-lift truck whose fork can be moved forward and backward as well as up and down.

1962 *Engineering* 2 Nov. 584/1 Until the reach truck appeared, the provision of two hydraulic functions in a fork truck was considered difficult. **1963** *Times Rev. Industry* May 91/3 Reach types—The fork carriage is movable in a horizontal plane, with forks reaching beyond the front wheels to withdraw the load to a position within the wheelbase.

reach, *v.*[1] Add: **I. 6. c.** *U.S. slang.* To bribe.

1906 A. H. LEWIS *Confessions of Detective* 72 I'd been squared; it was known that I could be reached. **1912** A. TRAIN *Courts, Criminals & Camorra* III. ix. 234 In America, if the criminal can 'reach' the complaining witness or 'call him off' he has nothing to worry about. **1929** C. F. COE *Hooch!* v. 105 You could reach the..Attorney without tippin' your hand to him at all. **1967** L. KATCHER *Earl Warren* xvi. 124 It is impossible..to open a big, notorious gambling operation without buying off public officials... This does not necessarily mean a sheriff or a District Attorney or a chief of police is being reached. **1968** W. SAFIRE *New Lang. Politics* 373/1 *Reached*, bought off; corrupted. A public official may be *approached* with no implication of commitment on his part; when he has been *spoken to*, the implication is that he is neutralized or partially persuaded pending a final decision; when he is *reached*, however, he has been bought and sold.

8. b. (Later examples.) Now *esp.*, to communicate with (a person).

1919 E. O'NEILL *Moon of Caribbees* 113 Ut is only from your chance meetin' wid Harry..that I happen to know where to reach you. **1967** D. FRANCIS *Blood Sport* v. 55 The two drivers, reached by telephone, met us by appointment. **1973** R. LUDLUM *Matlock Paper* xiii. 122 I'm off the phone now. Would you like to try reaching Miss Ballantyne?

II. 12. c. (Later examples.) *to reach for the roof, sky*, etc. (orig. *U.S.*), of a person held at gunpoint: to raise the hands above the head; *to reach for one's gun*, etc., used *fig.* for: to react with extreme hostility.

The statement in quot. 1953 is commonly attributed to the German Nazi leader H. Goering (1893–1946), but it has been traced (in a slightly different form) to the nationalistic play *Schlageter* (1933) by the German dramatist H. Johst (1890–): see *Oxf. Dict. Quotations* (ed. 3, 1980).

1904 L. TRACY *King of Diamonds* iii. 39 He reached over for the stone. **1910** W. M. RAINE *B. O'Connor* ii. 25 Now reach for the roof. **1927** *Ladies' Home Jrnl.* Dec. 6/3, I reached for the stars pronto, without even turning my head. **1931** W. JAMES *Sun Up* 42 'Stick em up,' I says... One of 'em flinches some but finally reaches for the sky. **1953** in *Oxf. Dict. Quotations* (ed. 2) 223/2 When I hear anyone talk of Culture, I reach for my revolver. **1959** *Spectator* 9 Oct. 480/2 Cherwell was not a cultured man; indeed he seems almost to have reached for his gun when 'culture' was in the air. **1967** *Guardian* 12 Oct. 9/6 This is the point at which Laing's critics reach for their guns. **1968** R. F. ADAMS *Western Words* (ed. 2) 245/2 *Reach for the sky!*, a gunman's command to raise the hands in the air. **1980** *Listener* 14 Aug. 200/1 Members of PRO Dogs..will..be reaching for their choke-chains because..criticism of..dogs is a treasonable activity.

e. (Later example.)

1935 W. G. HARDY *Father Abraham* IV. i. 349 But Abraham strode along and snuffed the air and was tender to Sarai as he helped her on and felt his whole heart reaching out to her.

f. To make an unwarranted inference; to jump to a conclusion; to guess. orig. and chiefly *U.S.*

1960 'E. MCBAIN' *Give Boys Great Big Hand* x. 106 This may be reaching, but here it is anyway, for what it's worth. **1963** 'G. BAGBY' *Murder's Little Helper* xii. 149 Anderson moaned. 'Inspector,' he said, 'Isn't that reaching?' **1964** L. TREAT in H. Waugh *Merchants of Menace* (1969) 11 The way he saw things, the Lieutenant was sure reaching for it—far out. **1973** G. MOFFAT *Lady with Cool Eye* xi. 130 Dawson..might very well be visiting Mrs Wolkoff..but no: as the Americans say, we're reaching. **1978** R. LUDLUM *Holcroft Covenant* xviii. 212 'Aren't you reaching, Miles?'.. 'I said it was a theory, but not without some support.'

14. b. (Later example.)

1935 B. MALINOWSKI in M. Black *Importance of Lang.* (1962) 90 A word rich in associations and reaching out in many directions.

c. (Later example.)

1951 M. MCLUHAN *Mech. Bride* (1967) 132/2 Some interesting assumptions that reach back more than two centuries.

16. a. Also *absol. spec.* in *Baseball*: to reach first base.

1891 *Young Man* Apr. 128/1, I sent letter upon letter after him, but they don't seem to reach. **1974** *Anderson* (S. Carolina) *Independent* 20 Apr. 6A/6 The Cavs tied it in their half of the inning as Duval White reached on an error, stole second, went to third on Dan Berstein's first of four hits and scored on Jonathan Williams' fly ball. **1976** *Billings* (Montana) *Gaz.* 6 July 1-C/3 Dan Fuchs reached on an error, Rich Popp singled to score Knudtson, and Mike Klunder brought Fuchs home on a sacrifice fly.

reachable, *a.* Add: **2. a.** (Later examples.) Also, as *sb.*, one who may be reached (in quot. 1974, denoting a person who can be bribed).

1914 R. & E. SHACKLETON *Four on Tour in Eng.* xviii. 186 Few visitors go to Runnimede [*sic*], because it has not been a readily reachable place by rail. **1974** *Publishers Weekly* 27 May 31 (Advt.), The secret deals behind the rip-off, put-down and sell-out of the American people..to Big Money interests..with the help of the reachables in office! **1978** *Detroit Free Press* 5 Mar. A4/1 Most buds and twigs and other reachable food are gone. If snow is deep enough, deer cannot escape.

b. *Math.* That may be reached (from a specified point) by passing along the lines of a graph.

1959 *Sociometry* XXII. 143 The matrix *M* contains all these paths and also a path of length *l* from each point to itself. Thus each point is reachable from itself. **1965** F. HARARY et al. *Structural Models* ii. 43 Point *v* is reachable from *u* in a digraph *D* if and only if there is a sequence from *u* to *v*. **1978** D. D. ŠILJAK *Large-Scale Dynamic Syst.* iii. 149 A reachable set $V_i(v_j)$ of a point v_j is a set of points v_i reachable from v_j.

Hence **reachabi·lity** *Math.*, the possibility of reaching one point of a graph from another; freq. *attrib.*

1959 *Sociometry* XXII. 141 We present a logical sequence of theorems that characterize strengthening and weakening group members... We..find it convenient to introduce the concept of the 'reachability matrix' of a group. **1965** F. HARARY et al. *Structural Models* ii. 43 Reachability is reflexive since every point of *V* is reachable from itself by a path of length 0. *Ibid.* 45 The difference between reachability and joining is that in the latter instance we ignore the direction of the lines. *Ibid.* v. 117 The reachability matrix *R*(*D*) whose entries are denoted r_{ij} and defined as follows: $r_{ij} = 1$ if v_j is reachable from v_i; otherwise $r_{ij} = 0$. **1978** D. D. ŠILJAK *Large-Scale Dynamic Syst.* iii. 149 The reachability concept of digraphs.

reacher. Add: **3.** *Yachting.* (See quot. 1903.)

1903 *Outing* XLII. 646/2 Intermediate between the baby and the balloon are various jib-topsails called 'reachers' and numbered 1, 2, 3, according to the size. **1977** P. JOHNSON *Offshore Manual Internat.* 152 Under the rule 'jibs' includes all fore and after headsails such as genoas, staysails, bigboy/bloopers, reachers and drifters.

reaching, *vbl. sb.*[1] Add: **3.** (In sense 15 c of the vb.) *reaching foresail, jib, sail, staysail.*

1948 R. DE KERCHOVE *Internat. Maritime Dict.* (ed. 2) 581/2 *Reaching foresail*, a triangular sail which sets on the forestay... Also called Genoa foresail, Genoa jib. **1924** G. H. P. MUHLHAUSER *Cruise of Amaryllis* vii. 273 There is now rather more wind and we are carrying reaching jib and staysail. **1962** D. F. SOUTHERN in A. Garrett *Roving Commissions* 11 It was sunny, warm and most pleasant running under our large reaching sail. **1924** G. H. P. MUHLHAUSER *Cruise of Amaryllis* vii. 273 At sunset I changed to the working jib but left the reaching staysail.

reaching, *vbl. sb.*[2] (Later example.)

1791 J. WOODFORDE *Diary* 7 June (1927) III. 275 She was..very much swelled in the face by reaching and very weak.

reach-me-down, *a.* and *sb.* Add: **A.** *adj.* **b.** *transf.* and *fig.* Ready-made, stock; derivative, inferior.

1907 G. B. SHAW *Let.* 11 July (1972) II. 700 You are not.. one of these reach-me-down people. **1914** —— in *New Statesman* 14 Nov. 19/2 Europe has a stock of ready-made constitutions... It is therefore quite possible that a reach-me-down constitution proposed..by an international congress..might prove acceptable. **1932** V. WOOLF *Common Reader* 2nd Ser. 230 There are a dozen occasions on which a reach-me-down character will satisfy him well enough. **1951** C. DAY LEWIS *Lyrical Poetry of Thomas Hardy* in *Proc. Brit. Acad.* XXXVII. 158 Often..Hardy seems to lose all touch with his medium, and will dress up his subjects in the shoddiest, reach-me-down verse. **1962** *Times* 14 Jan. 12/5 The clergyman full of reach-me-down psychology. **1975** *Listener* 4 Dec. 760/1 The role he has chosen is that of a reach-me-down James Bond. **1976** *Glasgow Herald* 26 Nov. 5/5 Daniel Wayenberg's programme of works by Brahms, Bartok, Ravel and Mussorgsky proved an admirable one with not a reach-me-down sonata in sight.

B. *sb.* **1. a.** (Earlier and later examples.)

1862 F. SINNETT *Acct. Colony S. Australia* 53 Waxen dummies, in their model reach-me-downs. **1922** MRS. A. SIDGWICK *Victorian* i. 11 She has evidently bought a reach-me-down at one of the cheap shops, and as for her hat it's the limit. **1926** A. BENNETT *Lord Raingo* I. xxxv. 165 He had said stiffly that he would enter the House of Lords in no hired reach-me-down. **1928** D. BYRNE *Destiny Bay* i. 117 A small rat-faced man in a suit of reach-me-downs. **1931** R. CHURCH *High Summer* IV. vi. 322 'Buy a..ready-made suit'... 'Not even the prospect of saving Filosilk from irretrievable ruin could induce me to wear a reach-me-down.' **1981** *Times* 12 Mar. 10/8 The costumes..look..like tattered reach-me-downs from the Royal Shakespeare Company.

b. *transf.* and *fig.*

1916 G. B. SHAW *Pygmalion* 191 The rest of the story.. would hardly need telling if our imaginations were not so enfeebled by their lazy dependence on the ready-mades and reach-me-downs of the ragshop in which Romance keeps its stock of 'happy endings' to misfit all stories. **1958** *Spectator* 31 Jan. 136/3 This second-hand reach-me-down of a musical comedy. **1963** *Times* 28 Jan. 6/3 Ministers realize..that there would be acute political difficulties in dressing the shop window with the cast-off reach-me-downs of policy from years ago. **1977** *Gramophone* Dec. 1015/1 My particular ration of reviews usually spares me the necessity of sitting in judgement on the familiar reach-me-downs of the classical repertoire, and the past year has been no exception.

2. *pl.* Trousers.

1877 [in Dict.]. **1905** *Westm. Gaz.* 20 Apr. 2/1 There is a gentleman in pegtop reach-me-downs (I believe this is the correct method in America of describing that portion of gentleman's attire which a lady is never supposed to notice). **1979** G. MITCHELL *Mudflats of Dead* ix. 96 Tatty old reach-me-downs..and a gosh-awful dirty sweater.

reachy, *a.* Delete *rare* and add later examples.

1902 *Rep. Evolution Committee R. Soc.* I. 96 Though not so 'reachy' as a fine Indian Game, they never have the general appearance of Leghorn. **1952** A. W. HUNTER *Leighton's Compl. Bk. Dog* xvi. 227 *Neck* [of Kerry Blue Terrier]: Strong and reachy.

reacquaint, *v.* (Later examples.)

1973 M. AMIS *Rachel Papers* 20, I wondered if there were any important lies I had told her which it would be worth reacquainting myself with, but could think of none. **1977** *National Observer* (U.S.) 1 Jan. 6/5 One purpose of the tests is to give owners fun with their dogs and reacquaint them with their pets.

reacquisi·tion. [f. RE- 5 a + ACQUISITION.] The action of reacquiring; a thing which or a person who is reacquired.

1904 *Lancet* in *Westm. Gaz.* 30 Sept. 10/1 The man on his holiday..rises to the occasion by the reacquisition of powers which belong not to the town. **1959** *Times* 10 Jan. 8/5 He paid tribute to the Socratic wisdom which had rendered Mr. Forster so valuable a reacquisition to the college. **1977** *Word 1972* XXVIII. 194 It looks as if we have a reacquisition here.

react, *v.*[1] Add: **1. c.** *trans.* To cause to react chemically or immunologically *with* or *together*.

1944 [see *ADDUCT *sb.*]. **1949** [see *OXO(-) 2 c]. **1962** J. C. WRIGHT *Metallurgy in Nuclear Power Technol.* v. 91 In the Degussa process fine beryl is reacted with excess lime at 1,500°C. **1963** *Listener* 14 Mar. 459/2 A team of workers.. showed that xenon and fluorine could readily be reacted together to produce xenon-tetrafluoride. **1971** *Nature* 21 May 195/1 These, and several antisera previously made against Australasian marsupial sera, were reacted with a range of sera from Australasian and American marsupials in immunoelectrophoretic tests. **1972** *Sci. Amer.* Aug. 34/1 It is fairly easy to react unsaturated molecules with a variety of chemical reagents.

2. (Later examples.) Also, of a person: to respond; to behave in response *to* an event, a statement, etc.

1913 H. JAMES *Small Boy & Others* xv. 212 What tenuity of spirit it argues that I should neither have enjoyed nor been aware of missing..a space wider than the schoolroom floor to react and knock about in. **1921** G. B. SHAW *Back to Methuselah* p. xlviii, The assumption that he may safely cross Oxford Street in a state of unconsciousness, trusting to his dodging reflexes to react automatically and promptly enough to the visual impression produced by a motor bus. **1928** E. O'NEILL *Strange Interlude* I. 25 My heart pounding!..seeing Nina again!..how sentimental..how she'd laugh if she knew! and quite rightly..absurd for me to react as if I loved..that way. **1931** —— *Haunted* II, in *Mourning becomes Electra* (1932) 251 *Lavinia*... I have a right to love! *Orin* (reacting as his father had—his face grown livid—with a hoarse cry of fury grabs her by the throat). You—you whore! **1953** *Times* 13 May 3/5 Mr. Selwyn Lloyd said the Siamese Government..was reacting to this threat by taking precautionary measures on the north-eastern frontier. **1966** *Guardian* 11 Aug. 8/2 Pictures not only of the member addressing the House..but of other members reacting to his speech. **1979** *Economist* 28 Apr. 28/2 A firework lobbed by a demonstrator caused the police to react.

4. *spec.* of share prices: to fall after rising.

1896 [see Dict.]. **1908** *Daily Chron.* 10 Jan. 1/7 In one or two directions Stock Markets were again heavy, and prices further reacted. **1927** *Daily Tel.* 22 Nov. 2 Cairn line reacted 9d and P. and O. fell 2. **1972** *Ibid.* 29 Apr. 17/6 The shares reacted to 222p before rallying to 228p, a net loss of 2.

reactance (ri,æ·ktǎns). *Electr.* [ad. F. *réactance* (É. Hospitalier 1893, in *L'Industrie Électrique* 10 May 210/1), f. *réaction* REACTION: see -ANCE and cf. Eng. *resistance, impedance.*]

1. a. The non-resistive component of impedance, arising from the effect of inductance or capacitance or both and causing the current to be out of phase with the e.m.f. causing it. Cf. IMPEDANCE in Dict. and Suppl.

1893 *Trans. Amer. Inst. Electr. Engineers* X. 413 The term 'impedance' is suggested for the denominator..and for the quantity enclosed between the brackets, the term 'reactance' is proposed. **1896** F. BEDELL *Princ. Transformer* iv. 68 The reactance is, accordingly, equal to the component of the impressed electromotive force at right angles to the current, divided by the current. Reactance is measured in ohms. **1902** W. G. RHODES *Alternating Currents* 62 We propose to determine the equivalent resistance *R*, and the equivalent reactance *S*, of the combination. **1940** *Amateur Radio Handbk.* (ed. 2) i. 10/2 The reactance of a condenser increases as the frequency of alternating current decreases... The reactance of an inductance decreases as the frequency decreases, which is the opposite effect to that of a condenser. **1970** D. F. SHAW *Introd. Electronics* (ed. 2) ii. 33 The general definition of complex impedance is $Z = R + jX$, where *R* is the resistance and *X* is the reactance of the circuit. **1975** D. G. FINK *Electronics Engineers' Handbk.* VII. 8 The reactance of a capacitor is given by $X_C = 1/2\pi fC = 1/\omega C$ (ohms) where $f = \omega/2\pi$ is the frequency in hertz.

b. = *REACTOR 2 a.

1923 *Mod. Wireless* I. 263 Try reversing the connections of the Armstrong inductance *or* reactance. **1947** R. LEE *Electronic Transformers & Circuits* vi. 150 To avoid introducing losses and attenuation in the transmission bands, reactances as nearly pure as practicable are used in the elements of a wave filter. **1961** [see *REACTOR 2 a].

2. *Mech.* and *Acoustics.* The imaginary component of a mechanical or acoustic impedance, producing a phase difference between a driving force and the resulting motion but no dissipation of energy.

1925 *Physical Rev.* XXV. 91 In the acoustic filters the impedances were combinations of the reactances, $iM\omega$ and $i/C\omega$, ω being 2π times the frequency, *M* the inertance and *C* the capacitance. **1932** W. WEST *Acoustical Engin.* i. 3 Any impedance may be expressed as the vectorial sum of two components, a resistance and a reactance, whose phases differ by 90°. *Ibid.* iv. 54 The impedance comprises a resistance component, which depends on the rate of absorption of sound by the walls of the cavity..and an elastic reactance, in parallel, which depends on the volume of the cavity. **1950** KINSLER & FREY *Fund. Acoustics* viii. 202 The acoustic reactance *x* of a sound medium..is the component that results from the effective mass and stiffness of the medium. **1958** CONDON & ODISHAW *Handbk. Physics* II. iii. 22/2 The reactance is the sum of the two contributions: $-ik/\omega$, the elastic reactance, and $i\omega m$, the inertial reactance. **1968** H. J. PAIN *Physics of Vibrations & Waves* ii. 38 Mass, like inductance, produces a positive reactance, and the stiffness behaves in exactly the same way as the capacitance.

3. *Psychol.* A term sometimes used for the type of response aroused in a person who feels his freedom of choice is threatened or impeded.

1966 J. W. BREHM *Theory of Psychol. Reactance* i. 2 Since this hypothetical motivational state is in response to the reduction (or threatened reduction) of one's potential for acting, and conceptually may be considered a counterforce, it will be called 'psychological reactance'. **1970** *Jrnl. Personality & Social Psychol.* XIV. 18 If the communication arouses reactance, the individual will tend to reject its position in order to demonstrate his freedom to decide for himself. **1972** *Harvard Law Review* LXXXVI. 399 'Reactance' is conceived to be an aversive state created in the individual by a threatened loss of his freedom to act or choose.

4. *attrib.* and *Comb.*

1921 *Wireless World* IX. 187/1 Reactance coils are used in conjunction with valve sets. **1964** R. F. FICCHI *Electr. Interference* x. 203 A reactance-grounded system is one in which a reactance is inserted in the connection to ground. **1967** *Electronics* 6 Mar. 186/1 For slow scan applications, however, the reactance components would become excessively large and difficult to stabilize with temperature. **1972** L. S. WRIGHTSMAN *Social Psychol. in Seventies* x. 306 Reactance theory concerns itself with situations where one's freedom of choice is threatened. **1976** TEDESCHI & LINDSKOLD *Social Psychol.* viii. 360/1 Numerous experiments have shown reactance-like effects in the laboratory. *Ibid.* 361/1 Reactance studies in which subjects are told they are being evaluated for leade ship.

reactant (ri,æ·ktǎnt), *sb.* (*a.*) *Chem.* [f. REACT *v.*[1] + -ANT[1].] A reacting substance or species. Also *attrib.* or as *adj.*

1928 *Chem. Rev.* V. 67 In hydrogenation there is an optimum ratio to the partial pressures of the reactants. **1936** T. J. WEBB *Elem. Princ. Physical Chem.* viii. 253 In general the rate of a given reaction depends upon the instantaneous concentration of the reactants. **1948** *Ann. Rep. Progr. Chem.* XLV. 10 The immediate consequence of absorption of some of the energy of the incident radiation is the conversion of the absorbing reactant molecule into the product. **1950** *Sci. News* XV. 65 Once a layer of oxide has formed, subsequent reaction must take place by the reactants.. diffusing through it. **1971** *Jrnl. Oil & Colour Chemists' Assoc.* LIV. 849 The necessary reactants, ammonia and sulphur dioxide, appeared to be absorbed from the atmosphere by droplets of water condensed on the paint surface. **1973** J. G. TWEEDDALE *Materials Technol.* II. ii. 23 With the majority of materials suitable for melting and freeze casting, gases such as oxygen, hydrogen and nitrogen..are much more soluble in, or reactant to, the liquid state of a material than they are to the solid state.

reaction. Add: **2. b.** (i) (Further examples.) Also, any chemical change. Also extended to transformations of atomic nuclei and other particles.

1926 H. G. RULE tr. *J. Schmidt's Text-bk. Org. Chem.* 131 The Hofmann method, in which bromine and potassium hydroxide are brought into reaction with acid amides. **1936** *Nature* 29 Feb. 344/1 The typical features of nuclear reactions are therefore perhaps most clearly shown by neutron impacts. **1950** N. V. SIDGWICK *Chem. Elements* I. 397 The reaction of boron trichloride with an alcohol is quite violent. **1956** A. H. COMPTON *Atomic Quest* i. 53 The amount of U-235 needed to bring about a chain reaction was many times smaller than earlier measurements had indicated. **1972** R. A. JACKSON *Mechanism* i. 5 Unimolecular reactions occur as a result of reorganization of the bonds within a molecule, with or without rupture into fragments. *Ibid.* 6 Bimolecular reactions take place during a collision of two molecules. **1977** J. NARLIKAR *Struct. Universe* ii. 36 The star's nuclear reactions generate energy which goes towards providing the necessary pressure to support the star against its tendency to contract with gravitation.

(ii) *spec.* (usu. with qualifying adj.) a reaction characteristic of acid or alkali; hence, acidity, neutrality or alkalinity.

1856 W. A. MILLER *Elem. Chem.* II. x. 710 A salt which affects neither the blue of litmus nor the yellow of turmeric is said to have a neutral reaction. **1899** *Jrnl. Physiol.* XXIV. 289 On the addition of acid a dispersion of the flakes of coagulum occurs with production of an opalescent fluid having an acid reaction. **1900** *Proc. R. Soc.* LXVI. 116 The effect of the acid or basic reaction of the salt on the hydrosol. **1938** *Jrnl. Inst. Brewing* XLIV. 466/1 The highest grade of asbestos is a completely insoluble material, neutral in reaction and tasteless. **1956** K. IMHOFF et al. *Disposal of Sewage* iv. 23 The 'Reaction' of aqueous wastes may be described as acid, neutral, or alkaline, depending on the concentration of hydrogen ions. Pure water is neutral in reaction. **1968** PASSMORE & ROBSON *Compan. Med. Stud.* I. vi. 2/2 It follows that the reaction of an aqueous solution may be expressed either in terms of $[H^+]$ or $[OH^-]$.

3. c. *Psychol.* A response to a stimulus which can be observed, estimated, or measured.

1887 *Jrnl. Mental Sci.* XXXII. 604 The reaction is found to occupy less time in the insane than in the sane. **1943** C. L. HULL *Princ. Behav.* xviii. 326 Many reactions.. approach the all-or-none type, which differs appreciably from the galvanic skin reaction,..etc. *Ibid.*, Reaction is a joint multiplicative function of habit strength and drive. **1968** R. F. C. HULL tr. *Jung's Analytical Psychol.: Tavistock Lectures* ii. 54 Other characteristic disturbances are:.. reaction expressed by facial expression, laughing, movements of the hands or feet or body..insufficient reactions like 'yes' or 'no'.

d. In general use: a response (to an event, a statement, etc.); an action or feeling that expresses or constitutes a response.

1914 H. JAMES *Notes of Son & Brother* v. 117 His [*sc.* William James's] letters..mark the beginning of those vivacities and varieties of intellectual and moral reaction which were for the rest of his life to be the more immeasurably candid and vivid. **1922** JOYCE *Ulysses* 650 Did Bloom discover common factors of similarity between their respective like and unlike reactions to experience? **1932** KIPLING *Limits & Renewals* 134 Only the speed of my reactions saved me from bumping into Bunny when he pulled up without warning beside a lorry. **1946** E. O'NEILL *Iceman Cometh* I. 89 They all hoot him down in a chorus of amused jeering. Hugo is not offended. This is evidently their customary reaction. **1980** D. BRIERLEY *Blood Group O* 43 Reaction to the death of Desnos had set in.

e. *Radio.* A former name for positive feedback. Also *ellipt.*, a reaction coil.

1917 R. D. BANGAY *Elem. Princ. Wireless Telegr.* II. 205 We now come to the final and most efficient method of utilising the properties of the magnifying valve for the purposes of reception of spark signals. It is known as the reaction method. **1920** *Wireless World* 24 July 327/2 The reaction may cause some howling if it is not in phase with the frame. **1922** A. C. LESCARBOURA *Radio for Everybody* i. 32 This small coil is frequently called the 'tickler' or reaction. **1923** *Radio Times* 28 Sept. 22 Two-valve long range receiving set with anode tuning and reaction. **1933** *Boys' Mag.* XLVII. 117/2 To modernize an old set.. swinging reaction can easily be altered to Reinartz reaction. **1943** C. L. BOLTZ *Basic Radio* xi. 184 Other names for positive feed-back are reaction and regeneration. *Ibid.* xiv. 222 Reaction in the hands of the inveterate knob twiddler is a curse to everybody.

4. a. (Earlier and later examples.)

1792 A. YOUNG *Trav. France* I. 557 A most curious political combination, which seems to shew, that..where evils are of the most alarming tendency, there is a re-action, an undercurrent, that works against the apparent tide, and brings relief. **1965** *New Statesman* 7 May 724/2 In spite of his achievements as a social reformer, he became a symbol of black reaction to organised labour. **1969** A. G. FRANK *Latin Amer.* (1970) xxii. 341 After eliminating popular leadership in labor, student, and other organizations..reaction settled back into comfort. **1974** tr. *Sniečkus's Soviet Lithuania* 29 Operating under conditions of extreme political reaction at home, the Communist Party of Lithuania skilfully combined legal and illegal forms of political activity.

b. *Econ.* A downward movement (of share prices, etc.) following an upward one.

1841 [see *INFLATION 6]. **1925** *Scribner's Mag.* Sept. 338/1 The mercurial American..sees either a coming 'business boom' or a season of 'reaction', and he usually bases his belief on visible tendencies in trade and industry. **1930** *Daily Express* 8 Sept. 10/2 It is safer to buy on reactions than on the top of a rise.

5. *reaction drive, experiment, force, mechanism, period* (earlier example), *potential, rate, speed, threshold, time* (later examples), *velocity, vessel, word*; **reaction chamber,** (*a*) a vessel in which a chemical reaction occurs, esp. in an industrial process; (*b*) the combustion chamber of a rocket; **reaction circuit,** that part of the anode circuit of a thermionic valve which produces positive feedback in the grid circuit; **reaction coil,** an inductance coil included in the anode circuit of a thermionic valve so as to cause positive feedback in the grid circuit; **reaction engine,** substitute for def.: any engine in which motive power is derived from the reaction exerted by a jet of escaping fluid (usu. gas); (further example); **reaction formation,** a term originally used by Freud for the tendency of a repressed wish or feeling to be expressed in a contrasting or opposite form; **reaction index** *Broadcasting* (see quots.); **reaction jet,** a jet engine used to provide intermittent thrust for changing or correcting the velocity of a craft or the like; **reaction machine** (further example); **reaction motor** = **reaction engine*; **reaction pattern,** an assumed pattern of behaviour or response established in the nervous system; **reaction propulsion,** any form of propulsion which utilizes the reaction exerted by escaping fluid as the source of motive power; *spec.* jet or rocket propulsion; **reaction rim** *Petrol.*, a zone of one mineral enclosing another and formed by reaction of the latter with its surroundings; **reaction shot** *Film* and *Television,* the photographing of a person responding to an event or to a statement made by another; **reaction time,** the time taken by a person (or any living organism) to respond to a stimulus; **reaction turbine,** a turbine which is driven by the pressure drop experienced by the working fluid in passing across or through the rotor; **reaction type,** a physical or personality type whose members are expected to react in specific ways; **reaction wood,** modified wood that forms in branches and leaning trunks and tends to restore upward direction of growth.

1924 *Chem. Abstr.* XVIII. 2426 Liquid hydrocarbons are heated under pressures of 100–300 lbs. per sq. in. at temps of 350–550° and after partially cooling are passed through a series of vaporizing or reaction chambers of successively diminishing pressure. **1952** E. BURGESS *Rocket Propulsion* iii. 61 The combustion chamber in which the burning takes place is sometimes known as the 'blast' or 'reaction' chamber. **1966** H. O. RUPPE *Introd. Astronautics* I. i. 10 Usually, an oxidizer and a fuel are stored in separate tanks, and transported by a feed system to the reaction chamber. **1969** H. T. EVANS tr. *G. Hägg's Gen. & Inorg. Chem.* xxi. 529 The nitrose is pumped up to a denitrating and concentrating tower..where it is combined with the chamber acid pumped up from the reaction chamber. **1919** *Sci. Abstr.* B. XXI. 291 The case of reaction circuits is also dealt with, and conclusions are drawn as to the audion characteristics of importance in a particular arrangement. **1931** *Boys' Mag.* XLV. 125/1 A simple capacity coupled inductive reaction circuit, better known as 'swinging' reaction. **1917** R. D. BANGAY *Elem. Princ. Wireless Telegr.* II. 207 The amount of this extra E.M.F. induced in the grid coil by the reaction coil can be controlled by adjusting the coupling between the two windings. **1943** C. L. BOLTZ *Basic Radio* xiv. 221 With telephones on head hold the reaction coil in the hand and move towards the aerial coil. **1957** 'T. STURGEON' *Thunder & Roses* 122 They fired up the reaction drive and began to move toward the sun. **1967** N. E. BORDEN *Jet-Engine Fundamentals* 9 All gas-turbine engines, together with pulsejets, ramjets, and rocket motors, belong to a class of power plants called reaction engines. **1893** *Amer. Jrnl. Psychol.* VI. 242 Is the sensorial-muscular difference entirely conditioned by the technique of the ordinary reaction-experiment? **1933** J. C. FLUGEL *Hundred Years Psychol.* viii. 186 The reaction experiment was..a legacy both from the personal equation problems of the astronomers and from Helmholtz's measurement of the speed of the nervous impulse in the sensory nerves. **1965** C. N. VAN DEVENTER *Introd. Gen. Aeronaut.* ix. 201/2 The reaction force, which is equal to the acceleration force, propels the balloon in the westerly direction shown. **1910** A. A. BRILL tr. *Freud's Three Contributions to the Theory of Sex* iii. 83 A sub-species of sublimation is the suppression through reaction-formation, which..begins even in the latency period of infancy. **1924** [see **character-trait*]. **1934** *Mind* XLIII. 113 How rare is that love of virtue which does not bear the trace of neurotic reaction-formation. **1960** *Encounter* XV. v. 25 A 'reaction-formation' in the psychoanalytic sense. **1974** W. B. ARNDT *Theories of Personality* xvii. 349 Another common example of reaction formation is where repressed hostility for a person, say a mother's hostility toward her child, is converted by the ego into excessive concern for his well being. **1967** *Listener* 17 Aug. 195/3 The reaction index? This is supposed to measure what the audience thought about the show. **1972** *Ibid.* 7 Sept. 295/3 If radio had existed in the mid-1820s, a series of late Beethoven quartets would have had..a 'Reaction Index' (that's the measure of appreciation) too low to be mentioned. **1972** P. MOORE *Can You speak Venusian?* xv. 153 Dr. Barber..proposes to fit large reaction jets to the tops of mountains on opposite sides of the world... When the tilt begins, one simply switches on the jets. **1978** *Nature* 5 Oct. 378/2 Reaction jets are fired once or twice daily to reduce wheel momentum that accumulates due to disturbance torques on the spacecraft. **1972** D. G. SHEPHERD *Aerospace Propulsion* i. 4 It should also be recognized that the propeller operates by the same basic principle... Thus all propulsion systems are reaction machines, although this is often popularly attached only to jet engines. **1972** R. A. JACKSON *Mechanism* v. 80 Stereochemical studies allow us further insight into the details of a reaction mechanism by providing information about the direction of approach of a reagent or of the movement of groups during a reaction. **1935** C. G. PHILP *Stratosphere & Rocket Flight* xi. 54 In its simplest terms the reaction motor most favoured at present takes the form of a rocket. **1962** F. I. ORDWAY et al. *Basic Astronautics* ii. 13 Archytas devised a wooden pigeon propelled by a steam reaction motor. **1923** K. DUNLAP in *Psychol. Rev.* XXX. 94 A feeling is always a real stimulus pattern which is the beginning of a reaction pattern. **1926** W. MCDOUGALL *Introd. Social Psychol.* (ed. 20) 417 Those who..imply that they can explain alleged instinctive behaviour by postulating in vague general terms a 'reaction pattern' in the nervous system corresponding to every movement and attitude displayed..have never succeeded in demonstrating the validity of such interpretation in any single case of instinctive behaviour. **1946** F. P. CHISHOLM in W. S. Knickerbocker *20th Cent. English* 177 Understanding the nature of language-situations is itself a very powerful developer of more mature reaction-patterns, and hence of more adequate 'command of the language'. **1959** *Times Lit. Suppl.* 27 Mar. 181/3 A psychic organism that..is bound up with instincts and emotions and is the source of innate reaction-patterns which go much farther to determine the behaviour of the individual than he cares to recognize. **1887** *Jrnl. Mental Sci.* XXXII. 604 Guicciardi and Tanzi have made a series of observations on the 'reaction period' in fourteen cases where there were hallucinations of hearing. **1952** C. L. HULL *Behavior System* i. 12 Absolute zero of reaction potential. **1972** G. R. LEFRANCOIS *Psychol. Theories Human Learning* vi. 129 Reaction potential, sometimes called excitatory potential, is a measure of the potential that a stimulus has for eliciting a specific response. **1935** C. G. PHILP *Stratosphere & Rocket Flight* ii. 5 Reaction propulsion may be said to date from 1919, in which year Professor Goddard..announced to the world the results of his researches made with rockets. **1962** F. I. ORDWAY et al. *Basic Astronautics* ii. 18 Konstantin Tsiolkovsky..seems to be the first scientist who realized that it is only possible to travel in space by means of reaction propulsion. **1971** P. J. MCMAHON *Aircraft Propulsion* iii. 80 Combining the thermodynamic and propulsion efficiencies gives the overall efficiency of the reaction propulsion engine. **1946** *Nature* 6 Apr. 439/1 This is strong evidence for the conclusion that the decrease in the bimolecular reaction-rate as the reactive carbon atom changes from primary to secondary is due to an increase in steric hindrance. **1972** WESTON & SCHWARZ *Chem. Kinetics* i. 3 Experimental studies of reactions generally involve the determination of reaction rates as a function of several variables: chemical composition, temperature, pressure, or volume. [**1886** *Bull. U.S. Geol. Survey* No. 28. 52 Wherever it comes in contact with the olivine, the peculiar reactionary rims of amphibole described by Törnebohm..are finely developed.] **1892** *Amer. Jrnl. Sci.* CXLIII. 516 The attention of the writer was repeatedly attracted by a fibrous growth around olivine, that resembles..the reaction rims that have been described as existing between garnet and serpentine. **1921** *Mineral. Mag.* XIX. 145 If the corona can be shown to be due to alteration or modification of the nucleus the term reaction rim is preferred. **1960** TURNER & VERHOOGEN *Igneous & Metamorphic Petrol.* (ed. 2) vi. 145 The very existence of solid-solution series in so many groups of igneous minerals, and the frequent development of reaction rims (coronas) of one mineral around central cores of another, are evidence of reaction. **1953** Reaction shot [see *OFF SCREEN, OFF-SCREEN *adv.* (*phr.*) and *a.*]. **1966** *Guardian* 11 Aug. 8/2 The Select Committee on televising the House of Commons..was understandably cautious about 'reaction shots', by which the committee meant pictures not only of the member addressing the House..but of other members reacting to his speech. **1930** G. R. DE BEER *Embryol. & Evolution* xv. 105 Atavism is..due to the reproduction of a set of conditions (a definite system of reaction-speeds) which obtained in the ancestor. **1964** A. EDEL in I. L. Horowitz *New Sociology* xiv. 224 The comparable discovery of color blindness or different reaction-speed or influence of drugs or alcohol affects the concept of a reliable observer in other fields. **1970** W. SAHAKIAN *Psychol. Learning* xi. 230 The concept of the reaction threshold is well established. **1879** Reaction-time [see *PSYCHOMETRY 2]. **1883** *Mind* Apr. 177 (*heading*) Reaction time and attention in the hypnotic state. **1908** J. M. CATTELL in *Essays in Honor of W. James* 574 The incoming currents and the pre-existing structure of the centres cause the discharge, and the perception, in my opinion, usually follows the discharge in time. This time order I pointed out more than twenty years ago in the case of the reaction-time. **1923** R. A. KNOX *Memories of Future* v. 73, I went round to his house, where he looked at my tongue, X-rayed me, felt my pulse, took my reaction-times, and shook his head importantly. **1971** J. W. KLING et al. *Woodworth & Schlosberg's Exper. Psychol.* (1972) ix. 309/2 The simple reaction time of human subjects..is one form of latency measure. **1972** K. BONFIGLIOLI *Don't point that Thing at Me* xiii. 96 Another shot rang out, followed one fifth of a second later by the bang of the car door... There is still nothing wrong with the Mortdecai reaction-time. **1881** *Encycl. Brit.* XII. 524/1 Turbines in which part only of the available energy is converted into kinetic energy, before the water enters the turbine wheel, may be termed Reaction Turbines. **1929** T. M. NAYLOR *Steam Turbines* i. 3 The only pure reaction turbines in use are of very small power, and are used for fluids other than steam, e.g. the garden sprinkler.., distributors on sewage filter beds, [etc.]. **1969** W. THOMSON *Thrust for Flight* 111 The reaction turbine is one in which the whole of the pressure drop and the velocity increase occur as the gas flows through the rotor blade passages. **1904** *Psychol. Bull.* I. 230 The chief directions in which Kraepelin has stimulated his associates to work psychologically, are a number of more biological than purely psychological reaction-types, such as retardation and inhibition, flight of ideas, etc. **1917** C. E. LONG tr. *Jung's Analytical Psychol.* iii. 158 Relatives, and especially related women, have therefore on the average, resemblance in reaction-type. **1917** A. MEYER *Coll. Papers* (1951) II. 44 The organic reaction types. **1922** [see *ECOPHENE]. **1934** E. B. STRAUSS tr. *Kretschmer's Text-bk. Med. Psychol.* xiii. 184 In our description of the various reaction-types we shall make use of psychopathological instead of normal material. **1953** H. READ *True Voice of Feeling* II. iii. 262 The artist..reveals an inward unity and concentration of personality in marked contrast with the extraneous dissipations and diversities of the average reaction-type. **1904** *Brit. Med. Jrnl.* 10 Sept. 564/2 The reaction velocity of the chemical or physical processes that result in the agglutination of bacteria, is a very variable factor. **1926** *Jrnl. Inst. Petroleum Technologists* XII. 202A When the apparatus is shut down for cleaning, the reaction vessel is opened and steam or water is pumped through the tubes. **1973** *Materials & Technol.* VI. viii. 504 The mixture is stirred in a reaction vessel and the monomer becomes suspended as an emulsion of tiny droplets. **1949** H. P. BROWN et al. *Textbk. Wood Technol.* I. xii. 288 The existence of internal forces in living trees, independently of the presence of reaction wood, has also been suggested. **1980** *Family Handyman* Sept. 70/3 The fruitwoods (cherry, apple) are more difficult [to dry out], depending upon the size of the log and the presence or absence of reaction wood. **1920** T. P. NUNN *Educ.* v. 44 The subject's memory does not throw up a number of suggestions from which a suitable reaction-word is consciously selected.

rea·ctionarily, *adv.* [f. REACTIONARY *a.* + -LY².] In a reactionary manner.

1966 *Economist* 23 July 329/1 Mr Wilson's Government is now following a right-wing policy of deflation more resolutely, more ruefully, more reactionarily..than any of its predecessors since the war. **1970** R. A. H. ROBINSON *Origins of Franco's Spain* 301 Prieto, leader of the Bilbao Socialists,..called the Statute reactionarily anti-liberal: 'Spain cannot tolerate that territory turning itself into a Vaticanist Gibraltar.'

rea·ctionariness. *rare.* [f. REACTIONARY *a.* + -NESS.] Reactionary character.

1923 U. L. SILBERRAD *Lett. Jean Armiter* vi. 149, I believe he felt almost kindly..towards me and my antiquated reactionariness.

reactionary, *a.* and *sb.* Add: **A.** *adj.* **2.** (Earlier and later examples.) Also, in Marxist use, unfavourably contrasted with *revolutionary*.

1840 J. S. MILL in *London & Westm. Rev.* Mar. 276 The philosophers of the reactionary school—of the school to which Coleridge belongs. **1953** R. LEHMANN *Echoing Grove* iii. 156 The British Government's iniquitous non-intervention policy playing into the hands of Franco's abominable reactionary conspiracy. **1957** *Economist* 28 Dec. 1134/1 Hungarians are to have both the 'true freedom' and the bananas. Mr Kadar's masters were shrewd enough to realise that, in this reactionary country, the latter is appreciated more than the former. **1974** tr. *Sniečkus's Soviet Lithuania* 23 The bourgeois nationalists set up various kinds of reactionary armed organisations to combat the revolutionary movement. **1975** J. PLAMENATZ *K. Marx's Philos. of Man* xi. 299 Ideas and practices adopted by the bourgeois when they put themselves forward as the champions of society as a whole against irresponsible power and a reactionary nobility can become a nuisance to them once they are installed as the dominant class and their position comes to be challenged.

B. *sb.* (Later examples.) Also, in Marxist use, an opponent of communism.

1908 *Nation* 1 Oct. 302/2 Part of Wall Street will vote for Taft because it believes him at heart a 'reactionary', or, at least, the less of two evils. **1921** G. B. SHAW *Back to Methuselah* II. 52, I can find you hundreds of the most sordid rascals, or the most densely stupid reactionaries, with all these qualifications. **1951** G. MIKES *Down with Everybody!* I. i. 15 'A reactionary and a foreign spy is a man who is not pleased when his wages are cut or when he is asked to work more for the same wages and who is not pleased to starve.' 'Very good, Comrade Barna, very good indeed.' **1967** tr. *Quotations from Chairman Mao Tsetung* (ed. 2) 75 The reactionaries in all countries are fools of this kind... Their persecution of the revolutionary people only serves to accelerate the people's revolutions. **1981** L. DEIGHTON *XPD* ii. 5 Literally *pogoni* means epaulette, but for a citizen of the USSR..it is a symbol of the hated reactionary.

rea·ctionaryism. Also **reactionarism.** [f. REACTIONARY *a.* and *sb.* + -ISM.] = *REACTIONISM. Hence **rea·ctionarist.**

1911 GALSWORTHY *Patrician* I. i. 11 His common sense continually impelled him, against the sort of reactionaryism of which his son Miltoun had so much, to that easier reactionaryism, which..makes what material capital it can out of its enemy, Progress. **1922** *Contemp. Rev.* Aug. 240 His party had previously been coloured by monarchism and reactionarism. **1924** *Glasgow Herald* 22 May 7 The advent of the Labour Government was heralded by the reactionarists as the end of all things. **1965** *Listener* 4 Nov. 723/1 Reactionaryism, whether in politics or art, is never pleasant to contemplate.

rea·ctionism. [f. REACTION + -ISM.] Reactionary principles or practice.

1891 J. M. ROBERTSON *Mod. Humanists* 91 For the Bentham group Burke finally represented sheer reactionism. **1930** A. I. NAZAROFF *Tolstoi* vi. 90 This lack of 'social sensibility' shocked them. They even mistook it for the mortal sin of 'reactionism'.

reactionist, *sb.* Add: (Earlier and later examples.) Also, a person who reacts *against* something.

1857 J. F. MAGUIRE *Rome: its Ruler & its Institutions* p. ix, I trust I have done sufficient to enable the reader..to estimate, at their right value, the accusations which have been made against him [*sc.* Pope Pius IX], as a reformer of the one day, and a reactionist of the next. **1861** *Q. Rev.* CIX. 294 The utter weariness of spirit which this unresting scepticism has bred in most minds of the highest order of thought; the deep study into which it has driven the noble reactionists who have arisen there..have entirely altered the whole tone of religious feeling amongst our Teutonic brethren. **1900** *Dublin Rev.* Jan. 35 Reactionists..signatories to the Royal supremacy in 1559, who in 1579 appeared in prison as recusants. **1902** G. B. Shaw *Mrs. Warren's Profession* p. xxx, Clergymen's sons are often conspicuous reactionists against the restraints imposed on them in childhood. **1909** [see *baby *sb.* 1 e].

reactivate (ri,æ·ktivē^i^t), *v.* [Re- 5 a.] *trans.* To make active or operative again.

1903 *Med. Rec.* (N.Y.) 14 Feb. 251/2 The serum can be reactivated by a little fresh serum not only from a normal rabbit, but from the goat and the rat. **1949** M. Mead *Male & Female* viii. 176 Menstruation..is itself believed to be reactivated by marriage. **1953** *Times* 13 May 3/5 The importance of maintaining the base there in such condition that it could be reactivated immediately in case of war. **1957** *Observer* 27 Oct. 12/2 An American recession may also cause trouble by reactivating the dollar problem. **1958** *Engineering* 14 Mar. 352/3 In this building humidity control is accomplished automatically by passing the air required for ventilation, plus a percentage of recirculated air, through desiccant driers automatically reactivated by gas. **1976** A. White *Long Silence* xx. 179 Please reactivate the plan to surround the station. **1977** *Living with Tanker Surplus* (Shell Internat. Petroleum Co.) 6 A ship in lay-up cannot easily or quickly be reactivated.

Hence **reactiva·tion**, the action or result of reactivating.

1903 *Med. Rec.* (N.Y.) 14 Feb. 251/1 It has been found that this 'reactivation' of the serum, as it has been called, can often be brought about by the serum of various animals. **1919** *Lancet* 26 Apr. 705/2 Professor Chauffard and M. L. Girard brought forward a new and striking proof of the tuberculous nature of erythema nodosum—the reactivation of the disease when nearly extinct by injection of tuberculin. **1926** *Glasgow Herald* 1 May 4 Very characteristic of spring is what may be called reawakening, if we may use the word to include reactivation from a rest that is deeper than sleep. **1957** *Times* 18 Nov. p. i/1 Sophisticated arguments about the 're-activation' of bank deposits or the velocity of circulation. **1970** H. Trevelyan *Middle East in Revolution* 12 The Agreement provided for the reactivation of the Base for defence against the invasion of any Arab State or Turkey by a State other than Israel.

reactive, *a.* Add: **3. a.** (Further examples.) Also *reactive formation* = *reaction formation* s.v. *reaction 5; *reactive inhibition*, the inhibiting effect of the supervention of fatigue or boredom on the response to a stimulus.

1925 J. Strachey tr. *Freud's Case of Hysteria* in *Coll. Papers* III. 67 Repression is often achieved by means of an excessive reinforcement of the thought contrary to the one which is to be repressed. This process I call *reactive* reinforcement. *Ibid.* 68 The thought which asserts itself exaggeratedly in consciousness and (in the same way as a prejudice) cannot be removed I call a *reactive thought.* **1943** C. L. Hull *Princ. Behavior* xviii. 327 Uniform time intervals between reinforcements great enough to prevent the accumulation of appreciable amounts of reactive inhibition. **1968** *Globe & Mail* (Toronto) 3 Feb. 11/6 These young people can join 'negative identity' groups and become..therapeutically involved in extreme reactive kinds of activity. **1974** Chaplin & Krawiec *Systems & Theories of Psychol.* vii. 263 In and of itself fatigue will generate a form of inhibition which Hull calls reactive inhibition, and the animal will cease to respond. **1975** *Way* Suppl. No. 25. 67 Dynamic psychology might interpret this as evidence for reactive formation, which is a technical term suggesting that we control an unacceptable impulse by exaggerating the opposite tendency. **1977** G. H. Sage *Introd. Motor Behav.* (ed. 2) xvi. 359 The first of these is an inhibition (reactive inhibition) caused by a reluctance to repeat a response.

b. Also, characterized by reaction to a stimulus.

1927 C. Spearman *Abilities of Man* iv. 47 Stern's division of persons into the 'spontaneous' and the 'merely reactive'. **1952** M. K. Wilson tr. *Lorenz's King Solomon's Ring* xi. 171 A few birds—usually old, strongly reactive ones—take off, emitting 'Kiaw' cries and thereby provoking the whole flock to leave the ground with them.

c. *Psychol.* Of mental illness: thought to be caused by reaction to environmental stress; exogenous; so *reactive schizophrenic*, a person with reactive schizophrenia (cf. *process schizophrenia* s.v. *process *sb.* 13 a).

1924 A. A. Brill *Bleuler's Textbk. Psychiatry* xii. 537 Reactive *depressions*, which become aggravated to a mental disease, are quite rare in the light of present views. **1955** McCarthy & Corrin *Med. Treatment of Mental Dis.* xix. 326 Reactive depressions are the mild, brief depressions, the result of situations depressing in themselves, and not out of proportion to circumstances. **1958** H. Weiner in L. Bellak *Schizophrenia* iv. 157 Whether such reactive psychoses actually imply a different series of etiologic contributing factors, i.e., 'non-organic', is highly speculative. **1962** *Lancet* 10 Jan. 105/1 Two were middle-aged men with anxiety states... The third was a middle-aged lady with a reactive depression. **1962** *Psychol. Bull.* LIX. 329/1 Reactive schizophrenia indicates a good prognosis..with notable stress precipitating the psychosis. *Ibid.* 332/1 If the Rorschach diagnosis is followed, then it appears that reactive schizophrenics are not psychotic. **1965** J. Pollitt *Depression & its Treatment* 95 The terms 'endogenous' and 'reactive'.. differentiate types of depression on the basis of presence or absence of an external cause. **1966** I. B. Weiner *Psychodiagnosis in Schizophrenia* vi. 94 A group of process schizophrenics made no more frequent errors than the reactive schizophrenics. **1971** *Brit. Med. Bull.* XXVII. 77/2 One school of thought..allocates such cases to a special category of 'reactive psychoses'. **1974** M. C. Gerald *Pharmacol.* xvi. 310 When the cause of depression can be identified,..we term this reactive or exogenous depression. **1976** L. J. West et al. *Treatment of Schizophrenia* vi. 278 The good premorbid/bad premorbid, and process/reactive dimensions do seem to identify significant characteristics.

5. a. *Chem.* Readily susceptible to chemical reaction.

1888 *Nature* 22 Mar. 503/1 The unsaturated hydrocarbons ..are..more reactive than the paraffins. **1942** G. Wendt *Chem.* vii. 179 As in the other families of elements we shall meet, the lightest of the group—in this case fluorine—is the most reactive. **1957** G. E. Hutchinson *Treat Limnol.* I. xi. 708 It is not clear, however, in what form this reactive iron is actually present in the lake water. **1972** R. A. Jackson *Mechanism* iv. 78 A trapping or inhibiting agent may be insufficiently reactive towards a particular intermediate to divert it from its normal course of reaction, or the agent may react in such a way as to regenerate another reactive intermediate.

b. Of a process: involving chemical reaction.

1950 *Chem. Abstr.* XLIV. 8190 (*heading*) Reactive diffusion in metals. **1960** *Ibid.* LIV. 23646 The reactive diffusion in a system Nb-B is accomplished by diffusion of B atoms through the reaction products toward the metal. **1971** *New Scientist* 8 Apr. 96/1 Reactive evaporation..is often used for depositing metal oxides. **1973** R. L. Burwell in Basolo & Burwell *Catalysis* 11. 72 Ethylene is adsorbed by reactive adsorption. Perhaps it first adsorbs as a π-complex and then reacts to monoadsorbed ethane. **1978** Felder & Rousseau *Elem. Princ. Chem. Processes* x. 384 In this chapter we show..how calculated enthalpies of reaction are incorporated in energy balances on reactive processes.

c. Of a dye or other colouring material: designed to react chemically with the substrate, usu. in order to become fixed.

1957 *Jrnl. Soc. Dyers & Colourists* LXXIII. 238/2 The search for more practical methods of using reactive dyes has continued, and this work has now culminated in the production of a new range of dyes—the Procion (ICI) dyes—which are water-soluble but contain a reactive group capable of combining with cellulose under alkaline conditions. **1973** *Materials & Technol.* VI. iv. 310 The direct, basic, sulphur, vat, azoic and reactive dyes are all suitable for colouring the fibre [*sc.* rayon]. *a* **1977** *Harrison Mayer Ltd. Catal.* 39/1 *Reactive colours*, a new range of leadless colours for underglaze, on-glaze or in-glaze decoration... On firing, these colours react with the glaze to give interesting and variegated effects.

d. Of coke or coal: having a high reactivity (sense *b).

1963 *Economist* 21 Dec. 1284/1 Reconciling the clean air policy with the British love of open fires means trying to produce enough smokeless fuel of the sort that can be burnt in the fireplaces of smokeless zones. But the Minister of Power now estimates that there will be a gap..between the demand for such 'reactive' smokeless fuels and the supply. **1974** *Encycl. Brit. Macropædia* IV. 783/2 Coals of medium rank are used for low-temperature carbonization because they yield reactive cokes.

6. a. *Electr.* Possessing or pertaining to electrical reactance; *spec.* applied to the vector component of an alternating current (or voltage) which is 90° out of phase with respect to the associated voltage (or current), i.e. wattless; *reactive power*, the product of the voltage and the reactive current, or of the current and the reactive voltage; *reactive volt-ampere*, a unit of reactive power.

1892 J. A. Fleming *Alternate Current Transformer* II. ii. 269 Reactive Coil or Dimmer.—This is a device used in alternating current work to serve the same ends as rheostats in direct current plants. **1892** S. P. Thompson *Dynamo-Electr. Machinery* (ed. 4) xxii. 628 We have here two electromotive-forces, the impressed O A and the reactive A E.. with their resultant the effective electromotive-force O E, with an angle E O A..between them. **1914** J. H. Morecroft *Continuous & Alternating Current Machinery* vi. 205 The component of voltage 90° out of phase with the current we shall call the reactive component of the voltage or reactive voltage. **1916** *Standardization Rules Amer. Inst. Electr. Engineers* 15 *Reactive volt-amperes*, the product of the reactive component of the voltage by the total current, or of the reactive component of the current by the total voltage. **1920** *Whittaker's Electr. Engineers's Pocket-Bk.* (ed. 4) 222 The reactive current changes from leading to lagging as the field excitation is reduced. **1951** W. Sluckin *Princ. Alternating Currents* ix. 225 In an induction motor, neglecting heating losses, the active component provides the useful mechanical power delivered by the motor, while the reactive component is associated with the production of the alternating magnetic field necessary for the operation of the motor. **1956** C. S. Siskind *Electr. Circuits* xi. 265 The vertical component—the quadrature component—is $EI \sin \theta$. The latter, acting adversely to lessen the power factor, is expressed as the reactive volt-amperes, abbreviated R-va. **1961** *Listener* 9 Nov. 768/2 There is also the problem, with direct current lines, of providing what is called the reactive power—power where the current is out of step with the voltage—for the operation of converter equipment. **1970** J. Earl *Tuners & Amplifiers* iv. 83 The source itself can be mostly resistive or mostly reactive. **1978** *Gramophone* May 1958/1 It is claimed to have an output of 100 watts RMS working into an 8-ohm inductive or reactive load.

b. *Mech.* and *Acoustics.* Possessing or pertaining to mechanical or acoustic impedance.

1934 Olson & Massa *Applied Acoustics* ii. 32 (*caption*) Resistive and reactive air load per unit area on one side of a vibrating piston of radius R centimeters set in an infinite baffle. **1963** [see *impedance 2]. **1976** A. H. Benade *Fund. of Musical Acoustics* xxi. 457/2 The other register hole on my special clarinet can be called a reactive register hole, i.e., an aperture in which the flow depends mainly on the inertia of the air moving through it.

7. *Gram.* (See quot.) *rare.*

1957 R. W. Zandvoort *Handbk. Eng. Gram.* v. ii. 224 To express the speaker's reaction to a previous statement by the person addressed which is repeated by the speaker (*reactive questions*)... You can't catch me.—I can't, can't I? said Philip.

reactivity. Add: **a.** (Further examples.)

1907 *Chem. Abstr.* I. 1395 Transformation of open chains to cyclic compounds enhances their reactivity. **1934** *Jrnl. Theol. Stud.* XXXV. 402 The author would establish that religion consists in simultaneous reactivity of the affective, conative and cognitive elements of mentality. **1949** *Brit. Jrnl. Psychol.* Dec. 86 When the individual's P.G.R. [psychogalvanic reflex] scores are obtained for a given attitude they must be expressed for each person relative to his own general P.G.R. reactivity. **1950** *Sci. News* XV. 70 Consideration of the chemical reactivity of crystals will obviously be focussed primarily on the surfaces. **1956** *Nature* 10 Mar. 477/2 It is assumed that the reactivity of the anhydride is not increased by adsorption. **1972** DePuy & Chapman *Molec. Reactions & Photochem.* vii. 137 Electronic effects are more important than the steric effects in determining the relative reactivity of dienophiles.

b. The rate of reaction of a coke or coal with (orig.) carbon dioxide, or with oxygen, under specified conditions.

1926 *Rep. Fuel Res. Board 1925* (Dep. Sci. & Industr. Res.) 23 A method has been designed which gives an empirical figure for reactivity to carbon dioxide. **1930** *Engineering* 22 Aug. 251/4 A convenient distinction has been drawn between the combustibility of a coke, denoting the rate at which it burns in oxygen or air, and its reactivity, meaning the rate at which it reacts with carbon dioxide and produces the reducing atmosphere in which the metallic iron is extracted. **1947** G. W. Himus *Elem. Fuel Technol.* xv. 296 The 'Reactivity Value' of coke is defined by the Fuel Research Board as 'the number of millilitres of carbon monoxide formed from 100 millilitres of carbon dioxide' under certain definitely specified conditions. **1971** *Materials & Technol.* II. x. 601 Gas coke..has a lower reactivity than most coals and is not suitable for use on open fires. *Ibid.* 604 The reactivity of coke with respect to oxygen is often measured by the Critical Air Blast (C.A.B.) method.

c. *Nuclear Physics.* A measure of the extent to which a reactor (or part of it) deviates from a steady critical condition (see quot. 1962).

Orig. in a broader sense.

1945 H. D. Smyth *Atomic Energy* viii. 89 The reactivity of the pile was so far above expectations that it would have been beyond the capacity of the control rods to handle if the remainder of the heavy water had been added. **1947** *Physical Rev.* LXXII. 17/1 The reactivity of a chain-reacting pile depends critically on the balance of neutron production, absorption, and leakage. **1954** R. Stephenson *Introd. Nuclear Engin.* vii. 270 In order to operate at any appreciable power, some excess reactivity must be available to overcome the various factors which act to reduce the ability of the chain reactor to multiply neutrons. **1960** *Gloss. Atomic Terms* (U.K.A.E.A.) 44 At any steady state of operation the reactivity is zero. **1962** *Gloss. Terms Nuclear Sci.* (*B.S.I.*) 97 *Reactivity*, the value of the expression $(k_{\text{eff}} - 1)/k_{\text{eff}}$, which is a measure of the departure of a reactor from the critical condition... k_{eff} is the multiplication constant (effective). **1963** B. Fozard *Instrumentation Nuclear Reactors* xii. 149 A sudden change in reactivity in either direction is liable to produce thermal shock in the fuel elements. **1974** *Encycl. Brit. Macropædia* XIII. 3142 The reactivity of the core increases when the rods..are withdrawn.

reactor (ri,æ·ktəɹ). Also (*rare*) **reacter.** [f. React *v.*[1] + -or.] **1.** A person, animal, or organism that reacts to a stimulus, esp. under test or experimental conditions; *spec.* one showing an immune response to a specific antigen.

1890 W. James *Princ. Psychol.* I. xi. 433 One must bear in mind that in these experiments the reacter always knew in advance in a general way the *kind* of question which he was to receive. *Ibid.* xiii. 525 The reacter awaits the signal and reacts if it is of one sort, but omits to act if it is of another sort. **1895** E. B. Titchener in *Amer. Jrnl. Psychol.* VII. 83 *Reagent*, reagent *or* reactor. **1907** *Psychol. Rev.* (Monogr. Suppl.) VIII. iii. 314 In Series III. the reaction consisted in stopping a vertical movement... The reactor moved the pencil up and down against this vertical guide. **1928** *Daily Tel.* 6 Nov. 7/7 Out of 835 animals..122 reacted to the double intradermal test, and 94 of these reactors proved tuberculous at autopsy. **1932** *Amer. Rev. Tuberc.* XXV. 367 In this case the reactor was the sanatorium chef, who has never had tuberculosis. **1932** [see **Schick-negative* adj.]. **1961** *Listener* 30 Nov. 933/1 There may be some value in recording people's reactions to events and also the appearance of the reactors at any given moment. **1969** Myers & Steele *Bovine Tuberculosis* vi. 351 Since 1961, the [N.Z.] Government has provided the funds to pay for the tuberculin testing costs, and compensation for reactors sent to slaughter. **1973** *Black Panther* 10 Nov. 3/4 They are not actors, but reactors, and not leaders, but followers. **1976** *Nature* 13 May 144/1 Among the other categories of patients tested, the percentage of negative reactors varied from 3 to 14%.

2. a. *Electr.* A coil or other piece of equipment which provides reactance in a circuit.

1915 H. B. Dwight *Constant-Voltage Transmission* iii. 14 The name 'synchronous condenser'..is not quite so appropriate when the machine is used with a constant-voltage transmission line, because for a large share of the time the current in the machine is not leading, but lagging, and the machine at that time does not behave as a condenser, but would more accurately be called a 'synchronous reactor'. **1920** *Chem. Abstr.* XIV. 2756 The cast-in-concrete air-core reactor is recommended for furnace work. **1951** *Engineering* 9 Nov. 584/2 Each pair of ignitrons is capable of supplying a rectified current of 650 amperes at 600 volts, the 30 per cent ripple in which is reduced by the smoothing reactor. **1958** J. Shepherd et al. *Higher Electr. Engin.* xvi. 389 Current-limiting reactors may be connected in series with each generator, in series with each feeder, or between each bus-bar section. **1961** G. F. Tagg *Pract. Electr. Engin* I. 33 One method of reducing short-circuit current is by the employment of reactances or inductance coils which, for arge a.c. power systems, are known as reactors.

b. A vessel or apparatus in which substances are made to react chemically, esp. one in an industrial plant.

1935 *Industr. & Engin. Chem.* Sept. 1072/2 In the pyrolysis of ethane and propane best results were obtained when using a reactor consisting of a helical coil of KA2S tubing... This reactor was placed in a radiant-type electrically heated furnace. **1939** *World Petroleum* May 42/2 The plant consists essentially of an assembly of three polymerization reactors, debutanizer, rerunning column for separation of polymer into dimer..and trimer.., with two nickel catalyst hydrogenation reactors for conversion of the dimer to finished iso-octane. **1974** *Daily Tel.* 17 July 19/4 The kettle he should have been watching was a three-ton reactor heating synthetic resin. The reactor..was just two degrees under 100 degrees centigrade when it was seen and could have cracked..or exploded. **1975** *Sci. Amer.* Nov. 107/1 Using air to remove the graphite from the diamond surface enables us to carry out both operations in a single reactor. **1978** *Nature* 22 June 582/1 The accident happened in a reactor used for the production of trichlorophenol.

c. = *nuclear reactor* s.v. *Nuclear *a.* 4. Freq. *attrib.*

1945 [see **nuclear reactor*]. **1947** *Newsweek* 8 Sept. 76/3 The tight-lipped Atomic Energy Commission did not tell all it knows about the new 'reactor'. The active substance is plutonium. **1950** *Chemical Engin. Progress* XLVI. 110/1 It behoves this nation to keep in the forefront of reactor technology. *Ibid.*, The enormous cost of the reactor program. **1957** *Economist* 19 Oct. 256/1 A maximum limit of 20 per cent enrichment with uranium 235 ..is usually imposed on uranium exports from the US, and the limit is exceeded only in such special cases as the fuel core for Harwell's Dido research reactor. **1963** B. Fozard *Instrumentation Nuclear Reactors* xii. 144 Most of the neutrons in a reactor core..are produced at the instant of fission as the products of a reaction of great violence. **1971** *Materials & Technol.* II. xii. 734 Reprocessing..is essential if plutonium is to be utilized in a mixed national power system of fast and thermal reactors. **1975** *Nature* 16 Oct. 525/3 The air in the reactor room is maintained at a lower pressure than the air outside, so that if radioactivity were released from the reactor, it would not immediately be dispersed into the atmosphere.

read, *sb.*[2] Add: (Earlier and later examples.) Also *transf.*, something for reading, esp. with ref. to its value as entertainment or information (freq. with qualifying adj.).

1825 Jamieson Suppl. s.v., Will ye gie me a read of that book? **1902** J. Milne *Epistles Atkins* i. 8 The soldiers..have 'another good read'. **1958** *Observer* 9 Feb. 15/3 A.G.'s usual solid, lively read. **1961** *John o' London's* 21 Sept. 327/3 *My Friend Sandy* can be hugely recommended..as a pleasantly light, bright sophisticated read. **1963** T. Parker *Unknown Citizen* v. 136 He'd come back to the prison, had his tea, and gone to bed to lie down and have a read. **1975** L. Trilling in *Times Lit. Suppl.* (1976) 5 Mar. 250/4 Was she [*sc.* Jane Austen] perhaps to be thought of as nothing more than a good read?.. Now that we have before us that British locution, which Americans have lately taken to using, the question might be asked why the phrase should have come to express so much force of irony and condescension. **1977** J. I. M. Stewart *Madonna of Astrolabe* xviii. 256 *Tamburlaine* is a tolerable read... As a stage play it is pretty hopeless. **1981** *Times* 2 Mar. 12/6 The labels are informative to the point of saturation. If you do not like the wine, you might at least enjoy the read.

read, *v.* Add: **5. a.** Also, to understand (musical notation); *spec.* = *sight-read* s.v. *Sight *sb.*[1] 17.

1792 H. Newdigate *Let.* Mar. in A. E. Newdigate-Newdegate *Cheverels* (1898) ix. 133 Her Voice was not strong but..they are quite astonish'd with her knowledge of Music & facility in reading it. **1894** G. B. Shaw in *Fortn. Rev.* Feb. 258 To do half-a-dozen things much more difficult than reading music. **1918** —— in *Nation* 22 June 308/1 To wile away the time by reading at sight a bundle of band parts and vocal scores of a rather difficult opera. **1938** D. Baker *Young Man with Horn* I. v. 56 Jeff's band didn't play from music, though they could all read music. **1974** *Listener* 24 Jan. 106/3, I could read the music and be able to make it work right away with five minutes' rehearsal.

b. *spec.* to peruse books, newspapers, etc., for quotations suitable for inclusion as illustrative examples in a dictionary.

1876 J. A. H. Murray *Let.* 29 Nov. in K. M. E. Murray *Caught in Web of Words* (1977) vii. 146, I dont for words of that kind believe in the quotation test at all..because you know that not one millionth of current literature is read, & that it is the veriest chance or succession of chances which has caught *carriageless*..& missed a thousand others as good. **1961** R. W. Burchfield in *Essays & Studies* XIV. 39 A large number of literary sources..are being systematically read against an Oxford dictionary. **1977** K. M. E. Murray *Caught in Web of Words* xii. 235 Lowell's book of literary essays, *My Study Windows*, was one of those read for the Dictionary.

c. (Later examples.)

1921 P. L. Haworth *Trailmakers of Northwest* 206 As Brennan had lost one eye and could not see any too well out of the other, he was glad to have one of us ride in his canoe and read water for him. **1932** L. Golding *Magnolia St.* II. ii. 300 In the little town in..Lancashire where she was born quite as many people read tea-leaves as read their ABC. **1951** E. Rickman *Come racing with Me* iii. 19 We are talking about 'reading' a race, which is the practice on the spectator's part of a comprehensive and discriminating view of a field of horses from start to finish, so that the performance of all or most of the runners, and their relative positions at various stages, are intelligently observed and memorised. **1965** Priestley & Wisdom *Good Driving* xi. 81 You get into the habit of registering mentally all the signs..which enable you to 'read' the road in front of you. **1967** *Boston Sunday Herald* 26 Mar. iv. 3/8 An optical scanner..may eliminate the sorting machines by 'reading' the zip code on the letter and dispatching it accordingly. **1967** Karch & Buber *Offset Processes* ii. 20 An optical system 'reads' the photograph, and a heated stylus is directed to penetrate the plate to be printed, producing halftone dots. **1969** R. Welsh *Beginner's Guide Curling* xvii. 120 The ability to read strange ice..and knowing exactly when to sweep are other qualities of a good skip. **1970** G. F. Newman *Sir, You Bastard* vi. 159 Ambition drowning the man was how she would read his promotion. **1971** *Sunday Express* (Johannesburg) 28 Mar. 17/1 You read a putt, stroke it properly along the line you have chosen, and then the ball breaks off in the opposite direction. **1972** *Daily Tel.* 5 May 3/3 A meter reader rang the bell and told my wife he wanted to read the meter in the garage. **1974** *Times* 19 Feb. 15/3 Most people are not used to 'reading' plans..and have only slightly less difficulty with architectural photographs. **1977** *Time* 14 Nov. 48/1 They broke down and then analyzed the RNA in the archaebacteria's ribosomes, the structures that 'read' the message of the master molecule DNA and produce the protein necessary for life. **1978** *Monitor* (McAllen, Texas) 12 Feb. 1-B/1 This generation of Gypsies..will wake up to modern life and give up many of the old customs... My job was supposed to be reading palms. **1979** *SLR Camera* Jan. 36/3 Like the now discontinued EF the AE-1 uses a silicon photocell to read the light.

e. To interpret (a design) in terms of the setting up needed to reproduce it on a loom. Also with *in*.

1839 Ure *Dict. Arts* 267 In both modes of manufacture, the piece is mounted by reading-in the warp for the different leaves of the heddles. **1895** T. F. Bell *Jacquard Weaving & Designing* i. 9 The straight-edge EE..will slide up and down in the frame, to mark the line on the design paper that is next to be read by the lasher. **1897** [see *reading-machine* s.v. Reading *vbl. sb.* 10 b]. **1924** T. Woodhouse *Jacquards & Harness* iv. 107 Before describing the remaining parts of the machine, it will..be best to indicate how the design is read. **1958** A. Hindson *Designer's Drawloom* xi. 105 The weaver can tie up the pattern single-handed, but it can be done more easily and quickly if there is a helper to read the pattern draft.

f. To study (a subject, a 'school') at a university; to read for (a degree). Cf. sense 15 c.

1884 [see *Greats* s.v. Great C. 10]. **1955** *Times* 23 May 6/1 Agriculture is no longer a subject to be ashamed of; it produces no inferiority complex in those who read it. **1966** *Rep. Comm. Inquiry Univ. Oxf.* II. 49 Graduates reading first degrees. *Ibid.* 85 Women undergraduates reading arts. **1970** [see *English *sb.* 3 d]. **1977** *Professional Careers Bull.* Autumn 1/1 Partially it has been due to an ever increasing demand from sixth formers to read law.

g. Phr. *to read one's shirt* (see quot. 1925). *slang.*

1918 *Nat. Geogr. Mag.* June 499 They..speak of 'reading their shirts'. **1925** Fraser & Gibbons *Soldier & Sailor Words* 237 *To read a shirt*, to search it for lice. **1931** 'D. Stiff' *Milk & Honey Route* xiii. 144 It is said, for instance, that the hobo spends a great deal of his time reading his shirt, seeking certain animals known as 'seam squirrels'.

h. *Computers.* To copy or extract data on or in (any storage medium or device); to copy, extract, or transfer (data). Also const. *into, out of*.

1940 W. J. Eckert *Punched Card Methods Scientific Computation* 4 The number are..read into the machines by..electrical contacts made through the holes. **1945** *Jrnl. Franklin Inst.* CCXL. 277 When the punched tapes are ready, the problem is placed on the machine by automatic controls which 'read' the first tape and make the specified assembly. **1948** *Math. Tables & Other Aids to Computation* III. 123 The speeds at which words can be read (or written) by the machine will be much less than the speeds at which the machine can transfer words internally. *Ibid.* 124 When additional instructions are received they can be read into the machine from an instruction tape. **1950** *High-Speed Computing Devices* ix. 151 The tape reader automatically reads punched tape..and transcribes the data represented by the holes in the tape to a deck of cards. Other equipment can perform the reverse operation, reading the holes punched in the cards and producing a tape. **1959** E. M. McCormick *Digital Computer Primer* ix. 135 The tape is then connected into the computer system and the information read from it to the computer. **1964** F. L. Westwater *Electronic Computers* i. 2 The card or tape is then 'read'. This may be done by allowing the holes to pass under tiny wire brushes. *Ibid.* iv. 59 To read a word out of the store we have to open a gate at the end, and this permits pulses to escape. **1964** *Ann. N.Y. Acad. Sci.* CXV. 654 The length of time required to read information from or store information into one of the 1,024..12-bit memory locations. **1970** O. Dopping *Computers & Data Processing* xiv. 226 The computer time for file maintenance..is often mainly determined by the time for reading and writing magnetic tape. **1972** *Computer Jrnl.* XV. 201/1 The commonest way of reading a file into the system. **1972** *Guardian* 14 Aug. 10/3 Computers can already 'read' a high speed disc-store at around 500,000 characters a second. **1978** J. K. Atkin *Basic Computer Sci.* vii. 92 To read a bit from the memory it is necessary to interrogate a particular core by sending current pulses.. along the appropriate x- and y-wires.

i. To receive and understand the words of (a person) by radio or telephone, to hear; to detect (an object) by sonar; *transf.*, to understand the words or intentions of (a person).

1956 *Amer. Speech* XXXI. 228 [U.S.A.F. slang] *Do you read me?* As in conversation by radio, this means 'Do you understand me?' The answer might be, 'Yes, *five by five*', meaning loud and clear. **1956** 'E. McBain' *Cop Hater* (1958) ix. 85 'Are you stoned now, or can you read me?' 'I hear you,' Ordiz said. **1960** *Master Detective* July 83/1 Static-laced code crackle sounded from the speaker. 'Poelzell. I read you. Keep the Dodge in sight.' **1963** *Times* 25 May 10/7 'Does *anyone* read poor Philip?' A comforting voice from a glider, still airborne: 'Humphrey to Philip. Loud and clear.' **1967** R. J. Serling *President's Plane is Missing* (1968) ix. 164 'Don't be so oversolicitous, Rod. It's as bad for a marriage as being too inconsiderate. Do you read me?' 'I read you, Nancy.' **1968** R. Severn *Game for Hawks* x. 120 'How d'you read her, Cass?' he asked, sourly. 'Could she be taking you for a ride?' **1970** B. Knox *Children of Mist* v. 103 'If you can hear..this is an emergency call.'.. Thane pressed the microphone button. 'Fenn, we read you.' **1972** J. Porter *Meddler & her Murder* x. 131 The girl friend listening?.. Oh, I read you. Well, I'll make it short and sweet. **1974** L. Deighton *Spy Story* xviii. 193 A couple of conventional subs steaming a parallel course... We read them on the sonar and ranged them. **1977** D. Bennett *Jigsaw Man* xi. 203 As from the end of this call, this number will be discontinued. I am reading you back for the fast time.

6. c. (*fig.* example.)

1956 E. H. Hutten *Lang. Mod. Physics* vi. 262 The empiricist prejudice..is, indeed, very strong, but it is obviously not true that we simply read off our hypotheses from data.

e. *to read up*: to study (a subject, a topic, etc.) intensively and systematically; to familiarize oneself with (a subject) by reading.

1842 J. S. Mill *Let.* 22 Aug. in *Wks.* (1963) XIII. 542, I began to *read up* the subject. **1856** C. M. Yonge *Daisy Chain* II. xxvii. 657, I dread reading up all I must read presently. **1869** 'Mark Twain' *Innocents Abroad* xv. 147, I shall throttle down my emotions hereafter, about this sort of people, until I have read them up. **1894** 'R. Andom' *We Three & Troddles* xvii. 149 Those miserable, hollow shams who read up the cricket news..in the evening papers. **1915** R. Brooke *Coll. Poems* p. cxxxvii, I've been peacefully reading up the countryside all the morning. **1921** K. Macaulay *Dangerous Ages* v. 103 You should read it up beforehand, and try if you can understand it. **1962** D. Lessing *Golden Notebk.* II. 280 Those Russians, they're pretty well up in my field, I read them up. **1977** F. Branston *Up & Coming Man* xiv. 152 He would have covered his interests by reading up the minutes of all committees.

f. Computers. *to read out*, to extract (data); to transfer from internal storage; so *to read in*.

1946 *Ann. Computation Lab. Harvard Univ.* I. 62 The storage counter cams..control the number impulses for reading out either from a switch or from a storage counter. Figure 26 shows the circuits for a read-out. *Ibid.* 159 The number of columns shifted is recorded in a counter and a predetermined number of significant digits and a power of ten are read out. **1957** [see *off-line *a.* and *adv.* A. 2]. **1959** E. M. McCormick *Digital Computer Primer* ii. 7 When the problem is completely solved..the calculation is stopped, and the output, or answer, is read out. **1961** [see *read-out 1 a]. **1968** *Times* 10 Dec. 6/8 On each orbit the storage system reads out the information to a ground station. **1970** O. Dopping *Computers & Data Processing* xiv. 222 When all the records have been read-in, all that is needed then is to print the contents of the 50 cells. **1971** *Physics Bull.* Mar. 158/3 It covers those devices in which information can be stored for a limited or controlled time and then read out leaving the device capable of repeated use.

7. b. (Later examples.) Also, to interpret or comprehend.

1962 *Listener* 22 Nov. 886/3 When East removed the double into One Spade, West read his partner for a psychic opening and bid Three No Trumps. **1967** *Ibid.* 28 Dec. 846/3 He..wants..the celebration of the Eucharist (so I read him) to take the form of a prayer meeting. **1970** *Sunday Tel.* 20 Dec. 21/7 Gleeson mesmerises batsmen unable to read him, not into error but into strokelessness.

8. b. Also with *in*.

1903 *Westm. Gaz.* 13 Nov. 7/2 The learned counsel argued that his lordship must read in a negative... In a contract for personal service you must have in it a negative, express or implied. **1919** 'C. Dane' *Legends* 96 She said to me once that the critics had 'read in' things that she had never dreamed of—that it made her doubt her own motives. **1966** G. N. Leech *Eng. in Advertising* xv. 141 In 'lovely, oveny biscuits', 'oveny' can only be made denotatively meaningful by reading in something extra. **1979** E. H. Gombrich *Sense of Order* iv. 99 Finding it difficult, if not impossible, to tell at any point where we see elements and where texture..; where we are reading and where we are 'reading in'.

9. a. Also, to convey (a statement) when read; to say. Cf. sense 18 b below.

1894 [see *It *pron.* 3 f]. **1904** G. Parker *Ladder of Swords* xvi. 229 A footman..came to Angèle, bearing a note which read: 'Your friend is very ill, and asks for you.' **1916** G. B. Shaw *Androcles & Lion* p. lxvi, Your examination paper will read 'The time of Jesus was worth nothing... Dr. Crippen's time was worth, say, three hundred and fifty pounds a year. Criticize this arrangement.' **1946** Bible (Rev. Standard Version) *Mark* xv. 26 And the inscription of the charge against him read, 'The King of the Jews.' **1961** New English Bible *Rom.* xii. 19 There is a text which reads, 'Justice is mine, says the Lord, I will repay.'

11. e. Phr. *to take* (something) *as read*: to treat (a statement, a subject, etc.) as if it has been agreed, without having a discussion about it; to take for granted. Occas. with other introductory vbs.

1886 G. M. Hopkins *Lett. to R. Bridges* (1955) 244 Objections on your part, if any, are now too late and will be 'taken as read'. **1928** D. L. Sayers *Unpleasantness at Bellona Club* iii. 22 Don't let's harrow our feelings. Take it as read. **1930** E. M. Brent-Dyer *Chalet Girls in Camp* x. 151 'It's really I who ought to say 'sorry', you know.'.. 'We'll take it all as read,' put in Miss Wilson hastily. **1938** M. Allingham *Fashion in Shrouds* xxi. 397, I think we can almost take that as read, don't you? **1959** 'M. M. Kaye' *House of Shade* v. 59 I'll take it as read. **1973** H. Miller *Open City*

xvii. 187 You can regard your complaint of boorishness..as read.

12. a. Also const. *with*.

1885 A. Edwardes *Girton Girl* I. iii. 68 Geoffrey Arbuthnot, B.A. Cantab., is willing to read classics and mathematics with Miss Bartrand. Terms, five shillings an hour.

13. a. Also *transf.*

1977 F. Branston *Up & Coming Man* xiv. 152 What could be more natural than for a keen new councillor to read himself in on past decisions?

b. *to read out of* (earlier and later examples); also *refl.*; *to read in*: to admit or induct formally; to make (a person) a member of an armed service, to conscript.

1836 W. Dunlap *Thirty Years Ago* I. xxi. 201 By the death of his parents, he was left in possession of some property, which he dissipated even before he 'was read out of meeting'. **1841** *Congress. Globe* 30 June 133/2 Mr. Alford concluded by warning the 'tariff boys' of the South, that instead of their reading him out of church, if they did not mind he would read them out of church. **1890** *Harper's Mag.* Feb. 349/2 They said I wasn't no Christian; and so they got together and read me out o' the church. **1915** F. Hopwood *Let.* 20 May in M. Gilbert *Winston S. Churchill* (1972) III. Compan. II. 920 It is plain that a First Sea Lord remains in office until the new Patent appointing his successor is passed the Seal & he is 'read in' at the Board. **1938** C. S. Forester *Ship of Line* viii. 110 Excellent, Mr. Bush. Read 'em in. **1942** E. Paul *Narrow St.* xxii. 186 Men..who may be read into the army and shot as traitors if they try to strike, are difficult material. **1976** *Time* 27 Dec. 14/2 Arafat also warned that any Palestinian group that rejected the idea..must read itself out of the P.L.O.

II. 15. a. Also, to read (sense *5 a) music.

1889 G. B. Shaw in *Star* 24 May 4/2 The few who are really able to read at sight. **1976** *Star* (Sheffield) 3 Dec. 16/7 (Advt.), Organist required for a 9-day period at Christmas. Must be able to read.

c. (Earlier and further examples.)

1823 M. Wilmot *Let.* 1 Oct. (1935) 202, I trust that Edw[d] may obtain the gold medal which he is reading for. **1863** Mrs. Gaskell *Dark Night's Work* xv. 271 You knew him at Hamley, I suppose? I remember his reading there with Mr. Ness. **1874** J. Codman *Mormon Country* i. 2 They buy a big book..and, having read up thoroughly, fill the cavities of their minds with details from these to supply what they did not learn from their extended visit of half a day. **1890** C. M. Yonge *More Bywords* 129 The two sisters are reading up for the Oxford exam. **1911** J. London *Let.* 17 Aug. (1966) 350, I should advise you..to read up on socialism. **1938** E. C. Lodge *Terms & Vacations* iv. 51 Those of us who read for University schools went to the different Colleges to lectures. **1962** [see *litteræ humaniores]. **1976** 'M. Albrand' *Taste of Terror* xviii. 103 Why don't you read up on it in the *Britannica*?

d. To act as a publisher's reader.

1850 Thackeray *Pendennis* II. iii. 27 Warrington artfully inspired the two gentlemen who 'read' for Messrs. Bacon and Bungay with the greatest curiosity regarding 'Walter Lorraine'. **1891** G. Gissing *New Grub Street* I. vi. 122 She.. liked to know who 'read' for the publishing-houses. **1956** P. Scott *Male Child* II. i. 112, I..asked her whether she had ever read for a publisher. **1978** S. Hodge *Gollancz* iii. 64 They went on reading for him.

e. To receive and understand a message by radio, telephone, etc.

1930 *Amer. Speech* V. 289 The receiving operator 'receives', 'copies' or 'reads'. **1962** J. Glenn in *Into Orbit* 213 *Schirra*: 'John, leave your retro-package on through your pass over Texas. Do you read?' *Glenn*: 'Roger'. **1963** *Times* 25 May 10/7 'Philip to Kitty—do you read?' No reply. **1966** D. Francis *Flying Finish* ii. 26, I said, 'Port Ellen tower this is Golf Alpha Romeo Kilo November, do you read?'

16. c. *you wouldn't read about it*: exclamation used to express a mixture of incredulity and disgust. *Austral.* and *N.Z. colloq.*

1950 J. Cleary *Just let me Be* xiv. 135 Everything I backed ran like a no-hoper. Four certs I had, and the bludgers were so far back the ambulance nearly had to bring 'em home. You wouldn't read about it. **1962** D. Cusack *Picnic Races* xxi. 249 He drew a deep breath. 'You wouldn't read about it.' **1973** H. Williams *My Love had Black Speed Stripe* x. 69 You wouldn't read about it. A bloke his missus reckons was a doctor of philosophy, whatever that was, and just about the biggest dill you could meet.

18. a. (Later examples.)

1887 A. Birrell *Obiter Dicta* 2nd Ser. viii. 260 When the dish is served, we only ask, Is it good?..when the book comes out, Does it read? **1931** *N. & Q.* 17 Oct. 287/2 The translation is oddly unequal. It is often conspicuously clear and vigorous; sometimes it is halting and dull; occasionally, it does not 'read'.

b. Also, to convey a statement when read.

1891 F. H. Williams *Atman* v. 270 The letter reads as follows.

d. Of a measuring instrument: to have a graduated scale of a specified kind.

1862 *Catal. Internat. Exhib., Industr. Dept., Brit. Div.* II. No. 2941, Standard barometer on Fortin's principle, reading from an ivory zero point in the cistern.

19. e. Of an actor: to audition *for*, to rehearse *for* a role. Also, *to read in for*, to take the part of (another actor) at a rehearsal.

1943 S. Lewis *Gideon Planish* 71 'And will you read for it?'.. 'You mean try and see if I can act one of the parts?' 'Professionally, we call it "read for a part".' **1966** A. E. Lindop *I start Counting* ii. 44 She'd had a letter..asking her to report to the Jubilee Hall, where she was to read for the Amateur Dramatic Society. **1968** J. Bingham *I love, I Kill* iii. 32 Shirley, you read in for Sarah... You'll be understudying her anyway. **1970** E. Berckman *She asked for It* ii. 18 'How's it done?' 'You ring your agent, and say you'll read for the part.' *Ibid.* 19, I stood over her, literally, till she'd rung and said she'd read for the producer. **1971** *Guardian* 10 Dec. 10/5 The [play] reading is on again... Somebody can read in for Graham.

III. 22. *Computers.* The infin. used *attrib.* and in *Comb.* with the sense 'reading'.

1953 A. D. & K. H. V. Booth *Automatic Digital Calculators* xii. 115 Mounted close to the drum are a series of read/record heads. **1960** *Proc. Inst. Electr. Engineers* (VII. B. 56) (*heading*) A digital computer store with very short read time. **1964** F. L. Westwater *Electronic Computers* iv. 77 The resulting change of flux as the core switches will cause an electromotive force in the read wire which we can recognise. **1965** *Wireless World* July 340/1 The read/write cycle time is 600 nsec. **1971** J. H. Smith *Digital Logic* vi. 126 In practical core memories the *X* and *Y* co-ordinates are only used for identifying the core required and each core in the plane is threaded with additional 'read' and 'write' wires. **1979** J. E. Rowley *Mechanical In-House Information Syst.* i. 64 Read-write heads..give direct access to the opposite track, and then this track may be searched sequentially.

23. read-around ratio *Computers*, the number of times that a particular bit in an electrostatic store can be read without degrading bits stored nearby.

1953 *Math. Tables & Other Aids to Computation* VII. 112 The inherent coupling between adjacent storage locations on the face of any cathode ray tube places a limit on the number of times any point on the raster may be consulted before its neighbors are regenerated. For the Institute machine this number, called the 'read around' ratio, is in the neighborhood of 30. **1969** P. B. Jordain *Condensed Computer Encycl.* 415 A high read-around ratio means greater reliability.

read, *ppl. a.* Add: **2.** Also *read up*.

1873 'Mark Twain' *Gilded Age* xi. 112, I *am* better read up in most sciences, maybe, than the general run of professional men. **1883** H. E. Manning *Eternal Priesthood* xx. 277 He is a welcome visitor..a ready and amusing guest, read up in the newspapers, and full of the events of the day.

readability. Add: (Earlier and later examples.) Also in extended sense, the quality of, or capacity for, being read with pleasure or interest, considered as measured by certain assessable factors, as ease of comprehension, attractiveness of subject and style.

1843 S. Coleridge *Let.* July in *Mem. & Lett.* (1873) I. xi. 281 If bad arrangement in S.T.C. is injurious to readibility, in S.C. it will be destructive. **1899** J. Southward *Mod. Printing* II. i. 4 A book..is not a good book because it is a pretty one; readability is of far more importance than picturesqueness. **1935** Gray & Leary *What makes Book Readable* ii. 38 The weight of opinion of all judges is that an informal.., non-technical.., adult..vocabulary is an important contribution to readability, whereas a vocabulary limited to 1,000–1,500 words.., is not essential. **1948** R. Flesch in *Jrnl. Appl. Psychol.* XXXII. 228 To measure the readability ('reading ease' and 'human interest') of a piece of writing, go through the following steps. **1953** *Journalism Q.* XXX. 417/1 One can think of cloze procedure as throwing all potential readability influences in a pot, letting them interact, then sampling the result. **1958** H. B. & A. C. English *Dict. Psychol. & Psychoanal. Terms* 441 The criteria brought forward for determining readability suggest that it is not a single variable but a combination of at least three or four. **1963** R. Morris *Success & Failure in Learning to Read* iv. 97 The attempts that have been made to implement [E.L.] Thorndike's 'readability-control' programme have added considerably to the resources available to the teachers of reading today. **1975** *Language for Life* (Dept. Educ. & Sci.) xiv. 218 The writers would be able to refashion their stories to adjust readability levels. **1977** *N.Y. Rev. Bks.* 23 June 4 (Advt.), One might define a great essay as a short excursion which has infinite readability.

readable, *a.* (and *sb.*) Add: **2. a.** (Earlier examples.)

1771 *Monthly Rev.* Dec. 493 The real Author of these Letters..chose to turn it to what literary advantage he might make of a couple of very *readable* volumes. *a* **1817** Jane Austen *Northanger Abbey* (1818) I. vi. 74 Sir Charles Grandison! That is an amazing horrid book... I thought it had not been readable.

b. (Later example.)

1977 *New Yorker* 1 Aug. 13/3 Sales clerks..stacked giant displays of discounted readables.

readapt, *v.* Add: **b.** *intr.* To become adapted anew.

1961 Webster, *Readapt*.., to become adapted again. **1971** N. Freeling *Over High Side* III. 226 The little flat..had become 'working woman alone' instead of 'married couple'. ..'I'm glad to see you're re-adapting with no trouble.'

reader. Add: **2. c.** (Examples.) Also, one similarly employed by a theatre to read plays offered for production.

1829 H. Foote *Compan. Theatres* 146 Drury-Lane.—Season 1828–9. Lessee and Manager—B. Price, Esq.—Reader of Plays—Mr. Frederick Reynolds. **1859** E. Fitzball *Thirty-Five Years Dram. Author's Life* I. vii. 262, I have been dramatic reader myself, in the Theatre Royal, Covent Garden,..some years. **1891** G. Gissing *New Grub Street* II. xiii. 4 One of Mr Jedwood's 'readers'..was expressing a doubt whether Fadge himself was the author of the review. **1895** G. B. Shaw in *Sat. Rev.* 2 Mar. 280/2 The Lord Chamberlain's reader is not selected by examination either in literature or morals. **1924** J. Galsworthy *White Monkey* II. vi. 168 Here were manuscripts, of which the readers to Danby and Winter had already said: 'No money in this.' **1956** P. Scott *Male Child* II. iv. 153 He told me.. he'd get another reader..in your place. He thought your illness had impaired your judgment. **1976** M. Green *Children of Sun* v. 171 J. B. Priestley..became..a publisher's reader for John Lane.

d. One who reads designs in weaving (see *read *v.* 5 e).

1839 Ure *Dict. Arts* 267 The weaving of imitation shawls is executed, as usual, by as many shuttles as there are colours in the designs, and which are thrown across the warp in the order established by the reader. **1932** L. Hooper *New Draw-Loom* II. ix. 82 The reader, looking carefully at the line, No. 1 of the design at the side next to the numerals, must count the number of dark squares with which it begins ..and call 'Take 1'. **1970** *Classification of Occupations* (Office of Population Censuses & Surveys) 70/1 (Index), Reader: design; textile.

e. One who reads music; a sight-reader.

1947 G. B. Shaw in *Mus. Times* Jan. 10/1 It takes years of practice to train a group of good readers to sing in tune not only passably but exactly. **1977** *Grimsby Even. Tel.* 5 May 3/3 (Advt.), Pianist wanted also Trombonist by local rehearsal dance band. Must be readers.

3. a. (Examples in Jewish context.)

1872 *Minutes S. Manch. Hebrew Congreg.* 29 Sept. in I. W. Goldberg *South Manch. Hebrew Congreg.: 80 Years of Progress* (1952) 8 That the Reverend H. D. Marks be elected Reader, Stipendiary Secretary and Minister to the Congregation. **1973** *Jewish Chron.* 2 Feb. 43/1 A memorial service for Mr. Victor Schiller, honorary reader of the Lecton Synagogue..was held at the synagogue.

b. reader-aloud, one who reads (a literary text, etc.) aloud, esp. to an audience. Also *reader-alouder*. Cf. Read *v.* 11 a.

1938 *Times* 16 Sept. 13/4 Fountains are less trouble in bedrooms than readers-aloud or raconteurs. **1952** G. Raverat *Period Piece* viii. 145 Aunt Etty was the best reader-aloud I have ever known. **1952** *Sat. Rev.* (U.S.) 13 Sept. 6/3 Hemingway is a reader-alouder, it appears. **1977** *Listener* 10 Nov. 624/4 Lots of subordinate clauses can make life very difficult for the reader-aloud.

6. a. (Earlier examples.)

1718 C. Hitching *Regulator* 20 A reader, *alias* pocket-book. **1789** G. Parker *Life's Painter Varieg. Char.* xv. 151 *Reader.* Is a pocket-book; a person cannot be too careful of this article, particularly if he should have..any rum screens in it, that is, bank notes.

b. (Further example.)

1977 'L. Egan' *Blind Search* iv. 57 McAllister was a gambler... This is a deck of readers—marked cards.

c. *U.S. Criminals' slang.* (See quot. 1926.)

1926 *Clues* Nov. 162/1 *Reader*, a circular notifying police officers to arrest the party described thereon. **1955** *Publ. Amer. Dial. Soc.* xxiv. 150 Sometimes there is a 'detainer' issued for a thief... This is called a *reader* or a *dipsy*.

7. A device for obtaining data stored on tape, cards, or other media (usu. converting the data into coded electrical signals).

1946 *N.Y. Times* 15 Feb. 16/3 When the problem is punched on the cards they are dropped into a slot in a 'reader'. **1964** F. L. Westwater *Electronic Computers* iv. 80 Even with the faster types of card reader it is difficult to exceed 800 digits per second. **1968** *Brit. Med. Bull.* XXIV. 205/1 It may be possible to eliminate the stage of transfer onto punched cards by using an optical reader, for there is now a rapid development in this type of device. **1972** M. Woodhouse *Mama Doll* xi. 145 Some people at Admiralty ran the tape through a five-hole reader for us, and gave us back seven hundred and eighty-four groups of digits.

8. A machine for producing on a screen a magnified, readable image of any desired part of a microfilm or other microform.

1950 *Amer. Documentation* I. 141/2 A new reading machine just announced..holds much promise. This reader giving a clear, sharp image..is relatively inexpensive. **1962** A. Günther *Microphotogr. in Lib.* (Unesco) 7 Micro-opaque cards..may be readily filed. However, they need much more light for projection and, therefore, a more complicated and more expensive reader, which must be equipped with a blower for cooling. **1975** P. G. New *Reprography for Librarians* iv. 48 The librarian committed to exploiting micro materials must not only consider investing in a multitude of portable readers for loan, but must also ensure that his library is fully equipped with..viewers for use on the premises.

9. *attrib.* and *Comb.*, as *reader group*, *participation*, *response*; *reader-contributor*, *-writer*; (sense 2 c) *reader's report*; **reader-printer**, a reading machine (sense *(*b*)) that can also produce enlarged, readable copies.

1946 *R.A.F. Jrnl.* May 146 The success of the new magazine will depend on the continuance of the excellent reader-contributor relationship which was fostered. **1951** M. McLuhan *Mech. Bride* (1967) 112/2 These magazines, carefully geared to both the purse and heart strings of their respective reader groups, feature houses and rooms in which almost nobody ever lives. *Ibid.* 5/2 This kind of newspaper invites reader participation in its triumphs. **1959** H. W. Ballou *Guide to Microreproduction Equipment* 167 Thermo-Fax Brand Microfilm Reader-Printer... Special Features: Reader and Printer combined in one machine for automatic push-button copying or reading. **1971** *Ann. Rep. Curators Bodl. Libr. 1969–70* 47, 4,011 prints were made on the microfilm reader-printer. **1940** *Kenyon Rev.* II. 274 The reader-response has been altered through a lessening of the pleasure with which the utterance is received. **1979** *Maledicta* III. 83 Among those critics who use psychoanalytical theory there is little agreement over what one can say legitimately about 'reader response'. **1897** 'S. Grand' *Beth Bk.* (1898) xlvii. 460 Mr. Kilroy took the manuscript himself to a publisher..who..accepted it... Beth..heard the reader's report. **1978** E. Tidyman *Table Stakes* II. v. 241 Each morning a mailboy would arrive with a stack of scripts..Attached were the readers' reports. **1951** S. Spender *World within World* 310 Reader-writer walk together in a real-seeming dream-alliance leading into gardens inhabited by Stephen Daedalus and Marcel.

readership. Add: **3.** The total number of (regular) readers of a periodical publication, as a newspaper or magazine; all, or a section, of such readers considered collectively. Also *attrib.* orig. *U.S.*

1923 O. G. Villard *Some Newspapers & Newspapermen* 189 The appeal of the *News* to the masses has been so successful that it now has a readership of some forty thousand. **1947** C. L. Allen (*title*) A readership study of 3 typical Wisconsin hometown dailies. **1951** *Sunday Times* 2 Dec. 1/3 Mr. Stephen's..experienced counsel and reflections [will] become available to the whole Sunday Times readership. **1958** *New Statesman* 30 Aug. 241/1 It holds its vast circulation..by grace of Mr. Gilbert Harding, whose weekly column (according to readership surveys) is the *People's* biggest pulling feature of all. **1963** *Guardian* 10 Apr. 7/2 Another variation, reflecting different readership, is the background of the characters. **1971** *Nature* 2 Apr. 310/3 In view of the intended readership the selection of topics seems reasonable enough. **1979** *London Rev. Bks.* 25 Oct. 2/3 The obvious difference will relate to the subjects generated by the nationality of the *London Review*'s readership, and by that of its contributors.

read-in (rī·dˌin). *Computers.* [f. vbl. phr. *to read in* (*READ *v.* 6 f).] The input of data to a computer or storage device.

1946 *Ann. Computation Lab. Harvard Univ.* I. 63 If a quantity is standing in the counter at the time of read-in so that addition must be performed, the carry circuits are utilized. **1952** [see *MATRIX 6 d]. **1959** E. M. McCormick *Digital Computer Primer* ii. 8 When the storage..comprises relays and vacuum tubes,..special read-in equipment is required so that the information will be in a form the computer can use. **1970** *Computers & Humanities* IV. 166 Only the read-in statements of the program set would need to be changed to accommodate this programming.

readiness. Add: **4. b.** *Psychol.* The stage of physiological or developmental maturity at which an organism is able to take in new learning with ease. Also *attrib.*

1948 E. R. Hilgard *Theories of Learning* ii. 22 There is another kind of readiness familiar to educators. This is illustrated by the use of such a term as 'reading readiness' to refer to the child's reaching a maturity level appropriate to the beginning of reading. **1956** H. C. Lindgren *Educ. Psychol.* ix. 236 Many schools postpone the teaching of reading for first-graders who do not demonstrate 'reading readiness' on standardized tests. **1967** J. C. Nunnally *Psychometric Theory* iii. 77 In schools, predictive validity is at issue in measures of 'readiness'. **1976** *Woman's Day* (U.S.) Nov. 58/2 Clare Pederson..takes a particularly dim view of readiness tests... 'Why don't school systems take the money they waste on readiness tests and spend it on books instead?' **1977** P. R. Ammon in Hom & Robinson *Psychol. Processes in Early Educ.* vii. 184 The question of readiness pertains not only to *how* children can learn, but also to *what* they can learn.

Reading (re·diŋ). [The name of the county town of Berkshire.] **1.** *Reading Beds*, a set of beds of sand, clay, and gravel of fluviatile origin underneath the London clay in the London and Hampshire basins.

1817 *Trans. Geol. Soc.* IV. 283 In many parts of this great valley or trough of chalk [*sc.* the Thames valley] we recognized our Reading beds in their proper place, as the inferior strata of the plastic clay formation. **1854** *Q. Jrnl. Geol. Soc.* X. 164 The leaves preserved in the Reading beds. **1882** A. Geikie *Text-bk. Geol.* 844 The Woolwich and Reading Beds, or 'Plastic Clay' of the older geologists, consist of lenticular sheets of plastic clay, loam, sand, and pebble-beds. **1923** [see *LANDENIAN *a.*]. **1969** Bennison & Wright *Geol. Hist. Brit. Isles* xv. 336 The Reading Beds facies is the most extensive of the three in the London Basin.

2. a. *Reading onion*, a variety of onion developed by the firm of Sutton & Son (formerly of Reading). Also *absol.*

1845 E. Acton *Mod. Cookery* (ed. 4) xxii. 508 The Reading onion is the proper kind for pickling. **1885** W. Robinson tr. *Vilmorin-Andrieux's Veg. Garden* 366 White Spanish, or Reading, Onion... Bulb quite flat, 3 to 4 inches in diameter. **1963** *Sutton's Seed Catal.* 66/1 Sutton's Improved Reading. A maincrop onion.

b. *Reading sauce*, a sharp sauce flavoured with onions, spices, and herbs.

1861 Mrs. Beeton *Bk. Househ. Managem.* 240 *Reading sauce*,..walnut pickle..shalots..Indian soy..bruised ginger [etc.]... *Seasonable.*—This sauce may be made at any time. **1862** 'L. Carroll' in *College Rhymes* III. 114 There are epithets That suit with any word—As well as Harvey's Reading Sauce With fish, or flesh, or bird. **1878** M. Jewry *Warne's Model Cookery* 46/1 A large spoonful of sauce, either Worcester or Reading. **1907** *Yesterday's Shopping* (1969) 33/2 *Sauces* (Other Makers')... Reading.

3. Designating the gypsy caravan of traditional design, supposedly first built in Reading (see quots.). Chiefly in *Reading wagon.*

1940 F. G. Huth in *Jrnl. Gypsy Lore Soc.* XIX. 117 The Reading Waggon, or old type of Gypsy *vardō*, with large wheels running outside the body of the van. **1951** *Archit. Rev.* CIX. 317 There are five distinct types of gypsy wagon in use on the roads today... Reading wagon. Originally built by the Dunton family at Reading, this is probably the oldest type of van and is generally accepted as the 'gypsy shape'. **1972** Ward-Jackson & Harvey *Eng. Gypsy Caravan* ii. 43 The Reading type of van had certainly been evolved by the 1860's. **1975** *Country Life* 2 Oct. 840/1 We thought we might buy an old gypsy wagon... I found the ruin of a 'Reading' or showman's wagon. **1976** *Horse & Hound* 3 Dec. 68/4 (Advt.), Gypsy Caravan of Reading style for sale.

reading, *vbl. sb.* Add: **1. e.** *Computers.* The copying, extraction, or transfer of data. Also with *in*, *out.* Also *transf.* Freq. *attrib.* Cf. *READ *v.* 5 h, 6 f.

1949 E. C. Berkeley *Giant Brains* iv. 44 The reading of a hole in a column of a punch card is done by a brush of several strands of copper wire pressed against a metal roller. **1950** *High-Speed Computing Devices* ix. 155 The input to the Tabulator is from a single feed with reading stations examining the two most advanced cards simultaneously. **1964** F. L. Westwater *Electronic Computers* iv. 65 When the magnetised spot of wire passes under the reading head there will be a change of magnetic flux through the coils on the head. **1964** J. Z. Young *Model of Brain* xiii. 217 We can thus say that the vertical lobe system is necessary for 'reading-out' of the memory as well as for 'reading-in'. **1970** O. Dopping *Computers & Data Processing* viii. 122 After a few milliseconds, the beginning of the tape block reaches the reading head and the buffer register in the channel starts to be filled with information.

2. a. Also with *aloud, out.*

1936 F. R. Leavis *Revaluation* ii. 44 Here, if this were a lecture, would come illustrative reading-out—say of the famous opening to Book III. **1960** C. Day Lewis *Buried Day* iv. 64, I don't remember much reading-aloud, before I could read to myself.

b. Also with *aloud.*

1960 C. Day Lewis *Buried Day* vii. 149 These were H.R.K.'s incomparable readings-aloud from Jane Austen, Thackeray, Dickens or the poets. **1974** *Listener* 14 Mar. 347/2 The least we can ask from a reading-aloud of poetry we know is that it adds to our gain from private reading.

e. (Earlier and later examples.)

1787 J. Cobb *Eng. Readings* 5 But tell me, Kitty, how did this *rage* for English Readings reach a town so far from London? **1813** M. Edgeworth *Let.* 16 May (1971) 55 We have been to one of Mrs. Siddons readings—*Measure for Measure*... In settling with Sheridan she came short 10 or 12 thousand pounds and her Readings are to make up this defalcation. **1916** M. B. Lowndes *Diary* 12 Apr. (1971) 71, I went to the most remarkable Poets' Reading I have ever attended... I was moved by Mr de la Mare reading five poems of great beauty. **1953** *Ann. Reg. 1952* CXCIV. 377 The Hell scene in Shaw's *Man and Superman* had been staged with elaborate simplicity as a 'reading'.

7. c. An extract from a previously printed source; in *pl.* freq. denoting a particular selection of such extracts intended to be read at one time or as a unit.

1835 C. Fry (*title*) Daily readings. Passages of Scripture, selected for social reading. **1865** Ctess. of Cawdor (*title*) Short Sunday evening readings selected and abridged from various authors. **1908** Robinson & Beard (*title*) Readings in modern European history. A collection of extracts from the sources. **1931** W. L. Valentine *Readings in Exper. Psychol.* p. xiv, The original purpose was to include as a single reading only a single experimental paper. **1947** *Mind* LVI. 278 This joint work is intended to be read in conjunction with a companion volume of 'readings' culled from the classics of ancient and modern philosophy. **1972** *Sci. Amer.* Feb. 117/1 *The Science of Matter* offers more than 160 samples, averaging a couple of pages each; *A History of Medicine*..gives us a couple of dozen readings some 10 or 12 pages in length.

9. (Further examples.)

1814 *Morning Herald* 14 Mar. in J. Agate *These were Actors* (1943) 31 Mr. Kean thought fit to leave out the whole of the first line in this declaration... This, in the saucy jargon of the day, may be called 'a new reading'. **1865** Dickens *Mut. Friend* II. III. x. 94 By-the-by, that very word, Reading, in its critical use, always charms me. An actress's Reading of a chambermaid, a dancer's Reading of a hornpipe, a singer's Reading of a song, a marine-painter's Reading of the sea, the kettle-drum's Reading of an instrumental passage, are phrases ever youthful and delightful. **1929** A. Carse *Orchestral Conducting* III. i. 96 The personality of a conductor, the individuality of his readings ..count for more than technical correctness. **1945** H. Wood *About Conducting* 105 Every aspirant to a conductor's career should..make himself acquainted with the traditional readings of the classical repertoire. **1969** *Listener* 13 Mar. 360/2 The structure of his film implies one reading of Isadora's life, while its content implies a quite contrary interpretation. **1977** M. Allen *Spence in Petal Park* iv. 16 Someone turned him over..after death, I would say. The pathologist will tell us for sure, but that's my reading.

10. a. *reading-circle, clinic, habit, -lamp* (earlier and later examples), *light, list, material, matter* (earlier and later examples), *party* (earlier and later examples), *rate, -readiness, scheme, society* (earlier and later examples), *table* (earlier examples).

1871 Mrs. Stowe *Pink & White Tyranny* xi. 124 They would get up their reading-circles, and he would set her to improving her mind. **1926** R. Macaulay *Crewe Train* II. v. 118 A reading circle. You all study some book together, and meet and talk about it. **1963** R. I. McDavid *Mencken's Amer. Lang.* 320 Minton points out the spread of technical medical terminology to education, as *clinic* (yielding *reading clinic* and *speech clinic*). **1975** *Language for Life* (Dept. Educ. & Sci.) xxvi. 514 There should be a reading clinic or remedial centre in every L.E.A. **1940** R. S. Lambert *Ariel & all his Quality* v. 131 You could hear complaints..that broadcasting was undermining the reading habit. **1963** D. Pryce-Jones in Sissons & French *Age of Austerity* 212 The war may have enlarged the reading habits of a great many people. **1975** *Language for Life* (Dept. Educ. & Sci.) xxi. 304 The reading habit should be established early. **1782** *Catal. Stock in Trade Benjamin Martin* 14 A reading lamp, with magnifying glass and shade. **1908** Mrs. H. Ward *Diana Mallory* II. x. 212 She was bending over the fire..a reading-lamp beside her. **1960** T. Cooper *Winter's Day* II. v. 134 Do..switch off the big light; this reading-lamp on the desk is ample. **1936** M. Allingham *Flowers for Judge* xix. 273 The green reading light..shining down upon his papers. **1945** Wilson & Wright *Tomorrow's House* xi. 116/2 Getting a decent reading light is by no means a matter of setting a table lamp on the night table. **1981** L. Deighton *XPD* xli. 329 He had a small reading light by which to read the documentation. **1925** *Scribner's Mag.* July 61/1 Books on fishing..should, in my opinion, have a place on every reading list. **1981** *Times Lit. Suppl.* 6 Feb. 136/4 The names of these daunting authors..make an occasional modest appearance on reading-lists. **1961** *Educ. in Scotland 1960* (HMSO) 44 A welcome increase in the provision of supplementary reading material. **1975** *Language for Life* (Dept. Educ. & Sci.) xvii. 253 Her first task is to assess the attainment level of every child and provide each with reading material of the right level of readability. **1848** Thoreau in *Union Mag.* Aug. 79/2 An odd leaf of the Bible,..Emerson's Address on West India Emancipation..an odd number of the Westminster Review... This was the readable, or reading matter, in a lumberer's camp in the Maine woods. **1923** R. Macaulay *Told by Idiot* II. i. 68 Wise men and women would derive such pleasure as they could from the writings of others, without putting themselves to the trouble of providing reading matter in their turn. **1972** 'E. Ferrars' *Breath of Suspicion* xi. 185 I'm leaving the choice of some reading-matter for you to Bernard. **1785** B. Sheridan *Jrnl.* (1960) i. 43 Yesterday evening we spent at Mr Vesey's—a sort of conversationé—and reading party. **1930** J. S. Huxley *Bird-Watching & Bird Behaviour* iii. 61, I was spending some of the spring vacation with a reading-party on the coast of North Wales. **1980** D. Newsome *On Edge of Paradise* ii. 59 A meeting there with a reading-party was usually the prelude to some summer expedition abroad. **1960** *Bookseller* 17 Dec. 2330/3 A 'reading-rate controller'.., an inverted T-square with the handle part moving down the page of a book,..is attached to a sloping desk... A ready reckoner shows the number of..[lines] read in a minute, and the pupil can set the speed of this and then try to read faster. **1975** *Broadcast* 28 July 11/3 Our videodisc player's reading rate is 30 million bits per second. **1948, 1956** Reading-readiness [see *READINESS 4 b]. **1964** M. Critchley *Developmental Dyslexia* iv. 15 Bound up with the problem of when a child should first receive formal instruction in reading is the notion of a state of 'reading-readiness'. **1976** *Woman's Day* (U.S.) Nov. 58/2 How can reading-readiness scores have meaning when reading experts are still debating what skills are needed for beginning reading? **1974** *Education & Community Relations* Jan. 3 Several multiracial primary schools foresaw a major change 'in the selection of reading schemes and supplementary readers'. **1975** *Language for Life* (Dept. Educ. & Sci.) vii. 104 The reading scheme is at the centre of this material in most young children's early experience of reading. **1775** T. Campbell *Diary* 21 Mar. (1947) 58 Strolled into the Chapter Coffee-house..remarkable for a large collection of books, & a reading Society &c—I subscribed a shilling for the right of a years reading. **1828** M. O'Brien *Jrnl.* 28 Oct. (1968) iii. 21, I hope we shall manage the reading society, though we can only muster three members at Present. **1890** G. B. Shaw in *Star* 28 Feb. 2/4, I repaired to the London Institution to see 'The Shakespere Reading Society' recite 'Much Ado'. **1794** T. Sheraton *Cabinet-Maker & Upholsterer's Drawing-Bk.* II. III. Pl. 44 (*caption*) A Reading & Writing Table. **1855** Trollope *Warden* ix. 134 A huge arm-chair fitted up with candlesticks, a reading table, a drawer, and other paraphernalia.

b. reading age, reading ability expressed in terms of the age (during the period of development) for which a comparable ability is calculated as average; **reading chair**, a chair designed to facilitate reading; *spec.* one equipped with a book-rest upon one arm; **reading copy**, a copy of a book that is usable although in less than perfect condition; **reading-glass**, (*b*) in *pl.*, a pair of spectacles for use when reading; **reading-machine**, (*b*) a device for producing an enlarged, readable image from microform; (*c*) a device for automatically producing electrical signals corresponding to the characters of a text; **reading notice** *U.S.* (see quot. 1909).

1921 C. Burt *Mental & Scholastic Tests* III. iii. 271 Consequently, a score of sixty words indicates a mental age for reading at ten;..according to the formula:—Reading Age $= (4 + \frac{\text{Words}}{10})$ years. *Ibid.*, The reading ages of four and five pretend to little more than a conventional significance. **1945** F. J. Schonell *Psychol. & Teaching of Reading* i. 21 There is always a great increase in eye movements as the reading material increases in difficulty for particular reading ages. **1952** Anderson & Dearborn *Psychol. of Teaching Reading* i. 10 If the reading age is appreciably below the mental age, the child is regarded as a reading problem. **1961** *Guardian* 28 Apr. 13/3 He looks a dissipated 20... His reading age is 8·2. **1975** *Language for Life* (Dept. Educ. & Sci.) ii. 11 There are at least a million adults with a reading age of below 9·0 who cannot read simple recipes. **1803** T. Sheraton *Cabinet Dict.* 17 *Arm-chair* for a library, or a reading chair... These are intended to make the exercise easy, and for the convenience of taking down a note or quotation... The reader places himself with his back to the front of the chair, and rests his arms on the top yoke. **1853** A. J. Downing *Architect. Country Houses* xii. 426 Fig. 218 is a reading-chair of a simple and good form,..having a desk for a book on one arm, and a stand for a candle on the other—both being..easily lifted out.., when not in use. **1951** E. Paul *Springtime in Paris* iii. 54 There was a long table, and ranged on both sides, good reading chairs. **1977**

J. Hodgins *Invention of World* iii. 44 The tall green reading chair that had recipes..shoved under its cushion. **1952** J. Carter *ABC for Book-Collectors* 164 Reading copy, a usually apologetic, but occasionally slightly defiant, term meaning that the book is not in collector's condition. **1977** J. Wilson *Making Hate* iv. 52 The *Just So Stories*. I had an early edition, a torn reading copy, but quite clean. **1853** Dickens *Bleak House* xli. 405 The green lamp is lighted, his reading-glasses lie upon the desk. **1972** G. Bill *Villains Galore* i. 1 Clara..needed reading glasses for all but the largest print. **1937** M. L. Raney *Microphotogr. for Libraries* 76 There is today plenty of work for reading machines to do, since the entire contents of great libraries that have filming cameras lie open to order in so far as copyright allows. **1940** A. Huxley *Let.* 14 Oct. (1969) 461, I would like to have.. micro-photographs suitable for reading by means of a reading machine. **1959** *Library Resources & Technical Services* III. 90 The average library user does not meet the microcopy until he has to use it on the reading machine. **1964** *Litho-Printer* Aug. 34/2 Even optical reading machines, which are now entering the field of practicability cannot quite dispense with human work: they need clean copy, at least re-typed from edited manuscripts. **1965** R. R. Karch *Graphic Arts Procedures* (ed. 3) xiii. 338 Specially-designed figures printed at the bottoms of bank checks are printed with ink capable of being magnetized and read by electronic reading machines for routing the checks to proper places. **1980** J. Drummond *Such a Nice Family* viii. 38 Would you like us to fix up a reading-machine for you?.. It'll throw up an enlargement of the text. **1909** Webster, *Reading-notice*, in a newspaper or periodical, a paid advertisement so set up as to have the appearance of regular news or editorial or contributed matter. **1970** R. K. Kent *Lang. Journalism* 109 *Reading notice*, an advertisement in a newspaper or magazine that is set in body type and in columns so as to appear the same as editorial matter.

reading, *ppl. a.* **2.** (Further examples of (*the*) *reading public*.)

1877 M. W. Chapman in *Harriet Martineau's Autobiogr.* III. 99 The reading public..were longing to express their grateful acknowledgements. **1916** E. Pound *Let.* 17 Nov. (1971) 99 That many-eared monster with no sense, the reading public. *a* **1936** Kipling *Something of Myself* (1937) iii. 47 Our reading public..were..as well educated as fifty per cent of our 'staff'. **1962** M. McLuhan *Gutenberg Galaxy* 132 There was no reading public in our sense... Under manuscript conditions an author would..have no public. An advanced scientist today has no public. **1975** S. Schoenbaum *W. Shakespeare* xi. 120 A dramatist had least to say about..publication... He strove, after all, to please audiences in the theatre, not a reading public.

readjustment. Add: **2.** *Comb.*, as **readjustment rule** *Linguistics* (see quot. 1972).

1968 Chomsky & Halle *Sound Pattern Eng.* i. i. 10 The 'readjustment rules' relating syntax to phonology make various other modifications in surface structures. **1972** R. A. Palmatier *Gloss. Eng. Transformational Grammar* 141 *Readjustment rule*,..one of a set of special rules which prepare the syntactic surface structure of a sentence for inputting to the phonological component; one of the types of phonological rules..which determine admissible, or possible, and inadmissible, or impossible, classificatory matrices. **1977** *Canad. Jrnl. Linguistics 1976* XXI. ii. 215 He also includes the suggestion, discussing Trager's similar analysis of short *a* in New Jersey English in 1940.., that such factors may be handled as a type of readjustment rule in the historical development of the phonology of a language.

readmire, *v.* (Later example.)

1930 O. W. Holmes *Let.* 12 May (1953) II. 1246, I finished it [*sc.* a book] a few days ago. I readmired the Rousseau and Machiavelli and believed without adequate knowledge what you say about foundations.

read-mostly (rīdˌmōu·stli), *a.* *Computers.* [f. Read *v.* + Mostly *adv.*] Applied to a memory whose contents can be changed, though not by program instructions, but which is designed on the basis that such changes will be very infrequent compared with the number of occasions when the contents are read.

1971 *New Scientist* 1 Apr. 29/3 Initially, read-mostly memories will be used for semi-permanently stored computer instructions, such as in process control computers. **1977** *Sci. Amer.* Sept. 139/1 Another variation on the read-only memory is the read-mostly memory... Read-mostly memories have two forms. The commonest is the optically erasable read-only memory. *Ibid.*, An alternative form of read-mostly memory is the electrically alterable read-only memory.., which can be altered without the necessity of erasing the entire array.

read-only (rīdˌōu·nli), *a.* *Computers.* [f. Read *v.* + Only *adv.*] Applied to a memory whose contents cannot be changed by program instructions but which can usually be read at high speed; also *ellipt.* Abbrev. ROM s.v. *R II. 2 a.

1961 H. R. Foglia et al. in *IBM Jrnl. Res. & Development* V. 67/1 Another form of memory can be used that may be read at these high speeds, with capability of being changed in a few minutes. Memories of this type, in which the fast-read cycle is of prime importance, may be called read only memories. **1969** P. B. Jordain *Condensed Computer Encycl.* 416 Read-only storage is used for rapid access to information of a permanent nature. *Ibid.*, Read-only stores are not to be confused with nondestructive read-out memories, memories that may be altered but can be repeatedly read without loss of data. **1970** O. Dopping *Computers & Data Processing* x. 135 Read-only memories are sometimes used in the internal organization of a computer, but in some machines they are also used for the permanent storage of standard programs. **1977** *Engineering Materials & Design* Aug. 9/3 The function program for the device is held in a 16 kilobit read only memory. **1979** R. Mutch *Gemstone* viii. 96 Probably only need one read-only.

read-out (rī·dˌaut). Also **readout.** [f. vbl. phr. *to read out* (*read *v.* 6 f).] **1. a.** *Computers.* The extraction or transfer of data from a storage medium or device. Also *transf.*

1946 [see *read *v.* 6 f]. **1952** [see *matrix 6 d]. **1961** *IBM Jrnl. Res. & Development* V. 67/1 During readout the voltage pulse will be applied to a selected conductor corresponding to the word to be read out. **1970** O. Dopping *Computers & Data Processing* x. 151 Read-out is effected when a desired word passes through the pulse-shaping circuits. **1971** J. Z. Young *Introd. Study Man* xxii. 302 This reprogramming of the read-out of the DNA may serve to bring into play a new complex of enzyme systems.

b. The display of data by an automatic device in an understandable form. Also *transf.*

1961 *Aeroplane & Astronautics* CI. 573/2 The range indicator displays have a six-figure readout correct to the nearest 25 m. **1965** *Wireless World* July 35 (Advt.), For rapid transistor measurements, it can be set up for direct meter readout. **1971** *Engineering* Apr. 44/2 (*caption*) The new Sangamo extensometer which offers direct readout plus great sensitivity. **1971** *Nature* 13 Aug. 443/3 Displays have been selected during evolution to provide an accurate 'read out' of an animal's internal state to another animal.

c. (See quot. 1966.)

1966 *Britannica Bk. of Year 1965* 807/2 *Readout*, the radio transmission of data or pictures from a space vehicle either immediately upon acquisition or later by means of playback of a tape recording. **1970** N. Armstrong et al. *First on Moon* iii. 66 There was still work to do, starting with spacecraft-to-ground readouts.

2. A device for extracting or displaying data.

1954 *IRE Trans. Electronic Computers* Dec. 12 (*heading*) A radio-frequency nondestructive readout for magnetic core memories. *Ibid.* 15/1 It was possible to sense any core in this array plane using the rf readout. **1967** *Electronics* 6 Mar. 114/1 (Advt.), Our all-new nixie tube—the industry's lowest-cost electronic readout, and one sure to usher in a whole new generation of low-cost digital instrumentation. **1969** A. C. Marin *Rise with Wind* i. 4 Any efforts..to create an identity for the Director always fell flat, killed by the ever-present awareness of the computerlike brain... You could almost sense the logic circuits working, the tapes running on the reels, the punch cards appearing on the read-out. **1972** *Physics Bull.* July 418/3 An easy to read 2½ digit led readout reduces error when interpreting the measurements, particularly in low light conditions. **1976** M. Machlin *Pipeline* liii. 538 She was pleased to see that Schultheiss was alone in the control shack, which was a large building filled with a complicated set of flashing lights, meters, and digital readouts.

3. A record of its output produced by a computer or scientific instrument.

1967 *Economist* 11 Feb. 542/1 The computer read-out is fed into the draughting machine which should then draw the correct shape of the ship for the designer to check. **1970** H. Harrison *Captive Universe* 142 Just look at these figures... These are from a machine, a readout. **1971** *Daily Colonist* (Victoria, B.C.) 11 Dec. 17/5 The echogram—the read-out of an electronic device that is useful in diagnosing such abnormalities as tumours. **1977** *Daily Tel.* 25 Jan. 15/3, I left behind at the institute about 100-yards of paper read-outs, my metabolic processes recorded in squiggly lines.

4. *attrib.*

1965 *Wireless World* July 352/3 The average readout time is two seconds but for maximum readout it is five seconds. **1966** *Times Rev. Industry* Oct. 52/1 The units in the range—sample injection systems, oven and temperature controllers, columns, detectors and read-out units—are of modular design. **1968** H. Harris *Nucleus & Cytoplasm* iv. 68 Our text-books are full of diagrams showing ribosomes rolling along a messenger tape and thus fulfilling their role as a 'read-out' mechanism. **1976** *Offshore Platforms & Pipelining* 57/1 Readout gauges on the control panel will display tension in each line. **1976** B. Bova *Multiple Man* (1977) i. 16 The computer was humming to itself, lights flickering on its read-out console.

rea·d-through. Also **readthrough, read through.** [f. Read *v.*] **1.** An act of reading through; spec. *Theatr.*, an initial rehearsal at which actors read their parts from scripts.

1961 A. Wilson *Old Men at Zoo* ii. 95 She has to go to a read-through whatever that may be. **1963** E. Humphreys *Gift* ii. i. 209 He was late for the read through... Started talking loudly to the actress next to him and greeting everybody when we had already begun to read. **1966** 'O. Norton' *School of Liars* vii. 113, I..came back for the first read-through, and the acting notes. **1971** *Guardian* 3 July 9/3 'This script is a mess..' said Adrienne Corri the other day at a read-through for my TV series. **1976** J. Grenfell *Joyce Grenfell requests Pleasure* xvi. 230 Our spirits went up and down..after the usual enthusiastic read-through when the material seemed so original and imaginative.

2. *Biochem.* The continued transcription of genetic material by RNA polymerase that has overrun a termination sequence.

[**1970** Goff & Minkley in L. Silvestri *RNA-Polymerase & Transcription* 134 One interesting interpretation of these results is that the largest RNA class is produced when rho fails to function at the first termination signal used *in vivo* and the polymerase reads through to a second 'stop signal'.] **1970** A. A. Travers in *Nature* 14 Mar. 1011/2 (*caption*) Fig. 3. Readthrough by *E. coli* σ initiated RNA polymerase into sequences transcribed by σ^{T4} initiated polymerase. **1971** *Ibid.* 15 Dec. 207/2 These sequence data strongly suggest that the II*b* protein is a read-through product resulting from polypeptide chain elongation. **1978** *Ibid.* 30 Mar. 417/2 One of these..is the only oligonucleotide consistent with transcriptional 'read-through' of the termination site.

readva·nce, *sb.* Chiefly *Geol.* [f. the vb.] A renewed advance.

1879 *Geol. Mag.* Decade II. VI. 250 The recurring glacial conditions were too insignificant to cause a re-advance of the ice-sheet. **1927** Peake & Fleure *Apes & Men* 29 With the re-advance of the temperate forest in Europe, as the climate improved, most of them [*sc.* the mammals] finally disappeared. **1975** J. G. Evans *Environment Early Man. Brit. Isles* ii. 45 In the north of the British Isles, three readvances during the general retreat of the ice are marked by 'moraines'.

readvertise, *v.* Add: Now *spec.* to give further notice of (a job vacancy). Hence **rea·dvertised** *ppl. a.*; **rea·dvertising** *vbl. sb.*; **readve·rtisement.**

1934 Webster, Readvertisement. **1963** *Times* 19 Apr. 7/1 The decision to readvertise the post of Chief Constable of Glamorgan was 'reluctantly' agreed to by the standing joint committee of the county council today. **1964** A. Battersby *Network Analysis* x. 153 The table could obviously be extended to include reprinting, re-advertising, and later royalty payments. **1971** *Engineering* Apr. 124/2 Previous candidates for the second post (now re-advertised) will be reconsidered if they so indicate. **1977** *Times Educ. Suppl.* 21 Oct. 46/1 (Advt.), Headteachers; (1) Balderston Comprehensive Community School (readvertisement). **1978** *Nature* 9 Nov. 109/1 It would like to readvertise the head of technology post inviting both engineers and astronomers to apply.

ready, *a.*, *adv.*, and *sb.* Add: **A.** *adj.* **I. 1. e.** *U.S. slang.* Excellent, first-rate; mature, fully competent. Chiefly of music or musicians.

c **1938** N. E. Williams *His Hi De Highness of Ho De Ho* 35/2 When an individual or a piece of music is high class or greatly admired, we indicate it by saying, 'He's ready!' or 'That's ready!' **1944** C. Calloway *Hepsters Dict.*, *Ready*,.. 100 per cent in every way. Ex., 'That fried chicken was ready.' **1945** *Tomorrow* June 27/3 This time he was *ready*, so to speak, for it was on this second sojourn..that he began to impress his musical contemporaries. **1968** in R. Russell *Jazz Style in Kansas City* (1971) 183 When he came back, several months later, he was a new musician. *He was ready.*

f. *ready room*, a room in an aircraft-carrier where pilots are briefed and await orders to fly. *U.S. Mil.*

1945 in Webster Add. **1953** P. C. Berg *Dict. New Words* 134/2 *Ready room*,..the room of an aircraft-carrier where pilots ready for flight assemble to receive their briefing. **1971** W. H. Cracknell in *Profile Warship* iii. 55/2 Below the flight deck..was the gallery deck. Here were a rudimentary combat intelligence centre, squadron ready rooms, and other air department offices. **1977** *Time* 2 May 1/1 Stamped indelibly inside my head is what used to be on Navy ready-room walls—'Flying itself is not inherently dangerous, but like the sea, it is unmercifully unforgiving of human error.'

6. d. *U.S. Blacks.* (See quots.)

1967 J. Horton in *Trans-Action* Apr. 5/2 One either knows 'what's happening' on the street, or he is a 'lame', 'out of it', 'not ready' (lacks his diploma in street knowledge), a 'square'. **1970** C. Major *Dict. Afro-Amer. Slang* 96 *Ready*, hip; receptive. **1973** T. Kochman *Rappin' & Stylin' Out* 163 Another term such as 'ready' is descriptive of the person who 'has his diploma in street knowledge', which means knowing what's happening, taking advantage of opportunities, avoiding pitfalls, and being prepared to move where the action is.

IV. 16. a. (Further examples.)

1767 J. Woodforde *Diary* 24 July (1924) I. 64 My father sent me down a couple of fowls ready roasted. **1775** P. Freneau *Poems* (1902) I. 169 How could the wretches help but marching on, When at their backs your swords were ready drawn? **1796** J. Woodforde *Diary* 15 Oct. (1929) IV. 314 They have let their House ready furnished to a Revd. Mr. Beevor. **1868** *E. Acton's Mod. Cookery* (rev. ed.) xxx. 590 Never purchase it [*sc.* coffee] ready ground unless compelled to do so. **1930** H. Nicolson *Let.* 2 Jan. (1966) 40, I suppose that I shall get into the way of finding these paragraphs leaping ready-armed to the mind. **1952** J. B. Oldham *Eng. Blind-Stamped Bindings* 3 Sale of books ready-bound. **1960** *Farmer & Stockbreeder* 23 Feb. 123/3 Sold, ready-cooked in foil containers, the pies are in two sizes. **1976** *Glasgow Herald* 26 Nov. 16/3 Food can be bought ready prepared if not for the table at least for the oven or the saucepan.

b. *ready-carved, -cooked, -folded, -ground, -prepared* (further examples), *-roasted, -shelled, -sliced, -traced, -trained, -written* (later example). (See also *ready-mixed *a.*)

1803 M. Wilmot *Let.* 31 May in Londonderry & Hyde *Russian Jrnls.* (1934) i. 13 Then ready carved bouillé, ready carved fricassées etc. **1974** L. Deighton *Spy Story* xi. 112 She put some ready-cooked pizzas into the oven. **1964** *McCall's Sewing* xiii. 234/2 *Ready-folded braid*, these braids are of a woven bias construction. **1960** *Farmer & Stockbreeder* 15 Mar. (Suppl.) 11/2 Put the almonds through a nut mill (neither minced nor ready-ground almonds will do.) **1875** T. Seaton *Fret Cutting* vii. 71 The high price he has had to pay..for ready-prepared wood. **1959** *Times* 9 Mar. (Suppl.) p. vii/7 Ready-prepared vegetables and other fresh produce are now being offered in the supermarkets. **1754** Richardson *Grandison* IV. xviii. 144 He makes her.. become herself the cat's paw to help him to the ready-roasted chestnuts. **1909** *Daily Chron.* 14 Dec. 6/3 Pound boxes of ready-shelled walnuts at 1s. 3d. **1958** *Times Lit. Suppl.* 23 May 281/2 Bud Floyd and his wife Debbie tortured in their antiseptic, ready-shelled, air-conditioned inferno. **1960** *Times* 11 Feb. 3/5 Every day on television one can see the new styles ingeniously used to advertise instant coffee and ready-sliced bread. **1977** J. Wainwright *Day of*

Peppercorn Kill 17 Ready-sliced bread—because if she ever handled a bread-knife she'd cut her damn-fool fingers off. **1967** E. SHORT *Embroidery & Fabric Collage* iv. 94 As the firm also sold ready traced materials and supplied the threads for working them, Morris's influence was widespread. **1946** *Nature* 5 Oct. 491/1 Sir Reginald pointed out first that in research on the problems of an old traditional industry there are usually no ready-trained scientific workers. **1977** *Belfast Tel.* 22 Feb. 4/1 (Advt.), With the full library of ready-written, ready-to-use application packages available in the U.K., the System Ten 220 Series can be quickly harnessed to your work.

d. Const. with infin. or with *for* and following noun, and used as attrib. phrases expressing preparedness for the action indicated, as *ready-to-eat, -use*, etc. (See also *READY-TO-WEAR *a.* (and *sb.*).)

1887 G. M. HOPKINS *Let.* 12 May (1956) 379 Publishers 'tapped a stratum'..of almost untouched reading or ready-to-read public. **1897** *Sears, Roebuck Catal.* 294/3 (*heading*) Ready-to-use table cloths. **1907** *N.Y. Times* 14 Sept. 4 Through this store's efforts a new attitude toward ready-for-service clothing has been adopted by hundreds of men. **1909** H. N. CASSON *C. H. McCormick* 237 Certain ready-to-eat foods are now being made from wheat. *c* **1938** *Fortnum & Mason Price List* 72/1 'Ready to serve' dishes. **1959** *Times* 9 Mar. (Suppl.) p. vi/3 Preparing cartons of frozen ready-to-cook chickens. **1972** *Listener* 7 Sept. 292/3 A range of ready-to-serve fish dishes with shrimp and lobster sauces. **1976** N. ROBERTS *Face of France* v. 66 A civilisation of leisure will be raring for ready-to-eat pork products. *a* **1977** *Harrison Mayer Ltd. Catal.* 98/2, 1 of 0·28 litre pack of the following liquid, ready-to-use glazes.

e. With sbs. used attrib. in sense 7, as *ready-reference, -use*.

1928 G. CAMPBELL *My Mystery Ships* xiv. 250 A lucky shot from her might 'touch off' any of the ready-use ammunition which was at the guns. **1955** 'N. SHUTE' *Requiem for Wren* iii. 69, I give her a coconut out of the ready-use locker. **1963** *Amer. N. & Q.* Jan. 77/1 The book..can be used as a ready reference tool to answer questions about nearly all basic biological research in modern times. **1971** *Engineering* Apr. 122/2 Here's the tough, expanding, ready-reference file.

17. a. *ready-hearted*; also *ready-smiling*.

1937 A. L. ROWSE *Sir Richard Grenville* ii. 31 So ready-hearted, so busy and generous about life's affairs. **1940** BLUNDEN *Poems 1930–40* 252 Bright-tressed, ready-smiling, April-eyed.

C. *sb.* **1.** Also in *pl.*, bank notes.

1937 PARTRIDGE *Dict. Slang* 690/2 *Readies*, money in bank..notes. **1968** [see *GREEN *sb.* 7 d]. **1974** D. FRANCIS *Knock Down* xiv. 157 He sort of winks at me and gives me a thousand quid in readies. **1977** *Private Eye* 4 Mar. 9/1 Send £50 to the address below, preferably in readies.

2. a. Now usu. in phr. *at (the) ready*. Also *transf.* (Further examples.)

1931 A. CURTAYNE *St. Anthony of Padua* viii. 78 Galloping full tilt with vizor down and lance couched at the ready. **1955** *Times* 22 July 10/5 Others were more cautious, with fur capes or dark coats over their frocks and umbrellas at the ready. **1978** J. CARROLL *Mortal Friends* I. iii. 30 The troops in the lorries were standing, rifles at ready.

b. *U.S. colloq.* The condition of being prepared to start (something). Freq. in phr. *to get a good ready* and varr., to assume a favourable stance or position for this. Also *transf.* Now *rare*.

[**1855** 'Q. K. PHILANDER DOESTICKS' *Doesticks; what he Says* xviii. 153 The music got 'good ready' for a fair start, and at the word 'go' they went.] **1872** 'MARK TWAIN' in *Buyers' Man. & Business Guide* 76, I could have ketched them cats if I had had on a good ready. **1878** B. F. TAYLOR *Between Gates* 71 A time hardly long enough for a century plant to get a good ready for blossoming. **1897** A. H. LEWIS *Wolfville* i. 2 So we begins to draw in our belts an' get a big ready.

3. *Rope-making.* A strand in a rope or cable.

1857 R. CHAPMAN *Treat. Ropemaking* 84 The only method to be obtained is to give one turn or twist to the strand or readie, while the machine draws it a certain length. **1883** *Man. Seamanship for Boys' Training Ships* (Admiralty) (1886) 125 You now commence to form the long-splice, by unlaying one strand, and filling up the space it leaves with the opposite strand next to it..these strands being composed of three small strands, which are called readies. **1957** *Encycl. Brit.* XIX. 546/1 As the strand is twisted it is wound on a large reel and appears as a smooth, round strand composed of a number of individual yarns. This is known as the 'ready'.

4. *ready-up*, a conspiracy or swindle; a case of fraudulent manipulation; a fake. Cf. READY *v.* 4 b. *Austral. slang.*

1924 *Truth* (Sydney) 27 Apr. 6 *Ready up*, a fake. **1926** J. DOONE *Timely Tips for New Australians* 7 *Ready-up*, a conspiracy. **1945** BAKER *Austral. Lang.* xv. 267 *Ready-up*, a case in which illegal methods are used to influence the outcome of a decision or an action. **1961** H. R. F. KEATING *Rush on Ultimate* v. 85, I don't accept all the pretences and ready-ups you people put out.

ready, *v.* Add: **1. b.** *intr.* or *absol.* To make oneself ready or prepare in any way. *U.S.*

1967 *Wall St. Jrnl.* 12 Dec. 1 Machinists Union President Roy Siemiller, readying for national bargaining, and Steelworkers chief I. W. Abel feel they must match the big rubber and auto settlements. **1972** *Time* 17 Apr. 22 (*caption*) In a cloud of catapult steam, a U.S. jet readies to attack Viet Nam.

3. a. For 'Now only *dial.*' in Dict. read 'Now chiefly *N. Amer.*' and add further examples. Also const. *up*.

Perh. influenced in early use by REDD *v.*[2] 6, to put in order, make neat.

a **1849** J. KEEGAN *Legends & Poems* (1907) 111 Hould your gob..and go ready the room for the dacint boys to sit down. **1864** *Harper's Mag.* Apr. 616/1 The pot ought to be a-bilin' for dinner, and the Kitchen to be readied up. **1900** H. LAWSON *On Track* 73 Anyway, she'll have one readied up somehow. **1926** *Amer. Mercury* Dec. 464/2 The report that a certain man '*authored* the show, which will be *readied* next Fall, when it will be *hoked up* (from *hokum*)'. **1934** *Bulletin* (Sydney) 25 July 38/1 This has invited the All-Blacks to call in on their way back from their tour of Britain next year and get what is being readied up for them. **1937** V. MCNABB *God's Way of Mercy* xxi. 185 You have come apart from the world to ready your soul for the doings of that great week. **1958** *Observer* 2 Mar. 6/6 It can be readied in 15—in less if we have some warning—not in two hours. **1959** R. E. WATTERS *Check List Canad. Lit.* p. xiii, To the Editor, Miss Francess G. Halpenny, who readied the manuscript for the printers,.. I am heavily indebted. **1968** 'E. LATHEN' *Stitch in Time* xvi. 141 The tax people were readying an attack on Martin. **1969** *Sun* 22 July 3/8 American scientists are readying the first space station for lift-off into earth orbit in 1971. **1971** J. Z. YOUNG *Introd. Study Man* ii. 28 These ions are pumped back, readying the system for further signalling. **1978** J. A. MICHENER *Chesapeake* 303 She asked her slaves to ready the small shallop. **1979** *Arizona Daily Star* 5 Aug. A 10/2 An army of scientists and engineers readied a 2-mile floating defense line yesterday.

c. Of a person. Also const. *up*. Now chiefly *N. Amer.*

1846 *Swell's Night Guide* 78 He's to be readied at any downey move, and knows how to work it. **1895** J. BARLOW *Strangers at Lisconnel* 303 Nothin' else 'ud suit them except gettin' all readied up for us to be slinkin' out in the evenin' late. **1900** H. LAWSON *Over Sliprails* 162 The girl's relations..had a parson readied up, and they were married the same day. **1924** J. GALSWORTHY *White Monkey* II. ix. 198 I'll put you wise about our authors, and ready you up to go before Peter. **1940** *Sun* (Baltimore) 27 Feb. 13/2 Johnny Paycheck already has been matched with him. Lee Savold is being readied for a shot at him. **1968** *Globe & Mail* (Toronto) 17 Feb. 4 (Advt.), An exercycle..to ready you for a party, or extra work.

4. a. (Further example.)

1927 E. WALLACE *Mixer* iv. 58 He sat..in his office.. deploring inwardly the tendency of owners to 'ready' their horses for Epsom.

b. (Further example.)

1933 *Bulletin* (Sydney) 15 Nov. 33/1 All readied-up, I thought, though not bad fun.

ready-made, *ppl. phr.*, *a.*, and *sb.* Add: **3. b.** (Earlier example.)

1777 P. THICKNESSE *Year's Journey* II. lii. 153 The principal manufacture of the city [*sc.* Paris]; i.e. *ready-made love*.

5. Also *transf.* and *fig.* (Earlier and later examples.)

1831 M. EDGEWORTH *Let.* 29 Mar. (1971) 501 Then she is so fond of..her own family. She seems as if she was a ready-made for Fanny. **1905** *Daily Chron.* 22 Nov. 10/2 Wholesale manufacturers and confectioners rejoice greatly as they see their trade in Christmas 'ready mades' annually swelling. **1933** C. ST. J. SPRIGG *Fatality in Fleet St.* vii. 86 He looked like a film Cossack jammed into an East End ready-made. **1967** *Economist* 10 June 1142/1 The typical Italian clothing shop cannot afford to carry a big enough range to demonstrate the advantages of readymades.

b. The term introduced by Marcel Duchamp (1887–1967), French artist, to denote representatives of a dadaistic art-form created by him, in which simple manufactured objects are exhibited as works of art; the art-form itself.

[**1915** M. DUCHAMP in A. Schwarz *Marcel Duchamp* (1969) 54 Précises les 'Readymades'. En projetant pour un moment..à venir..'*d'inscrire* un readymade'.] **1935** D. GASCOYNE *Short Survey of Surrealism* ii. 28 Such was Marcel Duchamp's disgust for 'art' that he invented a new form of expression, which he called *Ready-Made*. A Ready-Made was any manufactured object that the artist liked to choose. **1958** *Times* 20 May 3/7 The 'ready-mades' in which Marcel Duchamp parodied the exhibition work of art, signing his name on such manufactured objects as a wash-basin or a snow shovel. **1968** *N.Y. City* (Michelin Guide) 17 Marcel Duchamp..created his provocative 'ready-mades', which consist of simple..objects, which the artist exhibits as works of art (having intervened only to give them names); thus, he displayed..A Fountain, which was..a can bought in a department store. **1972** C. W. E. BIGSBY *Dada & Surrealism* ii. 11 The ready-mades were simply objects which he [*sc.* Marcel Duchamp] himself had selected as being commonplace.

rea·dy-mix, *a.* (and *sb.*) orig. *U.S.* [f. READY *a.* + MIX *sb.*[2]] = *READY-MIXED *a.* (and *sb.*) Also *fig.*

1950 M. MCCARTHY in *Reporter* 18 July 39/1 The ready-mix cake turns out 'terrific'. **1958** [see *INSTANT *a.* 4 c]. **1963** *Punch* 28 Aug. 322/3 A studio audience complete with ready-mix mirth and instant appreciation. **1966** *Guardian* 28 Apr. 4/2 Factory food, in the form of ready-mixes, was certainly better than that produced by 'the multitude of indifferent cooks..now wandering around the country'. **1976** E. WARD *Hanged Man* iii. 13 A ready-mix concrete truck marked Metro Concrete jolted along the access road. **1980** *Times Lit. Suppl.* 30 May 608/4 Germaine is the principal new ingredient in the Barthian narrative ready-mix.

ready-mixed, *a.* (and *sb.*) orig. *U.S.* [f. READY *a.* 16.] Of paints, concrete, and other artificial compound substances, having some or all of the constituents already mixed together. Also *ellipt.* as *sb.*

1895 *Montgomery Ward Catal.* Spring & Summer 254/2 Japanese Ready Mixed Paints and Enamels. **1908** *Sears, Roebuck Catal.* 71/1, 85 cents per gallon buys our guaranteed Seroco Ready Mixed House Paint. **1930** *Engineering* 16 May 631/3 The practice of selling ready-mixed concrete was introduced in the United States about ten years ago. **1960** *Farmer & Stockbreeder* 22 Mar. (Suppl.) 10/2 You can make up your own flooring compounds, but probably the simplest way is to buy a tin of ready-mixed material. **1973** M. TRUMAN *H. S. Truman* iii. 72 Mr. Pendergast owned the Ready-Mixed Concrete Company which in the past had been used almost exclusively by contractors paving Jackson County roads. In Judge Truman's 225-mile road-building program, only three-fourths of a mile were paved with Ready-Mixed. **1977** J. I. M. STEWART *Madonna of Astrolabe* iii. 51 To what extent should we be justified in pouring unexpected wealth, as if it were so much ready-mixed concrete, into shoring up a mere sense-of-beauty-occasioning object?

ready-to-wear, *a.* (and *sb.*) orig. *U.S.* Also **ready-for-wear.** [f. *READY *a.* 16 d.] **1.** Of clothing: = READY-MADE *a.* 2, 4.

1895 *Montgomery Ward Catal.* 276/1 (*heading*) Ready to wear clothing. **1905** *Daily Chron.* 27 Feb. 8/3 A more exclusive type of ready-to-wear hat is the..sailor turban, toque, or narrow boat shape. **1930** *Times* 17 Mar. 9/4 The ready-to-wear sections bring the new styles within the reach of modern purses... A new spring catalogue giving illustrations of their ready-for-wear clothes has been prepared. **1953** *Manch. Guardian Weekly* 30 July 7/1 They ..announced the premature birth of Neiman-Marcus as 'the South's finest and only exclusive women's ready-to-wear shop'. **1977** M. SOKOLINSKY tr. *R. Merle's Virility Factor* xvi. 315 She..had skillfully managed a ready-to-wear business. **1981** *Country Life* 12 Feb. 414/2 The ready-to-wear collections for spring and summer.

2. as *sb.* (An article of) ready-made clothing. Chiefly *pl.*

1923 *Blackw. Mag.* Apr. 503/2 There was a young person, looking quite the little man in a suit of ready-to-wears. **1973** 'J. ASHFORD' *Double Run* iii. 21 His clothes had the hangdog look of cheap ready-to-wears which had had a hard life. **1974** *Country Life* 3/10 Jan. 54/3 He has private clients, as well as selling ready-to-wear in boutiques. **1977** *South China Morning Post* (Hong Kong) 13 Apr. 14/8 A vice-president of Bloomingdales..commented that the ready-to-wear is wonderful for the film industry.

reafference (ri,æ·fĕrĕns). [ad. G. *reafferenz* (von Holst and Mittelstaedt 1950, in *Naturwissenschaften* XXXVII. 464). Cf. AFFERENT *a.*] Sensory stimulation in which the stimulus changes as a result of the individual's movements in response to it.

1965 *Sci. Amer.* Nov. 85/1 A key to its operation is the availability of 'reafference'. This word was coined by the German physiologists Erich von Holst and Horst Mittelstädt to describe neural excitation following sensory stimulation that is systematically dependent on movements initiated by the sensing animal. **1971** J. S. BRUNER *Beyond Information Given* (1974) xiv. 249 The crucial issue in the regulation of intentional action is the opportunity to compare what was intended with what in fact resulted, using the difference between the two as a basis of correction. It is immediately apparent that this is the concept of reafference as a source of regulation in behavior. **1973** R. MARTIN tr. *von Holst's Behav. Physiol. of Anim. & Men* I. iii. 141 Rather than asking about the relationship between a given afference and the evoked efference (i.e. about the reflex), we set out *in the opposite direction*..asking: What happens in the CNS with the afference (referred to as the 'reafference') which is evoked through the effectors and receptors by the efference? **1973** C. D. KERNIG *Marxism, Communism & Western Soc.* VII. 103/2 As early as 1935 Anokhin..had discovered a phenomenon corresponding to the reafference principle. **1979** S. COREN et al. *Sensation & Perception* xvi. 391/1 It has been suggested that reafference is necessary for the development of accurate visually guided spatial behavior.

re-a·fferent, *a.* [f. RE- + AFFERENT *a.*] Of or pertaining to reafference.

1965 *Sci. Amer.* Nov. 87/1 This kind of movement, with its contingent reafferent stimulation, is the critical factor in compensating for displaced visual images. **1965** N. CHOMSKY *Aspects of Theory of Syntax* i. 34 Under certain circumstances reafferent stimulation (that is, stimulation resulting from voluntary activity) is a prerequisite to the development of a concept of visual space. **1971** R. MARTIN tr. *Lorenz's Stud. in Anim. & Hum. Behav.* II. 300 Such sensory signals directly produced by inherent movements of the organism are referred to as *reafferent signals*, and the signal relating to the outgoing motor command which is transmitted to the perceptual mechanism is the efferent signal copy. **1973** —— tr. *von Holst's Behav. Physiol. of Anim. & Men* I. iii. 149 There is absence of the reafferent 'stop'..which normally arrests the correcting movement. **1975** L. GANZ in A. H. Riesen *Developmental Neuropsychol. of Sensory Deprivation* vi. 198 They believe that the reafferent perception of a moving part of the body is essential for the development of coordination.

Reaganism (rē[1]·găniz'm). [f. the name of Ronald W. *Reagan* (b. 1911), American Republican politician, Governor of California 1967–75, and President of the United States 1981– + -ISM.] The policies and principles advocated by Ronald Reagan; adherence to or support of these. Also **Rea·ganite**, a supporter of Reagan; also *attrib.* or as *adj.*

1966 *Punch* 7 Dec. 832/3 Reaganism is really rampant now. **1975** *Financial Times* 20 Nov. 5/8 Wits have suggested that 'Reaganism is extremism in defence of Fordism'. **1976** *Times* 21 Feb. 6/7 The Reaganites..have moved on... If organization was the key to success, Mr Ford would never stand a chance. **1977** *Time* 3 Jan. 22 (*caption*) Reaganite at G.O.P. convention. **1981** *Economist* 24 Jan. 13/2 The right way lies through greater scope for bodies like the International Monetary Fund..which lends its money tied to almost Reaganite advice. **1981** *Times* 31 Jan. 13/3 Mrs Thatcher approximates on occasions to the tones of Reaganism.

reagent. Add: **1.** Now applied to any substance employed in chemical reactions (cf. sense 2). (Further examples.)

1904 L. W. Riggs *Elem. Man. Chem. Laboratory* III. 82 Any positive ion..when separated from other cations..will exhibit with reagents certain phenomena characteristic of that ion. **1929** C. R. Hayward *Dict. Metall. Pract.* xxii. 487 Recarburizing..may be accomplished by adding the reagents to the converter. **1948** Currier & Rose *Gen. & Appl. Chem.* xix. 151 Nitric acid..is a very important substance: in the laboratory as an oxidizing reagent, and in industry for the manufacture of explosives. **1964** N. G. Clark *Mod. Org. Chem.* v. 65 Traditional reagents and reaction conditions rarely affect the paraffins, but they exhibit useful reactivity at high temperatures. **1973** *Materials & Technol.* VI. viii. 545 To make a bonded joint, the PTFE is first etched with a reagent.

3. *Comb.* **reagent grade**, a grade of commercial chemicals characterized by a high standard of purity; freq. *attrib.*; **reagent paper**, paper treated with a reagent for use in chemical tests.

1935 *Jrnl. Amer. Chem. Soc.* LVII. 408/2 Baker and Adamson $CuSO_4.5H_2O$, Reagent Grade, was recrystallized twice from distilled water. **1945** *Ibid.* LXVII. 1096/1 Reagent grade ammonium sulfate was heated at 75° for several days. **1966** A. S. Prasad *Zinc Metabolism* xv. 275 Six of..[the patients] received reagent grade zinc sulfate 90 mg daily, and three received reagent grade ferrous sulfate 1 gm orally daily. **1973** *Jrnl. Amer. Chem. Soc.* XCV. 1913/1 All reagents and solvents used were reagent grade and, unless noted otherwise, were used without further purification. **1908** *Practitioner* Mar. 410 A pea-sized piece being rubbed up with 2 c.c. of water, and the reagent-paper dipped into this.

reaggregate, *v.* Add: **b.** *intr.* To come together again.

1962 H. Bloemendal et al. in A. Pirie *Lens Metabolism Rel. Cataract* 300 The subunits..reaggregate after removal of urea.

reagin (riˌēⁱ·dʒin). *Immunol.* [a. G. *reagin*, f. *reag-ieren* to react + *-in* -INE⁵.] **a.** The complement-fixing substance in the blood of persons with syphilis which is responsible for the positive response to the Wassermann reaction.

1911 R. W. Matson tr. *A. Wolff-Eisner's Clin. Immunity & Sero-Diagnosis* iii. 33 To avoid errors, it is..best to use the term 'reactive substances' (reagins) rather than 'antibodies', since the latter implies a neutralization in the sense of an antitoxin. **1915** J. E. R. McDonagh *Biol. & Treatm. Venereal Dis.* x. 71 Owing..to the fact that a positive Wassermann reaction may be obtained in conditions other than syphilitic ones, the reaction ceases to be a specific reaction. Therefore the third factor ought not to be called an antibody, since it is in no wise specific, hence it is best called reacting substance, or Reagin. **1937** H. Eagle *Lab. Diagnosis Syphilis* i. 24 There is reason to believe that Wasserman's first theory was correct, and that the active component of syphilitic serum, so-called reagin, may well be an antibody to *Spirochaeta pallida* despite its reactivity with normal tissue lipoids. **1942** *Jrnl. Lab. & Clin. Med.* XXVII. 729 It seems controversial as to whether reagin is an antibody to lipid haptens of the host..or an antibody to the spirochete. **1976** A. E. Wilkinson in Catterall & Nicol *Sexually Transmitted Dis.* 215 Although the function of reagin is still uncertain, its level seems to be roughly related to the amount of tissue reaction by the host, rising rapidly with increasing numbers of treponemes in early syphilis and later falling as the number of organisms declines with developing immunity.

b. The antibody which is involved in allergic reactions, causing the release of histamine and similar agents when it combines with antigen in tissue and capable of producing sensitivity to the antigen when introduced into the skin of a normal individual.

1925 [see *atopy]. **1963** *Advances in Immunol.* III. 181 Reagin still represents a nebulous concept to many immunologists, some doubting the legitimacy of its classification as an antibody. **1969** R. S. Weiser et al. *Fund. Immunol.* xv. 163 The antibodies responsible for P-K type sensitivities, the so-called 'reagins' or P-K antibodies, have long been a mystery. **1977** *Nature* 16 June 618/1 Allergic diseases such as hay fever, extrinsic asthma, drug hypersensitivities and some forms of urticaria are mediated by allergen-specific antibodies of the IgE class, known also as reagins.

Hence **reagi·nic** *a.*, of, pertaining to, or being (a) reagin.

1931 A. F. Coca *Asthma & Hay Fever in Theory & Pract.* I. xvii. 332 Bona fide reaginic reactions are indicative of past, present or potential sensitivities in the atopic individual. **1945** *Vet. Rec.* LVII. 339/2 (*heading*) Reaginic allergy in cattle. **1975** *Nature* 6 Feb. 475/1 In the rat, reaginic antibodies were reported and their possible significance in *S*[*chistosoma*] *mansoni* infection considered. **1977** A. M. Denman in Holborow & Reeves *Immunol. in Med.* x. 295 IgE constitutes the major class of reaginic antibody but it seems likely that some IgG..antibodies also contribute.

real, *a.*², *adv.*, and *sb.*³ Add: **A.** *adj.* **I. 1. c.** *real money*: (*b*) *colloq.* A large sum of money.

1918 R. W. Lardner *Treat 'em Rough* 120, I could go out and pitch baseball and make real money. **1939** A. Huxley *After Many Summer* I. iv. 46, I did some business this morning... Might make a lot of money. *Real* money. **1964** L. Deighton *Funeral in Berlin* iii. 21 'Whom do you feel like?' I liked that 'whom'—you've got to pay real money these days to get a secretary that could say that.

(*c*) *colloq.* The coinage or currency in which one habitually reckons, freq. as opp. to foreign currency.

1973 L. Meynell *Thirteen Trumpeters* iv. 50 So I'm paying one thousand seven hundred and ten lire for my Pimms?.. What's it mean in real money? **1977** *Vole* No. 2. 17/2 Just before the demise of real money and the introduction of decimal coinage, the officials of Gloucester Shoveha'penny League invested £10 in old-style halfpennies. **1977** *Zigzag* Mar. 7/1 They charged me three hundred francs. Well, that's..quite a lot in real money.

d. (Further examples.)

1875 *Encycl. Brit.* I. 544/2 Every quadratic equation has always two roots, real or imaginary. **1910** *Ibid.* I. 613/1 The development of the theory of equations leads to the amplification of real numbers, rational and irrational, positive and negative, by imaginary and complex numbers. **1952** S. C. Kleene *Introd. Metamath.* i. 6 That there are infinite sets considered in mathematics which cannot be enumerated was shown by Cantor's famous 'diagonal method'. The set of the real numbers is non-enumerable. **1965** Patterson & Rutherford *Elem. Abstract Algebra* iii. 85 The real number *a* is called the real part of the complex number (*a*, *b*) and the real number *b* is called the imaginary part. **1972** S. W. P. Steen *Math. Logic* iii. 178 Having defined the integers we can then define rational numbers as triplets of integers, then real numbers as Dedekind Sections of rational numbers and lastly complex numbers as ordered pairs of real numbers.

f. *real time*, the actual time during which a process or event occurs, esp. one analysed by a computer, in contrast to time subsequent to it when computer processing may be done, a recording replayed, or the like.

1953 *Math. Tables & Other Aids to Computation* VII. 73 With the advent of large-scale high-speed digital computers, there arises the question of their possible use in the solution of problems in 'real time', i.e., in conjunction with instruments receiving and responding to stimuli from the external environment. The criteria for satisfactory operation in such real-time service are different from those generally encountered. **1964** *Listener* 19 Nov. 784/1 A higher speed in computers means that their complexity can increase very rapidly, too, and that they can more easily engage in activities in what we call 'real time'. That is to say, they can calculate at the actual speed of the events taking place. **1968** *Times* 10 Dec. 6/8 The data gathered by the telescopes are stored on board the satellite by magnetic tapes and discs... The Smithsonian experiment can also be used in real time, transmitting information as it gathers it. **1970** *Nature* 20 June 1110/2 The data are telemetered to ground-based stations which record the information on magnetic tape and provide a digital print-out in real time. **1973** *Sci. Amer.* May 115/2 It is wrong to detail a suspense plot, even though we all recall from real time how *Apollo 13* limped back safely. **1973** *Nature* 12 Oct. 294/1 As we are working in scientific 'real time', we have to ask at what stage the work will be when filming is in progress. **1979** R. Hawkey *Side-Effect* xi. 83 The Real Time was three hundred milliseconds, but it was shot in slow motion.

attrib.

1953 [see above]. **1960** *N.Y. Times* 17 July 13/4 As an experiment, Air Force and Weather Bureau meteorologists attempted to use the pictures to make 'real time' forecasts of the weather—forecasts fresh enough to be useful. **1968** *Times* 1 Nov. 23/6 Computers have been slow to conquer the real-time control of industrial processes and traffic flows. **1970** O. Dopping *Computers & Data Processing* vi. 96 An example of a real-time process is a cheque account system in a bank where all transactions, e.g. withdrawals, are reported to the computer before they are finished. **1972** *Guardian* 9 Feb. 3/8 We do think we know how to develop a satellite with a near real-time (instantaneous) capability. **1975** *Offshore Engineer* Sept. 52/2 Sea & Storm is also..showing a wave data processing unit..which will give virtually realtime treatment of data from wave buoys. **1977** *Navy News* June 44 (Advt.), To undertake training of our customers' engineers/programmers/technicians on all aspects of software applicable to real-time radar systems.

2. a. Phr. *real life, real world* (passing into senses 3 and 4). Also *attrib.*

1771 T. Jefferson *Let.* 3 Aug. in Koch & Peden *Life & Selected Writings* (1944) viii. 358 Considering history as a moral exercise, her lessons would be too infrequent if confined to real life. **1801** M. Edgeworth *Belinda* I. iii. 70 Nothing is more unlike a novel than real life. **1836** Dickens *Pickw.* (1837) v. 44 A curious manuscript..curious as a leaf from the romance of real life. **1838** J. S. Mill in *Westm. Rev.* XXXI. 28 The writers and readers..in France have..a thirst for something which shall address itself to their real-life feelings. **1852** [in Dict.]. **1876** C. M. Yonge *Womankind* v. 34 Insolence to a governess is an old stock complaint. In real life, I never heard of it from anyone by birth and breeding a lady. **1909** *Daily Chron.* 16 Apr. 3/5 Jocelyn Johnstone..showed..humour in her sketches of..'real life' scenes. **1923** C. D. Broad *Sci. Thought* xiii. 536 Now, in real life, there are no examples of pure creation. **1937** 'G. Orwell' *Road to Wigan Pier* ix. 182 One could..give everything away, change one's name and start out with no money... But in real life nobody ever does that kind of thing. **1957** P. Suppes *Introd. Logic* xii. 286 Textbook problems (as opposed to real-life problems). **1963** *Amer. Speech* XXXVIII. 296 The instances in which its selection depends on real world context. **1966** *Listener* 19 May 727/1 The Vice Chancellor of Lancaster University strongly believes 'that the university must keep contact with the real world outside'. May I take this opportunity to ask..: (*a*) what is real about the real world? (*b*) why it is always outside? **1977** *National Observer* (U.S.) 15 Jan. 13/1 The roles each of us plays on the revolving stage of the real world have been well described. **1978** P. Marsh et al. *Rules of Disorder* ii. 33 In the perception of our non-academic pupils, school is..a waste of time..not..a part of their 'real' lives.

4. a. spec. *Econ.* Reckoned by purchasing power rather than monetary or nominal value.

1775 Johnson *Journey to Western Islands* 368 Lesley.. related so punctiliously, that a hundred hen eggs, new laid, were sold in the Islands for a peny... Posterity has since grown wiser; and having learned, that nominal and real value may differ, they now tell no such stories. **1776** Adam Smith *Wealth of Nations* I. I. v. 39 Labour, like commodities, may be said to have a real and a nominal price. Its real price may be said to consist in the quantity of the necessaries and conveniences of life which are given for it; its nominal price, in the quantity of money. **1882** R. Bithell *Counting-House Dict.* 208 The nominal value of a coin is that value which is assigned to it by law, and often differs very materially from its *real* or *metallic* value. **1885** J. L. Joynes tr. *Marx's Wage-Labour & Capital* 10 The real wage expresses the price of labour in relation to the price of other commodities... Real wages may remain the same, or they may even rise, and yet the relative wages may none the less have fallen. **1929** *Soc. Sci. Abstracts* 23 The close similarity of the general price level.. substantiates its use as a measure of 'real income'. **1936** K. A. H. Egerton *Dict. Econ. Terms* (ed. 2) 131 Real wages at such times change at a very different rate, and sometimes in the opposite direction, from nominal or money wages; being based on the purchases a wage at any given time will make. **1964** Gould & Kolb *Dict. Soc. Sci.* 454/1 If a series of national product estimates for several years is divided by a price index, each year's national product being divided by the price index for that year, the resulting series is known as *deflated* or *real* national product, or national product in *real terms*. **1976** *Glasgow Herald* 26 Nov. 1/6 Real earnings have fallen in the past few years and there is no way we can agree to any further reduction in the purchasing power of our members. **1981** *Sunday Times* 26 Apr. 13/4 Despite an urgent maintenance and restoration programme, it [*sc.* the National Trust] is spending less in real terms on looking after its property than it was two years ago.

b. *real ale*, a name sometimes applied to draught beer that has been brewed and stored in the traditional way, and which has undergone secondary fermentation of the yeast in the container from which it is dispensed; also called 'cask-conditioned' beer; *real coffee*, coffee made directly from ground coffee beans, as opposed to 'instant' coffee.

1964 L. Deighton *Funeral in Berlin* iv. 281 Could you find us a little cup of real coffee? **1972** *What's Brewing* Oct., Mr A— B—..is ripping out the keg taps and replacing them with real ale from wooden barrels. **1973** C. Hutt *Death of Eng. Pub* i. 25 The beer-drinker who feels strongly about the declining quality of his pint has two organisations he can turn to..—the long-established Society for the Preservation of Beers from the Wood, and the more recently formed, more militant CAMRA (Campaign for Real Ale). **1974** N. Freeling *Dressing of Diamond* 201 'Where's the patrol, Gilbert?' 'Be back any minute.' 'Then you might make us some real coffee.' **1974** *Good Beer Guide* (CAMRA) 2 The real ale we are talking about has to stand up to three tests; in the way it is brewed, the way it is stored and the way it is served. **1976** *Evening Standard* 29 Dec., The most popular of about a dozen real ales brought in from distant parts to a growing number of pubs in the capital. **1980** *Times* 23 Sept. 8/3 In the 1970s..the 'real ale' fashion took hold.

c. (*a*) (Further examples.)

1846 *Punch* 20 June 272/2 You, who will not subscribe to the real thing; come, pull out your purse to the *name*:.. although you know that you ask for the 'Ragged Schools',.. beg subscriptions for the 'Youths of Limited Circumstances'. **1884** *Art Amateur* Dec. 23/1 Those persons who indulge in.. having..Japanese rooms in their houses, but have only a ludicrous imitation, will be interested in seeing here the real thing. **1902** T. W. H. Crosland *Outlook Odes* 31 My tobacco merchant, who sells me two ounces of the real thing every week. **1939** *War Illustr.* 2 Dec. 365 The 'stand-by' atmosphere of the first few weeks of war may be lost at any moment in the urgency of the 'real thing'. **1977** *Time* 22 Aug. 40/2 But the copied Coke may not work. India's soft-drink fanciers have learned to distinguish between ersatz Coke, which is peddled everywhere on the Indian market, and the Real Thing.

(*b*) *spec.* True love as distinct from infatuation, flirtation, etc.

1857 C. M. Yonge *Dynevor Terrace* I. xi. 173, I could not part with you where we were not sure the 'real thing' was felt for you. **1906** J. Galsworthy *Man of Property* III. iii. 302 This was none of those affairs of a season that distract men and women about town... This was the real thing! **1919** Wodehouse *Damsel in Distress* v. 61 It had come at last. The Real Thing. George had never been in love before. Not really in love. **1931** J. Cannan *High Table* x. 152 He was afraid that she would think he was just flirting—that it wasn't the Real Thing. **1941** M. McCarthy in *Partisan Rev.* VIII. 327 All that conjugal tenderness had been a brightly packaged substitute for the Real Thing. **1955** E. Waugh *Officers & Gentlemen* II. ii. 189, I thought of you at the last. Ever since we met I've known I had found the real thing. **1960** *Woman's Own* 19 Mar. 17/2 Once these phases are over, you should be ready for the Real Thing..the man who will be exactly right for *you*. **1973** G. Scott *Water Horse* (1974) xvi. 109 A girl..whom she knew to be looking for the Real Thing in Spain.

d. *the real McCoy*: see *McCoy.

e. *real tennis* = Tennis *sb.* 1. Also *attrib.*

The usage distinguishes the original game from the modified form which became the more popular after 1874; see

Lawn-tennis and Tennis *sb.* 2. Derivation from Real *a.*^{1} is a folk etymology.

1880 [see *jeu de paume* s.v. *jeu c]. **1902** [see *royal tennis* s.v. *royal *a.* 15 a]. **1954** A. S. C. Ross in *Neuphilol. Mitteilungen* LV. 22 The games of real tennis and piquet.. are still perhaps marks of the upper class. **1966** *Oxford Mag.* Michaelmas, No. 8, p. 149 A splendid exhibition of real tennis was given at the Merton Street court on Sunday. **1972** *Daily Tel.* (Colour Suppl.) 14 Jan. 25/4 There are 17 Real Tennis courts in use in the country. **1975** *Country Life* 30 Jan. 258/1 Today tennis means to most people lawn tennis, while its..ancestor..has survived under the title 'real tennis'... Only one public school boasts a real tennis court... Canford in Dorset.

5. c. (Later examples.) Also *loosely*, aware of, or in touch with, real life.

1961 *Noble Savage* Fall 12 He [*sc.* Seymour Krim] alludes to something called 'direct writing', and he finds that criticism gets in the way of his 'truer, realer, imaginative bounce'. **1964** *Sunday Express* 1 Mar. 22/5 Most [actors]..are so insincere... Albie..is an exception... He's a real person. **1966** *New Statesman* 17 June 873/2 This was a realler America than I had known in the past, hitching on this or that bandwagon or presidential campaign. **1967** P. Welles *Babyhip* (1969) xxviii. 179 Sometimes I wish I were back in Paris. The people seemed realer. **1969** *Newsweek* 9 June 95 Why suffer all the bad hotels and rotten food and accountants and taxes if you waste the opportunity on stage to be real? **1973** *Scotsman* 7 Aug. 8/5, I notice..the editor-designate of the much discussed 'Scottish International' review telling us that Glasgow is a 'realler' city than Edinburgh. **1976** *New Yorker* 1 Mar. 35/1 'Ellen. Be real for once. I said we'd get together.' 'In your letter you said we'd have dinner.' **1977** *Time* 25 July 45/2 Billy is very sweet and very gentle and very real.

6. c. *real estate*: also *attrib.*

1840 *Spirit of Times* 25 Jan. 562/1 A negro, the holder of a ticket in the grand real estate lottery.., came pushing into a lottery office in great excitement. **1843** *Niles' Nat. Reg.* 4 Mar. 5 Real estate bank... A committee of the legislature of Arkansas have reported the facts connected with the management of this institution. **1849** *Knickerbocker* XXXIII. 174 His father had recently made some heavy real-estate purchases. **1854** H. D. Thoreau *Walden* 88 This experience entitled me to be regarded as a sort of real-estate broker by my friends. **1880** *Harper's Mag.* Sept. 562 This region was ..seized upon by real-estate speculators. **1892** Kipling *Lett. of Travel* (1920) 85 The packed real-estate offices; the real-estate agents themselves. **1903** *Westm. Gaz.* 11 Sept. 2/3 The law might almost be forgiven for making no provision for dealing with real-estate-owning paupers. **1965** H. T. Ansoff *Corporate Strategy* (1968) vi. 104 A company which primarily buys and sells..may be an investment trust, a pension fund, or a real estate syndicate. **1969** *Sydney Morning Herald* 24 May 30/1 (Advt.), The Real Estate Institute of New South Wales..will commence the next evening course of lectures in Real Estate and Valuation Practice. **1972** *Accountant* 17 Aug. 193/2 The cannibalization of assets, particularly of real estate subsidiaries. **1978** S. Brill *Teamsters* vi. 208 He sincerely believed that real-estate investments were the gold mines of the future.

III. 11. *real-seeming* adj.

1948 E. Bowen *Why do I Write?* 24 You and I, by writing a story, impose shape—on fictitious life, it's true, but on life that is real-seeming enough to be familiar and recognisable. **1951** S. Spender *World within World* 310 Reader-writer walk together in a real-seeming dream-alliance leading into gardens inhabited by Stephen Daedalus and Marcel.

B. *adv.* **1.** (with adjs.) For 'chiefly *Sc.* and *U.S.*' read 'orig. *Sc.* and *U.S.*' and add further examples.

Not common in standard use in southern England.

1939 *War Illustr.* 28 Oct. 219/1 If I had not been on fire I could easily have shot down two more. It was real bad luck, but my pals accounted for three besides the one I hit. **1943** K. Tennant *Ride on Stranger* viii. 77 He's real clever. **1959** J. Ludwig in *Tamarack Rev.* Summer 7 Some day she'd get real tough with her son Sidney. **1968** *Globe & Mail* (Toronto) 17 Feb. 50/3 (Advt.), Austin Healey Sprite black, radio, a real nice car. **1968** K. Weatherly *Roo Shooter* 111 It was real heavy going, and I must have dried the flamin' plugs and points twenty times. **1976** *Daily Mirror* 18 Mar. 24/4 I'm havin' a rest—I feel real listless.

2. (with advbs.) *colloq.* (chiefly *N. Amer.* and *Austral.*).

1893 H. A. Shands *Some Peculiarities of Speech in Mississippi* 52 Real down... Used by cultivated whites to mean *exceedingly* or *extremely*. A thing that is extremely nice is said to be *real down* nice. **1924** J. C. French *Writing* x. 290 Avoid: They live *good* in that camp (say live *well*), I *sure* will write *real* soon (say *surely* will, *really* soon). **1933** R. L. Pooley in *Amer. Speech* VIII. 61/2 One such [grammarian], commenting on the sentence, 'I will write *real* soon,' corrects *real* to read *really*. This is utter nonsense. No one ever says *I will write really soon*... It simply isn't English. **1942** Z. N. Hurston in A. Dundes *Mother Wit* (1973) 225/1 De man looked at me real hard for dat. **1947** K. Tennant *Lost Haven* xix. 317 Everyone said she was lucky... Everything fell out 'real nice' for her. **1959** *Weekly Times* (Melbourne) 30 Sept. (Advt.), How about picking up your phone and asking your B.F.E. dealer to arrange a free demonstration of a '35' on your property real soon? **1967** G. Jackson *Let.* 13 July in *Soledad Brother* (1971) 121, I felt real bad about that. **1975** D. Lodge *Changing Places* ii. 57 You and I must have lunch together real soon.

C. *sb.*^{3} **4.** *Math.* A real number.

1866 W. R. Hamilton *Elem. Quaternions* I. i. 10 Such scalars are..simply the reals (or real quantities) of Algebra. **1940** W. V. Quine *Math. Logic* 273 The fact that every bounded class of reals has a least bound is the basic formal difference between the reals and the ratios. **1967** Condon & Odishaw *Handbk. Physics* (ed. 2) I. ii. 22/1 Apart from the reals and the complex numbers they are the only associative hypercomplex systems with real coefficients and no divisors of zero. **1979** *Proc. London Math. Soc.* XXXVIII. 367 Let x, h, Q denote large reals with $x \geqslant h > Q$.

D. In colloq. phr. *for real* (orig. *U.S.*). **a.** as *adj. phr.* Genuine, (in) earnest, true, sincere.

1956 [see *pick *v.*^{1} 20 p]. **1972** M. J. Bosse *Incident at Naha* 55 Was that kid for real? I mean, he didn't look as if he could fight his way out of a paper bag. **1973** *Black Panther* 17 Mar. 8/1 This is no 'scare tactic', it is for real. **1973** W. Fairchild *Swiss Arrangement* vii. 78, I told him I was staying with Mom and that's for real. **1977** B. Randall *Fan* 34 Dear Mr. Breen. Are you for real?.. Give us a rest.

b. *adv.* Really, truly, actually; in reality.

1962 J. Glenn in *Into Orbit* 183 Everyone seemed to sense that we were going for real this time. **1964** M. McLuhan *Understanding Media* (1967) II. xxx. 320 It was Hitler who gave radio the Orson Welles treatment for real. **1970** E. Bullins *Theme is Blackness* (1973) 179 Yeah! For real! Shoot me! That's what she says. **1972** J. E. Franklin in W. King *Black Short Story Anthol.* 355 'We'll let her in on our team, see?' 'For real?' 'Not for real, just play-like.' **1977** *R. Air Force News* 22 June–5 July 11/2 Two pilots have in fact done the job 'for real'—both Sqn Ldr Marshall and Flt Lt Dave Fischer have put Harriers down on the deck of HMS Bulwark.

real estate: see Real *a.*^{2} 6 c in Dict. and Suppl.

‖ **realia** (reˌā·liă, riˌeⁱ·liă). [neut. pl. of late L. *reālis* actual, real.] **1.** *Educ.* Objects which may be used as teaching aids but were not made for the purpose. *N. Amer.*

1950 J. S. Kinder *Audio-Visual Materials & Teaching Techniques* xiii. 333 Realia include such items as objects, specimens, samples, relics, artifacts, souvenirs, and even models and dioramas. **1962** *Library Jrnl.* LXXXVII. 819/1 They ignore the miniature models, facsimiles, mock-ups, and realia which one used in construction of exhibitions and bulletin boards. **1970** J. Riddle et al. *Non-Book Materials* (prelim. ed.) 44 Realia are entered under title. The title may be taken from the box or accompanying data. Where no title can be found, the catalogues will supply one, e.g. [Robin's egg] (Realia). **1975** *Ontario Libr. Rev.* LIX. 243 The study encompassed seventeen types of audio and visual materials;..microforms, overhead projectors, sculpture replicas and realia, media kits and simulation games.

2. Real things, actual facts, esp. as distinct from theories about them.

1952 G. Sarton *Hist. Sci.* I. xiv. 362 The *realia*, we should always remember, cannot be learned in books but only in the practice of a scientific profession. *Ibid.* xix. 480 There is a real need of new translations..fully explained by a scholar..acquainted not only with philologic details but with all the realia expressed or implied. **1962** Y. Malkiel in Householder & Saporta *Probl. Lexicogr.* 5 Attention is focused on..strictly lexical data (at the expense of *realia*, proper names, and the like). **1975** *Times Lit. Suppl.* 25 Apr. 464/1 Takes Christian scholars to task for being too theological about Judaism, for ignoring its *realia*.

realign (riˌălǝi·n), *v.* [f. Re- 5 a + Align *v.*] **a.** *intr.* for *refl.* To fall into line again; to return to previously aligned positions.

1923 *Glasgow Herald* 14 Aug. 7 If France does not meet us half way, enabling the Allied front to realign, there will be a separate reply to Germany.

b. *trans.* To align again or anew. Also *fig.*

1957 V. W. Turner *Schism & Continuity in African Soc.* v. 131 Private intrigues provide means whereby individuals seek to realign the social structure in pursuit of their own advantage. **1967** Cox & Grose *Organization & Handling Bibl. Rec. by Computer* IV. 93 There is a Restructure program which realigns and copies the data base files. **1973** *Computers & Humanities* VII. 139 The texts are realigned at the place where the match was found.

realignment. For 'Chiefly *U.S.*' read 'orig. *U.S.*' and add further examples.

1929 P. Hughes *Catholic Question 1688–1829* III. ii. 197 A re-alignment in English political life suddenly brought uncertainty to an end. With that re-alignment the Catholic Question emerges. **1935** A. P. Herbert *What a Word!* iv. 92 Comment in the Lobbies centred round the re-alignment of, etc., etc. **1957** *Times Lit. Suppl.* 20 Dec. 766/2 Clear and virtually immeasurable material benefits, widespread realignments of jobs, changes of thinking and attitudes, and alteration of ways of working. **1959** *Economist* 3 Jan. 11/2 The chance thus arose of the concerted realignment of European currencies. **1964** *Ann. Reg. 1963* 78 Externally, political realignments with the Pacific and South East Asia continued, a number of official visits being exchanged. **1979** *Time* 2 Apr. 10/2 In the scramble for realignment in the face of the impending treaty, Hussein has even reconciled with Yasser Arafat..with whom he has been at bloody odds since 1970.

realism. Add: **1. a.** (Earlier and later examples.)

1826 R. Whately *Logic* 299 Nothing, perhaps, has contributed more to the error of Realism than inattention to this ambiguity. *Ibid.* 300 All these absurdities are in fact but the extreme and ultimate point of Realism. **1828** J. S. Mill in *Westm. Rev.* IX. 155 Their [*sc.* Aristotelian logicians'] classification of names according to the *mode of their signification* (of which the doctrine of the Predicables forms a part) when purified from the taint of Realism which adheres to the expression but without infecting the substance, constitutes a prodigious step in the theory of naming. **1948** C. Hartshorne *Divine Relativity* iii. 122 Even if one takes the 'conceptualist' solution of the problem of nominalism and realism, one need not therefore deny that God may have something corresponding to concepts. **1970** N. Wolterstorff *On Universals* vii. 170 Our position is that of realism and 'nominalism'. Is rapprochement between two such ancient armies possible?

b. (*a*) (Earlier examples.)

1830 W. Hamilton in *Edin. Rev.* LII. 169 If the veracity of consciousness be unconditionally admitted..the doctrine is established which we would call the scheme of Natural Realism or Natural Dualism. *Ibid.* 180 The scheme of Natural Realism, which it is Reid's immortal honour to have been the first..to embrace.

(*b*) In the 20th century, applied to philosophical theories reacting against 19th-century idealism which, while they agree in affirming that external objects exist independently of the mind, differ in their accounts of appearance, perception, and illusion. More recently (opp. to *verificationism), the theory that the world has a reality that transcends the mind's analytical capacity, and hence that propositions are to be assessed in terms of their truth to reality, rather than in terms of their verifiability. Cf. also *naïve realism* s.v. *naïve *a.* 1 b, *New Realism.

The quotations are chosen to give some idea of the range and diversity of views in modern theories of realism.

1906 *Mind* XV. 308 Some of the leading supporters of the new Realism (especially Mr. Moore and Mr. Russell) connect it with an extremely nominalistic type of Logic... This Logic, however, seems to be quite capable of recognising types such as those of Plato. **1920** D. Drake et al. *Ess. Critical Realism* p. vi, Our realism is not a physically monistic realism, or a merely logical realism... To find an adjective that should connote the essential features of our brand of realism seemed chimerical, and we have contented ourselves with the vague, but accurate, phrase *critical realism*. **1920** J. Laird *Stud. in Realism* i. 13 Any realism of this kind, even if it defends common sense, defends a common sense which is very sophisticated indeed. **1938** G. D. Hicks *Critical Realism* p. xiii, Realism, as Professor Perry has defined it, stands for the principle that 'things may be, and are, directly experienced without owing either their being or their nature to that circumstance'. **1954** M. R. Cohen *Amer. Thought* ix. 271 The practical consequence of Peirce's realism is his sharp distinction between what is useful and what is true. **1963** J. Macquarrie *Twentieth-Cent. Relig. Thought* xvii. 259 In German realism, which stands rather apart from the Anglo-American brand, the influence of phenomenology is noticeable. **1967** *Encycl. Philos.* VII. 80/2 Representative realism also accounts for illusions, dreams, images, hallucinations, and the relativity of perception... [It] is the easiest inference from the scientific account of the causal processes up to the brain in all perceiving and fits other scientific evidence. **1969** L. W. Forguson in K. T. Fann *Symposium on J. L. Austin* III. 328 Austin's purpose with regard to both the sense-datum theory and philosophic realism was entirely negative... In his view, the problems..either aren't problems at all or.. aren't philosophical..but scientific problems. **1972** K. R. Popper *Objective Knowl.* p. vii, While I am prepared to uphold to the last the essential truth of commonsense realism, I regard the commonsense theory of knowledge as a subjectivist blunder. **1973** M. Dummett *Frege: Philos. Lang.* xiii. 466 The fundamental tenet of realism is that any sentence on which a fully specific sense has been conferred has a determinate truth-value independently of our actual capacity to decide what truth-value is. **1979** *Sci. Amer.* Nov. 139/1 Realism can be stated formally as the belief that a mere description of data is not all that should be required of a theory.

2. c. orig. *U.S.* (*a*) In legal theory, the doctrine that the law is to be discovered by studying actual legal decisions and procedures, rather than by recourse to enactments or statutes; (*b*) more loosely in political theory, the view that actual political power is the subject-matter of politics, as opp. to doctrine, law, rights, or justice.

1930 J. Frank *Law & Modern Mind* v. 42 (*heading*) Legal realism. **1930** K. N. Llewellyn in *Columbia Law Rev.* XXX. 449 A sophisticated reversion to a sophisticated realism. Gone is the ancient assumption that law is because law is. *Ibid.* 461 (*heading*) Realism as to 'society'. **1951** J. H. Herz *Polit. Realism & Polit. Idealism* ii. 24 Political Realism has at all times insisted that the nature of politics is fundamentally determined by the struggle for power. **1959** B. Crick *Amer. Sci. of Polit.* v. 85 The popular character of pragmatic realism as reformism can be seen most vividly in the literature of the era. **1960** G. Schubert *Public Interest* iv. 148 A second thread of Legislative Realism emphasizes the effect of each chamber..in conditioning the behavior of the individual members. **1961** O. Kirchheimer *Polit. Justice* v. 216 Through the psychological variant of legal realism we have become conscious of all the numerous factors in the judge's personality structure which might become determinative factors of judicial action. **1962** B. C. Borning *Polit. & Soc. Thought C. A. Beard* ii. 19 The very spirit of science that stimulated Beard and others to aim at realism was closely related to the premise that man by using reason could not only understand but also control his environment. **1968** W. Twining *Karl Llewellyn Papers* I. ii. 5 At Oxford, American Realism was just another Aunt Sally. **1977** M. Clanchy in E. Attwooll *Perspectives in Jurisprudence* x. 176 Realism has been given a special meaning in jurisprudential thinking to distinguish between real rules of law and paper rules.

3. (Further examples.)

1894 C. L. Morgan *Psychol. for Teachers* ix. 203 Realism ..involves the introduction of such details as shall assimilate the representation to actual fact, and the incorporation of the results of generalisation in individual persons or concrete things. **1912** Laran & Gaston-Dreyfus *Courbet* 51 Gautier was astonished at seeing Realism in a shed. **1924** [see *expressionism]. **1937** H. Read *Art & Society* iv. 180 My underlying contention, that there is an inherent contradiction between art and vulgarism (or, to confine ourselves to æsthetic terms, between art and realism). *Ibid.* vii. 247 There are, in fact, only these three basic modes—realism, idealism and expressionism. **1957** B. S. Myers *Art & Civilization* xxvi. 645 The late-nineteenth- and early-twentieth-century realism reappeared in the United States during the depression years after 1929 as a school of Social Realism. **1957** *Observer* 3 Nov. 14/2 Realism was Courbet's answer to the quarrelling schools of French Classicism (Ingres) and Romanticism (Delacroix). **1970** F. Marti-Ibañez *Adventure of Art* xii. 571/1 Some interpreters regard personal intimacy as the catalyst for Picasso's return to realism. **1977** T. Neville *Challenge of Mod. Thought* xix. 117 It is precisely by means of this extreme realism that Kafka points the inadequacy of the known facts as a guide to ultimate truth.

realist, *sb.* (and *a.*). Add: **3. c.** One who adheres to or is influenced by principles of realism (sense *2 c).

1930 K. N. Llewellyn in *Columbia Law Rev.* XXX. 463 The problem calls for exploration, from the realist's angle, by cautious study of detail. **1954** M. R. Cohen *Amer. Thought* ii. 64 The realists insist that any theory of value that is not arbitrary must be based on actual experience. **1960** G. Schubert *Public Interest* iv. 142 Political scientists generally..appear to agree with those Realists who insist that there must be a general consensus to accept the decisions of public officials, if a democratic polity is to exist. **1971** Chambliss & Seidman *Law, Order & Power* i. 2 The American legal realists, who insisted that we must study the *law in action* as well as the *law in the books.* **1977** M. Clanchy in E. Attwooll *Perspectives in Jurisprudence* x. 176 The historian of law will tend to be a realist.

4. (Later examples.)

1931 R. Pound in *Harvard Law Rev.* XLIV. 697, I approach the subject of the call for a realist jurisprudence.. with some humility. **1959** Hart & Honoré *Causation in Law* iv. 92 The general scepticism as to the possibility of framing rules which developed into the 'Realist' movement of the 1930's. **1977** *Dædalus* Summer 58 We may discover that the realist paradigm, which stresses the primacy of foreign policy, has to be seriously amended, not only for the present but for the past.

realistic, *a.* Add: **1. a.** (Earlier and later examples.)

1829 H. C. Robinson *Diary* 13 Aug. (1967) 102 [Goethe] repeated the remark which is one of his fixed ideas that it is by..facts that even a poetical view of nature is to be.. authenticated... It is this which had made Goethe a *realistic* poet, as opposed to the idealism of such poetry as Wordsworth's. **1943** *Ulster: Brit. Bridgehead* (H.M.S.O.) 6 (*caption*) This realistic picture shows British troops in training in Northern Ireland. **1971** *Hi-Fi Sound* Feb. 67/3 High fidelity stereo at its most successful is wide-ranging and realistic, analytical and rich in detail.

2. a. (Later examples.)

1936 *Sun* (Baltimore) 26 Feb. 1/5 Mr. Eden, although doubting his wisdom, wished Chamberlain success in his 'realistic' search for lasting peace. **1962** *Listener* 12 Apr. 626/2 Neither a minimum property qualification nor even a simple educational test..would be realistic or just in the present situation of South Africa. **1963** *Observer* 3 Nov. 33/3 'Realistic' can vary from its theatre meaning of 'with damp washing' to its place at the top of the conjugation 'I am realistic, you have compromised, he has sold out'. **1973** *Howard Jrnl.* XIII. 321 Realistic payment of prisoners is a novel idea to students of the British penal system.

3. (Earlier example.)

1843 J. S. Mill *Logic* I. I. viii. 197 The philosophers who overthrew Realism..retained long afterwards, in their own philosophy, numerous propositions which could only have a rational meaning as part of a Realistic system.

reality. Add: **7.** *attrib.* and *Comb.*, as *reality content, control, -revealer, value*; *reality-based, -centred* adjs.; **reality principle,** the principle propounded by Freud that the actual conditions of living modify the pleasure-seeking activity of the libido; **reality-testing,** the testing of an emotion or thought in a real-life context; also *attrib.*; hence **reality-test** *sb.* and *v.*, **-tested** *ppl. a.*

1960 L. Pincus *Marriage* I. 25 A challenge to move forward to fuller and more reality-based relations. **1962** *Listener* 19 Apr. 683/1 These concepts themselves keep the child's thinking 'reality-centred'. **1951** J. M. Fraser *Psychol.* x. 112 When we find someone in whose life.. phantasy achievements occupy a very large place, we are probably justified in thinking that the reality-content of his motivation is a little low. **1949** 'G. Orwell' *Nineteen Eighty-Four* I. 37 Whatever was true now was true from everlasting to everlasting... All that was needed was an unending series of victories over your own memory. 'Reality control', they called it: in Newspeak, 'doublethink'. *Ibid.* 54 It's merely a question of self-discipline, reality-control. **1921** R. Macaulay *Dangerous Ages* xii. 236 Your ego is at present in..an impermanent stage in its struggle towards the adult level of the reality-principle. **1922** C. J. M. Hubback tr. *Freud's Beyond Pleasure Princ.* i. 5 Under the influence of the instinct of the ego for self-preservation it [*sc.* the pleasure-principle] is replaced by the 'reality-principle'. **1954** D. Riesman *Individualism Reconsidered* xxii. 345 By the reality principle alone, mankind could not be governed. **1957** N. Frye *Anat. of Criticism* (1971) ii. 75 In literature, what entertains is prior to what instructs,.. the reality-principle is subordinate to the pleasure-principle. **1968** *Listener* 22 Feb. 244/1 The real world—where there are limits on what is possible..where..the reality principle operates. **1976** S. Hynes *Auden Generation* vi. 185 It is the existence of Europe, and not any political doctrine that is the reality principle here. **1962** A. Huxley *Island* ix. 136 Murugan calls it dope... We, on the contrary, give the stuff good names—the *moksha*-medicine, the reality-revealer, the truth-and-beauty pill. *Ibid.* 141 'Which is the easy way?' Will asked. 'Education and reality-revealers.' **1925** J. Riviere tr. *Freud's Papers on Metapsychol.* in *Coll. Papers* IV. 20 Their entire disregard of the reality-test. **1968** N. N. Holland in Levine & Madden *Art Victorian Prose* 333 The more we reality-test a work of literature, the more we become aware of the reality of ourselves as separate beings. **1960** L. Pincus *Marriage* I. 19 Some remnants of ego (reality-tested experience) may..be repressed. **1925** J. Riviere tr. *Freud's Papers on Metapsychol.* in *Coll. Papers* IV. 16 One mode of thought-activity was split off; it was kept free from reality-testing and remained subordinated to the pleasure-principle alone. **1953** J. Strachey tr. *Freud's Interpretation of Dreams* II. in *Coll. Works* V. 566 In other words it becomes evident that there must be a means of 'reality-testing' (i.e. testing things to see whether they are real or not). **1955** M. Laserowitz *Struct. of Metaphysics* ii. 72 These then contribute their psychic charge, which both intensifies our feeling of disquietude and weakens our reality-testing abilities. **1960** L. Pincus *Marriage* I. 20 The more healthy process of reality-testing and reassimilation. **1974** S. A. Renshon *Psychol. Needs & Polit. Behav.* iv. 44 The principle of adequate reality testing allows us to come to grips with this problem. **1923** Reality-value [see *image *sb.* 5 a]. **1961** *Listener* 23 Nov. 856/2 From the point of view of emancipation, as opposed that is to the point of view of truth or (as he called it) reality value, Freud was deeply affected by two considerations.

realizability. (Example.)

1975 *Nature* 20 Mar. p. xiv (Advt.), The emphasis throughout is on the theoretical foundations of optimum source synthesis, including conditions for physical realizability and mathematical methods for satisfying them.

realization. Add: **1. b.** (Later examples.)

1966 *Guardian* 1 Sept. 7/3 Ralph Ortiz, American and destroyer of pianos..doesn't call them happenings any more, he drawls them 'realisations'. **1976** *Southern Even. Echo* (Southampton) 6 Nov. 7/8 Another well-made film, John Huston's realisation of the Rudyard Kipling short story 'The Man Who Would Be King', is showing at the end of next week at the Palace, Bordon.

c. *Math.* An instance or embodiment of an abstract group as the set of symmetry operations or the like of some object or set.

1954 Beaumont & Ball *Introd. Mod. Algebra & Matrix Theory* iv. 135 Find a realization in geometry of the group consisting of the elements e, a, a^2, a^3, a^4, a^5 where $a^6 = e$, the identity of the group. **1965** Patterson & Rutherford *Elem. Abstract Algebra* ii. 52 A particular member of an equivalence class is called a realisation..of the corresponding abstract group. **1979** *Proc. London Math. Soc.* XXXVIII. 260 But this coequalizer, if computed in $\mathscr{T}$ (or in $\mathscr{F}$), would yield precisely the geometric realization $|K|$ of K..so we have simply to prove that the coequalizer is preserved by the embedding $\mathscr{F} \to \mathscr{E}$.

d. *Statistics.* A particular series which might be generated by a specified random process.

1957 Kendall & Buckland *Dict. Stat. Terms* 242 A realisation of a stochastic process $\{x_t\}$ is one of the series of values $(.. x_{-2}, x_{-1}, x_0, x_1, ..)$ to which it may give rise. The realisation may be regarded as a 'member' of the process in the same way that an individual observation is regarded as the member of a population. **1965** Cox & Miller *Theory Stochastic Processes* i. 9 The realization illustrates well the very irregular behaviour of the system. **1975** D. R. Brillinger *Time Series* ii. 18 Once a θ has been generated (in accordance with its probability distribution), the function $X(t, \theta)$, with θ fixed, will be described as a realization, trajectory, or sample path of the time series.

2. b. *Linguistics.* The phonetic, phonological, graphic, or syntactic manifestation of a linguistic unit, structure, or set of features. Also *attrib.*

1954 Pei & Gaynor *Dict. Linguistics* 6 *Actualization*, the perceptible result of the articulation of the phonemic variants or of the archiphoneme... Also called *realization.* **1968** *Language* XLIV. 285 A transformation places an element in position, and a realization rule provides a spelling in terms of the alphabet of the neighboring component. **1971** R. Fowler in *Archivum Linguisticum* II. 131 If I understand the implications of Chomsky's rule, it would seem that his presentation of deep structure has been misleadingly influenced by accidents of surface-structure realization. *Ibid.* 133 TG theory..offers a pattern for what I call 'realization rules'—rules which effect the transition between combinations of feature sets and strings of morphemes. **1971** B. Mafeni in J. Spencer *Eng. Lang. W. Afr.* 102 The two words 'de' in 'de way' and in 'you de waste' are spelt alike, but they are actually two different lexical and grammatical items with different phonetic realisations. **1972** *Language* XLVIII. 384 All speakers clearly simplify to a certain extent the phonetic realization of words derived from their own languages, and yet pronounce them with their sound structures more intact than do non-native speakers. **1977** *Canad. Jrnl. Linguistics 1976* XXI. II. 198 Important questions remain about Halliday's model, particularly as regards the precise relationship between meaning potential and its realization at the level of form and the nature and details of the realization rules which connect the two.

4. *Mus.* The action of completing or enriching the texture of a piece of music left sparsely notated by a composer; also a piece of music so completed or enriched.

1911 E. Newman tr. *Schweitzer's J. S. Bach* II. xxxv. 447 The only original instrument to be considered in connection with the realisation of the thorough-bass is the organ. **1946** *Penguin Mus. Mag.* Dec. 92 There is an atmosphere about these 'realisations' by Nadia Boulanger which is usually absent from our choral recordings. **1954** *Grove's Dict. Mus.* (ed. 5) VII. 69/1 *Realization*, a useful modern term for the setting forth of a thorough-bass in full harmony, with more or less elaborate textures, from a continuo part, either at sight in performance or in editing old music. **1958** *Listener* 4 Dec. 964/3 His [*sc.* Roman's] realization of Leo's *Dixit*, which he conducted in 1747, shows how far his predilection for the Italians went. **1959** *Collins Mus. Encycl.* 534/1 *Realization*, the act of completing the harmony of a 17th- or 18th-cent. work by providing a keyboard accompaniment based on the indications afforded by the figured bass. **1966** *Listener* 10 Mar. 364 Deryck Cooke's fine realization of Mahler's tenth symphony hardly received its due on Wednesday. **1980** *Early Music* Jan. 109/2 The continuo realization by Claire Caillard follows the principles of Saint Lambert.

Hence **realiza·tional** *a.*

1965 Ld. Northbourne tr. *Schuon's Light on Ancient Worlds* 66 The Biblical, mystical and 'realizational' character of Christianity. **1968** *Language* XLIV. 574 Working with Potawatomi, I found the rewrite format surprisingly easy to set up. The realizational format was rather more difficult. **1972** *Ibid.* XLVIII. 373 The realizational rule that, in his analysis, provides the input for the vowel-reduction rule by also converting *o* to *ö*..would have to re-apply in order to convert *u* to *ü* again. *Ibid.* 408 The present article sets the frame for a wider study of suffixal *j* in Germanic by linking the realizational rules of underlying *j* in two Germanic dialects—Old English and Gothic. **1979** *Trans. Philol. Soc.* 203 Vowel-inventories are much less varied than those of the consonants, but there is one realizational difference which suggests interesting patterns of historical change.

realize, *v.*[2] Add: **1. b.** (Earlier example.)

1769 A. Ferguson *Inst. of Moral Philos.* VI. v. 257 Peevishness..tends to realize imaginary evils.

d. *Mus.* To complete a piece of music left sparsely notated by a composer; to enrich the texture of a work, esp. by orchestrating music written for a single voice or instrument.

1911 E. Newman tr. *Schweitzer's J. S. Bach* II. xxxv. 451 Our forces are different from those of Bach's day. Orchestra and choir are much larger..; if we realise the thorough-bass on the same scale it sounds too loud. **1947** A. Einstein *Mus. in Romantic Era* ix. 98 To interpret the role of the piano in orchestral form, to 'realize' it—which means to coarsen it naturalistically. **1958** A. Jacobs *New Dict. Mus.* 304 *Realize*, to work out in full and artistically such music as was originally left by its composer in a sparsely-notated condition... Though lacking the advantage of being self-explanatory, 'realize' is superior to 'arrange' in this context since it avoids the implication of alteration. **1980** *Early Music* Jan. 111/2 Other reconstruction work has involved realizing short score into full score (as in parts of the Overture in D).

3. a. Also, to become aware of the presence of (a person).

1916 H. S. Walpole *Dark Forest* II. iv. 269 The moment I realized him I felt afraid.

realized *ppl. a.*, spec. in phr. *realized eschatology* Theol. (see quot. 1946).

1936 C. H. Dodd *Apostolic Preaching & its Devel.* iii. 156 This promise of a second coming is realized in the presence of the Paraclete..in the life of the Church... The evangelist, therefore, is deliberately subordinating the 'futurist' element in the eschatology of the early Church to the 'realized eschatology' which..was from the first the distinctive and controlling factor in the *kerygma.* **1946** E. L. Mascall *Christ, Christian, & Church* vi. 101 In recent years much stress has been laid upon the notion of 'realized eschatology', ..the view that..the last Day and the Final Judgment are actually present to Christians now. **1977** G. W. H. Lampe *God as Spirit* i. 27 It has been argued convincingly that T. W. Manson, C. H. Dodd, and other exponents of 'realized eschatology' offered a one-sided interpretation of the evidence.

reallocate (riˌæ·lŏkēɪt), *v.* [f. Re- 5 a + Allocate *v.* 1.] *trans.* To apportion or assign again.

1957 *Economist* 7 Sept. 863/1 When the French Government reallocates next month the oil prospecting rights over a 25,000 square mile tract of the Sahara Desert, several major British and American oil companies are likely to be committed to carry out intensive exploration in the area. **1964** A. Battersby *Network Analysis* i. 9 It [*sc.* network analysis] reduces the examination of a large project to three stages:..(c) Re-allocating money or other resources to improve the schedule.

realloca·tion. [f. Re- 5 a + Allocation.] **a.** The action of apportioning or assigning again. **b.** A case or example of this.

1948 E. Gowers *Plain Words* 48 We might find that, even though the Board of Trade could still not resist announcing that certain surplus government factories are now 'available for re-allocation', they would not leave it at that. 'In short,' they would add in a burst of confidence, 'they are to be relet.' **1960** *Farmer & Stockbreeder* 16 Feb. 122/3 Should there be any re-allocation of profitable pennies from corn, milk and sugar beet, the cattle producer is first in the queue. **1962** A. Battersby *Guide to Stock Control* 108 No figure in the third column is less than any in the fourth column; this means any further re-allocation of orders must of necessity increase the total stock value. **1964** *Ann. Reg. 1963* 124 In 1963 this amounted to 81,563 tons, with sizeable additional reallocations. *a* **1974** R. Crossman *Diaries* (1975) I. 626 We soon found that some of the 130 select authorities were not using up their allocation and we had some very nice re-allocations to do in order to make sure that our total didn't fall down.

really, *adv.*[2] Add: In adj. phr. **really truly** chiefly *N. Amer. Children's speech*, authentic, genuine.

1908 L. M. Montgomery *Anne of Green Gables* xi. 114 They all had puffed sleeves..it was awfully hard there among the others who had really truly puffs. **1909** M. Diver *Candles in Wind* xxxiii. 348 Such a really truly knight! **1911** G. Stratton-Porter *Harvester* xvi. 356 There are fairies! Really truly ones! They have found the remainder of the willow dishes. **1911** T. Dreiser *Jennie Gerhardt* 249

She thinks you are her really truly uncle. **1942** *Post* (Morgantown, W. Va.) 2 May 5/7 The [family] have one of the prize sites with a really, truly beach.

realm. 2. b. (Further example.)

1924 W. B. SELBIE *Psychol. Relig.* 80 Though the term unconscious is used very loosely by Freudians it generally means a 'realm' where various emotions which have from time to time been repressed, lie hidden.

‖ **Realpolitik** (re͵ā:lpoliti·k). Also **real-politik.** [Ger.] Practical politics; policy determined by practical, rather than moral or ideological, considerations. Also *transf.* Cf. *practical politics* s.v. *PRACTICAL *a.* (*sb.*) 6.

1914 G. B. SHAW in *New Statesman* 14 Nov. (Suppl.) 5/2 He [*sc.* Friedrich von Bernhardi] prophesies that we, his great masters in *Realpolitik*, will do precisely what our Junkers have just made us do. **1915** E. B. HOLT *Freudian Wish & its Place in Ethics* iv. 151 This science is '*Realpolitik*', the Politics of Reality. **1920** *Times* 19 Jan. 13/2 An over-strong Russia..might not altogether suit the *Realpolitik* of this country. **1926** A. HUXLEY *Jesting Pilate* IV. 275 Freudism became the *realpolitik* of psychology and philosophy. **1928** C. H. DODD *Authority of Bible* xii. 266 In the last days of the monarchies Israel became involved to its cost in the large 'Realpolitik' of the time. **1931** *Times Lit. Suppl.* 4 June 433/2 The conflict between these two ideals—*Realpolitik* and a policy founded upon principles of justice and morality. **1948** R. ROBINSON tr. *Jaeger's Aristotle* II. v. 113 The letter that we possess is the solemn record of this peculiar pact between *Realpolitik* and theoretical schemes of reform. **1952** J. D. MACKIE *Earlier Tudors* x. 351 [Thomas Cromwell] had little belief in the omnipotence of the papacy and pinned his faith to *Realpolitik*. **1958** *New Statesman* 19 Apr. 494/2 But the bare-faced hypocrisy with which they have attempted to conceal their military *realpolitik*, and which has now been devastatingly exposed, is a serious tactical error. **1961** *Listener* 27 Apr. 731/2 Writing in the eighteen-fifties—the decade which saw the birth of the name and concept of *Realpolitik*—Mommsen was imbued with the sense of need for a strong man. **1970** G. GREER *Female Eunuch* 109 Even the best educated of them [*sc.* women] know that arguments with their men-folk are disguised real-politik. **1979** *N.Y. Rev. Bks.* 25 Oct. 49/2 Soviet policy may have sprung neither from revolutionary ideology nor from traditional *Realpolitik*.

Hence **realpoli·tiker**, one who believes in, advocates, or practises *Realpolitik*.

1930 C. SFORZA in *Time & Tide* 4 Apr. 435/2 'The United States of Europe!' sneered..the *real-politikers*, whom, by a strange legerdemain, the defeat of Hohenzollern Germany has conjured up again in France. **1931** *Times Lit. Suppl.* 22 Jan. 53/1 Both [Cavour and Bismarck] were *Realpolitiker*, endowed with an extraordinary capacity for gauging the forces with which they had to deal. **1958** *Times* 14 June 8/5 In all this he [*sc.* Pierre Flandin] took the line of a French *Realpolitiker*. **1963** *Observer* 1 Dec. 21/4 He learned the lesson, and applied it in Laos—and not in the sentimentally tough way supposed by the *realpolitikers*. **1976** *Survey* Winter 16 Czechoslovakia may look even more remote than Angola..but its fate counts in the over-all balance, whatever the *Realpolitiker* may think.

‖ **Realschule** (re͵ā·lʃū:lə). Also **realschule.** Pl. **Realschulen.** [Ger.] In Germany and Austria, a secondary school in which sciences and modern languages are taught. Cf. *real school* s.v. REAL *a.*² 10.

1833 [see REAL *a.*² 10]. **1879** *Encycl. Brit.* X. 471/1 Of more recent growth is the system of *realschulen*, where Latin is the only ancient language taught, the other branches being modern languages, especially French and English, mathematics and natural philosophy, geography and modern history. **1949** R. K. MERTON *Social Theory & Social Structure* xiv. 343 Hecker, who first actually organized a *Realschule*. **1969** *Listener* 10 Apr. 480/2 Experimental step towards comprehensive education: class in a Realschule. **1980** *Jewish Chron.* 23 May 14/2, I later taught in the Realschule, founded by his grandfather, Rabbi Samson Raphael Hirsch.

Realtor (rī·ăltǫɹ). *U.S.* Also **realtor.** [f. REALT(Y² + -OR.] A proprietary term in the U.S. for a real-estate agent or broker who belongs to the National Association of Realtors (formerly the National Association of Real Estate Boards). Also *gen.*, an estate agent.

1916 C. N. CHADBOURN in *Nat. Real Estate Jrnl.* 15 Mar. 111/2, I propose that the National Association adopt a professional title to be conferred upon its members which they shall use to distinguish them from outsiders. That this title be copyrighted and defended by the National Association against misuse... I therefore, propose that the National Association adopt and confer upon its members, dealers in realty, the title of *realtor* (accented on the first syllable). **1922** S. LEWIS *Babbitt* xiii. 157 We ought to insist that folks call us 'realtors' and not 'real-estate men'. Sounds more like a reg'lar profession. **1925** O. W. HOLMES *Let.* 17 Dec. in *Holmes–Laski Lett.* (1953) I. 807 These realtors, as they call themselves, I presume are influential. **1929** *Sun* (Baltimore) 8 Jan. 26/3 (*heading*) Realtors doubt plan for Fox Theater here. **1931** *Evening Standard* 25 Apr. 15/2 (*heading*) 'Realtor' recommends Surrey. **1934** E. POUND *Eleven New Cantos* xxxv. 23 His Wife now acts as his model and the Egeria Has, let us say, married a realtor. **1942** *Amer. Speech* XVII. 209/2 The ambitious realtor's favorites, the overworked [street names] Grand, Broadway, and Inspiration. **1948** *Official Gaz.* (U.S. Patent Office) 14 Sept. 340/2 National Association of Real Estate Boards, Chicago, Ill... Service Mark. *Realtors.* For services in connection with the brokerage of real estate... Claims use since Mar. 31, 1916. **1962** R. BUCKMINSTER FULLER *Epic Poem on Industrialization* 139 The organized religions The world's premier realtors. **1969** *Parade* (N.Y.) 14 Dec. 18/2 The realtor who sold most of the property to the hippies has had her office windows smashed. **1970** *Globe & Mail* (Toronto) 25 Sept. 40/2 (Advt.), Metro wide established realtor with country wide referral contacts. **1973** R. C. DENNIS *Sweat of Fear* ix. 59 The realtor said... 'Let me point out some of the features of this lovely, lovely home.' **1979** *Tucson Mag.* Apr. 33/3 Included are..bankers and lawyers; social and political activists; professors and artists, renovators and historians, journalists and realtors.

realty². Add: **4.** Also *attrib.*

1888 A. RANDALL-DIEHL *Two Thousand Words* 175 *Realtyman*, a dealer in real estate. **1908** E. WHARTON *Hermit & Wild Woman* 135, I chanced on a record of the transaction in the realty column of the morning paper. **1934** E. POUND *Eleven New Cantos* xi. 48 Beecher's church organized by realty agents. **1947** E. HODGINS *Mr Blandings* iii. 45 As a grizzled veteran of realty values, he would discuss his one time innocence with the real estate man. **1963** C. D. SIMAK *They walked like Men* viii. 47 People were storming realty offices in a mad attempt to find a place to live. **1968** *Globe & Mail* (Toronto) 17 Feb. 51 (Advt.), Lawyer to manage litigation, realty transactions by property development corporation. **1972** J. GORES *Dead Skip* (1973) xiv. 100 The tract home had been rented from the realty office by phone. **1975** *New Yorker* 1 Sept. 20/3 The realty company that is the agent for U.S. Steel gave us thirty days to get out.

ream, *sb.*² Add: **4.** (See quots.)

1962 *Gloss. Terms Glass Industry* (*B.S.I.*) 39 *Ream*, a non-homogeneous layer in flat glass. **1971** *Materials & Technol.* II. vi. 408 In the drawing of sheet the outer layers of glass may have come from the glass originally on the surface..and may be somewhat deficient in alkali compared with the main glass... This results in a type of inhomogeneity known as 'ream', in which the inhomogeneity is in a direction at right angles to the plane of the glass.

ream, *sb.*³ Add: **d.** *transf.* in *pl.* A large quantity.

1913 D. H. LAWRENCE *Love Poems & Others* 54 Eh, what a shame it seems As some should ha'e hardly a smite o' trouble An' others has reams. **1927** J. S. HUXLEY *Relig. without Revelation* iv. 113 This simple personal fact illustrates, better than could whole reams of argument, the extreme complexity of religion. **1976** *San Francisco Examiner* 30 May (This World Suppl.) 19/1 Spacecraft sent there in recent years have dispelled legends and added reams of sound, ordered data, yet the charisma of Mars remains.

ream, *v.*³ Add: **I. 3. a.** Also, to clear (something of an obstruction); to excavate. Also without *adv. U.S.*

1967 'T. WELLS' *Dead by Light of Moon* x. 99 The toilet.. flowed over and Mr. Hawthorne had to come up and ream out the pipes. **1978** J. A. MICHENER *Chesapeake* 642 At the bottom of the Chesapeake..this primeval riverbed existed, sixty feet deeper than the shallow waters surrounding it, but as clearly defined as when first reamed out by tumbling boulders. **1978** J. UPDIKE *Coup* (1979) v. 200 The pipe came into even more elaborate play, the amber stem pointing this way and that as Craven knocked, blew into and rapidly reamed this little instrument of pleasure. **1980** *Nature* 19 June 532/3 As this plinian eruption column formed, it reamed out the volcanic conduit, forming a central crater more than 1·5 km in diameter.

II. *fig.* **4.** *U.S. slang.* To cheat, to swindle. Cf. *RIM *v.*³ 2.

1914 'HIGH JINKS, JR.' *Choice Slang* 17 *Ream one* (*to*), to swindle one. **1938** A. J. LIEBLING *Back where I came From* 84 He had invented a new technique for reaming the customers. **1942** BERREY & VAN DEN BARK *Amer. Thes. Slang* §314/8 Cheat; defraud,..*ream.* **1952** S. KAUFFMANN *Philanderer* (1953) xiii. 216 Yeah, I smell the rat. Joe Bass's new relatives. Well, palsy, they're liable to ream you yet.

5. Usu. with *out.* To reprimand. *U.S. colloq.*

1950 E. HEMINGWAY *Across River* xii. 117 You ream out people you respect, to make them do what is fairly impossible, but is ordered. **1972** R. BUSBY *Reasonable Man* xvi. 145 Banner's back—reamed you out as well, has he? **1973** J. RYDER *Trevayne* (1974) xi. 89 I'll get my ass chewed... I'll get reamed anyway for letting you make this tour. **1979** 'A. HAILEY' *Overload* IV. xvii. 380 A half-wit in my department has been sitting on the thing all morning. I'll ream her out later.

reamed (rīmd), *ppl. a.* [f. REAM *v.*³ + ED¹.] Of a hole: enlarged by reaming.

1909 *Westm. Gaz.* 9 Nov. 5/1 Two bolts..engage in two carefully reamed holes in the pivot and lever, and are secured by castellated nuts and split pins.

reamer (rī·məɹ), *v.* [f. the sb.] *trans.* To use a reamer on; to clear *out* with a reamer.

1934 WEBSTER, *Reamer*,..v.t., to cut with a reamer, as in enlarging diamond dies. **1935** tr. *H. Mignet's Flying Flea* (Air League Brit. Empire) xiii. 237 It may happen..that the platinum points..have seized up... Reamer this out, a very little, with a metal rod covered with a strip of emery cloth. **1938** J. HEALEY *Metal Aircraft for Mechanic* ii. 14 Tubular rivets are a reamer fit, so having reamered the hole to size, radius the edge of the metal slightly.

reaming, *vbl. sb.* Add: **2.** *fig.* A reprimand. *colloq.*

1973 M. WOODHOUSE *Blue Bone* xi. 111 One major stink... Massive reamings are being handed out. **1976** 'J. CHARLTON' *Remington Set* xxiii. 119 You're bloody cheerful..for a bloke that's headed for a number one reaming from the CO.

re-a·nalyse, *v.* [RE- 5 a.] *trans.* To analyse again.

1934 in WEBSTER. **1946** *Nature* 17 Aug. 243/2 As commercial penicillins recently have contained much more penicillin *K* than was formerly the case, the statistics of the Johns Hopkins Hospital were re-analysed as regards the time factor. **1964** K. G. LOCKYER *Introd. Critical Path Anal.* ix. 88 By taking the original network and inserting into it the *actual* times..it is simple to re-analyse the network. **1973** J. J. MCKELVEY *Man against Tsetse* iii. 200 Ehrlich rushed to Liverpool, confirmed the results of Thomas and Breinl, returned to Germany, and with his colleague Alfred Bertheim reanalyzed atoxyl. **1977** *Word 1972* XXVIII. 93 Yet, because of changes elsewhere in the adjective system, they must be reanalyzed synchronically as NPs.

reana·lysis. [Cf. prec. and ANALYSIS.] A second, or further, analysis.

1934 in WEBSTER. **1962** H. A. GLEASON in Householder & Saporta *Probl. Lexicogr.* ii. 92 In some cases no kind of analysis or reanalysis can force the material into the sort of model that descriptive linguistics find appropriate to grammatical statements. **1968** CHOMSKY & HALLE *Sound Pattern Eng.* I. i. 10 If the syntactic component were to be connected to an orthographic rather than a phonetic output system, the reanalysis into phonological phrases would be unnecessary. **1977** *Times* 19 Nov. 14/4 The Bancroft Library..decided to submit the plate to detailed re-analysis.

reanneal (rī͵ănī·l), *v.* [RE- 5 a.] *trans.* To anneal again; in *Biochem.*, to change (single-stranded nucleic acid) back into a double-stranded form; also *intr.*, to change from a single-stranded to a double-stranded form. Hence **reannea·ling** *vbl. sb.*

1963 J. OSBORNE *Dental Mech.* (ed. 5) x. 212 If a considerable amount of bending and re-bending has to be done the wire must be re-annealed from time to time. **1971** *Nature* 25 June 503/1 Mouse satellite DNA..consists of highly repetitive nucleotide sequences which therefore reanneal relatively rapidly after denaturation with alkali. **1980** *Sci. Amer.* Apr. 77/3 The first step of this process is called denaturation, the second step reannealing. *Ibid.*, When the DNA is denatured and reannealed to radioactive RNA, only the remains of those colonies that contained a plasmid whose sequence matches the messenger become radioactive.

reanswer, *v.*² For *Obs.*⁻¹ read *rare* and add later examples.

1933 J. CLAYTON *Sir Thomas More* v. 87 From the time of S. Anselm..the most profound and subtle philosophical questions had been raised and answered, and again re-considered and reanswered. **1977** *Word 1972* XXVIII. 78, I am grateful for her patience in answering and reanswering countless questions and either producing or approving almost all the sentences included in this article.

reap, *sb.*² Add: **3.** *Judo.* (See quot. 1968.) Cf. next.

1968 K. SMITH *Judo Dict.* 167 *Reap*, an action of the leg or foot to sweep away the legs or feet of an opponent in execution of a throw. **1975** R. BUTLER *Where All Girls are Sweeter* ii. 8, I..locked his arm and gave him what the judo boys call a 'reap' and his arm cracked loudly as he went down on his back.

reap, *v.*¹ Add: **B. 2. e.** *Judo.* To sweep (one leg or both legs) from under one's opponent.

1950 E. J. HARRISON *Judo* iii. 56 When reaping your opponent's leg..you should turn your head..and gaze upwards at the ceiling. **1954** E. DOMINY *Teach Yourself Judo* vii. 73 Now bring your right hip past his right and reap his leg away as already described. **1956** K. TOMIKI *Judo* iii. 74 Making a sickle of your leg, apply the back of your right knee to that of *uke's* left knee, crosswise. Sharply reap his left leg toward your right oblique back corner.

reaper. Add: **1. b.** fig. *the* (*Great, Grim, Old*) *Reaper*: Death personified.

The expression arises from the iconographic portrayal of Death wielding a scythe: cf. SCYTHE *sb.* 2.

1839 LONGFELLOW in *Baltimore Lit. Monument* May 17/1 O, not in cruelty, not in wrath, The reaper came that day. **1931** *N. & Q.* 5 Sept. 180/2 One is startled by the inroads which the great reaper has made in the ranks of the Knights since the 15th Edition. **1940** A. UPFIELD *Bushranger of Skies* xiv. 161 That he happened to be the seventh son of a seventh son..was said..to account for his escapes from The Reaper. **1976** R. LEWIS *Witness my Death* v. 182 The old house had been silent, waiting with him for the Old Reaper to come again. **1977** *New Statesman* 2 Sept. 304/1 The Grim Reaper has been rather too vigorously at work among us... At least ten of the best have gone.

2. a. (Earlier and further examples.)

1844 *Let.* 8 Nov. in *Ohio Cultivator* (1845) 15 Mar. 47, I intended..to have written you immediately after harvest, respecting the performance of your Reaper. **1845** *Ohio Cultivator* 1 Jan. 8/3 (*heading*) McCormick's Virginia Reaper. This is another valuable invention for wheat growers. **1847** *Monthly Jrnl. Agric.* June 583 In what consists the difference between their [*sc.* Hussey's and McCormick's] Reapers we are not exactly advised. **1868** *Iowa State Agric. Soc. Rep. 1867* 237 By the folding arrangement the driver can fold the reaper-bar..rendering it perfectly portable. **1923** R. HERRICK *Homely Lilla* xvi. 238 But there are tractors and reapers and sprayers. **1981** *Country Life* 7 May 1266/1 Meadows were mown by horse-drawn reaper.

b. reaper-(and-)binder = SELF-BINDER.

1895 C. D. WARNER *Golden House* ix. 116 He's got no more feeling in business than a reaper-and-binder. **1901** G. B. SHAW *Three Plays for Puritans* p. xxxii, Fools who go laboriously through all the motions of the reaper and binder in an empty field. **1915** C. MACKENZIE *Guy & Pauline* 238 Close at hand was the hum of a reaper-and-binder. **1953** E. HYAMS *Gentian Violet* 54 A reaper-binder was cutting oats.

reaping, *vbl. sb.* Add: **1. b.** *Judo.* The action of reaping (*REAP *v.*^{1} 2 e) the leg or legs of one's opponent.

1954 E. DOMINY *Teach Yourself Judo* vii. 70 The Major Outer Reaping. This is one of the most effective and popular throws in judo. **1956** K. TOMIKI *Judo* iii. 68 *O-soto-gari* (Major Outer Reaping Leg Throw). **1976** *Oxf. Compan. Sports & Games* 547/2 The most successful throws have proved to be..*o-soto-gari* (major outer reaping throw), [etc.].

reapprai·sal. [RE- 5 a: cf. next.] A second appraisal; a reassessment (of something) esp. in the light of new facts.

1911 in WEBSTER. **1953** [see *agonizing reappraisal* s.v. *AGONIZING *ppl. a.* 1 b]. **1959** *Listener* 17 Dec. 1063/1 The Government of Signor Segni has found it necessary to make a reappraisal of the Vanoni plan. **1971** C. M. KERNAN *Lang. Behavior in Black Urban Community* i. 2 It promotes an informed reappraisal of the linguistic abilities of Black students. **1976** *Morecambe Guardian* 7 Dec. 15/4 Local government was reorganised by them without any re-appraisal of the whole basis of local government finance.

reapprai·se, *v.* [RE- 5 a.] *trans.* To make a fresh valuation of, to revalue; to reassess, freq. in the light of new facts. Hence **reapprai·sed** *ppl. a.*, **reapprai·sement, reapprai·ser.**

1895 *U.S. Customs Guide* 124 As I consider the appraisement made by the United States appraisers too high..I have to request that the same may be reappraised..with as little delay as your convenience will permit. *Ibid.* 125 Re-appraisement should take place immediately. **1903** *Daily Chron.* 3 Nov. 5/3 Mr. Low..arranged to have the rental reappraised every twenty-five years. **1906** *Westm. Gaz.* 1 Sept. 2/1 The August circular issued by the United States Government, and dealing with 'Reappraisements of Merchandise by U.S. General Appraisers'. *Ibid.*, Autograph bats specially selected, entered at 15*s.* 6*d.*, reappraised at 21*s.* per each... Entered value is net. Reappraised value less 20 per cent. and 5 per cent. *Ibid.*, The appraisers put a higher value upon them; the reappraisers decide that the true value is 21*s.*, less 20 per cent. and 5 per cent. **1961** *Lancet* 22 July 213/1 There is singularly little evidence that sufficient thought has been devoted to the problem of re-appraising the treatment. **1976** *New Yorker* 8 Mar. 127/1 His subject—finding appropriate uses for technology, and reappraising the engineer's role in society—is important.

reap-silver. For † *Obs. rare* read *Obs.* exc. *Hist.* and add later examples.

1843 CARLYLE *Past & Present* II. x. 123 The Lakenheath eels cease to breed squabbles between human beings; the penny of reap-silver to explode into the streets of the Female Chartism of S^t. Edmundsbury. **1929** F. M. POWICKE in *Cambr. Med. Hist.* VI. vii. 229 The definition of the competence in jurisdiction of the monastic cellarer and the borough reeve, the wrangles about reapsilver and other dues.

rear, *sb.*^{3} (and *a.*^{1}). Add: **I. 2. b.** The buttocks or backside. *colloq.*

1796 *True Briton* 26 Oct. 3/3 Lord Camelford can boast of a power which rivals that of the First Lord of the Admiralty. He has made Captain Couver a *yellow rear*. **1851** H. MELVILLE *Moby Dick* I. xxi. 159 He put his hand upon the sleeper's rear. **1876** 'MARK TWAIN' *Adv. Tom Sawyer* ii. 28 In another moment he was flying down the street with his pail and a tingling rear.., and Aunt Polly was retiring from the field with a slipper in her hand. **1949** N. R. NASH *Young & Fair* I. ii. 16 Just once is enough, Baby. (*She slaps her on the rear*) Come on—get to work. **1965** H. GOLD *Man who was not with It* vi. 49 You used to have some fat, some curves there. Quite a rear you used to have—quite a rear.

3. a. *spec.* The back part of a motor vehicle.

1966 *Publ. Amer. Dial. Soc.* 1964 XLII. 8 *Rear*,..the aft suspension of a car; the differential of a car; the entire aft of an automobile. **1976** *Evening Post* (Nottingham) 16 Dec. 8/2 The 38-ton Bedford TM costs £16,887 for the tractor business end and trailers or huge van-type rears are £1,100 to £1,700 extra.

b. A (public or communal) water-closet, lavatory, or latrine. Also *pl.* (const. as *sing.*). orig. *School* and *University slang.*

1902 FARMER & HENLEY *Slang* VI. 4/2 *Rear*..(University), a jakes. **1907** H. NICOLSON *Let.* 31 Apr. in J. Lees-Milne *Harold Nicolson* (1980) I. ii. 29 The usual bad rears with its hook and eye lock. **1940** [see *LAT^3]. **1946** B. MARSHALL *George Brown's Schooldays* xliii. 170 And now let's raid the rears and rout out any of the other new swine that are hiding there. **1969** VISCT. BUCKMASTER *Roundabout* ii. 30 We also had to know a Latin description of the rear, which we called Foricas.

II. 7. a. *rear-line* (later example), *-link.*

1971 C. BONINGTON *Annapurna South Face* iii. 40 Lieutenant Bishnuparsad, our rear-link wireless operator, was already installed there. *Ibid.*, He was to stay here at the pension paying-post throughout the expedition, acting as rear link and also handling all our mail. **1974** T. P. WHITNEY tr. *Solzhenitsyn's Gulag Archipelago* I. iv. 167 They were vehement in their rear-line wrath (the most intense patriotism always flourishes in the rear).

b. (Later examples.)

1920 Rear pocket [see *custard pie* s.v. *CUSTARD 2 b]. **1920** *T. Eaton & Co. Catal.* Spring & Summer 395/3 Rear Tire Carrier suitable for all models of Ford touring cars. **1925** F. SCOTT FITZGERALD *Great Gatsby* i. 10 Then there was a boom as Tom Buchanan shut the rear windows and the caught wind died out about the room. *Ibid.* 12 All the cars have the left rear wheel painted black as a mourning wreath. **1931** E. S. GARDNER in *Detective Fiction Weekly* 7 Mar. 325/1 One of the officers..ensconced himself in the rear seat. **1951** *Catal. Exhibits, Festival of Britain* p. xxix, This new Foden rear-engine chassis has revolutionised normal design practice. **1952** V. CANNING *House of Seven Flies* 5 A second sailor opened the rear door of the car for him. **1964** V. J. CHAPMAN *Coastal Vegetation* vi. 170 Whether one is investigating fore-, mid- or rear-dunes, it will be found that the water is fresh. **1966** 'A. HALL' *9th Directive* xx. 184 The car..was gathering speed..when I..got the rear door open and lurched inside. **1968** *Listener* 26 Dec. 868/3 Following the coffee-table book comes the rear-window book: the huge unread, unreadable volume that lies on the shelf behind the back seat. **1969** B. KNOX *Tallyman* vi. 120 Rear-wheel skids should be steered into, said the rule-book. **1973** *Country Life* 1 Mar. 540/2 Rear-seat passengers are not too badly off for leg room. **1975** *Ibid.* 2 Jan. 32/2 A real omission here is a heated rear window... Rear wipers are likewise unknown. **1976** P. R. WHITE *Planning for Public Transport* iii. 56 The rear-engine layout was also adopted for single-deckers. **1978** *Dumfries Courier* 20 Oct. 22/1 (Advt.), All are quality cars with spacious reclining seats, fitted carpets,..heated rearscreen, radial tyres, etc.

8. a. *rear-facing.*

1978 *Cornish Guardian* 27 Apr. 24/5 (Advt.), 1973 Volvo 145 D/L Estate... Rear-facing child seats.

b. *rear-driven* (so *-drive*), *-lit*; *rear-illuminate, -project* vbs.

1904 Rear-driven [Listed in Dict.]. **1961** *Twentieth Century* Feb. 124 Rear-lit cloths become more common [in the theatre]. **1970** *Nature* 19 Dec. 1217/1 A number of test-areas in the form of circular holes in a metal plate are uniformly rear-illuminated to a supra-threshold luminance. **1972** *Country Life* 26 Oct. 1060/3 The rack and pinion steering is responsive yet without quite the feel of a rear-drive car. **1973** *Jrnl. Genetic Psychol.* June 255 The stimuli ..were rear-projected onto a 27·9 cm^2 opaque glass screen. **1977** *Lancashire Life* Jan. 79/1 No rear drive Citroen has been made since the 1930s.

c. At the rear, as *rear-engined, -mounted.*

1933 *Motor* 10 Oct. 524/1 The rear-engined Trojan. **1957** *Sci. News Let.* 23 Mar. 190/1 Rear-engined cars are here to stay. **1960** *Farmer & Stockbreeder* 19 Jan. 90/1 In this country the accepted method of handling silage has been by means of a rear-mounted buckrake. **1975** *Drive* New Year 102/2 The protesting chatter from the air-cooled rear-mounted engine is more a symptom of asthma than mechanical stress. **1976** P. R. WHITE *Planning for Public Transport* iii. 56 The higher maintenance costs and poorer availability of the rear-engined models.

9. rear echelon *U.S. Mil.*, that section of an army concerned with administrative and supply duties; also *transf.*; **rear end,** (*a*) the back part or section (of anything, esp. a vehicle); (*b*) *slang*, the backside or buttocks (of a person); hence as *v. trans.* (N. Amer.), to collide, or cause (one's vehicle) to collide, with the rear end of another vehicle; **rear-ender,** a rear-end collision; **rear gunner,** a member of the crew of a military aircraft who operates a gun from a compartment or turret at the rear of the aircraft; **rear-lamp, -light,** a (usu. red) lamp at the rear of a vehicle which can be switched on to serve as a warning light in the dark; **rear mirror,** a rear-view mirror (see **rear-view* attrib.); **rear pillar** (see quot. 1930); **rear projection** = *back projection* s.v. *BACK-B; **rearsight,** a part of a camera viewfinder, situated at the back, to which the eye is applied; **rear-view** *attrib.*, giving a view to the rear; *spec.* of a mirror inside a motor vehicle in front of the driver.

1934 WEBSTER, Rear echelon. **1947** *Amer. Speech* XXII. 55 *Rear echelon commando*, a soldier assigned to the rear. **1967** *Boston Sunday Herald* 7 May III. 14/2 The number [of servicewomen] in Vietnam will remain small, chiefly because there is no large 'rear echelon' setup of the kind maintained in Europe in World War II. **1977** P. JOHNSON *Enemies of Society* xii. 165 This shaky argument, of the type which convinced the rear echelons of the Gadarene swine, carried the day. **1868** Rear end [see sense 7 b in Dict.]. **1926** *Daily Colonist* (Victoria, B.C.) 19 Jan. 5/3 Two passengers were killed and fifty injured today in a rear-end collision of..two subway trains. **1937** J. WEIDMAN *I can get it for you Wholesale* xxviii. 268 She's a pain in the rear end. **1961** *Amer. Speech* XXXVI. 273 *Rear end*,..the differentials of a tractor. **1967** G. KELLY in *Coast to Coast 1965–6* 95 Blokes my age are sitting on their rear-ends ordering the rest.. around. **1976** *Islander* (Victoria, B.C.) 1 Aug. 3/4 A driver came to an abrupt stop in front of me. I slithered all over the wet road but did I rearend her? Of course not. **1978** *Detroit Free Press* 2 Apr. 3A/1 The men, who were on a chartered city bus traveling to a football game in 1972 when it was rear-ended by another bus, rejected a settlement of $500 apiece and took their case to the jury. **1932** *Erie Railroad Mag.* Apr. 46/1 With all his fast running I never knew of him piling them up, of any but a few derailments and never a rear-ender. **1920** *Flight* XII. 11/1 A central passage leads through to what in the military machine was the rear gunner's cockpit, which is now occupied by the 'postman'. **1944** 'N. SHUTE' *Pastoral* i. 3 He had developed into a very good rear-gunner in the Wimpey. **1977** *R.A.F. News* 27 Apr.–10 May 8/2 The aircraft was hit again and again and the rear gunner was wounded. **1907** *Westm. Gaz.* 17 Sept. 4/2 When the compulsory carrying of rear-lamps has been suggested the proposal has always been violently resisted. **1937** *East London Rubber Co. Ltd. Motor Catal.* 154/2 Top covers for rear lamps. **1918** A. QUILLER-COUCH *Foe-Farrell* iii. 54 The car purred and glided away... We watched the rearlight turn the corner. **1967** N. FREELING *Strike out where not Applicable* 159 There is nothing that looks so like the rear lights of a car as the rear lights of another car. **1968** Rear mirror [see G.T. s.v. *G III. f]. **1930** *Motor Body Building* LI. 105/1 *Rear pillar*, a vertical frame member at the back corner of the body. **1977** Rear pillar [see *PILLAR *sb.* 2 c]. **1960** *Practical Wireless* XXXVI. 316/2 A team of demonstrators who operated the sequence of exhibit animations, rear projection films and synchronised sound and provided a live commentary. **1976** BOTHAM & DONNELLY *Valentino* xii. 93 Working behind the screen, with rear-projection to help them follow the story. **1971** *Amateur Photogr.* 13 Jan. 50/3 The rearsight is quite large, has a permanently attached rubber eye-cup and is adjustable between +1 to −4 dioptres to suit individual eyesight. **1978** *Ibid.* 2 Aug. 79/2 Accessories included: carrying strap, body cap, rearsight rubber eyecup, etc. **1926** Rear-view [see *DRIVING *vbl. sb.* 3 a]. **1959** H. NIELSEN *Fifth Caller* xiii. 195 His face had been in the rearview mirror. **1969** G. MACBETH *War Quartet* 17 For the moment they were framed In rear-view mirrors. **1974** V. NABOKOV *Look at Harlequins* (1975) IV. iv. 173, I see today..the rearview reflection of that sweet wild past.

rear, *v.*^{1} Add: **II. 9. c.** Also const. *into.*

1871 BROWNING *Prince Hohenstiel-Schwangau* 52 To play at horticulture, rear some rose Or poppy into perfect leaf and bloom.

III. 10. b. *fig.* phr. *to rear its* (*ugly*) *head*, and varr. = *to raise its* (*ugly*) *head* s.v. *RAISE *v.*^{1} 17 e.

1857 TROLLOPE *Barchester T.* II. viii. 124 Rebellion had already reared her hideous head within the [bishop's] palace. **1946** K. TENNANT *Lost Haven* (1947) vii. 96 Another problem reared its ugly head. **1966** B. KIMENYE *Kalasanda Revisited* 21 Scandal of even the mildest type failed to rear its head. **1971** *Daily Tel.* 5 July 1 The problem of broken rails is rearing its ugly head again in the current spate of railway accidents. **1976** *0–10 Cricket Scene* (Austral.) 21/1 They crumbled as their inexperience reared its ugly head.

rear-guard^1. Add: **2. b.** *rear-guard action*, a defensive stand by the rear-guard of a retreating army. Also *fig.*

1898 [in Dict., sense 2]. **1946** *Ess. & Stud.* XXXI. 46 Yet this scene is a magnificent rear-guard action by Cleopatra. **1954** F. C. AVIS *Boxing Ref. Dict.* 93 *Rearguard action*, defensive boxing. **1977** *World of Cricket Monthly* June 29/1 It was left to Murray and Roberts to provide a defiant rearguard action which postponed the end

reargue, *v.* Add: Also *absol.* or *intr.*

1972 *N.Y. Law Jrnl.* 31 Oct. 15/5 The informal motion to reargue is granted. **1973** *Ibid.* 31 Aug. 2/5 A letter from counsel for South Wall Associates, which shall be deemed a motion to reargue.

rear-horse. (Earlier and later examples.)

1869 *Rep. U.S. Comm. Agric. 1868* 308 The *Mantes* or 'rear-horses' prey upon other insects. **1900** *Everybody's Mag.* July 21 Most people are acquainted with the praying mantis—otherwise known as the 'rearhorse'. **1935** H. T. FERNALD *Appl. Entomology* (ed. 3) xvi. 87 They [*sc.* mantids] are often called rearhorses, devil-horses,..or mule killers.

rearing, *vbl. sb.* Add: **5. b.** (Further example.)

1967 K. M. SMITH *Insect Virol.* x. 184 The hot medium is poured into rearing jars.

6. rearing-house, a building in which young chickens are kept.

1824 J. H. BARLOW *Hatching Poultry by Steam* 15 The Rearing House is of the same size and dimensions as the Hatching House, in which Fowls are kept until they are three weeks or a month old. **1948** L. ROBINSON *Mod. Poultry Husbandry* xi. 227 When growing stock are first placed in arks or other types of range rearing-house, a temporary run of wire netting should be erected. **1962** D. DE SAULLES *Pictorial Poultry Keeping* (ed. 2) This pullet is just about ready to be taken from the rearing house and put into laying quarters. **1975** T. ALLBEURY *Special Collection* xxiii. 168 The lights were on in the rearing house... He could hear the shrill noise of eight thousand week-old chicks.

rearing, *ppl. a.* Add: **3.** = *raring* adj. s.v. *RARE *v.* 1 b.

1926 G. FRANKAU *My Unsentimental Journey* viii. 104 A good many of the eight hundred other diners were 'raring' (Anglicé—rearing) 'to go'. **1947** H. WALSH *Fourth Point of Star* 34, I am rearing to talk this business over with her. **1963** *Listener* 28 Feb. 393/3 Inside most liberal Lincolnographers there seems to be a Lincolnolater rearing to genuflect.

rearing crew. *N. Amer.* [app. f. REAR *sb.*^{3}] = *rear-crew* s.v. REAR *sb.*^{3} 9.

1963 R. D. SYMONS *Many Trails* xviii. 184 The last men.. will form the nucleus of the 'rearing crew'—that is, the crew which will bring up the rear of the drive, taking care to roll into the water any logs left stranded on the banks. **1971** *Daily Progress* (Charlottesville, Va.) 6 May 7-D/5 Freeing stranded logs is the job of a 32-man 'rearing crew', which works seven days a week with power boats, winches and occasionally a stick of dynamite.

rearmament. (Later examples.)

1905 *Daily Chron.* 14 Mar. 1/7 The artillery rearmament scheme accounts for £1,213,000. **1935** *Hansard Commons* 22 May 363 Re-armament that could not fail to cause all lovers of peace considerable anxiety. **1938** *Encycl. Brit. Bk. of Year* 60/2 In Great Britain the economic consequences of re-armament are..rather intangible and remote. **1938,** etc. [see *Moral Rearmament* s.v. *MORAL *a.* 7 f]. **1961** *Daily Worker* 25 May 2 Without Britain's tolerance German rearmament in the air would be jeopardised.

rearou·sal. [f. RE-AROUSE *v.*] A second or further arousal.

1934 in WEBSTER. **1949** M. MEAD *Male & Female* IV. xiv. 293 The demon to be avoided..is lack of potency, defined in a number of quantitative ways—frequency, time, interval before rearousal.

re-arrange, *v.* (Earlier example.)

1824 DE QUINCEY in *London Mag.* Jan. 5/2, I have therefore abstracted, re-arranged, and in some respects..have improved, the German work on this subject.

re-arti·culate, *v.* [RE- 5 a.] To articulate for a second or further time. So **re-arti·culated** *ppl. a.*

1963 *Economist* 21 Sept. 987/2 A wholly rearticulated Office of External Relations. **1964** *Language* XL. 78 Verbs with rearticulated root vowel often appear in apocopated form in rapid speech. **1964** E. PALMER tr. *Martinet's Elem. General Linguistics* ii. 45 The necessity..of re-articulating a foreign mode of experience to conform to the model which is familiar to us. **1973** MATIAS & WILLEMEN tr. M. Cegarra in *Screen* Spring/Summer 177 It is clearly the whole notion of film rhetoric which needs to be re-articulated.

rearward, *adv.* Add: **1. c.** *Comb.*, as *rearward-facing, -hinged* adjs.

1955 *Times* 23 June 4/4 It had been decided in Australia to have rearward-facing seats. **1959** *Economist* 13 June 1042/1 The engine drives a ducted fan, which supplies compressed air to two concentric rings of jet openings facing downward..while rearward-facing jets propel it. **1967** *Jane's Surface Skimmer Systems 1967–68* 25/1 There is a rearward-hinged car-type door on each side of the cabin.

rearwardly, *adv.* (Later examples.)

1888 *Engineer* 4 May 374/3 Having a handle..extending rearwardly beyond the suction tube. **1934** *Canad. Patent Office Rec.* 30 Oct. 2464/1 Beams extending..rearwardly of the rear axle. **1946** A. W. JUDGE *Mod. Petrol Engines* vi. 237 The cooling air..leaves the engine cowling through a rearwardly inclined exit. **1973** *Times* 30 Oct. 17/8 A reasonable proportion of the water is thrown rearwardly.

rearwardness (rīə·ɹwəɹdnės). *rare.* [f. REARWARD *a.* + -NESS.] The state of being in the rear or in arrears.

1903 *T.P.'s Weekly* 16 Oct. 621/2 It is advantageous to keep oneself quite a year behind contemporary literature; this rearwardness saves both time and money.

re-ascе·nded, *ppl. a.* [f. REASCEND *v.* + -ED[1].] That has ascended again.

a **1838** R. GRANT *Sacred Poems* (1839) 8 Oh! from earth to heav'n restor'd, Mighty re-ascended Lord. **1906** *Westm. Gaz.* 14 Apr. 6/2 Rise, O saints..Round your re-ascended Sun circling soar!

reason, *sb.*[1] Add: **II. 5. c.** Phr. *for reasons best known to oneself,* for seemingly perverse reasons.

1638 W. CHILLINGWORTH *Relig. Protestants* 84 Yet it hath pleased God (for Reasons best known to himselfe) not to allow us this convenience. **1743** FIELDING *Jonathan Wild* IV. xiii. 383 Indeed those, who have unluckily missed it, seem all their Days to have laboured in vain to attain an End, which Fortune, for Reasons only known to herself, hath thought proper to deny them. **1847** A. BRONTË *Agnes Grey* xiii. 191 If they chose to 'take' me, I went; if, for reasons best known to themselves, they chose to go alone, I took my seat in the carriage. **1894** SOMERVILLE & 'Ross' *Real Charlotte* III. xli. 133 Removing his pipe and the hat which, for reasons best known to himself, he wore while at work. **1938** G. GRAHAM *Swiss Sonata* vi. 250 She tried very hard to adopt me, but my father, for reasons best known to himself, wouldn't give me up.

III. 10. e. *the age of reason, (a)* (freq. with capital initials) the late seventeenth and eighteenth centuries in Western Europe, during which cultural life was characterized by faith in human reason; the Enlightenment (cf. ENLIGHTENMENT 2); *(b) R. C. Ch.*, the age at which a child is capable of discerning right from wrong and can be held responsible for his or her actions; also *loosely.*

(a) **1794** T. PAINE *(title)* The age of reason; being an investigation of true and fabulous theology. **1902** CHESTERTON *Twelve Types* 129 Carlyle..denied every one of the postulates upon which the age of reason based itself. **1926** R. H. TAWNEY *Relig. & Rise of Capitalism* i. 61 The sanguine optimists of the Age of Reason. **1971** R. J. WHITE *Second-Hand Tomb* xviii. 200 You medieval scholars suffer from a double dose of spiritual pride where the Age of Reason is concerned.
(b) **1884** ADDIS & ARNOLD *Cath. Dict.* 17/1 The age of reason is generally supposed to begin about the seventh year... At that time a child becomes capable of mortal sin. **1947** E. SUTTON tr. *Sartre's Age of Reason* viii. 126 You have..reached the age of reason, my poor Mathieu...but you try to dodge that fact too, you try to pretend you're younger than you are. *Ibid.* xviii. 360 He yawned again as he repeated to himself: 'It's true, it's absolutely true: I have attained the age of reason.' **1955** tr. *Maupassant's Compl. Short Stories* 1237, I am seven years old today. As it is the age of reason, I want to thank you for having brought me into this world. **1974** *Oxf. Dict. Chr. Ch.* (ed. 2) 24/1 The attainment of the age of reason is commonly marked by a child's First Communion.

V. 23. *reason-monger; reason-contained, -giving, -wrought* adjs.

1973 *Art Internat.* Mar. 75/2 The frost of the passage, its chill, reason-contained fire is even more remarkable. **1855** BAGEHOT in *Nat. Rev.* July 36 The strong analytic, comprehensive, reason-giving powers..were utterly foreign to his mind. **1933** DELL & BAYNES tr. *Jung's Mod. Man in Search of Soul* viii. 186 In works of art of this nature..we cannot doubt that the vision is a genuine, primordial experience, regardless of what reason-mongers may say. **1906** HARDY *Dynasts* II. I. ii. 152 Here, then, ends My hope for Europe's reason-wrought repose!

reason, *v.* Add: **6. b.** (Later example.)

1900 *Outrageous Fortune* x. 117 There is little need now to recapitulate those arguments with which I reasoned down the dictates of my better nature.

c. To drive *away* or *off* by reasoning.

1839 E. A. POE in *Burton's Gentleman's Mag.* (Philadelphia) Sept. 150, I struggled to reason off the nervousness which had dominion over me. **1854** M. L. CHARLESWORTH *Ministering Children* ix. 139 Let the sinner then beware how he reasons away and rejects the awful Word of God. **1866** M. C. HARRIS *Christine* xiv. 74 It was very natural, the doctor said to himself, trying to reason away the pain he felt.

reasonability. (Further example.)

1973 *Atlantic Monthly* June 58/2 In those early days of knowing him, I still believed in reasonability.

reasonable, *a.* Add: **8.** *reasonable-sized* adj.

1965 E. JUTIKKALA in Glass & Eversley *Population in Hist.* xxiii. 554 The only reasonable-sized city in Finland, Turku,..must be discussed separately from the surrounding province.

reasonably, *adv.* Add: **5.** *Comb.*, as *reasonably-priced, -sized* adjs.

1902 *Daily Chron.* 22 June 3/3 See that reasonably-priced meals are provided. **1960** *Farmer & Stockbreeder* 8 Mar. 77/3 A reasonably-priced flowmeter was necessary. **1968** FOX & MAYERS *Computing Methods for Scientists & Engineers* v. 76 That is if the elements of the inverse matrix A^{-1} are large for reasonably-sized A.

reasoned, *ppl. a.* Add: **a.** (Later example.)

1904 E. F. BENSON *Challoners* vii. 146 He would sooner have mated her with a thief or an adulterer..than with a reasoned atheist.

b. *reasoned amendment,* an amendment to a bill in Parliament that seeks to prevent a further reading by proposing reasons for the alteration or rejection of the bill.

1909 *Times* 9 Nov. 10/3 Such an amendment would..have obvious advantages over the longer form which is known as a reasoned amendment. **1975** *Daily Tel.* 23 July 1 The Conservative 'reasoned amendment'..supported the Government's belated commitment to reduce the disastrous rate of inflation.

c. *reasoned bibliography* [cf. *CATALOGUE RAISONNÉ], a descriptive survey of relevant books and articles appended to an essay or the like.

1958 *Listener* 11 Sept. 392/3 The fourth essay..which..is accompanied by a reasoned bibliography of formidable fullness. **1969** *Archiv* CCV. 490 Her reasoned bibliography ranges as far afield as Calcutta and Hiroshima.

re-aspire, *v.* (Later example.)

1936 R. CAMPBELL *Mithraic Emblems* 17 From the sacred flames they feast In hymns of incense re-aspire To praise His throne of silver fire.

reassemble, *v.* Add: **2.** Also *fig.*

1945 P. LARKIN *North Ship* 9 The meadows are bright With the coldest dew; The dawn reassembles.

reasse·mbled, reasse·mbling *ppl. adjs.*

1904 *Westm. Gaz.* 21 Oct. 2/3 The first sitting of the reassembled Chambers. **1906** *Macmillan's Mag.* Apr. 438 To my reassembling senses..came the realisation of a greater tragedy. **1977** W. M. SPACKMAN *Armful of Warm Girl* 88 Nicolas collected his wits enough to follow, with a re-assembled smile.

reassertion. (Earlier example.)

1843 MILL *Logic* I. II. i. 221 That cannot be called reasoning or inference which is a mere reassertion in different words of what had been asserted before.

reassignment. (Examples.)

1884 [see RE- 5 a]. **1960** *Amer. Speech* XXXV. 216 Hoenigswald recognizes the following types of sound change:..split from reassignment of noncontrasting phones. **1976** *National Observer* (U.S.) 18 Dec. 2/4 The Appeals Court..ordered reassignment of 20,000 to 30,000 students—up to half the student total—to achieve racial balance. **1978** *N.Y. Times* 29 Mar. B4/4 Sent..Sam Perlozzo, second baseman, to minor leagues for reassignment.

reassimilate, *v.* (Example.)

1952 G. SARTON *Hist. Sci.* I. xvi. 395 Another result of the long wars was the existence of a relatively large body of veterans who..could not be easily reassimilated.

reassociate, *v.* (Later example.)

1964 G. H. HAGGIS et al. *Introd. Molecular Biol.* xi. 293 When the pH is brought back to neutrality the α and β pairs reassociate into the four-unit molecule.

Hence **re:associa·tion.**

1923 J. S. HUXLEY *Essays of Biologist* iv. 152 Dissociation in most cases is not complete;..now and again re-association of the parts [of the mind] occurs. **1953** HINSIE & CAMPBELL *Psychiatric Dict.* (ed. 2) 738/2 *Reassociation,* a process of renewed or refreshed association occurring in hypnoanalysis of the war neurosis, during which the patient relives the traumatic event with emotional vividness. Such forgotten experiences will then become a part of his normal personality and consciousness. **1977** *Proc. R. Soc. Med.* LXX. 560/1 Nucleic acid reassociation experiments indicate that at least a proportion of tumour cells carry virus genetic material.

reassortment. (Later examples.)

1959 B. WOOTTON *Social Sci. & Social Path.* xi. 330 He may break down under the stress of the eleven-plus reassortment. **1971** D. J. COVE *Genetics* i. 8 The formation of a zygote by the gametes of the two different strains, followed by the production of ascospores must provide an opportunity for the shuffling or reassortment of genetic information affecting different characters.

reassurer. (Earlier example.)

1787 J. A. PARK *Marine Insurances* xv. 315 Re-assurance..may be said to be a contract, which the first insurer enters into, in order to relieve himself from those risks which he has incautiously undertaken, by throwing them upon other underwriters, who are called re-assurers.

reassu·ring, *vbl. sb.* [f. REASSURE *v.* + -ING[1].] The action of the verb REASSURE.

1865 in WEBSTER. **1902** 'MARK TWAIN' in *Harper's Weekly* 6 Dec. 5/2 Alfred..did what he could..to respond with some show of heart to the Major's kindly pettings and reassurings.

reasty, *a.* For '† *Obs.* exc. *dial.*' read 'chiefly *dial.*' and add: **1.** (Later examples.)

1914 C. MACKENZIE *Sinister Street* II. IV. ii. 859 A luxurious mournfulness was in the view, and he leaned out over the sill scenting the reasty London air. **1959** *Listener* 10 Dec. 1035/2, I paid for all mistakes with drops of sweat Strained from the reasty gammon of my pain. **1964** J. HALE *Grudge Fight* v. 76 What you'll do is shut your trap and get back to your reasty pit. **1974** P. WRIGHT *Lang. Brit. Industry* xvii. 166 In some homes..bacon with a strong nasty taste is not rancid but *reasty.* **1978** *Jrnl. Lancs. Dial. Soc.* XXVII. 13 Please, Looard, send summat good to eyt; Not reeasty bacon or fatty meyt.

reattach, *v.* Add: **2.** (Later examples.)

1921 O. E. INGLIS *Burchard's Textbk. Dental Path. & Therapeutics* (ed. 6) VI. xxviii. 777 The first indication [of when a tooth has been forced out by accident] has ever been acted upon by parents who have quickly pressed teeth into their places where they became reattached. **1952** W. H. ARCHER *Manual of Oral Surg.* i. 41/2 The tooth became re-attached, and circulation into the pulp tissue was re-established. **1957** G. RYLE in C. A. Mace *Brit. Philos. in Mid-Century* 254 The notion of meaning had been.. partly detached from the notion of naming and re-attached to the notion of saying.
refl. **1953** I. GLICKMAN *Clin. Periodontol.* xxxvii. 609 The problem hinges upon the question of whether the periodontal tissues reattach themselves to tooth surface previously denuded by disease..or whether they are attached at the level of the pre-existent pocket. **1980** D. WILLIAMS *Murder for Treasure* v. 45 The guard..had re-attached himself to Treasure's entourage.

Hence **reatta·ched** *ppl. a.*

1928 H. K. BOX *Treatm. Periodontal Pocket* III. 117 The arrangement of the reattached tissues on the curetted cemental surface.

reattachment. Add: **b.** *Dentistry.* The re-establishment of the connections between a tooth and the jaw.

1908 O. E. INGLIS *Burchard's Textbk. Dental Path. & Therapeutics* (ed. 3) IV. xv. 410 Kirk records a case of immediate replantation in early life, followed in old age by root resorption. The tooth when extracted contained secondary dentine, which could only have formed as the result of a reattachment of the pulp. **1928** H. K. BOX *Treatm. Periodontal Pocket* III. 103 Gentle digital pressure..appeared to be the only precaution taken to insure reattachment. **1953** I. GLICKMAN *Clin. Periodontol.* xxxvii. 609 The term 'reattachment' is to be used here to connote the restoration of gingival contour effected by the re-embedding of the periodontal membrane into newly formed cementum, and attachment of gingival epithelium to tooth surface denuded by periodontal disease. **1962** BLAKE & TROTT *Periodontol.* x. 96 By combined cementum and soft tissue curettage, it is possible to obtain a degree of attachment of soft tissue to cementum with a consequent real reduction in pocket depth... This is..called 'reattachment'.

reattempt, *v.* (Later examples.)

1861 M. ARNOLD *On Translating Homer* iii. 102, I think that the task of translating Homer into English verse both will be re-attempted, and may be re-attempted successfully. **1895** HARDY *Jude the Obscure* III. vi. 198 He had begun to sit in his parlour during the dark winter nights and re-attempt some of his old studies.

Réaumur. Delete ‖ and add after 'physicist': René-Antoine Ferchault de *Réaumur.*

a. Used *ellipt.* (in Dict.: further examples).

1799 MALTHUS *Jrnl.* 30 May (1966) 39 In the summer of 1793 the therm was 25 Reaumur. **1832** S. AUSTIN tr. *H. Pückler-Muskau's Tour in Germany, Holland & England* III. 196 The room..is regularly heated to a temperature of fourteen degrees Reaumur. **1950** 'G. ORWELL' *Shooting Elephant* 18, I had been unequal to translating Réaumur into Fahrenheit, but I know that my temperature was round about 103.

b. Used in the possessive and *attrib.* to designate various processes, materials, and concepts developed by him, as **Réaumur malleable iron,** a name for white-heart malleable cast iron; **Réaumur's porcelain,** a devitrified form of glass produced by prolonged exposure to heat near but below the fusion temperature, formerly used for chemical vessels; **Réaumur process,** a process for annealing iron leading to the production of white-heart malleable iron, first published by him in 1722; **Réaumur('s) scale,** his temperature scale (see Dict.).

1912 W. H. HATFIELD *Cast Iron* xiii. 195 Sample J..was a..sample of English Réaumur malleable cast iron. It consisted mainly of well-laminated pearlite, in which was immersed the remaining annealing carbon, with a skin of well-developed ferrite. **1832** G. R. PORTER *Porcelain & Glass* xvi. 317 M. Reaumur,..in..1739, communicated the result of these to the Royal Academy of Sciences in Paris. The subject becoming by this means more generally known, glass, when thus converted, obtained, and has since kept the name, of Reaumur's porcelain, a designation which it owes to its appearance rather than to its real properties. *Ibid.* 325 Glass has been converted into Reaumur's porcelain during volcanic eruptions, by being enveloped in burning lava. **1868** C. L. EASTLAKE *Hints Househ. Taste* x. 219 In the production of what is called Réaumur's porcelain, the formation of crystals may be determined by the application of heat lower than that necessary to effect the perfect fusion of the glass. **1918** P. MARSON *Glass* iii. 17 'Réaumur's Porcelain' is a glass in a devitrified state, and is used for pestles and mortars, devitrified glass being less brittle than ordinary glass and similar to vitrified porcelain. **1911** B. STOUGHTON *Metall. of Iron & Steel* (ed. 2) xiii. 356 In the original Réaumur process the castings are packed in iron oxide during the anneal, and this operation is carried on at a temperature of about 800 to 875°C..for a period of four or five days. **1949** J. E. GARSIDE *Process & Physical Metall.* xxi. 374 Malleable cast-irons are made by two methods—..(2) The Whiteheart process, also known as the European or Réaumur process. **1795** W. NICHOLSON *Dict. Chem.* II. 935 In Reaumur's scale, the number of degrees between these two points is 80. **1863** E. ATKINSON tr. *Ganot's Elementary Treatise on Physics* vi. i. 194 Besides the centigrade scale two others are frequently used—Fahrenheit's scale and Réaumur's scale. **1958** S. PETTERSSEN *Introd. Meteorol.* (ed. 2) ii. 20 The Reaumur scale was much used in Central Europe until the beginning of this century but has since gone out of use.

reave (rīv, rēⁱv), *sb. Archæol.* [Origin unknown: perh. f. OE. *rǣw* REW *sb.*[1]] A long low bank or wall found on Dartmoor.

1848 J. H. MASON in S. Rowe *Perambulation of Dartmoor* 130 In tracing the northernmost *reave* from Hamildon..we lost it in a tin-work. **1976** *Current Archaeol.* V. 250/2 Four major walls on the moor... The walls were known as reaves in local dialect (pronounced 'raves'). *Ibid.* 252/1 The lynchets seem to show that the reaves..were built by a people who already had fields laid out in parallel strips. **1978** *Antiquity* Mar. 16/1 Dartmoor reaves..(the word derives from the Old English *raew*, meaning a row) are long, low banks, constructed mainly of stone, and often covered in vegetation. These may run for any distance up to 15 km, and they may reach 0·5 m or more in height.

reb[1]**.** For *U.S.* read 'Chiefly *U.S.*' and add: (Further examples.) Also *spec.* = *REBEL *sb.*[1] 1 e; cf. *Johnny Reb* s.v. *JOHNNY, JOHNNIE 3. Also *attrib.*

1897 KIPLING *Captains Courageous* iii. 62 Earnin' my bread on the deep waters, an' dodgin' Reb privateers. **1904** —— *Traffics & Discoveries* 31 Then we got into the Colony [*sc.* Orange Free State], and the rebs—ministers mostly and schoolmasters—came round the cars with fruit and sympathy and texts. **1909** 'O. HENRY' *Options* (1916) 81 The alleged aristocratic superiority of a 'reb' ought to be visible to him at once. **1916** 'TAFFRAIL' *Pincher Martin* v. 73 They wanted me to order the rebs. to shove off. **1928** S. V. BENÉT *John Brown's Body* 181 'Hello, Charley,' he said, 'Where you been?'..'Out hearing the Rebs,' he said. **1938** J. DANIELS *Southerner Discovers South* xxxv. 346 The boy..insisted in the hospital that he was the best alligator catcher on the coast of Georgia. Perhaps he was. Maybe still one Reb can beat ten Yankees. **1947** *Sierra Club Bull.* May 80 The stars and stripes, the flag of our now united country raised in honor of our visit, and I, an old battle-scarred and weather-worn Reb. **1963** *Amer. Speech* XXXVIII. 45 *Reb*, a Southern driver or a Southern trucking firm. **1979** S. SHEPPARD *Four Hundred* i. 4 A certain scheme for separating some of the Rebs from their money.

reb[2] (reb). Also **rebb** and with capital initial. [Yiddish, *abbrev.* of *rebbe* *REBBE.] A traditional Jewish courtesy title prefixed to a man's first name or surname.

1882 [see *KEHILLA]. **1892** I. ZANGWILL *Childr. Ghetto* I. 147 'Well, how goes it, Reb Moshé?' said Reb Shemuel.., noticing Moses loitering. He called him 'Reb' out of courtesy and in acknowledgement of his piety. The real 'Reb' was a fine figure of a man. **1932** L. GOLDING *Magnolia Street* I. v. 84 The beard of Reb Berel, the beadle, was in attendance. **1967** C. POTOK *Chosen* i. 15 Reb Saunders ordered them never to lose because it would shame their yeshiva. **1975** *Publishers Weekly* 3 Feb. 75/3 A ragged stranger stands by the door of the synagogue... The boy whispers to the woman that the stranger, reb Naftoli, is a *badchen*, a merrymaker, who speaks in rhymes. **1978** I. B. SINGER *Shosha* ix. 170 We had a preacher in our family—Reb Zekele Preacher, they called him.

rebab (rĭbæ·b). Also **rabab(a, rabap, rebaba, rubabah,** etc. [a. colloq. Arab. *rebāb*, classical Arab. *rabāb* in the same sense: cf. RIBIBE *sb.*] A plucked or bowed stringed instrument of Arabian origin, now in use in North Africa and the Middle East, and among the Islamic populations of the Indian sub-continent, Malaysia, and Indonesia.

1738 [see *OUD]. **1802** *Jrnl. F. Horneman's Trav.* iii. 72 The song of these Fezzan girls is Soudanic. Their musical instrument is called *rhababe*. **1836** E. W. LANE *Acct. Manners & Customs Mod. Egyptians* II. v. 73 A curious kind of viol, called rabab, is much used by poor singers, as an accompaniment to the voice. **1856** R. F. BURTON *Personal Narr. Pilgrimage to El-Medinah* III. ii. 76 They have the one-stringed Rubabah, or guitar. **1925** *Blackw. Mag.* Feb. 217/2 Zakka Khel the *Subedar* played cunningly, on the rebab, an instrument like a mandoline. **1929** F. STARK *Let.* 22 Dec. (1974) I. 226 Mahmud..got his *rebaba*, played with the fingers and a bow on one string, and they [*sc.* Bedouin tribesmen in Iraq] showed us the four different modes of their music. **1937** M. COVARRUBIAS *Island of Bali* (1972) viii. 213 There are other instruments, such as..the two-string violin (*rebab*), which are used mainly as a lead for the melody. **1958** O. CAROE *Pathans* xix. 309 There were performers who chanted to the *rabap*. **1960** G. E. EVANS *Horse in Furrow* xiii. 177 In Arabia the poet singer to the 'rebab' (lute with one string and a bow) is a recognised authority who dare not for his life deviate by a word from the known facts. **1967** I. DIQS *Bedouin Boyhood* xi. 104 Long minutes later I heard some broken tunes sent up by the *rababa*. **1972** M. SHEPPARD *Taman Indera* iii. 57 (*caption*) A [Malay] maker of musical instruments, working on a *rebab*. **1976** *Listener* 17 June 784/2 A musician in eastern Afghanistan who played a rebab, a bowed string instrument he had made out of a biscuit tin and a broom handle.

reback (rībæ·k), *v.* [f. RE- 5 a + BACK *v.* 2.] *trans.* To replace the damaged spine of (a binding or book). So **reba·cked** *ppl. a.*, **reba·cking** *vbl. sb.*

1901 D. COCKERELL *Bookbinding* xxii. 305 Re-backing. Bindings that have broken joints may be re-backed. **1952** J. CARTER *ABC for Book-Collectors* 150 Re-backed. This means that the binding of the book has been given a new backstrip or spine. **1970** *Bodl. Libr. Rec.* VIII. 192 Although it [*sc.* an eighteenth-century New Testament] has been rebacked and repaired..it is now very worn. **1981** *Sotheby's Catal. Printed Bks.* 16 Mar. 34, 179 Lambarde (W.), Dictionarium Angliae Topographicum & Historicum, portrait, calf, rebacked, 1730.

re-bar (rī·bāɹ). *U.S.* [f. RE(INFORCING *ppl. a.* + BAR *sb.*[1]] A steel reinforcing rod in concrete.

1961 *Publ. Amer. Dial. Soc.* XXXVI. 29 *Re-bar*,..abbreviated term for reinforcing steel, which is used to strengthen nearly all concrete structures. **1974** *Spartanburg* (S. Carolina) *Herald* 24 Apr. A1/6 Reinforcing steel bars, known in the industry as re-bars, are used to reinforce concrete in the construction of highways, bridges, buildings and other structures. **1979** *Civil Engineering* Nov. 39/2 A rebar bolt has exponential load transfer characteristics.

rebarbarization. (Further example.)

1949 WELLEK & WARREN *Theory of Lit.* 340 For the 'rebarbarization' of literature, cf. the brilliant article, 'Literature' by Max Lerner and Edwin Mims.

rebarbative, *a.* Delete *rare* and substitute for def.: Repellent, forbidding; unattractive, dull; unpleasant, objectionable. (Further examples.)

1927 *Observer* 1 May 20 The small minority that is not put off by the dry and rebarbative quality of the tuition. **1946** BEERBOHM *Mainly on Air* 67 Even A. B. Walkley..found Ibsen rather rebarbative. **1958** I. MURDOCH *Bell* iv. 48 Still, everyone appeared to be extremely nice, except that that Dr. Greenfield man was a trifle rebarbative. (This was a word which Toby had recently learnt at school and could not now conceive of doing without.) **1958** J. PRESS *Chequer'd Shade* i. 12 Unless he commands sufficient poetic authority to compel the general acceptance of his minted coinage his work will inevitably be judged rebarbative and obscure. **1963** *Listener* 7 Mar. 436/1 Some rebarbative club member does seem to have opened one or two windows in the smoking-room. **1971** P. D. JAMES *Shroud for Nightingale* iii. 63 Her face matched her personality, rebarbative and defensive. **1976** *Gramophone* Aug. 266/1 An accessible musical language can be equally deceptive and pose as many (though of course different) problems as an entirely novel and rebarbative idiom.

Hence **reba·rbatively** *adv.*; **reba·rbativeness**; **rebarbati·vity.**

1947 I. BROWN *Say Word* 102 Is Max our only dealer in rebarbativity? **1966** *Punch* 16 Nov. 754/3 A veritable drummer boy, all knobbly North Country rebarbativeness and almost incomprehensible obsolete dialect. **1968** I. MURDOCH *Nice & Good* vii. 57 Beyond Uncle Theo were some alien holiday-makers,..of whom this part of the beach happily attracted few, because of its rebarbatively stony nature. **1975** M. AMIS *Dead Babies* lvii. 214 During the Americans' twenty-minute absence from the sitting-room Celia joined in her husband's wholly successful attempt..to moderate Roxeanne's rebarbativeness to the odd aside. **1976** *Listener* 22 Apr. 495/1 A rejection of formal logic and with it of a rebarbatively technical foundation and medium for philosophical thinking.

rebat(e, varr. *RABAT *v.*

rebate, *sb.*[1] Add: Now usu. with pronunc. (rī·bēⁱt). (Further, incl. *attrib.*, examples.) Also *Comb.*

1869 *Bradshaw's Railway Man.* XXI. 448 Rebate account..£1,348. **1907** *Daily Chron.* 9 Dec. 4/3 They cannot dislodge the Welsh makers [of tin-plates] from their hold of the rebate trade. **1908** *Times* 1 Feb. 5/2 The rebate-taker, the franchise-trafficker, the manipulator of securities..and the man-killer all alike work at the same web of corruption. **1908** *Daily Chron.* 1 Feb. 5/3 The President [*sc.* Roosevelt] attacks by name..the Atchison and Santa Fé Railway..for its rebate practices and intervention in the money market. **1955** *Times* 10 May 15/3 An interesting feature of German price lists for the outside world is the appearance of rebates to shipbuilders—rebates for indirect exports, which recall the cartel. **1957** CLARK & GOTTFRIED *University Dict. Business & Finance* 292 In current usage, a rebate is distinguished from a discount in that the former is not taken out or deducted in advance, but is handed back after payment of the full amount. **1965** H. K. COMPTON *Gloss. Purchasing & Supplies Managem. Terms* 115 *Rebate*, an allowance (or discount) on price, usually given after the completion of the contract, and most frequently based on some relationship with the business turnover. **1965** *McGraw-Hill Dict. Mod. Econ.* 426 Rebates to large and more favored shippers were used extensively in the U.S. railroad industry in the nineteenth century as a form of price discrimination. **1976** *Milton Keynes Express* 2 July 21/2 The decision to ban rebate tenants at Fishermead was revealed in this month's issue of the magazine 'City Limits'.

rebate *v.*[1] Add: **2. d.** To pay back (a sum of money) as a rebate; to give a rebate on.

1957 CLARK & GOTTFRIED *University Dict. Business & Finance* 292/2 Under customs regulations..import duties paid on goods which are later re-exported may be rebated in part or in full. **1977** *Time* 21 Feb. 49/1 Much of the energy tax would have to be rebated in some form to the poor to help them meet higher living expenses.

Hence **rebatable** (rĭbēⁱ·tăb'l, rī·bēⁱ:tăb'l), *a.*

1972 *Daily Tel.* 15 Feb. 17 The CBI's two main recommendations are a 2½ p.c. cut in corporation tax..and a halving of the rebatable heavy oil duty.

rebb, var. *REB[2].

rebbe (re·bə). Also with capital initial. [Yiddish, f. Heb. *rabbī* RABBI *sb.*] A rabbi; *spec.* a Chasidic religious leader.

1881 *Encycl. Brit.* XIII. 681/2 The Zaddikim (or 'righteous') and Rebbés, as their leaders are called, live in magnificence upon the contributions of the most ignorant of the people. **1882** [see *CHEDAR]. **1965** J. A. MICHENER *Source* (1966) 45 Two others prayed in loud voices on a line of their own, while the old rebbe, incredibly ancient, Cullinane thought, mumbled prayers that no one else could have heard. **1967** *N.Y. Times* 22 Mar. 29 (Advt.), The Lubavitcher Rebbe, Rabbi..Schneerson, has issued his annual call to world Jewry to observe the Purim festival. **1978** I. B. SINGER *Shosha* xiv. 243 To me..you are my rebbe. Your every word is filled with wisdom and love of God as well.

rebbitzin (re·bitsin). Also **rebbetzin, rebbitzen** and with capital initial. [Yiddish, fem. of *REBBE.] The wife of a rabbi.

1892 I. ZANGWILL *Childr. Ghetto* I. iv. 110 'His third wife was Kitty Green..,' persisted the Rebbitzin. **1926** S. ASH *Kiddush Ha-Shem* II. ii. 109 She was standing in the next room together with her mother, the *rebbetzin*. **1965** J. A. MICHENER *Source* (1966) 670 For the next ten years Leah, the young rebbetzin of Eliezer bar Zadok, knew only the Judenstrasse. **1966** H. KEMELMAN *Saturday Rabbi went Hungry* (1967) xxxvii. 236, I just called the hospital and they told me the rebbitzen had a boy. **1972** —— *Monday Rabbi took Off* v. 43 Believe me, the *rebbitzin* is real class, a Wellesley graduate. **1978** I. B. SINGER *Shosha* xii. 212 Mother's old-fashioned clothes brought a condescending expression from the rebbitzen.

rebec. Now the usual form of REBECK *sb.*[2] a (in Dict. and Suppl.).

1755 [see REBECK *sb.*[2] a]. **1915** A. DOLMETSCH *Interpretat. Mus. 17th & 18th Cent.* vii. 463 A little band consisting of a bass-viol, a tenor viol, a violin or rebec..and a flute. **1932** R. DONINGTON *Work & Ideas A. Dolmetsch* 15 It is probably the rebecs that are the nearest relatives of the violins... A number of fine rebecs have recently been finished... Now that the difficulties of the preliminary research work have been overcome..the rebecs are not difficult or costly to make. **1955** *Times* 20 May 3/5 A concert for children will consist of recorder and harpsichord pieces..and 'French brawls' for rebec and tambourin. **1980** *Early Music* Jan. 87/3 Progress Instruments, by applying modern plastics to make the backs of rebecs and plucked stringed instruments, are seeking to bring them within everyone's purse without sacrificing their authenticity of tone.

Rebecca. Add: **a.** (Further examples.)

1843 *Times* 10 Jan. 6/3 There has been..a mob of lawless depredators..who assembled nightly for the purpose of destroying the turnpike gates... These ruffians are headed by a very tall man, dressed for disguise as a female who goes by the name of Rebecca, and, as many of his associates are likewise dressed as females, the whole gang have been christened 'Rebecca and her daughters'. *Ibid.* 22 June 5/5 (*heading*) Rebecca riots.

c. Var. *REBEKAH.

Rebeccaite (earlier examples); also *transf.*

1843 A. SEDGWICK *Let.* 23 June in *Life* (1890) II. i. 56 Dress me like one of the Welsh Rebeccites [*sic*], and call me a water-nymph. **1878** F. KILVERT *Diary* 25 Nov. (1940) III. 434 A large party of Rebaccaites being out spearing salmon below Rhayader Bridge.

rebeck, *sb.*[2] For 'Now only *Hist.* or *poet.*' read 'Chiefly *Hist.*' See *REBEC.

re-become, *v.* (Further examples.)

1920 A. HUXLEY in E. Sitwell *Wheels* (Fifth Cycle) 35 And the stretched gargoyles re-become Women and men! **1938** L. MACNEICE *I crossed Minch* II. ix. 131 It is useless to ask you..to re-become your ancestor the Irish peasant.

re-beget, *v.* (Later example.)

1935 W. EMPSON *Poems* 19 Searching the cave gallery of your face My torch meets fresco after fresco ravishes Rebegets me.

re-begin, *v.* (Later example.)
1930 AUDEN *Poems* 44 And love's worn circuit re-begun.

Rebekah (rī·be·kă). *U.S.* Also **Rebecca.** [The form, in the Authorized Version of the Bible, of the name *Rebecca*, used in allusion to Gen. xxiv. 60.] A member of a society or 'order' of women, founded in Indiana in 1851 as a complementary organization to that of the Odd Fellows. Also *attrib.*
1860 C. E. DE LONG *Jrnl.* 27 July in *Calif. Hist. Soc. Q.* (1931) X. 252 Met in the Lodge Room. Rebeccas & Brothers & had a free & easy. **1913** *Chicago Record-Herald* 16 Mar. v. 6/5 The staff of Maple Leaf Rebekah Lodge, No. 369, will confer the Rebekah degree on a large class of candidates. **1930** *Randolph Enterprise* (Elkins, W. Va.) 16 Jan. 5/4 They sure have a fine bunch of Odd Fellows and Rebekahs down there. **1949** *Milwaukie* (Oregon) *Rev.* 28 July 6/3 Mrs. Wanda Million and Mrs. Esther Lineagar were initiated into the Milwaukie Rebekah lodge at last week's meeting in the city hall. **1972** *Fairbanks* (Alaska) *Daily News-Miner* 3 Nov. 7/2 (*caption*) Rebekahs—Members of the Rebekahs are interested in forming an Independent Order of the Odd Fellows in Fairbanks.

rebel, *a.* and *sb.*[1] Add: **A.** *adj.* **1. a, b.** (Further attrib. examples.)
1861 O. W. NORTON *Army Lett., 1861–65* (1903) 24 The rebel camps are within two miles of us. **1937** *Granta* 3 Feb. 219/1 Seeing the contrast between the military efficiency of the rebel army and the unpreparedness of the people for war [at the time of the Spanish Civil War 1936–39]. **1944** H. FAST *Freedom Road* 167 It was not essentially a problem of reconstruction, not even a problem of readmission of the rebel states into the Union. **1963** *Times* 11 May 11/5 Dubbed the Rebel City for espousing the cause of Perkin Warbeck in 1492, Cork has always maintained a fighting reputation. **1980** *Times* 3 Jan. 1/7 The sources said..that the Russians were using sophisticated M124 helicopter gunships against rebel strongholds.

2. a. (Later examples.)
1931 *Ann. Reg. 1930* II. 49 The Prime Minister's speech, as was to be expected, was considered unsatisfactory by the 'rebel' group in the Labour Party. **1976** *Southern Even. Echo* (Southampton) 18 Nov. 17/5 Action would now be concentrated on Albert Johnson quay where most of the rebel dockers worked.

B. *sb.*[1] **1. a.** (Further examples.)
1902 KIPLING *Traffics & Discoveries* (1904) 32, I shot my Bible full of bullets after Bloemfontein went... Take it and pray over it before we Federals help the British to knock hell out of you rebels. **1966** *BBC Handbk. 1966* 97 Stanleyville radio was in the hands of the rebels in the Congo (Leopoldville) Republic. **1976** *Daily Tel.* 20 July 4/2 Armed men, believed to be Moslem rebels, ambushed a bus in the southern Philippines on Sunday.

d. A supporter of the American cause during the War of Independence (1775–83). **e.** A supporter of the Southern, or Confederate, cause during the American Civil War (1861–5); hence, by extension, used colloq. for SOUTHERNER 2. Chiefly *U.S.*
1775 *Massachusetts Spy* 3 May 3/1 The commanding officer accosted the militia in words to this effect, 'Disperse you damn'd rebels!' **1788** *Ann. Reg. 1776* I. 181 Gen. Clinton, with two brigades of British..were sent to make an attempt upon Rhode Island... The rebels having abandoned the island at their approach, they took possession of it without the loss of a man. **1847** *Knickerbocker* XXIX. 54 Mrs. Mowatt is..a great granddaughter of one of those old 'rebels' who signed the Declaration of Independence. **1861** E. COWELL *Diary* 15 Apr. in *Cowells in Amer.* (1934) 290 [The] proceeding caused the necessary diversion of 'the rebels'' course. **1864** [in Dict., sense 1 a]. **1895** W. H. CHAMBLISS *Diary* 305 The malignant epithets, 'Yankee' and 'Rebels',..were invented by fanatics and foreigners to aggravate our interstate quarrel. **1905** A. C. RICE *Sandy* 123 'Was he a rebel?'.. 'He was a Confederate, sir! I never knew a rebel.' **1929** *Amer. Speech* IV. 344 *Rebel*, a Southerner. **1938** *Oklahoma Supreme Ct. Rep.* CLXXXIII. A. 509/2 The Northern man is often referred to as 'Yankee' and the Southern man as 'Rebel'. **1959** W. PETERS *Southern Temper* xiii. 211 [The] publisher of the Augusta *Courier*.. exudes pleasantness and good will, even when his caller is a Northern newspaperman or writer. 'Well,' he said to one such not long ago, 'I guess you've come down here to give us rebels hell.'

2. a. (Later example.)
1955 *N.Y. Times* 27 Oct. 28/2 Mr. Dean..is a mixed-up rebel because his father lacks decisiveness and strength.

b. *rebel without a cause*: the title of a cinematographic film released in the U.S. in 1955, applied to a (young) person whose aggressive behaviour is attributed to feelings of frustration or insecurity rather than to loyalty to a particular cause.
[**1955** *N.Y. Times* 27 Oct. 28/2 It is a violent, brutal and disturbing picture of modern teenagers that Warner Brothers presents in its new melodrama..'Rebel Without a Cause'. Young people neglected by their parents or given no understanding and moral support by fathers and mothers who are themselves unable to achieve balance and security in their homes are the bristling heroes and heroines.] **1963** *Times* 30 May 15/6 It is a story of a rebel-without-a-cause.. and of the gradual disillusioning of a younger man..with the romantic image that at first glance he presents.

3. *rebel-hearted, -held* adjs.; **rebel yell,** a characteristic shout or battle-cry uttered by Confederate soldiers during the American Civil War; also *transf.*
1926 C. DAY-LEWIS in *Oxford Poetry* 19 What sense Have they the pioneer-minded, the rebel-hearted, If man's fulfilment rest on no 'perhaps' Outside him? **1966** *BBC Handbk. 1966* 98 The Service's East African Unit..became..the only source of news from rebel-held territory [in the Congo Republic]. **1863** A. J. L. FREMANTLE *Jrnl.* 2 July in *Three Months in Southern States* 265 The Southern troops, when charging, or to express their delight, always yell in a manner peculiar to themselves... The Confederate officers declare that the rebel yell has a particular merit, and always produces a salutary and useful effect upon their adversaries. A corps is sometimes spoken of as a 'good yelling regiment'. **1868** *Harper's Mag.* Sept. 488/1 A tall woman..uttered a long, piercing cry, which Humphreys afterward described as 'a rebel yell', and Alec as 'a keen whoop'. **1936** M. MITCHELL *Gone with Wind* vi. 121 Stuart Tarleton's voice rose, in an exultant shout, 'Yee-aay-ee!' as if he were on the hunting field. And she heard for the first time..the Rebel yell. **1945** S. LEWIS *Cass Timberlane* (1946) xxix. 193 No dance at the Heather Country Club was canonical without the presence of Jay Laverick, emitting the rebel yell. **1974** P. RUELL *Death takes Low Road* x. 126 For God's sake, lassie, can you no' keep your voice down to less than a rebel yell?

rebel, *v.* **2.** For † *Obs. rare*—[1] read *rare* and add later example.
1908 A. S. M. HUTCHINSON *Once aboard Lugger* IV. ii. 219 To-day the empress sway of conventionality is rarely rebelled.

rebeldom. 1. (Further examples.)
1887 J. D. BILLINGS *Hardtack & Coffee* 280 Afterwards [soldiers] went by thousands into other sections of Rebeldom. **1893** [see *CHINCAPIN].

† **rebelism** (re·bĕliz'm). *U.S. Obs.* [f. REBEL *sb.*[1] + -ISM.] Adherence to the principles or practice of the Confederates during the American Civil War (1861–5).
1862 *Constitution* (Middletown, Conn.) 26 Mar. 4/1 There is a good deal of rebelism in the *Old Bailie*. **1864** *Harper's Mag.* July 271/1 He..is silent or pretends to rebelism when his mistress..is by. **1867** *Congress. Globe* 10 Dec. 103/3 The action of Congress can have no other effect than to embarrass the work of reconstruction,..to feed the spirit of rebelism and incite insubordination.

rebelly, *a.* Delete *rare* and add later examples.
1936 'F. O'CONNOR' *Bones of Contention* 179 The child and grandchild of rebelly men. **1959** *Manch. Guardian* 2 July 5/4 Finsbury..seems always to have been a fairly rebelly quarter.

rebid (rībi·d, rī·bid), *v. Bridge.* [RE- 5 a.] *trans.* and *intr.* To bid (*BID *v.* 3 c) again. Hence **re·bid** *sb.*; **rebi·ddable** *a.*
1923 *Daily Mail* 6 Oct. 6/4 Z has called '3 clubs'. A bids '2 spades'. Y or Z may point out the insufficiency or may in turn re-bid 3 clubs. **1927** M. C. WORK *Contract Bridge* iii. 27 It is not the one-bids, or the ones jumped to twos, which produce the heavy sets in Contract; it is the game-going jumps and the rebids to reach game-going declarations that do the damage. **1929** —— *Compl. Contract Bridge* iv. 25 One of them being strong enough to bid two of a major, and East not being able to rebid. **1945** PHILLIPS & REESE *How to play Bridge* vi. 45 If your hand is weak, but your suit is rebiddable, you should bid Three of it. **1958** *Listener* 9 Oct. 572/3 The Diamonds are not rebiddable. **1971** *Daily Tel.* 21 Aug. 8/3 East contested the part score with 3 diamonds, judging that his two honours would be adequate support opposite the rebid suit. **1975** *Times* 11 Jan. 7/5 By rebidding his suit he imagined that he was asking his partner to choose between Hearts and Spades. **1976** *Cumberland News* 26 Nov., In many respects rebids are more important than opening bids or first responses for very rarely do these bids give precise information about the hands.

rebind, *v.* (Earlier and later examples.)
1820 *Rep. Comm. Public Rec. 1800–1819* 525 The total sum of £1,000 per Annum..to the Purposes of maintaining ..and..occasionally re-binding..the Public Records. *Ibid.* 527 Many different Series of Records..have been carefully repaired and suitably rebound. **1901** D. COCKERELL *Bookbinding* i. 18 Nearly all librarians complain that they have to be continually rebinding books. *Ibid.* xxii. 306 When the sewing cords or threads of a book have perished it should be re-bound. **1946** H. J. PLENDERLEITH *Preservation of Leather Bookbindings* 10 Some [volumes of a catalogue] have actually had to be rebound. **1963** B. C. MIDDLETON *Hist. Eng. Craft Bookbinding Technique* ii. 8 Thousands of old books..were rebound in modern morocco.

rebinding, *vbl. sb.* (Earlier and later examples.)
1857 D. LAING *Penni Worth of Witte* p. iii, It must have suffered in the rebinding, by being rather unsparingly cut in the edges. **1931** A. ESDAILE *Student's Man. Bibliogr.* vi. 178 Most bibliographers are aware of the great mass of important knowledge which has been destroyed by careless re-binding.

‖ **reblochon** (rəblɔʃɔ̃). [Fr.] The name of a soft French cheese made originally and chiefly in Savoy.
1908 DOANE & LAWSON *Varieties of Cheese* 43 *Reblochon.* This is a soft French cheese weighing 1 to 2 pounds. It is made from fresh whole milk which is curdled with rennet at a temperature of 80 °F. or above, the time allowed being about thirty minutes. **1931** F. COLCHESTER-WEMYSS *Pleasures of Table* vii. 70 Reblochon is a delightful cheese, and not at all awkward as regards keeping. **1935** O. BURDETT *Little Book of Cheese* iv. 59 Though not often to be had in England, and, perhaps, not very often beyond the borders of Savoy, *Reblochons* must be mentioned. It makes a convenient postscript to Brie, for it is a smallish round, flat cheese, very creamy and rich in flavour. **1967** *House & Garden* Apr. 96/3 Fertilizers mask the taste of grass... Reblochon is losing its hint of gentian. **1971** *Sunday Times* 28 Mar. (Colour Suppl.) 34/4 *Reblochon*, the most distinguished of the cheeses of the Haute Savoie. Made with the yield of the second milking of the fawn Tarentais cow (*rebloche* in the local patois means 'second milking'). **1973** J. M. WHITE *Garden Game* 44 He cut off a sliver of *reblochon* and sampled it... He waved the cheese-knife.

reboa·ntic, *a.* Chiefly *poet.* [f. REBOANT *a.* + -IC.] = REBOANT *a.*
1903 KIPLING *Five Nations* 124 When the Conchimarian horns Of the reboantic Norns Usher gentlemen and ladies With new lights on Heaven and Hades. **1907** *Academy* 23 Mar. 298/1 Even then the Norns couldn't be reboantic, supposing that word to be correctly derived from *reboo* = to bellow back.

reboard, *v.* Delete *rare* and add later examples. Also *absol.*
1906 *Westm. Gaz.* 24 Mar. 10/2 Her bulwarks kept her afloat, and the crew reboarded her and brought her safely to Milford Haven. **1977** *R.A.F. News* 5–18 Jan. 3/2 He was winched to safety and later put down on the tanker to..reboard the catamaran. **1977** *Western Living* (Vancouver) Apr. 33/2 The conductor ordered all to reboard.

rebody, *v.* Restrict † *Obs.*—[1] to sense in Dict. and add: **2.** *trans.* To furnish (a motor vehicle, etc.) with a new body. Hence **rebo·died** *ppl. a.*
1963 *Times* 19 Jan. 3/6 His car had to be rebodied. **1977** *Custom Car* Nov. 30/3 Their Rio was slated by the press, who saw it as nothing more than a rebodied Dolomite.

reboiler (rībɔi·ləɹ), *v.* [RE- 5 c.] *trans.* To fit with a new boiler.
1889 [in Dict. s.v. RE- 5 c]. **1908** *Westm. Gaz.* 25 Apr. 2/3 The Banter Line decided to reboiler the *Caesar* and go for the Atlantic record. **1961** *Guardian* 5 June 10/6 One of the two original engines..was..reboilered just a year before the line closed.

reboiler (rībɔi·ləɹ), *sb.* [f. REBOIL *v.*[2] + -ER[1].] A heater for vapourizing the liquid at the bottom of a fractionating column.
1956 MCCABE & SMITH *Unit Operations of Chem. Engin.* xii. 685 The liquid feed flows down the column to the still, which in this type of plant is called the 'reboiler', and is subjected to rectification by the vapor rising from the reboiler. **1966** *McGraw-Hill Encycl. Sci. & Technol.* XIII. 185/2 Many [stripping] processes employ a combination of all three; that is, after absorption at elevated pressure, the solvent is flashed to atmospheric pressure, heated, and admitted into a stripping column which is provided with a bottom heater (reboiler). **1977** F. G. SHINSKEY *Distillation Control* ix. 273 Multiple reboilers are generally used in severe fouling service, so that they may be individually cleaned without interrupting operation of the column.

re-book, *v.* (Further examples.)
1898 G. GISSING *Let.* 27 Jan. in R. A. Gettman *G. Gissing & H. G. Wells* (1961) 85 The trunk..will have to be..rebooked to Rome. **1906** *Westm. Gaz.* 6 Sept. 8/3 Such a by-law..compels a passenger to get out and rebook, even though he miss his train. But he would still have to rebook if going by a later train. **1978** 'S. WOODS' *Exit Murderer* 55 I've re-booked your room for you.

rebop: see *BEBOP.

rebore (rī·bōᵊɹ), *sb.* [f. the vb.] A re-boring of one or more cylinders of an internal-combustion engine; also, an engine which has had its cylinders re-bored.
1954 'TORRENS' *Motor Cyclist's Workshop* (ed. 6) xx. 126 When your piston is 'worn out', your cylinder is sorely in need of a rebore or..regrinding. **1967** J. MILLS *Low-Cost Car Repairs* iii. 75 The check is to determine whether a recon-set can be used or whether a rebore is needed. **1970** K. BALL *Fiat 600, 600D Autobook* i. 13 A rebore will require new pistons and rings a size larger than the original and these will usually be supplied by the garage..undertaking the rebore. **1977** *S. Wales Echo* 18 Jan. (Advt.), Exchange crankshafts, camshafts, short engines, rebores, pistons.

reborrowing (rībǫ·rouiŋ), *vbl. sb.* [f. REBORROW *v.* + -ING[1].] The action of the vb. REBORROW (esp. in *Philol.*); also, that which is reborrowed.
1869 *Bradshaw's Railway Man.* XXI. 221 Pay off and create in lieu of reborrowing. **1933** L. BLOOMFIELD *Language* xxv. 452 The same re-borrowing of this last word appears in Old English. **1953** K. JACKSON *Lang. & Hist. Early Brit.* II. 332 Förster notes that the AS. form of Nene is spelt five times in Peterborough documents as *Nyn*, and regards this as a re-borrowing. **1979** *Amer. Speech* LIV. 29 Of the 6 pure reborrowings, 4 are from *cent*: Indonesian *sen*, Samoan *sene*, Tongan *seniti*, and Swahili *senti*.

rebound, *sb.* Add: Now usu. with pronunc. (rī·baund). **3. a.** *spec.* in *Basketball, Football,* etc., the return of a ball from the backboard, goal-post, etc., after an unsuccessful shot; a ball that rebounds in this manner. Also *attrib.*
1922 W. E. MEANWELL *Basket Ball for Men* vi. 61 The opposing attack is following in hard for the rebound. *Ibid.*, The hook pass..permits the guard to reverse and present his back to the oncoming rebound man. **1948** *Sun* (Baltimore) 7 Jan. 11/1 Jimmy Kirby..tapped in four field goals when taking rebounds. **1954** *Basketball* ('Know the Game'

Series) 35 When a shot is missed obtaining the rebound is vital... Although defensive players usually start with the best position for the rebound offensive, players must make every effort to beat the defender to the best rebound positions. **1955** *Sun* (Baltimore) 4 Feb. 15/1 He is an outstanding rebound man and the team's third leading scorer. **1969** *Eugene* (Oregon) *Register-Guard* 3 Dec. 1D/3 'It was the board play that killed us,' continued Belko, pointing to Wichita's 62–43 edge in rebounds. **1971** *N.Y. Times Guide Spectator Sports* iii. 78 A man much taller than the rest..had the best chance to retrieve the 'rebound' over the heads of smaller players. **1976** *Western Mail* (Cardiff) 22 Nov. 16/3 Preece was on hand to fire home the rebound from close range. **1978** *Dumfries Courier* 13 Oct. 4/6 Milligan levelled the scores for Girvan connecting with a rebound after a shot had been blocked in the goalmouth.

c. (Examples in *Med.*) Freq. *attrib.*

1951 *Jrnl. Clin. Endocrinol.* XI. 235 (*heading*) Spermatogenic rebound phenomenon after administration of testosterone propionate. **1954** *Jrnl. Nerv. & Mental Dis.* CXX. 46 (*heading*) Abstention [from addictive drugs], rebound, and readjustment. **1974** M. C. Gerald *Pharmacol.* vi. 115 The relief produced by the shrinkage of swollen nasal membranes is merely temporary and is followed by rebound congestion. *Ibid.* xv. 288 More often death has been attributed to secondary causes such as..suicides arising from rebound depression during periods of drug withdrawal or abstinence. **1977** *Lancet* 9 Apr. 774/1 Thrombocytopenia caused by alcohol is reversible after alcohol withdrawal, and is followed by rebound thrombocytosis. **1978** M. G. Harmatz *Abnormal Psychol.* vii. 162/1 Patients felt even more deeply depressed when drug action wore off than before they had treatment (a rebound effect). Modern antidepressants..avoid these side effects.

d. Restrict † *Obs.* to phrases in Dict. and add: Also † *in* or *on the rebound*: during a period of reaction following an emotionally disturbing experience, esp. a broken engagement or a refusal of marriage. Also used without *prep.*

1853 Mrs. Gaskell *Ruth* III. iv. 129 His first rebound to Jemima. **1859** *Harper's Mag.* Aug. 341/1 Ellen Bond caught his heart 'in the rebound', as somebody says. **1861** C. M. Yonge *Young Step-Mother* xxi. 295 We may steer her safely through, above all, if one of the six cousins will but catch him in the rebound. **1864** G. J. Whyte-Melville *Queen's Maries* II. xxxviii. 234 It is an old saying that 'many a heart is caught on the rebound'. *a* **1899** V. S. Lean *Collectanea* (1904) IV. 41 Many a heart is caught in the rebound, *i.e.* after a repulse by another. **1921** Galsworthy *To Let* III. x. 290 Ah! it was strange—this marriage. The young man, Mont, had caught her on the rebound, of course, in the reckless mood of one whose ship has just gone down. **1931** H. S. Walpole *Judith Paris* III. i. 428 She has but accepted him on the rebound from her trouble with Beaminster. **1969** A. Glyn *Dragon Variation* ix. 283 Maybe the girl had had a fight with Carl, and had turned to Jeff on the rebound. **1977** A. Morice *Murder in Mimicry* I. ix. 91 Her passion for Gilbert was already on the wane... The rebound was in full swing. **1978** *Lancashire Life* Sept. 47/2 Perhaps it was on the rebound from this disappointment that he contracted his disastrous first marriage.

rebound, *v.* Add: **1. b.** (Further examples.)

1955 *Times* 9 Aug. 12/2 Equities rebounded sharply yesterday after their reaction last week although they did not always fully hold their gains. **1979** *Arizona Daily Star* 1 Apr. D2/3 Coal prices just don't seem to want to rebound.

e. *Basketball.* To catch a rebound (*rebound *sb.* 3 a).

1954 *Sun* (Baltimore) 20 Dec. B18/2 Pollard is the best balanced basketball player I have ever seen;..he can rebound with the best big men in the business. **1974** *State* (Columbia, S. Carolina) 3 Mar. 1-D/1 Kelley went to the line for a one-and-one at 1:04 and missed. Stewart rebounded and McCurdy failed to connect twice.

reboundant (rĭbau·ndănt), *a.* *Her. Obs.* (exc. *Hist.*). [f. Rebound *v.* + -ant[1].] = Reverberant *a.* 1.

1688 [see Reverberant *a.* 1]. **1828** W. Berry *Encycl. Heraldica* I., *Reboundant, or Rebounding*, a term sometimes used, in ancient heraldry, for the tail of a lion, when turned up like the letter S, the end of the tail being outwards, which was called *reverberant, beaten back*, or *reboundant*, as if the animal had beaten it to his back and it had rebounded; the usual way of turning the end of the tail, in ancient times, being inwards; but it is now seldom borne otherwise than outwards, and, therefore, not noticed in the blazon. **1878** B. Burke *General Armory* p. xliv, *Reboundant*, an ancient term for the tail of a lion when turned up and bent in the form of a letter S with the point outwards, the ancient way of depicting the tail was usually with the point turned towards the back, unless blazoned reboundant. **1910** W. A. Copinger *Heraldry Simplified* 368/1 *Reboundant*, or Rebounding, formerly applied to the tail of a lion when turned up like the letter S.

rebounder. Add: **b.** *Basketball.* A player who is skilled in catching rebounds (*rebound *sb.* 3 a).

1949 *Sun* (Baltimore) 28 Dec. 14/6 Dolhou goes on the injured list with..a growing reputation as an adept floorman, rebounder and set shot. **1954** *Ibid.* 20 Dec. B18/3 What more do you want..shooter, playmaker, rebounder, durability. **1974** *Spartanburg* (S. Carolina) *Herald-Jrnl.* 21 Apr. B1/1 He started on the basketball team..playing the point position as playmaker and still being one of the leading rebounders for Coach Bill Hinson's Viking team. **1979** *N.Y. Times* 25 Nov. v. 10/3 In winning the Southeastern Conference regular-season title and posting a 23–8 mark, Dale Brown had size, quickness, shooters, ballhandlers, rebounders and experience.

rebounding, *vbl. sb.* Add: **b.** *spec.* in *Basketball*, the action of catching a rebound (*rebound *sb.* 3 a). Also *attrib.*

1954 *Basketball* ('Know the Game' Series) 35 (*heading*) Rebounding. **1957** *Encycl. Brit.* III. 181 *Rebounding*,..the fundamental ability to get proper position, time the jump and properly retrieve rebounds is a vital part of the game. **1969** *Eugene* (Oregon) *Register-Guard* 3 Dec. 1D/4 The rebounding was that close only because the hosts had trouble getting going on the backboards. **1972** *N.Y. Times* 4 June 7/4 Bill Moore, who holds most of Susquehanna University's rebounding records, has been appointed assistant basketball coach at the university. **1976** *Springfield* (Mass.) *Daily News* 22 Apr. 39/1 We lost this game chiefly for two reasons: offensive rebounding (16–10 Celts with Cowens pulling nine) and turnovers (the Braves coughing up 30 to 17).

rebours, *a.* and *sb.* Restrict † *Obs.* to senses in Dict. and add: **B.** *sb.* Also in phr. ‖ *à rebours* (a rəbūr), in the wrong way, perversely; through perversity.

1906 W. James *Let.* 3 Apr. in R. B. Perry *Thought & Character W. James* (1935) II. 393 How lamely I, for one, must have expressed myself to be taken so *à rebours*. **1939** T. S. Eliot *Idea Christ. Society* i. 19 It [*sc.* a dislike of everything maintained by Germany or Russia] may..lead us to be mere imitators *à rebours*, in making us adopt uncritically almost any attitude which a foreign nation rejects. **1949** I. Deutscher *Stalin* iv. 96 In making a fetish of the underground, in shying away from the broader opportunities for action, they tended to reduce the resolution to impotence. They were liquidators *à rebours*. **1951** M. Lowry *Let.* 25 Aug. (1967) 262 While he took no human action at all.. some principle of tyrannic yet thwarted force in his feeling has worked against him, *à rebours*: now he does take action ..mysteriously the thing begins to work for him.

rebozo, reboso. (Earlier and later examples.)

1807 J. Pinkerton *Mod. Geogr.* (rev. ed.) III. 185 The Mexican ladies..when they are at home, or go out in a carriage,..wear what is called the *rebozo*, or muffler, like the shawls now used at Madrid. **1844** J. Gregg *Commerce of Prairies* I. 216 A Mexican female is scarcely ever seen without her rebozo or shawl. **1927** W. Cather *Death comes for Archbishop* I. ii. 25 She was dressed in black, with a white apron, and a black reboso over her head, like a Mexican woman of the poor. **1947** J. Steinbeck *Wayward Bus* 235 The little modest dark girls in blue *rebozos*. **1956** R. Bradbury *October Country* 19 Behind him came women in black rebozos. **1977** *Guider* July 310/3 The dancers wear white dresses with coloured belts and rebozos tied from hand to hand.

rebranch (rībrɑ·nʃ), *v.* [f. Re- 5 a.] *intr.* To ramify; to branch again. Hence **rebra·nching** *vbl. sb.*

1888 J. Le Conte *Evolution* I. i. 14 A growing tree branches and again branches in all directions... Even so the tree of life, by the law of differentiation, branches and rebranches continually. **1895** W. H. Hudson *Introd. Philos. H. Spencer* i. 19 That doctrine of the gradual branching and rebranching of species..went somewhat vaguely by the name of the development hypothesis. **1935** Huxley & Haddon *We Europeans* v. 161 Evolutionary branches may ..unite again after they have diverged and then either rebranch or remain united.

rebreathe *v.* Add: Hence also **rebrea·thing** *vbl. sb.* (freq. *attrib.*).

1897 W. Marcet *Contrib. Hist. Respiration in Man* 109 Curves were taken showing the effects produced by the re-breathing of six litres of air during two minutes. **1935** *Sun* (Baltimore) 17 May 5/2 Their faces are covered with four layers of gauze, muffling nose, mouth, eyes and ears. One purpose of the gauze is to increase slightly the rebreathing of exhaled carbon dioxide. **1960** *Brit. Jrnl. Anaesthesia* XXXII. 256 (*heading*) A rebreathing technique for the determination of arterial Pco_2 in the apnoeic patient. **1976** H. MacInnes *Death Reel* xxiii. 184 He was pulled in..by a diver using re-breathing apparatus.

rebroadcast (rī-), *v.* [Re- 5 a.] *trans.* To broadcast again; *spec.* to broadcast (a programme received from another station).

1923 *Daily Mail* 14 Aug. 5/3 A special orchestral concert ..will be relayed to all the broadcasting stations in Britain, and thence be re-broadcast by them on their own particular wave-lengths. **1939** *Sun* (Baltimore) 9 Feb. 1/2 Several hours after the vessel's first distress call, she rebroadcast her SOS appeal. **1948** *John o' London's Weekly* 10 Dec. 598/3 The difficulty in receiving the Scottish station makes it unlikely that more than a handful of Scott's English admirers will be able to judge how *Waverley* sounds on the air, but perhaps the serial will be re-broadcast later on another wavelength. **1951** A. C. Clarke *Sands of Mars* viii. 94 It was a live programme, beamed to Mars..picked up and rebroadcast. **1965** *Economist* 9 Oct. 152/3 Plays supplied by the networks to their provincial affiliates, and already censored in Madrid, must be recensored before being rebroadcast. **1974** P. Gzowski *This Country* 12/2 What I said live to the Maritimes was recorded in Toronto and rebroadcast an hour later, then recorded in Winnipeg and so on.

Hence **rebroa·dcast** *ppl. a.*, **rebroa·dcasting** *vbl. sb.*; also **rebroa·dcaster**, a station that rebroadcasts material received from elsewhere.

1956 *Nature* 10 Mar. 451/2 There are fuller accounts of the External Services and of the re-broadcasting of the B.B.C. programmes throughout the world. **1957** *BBC Handbk.* 38 Programmes of this kind may be conveyed to the rebroadcaster either by short-wave transmission or as recordings by sea or airmail. **1962** *Ibid.* 102 The local station may record the BBC transmission for rebroadcasting later. **1969** *Listener* 17 July 91/3 The rebroadcast *Morals and Medicine* debate on abortion was a sterilised, factual affair by comparison. **1973** *Ibid.* 13 Sept. 348/3 No one could tell which programmes might one day be required..for rebroadcasting. **1974** *BBC Handbk.* 273/1 Every programme chosen for distribution to re-broadcasters is of the highest quality.

rebroa·dcast (rī-), *sb.* [f. the vb.] A repeat broadcast, esp. one of a programme received from another station; also, the action of broadcasting again.

1927 *Observer* 24 July 4/5 Rebroadcasts can be made on both sides of the Atlantic and..though they are interesting the quality is usually painful and always bad. **1939** *Sun* (Baltimore) 9 May 2/4 Thousands of British subjects heard the message as broadcast by the French stations or picked up through the short-wave rebroadcast from the United States. **1940** *Ibid.* 23 Feb. 1/4 Explaining the experiment, involving receipt of National Broadcasting Company programs from New York city by a receiver 130 miles distant, and simultaneous rebroadcast by Station W2XB, Dr. Baker said [etc.]. **1943** R. Chandler *High Window* x. 79 This ball game is a studio re-broadcast. **1963** *Guardian* 19 Apr. 12/2 The National Aeronautics and Space Administration had promised to allow some broadcasts direct from the capsule as well as the rebroadcast of television tapes. **1965** *Economist* 9 Oct. 152/2 Even [Spanish] commercials taped for rebroadcast day after day must be vetted daily. **1974** *Radio Times* 14 Mar. 30/3 Re-broadcasts of programmes from a fortnightly series on the arts.

rebuff (rĭ₁bʊ·f), *v.*[2] *rare.* [f. Re- 5 c + Buff *a.* or *buff *v.*[3] 2.] *trans.* To restore to a buff colour.

1924 Galsworthy *White Monkey* III. x. 281 On both sides flat houses, recently re-buffed.

rebuffer (rĭbʊ·fəɹ). *rare.* [f. Rebuff *v.* + -er[1].] One who rebuffs others.

1950 O. Nash *Family Reunion* (1951) 109 The medica tyrant, the social rebuffer.

rebuild, *v.* Add: (Further examples.)

1927 *Scribner's Mag.* Apr. 356/1 Another boy..wore a black silk handkerchief across his face because he had no nose then and his face was to be rebuilt... They rebuilt his face, but..they could never get the nose exactly straight. **1961** M. Beadle *These Ruins are Inhabited* (1963) ii. 19 The fire..had gone out... While George rebuilt it, I set about frying bacon and eggs.

rebuild *sb.* (further examples); **rebuilt** *ppl. a.* (further examples); hence also **rebui·lded** *ppl. a.* (*poet.*).

1924 R. Campbell *Flaming Terrapin* iii. 48 Sodom, rebuilded, scorns the wilting power. **1934** Webster, *Rebuilt*.., of factory products, as typewriters, disassembled, reconstructed with new parts replacing those that are worn, and refinished. **1959** J. Thurber *Years with Ross* vii. 124 A rebuilt typewriter I had been using. **1960** K. M. Kenyon *Archæol. in Holy Land* iv. 106 Sometimes the collapsed wall survived in the shape of an inverted U, and the rebuild consisted of a capping which might have foundations on the same level as the original wall. **1972** *World of Wild Wheels* (Custom Car) 10/1 As the moulding drops off they tend to leave it off. It's less work in the re-build. **1973** *Country Life* 1 Mar. (Suppl.) 11 Modern house being a rebuild of the original manor house. **1976** *Evening Post* (Bristol) 23 Apr. (Advt.), Bodywork, resprays, engine re-build, reasonable prices. **1978** *Gramophone* July 173/3 The Canterbury organ was ailing and unfit (in fact a rebuild is about to begin).

rebu·kative, *a.* *rare.* [f. Rebuk(e *v.* + -ative.] Disapproving, rebuking. So **rebu·katively** *adv.*

1924 'O. Douglas' *Pink Sugar* iii. 30 Miss Dickson.. asked if we had called yet..and added, rather rebukatively, that Mr. M'Clandish had called at once. **1950** —— *Farewell to Priorsford* 219 Do you suppose she meant gangsters or only what Jane Austen called 'less worthy females'? No, Janet, I'm not backbiting, so don't look so rebukative.

rebunk (rībʊ·ŋk), *v.* [f. Re- 5 a + *bunk *sb.*[4], after *debunk *v.*] *trans.* To restore the reputation of or regard for (a person who has been debunked). So **rebu·nking** *vbl. sb.*

1960 *Times Lit. Suppl.* 6 May 291/4 We live in an age of rebunking, when it has become fashionable once more to take the Victorians almost as solemnly as they took themselves. **1962** *Ibid.* 11 May 341/1 Mr. Swanberg sets out neither to debunk nor to rebunk 'the Chief', but to describe him..as a social and political phenomenon.

rebunker (rībʊ·ŋkəɹ), *v.* [f. Re- 5 a + *bunker *v.* 1 b.] *intr.* To take in a further supply of coal or oil for consumption on a voyage.

1899 C. J. C. Hyne *Further Adv. Capt. Kettle* iii. 60 But wood, as compared with coal, is bulky stuff to carry, and as the stowage capacity of these stern wheelers is small, they have to make frequent calls to rebunker. **1929** *Daily Express* 14 Jan. 11/1 The Wimpole rebunkered and provisioned here and sailed for Grimsby on the midday tide.

rebu·rgeoning, *vbl. sb.* [f. Reburgeon *v.* + -ing[1].] A renewed budding or sprouting (in quot. *fig.*).

1929 'M. B. Eldershaw' *House is Built* ix. 210 The reburgeoning of life throughout the country did not leave this household quite untouched.

rebu·rial. [RE- 5 a.] A second interment (of a corpse).

1922 Z. GREY *To Last Man* viii. 185 It struck Jean as singular that neither Esther Isbel nor Mrs. Jacobs suggested a reburial of their husbands. **1980** J. BARNETT *Palmprint* v. 50 I've arranged for a re-burial service by the Reverend Solomon.

rebus, *sb.* (Later *attrib.* examples.)

1928 O. JESPERSEN *Internat. Lang.* II. 170 The number of roots admitted in primitive Esperanto was extremely small, and a good deal of ingenuity was used to express as much as possible by means of compounds and derivatives... The great number of these rebus-words..has deterred many intelligent people from Esp. **1969** A. PARPOLA et al. *Decipherment of Proto-Dravidian Inscriptions of Indus Civilization* ii. 8 It now appears that it [*sc.* the Indus script] is a purely logographic script, based on the so-called rebus principle. This means that each sign represents a whole word, which may comprise one or more syllables, and that a given word is expressed by a clearly recognizable picture of a quite different thing, which has, however, the same phonetic value.

re-bush (rību·ʃ), *v.* [f. RE- 5 c + BUSH *v.*^{3}] *trans.* To provide with a replacement bush. Hence **re-bu·shing** *vbl. sb.*

1885 C. G. W. LOCK *Workshop Receipts* 4th Ser. 331/2 It is important..that enough metal is left round these holes to admit of their being re-bushed if necessary. **1970** K. BALL *Fiat 600, 600D Autobook* ix. 110/2 If this clearance is exceeded, replace either the roller shaft or rebush the shaft bore. *Ibid.* 112/1 Rebushing must be followed by reaming to a uniform internal diameter of ·867 inch ±·0004 inch.

‖ **rebus sic stantibus** (rēⁱ·bʊs sik stæ·ntibʊs), *phr.* [mod.L.] Things standing thus; provided that conditions have not changed; *spec.* in *International Law* used of the principle that a treaty lapses when conditions are substantially different from those which obtained when it was concluded; *clausula rebus sic stantibus* [*CLAUSULA], a clause to this effect.

[**1598** A. GENTILI *De Iure Belli Libri Tres* III. xiv. 599 Et tandem facto, ac silentio hîc quoque, vt in priuatis, dices ratificari foedus... Item excipitur de rerum statu immutatio. Si mutatio nequit praeuideri. Etiam & adiecto iureiurando subintelligi clausula, *Rebus sic stantibus.* **1760** tr. *de Vattel's Law of Nations* I. II. xvii. 230 The only state of things, on account of which the promise is made, is essential to it, and the change of that state alone can lawfully hinder or suspend the effect of that promise. This is the sense which ought to be given to that maxim of the civilians, *Conventio omnis intelligitur rebus sic stantibus.*] **1849** R. WILDMAN *Institutes Internat. Law* I. iv. 175 The doctrine, that every treaty implies a condition of defeasance on any material change of circumstances, which is usually called the rule de rebus sic stantibus, is rejected by Grotius and Bynkershoek as calculated to destroy the obligation of all compacts. **1883** *Wharton's Law-Lex.* 693/2 *Rebus sic stantibus*, at this point of affairs. **1927** *Amer. Jrnl. Internat. Law* XXI. 509 The principle of *rebus sic stantibus* was invoked by Austria-Hungary in 1908 as a justification..for the annexation of Bosnia and Herzegovina. **1939** E. H. CARR *Twenty Years' Crisis* xi. 233 International lawyers evolved the doctrine that a so-called *clausula rebus sic stantibus* was implicit in every treaty, i.e. that the obligations of a treaty were binding in international law so long as the conditions prevailing at the time of the conclusion of the treaty continued, and no longer. **1973** I. M. SINCLAIR *Vienna Convention on Law of Treaties* iv. 105 All international lawyers are aware of the pitfalls surrounding the application of the *clausula rebus sic stantibus* and the controversies which have raged as to its admissibility as a ground for the unilateral denunciation or termination of a treaty. **1975** D. FISICHELLA in S. E. Finer *Adversary Politics & Electoral Reform* III. 264 It seems probable that the second ballot would create '*rebus sic stantibus*' further incentives to manipulation from outside and therefore increased factionalization.

rebuttable, *a.* (Later examples.)

1908 *Westm. Gaz.* 28 Jan. 8/3 Will you state when you think it is rebuttable and when you think it is irrebuttable? **1971** *Daily Tel.* 25 May 3/3 If the gift is substantial..there should be a rebuttable presumption that the witness exercised undue influence on the testator.

rebuttal. Add: Also *attrib.*

1925 *North Western Reporter* CCII. 898/2 Rebuttal evidence properly is that which explains away, contradicts, or otherwise refutes the defendant's evidence 'by any process which consists merely in diminishing or negativing the force of' it. **1971** *N.Y. Law Jrnl.* 23 Nov. 18/3 Petitioner's rebuttal affidavit..was received by the court after the court's decision had been published. **1976** *Billings* (Montana) *Gaz.* 17 June 3-H/8 Smith's attorney..presented John L. Agro..as a rebuttal witness. **1976** *Southern Even. Echo* (Southampton) 11 Nov. 4/4 So bitter was the resentment in Southampton of the criticism contained in the late Sir John Hodsoll's report, that the Public Records Office took the unique step of including rebuttal evidence in the State Archives.

rec, rec. (rek), colloq. abbrev. of RECREATION^1. Also *attrib.* and *ellipt.* (= *recreation ground*).

1929 'R. CROMPTON' *William* iv. 86 Somehow or other the Outlaws got through the lessons before 'rec'. **1931** E. RAYMOND *Mary Leith* v. 170 You saw the mounted specials clear the Rec. **1948** PARTRIDGE *Dict. Forces' Slang* 153 *Rec space*, the ratings' recreation spaces on board ship. **1950** P. TEMPEST *Lag's Lex.* 176 *Rec*, used in some prisons instead of the word 'association'. The prisoners' recreation time. **1960** J. R. ACKERLEY *We think the World of You* 46 The only open space, besides the Rec., in the neighbourhood. **1962** W. GRANVILLE *Dict. Sailors' Slang* 94/2 *Rec room, recreation room* at Osborne, now closed. **1967** *Boston Sunday Globe* 23 Apr. B 41/1 (*heading*) A rec hall for patients. **1972** *Sat. Rev.* (U.S.) 24 June 18/3 The dance was held in the games room of the rec center. **1975** 'E. LATHEN' *By Hook or by Crook* xiii. 129 The wedding presents were supposed to go on the Ping-Pong table in the rec room. **1977** J. SAVAGE *Nemesis Club* vi. 75 He often goes to the rec. after school.

recado. Add: **2.** Also, a saddle-cloth.

1961 G. DURRELL *Whispering Land* vii. 180 Using our saddles and the woolly sheepskin saddle-cloth, called a *recado*, as back-rests.

recalcitrant, *a.* and *sb.* Add: **B.** *sb.* Also *transf.*

1918 *Oxf. Mag.* 21 June 343/2 The American Universities have generally adopted the 'Elective System'... There is, however, a distinguished recalcitrant in the University of Princeton.

Hence **reca·lcitrantly** *adv.*

1976 *Gramophone* Apr. 1603/1 A dialogue between God and a recalcitrantly sinful soul.

reca·lculation. [f. RECALCULATE *v.*: see -ATION.] The action of recalculating.

1848 M. SOMERVILLE *Phys. Geogr.* (1849) App. II. 425 The height here assigned to the Peak of Aconcagua differs 700 feet from that given by Captain Fitzroy. A re-calculation..of his elements has led us to adopt a much greater elevation for the giant of the Chilian Andes. **1872** H. WRAY *Some Applic. of Theory to Practice of Construction* 150 This gives a weight rather less than was provided for, but the difference is not enough to render recalculation necessary.

recalescence. Add: The temporary generation of heat associated with a change in crystal structure when a solid is cooled through a transformation temperature (sometimes sufficient to produce a brief rise in temperature). (Earlier and further examples.) So **recale·scent** *a.*

1873 W. F. BARRETT in *Phil. Mag.* XLVI. 477 Wherever the momentary expansion of the wire is feeble or absent, there likewise this recalescence, as it might be termed, is also feeble or absent. **1912, 1916** [see *DECALESCENCE]. **1973** J. G. TWEEDDALE *Materials Technol.* II. ii. 15 Once nucleation is really started solidification may proceed quite quickly and is then likely to be associated with release of thermal energy as recalescence.

recall, *sb.*^{1} Add: Also with orig. U.S. pronunc. (rī·kǭl). **1.** (Further examples.)

1869 *Sphinx* 27 Nov. 274/2 Even the gods forgot to applaud—the highest compliment which could be paid to the actor, and worth fifty recalls. **1964** *Financial Times* 3 Mar. 13/1 Several hundred were called back yesterday, and the recall will continue this week and next. The final assembly tracks for bicycles..are being restarted. **1969** T. PARKER *Twisting Lane* 197 What's more I did a Borstal recall as well; that's like an extension of it. **1972** *Sat. Rev.* (U.S.) 17 June 6/3 The previous December, General Motors had announced the biggest recall ever—6·7 million Chevys were called in for breaking engine mounts. **1976** *Globe & Mail* (Toronto) 15 Dec. 5/1 More glass has been found in Coca-Cola bottles and..he expects the soft drink company will have to issue another recall.

c. (Earlier and later examples.)

1835 J. E. ALEXANDER *Sketches in Portugal* vii. 160 The bugle sounds the recal for the skirmishers. **1880** J. H. SHORTHOUSE *John Inglesant* xxii. 283 The horn below sounding the recall.

2. Delete *rare.* In *Psychol.*, the act of calling to mind something previously learned or experienced, esp. in memory tests, usu. distinguished from recognition; also *attrib.*; *total recall*, the ability to call to mind every detail that caught the attention.

1894 M. W. CALKINS in *Psychol. Rev.* I. 480 The likelihood of recall increases, therefore, by the recency of the position. **1901** *Ibid.* VIII. 363 A somewhat similar feeling had that day been generated by wholly different content.. and..there had been direct emotional recall through emotion. **1932** F. C. BARTLETT *Remembering* xv. 256 The matter of recall is mainly a question of interest, while the manner of recall is chiefly one of temperament and character. **1934** R. MACAULAY *Going Abroad* xvii. 134 Total Recall is always subject to the gaps in one's memory. **1953** *Columbia-Viking Desk Encycl.* 805/2 His complicated style seeks by total recall to recapture the minutest psychological and sensory detail. **1953** MILLER & SELFRIDGE in Saporta & Bastian *Psycholinguistics* (1961) 203/1 The same data are replotted to show the relation of the recall-score to the length of the list. **1963** J. D. SALINGER *Seymour: an Introduction* 238, I was not..the least bit intoxicated by my own powers..of almost total recall. **1970** *Jrnl. Gen. Psychol.* Oct. 236 Part-whole learning interferes with motor recall just as it does with verbal recall. **1971** *Ibid.* Oct. 215 Recall-memory tests call for reproduction of previous input–output events. **1976** GHATALA & LEVIN in Levin & Allen *Cognitive Learning in Children* iii. 62 The possibility has been raised that the processes and/or types of stored information utilized in recognition decisions differ from those utilized in recall. **1977** M. W. EYSENCK *Human Memory* ii. 35 On a subsequent, unexpected recall test, semantically processed material was much better recalled than phonemically or structurally processed material. **1977** *Lancashire Life* Feb. 70/3 Clara's memory may be less than the total recall she would have wished.

3. c. *U.S.* Removal of an elected government official from office by a system of petition and vote; this method of terminating a period of office. So *recall election.*

1902 *Arena* XXVIII. 470 If the Recall was in force in any locality, whenever a petition signed by any number over one-half of the registered voters of that locality for the recall of any officer of that locality was filed, that office would become vacant. **1911** *Ann. Amer. Acad. Pol. & Soc. Sci.* XXXVIII. 163 (*heading*) Popular control under the recall. **1970** *Internat. & Compar. Law Q.* 4th Ser. XIX. II. 188 Electoral laws..or the right of recall, or the right to be elected to public office. **1976** *Billings* (Montana) *Gaz.* 16 June 3-B/1 *Philadelphia* (AP)—Critics of Mayor Frank L. Rizzo..filed petitions Tuesday asking for his recall. **1978** *Detroit Free Press* 16 Apr. 8A/4 Five suburban politicians have lost their jobs because they supported a MSHDA-backed housing program, and three more are facing a recall election in Birmingham next month. **1979** *Tucson* (Arizona) *Citizen* 3 Oct. 5A/1 A near-loss in a bitter recall election.

4. *attrib.* and *Comb.*, as *recall clause, coverage, signal, telegram.*

1976 *Sunday Times* 30 May 8/3 If by June 15 they can collect 145,448 signatures..then Rizzo has 10 days to resign or face a referendum... Hence, the procedure is known as the 'recall clause'. **1971** *Wall St. Jrnl.* 11 Aug. 28/1 Practically every week now brings news that a potentially faulty or dangerous product is being recalled... Many manufacturers are increasingly interested in.. product recall coverage. **1904** *Daily Chron.* 11 June 5/4 The eight blocking ships saw the recall signal right enough, but.. disregarded it. **1916** H. G. WELLS *Mr. Britling sees it Through* I. i. 27 He wished he knew of somebody who could send a recall telegram from London.

recall, *v.*^{1} **3. c.** (Earlier example.)

1671 LOCKE *Essay Draft B* (1931) 264 The mind can repeat..those ideas..by the power it has of recalling and bringing in view any of its own ideas.

Récamier (rēⁱkæ·myēⁱ, ‖ rekamye). [Name of Jeanne Françoise Julie Adélaïde *Récamier* (1777–1849), French hostess.] **a.** (Also *Madame Récamier* and with small initial.) Used *attrib.* and *absol.* to designate a *chaise-longue* of the type on which Madame Récamier is portrayed reclining in a painting by David. **b.** Used *attrib.* and *Comb.* to designate a reclining position similar to that in which Madame Récamier is portrayed.

1924 M. J. MURRY *Voyage* ix. 168 Mrs. Tancred got up from her Récamier and stretched out both hands to him. **1936** H. NICOLSON *Let.* 19 Feb. (1966) 244 Draped curtains and Madame Récamier sofas and wall-paintings. **1938** E. BOWEN *Death of Heart* I. iii. 66 Anna, on the sofa in a Récamier attitude. **1944** 'P. QUENTIN' *Puzzle for Puppets* i. 9 A Madame Récamier couch and a huge mirror. **1964** H. GRISEWOOD *Last Cab on Rank* i. 7 A charming récamier sofa. **1966** J. AIKEN *Trouble with Product X* v. 88 She herself was disposed, Recamier-fashion, on one of the twin beds, against a pile of pillows. **1971** M. SMITH *Gypsy in Amber* vii. 53, I don't understand..how a man of your obvious good taste could put a récamier in this room. **1972** J. AIKEN *Butterfly Picnic* x. 180, I had adopted a sort of Récamier posture, reclining on my elbows. **1974** H. MCCLOY *Sleepwalker* iv. 49 She..sat on a Récamier couch. **1979** *N.Y. Times Mag.* 16 Dec. 142/3 The smaller studio at the north end of the space is more formal, primarily because of the major furnishings—a matching pair of *récamiers* (Empire-style lounges).

recap (rī·kæp), *sb.*^{1} orig. *U.S.* [f. RECAP *v.*] A pneumatic tyre that has been recapped.

1939 in WEBSTER Add. **1940** in *Amer. Speech* (1944) XIX. 63/2 In recapping it is necessary to make a distinction between a full recap and a top-cap. **1943** *Sun* (Baltimore) 28 Apr. 7/1 The 'recaps for all' announcement had given the public the impression we are over the hump in the rubber situation. **1968** *Wanganui* (N.Z.) *Chron.* 15 Nov. 10/6 (Advt.), If it's tyres or Recaps you need, then try our 10-minute exchange service. **1969** *Truth* (Melbourne) 12 July 31/7 (Advt.), Guaranteed recaps from only $6.50.

recap (rī·kæp), *sb.*^{2} Colloq. abbrev. RECAPITULATION^1 I.

1950 in WEBSTER Add. **1955** POHL & KORNBLUTH *Space Merchants* ii. 22 A brief recap of the extensive plans his lecture agent had made. **1959** *Times Lit. Suppl.* 2 Oct. 561/1 Comments and 'recaps', hints of tragedies to come or to be overcome, helped to give to oral narrative both atmosphere and shape. **1969** *Morning Star* 1 Nov. 3/8 Three films by John Lennon and Yoko Ono were shown to the Press this week—a recap of a recent New Cinema programme and a foretaste of two new John–Yoko programmes. **1973** *Times* 13 July (Motor Racing Suppl.) p. vi/1 A quick recap on my instructor's words. **1977** *N.Y. Rev. Bks.* 24 Nov. 42/4 Instant observation, like sports' reporting, is seldom more than re-cap, resumé, or the usual proclamation of personal preference.

recap, *v.*^{1} (Earlier and further examples.)

1856 'STONEHENGE' *Brit. Sports* I. ii. 21 The cases may easily be recapped, and used many times. **1967** KARCH & BUBER *Offset Processes* ix. 375 Fill the fountain bottle with the fountain solution and re-cap it.

2. *trans.* To renew (a worn pneumatic tyre) by cementing, moulding, and vulcanizing a strip of camel-back on the tread. orig. *U.S.*

1939 in WEBSTER Add. **1943** *Sun* (Baltimore) 28 Apr. 7/1 Any civilian can get his tires recapped. **1946** W. H. GROUSE *Automotive Mechanics* xxvii. 579 Worn tires that have good casings without separated plies or broken or damaged cord can be recapped so that they will have considerably longer life.

Hence **reca·ppable** *a.*, that can be recapped; **reca·pper,** (*b*) one who recaps tyres; **reca·pping** *vbl. sb.*

1939 WEBSTER Add., Recappable. **1940** Recapping [see *RECAP *sb.*^{1}]. **1942** *Sun* (Baltimore) 9 Apr. 26/5 Camelback would be released to retreaders and recappers for passenger tires. **1959** L. E. ONEACRE in M. Morton *Rubber Technol.* iv. 104 The main advantage of an electric mold is that the recapper does not have to install a steam boiler to supply heat that would be needed for steam molds. **1967** H. J. STERN *Rubber* (ed. 2) ix. 401 Many of the tyres produced are retreaded when worn. Sometimes the process is described as recapping, or remoulding, according to the external area which is renewed. **1973** *Black Panther* 24 Nov. 11/3 Rebozo was the largest tire re-capper in Florida. **1976** *Billings* (Montana) *Gaz.* 30 June 7-E/4 (Advt.), Plus ·32 to ·58 federal excise tax each and recappable tire.

recap (rī·kæp), *v.*^{2} Colloq. abbrev. RECAPITULATE *v.* 1. Also *absol.*

1950 in WEBSTER Add. **1958** 'N. BLAKE' *Penknife in my Heart* ii. 36 Let me recap. the situation. **1959** H. HOBSON *Mission House Murder* xviii. 183 Let us recap, Mr. Ford, and assess your position. **1971** *New Scientist* 1 July 44/1 The computer résumé they use when she recaps the results to the other scientists. **1976** 'A. HALL' *Kobra Manifesto* ix. 129 'Want to recap anything?' 'No, I've got it.'

recapacitate, *v.* Restrict *rare* to sense in Dict. and add: **2.** *trans. Physiol.* To restore potency to (a spermatozoon). Cf. *CAPACITATE *v.*, *CAPACITATION.

1959 M. C. CHANG in C. W. Lloyd *Rec. Progress Endocrinol. & Reproduction* 153 Decapacitated rabbit sperms can be recapacitated again. *Ibid.* 161 The capacitated sperms can be decapacitated by treatment with seminal plasma.. but can be recapacitated if they remain longer in the female tract. **1969** *New Scientist* 31 July 234/1 Such sperm were said to have suffered decapacitation, and could regain fertilizing ability (be 'recapacitated') by spending a second period in the female tract.

Hence **re:capacita·tion.**

1970 [see *DECAPACITATED *ppl. a.*]. **1974** *Jrnl. Reproduction & Fertility* XLI. 243 It was possible to demonstrate sperm recapacitation.

reca·pitalize, *v.* [RE- 5 b.] *trans.* and *intr.* To capitalize (shares, etc.) again. Also *fig.* So **re:capitaliza·tion**; **reca·pitalized** *ppl. a.*

1927 *Sunday Express* 11 Sept. 1/1 The 'recapitalisation' bubble..is still crowding northern Bankruptcy courts with failures affecting thousands of people. **1928** *Observer* 15 July 20/3 Does anybody suppose that the recapitalised mills are paying their shareholders any such return? **1945** *Richmond* (Va.) *News-Leader* 1 Aug. 13/2 Thomas E. Wilson, chairman of the Board of Directors of Wilson & Co., Inc., today announced plans to recapitalize the company's 274,085 outstanding shares of $6 preferred stock. **1947** J. HAYWARD *Prose Lit. since 1939* 25 The break with the pre-war period was irreparable, and..a reorientation of intelligence and sensibility, a recapitalisation of experience, was inevitable. **1979** *Beautiful British Columbia* Spring 16/1 Bishop declared bankruptcy, re-capitalized, and Secrets of Chinatown was released the following year.

recapitulant (rīkăpi·tiŭlănt), *a. rare.* [f. RECAPITULATE *v.*: see -ANT^1.] = RECAPITULATORY *a.*

1929 W. FAULKNER *Sound & Fury* 378 He repeated his story, harshly recapitulant. **1932** —— *Light in August* xii. 269 The boys' diction was slow now, recapitulant. **1939** —— *Wild Palms* 244 You expressed gratitude almost tediously recapitulant.

recapitulate, *v.* Add: **1. c.** *Mus.* To restate, usu. in similar but distinct form, a musical theme which has been developed in an intervening section. Cf. *RECAPITULATION^1 1 c.

1959 D. COOKE *Lang. Music* v. 250 The second subject of the finale picks up the six-note chromatic scale..; when it is recapitulated, the same notes are used in the bass.

recapitulation^1. Add: **1. b.** (Further examples.)

1904 G. S. HALL *Adolescence* I. p. viii, Realizing the limitations and qualifications of the recapitulation theory in the biologic field, I am now convinced that its psychogenetic applications have a method of their own. **1919** J. B. WATSON *Psychol.* vii. 266 The recapitulation theory.. holds..that ontogeny repeats phylogeny—that the developing child must pass through all the stages that the race has passed through. **1924** R. M. OGDEN tr. *Koffka's Growth of Mind* ii. 48 He can dismiss both the recapitulation- and the utility-theories. **1957** P. HALMOS *Towards Measure of Man* i. 19 Today, the theory of recapitulation is, on the whole, discredited.

c. *Mus.* The section of a composition or movement (esp. one in sonata form) in which some or all of the themes presented in the exposition are repeated, usu. in a modified form. Also *attrib.*

1879 GROVE *Dict. Music* I. 551/1 In the recapitulation of his [*sc.* Beethoven's] subjects,..there is a growing tendency to avoid the apparent platitude of repeating them exactly as at first. **1898** G. B. SHAW *Perfect Wagnerite* 3 In classical music there are, as the analytic programs tell us, first subjects and second subjects, free fantasias, recapitulations, and codas. **1934** C. LAMBERT *Music Ho!* II. 127 His [*sc.* Satie's] unusual employment of what might be called interrupted and overlapping recapitulations. **1947** A. EINSTEIN *Music in Romantic Era* vii. 70 Beethoven had been criticized for having held too fast to the sonata form in his third *Leonore* Overture, or—more precisely—that he had not foregone the recapitulation. **1947** *Penguin Music Mag.* Dec. 29 After the climax Mendelssohn duly modulates to his 'recapitulation-section'. **1959** *Collins Music Encycl.* 613/2 The procedures denoted by the names of its [*sc.* sonata form's] three sections—Exposition (*i.e.* presentation), Development (*i.e.* discursive treatment), and Recapitulation (*i.e.* return)—were present in earlier music. *Ibid.* 614/1 The Recapitulation may differ from the Exposition in details, *e.g.* in orchestration and in the use of new accompaniments to themes. **1959** *Listener* 23 July 152/1 The first theme of the sonata-form opening movement, expounded in three-four time, is transformed in the abbreviated recapitulation to four-four. **1979** C. DEXTER *Service of all the Dead* iii. 22 He had sedulously drilled the set works into them—their themes, their developments and recapitulations.

2. For *rare*$^{-1}$ read *Theol.* and add later examples.

1913 E. GRUBB *Doctrine of Person of Christ* iv. 28 This idea of 'recapitulation'..is one of the deepest and most pregnant thoughts contributed by Irenæus. **1957** *Oxf. Dict. Chr. Ch.* 1142/1 The conception of recapitulation was elaborated esp. by St. Irenaeus, who interpreted it as both the restoration of fallen humanity to communion with God through the obedience of Christ and as the summing-up of the previous revelations of God in past ages in the Incarnation. **1969** J. ATKINSON in *Dict. Chr. Theol.* 285/2 The recapitulation in Christ connotes the total work of God for man's redemption.

reca·rbon, *v.* [f. RE- 5 c + CARBON *sb.*] *trans.* To fit (an arc-lamp) with new carbon electrodes. So **reca·rboning** *vbl. sb.*

1902 W. J. DIBDIN *Public Lighting* 445 There are two pairs of carbons in each lamp, such being necessary to allow of the lamp burning throughout the whole of a winter night without being re-carboned. **1902** *Encycl. Brit.* XXVIII. 86/2 The cost of carbons and the labour of recarboning. **1917** C. N. BENNETT *Guide to Kinematogr.* xi. 185 If someone will..kindly re-carbon the arc for us and turn on the electric current we shall be ready to start showing.

recarbonate (rīkā·ɹbŏneɪt), *v.* [f. RE- 5 c + CARBONATE *v.*^{1}] To charge (water) with carbon dioxide after softening. Hence **reca·rbonated** *ppl. a.*; **re:carbona·tion.**

1907 CROSS & BEVAN *Paper-Making* (ed. 3) xv. 356 In order to retain this carbonate in a more permanently soluble form the Archbutt-Deely plant is provided with means for re-carbonating the softened water by the injection of carbon dioxide. **1926** *5th Ann. Rep. Ohio Conf. Water Purification* 60 (*heading*) Methods of recarbonation of lime-soda softened water. **1936** E. S. HOPKINS *Water Purification Control* ix. 163 The lime-softened water may be satisfactorily stabilized at low cost by recarbonating it with carbon dioxide gas. **1969** *Civil Engin.* (N.Y.) June 40/1 The recarbonated water then flows through two ballast ponds in series. **1978** R. WALKER *Water Supply, Treatment & Distribution* xv. 183 The recarbonation chamber must be sized and baffled to provide between 15 and 30 minutes retention time.

recarburization (rīkā:ɹbiŭrəizē·ʃən) *Steel-making.* [RE- 5 c.] Addition of carbon (in the form of coke, anthracite or a carbon-rich alloy such as pig iron) to steel to produce the desired composition after refining.

1888 *Jrnl. Iron & Steel Inst.* 331 The recarburisation of the bath of iron gives rise, in the case of basic or neutral open hearth furnaces, to a very considerable loss of metal. **1924** E. L. RHEAD *Metallurgy* (ed. 3) xi. 222 Recarburisation is now often effected by the use of anthracite. This is put at the bottom of the ladle or thrown into the stream of metal as it runs from the furnace. **1940** SIMONS & GREGORY *Steel Manuf. simply Explained* xv. 105 Anthracite coal is used if the recarburization is carried out in the ladle.

Also **reca·rburize** *v. trans.*; **reca·rburizing** *vbl. sb.*

1888 *Jrnl. Iron & Steel Inst.* 332 This recarburising material consisted in the case of the first charge of 0·145 ton of ferro-manganese and 0·030 ton of ferro-silicon. **1929** C. R. HAYWARD *Outl. Metall. Pract.* xxii. 475 Deoxidize and recarburize the bath. **1950** *Engineering* 30 June 738/3 When making high-carbon steels..it was formerly common practice to run the carbon down in the furnace and then to recarburise to the composition required by the addition of coke or anthracite to the ladle. **1974** *Encycl. Brit. Macropædia* XVII. 645/1 For a long time, high-carbon steels such as rails were made by recarburizing the steel with hot metal. **1974** D. M. CONSIDINE *Chem. & Process Technol. Encycl.* 654/1 Deoxidizing, recarburizing, or alloying additions are made to the ladle during steel tapping from the furnace to adjust the final composition of the steel to the desired specification.

re-ca·se, *v.* [RE- 5 c.] *trans.* To furnish with a new case; to case again; *spec.* to rebind (a book) using its original case or a new one. Hence **reca·sed** *ppl. a.*; **reca·sing** *vbl. sb.*

1853-8 [see RE- 5 c in Dict.]. **1920** T. J. WISE *Bibliogr. Writings J. Conrad* 1. 4 It is clear that ex-library copies of *Almayer's Folly*..have recently been made attractive and marketable by the apparently simple process of re-casing them in cloth. *Ibid.*, when the binding looks very green and new..the book is probably a re-cased one. **1952** J. CARTER *ABC for Book-Collectors* 150 A book which, being shaken or loose, has been taken out of its covers and re-settled in them more firmly is said to be re-cased. *Ibid.*, Most re-casing is not hard to detect. **1977** *Shotton's* (Durham) *Catal.* Oct., Recased into orig. cloth.

recast, *v.* **1.** Delete *rare*$^{-1}$ and add later examples.

1894 E. FAWCETT *New Nero* 17 He recast a sudden look upon Fanshawe and his face drearily brightened. **1899** P. H. WICKSTEED tr. *Dante's Paradiso* ii. 21 Now thou wilt urge that the ray here is darkened rather than in other parts, because here it is recast from further back.

2. c. *Theatr.* To assign (an actor) to another part; to cast (a role, etc.) again. Also *fig.* Cf. CAST *v.* 48.

1951 N. MARSH *Opening Night* vii. 163 A lively and almost cosy discussion about recasting had developed. **1962** L. PAYNE *Too Small for his Shoes* viii. 162 I'll have to recast the part and re-shoot every sequence he was in. **1979** A. SCHOLEFIELD *Point of Honour* 80 My father was recast as a hero..saviour of lives in the face of the enemy. **1981** N. J. CRISP *Festival* vi. 143 Should the play..justify..a possible transfer to the West End, it will..have to be recast.

recategorize (rīkæ·tĕgŏrəiz), *v.* [RE- 5 a.] *trans.* To assign to another category; to reclassify. So **recategoriza·tion**; **reca·tegorizing** *vbl. sb.*

1949 M. MEAD in M. Fortes *Social Structure* 32 We may find ..a recategorizing of cultural experience into such characteristic American forms as fraternities. **1957** PARTRIDGE *English gone Wrong* i. 12 Those..horrifics, *recategorize* and *recategorization*, have..fascinated the combatant services and the Civil Service. **1970** *Jrnl. Gen. Psychol.* Apr. 151 The meaning properties tend to be exhausted rather rapidly by the recategorization instructions. **1977** *Guardian Weekly* 19 Sept. 6/3 He claims there are no political detainees in Chile. (Those left in gaol have been recategorised as common criminals.)

recce (re·ki), *sb.* orig. *Mil. slang.* Also **reccy.** Shortened form of RECONNAISSANCE. Freq. *attrib.* Cf. *RECCO.

1941 *Illustr. London News* CXCVIII. 802 (*caption*) A motor-cycle 'reccy' unit (special reconnaissance troops of armoured force). **1942** E. WAUGH *Put out more Flags* 151 The C.O. has just gone forward with his recce group to make his recce. **1944** *R.A.F. Jrnl.* Aug. 260 We aren't likely to do any serious fighting unless..we are faced by recce patrols by the enemy. **1951** R. CAMPBELL *Light on Dark Horse* iv. 71 My lads became truly proficient in practical recce-work. **1958** G. USHER *Death in Bag* vi. 56, I did a bit of a recce. **1961** W. VAUGHAN-THOMAS *Anzio* iii. 45 No recce plane tried a quick dash to capture a tell-tale photograph. **1968** *Listener* 19 Dec. 812/1 In a side-street we stopped. 'I'll just do a bit of a recce,' the Fiddler said. **1974** *Observer* (Colour Suppl.) 28 Apr. 25/4 We were interrupted by a knock at the door of the mews flat in Belgravia, where Deighton had set up temporary headquarters during his London recce. **1977** 'E. CRISPIN' *Glimpses of Moon* xii. 235 He had had it off all right, thanks..to making careful reccys. **1979** 'A. HAILEY' *Overload* 1. xvii. 102, I sometimes think about two guys in Korea, close buddies of mine. We were on a recce patrol near the Yalu river.

recce, *v.* orig. *Mil. slang.* Also **reccy.** [Shortened f. RECONNOITRE *v.*] *trans.* and *intr.* To reconnoitre (a place, etc.).

1943 J. H. FULLARTON *Troop Target* xxiv. 175 We're even reccying alternative positions twenty miles back to withdraw to. **1944** M. STANDING in *War Report* (B.B.C.) (1946) II. iv. 106 Do not unload until waders have recce'd the water in front of your door. **1945** *Comment from Italy* (Three Arts Club) 48 So I find four bottles and start out across the fields to recce for a farmhouse. **1945** E. WAUGH *Brideshead Revisited* 299 I'm going out myself with the adjutant to recce training areas. **1958** P. SCOTT *Mark of Warrior* 1. 59 I'll know better to-day when I've recced it. **1959** 'J. CHRISTOPHER' *Scent of White Poppies* x. 156 These two recce'd up here, and found them gone. **1968** *Listener* 11 July 40/3 He was..recce-ing the new tourist 'firsts' like the Canadian North-West Passage. **1972** *Shooting Times & Country Mag.* 4 Mar. 21/2 'Lofters'..come over to recce the food situation in the more populated areas. **1976** *Listener* 8 Apr. 438/1 Neither of us had seen any of his architecture in Virginia, so I set off to recce Richmond and Charlottesville.

recco (re·ko). *Mil. slang.* Abbrev. of RECONNAISSANCE. Also *attrib.* Cf. *RECCE *sb.*

1917 A. G. LEE *Let.* 24 May in *No Parachute* (1968) 19 They were still flying two-seater Nieuports, doing..reccos and photography. **1934** *Flight* 18 Jan. 51/1 A shorter 'recco' is also done to the north, if trouble is brewing. **1942** in Forbes & Allen *Ten Fighter Boys* 60 Green section were detailed to..proceed to Chatham, where a recco-machine was hanging around. *Ibid.* 155 My next trip was a scramble to intercept some Hun machines on recco off Dungeness. **1942** W. SIMPSON *One of our Pilots is Safe* ii. 19 That was the last 'recco.' flight we made, and for months we had to content ourselves with mock air battles. **1943** *Life* 9 Aug. 100/2 (*caption*) Armed recco over Rabaul. **1966** P. DERRIG *Pride of Green Berets* 61 Civil Guard recco units.

reccy, var. *RECCE *sb.* or *v.*

recd. Also **rec'd.** Abbrev. of *received* pa. t. and pa. pple. of RECEIVE *v.*

1599 J. DAY in P. Henslowe *Henslowe's Diary* (1904) I. 57 Rec^d of m^r Hinchloe more in ernest of The Tragedy of Thomas Merrye 20^s Joh. Day. W Haughton. **1775** D. GARRICK *Let.* 1 Nov. (1963) III. 1044 In the middle of the play last night I rec^d your very extraordinary Note. **1851** J. CHAPMAN *Diary* 23 Apr. in G. S. Haight *Geo. Eliot & J. Chapman* (1940) 158 Rec^d a letter from Susanna giving a better account of Beatrice. **1876** W. WHITMAN *Daybks. & Notebks.* 12 Mar. (1978) I. 6 Sent & recd. **1934** E. POUND *Eleven New Cantos* xxxiv. 17 And on his return was recd. by Gouverneur Morris and Mr Astor with a pubk. dinner at Tammany Hall. **1965** H. GOLD *Man who was not with It* xi. 86 It had cost me to go back to Pittsburgh, although I had rec'd value.

recede, *v.*[1] Add: **1. e.** Of a colour: to appear to be more distant from the eye than another in the same plane; = RETIRE *v.* 3 b. Cf. *ADVANCE *v.* 2 b.

1935 A. H. RUTT *Home Furnishing* iv. 35 Advancing and receding qualities in colors are a reality, as psychologists have proved. The warm hues seem to advance and the cool ones to recede. **1951** *Good Housek. Home Encycl.* 152/1 The cool tints..tend to 'recede' and will give a feeling of space.

5. a. (Earlier example.)

1788 E. SHERIDAN *Let.* 27 July in *Betsy Sheridan's Jrnl.* (1960) iv. 107 And now to *recede*—I had just sent off my letter yesterday when Mrs Angelo call'd, as usual all life and spirits and full of news.

Hence **rece·ded** *ppl. a.*

1909 M. B. SAUNDERS *Litany Lane* I. vi. 69 Her attendant lady.., Augusta of the receded fringe.

receding, *ppl. a.* (Further examples.)

1895 A. W. PINERO *Second Mrs. Tanqueray* III. 103 A man..with a low forehead, a receding chin, a vacuous expression. **1956** *Jrnl. Theol. Stud.* VII. 18 The incidence of the gradually receding preposition παρά supports the impression. **1958** [see *ADVANCE *v.* 2 b]. **1977** *Transatlantic Rev.* LX. 183 If I have learned anything it is that the past is not a receding dream but an ever burgeoning presence at our backs that sustains us.

receipt, *sb.* **VI. 17.** *receipt tax* (earlier example).

1787 DUKE OF DORSET in O. Browning *Despatches from Paris* (1909) I. 217 It is fear'd that the Duty is intended to include Stamp-receipts after the plan of the Receipt-Tax in England.

receipt, *v.*[2] Add: **2.** Also *fig.*

1938 E. BOWEN *Death of Heart* III. i. 327 She receipted Portia's remark with an upward jerk of the chin.

3. (Earlier and later examples.)

1832 *Sen. Doc. 23rd U.S. Congress I Sess.* No. 512 (1835) II. 829 [Stock] will be delivered..to an issuing officer,..who will receipt therefor. **1862** O. L. JACKSON *Colonel's Diary* (1922) v. 96 Major Lyford..receipted to me for the safe delivery of the cargo. **1913** J. LONDON *Valley of Moon* 503 These two assistants had..been receipted for by the local deputy sheriff.

receipted *ppl. a.* (further example).

1979 *Daily Tel.* 21 Nov. 3/3 Drivers would need to present full log sheets of receipted bills to support their case for relief.

receiptor. (Earlier and later examples.)

1814 *Mass. Supreme Court Rep.* XI. 319 The receiptors are precluded, by their own act, from calling in question the validity of the attachment. **1914** F. RAWLE *Bouvier's Law Dict.* III. 2824/2 The officer taking the goods often.. delivers them to some third person, termed the 'receiptor', who gives his receipt for them.

receivable, *a.* Add: **A.** *adj.* **1. d.** Of a broadcast signal or a broadcasting station.

1962 *Rep. Comm. Broadcasting 1960* 196 in *Parl. Papers 1961–2* (Cmnd. 1753) IX. 259 Both the BBC and the ITA.. accept it as their duty to see that their present services are as nearly as possible available to everybody in the country. Not only should they be receivable; they must also be technically acceptable.

B. *sb. pl. Comm.* Debts owed to a business, esp. regarded as assets. Cf. *PAYABLES *sb. pl.*

1863 'E. KIRKE' *My Southern Friends* xxii. 231 When I went home..we had only nineteen thousand in bank. I had exhausted all our receivables. **1947** *Sun* (Baltimore) 30 Sept. 19/1 A move to..take care of a steadily expanding volume of receivables acquired. **1955** *Times* 10 May 17/2 Long-term receivables have been separated from current receivables, and a new item, short-term borrowings, appears under current liabilities. **1978** *Daily Tel.* 21 Mar. 3 (Advt.), The HP 3000 will run your payroll, process invoices, print out receivables and take care of general ledger work.

receive, *v.* Add: **I. 4. a.** (Further example.)

1861 D. G. ROSSETTI tr. *Dante's Vita Nuova* 299 The sonnet has two parts... It might well receive other divisions also.

d. Also of other, non-recording, apparatus.

1957 *Encycl. Brit.* XXI. 912I/2 The television signal is received on a short wave antenna and carried by a transmission line to the receiver.

e. Of a radio or television set: to reproduce the sound or picture transmitted by (a station or a person). Also *transf.*, of the user, and *absol.*

1908 *Rep. Brit. Assoc. Adv. Sci. 1907* 621 In this way it is possible to receive at Hythe from Elmers End. **1930** *Morn. Post* 18 Aug. 3/4 In order to receive foreign stations consistently it is necessary to employ a powerful receiver. **1969** M. PUGIT *Last Place Left* xxv. 187 Get what I mean, now? You receiving me, strength four? **1970** J. EARL *Tuners & Amplifiers* iii. 75 If you are proposing to try receiving distant stations..you will need a tuner of the best possible selectivity.

II. 13. a. Also in phr. *to receive in marriage* = *to take in marriage* s.v. TAKE *v.* 14 b.

1835 O. PRATT in *Utah Gen. & Hist. Mag.* (1938) XXIX. 34, I baptized Sarah Marinda Bates, near Sacketts Harbor, whom I received in marriage upwards of one year after.

14. b. (Later example.)

a **1817** JANE AUSTEN *Persuasion* (1818) III. iv. 58 He thought it a very degrading alliance; and Lady Russell.. received it as a most unfortunate one.

IV. 24. Also, to receive visitors.

1902 H. JAMES *Wings of Dove* IX. xxxii. 499 'I'm commissioned to ask you from her to go and see her.'.. He was.. bewildered. 'Then she can receive—?'

25. The infin. used, usu. *attrib.*, to designate the receiving mode, controls, etc., of a radio or telecommunication system.

1920 *Wireless World* 7 Aug. 356/1 A send–receive switch. **1966** 'A. HALL' *9th Directive* xiii. 121 Loman was buzzing for me so I switched the radio to 'receive'. 'Do you hear me, Quiller?' **1970** *New Scientist* 24 Dec. 554/3 The Applications Technology Satellite 3..provided two transmit and two receive voice channels.

received, *ppl. a.* Add: **1. a.** (Further examples.) Also *received idea* = *idée reçue* s.v. *IDÉE. Cf. also *received text* s.v. TEXT *sb.*[1] 1 d.

1608 E. TOPSELL *Serpents* 219 Suidas followeth the common received opinion, that the Salamander quencheth the fire. **1959** *Times Lit. Suppl.* 20 Feb. 94/4 The error he has discovered in the received reference books..deserves special note from all those concerned with the period. *Ibid.* 20 Mar. 159/1 Her neat and tidy balance sheets are summaries of received ideas into which she ventures to inject no new thought. **1960** J. BAYLEY *Characters of Love* ii. 52 The appearance of Courtly Love..has left an immense legacy of received ideas about sex and society. **1973** *Howard Jrnl.* XIII. 330 In former days, the received view was accepted more readily and unquestioningly. **1973** *Times* 13 Dec. 13/4 It is a received idea that television is the most powerful medium ever devised. The proposition is hardly ever questioned. **1976** E. MACLAREN *Nature of Belief* iv. 39 His formal education may help him to be critical or sceptical about quite a lot of 'received opinion'.

b. Of language or pronunciation: *received pronunciation*, the pronunciation of that variety of British English widely considered to be least regional, being originally that used by educated speakers in southern England; also, the 'accepted', standard pronunciation of any specified area, Received Standard; *Received Standard* (*English*), the spoken language of a linguistic area (usu. Britain) in its traditionally most correct and acceptable form. Hence in other derived uses.

[**1818** *Trans. Amer. Philos. Soc.* I. 259 According to its most generally received pronunciation, it is more properly a diphthong.] **1869** A. J. ELLIS *On Early Eng. Pronunc.* I. 13 The alphabet required for writing the theoretically received pronunciation of literary English. **1874** —— *Ibid.* IV. 1095/1 The tip of the tongue for received English is not so advanced towards the teeth or gums, as for the continental sound. **1882** —— in *Trans. Philol. Soc.* 21 We say they are dialectal forms of the received *down*. **1889** [see *RP* s.v. *R II. 2 a]. **1890** *Dialect Notes* I. 26 For the study of pronunciation the received spelling is very ill adapted. **1913** H. C. WYLD in *Mod. Lang. Teaching* IX. 261/2 When he speaks of *Standard English*, he is, I believe, referring to what I now call *Received Standard*. **1914** M. MONTGOMERY in *Ibid.* X. 11/2 Yet in that country [*sc.* Germany], as time goes on, a process of assimilation towards a single 'Received Standard' is said to be growing more, rather than less, marked. **1932** D. JONES *Outl. Eng.* xviii. 148 In Received English there are six affricates which may be represented phonetically by.. diagraphs. **1932** *S. P. E. Tract* XXXVII. 542 These authors.. define the 'Received Pronunciation' as that of 'the great public schools, the Universities, and the learned professions'. **1936** *Trans. Philol. Soc.* 80 My own recollection of this opposition to Received Speech is that the dialect speaker acquires a consciousness of 'correctness' in speech accompanied by a powerful objection to being caught..'talking fine'. **1937** D. JONES in *Le Maître Phonétique* Apr.–June (Suppl.), I take the view that foreigners learning English should be free to choose whatever pronunciation they prefer. Many naturally choose what has been termed 'received' pronunciation (R.P.), as being a widely understood type of English. **1940** J. H. JAGGER *Eng. in Future* i. 15 The influence of the various forms of Modified Standard—to accept Professor Wyld's terms—upon each other and upon Received Standard. **1962** A. C. GIMSON in R. Quirk *Use of Eng.* 281 *Received Pronunciation*, or RP, suggesting..the result of a collective social judgment rather than of a conscious, prescriptive agreement. **1964** C. BARBER *Ling. Change Present-Day Eng.* ii. 20 The influence of the mass-media and of mass-education..does not necessarily produce speakers of Received Standard English. **1969** S. POTTER *Changing Eng.* i. 14 Other cities, notably Edinburgh and Dublin, have their received pronunciations, and so have other regions of the English-speaking world. **1973** G. W. TURNER *Stylistics* v. 147 Even now 'received pronunciation' will help its user to obtain credit when ordering goods by telephone. **1974** J. I. M. STEWART *Gaudy* x. 179 There is no such thing as an Oxford accent, since what phoneticians call Received Standard English came into existence without the university's playing any very identifiable part in the process.

receiver[1]. Add: **1. c.** (*a*) *Amer. Football*, an offensive player eligible to catch a pass; also, a defender designated to receive a kick-off or punt, a safety man; (*b*) *U.S. Baseball*, a catcher. Cf. *wide receiver* s.v. *WIDE *a.*

1897 *Encycl. Sport* I. 421/2 The direction of a pass must depend upon where the prospective receiver is. **1908** *Baseball Mag.* Aug. 16/1 Flint was a wonderful catcher and the amount of work he could stand would make some of the receivers of today take notice. **1921** *Outing* Jan. 156/3 (*caption*) Crangle of Illinois was..a sure receiver of the forward pass. **1935** L. LITTLE *How to watch Football* vii. 140 The passer..would be helpless without the receiver who is able to get into position. **1940** D. HILL *Football through Years* 64/2 The accompanying illustrations.. show what a split second can mean to the receiver of the ball in fast brilliant play. **1957** *Encycl. Brit.* IX. 474/2 Eligible receivers were the players at the end of the line of scrimmage. **1967** *Ebony* June 128/3 Battey has been Howard's chief rival as the American League's premier receiver. **1972** J. MOSEDALE *Football* i. 7 A great receiver like Paul Warfield..loafs through his pass patterns until the defender relaxes. **1981** *Sports Illustr.* 12 Feb. 28 The Irish set up one touchdown by Walker when their kickoff receivers got their signals crossed.

2. c. (Further example.)

1977 *N.Z. Herald* 8 Jan. 1–3/10 Meanwhile, the Nelson receiver of wreck, Mr R. K. Watson, said no legal action would be taken against the three men who boarded the boat and claimed salvage rights.

d. An official of the Metropolitan Police Force (see quot. 1966).

1829 *Act* 10 *Geo. IV.* c. 44 § 10 It shall be lawful for His Majesty to appoint a proper Person to receive all Sums of Money applicable to the Purposes of this Act, who shall be called 'The Receiver for the Metropolitan Police District'. **1902** *Encycl. Brit.* XXXI. 818/1 The county council of any county within the Metropolitan Police District has to transfer to the receiver of police a sum bearing..proportion to the police rate. **1928** *Daily Mail* 7 Aug. 17/2 The Receiver is concerned with equipment and so forth..of..the Metropolitan Police. **1966** J. D. DEVLIN *Police Procedure, Administration & Organisation* iii. 20 The police authority of the Metropolitan Police Force is the Home Secretary, and the official responsible for police property, buildings and finance is the Receiver for the Metropolitan Police.., who is appointed by the Crown. *Ibid.*, In provincial forces, the duties and functions of the Receiver fall on the police authority.

4. d. (See quot. 1970.)

1938 M. LANGLEY *Refuelling in Flight* 18, I insisted that the tanker (giver) should formate on the liner or bomber (receiver). **1970** *Gloss. Aeronaut. & Astronaut. Terms* (*B.S.I.*) x. 17 *Receiver aircraft*, an aircraft which is being refuelled in the air.

7. b. (Further examples.) Also occas. applied loosely to the complete telephone receiving-unit.

1897 *Sears, Roebuck Catal.* 472/2 (Advt.), The improved long distance battery telephone of the regular Bell telephone style with..compound pole receiver. **1918** S. LEACOCK *Frenzied Fiction* iv. 52 'Great-grandfather,' I said, as I hung up the receiver in disgust, 'you are a Mutt!' **1936** DYLAN THOMAS in *New Verse* Dec. 17 The parting of hat from hair, Pursed lips from the receiver. **1971** *Daily Tel.* 11 June 32/6 The amount of telephoning which has to be done does not justify two receivers at the charity's office. **1980** A. N. WILSON *Healing Art* xvi. 195 He had a telephone receiver to his ear.

c. An apparatus for receiving radio or other signals transmitted as electromagnetic waves; now *spec.* a combined tuner and amplifier (without a loud-speaker).

1891 *Rep. Brit. Assoc. Adv. Sci. 1890* 757 To calculate the force between two neighbouring Hertzian receivers. **1912** *Chambers's Jrnl.* Jan. 60/2, I had got our receiver into 'tune' with the transmitter on board a steamer some miles away. **1927** *Radio Assoc. Official Handbk.* 50 The ultimate Television receiver will be a simple piece of apparatus. **1930** *Morning Post* 18 Aug. 3/4 With any good receiver..several foreign stations may be regularly well received. **1933** [see *LOOKER *sb.* 1 d]. **1955** *Radio Times* 22 Apr. 3/2 The F.M. receiver is designed to take advantage of the full frequency range transmitted. **1966** *McGraw-Hill Encycl. Sci. & Technol.* XI. 200/1 In most pulse-radar systems a single antenna serves for both transmission and reception... The duplexer protects the sensitive receiver by disconnecting it from the antenna during the presence of the powerful transmitter pulse. **1973** *Daily Tel.* (Colour Suppl.) 12 Oct. 31/4 Other products not listed include radio tuners and tuner/amplifiers (known now as 'receivers'). **1976** A. WHITE *Long Silence* 31 By the time Dick was thirteen, he'd built his own radio receiver and transmitter. **1978** *Gramophone* May 1958/1 Trio (B. H. Morris) plan to demonstrate several new amplifiers, tuners, receivers and turntables.

d. A detector of sound or other compressional waves.

1920 *Physical Rev.* XV. 178 A pair of receivers mounted on a horizontal rod which may be rotated..is an efficient device for getting the direction of a source of sound. **1931** STEWART & LINDSAY *Acoustics* x. 261 The earliest type of acoustic receiver was the so-called Broca tube, consisting.. of a sphere or nipple *C* of rubber or sheet metal attached to the end of a listening tube *T*. **1957** NOLTINGK & TERRY in E. G. Richardson *Technical Aspects of Sound* II. ii. 111 Magnetostrictive and piezoelectric receivers may be designed. **1973** *Nature* 30 Nov. 297/1 This communication describes the results of a reversed seismic refraction line carried out with explosives and seabed receivers in the median valley of the Mid-Atlantic Ridge.

receiver-general. Add: † **2.** *transf.* **a.** *slang.* A prostitute. *Obs.* **b.** *Pugilists' slang.* (See quot. 1903.) *Obs.*

1811 *Lexicon Balatronicum*, *Receiver General*, a prostitute. **1821** P. EGAN *Boxiana* III. 356 It was evident M'-Dermot was doomed to be a Receiver-General; although he had nobbed Purcell over the right eye..Purcell had the best of it. **1829** *Ibid.* 2nd Ser. II. 180 Dick was now a receiver-general, and his mug was severely bruised. **1903** FARMER & HENLEY *Slang* VI. 5/1 *Receiver-general*..(pugilists'), a boxer giving nothing for what he gets.

receivership. Add: **1.** Also in extended use.

1934 H. G. WELLS *Exper. Autobiogr.* II. ix. 732 Lenin's reconstructed Communist Party was a much more effective step towards an organized receivership.

2. (Further examples.)

1929 *Times* 30 Oct. 14/2 After the close of the market it became known that the receivership in the Cuba Cane Sugar Company had been made permanent. **1967** R. Stein *Great Cars* 222/2 Other troubles piled up. In 1921, Lincoln was forced into receivership, and Ford bought the company. **1976** F. Zweig *New Acquisitive Society* ii. v. 113 The sinking enterprise finally ends up in receivership.

receiving, *vbl. sb.* Add: **1.** (Later examples.)
1931 *Writer's Digest* Oct. 28 (*To*) *fall for receiving*, to be convicted to having stolen property in one's possession... 'He caught me with the rocks, so I fell for receiving.' **1956** E. Grierson *Second Man* ii. 37 He was also in trouble again with the police: a little receiving. **1979** *Tucson* (Arizona) *Citizen* 20 Sept. 11d/7 Paul Jones of Cal, who caught 10 passes against Arizona last Saturday, leads in receiving with 13.

2. a. (Further examples of *receiving order.*)
1930 *Daily Express* 30 July 2/7 Receiving Orders are announced in the 'London Gazette'. **1977** *Private Eye* 1 Apr. 4/1 Harry Alan's financial affairs last attracted attention in 1973 when Air Express Travel obtained a receiving order against him for £700.

b. *receiving country, depot, home, -house* (earlier and later examples), *office* (examples), *pen, -room* (further examples), *-ship* (further examples), *-station* (further examples), *-yard* (further example).
1938 *Washington Post* 21 Dec. 6/1 Refugees would be allowed to leave Germany for a 'receiving country'. **1958** J. J. Spengler in B. Thomas *Economics of Internat. Migration* ii. 17 (*title*) Effects produced in receiving countries by pre-1939 immigration. **1970** *Soviet Weekly* 13 June 11 Our laundry has 32 receiving depots and washes for 150,000 people. **1967** *U.S. Supreme Court Reports* CCCLXXXVII. 27 The fact of the matter is that, however euphemistic the title, a 'receiving home'..for juveniles is an institution for confinement. **1973** *Washington Post* 13 Jan. a5/2 Under the plan children in 'predisposition status' and under Receiving Home authority will be transferred into one of five categories. **1824** E. Weeton *Jrnl.* May (1969) II. 280, I wished to see the General Post Office, so..I took that letter all the way there, instead of putting it into one of the receiving Houses nearer at hand. **1854** E. E. Hale *Kanzas & Nebraska* ix. 224 A boarding-house or receiving-house, in which three hundred persons may receive temporary accommodation on their arrival. **1900** S. A. Nelson *ABC of Wall St.* 157 *Receiving houses*, houses which make a business of receiving and selling cash grain. **1908** *Daily Chron.* 21 Apr. 1/6 He should..see that the receiving house clause was given the very fullest effect to. *c* **1865** in R. Whitehouse *London Album* (1980) Pl. 70, Midland Railway, Receiving Office. **1885** *List of Subscribers, Classified* (United Telephone Co.) 2 The Midland Railway Company will also receive Goods at the following Receiving Offices. **1972** *Classification of Occupations* (Dept. Employment) II. 366/2 *Receiving office assistant*, receives from customers articles requiring service and returns finished articles at a receiving office. **1931** Receiving pen [see *crush *sb.* 4 c]. **1846** G. Dodd *Brit. Manuf.* VI. 184 [The] sail-cloth is taken to a 'receiving-room', where it is examined, freed from lumps and irregularities, measured, and weighed. **1978** M. Puzo *Fools Die* v. xxix. 333, I noticed that most of the men threw their car keys on the table in the first receiving room. **1901** *Daily Colonist* (Victoria, B.C.) 3 Nov. 2/3 A third class ensign on the receiving ship Columbia lying at the New York Navy Yard. **1978** K. Bonfiglioni *All Tea in China* iv. xiii. 180 The only other vessels in the anchorage were the receiving ships. **1939** *War Illustr.* 28 Oct. 219/1 From his bed in an R.A.F. medical receiving station hidden away in the woods 'somewhere in France'. **1977** G. W. H. Lampe *God as Spirit* ii. 54 Divine communications at the subconscious level, for which the actual recipients had acted simply as passive receiving stations. **1923** Receiving yard [see *forcing *vbl. sb.* 3 a].

c. Of things: designed for the reception of radio signals or the like, as *receiving aerial, apparatus, circuit, set* (also *fig.*), *station.*
1923 E. W. Marchant *Radio Telegr. & Teleph.* iii. 24 The exact arrangement of the receiving aerial may be varied within fairly wide limits. **1962** A. Nisbett *Technique Sound Studio* 267 This highly inefficient transformer action is improved if the receiving aerial is so constructed as to resonate at the desired frequencies of reception. **1908** Receiving apparatus [see *pick *v.*[1] 20 f]. **1925** *Times* 28 May 20/4 Such a standard must obviously be based upon a consideration of two factors—namely, the limitations of the present transmitting and receiving apparatus; and, secondly, the æsthetic element. **1923** E. W. Marchant *Radio Telegr. & Teleph* iv. 38 When the coherer was first used in connection with receiving circuits, it was connected between the aerial and the ground. **1955** *Radio Times* 22 Apr. 3/2 A special type of receiving circuit is necessary for F.M. **1916** *Lit. Digest* (N.Y.) 1 Jan. 13/2 His outfit comprised only a cheap home made receiving set! But it did the work, just the same. **1937** *Discovery* Nov. 334/2 His [*sc.* the shrew's] bewhiskered snout is a receiving-set fitted to pick up any broadcast interesting to a shrew. **1953** A. Huxley *Let.* 9 Aug. (1969) 682 Receiving sets grafted into the tissues of animals, so as to make them robots responsive to the radioed will of their masters. **1975** *Listener* 4 Dec. 738/2 A fee required of each owner of a receiving set. **1923** E. W. Marchant *Radio Telegr. & Teleph.* iii. 23 A number of vertical wires are attached to a suspended horizontal wire and brought down in a fan-shape to the receiving station.

3. Special combinations. **receiving barn** *U.S.*, a stable in which horses are placed before a race to prevent tampering; **receiving blanket** *N. Amer.*, a soft blanket in which to wrap a baby (cf. Receiver[1] 6 a); **receiving line** orig. *U.S.*, a row of persons by whom guests are greeted in turn on arrival.
1946 *Sun* (Baltimore) 26 Oct. 8/4 Refusal of George D. Widener to allow his equine star, Lucky Draw, to compete in the Pimlico Special simply because of the receiving barn is to be regretted. **1949** *Ibid.* 29 Apr. 18/4 There has been no doping case since the rules governing the receiving barn were revised last fall. **1974** Tilley & Plowden *This is Horse Racing* 181 *Receiving barn*, facility where horses are isolated for certain period before post time, to minimize chances of tampering. **1926** *Infants' Dept.* Oct. 5028/1 *Layette...* 1 Receiving blanket. **1944** K. Hardy *Sewing for Baby* viii. 214 You will need two cotton receiving blankets. **1970** *Globe & Mail* (Toronto) 26 Sept. 12/8 (Advt.), Since mid-summer we have paid out Four Hundred and Twenty-one Dollars for the basic essentials in layettes; shirts, diapers, gowns, and receiving blankets. **1933** H. L. Ickes *Diary* 17 Nov. (1955) I. 125 He told Anna in the receiving line last night that he was going to order me down there. **1971** M. Lee *Dying for Fun* xl. 189 Millie Panhard Geltzer went to the Woman of the Year Luncheon... She shook hands with the receiving line.

receiving, *ppl. a.* Add: **2.** *receiving end*, the position that receives a transmitted signal or discharged object. Usu. *fig.*, used loosely in colloq. phr. *to be on* (or *at*) *the receiving end*, to be the (unfortunate) recipient of some action, event, etc.; to bear the brunt, to suffer.
1933 [see *invert *v.* 2 g]. **1937** H. L. Ickes *Diary* 2 Oct. (1955) II. 219, I shall refuse to be at the receiving end of any more brickbats. **1942** Berrey & Van den Bark *Amer. Thes. Slang* § 674 *Catcher's position*, receiving end. **1946** B. Pemberton in S. H. Adams *Alexander Woollcott* xiv. 142 But it [*sc.* the nature of Woollcott's criticism] was hell for those on the receiving end. **1949** J. Szigeti *With Strings Attached* xxxiii. 302 It cannot be the love of music pure and simple, for we share this with multitudes who either are on the receiving end alone or, not content with this, also aspire to the satisfaction of making music themselves. **1955** W. C. Gault *Ring around Rosa* vi. 78 Jan had just brought a right hand from right field and the wrestler had been on the receiving end. **1958** P. Kemp *No Colours or Crest* viii. 151 His experience of guerrilla warfare had been, as it were, on the receiving end; for he had served before the war on the North-West Frontier and in Palestine. **1962** A. Nisbett *Technique Sound Studio* x. 176 Dialling is rather more of a performance than being on the receiving end of a phone call. **1968** G. Jones *Hist. Vikings* iii. ii. 202 As in Scandinavia, so at the receiving end in Europe the times were favourable to the art and practice of *viking*. **1976** J. Snow *Cricket Rebel* 134 The wrist had been on the receiving end of a Dennis Lillee bouncer.

re-cement, *v.* Add: Hence **re-cemented** *ppl. a.*
1946 *Nature* 13 July 58/1 The lower part of the profile consists, according to the district, either of re-cemented chalk or compact sand, both of which are very water-retentive. **1965** G. J. Williams *Econ. Geol. N.Z.* iii. 26/2 Re-cemented brecciated quartz is occasionally seen.

recency. Add: **a.** (Further examples.)
1882 C. E. Dutton *Tertiary Hist. Grand Cañon District* v. 83 Even here where historic antiquity merges into geologic recency the one gives us no measure of the other. **1948** H. Nicolson *Diary* 23 Sept. (1968) 149 Frank Pakenham tells me that I was on the list for peerages last December... I might have come up again had it not been for the recency of Croydon. **1964** *Language* XL. 204 The recency and taxonomic character of paralinguistics and kinesics are not sufficient cause for overlooking them. **1976** *Nature* 5 Feb. 395/2 Genetic similarity may serve as direct measure of the recency of the cladistic event which separated the two compared lines of descent.

b. *Psychol.* The fact of being recent as it affects the facility with which learned material or an experience is recalled; freq. *attrib.* Cf. *primacy 1 b.
1894 M. W. Calkins in *Psychol. Rev.* I. 482 The influence of recency, too, can be studied. **1916** J. B. Watson in *Psychol. Bull.* XIII. 77 Other investigators hold that the stamping in of a successful act depends upon the principles of *recency* and *frequency* and is not dependent upon the pleasantness or unpleasantness resulting from the activity. **1929** K. S. Lashley in C. Murchison *Found. Exper. Psychol.* xiv. 555 It seems probable that primacy and recency are effective only when they increase the intensity or stimulating value of the situations. **1938** R. S. Woodworth *Exper. Psychol.* ii. 38 The wrong name recalled acquires recency value and blocks the correct name. **1948** E. R. Hilgard *Theories of Learning* vii. 183 As it applies to memory, the law of proximity becomes a law of recency. **1964** W. K. Estes in A. W. Melton *Categories of Hum. Learning* 98 The suggestion has been put forward..that the negative recency function results largely from response tendencies the *S*s bring with them to the experiment. **1971** *Sci. Amer.* Aug. 85/1 There is considerable evidence that the recency effect is due to retrieval from short-term storage.

recensionist. (Example.)
1962 *Listener* 29 Nov. 920/1 Mr Edel is a recensionist, reconstructing the life of his hero from a myriad documents.

recent, *a.* Add: **1.** (Later examples.)
1966 *Listener* 29 Sept. 479/2 Gerhard's Op. 1..its beauty [is] marred only by a lack of variety and a tendency to go on too long. Nearly fifty years more recent, the *Duo Concertante* for violin and piano shows neither quality. **1976** *Encounter* June 72/2 Professor Daiches' method, then, consists partly of summarising the results of recent research on the ancient Near East, and partly of commentary on the Pentateuch. **1976** *Daily Tel.* 20 July 1/1 The four countries had agreed on the ban during their recent economic summit in Puerto Rico.

2. b. (Further example.)
1877 *Encycl. Brit.* VI. 134/2 If not set when either moist or recent, they [*sc.* beetles' legs] may be softened by being placed for a night in any small vessel containing a layer of wet sand.

4. b. Also = *Holocene *a.* (Later examples.)
1882 A. Geikie *Text-bk. Geol.* 883 Above them [*sc.* glacial deposits] lie younger accumulations such as river-alluvia, peat-mosses, lake-bottoms,..raised lacustrine and marine terraces, which, merging insensibly into those of the present day, are termed Recent or Prehistoric. **1927** [see *Holocene *a.*]. **1959** J. D. Clark *Prehist. Southern Afr.* ii. 49 A.. method of correlating the succession of events in Africa with those in Europe during the Pleistocene and early Recent times. **1975** *Nature* 20 Mar. 209/2 Sterols..have been identified in Recent and ancient sediments.

recently, *adv.* **b.** (Further examples.)
1922 Joyce *Ulysses* 123 What is it?..—A recently discovered fragment of Cicero's. **1937** *Granta* 3 Feb. 219/1 He was off with the five survivors of our English group to join the recently formed English Battalion. **1960** *Farmer & Stockbreeder* 19 Jan. 102/3 Females changed hands at prices ranging to 130 gs, paid for a recently-calved C.M. cow. **1979** *Tucson* (Arizona) *Citizen* 20 Sept. 3c/6 It already has been replaced by the recently-completed 254-bed West Wing.

recep. (rɪ̆se·p). **1.** Abbrev. of *reception room(s)* s.v. Reception 10. (Freq. used in advertisements.)
1920 *Evening News* 2 Mar. 7/2 (Advt.), Exchange tenancy houses,..4 bed. 2 recep. bath. **1926** [see *bed *sb.* 1 e]. **1950** *Evening Standard* 21 Mar. 12/3 (Advt.), At Harrow... Charm. mod. hse... 2 recep., kit. **1976** 'Z. Stone' *Modigliani Scandal* i. iv. 41 The house..was small—three bedrooms, two recep. and a study.

2. *Theatr.* See *reception 5 c.

reception. Add: **2. d.** (Further examples.) Now usu. a party at which guests are formally greeted, esp. after a wedding.
1865 Ld. Broughton *Recoll. Long Life* (1911) VI. ix. 54 On March 5 [1842] I dined at Lord Palmerston's... Lady Palmerston had a reception afterwards. **1906** *Mrs. Beeton's Bk. Househ. Managem.* 1680 The orthodox wedding breakfast seems likely to become a thing of the past, so much has it been superseded by the tea and reception which usually follow afternoon weddings. **1907** *St. Nicholas* Oct. 1119/1 The 'happy couple'..will hurry back to Red Feather's house to the reception. **1928** J. Sykes *M. A. Disraeli* 3 Lord Broughton ('Recollections of a Long Life') says it was in Lady Palmerston's day that an evening party at a Minister's house began to be called a reception. **1944** J. Lees-Milne *Prophesying Peace* (1977) 72 We went together to the Dorchester reception given by the bride's mother. **1965** *Proc. Classical Assoc.* LXII. 35 During the Reception a gavel was presented for the use of the Association by Miss D. J. Wood, Joint Hon. Secretary of the Manchester and District Branch. **1977** *Times* 14 July 16/6 *Receptions...* Lord Grey of Naunton, accompanied by Lady Grey, entertained members of the Royal Over-Seas League at a reception in the House of Lords last night.

e. A place where guests register on arriving at a hotel, etc., or where an organization's clients, etc., are received. Usu. without article and with capital initial.
1917 E. Fenwick *Diary* 13 Nov. in *Elsie Fenwick in Flanders* (1981) 183 The reception was a regular Hades of women and children and men..all terribly wounded. **1930** E. Waugh *Vile Bodies* x. 169 'Bless you,' said the woman at the counter marked 'Reception', 'all our rooms have been booked for the last six months.' **1958** 'Castle' & 'Hailey' *Flight into Danger* viii. 107 Those cars.. were promptly waved..to parking spaces well clear of the entrance to Reception. **1969** D. Clark *Nobody's Perfect* iii. 110 Not one gets past me or Bert. We hold them in reception, phone up the one they want to see, and make them wait till they're fetched. **1970** G. F. Newman *Sir, You Bastard* v. 148 A sister met him in the reception of the decaying building. **1975** M. Drabble *Realms of Gold* iv. 246 Frances had a call from Reception telling her that it would take at least two hours to put a call through to London.

f. Shortened f. *reception room* s.v. Reception 10. Cf. *recep. 1.
1929 *Daily News* 13 Sept. 11/5 Semi-detached Houses... Attractive Elevations... Large hall, 2 reception, 3 bedrooms. **1977** *Evening Post* (Nottingham) 27 Jan. 14/3 (Advt.), An extremely good two double bedroomed semi-detached house with garage, two receptions, kitchen, bathroom, gardens. **1980** *Daily Tel.* 29 July 1/8 The 18th century house has four receptions, nine bedrooms and eight bathrooms.

5. c. *Theatr.* An ovation granted a popular actor on taking the stage. Also abbrev. *recep.*
1847 F. A. Kemble *Let.* 15 Feb. in *Records Later Life* (1882) III. 160, I wish I could avoid my 'reception', as it is called, because any loud sound shakes me from head to foot. **1936** W. H. Lane Craufurd *Murder to Music* vii. 104 'Did you hear my little recep.!' he cried ecstatically.

d. The receiving of broadcast signals; the efficiency with which this is done, as regards audibility, picture quality, freedom from interference, etc.
1907 *Rep. Sel. Comm. Radiotelegr. Convention* 129/2 in *Parl. Papers* VIII. 1 Receivers tuned for the reception of waves of such lengths..can be rendered quite immune from influence by..longer and more powerful waves. **1923** E. W. Marchant *Radio Telegr. & Teleph.* ix. 104 For the long wave-lengths the change in the spacing produces less effect on the efficiency of reception than it does for shorter wave-lengths. **1943** C. L. Boltz *Basic Radio* xiii. 203 We are here concerned with the reception of C.W., I.C.W., and amplitude-modulated carriers. **1949** *Radio Times* 15 July 6/3, I expected the television to be perfection, but..the same excuses everywhere—'Of course, reception isn't so good here because of the electrical appliances in the district.' **1962** [see

*RECEIVING *vbl. sb.* 2 c]. **1968** A. MARIN *Clash of Distant Thunder* (1969) ix. 63 We can get the Television Français... The reception is not very good. **1972** *Times* 21 Sept. (Ireland Suppl.) p. ii, At that time television was only just getting off the ground..and many areas still did not have reception.

6. (Further example in *Amer. Football.*)

1976 *Billings* (Montana) *Gaz.* 16 June 5-c/3 Bell is expected to have a chance at several receptions, with two top passing quarterbacks on hand.

10. (sense 2) *reception area, camp, -clerk, committee, counter, day* (earlier examples), *desk, evening, hall, night, room* (further examples), *town*; **reception centre,** a centre for the reception of newcomers or visitors; *spec.* a hostel providing temporary accommodation for the destitute; **reception class,** the lowest class in an infant school, into which children going to school for the first time are admitted; **reception statute** *U.S. Law*, a statute passed by an American state after Independence providing that the common law of England be received as binding in that state, subject to repeal and local interpretation.

1939 *Times* 2 Nov. 8/7 While anxiety was expressed about the effects of breaking up home life, tributes were paid to householders and others in the reception areas for their friendly helpfulness. **1971** F. FINLAY *Boy in Prison* vi. 79, I was handed over to one of the Grendon officers, who greeted me pleasantly and took me down an open pathway to the reception area. **1979** *Tucson Mag.* June 40/1 There was..a wedding performed in an airplane followed by a sky dive to the reception area. **1918** W. OWEN *Let.* 13 Sept. (1967) 576 Write to the 2nd Man., not this Recep. Camp as I'll be joining about Sunday. **1954** *Encounter* Feb. 39/2 It is when the fugitive succeeds in moving to the reception camps of Western Germany, and..back into civil life, that his enthusiasm turns to disgust. **1942** *Nation* 27 Apr. 41 Men passing the 'screening test' will be ordered promptly to reception centers for final examination and induction. **1948** *Act* 11 & 12 *Geo. VI*. c. 29 § 17 It shall be the duty of the [National Assistance] Board to make provision whereby persons without a settled way of living may be influenced to lead a more settled life, and the Board shall provide and maintain centres, to be known as reception centres, for the provision of temporary board and lodging for such persons. **1957** H. ROOSENBURG *Walls came tumbling Down* ix. 199 We were waiting for a truck to take us to a DP reception centre. **1978** C. A. BERRY *Gentleman of Road* ix. 69 Normal folk who live on the other side of the soup enjoy reception centres close to their doors as little as they favour Salvation Army hostels or prisons. **1972** *Where* Jan. 10/1 If a few children in each reception class could already read well, teachers would be forced to make more flexible arrangements. **1980** *Guardian* 24 June 11/2 Children with problems are very often referred as priority cases to..reception classes in infants schools. **1934** T. F. TWEED *Blind Mouths* ii. 11 The reception-clerk, who had been placidly reading his newspaper, dropped it and became suddenly alert. **1981** L. DEIGHTON *XPD* xxvii. 220 [He] walked quickly across to.. the lift... The reception clerk looked up. **1851** W. K. NORTHALL *Before & Behind Curtain* 89 We believe Mr. Marks consulted some members of the reception-committee. **1920** [see *EXTREMIST]. **1960** C. MACINNES *Mr. Love & Justice* 96 If you've got any ideas of seeing a lawyer, or having any sort of reception committee for me, that's up to you. **1978** *Navy News* Oct. 2/1 Among the 'reception committee' were the mayor and treasurer of the town of Ajax, Ontario. **1975** N. LUARD *Robespierre Serial* xv. 133 The hotel manager was behind the reception counter. **1853** E. TWISLETON *Let.* 16 Jan. (1928) iv. 67 It was Mrs. Crawford's reception day, and I was struck with her excellent, easy manners. **1884** G. MEREDITH *Let.* 30 May (1970) II. 738, I.. hope to present my respects on one of her reception days. **1936** 'J. TEY' *Shilling for Candles* xxiv. 263 He shot into the darkness of the great lounge and across it to the green light of the reception desk. **1940** E. GILL *Autobiogr.* vi. 180, I went to the hotel and managed to make myself understood at the Reception Desk. **1978** S. SHELDON *Bloodline* xliii. 363 Alec followed the waiter out of the large dining room into the small office behind the reception desk. **1846** J. K. POLK *Diary of President* (1929) 70 These informal reception evenings are very pleasant. **1938** D. DU MAURIER *Rebecca* iii. 17 A certain sofa..midway between the reception hall and the passage to the restaurant. **1976** *Washington Post* 19 Apr. C17/6 (Advt.), First floor has a very large reception hall, spacious living room [etc.]. **1848** S. THORNE *Jrnl. Boy's Trip* (1936) 30 To night being reception night I went to see the President and his lady again. **1846** S. S. MAGOFFIN *Diary* 7 Aug. in S. M. Drumm *Down Santa Fé Trail* (1926) 70 My dirt-floored chamber, dining-room, parlour, reception room &c. &c. *is* quite dessolate. **1906** C. H. B. QUENNELL *Mod. Suburban Houses* p. vii, The accommodation generally required is the three usual reception rooms—sometimes Drawing and Dining Rooms will suffice with what is known to the House Agent as the Sitting Hall in addition. **1961** *Times* 18 Oct. 20/2 More often than not, reception-room heating is inadequate. **1931** *Columbia Law Rev.* XXXI. 416 The so-called reception statutes vary in form, in the date chosen as a deadline, and as to the implications of the extent of reception. **1956** E. H. POLLACK *Fundamentals of Legal Research* i. 10 The 'reception' statutes, enacted by most American states in the eighteenth and nineteenth centuries, gave special recognition to the English common law and statutes..as of 1607, the date of the earliest English settlement at Jamestown. **1976** J. K. LIEBERMAN *Milestones!* i. 19 Reception statutes did not freeze into place the particulars of the common law of England... What was received..was the *process* of the common law..not the particular results that English judges had reached. **1958** *Times Rev. Industry* Feb. 24/1 Some 70,000 people are to be 'overspilled' from Glasgow City over the next 10 to 15 years into the new towns..and other reception towns.

receptionist. Add: **b.** A person employed by a hotel, medical surgery, or other organization, to receive clients, etc. Cf. *RECEPTION 2 e.

1901 *Girl's Own Paper* 12 Jan. 234/1 She answered an advertisement of a Kensington photographer who needed a 'receptionist' and saleswoman—shop-woman in fact. **1927** *Daily Express* 19 Feb. 2/4 An operation which she underwent..for the purpose of advertising the [plastic surgery] business, and on condition that she would continue to be employed as secretary and receptionist. **1932** D. L. SAYERS *Have his Carcase* iii. 41 'Ai'm afraid,' said the receptionist..'that all our rooms are engaged.' **1956** *Times* 21 Jan. 7/5 Such a qualification would ensure that the secretary ..could, in her employer's absence, conduct responsible interviews on his behalf, as opposed to receptionist duties. **1960** M. SPARK *Bachelors* vii. 99 Dr Lyte sat in his consulting room after the last of the evening surgery had departed and his receptionist had locked up and gone home. **1976** B. BOVA *Multiple Man* (1977) vi. 66 The reception lobby was equally quiet... A curved desk with all the paraphernalia of a busy receptionist... But no people.

receptive, *a.* Add: **1. a.** Also of sensory processes in an organism.

1906 C. S. SHERRINGTON *Integrative Action of Nerv. Syst.* iii. 90 The flexion-reflex has a 'receptive skin-field' which though extensive is characteristic for it. **1934** A. FORBES in C. Murchison *Handbk. Exper. Psychol.* iii. 175 When the receptive substance is excitatory the combination causes contraction of the muscle cell. **1975** M. &. N. SAMUELS *Seeing with Mind's Eye* xi. 152 Receptive visualization provides us with the means for getting in touch with images from our inner center.

c. *Med.* and *Psychol.* Affecting or relating to the comprehension of speech or writing, esp. as impaired by a brain disorder.

1926 H. HEAD *Aphasia* I. II. iii. 204 Closer observation showed that the 'receptive' aspect of her use of language had not in reality escaped. *Ibid.* 207 These defects..are entirely inexplicable on any theory..of separate loss of the 'emissive' and 'receptive', 'motor' and 'sensory' functions, which are supposed to accompany speech. **1955** R. JAKOBSON in Saporta & Bastian *Psycholinguistics* (1961) 423/2 The classical distinction between the so-called emissive (or expressive) aphasia on the one hand, and the receptive (or sensory) aphasia on the other. **1963** OSGOOD & MIRON *Approaches to Study of Aphasia* iii. 60 Patients displaying breakdown..in the comprehension of speech and word meanings, but without impairment of hearing per se (i.e., the classical 'sensory' or 'receptive' aphasia), are most likely to have lesions in the left temporal zone. **1961** R. BRAIN *Speech Disorders* vii. 93 Central aphasia is characterized by both receptive and expressive disturbance. **1973** J. W. BROWN *Pick's Aphasia* p. xi, With regard to 'receptive' disturbances, Pick assumed a complementary mental structure underlying the transition of heard sound to thought. **1977** W. H. PERKINS *Speech Path.* (rev. ed.) v. 132/2 By the same token, receptive aphasia, sensory aphasia, posterior aphasia, and fluent aphasia identify essentially the same language disorder as Wernicke's aphasia, or pragmatic aphasia. *Ibid.* xv. 341 The North-western Syntax Screening Test..of receptive and expressive grammatical ability has become available.

receptivity. Add: (Further examples.) Also, in the philosophy of Kant, a passive quality contrasted with spontaneity or activity.

1796 F. A. NITSCH *View of Kant's Princ.* 74 That a given variety can occur in our perceptions, knowledge, &c. supposes a..Receptivity which is totally Passive. *Ibid.* 75 The Receptivity, as far as it receives varieties of the first description, may be called external sense, and as far as it receives varieties of the second description, internal sense. **1950** M. PEAKE *Gormenghast* xxiv. 159 This poem..shall be addressed to as many as are here present in all the variance of their receptivity, status and acumen. **1956** C. MORRIS *Var. of Human Nature* i. 17 Receptivity should be the keynote of life. *Ibid.* ix. 191 In Factor D receptivity is directed toward nature, toward the man-cosmos relation, or to the needs of other persons. **1958** B. BERNSTEIN in J. A. Fishman *Readings in Sociol. of Lang.* (1968) 234 It is now necessary to show how this mode of perceiving and the attendant structuring of receptivity conflicts with and induces a resistance to formal education. **1973** CHURCHILL & AMERIKS tr. *Husserl's Experience & Judgment* I. i. 79 This phenomenologically necessary concept of receptivity is in no way exclusively opposed to that of the activity of the ego. **1974** A. E. BLUMBERG tr. *Schlick's Gen. Theory of Knowl.* iii. § 40. 371 The introduction of the antithesis between spontaneity and receptivity—in modern terms, between activity and passivity—is entirely inappropriate at this point.

receptor. 3. a. For def. read: The region of an antibody molecule which shows specific recognition of an antigen. Also *attrib.* and *Comb.*, as *receptor group*; *receptor-destroying* adj. (Further examples.) [The sense is due to P. Ehrlich, who coined the G. *receptor* (*Berlin klin. Wochenschr.* (1900) 21 May 453/2.)]

Ehrlich's theory of receptors originally took a broader form than that in which it is now accepted; hence in the first part of this century there was some overlap between this sense and sense c below.

1903 J. COATS *Man. Path.* (ed. 5) 151 By careful and increasing dosage the protoplasm of the cell may be gradually stimulated to form more and more receptor groups. **1935** F. P. GAY *Agents of Dis. & Host Resistance* xix. 377 The entire receptor hypothesis of Ehrlich rests on a purely imaginary misconception... There is no particular objection in referring to this absorption as due to certain chemical units that one may call the 'receptors' of the susceptible cell. .. It is another matter to assume..that the hypothetical receptors.., when injured or destroyed, are reproduced in excess and poured into the blood stream as specific antibodies to those foreign incitants that have engendered their production. **1941** KOLMER & TUFT *Clin. Immunol. Biotherapy & Chemotherapy* iii. 63 This [*sc.* Ehrlich's side-chain theory] is now regarded as untenable because of the physiologic improbability that there can exist a sufficient number of specific receptors for an innumerable number of antigens. **1951** WHITBY & HYNES *Med. Bacteriol.* (ed. 5) xii. 221 The enzyme is best known..as the receptor-destroying enzyme (RDE) which has helped to elucidate the phenomenon of hæmagglutination by viruses of the mumps–influenza group. **1967** *Cold Spring Harbor Symp. Quantitative Biol.* XXXII. 431/1 We assume first that nothing except antibody recognizes antigen, and we must therefore assume that the receptor for antigen is antibody already present at a site, in or on the cell, prior to exposure to antigen. **1970** FENNER & WHITE *Med. Virol.* iii. 45 The importance of glycoprotein receptors for the attachment of influenza virus has been demonstrated in experiments in which they have been destroyed by bacterial neuraminidase ('receptor-destroying enzyme'). **1973** *Sci. Amer.* June 82/3 The essential initial step in the immune response is the contact of an antigen—a foreign substance—with receptors on the surfaces of lymphocytes derived from the bone marrow, the so-called *B*-lymphocytes.

b. *Biol.* Any organ or structure which on receiving stimuli of a certain kind from its environment generates nerve impulses that convey information about that aspect of the environment. Freq. *attrib.*

1906, etc. [see *EFFECTOR 2]. **1906** C. S. SHERRINGTON *Integrative Action Nerv. Syst.* i. 13 Electrical stimuli applied to receptor organs are..efficient excitors of reflexes. *Ibid.* ix. 309 The branching at the receptive end places it in communication not with one but with several receptor cells. **1919** W. M. BAYLISS *Introd. Gen. Physiol.* iv. 112 The eye may be said to be the most accurately adjusted of all our receptor organs. **1920** T. P. NUNN *Education* xiii. 170 To pick out and distinguish the different elements and qualities of which the world is composed..is more possible for higher animals by the enormous development of the receptor-system. **1934** *Nature* 22 Sept. 445/1 Normal vision may be due to a receptor which gives rise to a red sensation, one which gives rise to a blue sensation and one which gives rise to a not blue, not red sensation which, of course, corresponds to a green sensation. **1962** *Listener* 8 Nov. 779/2 The use of the eye instead of the ear as the principal receptor for information probably has produced some consistent concomitant psychological changes. **1971** *Jrnl. Gen. Psychol.* LXXXV. 87 Reason..has proposed that susceptible persons are more highly receptive to incoming stimuli, and that this receptivity is global rather than being confined to one receptor system alone. **1974** D. & M. WEBSTER *Compar. Vertebr. Morphol.* x. 197 A blow on the head mechanically stimulates the eye's receptor cells. **1975** *Sci. Amer.* July 108/2 There are other receptors on the antennae of mosquitoes that respond to chemical stimuli.

c. *Physiol.* A region of a neurone or other tissue which specifically recognizes and responds to a neurotransmitter, hormone, or other substance. Freq. *attrib.*

1912 E. H. STARLING *Princ. Human Physiol.* vi. 312 The existence of..a 'receptor' substance, as he calls it, has been furnished by Langley. *Ibid.* 314 Receptor substances may act as intermediaries in every case of propagation of an impulse across a synapse of whatever description. **1939** M. A. GOLDZIEHER *Endocrine Glands* ii. 7 The organotropic hormones of the pituitary..are supposed to act upon the cells of the individual endocrine glands which constitute their receptor organs. **1955** *Biochim. & Biophys. Acta* XVI. 268 The picture which has emerged, assumes that acetycholine is stored in an inactive bound form. Stimulation releases the ester which combines with a receptor protein. **1961** R. D. BAKER *Essent. Path.* iii. 38 Materials from the infarct stimulate the bone marrow and cause leukocytosis, and their influence on central nervous system receptors may cause fever. **1973** *Nature* 20 Apr. 497/2 Receptors can be defined as components of a tissue which specifically react with a drug or hormone. *Ibid.*, The meaning of 'receptor' is becoming very diffuse and a clearer definition of the word is necessary. **1975** *N.Y. Times* 27 Mar. 9/1 The test shows whether the tumor cells contain receptors, or 'landing sites', for estrogen molecules, which are then taken into the cells and stimulate their growth.

recess, *sb.* Add: Now also with pronunc. (rī·ses). **3. a.** Chiefly *N. Amer.* exc. in Parliamentary use. (Earlier and further examples.)

1620 *Jrnls. House of Lords* 22 Mar. 61/1 They [*sc.* the Commons] humbly desire to know the Time of the Recess of this Parliament, and of the Access again, as they may accordingly depart and meet again at the same Time their Lordships shall. **1851** K. QUENTIN *Reisebilder & Studien* II. 58 Um 12 Uhr verliess ich mit den Kindern die Schule. Sie haben eine Pause (Recess) von einer Stunde. *c* **1860** E. DICKINSON *Poems* (1955) I. 117 Whose Beryl Egg, what School Boys hunt In 'Recess'—Overhead! **1913** A. HUXLEY *Let.* 3 Feb. (1969) 47, I had a very good vacation, or do you call it Ree-cess?, as one (female) American asked me. **1942** *Amer. Mercury* July 91 Must be a recess in Heaven—pretty angel like that out on the ground. **1951** E. PAUL *Springtime in Paris* ii. 27, I could not possibly hope to reach the cage before the bank closed at 12 o'clock noon, for the two-hour lunch recess. **1975** *Weekend Mag.* (Montreal) 1 Nov. 22/1, I watched him carefully as he won game after game at recess one day.

9. e. *Criminals' slang.* The lavatory in a prison. Usu. *pl.*

1950 P. TEMPEST *Lag's Lexicon* 177 *Recess*, the lavatory and urinal, which are generally situated in a recess (two cells knocked into one). **1958** F. NORMAN *Bang to Rights* III. 103 The recesses are give [*sic*] a good clean out. **1974** *Observer* (Colour Suppl.) 10 Feb. 17/1 Locked in their cells [*sc.* in Winson Green Prison, Birmingham] at 5.30., with one opening later to go to the recesses (lavatories) and to have a hot drink.

f. = *recess printing* below.

1971 D. POTTER *Brit. Eliz. Stamps* iii. 36 This different-size stamp, printed by recess, interrupted the unity of the set.

11. Also *Comb.* *recess time* (earlier and later examples); **recess printing,** a method of printing used in the production of postage stamps (see quot. 1951); hence **recess-print** *v.* (usu. as pa. pple.).

1930 *Times Educ. Suppl.* 26 July p. iv/1 All [stamps] are recess-printed in designs appropriate to the occasion. **1976** *Times* 30 Aug. 6/7 The first issue, containing a finely drawn head of Queen Victoria..and recess printed by Bradbury Wilkinson. **1914** A. B. CREEKE *Stamp-Collecting* iii. 66 *Recess-printing.* The design is cut into the plate, and the ink stands up slightly on the stamp. **1951** R. J. SUTTON *Stamp Collector's Encycl.* 190 Recess Printing: Strictly speaking, any process where the inked image is below the plane surface of the plate, cliché, block or cylinder; but in modern philatelic parlance refers to the present-day machine-printed, photo-mechanically engraved plate method of reproduction, which in its essentials is similar to the line-engraving by which most of the first and early stamps were printed. A 'recess' printed stamp has a distinct raised image. **1869** MRS. STOWE *Oldtown Folks* xxxiii. 431 At recess-time she strolled out with me into the pine woods back of the school-house. **1946** G. WILSON *Fidelity Folks* III. 84 A half dozen biscuits soaked in it ought to keep starvation away until recess time.

recess, *v.*² Add: Now also with pronunc. (rī·ses). **3. a.** For *U.S.* in Dict. read 'Chiefly *U.S.*' and add further examples.

1933 W. J. ABBOT *Watching World go By* xvii. 316 The convention was thrown into confusion. It recessed almost in a riot. **1943** *Sun* (Baltimore) 12 Feb. 17/1 Tomorrow's holiday on which the country's major securities and commodities exchanges will recess. **1970** *Daily Tel.* 6 July 9 The French Parliament recessed for its three-month summer holiday last week. **1977** *Ibid.* 4 May 19/1 A Turin court trying 53 Leftist 'Red Brigade' guerillas recessed indefinitely yesterday for lack of citizens willing to serve on the jury. **1977** *New Society* 7 July 23/2 The inquiry recessed earlier this month so that the contending parties would have a chance to wade through transcripts. **1977** *Time* 26 Dec. 22/1 Congress recessed last week for a month-long holiday without enacting his energy bill.

b. *trans.* Chiefly *U.S.* To put (a meeting, etc.) into recess; to adjourn, suspend.

1954 W. FAULKNER *Fable* 80 It takes more ammunition to recess a war for ten minutes than to stop a mere offensive. **1967** *Guardian* 12 June 8/4 Hans Tabor recessed the meeting and told them to 'stand by' for any urgent call. **1970** W. WAGER *Sledgehammer* xxv. 213 When Gillis recessed the proceedings..not a single juror had been picked. **1978** *Detroit Free Press* 2 Apr. 10A/5 Exhausted negotiators agreed to recess formal talks for the weekend and meet in private.

recession, *sb.*¹ Add **1. d.** *Philol.* The transference of accentuation towards or on to the first syllable of a word.

1886 *Amer. Jrnl. Philol.* VII. II. 246 A tendency existed to recession from the end of the word. **1929** *S.P.E. Tract* XXXII. 388 This condition, which lightens the syllable, allows and even invites loss and recession of accent.

4. *Econ.* A temporary decline or setback in economic activity or prosperity.

1929 *Economist* 2 Nov. 806/1 The material prosperity of the United States is too firmly based, in our opinion, for a revival in industrial activity—even if we have to face an immediate recession of some magnitude—to be long delayed. **1930** *Engineering* 3 Jan. 21/2 The paramount problem is now whether this recession is yet at an end. **1938** E. AMBLER *Cause for Alarm* i. 16 'Trade recession' they called it... As far as I could see there wasn't a great deal of difference between a trade recession and a good old-fashioned slump. **1958** *Spectator* 30 May 676/2 This is partly due to the continued inability of the United States to pull itself out of recession. **1976** F. ZWEIG *New Acquisitive Society* II. iii. 99 The private sector, particularly in the throes of recession, is limited in its ability to pay by the discipline of the market system. **1981** *Times* 11 Mar. 19/4 The economy is now in deep recession.

recessional, *a.* and *sb.* Add: **A.** *adj.* **1. a.** (Further examples.)

1932 CHESTERTON *Coll. Poems* (1933) 45 We fancied heaven preferring much Your rowdiest song..to such Very recessional repentance. **1973** *Times* 15 Nov. 6/6 Timothy Farrell, sub organist of Westminster Abbey, thundered recessional music.

3. *recessional moraine* (Geol.), a form of moraine which is deposited during a temporary halt or minor readvance of a receding glacier or ice sheet, similar in appearance to a terminal moraine.

[**1897** *Jrnl. Geol.* V. 427 To account for the moraines of recession by any scheme of ups and downs of the solid earth.] **1907** R. D. SALISBURY *Physiogr.* v. 277 As the edge of the ice was melted back, it sometimes halted for a time far back from the position of its maximum advance. Beneath the edge in such positions, terminal moraines were made. Such terminal moraines are sometimes called recessional moraines. **1925** W. J. MILLER *Introd. Physical Geol.* viii. 255 Recessional moraines, forming a great succession of curving ridges, are wonderfully displayed to the south of Lakes Michigan and Erie. **1957** G. E. HUTCHINSON *Treat. Limnol.* I. i. 82 The terminal or recessional moraines of valley glaciers may persist, in certain circumstances, in a sufficiently well-preserved state that they can dam the stream that replaces the glacier. **1976** C. L. MATSCH *N. Amer. & Great Ice Age* vii. 84 Recessional moraines are valuable aids to the glacial geologist because their spacing might allow the calculation of rates of melting if appropriate materials are available for radiocarbon dating.

recessionary (rīse·ʃənări), *a.* [f. RECESSION *sb.*¹ + -ARY¹.] Of, pertaining to, or characterized by (economic) recession.

1958 *Times* 24 Nov. 15/2 Moreover, there are several factors that have so far provided a cushion against recessionary forces. **1970** *Times* 22 May 8 He admits himself baffled by the combination of high inflationary symptoms in prices and interest rates with recessionary symptoms in output. **1974** *Daily Tel.* 19 July 19 The outlook is clearly recessionary, but it is still doubtful if the Chancellor could afford to put back more than £500 million into the economy. **1979** *Nat. Westm. Bank Q. Rev.* Aug. 4 The desire to keep the economy at a high level of activity in general world wide recessionary conditions.

recessive, *a.* Add: **A.** *adj.* **1. a.** Also of persons, retiring, reserved. *rare.*

1925 T. DREISER *Amer. Tragedy* I. I. xiii. 95 She, for her part, felt recessive and thence evasive.

b. Philol. *recessive accent*, stress transferred towards or on to the first syllable of a word.

1879 W. W. GOODWIN *Elem. Gr. Gram.* (ed. 2) I. 19 When a word throws its accent as far back as possible..it is said to have *recessive* accent. **1926** FOWLER *Mod. Eng. Usage* 168/1 He [*sc.* the latinist] has still to reckon with the recessive-accent tendency, which has as good a right to a voice in the matter as his erudition. **1955** *Sci. Amer.* Aug. 82/3 Add to these specimens the 'recessive accent'—stressing of the first syllable of a word which has previously been accented on the second or third syllable. **1973** A. H. SOMMERSTEIN *Sound Pattern Anc. Gr.* v. 171 *Action* nouns..have recessive accent if masculine but final accent if feminine.

c. *Philol.* That tends to recede from use or fall into desuetude.

1935 *Univ. Mich. Publ. Lang. & Lit.* XIII. 14 Inasmuch as the *-eth* plural was a recessive characteristic, we naturally find the *-e(n)* form as well as the *-eth* form occurring south of this line. **1962** *Amer. Speech* XXXVII. 172 Possibly *coal hod* is a recessive form on the Banks. **1972** M. L. SAMUELS *Linguistic Evol.* vi. 92 The isogloss for a given feature may or may not shift. If it does shift, there may be complete levelling resulting in the elimination of the recessive form.

2. *Biol.* [tr. G. *recessiv* (Mendel, *Versuche über Pflanzenhybriden*, in *Verh. d. Naturforsch. Ver., Brünn* (1865) IV. 10).] Applied to a hereditary trait which is not perceptibly expressed in heterozygotes, being masked by a dominant allele of the gene that determines it; hence applied also to an allele which can affect the phenotype only in the absence of some other, dominant, allele. Const. *to* the dominant allele.

1900, etc. [see *DOMINANT *a.* 7]. **1920** *Glasgow Herald* 21 Aug. 4 The characters of tallness and dwarfness were thus separating out again. One of them, dwarfness, had temporarily disappeared in the first filial generation, and for that reason was called by Mendel the recessive character. **1930** R. A. FISHER *Genet. Theory Nat. Selection* iii. 52 The pronounced tendency of the mutant gene to be recessive, to the gene of wild type from which it arises, calls for explanation. **1950** *Science News* XV. 124 The research worker may find blood group inheritance a convenient field for study... Recessive characters, even in the presence of dominant ones, are quite easily recognised, for the heterozygotes can be distinguished from the homozygotes by using the appropriate antibodies. **1964** M. ARGYLE *Psychol. & Social Probl.* vi. 78 A single recessive gene produces the phenomenon of skipping generations and of carriers who do not show the condition themselves; certain kinds of mental deficiency are like this. Schizophrenia is thought by some to be inherited by two or more recessive genes. **1971** D. J. COVE *Genetics* ii. 14 If a heterozygous strain..resembles the strain homozygous for the *A* allele.., thus the *A* allele is said to be dominant to the *a* allele, or conversely the *a* allele is said to be recessive to the *A* allele.

B. *sb.* *Biol.* **a.** An individual in which a particular recessive allele is expressed. **b.** A recessive allele or character.

1900 W. BATESON in *Jrnl. R. Hort. Soc.* XXV. 58 Mendel discovered that in this generation the numerical proportion of dominants to recessives is approximately constant, being in fact as three to one. **1902** *Rep. Evolution Committee R. Soc.* I. 8 The recessives are thenceforth not only apparently but *actually pure*, and if allowed to fertilise themselves give rise to recessives only, for any number of generations. **1905** R. C. PUNNETT *Mendelism* 15 This condition behaves as a single recessive to the normal state. **1916** W. BATESON *Probl. Genetics* iv. 91 We find that..a diversity of recessives may appear within a moderately short period. **1931** E. B. FORD *Mendelism & Evolution* II. iii. 47 The first gene to be discovered in *Drosophila simulans* was that for yellow body-colour. It is a sex-linked recessive. **1949** W. C. ALLEE et al. *Princ. Animal Ecol.* xxxiv. 655/1 Deleterious autosomal recessives are strikingly abundant in certain wild populations of *Drosophila.* **1972** J. MURRAY *Genetic Diversity & Natural Selection* ii. 5 The lowered fitness is the result of the unmasking of deleterious recessives.

recessiveness (rīse·sivnės). *Biol.* [f. prec. + -NESS.] The state or property of being recessive. Opp. *DOMINANCE 2.

1909 W. BATESON *Mendel's Princ. Heredity* 71 Basing his procedure on a knowledge of the dominance or recessiveness of each character the breeder may thus guide his operations with certainty. **1938** L. RIDE *Genetics & Clinician* ii. 17 In the case of the red and white four o'clocks, the dominance of 'red' is but 50% as is also the recessiveness of white, i.e., neither character is definitely dominant nor recessive. *Ibid.*, The dominance of some characters in the echinoderm may be changed to recessiveness by altering the chemical nature of the sea-water. **1975** J. B. JENKINS *Genetics* iii. 83 Bateson..proposed his presence-and-absence hypothesis.. which stated that dominance is due to the presence of a particular gene and that recessiveness results from the loss of that gene.

recharge, *sb.* **1.** Delete *rare* and add: *spec.* in *Hydrology*, the replenishment of the water content of an aquifer as a result of the absorption of water into the zone of saturation (freq. induced artificially by sinking wells into the aquifer); the water so added. Also (*rare*), the action of recharging a battery. (Further examples.)

1928 M. ARENDT *Storage Batteries* vii. 146 This is a common feature of all high rate recharges, as the more dense electrolyte formed by the electrolytic action within plate pores and at plate surfaces does not have time to diffuse throughout the electrolyte during the earlier part of the recharge period. **1931** *Trans. Amer. Geophysical Union* XII. 208 At eight of the plats some recharge was indicated, but some of these had been irrigated in the previous summer. **1942** O. E. MEINZER *Hydrol.* x. 404 The recharge is increased if the intake area receives not only the local precipitation but also the surface flow of a tributary catchment area. **1965** R. G. KAZMANN *Mod. Hydrol.* v. 139 When the supply of soil moisture in a given place is fully replenished, any additional water received from the surface is carried downward under the influence of gravity, either directly to the water table or to the intermediate belt of the zone of aeration: this phenomenon is termed the 'recharge' of an aquifer. **1976** J. D. BREDEHOEFT et al. in J. C. Rodda *Facets of Hydrol.* ix. 241/2 Variations in recharge change the inflow as well as the saturated thickness of the aquifers to the west of Barstow.

4. Special Comb. in *Hydrology*: **recharge area,** an area of ground surface through which is absorbed the water that will percolate into a zone of saturation in one or more aquifers; **recharge basin,** an artificially constructed basin, freq. in sandy material, used to collect water for artificial recharge of an aquifer; **recharge well,** a well used to inject water into an aquifer by artificial recharge.

1951 H. E. THOMAS *Conservation of Ground Water* ii. 29 The ground-water phase of the hydrologic cycle is one of movement from the places where water enters the aquifer—the 'recharge' areas—to the place where the water is discharged from the ground. **1978** BETSON & ARDIS in M. J. Kirkby *Hillslope Hydrol.* viii. 308 The impact upon streamflow of paving over a thin-soil primary source area..would be far less than a similar amount of paving over a primary recharge area. **1951** H. E. THOMAS *Conservation of Ground Water* iii. 143 The city has recharge basins totaling 65 acres which permit infiltration of up to a million gallons a day into the ground. **1970** *Daily Tel.* 18 Sept. 5/2 Long Island is combating the threat [of drought] by constructing 'recharge basins' capable of retaining about 10 per cent. of the water now being lost to the sea. **1951** H. E. THOMAS *Conservation of Ground Water* iii. 125 Permits were issued with the proviso that water used for cooling and air conditioning be returned to the same aquifer through recharge wells. **1976** RAUDKIVI & CALLANDER *Analysis of Groundwater Flow* iii. 58 Water is pumped through the aquifer from the recharge well to the well.

recharge, *v.* **1. b.** Add to def.: *spec.* to replenish the water content of (an aquifer). (Further examples.)

1942 A. C. SWINNERTON in O. E. Meinzer *Hydrol.* xiv. 698 It is possible to recharge basalt by running water down drilled wells. **1966** DAVIS & DE WIEST *Hydrogeol.* xii. 425 Where infiltration is most vigorous, underlying aquifers may be recharged. **1976** RAUDKIVI & CALLANDER *Analysis of Groundwater Flow* v. 108 If the well is at the centre of an island,..the aquifer is recharged from the lake surrounding the island.

5. a. *trans.* To restore an electric charge to (a battery). **b.** *intr.* Of a battery: to acquire an electric charge again, to become recharged.

1876 [in Dict., sense 1 b]. **1893** J. T. NIBLETT *Portative Electricity* III. 188 As a rule the user of a secondary battery knows..at what rate his battery is intended to be recharged. **1928** M. ARENDT *Storage Batteries* vii. 143 A partial charge.. may be given to recharge a battery sufficiently to meet some special demand. **1960** *Farmer & Stockbreeder* 22 Mar. (Suppl.) 8/2 The battery runs for 2½ hours on a single charge and is recharged for a few pence with a trickle charger. **1974** *Sci. Amer.* Nov. 134/2 The fully discharged battery would recharge..in about 40 hours. **1976** *Country Life* 22 Jan. 200/3 Batteries for a lawnmower..have been recharged.

c. In *fig.* phr. *to recharge one's* or (*the*) *batteries*, to restore fitness and mental composure by means of changed circumstances, esp. rest; also *absol.*

1921 W. S. CHURCHILL *Let.* 9 Feb. in M. Soames *Clementine Churchill* (1979) xiii. 194 Subordinate everything in yr life to regathering yr nervous energy, and recharging yr batteries. **1971** A. PRICE *Alamut Ambush* x. 127 His London existence had been frenetic, and Firle was where he recharged his batteries. **1976** J. SNOW *Cricket Rebel* 83, I felt that I was at the halfway stage of my career and needed the rest to recharge the batteries. **1976** G. MOFFAT *Short Time to Live* xii. 136 London's..overwhelming... You come home to recharge, and go back.

Hence **recha·rgeable** *a.*, that may be recharged; **recharging** *vbl. sb.* (further examples).

1893 J. T. NIBLETT *Portative Electricity* III. 187 Nearly all cases of failure of secondary batteries are due to lack of sufficient knowledge on the part of the user for properly conducting the operation of recharging. *Ibid.* 188 The rate at which a secondary battery receives the recharging current may be allowed to vary considerably without fear of damage to any of its parts. **1926** C. CONNOLLY *Let.* 8 June in

Romantic Friendship (1975) 139, I need recharging. I expect we both do. **1942** PARTRIDGE *Usage & Abusage* 170/2 The invention of either new words or new senses (i.e., the re-charging of old words). **1949** *Econ. Geol.* XLIV. 523 In considering sites for water storage, the hydrologic engineer and the economic geologist should not overlook rechargeable aquifers. **1964** T. L. KINSEY *Audio-Typing & Electric Typewriters* iii. 16 The batteries, like accumulators, are rechargeable. **1972** *New Scientist* 11 May 321/1 These newcomers have provided..new electrical devices—such as..a rechargeable battery with an energy-to-weight ratio some 10 times higher than that of the familiar lead and sulphuric acid system. **1977** *Sci. Amer.* May 27/2 More expensive techniques are to build infiltration pits..and recharging wells, by means of which water is pumped into the ground rather than drawn from it. **1978** *Nature* 15 June p. xv/1 The recorders are..supplied with rechargeable fibre tipped pens.

‖ **réchaud** (reʃo). [Fr., f. stem of *réchauffer* *RÉCHAUFFER *v.*] A receptacle in which food is warmed or kept warm.

1925 B. RACKHAM tr. *E. Hannover's Pottery & Porcelain* III. viii. 185 The factory hardly created much in the way of new forms..beyond a series of '*Réchauds*' (foodwarmers). **1955** H. NEWMAN in *Apollo* Feb. 35 The pedestal of a food-warmer (*réchaud*) is usually cylindrical or slightly conical, and is of greater diameter than that of a tea-warmer. **1958** R. GODDEN *Greengage Summer* ix. 106 The rose-coloured wine, the réchaud flame, the lights were reflected in the windows over and over again.

rechaufe, *v.* Delete † *Obs.* and add: Now in form **rechauffe.** Also *fig.* Cf. *RÉCHAUFFER *v.*

1836 DISRAELI in Monypenny & Buckle *Life Disraeli* (1910) I. App. B. 387 Canning irritated by Copley's rechauffing in a speech Philpotts'..pamphlet. **1931** R. CAMPBELL *Georgiad* I. 18 His melancholy recipès [*sic*] For 'happiness'... How to 'rechauffe' the stock-pot of desire.

réchauffé. Add: Also **rechauffe, réchauffée.**

A. *sb.* (Further *lit.* and *fig.* examples.)

1851 E. WARD *Jrnl.* 5 Feb. (1951) 123 Took tea with the Godleys, met the Russells, and had a *rechauffe* both of the ball supper and the ball gossip. **1976** *Times Lit. Suppl.* 26 Mar. 337/2 The main objection to the book is that it is a *réchauffé*... Stevenson's contribution now bears a family resemblance to his piece then. **1977** *Times* 3 Sept. 10/5 Cru de Meynas..is a useful bottle for casual meals of cold game or réchauffées.

B. *adj.* Of food: reheated. Also *fig.*, rehashed.

1909 WEBSTER, *Réchauffé*..p.a. masc., *réchauffée*..p.a. fem... Warmed over;—of a dish food. Also fig. **1921** *Sat. Westm. Gaz.* 17 Sept. 14/1 Professor Wendell..frequently inserts what the dust-cover or jacket of the English edition denominates his 'humanity' between a hackneyed quotation and a platitude tastefully rechauffé. **1977** *Gramophone* Feb. 1307/1 These, then, are humdrum, *rechauffé* performances full of gestures by rote. **1977** *Broadcast* 19 Dec. 16/2 Canned laughter: Artificial sauce used to season rechauffe mirth.

Hence **rechauffeed** *ppl. a.* = sense B above.

1883 E. W. HAMILTON *Diary* 3 Feb. (1972) II. 395 The programme, to which he leans in addition to the unexciting non-contentious, *rechauffeed* bills, is Metropolitan Government and Local Government for Ireland.

‖ **réchauffer** (reʃofe), *v.* [Fr.: see RÉCHAUFFÉ.] Usu. as *infin.*, to warm up again; *fig.*, to rehash. Hence ‖ **réchauffage** (-āʒ) [Fr. suff. *-age*: cf. -AGE], a rehash.

1965 *Punch* 31 Mar. 473/3 This plan to store up the dead at minus two hundred degrees C. and then *rechauffer* them to life when medical science has learned how to put right whatever it was they died of. **1967** *Punch* 28 June 961/3 In telling the story of her career Lady Summerskill has fallen into the Politician's Pitfall of believing that it is possible to *réchauffer* old Parliamentary speeches. **1972** E. LUCIE-SMITH in Cox & Dyson *20th-Cent. Mind* III. xvi. 466 Most of what they produced was a mere *réchauffage* of pre-war ideas.

re·check, *sb.* [f. the vb.] A renewed or second examination or investigation.

1926 *Amer. Jrnl. Med. Sci.* CLXXI. 851 A recheck showed that no fermentation test had been done on the urine, which vitiated the value of the result. **1972** T. ARDIES *This Suitcase is going to Explode* xvii. 190 Those rechecks on the refugee scientists were *supposed* to be thorough. **1977** J. M. JOHNSON in Douglas & Johnson *Existential Sociol.* viii. 243 Upon receiving the reports and memo, the supervisor of Unit Two did not return the forms to the workers for a recheck.

reche·ck, *v.* [RE- 5 a.] *trans.* and *intr.* To check again. Hence **reche·cking** *vbl. sb.*

1902 'MARK TWAIN' in *Harper's Weekly* 6 Dec. 4/2 Your luggage..rechecked, fare-ticket and sleeper changed. **1957** J. S. HUXLEY *Relig. without Revelation* iii. 51 Constant checking and rechecking against fact. **1962** L. DEIGHTON *Ipcress File* xi. 71, I decided to recheck his security clearance. **1967** KARCH & BUBER *Offset Processes* x. 469 Retighten the sprocket and recheck by running sheets. **1977** 'E. TREVOR' *Theta Syndrome* ii. 27 A young intern rechecked the patient. **1977** P. G. WINSLOW *Witch Hill Murder* II. 215 All that's left to us is to check and re-check on every aspect of the case.

recherché, *a.* (Later examples.)

1939 JOYCE *Finnegans Wake* (1964) 149 The fiery goodmother Miss Fortune (who the lost time we had the pleasure we have had our little *recherché* brush with, what, Schott?). **1946** A. CHRISTIE *Come, tell me how you Live* viii. 148 We have a very delicious and recherché lunch with the French Commandant. **1955** *Times* 16 May 11/4 The more recherché of whose oratorios ought to be remembered for future eighteenth-century festivals. **1970** I. MURDOCH *Fairly Honourable Defeat* I. v. 55 The smell..was fresh and bitter and at the same time nauseating. Hilda wondered if it were not caused by some extremely recherché form of dry rot. **1978** *Dædalus* Fall 4 Our perception of a lifetime has become increasingly recherché.

‖ **recherche du temps perdu** (rəʃęrʃ dü taṅ pęrdü). [ad. F. *à la recherche du temps perdu* (also used), lit. 'in search of the lost time', used by Marcel Proust (1871–1922) as the title of a reminiscent novel (1913–27).] The remembrance of things past; the narration or evocation of one's early life.

1946 L. P. HARTLEY *Sixth Heaven* xi. 233 A feeble poor-spirited attempt to revive the joys of childhood, a journey à la recherche du temps perdu. **1952** *Spectator* 19 Dec. 854/2 Like so many sensitive novels by contemporary women novelists, it is a *recherche du temps perdu.* **1966** M. STEEN *Looking Glass* x. 217, I..listened to the two old friends sharing their *recherche du temps perdu.* **1975** *Broadcast* 3 Nov. 14/3 Old Times by Harold Pinter..is, of course, a play about *recherche du temps perdu.*

‖ **Rechtsstaat** (re·χʸtsˌʃtāt). Also (*erron.*) **Rechtstaat.** [Ger., f. *rechts* gen. of *recht* RIGHT *sb.*¹ + *staat* STATE *sb.*] A country in which the rule of law prevails.

1935 J. D. LEWIS *Genossenschaft-Theory of Otto von Gierke* vi. 69 Being a *Rechtstaat*, the modern state, the German state for example, stands within law and recognizes legal limitations upon its own sovereign will. **1944** F. A. HAYEK *Road to Serfdom* vi. 54 The early nineteenth-century discussions in Germany about the nature of the *Rechtsstaat.* **1948** [see *kulturstaat* s.v. *KULTUR]. **1963** *Economist* 5 Oct. 5/1 In a' *Rechtsstaat* (state based on law) only the judgements of a competent court are valid and binding. **1977** *Times Lit. Suppl.* 1 July 809/2 Try as the lawyers might.. to make Franco Spain a *Rechtstaat.*

‖ **recibiendo** (reþivie·ndo). *Bullfighting.* [Sp., lit. 'receiving', f. *recibir* (see next).] A method of killing the bull by which the bullfighter receives the charging bull on the point of his sword. Also as quasi-*adv.*

1902 *Encycl. Brit.* XXVI. 460/1 If the *matador* remains without moving, or rather moving only his body to avoid the stroke of the horns, the thrust is known as *recibiendo.* **1932** E. HEMINGWAY *Death in Afternoon* ix. 88 He did kill several times recibiendo, receiving the bull on the sword in the old manner. **1976** E. P. BENSON *Bulls of Ronda* iv. 30 'He's going to receive the bull. What they call a *recibiendo.*' .. The bull..propelled itself against the waiting man... The sword plunged deep into the entrails of the bull.

‖ **recibir** (reþivi·r). *Bullfighting.* [Sp., lit. 'to receive'.] The action on the part of a bullfighter of receiving a charging bull while remaining stationary.

1838 *Q. Rev.* LXII. 411 The picador, holding his lance under his right arm, pushes to the right, and pulls his horse to the left; the bull is thus turned from his plunge, and passes on to the next horseman. This is called 'recibir', 'hoc habet'. **1932** R. CAMPBELL *Taurine Provence* iii. 76 There are several forms of estocada... Some..are attacks on stationary bulls, others, as in the Recibir, are performed by the stationary man on the charging bull.

recidivism. (Later examples.)

1971 *Sci. Amer.* May 51/1 There is no strong evidence.. that recidivism increases with leniency of sentence. **1977** *Listener* 15 Dec. 803/2 But though the problem of recidivism and rehabilitation still remains, it can hardly be the chief cause of today's overcrowded prisons.

recidivist. Add: **a.** (Later examples.)

1931 *Sun* (Baltimore) 20 Jan. 10/2 This creates a body of recidivists who are being constantly released and as constantly returned. **1964** *Listener* 26 Mar. 507/1 The Reader in criminology at Oxford has given me the following definition of a recidivist: A recidivist is the offender who neither mends his ways spontaneously nor learns to avoid detection, and who is neither deterred by the experience of conviction nor reformed by any of the methods in the courts' repertoire. **1981** W. EBERSOHN *Divide Night* ii. 26 Old recidivists who felt at home only in jail and would be back again and again.

b. *attrib.* or as *adj.*

1920 *Contemp. Rev.* Nov. 684 It is the source of depraved, unchastened, even of recidivist, tendencies, as well as of those which point towards a wider and more perfect life. **1931** J. S. HUXLEY *What dare I Think?* iii. 88 Sterilization has been suggested, but this seems disproportionate save in recidivist cases of philoprogenitiveness which seem otherwise incurable. **1950** *Chambers's Jrnl.* 230/1 Often..he had the opportunity of seeing the overcrowded masses of recidivist (frequent offender) prisoners, many of them unprepossessing and hardened-looking roughs, with whom he was glad he had not to mix. **1962** *Lancet* 15 Dec. 1278/1 My work as a probation officer among recidivist alcoholics in Pentonville Prison.

recidivity. (Example.)

1937 G. FRANKAU *More of Us* xii. 123 Man asks you..not to nag him for his recidivities.

recipe, *v. imper.* and *sb.* Add: **B.** *sb.* **2.** (Earlier and later examples.) Also *fig.*

1716 T. CAVE *Let.* 5 Oct. in M. M. Verney *Verney Lett. 18th Cent.* (1930) II. xxii. 45 Sister Lovett and I greatly admire the Ink you wrote last with,..but dare not wish for the Recipe it being no doubt a Secrett. **1947** [see *PROMOTING *vbl. sb.* 2 b]. **1969** *Times* 12 May 16/3 The D.N.A. molecules in the cells of normal people contain a chemical recipe for manufacturing ordinary haemoglobin. **1981** *Times* 9 Apr. 9/7 Another recipe made especially for Easter is fritters of soft ricotta cheese.

4. *Comb.*, as **recipe-book,** a book containing recipes, a cookery-book; also *fig.*

1872 *Young Englishwoman* Dec. 662 Recipes of practical utility will appear..to be neatly copied into their recipe-books. **1952** M. LASKI *Village* iii. 62 To have read the recipe-books and produced appetising meals for her family would have meant, to her, willing acceptance of..servitude. **1964** P. STREVENS in D. Abercrombie et al. *Daniel Jones* 125 Teaching grammars in the future..will be superior..to those of the past which have simply been grammar-teaching recipe-books. **1976** L. DEIGHTON *Twinkle, twinkle, Little Spy* xiv. 140 Bessie Mann was asking me how many kids we were going to have, and I found myself looking at recipe books and baby carriages.

reci·pher, *v.* Also **recypher.** [RE- 5 a.] *trans.* To encipher again (a message that is already in cipher). Hence **reci·pher** *sb.*; **reci·phering** *vbl. sb.*

1961 in WEBSTER. **1963** *Times* 21 May 7/3 He said the purpose of such a table would be to convert plain language letters or punctuation into figures which could then be subsequently reciphered on a reciphering pad. **1975** C. MOTT-RADCLYFFE *Foreign Body in Eye* ii. 28, I remember one telegram, all in re-cypher, beginning, 'I saw the Minister of Foreign Affairs on return from leave yesterday. His Excellency remarked how sunburnt I was looking after my recent holiday in Ireland.'

recipiangle. (Later example.)

1939 *Nature* 22 Apr. 673/2 The seventy objects which comprise Mr. Court's most recent benefaction include an Italian recipiangle of about 1600. This is an instrument used for measuring angles in surveying, and it is also marked with lines and scales which can be used for making calculations.

recipience. Add: **b.** Recipient state or condition.

1902 in WEBSTER. **1906** S. S. LAURIE *Synthetica* I. 7 The subject-reality..appears to be a mere potency of recipience and reaction. **1923** *Times Lit. Suppl.* 29 Nov. 801/2 Their [*sc.* the neo-realists'] insistence on the independent reality of the physical world and the passive recipience of the mind in knowing it.

recipient, *a.* and *sb.* Add: **B.** *sb.* **4.** *Linguistics.* The indirect object of a verb or the complement of an adjective.

1937 O. JESPERSEN *Analytic Syntax* xxxviii. 156 In conventional grammar the term *object* is further used for what is governed by an adjective. Here, too, I have avoided the term object..and have adopted instead the term *Recipient*, abbreviated R... R is seen to be chiefly used where Latin, German, etc. have a dative which is not governed by a transitive verb. **1972** R. QUIRK et al. *Gram. Contemp. Eng.* vii. 350 The most typical function of the indirect object is that of *recipient* (or 'dative' participant); *ie* of animate being passively implicated by the happening or state: I've found *you* a place. *Ibid.* 353 The subject may also have a recipient (or 'dative') role with verbs such as *have, own,* [etc.] .., as is indicated by the following relation: Mr Smith has bought/given/sold his son a radio→So now his son has/owns/possesses the radio.

reciprocal, *a.* and *sb.* Add: **A.** *adj.* **3. c.** *reciprocal innervation* or *inhibition* (Physiol.): an arrangement of nerve stimulation as a result of which contraction of one muscle or group of muscles to produce movement is accompanied by simultaneous inhibition of an antagonistic muscle or group of muscles, whose contraction would tend to produce the opposite movement.

1897 C. S. SHERRINGTON in *Jrnl. Physiol.* XXII. 327 It has revealed to me an almost unexpectedly significant number of examples of depressor effect generally, perhaps always, in combination with pressor effects, that is to say, in the form of reciprocal innervations. **1906** —— *Integrative Action Nervous Syst.* iii. 83 (*heading*) Reciprocal inhibition. **1942** JOHNSTON & WHILLIS *Gray's Anat.* (ed. 28) 942 Experimental evidence shows that all the fundamental reflexes of posture.., the reciprocal innervation of antagonists, and the elementary combination of synergists, can still occur without the cerebellum. **1960** W. B. CROW *Synopsis of Biol.* lxv. 445 Neurons connect up two or more efferent paths so that two or more muscles come into action together, or one is inhibited when another comes into operation (reciprocal innervation). **1971** *Sci. Amer.* Aug. 75/1 One principle Sherrington discovered was 'reciprocal innervation'. **1977** G. H. SAGE *Introd. Motor Behav.* (ed. 2) viii. 157 The flexion reflex consists of a contraction of the flexor muscles while reciprocal connections with the antagonistic extensor muscles cause reciprocal inhibition.

d. *Genetics.* Of each of a pair of crosses: complementary to another in that the male parent in each is of the same kind as the female parent in the other.

1902 W. BATESON *Rep. Evolution Comm. R. Soc.* I. 21 Reciprocal crosses..showed clearly that of the two pairs of antagonistic characters, the violet colour is dominant. **1909** —— *Mendel's Princ. Heredity* xi. 203 When the cross is in the form pure single ♀ × double-throwing ♂, all the F_1 plants give a mixture of doubles and singles in F_2; but when the reciprocal cross is made, namely double-thrower used as ♀ × pure single used as ♂, it is found that the F_1 plants are of two kinds. **1948** H. P. RILEY *Genetics & Cytogenetics* vi. 88 The cross curved × wild type is known technically as the reciprocal of the cross wild type × curved. *Ibid.* vii. 96

When genes are in autosomes reciprocal crosses normally give identical results, but when genes located in the X chromosome are dealt with, the results of reciprocal crosses are different. **1971** D. J. Cove *Genetics* viii. 111 If some genetical information is also carried in the cytoplasm, the unequal contribution of cytoplasm to the zygote by the two gametes should provide a way of detecting it. The technique used for this is the reciprocal cross.

e. *Physics.* In the names of quantities defined as reciprocals of standard physical units, as *reciprocal centimetre, ohm, second* (see quots.).

1934 H. E. White *Introd. Atomic Spectra* i. 6 Wave numbers..are units with the dimensions of reciprocal centimeters, abbreviated cm^{-1}. **1960** Brand & Speakman *Molecular Struct.* i. 8 The passage of energy between matter and radiation occurs in quanta of magnitude ΔE, where $\Delta E = h\nu$. When ΔE is expressed in terms of the erg and ν as reciprocal seconds, Planck's constant, h, has the value $6{\cdot}6256 \times 10^{-27}$ erg sec. **1960** A. D. Cross *Introd. Pract. Infra-Red Spectroscopy* i. 2 Band positions are quoted in units of wave number (ν) which are expressed in reciprocal centimetres (cm^{-1})... However, the true unit of frequency ($\bar{\nu}$) is given in reciprocal seconds (sec^{-1}). **1978** *Sci. Amer.* Dec. 66/1 The maximum conductivity is somewhat greater than 2,000 reciprocal ohms per centimeter (equivalent to a resistivity of less than ·0005 ohm per centimeter).

f. *reciprocal course*: a path followed by a person or craft which is opposite in direction to one with which it stands in relation, e.g., to the one desired or the one which was followed immediately before.

1946 *Happy Landings* (Air Ministry) July 5/3 The immediate action is to turn on the reciprocal course. **1958** 'N. Shute' *Rainbow & Rose* ii. 57, I..flew out to sea..on the reciprocal course, and then turned in again and flew towards the coast on 110°. **1961** B. Fergusson *Watery Maze* ii. 49 All these craft had lately been 'degaussed'..with unexpected effects on their compasses, and some of the shoreward-bound parties were steering on a reciprocal course.

7. Phonetics. *reciprocal assimilation* (see quot. 1972).

1915 G. Noël-Armfield *General Phonetics* ix. 32 If the adjacent sounds act upon each other more or less equally the influence may be called reciprocal. *Ibid.* 33 Reciprocal assimilation is common in diphthongs. **1939** L. H. Gray *Foundations Lang.* iii. 68 It [*sc.* assimilation] may be reciprocal, when the modification is mutual. **1972** Hartmann & Stork *Dict. Lang. & Linguistics* 21/2 If two sounds influence each other mutually the term *reciprocal assimilation* (alternative term: *coalescent assimilation*) is used, e.g. English *seven* pronounced as [sebm̩] where the labio-dental [v] has become bilabial [b] which in turn influences the alveolar nasal [n] changing it to the bilabial nasal [m].

B. *sb.* **3.** Restrict † *Obs.* to sense in Dict. and add: **b.** A noun, pronoun, or verb that expresses mutual action or relationship.

1961 R. B. Long *Sentence & its Parts* xvi. 357 Reciprocals can refer only to plural nouns, pronouns, or nounal units; reflexives can refer to singulars as well. **1965** *Canad. Jrnl. Linguistics* Spring 175 Especially reflexives, reciprocals, iteratives, passives, and the Eyak progressive almost always take the vocalic forms.

reciprocate, *v.* Add: **2. b.** (Later examples.)

1903 G. B. Shaw *Man & Superman* III. 97 He..is peevish and sensitive when his advances are not reciprocated. **1922** Joyce *Ulysses* 717 Hospitality extended and received in kind, reciprocated and reappropriated in person. **1924** C. Mackenzie *Old Men of Sea* viii. 131, I was rather disappointed to hear that she was unlikely to reciprocate Dick Duffy's affection.

3. b. Also *gen.*, to return love or liking.

1883 'Mark Twain' *Life on Mississippi* iv. 542 He had loved one 'too fair for earth', and she had reciprocated. **1916** G. B. Shaw *Androcles & Lion* p. xxx, Unless you love your neighbor as yourself and he reciprocates you will both be the worse for it. **1922** Joyce *Ulysses* 679 In what manners did she reciprocate? She remembered... She provided... She admired. **1936** L. C. Douglas *White Banners* xi. 235 Hannah liked her, and felt that the girl heartily reciprocated.

reciprocating, *ppl. a.* **2. b.** Add to def.: Applied *spec.* to engines in which the working fluid drives an oscillating piston. (Earlier and later examples.)

1822 J. Robison *Syst. Mech. Philos.* II. 577 When water is to be driven along a main by the strokes of a reciprocating engine, it should be forced into an air-box. **1901** *Trans. Inst. Engineers & Shipbuilders in Scotland* XLV. I. 25 An ordinary reciprocating engine performs one complete cycle of operations..in two strokes of the piston. **1911** *Encycl. Brit.* XXV. 824/1 The rapid development of the marine steam turbine makes it probable that it will displace the reciprocating engine in all large and fast ships. **1948** *Daily Tel.* 9 Apr. 4/4 The aircraft developed in recent years in America were..of conventional design. Their engines were reciprocating engines, and they were designed to fly at normal speeds. **1973** *Times* 13 Dec. 35/2 The Wankel still relies on petrol and unfortunately uses rather more of it than a comparable reciprocating engine.

reciprocator. Add: **b.** A reciprocating engine forming part of a composite power plant.

1907 *Westm. Gaz.* 16 Sept. 4/1 Not an ounce of steam will be wasted, the principle being to carry the exhaust steam from the high-pressure reciprocators to the low-pressure turbines. **1931** *Times* 24 Jan. (Trade & Engin. Suppl.) p. iv/3 Another alternative, in which the exhaust steam from the reciprocator is led to a turbo generator which delivers its current to a motor on the propeller shafting, has been applied to the existing 'City' ships of the Ellerman Line. **1952** Fox & McBirnie *Marine Steam Engines & Turbines* xi. 197 Only the reciprocator is used while entering or leaving port.

reciprocitarian. Add: (Later example.) Also *attrib.* or as *adj.*

1906 *Athenæum* 3 Feb. 134 To these he appeals on reciprocitarian lines by offering a reduction of our wine duties. **1932** *Times Lit. Suppl.* 1 Dec. 909/4 Dilke asserts that he [*sc.* Joseph Chamberlain] was a strong 'Reciprocitarian' and had already the notion of a 'British Zollverein'.

reciprocity. Add: **1. a.** Also in *Social Science* (see quots. 1960, 1972).

1904 W. T. Mills *Struggle for Existence* xx. 262 Reciprocity is a new word in politics, but it expresses an old fact in real life. **1952** T. M. Newcomb *Social Psychol.* ix. 308 The last stage in acquiring roles involves recognizing reciprocity between oneself and others. **1960** G. W. Allport *Personality & Soc. Encounter* xi. 175 The child understands that members of other countries are as attached to their own lands as he is to his; this is the principle of reciprocity. **1967** E. A. Hoebel in P. Bohannan *Law & Warfare* II. 187 In Comanche society reciprocity is not developed to an exaggerated degree. **1971** E. Ardener *Soc. Anthrop. & Lang.* p. lv, Maussian systems of exchange and reciprocity are analogous to systems of communication, of which language is also one. **1972** *Jrnl. Social Psychol.* LXXXVII. 89 Gouldner has postulated the existence of a universal norm of reciprocity which stipulates that..people should help those who help them.

2. b. (Earlier example.)

1838 F. Haywood tr. *Kant's Critick Pure Reason* I. II. ix. 76 Both the Judgments, the relationship of which forms the hypothetical judgment.., in whose reciprocity likewise the disjunctive consists.

3. *attrib.* and *Comb.*, as *reciprocity-monger, technique, treaty*; **reciprocity failure** *Photogr.*, departure from adherence to the reciprocity law, found with all emulsions, in which greater exposure than that predicted by the law is required at both very low and very high light intensities; **reciprocity law** *Photogr.*, the statement that the degree of blackening of an ideal emulsion is constant for a given incident energy, i.e., for a given product of light intensity and exposure time; **reciprocity theorem** *Physics*, a theorem which states that the response of a given physical system is unchanged under interchange of the locations of a constant excitation and of the measured response; also called the Onsager principle; *spec.* (*a*) *Electr.* (see quot. 1957); (*b*) *Nucl. Physics*, the statement that time-reversal leaves the transition rate for a nuclear reaction unchanged.

1923 *Jrnl. Optical Soc. Amer.* VII. 1110 In order to show in a different way the magnitude of the reciprocity failure, the values of sensitivity have been computed. **1966** D. G. Brandon *Mod. Techniques Metallogr.* 13 Emulsions produced specifically for metallography are designed to retain their speed for long periods, that is, to have a low reciprocity failure, while emulsions for astronomical applications, involving exposure times of several hours, show almost no reciprocity failure at all. **1973** *Sci. Amer.* Dec. 122/3 Lowering the temperature of the emulsion tends to suppress the recombination of the ions and hence to suppress reciprocity failure. **1979** *SLR Camera* May 11/1 Unless the meter takes into account reciprocity failure then the film cannot be correctly exposed. [**1900** *Astrophysical Jrnl.* XI. 89 Scheiner, in 1891, proved that the increase in the number of fainter stars on prolonging the exposure fell far below what would be expected according to the law of reciprocity.] **1907** Sheppard & Mees *Investigations Theory of Photogr. Process* II. vi. 214 A reversing action of the released bromine may..be deduced from the failures of the Bunsen and Roscoe 'reciprocity law'. **1942** C. E. K. Mees *Theory of Photogr. Process* vi. 236 Bunsen and Roscoe laid down a general law for photochemical reactions which states that the product of a photochemical reaction is dependent simply on the total energy employed... From the reciprocal relation between time and intensity in the Bunsen–Roscoe expression, it was called the reciprocity law. **1974** Dainty & Shaw *Image Sci.* ii. 35 For very long or very short exposure times the process of latent image formation is less efficient, and this is known as reciprocity law failure. **1885** A. Crump *Formation Polit. Opin.* 198 The declamations of the Fair Traders and the reciprocity-mongers..fail to disturb the convictions of the sound thinkers in the country. **1973** *Times* 18 Oct. (Brazil Suppl.) p. ii/4 There is a dependence on imported technology and design, as well as insufficient use of reciprocity techniques. [**1876** *Proc. R. Soc.* XXV. 118 Although the principle of reciprocity appears to be firmly grounded on the theoretical side, instances are not uncommon in which a sound generated in the open air at a point A is heard at a distant point B, when an equal or even more powerful sound at B fails to make itself heard at A.] **1938** G. P. Harnwell *Princ. Electricity & Electromagnetism* xiii. 451 The reciprocity theorem is a consequence of the symmetry of the determinant and is generally stated in a limited form involving the current in one branch and the emf. in another. **1952** Blatt & Weisskopf *Theoret. Nucl. Physics* x. 529 We obtain the reciprocity theorem... This theorem states that the probability for a transition proceeding one way in time is equal to the probability for the same transition but with the sense of time reversed. **1957** B. I. & B. Bleaney *Electr. & Magnetism* iii. 69 We have the Reciprocity Theorem, which states that a given e.m.f. in the *p*th branch will produce the same current in the *q*th branch of a circuit as the same e.m.f. in the *q*th branch would produce in the *p*th branch. **1968** [see *Onsager]. **1970** I. E. McCarthy *Nuclear Reactions* ii. 31 The reciprocity theorem or time-reversal invariance is an essential property of nuclear systems. **1847** H. Clay in *Whig Almanac 1848* 22/1 Out of these acts have sprung a class..of treaties,.. commonly called Reciprocity Treaties.

recirculate, *v.* [Re- 5 a.] To circulate again. **a.** *trans.* To make available for reuse. **b.** *intr.* Of material: to take part in recirculation.

1916 Harding & Willard *Mech. Equipment Buildings* I. xv. 349 The air is simply re-circulated, no fresh air being taken into the heating system from the outside. **1934** W. Trinks *Industrial Furnaces* (ed. 3) I. vi. 392 In several designs of fuel-fired furnaces, burned gases are drawn from the heating chamber by a fan and recirculated, mixing with the fresh combustion gases. **1958** *Jrnl. Amer. Water Wks. Assoc.* L. 1025/2 Treated sewage can be recirculated from the bottom of the final tank to the wet well where it is mixed with the incoming raw sewage. **1959** *Motor Manual* (ed. 36) v. 107 The balls recirculate (thereby reducing the rate of wear) and their use reduces friction in the mechanism to a minimum. **1964** *Proc. R. Soc.* B. CLIX. 262 The few large lymphocytes which re-circulate from the blood to the lymph do so for only a brief period. **1967** E. Chambers *Photolitho-Offset* ix. 127 The machine has a unique roller-jet agitation..allowing for the developer to be recirculated. **1977** *Jrnl. Neuropath. & Exper. Neurol.* XXXVI. 471 Microglial cells are continually replaced by circulating mononuclear cells and may, themselves, also recirculate.

Hence **reci·rculated** *ppl. a.*, **reci·rculating** *vbl. sb.*

1916 Harding & Willard *Mech. Equipment Buildings* I. xvi. 442 This apparatus is designed for use where maximum cooling of the air by evaporation in addition to air cleansing is desired with recirculated spray water. **1947** T. N. Adlam *Radiant Heating* 5 It can be arranged to discontinue recirculating and admit all fresh air after the correct room temperature has been attained. **1967** *Punch* 5 July 22/2 Once he has overcome in training the psychological objection to drinking recirculated fluids, the astronaut will not be bothered by such trivialities.

reci·rculating, *ppl. a.* [f. prec. + -ing².] **1.** Circulating again or continuously, in senses of the vb.

1916 Harding & Willard *Mech. Equipment Buildings* I. xiv. 337 The use of recirculating ducts, through which part or all of the air delivered to the rooms is returned to the furnace to be reheated, will greatly reduce the cost of operation. **1954** G. M. Fair et al. *Water Supply & Waste-Water Disposal* xxx. 908 The recirculating system generally includes pumps, hair-catchers, chemical feeds.., filters, disinfecting equipment.., and heaters. **1964** *Proc. R. Soc.* B. CLIX. 262 Some of the large lymphocytes in thoracic duct lymph divide..but..the number of new small lymphocytes which they contribute to the total re-circulating pool is extremely small. **1975** *Offshore* Aug. 3/1 (Advt.), Even the initial lead slurry, when you use our patented recirculating mixer, will be to the desired weight.

2. *recirculating ball*, a ball-bearing running in a closed ball race; usu. *attrib.* with reference to a form of automotive steering mechanism in which a half-nut containing an eccentrically mounted ball race can be made to move along a helical cam by rotation of the cam.

1946 W. H. Crouse *Automotive Mech.* xxiii. 494 The recirculating ball-and-nut type of steering-gear mechanism that uses a grooved ball nut, ball bearings, and a gear sector. **1956** E. Molloy *Automobile Engineer's Ref. Bk.* xv. 37 Screw-and-nut gears incorporating balls between the screw and nut, and known as recirculating ball steering gears, are widely used on all classes of vehicles above the 12-h.p. range. **1960** *Farmer & Stockbreeder* 23 Feb. 45/2 Light, responsive, re-circulating ball type steering. **1970** *A.A. Bk. of Car* 151/4 (*caption*) Recirculating balls are used to reduce friction between a rotating worm and a nut moving along it. **1980** *Times* 9 May 26/2 Instead of rack and pinion Toyota has decided to stick with recirculating ball steering.

recirculation. Add to def.: *esp.* the process of making available for reuse waste products or other material. (Further examples.)

1916 Harding & Willard *Mech. Equipment Buildings* I. xiv. 330 All of the air is brought in from the outside to warm the building, and no recirculation is allowed. **1934** W. Trinks *Industr. Furnaces* (ed. 3) vi. 394 (*caption*) Furnace designed for recirculation of products of combustion. **1954** G. M. Fair et al. *Water Supply & Waste-Water Disposal* xxx. 905 Modern swimming pools are designed for the recirculation of pool water and its continuous repurification, reheating, and redisinfection. **1964** *Proc. R. Soc.* B. CLIX. 280 It seems likely that a re-circulation through the lymph nodes is a feature of the life-history of small lymphocytes among mammals generally. **1975** *Nature* 20 Mar. 175/2 Recirculation of metal and other wastes could save an increasing proportion of the total energy used in Sweden.

recirculatory (rīsɜ̄·ɹkiulĕtəri, rīːsɜ̄ɹkiulēi·-təri), *a.* [Re- 5 a.] Involving recirculation; recirculating.

1951 *Engineering* 23 Nov. 664/1 The steering gear is of the recirculatory-ball pattern. **1959** *Motor* 23 Sept. 179/2 Available as an extra is a recirculatory interior heater.

‖ **récit** (resi). [Fr.] **1.** *Mus.* (See quots.)

1884 F. Niecks *Conc. Dict. Mus. Terms* 201 *Récit* (Fr.), (1) what is performed by one singer or one instrumentalist, a vocal or instrumental *solo.* (2) The principal part in a piece of concerted music. (3) One of the manuals and corresponding stops of the organ, the Swell Organ. **1924** L. J. De Bekker *Black's Dict. Mus. & Musicians* 538/1 *Recit*, Fr. solo part; principal of several parts. **1954** *Grove's Dict. Mus.* (ed. 5) VII. 72/1 *Récit*.., a 17th-century term for a declamatory melody supported by simple accompaniment,..but also, by analogy, an instrumental piece, such as an organ piece with the tune played on a solo stop. **1968** A. Niland *Introd. to Organ* 109 Cavaillé-Coll never really took to the swell box, being content to enclose only the récit expressif, even in a five manual organ. **1975** *New Yorker* 28 Apr. 133/2 The *Récit* [*sc.* a rank of organ pipes] is in mysterious darkness, behind the louvres of the box that encloses it.

2. *Lit.* Narrative, account (freq. opposed to dialogue); a relating of events. Also, a book or passage consisting largely of narrative.

1944 'G. Orwell' in *Horizon* X. 237 The whole book, *récit* as well as dialogue, is written in the American language. **1959** *Times Lit. Suppl.* 27 Mar. 173/1 The *récit*..studies always to keep an uncluttered foreground where only one or two characters are permitted to disport themselves; for the most part it sticks to narrative and reported speech. **1960** *Ibid.* 18 Nov. 737/3 The four *récits* which compose his latest work are set as far apart as Ethiopia, Spain, Italy and the Midi. **1964** *New Statesman* 17 Apr. 610/2 Its form is French: a flowery *récit* by an ageing recluse describing his attempts to make life and thought converge. **1978** *Observer* 26 May 30/1 The rhythms of his *récit*—his dialogue is a different matter—are terribly unvarious.

recital. Add: **3. b.** Now also in wider sense, a performance of instrumental music or of music and songs, freq. from the works of several composers.

1929 *Radio Times* 8 Nov. 417/2 A Recital of Gramophone Records. **1962** *Amer. Speech* XXXVII. 19 New York City boasts of many fine museums, art galleries, and recital halls. **1981** *Early Music News* Mar. 2 Gillian Weir..will give a joint harpsichord and organ recital, conceived as a salute to Couperin and Bach.

recitation. Add: **3.** (Earlier examples.)

1770 P. Fithian *Let.* 30 Nov. in *Jrnl. & Lett.* (1900) 8 At nine the Bell rings for Recitation, after which we study till one, when the Bell rings for Dinner. **1780** E. Parkman *Diary* 9 Feb. (1899) 208 He has been absent from ye Recitations so long, that he ought to be one of ye first that returns at this Term.

4. (sense 3) *recitation bench* (further example), *-method*, *-room* (earlier and later examples); (sense 2) *recitation music*, *-note* (earlier example).

1949 'J. Nelson' *Backwoods Teacher* 48 Likely-looking ones I placed on the table..beside the four, long, recitation benches. **1899** W. James *Talks to Teachers* i. 4 Traditions of instruction..evolved from the older American recitation-method. **1927** *Grove's Dict. Mus.* (ed. 3) III. 371/2 A long series of 'Recitation Music', *i.e.* compositions for piano intended to accompany the declamation of various well-known poems, was written by Stanley Hawley. **1844** W. B. Heathcote *Canticles* p. iii, The first half of the verse is said on the recitation-note G. **1827** *Harvard Reg.* Sept. 202 We hurry to the Chapel, and then crowd to the recitation room. **1899** W. James *Talks to Teachers* xiv. 161 The flowing life of the mind is sorted into parcels suitable for presentation in the recitation-room.

recitative, *a.*[1] and *sb.* Add: **B.** *sb.* **3. b.** Also *fig.*

1957 M. Spark *Comforters* iii. 42 It said: On the whole she did not think there would be any difficulty with Helena... There seemed, then, to have been more than one voice: it was a recitative, a chanting in unison.

4. *Comb.*, as *recitative-like* adj.

1947 A. Einstein *Mus. in Romantic Era* xi. 143 Characteristically Lisztian recitative-like interjections. **1963** *Times* 28 Feb. 16/3 It was especially in his perfect shaping of the recitative-like passages that Mr. Frank demonstrated his cultivated musicianship.

recitative, *v.* **2.** (Later example.)

1932 [see *preludingly *adv.*].

recitativo. Add: **2.** Used in certain Italian phrases designating varieties of recitative, as **recitativo accompagnato** (akǫmpanyā·to): in which the vocalist is accompanied by an orchestra; **recitativo secco** (se·ko) [lit. 'dry recitative']: in which the vocalist has little or no musical accompaniment; **recitativo stromentato** (strǫmentā·to) [lit. 'accompanied recitative'] = *recitativo accompagnato* above.

[**1771** C. Burney *Present State of Mus. France & Italy* 285 Signor Rinaldo di Capua has at Rome the reputation of being the inventor of accompanied recitatives. **1801** T. Busby *Dict. Mus.*, *Recitative accompanied*, a *recitative* is said to be *accompanied* when besides the bass there are parts for other instruments.] **1866** [see *recitativo stromentato* below]. **1947** A. Einstein *Mus. in Romantic Era* ix. 96 The genuine melodrama, in which the spoken word, usually an emotional monologue, was given an orchestral background in the manner of a *recitativo accompagnato*. **1963** *Listener* 14 Feb. 313/1 *Recitativo accompagnato* began to encroach more and more on the traditional *secco*. **1828** T. Busby *Mus. Man.* 144 *Recitativo secco*, (Ital.) unaccompanied recitative. **1876, 1883** [see Secco *a.*]. **1891** G. B. Shaw in *World* 13 May 27/2 Start on the *recitativo secco* by entirely expunging the first two lengths after the duel. **1955** E. Dent in H. Van Thal *Fanfare for E. Newman* 105 It is practically a reversion to *recitativo secco* in a more pretentious form. **1963** Auden *Dyer's Hand* 524 Ariel *is* song; when he is truly himself, he sings. The effect when he speaks is similar to that of *recitativo secco* in opera. **1977** *Listener* 26 May 692/1 The vocal line is written in the customary *recitativo secco* style. [**1828** T. Busby *Mus. Man.* 144 *Recitativo istromento*, (Ital.) accompanied recitative.] **1837** J. A. Hamilton *Dict. Two Thousand Italian, French, German, Eng. & Other Mus. Terms* 58 *Recitativo stromentato* (Italian) recitative accompanied by the orchestra. **1866** *Chambers's Encycl.* VIII. 140/2 It is termed *recitativo accompagnato, strumentato*, or *obbligato*. **1905** E. J. Dent *Alessandro Scarlatti* ii. 45 Here we have an unmistakable *recitativo stromentato*, the earliest (1686) that I have been able to find.

recite, *v.* **7.** (Earlier Amer. examples.)

1742 E. A. Holyoke *Diary* 22 Aug. (1911) 32 This day began to recite to Mr Flynt & Mr Appleton in Tully and virgill & Greek testament. **1759** S. Gardner *Jrnl.* 21 Mar. in *Essex Inst. Hist. Coll.* (1913) XLIX. 6 Finished reciting, the Dr. gave us good advice. **1815** *Niles' Weekly Reg.* IX. 18/1 Those not immediately engaged in reciting to some one or other of the professors, remain in their own chambers.

Reckitt (re·kit). Also *erron.* **Reckett.** [See quot. 1877.] Used in the possessive as the proprietary name of a blue (*blue *sb.* 2 c) for laundry use; also as the name of the colour of this substance, a clear cobalt blue, esp. *transf.* Hence **Reckitt's bluebag**, the bag in which this product is marketed.

1877 *Trade Marks Jrnl.* 19 Feb. 471 Reckitt's Blue in squares will be found far more beautiful & much more economical than any other... Francis Reckitt, of Hull, Yorkshire, on behalf of self and partner, James Reckitt, trading as I. Reckitt and Sons, at..London, and as Isaac Reckitt and Sons, at Hull, Yorkshire; starch manufacturers. **1893** S. R. Crockett *Stickit Minister* 46 The book..was bound in a peculiarly deadly blue, of a rectified Reckitt tint, which gave you dazzles in the eye. **1898** G. B. Shaw *Let.* 25 Apr. (1972) II. 37 Mud & fog are not so fatal as sciroccos [*sic*]..& Reckitt's blue. **1920** E. Sitwell *Wooden Pegasus* 83 Then (Recketts' blue) a puff of wind. **1925** 'H. H. Richardson' *Way Home* ii. i. 113 As for the sky, Mahony declared it made him think of a Reckitt's bluebag. **1930** E. V. Lucas *Down Sky* 138 A bunch of yellow-haired girls lying on marble slabs looking at a sea of Reckitts. **1969** R. Harris *Nat. Hist. Collecting* 49 Some sponges are brightly coloured. One is called the Reckitt's blue, not without reason. **1971** *Guardian* 6 Feb. 3/3 The flies zoom between the Reckitt's Blue walls. **1976** *Trade Marks Jrnl.* 1 Dec. 2497/2 Reckitt's Bag Blue. Ready for use... Laundry blue for sale in the United Kingdom and for export to the Irish Republic. Reckitt & Colman Products Limited, trading as Reckitt & Colman,..Hull, Yorkshire; manufacturers and merchants.

Recklinghausen's disease, var. *von Recklinghausen's disease.

reckon, *v.* Add: **I. 5. d.** *colloq.* To rate highly, to esteem. Usu. in negative phrases.

1957 *Evening News* 12 Nov. 6/4 If..an East Ender wants to say that he does not consider the character of another to be worth while he says 'I don't reckon him'. **1977** *Sunday Times* 52/3, I don't reckon the chances of *Young Scientists of the Year*..against *Just William*.

6. a. Now usu. *colloq.*, esp. in the U.S. (formerly chiefly in southern States).

1810 M. Dwight *Jrnl.* 9 Nov. in *Journey to Ohio in 1810* (1912) 37 The people here talk curiously, they all reckon instead of expect. **1863** *Congress. Globe* 7 Feb. 783/3 If you can take this property by compact, I reckon you cannot take it against the consent of the owners. **1893** H. A. Shands *Some Peculiarities of Speech in Mississippi* 53 *Reckon*,..this word is almost always used in the ordinary conversation of our best educated people for *think* or *suppose*, and corresponds to a like use of *guess* in the Northern States. **1900** *Cosmopolitan* Feb. 389/1 She met Sam on the way out, and says she: 'Sam, what do you reckon? My quilt took the premium.' **1963** *Social Problems* Spring 367/1, I reckon it'll always be lucky. **1977** I. Shaw *Beggarman, Thief* iii. ii. 193, I don't reckon I've had a fare there for more than ten years.

II 11. b. (Further examples.)

1902 Kipling *Five Nations* (1903) 63 We reckon not with those Whom the mere Fates ordain. **1945** T. S. Eliot *What is a Classic?* 8 We may say confidently that it [*sc.* the definition] must be one which will expressly reckon with him.

Hence as *sb.*, an act of consideration; a 'think'. *colloq.*

1949 F. Sargeson *I saw in my Dream* vii. 57 He reckons he's going to... Then he'd better go and have another reckon, the girl said.

reckonable, *a.* Delete *rare* and add: Also, admissible for the purposes of reckoning. (Further examples.) Hence **reckonabi·lity**, the quality of being reckonable.

1905 *Daily Chron.* 21 July 4/4 Its only drawback is that it is called 'Hardy's country' by those fiction-enthusiasts who now form so reckonable a section of Weymouth guests. **1967** *Encycl. Philos.* VII. 94/1 (*heading*) Reckonability. **1971** *Daily Tel.* 15 Sept. 6/8 This means that for every £1,000 of reckonable earnings the pension offered must amount to at least £10 for each year of service. **1973** *Times* 29 Nov. 16/3 There were bound to be practical difficulties and problems of definition in reopening at this late stage the question of reckonable service of teachers who joined the profession immediately after the war.

reckoning, *vbl. sb.* Add: **9.** *reckoning tablet.*

1930 T. S. Eliot tr. *St.-J. Perse's Anabasis* 67 He who has spread on the ground his reckoning tablets.

reclaim, *sb.*[1] Restrict 'Now *rare*' to senses in Dict. and add: **II. 5.** = **reclaimed rubber*.

1935 Dawson & Porritt *Rubber* 208/2 Although reclaim as compared with new rubber definitely leads to inferior mechanical properties in vulcanisates,..it has important applications in rubbers where mechanical strength and abrasion resistance are of secondary significance. **1954** H. J. Stern *Rubber* vi. 200 Small differences in temperature from one part of the rubber to the other greatly affect the uniformity of the reclaims. **1971** R. Singleton in C. M. Blow *Rubber Technol. & Manufacture* vi. 207 First-quality reclaim made from whole tyres contains about 45% rubber hydrocarbon by weight. The remaining 55% consists of valuable carbon black, a little mineral filler, and softeners.

reclaim, *v.* Add: **I. 3. d.** (Further examples.)

1903 G. B. Shaw *Man & Superman* p. xi, Far beyond mere lovemaking into politics, high art, schemes for reclaiming new continents from the ocean. **1922** Joyce *Ulysses* 68 Reclaim the whole place. Grow peas in that corner there. **1943** J. S. Huxley *TVA* vi. 30 Gullied and badly eroding land reclaimed in the Valley. **1966** *Listener* 26 May 751/2 You could take advantage of this fact by reclaiming a large area of the Wash itself.

e. To recover (rubber) for reuse by freeing it from impurities and rendering it plastic again; more widely, to make (re)usable (what has been used or rendered unusable). Also *absol.*

1895 *Sci. Amer.* 26 Oct. 267/1 Methods of reclaiming rubber. **1898** *India-Rubber & Gutta-Percha & Electr. Trades' Jrnl.* XVI. 184/1 Prior to that time [*sc.* 1870] the use of rubber reclaimed from fibrous wastes had been confined practically to one large factory in Boston and one near New York. **1937** H. Barron *Mod. Rubber Chem.* xxi. 254 Miller carried out four cycles of reclaiming starting from a reclaim. That is, he vulcanised, reclaimed, added sulphur, revulcanized, reclaimed, etc. **1937** *Iron Age* 5 Aug. 38/3 Many new parts of Monel rendered unserviceable as a result of being turned undersize or bored oversize in the process of manufacture are readily reclaimed by spraying. **1962** A. Nisbett *Technique Sound Studio* vi. 113 The tape is finally wiped and reclaimed. **1970** [see *reclamation 2 d]. **1972** P. W. Allen *Natural Rubber & Synthetics* v. 121 About 90 per cent of the world's supply of new rubbers is not reclaimed but ends up as unwanted waste products. **1976** *Conservation News* Nov./Dec. 18/2 It cost twice as much to reclaim bottles as it did to buy new ones. **1977** *Lancashire Life* Dec. 92/4 It is particularly annoying to see stones from old property bulldozed aside instead of being reclaimed for future use.

reclaimed, *ppl. a.* Add : **1.** (Further examples.)

1961 D. M. Disney *Mrs. Meeker's Money* vii. 77 A reclaimed island of land-scaped brick and glass on the fringe of the business district. **1974** W. J. Burley *Death in Stanley St.* ix. 164 The new waste-disposal unit, pride of the city, had been built on a promontory of reclaimed land.

2. Rendered reusable; *reclaimed rubber*, rubber obtained from used vulcanized rubber by treating it to remove free sulphur and foreign substances and to render it plastic, chiefly used mixed with crude rubber in low-grade rubber goods.

1897 *Sci. Amer.* 25 Sept. 196/2 The reclaimed rubber of commerce is obtained by steaming or devulcanizing old rubber waste, generally shoes, freed more or less perfectly from fiber. **1913** B. D. Porritt *Chem. Rubber* v. 66 The consumption of reclaimed rubber..is probably equal to the world's production of raw rubber. **1942** *Time* 2 Feb. 63/3 Reclaimed rubber, ordinarily bypassed by manufacturers because it wears out faster than natural rubber. **1958** *Jrnl. Amer. Water Works Assoc.* L. 1021 (*heading*) Emergency use of reclaimed water for potable supply at Chanute, Kan. **1971** R. Singleton in C. M. Blow *Rubber Technol. & Manufacture* vi. 203 Reclaimed rubber has become widely accepted as a raw material which possesses processing and economic characteristics that are of great value in the compounding of natural and synthetic rubber stocks. **1976** *Lancs. Evening Post* 7 Dec. 13/5 (Advt.), Demolition materials. Reclaimed timber (cut to your requirements)... Reclaimed stone.

reclaiming, *vbl. sb.* Add: **a.** (Further examples.)

1892 *Sci. Amer.* 7 May 293/3 These [*sc.* old boots and shoes] are sorted roughly, put up in bales, and shipped to the companies who make a business of reclaiming. **1913** B. D. Porritt *Chem. Rubber* v. 60 'Reclaiming' at the present time is an industry by itself, several large works being exclusively engaged on this work. **1971** R. Singleton in C. M. Blow *Rubber Technol. & Manufacture* vi. 203 The raw material for reclaiming is scrap rubber in a wide variety of forms, but tyres..form the major quantity.

b. (Further examples.)

1895 *Sci. Amer.* 26 Oct. 267/1 Rubber reclaiming factories. **1954** H. J. Stern *Rubber* vi. 200 Peptising agents accelerate the reclaiming process and are useful with both natural and synthetic rubbers. **1957** *Times* 20 Dec. 17/6 In our reclaiming plant overtime working was in force from October.

reclamation. Add: **2. c.** (Earlier and later examples.) Cf. also *land reclamation* s.v. *land *sb.*[1] 10 a.

1848 J. S. Mill *Let.* 3 Feb. in W. Ward *Aubrey de Vere* (1904) iv. 132, I look much more than you do to reclamation of waste lands. **1955** *Times* 24 May 8/3 The United Nations Relief and Works Agency is soon to present..a report on the feasibility of an ambitious reclamation scheme known as the Sinai strip. **1970** *New Yorker* 15 Aug. 32/1 The Dutch.. knew..how difficult and dirty any sort of reclamation work could be.

d. The action or process of reclaiming used or unusable objects or materials.

1937 *Iron Age* 5 Aug. 36/2 This..has been largely responsible for the extended use of the spray process in applying this metal both for the protection of new parts and for the reclamation of worn or unserviceable items. **1954** *Publ. Calif. State Water Pollution Control Board* No. 9. i. 13 Implicit in the study of waste water reclamation and utilization is the idea that eventually it will be of economic value as a water source. **1962** A. Nisbett *Technique Sound Studio*

vii. 133 In BBC practice reclamation also includes not only checking through the tape to remove spacers, trailers, etc... but also removing all temporary joints and replacing them by cemented joints. **1970** *New Society* 5 Mar. 387/3 The reclamation industry reckons it saves Britain £1,000 million by reclaiming otherwise imported material.

6. Special *Comb.*: **reclamation disease** [tr. G. *urbarmachungskrankheit* (B. Sjollema 1933, in *Biochem. Zeitschr.* CCLXVII. 151)], a disease affecting crops, esp. cereals, grown on reclaimed land, caused by a deficiency of copper and distinguished by discoloured leaves and the failure of affected plants to produce seed.

1937 F. T. Heald *Introd. Plant Pathol.* xviii. 365 The curative value of boron has also been demonstrated for the 'reclamation or bog disease', a trouble characteristic of swampy heath soils in European countries. **1949** Butler & Jones *Plant Pathol.* ix. 312 Among the group of crop disorders..owing to the active measures taken during modern times to reclaim peat moor, swamp, and polder soils, that which eventually became widely termed 'reclamation disease' is one of the most important. **1961** W. Stiles *Trace Elements in Plants* (ed. 3) iii. 99 Reclamation disease.. affects oats and other cereals.

réclame. Add: (Earlier example.) Also, popular acclaim, notoriety, glory, fame.

In quot. 1870 the sense seems to be 'an advertisement'.

1870 O. Logan *Before Footlights & behind Scenes* xxii. 255 Perhaps you think I mean this as a *reclame* for the Sherman House. **1906** R. Fry *Let.* 16 Mar. (1972) I. 257 Pictures.. which he offered at ridiculous prices for the *réclame* of getting into the Museum. **1945** R. Hargreaves *Enemy at Gate* 105 The effulgent *réclame* of the conqueror of Wurmser and the Archduke Charles. **1977** *Times Lit. Suppl.* 25 Feb. 200/2 The author of a novel..which the serious papers denounced as prurient, so adding both to the number of copies sold and to his réclame among his colleagues.

reclassify (rīklæ·sifəi), *v.* [Re- 5 a.] *trans.* To classify again; to alter the classification of.

1920 in Webster. **1928** *Daily Tel.* 27 Nov. 8/2 They will have an opportunity of reclassifying their institutions. **1946** *Nature* 28 Sept. 439/1 Existing roads should be reclassified and the design of new roads should not be attempted before their purpose was clearly determined. **1953** *Times* 8 June 7/4 Whether the Government will consider the advisability of reclassifying crash helmets as motor-cycle accessories. **1972** W. McGivern *Caprifoil* iii. 47 'Those files aren't available.' 'They've been reclassified?' **1977** *Evening Post* (Nottingham) 27 Jan. 2/8 Re-classify their status—they are part retired, but certainly not wholly unemployed.

reclinable, *a.* (Further example.)

1957 *Archit. Rev.* CXXII. 351 (*caption*) In both, seats are reclinable and the windows are double-glazed.

recline, *v.* Add: **1. a.** (Later example.)

1972 *Daily Tel.* (Colour Suppl.) 25 Aug. 19/2 A back-row, next-to-bulkhead seat is often fixed, i.e. the backrest cannot be reclined.

3. d. Of a seat: to admit of mechanical inclination of the back to a reclining or recumbent position.

1972 *N. Y. Law Jrnl.* 24 Oct. 3/2 The company is engaged in the manufacture and sale of upholstered furniture, principally medium priced chairs that recline. **1974** *Trafford's Catal.* 963/3 Multiposition metal reclining chair... Can recline to many positions.

recliner. Add: **2.** A chair in which one may comfortably recline; a reclining chair or seat. Also *Comb.*, as *recliner chair, seat.* orig. *U.S.*

1928 E. O'Neill *Strange Interlude* ix. 275 There is a stone bench at center, a recliner at right. **1948** Partridge *Dict. Forces' Slang* 153 *Recliners*, Navy 'issue' armchairs. (Ward-room.) **1970** *Globe & Mail* (Toronto) 25 Sept. 31/2 (Advt.), The comfort of hushed travel in recliner seats. **1977** E. Leonard *Unknown Man No. 89* xx. 192 Jay Walk, in his desk-chair recliner, had his shoes off. **1978** *Lancashire Life* Oct. 115/2 Buoyant Upholstery have just introduced the Wellbeck Chameleon range of fourteen interchangeable items, made up of Chesterfields, unit pieces, settees, recliner chair, wing chair, [etc.].

reclining, *ppl. a.* (Further examples.)

1883 L. M. Mitchell *Hist. Anc. Sculpture* xix. 354 By a recent correction in the placing of the reclining figure..lines of unexpected beauty in the composition of Pheidias have been revealed to us. **1966** D. Hall *Henry Moore* iv. 72 He exploited his stone-carving breakthrough in a series of female figures: upright busts, reclining figures.

reclining, *vbl. sb.* Add: **reclining chair** (examples); **reclining seat,** a seat which may be adjusted to a reclining position, esp. in a motor vehicle or aeroplane.

These combinations can equally be seen as examples of the *ppl. a.*

1863 Geo. Eliot *Let.* 26 Dec. (1956) IV. 124 Another munificent friend has given me the most splendid reclining chair conceivable. **1907** *Yesterday's Shopping* (1969) 276/2 Improved portable suspensory Reclining Chair, with leg rest in canvas. **1976** B. Bova *Multiple Man* (1977) xiv. 148 We sat side by side in the most luxurious reclining chairs I'd ever flown in. **1943** S. C. Menefee *Assignment: U.S.A.* i. v. 117 She settled her ample proportions into the reclining seat next to me. **1974** 'D. Craig' *Dead Liberty* xix. 108 Boxanford arranged..to change his car... He wanted reclining seats.

reclude, *v.* Add: **2. b.** Also *refl.*

1911 M. Beerbohm *Zuleika Dobson* ii. 22 No woman who knows that of herself can be rightly censured for not recluding herself from the world.

reclusage. Restrict † *Obs.* to sense in Dict. and add: **2.** Retirement, reclusion.

1960 *Times Lit. Suppl.* 18 Nov. 742/3 For more than half a lifetime..he had enjoyed a voluntary reclusage on the Riviera di Levante.

recluse, *a.* and *sb.* Add: **c.** *Comb.*, as *recluse-like* adj.

1946 E. Blunden *Shelley* xvii. 213 The fashionable round ..did not prevent her from falling under the spell of the recluse-like Shelley.

reclusion. 1. a. (Further examples.)

1908 E. Wharton *Hermit & Wild Woman* 33 In a life of penance and reclusion her eyes might be opened to her iniquity. **1971** T. Merton *Contemplation in World of Action* ii. v. 300 It must not be imagined that these problems of order rose exclusively from a lack of legislation and from a too-free development of 'charisms' of pilgrimage, hermit-solitude or reclusion.

reclusive, *a.* Add: Now freq. of persons. (Further examples.)

1965 *Listener* 16 Sept. 426/2 A reclusive New Englander who wrote but did not flourish in the literary climate of Transcendentalism. **1971** *Wall St. Jrnl.* 13 Aug. 1/6 Esquire ..ran a cover showing the reclusive Howard Hughes. **1979** *Daily Tel.* 1 Sept. 21/3 Equal partnership deals are not common in the business career of the reclusive Mr Ludwig.

Hence **reclu·sively** *adv.*, in the manner of a recluse; **reclusiveness** (further examples).

1925 C. Connolly *Let.* 25 Jan. in *Romantic Friendship* (1975) 56 The last week of Minehead..left me with an intense reclusiveness. **1963** *Punch* 13 Feb. 249/1 His life was spent uneventfully, reclusively almost. **1976** *National Observer* (U.S.) 14 Feb. 15/2 My symptom was reclusiveness. **1979** *N. & Q.* June 240/2 W. S. W. was both a Scholar and subsequent Fellow of Trinity College, Cambridge, where he lived reclusively.

recode (rīkōᵘ·d), *v.* [Re- 5 a.] *trans.* To put into another or different code; *spec.* in *Psychol.*, to rearrange mentally (information presented by a problem, situation, or test).

1951 [implied in *recoding *vbl. sb.*]. **1957** J. S. Bruner *Contemp. Approaches in Psychol.* 59 All the measurements can be recoded into a simple rule. **1964** M. McLuhan *Understanding Media* (1967) viii. 90 The human ear can be compared to a radio receiver that is able to decode electromagnetic waves and recode them as sound. **1971** *Jrnl. Gen. Psychol.* LXXXV. 213 There are often possibilities for *S* to encode the information in one of the languages not intended or to recode the information in a second language. **1977** J. M. Scandura *Problem Solving* vii. 301 In order to recover the original elements..they must be recoded. *Ibid.* 309 Extraneous processes may reduce memory load..where two digits are recoded..as one unit.

So **reco·ding** *vbl. sb.*

1951 G. A. Miller *Lang. & Communication* xi. 233 The task also illustrates something we can call recoding, and in many problems it can be shown that the restructuring process is, in whole or in part, a matter of coding the information in a new form. **1957** J. S. Bruner *Contemp. Approaches to Cognition* 60 Once a system of recoding has been worked out whereby information is condensed into more generic codes, the problem of mastery becomes one of mastering the recoding system. **1964** J. Z. Young *Model of Brain* ii. 21 The conversion from one sort of physical system to another is called re-coding (e.g. speech into writing). Information is thus that feature of the system that remains invariant under re-coding. **1970** B. Milner in Pribram & Broadbent *Biol. of Memory* 42 This maze has 28 choice-points, so that, even with recoding, the sequence of turns to be remembered cannot be encompassed within the span of immediate memory. **1977** J. M. Scandura *Problem Solving* vii. 304 Even on simple tests of memory span, recoding and rehearsal processes tend to be highly dependent on individual preference.

recogitate, *v.* **1. b.** (Later examples.)

1920 in Webster. **1932** H. Crane *Let.* ?Feb. (1965) 401, I had to spend the rest of the day and evening cogitating and recogitating.

recognition. Add: **7. c.** *Psychol.* In the study of thinking and memory, the mental process whereby things are identified as having been previously apprehended or as belonging to a particular known category, usu. distinguished from the process of recall.

1894 Creighton & Titchener tr. *Wundt's Hum. & Anim. Psychol.* xx. 297 The simplest case of assimilation is the cognition of an object; the simplest case of successive association, its recognition. **1894** *Psychol. Rev.* I. 608 There were some incidental illustrations of false recognition. **1923** C. Spearman *Nature of Intell.* xix. 313 Recognition..is often traceable to nothing more than an awareness of similarity. **1951** G. A. Miller *Lang. & Communication* vi. 121 It is a general rule of verbal learning that recognition is easier than recall. **1965** E. E. Harris *Foundation of Metaphys.* in *Sci.* xix. 380 There are two kinds of problems..in attacking which the cybernetic approach has been used... The second are problems of transmission and of recognition. **1965** K. M. Sayre (*title*) Recognition: a study in the philosophy of artificial intelligence. *Ibid.* i. 33 The task of achieving mechanical recognition of letter-patterns brings up problems of both sorts. **1973** A. J. Pomerans tr. *Piaget & Inhelder's Memory & Intelligence* 1 It is difficult to decide whether his [*sc.* the subject's] recognition is based on the remembrance or conservation of perceptive schemata..or whether it reflects the organization of the sense data by these schemata.

d. *out of* (or *beyond*) *recognition*, to such a degree as to be unrecognizable.

1901 G. B. Shaw *Three Plays for Puritans* 202 The world, instead of having been improved in 67 generations out of all recognition, presents, on the whole, a rather less dignified appearance. **1916** —— *Androcles & Lion* p. xli, Jesus is refined and softened almost out of recognition. **1964** M. Drabble *Garrick Year* ii. 33 After she was born,..things improved out of all recognition. **1977** *Rolling Stone* 5 May 30/5 Futuristic explorers..returning to their own world to find it changed beyond recognition.

8. (sense 7 a) *recognition-call, scene*; (sense *7 c) *recognition habit, learning, memory, schema, test, vocabulary, word*; **recognition colour**: also *transf.* in *Mil.* use; **recognition grammar** *Linguistics*, a grammar based on the analysis of given sentences in a corpus (opp. generative grammar); **recognition mark** (later examples); **recognition marking**: also *transf.* in *Mil.* use; **recognition picketing** *U.S.*, the picketing of an employer to obtain union recognition; **recognition signal** *Mil.* (see quot. 1963).

1911 J. A. Thomson *Biol. Seasons* ii. 155 Love-calls and song probably had their roots in the simple recognition-call or characteristic signal of the species. **1944** *Return to Attack* (Army Board, N.Z.) 32/2 Three tanks, displaying British recognition colours, climbed the hill. **1966** A. F. R. Brown in *Automatic Transl. of Lang.* (NATO Summer School, Venice 1962) 49 A recognition grammar will turn out to be a thousand times more complicated than a conventional descriptive grammar. **1968** J. Lyons *Introd. Theoret. Ling.* vi. 230 We have put the categorial system in the form of a 'recognition' grammar and the 'rewrite' system in the form of a 'production' grammar. **1920** T. P. Nunn *Educ.* xiii. 169 Learning to read involves, in fact, building up recognition-habits. **1970** M. R. Amato *Experim. Psychol.* xii. 550 The simplest case of recognition learning is verbal discrimination in which an arbitrarily selected 'correct' item is to be identified from an accompanying, but incorrect, item. **1906** M. C. Dickerson *Frog Bk.* 26 These brilliant colours..may act as recognition marks for others of the same species. **1939** A. S. Pearse *Anim. Ecol.* (ed. 2) iii. 31 He [*sc.* E. S. Poulton] cites the conspicuous white tails of the rabbit and antelope as examples of recognition marks. **1960** M. Burton *Wild Animals Brit. Isles* 121 A patch of white around the short tail [of the red deer] furnishes a 'recognition mark', common to most of the deer family. **1977** T. I. Storer et al. *Elements Zool.* (ed. 4) xiii. 220/2 Recognition marks and other signals are often important in intraspecific communication. **1940** in *Brit. Aviation Colours of World War Two* (R.A.F. Museum Series) (1976) III. 9 (*heading*) Aircraft colouring and recognition markings. **1975** Gander & Chamberlain *German Tanks of World War 2* vi. 53/2 Perhaps the most universally applied markings used on German tanks was the tactical national recognition marking. This was usually a black cross outlined in white. **1955** H. E. Garrett *Gen. Psychol.* x. 396 Students do not always distinguish between those facts which should be learned for recall and those for which recognition memory is sufficient. **1973** J. G. Greeno in B. B. Wolman *Handbk. Gen. Psychol.* viii. 150/2 The agreement between the data and the theory demonstrates that it is appropriate to analyze recognition memory in terms of a concept of trace strength. **1960** *U.S. Statutes at Large 1959* LXXIII. 542 (*heading*) Boycotts and recognition picketing. **1962** N. S. Falcone *Labor Law* xi. 345 Recognition picketing is generally defined as picketing an employer's establishment to force the employer to recognize and bargain with the union. **1932** T. S. Eliot *Selected Ess.* 194 The Recognition Scene, so important in Shakespeare's later plays. **1971** *Jrnl. Gen. Psychol.* Jan. 166 Recognition schema operating on coded features are entirely possible. **1958** P. Scott *Mark of Warrior* ii. 149, I want you to set up your recognition signals on the D[ropping]. Z[one]. itself. **1963** *Dict. U.S. Mil. Terms* (U.S. Dept. Defense) 180 *Recognition signal*, any prearranged signal by which individuals or units may identify each other. **1978** R. V. Jones *Most Secret War* v. 48 You have to shoot your opponent out of the ocean..if he does not make the right recognition signal. **1923** P. B. Ballard *New Examiner* vii. 81 The third and last test was a Recognition Test... The candidate..had to underline the one word or phrase which would make each statement true. **1966** J. M. Brown et al. *Applied Psychol.* xii. 418 Recognition tests..were used to evaluate the memorability of advertising messages. **1966** J. Derrick *Teaching Eng. to Immigrants* ii. 99 Most stories will contain far more material than the pupils are expected to reproduce themselves (i.e. relying on and helping to build up their 'passive' or recognition vocabulary). **1977** P. Strevens *New Orientations Teaching Eng.* v. 62 Recognition vocabulary..can lie outside the confines of controlled vocabulary, grammar, etc., as long as the learner understands it when he meets it. **1957** Partridge *Eng. gone Wrong* ii. 44 *Monolithic*, especially perhaps in *monolithic unity*, is a recognition-word, a keyword, a badge.

recognitive, *a.* (Further examples.)

1930 *New Statesman* 16 Aug. 593/1 Its function appears to be mainly critical and recognitive. **1977** *Maledicta* Summer 33 The relatively passive attitude of acceptance of good or evil we call *recognitive.*

recognitory, *a.* Add: (Further example.) Now *rare.*

1964 R. Perry *World of Tiger* iii. 42 It is difficult to think of any recognitory purpose this marking could serve.

recognizability. (Further examples.)

1938 [see *extruder 2]. **1979** *Sci. Amer.* June 42/2 The transformation of an embryo into a fetus..is a transformation from external recognizability only as human to increasing recognizability as an emergent person.

recognize, *v.*[1] Add: **4. a.** Also *absol.*

1974 M. PENDYRE *Breach of Security* xxiii. 132 Our customary criteria for recognition are that the government should control the whole country... But..those raving Afro-Asian countries have recognized already. **1977** D. BEATY *Excellency* v. 66 The State Department isn't going to recognize until they *do* have the details.

recognized, *ppl. a.* (Further examples.)

1945 *Guide to Educ. System Eng. & Wales* (Min. of Educ.) 60 *Recognised Efficient School*, independent school inspected by H.M.I.s and regarded as efficient by the Ministry. **1966** *Rep. Comm. Inquiry Univ. Oxf.* I. i. 47 We recommend that the existing university category of 'Recognized Student' should be revised. **1974** G. HUBBARD *Quaker by Convincement* IV. i. 180 Until recently we were a Recognized Meeting, part of the Preparative Meeting of Kingston upon Thames, some three miles away.

recognizer. Add: **2.** A device which can interpret speech by identifying the sounds and assigning them the correct meaning.

1952 *Jrnl. Acoustical Soc. Amer.* XXIV. 637 The recognizer discussed will automatically recognize telephone-quality digits spoken at normal speech rates by a single individual, with an accuracy varying between 97 and 99 percent. **1958** *Listener* 11 Dec. 984/2 One aspect of this work..is that of Drs. Ahmed and Fatehchand..on the direct recognition of the spoken word [by a computer]... It is safe to predict that a recognizer of 95 per cent. accuracy could be built within five years. **1973** *Physics Bull.* May 281/1 Ideally the recognizer should perform this action irrespective of the speaker and the acoustic environment in which he is speaking. This means that the machine not only has to recognize the speech sounds it receives, but it also has to ignore those facets of the signal that convey information irrelevant to the task of recognizing the speech. **1976** W. A. AINSWORTH *Mechanisms of Speech Recognition* x. 104 An automatic speech recognizer may be defined as any mechanism, other than the human auditory system, which decodes the acoustic signal produced by the human voice into a sequence of linguistic units which contain the message that the speaker wishes to convey. *Ibid.* 111 If the world of discourse of the speech recognizer is sufficiently restricted it is sometimes possible to employ semantic information to choose between words or phrases which seem equally likely on phonetic, syntactic or other grounds.

recoil, *sb.* Add: **3*.** *Nucl. Physics.* The result of a collision between two sub-atomic particles, or of spontaneous decay of a single particle, in which the two resulting particles move in opposite directions with speeds determined by conservation of momentum.

1909 *Nature* 24 June 490/1 Rutherford..suggests the possibility of the phenomenon being due to a recoil effect rather than to a volatility possessed by the product radium B. **1912** *Phil. Mag.* XXIV. 622 It is well known..that the emission of α particles from radioactive substances is accompanied by a vigorous recoil of the residual atoms. **1933** *Discovery* Apr. 107/2 The energy of recoil is greatest when it [*sc.* a neutron] strikes a hydrogen nucleus, and the recoiling atom may travel 30 c.m. or more in air before it is brought to rest. **1964** J. B. HASTED *Physics of Atomic Collisions* iii. 107 Since the angle of recoil is related to the velocity, a suitable positioning of slits should serve to select atoms of a certain velocity.

4. a. Further names of devices intended to diminish or absorb recoil, as *recoil box, pad, reducer, spring* (in Dict.: examples); also, names of devices used to measure the force or energy of the recoil of a firearm, as *recoil gauge, machine, recorder*; also *recoil action.*

1908 *Westm. Gaz.* 13 Feb. 4/2 The recoil action of the spring..closes these valves. **1892** W. W. GREENER *Gun & its Development* (ed. 5) 480 Recoil breeching of rope is..the simplest gear for taking the recoil. Others in use are..the indiarubber breeching, or the recoil box of Mr. E. T. Booth. **1890** *Field* LXXVI. 461/1 Ascertaining, by chronograph and recoil-gauge, what the forward velocity of the shot and the backward movement of the gun respectively amount to. **1896** W. W. GREENER *Gun & its Development* (ed. 6) xii. 316 (*caption*) New mechanical gun-rest and recoil-gauge. **1900** G. T. TEASDALE-BUCKELL *Experts on Guns & Shooting* xii. 138 We cannot follow Mr. Toms..in his remarks about the recoil gauge. **1896** *Field* 28 Mar. 457/1 There would thus be an increase of the back-thrust registered on the recoil machine. **1931** G. BURRARD *Mod. Shotgun* I. vi. 145 A recoil pad can be a great boon to those who are at all sensitive to recoil or to almost anyone who uses a gun in a hot climate where one frequently has to shoot in nothing but a thin shirt. **1974** R. DUNLAP *Gun Owner's Bk. of Care, Repair & Improvement* xiii. 207 We have the obvious changes in original wood fittings for firearms: fitting recoil pads to shotguns and rifles, which more or less combines with the desire for shortening or lengthening buttstocks. **1976** *Shooting Times & Country Mag.* 18–24 Nov. (Advt.), Beavertail fore-end in walnut, pistol grip stock with recoil pad. **1906** H. SHARP *Mod. Sporting Gunnery* v. 123 The sportsman does not appear to have attached very much importance to these recoil recorders, possibly for the reason that machines devised on the above lines tell only the weight of recoil. **1942** *R.A.F. Jrnl.* 3 Oct. 29 The compensator or recoil reducer was very effective. **1975** G. T. GARWOOD *Shotguns & Cartridges for Game & Clays* (ed. 3) xvi. 155 In the USA various proprietary 'recoil reducers' are advertised, the best known being the Edwards. This is a sealed device, and the working principle is not disclosed. **1859** H. C. FOLKARD *Wild-Fowler* xxii. 126 The best plan of all is Colonel Hawker's invention of a steel spiral recoil-spring. **1882** 'MARKSMAN' *Dead Shot* (ed. 5) 331, I have recently seen several attached to heavy breech-loaders, in which the recoil-spring and fittings were so short and cramped, as to be only twelve or fourteen inches in length. **1971** G. T. GARWOOD *Gough Thomas's Second Gun Bk.* xi. 211 If it were not for the friction device and the recoil spring, the parts of the gun with which the shooter makes contact..would not commence to recoil at all.

a*. In *Nucl. Physics.* (cf. sense 3* above), as *recoil atom, electron, energy, momentum, nucleus, proton, ray, track.*

1912 *Phil. Mag.* XXIV. 622 Recoil atoms produce a strong ionization in the gas they traverse. **1942** POLLARD & DAVIDSON *Appl. Nucl. Physics* iii. 40 A cloud chamber for observation of alpha particles, protons, and heavy recoil atoms is not hard to construct. **1923** *Physical Rev.* XXI. 483 The velocity of secondary β-rays excited in light elements by γ-rays agrees with the suggestion that they are recoil electrons. **1966** S. E. LIVERHANT *Outl. Atomic Physics* iv. 111 In an experimental arrangement designed to measure the coincidences between the scattered photon and the recoil electron in Compton scattering, the detectors are to be placed symmetrically about the direction of the incident X-ray beam. **1949** FRIEDLANDER & KENNEDY *Introd. Radiochem.* xi. 253 Neutron capture is always followed by γ-ray emission, and the nucleus receives some recoil energy in this process. **1963** *Radiochem. Man.* (Radiochemical Centre) II. ii. 5 When an atom in a chemical compound captures a neutron, by an (n, γ) reaction, the atom recoils with an energy usually greater than that of the chemical binding forces: recoil energies are usually in the range of a few MeV whilst chemical bond energies are usually only a few eV. **1950** D. HALLIDAY *Introd. Nucl. Physics* iii. 106 The recoil momentum of a disintegrating nucleus will be influenced in magnitude and direction by the presence of a neutrino. **1962** SEMAT & ALBRIGHT *Introd. to Atomic & Nuclear Physics* (ed. 4) xiv. 470 The mass to which the recoil momentum is transferred can be considered infinite in comparison with that of an atom, so that the velocity of recoil is zero. This phenomenon is sometimes called recoilless emission of radiation. **1934** *Proc. Cambr. Philos. Soc.* XXX. 99 The ionisation due to recoil nuclei of the energies here concerned is almost entirely primary. **1949** O. OLDENBERG *Introd. Atomic & Nuclear Physics* xxi. 237 The two tracks so produced, that of the original alpha particle deflected by the collision and that of the 'recoil nucleus', are both well defined. **1942** POLLARD & DAVIDSON *Appl. Nucl. Physics* iii. 41 The recoil protons caused by neutrons in a gas containing hydrogen can..be detected with such equipment. **1949** O. OLDENBERG *Introd. Atomic Physics* xix. 195 When the cloud chamber is filled with CH_4 and subjected to neutron bombardment, the short, straight tracks of recoil protons show up. **1913** E. RUTHERFORD *Radioactive Substances* iv. 178 By observing the deflections of a pencil of recoil rays, both in a magnetic and electric field, the velocity and value of *e/m* of the recoil atoms can be deduced. **1926** R. W. LAWSON tr. *Hevesy's Man. Radioactivity* vi. 59 In consequence of their smaller velocity, the phenomenon of scattering occurs in a much more marked degree with recoil rays than with α-particles. **1927** *Proc. R. Soc.* A. CXVI. 664 This paper describes the measurement of the mobility of a single atom of actinium A immediately after it reaches the end of its recoil track. **1930** E. RUTHERFORD et al. *Radiations from Radioactive Substances* vi. 155 At ordinary pressure, the recoil track is shown by a knob at the end of the track. As the pressure is reduced, the recoil track becomes longer and often shows evidence of a marked scattering.

b. recoil escapement (earlier example); **recoil gear** *Mil.* (see quot. 1940); **recoil starter,** a device for starting a small internal-combustion engine in which a cord, wound round a pulley, is rewound by a spring after being pulled for the starting cycle.

1838 *Penny Cycl.* XII. 299/1 [This] motion is called the recoil, and this escapement is thence called the recoil escapement. **1904–5** *Jrnl. R. Artillery* XXXI. 303 Recoil gear. **1911** H. A. BETHELL *Mod. Artillery in Field* i. 26 (*heading*) Hydropneumatic recoil gear. **1940** *Chambers's Techn. Dict.* 706/2 *Recoil gear* (Artillery), The whole recoil mechanism, embracing both buffer and recuperator. **1960** *Farmer & Stockbreeder* 16 Feb. 106/2 (Advt.), Petrol-engine model with..two-stroke engine;..automatic recoil-starter eliminating the use of loose starting rope. **1972** P. DEMPSEY *How to repair Small Petrol Engines* vii. 235 Rewind starters. Sometimes called recoil starters, these devices are found on outboards, lawnmowers, go-karts.

recoiling, *ppl. a.* (Examples in *Nucl. Physics.*)

1911 *Ann. Rep. Progress of Chem.* VII. 272 A coating of silver 20μμ in thickness stopped the recoil completely, while 10μμ allowed some 60 per cent of the recoiling atoms to pass through. **1950** D. HALLIDAY *Introd. Nucl. Physics* iii. 107 Allen tried to detect recoiling Li^7 ions formed during the disintegration by *K*-capture of Be^7. **1963** BOWEN & GIBBONS *Radioactivation Analysis* vii. 109 The recoiling atom travels for a short distance before it gives up all its excess energy, and may undergo various chemical reactions in the process.

recoilless (rĭkoi·l,lės), *a.* Also **recoil-less.** [f. RECOIL *sb.* + -LESS.] Having no recoil.

a. *Mil.* Applied to a firearm in which recoil is reduced or eliminated by deflection of much of the combustion gas to the rear.

1948 *Jrnl. British Interplanetary Soc.* July 163 There were two types [of rocket-firing guns] scheduled for development, one static.., the other a portable 'recoilless' model on a wheeled chassis. **1953** *Times* 28 May 5/4 Both the United States and the French armies have produced admirable recoilless guns since 1946. **1957** *Economist* 7 Sept. 855/1 Recoilless anti-tank rifles could knock out any tank built in the Soviet Union. **1972** M. KENYON *Shooting of Dan McGrew* i. 9 You'll be wanting a recoil-less rifle to defend your honour. **1975** *Times* 10 Apr. 8/7 Mortar and recoilless rifle fire has been used against the international airport.

b. *Nucl. Physics.* Applied to transitions occurring in an atomic nucleus bound in a crystal lattice in which a photon is emitted from the nucleus without recoil (the Mössbauer effect: see *MÖSSBAUER).

1960 *Physical Rev.* CXX. 1093/1 Mössbauer's observation rests on the fact that in the case of a nucleus bound in a crystal, a γ ray can be emitted or absorbed without any energy transfer to and from the lattice. The probability of such a recoilless transition is, in most cases, small. **1962** [see *recoil momentum* s.v. *RECOIL *sb.* 4 a*]. **1971** GREENWOOD & GIBB *Mössbauer Spectrosc.* i. 11 Mössbauer experiments usually utilise the recoilless emission of γ-rays by a radioactive source followed by their subsequent resonant recoilless reabsorption by a non-active absorber. **1974** *Nature* 19 Apr. 638/2 The 13·3-keV transition to the ground state has long been one of the most attractive candidates for high resolution experiments because..the low energy of the γ photon assures that a high probability of recoil-less transitions will result even at room temperature.

recollating, *vbl. sb.* (Further example.)

1881 P. FITZGERALD *World behind Scenes* III. 177 This [painting] represents Farren & Farley, but the recollating with Zoffary's work makes this picture comparatively feeble.

recolonization. Add: **2.** *Ecol.* The return of an animal, plant, or other organism to an area once inhabited by the species or group concerned.

1923 *Jrnl. Ecol.* XI. 242 In places re-colonisation by *Saxifraga oppositifolia* of such 'blow-outs' was observed. **1956** *Nature* 11 Feb. 282/1 By recolonization, the yield of a sprayed plot may be diminished. **1958** *New Biol.* XXVII. 47 The 'homing' instinct of the injected cells is so remarkable that the recolonization hypothesis was not at first accepted. **1973** *Nature* 3 Aug. 254/2 Factors inhibiting the recolonization by plants of colliery spoil..were reviewed by American and British workers.

recolonize, *v.* Add: **1.** (Later example.)

1976 *Listener* 18 Mar. 329/2 The Europeans are back, recolonising Africa.

2. *Ecol.* Of a plant, animal, or other organism: to return to (a former habitat of the species or group concerned).

1943 J. S. HUXLEY in *Discovery* Jan. 9/1 Mountain regions..have become re-colonized since the retreat of the ice. **1954** *New Biol.* XVII. 18 The best that can be done is to allow the elephant-grass, *Pennisetum*, to recolonize a fallow plot. **1958** *Ibid.* XXVII. 47 The appropriate cells.. then find their way into the damaged tissue to recolonize it. **1961** *Times* 19 Apr. 14/7 The hares have recolonized the fields. **1963** *Lancet* 19 Jan. 133/1 This pattern suggested that the patients' skin had been recolonised by normal commensal organisms. **1967** *Oceanogr. & Marine Biol.* V. 320 It [*sc.* a sea-urchin]..became extinct during the glacial periods, though surviving in Australia, and recolonizing New Zealand in interglacial periods.

recolt. Substitute for entry:

‖ **récolte** (rekǫlt). Also 8 recolt. [Fr.] A harvest or crop. (Chiefly in France.)

1788 [in Dict. s.v. RECOLT]. **1865** M. EYRE *Lady's Walks* xxix. 311 Chesnuts are also a *récolte*, they are..commonly sold ready roasted and stripped of the husk in the markets. **1971** *Country Life* 2 Dec. 1557/2 Much of this surplus..has now been re-classified to help the meagre *récolte* in 1971.

recombi·nable, *a.* [f. as next + -ABLE.] Capable of recombining or being recombined.

1964 D. MICHIE in G. H. Haggis *Introd. Molecular Biol.* x. 272 The most important conclusion from this work concerns the attempt to relate the size of the recombinable units, as measured genetically, to the dimensions of the DNA molecule. **1970** J. S. BRUNER in K. Connolly *Mechanisms Motor Skill Development* 79 It is in the altered nature of failure that one sees most vividly the differentiation of a gross act into a set of recombinable constituents.

recombinant (rĭkǫ·mbinǣnt), *a.* and *sb.* *Genetics.* [f. RECOMBIN(E *v.* + -ANT[1].] **A.** *adj.* Formed by recombination.

1942 *Jrnl. Genetics* XLIII. 320 Double and higher recombinant types were neglected. **1960** *New Biol.* XXXI. 71 A daughter chromosome might be formed by copying first the ab fragment and then the C portion of the original chromosome so that we now have a recombinant chromosome, abC. **1971** D. J. COVE *Genetics* iii. 21 If a yellow-conidiospored strain is crossed to a strain requiring the vitamin biotin, it is found that a considerable excess of parental types over recombinant types is obtained. **1975** *Nature* 18 Dec. 562/3 The hazards associated with cloning recombinant DNA molecules can only be speculated about, since there is no experimental evidence to prove or deny that they exist. **1977** *Time* 7 Mar. 51/1 Should Harvard and M.I.T. be permitted to go ahead with experiments in so-called recombinant DNA-experiments involving the implantation, in cells of a common bacterium, of alien DNA-borne genes? **1978** *Daedalus* Spring 39 Much of the discussion about recombinant DNA research has centred on whether the work is likely to create hazardous organisms.

B. *sb.* A recombinant organism or cell.

1951 *Jrnl. Gen. Microbiol.* V. 59 Produce a double infection and..obtain in the population of virus units resulting a proportion of recombinants. *Ibid.*, The existence of recombinants can..only be demonstrated if conditions can be so arranged as to favour their selective proliferation. **1969** A. M. CAMPBELL *Episomes* ix. 124 Crosses between lambda and 434 fail to produce any recombinants that generate one immunity and respond to another. **1976** *Nature* 1 July 2/3 Foreign genes are inserted into the bacterium by splicing them into a plasmid..and reintroducing the recombinant into the bacterium.

recombinase (rīkǫ·mbinēiz). *Biochem.* [f. RECOMBIN(ATION + *-ASE.] An enzyme or enzyme system which promotes genetic recombination.

1964 A. W. & P. B. KOZINSKI in *Proc. Nat. Acad. Sci.* LII. 211 We postulated..that recombination between T4DNA molecules requires a specific enzyme, 'recombinase'. **1969** A. M. CAMPBELL *Episomes* ii. 18 These two proteins seem to function in a recombinase system. **1970** *Austral. Jrnl. Biol. Sci.* XXIII. 1237 The product of *rec-w*+ could be a regulator specifically controlling the recombinase which initiates recombination at the *cog* locus.

recombination. Add: **1.** (Earlier examples.)

1828 in WEBSTER. **1847** A. DE MORGAN *Formal Logic* xi. 218 It is good against those who confound analysis and recombination of existing materials with introduction of them.

2. *Physics.* The recombining of ions and electrons to form neutral atoms. Freq. *attrib.*

1897 *Phil. Mag.* XLIV. 424 When a gas is acted on by the Röntgen rays a steady state is reached when the rate of production of the ions by the rays is equal to their rate of recombination. **1942** J. D. STRANATHAN *'Particles' Mod. Physics* i. 8 Let us suppose that there are *n* pairs of ions present per cc. at any time, *n* positive ions and *n* negative ions... The number of recombinations *R* per cc. per second is then given by $R = \alpha n^2$ where α is a constant called the coefficient of recombination. **1962** *Guardian* 10 July 9/5 Atoms in the atmosphere would be broken up in extremely large numbers, so that this recombination light would be visible even to the naked human eye. **1969** J. J. SPARKES *Transistor Switching* i. 13 It will first have to supply the recombination current for any charge already present. **1974** *Encycl. Brit. Macropædia* XIV. 506/2 Other forms of radiation met with in plasma physics include line and recombination radiation.

3. *Genetics.* **a.** The formation by a sexual process of genotypes that differ from both the parental genotypes.

1903 *Proc. Cambr. Philos. Soc.* XII. 53 Since the resolution of a compound character may be spoken of as an analysis leading to a distribution of the components among the gametes, the term synthesis should surely be reserved for a recombination that has taken place in such a way that the gametes become bearers of the compound character again, as they were in the pure compound form. **1909** W. BATESON *Mendel's Princ. Heredity* iii. 71 These cases of novelties resulting through a re-combination of the factors brought in by the original pure types are striking because it is not at first sight evident how the novelty has been produced. **1941** J. S. HUXLEY *Uniqueness of Man* iv. 107 Recombination—*i.e.*..reshuffling of old genes in new constellations owing to independent assortment after a cross. This accounts for most of the differences observed between brothers and sisters in the same family. **1976** *Times Lit. Suppl.* 6 Aug. 985/2 Recombination was an idea that Darwin had lacked in his attempt to explain how natural selection and breeding were connected.

b. The formation by crossing-over of chromosomes that differ from both the chromosomes from which they derive. Also *attrib.*

1923 BRIDGES & MORGAN *Third-Chromosome Group of Mutant Characters of Drosophila Melanogaster* i. 9 If Dichæte is crossed to pink, and the F_1 female is back-crossed to a pink male, most of the flies are of the two original types, Dichæte or pink; but a small number of the offspring are both Dichæte and pink or neither (i.e., wild-type). These two latter classes are called 'recombination classes' and the 'percentage of recombination' may be found... The use of the term 'recombination' in this technical sense is a shortening of the full term 'recombination of linked characters'. **1939** C. D. DARLINGTON *Evolution of Genetic Systems* xiv. 77 This recombination we now see is more profound than Weismann imagined. It extends beyond the chromosomes to the genes. The number of units capable of recombination is not five or even fifty, but five thousand or fifty thousand. *Ibid.*, Taking the sum of the haploid number of chromosomes and of the average chiasma frequency of all the chromosomes in a meiotic cell as a recombination index. **1940** *Jrnl. Genetics* XL. 429 Let *x* be the recombination frequency. **1943** *Biol. Rev.* XVIII. 50 In one set of individuals AB and ab may be more favoured than Ab and aB, the reverse may be true elsewhere and, as recombination is the only means short of mutation of changing the arrangement, this inconstancy of advantage must favour some degree of recombination. **1955** *Jrnl. Gen. Microbiol.* XIII. 346 Genetic recombination has now been demonstrated amongst several viruses. **1965** *Proc. Nat. Acad. Sci.* LIII. 457 The term 'recombination' when used in the context of bacterial genetics connotes to many either the process of DNA transmission known as conjugation or the formation by conjugation of any progeny which inherit phenotypic traits derived from both parents. It can, however, be used more strictly to denote the series of physical and chemical events which serve to link genes derived from one parental DNA with those derived from another parental DNA. **1976** *National Observer* (U.S.) 5 July 6/1 The object of these guidelines is to ensure that experimental DNA recombination will have no ill effects on those engaged in the work, on the general public, or on the environment. **1977** A. W. F. EDWARDS *Foundations Math. Genetics* viii. 94 Linkage is not complete, and its magnitude is measured by the recombination fraction, *r*, between the two loci.

recombina·tional, *a.* *Genetics.* [f. prec. + -AL.] Of or pertaining to recombination.

1959 *Nature* 14 Nov. 1593/1 (*heading*) Recombinational lethals in a polymorphic population. *Ibid.* 1594/1 A recessive lethal can be produced by recombinational instead of mutational change. **1969** *Genetics* LXI. 298 The problem of recipient culture variability during recombinational analyses. **1977** *Jrnl. Protozool.* XXIV. 27/2 The duplex forms could have arisen as a consequence of a prior mutational or recombinational event.

Hence **recombina·tionally** *adv.*, by or as a result of recombination.

1969 W. D. STANSFIELD *Theory & Probl. Genetics* ix. 184 Recombinationally separable forms of a gene within a cistron are referred to as heteroalleles.

recombina·tionless, *a.* *Genetics.* [f. as prec. + -LESS.] That does not show recombination.

1969 L. LEVINE *Biol. of Gene* v. 101/2 They were able to isolate two recombinationless (Rec) mutants in an F strain of *Escherichia coli* K12. **1974** *Nature* 4 Jan. 44/1 Recombinationless bacterial mutants are highly sensitive to near-ultraviolet, suggesting that DNA may be an indirect target of the action of near-ultraviolet.

recombine, *v.* **2.** (Earlier and later examples.)

1859 MILL *Liberty* ii. 85 With what a salutary shock did the paradoxes of Rousseau explode like bombshells in the midst..of onesided opinion..forcing its elements to recombine in a better form. **1910** W. M. WHEELER *Ants* viii. 131 These characters..are relatively stable in particular races or varieties and have a tendency to combine and recombine in endless permutation. **1942** J. D. STRANATHAN *'Particles' Mod. Physics* i. 27 Ions formed in a gas have a tendency to recombine. **1974** *Encycl. Brit. Macropædia* IX. 811/2 Nitrogen ions may recombine similarly.

recombinogenic (rīkǫ:mbinodʒe·nik), *a.* *Biol.* [f. RECOMBIN(ATION + -O + *-GENIC.] Tending to cause genetic recombination.

1965 *Genetics* LII. 107 (*heading*) The recombinogenic effect of thymidylate starvation in *Escherichia coli* merodiploids. **1971** *Nature* 12 Nov. 71/3 It is not unreasonable to assume that the protein plays an important part in some facet of meiosis, and in view of the T_4 evidence, neither is it unreasonable to suppose that it has some recombinogenic activity.

recommend, *sb.* For '*dial.* and *U.S.*' read '*colloq.* (orig. *U.S.*)' and add earlier and later examples.

1806 L. DOW *Travels* I. iv. 110 This morning, I went on shore, having no proper recommends with me. **1832** J. J. STRANG *Diary* 19 Feb. in M. M. Quaife *Kingdom of St. James* (1930) 202 There is no complaint against me and they offer me a good recommend. **1892** B. POTTER *Jrnl.* (1966) 227 Miss Emmet..wedged in a recommend of farm-house lodgings of her cousins. **1908** *Practitioner* Nov. 731 The Committee pays for out-patient 'recommends' at the rate of one guinea for six. **1924** J. GALSWORTHY *White Monkey* I. viii. 65 They'll give you a good recommend, won't they? **1967** [see *book-society* s.v. *BOOK *sb.* 18]. **1977** *Listener* 30 June 867/4 William McIlvanney's *Laidlaw* comes with a recommend from Ross Macdonald.

recommend, *v.*[1] **7. c.** (Earlier example.)

1813 JANE AUSTEN *Pride & Prej.* I. xviii. 217 Let me recommend you, however, as a friend, not to give implicit confidence to all his assertions.

recommendation. Add: **4. a.** Also, that which is recommended; a proposal or suggestion.

1911 G. B. SHAW *Doctor's Dilemma* 299 How this was effected may be gathered from the recommendations finally agreed on. **1929** *Star* 21 Aug. 19/1 It is interesting to record that some of our recommendations have duly improved in capital value. **1976** *Daily Tel.* 20 July 2/3 A report following a public enquiry into the disaster made a number of observations and recommendations.

recommended, *ppl. a.* Add: Also, advised, prescribed.

1968 *Globe & Mail* (Toronto) 3 Feb. 10/7 Sulphur dioxide levels in the smelter were 40 times the recommended safe level. **1977** *Sniffin' Glue* July 17 Recommended reading: Anything by Colin Wilson.

recommission, *v.* Add: **b.** *intr.* for *pass.* Of a ship. Hence **recommi·ssioning** *vbl. sb.*

[**1909** *Army & Navy Gaz.* 1 May 431/2 Fleet Surg. H. B. Marriott to Doris on recommis.] **1922** *Daily Mail* 3 Nov. 12/5 Naval Appointments..to Emperor of India on recommissioning. **1928** *Observer* 15 July 12/4 It was intended that she should return home at the end of the present cruise to re-commission. **1977** *Navy News* June 15/1 The Arethusa recommissioned at Portsmouth in April.

recommittal. (Earlier example.)

1837 *Second Rep. Inspectors of Prisons* I. 90 in *Parl. Papers* XXXII. 1 Judging from the immense number of recommittals, it would almost seem that the effect produced by imprisonment..is not such as materially to deter from the commission of crime.

recompensive, *a.* For † *Obs. rare*—1 read *rare* and add later example.

1924 *Brit. Weekly* 21 Aug. 443/2, I am glad to tell that I am having recompensive explorations here.

recomposition. Add: **b.** *Linguistics.* (See quots.)

[**1933** J. MAROUZEAU *Lexique Terminol. Linguistique* 158 *Recomposition*..Procédé par lequel on restitue à l'un des éléments d'un composé la forme qu'il avait à l'état autonome; ainsi quand on donne à lat. *recludo* la forme *reclaudo* d'après le simple *claudo*.] **1935** T. HUDSON-WILLIAMS *Short Introd. Study Compar. Gram.* 8 *Recomposition* is a species of analogy; the form of a compound verb is affected by that of the simple verb; the simple form is restored or, occasionally, retained consciously in the compound; e.g. *sē+paro* should give..*sēpero*; but the literary dialect reformed it to *sēparo*... *Decomposition* is the opposite process, the simple verb being affected by the compound. **1964** A. MARTINET *Elements of General Linguistics* iv. 126 An element like *tele-*..which today combines freely with monemes and syntagms that exist outside the combinations in question.. behaves in fact like an affix... Perhaps in the case where a new syntagm is formed we might speak of 'recomposition' from elements which are extracted by analysis. **1972** HARTMANN & STORK *Dict. Lang. & Linguistics* 192/2 *Recomposition*, the process or result of using a borrowed element as an affix to form new words, e.g. *tele* in *telecast, teleview, teleprinter*.

recompress (rīkǫmpre·s), *v.* [RE- 5 a.] *trans.* To compress again; to increase again the pressure of air or other gas in (a vessel) or acting on (a person); *esp.* to subject (an aircraft pilot, diver, etc.) to increased pressure again.

1945 *Jrnl. Gen. Physiol.* XXVIII. 220 The frogs..were recompressed within 30 seconds. **1950** *Ibid.* III. 255 The chamber was recompressed at free-fall rate. **1951** A. R. BEHNKE in J. F. Fulton et al. *Decompression Sickness* iii. 87 Should symptoms recur.., recompress the diver to a depth giving relief. **1967** P. D. GRIFFITHS in R. I. McCallum *Decompression of Compressed Air Workers* 230 The patient must be observed constantly and recompressed at once should symptoms return, preferably to the minimum effective pressure. **1969** HAXTON & WHYTE in Bennett & Elliott *Physiol. & Med. of Diving* i. 12 It is sometimes necessary to recompress a patient to a pressure slightly higher than that at which he has been working.

recompression (rīːkǫmpre·ʃən). [RE- 5 a.] **1. a.** The state of being compressed again. **b.** The action of compressing again, *esp.* by exposure to increasing air pressure (e.g. during descent from a high-altitude flight without pressurization or following decompression after a dive).

1939 *Jrnl. R. Aeronaut. Soc.* XLIII. 822 After the shock the speed again becomes subsonic, so that the consequent divergence of the streamlines on the back part of the upper surface generates a recompression. **1943** M. A. & F. A. HITCHCOCK tr. *Bert's Barometric Pressure* I. II. iv. 501 M. Bucquoy mentions..the cure of muscular swellings by recompression. **1951** FERRIS & ENGEL in J. F. Fulton et al. *Decompression Sickness* ii. 23 The pain of bends is immediately relieved by recompression of 3000- to 6000-foot equivalents and recurs upon reascent to the original altitude. **1969** A. R. BEHNKE in Bennett & Elliott *Physiol. & Med. of Diving* xi. 227 Hoppe-Seyler (1857) described blockage of pulmonary vessels by nascent bubbles and the inability of the heart to propel blood under these conditions. He proposed recompression to absorb the liberated gas and re-establish circulation. **1973** *Nature* 21–28 Dec. 523/1 These did not occur at maximum altitude, but during the re-compression. The other runs gave clear heart signals throughout. **1977** *Hongkong Standard* 14 Apr. 16/3 Mr Ng was later sent to Queen Mary Hospital, after the specialists were satisfied there was no need for further recompression.

2. recompression chamber or **lock,** a chamber in which a person can be subjected to an air pressure above that of the atmosphere.

1951 A. R. BEHNKE in J. F. Fulton et al. *Decompression Sickness* iii. 87 Individuals believed to be 'cured'..have been rushed to the recompression chamber in a state of collapse. **1967** P. D. GRIFFITHS in R. I. McCallum *Decompression of Compressed Air Workers* 229 An important factor is that medical recompression locks often have a safe working pressure..of only 45–50 p.s.i.g. **1976** *Daily Tel.* 27 Jan. 15/1 A 14-year-old boy, critically ill with carbon monoxide poisoning, recovered consciousness yesterday in the Royal Navy's recompression chamber at Rosyth dockyard. **1977** *Proc. R. Soc. Med.* LXX. 503/2 This involves being able to carry out a detailed examination of the patient, and to put up infusions, give injections or insert catheters in the confined, noisy and pressurized space of a recompression chamber.

recon (rīkǫ·n), *v.*[2] *U.S. Mil. slang.* *trans.* and *intr.* Abbrev. of RECONNOITRE *v.*

1966 *National Observer* (U.S.) 26 Dec. 1/4 We launched a small operation and while reconning the area, saw a bunch of color near a tree line. **1969** I. KEMP *Brit. G.I. in Vietnam* v. 96 Our orders are to recon only, and avoid all contact with the enemy whatsoever.

recon (rīkǫ·n), *sb.*[1] *U.S. Mil. slang.* Abbrev. of RECONNAISSANCE; a reconnaissance unit. Freq. *attrib.*, as *recon company, unit* (etc.). Cf. *RECCE *sb.*

1918 E. M. ROBERTS *Flying Fighter* 337 *Long Recon*, a trip of from 20 to 80 miles behind the Hun lines to gather information. **1942** *Yank* 25 Nov. 21 He was temporarily with the recon. **1943** J. GOODELL *They sent me to Iceland* ii. 31 Convoyed by jeeps and recon cars we sped through the town. **1946** *Sun* (Baltimore) 27 July 12/1 (*heading*) Ex-Patton recon unit to parade in Cumberland. **1948** N. MAILER *Naked & Dead* I. ii. 20 The men in recon looked small and lost in comparison to the other platoons. **1950** 'D. DIVINE' *King of Fassarai* xiv. 108 Should have the recon reports by now. Get through to Air Command again. **1968** *Globe & Mail* (Toronto) 13 Feb. 4/1 It is recon's bad luck to live in an area bordered by an ammunition dump, a flightline loading area and the 26th Marine Regiment's command post. *Ibid.* 4/3 The survivors of the recon company are frightened but uncowed. **1975** A. PRICE *Our Man in Camelot* v. 93 'He was a pilot in recon.'..'Photographic reconnaissance,' he explained. **1977** 'E. MCBAIN' *Long Time no See* xiii. 208 Our recon patrol found an enemy base camp.

recon (rī·kǫn), *sb.*[2] *Biol.* [f. REC(OMBINATION + *-ON[1].] A piece of genetic material which can be exchanged but not divided by genetic recombination; thus the shortest piece which can be so exchanged.

1957 S. BENZER in McElroy & Glass *Symposium on Chem. Basis of Heredity* 71 The unit of recombination will be defined as the smallest element in the one-dimensional array that is interchangeable..by genetic recombination. One such element will be referred to as a 'recon'. **1969** A. M. CAMPBELL *Episomes* iii. 38 The 'unit factor' of the classical geneticist is replaceable by the muton, the recon, the cistron, or even a collection of linked cistrons, each in the appropriate operational context. **1978** N. JARDINE in Hookway & Pettit *Action & Interpretation* 122 The operons, cistrons, recons and mutons of the molecular geneticist.

reconcentration. (Further examples.)

1956 *Nature* 21 Jan. 126/2 Kunkel and Tiselius were not able to demonstrate the heterogeneity of serum albumin by their method, and the ability of the method here described to do this may also be due to this reduction of diffusion by reconcentration. **1972** *Times* 26 June 12/3 Biological reconcentration of filter feeding organisms..invalidates the dilution hypothesis.

reconcile, *v.* Add: **I. 5. b.** (Further example.)

1840 *Act* 3 & 4 *Vict.* c. 52 § 6 If..Prince Albert shall..be reconciled to or shall hold Communion with the See or Church of Rome.

II. 10. b. *Accountancy.* To establish the consistency of (one account) *with* another, esp. by allowing for transactions made or begun but not yet fully recorded (as when a cheque has been issued but not yet presented for payment). Cf. *RECONCILIATION 4 b.

1900 W. W. SNAILUM *Fifteen Studies in Book-Keeping* xi. 122 At the end of each financial period it will be necessary to 'reconcile' the bank account... This is effected by means of a 'reconciliation statement'. **1930** A. PALMER *Munro's Book-Keeping & Accountancy* (ed. 10) 26 The Bank Pass Book..would show a balance at the credit of £174, which would be reconciled as follows. **1947** [see *RECONCILIATION 4 b]. **1970** R. W. WALLIS *Accounting* v. 66 Reconciliations may also establish the accuracy of the different parts of the accounting system within an organization, for example by reconciling the debtors' control account in the ledger with the total of the individual accounts in the sales (debtors) ledger.

reconciliate, *v.* (Later example.)

1922 *Glasgow Herald* 26 Apr. 11/5 The question of reconciliating the two wings of the army.

reconciliation. Add: **4. b.** *Accountancy.* The action or practice of rendering one account consistent with another by balancing apparent discrepancies; *reconciliation statement,* a statement of account whereby such discrepancies are adjusted.

1895 J. THORNTON *Man. Bookkeeping* xi. 187 See that all Banker's charges..are duly entered in your own books, or you will have difficulty with your Reconciliation. **1929** L. C. CROPPER *Book-Keeping & Accounts* iv. 46 In order to explain this divergence it is necessary to construct a statement, known as a 'Reconciliation Statement'... A specimen example is appended showing how this 'reconciliation' is arrived at. **1947** F. H. JONES *Jordan's Mod. Book-Keeping* I. iii. 33 In order to reconcile the Cash Book balance with the statement of Account balance a Bank Reconciliation Statement is compiled. **1957** W. W. BIGG *Cost Accounts* xiii. 231 Assuming that it is desired to keep the Cost and Financial Accounts entirely distinct it is still imperative that they be rendered capable of reconciliation one with the other. **1973** A. & E. E. FIELDHOUSE *Elem. Book-Keeping* 80 If the balances of the two books should disagree a Reconciliation Statement should be made out.

recondi·tion, *v.* [RE- 5 a.] *trans.* **1.** To restore to a proper, habitable, or usable condition; to repair or rehabilitate.

1920 *Glasgow Herald* 29 Apr. 7/1 The Agamemnon..is being reconditioned at the Brooklyn Navy Yard. **1922** *Flight* XIV. 366/1 In the name of economy, the R.A.F. has had to be content with machines built during the War and 'reconditioned', or, at best, with designs got out during the War. **1930** S. RUNCIMAN *Hist. First Bulgarian Empire* II. i. 53 A strong line of Imperial fortresses..had probably been reconditioned by Constantine Copronymus. **1935** *Punch* 27 Mar. 346/2, I see with shame that H.M. Gov. propose in a White Paper to 'recondition' the Navy. But I see with delight and surprise that for once the *Shorter O.E.D.* does not acknowledge the existence of the filthy verb. **1966** J. S. COX *Illustr. Dict. Hairdressing* 125/2 *Recondition* (Hair),.. to restore hair by means of suitable substances and/or treatments to its normal condition.

2. *Forestry.* To reduce warping and collapse in (timber) by heating in a steam-filled atmosphere for several hours.

1932 *Rep. Forest Products Res. Board 1930* iv. 42 Experiments have been made during the year to ascertain the possibility of reconditioning or restoring collapsed Tasmanian oak. **1938** H. E. DESCH *Timber* x. 127 Timber that is badly warped or cupped, without showing any visible signs of collapse, may also be successfully re-conditioned. **1979** J. G. WILKINSON *Industr. Timber Preservation* vii. 198 Conventional kilns can also be used to: 1. Recondition timber which has collapsed. 2. Destroy fungal growth and insect infestations.

3. *Psychol.* To alter the responses of (a person) by means of conditioning techniques; to replace (existing responses) in this manner.

1935 [implied in *RECONDITIONING *vbl. sb.* 3]. **1942** *Sun* (Baltimore) 4 Nov. 9/5 The army has been consistently uninterested in taking the rejects into conditioning battalions and reconditioning them. **1957** W. SARGANT *Battle for Mind* x. 220 It is very difficult indeed to condition or recondition such persons [*sc.* psychopaths], some of whom are criminals, until later in life when their brainwave patterns become much more normal. **1967** J. A. HADFIELD *Introd. Psychotherapy* xiv. 88 The objection then to treatment by re-conditioning the symptoms alone is..that we are not dealing with the real illness.

Hence **recondi·tioned** *ppl. a.*

1932 KIPLING *Limits & Renewals* 374 Our pernicious system of employing reconditioned souls on such delicate duties. **1933** *Sun* (Baltimore) 21 Apr. 19/3 (Advt.), Guaranteed reconditioned cars. **1944** AUDEN *For Time Being* (1945) 52, I moved the vices out of the city into a chain of re-conditioned lighthouses. **1957** L. F. R. WILLIAMS *State of Israel* ix. 155 Israel's first elected Parliament, which met in a reconditioned cinema. **1977** *Western Mail* (Cardiff) 5 Mar. 14/3 (Advt.), Massey Ferguson 35, 4-cylinder Tractor. Reconditioned engine.

recondi·tioning, *vbl. sb.* [f. prec. + -ING[1].] The action or process of the vb. **1.** Restoring to proper or adequate condition; rehabilitation, repair. Also, conversion or modernization (of houses, etc.).

1920 *Sphere* 27 Mar. 339 (*heading*) *Reconditioning.* A present striking phase of the great British shipping industry. *Ibid.* (*caption*) The word at the top of this page—'Reconditioning'—may be unfamiliar to the general public, but it is to-day well known to all the shipping world. **1926** *Manch. Guardian Weekly* Feb. 104/2 Measures are being considered for the improvement and reconditioning of existing rural cottages. **1936** *Discovery* Apr. 117/1 Systematic re-conditioning of working-class houses throughout the country. **1944** M. LASKI *Love on Supertax* x. 95 You really ought to let me give your hair a thorough re-conditioning.

2. *Forestry.* The steaming of timber to reduce warping and collapse (see *RECONDITION *v.* 2).

1932 *Rep. Forest Products Res. Board 1931* ii. 11 The treatment, which has been called re-conditioning, consisted essentially of warming the timber, which was first dried to a moisture content of 15 per cent.,..to 210 °F in saturated air. **1948** *New Biol.* IV. 89 The kiln load is given a stress-relieving or reconditioning treatment. **1979** J. G. WILKINSON *Industr. Timber Preservation* vii. 198 Reconditioning typically involves heating defective boards for between four and eight hours at 100 °C in a steam-filled atmosphere.

3. *Psychol.* The replacement through conditioning of one conditioned response by another; the re-establishing of a conditioned response after its extinction.

1935 J. E. WALLIN *Personality Maladjustments* xi. 461 Such bonds must be loosened or dissipated by substituting other emotional bonds that are more potent by a process of emotional reconditioning. **1940** HILGARD & MARQUIS *Conditioning & Learning* 349/1 *Reconditioning,* the re-establishment of a conditioned response after it has been diminished by extinction or forgetfulness. **1957** W. SARGANT *Battle for Mind* x. 221 The need to vary methods of conditioning and reconditioning according to the different temperaments is clearly shown by a study of the way prison sentences affect various types. **1967** J. A. HADFIELD *Introd. Psychotherapy* xiv. 88 One could not deal with this guilt by re-conditioning because neither she nor we knew of its existence. **1972** J. W. KLING et al. *Woodworth & Schlosberg's Exper. Psychol.* xiv. 570/2 Reconditioning: if extinction trials are followed by a single presentation of the CS–US combination much or all of the effects of extinction will be overcome.

reco·njure, *v.* [RE- 5 a; cf. F. *reconjurer* (Cotgr.).] *trans.* To conjure again; to reconstruct in imagination; to recall.

1611 COTGRAVE *Dict., Reconjurer,* to reconiure, to coniure againe. **1904** *Edin. Rev.* Jan. 53 Nor can the antiquarian reconjure their image in the past from their ruins of today. **1915** C. MACKENZIE *Guy & Pauline* i. 57 There was neither passion nor sentiment in the music..yet in solitude when Guy reconjured the sound afterward, it returned to his memory like fire.

reconnaissance. Add: **1.** (Further examples.)

1944 *Return to Attack* (Army Board, N.Z.) ii. 7 When he [*sc.* Rommel] attacked, Maryland bombers of the RAF caught his tanks... He withdrew, calling his attack a 'reconnaissance in force', a phrase which he was to use again.

attrib. **1950** 'D. DIVINE' *King of Fassarai* vii. 46 One of the big four-engined aeroplanes that came past them occasionally on reconnaissance flights. **1966** *Daily Tel.* 19 Apr. 32/5 A multi-million-pound order for a British EMI 'reconnaissance pod'. **1976** H. TRACY *Death in Reserve* xxi. 167 They should have a light aircraft going to take reconnaissance photographs.

reconnoitre, *v.* Add: Also *U.S.* **reconnoiter.** **2. a.** (Later example.)

1948 N. MAILER *Naked & Dead* III. v. 523 He could not reconnoiter the pass.

reconnoitrer (earlier example).

1860 C. M. YONGE *Hopes & Fears* III. xiii. 254 Tearfully she thanked the trusty reconnoitrer.

reconnoitring, *ppl. a.* Add: (Earlier example.)

1759 LD. G. SACKVILLE *Let.* 16 June in *Rep. MSS. Mrs. Stopford-Sackville* 307 in *Parl. Papers 1904* (Cd. 1892) XLVII. 1 Prince Ferdinand's and Marshal Contades' reconnoitering partys met this morning.

Hence **reconnoi·tringly** *adv.,* in a reconnoitring manner. *rare.*

1924 A. D. SEDGWICK *Little French Girl* IV. iii. 324 Giles could almost see him nibbling reconnoitringly at the edge of the stained oak mantelpiece.

reconstitute, *v.* Add: **1.** *trans.* **a.** (Further examples.)

1944 J. LEES-MILNE *Prophesying Peace* (1977) 68 Thurstan wants to pull down some Georgian dwellings of little intrinsic worth, and to reconstitute some medieval overhangs and fronts. **1977** *Church Times* 5 Aug. 16/3 Bishop Runcie said he thought that, if the Orthodox were dissatisfied with the reactions of the Conference, the dialogue might have to be reconstituted.

b. *spec.* to restore the previous constitution of (dehydrated food) by the addition of liquid.

1917 *Nat. Food Jrnl.* 24 Oct. 59/1 The total amount of dried milk (full cream) that may be available equals approximately 2,200 tons, and would represent nearly 4,000,000 gallons of whole milk when reconstituted. **1945** *ABC of Cookery* (Min. of Food) vii. 22 It is not always necessary to reconstitute dried eggs before use. **1951** L. NICHOLLS *Trop. Nutrition & Dietetics* (ed. 3) x. 202 Vegetables, fish or meat dried by this method are easily reconstituted with good retention of flavour and colour. **1960** *Times Rev. Industry* July 18/1 Fruits..stored..in the dried state and..reconstituted..by soaking in water and cooking. **1972** *Homes & Gardens* Aug. 98 Ice cream powders..can be reconstituted with water, or with milk and cream.

2. *intr.* To undergo or take part in reconstitution.

1974 *Sci. Amer.* June 77/3 Both sodium and potassium reconstitute into feldspars during metamorphism or igneous melting.

reco·nstituted, *ppl. a.* [f. RECONSTITUTE *v.* + -ED[1].] That has been constituted or formed anew; applied *spec.* to food which has been dehydrated and subsequently made ready for use by adding liquid. *reconstituted stone* = *reconstructed stone* s.v. *RECONSTRUCTED *ppl. a.* a.

1850 H. MARTINEAU *Hist. Peace* II. IV. xii. 157 The first act of the reconstituted government was to carry a new Coercion Bill. **1925** *Chem. Abstr.* XIX. 545 Acidity of the reconstituted milk was a little lower than that of raw milk. **1928** *Daily Mail* 30 July 13/3 Reconstituted and synthetic cream. **1946** *Daily Tel.* 30 Jan. 2/1 Dark fruit cake... 6 oz fruit, 2 reconstituted eggs, [etc.]. **1951** *Good Housek. Home Encycl.* 348/2 Reconstituted dried egg may be used in making batter. **1966** D. FRANCIS *Flying Finish* vi. 77 The floors were some sort of reconstituted stone heated from underneath. **1969** *Guardian* 20 Sept. 9/7 Mother and father eating fish fingers and reconstituted potatoes in gloomy silence. **1976** A. DAVIS *Television* ii. 32 The BBC converter ..works by storing the signals relating to each line of the picture and releasing them at the right moment to take their place in a reconstituted picture at the new standard. **1977** A. HALLAM *Planet Earth* 159/3 Reconstituted stone, where the natural material is crushed and recast in blocks simulating the original in color and texture, with the advantage that the blocks are of uniform size.

reconstitution. Add: **1. a.** (Earlier example.)

1848 E. A. POE *Eureka* 141 The regathering of..Matter and Spirit will be but the re-constitution of..God.

2. The restoration of dehydrated food to its original constitution by the addition of liquid.

1920 *Nat. Food Jrnl.* II. 595/1 The Clauses..prohibiting the addition to milk of colouring matter or water, the reconstitution of milk [etc.]..will remain in force. **1945** *ABC of Cookery* (Min. of Food) xvii. 59 If dried eggs are used they may be added dry with the other dry ingredients and the water needed for reconstitution added with the mixing liquid.

reconstruct, *v.* Add: **2.** (Further examples.) Also *spec.* in *Philol.,* to reform hypothetically (part of) a protolanguage by deduction from (later) recorded languages.

1917 *Science Progr.* XI. 682 Not only is the past retrieved in fragments; in some museums and exhibitions, and to a certain extent in historical plays, it is actually reconstructed. **1930** *Language* VI. 164 It is a well-known fact that it is impossible to reconstruct a complete paradigm of Indo-European personal pronouns. **1965** *Ibid.* XLI. 19 The younger protolanguages which we can reconstruct within the Indo-European family..cannot be placed in an identical frame of reference with Proto-Indo-European. **1976** E. MACLAREN *Nature of Belief* ii. 11 We can reconstruct how the process must have gone on.

Hence **reconstru·ctable, -ible** *adjs.,* capable of being reconstructed.

1961 WEBSTER, Reconstructible. **1965** *Language* XLI. 19 [Proto-Indo-European] is reconstructible only on the basis of internal evidence. **1978** *Ibid.* LIV. 285 Morphology is harder to recapture, and syntax is even more slippery—if indeed it is reconstructable at all beyond a rather shallow level. **1978** *Nature* 13 Apr. 605/2 By using chronologies recording different elements of climate a greater range of climatic variables will be reconstructable.

reconstructed, *ppl. a.* Add: **a.** (Further examples.) *reconstructed stone* (see quot. 1950).

1909 W. G. RENWICK *Marble & Marble Working* xv. 175 Reconstructed Sicilian marble was selected for lining the walls of the operating-rooms at the Manchester Royal Infirmary, opened last year. *Ibid.* 176 (*caption*) The first building to be erected in Reconstructed Portland Stone.

1933 Bloomfield *Language* 302 Students of the Romance languages reconstruct a Primitive Romance ('Vulgar Latin') form before they turn to the written records of Latin, and they interpret these records in the light of the reconstructed form. **1935** *Specification* XXXVII. 245/1 Reconstructed stone is natural stone—reconstructed, and is to be distinguished from artificial stone, which may be described as high-grade concrete. **1950** *Ibid.* LII. 343/1 Reconstructed stone is natural stone crushed and moulded into the required shape after it has been formed into a plastic mass by the addition of cement and water. **1951** E. E. Evans-Pritchard *Social Anthrop.* iii. 43 The reaction against the attempt to explain social institutions by their reconstructed past..came at the end of last century. **1957** *Gloss. Terms Stone in Building* (*B.S.I.*) 30 *Reconstructed stone*, a building material manufactured from cement and natural aggregate for use in a manner similar to and for the same purpose as natural building stone. **1959** *Language* XXXV. 425 We..agree on the essential artificiality of Reconstructed Proto-Indo-European.

b. *U.S.* Converted from (a form of) Communism.

1966 *New Statesman* 14 Oct. 549/1 (Vietnam) As reconstructed peasants sleep Upon their AID-assisted beds. [**1973** R. Hayes *Hungarian Game* viii. 63 All 10 seem to be unreconstructed Stalinists, somewhat to the fanatical left of both Rákosi and Gerö.]

reconstruction. Add: **1. b.** Usu. with capital initial. Also, the period during which this process occurred. (Further examples.)

A fuller treatment of this sense (also in derivative forms) may be found in M. M. Mathews *Dict. Americanisms* (1951).

1890 C. L. Norton *Political Americanisms* 93 *Reconstruction.* After the Civil War the question of restoring the lately seceded States..became the leading civil problem of the time. The measures introduced into Congress were popularly known as Reconstruction Bills. **1949** D. S. Freeman in B. A. Botkin *Treas. S. Folklore* p. x, The existing general pattern of Southern folklore probably was set in late 'slave days' and during the Reconstruction. **1967** *Freedomways* VII. 133 In history the horrors of slavery are watered down and sketchily covered so as not to enrage the complacent black student, while the period following Reconstruction is covered as if the Negro had strangely disappeared from the face of the earth. **1978** *Names* Mar. 106 In much of the South it [*sc.* the township] is an artifact of Reconstruction governments after The War.

c. The rebuilding of an area devastated by war. Also, the restoration of economic stability to such an area.

1925 A. J. Toynbee *Survey of Internat. Affairs 1920–23* I.39 Austrian reconstruction (scheme drafted; protocols signed). *Ibid.* 40 Hungarian reconstruction (collaboration decided on). **1933** *Radio Times* 14 Apr. 75/1 Several grandiloquently named new departments of State, such as the Ministry of Supply and the extremely short-lived Ministry of Reconstruction. **1940** *Economist* 31 Aug. 280/1 Those who did not find work before August 1st were assembled in reconstruction camps. **1946** *R.A.F. Jrnl.* May 172 All the women were free to return to their interrupted training, to resume their pre-war occupation or to help with the gigantic task of reconstruction. **1953** P. C. Berg *Dict. New Words* 135/1 *Reconstruction area*, an area which has to be redeveloped as a whole, on account of war damage. **1974** tr. *Sniečkus's Soviet Lithuania* 51 As soon as the nazis had been expelled, the working people plunged into the task of reconstruction.

2. (Later examples.)

1930 *Language* VI. 185 The scarcity of material for dual forms to substantiate the I[ndo-]E[uropean] reconstruction is not surprising. **1937** 'M. Innes' *Hamlet, Revenge!* II. vi. 166 You must do that reconstruction all over again. **1959** *Language* XXXV. 423 No reputable linguist pretends that Proto-Indo-European reconstructions represent a reality. **1977** M. Goulder in J. Hick *Myth of God Incarnate* iv. 65 As with the account I have given of Jesus, we are forming a reconstruction of history, and such reconstructions can never be more than probable.

Hence **reconstru·ctional** *a.*, of or pertaining to reconstruction; reconstructionary; **reconstructionist,** (*b*) one who reconstructs the past mentally (see Reconstruct *v.* 2); also *attrib.* or as *adj.*

1864 M. H. Throop *Future* 119 The act of secession extinguished the Union party as soon as it was adopted, except as a *reconstructionist* party. **1920** G. S. Gordon *Let.* 21 Jan. (1943) 133 Now—in this reconstructional mood—Professors are no longer Scholars or Professors, but 'Heads of Depts.'. **1925** E. F. Norton *Fight for Everest: 1924* vi. 131 These were undoubted signs of reconstructional work. **1949** Wellek & Warren *Theory of Lit.* iv. 32 We must, these literary reconstructionists argue, enter into the mind and attitudes of past periods. **1958** *Archivum Linguisticum* X. I. 8 The..prism of literature..may twist the actual sequence of events, as the reconstructionist is tempted to envision it. **1966** M. Scriven in W. H. Dray *Philos. Analysis & Hist.* 255 The difference between this analysis and the reconstructionist approach. **1978** *Language* LIV. 470 The reconstructional changes he suggested have withstood the test of time. **1979** *Jrnl. R. Soc. Arts* Apr. 262/2 Rationality, objectivity, universalism and abstract analysis are features of the reconstructionist approach.

reconstructive, *sb.* Add: (Further example.) *rare.*

1927 *Daily Express* 24 Nov. 5 (Advt.), The prescribed reconstructive which creates the good red blood in which *no* germ can obtain a footing.

reconte·st, *v.* [Re- 5 a; cf. F. *recontester* (Cotgr.).] *trans.* To contest again.

1611 Cotgrave *Dict.*, *Recontester*, to recontest; make new protestation of, or complaint vnto. **1897** W. J. Locke *Derelicts* xviii. 239 The old man vaunting the ancients and Joyce defending the moderns, until a veritable Battle of the Books was recontested. **1922** *Glasgow Herald* 11 Nov. 9 Both are recontesting the seats they have occupied in Parliament.

reconvene, *v.* Add: (Later examples.) Hence **reconve·ning** *vbl. sb.*, a renewed convening.

1903 *Westm. Gaz.* 20 June 7/1 A prominent delegate.. urges the reconvening of the Joint High Commission. **1906** *Ibid.* 11 Apr. 5/1 The anthracite operators..made a counter-proposal—namely, to re-convene the Coal Commission. **1972** *Maclean's Mag.* Sept. 10/2 The Select Committee..which he reconvened. **1977** *Time* 17 Jan. 12/2 To break the deadlock when and if the talks reconvene.. Richard last week made firm Britain's readiness to accept a major role in the transition period from white to black rule.

reconversion. Add: **1. b.** (Further examples.) *spec.* alteration (of industry, etc.) to peacetime requirements after war. In recent use, conversion by adaptation of function, modernization; also, an object so converted.

1944 *Sun* (Baltimore) 21 Jan. 7/2 'Reconversion' in the foreign field.., like the reconversion of domestic industry from war to peace production, is one of our major problems. **1946** *News Chron.* 2 Mar. 2/2 The difficulties of demobilisation and of industrial re-conversion. **1956** *Planning* XXII. 239 Reconversion in industry is an essential consequence of the introduction of the common market... Reconversion as defined in the [Spaak] report means modernisation or rationalisation of production methods to cope with increased competition. **1976** *National Observer* (U.S.) 28 Aug. 14-B/4 (Advt.), He covers reconversions as well as new buildings.

reconvey, *v.* **2.** (Earlier *absol.* example.)

1838 W. Bell *Dict. Law Scotl.* 67 When he [*sc.* the assignee] reconveys to the cedent, it [*sc.* the deed] is called a *retrocession.*

reconviction. (Further examples.)

1909 *Rep. Commissioners of Prisons* I. 15 in *Parl. Papers* (Cd. 4847) XLV. 133 The highest proportion of re-convictions is in this class no less than 40 per cent. **1968** *Economist* 3 Feb. 16/2 Reconvictions bring those under suspended sentences into prison after all. **1976** *Howard Jrnl.* XV. I. 7 Striking variations in reconviction rates.

record, *sb.* Add: **I. 1. a.** (Further example.)

1870 'Mark Twain' in *Galaxy* Oct. 575/1 That verdict is of record, and holds good to this day.

2. *on record* (further examples). Also, *to go on record*: to give oneself a place on a formal record, to be recorded (*as* favouring a given course of action, etc.); to express one's opinion. Also, *to be on record, to put* (oneself, etc.) *on record.* orig. *U.S.*

1900 *Congress. Rec.* 11 Jan. 785/1, I would be perfectly contented if Senators would put their vote on record. **1920** H. G. Wells *Outl. Hist.* 169/1 Greece had suddenly begun to produce literature, and put itself upon record as no other nation had ever done hitherto. **1930** E. M. Brent-Dyer *Chalet School & Jo* v. 64 It is on record that seventeen people had to go and remake theirs [*sc.* beds]. **1930** *Daily Express* 8 Sept. 10/4 President Parsons of Woolworths has also gone on record with the statement that [etc.]. **1940** *Publishers' Weekly* 1 May 3007/1 The Association has previously been on record against legislation of this kind. **1967** *N.Y. Times* (Internat. Ed.) 11–12 Feb. 1/1 West German Vice Chancellor Willy Brandt put the Bonn Government on record today as being willing to bar any nuclear explosions. **1975** J. Grady *Shadow of Condor* vii. 116 I've hardly heard anything of what's being done..and I would like to go on record right now to that effect. **1978** *Lancashire Life* July 43/2 It is on record that soldiers from the 6th Manchester Regiment in Egypt provided enough eager players to hold a Lancs. v Cheshire match shortly before going on to Gallipoli.

II. 5. d. (Further examples.)

1887 M. Shearman *Athletics & Football* v. 143 T. G. Little and J. H. T. Roupell..tied at 5ft. 9in., a height which remained the 'record' for the next five years. **1924** C. Mackenzie *Heavenly Ladder* xxiii. 286 The various 'records' we've broken..were not of our own seeking. **1955** N. & R. McWhirter (*title*) Guinness book of records. **1975** *Oxf. Compan. Sports & Games* 734/1 Thin air, a handicap in the endurance events, contributed to the shattering of world records in 11 track and field events with a premium on explosive effort.

e. (i) A disc or, formerly, a cylinder from which recorded sound or television pictures can be reproduced. Occas. also, a recording made on magnetic tape.

1878 *Design & Work* 19 Jan. 72/2 The vibrations resulting when a voice..utters certain words or other sounds, instead of being caused to transmit corresponding vibrations to a distance, are caused to produce a material record... The record can also be multiplied precisely as a photographic portrait can be multiplied. **1878** *Cassell's Family Mag.* June 443/1 Mr. Edison is now engaged in devising a finished instrument capable of storing up speeches and music of all kinds, and of allowing the records to be sent by post. **1892** W. Gillet *Phonograph* ii. 11 Previous to taking a record the cylinder has a sheet of tinfoil carefully wrapped round it. *Ibid.*, The record being finished, to reproduce it we have but to bring the cylinder back to the point of starting, and again rotate it. **1897** *Sears, Roebuck Catal.* 485/2 One graphophone talking machine... 12 Musical and Talking Records, your own selection. **1919** H. L. Wilson *Ma Pettengill* i. 20 With a..hired help to bring him his breakfast in bed and put on another record and minister to his lightest whim. **1919** Wodehouse *Damsel in Distress* xxiii. 278 I've been dancing to your music for years! I've got about fifty of your records on the Victrola at home. **1949** Frayne & Wolfe *Elem. Sound Recording* xxix. 601 The making of very high-quality magnetic records has become possible commercially. **1966** *Listener* 3 Nov. 646/1 Musicians' Union..objects to any new broadcast popular music programmes relying mainly on records. **1975** G. J. King *Audio Handbk.* vii. 154 Although there are still a few mono releases, the basic record is cut for two-channel stereo. **1976** *National Observer* 13 Nov. 8/2 Video-disc players, which attach to your television and broadcast shows from records, are being developed by several major manufacturers. **1978** *Gramophone* June 136/3 The programme is recorded digitally using the well proved PCM (pulse code modulation) encoding system... Philips are forecasting that players and disc records will be available in the early 1980s.

(ii) *fig.* (See quots.)

1926 Maines & Grant *Wise-Crack Dict.* 12/2 *Put on a new record*, change the subject. **1976** W. Goldman *Magic* III. xii. 207 'There's something crazy here..and I care.' 'Oh Jesus, I'm sick of that record.' **1977** Partridge *Dict. Catch Phr.* 177/2 *Put another record on!* and *change the record!*.. Addressed to..anyone..'going on about something'.

f. An account of a person's conduct in a particular sphere, preserved for reference; *spec.* a record (or history) of criminal convictions or prison sentences. orig. *U.S.*

1901 *Land of Sunshine* Apr. 234 In that crowded hall were many men with 'records'. *a* **1911** [see *pedigree *sb.* 2 d]. **1918** A. Woods *Crime Prevention* vii. 87 The convict has a hard enough row to hoe when he gets out to overcome his record, even if he is mechanically capable. **1938** [see *arm *sb.*[1] 2 b]. **1952** M. Allingham *Tiger in Smoke* x. 168 Not one of you has got a real record..and you don't want to spoil it, eh? **1954** *Manch. Guardian Weekly* 18 Mar. 3 McCarthy had described her as a 'code clerk' whose 'Communist record' was known to the country. **1969** [see *moderate *sb.* a]. **1973** 'E. Ferrars' *Foot in Grave* viii. 144 'You didn't know..that he'd got a record.' 'A police record?' 'Yes.'

g. In various phrases: *off the record* (orig. *U.S.*): unofficially, confidentially; also as adj. phr.; also, *for, on the record*, for the sake of having the facts recorded or known; also, *to put* (*set*, etc.) *the record straight*: to achieve a proper record of the facts; to correct a misapprehension.

1933 H. L. Ickes *Secret Diary* 24 Mar. (1953) I. 9 He met and answered every question, although in some instances his answers were off the record. **1935** *Time* 2 Sept. 16/2 Only a very few Canadian tycoons took a calmer off-the-record view. **1939** *Time* 16 Oct. 101/1 By such slightly off-the-record stunts as burglarizing the plane factory..the Major sleuths out a sabotage gang. **1943** M. Asquith *Off Record* 10 If it is an Americanism, all the better. They are our allies, and if no one else understands the meaning of 'Off the Record', they will. **1949** *Manch. Guardian Weekly* 31 Mar. 2/3 Professor Schuman, who is a tidy-minded man, wanted to keep the record straight. **1949** R. Chandler *Little Sister* xxxi. 226 Off the record—we were always sure. We just didn't have a thing on him. **1951** *N.Y. Times Book Rev.* 22 Apr. 35/4 (*heading*) For the record. **1953** A. C. Clarke *Prelude to Space* viii. 43, I thought you might like to come along. For the record, you can be one of our legal advisers. **1965** A. Nicol *Truly Married Woman* 34 Look here, Olu, do you chaps hate us?.. Of course, this is all off the record. We are speaking as man to man. **1967** N. Freeling *Strike out where not Applicable* 30, I said we'd get the gendarmerie to look at things, just to get the record straight, what? **1971** *Daily Tel.* 24 Apr. 9/6 Our Saxon forebears..[regarded] all smithy conversations as off-the-record and therefore not slanderous at law. **1972** *N.Y. Times* 3 Nov. 35/1 Sir Rudolf is a spirited and independent man who feels he is obligated to put the record straight. **1973** D. Westheimer *Going Public* i. 15, I wouldn't..advise you to lower your standards. I'll say for the record I'm not advising that. **1973** *Times* 17 Dec. 14/4 An unattributable criticism of the oil companies by one minister was followed next day by an on-the-record reversal. **1976** J. Snow *Cricket Rebel* 76, I was impressed by the fact that he had bothered to get in touch with me to put the record straight. **1977** *Oxford Consumer* Mar. 5/1 Mr. Shergold made further investigations and sent us the following letter which should help to set the record straight. **1978** *Church Times* 1 Sept. 10 I'd be surprised if they didn't get down to some pretty forthright talking about women priests—not necessarily on the record, but among themselves. **1978** R. V. Jones *Most Secret War* iv. 41 Our discussion, which he had assured me was 'off the record', was reported back to the Air Ministry.

h. *pl.* Used *absol.* and *attrib.* (with capital initial) to designate a place where official records are kept; *spec.* a criminal records office or department (cf. sense *5 f).

1934 *Discovery* Nov. 319/2 The buildings under observation were the Great Temple, the Records Office and the Police Barracks. **1937** M. Allingham *Dancers in Mourning* xxvi. 314 Yeo had become a new man since the message from the [Police] Records Department. **1958** 'J. Byrom' *Or be he Dead* iii. 52 'I'll send you a copy..so that you can bring your files up to date.'.. 'I'm sure Records will be much indebted to you.' **1973** 'C. Aird' *His Burial Too* iv. 38, I did a person check with Records before I left the Station... Criminal Records Office have no knowledge of him.

i. *Computers.* A number of related items of information which are handled as a unit.

1957 *Proc. Western Joint Computer Conf.* 215/1 A record might be defined as all of the individual items of information (or words) about a given file unit. **1963** *Communications* (Assoc. Computing Machinery) VI. 267/1 Suppose each record of an input tape contains up to 50 fields.., some of which may be missing in any given input record. **1964** T. W. McRae *Impact of Computers on Accounting* vi. 189 A tape reel holds a certain number of records just as a ledger holds a certain number of accounts. **1966** C. J. Sippl *Computer Dict. & Handbk.* 265/1 The most basic subdivision of a record is called a field. **1970** O. Dopping *Computers & Data Processing* i. 14 We know that the first word in this record is always the last name of the subscriber, the second one is his first name, etc. **1973** C. W. Gear *Introd. Computer Sci.* i. 13 To avoid confusion we will refer to the set of information on each card (name and phone number) as a record.

IV. 13. a. (sense 5 a) *record-keeping*; (sense 5 d) *record-breaker, -breaking* (further examples), *-holder, -setting, -smasher, -smashing*; (sense *5 e) *record-buying, -collecting, collector*.

1894 *Rep. Vermont Board Agric.* XIV. 93 Raising trotters for sporting men..has been done with the one idea of producing a record breaker, regardless of every other qualification. **1929** A. Huxley *Do what you Will* 145 Modern record-breakers have been ready to undergo.. hardships for the sake of money. **1976** *Liverpool Echo* 7 Dec. 7/3 A Birkenhead company is making a name for itself as record breakers in the shipping world. **1929** A. Huxley *Do what you Will* 147 The record-breaking was to have a numerous audience. **1937** C. Isherwood *Sally Bowles* 66 Huge contracts for Sally, record-breaking sales for the novels I should one day write. **1950** *Sport* 22–28 Sept. 20/4 Not satisfied with his record-breaking average of 23 m.p.h., Joy rode again last weekend in vain hope of lowering his hundred mile time. **1949** L. Feather *Inside Be-Bop* i. 5 Lester's introduction to the record-buying jazz public. **1970** *Guardian* 7 Aug. 8/2 The two orchestras..are..little known..by the record-buying public. **1956** M. Stearns *Story of Jazz* (1957) xvii. 216 To the record-collecting converts known as 'moldy figs', however, this was not 'authentic' jazz. **1932** *New Yorker* 14 May 57/1 Mme. Ljungberg, hitherto accessible to record-collectors principally in opera albums, introduces herself as a singer of Strauss. **1946** *Penguin Music Mag.* Dec. 91 The record collector, who has built up his library.., really gets to know the music to which he listens. **1934** *Discovery* Dec. 352/1 The record holders of the fastest time between England and Australia. **1963** *Times* 30 Jan. 4/3 That graceful and intelligent runner, Johnson, is still the United Kingdom recordholder over 800 metres. **1977** *Whitaker's Almanack 1978* 584/2 Terry Paine, ..the Football League's appearance record-holder, played his..final League match against Southampton. **1965** D. E. C. Eversley in Eversley & Glass *Population in Hist.* I. 34 Where central legislation..enforces record-keeping, the change tends to be abrupt. **1977** J. M. Johnson in Douglas & Johnson *Existential Sociol.* viii. 246 Those typifications of the daily work of intake workers that did not result in an official 'case' for record-keeping purposes. **1969** *Jane's Freight Containers 1968–69* 112/2 Time required to unload a trailer has been reduced from 10 minutes to a record-setting 90 seconds. **1972** J. Mosedale *Football* ii. 21 The Eagles won 14–0, a record-setting two playoff shutouts in a row. **1928** *Daily Sketch* 7 Aug. 22/3 Arne Borg, the record-smasher at all distances in the swimming world, was at work again yesterday. **1889** *Puck* (N.Y.) 7 Aug. 399/2 We will soon have as many record-smashing ocean-steamers as we now have champion pugilists.

b. (sense 5 a) *record book, card, office* (further example); (sense *5 e) *record cabinet, case, company, deck* (*deck *sb.*[1] 3 f), *groove, label* (*label *sb.*[1] 7 c), *library, needle, rack, shop, storage, store*.

1961 *Evening Standard* 6 Feb. 22/3 A further step toward deathless record-book fame in its dreariest form. **1976** *0–10 Cricket Scene* (Austral.) 5/1 That was the start of the climb..which was to re-write the record books and lift Australia to the peak of performance. **1967** H. Pinter *Basement* 70 Law goes to the record cabinet. He examines record after record. **1934** *Burlington Mag.* Sept. 142/1 Prolonged study of the data which record-cards may provide. **1960** M. Spark *Bachelors* i. 6 The specialist himself would possibly remember only the gist, and then only with the aid of his record cards. **1977** *News of World* 17 Apr. 7/2 Details..noted down by teachers on their pupils' record cards. **1908** *Sears, Roebuck Catal.* 201/1 Disc Record Cases..made from wood covered with black seal grain imitation leather... No. 1 holds 50 7-inch disc records. **1949** D. Smith *I capture Castle* xiii. 245 A wireless and a gramophone combined..[and] a record case to match. **1938** D. Baker *Young Man with Horn* iv. vii. 278 The record company went broke before any of their records were issued. **1978** *Lancashire Life* Apr. 29/3 Life after death is a tall order, but this month a record company comes near to meeting it by supplying the next best thing. **1976** A. Hope *Hi-Fi Handbk.* 116 If you intend giving your record deck a fairly hard working life [etc.]. **1946** E. Hodgins *Mr. Blandings* i. 9 He lowered the rusty tone arm, complete with needle, on to the record groove. **1976** M. Maguire *Scratchproof* xi. 172 'The record labels too, I suppose.' 'Steaming off and switching?' **1977** *Listener* 25 Aug. 247/2 Elvis had been doing it..already, on a little Tennessee record label. **1961** *Times-Picayune* (New Orleans) 19 June III. 11/3 A stereo series called 'Adventures in Music', which is an instructional record library for elementary schools. **1974** E. Ambler *Dr. Frigo* i. 50 On shelving built along the inner wall was..hi-fi equipment and a record library. **1918–19** *T. Eaton & Co. Catal.* Fall & Winter 369/2 Record Needles, 100 for 15c. **1904** G. B. Shaw *Let.* 23 Nov. (1972) II. 467, I was startled to hear that Edith Livia was getting..twenty-five shillings a week for work at the Record Office. **1973** A. Roy *Sable Night* ii. 22 The bookcase and record-rack yielded nothing. **1975** R. Butler *Where All Girls are Sweeter* ii. 17, I looked through his record racks... There was a nice mixture from Bach to Vivaldi. **1960** *Twentieth Cent.* Apr. 341 Record-shops..have mushroomed all over Britain in the last five years. **1975** *Guardian* 22 Jan. 14/5 The top 40 singles are based on local record shop returns. **1939–40** *Army & Navy Stores Catal.* 838/2 Radiogramophone..with five record albums and..extra record storage. **1974** *Times* 8 Apr. 13/3 A record storage cabinet in a Queen Anne style. **1949** *Billboard* 2 Apr. 34 Albums listed are those classical and semi-classical albums selling best in the nation's retail record stores. **1977** D. Westlake *Nobody's Perfect* (1978) 107 A branch of a major department store..the record stores, the shoe stores, the ladies' clothing stores.

c. (Further examples.)

1912 Chesterton *Manalive* ii. i. 194 Smith was one of the University's record men for shooting. **1922** *Brit. Med. Jrnl.* 2 Sept. 412/1 During 1919,..3,420 new students were registered, being 1,105 greater than the 'record' entry of 1891. **1937** *Discovery* Sept. 264 His 'dash'..was accomplished in record time. **1948** 'J. Tey' *Franchise Affair* viii. 86 If you could have seen your face when I introduced you to her... It cured me of her in record time. **1960** *Farmer & Stockbreeder* 16 Feb. 83/1, 27,000 gn record-priced bull. **1978** *Lancashire Life* Apr. 69/2 Visitors numbered a record 114,000 in 1977, and it is hoped that this trend will continue.

14. Special combinations. **record album,** † (*a*) a holder for gramophone records, *obs.*; (*b*) = *album[1] 6; **record changer,** a device for automatically placing another record on the turntable of a gramophone when the preceding record has ended; also **record-changing** *a.*; **record club,** a society which enables members to purchase selected gramophone records at reduced prices; **record hop** *slang,* a dance at which the music is provided by gramophone records; a place where such entertainment is held; **record jockey** *U.S. slang* (immediately supplanted by *disc jockey*: see *disc 8 f); **record linkage,** the process of combining items of information or sets of data relating to the same subject; **record player,** orig. a turntable and pick-up unit designed to be plugged into and played through a radio; now usu. a gramophone; **record sleeve,** a stiff envelope in which a gramophone record may be stored (cf. *sleeve *sb.* 7); **record token,** a voucher exchangeable in a shop for a gramophone record or records; **record type,** a type-face including special sorts reproducing the contractions or particular letter forms found in mediæval manuscripts.

1925–6 *T. Eaton & Co. Catal.* Fall & Winter 391/1 These Record Albums are made with strong cardboard covers... Each album will hold 12 records. **1945** *Billboard* 24 Mar. 18/2 (*heading*) Best-selling record albums by classical artists. **1955** Keepnews & Grauer *Pictorial Hist. Jazz* viii. 87/2 When people got around to..dissecting it [*sc.* a variety of jazz] in books and record-album notes,..it became known as 'Chicago style'. **1931** *N.Y. Times* 12 July 4/8 The Capehart 400 series..has several novel features... The record changer is equipped with a special constant-speed electric motor which operates both the turn-table and the record-shifting mechanism. **1947** *Gramophone* Nov. 88/1 The amplifier and record changer are contained in a small chair-side consol. **1977** *Times* 18 Apr. (Gramophone Suppl.) p. i/2 A radio-gramophone, with automatic record changer, was installed in our living room. **1931** *Wireless World* 23 Sept. 349/3 H.M.V.'s ace set is the model 531, being a nine-valve superheterodyne with automatic record-changing radio-gramophone. **1943** *Gramophone* Dec. 107/1 The spindle and turntable move left and down, which leaves the area free for the first record to drop upon the 'floor' of the record-changing unit. **1958** *Manch. Guardian* 21 Jan. 6/6 If anything the record club is likely to spread an interest in records of serious music rather than reduce the profits of the big companies. **1961** G. Smith *Business of Loving* xi. 229 We started as a record club... The first discs ..were fifteen shillings. **1960** *Punch* 9 Mar. 345/1 Akin to the juke-box joints are the record-hops. **1966** *Wall St. Jrnl.* 25 July 1 'Record hops'..are dances often organized by a disc jockey and plugged by him over the air, as a means of supplementing his income. **1940** *Variety* 3 Apr. 39/3 [Quoting J. Kapp] The name bands are come on for the record jockeys who ride herd over not only Decca records but all the others. **1946** H. L. Dunn in *Amer. Jrnl. Public Health* XXXVI. 1412/2 In the process of record linkage the uniting of the fact-of-death with the fact-of-birth has been given a special name, 'death clearance'. **1959** *Science* 16 Oct. 954/1 The term record linkage has been used to indicate the bringing together of two or more separately recorded pieces of information concerning a particular individual or family. **1968** *Brit. Med. Bull.* XXIV. 208/2 If birth and marriage records are included in the system, it is possible to use record linkage to assemble sibships, parent-offspring groups and eventually pedigrees. **1934** *Wireless World* 5 Jan. 10/3 (*caption*) The Collaro record player incorporated in a radio-gramophone cabinet. **1939** *New Regal-Zono Records* Feb. 4 (Advt.), The thousands already sold of the Columbia electric record-player prove conclusively how many fully appreciate the facility of playing their records through their radio sets. **1958** *Sunday Times* 3 Aug. 3/6 Now that the station has bought a new record-player and gets all its music in prerecorded tapes, the personal touch is all but gone. **1960** *Practical Wireless* XXXVI. 377 (Advt.), Turns any gramophone into a first-class tape-recorder and back into a record-player in a moment. **1973** M. Amis *Rachel Papers* 68 You mean to tell me that it's only made in stereo?..What about the people who don't own stereo record-players? **1977** *Gramophone* July 241/1 The humble record player of earlier years could still be found in a few places. **1954** *Gramophone Record Rev.* July 415 On the record sleeve, the user is extolled to play the record at full room volume. **1963** L. Deighton *Horse under Water* xviii. 74 The brightly coloured record sleeves that are the folk art of the new world. **1978** P. Porter *Cost of Seriousness* 47 An old woman, So the record sleeve denotes, Is singing of death In a young world. **1958** M. Kelly *Christmas Egg* ii. 76 The envelope that had held his brother's record token. **1977** *Radio Times* 26 Nov.–2 Dec. 56/1 EMI Record Tokens ..can be exchanged at over 5,000 leading record shops. **1886** F. W. Maitland *Let.* 24 Apr. (1965) 19 As regards mode of printing:—The use of 'record type' seems undesirable. **1934** V. H. Galbraith *Introd. Use of Public Records* v. 77 A century ago the Record Commission in its publications tried by means of 'record type' virtually to reproduce the document, with all its abbreviations. **1972** C. R. Cheney in A. Campbell *Charters of Rochester* p. vi, Originals and early copies are reproduced as faithfully as is possible, without going to the extreme of using 'record type'.

record, *v.* Add: **III. 9. c.** To convert (sound or visual scenes, esp. television pictures) into a permanent form from which they can afterwards be reproduced by machine. Also *absol.*

1892 W. Gilbert *Phonograph* ii. 31 The instrument is now ready to register any sound... While the handle is steadily turned.., speak slowly and distinctly the words you wish to be recorded. **1902** *Encycl. Brit.* XXXI. 680/2 When the phonograph records the sound of an orchestra, it does not record the tones of each instrument. **1935** H. C. Bryson *Gramophone Record* iv. 70 A good modern recorder is designed to record frequencies between 250 and 5,000 without discrimination. **1960** *How TV Works* 37/1 A video-tape machine recording the opening of Parliament. **1967** S. Beckett *Eh Joe* 15 Joe's opening movements followed by camera at constant remove... No need to record room as a whole. **1972** *Daily Tel.* 29 Jan. 3 The full proceedings of an inquest were recorded for broadcasting for the first time yesterday. **1978** *Radio Times* 9–15 Dec. 81/4 Most people who record and play back BBC television programmes using videocassette equipment do not realise they infringe copyright. **1980** S. Brett *Dead Side of Mike* xiii. 145 I'd better go. We're about to record.

d. *intr.* Of a performer or instrument: to be suited to sound recording.

1923 O. Mitchell *Talking Machine Industry* viii. 88 It has been complained by some that, in technical phrase, she does not record well. **1925** P. A. Scholes *Second Bk. Gramoph. Rec.* p. xviii, The Piano, as an instrument, records less well than other instruments.

e. *trans.* and *intr.* Of a performer: to give a performance, or a performance of (a work), that is recorded.

1927 *Daily Tel.* 12 Feb. 7 She has recorded the Ave Maria from 'Otello'..as if she had recorded all her life! **1928** *Melody Maker* Feb. 155/3 The band..has recently jumped into prominence, having already recorded for Edison Bell. **1966** *Listener* 10 Mar. 345/1 Mostly they recorded at the end of their careers, and violinists seem to deteriorate much earlier than pianists.

V. 12. The infin. used in the sense 'recording'. **a.** *attrib.* (often as a name of a part), as *record button, head*; also *record–reproduce* adj.

1950 Godfrey & Amos *Sound Recording & Reproduction* (1952) vi. 162 When the *Record* button is depressed, current is fed to the wiping head. **1973** *Times* 28 Nov. 6/7 Miss Woods..pressed the 'record' button (it was next to the 'stop' button). **1975** P. G. Winslow *Death of Angel* ix. 186 He pushed the record button. But the heads of his machine were too old. They didn't erase the music. **1946** *Trans. Amer. Inst. Electr. Engineers* LXV. 216/2 The playback head is located a few feet along the wire from the record head so that in listening tests it is possible to get a quick comparison between a few bars of music as recorded and played back. **1950** G. A. Briggs *Sound Reproduction* (ed. 2) xix. 135 For reproduction, the erase and record heads are switched off and the play-back head is brought into use. **1976** I. R. Sinclair *Master Stereo Cassette Recording* i. 9 Though some high quality reel-to-reel machines use separate record and replay heads,..it is usual on cassette recorders to have only one head used for both recording and for replay. **1951** *Bell Syst. Technical Jrnl.* XXX. 1146 The ring-type record–reproduce head. *Ibid.*, The process was repeated..for several record–reproduce speeds.

b. Not *attrib.*

1950 G. A. Briggs *Sound Reproduction* (ed. 2) xix. 136 By suitable switching of output circuits, one amplifier may be arranged to function for both record and replay. **1968** C. N. G. Matthews *Tape Recording* iv. 36 During record or reproduce it [*sc.* the tape] is kept in close contact with the heads by pressure pads or by its own tension. *Ibid.* 38 Equalization is switched automatically as the machine is switched from record to playback. **1971** *Hi-Fi Sound* Feb. 49/2 (Advt.), 4 track stereo record and replay using popular Compact Cassettes. **1976** K. Bonfiglioli *Something Nasty in Woodshed* x. 119 Even on virgin tape I still got the gentle muttering if it was played through on 'record'..at a nil recording level.

recordable, *a.* Add: (Further examples.) Also, worthy of record, memorable.

1917 *Wireless World* May 87 It might prove useful when signals of recordable strength are obtainable. **1971** *Jrnl. Gen. Psychol.* Jan. 168 Psychologists sometimes deal with body process in either recordable terms or in hypothetical body-process terms. **1974** 'M. Innes' *Appleby's Other Story* viii. 62 Everything recordable about this room had been recorded.

Recordak (rī·kǭ·ɪdæk). Also with small initial. The proprietary name of an apparatus manufactured by Kodak Ltd. for producing a photographic record of a series of documents, as bank cheques, etc.

1929 *Encycl. Brit.* XVII. 805/1 G. L. McCarthy..has designed a camera intended to photograph upon a strip of motion picture film all the checks passing through a bank. This camera, which is known as the 'Recordak', provides a permanent record which greatly diminishes the risk of fraud. **1937** *Trade Marks Jrnl.* 31 Mar. 360/2 Recordak... Photographic apparatus and parts thereof,..and films prepared for exhibition. Kodak Limited,..London,..; manufacturers. **1942** *R.A.F. Jrnl.* 2 May 11 The Recordak machine has replaced the clumsy methods of the Tours' post office. The airgraph service is now established. **1948** E. L. Irey *Tax Dodgers* xiii. 251 It was the only bank in Atlantic City which used a recordak. **1967** Cox & Grose

Organization & Handling Bibl. Rec. by Computer 185 In 1956 we installed a 'magnetic tape to microfilm' device..and decentralized the whole file, using about forty Recordak readers, each containing all of the 160 million names.

recordant, *a.* For *rare*—1 read *rare* and add further example.

1877 Ruskin *St. Mark's Rest* II. iv. 42 They are merely shapes of amphora..usefully recordant of different ages of the wine.

recordation. Add: **2.** (Later example.)

1881 Meredith *Tragic Comedians* I. iii. 40 She was prepared to express her recordation of the circumstance in her diary.

4. (Further examples in *U.S. Law.*)

1924 G. W. Thompson *Commentaries on Mod. Law of Real Property* VIII. liv. 274 The majority rule holds to the tenet that the recordation of an instrument void on its face is not of itself constructive notice. **1938** *U.S. Statutes at Large* LII. 1006 Recordation of Aircraft Ownership. *Ibid.*, Every such conveyance so recorded..shall be valid as to all persons without further recordation. **1948** *Columbia Law Rev.* Dec. 1248 Recordation of title to chattels is normally governed by local laws. **1962** *Iowa Law Rev.* Winter 227 Was his recordation at that time at such place in the records that it should be concluded [etc.]? **1976** *Washington Post* 19 Apr. C10/4 All costs incident to settlement and conveyancing, including..recordation costs and taxes..will be at the cost of the purchaser.

recorded, *ppl. a.* Add: **1. b.** Also, *recorded delivery*, a Post Office service whereby the safe delivery of an item of mail is recorded in a register signed by the recipient; also *ellipt.*, a letter or package sent by recorded delivery.

1961 *Use Recorded Delivery* (G.P.O. Leaflet P.L. 140) 2 Recorded delivery is designed for the customer who wants to be able to prove, if necessary, that a letter or packet has been delivered. **1968** R. Petrie *MacLurg goes West* I. iv. 31 There was this package, see. Registered. No. I'm wrong there; it was that other thing. Recorded delivery, with a little orange sticker on the top. **1969** W. J. Burley *Death in Willow Pattern* i. 8 The post—two recorded deliveries among the rest. **1977** 'E. Crispin' *Glimpses of Moon* xii. 256 A letter marked in one place 'Special Delivery', and in another, 'Recorded Delivery'.

2. a. Of sounds or images: converted into a durable form (e.g. on disc, tape, or film) from which the original can be reproduced by suitable apparatus.

1932 *Radio Times* 29 July 242/1 The B.B.C...[has] decided to supplement with recorded programmes the proposed broadcasting service from the new Empire shortwave transmitter at Daventry. **1949** *Ibid.* 15 July 13/1 Stand Easy... (Wednesday's recorded broadcast). **1958** M. Kelly *Christmas Egg* III. 106 He was addicted to the collection of recorded music. **1962** A. Nisbett *Technique Sound Studio* 167 Recorded effects consist principally of those which cannot conveniently be created in the studio: cars, aircraft, birdsong,..and so on. **1975** *Sci. Amer.* May 45/1 A 'videodisc' system that presents recorded pictures and sound on a standard television set will be put on the home-appliance market next year.

b. Of a recording medium: bearing a recording.

1962 A. Nisbett *Technique Sound Studio* 243 A little of the bias signal can still be heard if recorded tape is pulled slowly over the reproducing head.

recorder[1]. Add: **1.** (Later examples.) Now in England and Wales, a part-time judge presiding over certain Crown Courts (see quot. 1971).

1955 *Times* 3 May 6/3 At the first trial before the Recorder (Sir Gerald Dodson) earlier in the session the jury had failed to agree. **1965** *Modern Law Rev.* XXVIII. v. 563 The Recorder of Manchester..interrupted a case..to address us on the iniquitous way in which his court was being used. **1971** *Act* 19 & 20 *Eliz. II.* c. 23 §. 21 Her Majesty may from time to time appoint qualified persons, to be known as Recorders, to act as part-time judges of the Crown Court and to carry out such other judicial functions as may be conferred on them under this or any other enactment... Every appointment of a person to be a Recorder shall be of a person recommended to Her Majesty by the Lord Chancellor, and no person shall be qualified to be appointed a Recorder unless he is a barrister or solicitor of at least ten years' standing. **1972** *Daily Mail* 2 Aug. 6/4 Judges' itineraries can be changed, solicitors can sit as recorders. **1979** T. Skyrme *Changing Image Magistracy* 219 New-style Recorders differed from their predecessors in that they were not affiliated to any borough, or to any other local government area, but might be required to sit in any part of the Circuit. They were also required before appointment to undertake to sit on not less than twenty days a year.

4. (Further examples.) Also, † the recording part of an early gramophone or phonograph; now *spec.* a tape-recorder.

1899 *T. Eaton & Co. Catal.* Spring & Summer 191/2 A Columbia Graphophone, with clockwork motor, recorder, reproducer, hearing tube, speaking tube and horn. *Ibid.* 191/3 Recorder, with sapphire point, $5.00. Reproducer, with sapphire point, $5.00. **1902** *Encycl. Brit.* XXXI. 680/1 The recorder describes a series of spirals diminishing from the circumference to the centre of the disc. **1908** *Sears, Roebuck Catal.* 201/3 Recorder, for..our special home graphophone. **1914** *Cassier's Engineering* XLV. 414/2 Typical thermoelectric recorders were..described. **1935** *Discovery* Nov. 324/1 The necessary constancy of motion of cinematographic film in recorders, reproducers, printers, and associated apparatus. **1948**, etc. [see *flight recorder* s.v. *flight *sb.*[1] 15]. **1957** *Times* 13 Dec. 18/2 The Minifon pocket recorder is..regarded as an essential item for everyday use in the office. **1959** W. S. Sharps *Dict. Cinemat.* 109/1 A magnetic recorder is equipment incorporating an electromagnetic transducer..for recording electric signals as magnetic variations in the medium. **1971** *Engineering* Apr. 105/1 (Advt.), One of Bell & Howell's portable, multichannel recorders is the answer. **1973** A. Broinowski *Take One Ambassador* iii. 32 She cocked an eyebrow over her mini-cassette recorder.

5. *attrib.* and *Comb.*, as *recorder–reproducer*.

1937 *Jrnl. Soc. Motion Picture Engineers* XXIX. 217 (*caption*) Magnetic recorder–reproducer. **1970** *Proc. IEEE* LVIII. 886 (*heading*) Signal recorder–reproducer using a coherent light source and a photographic film record.

recorder[2]. Restrict *'Obs.* exc. *Hist.'* to senses b, c in Dict. and add: **a.** (Later examples.)

The popularity of the instrument spread in the twentieth century after its revival by Arnold Dolmetsch in 1919.

1920 *Glasgow Herald* 10 Aug. 6 One was able to understand why the Greeks went into battle to the soft strains of solemn music rendered on flutes and recorders. **1932** R. Donington *Work & Ideas A. Dolmetsch* 16 The first group of early instruments to regain something of its original popularity has been the family of recorders, or English flutes. Many hundreds of Dolmetsch recorders are already in use. **1958** M. Dolmetsch *Personal Recoll. A. Dolmetsch* viii. 88 Our broken consorts now, for the first time, included the recorder, the instrument employed being, of course, the ancient boxwood and ivory recorder which Arnold had brought over from England. It was played by his first recorder pupil, namely the Harvard Professor Peabody. **1962** E. Hunt *Recorder & its Music* 7 The present-day meteoric return to popularity of the recorder—whose seductive tone charmed the ears of Henry VIII, Shakespeare and Pepys—is a development unparalleled in the history of any other musical instrument. **1976** D. Munrow *Instr. Middle Ages & Renaissance* i. 14/1 The essential features of the recorder are its beak-shaped mouthpiece and the number of its finger-holes: seven finger-holes plus a thumb-hole.

recordership. (Later example.)

1975 *Daily Tel.* 5 Nov. 12/5 (*heading*) Recordership for woman solicitor.

recording, *vbl. sb.* Add: **3. b.** The action or process of recording sound or television pictures.

1904 S. R. Bottone *Talking Machines & Records* 67 Male voices generally come out more true to the singer's timbre than ladies', the delicate overtones of these latter being more altered in recording. **1923** O. Mitchell *Talking Machine Industry* ii. 15 Mr. Fenby,..in 1863, took out a patent for the electrical recording and reproducing of sound. **1935** *Discovery* Oct. 309/1 The air plant has to be shut off for a few minutes during an actual recording, on account of the noise of the air being forced through the ventilators. **1976** I. R. Sinclair *Master Stereo Cassette Recording* i. 5 Magnetic recording..is almost as old in concept as disc recording, but has had to wait for modern technology to be developed to the stage at which it could be used successfully.

4. A representation of sounds or pictures in a form from which the original can be reproduced by suitable apparatus.

1932 *New Yorker* 11 June 46/3 Accepting the recordings as accurate, I venture that Mme. Leider is a musicianly performer with a fine sense of text. **1949** *Radio Times* 15 July 13/1 Sandy Macpherson takes you to 'The Chapel in the Valley' (BBC recording). **1958** J. Moir *High Quality Sound Reproduction* vii. 130 The standards adopted for 78-r.p.m. recordings have proved unnecessarily robust for electrical reproducers. **1968** *Listener* 18 July 91/1 The Seekers, lugubriously watching a recording of themselves singing 'The Carnival is Over'. **1977** *Times* 24 Aug. 14/4 The basis of the library will be its gradual acquisition of recordings by poets of their verse at the time of its publication.

5. *attrib.* and *Comb.*, as (sense 3 a) *recording fee*; (sense *3 b) *recording deck* (*deck *sb.*[1] 3 f), *right, room, session, studio, tape, van*; **recording amplifier,** one provided to amplify the signals supplied to the cutter (in disc recording) or to the recording head (in tape recording); **recording channel,** a circuit or set of equipment used for sound or video recording; **recording engineer,** an engineer responsible for the technical aspects of recording when a sound or video recording is made; **recording head,** a head (*head *sb.* 11 g) for recording on to magnetic tape or wire; **recording level,** a measure of the average strength of a recorded signal.

In some cases not clearly distinguishable from the ppl. adj.

1934 *Wireless World* 5 Jan. 9/3 The recording amplifier is specially designed to amplify the currents delivered by the microphone or 'A' amplifier to a degree suitable for the electrical conditions as determined by the recording head. **1964** A. A. McWilliams *Tape Recording & Reproduction* ix. 185 The purpose of the recording amplifier is to deliver sufficient current to the record head to magnetize the tape correctly over the working frequency range. **1975** G. J. King *Audio Handbk.* vii. 160 The difference signals are finally mixed with the sum signals and pass with the latter through the RIAA equaliser and hence to the cutter head, via the recording amplifier. **1938** *Motion Pict. Sound Engin.* (Acad. Motion Pict. Arts & Sci.) v. 69 A stage recording channel uses one or more transmitters on the stage to initiate the electrical energy necessary for recording either on film or on disc. **1949** Frayne & Wolfe *Elem. Sound Recording* xi. 184 A complete recording system is known as a recording channel. **1975** G. J. King *Audio Handbk.* x. 237 The controlled amplifier in the recording channel is adjusted in gain by rectified signal from a control amplifier fed from the recording amplifier. **1977** *Times* 24 Aug. 14/2 Three superior recording decks would cost £8,000. **1962** A. Nisbett *Technique Sound Studio* 268 *Recording engineer* (BBC), professional engineer whose job includes the technical recording of sound and the editing of tape, but not microphone balance and control. **1977** *Gramophone* Mar. 1453/1 It is indifferently balanced, with the recording engineer conspicuously experimenting with his levels. **1898** Recording fee [in Dict., sense 3]. **1934** *Wireless World* 5 Jan. 9/2 The 'recording' and 'reproducing' heads are each provided with a micrometer adjustment for controlling the separation of the pole pieces. **1971** *Physics Bull.* June 359/1 Magnetic tapes of the kind used in computers or as videotapes in television vary in abrasiveness so that some tapes cause excessive wear of expensive recording heads. **1934** *Wireless World* 5 Jan. 10/2 Provided that the maximum recording level of 10 dbs. below 1 milliwatt is not seriously exceeded when recording, the distortion due to non-linear magnetic effects is hardly noticeable aurally. **1975** G. J. King *Audio Handbk.* vii. 157 Recording level may be given in terms of amplitude or velocity. **1962** Recording right [see *gear *v.* 4 a]. **1907** *Westm. Gaz.* 12 Dec. 9/4 Employees ..assisted many of the frightened girls to cross from the blazing building to the Gramophone recording-rooms. **1975** *Language for Life* (Dept. Educ. & Sci.) xxv. 425 Almost a quarter of the schools had a projection room and 14 per cent a recording room. **1927** *Melody Maker* Sept. 923/1 All their days..appear to be occupied with recording sessions. **1962** *Times* 5 July 15/4 The raw product of a recording session is a magnetized length of tape. **1928** *Gramophone* Apr. 451 (*heading*) Round the recording studios. **1958** [see *cut *v.* 23 d]. **1977** *Times* 18 Apr. (Gramophone Suppl.) p. iv/2 Contemporary popular music is to a large extent a child of the recording studio. **1960** *Guardian* 9 Nov. 11/2 The biggest manufacturer of recording tape in Europe. **1977** *Times* 24 Aug. 14/1 Imagine 10 shelves..holding 380 reels of 10½ in polystyrene recording tape. **1940** P. Fleming *Flying Visit* i. 17 Wires..poured into the streamlined flanks of a..lightly armoured recording van.

recording, *ppl. a.* Add: **a.** (Further examples.)

In some cases not clearly distinguishable from the vbl. sb. used *attrib.* (see prec., sense *5).

1892 W. Gilbert *Phonograph* III. 82 Adjust the screw on the guide rod until the recording stylus makes a slight groove on the revolving wax cylinder. **1937** 'M. Innes' *Hamlet, Revenge!* III. iii. 249 Phonetic nicety apart..the machine..combined recording and reproducing units in an unusually compact way. **1949** *Radio Times* 15 July 14 Richard Dimbleby, with the BBC Mobile Recording Unit. **1962** A. Nisbett *Technique Sound Studio* 260 The Peak programme meter (PPM) is used by the BBC and most recording companies.

b. Of measuring instruments: able to produce a record of readings obtained.

1873 [in Dict.]. **1904** R. M. Walmsley *Electr. in Service of Man* I. ix. 357 A recording wattmeter, which would record the number of watts at every instant, so that..the total energy could be measured up or calculated. **1930** C. J. Stewart *Aircraft Instruments* viii. 146 It is sometimes necessary to record the temperature of the air during flight, and for this purpose recording thermometers are used. **1961** R. Rawlinson in G. F. Tagg *Pract. Electr. Engin.* III. 363 Situations demanding the use of a recording ammeter are fortunately not common.

recordist (rĭkǭ·ɹdist). [f. Record *v.* + -ist.] One who records or makes recordings.

1931 L. Cowan *Recording Sound for Motion Pictures* 384 *Recordist*, person engaged in recording sound. **1938** *Nature* 5 Feb. 226/2 That highly skilled, imaginative, ingenious, agile and patient collaborator in film-making who bears the regrettable though comprehensible title of 'recordist'. **1956** *B.B.C. Handbk. 1957* 65 The Corporation has made steady progress in securing world-wide sources of news in pictures... It maintains a staff of newsreel film cameramen and recordists in this country. **1958** *Times* 2 Dec. 3/2 (Advt.), Electro-Encephalography Recordist (single-handed) required. **1960** *Guardian* 9 Nov. 11/1 The federation issued a policy statement for the guidance of amateur recordists. **1966** V. C. Lewis *Bird Recognition* III. 3/1 The recordist of the 'songs' and 'calls' illustrated herewith is of the opinion that the use of sound concentrators..tends to detract from 'naturalness' of the recorded sounds. **1978** *Daily Tel.* 23 Sept. 1/3 All BBC television programme production is threatened from today by an unofficial overtime ban by cameramen and sound recordists.

Recordite (re·kǭɹdəit), *sb.* (and *a.*) *Obs.* exc. *Hist.* [f. the name of the *Record* newspaper + -ite[1].] One who subscribes to views represented by the evangelical Church of England newspaper, the *Record* (1828–1949). Also *attrib.* or as *adj.*

1853 W. J. Conybeare in *Edin. Rev.* XCVIII. 284 This exaggeration of Evangelicanism, sometimes called the Puritan, sometimes, from its chief organ, the Recordite party, we shall now endeavour to describe. *Ibid.*, Thus from *justification by faith* the Recordite infers the worthlessness of morality. **1875** F. Arnold *Our Bishops & Deans* I. i. 11 We suspect we may supply the ellipse by the words 'Protestants' or 'Recordites'. **1965** W. R. Ward *Victorian Oxford* x. 224 Gladstone arranged with Vice-Chancellor Jeune to delay the by-election till the last possible moment, but his legal adviser Phillimore was still on tenterhooks that 'some *Recordite* would be put up to poll two or three votes and claim to be returned before a committee'.

recordless, *a.* (Earlier example.)

1854 'G. Greenwood' *Haps & Mishaps* 116 That old, old city of a forgotten and recordless past.

re-cork, *v.* Add: (Later examples.) Also *fig.*

1906 *Daily Chron.* 3 Apr. 7/4 While he was recorking the bottle Dunstan picked up the glass. **1922** Joyce *Ulysses*

523 (He uncorks himself behind: then, contorting his features, farts loudly.) Take that! (He recorks himself.) **1969** E. PENNING-ROWSELL *Wines of Bordeaux* xviii. 271 The leading châteaux re-cork their reserves of old wines roughly every twenty-five years.

‖ **recorte** (reco·rte). *Bull-fighting.* [Sp., lit. 'cutting, trimming'.] A pass by which the torero cuts short the bull's charge.

1925 E. HEMINGWAY in *This Quarter* I. II. 217 A series of acceptable veronicas ending in a very Belmontistic recorte. **1932** —— *Death in Afternoon* vii. 67 A recorte is any pass with the cape that..stops him brusquely. **1932** R. CAMPBELL *Taurine Provence* iii. 71 The cape, the use of which varies from the vulgar vuelta and recorte to the most perfect designs. **1967** MCCORMICK & MASCAREÑAS *Compl. Aficionado* ii. 54 The banderillero..performs a rough *recorte* to fix the toro gently before he disappears behind a burladero.

recount, *sb.*[1] For † *Obs.* read *rare* and add later example.

1905 *Daily Chron.* 20 July 3/1 We..are not bored by the intolerable recount of flukey rounds.

recounter, *sb.*[1] (Later example.)

1953 PARTRIDGE *Shaggy Dog Story* ii. 17 But not even the most cavalier of casual recounters may omit two extremely significant and pertinent literary examples.

recoup, *sb.* Add: Also *attrib.*

1904 H. G. TURNER *Hist. Colony Victoria* II. ix. 276 The too general use of the recoup system under which public works were authorised to be paid for out of future loans. **1966** *Public Administration* XLIV. 411 If the recoup mechanism is to do its job.

recoup, *v.* Add: **3. b.** Also *absol.* or *intr.*

1906 L. J. VANCE *Terence O'Rourke* I. iii. 19 Each..had seemed to be broken in fortune, and..ready to seize upon any chance to recoup. **1976** C. BERMANT *Coming Home* II. vii. 218, I had..acquired so many debts that if I didn't return to England to recoup, we might have to run for it.

c. *intr.* To regain lost health, vitality, etc.; to recuperate.

Prob. arising from confusion with *recuperate.*

1939 M. SPRING RICE *Working-Class Wives* iv. 79 We have sent her away for two years running to help her to recoup. **1955** W. GADDIS *Recognitions* I. ii. 66 The Society recouped: found its own Marguerite.

recoupe, *sb.* **b.** For 1835 read 1810 as date of quot.

recouperation (rĭkūpĕrēⁱ·ʃən). *nonce-word.* [App. blend of RECOUP *v.* and RECUPERATION.] = RECOUPMENT.

1904 G. B. SHAW *Let.* 23 Nov. (1972) II. 466 It seems to me that unless you were living quite madly beyond your income in the old days, the economies of the last few years ought by this time to have produced some degree of recouperation.

recouple, *v.* Add: Hence **recou·pling** *vbl. sb.*, a repeated joining in pairs or linking.

1890 W. JAMES *Princ. Psychol.* I. ii. 76 The multiplicity of emotional and instinctive reactions in man, together with his extensive associative power, permit of extensive recouplings of the original sensory and motor partners.

recoupment. (Earlier and later examples.)

1839 *N.Y. State Supreme Court Rep.* (Wendell XXII, 1840) 156 The offer came under the third category, *recoupment.* **1905** *Daily Chron.* 18 July 5/5 The full effect of 'recoupment' and 'betterment' would reduce it [*sc.* net cost]. **1953** *Words & Phrases* (St. Paul, Minn.) XXXIX. 28/2 A 'recoupment' is a counterclaim arising out of the contract sued upon, whereas a 'set-off' is a counterclaim arising from an independent transaction. **1977** *Times Educ. Suppl.* 21 Oct. 3/1 A nationwide recoupment scheme to equalize the burden of financing advanced further education.

recourse, *sb.*[1] Add: **4. c.** *Law.* Phr. *without recourse,* used to indicate that the endorser of a bill, etc., shall not be held liable for its non-payment.

1800 *U.S. Supreme Ct. Rep.* (1816) VII. 160 Pay the within to James Welch, on order, without any recourse whatever. **1805** *Ibid.* (1807) III. 203 The words *without recourse* do not imply *without value.* **1839** J. BOUVIER *Law Dict.* I. 499/1 The words commonly used are *sans recours,* without recourse. **1878** M. D. CHALMERS *Digest of Law of Bills of Exchange* iv. 97 It is held in America that an indorser 'without recourse' is responsible..*e.g.,* where the bill is a forgery. **1948** D. RICHARDSON *Simple Guide Bills of Exchange Acts* II. 56 When a party adds to his signature the words *sans recours* (*i.e.,* without recourse to me)..he means that, should the bill be dishonoured, the holder cannot look to him for repayment.

recover, *sb.* **4. a.** Delete † *Obs.* and add later example.

1915 KIPLING *New Army in Training* ii. 10 The squads at bayonet-practice had their balance, drive, and recover already.

b. (Earlier example.)

1818 'T. BROWN' *Brighton* III. ii. 123 'I hold it that a *prime* coachman's a better fellow than a paltry—' peer he was going to say, but he knew how to pull up to a hair; so, making a recover, he added—'man of fortune'.

recover, *v.*[1] Add: **I. 1. f.** To remove (certain substances) from industrial waste in order that they may be reused.

1906 R. W. SINDALL *Paper Technol.* iv. 37 About 75 to 85 per cent. of the soda used in the treatment of esparto can be recovered. **1929** CLAPPERTON & HENDERSON *Mod. Paper-Making* xxii. 315 In almost all mills a large quantity of fibre and clay may be recovered from the back waters of the machines. **1929** *Industr. & Engin. Chem.* May 446 (*caption*) Air filters recover dust from gyratory crushers... This dust is sold as agricultural limestone. **1941** *Coke & Smokeless-Fuel Age* III. 285/1 All coke producers are required to recover benzole from their gas. **1969** D. STEWART *Paper* 33 The caustic soda is recovered in the following way.

8. b. For † *Obs.* read *rare* and add earlier and later examples.

1602 JONSON *Poetaster* III. i. D3, Did you neuer heare any of my verses? *Horace.* No, Sir; but I am in some feare, I must, now. *Crisp.* Ile tell thee some (if I can but recouer 'hem). **1957** L. DURRELL *Justine* IV. 233 It is strange when everything about Alexandria is so vivid that I can recover so little of that lost period.

9. b. (Later examples.)

1816 JANE AUSTEN *Emma* III. iii. 39 A young lady who faints, must be recovered. **1940** W. FAULKNER *Hamlet* III. i. 179 This legal dollar which would be little enough compensation, not for the time he had spent recovering the cow. **1967** *Listener* 7 Sept. 302/3 Well, I think Mr Wilson would put one well on the way to convalescence, and the Queen would recover one completely.

III. 18. a. Also *fig.*

1921 H. CRANE *Let.* 19 Sept. (1965) 64 *The L[ittle] R[eview]*, I was informed..is recovering, will shortly re-appear as a quarterly under Pound, Picabia, etc.

recoverability. (Further examples.)

1964 N. CHOMSKY *Current Issues in Linguistic Theory* ii. 46 But if there are several alternative designated elements, the comments on 'recoverability' must be slightly revised. **1965** G. J. WILLIAMS *Econ. Geol. N.Z.* xviii. 286/1 The recoverability of coal from a thick seam by underground mining is, of course, low. **1968** *Language* XLIV. 234 It will consist of..deletion of the subject of the embedded sentence, subject to the recoverability condition (i.e. only in those cases where it is identical with that of the matrix sentence). **1979** *Sci. Amer.* Jan. 29/3 Estimates of ultimate recoverability vary from one coalfield to another depending on the accessibility of the coal.

recoverable, *a.* Add: **1. a.** (Further examples.)

1952 F. H. NORRIS *Paper & Paper Making* xiv. 222 Water derived from boiler washings and the rag washers is not recoverable. **1964** N. CHOMSKY *Current Issues in Linguistic Theory* ii. 41 A deleted element is, therefore, always recoverable. **1974** *Canad. Jrnl. Linguistics* XIX. 147 It is clear that not every instance of the operation of vowel deletion in Canadian French results in a recoverable vowel.

c. Designating mineral reserves which by reason of their location and purity may be extracted economically.

1950 E. AYRES in L. M. Fanning *Our Oil Resources* vii. 234 The oil-shale regions of Colorado, Utah, and Wyoming.. contain the bulk of recoverable shale oils as well as the bulk of total shale oils. **1959** D. L. KATZ et al. *Handbk. Natural Gas Engin.* xi. 462/2 The initial gas content [of a natural reservoir] minus the content at a selected abandonment pressure gives the recoverable gas. **1973** E. N. TIRATSOO *Oilfields of World* xii. 336 Those volumes of hydrocarbons technically recoverable, to a high degree of certainty, but the exploitation of which is deemed uneconomic. **1976** *Conservation of Resources* (Chem. Soc.) 20 So far we have used up some 16 % of total possible recoverable oil reserves, and only about 4 % in the case of coal. **1979** *N.Y. Rev. Bks.* 17 May 14/4 The world's recoverable coal reserves are several times those of oil.

2. b. (Later example.)

1962 *Times Lit. Suppl.* 28 Sept. 759/1 It was realized that many severe mental disturbances were more recoverable than had previously been supposed.

recovered, *ppl. a.* Add: (Further examples, in sense *1 f of the vb.) † *recovered rubber* = *reclaimed rubber* s.v. *RECLAIMED *ppl. a.* 2.

1892 *Sci. Amer.* 7 May 293/2 Of all the materials used in rubber compounding, none was found to be as effective as recovered rubber, and this for the simple reason that when carefully prepared it *is* rubber. **1897** *India-Rubber & Gutta-Percha & Electr. Trades' Jrnl.* 12 Apr. p. vi (Advt.), G. W. Laughton & Co., manufacturers of recovered rubbers. *Ibid.* p. vii (Advt.), The Recovered Rubber Works, Ltd., Clayton, Manchester. **1902** *Chambers's Jrnl.* Oct. 683/2 This rejuvenated substance is known in New York as 'recovered' rubber. **1906** R. W. SINDALL *Paper Technol.* iv. 37 The organic matter is burnt off, and the mass left behind consists mainly of impure carbonate of soda. This residue is known as 'recovered ash'. **1929** CLAPPERTON & HENDERSON *Mod. Paper-Making* xxii. 317 Most of the recovered stuff will have to be used in a paper of a lower grade. **1952** F. H. NORRIS *Paper & Paper Making* xiv. 225 The most important point is the final recovery cost as compared with the value of the recovered fibre.

recoveree. Restrict 'now *rare* or *Obs.*' to sense in Dict. and add: **2.** One who is recovering from a disease or an illness.

1957 *Times* 15 Oct. 3/4 There was the Asian influenza casualty..who was replaced gallantly by an influenza recoveree, Mr Robert Harben. **1973** *Washington Post* 5 Jan. B5/2 The survey also showed that employers will hire wheelchair people, ex-convicts, T.B. recoverees, the deaf and the blind ahead of epileptics.

recoverer[1]. **1.** (Later examples.)

1884 TENNYSON *Becket* III. iii. 135 Our recoverer and upholder of customs hath in this crowning of young Henry by York and London..violated the immemorial usage of the Church. **1978** A. PRATT *Directory of Waste Disposal & Recovery* 107 This list does not cover in great depth the more traditional areas of recovery—metals, paper, textiles etc. In these fields there are many recoverers and merchants.

recovering (rĭkʌ·vəriŋ), *vbl. sb.*[2] [f. RE-COVER *v.*[2] + -ING[1].] The action of RECOVER *v.*[2]

1904 *Daily Chron.* 28 July 8/5 His umbrella..may want re-covering. **1930** A. D. STUBBS *Pastimes that Pay* 45 When your dining room chairs require re-covering there is no need to send them to the upholsterer. **1967** M. HOLFORD *Photogr. Handbk.* 147 Send them to the local umbrella recovering shop.

recovery. Add: **I. 2. d.** In general use, the act of regaining an original position, esp. after rhythmic movement.

1876 [see *RECURB]. **1949** SHURR & YOCOM *Mod. Dance* 173 Practice slowly at first. Fall: *one, two, three, four*: Recovery. *Ibid.* 190 *Recovery,* a series of movements used in order to return to position after a full sequence.

e. Reversion of a material, object, or property to a former condition following removal of an applied stress or other influence.

1885 P. G. TAIT *Properties of Matter* xi. 218 All elastic recovery in solids is gradual. **1895** *Proc. R. Soc.* LVIII. 132 Recovery of elasticity which the overstrained material undergoes with the mere lapse of time. **1939** WILLIAMS & HOMERBERG *Princ. Metallography* (ed. 4) iii. 73 Complete recovery cannot be attained in polycrystalline metals. **1966** C. R. TOTTLE *Sci. Engin. Materials* vii. 164 Recovery can also take place by annihilation of positive and negative dislocations, with or without the added movements in climb or cross-slip. **1975** E. R. TROTMAN *Dyeing & Chem. Technol. of Textile Fibres* (ed. 5) vi. 129 Recovery from strain [of polynosic fibres] gives good dimensional stability to fabrics which contain them.

3. b. Also, cf. *on the mend* s.v. MEND *sb.* 5. (Further example.)

1834 H. EVANS *Diary* 27 July in *Chrons. Oklahoma* (1925) III. 206 We found this Camp in a desolate situation... The sick some little on the recovery.

II. 4. a. (Later *attrib.* example.)

1951 KOESTLER *Age of Longing* I. i. 9 Your hand..is on lend-lease to a vicious old man; it is my recovery grant, or whatever you call it.

5. c. (Later examples.)

1922 JOYCE *Ulysses* 710 The dun for the recovery of bad and doubtful debts. **1964** W. D. PARK *Collection of Debts* (ed. 2) iii. 37 The court has power, in any action for the recovery of a debt or damages, to order interest at such rate as it thinks fit on the whole or part of the debt for the whole or part of the period it has been due.

e. The extraction of reusable substances from the waste produced by a process; also, the original extraction of a useful substance from a mixture, raw material, etc.

1885 *Jrnl. Iron & Steel Inst.* I. 216 (*heading*) Recovery of residuals from furnace gases. **1906** R. W. SINDALL *Paper Technol.* iv. 37 (*heading*) Soda recovery. **1923** S. J. TRUSCOTT *Textbk. Ore Dressing* 3 With copper,..though ore containing as little as 2·5 per cent may exceptionally be successfully smelted, a better recovery is obtained when the content is higher. **1923** W. H. WALKER et al. *Princ. Chem. Engin.* vii. 228 (*heading*) Recovery of waste heat from furnaces. **1951** K. K. LANDES *Petroleum Geol.* xi. 621 Modern production methods..result in a much higher percentage of ultimate recovery and, conversely, a lower percentage of residual oil left underground. **1962** F. T. DAY *Introd. Paper* iv. 40 The excess water which falls through the machine wire bed flows away for recovery. **1978** J. UPDIKE *Coup* (1979) vi. 247 Engineer's my title; recovery's my racket... Better recovery in the established fields is the name of the game... It's a miracle, what you can squeeze out of a rock if you know where to pinch it.

f. The return or capture of a ringed or tagged animal after its release; = *RETURN *sb.* 15 b.

1909 *Brit. Birds* III. 180 Turning now to..the recovery of marked birds, it is as yet too early perhaps to expect many results of interest. The most interesting recovery that has as yet been reported is ring No. 4308. **1940** H. F. WITHERBY et al. *Handbk. Brit. Birds* III. 23 Twenty-five recoveries of British ringed nestlings indicate movements of comparatively short distances only. **1959** *Listener* 19 Feb. 321/1 We have been marking young seals with identity tags since 1951..and we have had some good recoveries. **1965** P. WAYRE *Wind in Reeds* iii. 36 Of the 284 ducks I ringed at Mileham, forty-five were recovered... Thirteen recoveries were from abroad. **1976** L. BROWN *Brit. Birds of Prey* ix. 114 Most of the recoveries are of birds which died unnatural deaths.

g. An amount recovered, usu. in contrast with that expended or initially available.

1931 *Economist* 17 Jan. 112/2 Total recoveries for December were, for the first time for over three years, slightly (30,000,000 francs) below the expected level. **1958** *N.Z. Timber Jrnl.* May 56/1 *Recovery,* the ratio of final product to log volume in timber conversion. **1973** J. L. GREGOIRE in V. S. White *Mod. Sawmill Techniques* v. 118 Figure 5.2 shows typical recovery on a 9-inch-diameter log 16 feet long with 1/16-inch taper per foot... From this log we are able to obtain a 1×4 14 feet long and six pieces of 2×4 16 feet long.

h. The retrieval of a satellite or spacecraft after a flight. Freq. *absol.* and *attrib.*

1949 *Jrnl. Brit. Interplanetary Soc.* VIII. 197 Two possibilities for increasing the chances for physical recovery after impact seemed worthy of investigation. **1960** D. E. BAILEY in K. W. Gatland *Spaceflight Technol.* 220 The main problems of satellite recovery are associated with deceleration, heating and tracking. **1961** *Ann. Reg. 1960* 385 Subsequently the U.S. Air Force made two further recoveries of the smaller Discoverer satellites by snatching them in mid-air as they floated down towards the sea by parachute. **1962** D. SLAYTON in *Into Orbit* 22 The recovery techniques which we would put into play to find and rescue the Astronaut and his capsule after they had landed. **1967** *Technol. Week* 20 Feb. 10/3 Orbital telemetry indicated that the capsule battery should have sufficient charge to operate the radio beacon and flashing light that serve as recovery aids.

7. a. (Later examples.) Freq. in economic contexts.

1932 A. SALTER *Recovery* IV. i. 282 Here what is needed is a moratorium of several years, say four or five, to cover the depression and a period for Germany's recovery after it. **1940** G. CROWTHER *Outl. Money* iii. 115 Prices rose with staggering rapidity, until..they were one million million times the pre-war level. This is 'inflation without recovery'. **1958** *Times* 28 June 11/7 The pound staged a remarkable recovery against the United States dollar. **1974** B. PEARCE tr. *Amin's Accumulation on World Scale* II. iv. 497 In order to explain world recovery, all that remains is to analyze the effects of new techniques.

c. The restoration to working condition of a disused mine.

1932 *Trans. Inst. Mining Engineers* LXXXII. 452 The recovery of two separate underground districts which had been sealed off for several years due to the occurrence of fire.

III. 10. *attrib.* and *Comb.*, as (sense 3) *recovery area, room, school, unit, ward*; (sense 5) *recovery airfield, area, crew, fleet, line, ship, team, vehicle*; (sense 5) *recovery furnace, plant*; (sense 7) *recovery area, party*; **recovery time,** (*a*) the time required for an object or material, esp. an item of electronic equipment, to return to some specified condition following an action, e.g. the passage of a current; (*b*) *Railways,* time allowed in a schedule in excess of that which would be required in normal running.

1963 *Dict. U.S. Mil. Terms* 11 It is not expected that combat missions would be conducted from a recovery airfield. **1965** *Guardian* 23 Aug. 1/2 It was taken for granted that the astronauts would be brought down in the Bermuda 'recovery area' at 12 22 a.m. **1971** *Ibid.* 1 July 1/5 The Soyuz made a..soft landing in the expected recovery area. **1976** *Scotsman* 27 Dec. 2/7 An attempt to have South Ayrshire designated as a recovery area. **1977** *Times* 25 Aug. 2/6 After transfer to the recovery area he [*sc.* a baby] was left in the care of a pupil nurse. **1971** *Guardian* 1 July 1/5 A helicopter-borne recovery crew..found the cosmonauts.. without any signs of life. **1976** *Daily Times* (Lagos) 26 Aug. 9/3 Landings in darkness are generally avoided by Soviet space controllers as they hamper the work of recovery crews. **1968** *Guardian* 23 Sept. 1/2 The splash-down appears to have been some way from the recovery fleet. **1942** G. S. WITHAM *Modern Pulp & Paper Making* (ed. 2) viii. 215 The Wagner Recovery Furnace..embodies an attempt to greatly increase the efficiency of heat utilization in the recovery furnace over what is possible with the traditional rotary furnace. **1963** R. R. A. HIGHAM *Handbk. of Papermaking* v. 107 There are various designs of rotary recovery furnaces although these are generally of the horizontal type. **1976** J. D. LEE *Ninth Man* I. i. 8 One of the deck crewmen started paying out the recovery line, and the rubber boat bobbed away from the submarine. **1933** *Sun* (Baltimore) 7 Oct. 1/8 McKee named his ticket the 'Recovery Party'. **1929** CLAPPERTON & HENDERSON *Mod. Paper-Making* xxii. 318 The water goes to waste, or back into use, or to a further recovery plant. **1970** *Adv. in Chem.* XCVII. 223 The performance of butadiene recovery plants improves as solvent selectivity increases. **1916** S. S. GOLDWATER in *Trans. Amer. Hospital Assoc.* XVIII. 476 A large ward designed for an acute surgical service should have recovery rooms, where postoperative cases may be cared for. **1951** *Anesthesiology* July 476 The use of the recovery room has without question saved lives. **1964** G. L. COHEN *What's Wrong with Hospitals?* iii. 51 She wanted a post-operative recovery room, to avoid crises on a ward ill equipped to deal with them. **1979** *Arizona Daily Star* 1 Apr. K10/1 Hospital auxiliary needs volunteers to make infant sweaters,..blankets and stuffed toys for children coming from the recovery room. **1909** *Westm. Gaz.* 11 Sept. 9/4 The establishment of open-air recovery schools. **1962** D. SLAYTON in *Into Orbit* 23 The Navy stuck most of its recovery ships in these big areas. **1976** B. JACKSON *Flameout* (1977) vi. 108 Red Cross volunteers were still carrying coffee and Coke to the recovery teams. **1944** *Princ. Radar* (Mass. Inst. Technol. Radar School) xi. 18 The time required for elimination of these free ions after disappearance of the main pulse signal is referred to as the recovery time of the device. **1959** G. R. PARTRIDGE *Princ. Electronic Instruments & Instrumentation* xix. 373 The interval from the end of the dead time to the moment when another full-size pulse can be produced is known as the recovery time. **1961** *Trains Illustrated* Nov. 684/1 Time regaining soon began and by Doncaster, with the joint help of 4 min recovery time and a top speed of 85 m.p.h. on the level at Moss, 6 min had been picked up. **1964** *Proc. IEEE* LII. 1301/1 The time required for full recovery of a gap between silver contacts in vacuum..ranged from about 1 μ sec to 30 μ sec... This short recovery time is to be contrasted with the much longer recovery time in gases which is of the order of milliseconds. **1967** R. K. RICHARDS *Electronic Digital Components & Circuits* ii. 31 The time for removal of the minority carriers is called the 'recovery time' of the diode. **1977** *Modern Railways* Dec. 481/3 Nothing more than 81 mile/h was sufficient for even time to Stowmarket and the ensuing sharp 14 min to Diss was just kept from where recovery time should have balanced the arrears. **1965** *Nursing Times* 5 Feb. p. iv/2 (Advt.), Recovery Unit. *a* **1944** K. DOUGLAS *Alamein to Zem Zem* (1946) 10 Field workshops with huge recovery vehicles and winches. **1974** A. DOUGLAS *Noah's Ark Murders* i. 6 The recovery vehicle was positioned directly opposite the car. **1965** *Nursing Times* 5 Feb. p. lxii (Advt.), Enrolled Nurses..For Recovery Ward to do full-time day duty. **1970** H. MCLEAVE *Question of Negligence* i. 14 Cameron strolled around the recovery ward to inquire, as always, about the patients he had done that day.

recreance[2]. (Later example.)

1897 F. THOMPSON *New Poems* 103 To give the pledge, and yet be joined That a pledge should have force to bind, This, O Soul, too often still Is the recreance of thy will!

recreate, *v.*[1] Add: **5.** (Later examples.) Now chiefly *U.S.*

1978 *Verbatim* Winter 6/1 The President plans to recreate on Labor Day. **1979** *Sunset* Apr. 16/3 (Advt.), Recreate. It's fun in Colorado. For the best in summer fun take yourself and your family away.

recreation[1]. Add: **5.** *attrib.* and *Comb.*, as *recreation area, centre, ground, hall, home, leader, leadership, league, officer, ramble, room, tent, therapy, time, vehicle.*

1961 *Recreation* Dec. 531/1 Recreation areas are never too large for the future. **1978** *N.Y. Times* 29 Mar. B2/3 Ocean Beach Park, a recreation area on Long Island Sound. **1943** J. S. HUXLEY *TVA* 17 Guntersville, formerly a sleepy market town..is now becoming..an important recreation centre. **1974** M. G. D. DIXEY *Local Recreation Centres* 1. 10 Most local authorities recognise the need for indoor recreation centres. **1859** Recreation ground [see sense 3 a in Dict.]. **1898** E. HOWARD *Tomorrow* xiv. 147 These wretched slums will be pulled down, and their sites occupied by parks, recreation grounds, and allotment gardens. **1969** I. & P. OPIE *Children's Games* xii. 341 The merry-go-round is a type of swing placed in the recreation ground by the local council. **1981** J. B. HILTON *Playground of Death* iv. 42, I learned on an Essex Recreation Ground. **1943** J. S. HUXLEY *TVA* 75 This method of sectional prefabrication has now been successfully applied to larger buildings, such as..recreation halls. **1976** *National Observer* (U.S.) 10 July 6/2 Add to this the boom in recreation and leisure homes and you have Ozark hills and hollows chock full of people. **1923** *Playground* Apr. 35/2 A recreation leader should be active in the social work program of his city. **1936** H. R. CLARK *Playground Man.* ii. 32 Discuss the future possibilities for playground and recreation leaders. **1953** H. D. CORBIN *Recreation Leadership* ii. 20 The recreation leader is responsible for the organization, direction, and supervision of recreational activities. **1924** *Playground* Apr. 118 The marked increase in employed recreation leadership. **1976** *National Observer* (U.S.) 22 May 14/4 (Advt.), Liberal Arts Career Studies... Recreation Leadership. *Ibid.* May 17/2 We were told to scrounge up our own games through local recreation leagues to get as much experience as possible. **1976** *Evening Times* (Glasgow) 1 Dec. 3/1 The Carstairs patient who died attempting to defend recreation officer Neil McLellan. **1853** Recreation ramble [see sense 3 a in Dict.]. **1854** Recreation room [see *coconut matting* s.v. *COCO, COCOA 4 d]. **1890** *Harper's New Monthly Mag.* Feb. 342/1 An excellent canteen and a recreation-room are, however, now provided in almost every barrack. **1978** J. WAINWRIGHT *Thief of Time* 99 I'm in the Recreation Room. Playing Ludo. **1930** E. M. BRENT-DYER *Chalet Girls in Camp* v. 75 The two big tents for the commissariat and recreation tents had ridge-poles. **1977** M. EDELMAN *Polit. Lang.* iv. 60 If they play volleyball, that is recreation therapy. **1909** 'MARK TWAIN' *Is Shakespeare Dead?* iv. 45 It seriously shortened his..recreation-time. **1974** *State* (Columbia, S. Carolina) 15 Feb. 17-B/1 (Advt.), Home sites. Mobile Homes. Recreation vehicles. **1977** *Globe & Mail* (Toronto) 27 Apr. 35/2 He predicted sales of RVs will continue to rise, 'because the recreation vehicle looks solid when compared with other vacation forms'.

recreational, *a.* Add: **a.** (Later examples.) Also, used for, or as a form of, recreation; concerned with recreation.

1890 *Century Mag.* June 176 The recreational section has been a most unequivocal Success, and has already proved a boon to East London. **1946** *Q. Jrnl. Forestry* XL. 2 The Americans have a word for it: the 'recreational' use of land. This is primarily what National Parks are for. **1946** *R.A.F. Jrnl.* May 173 There is an extensive technical and recreational library. **1956** A. H. COMPTON *Atomic Quest* 110 The Cook County recreational area. **1973** *Times* 2 Mar. 16/5 Proposals to create the first protected nature reserve..are being discussed by Deal town council with..recreational societies. **1976** *Billings* (Montana) *Gaz.* 20 June 1-F/1 We used to hear about recreational shopping—it was sort of a lark and a lot of fun—but I think now it is a pretty grim, serious business. **1977** *Age* (Melbourne) 18 Jan. 24/1 (Advt.), Caravan Owners!..Recreational vehicle reports include a 24 ft. Glendale, pronounced ideal for a young couple's first home.

b. *recreational mathematics,* mathematics studied or indulged in for pleasure or amusement.

1940 KASNER & NEWMAN *Math. & Imagination* 156 Researches in recreational mathematics sprang from the same desire to know, were guided by the same principles, and required the exercise of the same faculties as the researches leading to the most profound discoveries in mathematics and mathematical physics. Accordingly, no branch of intellectual activity is a more appropriate subject for discussion than puzzles and paradoxes. **1973** *Sci. Amer.* Sept. 176/1 It would..be hard to imagine two problems in combinatorial point-set geometry more remote from foreseeable practical applications unless one thinks of recreational mathematics (with its two virtues: amusement and instruction) as a branch of applied mathematics.

Hence **recrea·tionalist,** one who advocates or promotes the provision of facilities for recreation; **recrea·tionally** *adv.*

1970 *Daily Tel.* 31 Mar. 14 Landowners, farmers, residents, recreationalists, preservationists, conservationists, naturalists, sportsmen and many others have to be considered. **1975** *Nature* 18 Sept. 185/1 Extracts of the poppy plant have been used since the days of the Homeric epics medically and recreationally. **1977** *Jrnl. R. Soc. Arts* CXXV. 257/1 The NCC [*sc.* Nature Conservancy Council] is trying to achieve a revolution in attitudes reconciling the needs of the recreationalists and the conservationists. **1979** *Sci. Amer.* Feb. 52/2 The diver's work is far more demanding than might be supposed by someone who has dived recreationally in clear, warm water.

recreationist (rekrĭ,ē[1]·ʃənist). [f. RECREATION[1] + -IST.] **a.** One who pursues a recreation. **b.** = *RECREATIONALIST. (See also quot. 1952.)

1904 *Daily Chron.* 13 Sept. 6/6 The campers had relaxed their vigilance... At a sudden startled shout of 'Police,' the Recreationists discovered helmeted and uniformed stalwarts advancing on them. **1952** D. RIESMAN in *Antioch Rev.* Dec. 420 Students of leisure—'recreationists' perhaps we'd better call them. **1963** *Times* 6 Nov. 13/3 A useful exercise..to bring poachers..round a table with gamekeepers..together with naturalists, architects, town planners, industrialists, and recreationists (if the word will serve). **1977** *Daily Colonist* (Victoria, B.C.) 8 July 13/4 Cougar Air..will be relying heavily on lumber and mining companies for business as well as recreationists.

recredence (rĭkrī·dĕns). *rare*—[1]. [Prob. back-formation on RECREDENTIAL *a.* and *sb.*, infl. by CREDENCE *sb.* 4 b.] In phr. *letters of recredence* = RECREDENTIAL *sb. pl.*

1855 E. C. GRENVILLE MURRAY *Embassies & Foreign Courts* xxii. 345 In this audience the ambassador presents his letters of recall to the sovereign, and usually makes a farewell speech... He receives at the same time his letters of recredence.

recredential, *a.* and *sb.* For † *Obs.* read *Obs.* exc. *Hist.* and add: **B.** *sb.* (Later example.)

1909 *Eng. Hist. Rev.* XXIV. Apr. 256 He obtained his recredentials on 18 October 1666.

recrudency. For † *Obs. rare*—[1] read *rare* and add later example.

1903 *Jrnl. Hellenic Stud.* XXIV. p. lxii, This success is all the more notable as it synchronises with the recrudency of efforts to circumscribe Greek studies.

recrudescence. Add: **2.** *transf.* A revival or rediscovery (of something regarded as good or valuable).

1906 H. W. & F. G. FOWLER *King's Eng.* i. 15 A literary tour de force, a *recrudescence,* two or three generations later, of the very respectable William Lamb. **1973** *Times Lit. Suppl.* 3 Aug. 900/2 The first fruit of this act of recrudescence was the catalogue of drawings.

recruit, *sb.* Add: **I. 3. a.** (Later example.)

1866 *Harper's Mag.* Apr. 677/1, I had gone in for a new recruit of clocks—for you must know I'm a clock peddler.

e. *Ecol.* An animal which has recently reached the size that qualifies it to be counted as a member of the population to which it belongs.

1938 *Jrnl. du Conseil* X. 269 It has been assumed that the same number of recruits would be found. **1948** M. GRAHAM *Rational Fishing of Cod of N. Sea* iii. 86 Codling from the deeper areas of the North Sea grow more slowly and will not enter as recruits until they are..2–3 years old. **1977** J. L. HARPER *Population Biol. of Plants* v. 141 Order and organization appear in populations because of feedback from existing populations to new recruits and because these recruits themselves interact.

II. 8. *recruit drill, training.*

1909 A. HUXLEY *Let.* 14 Dec. (1969) 32, I have,i n company with Gielgud, accomplished forty recruit drills this half and am now very nearly a full fledge[d] territorial. **1914** (*title*) Recruit training (infantry), 1914: an aid to all instructors. By two Officers of the Dorsetshire Regiment. **1976** *Billings* (Montana) *Gaz.* 30 June 3-B/3 Navy Fireman William G. Jones,..has completed recruit training at San Diego, Calif.

recruit, *v.* Add: **I. 3. e.** To become a member of (a natural population). Also *intr.* (const. *to*). Cf. sense 6 d below.

1965 *Oceanogr. & Marine Biol.* III. 357 The stock to which an individual recruits is solely determined by the time at which it attains the critical size. **1967** *Ibid.* V. 415 Before 1950 only a part of each year-class recruited the fishery at three years of age, the remainder recruiting it at age four, but in later years most, if not all, of the members of each year-class recruited at three years of age.

6. a. (Later *transf.* examples.)

1936 [see *MONTARÍA]. **1961** NEW ENGLISH BIBLE *Acts* xvii. 5 The Jews..recruited some low fellows from the dregs of the populace. **1974** *Economist* 11 May 36/2 The neo-fascists among whom many of the stewards at his meetings were recruited.

b. *U.S.* To (attempt to) induce (an athlete) to sign on as a student at a college or university.

1913, etc. [implied in *RECRUITED *ppl. a.*]. **1974** *Time* 21 Jan. 62/1 With impressive speed he recruited new talent and turned out a winner his first season. **1979** *Arizona Daily Star* 1 Apr. (Parade Suppl.) 23/1 Like her fellow junior from West Virginia, Earl Jones.., Ostrowski already is being heavily recruited by the country's top college coaches.

c. *Physiol.* To bring (additional muscle fibres or muscular activity) into play by the recruitment of their neurones.

1938 *Amer. Jrnl. Physiol.* CXXII. 49 The manner of recruiting mechanical energy during hyperpnea was extremely variable. **1979** *Sci. Amer.* Sept. 148/3 Slow-twitch units, resistant to fatigue and generating relatively little tension, are the first to be recruited.

d. *Ecol.* Of a natural population: to acquire by recruitment (sense *2 c). Cf. sense 3 e above.

1977 J. L. HARPER *Population Biol. of Plants* v. 116 Even in a controlled, 'homogeneous' environment the numbers of seeds that are recruited into a germinating population are determined by the individual properties of each seed.

II. 9. (Later examples.) Also with *up.*

1860 H. J. HAWLEY *Diary* 10 May in *Wisconsin Mag. Hist.* (1936) Mar. 336 We..stoped [*sic*] giving the teams a fine chance to recruit up a little which they need. **1896** E. DOWSON *Let.* 19 Mar. (1967) 346, I believe I have recruited a little since I came here.

recruital. **1.** (Later example.)

1889 W. R. SMITH *Relig. Semites* i. 12 The urban population is maintained only by constant recruital from the country.

recruited, *ppl. a.* (Later examples in sense *6 b of the vb.)

1913 *Collier's* 1 Mar. 20/2 None of them belongs to the class of 'recruited' athletes, so common in our colleges twenty years ago. **1974** *Anderson* (S. Carolina) *Independent* 19 Apr. 5B/3 One of the most heavily recruited South Dakota schoolboys in history. **1979** *Tucson* (Arizona) *Citizen* 28 Apr. 1B/2 He was one of the state's most highly recruited athletes this season, with every major college swimming power after him.

recruiter. **1.** For † *Obs.* read *Obs.* exc. *Hist.* and add later example.

1954 BRUNTON & PENNINGTON *Members of Long Parl.* i. 2 The constituency concerned was short of a member until the election of the 'Recruiters'—that is, the members elected from 1645 onwards.

2. (Later examples.) Also, one who recruits employees.

1899 A. CONAN DOYLE *Duet* 301 Frederick William, the half-mad recruiter of the big Potsdam grenadiers. **1944** *Living off Land* viii. 159 The recruiter takes them to District Headquarters. **1970** *Wall St. Jrnl.* 30 Mar. 1/1 One reason for the recent increase in executive recruiters seems to be their value in haggling over perks. **1977** *Graduate* 9 Dec. 15/3 It is also, incidentally, the recruiter's intention to deal with all applicants in an efficient and courteous manner.

recruiting, *vbl. sb.* Add: **b.** *recruiting bill, campaign, drive, -market, office, poster, -schooner, sergeant, station.*

1708 ADDISON *Let.* 24 Jan. (1941) 89 The next day,..they cramped the former Recruiting Bill by a new clause. **1976** *Sunday Mail* (Glasgow) 28 Nov., There have been recruiting campaigns for both police and teachers since regionalisation. **1956** *Railway Mag.* May 345/1 A big recruiting drive for staff..has been launched by British Railways. *a* **1971** R. WHYATT in J. Burnett *Useful Toil* (1974) I. 126 A recruiting drive was on, and her brothers might have to go. **1901** *Macmillan's Mag.* Apr. 476/1 The recruiting-market is in direct competition with all other avenues of employment. **1848** J. R. LOWELL *Biglow Papers* 1st Ser. viii. 115 He looked through the dirty pane of the recruiting-office window. **1919** G. B. SHAW *Augustus does his Bit* 244 This is the Town Hall Recruiting Office. Give me Colonel Bogey, sharp. **1909** *Regulations for Recruiting for Regular Army & Special Reserve* (War Office) I. 8 Illustrated recruiting posters may, with the concurrence of the local postmasters, be exhibited outside post offices. **1940** 'G. ORWELL' *Inside Whale* 184 After the bombs and the food-queues and the recruiting-posters, a human voice! **1971** P. D. JAMES *Shroud for Nightingale* i. 23 She was attractive enough for a recruiting poster. **1923** 'R. DALY' *Enchanted Isl.* i. 16 But you'd have had a more comfortable trip if you'd let him send his recruiting-schooner for you. **1849** *Whig Almanac & U.S. Reg. for 1850* 26/2, 23 cents per day, hardships in war, and no hope at all, require the aid of a recruiting sergeant. **1948** *Contact Books* XI. 62/1 When first, as a boy, I got to know boxers, unemployment and hardship were the greatest recruiting sergeants for the ring. **1845** J. C. FRÉMONT *Rep. Exploring Exped. Rocky Mts.* 160 The bottoms of this river, (the Bear), and of some of the creeks.. form a natural resting and recruiting station for travellers. **1907** G. B. SHAW *John Bull's Other Island* p. xxxv, Every school is a recruiting station; every church is a barrack.

recruitment. Add: **2. a.** (Later examples.)

1945 in *Amer. Speech* (1946) XXI. 78/2 The material included with this letter describes..the availability of recruitments from this company. **1958** *Times* 26 Mar. (Careers in Industry Suppl.) p. xxiii, One may study the recruitment literature of many employers. **1971** M. E. RAY *Recruitment Advertising* i. 9 Recruitment advertising is but a small part of the wide and varied duties of a Personnel Officer.

c. *Ecol.* Increase in a natural population as progeny grow and become recruits (sense *3 e); the extent of such increase.

1938 *Jrnl. du Conseil* X. 266 A stock will be in equilibrium with fishing when..C = A+G−M where C is capture, A is recruitment, G is growth, M is natural mortality. **1938** H. G. CHAMPION in Champion & Trevor *Man. Indian Silviculture* I. v. 146 The extension over the regeneration area as a whole of the light conditions appearing most favourable to regeneration is..the correct first step, always bearing in mind the possibility of different requirements for recruitment, i.e. new seedlings, and establishment, i.e. the further development of seedlings already present. **1954** W. E. HILEY *Woodland Managem.* xx. 357 A number of trees will be included, which have grown..but were omitted from the earlier enumeration because they had not then reached this size. These are called 'recruited trees'... It has been claimed that the volume of these trees—the recruitment—should be omitted from the calculation. **1965** *Oceanogr. & Marine Biol.* III. 357 A problem which has recently received considerable attention is the mechanism underlying recruitment of adolescent fish to the various North Sea Summer–Autumn spawning stocks. **1970** S. H. GARDINER tr. *Assmann's Princ. Forest Yield Study* 459 The lower the threshold of measurable diameter the smaller is the amount of recruitment. **1977** J. L. HARPER *Population Biol. of Plants* v. 144 Changes in the composition of light after it has passed through a leaf canopy may be one of the critical factors hindering the recruitment of seedlings under vegetation.

d. *Anat.* The incorporation into a tissue or region of cells from elsewhere in the body.

1973 *Laboratory Investigation* XXVIII. 56/1 Small bronchioles, bronchi, and tracheas showed cells distributed within all three layers which suggested recruitment by movement of cells from capillaries through the epithelium to airway lumina. **1978** *Nature* 2 Feb. 403/1 These compartments have the property that once the boundary has formed, the cells from the neighbouring compartments can never cross it, so each develops by further subdivision but not by recruitment of cells from outside.

3. *Physiol.* **a.** The involvement of successively more motor neurones in response to an unchanging stimulus.

1923 LIDDELL & SHERRINGTON in *Proc. R. Soc.* B. XCV. 335 The several forms assumed by the course of the ascent indicate the various time relations exhibited by the progressive involvement of additional motoneurones during the development of the reflex. That process may, for convenience of statement, be designated 'recruitment'. **1937** BEST & TAYLOR *Physiol. Basis Med. Pract.* lxv. 1278 Many reflexes gradually increase to a maximum when a stimulus of *unaltered* intensity is merely prolonged. This is due to the activation of a progressively greater number of motoneurons. The phenomenon is called recruitment and is figuratively spoken of as 'inertia' by Sherrington. **1975** A. VANDER et al. *Human Physiol.* (ed. 2) viii. 210 The tension of the muscle can be controlled by the recruitment of additional motor units.

b. The phenomenon shown by an ear which, while having a relatively high threshold for the perception of quiet sounds, perceives louder sounds with undiminished intensity, i.e. increases in objective intensity of sound result in abnormally great increases in perceived loudness.

1937 E. P. FOWLER in *Arch. Otolaryngol.* XXVI. 517 When there is no recruitment of loudness in the poorer ear, i.e., no change in the differences in hearing at the thresholds required to balance the loud sounds binaurally, it means that there is an impedance (conduction) lesion in the poorer ear. **1948** *Proc. R. Soc. Med.* XLI. 517 The deafness of the affected ear present at threshold disappears at higher intensities, and this in its simplest terms constitutes the phenomenon of Loudness Recruitment. **1960** *Jrnl. Speech & Hearing Res.* III. 15/1 The classical technique for the direct measurement of loudness recruitment in subjects with unilateral hearing loss is performed by having the subject equate the loudness of a pure tone on one ear with the loudness of a pure tone of identical frequency on the other ear. **1971** D. E. ROSE *Audiol. Assessment* x. 332 Recruitment came to be viewed..as the distinguishing feature of an ear with a cochlear lesion.

recruity. (Earlier example.)

1890 [see *ONCE *adv.* A. δ].

recrystallization. Add: **1.** (Earlier and further examples.) *spec.* in *Metallurgy,* a rearrangement of the crystalline structure of a metal at high temperatures which tends to reduce distortion of the lattice.

1793 *Trans. Soc. Improv. Med. & Chirurg. Knowledge* 30 (*heading*) A process for preparing pure emetic tartar by re-crystallization. **1925** *Jrnl. Iron & Steel Inst.* CXII. 474 A formula is derived for establishing the relation between the progress of recrystallisation and the degree of deformation in the hot state. **1937** *Discovery* Feb. 35/2 The firn consists of granular particles of ice..formed by recrystallisation of the snow. **1947** J. C. RICH *Materials & Methods Sculpture* iv. 67 The setting of plaster of Paris after it has been mixed with water is also referred to as a rehydration and occasionally as a recrystallization of the calcined gypsum back to its original hydrated rock form. **1973** B. J. HAZZARD tr. *Becker's Organicum* ii. 38 The most important method for purifying solids is recrystallization. **1976** M. C. NUTT *Metallurgy & Plastics for Engineers* v. 78 Recrystallization occurring at elevated temperatures is a process of the formation and growth of unrestrained grains, supplanting entirely the cold-worked structure.

2. Special Comb.: **recrystallization temperature** *Metallurgy,* the temperature at or above which recrystallization of the crystal lattice of a metal takes place (see quots.).

1927 *Carnegie Scholarship Mem.* XVI. 166 No systematic investigation has been made..into the relation between the degree of cold-work and the recrystallisation temperature. **1948** J. E. GARSIDE in H. W. Baker *Mod. Workshop Technology* I. vi. 135 More precisely, cold working is defined as that process of deformation which is conducted below the recrystallization temperature of the metal or alloy. **1961** G. E. DIETER *Mech. Metallurgy* v. 155 For practical considerations a recrystallization temperature can be defined as the temperature at which a given alloy in a highly cold-worked state completely recrystallizes in 1 hr. *Ibid.*, The recrystallization temperature decreases with increasing purity of the metal. **1976** M. C. NUTT *Metallurgy & Plastics for Engineers* v. 78 When a metal is heated, the internal force changes only slightly, but the movement of the atoms increases sharply. In time a temperature is reached at which movement of the atoms can start, and they can arrange themselves into lattices that are not distorted. This degree of heat is known as the recrystallization temperature.

recrystallize, *v.* Add: Also *intr.* (Further examples.)

1935 G. E. DOAN *Princ. Physical Metallurgy* iii. 103 Lead ..recrystallizes spontaneously at room temperature, even if only slightly deformed. **1946** *Nature* 5 Oct. 482/2 The hard rolled silver specimens when heated to about 900 °C. recrystallized very rapidly. **1956** *Ibid.* 3 Mar. 429/2 Tyrosine was recrystallized from hot water. **1963** D. W. & E. E. HUMPHRIES tr. *Termier's Erosion & Sedimentation* xvii. 338 Certain rocks are dissolved and recrystallized so readily under the effect of differential pressures, that they can flow as plastic substances toward zones where the pressure is lowest. **1971** I. G. GASS et al. *Understanding Earth* iii. 60/2 The mineral can recrystallize to different and denser crystalline structures.

Hence **recry·stallizable** *a.*, that may be crystallized again; **recrystallized** *ppl. a.* (further examples); **recry·stallizing** *ppl. a.*

1859 *Proc. R. Soc.* IX. 653 The gold-salt is a bright yellow crystalline precipitate, difficultly soluble in boiling water, and not recrystallizable without some alteration. **1908** [see *IDIOBLASTIC *a.*]. **1962** SIMPSON & RICHARDS *Junction Transistors* iii. 48 This recrystallized germanium forms a single crystal of the same orientation as the germanium disk and, except for the *p*-type impurity, is indistinguishable from it. **1976** COTTERILL & MOULD *Recrystallization & Grain Growth in Metals* iii. 40 The recrystallized grain size depends chiefly on the degree of deformation and to a lesser extent on the annealing temperature. *Ibid.* 54 'Recovery' will continue until the entire specimen has been consumed by the recrystallizing grains.

rect, *a.* Add: **d.** *fig.* Upright.

1890 E. JOHNSON *Rise Christendom* 102 A rect and good and great soul, what is this but God sojourning in the body of man?

Hence **re·ctly** *adv.*, directly. *rare*$^{-1}$.

1922 JOYCE *Ulysses* 208 Swiftly rectly creaking rectly rectly he was rectly gone.

rectal, *a.* Add: *rectal gland,* a gland that excretes into the rectum; *esp.* in cartilaginous fishes, a gland that excretes salt so as to maintain the osmotic balance.

1887 MARSHALL & HURST *Pract. Zool.* xi. 217 The rectal gland is a thick-walled tube, about three quarters of an inch long, lying in the body-cavity dorsal to the rectum. **1925** R. E. SNODGRASS *Anat. & Physiol. Honeybee* vi. 165 Nothing definite is known of the function of the rectal glands. **1974** D. & M. WEBSTER *Compar. Vertebr. Morphol.* xvii. 442 Excess salt is actively excreted by the rectal, or digitiform gland [of chondrichthyeans].

Hence **re·ctally** *adv.*, by way of the rectum.

1906 *Practitioner* Nov. 645 This serum was injected rectally. **1977** *Lancet* 16 Apr. 857/2 We have measured the effect of rectally administered cimetidine on acid secretion in the canine stomach.

rectangle, *sb.* Add: **1. a.** Also, something that has the shape of a rectangle.

1898 G. B. SHAW *Arms & Man* I. 8 For an instant the rectangle of snowy starlight flashes out. **1901** 'LINESMAN' *Words by Eyewitness* iii. 60 The indistinct rectangles of the companies shook themselves out into a single rank. **1925** F. SCOTT FITZGERALD *Great Gatsby* vii. 174 A small rectangle of light which I guessed was the pantry window. **1940** W. FAULKNER *Hamlet* III. i. 168 As if a rectangle of opaque glass had been set into nothing's self. **1965** A. LURIE *Nowhere City* (1977) ix. 103 The shop windows had been painted over in irregular rectangles of red, blue, green and white.

rectangle, *a.* (Later example.)

a **1796** BURNS *Caledonia* in *Works* (1800) IV. 356 Rectangle-triangle, the figure we'll chuse.

rectangular, *a.* **1. a.** (Later *Comb.* examples.)

1960 *Farmer & Stockbreeder* 8 Mar. (Suppl.) 10/3 Rectangular-shaped pods which should be gathered when 1 to 1½ in long. **1976** *Private Eye* 24 Dec. 8/1 They must be true, rectangular-type icebergs, without cracks or crevasses.

rectangularism (rektæ·ŋgiŭlăriz'm). *rare.* [f. RECTANGULAR *a.* + -ISM.] A tendency towards or preference for rectangular forms.

1954 *Archit. Rev.* CXVI. 88/2 But in Holland there was no convulsion change; *de Stijl* won common acceptance by compromise..with existing styles, as in the case of Dudok's romantic rectangularism.

‖ **recte** (re·kte), *adv.* [L., lit. 'in a straight line, rightly'.] **1.** Correctly: used to indicate that the word or phrase following it within a parenthesis is the correct version of that which immediately precedes the insertion.

1886 *Trans. Philol. Soc.* 621 Leg. *contini* (recte *cointinni*) gen. of *cointinn* s.f. 'strife, controversy'. **1934** *Times Lit. Suppl.* 3 May 325/2 'Tithreks Saga' (*recte* 'Thithriks Saga af Bern'). **1939** JOYCE *Finnegans Wake* (1964) III. 543 The villa of the Ostmanorum to Thorstan's, *recte* Thomars Sraid. **1979** *Trans. Philol. Soc.* 184 Kent translates the portion after my square brackets 'This indeed..(is) my activity (*recte* physical-dexterity).'

2. *Mus.* In phr. (*per*) *recte et retro* [med.L., in the right way and backwards], applied to the movement of a canon cancrizans (see *CANCRIZANS *a.*).

[**1801** T. BUSBY *Compl. Dict. Mus.*, *Recte*,..a word signifying forwards and particularly pertaining to the *Canon*.]

1836 *Penny Cycl.* VI. 243/1 The canon *Recte et Retro* has but one peculiarity, and pretends to only one merit, namely, that it may be sung either forwards or backwards. **1876** [see *CANCRIZANS *a.*]. **1909** R. Dunstan *Composer's Handbk.* x. 155 A Canon 'per Recte et Retro' is one that may be sung *forwards* and *backwards* at the same time, producing two parts in one. **1922** R. O. Morris *Contrapuntal Technique* 50 In each pair of voices the part of the lower is that of the upper begun at the end and sung backwards, i.e. a canon *per recte et retro.* **1954** *Grove's Dict. Mus.* (ed. 5) V. 79 Stainer wrote a hymn-tune 'per recte et retro' in 1898.

rectenna (rekte·nă). [f. *rect(ifying ant)enna.*] A unit combining a receiving aerial and a device for rectifying the current it produces.

1975 *Pop. Sci.* Sept. 66/2 Transmitting electric power from outer space to earth... The rectifying units could be coupled to the receiving antenna or built into it—a combination now called a rectenna. **1977** *Indian Express* 18 Aug. 6 A micro-wave beam is directed to rectenna on the ground. **1978** *Times* 8 Sept. 19/6 The ground antenna which will receive the microwave beam and rectify this energy to direct-current electricity—the name 'rectenna' has been coined—will consist of a grid of wires carried on insulated posts.

rectification. Add: **1. a.** Also *spec.* in Chinese communism, the correction of errors in ideology and practice within the communist party. Also *attrib.*, as *rectification campaign, drive, movement.*

1956 tr. *Sel. Wks. Mao Tse-Tung* IV. 111 In the rectification campaign of 1943 all bureaux..of the Central Committee of the Party, all regional and district Party Committees should..endeavour to gain experience. **1959** *New Statesman* 17 Jan. 64/3 We make sure that..any professor or student who needs rectification is encouraged to volunteer for three or four weeks of unskilled labour in the steel works. **1962** E. Snow *Red China Today* (1963) xlvii. 376 It was the opening shot of an official 'rectification' or *cheng-tung tso-feng* movement. **1967** tr. *Quotations from Chairman Mao Tsetung* (ed. 2) 4 As we used to say, the rectification movement is 'a widespread movement of Marxist education'. Rectification means the whole Party studying Marxism through criticism and self-criticism. **1971** J. J. Taylor in D. J. Dwyer *China Now* (1974) xxii. 425 The Cultural Revolution is to the international united front what the rectification drives within the CCP in 1941 and 1942 were to the anti-Japanese front in China: an effort to maintain purity and fervour in the revolutionary nucleus. **1977** *Time* 21 Mar. 22/3 Mao's.. willingness periodically to shake up the bureaucracy in 'rectification campaigns'.

c. *Photogrammetry.* The process of preparing a plan view from an aerial photograph taken at an oblique angle.

1920 M. N. MacLeod *Mapping from Air Photographs* II. iv. 54 The rectification, or plotting of photos by comparison with fixed points, is at best a roundabout method. **1921** *Geogr. Jrnl.* LVII. 141 The theory of the rectification of photographs that should have been taken vertically, but are really tilted several degrees in an unknown direction, involves propositions in the theory of perspective which are not readily accessible in convenient form. **1928** *Ibid.* LXXI. 589 Whether the tilt is to be eliminated by photographic 'rectification', or by transferring the map grid to the photograph in perspective,..it is first necessary to find the tilt and the height at the moment of exposure. **1944** P. G. McCurdy et al. *Man. Photogrammetry* ii. 54 Optical rectification is the process of projecting the image of a tilted photograph into a horizontal plane. **1968** *Times* 1 Nov. 6/8 A process known as rectification is already standard practice. This is an automatic method of giving correct positions in plan to elevated features such as hills.

4. The process or act of permitting an electric current to flow preferentially in one direction; *esp.* in *Electr.*, the conversion of an alternating current into a direct current; also in *Physiol.*, the action of nerve membranes in allowing electrical impulses to be conducted preferentially in one direction.

anomalous rectification (Physiol.), the phenomenon of permitting current to flow preferentially from low to high ionic concentrations.

1895 *Electrician* 9 Aug. 488/1 A commutator..to which current is led and from which it is taken, after rectification. **1905** *Proc. R. Soc.* LXXIV. 485 The rectification is less complete in proportion as the temperature of the carbon filament increases. **1922** *Encycl. Brit.* XXXII. 1027/2 The remainder of the plate voltage is created by the rectification by the valve of the speech currents induced in the secondary circuit. **1941** *Jrnl. Gen. Physiol.* XXIV. 562 The most convenient specification of the rectification characteristics of the membrane. **1949** A. L. Hodgkin et al. in *Arch. Sci. Physiol.* III. 139 There is a marked rectification but it evidently takes some time to develop... We therefore propose the use of the term 'delayed rectification' to describe this effect. **1962** *Jrnl. Physiol.* CLXIII. 61 A fall in the membrane conductance when the membrane current flows from the inside to the outside of the fibre, and rise in conductance when the current is in the opposite direction has been called anomalous rectification. **1965** *Math. in Biol. & Med.* (Med. Res. Council) vi. 258 In 1941, Cole and Curtis showed that, in the steady state, the membrane of squid nerve has a much lower resistance to outward (depolarizing) currents than to inward (hyperpolarizing) currents. By analogy with the behaviour of electrical rectifiers this phenomenon was called rectification and the term 'delayed rectification' was introduced—emphasizing the fact that the changes in resistance take an appreciable time (a few milliseconds) to occur. *Ibid.*, Rectification can occur in the absence of [ionic] concentration gradients.., and in skeletal muscle fibres..and in cardiac muscle fibres..rectification in the opposite direction to that predicted from simple changes in membrane ion concentration occurs. **1966** R. G. Kloeffler *Electron Tubes* x. 209 For the purpose of analysis of rectification by diodes, a clear concept may be obtained by assuming that both the device and the load are linear. **1970** J. Shepherd et al. *Higher Electr. Engin.* (ed. 2) xxv. 798 The semiconductor diode rectifier is now replacing the mercury-arc rectifier for polyphase rectification in all applications except those involving the highest voltages.

rectified, *ppl. a.* Add: **1. b.** *Photogrammetry.* Designating a plan or photograph which has been corrected for errors of perspective (cf. *RECTIFY *v.* 1 c).

1920 M. N. MacLeod *Mapping from Air Photographs* I. iv. 27 A 'rectified' print of the negative is obtained which is true to scale all over and can be traced on to the map. **1969** G. C. Dickinson *Maps & Air Photographs* xv. 245 All five or nine photographs are printed fused together into one image, the obliques being 'transferred' or rectified into vertical views before printing.

3. b. (Examples.)

1892 S. P. Thompson *Dynamo-Electric Machinery* (ed. 4) iii. 38 The currents are now 'rectified', or 'redressed', as our continental neighbours say, but are not continuous. *Ibid.* (*caption*) Curve of rectified or commuted alternating current. **1910** G. W. Pierce *Princ. Wireless Telegr.* xviii. 197 The rectified current obtained by applying the alternating voltage *V* could be read on the galvanometer. **1947** R. Lee *Electronic Transformers & Circuits* iii. 48 With large values of capacitance, the rectified voltage..increases to within a few per cent of the peak voltage. **1958** *New Scientist* 10 July 342/2 A wire 'tickled' a crystal of silicon, and when the alternating radio signal was applied to the combination the current would flow only in one direction: this 'rectified' current could then be used to work a Morse receiver. **1965** *Wireless World* July 335/1 The rectified current does not then cause potential changes in the source.

4. Of tulip flowers: having variegated colouring caused by a virus affecting the plant.

1659 T. Hanmer *Garden Bk.* (1933) 21 When they [*sc.* the colours of tulips] streame away, as they doe ever wholly in flowers perfected, or rectified (as the tearme is) the leaves retaine not the least blew or yellow in them. **1850** *Beck's Florist* 23 Some say, that as they broke or became rectified, another number was given them. **1881** *Encycl. Brit.* XII. 259/2 The breeder bulbs and their offsets may grow on for years producing only self-coloured flowers, but after a time.. some of the progeny 'break', that is, produce flowers with the variegation which is so much prized. The flower is then said to be 'rectified'. **1911** [see *REMBRANDT]. **1929** A. D. Hall *Bk. Tulip* v. 99 This change [in colouring] is called 'breaking', the flower is termed 'broken' or 'rectified', while the original form is known as a 'breeder'. **1948** [see *REMBRANDT].

rectifier. Add: **1. b.** *Photogrammetry.* A device for preparing, by optical or other means, a plan view from an oblique aerial photograph.

1921 *Geogr. Jrnl.* LVII. 141 The construction of the photographic 'rectifier'..embodies some curious properties of the lens with a flat field. **1932** McCaw & Cazalet tr. *O. von Gruber's Photogrammetry* xi. 277 If a photograph is projected on a plane (map plane) oriented in a definite manner such that the projection also indicates a definite scale, it is customary to describe the process as rectification and the apparatus therefore as a rectifying camera or simply a Rectifier. **1962** *Photogrammetric Record* IV. 84 The great increase in setting accuracy and definition available in the SEG V (and other modern rectifiers). **1964** *Exhib. Guide 10th Internat. Congr. Photogrammetry* 76 Wild E4 Rectifier-enlarger... Rectification elements: Inclination of table in *x* and *y* directions or across the diagonals.

2. b. Substitute for def.: A device or substance which permits an electric current to flow preferentially in one direction; *esp.* in *Electr.*, a device for converting an alternating current into a direct current; also applied in *Physiol.* to a nerve membrane which conducts electrical impulses preferentially in one direction. (Earlier and further examples.)

1895 *Electrician* 9 Aug. 488/1 An efficiency of 96 per cent. is claimed for the rectifier. **1911** *Encycl. Brit.* XXVII. 835/1 A common type of rectifier is another tube containing gas at a low pressure. **1926** R. W. Hutchinson *Wireless* 119 Fig. 96 shows a method of using a crystal as a detector or rectifier. **1941** *Proc. Soc. Exper. Biol. & Med.* XLVIII. 293 In a nerve fiber membrane, current may pass more easily in one direction than in the other,..the nerve fiber membrane behaves as a rectifier rather than a simple resistance. **1955** *Amer. Jrnl. Physiol.* CLXXXIII. 671/1 (*heading*) Rectifier properties of Purkinje fibers. **1958** *Times* 11 Feb. 15/2 Thirty years ago we started with the copper oxide rectifier, and 10 years later we introduced the Westalite selenium rectifier. Last year we added the germanium-type rectifier to our range. **1961** [see *INVERTER 2 a]. **1970** J. Shepherd et al. *Higher Electr. Engin.* (ed. 2) xxv. 795 In its single-phase form the mercury-arc rectifier consists of a graphite or carbon-coated iron anode and a mercury-pool cathode enclosed in an envelope from which all air has been removed.

4. rectifier (photo-)cell, rectifier photo-electric cell, a photovoltaic cell.

1933 *Sci. Proc. R. Dublin Soc.* XX. 538 The selenium rectifier cell of Bergmann. **1935** *Discovery* July 214/2 The so-called rectifier cell has been developed, with its great convenience of being able to dispense with batteries. **1936** [see *light-sensitive* s.v. *LIGHT *sb.* 15]. **1952** *Jrnl. Sci. Instrum.* XXIX. 137 Correcting the deviation from the theoretical value of the response of selenium rectifier photo-cells to obliquely incident light.

rectify, *v.* Add: **1. c.** *Photogrammetry.* To correct errors of perspective in (an oblique aerial photograph, or a position derived from one) in order to obtain a plan view.

1919 *Geogr. Jrnl.* LIII. 390 This method..is..not so satisfactory as our method of rectifying the print in a camera. **1928** *Ibid.* LXXI. 591 The photographed positions of two control points are rectified. **1944** P. G. McCurdy et al. *Man. Photogrammetry* x. 440 (*heading*) Control and computation to rectify the individual photographs. **1979** *Sci. Amer.* Apr. 28/3 Essentially an orthophoto is an aerial photograph which has been rectified and on which contour lines, spot heights, and other information are superimposed.

7. c. Substitute for def.: To permit (an electric current) to flow preferentially in one direction; *esp.* in *Electr.*, to convert (an alternating current) into a direct current. (Earlier and further examples.)

1892 S. P. Thompson *Dynamo-Electric Machinery* (ed. 4) xxiii. 652 A commutator, which rectified the alternations. **1895** *Electrician* 9 Aug. 488/1 The town supply of current at a pressure of 3,000 volts is transformed down to 65 volts and rectified. **1922** *Encycl. Brit.* XXXII. 1024/2 It [*sc.* the valve] can..be used to separate out the two constituents of a high frequency alternating current and 'rectify' them into a direct current. **1962** *Jrnl. Physiol.* CLXIII. 111 The 2–3 membrane was assumed to be permeable only to potassium and to rectify anomalously: the extent of this rectification is illustrated. **1962** A. Lytel *Industr. Electronics* ii. 38 These rectifiers are two-element tubes and are used in power supplies to rectify or convert alternating current to direct current. **1964** B. V. Rollin *Introd. Electronics* v. 65 To rectify a signal by mixing it with a reference voltage of the same frequency and observing the resulting d.c. output.

rectifying, *vbl. sb.* (Later examples.)

1845 G. Dodd *British Manufactures* V. iii. 63 This distillation is the rectifying of the spirit, by which a certain portion of essential oil is removed from it. **1928** *Geogr. Jrnl.* LXXII. 383 When we come to what should be the most interesting chapter on map-plotting, contouring, and rectifying, we find it composed of chunks taken mostly from German propagandist pamphlets. **1960** *Nature* 5 Nov. 495/1 (*heading*) Rectifying properties of heart muscle. **1962** D. F. Shaw *Introd. to Electronics* xii. 246 The rectifying property of a semi-conductor diode is a consequence of the asymmetrical conduction across the contact between a metal and a semi-conductor.

rectifying, *ppl. a.* Add: **1.** (Further examples.)

1892 S. P. Thompson *Dynamo-Electric Machinery* (ed. 4) xxiii. 659 A rectifying commutator. **1906** *Proc. Physical Soc.* XX. 182 Wehnelt..proposed to employ vacuum-tubes with one electrode covered with..oxides and heated, as rectifying valves for alternating currents. **1932** *Geogr. Jrnl.* LXXX. 463 The Panorama-camera..consists of nine lenses working through prisms, and, in conjunction with a special rectifying printing apparatus, produces the equivalent of a photograph taken with a very wide-angled lens. **1944** P. G. McCurdy et al. *Man. Photogrammetry* ii. 54 Rectifying apparatus is often designed so that a change in scale and tilt removal can be made simultaneously. **1947** R. Lee *Electronic Transformers & Circuits* iv. 86 This circuit requires more rectifying tubes.

2. *rectifying column*, a distillation column in which the distillate is subjected to successive stages of purification by continually condensing and redistilling the vapour.

1891 S. P. Sadtler *Handbk. Industr. Org. Chem.* vi. 216 An improved Savalle rectifying column as used generally in French and Belgian distilleries. **1923** W. H. Walker et al. *Princ. Chem. Engin.* xvii. 557 An apparatus in which this direct interchange of heat and consequent condensation and evaporation can take place is called a rectifying column. **1946** *Nature* 20 July 105/1 The work..included the design and construction of..a liquid methane rectifying-column. **1955** Coulson & Richardson *Chem. Engin.* II. xviii. 611 A column apparatus may be used for batch or continuous operation. In the former case the column is mounted on a large boiler or still which holds the charge, and the column is said to be a rectifying column.

rection. Delete *rare* and add later examples.

1953 [see *intraverbal* s.v. *INTRA-[1]]. **1968** J. Lyons *Introd. Theoret. Linguistics* vi. 241 Concord..is usually distinguished from *government* (or 'rection', in the usage of some authors).

Hence **re·ctional** *a.*

1938 *Trans. Philol. Soc.* 115 Where..a given declension implies a given gender, the inflexion may be said to express a rectional category in addition to the categories of case and number. **1949** *Archivum Linguisticum* I. II. 167 Notionally noun compounds are either attributive or rectional (governing).

rectitudinous, *a.* Add: (Later examples.) Also as *sb.*

1906 F. S. Oliver *Alexander Hamilton* v. ii. 381 The rectitudinous inquisition that is enjoyed under the freedom of the press. **1966** 'W. Cooper' *Mem. New Man* I. ii. 27 We were both wearing soberly rectitudinous dark clothes. **1978** *N.Y. Rev. Bks.* 18 May 23/1 It is not so much an appetite for hypocrisy as for the sententious and rectitudinous—for 'expressin' right'—that is a vital impulse in the American folk character.

‖ **rectius** (re·ktiŭs), *adv.* [L., compar. of *RECTE *adv.*] More correctly: used similarly to *RECTE *adv.* 1.

1932 *N. & Q.* 6 Feb. 103/1 'Gallinatia': (*rectius* 'Galimatia(s)')... The more correct spelling is Galimatia(s). **1965** J. S. Roskell *Commons & their Speakers* i. 12 A London chronicle says that he was..replaced by William (*rectius* John) Doreward. **1980** *Daily Tel.* 13 Aug. 14, I am by no means sure that Mr Anthony Powell should be allowed to rebuke the editors..for 'oddly' referring to Garter King at Arms (*rectius*, Garter King of Arms).

recto, *sb.* and *adv.* Add: **A.** *sb.* Also in *Palæography*, the front of a leaf of manuscript.

1849 D. Rock *Ch. of Fathers* I. I. iii. 280 The verses, in a very old hand, at the recto of fol. 258. **1964** F. Bowers *Bibliogr. & Textual Crit.* III. vi. 84 A textual critic can find the most desirable combination of recto and verso settings. **1978** *Bodl. Libr. Record* IX. 324 The writing exercises..are confined to the rectos of the pages.

recto-. Add: Also more widely in *Surg.* with the sense 'of or pertaining to the rectum', as **re·ctopexy** [*-pexy], the fixation of a prolapsed rectum; **re·ctoscope** [-scope], an instrument for use in rectoscopy; **recto·scopy,** visual examination of the rectum.

a **1898** *Syd. Soc. Lex.*, Rectopexy. **1902** J. P. Tuttle *Treat. Dis. Anus* xvii. 691 (*caption*) Rectopexy for procidentia recti—the incision. **1977** *Lancet* 22 Jan. 170/2 On 10 patients a transabdominal rectopexy was performed, using a modified Ripstein procedure. **1890** Billings *Med. Dict.* 442/2 *Ractoscopo*, speculum for the rectum. **1906** F. L. Mummery *Sigmoidoscope* i. 7 There are several patterns of pneumatic sigmoidoscope or rectoscope now in use. **1977** *Time* 17 Jan. 51/1 The surgeon cuts directly through the urethra with a marvellous combination of scalpel and fibre-optics looking glass called a rectoscope. *a* **1898** *Syd. Soc. Lex.*, Rectoscopy. **1909** *Index-Catal. Library Surgeon-General's Office, U.S. Army* XIV. 343/1 Rectoscopy. *See* Rectum (Exploration of). **1967** N. S. Kapany *Fiber Optics* vii. 171 The application of flexible fiberscopes not only to gastroscopy, but also to..rectoscopy.

rector. Add: **3. a.** Now also in the Church of England, the leader of a team ministry. In the Roman Catholic Church, a parish priest.

1923 S. Kaye-Smith *End of House of Alard* II. 117 They came to the cottage where the Rector lived, instead of in the twenty-five roomed Rectory. **1927** *Catholic Times* 11 Feb. 21/2 In 1901 he became rector of St. Joseph's, Birkenhead. **1972** *Daily Tel.* 7 Aug. 10/5 Only the leader of the team, usually called 'Rector', is the beneficed freehold incumbent. **1977** Macmorran & Elphinstone *Handbk. for Churchwardens* (new ed.) vii. 66 In the context of a team ministry.. the incumbent of the benefice or benefices to which a team ministry extends is always styled 'rector'... The other members of the ministry are styled 'vicars'.

4. a. (Later examples.)

Now used more widely in Eng. to designate the principal of a higher educational institution, as the Royal College of Art, the Imperial College of Science and Technology, Liverpool Polytechnic, etc.

1916 Joyce *Portrait of Artist* (1969) i. 55 All the fellows would make fun and talk about young Dedalus going up to the rector to tell on the prefect of studies. **1950** *Chambers's Encycl.* XIII. 658/2 [Sir H. T. Tizard] was..rector of the Imperial College of Science and Technology 1929–42. **1973** *Stornoway Gaz.* 3 Mar. 1/4 The Nicolson [School] has had its share of brilliant rectors, teachers and pupils.

rectoral, *a.* Delete '(Said only of God.)' and add further examples.

1754 *Session Papers, Petition T. Tullidelph* (Court of Session, Scotland) 5 Mar. 4 The University Meeting requested the Rector to hold a Rectoral Court against the next Day [at St. Andrews]. **1919** A. Gordon *Cheshire Classis* 121 Some of the above provisions cannot fail to remind us of Richard Baxter's 'rectoral' theory of the ministerial office.

rectorial, *a.* Add: **B.** *sb. Sc.* A rectorial election.

1899 *Student* (Edin. Univ.) 2 Nov. 41 One student writes protesting against the enormities of the Rectorial. **1920** *Glasgow Herald* 27 Nov. 6 The Scottish Universities, to whose noisy 'Rectorials' Viscount Bryce made reference. **1923** *Ibid.* 26 July 6 St David's Day..is March 1, the day of the Rectorial. *Ibid.*, The torchlight procession on the night of the Rectorial. **1968** *Guardian* 30 Oct. 16/4 Edinburgh has never known a rectorial like this.

rectorite (re·ktŏrəit). *Min.* [See quot. 1891 and -ite[1].] An aluminosilicate of sodium that is a clay mineral of the montmorillonite group and occurs as large, soft white leaves or plates.

1891 Brackett & Williams in *Amer. Jrnl. Sci.* CXLII. 16 The second hydrous silicate of alumina..is found in the Blue Mountain mining district in Marble Township, Garland county [Arkansas]... We propose the name Rectorite for this,..in honor of Hon. E. W. Rector, of Hot Springs, Ark., who originated and has so unceasingly supported..the bills providing for the Geological Survey of Arkansas. **1950** *Amer. Mineralogist* XXXV. 590 The structural scheme of rectorite consists of contiguous pairs of pyrophyllite-like units separated by pairs of layers of water molecules. An equally apt description would be the alternation of one pyrophyllite unit with one vermiculite unit. **1970** *Clays & Clay Minerals* XVIII. 239 Pyrophyllite is widespread in pelitic rocks of the Manning Canyon Shale in north central Utah, and the association of this mineral with other clay minerals, especially rectorite, is related to the origin. The regular mixed-layer clay mineral rectorite seems to form as a result of the alteration of muscovite–paragonite during late stages of diagenesis... Pyrophyllite subsequently formed from the alteration of rectorite during advancing metamorphism.

rectory. **1.** For † *Obs. rare*—[1] read '*Obs.* exc. *Hist.*' and add later example.

1919 J. E. H. Thomson *Mem. T. Dunlop* ii. 19 All that remained of the Rectory or Pedagogy, that in pre-Reformation days represented the later University.

rectosigmoid (rektosi·gmoid), *sb.* and *a.* *Med.* [f. Recto- + Sigmoid.] **A.** *sb.* The region of the junction of the rectum and the sigmoid. **B.** *adj.* Of, pertaining to, or being this region.

1912 *Trans. Amer. Surg. Assoc.* XIII. 159 Carcinoma of the rectum and rectosigmoid remains a local condition until a late stage. **1913** *Jrnl. Amer. Med. Assoc.* 18 Oct. 1489/1 (*heading*) Villous polypus of recto-sigmoid juncture removed by ligation and clamp. **1961** *Lancet* 16 Sept. 624/2 Barium-enema showed a narrow rectosigmoid, with the calibre increasing near the level of the iliac crest. **1962** *Ibid.* 5 May 951/2 Neoplasm of the rectosigmoid region and sigmoid colon. **1977** *Proc. R. Soc. Med.* LXX. 273/1 Anterior resection of the rectum..for..adenocarcinoma of the recto-sigmoid.

Also **re:cto-sigmoi·dal** *a.*

1902 J. P. Tuttle *Treat. Dis. Anus* xvii. 678 Any neoplasm of the sigmoid or upper portion of the rectum may induce a gradual descent until the growth reaches a resting-place in the ampulla of the rectum... Thus, unusual contracture at the recto-sigmoidal juncture..will cause the arrest of the faecal masses. **1914** *Brit. Jrnl. Surg.* I. 683 (*caption*) Small but well-marked recto-sigmoidal anastomosis.

rectress. Add: **3.** = Rectoress 2. *rare.*

1906 *Month* July 66 The rector and rectress, and their two delicate-looking, perfectly-dressed daughters.

‖ **rectus** (re·ktŏs). [L., = straight, right.] **1.** *Mus.* In a fugal composition, the version of a theme performed in the basic or original, as opposed to the reversed or inverted, order. *rectus et inversus* [L., 'inverted'] = *recte et retro* s.v. *recte *adv.* 2.

1931 D. F. Tovey *Compan. to 'Art of Fugue'* 31 The next two fugues are *tours de force*, being compositions that can be inverted note for note from beginning to end. For purposes of comparison Bach writes his *Inversus* under his *Rectus.* **1938** *Oxf. Compan. Mus.* 134/2 The Canon Cancrizans.. other names for it are Canon Recte et Retro or Rectus et Inversus. **1959** *Listener* 30 July 189/3 The English Rite puts the *Gloria* at the end. Rubbra starts it as an elaborate double fugue *rectus et inversus.* **1960** *Times* 30 Nov. 17/3 Fugue, *rectus et inversus*, canon, ostinato..shall these dry bones live? Britten..uses them all. **1962** *Listener* 27 Dec. 1109/2 The rectus versions of the 'mirror' fugues XII and XIII.

2. *Law.* Phr. *rectus in curia* [lit. 'right in court'], innocent, acquitted, set right in point of law.

[*a* **1135** in B. Thorpe *Anc. Laws & Inst. Eng.* (1840) I. 240 Omni domino licet submonire hominem suum, ut ei sit ad rectum in curia sua.] *a* **1577** T. Smith *De Republica Anglorum* (1583) II. iii. 46 Yet with a clause, *modo stet rectus in curia*, that is to say, that no man obiect against the offendor. **1645** J. Howell *Lett.* III. vii. 59 He is now come to be again *rectus in curia*, absolutely acquitted and restor'd to all things. *a* **1706** Evelyn *Diary* an. 1680 (1955) IV. 229 Saturday came other Witnesses of the Commons.. who tooke off all the former days objections, & set the Kings Witnesses *recti in Curia.* **1816** *Edin. Rev.* XXVII. 122 He must come *rectus in curia*, and swear to the falsehood of the libel. **1866** J. G. Murphy *Crit. Comm. Exodus* 310 We meet with the propitiation or atoning sacrifice, by which they become *recti in curia*, right in point of law. **1934** E. Pound *Eleven New Cantos* xxxii. 7, I pray you place me rectus in curia in this business with the Emperor.

recueillement. Delete *rare* and add later examples.

1897 G. du Maurier *Martian* I. 35 The deep stillness and studious *recueillement* that brood over the scene. **1903** E. Wharton *Sanctuary* II. v. 150 The silence, the *recueillement*, about her. **1931** R. Fry in W. Rose *Outl. Mod. Knowledge* 936 It succeeds in arousing a mood of *recueillement* not unlike that which emanates from some of Giorgione's compositions. **1977** *Times Lit. Suppl.* 20 May 610/4 Every writer required his *recueillement* (a word that appears several times in his letters), his time of in-gathering and collecting.

‖ **reculer pour mieux sauter** (rəküle pur myö sote), *phr.* [Fr., lit. 'to draw back in order to leap better'.] Making use of a withdrawal or setback in such a way as to advance or succeed all the more.

[*c* **1500** J. D'Arras *Mesuline* (1895) xx. 113 Alwayes wyse men goo abacke for to lepe the ferther.] **1820** Lady Granville *Let.* 30 Aug. (1894) I. 170 'Yes,' he said, 'with people in general it is *reculer pour mieux sauter*, with her *sauter pour mieux reculer*.' **1907** G. B. Shaw *Let.* 21 Mar. (1972) II. 675 The sales that are influenced by my name go up steadily from year to year; and all the apparent slumps are cases of 'reculer pour mieux sauter'. **1920** D. H. Lawrence *Women in Love* i. 6, I think my coming back home was just *reculer pour mieux sauter*. **1951** R. F. Harrod *Life J. M. Keynes* x. 431 This was, in his mind, a case of *reculer pour mieux sauter.* **1972** *Times* 30 May (Hongkong Suppl.) p. v/4 The hesitation in currency circulation in 1967–1968 following the fall in deposits was a matter of *reculer pour mieux sauter*: growth..took off again.

recultivation. (Earlier example.)

1850 *Proc. Philol. Soc.* IV. 208 It is now just about a hundred years ago that Klopstock paved the way to the recultivation of German.

recumb, *v.* For † *Obs.* read *rare* and add later examples.

1906 M. Dods *Later Lett.* (1911) 213 Will you excuse pencil, as I am in a run down condition and my doctor bids me 'recumb' as much as I can. **1925** O. W. Holmes in *Holmes–Laski Lett.* (1953) I. 693 Now I shall recumb with a hot bottle at my back.

recumbent, *a.* (and *sb.*) Add: **A.** *adj.* **1. b.** (Later examples.) *recumbent stone circle*, in *Archæol.*, a stone circle characterized by the presence of one large stone lying flat flanked by two tall uprights.

1933 V. G. Childe in *Proc. Soc. Antiquaries Scotland* LXVII. 51 Recumbent Stone Circles may have been erected in late Hallstatt times. **1943** J. & C. Hawkes *Prehist. Britain* iii. 59 Their adaptation of a passage-grave tradition in the remarkable 'Recumbent Stone' circles of north-east Scotland. **1962** Gordon & Lavoipierre *Entomol. for Students of Med.* xx. 134 Like the head and thorax the abdomen is covered with long hairs; on the dorsal aspect of the abdomen the hairs may either lie flat (a condition described as recumbent) or they may be raised. **1963** *Field Archaeol.* (Ordnance Survey) (ed. 4) 40 There is an eccentric type found in North-east Scotland... This is the 'Recumbent' stone circle which has more than seventy examples in this area.

3. Geol. *recumbent fold*, a fold whose axial plane is nearly horizontal; so *recumbent anticline, syncline.*

1909 *Summ. Progr. Geol. Surv. 1908* 52 A discrepancy between the two limbs of the recumbent fold. **1910** *Q. Jrnl. Geol. Soc.* LXVI. 617 The sliding is not confined to the lower limbs of recumbent anticlines. *Ibid.*, The schists of the Highlands of Scotland are disposed in a succession of recumbent folds of enormous amplitude. **1922** [see *nappe 2]. **1937** [see *fan *sb.*[1] 10 f]. **1962** Read & Watson *Introd. Geol.* I. viii. 451 A recumbent anticline..faces laterally and a recumbent anticline in which the hinge-region sags or droops faces downwards. **1964** W. C. Putnam *Geol.* vi. 131/1 In an extreme case, the whole fold may be forced over on its side so that its axial plane..is horizontal, or very nearly so... Such a structure is called a recumbent fold. **1969** H. Robinson *Morphology & Landscape* iii. 34 Sometimes the pressure exerted upon a recumbent fold is sufficiently great to cause it to be torn from its roots and to be thrust forward.

recuperate, *v.* Add: Also with pronunc. (rĭkū·pĕrēɪt). **1. a.** Delete † *Obs.* and add later examples.

1896 J. A. H. Murray *Let.* 22 Apr. in K. M. E. Murray *Caught in Web of Words* (1977) xiv. 279 We reached the summit however, & recuperated our energies. **1977** *Guardian Weekly* 7 Aug. 11/5 No plant in the world has shown that it can recuperate plutonium on an industrial scale from oxide-bearing fuel.

b. (Later example.)

1924 *Proc. Classical Assoc.* 13 Both these Associations have fully recuperated any loss which they had made during the war.

Hence **recu·perating** *vbl. sb.* and *ppl. a.*

1894 'R. Andom' *We Three & Troddles* xix. 174 We each mentioned our favoured recuperating localities. **1979** B. Parvin *Deadly Dyke* xxiv. 128 Recuperating firemen stood watching the thick palls of smoke.

recuperation. Add: **3.** *Gunnery.* The action of a recuperator (sense *4).

1922 *Encycl. Brit.* XXXI. 1185/2 As the buffer flow-space is greatest at the termination of recuperation, some check is required to prevent a metal-to-metal blow. *Ibid.* 1186/1 Recuperation may be by means of steel springs or compressed air.

recuperative, *a.* (and *sb.*) Add: **A.** *adj.* **5.** Of, pertaining to, or being a recuperator (sense 2), or an air heater using the same principle.

1906 A. L. J. Queneau tr. *Damour's Industr. Furnaces* x. 142 The volume..of the recuperative chambers should be calculated to suit the exchange of the calories to be effected, according to the specific heats of the recuperating refractory bricks. **1923** *Iron Age* CXI. 1782 The recuperative installation is adopted where blast furnace or coke oven gas is available. **1930** *Engineering* 31 Jan. 155/2 Two methods of transferring heat from a hot gas to a cold one were in use, and might be distinguished as belonging, respectively, to the recuperative and to the regenerative type. In the recuperative type, the cool and the hot gases were separated by a conducting wall through which the transfer of heat took place. **1938** *Jrnl. Iron & Steel Inst.* CXXXVIII. 327P Of the 848 pit holes surveyed,..6·2 % are of the one-way-fired recuperative type, 2·1 % are of the bottom-fired recuperative type. **1962** [see *recuperator 2]. **1971** B. Scharf *Engin. & its Language* xiv. 204 Air heaters are classified as recuperative or regenerative, and the recuperative heaters are further subdivided into tubular or plate-type heaters.

recuperator. Add: **2.** (Further examples.) Now restricted to a form of heat exchanger in which hot waste gases, being conducted continuously along a system of flues, impart heat to incoming air or gaseous fuel flowing in the opposite direction in parallel flues by conduction through the dividing walls. Cf. Regenerator 2.

1906 A. L. J. Queneau tr. *Damour's Industr. Furnaces* ii. 47 Two systems are still in practice—the Siemens recuperator with inversion, and recuperation without inversion, by parallel counter currents. **1911** F. W. Harbord *Metallurgy of Steel* II. xxi. 541 Gorman's furnace..formed a further step in advance, as the waste gases on their way to the chimney passed around horizontal fireclay pipes or 'recuperators'. **1938** H. Etherington *Mod. Furnace Technol.*

vii. 314 In a recuperator, the hot waste gases and the cold air are led through separate channels in close contact.. Regenerators operate on a different principle. **1953** D. J. O. BRANDT *Manuf. Iron & Steel* xxviii. 203 Soaking pits are of two kinds, regenerative pits, which are fired in two directions, being reversed at intervals, and recuperative which are fired in one direction only, the heat in the outgoing gases being as far as possible transferred to the incoming air and fuel in a recuperator. **1962** G. R. BASHFORTH *Manuf. Iron & Steel* IV. ii. 39 In the recuperative type of soaking pit, the flow of fuel and air is maintained in one direction... The waste products of combustion pass through a recuperative chamber... These recuperators may either be of the refractory or metallic type.

3. That which restores one's health or spirits.

1905 *Smart Set* 17 Sept. 24 A/2 (Advt.), A day trip on these steamers is calculated to brace the entire system, and the jaded business man will find them a splendid recuperator.

4. *Gunnery.* (See quot. 1922.)

1918 E. S. FARROW *Dict. Mil. Terms* 498 *Recuperator gauge,* in artillery, a gauge for verifying the charge of the recuperator, in liquid and in compressed gas. **1922** *Encycl. Brit.* XXXI. 1184/1 The recuperator returns the gun to the firing position after it has come to rest under the action of the recoil resistance. **1925** *Jrnl. R. Artillery* LII. 38 The recuperator question was taken in hand early on in the war,a nd by the end of 1918 all springs had been replaced by air recuperators. **1962** *Ordnance Techn. Terminol.* (U.S. Army Ordnance School) (AD 660 112) 86/1 *Counterrecoil mechanism,* a hydraulic, pneumatic, or mechanical system that returns a gun into battery, or firing position, after recoil; a recuperator.

Hence **recu:perato·rial** *a.*

1976 J. M. KELLY *Stud. in Civil Judicature of Roman Republic* ii. 47 If then we discard the dominant theory, how are we to explain the special recuperatorial jurisdiction otherwise?

recurb (rĭkɔ̄·ɹb). *rare*⁻¹. [f. RE- + CURB *sb.*: cf. F. *recourber* vb., L. *recurvāre* RECURVE *v.*] The curved shape produced at the repeated climax of systematic oscillation.

1876 G. M. HOPKINS *Wreck of Deutschland* xxxii, in *Poems* (1967) 62 The recurb and the recovery of the gulf's side, The girth of it and the wharf of it and the wall.

recurrable (rĭkɔ̄·răb'l), *a.* [f. RECUR *v.* + -ABLE.] That can recur.

1935 E. POUND *Let.* 17 Apr. (1971) 273, I don't know that I have been clear enough re *recurrable* epithets—either to be simple and natural so that repeat don't worry one, or else strange and part of definite intended stylization.

recurrence. Add: **6.** *attrib.* and *Comb.*, as *recurrence frequency, interval*; **recurrence formula, relation** *Math.*, an expression which defines the general member of a series in terms of the preceding members; **recurrence surface** [tr. Sw. *rekurrensyta* (E. Granlund 1932, in *Sveriges Geologiska Undersökn.* Ser. C. No. 373. viii. 73)], a horizon in a peat bog between highly decomposed and slightly decomposed peat, indicating the commencement of a period of active peat growth; **recurrence time** *Math.*, the time between two successive occasions when a Markov process enters any given state.

1902 E. T. WHITTAKER *Course Mod. Analysis* x. 210 The recurrence-formulae. We proceed to establish a group of formulae which connect Legendre functions of different orders. **1925** *Biometrika* XVII. 165 (*heading*) Recurrence formulae for the moments of the point binomial. **1965** *Wireless World* Sept. 431/1 It remains now to provide a suitable pulse generator of variable recurrence frequency to fire the thyristor. **1965** R. G. KAZMANN *Mod. Hydrol.* iv. 76 Statistical studies made to determine the recurrence interval of this design-flood resulted in figures ranging from 1000 to 90,000 years. **1933** *Biometrika* XXV. 420 (*heading*) On a recurrence relation connected with..double Bessel functions. **1961** M. M. NICOLSON *Fund. & Tech. Math. for Scientists* xvi. 369 A set of formulae relating Legendre polynomials of different orders n; such relations are called recurrence relations. **1979** PAGE & WILSON *Introd. Computational Combinatorics* ii. 5 If such a recurrence relation can be produced, it can usually be made the basis of an algorithm for computing values of the desired function. [**1934** *Irish Naturalists' Jrnl.* V. 134 To look for Granlund's 'rekurrenz-surfaces'.] **1938** *New Phytologist* XXXVII. 452 Granlund suggests that such layers are due to slowing up of bog growth by unfavourable conditions, and to the level marking the sudden renewal of growth he gives the name 'Rekurrenzflache [*sic*]', which has been translated by Jessen as Recurrence-surface. **1956** H. GODWIN *Hist. Brit. Flora* iii. 34/2 In his work on the raised bogs of Scania, Nilsson..has been able to identify no fewer than nine recurrence surfaces between *c.* 3500 B.C. and the present day. **1975** J. G. EVANS *Environment Early Man Brit. Isles* iv. 77 Resumption of peat growth, leading to the formation of 'recurrence surfaces', takes place when conditions of high rainfall return. [**1943** *Rev. Mod. Physics* XV. 54/2 (*heading*) The average time of recurrence of a state of fluctuation in which the molecular concentration in a sphere of air of radius a will differ from the average value by 1 percent.] **1949** *Trans. Amer. Math. Soc.* LXVII. 99 A new method of finding the second moment of the recurrence times of finite or infinite Markov chains. **1971** R. A. HOWARD *Dynamic Probabilistic Syst.* I. v. 287 θ_{ii} is the number of transitions between a departure from state i and the first return to i; it is called the first passage time from state i to state i, or the recurrence time of state i.

recurrency. 2. For † *Obs.* read *rare* and add later example.

1928 H. POUTSMA *Gram. Late Mod. Eng.* (ed. 2) I. I. i. 83 The principal verbs used to express recurrency, i.e. the iterative aspect of an action..are *can, to use* and *will.*

recurrent, *a.* and *sb.* Add: **A.** *adj.* **3. d.** Math. *recurrent relation* = **recurrence relation.*

1896 *Phil. Trans. R. Soc.* A. CLXXXVII. 522 These recurrent relations between the functions for different values of n hold for general complex values of m and n. **1931** E. W. HOBSON *Theory Spherical & Ellipsoidal Harmonics* ii. 67 Recurrent relations..between the functions $Q_n(\mu)$ for different values of n.

recurring, *ppl. a.* and *vbl. sb.* The stressed syllable now usually has the same sound as the infinitive, not that of *recurrent.*

recurringly (rĭkɔ̄·riŋli), *adv.* [f. RECURRING *ppl. a.* + -LY².] In a recurring manner; repeatedly.

1915 'A. HOPE' *Young Man's Year* xxix. 272 It pointedly and recurringly reminded him that there were more women than one in the world. **1923** *Daily Mail* 10 Aug. 4/2 A bogus manager..is 'a manager who engages artists and recurringly fails to pay their salaries'.

recursion. Restrict 'Now *rare* or *Obs.*' to sense in Dict. and add: **2. a.** The application or use of a recursive procedure or definition; *primitive recursion* [tr. G. *primitive rekursion* (R. Péter 1934, in *Math. Ann.* CX. 613)], definition of a function of natural numbers by induction on a single argument or (equivalently) by simple recursion formulæ; *recursion formula,* an equation relating the value of a function for a given value of its argument (or arguments) to its values for other values of the argument(s).

[**1871** *Math. Annalen* IV. 113 Man hat also für die Funktion $R^{m,\nu}$ folgende Recursionsformel: $2(\nu-1)/z \cdot R^{m,\nu} = R^{m+1,\nu-1} + R^{m-1,\nu+1}$.] **1930** *Proc. London Math. Soc.* XXX. 267 For other values of r we define $f(r, n, k)$ by recursion formulae. **1933** *Ann. Math.* XXXIV. 863 The recursion formulas, $m+1 = S(m)$, and $m+(k+1) = S(m+k)$. **1934, 1974** [see *RECURSIVE *a.* 2 a]. **1943** *Trans. Amer. Math. Soc.* LIII. 42 Schema (I) introduces the successor function,..and Schema (V) the schema of primitive recursion. **1961** *Commun. Assoc. Computing Machinery* IV. 65/1 The growing extent and direction of application of recursion in programming research. **1964** E. BACH *Introd. Transformational Gram.* iii. 46 Care must be taken to ensure that unwanted recursion (looping) does not occur. **1967** KLERER & KORN *Digital Computer User's Handbk.* i. 167 Even if recursive procedures are explicitly outlawed,..recrsuion can take place unwittingly. **1972** R. A. PALMATIER *Gloss. Eng. Transformational Gram.* 142 Recursion is restricted to the transformational component of the grammar. **1973** C. W. GEAR *Introd. Computer Sci.* v. 232 FORTRAN does not allow recursion. **1975** F. R. PALMER in W. F. Bolton *Eng. Lang.* i. 34 The structure of language involves 'recursion' of the kind illustrated by 'This is the house that Jack built', 'This is the mouse that lived in the house that Jack built' and so on—if necessary *ad infinitum.*

b. A recursive definition.

1936 *Math. Ann.* CXII. 727 There are other definitions of this sort, e.g. certain recursions with respect to two or more variables simultaneously, which cannot be reduced to a succession of substitutions and ordinary recursions. **1963** W. V. QUINE *Set Theory* § 11. 79 There are the familiar so-called recursive definitions or recursions. **1966** N. CHOMSKY *Topics Theory Generative Gram.* ii. 33 An utterly fantastic proposal, namely, that a grammar should contain no recursions in its system of rules. **1971** *Computers & Humanities* V. 155 ALGOL is more powerful in that it allows recursions, has block structure, and permits expressions in many places.

recursive (rĭkɔ̄·ɹsiv), *a.* [f. L. *recurs-* (see RECURSANT *a.*) + -IVE.] **1.** Periodically or continually recurring. Now *rare* or *obs.*

1790 *Loiterer* 13 Mar. 7 Till your ear be so attuned to one particular measure, that your ideas may be spontaneously absorbed into the same revolving eddy of recursive harmony.

2. a. *Math.* and *Logic.* [after similar uses of G. *rekurrent* (D. Hilbert 1904, in *Verhandl. des dritten Internat. Math. Köngr.*), *rekursiv* (K. Gödel 1931, in *Monatshefte f. Math. u. Physik* XXXVIII. 179).] Involving or being a repeated procedure such that the required result at each step except the last is given in terms of the result(s) of the next step, until after a finite number of steps a terminus is reached with an outright evaluation of the result; *recursive definition,* a definition (of a function) which is either primitive recursive or (now usu.) general recursive; *recursive function,* a function which has or which may be given a recursive definition; *recursive relation,* a property of, or relation between, natural numbers whose truth value for all arguments is a recursive function; *recursive set,* a set of natural numbers whose defining property is recursive; *general recursive* adj. phr., applied to a function or relation which is recursive and is defined for all natural number values of its arguments; *partial recursive* adj. phr., applied to a function defined by a recursive process which for some or all values of the arguments does not terminate, leaving the value of the function undefined; *primitive recursive* adj. phr., applied to a function or relation which can be generated by primitive recursion and substitution from the zero, successor, and identity functions.

1934 KLEENE & ROSSER *Gödel's Undecidable Propositions Formal Math. Syst.* (typescript) 3 We define the class of recursive functions to be the totality of functions which can be generated by substitution..and recursion..from the successor function $x+1$, constant functions.., and identity functions. *Ibid.*, A relation R shall be recursive if the representing function is recursive. *Ibid.*, Recursive functions have the important property that, for each given set of values of the arguments, the value of the function can be computed by a finite procedure. Similarly, recursive relations (classes) are decidable in the sense that, for each given set of natural numbers, it can be determined by a finite procedure whether the relation holds or does not hold... The functions $x+y$, xy, x^y and $x!$ are clearly recursive. **1936** *Math. Ann.* CXII. 727 In this paper we offer several observations on general recursive functions, using essentially Gödel's form of the definition. *Ibid.*, Ordinary or 'primitive' recursive functions. *Ibid.* 729 A recursive function (relation) in the sense of Gödel..will now be called a primitive recursive function (relation). **1938** *Jrnl. Symbolic Logic* III. 151 If we omit the requirement that the computation process always terminate, we obtain a more general class of functions, each function of which is defined over a subset (possibly null or total) of the n-tuples of natural numbers... These functions we call partial recursive. **1940** *Mind* XLIX. 240 Preliminary considerations, such as..the exact specification of the rules for the use of recursive definitions. **1943** *Mind* LII. 268 Quite elementary theorems, requiring for their proofs recursive arguments to take care of the indefinite number of variables involved. **1943** *Trans. Amer. Math. Soc.* LIII. 44 A system E of equations defines recursively a general recursive function of n variables if, for each set $x_1, \ldots, x_n$ of natural numbers, an equation of the form $f(x_1, \ldots, x_n) = x$, where f is the principal function symbol of E, and where $x_1, \ldots, x_n$ are the numerals representing the natural numbers $x_1, \ldots, x_n$, is derivable from E..for *exactly* one numeral x. **1944** *Bull. Amer. Math. Soc.* L. 285 In the present paper, 'recursive function' means 'general recursive function'. *Ibid.* 288 Closely related to the technical concept [of a] recursively enumerable set of positive integers is that of a recursive set of positive integers. This is a set for which there is a recursive function $f(x)$ such that $f(x)$ is say 2 when x is a positive integer in the set, 1 when x is a positive integer not in the set. We may also make this the definition of the set being recursively soluble. For 2 and 1 may be regarded as the two possible truth-values, true, false, of the proposition 'positive integer x is in the set'. **1962** R. B. BRAITHWAITE in B. Meltzer tr. *Gödel's Formally Undecidable Propositions* 12 An arithmetical function is recursive if it is the last term in a finite sequence of functions in which each function is recursively defined by a rule involving two functions preceding it in the sequence (or is the successor function or a constant or obtained by substitution from a preceding function). **1964** E. MENDELSON *Introd. Math. Logic* 125 Relations obtained from primitive recursive (or recursive) relations by means of the propositional connectives and the bounded quantifiers are also primitive recursive (or recursive). **1965** HERMAN & PLASSMAN tr. *H. Hermes' Enumerability, Decidability, Computability* i. 29 Today it is generally believed that *every* system of algorithms can be defined by recursive functions. This gives a deeper meaning to Gödel's result. *Ibid.* iii. 82 The essence of Ackermann's proof of the existence of a computable function which is not primitive recursive consists in defining a computable function which increases in a certain sense faster than any primitive recursive function. **1967** *Encycl. Philos.* VII. 92/1 This Herbrand–Gödel–Kleene notion of general recursive function can be put in the context of instructions and computations discussed above. **1970** *Nature* 19 Dec. 1234/1 Turing formulated his concept of an abstract computing machine; the functions computable by these machines are exactly the recursive functions. **1974** A. KENNY tr. *Wittgenstein's Philos. Gram.* 34 Is there a further step from writing the recursive proof to the generalization? Doesn't the recursion schema already say all that is to be said?

b. *Linguistics.* Applied to a grammatical feature or element which may be involved in a procedure whereby that feature or element is repeatedly reintroduced; applied to a grammatical rule in which part of the output serves as input to the same rule.

1955 N. CHOMSKY *Logical Struct. Linguistic Theory* (microfilm, Mass. Inst. Technol.) vi. 248 We will find many other reasons to question the validity of the extension of the notion of *production* to *recursive production.* **1957** —— in *Janua Linguarum* IV. 57 Bar-Hillel has suggested..that Pike's proposals can be formalized without the circularity that many sense in them by the use of recursive definitions. **1968** J. LYONS *Introd. Theoret. Linguistics* vii. 326 The adverb is a recursive category..in the sense that one adverb may modify another. **1970** —— *Chomsky* viii. 90 It will be observed that rules (2), (3) and (4) are recursive, but in different ways. Rule (2) is left recursive; rule (3) is right recursive; and rule (4) is self-embedding. **1972** R. A. PALMATIER *Gloss. Eng. Transformational Gram.* 142 A recursive rule is a rule which reapplies indefinitely to its own output... The recursive power of a grammar, which resides entirely in the syntactic component, is its ability to generate an infinity of sentences... The recursive mechanism is the system of rules which account for the infinite properties of language... A recursive element is one from which strings can be derived that contain the same element... The recursive property of a grammar..is its provision for embedding sentences within other sentences. **1977** *Word 1972* XXVIII. 336 Logicians of the first half of the century had developed and used recursive grammars with such clarity that Chomsky's 'application' can hardly be regarded as a *tour de force*.

c. *Computing.* Applied to a statement, definition, subroutine, or the like, some part of which makes use of the whole of itself, so that its explicit interpretation requires in general many successive executions; applied also to languages, compilers, etc., which allow of such techniques.

Quot. 1958 uses the word in a context where 'iterative' would now be usual.

1958 *Commun. Assoc. Computing Machinery* Aug. 10 The idea of recursive curve fitting has been in use for some time as a graphical technique for fitting curves 'by eye' to observational data. **1959** *Numerische Math.* I. 45 The definition of expressions, and their constituents, is necessarily recursive. **1960** *Ibid.* II. 312 It is then impossible to call in a subroutine while one or more previous activations of the same subroutine have not yet come to an end... We intend to describe..a means of removing the..restriction..; hence the name 'recursive programming'. **1973** C. W. Gear *Introd. Computer Sci.* v. 233 We can understand recursive procedures by imagining that many different copies of the procedure are available. **1979** Page & Wilson *Introd. Computational Combinatorics* vi. 136 Since backtrack programming is closely related to tree searching we can consider using recursive techniques in our implementations.

3. *Phonetics.* A term sometimes used to refer to consonants accompanied by glottal closure or implosion. Also as *sb.*

1924 R. L. Turner in *Bull. School Oriental Stud.* III. 304 According to one of my informants, an *m* accompanied by glottal closure and distinguished from ordinary *m*, exists in Magarkurā, one of the Mongolian languages of Nepal. Prince Troubetzkoy refers to consonants in the Caucasian languages accompanied by complete closure of the glottis. These he calls 'recoursives', a convenient term I have anglicized as 'recursives'; he indicates them by a dot above or below the letter. **1934** Webster, *Recursive*, adj.,.. formed with an inward movement of air caused by lowering the larynx with closed glottis;—said of certain consonants in Sindhi (*g*, *j*, *d*, *b*). **1974** *Encycl. Brit. Macropædia* IX. 448/1 One major feature distinguishing Sindhi from the rest of the northwest group is the development of a series of imploded stops (also called suction stops and recursive stops), for *b*, *d*, *j*, and *g*.

recursively (rĭkɒ̄·ɹsivli), *adv.* [f. prec. + -ly².] In a recursive manner: esp. *recursively defined*, having a recursive definition; *recursively enumerable*, (of a set of natural numbers) generated by a general recursive function having one parameter which ranges through all possible values.

1934 Kleene & Rosser *Gödel's Undecidable Propositions Formal Math. Syst.* (typescript) 21 These are arithmetic propositions which involve only recursively defined functions. **1943, 1944** [see *recursive *a.* 2 a]. **1944** *Bull. Amer. Math. Soc.* L. 285 A set of positive integers is said to be recursively enumerable if there is a recursive function $f(x)$ of one positive integral variable whose values for positive integral values of x, constitute the given set. **1961** *Commun. Assoc. Computing Machinery* IV. 10/2 Many of the constituents of the Algol language are defined recursively. **1962** B. Meltzer tr. *Gödel's Formally Undecidable Propositions* 46 A number-theoretic function $\phi(x_1, x_2, \ldots x_n)$ is said to be recursively defined by the number-theoretic functions $\psi(x_1, x_2, \ldots x_{n-1})$ and $\mu(x_1, x_2, \ldots x_{n-1})$ if for all $x_2, \ldots x_n$, k the following hold:

$$\phi(0, x_2, \ldots x_n) = \psi(x_2, \ldots x_n),$$
$$\phi(k+1, x_2, \ldots x_n) = \mu(k, \phi(k, x_2, \ldots x_n), x_2, \ldots x_n).$$

1964 *Mem. Amer. Math. Soc.* LI. 8 An index of ϕ_2 is obtainable primitive recursively from an index of ϕ_1, and vice versa. **1968** [see *nest *v.* 4 b]. **1968** *Language* XLIV. 571 The set of all sets of integers is non-denumerable; the set of all Turing machines is denumerable; each recursively enumerable set corresponds to a Turing machine; therefore there are sets of integers which are not recursively enumerable. **1970** *Ibid.* XLVI. 787 Sentence margins are slots where nuclear sentence patterns may recursively be embedded within other sentences. **1970** Eilenberg & Elgot *Recursiveness* 84 The class of all recursively enumerable sets is countable. **1974** Kernighan & Plauger *Elem. Programming Style* iii. 54 Learning to think recursively takes some effort, but that is repaid with smaller and simpler programs... Use recursive procedures for recursively-defined data structures.

recursiveness (rĭkɒ̄·ɹsivnės). [f. as prec. + -ness.] The property of being recursive.

1936 *Amer. Jrnl. Math.* LVIII. 346 Since the results of the present paper were obtained, it has been shown by Kleene.. that analogous results can be obtained entirely in terms of recursiveness, without making use of λ-definability. **1962** R. B. Braithwaite in B. Meltzer tr. *Gödel's Formally Undecidable Propositions* 11 The notion of recursiveness has played a central part in metamathematics since Gödel's work on it. *Ibid.* 12 The importance of recursiveness for metamathematics in general lies in the fact that recursive definition enables every number in a recursively defined infinite sequence to be *constructed* according to a rule, so that a remark about the infinite sequence can be construed as a remark about the rule of construction and not as a remark about a given infinite totality. **1964** E. Bach *Introd. Transformational Gram.* ii. 16 In order to provide for an infinite number of terminal strings, a grammar must have a basic property called recursiveness. **1970** *Nature* 19 Dec. 1234/1 The concept of recursiveness was formulated in Gödel's sensational work in 1931 on the limitations of mechanical languages. **1975** G. Sampson *Form of Lang.* v. 89 As soon as we allow 'S' to appear on the right-hand side of one of the rules, the grammar acquires the property of 'recursiveness'.

re·curve, *sb. Archery.* [f. the vb.] A backward-curving end of the limb of a bow; a bow designed with this feature. Also *attrib.*

1961 E. Burke *Archery* i. 10 (*caption*) Named parts of the bow..recurve..upper limb..bowsight..lower limb.. nock. **1962** G. H. Gillelan *Young Sportsman's Guide to Archery* ii. 19 The other important bow design is the recurve, so named because its tips have a reverse curl. **1979** *Country Life* 26 July 287/1 The 'Bowhunter' style involves any type of bow, usually of a recurve construction, that is a combination of glass-fibre and wood..to buy a new bow works out as follows: long bow, £20–£50; recurve, £150–£180. **1980** *Hunting Ann. 1981* 81/3 For targets of opportunity, a recurve or long bow can be handled faster.

recurved, *ppl. a.* Delete 'in 19th c.' and add later examples.

1925 E. H. Wilson *Lilies E. Asia* 23 Flowers white, fragrant, funnel-shape, dilated, more or less recurved at the apex. **1936** D. Wilkie *Gentians* vi. 33 The calyx is tubular, and the lobes..are ovate and recurved. **1961** J. E. Collin *Brit. Flies* VI. i. 71 Proboscis not very stout nor much recurved. **1980** *Plantsman* I. 251 Both [lilies]..have delicate pendant flowers with slightly recurved petals.

recusal (rĭkiū·zăl). [f. Recuse *v.* + -al.] An objection to a judge as prejudiced.

1958 *Manch. Guardian* 5 Aug. 5/7 The submission to recusal was based on reports that incorrectly stated the facts. **1980** *Times* 30 Oct. 6/8 They should not feel that by making their applications for his recusal they had prejudiced their case.

recyclable (rīsəi·klăb'l), *a.* [f. *recycle *v.* + -able.] Capable of being recycled.

1971 *New Yorker* 4 Dec. 177 Publishers might do well to encase their pages and bindings in some sort of ersatz (but recyclable) horn. **1972** *Guardian* 30 Oct. 12/1 The shape of cars to come—a disposable commuter car which would be 'recycleable' after perhaps two years. **1976** *Nature* 6 May 66/2 Evidence suggests that net water flow from the rectal lumen to haemolymph results from increases in intercellular space osmotic pressure due to the transport across lateral cell membranes of recyclable intracellular solutes. **1979** *Observer* 30 Dec. 3/8 Theoretically they [*sc.* big plastic bottles] are recyclable, but actually they are constructed so as to make reclamation highly improbable.

Hence **recy:clabi·lity.**

1973 *Sci. Amer.* July 1 In terms of its attributes, its utility and recyclability, glass is a natural. **1978** *Jrnl. R. Soc. Arts* CXXVI. 609/2 Lifetime and recyclability of the product.

recycle (rīsəi·k'l), *v.* Also **re-cycle.** [Re- 5 a.] **1.** *trans.* **a.** To reuse (a material) in an industrial process; to return to a previous stage of a cyclic process.

1926 [implied in *recycling *vbl. sb.*]. **1928** *Jrnl. Inst. Petroleum Technologists* XIV. 766 It is economically more advantageous to stop cracking in the first cycle when coke formation begins and produce more gasoline by re-cycling those fractions which do not form great quantities of coke during cracking. **1929** *Proc. R. Soc.* A. CXXIV. 43 It ought to be possible to obtain nearly the theoretically possible yield by returning to the reaction chamber or 'recycling' all the products formed except the gasoline. **1945** H. D. Smyth *Gen. Acct. Devel. Atomic Energy Mil. Purposes* ix. 100 Any given sample of material is recycled many times. **1958** *Times* 17 Oct. 5/1 It is envisaged that plutonium produced in the working of the reactor will later be recycled through it. **1964** N. G. Clark *Mod. Org. Chem.* iv. 62 Using only a small volume of solvent, which is continually recycled, it is possible to carry out the equivalent of many hundreds of separate extractions. **1972** *Sci. Amer.* Oct. 69/1 Their new process is the first closed-loop, spray-etching system that electrolytically reverses the chemical reaction of etching. It continuously recycles cupric chloride and has reduced the cost of etching wiring boards by over 90%. **1980** *Times* 7 Mar. 25/3 The uranium is recycled back to an enrichment plant to make new thermal-reactor fuel, and the plutonium is stored.

b. *spec.* To reuse (a waste material), to convert (waste) into or *into* a usable form; also, to reclaim (a material) from waste.

1960 *Aeroplane* XCIX. 521/2 It has systems which reduce all organic waste to a small amount of ash and recycle urine and waste water into drinkable water. **1967** *Technology Week* 23 Jan. 34/3 It would allow us to economically desalt sea and brackish water, recycle water from sewage. **1971** *Sci. Amer.* May 95/1 (Advt.), You bring us the cans and we'll recycle them. **1971** *New Yorker* 16 Oct. 33 What you ecology-minded ladies don't realize is that before a bottle can be recycled it has to be emptied. **1973** *Guardian* 22 Mar. 15/1 The Liberals of Kew..have been recycling paper, and have managed to scrape a regular £25 a month. **1974** *Listener* 28 Feb. 278/1 Such a plant would recycle steel, aluminium, zinc, lead and copper from scrap. **1979** *China Now* Mar./Apr. 31/3 The report covers all methods of recycling organic materials.

c. *transf.* in connection with natural processes. Usu. in *passive.*

1965 G. J. Williams *Econ. Geol. N.Z.* i. 2/2 These [beds of sediment] are of considerable interest to economic geologists for through them much detrital gold was recycled within and beyond the primary gold-bearing areas. **1970** *Nature* 17 Oct. 273/2 The annual discharge of dissolved sodium in rivers is about 20×10^7 tons, of which 9×10^7 tons have been recycled from the sea through the atmosphere. **1971** I. G. Gass et al. *Understanding Earth* iii. 68/2 Much of the ocean will be recycled in the ocean-floor spreading process. **1973** *Sci. Amer.* Apr. 61/1 Stars continually recycle their material through the interstellar medium.

d. *fig.*

1969 *Guardian* 12 May 1/5 (*heading*) Bankers find way to recycle hot money. **1970** *Nature* 25 July 321/2 It is not possible to recycle the output of the secondary schools without there being some intermediate opportunity for broadening the intellectual experience of the young men and women concerned. **1973** *Ibid.* 2 Mar. 4/2 A further five [cases] may be the result of the virus being recycled in swill. **1973** *Black Panther* 4 Aug. 7/3 Those workers finding themselves without jobs..are re-cycled back to their former jobs at the reduced wages. **1974** *Weekend Mag.* (Montreal) 16 Mar. 2/2 The kids are appropriating the Fifties, proving once more that fads (like garbage) can be recycled. **1974** *Newsweek* 7 Oct. 52/1 A new international banking system to recycle OPEC funds into loans to the poorer nations. **1978** *Washington Post* 8 Aug. C4/5 Many juveniles, he adds, are repeat offenders, 'recycled' through the system.

2. a. *trans.* To repeat (a process) on a computer or counting device; also *absol.* **b.** *intr.* Of a computer: to repeat a procedure.

1962 A. Shepard in *Into Orbit* 103 Walt decided to recycle the count—or set it back—to allow for this delay. **1973** *Sci. Amer.* May 110/3 The three input terminals of a nand gate connected to Q_e, Q_d and Q_a of a series of five flip-flops would cause the apparatus to recycle on the count of 25 (11001). **1970** A. Cameron et al. *Computer & O.E. Concordances* 47, I made a preliminary run and found a large number of keypunch errors that I had missed originally... I decided therefore to recycle.

3. *intr.* To undergo recycling.

1970 *Nature* 28 Nov. 856/2 The inability of most newly formed lymphocytes to recycle from blood to lymph could explain their truncated life span. **1975** *Ibid.* 24 July 247/1 The PhD degree is a relatively easy target to attack because its recipients do not seem to confer on society the same sort of benefits as, say, medical doctors. More recycle into the educational system than go elsewhere. **1978** *Amat. Photographer* 29 Nov. 128/3, I had noticed the unit appeared to be taking longer than usual to recycle after each shot, but assumed the battery was getting low.

Hence **recy·cled** *ppl. a.*; **recy·cling** *vbl. sb.*; *recycling time* (Photogr.), the time required to recharge the capacitor of a flash unit.

1926 *Petroleum Devel. & Technol. 1925* 338 With the use of higher pressures and temperatures permitting the ultimate cracking of this cut, more recycling of this fraction may be practiced. **1958** *Amat. Photographer* 31 Dec. 2/2 (Advt.), Angle 60°, recycling time 6 sec. **1964** M. Gowing *Britain & Atomic Energy 1939–1945* ix. 258 There were heavy losses of the product and of time in recycling and in washing and cleaning the machines. **1969** *Focal Encycl. Photogr.* (rev. ed.) 636/2 The recycling time and the number of flashes obtainable from a set of batteries..are also the subject of specific measurement methods. **1970** C. S. Russell et al. *Drought & Water Supply* viii. 68 Only 46 percent ..indicated a willingness to drink recycled domestic water. **1970** *Daily Tel.* 12 Sept. 5/7 They lived off their recycled body wastes. **1971** *Ibid.* 29 Apr. 14/6 The more than 9·1 million aluminium cans represent about 460,000 lb of litter and solid waste removed for complete recycling. **1972** *Guardian* 6 June 15/4 Recycling enthusiasts are..collecting ..old bottles and tin cans. **1975** *Nature* 17 Jan. 149/2 There is little commercial future for recycled glass in high grade uses at present. **1975** *N.Y. Times* 25 Oct. 27/3 The recycling boom is waning because of unfavorable economic conditions. **1977** *Financial Times* 4 June 5/3 Retreading is a form of recycling, which should be encouraged. **1978** D. Bloodworth *Crosstalk* xxiii. 180 He had driven the Deputy Director..half mad with his hesitation, his recycled arguments for accepting and not accepting.

recycle (rīsəi·k'l), *sb.* Also **re-cycle.** [f. the vb.] The operation or process of recycling a material, etc.; also, the material itself. Orig. and freq. *attrib.*, usu. denoting material subjected to or set aside for recycling.

1926 *Petroleum Devel. & Technol. 1925* 339 The gas oil was returned to the cracking system as recycle charging stock. **1936** W. L. Nelson *Petroleum Refinery Engin.* iii. 19 Recycle stock has about the same boiling-range and.. physical characteristics as gas oil. **1939** *World Petroleum* Mar. 104/3 The asphalt bottoms produced are released through exchangers against reduced crude. They are blended with the cracked recycle gas oil and thence through the tar coolers to tankage. **1946** *Nature* 30 Nov. 800/1 The gradual deterioration in the quality of re-cycle benzene is due to the preferential accumulation of paraffins. **1961** *Engineering* 2 June 781/1 Reduce the cost of fuel burned by using plutonium recycle or spikes of fully enriched uranium. **1966** *McGraw-Hill Encycl. Sci. & Technol.* XIII. 185/2 The rich solution from the absorption step must be stripped in order to permit recovery of the absorbed solute and recycle of the solvent. **1975** *Nature* 13 Feb. 496/3 Recycle, or reuse of materials, is an important aspect of the proper management of these resources. *Ibid.* 2 Oct. 369/1 There is a great variety of possible schemes for incorporating a converter, or heat engine, into the heat recycle.

recycler (rīsəi·klə.ɹ). [f. *recycle *v.* + -er¹.] One who or that which recycles (waste products, etc.).

1973 *Nature* 13 Apr. 483/3 Exhaust gas recyclers which cause an increase in the fuel consumption. **1974** *Ibid.* 19 Apr. 641/3 Developing..new manufacturing designs congenial to recyclers. **1976** *National Observer* (U.S.) 13 Mar. 8/2 With the emergence of the week-end home mechanic, the industry has tried to change its image from that of 'junk-yards keepers' to 'recyclers'.

recyclist (rīsəi·klist). *rare.* [f. as prec.

+ -IST.] An advocate of the recycling of waste products; a recycler.

1973 *Times* 1 Aug. 12/1 Perhaps pop artists were the first Recyclists.

red, *a.* and *sb.*[1] Add: **A.** *adj.* **I. 1. b.** *fig.* (Later examples.)

1795–1804 W. BLAKE *Four Zoas* in *Compl. Writings* (1972) 336 Red rage redounds. **1892** W. B. YEATS *Countess Kathleen* ii. 34 God's red anger seize them. **1938** —— *Herne's Egg* iii. 28 The Great Herne himself And he in a red rage. **1952** DYLAN THOMAS *Coll. Poems* p. x, Of fear, rage red, manalive.

g. *red, white, and blue*: the colours of the Union Jack, hence, the flag itself; also *attrib.* or as *adj.*, patriotic, devoted to the service of Britain.

1855 D. T. SHAW *Britannia, Pride of Ocean* 1 May the Service United ne'er sever, And both to their Colours prove true, The Army and Navy for ever! Three cheers for the Red, White and Blue! **1912** R. BROOKE *Lett.* (1968) 387 Aren't you, perhaps, going to lecture..about the British Empire, on 'Heart-Cries under the Red White and Blue', or some such title? **1971** *Scope* (S. Afr.) 19 Mar. 30/1 They were all that he was not; British in tradition; red-white-and-blue in sentiment. **1972** P. LOVESEY *Abracadaver* xv. 191 Our careers are *dedicated* to the red, white and blue. There is no need to remind us where our duty lies. **1974** *Times* 24 Aug. 2/2 Anyone joining his organization had his background checked 'to avoid communist infiltration... If the man has a red, white and blue background, then he is okay'. **1977** *Sniffin' Glue* July 21 He just averts his gaze to the red white and blue and exchanges nothings with the silly mayor.

h. *to paint the town red*: see PAINT *v.*[1] 9.

3. (Further examples.)

1865 SWINBURNE *Chastelard* v. i. 141 The men of Pharaoh's, beautiful with red And with red gold. **1892** W. B. YEATS *Countess Kathleen* i. 18, I am half mindful to go pray to him To cover all this table with red gold. **1931** M. ALLINGHAM *Look to Lady* xiii. 144 The real Chalice..is made of English red gold.

b. (Further example.) Also *red 'un*, a sovereign.

1816 SCOTT *Antiq.* I. xv. 325 It's a red half-guinea to him every time he mounts his mare. **1890** in Barrère & Leland *Dict. Slang* II. 175/1 The youth, her wish obeying, placed a coin down—gently saying—'There's a red 'un—or in other words "a quid!"' **1899** C. ROOK *Hooligan Nights* ii. 25 Honest work..will bring in but a few shillings a week; and what is that compared to the glorious possibility of nicking a red 'un? **1901** G. B. SHAW *Capt. Brassbound's Conversion* II. 265 E'll give huz fawv unnerd red uns. **1905** *Hackney & Kingsland Gazette* 15 Sept. 3/7 He said 'Here comes a German with a red lot (gold chain, etc). If you have heart, pull it.' **1981** A. HEWINS *Dillen* iii. 20, I don't think much o' that stone you got. I'll give you a nice red un for it.

c. For *U.S.* read 'orig. *U.S.*' (Earlier and later examples.) Also (*U.S.*) in phr. *nary (a) red (cent)*: see *NARY *a.*

c **1839** J. S. JONES *People's Lawyer* (1856) I. i. 8 It would not have cost you a red cent. **1900** W. ARCHER *Let.* 1 Feb. in C. Archer *William Archer* (1931) xii. 263 We have never agreed about plays, and we never will... I have never given a red cent for the ideas in plays. **1904** KIPLING *Traffics & Discoveries* 23 I'd turned in every red cent on the Zigler. **1943** K. TENNANT *Ride on Stranger* xvii. 188 'To think of it,' groaned George Benson. 'We don't get a red cent, not a flaming red cent.' **1958** J. CAREW *Black Midas* ix. 193 He will pay you seven dollar..and not a red cent extra. **1976** T. SHARPE *Wilt* xiii. 135 'I'll alimony you for all the money you've got.' 'Fat chance. You won't get a red cent.' **1979** *Tucson Mag.* Apr. 34/3 In ten years, the city has not spent one red cent from any federal funds for Barrio Historico.

5. a. (Later example.)

1922 JOYCE *Ulysses* 23 You know that red Carlisle girl, Lily?

c. *Red Indian*: see INDIAN *sb.* 2 b in Dict. and Suppl.

7. esp. in phr. *red face*, a sign of embarrassment or shame.

1937 PARTRIDGE *Dict. Slang* 692/1 *Red face* (or *neck*), *have a*, to be ashamed. **1973** *Listener* 14 June 786/1 Mediterranean weather caused red faces among long-range weathermen who had to confess they'd got June wrong so far. **1977** *Listener* 30 June 865/1 The celebrated Samuel Palmer fakes ..that have left so many red faces in the world of fine art. **1980** B. PARVIN *Death in Past* v. 30 She..grabbed me and said: 'It's true—I'm going to have a baby!' Was my face red! **1981** L. DEIGHTON *XPD* iii. 13 There was secret material..[that] would have caused a few red faces here in Whitehall.

9. b. (Earlier and further examples.) Also, Bolshevik, communist; freq. *spec.* of or pertaining to the U.S.S.R.; *red revolution*, a socialist or communist revolution.

1848, etc. [see *RED REPUBLIC]. **1917** [see *RED GUARD 1 a]. **1919** *Times* 7 Oct. 4/3 That I was prepared to create a Red Revolution in England..is something which I have never said. **1920** *Blackw. Mag.* Sept. 404/2 The Red Government, still bent upon the destruction of Europe, was..recognised. **1924** R. MACAULAY *Orphan Island* xix. 252 It is mainly a catalogue of grievances, together with rousing addresses... 'What we call Red journalism.' **1926** *Brit. Gaz.* 12 May 3/6 After an attempt to hold a 'Red' Meeting in Edgware-road, a crowd of about 2,000 people was said to have collected and arrests were made by the police. **1927** W. E. COLLINSON *Contemp. Eng.* 85 The spread of the Bolshevistic propaganda has led to the fear, lest Labour should go red. **1929** J. BUCHAN *Courts of Morning* I. 129 The Scotsman had become their special intimate... Judson, who seemed to have known him before, called him Red Geordie. **1934** *Discovery* Feb. 55/2 All along that frontier, every three hundred yards, there are Red soldiers with rifle and machine-gun. **1940** W. EMPSON *Gathering Storm* 49 Revolt and mercy fired no sparks In the Red argument at all. **1948** E. B. WHITE *Let.* 24 Jan. (1976) 290 My desk got so deep in Red literature that I had to fumigate myself every night before going home. **1951** *Sun* (Baltimore) 19 June 7/1 Count Wolf von Westarp, co-founder of the band of neo-Nazis,..has indignantly denied any Red ties. **1958** *Spectator* 6 June 723/2 There are still hundreds of writers in gaol all over the Red Empire, not to mention Franco's or Salazar's prisons. **1965** B. PEARCE tr. *Preobrazhensky's New Econ.* 189 The red managers, proletarian engineers, and business executives have no monopoly of the means of production. **1970** M. O'BRINE *Crambo* lii. 193 He is still a Red Navy man. He has the right to be buried at sea. **1972** D. BLOODWORTH *Any Number can Play* ii. 9 He infuriated the communists because he ran too just and egalitarian a kingdom to suit the sacred cause of red revolution. **1976** G. MANSELL *Why External Broadcasting?* 18 Other totalitarianisms, whether of the red or the black variety. **1981** *Times* 3 Mar. 13/2 Anything is better than the horrors of nuclear war..better red than dead. **1981** *Time Out* 24–30 Apr. 7/4 Rosenthal and her fellow-candidates will be..hoping that Sir Horace Cutler's deepest fears of a 'red' London are realized.

II. 12. *red-blood* (fig.), *-fire, -roof, -rose* (later examples), *-wine* (later examples).

1915 J. LONDON *Let.* 5 Nov. (1966) 463, I go ahead content to be admired for my red-blood brutality. **1925** V. WOOLF *Common Reader* 262 The high-brow public and the red-blood public. **1943** WYNDHAM LEWIS *Let.* 8 Aug. (1963) 360 The vulgarly red-blood American attitude (the lady and gentlemen complex). **1976** A. J. RUSSELL *Pour Hemlock* (1979) ii. 19 I'm not their kind of people... This is a Redblood administration, I'm a Mollycoddle. **1918** D. H. LAWRENCE *New Poems* 15 As it guards the wild north cloud-coasts, red-fire seas running through The rocks. **1913** —— *Love Poems & Others* 33 The subtle, steady rush..of advancing God..Is heard..In the tapping haste of a fallen leaf, In the flapping of red-roof smoke. **1895** W. B. YEATS *Poems* 234 The red-rose-bordered hem. **1942** W. STEVENS *Notes toward Supreme Fiction* 36 The channel slots of rain, the red-rose-red. **1877** E. S. DALLAS *Kettner's Bk. of Table* 376 *Matelote Relish*, small onions and mushrooms in a red-wine sauce. *Ibid.* 483 It is difficult to procure the mild red-wine vinegar in London. **1943** E. M. ALMEDINGEN *Frossia* iv. 192 A nice plump partridge, red wine sauce, and cranberry jelly. **1971** *Vogue* 15 Sept. 125/2, I had chicken in red wine sauce with mushrooms and bacon.

13. *red-black, -gold* (earlier and later examples), *-golden, -pink, -purple* (further examples), *-rose, -white* (later example), *-yellow* (later example).

1910 *Westm. Gaz.* 25 Jan. 5/2 The material employed is the finest red-black rubber. **1975** R. H. RIMMER *Premar Experiments* II. 174 Even before I touched her, her nipples were engorged, red-black and demanding. **1607** E. TOPSELL *Four-footed Beasts* 661 This beast is of red-gold-colour. **1871** SWINBURNE *Songs before Sunrise* 237 Till the red-gold harvest-rows, Full-grown, are full of the light. **1923** D. H. LAWRENCE *Birds, Beasts & Flowers* 98, I have..seen..His red-gold, water-precious, mirror-flat bright eye. **1973** J. CLEARY *Ransom* i. 21 She was..beautiful, with that red-gold hair that was a sensation on colour television. **1962** I. MURDOCH *Unofficial Rose* 12 Her red-golden hair. **1880** E. GLAISTER *Needlework* ix. 101 If the flowers be another colour than yellow, say red-pink, or blue, the darning may be the same colour. **1951** E. PAUL *Springtime in Paris* xv. 268 The pharmacy had large old-fashioned globes of coloured liquid, red-pink like Corsican wine and transparent blue-green. **1851** *Southern Planter* (Richmond, Va.) July 197/2 Improved Red Purple Straw on corn land. **1929** A. CLARKE *Pilgrimage & Other Poems* 15 Vats of red-purple dye. **1917** G. FRANKAU *Inn of Thousand Dreams* in *City of Fear* 26 Once more I press..Your finger-tips against these lips Your own red-rose lips knew. **1920** J. MASEFIELD *Enslaved* 9 Little red-white blossoms flecked me. **1937** V. WOOLF *Years* 333 There was a red-yellow glow... The sun was sinking through the London dust.

14. a. *red-belted* (see also sense 14 b in Dict.), *-bordered, -carpeted, -checked, -clayed, -cloaked* (further examples), *-coloured* (later example), *-eared* (see also sense 14 b below), *-eaved, -edged, -ensigned, -flowered* (see also sense 14 c in Dict.), *-furred, -hatted* (earlier and later examples), *-labelled, -lipped* (further example), *-mouthed* (see also sense 14 b in Dict.), *-rimmed, -screened, -striped, -tabbed, -tied, -tiled* (later example), *-toothed, -veined* (see also sense 14 c in Dict.). See also *RED-BLOODED etc. as main entries in Suppl.

1925 F. SCOTT FITZGERALD *Great Gatsby* iv. 81 A glimpse of red-belted ocean-going ships. **1922** JOYCE *Ulysses* 657 Dry them..in a long redbordered holland cloth passed over a wooden revolving roller. **1905** *Westm. Gaz.* 6 Sept. 6/2 There were waiting on the red-carpeted platform.. officials representing the railway company. **1922** JOYCE *Ulysses* 484 They appear on a redcarpeted staircase. **1948** M. LASKI *Tory Heaven* viii. 106 He climbs the red-carpeted steps under the gay awning. **1976** N. ROBERTS *Face of France* xvi. 165 A red-carpeted dais. **1973** M. AMIS *Rachel Papers* 170 My sister, a swirl of red-checked nightie, flew through the doorway. **1978** R. LUDLUM *Holcroft Covenant* xxiv. 277 Running across the fronts of the booths were brass rods holding red-checked curtains. **1913** J. MASEFIELD *Daffodil Fields* 2 Some short-grassed fields begin, Red-clayed and pleasant. **1910** W. B. YEATS *Green Helmet* 21 A tall red-headed red-cloaked man stands upon the threshold. **1980** *Jrnl. R. Soc. Arts* Mar. 241/2 Max Ernst's red-cloaked, bird-masked lady in *The Robing of the Bride*. **1942** S. SPENDER *Life & Poet* 12 Since we believe socialism to be just, novels should preach socialism and see everything through red-coloured spectacles. **1900** W. B. YEATS *Shadowy Waters* 46 A red-eared hound follows a hornless deer. **1881** O. WILDE *Poems* 80 The dusky red-eaved sheds. **1918** G. FRANKAU *Judgement of Valhalla* 6 (*title*) The song of the red-edged steel. **1922** JOYCE *Ulysses* 221 Father Conmee..took his rededged breviary out. **1942** E. SITWELL *Street Songs* 7 Man's threatening shadow Red-edged by the sun like Cain, has a changing shape. **1965** G. MCINNES *Road to Gundagai* xiii. 239 The navy blue red-edged flag. **1892** D. SLADEN *Japs at Home* (ed. 2) xxvi. 283 While in the distance looms the harbour of Yokohama, full of the mighty red-ensigned steamers of the England he pined for night and day. *a* **1915** JOYCE *Giacomo Joyce* (1968) 16 Poised on its edge a woman's hat, red-flowered. **1932** BLUNDEN *Face of England* 66 Where the sheep's parsley tops a red-furred stem. **1863** GEO. ELIOT *Romola* I. xiii. 222 The boy-cardinal Giovanni de Medici, youngest of the red-hatted fathers. **1918** A. BENNETT *Pretty Lady* x. 52 The young red-hatted officer. **1930** BLUNDEN *Poems* 185 Where the red-hatted cranks Have fixed a portcullis With notice-board—thanks! **1922** JOYCE *Ulysses* 95 The redlabelled bottle on the table. **1881** O. WILDE *Poems* 70 An amorous red-lipped boy. **1913** KIPLING *Songs from Books* 239 And red-mouthed shadows racing By, that thrust me from my food. **1934** DYLAN THOMAS *Let.* c 26 May (1966) 133 I've wasted some of my tremendous love for you on a lank, redmouthed girl with a reputation like a hell. **1916** JOYCE *Portrait of Artist* (1969) 252, I fear his redrimmed horny eyes. **1962** I. MURDOCH *Unofficial Rose* xii. 115 The red-rimmed eyes. **1977** P. HILL *Liars* vii. 91 Her eyes were red-rimmed, as if she had been crying. **1930** BLUNDEN *Poems* 134 The red-screened windows of schoolhouse and inn. **1955** E. POUND *Classic Anthol.* II. 94 Fang Shu's black-dappled team of four Drew his red-screen'd car to the war. **1865–6** W. WHITMAN *Sequel to Drum-Taps* 19 The red-striped artilleryman. **1940** BLUNDEN *Poems 1930–40* 209 He.. damned, at each pause, red-tabbed Brigade, Whose orders for grimness more than the frost-spell made us shiver. **1948** W. FORTESCUE *Beauty for Ashes* xxvii. 207, I accosted a red-tabbed English officer who directed me to it at once. **1977** J. CLEARY *High Road to China* iv. 107 Johnny Silversmith, red-faced and red-tabbed, came to our table. **1911** G. K. CHESTERTON *Innocence of Father Brown* iv. 105 The red-tied youth. **1960** D. POTTER *Glittering Coffin* iii. 38 Red-tied adolescent poets. **1977** H. OSBORNE *White Poppy* viii. 69 An iron bedstead on a red-tiled floor. **1881** O. WILDE *Poems* 178 The red-toothed lightning. **1925** BLUNDEN *Eng. Poems* 123 Through red-toothed nettles. **1877** C. PATMORE *Unknown Eros* xi. 51 He had put, within his reach, A box of counters and a red-vein'd stone. **1907** *Daily Chron.* 18 Mar. 6/2 His face is clear, with the red-veined cheeks of a sailor. **1956** R. FINLAYSON in C. K. Stead *N.Z. Short Stories* (1966) 22 He was a thickset florid man with a red-veined nose.

b. *red-eared* (see also sense 14 a above), *-lipped.*

1937 *Jrnl. Tennessee Acad. Sci.* XII. 45 (*caption*) The Red-Eared Sunfish. Only the males have the red tip on the opercular flap. **1952** A. CARR *Handbk. Turtles U.S. & Canada* II. 251 The red-eared turtle can usually be recognized..by the long, oval expansion of the broad supra temporal stripe, which is usually bright red. **1910,** etc. Red-lipped snake [see *HERALD *sb.* 5].

c. *red-leafed* (later examples; also *fig.*).

1911 E. POUND *Canzoni* 1 Ah! red-leafed time hath driven out the rose. **1923** BLUNDEN *To Nature* 47 There shone the Ancre, red-leafed woods above it.

15. a. *red-decked, -flushed, -gilded, -lined* (earlier and later examples; see also *RED-LINE *v.*), *-lit, -polished, -struck, -washed.*

1923 D. H. LAWRENCE *Birds, Beasts & Flowers* 66 Red-decked socialists, Hibiscus-breasted. **1871** W. WHITMAN *Passage to India* 18 The red-flush'd cheeks, and perfumes. **1943** V. WOOLF *Haunted House* 124 The red-flushed clouds. **1949** E. POUND *Pisan Cantos* lxxix. 77 The mountain forest is full of light The tree-comb red-gilded. **1820** KEATS *Lamia & Other Poems* 57 Why were they proud? Because red-lin'd accounts Were richer than the songs of Grecian years? **1921** W. DE LA MARE *Crossings* 31 Unlocks the trunk and pushes back its red-lined lid. **1966** *Sunday Times* (Colour Suppl.) 4 Dec. 73/3 [GI Jargon] *Red-lined*, cancelled or classified unserviceable. **1979** *N.Y. Times* 24 Jan. B 18/1 Redlining has an undeniable racial component whereby redlined neighborhoods often coincide with nonwhite neighborhoods. **1930** R. CAMPBELL *Gum Trees*, Along the red-lit rim of space In lofty cadences they rhyme. **1934** V. G. CHILDE *New Light Most Anc. East* iv. 89 Household vessels, always the most sensitive indicator of ethnic change, are radically altered. Though Black-topped and Red-polished ware continue to be manufactured they are no longer the vehicle for new shapes. **1977** *Jrnl. R. Soc. Arts* CXXV. 476/2 The most important items found in the tombs of *Kotchati* and acquired by the Cyprus Museum are two clay (Red Polished ware) models of sanctuaries. **1923** D. H. LAWRENCE *Birds, Beasts & Flowers* 82 Since the Lamb bewitched him with that red-struck flag His fortress is dismantled. **1932** BLUNDEN *Face of England* 50 Red-washed cottages.

b. *red-glowing, -panting.*

1936 R. CAMPBELL *Mithraic Emblems* 24 A sombre grape, whose heart, Red-glowing to the hilted dart, Seems a lit furnace that he fans. **1922** JOYCE *Ulysses* 47 Unheeded he kept by them.., a rag of wolf's tongue redpanting from his jaws.

III. 16. e. Applied to hearts and diamonds in a pack of cards.

1764 [in Dict., sense 16 a]. **1908** R. F. FOSTER *Auction Bridge* 50 Here is an example of a hand which is not a good red declaration. **1910** W. DALTON *'Saturday' Bridge* vii. 100 Doubling an original red-suit declaration cannot be recommended on anything very short of a certainty. **1973** *Times* 29 Sept. 11/7 He needed to find both red aces on the left... His game bid was against the odds.

f. Applied to the representation of British territories on maps: see sense *1 e of the sb.

1916 J. BUCHAN *Greenmantle* iv. 52 You see that map... South Africa is coloured green. Not red for the English, or yellow for the Germans. **1934** A. HUXLEY *Beyond Mexique Bay* 36 The non-existent young lady in fancy dress would be mortally offended by the suggestion that the place [*sc.* British Honduras] should be painted anything but red on the map. **1964** *Critical Q.* Winter 320 You shook your finger at the map and said..'Africa, I want it red.' **1975** *Listener* 4 Sept. 297/1 At the beginning of the 20th century, practically every country exporting spices was marked red on the map. **1977** A. WILSON *Strange Ride R. Kipling* iv. 212 Rhodes arranged for Rudyard to make a visit up to the territory of Rhodesia, which he saw as the first step in his dream of an all-red British route from Cape Town to Cairo.

17. a. *Animals*, as **red buck,** substitute for def.: = *IMPALA, *ROOIBOK; (earlier and later examples); **red bug,** (*b*) substitute for def.: = JIGGER *sb.*[2] in Dict. and Suppl.; (examples); **red cat** *S. Afr.* = *ROOIKAT; (earlier and later examples); **red crab** (earlier example); **red dog,** the dhole, *Cyon* (or *Cuon*) *alpinus*; **red fox** (*b*) (earlier and later examples); **red hare,** (*b*) a southern African hare belonging to the genus *Pronolagus*, distinguished by speckled buff and black fur, with reddish fur beneath the body and a red-brown tail; **red hartebeest,** a variety of hartebeest, *Alcelaphus bucelaphus caama*; **red howler,** a howler monkey, *Alouatta seniculus*, found in forested areas of South America and distinguished by long red-brown fur; **red mite,** (*a*) a blood-sucking mite, *Dermanyssus gallinæ*, which attacks poultry; (*b*) = RED SPIDER; **red panda** = PANDA; **red river hog,** a West African race of the bush pig, *Potamochœrus porcus*; **red setter,** an Irish setter belonging to the breed sometimes so called, distinguished by a long, silky, dark red coat, drooping ears, and a long feathered tail; **red squirrel,** (*a*) substitute for def.: a small North American squirrel, *Sciurus hudsonicus*, also called the chickaree; (earlier and later examples); (*b*) the common European squirrel, *Sciurus vulgaris*, now relatively rare in Britain; **red wolf,** (*b*) substitute for def.: a North American wolf, *Canis rufus*, native to parts of the south-western states, where it is rare; (later examples); (*c*) a variety of the common wolf, *Canis lupus*.

1813 J. CAMPBELL *Jrnl.* 30 Oct. in *Trav. S. Afr.* (1815) xl. 484 The following are the number of creatures killed by our people during the journey..Redbucks..6..Rhebucks..3. **1965** Red-buck [see *IMPALA]. **1804** D. MCKINNEN *Tour Brit. W. Indies* x. 171 The red bug..has stained the cotton so much in some places this year as to render it of little or no value. **1827** J. L. WILLIAMS *View W. Florida* 29 Red bugs are numerous, especially in mossy woods. **1856** *Rep. Comm. Patents 1855: Agric.* (U.S.) 104 The 'red-bugs', or..'cotton-stainers', generally make their appearance about August. **1909** Red bug [see *BÊTE ROUGE]. **1939** *Sun* (Baltimore) 18 Aug. 11/2 The chiggers—'red bugs' to some—were terrific. **1955** *Sci. News Let.* 16 July 42/1 Chiggers, called red bugs down South, cause the most exquisite itching. **1731** G. MEDLEY tr. *Kolb's Present State Cape Good-Hope* II. 127 A few that are call'd Wild Red Cats..have a streak of bright Red running along the ridge of the back. **1947** *Cape Times* 3 May 14 Buck which used to be plentiful have been almost exterminated by wild red cats. **1966** E. PALMER *Plains of Camdeboo* x. 180 There could have been lynx or red cats in the mountain behind us... Even in a zoo these animals are wonderful, the size of a small leopard, not spotted but brick red with jet-black pointed ears and emerald eyes. **1825** C. WATERTON *Wanderings S. Amer.* 285 Amongst the bare roots of the trees..a red crab sometimes makes its appearance. **1862** *Chambers's Encycl.* III. 528/2 The name Dhole is extended to some other very similar species or varieties, natives of Ceylon, Nepaul, and other parts of the East, to which the common name Red Dogs has been sometimes applied. **1894** KIPLING *Second Jungle Bk.* 178 'What moves?' said Phao...'The dhole, the dhole of the Dekkan—Red Dog, the Killer!' **1957** P. J. DARLINGTON *Zoogeogr.* vi. 394 *Cuon* (the Dhole or Red Dog), widely distributed in southern and eastern Asia. [**1637** T. MORTON *New Eng. Canaan* II. v. 79 The Foxes are of two coloures; the one redd, the other gray.] **1778** in *Essex Inst. Hist. Coll.* (1913) XLIX. 109 Sold..38 red fox skins. **1917** H. E. ANTHONY *Mammals Amer.* 72/2 The Red Fox mates in February or early in March. **1974** *Harper's & Queen* Sept. 37/3 (*caption*) Red Fox Jacket £450. **1844** J. BACKHOUSE *Narr. Visit Mauritius & S. Afr.* xxviii. 485 The Red Hare or Roode Haas..is smaller than the Common Hare. **1912** J. STEVENSON-HAMILTON *Animal Life Afr.* xvi. 252 The red hare..has only recently acquired the dignity of a separate genus. **1939** [see *KLIPBOK]. **1971** C. M. VAN DER WESTHUIZEN in D. J. Potgieter et al. *Animal Life S. Afr.* 396/1 The red hares (*Pronolagus* spp.) are peculiar to Southern Africa, where they inhabit elevated and hilly country. **1947** J. STEVENSON-HAMILTON *Wild Life S. Afr.* xii. 80 The Cape or red hartebeest..is now found only in the remoter parts of the north-west of the Cape Province and portions of the deserts of Bechuanaland and South-West Africa. **1966** E. PALMER *Plains of Camdeboo* viii. 134 The red hartebeest was almost certainly here for it was once one of the commonest antelope in the Cape. **1979** DELANY & HAPPOLD *Ecol. Afr. Mammals* vii. 152 Blue wildebeest, red hartebeest and eland..are elements of a fauna found further to the south. **1865** Red howler [see HOWLER 1 b]. **1894** H. O. FORBES *Hand-bk. Primates* I. 194 The Red Howlers always travel in large companies. **1958** J. CAREW *Wild Coast* viii. 109 The forest was full of noises—the roar of red howlers. **1894** *Rep. Vermont Board Agric.* XIV. 176 A little kerosene on the roosts will destroy the red mites that are so troublesome. **1912** J. H. ROBINSON *Princ. & Pract. Poultry Culture* xx. 342 Red mites..secrete themselves about the roosts. **1950** *N.Z. Jrnl. Agric.* Feb. 146/3 Some vegetable crops, including beans, are liable to become severely infested with red mite. *Ibid.* 182/3 Infestations of body lice, red mite, and intestinal worms all weaken the birds' constitution. **1976** WALTERS & PARKER *Keeping Chickens* vi. 61 Red mites. These are in fact greyish in colour, about the size of a pinhead and live in cracks and joints in the woodwork of the house. **1955** F. BOURLIÈRE *Mammals of World* vi. 184 The Red Panda is a solitary animal. **1971** L. H. MATTHEWS *Life of Mammals* II. ix. 266 The red or lesser panda..inhabits parts of western China and the slopes of the Himalayas. **1868** Red river hog [see RIVER *sb.*[1] 5]. **1953** G. M. DURRELL *Overloaded Ark* i. 38 A fully grown pair of Red River Hogs fled... They were the most vivid orange colour with long white tufts on their ears, and a flowing mane of white hair along their backs. [**1872** 'IDSTONE' *Dog* xii. 108 The Irish Setter should be of a pure rich mahogany red.] **1885** [see SETTER *sb.*[1] 11 a]. **1893** R. B. LEE *Hist. & Descr. Mod. Dogs* (*Sporting Div.*) xvii. 343 One cannot say that the Irish red setter, the Irish terrier, and the water spaniel of Ireland, came at any recent date from one stock. **1912** A. HUXLEY *Let.* 23 June (1969) I. 46 For the past week the..beautiful red setter has been ill, refusing nourishment. **1954** M. K. WILSON tr. *Lorenz's Man meets Dog* viii. 78 A Red Setter or a dog of a similar long-haired, long-eared breed. **1977** *Irish Press* 29 Sept. 16/2 (Advt.), Red Setter pups 6 weeks old, male and female, parents F.T.C. [**1637** T. MORTON *New Eng. Canaan* II. v. 81 There are Squirils of three sorts, very different in shape and condition; one..is red, and hee haunts our howses, and will rob us of our Corne.] **1682** T. ASH *Carolina* 22 There are.. the Red, the Grey, the Fox and Black Squirrels. **1795** *Stat. Acct. Scotland* XV. xxi. 439 The red squirrel..has become extremely common of late years. **1902** W. D. HULBERT *Forest Neighbors* 102 Other sounds there were..the scolding of the red squirrel, disturbed and angry. **1935** [see *GREY SQUIRREL]. **1971** *Country Life* 17 June 1538/1 It is not within my memory when red squirrels were about in fair numbers. **1972** *Ecology* LIII. 1142/1 Pasture juniper fruits provide winter food for red squirrels. **1942** G. M. ALLEN *Extinct & Vanishing Mammals* 229 The typical form of red wolf was slightly the smallest of the three races. **1964** [see *grey wolf* s.v. *GREY, GRAY *a.* 8 b]. **1969** J. FISHER et al. *Red Bk.* 75/2 It [*sc.* the giant panda] appears to be without natural enemies, with the possible exception of the leopard and the red wolf. **1978** B. H. LOPEZ *Of Wolves & Men* 279 My wife and I raised two hybrid red wolves.

b. *Birds*, as **red bishop (bird),** an African weaver belonging to the genus *Euplectes*, esp. *E. orix*; **red grouse** (examples); **red mavis** *U.S.*, the common ground thrush, *Toxostoma rufum*; = *brown-thrasher* s.v. BROWN *a.* 6.

1884 E. L. LAYARD *Birds S. Afr.* (ed. 2) 462 Red Bishop Bird..though not an uncommon bird, is certainly a very local one. **1939** *Nature* 1 Apr. 566/1 The red bishop has never been found to have more than three wives in his large territory. **1955** MACKWORTH-PRAED & GRANT *Birds E. & N.E. Afr.* II. 951 Zanzibar Red Bishop..differs from the South African and Tanganyika Territory races of the Red Bishop. **1966** E. PALMER *Plains of Camdeboo* xii. 197 Here would be red bishop birds in summer plumage, the grenadier of Barrow... Sita saw a bird like a jewel sail past her... It was a red bishop bird, black and glowing scarlet, on its way to the reeds with its drab-coloured harem. **1776** T. PENNANT *Brit. Zool.* (ed. 4) I. 269 Grous..Red... The plumage on the head and neck is of a light tawny red. **1910** MALCOLM & MAXWELL *Grouse* i. 1 We shall be almost exclusively concerned with the red grouse. **1927** S. GORDON *Days with Golden Eagle* xiv. 93 The grey or hooded crow is a far more deadly enemy to red grouse than the golden eagle. **1971** *Country Life* 12 Aug. 390/1 It [*sc.* heather] provides the main food of that highly famed bird, the Scottish red grouse. **1854** THOREAU *Walden* 171 Upon the topmost spray of a birch sings the brown-thrasher—or red mavis, as some love to call him. **1858** *Atlantic Monthly* Dec. 869/2 The Red Mavis..has many habits similar to those of the Cat-Bird. **1917** T. G. PEARSON *Birds Amer.* III. 179 Brown Thrasher... Other names..Mavis; Red Mavis; Song Thrush.

c. *Fishes*, etc., as **red bream** (later examples); **red drum** (earlier and later examples); **red groper,** a red-skinned form of the blue groper, *Achœrodus gouldii*, a marine fish found off the coast of southern Australia; **red grouper,** delete 'Mexican' and add: found off the coast of south-eastern North America; (earlier and later examples); **red snapper,** substitute for def.: one of several important marine food fishes belonging to the family Lutjanidæ, esp. *Lutjanus campechinus* of eastern North and Central America; (earlier and later examples).

1924 *Truth* (Sydney) 27 Apr. 6 *Red bream*, name given to young schnapper. **1969** *Man* (Austral.) Mar. 87/2 Another prize for the table is the snapper or red bream. **1709** J. LAWSON *New Voy. Carolina* 156 Black Drums are a thicker-made fish than the Red Drum. **1969** *Daily Progress* (Charlottesville, Va.) 25 May 5 B/1 A big Channel Bass, or Red Drum as it is called in some circles, lay on the charmingly beautiful wild-beach. **1893** J. D. OGILBY *Edible Fishes & Crustaceans N.S.W.* 134 (*heading*) Red Groper. **1962** L. WEDLICK *Fishing in Austral.* iv. 159 The red groper is now considered to be the female of the species. **1829** Red grouper [see GROUPER 1]. **1976** *National Observer* (U.S.) 23 Oct. 19/4 This is the place for exotic fish eating, with surprises like..Florida red grouper. **1775,** etc. [see SNAPPER *sb.*[1] 6 b]. **1973** *Nature* 6 July 49/1 The red snapper, *Etelis marshi* (an Indian Ocean fish). **1978** *Detroit Free Press* 16 Apr. (Detroit Suppl.) 28/2 There is a respectable number of fish dishes, ranging from the irreproachable Florida red snapper to frog legs, scallops and deviled crab. **1978** *Times* 4 Nov. 13/3 Red Snapper baked in a sauce of fresh tomatoes, onions, celery.

d. *Plants*, as **red alder** = *red els*, *ROOI-ELS; **red ash,** (*a*) for *pubescens* substitute *pennsylvanica*; (earlier and later examples); (*b*) (later example); **red bay,** for *carolinensis* substitute *borbonia*; (earlier and later examples); **red bean** (see sense 19 below); **red beech,** (*a*) substitute for def.: the common North American beech, *Fagus grandifolia*; (earlier and later examples); (*c*) a southern beech of New Zealand, *Nothofagus fusca*; **red birch** (earlier and later examples); **red elm,** substitute for def.: one of several elms, esp. the American slippery elm, *Ulmus fulva*; (earlier and later examples); **red fir,** (*b*) substitute for def.: a fir of western North America belonging to the genus *Abies*, esp. *A. magnifica*; (examples); (*c*) add = *Douglas fir* s.v. *DOUGLAS[1]; (examples); **red grass** *S. Afr.*, one of several reddish pasture grasses, esp. *Themeda triandra*; **red iron bark** (earlier and later examples); **red mahogany** (earlier and later examples); **red maple** (earlier and later examples); **red oak,** substitute for def.: a North American oak, *Quercus borealis* (or *Q. rubra*), or a closely related species; (earlier and later examples); **red osier,** substitute for def.: (*a*) *N. Amer.* in full, *red osier dogwood*; one of several species of dogwood, esp. *Cornus stolonifera*; (earlier and later examples); † (*b*) the basket willow, *Salix* × *rubra*; **red pine,** (*a*) (earlier and later examples); (*b*) (later examples); (*c*) (earlier and later examples); (*d*) the Japanese pine, *Pinus densiflora*; cf. *MATSU; **red sandal wood** (earlier example); **red spruce,** for *rubra* substitute *rubens*; delete rest of def.; (earlier and later examples); **red willow,** one of several North American willows with reddish bark, esp. *Salix lævigata*; also = *red osier*.

1907 T. R. SIM *Forests & Forest Flora Cape of Good Hope* xiv. 217 Red Alder or Red Els. **1784** *Mem. Amer. Acad.* I. 492 *Fraxinus*..The White Ash. The Red Ash. The Black Ash. The Prickley Ash. **1965** *Austral. Encycl.* I. 165/2 The red almond (also called red ash, white-leaf, leather-jacket and cooper's wood), is a smooth-barked tree. **1969** T. H. EVERETT *Living Trees of World* 286/2 The red ash forms an irregular head with stout, erect branches. **1731** M. CATESBY *Nat. Hist. Carolina* I. 63 The Red Bay... The wood is fine grain'd, and of excellent use for Cabinets. **1734** [see *hand-board* s.v. *HAND *sb.* 63]. **1938** M. K. RAWLINGS *Yearling* iv. 35 The red bay thicket seemed impenetrable. [**1637** T. MORTON *New Eng. Canaan* II. ii. 63 Beech there is of two sorts, redd and white.] **1810** F. A. MICHAUX *Hist. Arbres Forestiers de l'Amérique Septentrionale* I. 27 Red beech.. dans les Etats du nord. **1894** *Amer. Folk-Lore* VII. 99 *Fagus sylvatica*, white beech, red beech. **1928** COCKAYNE & TURNER *Trees N.Z.* 83 *Nothofagus fusca*..Red-beech. A tall, massive tree. **1970** R. M. LOCKLEY *Man against Nature* x. 204 The native red beech *Nothofagus* takes a hundred.. years to mature. **1785** H. MARSHALL *Arbustrum Americanum* 19 Red birch..grows to a pretty large size. **1918** N. DUNCAN *Battles Royal* I. ii. 41 The crew was gathered close about a roaring red birch fire. **1949** COLLINGWOOD & BRUSH *Knowing your Trees* 172 River birch is also called red birch. **1805** M. LEWIS *Jrnl.* 12 Apr. in *Orig. Jrnls. Lewis & Clark Exped.* (1904) I. vii. 299 Some timber..consists of Cotton-wood red Elm, with a small proportion of small Ash. **1810** [see *moose elm*]. **1956** *Handbk. of Hardwoods* (Forest Prod. Res. Lab.) 88 Elm, English..Other Names. Red elm, nave elm. *Ibid.* 92 Commercial white elm may include some slippery elm (*Ulmus fulva*) also known as red elm. **1844** LEE & FROST *Ten Years in Oregon* 81 The red fir constitutes the greater part of the timber of the country. **1884** [see *DOUGLAS[1]]. **1884** [see *mountain hemlock* s.v. *MOUNTAIN 9 d]. **1949** COLLINGWOOD & BRUSH *Knowing your Trees* 106 In close stands the trunks of red fir are clear of branches from sixty to eighty feet. **1957** M. HADFIELD *Brit. Trees* 32 Douglas fir,..Oregon pine, red fir. **1974** *Country Life* 12 Dec. 1855/1 A fine Red fir (*Abies amabilis*) a rather rare tree from Washington State and British Columbia. **1929** J. W. BEWS *World's Grasses* vi. 253 The most important grass in enormous areas of African savanna..is the 'Rooi gras' or 'Red grass' of S. Africa. **1955** J. COPE *Fair House* ii. 37 He [*sc.* a horse] likes the red-grass down here. **1884** A. NILSON *Timber Trees N.S.W.* 65 *E*[*ucalyptus*] *leucoxylon*.—Red-flowering Ironbark; Black Ironbark; Red Ironbark. **1944** *Living off Land* vii. 137 Slow growers with a dense grain.. include..Snow Gum, Red Ironbark. **1884** Red mahogany [see *forest mahogany* s.v. *FOREST *sb.* 5]. **1965** *Austral. Encycl.* IV. 404/2 Phillip's 'gum-tree' was the red mahogany, *E*[*ucalyptus*] *resinifera*. **1770** J. R. FORSTER *Trav. N. Amer.* I. 167 The red Maple, or *Acer rubrum*, is plentiful in these places. **1955** [see *PACE *v.* 2 a]. **1976** *Sci. Amer.* Nov. 111/3 There were other valley species, among them..the sugar maple..and its relatives the silver maple.., the red maple (*A. rubrum*) and the box elder. **1634** W. WOOD *New Englands Prospect* 16 Of Oakes there be three kindes, the red Oake, white, and black. **1663** *Rec. Town of Plymouth* (Mass.) (1889) I. 64 Lott lyeth on the easterly side of the fourth lott and att the south end bounded with a Rid oake stake. **1901** H. ROBERTSON *Inlander* 310, I des gwine down to de branch to git me some red-oak bark. **1958** G. A. PETRIDES *Field Guide Trees & Shrubs* 294 The barks of many red oaks are dark in color. **1976** *Sci. Amer.* Nov. 112/1 The red oak and the white oak, which put down a deep tap root, seldom survive the process of transplantation. **1807** F. PURSH *Jrnl. Bot. Excursion* (1923) 48 Cornus several sorts, among which is the Osier rouge or Red Osier. **1857** THOREAU *Maine Woods* (1864) 174 There grew..*Cornus stolonifera*, or red osier. **1864** *Ibid.* 314 *Cornus stolonifera* (red-osier dogwood), prevailing shrub on shore of West Branch. **1946** T. M. STANWELL-FLETCHER *Driftwood Valley* 112 The moose browsed on young twigs of willow and red-osier dogwood. **1971** *Islander* (Victoria, B.C.) 30 May 3/1 A red osier dogwood..shaded our tents. **1972** FREDERICKSON & EAST

Silence of North xx. 182 His [*sc.* a bear's] broad burly rump was vanishing in a thick tangle of red osier halfway down the slope. **1809** E. A. KENDALL *Trav. U.S.* III. 145, I have referred the sapling of the lumberers to the yellow, red or Norway pine. **1829,** etc. [see *NORWAY[1]]. **1884,** etc. [see *MATSU]. **1884** A. NILSON *Timber Trees N.S.W.* 81 *F[renela] Endlicheri.*—Red Pine; Black Pine. **1900** A. H. KENT *Veitch's Man. Coniferæ* (new ed.) 145 Two of the species are of great importance in their native countries on account of their valuable timber, viz., the Rimu or Red Pine of New Zealand, *Dacrydium cupressinum*, and the Huon Pine. **1911** [see *Moreton Bay pine* s.v. *MORETON BAY a]. **1916** E. POUND *Lustra* 89 The red-pine-tree god looks on him and wonders. **1970** R. M. LOCKLEY *Man against Nature* x. 204 The rimu or red pine *Dacrydium* [takes] two hundred years to mature to the milling stage. **1840** J. PEREIRA *Elem. Materia Medica* II. 1142 Red Sandal or red Sander's wood (*lignum santali rubri*; *lignum santalinum rubrum*) is imported in roundish or somewhat angular billets, which are blackish externally, but of blood-red internally. **1777** *Quebec Gaz.* 17 Apr. 2/1 The logs covering the sleepers, shall be of ash or red spruce. **1943** R. PEATTIE *Great Smokies* 157 The red spruce..crowns only our highest peaks. **1977** J. L. HARPER *Population Biol. Plants* xx. 622 At least 50% of the trees in the upper canopy were red spruce. **1784** *Mem. Amer. Acad.* I. 491 *Salix*... The White Willow. The Red Willow. The Rose Willow. The Dogwood. **1855** LONGFELLOW *Hiawatha* i. 12 The bark of the red willow. **1895** *Outing* XXVII. 211/1 The lake..was covered with a growth of red willows and rushes. **1969** T. H. EVERETT *Living Trees of World* x. 96/1 Among lower-growing American willows the following are of tree size: the red or polished willow [etc.].

e. *Minerals* etc., as **red clay,** (*a*) in general use; (*b*) a fine-grained, red or reddish-brown, abyssal clay of diverse origins, containing windblown particles, meteoric and volcanic dust and debris, and insoluble organic remains; **red earth,** † (*a*) (in Dict., sense 19); (*b*) a red soil of the tropics and sub-tropics, usu. clayey and highly leached, and coloured by iron; cf. *red loam* (next entry); **red loam,** a red soil of the tropics, usually friable and highly leached; cf. *red earth* (*b*) above; **red mud,** (*a*) a marine mud of terrigenous origin, found on continental shelves and in other shallow waters, and coloured by iron oxides; (*b*) a residue from the extraction of alumina from bauxite, coloured red by ferric impurities; **red rock,** (*a*) *U.S.* (see quot. 1904); (*b*) *Geol.*, a predominantly or wholly granophyric rock of red colour associated with some large gabbroic masses; **red soil,** a general name for leached soil of the tropics and sub-tropics, coloured red by ferric compounds; cf. sense A. 1 f in Dict.

1387 Red clay [in Dict.]. **1827** J. L. WILLIAMS *View of W. Florida* 89 In the gulf [of Mexico], the..red clay lands approach within eighteen or twenty miles of the coast. **1874** *Proc. R. Soc.* XXII. 427 The bottom consists of '*Globigerina*-ooze' or of the red clay produced by the decomposition of the shells of Foraminifera. **1916** H. F. CLELAND *Geol.* vi. 242 Radiolarian ooze and red clay shade into each other in certain places, the deposit being called radiolarian ooze when these organic remains constitute 25 per cent. of the mass. **1926** *Jrnl. Geol.* XXXIV. 140 The *terra rosea* of the Istrian Peninsula, Dalmatia, and Greece consists of red clay, residual from a limestone basement. **1964** W. C. PUTNAM *Geol.* xiv. 371/2 Some workers once thought the red clay consisted mostly of meteoritic dust... Now the evidence appears more convincing that the red clay has a land-derived origin, and that it consists for the most part of the very finest clay and related particles. **1976** *National Observer* (U.S.) 23 Oct. 9/3 But Cooper and his boys are a long way from the red-clay farm he describes so vividly in *Families*. *a* **1977** *Harrison Mayer Ltd. Catal.* 14/2 *Red clay*, a term applied to all the ferruginous bodies, high in iron and manganese. Typified by the clay known as Etruria Marl. **1877** C. W. THOMSON *Atlantic* I. iv. 315 Wherever, throughout the islands, a section of the limestone is exposed of any depth, it is intersected by one or two horizontal beds of an ochre-like substance, called locally 'red earth'... This 'red earth', mixed with varying proportions of decayed vegetable matter and coral-sand, forms the surface layer of vegetable soil. **1889** *Bull. U.S. Geol. Survey* No. 52. 25 The red earth of the southern portion of the Great Appalachian Valley is apparently identical, both in composition and in the method of accumulation, with the 'terra rossa' of southern Europe, the 'laterite' of India, and the 'red earth' of Bermuda. **1932** [see *red loam* below]. **1958** C. ACHEBE *Things fall Apart* xxv. 184 There was a small bush behind Okonkwo's compound. The only opening into this bush from the compound was a little round hole in the red-earth wall through which fowls went in and out. **1966** *Official Yearbk. Australia* LII. 878 Red earths associated with old land surfaces are widely distributed throughout the semi-arid areas. **1932** H. GREENE tr. *Vageler's Introd. Tropical Soils* v. 163 The younger the soil, the greater the predominance of unchanged siallitic material, and the soil has then the character of a more or less plastic red loam. **1932** G. W. ROBINSON *Soils* xiii. 271 P. Vageler draws a distinction between red loams and red earths... In comparatively young soils..the clay is of a siliceous type and the soil is described as a red loam. In the red earths, removal of silicic acid or accession of sesquioxides has proceeded sufficiently to give a weathering complex of a predominantly sesquioxidic character. **1885** *Rep. Sci. Results Voy. H.M.S. Challenger: Narrative* I. xxi. 918 Red muds. **1926** *Jrnl. Geol.* XXXIV. 140 The red muds which Murray found in such quantities in the Atlantic Ocean off the mouth of the Amazon River. **1936** *Metals Handbk.* (Amer. Soc. Metals) 902 The Bayer process is almost universally employed for the purification of bauxite. In this process the bauxite is digested with caustic soda solution under pressure and the alumina dissolved out as a solution of sodium aluminate. The residue, known as red mud, contains the oxides of iron, silicon, and titanium [etc.]. **1972** *Daily Tel.* (Colour Suppl.) 27 Oct. 25/1 There are tentative hopes for a new industry based on 'red mud'. This is the unpleasant-looking residue of the aluminium process... Red mud may yet be pay dirt. **1880** J. F. CARLL *Geol. Oil Regions* vi. 72 In this record we have two important facts to work upon—the top of the conglomerate and the presence of red rock beneath it and not far below its base. **1893** *Bull. U.S. Geol. Survey* No. 109. 23 The red rock..is found in three distinct though indefinitely outlined areas... It occupies a position between the gabbro and the fragmental rocks. **1904** *Dialect Notes* II. 387 *Red rock*, the drillers' name for the red shale underlying the Panama Conglomerate. **1908** *Jrnl. Geol.* XVI. 774 The 'red rock dike' of analysis No. 12 is called gabbro-aplite by the author. **1918** *Ibid.* XXVI. 632 The 'red rock' has purposely been left out of the discussion of variations from the gabbro,..because its geologic relations are very different... The gray gabbro rapidly gives place to a bright red rock... The 'red rock' has become widely known under this name because of its brilliant color and the difficulty of giving it a more accurate classification... The rock here discussed is intrusive and granitoid. **1969** BENNISON & WRIGHT *Geol. Hist. Brit. Isles* xi. 268 Red rocks of Permian and Triassic age outcrop in south-west England. **1889** *Bull. U.S. Geol. Survey* No. 52. 29 It closely resembles the similar red soils of Virginia and of many other regions. **1906** E. W. HILGARD *Soils* iii. 34 The 'red' soils formed from the so-called granites and slates of the western slope of the Sierra Nevada of California. **1932** G. W. ROBINSON *Soils* xvi. 323 The red soils which occupy most of southern India outside the black cotton area..are probably similar to the red loams and red earths of East Africa. **1940** G. TAYLOR *Australia* v. 77 All rocks in the west which are not very poor in iron (and not situated in a basin) yield red soils, since the paucity of organic matter allows for a rapid oxidation of the iron in the clay. *Ibid.* viii. 181 The red soils indicate that the material has been peroxidized under a hot sun in an arid climate not subjected to periodic flooding. **1970** *E. Afr. Standard* (Nairobi) 23 Jan. 16/8 (Advt.), Freehold red-soil plot in the most desired residential area.

f. Combined with other colours, as **Red and White Friesian,** a cow or bull belonging to the breed so called, distinguished by its red and white coat from the black and white animals of the older Friesian breed; also *ellipt.*

1962 *Guardian* 23 Oct. 2/5 A breed of cow making its first appearance at the [Royal Dairy] show this year is the Red and White Friesian. *Ibid.*, One of the Red and Whites has given 8·62 gallons in three milkings at the show. **1975** *N.Z. Jrnl. Agric.* Sept. 65/2 Breeders began experimenting by crossing their purebred cattle with Red and White Friesian and Danish Red bulls.

18. Prefixed to the name of a part (or some distinctive feature) used to denote the whole: **a.** of persons, as **red-beard** (later example); **red-hat,** (*b*) a staff officer (*Mil. slang*).

1868 W. MORRIS *Earthly Paradise* I. 194 Thou laughest—hast thou never heard Of this same valorous Red Beard, And how he died? **1916** W. OWEN *Let.* 3 July (1967) 398 Red-Hats gallup up to us at startling speed.., but they never stay long, or criticise. **1918** A. BENNETT *Pretty Lady* xxii. 146 It was the red hat put me off. **1919** W. DEEPING *Second Youth* xxxiv. 288 When the real job's finished we just throw up our caps and shout. I wish the red-hat element would try to understand that. **1978** A. WAUGH *Best Wine Last* xv. 179 A number of very high-ranking officers were invited... The visiting red hats were not impressed.

b. *spec.*, forming the names of certain birds, fishes, plants, etc., as **red-ear,** (*a*) in full, *red-ear sunfish*; a North American freshwater fish, *Lepomis microlophus*, which has a red patch on its operculum; (*b*) in full, *red-ear turtle*; a small North American turtle, *Pseudemys scripta elegans*, distinguished by a reddish stripe behind the eye; also called a slider; **red fin,** (*c*) the Australian name for the English perch, *Perca fluviatilis*, which was introduced into Australia in 1868; **red-root,** (*a*) (earlier and later examples). See also *RED-HEART etc. as main entries in Suppl.

1948 *List Common Names Fishes U.S.* (Amer. Fisheries Soc.) 1. 16 Redear Sunfish *Lepomis microlophus*. **1957** M. B. TRAUTMAN *Fishes of Ohio* iv. 518/1 Three years later the offspring of these 14 Red ears appeared to be..numerous. **1958** R. CONANT *Field Guide Reptiles & Amphibians* 58 Baby Red-ears, commonest of all pet turtles, are sold in enormous numbers. **1977** *N.Z. Herald* 8 Jan. 4–9/5 (Advt.), Miniature red ear turtle, tank, element and thermostat. **1979** *Arizona Daily Star* 1 Apr. c 11/4 A state-record redear sunfish has been reported from Parker Canyon Lake... The big redear was identified by Ft. Huachuca fisheries biologist Bruce Halsted. **1951** T. C. ROUGHLEY *Fish & Fisheries Austral.* 152 English perch (Redfin—*Perca fluviatilis*). **1969** *Southerly* XXIX. 127 Twice, in the dusk, he caught a redfin. **1709** J. LAWSON *New Voy. Carolina* 78 The Red-Root whose Leaf is like Spear-mint, is good for..sore Mouths. **1941** R. S. WALKER *Lookout* 59 The commonest shrub..is New Jersey tea or red-root.

19. a. With miscellaneous sbs., as **red alert,** a warning of danger; an instruction to be prepared for an emergency, or, in hospitals, to admit only emergency cases; also, a state of readiness for an emergency; also *fig.* and (with hyphen) *attrib.*; **red anchor,** used *attrib.* to designate that period in the history of the Chelsea porcelain factory during which it produced high-quality porcelain with a distinguishing red anchor mark; also applied to porcelain of this period; **Red Arrow,** a familiar name for the nightly express train from Moscow to Leningrad; **red-arse** *Mil. slang*, a recruit; **Red Astrachan,** a red-skinned variety of eating apple; **red atrophy** *Med.*, a later stage of massive necrosis of the liver, in which the organ is red rather than yellow; **red ball** *U.S. slang*, a fast freight train or truck; high priority freight; also *attrib.*; **red-band** *Prison slang* (see quot. 1950); **Red Bank,** the name of an oyster bed in Co. Clare, Ireland, used attrib. in *Red Bank oyster*; **red banner** = *RED FLAG 1, 3 a; also used in the title of various distinctions and orders in the U.S.S.R.; **red bean,** (*a*) the red-skinned seed of one of several legumes; (*b*) an Australian timber tree, *Dysoxylum muelleri*, of the family Meliaceæ; **red beds** *Geol.*, add: more widely, sedimentary strata deposited at any period in a continental environment, composed largely of sandstone, siltstone, or shale, and coloured red by iron compounds which usu. coat individual grains; also *attrib.* in *sing.*; (earlier and further examples); **red-berry,** (*a*) substitute for def.: one of several North American plants, esp. the red baneberry (*Actæa rubra*); (earlier and later examples); (*b*) (later example); **red biddy** *colloq.*, a drink consisting of methylated spirits and cheap red wine; also, inferior red wine; **red blanket** *Austral. slang* (see quot.); **red blood cell** or **corpuscle** = *RED CELL; **red board** *U.S. slang*, (*a*) a stop signal on a railway; (*b*) (see quot. 1935); **red body,** also, the gland that this aggregation supplies, or both structures together; = *red gland* below; (earlier and later examples); **Red Branch [**tr. Gael. *Craebh Ruaid*], in Irish epic tradition, the name of the most famous of the royal houses of Ulster; **Red Brigade(s),** a left-wing extremist terrorist group operating in Italy from the early 1970s; hence **Red Brigader,** a member of this group; **red carpet,** the carpet of this colour traditionally laid down on formal occasions to greet important visitors, used *fig.* to indicate a ceremonial welcome or lavish reception; freq. *attrib.*, as *red carpet treatment*, etc.; **red caviar,** the red roe of fish other than the sturgeon; **Red Centre,** the remote interior of Australia; cf. *CENTRE *sb.* 11 h; **Red Chamber,** the Senate chamber of the Canadian Parliament Building, Ottawa; hence, the Senate itself; **red channel,** at a port, airport, etc., the channel through which passengers should pass who have goods to declare; † **red children,** North American Indians considered as under the guardianship of a white person or agency (*obs.*); **red-cooking** *vbl. sb.*, a form of Chinese cookery in which meat is fried quickly and then stewed in soya sauce; hence (as a back-formation) **red-cook** *v. trans.*; **red core,** a disease of strawberries caused by the fungus *Phytophthora fragariæ*, which attacks the roots, staining the central part of them and making affected plants wilt; **red corpuscle** = *RED CELL; **red country,** large tracts of red sand, *spec.* in Australia; **Red Crescent,** also, the equivalent of the Red Cross in other Muslim countries; (earlier and later examples); **red Devon,** a large red-brown bull or cow of the breed so called, usually kept for the production of beef; = *DEVON (*a*); **red duster** *slang* = *red ensign*; **red dwarf** *Astr.*, an old, relatively cool star lying on the main sequence; also *attrib.*; **red emperor,** an Australian marine fish, *Lutjanus sebæ*, found off parts of the northern coast; **red ensign** (examples); **red figure** *Archæol.*, used *attrib.* and *absol.* to designate a technique of vase painting devised in Athens in the late sixth century B.C. in which figures and patterns are outlined and detailed with lines of black paint on a red clay ground and the background filled in with black; so **red-figured** *a.*; **red flannel,** flannel dyed red and formerly used esp. for making underwear, nightwear, etc.; also used *colloq.* in *pl.* to designate clothing made from red flannel; also *fig.*; **red flannel hash** *U.S.*, a hash (HASH *sb.* 1) made with beetroot; **red giant** *Astr.*, a relatively cool giant star; **red gland** *Zool.*, a gland in the wall of a swim bladder which secretes gas into the bladder so as to increase the buoyancy of the fish; also, esp. formerly, the rete mirabile that supplies the gland, or both structures together; **red hardness** *Metallurgy*, the property, exhibited by some steels used for machine tools, of retaining a high degree of hardness up to a low red heat; **red hat,** the symbol of a cardinal's office; (see also sense 18 a); **red Indian,** (*a*) (see INDIAN *sb.* 2 b); (*b*) an Australian marine fish, *Patæcus fronto*, which resembles a blenny; **red judge,** *spec.* a high court judge (later examples); **Red Kaffir** *S. Afr.* (see quot. 1904); **red lamp,** (*b*) = *RED LIGHT 2; **Redland** *sb.* and *a.*, the Soviet Union, Russian (*slang*); **red lane** (earlier example); **red lantern** = *RED LIGHT 2; **red lead** *Naval slang*, (*a*) tomato ketchup; (*b*) tinned tomatoes; **red leg** *Zool.*, a bacterial disease of frogs causing hæmolytic septicæmia and a red flush on the ventral surfaces of the hind legs; **red meat,** dark-coloured meat, as beef or lamb (as opposed to chicken, veal, etc.); also *fig.*; **red menace,** the political or military threat regarded as emanating from the Soviet Union; **red morocco** (later examples); **Red Ned** *Austral.* and *N.Z. slang*, inferior red wine or other similar drink; **red noise** (see quots. 1961); **red nucleus** *Anat.*, each of a pair of nuclei in the tegmentum of the midbrain, dorsal to the substantia nigra, which form part of the extra-pyramidal motor system; **Red Paint,** applied to an ancient North American Indian people known from burials in which large quantities of red ochre were used; **red palm oil,** palm oil having a red colour, obtained by boiling the fruit in water instead of by fermentation; **red-pencil** *v. trans.*, to mark (in red) as erroneous or unacceptable; to correct (a piece of written work); **red peril** = *red menace* above; **red planet** (with def. article), the planet Mars; **red poley** = REDPOLL[2] in Dict. and Suppl.; **Red Prince,** nickname of Prince Frederick Charles of Prussia (1828–85); **red rain,** rain that is red or reddish in colour because of suspended dust or, rarely, red algæ; **red reflex** *Ophthalm.*, a red glow, seen in ophthalmoscopy when the interior of the eye is illuminated, caused by the light reflected from the fundus having passed through the choroid; **red ribbon,** (*a*) also **riband** (later example); (*c*) *U.S.* as a symbol of temperance; **Red Riding Hood** [f. the fairy tale *Little Red Riding Hood*], used *attrib.* to designate a type of cape with a hood; **red robin,** (*c*) *U.S.*, a perennial herb, *Castilleja coccinea*, which has bright red bracts surrounding small greenish-yellow flowers; **red rock fault** *Geol.*, a fault in Permian red beds, forming part of the boundary of the Cheshire Basin; **Red Rover,** a children's chasing game; also, the child who is 'it' in this game; **red sable,** the fur of the Japanese mink (kolinsky), used esp. for artists' brushes; a brush made from this fur; **red squill** (see SQUILL); **red star,** a symbol of the Soviet Union; **red steer** *Austral. slang* (see quot. 1941); **red-stone** (later examples); **red tabby,** a cat, esp. a long-haired one, with a reddish-orange coat patterned in a deeper red; **red tag,** name of an artificial fly used in angling; **Red Terror,** the persecution of opponents by the Bolsheviks after the Russian revolution of 1917; also *transf.*; **red tide** = *RED-WATER 4; **Red Tory** *Canada*, one of a political group who, while maintaining some conservative principles, yet support many liberal and socialist policies; so **Red Toryism**; **red vision** *Ophthalm.* = *erythropsia* s.v. *ERYTHRO-; **red warning** = *red alert* above.

See also as main entries in Suppl.: *RED ARMY, *RED BELT, *RED BOOK, etc.

1961 WEBSTER, Red alert. **1962** 'K. ORVIS' *Damned & Destroyed* xxvii. 203 His every move will be under red-alert watch. **1967** *Guardian* 29 Dec. 1/1 The emergency bed service..has put out a 'red alert' to more than 200 hospitals in the London area. **1970** *Daily Tel.* 26 Sept. 1/6 Fearing that the Arabs will attempt to seize another British plane.. the Government sent out a 'red alert' to airlines yesterday, warning them to exercise stringent anti-skyjacking precautions. **1972** 'G. BLACK' *Bitter Tea* (1973) xii. 188 It looked as though a phone call to me had resulted in a red alert. **1973** M. AMIS *Rachel Papers* 98 Fortunately, my room was in a state of red alert nowadays and Rachel's telephone call hadn't caught me with my pants down. **1975** *Times* 26 Nov. 1/4 The health authorities at Croydon yesterday put out a 'red' alert of hospital beds... Hospitals in its area will take only emergencies. **1981** W. SAFIRE in *N.Y. Times Mag.* 22 Feb. 9/1 The red alert flashed here a few weeks ago—warning of incoming semantic missiles from the new Secretary of State, Al Haig. **1957** MANKOWITZ & HAGGAR *Conc. Encycl. Eng. Pott. & Porc.* 49/2 Work of the 'raised' (i.e. embossed) and 'red anchor' periods enjoys the highest esteem. *Ibid.*, The resulting quality..was perhaps inferior to 'red anchor' Chelsea. **1966** *Daily Tel.* 26 Oct. 16/4 A Chelsea figure of a Chinaman, Red Anchor period, was sold for £4,200. **1975** *Oxf. Compan. Decorative Arts* 140/2 This factory's [*sc.* Chelsea's] figures of the 'red anchor' period (1748–55 when the factory mark was an anchor painted in red) are among the loveliest in the whole range of European porcelain. **1973** J. SHUB *Moscow by Nightmare* viii. 87 The Krasnaya Strela—the Red Arrow—leaves Moscow at 11.53 every night. **1974** A. WILLIAMS *Gentleman Traitor* v. 94 You'll be given your ticket on the Red Arrow Express for Leningrad. **1946** R. GRINSTEAD *They dug Hole* I. i. 13 And so it goes on. The everlasting bickering between old sweat and red-arse! **1947** D. M. DAVIN *Gorse blooms Pale* 193 You were only a bloody redarse in those days. **1847** J. M. IVES *New England Bk. Fruit* 36 Red Astracan.—This beautiful apple is of medium size, of a round and rather flat form. **1860** R. HOGG *Fruit Man.* 21 Red Astrachan... Flesh white, and richly flavoured. **1876** J. BURROUGHS *Winter Sunshine* 128 The red astrachan [is] an August apple. **1948** *Newsweek* 30 Aug. 32/1 The best and most popular American apples are descended from Russian apple trees—Borominka, Titovka, Red Astrakhan, Alma Ata—imported into the United States a hundred years ago. **1977** *N.Z. Herald* 8 Jan. 1–5/5 One store was selling a New Zealand apple, red astrachan, at 33c a pound. **1849** E. SIEVEKING tr. *Rokitansky's Man. Path. Anat.* II. I. ii. 122 Atrophy of the liver, independent of the *marasmus senilis* of the organ, appears in various forms. We first draw attention to two distinct forms which have not been remarked hitherto... Owing to their distinctive colouring, they may be appropriately termed yellow and red atrophy. **1961** R. D. BAKER *Essent. Path.* xvi. 409 Massive necrosis... If the patient lives several weeks after the onset of jaundice subacute red atrophy is found at autopsy. **1927** *Amer. Speech* II. 388/2 Fast freights are known as *red balls*. **1934** *Sun* (Baltimore) 3 May 12/6 Several who have worked on these 'red ball' runs told me that after a man has been on a truck twenty-four hours he's tired and unstrung. **1944** *N.Y. Times* 8 Oct. IV. 5/4 The famous Red Ball highway—a belt of one-way roads for truck convoys that actually kept pace with General Patton's advance. *Ibid.* 5/5 It was assumed that bullets and butter, and gasoline as important as either, would be delivered. It was—once the Red Ball got rolling. **1968** *T.V. Times* (Austral.) 29 May 18/3 In railway language 'Red Ball' means top priority freight. **1950** P. TEMPEST *Lag's Lexicon* 178 *Redband*, a privileged prisoner. He is allowed to travel freely about the prison in pursuance of his duties. **1952** J. HENRY *Who lie in Gaol* x. 143 That prisoners could walk through the house unaccompanied by a red-band or an officer seemed to her little short of madness. **1976** A. MILLER *Inside Outside* 3, I would then have a cup of coffee brought to me by a 'red band'. **1876** *Encycl. Brit.* V. 803/1 Near Pooldoody is the great Burren oyster bed called the Red Bank,..from which a constant supply of the excellent Red Bank oysters is furnished to the Dublin and other large markets. **1922** JOYCE *Ulysses* 325 He spat a Red bank oyster out of him. **1935** S. & B. WEBB *Soviet Communism* II. ix. 759 The Red Banner of Toil is awarded 'by special decision' of the Central Executive Committee (TSIK) of the All-Union Congress of Soviets. **1957** *Encycl. Brit.* XXII. Pl. iv, following p. 704, *Order of the Red Banner*: For conspicuous bravery or self-sacrifice in time of war, special capacity for leadership or some action contributing decisively to the success of soviet arms (military or civil). **1966** tr. Lin Piao in *Quotations from Chairman Mao Tse-tung* (Foreword), The most fundamental task in our Party's political and ideological work is at all times to hold high the great red banner of Mao Tse-tung's thought. **1974** tr. *Snieċkus's Soviet Lithuania* 28 New fighting patriots took the places of those that were killed or jailed, keeping the red banner of revolution flying. **1977** *N.Y. Rev. Bks.* 26 May 24/3 The pilgrims move in ranks, by sections, red banners flying. **1892** T. F. GARRETT *Encycl. Pract. Cookery* 93/2 Red Haricot Beans à la Bourguignonne...Take 1 qt. of Red Beans, pick out any stones. **1895** [see *black bean* s.v. *BLACK *a.* 19]. **1908** J. H. MAIDEN *Forest Flora N.S.W.* III. 115 'Red bean' is, however, the commonest name..because it is supposed to resemble the timber of the Black Bean.. except in colour. **1931** E. SHERSON *Bk. Vegetable Cookery* viii. 161 Boil the little red beans in the usual way. **1932** [see *pencil cedar* s.v. *PENCIL *sb.*[2] 7 b]. **1965** *Austral. Encycl.* I. 468/2 Other trees to which the name [bean] is applied are the red bean.., walnut bean.., and yellow bean. **1977** *Sunday Times* (Colour Suppl.) 4 Dec. 19/1 *Afters*: 'toffee apple', red-bean pancakes. **1980** *Times* 21 June 11/6 Red-bean salad in a sweet, spicy dressing. **1849** *Q. Jrnl. Geol. Soc.* V. 25 The appearance at certain points of the series of stratified deposits of red sandstones and other rocks coloured by the peroxide of iron, in regions where the older formations contain comparatively few red beds, is a fact observed in many countries. **1922** *Bull. Geol. Soc. Amer.* XXXIII. 107 The thickest beds of such [iron] ore in the Appalachian district are in areas where the underlying red beds of Upper Ordovician age are either very thin or are entirely eroded away. **1946** L. D. STAMP *Britain's Structure & Scenery* xii. 124 In early Permian times conditions repeated those found in early Old Red Sandstone times. The older geologists who used the term New Red Sandstone for the red beds of the Permian and Trias introduced this very useful comparison. **1974** *Encycl. Brit. Macropædia* XVIII. 694/1 Continental sediments, especially of red-bed facies often associated with evaporite deposits, are especially widespread and characteristic of the Triassic. Throughout Eurasia north of Tethys, such rocks are a conspicuous part of the rock record. **1785** G. WASHINGTON *Diary* 28 Jan. (1925) II. 338, I discovered.. the red berry of the Swamp. **1805** M. LEWIS *Jrnl.* 12 Apr. in *Orig. Jrnls. Lewis & Clark Exped.* (1904) I. vii. 299 The under brush is willow, red wood,..the red burry [*sic*], and Choke cherry. **1951** *Dict. Gardening* (R. Hort. Soc.) IV. 1754/1 Rhagodia..Australian Red Berry. **1973** E. GOUDIE *Woman of Labrador* p. xix, Well fortified with her never-ending supply of tea and redberry pie. **1928** *Daily Express* 5 Dec. 13/2 Glasgow has not relaxed its war-time drink restrictions..but nothing is being done to make the sale of this horrible 'Red Biddy' punishable by prison. **1939** JOYCE *Finnegans Wake* (1964) I. 39 Blotto after divers tots of hell fire, red biddy, bull dog, blue ruin and creeping jenny. **1950** E. HYAMS *From Waste Land* 204 Pamphlets issued by the French wine trade..to persuade the customer that the Red Biddy he is drinking is something very special and fine indeed. *a* **1953** DYLAN THOMAS *Adventures Skin Trade* (1955) 85 'I suppose he thinks red biddy's like bread and milk,' Mr. Allingham said. **1961** C. WILLOCK *Death in Covert* iii. 67 Any idea where we could get any of the hard stuff? This flipping red biddy's burning a hole in my stomach. **1977** M. KENYON *Rapist* v. 58 Next time it'd be Majorca..and what if he was not a red biddy man? At five bob a bottle he bloody soon would be. **1926** A. GILES *Exploring in Seventies* 127 Tinned meat in 6 lb tins ('red blanket' we called it). The tins were painted red without labels or description of contents. **1846** *Phil. Trans. R. Soc.* CXXXVI. 66 Professor Rudolph Wagner was the first to point out the circular form of the red blood-corpuscle of the Lamprey, but he does not appear to have noticed the existence of a nucleus. **1910** H. W. ARMIT tr. *Ehrlich & Lazarus' Anæmia* i. 3 Tarchanoff proposed that by determining the loss of water during profuse sweating, and by comparative red blood cell counts both before and after the sweating, an estimate of the quantity of blood could be arrived at. **1950** *Sci. News* XV. 87 Thanks to the hæmoglobin in them, the red blood corpuscles of our blood carry oxygen from lungs to muscles and brain, which all the time use it up. **1971** W. M. DOUGHERTY *Introd. Hematol.* v. 135/2 The hematocrit (packed cell volume) is the determination that equates what volume of a given unit of blood is composed of red blood cells (erythrocytes and reticulocytes). **1929** *Bookman* (U.S.) July 527/2 *Red board*, when..a train has to stop for orders. **1935** A. J. POLLOCK *Underworld Speaks* 96/1 *Red board*, board facing the grandstand on which a horse race is declared official by the judges. **1946** *Sun* (Baltimore) 5 Apr. 18/1 After each race there was much 'red board' speculation and betting as to which horse had won. **1968** *Wall St. Jrnl.* 31 Jan., 'One thing about Sam,' he says. 'He never bet the red board.' (In track jargon, to bet the red board is to claim you picked the winner—after the race is over.) **1973** *Amer. Speech* 1969 XLIV. 259 *Red board*, stop signal on an overhead signal bridge. **1785** A. MONRO *Struct. & Physiol. Fishes* iii. 28 A red-coloured organ..is found on the inner side of the air-bag of the cod, haddock, etc.: but in those fishes where the air-bag communicates with the alimentary canal, this red body is either very small and simple..or entirely wanting. **1911** *Proc. Zool. Soc.* I. 184 In the vast majority of cases 'red body' includes both rete mirabile and gas gland. **1963** L. BIRKETT tr. *Nikolsky's Ecol. Fishes* i. 7 In the two red bodies in the swim-bladder of the eel, there are 88,000 venous and 116,000 arterial capillaries. **1723** D. O'CONNOR tr. *Keating's Gen. Hist. Ireland* 91 The Lodge of *Teagh na Craoibhe Ruadhe*, which signifies in English the House of the *Red Branch*, where the most renowned Champions lodged their arms... The Champions.. were distinguished by the Title of Champions of the Red Branch. **1772** S. O'HALLORAN *Introd. Study Hist. Ireland* I. v. 40 Long before the birth of Christ we find an *hereditary* order of chivalry in Ulster, called *Curaidhe na Craoibhe ruadh*, or the Knights of the Red Branch, from their chief seat in Emania, adjoining to the palace of the Ulster kings, called Teagh na Craoibhe ruadh, or Academy of the Red Branch. **1879** *Encycl. Brit.* IX. 75/1 Ulster, whose warriors of the *Craebh Ruaid* or Red Branch are the most prominent figures in the Heroic period, had no Fenians. **1889** W. B. YEATS *Wanderings of Oisin* III. 41 Came by me the Kings of the Red Branch with roaring of laughter and songs. **1892** —— *Countess Kathleen* iv. 73 And on tales Of Finian labours and the Red-Branch Kings. **1970** N. CHADWICK *Celts* ix. 268 The ruling king in the [Tain] cycle is Conchobar mac Nessa of the House of the Red Branch at Emain Macha in Ulster. **1973** *Times* 11 Dec. 1/2 Messages found this morning in a telephone booth said that Dr Amerio would be kept in a 'people's jail' as a reprisal against dismissals at Fiat. The messages claimed that the kidnapping was the work of the 'Red Brigades'. **1977** *Time* 18 July 29/1 Some unemployed university graduates..have joined in the terrorism of groups like the 'Red Brigades'. **1978** *Ann. Reg.* 1977 136 Terrorist action with a political flavour was also carried on by other extremist groups, in particular by the left-wing Red Brigade. *Ibid.*, In their efforts to spread terror the Red Brigaders resorted to shooting in the legs or kneecap a number of fairly prominent persons. **1979** *Rolling Stone* 11 Jan. 79 Outside..the Red Brigades are blowing people's knees off. **1934** S. LEWIS *Work of Art* 72 He's got to be a certified public accountant,..or one-night-stand lecturer that blows in and expects to have the red carpet already hauled out for him. **1938** N. MARSH *Artists in Crime* ii. 28 Be sure to have the red carpet out. **1952** *N.Y. Times* 21 Aug. 21/6 (*heading*) Englewood rolls out red carpet for little baseball league teams. **1960** *Daily Mail* 13 Dec. 7/8 A champagne party was laid on for Mr. Steven Mueller, **2,000,000**th passenger to leave London in a TWA jet airliner... There was a hitch when Mr. Mueller arrived. He is just two years and four months old. The red carpet treatment went to his mother. **1966** J. A. MORRIS *Bird Watcher* (1968) ii. 30 We're rolling out the red carpet for him. Nothing will be too good for good old Congressman Herper. **1969** 'G. BLACK' *Cold Jungle* viii. 122 A complete breakdown in red carpet reception arrangements. **1975** *Evening Standard* 23 Sept. 12/1 (Advt.), May we give you the red carpet treatment? Why get footsore and weary comparing notes at all the carpet stores? **1977** *New Yorker* 10 Oct. 67/2 Eaton's interest in the Soviet Union—to which he has made eight red-carpet journeys since 1958—was indirectly whetted by John D. Rockefeller, Sr. **1894** T. F. GARRETT *Encycl. Pract. Cookery* 324/1 *Red Caviare*, this is a very inferior quality, made from the roe of any fish, such as the grey mullet, or carp. **1927** A. MARTINEAU *Caviare to Candy* iii. 31 *Red Caviare*. This is made from the roe of a hen pike. **1946** G. STIMPSON *Bk. about Thousand Things* 80 Virtually all the red caviar..is displayed as of Russian origin. **1957** V. NABOKOV *Pnin* i. 10 Those stupendous Russian ladies..infuse a magic knowledge of their difficult and beautiful tongue..in an atmosphere of Mother Volga songs, red caviar, and tea. **1964** A. LAUNAY *Caviare & After* i. 21 Red caviare (*Keta*) is made from the salmon roe..bright orange in colour. **1974** M. G. EBERHART *Danger Money* (1975) v. 57 They bought..some red caviar. 'It would be good with rye bread,' Susan suggested. **1935** H. H. FINLAYSON (*title*) The red centre: man and beast in the heart of Australia. *Ibid.* ii. 22 The Luritja Country—the south-west portion of Central Australia and contiguous tracts in the adjoining States—..might well be known as the Red Centre. Sand, soil, and most of the rocks are a fiery cinnabar. **1979** *Jrnl. R. Soc. Arts* Apr. 293/1 Nearly a decade of good rains have turned the famous Red Centre into something approaching a Green Centre. **1905** *Eye Opener* (Calgary, Alberta) 25 Feb. 1/6 The innocent haw-buck who imagines that the red chamber is full of dignity and high thoughts has never listened to the debates from the galleries. **1948–9** *Parl. Affairs* II. 50 The Senate Chamber at the east end, known from its bright leather upholstery as the 'Red Chamber', is similar in design to the Commons Chamber but is much smaller and has no side galleries. **1955** *Chatelaine* Apr. 13 Canada's first woman senator is Mrs. Norman F. Wilson, who shattered a fifty-year-old tradition that had preserved the Red Chamber as an exclusively men's club when she stepped over the threshold in 1930. **1965** *Globe & Mail* (Toronto) 6 Dec. 6/5 Mr. Pearson..could make no better beginning than to appoint to the Red Chamber 12 such Canadians. **1968** Red channel [see *GREEN *a.* 1 i]. **1979** *Guardian* 2 Aug. 1/8 Customs staff will examine in detail the baggage of all passengers going through the red channel and carry out more spot checks..on those using the nothing-to-declare green channel. **1801** B. HAWKINS *Lett.* (1916) 379 Your father is desirous that his red children would consent to establish houses of entertainment and ferries on these roads. **1855** J. H. CHAMBERS in *Montana Hist. Soc. Contrib.* (1940) X. 136 Col Vaughan gave his red children a talk. **1871** *Weekly Manitoban* 5 Aug. 2/4 She wishes her Red children, as well as her White people, to be happy and contented. **1972** K. LO *Chinese Food* I. 23 We red-cook it [*sc.* fish], quick-fry it, clear-simmer it, deep-fry it, steam it, and hot-plunge it. **1956** B. Y. CHAO *How to cook & eat in Chinese* I. vi. 65 Red-cooking is stewing with soy sauce, some materials needing pre-frying, some not. It is so-called because the soy-sauce juice gives a reddish colour. **1972** K. LO *Chinese Food* I. 12 In red-cooking the meat or poultry is first quick-fried and then simmered in broth or water along with soya sauce and other constituents of the soya herbal sauce. **1936** *Ann. Rep. E. Malling Res. Station 1935* 144 The roots of the affected [strawberry] plants showed the 'red core'. **1952** E. RAMSDEN tr. *Gram & Weber's Plant Dis.* III. 364/1 No method of soil treatment has proved effective against red-core disease. **1970** *Countryman* Spring 111 Red core was first known as a disastrous disease in 1921 in Scotland. **1846** *Phil. Trans. R. Soc.* CXXXVI. 64 The well-known red corpuscle of the blood of the Frog. **1871** *Q. Jrnl. Microsc. Sci.* XXII. 361 The chemical and formal structure of the red corpuscle. **1911** C. E. W. BEAN '*Dreadnought*' *of Darling* x. 89 The river came down in flood. People had been forced to clear out of some of the 'frontages' and camp back in the red country. *Ibid.* xv. 142 The mallee..covers thousands of square miles of red country in Victoria, New South Wales, and South Australia. **1936** A. RUSSELL *Gone Nomad* viii. 60 Picture great wind-scoured plains of red sand..; a sun glaring wanly day after day from a sky reddened with the dust of incessant sand-storm..—and you will see the great 'Red Country' of the West Darling in the big seven years' drought of 1897–1903. **1877** H. PONSONBY *Let.* 6 Sept. in A. Ponsonby *Henry Ponsonby* (1942) 376 The Red Cross or Crescent is a valuable association in its attempts to protect the sick and wounded in time of war. **1959** *Chambers's Encycl.* XI. 552/1 The League of Red Cross Societies (founded 1919) is a federation of national Red Cross and Red Crescent societies. **1970** *Times* 3 Apr. (Arab League Suppl.) p. viii/3 Their own Palestinian Red Crescent facilities. **1971** *Shankar's Weekly* (Delhi) 4 Apr. 10/4, I think it will be a better idea to get some business men and others contribute money, buy medicines and other equipment with that and donate it to the East Pakistan Red Crescent or some other organisation. **1976** G. SEYMOUR *Glory Boys* ii. 23 The big tanks had rumbled into..Nablus. He recalled..the wail of the Red Crescent ambulances. **1912** R. LYDEKKER *Ox & its Kindred* v. 101 Attention may be directed to the well-known red Devons. **1979** V. CANNING *Satan Sampler* ix. 197 A colour gravure of a red Devon heifer. **1925** FRASER & GIBBONS *Soldier & Sailor Words* 237 *Red duster, the*, the Red Ensign of the Mercantile Marine. **1928** *Daily Express* 10 Aug. 15/1 His papers have not yet come through allowing him to fly the White Ensign, so, meanwhile, the Vita sails under the 'red duster'. **1944** *Times* 7 June 6/7 A glance at the ships, with their different flags, the Red Duster of the Merchant Navy, the Stars and Stripes, [etc.]. **1977** *Jrnl. R. Soc. Arts* CXXV. 216/1 Today even the Red Duster is to some extent a flag of convenience. [**1916** *Proc. Nat. Acad. Sci.* II. 17 Differing from the dwarf red stars most conspicuously in density, dimensions, and total brightness.] **1929** J. H. JEANS *Universe around Us* v. 293 The great gulf which lies between the red giants and the red dwarfs. **1959** *Listener* 26 Feb. 370/1 Instead of cooling steadily down towards the Red Dwarf stage..the Sun is becoming more energetic as it ages. **1978** *Nature* 22 June 645/1 The energies of even the weak radio flares emitted by a red dwarf star are several orders of magnitude greater than those from large and infrequent solar outbursts. **1951** T. C. ROUGHLEY *Fish Austral.* 68 The red emperor or king snapper..grows to a weight of at least 40 pounds. **1956** M. WEST *Gallows on Sand* xiii. 145 Fillets of red emperor, caught while we were at the bottom of the sea. **1965** *Austral. Encycl.* IX. 41/1 The juvenile form of the red emperor.. bears a red broad-arrow mark, from which it derives its name of government bream. **1730** *Royal Navy Orders & Instructions* 12 Merchant-Ships are to wear a Red Ensign; with the Union Jack in a Canton at the upper End next the Staff; and a white Jack, with a red Cross, commonly called *St. George's Cross*, passing quite through the same. **1910** *Encycl. Brit.* X. 459/1 The red ensign is the distinguishing flag of the British merchant service. **1961** B. FERGUSSON *Watery Maze* vi. 123 Red Ensign ships—merchant ships with Merchant Navy crews, requisitioned for Admiralty service—were administered by the Director of Sea Transport. **1976** *Oxf. Compan. Ships & Sea* 695/2 The Red Ensign ..is today flown by all British merchant vessels and also by many yachts. **1893** P. GARDNER *Catal. Greek Vases in Ashmolean Mus.* iv. 22/1 The natural advantages..of the red-figure method caused it to speedily supersede the older style. **1899** R. GLAZIER *Man. Hist. Ornament* 77 The Transitional period (B.C. 500–470), when the black silhouette figures on a red ground gave way to the red figure period on a black ground. **1918** J. D. BEAZLEY *Attic Red-Figured Vases in Amer. Museums* i. 5 The earliest red-figure vases are mostly amphorae or cups. **1936** *Burlington Mag.* May 253/1 Amongst the fifth-century red-figure vases there are many of high artistic merit. **1960** R. G. HAGGAR *Conc. Encycl. Continental Pott. & Porc.* 211/1 Greek pottery is generally classified by style: Geometric, Oriental influence, Black-figure, Red-figure and mixed styles. **1975** J. BOARDMAN *Athenian Red Figure Vases: Archaic Period* ii. 11 Red figure is the reverse of black figure. *Ibid.* 12 Relief line is so important in early red figure that..a word about it is called for. **1978** K. J. DOVER *Greek Homosexuality* I. 10 An Attic red-figure vase of the early fifth century depicts a man at a dinner party. **1890** Red-figured [in Dict., sense 14 a]. **1918** J. D. BEAZLEY *Attic Red-Figured Vases in Amer. Museums* p. v, The Andokides painter, one of the first artists to use the red-figured style. **1919** J. C. HOPPIN (*title*) Handbook of Attic red-figured vases. **1960** E. H. GOMBRICH *Art & Illusion* i. 40 The Greek vase painters made use of this principle of reversal when they switched over from the earlier black-figured technique ..to the red-figured style. **1977** *Jrnl. R. Soc. Arts* CXXV. 96/2 It [*sc.* the *anthemion*] was a favourite border design, too, with the painters of Greek pottery of the period, particularly of the red-figured Attic ware. **1848** *Santa Fé* (New Mexico) *Republican* 28 June 2/4 A proportionate lot of..Cinto laces, Red flannel shirts, [etc.]. **1860** *Times* 15 Sept. 10/1 Most of us wear no linen.., the red flannel shirt answering all purposes of outward and inward raiment. **1906** E. NESBIT *Railway Children* vi. 137 'How lucky we *did* put on our red flannel petticoats!' said Phyllis. **1940** L. I. WILDER *Long Winter* (1962) ix. 83 Her red flannel underwear was so hot. *Ibid.* 84 It's too hot for my red flannels, Ma! **1943** *Sun* (Baltimore) 24 Nov. 17/5 It is time for Kent countians to 'get into their red flannels'. **1978** WALKLEY & FOSTER *Crinolines & Crimping Irons* ii. 46 Both natural wool and red flannel became favourite materials for underwear and nightwear. **1907** *Dialect Notes* III. 248 *Red flannel hash*,.. beet hash. **1951** E. GRAHAM *My Window looks down East* vii. 59 She had a real hankerin' for red-flannel hash. **1977** J. CHEEVER *Falconer* 60 His mother..served the red flannel hash with poached eggs. **1916** *Proc. Nat. Acad. Sci.* II. 17 The brightest stars in the cluster are the red and yellow giants. **1929** J. H. JEANS *Universe around Us* v. 272 The stars of large diameter shewn in the table..are red and have very high luminosities; they are red giants. **1966** *Random House Dict.* 142/3 *Betelgeuse*, a first magnitude red giant star in the constellation Orion. **1977** J. NARLIKAR *Struct. Universe* ii. 39 The red-giant reactions do not take as long to complete as the reactions during the main-sequence stage. **1896** *Jrnl. Anat. & Physiol.* XXX. 550 The red glands occupy about the anterior half of the internal surface of the ventral wall of the swim-bladder. **1926** H. M. KYLE *Biol. Fishes* xi. 276 The fish is able to exercise some selection of gases, and the 'red glands' or retia mirabilia of the Physoclists are evidently used for this purpose. **1931** J. R. NORMAN *Hist. Fishes* ix. 174 The walls of the bladder are richly supplied with fine blood-vessels, and at certain areas these are accumulated to form the so-called red bodies or red glands, masses of interlacing and tightly packed arteries and veins. **1974** D. & M. WEBSTER *Compar. Vertebr. Morphol.* xv. 368 The rete mirabile here [in teleosts] produces gas, which the red gland secretes into the gas bladder. **1910** H. P. TIEMANN *Iron & Steel* 312 Red hardness is the name they give to the property of a tool when it maintains its cutting edge after its nose is red hot. **1925** *Trans. Amer. Soc. Steel Treating* VIII. 693 Molybdenum when present in sufficient amounts imparts to steel the properties of 'red hardness'. **1937** *Discovery* May 153/1 The forerunner of self-hard steel,..Musket self-hard steel, employed [carbon and tungsten]..to confer the then new so-called red hardness... Tungsten contributes to high speed steel the property of red hardness. **1819** *Orthodox Jrnl.* May 175/2 [He] laboured afterwards most earnestly to counteract its contents, and was honoured with the red hat by his holiness. **1863** GEO. ELIOT *Romola* I. i. 36 Men who love to see avarice and lechery under the red hat and the mitre. **1969** R. H. BAINTON *Erasmus of Christendom* (1970) i. 44 To receive the red hat he must go to Rome. **1975** R. PLAYER *Let's talk of Graves* vi. 217 Cardinal Cavalle..had got his red hat from Pius the Ninth. **1934** *Bulletin* (Sydney) 16 May 20/3 Someone identified the thing as *Patæcus fronto*, better known as the 'Red Indian' in N.S.W., where it is sometimes caught on the reefs. **1965** *Austral. Encycl.* VII. 395/2 Red Indian fish (*Pataecus fronto*), a fish of the southern Australian rocky shore-lines. Its high dorsal fin forms a crest like the feathers of a Red Indian's head dress. **1963** 'J. PRESCOT' *Case for Hearing* viii. 125 There's precious little point in letting him out on bail when a red judge is going to send him back again for at least a couple of years. **1972** *Times* 20 May 3/7, I would very much like to see more work being committed for trial by the red judge. **1977** *Daily Tel.* 19 Oct. 6/5 Since May there have been no visits by 'Red judges' because of a shortage of accommodation. Arrangements have been made for the more important criminal cases —murder and manslaughter—to be tried either at the Old Bailey or Maidstone. **1812** W. J. BURCHELL *Jrnl.* 27 May in *Trav. Interior S. Afr.* (1822) II. viii. 160 They had intended going to the *Roode Kaffers* (Red Caffres). **1879** R. M. BALLANTYNE *Six Months at Cape* iii. 44 This red-Kafir is in truth a savage. **1904** D. KIDD *Essential Kafir* i. 31 Red ochre and oil are rubbed into the skin, and frequently into the blanket. When this latter is done by a tribe the people are called Red Kafirs. **1846** *Blackw. Mag.* Nov. 595/1 Almost any serial will give hints enough to an acute boy, [and]..guide him to the door with the red lamp. **1927** W. E. COLLINSON *Contemp. Eng.* 96 The red lamp as the sign of a '*maison tolérée*'. **1929** J. L. HODSON *Grey Dawn* II. ii. 159 You should have seen the queue at the Red Lamp. **1962** H. MYERS tr. *Pingaud's Holland* 51 The dirty little canals near the harbour in the 'red lamp' district. **1942** BERREY & VAN DEN BARK *Amer. Thes. Slang* § 49/1 Redland, *Russia*. **1966** J. GARDNER *Amber Nine* iii. 44 If Redland have got a finger in the pie then that part of the world could be warmish. **1969** W. GARNER *Us or Them War* i. 15 Morton picked up the camera... He said, 'Exacta. Made in Dresden. East Germany. A favourite with Redland agents.' **1977** C. WOOD *James Bond* iv. 40 'You can imagine who the first suspects are?' Bond could. 'Redland.' **1821** M. WILMOT *Let.* 17 Jan. in *More Lett.* (1935) 92 Melodious clang of knives forks and plates to flourish *down the red Lane* the most magnificent supper that Gourmands ever guttled. **1958** L. DURRELL *Mountolive* xv. 286 The quarter lying beyond the red lantern belt. **1973** *Whig-Standard* (Kingston, Ontario) 11 Aug. 7/3 He was on the loose and cutting a swathe in the red lantern district. **1918** R. W. KAUFFMAN *Our Navy at Work* 6 'Red lead' is catsup, which it hugely resembles. **1919** G. M. BATTEY *70,000 Miles in Submarine Destroyer* 261 Beans and 'red lead' for breakfast. **1945** 'TACKLINE' *Holiday Sailor* v. 55 Everything went into a pot-mess—meat, spuds, peas, beans, rice, oxo, 'red-lead' (tinned tomatoes)—and the result was invariably good. **1959** W. L. CORZINE *Sailors in Nightgowns* vii. 100 We were having those delicious beans for breakfast, which we always camouflaged with red lead (catsup). **1905** EMERSON & NORRIS in *Jrnl. Exper. Med.* VII. 34 The name often given to the disease in these letters is 'red-leg', and this is also the name used by the frog-catchers. **1964** G. DURRELL *Menagerie Manor* iii. 75, I sent them [*sc.* toads] away for post-mortem, and the report came back that they were suffering from an obscure disease called red-leg. **1974** *Amer. Jrnl. Vet. Res.* XXXV. 1243 Since 1890, septicemic frog disease (red-leg) has had a devastating effect on frogs kept under laboratory conditions. **1898** Red meat [see sense 8 c]. **1933** E. O'NEILL *Ah, Wilderness!* I. 24 Poetry's his red meat nowadays, I think—love poetry—and socialism, too, I suspect. **1972** *Times* 3 July 12/2 Colin Carr chose..a lollipop, a Popper Polonaise, rather than good red meat, but it served to show off an enviable fluency on the instrument. **1977** *Jrnl. R. Soc. Arts* CXXV. 369/1 Dairy products, cereal products and red meat account for 60 per cent and 75 per cent respectively of the energy and protein intake of the population. **1925** B. COAN *Red Web* 6 It is time, right now, to get down to cases about this thing we hear called the 'red menace'. **1932** J. F. CARTER *What we are about to Receive* xviii. 204 But once the election is over..we shall quietly lay aside our witch hunting, put the Red Menace in cold storage. **1934** R. V. C. BODLEY *Japanese Omelette* xvii. 174 The substance of his words did not confirm the rather pessimistic views of my soldier friends in Changchun on the subject of the 'Red Menace'. **1977** *Time* 14 Feb. 17/1 Young..was quick to warn Smith that his efforts to gain U.S. support by invoking the 'Red menace' would not succeed. **1819** J. TAYLOR *Naturales Curiosæ* 129 Adonis—Red Morocco... Its flowers are of a bright scarlet, with a black spot or eye at the bottom, and are frequently sold in London under the name of red-morocco. **1931** M. GRIEVE *Mod. Herbal* I. 389/1 'Red Morocco' was a somewhat strange old English name for this plant [*sc.* pheasant's eye]. **1941** BAKER *Dict. Austral. Slang* 59 *Red Ned*, cheap red wine. **1941** —— *N.Z. Slang* vii. 62 Such terms for strong drink as.. *red Ned*. **1972** I. HAMILTON *Thrill Machine* xxvi. 120 Jo clutched the glass of Red Ned that I thrust at him. **1961** WARD & SHAPIRO in *Jrnl. Meteorol.* XVIII. 642/1 The only other characteristic of these spectra is their resemblance to 'red noise', that is, generally higher variance at the lower frequencies (longer periods). [*Note*] The term 'red noise' was suggested by Prof. E. N. Lorenz to describe this phenomenon. *Ibid.* 646/1 The spectrum of a time series of random numbers, which has been modified so that there is a moderate correlation between successive values, exhibits a characteristic damping of the higher frequencies. This type of spectrum, having more power (or variance) at lower frequencies can, by analogy to the spectrum of light, be called a 'red noise'. **1963** *Jrnl. Atmospheric Sci.* XX. 182/1 A general suppression of relative variance at higher frequencies and consequent inflation at lower frequencies, as compared to the even distribution of relative variance across all frequencies shown by the 'white noise' spectrum. Following a suggestion by E. N. Lorenz, Shapiro and Ward have called this phenomenon 'red noise'. **1979** *Nature* 23 Aug. 672/1 The spectra were calculated using a fast Fourier algorithm, the spectral estimates were smoothed, and a white or red noise null continuum was assumed in a significance testing. **1890** W. H. VITTUM tr. *Edinger's Twelve Lect. Struct. Cent. Nerv. Syst.* vi. 93 Below the thalamus is a rounded ganglion,—the nucleus ruber, the red nucleus of the tegmentum. **1942** F. A. METTLER *Neuroanat.* xiii. 302 The red nuclei are important extrapyramidal relay stations. **1972** M. L. BARR *Human Nerv. Syst.* vii. 110/1 The red nucleus is..involved in pathways through which the cerebellum is able to influence motor function. **1974** D. & M. WEBSTER *Compar. Vertebr. Morphol.* xii. 294 These fibers decussate in the midbrain and then form a large capsule around the red nucleus. **1917** W. K. MOOREHEAD *Stone Ornaments used by Indians in U.S. & Canada* 53 Oval forms occasionally found in the Red Paint People's graves in Maine are much weathered and appear very old. **1947** R. P. T. COFFIN *Yankee Coast* 225 Before the dawn and the Dawn People, there were the Red Paint Men... They had been gone so long now that not even the teeth of them are left, only the red paint, color of life, they smeared their bodies with. **1970** S. TRUEMAN *Intimate Hist. New Brunswick* iii. 43 'Red Paint' Indian burial ground dating back 3,500 to 4,000 years; in the bottom of each grave is a covering of red ochre, bright red oxide. **1933** *Discovery* May 158/1 Red palm oil and some samples of maize oil are good sources [of vitamin A]. **1975** *Sci. Amer.* June 126/1 Cereal and vegetable oils are generally poor in carotene—except for red-palm oil, which is very rich. **1959** *Encounter* Dec. 29/1, I have been red-pencilling student papers for a good many years. **1966** *Eng. Stud.* XLVII. 116 There are many teachers of English who look upon the adjective *corny* as a word to be red-penciled whenever it turns up in a student paper. **1979** *Verbatim* Summer 2/2 To red-pencil is 'to censor or correct'. **1927** *Observer* 4 Dec. 13/1 We have to guard against the Red Peril on our borders. **1973** *Sat. Rev. Society* (U.S.) Mar. 48/3 At the end of the Fifties the red peril slunk off. **1873** *Punch* 4 Jan. 1/2 Mars. The Red Planet salutes you. But you are a slow lot. **1894** J. E. GORE tr. *Flammarion's Pop. Astron.* IV. iv. 374 The red planet varies in brightness according to its position in the sky. **1972** *Nature* 4 Feb. 251/2 They show clearly that the red planet is far from being dead, and that weathering and volcanic activity are taking place on Mars to a significant degree. **1977** *Time* 17 Oct. 45/1 The two Viking landers and their orbiters have spent much of the 15 months since the arrival on Mars snapping pictures of the Red Planet. **1941** *Coast to Coast* 22 The mounted trooper found a couple of red poley steer skins in Jo Wiggins's slaughter-yard. **1878** DISRAELI *Let.* 13 June in Monypenny & Buckle *Life Disraeli* (1920) VI.

ix. 318 Lord B. mistook His Royal Highness for the father of the bride, who soon appeared as 'The Red Prince'. **1888** *Random Recoll. Courts & Society* vi. 140 The wedding of the Princess of Dessau with Prince Frederick Charles—the Red Prince—in September, 1857, was solemnized in the evening at the Palace with all the customary formalities. **1958** *Everyman's Encycl.* V. 494/1 Frederick Charles of Prussia.., known as the 'Red Prince' because of the uniform he usually wore. **1885** ETHERIDGE & SEELEY *Phillips' Man. Geol.* (ed. 2) I. ii. 18 In the Arctic regions minute spherical particles of iron are sometimes brought down from the air in snow, as though the earth occasionally entered clouds of meteoric dust. A like cause must account for the red rain which fell at Blankenburg in 1819, and owed its colour to cobalt chloride. **1904** G. S. WEST *Treat. Brit. Freshwater Algæ* 189 *Sph*[*ærella*] *lacustris*..is abundant all over the country in ditches, rain-pools, and bog-pools. The cells..frequently become brick-red in colour owing to the presence of hæmatochromin... The curious phenomenon known as 'Red Rain' owes its colour in a few instances to the presence of this Alga. **1933** E. HAWKS *Bk. of Air & Water Wonders* iv. 102 Red rain, accompanied by sand, fell on March 10, 1901, at Vienna and in Italy. **1884** H. E. JULER *Handbk. Ophthalmic Sci. & Pract.* xiv. 364 If the mirror be held at a considerable distance from an emmetropic eye no image of any details of the fundus is seen, but only a red reflex. **1954** S. DUKE-ELDER *Parsons' Disease of Eye* (ed. 12) vii. 94 If the fundus reflex is seen as a uniform red glow (the red reflex), the eye is emmetropic or approximately so. **1971** *Brit. Med. Bull.* XXVII. 69/1 The 'red reflex' coincides with a very early stage of development of a retinal neoplasm. **1853** DISRAELI in *Hansard Commons* 30 June 1045 The very next day his Sovereign elevated him [*sc.* Lord Ellenborough] in the Peerage, and decorated him with the Red Riband. **1879** 'MARK TWAIN' *Lett.* (1917) I. 355 He couched his lance and ran a bold tilt against total abstinence and the Red Ribbon fanatics. **1908** *Costumes Classical & Fashionable* (Liberty & Co.) 16 Red Riding Hood Cloak in cloth. **1936** N. STREATFEILD *Ballet Shoes* vii. 110 Pauline wore shorts and a shirt, and Petrova an apron and a red-riding-hood cloak over her frock. **1964** M. LASKI in S. Nowell-Smith *Edwardian England* iv. 204 White dresses with sashes..topped, for transit, by a red velvet Red Riding Hood cloak. **1966** M. STEEN *Looking Glass* i. 14, I was taken to parties..in my Red Ridinghood cape. **1826** W. DARLINGTON *Florula Cestrica* 72 *E*[*uchroma*] *coccinea*... Painted Cup. Red Robin. **1855** J. PHILLIPS *Man. Geol.* viii. 190 One [fault] stated to cause a dislocation to the extent of 1,000 yards, is called the 'red rock fault', north of Pendleton near Manchester. **1942** E. M. ANDERSON *Dynamics of Faulting* v. 76 The 'North Staffordshire Boundary Fault'.. is not a single fault, as two separate north-north-easterly fractures bound the coalfield... The northern of these is known as the Red Rock Fault. **1969** BENNISON & WRIGHT *Geol. Hist. Brit. Isles* xi. 268 The thickness of the beds in the Cheshire Basin indicates a great amount of downwarping which continued into Triassic times. The basin may have been bounded by faults, such as the Red Rock Fault, which continued to move during Permian times. **1891** *Amer. Folk-Lore* IV. 224 Red Rover. The boy who is 'it' is called the 'Red Rover', and stands in the middle of the street, while the others form a line on the pavement on one side. **1898** A. B. GOMME *Trad. Games* II. 107 The players, except one, take their stand at one side, and one stands at the other side in front of them. When all are ready, the one in front calls out 'Cock', or 'Caron', when all rush across to the other side, and he tries to catch one of them in crossing. This game is called 'Red Rover' in Liverpool... 'Red Rover' is shouted out by the catcher when players are ready to rush across. **1974** J. KEATS *Of Time & Island* v. 82 The little children played Red Rover. **1892** A. G. THORNTON *Illustr. Catal. Drawing & Surveying Instruments & Materials* 107 Finest Red Sable Brushes, Round Black Handles, plated ferrules. **1899** M. MARKS *Cycl. Home Arts* 62/2 The red sables are somewhat too strong for water-colour. **1910** *Encycl. Brit.* XI. 350/2 The fur [of the kolinsky] has often been designated as red or Tatar sable. **1948** F. A. STAPLES *Watercolour Painting* i. 3 The best red sable brushes should be used. **1970** *Oxf. Compan. Art* 169/2 The best soft brush for water-colour is the red 'sable', made from the fur of the Siberian mink. **1927** M. DEKOBRA tr. *Wainwright's Madonna of Sleeping Cars* xiv. 186 The gorilla with the pallid brow, marked with a Red star. **1969** G. MACBETH *War Quartet* 73 In his coat He wore the red star. **1979** J. BARNETT *Backfire is Hostile!* xiv. 158 This strange aeroplane ..with a red star on its tail. **1941** BAKER *Dict. Austral. Slang* 59 *Red steer, the*, fire, esp. a bush-fire. **1963** J. CANTWELL *No Stranger to Flame* 12 The cane-cutters, made negro by sun and by soot from fires (Red Steers, they called them). **1971** F. HARDY *Outcasts of Foolgarah* 118 Like the bushfires: hadn't he patented the special extinguisher to end the blight of the red steer for all time? **1947** J. C. RICH *Materials & Methods of Sculpture* viii. 222 Many kinds [of sandstones] receive their names from their colors, i.e. bluestone, brownstone, and redstone. **1959** N. SLUMAN *Blackfoot Crossing* 38 On it Sikimi placed a fine revolver, some otter skins, a redstone pipe, and several small sacks of rare pigments. **1976** *Burnham-on-Sea Gaz.* 20 Apr. (Advt.), An attractive redstone detached cottage conveniently close to the town centre. **1876** G. STABLES *Domestic Cat* vi. 51 The first cat of the Tabby kind which claims our attention is the Red or Sandy Tabby. **1903** F. SIMPSON *Bk. of Cat* xxv. 288/2 Red tabbies..are one of the difficult varieties to obtain. **1948** P. M. SODERBERG *Cat Breeding* 248 Red Tabbies cannot compete with several other breeds for popularity. **1977** D. S. RICHARDS *Handbk. Pedigree Cat Breeding* vii. 107 Ginger cats, or more correctly red tabbies, will invariably be male. **1898** Red tag [see ZULU *sb.* and *a.* 3]. **1923** *Daily Mail* 11 Aug. 7 Dace..have been caught with fly..and upper parts of the Lea should yield some good specimens of these fish to the black gnat, Zulu, red tag, and coachman. **1918** in J. Degras *Soviet Documents on Foreign Policy* (1951) I. 130, I wish to emphasise that the so-called 'Red Terror'—which is grossly exaggerated and misrepresented abroad—was not the cause but the direct result and outcome of Allied intervention. **1922** 'SAPPER' *Black Gang* xvi. 267 Experts of the Red Terror..butcheries of women and children. **1930** *Morning Post* 13 Aug. 13 Never before, even in 1918–19, when the Red Terror was at its height, have persecutions reached such a terrible level. **1957** *Encycl. Brit.* XIX. 713/1 The beginning of the Red terror coincided with the period of greatest food shortage, before the harvest. **1977** *Socialist Press* 2 Mar. 7/1 His Committee of Public Safety directs accelerating repression (the 'red terror') against 'enemies of the people'. **1947** *Sun* (Baltimore) 3 Sept. 3/4 A tiny sea creature was blamed today for the 'red tides' which destroyed fish. **1970** T. D. BROCK *Biol. Microorganisms* xix. 655 The red tide, an occasional occurrence in inshore areas, results from extensive blooms of red-pigmented dinoflagellate species. Red tides, which probably develop when the seawater becomes unusually enriched with nutrients, are of practical significance because some dinoflagellates produce fish toxins that may cause extensive and unsightly fish kills. **1980** *N.Y. Times* 13 Sept. 8/2 The red tide..usually occurs in much milder form each year in late summer or fall. **1975** *Globe & Mail* (Toronto) 22 Jan. 29/8 But the choice is not merely between the two levels of government; it is between two kinds of conservatism. Red Tory, blue Tory. **1976** *Weekend Mag.* (Montreal) 10 Jan. 2/1 All good Canadians are on the side of the Red Tories, the Dalton Camp forces who favor family allowances and the welfare state, Canadian nationalism, immigration, bilingualism and multiculturalism, the obviously good and liberal things that keep Canada great. **1974** *Globe & Mail* (Toronto) 29 Oct. 5/3 David Smith could outpace Alderman Anne Johnston in Ward 11, depending on how that ward buys her Red Toryism as opposed to his knee-deep Liberalism. [**1879** X. GALEZOWSKI in *Recueil d'Ophtalmologie* I. 534 (*heading*) Sur la vision rouge des opérés de cataracte.] **1883** *Ophthalmic Rev.* II. 281 Purtscher suggests that red-vision would probably be heard of more frequently..after cataract operations, were it not for the careful protection of the eyes. *Ibid.* 278 He went into the open air and the red vision disappeared. **1959** S. DUKE-ELDER *Parsons' Dis. Eye* (ed. 13) xxiv. 373 Erythropsia (red vision) occurs particularly after cataract extraction if the eyes are exposed to bright light. **1940** Red warning [see *ALERT *sb.* 1 b]. **1963** *Times* 22 Jan. 10/3 Commander J. R. E. Langworthy, secretary of the Emergency Bed Service, said last night that if the cold spell continues a 'red warning' might have to be considered. Under this hospitals are asked to stop admitting any but emergency cases. **1969** *Daily Tel.* 14 Jan. 1/6 The next step, if the position worsened, would be a red warning. This stops all but very urgent admissions, reserves of local nurses are called in, and extra beds are put up in wards.

b. With adjs. (and derived sbs.), as **red-green** *a.*, pertaining to or affecting the ability to distinguish between red and green; **red-raw** *a.*, rubbed or irritated until the flesh is exposed and inflamed; also *fig.*; **red-sensitive** *a.*, sensitive or responding to the colour red; **redward** *a.* and *adv.* (further examples); also **redwards.**

1888 Red-green-blindness [in Dict.]. **1935** *Discovery* Aug. 231/1 According to this theory red-green blindness is due to the red-green nerve being atrophied, leaving the yellow-blue nerve still in action. **1956** C. AUERBACH *Genetics in Atomic Age* 56 A good example for a sex-linked recessive gene in man is red-green colour-blindness. This abnormality is much more frequent in men than in women. **1958** *Listener* 6 Nov. 730/1 He, too, was a red-green colour-defective. **1964** S. DUKE-ELDER *Parsons' Dis. Eye* (ed. 14) xxiv. 364 The red-green cases fall into two main groups, protanopes and deuteranopes. **1971** J. Z. YOUNG *Introd. Study Man* xxxviii. 553 Those who are red-green blind cannot identify ripe or rotten fruit or even see red berries among the leaves! **1924** A. J. SMALL *Frozen Gold* 184 A red-raw panic. **1957** T. HUGHES *Hawk in Rain* 13 All day he stares at his furnace With eyes red-raw. **1936** *Discovery* May 151/2 This..was an advantage in the days of blue-sensitive materials when actinometers were first put forward, but has lost this advantage now green-sensitive and red-sensitive materials are so universally employed. **1967** KARCH & BUBER *Offset Processes* v. 149 Although it [*sc.* orthochromatic film] is insensitive to red, dyes can be added to make it red-sensitive. **1927** *Publ. Allegheny Observatory* VI. 136 The redward shifts of the solar lines. **1946** *Nature* 10 Aug. 205/2 The departure from the normal redward shift must be due to changes in the sun, and may readily be attributed to movements of the sodium vapour. **1973** *Sci. Amer.* May 118/1 A scarlet pigment, mercuric sulfide, is in fact a low-frequency reflector, reflecting about equally everything redward of a half-reflecting point in the orange. **1979** *Nature* 19 Apr. 719/1 The IR line moved redwards by ~150 Å and the red line bluewards by ~70 Å.

B. *sb.*[1] **1. c.** For 'in billiards' read 'in billiards and related games'. (Earlier and later examples.)

1857 J. E. RITCHIE *Night Side of London* 128 'Good stroke'—'Bad flewke'—'On the red'. **1895** [see *CUSH]. **1928** C. BERGENER *Contrib. Study of Conversion of Adjectives into Nouns* 135 The reds must be potted before you take the colours [in snooker]. **1974** *Rules of Game* 79 Three points if the cue ball hits the red into a pocket. **1977** *Cleethorpes News* 6 May 29/4 Hood potted the last red and this left Barnes in trouble, needing all the colours and a snooker to boot to pull off a win.

e. The red colour conventionally used in map-making to represent British territories.

1899 *Manch. Guardian* 2 May 7/1 The destruction of the Transvaal's independence..would blot out from the mass of red on the map of South Africa a spot of brown. **1966** *Observer* (Colour Suppl.) 27 Feb. 5/1 Red on the map tends to be spots, not splashes nowadays—but there are still more than 1,500 British islands. **1975** P. MASON *Kipling* vi. 150 A busy talkative man..preaching war..wanting to paint the map red.

f. *to see red*: to get very angry; to lose self-control.

[**1900** J. K. JEROME *Three Men on Bummel* xiii. 292, I began, as the American expression is, to see things red.] **1901** 'L. MALET' *Hist. Sir R. Calmady* I. v. 39 Happily violence is shortlived, only for a very little while do even the gentlest persons 'see red'. **1923** *Daily Mail* 19 June 15 It maddened me, I think, and I saw red—and before I knew what I was doing I stabbed him. **1937** A. CHRISTIE *Death on Nile* xi. 119 Why—? Because she thinks I'm not her social equal! Pah—doesn't that make you see red? **1953** J. WAIN *Hurry on Down* x. 221 Instead of answering he leaned across and snatched at the packet Charles held in his hand. Charles saw red. His livelihood was in danger. **1974** *Times* 31 Jan. 2/6 'The village was incensed when a woman was left to die in her bath because an ambulance man on a go-slow refused to come out,' he said. 'We saw red and said we would form an action group to drive ambulances and cars.' **1977** *Daily Mirror* 15 Mar. 2 (*heading*) MPs see red over soaring prices.

g. The colour conventionally (now less commonly) used to indicate debit items and balances in accounts, used esp. in phrases *in the red*: in debt, overdrawn, losing money (also *fig.*); *out of the red*: in credit, making a profit. Hence, debt, an overdraft. Cf. *BLACK *sb.* 2 d.

1926 MAINES & GRANT *Wise-Crack Dict.* 10/1 *In the red*, losing money in show parlance. **1927** *Scribner's Mag.* Apr. 380/2 'We've got to put forth our best efforts from now till the end of the month, or we'll be in red on the books,' he announced. **1928** *Publisher's Weekly* 10 Nov. 1957/2 About 966 copies more and the title will be out of the red. **1931** F. L. ALLEN *Only Yesterday* viii. 212 The Philadelphia Sesquicentennial was sinking deeper and deeper into the red. **1949** *Harper's Mag.* Mar. 62/2 The corporation was nearly a million dollars in the red. **1955** *Times* 28 June 3/3 With Tordoff and Saeed opening Somerset's second innings with commendable vigour, Leicestershire went further into the red. **1960** *Times* 15 Feb. 11/6 The British Transport Commission is already in the red to the tune of at least £30m. **1966** O. NORTON *School of Liars* i. 5, I don't think the manager at Barclays has ever heard of the Married Women's Property Act,..my red is Andrew's red. **1977** D. WILLIAMS *Treasure by Degrees* xviii. 169 A quarter of a million pounds..would be more than sufficient to keep the College out of the red for the foreseeable future. **1978** S. BRILL *Teamsters* vii. 268 CCC has never run in the red.

h. A red light, lamp, etc., meant as a signal to stop. Also *fig.*

1970 'W. HAGGARD' *Hardliners* xiv. 155 At the top of Whitehall he jumped his first red, slipping left to the Mall against the signal. **1972** D. BLOODWORTH *Any Number can Play* xvi. 153 'We go by the position of the lights, not the colours,' soothed Ivansong, as they roared through a red. **1976** 'P. B. YUILL' *Hazell & Menacing Jester* vi. 67, I was doing over fifty and jumping reds.

3. b. (Later examples.)

1927 E. HEMINGWAY *Men without Women* 207 You tried the red?..we'll have a round of the red. **1961** J. B. PRIESTLEY *Saturn over Water* viii. 113 We drank a bottle of Chilean red, and she made coffee. **1969** *Listener* 27 Mar. 417/3 A bottle of red with this, which lasted right through the half-pound of Brie cheese that followed. **1974** K. MILLETT *Flying* (1975) III. 286 Nell goes off to seek another bottle of red.

5. b. (Further examples.) Also, a variety of potato bearing red-skinned tubers or the tubers themselves.

1829 G. GRIFFIN *Collegians* II. xxx. 333 The English reds are a nate piatie. **1902** A. BENNETT *Grand Babylon Hotel* xxii. 251 The 'Spanish reds' from Catalonia, including the dark 'Tent' so often used sacramentally. **1926** R. N. SALAMAN *Potato Varieties* v. 28 A red,..when selfed, gives rise to three plants bearing red tubers to one bearing white. **1929** W. FAULKNER *Sartoris* II. v. 125 Got an old red we been saving for you... John would have enjoyed that fox. **1961** *Guardian* 24 Oct. 8/6 Some Russian dry whites and reds, selling at as little as 7s. 6d. a bottle. **1968** *Ibid.* 23 Feb. 9/6 No Swiss reds are of real distinction. **1968** K. WEATHERLY *Roo Shooter* 8 A number of roos were resting. The big buck was typical of the reds, standing on his tips about seven feet. **1972** E. HARGREAVES *Fair Green Weed* vii. 93 I'm to buy in more cattle, good reds, in the herd book. **1976** *Southern Evening Echo* (Southampton) 18 Nov. 16/6 Least wastage was 1½oz. from a pound of 'Reds'. **1977** *Age* (Melbourne) 18 Jan. 13/2 Let me forecast in no uncertain terms that this policy can lead only to a severe shortage of high quality reds in five years' time. **1977** *Grimsby Even. Tel.* 24 May 12/4 Principal sorts were: Cod.., coley.., rockfish.., reds.

6. b. (Earlier example.) Also, a Russian Bolshevik; a communist, or extreme socialist. Phr. *reds under the bed*, used to denote an exaggerated or obsessive fear of the presence and harmful influence of communist sympathizers in a particular society, institution, etc.

1851 *Punch* XX. 245/2, I dreamt that I stood in the Crystal Halls, With Chartists and Reds at my side. **1922** S. LEWIS *Babbitt* v. 56 Say, juh notice in the paper the way the New York Assembly stood up to the Reds? **1928** D. L. SAYERS *Lord Peter views Body* iii. 44 I'm a Tory, if anything. I'm certainly not a Red. Why should I help to snatch the good gold from the Primrose Leaguers and hand it over to the Third International? **1931** P. HODGES *Britmis* i. 20 The Orenburg Army,..had been operating against the Reds south of the Trans-Siberian Railway. **1940** [see *LIBERAL *sb.* 1 c]. **1947** *Partisan Rev.* XIV. 354 'All those guys,' he said, 'are just sore because they are not rich. Give any one of them a million dollars and they would forget all about being reds.' **1957** *Economist* 7 Dec. 882/2 Dr Villeda..has been at pains to show the Americans that he is no red. **1972** *Times* 24 May 16/3 This sort of 'reds under the bed' scare.. could only be counter-productive. **1974** *Socialist Worker* 23 Nov. 16/1 The question now is whether the Broad Left leadership has the guts to campaign openly against the Social Contract and for a £30 a week claim in the face of mounting hostility from the government and an increasingly bitter Reds under the Bed campaign from the forces of reaction inside and outside the NUM leadership. **1976** C. BERMANT *Coming Home* I. i. 16 There came the depredations of the Russian civil war, first from the Reds then the Whites. **1976** *West Lancs. Evening Gaz.* 15 Dec., Apparently it is usual practice for Tory writers, if they think an election is imminent, to re-hash previous pre-election writings, same methods, reds under the bed, Communists, or other disguises becoming members of the Labour Party. **1977** 'J. LE

CARRÉ' *Hon. Schoolboy* xiii. 303 There's a story that you people had some local Russian embassy link... Any Reds under your bed..if I may ask?

7. chiefly *U.S.* A red cent (see sense 3 c of the adj. in Dict. and Suppl.).

1849 *Alta California* (San Francisco) 12 July 1/5 Silver is not Plenty on the Pharaoh and his host's Tables, and any body can sea it, and bet a red on any card he chuses. **1856** 'OCKSIDE' & 'DOESTICKS' *Hist. & Rec. Elephant Club* 244 Judge—'Have you got ten dollars?' Mr. W.—' 'Tis true, I hain't a red.' **1865** 'MARK TWAIN' in Harte & 'Twain' *Sk. Sixties* (1926) 199 Greely would ante up money on him as long as he had a red. **1905** J. LONDON *Let.* 1 June (1966) 173, I don't care a red how much the Lazar-sheets roast me. **1922** JOYCE *Ulysses* 151 Didn't cost him a red. **1936** J. A. MCKENNA *Black Range Tales* 267 Many who came into Frisco had not a dad-blasted red left to their name.

8. ellipt. for *red alert* (sense *19 a of the adj.).

1943 B. NIXON *Raiders Overhead* iii. 28 Every night, and all night, there were raids. On the evening of the 16th the 'red' came up at 8.5 p.m. **1943** G. GREENE *Ministry of Fear* IV. i. 223 Yellow's up... About time for the Red I should think.

9. *Naut.* The port side of a ship. Also quasi-*advb.*

1948 PARTRIDGE *Dict. Forces' Slang* 153 *Red, the,* the port side of a ship. It shows a red light. **1956** 'TAFFRAIL' *Arctic Convoy* xi. 103 Someone shouted: 'There they are, sir! Bearing red nine-oh!'—otherwise ninety degrees on the port beam. **1958** W. KING *Stick & Stars* 66 Object bearing red five oh.

10. = *RED-BIRD 2, *RED DEVIL 3. *slang.*

1967 W. MURRAY *Sweet Ride* vii. 107 It's pills, mostly. Reds, goofballs, all kinds. And grass, of course. **1969** *Oz* May 21/1 Mixing 'reds' & alcohol can lead to a one way trip because the two drugs potentiate each other, i.e. 1+1 = more than 2. **1972** J. WAMBAUGH *Blue Knight* (1973) xvi. 293 What've you got, boy? Bennies or reds? Or maybe you're an acid freak?

11. *Comb.,* as (sense *6 b) *red-hunting* vbl. sb. and ppl. a. See also *RED-BAITING *vbl. sb.*

1927 U. SINCLAIR *Oil!* 313 Sure thing! He's nuts on this red-hunting business, and the pinks are worse than the reds, he says. **1935** H. L. ICKES *Secret Diary* (1953) I. 402 He feels about Red hunting just as I do and thinks it is absurd to deny communists an opportunity to express themselves or to have a ticket on the ballot. **1962** M. MCCARTHY *On Contrary* 37 Such Red-hunting publications as *Counter-attack.*

redacter, var. REDACTOR.

1816 SCOTT *Tales of my Landlord* 1st Ser. I. 8, I am not the writer, redacter, or compiler, of the Tales of my Landlord.

rédacteur. (Further examples.)

1848 J. G. LOCKHART *Let.* 4 Jan. in *N. & Q.* (1946) 9 Mar. 90, I wrote only yesterday to thank him for the Life of the Chancellor..tho' not to congratulate him on his redacteur. The book is awfully ill done. **1883** *Daily News* 2 Oct. 5/6 Other *rédacteurs* of the once famous *Journal des Débats.* **1962** *Economist* 27 Jan. 334/3 In the French tradition, the *Dépêche*..hands the big news of the day to a star rédacteur who comments on the story as he tells it.

redaction. Add: **2. a.** (Earlier example.)

1785 T. JEFFERSON *Writings* (1894) IV. 68 The English of which is, that the redaction of the paper had been taken from the imprisoned culprit, and given to another.

b. Also, an adaptation; a shortened form, an abridged version.

1948 *Observer* 30 May 3/3 Finally, we have..what is described as a 'redaction' or compression—this dangerous device grows in popularity—of Lytton's *The Last Days of Pompeii,* by S. Fowler Wright. **1977** *New Yorker* 8 Aug. 2/3 Vinnette Carroll's singing-and-dancing redaction of the Book of Matthew. **1978** *Amer. N. & Q.* Mar. 103/2 In 1661 Samuel Smithson produced a prose redaction of the old metrical romance of Guy of Warwick.

4. *attrib.* and *Comb.,* as **redaction criticism** (see quot. 1976); hence *redaction critic, redaction-critical* adj.

1970 N. PERRIN *What is Redaction Criticism?* i. 22 Although he does not use the term, Lightfoot was actually the first redaction critic. **1976** *Christian Believing* 47 The redaction critic returns by way of the work of form criticism to the Synoptic Gospels as wholes. **1976** *Times Lit. Suppl.* 8 Oct. 1285/3 As far as I know, all redaction critics begin by considering how Luke or 'Matthew' has altered the Marcan narrative. **1968** D. M. BARTON tr. *Rohde's Rediscovering Teaching of Evangelists* i. 15 Various basic theological ideas in the individual gospels were presented through redaction-critical work on the synoptic gospels. **1970** N. PERRIN *What is Redaction Criticism?* ii. 27 Bornkamm's article..is the first thoroughgoing redaction-critical investigation of the theological peculiarities and theme of Matthew's Gospel. **1966** KECK & MARTYN *Stud. in Luke-Acts* (1968) I. 65 At the present time the method called redaction-criticism is luring us into a one-sided concentration on the work of editors. **1968** D. M. BARTON tr. *Rohde's Rediscovering Teaching of Evangelists* ii. 37 Redaction criticism..endeavours to understand the gospels in their entirety against the background of a definite theological situation in the church. **1970** N. PERRIN *What is Redaction Criticism?* i. 1 Redaction criticism is an attempt to represent in English the German word *Redaktionsgeschichte,* which Willi Marxsen proposed as the designation for a discipline within the field of New Testament studies. **1976** *Times Lit. Suppl.* 8 Oct. 1285/3 What is called redaction criticism, the attempt to discover the theological and cultural presuppositions of the gospel writers by examining how they have edited ('redacted') their material.

redactional *a.* (later examples); also, of or belonging to a particular redaction.

1968 *Language* XLIV. 15 In this theory also, RV [*sc.* Rigvedic] *deyām* would probably be redactional for original **dāyām.* **1971** *Ibid.* XLVII. 65 Emeneau's hunch was that some forms beginning with *dy-* which occur in environments interdicted by the Sievers–Edgerton theory might actually be puristic redactional substitutions for Middle Indicisms in *j-.* **1971** *New Testament Abstracts* XV. 285 A minute analysis of vocabulary in this parable shows that before redactional activity it dealt with a king (God) who acted like a shepherd who separated the sheep from the goats with sure judgment.

redactoral (rĭdæ·ktŏrăl), *a.* [f. REDACTOR + -AL.] = REDACTORIAL *a.*

1970 R. S. FOSTER *Restoration of Israel* v. 110 The first redactoral addition in [2 *Kings* xvii.] v. 24–28 explains that the Samaritans were a mixed race.

red alert: see *RED *a.* 19 a.

Red Army. [see RED *a.* 9 b in Dict. and Suppl.] **a.** The name given to the Russian Bolshevik army and later to that of the Soviet Union.

1918 *Manch. Guardian* 13 Dec. 7/4 The Bolshevik Government..is engaged in creating a Red Army of over a million men. **1935** N. MITCHISON *We have been Warned* II. 172 In Moscow..on May Day there are great processions.. and marching by the Red Army. **1943** J. B. PRIESTLEY *Daylight on Saturday* viii. 51 The Red Army is still showing what a workers' republic can do. **1976** 'M. BARAK' *Secret List H. Roehm* viii. 81 After the Revolution he remained an officer in the Red Army. **1978** *Detroit Free Press* 16 Apr. (Record) 15/3 At last, in January 1944 the Red Army advance made it safe for the Kranzbergs and little Miriam to leave their hiding place. **1980** M. BAR-ZOHAR *Deadly Document* x. 164 The band chimed in with..the Red Army song.

b. Adopted as the name of the army in other, esp. communist, countries.

1926 *Encycl. Brit.* II. 393/1 The [Hungarian] Red Army was organised, primarily to ensure the maintenance of the dictatorship. **1934** tr. *Mao Tse-Tung's Red China* 21 The Chinese Soviets and their Red Army have grown out of the development of the agrarian revolution, which liberates the masses of the peasants from oppression and exploitation. **1965** M. MICHAEL tr. *J. Myrdal's Report from Chinese Village* i. 4 The peasants of northern Shensi..set up their own soviet republic and formed their own Red Army. **1974** tr. *Sniečkus's Soviet Lithuania* 20 Many joined the ranks of the Lithuanian Red Army. **1975** *Times Lit. Suppl.* 14 Feb. 163/2 Horthy came to power in the winter of 1919–20.. after Romania's military victory over the Hungarian Red Army. **1977** *Time* 21 Mar. 26/3 The Communists' Red Army had just completed its epic Long March from the Southeast to its new headquarters at Yenan in remote northern Shensi province.

c. The name of a left-wing extremist terrorist organization in Japan.

1972 *Sat. Rev.* (U.S.) 24 June 30/1 The Red Army, an extremist terrorist group in Japan, sponsored and trained by the radical Popular Front for the Liberation of Palestine. **1974** *Times* 7 Feb. 5/1 The Popular Front for the Liberation of Palestine and the Red Army of Japan in a statement issued yesterday sought to justify the attack on the Singapore oil storage tanks—where it is claimed 15 tanks were blown up. **1976** K. BENTON *Single Monstrous Act* iii. 19 The Libyans..seem to have dished out money to every revolutionary group there is, from the Japanese Red Army to the Provos.

d. Red Army Faction, the name of a terrorist organization of West Germany.

1977 *Time* 19 Sept. 8/3 The initials represent the now familiar Red Army Faction, which had murdered both Buback and Ponto. **1979** R. PERRY *Bishop's Pawn* ix. 174 The terrorists..were definitely operating under the Red Army Faction umbrella.

reda·te, *v.* [RE- 5 a.] *trans.* To change the date of; to assign a new date to. Hence **reda·ting** *vbl. sb.*

1611 COTGRAVE *Dict., Redater,* to redate, or adde a new date vnto. **1864** *Spectator* 31 Dec. 1498 Instead of rewriting or redating the previous part of my letter I prefer to send it as it was written. **1935** HUXLEY & HADDON *We Europeans* ii. 54 A recently propounded re-dating of a fragment of a skull. **1980** *Early Music* Jan. 103/2 The new madrigal was not really published in appreciable quantity until the late 1530s, and the re-dating of a central group of manuscript sources shows that dissemination in manuscript was the main way in which the repertory circulated during the years 1520–40.

red-back. 1. (In Dict. s.v. RED *a.* 18 b.)

2. *Austral.* In full, *red-back spider;* = *jockey spider* s.v. *JOCKEY *sb.* 9.

1933, etc. [see *jockey spider* s.v. *JOCKEY *sb.* 9]. **1936** K. C. MCKEOWN *Spider Wonders Austral.* xi. 152 The Red-back Spider..has adapted itself to a life in close association with man. **1953** A. UPFIELD *Murder must Wait* xiv. 130 Five red-back spiders..lying in wait to inject their poison. **1956** *Coast to Coast 1955* 59 Look, there's a red-back in it. **1978** *Telegraph* (Brisbane) 11 Aug. 4/4 The six were victims of a wolf spider—of a type previously unknown and potentially as dangerous as a redback. **1979** *Ibid.* 22 Feb. 3/1 It's a battle to the death. Redback spider versus poisonous dugite snake.

red-backed, *a.* For the Latin name of the red-backed sandpiper substitute *Erolia alpina;* also, the red-backed mouse or vole (*Clethrionomys gapperi*), and the Australian red-backed spider (= *RED-BACK 2). (Earlier and further examples.)

1709 J. LAWSON *New Voy. Carolina* 126 The Red-back'd Snake [is found in Carolina]. **1897** *Proc. Biol. Soc. Washington* XI. 113 The following brief synopsis of the Red-backed Voles is based on a study of specimens in the collection of the U.S. Biological Survey. **1934** *Bulletin* (Sydney) 6 June 20/3 In the Chillagoe..district the red-backed spider is known as 'the jumping red-back'. **1936** D. MCCOWAN *Anim. Canad. Rockies* viii. 71 The Red-backed mouse is a forest dweller..of medium size and has a coat that is marked by a fairly broad belt of chestnut brown hair over the spine. **1940** GABRIELSON & JEWITT *Birds Oregon* 263 The handsome Red-backed Sandpiper is a common migrant on the coast. **1942** Red-backed spider [see *KATIPO]. **1962** M. E. MURIE *Two in Far North* II. iii. 117 Olaus was interested in learning all he could about the distribution of..the red-backed mouse. **1963** *Times* 5 June 14/4 There was still to come the red-backed shrike. **1966** 'J. HACKSTON' *Father clears Out* 134 Safe from..red-backed spiders, and spiders without red backs. **1977** J. L. HARPER *Population Biol. Plants* xv. 465 The seed was collected and buried mainly by..redbacked voles.

red-bait (re·dbēɪt). *S. Afr.* [tr. Afrikaans *rooiaas.*] A large sea-squirt, *Pyura stolonifera,* an ascidian which is used as bait by anglers.

1895 *Agricultural Jrnl.* (Dept. of Agric., Cape Colony) 912 The bait most in use is crayfish, and 'rooiaas' (red bait) a species of Zoophyte. **1905** J. GILCHRIST in Flint & Gilchrist *Science in S. Afr.* III. iv. 192 One of the features of the rocky parts of the coast line from Cape Point eastwards is the clusters of 'rooias' or 'red-bait'. **1930** C. L. BIDEN *Sea-Angling Fishes of Cape* xii. 217 The name 'red-bait' is the English interpretation of the Dutch 'rooi aas'. **1945** *Cape Times* 20 Oct. 7 Red bait could be cut by the sackful. **1957** S. SCHOEMAN *Strike!* iii. 29 Not a single fish would take redbait or mussel. **1971** *Stand. Encycl. S. Afr.* III. 205/2 'Sea-squirts', including the common 'red-bait' (*Pyura*) and the transparent *Ciona,* live permanently attached to rock surfaces.

Re·d-baiting, *vbl. sb.* orig. *U.S.* Also with small initial. [*RED *sb.*[1] 6 b.] Harassment of those of known or suspected communist sympathies; also *attrib.* So (as a back-formation) **re·d-bait** *v. trans.* and *intr.,* to oppose, thwart, or persecute because of communist associations; **Re·d-baiter, red-baiter,** one who seeks out and harasses supposed communists.

1929 *Nation* 2 Oct. 343/1 Red-Baiters... Mr. Woll and his underlings have become..obsessed with an anti-Communist spirit. **1934** M. H. WESEEN *Dict. Amer. Slang* 386 *Red-baiting,* looking for communists. **1937** *Nation* 14 Aug. 167/2 A new red-baiting campaign. **1939** *Sun* (Baltimore) 22 Mar. 12/1 It was well-nigh impossible to say a word for capitalism and against the vagaries of Communism without being accused of Red-baiting. **1940** G. SELDES *Witch Hunt* p. xi, Nevertheless, that program was redbaited into compromise and failure. **1943** F. SCULLY *Rogue's Gallery Hollywood* 83 Fugitives from red-baiting America..they all rallied 'round leaders like Pirandello. **1946** *Sun* (Baltimore) 19 July 20/1 The War Department hasn't gone off half-cocked to 'witch hunt, red bait or to bust' unions. **1950** *Manch. Guardian Weekly* 15 June 15 The 'Amerasia' case is something that the Red-baiters have wanted to open up again ever since the conviction of Alger Hiss. *Ibid.* 16 Nov. 9 The defeat of the Liberals..suggests that vociferous 'Red-baiting' is, however silly, good politics. **1962** D. LESSING *Golden Notebk.* IV. 483 The fanciest bit of red-baiting I've heard in a long time. **1969** *Listener* 13 Feb. 214/2 One might sneer away the Red-baiting of the Hearst press and shrug off the ceaseless cries of 'Fascists!' from the Left, and yet be uneasy about the future. **1974** *Socialist Worker* 2 Nov. 12/5 The information could be used to red-bait or victimise workers involved in the present disputes. **1976** *Times Lit. Suppl.* 23 Jan. 89/1 Professor Nove may be in danger of incurring from some of our red-baiters the ludicrously unjustifiable charge of being an apologist for Stalin. **1977** *Time* 7 Feb. 46/3 Boyle, 40, stars as the Red-baiting chairman of the Senate Permanent Subcommittee on Investigations.

red-bellied, *a.* (Earlier and later examples.)

1709 J. LAWSON *New Voy. Carolina* 126 Red-bellied Land-Snakes. **1731** M. CATESBY *Nat. Hist. Carolina* I. 19 The Red-bellied Wood-pecker... The belly near the vent.. is stained with red. **1917** T. G. PEARSON *Birds Amer.* II. 161/2 The Red-bellied Woodpecker..evinces a decided taste for fruit. **1934** DYLAN THOMAS *Let.* 15 Apr. (1966) 108 If there must be a worm in our letters let it be the jolly, red-bellied one you told me about. **1965** MRS. L. B. JOHNSON *White House Diary* 3 June (1970) 281 Most startling of all was a fish whose every scale stood out..the red-bellied angelfish. **1973** M. CROWELL *Greener Pastures* 109 It is the red-bellied woodpecker that visited the feeder last week. **1977** C. MCCULLOUGH *Thorn Birds* iv. 75 Of snakes the variety was almost endless..red-bellied black snakes.

red belt. 1. [*RED *a.* 9 b.] **a.** Territory under the political control or influence of the U.S.S.R. **b.** Elsewhere, an area of communist strength or influence.

1947 *Sun* (Baltimore) 22 Dec. 2/1 The 'Red Belt' states of Europe are moving into a fairly solid bloc. **1966** M. R. D. FOOT *SOE in France* ix. 257 The French communist organizations in the 'red belt' round Paris. **1969** P. ALLUM in Henig & Pinder *European Political Parties* 233 The DC is strongest in the 'white provinces' where it regularly polls half the vote and it is weakest in the 'red belt' where its vote is only around 30 per cent. **1977** *Time* 4 Apr. 22/3 But much as Moscow might like a Red belt across Africa, even Angola and Mozambique are not anxious to be totally under Soviet control. **1978** *Sunday Star* (Toronto) 26 Feb. A4/3 When voters of the Paris red-belt suburb of Kremlin-Bicetre attend election meetings, the gloves are off.

2. [Red *a.* 16.] A belt worn by one who has attained a certain degree of proficiency in judo or karate; also, a person qualified to wear such a belt.

1952 E. J. Harrison *Judo* i. 14 A black belt is worn in the first five Dan grades..and a red belt in the tenth and higher Dan grades. **1958** *Radio Times* 7 Feb. 9/4, I am only a Red Belt. **1967** P. Urban *Karate Dojo* 44 A solid red belt is worn by the highest grand masters. **1971** *Rand Daily Mail* 27 Mar. 6/8 Executive members of the South African division of the Japanese Karate Association put their heads together and came up with a new belt—a red one symbolising a junior brown belt. **1976** B. Jacks *Judo* 8 The adult beginner wears a white or red belt and the grades then progress.

red-belted: see *red *a.* 14 a, Red *a.* 14 b.

red-berried, *a.* **1.** (Earlier and later examples.)

1731 P. Miller *Gardeners Dict.* s.v. *Sambucus*, The Mountain red-berry'd Elder. **1930** J. Masefield *Wanderer of Liverpool* 19 Red-berried blackthorn. **1972** *Hilliers' Man. Trees & Shrubs* 360 *Sambucus..racemosa* L. 'Red-berried Elder'. A medium-sized to large shrub.

red-bird. **1.** For *Piranga æstiva* substitute *Piranga rubra*; for *P. rubra* substitute *P. olivacea*. Add Latin names of the Baltimore oriole (*Icterus galbula*) and the cardinal (*Richmondena cardinalis*). (Earlier and later examples.)

1669 [see *Baltimore]. **1929** W. Faulkner *Sartoris* iv. iv. 337 They saw redbirds darting like arrows of scarlet flames. **1938** M. K. Rawlings *Yearling* ix. 81 A red-bird swung in an arc across the sink-hole. **1959** E. B. White *Let.* Feb. (1976) 459 It's a nice place to be, what with the..red-bird saying 'Portugee, Portugee'.

2. The drug secobarbital (Seconal); also, a tablet of this drug (coloured red). *slang.*

1969 R. R. Lingeman *Drugs from A to Z* 219 *Seconal*... Slang names: red birds, red devils, reds. **1976** *Billings* (Montana) *Gaz.* 11 July 9-A/1 In order on DAWN's list of drugs most frequently recorded in crisis situations—in which a drug user sought help or died—were heroin, marijuana, aspirin, LSD, secobarbital (marketed as Seconal and known as 'red devils, Mexican reds and red birds'), [etc.].

re·d-blooded, *a.* [Red *a.* 14 a.] **1.** Having red blood.

1802, 1840 [see Red *a.* 14 a].

2. Restored to health and strength after weakness or exhaustion.

1877 Tennyson *Harold* iv. iii. 131 Sit down, sit down, and eat, And, when again red-blooded, speak again.

3. *transf.* Virile, vigorous, full of life, spirited.

1881 A. A. Hayes *New Colorado* xi. 155 [Nothing] can be conceived more exasperating to a strong red-blooded man than to..have a villain take his watch and money. **1888** W. Whitman in *Cent. Mag.* (1911) Dec. 254/2 John's letter appeals to me..because of its uncompromising red-blooded espousal of the book. **1914** E. R. Burroughs *Tarzan of Apes* xix. 257 Tarzan..did what no red-blooded man needs lessons in doing. **1923** *Daily Mail* 28 Feb. 10 (Advt.), It's a rip-roaring, red-blooded yarn that no man or woman will be able to read unmoved. **1941** B. Schulberg *What makes Sammy Run?* vii. 159 The play was..about two red-blooded guys who are always scrapping. **1966** Wodehouse *Plum Pie* i. 11 A redblooded loony doctor under the influence of the divine passion ought surely to have put the thing through months ago. **1978** M. Puzo *Fools Die* xxxiii. 387 To me he sounded like any red-blooded American businessman.

re·dbone. *U.S.* A hound belonging to a variety distinguished by a red or red and tan coat, which was once used to hunt racoons. Also *attrib.*

1916 W. H. Miller in *Field & Stream* XXI. 177/1 Good Redbone, Pennsylvania or Portsmouth hound stock is what we want up North. **1919** —— *Amer. Hunting Dog* iii. 57 Two strains are well known, the Redbone, an ancient breed of Southern coon-hound, and the J. E. Williams dogs. **1948** W. Faulkner *Intruder in Dust* i. 5 A true rabbit dog, some hound, a good deal of hound, maybe mostly hound, redbone and black-and-tan. **1975** E. Wigginton *Foxfire 3* 38, I had a *good* stock a' dogs—blue tick and redbone mix.

red book, red-book. Add: **4.** *Little Red Book*: a popular name used in Western countries for 'Quotations from Chairman Mao Tse-tung' (published in English in 1966). Also in extended and allusive use.

1967 [see *Maoism]. **1970** G. Jackson *Let.* 17 Apr. in *Soledad Brother* (1971) 225 Burn it; all the fascist literature, burn that too. Then equip yourself with the Little Red Book. **1971** D. Bagley *Freedom Trap* viii. 193 Communist Albania has ceased to hew to the Moscow line. Enver Hoxha, the Albanian party boss, has read the Little Red Book and thinks the thoughts of Mao. **1974** *Times* 21 Oct. 12/8 A hotelier in..Lübeck has arranged to provide in all bedrooms..a German translation of Chairman Mao's little red book. **1976** J. Crosby *Nightfall* x. 47 If I write my own little Red Book, that will be in it. Hit the pricks—or they get ideas. **1977** *N.Y. Rev. Bks.* 12 May 22/3 Photos showed rampaging teenagers waving their little red books of Mao quotations.

redbreast. Add: **3.** *U.S.* The long-eared sunfish, *Lepomis megalotis.*

1888 G. B. Goode *Amer. Fishes* 66 In Pennsylvania it [*sc.* the long-eared sun-fish] is called 'Sun Perch' and 'Red Headed Bream', elsewhere it is the 'Red Breast'. **1948** *New Hanover Fishing Club Prize List* 30 Annual prizes for fresh-water fish..Red Breast.

red-brick. Also red brick, redbrick. **1.** A red building-brick. Freq. *attrib.*

1712 J. Mortimer *Whole Art Husbandry* II. 150 The black Mould..will in time degenerate into a red-brick Earth. **1835** J. Romilly *Diary* 11 Mar. (1967) 70 They are nasty red-brick churches, in the worst stile of 1760. **1839** [in Dict. s.v. Red *a.* 16 a]. *a* **1847, 1888** [in Dict. s.v. Red *a.* 12 a]. **1916** E. F. Benson *David Blaize* v. 101 His horizon and aspirations stretched no farther than this red-brick arena. **1943** 'B. Truscot' *Redbrick University* 17 The material used in them [*sc.* universities] was..a hideously cheerful red brick suggestive of something between a super council-school and a holiday home for children. **1960** J. Betjeman *Summoned by Bells* v. 46 But for me, Less academic, red-brick Chalfont Road Meant great-aunt Wilkins, tea and buttered toast. **1977** *Western Mail* (Cardiff) 5 Mar. 7/3 For the Opposition leader, it was a nostalgic return to the red brick establishment of Kesteven and Grantham girls' school which she left 34 years ago.

2. (Also with capital initial.) Used *attrib.* or quasi-*adj.* to denote a British university founded in the late nineteenth or early twentieth century in a large industrial city, with buildings of red-brick, as distinct from the older universities (esp. Oxford, Cambridge, the ancient universities of Scotland, and some of the London colleges) built predominantly in stone, and also as distinct from the new universities founded after the 1939–45 war; of or pertaining to such a university; also *ellipt.*, a red-brick university; *collect.*, such universities in general. Also *transf.*

1943 'B. Truscot' *Redbrick University* 18 The range of interests represented in a Redbrick staff common-room. *Ibid.* 19 It may be natural enough for him to go on to Redbrick, but to..enter Oxbridge is something infinitely more exciting. **1944** 'H. Ashton' *Yeoman's Hospital* ix. 197 Marriner took his professorship at that frightful red-brick university. **1950** *Times Educ. Suppl.* 10 Mar. 183 (*heading*) Redbrick criticized. **1958** *Times Lit. Suppl.* 17 Jan. 30/4 Talk of..'the red-brick intellectuals', though no Movement founder-member had done more than *teach* at one of the provincial universities. **1958** *Observer* 16 Feb. 12/3 One of the new 'redbrick actors', neither actorish in aspect nor conventionally po-voiced. **1958** *New Statesman* 22 Feb. 233/1 Under education, the correct entry is: 'Educated Thomas Cooks, American Express, Wayfarers, etc., etc.' Europe has been my Redbrick. **1960**, etc. [see *Oxbridge]. **1966** G. Sinstadt *Whisper in Lonely Place* iii. 33 He's a research engineer, degree from one of the red-bricks, middle twenties. **1975** D. Lodge *Changing Places* i. 9 Rummidge.. had lately suffered the mortifying fate of most English universities of its type (civic redbrick). **1976** M. Hinxman *End of Good Woman* i. 13 They kept introducing her to eligible mates. Revolutionaries at the London School of Economics, posh chums from Oxford..budding scientists and engineers at the 'red-brick' universities. **1977** *Jrnl. R. Soc. Arts* CXXV. 670/1 Some of the best safety managers I know left school at 14 or 15 years of age. Conversely, we have seen people who come from red bricks and grey stones but are quite unable to do the job at all.

red-bud. Add: **a.** (Earlier and later examples.) Also *attrib.*

1705 R. Beverley *Hist. & Present State Virginia* iv. 56 They dish up [roots, herbs, etc.] various ways, and find them very delicious Sauce to their Meats;..such are the Red-buds, Sassafras-Flowers, Cymnels, Melons, and Potatoes. **1709** J. Lawson *New Voy. Carolina* 100 The Red-Bud-Tree bears a purple Lark-Heel. **1931** W. Faulkner *Sanctuary* xviii. 164 Lilac and wistaria and redbud..had never been finer. **1946** D. C. Peattie *Road of Naturalist* v. 58 The red-bud trees begin to bloom. **1977** *New Yorker* 2 May 51/2 The dogwoods and redbuds blossomed.

redcap, red-cap, red cap. Add: **4.** *Mil. slang.* A military policeman.

1919 *Athenæum* 1 Aug. 695/1 In your July 18 issue a correspondent mentions 'red-hat' as an army policeman. I have always found 'red-cap' to be the more familiar term. **1949** G. Cotterell *Randle in Springtime* 7 'Mind yourself, there are some redcaps in that jeep.' 'I seen 'em,' the driver grinned, slowing down to below forty miles an hour, as another jeep, containing three Military Policemen, approached and passed them. **1964** J. Hale *Grudge Fight* viii. 127 The redcaps and the R.A.F. police. **1976** J. O'Connor *Eleventh Commandment* iv. 53 She used to take me to night-clubs tucked away where no officers or redcaps knew about.

5. Chiefly *U.S.* A porter at a railway station.

1919 S. Lewis *Free Air* xxiv. 245 A factory illuminated by arc-lamps,—the baggage—the porter..red caps. **1929** M. de la Roche *Whiteoaks* x. 145 A 'redcap' darting into the throng, the bag clutched in his hand. **1931** W. Faulkner *Sanctuary* xxi. 227 A man shouted 'taxi' at them; a redcap tried to take Fonzo's bag. **1942** *Sun* (Baltimore) 10 Oct. 10/2 There are only thirty-five red caps to help the anxious passengers with their luggage. **1960** B. Keaton *Wonderful World of Slapstick* iii. 59 Kelly didn't explain that there were no redcaps at Victoria Station. **1969** J. A. McPherson in A. Chapman *New Black Voices* (1972) 156 He had redcaps in the Chicago stations telling the soldiers who to ask for on the train. **1977** *Times* 19 Apr. 15/7 In France and Switzerland the larger stations have 'red cap' porters who shift baggage on a prescribed tariff.

red carpet: see *red *a.* 19 a.

red cedar. **a.** Substitute for def.: A North American species of juniper, esp. *Juniperus virginiana*, or the western conifer, *Thuja plicata*. Also *attrib.* (Earlier and further examples.)

1682 S. Wilson *Acct. Province Carolina in Amer.* 12 This Country hath..divers sorts of lasting Timber that England hath not, as Cedar white and red, Cypress, Locust, Bay and Laurel Trees. **1797** *Deb. Congress U.S.* 10 Feb. (1849) 2113 It would be expedient ..to secure some of the lands in South Carolina and Georgia, well clothed with live oak and red cedar timber, for the purpose of building ships of war. **1851** *Knickerbocker* XXXVII. 377 The country-bred traveller..inhales the odor of the red-cedar buckets. **1884** C. S. Sargent *Rep. Forests N. Amer.* 7 The hemlock, and the red cedar (*Thuya*) are still important elements of the forests. **1904** E. Step *Wayside & Woodland Trees* 81 The Virginian Juniper..or 'Red Cedar', as it is called on the American continent, is..frequently planted in our parks and gardens. **1958** G. A. Petrides *Field Guide Trees & Shrubs* 22 The junipers (including the Red Cedar) may bear either scaly or hollowed 3-sided needles. **1969** T. H. Everett *Living Trees of World* iv. 63/1 Western red-cedar.. is native along the Pacific Coast of North America. **1972** *Ecology* LIII. 1141/2 'Fruits' of pasture juniper and red cedar are important foods for red squirrels.

red cell. A blood cell containing hæmoglobin; an erythrocyte; = *red blood cell, red corpuscle*, both s.v. *red *a.* 19 a.

1885 Delafield & Prudden *Handbk. Path. Anat. & Histol.* (ed. 2) ii. 50 In the extravasation of blood by diapedesis, the white blood-cells may pass through the walls of the vessels..; the red cells, on the other hand,..are.. carried passively through the walls by minute amounts of fluid. **1896** *Boston Med. & Surg. Jrnl.* CXXXV. 131/2 Nucleated red cells have usually been classified as microblasts, normoblasts, megoblasts..and those with dividing nuclei. **1936** *Lancet* 11 July 88/2 A..study of the permeability of red cells. **1968** Passmore & Robson *Compan. Med. Stud.* I. xxvi. 2/1 The red cells are by far the most numerous of the blood cells; for every white cell there are about 500 red cells and about 30 platelets.

2. *attrib.*

1917 C. Price-Jones *Blood Pictures* i. 11 Assuming the average red-cell count of a woman to be 4,450,000 per c.mm. **1941** *Science* 24 Jan. 87/1 (*heading*) Red cell volume circulating and total as determined by radio iron. **1947** *Radiology* XLIX. 303/2 After acutely toxic doses of such agents as Sr^{89} and Pu^{239}, the minimum red cell count occurs in survivors at a period later than the time of death of non-survivors. **1968** Passmore & Robson *Compan. Med. Stud.* I. xxvi. 5/1 Red cell precursors normally account for one third to one tenth of the bone marrow cells. **1976** *Med. Clin. N. Amer.* LX. 945 Pure red cell aplasia is a disorder in which patients cease making new red cells. **1976** I. Chanarin et al. *Blood & its Dis.* ii. 11 The normal..red cell count at sea level is..$10^6/\mu l$ 5·0±0·6 [for men].

red cent: see *red *a.* 3 c in Dict. and Suppl.

red-cheeked, *a.* (Earlier and later examples.)

1602 Marston *Antonio's Revenge* v. iv. sig. K1 Red cheekt Bacchus. **1872** Geo. Eliot *Middlemarch* II. xxxvii. 254 Pratt, a red-cheeked man. **1923** E. O'Neill *Anna Christie* i. 7 He is a boyish, red-cheeked, rather good-looking young fellow of twenty or so. **1960** *Farmer & Stockbreeder* 16 Feb. (Suppl.) 3/1 From the car he waved goodbye to her. Red-cheeked, in her felt shoes, one hand clutching her dress at the neck, she waved back.

Red China. [*red *a.* 9 b.] Communist China; the People's Republic of China. Hence **Red Chinese** *sb.* and *adj. phr.* Cf. *mainland China* s.v. *mainland 2 b.

1934 tr. Mao Tse-Tung (*title*) Red China. **1937** E. Snow *Red Star over China* i. 17 There has been perhaps no greater mystery among nations, no more confused an epic, than the story of Red China. **1966** 'G. Black' *You want to die, Johnny?* viii. 151 You couldn't stop junks landing... I'm thinking of Red Chinese. **1967** R. J. Serling *President's Plane is Missing* (1968) vii. 138 Is there any reason to suspect the Red Chinese or Russians? *Ibid.* 139 Suppose, sir, Red Chinese agents had somehow kidnaped Mr. Haines. **1971** J. Henderson *Copperhead* (1972) xv. 195 Targets inside Russia and Red China. **1972** J. Ball *Five Pieces of Jade* ii. 27 A systematic new campaign by the red Chinese to pump narcotics..into the United States. **1972** 'G. Black' *Bitter Tea* (1973) iii. 44 Plenty of people in Malaysia still hate Red China. **1978** *Listener* 8 June 721/1 The entry permit into what we used to call 'Red China' is stamped on your passport.

red-circle, *v.* To separate out by circling in red ink; usu. *fig.*; *spec.* (see quots. 1974 and 1977). Hence **red-circling** *vbl. sb.*

1965 E. Brown *Big Man* xxiii. 202 The night had been red-circled for pleasure and for entertainment. **1973** *Maclean's Mag.* July 63/1 This was not a problem peculiar to the Trudeau regime, but it grew worse when the Treasury Board approved a plan to 'red circle' my 28 senior officers, the heart of my department. *Ibid.*, He suggested that if a committee were set up, the impending red circling might be avoided. **1974** *Globe & Mail* (Toronto) 14 Feb. 1/2 [The secretaries] fear their position will be further downgraded by a reclassification scheme undertaken by the Treasury Board, whereby secretaries could be red-circled—held in their current pay bracket until the new secretarial classifications catch up to them. The possibility of red-circling has stalled salary negotiations between the Treasury Board and the Public Service Alliance of Canada. **1976** *Ibid.* 15 Sept. 1/2 The alliance said red-circling is not permitted and that an employee can only be demoted if he is proved to be incompetent or incapable of performing the duties of his position. **1977** *Spare Rib* May 22/1 Certain men at Vauxhall's were 'red circled', placed in a special category to preserve their higher rate of pay. (It is called 'red circling' when workers moved on to a job with a lower rate of pay take their previous higher rate with them.)

redcoat, red-coat, red coat. Add: **1. c.** A steward at a Butlin's holiday camp.

1950 L. BLAIR *Butlin Holiday Bk. 1949–50* 66 The snow eventually disappeared and the 'Redcoats' prepared to return to the Holiday Villages. **1962** R. NORTH *Butlin Story* v. 61 Charlie was a Redcoat at Filey for four seasons. **1966** P. J. KAVANAGH *Perfect Stranger* iii. 23 To counteract my snobbism, he sent me to Butlin's Holiday Camp to do a month as a Holiday Uncle, or Redcoat. **1979** *Daily Tel.* 2 Aug. 3/3 A holiday camp 'redcoat'..claimed a world record at Brighton yesterday, by eating 100 peanuts in 46 seconds.

d. The title of a particular attendant at the door of the House of Lords.

1972 *Times* 22 July 12/5 Redcoat is the only attendant dressed in red in the House, a reminder that his was a royal appointment of Charles II's originally. The King, visiting the Lords and finding no one to greet him, made his own appointment on the spot. **1974** *Daily Tel.* (Colour Suppl.) 6 Dec. 29/2 C. D. Maxted, known as Red Coat, is a familiar figure to all peers as they arrive at the Lords.

3. (Later example.)

1906 *Westm. Gaz.* 6 Sept. 2/1 The British markets want large, bright apples, preferably of the red-coat type.

red cross, red-cross. Add: **3. a.** *red cross flag* (further example).

a **1850** WORDSWORTH *Prelude* (1959) x. 385 The proud fleet that bears the red-cross flag.

b. *Red Cross work.*

1914 W. OWEN *Let.* 23 Sept. (1967) 284 There are already *too many* ladies offering to help with red cross work.

re·d-cross, *v. rare.* [f. the sb.] *trans.* To mark with a red cross.

1869 BROWNING *Ring & Bk.* IV. xi. 128 You would have ..forced me..find my way submissive to the fold. Be red-crossed on the fleece, one sheep the more.

red-crossed, *a.* (Later examples.)

1900 W. S. CHURCHILL in *Morning Post* 17 Feb. 8/1 White-hooded, red-crossed ambulance waggons. **1916** 'BOYD CABLE' *Action Front* 165 Another [ambulance wagon] was overturned,..and in the Red-Crossed canvas tilts of others gaped huge tears and rents. **1935** C. S. FORESTER *Afr. Queen* ii. 30 The Mediterranean squadron..with the red-crossed Admiral's flag in the van. **1962** J. B. PRIESTLEY *Margin Released* II. iv. 113 The starched and red-crossed debs.

red-currant. Add: **c.** *red currant jam, tart.*

1788 J. WOODFORDE *Diary* 8 July (1927) III. 36 We had for Dinner to Day some Peas and Beans, a Piggs Face..and black and red currant Tarts. **1861** MRS. BEETON *Bk. Househ. Managem.* 771 Red-currant jam. **1866** J. BLACKWOOD *Let.* 10 Sept. in *Geo. Eliot Lett.* (1956) IV. 307 My little boy..declined red currant tart. **1958** R. PAGE *Let.* 11 Oct. in R. McDouall *Clubland Cooking* (1974) 166 Another member had a weakness for Red Currant and Raspberry Tart.

redd, *sb.*[1] Add: **1.** Also with *up.* (See also quot. 1893–4.)

1893–4 R. O. HESLOP *Northumb. Words* II. 569 By inversion, 'A fine *red* up' is sometimes used to indicate a scene of disorder. **1917** 'H. H. RICHARDSON' *Fortunes R. Mahony* II. ii. 105 She herself, in proper wifely fashion, proposed to give her little house a good red-up, in its master's absence.

redd, *sb.*[2] **2.** (Earlier and later examples.)

1808 JAMIESON s.v. Red, Redd. With their snouts they form a hollow in the bed of the river, generally so deep, that, when lying in it, their backs are rather below the level of the bed. This is called the redd. **1913** F. M. HALFORD *Dry-Fly Man's Handbk.* III. i. 307 An observant man will detect the heaps of clean gravel or redds where the ova have been deposited by the trout... If there are salmon in the river, their redds too will be visible. **1916** *Trans. Inverness Sci. Soc.* VIII. 324 Salmon and all kinds of trout are very much alike in their spawning habits. The spawning bed, often called a 'redd', is composed of gravel or rough sand. **1960** *New Scientist* 2 June 1392/1 A study of the nature of redds—the gravel banks chosen by the female trout to receive her eggs—has shown that an essential feature is the presence of water currents. **1971** W. HILLEN *Blackwater River* xi. 105 The alevins emerge from the spawning nest, or redd, in late winter. **1977** *New Yorker* 2 May 47/2 Everywhere, in fleets, are the oval shapes of salmon. They have moved the gravel and made redds.

redd, *v.*[2] Add: **6. a.** Also in *U.S.* and general use.

1842 *Spirit of Times* (Philad.) 12 Aug. (Th.), I never used to red up their chamber without thinking of it. **1896** E. HIGGINSON *Flower that grew in Sand* 120 'You got your front room red up, Emarine?' 'No; I ain't had time to red up anything.' **1909** A. QUILLER-COUCH *True Tilda* xix. 258 They tumbled out and redded up the place in a hurry. **1912** MULFORD & CLAY *Buck Peters* i. 19, I guess you two men can take care of each other while I red up. **1951** L. CRAIG *Singing Hills* xix. 181 You take this baby while I redd up the room. **1977** J. AIKEN *Five-Minute Marriage* ix. 141 The rooms..are all clean and redd up, sir.

redden, *v.* Add: **2. d.** Of a pullet: to acquire a deeper shade of red in the comb and wattles as the bird approaches maturity and prepares to begin laying.

1909 T. W. STURGES *Poultry Man.* vii. 106 When a pullet is about to redden up and develop her comb previous to laying, the change from one pen to another will check this development. **1950** *N.Z. Jrnl. Agric.* Oct. 332/3 If any [pullets] appear unlikely to start 'reddening up' for a month or more, they should..be sold immediately. **1967** T. R. MORRIS in T. C. Carter *Environmental Control in Poultry Production* ii. 27 Once the flock has begun to 'redden up' it is usually too late to alter sexual maturity.

reddening, *vbl. sb.* [f. REDDEN *v.* + -ING[1].] The action of making or becoming red. Also *attrib.*

1847 T. T. STODDART *Angler's Compan. Scotl.* 116 Worms on their transference to the moss-jar still undergo the process of scouring..that of toughening, and..the further one of reddening. *Ibid.*, The reddening matter..is a species of high-coloured earth, reduced to a powder. **1927** HALDANE & HUXLEY *Animal Biol.* vii. 150 Impulses..run directly to the local vessels, which open up, causing reddening of the skin. **1978** PASACHOFF & KUTNER *University Astron.* xxiii. 579 Traditionally, studies of reddening and extinction have been used to find the distances to stars.

red devil. 1. A type of Italian hand grenade. Also *attrib.*

a **1944** K. DOUGLAS *Alamein to Zem Zem* (1946) vi. 44 The little tin 'red devil' grenades, bombastic little crackers that will blow a man's hand off and make a noise like the crack of doom. **1967** *Sunday Times* (Colour Suppl.) 10 Sept. 45/4 *Red devils*, Italian hand grenades painted red. They made a lot of noise but caused little damage.

2. *the Red Devils*: popular name for the Parachute Regiment of the British Army.

1943 in G. G. Norton *Red Devils* (1971) ii. 24 General Alexander directs that I Para Brigade be info[rmed] that [they] have been given name by Germans of 'Red Devils'. **1948** M. PACKE *First Airborne* vii. 78 They..inspired the German paratroops..to christen them the Red Devils. **1974** *Times* 19 Apr. 15/4 The Red Devils free-fall team is giving another display. **1977** *Times* 8 June 4/1 The Red Devils, the Army's daring freefall parachute team.

3. = *RED-BIRD 2.

1967 *Boston Sunday Herald* 26 Mar. I. 12/2 Friday's 'goof ball' raid in a South End apartment (where 3,600 so-called 'red-devils' were confiscated) was the result of three months investigatory work. **1971** 'D. SHANNON' *Murder with Love* (1972) iv. 67 Quite a collection of the pills..the Blue Angels and Red Devils and Yellow Submarines. **1974** M. C. GERALD *Pharmacol.* xi. 205 Short-acting barbiturates such as..secobarbital ('red devils').

redding, *vbl. sb.*[1] Add: **2.** *redding-out*: the process of undergoing or experiencing a red-out.

1933 *Jrnl. R. Aeronaut. Soc.* XXXVII. 407 The phenomenon of 'redding out' is essentially and solely ocular in origin due to postural congestion of the vascular retina. **1951** NAYLER & OWER *Flight To-day* (ed. 3) i. 24 Accelerations..in the other direction, i.e., upwards towards the pilot's head, of more than 2g [are common] in bunts, which lead to risks of 'redding out' in contrast to 'blacking out'. **1961** R. L. CHRISTY in H. G. Armstrong *Aerospace Med.* xvi. 250/2 Occasionally there may be a temporary loss of vision and there have been a few scattered reports that objects appear red and produce the phenomenon commonly referred to as 'redding out'.

reddingite (re·diŋəit). *Min.* [f. the name of *Redding* township, Fairfield County, Connecticut, where the mineral was first found: see -ITE[1].] A hydrated phosphate of ferrous iron and bivalent manganese (the latter predominating), $(Mn,Fe)_3(PO_4)_2.3H_2O$, which forms an isomorphous series with phosphoferrite and occurs as pinkish, yellowish, or colourless, translucent or transparent, orthorhombic crystals.

1878 BRUSH & DANA in *Amer. Jrnl. Sci.* CXVI. 35 In addition to the above minerals, as original constituents of the same deposit, are amblygonite (hebronite), and a phosphate of manganese isomorphous with scorodite which we shall describe under the name reddingite. **1955** [see *phosphoferrite* s.v. *PHOSPHO-]. **1964** *Amer. Mineralogist* XLIX. 1122 Landesite, a rare hydrated manganous-ferric phosphate, is an alteration product of reddingite which, in turn, is derived from the hydration and alkali-leaching of lithiophilite-triphylite at the Berry Quarry, Poland, Maine. **1971** *Mineral. Abstr.* XXII. 18/1 Iron-manganese phosphate minerals, new to the Congo are..reddingite-phosphoferrite, bermanite, phosphosiderite, [etc.].

reddish, *a.* Add: **1. b.** (Further examples of insect names.)

1889 *Cent. Dict.* 5018/3 *Reddish light-arches*, a British noctuid moth. **1907** R. SOUTH *Moths Brit. Isles* 1st Ser. 279 The Reddish Light Arches..occurs in beech woods. *Ibid.* 321 The Reddish Buff... The female is much smaller than the male. **1968** *Oxf. Bk. Insects* 82/1 It is easy to confuse this moth with the less common Reddish Light Arches.

2. a. *reddish-blue, -brown* (earlier and later examples), *-purple, -violet.*

1934 *Webster*, Reddish-blue. **1962** I. MURDOCH *Unofficial Rose* xviii. 179 A dark reddish-blue sky. **1964** S. DUKE-ELDER *Parsons' Dis. Eye* (ed. 14) xxi. 296 The anterior ciliary veins are dilated, and a reddish-blue zone surrounds the cornea. **1629** J. PARKINSON *Paradisi in Sole* l. 518 The scales..are eyther of a reddish browne, whitish, or greenish colour. **1855** J. PHILLIPS *Man. Geol.* 411 Over all is a continuous widely spread reddish-brown clay. **1980** *Catal. Fine Chinese Ceramics* (Sotheby, Hong Kong) 16 The unglazed stoneware burnt reddish-brown in the firing. **1629** J. PARKINSON *Paradisi in Sole* viii. 55/2 A white [flowring Tulipa], speckled with a reddish purple, more or lesse, of diuers sorts, with white, yellow, or blew bottomes. **1963** A. LUBBOCK *Austral. Roundabout* 108 The granite ridges round Cloncurry, reddish-purple and bare. **1971** L. A. BOGER *Dict. World Pott. & Porc.* 278/2 Inscriptions were often painted on the black background in red (or reddish purple). **1980** *Catal. Fine Chinese Ceramics* (Sotheby, Hong Kong) 92 Covered with a bright reddish-purple glaze attractively streaked and mottled in milky blue. **1856** *Rep. Comm. Patents 1855: Agric.* 273 The *Red-striped* [sugar] cane,..and the *Violet* or *Reddish-violet*, which is only a variation from the former,..will generally prosper..[in] the Southern States. **1964** S. DUKE-ELDER *Parsons' Dis. Eye* (ed. 14) x. 102 The ciliary form for the most part a diffuse reddish-violet blush.

Hence **re·ddishly** *adv.*

1946 R. CAPELL *Simiomata* II. 47 He is donnish, tall and reddishly fair.

reddition. Add: **1. d.** Recompense or restitution.

1929 R. BRIDGES *Testament of Beauty* IV. 143 And for her soilure make Reddition to Nature.

3. (Later example.)

1950 J. N. D. KELLY *Early Christian Creeds* ii. 36 This solemn rehearsal, or reddition, of the creed before baptism was universally observed in the West.

red dog. 1. (In Dict. s.v. RED *a.* 19 a.)

2. A low grade of flour.

1889 in *Cent. Dict.* **1931** *Hearings U.S. Congress House Comm. Ways & Means* 131 That would probably include 'red dog' flour, which is a very low grade flour which is considered feed. **1946** *Sun* (Baltimore) 14 Feb. 14/1 'Red dog' is fine bran particles and small quantities of wheat flour.

3. Either of two card games (see quot. 1934).

1930 *Sun* (Baltimore) 18 Aug. 6/1 Playing red dog for money. **1934** *Webster*, *Red dog*... 3. a. A game in which players hold each five cards and bet, for a pool, that they hold a higher card in the same suit than the top card of the stock. b. A variety of stud poker played with seven cards, the first two and the last one being dealt face down, in which all buried red cards are wild. **1935** *Encycl. Sports* 400/1 *Red dog.* This is a card game for any number of players from three to eight. **1938** J. D. CARR *Crooked Hinge* xxi. 290 It was, in the terms of an American pastime called Red Dog, 'high, low, jack, and the goddam game'. **1945** A. A. OSTROW *Compl. Card Player* 47 (*heading*) Red Dog (Also known as high-card pool). *Ibid.* 48 Six-Spot Red Dog... In this variant of red dog each player receives 3 cards. **1974** *Hoyle's Mod. Encycl. Card Games* 289 Despite its simplicity, red dog can build up to high stakes.

4. A manœuvre in American football, in which an opponent rushes the player who is passing the ball. Also as *v. trans.*, to rush (a player) in this way.

1959 *Washington Post* 17 Nov. C1/3 A variety of defenses which stress red-dogging the passer. **1959** *Time* 30 Nov. 56/2 Huff is at his rugged best when he knifes through the line and 'red-dogs' a quarterback as he fades to pass. The crash of Huff's tackle can stir the Giant bench to bellowing glee. **1966** ROTE & WINTER *Lang. Pro Football* iii. 132 *Red dog*,..surprise defensive maneuver where one or more linebackers..charge across line of scrimmage after ball carrier.

reddy, *a.* Add: **b.** (*b*) *reddy-brown* (further examples), *mauve.*

1946 G. MILLAR *Horned Pigeon* i. 1 A bedside light shone into her reddy-brown curls. **1968** D. IRELAND *Chantic Bird* i. 5 Ma's photos..were in a flat, wooden box, covered with flowered paper. Reddy brown. **1970** A. DRAPER *Swansong for Rare Bird* vi. 45 My best shirt was reddy mauve. **1977** 'M. UNDERWOOD' *Murder with Malice* ii. 24 The reddy-brown stain on the mushroom-pink carpet showed where her head had lain.

reddy, var. READY *sb.* 1 in Dict. and Suppl.

1962 R. COOK *Crust on its Uppers* i. 24 Not enough reddy in it in my case. *Ibid.* iii. 39 'Loot!'..'In reddy?' *Ibid.* viii. 65 Reddies which should be sailing into her African kick.

rede, *sb.*[1] Add: **5.** Comb. *rede-craft* (see quot.).

1880 W. BARNES (*title*) An outline of rede-craft (logic) with English wording.

redeal, *v.* [RE- 5 a.] To deal again. Also as *sb.*, a fresh deal.

1935 *Sun* (Baltimore) 11 Jan. 1/2 The New Deal is to be 'redealt'. **1959** T. REESE *Bridge Player's Dict.* 182 If the pack is deficient in any respect there must always be a redeal. **1964** *Official Encycl. Bridge* 287/2 When there is a redeal, the current deal is canceled; the same dealer deals again, unless he was dealing out of turn. *Ibid.* 450/1 Hands are never redealt at duplicate except in special cases.

red-eared: see also *RED *a.* 14 a, 14 b.

redeemed, *ppl. a.* Add: **b.** Of land: reclaimed. *rare.*

1838 H. COLMAN *1st Rep. Agric. Mass.* (Mass. Agric. Survey) 37 From one acre of redeemed meadow 4½ tons of English Hay were weighed and sold in 1836–7.

redefe·ction. [RE- 5 a + DEFECTION.] Return to a country from which one has previously defected. Hence (as a back-formation) **redefe·ct** *v. intr.*; **redefe·ctor.**

1957 *Britannica Bk. of Year* 814/1 *Redefection, n*, the returning of exiles to their native country. **1959** *Washington Post* 7 Apr. A 16/2 Many months before the Hungarian Revolution, the Communist propaganda mills began an elaborate campaign to encourage the 'redefection' of homesick or otherwise dissatisfied or disillusioned refugees from satellite countries. *Ibid.*, The destiny that awaited these 'redefectors' was of course easily predictable. **1963** *Punch* 13 Feb. 249/3 Defected Western scientist who wishes to redefect. **1963** *Daily Progress* (Charlottesville, Va.) 7 Aug. 36/2 West German social workers concede the justice of complaints by many of the re-defectors that they are treated as 'outcasts' in West Germany. **1974** 'J. Le Carré' *Tinker, Tailor* xxi. 179 What's Tarr supposed to be doing now: redefecting to us?

redefine, *v.* (Further examples.)
1946 *Nature* 14 Dec. 885/1 Since inequality in the number of filaments in *Spirographis* was the only positive character distinguishing it from *Sabella*, that distinction is no longer valid, and both should be united under *Sabella*, as re-defined. **1951** R. Firth *Elem. Social Organiz.* v. 163 Let us..re-define the notion of primitive. **1964** *Ann. Reg. 1963* 231 A Trades Union Council re-defined the duties of unions on 3 July. **1979** *Listener* 16 Aug. 212/3 The many attempts ..to get round the decline of religion and worship by re-defining them in various Pickwickian senses.

redefinition. Add: (Further examples.) Hence **redefini·tional** *a.*
1944 J. S. Huxley *On Living in Revolution* 13 A re-definition of the status of colonies. **1949** *Mind* LVIII. 146 It will be convenient to call a statement in which a word is used in a high or in a low sense a *redefinitional statement*. **1956** *Nature* 25 Feb. 370/2 Many, and perhaps all, scientific advances involve the re-definition of terms. **1970** S. L. Barraclough in I. L. Horowitz *Masses in Lat. Amer.* iv. 125 Another effect of changing technology is to force a redefinition of the traditional relations between peasants and management. **1977** *New Society* 5 May 225/1 There is a very close concern with the meanings of words and their definition or re-definition.

redemption. Add: **8. redemption yield,** the yield of a stock calculated as a percentage of the redemption price and allowing for any capital gain or loss which that price represents relative to the current price.
1948 G. Crowther *Outl. Money* (ed. 2) ii. 74 If the price of this bond in the market is 101, that means that for every £101 invested now, the purchaser will get £6 in interest, but he will also lose £1 in capital value—that is to say, the 'redemption yield' is 2½ per cent per annum. **1972** *Daily Tel.* 2 Dec. 24 The redemption yield is defined as that rate of interest at which the present price is made to equal the present discounted value of the future stream of interest payments plus the present discounted value of the eventual capital repayment. The rate of interest used for the purpose of discounting these future interest and capital values is the redemption yield rate of interest itself. **1973** *Ibid.* 7 Mar. 21 At the issue price of £99½ the 1980 stock will give a running yield of 9·05 p.c. and a gross redemption yield of 9·10 p.c. to 1980.

redemptionless, *a.* (Earlier example.)
1846 J. Brown *Let.* 12 Aug. (1912) 93 By the bye, is not he a redemptionless devil that Sir Robert?

redemptivism (rĭde·mptiviz'm). *rare.* [f. Redemptive *a.* + -ism.] The desire to redeem. So **rede·mptivist** *a.*
1924 C. Mackenzie *Heavenly Ladder* xxiii. 289 You are obsessed by redemptivist phantoms... I perceive you the victim of an absurd idea that you have to save other people. Even your own God Jesus Christ made no attempt to do that. *Ibid.* 290 You misunderstand what you call my redemptivism... I regard myself as an automatic purveyor of Almighty God's bounteous Grace by administrating His Sacraments.

redemptor. Add: **3.** = Trinitarian *sb.* 1.
1880 Mrs. Oliphant *Cervantes* ii. 25 The friar, Jorge Olivar, one of the Brothers of Mercy, and official Redemptor for the province of Aragon.

redemptorial (rĭdĕmptō·riăl), *a. rare.* [f. as Redemptory *a.* + -al.] = Redemptory *a.*
1900 R. W. Barbour *Thoughts* 6 He pleads His own crucified person. His very redemptorial existence is His plea.

Redemptorist. 1. (Earlier and later examples.)
1835 J. B. Robertson in *Schlegel's Philos. Hist.* I. p. xlii, In conjunction with..some of the Redemptorists—a most able, amiable, and exemplary body of ecclesiastics at Vienna—he established in 1820, a religious and political journal. **1840** J. R. Hope-Scott *Diary* in R. Ornsby *Mem. J. R. Hope-Scott* (1884) I. xii. 227 Viewed as instruments of the Church, he thinks that most of the orders are now of little use. Those of the Jesuits and Redemptorists, with one or two more of the same kind as the latter, he conceives to be the only effectual orders. **1915** *Encycl. Relig. & Ethics* VIII. 68/1 The Redemptorists have remained sturdily faithful to their primary work of giving missions and retreats. **1975** *Church Times* 27 June 14/5 It [*sc.* the Roman clerical collar] is still worn by Redemptorists, Passionists and Oratorians.

Redemptoristine. Add: (Further examples.) Also *attrib.* or as *adj.*
1886 T. Livius tr. *Saintrain's Our Lady of Perpetual Succour* (ed. 3) I. xxiv. 211 In the public chapel attached to the convent of the Redemptoristine Nuns, St. Alphonsus, Dublin, the Holy Picture has a beautiful shrine. **1931** *Tablet* 8 Aug. 183/2 The Redemptoristine nuns from Clapham went into their new home at Chudleigh in 1925. *Ibid.*, The Redemptoristines are established also in a number of convents in Canada, Italy, Austria, France, Belgium, Spain, Holland and Brazil. **1969** *Observer* (Colour Suppl.) 13 Apr. 54/1 *Redemptoristines.* Founded by St Alphonsus Liguori at Amalfi, Italy, in 1731.

redemptress (rĭde·mptrĕs). [After Redemptor.] A female redeemer; = Redemptrice.
1865 [see Restoress].

redeploy·, *v.* [Re- 5 a.] **a.** *intr.* To carry out redeployment; to change employment to increase overall efficiency. **b.** *trans.* To move (troops, labour, materials, etc.) from one area of activity to another.
1945 *Sunday Times* 27 May 7 Re-deploying to crush Japan. **1945** *Sat. Rev. Lit.* (U.S.) 16 June 12/1 Others stated that the plan to redeploy troops from Europe was a great mistake. **1948** *Picture Post* 3 Apr. 11/2 Labour forces had to be redeployed. **1949** *Manch. Guardian Weekly* 28 Apr. 3/3 A very extensive proportion of this industry could be redeployed within six months. **1958** *Times Lit. Suppl.* 22 Aug. 473/2 Organized labour cannot be induced to redeploy over the day-shift, thus releasing labour for a second day (and sometimes a third night) shift. **1966** *Hansard Commons* 20 June 628 Action is needed equally to deal with the problem of internal demand, public and private, and to redeploy resources, both manpower and capacity, according to national priorities, and check inflation. **1970** *New Society* 5 Mar. 389/1 The unification of hitherto separate services.. should make it easier to recruit and redeploy social service staff. **1971** *Brit. Jrnl. Industrial Relations* July 160 Some believed that there was a vast pool of under-used labour and that a short sharp burst of deflation would force companies to release surplus manpower which could then be redeployed into the essential export industries. **1980** *Times* 29 Feb. 19 Hawker's philosophy since aerospace nationalization has been to redeploy its resources into the electrical and mechanical engineering business it knows well.

Hence **redeploy·able** *a.*, available for redeployment, able to be redeployed.
1946 I. Shaw in *New Yorker* 2 Feb. 24/2 'I'm redeployable,' Olson sang.

redeploy·ment. [Re- 5 a.] Movement or reallocation (of troops, labour, resources, etc.); reorganization for greater efficiency; transfer to alternative employment.
1945 *Time* 12 Feb. 17/2 The new blueprint for U.S. redeployment calls for an army of 6,500,000 men to defeat Japan. **1945** *Newsweek* 28 May 28/3 The redeployment of three and four star generals from the European theater. **1949** *Manch. Guardian Weekly* 28 Apr. 3/3 Only by redeployment of labour can higher wages, greater productivity, and lower costs be achieved. **1955** *Times* 7 July 13/1 The growth of deposits had been checked (partly, as with Martins, by the redeployment of funds by large customers). **1959** *Economist* 3 July 42/1 Redeployment of liquid resources in this way, incidentally, can also keep directors and managers in the powerful style to which they are accustomed. **1966** *Daily Tel.* 2 Nov. 1/2 Temporary bridging finance for house purchase also has a special importance at a time when the redeployment of labour needs to be encouraged. **1970** *New Scientist* 24 Sept. 613/2 If they all have similar reserves of manpower, there should soon be no shortage for the Soviet Union's developing economy. The question may then be one of retraining and redeployment. **1974** *Financial Times* 20 Mar. 18/8 If they cancel the entire venture now, some 21,000 workers on the programme in Britain and a similar number in France will face either redundancy or redeployment.

redeposit, *v.* Add: (Further examples.) Also *absol.* Hence **redepo·sited** *ppl. a.*, **redepo·siting** *vbl. sb.*
1905 *Westm. Gaz.* 8 Feb. 9/3 The Bill which the Board proposes to redeposit in Parliament. *Ibid.*, The Board had decided to take an early opportunity of redepositing their bill. **1946** F. E. Zeuner *Dating Past* vi. 169 Re-deposited Younger Loess (probably result of ploughing), with Neolithic. **1963** A. J. Hall *Textile Sci.* vi. 282 At the same time that soil is passing out of the fabric into the main bulk of detergent liquor some of this soil is passing from this liquor into the fabric and there being re-deposited on the fibres. **1965** G. V. Williams *Econ. Geol. N.Z.* xix. 334/2 These rocks consist of conglomerates, black shales, re-deposited sandstones, mudstones and pseudo-tillites. **1975** *New Yorker* 17 Nov. 37/2 'I never heard of a bank saying "Do not redeposit",' she said. **1977** *Antiquaries Jrnl.* LVII. 235 There are tips of redeposited sands and loams..associated with features in the timber building sequence.

rederi·ve, *v.* [Re- 5 a.] To derive again.
1968 P. A. P. Moran *Introd. Probability Theory* vii. 293 It has probably been independently rederived by more writers than almost any other result. **1968** C. G. Kuper *Introd. Theory Superconductivity* xiv. 237 Thus all the results of Chapter 12 may be rederived.

redesign, *v.* Add: (Further examples.) Hence **redesi·gned** *ppl. a.*, **redesi·gning** *vbl. sb.*
1914 *Jrnl. Inst. Electr. Engineers* LIII. 94/2 It would be safe to re-design on a scientific basis all the cables mentioned in the British Standard Specification. **1930** G. B. Shaw *Apple Cart* p. xxix, Wren was not content to re-design and rebuild St Paul's: he wanted to redesign London as well. **1943** *Mind* LII. 63 Though minor improvements and modifications of traditional language and its categories are permissible, any radical 'redesigning' of them must necessarily distort reality and be ultimately unintelligible. **1946** *Nature* 21 Dec. 897/2 Many of the re-designed features were not amenable to accepted strength computation methods. **1969** *Jane's Freight Containers 1968–69* 185/1 This berth was re-designed and re-constructed to handle the London-Gothenburg passenger, car and cargo service of the England Sweden Line. **1973** *Sci. Amer.* Apr. 17/1 A further need is to redesign medical education so that physicians and other health personnel are trained and challenged to provide primary care and to deal with the chronic diseases. **1978** *Dumfries Courier* 20 Oct. 10/3 (*caption*) The 900 series has a 5 cm. longer wheelbase and a completely redesigned chassis.

redesi·gn, *sb.* [f. the vb.] A fresh design; designing again.
1930 *Daily Express* 6 Oct. 1/4 The re-design of the airship's hull. **1946** *Nature* 28 Sept. 439/1 Redesign of existing roads and the planning of new roads must serve two purposes, circulation and safety. **1963** *Guardian* 15 May 6/8 This is a redesign..of the regular Tuscan pattern. **1973** *Sci. Amer.* Sept. 69/1 Most of the work being done on the problem of air pollution resulting from the internal-combustion engine is focused on redesign of the engine or on adding emission-control devices to it. **1977** *Time* 15 Aug. 5/2 Our last redesign came in 1971.

redevelop, *v.* Add: **a.** (*intr.* examples.)
1967 *Oceanogr. & Marine Biol.* xiv. 363 After a short time polarity in growth redevelops. **1978** *SLR Camera* Nov. 9/2 The image will then re-develop to a warm brown tone.
b. *spec.* in *Town Planning.*
1936 E. E. Finch & C. G. Eve *Rep. Town Planning Scheme* (Corporation of London Publ. Health Dept.) 3 It therefore appears that nearly a quarter of the building site area has been redeveloped in the last 30 years. **1941** H. J. Manzoni in F. E. Towndrow *Replanning Britain* iv. 99 (*heading*) Relating the redeveloped units. **1947** *Act* 10 & 11 *Geo. VI.* c. 51 § 5(3) For the purposes of this section, a development plan may define as an area of comprehensive development any area which in the opinion of the local planning authority should be developed or re-developed as a whole. **1956** N. Lichfield *Econ. Planned Devel.* x. 129 Where an area is to be re-developed, demolition and clearance may be required. **1971** P. Gresswell *Environment* 91 *Comprehensive* development covers a large area, usually in towns—perhaps including a number of streets which are to be redeveloped to one comprehensive plan. **1976** *Star* (Sheffield) 29 Oct. 10/2 Our re-developed city has been advertised as a tourist and conference centre,..and yet the horrible menace of litter continues.

redevelopment. Add: *spec.* in *Town Planning.* Also *attrib.*
1935 *Act* 25 & 26 *Geo. V* c. 40 §13 It shall be the duty of the local authority to cause the area to be defined on a map, and to pass a resolution declaring the area so defined to be a proposed re-development area. **1938** *New Statesman* 25 June 1060/1 As to the great city itself, no satisfactory redevelopment of it is possible so long as population and business pour into it and its overall density is increasing. **1940** *Economist* 28 Dec. 794/2 The committee recommends that in cases where private ownership presents an obstacle to planned development, redevelopment or conservation on an economical basis, the areas should be bought outright by planning authorities. **1944** in D. Tyerman *Ways & Means of Rebuilding* iii. 59 Mr Cadbury had been considering plans of redevelopment schemes at thirty to the acre. **1952** L. Keeble *Princ. & Pract. Town & Country Planning* xvi. 345 In towns where a great deal of redevelopment overspill will have to be accommodated..it will often be possible to plan some completely new neighbourhoods for development at later stages. **1964** J. B. Cullingworth *Town & Country Planning* xii. 241 Housing, comprehensive redevelopment and traffic. **1966** N. Lichfield *Cost Benefit Anal. Town Planning Cambridge* iv. 26 The projects comprise a group of interrelated redevelopment areas, roads and car parks. **1972** R. Quilty *Tenth Session* 136, 61 Sainsbury Road is bang in the middle of a redevelopment area. One of those decaying streets back of Kentish Town. **1977** *Grimsby Even. Tel.* 13 May 1/3 The 'shocking conditions' they have to live in while their area goes through a redevelopment phase.

red-eye. Add: **3.** (Examples.)
1857 Thoreau *Maine Woods* (1864) 172 The birds sang quite as in our woods,—the red-eye, red-start, veery, wood-pewee, etc. **1917** T. G. Pearson *Birds Amer.* III. 103/2 Mr. Job..photographed several times a female Red-eye solicitously feeding two voracious young Cowbirds. **1953** D. A. Bannerman *Birds Brit. Isles* II. 252 The red-eye has been called 'preacher-bird' because of its unceasing vocal efforts.
4. (Earlier and later examples.)
1819 J. A. Quitman *Diary* in J. F. H. Claiborne *Life & Corr. J. A. Quitman* (1860) I. 42 Whiting and I had to treat to 'red-eye' or 'rot-gut', as whiskey is here called. **1838** *Yale Lit. Mag.* III. 12 An Indian tribe that..seldom ever passed the prairie except to sell their skins, and purchase 'red-eye'. **1903** *Sun* (N.Y.) 15 Nov., Ben made for the nearest red-eye plant, and inside an hour he was riotous and shooting up the town. **1910** in J. Lomax *Cowboy Songs* 305 Drink that rot gut, drink that rot gut, Drink that red eye, boys. **1911** C. E. Mulford *Bar-20 Days* viii. 95 Any-body'd think you was full of red-eye, th'way you act. **1949** A. Hynd *We are Public Enemies* ii. 44 Barrow put down a slug of red eye and walked up to her. **1957** J. Steinbeck *Short Reign of Pippin IV* 69 Serving red-eye in shot-glasses. **1976** *Observer* 5 Dec. (Colour Suppl.) 18 (Advt.), Most of the liquor to be had [in New Orleans] at that time [*sc.* 1865] was known as 'redeye'. Because that's what it did.
5. *U.S. slang.* Tomato ketchup.
1923 G. H. McKnight *Eng. Words* 56 *Red eye* for 'catsup'. **1947** *Sun* (Baltimore) 7 Aug. 10/3 Red-Eye..that great disguise, ketchup. **1960** Wentworth & Flexner *Dict. Amer. Slang* 423/2 *Redeye*.., ketchup. *W.W.I and W.W.II Armed Forces use.*
6. *Austral.* A cicada, *Psaltoda mœrens.* Also *attrib.*
1925 [see *floury *a.* d]. **1945** Baker *Austral. Lang.* xii. 214 Most noted among our appellations for cicadas are: baker, floury baker,..red eye and double drummer. **1965** *Austral. Encycl.* II. 379/2 (*caption*) Red-eye cicadas. *Ibid.* 380/1 Other well-known cicadas are the red-eye..and the aptly named cherry-nose.
7. *red-eye gravy*: gravy made by adding liquid to the grease from cooked ham or other lean meat. *U.S.*

1947 *Reader's Digest* Apr. 130/1 Pinky brown slices of cured ham that almost floated in red-eye gravy. **1949** *Newsweek* 11 July 6/2 Truman had..'good Missouri hams, red-eye gravy, and hominy grits'. **1959** *Washington Post* 29 Oct. D5/1 To the folks in the hominy grits and red-eye gravy belt there is only one game this week—Louisiana State vs. Mississippi. **1977** *Time* 24 Oct. 27/2 Dennis serves up his baked ham and red-eye gravy, grits, green beans, carrots, buttermilk biscuits and coffee.

8. *U.S. colloq.* Used *attrib.* to designate an aeroplane flight on which the traveller is unable to get adequate sleep because of the hour of arrival or because of differences in time zones.

1968 Mrs. L. B. Johnson *White House Diary* 31 Mar. (1970) 642 Lynda was coming in on 'the red-eye special' from California, about 7 A.M., having kissed Chuck good-by at Camp Pendleton last night as he departed for Vietnam. **1972** 'J. Lange' *Binary* 19 They all looked tired... Phelps had brought them out to California on a red-eye flight, let them sleep a few hours, then dragged them up for a meeting. **1973** *Time* 25 June 8/3 He took two 'red-eye' flights from Seattle to the capital. **1976** *National Observer* (U.S.) 4 Sept. 5/1 Schweiker..and Newhall took the red-eye special back to Washington that same night. Newhall just wanted to sleep, but Schweiker was, in Newhall's words, 'euphoric'.

9. *Canada.* A drink made from beer and tomato juice.

1973 *Daily Colonist* (Victoria, B.C.) 29 Aug. 2/2, I did manage to acquire a fair liking for 'red eye'..a mixture of beer and tomato juice. **1975** 'S. Marlowe' *Cawthorn Jrnls.* (1976) xiii. 107 'I'll have a redeye,' Lester told the barman, who mixed tomato juice and beer for him, half and half. **1976** *Maclean's Mag.* 22 Mar. 51/2 The red-eye, a murky combination of beer and tomato juice.

red-eyed, *a.* Add: **1.** (Later examples.)

1911 J. Masefield *Everlasting Mercy* 47 Old parson, red-eyed as a ferret. **1934** C. Carmer in B. A. Botkin *Treas. S. Folklore* (1949) III. ii. 490 Two-Toe is a red-eyed 'gator and about fourteen feet long.

2. b. In the names of certain insects.

1934 *Nat. Geogr. Mag.* May 612/2 Spiders and red-eyed flies are numerous. **1937** C. Longfield *Dragonflies Brit. Isles* 170 The Red-eyed Damsel-fly should be easy enough to tell by its eyes alone.

Red Fed (re·d fed). *N.Z. colloq.* Also **redfed.** [f. Red *a.* 9 b (in Dict. and Suppl.) + Fed-(eration.] A member of the Federation of Labour (founded 1909); now *gen.*, one who rebels against the established order, a left-winger. Hence **Re·d-Fed-ism.**

1914 *Evening Post* (Wellington, N.Z.) 14 Jan. 10/5 The charge you prefer against the 'Red Feds'. **1916** *Chrons. N.Z. Expeditionary Force* 15 Nov. 134/1 I'll poke the fellow in the jaw that calls me a 'Red Fed'. **1931** N. E. Coad *Such is Life* 24 They are on the look-out for Bolshevists, Red-Feds and I.W.W.s. **1948** D. W. Ballantyne *Cunninghams* I. xxxi. 152 That crazy young redfed..who landed himself in trouble over at the works with his gabbing. **1959** K. Sinclair *Hist. N.Z.* iii. 199 In contrast to the United Labour Party, the 'Red Feds' eschewed political action. *Ibid.*, The 'Red Fed's' rejection of the principle of industrial arbitration. **1959** *N.Z. Listener* 26 June 4/1 Those dark days when many a university lecturer and many a student were being hauled across the coals for radicalism, Communism, red-Fed-ism, and all sorts of other nonsense. **1969** F. Sargeson *Joy of Worm* iv. 134 And when besides he's Red Fed, Maoriland worker, not to mention *Das Kapital* all rolled into one—well, it's a toss-up whether he can continue to survive. **1970** D. M. Davin *Not Here, not Now* vi. i. 280 He sounded a bit of a red-fed, though. No time for Baldwin or any of that lot over in England.

Redfern (re·dfɜːn). [f. the name *Redfern*, Maddox.] (See quot. 1909.) Also *attrib.*

1909 J. R. Ware *Passing Eng.* 207/2 *Redfern* (*Soc.*, 1879), perfectly-fitting lady's coat or jacket. From the vogue obtained, 1879 on, by Redfern, Maddox, W. Regent Street, whose lady's tailoring became celebrated over the whole world. **1932** N. Coward *Cavalcade* I. iii. 24, I am now going home to have a bath and put on my new Redfern model.

Red Fife (red fəif). Also **Red Fyfe.** [f. Red *a.* + the name of David *Fife* (1804?–77), Canadian botanist.] A rust-resistant variety of spring wheat, developed in Canada during the 1870s by David Fife.

[**1851** *Watchman* (St. Thomas, Ontario) 1 Feb. 2/4 In another column will be found an article on the 'Fife Wheat' which is held in such high estimation..by all who have tried it.] **1883** *Prince Albert* (Saskatchewan) *Times* 3 Oct. 6/2 Try it and be convinced, and by all means give the 'red fyfe' the preference. **1889** *Experimental Farms: Rep. 1888* (Canada Dept. Agric.) 29 One sample of the Red Fyfe was grown in Ontario. **1900** *Westm. Gaz.* 28 Dec. 2/1 The quantity and quality of Red Fife..is as fine as ever. **1932** *Discovery* Mar. 73/2 The suitable wheat [for prairie farming], Red Fife, was discovered by accident. **1936, 1965** [see *Marquis 5]. **1973** H. Robertson *Grass Roots* iii. 56 Homesteaders were able to purchase high-quality Red Fife wheat.

red-fish. Add: **2. b.** After 'American' insert 'or North Atlantic'. (Earlier and later examples.)

1763 tr. *Le Page du Pratz's Hist. Louisiana* II. 26 This Gulf abounds with delicious fish; as..red fish, cod, sturgeon, ..and many other sorts. **1843** *Southern Lit. Messenger* I. 121/2 The waters too, furnished their finny..treasures,—the red fish, buffalo [etc.]. **1897** [see **channel bass*]. **1955** S. A. Grau *Black Prince* 190 He had not lifted his head from the redfish he was cleaning. **1962** K. F. Lagler et al. *Ichthyol.* viii. 247 The giant redfish (*Arapaima gigas*) of the Amazon is one of the largest freshwater bony fishes. **1969** A. Wheeler *Fishes Brit. Isles & N.-W. Europe* 480/1 The redfish is widely distributed in the North Atlantic.

4. *Austral.* = *nannygai.

1951 T. C. Roughley *Fish & Fisheries Austral.* 26 The nannygai, or redfish..occurs round the southern half of Australia. **1966** [see *nannygai]. **1979** *Verbatim* Summer 7/2 Australian fishermen found that redfish sold better than nannygai though the difference is entirely linguistic.

red flag. 1. (See Red *a.* 4 b.)

2. As a sign of danger, a warning, or a signal to stop. Also *attrib.* and *fig.*

1777 P. Thicknesse *Year's Journey* I. iii. 23 There is a red flag hoisted gradually higher and higher, as the water flows into the harbour [at Calais]. **1856** *N.Y. Herald* 12 Jan. 1/4 James Flood is road master of his section; any obstruction being on the track it is the duty of the flagman to exhibit his red flag. **1885** C. M. Yonge *Nuttie's Father* I. xiii. 153 They went into a hole and stuck fast, while the red-flag traction engineman prodded her with an umbrella. **1908** Kipling in *Flag* (Union Jack Club) 8 Thou didst flee up Cheepe, calling..for a red flag. **1968** J. Updike *Couples* ii. 146 You're sore as hell about some silly thing, maybe Harold's snubbing you, maybe you have the red flag out, but you're right there. **1973** 'C. Aird' *His Burial Too* iii. 32 The roadmen went and got into a muddle with their flags... One of them..apparently gets a power complex every time anyone puts a red flag into his hand. **1976** *Billings* (Montana) *Gaz.* 17 June 2-A/4 Time and time again, Eizenstat addressed the members and urged them to avoid 'red flag' words or issues—such as homosexual rights, amnesty, opposition to capital punishment, full federalization of welfare costs. **1977** *Time* 17 Oct. 39/3 He..warned present and future White House aides to be on the alert for 'red flags' of moral dilemmas that may arise while serving a President.

3. a. As a symbol of revolution, socialism, or communism, freq. *spec.* of Soviet Russian communism. Also *attrib.* and *fig.*

1848 A. H. Clough *Let.* 26 Feb. in T. Arnold *N.Z. Lett.* (1966) 78 The Red Flag flying at Paris. **1857** C. M. Yonge *Dynevor Terrace* I. xx. 322 Muskets and pikes were here and there seen, and once he recognized the sinister red flag. **1878** *Indianapolis Sentinel* 23 May 4/6 We denounce the red flag communism imported from Europe. **1888** E. Bellamy *Looking Backward* xxiv. 353 They were paid by the great monopolies to wave the red flag and talk about..blowing people up. **1889** J. Connell in *Justice* 21 Dec. 3/2 Then raise the scarlet standard high! Within its shade we'll live and die! Though cowards flinch, and traitors jeer, We'll keep the Red Flag flying here! **1891** [see Red *a.* 4 b]. **1909** *Westm. Gaz.* 19 Oct. 2/1 The Socialists who in such circumstances would be returned in many constituencies..would be the real thing, of the red-flag order. **1914** Chesterton *Flying Inn* xxiii. 274 A very coarse strip of red rag..had been tied round the wooden sign-post by way of a red flag of revolution. **1922** W. J. Locke *Tale of Triona* xvii. 199 The only positive ideal in England at the present moment is Bolshevism. The only flag waved..is the red flag. **1957** *Encycl. Brit.* XIX. 711/1 In the urban centres the victory was won under the red flag of class warfare. **1967** *Guardian* 4 Dec. 1/4 The purpose of the visit is political—to show the Red Flag over Cairo. **1973** *Times* 21 Nov. 6/8 Red flag on Cunarder. The former Cunard liner Franconia..left Southampton yesterday flying the hammer and sickle. She was bought..by..the Far Eastern Steamship Company, of Vladivostock. **1974** P. Gore-Booth *With Great Truth & Respect* 210 The country was infested with various hostiles, Red Flag Communists, White Flag Communists, Karens or simply dacoits. **1977** *Time* 4 Apr. 24/3 There was little of the tedious Red-flag waving 'revolutionary culture' with which visitors to Peking are entertained.

b. *the Red Flag*: a socialist song by James Connell (see quot. 1889 above).

1909 R. Brooke *Let.* 2 Jan. (1968) 154 Yes! yes! Herbert Samuel..is a Socialist... He used to sing *The Red Flag* after dinner every night instead of grace. **1935** H. Nicolson *Let.* 1 Nov. (1966) 222 He..left the hall while they sang the *Red Flag.* **1968** A. Diment *Bang Bang Birds* ix. 160 A covey of West German millionaires who were singing the Red Flag in a hypnotised dirge. *a* **1974** R. Crossman *Diaries* (1976) II. 507 As an outgoing member I went down to the last debate and took part in singing the 'Red Flag' and 'Auld Lang Syne'. **1976** *Whitaker's Almanack 1977* 361/1 Labour M.P.s in their jubilation sang 'The Red Flag', shouted, and waved order papers in the air.

4. = *red ensign* s.v. Red *a.* 19 a. See Ensign 5.

1901 W. C. Russell *Ship's Adventure* v. 78 He..had begun the sea life in the Royal Navy as midshipman, but..had quitted the white for the red flag.

Hence **red fla·gger,** one who carries a red flag, a communist; **red fla·ggery,** communist doctrines.

1920 R. Macaulay *Potterism* II. i. 54, I hate red-flaggery, and all other flaggery. **1921** *Times* 4 Feb. 11/6 The common enemy..what Belfast of today calls the 'red-flaggers'. **1923** *Glasgow Herald* 23 June 8/3 That modest pattern which ..Mr. Kirkwood is finding it so difficult to assimilate with Red Flaggery. **1934** G. B. Shaw *On Rocks* II. 231 That's the way to dish these Labor chaps and Red flaggers.

red-flowered: see *red *a.* 14 a, Red *a.* 14 c.

Red Fyfe, var. *Red Fife.

Red Guard. [Red *a.* 9 b in Dict. and Suppl.] **1. a.** A member of an organized detachment of workers during the Russian Bolshevik revolution of 1917; also, such units collectively.

1917 *Times* 12 Nov. 8/5 In Moscow, the 'Red Guard' was defeated. *Ibid.* 13 Dec. 8/5 The fighting at Tamarovka seems to have been between detachments of shock battalions..and local troops, with sailors, 'Red Guards', infantry, and armoured cars. **1943** E. M. Almedingen *Frossia* x. 407 At the corner of Sredny a red guard picket awaited them. **1957** *Encycl. Brit.* XIX. 710/2 Definitely expecting a crushing defeat of Trotsky's Red guards, the committee of public defense gave orders to the cadets of the military schools to arrest the military revolutionary committee. **1961** *Everyman's Conc. Encycl. Russia* 388 Kerenskiy's Provisional Government..was overthrown..with the aid of the Red Guards. **1977** *N.Y. Rev. Bks.* 9 June 46/3 The role of the Petrograd Red Guard in the October seizure of power has been greatly exaggerated.

b. A member of a paramilitary group of Russian soldiers and Finnish communist sympathizers who seized power in Finland in 1918; the group itself.

1922 *Encycl. Brit.* XXXI. 74/1 Whole trainloads of revolutionary *soldateska* arrived from Petrograd... They entered the so-called Finnish 'Red Guards', and ransacked the country. The reactionaries..organized the 'White Guards'. **1956** A. G. Mazour *Finland between East & West* iii. 43 In this manner there came into being the so-called Red Guard.

2. A name given to (*a*) the armed units of village people in the Second Revolutionary Civil War in China, 1927–37, (*b*) a youth movement during the Cultural Revolution in the People's Republic of China, 1966–76; also, a member of one of these movements.

1966 *Guardian* 24 Aug. 9/7 The teenage demonstrators, who are known as the 'Red Guard'..appeared to have taken over permanently the churches serving Peking's Christians. **1966** *Economist* 27 Aug. 813/1 The rioters were clearly identified as a new youth group of secondary school and university student activists called the Red Guard. The Red Guard made its first appearance at the monster rally on August 18th, when the students were publicly congratulated for their revolutionary zeal by Mao Tse-tung. **1967** *Listener* 19 Jan. 80 The Red Guards damaged a number of temples and old buildings, destroyed old books. **1971** T. W. Robinson *Cultural Revolution in China* p. vii, The Red Guard phase of the Great Proletarian Cultural Revolution began in the late summer of 1966. **1973** M. Lindsay in Yuan-li Wu *China* vi. 142 Mao insisted that the Red Guards (local village militia) had an important function in harassing small enemy forces and assisting the Red Army. **1977** *N.Y. Rev. Bks.* 12 May 22/3 To purge the party bureaucrats Mao mobilized these adolescents as Red Guards, but millions of them later had to be dispersed to the countryside. **1978** *China Now* July/Aug. 25/1 During the Cultural Revolution in the late 1960's, the influx of Red Guards from all over the country swelled the numbers to nine million.

3. *transf.* Applied to various other radical groups and their members.

1966 *Observer* 25 Sept. 1 In his winding-up speech to the Liberal Assembly..Mr Grimond yesterday hit back at the party's youthful 'Red Guard'. **1966** *Time* 4 Nov. 35 Japan's Red Guards are members of the Socialist opposition—aided by Communists and the *Komeito* (Clean Government Party). **1967** *Guardian* 17 July 14/3 The growing anger of the Liberal Party's leadership at the outspoken criticism by the party's young 'Red Guards'. **1968** *N.Y. Times* 10 Feb. 2 As in all such movements there is an extremist group, called 'Red Guards' in Turin, that seeks to eliminate virtually all traditional authority, to elect professors and to confer marks based on the findings of student committees. **1968** *Listener* 10 Oct. 482/2 A young Red Guard of British music recently expressed to me his concern about form in pop music. **1969** *Guardian* 20 Nov. 3/5 West Bengal's Red Guards, as the Marxist volunteers have been nicknamed. **1970** *Ibid.* 8 Apr. 12/3 India's most turbulent politician, Jyoti Basu, was addressing maybe 100,000 Marxists on the Maidan in Calcutta. He was surrounded by his own Red Guards; tough, supple, and enormously well-disciplined young men.

Hence **Red Guardism,** the Chinese Red Guard movement.

1967 *N.Y. Times* 5 Mar. 2 By November last year Red Guardism was in full cry, and zealous youths were swarming across China..holding aloft little red books containing quotations from Mr. Mao.

red gum[2]. Add: **2.** esp. *E. camaldulensis* or one of a group of closely related species. (Later examples.)

1911 E. M. Clowes *On Wallaby* ix. 249 Farther eastward iron bark and stringy bark prevail, and red gum follows the course of the Murray and its tributaries. **1920,** etc. [see *marri]. **1955** M. R. Jacobs *Growth Habits of Eucalypts* vi. 219 The red gums form one of the most widespread and stable groups of the eucalypts.

2*. *U.S.* The sweet gum, *Liquidambar styraciflua*, an important timber tree.

1839 *Southern Lit. Messenger* V. 113/2 Dislodge the rackoon from its lofty hole in the red-gum tree. **1916** E. T. Seton *Woodcraft Man.* 288 Sweet Gum, Star-Leaved, or Red Gum, Bilsted, Alligator Tree, or Liquidambar. **1942** W. M. Harlow *Trees Eastern U.S.* 193 Now that veneered furniture has so largely replaced solid pieces, redgum wood has come into prominence.

red-headed, *a.* **2. b.** (Earlier and later examples.)

1744 W. Ellis *Let.* 11 Aug. in *Mod. Husbandman* (1750) VI. xxi. 161 The red-headed Thistle is growing on the Hills. **1901** E. Mounts *Islands in Ocean of Memory* 58 You may throw the bait out within three feet of the boat and a red-headed hag or gony will make a dive at it. **1947** J. Stevenson-Hamilton *Wildlife S. Afr.* xxx. 249 The red-headed squirrel (*Paraxerus palliatus*), is distinguished by the rufous colour of the head and underparts.

re·d-heart. **1.** A cherry belonging to a variety bearing heart-shaped fruit with red flesh; also, the fruit of a tree of this kind. Also *attrib.*

[**1664** J. EVELYN *Kalendarium Hortense* 68 June.. Cherries,..Heart, Black, Red, White.] **1707** [see *black heart* s.v. *BLACK *a.* 19]. **1764** [see RED *a.* 12 b]. **1833** H. BARNARD *Let.* 25 May in *Maryland Hist. Mag.* (1918) XIII. 377 Here were..numerous trees of ripe cherries, black hearts and red hearts. **1887** *Harper's Mag.* Dec. 31/1 Under the largest of two red-heart cherry-trees sat a girl shelling pease. **1904** E. A. G. GLASGOW *Deliverance* 238, I used to cut round old Fletcher's pasture..to keep from passin' by his red-heart cherry-tree.

2. One of several trees with reddish bark or wood, esp. the western North American *Ceanothus spinosus*, an evergreen shrub or small tree belonging to the family Rhamnaceæ and bearing clusters of blue or white flowers.

1926 J. MASEFIELD *Odtaa* xiv. 231 He saw a footmark in some soft earth close to a red-heart. **1937** *Range Plant Handbk.* (Forest Service, U.S. Dept. Agric.) B39 The branches of a number of species [of *Ceanothus*], such as.. redheart, or spiny myrtle (*C. spinosus*), end in spines. **1951** W. L. JEPSON *Flowering Plants Calif.* 620 Red-heart. Straggling shrub 5 to 10 ft. high, or forming a small tree up to 24 ft. **1965** *Austral. Encycl.* V. 225/2 *Dissiliaria baloghioides* (hauer or redheart). **1973** G. M. CHIPPENDALE *Eucalypts W. Austral. Goldfields* 93/1 Redheart [sc. *Eucalyptus decipiens*] is a spreading, twisted, gnarled tree. **1973** *Stand. Encycl. S. Afr.* IX. 266/1 Red-heart..(*Acacia nilotica* = *A. benthami*) Thorn-tree with a spreading rounded canopy.

red herring. **2. b.** (Earlier and later examples.)

1884 *Liverpool Daily Post* 11 July 5/4 The talk of revolutionary dangers is a mere red-herring. **1928** *Manch. Guardian Weekly* 10 Aug. 105/1 Both the Opposition parties are trying to drag in the Protectionist red herring in the vain hope of causing dissension. **1956** [see *CHIVVY *v.*[1]]. **1967** G. F. FIENNES *I tried to run Railway* iv. 48 The Coroner's opinion that the detonators were 'something of a red herring'. **1975** M. RUSSELL *Murder by Mile* xi. 116 This could be a side-issue or red herring designed to..turn me from the genuine scent. **1976** *Southern Even. Echo* (Southampton) 13 Nov. 9/3 He accused Mr. Deacon of introducing a red herring into the issue.

red horse, red-horse. Add: **3.** *slang* (orig. *Mil.*). Corned beef.

1864 I. JACKSON *Let.* 28 June in *Some of Boys* (1960) 184 Supper..is coffee & Red Hoss. **1905** J. BOWE *With 13th Minnesota in Philippines* 24 Of bean-soup, hard-tack, and red horse..we have had our fill. **1920** W. B. ELLINGTON *Company 'A', 23rd Engineers* 27 We have red horse and rice pudding for dinner. **1941** J. SMILEY *Hash House Lingo* 46 *Red horse*, corned beef.

red-hot, *a.* (and *sb.*). Add: **2. a.** Also, outstanding, uninhibited, lively, sexy, passionate; esp. in phr. *red-hot momma*, (*a*) a woman who sings in a particular earthy style; (*b*) a girlfriend, lover. Also *transf.* in jazz; cf. *HOT *a.* 8 g.

1888 J. RUNCIMAN *Chequers* 116 You take the fellows in town that make their living after dark... There's some red-hot ones up—you know where—in Piccadilly. **1926** WHITEMAN & MCBRIDE *Jazz* viii. 169 A red hot mama song. **1934** S. R. NELSON *All about Jazz* ii. 58 Dorsey is a red-hot stylist and technician [on the saxophone]. **1934** C. LAMBERT *Music Ho!* III. 210 The negro associations of jazz, the weary traveller, the comforting old mammy, the red-hot baby, have become a formula of expression only, as empty and convenient as the harlequin and columbine of the nineteenth century. **1935** *Time* 21 Jan. 58 Sophie Tucker, famed as 'the last of the red hot mamas'. **1936** WODEHOUSE *Laughing Gas* ii. 24 The bride-to-be is probably some frightful red-hot mamma. **1940** O. NASH *Face is Familiar* 87 Affection..leads to breach of promise If you go round lavishing it on red-hot momise. **1942** Z. N. HURSTON in A. Dundes *Mother Wit* (1973) 223/2 A red hot pimp like you *say* you is, ain't got no business in the barrel. **1950** A. LOMAX *Mister Jelly Roll* 69 A red-hot bass player, seventy-nine years old, a proud Creole. **1957** R. HOGGART *Uses of Literacy* v. 132, I first heard 'Paper Doll' sung in the 'red-hot' fashion by an American star crooner. **1976** in D. Villiers *Next Year in Jerusalem* 204 (*caption*) 'The Last of the Red Hot Mommas', Sophie Tucker. **1977** J. WAINWRIGHT *Do Nothin'* xi. 183 It was jive and blues; either red-hot or smoochy.

b. Also, sensational, lively, exciting, intense. (Further examples.)

1887 *Lantern* 19 Feb. 6/1 A red-hot newsy journal. **1891** 'MARK TWAIN' in *Harper's Mag.* Dec. 97 Suddenly a red-hot new idea came whistling down into my camp. **1904** J. C. LINCOLN *Cap'n Eri* xi. 205 '"Fightin' Fred Starlight, the Boy Rover of the Pacific"', he read aloud. 'Humph! Is it good?' 'Bet your life! It's a red-hot story.' **1915** WODEHOUSE *Psmith Journalist* v. 33 My idea is that *Cosy Moments* should become red-hot stuff. I could wish its tone to be such that the public will wonder why we do not print it on asbestos. **1955** *Times* 16 May 3/3 Local propaganda on the virtues of nationalization has resembled rather the cooing of lethargic doves than the strident militancy of red hot Socialism. **1969** *John Edwards Mem. Foundation Q.* V. II. 60 An urban audience more accustomed to 'red hot' fox trots than to barn dances. **1977** *Belfast Tel.* 24 Jan. 18/6 The clinching of these red-hot finals must be hailed as another major breakthrough for the sport.

d. *Austral. slang.* Unfair, unreasonable.

1896 H. LAWSON *While Billy Boils* 281 When..she paused for breath, he drew a long one, gave a short whistle, and, said: 'Well, it's red-hot!' **1907** A. WRIGHT *Keane of Kalgoorlie* 107 'It's red 'ot,' put in Dave, 'th'way these 'ere owners makes er pore man give 'em a lump in th' sweep. **1941** BAKER *Dict. Austral. Slang* 59 A red hot price.

3. *red-hot poker*, substitute for def.: a tall perennial herb of the genus *Kniphofia* (formerly *Tritoma*), esp. *K. uvaria*, belonging to the family Liliaceæ, native to southern or tropical Africa, and bearing spikes of red, yellow, or white flowers. (Earlier and later examples.)

1887 'F. ANSTEY' *Talking Horse* (1892) 216 The dahlias and 'red-hot pokers' and gladioli..burnt with a sinister glow. **1916** M. HAMPDEN *Flower Culture* xvii. 206 Red-hot pokers are not over [in November]. **1934** G. A. R. PHILLIPS *Aristocrats of Flower Border* xiii. 191 Far more descriptive of its vivid beauty are the common names of torch lily and red hot poker. **1971** H. EVANS *How to cheat at Gardening* xi. 168 The Red Hot Poker..looks marvellous mixed with Sea Holly.

4. as *sb.* A frankfurter; a hot dog. *U.S. slang.*

1892 *Chicago Figaro* VI.157/2 The appetizing savors of 'red hots'. **1934** J. T. FARRELL *Calico Shoes* 46 Don leaned against the thrown-together red hot stand, munching at a hot-dog sandwich. **1971** B. MALAMUD *Tenants* 143, I got this redhot with mustard on it I'm gonna eat my meat.

redi·al, *v.* [f. RE- 5 a + *DIAL *v.* 4.] *intr.* and *trans.* To dial again.

1961 'E. LATHEN' *Banking on Death* (1962) viii. 70 His daughter broke the connection. He started to redial then put the phone down. **1966** 'A. HALL' *9th Directive* xiv. 132 All three lines were busy and I began redialling the numbers. **1973** 'E. MCBAIN' *Let's hear It* xiii. 193 In as long as it took for the caller to re-dial, the phone began to ring again. **1976** 'D. CRAIG' *Faith Hope & Death* xvi. 111, I re-dialled and still engaged, so it was not a wrong number.

redictate, *v.* Add: (Later example.) Also *absol.*

1964 T. L. KINSEY *Audio-Typing & Electric Typewriters* iii. 12 After a recording has been transcribed the dictator need only re-dictate over the existing work and it is automatically erased, the new dictation being recorded in its place. **1974** R. CROSSMAN *Diaries* (1975) I. 15, I decided therefore to re-dictate this whole first transcript in plain intelligible English.

rediffu·se, *v.* *Broadcasting.* [RE- 5 a.] *trans.* To disseminate, broadcast, or rebroadcast by rediffusion. So **rediffu·sed** *ppl. a.* Also **rediffu·ser,** a person who or company which rediffuses a programme.

1931 *Times Educ. Suppl.* 1 Aug. p. iv/1 In order to receive such rediffused signals the listener requires an ultra-short wave adapter. **1932** *B.B.C. Year-bk. 1933* 70 Apart from the purely copyright aspect..the BBC..may very reasonably question the equity of the public rediffuser being able to use its programmes for the same..fee as is paid by the private listener. **1948** *Architect Rev.* CIV. 131/2 A public address system enables broadcast programmes to be received and rediffused throughout the school. **1950** *Sport* 7–11 Apr. 22/4 It may not be long before television programmes are rediffused through cinemas.

rediffusion (rīdifiū·ʒən). *Broadcasting.* [RE- 5 a.] **a.** The dissemination, broadcasting, or rebroadcasting of a programme by (*a*) reproduction on loudspeakers and screens in public places, (*b*) transmission by a broadcasting company which was not responsible for making it, or (*c*) publication by other media of items from a radio or television programme.

1927 *Observer* 13 Nov. 19/5 The best programmes of the British service will be available for re-diffusion throughout the Continent as well as throughout the Empire and the rest of the world. **1933** *B.B.C. Year-bk. 1934* 28 It was found possible to apply the [Copyright] Act..to public loudspeaker 'rediffusion'. **1948** *Daily Tel.* 9 June 6/5 The Association for the Protection of Copyright in Sport set out to secure certain safeguards, particularly against general 'rediffusion' of television on big cinema screens. **1950** *Sport* 7–11 Apr. 22/4 Sporting events will, I think, be among the most popular types of rediffusion. **1967** W. SOYINKA *Kongi's Harvest* 2 Who but a lunatic Will bandy words with boxes With government rediffusion sets Which talk and talk and never Take a lone word in reply.

b. *spec.* The distribution of radio or television transmissions within a community by cable from a single receiver.

1935 *Nature* 2 Feb. 196/1 'Rediffusion' is a method of distributing a broadcast programme over an independent line network to a number of subscribers. **1968** BETHELL & BURG tr. *Solzhenitsyn's Cancer Ward* I. xix. 295 Vadim..was happily surprised to discover there was no radio... (The reason for this omission was that for years they had been planning to move the clinic into better-equipped quarters, and the new place..was going to be wired with rediffusion points throughout.) **1975** C. STUART in J. Reith *Diaries* ii. 179 Wireless or relay exchange (also called rediffusion) was the practice of wiring broadcast programmes to individual subscribers by commercial companies operating under licence from the Post Office.

redi·g, *v.* [RE- 5 a.] *trans.* To dig again. So **redi·gging** *vbl. sb.*

1907 *Church Q. Rev.* July 470 This division seems to entail some redigging of ground already trenched. **1922** G. BELL *Let.* 16 Feb. (1927) II. xxii. 633, I must tell you the Yusufiyah is one of the oldest canals in the world... Julian sailed down it to Ctesiphon and the Abbasids re-dug it. **1963** *Times* 4 June 12/5 A year later the tree can be lifted out after the trench is redug. **1965** J. A. MICHENER *Source* 892 Couldn't they have redug the tunnel?

Red Indian: see INDIAN *sb.* 2 b in Dict. and Suppl.

redingote. (Earlier and later examples.)

1793 F. BURNEY *Let. c* 9 Feb. (1972) II. 13 He was quite wet through his *redingotte*. **1802** C. WILMOT *Let.* 3 Jan. in *Irish Peer* (1920) 22 Benches..where servants are generally stretch'd in 'Redingotes' (Great coats) and cock'd hats. **1890** *Athenæum* 28 June 838/2 The Emperor [Napoleon], buttoned up in his legendary grey *redingote* and seated on a white horse stands motionless on a small rise of ground. **1930** *Times* 17 Mar. 9/4 Some of the new redingotes are made to give the effect of a coat and skirt with pleated lingerie vest. **1939** *Country Life* 11 Feb. p. xxxviii/2 This Matita two-piece redingote and dress is in a tone-on-tone effect in light and dark grey. **1965** [see *CLOQUÉ]. **1973** *Times* 14 Nov. 16/8 The Queen will wear a classic redingote of blue silk.

redingtonite (re·diŋtənait). *Min.* [f. the name of the *Redington* mine, Knoxville, Napa Co., Calif. + -ITE[1].] A hydrous sulphate of iron, magnesium, chromium, and aluminium occurring as fibrous masses of a white, yellowish, or purple colour.

1888 G. F. BECKER in *Monogr. U.S. Geol. Survey* No. 13. 279 A hydrous chromium sulphate occurs in fissures in silicified serpentine... It seems appropriate to give the name redingtonite to this hitherto unknown mineral. **1965** G. J. WILLIAMS *Econ. Geol. N.Z.* x. 149/1 He found deep lilac or purple earthy redingtonite associated with the folia of the fuchsite.

red ink. **1.** *slang.* Cheap red wine; also applied to some other inferior alcoholic drinks. Chiefly *U.S.*

1919 *Red Cross Mag.* Nov. 22/3 He at once took ten of his fellow students to a sixty-cent 'red-ink' and spaghetti dinner down on Tenth Street. **1926** J. BLACK *You can't Win* xii. 153 Barrels of the deadly 'foot juice' or 'red ink', as the winos called it. **1930** *N.Y. Times Mag.* 16 Feb. 19 Today's word 'rum' used in a broad sense to designate all kinds of forbidden liquors, may refer to..the 'red ink' of Greenwich Village. **1942** H. W. VAN LOON *Lives* 631 The wine problem was easily settled. Any kind of 'red ink'—any kind of that cheap Chianti..would be satisfactory. **1952** E. O'NEILL *Moon for Misbegotten* III. 140 You'd lie awake..with..the wine of passion poets blab about, a sour aftertaste in your mouth of Dago red ink! **1976** W. H. CANAWAY *Willow-Pattern War* iii. 28 Lunch..was a real workaday snack this time: *raclettes* and *rösti* with a half-bottle of red ink.

2. *U.S. colloq.* The debit side of an account: cf. *RED sb.[1] 1 g. Also in extended use.

1929 *Century* Mar. 605/2 Red ink returns were as prolific as asparagus, which meant you..dug deep for the freight money. **1939** S. BENT *Newspaper Crusaders* ii. 35 The long-drawn crusade whereby St. Louis was taken out of political red ink and put on the credit side of the electoral ledger merits examination. **1948** *Sun* (Baltimore) 31 Jan. 1/3 We cannot play with red ink when we're financing a great government. **1967** *Boston Sunday Herald* 7 May IV. 9/2 Give us enough red ink and make money plentiful enough and the economic skies will soon clear. **1977** *Time* 28 Feb. 26/1 Carter's projected $57·4 billion deficit is an improvement over the $68 billion in red ink anticipated for fiscal 1977, which ends on Sept. 30. **1979** *Financial Rev.* 19 Oct. 27/1 The company would report a loss of more than $US 3 million for the third quarter, bringing the red-ink figure for nine months close to $US 6 million.

redintegration. **2. c.** (Later examples.)

1912 B. DUMVILLE *Fund. Psychol.* x. 208 All suggestion of things not present is due to a process of redintegration; things found or put together in past experience tend to call one another up. **1920** H. L. HOLLINGWORTH *Psychol. Functional Neuroses* ii. 19 Redintegration is to be conceived as that type of process in which a part of a complex stimulus provokes the complete reaction that was previously made to the complex stimulus as a whole. This is not precisely Hamilton's use of the term 'redintegration', but the process is so similar that the term may be used here without injustice. **1938** G. W. ALLPORT *Personality* xix. 525 One variation of the associational theory is the doctrine of redintegration. **1947** G. MURPHY *Personality* viii. 172 If the term canalization marked off no specific kind of event but were purely an alternative for such terms as conditioning, positive adaptation, or redintegration, there would be no justification in using it.

redintegrative, *a.* Delete *rare*—[1] and add further examples. Hence **redi·ntegra:tively** *adv.*

1870 S. H. HODGSON *Theory of Practice* I. 370 States of consciousness which the redintegrative activity has the tendency to produce. **1890** W. JAMES *Princ. Psychol.* I. xiv. 581 The forms of its transitions, whether redintegrative, associative, or similar, are due to unknown regulative or determinative conditions. **1920** H. L. HOLLINGWORTH *Psychol. Functional Neuroses* ii. 18 The redintegrative mechanism, whereby a part reinstates a previous whole, is one of the most enlightening concepts ever offered to psychology. **1933** G. MURPHY *Gen. Psychol.* xviii. 352 All about us are objects to which we do not respond redintegratively because this would involve dozens of *conflicting* action patterns. **1941** *Brit. Jrnl. Psychol.* Oct. 167 Three of the six CO stimuli aroused reactions of a redintegrative character. Some of them went back to situations of childhood and early life. **1946** C. MORRIS *Signs, Lang. & Behavior* 292 The requirement for redintegrative (or 'part-whole') efficacy. **1960** *Encounter* Jan. 81/1 This book has been for me..a remarkable redintegrative experience.

rediscount, *sb.* Add: Also *attrib.*, as *rediscount rate.*

1927 *New Republic* 21 Sept. 108/2 The action of the Reserve Board in ordering the Chicago bank to reduce its rediscount rate from 4 to 3½ percent has resulted in a direct challenge of the Board's authority to compel such a change. **1929** *Times Lit. Suppl.* 21 Mar. 218/3 This..should be corrected by the raising of the Reichsbank rediscount rate and the forcing down of German prices. **1951** *N.Y. Herald Tribune* 15 Nov. 20/2 The rise in the Bank of England rediscount rate from 2 to 2½ per cent. **1970** G. JACKSON *Let.* 17 Apr. in *Soledad Brother* (1971) 223 The missionaries, with the benefits of christendom, school us on the value of symbolism, dead presidents, and the rediscount rate.

redisсou·ntable, *a.* [RE- 5 a.] That may be discounted again.

1964 *Economist* 8 Aug. 573/1 Restrictions on the eligibility of rediscountable paper.

redi·scounting, *vbl. sb.* [f. REDISCOUNT *v.* + -ING[1].] The action of discounting again. Also *attrib.*

1931 *Economist* 2 May 946/2 This, in its turn, has occasioned a very decided increase in rediscounting. **1961** *Ann. Reg. 1960* 491 Gerrard and Reid, discount brokers, were granted borrowing and rediscounting facilities at the Bank of England. **1974** B. PEARCE tr. *Amin's Accumulation on World Scale* II. iii. 429 The commercial banks in the under-developed countries do without rediscounting by the bank of issue.

redisperse, *v.* (Later examples.)

1946 *Nature* 28 Dec. 946/2 Elutriation methods of size separation redisperse coagulæ into their ultimate particles, thereby producing erroneous results. **1956** *Ibid.* 17 Mar. 521/2 The precipitates were then..redispersed by high-speed stirring.

redissolve, *v.* **a.** (Later examples.)

1941 J. S. HUXLEY *Uniqueness of Man* 98 The mineral framework of the bones is redissolved to be used up by the living cells. **1946** *Nature* 7 Sept. 350/2 The precipitates are.. redissolved in a 3 per cent solution of sodium dihydrogen phosphate. **1965** PHILLIPS & WILLIAMS *Inorg. Chem.* I. xv. 567 It dissolves in an excess of the base, and can then be reprecipitated by addition of thionyl chloride, but excess of this acid does not, however, redissolve the aluminium sulphite.

redistil, *v.* Add: Hence **redisti·lled** *ppl. a.*

1930 *Engineering* 21 Mar. 394/1 A parcel of redistilled magnesium of exceptional purity. **1956** *Nature* 21 Jan. 130/2 Using the normal procedure of shaking infective fluid with 20 per cent of freshly redistilled ether and leaving overnight.

redistillation. (Earlier example.)

1666 BOYLE *Orig. Formes & Qual.* 281 Neither do liquors, that have already been distill'd, obtain that colour upon redistillation.

redistributive, *a.* Add: Also of wealth, etc.

1931 G. B. SHAW *Fabian Ess.* p. viii, Redistributive taxation within Capitalist limits means dole for idleness. **1971** *Morning Star* 2 Sept. 3 Taxation structure should be much more progressive and redistributive and should include effective taxation of wealth, capital gains and gifts and a heavier tax on unearned income. **1974** *Guardian* 27 Mar. 15/4 The Budget is redistributive in favour of the working man.

redistrict, *v.* Add: (Further examples.) Hence **redi·stricting** *vbl. sb.* Also *attrib.*

1870 *Trans. Illinois Agric. Soc.* VII. 510 Mr. Flag moved that the subject of redistricting the State be referred to a special committee of nine. **1890** *N.Y. Weekly Tribune* 22 Oct. 12/3 Democratic rascalities in redistricting and in voting and counting will not prevent but will hasten and insure the passage of a bill to secure fair Congressional elections in future. **1949** *Illinois State Register* (Springfield) 1 Feb. 6/4 States throughout the nation are eyeing the Illinois plan for redistricting schools which has proved to be a tax saver as well as a more efficient means of educating youths. **1973** *Time* 25 June 18/3 He supports busing and the redistricting of the Richmond school system to achieve racial balance. **1977** *Time* 21 Mar. 57/2 The mock rebellion is a protest against a redistricting plan under which Martha's Vineyard will lose the seat that it has had in the Massachusetts legislature for 285 years. **1980** *Christian Sci. Monitor* (Midwestern ed.) 4 Dec. 5/1 The shift will be reflected in a gain of congressional seats by the region, when the US House of Representatives is redistricted on the basis of the 1980 census.

‖ **redivivus** (rediv*ī*·vŏs), *a.* Also fem. **rediviva,** fem. pl. **-æ.** [L., see REDIVIVE *a.*] Come back to life; = REDIVIVE *a.*

Always placed after the sb.

1675 R. HEAD (*title*) Proteus redivivus: or the art of wheedling. **1681** H. NEVILE (*title*) Plato redivivus. **1843** H. JAMES *Let.* 11 May in R. B. Perry *Tht. & Char. W. James* (1935) I. 47, I believe Jonathan Edwards *redivivus* in true blue would, after an honest study of the philosophy that has grown up since his day, make the best possible reconciler and critic of philosophy—far better than Schelling *redivivus.* **1856** C. M. YONGE *Daisy Chain* II. xxii. 589 He walked round and round his friend, called him Nicholas Randall *redivivus*, quoted Dogberry. **1937** *Mind* XLV. 492 Paton.. has written the sort of defence of Kant against his critics which a Kant *redivivus* might have written in self-defence. **1939** JOYCE *Finnegans Wake* (1964) III. 490 She's write to him she's levt by me, Jenny Rediviva! **1974** *Listener* 28 Feb. 284/3 The belligerent women of all parties, tricoteuses *redivivae.* **1975** *Times* 5 May 15/2 Some still believe in Stormont Redivivus. **1979** *Amer. N. & Q.* June 167 There isn't much more to say about this first volume of GW [sc. *Gesamtkatalog der Wiegendrucke*] *redivivus.*

Redjang, var. *REJANG. **red lead**: see also *RED *a.* 19 a.

red-legs, red-leg. Add: **3.** Also = RED-SHANKS 3 a. (Later examples.)

1886 BRITTEN & HOLLAND *Dict. Eng. Plant-Names* 399 Red Legs. From the general redness of the stems. (1) *Polygonum bistorta*... (2) *Polygonum Persicaria.* **1960** *Oxf. Bk. Wild Flowers* 126/1 Spotted Persicaria or Red-legs..can usually be easily recognized by the red stems and the dark blotch in the middle of the leaves. **1971** *Countryman* Winter 126 The redleg..was flowering in late summer.

4. *U.S. Mil. slang.* An artilleryman.

1900 P. REVERE *Cleveland in War with Spain* 164 The battery marched down the street... Cleveland's 'red-legs' were off. *Ibid.*, For once the 'dough boys' were envied by the 'red legs'. **1927** *Amer. Legion Monthly* July 16 Reilly's redlegs..admired the advance guard of Bengal lancers. **1969** S. N. SPETZ *Rat Pack Six* 71 Anyway, you'll get a chance to cool it down there, just guarding a bunch of Red Legs.

red letter. Add: **2. b. red-letter day** (earlier and later examples).

1704 S. KNIGHT *Diary* in *Amer. Speech* (1940) XV. 231/2 Red letter day. **1740** *Mock Campaign* 18 Their empty Eccho only now displays Great —'s Power on Red Letter Days. **1905** PROCTOR & FRERE *New Hist. Bk. Common Prayer* (ed. 3) ix. 338 It is difficult to see clearly the motive which determined the selection of the black letter Saints' Days. In the case of the red letter days it was clearly the desire to bring the festivals to the test of the Bible. **1919** *Granta* 1 May 4/1 January 18th, 1889 should be a red-letter day in the history of Cambridge University, for it was on that date that *The Granta*, like a new planet, swam into our ken. **1965** C. E. POCKNEE *Parson's Handbk.* (ed. 13) xvi. 145 The 1928 Book classifies days as holy, special, and ordinary. To *Holy* (or *Red-letter*) *Days* 1928 has added St. Mary Magdalene, 22 July, and the Transfiguration of our Lord, 6 August.

red-letter *v.* (later example).

1940 A. UPFIELD *Bushranger of Skies* xiv. 160 The history of his life was red-lettered with luck.

red light. 1. A warning light, esp. one instructing traffic to stop. Hence *fig.*, a sign of danger; a warning; a signal to pause or desist in some course of action or thought; esp. in phr. *to see the* (or *a*) *red light.*

1849 C. BRONTË *Shirley* III. iii. 44 He is one of Mrs. Yorke's warning-examples—one of the blood-red lights she hangs out to scare young ladies from matrimony. **1862** ANON. *Railway Traveller's Handy Bk.* 99 *Danger, to stop*, is shown by a red light fixed upon a pole being turned full upon the line... *Caution, to go slowly*, is shown..by a green light. *All right, to go on*,..by a white light. *c* **1864** BROUGH & HALLIDAY in M. R. Booth *Eng. Plays of 19th Cent.* (1973) IV. 239 There, that's our signal—that's the red light on our railway, and means 'danger'. **1907** A. QUILLER-COUCH *Major Vigoureux* xxiii. 234, I fancy the man has begun to see the red light. **1927** *Daily Tel.* 15 Nov. 9/3 Men see a red light when they find that things they have called their own—like intelligence—may be given to women too. **1931** E. WALLACE *On Spot* x. 120 If Con had been better acquainted with Tony he would have seen the red light. **1938** *Mag. Digest* Jan. 66 (*heading*) A red light for the pugnacious. **1946** *Sun* (Baltimore) 29 Jan. 11/1 What in fact the Associated Press has done is to put up the red light. **1948** G. V. GALWEY *Lift & Drop* vii. 190 Roberts' carelessness in getting pinched showed them the red light and they ceased operations. **1958** *Spectator* 28 Feb. 251/1 The French Government may see the red light. **1974** E. AMBLER *Dr. Frigo* II. 97 He's hit by a drunk driver running a red light and killed. **1977** *New Yorker* 24 Oct. 52/3 He drove through a red light in Pennsylvania and..was picked up by police.

2. The sign of a brothel. Freq. *attrib.*, as *red light district*, etc.

1900 *N.Y. Jrnl.* Nov. 19 (*caption*) Children of the 'red light district'. **1900** *Boston Transcript* 4 Dec. 14/3 The disorderly houses in the 'red-light' district were all closed last night. **1925** H. L. FOSTER *Trop. Tramp with Tourists* 276, I was amazed to find that about two thirds of every city consisted of red-light district. **1928** *Daily Express* 26 Sept. 11/1 It is further asserted that he has elevated the 'red light' houses to the level of a business in New York. **1947** [see *GEISHA]. **1951** E. PAUL *Springtime in Paris* xi. 205 Strangers in cities of Spain or Italy, who want to locate the red-light district, are advised to seek a point equidistant between the principal seminary and the main barracks of the Guardia Civil. **1962** *Coast to Coast 1961–62* 131 Harry was rough, tough and hairy, and he knew where to find a swy game, a sly-grog joint or a red light in every capital city. **1967** O. WYND *Walk Softly* vi. 91 He is reported to have sizeable interests in the Naboshima Red Light district, and many bars. **1973** *Islander* (Victoria, B.C.) 17 June 16/3 At one time there were about 2,000 men in the camp, and except for the red-light girls at the other end of town, only two women. **1978** *Detroit Free Press* 16 Apr. 11A/2 Besides, she said, a legal red-light district would probably be bad for business. **1981** *Observer* 2 May 3/4 The trial will seem far removed from the red-light districts and suburbs where Sutcliffe struck.

3. A children's game in which one participant turns his back on the others, who try to sneak up on him without being seen moving.

1953 P. G. BREWSTER *Amer. Nonsinging Games* 35 Red Light (Mississippi). The player who is 'It' counts rapidly to ten and then cries, 'Red Light!'.. At the cry of 'Red Light!' each must stop and hold the position in which he was when he heard it. **1969** I. & P. OPIE *Children's Games* vi. 195 Other names [for 'Peep behind the Curtain'] include.. 'Red Light' (Liverpool, Blackburn, Spennymoor, Peterborough, Helensburgh, and Edmonton, Alberta), [etc.]. **1975** *New Yorker* 10 Mar. 38/1 Evenings, screen doors bang behind children rushing out to meet each other for hide-and-seek, giant steps, dead dog, red light.

Hence **red-li·ghter**, a prostitute.

1913 A. STRINGER *Shadow* 37 He could hobnob with bartenders and red-lighters.

red line, *sb. phr.* Used to describe the British army, esp. in phr. *thin red line*; also *transf.*

1855 F. DUBERLY *Let.* 8 June in E. E. P. Tisdall *Mrs. Duberly's Campaigns* (1963) v. 147 They advance, supported by the impenetrable red line, our infantry. **1877** W. H. RUSSELL *Brit. Exped. Crimea* III. ii. 156 The Russians ..dashed on towards that *thin red line tipped with steel.* **1890** KIPLING *Departmental Ditties* (U.S. ed.) 61 It's 'Thin red line of 'eroes' when the drums begin to roll. **1935** 'G ORWELL' *Clergyman's Daughter* iv. 226 Napoleon Buona parte..soon found that in the 'thin red line' he had more than met his match. **1971** *Guardian* 24 Feb. 10/1 Trade unionists..are beginning to give physical support to the Union of Post Office Workers as their 'thin red line'. **1974** *Times* 19 Apr. 14 Home of the thin red (or khaki) lines... 'Home of the British Army', say the road signs leading into Aldershot.

re·d-line, *v.* Also **redline, red line.** To circle or mark in red ink; freq. *fig.* (see quots.). Hence **re·d-lining** *vbl. sb.* See also *red-lined* s.v. RED *a.* 15 a in Dict. and Suppl.

1942 *Yank* 23 Sept. 14/1 Who is it the yardbird sees when he gets red-lined on the payroll for signing his name wrong? **1945** *Amer. Speech* XX. 261 To *redline* a soldier is to cross off his name on the payroll for a particular month because of an improper signature or some other irregularity on anyone's part. **1961** *Richmond* (Va.) *Times-Dispatch* 18 Jan. 4/1 The American Automobile Association may 'red-line' Prince George county because of its policy toward traffic violators. 'Red-lining' is a method used by the AAA to warn motorists of possible speed traps. **1973** *Times* 7 Feb. 20/4 They found that Laurelton had been 'red-lined' by the bank, which meant that it was not possible to get a normal mortgage. **1973** *Black Panther* X. XXVIII. 4/4 'Red-lining' is a corrupt scheme whereby real estate developers..arrange unofficial agreements with banks to have them refuse to grant improvement loans for particular buildings. Eventually the homes fall into a state of such disrepair that the owner is willing to sell it. **1976** *In Common* VI. II. 4/1 Common Cause Governing Board..voted CC support of legislation aimed at discouraging 'redlining'—the practice by lending institutions of discriminating arbitrarily against certain city neighborhoods in making home mortgage loans. **1977** *Listener* 9 June 763/1 The policy of so-called 'red-lining', that is, drawing a line round certain undesirable areas and refusing to lend money on property within the red line. **1979** *Verbatim* Summer 2/2 To redline an aircraft, thus, is 'to ground' it.

redly, *adv.*[1] Add: **b.** *Comb.*, as *redly-lipped, -squirting* adjs.

1910 J. MASEFIELD *Ballads & Poems* 91 Maids that were redly-lipped and comely-skinned. **1930** R. CAMPBELL *Adamastor* 90 Its steel-shot bulk with redly-squirting Nose and lolling tongue.

red man. Add: **2. b.** One of the extinct Beothuk people of Newfoundland.

1955 L. E. F. ENGLISH *Historic Newfoundland* 9/2 They [*sc.* Beothuks] were described as of ordinary height—yet there are recorded instances of giant Red Men of seven feet in stature. **1969** H. HORWOOD *Newfoundland* xi. 78 The original Red Men, who, because of their attachment to red ochre, gave their nickname to all the other native tribes of North America.

4. = *ROMAN *sb.*[3] 2.

1966 E. PALMER *Plains of Camdeboo* xiv. 235 The Red Men come into the house at night... Of medium size—perhaps three inches with the legs fully spread..orange-red, hairy, fast, with great snapping beak-like jaws which, most horrifyingly, they can move at the same time up and down and from side to side.

Redmondite (re·dmǫndəit), *a.* and *sb.* [f. the name *Redmond* (see below) + -ITE[1].] **A.** *adj.* Of or pertaining to the Irish politician John Edward Redmond (1856–1918) or his nationalist ideas. **B.** *sb.* A supporter of Redmond or his policies.

1895 *Notes from Ireland* 2 Feb. 47 The Redmondite manifesto. *Ibid.*, The past week has seen the issue of two familiar appeals..one from the McCarthyites, and one from the Redmondites. **1905** T. D. SULLIVAN *Recoll. Troubled Times in Irish Politics* xxxvii. 339 At the first blush one might suppose that the Tory party would scoff at the Redmondite motion. **1910** *Westm. Gaz.* 9 Feb. 2/2 He cannot even pretend he is entitled to a Redmondite summons. **1913** *Times* 30 Dec. 3/2 Mr John MacNeill denies that his friends are actuated by hostility towards the Redmondites. **1928** T. M. HEALY *Lett. & Leaders of my Day* II. xxxi. 391 In the middle of the negotiations with the Liberal Cabinet as to the Home Rule Bill—which the Redmondites were certain to denounce as inadequate—Dillon tried to get control of the *Freeman.* **1962** GREENE & LAURENCE in G. B. Shaw *Matter with Ireland* 142 *Sinn Féin*, which..had already won two by-elections against Redmondite candidates. **1973** S. LEVENSON *James Connolly* xvii. 208 He accused the Redmondites of accepting partition without a struggle. **1978** D. MURPHY *Place Apart* ii. 17 My mother, whose ancestry was Redmondite at best.

Hence **Re·dmondism**, the ideas or policies associated with Redmond.

1914 R. CASEMENT *Let.* 29 July in R. MacColl *Roger Casement* (1956) vii. 133 Redmondism has no real support here at all.

red-mouthed: see *RED *a.* 14 a, RED *a.* 14 b.

re·dneck. Also **red-neck, red neck. 1.** *U.S.* **a.** A member of the white rural labouring class of the southern States; one whose attitudes are considered characteristic of this class; freq., a reactionary.

Originally, and still often, derogatory, but now also used with more sympathy for the aspirations of the rural American.

1830 A. ROYALL *Southern Tour* I. 148 This may be ascribed to the *Red Necks*, a name bestowed upon the Presbyterians in Fayetteville. **1893** H. A. SHANDS *Some Peculiarities of Speech in Mississippi* 53 *Red-neck*,..a name applied by the better class of people to the poorer inhabitants of the rural districts. **1904** *Dialect Notes* II. 420 *Redneck, n.*, An uncouth countryman. 'The hill-billies came from the hills, and the *rednecks* from the swamps.' **1913** J. DAVIS *Life & Speeches* iii. 42 If you red-necks or hill billies ever come to Little Rock be sure and come to see me—come to my house. **1936** W. FAULKNER *Absalom, Absalom!* 122 Rich and poor, aristocrat and redneck. **1959** *Times Lit. Suppl.* 28 Aug. 491/4 The ugly faces and, under prompting or provocation, the uglier actions of a handful of red-necks, crackers, tar-heels and other poor white trash here and there in the South. **1960** *Spectator* 15 Jan. 83/2 The old patrician families who are opposed to the graft, blackmail and demagogy by which the Boss, the tribune of the rednecks, keeps himself in power. **1969** *Observer* 7 Dec. 25/3 They [*sc.* communes] all shared two experiences: the search for new values, and attention from local rednecks and the police. **1971** J. BISHOP *Days of Martin Luther King, Jr.* IV. 329 The fearful Southern red-neck, committed to the credo that the black man is a bridge between the animal kingdom and the human, derided the speech as typical 'coon shouting'. **1973** *Black World* Mar. 56 Carload of rednecks came with the darkness to Slim's house. Blew the horn until Slim's daddy opened the door. **1975** *Daily Tel.* 15 Oct. 17/7 Was it because they might think his [*sc.* Governor George Wallace's] reputation as a Right-wing 'red neck' a political embarrassment? **1976** *Time* 27 Sept. 47/1 That was the point Carter was attempting to make when he said in 1970 that Maddox 'has compassion for the little man', and when he said that a Humphrey-Wallace ticket in 1972 'would do well in the South', and when he called himself 'basically a redneck'. **1977** D. JAMES *Spy at Evening* x. 71 Middle-class rednecks like you..get all worked up about it. **1978** J. UPDIKE *Coup* v. 192 Her momma's a washrag and her daddy's a redneck.

b. *attrib.* or as *adj.*

1961 D. ALEXANDER *Bloodstain* xi. 134 You should never have come out here alone. This is redneck country. Every man in every one of these houses is a Night Rider. **1965** *Listener* 20 May 730/2 His general manner and accent suggest a person who might hold the racist views of a red-neck Southern bigot. **1971** B. MALAMUD *Tenants* 60 'I' grows up in redneck Mississippi in pure black poverty. **1972** R. BLOCH *Night-World* (1974) vii. 43 See how far you can march through Georgia today before some redneck sheriff busts you for vagrancy. **1973** *Freedomways* XIII. 52 Even Faulkner's ability was distorted by the pervasive racism of his redneck traditionalism. **1974** *New Yorker* 25 Feb. 102/3 He seems Southern redneck—a common man who works outdoors in the sun—to the soul. **1976** *National Observer* (U.S.) 17 July 4/1 Quite possibly Mississippi's only self-avowed redneck Republican. **1979** *Arizona Daily Star* 22 July I. 5/4 Carter..ran on a virtually redneck platform for the 1970 nomination... After running a redneck campaign, [he] pledged an end to discrimination in his inaugural address.

2. (See RED *a.* 18 a.)

3. *S. Afr.* = *ROOINEK.

1900 A. H. KEANE *Boer States* p. xviii, *Rooinek*, 'Red-neck', in reference originally to some merinos introduced by an English farmer into the Free State, and marked with a red brand on the neck. These were spoken of as *red-necks*—an expression afterwards extended to the English themselves, and then as a term of contempt to the British troops in red uniform. **1921**, etc. [see *ROOINEK]. **1936** R. CAMPBELL *Mithraic Emblems* 111 To find a red-neck cheap upon this day You do not need to wander far away. **1972** J. McCLURE *Caterpillar Cop* ii. 18 What's with this Redneck?.. Another bloody English immigrant?

red-necked, *a.* Add: **a.** (Further examples.)

1782 J. LATHAM *Gen. Synopsis Birds* I. II. 558 (*heading*) Red-necked W[oodpecker]. **1847** P. H. GOSSE *Birds of Jamaica* 334 The red-necked gaulin—*Egretta ruficollis*. **1926** Red-necked wallaby [see *brush wallaby* s.v. *BRUSH *sb.*[1] 4]. **1971** *Country Life* 27 May 1292/3 The red-necked phalarope ..though still Ireland's rarest breeding bird, has shown an increase.

b. Holding redneck views; characteristic of a redneck (sense *1); conservative. orig. *U.S.*

1960 *Washington Post* 30 Apr. A6 'Uncle Earl' cavorted in typically 'red-necked' style at a fashionable luncheon. **1973** *Publishers' Weekly* 2 Apr. 58/2 A villain (red-necked political appointee with shady family connections to an equally red-necked but powerful Senator). **1977** *Arab Times* 13 Dec. 6/4 The white, red necked, blue collared worker is more interested in better wages, lower taxes, improved Social Security than justice in the Middle East.

redness. Add: (Further examples.) Also, the state or quality of being politically 'red'.

Under Chairman Mao the concept of 'redness' as opposed to 'expertness' was of great significance in the People's Republic of China.

1940 R. S. LAMBERT *Ariel & all his Quality* iii. 84 Press campaigns against alleged BBC 'redness'. **1973** R. TAYLOR *Educ. & Univ. Enrolment Policies in China, 1949–1971* 39 The subordination of expertise to ideology (or 'redness'). **1973** T. R. TREGEAR *Chinese* iii. 57 In the industrial field 'expertness' assumed greater importance than 'redness'. **1975** I. C. Y. HSÜ *Rise of Mod. China* (ed. 2) xxvi. 796 The government in 1957 initiated a 'socialist education movement' among the industrial and agrarian population, followed by the dispatch of military and civil leaders to physical labor as an example to the people. The importance of 'redness', i.e., ideology over expertise, was very much emphasized. **1976** *Lancs. Evening Post* 7 Dec. 3/9 He grabbed witness by the collar, causing scratches to the neck and redness. **1981** G. HAMMOND *Revenge Game* xii. 137 In Keith's mind, a set of vague ideas solidified into a herring of most extraordinary redness.

‖ **redningskoite** (re·dniŋzkoi:tə, re·dniŋzʃoi:tə). Also **redningschoite, redningsshöite,** and with capital initial. [Norw., f. *redning* rescue + *skøyte* a type of fishing vessel.] A kind of Norwegian lifeboat. Also *attrib.*

1906 H. W. SMYTH *Mast & Sail* 434 *Redningskoite*, a Norwegian sea-keeping lifeboat for assisting the Northland fishing fleets in bad weather. **1925** *Yachting Monthly* XXXVIII. 135/1 The original Redningschoites were designed, by the late Colin Archer, to be the best heavy weather boats in the world. **1935** C. E. T. LEWIS *Lifeboats & their Conversion* ii. 39 The cruising lifeboats of Scandinavia and Russia as typified by the Norwegian ketch-rigged redningsshöites. The main duty of these craft is to keep in touch with the herring fleets throughout the winter, and render any help required. **1937** *Yachting Monthly* LXII. 508/1, I wanted to try out the conventional *redningskoite* sail plan. **1962** D. PHILLIPS-BIRT *Fore & Aft Sailing Craft* vii. 177 The redningskoite is illustrated in Figs 89, 90, and 91. The Norwegian term is rendered literally as 'rescue sailing ship'.

re·do, *sb.* [f. the vb.] A doing over again (in various senses); a repetition.

a **1953** DYLAN THOMAS *Quite Early One Morning* (1954) 79 The decorators were in at the mortuary, giving the old home a bit of a re-do like. **1961** D. B. SHIELDS in *Webster* s.v., No pleasanter prospect than a redo of our South American trek. **1977** *Surgery* LXXXI. 41 (*heading*) 'Redo' surgery after operations for aneurysm and occlusion of the abdominal aorta.

redondite (rĕdǫ·ndəit). *Min.* [f. the name of *Redonda* Island, W. Indies + -ITE[1].] A hydrated phosphate of aluminium and iron, $(Al,Fe)PO_4.2H_2O$, occurring as whitish amorphous masses.

1870 C. U. SHEPARD in *Amer. Jrnl. Sci.* C. 96 Barrandite has gr. = 2·576. Redondite gives gr. = 2·019. **1964** *Amer. Mineralogist* XLIX. 445 *X*-ray powder data are given on redondite from Ponikla and Listenec, Czechoslovakia, from Redonda Island, and for tangaite from Tanganyika... Redondite (and tangaite) give patterns that are identical and distinct from those of variscite and clinovariscite... The authors feel that the name redondite should be used for all material of this type with Al $>$ Fe and the name tangaite is superfluous. **1975** *Mineral Abstr.* XXVI. 225/2 Variscite, crandallite, and redondite, relatively rare phosphate minerals, are found in phosphatic rocks associated with carbonatites and syenites in the Grande islet (Brava island) Cape Verde.

redouble, *sb.*[2] *Bridge.* [f. next.] A call that redoubles a bid.

1906 'CUT-CAVENDISH' *Compl. Bridge Player* 98 The redouble is the *rara avis* of the Bridge world. **1910** J. B. ELWELL *Auction Bridge* 103 The laws of Auction, as embodied for club play, limit the doubling feature to one double and one re-double. **1925** [see *BUSINESS 21 d]. **1964** *Official Encycl. Bridge* 450/1 Ill-judged doubles of game or slam contracts may lead to redoubles. **1975** *Times* 20 Dec. 10/7 The Double of a No trump is primarily for a penalty: what does the opener mean to convey by a Redouble?

redouble, *v.*[2] Add: **b.** *spec.* in Bridge, to double again (a bid which an opponent has already doubled). Also *absol.* or *intr.*

1894 'BOAZ' *Pocket Guide to Bridge* 6 The leader has then to ask the adversaries whether either of them wishes to redouble. **1898** [see *DOUBLE *v.* 1 g]. **1910** J. B. ELWELL *Auction Bridge* 102 The partner..may be well satisfied with the double, and, perhaps, in a position to redouble... The general Auction laws do not limit the number of times that a declaration may be doubled and re-doubled. **1921** *Sat. Westm. Gaz.* 1 Oct. 17/1 The player who doubles would not lose much if the rule was that *his* double could not be re-doubled. **1980** *Times* 12 Jan. 10/6 South doubles for a take-out and West redoubles.

redoubled, *ppl. a.* Add: **1. c.** *spec.* in Bridge.

1964 *Official Encycl. Bridge* 450/1 When the standard of play is high, redoubled contracts are rare.

redoubler. 1. For *rare*—[0] read *rare* and add example.

1959 T. REESE *Bridge Player's Dict.* 182 At the slam level the odds in favor of the redoubler are better yet.

redoubling, *vbl. sb.* Add: **1. c.** *spec.* in Bridge.

1899 A. DUNN *Bridge* 63 Doubling and Redoubling... After the trump suit is announced, the adversaries may 'double' the value of the suit selected... The dealer and his partner may redouble. **1908** *Laws of Auction Bridge* §55 Doubling and redoubling affect the score only, and not the value in declaring. **1963** G. F. HERVEY *Handbk. Card Games* 134 Doubling and redoubling do not..increase the size of a contract.

redoubt, *sb.* Add: **1. b.** (Later examples.)

1955 *Times* 16 May 3/4 Labour's most south-westerly redoubt is in acute danger. **1963** *Times* 30 May 13/2 It would be too embarrassing for all concerned if Ebbw Vale and the other Labour redoubts were to be presented on nomination day with official Labour candidates on top of the sitting 'independents'. **1970** R. LOWELL *Notebk.* 72 Let's face it, English is a racist redoubt. **1977** *Time* 21 Mar. 10/3 Like his predecessors, he has tried—and failed—to overcome the age-old linguistic dispute that makes Belgium the staunchest redoubt of tribalism in Western Europe.

3. (Earlier example.)

1787 [see *ASSEMBLÉE].

red-out (re·daut). [f. RED *a.* and *sb.*; cf. *BLACK-OUT.] A reddening of the vision resulting from an accumulation of blood in the head when the body is accelerated downwards.

1942 *Richmond* (Va.) *Times-Dispatch* 21 Dec. 13/1 The doctors learn airplane ambulance work... They learn about grayouts, blackouts and redouts. **1943** *Effects of Flight* (U.S. Navy Training Div., Bur. Aeronaut.) iv. 70 High numbers of *g*'s acting upward through the vertical axis of the body can be produced..and when these are excessive there may be the sensation of everything turning red, followed by unconsciousness. This has been called 'red-out'. **1946** R. A. McFARLAND *Human Factors in Air Transport Design* ix. 363 Values of -2 or $-3g$ produce fullness and a throbbing pain in the head. The vessels of the eyes become congested, and reddening of vision, or 'red-out', may occasionally occur. **1962** F. I. ORDWAY et al. *Basic Astronautics* xii. 463 If the acceleration is applied in the opposite direction, then a condition known as red-out occurs... The blood..increases in weight to the point where the heart can no longer pump it. **1970** *Daily Tel.* (Colour Suppl.) 10 July 25/2 With a severe bout of negative G you get a red-out, when so many vessels burst that your vision becomes crimson and you see through a haze of blood. **1980** *Verbatim* Winter 19/1 Too many positive G's may cause loss of consciousness—a *red-out*.

Hence **red ou·t** *v. intr.*, to undergo or experience a red-out. See also *REDDING *vbl. sb.*[1] 2.

1955 M. RELFER *Dict. New Words* 175 *Red out*, to experience a red field of vision, congestion of the face and, in particular, the eyes, pressure in the head, etc., as a result of blood rushing to the head in certain aerial maneuvers, such as a rapid climb, inverted spins, outside loops, etc. **1980** *Verbatim* Winter 19/1 A pilot is in danger of redding out when an aerial maneuver puts a strong positive-G stress on his body.

redowa. In etym. read 'ad. Czech *rejdovák*, f. *rejdovati* to steer, manipulate (as with a carriage pole), to wheel about'. Substitute for def.: A Bohemian folk dance, in Western Europe developed into a dance in relatively quick triple time; the music for such a dance. (Earlier and later examples.)

1845 J. R. PLANCHÉ *Graciosa & Percinet* II. 9 Charming Polka—Redowa Polka! Pink of Polkas thou'rt to me! **1855** E. R. SMITH *Araucanians* vi. 65 The schottisches and redowas of the modern ball-room. **1885** A. DODWORTH *Dancing* viii. 62 *Redowa*. When first introduced this dance had the time of a polka mazourka... Our beautiful waltz of to-day is a subdued redowa. **1903** W. LAMB *How & what to Dance* vii. 70 The Redowa, when first introduced, began with a promenade movement, but it is now generally commenced with the circular figure. **1960** P. J. S. RICHARDSON *Social Dances of 19th Cent. Eng.* ix. 99 As late as 1894 or 1895 I can clearly remember being present at a popular assembly in London when the Redowa was announced, but only about three veteran couples..were able to perform it.

redox (rī·dǫks, re·dǫks). *Chem.* [f. RED(UCTION + OX(IDATION.] A reversible reaction in which one species is oxidized and another reduced; usu. *attrib.*, indicating (some connection with) such a reaction, or a simultaneous oxidation and reduction, as *redox couple, electrode, indicator, potential, reaction,* etc.

1928 MICHAELIS & FLEXNER in *Jrnl. Biol. Chem.* LXXIX. 689 The success met on application of the theoretical fundamentals of oxidation-reduction potentials (hereinafter to be referred to by us as 'redox' potentials)..to organic redox systems..has given great impetus to more elaborate study of physiological materials. **1938** *Nature* 15 Oct. 723/1 Increasing use of redox indicators is being made with marked success in analytical chemistry. **1940** GLASSTONE *Text-bk. Physical Chem.* xii. 932 A reversible oxidation-reduction electrode..sometimes abbreviated to.. 'redox' electrode. **1959** *Engineering* 2 Jan. 25/2 A mercaptan modifier and redox catalyst are employed to obtain the desired molecular structure in the shortest possible reaction time. **1965** PHILLIPS & WILLIAMS *Inorg. Chem.* ix. 312 Since galvanic cells consist essentially of two redox couples opposed one against the other, it is convenient to choose one couple arbitrarily and regard it as having zero potential. **1970** AMBROSE & EASTY *Cell Biol.* ii. 66 Note..that a favourable redox potential does not necessarily mean that a particular reaction will take place, but simply that it is thermodynamically feasible. **1971** *Nature* 4 June 311/2 An internal redox apparently occurs, and the electron moves from cation to anion. *Ibid.* 12 Nov. 89/1 The red colour of Mars suggests the presence of ferric iron which is not readily explained by the redox state implied by the second hypothesis. **1978** P. W. ATKINS *Physical Chem.* xii. 362 In a redox titration a reduced form of an ion (e.g., Fe^{2+}) is oxidized by the addition of some oxidizer (e.g., Ce^{4+}).

redpoll[2], **-polled.** (Earlier and later examples.)

1891 J. MACDONALD *Stephens's Bk. Farm* (ed. 4) III. VI. 416/1 The Norfolk and Suffolk Red Polled breed stands highest for dairying purposes. The Red Polls are handsome symmetrical animals of medium size. **1949** *Caribbean Q.* I. II. 36 A small herd of grade red poll cattle was maintained. **1970** G. E. EVANS *Where Beards wag All* viii. 95, I have kept

Red Polls, because they are harmless, and the Suffolk breed for a Suffolk man.

red rag, red-rag. Add: **3.** (Earlier and later examples.)

1873 C. M. Yonge *Pillars of House* II. xviii. 151 Jack will do for himself if he tells Wilmet her eyes are violet; it is like a red rag to a bull. **1875** 'Mark Twain' in *Atlantic Monthly* Feb. 219 'What do you suppose I told you the names of those points for?' 'Well, to—to be entertaining, I thought.' This was a red rag to a bull. **1965** *Listener* 25 Nov. 874/3 Professor Allen has adopted more an 'inquiry programme' style to examine some of the sacred cows and red rags of American life.

4. *Naut. slang.* = *red ensign*, **red duster*.

1910 D. W. Bone *Brassbounder* 129 Pluggin' a Dutchman's naethin'; it's th' 'Rid Rag' that Kelly's doon oan. **1929** D. J. Munro *Roaring Forties* 23 Up went Old Glory... We followed suit with the 'Red Rag' waving in defiance.

redraw, *v.*[2] Add: **4.** *trans.* To draw up again, to compose again.

1815 A. Constable *Let.* 26 Apr. in J. Constable *Corr.* (1962) I. 126 My father has had his *will redrawn*, leaving *out* the objectionable clause.

Red Republic. Also with small initials. [Red *a.* 9 b.] A republic based on socialist principles, *spec.* the French Second Republic, proclaimed in 1848. So **Red Republican,** one who holds radically republican views and advocates the use of force to realize them, esp. a supporter of the European revolutions of 1848; **Red Republicanism,** the principles and views of Red Republicans.

1848 *Illustr. London News* 1 July 415/1 The 'Red Republicans' have justified their name. They have filled the streets of Paris with blood... The working classes, or 'Red Republicans', were imbued with the doctrines of Communism. **1848** *Tablet* 2 Sept. 566/4 The red republic is now in a situation somewhat analogous to that of the Jacobins under Bonaparte. **1850** (*title of newspaper*) The Red Republican. **1850** E. P. Whipple *Washington & Principles of Revolution* 29 We are proposing all those intricate problems which red republicanism so swiftly solves. **1857** C. M. Yonge *Dynevor Terrace* I. xx. 327 Raise our barricade for the rights of the Red Republic, and cry *La liberté, l'égalité, et la fraternité*. *Ibid.* II. ii. 23 All I am clear about is, that even a Red Republican is less red than he is painted. **1858** *N.Y. Tribune* 11 Jan. 2/5 When Mr. Bigler was in Kansas last summer, he was the known, open and enthusiastic advocate of what some hereabout call Red Republicanism. **1874** Trollope *Phineas Redux* I. xxxiii. 276 One..advocates the personal government of an individual ruler, and the other that form of State which has come to be called a Red Republic. **1875** P. K. O'Clery *Hist. Ital. Revolution* v. 185 The other [was] a soldier and nothing more, knowing nothing of politics beyond a rabid red-republicanism. **1960** R. K. Webb *Harriet Martineau* xi. 322 Only Cavour was capable..of steering his way between the reactionary agents and the red republicans. **1972** T. Coleman *Passage to Amer.* xiv. 221 Kossuth came to America in 1851... He came to be seen as a continental red republican.

redressive, *a.* For *rare*—1 read *rare* and add later example.

1965 H. Kahn *On Escalation* ii. 45 The first use of nuclear weapons..is likely to be less for the purpose of destroying the other side's military forces..than for redressive, warning,..or deterrence purposes.

redri·ll, *v.* [f. Re- 5 a + Drill *v.*[4]] *trans.* To drill (crops or ground) again in the same season. So **redri·lling** *vbl. sb.*

1959 *Times* 5 Aug. 4/1 (Advt.), Aldrin wettable powder, used as a seed dressing, has proved outstandingly successful against the Black Cutworm.., eliminating time and money-wasting re-drilling and reducing handling and application costs. **1961** *Times* 24 July 6/6 Wheat bulb fly is in some years a very serious pest. In 1953 the estimated total loss in this country, taking into account crops which had to be redrilled or patched, was estimated at £1,250,000.

Red River. *Canad.* The name of a river flowing from North Dakota, U.S.A., to Lake Winnipeg, Manitoba, Canada, used *attrib.* in **Red River cart** *Hist.* (see quot. 1875); **Red River fever,** typhoid fever; **Red River frame** *Hist.*, used in a particular style of architecture (see quot. 1921); **Red River jig,** a fast, intricate jig.

1857 J. Palliser *Jrnl.* 14 July (1863), The Red River cart is one admirably suited to the exigencies of the country. **1875** J. Carnegie *Saskatchewan & Rocky Mts.* ii. 13 Red River cart, a stout two-wheeled vehicle of the toughest quality though entirely made of wood, wheels, body, shafts, and all, being fitted together without a single particle of iron. **1968** [see *ox-train* s.v. *ox 5]. **1975** *Whig-Standard* (Kingston, Ontario) 21 Nov. 25/1 I've been here [*sc.* at Calgary] for three days and I haven't seen one buffalo, or a Red River cart or a redcoated Mountie or a saloon shoot-out. **1880** D. Currie *Lett. of Rusticus* 62/1 Red River fever was very prevalent at the Portage. **1889** J. G. Donkin *Trooper & Redskin in Far North-West* iii. 41 In fact it is the typho-malarial scourge known as Red River fever in Manitoba, jungle fever in India,..and Rocky Mountain fever in British Columbia. **1945** K. M. Haig *Brave Harvest* 40 Aunt Alice's heart sank. The Red River fever! **1966** M. Kavanaugh *Assiniboine Basin* xxxv. 223 Fisher spent six weeks in the hospital suffering from typhoid—sometimes called Red River fever. **1882** *Edmonton Bull.* 29 July 4/1 They are of the style known as Red River frame and are for use as storehouses. **1921** *Beaver* Feb. 15/2 The 'big house' was a two-and-a-half storey building, with a large kitchen behind, built from the same plan as the officers' dwellings in Fort Garry, and known as a Red River frame building. **1963** MacLeod & Morton *Cuthbert Grant of Grantown* 93 There on the western limit of his seigniory, Cuthbert Grant built the great log house, in the Red River frame style. **1872** *Canad. Monthly* Oct. 305/1 The principal dance, in fact the only one, is called a Red River jig, which somewhat resembles a horn-pipe, male and female participating in it. **1930** L. Munday *Mounty's Wife* iii. 44 The jigging by the men, known as the Red River jig, is really done very cleverly and is so swift. **1965** G. Shepherd *West of Yesterday* x. 74 Two compatriots came out on the floor and danced a Red River jig.

red rot. [f. Red *a.* + Rot *sb.*[1]] **a.** Fungal decay of standing trees or of timber characterized by red-brown rotted tissue; *esp.* that caused by *Trametes pini* in conifers.

1894 W. Somerville tr. *Hartig's Text-bk. Dis. Trees* 1 The damping-off of seedling beeches,..the red-rot of the spruce, &c., were known to foresters more than a hundred years ago. **1925** Hawley & Hawes *Man. Forestry* (ed. 2) vii. 127 The practice..of leaving for seed purposes trees diseased with red rot is unsafe because it tends to perpetuate the disease, not through the seed of the old trees, but by the fungus upon them. **1934** [see *conk *sb.*[2]]. **1950** R. Moore *Candlemas Bay* 119 The house was starting in to go right now, the way all the fine old houses went, as surely as if red rot had got into its solid beams and were eating it hourly down.

b. A fungal disease of sugar cane characterized by red patches within the canes.

1907 *Bull. Hawaiian Sugar Planters' Assoc. Exper. Station* VII. 25 The fungus is *Colletotrichum falcatum*, and the disease it causes is called the 'red rot' of the cane. **1928** F. S. Earle *Sugar Cane* v. 154 The red rot fungus gains entrance to the stalks through borer holes and other injuries. **1944** *Phytopathology* XXXIV. 210 The lesions produced on the inoculated leaves were in all ways similar to lesions produced by virulent red-rot cultures. **1975** *Mycologia* LXVII 56 Perithecia produced by *C*[*olletotrichum*] *graminicola* most closely resemble those of *Glomerella tucumanensis*, the causal agent of the red rot of sugarcane... Carvajal and Edgerton..connected the conidial state, *C. falcatum*, with *P*[*hysalospora*] *tucumanensis*. The perfect state of this fungus was transferred by von Arx and Müller..to the genus *Glomerella*, and the name generally accepted today is *G. tucumanensis*.

red-shank(s, redshank. Add: **2. a.** *to run* (etc.) *like a redshank*: also in other dialects and *N.Z.* (further examples).

1873 E. Waugh *Snowed-Up* v. 88 They're off like red-shanks! An' they'n come noan back to-neet, noather. **1891** G. Chamier *Philosopher Dick* 466 Without another thought or look behind us we were off like red shanks. **1901** W. F. Barry *Wizard's Knot* vi. 53 Don't be running from us that way like a redshank. **1903** *N.Z. Illustr. Mag.* VIII. 93 They would be off into the bush like redshanks.

red shift, *sb.* Chiefly *Astr.* Also **red-shift, redshift.** [f. Red *a.* and *sb.* + Shift *sb.*] Displacement of spectral lines towards the red end of the spectrum; increase in the wavelength of electromagnetic radiation. Also *fig.*

1923 A. S. Eddington *Math. Theory Relativity* v. 164 The red shift in the spiral nebulae. **1936** *Five Halley Lectures* 17 This telescope should penetrate to distances where the effects of red-shifts are so great that the requisite data will lie well above the threshold. **1958** *Listener* 11 Dec. 971/2 When we look at these distant regions we find that the light is reddened, indicating that the galaxies are receding from us. As far as we can see, the red shift of the most distant nebulae is still increasing linearly with distance. **1967** *Daily Tel.* 30 Jan. 10/4 The gigantic red-shift of quasars is therefore considered proof by some astronomers that they may be as much as six to eight thousand million light years away from our earth. **1971** *Sci. Amer.* May 56/3 Red shifts are commonly expressed as a fraction or percentage obtained by dividing the measured displacement of a line by the wavelength of the undisplaced line. **1973** A. Garner *Red Shift* 155 Next time it'll be all right, every time, and it isn't. Next time will make up for him—and me. Never... Galactic. Red shift. The further they go, the faster they leave. The sky's emptying. God, this wind's cold. **1976** *Pract. Electronics* Oct. 793/3 During 1975 two teams of astronomers in the United States recorded a red-shift of $z = 0{\cdot}5240$ in the optical spectrum of a quasar. **1979** *Nature* 11 Oct. 498/1 Hyperpolarisation of the membrane causes a blueshift of the spectrum when probe is applied to the inside and a redshift for probe bound to the outer surface.

Hence **red-shifted** *a.*, exhibiting a red shift; also *transf.*; (as a back-formation) **red-shift** *v. trans.*

1963 *Nature* 16 Mar. 1041/1 Some broad lines..may be red-shifted hydrogen lines. **1964** *Listener* 20 Aug. 266/2 Matthews and Greenstein were able to identify the lines of 3C 48, which they found to be red shifted by 37 per cent. **1973** *Nature* 3 Aug. 264/1 As the 3 cm radiation propagates through an expanding Universe it will be redshifted. *Ibid.* 21/28 Dec. 517/1 The report..seems to provide a rare parallel to the visual pigments of the freshwater Osteichthyes, and to raise the question whether its pigment is a porphyropsin or a redshifted rhodopsin. **1976** *Pract. Electronics* Oct. 793/3 They set up their apparatus to scan for the 21 cm line at what could be its redshifted wavelength. **1979** *Nature* 5 July 20/1 The apparent colours of the faint galaxy identifications (presumably at redshifts of about 0·5) are considerably bluer than expected from redshifting the spectrum of nearby giant ellipticals such as M87.

red shirt, redshirt. 1. a. A supporter of Garibaldi, esp. one of the thousand who sailed with him in 1860 to conquer Sicily.

1864 Young & Stevens *Garibaldi: Life & Times* lxxv. 200 Naples had gone mad with joy: men, women, ragamuffins, priests, Redshirts, ex-Bourbon *sbirri*, *lazzaroni*,..—all lent their voices to..the general cry of '*Viva Garibaldi!*' *Ibid.* lxxvi. 202 Some of them mended their lives when Garibaldi came, and fought well in the ranks of the Red-shirts before Capua. [**1868**: in Dict. s.v. Red *a.* 4.] **1948** F. Frenaye tr. *Levi's Christ stopped at Eboli* xvii. 168 When King Franceschiello had to leave Naples.., Garibaldi and his Red Shirts set out to attack him. **1979** *Guardian* 12 June 9/4 It took a march on Rome..—echoes of Garibaldi's thousand Red Shirts—to get water and elementary sewerage installed.

b. In more general use, a revolutionary, an anarchist, a communist.

1889 [in Dict. s.v. Red *a.* 18 a]. **1905** *Daily Chron.* 12 Sept. 3/2 Because I made a stand in my native town for municipal ownership of public utilities, I was branded a 'red-shirt', a 'dynamiter', and an 'Anarchist'. **1911** H. S. Harrison *Queed* xviii. 234 Queed wrote a stinging little article..holding up to public scorn journalistic red-shirts who curry-combed the masses. **1934** T. S. Eliot *Rock* i. 42 Enter *redshirts* in military formation. **1940** G. Greene *Power & Glory* I. i. 13 You remember this place—before the Red Shirts came?

c. *spec.* A member of a Pathan nationalist organization formed in North-West Province in 1921 and lasting until the creation of Pakistan in 1947; also *attrib.* or as *adj.*

1930 *Civil & Milit. Gaz.* (Lahore) 1 June 1/5 In Mardan and Charsadda..the activities of the 'Red Shirts' have again increased. **1932** *Ann. Reg. 1931* 156 An organisation closely allied with Congress, the 'Red Shirt' Army under Abdul Ghaffar Khan, was a source of much anxiety in the North-west Frontier Province. **1948** G. Cunningham *Diary* in N. Mitchell *Sir George Cunningham* (1968) vii. 152, I could tell he felt he was on rather weak ground in talking about the Red Shirt activities by the twiddling of his bare toes. **1968** N. Mitchell *Sir George Cunningham* v. 87 He records a recruiting meeting at Swabi..on 11th February, and the fact that four notorious ex-Red Shirts had publicly given him purses towards any war fund purpose.

2. *U.S.* A college athlete whose course is extended by a year during which he does not take part in university events, in order to develop his skills and extend his period of eligibility at this level of competition. Also *attrib.*, as *redshirt year*.

1955 *Life* 5 Dec. 144/2 Although he is what the pros call 'redshirt', a player with one more year of college eligibility, five pro clubs are eyeing him. **1970** *Time* 7 Dec. 78 He worked even harder in his sophomore year as a 'redshirt', practicing with the varsity but not playing in any games—so that he would have an additional year of eligibility. **1976** *Honolulu Star-Bull.* 21 Dec. H-2/1 Crowe was coming off a redshirt year last season while Bonup was going through one.

So as *v. trans.*, to keep out of university competition for a year for the above reasons; so **re·d-shirting** *vbl. sb.*

1950 *Birmingham* (Ala.) *News* 27 Sept. 35/1 He coached all the juniors and senior linemen and the boys red shirted. *Ibid.* 19 Nov. C1/2 There are not enough players to have a 'B' squad or red shirt promising sophomores. **1958** *Tuscaloosa* (Ala.) *News* 8 Jan. 6/8 An anticipated argument over 'red shirting'—the practice of holding athletes out of competition to prolong their eligibility—failed to develop. **1963** *San Francisco Chron.* 3 Dec. 44 He could have been red-shirted but he was an uncertain commodity last year. **1966** *Time* 14 Oct. 49 They [*sc.* the Big Ten] also are forbidden to 'red-shirt' prospects—putting them on a five-year program, keeping them out of action as sophomores in order to beef them up. **1968** *Daily Progress* (Charlottesville, Va.) 10 Apr. A10 Edwards supported continuation of red-shirting, a common practice that permits an athlete to use four years to complete three years of varsity eligibility.

redskin. Add: **2.** A variety of potato.

1908 *Chambers's Jrnl.* Oct. 702/1 The chief products grown are..potatoes... Tasmanian 'redskins' are..exported. **1973** *Courier & Advertiser* (Dundee) 21 Feb. 2/8 Scandinavia demands Redskin..and Maris Piper.

red snow. 1. (Further examples.)

1820 *Edin. Phil. Jrnl.* III. 307 (*heading*) Observations on the red snow of Mount St. Bernard. *Ibid.*, Some imperfect observations on the red snow of the Alps were made by M. Saussure in 1778, and the result of them appeared in the 3d volume of his Travels. **1894** J. W. Moore *Meteorol.* xx. 236 Red snow and green snow have been observed in the Arctic Regions and elsewhere. **1912** *Q. Jrnl. R. Meteorol. Soc.* XXXVIII. 220 The red snow first attracted attention because the hoof-prints of the pack animals..were observed to be 'splotched with red as if the snow-crust had cut the mules feet and dyed the snow with drops of blood'. **1933** E. Hawks *Bk. of Air & Water Wonders* vii. 145 Red snow was known to Pliny, and was attributed by him to a dust with which the snow became covered after it had lain for some time on the ground... The phenomenon of red snow is due to the presence of some genus of algæ, scientifically known as *Protococcus nivalis*. **1973** *Islander* (Victoria, B.C.) 17 June 5/2 The three explorers saw white ptarmigan, and the unique 'red snow' of the area.

red spot. 1. *Astr.* = *great red spot* s.v. *great *a.* 20.

1879 *Monthly Notices R. Astron. Soc.* XL. 86 The very remarkable red spot which has attracted the attention of every observer during the present opposition. **1962** *Listener* 26 July 136/1 After 1882 the Red Spot began to fade, and since then it has undergone various changes. **1977** *Times Educ. Suppl.* 21 Oct. 21/2 Neither is it true to say that with regard to the Red Spot on Jupiter, 'scientists do not know what causes it'.

2. A defect of cheese in which there are fine red spots throughout.

[**1900** *Bull. N.Y. Agric. Exper. Station* No. 183. 189 The evidence seems to be conclusive that the red spots are produced by the growth of a minute plant which finds its way into the curd before it is put to press.] **1932** *Discovery* Feb. 59/2 The trouble in cheese known as 'open-ness' is being investigated and red spot in cheese and oiliness in butter have been studied with some success. **1955** J. G. DAVIS *Dict. Dairying* (ed. 2) 662 The peculiar fault known as 'red spot' in Cheddar cheese is due to an organism biochemically resembling the mastitis streptococcus which apparently lives a saprophytic existence in the udders of certain cows.

redstart. 1. a. Substitute for first part of def.: A small European and North African bird belonging to the genus *Phœnicurus* of the family Turdidæ, esp. *P. phœnicurus.* (Later examples.)

1925 C. E. RAVEN *In Praise of Birds* vi. 76 Not far off was a Redstart's nest in a piece of old iron piping. **1950** J. BUXTON *Redstart* xi. 132 Am I to describe as redstarts only those species which are placed in the genus *Phoenicurus*? **1973** T. SOPER *New Bird Table Bk.* iii. 31 Redstarts and woodpeckers are hole-nesters.

2. (Earlier and later examples.)

1731 M. CATESBY *Nat. Hist. Carolina* I. 67 The Red-Start... These Birds frequent the shady Woods of Virginia. **1947** R. T. PETERSON *Field Guide to Birds* (ed. 2) 208 The Redstart is one of the most butterfly-like of birds.

red-tape, red tape. Add: **b.** (Earlier and later examples.)

1736 LD. HERVEY *Poet. Epistle to Queen* in *Mem.* (1848) II. 156 Let Wilmington, with grave, contracted brow, Red tape and wisdom at the Council show. **1837** C. G. F. GORE *Stokeshill Place* I. vii. 142 My dear, you mistake John Barnsley... Dearly as he loves a bit of red tape, you never saw him try to inspire any other man with the love of business. **1938** *Daily Progress* (Charlottesville, Va.) 18 Aug. 4/1 The trial time has been about cut in half by the preliminary clearing away of red tape. **1956** A. WILSON *Anglo-Saxon Attitudes* I. i. 4 He resigned from the Labour Party and the House of Commons to fight your battle without the restraints of red tape. **1977** *Time* 14 Feb. 24/3 Strawbossing the operation was Energy Chief James Schlesinger, who helped draft the natural gas bill and cut red tape to get gas supplies moving.

red-taped *a.*, also, restricted by red-tape (further examples); **red-ta·p(e)y** *a.* [-Y[1]] = RED-TAPISH *a.*

1889 *Columbus* (Ohio) *Dispatch* 21 Jan., Whether the newspaper reports are extravagant, or the official reports are too red-tapy or timid,..it is hard to say. **1905** D. SLADEN *Playing the Game* iv. 37 He'll be more red-tapey than ever, so as not to let the Japanese suspect anything. **1928** E. E. CUMMINGS *Enormous Room* iv. 61 The whole rotten red-taped Croix Rouge. **1954** *Sun* (Baltimore) 19 July 26/6 Red-taped—Jimmy Kennedy..wants to work but can't. **1975** *Daily Tel.* 21 July 5/8 There is..'a strictly Christian name approach' so that they are as different as possible to the 'red-tapey concept' of the social services.

red tapeworm. *joc.* [Blend of RED-TAPE and TAPEWORM.] Red-tapism or a red-tapist regarded as parasitic or as a disease of society.

1917 *Times* 26 Oct. 8/3 Send the papers to the Christchurch Museum in New Zealand as an example of the Red Tape-worm of England. **1918** *Studies* Dec. 664 The State ought to provide it; but the mechanism is clogged by the red-tapeworm. **1939** *Amer. Speech* XIV. 6 Others refer disparagingly to 'poluticians',..and 'red tapeworms'.

red-top. Add: **2.** (Earlier and later examples.) Substitute for def.: One of several pasture grasses, esp. *Agrostis stolonifera* or one of its varieties. Also *attrib.*

1790 S. DEANE *New-England Farmer* 115/1 The red top grass is so natural to every soil in this country, that all our old fields..are full of it. **1856, 1889** [see *FINETOP]. **1891** M. E. WILKINS *Humble Romance* 92 The whole yard..[was] covered with a tall waving crop of red-top. **1937** *Range Plant Handbk.* (Forest Service, U.S. Dept. Agric.) G8 It seems preferable to use redtop, as a generic name for most of the native range species of *Agrostis*. **1958** J. G. MACGREGOR *North-West of 16* v. 65 In bays, mostly on the west side and shaded from the afternoon sun, grew Red Top, the glory of the wild hay meadows. In places it was six feet high. **1972** *Daily Colonist* (Victoria, B.C.) 9 Mar. 5/3 The birds [*sc.* prairie chickens] would survive when redtop grass was raised, since it was combined in midsummer.

reduce, *v.* Add: **II. 17. c.** In mod. use, the opposite of OXIDIZE *v.* in Dict. and Suppl.; to cause to undergo reduction. (Further examples.)

1872 *Mining Mag. & Rev.* I. 250 When oxides are heated with carbon, the oxygen they contain combines with the carbon to form two invisible gases..which pass away into the air, the ore being thus 'reduced'. **1890** W. JAGO *Inorg. Chem.* iii. 48 There are other examples of reduction in which the bodies are simply reduced to a lower stage of oxidation. **1935** J. W. MELLOR *Comprehensive Treat. Inorg. & Theoret. Chem.* XIV. lxvii. 608 Cobaltic fluoride in hydrogen at 200° ..is reduced to cobaltous fluoride. **1955** *Sci. News Let.* 7 May 297/2 Using heats as high as 3,100 degrees Fahrenheit, quartzite rock is reduced with coke and charcoal. **1971** *Nature* 1 Jan. 13/1 The resulting electrons are used to reduce carbon dioxide to carbohydrate. **1974** *Sci. Amer.* Dec. 68/3 The molecule that has lost electrons is said to have been oxidized; the one that has received them is said to have been reduced. Thus in photosynthesis water is oxidized and carbon dioxide is reduced.

III. 21. f. *Photogr.* To decrease the density of (a negative or print).

1889 E. J. WALL *Dict. Photogr.* 158 Bromide prints may be reduced in exactly the same way as negatives. **1903** A. WATKINS *Photogr.* 118 Do not throw away paper prints which are too dark from over printing. They can be reduced. **1956** *Focal Encycl. Photogr.* 950/1 Before starting to reduce a negative or print it should be well soaked in water. **1963** P. MOYES *Murder à la Mode* iv. 65 'What does "reducing" mean, exactly?' 'Makin' the print lighter... If the neg's too contrasty, like you can't get the light part to print without the dark's too dark. So you reduce it. By nibbin' the dark part with cyanide.'

22. (Later examples without const.)

1941 *Sun* (Baltimore) 17 Feb. 18/4 He was a top sergeant there. His cooking career began in France in July, 1918, when he was 'reduced' and made a mess sergeant. **1948** PARTRIDGE *Dict. Forces' Slang* 154 *Reduced*, reduced in rank. (Services' colloquialism verging on jargon.) **1953** K. TENNANT *Joyful Condemned* xxiii. 220 The deputy-governor ..had been reduced..because of some trouble in a gaol of which he had been governor.

IV. 26. a. (Later examples.)

1903 E. A. ROSS in *Amer. Jrnl. Sociol.* IX. 197 There never has been a good reason for supposing we shall be able to reduce everything social to a single element. *Ibid.* 198 It is certain, nevertheless, we cannot reduce the whole man to a 'cell' in a 'social organism'. **1920** *Psychol. Rev.* XXVII. 71 The psychological simplification of human behavior, which reduces instinctive conduct to the functioning of psychical dispositions or impulses.

c. Also, to condense, come down *to*. (Further examples.)

1924 *Times Lit. Suppl.* 6 Nov. 704/2 His success or failure hangs..on the degree of intensity with which he fuses his material—and perhaps the old distinction between fancy and imagination reduces in the end to that. **1953** J. B. CARROLL *Study of Lang.* iii. 78 The problem of describing verbal behavior..reduces to the problem of describing the strengths..of verbal responses under various stimulus conditions. **1956** E. H. HUTTEN *Lang. Mod. Physics* iii. 109 The equations of motion for a material particle as given by the general theory reduce to the equations of motion of Newton, when we consider the simplest case of a Euclidean, limited, region of space. **1971** *Ideal Home* Apr. 69/1 The size of houses in sq. ft. has tended to reduce quite rapidly over the last few years. **1973** *Daily Tel.* 15 May 19 (Advt.), After only 8 years the amount you need to pay in cash will reduce and if present conditions continue you pay nothing after 10 years. **1978** *Amer. Polit. Sci. Rev.* Sept. 964/1 Over time those claims reduce to nothing more than rationalizations to maintain power. **1979** *Daily Tel.* 1 Dec. 27 (Advt.), The Company invests 98% to 113% of each payment (depending on your starting age), except in the first two years when these figures reduce to 73% to 89%.

d. To articulate (a speech sound) in a way requiring less muscular effort; to form (a vowel) in a more neutral, centralized articulatory position; to weaken, obscure.

1874 A. J. ELLIS *Early Eng. Pronunc.* IV. 1099/1 Reducing (r_0) from a consonant to a pure glide. *Ibid.* 1315 So that (oo') often falls into the juncture (AA), or else (ee', oo') are reduced to two syllables. **1892** W. W. SKEAT *Primer Eng. Etymol.* ii. 25 The *day* in *Monday* has been reduced to *-dy* (di) in familiar speech. **1909** D. JONES *Pronunc. Eng.* I. 46 Cases occur in which almost all other vowels may be reduced to ə when unstressed. **1934** C. DAVIES *Eng. Pronunc.* 12 Back-rounded vowels were unrounded and reduced to an indistinct sound similar to [ʌ] or [ə]. **1957** E. J. DOBSON *Eng. Pronunc. 1500–1700* II. x. 871 The unstressed back vowels seem not to have been reduced to [ə] as early as ME *ĕ*. **1962** A. C. GIMSON *Introd. Pronunc. Eng.* vii. 143 In present RP the secondary accent has been lost and the former [e] or [ɛ:] reduced to [ə] or elided.

e. *intr.* To lessen one's weight, to slim.

1926 MAINES & GRANT *Wise-Crack Dict.* 12/2 *Perpendicular your outline*, reduce a little. **1929** E. LINKLATER *Poet's Pub* xii. 145 'And how did they reduce?' asked Jean... 'They perspired without shame,' said the professor. **1958** *Times Lit. Suppl.* 13 June 334/5 A commendably simple and, at the same time, reliable guide for those who wish to 'reduce' without too much trouble. **1963** R. WOLFF *I, Keturah* (1964) II. xvii. 230 Miss Hawthorne said abruptly 'I think you ought to reduce, Keturah.' So she bought a book on dieting. **1971** *Homes & Gardens* Sept. 65/3, I try continually to reduce, but you cannot take a couple out for a gay evening and be on a diet.

reduced, *ppl. a.* Add: **4. e.** Mathematically modified to a more convenient form.

1862 E. ATKINSON tr. *Ganot's Elem. Treat. Physics* X. ix. 724 The resistance offered by the element and galvanometer is equal to the resistance of 4·08 yards of such copper wire, and this is said to be the reduced length of the element and galvanometer in terms of the copper wire. **1916** W. C. McC. LEWIS *Syst. Physical Chem.* II. iii. 90 It is more convenient to make use of the reduced form [of van der Waals' equation], i.e. pressures, volumes, and temperatures will be expressed as fractions..of their critical values. **1930** L. BRAND *Vectorial Mech.* xiv. 445 This is the same as the equation..for a simple pendulum of length $l = k^2/b$. For this reason l is called the reduced length of the pendulum. **1934** H. E. WHITE *Introd. Atomic Spectra* ii. 34 The preceding equations will apply to two masses m and M rotating about their center of mass, if m be replaced by $mM/(m+M) = m/(1+m/M) = \mu$. μ is called the reduced mass and approaches m as $M \to \infty$. **1950** CORBEN & STEHLE *Classical Mech.* iv. 54, μ is called the reduced mass of the system and is given by $\mu = m_1m_2/(m_1+m_2)$. **1973** *Sci. Amer.* July 25/2 The 'reduced', or simplified, form of the horn equation shows similarly that at any point in the horn the acoustic wavelength depends on the square root of the difference between the squared frequency and a 'horn function' U that depends in a rather simple way on the nature of the horn flare.

6. b. *Phonetics.* Of a vowel sound: articulated less distinctly than a stressed vowel; weakened and centralized; become more obscure than the vowel of which it is a reflex.

Much used in descriptions of the reduced grade of ablaut theory in Indo-European philology.

1894 V. HENRY *Short Compar. Gram. Eng. & German* I. iii. 76 To a normal grade *ĕy, ĕw*, there corresponds a reduced grade *ĭ, ŭ*. **1909** O. JESPERSEN *Mod. Eng. Gram.* I. xv. 423 Besides this 'full' [ə] we have a reduced [ə]. **1938** *Language* XIV. 41 Statements that the reduced grade preceded the accent and the zero grade followed it conflict with some of the best established and most pervading ablaut schemes. **1957** E. J. DOBSON *Eng. Pronunc. 1500–1700* II. x. 868 Gil uses *ĕ* as the symbol for the reduced vowel from ME *ŭ* in *oner* 'honour'. **1962** A. C. GIMSON *Introd. Pronunc. Eng.* vii. 120 As the great variety of spellings indicates, /ə/ may represent the reduced (obscured, 'schwa') form of any vowel or diphthong in an unaccented position. **1964** *Language* XL. 156 Indo-European reconstructions would require a consideration of laryngeals or reduced-grade vowels or both. **1968** CHOMSKY & HALLE *Sound Pattern Eng.* 28 The segment represented as ə will be referred to as the 'reduced vowel'. **1972** A. A. PRINS *Hist. Eng. Phonemes* i. 38 Indo-European had the following vowel system:..Reduced Vowels: $ə_1$, $ə_2$.

c. *spec.* Lowered in price.

1939 JOYCE *Finnegans Wake* (1964) I. 166 A real fur, reduced to 3/9. **1941** E. BOWEN *Look at all these Roses* 8 She came up to London..and bought reduced coats and shoes for the little girls. **1975** M. KENYON *Mr Big* xviii. 174 It's *reduced.* And it really fits.

reduceless (rĭdiū·slĕs), *a.* [f. REDUCE *v.* + -LESS.] Incapable of reduction, that cannot be lessened.

c **1864** E. DICKINSON *Poems* (1955) II. 641 As an Estate perpetual Or a reduceless Mine. **1954** W. FAULKNER *Fable* 16 They wore..the same regimental numerals, to the rest of the regiment which had not only preceded them by that reduceless gap but which had even seemed to be fleeing from them.

reducend. For † *Obs.* read *rare* and add later examples.

1847 G. BOOLE *Math. Anal. of Logic* 45 Reducend Mood, *Baroko.* **1880** W. H. S. MONCK *Introd. Logic* xvi. 181 Both extremes of the Reducend Syllogism occur in its conclusion.

reducer. Add: **1.** (Further example.)

1923 W. S. MAUGHAM *Our Betters* I. 23 He's the great reducer... What does he reduce?.. The Duchess of Arlington told me he'd taken nine pounds off her.

2. c. For *Photogr.* read *Chem.* (cf. sense 2 e below). (Further examples.)

1935 J. N. FRIEND *Text-bk. Physical Chem.* II. vii. 302 When E_0 is negative the ion in the lower state of oxidation.. functions as a reducer or reductant. **1973** *Sci. Amer.* Oct. 128/2 The oxidant, hydrogen peroxide, is stored in a plastic bag within the pressure vessel and mixed in the exit opening with reducer in the soap.

e. *Photogr.* A chemical used to reduce the density of a print or negative.

1897 E. J. WALL *Dict. Photogr.* (ed. 7) 500 Belitski's Reducer. This is the most convenient as it is one solution. *Ibid.* 501 If the negative has been dried, soak in water till wet, then cover with the reducer. **1905** *Westm. Gaz.* 25 Feb. 14/2 This [*sc.* Farmer's] reducer is compounded of potassium ferricyanide solution, and a solution of hypo. **1911** [see *BLEACHER 4]. **1960** G. A. GLAISTER *Gloss. Bk.* 342/2 Proportional reducers exert a uniform action on the negative, thus preserving the tone. **1977** J. HEDGECOE *Photographer's Handbk.* 242 Persulfate reducer..makes a better reducer for negatives which are over-developed and therefore need less density and contrast.

f. A means of reducing one's weight.

1903 E. SANDYS in *Athletics for Women* 99 For those able to dispense with a few pounds of surplus adipose tissue, it [*sc.* swimming] is one of the best of reducers.

g. *Printing.* (See quot. 1968).

1963 KENNEISON & SPILMAN *Dict. Printing* 161 *Reducers*, the addition of varnish, boiled oils, etc., to printing inks to enable them to work more easily. **1968** *Gloss. Terms Offset Lithogr. Printing* (*B.S.I.*) 26 *Reducer.* 1. A liquid, miscible with ink, used to reduce its consistency. 2. A substance for addition to a printing ink to reduce its colour strength without necessarily affecting its consistency.

reducibility. Add: spec. in *Logic*, as *axiom of reducibility* (see quot. 1952).

1910 WHITEHEAD & RUSSELL *Principia Math.* I. 168 (*heading*) The hierarchy of types and the axiom of reducibility. *Ibid.* 174 We assume, then, that every function of one variable is equivalent, for all its values, to some predicative function of the same argument. This assumption seems to be the essence of the usual assumption of classes; at any rate, it retains as much of classes as we have any use for... We will call this assumption the *axiom of classes*, or the *axiom of reducibility*. **1930** L. S. STEBBING *Mod. Introd. Logic* xxiii. 463 Ramsey has suggested a reconstruction of the system of *Principia Mathematica* in which the axiom of reducibility is no longer needed. **1942** D. D. RUNES *Dict. Philos.* 266/2 As an indication or rough description of the axiom of reducibility, it may be said that it cancels a large part of the restrictive consequences of the prohibition against impredicative definition..and, in approximate effect, reduces the ramified theory of types to the simple theory of types. **1952** S. C. KLEENE *Introd*

Metamath. iii. 44 To escape this outcome, Russell postulated his *axiom of reducibility*, which asserts that to any property belonging to an order above the lowest, there is a coextensive property (i.e. one possessed by exactly the same objects) of order 0. **1963** W. V. QUINE *Set Theory & its Logic* xi. 251 The axiom of reducibility regales us after all with attributes unspecifiable except by quantifying over attributes whose order is as high as their own.

reducible, *a.* **4. a.** (Later examples.)

1932 LEWIS & LANGFORD *Symbolic Logic* ix. 282 Functions like this one, which can be expressed in equivalent form by means of functions of a lower degree of generality, will be said to be *reducible*. **1967** R. A. GEORGE tr. *Carnap's Logical Struct. of World* I. 6 An object (or concept) is said to be reducible to one or more other objects if all statements about it can be transformed into statements about these other objects.

b. (Later examples in *Chem.*)

Absence of a const. is usual in this sense.

1903 H. C. JONES *Elem. Inorg. Chem.* xxii. 281 Cobaltous oxide..is a greenish powder, easily reducible to the metal. **1957** G. E. HUTCHINSON *Treat. Limnol.* I. xi. 707 Some of both oxidizable and reducible iron was no doubt in organic combination. **1976** *Nature* 15 Jan. 147/1 These bulk membranes, being less dense than water, separated aqueous reducing agents and potentially reducible substrates.

reducing, *vbl. sb.* Add: **2.** (in sense *26 e of the vb.) *reducing belt, pill, treatment*; **reducing gear** = *reduction gear* s.v. *REDUCTION 13; **reducing machine,** an apparatus for producing scale models.

1928 A. HUXLEY *Point Counter Point* v. 69 No idea how comfortable those rubber reducing belts are till you've tried them. **1917** E. BUTLER *Transmission Gears* iii. 66 The first use of a planetary reducing gear as a transmission between a petrol motor and the driving wheel of an automobile, was made in 1888–9 by Edward Butler on his petrol cycle. **1947** J. C. RICH *Materials & Methods of Sculpture* vi. 191 In using platinum or palladium for medals, the original model is first cast in a hard bronze, and by means of a reducing machine a small steel die is cut of the precise size of the medal. With this die the copies are struck. **1968** *Canad. Antiques Collector* July 10/1 Benjamin Cheverton's 'reducing machine' had been employed for the scale model. This ingenious machine kept proportions exact, so that a six-inch statuette would lose nothing of the artistry of the original. **1955** W. GADDIS *Recognitions* II. vii. 608 I'm taking *scads* of these marvelous reducing pills that simply take your appetite away. **1907** F. H. BURNETT *Shuttle* xix. 195 Mina is growing fat, and spends her days in taking reducing treatments.

reductant (rǐdʌ·ktǎnt). *Chem.* [f. REDUCT(ION + -ANT[1], after OXIDANT.] A reducing agent.

1925 *Chem. Rev.* II. 128 The heroic efforts to measure the potential of a pure solution of a reductant are evidence of the tenacity of a preconception. **1935** [see *REDUCER 2 c]. **1968** J. MARCH *Adv. Org. Chem.* xix. 853 In some cases both the oxidant and reductant are organic. **1976** *Sci. Amer.* July 71/2 The process is termed gaseous direct reduction or solid direct reduction depending on the state of the reductant.

reductase (rǐdʌ·ktēⁱz). *Biochem.* [ad. F. *réductase* (M.-E. Pozzi-Escot 1902, in *Bull. de la Soc. Chim. de Paris* XXVII. 559), f. *réduct-ion* REDUCTION: see *-ASE.] **a.** Any enzyme which promotes chemical reduction.

1902 *Jrnl. Chem. Soc.* LXXXII. I. 655 The author [*sc.* Pozzi-Escot] has discovered a new class of diastases which he calls 'reductases'. **1914** [see *DEHYDRASE a]. **1938** *Ann. Rev. Biochem.* VII. 112 The protein of acetaldehyde reductase has been obtained in a crystalline condition. **1974** *Nature* 13 Dec. 579/1 The enzymes responsible for the first step in nitrate assimilation and for nitrate respiration are the nitrate reductases, both these processes involving the conversion of nitrate to nitrite. **1977** *Proc. R. Soc. Med.* LXX. 617/1 Thurnham..measured the erythrocyte glutathione reductase activity.

b. reductase test, a method of estimating the bacterial content of a sample of fluid, usu. milk, by measuring its reducing power.

1910 *Analyst* XXXV. 207 (*heading*) Reductase test for milk. **1932** *Discovery* Feb. 59/2 In the north of Europe.. general use is made of the 'reductase' test, which takes the time required to decolourize a definite solution of methylene blue as a measure of the purity of milk. **1964** *Biol. Abstr.* XLV. 3876/1 Application of the reductase test to 261 randomly selected staphylococcus strains showing a positive plasma coagulase test yielded reductase times of 15 minutes or less in 96·6% of the cases.

‖ **reductio** (rǐdʌ·ktio). Pl. **reductiones** (rǐdʌktiōᵘ·nīz). [L., = REDUCTION.] Used in various Latin phrases: **1. reductio ad impossibile,** reduction to the impossible: a method of proving a proposition by drawing an absurd or impossible conclusion from its contradictory.

1552 T. WILSON *Rule of Reason* (ed. 2) f. 56 The other croked waye (called of the Logicians, *Reductio ad impossibile*) is a reduccion to that, whiche is impossible. **1843** J. S. MILL *Logic* I. II. iii. 265 We shall thus discover the error in our generalisation, by what the schoolmen termed a *reductio ad impossibile*. **1869** W. S. JEVONS *Substitution of Similars* 44 This indirect or negative method is closely analogous to the *indirect proof*, or *reductio ad absurdum*, so frequently used by Euclid and other mathematicians, and a similar method is employed by the old logicians in the treatment of the syllogisms called *Baroko* and *Bokardo*, by the *reductio ad impossibile*. **1884** J. N. KEYNES *Formal Logic* III. iv. 181 This method of reduction is called *Reductio ad impossibile*, or *Reductio per impossibile*, or *Deductio ad impossibile*, or *Deductio ad absurdum*. **1962** W. & M. KNEALE *Devel. Logic* i. 8 What Aristotle attributed to Zeno was presumably the discovery of the use of the *reductio ad impossibile* in metaphysics.

2. reductio ad absurdum: reduction to the absurd (see REDUCTION 9 b). Also with superl. **reductio ad absurdissimum** (the most absurd, the greatest absurdity).

1741 I. WATTS *Improvement of Mind* I. xiii. 181 *The Respondent* may be attack'd either upon a Point of his own Concession, which is call'd *Argumentum ex concessis*, or by reducing him to an Absurdity, which is call'd *Reductio ad absurdum*. **1824** J. S. MILL in *Westm. Rev.* II. 34 This we admit: and we regard it as a decisive *reductio ad absurdum* of his own argument. **1865** —— *Exam. Hamilton's Philos.* iv. 44 Hegel..has fairly earned the honour..of having logically extinguished transcendental metaphysics by a series of *reductiones ad absurdissimum*. **1896** G. B. SHAW *Our Theatres in Nineties* (1932) II. 170 Madame Sarah Grand's position is a *reductio ad absurdum* of our whole moral system. **1931** *Times Educ. Suppl.* 10 Jan. 9/4 A *reductio ad absurdissimum* is seen in the fact that an aspirant for employment in a business house, who has actually qualified for exemption from matriculation by virtue of the subjects endorsed on his school certificate, is not infrequently informed that his application cannot be entertained unless he produces the actual matriculation certificate. **1939** *Canadian Forum* July 126/2 It..may prove to be no more than the *reductio ad absurdum* of his own introspectiveness. **1955** *Times* 23 June 11/3 When the House of Commons regards even nationalized boards as little more than civil servants, and piles a committee on top of their committee we approach the *reductio ad absurdum*. **1963** [see *Christocentricity* s.v. *CHRISTO-]. **1969** L. RUBY *Art of Making Sense* (rev. ed.) viii. 84 Here is a more complex sample of the reductio ad absurdum. **1976** *Times Lit. Suppl.* 3 Dec. 1522/4 Whether the result represents anything more than a reductio ad absurdum of the traditional musicological pastime of theme-spotting. **1977** *Time* 7 Feb. 51/1 *Reductio* is always *ad absurdum*.

reduction. Add: **II. 6. e.** *transf.* The process of explaining behaviour, social or mental activity, etc., by reducing it to its component factors or to a simpler form; also by ascribing a complex result to the operation of a few or one of its factors.

1916 A. A. BRILL tr. *Freud's Wit & its Relation to Unconsc.* ii. 28 The briefest reduction of the meaning by which one could replace this joke would be..[etc.]. **1927** W. M. WHEELER in *Proc. 6th Internat. Congr. Philos., 1926* 34 The reduction of these new properties to those of the parts in the sense of identification, and the finding of a causal determination also in this sense is impossible. **1928** H. G. & C. F. BAYNES tr. *Jung's Contrib. to Analytical Psychol.* 56 When the unsuitable structures have been reduced, and the natural course of things restored, the possibility of a normal life being thus attained, reduction is not to be pushed further. **1950** H. HARTMANN *Ess. Ego Psychol.* (1964) vi. 112 We may refer to such simplifications as 'theories by reduction'. They see one specific phase..as the sole causative factor for a character type. **1960** J. STRACHEY in *Freud's Compl. Wks.* VIII. 23 Here and elsewhere in this work Freud uses the word 'reduction' in the sense of taking something back to its original form. **1960** R. F. C. HULL tr. *Jung's Gen. Aspects of Dream Psychol.* in *Coll. Wks.* VIII. 240 Obviously this reduction is quite unsatisfying from the scientific point of view... The discovery of a single antecedent is by no means sufficient.

f. *Computers.* The transformation of data into a simpler or more amenable form.

1958 *Jrnl. Assoc. Computing Machinery* V. 89 (*heading*) Special purpose analog machine for data reduction. **1969** P. B. JORDAIN *Condensed Computer Encycl.* 423 Reduction can take several forms: changing the encoding to eliminate redundancy, or extracting significant details from the data and eliminating the rest or choosing every second or third out of the totality of available points.

7. b. *reduction sentence*: a sentence giving conditions for the use of a concept less strict than a definition.

1936 R. CARNAP in *Philos. of Sci.* III. 441 We shall call R_1 and R_2 reduction sentences for 'Q_3' and '$\sim Q_3$' respectively. **1949** [see *non-dispositional* s.v. *NON- 3]. **1963** A. PAP *Introd. Philos. of Sci.* ii. 32 The virtue of the reduction sentence, then, is that it permits us to ascribe a disposition *D* to an object only if the relevant experiment has been performed and found to have a positive outcome. **1965** P. CAWS *Philos. of Sci.* viii. 54 Carnap..closes the loophole in the definition by rewriting it as a *reduction sentence*.

10. a. Also in *Chem.*, the opposite of OXIDATION (senses a and b in Dict. and Suppl.): the removal of oxygen from, or addition of hydrogen to, a compound; partial or complete donation of an electron to an atom or molecule; a decrease in the proportion of electronegative constituents in a molecule or compound. (Further examples.)

1900 W. A. SHENSTONE *Inorg. Chem.* 177 The terms oxidation and reduction are no longer confined to changes in which oxygen plays a part... The term reduction may be applied to any change which involves a decrease in the relative amount of the negative radicle present in a compound. **1913** J. B. COHEN *Org. Chem. Adv. Students* II. ii. 100 The difference between the two catalysts is also brought out in the case of heptine C_7H_{12}, copper giving heptene C_7H_{14} and polymerisation products.., and nickel effecting complete reduction to heptane. **1930** L. B. FLEXNER tr. *L. Michaelis's Oxidation–Reduction Potentials* 10 We shall simply collect together as equivalent processes (1) the addition of oxygen, (2) the loss of hydrogen, and (3) the loss of electrons and call them all oxidations, and their converses, reductions. **1950** N. V. SIDGWICK *Chem. Elements* II. 1327 Ferrous compounds are formed either from the metal or by the reduction of the ferric. **1964** N. G. CLARK *Mod. Org. Chem.* x. 177 Aldehydes readily undergo reduction to alcohols. **1970** AMBROSE & EASTY *Cell Biol.* ii. 62 Reduction is regarded conversely as involving a gain of electrons, and substances which have the characteristic of giving up electrons to other substances are called reducing agents. **1979** *Archaeology* July–Aug. 21/2 When there is a lack of oxygen in the 'reduction' the iron oxide constituent of the earthenware clay remains in its ferrous or black state.

d. *Philos.* In phenomenology, the process of reducing an object of consciousness or an idea to its pure essence through elimination of all reference to extraneous things, in particular by eliminating (or 'bracketing') all reference to the real world of material objects; esp. as *eidetic, phenomenological, transcendental reduction*. (See quot. 1943.)

1914 *Mind* XXIII. 590 He [*sc.* Husserl] deals in a most valuable section with the relation of consciousness to natural reality, with the province of pure consciousness, and with the phenomenological reductions. **1924** *Monist* XXXIV. 520 To carry out the 'phenomenological reduction', i.e., to isolate an object from its existential or systematic connections, is equivalent to considering it as it is originally given, without the distorting influences of 'theory'. **1931** W. R. B. GIBSON tr. *Husserl's Ideas* 44 The corresponding Reduction which leads from the psychological phenomenon to the pure 'essence', or,..from factual ('empirical') to 'essential' universality, is the eidetic Reduction. *Ibid.* 114 We propose to speak..of phenomenological reductions... From the epistemological viewpoint we would also speak of transcendental reductions. **1943** M. FARBER *Found. Phenomenol.* i. 20 The 'reduction' opens up a universal field for philosophical investigation which is free from all prejudgements and assumptions, hence its crucial methodological importance. Husserl is careful to distinguish eidetic reduction (proceeding from fact to essence) from transcendental reduction, according to which the phenomena are characterized as 'irreal'... The method of phenomenological reduction is applied in order to achieve the presuppositionless field of philosophy. **1966** A. GURWITSCH *Stud. Phenomenol. & Psychol.* v. 111 Performance of the transcendental without the eidetic reduction discloses the flow of 'my' transcendentally purified mental states in phenomenal time. **1970** A. GIORGI *Psychol. as Human Sci.* iii. 148 By means of the phenomenological reduction, i.e., by a change in attitude, the world can be considered as phenomenon. **1972** H. SPIEGELBERG *Phenomenol. in Psychol. & Psychiatry* ii. 76 He did not believe in a strict separation between the world of essences and the world of facts, thus rejecting Husserl's 'eidetic reduction'.

11. b. *spec.* of the size of a copy or photographic image in photography, microphotography, etc.

1889 E. J. WALL *Dict. Photogr.* 158 Whereas in enlargements the greater distance is between lens and sensitive surface, in the case of reduction the greater distance must be between the lens and negative. **1959** F. LUTHER *Microfilm* 1 Reductions greater than those now in common use were employed to produce microfilms that could meet the rule-of-thumb test of quality, that is, be enlarged back to original size without substantial loss of definition or legibility. **1962** A. GÜNTHER *Microphotogr. in Libr.* 5 The advantages of the use of photographic reduction in recording documents are so obvious that it is not surprising that the first microphotograph was made shortly after the invention of photography. **1965** *Focal Encycl. Photogr.* II. 1255/1 Reduction in printing, in copying and graphic arts work applies to reproduction at a scale of less than 1:1 or same size. **1973** D. A. SPENCER *Focal Dict. Photogr. Technol.* 518 A 1:3 reduction is a copy that is one-third of the linear size of the original.

c. *Photogr.* Diminution of the density of a print or negative.

1889 E. J. WALL *Dict. Photogr.* 158 Reduction will proceed in proportion to the amount of ferridcyanide [*sic*] present. **1902** A. WATKINS *Photogr.* 93 Where a rapid plate (of poor quality) does not seem to give sufficient contrast before it fogs over, a knowledge of reduction and intensifying will often give a good negative. **1956** *Focal Encycl. Photogr.* 951/2 The object of reduction is to make a very dense negative easier to print, or to lighten undesirably black areas of a print. **1977** J. HEDGECOE *Photographer's Handbk.* 242 Assess the progress of reduction by removing the negative at frequent intervals.

d. *Mus.* Transcription of a full orchestral score for a smaller number of instruments, esp. for piano; the reduced score thus produced.

1884 F. NIECKS *Dict. Mus. Terms* 273 *Riduzione*, reduction. **1966** [see *piano reduction* s.v. *PIANO *sb.*[2] 2 d]. **1973** L. LOCKWOOD in A. Tyson *Beethoven Stud.* 118 (*caption*) Reduction of *Sehnsucht*, bars 3–6. **1979** [see *open score* s.v. *OPEN *a.* (*adv.*) 22 c]. **1980** *Times* 28 June 9/7 Mahler songs, not in their familiar orchestral settings but in piano versions. Some are originals, some reductions, and some fall in between.

e. *Cytology.* The halving of the number of chromosomes per cell that occurs at one of the two anaphases of meiosis (cf. *POST-REDUCTION, *PREREDUCTION); chiefly *attrib.* in **reduction division,** the meiotic cell division during which reduction occurs. [The senses are due to A. Weismann, who used G. *reduktion, reduktionstheilung* (*Über die Zahl der Richtungskörper und über ihre Bedeutung für die Vererbung* (1887) i. 14, ii. 35).]

1891 *Jrnl. R. Microsc. Soc.* 461 There is a 'reduction-division', for twelve chromosomes are found in each new cell. **1896** E. B. WILSON *Cell* v. 182 The process of reduction is very obviously a provision to hold constant the number of chromosomes characteristic of a species. **1906** *Rep. Brit. Assoc. Adv. Sci. 1905* 570 Weissman predicted that a transverse division of the chromosomes would be found to take place by which the reduction would be brought about. *Ibid.*, A true reduction division is found to occur in the heterotype stage. **1927** HALDANE & HUXLEY *Animal Biol.* ii. 59 Instead of the chromosomes dividing, the members of a pair come to lie side by side; and at division one whole chromosome of a pair is separated from the other. This process is called the reduction of the chromosomes, for owing to it, each of the two cells produced at this division possess only half of the ordinary number of chromosomes for the species. **1931** E. B. FORD *Mendelism & Evolution* i. 12 Each chromosome must contain many factors. These will be inherited together for, at the reduction division, they will pass into the same germ cell without the opportunity of random assortment. **1948** H. P. RILEY *Genetics & Cytogenetics* iv. 65 The reduction division reduces the *number* of chromosomes and centromeres. **1971** D. J. COVE *Genetics* i. 7 This type of cell division whereby a diploid cell can give rise to haploid cells is called reduction division. **1979** *Sci. Amer.* Feb. 104/1 Meiosis, the 'reduction division' whereby one male germ cell divides to form four sperm cells, each of which has half the normal complement of chromosomes.

f. *Phonetics.* Weakening; obscuring (of a vowel); substitution of a sound which requires less muscular effort to articulate.

1909 O. JESPERSEN *Mod. Eng. Gram.* I. ix. 260 Weak /iu/ has in some words kept both sounds, though with an early reduction of /i/ to /j/. **1953** K. JACKSON *Lang. & Hist. Early Brit.* 293 The reduction of pretonic ǫ̆ to ŏ in Welsh. **1959** C. L. WRENN *Word & Symbol* (1967) 39 *Gerrans*..shows the regular Cornish reduction of the final *t* to *s*. **1962** A. C. GIMSON *Introd. Pronunc. Eng.* vii. 120 This reduction of unaccented vowels, typical of a stress-accent language such as English, has been a feature of the English sound system for over a thousand years. **1970** B. M. H. STRANG *Hist. Eng.* vi. 342 The reduction of vowels is a sign that these formal distinctions were no longer functionally important.

g. Reducing or limiting the use of addictive drugs. Usu. *attrib.*

1914 JACKSON & HELLYER *Vocab. Criminal Slang* 69 *Reduction*.., the reduction cure for a 'habit'. Example: 'The only sensible way of getting off is on the reduction'. **1953** W. BURROUGHS *Junkie* iii. 39 The 'thirty-day cure'. This is not a reduction cure. They don't give any junk... All they offer the addict is thirty days' detention. *Ibid.* viii. 73, I have never known one of these self-administered reduction cures to work. **1962** 'K. ORVIS' *Damned & Destroyed* ii. 18 You've tried everything with your daughter, haven't you?..Forced her to take cold-shock and reduction treatments.

13. reduction division: see sense 11 e above; **reduction gear** *Engin.*, a system of gear wheels in which the driven shaft rotates more slowly than the driving shaft; so **reduction gearing**; **reduction negative, print** *Photogr.*, a negative or print made from a larger original; so **reduction printing.**

1896 E. T. CARTER *Motive Power & Gearing* xxviii. 532 The double reduction gear used on the Frankfort-Offenbach tramcars. **1942** *R.A.F. Jrnl.* 3 Oct. 18 The port propeller amd reduction gear casing were wrenched off. **1971** B. SCHARF *Engin. & its Lang.* xii. 161 Any system of gears in which the speed of the driven shaft is lower than the speed of the driving shaft may be described as a reduction gear. **1896** E. T. CARTER *Motive Power & Gearing* 617/1 (Index), Reduction gearing. **1934** *Jane's Fighting Ships* 94 Turbines with single reduction gearing. **1942** J. LISTON *Aircraft Engine Design* viii. 146 The inherent tendency for the propeller efficiency to drop at high speeds can be offset by suitable reduction gearing. **1945** *Jrnl. Soc. Motion Picture Engineers* Apr. 290 This process [*sc.* reduction printing] is commonly used in making 16-mm negatives or prints from 35-mm originals. Film thus made is referred to as a reduction negative or reduction print, as the case may be. **1943** *Ibid.* Dec. 507 An effort was made to learn if the wows introduced into the reduction prints by the printer itself could be reduced by an increase in the speed of the printer. **1973** D. A. SPENCER *Focal Dict. Photogr. Technol.* 420 The assembly is also used to make reduction prints—e.g. by projecting 35 mm film on to 16 mm raw stock in the camera. **1945** *Jrnl. Soc. Motion Picture Engineers* Apr. 290 Reduction printing is the process of producing and recording photographically a smaller image, usually on a smaller film, from a larger image.

reductional *a.* (examples in *Cytology*: cf. sense 11 e above); **redu·ctionally** *adv.*

1903 *Biol. Bull.* IV. 266 Van Winiwarter..considers it probable that one of these divisions is reductional. **1905** *Proc. Acad. Nat. Sci. Philadelphia* LVII. 195 There is no evidence that chromosomes divide in different ways in the first maturation mitosis, some equationally and some reductionally. **1914** *Jrnl. Morphol.* XXV. 622 The univalent chromosomes..conjugate first in the equator of the first maturation spindle and there separate reductionally. **1920** etc. [see *EQUATIONAL *a.* 3]. **1939** SANSOME & PHILP *Rec. Adv. Plant Genetics* (ed. 2) vi. 183 Muller's Theory implies that the whole chromosome divides reductionally at the first division of meiosis. **1975** *Nature* 8 May 111/1 Normally fertilisation stimulates both the completion of the reductional first meiotic division and the subsequent equational second division.

reductionism (rĭdʌ·kʃəniz'm). [f. REDUCTION + -ISM.] In philosophy, the practice of trying to show that certain entities may be eliminated by reducing all reference to them to reference to some other entities. In more general use, the practice of describing a phenomenon (particularly one involving human thought and action) in terms of an apparently more 'basic' or 'primitive' phenomenon, to which the first is then said to be equivalent; for example, the practices of describing mental states in terms of the behaviour that expresses them, of describing organic processes in terms of the physicochemical reactions which underly them, of describing social and political transformations in terms of the economic changes which engender them. In each case it is supposed that 'reduction' both explains, and also simplifies; 'reductionism' is therefore often used as a term of abuse for those theories which simplify too much, by reducing one phenomenon to another that is too basic to explain it.

1948 A. L. KROEBER *Anthropol.* (rev. ed.) xv. 576 The whole problem of the double aspect of our phenomena can also be seen as hingeing on how far we wish..to carry or not to carry what might be called intellectual reductionism. **1952** R. M. HARE *Lang. Morals* 180 Nor am I committing the sin of 'reductionism' which, because of its excessive prevalence, has become a fashionable target for philosophical heresy-hunters. **1953** W. V. QUINE *From Logical Point of View* 20 The other dogma is *reductionism*: the belief that each meaningful statement is equivalent to some logical construct upon terms which refer to immediate experience. **1960** B. G. ANDREAS *Exper. Psychol.* viii. 212 In theory construction reductionism refers to the use of constants and laws from one scientific discipline to explain the relationship found in another realm of investigation. **1965** *Jrnl. Politics* XXVII. 783 Reductionism. In its belief that every major irritation in society has a simple cause, a simple explanation and a simple solution, the radical right reduces such irritations to Communism. **1969** *Daily Tel.* 1 Nov. 7/7 It [*sc.* the minute dissection of music's anatomical structure] can easily succumb to the kind of 'reductionism' which ..claims that any organism can be fully explained by a careful analysis of its smallest components. **1969** *Times Lit. Suppl.* 20 Nov. 1341/1 Reductionism..assumes that all properties of organisms..are ultimately reducible to physics and chemistry. **1971** R. F. MURPHY *Dialectics of Social Life* (1972) ii. 68 Durkheim..directed his critique against theories that sought to reduce social explanation to areas of psychology and biology that were not known at the time... Such 'reductionism' to the unknown is indeed a shallow gambit. **1976** *Nature* 3 June 439/1 Reductionism rests on the belief that the whole can be fully explained in terms of the parts. **1979** *Bull. Amer. Acad. Arts & Sci.* Apr. 20 What would be needed instead is what I once heard Etienne Gilson describe as a dogmatic basis for dogmatic tolerance. For that we must go beyond the reductionism that has shaped all of us to a historical awareness of the deepest issues that have divided the two communities. **1981** *Times Lit. Suppl.* 6 Feb. 137/4 Structuralism..has offered certain threats to reductionism.

reductionist. Add: **b.** An advocate of reductionism; one who attempts to analyse or account for a complex theory or phenomenon by reduction. Also *attrib.* or as *adj.*

1934 in WEBSTER. **1943** *Mind* LII. 129 The behaviour field which, as a whole, is molar from the reductionist's point of view. **1953** K. BRITTON *John Stuart Mill* iii. 86 Here it was Comte who maintained a reductionist view, holding that all the laws of psychology must find their ultimate explanation in terms of bodily changes. **1956** A. J. AYER in H. D. Lewis *Contemp. Brit. Philos.* 60 The reductionist's hero is the average man who is patently a logical construction. **1960** J. COHEN *Chance, Skill & Luck* i. 13 It does not follow that psychology lacks the status of an independent science and must be 'reduced' to neurophysiology, though this is what latter-day reductionists in effect demand. **1964** I. L. HOROWITZ *New Sociol.* 9 It succeeds in re-tooling the 'culture-lag' doctrine by making it conform to its own reductionist image of society. **1974** M. WILES *Remaking of Christian Doctrine* i. 5 Reductionists who in the face of the evolution of the human species want to say that man is really nothing but his animal ancestry in another form. **1977** *Times Lit. Suppl.* 1 Apr. 409/2 While the interpretation may be reductionist, it is a plausible one.

reductioni·stic, *a.* [f. REDUCTION + -ISTIC.] = REDUCTIONIST *a.* Hence **reductioni·stically** *adv.*

1960 B. G. ANDREAS *Exper. Psychol.* viii. 213 In psychology a theory may be considered reductionistic if, in addition to describing behavioral events, it employs constructs from physiology. **1965** *Jrnl. Politics* XXVII. 783 The list of problems and events treated reductionistically is enormous. **1971** *Jrnl. Gen. Psychol.* LXXXIV. 152 It is quite easy to see how each generation of reductionistically oriented theorizers was so easily seduced into using the most current, exciting, interesting, and potentially useful technology as the basis for its ideas. **1974** B. F. SKINNER *About Behaviorism* xiv. 240 A science of behavior has been said to dehumanize man because it is reductionistic. **1976** SMYTHIES & CORBETT *Psychiatry* i. 7 Current sociological theory is just as fragmented, disorganized and reductionistic as Freudian psychology.

reductive, *a.* and *sb.* **A.** *adj.* Delete 'Now *rare*' and add: **1. b.** *Psychol.* That leads back to an earlier state.

1928 H. G. & C. F. BAYNES tr. *Jung's Contrib. to Analytical Psychol.* 58 If now, by means of a reductive procedure, we uncover the infantile pre-stages of an adult psyche, we find as the ultimate foundation the infantile seeds. **1950** J. A. HADFIELD *Psychol. & Mental Health* xvi. 410 We style our method direct reductive analysis: it is reductive in that we analyse back to the deep-seated and predisposing causes as well as the more recent and precipitating causes. **1962** *Listener* 29 Mar. 568/2 Psychoanalysis is primarily historical and reductive, deducing the analysand's present situation from his past history. **1967** J. A. HADFIELD *Introd. Psychotherapy* xxii. 182 By reductive analysis I mean all those systems of psychotherapy whose methods are to go into the past to discover the causes of the neurosis in childhood experiences.

2. a. (Further examples.)

1924 C. E. MONTAGUE *Right Place* iii. 29 Calvin cast his reductive shadow over the naturally high spirits of Scotland. **1957** G. E. HUTCHINSON *Treat. Limnol.* I. ix. 626 Reductive organic sediments. **1969** *Listener* 14 Aug. 203/3 A British cinema..need not be one that seeks to indoctrinate foreigners in some reductive British image. **1974** *Times* 19 Nov. 9/4 Mr. Wilson..is not a reductive writer: he wants to recreate Crowley, not to explain him away. **1979** *Quarto* Oct. 3/4 There may be something reductive in Wolfe's constant harping on the rivalry and the petty resentments of the astronauts and their wives.

b. That tends to reduce, or is connected with reduction, esp. *REDUCTION 6 e and 7 b. (See also *REDUCTIONISM.)

1937 T. PARSONS *Struct. Social Action* v. 181 He [*sc.* Pareto] is thus free at the outset at least from the 'reductive' tendencies so prominent in the older positivism. **1957** P. LAFITTE *Person in Psychol.* v. 62 Reductive tendencies in social psychology can now be considered. The first of these is the tendency to see the person as an object which is pushed around in a field of force. **1966** O. WOJTASIEWICZ tr. *Kotarbinski's Gnosiology* IV. i. 221 All reasonings are usually divided into deductive and reductive, the former being from reason to consequence, and the latter, from consequence to reason. **1977** R. WILLIAMS *Marxism & Lit.* I. iv. 62 What is in fact idealized, in the ordinary reductive view, is 'thinking' or 'imagining'. **1979** *Dædalus* Summer 96 The search for a common denominator can prove fruitful—if it does not degenerate into a reductive maneuver.

c. *Art.* = *MINIMAL *a.* c.

1967 *New Yorker* 25 Feb. 99 To judge by art magazines and museum programs, nothing new has been done in the past few years but Happenings, optical displays, and so-called primary structures and reductive paintings. **1970** *Britannica Bk. of Year 1969* 798/3 *Rejective art*, a simplified and often depersonalized art (as painting or sculpture) based on the principle of the artist rejecting the various options open to him; called also *reductive art, reductivism, rejectivism.*

B. *sb.* For † read *rare* and add later examples.

1871 T. D. HAYE tr. *Taine's On Intelligence* I. II. i. 53 It is the *special reductive*, that is to say, the contradictory sensation, which fails in the conflict, and, instead of depriving the image of its externality, becomes itself effaced. **1890** W. JAMES *Princ. Psychol.* II. 125 The usual explanation of hypnagogic hallucinations is that they are ideas deprived of their ordinary reductives.

reductivism (rĭdʌ·ktiviz'm). [f. REDUCTIVE *a.* and *sb.* + -ISM.] **1.** *Art.* = *MINIMALISM.

1967 *Listener* 17 Aug. 220 Bernard Cohen's *White Plant* dates from the period when his earlier 'linguistic' style had degenerated into a hothouse aestheticism; the rather self-conscious reductivism of his recent exhibition was far less cloying. **1970** [see *REDUCTIVE *a.* 2 c].

2. = *REDUCTIONISM.

1972 *Village Voice* (N.Y.) 1 June 74/3 Dylan had been moving toward Duchamp's brand of Cartesian reductivism and public withdrawal. **1975** *Times Lit. Suppl.* 23 May 566/1 The reductivism implied in this enterprise—the reducing of ideas to another level of meaning or set of causes.

So **redu·ctivist** *a.* and *sb.* = *minimalist* s.v. *MINIMAL *a.* c.

1967 *Listener* 13 July 45/3 Harold and Bernard Cohen were the two foremost British painters during the early 'sixties who were trying to evolve a visual language to correspond to what 'the artist thinks'. Now both seem to have given this up as a bad job and fallen in line with current reductivist tendencies. **1967** *Sat. Rev.* (U.S.) 23 Sept. 23 New York..is dominated by large numbers of artists who swim in one or two schools producing closely related works—lately, the reductivists and the remainders of the Pop people.

red 'un: see *RED *a.* 3 b.

redund (rĭdʌ·nd), *v. rare.* [Shortened f. REDUND(ANT *a.* and *sb.*] **a.** *intr.* To be redundant; to contain a redundancy. **b.** *trans.* To make redundant.

1905 *Daily Chron.* 16 Jan. 4/7 The phrase 'inadvertently forgotten' does not redund so much as appears. **1959** *Guardian* 23 Dec. 4/1 'I've worked here before,' said another, 'but I was redunded in May.'

redundancy. Add: **2.** *spec.* **a.** *Engin.* The presence in a framework of more members than are needed to confer rigidity.

1904 J. B. JOHNSON et al. *Theory & Pract. Mod. Framed Structures* (ed. 8) I. xxv. 260 Another common example of redundancy is where two diagonals are used in the same quadrilateral. **1923** W. L. MARSH *Internat. Air Congr., London, 1923* 828 Owing to the extreme redundancy of the structure [of the airship] the calculations cannot be tackled by the graphical methods employed on most types of girder work construction. **1950** J. C. GRASSIE *Elem. Theory Structures* ix. 129 (*heading*) Conditions for internal and external redundancy in structures. **1966** J. L. MERIAM *Statics* iii. 81 For a truss that is statically determinate externally, there is a definite relation between the number of its members and the number of its joints necessary for internal stability without redundancy.

b. The condition of having more staff in an organization than is necessary. Hence, the state or fact of losing a job because there is no further work to be done; a case of unemployment due to reorganization, mechanization, loss of orders, etc.

1931 *Economist* 11 Apr. 780/1 Such economics create redundancy of staff and unemployment rather than increased employment. **1934** *Planning* II. xxvi. 3 The shipbuilding and wool textiles industries have succeeded in establishing common instruments with which to combat redundancy. **1952** *Economist* 12 July 77 The strike against redundancy is a comparatively new phenomenon in industrial relations. **1955** *Times* 31 Aug. 4/6 The men stopped work after a dispute..over the way to handle redundancy at the works because of a reorganization scheme. **1956** *Economist* 7 July 12/2 The unions now appear ready to lay rather more emphasis on bargaining for higher severance pay, and rather less on demonstrations against the fact of redundancies. **1957** *Observer* 8 Sept. 9/4 This [*sc.* Gloucester] is a rather troubled city, with 15,000 people—nearly a third of the insured population—in the aircraft industry, and the prospect of substantial redundancy as defence contracts run out. **1972** *Accountant* 5 Oct. 420/1 Should a staff surveyor become redundant, redundancy pay would be considered, the maximum benefit being limited to one month's pay (based on salary at the date of redundancy) for every completed year's service. **1976** J. R. L. Anderson *Redundancy Pay* i. 11 The terms of the final merger called for heavy redundancies. **1977** M. Drabble *Ice Age* ii. 240 There isn't any work. There's large-scale unemployment. Redundancies everywhere. **1977** I. Shaw *Beggarman, Thief* iii. vi. 267 We live in the age of what the British call redundancy.

c. *Linguistics.* The element or degree of predictability in a language arising from knowledge of its structure; the fact of superfluity of information in a piece of language.

1948 *Bell Syst. Techn. Jrnl.* XXVII. 398 The redundancy of ordinary English, not considering statistical structure over greater distances than about eight letters, is roughly 50%. **1954** G. A. Miller et al. in J. S. Bruner *Beyond Information Given* (1974) iii. 59 When missing or ambiguous portions of a stimulus pattern can be supplied correctly..on the basis of the context alone, the missing portions carry little or no information. This fact is referred to as the redundancy of the language. **1972** J. L. Dillard *Black English* vii. 283 What the linguist calls redundancy—a technical term..which explains how we are able to understand sentences which we have not heard plainly or to read paragraphs in which a great deal of the print has been scrambled. **1977** A. Sheridan tr. *J. Lacan's Écrits* iii. 86 This notion of redundancy in language originated in research that was all the more precise because a vested interest was involved. **1979** E. H. Gombrich *Sense of Order* iv. 104 It is easy to understand how our grasp of ordinary language profits from high redundancies. We can afford to miss or mishear individual sounds or even words without losing the meaning.

d. *Engin.* The incorporation of extra parts in the design of a mechanical or electronic system in such a way that its function is not impaired in the event of a failure.

1962 J. Glenn in *Into Orbit* 38 The engineers had a word for this insistence on inserting backups into the system. They called it the principle of 'redundancy'. **1972** L. M. Harris *Introd. Deepwater Floating Drilling Operations* viii. 84 Redundancy implies that alternate methods of well control and operating subsea equipment will be available in the event of failure of any one component or group of components. **1972** *Sci. Amer.* Jan. 46/2 Perhaps the most unusual feature of the grand-tour spacecraft will be a computer called star ('self-test and repair'), provided with enough redundancy to operate for at least 10 years.

3. *attrib.* and *Comb.*, as (sense *2 b) *redundancy agreement, pay, payment, scheme*; (sense *2 c) *redundancy rule*; **redundancy check** *Computers*, a check on the correctness of processed data that involves a comparison with accompanying data derived from them prior to processing.

1951 *Public Administration* XXIX. 374/1 Examples, in the years between the two wars, of competitive industries being turned into monopolies, sometimes with the help of the State—the agricultural schemes, or the redundancy agreements, as in tinplate and shipbuilding. **1969** *Guardian* 3 July 12/1 The dockers and the port employers should start thinking about the sort of redundancy agreement that would meet their needs. **1962** *Gloss. Terms Automatic Data Processing* (*B.S.I.*) 33 *Redundancy check, redundant check*, a check that uses extra digits, which do not themselves fully represent the data concerned. **1970** O. Dopping *Computers & Data Processing* ii. 49 The most common form of redundancy check is the parity check. **1969** *Times* 7 Nov. 21/7 (*heading*) Redundancy pay. **1976** J. R. L. Anderson *Redundancy Pay* i. 11 The terms of the final merger called for heavy redundancies... There would be a bit of redundancy pay. **1980** *Times Lit. Suppl.* 31 Oct. 1240/4 Gus Baedecker, the London adman of *Events Beyond the Heartlands*, who uses his redundancy pay to take Kate and the children away from it all to a cottage on the Welsh coast. **1965** *Act* 13 & 14 *Eliz. II* c. 62 § 1 Where on or after the appointed day an employee who has been continuously employed for the requisite period—..is dismissed by his employer by reason of redundancy,..then,..the employer shall be liable to pay to him a sum (in this Act referred to as a 'redundancy payment'). **1966** *Listener* 17 Mar. 391/2 We carried out too, our pledge to introduce redundancy payments for those who were temporarily out of a job through the speeding of the process of industrial change. **1972** M. Jones *Life on Dole* ii. i. 98 The Redundancy Payments Act of 1965..compels the employer to pay out a lump sum..to each employee who is dismissed. **1965** N. Chomsky *Aspects of Theory of Syntax* 214 More generally the *phonological redundancy rules*, which determine such features as voicing of vowels.., can be supplemented by analogous syntactic and semantic redundancy rules. **1972** *Archivum Linguisticum* III. 14 A morphological feature.. must be recognized as being syntactically relevant, by means of a lexical redundancy rule. **1976** *Language* LII. 296 Lexical redundancy rules define the set of possible underlying morphemes in a language, in addition to minimizing the feature specifications required in the lexicon. **1969** *Guardian* 3 July 12/2 A generous redundancy scheme for dockers could save money.

redundant, *a.* and *sb.* Add: **A.** *adj.* **1. d.** *Engin.* Of a component of a framework, or a force or moment on it: capable of being removed without causing loss of rigidity. Hence of a framework: containing more than the minimum number of components necessary for rigidity.

1890 *Jrnl. Assoc. Engin. Societies* IX. 242 (*heading*) Deflection of framed structures and the distribution of stresses over redundant members. **1908** E. S. Andrews *Theory & Design of Structures* xi. 290 Redundant frames have the following disadvantages:—(1) Any stress in one member caused by bad fitting or change of temperature causes stress in all the other members. **1929** Niles & Newell *Airplane Structures* xiv. 316 In any redundant structure, the distribution of stresses will be such that not only are the conditions of equilibrium satisfied, but also that the deformations of all parts of the structure will be consistent with respect to each other. **1953** C.-K. Wang *Statically Indeterminate Structures* i. 4 In analyzing indeterminate structures it is necessary to have as many extra conditions, in addition to those of statics, as there are redundant reactions. **1976** A. C. Palmer *Structural Mech.* vii. 147 Determine the number of redundant forces (or moments) for each of the plane frames in Figure 7.22.

e. Of a person: no longer needed at work; unemployed because of reorganization, mechanization, change in demand, etc.

1928 *Britain's Industr. Future* (Liberal Industr. Inquiry) xxv. 358 We reach, finally, the pressing, but difficult, problem of the redundant workers. When everything possible has been done..there is little doubt that we shall still have to deal with a large surplus of labour in the coal-mining industry. **1934** J. B. Priestley *Eng. Journey* x. 346 You may do a good stroke of work by declaring the Stockton shipyards 'redundant', but you cannot pretend that all the men who used to work in those yards are merely 'redundant' too. **1956** *Times* 21 July 7/5 Redundant workers..workers dismissed on the score of redundancy. **1958** *Spectator* 30 May 713/3 Over five thousand other men were rendered redundant. **1969** H. E. Bates *Vanished World* xii. 156 Nowadays,..it would no doubt be said that I became redundant. I prefer the old way: I was unexpectedly sacked. **1974** C. Hill *Scorpion* 49, I rang his office... He doesn't work there any more. He was made redundant about two months ago. **1976** *Milton Keynes Express* 30 July 9/3 He had been made redundant and needed money.

f. Of a language: containing material which is predictable from context or a knowledge of its structure; also of a language feature, predictable in this way.

1954 G. A. Miller et al. in J. S. Bruner *Beyond Information Given* (1974) iii. 59 If a language is highly redundant, the relative information per symbol is much lower than it would be if successive symbols in a message could be chosen independently. **1965** W. S. Allen *Vox Latina* 78 Towards the end of a word sounds tend to become more 'redundant', i.e. predictable in terms of what has already been uttered. **1979** E. H. Gombrich *Sense of Order* iv. 104 If the message reads that the meeting was suspended for lack of a q.u.o.r.u.m. every successive letter can be said to be increasingly redundant.

B. *sb.* Restrict † *Obs.* to sense in Dict. and add: **1. b.** *Engin.* A redundant component of a framework (see sense A. 1 d above).

1953 C.-K. Wang *Statically Indeterminate Structures* i. 5 When the equations are solved and the redundants found, they can be put back on the given indeterminate structure and the remaining reactions solved by the equations of statics. **1976** A. C. Palmer *Structural Mech.* vii. 138 Although the frame was three times redundant, this extra piece of information enabled us to reduce the number of unknown redundants to two.

2. A person who leaves his job because of redundancy (sense *2 b); = *redundantee.

1975 *Times* 4 Aug. 12/1 A call for volunteer redundants has not fallen on deaf ears.

Hence **redu·ndantize** *v. trans.*, to make (a person) redundant.

Fortunately *rare*.—Ed.
1949 *Picture Post* 19 Nov. 22/1 The blameless little men, so many of whom have been and will be 'redundantised'.

redundantee (rĭdʊ:ndăntī·). *rare.* [f. Redundant *a.* + -ee[1].] A person who has been made redundant.

1963 *Times* 8 May 13/7 Could not redundancies due to the Beeching plan be handled in a similar way? I am sure that industrialists would cooperate to try to find work for these men, possibly on the basis of one redundantee (?) to so many regular employees. **1971** *Selling Today* Sept. 8/2 Much is offered by way of genius. Like the recent 'redundantee' who offered a world of experience, expertise, exuberance and enthusiasm.

reduplicate, *v.* **2.** (Later example.)

1973 *Sci. Amer.* Feb. 59/1 The manner in which two-syllable adjectives reduplicate is different... A verb reduplicates by the entire word, but the adjective reduplicates in terms of its constituent syllables.

reduviid, *a.* and *sb.* Insert in etym. after *Reduvius* (J. C. Fabricius *Systema Entomologiæ* (1775) 729). (Earlier and later examples.)

1888 J. S. Kingsley *Riverside Nat. Hist.* II. 267 These are strongly suggestive of certain tropical forms of Reduviids. **1909** *Lancet* 20 Nov. 1495/2, I have recently suspected a reduviid bug..as having some relationship with the causation of kala-azar in Madras. **1962** Gordon & Lavoipierre *Entomol.* xxxix. 237 Triatomines may be distinguished from other reduviid bugs. **1965** B. E. Freeman tr. *Vandel's Biospeleol.* xii. 182 Certain reduviid bugs are frequently found in the entrances of tropical caves.

redux, *a.* Add: **2.** Brought back, restored.

[**1662** Dryden (*title*) Astraea Redux. A poem on the happy restoration and return of His Sacred Majesty.] **1873** Trollope (*title*) Phineas redux. **1971** J. Updike (*title*) Rabbit redux.

red-veined: see *Red *a.* 14 a, Red *a.* 14 c.

redward, *a.* and *adv.*: see Red *a.* 19 b in Dict. and Suppl.

red ware[2]. Add to def.: Also, a type of fine, glazed pottery. (Earlier and later examples.)

1699 M. Lister *Journey to Paris* 139 As for the Red Ware of China, that has been and is done in England, to a far greater perfection than in China, we having as good Materials. **1934** *Discovery* June 166/2 Plain burnished red ware. **1959** *Chambers's Encycl.* XI. 137/2 Unglazed redware was made till about 1770... Thomas Astbury (1688–1743) is supposed to have been the first to glaze this finely potted red ware and to decorate it with pads of white clay stamped in patterns. **1965** E. Tunis *Colonial Craftsmen* v. 121 Redware as it came from firing was no harder than a modern flowerpot and it was just as porous. To make it useful, the potters glazed it. **1975** *Country Life* 26 June (Suppl.) 56/2 Christie's... Fine English Porcelain and Pottery..Astbury glazed redware..bell-shaped mug. **1977** *New Hampshire Times* 27 July 17/2 The potter had only one type of clay available, the local glacial clay underlying most of the coastal area. This clay fires in a kiln to a red color and therefore is called redware. Redware collapses past a certain firing temperature.

red-water. Add: **3.** (Earlier example.)

a **1759** N. Owen *Jrnl. Slave-Dealer* (1930) 30 If they are found out they are obliged to drink a large quantity of poyson, comonly caled red watter, which soon puts an end to thier days.

4. A mass of water made red by pigmented plankton, esp. dinoflagellates.

1856 *Edin. New Philos. Jrnl.* IV. 264 Alphonse Albuquerque..saw, from the stern of his vessel, issuing from the strait, and expanding outside, a stream of red water, which flowed towards Aden. **1902** *Amer. Naturalist* XXXVI. 189 The 'red water' occurred for two hundred miles..along the coast, from the region of Santa Barbara to San Diego. **1933** *Science* 7 July 13/1 *Provocentrum* is more frequently prominent in production of 'red water' than reports have indicated. **1948** *Jrnl. Marine Res.* VII. 57 The presence of this [human respiratory] irritation was reported as associated with 'red water', dying fish and onshore winds. *Ibid.* 60 'Red water' containing 56×10^6 dinoflagellates per liter.

red, white, and blue: see *Red *a.* 1 g.

redwing. 1. a. Substitute for def.: A European thrush belonging to one of the subspecies of *Turdus musicus* (or *T. iliacus*), distinguished by red patches on the flanks and under sides of the wings. (Later examples.)

1894 A. Newton *Dict. Birds* 778 The notes of the Redwing are indeed pleasing in places where no better songster exists. **1954** D. A. Bannerman *Birds Brit. Isles* III. 192 To these islands the Continental redwing is a winter visitor. **1977** J. L. Harper *Population Biol. Plants* ii. 47 Redwings..eat the fleshy receptacles [of rose hips].

b. For *Agelæus* substitute *Agelaius*. (Earlier and later examples.)

1778 J. Carver *Trav. N. Amer.* 474 The second sort [of blackbird] is the red wing, which is rather smaller than the first species. **1947** *Chicago Tribune* 2 Sept. 7/3 The grackles and redwings also are having a high old time these days roaming around the country. **1974** A. Dillard *Pilgrim at Tinker Creek* xi. 201 By the creek, where..redwings scatter.

c. (Earlier and later examples.)

1878 T. J. Lucas *Camp Life & Sport S. Afr.* vi. 85 We had a sprinkling of 'red wing', but the game grey partridge was more predominant. **1962** Mackworth-Praed & Grant *Birds Southern Third Afr.* 208 Red-wing... Top of head brown with darker centres to feathers.

redwood. Add: **1. a.** (Earlier and later examples.)

1619 W. Phillip tr. *Schouten's Relation Wonderfull Voiage* 37 In each Canoe..there lay two whole broad planckes of fayre redde wood. **1957** *Handbk. Softwoods* (Forest Prod. Res. Lab.) 42 Timber of this species [sc. *Pinus sylvestris*] imported from the Continent is commonly called redwood, red deal, or simply 'red'. **1963** [see *kapur].

b. Delete *Sc.*; = *compression wood* s.v. *compression 6. (Later example.)

1925 [see **compression wood*].

Redwood[2] (re·dwud). [The name of Sir Boverton *Redwood* (1846–1919), British chemist.] **a.** *Redwood viscometer*: either of two types of viscometer (differing in the ranges of viscosity for which they are suitable), which were designed by Redwood and are used esp. to measure the viscosity of petroleum and its products.

[**1886** *Jrnl. Soc. Chem. Industry* 29 Mar. 131/1 He had been in the habit of using one of Mr. Redwood's instruments for determining viscosities.] **1896** B. Redwood *Petroleum* II. ix. 605 The Redwood viscometer..is a modification, designed by the author in 1885, of the instrument formerly used at the Battersea Works of Price's Patent Candle Company. **1931** G. Barr *Monogr. Viscometry* iv. 96 Liquids for which the Redwood No. II viscometer is specified..are difficult to free from suspended impurities. **1949** A. C. Merrington *Viscometry* v. 58 The calibration of a Redwood viscometer with a number of oils using an apparatus of the Thorpe and Rodger type. **1972** Harker & Allen *Fuel Sci.* vii. 98 The instrument most commonly used in the United Kingdom to measure viscosity is the Redwood Viscometer... The two standard instruments are the No. 1 and the No. 2 Redwood viscometers. The former is used for thin oils having viscosities of less than 2,000 Redwood seconds, and the latter for more viscous oils. **1973** A. L. Mills in Hobson & Pohl *Mod. Petroleum Technol.* (ed. 4) xx. 730 These instruments are now rarely used except perhaps for black oils... In fact, the method of viscosity determination using the Redwood viscometer has been deleted from the Institute of Petroleum 'Standard Tests'.

b. *Redwood second* (also *second Redwood*): a unit of viscosity used in conjunction with Redwood viscometers and equal to one second of the time required for a given quantity of fluid to pass through a capillary in the instrument. So *Redwood time, unit, viscosity,* etc., and with ellipsis of second word.

1913 *Petroleum World* June 272/1 The remaining three columns respectively give their colour, density at 20° C. and viscosity at 20° in Redwood units. **1930** *Engineering* 5 Sept. 308/1 The fuel used throughout this test was Mexican boiler oil with..a viscosity of 200 secs. Redwood. **1949** A. C. Merrington *Viscometry* v. 57 The results are normally expressed as 'Redwood seconds' at the temperature of the test. *Ibid.* A Redwood time of T_R seconds. **1967** A. S. Brunjes in Bland & Davidson *Petroleum Processing Handbk.* xii. 32 The Kinematic, Saybolt, Universal, redwood [*sic*] No. 1, and Engler scales. **1973** P. J. King et al. in Hobson & Pohl *Mod. Petroleum Technol.* (ed. 4) vi. 215 Reference to..viscosities expressed in terms of Redwood seconds..is still found in the literature. **1973** J. G. C. Pope in *Ibid.* xviii. 654 The viscosity of relatively mobile oils is recorded as so many seconds Redwood I @ 100° F. **1973** W. H. Thomas in *Ibid.* xxv. 860 When the Redwood viscosity requirements are quoted in specifications the usual procedure is to determine viscosity in kinematic or dynamic units and to convert these into Redwood by means of a conversion chart.

red-worm. Add: **3.** A parasitic nematode worm belonging to the family Strongylidæ, esp. to the genus *Strongylus,* which infests the intestine and other organs of many vertebrate animals, causing severe anæmia and general debility.

1891 R. Wallace *Rural Econ. Austral. & N.Z.* xxviii. 374 Sheep also suffer from the red worm..in their fourth stomach. **1951** *Chambers's Jrnl.* Oct. 587/1 Red-worms belong to the Strongyle family. **1970** Miller & West *Black's Vet. Dict.* (ed. 9) 768/1 Thiabendazole is a useful drug for the removal of red worms in horses.

reed, *sb.*[1] Add: **I. 1. b.** (Further examples.)

c **1593** T. Deloney *Garland of Goodwill* (1631) iii. sig. B1, But senselesse man, what de I meane, Upon a broken reede to leane. **1617** J. Chamberlain *Let.* 20 Dec. (1939) II. 123 Yf you trusted to him you trusted to a rotten reede who wold have failed you in the end. **1621** *House of Lords Jrnls.* 30 Apr. 101/1 Their lordships..reported, That they.. demanded of his lordship [*sc.* F. Bacon] whether it were his Hand..who answered 'My lords, it is my Act, my Hand..I beseech your Lordships, be merciful unto a broken Reed.' **1757** Smollett *Reprisal* i. i. 7 You lean upon a broken reed if you trust to their compassion. **1926** R. H. Tawney *Relig. & Rise of Capitalism* ii. 108 Human efforts, social institutions, the world of culture, are at best irrelevant to salvation, and at worst mischievous. They distract man from the true aim of his existence and encourage reliance upon broken reeds. **1961** I. Murdoch *Severed Head* xiii. 118 A nervous shrinking which was not exactly dislike made me hesitate to probe the motives of such a being. Therewith some vague yet powerful train of thought led me to say, 'I'm a broken reed after all.' **1973** *Times Lit. Suppl.* 23 Mar. 311/3 The history of the opposition shows what bruised reeds the generals were.

II. 8. a. *double reed* (earlier and later examples); also (with hyphen) *attrib.*

1876 Stainer & Barrett *Dict. Mus. Terms* 137/2 *Double reed,*..the vibrating reed of instruments of the oboe class. **1879** Grove *Dict. Mus.* I. 151/2 *Bassoon*.., a wooden double-reed instrument of eight-foot tone. **1931** G. Jacob *Orchestral Technique* iii. 26 The bassoon also agrees well with its double-reed cousin the oboe. **1961** A. Baines *Musical Instruments* ix. 233 The European shawm reed is of harder material prepared like all Western double reeds by folding over a strip of seasoned cane, shaping and binding the ends together, and paring down and finally separating the tip. **1974** *Encycl. Brit. Macropædia* XIX. 848/1 The human voice..may be classified as a double-reed aerophone in which the vocal chords act as a double reed.

d. (Earlier and later examples.) *double reed*: see sense 8 a.

1838 C. Fox *Jrnl.* 5 June (1972) 50 Professor Wheatstone ..then played the Chinese reed, one of the earliest instruments constructed. **1871** H. Calderwood *Let.* 23 June in Calderwood & Woodside *Life H. Calderwood* (1900) 216 The orchestra mostly reeds and strings. **1877** G. B. Shaw *How to become Musical Critic* (1960) 26 The strings and reeds were a little better than usual. **1926** Whiteman & McBride *Jazz* ix. 199 In the double reeds, I am planning to add a bassoon. **1939** Joyce *Finnegans Wake* (1964) 408 Brass and reeds, brace and ready! **1959** 'F. Newton' *Jazz Scene* vi. 107 Three trumpets, three trombones, four reeds, piano. **1961** J. A. MacGillivray in A. Baines *Musical Instruments* x. 244 The clarinet..marked (like the oboe among the double reeds) the arrival of the fully lip-controlled instrument. **1974** *Encycl. Brit. Macropædia* XIX. 855/1 Shawms were a particularly important family of loud double reeds. **1975** *New Yorker* 19 May 6/3 Joe Muranyi on reeds, and Bobby Pratt on trombone.

12. (Later example.) *reed-and-tie,* used of a style resembling reeds bound together.

1875 T. Seaton *Man. Fret Cutting & Wood Carving* vi. 68 Make a little reed round the uncarved or T part of the bracket and the support... This will form a neat reed, and give a pretty finish to your work. **1960** H. Hayward *Antique Coll.* 235/1 *Reed-and-tie moulding,* an ornament composed of contiguous parallel convex mouldings bound together by straps simulating ribbons. **1971** *Country Life* 1 Apr. 766/1 The grandiloquence of Louis XVI's France, with heavy reed-and-tie borders..also had a place at fashionable West-End silversmiths.

13. a. *reed boat, -swamp, -whistle*; (sense 8) *reed cap, section*; (sense 10) *reed hook, space.*

1902 *Encycl. Brit.* XXV. 377/1 The catamaran and the reed boat were known to the Peruvians. **1977** *Time* 28 Nov. 60/1 Now Heyerdahl is about to take a reed boat down the Tigris River. **1964** S. Marcuse *Musical Instruments* 441/1 *Reed cap,* a small wooden cap with a blowhole on top; it enclosed the reed of some 16th-c. double-reed instrs. **1976** Reed-cap [see *rauschpfeife]. **1910** L. Hooper *Hand-Loom Weaving* (1920) 328 *Reed hook,* hook for entering reed. **1914** H. Nisbet *Preliminary Operations of Weaving* I. ix. 359 The reacher, with the right hand, then proceeds to select the warp threads from a bunch held in the left hand, and delivers them in consecutive rotation to a reed-hook which is inserted through successive eyes of the harness by the drawer-in. **1957** Simpson & Weir *Weaver's Craft* (ed. 8) viii. 97 (*caption*) Reed hooks. **1939** D. Baker *Young Man with Horn* iii. i. 117 Rick..started setting chairs together the way they should go, in threes: reed section, brass section, rhythm section, and the extras one on top of another. **1975** *New Yorker* 21 Apr. 8/3 Billy Harper, a young and very exciting tenor saxophonist..steams up the reed section of the Thad Jones-Mel Lewis band. **1919** *Brit. Manufacturer* Nov. 35/2 Wide hand looms of high reedspace scarcely require more effort than those for narrower weaving. **1971** *Nature* 11 June 364/2 Here the invasion of reedswamp from the north and west was incomplete. **1975** J. G. Evans *Environment Early Man Brit. Isles* iii. 58 The vegetation.. passes through a variety of stages—reed swamp, carr..and raised bog. **1864** J. A. Grant *Walk across Afr.* xi. 245 On his arm he carried a reed-whistle three inches long, but it seemed to be more for ornament than use. **1962** R. P. Jhabvala *Get Ready for Battle* ii. 101 A toyman with toys stuck on the end of a long pole.., blowing on a reed-whistle.

b. *reed-cutter* (later example); *reed-cutting, -drawing* (earlier and later examples).

1974 *Country Life* 3 Oct. 922/1 In winter..the reed cutters took the harvest that served for thatch all over Britain. **1973** R. Adams *Watership Down* xxxiii. 260 The 'boat' was a miniature punt, used for reed-cutting. **1874** Hardy *Far from Madding Crowd* I. vi. 74 Oak seized the cut ends of the sheaves, as if he were going to engage in the operation of 'reed-drawing'. **1946** N. Wymer *Eng. Country Crafts* v. 50 The preparation of the straw—variously known as yelming, reed-drawing, or gabbling—consists of removing all unsuitable pieces and arranging the strands level.

c. (Also parasynthetic) *reed-bottomed, capped, -choked, -encumbered, -fringed, -stemmed, -throated.*

1835 C. Mathews *Let.* 7 Feb. in A. Mathews *Mem. Charles Mathews* (1839) IV. 343 Then behold six reed-bottomed, ragged, ricketty chairs. **1977** *Early Music* July 342/2 A rauschpfeife, a relatively easy (i.e. non-embouchure) instrument, presumably derived from a reed-capped bagpipe chanter. **1952** V. Canning *House of Seven Flies* viii. 125 The narrow, reed-choked mouth of an old cut. **1892** W. B. Yeats *Countess Kathleen* iii. 55 Leave marshes and the reed-encumbered pools. **1906** A. B. Cooper *Flood-Tides* 4 By wold and wilderness, by reed-fring'd lake. **1952** V. Canning *House of Seven Flies* viii. 124 Flat, reed-fringed islands. **1942** W. Faulkner *Go down, Moses* 266 She held a reed-stemmed clay pipe but she was not smoking it. **1914** W. B. Yeats *Responsibilities* 76 From that reed-throated whisperer Who comes at need.

14. reed bat = *reed legget* below; **reed-horn,** (*a*) a fog-horn in which the sound is produced by a current of air blowing on a reed (sense 8 c); (*b*) *slang,* a saxophone; **reed-knife,** a knife-like instrument used in tuning a reed-organ; **reed legget** = *legget; **reed-man,** (*a*) a player of a reed instrument; (*b*) one who works with reeds; **reed-mark** (see quots.); **reed-marked** *a.,* of cloth, having the warp threads lying unevenly; **reed relay** *Electr.,* a small, high-speed, switching device consisting of a pair of contacts, enclosed in a glass tube, which can be brought together by an external magnetic field.

1969 Reed bat [see *legget]. **1902** *Encycl. Brit.* XXX. 266/2 At the Trinity House experiments with fog signals at St. Catherine's (1901) several types of reed-horn were experimented with. **1936** *Metronome* Feb. 61/2 *Reed horn,* sax. **1876** Stainer & Barrett *Dict. Mus. Terms* 339/2 An organ is tuned by means of hollow cones and reed-knives. **1961** *Thatcher's Craft* (Rural Industries Bureau) vii. 205/1 (*caption*) Norfolk reed leggett used for dressing reed into position. **1872** Reed-man [see *brass-man* s.v. *brass *sb.* 6]. **1938** D. Baker *Young Man with Horn* i. v. 47 There was the band playing 'Home, Sweet Home' as a one-step with the reed man getting into clear and going absolutely wild on a clarinet. **1951** Wallace & Bagnall-Oakley *Norfolk* vii. 84 The old villages..began as trading places for the eel-fishers, the reed-men and the smugglers from the sea. **1977** *New Yorker* 6 June 128/2 It consists of eleven Laurence studio performances (about forty minutes in all), backed by two reedmen (Paul Quinichette or the late Bobby Jaspar) and two rhythm sections. **1931** E. Midgley *Techn. Terms Textile Trade* I. 261 *Reed marks,* a type of defect in woven fabrics due to the warp threads running in 'twos' or 'threes'. **1961** Blackshaw & Brightman *Dict. Dyeing* 145 *Reed marks,* marks or streaks running the warp of a cloth and caused by defects in the functioning of the reed during weaving. **1894** T. W. Fox *Mechanism of Weaving* iii. 37 Sometimes warp threads are allowed to run in pairs throughout the piece without being looked upon as a serious defect; such material is said to be reed-marked, or without cover. **1947** *Electr. Engin.* LXVI. 1104 (*heading*) Glass enclosed reed relay. **1966** *Times* 16 Dec. 11/6 The key component in the Ambergate exchange is a miniature reed relay. **1975** Fink & McKenzie *Electronics Engineers' Handbk.* xxiii. 41 Figure 23–46 shows the reed relay, combining small size and high reliability. A magnetic field induced by an external coil follows the path of the encapsulated contact arm, causing a force to pull the two arms together.

reed, *v.* Add: **4.** *Weaving.* To pass (warp threads) through the splits of a reed.

1894 T. W. Fox *Mechanism of Weaving* ii. 17 It will be noticed that the threads from shaft 4 are reeded two in a dent, and those from the remaining shafts three in a dent. **1957** *Textile Terms & Definitions* (Textile Inst.) (ed. 3) 79 *Reed, v.,* to draw ends through a reed (local, to sley, to bob the reed or to enter the reed).

reeded, *ppl. a.* Add: **2.** (Earlier example.)

1778 J. Bampfylde *Sixteen Sonnets* 16 Counting the frequent drop from reeded eaves.

3. (Earlier and later examples.)

1829 H. Foote *Compan. to Theatre* 36 The upper circle and tiers, including both the slips and lower gallery, are each supported in part by 14 slender shafts, reeded, of iron. **1935** *Archit. Rev.* LXXVIII. 33 The window is glazed with reeded glass. **1952** [see *agba]. **1978** R. Rendell *Sleeping Life* ii. 14 No one came when they rang the bell on the neighbouring front door, a far more trendy and ambitious affair of wrought iron and reeded glass.

5. Of wood: having a specified kind of reed.

1839 Ure *Dict. Arts* 972 A quantity of well-seasoned and clean reeded deal is required for forming the joints.

6. *fig.*

1926 T. E. Lawrence *Seven Pillars* (1935) lxxxix. 495, I knew that Sherif Abd el Main should be still at Shobek, so rode boldly up the silent street in the reeded starlight, which played with the white icicles.

reediness. (Earlier and later examples.)

1844 H. Stephens *Bk. Farm* II. 365 The straw of the former kind is strong and inclined to reediness. **1931** E. Midgley *Techn. Terms Textile Trade* I. 20 The warp threads..must lie in the cloth an equal distance apart, or a defect known as 'reediness' is created.

re-edit *v.*, **re-editing** *vbl. sb.* (Examples in *Cinemat.*) Cf. *edit *v.* 2 d, *editing *vbl. sb.* b.

1953 K. Reisz *Technique Film Editing* ii. 168 The picture and words were slightly re-edited to fit in with the music. **1975** *Listener* 21 Aug. 242/2 Not as severely compromised by studio re-editing and reshooting as some of his earlier films had been.

reedmergnerite (rīdmɜ̄·ɹgnərəit). *Min.* [See quot. 1954 and -ite[1].] A colourless triclinic silicate of sodium and boron, $NaBSi_3O_8$.

1954 C. Milton et al. in *Bull. Geol. Soc. Amer.* LXV. 1286 Cores and cuttings from the Green River formation in Utah contain two new minerals, reedmergnerite and eitelite,..in dolomitic shale. Reedmergnerite..occurs in many wells in Duchesne and Uintah counties as crystals rarely more than 1 mm long, colorless, triclinic..; habit stubby prismatic... The name honors Frank S. Reed and John L. Mergner, technicians of the Geological Survey. **1974** *Amer. Mineralogist* LIX. 79/1 This study was undertaken to determine more precisely the bond lengths and angles of danburite.. for comparison with topologically similar paracelsian ($BaAl_2Si_2O_8$) and hurlbutite ($CaBe_2P_2O_8$) and with structurally similar feldspars: anorthite ($CaAl_2Si_2O_8$)..; albite ($NaAlSi_3O_8$); and reedmergnerite ($NaBSi_3O_8$).

Reed–Sternberg (rīd stɜ̄·ɹnbɜ̄ɹg). *Path.* [The names of Dorothy M. *Reed* (1874–1964), U.S. pathologist, and C. *Sternberg* (1872–1934), Austrian pathologist, who described the cell in 1902 and 1898 respectively.] *Reed–Sternberg cell*: a binucleate or multinucleate giant cell characteristic of Hodgkin's disease.

[**1937** *Surg., Gynecol. & Obstetr.* LXIV. 466/1 Hodgkin's disease,..with its Sternberg Reed cells, fibrosis, necrosis, and eosinophilic infiltration, needs no introduction.] **1947** Jackson & Parker *Hodgkin's Dis. & Allied Disorders* i. 7 The fact that the Reed–Sternberg cells are frequently scattered, isolated, and often separated widely by cells of other cell types favors an inflammatory process rather than a neoplasm. **1980** *Brit. Med. Jrnl.* 29 Mar. 903/1 The dermis was infiltrated by lymphocytes,..mononuclear Hodgkin's cells, and classical binucleate Reed-Sternberg cells.

re-educate, *v.* Add: (Further examples.) Now often *spec.* with the object of changing political beliefs or social behaviour.

1947 *Hansard Commons* 15 Dec. 1434 The work of the *Kulturbund zur demokratischen Erneuerung Deutschlands* in re-educating the German people in the spirit of democracy and international understanding. **1955** *Treatment of Brit. P.O.W.'s in Korea* (H.M.S.O.) 4 'Re-educating' the prisoners. The Chinese technique of 're-education' embraced every phase of daily life in the prison camps. **1967** *Listener* 18 May 653/1 The aim..is to re-educate the prisoner rather than to punish him. **1975** *Chinese Econ. Stud.* VIII. iv. 3 Chairman Mao teaches us that 'it is necessary for educated youths to go to the countryside to be reeducated by the poor and lower-middle peasants'. **1976** *New Yorker* 26 Jan. 110/2 The Chinese considered him sufficiently important to be spared and 'reëducated', or brainwashed. **1976** W. H. Canaway *Willow-Pattern War* vi. 64 Agricultural communes which specialized in re-educating professors and other intellectuals as labourers.

re-education. Add: (Further examples: cf. prec.) Also *attrib.*

1906 *Trans. Assoc. Amer. Physicians* XXI. 724 Re-education is undoubtedly one of the most important factors in producing lasting cures. **1944** J. S. Huxley *On Living in Revolution* 151 This gang has succeeded in imposing its ideas on a considerable minority of the German people, and..this constitutes a grave problem of re-education. **1945** 'G. Orwell' *Animal Farm* iii. 26 He formed..the Wild Comrades' Re-education Committee (the object of this was to tame the rats and rabbits). **1945** *Times* 8 May 7/5 It is becoming clear that the 're-education' of Germany by the allies will not be a pious aspiration, but an unavoidable duty. **1951** Koestler *Age of Longing* ix. 337 You don't like revolutionary vigilance,..and discipline, and re-education camps. **1974** N. Freeling *Dressing of Diamond* 133 A year of physiotherapy..in a re-education centre. **1976** Scott & Koski *Walk-In* (1977) xiii. 79, I am once again politically unreliable. I once again face re-education. **1977** *Time* 9 May 22/1 Also targetted for resettlement are most of the 30,000 political prisoners the regime admits are still interned in 're-education' camps.

reedy, *a.* Add: **3. a.** (Later example.)

1890 G. Meredith *Let.* 26 Mar. (1970) II. 993 A reedy state of health forbids my going to Dinners.

b. (Earlier example.)

1743 W. Ellis *Mod. Husbandman* Dec. viii. 410 As.. they make good Part of their Rent by the Sale of their Wheat Straw, they are very careful to preserve it as reedy or long as they can.

c. Of cloth: having the warp threads unevenly distributed.

1931 E. Midgley *Techn. Terms Textile Trade* I. 261 *Reedy*, a term applied to a cloth which shows reed marks.

5. *Comb.* (Later example.)

1905 *Westm. Gaz.* 1 Nov. 1/3 The valley of the reedy-voiced little Ervola.

reef, *sb.*[1] Add: **1.** (Earlier and later *transf.* examples.)

1846 *Swell's Night Guide* 48 Ruttum turned out a quid as big as a moke's egg, took a reef in his patter trap. **1884** 'Mark Twain' *Huck. Finn* xxxi. 316, I lit out, and shook the reefs out of my hind legs. **1903** Somerville & 'Ross' *All on Irish Shore* i. 2 'I dunno, Master Freddy; it might be 'twas a hare,' returned Patsey, taking in a hurried reef in the strap that was responsible for the support of his trousers. **1924** E. Pound *Let.* 3 Dec. (1971) 190 Am also letting out another reef in my long job. Installment of which should soon be inspectable.

3. *reef-earing* (further examples); **reef-knot,** (*b*) (later example); **reef-knot** *v.* (earlier example); **reef net** *N. Amer.*, a type of net used for catching salmon; also *attrib.*; hence **reef netter,** a fisherman who uses a reef net.

1883 *Man. Seamanship for Boys' Training Ships R. Navy* (Admiralty) (1886) 51 Reef-earrings are pieces of rope, in size according to the size of the leech-rope, as when a topsail is reefed the reef-earring, when passed is supposed to bear the same amount of strain as the leech-rope. **1974** P. Wright *Lang. Brit. Industry* xv. 148 Over the mainsail came, broke all the reef-ear-rings, an' then we'd full sail on. **1974** *Maclean's Mag.* Nov. 10/1 Show the other lads the difference between a reef knot and a granny. **1883** *Man. Seamanship for Boys' Training Ships R. Navy* (Admiralty) (1886) 87 For a topgallant sail or royal,..[a roband-hitch] is ..not clove-hitched, the two nearest robands being reef-knotted together. **1917** *Pacific Fisherman Yearbk.* 60 (*heading*) The Siwash reef net. *Ibid.*, Reef net fishing was confined to the flood tide. **1970** *National Fisherman* Feb. 21-B/1 In 1969 there were 63 pairs of reefnet vessels registered in Puget Sound. **1974** B. & R. Hill *Spirit in Stone* iii. 35 A man whom we will call the ritualist and several assistants are fishing for salmon with a reef net. **1939** *Pacific Fisherman* June 45/2 With the increase in gear, considerable friction arose between purse seiners and reef netters.

reef, *sb.*[2] Add: **2. a.** (Earlier and later examples.)

1857 in *Occasional Papers Univ. Sydney Austral. Lang. Res. Centre* (1966) No. 9. 21 On this gold-field the word reef shall be taken to mean any seam of quartz, the average thickness of which..shall exceed three (3) feet. **1939** C. W. Towne *Her Majesty Montana* 114 Even before the end of placer mining, Butte prospectors had located quartz on a black-stained reef. **1955** *Times* 9 May 18/3 The total development footage driven was 48,295 ft., and of the 21,085 ft. on basal reef and sampled 12,990 ft., or 62 per cent., proved payable. **1966** 'J. Hackston' *Father clears Out* 16 An offshoot from our old reef provided the quartz.

c. *S. Afr.* (With capital initial.) = *Rand *sb.*[2] 1 b. Also (usu. with small initial), rock in a mine which is not gold- or diamond-bearing.

1893 T. Reunert *Diamonds & Gold S. Afr.* i. 21 The surface shales and basalt surrounding the pipes are called 'Reef'. *Ibid.* 22 In the upper levels of the mines intrusive masses of shale and igneous rock are met with, called 'Floating Reef'. They are destitute of diamonds. *Ibid.* 28 The encasing rock of the mine (or the 'Reef', as the diggers called it) being exposed by the removal of the diamondiferous ground, began to disintegrate, and fall into the mine... The reef troubles..more than once threatened to involve the whole mine in ruin. **1905** L. Phillips *Transvaal Probl.* ii. 49 Meetings took place along the Reef from Boksburg to Krugersdorp. **1926** S. G. Millin *S. Africans* 77 The richest road in the world, whose sixty miles run over the gold-mines of the Reef. **1970** W. Smith *Gold Mine* xvi. 44 Free gold.. rapidly worked its way down..its journey accelerated by the vibration of the conveyor and bin as mine reef was dropped. **1975** 'D. Jordan' *Black Account* xvii. 89 One of the houses with the Reef's pre-war style of flat roofs and enormous bay windows.

4. (sense 1) *reef-forming, -making, -strewn* adjs.; (senses 2 a and *2 c) *reef development, town, value*; **reef-break** *Surfing* (see quot. 1970); **reef-builder,** for 'coral insect' read 'cœlenterate or other marine organism' (earlier and later examples); **reef flat,** the horizontal upper surface of a reef; **reef-knoll,** a hillock, usu. of limestone, formed from ancient coral; **reef-limestone,** limestone which was formed in reefs.

1966, 1968 Reef break [see *point break* s.v. *Point *sb.*[1] B. 14]. **1970** *Studies in English* (Univ. of Cape Town) I. 26 A reef break, surf breaking over a reef, will provide a good, fast ride. **1869** *Amer. Naturalist* III. 352 We could find no evidence that the reef-builders at the present time.. are working upon so high a northern line. **1972** *Sci. Amer.* June 54/1 The chief animal reef-builders today are the corals, but many other marine invertebrates are important members of the reef community. **1971** *Daily Tel.* 11 Oct. 17 A limited amount of reef development in the lower western portion of the mine yielded reasonable values. **1886** *Trans. R. Soc. Edin.* XXXII. 557, I..came upon the coral rock exposed in flat surfaces resembling those of the ordinary reef-flat. **1931** J. S. Gardiner *Coral Reefs & Atolls* ii. 35 Such rock masses as are visible on the reef flat do not stand up above the high tide level. **1976** R. C. Selley *Introd. Sedimentol.* viii. 297 There are three main morphological elements to a reef: the fore-reef, the reef flat and the back-reef. *Ibid.* 299 Tidal channels ..traverse the reef-flat. **1967** *Oceanogr. & Marine Biol.* V. 330 Tethyan corals include such reef-forming genera as *Stylina*, *Isastraea*, and *Thamnastrea.* **1890** R. H. Tiddeman in *Rep. Brit. Assoc. Adv. Sci. 1889* 602 At the foot of these mounds, or reef-knolls as I would call them, we have in many places a breccia formed of fragments of the limestone. **1969** Bennison & Wright *Geol. Hist. Brit. Isles* ix. 211 Extensive sheet reefs, not necessarily primarily organic in origin, as well as reef-knolls are widespread, the reef-knolls occurring on the flanks of massifs. **1893** P. Lake tr. *E. Kayser's Textbk. Compar. Geol.* iii. 225 In these reef limestones..the greater part of the rock is formed not by corals, but by the rock-building algae..*Gyroporella* and *Diplopora.* **1938** M. Black *Hatch & Rastall's Petrol. Sedimentary Rocks* (ed. 3) viii. 163 The term 'reef limestone' has been used in geological literature with varying significance. In this discussion, shelly or structureless, unbedded limestones which show no clear connection with sessile benthonic organisms will be left out of consideration. **1956** W. Edwards in D. L. Linton *Sheffield* 6 Shirley and Horsfield..have described the reef-limestones of the northern fringe of the main outcrop near Castleton. **1855** J. Phillips *Man. Geol.* xvi. 491 The reef-making madrepores are seldom found below 100 feet. **1961** *Times* 14 Dec. 17/5 Ice and reef-strewn channel. **1938** N. Devitt *Spell of S. Afr.* 185 At a military court held in a certain Reef town, a civilian was charged with murder. **1955** *Times* 3 May 17/2 Reef values to the south-west of the fault are expected to be similar to those encountered in the President Brand and Western Holdings mines.

reef, *v.*[1] Add: **1. b.** (Further examples.) *Criminals' slang*, to pull up (the lining of a pocket) so as to steal the contents; to pick (a pocket); hence, to steal or obtain dishonestly in any fashion; also more *gen.* to remove, to take or strip *off*, to pull *down*.

1899 [see *Leather *sb.* 2 e (*a*)]. **1901** M. Franklin *My Brilliant Career* xvii. 142 She was the only one who bothered with a bathing-dress. The rest of us reefed off our clothing. **1903** Farmer & Henley *Slang* VI. 10/1 *Reef*..(thieves'), to draw up a dress-pocket until the purse is within reach of the fingers. **1926** *Variety* 29 Dec. 7/4 The cleverest wire who ever reefed an insider would be astonished to hear that a 'milk man' was a hambo, who stole more bows than the applause warranted at the finish of his act. **1938** *Surg., Gynecol. & Obstetr.* LXVI. 200/2 An attempt was made to shorten the quadriceps by reefing the tendon and fastening the aponeurosis of the internal vastus to the patella under tension. **1944** L. Glassop *We were Rats* xviii. 102 'Where'd you get all the smash?' asked Pat. 'The Harday organization,' said Gordon, 'works fast. I reefed it off a few Parsees like steam.' **1949** —— *Lucky Palmer* xiv. 124 Mugs deserve to have their dough reefed off them. **1953** K. Tennant *Joyful Condemned* xxiii. 223 They vowed it [*sc.* a magpie] ran squawking to inform on anyone who was reefing down a bit of lightning conductor to make an aerial. **1955** *Publ. Amer. Dial. Soc.* xxiv. 95 Some careful tools reef every score. **1959** *Economist* 7 Feb. 505/1 Where public servants..feather their nests when they are not reefing money off honest citizens. **1967** K. Giles *Death in Diamonds* vi. 104 If I go near the car pool they'll reef it off me. **1976** *Courier-Mail* (Brisbane) 17 July 24/9 Collins 'reefed' his $140 watch from his left hand. **1977** *Times* 13 July 5/4 As the talent suckers chummy, the wire reefs his leather... A slick pickpocket team has a private language for its dirty work.

c. To feel the genitals of (a person). *coarse slang.*

1962 Parker & Allerton *Courage of his Convictions* i. 33, I enjoyed reefing girls much more than lessons. The girls enjoyed it too. **1972** B. Rodgers *Queens' Vernacular* 101 Cop a feel..reef (Brit gay sl); take somebody's pulse.

B. *Comb.* **reef-topsail,** used *attrib.* to designate a breeze of a strength in which topsails are reefed; also *fig.* ? *obs.*

1840 R. H. Dana *Two Yrs. before Mast* xxxi. 235 We had a steady 'reef-topsail breeze' from the westward. **1849** H. Melville *Redburn* 1648 By night it was a reef-topsail-breeze. **1909** B. Lubbock *Deep Sea Warriors* 16 The sail-maker's reef-topsail voice drowned my question.

reef, *v.*[2] Add: So **ree·fing** *vbl. sb.*[2]; also *attrib.* (Further examples.)

1865 *Mining Surveyors' & Registrars' Rep.* (Dept. Mines, Victoria) Sept. 46 The southern or Gipps Land slope of the Great Dividing Range..will become one vast reefing district. **1874** A. Bathgate *Colonial Experiences* viii. 95 Quartz crushing for gold..gives abundant promise for the future, notwithstanding that the interest of the speculating public has been somewhat shaken in 'reefing'. **1874** C. Holloway *Jrnl. Visit N.Z. 1873–75* I. 121 (typescript), These Block's [*sic*] are distant about 20 miles from the rising reefing district of Lyell. **1906** J. M. Bell in P. Galvin *N.Z. Mining Handbk.* 5 Reefing is being carried out at a number of places.

reefable (rī·făb'l), *a.* [f. Reef *v.*[1] + -able.] Capable of being reefed.

1909 *Westm. Gaz.* 26 Oct. 5/1 Instead of having two rigid planes or wings, set one on either side of the body, it has a single transversal span of canvas which is reefable, like that of the sail of a ship.

reefed, *ppl. a.* Add: **2.** Also with *up*, and *transf.*

1874 K. H. Digby *Temple of Memory* iv. 78 The windmills with the reef'd-up sails. **1962** *Into Orbit* 245 *Reefed*, the condition of a parachute which is not fully deployed, in order to reduce the initial stress.

reefer[1]. Add: **1.** (Earlier and later examples.)

1818 'A. Burton' *Adventures J. Newcome* i. 40 'Hoy! Reefers! Reefers!—with your sport you seem to make a *Dover Court.*' **1939** Joyce *Finnegans Wake* (1964) 323 Reefer was a wenchman.

2. (Earlier and later examples.) Also (*N Amer.*), an overcoat.

1878 C. Hallock *Amer. Club List & Sportsman's Gloss.* p. ix/2 *Reefer*, a short jacket worn by sailors. **1921** [see *covert *cloth*]. **1935** A. J. Pollock *Underworld Speaks* 96/1 *Reefer.* an overcoat. **1947** *Words: New Dict.* 480/1 *Reefer, n. Slang.* 2. A short, double-breasted overcoat. **1968** [see *Lounge *sb.* 2 c]. **1970** J. H. Gray *Boy from Winnipeg* 47 Our winter overcoats—'reefers' we called them—lasted so well that one might serve as many as three boys before being discarded.

attrib. (Further examples.)

1901 G. B. Shaw *Capt. Brassbound's Conversion* ii. 241 Sprawl supine on the floor, with their reefer coats under their heads. **1928** R. Macaulay *Keeping up Appearances* xv. 170 Cary spoke with a hint of nervous defiance, thrusting her hands into the pockets of her reefer coat. **1936** N. Streatfeild *Ballet Shoes* x. 161 On the day of the interview, Nana cleaned Pauline's reefer coat, and blue beret. **1955** *Times* 20 Aug. 3/3 He was wearing a reefer jacket and uniform trousers under a blue naval raincoat. **1969** N. W. Parsons *Upon Sagebrush Harp* i. 4 Rena and I shivered in our white serge reefer coats. **1978** *Jrnl. R. Soc. Arts* CXXVI. 702/2 Pugin shocked his contemporaries by attending important meetings with aristocratic clients dressed in a seaman's jersey and reefer jacket.

3. [Or perh. ad. Mexican Sp. *grifo* marijuana, one who smokes marijuana.] A cigarette containing marijuana; marijuana; one who smokes marijuana. Also *attrib. slang* (orig. *U.S.*).

1931 [see *camp *a.* (and *sb.*[5])]. **1932** *Melody Maker* Sept. 749/2 'Song of the Weed', 'Got the South in my Soul', 'I Heard', and 'Reefer Man' are all worth your half-crowns. **1933** *Chicago Defender* 2 Dec. 5 The humble 'reefer', 'the weed', the marijuana, or what have you by way of a name for a doped cigarette has moved to Park Ave. from Harlem. **1940** R. Chandler *Farewell, my Lovely* xxxiii. 256 He sold reefers... With the right protection behind him. **1946** S. Jackson *Indiscreet Guide to Soho* 120 'Reefers' (cigarettes made from marihuana) used to sell in thousands in the West End before the war. **1952** *Amer. Speech* XV. 335/2 One who smokes is a nicotine-hound or a reefer (especially a smoker of marihuana). **1952** M. Tripp *Faith is Windsock* ix. 137 Got any reefers?..Gimme some skin man. **1956** 'N. Shute' *Beyond Black Stump* 279 And then we got to smoking those reefers... Those cigarettes! **1959** *News Chron.* 26 Aug. 1/2 'Reefer' cigarettes, made up from hashish, are sold in the West End and in Notting Hill at 5s. apiece. **1967** M. M. Glatt et al. *Drug Scene* iv. 49 Quite a few were on heroin and cocaine, most smoked reefers, but not too many were on Purple Hearts. **1972** W. Labov *Lang. in Inner City* p. xxii, Reginald then makes another disruptive move, suggesting that they get a bag of reefer (marijuana). **1976** *Milton Keynes Express* 2 July 9/6 [He]..was fined £100 after three ounces of cannabis, enough to make 240 'reefers', was found at his home. **1979** *High Times* Mar. 25 Louisiana state cop displays a pot of pot discovered among 30 tons of Columbian reefer.

4. *Criminals' slang.* (See quots.)

1935 N. Ersine *Underworld & Prison Slang* 62 *Reefer*,..a pickpocket. **1941** Baker *Dict. Austral. Slang* 59 *Reefer*... (2) A pickpocket's accomplice.

reefer[2]. Add: **1.** (Earlier example.) Also *N.Z.*

1859 *Adelong Mining Jrnl.* 15 Apr. 4/2 On Monday last he made known to a few of our old reefers his discovery. **1940** Baker *N.Z. Slang* iv. 28 Gold-fields brought [to N.Z.] the reefer, the deep lead, the gutter, the monkey shaft.

3. *Austral.* One associated with the Great Barrier Reef.

1951 J. Devanny *Travels N. Queensland* xv. 78 We plunged into the water up to our knees..holding the sticks which experienced 'reefers' invariably carry.

ree·fer[3]. Alteration of Refrigerator. Usu. = *refrigerator car* or *ship*. Also *attrib.*, and as *adj.* = Refrigerated *ppl. a.*

1914 *Wells Fargo Messenger* III. 39 Ten thousand halibut must be packed in Wells Fargo 'reefers' between sun-up and sunset. **1924** 'DIGIT' *Confessions 20th Cent. Hobo* 12 *Reefer*, a refrigerator box car for perishable goods with an ice-box at each end. **1926** *Amer. Speech* I. 652/2 *Reefer*, refrigerator. **1951** *Manch. Guardian* 27 Sept. 14/2 Denmark also provides examples of English, or rather American naming, in the African Reefer and the Indian Reefer—'Reefer' being an Americanism for a vessel carrying refrigerated cargo. **1953** *Sun* (Baltimore) 7 Nov. (B ed.) 6/3 Then..to San Francisco for 'reefer' cargo—refrigerated fruit. **1958** J. KEROUAC *On Road* I. 19 We didn't know..what boxcars and flats and de-iced reefers to pick. **1961** *Amer. Speech* XXXVI. 273 *Reefer box*, a refrigerated trailer. **1963** *North* (Ottawa) May–June 14/1 Price had been showing them how to can the local fruit and prepare it for freezing in the Indian Affairs reefer. **1963** T. PYNCHON *V.* i. 22 To the mezuzah nailed up over the vegetable reefer and the Zionist banner hanging in back of the salad table Da Conho added this prize. **1965** R. B. ORAM *Cargo Handling* (1969) vi. 99 Refrigerated space is now commonly referred to as 'reefer' space. **1968** P. DURST *Badge of Infamy* iv. 32 Steaks are in the reefer, the french fries are all out and in the wire basket. **1971** *Maclean's Mag.* Sept. 34/1 Reefers are insulated vans with Thermo King refrigerated units on them. They can carry anything from ice cream to corpses. **1976** *Times* 6 Oct. 21 The underlying strength of the refrigerated ship (reefer) business. **1978** *Jrnl. R. Soc. Arts* CXXVI. 186/1 At present in the Dry Cargo Fleets of the World the United Kingdom is first in Reefers, second in Containers and, it would seem, is leaving Bulkers and General Cargo to others. Reefer and Container ships certainly need high grade officers who are good navigators and capable ship handlers in traffic.

reefing, *vbl. sb.*[1] Add: **b.** *reefing breeze* (later example), *gear, hook, spindle, wheel.*

1956 A. F. LOOMIS *'Hotspur' Story* 118, I was sailing in a reefing breeze. **1911** J. BARTEN *Compl. Naut. Pocket Dict.* 156/2 *Reefing gear*, Mechanismus zum Segelreffen. **1961** F. H. BURGESS *Dict. Sailing* 169 *Reefing gear*, patent roller fittings used in some small sailing boats, to dispense with the use of reef points. **1860** 'VANDERDECKEN' *Yarns* 36 The topmast shrouds..should have..reefing hooks and thimbles. **1962** *Roving Commissions 1961* 43 Mr 'Christie' Mahoney arranged for our reefing spindle to be mended. **1840** *Civil Engin. & Archit. Jrnl.* III. 104/1 This vessel..has the reefing wheels after Mr. Hall's patent.

Reek (rīk), *sb.*[3] *Ireland.* [Var. of RICK *sb.*[1]: cf. REEK *v.*[3]] A mountain, used *spec.* in *pl.* in *Macgillicuddy's Reeks* (also, *the Reeks*), county Kerry. Also in *sing.*, as pop. name for Croaghpatrick, county Mayo. *Reek Sunday*, the last Sunday in July, on which pilgrimages are made to Croaghpatrick.

1780 A. YOUNG *Tour in Ireland* I. 381 Nothing stops the eye till Mangerton and Macgilly Cuddy's Reeks point out the spot where Killarney's lake calls for a farther excursion. *Ibid.* II. 3 Mangerton, and the Reeks, in Kerry; the Galbies in Corke..these are the principal in Ireland. **1808** J. MILNER *Let.* 22 Sept. in *Inquiry concerning Ireland* (ed. 2, c 1810) 326 The forked, cloud-capped Reeks, overlooking the Atlantic Ocean. **1870** P. W. JOYCE *Irish Local Names* 36 Croagh; *Cruach*, a rick or stacked up hill... Croaghpatrick; St. Patrick's rick or hill. **1871** T. C. POPE *Council of Vatican* 236 He required a period of nearly six weeks to complete the remaining portion of the journey to Rome. He commenced the ascent of the Alpine reeks on a Friday. **1922** JOYCE *Ulysses* 290 From the streamy vales of Thomond, from M'Gillicuddy's reeks the inaccessible and lordly Shannon the unfathomable. **1930** *Irish Rosary* May 321 From our drawing-room windows one had a perfect view of the Reek. **1959** D. D. C. P. MOULD *Peter's Boat* iii. 31 Carrauntual, the 3414 foot height at the western end of the great ridgeway of the MacGillycuddy's Reeks. *Ibid.* 32 The ridge of the Reeks springs up suddenly, a wall of rock, from the plains of Kerry. **1960** [see *GARLAND *sb.* 9]. **1964** B. WHELPTON *Unknown Ireland* vii. 98 The Gap of Dunloe between the Reeks and the Purple Mountains.

reek, *v.*[1] Add: **3. b.** (Later examples.)

1961 *Newark Evening News* 21 Nov. 12 The day before Election Day, to which we are entitled as a legal holiday, we were informed to report to our respective polls to work as 'workers of the party'. .. Such tactics reek of totalitarianism! **1969** *Listener* 3 Apr. 467/3 The plot fairly reeks of the confessional.

reel, *sb.*[1] Add: **2. c.** *off the reel* (further examples); also, immediately, quickly; also *right* (or † *sharp*) *off the reel.*

1825 J. NEAL *Bro. Jonathan* I. vi. 156 So then, says he to me, says he; sharp off the reel; —as 'cute a feller, that, as ever you seed. **1833** J. K. PAULING *Banks of Ohio* II. v. 78 I'd as good a mind as I ever had to shoot a wild deer, to have a fight with him off the reel, and settle the right of soil at once. **1835** *Gentleman's Vade-Mecum* (Philadelphia) 14 Feb. 3/1 Where's my old man—tell me that..where's Tom Bloomberg—tell us right off the reel. **1900** ADE *Fables in Slang* 27 He could tell you quick—right off the reel. **1927** *Daily Tel.* 3 May 17/2 The Eton XI..were undefeated, having scored four victories off the reel. **1941** J. SMILEY *Hash House Lingo* 40 *Off the reel*, added to an order to signify a 'rush order'. **1946** *Sunday Dispatch* 8 Sept. 6/5 Won six races off the reel for Wembley Cubs. **1951** F. YERBY *Woman called Fancy* ii. 44 'You want to bring me back?' Court said. 'Why, little Fancy?' 'Can't answer that —not right off the reel. Don't rightly know myself.'

3. b. *spec.* The flanged cylinder or core on which magnetic tape or punched paper tape is wound; also *transf.*, a length of tape wound on such a cylinder. (Further examples.)

1939 *Wireless World* 19 June 611/2 (*caption*) The necessary controls, together with the reels of steel tape, are mounted on top of the [recording] cabinet. **1953** E. T. CANBY *Home Music Syst.* xiii. 227 The reel size is seven inches. **1956** *RCA Rev.* XVII. 366 The tape is unwound from a reel..and after passing over the video heads, is pulled by the capstan. **1958** H. G. M. SPRATT *Magnetic Tape Recording* iii. 55 The tape..when wound on the normal type of spool employed, will result in a reel ranging from 5–12 in. in diameter. **1964** *Communications Assoc. Computing Machinery* VII. 630/1 This standard covers the physical dimensions of take-up (or storage) reels, with either fixed or separable flanges, so that reels of perforated tape may be interchanged among machines of various manufacturers. **1977** T. ALLBEURY *Man with President's Mind* ix. 101 The video tapes..were..sent in a special top priority diplomatic bag to Moscow. The priority was so high that the reels were not even rewound before despatch.

c. *Cinemat.* and *Photogr.* A flanged cylinder on which film is wound; usu. *transf.*, a length of film wound on such a cylinder; *loosely*, a (long) portion of a motion picture; also, † the spool on which photographs were mounted in a mutoscope (see quot. 1901).

In early usage in Cinemat., *reel* was restricted in signification to a fixed length of film, normally one thousand feet at 35 mm. gauge, complete films being called *two-reelers*, etc. (see *REELER[1] 3). The word is now used of other fixed lengths, of standard lengths of film at other gauges, and also without regard to length.

1896 QUEEN VICTORIA *Jrnl.* 3 Oct. (1980) 222 The new cinematograph process,—which makes moving pictures by winding off a reel of film. **1901** *Everybody's Mag.* Aug. 230/2 Ordinary photographs are printed from the negative film and mounted on a central spool, from nine hundred to twenty-seven hundred pictures to a 'reel', as it is called. **1912** *Maclean's Mag.* Apr. 634/1 It is comprised in three 'reels', which means that there are 3,000 feet of film, requiring a full hour to run. **1915** *Chicago Herald* 1 Nov. 8/5 'The Sentimental Lady' is five reels of whipped cream lightness and frothy texture. **1916** F. H. RICHARDSON *Motion Picture Handbk.* (ed. 3) 198 There has been some inclination to increase the size of reels to two and even three thousand feet... One thousand feet of film has been and should continue to be the standard reel of film. **1921** B. SCHULBERG *What makes Sammy Run?* iv. 51 People..become characters in Hollywood movies... In the last reel the good brother has to be killed off so that the bad brother can be regenerated. *Ibid.* xi. 193 Two-reel horse-operas. **1968** *Tamarack Rev.* Spring 9 He was waiting for the others to arrive so they could run through the second reel together. **1972** *Daily Tel.* 19 June 24/4, I don't know what I took. I know I shot three reels—36 pictures on each—but don't ask me what is on them.

d. *reel-to-reel* attrib. phr.: applied to a form of tape-recorder in which tape passes between two reels which are mounted separately on the recorder (cf. *open-reel* s.v. *OPEN *a.* 22 c; contrast *CASSETTE d and *CARTRIDGE 1 d (iii)); also to the tape used in such a machine; also *absol.*

1961 *N.Y. Times* 10 Sept. II. 15/3 'Reel-to-reel' machines move the tape..from an open supply reel to a take-up reel. **1967** *Tape Recording Mag.* Jan. 12/2 Transferring recording material on to an orthodox quarter-inch tape reel-to-reel model. **1975** *Gramophone* Jan. 1389 (Advt.), It will make going in for tape much more worthwhile—cassette or reel-to-reel or both. **1976** *Broadcast* 29 Nov. 15/1 Capitol Records..wants..listeners..to send cassettes or reel-to reel tapes of their vocal efforts. **1977** *Design Engin.* July 97/2 A range of two and four channel cassette tape recorders offers recording facilities usually associated with reel-to-reel instruments.

6. *reel line* (earlier example), *stand*; **reel-backing** *U.S. local* (see quot. 1976); **reel barge,** a barge, carrying extended lengths of pipe coiled on a reel, which is used to lay submarine pipelines; also *attrib.*; **reel boy,** a boy attending to the reeling of yarn, etc.; **reel-fed** *a. Printing*, using reeled paper; **reel-land** *nonce-wd.*, the world of the cinematograph; **reel man,** a sailor who holds the reel from which a log-line depends; **reel-room,** the room in a cinema where reels of cinematographic films are kept; **reel ship,** a self-powered ship performing the function of a reel barge; **reel timing,** a method of playing certain kinds of slot machine (see quot.).

1959 W. FAULKNER *Mansion* xii. 346 His uncle had the gun..a black strong small-gauge length of reel-backing running from the trigger through a series of screw eyes to the sash of the window screen. **1976** C. S. BROWN *Gloss. Faulkner's South* 161 *Reel-backing*.., a heavy (often old) length of fishing-line wound as the first layer on a fishing reel, and hence the last piece if the entire line is reeled out. **1972** *Study of Potential Benefits Offshore Oil & Gas Devel.* (Internat. Managem. & Engin. Group of Brit. Ltd.) x. 80 There is also the highly promising reel-barge technique, which, however, has so far been limited to comparatively small diameter pipe. **1975** *Offshore* Aug. 121/1 Santa Fe International Corp's reel barge Chickasaw has successfully laid a 10-in pipeline in more than 1,000 feet of water. **1975** [see *PIPE-LAY *sb.*]. **1975** *Offshore Progress* (Shell Internat. Petroleum Co.) 17 Another technique which has been used for some time in the Gulf of Mexico for small-diameter pipelines is the reel barge: the pipe is welded together onshore (thereby minimizing expensive offshore time) and coiled on a reel. The barge is then pulled along the right of way, unreeling pipe behind it. **1918** *Nation* (N.Y.) 7 Feb. 130/1 Defeating the man in whose flax mill he had worked as a reel boy. **1946** V. S. GANDERTON in H. Whetton *Pract. Printing & Binding* xii. 153/1 Multi-colour rotaries and methods have been brought to a high degree of perfection... They are either sheet- or reel-fed, but the delivery is flat. **1971** D. POTTER *Brit. Eliz. Stamps* xiv. 150 Reel-fed printing takes the paper into the press on a continuous reel, and the printed sheets are later divided. **1926** *Chambers's Jrnl.* Aug. 605/1 Some..would fain have treated her much in the style of those who at the present day mob the stars of reel-land. **1837** J. KIRKBRIDE *Northern Angler* 3 With regard to the reel and reel-line I need say nothing. **1851** H. MELVILLE *Moby Dick* III. xxxix. 226 The towering resistance of the log caused the old reelman to stagger strangely. **1928** *Daily Express* 8 Oct. 2/1 Hundreds of children..filed from the..Cinema..while the staff tackled a fire in the reel-room behind the gallery. **1976** *Offshore Platforms & Pipelining* 143/2 Santa Fe expects to launch its new reel ship in 1977. **1889** *Cent. Dict.*, Reel-stand. **1961** *World's Press News* 6 Jan. 7 (Advt.), A..Rotary Newspaper Press. The machine will be arranged with..six 3-arm magazine reelstands. **1969** E. H. PINTO *Treen* 320 The silk on the spool of the cocoon winder was then transferred to the lead-weighted reel stand. **1964** A. WYKES *Gambling* iii. 71 But another method, called 'reel timing', was not easy to track down... First, the player had to determine the exact number of seconds that each reel spun before coming to rest after the handle was pulled. Secondly, he had to memorize the sequence of all 60 symbols on the three reels.. He had to be able to count..a certain number of seconds between the insertion of the coin and the pulling of the lever.

reel, *sb.*[3] Add: **1.** (Further examples.) *Virginia reel*: see also VIRGINIA 1 d.

1745 in R. Forbes *Lyon in Mourning* (Scott. Hist. Soc. Ser.) (1895) I. 208 He..took his share in several dances, such as minuets, Highland reels (the first reel the Prince called for was, 'This is not mine ain house'). **1788** J. O'KEEFE (*title*) The Highland reel. **1814** [see FOURSOME *a.* 2]. **1818** B. DUN *Nine Quadrilles* Pref., There are two kinds of music to which the Scotch reel is danced, viz. the reel properly so called, and the strathspey. **1840** LYTTON *Money* III. v. 85 Do you remember her dancing the Scotch reel with Captain Macnaughten? **1843** [see EIGHTSOME *a.* or *adv.*]. **1913** *Times* 3 June 11/3 The old Scotch reel is rarely danced today, as the young folk prefer eight-somes as more 'romping'. **1950** *Oxf. Jun. Encycl.* IX. 278/2 The chief dances performed at the [Highland] Games are the Sword Dance, the Foursome Reel, the Reel of Tulloch, the Highland Fling, and the Seann Triubhas. **1955** *Highland Dancing* ii. 61 During the Highland Reel the distance between the points may be reduced. **1964** W. G. RAFFE *Dict. Dance* 414/2 *Reel o' Tulloch*... This and other Scottish Reels in 4/4 time, come from ancient periods. *Ibid.*, This Reel is a variant of the Foursome Reel. **1971** *Country Life* 23 Dec. 1790/1 Get up and take a whirl in an eightsome reel. **1974** *Encycl. Brit. Micropædia* VIII. 468/3 Popular reels include the Irish Sixteenhand Reel and the Scottish reels Maury's Wedding and the Duke of Perth.

2. (Later examples.) Also *U.S. dial.*, a song for such a dance.

1818 [see sense 1 above]. **1883** GROVE *Dict. Mus.* III. 92/1 The Irish reel is played much faster than the Scotch. **1964** *Amer. Folk Music Occasional* I. 61 From such a man you will hear ballads, breakdowns, reels. **1968** J. ARNOLD *Shell Bk. Country Crafts* 320 In the form of the reel, strathspey, or pibroch it has a primitive echo which is evocative for all its convention and sophistication.

reel, *v.*[2] Add: **2. b.** Also const. *out* (*rare*). Also (const. *off*), to cover (a distance, etc.) rapidly; to accomplish or perform without pause or effort.

1870 'MARK TWAIN' in *Galaxy* Dec. 883/2 The hands [of my watch] would straightway begin to spin round and round... She would reel off the next twenty-four hours in six or seven minutes. **1872** —— *Roughing It* iv. 46 We reeled off ten or twelve miles. **1928** *Granta* 30 Nov. 172/2 Milton just reeled out bits about Christmas when he was up here. **1961** *Trains Illustr.* Nov. 685/2 The 11 miles between posts 137 and 148 were reeled off at an average of 93.8 m.p.h. **1972** J. MOSEDALE *Football* iv. 50 The Rams became the most exciting team in football, reeling off six straight victories. **1976** *0–10 Cricket Scene* (Austral.) 33/2 In a fine performance in which he reeled off 35.5 overs, he captured 5–148 in the Third Test in Australia at Adelaide in 1974.

3. a. (Later examples.) Also, to draw *in*, as with a reel.

1942 *Tee Emm* (Air Ministry) II. 57 A large passenger aircraft was struck while its trailing aerial was still reeled out. **1975** *Offshore* Aug. 121/1 The test pipeline was reeled from the Chickasaw into water depths of approximately 1,000 to 1,040 feet. **1978** *Sci. Amer.* Feb. 158/1 To launch a kite hold it about 20 degrees forward of the vertical and in approximately the correct flying attitude, release it as a gust of wind passes and slowly reel out line. *Ibid.* 158/2 To bring the kite down you probably will reel in the kite line. **1979** *Amat. Photographer* 10 Jan. 73/2 It's also dangerous, and illegal, to have permanent power points in a bathroom, so you must reel in an extension cable each time so you can use your enlarger, safelights, etc.

b. *intr.* Const. *out*: to become uncoiled from a reel. So **ree·l-out** *sb.*

1975 *Daily Tel.* 11 Sept. 3/7 Three cases of seat belts reeling out with no load being taken by the belt until all the webbing was off the reel, and four cases of excessive reel-out.

re-elect, *v.* Add: Hence **re-ele·cted** *ppl. a.*

1838 J. L. ADOLPHUS in J. G. Lockhart *Life Scott* VII. vi 221 He spoke very beautifully and warmly of the re-elected candidate who sat by him. **1974** *Times* 4 Mar. 2/7 Re-elected Conservatives are anxious to make their views known.

reeler[1]. **2.** Delete *Obs. rare*[—1] and add: In mod. use, a machine which winds paper, yarn, etc., on to reels. (Later examples.)

1906 [see *RE-REEL *v.*]. **1907** [see *cop-winder* s.v. *COP *sb.*[2] 8]. **1929** CLAPPERTON & HENDERSON *Mod. Paper-Making* xvi. 246 Many defects in the paper..will..cause a break at the reeler, owing to the high tension of the paper as it passes from the roll to the reeler bar. **1952** F. H. NORRIS *Paper & Paper Making* xvii. 246 The reeler is equipped with a yardage counter and may have four winding drums. **1955** S. C. GILMOUR *Paper* vi. 59 On most modern machines..a drum reeler is more common.

3. *Cinemat.* Used with a qualifying number, as *two-reeler* or *two reeler*, to designate a film consisting of the given number of reels. orig. *U.S.* Cf. *REEL *sb.*[1] 3 c.

1916 *Chicago Herald* 17 Feb. 3/4 Essanay will make an international release of the eight-reeler. **1922** H. L. WILSON *Merton of Movies* v. 90, I got another two reeler to pull off after this one. **1938** F. H. RICKETSON *Managem. Motion Picture Theatres* 121 Coming-attraction trailers can be spotted after the newsreel. A two-reeler, if the length of the feature permits, or a one-reel comedy can follow. **1976** L. KENNEDY *Presumption of Innocence* ii. 88 A kind of mad, surrealistic quality, like an early Chaplin two-reeler.

Hence **ree·lerman**, one who operates a reeler (sense *2).

1929 CLAPPERTON & HENDERSON *Mod. Paper-Making* xvi. 247 The yardage is kept on two different tickets by the reelerman.

reeler[2] (rī·ləɹ). [f. REEL *v.*[1] + -ER[1].] **a.** A stagger; esp. in slang phr. *to cop a reeler*, to get drunk. **b.** One who sways or staggers; a drunken person.

1937 J. CURTIS *You're in Racket, Too* v. 60 Make him swear blind he'll be quiet as he comes up the stairs, see? Of course, if he's copped a reeler you'll have to skip it. **1960** A. CLARKE *Later Poems*(1961) 76 Though every firework has been banned, Student or reeler from a band Flung it.

reeling, *vbl. sb.*[2] Add: **1. a.** (Further examples.) Also *concr.*, reeled yarn or the like.

1894 *Cassell's New Technical Educator* IV. 369/1 The reelings are then weighed and made up into bundles. **1906** W. MACFARLANE *Princ. & Pract. Iron & Steel Manuf.* iv. 47 Bars for certain purposes are straightened by reeling. **1952** F. H. NORRIS *Paper & Paper Making* xvii. 246 There are also the faults..which in turn will add their quota of troubles in supercalendering and reeling. **1973** J. G. TWEEDDALE *Materials Technol.* II. iv. 95 A simplified form of a two-high mill of this kind can be used for straightening rolls and tubes by causing spiral flexture [*sic*] in the cold condition, a process called reeling. **1974** *Encycl. Brit. Macropædia* XVIII. 173/2 Reeling is the process of unwinding raw silk filament from the cocoon directly onto a holder.

b. *reeling drive, machine* (later examples).

1962 G. A. T. BURDETT *Automatic Control Handbk.* vii. 9 This is the basis of a large number of electronic control schemes embracing..coiling and reeling drives [etc.]. **1904** HARBORD & HALL *Metallurgy of Steel* xxxii. 506 Both are passed through the reeling machine. This consists of a pair of conical rolls, revolving both in the same direction, and lying side by side, their axes being placed, not horizontally, but inclined to the horizon a few degrees in opposite directions, so as to cross each other at a slight angle in the middle of their length. **1926** J. B. WALKER *Story of Steel* xii. 117 The next step is to pass the tube..through what is known as the reeling machine... In this operation any mill-scale is removed; the tubes are given a smooth, burnished surface. **1971** W. K. V. GALE *Iron & Steel Industry: Dict. Terms* 168 *Reeling machine*, a machine which straightens round steel bars by passing them between specially shaped rollers which induce reverse bending.

reely, reelly (rī·li). Representing a vulgar pronunciation of REALLY *adv.*[2]

In quot. 1792 representing the pronunciation of a German speaker.

1792 F. BURNEY *Jrnl.* May (1972) I. 152 Mrs. Schwellenberg exclaimed 'But, Miss Berner, I hear it bin reelly true you will Marry!' **1910** H. G. WELLS *Hist. Mr. Polly* vi. 158 Thought my bicycle was on fire... All right reely. **1933** E. A. ROBERTSON *Ordinary Families* x. 222 'E's a good boy to us, reelly, Ted is. **1939** JOYCE *Finnegans Wake* (1964) II. 527 Of course it was downright verry wickred of him, reely meeting me disguised. **1967** N. MARSH *Death at Dolphin* i. 9 'Well—I don't know, reely, if we've anybody free at the moment,' said the clerk.

re-embarkment. Add: Also 8 re-im-. (Earlier and later examples.)

1728 G. CARLETON *Mem. Eng. Officer* 95 The heavy artillery landed for the siege was return'd aboard the ships, and everything in appearance prepar'd for a re-imbarkment. **1915** J. CHURCHILL *Jrnl.* 21 Mar. in M. Gilbert *Winston S. Churchill* (1972) III. Compan. I. 722 The re-embarkment would take longer.

re-embo·died, *ppl. a.* [f. RE-EMBODY *v.* + -ED[1].] Reincarnated. So **re-embo·diment.**

1901 'A. HOPE' *Tristram of Blent* xiii. 175 That re-embodiment or resurrection of her in the girl who moved and talked and sat like her, who had her ways though not her face. **1924** W. B. SELBIE *Psychol. Relig.* 271 In Indo-European folk-lore, dogs, wolves, and hares represent such re-embodied spirits.

re-embroi·der, *v.* [RE- 5 a.] *trans.* To ornament with additional embroidery. So **re-embroi·dered** *ppl. a.*; **re-embroi·dering** *vbl. sb.* (also *attrib.*).

1927 *Daily Express* 8 Apr. 5 The gown is of ivory silk lace, re-embroidered with small china beads. *Ibid.*, Interesting example of the re-embroidering vogue. In this case an embroidery of coloured taffeta and bugle beads was applied to black Spanish lace. **1963** *Times* 24 Jan. 12/4 Re-embroidered white lace is used. **1968** J. IRONSIDE *Fashion Alphabet* 235 *Re-embroidered*: This is a lace with an all-over motif outlined and emphasised by re-embroidering either with silk thread, ribbon, braid or metallic yarns. **1974** *Times-Picayune* (New Orleans) 15 Aug. v. 6/1 The bride.. wore a peau de soie gown styled with a sculptured yoke of re-embroidered lace and a cameo neckline.

re-emission. (Further examples.)

1955 FRIEDMAN & WEISSKOPF in W. Pauli *Niels Bohr* 136 These states..have a finite lifetime, since they can decay by the re-emission of the incident particle. **1968** G. M. B. DOBSON *Exploring Atmosphere* (ed. 2) iii. 62 As a result of this complicated process of constant absorption and re-emission of radiation,..the ground..absorbs about half of the incoming solar radiation.

re-emit, *v.* (Further examples.)

1924 *Proc. Physical Soc.* XXXVI. 422 It is possible that the α-particle is in some way attached to the residual nucleus. Certainly it cannot be re-emitted with any considerable energy, or we should be able to observe it. **1955** *Bull. Atomic Sci.* Mar. 92/1 Several neutrons are re-emitted when a uranium atom is exploded by one neutron. **1969** *Times* 19 Feb. 13/6 Atoms and molecules of the atmosphere absorb sunlight and then reemit the energy at wavelengths which are characteristic of the particular type of atom or molecule.

re-e·mphasize, *v.* [RE- 5 a.] *trans.* To emphasize again, to place renewed emphasis on. So **re-e·mphasis.**

1857 E. B. BROWNING *Aurora Leigh* I. 26 From many a volume, Love re-emphasised. **1894** J. R. ILLINGWORTH *Personality, Human & Divine* i. 18 This intimacy and immediacy of possible union between the soul and God..had long vanished from the popular religion. Luther re-emphasized it. **1934** WEBSTER, Re-emphasis. **1948** J. TOWSTER *Polit. Power in U.S.S.R.* viii. 174 The changes or re-emphases that took place. **1971** *Nature* 23 Apr. 490/3 He also reemphasizes his original contention that an anomalous situation does exist.

Reemy, var. *R.E.M.E., REME.

re-enclo·se, *v.* [RE- 5 a.] To enclose again.

1598 FLORIO *Worlde of Wordes* 307/2 *Racchiúdere*,..to re-enclose or shut vp againe. *Racchiuso*, re-enclosed or shut vp againe. **1849** E. A. POE *Let.* 13 Jan. (1948) II. 416 Please re-enclose me the printed papers. **1870** 'MARK TWAIN' *Lett. to Publishers* (1967) 31, I re-enclose the Express letter, as you desire. **1907** R. BROOKE *Let.* 29 Oct. (1968) 114 You probably know all this already from Mrs Leon. I re-enclose her letter.

re-encounter, *sb.* **b.** (Later examples.)

1904 *Daily Chron.* 28 July 8/5 If she is wise she will.. avoid disenchanting re-encounters in the flesh. **1948** *Times Lit. Suppl.* 18 Sept. 526/3 Mr. Sassoon..sets down his personal experience of the re-encounter. **1974** FRITH & MCLAUCHLAN in R. K. Harris *Nuclear Magnetic Resonance* (Chem. Soc. Specialist Periodical Rep.) III. xii. 387 This.. broadens our definition of cage recombination to include reaction of the original partners in the radical pair on re-encounter after their initial diffusive separation.

re-enforcer. (In Dict. s.v. RE-ENFORCE *v.*) Add: Also, something which re-enforces.

1914 W. MCDOUGALL *Social Psychol.* 404 The energy of the sex impulse..may function as a re-enforcer of purely intellectual activities.

re-engine, *v.* Add: (Later examples.) Also of an aeroplane. Hence **re-e·ngined** *ppl. a.*; **re-e·ngining** *vbl. sb.*

1941 *Sun* (Baltimore) 20 Jan. 2/7 Reengined and rearmed Hurricanes, new Tornadoes..and improved Defiants. **1955** *Times* 23 Aug. 5/1 The Grants Scheme should be extended to include the re-engining and re-conditioning of suitable trawlers. **1967** *Jane's Surface Skimmer Syst.* 1967–68 36 (*caption*) A re-engined version of the BHC SR.N5. **1973** *Stornoway Gaz.* 2 June 2/5 The cruising speed will be 14½ knots—she has not been re-engined.

re:-enginee·r, *v.* [RE- 5 a.] *trans.* To design and construct anew; also *transf.* and *fig.*, to arrange or contrive anew.

1944 *Sun* (Baltimore) 14 Dec. 4-0/3 Management and labor should decide now..whether jobs re-engineered for women will be restored to provide work for servicemen. **1946** *Jrnl. Inst. Electr. Engineers* XCIII. IIIA. 59/2 It was decided therefore to re-engineer the system using aerial arrays. **1958** J. K. GALBRAITH *Affluent Society* xiii. 194 The first task of the public relations man is to 're-engineer' his image to include something besides the production of goods. **1974** W. REES-MOGG *Reigning Error* v. 104 The most fundamental relationships of human life have been re-engineered in order to prevent sufferings which turned out to represent the unavoidable limitations of human existence. **1977** *Gramophone* Feb. 1346/2 The new GT55P arm has been completely re-engineered.

So **re-enginee·red** *ppl. a.*, **re-enginee·ring** *vbl. sb.*

1962 *Rep. Comm. Broadcasting 1960* 337 in *Parl. Papers 1961–2* (Cmnd. 1753) IX. 259 The importance..of planning the use of Bands IV and V (and when the time comes the re-engineered Bands I and III)..as an integrated whole. **1973** C. SAGAN *Cosmic Connection* (1974) xxii. 150 Our motivations for planetary re-engineering must be clear. **1977** *Time* 18 Apr. 46/2 What would happen, they ask, if by accident or design, one variety of re-engineered *E. coli* proved dangerous?

re-enli·ster. [f. RE-ENLIST *v.* + -ER[1].] A person who enlists again.

1908 *Daily Chron.* 8 May 8/2 The majority of the re-enlisters 'are the discontented, the thriftless, the criminal class'.

re-enlistment. Add: Also *attrib.*

1953 R. WELLS (*song-title*) Re-enlistment blues. **1970** *Times* 28 May 7/7 A source of much resentment is the iniquitous system whereby the Army maintains a high re-enlistment rate.

re-enslavement. (Earlier example.)

1859 LD. LYONS *Let.* 6 Dec. in Ld. Newton *Lord Lyons* (1913) I. ii. 19 The reenslavement of all the emancipated negroes.

re-enter, *v.* Add: **1. c.** (Later example.) Also in wider contexts.

1803 G. COLMAN *John Bull* IV. i. 56 Re-enter Dan booted. **1937** 'M. INNES' *Hamlet, Revenge!* II. iii. 137 And so—just conceivably—re-enter the spies.

2. c. *spec.* of spacecraft. Also *absol.*

1961 *Times* 6 May 8/2 Seven minutes after take-off the report came through that the capsule was beginning to reenter the earth's atmosphere. **1962** S. CARPENTER in *Into Orbit* 56 The capsule should not re-enter too quickly or the deceleration will be too great. **1968** *Times* 16 Dec. 7/3 A second crucial phase begins when Apollo 8 reenters the earth's atmosphere. **1977** G. SCOTT *Hot Pursuit* x. 90 The Americans..spotted it... It looked as though it was about to reenter.

d. In the drilling of offshore oil wells and similar holes: to enter (a borehole) again with a drilling bit.

1961 W. BASCOM *Hole in Bottom of Sea* xii. 244 Two parallel guide lines, stretched between the ship and fittings on the bottom, had a sliding crossbar to guide the bit so that the hole could be re-entered at will. **1967** *Ocean Industry* June 15/1 Sonar system for hole re-entry which makes it possible to re-enter a small diameter borehole in three-mile-deep water. **1968** *Proc. Offshore Exploration Conf.* 241 The drilling personnel have found it necessary to remove the drill string and desire to reenter it at a later time. **1975** *Proc. Offshore Technol. Conf.* I. 27/1 One beacon..is attached to the object being re-entered (well head) and the other beacon..is attached to the re-entry tool.

4. (Earlier example.)

1838 W. HOWITT *Rural Life Eng.* I. I. v. 81 On applying to the steward he found that he was actually re-entered as tenant to the farm.

Hence **re-e·nterable** *a.*, capable of being re-entered.

1969 P. B. JORDAIN *Condensed Computer Encycl.* 423 A reenterable program can service several tasks concurrently by switching from one task to another task at high speed.

re-entering, *ppl. a.* **2.** (Further examples.)

1958 *Punch* 17 Sept. 361/1 Re-entering nose-cones. **1959** *Daily Tel.* 14 Apr. 1/7 The proposed American attempt to catch a re-entering satellite is a very long shot indeed. **1974** *Encycl. Brit. Macropædia* XV. 938/2 In the early 1960s a new technique..was developed, using materials similar to those employed as heat shields for re-entering space vehicles.

re-e·ntrancy. [f. RE-ENTRANCE + -Y[3].] **a.** *Electr.* The state of being re-entrant; also, a measure of the number of complete turns required to trace out an armature winding (see *RE-ENTRANT *a.* 2 a).

1901 SHELDON & MASON *Dynamo Electr. Machinery* iii. 47 Any closed-coil winding, single or multiple, may be singly or multiply re-entrant, the re-entrancy being reckoned as great as that of any single winding on the armature. **1902** *Jrnl. Inst. Electr. Engineers* XXXI. IV. 933 A few writers.. take the re-entrancy as being the number of times we must go around the armature in tracing out the whole winding. *Ibid.* 935 Condition of Re-entrancy.—The first condition to be fulfilled by a proposed winding is that it should re-enter upon itself. **1907** HOBART & ELLIS *Armature Construction* viii. 157 Multiplicity and re-entrancy of multiplex windings.

b. The capability of being entered again.

1976 P. C. SANDERSON *Minicomputers* iv. 72 For some applications, hardware should allow re-entrancy. This allows the same procedures to be performed on different blocks of data. **1976** *Nature* 11 Mar. 176/2 There is an absence of detailed comment on..modern programming techniques which are important for memory-starved mini-computers, such as subroutine re-entrancy.

re-entrant, *a.* (and *sb.*) For **b** read **B** and add: **A.** *adj.* **1. a.** (Further examples.)

1967 M. CHANDLER *Ceramics in Mod. World* iv. 122 It is difficult to form reentrant shapes between two dies. **1973** J. G. TWEEDDALE *Materials Technol.* II. iv. 94 There are limits on the shapes of the grooves in grooved rolls, re-entrant angles are completely unusable. **1975** D. G. FINK *Electronics Engineers' Handbk.* IX. 49 Magnetron oscillators are single-port devices. Both the slow-wave circuit and the electron stream are reentrant; i.e., the circular geometry is always used.

b. *Mus.* Designating a form of tuning of the open strings of the citole, cittern, and ukulele, in which the fourth course is tuned to a higher pitch than the third, as e′, d′, g, b or e′, d′, g, a for the cittern.

1948 *Galpin Soc. Jrnl.* I. 48 The cittern's curious re-entrant tuning gives simply-fingered versions of all the chords commonly used in contemporary music. **1961** A. BAINES *Mus. Instruments* vii. 166 Its [*sc.* the cittern's] tunings..were re-entrant, with the fourth course higher in pitch than the third, as on the modern ukelele. **1976** D. MUNROW *Instruments Middle Ages & Renaissance* iv. 27/1 The instrument which Tinctoris describes [*c.* 1487] is unquestionably the ancestor of the renaissance cittern, with.. a re-entrant tuning for its four metal strings. *Ibid.*, The earliest account of the tuning of any stringed instrument, that of Jerome of Moravia (*c.* 1250), described three fiddle tunings, one of which is re-entrant.

2. a. Of or pertaining to something which returns upon itself, as in *Electr.*, applied to a form of armature winding (see quot. 1901); in *Acoustics*, applied to a form of horn loudspeaker in which the bore is divided and folded upon itself before expanding to the flare, in order to reduce space.

1901 SHELDON & MASON *Dynamo Electr. Machinery* iii. 46 A singly-re-entrant winding is one in which, by successive angular advances, all the coils have been laid when an advance of 360° has been made. To be doubly-re-entrant wound the angular advance between successive coils, in the order of their winding, is doubled; and the whole winding is not complete until the armature has been gone around, angularly, twice, i.e., through an advance of 720°. **1902** *Jrnl. Inst. Electr. Engineers* XXXI. IV. 933 A winding is re-entrant if it comes back to the starting point and is then complete. **1928** *Gramophone* Jan. 345/1 There are now listed three models (called 're-entrant') in which a relatively broad acoustic system is, by means of embodying a double reflexion of tone, enabled correctly to expand to quite a wide-mouthed horn in no greater depth from front to back than is allowable in the relatively shallow American pattern cabinet. **1940** *Chambers's Techn. Dict.* 710/1 The majority of windings are singly re-entrant. **1960** *Practical Wireless* XXXVI. 395/2 Speakers of the re-entrant type will be found most suitable. **1961** BRIGGS & COOKE *A to Z in Audio* 79 One of the earliest applications of this principle [*sc.* that of the exponential horn] to sound reproduction was probably the re-entrant gramophone produced by HMV in 1927.

b. *Computers.* Of, pertaining to, or designating a program or subprogram which may be called or entered many times concurrently from one or several programs without alteration of the results obtained from any one execution.

1964 *Proc. Fall Joint Computer Conf.* I. 45 (*heading*) Method of control for re-entrant programs. *Ibid.* 45/1 A routine which permits unlimited multiple entrances and executions before prior executions are complete is called a re-entrant routine. **1970** O. DOPPING *Computers & Data Processing* xiv. 221 A form of programming which allows re-entry into a partially used subroutine is called re-entrant programming. **1976** H. D. BAECKER in *Virtual Storage* (Infotech International Ltd.) 195 Allocation of and access to local variables in recursive or re-entrant environments. *Ibid.*, Re-entrant programs are not only a good thing because of their alleged economy of space.

B. *sb.* **b.** *Geogr.* A prominent, angular indentation into a landform, such as an inlet between two coastal promontories or a valley extending into a hill or mountain side.

1893 [see *pocket-beach* s.v. *POCKET *sb.* 13]. **1899** R. T. HILL *Geol. Jamaica* i. 18 The interior mountains are marked by deeply etched knife-edged salients..and angular re-entrants. **1936** *Bull. Amer. Assoc. Petroleum Geologists* XX. 1224 The profound reëntrant between the escarpment of the Serra das Furnas and that of the Serra de São Joaquim. **1962** J. ONSLOW *Bowler-Hatted Cowboy* v. 53 Dense spruce spread from the valley upwards, following the big re-entrants. **1973** C. BONINGTON *Next Horizon* xviii. 248 The road was like a switchback gone mad, as it bucked from valley floor, over spurs, round re-entrants and down again.

re-entry. Add: **2. b.** *card of re-entry*: also, in Bridge, a card which by winning a trick gives the lead (in his own hand or in dummy) to a player who has previously had it. Also *re-entry card* and *ellipt.* as *re-entry*.

1899 A. DUNN *Bridge* 22 If the long suit hand has no card of re-entry, he will be prevented from bringing in his suit. **1905** [see *DUCK *v.* 6]. **1908** R. F. FOSTER *Auction Bridge* 84 In planning the play of a no-trumper, the declarer must be careful to provide for re-entry cards. **1958** *Listener* 9 Oct. 572/1 If he had a suit headed by K Q J and a re-entry he would pass, not overcall. **1967** COHEN & BARROW *Bridge Players' Encycl.* 405/1 *Re-entry*, a card by which a player who had the lead (including the opening lead) can regain it.

c. *Astronautics.* The return of a spacecraft into the earth's atmosphere.

1948 *Jrnl. Brit. Interplanetary Soc.* VII. 34 The technique of atmospheric re-entry will be developed from progressively daring excursions into space. **1961** *Guardian* 6 May 1/3 The vapour trail caused by the re-entry of the capsule. **1968** *Times* 16 Dec. 7/2 The reentry of the first rocket stage into the atmosphere. **1970** *Guardian* 18 Apr. 1/1 The spacecraft ..appeared to be badly scarred by the heat of re-entry. **1977** G. SCOTT *Hot Pursuit* x. 89 Clearly it had not been programmed to come down where it did; you've seen how it was damaged in re-entry and landing.

d. The act of re-inserting a drilling bit into a borehole during the drilling of an offshore oil well or similar hole.

1961 W. BASCOM *Hole in Bottom of Sea* xiii. 271 There would be no riser pipe or other means of hole re-entry. If the bit were once withdrawn, the hole would be lost. **1962** *Design of Deep Ocean Drilling Ship* (U.S. Nat. Research Council) 64 A riser pipe may be the best means of hole re-entry... When re-entry is attempted—after a bit change, for example—as the pipe tip approaches bottom a sensing sonde will be lowered into position at the bit which will be able to sense the tip of the projecting casing. **1968** *Proc. Offshore Exploration Conf.* 242 Reentry was attempted by two engineers with only one reentry for a number of attempts. **1974** *Geotimes* Dec. 16/2 The casing broke just below the reëntry core, and was displaced downward.. after 4 successful reëntries, eventually preventing further reëntry.

e. *Surfing.* (See quot. 1968.)

1968 W. WARWICK *Surfriding in N.Z.* 14/1 A re-entry is a roller coaster, taken a stage further. To perform this tactic, your board must be moving roughly parallel to the top of the wave and as the wave begins to break, kick your board to the top so that it is sitting on top of the curl with virtually no water covering its deck. Your board will appear to have stalled at the top of the wave for a second then it will be sucked back down with the curl. **1970** *Surf* I. x. 11/2 Finishes it off with a re-entry.

f. Return to one's usual place or mode of living.

1972 *Listener* 31 Aug. 270/1 The standard pattern of war veterans..a difficulty in what is called 're-entry', in getting back into the civilian society. **1974** *N.Y. Times* 8 July 1/3 'Country' is where you go..to escape from your city responsibilities, and when country-time ends, re-entry can be traumatic.

4. b. *Philately.* (See quots.)

1916 F. J. MELVILLE *Postage Stamps in Making* I. ix. 96 The varieties of the first British stamps which are best described as having had the roller applied twice, or 're-entries' known to have existed on Plate 145 of the 1d., Small Crown, imperforate, and other plates of Great Britain. **1951** R. J. SUTTON *Stamp Collector's Encycl.* 191 *Re-entry*, duplication of part of a stamp design due to a first impression having been inadequately erased, and thus enabling traces of its 'entry' to appear in conjunction with the new impression, causing a doubling of a part of the image... Known in the U.S.A. as 'shift'. **1971** D. POTTER *Brit. Eliz. Stamps* xiv. 159 On recess-printed stamps the entry die may momentarily make contact in part, twice, and slight doubling of the design results. This is known as a re-entry. **1972** D. & M. PATRICK *Hodder Stamp Dict.* (1973) 204/1 *Re-entry*, a second attempt to rock in the stamp design on a steel plate for engraving postage stamps... A perfect re-entry leaves no second line on the stamps. **1975** B. GUNSTON *Philatelist's Compan.* 247 *Re-entry*, characteristic doubling or thinning of portions of the design of a line-engraved stamp caused by the impression having been entered more than once on the plate.

5. *attrib.* (*a*) in sense *2 c, as *re-entry angle, black-out, capsule, heating, parachute, problem, vehicle*; (*b*) in sense 'giving permission for re-entry into a country', as *re-entry permit, visa*; **re-entry card**: see sense 2 b above; **re-entry point** *Computers* (see quots.).

1970 *Daily Tel.* 17 Apr. 6/1 Without this burn, the spacecraft would miss by 100 miles the critical re-entry angle, between 5·6 and 7·2 degrees. **1966** *Electronics* 14 Nov. 54 Reentry blackout has plagued every flight in the Mercury and Gemini series. **1967** *Technology Week* 20 Feb. 10/2 *Biosatellite I's* re-entry capsule containing biological specimens and data on magnetic tape..is believed to have re-entered in or near Australia. **1962** F. I. ORDWAY et al. *Basic Astronautics* i. 5 A review of the problems of reentry heating. **1976** P. CAVE *High Flying Birds* i. 11 Originally designed as a possible re-entry parachute device for space capsules, the flying sail designed by Francis M. Rogallo in the early sixties has come a long way. **1948** F. FRENAYE tr. *Levi's Christ stopped at Eboli* xiii. 123 Before they are aware of it.. their re-entry permit [to the US] has expired, and they have to stay at home. **1972** R. PERRY *Fall Guy* iv. 73 Wondering whether I'd be granted a re-entry permit. **1922** *Gloss. Terms Automatic Data Processing* (*B.S.I.*) II. 39 The point at which a routine is re-entered from a subroutine is a re-entry point. **1977** *Gloss. Terms Data Processing* (*B.S.I.*) VII. 8/1 *Reentry point*, the address or the label of the instruction at which the computer program that called a subroutine is reentered from the subroutine. **1957** *Times* 9 Nov. 6/5 The President's positive claim that the United States has solved the so-called re-entry problem of bringing space missiles back to earth. **1965** *New Scientist* 2 Dec. 638/1 Further improvement is being made with re-entry vehicles which embody penetration aids against anti-missile defence. **1973** *Times* 26 Feb. (Arms for Peace Suppl.) p. ii/4 The United States, by possessing the ability to put multiple independently targeted reentry vehicles on her launchers, has many more nuclear warheads than the Soviet Union. **1973** J. SHUB *Moscow by Nightmare* xi. 125 I'm not coming back... The Soviet Embassy called me yesterday. They've cancelled my re-entry visa. **1977** *Times* 11 May 7/8 The Soviet authorities had given him a permanent reentry visa so that he can return to Moscow.

re-equip, *v.* (Later examples.)

1919 J. L. GARVIN *Econ. Foundations Peace* viii. 158 Their industrial centres, wherever existing, have to be re-equipped. **1944** J. S. HUXLEY *On Living in Revolution* 148 Neither the profit motive nor political considerations should be allowed to interfere with the job of re-equipping Europe. **1960** *Farmer & Stockbreeder* 19 Jan. (Suppl.) 6/1 Currently engaged in re-equipping many leading breeding and research farms.

re-e·scalate, *v.* [f. RE- 5 a + *ESCALATE *v.* 2.] *trans.* To escalate (a war or conflict) again. Also *absol.*

1965 H. KAHN *On Escalation* xii. 237 Further bargaining is rarely successful unless the conflict is re-escalated. **1965** *Punch* 4 Aug. 165/1 Up and down this ladder nations may escalate, de-escalate and re-escalate. **1972** *Sat. Rev.* (U.S.) 6 May 34/1 President Nixon has always kept for himself the option of re-escalating the war.

So **re-escala·tion**, the act or process of re-escalating. Also *attrib.*

1965 H. KAHN *On Escalation* xii. 231 De-escalation dominance might also involve being in a good position to resume fighting if the other side forced further action. The latter property could also be called 're-escalation dominance'. *Ibid.* 234 Of course, de-escalation cannot guarantee that re-escalation will not occur.

re-estate, *v.* Delete † *Obs.* and add later example.

a **1945** E. R. EDDISON *Mezentian Gate* (1972) ix. 82 Kallias's meaning was by this alliance to re-estate his power in the Meszrian Marches.

reet (rīt), *a.* U.S. dial. var. RIGHT *a.* (usu. in sense 8).

Also a common dial. var. in the U.K.: see *Eng. Dial. Dict.*

1934 in WEBSTER. **1942** *Amer. Mercury* July 85 Jelly got into his zoot suit with the reet pleats. **1943** *Crisis* July 201/2 Negro youths will crack at anyone of any race who is nice looking. They will say, 'A fine queen..a reet cheet'. **1946** B. TREADWELL *Big Bk. Swing* 125/1 *Reet*, fine, O.K. **1977** *Hot Car* Oct. 42/3 People I've spoken to who went last year said it was reet good and very alcoholic.

re-eva·luate, *v.* [RE- 5 a.] *trans.* To evaluate again.

1945 *Physiol. Rev.* XXV. 126 Those same changes which were originally considered slight and of no consequence have more recently been re-evaluated in the light of new experiments and are now spoken of as 'worthy of emphasis'. **1964** M. A. K. HALLIDAY et al. *Linguistic Sci.* p. xiii, As theories develop so must applications thereof be re-expounded, and books continually re-evaluated. **1972** *Jrnl. Social Psychol.* LXXXVII. 145 The modified semantic differential was translated into Afghan colloquial speech and reevaluated according to the criteria of excellence. **1976** *Nature* 29 Apr. 740/2 It asked the Secretary of the Department of Health, Education and Welfare (of which NIDA is a part) to reevaluate the project and determine whether Rubin is suitably qualified to conduct the research. **1979** *Time* 2 Apr. 2/3 Their music has the power to force people to reevaluate their ideas and institutions.

Hence **re-evalua·tion**, a second or further evaluation.

1946 *Nature* 16 Nov. 689/2 In view of the great progress made in recent years on the pancreatic enzymes, there is no doubt that much of the older work on the peptidases, etc., of the intestinal canal will need re-evaluation. **1959** *Encounter* Sept. 58/1 These re-evaluations called into question the accepted idea of the populist basis of American radicalism. **1970** *Publishers' Weekly* 8 June 152/1 This capability is worth noting; it may cause a reevaluation of short-run publishing. **1972** *Maclean's Mag.* Sept. 12/2 It is too much to hope that it will cause a re-evaluation in the selection of officers from the top down. **1976** *Nature* 29 Apr. 740/2 The reevaluation was carried out on March 11 at a closed meeting.

reeve, *sb.*[1] **2. d.** (Earlier and later examples.)

1853 S. STRICKLAND *27 Yrs. Canada West* II. 271 Counties..choose their reeves, and deputy reeves where the population admits of it, and these form the county council. **1884** *Brandon* (Manitoba) *Blade* 17 Jan. 8/3 The Reeve, in a few well chosen remarks, dwelt on the duties and responsibilities devolving on them as servants of the people. **1945** G. W. BROWN *Canad. Democracy in Action* vii. 89 The town council consists of a mayor, a reeve, and two or three councillors elected for each of the wards. **1965** *Victoria* (B.C.) *Daily Times* 20 July 11/8 The reeve said the general principle of regional planning is good but the mechanics need improving. **1968** *Globe & Mail* (Toronto) 5 Feb. 1/3 Dresden Reeve Wilfred Shaw said 61 families had been removed from their houses by firemen and other town employees.

reeve, *v.*[1] Add: **3. d.** *fig.* To gather together.

1876 G. M. HOPKINS *Wreck of Deutschland* xii, in *Poems* (1967) 55 Yet did the dark side of the bay of thy blessing Not vault them, the millions of rounds of thy mercy not reeve even them in?

Reeves (rīvz). The name of John Reeves (1774–1856), English naturalist, used *absol.*, *attrib.*, or in the possessive in **Reeves('s) pheasant** to designate a long-tailed Chinese pheasant, *Syrmaticus reevesii*, introduced to Europe by him and named in his honour by J. E. Gray in 1829.

1829 J. E. GRAY in E. Griffith et al. tr. *Cuvier's Anim. Kingdom* VIII. 25 (*heading*) Reeves' Pheasant, *Phasianus Reevesii*. **1834** G. BENNETT *Wanderings in N.S.W.* II. iv. 55 In the aviary [at Macao], the beautiful..Reeves's Pheasant, was seen. **1922** W. BEEBE *Monogr. Pheasants* III. 146 Then came my first view of a live Reeves in its wild home. **1926** J. S. HUXLEY *Ess. Pop. Sci.* 47 If a female Reeves pheasant is crossed with a male of another race, the males among the hybrid offspring show many characters of the male Reeves pheasant. **1951** J. DELACOUR *Pheasants of World* ix. 227 Reeves's Pheasants are found on all the higher wooded hills of Central China north of the Yangtze River. **1975** *Islander* (Victoria, B.C.) 19 Oct. 4/3 We now have..the rare Reeves pheasant. **1976** *Shooting Times & Country Mag.* 18–24 Nov. 28/2 He is, however, incorrect in his remarks about the Reeves pheasant.

reevesite (rī·vzəit). *Min.* [f. the name of Frank *Reeves*, Australian geologist + -ITE[1].] A hydrated basic carbonate of nickel and iron, $Ni_6Fe_2CO_3(OH)_{16}.4H_2O$, occurring as yellowish plates.

1967 J. S. WHITE et al. in *Amer. Mineralogist* LII. 1182 Reevesite: This mineral occurs as bright yellow fine-grained aggregates lining cavities and cracks in the weathered meteorites. *Ibid.* 1193 The mineral is named reevesite in honor of Dr. Frank Reeves, who was responsible for the discovery of the Wolf Creek meteorite crater in 1947. **1971** *Ibid.* LVI. 1077 Reevesite..has been found in the nickel ore from the Bon Accord area in the Barberton Mountain Land, South Africa.

reeving, *vbl. sb.*[1] (Further *attrib.* examples.)

1969 E. H. PINTO *Treen* 266 The pear-shaped, elm object is a reeving block. **1971** *Gloss. Terms Materials Handling* (*B.S.I.*) v. 18 *Reeving thimble*, a thimble..of sufficient internal length and breadth for one thimble to pass through another. **1975** *Offshore* Sept. (Dutch Suppl.) 49–12/3 The actual pulling wires, also 57-mm diameter, ran from the Pontra Maris to a sheave pontoon anchored 2 km away by eight 7·2-ton capacity delta anchors. The reeving system allowed a total pulling force of 600 tons.

re-excite, *v.* Add: (Earlier example.) Hence **re-exciting** *vbl. sb.* and *ppl. a.*

1697 J. SERGEANT *Solid Philos.* 195 Some short time must be allow'd for the coming of Impressions from without ..and the Re-exciting them in the Fancy. *Ibid.* 438 Such Sounds, thro' the *use* of the Words are apt to re-excite the Memory. **1964** J. Z. YOUNG *Model of Brain* xiii. 211 Here we may notice that because it contains re-exciting circuits it could provide an increase in the 'command to attack' by what amounts to a positive feed-back.

re-existence. (Later example.)

1973 *Times Lit. Suppl.* 14 Dec. 1536/2 He builds up imaginary examples of transmigration, re-existence, etc.

re-export, *sb.* **2.** (Earlier examples.)

1761 J. GLEN *Descr. S. Carolina* 48 The Exports of South Carolina Produce are inserted in one Account, and the Re-exports of imported Commodities and Manufactures in another. **1775** *Jrnls. Continental Congress U.S.* (1905) III. 502 The reëxport employs ships, sailors [etc.].

ref (ref), *sb.*[1] Colloq. abbrev. of REFEREE *sb.* 3 b.

1899 R. H. BARBOUR *Halfback* xxii. 233 De Farge (the referee) is awfully down on holding and off-side plays. Last year he penalized us eight times during the game. But he's all right... He's the finest little ref that ever tossed a coin. **1939** *War Illustr.* 9 Dec. 394/3 Prisoners taken from U-boats and merchant ships are spending a happy hour kicking the ball about... An armed guard stands by, but not to protect the 'ref'. **1941** *London Opinion* Sept. 45/2 The referee goes to examine the eye while the crowd roars. Can he go in? The ref. moves away. He can. He does. **1957** I. CROSS *God Boy* (1958) 108 You're a pretty good ref, Sister. **1962** *Observer* 9 Sept. 16/2 A mob stormed outside the club offices shouting: 'We want the ref.' **1966** F. SHAW et al. *Lern Yerself Scouse* 51 *Buy a bewk, ref!* The referee appears to have forgotten the rules of the game. **1972** A. DRAPER *Death Penalty* iii. 18 He detested referees who were continually blowing their whistles... A ref could make or mar a game. **1976** *Listener* 29 Jan. 117/1 Adam is able to make good jokes about Cambridge..and there is no ref to blow the whistle on him.

ref (ref), *sb.*[2] Colloq. abbrev. of REFERENCE *sb.* (in Dict. and Suppl.) **a.** In sense 3.

1926 F. M. FORD *Let.* 9 Mar. (1965) 168 Yours of the 23d ult. Ref German Translation of *No More Parades.* **1967** WODEHOUSE *Company for Henry* ix. 149 'I want his advice.' 'With ref. to what?' 'Oh, something that's coming up'. **1971** —— *Much Obliged, Jeeves* xi. 108 It's with ref to that book you pinched from the Junior Ganymede.

b. In sense *6 b.

1901 [see *BOVRILIZE *v.*]. **1907** WESTBROOK & WODEHOUSE *Not George Washington* xvii. 183 Your refs. must be A1, or you don't stand an earthly. **1934** H. G. WELLS *Exper. Autobiogr.* I. iv. 161 Such questions seemed to me already of far more importance than satisfying J.K. or securing a satisfactory 'ref.' when my apprenticeship was up. **1974** P. WRIGHT *Lang. Brit. Industry* xii. 102 *Refs* (references).

ref (ref), *v. trans.* and *intr.* Colloq. abbrev. of REFEREE *v.*

1929 R. C. SHERRIFF *Journey's End* II. i. 50 *Raleigh.* Did you play Rugger? *Osborne.* Yes. But mostly reffing at school in the last few years. **1964** J. HALE *Grudge Fight* viii. 125 A scrum developed while Windy who was supposed to be reffing blew his whistle and went red in the face and didn't dare come too close. **1968** *Punch* 2 Oct. 457/3 Who says the game was badly reffed? The sending-off of Nobby Stiles, For nothing, was supremely deft. **1975** *Times* 4 Jan. 12/3 Muhammad Ali..was fighting Mildenberger and Teddy Waltham was reffing. **1977** *Gay News* 24 Mar. 2/2 Norman has recently been booked to ref games in California.

reface, *v.* Add: **3.** To face (a person, a concept) again.

1906 *Daily Chron.* 18 Apr. 3/4 Rather than re-face Mag McGhie..David prefers to 'face an angry Maker'. **1979** R. RENDELL *Make Death love Me* xii. 106 It would teach her to assume responsibility and re-face reality.

refained (rĭfē^i·nd), *a.* Also **refaned, refayned, refeened** (-fī·nd). Repr. an affected pronunc. of REFINED *ppl. a.* (with reference to sense 2). Freq. joc. or derogatory.

1930 A. HUXLEY *Brief Candles* 25 Altogether too much the lady—refained; you know the type. A Governess;..the genteel, Jane Eyre, daughter-of-clergyman kind. **1932** *New Statesman* 9 Jan. 36/2 Few audiences could take seriously a performance of *Hamlet* in which..Horatio [spoke] in what is known as the 'refaned' accent. **1939** R. CAMPBELL *Flowering Rifle* II. 46 The most 'refayned' of all that breed. **1940** W. DE LA MARE *Pleasures & Speculations* 137 His [*sc.* the advertiser's] tone is usually genteel and refaned. **1940** H. G. WELLS *New World Order* 53 A friendly adviser..protests against 'the wombs of associated labour'... My adviser produces.. 'the lap of social labour', which is more refained but pure nonsense. **1940** *John o' London's* 3 May 149/3 Edinburgh being very 'refained', the word [*sc.* keelie] is seldom used in the more polite society. **1941** V. WOOLF *Between Acts* 122 The old lady..looked too refined. 'Refeened'—Mrs. Manresa qualified the word to her own advantage... She could span the old lady's 'refeenment'. **1961** *Radio Times* 27 Apr. 63/4 *The Kilt Is My Delight* is indeed a delightful programme, but..may I suggest that it sometimes takes on a less 'refaned' air? Always these immaculately dressed ladies and gentlemen prance around in some 'stately home'. **1962** N. MARSH *Hand in Glove* i. 28 Nicola..wondered if Mr. Period would find the phrase 'refeened,' a word he often used with humorous intent. **1962** *Punch* 14 Feb. 297/3 An appalling gold-digger with a refained accent. **1969** M. O'BRINE *Mills* xi. 43 The Sangsters were much too 'refained to argue with someone they were meeting for the first time. **1972** A. MACVICAR *Golden Venus Affair* v. 53 Her accent was 'refained', but it betrayed a Glasgow East End origin. **1976** *Listener* 25 Mar. 386/4 The blowzy, mini-skirted divorcee with a loutish son and an impossibly 'refeened' mother.

Hence **refai·nment, refee·nment** (with reference to REFINEMENT 2).

1933 H. MATHESON *Broadcasting* iii. 63 Universal education may mean a universal hybrid speech..often overlaid with a veneer of what can only be called 'refainment'. **1941** [see above]. **1960** J. MITFORD *Hons & Rebels* i. 17 Nancy [Mitford], even in those early days preoccupied with U and Non-U usage, made up a poem illustrative of the main 'refainments' of Miss Broadmoor's speech.

refan, *v.* Add: **2.** [RE- 5 c.] *Aeronaut.* To fit (a turbo-fan) with a new fan. So **refa·nned** *ppl. a.*, **refa·nning** *vbl. sb.*

1973 *Internat. Aerospace Abstr.* XIII. 2222/1 (*heading*) Refanned commercial gas turbine engines. **1974** *Ibid.* XIV. 2236/1 (*heading*) Reduction of JT8D powered aircraft noise by engine refanning. **1975** *Times Lit. Suppl.* 21 Mar. 318/3 Improved engine design has produced a new generation of quieter aircraft, earlier and noisier types can be refanned and further progress in the direction of peace and quiet may be expected. **1978** *Flight Internat.* 18 Feb. 429/1 United Airlines' flirtation with the refanned 727-300B in 1975 marked the end of this transport's major development.

refan (rī·fæn), *a.* and *sb. Aeronaut.* [f. prec. vb.] **A.** *adj.* **a.** = *REFANNED *ppl. a.* **b.** = *REFANNING *vbl. sb.* (used *attrib.*). **B.** *sb.* A refanned engine.

1974 *Internat. Aerospace Abstr.* XIV. 2236/1 This would be accomplished by retrofitting the existing fleet with quieter refan engines and new acoustically treated nacelles. **1975** *Ibid.* XV. 2764/2 The objective of the refan program is to demonstrate the technical feasibility of substantially reducing the noise levels of existing JT8D powered aircraft. **1978** *Flight Internat.* 18 Feb. 428/2 The principal advantage of refans (whether cropped or sized up) over new engines can be summarized as lower development, acquisition and ownership costs; [etc.].

refect, *v.* Add: **2.** *trans.* To eat (fæcal pellets).

1960 M. BURTON *Wild Animals Brit. Isles* 60 The droppings refected are different from those discarded. **1964** R. M. LOCKLEY *Private Life of Rabbit* x. 102 Termites may refect food as much as six times.

refection, *sb.* Add: **2. d.** The eating of fæcal pellets, practised by rabbits and some other animals.

1939 *Nature* 10 June 982/1 The pellets frequently constitute more than one third of the stomach contents [of the rabbit] and refection to such a degree seemed too improbable. **1952** L. H. MATTHEWS *Brit. Mammals* vi. 136 In 1939 the habit of 'refection' was rediscovered in the rabbit. **1964** R. M. LOCKLEY *Private life of Rabbit* x. 102 Many animals, including insects as well as hares and rabbits, have this habit of refection. **1973** *Bk. Brit. Countryside* (Automobile Assoc.) 367/2 Feeding is by refection, a similar method to chewing the cud. Food is eaten then excreted in semi-digested form as soft moist pellets. These are eaten again and passed through the intestines to be fully digested.

refectory, *sb.* Add: (The pronunc. re·fĕktəri is still used by some Roman Catholics.) **b.** *refectory table* (also with ellipsis of *table*): see quots. 1948, 1960.

1913 L. V. LOCKWOOD *Furniture Collector's Gloss.* 51/2 *Refectory*, an early long, narrow table upon which was served a meal. **1923** H. STANLEY-BARRETT *Old World Galleries A.B.C. Hist. Eng. Antique Furnit.* (ed. 2) 118 The Elizabethan trestle refectory table usually had heavily carved bulbous legs. **1928** *Daily Express* 18 Apr. 4. Refectory tables ..were the principal pieces of furniture in medieval and Tudor times. **1948** *Antique Collector* Aug. 127/1 In the late 16th and 17th centuries the common dining-table was an oblong one with either four or six turned legs connected by square sectioned stretchers. In contemporary inventories it was usually called a 'long table', but in order to conjure up a picture of jovial monks dining, the long table has been renamed a 'refectory table', which inaccurate term is often used today. **1960** H. HAYWARD *Antique Coll.* 235/1 *Refectory table*, popular modern term for a long table of the type in use in the second half of the 16th cent. until the Restoration. **1971** D. FRANCIS *Bonecrack* iv. 51 We sat..with our feet up on a sixteenth century Spanish walnut refectory table. **1976** *Cumberland News* 3 Dec. 29/5 (Advt.), We are most interested in old oak furniture—dressers, court cupboards—kitchen presses, bedding chests, kitchen and refectory tables as well.

refeed (rīfī·d), *v.* Also **re-feed.** [RE- 5 a.] *trans.* To feed again, esp. after a period of starvation.

1884 [in Dict. s.v. RE- 5 a]. **1943** *Nutrition Abstr. & Rev.* XII. 637/2 [The birds] were then refed on maize until the original weight was regained. **1971** *Jrnl. Nutrition* CI. 1564/2 Rats were starved 48 hours and were refed the high carbohydrate diet for 0, 1, 2, 3, 4, and 7 days.

So **refe·d** *ppl. a.*, **refee·ding** *vbl. sb.*

1932 *Biol. Abstr.* VI. 410/2 (*heading*) Re-feeding after starvation. **1950** *Arch. Biochem.* XXVII. 177 The percentage of nitrogen in the extracts obtained from the livers of the rats refed with a high-carbohydrate diet was significantly lower than the percentage of nitrogen in the extracts obtained from the pellet-refed and the fat-refed rats. **1964** *Proc. Soc. Exper. Biol. & Med.* CXV. 441/1 The data for refed rats reflect a marked increase in liver lipid upon refeeding. **1967** M. KENYON *Whole Hog* viii. 94, I put them [*sc.* laboratory animals] on controlled feeding after a period of starvation and their reactions to the re-feeding.. would be similar to human reactions.

refer, *v.* Add: **7. f.** To postpone the passing of (a candidate) in an examination or the acceptance of (an application for a degree), provision being made for re-examination at a later date.

1907 *Practitioner* June 795 A student, who should venture to put upon an examination paper what is the only logical outcome of the teaching of text-books, ought, without hesitation, to be referred. **1908** A. S. M. HUTCHINSON *Once Aboard Lugger* I. i. 32 'I had forgotten. Your examination?' ..'I failed. I was referred for three months.' **1927** *Univ. Oxford Examination Statutes* vi. 227 The examiners shall have power..to recommend the Board to refer the Student's application for leave to supplicate back to him in order that he may present himself for re-examination. **1976** *Daily Times* (Lagos) 3 Nov. 31/2 Twenty-four students drawn from the states and the Armed Forces passed the prescribed test while four students were referred. **1979** *Jrnl. R. Soc. Arts* Dec. 9/1 The candidates for this session's examination were exclusively restricted to those who had been referred in a previous examination or who were resitting in order to obtain higher grades.

8. a. (Further examples.) Also const. *back to*.

1927 W. E. COLLINSON *Contemp. Eng.* 123 The elements of committee English which I had picked up in the Debating Society were soon reinforced by the constantly heard expressions: standing orders, terms of reference (defining the scope of a committee's labours), to refer back (to a committee for further consideration). **1934** G. B. SHAW *On Rocks* II. 267, I must really refer you back to him for further consideration and report. **1961** NEW ENG. BIBLE *Luke* xxiii. 15, I have myself examined him in your presence and found nothing in him to support your charges. No more did Herod, for he has referred him back to us. **1976** [see sense 8 d below].

d. To send or direct (a person) to a medical consultant or institution for specialist treatment.

1961 *Lancet* 2 Sept. 517/2 We are indebted to Dr. J. F. O'Connell for referring this patient. **1970** H. MCLEAVE *Question of Negligence* xxii. 186 She did consult me, but she was referred by someone else. **1973** *Guardian* 9 Mar. 13/2 The slum Doctor round the corner who never examines his patients before referring them. **1973** *Listener* 19 Apr. 507/1 They're all referred by the GP... They're all psychogeriatrics. **1976** *Women's Report* Sept./Oct. 2/1 Yet the clinic makes use of the NHS because all clients needing surgery or expensive treatment have to be referred back to NHS hospitals or clinics.

referring *vbl. sb.* and *ppl. a.* (later examples).

1950 P. F. STRAWSON in *Mind* LIX. 320 We very commonly use expressions of certain kinds to mention or refer to some individual person or single object or particular event or place or process... I shall call this way of using expressions the 'uniquely referring use'. *Ibid.* 326 'Mentioning', or 'referring', is not something an expression does; it is something that some one can use an expression to do.

referability (re:fĕrăbi·liti). *rare.* [f. REFERABLE *a.* + -ILITY.] The fact or quality of being referable.

1964 R. H. ROBINS *Gen. Linguistics* vi. 233 Non-favourite sentences of class I have no such referability to a longer sentence in which they may be incorporated.

referee, *sb.* Add: **3. b.** (Earlier and further examples.)

1840 *Spirit of Times* 25 Jan. 559/3 He was a general referee and umpire, whether it was a horse swap, a race, a rifle match, or a cock fight. **1856** *Porter's Spirit of Times* 6 Dec. 229/1 In [baseball] matches, an umpire is chosen on each side, and a referee to decide, when the umpires cannot agree. **1887** G. A. HUTCHISON *Football* ii. 11 In case of infringement, the referee shall..order a scrummage to be formed. **1906** *Daily Chron.* 7 Sept. 9/4 No great blame attaches to the referee, who probably did not notice the forward till he was apparently off-side. **1936** H. B. T. WAKELAM *Game goes On* 17 Other innovations during the Daring 'Eighties were the appointment of neutral referees and the provision of whistles for those functionaries. **1951** F. N. S. CREEK *Soccer for Boys* iii. 18 The duration of the game is mainly the responsibility of the referee. **1977** *Times* 16 Mar. 12/1 The main topic of conversation..was the alleged attempt to bribe the Danish referee before the first leg.

c. A person appointed to examine a scientific or other learned work and comment on its suitability for publication.

1884 *Proc. London Math. Soc.* XV. 160 The original paper has been divided into two..at the suggestion of the referee. **1926** A. E. HOUSMAN *Let.* 14 Oct. (1971) 242 A report of mine ..decided the Syndics not to accept a treatise of Richmond's. ..A. W. Ward..told him that I was the referee. **1970** *Physics Bull.* Jan. 2/2 The majority of authors expressed their appreciation of the value of the constructive criticism of the referees in improving the quality of their papers. **1971** *Nature* 22 Oct. 571/3 Each paper was carefully scrutinized by one senior referee and by one of the two distinguished editors-in-chief.

4. A person who may be referred to for information or guidance on the character or other qualities of someone, *spec.* of an applicant for employment, for an academic or other award, or the like.

1862 H. MAYHEW *London Labour* IV. 12 Classification of the workers and non-workers of Great Britain... Referees, or those who give characters to professional beggars when a reference is required. **1882** *Sydney Slang Dict.* 7/2 *Referees*, those who give characters to enable dishonest persons and thieves' accomplices to obtain situations. **1944** *Oxf. Univ. Gaz.* LXXIV. 316/1 Candidates are requested to send in their names with eight copies of any statement that they may wish to make..giving the names of not more than three referees. **1971** *Reader's Digest Family Guide to Law* 689/2 One way an employer can assess the abilities of an applicant is to ask for references from former employers. It may also be useful to telephone the referee, who may be prepared to give more information informally than he can provide in writing. **1972** *Library Assoc. Record* Nov. 224/1 On three occasions lately I have sent for an application form and job description only to find that these did not arrive until two or three days before the closing date, this making it very difficult..to arrange referees, etc. **1976** *Oxf. Univ. Gaz.* CVII. 209/1 Applications, including a *curriculum vitae*,..and the names of two academic referees, should be sent to the Secretary of the Marjory Wardrop Fund.

referee, *v.* Add: **2.** *trans.* and *intr.* To examine and evaluate (a scientific paper, thesis, or book); to act as referee (in sense *3 c of the sb.). **refereeing** *vbl. sb.* (later examples). Hence **referee·d** *ppl. a.*

1966 *Rep. Comm. Inquiry Univ. Oxf.* II. 452 Editing or refereeing for journals. **1970** *Physics Bull.* Jan. 2/2 (*heading*) Refereeing of research papers. *Ibid.* 3/1 If a referee is unable to referee a paper himself, he is invited to pass it to an appropriate colleague. **1970** *Computers & Humanities* IV. 312 All submitted papers will be refereed. **1971** *Nature* 24 Sept. p. xvi/2 (Advt.), All papers are scrupulously refereed and the journal is guided by an editorial board of distinguished scientists whose activities cover all aspects of polymer research. **1975** *Ibid.* 6 Nov. 1/1 The Scientific Information Committee of the Royal Society has recently put forward a set of guidelines for the refereeing of papers for publication. **1978** *Maledicta* II. 10 Unfortunately for them, our journal is not a 'refereed' academic publication.

reference, *sb.* Add: **3. d.** *Logic* and *Linguistics.* The act or state of referring through which one term or concept is related or connected to another or to objects in the world; also as *objective reference,* and *attrib.* as *reference class, property.*

1883 F. H. Bradley *Princ. Logic* I. I. ii. 55 Judgment is not the synthesis of ideas, but the reference of ideal content to reality. *a* **1914** C. S. Peirce *Coll. Papers* (1933) III. xix. 366 Dyadic relations..which can only subsist between two subjects of different categories of being..may advantageously be termed a reference. **1927** Ogden & Richards *Meaning of Meaning* (ed. 2) i. 9 It is Thought (or, as we shall usually say, *reference*) which is directed and organized, and it is also Thought which is recorded and communicated. **1946** C. I. Lewis *Knowledge & Valuation* x. 270 This property *ψ* may be called the *reference property. Ibid.* 271 The class of things having it [*sc.* a property] may be called the *reference class.* **1951** G. Humphrey *Thinking* viii. 228 In its original form as the 'problem of meaning' the question has to be obscured by the invention of new descriptive terms such as *transcendent reference, objective reference* or *context* in order to satisfy the scientific conscience. **1956** G. Ryle in A. J. Ayer *Revol. in Philos.* 7 Both [Frege and Bradley] saw that it is..intrinsic to a thought to be true or false, or to have 'objective reference'. **1959** K. R. Popper *Logic Sci. Discovery* viii. 155 This class *α*, which is assumed to be *non-empty*, serves, as it were, as a frame of reference, and will be called a (finite) *reference-class.* **1972** *Language* XLVIII. 446 In order to understand problems of semantic theory, it is crucial to understand why most philosophers think of the notion of reference as the key element in such theories. Reference is the relation between singular term and bearer, as well as between general predicate and the entities of which the predicate is true. With the notion of reference go the notions of naming, describing, and—therefore—truth. **1974** P. F. Strawson *Subject & Predicate* ii. 47 Hearer and speaker should each understand the name..as having a certain unique reference; and..the reference should be the same for each of them.

e. *Sociol.* and *Psychol.* The process by which or the extent to which an individual establishes a relation with elements in society as a standard for comparing status and values (see also *frame of reference* s.v. *frame *sb.* 4 d (ii)). Freq. *attrib.* (see also *reference group* in sense 8 a below).

1937 G. Murphy et al. *Exper. Social Psychol.* (rev. ed.) iv. 220 A laboratory situation is set in which social factors determine a reference frame which must be used by the subject in perceiving. **1947** Sherif & Cantril *Psychol. of Ego-Involvements* vi. 137 Judgments of the physical characteristics of others..become..ego-involving judgments in which an individual uses himself..as a central point of reference. **1948** M. & C. Sherif *Outl. Social Psychol.* xviii. 621 This ordering of responses held whether a respondent made as many as nineteen consensual references or as few as one. **1956** Gardner & Thompson *Social Relations & Morale* v. 23 Displacements of the distributions of scores along the reference continuum. *Ibid.* vii. 43 The most general reference population..would be: 'All the persons (living or dead) you have..known in any way'.

6. a. *spec.* = *referee *sb.* 4.

1837 Dickens *Let.* 24 Feb. (1965) I. 238, I have..taken the liberty of mentioning your name, among those of other references, to testify to my being 'sober and honest'. **1865** [in Dict.]. **1934** D. L. Sayers *Nine Tailors* II. ii. 95 'Did he give you any references?'..'Yes..he did. He give me the name of a garridge in London..and..said if I was to write to the boss, he'd put in a word for him.'

b. A (usu. written) report produced by a referee (*referee *sb.* 4); a testimonial.

1895 in *Funk's Stand. Dict.* **1924** Galsworthy *White Monkey* II. ix. 197 That was my first job since the war, so I can whistle for a reference. **1936** *Punch* 21 Oct. 467/1 'I have references, excellent references... Here is one from a lady in Eaton Square.' (Hands it to the employer.) **1940** G. D. H. & M. Cole *Counter-Point Murder* viii. 85 Corcoran said he wrote to us taking up the reference, and got back a letter speaking very highly of the firm. **1976** 'P. B. Yuill' *Hazell & Menacing Jester* ii. 27 'Did Thornton get another job?' 'Nobody's asked me for a reference.'

8. a. *reference librarian, library* (further examples), *point*; **reference book,** (*a*) a book used for reference purposes; cf. *book of reference* in sense 7; (*b*) *S. Afr.*, an identity document or group of documents officially introduced in 1952 or the name for a pass (see *pass *sb.*[2] 8 f), regulating movement in particular areas, which all non-white residents must carry (replaced in 1977 by 'travel documents': see quot. 1977 s.v. *pass *sb.*[2] 8 f); **reference electrode** *Electr.*, an electrode the potential of which can be accurately maintained and reproduced, and in relation to which other potentials can be measured; **reference frame** = *frame of reference* s.v. *frame *sb.* 4 d; occas. *transf.*; **reference group** *Sociol.* and *Psychol.*, a group to which a person may or may not belong but which he, perhaps subconsciously, refers to as a standard in forming his attitudes and behaviour; **reference tube** *Electr.*, a cold-cathode gas-filled tube which can maintain an accurately fixed voltage across itself for long periods.

1889 *Cent. Dict.*, Reference book. **1952** [see *pass *sb.*[2] 8 f]. **1954** L. G. Green *Under Sky like Flame* xii. 174 On the Gold Coast cooks carry a reference book. **1960** *Observer* 27 Mar. 16/4 Failure to produce a reference book on demand is a criminal offence. **1967** [see *author *v.*]. **1969** *Golden City Post* July 3 The thugs..robbed him of his money, reference book and personal documents. **1970** C. L. Cline *Lett. George Meredith* I. p. xxxii, The inaccessibility of reference books in provincial towns may also have contributed to the slothfulness of the editing. **1971** *Drum* Mar. 4 They walked purposefully towards the women who searched themselves for their reference books. But it was not the reference books the policemen wanted. **1971** *Rand Daily Mail* 27 Mar. 2/2 The vast majority of short-term prison sentences are for minor statutory offences connected with Bantu influx control, taxation and reference book regulations. **1972** *Physics Bull.* Apr. 225/2 For a reference book the index is inadequate. **1926** *Jrnl. Amer. Chem. Soc.* XLVIII. 34 The effect of temperature upon the potential of reference electrodes. **1948** Glasstone *Textbk. Physical Chem.* (ed. 2) xii. 940 There is no reliable method known for determining the absolute potential of a single electrode. The only sound procedure is to combine the electrode with a reference electrode of known potential difference and to measure the E.M.F. of the resulting cell. **1975** M. R. Jenkins in Williams & Wilson *Biologist's Guide to Princ. & Techniques Pract. Biochem.* vii. 202 Calomel electrodes..are the most common reference electrodes and they consist of a solution of mercurous chloride (calomel) and potassium chloride in contact with solid mercurous chloride and mercury. **1921** J. M. Bird *Relativity & Gravitation* ii. 36 (*heading*) The reference frame for space. **1940** C. S. Sherrington *Man on his Nature* ii. 62 There was as yet no reference-frame of natural law, of chemistry or physics, by help of which to orientate the natural fact. **1967** [see *frame *sb.* 4 d (i)]. **1970** *Nature* 17 Oct. 272/2 In deriving the equations of the electromagnetic field in a rotating reference frame, Schiff used the explicit transformation to rotating coordinates. **1942** H. H. Hyman *Psychol. of Status* ii. 37 Satisfaction with status is consequently also a function of the reference group, since the reference group is a variable of the judgment. **1957** *Jrnl. Abnormal & Social Psychol.* LV. 360/1 Attention has also been given to the influence of his reference groups: the groups in which he aspires to attain or maintain membership. **1969** *Times* 14 Apr. 7/3 The two groups of farmers have different reference groups, a different set of individuals with which they will compete for status and recognition. **1970** C. T. Restrepo in I. L. Horowitz *Masses in Lat. Amer.* xiv. 542 The absence of contacts—and hence the lack of visibility of reference groups—has kept the peasants unaware even of their own needs. **1973** 'J. Patrick' *Glasgow Gang Observed* xiii. 115 Tim's reference group for clothes was the teenage record scene. **1977** R. Holland *Self & Social Context* v. 119 The area of social theory most closely related to that of role, namely 'reference group' research. **1951** L. I. Edwards in J. D. Stewart *Reference Librarian* iii. 61 Theoretically the reference librarian should know something about everything because of the varied nature of the queries received. **1978** W. White in *W. Whitman's Daybks. & Notebks.* I. 87 For this information and other help I am grateful to George A. Masterton, reference librarian at Wayne State University. **1860** Reference library [see *art gallery* s.v. *art *sb.* V]. **1976** *Nature* 1 Apr. 466/3 This book is a 'must' and it certainly deserves space on a shelf of every reference library. **1977** *Evening Post* (Nottingham) 24 Jan. 3/2 Now there is a reference library, a craft work base, and two other areas into which children can move for private reading and study. **1884** Reference-point [see *bench-mark b]. **1936** M. Sherif *Psychol. of Social Norms* vi. 96 This subjectively established standard or norm serves as a reference point with which each successive experienced movement is compared and judged to be short. **1977** *Rolling Stone* 5 May 33/1, I really do think Rod Stewart, Bruce Springsteen and the Who are the most appropriate reference points for rock and roll. **1960** *Electronic Engin.* XXXII. 218 Studies were confined to neon-filled tubes..having molybdenum anodes and cathodes and employing high-stability reference-tube manufacturing techniques. **1962** G. A. T. Burdett *Automatic Control Handbk.* vii. 23 The primary duty of the reference tube..is to provide voltage which can be accurately maintained within close limits for long periods.

b. In extended scientific and technical use denoting an object, property, value, or the like, used as a basis for comparative measurement or standardization. Also *absol.*

1878 J. W. Draper *Sci. Mem.* ii. 57, I had previously passed through the slit a beam of sunlight reflected from a mirror, so as to have a reference spectrum with fixed lines. **1901** *Shop & Foundry Pract.* III. xxvii. 23 Reference gauges are gauges that represent either an accurate subdivision of the imperial yard, or some arbitrary size or shape adopted for some purpose and required to be preserved. **1941** C. O. Fairchild et al. *Temperature* 305 It is not always possible to maintain the reference junctions..at a desired temperature during the calibration of a thermocouple. **1941** K. Henney *Radio Engin. Handbk.* (ed. 3) xxi. 775 A conveniently and consistently accurate method of measuring the amplitude of the signals is required, as well as a reference level common to the entire system. **1952** Markus & Zeluff *Electronics for Communication Engin.* ix. 342/1 This cavity has a high Q and is used as the frequency reference. **1953** Amos & Birkinshaw *Television Engin.* I. i. 20 D.c. restoration is only possible provided the picture signal contains a reference signal related to black level and the television waveform therefore includes such a signal. **1966** Williams & Fleming *Spectrosc. Methods Org. Chem.* iv. 81 The positions of proton resonances in an NMR spectrum are measured relative to the resonance position of the twelve equivalent protons of an arbitrary reference substance, tetramethylsilane. **1975** D. G. Fink *Electronics Engineers' Handbk.* xix. 3 The reference pressure for sounds in air, corresponding to 0 dB, has been defined as a sound pressure of 0·0002 microbar. **1978** P. W. Atkins *Physical Chem.* xxix. 968 The potentiometer reading is used in the normal way to find its new potential relative to the reference.

reference, *v.* Add: **1. b.** To relate (a measurement) *to* a defined base or zero level.

1971 *Nature* 3 Sept. 51/2 A complete separation of the explosion population from the earthquake population is obtained when referenced to the arbitrary decision line. **1972** *Science* 23 June 1349/3 The intensity of the sound was as high as 80 db (referenced to 0·0002 dyne/cm^2).

2. (Further examples.)

1971 *Nature* 3 Sept. 71/3 Each chapter is very fully referenced. **1972** *Physics Bull.* May 295/3 The book is well produced and well referenced. **1975** *Nature* 3 Apr. p. iv (Advt.), Published as a two-book set for easier handling, each part is fully referenced and illustrated. **1977** *Jrnl. R. Soc. Arts* CXXV. 451/2 One BCS paper is referenced on page 35 of the White Paper Cmd. 6354. **1978** *Sci. Amer.* Jan. 28/3 The version we see (not explicitly referenced) is probably from an edition of about 100 years ago or from a 20th-century reprint. **1980** *Encounter* May 16/2 It is enough to remember that Ferrar and Debenham's formulation of the sequence of Beacon rocks is still referenced today.

Hence **re·ferenced** *ppl. a.*, **re·ferencing** *vbl. sb.*

1884 Referencing [see sense 3 in Dict.]. **1971** *Nature* 30 Apr. 602/1 It is a very good book indeed—but it could have been excellent if just a little extra thought had gone into the original plan and an extra month into the final editing and referencing. **1972** *Science* 5 May 503/3 The authors..give an additional line of the frequently quoted but never referenced turbulence poem by Richardson (1922) beginning 'Big whorls have little whorls'. **1978** *Nature* 14 Dec. 739/2 The referencing, which includes entries up to the first half of 1976, is impressive.

referend (re·fĕrend, refĕre·nd). [ad. L. *referend-um*, gerund or neut. gerundive of *referre* to Refer.] That by which or, more commonly, to which reference is made, *spec.* that which is signified by a particular sense of a word.

1925 *Monist* XXXV. 427 By the content of a judgment is meant the referend plus that which is predicated of the referend, and by the referend is meant that to which the judgment refers. **1930** L. S. Stebbing *Mod. Introd. Logic* ii. 13 We shall find it convenient to use the word 'referend' to stand for that which is signified. *Ibid.*, It is perhaps unfortunate to have to introduce new terminology, but the word 'object' is not suitable for the purpose for which I use the technical term 'referend'. The referend is that which is being referred to. **1939** *Trans. Philol. Soc.* 74 How can we disentangle ourselves from the close meshwork of our native language and find a *tertium quid* or set of neutral referends to serve as a measure for both languages compared? **1940** *Kenyon Rev.* 269 The monosign is referential in the sense that what it means.., its referend, is something distinct from itself. **1941** *Mind* L. 151 He thinks he is holding fast to some identical referend throughout, whereas in truth he has only an identical symbol which is changing its referend. **1956** J. Whatmough *Language* 262 Referend. That which is symbolized or referred to by a verbal symbol, e.g. the referend of *rain* is 'the moisture of the atmosphere condensed and falling in visible drops'. **1957** S. Potter *Mod. Linguistics* vii. 141 The bird, the living creature that we see with our eyes, we may call the *referend*, and the picture of it that we have in our minds as we speak..may be called the *image.* **1977** *Word 1972* XXVIII. 162 The auxiliary is invariably present when the referend is not the subject of the clause.

referendum. Delete ‖ and add earlier and further examples. Pl. **referendums, -enda.**

In terms of its Latin origin, *referendums* is logically preferable as a modern plural form meaning ballots on one issue (as a Latin gerund *referendum* has no plural); the Latin plural gerundive *referenda*, meaning 'things to be referred', necessarily connotes a plurality of issues. Those who prefer the form *referenda* are presumably using words like *agenda* and *memoranda* as models. Usage varies at the present time (1981), but *The Oxford Dictionary for Writers and Editors* (1981) recommends *referendums*, and this form seems likely to prevail.

1847 G. Grote *Let.* 25 Sept. in *Seven Lett. concerning Politics Switzerland* (1847) iv. 81 The clergy made efficient use of their influence over the popular *referendum.* **1870** *Sat. Rev.* 7 May 602/1 The *veto* or *referendum* has this much in common with the Bonapartist *plebiscitum*, that it is submitted to a body which is not an assembly and which cannot discuss. **1870** *Rep. Mass. Bureau of Statistics of Labor* I. 358

We want the referendum. **1889** F. O. Adams *Swiss Confederation* vi. 77 In Federal matters there are now two Referendums. **1911** W. S. Churchill *Let.* 29 Mar. in R. S. Churchill *Winston S. Churchill* (1969) II. *Companion* II. xiv. 1061 The collapse of the Referendum policy in the House of Lords was the subject of comment in the Lobbies yesterday. **1945** —— in *Times* 22 May 4/1 If you should decide to stand on with us, all united together until the Japanese surrender is compelled, let us discuss means of taking the nation's opinion, for example, a referendum, on the issue whether in these conditions the life of this Parliament should be further prolonged. **1945** C. Attlee in *Ibid.* 4/2, I could not consent to the introduction into our national life of a device so alien to all our traditions as the referendum, which has only too often been the instrument of Nazism and Fascism. Hitler's practices in the field of referenda and plebiscites can hardly have endeared these expedients to the British heart. **1965** H. V. Wiseman *Britain & Commonwealth* II. iii. 86 Referenda have been held in New Zealand on the question of prohibiting the sale of intoxicating liquors. **1975** *Referendum on U.K. Membership of European Community* (Cmnd. 5925) i. 3 The present White Paper is concerned only with the organisation of the referendum. *Ibid.* iii. 5 The Government propose to ensure that the postal and proxy voting facilities which are available for general elections are also available for the referendum poll. **1975** *Times* 10 Apr. 5/1 The Liberals think that Referendum Day should be a public holiday. **1975** *Act Eliz. II* c. 33 § 1 A referendum shall be held on the question whether the United Kingdom is to remain a member of the European Economic Community. **1976** H. Wilson *Governance of Brit.* iii. 75 There was great interest in constitutional circles in my announcement on 23 January 1975 that collective responsibility would be relaxed for the period of the referendum campaign on membership of EEC—the famous 'agreement to differ'. **1976** *Ann. Reg. 1975* 53 Two referenda had already been held in Wales in 1975. **1976** *Times* 22 Dec. 11/7 Since we are now likely to hear much about referendums, could we ask the BBC not to continue calling them referenda? **1977** *Daily Tel.* 16 Feb. 1/3 Proposed referenda on the plan for Scottish and Welsh Assemblies should be consultative only and not binding on Parliament. **1977** *Times* 17 Mar. 19/3 They did not tell us at the time of the referendum that Brussels was to reform the English language. **1977** *Time* 21 Nov. 28/2 The many referendums on the ballots reflected a growing public demand for more efficient and less meddlesome government.

referent, *sb.* and *a.* Delete *rare* and add: **1.** (Further example.)

1921 *Contemp. Rev.* Mar. 315 The whole administration is conducted by the provincial government in Bratislava (Pressburg), under the Minister for Slovakia and his thirteen 'Referents' or State Secretaries.

2. c. *sb.* That to which something has reference; *spec.* that which is referred to by a word or expression. Also in *Comb.* (*appositively*), as *referent-object*.

1923 Ogden & Richards *Meaning of Meaning* i. 13 The word 'thing' is unsuitable for the analysis here undertaken, because in popular usage it is restricted to material substances—a fact which has led philosophers to favour the terms 'entity', 'ens' or 'object' as the general name for whatever is. It has seemed desirable, therefore, to introduce a technical term to stand for whatever we may be thinking of or referring to. 'Object', though this is its original use, has had an unfortunate history. The word 'referent', therefore, has been adopted. **1931** F. C. S. Northrop *Sci. & First Principles* ii. 49 This theory [*sc.* the physical theory of nature] is untenable unless there is a referent for atomicity and motion in something other than the microscopic particles. **1937** *Harper's Monthly Mag.* Dec. 49/2 Knowledge about technological unemployment..is not advanced by the syllogisms of classical economists. The classicists treat the term as a thing-in-itself without finding the referents which give it meaning. **1938** *Mod. Lang. Rev.* Oct. 547 The reinterpretation of the term [*baroque*] has sprung, not.. from the feeling that it could be better applied to some other type of art, but from the revaluation of its original referent. **1950** *Papers Mich. Acad. Sci., Arts & Lett.* XXXVI. 323 The same question may..be phrased by asking how to bridge the gap between..sign and referent. **1958** S. Stubelius *Airship, Aeroplane, Aircraft* 7 As a rule, there has been no difficulty in ascertaining the referents in my linguistic material, with the aid of context. **1964** *Eng. Stud.* XLV. 385 Gender distinctions had always been functional in English as indicating either the sex of the referent or the non-significance of sex-distinction of the referent. **1964** *Language* XL. 229 The much-studied relations of words to their referent-objects. **1968** [see *denotatum]. **1970** *New Society* 5 Mar. 394/2 Clearly, if the ongon is to have any meaning at all, there must be some way of knowing at what level the symbols are to be interpreted, bearing in mind that each drawing or material object will have several referents. **1973** *Times Lit. Suppl.* 26 Oct. 1306/3 Canada often provides the landscape for his fable or the referents of his argument. **1976** *Archivum Linguisticum* VII. 17 Most Castilian loanwords from other languages have been borrowed to refer to referents, or fulfil functions, when Latin had originally an apparently good word for the same purpose. **1979** *Dædalus* Summer 97 'Official' discourse is reproached for being without a referent in psychic or social reality.

3. *Logic.* Any member of the class of all terms bearing a given relation to any term. (The correlative of *relatum*.)

1903 [see *domain *sb.* 4 f]. **1933** L. S. Stebbing *Mod. Introd. Logic* (ed. 2) vii. 111 Every relational proposition has a converse, which consists in interchanging the terms with, or without, a change in the relation asserted to hold between them. The term *from* which the relation proceeds is called the referent; the term *to* which it proceeds is called the relatum. **1947** H. Reichenbach *Elem. Symbolic Logic* iii. 115 There will be more than one relatum with respect to Peter if Peter has other children... The class of referents is also called the domain of function, and the class of relata is called the converse domain. **1967** R. A. George tr. *Carnap's Logical Struct. of World* III. 60 A relation extension is called one-many if, for each relatum, there exists only one referent.

referential, *a.* Add: **b.** Of or pertaining to a referent (sense *2 c); *spec.* of language or symbolism: that indicates a referent or has a referent as object.

1884 [in Dict.]. **1923** Ogden & Richards *Meaning of Meaning* i. 13 Besides this referential use which for all reflective, intellectual use of language should be paramount, words have other functions which may be grouped together as emotive. *Ibid.* ix. 318 Unless the referential and the affective-volitional aspects of mental process are clearly distinguished, no discussion of their relation is possible. **1922** T. C. Pollack *Nature of Lit.* IX. 195 In *phatic communion*, one person uses words to come into relation with another. In *referential symbolism*, one person uses words to direct the attention of another to certain referents... In *evocative symbolism*, one person uses words to evoke a controlled experience in another. **1946** C. Morris *Signs, Lang. & Behavior* 60 The current distinction between 'referential' and 'emotive' terms, a basic distinction in the work of C. K. Ogden and I. A. Richards. **1946** H. Jacob *On Choice of Common Lang.* 116 The never entirely separable functions of language roughly classified as 'emotive' and 'referential'. **1964** [see *extrasomatic *a.*]. **1964** S. Jacobson *Adverbial Positions in Eng.* i. 38 Several adverbs and adverbial phrases, especially such as express restriction or particularization, refer to, i.e. direct attention to, some particular constituent within the sentence. They may be called referential adverbials, and together with the constituent referred to, which may be a word, phrase, or clause, they form a structure of reference... Thus..'Only a Person can forgive'.., where *only* refers to *a Person*. **1964** R. H. Robins *Gen. Linguistics* 29 Word translation, or the finding of lexical equivalents, is easiest.. with words in other languages which are such as to have a referential meaning more or less uniform in all cultures. **1971** *Archivum Linguisticum* II. 40 Nor is there any compulsion to believe in the primacy of any subdivision of meaning, for instance in the referential 'table'-ness of 'table'. **1980** *Mind* LXXXIX. 601 The truth of the speaker's belief q is neither necessary nor sufficient for the referential use of his definite description.

referentially *adv.* (examples).

1922 W. E. Johnson *Logic* II. 120 Those so-called constants which are dependent upon context are only referentially constant. **1963** J. Lyons *Structural Semantics* iii. 39 Each of the [colour-]terms is referentially, or denotationally, vague in the sense that it denotes an area of the spectrum whose boundaries are not fixed precisely. **1966** *Philos. Rev.* LXXV. 11 Some of Socrates' substitutions are within intensional or referentially opaque contexts. **1975** *Nature* 10 Apr. 510/1 [He] is not bound by referentially constrained situations in his use of VIC [*sc.* Visual Communication, a therapeutic programme]. **1980** *Mind* LXXXIX. 599 Has the definite description been used referentially? No doubt the students took it in the attributive way... They do not even realize that the teacher intends his description referentially.

referral (rĭfɔ̄·răl). [f. Refer *v.*: see -al II. 5.] **a.** The act of referring; *spec.* the referring to a third party of personal information concerning another.

1934 in Webster. **1943** *Sun* (Baltimore) 27 Nov. 6/3 The publication by Senator Butler of his report and his referral of it to the Truman Committee. **1968** *Globe & Mail* (Toronto) 15 Jan. 24/7 (Advt.), Television and newspaper advertising will supply starting work followed by constant referral jobs. **1969** *Ithaca* (N.Y.) *Jrnl.* 27 Nov. 32/2 The name of the woman who was two months pregnant was apparently given secretly to the..company by one of her friends, who was paid for the 'referral' with a vaporizer or other small appliance. **1971** *Nature* 30 Apr. 545/1 The Unisist committee asks that associated countries should survey information services of national, regional or international scope and make plans to integrate these into a 'world referral network'. **1971** *N.Y. Law Jrnl.* 23 Nov. 20/4 After referral to me by order of Mr. Justice McInerney, this motion for a withdrawal order is granted. **1981** *Times* 10 Mar. 18/6 The senior management of these businesses comes out well from these referrals.

b. The referring of an individual to an expert or specialist for advice; *spec.* the directing (usu. by a general practitioner) of a patient to a medical consultant for specialist treatment (see *refer *v.* 8 d). Also *attrib.*

1955 D. M. Deed in C. Morris *Social Case-Work in Gt. Brit.* (ed. 2) iii. 70 At the time of referral [to a family caseworker] the child was in a temporary hostel. **1958** *Times* 8 Nov. 7/5 The public..is in turn increasingly unwilling to trust themselves to the care of their N.H.S. practitioner, thus reinforcing the habit of unnecessary referral to hospitals. **1960** in L. Pincus *Marriage* II. 58 At the time of their referral to the Bureau, they had been married for nine and a half years. **1966** *Lancet* 24 Dec. 1403/1 The referral system, whereby consultants see patients only at the request of the family doctor, came into being at the end of the 19th century. **1968** *World Medicine* 26 Nov. 35/1 The referral diagnosis was Addison's disease. **1972** *Where* May/June 136/3 He can go to his family doctor who will either examine him and take the necessary tests to establish the diagnosis before giving treatment, or will send him to the nearest hospital clinic with a letter of referral. **1976** *Proc. R. Soc. Med.* LXIX. 949/1 Our surgical unit is no less busy than most in the country: it has its share of medical ward referrals, urgent admissions and emergencies. **1978** *Times* 2 Nov. 14/2 They [*sc.* the Samaritans] can, and do, act as a medical or psychiatric referral agency.

reffo (re·fo). *Austral. slang.* [Abbrev. Refugee *sb.*] A European refugee; *spec.* a refugee who left Germany or German-occupied Europe before the war of 1939–45. Now *Obs.* exc. *Hist.*

1941 Baker *Dict. Austral. Slang* 59 *Reffo*, a refugee from Europe. **1951** Cusack & James *Come in Spinner* 278 'The woman's a Viennese.' 'Oh, a reffo?' **1955** J. Cleary *Justin Bayard* x. 137 She talked even now in her letters of the Dagoes and Balts and reffos, the New Australians, who were taking over the country. **1960** *Times Lit. Suppl.* 3 June 349/3 Stefan is the refugee—from Bulgaria... Lionel.. considers Stefan 'a bloody reffo' and a nuisance. **1961** P. White *Riders in Chariot* 221 He was..a blasted foreigner, and bloody reffo, and should have been glad he was allowed to exist at all. **1965** *Listener* 2 Sept. 339/2 Australians.. had their full quota of terms such as wogs, dagos, and so on, and refugees were commonly referred to as 'bloody reffos'. **1976** *Australasian Post* 8 Apr. 54/2 Several decades ago, the normal expression for migrants was 'reffo', which was then officially changed to 'migrant'.

refill, *sb.* Add: **b.** The renewed contents of a glass; a second or further drink.

1929 'E. Queen' *Roman Hat Mystery* iii. 53, I asked her if it was time to go in for my orangeade refills. **1960** C. MacInnes *Mr Love & Justice* 79 The star ponce beckoned for refills... The girl..brought the glasses. **1966** M. Sharman *Seeds of Violence* ii. 11 'I think we'd better have refills.' He busied himself with the drinks. **1968** 'R. Raine' *Night of Hawk* xxxiii. 156 Drink up and I'll give you a refill. **1977** *Rolling Stone* 30 June 25/1 She lets go with a loud, decidedly unsentimental laugh that startles a room-service waiter trying to set down refills on a coffee table hopelessly cluttered with empty glasses and Heineken bottles.

c. *adj.* That requires or serves as a refill.

1907 *Yesterday's Shopping* (1969) 345/1 Nickel Pencil.. 4 in. long, with refill leads. **1918** W. Owen *Let.* 9 Sept. (1967) 574 I'd like a parcel with re-fill battery, cigarettes, & chocolate. **1921** *Edin. Rev.* Jan. 158 Perhaps in time each party will provide not only its own refill ministers and kitchenmaids but even its own king. **1961** *Lebende Sprachen* VI. 103/2 *Refill cartridge*, die Nachfüllmine..für Kugelschreiber.

refillable (rīfi·lăb'l), *a.* [f. Refill *v.* + -able.] Capable of being refilled.

1920 in Webster. **1961** R. A. Foresman in H. R. Shepherd *Aerosols* iii. 48 Although disposable aerosols are the only real market factor at this writing, the refillable units were of some consumer importance as late as 1958. **1962** *Harper's Bazaar* Aug. 65 An elegant new black and gold refillable atomiser. **1971** *Nature* 23 July 274/1 For electrophoresis, refillable glass cannulae containing 25 % KCl and a coiled silver wire were implanted chronically. **1977** *Private Eye* 13 May 23/3 (Advt.), Refillable ballpens and cartridge pens that look good and feel good.

refi·nance (*also* -finæ·ns), *v.* [Re- 5 a.] *trans.* To finance again; to provide with further capital. So **refi·nanced** *ppl. a.*; **refi·nancing** *vbl. sb.* and *ppl. a.*

1908 *Standard* 6 Apr. 6/4 Plans have been drafted for the refinancing of the Erie Railway Company. **1921** *Glasgow Herald* 6 July 8/2 The first important refinancing operation, since the Funding and Victory issues, was the Conversion Loan announced with the Budget statement. **1922** *Daily Mail* 26 Oct. 3 The conditions of the Government guarantee and the details of the scheme for re-financing the company were first officially announced. **1930** *Times Lit. Suppl.* 30 Oct. 893/1 Oscar, generously refinanced through 'Gamy', is sailing..safely into harbour. **1934** *Planning* I. xix. 3 Refinancing in the post-war boom had left an evil legacy: the practices of local finance, of the issue of part-paid shares and of calling up unpaid capital had intensified the problem and to a large extent control had passed into the hands of the banks. **1971** *Flying* Apr. 25/2 The R. J. Enstrom Helicopter Company..is being reactivated and refinanced as a wholly owned subsidiary of Franklin Capital Corp. of Michigan. **1976** *Economist* 16 Oct. 102/2 Instead of forcing foreigners to convert their sterling holdings into other reserve assets once and for all, such a scheme would allow Britain to refinance any rundown in its sterling balances, both private and official, as and when it occurred. **1979** *Jrnl. R. Soc. Arts* CXXVII. 428/1 There would be danger, if interest rates fell substantially, that mortgages would be redeemed and refinanced.

Hence **refi·nance** *sb.*, renewed or additional finance; chiefly *attrib.* in *refinance credit* (see quot. 1970); **refina·nceable** *a.*, capable of being refinanced.

1959 *Economist* 28 Feb. 817/1 The authorities have not lifted the ban on 'refinance' credits... These are usance credits, usually of three months' duration, opened in order to meet sight drafts payable in London. **1965** *Ibid.* 19 June p. ix/1 What of 'refinanceable credits'—the portions of medium-term advances for export credits which now allow the banks to grant such advances with no impact on their liquidity ratio? **1970** *Penguin Dict. Commerce* 276 *Refinance credits*, credits obtainable by an overseas buyer, where the exporter cannot provide credit and the buyer does not wish to pay cash. **1976** *Bank of England Q. Bull.* XVI. 194 Cash flow may well be negative in the earlier years, thus requiring refinance at uncertain interest rates.

refinedness. Delete ? *Obs.* and add further examples.

1717 *Censor* II. sig. A4ᵛ, The sensible Part of the World in their Pleasures, as well as graver Conduct, are proud of being influenc'd by Examples that give them the Credit of Discernment, and a Refinedness of Taste. *a* **1945** E. R. Eddison *Mezentian Gate* (1972) xxxviii. 227 'Your son, I said. There are other names for bastards.' 'I have always admired the refinedness of your language.'

refiner. Add: **1. b.** *spec.* A machine used in paper-making in which knots and lumps in the pulp are broken down by scissoring between blades or discharged by centrifugal action.

1902 *Encycl. Brit.* XXXI. 458/2 One form of beater [for paper making] has already been referred to..but engines of quite a different construction are now used largely in

American mills, and also to some extent in Great Britain. These are known as 'refiners'. *Ibid.* 459/1 By the use of the refiner the time occupied in the beater can be reduced by nearly one half. **1929** CLAPPERTON & HENDERSON *Mod. Paper Making* vi. 68 The final clearing of knots, and the reduction of the longer fibres to a uniform length, are often performed by a refiner or perfecting engine. **1963** R. R. A. HIGHAM *Handbk. Papermaking* ii. 55 The Bauer refiner consists of two discs which rotate in opposite directions, the bars of which form a variety of cutting surfaces according to the character of the stock and the grade of paper to be manufactured.

refinery. Add: **1.** (Later examples.) Also *attrib.*

1939 *Thorpe's Dict. Appl. Chem.* (ed. 4) III. 348/2 The largest refinery plant in this country is at Prescot, where copper is refined..from blister copper. **1951** DYLAN THOMAS *Let.* Jan. (1966) 351 Today I was taken to see a great new black-towered hissing and coiling monster, just erected in the middle of the refinery. **1954** *Thorpe's Dict. Appl. Chem.* (ed. 4) XI. 187/1 Refined sugar presupposes treatment with bone charcoal in refineries as distinct from factories dealing with sugar beet or sugar cane. **1959** *Listener* 2 Apr. 582/1 Refinery gases, oil, and now refrigerated methane. **1970** W. G. ROBERTS *Quest for Oil* ix. 93 The newest refineries use desulphurisation processes of this kind to treat a wide cut from the light end of the crude oil right up to kerosine or gas oil. **1981** J. SIMPSON *Moscow Requiem* II. v. 159 The coast of Saudi Arabia and the peninsula where stood the second largest oil refinery in the world.

refit, *sb.* (Further examples.)

1945 *Jane's Fighting Ships 1944–45* 432 A contract was signed..for the repair and refit of this battle-cruiser. **1955** *Times* 7 May 8/1 An explosion occurred last night in the diesel room of H.M.S. Daring under refit in Devonport dockyard. **1975** *Drive* New Year 28/2 Is it more economical to write off a damaged car and pay the client out or make him wait for a re-fit? **1976** *Gramophone* Sept. 453/3 The Canterbury instrument is now in need of a refit.

reflate (rīflēɪ·t), *v.* [f. RE- 5 a after *DEFLATE *v.* 3, *INFLATE *v.* 4.] **a.** *absol.* To raise the pressure of demand (in an economy) after a period of falling pressure. Also *trans.*, to expand (the money supply or the flow of expenditure) or raise (prices) after a period of contraction or reduction. **b.** *intr.* for *pass.* Of an economy: to be affected by or subject to reflation. Hence **refla·ting** *vbl. sb.*

1932 *Sun* (Baltimore) 12 Apr. 10/2 There are plenty of ways to inflate or 'reflate' without putting the Federal Government $2,000,000,000 more into debt to accomplish the purpose. **1939** *Ibid.* 18 Dec. 13/6 The Administration was pleased to see farm prices on the rise for the New Deal dedicated a large part of its recovery promotion energies to schemes for 'reflating' commodity quotations. **1958** *Engineering* 21 Mar. 354/2 The rest of the world is afraid that the American determination not to reflate is going to start a deflation abroad. **1960** *Economist* 15 Oct. 220/2 Britain's present poor export performance makes it imperative that we should not reflate too early. **1966** *Daily Tel.* 2 Nov. 1/1 It is not a sign that the Government has begun to reflate the economy to halt unemployment and start industrial production moving forward. **1971** *Ibid.* 10 Sept. 19 The banks have 'saved' £600 million and..the authorities will probably want a substantial slice of it locked up again in case the economy reflates too fast again. *a* **1974** R. CROSSMAN *Diaries* (1976) II. 134 If we wait until the officials tell us it's wise to reflate, the results won't show for years ahead and we'd have no prospect of winning the election. **1975** *Washington Post* 31 Aug. c7/4 The French and Germans are now having to reflate their economies by massive government expenditures. **1979** *Dædalus* Spring 43 Governments are..taking pains not to reflate the economy enough to wipe out unemployment for fear of rekindling inflation and a balance of payments crisis.

reflation (rīflēɪ·ʃən). [f. RE- 5 a after *DEFLATION 3, *INFLATION 6.] The process of reflating or taking measures designed to allow an expansion in economic activity to be resumed.

1932 *Economist* 20 Feb. 394/2 Its purpose has been aptly described as 'reflation', to prevent further deflation..and to undo some of the present extreme deflation. **1932** *Sun* (Baltimore) 12 Apr. 10/2 It does seem in order to ask why, if inflation or 'reflation' or whatever they may choose to call it is really the principal concern, they do not..come forward with a straight inflation or 'reflation' project. **1932** *Hansard Commons* 20 Apr. 1582, I propose a different thing altogether [from inflation]. I would describe it as reflation, which I would define as controlled expansion of the note issue to keep pace with increased production. **1933** *Daily Tel.* 24 Apr. 11/3 The fight in Congress to beat depression by inflation—reflation, as some call it—grows more heated. **1940** G. CROWTHER *Outl. Money* iii. 116 The custom has grown up of referring to what happens during the upward phase of the normal trade cycle not as 'inflation' but as 'reflation'. For the present, we can think of 'reflation' as being restricted to a rise of prices that merely restores the *status quo ante*—the position before the start of the preceding deflation—and inflation to any further rise in prices after this point. **1959** *Economist* 17 Jan. 194/2 Every pound's worth of income tax relief this year would bring less risk to sterling than every ten shillings' worth of reflation made in any other way. **1971** *New Scientist* 10 June 606/1 A reflation stimulus is urgently needed now to fill the yawning gap in consumer demand. **1975** *Evening Standard* 24 July 36/2 (*heading*) It's reflation time says EEC. **1977** *Times* 29 Aug. 9/3 An electorally opportunistic government..might be strongly tempted to chance some reflation in the run up to a general election next year.

reflationary (rīflēɪ·ʃənări), *a.* [f. *REFLATION + -ARY[1].] Characterized by, suggestive of, or tending to reflation.

1932 *Times Lit. Suppl.* 8 Dec. 931/3 The 'reflationary' policy of the American Government will in the end, he thinks, set prices rising again. **1940** *Economist* 7 Dec. 704/2 As long as the bulk of the gold inflow in the United States was the counterpart of a movement of capital there was no inherent reflationary or inflationary virtue to be found in it. **1957** *Ibid.* 26 Oct. 286/1 No small reflationary measures taken by Britain now, however, would make the situation then any better. **1963** *Indian Econ. Rev.* Feb. 32 As it proved, what expansion of the money supply there was in the 1930s was not inflationary but..reflationary—that is, it served to increase national income without inducing a significant rise in prices. **1969** *Daily Tel.* 28 Oct. 16 An election just after a reflationary Budget would be cynically received. **1974** *Guardian* 27 Mar. 15/3 The TUC wanted a mildly reflationary Budget and Mr Healey has given them.. a mildly deflationary one. **1976** LD. SELWYN-LLOYD *Mr. Speaker, Sir* vii. 150 Many heads had already been shaken at the reflationary measures of the first two years or so of the Parliament and the idea of bursting through to growth and success.

reflationist (rīflēɪ·ʃənist). [f. *REFLATION + -IST.] One who supports or advocates a policy of reflation.

1959 *Economist* 31 Jan. 393/1 The next questions that eager reflationists put to him should presumably be about the date of that budget and about investment allowances. **1972** *Guardian* 24 Jan. 6/8 Mr Macleod was a natural reflationist. **1980** *Spectator* 1 Nov. 4/2 What *is* unique to Britain is the great strength of the reflationists in the party of the Right.

reflect, *v.* Add: **I. 4. b.** Also used with reference to other forms of wave or radiation. (Further examples.)

1902 *Chem. News* 24 Jan. 47/2 (*heading*) Rays capable of being reflected in radiation emitted by a mixture of chlorides of radium and barium. **1909** *Proc. R. Soc.* A. LXXXII. 495 The fraction of the incident α-particles which are reflected. **1937** *Discovery* Jan. 3/2 The ionosphere—that region in the upper atmosphere where free electrons reflect wireless waves. *Ibid.* 4/1 Pulses are radiated in all directions: some reach the receiver by travelling direct along the ground, others by travelling high up into the atmosphere, where they are reflected downwards by one or more of the conducting layers. **1950** D. HALLIDAY *Introd. Nuclear Physics* vi. 247 A substance with a positive scattering length should..reflect neutrons totally at small external glancing angles. **1960** K. N. TONG *Theory Mech. Vibration* iv. 308 If the bar has an end, the disturbance wave will be reflected as it reaches that end. In a certain subsequent time period the reflected wave and the incident wave coexist in the bar. Afterward, only the reflected wave remains. The manner in which the reflection takes place depends on the end condition. **1974** S. W. FLAX et al. in R. S. Reneman *Cardiovascular Applications Ultrasound* ii. 19 Another factor is how blood cells reflect ultrasound.

c. *Physiol.* To give out (an impulse) along a motor nerve, in response to one received along a sensory nerve. Usu. *pass.*

1833, 1855 [in Dict., sense 4 a]. **1859** J. C. DALTON *Treat. Human Physiol.* II. i. 314 The function of the gray matter is..to receive the impulse conveyed to it, and to reflect or send back another. **1906** H. W. SYERS tr. *J. P. Morat's Physiol. of Nerv. Syst.* ii. 218 The impulse is reflected from the posterior roots to the tracts of the spinal cord, in conscious impressions. **1931** H. G. WELLS et al. *Sci. of Life* I. iii. 86/1 The impulse may be wholly reflected in a reflex or pass on in part and more or less modified to the hemispheres. **1950** P. D. F. MURRAY *Biol.* vii. 68 The term 'reflex'.. refers to the manner in which the impulse, having passed in to the central nervous system, is 'reflected' outwards from it.

7*. With direct statement, question, or exclamation as obj. (For indirect uses, see sense 12 b in Dict.)

1862 MRS. H. WOOD *Channings* II. vii. 102 'No, no; it would not be right of him to make me his wife now,' she reflected. **1881** MRS. J. H. RIDDELL *Senior Partner* II. xi. 223 'She has the Pousnett kind of talk,' he reflected, 'and the same uppish way with her.' **1906** E. PHILLPOTTS *Portreeve* I. vi. 50 'Let what will come, there's amusement in it,' she reflected. ''Tis hunting of a sort. Fox-hunting—man-hunting—what more has life for me?' **1919** V. WOOLF *Night & Day* xxxiii. 506 Even if she started the very moment that she got it [*sc.* a letter], he reflected, she would not be home till Tuesday night.

II. 12. a. Also occas. with *over*.

1906 W. S. MAUGHAM *Bishop's Apron* ix. 137 Winnie reflected over this for a moment.

14. b. (Further example.)

1979 *Nature* 11 Jan. 84/1 If the flight control centre was indeed 'astounded', this surely reflects on the rate at which the Soviet team get access to the data from US missions.

reflectance (rĭfle·ktăns). *Physics.* [f. REFLECT *v.* + -ANCE.] The proportion of the light incident upon a surface, which is reflected or scattered by it; *spec.* a complex number whose modulus is the proportion of the radiant flux (at some specified wavelength or range of wavelengths) which is reflected, and whose argument indicates the change of phase undergone by the reflected light. Cf. **reflection coefficient, factor*. Also *attrib.*

1926 *Jrnl. Optical Soc. Amer.* X. 178 Reflectance..is the ratio of reflected to incident radiant energy. **1932** [see *INFRA-RED *a.* and *sb.* A. 1]. **1956** *Nature* 14 Jan. 74/2 The assessment of particular reflectance characteristics of cotton may be made on the automatic Nickerson–Hunter cotton colorimeter. **1957** V. J.-R. KEHOE *Technique Film & Television Make-Up* viii. 96 Black velvet has approximately 2 per cent reflectance, while some white paper is as high as 90 per cent. **1960** *Illuminating Engin.* LV. 228/1 The concepts of transmittance and reflectance can be extended to cover the separation of specular and diffuse components which are functions of angles. **1975** D. H. BURRIN in Williams & Wilson *Biologist's Guide to Princ. & Techniques Pract. Biochem.* v. 138 Reflectance spectrophotometers, which measure the radiation absorbed when a light beam is reflected by the sample, allow the determination of absorption spectra of pastes and suspensions of microorganisms which are too opaque to transmit radiation. **1977** J. HEDGECOE *Photographer's Handbk.* 132 (*caption*) Meter reads direct off mid-gray (ideally 16 percent reflectance) card which simulates subject mid-tone.

reflected, *ppl. a.* Add: **2. b.** Also used of other waves and radiations (cf. *REFLECT *v.* 4 b). (Further examples.)

1830 *Encycl. Metrop.* II. 753 A tendency in the reflected Sound to confine itself to the direction which a ray of Light regularly reflected at the echoing surface would follow. **1862** R. MALLET *First Princ. Observational Seismol.* II. III. xvi. 356 Ottajano and Somma..sustained the subordinate shock, of reflected waves from the N.E. flank of Vesuvius. **1909** *Proc. R. Soc.* A. LXXXII. 497 For β-particles the number of reflected particles..decreases with the atomic weight of the reflector. **1925** *Year-bk. Wireless Telegr. & Telephony* 13 A system of telegraphy employing reflected beams was not only possible, but possessed very many advantages. **1960** [see *REFLECT *v.* 4 b]. **1975** LEOPOLD & ASHER *Fund. Abdominal & Pelvic Ultrasonography* p. vii, One can obtain information from all areas of the body by suitably observing the reflected ultrasound pulses.

reflecting, *ppl. a.* Add: **1. a.** Also, that reflects waves or radiation of other kinds (cf. *REFLECT *v.* 4 b). (Further examples.)

1850 W. & R. CHAMBERS *Nat. Philos. Acoustics* 26 The reflected [sound] waves have the same form as if they diverged from a point on the other side of the reflecting surface, directly opposite to the origin of the waves and equally distant from the surface. **1869** J. TYNDALL *Sound* (ed. 2) i. 13 Like sound also, light and radiant heat, when sent through a tube with a reflecting interior surface, may be conveyed to great distances with comparatively little loss. **1937** *Discovery* Jan. 3 The reflecting ionosphere layer. **1953** REED & RUSSELL *Ultra High Frequency Propagation* 513 The amplitude of the reflected energy is dependent.. upon the dynamic mechanics of the reflecting media.

reflection, reflexion. Add: **2. a.** Also, the similar action of surfaces on other waves and radiations (cf. *REFLECT *v.* 4 b). (Further examples.)

1902 *Chem. News* 24 Jan. 47/2 Certain rays existed in the radiation emitted by certain radio-active bodies which were capable of reflection. **1909** *Proc. R. Soc.* A. LXXXII. 497 The diffuse reflection of the α-particles is a consequence of their scattering. **1929** *Jrnl. Sci. Instruments* VI. 34 Sound has all the properties of a wave motion..and exhibits the phenomena of reflection, interference, diffraction and resonance. **1941** A. B. WOOD *Textbk. Sound* (ed. 2) iii. 311 The direct reflection of a sound of short duration from a surface of large area such as the wall of a building or a cliff is generally described as an echo. **1960** [see *REFLECT *v.* 4 b]. **1969** *Times* 28 Aug. 3/3 Seismic reflections indicate the thickness of the rocks.

9*. *Cryst., Math., Physics.* The conceptual operation of inverting a system or event with respect to a plane, each element being transferred perpendicularly through the plane to a point the same distance the other side of it. Freq. *attrib.*

1899 W. J. LEWIS *Treat. Crystallogr.* iii. 18 We shall often express the relation of two planes, or two lines, to a plane of symmetry bisecting the angle between them by the statement that they are reciprocal reflexions in the plane. **1910** *Nature* 26 May 368/1 Its 880 known solutions (8 × 880, if we admit reversals and reflections of the same square to be 'different'). **1955** W. PAULI *Niels Bohr* 30 The mathematical group was further amplified by including the reflections of space and time. *Ibid.* 33, I am restricting myself..to the discussion of the reflection of all coordinates simultaneously while I do not consider the reflection of space or time separately. **1965** A. F. BROWN tr. *Zhdanov's Crystal Physics* v. 144 Symmetry groups containing only the operations of reflection, rotation and inversion, and not containing any translations, are called point groups. **1965** *Sci. Amer.* Dec. 28/1 Until December, 1956, they [*sc.* physicists] had assumed that if an event is possible, its mirror image is also possible, and that if one looks at some real event in a mirror, what one sees could also actually happen. This was known as reflection symmetry. **1971** I. G. GASS et al. *Understanding Earth* i. 19/1 The stereogram of zircon..shows a four-fold rotation axis in the centre and also shows a number of reflection planes. **1972** F. J. BUDDEN *Fascination of Groups* xxvi. 507 The two-dimensional pattern of fig. 26·051 contains translations and glide reflections, but no rotations.

10. *reflection oscillator*; *reflection-reducing* adj.; **reflection coefficient, factor** *Physics* = *REFLECTANCE; **reflection nebula** *Astr.*, a nebula which is visible only by virtue of the light which it reflects; **reflection profiling** *Geol.*, profiling (sense *3) by means of reflection shooting; **reflection shooting** *Geol.*, seismic prospecting in which shock waves generated at the earth's surface are detected up to a mile away after having been reflected at the interface between strata, the depth of which is deduced from their time of arrival.

1942 A. HUND *Frequency Modulation* i. 139 The reflection coefficient for horizontal polarization. **1959** BORN & WOLF *Princ. Optics* xiii. 627 The complex reflection and transmission coefficients of the film may immediately be evaluated. **1975** E. HEIGHT *Optics* iii. 43 Determine the values of the amplitude reflection coefficients for light incident at 30° on an air-glass interface. **1920** Reflection factor [see *REFLECTOMETER]. **1971** E. SKUDRZYK *Acoustics* xv. 302 The amplitude reflection factor represents the ratio of the reflected to the incident pressure wave with respect to magnitude and phase. **1936** *Astrophysical Jrnl.* LXXXIV. 219 (*heading*) Reflection nebulae. **1974** *Sci. Amer.* Oct. 34/3 These reflection nebulas are useful for studying the properties of the interstellar dust grains, but they are distinguished from the true emission nebulas, which shine as a result of the atomic processes going on within them. **1938** B. MCCOLLUM in A. E. Dunstan et al. *Sci. of Petroleum* I. VIII. 396/2 (*heading*) Accuracy of reflection profiling. **1964** CURRAY & MOORE in van Andel & Shor *Marine Geol. Gulf of Calif.* 193 The sedimentary structure of the continental terrace of the Costa de Nayarit..has been investigated geophysically by means of continuous acoustic reflection profiling. **1971** I. G. GASS et al. *Understanding Earth* xvi. 243/2 Reflecting horizons..can be mapped over vast areas by continuous reflection profiling. **1962** CORSON & LORRAIN *Introd. Electromagn. Fields* xi. 406 Do reflection-reducing coatings on lenses improve the transmission significantly? **1929** *Trans. Amer. Inst. Mining & Metall. Engineers* LXXXI. 606 The distances are short in reflection shooting compared with those in refraction shooting. **1951** K. K. LANDES *Petroleum Geol.* ii. 48 Refraction shooting has recently become important again as a method of detailing rock structure where reflection shooting is not practicable. **1973** R. E. CHAPMAN *Petroleum Geol.* ii. 45 More detailed structural information is obtained from reflection shooting, in which the elastic waves are partly reflected by surfaces of contrasting density. **1971** *Physics Bull.* June 333/1 Reflection spectroscopy concerns the measurement of the frequency dependence of the specular reflectivity of the material to determine either the positions and strengths of features in its absorption spectrum or its optical constants.

reflectionless *adv.*, also as *adj.*, not giving rise to any reflection.

1951 *Rev. Sci. Instruments* XXII. 828/1 A reflectionless wave-guide termination. **1956** *Nature* 25 Feb. 392/1 A thin transverse film having a surface resistivity equal to the wave impedance of the waveguide forms a reflexion-less termination when [etc.].

reflectious (rĭfle·kʃəs), *a. nonce-wd.* [f. REFLECT *v.* + -IOUS. Cf. REFLEXIOUS *a.*] = REFLECTIVE *a.*

1874 HARDY *Far from Madding Crowd* II. xxv. 311 'Justice is come to weigh him in the balance,' I said in my reflectious way.

reflective, *a.* and *sb.* Add: **A.** *adj.* **4. c.** (Further examples.)

1934 M. BODKIN *Archetypal Patterns in Poetry* 314 An hypothesis..that archetypal patterns, or images, are present within the experience communicated through poetry, and may be discovered there by reflective analysis. **1961** *Manas* 5 Apr. 1/2 Mr. Lyford gives voice to a temper that represents..an achieved plateau of reflective thinking.

reflectivity. Add: Also (*a*) the degree to which anything incident on a surface is reflected; (*b*) the degree to which a surface reflects what is incident upon it. (Further examples.)

1916 *Physical Rev.* VIII. 152 The reflectivity of metal atoms striking surfaces of the same metals at room temperature (or lower) is zero. **1936** *Discovery* Aug. 237/1 Steel mirrors of high reflectivity. **1946** [see *ALUMINIZE *v.* 2]. **1966** *McGraw-Hill Encycl. Sci. & Technol.* XI. 395/1 Typical curves of the reflectivity of the polarized components versus angle of incidence are given in Fig. 7. **1974** *Mineral. Abstr.* XXV. 267/1 Reflectivities of pyrite..and sphalerite were measured with POH microscope and SPS-1 microscope photometer.

reflectometer. Substitute for def.: Any of various instruments for measuring quantities associated with reflection; *spec.* (*a*) one for measuring the critical angle of a transparent solid so that its refractive index may be calculated; (*b*) one for measuring the intensity of light reflected or scattered by a surface so that its reflectance may be calculated. (Earlier and later examples.)

1891 *Jrnl. Chem. Soc.* LX. 513 (*heading*) Measurement of refractive indices at high temperatures by means of the total reflectometer. **1920** *Sci. Papers U.S. Bureau of Standards* XVI. 435 The use of an incomplete sphere as a reflectometer furnishes two new absolute methods for the determination of diffuse reflection factors. **1935** *Sci. Abstr.* A. XXXVIII. 1223 (*heading*) Ultrasonic total reflectometer to measure speed of sound and elastic constants of solids. **1962** R. H. KAY in J. Thewlis *Encycl. Dict. Physics* VI. 240/1 Instruments primarily designed to measure reflecting power of materials are known as reflectometers and usually compare the test specimen against such a standard as magnesium oxide or aluminium. **1977** *Sci. Amer.* Feb. 88/3 (Advt.), A time domain reflectometer (TDR) works in a manner similar to radar. It generates repetitive pulses of energy that are sent down a cable and displayed on a cathode-ray tube screen. Any cable faults (impedance changes) cause pulse reflections. **1977** BOXALL & VON FRAUNHOFFER *Conc. Paint Technol.* ix. 193 The contrast ratio is the reflectometer reading obtained over the black tile after the reflectometer has been set to 100 % over the white tile.

Hence **reflecto·metry.**

1967 *Jrnl. Optical Soc. Amer.* LVII. 445 (*heading*) Terms, definitions, and symbols in reflectometry. **1977** *Sci. Amer.* Feb. 88/2 (Advt.), I knew that the TV industry used time domain reflectometry a lot.

reflector. 1. Delete † *Obs.* in Dict. and add further examples.

1790 T. WILKINSON *Mem.* IV. 132 By which means [*sc.* comparing cast lists of 1747 and 1789] the unprejudiced reflector may draw a fair conclusion. **1921** W. C. BOOTH *Rhetoric of Fiction* I. vi. 157 It was not until authors had discovered the full uses of the third-person reflector that they could effectively show a narrator changing *as he narrates*.

4. a. *spec.* in *Geol.*, a stratum or interface that reflects seismic waves.

1933 *Bull. Amer. Assoc. Petroleum Geologists* XVII. 258 The geologic section contains many strata which act as good reflectors of wave energy. **1952** C. H. DIX *Seismic Prospecting for Oil* xi. 217 In areas where the reflectors are almost planes with small dip and small variations of dip, the reflections carry across the records with little change in character or amplitude. **1965** *Bull. Amer. Assoc. Petroleum Geologists* XLIX. 352/1 Lateral continuity of these reflectors appears to be large compared to those within the..aprons and sea fans of the basins. **1978** *Nature* 29 June 744/1 The tilt of the terraces parallels a northwards dip of subsurface reflectors toward a sedimentary basin off Hudson Strait.

b. Also, something designed to reflect other forms of radiation (as radio waves or neutrons); e.g. part of a nuclear reactor designed to reflect escaping neutrons back into the core. (Further examples.)

1897 *Strand Mag.* Mar. 277/1 How far have you sent a telegraphic despatch on the air?.. Did you use a reflector? **1909** *Proc. R. Soc.* A. LXXXII. 496 The zinc sulphide screen S..was fixed behind the lead plate P, in such a position that no α-particles could strike it directly. When a reflector was placed in the position RR at about 1 cm. from the end of the tube, scintillations were at once observed. **1923** E. W. MARCHANT *Radio Telegr. & Telephony* i. 11 The strength of the signal received, when reflectors were used, was estimated to be about 200 times as great as when there were no reflectors. **1943** *Gloss. Terms Telecomm.* (*B.S.I.*) 66 A passive aerial placed behind an active aerial is usually called a reflector. **1945** *Chemical Age* 27 Oct. 390/1 And the escape of neutrons from the system can be reduced (relatively) by increasing the size of the system, and by a reflector (*e.g.*, a layer of graphite). **1958** *Times* 1 July 7/3 It consists of an arrangement of enriched reactor fuel in ordinary water and will be used to investigate..the use of different materials as 'reflectors' (to reflect neutrons, which might otherwise escape, back into the core). **1977** N. FREELING *Gadget* I. 21 Cast a near-crit mass... Put a high-class reflector round it. **1978** *Nature* 9 Feb. 497/3 Chain reaction is unlikely, since the mass of uranium used in such satellites is normally subcritical, and special methods, e.g. a reflector, must be used to keep sufficient neutrons within it to maintain a chain reaction.

c. A piece of reflective material, now commonly a red disc, mounted at the rear of a vehicle or by the roadside so as to show its presence by reflecting the light from headlights.

1909 *Cyclist Touring Club Gaz.* Dec. 544/1 If a rearward indication is considered desirable, the Lea Reflex reflector and lens does everything needful... It throws back the light of the overtaking vehicle in a red glow through a wide angle. **1931** *Highway Code* 13 If you do not use a red rear lamp remember to keep your red reflector clean and properly fixed. **1962** *Which? Car Suppl.* Oct. 133/1 We checked the position of all lamps and reflectors. **1972** A. PRICE *Colonel Butler's Wolf* vii. 68 'He came directly down the road... His headlight 'ud pick up the first of the reflectors. Even my bicycle light picks 'em up.'.. 'Then supposing a car came round the corner as he was approaching it—could it have cut off the reflectors and then blinded him?' 'Mmmm—it could have, I suppose—but it would have lit 'em all up first and warned him there was a corner here.' **1978** *Highway Code* 35 Make sure your cycle is safe to ride. At night you must have front and rear lamps and a rear reflector.

Hence **refle·ctored** *a.*, of a lamp: fitted with a reflecting surface or surfaces.

1916 A. BENNETT *These Twain* xix. 429 The glittering light of the latest triple-jetted and reflectored gas-lamps which the corporation..had placed in Crown Square. **1978** *Amer. N. & Q.* Dec. 65/2 Pierre Patte's early advocacy of reflectored lights in the auditorium.

reflectorize (rĭfle·ktǫ̆raiz), *v.* orig. *U.S.* [f. REFLECTOR + -IZE.] *trans.* To treat or coat with a substance that reflects light. Chiefly as **refle·ctorized** *ppl. a.*

1942 *New Hampshire Highway Signs & Road Marking* 56 Route markers 24″ × 24″ white or black. Plain or reflectorized. **1947** *Sun* (Baltimore) 22 May 2/5 A bus accident in Texas has resulted in one of several attempts by that state to reflectorize curb surfaces to enhance driving safety. *Ibid.*, A traffic circle where the reflectorized surface now warns fast drivers that the road does not go straight on. **1951** *Richmond* (Va.) *Times-Dispatch* 15 Feb. 7/6 More and more 'reflectorized' paint—the kind that gleams brilliantly under automobile lights at night—is being used to mark traffic lanes on Virginia highways. **1959** *B.S.I. News* Mar. 4/2 (*caption*) Left to right: sign with button reflectors, sign reflectorized all-over, painted sign. **1961** *Evening Star* (Dunedin, N.Z.) 28 Mar. 1/7 They signalled with torches and skipped out of the path of the oncoming traffic which even knocked down large reflectorised stop signs. **1967** *New Scientist* 26 Jan. 225/2 A great improvement on the type of number plate now in use in Britain would be one with black letters on a white, 'reflectorized' background. **1973** *Houston Chron.* 21 Oct. 9 (Advt.), Bicycle has black saddle and grips. 20″ × 1·75″ tires. Fully reflectorized for safety. **1978** *Highway Code* 15 Watch out for blind people who may be carrying white sticks (white with two red reflectorised bands for deaf/blind people).

reflectoscope (rĭfle·ktŏskōᵘp). [f. REFLECT *v.* + -O + -SCOPE.] An instrument for investigating opaque bodies by transmitting ultrasound into them and measuring its reflection.

1944 *Sun* (Baltimore) 26 May 9/1 The invention, credited to Dr. Floyd A. Firestone, physicist and acoustics expert, is known as the 'supersonic reflectoscope'... The machine can gauge thickness of metal when one side is inaccessible. **1964** I. EDLER in D. Gordon *Ultrasound as Diagnostic & Surg. Tool* xiv. 124 The apparatus used for ultrasound-cardiography is an ultrasound reflectoscope.

reflex, *sb.* Add: The pronunc. (rī·fleks) is now standard. **2. c.** *Linguistics.* A form (word, sound unit, etc.) corresponding to, or derived from, another comparable form.

1890 S. PRIMER in *PMLA* V. II. 196 It is doubtful whether it [*sc.* the *a*-sound] is a reflex of the older pronunciation. **1945** Y. MALKIEL in *Univ. Calif. Publ. Linguistics* I. IV. iii. 51, -entia seems to have taken root in Italy more than anywhere else, as follows from the..reflexes of *absentia, haerentia, licentia, negligentia, scientia*. **1965** A. ZETTERSTEN *Stud. Dial. & Vocab. Ancrene Riwle* 67 It is necessary to emphasize that this Mercian sound coalesced with the reflexes of /æ/ and /a/ in ME. **1970** *Publ. Amer. Dial. Soc.* LIV. 4 This chapter presents the regionally divergent reflexes of Middle English parent phonemes. **1971** J. ANDERSON in A. J. Aitken et al. *Edin. Stud. Eng. & Scots* 110 The permutation of *may* and the subject [in *May your cabbages wither away*] is the superficial reflex of this underlying structure [*I wish that your cabbages may wither away*]. **1975** *Language* LI. 983 The assumption is..that the different reflexes of the same unit are due to phonetic change, either in the lending or the borrowing language, and that therefore the borrowings took place at different times.

6. a. Also in literary use.

1921 G. B. SHAW *Back to Methuselah* v. 238 Martellus: Control your reflexes, child. The Newly Born: My what! Martellus: Your reflexes. The things you do without thinking.

b. *attrib.*, as *reflex apparatus, mechanism, movement, stimulus, therapy, time*; **reflex arc,** the connected set of nerves concerned in the production of a reflex action. Cf. REFLEX *a.* 5.

1924 R. M. OGDEN tr. *Koffka's Growth of Mind* iii. 77 This statement..agrees..with what we have already learned about the reflex-apparatus. **1882** B. BRAMWELL *Dis. Spinal Cord* i. 24 Every half segment of the spinal cord with its sensory and motor nerve roots is, in theory and probably also in fact, a perfect reflex arc. *Ibid.* 25 The multipolar nerve cells of the anterior cornua probably constitute the centre of this reflex arc. **1924** R. M. OGDEN tr. *Koffka's Growth of Mind* iii. 69 Always beginning with a sensory neurone and ending with a motor neurone, this apparatus is called a reflex-arc. **1976** *Radiol. Clin. N. Amer.* XIV. 432/2 The reflex arcs controlling normal esophageal motility are interrupted by disease of the medullary nuclei. **1885** *Encycl. Brit.* XIX. 29/1 Stimulation of a sensory surface may simultaneously produce, by a reflex mechanism, movement, secretion and consciousness. **1924** R. M. OGDEN tr. *Koffka's Growth of Mind* iii. 69 A reflex-mechanism is..conceived as a pre-determined, inherited connection between afferent (receptor) and efferent (effector) pathways. *Ibid.* 91 A stimulus excites a reflex-movement. **1937** *Discovery* Nov. 341/1 When the reasoning powers are great, as in man, the mind is less responsive to outside influences or reflex stimuli. **1956** A. HUXLEY *Adonis & Alphabet* 31 Unorthodox medicine tries to influence the autonomic system by direct mechanical action in the form of osteopathy, chiropractic, reflex therapy and acupuncture. **1913** *Amer. Jrnl. Physiol.* XXXI. 309 How soon, after administering a minimal and also stronger dose of alcohol, does a change in reflex time appear? **1964** L. MARTIN *Clin. Endocrinol.* (ed. 4) iii. 135 Delayed tendon reflexes are characteristic, and particularly the ankle jerks. Sherman *et al.* (1963) measured the reflex-time in 50 hypothyroid cases and considered that the increase had a diagnostic significance.

7. *Photogr.* A reflex camera. Cf. *REFLEX *a.* 7.

1926–7 *Army & Navy Stores Catal.* 969/2 Reflex cameras. The 'Mentor' Folding Reflex is constructed..of the finest materials. **1940** *Wall's Dict. Photogr.* (ed. 15) 548 A twin-lens reflex consists of a rigid box which forms the camera, on top of which is mounted a structure such as that shown in the sketch, but with the mirror fixed in position. **1948** H. S. NEWCOMBE *Twin-Lens Camera Compan.* 15 Other people also find it difficult to hold a normal reflex steady. **1958** *Oxford Mail* 19 May 7/3 In the single-lens reflex you actually focus by looking through the camera lens with a mirror. **1977** J. HEDGECOE *Photographer's Handbk.* 14/1 The single lens reflex is the most highly developed and deservedly popular camera for advanced work.

reflex, *a.* Add: **5. a.** *reflex action*: also in extended or *fig.* use.

a **1846** B. R. HAYDON *Autobiogr.* (1927) III. xv. 278 He [*sc.* Wordsworth]..had a portion of the spirit of the mighty ones..but..did not possess the power of using that spirit otherwise than with reference to himself and so as to excite a reflex action only. **1917** KIPLING *Diversity of Creatures* 159 Only the Lord can understand..How much is reflex action and How much is really sin.

7. *Photogr.* Applied to a camera in which the image from the main lens (or from a duplicate of it) is reflected by means of a mirror on to a glass screen and can be seen and adjusted up to the moment of exposure.

1895 W. DE W. ABNEY *Instantaneous Photogr.* p. v (Advt.), The 'Reflex' Manufacturing Company..Patentees and Sole Manufacturers of the 'Reflex' Camera... The actual working lens also serves for the finder. **1911** *Encycl. Brit.* XXI. 505/2 Although reflex cameras are rather heavy and bulky as hand cameras, they have many advantages over the ordinary hand camera. **1946** R. J. C. ATKINSON

Field Archaeol. v. 157 The chief advantage of the reflex type of camera is the full-sized focusing-screen, which is a valuable aid to composing the photograph and to exact focusing. **1976** *Daily Mail* (Hull) 30 Sept. 2/6 (Advt.), Edixa SL, 35 mm. Reflex Camera, flash gun, quartz, cine camera, lenses, etc; £32. **1976** J. Tate tr. *A. Bodelsen's Operation Cobra* v. 27 As neither his mother nor his father earned so much money now, he knew he could not reckon on getting a reflex camera.

8. *Electronics.* **a.** Applied to a circuit, amplifier, etc. in which the same valves or transistors are used for amplification of both high- and low-frequency signals (usu. the radio and audio frequencies respectively); also applied to the action of such a device.

1923 *Radio News* Feb. 1455/1 Very much discussion has been carried on as to the practicability of the so-called reflex circuit—a circuit designed, developed and patented in April and November of 1917 by Mr. Marius Latour, a French radio engineer. **1924** W. James *Construction Two-Valve & Crystal Reflex Receiver* 3 The first valve is connected to operate as a dual or reflex amplifier; that is, it gives high-frequency and low-frequency-amplification. **1928** Lauer & Brown *Radio Engin. Princ.* (ed. 2) vii. 163 (*heading*) Reflex amplification. **1934** *Pract. Wireless* 1 Sept. 723/1 Reflex circuits are rarely used at the present time, although they were extremely popular between 1922 and 1924. *Ibid.*, It is possible to obtain the same output from two valves wired in a reflex arrangement as from three valves connected in a more conventional circuit. **1957** R. F. Shea *Transistor Circuit Engin.* xi. 375 When size and cost are of extreme importance, reflex circuits may be used. **1961** J. M. Carroll *Design Man. for Transistor Circuits* viii. 154 Reflex circuits in which i–f and a–f gain are achieved in the same transistor stage have recently been incorporated into economy broadcast receivers.

b. Applied to an oscillator, esp. a klystron, in which the same resonant cavity serves to modulate the electron beam and to produce an amplified microwave signal.

1942 J. G. Brainerd et al. *Ultra-High-Frequency Techniques* x. 339 A reflex klystron oscillator, in which a single resonator acts both as the buncher and the catcher. **1945** *Proc. IRE* XXXIII. 112/2 Reflex oscillators can be considered as oscillators in which an electron stream passes through a longitudinal radio-frequency field across a 'gap' between two electrodes, then into a drift space in which there is a retarding electric field produced by a negative repeller electrode, and finally returns through the radio-frequency field across the gap. **1969** *IEEE Trans. Industr. Electronics* XVI. 103/1 The oscillation frequency of a reflex klystron is determined by..the size of the cavity resonator. **1975** D. G. Fink *Electronics Engineers' Handbk.* ix. 31 Reflex Klystrons are used as test signal sources, receiver local oscillators, pump sources for parametric amplifiers, and low-power transmitters for FM line-of-sight relays.

9. Applied to a photocopying process in which the original document is illuminated by light passing through a piece of sensitized paper placed in contact with it, a negative image being formed on the paper according to the amount of light reflected by the original; also applied to equipment or materials connected with such a process.

1943 *Jrnl. Sci. Instruments* XX. 18/1 The Kodak Reflex plate has been introduced to solve the problem of the exact preservation of scale in copying maps, machine drawings and other line diagrams. *Ibid.*, The latter [distortion] is eliminated by the nature of reflex copying. *Ibid.*, Reflex printing has been carried out with photographic paper for a number of years. **1947** *Jrnl. R. Aeronaut. Soc.* LI. 318/1 The exposure is made through the paper with a yellow reflex screen. *Ibid.*, A plasticising solution is applied to the cellulose film and the exposed reflex paper is then laminated on to the material. **1956** 'C. Blackstock' *Dewey Death* vii. 149 We then take a piece of..reflex contact document paper—the shiny side is the business end. **1958** T. Landau *Encycl. Librarianship* 267/2 The principle of reflex copying was established by Albrecht Breyer of Berlin,..who in 1839 produced reflex prints by placing silver chloride papers in contact with printed pages. **1972** A. Tyrrell *Basics of Reprography* xiii. 210 Reflex printing by the diffusion-transfer technique has been very popular... Attempts have been made to use diazo-sensitizers in reflex copying.

re·flexing, *vbl. sb. Electronics.* [f. Reflex *a.* + -ing[1].] The use or action of a reflex circuit.

1925 A. H. Morse *Radio* ii. 60 The modern practice of 'reflexing', or amplifying both audio and radio-frequency in a single triode. **1939** *A. W. A. Techn. Rev.* IV. 37 Reflexing does not appreciably reduce the higher audio note response. **1961** J. M. Carroll *Design Man. for Transistor Circuits* viii. 154/1 The reflexing circuit, normally used as a second i–f amplifier and first audio amplifier, can provide gain from a single transistor only a few db less than the gain obtained from two transistors in conventional circuits.

reflexive, *a.* and *sb.* Add: **A.** *adj.* **2.** Restrict † *Obs.* to senses in Dict. and add: **c.** *Social Sciences.* Applied to that which turns back upon, or takes account of, itself or a person's self, esp. methods that take into consideration the effect of the personality or presence of the researcher on the investigation.

1934 G. H. Mead *Mind, Self & Society* xxi. 173 Cooley and James..endeavor to find the basis of the self in reflexive affective experiences, i.e., experiences involving 'self-feeling'. **1957** P. Lafitte *Person in Psychol.* 17 All learning depends on the reflexive interpretation of one's experience together with the experience of others. *Ibid.* 21 The psychologist's reflexive judgements will be limited by his knowledge of himself in some of the ways that his subjects' reports are limited. **1970** A. Gouldner *Coming Crisis of Western Sociol.* xiii. 489 The historical mission of a Reflexive Sociology is to transcend sociology as it now exists. *Ibid.* 490 A Reflexive Sociology means that we sociologists must.. acquire the ingrained *habit* of viewing our own beliefs as we now view those held by others. **1972** M. Landau *Polit. Theory & Polit. Sci.* i. 32 A reflexive prediction is one in which the prediction is itself a factor which may materially alter the projected or anticipated outcome. **1977** Douglas & Johnson *Existential Sociol.* p. xiii, Our emphasis on the problematic and situated nature of meaningful experience contrasts..with the structuralism of Alvin Gouldner's 'reflexive sociology'. **1977** R. Holland *Self & Social Context* v. 82 In both cases the person producing the theory is included within the subject matter he attempts to understand. The usual term for this kind of approach is 'reflexive', a word which has begun to appear in the human sciences.. but which has long been implicit in social theory.

5. (Further example.) Also of phrases, esp. in *Linguistics.*

1933 L. Bloomfield *Language* xii. 193 In English we say *he washed him* when actor and goal are not identical, but *he washed himself* (a *reflexive* form) when they are the same person. **1979** *Trans. Philol. Soc.* 11 We might of course propose to handle such facts by a purely local reflexive deletion rule.

6. (Later examples in *Physiol.*) Also in extended use.

1927 *Jrnl. Nerv. & Mental Dis.* LXV. 463 We..succeeded in producing in apes..a reflexive contraction of the adductor muscles of the thigh. **1971** L. Koppett *N.Y. Times Guide Spectator Sports* i. 13 To have any chance at all, the batter, whose action must be entirely reflexive, needs protection from additional trickery. **1971** *Sci. Amer.* Aug. 74/1 A number of biologists..adopted the radical hypothesis that animal behavior was almost wholly reflexive. On this view the continually changing array of stimuli that an animal encounters as it moves through its environment was thought to produce a large part of the animal's repertory of behavior by reflexes and their mutual interactions. **1975** *New Yorker* 13 Jan. 30/2 At the end, the audience rose in an ovation—but at concerts like this one standing ovations have become reflexive. **1976** *Nature* 1 Apr. 392/1 To suggest ..that the evolutionary considerations which determine the mating systems of mammals and birds have any light.. to shed on the tensions and asymmetries commonly observed in human sexual relationships is to invite reflexive dismissal as a 'sexist'.

7. *Math.* and *Logic.* Applied to any relation which always holds between a term and itself. [The sense is due to G. Vailati, who used It. *riflessività* reflexivity (*Rivista di Matematica* (1891) I. 134).]

1903 B. Russell *Princ. Math.* xix. 159 All kinds of equality have in common the three properties of being reflexive, symmetrical, and transitive. **1937** R. Carnap *Logical Syntax of Lang.* iv. 261 Conditions which require for symmetrical, reflexive, and transitive relations the property of non-emptiness. **1953** A. A. Fraenkel *Abstract Set Theory* i. 34 Any set is equivalent to itself... Equivalence is a reflexive relation. **1972** F. J. Budden *Fascination of Groups* xx. 374 Conjugacy is a relation between the elements of a group. It is evidently reflexive (since $y = 1y1^{-1}$).

reflexively, *adv.* Add: **b.** = Reflexly *adv.*; in the manner of a reflex action, automatically. *rare.*

1952 *Mind* LXI. 252 As is usual with such reflexively repeated dicta, this one is true but never practical to follow. **1966** D. F. Galouye *Lost Perception* xvi. 172 Instantly the three men twisted round. The closest was Wellford. Reflexively, he loosed a laser discharge.

reflexiveness. (Further examples.)

1903 B. Russell *Princ. Math.* xxvi. 219 The property of a relation which insures that it holds between a term and itself is called by Peano *reflexiveness.* **1933** *Mind* XLII. 36 In the *Principia Mathematica* $p \supset p$ assigns to the relation $\supset$ the property of reflexiveness. **1968** *New Scientist* 16 May 339/1 Three properties of conditions are frequently mentioned: reflexiveness, symmetry and transitivity... A reflexive condition is a relation between an idea and itself... An example is equality.

reflexivity (further examples).

1940 W. V. Quine *Math. Logic* iii. 138 A natural extension of the notions of reflexivity and commutativity which were applied to a statement composition. **1950** L. M. Hammond et al. tr. *Hilbert & Ackermann's Princ. Math. Logic* iv. 135 The properties of reflexivity, symmetry, and transitivity of dyadic predicates. **1965** *Canad. Jrnl. Linguistics* X. 175 They [*sc.* classifiers] refer most clearly to the voice of the verb:..passivity, reflexivity. **1977** Douglas & Johnson *Existential Sociol.* v. 172 Reflexivity refers to the mutual interdependence of observer or knower to what is seen or known.

reflexivization (rĭfle:ksivəizēⁱ·ʃən). *Linguistics.* [f. next + -ation.] The action of making (a verb, noun phrase, etc.) reflexive; the process or fact of being made reflexive. Cf. Reflexive *a.* 5 in Dict. and Suppl.

1965 N. Chomsky *Aspects of Theory of Syntax* iii. 145 In a sentence such as..'the boy hurt the boy', the two phonetically identical Noun Phrases are necessarily interpreted as differing in reference; sameness of reference requires reflexivization of the second Noun Phrase. *Ibid.*, The reflexivization rule can be formulated as an erasure operation that uses the Noun Phrase to delete another. *Ibid.* 146 The reflexivization rule..will apply only when the integers assigned to the two items are the same. **1966** P. M. Postal in F. P. Dinneen *Rep. 17th Round Table Meeting Linguistics & Lang. Stud.* 182, I view the process of reflexivization as a complex of a number of partially independent operations. **1972** *Language* XLVIII. 390 The interactions of other pronominals with indirect object, shown in reflexivization properties for example, suggest that postpositions are two-place predicates rather than one-place (intransitive) predicates. **1978** *Studies in Eng. Lit.: Eng. Number* (Tokyo) 65 Reflexivization, which converts the simple personal pronoun into the compound refl. pronoun in *-self*, is apparently optional in ME.

reflexivize (rĭfle·ksivəiz), *v. Linguistics.* [f. Reflexive *a.* + -ize.] **a.** *trans.* To make (a verb, noun phrase, etc.) reflexive. **b.** *intr.* To become reflexive. Hence **refle·xivizing** *ppl. a.*

1965 S.-Y. Kuroda *Generative Gram. Stud. in Japanese Lang.* (Mass. Inst. Technol. thesis) v. 144 The object of a subordinate clause which is coreferential with the matrix subject will be Provincialized rather than Reflexivized. **1967** J. R. Ross *Constraints on Variables in Syntax* (Mass. Inst. Technol. thesis) vi. 254 It would be expected that the leftmost occurrence of *Bill* would be able to reflexivize the rightmost. **1971** *Language* XLVII. 160 It appears that in Japanese the subject can optionally reflexivize (with *zibun*) an identical NP [= noun phrase] in an embedded sentence, if that embedded sentence is a part of the VP. **1976** J. S. Gruber *Lexical Struct. Syntax & Semantics* i. iii. 73 The expression of Accompaniment must, like the expression of Location, not be generated in construction with the verb. This follows from phrase order and also the fact that they do not reflexivize. **1978** *Language* LIV. 142 Level III DA usages in our data always include *on-* along with the reflexivizing apparatus and reverential elements.

reflexly, *adv.* Add: Now usu. stressed **re·flexly.** (Further examples.)

1932 S. Zuckerman *Social Life Monkeys & Apes* ix. 146 It seems reasonable to surmise that when the sexual skin is swollen with oedema, its sensory nerve endings are stimulated by pressure and that this reflexly rouses the animal to sexual behaviour. **1961** *Lancet* 12 Aug. 367/2, I thought of..Superdiagnostex, lying in the cupboard where I hurled it reflexly when a salesman left it on trial last month. **1974** *Sci. Amer.* Oct. 100/1 A coordinated motor performance could be described as being differentiated into many parts along the time dimension, so that each part is reflexly triggered by the sensory components of its predecessor.

reflexogenous, *a.* Add: (Further examples.) **reflexogenic** *a.* (example).

1933 *Ann. Rep. London Co. Council* IV. iii. 133 Sometimes the epileptic fit is intimately bound up with the appropriate stimulus... Much depends on the nature of the reflexogenous stimulus. **1969** *Jrnl. Compar. Neurol.* CXXI. 124/2 Stimulation of the skin of the head and of the rostral half of the belly elicited reflex movements of the ipsilateral forelimb, and this area is referred to as the forelimb reflexogenous zones. **1973** *Nature* 3 Aug. 310/1 These calculations ..predict very high pressures in the aorta, and imply reflexogenic control over cerebral perfusion pressures.

reflexology (rī:fleksǫ·lŏdʒi). *Psychol.* [f. Reflex *sb.* + -ology; cf. G. *reflexologie.*] **a.** The theory that the behaviour of organisms is made up of established patterns of simple or complex reflex responses; the scientific study of reflex action as it affects behaviour.

[**1912** W. von Bechterew in *Deutsche Med. Wochenschr.* 8 Aug. 1481 (*heading*) Was ist Psychoreflexologie?] **1927** *Psychol. Abstr.* I. 590 Thanks to its objective method, reflexology has rendered service to applied sciences, psychiatry and pedagogy. **1933** E. & W. Murphy tr. A. Gerver in *Bechterev's Princ. Human Reflexology* 8 Bechterev..founded this Institute in 1918, and its chief aim was the study of the anatomy and physiology of the central nervous system and also the study of the principles of reflexology, a new branch of science created by him... The Institute is now called the Reflexological Institute for the Study of Brain. **1957** T. Kilmartin tr. *Aron's Opium of Intellectuals* vi. 198 'Reflexology' does not solve the riddle of existence any more than materialistic sociology. **1973** C. D. Kernig *Marxism, Communism & Western Society* VII. 144/1 (*heading*) Results of recent research in reflexology. **1975** C. Burt *ESP & Psychol.* iv. 54 The physiological psychologists (materialistic monists) who adopted Huxley's reflexology.

b. A technique for relaxing nervous tension through a method of foot massage.

1976 M. Segal *Reflexology* 1 Known also as compression foot massage, reflexology is a natural art of healing. *Ibid.*, Like acupuncture, reflexology has been used by the Chinese for 5,000 years. **1976** *Seed* V. v. 31 (Advt.), Reflexology (compression massage of the feet). **1977** D. Berkson *Foot Bk.* ii. 13 Various kinds of pressure-point therapy and reflexology as well as shiatsu.

Hence **re:flexolo·gical** *a.*; **re:flexo·logist.**

1927 *Psychol. Abstr.* I. 650 Therapeutics ought to investigate..the methods of reflexological orthopedics applicable to the cure of mental diseases. **1933** Reflexological [see sense a above]. **1933** E. & W. Murphy tr. A. Gerver in *Bechterev's Gen. Princ. Human Reflexology* 13 Not only have psychiatrists, reflexologists, and neuropathologists been in close touch with him [*sc.* Bechterev], but also teachers, both rural and urban, have always given him a ready ear. **1938** *Brit. Jrnl. Psychol.* Jan. 337 Behaviourists and reflexologists who do not believe that a rat has any mental life involving anticipations or foresights which govern his behaviour. **1957** *Listener* 31 Oct. 689/1 Another analogy was suggested by the experiments of the Russian reflexologists, Bechterev and Pavlov. **1976** M. Segal *Reflexology* i. 3 We, as reflexologists, do the same by trying to relax the patient and relieve nerve tension.

refloat, *v.*[2] Add: **a.** Also *transf.* in *Econ.* (Further examples.)

1973 *Oxf. Mag.* 1 June 1/2 He gallantly accepted the responsibility of re-floating it [*sc.* the *Magazine*]. **1974** B. Pearce tr. *Amin's Accumulation on World Scale* II. iii. 434

If a slump in cotton sales should occur, the central bank would refloat the producers through an additional issue. **1977** *Economist* 3 Sept. 67/1 Portugal refloats the escudo downwards.

b. *intr.* To float again.

1906 *Daily Chron.* 23 June 6/3 On the rising tide the Talisman refloated.

reflow, *sb.* **b.** *fig.*

1969 *Daily Tel.* 4 Sept. 1/4 The re-flow of funds into London after the wave of speculation which followed devaluation was not as large as the initial outflow. **1975** *Washington Post* 19 Feb. A15/2 May I ask at that point if you have had an opportunity to examine the reflow in the purchase of goods and services.

reflower, *v.* Add: **2.** Also *fig.* (Examples.)

1878 Swinburne *Poems & Ballads* 2nd Ser. 178 Out of the herbs on the walls reflowering. **1977** *Arab Times* 13 Dec. 7/3 This technology has reflowered in the sports hall, where highly specialised surfaces are needed.

Hence **reflo·wered** *ppl. a.*, covered with flowers again.

1907 E. Nesbit in *Daily Chron.* 19 Feb. 6/7 Hark to the sigh of the reflowered tomb: 'Ah, live, live, live, for Spring goes by, goes by!'

reflux. Add: **1. c.** Also, of the contents of the stomach or intestine.

1937 R. Schindler *Gastroscopy* xiv. 275 The continuous unregulated reflux of intestinal juice containing bile and pancreatic juice may play the greatest role. **1978** T. C. Jewett in E. Lebenthal *Digestive Dis. Children* 414 The redundant mucosa which forms a rosette at the cardio-esophageal area may also act as a barrier to reflux of gastric contents up the esophagus.

d. *Chem.* The condition, process, or action of refluxing; also *concr.*, the condensed vapour involved in this. Freq. in adverbial phr., as *at* or *under reflux*, in a vessel fitted with a reflux condenser.

1897 *Jrnl. Chem. Soc.* LXXI. 1036 The operation is carried out under reflux. **1923** H. M. Bunbury *Destructive Distillation of Wood* xii. 213 It is sometimes necessary to make a total reflux, i.e. to return all the condensed vapours to the column. **1936** W. L. Nelson *Petroleum Refinery Engin.* xv. 278 The reflux flows down the column but it changes composition from plate to plate so that all of the material that is originally put into the top of the column as reflux is vaporized and returns to the product storage tank. **1958** F. H. Garner et al. in H. W. Cremer *Chem. Engin. Pract.* V. vii. 422 Liquid-liquid extraction with reflux is usually applied to the separation of homologous substances where both the separation factor and distribution coefficient are low. **1959** *Petroleum Handbk.* (Shell Internat. Petroleum Co.) (ed. 4) 172 The light product returned in this manner to the top of the column is called the reflux. **1962** J. T. Marsh *Self-Smoothing Fabrics* xxii. 372 Melamine..may be determined gravimetrically after hydrolysing a known weight of the treated fabric in 0·2N HCl for 30 min. under reflux. **1968** *Inorg. Syntheses* XI. 20 The mixture is stirred at reflux for 6 hours. *Ibid.* 38 The reflux and stirring are continued for an additional 5–6 hours. **1975** *Jrnl. Chem. Soc.: Perkin Trans.* I. 297/1 The mixture..was heated at reflux under nitrogen. *Ibid.* 344/2 Ethyl cyclo-oct-4-enylideneacetate (1·0 g) was added to sodium hydroxide solution (20 ml; 2N) and brought to reflux.

2. reflux condenser *Chem.*, a condenser so mounted or designed that condensed vapour runs back into the stock of boiling liquid; **reflux œsophagitis** *Med.*, œsophagitis caused by the flow of fluid into the œsophagus from the stomach or intestine; **reflux valve** = *check-valve* s.v. *check-.

1891 F. W. Streatfield *Pract. Work in Org. Chem.* 64 The operation is most conveniently conducted in a tubulated retort to the neck of which is attached a reflux condenser. **1939** *Inorg. Syntheses* I. 82 The mixture is placed in a small flask fitted with a reflux condenser and kept at a temperature of about 40 °C. for approximately 48 hours. **1962** J. T. Marsh *Self-Smoothing Fabrics* xxii. 368 The flask is then cooled and the reflux condenser washed down with about 50 cc of distilled water. **1952** R. Belsey in F. A. Jones *Mod. Trends Gastro-Enterol.* I. vii. 144 Reflux oesophagitis leads to thickening of the oesophageal wall, not penetration or perforation. **1980** *Brit. Med. Jrnl.* 29 Mar. (Advt. facing p. 946) 'Tagamet' represents a mark of reliability in reducing gastric acid, and has revolutionised the treatment of disorders such as peptic ulcer and reflux oesophagitis, where acid plays a part. **1888** *Lockwood's Dict. Mech. Engin.* 282 *Reflux valve*,..a flap valve used for the purpose of taking off the pressure of a head of water acting in a backward direction against a set of pumps. **1893** Turner & Brightmore *Princ. Waterworks Engin.* vi. 375 'Re-flux' valves are introduced at such points as the inlets to reservoirs or towards the 'delivery' sides of deep depressions in the pipe-line. **1962** L. B. Escritt *Pumping Station Equipment & Design* vii. 72 If a reflux valve sticks open.. water will rush backwards from the rising main.

reflux (rī·flɒks), *v. Chem.* [f. the sb.] **a.** *intr.* Of a liquid: to boil in circumstances such that the vapour returns to the stock of liquid after condensing. **b.** *trans.* To boil (a liquid) in this way, esp. in a flask fitted with a reflux condenser; also *absol.*

1923 H. M. Bunbury *Destructive Distillation of Wood* xii. 229 The steam is then almost completely shut off and the contents allowed to reflux gently for about two hours. **1926** Lowy & Baldwin *Lab. Bk. Elem. Org. Chem.* 45 After all the alcohol or acetone has been added, reflux the mixture on a water bath for half an hour. **1938** A. A. Morton *Lab. Technique in Org. Chem.* iv. 83 The stopcock is closed, and the liquid allowed to reflux until the thermometer records the lowest temperature possible. **1958** A. I. Vogel *Elem. Pract. Org. Chem.* xvii. 420 Place 0·5 g. of the dry acid..into the flask, add 2·0–2·5 ml. of redistilled thionyl chloride and reflux gently for 30 minutes. **1965** Adams & Raynor *Adv. Pract. Inorg. Chem.* v. 49 Reflux equimolar quantities of vanadyl acetylacetonate and pyridine in ether. **1973** *Nature* 9 Mar. 113/2 The reincorporation of 1 molecule of H_2O into the partially dehydrated talc was achieved by refluxing the material with 50 volumes of benzene/water azeotropic mixture.

Hence **re·fluxing** *vbl. sb.* and *ppl. a.*

1923 H. M. Bunbury *Destructive Distillation of Wood* xii. 213 The bulk or the whole of the condensate from the rectifier, which contains most of the less volatile constituent, is returned to the column; this operation is termed 'refluxing'. **1959** R. J. Hengstebeck *Petroleum Processing* iii. 49 If bubble-cap trays are used, actual tray requirements are usually estimated by means of empirical correlations of 'tray efficiency' against the properties of the refluxing liquid. **1962** J. T. Marsh *Self-Smoothing Fabrics* xxii. 368 Refluxing for 30 min. is generally enough to hydrolyse the amino-aldehyde. **1975** L. F. & M. Fieser *Reagents for Org. Synthesis* V. 381 Raney nickel which had been deactivated by treatment with refluxing ethanol.

refocus, *v.* Add: *trans.* and *intr.* (Further examples.)

1943 A. W. Judge *Automobile Electr. Maintenance* (ed. 2) viii. 222 Provided the correct bulb is used as a replacement it should be unnecessary to re-focus after bulb renewal. **1971** S. Hill *Strange Meeting* i. 55 Then, he seemed to come to abruptly, and his eyes re-focused. **1981** J. Gardner *Licence Renewed* vi. 70 Bond just had time to refocus his glasses. The horses were off.

reforest, *v.* Add: = Reafforest *v.* 2. Chiefly *N. Amer.* (Further examples.)

1918 *Jrnl. Forestry* XVI. 335 It has been assumed that 75 per cent of the State-owned land must be reforested artificially. **1939** *Geogr. Jrnl.* XCIV. 178 The French have spent 317 million francs on reforesting over a million acres. **1969** S. M. Jepsen *Trees & Forests* i. 27 During 1965, more acres..of national forest land were reforested by planting and seeding than in any previous year.

reforestation (further examples).

1918 *Jrnl. Forestry* XVI. 889 It is absolutely essential to ameliorate the rivers, especially the Hun Ho, in the mountainous collecting basin, by reforestation. **1976** T. Walker *Spatsizi* xi. 121 Natural re-forestation was well advanced in the burn with pines ten feet high.

reform, *sb.* Add: **1. c.** *ellipt.* (with capital initial), the Reform Club (see 6 a below).

1853 *London Clubs* 51 *The Reform Club.* Next [to Boodle's] in order amongst political clubs stands the *Reform*, although we are not sure that it is not surpassed in seniority by its great rival..the *Carlton*. Both had their origin in the exciting era of 1830, and the Reform Bill. **1860** A. J. Munby *Diary* 18 Mar. in D. Hudson *Munby* (1972) 56, I feel no interest in..Reform and Carlton conflicts. **1886** B. Potter *Jrnl.* 14 Jan. (1966) 163 It was rumoured yesterday, 13th, that Morley was going to leave the Reform. Harrison has left the Athenaeum. **1940** H. Nicolson *Let.* 14 July (1967) 102, I dined..at the Reform and we listened afterwards to Winston. **1978** G. Greene *Human Factor* III. i. 97 They made a habit of lunching alternately at the Reform and the Travellers once a month on a Saturday.

2. b. *reform through labour* [tr. Chinese *láodòng gǎizào*], in China, an element of ideological reformation whereby criminals and dissidents are made to work as a part of their political reeducation.

1957 P. S. H. Tang *Communist China Today* v. 247 The theoretical basis for the policy of 'reform through labor' was stated by Mao Tse-tung in his 1949 report *On People's Democratic Dictatorship*..promising that 'reactionaries' who desisted from counter-revolutionary activities would not be put to death but would be given work in order to 'reform themselves through labour so as to become new men'. **1962** E. Snow *Red China Today* (1963) xxi. 156 He inspects reform-through-labour farms. *Ibid.* xlvii. 361 No one is entitled to assume that 'reform through labor' in China is administered by humanitarians. **1977** *China Now* July/Aug. 13/3 Bao spent seven years undergoing Reform Through Labour (Lao Dong Gai Zao) having been arrested in 1957.

4. a. Also (with capital initial) preceded by designating adj.

1873 Lady G. Fullerton *Life L. de Carvajal* II. viii. 243 Her beloved friends..were both nuns of the Augustinian Reform. **1893** *Mod. Lang. Notes* VIII. 344 (*heading*) History and texts of the Benedictine reform of the tenth century. **1911** A. Brennan *St. Lawrence of Brindisi* xvi. 147 The Fathers of St. Giles, who belonged to the Alcantarine Reform, were delighted to receive him [*sc.* Father Lawrence] as their guest. **1953** K. Sisam *Stud. Hist. Old Eng. Lit.* VI. ii. 106 The second half of the tenth century was the period of the Benedictine Reform.

6. a. (Also with initial capital.) *reform Convention, Democrat, mayor, movement, party* (earlier and later examples), *politician*; **Reform Club**, a club instituted to promote (usu. political) reform; *spec.* the name of a London club in Pall Mall founded in 1836; **Reform(ed) Neutral** *Philol.*, an international language developed by Rosenberger and de Wahl from *Idiom Neutral* (see *idiom 5); **reform school** orig. *U.S.*, a reformatory for young persons.

1835 *Times* 16 June 5/6 People have heard of the Middlesex Reform Club. It seems that this formidable 'corporation' is on the eve of dissolution. **1837** *Times* 27 Nov. 5/1 A numerous meeting of Whig-Radical members of the House of Commons was held to-day (Saturday), at 12 o'clock, at the Reform Club-house, Pall-mall. **1877** *Public Acts Michigan* 42 Reform club temperance societies may be incorporated in pursuance of the provisions of this act. **1884** B. Potter *Jrnl.* 22 Feb. (1966) 68 Lord Rollo..is a member of the Reform Club, but seldom goes. *a* **1974** R. Crossman *Diaries* (1975) I. 42 One of the Reform Club dinners at which Charles Snow took the chair and captivated Harold Wilson. **1851** *Documentary Hist. Amer. Industr. Society* (1910) VIII. 317 A National Reform Convention is however to be held. **1887** *Courier-Jrnl.* (Louisville, Kentucky) 8 Feb. 1/2 (*heading*) The Reform Democrats manage to get Mr. Randall into very deep water. **1968** *Listener* 5 Sept. 290/1 His machine had just taken a terrible beating at the hands of a reform mayor. **1839** J. S. Mill in *Westm. Rev.* XXXII. 476 The question is not now about particular reforms, but how to carry on the Reform movement. **1922** A. L. Guérard *Short. Hist. Internat. Lang. Movement* II. vi. 139 Reformed-Neutral of 1907 looked more natural than the primitive form. The restitution of international *c* wherever it had been replaced by *s* or *k* greatly improved the appearance of the language. But one of the most obvious blemishes of the Idiom was not corrected: the accumulation of final consonants as in *nostr*. *Ibid.* viii. 172 He [*sc.* Prof. Peano] is, like Dr. Molenaar, and like Messrs. Rosenberger and de Wahl in their Reform-Neutral, a radical, a posteriorist. **1946** H. Jacob *On Choice Common Lang.* iii. 27 Idiom Neutral, the early product of the Akademi, under the influence of Rosenberger and de Wahl, soon became Reform-Neutral, and when Rosenberger died de Wahl carried on his studies until, in 1922, he published his own system, Occidental. **1839** J. S. Mill in *Westm. Rev.* XXXII. 477 No reformer can hope to realize any reforms of importance, but by means of a strong and united Reform party. **1970** D. Goldrich et al. in I. L. Horowitz *Masses in Lat. Amer.* v. 189 It is much more common for 'reform' parties to symbolize the *peasant* as the forgotten. **1904** A. French *Barrier* iii. 22 The reform politicians, those bees who buzzed continually and occasionally stung, had been after the young man. **1859** Reform school [in Dict.]. **1860** C. E. DeLong *Jrnl.* 7 Dec. in *Calif. Hist. Soc. Q.* (1931) X. 258 In the afternoon a crowd of us went out to view the site of the [state] Reform School [for boys]. **1913** J. London *Valley of Moon* I. 3 An' her with seven, an' two of 'em in reform school. **1958** *New Statesman* 6 Sept. 294/3 A reform-school boy whose criminal side has been straightened up by the analysts. **1973** J. Cleary *Ransom* i. 12 Even the Police Commissioner's wife didn't go to finishing school—some of us reckon he found her in a reform school.

b. Reform Judaism, a liberalizing movement initiated in Germany by the philosopher Moses Mendelssohn (1729–86), to accommodate the Jewish faith to the European intellectual enlightenment. Also in various related *attrib.* collocations, as *Reform Jew, party, Synagogue*, etc. Occas. *ellipt.* as predic. adj.

In Britain, Reform Judaism occupies a middle position between Orthodox and Liberal Judaism.

1843 *Voice of Jacob* 27 Oct. 21/2 The Frankfort Reform Association..meets with great sympathy among a large portion of the Jews here... The Anti-reform party.. seriously proposes to counteract the..'reformers' in an honourable manner. **1844** *Southern Q. Rev.* Apr. 325 The Reform party maintain that the old written law,—the law of Moses and the Prophets, is the only divine..law, but that the Talmud and the decisions of the Rabbins..are not divine. *Ibid.* 333 An important effort was made in London.. establishing a Reform Synagogue. **1845** *Voice of David* 15 Aug. 219/1 The 'Berlin Reform Association'..is said to have declared..that should the Synod not agree with its (the Reform Association's) views, the latter would independently pursue its own course. **1860** *N.Y. Times* 6 Aug. 8/3 The innovations of the 'reform party'..which he [*sc.* Rabbi Isaacs] attributed to religious pride... The congregation.. remained uncontaminated by these pretended reforms. **1870** R. D-C. Lewin *What is Judaism?* 8 The signal triumphs which have attended the efforts of the Reform School of Judaism. *Ibid.*, Charitable institutions which are so largely supported by Reform Jews. **1892** I. Zangwill *Childr. Ghetto* III. 36 The paper was founded to inculcate..the principles of true Judaism... But this is rank Reform; it's worse than the papers we came to supersede. *Ibid.* 143 The Reform Synagogue, though a centre of culture and prosperity, was cold, crude, and devoid of magnetism. **1916** H. Sacher *Zionism & Jewish Future* 48 Why should not all Jews recover their spiritual unity through Reform Judaism? **1959** *Tamarack Rev.* Summer 12 Try to convince Gershon that she'd joined the Orthodoxes in protest against her sons' becoming Anglican-like Reform Jews. **1966** 'A. Blaisdell' *Date with Death* xvi. 208, I never was very religious, we were Reform but not much given to..keeping up with temple. **1977** H. Fast *Immigrants* IV. 238 What about the Reform Jews? The capacity of the rich is always larger than the capacity of the poor. **1980** *Times* 18 July 4/3 It is intended to broadcast a service from a Reform synagogue in London..the first occasion that an established non-Christian religious service has been included in the regular output.

reform, *v.*[1] Add: **12.** Also **re-form.** To subject (petrol, hydrocarbons, etc.) to *reforming *vbl. sb.* 2.

1924 *Proc. 31st Ann. Convention Pacific Coast Gas Assoc.* 724 The artificial gas portion of the commercial mixture may be manufactured by 'reforming' natural gas rather than by producing this gas from oil. **1931** *U.S. Bureau of Mines Techn. Paper* No. 483. 1 There is a definite demand for a means and process for re-forming hydrocarbon gases, including refinery gas. **1941** W. L. Nelson *Petroleum Refinery Engin.* (ed. 2) xxiv. 527 These authors conclude that it is not economical to top the light gasoline and reform the naphtha separately. **1966** *McGraw-Hill Encycl. Sci. & Technol.* XI. 403/2 In a typical operation, a Pennsylvania straight-run gasoline of 44 octane number may be reformed to give a product with an octane number of 80.. with a yield of 66 %. **1974** *Sci. Amer.* Oct. 67/2 The carbohydrates decay exoergically to form fossil fuels such as methane..which can then be re-formed endoergically to yield hydrogen gas.

reformabi·lity. *rare.* [f. REFORMABLE *a.*: see -ITY.] Capacity for being reformed.

1904 *Daily Chron.* 29 Nov. 6/1 The Council has made provision for all women sent from London courts, regardless of the question of reformability.

reformate (rĭfǭ·ɹmēit). [f. REFORM(ING *vbl. sb.* + *-ate*, after *distillate, filtrate*, etc.] The end-product of the process of reforming petroleum products.

1949 *Industr. & Engin. Chem.* Oct. 2185/1 The crude reformate was condensed at 32° F. **1951** *World Petroleum* Nov. 73/2 In recent weeks two new processes have been announced for separating and purifying the aromatics from reformate. **1958** W. L. NELSON *Petroleum Refinery Engin.* (ed. 4) xxi. 813 Reformate normally has an end point 15 to 30°F higher than that of the feedstock. **1973** HADLEY & TURNER in Hobson & Pohl *Mod. Petroleum Technol.* (ed. 4) xii. 442 Catalytic reforming of straight-run material yields a C_6–C_8 reformate rich in the aromatic hydrocarbons, benzene, toluene, ethylbenzene, and the xylenes.

reforma·tionist. [f. REFORMATION + -IST.] One who supports or advocates reformation.

1906 *Macmillan's Mag.* June 589 One who is proved incorrigible..may indeed be secluded, but..if the reformationists are right, his seclusion should have no penal character. **1928** *Sunday Express* 17 June 12/5 The chaos in the Church may harden into bitter anarchy and disintegrating conflict between Reformationists, Adorationists, and Modernists. **1969** *Listener* 17 July 87/3 'To make them better citizens,' says the Reformationist.

reformatory, *a.* and *sb.* Add: **A.** *adj.* (Later examples.)

1932, etc. [see *APPROVED *ppl. a.* 5]. **1933** J. MASEFIELD *Conway* II. 61 H.M.S. reformatory-ship *Clarence* was fired and burned by the boys on board her.

B. *sb.* (Earlier and further examples.) Also *N. Amer.*, a reforming institution for women or for first offenders.

1834 J. S. MILL in *Monthly Repos.* VIII. 735 He proposes that those who are convicted of offences..should be no otherwise ill-treated than by being compelled to live as a community apart... If all who, in any manner violated the laws, were removed into such a place of reformation, the inhabitants of the reformatory would speedily outnumber the remainder of the community. **1870** *N.Y.* (State) *Laws* I. 320 The action of the commissioners..in locating said prison or industrial reformatory..at Elmira..is hereby approved. **1878** *Harper's Mag.* Dec. 109/1 Our reformatories..do not check the first steps in wrong-doing. **1912** M. NICHOLSON *Hoosier Chron.* iii. 53 They were going to cut down the Reformatory's appropriation last winter. **1950** *Times* 20 Mar. 5/3 As the result of the laudable impulse for reformatory treatment, the expectation may have been fostered among criminals that they will find that the salutary discomforts of prison have been reformed away. **1970** *Globe & Mail* (Toronto) 26 Sept. 2/2 [He] was sentenced to two years less a day definite and 18 months indeterminate in reformatory after admitting that he stole about $50,000 from Sunnybrook Hospital. **1975** *Washington Post* 27 Feb. B1/7 Michael Craddock..thinks the reformatory is a danger, a 'public nuisance'. **1977** *Ibid.* 25 Feb. A2/1 About 200 inmates at the Ohio State Reformatory hurled trays and food and fought guards during a disturbance today in the institution dining room.

reformed, *ppl. a.* and *sb.* Add: **A.** *ppl. a.* **1. a.** (Further examples.) Also *U.S.*

With capital initial still used widely to denote Calvinist (as opp. Lutheran) Protestantism.

1794 T. COXE *View U.S.* ix. 373 There are and have been in the legislative, executive and judicial branches of the general government, persons of the following denominations —Episcopalian,..Reformed, Roman, and probably others. **1837** J. M. PECK *Gazetteer Illinois* (ed. 2) 73 A Seminary is about being established in a settlement of Reformed Presbyterians. **1844** I. D. RUPP *He Pasa Ekklesia* 466 The Reformed Methodists took their origin from a feeble secession from the Methodist Episcopal Church, in..1814. **1847** R. DAVIDSON *Hist. Presbyterian Church Kentucky* viii. 216 Campbellites..affected the title of Reformers, or Reformed Baptists, and spoke of 'The Reformation' as if there had never been any Reformation before. **1928** W. D. BROWN *Hist. Reformed Church in Amer.* i. 7 The Reformed Church in America is the direct outgrowth of the emigration from the Netherlands. **1954** *Collier's* 20 Aug. 21/3 Three allocations were decided upon—..the third to an Evangelical Reformed Church. **1967** R. MCA. BROWN *Ecumenical Revolution* viii. 142 In 1934 the Evangelical Synod of North America merged with the Reformed Church in the United States to form the Evangelical and Reformed Church, while a few years later both of these new groups merged to form what is now the United Church of Christ. **1969** T. F. TORRANCE *Theol. Sci.* ii. 87 So far we have been thinking of this mainly in terms of strictly Reformed theology but in some respects it had an even greater development in Lutheran theology. **1977** *Washington Post* 18 Mar. D18/3 The signers included Billy Graham and leaders of the.. Reformed Church in America. **1978** *Church Times* 29 Dec. 1/3 The consultation is proposing to the sponsoring bodies that a dialogue programme at world level be implemented between the Anglican and Reformed traditions.

d. *Judaism.* (With capital initial.) Subscribing to, or characteristic of, Reform Judaism (see *REFORM *sb.* 6 b).

1844 *Voice of Jacob* 19 July 188/2 There is a 'reformed Synagogue at Liverpool'..that..is to take no part in the election of a Chief Rabbi. **1859** *N.Y. Times* 30 Sept. 1/5 At the tabernacle of the Reformed Society..Dr. Adler preached in German. **1876** GEO. ELIOT *Dan. Der.* II. IV. xxxii. 298 He was affectionately directed by a precocious Jewish youth, who entered cordially into his wanting not the fine new building of the Reformed but the old Rabbinical school of the orthodox. **1898** W. J. LOCKE *Idols* vi. 70 Think of Simeon Goldberg, a good friend, a man..of the Reformed faith. **1918** H. BARNETT *Canon Barnett* II. xxxiv. 65 Minister of Reformed Synagogue in New York. **1971** *Guardian* 16 Nov. 8/6 Grandfather had been a warden of a reformed synagogue. **1977** *Church Times* 12 Aug. 5/5 On our last day we went with a party to a service in the Reformed synagogue in Haifa.

3. b. Also **re-formed.** Of petroleum products: subjected to or obtained by *RE-FORMING *vbl. sb.* 2.

1924 *Proc. 31st Ann. Convention Pacific Coast Gas Assoc.* 725 Reformed natural gas. **1931** *U.S. Bureau of Mines Techn. Paper* No. 483. 2 The natural gas employed was composed almost entirely of methane (CH_4) and ethane (C_2H_6), but the re-formed product comprised methane.. and hydrogen..as the chief combustible constituents. **1952** KIRK & OTHMER *Encycl. Chem. Technol.* VIII. 793 Generally a greater part of the natural gas is re-formed, and a smaller amount is mixed with air and added to the re-formed gas in order to control the specific gravity and burning characteristics of the mixture. **1966** *Petroleum Handbk.* (Shell Internat. Petroleum Co.) (ed. 5) 73/2 Reformed natural gas..can usually be blended to give a gas interchangeable with manufactured gas.

reformer[1]. Add: **3. b.** (Earlier example.)

1780 G. SELWYN in *15th Rep. R. Comm. Hist. Manuscripts* App. VI. 443 in *Parl. Papers 1897* (C. 8551) LI. 1 My best and ablest friends here are dead; their survivors supine and superannuated; their connections new Whiggs and Reformers, and Associators.

c. *U.S.* A member of one of the reformed sects of various Protestant denominations in the 19th century, *esp.* the Campbellite Baptists. *Obs.* exc. *Hist.*

1831 J. M. PECK *Guide for Emigrants* 258 The Reformers, or Methodist Protestant church, have several societies and preachers in the State [of Illinois]. **1834** [see *CAMPBELLITE 1]. **1871** E. EGGLESTON *Hoosier Schoolmaster* xii. 101 Squire Hawkins..had become a member of the 'Reformers'..who now call themselves 'Disciples', but whom the profane will persist in calling 'Campbellites'. **1931** W. W. SWEET *Relig. on Amer. Front* I. ii. 26 Between 1829 and 1832, something like 10,000 Kentucky Baptists withdrew to form the Disciples Church. Besides the Campbell followers, who were known as *Reformers*, there were several thousand anti-mission Baptists in Kentucky.

d. An advocate or adherent of Reform Judaism (cf. *REFORM *sb.* 6 b).

1855 *Jewish Chron.* 20 July 245/3 The two parties, orthodox and reformers. **1870** *N.Y. Times* 3 Apr. 3/3 The tenets of Mr. Lewin represent the most advanced opinions of the Reform School, and are therefore shared in full by a minority only of the Reformers themselves. **1892** I. ZANGWILL *Childr. Ghetto* III. II. iv. 39 'By worshipping bare-headed, and by seating the sexes together, they have defiled Judaism.' 'Stop..who told you the Reformers do this?' **1934** *Times Lit. Suppl.* 10 May 334/3 The 'Reformers', too, are unlikely to have much material earlier than their foundation, though, no doubt, their papers throw light on the schism and their *ritualia* are of great beauty. **1976** B. WILLIAMS *Making of Manchester Jewry* iv. 105 To Reformers the future of Judaism..appeared to depend upon..a degree of accommodation to the values of the surrounding milieu.

5. An installation or apparatus for the re-forming of petroleum products (*REFORMING *vbl. sb.* 2).

1934 *Jrnl. Inst. Petroleum Technologists* XX. 347 One of the new refineries in France..includes a cracking still, a viscosity breaker and a naphtha reformer. **1958** *Times Rev. Industry* May 24/3 The pilot scale installation incorporates ..a catalytic reformer in which gaseous hydrocarbons interact with steam to produce the hydrogen. **1971** *Daily Tel.* 6 Dec. 6/7 The board found it necessary to retain specialist workers employed on a hydro-carbon reformer plant. **1974** *Times* 22 Mar. 21/4 A 'reformer' unit which processes the fuel (natural gas or propane) to produce a hydrogen-rich feed for the fuel cell. **1978** *Trends in Oil & Gas Refining* (Shell Internat. Petroleum Co.) 3 In a simple refinery there are few secondary units—perhaps..a catalytic reformer (for the improvement of octane quality of motor gasoline).

reforming, *vbl. sb.* Add: **2.** Also **re-forming.** The treatment of hydrocarbons so as to produce changes in composition; *spec.* (i) increasing the octane number of petrol by heating it under pressure over a catalyst (the major effects being an increase in the proportions of aromatic and other unsaturated cyclic compounds, and loss of hydrogen); (ii) partially or completely converting gaseous hydrocarbons to carbon monoxide and hydrogen by heating with steam over a catalyst.

Not all the early reforming processes used a catalyst.

1924 *Proc. 31st Ann. Convention Pacific Coast Gas Assoc.* 724 The 'reforming' or 'cracking' of natural gas is a process of much interest to several of the Southern California gas utilities. **1932** *Jrnl. Inst. Petroleum Technologists* XVIII. 262 In the cracking or 're-forming' of gasoline, one company uses a De Florez furnace, heating the gasoline to 925° F. at about 1000 lb. pressure, obtaining a recovery of 86 to 88 per cent. of gasoline of high octane number from a straight-run paraffin type gasoline. **1941** *Oil & Gas Jrnl.* 27 Mar. 87/1 A catalytic process for the 'reforming' or converting of low-octane to high-octane gasolines at high temperatures in the presence of hydrogen gas. **1966** *Kirk-Othmer Encycl. Chem. Technol.* (ed. 2) X. 417 A basic problem in catalytic steam reforming and cracking is that the pyrolysis reactions..compete with the steam-hydrocarbon reactions. **1971** *Sci. Amer.* Dec. 57/2 During the 1950's new platinum-alumina-halogen catalysts were introduced to carry out the catalytic reforming of low-octane oil fractions. **1974** *Ibid.* Oct. 68/2 In the U.S. methane is the customary commercial source of hydrogen. In the process called re-forming it is treated with high-temperature steam, producing carbon monoxide (CO) and molecular hydrogen.

reformism (rĭfǭ·ɹmiz'm). [f. REFORM *sb.* + -ISM.] A policy of social, political, or religious reform, *spec.* in *Politics*, the theory that socialism can be established in an evolutionary way by reforms within a country's existing legislative system rather than by revolution. Cf. *REVISIONISM.

1904 R. C. K. ENSOR *Mod. Socialism* p. xxvi, The germs of all Von Vollmar's reformism may be found in his own speeches before Bernsteinism appeared. *Ibid.* p. xxvii, The concrete spirit of reformism, which is careful of national peculiarities in its domestic politics, cannot overlook them wholly in foreign affairs. **1920** *Contemp. Rev.* Dec. 872 Your Right leaders are favouring reformism on those questions which I have called fundamental and decisive. **1926** *Socialist Rev.* Jan. 317 Industrial Conferences where working men..are learnedly lectured by middle-class apostles of reformism. **1937** 'C. CAUDWELL' *Illusion & Reality* xii. 309 Since this Kingdom of Heaven was to be achieved by non-resistance, by heavenly forces and a general change of heart, it was bound to become mere reformism and end as a machine for tying the oppressed of the Empire to the throne of Constantine. **1957** R. N. C. HUNT *Guide to Communist Jargon* xli. 139 Reformism was the view..that the evils of the capitalist system could be exorcised by reforms. **1964** P. G. CASANOVA in I. L. Horowitz *New Sociol.* 72 The transformation of social structures in the twentieth century has brought both sides to make partial concessions to reformism. **1970** F. C. WEFFORT in I. L. Horowitz *Masses in Lat. Amer.* xi. 403 Reformism was conceived within an ideological framework of consecration of the State as the only solution to social and economic problems. **1973** C. D. KERNIG *Marxism, Communism & Western Society* VII. 154/2 On the international level contemporary reformism is represented by the Socialist International founded in 1951. **1976** *Times* 9 Aug. 11/3 Their convictions, constancy and devotional practices form in fact a needed counterweight within the church to the prevalence of reformism.

reformist. Add: **1. b.** *spec.* an advocate or supporter of *REFORMISM. Also as *adj.*

1904 R. C. K. ENSOR *Mod. Socialism* 164 We are revolutionaries, because..we are not at all sure, Citizen Millerand, of attaining our desired solution by the reformist method. **1906** M. MINTURN tr. *Jaurès's Stud. in Socialism* p. vi, The situation reached its climax in 1899 with the entrance of the Reformist Millerand into the Waldeck–Rousseau coalition cabinet. **1913** V. G. SIMKHOVITCH *Marxism versus Socialism* 292 Whether they call themselves revisionists, reformists, laborites or plain socialists..the overwhelming majority of the socialists of today are tending to be reformers. **1920** *19th Cent.* Aug. 206 England..allowed the right of private judgment to her middle classes in the seventeenth century and allowed every kind of Reformist literature to enter the country. **1927** H. J. LASKI *Communism* i. 39 The growth of capitalism..seemed to suggest that the day of its end was far distant. Everywhere there grew up reformist socialism. **1941** KOESTLER *Scum of Earth* xi. 113 The sectarian hatred between Stalinists, Trotskyists, and Reformists still existed. **1950** E. H. CARR *Bolshevik Revolution* I. i. 12 The 'Economists'..reached the same practical conclusion as the legal Marxists that it was necessary to postpone to an indefinite future the revolutionary socialist struggle of the proletariat and to concentrate meanwhile on a reformist democratic programme in alliance with the bourgeoisie. **1969** *Daily Tel.* 1 Feb. 19/3 An article published in Soviet newspapers yesterday blamed 'reformist' journalists for the 'moral tenor' in Czechoslovak life. **1974** tr. *Sniečkus's Soviet Lithuania* 12 A reformist opportunist trend..had developed on the basis of the petty-bourgeois nationalistic ideology. **1977** *Time* 14 Nov. 16/3 The situation in Italy is too critical for a reformist policy like the one the Communists propose.

reformulate, *v.* Add: (Further examples.)

1962 E. E. EVANS-PRITCHARD *Ess. Social Anthropol.* 9 Our knowledge has increased and some of our theoretical propositions have had to be reformulated accordingly. **1968** C. G. KUPER *Introd. Theory Superconductivity* iv. 55 These questions must be carefully reformulated before they can be answered. **1970** *Times* 20 Apr. 4/4 It might be necessary to reformulate existing trace mineral mixtures where this material was used. **1970** G. GERMANI in I. L. Horowitz *Masses in Lat. Amer.* xvi. 586 Class and mass theories must be reformulated within a more general framework.

Hence **refo·rmulated** *ppl. a.*

1965 *Mod. Law Rev.* XXVIII. 536 Alternative policies.. embodied in a reformulated principle.

reformulation. (Later examples.)

1922 A. G. HOGG *Redemption from this World* iv. 135 We are keeping well within the limits of legitimate reformulation when we say [etc.]. **1951** E. E. EVANS-PRITCHARD *Social Anthropol.* v. 86 The theories have been shaped and reshaped by this steady growth in knowledge and they have .., in each reformulation, directed observation into deeper layers. **1957** J. S. HUXLEY *Relig. without Revelation* (rev. ed.) ix. 220 The crude distinction in terms of ethical absolutes like 'good' and 'evil' requires reformulation in the light of psychology and history. **1968** FOX & MAYERS *Computing Methods for Scientists & Engineers* x. 195 For this purpose we would prefer a reformulation of the problem. **1970** G. GERMANI in I. L. Horowitz *Masses in Lat. Amer.* xvi. 586 Such reformulation has been suggested by the mass and 'national-popular' movements in Latin America. **1979** *Dædalus* Winter 38 The deeper cause of this popular success surely lies in the new philosophy's reformulation of the antipolitics of May.

refract, *v.* Add: **1.** (Examples relating to waves other than light.)

1874 *Proc. R. Soc.* XXII. 532, I have dealt with the effect of the atmosphere to refract sound upwards. **1944**

A. Holmes *Princ. Physical Geol.* xiv. 284 The waves advance more rapidly through the deeper water opposite a bay than through the shallower water opposite a headland... The waves thus become curved or refracted..towards parallelism with the shore line. **1966** *McGraw-Hill Encycl. Sci. & Technol.* XI. 408/1 Waves propagated through the solid earth are refracted by changes of material or changes of density. **1974** Harvey & Bohlman *Stereo F.M. Radio Handbk.* vii. 144 The sky-wave..may be refracted back towards the earth by the layers of ionized gas.

c. *intr.* To undergo refraction.

1964 *Oceanogr. & Marine Biol.* II. 84 If waves reach the beach unaffected by offshore underwater topography one has an easier task than if waves are breaking and refracting around an offshore bar.

4. *Ophthalm.* To measure the focusing characteristics of (an eye) or of the eyes of (a person). Also *absol.*

1897 J. Thorington *Retinoscopy* v. 45 To give a patient thus refracted with the retinoscope his emmetropic correction..an allowance must always be made, in all meridians, of one diopter. **1904** —— *Refraction & how to Refract* (ed. 3) ix. 235 If a young subject must be refracted without drops, then the fogging method must be followed. *Ibid.*, The [manifest] method by which the eyes of patients past forty-five years of age are refracted. **1953** N. Bier *Contact Lens Routine & Pract.* iv. 56 If the measurements..in the corneal fit were 8·75/13, do not refract with a trial lens of 8 mm radius and 13 mm diameter. **1968** *Sci. Jrnl.* Dec. 21/1 Normally when 'refracting' human patients an ophthalmologist relies on verbal reports and applies corrective lenses until the subject says that he sees most clearly.

refraction. Add: **2.** More widely, change in direction of propagation of any wave as a result of its travelling at different speeds at different points along the wave front. (Further examples.)

1874 *Proc. R. Soc.* XXII. 532 This refraction explains the well-known difference which exists in the distinctness of sounds by day and by night. **1914** [see *absorption 4 (*d*)]. **1944** A. Holmes *Princ. Physical Geol.* xiv. 297 (*caption*) Diagram to illustrate the development of a hooked spit by the refraction of oblique waves. **1971** *Nature* 12 Feb. 452/2 T. D. Krishna Kartha describes his work on the variation of velocity (refraction) of microseisms approaching Cochin in southern India. **1974** Harvey & Bohlman *Stereo F.M. Radio Handbk.* vii. 144 Refraction of the radio wave occurs due to the effects of the varying density of the gas layers in which the wave is travelling.

6*. *Ophthalm.* Measurement of the focusing characteristics of eyes. Also *attrib.* Cf. *refract *v.* 4.

1900 J. Thorington *Refraction & how to Refract* ix. 229 The great danger in any refraction..is an overcorrection. **1928** W. S. Duke-Elder *Pract. Refraction* xxi. 302 Test.. the depth of cycloplegia by testing the accommodation before the refraction is done. **1953** N. Bier *Contact Lens Routine & Pract.* iv. 56 The practitioner's contact lens refraction set. *Ibid.*, An alteration of 0·5 mm in the corneal radius is approximately equivalent to 3·00 D.S. in refraction. **1961** *Lancet* 30 Sept. 760/2 An ophthalmologist holds refraction clinics weekly in the surgery. **1975** M. Ruben *Contact Lens Pract.* iv. 67/2 The cylinder found by refraction is −3·00 D.

7. refraction profiling *Geol.*, profiling (sense *3) by means of refraction shooting; **refraction shooting** *Geol.*, seismic prospecting in which shock waves generated at the earth's surface are detected at several points along a line some miles long, the relation between the time of arrival at each point and its distance giving information about the nature and depth of the underlying strata.

1929, 1963 Refraction profiling [see *profiling *vbl. sb.* 3]. **1929, 1951** Refraction shooting [see *reflection shooting* s.v. *reflection 10]. **1960** C. Gatlin *Petroleum Engin.* iii. 37/1 Refraction shooting is used primarily as a reconnaissance tool to select areas and obtain interpretative data for the more detailed reflection method. **1978** *Nature* 27 Apr. 789/1 Seismic refraction shooting near the Isle of Lewis in the Outer Hebrides has shown the presence of major sedimentary units.

refractive, *a.* Add: **3.** (Later examples corresponding in sense to *refraction 6*.)

1953 N. Bier *Contact Lens Routine & Pract.* iv. 58 [Temporary spasm of accommodation] may persist throughout the refractive examination. **1969** J. R. Gregg *How to communicate in Optometric Pract.* iii. 31 At key spots along the refractive procedure, build in ways of showing confidence and understanding.

refractometry (rĭfræktǫ·metri). [f. Refract *v.* + -o + -metry.] The measurement of refractive indices of media.

1902 *Encycl. Brit.* XXX. 239/2 Refractometry by total reflection. **1950** *Engineering* 10 Feb. 143/2 Increased attention has been devoted to methods of high-precision refractometry. **1958** *Oxf. Univ. Gaz.* 23 Apr. 892 Studies in refractometry of living cells with particular reference to the investigation of osmoregulatory function. **1974** *Encycl. Brit. Macropædia* IX. 633/2 Of the many laboratory principles employed in the process analytical instruments, the three in widest use today are refractometry, absorption spectroscopy, and gas chromatography.

Hence **refractome·tric** *a.*, of or pertaining to a refractometer; made by means of refractometry; **refractome·trically** *adv.*

1904 *Nature* 4 Feb. 334/2 A simple thermostat for use in connection with the refractometric examination of oils and fats. **1920** *Amer. Jrnl. Physiol.* LI. 278 Reading refractometrically the serum non-protein increase after the intravenous injection of a known amount of acacia or gelatin solution. **1929** *Canad. Jrnl. Res.* I. 13 The total solid content was determined refractometrically. **1937** *Discovery* June 180/2 The application of refractrometric work to observe the progress of essential processes in the production of plastics may not be so commonly known. **1970** *Nature* 26 Dec. 1269/1 The relative values [of purity] given by the four methods were: Lowry, 1·0; gravimetric, 0·93; refractometric, 0·87; ultraviolet absorption, 0·32. *Ibid.*, The protein concentration..was also determined refractometrically and gravimetrically.

refractor. Add: **4.** *Geol.* A stratum, or an interface between strata, detected in refraction shooting.

1946 *Geophysics* XI. 40 The production in refraction shooting varies widely, depending on the surface conditions and also on the depth of the refractors. **1976** W. M. Telford et al. *Appl. Geophysics* iv. 365 Where a single refractor is being followed, a series of short refraction profiles are often shot rather than a long profile.

refractoriness. Add: **1. c.** *Physiol.* Temporary inability to respond fully to nervous or sexual stimuli.

1932 W. Burridge *Excitability* xxi. 172 Refractoriness is here defined as a condition of inexcitability of an excitable tissue which follows the receipt of an adequate stimulus. **1937** *Wilson Bull.* XLIX. 251 Birds invariably passed the climax of activity after a time and underwent regression. This was due to 'throwing out of gear' or development of refractoriness at some part of the sexual mechanism. **1949** *Ibid.* LXI. 221 This refractoriness must 'wear off' before external stimuli can induce a new gonadal activation. **1963** S. Ochs in E. E. Selkurt *Physiol.* ii. 28 In the alpha group of A fibers of the frog sciatic nerve, this period of absolute refractoriness lasts only a little longer than 1 msec.

refractory, *a.* and *sb.* Add: **A.** *adj.* **5.** *Physiol.* Temporarily unresponsive or not fully responsive to nervous or sexual stimuli; *esp.* in *refractory period*, a period of reduced responsiveness following a response to such a stimulus.

1879–80 *Jrnl. Physiol.* II. 400 The same absence of response was observed whenever the second excitation occurred 'during the commencement of the systole of the ventricle' (termed by Marey the 'refractory period'). **1900** J. Burdon-Sanderson in E. A. Schäfer *Text-bk. Physiol.* II. 449 This rhythmicality is attributed to the liability of the heart to be 'refractory' for a certain period after each excitation. **1937** L. V. Heilbrunn *Outl. Gen. Physiol.* xxxvi. 415 In skeletal muscle, the refractory period is much shorter than in cardiac muscle. **1950** *Nature* 16 Dec. 1034/2 During this time, experimental birds are 'refractory'—they cannot be forced into spermatogenesis by means of photostimulation. **1952** *Jrnl. Physiol.* CXVII. 534 After the earliest stimulus the membrane potential falls again with hardly a sign of activity, and the membrane can be said to be in the 'absolute refractory period'. The later stimuli produce action potentials of increasing amplitude, but still smaller than the control; these are in the 'relative refractory period'. **1967** J. L. McCary *Human Sexuality* xi. 176 After orgasm, the man enters the refractory period..; the sexual stimulation that was previously effective and pleasurable now becomes unavailing and distasteful. Women, on the other hand, usually do not go into a refractory period. **1971** M. B. V. Roberts *Biol.* xviii. 268 The importance of the refractory period is that, together with transmission speed, it determines the frequency at which an axon can transmit impulses. **1972** *Nature* 18 Feb. 366/1 A substance from the male accessory glands..rendered the female permanently refractory to further insemination. **1974** P. Svendsen *Introd. Animal Physiol.* xi. 119 The very long action potential and refractory period in cardiac muscle are of great importance. They ensure that..two successive contractions cannot add together without a period of relaxation between them.

B. *sb.* **1.** (Later example.)

1860 Dickens *Uncomm. Trav.* in *All Year Round* II. 394/1 The Refractories were picking oakum... The oldest Refractory was, say twenty; youngest Refractory, say sixteen.

2. More widely, any refractory material. (Further examples.)

1907 *Jrnl. Iron & Steel Inst.* LXXIII. 384 The plant, which has only recently been laid down by the American Refractories Company at Joliet, represents the first successful attempt at manufacturing refractory materials in the west of America. **1931** *Daily Express* 15 Oct. 14/1 For many months manufacturers of refractories have had to struggle against the dumping of large quantities of Belgian sand. **1957** *New Scientist* 9 May 44/1 It was inevitable that factories making fire-bricks—the original refractory—should spring up alongside iron- and steel-works. **1962** *Science Survey* III. 344 The tundish that evens out the flow between the ladle and mould is usually a simple refractory-lined box. **1967** M. Chandler *Ceramics in Mod. World* v. 140 A high proportion of refractories must serve also as structural materials.

refra·cture, *sb.*[2] [Re- 5 a.] Renewed fracture (of a bone).

1908 *Practitioner* Oct. 535 Instances of refracture in long bones, at an old site of previous similar injury.

refresh, *sb.* Delete 'Now *colloq.*' and add: **3.** The process of renewing the data stored in a memory device or displayed on a cathode-ray tube. Usu. *attrib.*

1967 *Technology Week* 20 Feb. 22/3 The complete refresh memory is made up of 16 parallel magnetostrictive delay-line loops that store all of the picture elements for one frame. **1972** D. Lewin *Theory & Design of Digital Computers* vii. 264 To produce a steady picture on the CRT the contents of the display file must be periodically cycled through (a word at a time) and passed to the display unit; this procedure is known as the refresh cycle. **1977** J. C. Boyce *Digital Computer Fundamentals* viii. 211 Typically the refresh operation must be performed about every 2 milliseconds. **1977** *Sci. Amer.* June 57/2 (Advt.), Every [memory] board is fast. With 'hidden refresh' and *no* 'wait state'.

refresh, *v.* Add: **1. a.** (Further examples.) Also, to plunge (cooked vegetables, etc.) into cold water as part of the cooking process.

1861 Mrs. Beeton *Bk. Househ. Managem.* xxv. 591 Let the herbs be as fresh as possible for a salad, and, if at all stale or dead-looking, let them lie in water for an hour or two, which will very much refresh them. **1877** E. S. Dallas *Kettner's Bk. of Table* 45 Some..prefer to eat them [*sc.* asparagus] with oil and vinegar. In this case they are, as the French say, to be *refreshed* with cold water. **1972** *Guardian* 18 Aug. 11/3 Lasagne... Boil the pasta for ten minutes then drain and run under the cold tap, and drain again... Cannelloni: these are boiled like lasagne, and refreshed in the same way.

5. (Further examples.)

1977 A. P. Malvino *Digital Computer Electronics* vii. 180 Because capacitor charge leaks off, the stored data must be refreshed every few milliseconds. **1977** *Sci. Amer.* Sept. 139/3 A memory used to refresh the information presented in a conventional video display, which is scanned point by point in a repeating linear pattern, does not require a memory with random access.

refresher. Add: **3. a.** (Earlier examples.)

1826 F. Reynolds *Life & Times* I. iv. 148 For the cause, after refresher on refresher, came on within the space of a few months. **1831** —— *Playwright's Adventures* vi. 108 He also knew that barristers..can only be kept alive by refreshers.

4. *attrib.*, applied to training or instruction provided as a review of material previously studied or to instruct a person in new developments, techniques, etc., esp. in *refresher course*; *refresher leave*, leave granted for the purpose of attending a refresher course.

1907 *Interim Rep. War Office Comm. Provision of Officers* 10 Given a short term of liability, and short periods of recall to the Colours for 'refresher' training, many officers.. would remain therein. **1914** Hamel & Turner *Flying* x. 209 Others..go direct into the Royal Flying Corps Reserve ..where they are available for periodical 'refresher' courses and for employment in the event of war. **1930** *Times Educ. Suppl.* 20 Sept. 403/4 Refresher courses for teachers. **1945** *Jrnl. Amer. Med. Assoc.* 12 May 141/1 A clinical refresher training program for..medical officers. **1959** *Listener* 17 Dec. 1085/1 This is not an introduction to Kipling, but a splendid refresher course. **1972** *Accountant* 17 Aug. (Suppl.) 14/3 (Advt.), Terms of appointment include generous refresher leave periods. **1976** H. Wilson *Governance of Britain* vi. 121 A major conference would involve one or two, or more, full briefing meetings at No. 10..with refresher briefings to review the progress of the conference and decide tactics to meet a changing situation. **1977** *New Yorker* 12 Sept. 103/1 A refresher training course in the basic sciences that I was teaching at the Armed Forces Institute of Pathology in the fall of 1969. **1980** R. Perry *Grand Slam* v. 42 [He] was making a complete pig's ear of shadowing me... He was in dire need of a refresher course.

refreshing, *vbl. sb.* Add: **1.** Also, the plunging of cooked vegetables, etc., into cold water.

1961 S. Beck et al. *Mastering Art of French Cooking* viii. 422 A second important French technique is that of refreshing. As soon as green vegetables have been blanched.. they are plunged for several minutes into a large quantity of cold water.

refreshing, *ppl. a.* **3.** (Earlier example.)

1716 *Parish Rec. Kenilworth* in *Mod. Lang. Rev.* (1951) XLVI. 327 Paid to Mr. Palmer a Refreshing fee at Christmas Sessions.

refreshment. Add: **7.** *refreshment bar, counter, room* (earlier and later examples), *saloon, stand, station, stop, table, tent*; **Refreshment Sunday** (later examples).

1860 Dickens *Uncomm. Trav.* in *All Year Round* II. 418/2 Crowds of us had sandwiches and ginger-beer at the refreshment-bars..in the Theatre. **1889** E. Dowson *Let.* 17 Mar. (1967) 50, I..searched through the Law Court refreshment bars. **1973** 'B. Mather' *Snowline* vi. 68 The first class refreshment bar at Sealdah Station. **1908** *Busy Man's Mag.* Jan. 89/2 The dance over, he took them to the refreshment counter for a cup of coffee and a sandwich. **1979** *National Trust* Spring 14/3 Nowhere perhaps is the transformation more apparent than in the Tea Room, now freed from the unsightly refreshment counter. **1835** Dickens in *Evening Chron.* 7 Mar. 3/4 The Militia-man..repaired to Bellamy's kitchen—a refreshment room where persons who are not members [of the House of Commons] are admitted on sufferance, as it were. **1966** G. W. Turner *Eng. Lang. in Austral. & N.Z.* vii. 157 Because the narrow-gauge lines necessary for a mountainous country preclude corridors, and therefore dining cars, in our trains, the New Zealand *refreshment rooms* on railway stations are notable. **1976** *Flintshire Leader* 10 Dec. 3/5 Mrs Parry worked in the refreshment room at Chester railway station. *a* **1828** J. Bernard *Retrospections of Stage* (1830) II. x. 318, I..purchased a cottage..surrounded by.. meadowland; the former being small enough for a refreshment saloon. **1936** A. Russell *Gone Nomad* ii. 8, I.. sauntered down the corridors to the refreshment saloon at the first suggestion of thirst. **1976** *Honolulu Star-Bull.* 21 Dec. A-3/1, I have two gripes about the refreshment stand operation at Blaisdell Center Arena. **1860** Dickens *Un-*

comm. Trav. in *All Year Round* II. 513/2, I travel by railroad... I am hungry when I arrive at the 'Refreshment' station where I am expected. **1977** C. McCullough *Thorn Birds* iii. 67 Our next refreshment stop is a place called Blayney. **1912** *Encycl. Relig. & Ethics* V. 770/2 The fourth Sunday in Lent, when the Gospel for the day narrates the Feeding of the Five Thousand, has long been called *Dominica Refectionis*, or 'Refreshment Sunday'. **1974** [see *Lætare]. **1977** *Church Times* 1 Apr. 5/4 'The God of love my Shepherd is' set in *The English Hymnal* for Refreshment Sunday. **1860** Dickens *Uncomm. Trav.* in *All Year Round* II. 514/2 You are going off by railway, from any Terminus... You present to your mind, a picture of the refreshment-table at that terminus. **1885** A. Edwardes *Girton Girl* I. xiv. 276 Let us bend our steps to the refreshment tent. **1928** E. Waugh *Decline & Fall* I. ix. 94 The refreshment tent looked very nice.

refrigerant, *sb.* Add: **3.** Also, a substance used as the working fluid in a refrigerator. (Further examples.)
1901 [see *champagne gas*]. **1926** *Encycl. Brit.* III. 319/1 In the refrigerating cycle, the refrigerant is made to pass into the evaporating coils so as to enable heat to be absorbed from the commodity to be cooled. **1964** *Listener* 7 May 776 (Advt.), ICI salesmen are today successfully selling..refrigerants to Icelanders (where you'd think it would be cold enough already). **1970** *Times* 16 June 2/7 The water is mixed with a liquid hydrocarbon freezing agent such as butane. The refrigerant takes heat from the water which in turn produces ice crystals and concentrates unwanted solids and salts into a brine slurry.

refrigerate, *v.* Add: **1. c.** (Later examples.)
1957 *Times* 1 Nov. 11/7 Operations which cannot be undertaken at normal temperature may be performed if the body is refrigerated. **1979** *Arizona Daily Star* 5 Aug. J 5/2 Refrigerate overnight before using.
2. (Earlier example.)
1559 P. Morwyng tr. *Gesner's Treasure of Evonymus* 151 A man must put les wyne to new routes then to dry: and perauentur, les also to them whiche ought to refrigerat and coule.

refrigerated, *ppl. a.* Add: Also applied, by extension, to the container in which food is kept, displayed, transported, etc., in a refrigerated condition.
1943 J. S. Huxley *TVA* xv. 128 TVA, in collaboration with the University of Tennessee, designed and built refrigerated barges..to encourage the fruit and vegetable freezing industry in the Valley. **1958** *Brit. Standard Specification* No. 3053 (*title*) Open and closed refrigerated display cabinets (for the retail sale of frozen packaged foods in temperate climates). **1962** [see *gondola 4 d]. **1967** *Economist* 7 Jan. 29/2 Bulgaria has bought a fleet of..long-distance refrigerated trucks (built on the standard American pattern)... There has been heavy investment in refrigerated rail cars bought from Hungary and Poland. **1967** *Commercial Fisheries Rev.* Dec. 53/1 The catch of the refrigerated tuna boats was 7,985 tons in 1966. **1976** *Southern Even. Echo* (Southampton) 3 Nov. (Advt.), Cunard have bought 10 fast refrigerated ships.

refrigerating, *vbl. sb.* Add: Also *attrib.*
1909 *Chambers's Jrnl.* Jan. 23/1 The refrigerating-engineer..claims to play the chief part in the successful maintenance of the overseas trade in chilled meat.

refrigeration. Add: **3.** *attrib.* and *Comb.*, as *refrigeration company, machinery, unit.*
1976 *National Observer* (U.S.) 28 Aug. 7/2 Les Whitely, who owns a refrigeration company in the San Francisco Bay area. **1943** J. S. Huxley *TVA* 30 The production of new refrigeration machinery. **1969** *Coast to Coast 1967–68* 103 The Natwicks sat on the front veranda to watch the traffic.. the semi-trailers and refrigeration units, the decent old-style sedans, [etc.]. **1979** *Tucson* (Arizona) *Citizen* 20 Sept. 1B/4 We have two refrigeration units in our house.

refrigerator. Add: **2.** (Further examples.)
1841 C. Cist *Cincinnati in 1841* (Advt.), Refrigerators or Ice Chests. **1958** *Times* 13 Jan. 11/2 Only 10 per cent. of the population of this island have refrigerators, against 90 per cent. in the United States. **1975** *N.Z. Jrnl. Agric.* Sept. 39/1 My first impression was that the New Zealand farm equipment manufacturers were attempting to 'sell refrigerators to the Eskimos', because, among the massive displays by the British manufacturers, a comparative handful of New Zealand firms were trying to enter an overcrowded market.
b. *refrigerator engineer, -freezer, -maker, ship, truck.*
1909 *Westm. Gaz.* 6 Sept. 5/3 The second refrigerator-engineer..informed us that the boats had put off. **1960** M. Spark *Ballad of Peckham Rye* ii. 27 Humphrey Place, refrigerator engineer of Freeze-eezy's. **1963** *Which?* 6 Feb. 42/1 The combined refrigerator-freezer..will hold more frozen food than a refrigerator's freezing compartment. **1976** *Woman's Day* (U.S.) Nov. 125 Self-defrosting refrigerator-freezer has built-in energy-saving condenser. **1950** *Manch. Guardian Weekly* 7 Dec. 15/3 The Sullivan tunes in the interest of the butcher and baker and refrigerator-maker. **1877** in *Sci. Amer.* (1977) Jan. 14/3 A despatch from M. Tellier to the French Academy of Sciences announces the arrival of the refrigerator ship *Frigorific* at Pernambuco, Brazil. **1921** *Daily Colonist* (Victoria, B.C.) 21 Oct. 12/5 The Moliere, another refrigerator ship..is at Seattle loading. **1976** *Islander* (Victoria, B. C.) 12 Sept. 10/1 A refrigerator ship carrying, eggs, bacon and steel to England. **1971** P. O'Donnell *Impossible Virgin* x. 211 Get Brunel boxed up and put in the refrigerator truck. **1974** R. B. Parker *God save Child* vi. 48 A big refrigerator truck lumbered by on the highway.

refry (rīfrəi·), *v.* [Re- 5 a.] *trans.* To fry again. So **refrie·d** *ppl. a.*, esp. in *refried beans* (U.S.) [Sp. *frijoles refritos*], a dish consisting of pinto beans boiled and fried in advance and refried when required; also *fig.*
1957 *House Beautiful* Sept. 126/2 Main course is a barbecue, Yucatan fashion, accompanied by refried beans. **1960** *N.Y. Times Mag.* 1 May 72/1 The sales of such canned items as tortillas, refried beans and green chilies..have shown marked increases in recent months. **1967** V. Bennett *Compl. Bean Cookbk.* iv. 117 To refry the beans: heat them in the balance of the bacon drippings. **1976** *Sat. Even. Post All-Amer. Cookbk.* 130/2 California refried beans with cheese. This is one of the best and heartiest dishes for which we have to thank the Spanish and the Mexicans. *Ibid.*, The beans are ready to refry at your convenience. **1977** McKnight & Tobler *Bob Marley* ix. 113 Of the ten songs, three are re-fried oldies.

refuel, *v.* Add: **1.** Also, to fill up the fuel-tank of (a car, an aircraft, etc.); now the usual sense.
1973 D. Robinson *Rotten with Honour* 186 He refuelled the middle-aged Saab. **1974** *Guardian* 25 Jan. 13/1 The Italian attitude has been one of reciprocity: you refuel our aircraft and we'll refuel yours. **1976** C. Egleton *State Visit* iii. 31 A tanker would roll out of the BP hangar to refuel a Trident which was on turn round for Amsterdam.
2. *absol.* or *intr.* To take on more fuel.
1940 N. Monks *Squadrons Up!* i. 18 They [*sc.* the pilots] dropped down to reload, refuel, and grab a sandwich. **1958** *Sat. Even. Post* 20 Sept. 129/1 The first waves of F-100 and F-101 fighters have already passed through.., the second waves are air-refueling. **1973** D. Kyle *Suvarov Affair* xiv. 173 He..decided to drop down to the seaplane station at Port Hardy, refuel and report. **1977** *R.A.F. News* 11–24 May 4/5 Flt Lt Hermer then flew to the Olna to refuel... He was unable to shut down his aircraft while refuelling.

refu·elling, *vbl. sb.* [f. prec. + -ing[1].] The action of the verb. Freq. *attrib.*
1917 W. S. Churchill in M. Gilbert *Winston S. Churchill* (1977) IV. Compan. I. 93 A sheltered anchorage with refuelling facilities, the whole properly netted and surrounded by an extensive system of mines, will have been created. **1930** *Engineering* 9 May 612/1 If we permit refuelling in flight. **1935** *Jrnl. R. Aeronaut. Soc.* XXXIX. 267 The refuelling system in the centre portion of the wing is an interesting time saving device. **1954** W. Tucker *Wild Talent* (1955) xv. 203 They're setting up refuelling bases and they hope to send that ship completely around the world. **1955** *Times* 12 July 7/5 An R.A.A.F. Canberra jet bomber will make a round-Australia flight to-morrow, making only two refuelling stops. **1968** J. Sangster *Touchfeather* xviii. 205 The other crewman was standing with the refuelling mechanic. **1978** R. Ludlum *Holcroft Covenant* 9 It was a refueling station never detected by Allied Intelligence.

refuge, *sb.* Add: **3. a.** Also *spec.*, an establishment that offers shelter to a woman who has been physically ill-treated by her husband (or another man with whom she has cohabited).
1976 *Lancaster & Morecambe Guardian* 7 Dec. 27/3 (Advt.), Battered Women's Refuge—Women's Information Centre. **1977** *New Society* 25 Aug. 389/1 The Hastings Refuge Group began campaigning in January 1976 in the hope of getting a house from the council to use as a refuge. Meanwhile they set up an emergency service for battered wives.
c. (Earlier and later examples.)
1869 [see *island *sb.* 2 c]. **1930** V. Sackville-West *Edwardians* iii. 122 Standing upon the refuge waiting to cross Park Lane, he had seen her drive out of Stanhope Gate. **1976** *Cumberland & Westmorland Herald* 4 Dec. 1/1 It was ludicrous that Belisha beacons could not be erected. People would be running the gauntlet from the pavement to the central refuge.
d. A mountain hut in which climbers and walkers can shelter.
1817 H. C. B. Campbell *Jrnl.* 4 Sept. in G. de Beer *Journey to Florence* (1951) 62 We were eight hours in reaching the top of this wondrous mountain... We stopped at the Refuge No 2. **1873** *Young Englishwoman* Nov. 524/2 Napoleon appointed that ten or twelve 'refuges' should be built for storm-harassed travellers here. **1899** G. Bell *Let.* 28 Aug. (1927) I. 51 We..walked up to the Refuge de l'Alpe in two hours. Two German men turned up at the Refuge. **1933** G. D. Abraham *Mod. Mountaineering* i. 8 The hut is situated less than an hour below the Shoulder... To use this refuge for ordinary mountaineering is an abuse; it is only intended and equipped for special parties *in extremis*. **1956** G. Rébuffat *Mont Blanc to Everest* 42 'There's the refuge. Look, they're signalling to us with lanterns!' How I wished they were. But I knew that the Solvay hut was at least 600 feet lower. **1967** 'G. Carr' *Lewker in Tirol* vi. 84 He had not been inside an Alpine hut for years, but this one was very different from the penitential refuges he remembered in Haute Savoie. **1973** *Guardian* 25 Apr. 1/8 The boys had only to be a short distance off route to walk right past their assessors, who were waiting in the safety of the mountain refuge on Foel Grach's summit.
e. *Biol.* A region in which a natural population can survive through a generally unfavourable period.
1929 *Bull. Geol. Soc. Amer.* XL. 663 On the west coast of Norway the ice seems to have reached out into the sea, but it was probably so thin that many islands and high peninsulas rose above it and formed places of refuge for arctic plants and animals. **1946** *New Phytol.* XLV. 235 The tundra refugees could survive only in the tundra refuges but not in those offered by the coastal mountains. **1954** A. J. Cain *Animal Species* v. 60 Its [*sc.* the arid period's] effect was to confine forest-living animals of all sorts to several refuges where rainfall was sufficient to maintain the sort of habitat necessary for them. **1979** *Guardian* 28 Aug. 3/2 The Dartford warbler..suffered population crashes seven times between 1860 and 1945, but recovered each time because a breeding population of several dozen pairs remained in a habitat refuge.
f. *U.S.* A bird sanctuary.
1933 *Sun* (Baltimore) 9 May 14/5 The refuge..is under the supervision of Mrs. R. L. Duke, who since 1931 has played host to the waterfowl which make it a winter 'resort'. **1956** Peterson & Fisher *Wild Amer.* xxix. 320 At the Refuge headquarters they told us that their census of nesting grebes on Tule Lake..showed 3500 pied-bills. **1976** *National Observer* (U.S.) 24 Jan. 9/4 The conservation group..succeeded in setting up a 150-acre refuge in central Wisconsin... It is a roosting site where eagles have been stopping..as they migrate southward.
5. refuge room, a gas-proof room.
1938 *Times* 10 Mar. 11/1 An internal passage will form a very good refuge-room if it can be closed at both ends. **1940** [see *goof *v.* 1 a].

refuge, *v.* Add: **2.** (Further *fig.* example.)
1929 R. Bridges *Testament of Beauty* III. 85 What grave lore had refuged with the Ishmaelite was stealing back from exile to its western home.

refugee, *sb.* Add: **1. d.** Someone driven from his home by war or the fear of attack or persecution; a displaced person. Also *fig.*
1914 E. A. Powell *Fighting in Flanders* vii. 190 The road from Antwerp to Ghent..was a solid mass of refugees. **1926** T. E. Lawrence *Seven Pillars* (1935) vi. lxxix. 436 Then there were the guests and refugees whom we might expect so soon as the news of our establishment was rumoured in Damascus. **1944,** etc. [see *displaced *ppl. a.* b]. **1957** L. Durrell *Justine* I. 39 You are a mental refugee of course, being Irish. **1976** *National Observer* (U.S.) 6 Mar. 18/4 Robert MacNeil, a 44-year-old refugee from NBC and the British Broadcasting Corp., opens with a succinct summary of the program's topic.
3. a. *refugee family, scholar*; **refugee capital** = *hot money* s.v. *hot *a.* 12.
1936 Refugee capital [see *hot money* s.v. *hot *a.* 12]. **1950** *N.Y. Times* 12 Sept. 11/2 Since the Korean invasion began, as much as $300,000,000 to $400,000,000 in 'refugee capital' has flowed here from Europe. **1940** *Manch. Guardian Weekly* 23 Feb. 147 Contracts have just been signed admitting 500 refugee families from Germany and Poland to San Domingo. **1936** *Discovery* Apr. 98/1 The most distinguished of the refugee scholars. **1978** P. Sutcliffe *Oxf. Univ. Press* vii. iv. 260 Some of the refugee scholars eventually made their way to America.
b. Also, of or pertaining to a refugee or refugees, as *refugee camp, centre, colony, project, style, train.*
1902 J. Buchan in J. Adam Smith *J. Buchan & his World* (1979) 38/2 [Milner] has turned over to me..the Boer refugee camps. **1906** *Westm. Gaz.* 23 Apr. 7/1 In the refugee camps yesterday rude altars were erected. **1953** *News Chron.* 2 June 1/4 The Mall looked like a gigantic refugee camp. Over 30,000 people were bedding down along the pavements. **1975** O. Sela *Bengali Inheritance* ii. 18 Kids, spawned in refugee camps, brought up in squalor. **1941** Koestler *Scum of Earth* 177 Refugee-centre besieged by crowd but said there is some British ambulance in Périgueux. **1940** *Manch. Guardian Weekly* 23 Feb. 147 This is the first step in an ambitious plan for a large refugee colony..that will be one of the most important refugee projects in the New World. **1864** K. Cumming *Jrnl. Hospital Life* (1866) ix. 146/2 His two daughters were with him, and were keeping house in *two* rooms, refugee style. **1888** M. Grigsby *Smoked Yank* xxvi. 224 General Hazen asked me to take charge of the refugee train that was assigned to his division.

refugee, *v.* Substitute for def.: **a.** *trans.* To cause (someone) to become a refugee. **b.** *intr.* To be or become a refugee; to depart or live as a refugee. Chiefly *U.S.* Hence **refugee·ing** *vbl. sb.*
1750 [in Dict.]. **1806** in B. Hawkins *Lett.* (1916) 429 It will be some time before the Greek young will get rid of the remains of that alloy which debased the agents and refugeed their associates. **1862** K. Stone *Jrnl.* 25 Aug. in *Brokenburn* (1955) 139 The planters generally are moving back to the hills as fast as possible. There are two families refugeeing in our neighbourhood. **1864** K. Cumming *Jrnl. Hospital Life* (1866) x. 157/2 Many of the citizens of Mobile..had *refugeed* from fear of an attack. **1866** W. Reid *After War* 250 Many of his pupils were..negroes that had been 'refugeed' from the Red River country. **1874** L. Collins *Hist. Sk. Kentucky* I. 162/1 [There have been] about 1,200 deaths..among the negroes refugeed at Camp Nelson. **1904** R. E. Lee *Recoll. & Lett. Gen. R. E. Lee* xv. 270 In the early years of the struggle, my mother and sisters, when 'refugeeing' had boarded..at his home. **1936** M. Mitchell *Gone with Wind* xviii. 324 The exodus of women, children and old people from the city began... Many..who took the train that night had already refugeed five and six times before. **1942** J. Lees-Milne *Ancestral Voices* (1975) 43 The two were very entertaining about their refugeeing with the niece of an old friend near Chedworth. **1965** 'Han Suyin' *Crippled Tree* xxix. 412 The house in which Aunt Number One refugeed herself when her husband, Uncle Liu, wanted to give her baby number twelve.

refugee·dom. [f. Refugee *sb.* + -dom.] The condition of (being) a refugee.
1967 P. E. H. Durston *Mortissimo* xv. 120 He had come to dislike the paraphernalia of refugeedom—votive masses for the unlikely deliverance of the homeland. **1968** *Guardian* 20 Sept. 9/3 Today, the possibilities of social refugeedom are just as great..but few if any parents are worth running away from.

refugium (rĭfiū·dʒiŏm). *Biol.* Pl. **-ia.** [a. L. *refugium* place of refuge (see Refuge *sb.*).] A refuge (sense *3 e), *spec.* one in which a species survived a period of glaciation.

1955 *Canad. Jrnl. Bot.* XXXIII. 442 (*heading*) Nature of the evidence in support of glacial refugia. 1967 M. E. HALE *Biol. Lichens* ix. 142 It occurs as a disjunct in the celebrated unglaciated refugium of south-western Wisconsin. 1976 *Islander* (Victoria, B.C.) 16 May 7/1 The presence of endemic mammals on the Island suggests that suitable survival areas (refugia) existed there during the peaks of the last two glaciations.

refund, *v.*[1] **1. c.** For † *Obs.* read *rare* and add later example.

1920 A. S. PRINGLE-PATTISON *Idea of God* i. 9 If any one prefers to use the term universe for the sum of created or dependent beings, he may, of course, refund the universe into God as its creative source.

refuse, *sb.*[2] Add: **2.** *refuse bin, can, cart, collection, collector, disposal, heap, sack, tip, tipping.*

1959 J. KIRKUP tr. *de Beauvoir's Mem. Dutiful Daughter* III. 212 In the evenings, there would be the refuse bin to empty. 1976 'W. TREVOR' *Children of Dynmouth* i. 14 The wind..rattled the refuse-bins on the ornamental lamp-posts. 1955 W. GADDIS *Recognitions* II. v. 539, I knew it, said Mr. Sinisterra, standing behind a refuse can. 1974 J. WAINWRIGHT *Hard Hit* 33 Along the street, the refuse cart is collecting the empties. 1945 *Listener* 12 July 35/1 For three months now there has been no refuse collection of any kind [in Berlin]. 1974 *Listener* 19 Sept. 368/3 There's a restaurant in Kensington Park Road. It needs six refuse collections a week. 1958 *Daily Mail* 25 Oct. 5/2 It happened to the rat-catcher (*he's now a rodent operator*), the dustman (*refuse collector*), and the sweeper (*street orderly*). 1976 BOTHAM & DONNELLY *Valentino* iii. 24 A string of unskilled jobs. Messenger, refuse collector, dishwasher and laundry assistant. 1906 *Westm. Gaz.* 10 Jan. 2/3 Owing to the narrow limits of Manhattan Island the problem of refuse-disposal is far more difficult in New York than in any other great city in the world. 1972 *Country Life* 28 Dec. 1790/2 Whereas refuse disposal will be a county function, refuse collection will be that of the district. 1816 W. PHILLIPS in *Trans. Geol. Soc.* III. 112 In 1805, I noticed some crystals of the oxyd of uranium on the refuse heaps of Tin Croft mine. 1921 R. A. S. MACALISTER *Text-bk. European Archaeol.* I. x. 556 Most Danish archaeologists..call these remains *affaldsdynger* (refuse-heaps) or *skaldynger* (shell-heaps). 1972 *Police Rev.* 1 Dec. 1557/2 Does he, at the moment of picking up your dustbin or refuse-sack, become the owner..of its contents? 1977 *Cornish Times* 19 Aug. 7/2 (Publ. Notice) Refuse sacks will be provided for premises which would normally receive a collection on these days. 1969 M. PUGH *Last Place Left* xviii. 132 We reached a quarry where we buried Nell's craft lightly in the refuse tip. 1981 *Observer* 17 May 3/3 Refuse tips are probably the richest wildlife refuges in cities. 1974 *Country Life* 3 Oct. 940/3 This valley..one of the loveliest in the south west..is threatened by refuse tipping.

refusenik (rɪfiū·znik). Also **refusnik.** [Partial tr. Russ. *otkáznik*, f. stem of *otkazát'* to refuse: see *-NIK.] A Jew in the Soviet Union who has been refused permission to emigrate to Israel.

1975 *Nature* 31 Jan. 297/2 If, as is often the case with scientists, the initial application is rejected, one may spend months or years as a 'refusnik', with neither the opportunity nor the necessary time to keep up one's reading or think about one's own research. 1976 *Listener* 26 Aug. 237/1 Hundreds of people all over Britain make regular telephone calls to refuseniks every week. 1978 *Daily Tel.* 19 Dec. 11/4 The couple..have recently been putting on a satirical show ..mainly to keep up the morale of their 'refusenik' friends. 1980 *Jewish Chron.* 18 July 18/1 The dissidents languishing in exile, in prison camps and insane asylums, and the refuseniks cut off from family and friends and..from their sources of livelihood. 1980 *Radio Times* 29 Oct. 63/4 Tonight Avital talks about her life since she left Russia, a life of waiting and campaigning to free her husband and other Jewish refusniks from jail in the USSR.

refusing, *vbl. sb.* (Later example.)

1901 *Chambers's Jrnl.* Sept. 663/2 He will, if not instantly checked, learn a lot of bad tricks, such as..slipping his head-collar at night, and 'refusing' in the hunting-field.

refusnik, var. *REFUSENIK.

refutability. For *rare*—[1] read *rare* and add later example.

1957 C. A. MACE *Brit. Philos. in Mid-Century* 160 One can sum up all this by saying that falsifiability, or refutability, is a criterion of the scientific status of a theory.

refute, *v.* Add: ¶ **5.** *trans.* Sometimes used erroneously to mean 'deny, repudiate'.

1964 C. BARBER *Ling. Change Present-Day Eng.* v. 118 For people who still use the word in its older sense it is rather shocking to hear on the B.B.C., which has a reputation for political impartiality, a news-report that Politician A has *refuted* the arguments of Politician B. 1978 *Observer* 7 May 4/9 Mr O'Brien, who was first elected general secretary three years ago, refutes the allegations. 1979 *Daily Mail* 17 Feb. 15/3 He refuted allegations that she took her own life because of police harassment. 1980 *Bookseller* 19 July 257/1, I refute Mr Bodey's allegation that it is our policy not to observe publication dates, and to display new titles in newsagents immediately on receipt from the publisher.

Reg.[1], abbrev. of *REGINA.

1792 W. BOSCAWEN *Treatise on Convictions on Penal Statutes* 48 *Reg.* v. *Matthews.* 1848 E. W. COX *Reports Cases in Criminal Law* II. 422 *Reg.* v. *Hawkes*..settles that question, about which some doubt had been previously entertained. 1976 *Law Rep. Queen's Bench Div.* 417 (*heading*) Reg. v. Michael (Crown Ct.).

reg[2] (reg). *Physical Geogr.* [N. African Arab.] A flat area of desert covered with gravel or boulders; stony desert.

1904 A. KNOX *Gloss. Geogr. & Topogr. Terms* 324 *Reg*, firm level ground, generally without vegetation, a barren, naked plain. 1926 *Chambers's Jrnl.* June 341/1 Beyond the harbour,..away to the east, lies open stony 'Reg', and thence the vast, empty desert. 1963 D. W. & E. E. HUMPHRIES tr. *Termier's Erosion & Sedimentation* ii. 38 *Regs* and *serirs* are planed areas with a covering of boulders, which tumble from the surface of the hamadas or from the plains below them. The term reg is generally reserved for the low plains used by caravans. Moreover, this term is applied commonly to all bouldery ground which has been subjected to deflation. 1966 M. WOODHOUSE *Tree Frog* xxvi. 196, I was somewhere near the edge of a *reg*, one of those huge flat plains of gravel which are, more than anything, the true desert. 1976 L. DEIGHTON *Twinkle, twinkle, Little Spy* xxiii. 226 The going changed to the gravelly surface of the 'reg' and then to rough 'washboard'.

reg[3] (reg), colloq. abbrev. of REGULATION.

1952 M. SHAARA in *Mag. of Fantasy & Sci. Fiction* Oct. 4 Wisher had decided..to follow the regs without question. For without the regs, the Mapping Command was a death trap. 1971 J. SANGSTER *Your Friendly Neighbourhood Death Pedlar* iv. 86 I'm sorry I can't do what you ask. Company regs. 1977 *Hot Car* Oct. 53/2 In Germany it will possibly do well because of their strict regs about modding a car.

regai·n, *sb.* [f. the vb.] **1.** An act of regaining; recovery. Also, an amount regained or recovered.

1927 *Observer* 2 Oct. 19/5 Take into consideration..wages cost, depreciation and interest on working capital, general expenses, discount, regain, and waste. 1927 *Morning Post* 4 Oct. 4/4 Progress of time will see..a regain of position of the horse in the ranks of industry.

2. The weight of moisture in a textile fibre or fabric expressed as a proportion of the weight of the material when thoroughly dry.

1904 J. M. MATTHEWS *Textile Fibres* iii. 46 The amount of normal wool is obtained by adding to the dry weight of the wool the amount of moisture supposed to be present in the air-dried material under normal conditions of humidity and temperature. The added amount is termed 'regain', and is officially fixed by the conditioning house. The permissible percentage of regain varies with the form of the manufactured wool. 1941 *Nature* 4 Oct. 408/2 Dry wool shows strong polarization under an applied potential, but as its regain is increased its conductivity increases exponentially. 1961 A. F. W. COULSON *Man. Cotton Spinning* II. I. ii. 285 The changes in moisture regain depend on temperature.

regal, *a.* and *sb.*[1] Add: **A.** *adj.* **4.** *regal lily* = *REGALE *sb.*[1] 4; *regal pelargonium*, a house plant belonging to a group of varieties of *Pelargonium* × *domesticum*, flowering in spring and early summer.

1925 E. H. WILSON *Lilies E. Asia* 38 The bulbs of the Regal Lily are often part yellow-brown or orange-coloured. 1939 D. T. MACFIE *Lilies* vii. 102 It is difficult to be moderate in the choice of words when talking of the regal lily. 1980 *Observer* 4 May 44/7 Charles Lyte..discovered in his research the extraordinary exploits of the men who introduced delights like the..Regal Lily into Britain. 1903 T. W. SANDERS *Amateur's Greenhouse* 311 Pelargonium.. Decorative and Regal Kinds. These are grown in great quantities for Covent Garden Market. 1951 J. E. CROSS *Bk. Geranium* xii. 104 The plant which still bears the name Pelargonium in commerce is *Pelargonium domesticum*, known in England generally as Show or Regal Pelargonium. 1955 *Times* 26 May 12/3 At Chelsea this year are several large groups of pelargoniums, both the zonal forms for outdoor bedding and the regal types for the greenhouse. 1962 R. PAGE *Educ. Gardener* ix. 260 Pots of palest pink regal pelargoniums..line the steps. 1966 ROCHFORD & GORER *Rochford Bk. Flowering Pot Plants* viii. 116 The Regal Pelargoniums..are generally known simply as Pelargoniums.

5. *regal* (*walnut*) *moth*, a large brown and yellow moth, *Citheronia regalis*, found in the eastern United States.

1854 E. EMMONS *Agric. N.Y.* V. 238 Regal Walnut-moth..feeds on the walnut. 1887 S. W. DENTON *Pages from Naturalist's Diary* (1949) 121, I have..caught eight sphinx moths, and many others, one like the regal walnut moth. 1912 *Country Life in Amer.* 1 Aug. 38 The blue horned hickory devil..turns into the Regal moth. 1972 SWAN & PAPP *Common Insects N. Amer.* xix. 270 Regal moth..Also known as hickory horned moth and royal walnut moth.

B. *sb.* **3. a.** (Later Hist. example.)

1905 R. H. BENSON *King's Achievement* III. xi. 482 He noticed for a moment a wonderful red stone on the thumb, and recognized it. It was the Regal of France that he had seen years before at his visit to St. Thomas's shrine at Canterbury.

regal, *sb.*[2] **2.** (Later examples.)

1944 W. APEL *Harvard Dict. Mus.* 633/2 The reed stops of the later organs are frequently called 'regal'. 1976 *Gramophone* Nov. 837/2 This is instanced by his almost spooky use of the 16-foot regal from the top manual coupled to the pedals.

regale, *sb.*[1] Add: **4.** The specific epithet of *Lilium regale*, used to designate a fragrant, white-flowered lily of the species so called, which was discovered in China by E. H. Wilson in 1903 and named by him in 1912 (*Horticulture* XVI. 110). Also *attrib.*

1935 WOODCOCK & COUTTS *Lilies* i. 3 Then came the epoch-making introduction of that choice representative of the genus, justly called *regale.* 1949 H. NICOLSON *Let.* 15 June (1968) 171 Out of this jungle growth I wish regale to rise. I know it means keeping regale seeds each year. 1962 R. PAGE *Educ. Gardener* viii. 236 The regale lilies open their cream-pink trumpets. 1963 W. BLUNT *Of Flowers & Village* 174 The Madonna lily is to the Regale lily as is the Parthenon to the Mansion House. *Ibid.*, Regale smells like a Bond Street hairdresser's.

regale, *sb.*[2] Add: **1. a.** (Later examples.)

1897 E. COUES *New Light Early Hist. Greater Northwest* I. 8 All were merry over their favorite regale, which is always given on their departure, and generally enjoyed at this spot, where we have a delightful meadow to pitch our tents, and plenty of elbow-room for the men's antics. 1922 E. R. EDDISON *Worm Ouroboros* xxxiii. 429 That night was supper set in Lord Juss's private chamber: a light regale, yet most sumptuous.

b. (Earlier example.)

1791 F. BURNEY *Jrnl.* Aug. (1972) I. 46 There was a grand regale of sweetmeats, fruits, & cakes.

regalia[1]. Add: **2.** Also erron. as sing.

1953 *Times* 29 May 15/4 The regalia which will be used at the Coronation..is that which is normally used at the Coronations of our kings.

regalia[2]. (Earlier example.)

1819 H. BUSK *Dessert* 379 Amber ginseng, and purified eringoes, Regalia's, and imperial's, and *maringoe's*.

regality[1]. **1. b.** For † *Obs. rare*—[1] read *rare* and add later examples.

1966 *New Statesman* 22 July 140/2 Her firmness is deeply satisfying and, in the final act, that excessive regality was lost in the gentle girlhood..which she can present when she chooses. 1979 *Daily Tel.* 4 Dec. 15/1 She is a narrator whose regality, though it is all natural style and never affectation, proves oddly inhibiting to those she interviews.

regard, *sb.* Add: **II. 10. c.** (Later examples.)

1847 DICKENS *Dombey* (1848) xxvi. 265 'Your regards, Edith, my dear?' said Mrs Skewton, pausing, pen in hand, at the postscript. 1978 W. J. BURLEY *Wycliffe & Scapegoat* ix. 160 Give my regards to your father and tell him not to worry.

IV. 16. *attrib.*, as **regard ring** (see quots.).

1889 in *Cent. Dict.* 1890 W. JONES *Finger-Ring Lore* viii. 414 'Regard rings', of French origin, were common even to a late period, and were thus named from the initials with which they were set forming the acrostic of these words: Ruby Emerald Garnet Amethyst Ruby Diamond Lapis lazuli Opal Verd antique Emerald. 1912 O. M. DALTON *Franks Bequest Catal. Finger Rings* 302 A 'regard ring', so called from the fact that the initial letters of the gems composing the bezel form that word. 1951 M. FLOWER *Victorian Jewellery* 253 *Regard ring*, a ring set with a row of small stones of different kinds, the initial letters of which spell a word. 1973 *Country Life* 29 Nov. (Suppl.) 56/1 A tiny antique 'Regard' ring, the word spelt by the first letters of the stones: ruby, emerald, garnet, amethyst, ruby and diamond. 1978 *Illustr. London News* Nov. 129/2 (*caption*) Early Victorian 'regard' ring, £140.

regard, *v.* Add: **I. 7. c.** Also, *as regarding.*

1884 BROWNING *Ferishtah's Fancies* 111, I am in motion, and all things beside That circle round my passage through their midst,—Motionless, these are, as regarding me.

regardless, *a.* Add: **1. c.** *ellipt.* (passing into *adv.*) for 'regardless of expense' or 'regardless of consequences', used postpositively. orig. *U.S.* Phr. *to press on regardless*: see *PRESS *v.*[1] 15 a.

1872 'MARK TWAIN' *Roughing It* xlvii. 334 We are going to get the thing [*sc.* a funeral] up regardless, you know. 1896 *Advance* (Chicago) 30 July 150 Miss Bond got herself up regardless, and came in resplendent in ruby velvet and white swansdown. 1898 J. D. BRAYSHAW *Slum Silhouettes* 40 Who do yer think is down 'ere, got up regardless? D'Arcy's mash, Daisy Chapman. 1911 H. QUICK *Yellowstone Nights* xi. 289 We got a bulletin from his doctors and messages from him to rush S.F. 41144 to its passage, regardless, or he'd accept a bid he'd got for the Bottle Imp. 1920 W. J. LOCKE *House of Baltazar* xvii. 205 I've a jolly good mind to set him up regardless, like a pre-war nut. 1928 T. E. LAWRENCE *Let.* 16 Apr. (1938) 587, I thought some plutocrat publisher was backing you, regardless: the price he offered was so fantastic. 1928 E. O'NEILL *Strange Interlude* II. 58 *Evans.* (*Blundering on regardless now.*) I know it's hardly the proper time—. 1940 M. DICKENS *Mariana* iii. 63 'It's a shilling. Is that too much?' He laughed at her. 'I told you—we're dining out regardless to-night.' 1960 *Observer* 24 July 17/6 What a marvellous feeling when you find the boat is sailing on regardless. 1962 *Listener* 19 Apr. 687/2 The microphone picks everything up, and transmits it regardless. 1980 J. SCOTT *Gospel Lamb* vii. 103 San fairy anne, as the Frogs used to say. He was clobbered, regardless.

regasify (rīgæ·sifəi), *v.* Also **re-gasify.** [RE- 5 b.] *trans.* To convert back into gas.

1926 [implied in REGASIFIED *ppl. a.* below]. 1940 *Gas Age* 24 Oct. 47/1 The liquefied natural gas would be stored in special insulated tanks, to be withdrawn..and regasified when need arose. 1946 *Nature* 20 July 105/2 The methane would be extracted and stored as liquid at periods of low demand, and re-gasified to enrich water gas at periods of high demand. 1967 *Sci. Amer.* Oct. 32/1 Natural gas is liquefied, stored and regasified for use in a city on days of peak demand.

So **rega·sified** *ppl. a.*; also **regasifica·tion,** the action or process of regasifying.

1926 R. W. LAWSON tr. *Hevesy & Paneth's Man. Radio-activity* xxiii. 167 The uncondensed impurities (nitrogen, hydrogen, rare gases) are then pumped off, and after removal of the liquid air, the regasified emanation is allowed to stream into the vessel in which it is to be used. **1940** *Oil & Gas Jrnl.* Oct. 51/1 We began an intensive study of natural-gas liquefaction, its storage and subsequent regasification. **1967** *Sci. Amer.* Oct. 32/1 Regasification involves heating liquid natural gas (*LNG*), which is at a temperature of −259 degrees Fahrenheit, so that it vaporizes and is raised to a safe temperature of 40 degrees F. **1978** *Liquefied Natural Gas* (Shell Internat. Petroleum Co.) 8 The heat required for re-gasification can be taken from a variety of sources—sea water, power station effluent or gas-fired heaters.

regathering, *vbl. sb.* (Later example.)

1955 *Times* 9 Aug. 10/2 They are kept together by a rule of life, by monthly meetings on the mainland, and a 10-day regathering on the island each June.

regatta. Add: **3.** A cotton fabric, usu. made in twill; a striped garment made in this fabric. Also *attrib.*, esp. as *regatta shirt*, an informal light-weight striped shirt.

1861 T. Baines *Jrnl.* 21 July in *Explorations S.-W. Afr.* (1864) 59, I gave Hendrick a couple of regatta shirts and elastic braces. **1910** *Westm. Gaz.* 7 Feb. 5/5 (Advt.), Woven Ginghams, Zephyrs, Regattas, and heavier grades, good for tub frocks. **1910** *Encycl. Brit.* VII. 278/1 *Regatta* is a stout, coloured shirt cloth similar in make to a jeanette. It was originally made in blue and white stripes and was used largely and is still used for men's shirts. **1962** *B.S.I. News* Jan. 8/2 The cloths are coloured-woven regatta fabrics, one of which is all cotton and the other a blend of cotton with one-third rayon staple. *Ibid.* 9/1 The blend has been evolved more recently; requirements for it have been based on regattas submitted to comprehensive trials by hospitals and local authorities. **1963** *New Yorker* 1 June 115 *These* shirts..in regatta, sky blue..navy or red. **1972** *Canad. Antiques Collector* Nov.–Dec. 10/1 The Langley records list substantial quantities of Chesterfields, frock coats, Scotch tweeds,..regatta shirts.

Régence[2] (rezɑ̃s). [Fr.: see Regence[1].] Used, chiefly *attrib.*, to designate the style of costume, furniture, and interior decoration, characteristic of the first third of the eighteenth century in France, during which occurred the French Regency (see Regency 5).

1919 H. Nicolson *Let.* 1 Feb. in J. Lees-Milne *H. Nicolson* (1980) vii. 114 A huge Régence writing table. **1930** R. Cuthill tr. *J. Schober's Silk & Silk Industry* iv. 272 *Regeance* [sic], a Jacquard fabric with small designs and also stripes in the warp direction; usually in striking colours. **1930** *Morning Post* 18 July 14/5 A Regence settee and four fauteuils. **1963** *House & Garden* Mar. 79/2 The term Régence ..is used for the period 1710 to 1730. **1968** *Ibid.* May 47 (*caption*) The sitting-room, showing one of the bergères, Régence overmantel and Austrian clock. **1973** *Country Life* 10 May 1307/1 Slender *Régence* ribbonwork displaced the more plastic forms of the Baroque. **1977** *Times* 16 June 18/6 An ormolu-mounted Régence commode at 53,000 francs..or £6,235.

regency. Add: **3. b.** (Later examples.) Also in *transf.* or extended senses: a group that manages or administers in the absence of a manager or political leader; an inside group or clique controlling affairs.

1940 *Sun* (Baltimore) 13 Aug. 15/5 Secretary Knox named a three-man 'regency' to publish and edit the *News* while he holds his Cabinet post. **1956** *New Republic* 9 Jan. 2/3 There's some evidence the Administration 'Regency' is using Ike's absence to even old scores. **1963** *Daily Tel.* 12 Jan. 15/3 Leading members of the Parliamentary Labour party have been angered by a suggestion..that a 'Regency' has been set up to rule in the absence of Mr. Gaitskell.

7. a. Regency point, a kind of lace (see quots.); also *attrib.*

1865 F. B. Palliser *Hist. Lace* xxx. 364 A 'point' lace, with the 'cloth' or 'toilé' on the edge, for many years was in fashion, and in compliment to the Prince, was named..'Regency Point'. It was a durable and handsome lace. **1900** E. Jackson *Hist. Hand-Made Lace* 193 Regency Point Lace. This lace, made in Bedfordshire, was in great demand during the Regency early in the nineteenth century. The edge is thick, the ground, a complicated réseau, or hand-made mesh. **1930** T. Wright *Romance of Lace Pillow* xv. 219 During the Regency (1810–1820) there was made in Northamptonshire a striking lace, with fillings of a bold character, which was called Regency Point.

b. Passing into *adj.* Applied to styles of architecture, clothing, furniture, etc., characteristic of the English Regency (sense 5 in Dict.), and, more generally, the late eighteenth and early nineteenth century.

The isolated early use in quot. *c* 1793 may possibly reflect the public controversy surrounding the Regency Bill of 1788.

c **1793** Jane Austen *Volume Third* in *Minor Works* (1954) 211 'She sends me a long account of the new Regency walking dress Lady Susan has given her... She says nothing indeed except about the Regency.' 'She *must* write well thought Kitty, to make a long letter upon a Bonnet & Pelisse.' **1880** E. Glaisher *Needlework* viii. 86 Shield-backed chairs of the Regency fashion. **1887** Regency cap [in Dict.]. **1909** *Cent. Dict. Suppl.*, Regency style. **1918** A. Bennett *Pretty Lady* vi. 25 He had furnished his flat in the Regency style of the first decade of the nineteenth century. *Ibid.* vii. 33 Regency furniture and china. **1936** *Discovery* Oct. 321/2 The short 'Brutus' curls of regency mock-classical beauties. **1938** C. Day Lewis *Overtures to Death* 18 We gaze At a Regency terrace, curved Like the ritual smile. **1954** J. Betjeman *Few Late Chrysanthemums* 43, I pulled aside the thick magenta curtains—So Regency, so Regency, my dear—. **1958** —— *Coll. Poems* 250 It's for Regency now I'm enthusing So we've Regency stripes on the wall. **1963** N. Freeling *Because of Cats* iii. 47 There were Regency-striped silk cushions. **1973** P. Moyes *Curious Affair of Third Dog* v. 57 The Regency-stripe wall-paper. **1976** *Denbighshire Free Press* 8 Dec. 16/7 (Advt.), Curtains... Regency stripe/gold, 2 width each side, length 53 in. £20. **1977** C. McCullough *Thorn Birds* iii. 64 The Louis Quinze sofa and chairs, the Regency escritoire. **1977** *S. Wales Echo* 18 Jan. (Advt.), Only four remaining on a small development of just 10 Regency style Detached Houses.

regenerable (rĭdʒe·nĕrăb'l), *a.* [f. Regener(ate *v.* + -able.] Capable of being regenerated.

1920 in Webster. **1927** A. Kocourek *Jural Relations* x. 140 Regenerable relations.. are mesonomic relations which are convertible into zygnomic relations by means of a jural act or event. **1976** *Nature* 24 June 660/1 Microparticles were needed in the thermally regenerable ion-exchange process to ensure rapid rates of ion-exchange.

regenerant, *a.* Restrict *rare*[—1] to sense in Dict. and add: **B.** *sb.* A regenerating agent.

1961 in Webster. **1963** *Engineering* 13 Sept. 338/3 The regenerant for the anion column can be either sodium carbonate or sodium hydroxide.

regenerate, *v.* Add: **2.** Also in *Biol.* (Further examples.)

1895 *Arch. für Entwicklungsmech. der Organismen* II. 122 The power of an adult animal to regenerate lost parts. **1909** R. H. Lock *Rec. Progress Study of Variation* iii. 61 The power of regenerating a lost part must clearly often be of service to the creatures which possess it. **1959** [see *regeneration 3]. **1961** Lenhoff & Loomis *Biol. Hydra* 409 Hydra treated with $10^{-5}M$ lipoic acid for short periods immediately after removal of their hypostomes and tentacles completely lose the capacity to regenerate those structures. **1970** Ambrose & Easty *Cell Biol.* i. 21 The capacity to regenerate certain tissues, possessed by most embryonic animals, is still present in some mature animals and plants.

3. (Later example.)

1962 *Which?* Oct. 294/1 After a time, the resin [in a water softener] has no sodium left, and has to be 'regenerated' by adding sodium chloride.

c. *Chem.* and *Textiles.* To re-precipitate (a natural polymeric substance, such as cellulose, proteins) following chemical processing, esp. in the form of fibres; to make (fibres) in this way. Cf. *regenerated *ppl. a.* 2.

1925 *U.S. Patent 1,528,219*, I..have invented certain new and useful Improvements in a Process of Regenerating Cellulose from Viscose. **1948** J. T. Marsh *Textile Sci.* i. 8 It has not been possible to regenerate fibres from wool, but successful attempts have been made with silk. **1950** R. W. Moncrieff *Artificial Fibres* 90 Some of the sodium cellulose xanthate decomposes, regenerating cellulose which is maintained in emulsion form by that part of the sodium cellulose xanthate which is still undecomposed. **1955** Cockett & Hilton *Basic Chem. of Textile Preparation* iv. 82 Attempts have been made to regenerate both silk and wool in which the protein raw material is in a linear or near linear form. **1972** M. A. Taylor *Technol. of Textile Properties* 30 Azlon is the generic term given..to fibres regenerated from natural protein, such as casein from milk. **1973** *Materials & Technol.* VI. iv. 277 The extruded filaments were injected into a bath of dilute sulphuric acid to re-precipitate, or 'regenerate', the original cellulose and form textile threads.

5. a. Also in *Biol.* (Further examples.)

1901 T. H. Morgan *Regeneration* i. 20 A piece of hydra regenerates without the formation of new material. **1928** J. S. Huxley *Ess. Pop. Sci.* 251 When small pieces of a planarian regenerate, they exhibit what we may call polarity. **1971** [see *regulate *v.* 5].

regenerate, *ppl. a.* and *sb.* Add: **A.** *ppl. a.* **4.** *Biol.* Formed or modified by regeneration.

1952 *Q. Rev. Biol.* XXVII. 169/2 Intimacy of morphological relation between the regenerate and the adult tissue has demanded that study of the process of regeneration be made against the background of the anatomy and physiology of adult tissues.

B. *sb.* Restrict †*Obs.* to sense in Dict. and add: **2.** *Biol.* A limb or other part formed by regeneration.

1952 *Q. Rev. Biol.* XXVII. 169/2 The histology of the regenerate emphasizes the continuity and interrelation between adult and regenerating tissue. *Ibid.*, The regenerate..is nourished by the adult blood stream. **1960** [see *dedifferentiation]. **1964** [see *melanogenesis* s.v. *melano-]. **1977** *Sci. Amer.* July 69/3 A graft between a proximal level of a host cockroach leg and a distal level of a donor leg gives rise to a normally oriented intercalary regenerate and forms a normal leg segment.

regenerated, *ppl. a.* Add: **2.** *Chem.* and *Textiles.* Of natural polymeric materials (as cellulose, proteins): re-precipitated (esp. in the form of fibres) following chemical treatment. Of fibres: prepared from a substance in this way.

1904 *Jrnl. Soc. Chem. Industry* 29 Feb. 177/1 The next operation..is one for the purpose of denitrating the cellulose, in order that the fibre may ultimately consist of what might be termed 'regenerated' cellulose. **1933** *Trans. Faraday Soc.* XXIX. 230 Regenerated celluloses are more highly activated than cotton which has merely been swollen. **1941** *Thorpe's Dict. Appl. Chem.* (ed. 4) V. 121/2 Viscose and regenerated cellulose rayons in general show a much higher moisture adsorption at all relative humidities than do native cellulose fibres. **1948** J. T. Marsh *Textile Sci.* i. 8 Regenerated fibres may be classified according to the nature of the parent material, cellulose or protein. **1963** A J. Hall *Textile Sci.* ii. 66 Several types of protein are satisfactory for the production of regenerated protein fibres and among those most used are casein..and the natural proteins..extracted from groundnuts and soya beans. **1964** N. G. Clark *Mod. Org. Chem.* xvii. 363 Regenerated fibres are derived from naturally occurring fibrous material by first converting it into a soluble derivative, forcing a solution of this through a minute jet to give a 'thread' of solution, and finally recovering the original or its derivative from solution as a solid thread or fibre. **1973** *Materials & Technol.* VI. iv. 277 Wool and silk are both protein fibres, and it is not surprising that attempts have been made to produce regenerated protein fibres.

regeneration. Add: **1. c.** *Forestry.* The natural regrowth of a forest which has been felled or thinned. Freq. *attrib.*

1888 E. E. Fernandez *Man. Indian Sylviculture* i. 6 The name regrowth will be specially given to the new crop obtained by coppice regeneration. **1909** P. T. Maw *Pract. Forestry* ix. 183 A Seed Felling or Regeneration Felling is made when a good seed year has come. As its name implies, it is the felling made for the actual regeneration of the area. It consists in the removal of all the trees except a few, which are left as mother trees, to seed the whole area; and also, to form a light canopy or shelter wood for the young crop. **1928** R. S. Troup *Silvicultural Syst.* iv. 38 Where regeneration is sufficiently well advanced it should be freed from overhead cover. *Ibid.* 45 The latter will be retained as regeneration areas under the revised working plan. **1979** *Biol. Abstr.* LXVII. 2139/2 The conditions of regeneration and growth of seedlings varied with stands and plots.

3. (Further examples.) Also in *Biol.*

1901 T. H. Morgan *Regeneration* i. 23 The word 'regeneration' has come to mean, in general usage, not only the replacement of a lost part, but also the development of a new, whole organism, or even a part of an organism, from a piece of an adult, or of an embryo, or of an egg. **1959** W. Andrew *Textbk. Compar. Histol.* xii. 478 While asexual reproduction is not common among the echinoderms, a high power of regeneration is present and a single arm can regenerate a whole starfish. **1978** *Nature* 27 July 374/1 Can re-innervation take place not only by regeneration of the original axons but also by collateral sprouting of..undamaged fibres?

4. *Electronics.* Positive feedback (see *feedback, feed-back *sb.* a).

1922 *Proc. IRE* X. 244 The effect of regeneration (that is, the supplying of energy to a circuit to reinforce the oscillations existing therein) is equivalent to introducing a negative resistance reaction in the circuit. **1943** [see *reaction 3 e]. **1957** *Practical Wireless* XXXIII. 694/1 The hole is used..in the next stage for a regeneration control. **1969** J. J. Sparkes *Transistor Switching* iii. 74 Regeneration will only commence provided the loop gain A_v..is greater than 1.

5. *Chem.* and *Textiles.* The action or process of regenerating fibres, etc. Cf. *regenerate *v.* 3 c.

1925 *U.S. Patent 1,528,219* The regeneration of cellulose from viscose solutions. **1950** R. W. Moncrieff *Artificial Fibres* ii. 20 The original cotton had consisted of short, hairy, nearly opaque fibres, and after regeneration it consisted of very long, smooth, transparent filaments, but it was still the same essential material. **1953** *Chem. Abstr.* XLVII. 643 (*heading*) Regeneration of egg albumins under pressure. **1972** M. A. Taylor *Technol. Textile Properties* 28 The regeneration and polymerisation of the cellulose occurs after the filament has been coagulated and stretched.

regenerative, *a.* (and *sb.*) Add: **2. b.** Applied to a principle or technique of refrigeration by which the uncooled portion of the working fluid loses some heat prior to the major cooling step by exchange with the cooled portion.

1896 *Proc. Chem. Soc.* XI. 222 In all continuously working circuits of liquid gases used in refrigerating apparatus the regenerative principle applied to cold first introduced by Siemens in 1857..has been adopted. *Ibid.* 231 If..hydrogen, previously cooled by a bath of boiling air, is allowed to expand at 200 atmos. over a regenerative coil..a liquid jet can be seen. **1922** Glazebrook *Dict. Appl. Physics* I. 565/1 The usual process [for the commercial liquefaction of gases] is a regenerative one, first successfully developed by Linde, in which the Joule-Thomson effect of irreversible expansion in passing a constrictive orifice..serves as the step-down in temperature, and a cumulative cooling is produced by causing the gas which has suffered this step-down to take up heat in a thermal interchanger from another portion of gas that is on its way to the orifice. **1961** F. E. Hoare et al. *Exper. Cryophysics* i. 4 Dewar was employing regenerative cooling to produce a jet of cold hydrogen gas which could be used for cooling other systems.

c. *Astronautics.* Applied to a method of cooling the walls of a rocket engine by circulating the fuel through them.

1947 *Amer. Jrnl. Physics* XV. 131/2 In the motor, between 2 and 3 percent of the heat due to combustion passes through the chamber and nozzle walls into the coolant, which returns again to the combustion chamber when regenerative cooling is utilized. **1949** G. P. Sutton *Rocket Propulsion Elements* vi. 142 In regenerative cooling the motor parts are cooled by means of a built-in jacket or cooling coil in which the oxidizer or the fuel are used as the coolant fluid. **1962** F. I. Ordway et al. *Basic Astronautics* x. 413 This regenerative cooling method serves two purposes. It cools the walls of the thrust chamber and adds thermal energy to the propellant. **1974** *Encycl. Brit. Macropædia* XV. 938/2 The conventional method of cooling [in rocket engines] is known as regenerative cooling.

3. Applied to any method of braking in which energy is extracted from the parts braked, to be stored and re-used.

1904 *Electrical Mag.* I. 600/1 The regenerative braking action comes into play automatically. **1930** *Engineering* 6 June 722/2 Regenerative braking had been adopted on the majority of the electric locomotives recently placed in service. **1958** *Ibid.* 14 Mar. 340/1 A bus using the regenerative transmission... In this system, when the vehicle is braked..energy is absorbed in accelerating a..flywheel... Then when the vehicle is restarted the energy of the flywheel is used to accelerate it, resulting in a saving of fuel. **1973** *Sci. Amer.* Dec. 23/2 A regenerative braking system would employ the vehicle's electric motors as generators during braking or downhill driving, thus putting the kinetic energy of the vehicle back into the storage system.

4. *Electronics.* Pertaining to or employing positive feedback (see *FEEDBACK, FEED-BACK *sb.* a); *regenerative feedback*, positive feedback.

1915 *Proc. IRE* III. 231 It is always better practice to use the cascade circuits for the radio frequencies, even if the regenerative circuits are not employed with each individual audion system. **1919** *Wireless World* Aug. 250/2 By using regenerative feed back much higher amplification can be realized, but the operation becomes less stable. **1922** *Sci. Amer.* Sept. 160/1 Armstrong's regenerative receiver, now so widely employed, is ever so much more sensitive than the ordinary vacuum tube receiver. **1947** R. LEE *Electronic Transformers & Circuits* ix. 254 The next pulse occurs when the negative grid voltage decreases sufficiently so that regenerative action starts again. **1969** J. J. SPARKES *Transistor Switching* iii. 59 The cross-coupling resistor..can be shunted by a capacitor..to speed up the regenerative switching of the circuit. **1971** *Physics Bull.* July 385/2 The high spectral intensity results from the fact that, since the laser is a regenerative oscillator, the oscillation linewidth decreases with increasing laser power—in contrast to the behaviour of any thermal source. **1975** G. J. KING *Audio Handbk.* ii. 35 Positive feedback means that the phase of the signal fed back is coincident with the phase of the source or input signal. This is regenerative feedback which results in sustained oscillation.

regeneratively *adv.* (further examples).

1947 *Amer. Jrnl. Physics* XV. 131/1 The coolant liquid absorbs heat as it circulates in ducts around the motor and is then injected into the combustion chamber (regeneratively cooled type). **1949** G. P. SUTTON *Rocket Propulsion Elements* vi. 142 The German Me 163 motor has a steel cooling jacket in which fuel cools the motor regeneratively. **1969** J. J. SPARKES *Transistor Switching* iii. 74 When T_2 is conducting, raising V_1 until it is about equal to V_{B2} turns T_1 on so that T_2 is switched off regeneratively.

regenesis. (Later U.S. example.)

1973 *Black World* June 90/2 Sister [Sherley Anne] Williams breaks her book [sc. *Give Birth to Brightness*] down into three major parts. Part 1 is called 'Regenesis'.

regent, *sb.* Add: **3. d.** (*a*) (Earlier and later examples.)

1813 *Niles' Reg.* V. 79/2 The regents of the university, expressly endeavored to effect this important object. **1969** *Morning Star* 13 Oct. 5/3 The Director of Afro-American Studies declares her sacking raises grave doubts about the Regents' desire to encourage black participation. **1976** *New Yorker* 26 Apr. 32/2 One of the Smithsonian's regents..is chairman of the House Appropriations Committee. **1977** *Detroit Free Press* 11 Dec. 11-D/1 Regents for Oklahoma State University Friday honoured Terry Miller by retiring his No. 43 football jersey and approving a commendation to be awarded at the next regents meeting.

4*. A variety of potato.

1846 [see *EARLY *sb.* a]. **1868** M. JEWRY *Warne's Model Cookery & Housekeeping Bk.* 14 Potatoes.—*We* think the best are..the regents for winter use. **1892** I. ZANGWILL *Childr. Ghetto* II. 6 'Kidneys or regents, my child?'..said Guedalyah the greengrocer. **1927** T. P. MCINTOSH *Potato* ii. 20 Not much appears to be known about Regent, which was a later introduction [*sc.* after 1836].

4.** A chairman of a branch of the Daughters of the American Revolution.

1890 *Constitution & Bye-Laws, Daughters Amer. Revolution* 4 When twelve or more members of the Society shall be living in one locality they may organize a Chapter. They may elect a presiding officer whose title will be Regent. **1928** *Harper's Mag.* Oct. 529/2 The Daughters upheld Mrs Brousseau and the contention of the Massachusetts State Regent. **1946** *Nat. Historical Mag.* Mar. 144/2 Please read over the foregoing statement again, Madam Regent. **1974** *Marlboro Herald-Advocate* (Bennettsville, S. Carolina) 18 Apr. 4/2 Mrs. Walter Hughes, local regent, also attended the Congress.

5. a. regent honeyeater, a bird, *Zanthomiza phrygia*, of the family Meliphagidæ, having black plumage with yellow bars and spots and found in the eucalyptus forests of south-east Australia.

1913 G. M. MATHEWS *List Birds Austral.* 270 *Zanthomiza phrygia phrygia.* Regent Honey-eater. **1967** A. RUTGERS *Birds Austral.* 262 Regent Honey-eaters make a lot of noise and have a loud laughing call.

reggae (re·gē[i]). Also **Reggae, Reggay.** [Origin unknown; perh. connected with Jamaican English *rege-rege* quarrel, row (in Cassidy and Le Page, *Dict. Jamaican Eng.* (1967) 380/1).] A kind of popular music, of Jamaican origin, characterized by a strongly accentuated off-beat and often a prominent bass; a dance or song set to this music. Also *attrib.*

1968 (*song-title*) Do the Reggay. **1969** *Daily Mirror* 10 Oct. 19/1 *Reggae*, West Indian music. **1969** *Observer* 23 Nov. 25/8 The visiting American executives ..dancing the Reggae, Jamaica's successor to the Ska. **1969** *Listener* 25 Dec. 905/2 A very dapper and jaunty Reggae group called the Pioneers. **1970** *Melody Maker* 3 Oct. 25/6 If I ever did reggae again, it would have to be darned good reggae, and there's not much of that around. It's such a blank type of music. **1971** *Advocate-News* (Barbados) 17 Sept. (Guyana Suppl.) p. vi (Advt.), A rum punch..served to an atmosphere of reggae, calypso and steelband music. **1973** G. SIMS *Hunters Point* xiii. 120 I'm a reggae fan. West Indian music. And early Beatles like 'From Me to You'. **1973** *Black World* Jan. 77/2, I heard the Rastas credited with starting everything from the island's most popular dance, 'Reggae', to the embryonic Black Consciousness movement. **1975** *Globe & Mail* (Toronto) 16 July 7/3 The reggaes..should be viewed as songs of social protest in which the dispossessed describe their personal experience and comment upon the social injustice of the system. **1976** *Telegraph* (Brisbane) 28 Apr. 58/4 As reggae grows in popularity, ever more artists are performing material with a reggae flavour. **1977** MC-KNIGHT & TOBLER *Bob Marley* iii. 42 So we come to reggae, which the British initially found difficulty in pronouncing, let alone understanding. **1978** *Sunday Times* 29 Jan. 43/2 Althea and Donna met at a reggae festival in Ochos Rios. **1979** *Spectator* 1 Dec. 13/3 The bulk of the reggae-blacks were born here and yet feel themselves to be foreigners.

Regge (rē[i]·dʒe). *Nuclear Physics.* The name of T. E. *Regge* (b. 1931), Italian physicist, used *attrib.* to designate certain concepts in the theory of the scattering of sub-atomic particles, as **Regge pole,** a pole of a complex function relating the scattered amplitude of partial waves to angular momentum; **Regge trajectory,** a path traced in the complex angular momentum plane by a Regge pole as the energy varies; esp. a plot of spin against the square of the rest mass for a group of particles.

1961 *Physical Rev. Lett.* VII. 394/2 We may satisfy Feynman's principle therefore by postulating that all poles of the *S* matrix are of this type (Regge poles). **1962** *Ibid.* VIII. 41/2 Each point is supposed to lie on a Regge trajectory. **1962** *Physical Rev.* CXXVI. 2204/2 This perturbation theory behavior is very different from that of the Regge case. *Ibid.*, Strongly interacting particles may exhibit the Regge behavior. **1973** [see *POLE *sb.*[2] 9*]. **1973** B. H. BRANSDEN et al. *Fundamental Particles* viii. 163 (*caption*) The Regge trajectories of some meson states. Mesons differing in spin by one unit appear to lie on the same Regge trajectory. **1973** L. J. TASSIE *Physics Elem. Particles* xii. 170 Most work on Regge theory is concerned with describing collision processes, and in this respect the Regge pole model is not a theory with a high predictive power. **1975** *Sci. Amer.* Feb. 62/3 The Regge trajectories turn out on observation to be nearly linear, meaning that the angular momentum of the particles on a particular trajectory is given to a good approximation by a linear function of the mass of the particle squared. **1977** P. D. B. COLLINS *Introd. Regge Theory* ii. 69 When such a Regge pole occurs for a physical integer value of *l* it will correspond to a physical particle or resonance. **1977** *Nature* 21 July 207/2 Hadrons on the same Regge trajectory have a remarkably simple relation between mass and angular momentum: $J = \alpha' M^2 + \alpha_0$, where J is the total angular momentum of the hadron, M is its mass and α' and α_0 are called the Regge 'slope' and 'intercept' respectively.

Reggeization (re:dʒeˌəizē[i]·ʃən). *Nuclear Physics.* [f. prec.: see -IZATION.] Treatment or modification in accordance with Regge theory.

1964 *Rev. Mod. Physics* XXXVI. 641/1 We have throughout considered the theory of spin ½ fermions, which as stated above shows the factoring property which is necessary for the success of the Reggeization procedure. **1975** *Physics Bull.* Jan. 25/2 Schnitzer's study of the Reggeization of non-abelian gauge theories is now seen to have been prophetic.

So **Re·ggeized** (also **r-**) *a.*

1971 N. DOMBEY in Cumming & Osborn *Hadronic Interactions of Electrons & Photons* ii. 37 Now assume instead that the pion is Reggeized; i.e. S_J has a moving pole at $J = \alpha_\pi(t)$. **1973** *Physics Bull.* Feb. 99/1 Reggeized baryon exchange models give poor quantitative agreement with the results. **1973** *Jrnl. Physics* A. VI. 506 A reggeized absorption model with no free parameters..is applied to spin-2+ production reactions.

Reggeon (re·dʒeɒn). *Nuclear Physics.* [f. as prec. + *-ON[1].] (A particle represented by a) Regge pole or trajectory, or a virtual particle regarded as exchanged in the type of scattering they represent. Hence **reggeo·nic** *a.*

1964 *Physics Lett.* IX. 269/1 Mandelstam has given some arguments that moving branching points may appear in a relativistic theory as a result of singularities to the right in the *j*-plane for particles with spin. These new singularities correspond to the production threshold of resonance states (reggeons) with negative orbital momenta. *Ibid.* XII. 153/2 If this fact is correct it would modify the reggeonic branch points and the elastic scattering asymptotic amplitude. **1974** *Physics Bull.* May 206/4 High energy backward scattering is studied by (i) covariant reggeization techniques, (ii) the use of a super multiplet reggeon propagator model to generate polynomial residues. **1977** P. D. B. COLLINS *Introd. Regge Theory* ii. 71 The power behaviour expected from the exchange of a Regge trajectory (sometimes called 'Reggeon')..may be contrasted with that from a fixed-spin (elementary) particle. **1978** *Nature* 19 Jan. 214/2 Reggeons with arbitrarily high spin can be exchanged with equanimity.

regiculture (re·dʒikɒ:ltiŭɹ). *rare.* [f. L. *rēgi-, rex* king + CULTURE *sb.*] Honour or homage to kings.

1880 SWINBURNE in T. H. Ward *Eng. Poets* III. 281 For all her evil report among men on the score of passive obedience and regiculture.

‖ **regidor** (reχido·r). Pl. **regidores, regidors.** [Sp. *regidor* alderman, f. *regir* to rule.] In Spain and the former Spanish dominions in America, a member of a cabildo or municipal council; a councillor; a village official.

1622 J. MABBE tr. *Aleman's Rogue* I. I. iii. 33 Thus it fared with a Regidor, who being espied by an old man,.. call'd him unto him. **1755** SMOLLETT *Cervantes' Don Quixote* I. p. xiv, Dedicated to the alcaides, regidors, and gentlemen of the noble town of Argamasilla. **1834** A. PIKE *Prose Sketches & Poems* 170 The Regidor, or Assistant Alcalde, Miguel Sena, has only perjured himself three times. **1848** E. BRYANT *What I saw in California* xxii. 283 The first of these pueblos is governed by its corresponding body of magistrates, composed of an alcalde or judge, four regidores or municipal officers, a syndic and a secretary. **1895** G. E. KING *New Orleans* vii. 115 Instead of a superior council, there was a cabildo, with regidores, alcaldes, [etc.]. **1934** *Hist. Soc. Southern California Publ.* XVI. 142 He was *regidor* of Los Angeles in 1838–39. **1950** G. BRENAN *Face of Spain* vi. 143 He introduced himself as the *regidor* of the village municipality. **1969** *Femina* (Bombay) 26 Dec. 41/1 One of the labourers summoned the *regidor*, a village official, to the scene. **1974** *Encycl. Brit. Micropædia* II. 422/1 In local affairs, each municipality in Hispanic America was governed by its *cabildo*, or city council... Its members, *regidores* (councillors) and *alcaldes ordinarios* (magistrates), along with the local *corregidor* (royally appointed judge), enjoyed considerable prestige and power.

‖ **régie** (reʒi). Also with capital initial. [Fr., f. *régir* to rule.] In France and certain other countries: a government department that administers a state-controlled industry or service; formerly *esp.*, one responsible for taxation, customs and excise, etc.; a government monopoly used as a means of taxation, *esp.* the tobacco monopoly in the former Turkish Empire. Also *attrib.*

1791 LD. GOWER in *Despatches Earl Gower* (1885) 61 The 4th [article of a decree] allows tobacco in leaves to be stored, for a year, in the ware-houses of the *Régie*. **1879** *Encycl. Brit.* IX. 738/1 Unfortunately, he [*sc.* Frederick the Great] adopted the French ideas of excise, and the French methods of imposing and collecting taxes,—a system known as the Regie. **1883** *Pall Mall Gaz.* 9 May 5/1 The Turkish tobacco régie..is designed to include a company having the exclusive right of preparing tobacco for home consumption and of selling it to the public. **1884** *Ibid.* 5 Sept. 6/2 Ladies.. smoke the strong régie cigar with evident enjoyment. **1890** *Athenæum* 11 Oct. 474/3 All the frequenters of a country inn [in France]..consume the tobacco of the *régie*. **1923** *Glasgow Herald* 26 Feb. 10 The exploitation of the railways of the Ruhr and the Rhineland by a Franco-Belgian 'regie' is believed to have been decided. **1929** W. RAY tr. *Hegemann's Frederick the Great* 122 The King indeed was thoroughly well satisfied with his Régie escapades... The patient Prussians had barely two more years to wait before death came to rid them of their great king, the extortions of the French *Régie*, [etc.]. **1958** G. T. MATTHEWS *Royal Gen. Farms 18th Cent. France* I. ii. 43 Prior to 1548 the various salt taxes and commercial concessions constituting the *grandes gabelles* were partly farmed to individual tax-farmers and partly managed by government *régies*. **1964** RIDLEY & BLONDEL *Public Administration in France* II. vii. 181 Finally we come to the revenue or, as the French call them, fiscal divisions. Until recently there were four more or less autonomous services (or *régies*). These had remained virtually unchanged since the Revolution and corresponded roughly to the main sources of state revenue: direct taxes, indirect taxes, customs duties, and registration fees, stamp duties and the national domain... After the war it was decided that the four *régies* should be transformed into two divisions of the ministry. *Ibid.* x. 239 Traditionally there were two ways of organizing a public service, the *régie* and the concession; the former operated by a government department or a local authority, the latter on contractual terms by private enterprise. **1977** S. J. & E. K. SHAW *Hist. Ottoman Empire & Mod. Turkey* II. iii. 233 In 1883 the Public Debt Commission turned the tobacco monopoly over to a private German-French company called the *Régie cointéressée de tabacs de l'Empire Ottoman*, which paid a fixed annual fee..in return and then divided the profits with the Ottoman treasury. The Régie had the sole right to buy and process all tobacco sold in the empire and regulate its cultivation... The tobacco..was stored in the Régie warehouses.

régime, regime. Add: **1.** (Later examples.)

1908 A. BENNETT *Old Wives' Tale* I. iii. 45 She was a shrivelled little woman, capable of sitting twelve hours a day in a bedroom and thriving on the *régime*. **1943** *Ann. Allergy* I. 33 Others in whom the psychic element is important are nevertheless improved by a hygienic régime or by symptomatic medication. **1973** *Daily Tel.* 13 Feb. 16 This is not a diet to enter upon without medical prescription... To embark on this régime without due regard to the consequences may delay diagnosis of other disorders.

2. a. (Later examples.) Now freq. applied disparagingly to a particular government or administration.

1955 *Times* 2 May 8/3 But none of us is prepared, either, to bolster up the aging régime of Chiang Kai-shek. *Ibid.* 11/5 Only King Saud and the régime in the Yemen (which recently survived in undiminished medieval splendour an abortive *coup d'État*) remain patently faithful to Egypt. **1973** *Guardian* 16 Apr. 1/6 The Smith regime in Rhodesia.

b. *old regime* (earlier and later *transf.* examples).

1816 W. SCOTT in *Q. Rev.* XIV. 192 A crime against sentiment which no author, of moderate prudence, would have hazarded under the old *régime*. **1842** GEO. ELIOT *Let.* 30 Aug. (1954) I. 144 There ought to be..a few spectral clingers to the memory of the old régime in the era of political regeneration. **1912** F. A. TALBOT *Moving Pictures* xii. 136 Under the old *régime* darkness prevailed from one end of the programme to the other, save, perhaps, during a short interval. **1971** R. Bendix in A. Bullock *20th Cent.* xv. 352/2 Their overthrow of an 'old regime' fulfils the first task of their [*sc.* revolutionary movements'] ideological mission. **1976** J. B. Hilton *Gamekeeper's Gallows* xv. 159 'Take her back home again tomorrow.'.. The old regime was over.

3. *Physical Geogr.* **a.** The condition of a watercourse with regard to changes that may be occurring in its form or bed and the possibility of an equilibrium in which there is neither erosion nor deposition; = *regimen 5.

[**1779** P. L. G. Du Buat *Principes d'Hydraulique* I. iv. 73 Ainsi, par le terme régime, nous entendons proprement la vitesse du courant, comparée à la résistance du terrain qui forme le lit.] **1856** *Min. Proc. Inst. Civil Engineers* XV. 241 The case of the River Clyde, at Glasgow, should be carefully examined, when considering any measure for the *régime* of the Thames. *Ibid.* 242 To regulate the low-water *régime*, by removing the shoals below London Bridge. **1895** *Ibid.* CXIX. 282 Observations were made at thirty sites... Each was known by long local experience to have been in a state of permanent regime, the canal having been flowing for years on its self-silted bed. **1925** F. Reeves *Notes & Data Rly. Engin.* 30 One frequently sees the results of this absence of accurate knowledge of the *régime* of the stream in washaways, bridges of unnecessary size, etc. **1927** *Min. Proc. Inst. Civil Engin.* CCXXIII. 268 The conditions of great rivers in unstable regime, presenting every kind of irregularity of flow. **1957** *New Scientist* 26 Dec. 30/3 The regime theory of canals was originally developed in India.. and stemmed from field observations of the self-adjusting character of these artificial alluvial canals. *Ibid.*, From the regime viewpoint the behaviour of a river is visualised as fluctuation about equilibrium or 'regime' dimensions. **1965** A. Holmes *Princ. Physical Geol.* (ed. 2) xviii. 543 The whole régime of sandbanks and inner channels eventually reaches an all-over width that meets the requirements of all but the very greatest floods.

b. The condition of a body of water with regard to the rates at which water enters and leaves it.

1874 *Chem. News* 27 Feb. 101/2 (*heading*) Pluvial régime of the torrid zone in the basin of the Atlantic Ocean. **1933** *Geogr. Jrnl.* LXXXII. 174 While some writers have thought the régime of the lake (the balance between gains and losses) to depend almost entirely on the precipitation on and evaporation from the lake-surface, Mr. Gillman finds that the mean inflow from tributary basins is by no means negligible. *Ibid.*, Theeuws held that the old régime of the lake was changed once and for all by the *débâcle* of about 1875.

4. The set of conditions under which a system occurs or is maintained.

1890 *Rep. Brit. Assoc. Adv. Sci. 1889* 502 We should expect that, after the change of loads has been frequently repeated so that a cyclic *régime* is established, the wire will, for any value of load between the two extremes, be longer during unloading than during loading. **1920** A. Fage *Airscrews in Theory & Exper.* xii. 176 The study of the working régime of a helicopter. **1942** *Electronic Engin.* XIV. 665/3 It has been found that the duration of this low voltage régime may be increased to..20–30 microseconds by connecting an additional condenser directly between anode and cathode. **1957** J. K. Charlesworth *Quaternary Era* II. xlviii. 1410 Pluvial conditions over vast areas of the world.. were replaced by a régime of desiccation. **1971** *Sci. Amer.* Sept. 118/1 Without altering the horticultural regime of keeping 90 percent of the land fallow the Tsembaga's 1,000 best acres might have supported a population of 200 or more per square mile. **1978** *Nature* 29 June 752/1 Anemones were..maintained in circulating seawater at 10 °C for 6 months before experimentation in a 12-h light and 12-h darkness regime.

regimen. Add: **5.** *Physical Geogr.* = *régime, regime 3 a.

1810 *Encycl. Brit.* XVIII. 65/1 We shall..learn the mutual action of the current and its bed, and the circumstances which ensure the stability of both. These we may call the regimen or the conservation of the stream, and may say that it is in regimen or in conservation. **1851** *Min. Proc. Inst. Civil Engineers* X. 231 Experiments and observations were made on the velocity and regimen of the stream. **1966** *McGraw-Hill Encycl. Sci. & Technol.* XI. 584/2 Most natural streams are in regimen. **1971** R. F. Flint *Glacial & Quaternary Geol.* iii. 47 It will be useful to follow the practice of engineers in reference to streams of water, and refer to the system or activity of the glacier as a whole, based on its meteorology, economy, rate and possible type of flow, and fluctuation, as the regimen of the glacier. The term, applied to glaciers as well as streams, is not quantitatively precise; it is broadly descriptive.

regimental, *a.* Add: **1.** (Earlier example.)

1659 J. Jones *Let.* 1 Dec. in J. Mayer *Inedited Lett. Cromwell & Other Regicides* (1861) 112 But crosse windes stayed the messenger at the water side till saturday last, soe that the tyme of meeteing at whitehall is come upon us before wee canne have any regimental meetings of o[u]r offic[e]rs.

2. *Mil. slang.* Maintaining or observing strict discipline.

1919 *Athenæum* 1 Aug. 695/1 *Regimental*, an Old Army adjective for a strict disciplinarian. **1948** Partridge *Dict. Forces' Slang* 154 *Regimental*... As an adjective, applied to an officer or N.C.O. who was a stickler for details. 'So-and-so's too regimental for words.'

regimentation. Add: (Later examples.) Also with ref. to a whole society.

1936 *Sun* (Baltimore) 6 July 8/4 Let us..take the word 'regimentation'.. One dictionary has its meaning as 'enforced socialism'. **1937** *Liberty* 10 July 4/2 The same sort of regimentation that we find in Russia. **1943** J. S. Huxley *TVA* i. 7 The possibility of obtaining the efficiency of a coordinated plan without totalitarian regimentation. **1958** A. Huxley *Let.* 15 Feb. (1969) 845 Uniformity and tidiness..are so admirable in a work of art or a scientific theory but..in human life spell regimentation.

Regina (rĭdʒəi·nă). [L. *rēgina.*] A queen; used to designate the prosecution in criminal proceedings during the reign of a queen, as in law reports.

1717 W. Salkeld *Rep. Cases adjudg'd in Court of King's Bench* I. 460 Domina Regina *versus* Wigg. **1792** W. Boscawen *Treat. on Convictions on Penal Statutes* 36 In the earliest case, indeed, upon the statute of 5 An. viz. *Regina* v. *Matthews*, the Court seem to have thought otherwise. **1976** *Law Rep. Queen's Bench Division* 372 Regina v. Kellett.

region. Add: **5. b.** A relatively large subdivision of a country for economic, administrative, or cultural purposes that freq. implies an alternative system to centralized organization; *spec.* one of the nine local government areas into which the mainland of Scotland has been divided since 1975, when the former system of counties was abolished. *Standard (administrative) region*: one of the eight (formerly nine) areas into which England is divided for industrial planning, demographic surveying, etc.

1921 G. D. H. Cole *Future of Local Govt.* ii. 15 What is really needed is..a systematic scheme of development including both towns and rural areas over the whole of a wide Region. **1933** H. Finer *Eng. Local Govt.* vii. 160 The largest area of government..which would comprehend the main large-scale services, to be managed or regulated by a Council popularly elected for the whole of the Region. **1950** Ormrod & Walker *Butterworth's Annotated Legislation Service: Statutes Suppl. No. 63* I. 10 England and Wales are divided into fourteen hospital regions, each administered by a Regional Hospital Board. Each region is based on a town in which there is a University Medical School. **1958** *Britain: Official Handbk. 1959* (H.M.S.O.) i. 14 Table 2 shows the distribution of the population by urban and rural districts and the populations of the standard administrative regions, of the seven major conurbations and of 16 large cities. **1959** W. Isard et al. *Industrial Complex Anal.* i. 6 Until the 'ultimate' is achieved in social science theory, analysts must be content with sets of regions—or hierarchies of sets of regions—which tend to differ from problem to problem. **1966** *Census 1961: Occupation Tables* p. xix, (*heading*) Areas for which statistics are given. Standard Regions. The constitution of the Standard Regions of England and Wales used in this volume is as follows. **1973** *Times* 23 May 16/6 The Government were confident of their ability to continue giving the regions the assistance they needed. **1973** *Act 21 & 22 Eliz. II.* c. 65 § 1 Scotland (other than Orkney, Shetland and the Western Isles) shall be divided into local government areas to be known as regions. **1976** *Scottish Daily Express* 23 Dec. 6/6 Even in booming Aberdeen and the thriving Grampian Region there are troubles between the two councils.

c. An area of the world made up of neighbouring countries that, from an international point of view, are considered socially, economically, or politically interdependent.

1925 W. S. Culbertson *Internat. Econ. Policies* App. ix. 549 Regional or world conferences..to establish in regions, or with respect to subjects in the agenda, 'a workable basis of coöperation among the nations of the earth'. **1948** G. A. Johnson in K. M. Panikkar et al. *Regionalism & Security* 45 There are..yet few who would..divide the world into regions, each a federation. **1959** W. Isard et al. *Industrial Complex Anal.* i. 5 For a long time economists, geographers, sociologists, political scientists, city and regional planners, and other social scientists have been concerned with the concept of 'region'. **1970** Cantori & Spiegel *Internat. Politics of Regions* i. 1 We will consider regions to be areas of the world which contain geographically proximate states forming, in foreign affairs, mutually interrelated units. **1977** M. Hudson *Global Fracture* xiii. 167 Regional consolidation is occurring within five broad geopolitical blocs... Each of these regions is characterized by a broad range of complementary products.

d. *Broadcasting.* A part of the country covered by a particular programme service or broadcasting company; *transf.*, the company itself.

1929 *Radio Times* 8 Nov. 442/1 The Northern Region—Manchester 22Y 797 kc/s. (376·4 m.) **1949** *Ibid.* 15 July 12/4 In Other Regions—Midland (296·2 m)..North (449·1 m), [etc.]. **1956** *B.B.C. Handbk. 1957* 124 The expansion of television resources in the Regions. **1968** *Listener* 25 July 123/2 This was a good effort by a small ITV region—Anglia—and the old companies of ITV have been putting on quite a brave show. **1974** *B.B.C. Handbk. 1975* 56/2 The Manchester site will eventually accommodate network production centre, television region and local radio station.

6. c. Phr. *in the region of*: round about, approximately.

1966 'A. Hall' *9th Directive* x. 97 The breech-pressure is in the region of 20 tons p.s.i. **1972** *Country Life* 5 Oct. (Suppl.) 7/2 Delightful house... Offers in the region of £40,000. **1979** *Solihull News* 26 May (Classified Section) 24/1 (Advt.), A superb and spacious centrally heated residence... Price: offers in the region of: £29,500.

8. (In sense *5 b) *region-planning.*

1921 G. D. H. Cole *Future of Local Govt.* ii. 14 What is really needed is plainly not mere town-planning, but region-planning. **1931** W. A. Robson *Devel. of Local Govt.* I. ii. 143 Similar problems are presented in connection with other fundamental region-planning requirements.

regional, *a.* Add: **1. b.** Geol. *regional metamorphism* [tr. F. *métamorphisme régional* (G. A. Daubrée *Études et Expériences Synthetiques sur le Métamorphisme* (1860) II. ii. 59)]: metamorphism affecting rocks over an extensive area as a result of the large-scale action of heat and pressure.

[**1859** T. S. Hunt in *Q. Jrnl. Geol. Soc.* XV. 489 We must commence by distinguishing between the local metamorphism which sometimes appears in the vicinity of traps and granites and that normal metamorphism which extends over wide areas and is apparently unconnected with the presence of intrusive rocks.] **1871** —— in *Amer. Naturalist* V. 494 The problem to be solved in regional metamorphism is the conversion of sedimentary strata..into aggregations of crystalline silicates. **1937** Wooldridge & Morgan *Physical Basis Geogr.* x. 133 Much more important are the great masses of metamorphic rock which have resulted from what is often called regional metamorphism, *i.e.* deep burial of rock masses..due to earth-movement. **1971** I. G. Gass et al. *Understanding Earth* i. 35/1 Regional metamorphism is accompanied by more or less intense deformation.

c. Of, pertaining to, or connected with a region (esp. in senses *5 b and c). So *regional board, planning*, etc.

1921 G. D. H. Cole *Future of Local Govt.* ii. 15 There is an overwhelming case, from the standpoint of public convenience and efficiency of service, for the regional planning of publicly owned road transport services. **1927** *Rep. Comm. Publ. Libraries Eng. & Wales* 151 in *Parl. Papers* (*Cmd. 2868*) XII. 231 Our conclusion is that a national system should be built up on..the grouping of public libraries round regional centres, which will generally be the great urban libraries. **1933** H. Finer *Eng. Local Govt.* vii. 164 If the regional solution were adopted it would..furnish an area large enough to include most of those services for which a large area has been found necessary. **1941** *Economist* 18 Jan. 68/2 Lord Nuffield..envisaged regional boards throughout the country which would co-ordinate hospital finance and policy. **1943** in J. S. Huxley *TVA* 5 The Tennessee Valley Authority initiated regional planning on a scale never before attempted in history. **1956** G. N. Flemming *Organisation of Technical Coll.* 1 There are at present three main types of technical college,..described in this circular as local, area and regional colleges. **1957** G. L. Goodwin *Brit. & United Nations* 459 The prospects of world peace will turn not on the United Nations but on the effectiveness of global and regional balances of power. **1959** W. Isard et al. *Industrial Complex Anal.* i. 6 The concept of regional structure has come to be relativistic. **1962** *Lancet* 27 Jan. 219/2 The unit would be organised on regional-board level. **1965** Haas & Schmitter *Polit. of Econ. in Lat. Amer. Regionalism* i. 1 One of the first prolonged attempts at regional economic integration between independent developing countries. **1969** *Times* 3 Feb. 10/8 Farming is not a subject which often enters the realm of regional planning. **1972** W. Isard et al. *Ecologic-Economic Anal. for Regional Development* p. xv, We constantly assert that no longer can regional development and regional planning be treated in their traditionally narrow contexts. **1976** C. A. Smith *Regional Anal.* I. p. xi, Careful field studies of markets and regional economics.. would have identified regional patterns not predicted by central-place theory..thereby stimulating the development of new regional system theories. **1977** M. Hudson *Global Fracture* xiv. 178 The currency-debt of a nation or regional grouping of nations not politically associated with the creditor central bank. **1978** *Dumfries Courier* 13 Oct. 2/6 The modernisation project at Templand had been praised by the Regional Planning Committee.

d. Of or pertaining to a broadcasting region (sense *5 d). Also, designating a B.B.C. radio service which operated during the 1930s.

1929 *Radio Times* 8 Nov. 403/3, 2BE *Belfast*..9.0 Regional News. **1930** *B.B.C. Year-bk.* 30 The Regional Stations of Daventry, London, and Manchester will cover about 75 per cent. of the population. **1962** *Rep. Comm. Broadc. 1960* 157 The four major companies having been appointed [by the ITA], this consideration prompted the appointment of the relatively large number of relatively small 'regional' companies. *Ibid.* 221 The present sound programmes of the BBC are..basically national programmes. Within them, regional programmes are accommodated. **1965** [see *national *a.* 1 d]. **1968** *Writing for BBC* (ed. 2) 12 A particularly worth-while opportunity for would-be contributors exists in the Regional editions of programmes.

B. *sb.* **1.** A B.B.C. radio service which operated during the 1930s.

1936 J. Reith *Diary* 20 Jan. (1975) iii. 185 We got it [*sc.* a statement] out at 9.38 as we had to collect all the Regionals and Empire. **1938, 1971** [see *national *a.* 1 d]. **1978** *Broadcast* 27 Feb. 4/2 A balance between the majors and regionals has emerged.

2. The part of a gravity anomaly or magnetic anomaly that is due to deep features and varies only gradually from place to place.

1940 L. L. Nettleton *Geophys. Prospecting for Oil* xii. 222 If this regional is properly estimated and removed,..the local features will show up in their proper form and relief. **1954** *Geophysics* XIX. 1 The problem of regionals and residuals arises in all geophysical methods which are based on measurement of a 'potential' field. **1967** *Bull. Amer. Assoc. Petroleum Geologists* LI. 2388/1 The 13th-order regional fits closely the observed data.

3. In general use, *ellipt.* for *regional* (*stock*) *exchange, newspaper, stamp*, etc.

1958 *Gibbons Stamp Monthly* 1 Sept. 2/3 Pictorials can be captioned—to most people these Regionals will be confusingly anonymous. **1965** *Time* 3 Sept. 58 Because of this growth..the cost of seats on the regionals has been rising steadily. **1969** *Times* 5 May (Wall Street Suppl.) p. v/7 Many of the regionals even encouraged institutional, or mutual fund, business...The major brokerage houses handling institutional transactions could thus buy a relatively inexpensive seat on a regional exchange. **1971** D. Potter *Brit. Eliz. Stamps* iv. 59 Jersey and Guernsey stamps were withdrawn on 1 October 1969, and the two islands issued their own stamps. But the regionals remained valid for postage elsewhere in the United Kingdom. **1974** *State* (Columbia, S. Carolina) 27 Feb. 3-B/4 The South Atlantic regional at Norfolk, Va. **1975** B. GUNSTON *Philatelist's Companion* 247 *Regional*, a stamp issued for use in only part of the territory under the authority of a postal administration (eg Scotland, in the case of the UK). **1975** *Times* 13 Aug. 12/1 While national newspaper managements were still thinking in the fifties of hot metal.. modernization ran across Britain and the regionals profited.

regionalism. Add: **1.** (Further examples.) Also, on a national or international scale: the theory or practice of regional rather than central systems of administration, or of economic, cultural, or political affiliation; the study of such phenomena as they relate to geographic factors.

1919 GEDDES & BRANDFORD in C. B. Fawcett *Provinces of England* p. ii, 'Regionalism' was, indeed, first a French word: and this not merely in geography, but also in politics, and long before the war. From Brittany to Provence its studies have been long preparing. **1923** G. M. TREVELYAN *Manin & Venetian Revolution* xiv. 244 He abandoned his Republican faith and his Venetian 'regionalism' in view of the new circumstances of Italy. **1931** E. C. MOWER *Internat. Govt.* v. 89 Regionalism, it is claimed, is justified both from the defensive value of natural frontiers and on sound economic principles, having regard to the needs of modern industrial life. **1934** *Encycl. Soc. Sci.* XIII. 208/2 Regionalism has been called a manifestation of 'world federalism' and an intermediate stage between administrative decentralization and federalism. **1936** *Columbia Univ. Quart.* Mar. 268 Regionalism can..be defined as the study of the relation of man to geographic areas, and the potentialities which this relation presents in terms of human welfare and progress. **1948** G. A. JOHNSON in K. M. Panikkar *Regionalism & Security* 45 Of these claims on behalf of regionalism the United Nations Charter is concerned directly with only one. **1959** A. H. ROBERTSON *Europ. Institutions* i. 4 As the idea of universalism waned,..that of regionalism developed. **1962** L. GOLDING *Dict. Local Govt.* 332 When War broke out in 1939 regionalism was applied in practice by dividing the country for purposes of civil defence and the administration of other emergency services into twelve large areas, each of which was placed in the charge of a Commissioner. **1965** HAAS & SCHMITTER (*title*) The politics of economics in Latin American regionalism. **1970** CANTORI & SPIEGEL *Internat. Polit. of Regions* i. 1 Sometimes 'regionalism' has been studied exclusively in terms of regional organization. **1977** M. HUDSON *Global Frontiers* xv. 195 (*heading*) The new regionalism.

2. A regional word, phrase, or peculiarity of pronunciation which is not part of the standard language of a country; regional distinctiveness in literature.

1953 S. A. BROWN in A. Dundes *Mother Wit* (1973) 40/1 We go then to what is called the New Negro Movement, then to Regionalism. **1954** F. G. CASSIDY *S. Robertson's Development Mod. English* v. 126 The third [sc. *you-all*] is a regionalism. **1955** *Times* 7 May 9/4 The regionalism of American writing falls into place beside that of Scotland or Ireland. **1964** *Language* XL. 93 Intellectual leaders of the Seicento..did not hesitate to use, as nonce-forms, regionalisms like *parapaglia* 'butterfly' (based on Bolognese *parpaja*..) and *sfragaro* 'wastrel' (Calabrese-Sicilian). **1974** R. A. HALL *External Hist. Romance Lang.* 216 Some lexical regionalisms have been inevitable in films made in, say, Mexico or Argentina. **1978** *Amer. Speech* LIII. 13 The layman applies the term imprecisely to a large body of lexemes including true slang, jargon, regionalisms, and colloquialisms, which are vaguely perceived as slang by such groups as college students.

regionalist. Add: Further examples with reference to geographical, administrative, or international regionalism. Also *attrib.*

1919 GEDDES & BRANFORD in C. B. Fawcett *Provinces of Eng.* p. iii, The most discerning..regionalists of to-day are also among the most appreciative of truly comprehensive politics. **1925** L. MUMFORD in *Survey* 15 Apr. 151/1 The regionalist attempts to plan such an area so that all its sights and resources..may be soundly developed. **1934** *Encycl. Soc. Sci.* XIII. 216/1 There was a revival of regionalist feeling in Italy after the World War. **1937** F. BORKENAU *Spanish Cockpit* i. 59 The Basque provinces, naturally, voted for the Basque regionalists. **1941** J. MASEFIELD *In Mill* 112 The Regionalist novel-writers. **1944** A. BRECHT in *Regionalism & World Organization* 11 The universalists want a world-wide organization; the major-regionalists recommend federations of continental scope; the minor-regionalists propose federal groupings of smaller countries; and the ideological unionists advocate a confederation of democracies or a league of the United Nations. **1977** *Economist* 23 Apr. 56/1 The three major regionalist parties [in Belgium]—the Walloon Rally, the Volksunie and the Francophone Front. **1977** G. P. ATKINS *Lat. Amer. in Internat. Polit. System* i. 9 Regionalists were primarily concerned with security arrangements for and keeping the peace in delineated geographical areas.

regionality (rīdʒənæ·liti). [f. REGIONAL *a.* + -ITY.] Nature or character connected with or pertaining to a region.

1961 in WEBSTER. **1966** *New Statesman* 8 Apr. 510/1 The zone of time-space that middle-class western man mostly inhabits is the continuous present of the Western World: the particularities of the particular place he happens to live in are often little more than a backdrop to home and work and leisure—unless he's feeling jolly, when he is sometimes prepared to wear his regionality as a mask or humour. **1976** *Amer. Speech 1973* XLVIII. 282 For obvious reasons, the concept of 'regionality' in regard to language is a preoccupation of the editors of the *Dictionary of American Regional English.* **1979** *Dictionaries* I. 27 Many of the statements about regionality are qualified in some way.

regionaliza·tion. [f. REGIONAL *a.* + -IZATION.] The action of adapting economic, political, social, or cultural organization to a geographical or administrative region.

1920 A. R. ORAGE in C. H. Douglas *Credit Power & Democracy* 152 The suggested regionalisation of the administration of the industry may be regarded as acceptable to the Miners' Federation. **1930** *Aberdeen Press & Jrnl.* 3 Nov. 5/6 We have just completed..what might be called the first try-out of programme regionalisation. **1938** ODUM & MOORE *Amer. Regionalism* I. ix. 216 The present regionalization of the country. **1952** *Property Owners' Jrnl.* Jan. 10/2 The other major factor is..regionalisation. Bricks are expensive things to carry... Consequently, brick houses must be built as near the brick-fields as possible. **1963** *Times* 23 Apr. 13/3 The fashion for regionalization is strengthening in Britain today. **1970** *Nature* 26 Dec. 1250/2 In regions..which have urban populations large enough for regionalization of intake to be a real possibility, less than half the students accepted in 1969 came from the region in which the universities are situated. **1975** *Church Times* 18 July 12/3 It may be believed that SCM is committing itself to increased regionalisation and student work from within. **1978** *Nature* 2 Feb. 403/2 The development of the adult fly involves first the regionalisation of the embryo into a number of territories.

regionalize (rī·dʒənăləiz), *v.* [f. REGIONAL *a.* + -IZE.] *trans.* To bring under the control of a region for administrative purposes; to divide into regions; to organize on a regional basis. So **re·gionalized** *ppl. a.*, **regionali·zing** *vbl. sb.*

1921 G. D. H. COLE *Future of Local Govt.* xii. 112 May it not be possible to escape the disadvantages of central ownership and control by regionalizing instead of nationalizing many industries and services. **1938** ODUM & MOORE *Amer. Regionalism* I. viii. 188 We have 'regionalized' our nation and subregionalized and districted our states. **1962** *Times* 23 Jan. 4/2 The draw for the second round of the F.A. Amateur Cup—to be played on February 3 and no longer regionalized. **1962** *Daily Tel.* 8 May 1/7 Miners' M.P.s repeatedly voiced suspicion that Lord Robens's real intention ..is to 'regionalise' the coal industry by creating autonomous boards in Scotland, Lancashire and elsewhere. **1972** *Times of India* 28 Nov. 1/2 Various service cadres will be regionalised. **1978** *Jrnl. R. Soc. Arts* CXXVI. 218/1 It costs just as much to broadcast to half a million people as to broadcast to fifty million, so that the more you regionalize your output the more expensive it becomes. **1978** *Radio Times* 11–17 Mar. 15/4 In future years Ceefax will offer regionalized news.

regionally, *adv.* (In Dict. s.v. REGIONAL *a.*) (Later examples.)

1886 *Science* 10 Sept. 233/2 The preservation of rock-oils in every formation, of every geological age, all over the world; subject, however, locally or regionally, to subsequent change or destruction. **1962** *Rep. Comm. Broadc. 1960* 151 We have examined the BBC on its allocation of money between its sound and television services, both nationally and regionally. **1974** *Nature* 1 Nov. 28/1 Viewed regionally, the area of greatest regressive tendency within the depositional regime can be identified as the central and northern North Sea.

‖ **regisseur** (reʒisǭr). *Theatr.* and *Ballet.* [Fr.] A stage manager or artistic director. Also *transf.* in *Cinemat.*

1828 J. EBERS *Seven Yrs. of King's Theatre* ii. 58 He had been a kind of manager of the Opera at Bologna, and subsequently Regisseur of the Théâtre Italien at Paris. **1925** *Daily Herald* 20 May 9/3 The three main streams of the revolutionary theatre..derive from the three *regisseurs.* **1935** A. REVUSKY *Jews in Palestine* x. 173 Piscator, the leading theatrical regisseur of Germany. **1949** *Ballet Ann.* III. 27 *Prince Igor*, revised by that experienced and excellent *régisseur*, Nicolas Beriosoff. **1954** 'E. Box' *Death in Fifth Position* i. 10, I was introduced to..the *regisseur* or director of the [ballet] company. **1965** *New Statesman* 16 Apr. 621/2 Shaw, Chekhov and Brecht wrote for a producers' theatre, intervening when necessary as their own *régisseurs* to bully their actors into subordination to their texts. **1968** *Listener* 14 Mar. 357/1 Zeffirelli is a *régisseur* in the grand 19th-century naturalistic manner. **1977** *New Yorker* 16 May 79/3 Serge Grigoriev, who was Diaghilev's regisseur, restaged it for the Royal Ballet.

register, *sb.*[1] Add: **I. 1. a.** Also, a record of attendance at a school.

1887 C. D. WARNER *Their Pilgrimage* (1888) vi. 165 Mr. King discovered by the register that the Bensons had been there. **1888** C. M. YONGE *Our New Mistress* ii. 14 She called over the names... The registers had got into a muddle, and there was no knowing who had left school and who was only absent. *a* **1930** D. H. LAWRENCE *Phoenix II* (1968) 22 One day my bread-stealer arrived at half past two, when the register was closed. **1955** E. BLISHEN *Roaring Boys* iv. 183, I called the register... The ginger-haired boy answered to the name of Grange. **1961** M. SPARK *Prime of Miss Jean Brodie* iii. 59, I must mark the register for today before we forget. There are two new girls. **1978** R. MILLS *Comprehensive Educ.* 44 His lessons..began with the calling of the register.

c. A person's face, regarded as an indication of feeling or emotion. *slang.*

1899 'J. FLYNT' *Tramping with Tramps* II. iv. 271, I hain't seen your register for many a day.

5. b. A quantity recorded or registered.

1904 T. HOLDICH *India* xii. 351 At this point the rainfall is extraordinary, 50 or 60 feet being a not unusual register at Cherra Punji on the edge of the plateau.

II. 8. c. *Art.* One of a number of bands or sections into which a design is divided.

1937 *Discovery* Sept. 287/1 As a rule these plant designs [on Jhukar pottery] were painted in black, or a deep purple, the red being used for the broad bands separating the registers. **1966** RONIGER & DUNN tr. *Lazarev's Old Russ. Murals & Mosaics* i. 39 In the middle register of the apse is the great monumental composition of the *Eucharist.* **1977** *Times Lit. Suppl.* 4 Feb. 137/3 The outside [of a conical drinking-horn] is decorated in paint or in enamel. There are two upper registers with scenes of animals and hunters. **1980** *Catal. Fine Chinese Ceramics* (Sotheby, Hong Kong) 222 Two groups of nine bosses arranged in three registers within rectangular enclosures, the registers alternating with bands of repeated curlicues.

d. *Linguistics.* A variety of a language or a level of usage, *spec.* one regarded in terms of degree of formality and choice of vocabulary, pronunciation, and (when written) punctuation, and related to or determined by the social role of the user and appropriate to a particular need or context.

1956 T. B. W. REID in *Archivum Linguisticum* VIII. 32 He will on different occasions speak (or write) differently according to what may roughly be described as different social situations: he will use a number of distinct 'registers'. **1962** *Canadian Jrnl. Linguistics* VII. 69 Interference may also vary according to the social role of the speaker in any given case. This is what the Edinburgh School has called *register.* **1966** G. N. LEECH *Eng. in Advertising* vii. 68 Varieties of English distinguished by use in relation to social context are called *registers.* **1971** P. YOUNG in J. Spencer *Eng. Lang. W. Afr.* 173 A novel, then, can be seen as an amalgam of registers within a wider register of literary endeavour. **1972** *N. & Q.* Dec. 446/2 Chaucer must therefore have used what was, for the London of his time, a more formal, possibly more archaic, register. **1977** P. STREVENS *New Orientations Teaching of Eng.* x. 119 They are aware..of the idea of 'varieties' of English, and they probably know the term 'register'—a variety related to a particular use of the language, a particular subject or occupation.

e. *Phonetics.* A type of phonation, essentially controlled by the larynx, but distinct from tone, employed contrastively in some languages (e.g. Cambodian).

1964 J. C. CATFORD in D. Abercrombie et al. *Daniel Jones* 34 'Register' differences..are associated with tone-differences in several S.E. Asian languages. **1967** D. ABERCROMBIE *Elem. Gen. Phonetics* 101 In Cambodian, for example, every syllable is spoken with one of two registers, which are mainly distinguished from each other by the position of the larynx in the throat. The same is true of Gujerati spoken in Surat, the difference here being between 'tight' and 'breathy' phonation.

9. a. (Further examples.)

Now used outside the U.S. in the sense 'perforated or open-work plate by which warm air is admitted'.

1920 E. FROST *Let.* Mar. in *Lett. R. & E. Frost* (1972) 86, I am writing to you with a pencil generally these days, because I can sit and warm my feet over the register at the same time if I use a pencil. **1950** R. MOORE *Candlemas Bay* II. 86 Two rooms were warmed by hot-air registers through the kitchen ceiling. **1957** V. NABOKOV *Pnin* vi. 145 A cranky-looking oil furnace in the basement did its best to send up its weak warm breath through registers in the floors. **1967** *Gloss. Terms Gas Industry (B.S.I.)* 91 *Register*, a fitment equipped with a damper or movable louvres which permit adjustment or closure. **1970** *Daily Tel.* (Colour Suppl.) 25 Sept. 14 (Advt.), Built-in ducts waft warm air to each room through small, skirting-level registers.

c. *Rope-making.* A disc containing concentric circles of holes through which the component yarns of a strand pass, the rotation of the disc serving to twist them together. Also *register plate.*

1793 J. HUDDART *Brit. Patent 1952* 5 The register is calculated to form the strand into shells of yarns, and therefore they must be made of different sizes. **1846** G. DODD *Brit. Manuf.* VI. 199 The system for attaining any required intensity of twist is called the 'register'. **1855** W. COTTON *Brief Memoir Capt. Joseph Huddart* 20 His great principle (concentric circles) was accomplished by what he called a register plate. **1950** A. E. HAARER *Ropes & Rope-Making* vii. 43 This..is what we call a register plate. Behind it you can see the yarns passing together into a short tube. **1957** D. HIMMELFARB *Technol. of Cordage Fibres & Rope* v. 127 Register plates are generally heavy castings of curved cross section, with holes approximately ½-inch to 1-inch in diameter.

10. b. = *cash register* s.v. *CASH *sb.*[1] 3 a. chiefly *U.S.*

1895 in *Funk's Stand. Dict.* **1911** *Daily Colonist* (Victoria, B.C.) 29 Apr. 13/4 Two robbers..took $160, all the money in the register, and made good their escape. **1976** 'E. McBAIN' *Guns* vii. 148 Colley wishes he could see into the open drawer of the register. **1977** *Transatlantic Rev.* LX. 40 He..then counted the cash in the register.

c. In mechanical calculators, a device in which numbers representing data or the results of arithmetical operations are stored or displayed; in an electronic computer or calculator, a location in store having a small capacity but negligible access time and used for a specific purpose (hence with qualifying sbs., as *address, control, storage register*).

1928 *Monthly Not. R. Astron. Soc.* LXXXVIII. 451 Their principal deficiencies were the absence of tens transmission in the multiplier register,..and the excessive labour of zeroising or clearing the registers. **1946** *Math. Tables & Other Aids to Computation* II. 151 The Brunsviga Dupla.. had two product registers..and had red and white figures as in the multiplier register. **1947** *Proc. I.R.E.* Aug. 759/1 The counter advances one stage on receiving a pulse, and hence is an adder as well as a register. **1956** [see *ADDRESS *sb.* 7 c]. **1959** *Commun. Assoc. Computing Machinery* Oct. 3/2 Besides the internal memory, the arithmetic unit has four fast access cells. In these cells, the words are stored in dynamic form, in registers. **1964** F. L. WESTWATER *Electronic Computers* i. 13 This number, when placed in a special register called the control register, will cause the machine to obey the instruction. **1973** *Sci. Amer.* Aug. 102/2 (Advt.), In addition to its computer-like operational stack, the HP-35 has a constant storage register which lets you store any number and recall it as often as you want for repeat operations, without ever having to re-enter it. **1977** *Ibid.* Sept. 86/3 In microprocessors registers are employed for the temporary storage of data, of partial results, of instructions and of the addresses where other data or instructions are to be found.

11. b. (Further examples.) More widely, exact coincidence of position of superimposed images, esp. in colour printing; so *in, out of register*. Also *transf.*

1683–4 J. MOXON *Mech. Exerc. Printing* (1962) 348 Out of register, bad register. **1771** P. LUCKOMBE *Hist. & Art of Printing* 500 *Out of register*, when pages are not worked even on each other. **1907** [see *DUOTONE]. **1915** [see *PRINT *v.* 14a]. **1947** *Electronics* Jan. 75/2 Color fringing..is also not present in the simultaneous system [of colour television], but a similar effect due to lack of register among the three simultaneous images may be present. **1950** *Proc. R. Soc.* A. CCI. 189 It [*sc.* a diffraction grating] is then cut in half, perpendicular to the rulings, and the two halves are put together face to face in register. **1966** H. WILLIAMSON *Methods Bk. Design* (ed. 2) xxii. 366 Colour printing usually costs more per colour than does black printing because of the laborious work of getting and maintaining register. **1967** V. STRAUSS *Printing Industry* xi. 735/2 Printers distinguish several kinds of register, depending on the intricacy of a job. No-register means that the several color areas are completely independent of each other, loose register that minor variations in their relations are inconsequential; tight, close, or hairline register indicates that these relations must be quite exact. **1975** J. B. HARLEY *O.S. Maps* ix. 138 Road casings were omitted..to assist with colour register when printing. **1975** *Nature* 25 Sept. 331/2 It is a rod-shaped, coiled-coil molecule, about 410 Å long, composed of two parallel α-helical chains which are in register. **1978** *Amat. Photogr.* 11 Jan. 69/2 A bas relief is made by printing through a negative and a positive, sandwiched together slightly out of register.

12. (sense 1) *register clerk*; **register board**, a flat surface with pegs or guides such that sheets of paper or film placed on it may be brought into the same relative position; **register mark** *Printing* (see quots.).

1967 KARCH & BUBER *Offset Processes* viii. 331 The register board..performs a very important part in obtaining accurate registration by providing a mechanism to jog each sheet into exactly the same position for entry into the head of the press. **1977** J. HEDGECOE *Photographer's Handbk.* 245 (*caption*) Take a negative 2¼ ins sq..and attach it to a strip of film which has been punched to fit the register board. **1887** C. D. WARNER *Their Pilgrimage* (1888) iii. 63 The register clerk stood fingering the leaves of the register with a gracious air. **1927** H. HUBBARD *Colour Block Print Making* 208 *Register marks*, in colour printing, marks for controlling the position of the paper in printing to ensure register. **1937** *Discovery* Oct. 300/2 Register marks are drawn on the stones just off the edge of the design. These the printer uses for placing the paper in exactly the right place on the stones used in subsequent printings. **1971** D. POTTER *Brit. Eliz. Stamps* xv. 174 Autotron marks, long bars, provide the electronic check for colour registration. Register marks..serve a similar purpose.

register, *sb.*[2] (Later examples in official titles.)

1948 *Daily Progress* (Charlottesville, Va.) 7 Apr. 13/7 He is the Register of Wills. That's what the state constitution calls him. **1972** *Publishers' Weekly* 21 Aug. 58/1 Now Acting Register of Copyrights on leave to UNESCO, Miss Ringer has been opposing appointment of George D. Cary as Register.

register, *v.* Add: **1. a.** (Later *fig.* examples.)

1891 'L. MALET' *Wages of Sin* I. iii. 53 He was always thinking, doing, feeling, experiencing something... Always registering impressions, making observations. **1946** D. C. PEATTIE *Road of Naturalist* iv. 49 All I could do was.. register on the one hand my sympathy with Abie and, on the other, the isolation of my own interests. **1955** W. HEISENBERG in W. Pauli *Niels Bohr* 22 The observer has.. only the function of registering decisions. **1972** *Daily Tel.* 31 Jan. 7 Those responsible for the television serialisation of Heinrich Mann's *Man of Straw*..worked hard to register the idea that the novel..prophesied the rise of the Nazis.

2. a. (Later *absol.* example.)

1930 N. R. STEPHENSON *Nelson W. Aldrich* iii. 48 The Senate passed the bill, Aldrich and Platt registering against it.

c. *trans.* and (now chiefly) *intr.* (for *refl.*) To enter the name of (a guest or visitor) in the register of a hotel or guest-house; to enter one's name in such a register. orig. *U.S.*

1848 *Lit. Amer.* 14 Oct. 237/1 Sixty miles down the Monongahela brought us to Pittsburgh, and about half past 7 P.M., I was registered at the 'Monongahela House'. **1850** M. REID *Rifle Rangers* I. v. 52 Take your supper, engage a snug room, and wait for me. Don't register till I come—I'll attend to that. **1891** 'MARK TWAIN' in *Harper's New Monthly Mag.* Dec. 96/2, I arrived in Washington, registered at the Arlington Hotel, and went to my room. **1905** A. BENNETT *Tales of Five Towns* II. 264 'You haven't registered,' Nina called to him... He advanced to sign. **1922** H. TITUS *Timber* xv. 136 She..stopped her car at the Commercial Hotel where she registered and was given a room. **1936** G. B. SHAW *Millionairess* IV. 187 You have allowed my husband to bring a woman to my hotel and register her in my name. **1967** BEAVIS & MEDLIK *Man. Hotel Reception* ii. 12 The receptionist should hand the pen to the guest when asking him to register. **1977** *Rolling Stone* 30 June 81/1 We then registered at the Airport Inn.

d. *intr.* (for *refl.*) To enter oneself or have one's name recorded in a list of people (freq. as a legal requirement), as being of a specified category or having a particular eligibility or entitlement.

1940 *Economist* 26 Oct. 521/2 Special delivery certificates have been issued for householders who must register with a single coal merchant. **1941** M. B. LOWNDES *Diary* 7 Nov. (1971) 225, I registered for my rations, sugar, bacon, butter, etc. at Fortnum's, where quality is *excellent*. **1952** B. PYM *Excellent Women* xxvi. 243, I told them of a laundry, a grocer and a butcher where they might register. **1965** *Listener* 10 June 875/3 To intimidate Negroes who might be tempted to register as voters. **1973** 'B. MATHER' *Snowline* vii. 85, I tried to get him to register..as an addict. You get a scrip to buy the damned stuff on prescription. **1975** S. BRIGGS *Keep smiling Through* 149/2 You could even..choose where to shop without being tied to the grocer where you were registered for basic rations. **1976** *Southern Even. Echo* (Southampton) 13 Nov. 8/4 The next day he registered as unemployed. **1977** *Time* 17 Jan. 24/2 This presumably would include all those civilians who fled the country to avoid the draft, simply failed to register or refused to submit to induction.

3. b. Of a person: to indicate or express (a particular feeling or emotion), esp. by facial expression.

1901 'L. MALET' *Hist. Sir R. Calmady* VI. viii. 568 The brightness died out of Honoria's face. She registered sharp annoyance against herself. **1915** WODEHOUSE *Something Fresh* iii. 56 A stage-director of a moving-picture firm would have recognized the look; Lord Emsworth was 'registering' interest. **1925** A. P. HERBERT *Laughing Ann* 32 For I don't have no adventure in the street, Men don't register emotion when we meet. **1977** *Private Eye* 29 Apr. 3/3 On being told, her face registered shock and horror.

c. *intr.* Of a person (orig. and esp. a film actor): to portray a particular role with conviction. Also of the ideas or feelings concerned: to communicate themselves successfully, to be convincing. Hence *gen.* of feelings, thoughts, utterances, etc.: to produce the desired effect, to make an appropriate impression on the person intended. Freq. const. (*up*)*on, with.*

1913 ESENWEIN & LEEDS *Writing Photoplay* 24 It is sometimes said that an effect, a bit of business, or an emotion which an actor is endeavoring to portray, 'will not register', meaning that it will not 'get across' or be understood by the audience in the way intended by the producer. **1915** *N.Y. Times* 1 Nov. 11 This new movie star 'registers', as the film folk have it. **1928** *Sunday Dispatch* 16 Dec. 14/4 It looks..as though the producers had not been willing to risk spending money on it in case Miss Eagels did not register well. **1934** H. G. WELLS *Exper. Autobiogr.* II. ix. 704 He never did as he intended or the hint was too feeble to register upon our minds. **1939** *Punch* 6 Sept. 255/1, I give a cough. A significant cough... The cough registers. Deep silence ensues. **1951** N. BALCHIN *Way through Wood* iv. 60 Even that didn't register. You see I didn't know *where* Joe had been knocked down. **1951** M. MCLUHAN *Mech. Bride* (1967) 141/2 The slick-chick and the corporation executive, as they now register on the popular imagination, are already inside the totem machine. **1964** 'A. GILBERT' *Knock, knock, who's There?* i. 14, I couldn't help seeing the name... I looked sharply at Ted, wondering if it was going to register with him. **1966** *Listener* 17 Feb. 253/1 Sixteen-year-old Alexandra can only hope to register with her mother, so she finds out sadly. **1977** *Daily Mirror* 16 Mar. 5/3 With the five-year-old it did not register.

d. *intr.* To appear or produce a response on a recording or measuring instrument.

1947 *Math. Tables & Other Aids to Computation* II. 356 When two pure imaginaries are multiplied together a minus sign will register. **1974** *Nature* 6 Sept. 19/1 The ion energies were too small to register.

4. b. (Further example.)

1976 *Physics Bull.* May 200/1 The images of the projected mask and the structure on the silicon wafer are superimposed and alignment is accomplished by registering the two images.

c. *Mil.* To adjust a gun in relation to (its target); to align (artillery) with its target.

1958 *Observer* 9 Feb. 11/4 The American Polaris..will free still further the Western nuclear deterrent from dependence on large static bases..which can be registered in advance. **1958** *Listener* 11 Sept. 386/3 The position had been liberally registered by Russian gunners from the city; hence the cannon balls. **1959** H. MACLENNAN *Watch that ends Night* IV. vii. 166, I had to spend ten hours in that hole with the body, for the machine guns were registered so close to the ground a rat couldn't have escaped.

6. *trans. Rope-making.* To form (a strand) by the use of a register. Cf. *REGISTER *sb.*[1] 9 c. Also *absol.*

1793 J. HUDDART *Brit. Patent 1952* 3 The spindle is turning in, registering the strand. **1800** *Remarks on Patent Registered Cordage* (Huddart & Co.) 3 He has invented a method of manufacturing cordage, whereby every yarn holds a situation in the strand, in which it bears its proportion of the strain of the rope. This is termed registering the strands. **1855** W. COTTON *Brief Memoir Capt. Joseph Huddart* 26 In order to render them impervious to water, it was necessary to register them at a higher angle. **1968** W. TYSON *Rope* I. iii. 10 In 1799 Huddart patented..a means of registering the strands at a short length from the tube and winding up the rope as made, thus preserving a uniformity of twist.

registered, *ppl. a.* Add: **1.** *spec.* of postal items recorded at the point of dispatch and indemnified against loss or damage. Also *ellipt.* as *sb.*

1837 *Act 1 Vict.* c. 34 § 25 All registered Letters shall be delivered to the Post Office, and also be delivered by the Post Office, under all such Regulations in every respect as the Postmaster General shall from Time to Time appoint. **1855** MRS. GASKELL *Let.* 21 July (1966) 359, I am going to send it by registered parcel post. **1864** D. G. ROSSETTI *Let.* 5 Feb. (1965) II. 498 It shall..fly in a registered letter to you as soon as may be. **1874** [in Dict.]. **1921** *Daily Colonist* (Victoria, B.C.) 9 Apr. 17/7 Three bandits..last night held up a United States mail truck here and robbed it of three pouches of registered mail. **1930** J. B. PRIESTLEY *Angel Pavement* xi. 553 Don't forget you've got three registereds there; bring me the receipts in the morning. **1946** W. STEVENS *Let.* 12 Nov. (1967) 537 The proofs..are being returned by registered mail today. **1962** *John o' London's* 11 Jan. 27/3 *Postman*..'Ere, I got a registered for yer. **1967** E. RUDINGER *Wills & Probate* ii. 85 He enclosed a short covering letter listing the enclosures, and sent it by registered post. **1976** *New Yorker* 8 Mar. 90/3 She found waiting for her on the kitchen table the mail in response to the registered letters she had sent to the United States senators. **1981** *Guardian* 15 May 4/3 The registered envelopes, posted in Dublin and Waterford, have been handed to police but most people have held on to the money.

2. *Rope-making.* Formed by means of a register. Cf. *REGISTER *sb.*[1] 9 c.

1800 *Remarks on Patent Registered Cordage* (Huddart & Co.) 5 But this loss of proportional strength, increases with the number of internal yarns contained in the first strands, while the registered strands bear a proportional strength to their number of yarns. **1846** G. DODD *Brit. Manuf.* VI. 199 A registered strand, or the strand produced by twisting the yarns together by this machine, is a smooth, uniform piece of cordage, all the yarns twisting round in one direction.

3. *registered nurse*, a nurse who has been entered on an official register. See also *state-registered nurse* s.v. *STATE *sb.* 41 a.

1896 *Brit. Med. Jrnl.* 18 Jan. 158/1 The precedent of the General Medical Council should be followed, and an analogous body created, composed of representatives of the nursing interests, the medical profession, the Privy Council, and the registered nurses. **1903** *Outlook* 14 Mar. 604/1 Such a person shall be given a Regents' certificate of proficiency and be privileged to bear the title of 'Registered Nurse' (R.N.). **1905** *Rep. Sel. Comm. Registration of Nurses* p. iv in *Parl. Papers* VII. 733 No person should be entitled to assume the designation of 'Registered Nurse' whose name is not upon the Register. **1949** *Reader's Digest* June 91/1 They passed with flying colors the examinations for registered nurse. **1976** L. HOCKEY *Women in Nursing* v. 50 After the age of twenty-five years, registered nurses are likely to move into a variety of other designations, mostly probably becoming ward sisters.

register office. Add: *spec.* the office of a registrar of births, marriages, and deaths.

The officially correct form in the U.K. at the present time (1981). Cf. *REGISTRY OFFICE 2.

1893 [in Dict.]. **1954** T. S. ELIOT *Confidential Clerk* III. 121 We'd meant to be married very quietly In a register office. **1976** *Southern Even. Echo* (Southampton) 2 Nov. 6/5 Colours are gradually creeping into the dresses in shades of palest pinks and blue satin ribbon edging, and cream is a favourite for register office weddings. **1980** *Times* 13 Aug. 1/8 Couples [in Russia] intending to get married apply to the local register office.

registrable, *a.* Add: Also **registerable.** (Later examples.)

1918 *Brit. Med. Jrnl.* 31 Aug. 212/2 In speaking of the minimum period, it is to be remembered that that time is only sufficient to gain a registrable qualification. **1960** *Times* 28 Apr. 3/3 (Advt.), Qualifications: Medical qualification registerable in New South Wales. **1962** *Economist* 20 Jan. 246/1 These agreements, which may become registrable. **1971** *Daily Tel.* 1 July 2/6 Places where Jews and Quakers celebrated marriage should become registerable in the interests of inter-religious harmony. **1976** *Sunday Times* (Lagos) 26 Sept. 11/1 At least, in some alert official's estimation, 4,000 registrable voters might just call at the centre. **1977** *Nature* 6 Jan. p. xiv/3 (Advt.), Applicants must have a veterinary qualification which is registerable in the United Kingdom.

registral, *a.* Delete *rare* and add later examples.

1967 E. SALZMAN *20th-Cent. Music* xiv. 173 Tiny, cell-like structures which retain their..identity through every kind of registral, rhythmic, dynamic, and color shift. **1970** *Language Sciences* Oct. 11/1 Rules that change this basic competence into dialect forms, into registral forms. **1980** *Dædalus* Spring 189 The expansion of registral sonority.. and the appoggiatura, G-sharp, strongly stress the arrival of the A.

registrant (re·dʒistrănt). orig. *U.S.* [f. REGISTER *sb.*[1] or *v.* + -ANT[1].] One who registers (in various senses), esp. one who thereby gains a particular entitlement.

1890 in WEBSTER. **1928** *Index Trade-Marks U.S. Patent Office 1927* 5 (*heading*) Alphabetical list of registrants of trade-marks for the year 1927. **1942** *Nation* (N.Y.) 27 Apr. 41 Up to Jan. 1, 1942, the Army rejected 8 per cent of the registrants passed as physically fit by Selective Service. **1955** W. W. DENLINGER *Compl. Boston* 65 The many registrants carrying this name in the studbooks since 1934. **1964** *Economist* 24 Oct. 360/2 The registrants are more likely to be Democrats. **1976** *Century of Trade Marks* (Patent Office) 8/2 The definition specifically includes marks 'proposed to be used'; though the Courts have held that this means that the registrant must have a 'present intention' to use the mark. **1977** E. AMBLER *Send no more Roses* ii. 18 The subject of that particular seminar was of fairly general interest.. and the number of registrants was high. **1979** *Rescue News* Mar. 2/6 The registration fee for the symposium is £4... Registrants will receive the definitive Symposium programme.

registrar. Add: (Also with pronunc. redʒistrā·ɹ.) **1.** *spec.* the title of (*a*) a senior officer with administrative responsibility in certain universities; (*b*) a local official responsible for maintaining an index of births, marriages, and deaths in the area under his authority.

(*a*) **1756** *Reply to Dr. Huddesford's Observations relating to Delegates of Press* 4 A Convocation being appointed to be held in the Theater on the second of July, the Vice-Chancellor gave directions to the Registrar to prepare the forms of nomination. **1797** [in Dict.]. **1870** D. P. CHASE *Registrarship of University* 5 The Registrar has been relieved of a great amount of labour connected with the University accounts. **1900** *Statuta et Decreta Univ. Oxon.* 283 The Registrar of the University shall be elected in Convocation. He..is required to attend..all meetings of the Houses of Congregation and Convocation and of the Congregation of the University,..and generally to perform all duties necessary for carrying on the business of the Houses. **1943** 'B. TRUSCOT' *Redbrick Univ.* iii. 59 After a pause for breath we come to the whole of the University [of Bristol] Council, the Deans of Faculties, the Professors and Professores Emeriti, the Librarian, the Registrar, twenty-nine representatives of Convocation, [etc.]. **1953** K. AMIS *Lucky Jim* i. 16 He'd been passing behind the Registrar's chair.., had stumbled and had knocked the chair aside just as the other man was sitting down. **1975** J. MANN *Captive Audience* i. 10 The crowd of students..far from being calmed by the duplicated communication which the registrar had delivered had become wild and agitated. **1980** *Times* 1 Aug. 15/7 (Advt.), In view of the forthcoming retirement of the present Registrar, applications are invited for the post of Registrar of the University of Wales.

(*b*) **1876** C. M. YONGE *Three Brides* II. xiii. 242 They put up their banns at the Union at Brighton, and were married by the Registrar. **1880** A. TROLLOPE *Duke's Children* II. xxvii. 325 None of your private chaplains... Just the registrar, if there is nothing better. **1892** I. ZANGWILL *Childr. Ghetto* II. I. xxv. 218 Let us be married honestly by a registrar. **1967** *Guardian* 1 Aug. 4/3 The shot-gun marriages tend to take place in the registrar's office under the mistaken impression that the church does not marry pregnant brides.

3. A doctor of a certain grade in a hospital: orig. a junior doctor whose duties included the maintenance of a register of patients; now usu. a senior officer undergoing training as a specialist or consultant. Cf. *RESIDENT *sb.* 3.

1862 *Med. Times & Gaz.* 18 Oct. 411/2 Besides these there are a Resident Medical Officer, or Physician's Assistant..; a Medical and Surgical Registrar at a salary of £25 a year; two House Surgeons. **1894** *Brit. Med. Jrnl.* 10 Nov. 1089/1 Rayner, Herbert E., F.R.C.S.Eng., appointed Surgical Registrar and Anæsthetist to the Hospital for Sick Children, Great Ormond Street. **1937** *Ibid.* 4 Sept. 470/2 Qualified students of the school can obtain appointments as house-physicians and house-surgeons, obstetric assistants, surgical, gynaecological, and medical registrars. **1961** *Lancet* 29 July 264/2 There would seem to be intra-professional divisions in which interests do not quite coincide—e.g., the unplaced registrars and the established consultants. **1965** P. FERRIS *Doctors* iii. 59 What senior registrars want is to be appointed consultants. **1977** *Western Morning News* 30 Aug. 3/3 Some new patients have to wait as long as two to three years before they are seen, because the consultant surgeons spend so much of their time with follow-up cases; these could be handled easily and effectively by registrars. **1980** *Times Lit. Suppl.* 1 Aug. 879/2 In interviews with residents (in Britain, registrars) she found that they expressed strong preference for the middle-class patient.

registrarship. Add: (Also stressed *registra·rship.*) (Further examples, with reference to *REGISTRAR 3.)

1889 *Brit. Med. Jrnl.* 9 Nov. 1077/1 London Hospital,..—Surgical Registrarship. Salary £100 per annum. **1937** *Ibid.* 4 Sept. 467/2 In addition, the following appointments are open to all qualified students of the hospital:..two medical registrarships at £100 per annum. **1963** *Lancet* 12 Jan. 117/2 After he was demobilised in 1946 he held registrarships in Bristol at Southmead Hospital and the Children's Hospital.

registration. Add: **1. b.** Also (occas. without article) *ellipt.*, = **registration number* below.

1973 J. PATTINSON *Search Warrant* vii. 111 A blue Chrysler... It had a New York registration. **1973** 'I. DRUMMOND' *Jaws of Watchdog* xii. 152 His car..was a Ferrari but with British registration. **1976** L. DEIGHTON *Twinkle, twinkle, Little Spy* x. 111 'The same registration!' said Mann excitedly. 'That makes four times the same number.'

c. *registration fee*; also (with reference to the registration of motor vehicles) *registration book, number, plate.*

1922 *Michelin Guide Gt. Brit.* III. 711 When disposing of his car the motorist must fill in the name and address of the new owner in the registration book. **1968** 'D. RUTHERFORD' *Skin for Skin* ii. 17 The Morris 1000 was parked at the kerbside... I had the registration book and the cover note ready. **1869** *Bradshaw's Railway Man.* XXI. 14 Certificates are required for transfers. Registration fee 2*s.* 6*d.* each deed and seller. **1967** *Post Office Guide* 85 The registration fee must be paid by postage stamps affixed to the cover. **1977** J. BINGHAM *Marriage Bureau Murders* ii. 24 There would be a down payment, a registration fee..and further annual payments. **1903** *Act 3 Edw. VII* c. 36 § 6 A person driving a motor car shall,..if an accident occur to any person,..or to any horse or vehicle..owing to the presence of the motor car on the road, stop and, if required, give his name and address, and also..the registration mark or number of the car. **1911** *Motor Man.* (ed. 13) viii. 260 A registration number once issued cannot be transferred to another car. **1959** M. GILBERT *Blood & Judgement* xii. 128 Are you the owner of a blue Riley saloon car, registration number GKR 692? **1977** B. PYM *Quartet in Autumn* v. 39 The car was an important status symbol and large sums of money could be paid for particularly desirable registration numbers. **1956** Registration plate [see *ALL OVER *advb. phr.* 1 b]. **1974** F. NOLAN *Oshawa Project* xviii. 170 A black Volkswagen with a Darmstadt registration plate. **1977** 'D. CORY' *Bennett* v. 133 Relatively few cars, and fewer still with foreign registration plates.

2. (Further examples.) Also used with reference to other keyboard instruments, esp. the harpsichord.

1921 G. A. AUDSLEY *Organ-Stops* 1 Haphazard methods of registration must be shunned. **1961** R. RUSSELL in A. Baines *Mus. Instr. through Ages* iv. 80 Undue preoccupation with such things as registration..tends to obscure the fundamental musical requirements of the instrument [*sc.* the harpsichord]. **1966** *Listener* 19 May 737/3 He is the most characterful harpsichord player since Landowska. Purists may question his frequent changes of registration. **1974** *Daily Tel.* 18 Feb. 11/1 The excesses to which Bach's 'Goldberg' Variations can easily lend themselves were strictly avoided by George Malcolm..on the harpsichord... Registration was also kept within reasonable limits. **1976** *Gramophone* May 1761/2 Chorzempa's [organ] registration balances happily with the orchestra.

3. Substitute for def.: The state of being in register (REGISTER *sb.*[1] 11 b in Dict. and Suppl.), or the action of obtaining this.

1901 *Chambers's Jrnl.* June 364/1 The skilled attendant replaces them in the clip, one upon another, taking a little care to ensure perfect 'registration'..and, lo! there is a finely painted lantern slide! **1949** *Electronics* Dec. 69/2 The three color images in camera and picture tube must be very precisely aligned, both electrically and optically, to secure accurate registration. **1959** HALAS & MANVELL *Technique Film Animation* III. xix. 218 Background artists should know what registration manipulation is possible under the camera. **1962** W. H. STEVENS in G. A. T. Burdett *Automatic Control Handbk.* viii. 61 Separate panels are now cut from the multiple boards, and the fixing and component holes are drilled or punched... Registration of the holes with the circuit is achieved by means of the pilot holes. **1967** *Listener* 30 Mar. 424/2 The three pictures are equally focused and accurately in registration one with the other. **1971** D. POTTER *Brit. Eliz. Stamps* iii. 37 The line was printed in two operations as part of the tricolour production, and the very accurate registration required was not forthcoming. **1975** J. B. HARLEY *O.S. Maps* i. 11 A second sheet of plastic material carrying an opaque coating is placed in exact registration with the first.

registrative, *a.* For *rare*—[1] read *rare* and add further example.

1878 W. JAMES in *Jrnl. Specul. Philos.* XII. 11 At one time, 'scientific' thought, mere passive mirroring of outward nature, purely registrative cognition..would seem to be his [*sc.* Spencer's] ideal.

registree (redʒistrī·). [f. REGISTER *v.* + -EE[1].] One who is registered (in various senses).

1923 G. B. SHAW in *Daily News* 18 Dec. 6/1 My refusal to credit the trade union known as the General Medical Council with the power to confer Omniscience and Infallibility on its registrees. **1966** *Punch* 28 Dec. 945/3 Miss Shuter at the desk had hysterics when an irate would-be registree broke into her glassy sanctuary and shook her by the shoulders.

re·gistry o:ffice. **1.** = REGISTER OFFICE; *spec.* † a place where a register of positions in domestic employment is kept (*obs.* exc. *hist.*).

1728 SWIFT *Let.* c 10 May in *Works* (1766) XVII. 169, I will take up the bones, and make of it a skeleton, and put it in my registry office. **1834** J. S. MILL in *Monthly Repos.* VIII. 439 Prying into the records of the..registry office. **1836** [in Dict.]. **1839** J. ROMILLY *Cambr. Diary* 16 Sept. (1967) 178 Lucy went..to the Registry Office..to get a place for Frances Wilderspin. **1892** C. M. YONGE *Cross Roads* xv. 157 She was in communication with the registry office there; but she would not take what the matron of the lodge called 'rackety situations'. **1910** E. M. FORSTER *Howards End* vii. 59 Would you come round with me to the registry office? There's a housemaid who won't say yes but doesn't say no. **1964** M. LASKI in S. Nowell-Smith *Edwardian England* iv. 144 Registry offices abounded, but for really high-class servants the best method was..use of the advertisement columns of the *Morning Post.*

2. = *REGISTER OFFICE.

1911 G. B. SHAW *Getting Married* 236 Marriages gave place to contracts at a registry office. **1931** J. S. HUXLEY *What dare I Think?* vi. 205 The marriage ceremonial among most primitive peoples..contains a religious motive, just as much as does a Christian wedding ceremony (and just as little as does a wedding in a registry office). **1974** 'R. TATE' *Birds of Bloodied Feather* iii. 67 Can't we just make a date? It only means slipping into a registry office. **1976** *Daily Times* (Lagos) 27 Aug. 16/4 Workers at the registry office explained to Ajar that according to the law his wife could retain her maiden name. **1980** J. CARTWRIGHT *Horse of Darius* ii. 27 They..were married in the registry office.

reg'lar (re·glăɹ), *a.* and *adv.* Repr. a colloq. pronunc. of REGULAR *a.* and *adv.*

1842 DICKENS *Let.* 17 Feb. (1974) III. 69 The Newhaven serenade was not so good; though there were a great many voices, and a 'reg'lar' band. **1843** —— *Martin Chuzzlewit* (1844) xxv. 306, I says 'my half a pint of porter fully satisfies; perwisin', Mrs. Harris, that it is brought reg'lar, and draw'd mild.' **1899** F. W. MAITLAND *Let.* 10 Oct. (1965) 201 Wherever I go I shall expect my E.H.R. 'reglar'. **1950** *Collier's* 6 May 56/2 (*caption*) I'm a 'real pal'—a 'reg'lar fellow'—a 'good scout'!

reglementary, *a.* (Later example.)

1937 M. COVARRUBIAS *Island of Bali* iii. 58 The independent village is called a *desa*, a term we shall employ to designate the legal, 'complete' village that has the three reglementary temples.

regnancy. Restrict *rare*—[1] to sense in Dict. and add: **2.** *Psychol.* In the sense of *REGNANT *ppl. a.* 2 c.

1938 [see *REGNANT *ppl. a.* 2 c]. **1963** S. R. MADDI in Wepman & Heine *Concepts of Personality* vii. 185 Murray..with his concept of regnancy, has gone a bit further than Allport in attempting to conceptualize relevant brain processes. **1964** GOULD & KOLB *Dict. Soc. Sci.* 352/2 The authors point to Allport's biophysical traits and Murray's regnancies as illustrations of hypothetical constructs.

regnant, *ppl. a.* Add: **2. c.** *regnant process* (Psychol.): in the theory of personality, a hypothesis that dominant brain processes exist which determine behaviour (see quot. 1938).

1938 H. A. MURRAY *Explor. Personality* ii. 45 It may prove convenient to refer to the mutually dependent processes that constitute dominant configurations in the brain as *regnant* processes; and, further, to designate the totality of such processes occurring during a single moment..as a *regnancy.* **1974** W. B. ARNDT *Theories of Personality* xii. 237 We must infer the characteristics of regnant processes from the behavior of organisms.

regolith (re·golĭþ). *Geol.* [erron. f. Gr. ῥῆγο-ς rug, blanket + -LITH.] The unconsolidated solid material covering the bedrock of a planet.

1897 G. P. MERRILL *Treat. Rocks* v. 299 This entire mantle of unconsolidated material, whatever its nature or origin, it is proposed to call the regolith, from the Greek words ῥηγος, meaning *a blanket*, and λιθος, *a stone.* **1935** *Jrnl. Geol.* XLIII. 745 'Regolith' was introduced by Merrill to include all unconsolidated surficial material and therefore embraces far more than residual weathered rock. **1949** F. J. PETTIJOHN *Sedimentary Rocks* ix. 282 Residual soils (regolith of Merrill, saprolith of Becker, and sathrolith of Sederholm) are the products of weathering formed *in situ.* **1970** *Nature* 24 Jan. 321/2 The solid rocks at Tranquillity Base are covered by a 4–6 m thick regolith or dust layer composed of local rock fragments..and spheres or fragments of glass. **1976** J. KLECZEK *Universe* iv. 155 The solid lunar globe is covered by a layer of loose broken rock material called regolith. **1977** A. HALLAM *Planet Earth* 16/1 Meteorite debris [on the moon] amounts to only about 2% of the sampled regolith.

Hence **regoli·thic** *a.*

1955 *Trans. R. Soc. N.Z.* LXXXII. 1015 Under the soil of the upland surface of the Belmont plateau there are arrested streams or sheets..of formerly regolithic debris now forming deposits of head on slopes. **1977** *Nature* 6 Jan. 38/2 Since the returned sample is of regolithic materials it could also contain basalt fragments.

regosol (re·gosǫl). *Soil Sci.* [erron. f. as prec. + *-SOL.] A poorly developed soil without definite horizons, overlying and formed from deep, unconsolidated deposits such as sand or loess.

1949 THORP & SMITH in *Soil Sci.* LXVII. 120 Soon after the definition of Lithosols was published in the 1938 Yearbook, it was realized that many weakly developed soils occur in deep soft-rock deposits, like loess and sand, that are not *stony* in the ordinary sense of the word. These nonstony soils were called lithosols for a time, but a practical need was felt for distinguishing deep soft soil materials from very stony ones. Hence the proposal of the name *Regosol.* This new term is not yet fully established in the literature, and it may prove desirable eventually to give the concept some other status than that of a great soil group. **1968** R. W. FAIRBRIDGE *Encycl. Geomorphol.* 523/1 Soil scientists sometimes use 'regosol' for soils developed without distinct horizons over deep unconsolidated 'rock', e.g., a mature alluvial formation. **1976** *Sci. Amer.* Sept. 174/3, ·7 billion hectares of sandy, undifferentiated soils called regosols are nonarable.

Hence **regoso·lic** *a.*

1956 *Proc. Soil Sci. Soc. Amer.* XX. 268/2 The Iowan loess is separated from the Farmdale loess by a regosolic buried soil.

regrade, *v.*[3] (Earlier and later examples.)

1826 A. MACOMB *Let.* 18 Nov. in *Reg. Deb. Congr. U.S.* (1829) III. 1572 The road..is to be regraded. **1869** *Rep. Comm. Agric. 1868* (U.S. Dept. Agric.) 362 They may be readily and rapidly leveled in the construction of a new road, or regraded when displaced by wear. **1960** *Farmer & Stockbreeder* 26 Jan. 70/2 The pigs are..regraded by the Association's own system of selective grading. **1977** *Times* 18 Mar. 4/5 Unless the corporation offers to regrade the cameramen there is little chance that their union..will allow the programme to go ahead.

Hence **regra·ded** *ppl. a.*, **regra·ding** *vbl. sb.*

1920 *Glasgow Herald* 1 Sept. 6 They have agreed to a conference to consider regrading. **1923** *Ibid.* 28 Mar. 10 Heavy extraordinary expenditure has to be budgeted for, including three-quarters of a million for arrears of regraded salaries. **1956** D. L. LINTON *Sheffield* 41 The regrading consequent on these changes would favour the Froggatt stream. **1962** A. BATTERSBY *Guide to Stock Control* 105 Transferring from one stock to another, e.g. re-grading.

regra·ss (rī-), *v.* [RE- 5 c.] To put (land) under grass again. So **regra·ssing** *vbl. sb.*

1901 *Yearbk. U.S. Dept. Agric.* 30 Experiments in regrassing were undertaken at Tucson, Ariz., in cooperation with the agricultural experiment station. **1940** *Advisory Bull. War Food Production* No. 1. 1 Ploughable grassland too poor to be initially cereal-worthy should..be ploughed and immediately re-grassed. *Ibid.* 28 Re-grassing properly and methodically undertaken enormously extends the effective grazing season.

regress, *v.* Add: **2. b.** *Psychol.* To return in one's mind to an earlier period or stage of life as a result of mental illness or through hypnosis or psychoanalysis. Also *trans.*, to induce regression in (a person). See also *REGRESSION 4 d.

1926 J. I. SUTTIE tr. *Ferenczi's Further Contrib.* xi. 137 Now the stage to which these two neurotics regressed seems to be the infantile stage of the first year of life. **1950** *Psychoanalytic Q.* XIX. 501 The immutability of a constant, passive environment forces him to adapt, i.e., to regress to infantile levels. **1956** AMBROSE & NEWBOLD *Handbk. Med. Hypnosis* vii. 146 If a child can be hypnotised and regressed with suitable suggestions, causing him to re-live the actual traumatic episode, much tension can be overcome. **1957** P. LAFITTE *Person in Psychol.* vi. 75 The person changes.. for the worse, perhaps regressing directly to infantile behaviour. **1960** *Times Lit. Suppl.* 3 June 356/3 Harry was later hypnotized by a friend of Dr. Puharich and 'regressed' through his life memories to see if he had any knowledge of Egyptian history, language, or religion. **1970** T. X. BARBER *LSD, Marihuana, Yoga & Hypnosis* vi. 259 When regressed hypnotically to the time of the original conditioning, all subjects again manifested the eye-blink response. **1976** F. H. FRANKEL *Hypnosis* v. 67 He was then regressed in time, and referred to business difficulties that he had experienced earlier that day and in recent weeks. **1978** GRIS & DICK *New Soviet Psychic Discoveries* ix. 104 A girl student..insisted that she be regressed by a co-student.

3. *intr. Genetics.* To tend or evolve towards the mean value for the population; to display regression to the mean (*REGRESSION 4 b).

1885 *Nature* 24 Sept. 509/2 The type is an ideal form towards which the children of those who deviate from it tend to regress. *Ibid.* 510/1 The stability of a type would, I presume, be measured by the strength of its tendency to regress. **1892** F. GALTON *Finger Prints* i. 21 There is a constant tendency in the offspring to 'regress' towards the parental type. **1909** *Westm. Gaz.* 21 Apr. 5/1 There is a tendency for children of exceptional parents to regress towards the average stock. **1953** SRB & OWEN *Gen. Genetics* xxiii. 497 Instead of showing the average value of their selected parents, the progeny regress from this value toward the original population mean, and in fact average only a little better than the population from which their parents came. **1975** A. SMITH *Human Pedigree* iii. 67 The reason why we have not ended up as uniform as tailor's dummies is that there is only a tendency to regress to the mean... The various genes involved in such a character as weight will combine, from time to time and to confound the general rule, in a manner that is unexceptional [*sic*]. A child will then be heavier than both its parents. It will not have regressed.

4. *trans. Statistics.* To calculate the coefficient(s) of regression of (a variable) *against* or *on* another variable. *colloq.*

1971 *Nature* 8 Oct. 407/1 These parameters were regressed on measurements made of site factors on five sampling sites from the fives dated flows. **1977** D. M. SMITH *Human Geogr.* vii. 170 Katzman..estimated several education production functions by regressing measures of output against measures of school input and local socio-economic status of residents.

regressed (rĭgre·st), *ppl. a.* [f. prec. + -ED[1].] That has regressed or been regressed.

1948 *Jrnl. Nerv. & Mental Dis.* CVII. 443 Lewis's observation goes back to 1926 when he saw a regressed schizophrenic patient reacquire a dorsiflexor response to plantar stimulation. **1965** B. E. FREEMAN tr. *Vandel's Biospeleol.* xxvi. 419 The variations in the regressed eyes of the mole may be noted.

regression. Add: **4. a.** (Later examples.)

1917 *Jrnl. Genetics* XXVII. 117 What is frequently called reduction in evolution, or, to use a less ambiguous term, regression. **1950** *Sci. News* XV. 136 They pointed out that the regression of tumours caused by Compound E did not generally last indefinitely. The tumours usually recurred. **1965** B. E. FREEMAN tr. *Vandel's Biospeleology* xxvi. 417 Regression of the eyes is more marked when it is phyletically ancient.

b. *Genetics.* The tendency for the mean value of a partially inherited quantitative character, among any class of relatives of an individual or a group chosen for their values of that character, to lie between the (mean) value for that individual or group and the mean value in the general population. Esp. as *regression to the mean.*

1885 F. GALTON in *Nature* 24 Sept. 507/1 The experiments showed further that the mean filial regression towards mediocrity was directly proportional to the parental deviation from it. **1889** [in Dict., sense 4]. **1912** J. A. THOMSON *Heredity* (ed. 2) ix. 321 The amount of the regression affords a useful measure of the intensity of the inheritance. If the regression is slight, it means that the intensity of the inheritance is high. **1952** SRB & OWEN *Gen. Genetics* xxiii. 497 This phenomenon, in which the progeny of selected parents slip back toward the average of the population from which the parents were chosen, has long been known. In this connection the phenomenon was called regression. Today, the term regression has a broader statistical connotation, but it is still applicable in its original sense to the problems we are discussing. **1975** A. SMITH *Human Pedigree* iii. 66 At this stage it is necessary to refer to the phenomenon known as the regression to the mean. Where random mating exists, and where there is no evolutionary pressure favouring any characteristic that is controlled by many genes, the offspring will have a tendency to be nearer average for that characteristic than their parents.

c. *Statistics.* The relationship between the mean value of a random variable and the corresponding values of one or more other variables; **coefficient of regression** = *regression coefficient* in sense 8 below.

1897 K. PEARSON in *Phil. Trans. R. Soc.* A. CLXXXVII. 259 The coefficient of regression may be defined as the ratio of the mean deviation of the fraternity from the mean offspring to the deviation of the parentage from the mean parent. *Ibid.*, From this special definition of regression in relation to parents and offspring, we may pass to a general conception of regression. Let A and B be two correlated organs (variables or measurable characteristics) in the same or different individuals, and let the sub-group of organs B, corresponding to a sub-group of A with a definite value *a*, be extracted. Let the first of these sub-groups be termed an array, and the second a type. Then we define the coefficient of regression of the array on the type to be the ratio of the mean-deviation of the array from the mean B-organ to the deviation of the type *a* from the mean A-organ. **1917** *Phil. Mag.* XXXIV. 205 When the regression of the first variable on the remaining $n-1$ variables is linear, the multiple correlation coefficient measures the dependence of the first variable on the others. **1925** R. A. FISHER *Statistical Methods for Res. Workers* v. 114 The following qualitative examples are intended to familiarise the student with the concept of regression. **1943** M. G. KENDALL *Adv. Theory Statistics* I. xiv. 328 In this chapter we shall mainly be concerned with the case in which regressions are linear or very nearly so. **1952** C. G. LAMBE *Elem. Statistics* vii. 56 This straight line which gives an estimate of the average value of *y* associated with any value of *x* is called the line of regression of *y* on *x* and p/σ_x^2 is called the coefficient of regression of *y* on *x*. **1972** T. H. & R. J. WONNACOTT *Introd. Statistics for Business & Economics* xiii. 287 Multiple regression is the extension of simple regression, to take account of the effect of more than one independent *X* variable on the dependent variable *Y*.

d. *Psychol.* The process of regressing, or a tendency to regress, in the sense of *REGRESS *v.* 2 b; *spec.* the tendency of the libido, under the stress of frustration, to return to a simpler and more satisfying stage of development; also, the state of returning mentally to an earlier period, esp. in hypnosis and psychoanalysis.

1910 tr. S. Freud in *Amer. Jrnl. Psychol.* XXI. 214 The flight from the unsatisfying reality into what we call.. disease, but which is never without an individual gain in pleasure for the patient, takes place over the path of regression, the return to earlier phases of the sexual life, when satisfaction was not lacking. **1913** C. G. JUNG *On Psychoanalysis* in *XVIIth Internat. Congr. Med.* § xii. 68 [Freud] called this phenomenon of reactivation or secondary exaggeration of infantile reminiscences 'Regression'. **1920** *Challenge* 21 May 44/3 The *libido*..in its regression to the collective unconscious, gives rise to the similation of archaic psychical adaptations. **1948** *Jrnl. Nerv. & Mental Dis.* CVII. 443 In regression to infantile levels the subject assumed the sleeping posture of an infant. **1961** *Economist* 11 Mar. 962/1 The poor layman who has laboriously got on to nodding terms with infantile sexuality, regression, Oedipal conflicts, displacement and the rest. **1970** T. X. BARBER *LSD, Marihuana, Yoga & Hypnosis* vi. 255 Under regression to infancy, the hypnotized person does not topple from his chair. **1971** *Jrnl. Gen. Psychol.* Apr. 208 In psychology the term 'regression' refers to a primitivization of behavior. **1978** GRIS & DICK *New Soviet Psychic Discoveries* ix. 105 Let me amplify on regressions. Whatever people think, their previous lives are not individual experiences.

7. *Geogr.* A retreat or withdrawal of the sea from the land.

1908 W. J. SOLLAS et al. tr. *Suess's Face of Earth* III. 364 Every new transgression (regression), in so far as the encroaching line of breakers itself has not denuded the land, will encounter an altered relief. **1937** *Bull. Amer. Assoc. Petroleum Geologists* XXI. 1436 Rhythmic transgressions and regressions of the sea continued throughout the period of Jackson sedimentation, evidenced by the interwedging of marine and non-marine sediments, as the strand line moved..back and forth. **1975** *Sci. Amer.* Feb. 90/3 The stratification of sedimentary deposits suggested successive marine transgressions onto the continents and regressions from them. The regressions could be attributed to the subsidence of the ocean basins and the transgressions to the partial filling of the basins with sediment eroded from the continents.

8. *attrib.* and *Comb.*, as (sense *4 c) *regression analysis, formula, function, theory*; **regression coefficient,** a coefficient in the regression equation; *esp.* the first-order coefficient, which is estimated by the covariance of the two variables divided by the variance of the independent variable; **regression curve,** a graph of the expected value of the dependent variable plotted against the value of the independent variable(s); **regression equation,** an equation which gives the expected value of the dependent variable as a function of the value(s) of the independent variable(s); **regression line** = *regression curve* above.

1948 *New Biol.* IV. 36 We can then use the technique of regression analysis to determine to what extent we can account for the variation in yield in terms of variation in rainfall. **1976** *National Observer* (U.S.) 19 June 18/3 It may seem absurd to label the probability of murder as 'P(M)' and subject it to the technique of regression analysis. **1903** *Phil. Trans. R. Soc.* A. CC. 20 Not only the slope (regression coefficient) of the line, but its position is identical. *Ibid.* 21 If an organ has been modified only by indirect selection, then its partial regression coefficients on any complex of other organs, however large or small, provided it includes all the directly selected organs, will remain unchanged by the selection. **1925** R. A. FISHER *Statistical Methods Res. Workers* v. 114 The regression coefficients are of interest and scientific importance in many classes of data where the correlation coefficient, if used at all, is an artificial concept of no real utility. **1964** R. VON MISES *Math. Theory Probability & Statistics* xi. 576 The correlation coefficient is the geometrical mean of the two regression coefficients. **1905** *Res. Mem. Drapers' Co.* XIV. 21 Yule's method of approaching the problem from the form of the regression curves is.. available and capable of very great extension. **1925** R. A. FISHER *Statistical Methods Res. Workers* v. 114 The function which represents the mean height at any age is termed the regression function of height on age; it is represented graphically by a regression curve, or regression line. **1943** M. G. KENDALL *Adv. Theory Statistics* I. xiv. 327 The means of arrays will in general lie more or less closely round smooth curves... Such curves are called regression curves and their equations..are called regression equations. **1972** G. P. BEAUMONT *Elem. Math. Statistics* xii. 152 We begin with a certain minimal property of the regression curves. **1897** *Proc. R. Soc.* LX. 480 The characteristic or regression equations which we have to find. **1943** Regression equation [see *regression curve* above]. **1978** *Nature* 18 May 184/2 The proportion of non-scientific staff [*A*]..is determined largely by the total staff employed (*S*) and the number of addresses amongst which it is dispersed (*D*) according to the regression equation $A = 22{\cdot}23 \log S - 1{\cdot}86D - 8{\cdot}77$. **1971** *World Archaeol.* III. 115 The regression formula predicts that a compound with five adults will have approximately ten huts. **1925** Regression function [see *regression curve* above]. **1904** *Biometrika* IV. 139 The actual degree of resemblance, our brothers being equally variable, is measured by the steepness of this regression line. **1925** Regression line [see *regression curve* above]. **1971** *World Archaeol.* III. 112 Variation away from the regression line is a function of wealth that is not used in this way. **1967** *Times Rev. Industry* Feb. 111/3 The lay reader should not be put off by the complicated language of regression theories, as Professor Kaldor's ideas are fascinating enough, and well enough argued in this lecture to be quite comprehensible to the non-economist.

regressive, *a.* Add: **1. c.** Also *spec.* of a tax, that bears proportionately harder on persons with lower incomes; *regressive assimilation* (examples).

1889 *Cent. Dict.*, Regressive assimilation. **1924** F. M. STENTON in Mawer & Stenton *Introd. Survey Eng. Place-Names* ix. 174 Some of these names, which enter into local nomenclature in considerable numbers, may be due to 'regressive assimilation'. **1939** [see *PROGRESSIVE *a.* 2 c]. **1964** C. BARBER *Ling. Change Present-Day Eng.* iii. 62 Regressive assimilation..in which the sound exerting the influence comes later in the word than the one influenced. **1976** *Hansard Commons* 9 June 1597 The [licence] fee is a poll tax and it is regressive. It bears very hard on the worse-off.

d. *Psychol.* Of, pertaining, or relating to psychological regression.

1926 J. I. SUTTIE tr. *Ferenczi's Further Contrib.* xi. 137 Besides this regressive trait that fetters the patients to their bed..there may also be at work..the 'secondary' function of the neurosis. **1957** P. LAFITTE *Person in Psychol.* xi. 161 Concentration camp life has plenty of examples of exceptional, as well as of regressive, behaviour. **1969** *Listener* 22 May 736/2 It [sc. *The Boston Strangler*] seeks to entertain by feeding us on clinical information about behaviour of the most regressive kind. **1970** R. F. BALES *Personality & Interpersonal Behav.* iii. 49 To..teach in such a way presumably helps one's normal defenses by providing in one's overt behavior a good example for the more regressive inner self.

4. *Geogr.* Of, pertaining to, or being a regression of the sea.

1937 *Bull. Amer. Assoc. Petroleum Geologists* XXI. 1436 Near the close of this regressive movement the Loma Novio, Government Wells, and Chernosky Sand members were deposited. **1950** *Ibid.* XXXIV. 284 The regressive type of bioherm or reef may contain within it back-reef types of sediments such as red shale and anhydrite, but the transgressive type does not. **1968** D. L. EICHER *Geologic Time* ii. 49 Transgressive and regressive sequences generally do not contain a complete sedimentary record of all environments that prevailed laterally at the time. **1978** *Nature* 29 June 749/2 There seems little reason to invoke oscillations in sea level..to account for any other transgressive or regressive sequences observed.

regressiveness (earlier example).

1853 W. BAGEHOT in *Prospective Rev.* IX. 421 There was a want of prospectiveness and a superfluous amount of regressiveness.

regressi·vity. [f. REGRESSIVE *a.* + -ITY.] The state of being regressive; regressiveness.

1904 G. S. HALL *Adolescence* I. ii. 55 Retarded development of an organ..is an indication of regressivity. **1972** *Times* 23 Oct. 18/6 VAT will have small regressivity.

regressor (rĭgre·səɪ). *Statistics.* [f. REGRESS *v.* + -OR.] Any of the independent variables in a regression equation. Also *regressor variable.*

1956 *Jrnl. R. Statistical Soc.* B. XVIII. 230 Two multiple correlations based on the same numbers of regressors. **1961** KENDALL & STUART *Advanced Theory Statistics* II. xxviii. 355 We understand by 'linear regression' that the conditional mean value of *y* is a linear function of the regressors $x_1, \ldots, x_p$. **1978** *Jrnl. Econometrics* VIII. 307 (*heading*) Posterior distribution for the multiple correlation with fixed regressors.

regret, *sb.* **2. b.** (Earlier U.S. example.)
1851 T. A. BURKE *Polly Peablossom's Wedding* 177 The invitations went out, and strange to say, not a single 'regret' was sent in; but all came.

regret, *v.* Add: **3.** *absol.* or *intr.* To feel regret.
1853 MRS. GASKELL *Ruth* II. x. 281 Those who had umbrellas were putting them up; those who had not were regretting and wondering how long it would last. **1883** 'H. CONWAY' *Called Back* vi. 77 'Do you regret, Mr. Vaughan?' 'No—not if there is a chance.'
regretting *vbl. sb.* (further example).
1907 G. B. SHAW *John Bull's Other Island* IV. 105 No more neglect, no more loneliness, no more idle regrettings and vain-hopings.

regretfully, *adv.* Add: **2.** It is to be regretted (that); = REGRETTABLY *adv.* (A regrettable use, prob. after *HOPEFULLY *adv.* 2.)
1976 *New Statesman* 20 Aug. 237/1 Regretfully, that is no ground for leniency towards him. **1977** *N.Z. Woman's Weekly* 10 Jan. 36/4 Regretfully I'm one of those who suffer from an odd compulsion. **1977** *Times Lit. Suppl.* 15 Apr. 468/4 The investigators, who must regretfully remain anonymous, have produced..a richness of archaeological potential which it will take years to absorb and assess. **1977** *Jrnl. R. Soc. Arts.* CXXV. 336/2 Regretfully, however, the editorial staff may justifiably be thought to stand criticized for what has been omitted.

regre·ttableness. [f. REGRETTABLE *a.* + -NESS.] Regrettable character.
1913 *Eng. Hist. Rev.* July 555 The regrettableness of the lapses from what might have been.

regrind (rī·graind), *sb.* [f. the vb.] An act of regrinding.
1952 L. J. ST. CLAIR *Design & Use of Cutting Tools* x. 187 Tool B_2 would require a metal removal of ·037" from the end per regrind. **1971** *Engineering* Apr. 8/1 (Advt.), You know a Dormer drill right down to the last regrind. **1975** *Drilling Technol. & Collet Chuck* (Bristol Erickson Ltd.) 9 'Stubbing' means that for short holes 3 diameters of drill plus one diameter for chip clearance gives four times more drill life with feeds increased by at least 33⅓%, equals more holes per re-grind.

regrou·nd, *v.* [RE- 5 c.] *trans.* To furnish with a new ground or basis for etching, painting, etc. So **regrou·nding** *vbl. sb.* Cf. GROUND *sb.* 6 and *v.* 8.
1831 J. CONSTABLE *Let.* 4 Dec. (1966) IV. 360, I know very well it can be blotched up, with dry point burr, regrounding, &c &c, but that is hatefull. **1832** *Ibid.* 28 Feb. (1966) IV. 368 It is necessary..to reground a plate. **1937** *Discovery* Mar. 76/2 To add to the plate he cleans it thoroughly, regrounds it, draws the new work and continues as before.

regroup, *v.* Add: Also *intr.*
a **1944** K. DOUGLAS *Alamein to Zem Zem* (1946) 69 We had all seen the enemy so disorganized that it did not seem possible he could regroup enough to give us much trouble. **1976** *National Observer* (U.S.) 22 May 10/3 It was very important for me to find day care so I could regroup psychologically. **1981** *Times* 25 Apr. 12/3 The host and the other men said their evening prayers. They regrouped around the fire.

regrou·pment. [f. REGROUP *v.* + -MENT.] Rearrangement in groups; a rearranged group. Also *attrib.*
1920 *Glasgow Herald* 1 July 6/4 A quiet continuance of the existing regime will allow..a regroupment without any definite break in development. **1961** *Encounter* Jan. 9/2 Villagers from the hills..have been 're-grouped' in new areas where they could be better protected and controlled—but only a third of these re-groupments were economically viable. **1961** *Guardian* 12 May 7/4 Algerians..who have been herded by the French into 'regroupment centres'. **1963** *Economist* 17 Aug. 562 India is thinking of rounding up the ..Nagas into 'regroupment villages'.

regrou·t, *v.* [RE- 5 c.] *trans.* To furnish with grouting again.
1967 *Do it Yourself* Nov. 1330/2 The joints between ceramic tiles can be re-grouted with grouting cement. **1974** *Sunday* (Charleston, S. Carolina) 28 Apr. 1-c/2 The tiles will be 'thoroughly cleaned and regrouted and restored to their original newness', he said.

regrow, *v.* Add: Also *trans.* (Further example.) **regrowth,** add def.: the phenomenon of growing or increasing again, *esp.* the renewed growth of vegetation after partial destruction by harvesting, fire, etc.; also *concr.*, the new vegetation that results; (earlier and later examples).
1741 W. ELLIS *Mod. Husb.* May v. 85 Folding Sheep..will likewise prevent the Regrowth of the Trefoil. **1920** A. S. PRINGLE-PATTISON *Idea of God* 72 The Tubularia, a kind of sea-anemone, re-grows its flower-like head. **1944** *Forestry Terminol.* (Soc. Amer. Foresters) 60/1 *Regrowth*, herbage that grows after grazing or after the plants have gone through a period of dormancy. **1956** PETERSON & FISHER *Wild Amer.* i. 17 Other great stretches, greener and fresher than their surroundings, showed where self-sown regrowth had reclaimed old cleared areas. **1977** J. L. HARPER *Population Biol. Plants* xiv. 438 The sward was then rested from grazing until the regrowth had approached 12·5 cm. *Ibid.* xx. 630 This form of regrowth may be more significant than seedlings as a means of recovery after fire. **1977** *Listener* 2 June 710/3 The National Union of Tailors and Garment Makers..see evidence of the regrowth of the sweat-shop.

regula. 2. For *rare*—¹ read *rare* and add later example.
1870 S. H. HODGSON *Theory of Practice* II. iv. 255 Logic is the regula of the sequences in meanings..; Grammar the regula of sounds and language.

regular, *a.*, *adv.*, and *sb.* Add: **A.** *adj.* **2. a.** (Further examples in *Astr.*)
1811 *Phil. Trans. R. Soc.* CI. 298 The arguments which I have given in the foregoing article, where only nebulæ of an irregular round figure were considered, need not be repeated when a regular circular form is presented to our view. **1922** *Astrophysical Jrnl.* LVI. 164 This state of affairs led Sir John Herschel to avoid the discussion of physical distinctions among nebulae and to elaborate his father's formal classification in an ingenious manner. All nebulous objects were divided into regular and irregular, and the latter alone into nebulae and clusters. **1926** *Ibid.* LXIV. 324 The characteristic feature of extra-galactic nebulae is rotational symmetry about dominating non-stellar nuclei. About 97 per cent of these nebulae are regular in the sense that they show this feature conspicuously. **1973** L. OSTER *Mod. Astron.* xx. 303 We can do little more than speculate at present as to why some spiral galaxies are barred and others are 'regular'.

d. *Math.* In various senses (see quots.).
1893 A. R. FORSYTH *Theory Functions Complex Variable* i. 12 A function which is monogenic, uniform and, except at poles, continuous, is called a meromorphic function. [*Note*] Sometimes regular, but this term will be reserved for the description of another property of functions. *Ibid.* iii. 52 A point *a* in the plane may be such that a function of the variable has a determinate finite value there, always independent of the path by which the variable reaches *a*; the point *a* is called an ordinary point [*Note.* Sometimes a regular point.] of the function. *Ibid.* viii. 163 The singularities..in the vicinity of which each branch of the function is uniform. [*Note*] These singularities will, for the sake of brevity, be called regular. **1908** H. HILTON *Introd. Theory Groups Finite Order* ii. 8 A permutation with the same number of symbols in each cycle—such as (1 4 3) (2 5 7) (9 6 8)—is called regular. **1968** P. A. P. MORAN *Introd. Probability Theory* iii. 117 It is convenient to use the words 'regular' and 'positively regular' for the cases where the vector $P^t p(0)$ converges to a vector independent of p(0), and where in addition this vector has all its elements positive. **1972** A. G. HOWSON *Handbk. Terms Algebra & Anal.* xxxi. 154 Some authors weaken the definition of an analytic function on a domain *S* by asking only that the function should be analytic (in the above sense) at all but a finite number of points of *S*. A function which is analytic in the stronger sense would be described by them as being regular on *S*. *Ibid.* xxxvi. 181 Those points..possess a tangent plane..and are called regular points. Points which are not regular are said to be singular. **1978** *Sci. Amer.* Oct. 96/2 A prime is regular if and only if it does not evenly divide the numerator of any of the first $p-3$ numbers in the series of fractions called the Bernoulli numbers... Of the primes smaller than 100 all but 37, 59 and 67 are regular.

3. d. Also *spec.* of a long-standing client or customer.
1841 DICKENS *Barn. Rudge* xi. 296 The regular Maypole customers..each..in..his allotted seat in the chimney corner. **1911** G. STRATTON-PORTER *Harvester* vii. 108, I have orders to fill for regular customers. **1966** H. MILLS *In Pursuit of Evil* vi. 59 'Is that a regular customer of yours?' I said to the..woman who owned the shop. **1973** 'H. HOWARD' *Highway to Murder* x. 125 Most of the ladies who patronize my salon are regular clients.

e. orig. *U.S.* Designating size or quality: average, medium; standard. (In quot. 1952 as *sb.*)
1952 *Amer. Speech* XXVII. 266 With regard to sizes of suits there are three basic divisions: regulars—for men of average height and weight; shorts..and longs. **1977** *Guardian* 11 June 14/7 If a Big Mac is too big for you then you might settle for a regular hamburger. **1978** *N.Y. Times Mag.* 23 July 22/2 In gasoline 'regular' has changed from meaning 'without tetraethyl lead' to its opposite—'with lead'.

6. c. (Further examples.)
1956 [see *BELSEN]. **1960** J. RAE *Custard Boys* II. xiii. 155 You're becoming a regular creeping Jesus. **1977** *Globe & Mail* (Toronto) 2 Mar. 6/6 Here we are today, being urged to go on a regular orgy of appeasement.

d. *regular fellow* (or *guy*), an agreeable, ordinary, or sociable person. Freq. as a term of mild approbation; a 'decent chap'. *colloq.* (chiefly *U.S.*).
A fortuitous juxtaposition in quot. 1840: cf GUY *sb.*² 2.
[**1840** BARHAM *Ingoldsby Legends* 1st Ser. 44 Did you see her..With her knees to her nose, and her nose to her chin, Leering up..You'd lift up your hands in amazement, and cry, '—Well! I never *did* see such a regular Guy!'] **1920** F. SCOTT FITZGERALD *This Side of Paradise* ii. 52, I know I'm not a regular fellow, yet I loathe anybody else that isn't. **1924** *Amer. Mercury* Jan. 51/2 He was just one of so many mute and inglorious Babbitts preparing to qualify as regular fellows. **1930** E. H. LAVINE *Third Degree* xiii. 161 So he [*sc.* a policeman] usually decides to become a 'regular guy'. **1936** C. S. LEWIS *Allegory of Love* iv. 173 Chaucer.. was not a 'regular fellow', *un vrai businessman*, or a rotarian. He was a scholar, a courtier, and a poet. **1936** H. L. MENCKEN *Amer. Lang.* (ed. 4) 254 When G. K. Chesterton made his first visit to the United States he was much upset when an admiring reporter described him as a regular guy. **1969** P. WILES in Ionescu & Gellner *Populism* 167 W. J. Bryan was to a degree exceptional even in the USA, a 'regular guy'. **1977** *Zigzag* June 17/1 He seems to be a regular, normal guy.

8. *Astr.* Of a satellite: (see quot. 1951).
1948 D. TER HAAR in *Kgl. Dansk. Vid. Selsk. Mat.-Fys. Medd.* XXV. No. 3. 63 This group has orbits which are all approximately in the equatorial plane of the primary and whose eccentricities are small. We shall call these satellites the 'regular' satellites. **1951** G. P. KUIPER in J. A. Hynek *Astrophysics* viii. 357 The satellite systems vary from the beautifully regular case of Uranus to a completely irregular system like Neptune... 'Regularity' is measured by low relative inclinations, low inclination with respect to the planetary equator, small orbital eccentricities, a common sense of motion—the same as that of planetary rotation—and some degree of regularity in the distances to the planet. **1960** *Jrnl. Brit. Astron. Assoc.* LXX. 35 Regular satellites, eighteen in number, travelling in almost circular orbits in the plane of the equator of the parent planet.

C. *regular-built* (earlier example).
1817 J. K. PAULDING *Lett. from South* I. 105, I can do this without forfeiting my character as a 'regular built' traveller, whose duty it is to tell all he sees, and more besides.

D. *sb.* **4. a.** (Example in *sing.*)
1917 W. OWEN *Let.* 23 Nov. (1967) 509 The C.O. is a terrible old 'Regular'.

b. (Later U.S. example.)
1894 'MARK TWAIN' *Let.* 28 Jan. (1917) II. 606 When the mind-curist is done with you, you *have* to call in a 'regular'.

c. (Earlier and later examples.)
a **1852** [see *CASUAL *sb.* 3 a]. **1872** 'MARK TWAIN' *Roughing It* xliii. 299, I struck up friendships with the reporters of the other journals, and we swapped 'regulars' with each other and thus encouraged work. 'Regulars' are permanent sources of news, like courts, bullion returns, 'clean-ups' at the quartz mills, and inquests. **1937** S. L. BERNSTEIN in C. Davy *Footnotes to Film* IV. 229 He can take the risk of alienating his 'regulars' in order to satisfy the requirements of the few. **1949** S. GIBBONS *Matchmaker* xx. 240 Mr. Waite was not a Regular at The Peal of Bells. **1959** 'A. GILBERT' *Death takes Wife* ix. 112 A woman entered his shop... She wasn't one of his regulars. **1970** *Daily Tel.* 28 Sept. 2/2 The Ministry of Technology does not plan at present to introduce coal rationing..but it believes that local coal merchants will limit supplies to 'regulars only'. **1978** *Dumfries Courier* 20 Oct. 16/3 Their popularity with the Edenbank regulars was demonstrated last week when the couple were presented with a framed colour aerial photograph of the hotel.

5. (Further examples.) Also in phr. *to go regulars*, to share profits. Now *Obs.*
1840 H. COCKTON *Valentine Vox, Ventriloquist* ii. 5 I'll hire the large concert room upon the Market Hill, and you shall go reg'lars in the profits. **1882** *Sydney Slang Dict.* 7/2 *Regulars*, a thief's share of plunder. *Ibid.* 10/1 A cross-cove, who had his regulars for stalling, cried 'Cop bung', as a pig was marking.

6. (Later example.)
1973 *Bodl. Libr. Rec.* IX. 11 Lines 1–2 are a list of solar regulars, sometimes called ferial regulars.

regularity. Add: **2.** *attrib.*
1925 C. D. BROAD *Mind & its Place* x. 457 The two conditions..are *not* jointly sufficient..to cause a memory even on the most extreme form of the regularity-theory of causation. **1935** *Aristot. Soc. Suppl. Vol.* XIV. 47, I accept the rationalist view, because it seems to me the only alternative to the so-called regularity view—that which reduces causal inference to a mere psychological habit or instinct. **1951** A. C. EWING *Fund. Questions Philos.* (1968) viii. 162 All this should make one hesitate very much before accepting the regularity theory merely because it is the simplest and keeps closest to what is empirically observed. **1954** A. J. AYER *Philos. Ess.* vi. 145 The same is true even on a 'regularity' view of causation. **1965** *Language* XLI. 186 The second breakthrough [in linguistics] was achieved in the 1870's, in the emergence of what I shall call the regularity hypothesis. **1977** M. MANDELBAUM *Anat. Hist. Knowl.* iii. 50 Hart and Honoré drew a sharp contrast between the plain man's notion of causation..and the regularity view, which they accepted as being..applicable in the sciences.

regularization. (Earlier example.)
1853 G. H. LEWES *Comte's Philos. Sci.* 289 The regularization of habitual or continuous intercourse.

re·gularizer. *rare.* [f. REGULARIZE *v.* + -ER¹.] A person or thing that produces regularity.
1921 LD. SHAW *Lett. to Isabel* xvii. 98 'There is a world elsewhere.' That is the secret... That it is which is the great regularizer.

regulate, *v.* Add: **5.** *refl.*, and *intr.* for *refl.* *Biol.* To exhibit regulation (sense *1 b).
1902 *Archiv für Entwicklungsmech. der Organismen* XV. 228 Pieces which are more active may be expected to regulate more widely. **1926** J. S. HUXLEY *Ess. Pop. Sci.* 235 The portion of substance which in its normal position would have developed into a half, has the power, if isolated, of regulating itself and its internal structure so as to give rise to a whole. **1971** *Nature* 24 Sept. 233/1 If half the optic tectum is removed and the optic nerve regenerates, the system regulates to preserve a retinotopic projection. **1977** *Sci. Amer.* July 67/1 Parts of the early embryo of various animals can be removed and the remaining parts will embryonically regulate to form a normal whole.

regulated, *ppl. a.* Add: **a.** Also *regulated tenancy*, a tenancy the rent of which is regulated by the terms of the Rent Acts (see quot. 1965).
1965 *Act Eliz. II* c. 75 § 1 In this Act 'regulated tenancy' means—a) a tenancy to which the Rent Acts apply by virtue of this section; or b) a statutory tenancy arising on the termination of such a tenancy as is mentioned in paragraph (a) of this subsection. **1970** *Internat. & Compar. Law Q.* 4th Ser. XIX. II. 206 Unfurnished tenancies under

the Rent Act being either (2) 'controlled' or (3) 'regulated tenancies'.

c. Proverb.

1819 'P. ATALL' *Hermit in America* i. 29 Accidents will happen in the best regulated families. **1850** DICKENS *David Copperfield* xxviii. 291 'My dear friend Copperfield,' said Mr. Micawber, 'accidents will occur in the best regulated families; and in families not regulated by that pervading influence..of Woman.' **1864** C. M. YONGE *Trial* II. iii. 60 Accidents will happen in the best regulated families. **1939** W. S. MAUGHAM *Christmas Holiday* x. 285 Accidents will happen in the best regulated families... If you find you've got anything the matter with you..go and see a doctor right away. **1961** M. KELLY *Spoilt Kill* iii. 159 Foul play... Even in the best regulated families.

regulating, *ppl. a.* Add: **3.** *Biol.* Of developing organisms or tissues (cf. *REGULATE *v.* 5).

1902 *Archiv für Entwicklungsmech. der Organismen* XV. 231 When a regulating piece is supplied with abundant food, growth and regulation are..very intimately connected. **1926** J. S. HUXLEY *Ess. Pop. Sci.* 259 This passage from a regulating to a non-regulating condition takes place during gastrulation, before the first structural differentiation, in the shape of the medullary plate, is visible at all.

regulation. Add: **1. b.** *Biol.* The property whereby a living organism can adapt the form of its body to accommodate for changes made or damage done to it, and whereby, in the normal course of development, the nature and growth of the various parts are so interrelated as to produce an integrated whole. Also *attrib.* [a. G. *regulation* (H. Driesch 1898, in *Ergebnisse d. Anat. und Entwickelungsgeschichte* VIII. 718).]

1902 *Archiv für Entwicklungsmech. der Organismen* XV. 187 The term regulation is employed here in the sense given by Driesch as including not only the actual regeneration of organs but any other changes, e.g., changes in the general form or outline and proportions of the body which may accompany or follow the replacement of lost parts. **1928** J. S. HUXLEY *Essays Pop. Sci.* 261 For Haldane, regulation places organisms in a different category from any non-living systems: for Driesch, it demands the intervention of vitalistic 'forces' such as his hypothetical entelechy. *Ibid.* 280 Once the tissues of the organism have become differentiated and it is capable of function, extraordinary powers of regeneration and regulation are developed. **1948** *New Biol.* V. 121 When the two cells resulting from the first cleavage division of a newt's egg are separated, at least one and often both form a complete though half-size individual. And conversely, two two-celled embryo newts can be fused to form a single large individual. This phenomenon of regulation, the adjustment of the entire developmental mechanism to disturbances of this sort, is a characteristic of the early stages of development of many kinds of animals. **1970** AMBROSE & EASTY *Cell Biol.* xiii. 422 Eggs of this type, which have the capacity to redevelop normally after a disturbance, are known as regulation eggs.

2*. *Electr.* The degree to which the output (or some other property) of an apparatus remains the same when the load varies, expressed as the percentage change in the former for a given change in the latter.

1899 FRANKLIN & WILLIAMSON *Elem. Alternating Currents* x. 129 A transformer of which the secondary e.m.f. falls off but little with increase of current is said to have good regulation. **1900** M. A. OUDIN *Standard Polyphase Apparatus & Systems* iii. 42 A certain three-phase unitooth machine of large output gave a regulation of 6¼ per cent, from full load to 10 per cent of the load. **1947** *Proc. IRE* XXXV. 444/2 The operations can be performed to any desired degree of precision, providing power supplies of excellent regulation and circuit components of high precision are used. **1975** *Physics Bull.* June 247/2 (Advt.), The 227 output is dependable, too. Excellent regulation of 0·005%, stability to 0·01% and low noise combine to assume high output resolution. **1977** *Design Engin.* July 81/1 Output regulation is specified as less than 0·1% for max to min load and for ±10% line voltage.

regulative, *a.* Add: **2.** *Biol.* Pertaining to or being regulation (sense *1 b); whose development is guided by regulation; opp. *MOSAIC *a.*[1] 5.

1902 *Archiv für Entwicklungsmech. der Organismen* XV. 229 Recognition of the fact that certain regulative processes are wholly or in part mechanical in nature is of importance for the future study of regulation. **1933** [see *MOSAIC *a.*[1] 5]. **1933** J. H. WOODGER tr. *L. von Bertalanffy's Mod. Theories Devel.* x. 143 In the regulative eggs cleavage occurs before segregation, so that every blastomere still contains the requisites for the formation of the whole organism. **1936** *Jrnl. Exper. Zool.* LXXIV. 91 The ability of the separated one-half blastomeres following the first cleavage to produce a one-half of normal size—so-called mosaic eggs—or a whole of one-half size—so-called regulative eggs. **1947** L. B. AREY *Developmental Anat.* (ed. 5) ix. 161 All gradations exist between determinative, mosaic eggs and indeterminate, regulative eggs. *Ibid.*, Even the mosaic egg of a tunicate is regulative before fertilization occurs. **1973** R. SEARLS in S. J. Coward *Developmental Regulation* ix. 241 A number of experiments indicate that the limb mesenchyme is completely regulative.

regulatively *adv.* (earlier and later examples).

1854 H. L. MANSEL *Man's Concept. Eternity* 10 A conception which is *speculatively* untrue may be *regulatively* true. **1952** *Mind* LXI. 554 Principles which function regulatively in ethical inquiry.

regulator. Add: **4. b.** *Econ.* A change in the rate of taxation which the Chancellor of the Exchequer may use to manipulate the economy between budgets; the power to operate such an alteration.

1961 *Daily Tel.* 18 Apr. 24/6 (*heading*) Economy 'regulators'. Changes without budget. *Ibid.*, This is the power he is taking to operate two new 'regulators' of the economy at any moment the Government thinks fit. *Ibid.* 7 July 1/8 Labour spokesmen maintained their objection to the Bill mainly on the grounds that excessive 'regulator' powers were left in the hands of the Government. **1968** *Times* 29 Nov. p. iv/4 The activation of the 10 per cent regulator has effectively doubled the tax..since the spring. **1976** *Daily Tel.* 1 Nov. 16 Full use of the regulator by itself would raise an extra £1,100 million of revenue in a full year and add 2½ p.c. to prices. The regulator currently permits value added tax to be raised by a quarter and specific duties such as those on drink, tobacco and petrol by a tenth between Budgets. **1977** *Whitaker's Almanack 1978* 354/1, I have decided to use my regulatory powers to increase by 10 per cent. all the revenue duties charged on tobacco and alcoholic drinks.

5. regulator gene *Genetics* [tr. F. *régulateur* (Jacob & Monod 1959, in *Compt. Rend.* CCXLIX. 1282)], a gene which codes for a polypeptide which can act as an operator to modify the frequency of initiation of transcription, so as to inhibit or stimulate the synthesis of mRNA (and hence of enzyme) on the structural genes of the operon.

1961 JACOB & MONOD in *Jrnl. Molecular Biol.* III. 334 A new type of gene, which we shall call a 'regulator gene'... A regulator gene does not contribute structural information to the proteins which it controls. The specific product of a regulator gene is a cytoplasmic substance, which inhibits information transfer from a structural gene (or genes) to protein. In contrast to the classical structural gene, a regulator gene may control the synthesis of several different proteins: the one-gene one-protein rule does not apply to it. **1969** A. M. CAMPBELL *Episomes* ix. 117 The regulator gene product has since been isolated. **1975** J. B. JENKINS *Genetics* xii. 527 There is some evidence for regulator genes and repressor substances in higher organisms, although their mode of operation appears to be quite different from those discussed under the operon concept.

regulatory, *a.* Add: **2.** *Biol.* Pertaining to, being, or involving regulation (sense *1 b).

1902 *Archiv für Entwicklungsmech. der Organismen* XV. 217 Morgan has proposed the name 'morphallaxis' for certain regulatory form-changes occurring in..lower animals, in consequence of which a piece gradually assumes more or less exactly the proportions of the whole organism. **1926** J. S. HUXLEY *Ess. Pop. Sci.* 302 This regulatory function of higher mechanisms is seen also in the domain of pure physiology. *Ibid.* 280 This period of non-regulation not only succeeds one regulatory phase, but precedes another. **1948** *New Biol.* V. 122 Many animals (especially those which undergo spiral cleavage) have little trace of profound regulatory power from the fertilised egg onwards. **1964** *New Perspectives in Biol.* IV. 246 A considerable amount is known about regulatory mechanisms in bacteria. *Ibid.* 259 The regulatory mechanisms that control cell differentiation in multi-cellular organisms may, in the not too distant future, cease to be one of the main unknown areas in biology.

Regulo (re·giŭlo). Also **regulo.** [a. L. *rēgulō* first pers. sing. pres. indic. of *rēgulāre* to regulate.] **a.** The proprietary name of a thermostatic control for a domestic gas oven.

1922 *Trade Marks Jrnl.* 29 Nov. 2182 Regulo... Taps and valves of ordinary metal... Radiation, Limited,..Birmingham; manufacturers. **1936** *Economist* 28 Mar. 738/1 The 'New World' cooker, with the 'Regulo'..revolutionised gas cooking. **1952** F. WHITE *Good English Food* II. i. 115 The oven..must be the right heat... Gas Companies provide Regulos at the side. **1968** S. E. ELLACOTT *Everyday Things in England 1914–68* ii. 33 About 1930 an oven-control dial was introduced for gas cookers. This was named 'Regulo'.

b. *attrib.*, esp. followed by a numeral indicating one of a scale of temperature settings marked on a Regulo. Also *fig.*

1926–7 *Army & Navy Stores Catal.* 291 'Regulo-controlled' gas cookers..fitted with the Regulo oven heat controller. **1936** LUCAS & HUME *Au Petit Cordon Bleu* 33 Cook in a fairly hot oven (Regulo Mark 6). **1958** *Spectator* 6 June 733/1 There was the Guildhall, where..a temperature approximating to Regulo 7, caused such breathiness among the woodwind. **1958** *Times* 6 Oct. 13/5 Place in well greased roasting-tin and cook for 45–60 minutes, according to size of bird. Regulo Mark 7. **1968** S. E. ELLACOTT *Everyday Things in England 1914–68* ii. 33 Cookery books..added the appropriate Regulo readings for their recipes. **1971** 'D. HALLIDAY' *Dolly & Doctor Bird* vii. 160 The permanently retired, stultifying in the sunshine at a low regulo setting. **1977** *New Society* 6 Oct. 22/1 The inevitable Tory tactic of keeping things low key by a regulo one campaign, which would let apathy take its toll. We went for regulo nine.

regulon (re·giŭlǫn). *Biol.* [f. REGUL(ATE *v.* + *-ON[1].] A unit comprising all the genetic material whose transcription is regulated by a single inducer or repressor.

1964 MAAS & CLARK in *Jrnl. Molecular Biol.* VIII. 365 The term *regulon* is proposed to describe such a system in which the production of all enzymes can be controlled by a single repressor substance. Two types of regulons can be distinguished, those in which the structural genes for the enzymes are adjacent to each other (histidine, tryptophan) and which thus consist of single operons, and those in which they are not (arginine) and which thus consist of several operons. **1976** *Ann. Rev. Microbiol.* XXX. 549 Because a single repressor regulates the specific expression of these operons with G3P as the inducer, the system has been referred to as the *glp* (for glycerophosphate) regulon. **1978** *Jrnl. Molecular Biol.* CXXIV. 359 (*heading*) Dominant constitutive mutations in *malT*, the positive regulator gene of the maltose regulon in *Escherichia coli*.

regur (re·gəɹ, rī̆·gəɹ). [ad. Hind. *regaṛ* black soil, ad. Telugu *rē-gaḍa*, *rē-gaḍi* clay.] Rich, dark, calcareous soil rich in clay, formed mainly by the weathering of basaltic rock and occurring extensively on the Deccan Plateau of India. Cf. *black cotton soil* s.v. *BLACK *a.* 19. Also *attrib.*

1828 *Edin. New Philos. Jrnl.* VI. 119 Immense deposits of a black alluvial clay are met with in various parts of India. It is denominated cotton ground, from the circumstance of that plant being always cultivated upon it. It is the regur soil of the ryuts. **1838** [see *black cotton ground* s.v. *BLACK *a.* 19]. **1879** MEDLICOTT & BLANFORD *Man. Geol. of India* I. xviii. 429 Regur, in its most characteristic form,.. preserves the constant characters of being highly argillaceous and somewhat calcareous, of becoming highly adhesive when wetted,..and of expanding and contracting to an unusual extent under the respective influences of moisture and dryness. **1906** E. W. HILGARD *Soils* xxi. 415 In view of the low rainfall and the closeness of the texture of regur, it is probable that little if any nitrates are currently washed out of the black cotton lands. *Ibid.*, The regur soil-sheet seems to be underlaid over the greater part of its area by a basaltic eruptive sheet. **1965** A. GOUREVITCH tr. *Gerasimov's Fund. of Soil Sci. & Soil Geogr.* xx. 326 In Asia, tropical black soils (regur) cover much of the Deccan plateau..and are widespread on the islands of Indonesia.

regurgitate. 1. a. (Earlier *fig.* example.)

1753 SMOLLETT *Count Fathom* II. lxii. 233 Renaldo's grief seemed to regurgitate with redoubled violence.

rehab (rī·hæb), *sb. slang.* (Not used in the U.K.) [abbrev. REHABILITATION.] **1.** = *REHABILITATION 2 d. Also *attrib. Austral.*, *N.Z.*, and *Canad.*

1948 K. STRONACH in A. E. Woodhouse *N.Z. Farm & Station Verse* (1950) 182 (*title*) Rehab. **1949** L. PETERSON *Chipmunk* 33 The car was completely theirs though; he'd paid cash for it out of his rehab money. **1953** M. SCOTT *Breakfast at Six* i. 12 This block's a Soldiers' Settlement. You know the sort of thing. Under Rehab. *Ibid.* vi. 53 It was the Rehab officer in charge of this settlement and others. **1959** G. C. SLATTER *Gun in my Hand* (1960) xi. 141 Rehab was the caper you jokers. **1964** *Canad. Weekly* 28 Nov. 12/3 By then I had a wife and child and my army rehab allowance was $90 a month. **1965** *N.Z. News* 27 Apr. 9/2 Rehabilitation assistance to returned war servicemen and women, a service known and respected throughout New Zealand as 'Rehab', officially ended on March 31. **1966** G. W. TURNER *Eng. Lang. in Austral. & N.Z.* viii. 172 A house may be bought with a rehab loan or a State advances loan.

2. = *REHABILITATION 2 c. Also *attrib. U.S.*

1961 PARTRIDGE *Dict. Slang* Suppl. 1246/2 *Rehab*, a rehabilitation ward or department in a hospital: since ca. 1945. **1970** *New York* 16 Nov. 45/2 The storefront drug-rehab center. **1976** *Amer. Speech 1973* XLVIII. 208 Afterward, alcoholics go to *rehab* 'the rehabilitation center' to readjust to a life free from the use of alcohol. **1977** *Chicago Tribune* 2 Oct. XII. 68/8 (Advt.), Rehab Nurse. Immediate position available in skilled nursing facility for Rehab Nursing Supervisor. **1978** *Tucson Mag.* Dec. 42/3 Hauling young people off to 're-hab' centers against their will may just be illegal.

3. = REHABILITATION 2 a. *U.S.*

1975 R. H. RIMMER *Premar Experiments* (1976) I. 125 If I can persuade him to sell for ten thousand dollars each, I'll toss this house in at ten thousand dollars. That will give us fifteen thousand dollars more for rehab. **1978** *New York* 3 Apr. 36/3 On the one hand, the re-habilitation provided work. Thomas was in touch with Peter Brennan, the building-trades leader, who was quite cooperative. The instructors in the re-hab program were often union members and the young trainees were doing jobs created only because of the program.

Hence as *v. trans.*; also **reha·bber.**

1977 *Archit. Rec.* Mar. 13/3 We can and should shorten time for developers and rehabbers. **1977** *Sat. Rev.* 23 July 9/2 The rehabilitation, into 28 apartments and several common rooms, of an abandoned tenement at 1186 Washington Avenue... 'rehab-ing' additional tenements in the vicinity of 1186. **1978** *Harper's Mag.* June 43 Solid 1890s structures built practically with slave labor, now rehabbed to perfection. **1979** *Arizona Daily Star* 1 Apr. J1/3 Rehabbing an older city home involves some special problems.

rehabilitate, *v.* Add: **3. b.** To restore (a disabled person, a criminal, etc.) to some degree of normal life by appropriate training.

1944 *New Statesman* 27 May 353/1, I think Dr. Rogerson's Patient would have had a very different outlook, had he been properly Rehabilitated. **1951** *Times* 20 Feb. 4/4 As soon as the wounded were rehabilitated they trained the new men, because of their valuable experience. **1968** *Listener* 19 Dec. 816/1 They want to rehabilitate us, but we think it is the rehabilitation officers who need rehabilitating, not us. **1978** *Lancashire Life* 51/1 The emphasis today is to rehabilitate old folk to enable them to remain active for as long as possible.

c. *absol.* for *refl.* To return from military to civilian status or purpose.

1945 *Daily Tel.* 29 June 4/3 Such assistance will be a precious aid to the first victims of the Axis—a people of 15,000,000 struggling to rehabilitate and develop, despite the grievous loss produced by the systematic murder by the Italians of the trained personnel and educated youth.

Also **rehabi·litating**, *vbl. sb.*

1924 *Glasgow Herald* 18 Mar. 6/3 The rehabilitating of Austria was carried a stage further.

rehabilitation. Add: **2. a.** (Further example.)

1973 *Detroit Legal News* 30 Aug. 13/8 Owner or interested party who appeared verbally granted a period of two weeks in which to..secure a building permit, and to immediately begin rehabilitation.

c. Restoration (of a disabled person, a criminal, etc.) to some degree of normal life by appropriate training. Cf. *REHABILITATE *v.* 3 b.

1940 M. J. MacDonald in *Hansard Commons* 17 Oct. 867 There is one..aspect of the healing of the wounded—.. which I should like to mention,..it is the secret of the maximum cure possible for the patient. It is the process known as rehabilitation. It is not sufficient that the wound should be healed; the wounded part of the patient must be enabled to function again so that he may once more play his part in society as a worker... I have appointed an adviser on rehabilitation. **1941** *Ann. Reg. 1940* 150 The principal questions for expert study being the..rehabilitation of men disabled in the war. **1952** *Rehabilitation* July (verso front cover). The British Council for Rehabilitation was founded in 1944... Rehabilitation was defined as 'the whole range of services from the time of the onset of the individuals' disability to the point at which he is restored to normal activity or the nearest possible approach to it'. **1974** *Science* 2 Aug. 423/2 People who are down on jails believe that the institutional setting is too dehumanizing for any meaningful rehabilitation to take place. **1979** *Internat. Rehabilit. Med.* I. 73/1 Mair..defined rehabilitation as implying the restoration of patients to their fullest physical, mental and social capability.

d. The retraining of a person, or the restoration of industry, the economy, etc., after a war or a long period of military service.

1941 *New Statesman* 15 Feb. 161/1 A military victory would be followed by the economic and democratic rehabilitation of France and Germany. **1941** *Times* (weekly ed.) 30 July 16/2 The possession of these..assets will ease the task of the Allied Governments when the time comes for the rehabilitation of European finance after the war. **1946** *R.A.F. Jrnl.* May 170 The career-finding agency..was inaugurated as one of the primary aids for rehabilitation of members. **1950** *N.Z. Jrnl. Agric.* May 458/2 (*heading*) Rehabilitation of Ex-servicemen. *Ibid.*, Land for the rehabilitation of returned servicemen has been..plentiful in Canada.

3. *attrib.*, as *rehabilitation area, camp, centre, counselling, grant, officer, programme, studies.* Also **rehabilitation medicine** (see quot. 1971).

1977 *Detroit Free Press* 11 Dec. 18-B/3 Improving city neighborhoods are excellent buys—especially rehabilitation areas where urban pioneers have turned the neighborhood around but buildings are still available at reasonable prices. **1967** W. Soyinka *Kongi's Harvest* 31 All the prostitutes were sent off to a rehabilitation camp. **1978** R. Ludlum *Holcroft Covenant* xx. 228 They were shocked beyond anything we can imagine when they learned about the 'rehabilitation camps'. Auschwitz, Belsen—it blew their minds. **1944** *Ourselves in Wartime* iii. 41 The Ministry of Labour..laid its plans for the rehabilitation of injured citizens. Men and women were trained at one of the Ministry of Labour's rehabilitation centres. **1967** R. Rendell *Wolf to Slaughter* vi. 64 What d'you do..? Start screaming like an addict in a rehabilitation centre? **1977** *Wandsworth Borough News* 16 Sept. 1/5 Government plans to erect a rehabilitation centre for 125 homeless men on the site of the old Battersea General Hospital. **1976** *Laurel* (Montana) *Outlook* 9 June 13/4 Graduate students received 94 master of science degrees, with 46 being in education, 31 in special education, and 15 in rehabilitation counselling. **1956** T. H. Raddall *Wings* 30 After I got my discharge from the army I took a forestry course at U.N.B., on my rehabilitation grant. **1969** *Jrnl. Amer. Med. Assoc.* 6 Jan. 137 (*heading*) Rehabilitation medicine's challenge for the 1970's. **1971** *Lancet* 27 Nov. 1207/2 A few years ago the University of New York announced that..they would no longer use the term 'physical medicine' in the context of rehabilitation but would replace it with the term 'rehabilitation medicine'. *Ibid.*, The following..relates to a World Congress to be held in Sydney, Australia, in August, 1972: 'Rehabilitation Medicine is a special area of medical practice traditionally concerned with the problems of the severely disabled and with the task of restoring them to a place of independence and dignity in society.' **1977** *Rehabilitation* Jan.–Mar. 8/1 With the recent international tendency to use the term 'Rehabilitation Medicine' instead of 'Physical Medicine' and, therefore, bringing in sociological and psychological factors, the pressing need for coordinated post-graduate study became the Council's challenge. **1979** *Internat. Rehabilit. Med.* I. 44/1 The ultimate goal is to establish rehabilitation medicine alongside diagnosis and treatments, as one of the three activities of all practising doctors. **1968** Rehabilitation officer [see *REHABILITATE *v.* 3 b]. **1950** *N.Y. Times* 20 Apr. 1/2 President Truman approved..a bill authorizing an economic rehabilitation programme for the Navajo and Hopi Indian tribes. **1973** *Brit. Med. Jrnl.* 17 Mar. 687/3 (*heading*) Chair of rehabilitation studies. **1974** *Ibid.* 15 June 622/1 Dr. Cairns Aitken, senior lecturer in the department of psychiatry, Edinburgh University, has been appointed to the newly founded chair of rehabilitation studies at that university.

rehabilitative (rīhăbi·lĭtātiv), *a.* [f. Rehabilitat(e *v.* + -ive.] Of or pertaining to rehabilitation; designed to rehabilitate.

1958 *Times* 8 Oct. 11/3 The rehabilitative process should begin with a man's arrival and should not stop short at the moment of release. **1963** T. & P. Morris *Pentonville* vii. 172 Many inmates are full of ideas about how prison could be improved, both as a deterrent and a rehabilitative technique. **1973** *Black Panther* 22 Sept. 5/2 There are no rehabilitative services offered in the Texas prisons. **1979** *Arizona Daily Star* 8 Apr. (Parade Suppl.) 4/1 This is short-term alimony, where the husband pays his former wife a monthly stipend for a limited period, generally two years, or even a lump sum. The term used by lawyers is 'rehabilitative alimony'. The idea is for the ex-wife to take advantage of the alimony period to return to school, to take a brushup course, or to launch a career. **1979** *Internat. Jrnl. Sociol. of Law* VII. 329 She feels that with the turn away from the rehabilitative model, indeterminate sentences and parole, we may inadvertently end up with a less discriminating system.

rehabilitee (rīːhăbiliti·). [f. Rehabilit(ate *v.* + -ee[1].] One who is (being) rehabilitated.

1972 *Rehabilitation* July–Sept. 7 Only in recent years would government seem to have begun to appreciate the importance of social aspects and the quality of life available for the rehabilitee, as opposed to concentrating on industrial aspects. **1978** *Jrnl. R. Soc. Med.* LXXI. 449 Two beds in the Lonsdale Unit were reserved for rehabilitees.

reha·logenize, *v.* *Photogr.* [f. Re- 5 b + Halogen + -ize.] *trans.* To convert the metallic silver in a developed image back to a silver halide (with the silver or the image as obj.). So **reha·logenizing** *vbl. sb.*

1940 F. J. Mortimer *Wall's Dict. Photogr.* (ed. 15) 549 *Rehalogenising*, the re-conversion of the silver image in a finished print or negative into silver chloride, bromide, or iodide. **1969** M. J. Langford *Advanced Photogr.* xi. 235 This bleach 're-halogenises' the silver image—the ferricyanide oxidises the silver which reacts with the bromide and reverts to a silver halide. **1977** J. Hedgecoe *Photographer's Handbk.* 324 *Bleach*, chemical bath capable of rehalogenizing black metallic silver.

Hence **reha:logeniza·tion**, the process of rehalogenizing.

1956 *Focal Encycl. Photogr.* 967/1 *Rehalogenization*, conversion of a silver image back into one of silver halide. **1958** *Newnes Compl. Amat. Photogr.* 323 As this process involves rehalogenisation of the silver image it is essential that the print and utensils used are completely free from hypo. **1967** E. Chambers *Photolitho-Offset* iv. 48 An improvement in the dot etching properties of the positives can be effected by tanning the gelatin in proportion to the silver image, resulting in a greater degree of lateral etching without loss of density. This process is known as rehalogenisation, or metallising.

rehash, *v.* Add: **2.** Chiefly *U.S.* To consider, mull over, discuss (an idea, performance, etc.) afterwards.

1965 Mrs. L. B. Johnson *White House Diary* 14 Dec. (1970) 340 Our houseguests..were all gathered around Lyndon rehashing the events of the evening. **1974** *Los Angeles Times* 13 Oct. III. 9/1 The Dodgers were anything but downtrodden as they rehashed the game. **1977** *Time* 31 Jan. 48/3 If he meets someone he knows after a session he may stop him on the street to rehash it.

rehear, *v.* **2.** (Earlier and later examples.)

1799 F. Burney *Jrnls. & Lett.* (1973) IV. 297 He has taken the amazing trouble & toil of copying the whole, from the pleasure the interview gave him! though he may always re-hear it *de vive voix*! **1947** *Observer* 28 Dec. 2/5, I long to rehear such great contrapuntal machines as the *Quoniam* and *Amen* choruses.

rehearsal. Add: **1.** *spec.* in *Psychol.*, the intentional repetition (mentally or verbally) of information in order to keep it temporarily in the memory.

1935 *Amer. Jrnl. Psychol.* XLVII. 66 Reminiscence..has not yet been demonstrated to occur independently of review, either intentional rehearsal or casual revival, during the interval between the two tests of retention. **1951** S. S. Stevens *Handbk. Exper. Psychol.* xvii. 654/1 Color naming has commonly been used during the rest interval in an attempt to reduce rehearsal. **1960** O. H. Mowrer *Learning Theory & Behavior* x. 365 A telephone number will be 'remembered', without rehearsal, for a short time after it is seen in a directory (or heard spoken), but will then usually be lost quite completely. **1976** [see *REHEARSE *v.* 1 d]. **1979** W. A. Wickelgren *Cognitive Psychol.* viii. 235 The classification of memory into learning, storage, and retrieval leaves the cognitive process of rehearsal somewhat in limbo.

2. a. Also, the act of practising any ceremony, e.g. a wedding or a state occasion. (Further examples.)

1953 Rodgers & Pearce *Altar Bound* 45 The rehearsal dinner takes place immediately before or after the rehearsal, and..is given by either the parents of the bride or groom. **1963** A. Vanderbilt *New Compl. Bk. Etiquette* ix. 93 It is becoming more and more popular for the wedding rehearsal to be held in the late afternoon the day before the wedding, followed by a rehearsal dinner, which may be scheduled for six-thirty or seven o'clock. In some sections of the country, mainly the South and Midwest, it is customary for the groom's parents to give the rehearsal dinner. **1977** *Times* 24 Mar. 2 (*heading*) Ulster trip by Princess becomes rehearsal for Queen's visit.

3. *attrib.*, as *rehearsal break, complex, hall, pianist, room*; **rehearsal band,** a band that meets to practise jazz, dance music, etc.; **rehearsal dinner** *U.S.*, a dinner held after a wedding rehearsal (usually in the evening before the wedding); **rehearsal script** (see quot.).

1969 *Down Beat* 17 Apr. 19/3 There have been any number of rehearsal bands around New York in the past 10 years. **1970** *New Yorker* 23 May 78/2 The so-called 'rehearsal' bands of Thad Jones–Mel Lewis, Clark Terry, [etc.]. **1957** *Sentinel* (Milwaukee) 14 Nov. II. 6/3 'That six minutes is beginning to look like an awful long time,' shivered Junie, chewing nonchalantly on a coffee cup during a rehearsal break. **1977** *West Briton* 25 Aug. 10/2 The dawning of a new and promising era for Redruth Amateur Operatic Society... The society took over its new rehearsal complex at Plain-an-Gwarry. **1953, 1963** Rehearsal dinner [see sense *2 a above]. **1974** *State* (Columbia, S. Carolina) 3 & 4 Mar. G8/6 The groom gifts his attendants at the rehearsal dinner or bachelor dinner. **1960** 'E. McBain' *Give Boys Great Big Hand* x. 107 Unfurnished rehearsal halls and the cubbyhole offices of music publishers. **1976** *Listener* 29 July 121/2 The last 17 hopefuls..gather together in the rehearsal hall. **1977** S. Brett *Star Trap* i. 11 There was a guy..who was rehearsal pianist for the show. **1959** M. Summerton *Small Wilderness* i. 18 Reading a part in a rehearsal room. **1979** *Jrnl. R. Soc. Arts* CXXVII. 500/1 The school housed an excellent theatre, a number of rehearsal rooms, a swimming pool, [etc.]. **1960** Rehearsal script [see *master-scene* s.v. *MASTER *sb.*[1] 29].

rehearse, *v.* Add: **1. d.** *Psychol.* To repeat, either mentally or orally (what it is desired to keep temporarily in the memory); to engage in rehearsal (sense *1).

1917 *Arch. Psychol.* XL. 103 Frequent reviews..throw into relief the portions [of memorised material] that are hazy, inexact and confused..because they fix more clearly in mind the material that is rehearsed. **1951** S. S. Stevens *Handbk. Exper. Psychol.* xvii. 654/1, 84 per cent of her younger subjects and 70 per cent of the older ones reported that they had rehearsed in the interval between learning and recall. **1964** *Jrnl. Exper. Psychol.* LXVIII. 414/2 The present experiment is designed to investigate the consequences for short-term memory of instructing *Ss* to rehearse a sequence of digits in groups of one, two, three, four, and five during presentation. **1976** G. R. & E. F. Loftus *Human Memory* iv. 56 Rehearsal can do two things: it can keep the information in short-term store for as long as we continue rehearsing, and it can also act as a mechanism by which information is transferred from short-term to long-term store. **1979** W. A. Wickelgren *Cognitive Psychol.* iii. 84 Time yourself reciting the alphabet verbally. Then time yourself while you go through the alphabet again, this time imaging each letter as if it were projected on a screen. It will take you about three times as long..as it did to rehearse each letter verbally.

rehearsed *ppl. a.*, restrict † to sense in Dict. and add: (*b*) that has been practised beforehand.

1871 L. Lockhart *Fair to See* I. vi. 167 He turned to confront them, on their entrance, with a carefully rehearsed mien.

reheat (rī·hīt), *sb.* [f. the vb.] **1. a.** The action or an instance of reheating; *spec.* artificial or spontaneous heating of the working fluid in a turbine taking place between stages. Also *attrib.*

1913 [see *reheat factor* below]. **1918** *Engineering* 6 Sept. 245/1 The case of a turbine consisting of two equal stages which, in order to avoid complications due to 'reheat', will be assumed to be operated by water. **1938** *Van Nostrand's Sci. Encycl.* 950/1 Many industrial processes in which heat plays a part, employ reheating, sometimes to the extent of several 'reheats'. **1953** Jennings & Rogers *Gas Turbine Analysis & Practice* iii. 104 One of the factors contributing to this lower efficiency is the..deleterious effect of reheat in the compressor. **1959** *Motor* 27 May 562/3 The resultant gases pass through the high-speed turbine, then a second, 're-heat' combustion chamber followed by the power turbine. **1965** *Economist* 17 Apr. 326/1 The main items needed..are another reheat furnace for the slabbing mill and a cold reduction line. **1966** *McGraw-Hill Encycl. Sci. & Technol.* XI. 425/2 Under suitable conditions of initially high steam pressure and superheat, one or two stages of reheat can be advantageously employed to improve thermodynamic efficiency of the cycle. **1975** J. B. Woodward *Marine Gas Turbines* ii. 44 The reheat step consists of a constant-pressure heating interposed between two expansion processes.

b. *Aeronaut.* = *AFTER-BURNING *vbl. sb.* 2. Also, an afterburner.

1949 [see *AFTER-BURNING *vbl. sb.* 2]. **1950** *Engineering* 6 Oct. 295/1 The performance of a jet engine may be changed by 'reheat' i.e., the burning of additional fuel with residual oxygen remaining in the combustion gases after they have passed through the turbine. **1957** *Ann. Reg. 1956* I. 14 The hero of the occasion was Mr. L. P. Twiss flying a Fairey Delta 2 research aircraft, powered by a Rolls Royce Avon turbo-jet fitted with reheat. **1959** *Spectator* 4 Sept. 295/1 A fighter making a 700-mile-an-hour run a few feet from the spectators, with re-heat ablaze, used to be a grand spectacle. **1972** D. Hart-Davis *Spider in Morning* ii. 21 The reheats were in and burning fuel at a terrifying rate. **1976** *Farnborough Internat. Exhibition* (Official Programme) 11/2 Such is the engines' thrust when reheat is on that fuel is burnt up at an incredible 20 tons an hour.

2. Special Comb.: **reheat factor,** a measure of the performance of a multistage steam turbine, usu. expressed as the ratio of the measured efficiency of the turbine and the (lower) efficiency expected on the assumption of adiabatic expansion of the steam.

1913 H. M. Martin *Design & Constr. of Steam Turbines* v. 44 It will be noted that after an expansion of one hundred-fold or so, the ratio ϵ/η becomes practically constant. This ratio..is known as the 'reheat factor'. **1950** J. K. Salisbury *Steam Turbines & their Cycles* i. 34 The sum of the stage available energies is greater than the turbine available energy by a small amount. The ratio of these two quantities is..the reheat factor. **1961** Fox & McBirnie *Marine Steam Engines & Turbines* (ed. 2) xviii. 438 The significance of the reheat factor is that in a multi-stage steam turbine any particular stage benefits somewhat from the inefficiency of the preceding stages.

reheated, *ppl. a.* Add: *spec.* in *Aeronaut.*, equipped with or augmented by afterburning. Cf. *REHEAT *sb.* 1 b.

1961 F. K. MASON *Hawker Aircraft since 1920* 74 Work started on a development using a fifty degree swept wing and a re-heated Avon of greatly increased power. **1976** *Farnborough International Exhibition* (Official Programme) 43/1 With a reheated take-off thrust of 38,000 lbs., this engine entered airline service in Concorde.

Reheboth, var. *REHOBOTH.

Rehoboam (rīhǒbōᵘ·ăm, rī͵ǒ-). [f. the name of *Rehoboam*, son of Solomon, King of Judah (I Kings xii–xiv).] †**1.** A shovel hat. *Obs. rare*—[1].

1849 C. BRONTË *Shirley* I. i. 11 A personage of short stature..bearing on broad shoulders a hawk's head,..the whole surmounted by a Rheoboam [**1850** Rehoboam] or shovel-hat, which he did not seem to think it necessary to lift.

2. A large bottle for wine or spirits, bigger than a JEROBOAM and smaller than a *METHUSELAH 2.

1895 *Brewer's Dict. Phr. & Fable* (new ed.) 1050/1 A rehoboam of claret or rum is a double jeroboam. **1959** *Gloss. Packaging Terms* (*B.S.I.*) 28 *Rehoboam*, a wine bottle—capacity 6 reputed quarts. **1960** *Times* 11 Jan. 17/2 A vigorous passing movement across the ground by three Frenchmen with a dummy rehoboam of champagne was ended only by a flagrant knock-on. **1972** [see *METHUSELAH 2].

Rehoboth (rī·͵ǒbǫþ). *S. Afr.* Also erron. **Reheboth.** [a. Heb. *rĕḥōbhōth* wide places.] A Biblical place-name (Gen. xxvi. 22), applied to a river, town, and district in Namibia (South West Africa), and used as the name of a people of mixed African and European descent. Also *attrib.* Hence **Re·hobother.** So **Rehobo·thian** *sb.*

1875 C. J. ANDERSSON *Notes of Trav. in S. Afr.* vi. 88 The cattle, etc., might have been retaken had our friends, the Rehobothians, at once accompanied me in pursuit of the marauders. **1926** S. G. MILLIN *South Africans* vii. 198 To-day self-governing half-caste tribes like the Bondelswarts and the Reheboths still exist in South-West Africa to trouble the souls of their white neighbours. **1930** C. G. SELIGMAN *Races of Africa* ii. 34 The old Hottentot population of the Cape has become largely absorbed by racial admixture with incoming Europeans and East Indian slaves, and has thus constituted the basis of the present.. 'Rehoboth' half-breeds. **1935** L. G. GREEN *Great African Mysteries* x. 125 The half-caste Rehoboths..set up nothing less than a civilised republic in a savage land. **1937** *Decisions High Court S.-W. Africa Jan. to Dec. 1936* 59 *Held*, that in this Territory the term 'Baster' when it is ascribed to a person's race is well known to refer to the members of the Reheboth Bastard Community. **1960** *State of Union 1959–60* lxv. 430 The *Rehobothers* whose number is estimated at 8,900, are of mixed origin, having immigrated from the Cape. **1970** *Standard Encycl. Southern Afr.* II. 191/2 The majority are..the descendants of early Basters and they insist on being called Rehoboth Basters, a term they reserve strictly to themselves. **1973** *Observer* (Colour Suppl.) 2 Sept. 56/1 Hereros, Ovambos, Damaras, Kakaovelders, Bushmen and Rehobothers (until recently known as the Bastards).

reho:spitaliza·tion. [f. RE- 5 a + *HOSPITALIZATION.] The act or the state of being admitted again to hospital.

1974 M. C. GERALD *Pharmacol.* xvi. 305 The remaining patients retain varying degrees of psychopathology, with many requiring periodic rehospitalization.

rehouse, *v.* (Later examples.)

1904 G. B. SHAW *Common Sense of Municipal Trading* viii. 75 The municipality bargains with the Local Government Board as to how many people it must rehouse. **1935** *Scrutiny* IV. 134 The problem of re-housing the inhabitants after slum-clearance is at present dealt with unsatisfactorily. **1966** *Listener* 6 Oct. 511/1 The first few years after the war.. saw the re-housing of Turner in the glory that he deserved. **1978** *Lancashire Life* Apr. 105/1 This trolley can be moved freely on its castors, then re-housed in its own base unit. **1980** *Jrnl. R. Soc. Arts* Mar. 186/2, 5½ per cent of London's total built up area was bought and developed for railway use without any statutory responsibility to re-house the displaced residents.

Hence **rehou·sed** *ppl. a.* Also *absol.* or as *sb.*

1927 *Scots Observer* 26 Feb. 2/5, I have seen the re-housed in their new environment. **1940** HARRISSON & MADGE *War begins at Home* xii. 331 Many of the re-housed families would go back to their old homes if they had not been pulled down.

rehousing, *vbl. sb.* (Later examples.)

1904 G. B. SHAW *Common Sense of Municipal Trading* viii. 76 The displaced have solved the rehousing problem by crossing the river into Battersea. **1936** 'G. ORWELL' *Diary* 27 Feb. in *Coll. Essays* (1968) I. 189 The re-housing is almost entirely the work of the Corporation. **1977** G. SCOTT *Hot Pursuit* iii. 31 Singapore's progressive rehousing policies.

rehydra·te, *v.* [RE- 5 a.] **a.** *intr.* To absorb water again, esp. after dehydration.

1923 J. W. MELLOR *Comprehensive Treat. Inorg. & Theoret. Chem.* III. 763 Crystals of the hemihydrate which practically re-hydrated on cooling. **1968** *Physics Bull.* Dec. 430 Technical advances..have resulted in good products which rehydrate quickly.

b. *trans.* To add water to again after dehydration; *esp.* to restore (dehydrated food) to a palatable state by the addition of water.

1962 F. I. ORDWAY et al. *Basic Astronautics* xiii. 521 The water necessary to rehydrate these processed foods can be recovered. **1965** *Listener* 10 June 875/1 We saw the astronauts learning to rehydrate their plastic bagfuls of strawberry cereal. **1969** *New Scientist* 16 Jan. 128/2 The food was shown to be fully dehydrated; and when later rehydrated it tasted excellent. **1971** *Sci. Amer.* Aug. 18/3 The patient is first rehydrated by intravenous injection, if necessary, and is then fed the oral solution at the rate at which fluid is lost by diarrhea. **1978** *Jrnl. R. Soc. Med.* LXXI. 223 He was given broad-spectrum antibiotics and rehydrated.

Hence **rehydra·table** *a.*, that may be rehydrated; **rehydra·ted** *ppl. a.*

1956 *Nature* 4 Feb. 239/2 When a flake of magnesium vermiculite, which has been partially dehydrated to the phase containing single sheets of interlayer water molecules .., is allowed to become rehydrated, a dark line is observed to enter the flake at the edges and gradually converge on the centre. **1969** *New Scientist* 16 Jan. 128/3 The rehydrated product should as far as possible be identical with the fresh product. **1970** N. ARMSTRONG et al. *First on Moon* vi. 127 U.S. choice beef was better for rehydratable meat cubes than prime, which had too much fat. **1975** *Radio Times* 12–18 July 40 Menu [for U.S. astronauts], rehydratable romaine soup,..rehydratable coffee. **1975** *Daily Colonist* (Victoria, B.C.) 12 July 1/2 The cosmonauts will dine on steak in plastic pouches, rye bread, cheese spread, rehydrated strawberries and tea with lemon and sugar [etc.].

rehydra·tion. [RE- 5 a.] The process of adding or taking up water again, usu. after dehydration.

1866 [in Dict. s.v. RE- 5 a]. **1923** J. W. MELLOR *Comprehensive Treat. Inorg. & Theoret. Chem.* III. 763 Special precautions are needed to remove water rapidly before it cools much below 130°, or rehydration sets in. **1936** *Discovery* Oct. 329/1 In summer influenza the protein particles of the blood plasm are subject to hydration, in early winter dehydration takes place while rehydration in late winter is followed closely by an epidemic in February and March. **1947** J. C. RICH *Materials & Methods of Sculpture* iv. 67 The setting of plaster of Paris after it has been mixed with water is also referred to as a *rehydration* and occasionally as a *recrystallization* of the calcined gypsum back to its original hydrated rock form. **1965** *New Scientist* 26 Aug. 498/3 Natural mayonnaise would not be used, since the emulsion separates on freezing giving an oil which, it was feared, would hinder re-hydration. **1979** *Nature* 29 Mar. 389/1 The possibility of oral rehydration has provided Third World health authorities with a very valuable breakthrough in the treatment of diarrhoeal diseases.

‖ **Reich** (rəiχʸ, rəik). Pl. **Reiche.** [Ger., = kingdom, realm, state: see RICHE, RIKE.] Chiefly during the period 1871–1945, the German state or commonwealth; also, one of a sequence of empires or régimes in Germany, esp. the *THIRD REICH.

Apart from *Third Reich*, collocations with an ordinal are rare and do not constitute recognized English historical terminology.

1921 *Times* 19 Jan. 11/2 All the States proclaim..their loyalty to the Reich. **1924** *Hansard Commons* 16 Jan. 152 We have always pointed out that,..if any part of the German Reich wished to set up an autonomous area for itself, they must utilise their own constitutional machinery. **1933** *Times* 15 Mar. 15/2 During the past week the Nazi steam-roller has passed over every one of the seventeen Federal States of the Reich. **1946** *Britannica Bk. of Year* (U.S.) 341/2 Germany was deprived not only of all Hitler's annexations of territory, but also of all former German reich territory east of the Oder and western Neisse rivers. **1972** F. FORSYTH *Odessa File* ii. 46, I have commandeered this ship in the name of the Reich. **1973** *Nature* 14 Sept. 107/2 A penetratingly sketched background of the fortunes and misfortunes of the Second and Third *Reiche*. *Ibid.*, The Jews had been emancipated in Prussia in 1812 and..had come to occupy high places in the Second Reich. **1974** J. WHITE tr. *Poulantzas's Fascism & Dictatorship* VII. v. 338 The dismembering of the State apparatus was also expressed in contradictions between the central authority of the Reich and the provincial authorities. **1976** *New Yorker* 8 Mar. 130/2 The villains here are a secret 'Comrades Organization' of ex-Nazis, who live in Brazil and hope to establish a Fourth Reich.

Also (f. the gen. sing.) **Rei·chsbank** [G. *bank* bank], the name of the central bank of the German Reich, 1875–1945; **Rei·chsbanner** [G. *banner* banner], a republican para-military organization in Germany from 1924 to 1933; **Rei·chsmark** [G. *mark* MARK *sb.*[2] in Dict. and Suppl.], the monetary unit of the German Reich, replaced in 1948 by the *DEUTSCHE MARK; **Rei·chsma:rschall, -ma:rshall** [Ger., in full *Reichsmarschall des Grossdeutschen Reiches* Marshal of the Greater German Reich], a title bestowed on Hermann Göring (1893–1946) in 1940 by Adolf Hitler; **Rei·chsrat** (formerly **-rath**) (-rāt) [G. *rat(h* council: cf. *BUNDESRAT], (*a*) the parliament of the Austrian part of the Habsburg Empire; (*b*) the council of the federated states of Germany between the end of the 1914–18 war and 1933; **Rei·chswehr** (-vēr) [G. *wehr* defence], the name of the German army between 1919 and 1935. See also *REICHSTAG.

All usu. with capital initial in Eng. as in German.

1879 *Encycl. Brit.* X. 466/1 The Imperial Bank (Reichsbank) ranks far above the others in importance. **1977** *New Yorker* 3 Oct. 85/1 Nazi archives at the Reichsbank.. yielded substantial data. **1924** *Times* 6 Dec. 11/1 Some scattered organizations..were amalgamated to be the nucleus of a united Republican guard, known as the Reichsbanner Black–Red–Gold.., the 'Great Germany' idea being invariably pushed into the foreground at Reichsbanner demonstrations. **1935** C. ISHERWOOD *Mr. Norris changes Trains* viii. 130 The newspapers were full of deathbed photographs of rival martyrs, Nazi, Reichsbanner and Communist. **1964** *Listener* 25 June 1038/2 The Reich authorities began..to condemn the Reichsbanner, an organization which existed solely to defend the Republic. **1874** *Anglo-Brazilian Times* (Rio de Janeiro) 23 Dec. 5/3 The business on Hamburg has been done at 448 reis per reichsmark at 90 days and 454 reis for sight drafts. **1924** *Times* 7 Nov. 11/6 The new banknotes of 10, 20, 50 and 100 Reichsmarks, which are part of the reformed and stabilized German currency..were exhibited at the Reichsbank this morning. **1978** *Time* 3 July 8/1 The old reichsmarks of the Nazi regime had become worthless. **1940** *R.A.F. in Action* 16 On the 20th May, 1940, the Reichsmarshal..was forced to promise that more guns would be provided immediately. **1976** J. WHEELER-BENNETT *Friends, Enemies & Sovereigns* ii. 36, I have always regretted that I was not present to see his defeat of Goering on that celebrated occasion when the Reichsmarschall had 'made a monkey' out of the chief American prosecutor, Robert Jackson, and David had deflated him. **1858** *New Amer. Cycl.* II. 392/2 The council of state, or *Reichsrath*, composed of 12 members, is a body coördinate to the ministry, and communicating immediately with the emperor. **1905** *Spectator* 11 Feb. 201 Meanwhile the Pan-German delegates in the Austrian Reichsrath are agitating for economic severance from Hungary and alliance with Germany. **1919** *German Constitution* (H.M.S.O.) I. 11 A Reichsrat is formed for the representation of the German States in Federal legislation. **1943** S. H. THOMSON *Czechoslovakia in European Hist.* ix. 180 The Vienna Parliament (Reichsrat) which functioned as the legislative body for the Austrian half of the Empire. **1969** E. WALL *Europe Unification & Law* iii. 72 Though the Reichsrat, representing the federated Länder, could object to a bill, the objection could be overridden by a two-thirds majority of the Reichstag or..by referendum. **1920** *Times* 30 Oct. 9/3 He depicted the Reichswehr as mainly a Royalist institution. **1934** *Ann. Reg. 1933* 182 A Heimwehr patrol [in Austria] shot dead a German Reichswehr soldier. **1976** J. WHEELER-BENNETT *Friends, Enemies & Sovereigns* iv. 100, I had had first-hand experience of the Seekt and Schleicher periods of the *Reichswehr* and of its brief honeymoon with Hitler which began to wane with the Night of the Long Knives in June 1934.

Reichert (rəi·χəɹt). The name of Emil *Reichert* (1838–94), German food scientist, used in the possessive and *attrib.* (freq. in *Comb.* with another name, as *Meissl, Polenske, Wollny*) with reference to standard procedures for determining the proportion of volatile water-soluble fatty acids present in butter, fats, and oils (one of which he published in *Zeitschr. f. anal. Chem.* (1879) XVIII. 68).

1885 *Analyst* X. 103 Reichert's process possesses every advantage over Hehner's, which is becoming replaced by the former. **1887** *Ibid.* XII. 203 (*heading*) On Reichert–Meissl's method of butter analysis. **1892** *Ibid.* VII. 171 Reichert..proposed to saponify 2·5 grammes of butter with caustic soda and alcohol, evaporate off the alcohol, add 50 c.c. of water and 2 c.c. dilute sulphuric acid, and to distil 50 c.c. in a weak current of air. This method, although Reichert himself calls it Hehner's method, is now known as the Reichert process. *Ibid.* 175 The Reichert–Wollny method is largely adopted in every country except France, and may be considered a standard method. **1894** *Ibid.* XIX. 189 Filtered butter-fat will give a constant Reichert–Meissl number for many weeks. **1901** *Ibid.* XXVI. 71 (*heading*) Note on the Reichert value of butter and other fats. **1906** [see *POLENSKE]. **1928** [see *KIRSCHNER]. **1936** *Analyst* LXI. 404 As the original Reichert process, using 2·5 g. of fat, and as the Reichert–Meissl process, using 5 g., have been obsolete since Wollny modified the Meissl process nearly 50 years ago, and as the name Reichert is common to the different forms, it may now be used alone in place of the indiscriminate use of the hyphenated forms, Reichert–Meissl, Reichert–Meissl–Wollny, Reichert–Wollny and Reichert–Polenske, when applied to the soluble volatile acids. **1957** *Encycl. Brit.* IV. 469/2 The Reichert–Meissel [*sic*] (Reichert–Wollny) value..is a valuable characteristic in butterfat analysis. **1973** [see *POLENSKE].

Reichian (rəi·χiăn), *sb.* and *a.* [f. the name of Wilhelm *Reich* (1897–1957), Austrian psychologist + -IAN.] **A.** *sb.* A supporter of the theories or practices of Wilhelm Reich, esp. those relating to sexual energy as vital energy (cf. *ORGONE), to its effect in determining character and mental health, or to his hypothesis that authoritarian regimes emerge in cultures that are sexually repressive. **B.** *adj.* Of, pertaining to, or following Reich or his theories.

1959 *Partisan Rev.* XXVI. 51 The Reichians want to believe in Socialism again. **1959** N. MAILER *Advts. for Myself* (1961) 295 The Yoga's *prana*, the Reichian's orgone, Lawrence's 'blood'. **1969** P. A. ROBINSON *Freudian Left* I. 10 The true Reichian is convinced that Reich's greatest contributions lay..in biophysics and astronomy. **1970** R. LOWELL *Notebook* 247 Such cures the bygone Reichian prophets swore to. **1976** *Listener* 8 Jan. 4/2 One of the unique features of present-day Portugal is the concurrence of political and sexual revolution. It provides a laboratory for Reichian radicals who see a causal relationship between sexual repression and totalitarianism, on one side, and sexual liberation and revolution, on the other. **1978** *N.Y. Rev. Bks.* 23 Feb. 29/4 The Victorian idea of TB as a disease of low energy..has its exact complement in the Reichian idea of cancer as a disease of unexpressed energy.

Reichstag (rəi·χʸsˌtāk, rəi·ksˌtāg). [Ger., f. gen. sing. of *REICH + *tag* diet: cf. *BUNDESTAG.] The diet or parliament of the German Empire (1871–1918) (formerly also, that of the North German Confederation) and of post-Imperial Germany until 1945; the building in Berlin in which this parliament met. Also *transf.*

1867 *Times* 3 Jan. 10/1 It is proposed to exclude Government functionaries, not from the future Diet of the Confederation (Reichstag), but only from the Parliament which is about to assemble. **1870** GEO. ELIOT *Let.* 3 Apr. (1956) V. 87 We went to the Reichstag one morning, and were so fortunate as to hear Bismarck speak. **1889** M. H. VAN DE VELDE *Cosmopolitan Recollections* I. v. 167 Will he attend the Reichstag? **1909** M. A. VON ARNIM *Caravaners* xiii. 220 She began to talk to me..about..our Reichstag. **1935** C. ISHERWOOD *Mr. Norris changes Trains* xvi. 263 We ought to be grateful to van der Lubbe, because the burning of the Reichstag had melted the snow. **1944** J. S. HUXLEY *On Living in Revol.* 138 In 1928..the Nazis had secured less than 2 per cent. of the seats in the Reichstag. **1975** *Times* 4 Mar. 1/2 From the Tory benches, there was a claim that the Commons was being turned into a Reichstag.

2. *attrib.*, as **Reichstag Fire**, a fire which destroyed the Reichstag building on 27 Feb. 1933, believed to have been engineered by the Nazi party in order to facilitate their seizure of power; **Reichstag Trial**, the subsequent trial of the alleged incendiary, Marinus van der Lubbe, and others; also *transf.*, as the type of a staged trial.

1933 *Times* 1 Mar. 13/2 A communication about the Reichstag fire was issued by the Prussian authorities. **1976** S. HYNES *Auden Generation* v. 143 The Reichstag fire appears as an emblem of public terror. **1968** D. HOPKINSON *Incense Tree* xii. 156 The trial was a travesty in the tradition of the Reichstag Trial at Leipzig. **1970** *Peace News* 17 Apr. 8/1 Bobby Seale has been sentenced to *four years* for contempt of court at Attorney General Mitchell's 'Reichstag Trial' in Chicago.

reide·ntify, *v.* [RE- 5 a.] **a.** *trans.* To identify again or in a new way; also *absol.* **b.** *intr.* To identify oneself with something again.

1934 WEBSTER, Reidentify, v.t. **1959** P. F. STRAWSON *Individuals* i. 32 We cannot attach one occasion to another unless, from occasion to occasion, we can reidentify elements common to different occasions. *Ibid.* 55 A condition..of the possession of a single, continuously usable framework..was the ability to *re*identify..some elements of the framework in spite of discontinuities of observation. **1964** C. M. WISE in D. Abercrombie et al. *Daniel Jones* 208 The second element..has been reidentified as a voiced postvocalic allophone. **1966** 'HAN SUYIN' *Mortal Flower* xii. 258 Others are longing to go back, to reidentify, but they are afraid of changing.

reification. Add: Also (rēⁱˌifikēⁱ·ʃən). (Further examples.) Also, depersonalization, esp. such as Marx thought was due to capitalist industrialization in which the worker is considered as the quantifiable labour factor in production or as a commodity.

1937 T. PARSONS *Struct. Soc. Action* xiii. 476 Positivistic empiricism has been predominantly a matter of the 'reification' of theoretical systems. **1941** H. MARCUSE *Reason & Revol.* II. i. 279 Marx's early writings are the first explicit statement of the process of reification (*Verdinglichung*) through which capitalist society makes all personal relations between men take the form of objective relations between things. **1954** H. J. EYSENCK *Psychol. Politics* viii. 262 Freud's reification of mental mechanisms is a literary rather than a scientific device. **1962** MACQUARRIE & ROBINSON tr. *Heidegger's Being & Time* I. i. 72 The Thinghood itself which such reification implies must have its ontological origin demonstrated. **1971** J. J. SHAPIRO tr. *Habermas's Toward Rational Soc.* iii. 39 The active assault upon culture is based on the same reification as the fetishism of those students who believe that by occupying university classrooms they are taking possession of science as a productive force. **1976** G. THERBORN *Sci., Class & Soc.* i. 26 The ugly consequences, in Friedrich's view, result from a 'reification' of the current epistemological stance of science. **1979** E. H. GOMBRICH *Sense of Order* v. 143 To see the [wavy] line as water, mountains or, perhaps, a fluttering ribbon might be described as 'reification', to see it as a living serpent as 'animation'.

reificatory (rĭ-, rēⁱˌifikēⁱ·tŏri), *a.* [f. REIFICAT(ION + -ORY².] Of, pertaining to, or characterized by, reification.

1951 Z. S. HARRIS *Methods in Structural Ling.* ii. 18 The reificatory question of what parts of human behavior constitute language. **1969** D. TRIESMAN in Cockburn & Blackburn *Student Power* 148 The International Student Conference..coalesced around the fundamental and reificatory tenet that it would only discuss problems of the 'student as such'.

reify, *v.* Add: Also with pronunc. (rēⁱ·ifəi). (Later examples.)

1931 M. R. COHEN *Reason & Nature* III. iii. 390 There is.. a fundamental philosophic issue: the extent to which the principle of unity should be hypostatized or reified (I wish the use of the ˌword *thingified* were more common). **1953** C. E. OSGOOD *Method & Theory in Experim. Psychol.* xvi. 680 The second hindrance to objectivity is the ubiquitous tendency to reify the word, to assume the word itself somehow carries its own meaning. **1971** *Times Lit. Suppl.* 31 Dec. 1619/3 To look upon them [*sc.* economic laws] as objective necessities, as bourgeois economists do, is to reify them. **1979** E. H. GOMBRICH *Sense of Order* x. 282 The temptation to 'reify' the shield into the open mouth of a gaping mask.. proved as irresistible as did the opportunity of turning spiralling volutes into suggestions of eyes.

Hence **re·ified** *ppl. a.*, **re·ifying** *vbl. sb.* and *ppl. a.*

1941 H. MARCUSE *Reason & Revol.* iv. 115 Lordship and bondage result of necessity from certain relationships of labor, which are, in turn, relationships in a 'reified' world. **1962** MACQUARRIE & ROBINSON tr. *Heidegger's Being & Time* II. vi. 487 Why does this reifying always keep coming back to exercise its dominion? **1965** B. PEARCE tr. *Preobrazhensky's New Economics* 47 One can..understand its laws in the spirit of vulgar economics, that is, by offering in the guise of science mere superficial description, complete with the reified relations of commodity production. **1969** R. BLACKBURN in Cockburn & Blackburn *Student Power* 207 An alienated society naturally encourages a re-ifying vocabulary. **1979** E. H. GOMBRICH *Sense of Order* ix. 242 It is surely not far-fetched to interpret its coiling frame as a reified flourish on a reified support.

reign, *sb.* Add: **4.** *attrib.*, as **reign mark**, a mark on a piece of oriental ceramic ware indicating in whose reign it was made; **reign name, title**, the symbolic name adopted by a Japanese or (formerly) Chinese ruler, by which his reign is known and dated.

1936 *Burlington Mag.* Jan. 10/2 Distinguished by a reign mark in blue or pink enamel. **1980** *Catal. Fine Chinese Ceramics* (Sotheby, Hong Kong) 6 Where a reign mark is given after the measurement no attribution to the period of this reign is intended unless the words '*and period*' are added. [**1834** C. GUTZLAFF *Sketch of Chinese Hist.* I. iv. 89 The Han Dynasty... The characters given after the emperors' names are the kwŏ-haou, 'national designations' of the emperors during their reigns. **1848** S. W. WILLIAMS *Middle Kingdom* II. xvii. 229 Kwoh Hiau, or Reigning Title.] **1935** C. P. FITZGERALD *China* xxiii. 457 Every Ming Emperor retained the same reign title for the full duration of his reign. **1974** *Encycl. Brit. Macropædia* X. 78/1 Mutsuhito, who took the reign name Meiji ('enlightened rule', 1863–1912). **1976** *Times* 10 Nov. 17/1 Reign titles disappeared from China with the fall of the empire in 1911: in Japan they still survive.

reigner. For † *Obs.* read *rare* and add later example.

1908 *Daily Chron.* 13 Feb. 4/4 Louis XIV., the record reigner, was never in his life clean all over from the natural exhalations of a monarch's skin.

Reil (rəil). *Anat.* [The name of Johann Christian *Reil* (1759–1813), German anatomist.] *island of Reil*: an area of the cerebral cortex which overlies the corpus striatum but is concealed within the lateral sulcus (the fissure of Sylvius).

Described by Reil in 1809 (*Arch. f. Physiol.* IX. 144).

1840 G. V. ELLIS *Demonstrations of Anat.* 31 The fissure [of Sylvius] divides above into two portions, one of which passes before, and one behind some small convolutions which constitute the island of Reil. **1888** W. R. GOWERS *Man. Dis. Nervous Syst.* II. IV. 6 Within the fissure of Sylvius lie the small convolutions of the island of Reil, or insula, four or five in number, which spread out like a fan. **1939** O. LARSELL *Textbk. Neuro-Anat.* XVIII. 219 The lateral fissure (fissure of Sylvius) opens to the hidden cortical surface of the island of Reil. **1961** A. R. BUCHANAN *Functional Neuro-Anat.* xxi. 173 The insular part of the cerebral cortex or island of Reil can be readily exposed by removal of the opercular portions of the frontal, parietal and temporal lobes of the cerebrum.

Reilly, var. *RILEY.

reim. Add: See also RIEM in Dict. and Suppl. (Earlier and later examples.)

1852 M. B. HUDSON *Feature in S. Afr. Frontier Life* I. v. 127 Their minister had with a reim round his neck Been dragged from his station by Bowker's command. **1862** *Colburn's United Service Mag.* III. 212 They have always what the Dutch call a 'forelouper'..who goes in front of the two leading oxen to pull them on with a strap or *reim*, as the Dutch call it. **1947** P. J. PRETORIUS *Jungle Man* vii. 86 When I secured a captive I took a reim, tied it round the neck of the animal, and the boy was then sent off to camp leading it.

reimbibe, *v.* Add: Also *fig.*

a **1960** E. M. FORSTER *Maurice* (1971) iii. 15 Then he would reimbibe the face and the four words.

reimbursabi·lity. [f. REIMBURSABLE *a.*] The quality of being reimbursable.

1978 *Nature* 16 Nov. 201/3 What this means is that Congress is limiting the reimbursability of salaries of the best faculty, the stars, the Nobel Prize winners, those people who make our institutions great.

reimmerse, *v.* Add: Also *fig.*

1905 *Speaker* 1 Apr. 18/1 It is to the desert that yearly pilgrimages bring hosts of the faithful..to re-immerse themselves in the original enthusiasm.

reimpje, reimpie, var. *RIEMPIE. (See also RHEIMPY.)

1891 B. MITFORD *Romance of Cape Frontier* xxiii. 419 Just slip off these bits of *reimpje*, Tambusa; and give me an assegai and a stick or something. **1923** O. SCHREINER *Thoughts on S. Afr.* 17 The great clean, bare 'voorhuis' (front room) with its mud floors and its chairs and sofa with reimpje seats. **1926** *Brit. Weekly* 27 May 158/4 Men and women sat on reimpje-seated chairs. **1927** *Glasgow Herald* 14 May 11/4 The sitting-room with its beautiful chairs and settee of native wood with 'reimpje' bottoms (criss-crossed thongs of home-cured leather), all in a simple old Dutch style, looked strangely unfamiliar.

reimplant, *v.*, **reimplantation.** (Later examples of both.)

1919 *Jrnl. Amer. Med. Assoc.* 26 July 301/1 Bonnefon's experiences confirm that if a small pathologic process can be cut out completely and then reimplanted in the old site, the environment being normal, it will be invaded by normal cells and lose its pathologic characteristics. **1955** *New Biol.* XVIII. 32 The reimplantation of stored infant tissues into the same animal, and..the observation of the reciprocal influences of host and implant, are technically practicable and established procedures. **1973** *Sci. Amer.* Feb. 28/3 We can transfer the eye into a tissue culture and change its orientation when we reimplant it in a host embryo, and correlate the result with the results of direct-transplantation experiments.

reimportation. (Earlier example.)

1857 MILL *Pol. Econ.* (ed. 4) II. III. xxiv. 229 The Bank reserves can replenish themselves without any re-importation of the gold.

reimpregnate, *v.* (Later example.)

1953 R. LEHMANN *Echoing Grove* 29 But still the stones seemed rocked, the unsterile mounds, reimpregnated, exhaled dust's fever.

reimpression. 2. (Later example.)

1924 W. B. SELBIE *Psychol. Relig.* 89 Every one is aware of unaccountable recollections of this kind. Such a re-impression of familiar things may take place even though there is no conscious recollection.

reimschoon, var. *REMSKOEN.

rein, *sb.*¹ Add: **4.** *rein-ring*; **rein-hand** (earlier example).

1843 *Ainsworth's Mag.* IV. 436 Our well-fed 'Phaeton' pulled his team together.., dropped his rein-hand, [etc.]. **1955** E. POUND *Classic Anthol.* III. 188 A leathered front-board with tiger-fell And metal rein-rings as well. **1968** J. ARNOLD *Shell Bk. Country Crafts* xxiii. 267 Attached to the hames are tug-hooks and rein-rings.

reincarna·tionism. [f. REINCARNATION + -ISM.] A belief in, or doctrine of, reincarnation.

1907 W. DE MORGAN *Alice-For-Short* viii. 75 This is an entirely unwarranted speculation, based upon no data; a neotheosophical reincarnationism without so much as a single Himalayan Brother to back you up! **1938** *Jrnl. Theol. Stud.* XXXIX. 192 We shall find ourselves emphasizing the subordinationism and the reincarnationism to such an extent that the Origenian theology may well appear to be merely one more form of Gnosticism.

reindeer. Add: **2.** *reindeer meat, skin* (later examples), *steak*; **reindeer lichen** (earlier example); **reindeer tongue**, the tongue of a reindeer, usu. smoked, considered as a delicacy.

1770 G. CARTWRIGHT *Jrnl.* 11 July (1792) I. 8 They [*sc.* caribou] find there many extensive tracts of land destitute of wood, and covered with plenty of Reindeer Lichen. **1926** *Daily Colonist* (Victoria, B.C.) 5 Jan. 2/4 Reindeer meat was the principal attraction on the menu. **1933** Reindeer-skin [see *KAMIK]. **1977** *Country Life* 13 Jan. 80/1 His wife makes..the soft reindeer-skin shoes for winter. **1958** W. BICKEL tr. *Hering's Dict. Class. & Mod. Cookery* 502 *Reindeer steak*,.. steak cut from a tender loin, sautéd in butter. **1973** D. FRANCIS *Slay-Ride* v. 67 She gave us reindeer steaks in a rich dark sauce. **1788** *Times* 1 Jan. 4/3 (Advt.), Smoked Salmon and Dutch Herring, Fine New French Olives, and New Rein Deer Tongues. **1857** J. H. WALSH *Economical Housekeeper* II. iii. 32 Reindeer Tongues, Pork Pies, and a whole host of similar commodities, are sold at the 'sausage shops' in London. **1935** M. MORPHY *Recipes of All Nations* 499 Reindeer are eaten in Norway, and smoked reindeer tongues are considered a great delicacy. **1973** J. FLEMING *You won't let me Finish* xvi. 129 I'm told I am to have some smoked reindeer tongue for my lunch.

reinduction. Delete † and add later example in sense of *INDUCTION 4 d.

1944 N. MAILER in *Cross-Section* 336 A half-year later, he was made (after reinduction school) a captain.

‖ **reine** (rẹn). *Cookery.* [Fr., lit. 'queen'.] Chiefly in phr. *à la reine* 'in the fashion of a queen', used to designate dishes prepared in some special way. Also used alone following the name of the dish.

1845 E. ACTON *Mod. Cookery* i. 37 (*heading*) Rabbit soup a la reine. Wash and soak thoroughly three young rabbits. **1884** MADAME VALERIE *Cookery for Amateurs* ii. 25 *Soups*...

À la Reine. Although this potage has a fine name it is easily made if you have the remains of cold fowl or turkey. **1930** H. BELLOC *New Cautionary Tales* 13 Turbot à la Reine, and Ices. **1958** W. BICKEL tr. *Hering's Dict. Class. & Mod. Cookery* 254 *Sole..quen style*, à la reine: poached, covered with creamed fish velouté, garnished with truffle slices and small fish dumplings. **1962** *Listener* 26 July 155/3, I had this dish in a tiny restaurant in the Dordogne Valley. It is called plaice *reine*.

Reinecke (rəi·nekə). *Chem.* The name of A. *Reinecke*, 19th-c. German chemist, used in the possessive or *attrib.* to designate (*a*) a red crystalline complex salt, ammonium diamminetetrakis(isothiocyanato)chromate(III), $NH_4[Cr(NCS)_4(NH_3)_2].H_2O$, which is used esp. in *Biochem.* to precipitate large cations, and (*b*) the parent acid of this salt, $H[Cr(NCS)_4(NH_3)_2]$, which can also be isolated as red crystals.

Reinecke described the preparation of the salt in 1863 (*Ann. d. Chem. u. Pharm.* CXXVI. 113).

1892 *Jrnl. Chem. Soc.* LXII. II. 798 Reinecke's salt crystallises in rectangular tables; it is insoluble in absolute ether, but dissolves in water to a ruby-red solution and in alcohol. **1928** *Chem. Abstr.* XXII. 764 The urine is slightly acidified and evapd. to ¼ its vol., purified with charcoal, and the creatinine pptd. with Reinecke Salt. **1928** *Brit. Chem. Abstr.* A. 542/2 The mixed potassium ammonium salt of Reinecke's acid, obtained by melting together potassium dichromate and ammonium thiocyanate. **1933** *Biochem. Jrnl.* XXVII. 157 Reinecke's salt, $[(NH_3)_2Cr(CNS)_4]NH_4$, is proving to be a valuable precipitant for a variety of basic substances, and its use is likely to extend. **1935** *Org. Syntheses* XV. 75 The undissolved residue from the second extraction consists chiefly of Morland salt (the guanidine salt of the Reinecke acid). **1965** tr. Hein & Herzog in G. Brauer *Handbk. Preparative Inorg. Chem.* II. xxiv. 1377 The total yield of air-dry Reinecke salt amounts to 250–275 g. *Ibid.* 1378 $H[Cr(SCN)_4(NH_3)_2]$... Synonym: Reinecke acid. **1966** PHILLIPS & WILLIAMS *Inorg. Chem.* II. xxvi. 322 The anion of Reinecke's salt..and that of K_2PtCl_6 are used to precipitate large organic cations.

Hence **reineckate** (rəi·nĕkēᶦt) [ad. G. *reineckat*: see -ATE[1]], (a salt of) the anion present in Reinecke's salt, $[Cr(NCS)_4(NH_3)_2]^-$.

1928 *Brit. Chem. Abstr.* A. 526/2 The cuprous 'Reineckate' is removed by filtration. **1939** *Thorpe's Dict. Appl. Chem.* (ed. 4) III. 115/1 Reinecke's salt... Its solution gives precipitates with the heavy metals and organic bases, alkaloids yielding characteristic crystalline compounds—reineckates. **1955** J. A. LOVERN *Chem. Lipids of Biol. Significance* ii. 61 Choline is estimated in a variety of ways. The simplest and most frequently used methods depend on the formation of a sparingly-soluble complex with the reineckate radical. **1957** *Jrnl. Antibiotics* X. 188 The antibiotic was..crystallized as its reineckate. **1964** *Oceanogr. & Marine Biol.* II. 152 The reineckate ion is removed with silver nitrate.

‖ **Reine Claude** (rę̄n klod). [Fr., perh. a. the name of *Claude* (1499–1524), daughter of Louis XII and wife of François I.] = GREENGAGE. Also *attrib.*

1731 P. MILLER *Gardeners Dict.* s.v. Prunus 16. La Reine Claude, i.e. Queen Claudia. This is a small round Fruit, of a yellowish Colour,..and its Juice is richly sugar'd. **1860** R. HOGG *Fruit Man.* 252 Reine Claude. See Green Gage. **1929** E. A. BUNYARD *Anat. Dessert* 118 In France it [*sc.* the greengage] is always known as Reine Claude, and the legend runs that it is thus named after the wife of François I. **1941** MRS. BELLOC LOWNDES *I, too, have lived in Arcadia* xvi. 299 A large old *Reine Claude*, of which the sweet luscious fruit was famed. **1962** *Harper's Bazaar* Aug. 37 Delicious though the *reine claude* can be. **1973** *Guardian* 20 Jan. 3/4 It is the land of..the honeyed Reine-Claude greengages.

reined, *ppl. a.* Add: **1.** Also *reined-back*.

1905 W. H. HUNT *Pre-Raphaelitism* II. vii. 174 At first acquaintance with the poet, I thought that later in my knowledge of him I should see some phases of the reined-back pose of Woolner's bust, but this I was unable to do. **1961** *New Statesman* 21 July 92/1 The reined-back rhythms of this verse are especially pleasing.

reinfect, *v.* (Later examples.)

1889 G. A. SMITH *Bk. Isaiah* (ed. 2) I. 422 Not only to find it [*sc.* sin] 'hindering, disturbing, complicating all', but reinfecting with the lust and odour of sin the will which gave it birth. **1928** L. E. H. WHITBY *Med. Bacteriol.* xxi. 210 Finally, the envelope of the corpuscle bursts and the merozoites are set free. These in turn reinfect red corpuscles and develop into trophozoites, thus carrying on the cycle. **1960** *Farmer & Stockbreeder* 12 Jan. 12 Loose smut re-infects growing corn and so perpetuates the disease.

reinfesta·tion. [RE- 5 a.] A second or further infestation.

1911 in WEBSTER. **1946** *Nature* 2 Nov. 636/2 One application of 0·5 per cent 'Gammexane' dust has been generally found to..prevent re-infestation for some time. **1968** *Times* 30 Oct. 12/2 A central portion of the sewer system was cleared of rats..and no attempt was made to prevent re-infestation.

reinforce, *v.* Add: **2. d.** *Psychol.* To strengthen (a response), usu. by repetition of a stimulus, esp. one that is painful or rewarding.

1906 C. S. SHERRINGTON *Integrative Action Nervous Syst.* v. 175 These widely separate reflex-arcs therefore re-inforce one another. **1927** G. V. ANREP tr. *Pavlov's Conditioned Reflexes* vii. 117 The second method consisted in contrasting the single definite conditioned stimulus..with different neighbouring stimuli which were never reinforced. **1951** S. F. NAGEL *Found. Social Anthropol.* iv. 58 To remain effective, however, the conditioning must be 'reinforced'. **1970** *Jrnl. Gen. Psychol.* July 3 Bugelski..notes that in the orthodox stimulus-response view of learning based on the reinforcement of an instrumental response, it is essential that the behavior appear first and then be..'reinforced by the psychologist (or someone) immediately'. **1973** *Howard Jrnl.* XIII. 281 A points system was used to pay the men for desirable behaviours that would be likely also to be reinforced in life outside the institution.

reinforced, *ppl. a.* Add: **2.** Special collocations: **reinforced concrete,** concrete with steel bars or network embedded in it to increase its tensile strength; **reinforced plastic,** plastic strengthened by the inclusion of a layer of fibre (esp. glass).

1902 *Min. Proc. Inst. Civil Engineers* CXLIX. 297 Reinforced concrete is extremely economical..where an imposing building is not required. **1906** *Daily Chron.* 27 Apr. 6/2 There is undoubtedly a great future for reinforced concrete. **1910** *Encycl. Brit.* VI. 837/2 The introduction of steel concrete (also known as ferroconcrete, armoured concrete, or reinforced concrete) is generally attributed to Joseph Monier, a French gardener. **1958** *Engineering* 14 Mar. 350/1 A sufficient number of reinforced-concrete buildings have now been in use for more than 50 years to show that, properly designed, reinforced concrete is as durable material as is likely to be required for most purposes. **1966** *McGraw-Hill Encycl. Sci. & Technol.* II. 337/1 Modern bridge abutments are usually made of reinforced concrete. **1974** *Encycl. Brit. Macropædia* III. 184/1 The towers are of reinforced concrete and the cables built up of strands of twisted wire. **1940** *Brit. Plastics* Aug. (Advt. section) 5 Two-piece housing in reinforced plastic material for electric hair drying unit. **1947** W. J. BROWN *Fabric Reinforced Plastics* iv. 76 The increasing use of reinforced plastics for engineering applications. **1959** *Engineering* 16 Jan. 86/1 The principal advantage of the reinforced plastics hull is the much reduced maintenance work and its easy repairability. **1971** *Nature* 30 July 305/1 If the exceptional properties of carbon fibres are to be utilized for engineering purposes they must be fabricated as a 'reinforced plastic'.

reinforcement. Add: **3. b.** *spec.* Increase in the intensity or amplitude of sound.

1879 [in Dict., sense 3]. **1937** A. T. JONES *Sound* viii. 198 When the stem of a vibrating tuning fork is placed on top of a wooden table or other extended wooden surface there is also a reinforcement of the sound. **1959** E. PULGRAM *Introd. Spectrography of Speech* vii. 58 This gain in amplitude is obtained in exchange for loss of duration, for a tuning fork thus placed for reinforcement will cease to operate more quickly than one not so placed. **1969** L. F. YERGES *Sound, Noise, & Vibration Control* 70 Today..deliberate 'electrical' amplification is the more significant means of sound reinforcement. *Ibid.* 145 Reinforcement is usually necessary in the following spaces: 1. Legitimate theaters with more than 1000 seats. 2. Lecture halls with more than 300 seats. 3. Almost all gymnasiums, arenas, and large assembly halls.

c. *Psychol.* (An act of) strengthening or establishing of a response, esp. in learning theory through the repetition of a rewarding or painful stimulus, or the satisfaction of a need; also *attrib.*

1876 W. JAMES *Coll. Ess. & Rev.* (1920) 31 The whole question of its predetermination relates to the intensity of the degree of reinforcement with which the triumphant representation occurs. **1906** C. S. SHERRINGTON *Integrative Action Nervous Syst.* v. 175 This reinforcement is significant of the solidarity of the whole spinal mechanism. **1927** G. V. ANREP tr. *Pavlov's Conditioned Reflexes* vii. 117 The first method consisted in repeating the definite conditioned stimulus a great number of times always accompanied by reinforcement. **1948** E. R. HILGARD *Theories of Learning* iv. 84 Primary reinforcement..is identified with diminution of need. Secondary reinforcement is mediated by a stimulus which has been closely and consistently associated with the need reduction. *Ibid.* xii. 347 Doubts about this basic pattern for reinforcement theory have been expressed frequently throughout the preceding chapters. **1953** C. E. OSGOOD *Method & Theory in Experim. Psychol.* ix. 376 The two crucial conditions for learning [in Hull's system] are thus contiguity and reinforcement. **1960** J. B. CARROLL in Saporta & Bastian *Psycholinguistics* (1961) 333/1 A purely Pavlovian or Watsonian view of language learning has been supplanted generally by some variety of reinforcement theory. **1963** *Listener* 7 Feb. 238/1 The pleasures of gambling, right up to the time the ruined rake rises from the table to shoot himself, are..due to 'the principle of intermittent reinforcement'. **1973** *Howard Jrnl.* XIII. 269 If reinforcement techniques can circumvent this double-bind situation, they may be justified.

5. The strengthening structure or material employed in reinforced concrete or plastic.

1905 G. J. FIEBEGER *Civil Engin.* xxi. 405 A beam may have its reinforcement on the tension side only, or on both the tension and compression sides of the neutral axis. **1958** *Engineering* 14 Mar. 350/1 Adequate cover to the reinforcement, including binding wires and stirrups, is essential, as is the elimination of all unnecessary steelwork. **1973** *Materials & Technol.* VI. viii. 521 The resin and the reinforcement, cut to size, are introduced separately into the mould. **1974** *Encycl. Brit. Macropædia* XIV. 519/1 Reinforcements [for plastics] include cotton and asbestos flocks; glass fibres, chopped or in the form of rovings, mats, or monofilaments; carbon fibres; and mineral whiskers.

reinforcer. Add: **b.** *Psychol.* That which serves to reinforce or strengthen a response.

1958 L. KRASNER in Saporta & Bastian *Psycholinguistics* (1961) 84/2 'Good' and a head shake were effective reinforcers. **1967** *Listener* 12 Jan. 55/2 By making reinforcers contingent on behaviour we can alter behaviour in a very effective way. **1974** B. F. SKINNER *About Behaviorism* 39 The behavior is said to be *strengthened* by its consequences, and for that reason the consequences themselves are called 'reinforcers'.

reinforcing, *vbl. sb.* Add: **2.** *concr.* = *REINFORCEMENT 5.

1966 *McGraw-Hill Encycl. Sci. & Technol.* XI. 426/1 As reinforcing for concrete, steel in several of the following forms may be used.

reinforcing *ppl. a.* (further examples).

1906 C. S. SHERRINGTON *Integrative Action of Nervous Syst.* v. 175 Gentle stimuli to the skin of a limb exerted a reinforcing influence on closely following stimuli applied to the limb region of the cortex of the brain. **1938** B. F. SKINNER *Behav. of Organisms* vi. 244 It is possible to show that an emotional or reinforcing stimulus..is effective without regard to various minor properties. **1948** E. R. HILGARD *Theories of Learning* iv. 108 Any stimulus which has been associated with need-reduction may itself serve as a reinforcing agent. **1949** POSTMAN & EGAN *Experim. Psychol.* xiv. 298 The instrumental response and the classical response have both been established through the same reinforcing stimulus—food. **1970** [see *homopolymer* s.v. *HOMO-]. **1973** *N.Y. Law Jrnl.* 31 Aug. 1/5 Three major steel companies.. were indicted yesterday..on charges of violating anti-trust law in the sale of reinforcing steel bars in Texas. **1973** P. DICKINSON *Gift* v. 75 The men and machines had dug a vast, rectangular wound in the clay;..half was still hummocked mud,..littered with grids of reinforcing rods.

reinfuse, *v.* Add: Hence **reinfu·sion.**

1963 *Lancet* 5 Jan. 61/1 We reviewed the problem of blood-transfusion for Jehovah's Witnesses and discovered that they will accept immediate reinfusion of their own blood.

‖ **Reinga** (re,i·ŋa). Also **reinga, Re-i-nga;** † **Treaingha.** [Maori, = 'place of leaping'.] In Maori tradition, the place where departed spirits make their way into the next world; hence, the land of departed spirits.

1822 *Proc. Church Missionary Soc.* 364 They say, that, at the death of a Chief, his soul goes to the Treaingha, at the North Cape. **1830** *New Zealanders* x. 236 Réinga signifies, properly, the place of flight; and is said, in some of the accounts, to be a rock or a mountain at the North Cape, from which, according to others, the spirits descend into the next world through the sea. **1884** M. A. MARTIN *Our Maoris* vi. 79 The natives in the north of the island still point out the cliff from which the spirits [of the dead] made their descent into the sea on their way back to the Island of Hawaii, from whence their forefathers came. This cliff was called the Re-i-nga, *i.e.*, the leaping-place. **1938** R. D. FINLAYSON *Brown Man's Burden* 48 Depart, O father, to the Reinga, to the far Hawaiki, to the Lord of the Dead. **1949** P. BUCK *Coming of Maori* IV. iv. 516 Thus death closed the account of the body, and the soul (*wairua*) entered the spirit land (*reinga*) with a clean sheet and without apprehension.

reinge·stion. [RE- 5 a.] = *REFECTION *sb.* 2 d.

1956 THOMPSON & WORDEN *Rabbit* iii. 27 It is difficult to believe that reingestion has not in fact been observed many times. **1964** H. N. SOUTHERN *Handbk. Brit. Mammals* 254 Utilization of food [by rabbits] assisted by reingestion, or refection, in which soft faecal pellets (mainly from caecum, where microbial digestion occurs) are swallowed. **1964** R. M. LOCKLEY *Private Life of Rabbit* x. 103 Reingestion was observed both out of doors by day and below ground.

reinikaboo: see *RANNYGAZOO.

reink, *v.* (Later examples.)

1937 *Discovery* Oct. 300/2 The stone being kept damp, and re-inked for each print. **1955** J. RYDER *Printing for Pleasure* v. 61 After taking the first print, and without re-inking, print onto the top sheet of the platen packing.

reinsman. Add: Also *Austral.* and *N.Z.*, spec. in *Trotting*. (Further examples.)

1904 *N.Y. Times* 13 Dec. 7 A number of well-known amateur reinsmen started from the Harlem River Speedway. **1930** W. BANNING in W. & G. H. Banning *Six Horses* 361 A reinsman was a master driver who..was able to drive each span of his complement wholly independent of the other. **1969** *Sydney Morning Herald* 24 May 27/1 Western Districts reinsman Gordon McWilliam lost a battle of tactics behind the hot favourite, Cocky Raider. **1977** *N.Z. Herald* 8 Jan. 1-9/4 The Cambridge reinsman R. F. Mitchell..had a farewell present at Cambridge last night when he drove Pompano Prince to victory.

reinstatement. Add: **1. c.** *Mil.* Re-establishment of a serviceman in a previously held civilian job after demobilization. Chiefly *attrib.*

1945 *Daily Herald* 17 May 4/3 The Reinstatement Act was working very smoothly—'and I believe I shall have very few cases to go to the reinstatement committees at all.' **1946** *R.A.F. Jrnl.* May 160 With the best will in the world, reinstatement regulations cannot help in such cases.

reinsure, *v.* Add: Also *intr.* or *absol.* (Earlier examples.)

1755 N. MAGENS *Ess. Insurances* I. 94 Such Insurer, his Executors, Administrators, or Assignees, may re-insure to the Amount of the Sum before insured. **1802** S. MARSHALL *Treat. Insurance* I. 115 At Marseilles..the insured, in such case, sues the insolvent insurer till he obtains a sentence authorizing him to re-insure at the expense of the insolvent.

reintegration. Add: **3.** (Later examples.)

It has supplanted *redintegration* as the usual form in this sense.

1973 *Times* 13 Feb. 7/2 Soviet consular officials have told them that their reintegration 'will take time'. **1977** *Sunday Times Mag.* (Perth, Austral.) 4/4 It was not the chattering of birds on the roof that set reintegration in process. **1979** *Internat. Rehabilit. Med.* I. 45/2 Intensive rehabilitation is indicated when..at least social reintegration into the family can be achieved.

reintegrative (rĭ,i·ntĭgrătiv), *a.* [f. RE-INTEGRATE *v.* + -IVE: see REDINTEGRATIVE *a.*] Tending to reintegration.

1957 V. W. TURNER *Schism & Continuity in Afr. Society* x. 303 A society continually threatened with disintegration is continually performing reintegrative ritual. **1974** *Gen. Systems* XIX. 67/2 But so brilliantly had Mayan..societies systematized their communications, that the patient's very gestures ('symptoms') had actuated the reintegrative liturgies. **1981** J. CAREY *John Donne* vii. 221 Donne's interest lies less in resurrection itself than in reintegration... His sole intent is to emphasize the power of the reintegrative act.

reinterpret, *v.* (Further examples.)

1920 A. S. EDDINGTON *Space, Time & Gravit.* ix. 141 It has been reinterpreted and has finally become merged in the conservation of energy. **1952** B. ULANOV *Hist. Jazz in Amer.* i. 7 The rhythmic base of music has been reinterpreted. **1979** *N.Y. Rev. Bks.* 25 Oct. 11/4 A seasoned cult member is assigned to the nascent convert..to reinterpret his old life according to the new beliefs.

reinterpretation (further examples).

1956 *Nature* 10 Mar. 443/2 For these reasons there should be a re-interpretation of humanism. **1974** R. A. HALL *External Hist. Romance Langs.* 6 The reinterpretation of an unfamiliar form or part of a form under the influence of another form with which it has been identified.

reinvention. (Further examples.)

1964 W. L. GOODMAN *Hist. Woodworking Tools* 38 It appears to be a re-invention of the Minoan and Roman tool. **1973** *Sci. Amer.* Apr. 85/1 James thought up the idea of the differential gear (actually a reinvention).

reinvert, *v.* (Later example.)

1907 J. H. PARSONS *Dis. Eye* iv. 43 Just as with a convex lens, the image is inverted. It is re-inverted psychologically in the brain.

reinvestment. (Further examples.)

1857 MILL *Pol. Econ.* (ed. 4) I. I. iv. 70 All property..is a part of capital, so soon as it..is set apart for productive reinvestment. **1931** *Economist* 3 Jan. 25/2 A fair amount of reinvestment business following the heavy dividend disbursements of this week sufficed..to give prices a firm tendency. **1980** W. ASH *Incorporated* vi. 61 Various proposals for the re-investment of the profits.

Reissner (rəi·snəɹ). *Anat.* The name of Ernst *Reissner* (1824–78), German anatomist, used in the possessive or with *of* to designate a thin vestibular membrane of the internal ear, separating the scala vestibuli from the central duct of the cochlea.

1872 [see *SCALA]. **1945** MCNALLY & STUART in C. & C. L. Jackson *Dis. Nose, Throat, & Ear* III. 366 (*caption*) Gross dilatation of the scala media has occurred with displacement of Reissner's membrane on to the wall of the scala vestibuli. **1974** D. & M. WEBSTER *Compar. Vertebr. Morphol.* x. 229 The scala media is separated from the scala vestibuli by a thin, epithelial structure, Reissner's membrane.

reissue, *sb.* Add: (Further examples.) Also, a reissued gramophone record.

1937 *Discovery* Oct. 320/1 Apart from this curious re-issue, Godwin's book was reprinted in the Harleian Miscellany in 1746. **1948** *Hansard Commons* 21 Jan. 217 American films.. were good enough to go on attracting cinema-goers even on re-issue. **1966** *Listener* 5 May 664/3 No reservations about a wonderful bargain HMV reissue. **1977** *Rolling Stone* 24 Mar., More people acquaint themselves with Fleetwood Mac and dig back to old reissues.

reistafel, var. *RIJSTTAFEL.

Reiter (rəi·təɹ). *Path.* The name of Hans *Reiter* (1881–1969), German bacteriologist, used in the possessive to denote a disease or syndrome first described by him in 1916 (*Deutsche Med. Wochenschr.* 14 Dec. 1535) which is characterized by arthritis, conjunctivitis, and urethritis, typically affects young men, and is usually caused by bacteria of the genus *Chlamydia*.

1923 STEDMAN *Med. Dict.* (ed. 7) 859/2 *Reiter's disease*, a fever of a more or less remittent type, lasting about seventeen days, accompanied with pains in the joints, conjunctivitis, iritis, cystitis, and enlargement of the spleen; it has been observed in the tropics, but its causation is unknown. **1946** *Jrnl. Infect. Dis.* LXXIX. 134 (*heading*) The possible relationship of the pleuropneumonia-like organisms to Reiter's disease, rheumatoid arthritis and ulcerative colitis. **1962** *Lancet* 26 May 1111/1 The symptom-triad of arthritis, conjunctivitis, and urethritis, generally known as Reiter's syndrome, has a striking predilection for young men in military service. **1972** [see *keratoderma* s.v. *KERATO-]. **1978** *Jrnl. R. Soc. Med.* LXXI. 335 In Reiter's disease, acute uveitis is usually asynchronous.

Reithian (rī·þiăn), *a.* Also **Reithean.** [f. the name of J. C. W. *Reith* (1889–1971), 1st Lord Reith of Stonehaven, Director-General of the British Broadcasting Corporation (1927–38) + -IAN.] Of, pertaining to, or characteristic of Reith or his principles, esp. relating to the responsibility of broadcasting to enlighten and educate public taste.

1961 *Guardian* 26 Oct. 10/5 The Reithian conception of broadcasting was barely in evidence at the time [*sc.* in 1923]. **1963** *Times* 12 Jan. 4/5 An elaborate compromise between past and present balancing Reithian principles against television's need to survive as show business. **1969** *Observer* (Colour Suppl.) 21 Dec. 38/1 From the great Reithean days the BBC had come to be taken for granted as a pillar of enlightened orthodoxy. **1973** *Times* 9 June 10/4 Nowhere has the Reithian prediction—offer the public what it wants and it will want what it gets—been vindicated more awesomely. **1977** *Punch* 31 Aug.–6 Sept. 327/3 The BBC..still retains at least something of the old Reithian sobriety or an image of established quality.

‖ **reja** (rē·ha). [Sp.] In Spain, a wrought-iron screen or grille used to protect windows, chapel tombs, etc.

1845 R. FORD *Hand-bk. Travellers in Spain* I. 252/2 The *coro*..is railed off by a fine *reja*, the work of Sancho Muñoz, 1519. **1870** R. H. BUSK *Patrañas* 147 Then night came: the *maja* stood at her *reja*, looking out for her serenader. **1914** BYNE & STAPLEY *Rejería of Span. Renaissance* p. vii, Renaissance Architecture in Spain could not be fully appreciated without examining the towering wrought-iron grilles, or Rejas, of the period. **1924** J. MASEFIELD *Sard Harker* IV. 289 The windows..were covered with old iron rejas. **1969** S. SITWELL *Gothic Europe* xii. 139 One remembers Spanish cathedrals very notably on account of their *rejas* or wrought iron screens which are a feature peculiar to Spain.

Rejang (rē^i^dʒa·ŋ). Also **Redjang.** [Native name.] An Indonesian people of southern Sumatra; a member of this people. Also, their language.

1783 [see *BATTA³ *a.* and *sb.*]. **1839** T. J. NEWBOLD *Straits of Malacca* II. xiv. 227 The Rejangs, a people inhabiting the interior of Sumatra. **1932** W. L. GRAFF *Lang. & Languages* xi. 423 The population of *Indonesian* tongue amounts to about 50 millions... About eight geographical groups can be distinguished... In the *Sumatra* group, *Achinese, Battak, Rejang, Lampong, Malay, Mentaway*. **1955** P. VOORHOEVE *Crit. Survey Stud. Lang. Sumatra* v. 20 We find in the language of Rejang another language which is undoubtedly independent although closely related to Malay.

reject, *sb.* Now with pronunc. (rī·dʒekt). **1.** Restrict † *Obs.* to sense in Dict. and add: **b.** [f. the vb.] One who is rejected or discarded by others, esp. as unsuitable for some activity (orig. for military service).

1925 *Glasgow Herald* 13 Mar. 8/7 Probably the large proportion of rejects is not so much a symptom of national decadence as a result of the fact that the right sort of men are not coming forward in sufficient numbers. **1942** *Sun* (Baltimore) 4 Nov. 9/4 He said that..the 'army has been consistently uninterested in taking the rejects into conditioning battalions and reconditioning them'. **1971** *Sunday Express* (Johannesburg) 28 Mar. 17/2 Time and again I have heard members at the turnstiles say that they would prefer to watch South African-born players rather than overseas rejects. **1974** E. TIDYMAN *Dummy* vi. 87 The misborn and the unwanted..society's rejects. **1979** R. RENDELL *Make Death love Me* ii. 21 He knew someone who..was also a reject of the University of Kent.

2. (Further examples.)

1935 H. C. BRYSON *Gramophone Record* ix. 234 If rejects are kept below 15 per cent. with rigid examination, then efficiency is high. **1949** J. DEKETH *Fund. Radio-Valve Technique* vii. 61 If this fusing method were applied to values of the dimensions of the A-technique..there would be a higher percentage of rejects in manufacture. **1952**, etc. [see *export reject*]. **1969** [see *CULLER 1 b].

3. *attrib.* **a.** Appositive.

1955 H. KURNITZ *Invasion of Privacy* (1956) ii. 17 This pioneer used a war surplus Eimo camera and 'reject' film which he developed in his bath tub. **1963** R. R. A. HIGHAM *Handbk. Papermaking* ii. 71 The lighter reject materials.. are ejected through a special automatically controlled V-notch slide valve. **1965** *Wireless World* July 22 (Advt.), *Antex* reduces operational fatigue, with resulting drop in reject output. **1977** 'M. YORKE' *Cost of Silence* ix. 69 His friends..had seen him with Madge and made a few cracks about reject models.

b. General attrib. uses.

1958 *Times* 26 Feb. 8/4 The reject figures of Army recruits has [*sic*] given some cause for concern here. **1963** R. R. A. HIGHAM *Handbk. Papermaking* ii. 71 Heavy material which will not pass through the screen is continuously forced downwards into a reject trough and is removed from a heavy reject box connected to the bottom of the volute trough.

reject, *v.* Add: **I. 6. d.** *Psychol.* Of a parent or guardian: to spurn (a child) by denying it the normal emotional relationship between parent and offspring.

1931 *Smith Coll. Stud. in Soc. Work* I. 407 Case histories are presented showing the attitude toward their parents.., husbands, and children of twelve mothers who rejected their children. **1932** *Ibid.* II. 237 This type of relationship cannot exist when a mother rejects her child. **1961** H. C. SMITH *Personality Adjustment* xviii. 513 Children raised in negligent and understaffed orphanages are not actively rejected but suffer severe deprivation of warmth and affection. **1973** A. JANOV *Primal Scream* vii. 74 But to feel really rejected means to..feel utterly alone and unwanted as that child.

10. *Med.* To show an immune response to (a transplanted organ or tissue) so that it fails to survive in the body of the recipient. Also *absol.*

1953 *Nature* 3 Oct. 603/1 Embryonic cells transplanted into embryos of different genetic constitutions may survive into adult life, although their hosts would almost certainly have rejected them if transplantation had been delayed until after birth. **1968** *Observer* 7 Jan. 1/1 Although he is now entering the crucial period where his body could begin to reject the implanted heart, today's hospital bulletin said there were no signs of rejection or infection. **1969** *Daily Progress* (Charlottesville, Va.) 12 Jan. A2/3 'The heart rejects like crazy,' Dr Shumway comments. **1974** R. M. KIRK et al. *Surgery* ii. 35/1 A graft that will be ultimately rejected at first appears to be accepted by the host tissues.

II. 11. The infin. used *attrib.*, designating a part of a record player by means of which the turn table is made to stop (and the pick-up arm usu. returned to its rest) before a side has ended. Also stressed (rī·dʒekt).

1947 *Gramophone* Dec. p. xi/2 Automatically plays eight 10-in. or 12-in. mixed records. Repeat and reject switch provided. **1975** J. GRADY *Shadow of Condor* ii. 34 Strains from *Carmen* came through the speakers. Malcolm..hit the reject lever. **1976** R. L. SIMON *Wild Turkey* xviii. 129 He shuffled over to the turntable and pushed the reject button.

rejecting *vbl. sb.* (later example); also as *ppl. a.*

1931 *Smith Coll. Stud. in Soc. Work* I. 407 The purpose of the study was to test part of the hypothesis..by a comparison of the case histories of a group of rejecting and non-rejecting mothers. **1939** P. M. SYMONDS *Parent–Child Relationships* i. 24 Attempts to define rejecting behavior are rare. **1970** H. EDELSTON *Found. & Growth of Character* III. ii. 117 We hear a great deal of the rejecting mother: not quite so much of the over-demanding child.

rejected, *ppl. a.* Add: **a.** Also spec. *Psychol.*, refused or denied the normal relationship between parent and child. Cf. *REJECT *v.* 6 d.

1931 *Smith Coll. Stud. in Soc. Work* I. 407 The problems for which the rejected child was referred were more frequently of the aggressive, rebellious type. **1961** H. C. SMITH *Personality Adjustment* xviii. 513 Such severely rejected children tend to develop a general apathy..to all human relationships.

c. Gram. *rejected condition* (see quots.).

1947 PARTRIDGE *Usage & Abusage* 80/2 Those sentences in which the principal clause speaks of what would be or would have been, and in which the *if*-clause states, or implies, a negative. Grammarians call this: Rejected Condition, as in 'If wishes were horses, beggars would ride'. **1957** R. W. ZANDVOORT *Handbk. Eng. Gram.* v. ii. 218 Clauses expressing a condition that is not, or is not likely to be, realized [I should not mind so much, if I was not so busy] are called clauses of *rejected condition.*

rejectee (rīdʒektī·). *U.S.* [f. REJECT *v.* + -EE¹, after *draftee*.] One who is rejected as unfit for military service. Also *transf.* Cf. *REJECT *sb.* 1 b.

1941 *Sun* (Baltimore) 18 June 3/1 Twenty-six youths rejected by selective service officials..began taking physical examinations..for admittance to the first camp in the United States to be established for 'rejectees'. **1942** *Nation* 27 Apr. 41 (*heading*) When the draftee becomes a rejectee. **1977** *Time* 20 June 48/2 Determined to become a doctor, Braun did what an increasing number of rejectees do each year: he looked abroad. **1978** J. A. MICHENER *Chesapeake* 637 'Grandpop, take a look at the kind of boys we want,' and when Cudjo continued pestering him, he pointed to rejectees half the old man's age.

rejection. Add: **1. c.** *Psychol.* The refusal or inability to accept emotionally the fact of being a parent to one's child; the state of rejecting a child or of being rejected by a parent. Cf. *REJECT *v.* 6 d.

1931 *Smith Coll. Stud. in Soc. Work* I. 407 Thirty-five cases of rejection were chosen in which staff members unanimously agreed to that diagnosis. **1939** P. M. SYMONDS *Parent–Child Relationships* i. 10 Such concepts and terms as rejection and overprotection seem to have emerged into common use out of the child guidance movement. *Ibid.*, Newell..reports on 33 children diagnosed as cases of maternal rejection. **1957** L. C. STECKLE *Probl. Human Adjustment* (rev. ed.) vi. 132 Rejection is most effective in building uncertainty. *Ibid.* 133 Parental rejection usually results in aggressively hostile behavior in the child. **1973** A. JANOV *Primal Scream* vii. 74 Once that is felt, there are no more feelings of 'rejection'.

2. *Electronics.* The process of attenuating an unwanted electrical signal. Freq. *attrib.*

1940 *Chambers's Techn. Dict.* 712/2 Rejection filter. **1950** LAWSON & UHLENBECK *Threshold Signals* xii. 346 Besides automatic biasing, rejection filters in the i-f amplifier can be used to reduce the effects of c-w interference. **1953** [see *DETECTION 3]. **1957** R. W. LANDEE et al. *Electronic Designers' Handbk.* xvi. 29 If the feedback network by itself does not have a complete null, the depth of the null for the rejection amplifier will be less than the depth of the null for the null network taken by itself. **1967** W. A. STOVER *Circuit Design for Audio, AM/FM, & TV* xiii. 227 The IF rejection is enhanced by placing a resonant circuit or filter near the tuner input.

3. *Med.* Failure of transplanted tissue to survive or function in the body of the recipient as a result of the immune response it evokes in the latter.

1954 *Proc. R. Soc.* B. CXLIII. 43 Incompatibilities (falling short of rejection) became apparent when homografts were exchanged between members of separate sublines which..stood only eight to twelve generations apart. **1974** *Times* 5 Apr. 18/3 Professor Shumway believes that heart-transplant patients, like those given kidney transplants, gradually develop a tolerance to the grafted organ and so become less likely to have to cope with severe rejection episodes. **1974** M. C. Gerald *Pharmacol.* i. 7 We are optimistic that..more effective drugs to prevent the rejection of organ transplants will be discovered in the present decade.

4. *Comb.*, as **rejection form** *rare* = *rejection slip* below; **Rejection Front**, an alliance of Arab groups, who refuse to consider a negotiated peace with Israel (see *rejectionist); **rejection slip**, a formal notice sent by an editor or publisher to an author with a rejected MS.

1907 Wodehouse *Not George Washington* ii. ii. 42, I papered the walls with editorial rejection-forms, of which I was beginning to have a representative collection. **1917** 'W. N. P. Barbellion' *Jrnl. Disappointed Man* (1919) 296, I used to file..rejection forms and meditated writing a facetious essay on them. **1975** *Financial Times* 23 Dec. 4/8 The 'Rejection Front', which is led by the PFLP, stands strongly opposed to efforts at a Middle East settlement and to conservative regimes in the Middle East, especially in Saudi Arabia and Iran. **1978** *Radio Times* 28 Jan.–3 Feb. 15/4 The Arab 'Rejection Front' nations of Iraq, Algeria, Libya and the People's Democratic Republic of Yemen were prepared to give finance, training facilities and arms to his group. **1906** J. London *Let.* 19 Nov. (1966) 223, I have just received from you, along with a rejection-slip, two poems.. which have evidently been submitted to you over my name. **1933** Dylan Thomas *Let.* 9 May (1966) 15 Forget the 'annihilative reverse' of the rejection slip. **1953** H. Miller *Plexus* II. xiii. 217 If they were thin envelopes it meant rejection slips, with a request to forward postage for the return of the scripts. **1978** P. Sutcliffe *Oxf. Univ. Press* iv. i. 108 He, Gerrans, and Doble soon settled upon a formula, a terse but dignified communication that might be a little more comforting to the author than a bare rejection slip, the use of which the Press has always eschewed. **1979** F. Adcock *Inner Harbour* 2 'Please send future work'—Editor's note on a rejection slip.

rejectionist (rĭdʒe·kʃənist). [f. Rejection + -ist.] An Arab who refuses to accept a negotiated peace with Israel. Also *transf.* Also *attrib.* or as *adj.* Hence **reje·ctionism**, the policy of a rejectionist.

1976 *Guardian* 2 June 2/2 If Mr Kosygin wants to engineer the format of an Arab 'rejectionist' coalition to confront American penetration of the area, he is unlikely to get much encouragement from President Assad. **1976** *Guardian Weekly* 19 Dec. 8/4 Condemned to death by the mainstream Arafat-led guerrilla leadership—'Fascist' he calls it—Abu Nidal is Palestinian rejectionism at its most uncompromising. **1977** *Time* 10 Jan. 22/1 Last week a prominent member of the rejectionist Popular Front for the Liberation of Palestine..and his wife..were found dead in their West Beirut apartment. **1977** *Listener* 18 Aug. 195/1 If..the peace moves collapse..he [*sc.* King Hussein] will be..helpless in a stormy sea of Arab rejectionism. **1977** *Times* 29 Nov. 15/4 It offends no previously declared principles—except those of the 'rejectionists' on both sides. **1979** *Economist* 1 Dec. 14/1 Khomeini would have remained a voice in the wilderness if his austere rejectionist doctrines had not caught the mood of a people whose religion is still young and vigorous.

rejective, *a.* (Examples.)

1957 *Publ. Amer. Dial. Soc.* xxviii. 87 The other clause must not be 'rejective' with regard to it [*sc.* the fronted clause]. Examples:..He likes it you think?..Is he coming do you doubt?.. (*doubt, forbid, disagree*, etc. are rejective). **1967** *New Yorker* 25 Feb. 108 Besides being called minimal art, it is known as..'rejective art', 'rejective art', [etc.]. **1970** *Britannica Bk. of Year 1969* 798/3 *Rejective art*, a simplified and often depersonalized art (as painting or sculpture) based on the principle of the artist rejecting various options open to him; called also *reductive art, reductivism, rejectivism.*

rejector. Add: **1. b.** *Electronics.* = *rejector circuit* below.

1923 *Wireless World* 7 July 441/1 Signals with the frequency of the aerial circuit will pass through the ordinary tuning device, and little will pass through the rejector. **1946** *Electronic Engin.* XVIII. 45/1 Methods of bass compensation in common use involving arrangements of chokes, condensers, tuned acceptors or rejectors..all fail where high fidelity is required. **1977** L. J. Giacoletto *Electronics Designer's Handbk.* (ed. 2) xxiv. 115 (*caption*) Complex frequency characteristic of..the admittance of a single-tuned circuit to which a rejector is coupled.

2. Special Comb.: **rejector circuit**, a circuit consisting of a capacitor and an inductor connected in parallel and having values chosen such that the combination offers a very high impedance to signals of a particular frequency.

1923 *Wireless World* 7 July 441/1 The smaller the damping of the rejector circuit, the better it will perform. **1929** *Daily Express* 7 Nov. 14/3 A rejector circuit, which acts as a by-path for unwanted stations. **1952** *Electronic Engin.* XXIV. 314/1 As the selectivity of the 50 kc/s amplifier is not sufficient to reject the 48 kc/s frequency completely, a separate rejector circuit is used. **1969** Nelkon & Humphreys *Electronics & Radio* viii. 170 The parallel *LC* circuit is known as a 'rejector' circuit because the main current is zero at f_0.

re·jig, *sb.* [Re- 5 c.] Reorganization, rearrangement.

1965 *New Statesman* 23 Apr. 630/1 The *Sunday Citizen*, for all its admitted demerits (which may yet be rectified if still another rejig..is accomplished effectively). **1974** *Guardian Weekly* 10 Aug. 5/1 The idea of the late-night front page rejig is unknown.

reji·g, *v.* [Re- 5 c.] *trans.* To refit or re-equip; to mend. Also *fig.*, to rearrange, refashion, alter.

1948 *Daily Express* 22 Apr. 1/6 Britain will send experts to help rejig French factories. **1958** *Spectator* 2 May 558/1 To alter the period of the action [of *Twelfth Night*], to rejig the entrances and exits of the characters..is really a kind of forgery. **1962** *Economist* 22 Sept. 1084/1 Schemes for rejigging the conditions of press competition. **1972** *Times Lit. Suppl.* 14 Apr. 419/4 Current attempts to rejig Spanish sixteenth and seventeenth-century literature in terms of racial influences, art history, and so on. **1976** A. White *Long Silence* iv. 34 Three [weeks]..he spent with Jean Duclerc, helping re-jig the wireless. **1979** *Economist* 13 Oct. 81/3 Last year, faced with slower-than-expected increases in electricity demand, Hydro-Québec rejigged part of the project to reduce overall capacity.

Hence **reji·gged** *ppl. a.*; **reji·gging** *vbl. sb.*

1960 *Times Lit. Suppl.* 30 Sept. 635/3 The subject is fascinating and the setting never dull, and re-jigged (as the technicians say) it might make an enthralling story. **1969** *Daily Tel.* 6 Oct. 1/1 Whitehall's structure will be considerably changed as a result of the Prime Minister's 'rejigging' of the machinery of government. **1972** *Guardian* 15 June 15/2 Who will take over the re-jigged RIBA? **1977** *New Statesman* 17 June 809/2 His rejigged Radio 4 *Today* programme is now packing the listeners in. **1980** *Jrnl. R. Soc. Arts* Feb. 152/1 This leads me to suggest that the industrial planning process needs re-jigging.

rejoicing, *vbl. sb.* Add: **1. c.** *Rejoicing of* (or *over*, etc.) *the Law* [tr. Heb. *Simchat Torah* (in Suppl.)], the Jewish feast at the conclusion of the Feast of Tabernacles, celebrating the gift of the covenant of the Law.

1861 J. T. Bannister *Temples of Hebrews* 390 *Tisri*.. [Day] 23. The rejoicing for the law, a solemnity in memory of the covenant that the Lord made with the Hebrews, in giving them the law by the mediation of Moses. **1892** I. Zangwill *Childr. Ghetto* I. 134 It was the Rejoicing of the Law, and the Sons of the Covenant had treated him to rum and currant cake. **1903** W. Rosenau *Jewish Ceremonial Institutions & Customs* v. 101 On the Day of Rejoicing Over the Law special inducements are held out to the younger members of the congregation to participate actively in the public service. **1925** *Jewish Encycl.* XI. 364/2 *Simḥat Torah* ('The Rejoicing over the Law'): Name given to the second day of *Shemini 'Azeret*; it falls on the 23d of Tishri and closes the Feast of Sukkot. **1953** T. H. Gaster *Festivals Jewish Year* vi. 100 Not impossibly, the custom of celebrating the Rejoicing in the Law as a *wedding* was inspired by the idea of sublimating to a more spiritual plane the..staging of a mock wedding at harvest festivals. **1962** B. Abrahams tr. *Life Glückel of Hameln* iii. 52 Her companions were not to return before *Simchat Torah*.. Festival of the Rejoicing of the Law, celebrated immediately after that of Tabernacles. **1978** J. Sacks in P. Moore *Man, Woman, & Priesthood* iii. 39 On *Simchat Torah*, the festival of 'Rejoicing in the Law', adults and children forget decorum and dance and sing around the synagogue in celebration of the ending of the yearly cycle of Torah-reading and the beginning of the new.

‖ **rejon** (rehǭ·n). *Bull-fighting.* Pl. **rejones.** [Sp. *rejón* lance, spear, f. *rejo* pointed iron bar, *reja* ploughshare (L. *rēgula* straight piece of wood, f. *regere* to keep straight).] A wooden-handled spear, usu. placed from horseback.

1838 *Q. Rev.* LXII. 397 These noble 'Bestiarii' fought with the '*rejon*', a short projectile spear, about four feet long. **1893** Chapman & Buck *Wild Spain* v. 57 The knight, mounted on fiery Arab steed, was armed only with the *rejon*, or short sharp lance of those days, five feet in length, and held at its extreme end. **1932** *Times Lit. Suppl.* 7 Jan. 11/1 Nobles and gentlemen, on horseback with long heavy spears (*rejones*)..awaited the bull's attack. **1934** R. Campbell *Broken Record* viii. 184 His *rejon* is nearly always mortal. **1957** A. MacNab *Bulls of Iberia* x. 99 The *rejón* act..is more popular in Portugal, but is also quite common in Spain. **1967** McCormick & Mascareñas *Compl. Aficionado* i. 19 The rider plays the bull with the horse itself, placing long banderillas, darts known as *rejones*, and killing with a long lance, also called a rejón. **1973** *Times* 5 Dec. 15/1 They attempt to finish him [*sc.* the bull] off with a *rejon*, a long-bladed, wooden-handled spear.

‖ **rejoneador** (rehoneado·r). *Bull-fighting.* Pl. **-es**; fem. **-a.** [Sp.] A mounted bull-fighter who places *rejones* (see prec.).

1926 *Blackw. Mag.* Sept. 290/2 No small skill in horsemanship is required to be a successful rejoneador. **1932** E. Hemingway *Death in Afternoon* iii. 31 A man who kills them [*sc.* bulls] on horseback with a javelin, using trained thoroughbred horses, is called a rejoneador or a caballero en plaza. **1957** R. Campbell *Portugal* vi. 114 The great Peruvian horsewoman, the beautiful Conchita Cintron, earned immortal fame as a *rejoneadora*. **1957** A. MacNab *Bulls of Iberia* x. 100 The *rejoneadores*..are technically deemed amateurs. **1967** McCormick & Mascareñas *Compl. Aficionado* i. 19 Rejoneo has little to do with the true art of toreo on foot; it is too showy, and the danger is risked by the horse, not the man (*rejoneador*). **1973** *Times* 5 Dec. 15/1 Women do fight in Spanish bull rings..but exclusively as *rejoneadoras*, from the backs of..horses.

‖ **rejoneo** (rehonē·o). *Bull-fighting.* [Sp.] The art of bull-fighting on horseback with *rejones* (see prec.).

1961 *John o' London's* 609/2 *Rejoneo*, the art of bull-fighting on horseback. **1965** *Pix* (Austral.) 13 Feb. 36/2 Conchita Cintron, first woman to master both rejoneo and the classic Spanish style on foot, was a matadora in her own right. **1967** McCormick & Mascareñas *Compl. Aficionado* i. 19 Alvarez cites further instances of corridas organized to celebrate marriages, all antedating the late mediaeval and renaissance practice of *rejoneo*, or knightly jousting against toros bravos. **1978** *Radio Times* 17–23 June 25/3 In the bull-ring he practises 'rejoneo', the aristocratic form of fighting bulls from horseback.

rejuvenate, *v.* Add: **2.** *Geol.* To restore to a condition characteristic of a younger landscape.

1903 H. Le R. Fairchild *Le Conte's Elements Geol.* (ed. 5) ii. 23 If the land area be lifted up the graded streams are rejuvenated—that is, their grade and power are increased. **1944** A. Holmes *Princ. Physical Geol.* xi. 195 When a river that has already established a flood-plain is rejuvenated, it cuts through its own deposits into the underlying rocks. **1954** W. D. Thornbury *Princ. Geomorphol.* vi. 143 During the low sea levels of the glacial ages streams presumably were rejuvenated in their lower courses.

rejuvenated *ppl. a.*, **rejuvenation** (examples of each in *Geol.*).

1936 *Geogr. Jrnl.* LXXXVII. 20 Before rejuvenation the river had developed an open mature valley in marked contrast to its present rugged canyon. **1954** W. D. Thornbury *Princ. Geomorphol.* vi. 142 Mature or old-age topography is likely to have superposed upon it youthful features as a result of rejuvenation. **1969** G. C. Dickinson *Maps & Air Photographs* xiii. 209 If, for reasons such as rise of the land, fall in sea level, or glacial overdeepening of the main valley, a river begins to cut down into its valley floor, a rejuvenation head will form at the upper limits of this downcutting, working its way progressively upstream. **1970** R. J. Small *Study of Landforms* iii. 105 In geologically active areas (such as New Zealand) it is possible that both fault- and fault-line scarps exist together. Indeed, it has been suggested that what are termed 'composite' and 'rejuvenated' scarps may be developed in these circumstances. **1971** *Nature* 19 Feb. 539/1 Further local rejuvenations of the main graben and step faults continued until mid-Pleistocene times, deepening the Lake Naivasha and Lake Natron sectors.

rejuvenatory (rĭdʒū·vĭnătŏri), *a.* [f. Rejuvenate *v.* + -ory².] Tending to cause rejuvenation.

1971 *Nature* 25 June 530/2 A reverse transcriptase would have 'rejuvenatory' potential if it could restore lost or masked primary information from secondary copies. **1972** *Ibid.* 15 Dec. 414/1 This may represent a special rejuvenatory function of sexual processes.

rejuvenescent, *a.* **2.** (Later example.)

1899 R. Fry *Let.* 9 June (1972) I. 173, I have very rarely had a more rejuvenescent visit to Cambridge than this last.

‖ **relâche** (rəlɑ̄ʃ). [Fr.] A period of rest, an interval; a break *from* something.

1863 A. J. Munby *Diary* 10 Apr. in D. Hudson *Munby* (1972) 155 Caldwell's is one of the few public dancing rooms in London, which is frequented by respectable women... When we arrived, the relâche was begun. **1905** G. Bell *Let.* 24 Oct. (1927) I. xi. 226 Tonight he has asked Yves Guyot to dinner because I said I wanted to see him, so we shall have a little 'relâche' from archaeology. **1910** W. S. Blunt *Let.* 19 Mar. in R. S. Churchill *Winston S. Churchill* (1969) II. Compan. ii. xv. 1159 Wd you rather have a *relâche* from politics?

relapsing, *ppl. a.* **6.** *relapsing fever*, substitute for def.: either of two similar kinds of fever characterized by relapses, caused by spirochætes of the genus *Borrelia* and transmitted respectively by lice and by ticks. (Earlier and later examples.)

1849 *Dublin Q. Jrnl. Med. Sci.* VIII. 50 This fever has been well called a relapsing fever; that is, it was made up of two parts, crisis being very generally present at the termination of each. **1936** *Lancet* 22 Feb. 448/1 Recent investigation of a small outbreak of relapsing fever in Kfar Vitkin, south of Hedera in the coastal plain, showed that all infections could be traced to a cave infested with *Ornithodorus papillipes*. **1966** Dunlop & Alstead *Textbk. Med. Treatment* (ed. 10) 218 Tetracycline..is the drug of choice, although subsequent relapses of tick-borne relapsing fever due to *Bor. duttoni* may be experienced. **1974** Passmore & Robson *Compan. Med. Stud.* III. xii. 75/1 The spirochaetes responsible for louse-borne relapsing fever is *Borr*[*elia*] *recurrentis* and for the tick-borne form, *Borr. duttoni*. *Ibid.*, Louse-borne relapsing fever is a disease of cold weather which occurs in epidemic form usually in the wake of disasters such as wars or earthquakes.

relata: see *relatum.

relatable, *a.* Add: **b.** Now usu. with *to.* Also, that may be shown to possess mutual relation. Hence **relatabi·lity.**

1937 *Burlington Mag.* July 58/2 The 'relatability' of pictorial forms..follows on the artist's realization of their basis, undifferentiated essentials. **1956** *Jrnl. Theol. Stud.* VII. 88 It is found that 38·5 per cent. of the elements of psalm language is certainly not relatable to psalm contents; the relatability of a large part of the remainder thus becomes questionable. **1964** *Language* XL. 244 A proposal for the relatability of two languages..has been traditionally based on the discovery of systematic sound correspondences between certain of their forms. **1975** T. F. Mitchell in W. F. Bolton *Eng. Lang.* iv. 165 *Blackboard* is less obviously relatable to *black board* than *blackbird* is to *black bird.*

relate, *v.* Add: **II. 9. c.** To feel affectively involved or connected with someone or something; to have an attitude of personal and sympathetic relationship *to.*

1950 *Childhood Educ.* Nov. 115/1 Group formation such as takes place in the classroom tends to be adult-centered and dependent upon the varying ways children relate to the teacher. **1965** *Listener* 10 June 864/2 Attitudes to other people at the unconscious level appropriate to an early stage of infancy, of the time before we learnt the capacity to relate. to whole persons. **1966** *New Statesman* 14 Oct. 549/1 The Civic Action now begins As friends and former foe relate. **1968** *Globe & Mail* (Toronto) 13 Feb. 33/8 (Advt.), Candidates should..be able to relate to senior officers of the University. **1969** C. DAVIDSON in Cockburn & Blackburn *Student Power* 361 If we only relate to on-campus issues, we run the risk of laying the counter-revolutionary groundwork. **1971** *Guardian* 7 Jan. 8/3 Married people can still relate. **1971** M. SPARK *Not to Disturb* iii. 89 'What do you mean, I don't relate?' she says. 'When you relate you don't ask what you mean. There's such a thing as a trend.' 'Who do you think you are, you—Chairman Mao?' **1977** J. L. HOULDEN *Patterns of Faith* ii. 20 It is possible to relate to him [*sc.* God] and..a Christian is one who finds that the relating is best done in ways that bear on the figure of Jesus.

relation, *sb.* Add: **3. d.** *Logic.* A constituent of a proposition or propositional function that connects two terms (a dyadic relation) or more (triadic, *n*-adic, etc.).

1870 C. S. PEIRCE *Coll. Papers* (1933) III. iii. § 47. 28 *Inclusion in* or *being as small as* is a *transitive* relation. **1885** W. JAMES in *Mind* X. 32 No relation-expressing proposition is possible except on the basis of a preliminary acquaintance with such 'facts'..as this. **1910** WHITEHEAD & RUSSELL *Princ. Math.* I. § 30. 245 Functions of this kind always mean 'the term having such and such a relation to *x*'. **1940** W. V. QUINE *Math. Logic* v. 201 Relations in the sense here considered are known, more particularly, as dyadic relations. **1956** H. REICHENBACH *Direction of Time* ii. 26 When the points are in a linear order, or serial order, they are governed by an asymmetrical and transitive relation. **1965** HUGHES & LONDEY *Elem. Formal Logic* xxxix. 272 Such relations are said to be non-symmetrical relations. Examples are: 'implies', 'brother of'... Such relations are said to be non-transitive relations. Examples are: 'one mile distant from', 'first cousin of'. *Ibid.* 274 Every dyadic relation must be either reflexive or irreflexive or non-reflexive. **1978** C. KIRWAN *Logic & Argument* i. 23 A binary relation such as hating, which holds from some but not all things to themselves, is neither reflexive nor irreflexive. Likewise many binary relations are neither transitive nor intransitive and many are neither symmetrical nor asymmetrical.

e. *Philos.*, esp. as *external relation*, a connection existing between one thing and another which is not intrinsic to the identity of the first; *internal relation*, a connection between one thing and another which is intrinsic to the identity of the first.

1893 F. H. BRADLEY *Appearance & Reality* iii. 31 Every quality in relation has..a diversity within its own nature, and this diversity cannot immediately be asserted of the quality. Hence the quality must exchange its unity for an internal relation. *Ibid.* iv. 40 This solid unit, existing only by virtue of external relations, is forced to expand. **1922** G. E. MOORE *Philos. Stud.* 288 Yet this last, according to me, is one of the things which the dogma of internal relations denies. **1935** A. J. AYER in *Aristotelian Soc. Suppl. Vol.* XIV. 179 The connexion between the proposition which Mr. Ryle mistakes for the dogma of internal relations and the dogma of internal relations as we understand it, is that they both follow from the proposition that all a thing's characters are intrinsic to it. **1956** R. A. WOLLHEIM in A. J. Ayer *Revolution in Philos.* ii. 22 In logic this view is known as the theory of 'internal relations'. All the relations in which an object stands are rooted in its nature as firmly as triangularity is rooted in the nature of the triangle. **1975** HARGREAVES & WHITE tr. *Wittgenstein's Philos. Remarks* iii. 63 The essential difference between the picture conception and the conception of Russell, Ogden and Richards, is that it regards recognition as seeing an internal relation, whereas in their view this is an external relation.

5. d. In phr. *no relation*, denying relationship by blood or marriage despite having the same surname.

1930 E. M. BRENT-DYER *Chalet Girls in Camp* xii. 175 Except..Ruth Wynyard, Lilli van Huysen, and Greta Macdonald—no relation!—all of them had been her [*sc.* Mrs. Macdonald's] pupils. **1977** *Private Eye* 13 May 14/1 We shall see much more of it now that Mr Moss Evans (no relation) has been elected to one of the two highest offices in the land, as General Secretary of the TGWU.

7. *Comb.*, as **relation-axis** *adj. phr. Gram.*, involving or consisting of a word expressing a relation and another with respect to which the relation holds; **relation-word** *Gram.*, a word expressing relation between other words or groups of words, e.g. a preposition or conjunction.

1933 L. BLOOMFIELD *Language* 267 They [*sc.* English substantive expressions] occur in the position of axis in the relation-axis construction (*beside John*), with a positional meaning of, say, 'center from which a relation holds good'. **1964** E. A. NIDA *Toward Sci. Transl.* iv. 57 In the phrases *through the house, behind the store,* and *in the shed,* the relationship between the prepositions *through, behind,* and *in* and the following immediate constituents (consisting of the noun with preposed determiner *the*) may be described as 'relation-axis'. **1925** GRATTAN & GURREY *Our Living Lang.* xii. 79 [The work of a preposition] is to show the relation in which a noun stands to some other part of the sentence... For this reason it is also known as a *Relation-word.* **1962** J. SÖDERLIND in F. Behre *Contrib. Eng. Syntax* 117 *Of*-groups where *of* is a pure relation-word.

relational, *a.* Add: **2.** (Further examples in *Gram.*)

1930 J. T. HATFIELD et al. *Curme Vol. Ling. Stud.* 37 The immaterial adnominal cases are the following;..relational—a man *in stature.* **1946** *Language* XXII. 219 A *relational phrase* has two immediate constituents. **1967** *Child Devel.* XXXVIII. 841 This study is concerned with the ability of preschool children to use the relational terms 'more', 'same', and 'less' when comparing the number, length, and weight of objects. **1979** *Trans. Philol. Soc.* 215 The element *-ai/ei-* is also found in association with one of the so-called 'relational particles'.

Hence (*Gram.*) as *sb.*, a conjunction or preposition considered as a relation-word; a relational particle.

1964 E. A. NIDA *Toward Sci. Transl.* iv. 62 There are four principal functional classes of lexical symbols: object words, event words, abstracts, and relationals. **1969** *Language* XLV. 485 Relationals are any units which function primarily as markers of relationships between other terms, e.g. *at, by, because, and, or.* **1978** *Ibid.* LIV. 80 Some English prepositions correspond to Japanese genitive constructions with *no* plus relationals.

relationism. a. (Further examples.)

1958 W. STARK *Sociol. Knowl.* viii. 338 By the concept of relationism he [*sc.* K. Mannheim] means that if we formulate a truth, we should not do so in abstract and absolute terms, but must always include in the formula the concrete conditions to which it is related. **1975** *Nature* 1 May p. iv (Advt.), The book is concerned with space and time as abstract relations which hold between objects and events (relationism), and as aspects of nature with causal properties of their own (absolutism).

relationist. Add: Also, one who holds that events are connected in a relative way. Also *attrib.* or as adj.

1885 W. JAMES in *Mind* X. 31 And may not the 'relationists' be right after all? **1923** C. D. BROAD *Sci. Thought* iii. 89 The former alternative is taken by the Relationist... Time just consists of the relations of before and after among events. **1974** L. SKLAR *Space, Time, & Spacetime* iii. 167 According to the relationist, the postulation of space, time, or spacetime as entities..is simply a confusion. *Ibid.*, The prerelativistic and relativistic versions of the relationist position. **1975** *Nature* 6 Feb. 485/3 Wishing to retain a pure relationist stance, he proposes that the statement 'is absolutely accelerated' is not a relational term, giving it instead the status of a complete assertion.

relationless, *a.* Add: **b.** Bereft of relation in general.

1889 'SCOTUS NOVANTICUS' *Metaph. Nova et Vetusta* (ed. 2) II. 86 The datum is not atomic or relationless. **1911** *Proc. Mus. Assoc.* May 121 Oneness and homogeneity could be evolved from such apparently relationless short-cut phrases.

relationship. Add: Also, an affair; a sexual relationship.

1944 M. LASKI *Love on Supertax* viii. 81 'Were you going to marry Lou?' asked Clarissa... 'We hadn't got further than a relationship,' Sid said. **1974** J. GARDNER *Corner Men* v. 41 Bob and I weren't hallo young lovers. We had a relationship, but I wasn't in love with him. **1975** R. RENDELL *Shake Hands for Ever* viii. 76 'Did Mr Hathall have a special friendship with any girl here?'..'Do you mean a relationship? D'you mean, was he *sleeping* with anyone?' **1977** *Rolling Stone* 30 June 62/2 People don't fall in love anymore, they have relationships. **1981** C. R. LAJEUNESSE *Dead Man Running* iii. 11 Rowena and I had a relationship at first, which had been a no-strings-attached affair. Then.. she became serious and I had shied away.

relative, *a.* and *sb.* Add: **A.** *adj.* **9.** Special collocations: *relative address* (Computers), an address (sense *7 c) which is defined only in relation to some other address; hence *relative addressing*, the practice of using relative addresses; *relative density* = *specific gravity* s.v. GRAVITY 4 c; normally defined using water or (for a gas) hydrogen as standard; (cf. quot. 1704 in sense A. 4 b); *relative deprivation* (Sociol.), deprivation as experienced by a person in respect of opportunities, standard of living, etc., which is relative to the circumstances of the group or society of which he is a member; *relative humidity* (Meteorol.): see HUMIDITY 1; *relative pitch*: (Mus.), the pitch of a note in relation to another; the ability to recognize or reproduce this; also in extended use in *Phonetics*; *relative sexuality* (Biol.) [tr. G. *relative sexualität* (M. Hartmann 1909, in *Arch. f. Protistenkunde* XIV. 325)], the phenomenon shown by those species of which an individual or gamete may act as either female or male, according as it is less or more male than its mate.

1956 BERKELEY & WAINWRIGHT *Computers* viii. 352/2 Relative addresses are translated into absolute addresses by adding some specific 'reference' address. **1970** O. DOPPING *Computers & Data Processing* xix. 312 The relative addresses should be tagged to show that they will later have to be modified. **1966** C. J. SIPPL *Computer Dict. & Handbk.* 268/1 Relative addressing is a feature of great significance in multiprogramming, time-sharing, and real time operations. **1967** KLERER & KORN *Digital Computer User's Handbk.* i. 20 Relative addressing is done with addresses that are generated relative to some preset location whose relative address is 0. **1879** J. D. EVERETT *Units & Physical Constants* iv. 30 The relative density of water at various temperatures.., the density at 4° C. being taken as unity. **1892** G. F. BARKER *Physics* III. i. 315 Relative density is the ratio of the absolute density of a gas or vapor to that of air or of hydrogen. **1957** A. EFRON *Basic Physics* I. ix. 105 The relative density of lead is 11·3. **1963** A. F. ABBOTT *Ord. Level Physics* ix. 115 The relative density of a substance is the ratio of the mass of any given volume of it to the mass of an equal volume of water. Numerically, specific gravity and relative density are identical. **1974** FOLIVI & GODMAN *New Certif. Physics* ii. 73/1 The ratio of the density of a substance divided by the density of water is the relative density of the substance. **1949** S. A. STOUFFER et al. *Amer. Soldier* I. iv. 125 To help explain such variations in attitude, by education, age, and marital condition, a general concept would be useful. Such a concept may be that of relative deprivation. *Ibid.* 126 The concept of relative deprivation may seem..not to be applicable to the educational differentials in attitude. **1966** *New Statesman* 8 July 55/2 In the expression 'relative deprivation', as Runciman uses it, the deprivation is largely imaginary and the emphasis..on the relativity. **1972** DOWSE & HUGHES *Polit. Sociol.* xiii. 411 When they cannot achieve these values..dissatisfaction, anger and often aggression occur. This type of situation is a quite usual one in any complex society and is termed 'relative deprivation', which may be defined as 'The tension that develops from a discrepancy between the "ought" and the "is" of collective value satisfaction'. **1926** D. C. MILLER *Sci. of Mus. Sounds* vii. 216 Many writers on the subject have held that the quality of a vowel, as well as that of a musical instrument, is characterized by a particular series of overtones accompanying a given fundamental, the pitches of the overtones varying with that of the fundamental, so that the ratios remain constant; this is the *relative-pitch theory.* **1929** *Melody Maker* Mar. 300/3 A person enjoying the ability to determine the interval between two or more musical sounds is said to possess Relative Pitch. **1933** L. BLOOMFIELD *Language* vii. 117 The Japanese language is said to distinguish two relative pitches, normal and higher. **1949** R-M. S. HEFFNER *Gen. Phonetics* vii. 213 It is the relative pitch of speech sounds which is a linguistic means of differentiation between meanings. **1969** H. L. SMITH in A. A. Hill *Linguistics Today* ix. 94 The four relative levels of stress in English.., the four relative pitch heights.., and the four *junctures* or *transitions*..form three independent but interdependent systems of *prosodic* or *suprasegmental phonemes.* **1977** *Proc. R. Soc. Med.* LXX. 134/1 There is a continuum of skills which ranges from 'tone deafness', through 'relative pitch', to 'absolute pitch'... Most people have relative pitch, in so far as they are able to say, when given a certain reference tone, that a second sound is higher or lower in pitch. **1948** F. E. FRITSCH *Struct. & Reprod. Algae* 327 Relative sexuality, in which one thread [of *Spirogyra*] behaves respectively as male and female to two others, is also on record. **1967** E. STEINER tr. *Esger & Kuenen's Genetics of Fungi* ii. 96 In the light of recent work certain older data are no longer to be interpreted as relative sexuality.

relativism. Add: **a.** (Earlier example.) Also, a name given to theories or doctrines that truth, morality, etc., are relative to situations and are not absolute.

1865 J. GROTE *Exploratio Philosophica* I. xi. 229 The notion of the mask over the face of nature is exactly that which I am sure Dr Whewell does not wish to fall into—it is what I have called 'relativism'. If 'the face of nature' is reality, then the mask over it, which is what theory gives us, is so much deception, and that is what relativism really comes to. [**1934** C. MORRIS in G. H. Mead *Mind, Self & Society* p. xix, Philosophically the position is here an objective relativism: qualities of the object may yet be relative to a conditioning organism. **1941** H. MARCUSE *Reason & Revolution* II. ii. 353 According to Comte, relativism is inseparable from the conception that sociology is an exact science dealing with the invariant laws of social statics and dynamics. **1959** A. BRECHT *Polit. Theory* v. 172, I do not intend to minimize the extent to which Comte's positivism actually contributed to preparing the ground for modern Scientific Method and Value Relativism. **1976** W. J. STANKIEWICZ *Aspects Polit. Theory* vii. 135 What is logically excluded is relativism as a methodology: a methodology demands fixity of purpose; a fixed purpose excludes relativism.

b. Special collocations: (*a*) *historical relativism*, the view that there can be no objective standard of historical truth, as the interpretation of data will be affected by subjective factors characteristic either of the historian or of the period in which he lives; (*b*) *ethical relativism*, the view that there are no universal or objective ethical standards; that each culture develops the ethical standards that it finds acceptable and that these cannot be judged by the ethical standards of another culture; (*c*) *cultural relativism*, the theory that there are no objective standards by which to evaluate a culture; that a culture cannot be understood except from the point of view of its own values or customs; the practice of studying a culture from such a standpoint.

(*a*) **1937** T. PARSONS *Struct. Soc. Action* xiii. 480 In place of a theory of dialectic evolution on the Hegelian model there emerges a complete historical relativism. **1945** K. R. POPPER *Open Society* II. xxii. 191 But this so-called 'historical relativism' by no means exhausts the historicist character of the Marxist theory of morals. **1956** W. KLUBACK *Dilthey's Philos. Hist.* iii. 58 The value of any age was true for that age but could not with validity be applied to other ages. For Dilthey historical relativism did not imply pessimism. On the contrary, it made man aware of his place in history. **1977** M. MANDELBAUM *Anat. Hist. Knowl.* vi. 150 Some of the conventional arguments for historical

relativism, and against the objectivity of historical knowledge, lose much of their force.
(*b*) **1937** T. PARSONS *Struct. Soc. Action* xi. 447 He [*sc.* Durkheim] was forced to define normality with reference to the social type alone, thus ending in a complete ethical relativism. **1944** *Brit. Jrnl. Med. Psychol.* XX. 113/1 This [empirical] point of view is distinct both from ethical absolutism and ethical relativism. **1964** M. RADER *Ethics & Human Community* ix. 236 There is a kind of incongruity in combining the two kinds of relativism. The methodological type requires tolerance..the ethical type condones the most intolerant of societies. **1968** *Internat. Encycl. Soc. Sci.* V. 158 The 'reductionist' form of ethical relativism, which presents the ethical beliefs of a people as functionally dependent on their other beliefs and practices.
(*c*) **1958** F. M. KEESING *Cultural Anthropol.* ii. 47 The scientific habit of looking at each people's standards and values objectively, seeing them as 'relative' to the particular view of life fostered within the culture concerned, has led some thinkers to a philosophic position often called 'cultural relativism'. **1968** *Internat. Encycl. Soc. Sci.* III. 543/2 The methodology of cultural relativism rests on the assumption that the ethnologist is able to transcend, or to eliminate for the moment, his own cultural conditioning and values and to assume the subjective..mentality of an adherent of..the culture. **1976** T. EAGLETON *Crit. & Ideology* iv. 134 Imperialism..bred an awareness of cultural relativism at precisely the point where the absolute cultural hegemony of the imperialist nations needed to be affirmed.

relativist, *sb.* Add: **1.** (Further examples.)
1935 K. KOFFKA *Princ. Gestalt Psychol.* 347 The relativist's argument rejects in the first place the distinction between the picture as a geographical and a behavioral object. **1953** M. GINSBERG *Ess. Sociol. & Soc. Philos.* I. vii. 124 Relativists generally stress the great diversity of morals. Yet the similarity is much greater. **1967** *Encycl. Philos.* III. 75/1 Writers who call themselves relativists always accept the first and second and sometimes accept the third of the theses. **1976** W. J. STANKIEWICZ *Aspects Polit. Theory* v. 97 If relativists are right in assuming that the analysis of values is complete when the latter are declared to be tastes, wishes or attitudes, it would seem impossible for moral statements to form any kind of pattern for either the individual or society.

2. A student or proponent of the theory of relativity.
1914 [implied in sense 3 below]. **1919** *Nature* 11 Dec. 374/2 The out-and-out relativist will not admit an absolute measure of acceleration any more than of velocity. **1922** A. S. EDDINGTON *Theory of Relativity* 16 The reason why the relativist resurrects this ancient truism is because it is only in this undissected combination of four dimensions that the experiences of all observers meet. **1968** *Amer. Jrnl. Physics* XXXVI. 1109/1 His [*sc.* Einstein's] great passion for the physical explanation of the laws of nature resulted in his abandoning ether and absolute time, thus radically modifying long-established Newtonian space-time. Thus, he was the first true relativist. **1977** *Listener* 24 Mar. 365/2 Newton's definitions of time and space..which were found to be implausible with the coming of the relativists at the end of the 19th century.

3. *attrib.* or as *adj.*
1914 C. D. BROAD *Perception* v. 286 It is no special objection to the relativist theory. **1921** *Nature* 8 Dec. 467/1 The differential equations which the relativist mathematicians use. **1939** V. A. DEMANT *Relig. Prospect* i. 12 Man has no criteria by which to guide himself in the movements of time. He resorts to beating back the forces that oppose what he conceives to be the most advanced phase. This attitude is completely relativist. **1949** *Scrutiny* XVI. 1. 26 It is commonly held that the essential point about totalitarian morality is the denial of a universal moral law binding on all mankind and its replacement by a relativist view of morals. **1962** *Listener* 10 May 821/1 We are usually too timid, too relativist, to be so vehement in our defence of righteousness today.

relativistic, *a.* **1.** Add: Of, pertaining to, or characterized by relativism or relativity. (Further examples.)
1917 A. S. PRINGLE-PATTISON *Idea of God* 212, I applied this specially to the case of the secondary qualities which are usually regarded as the stronghold of the relativistic theory. **1937** T. PARSONS *Struct. Soc. Action* xiii. 480 On the empirical plane one of the first radical representatives of this relativistic view is Dilthey. **1959** A. BRECHT *Pol. Theory* vi. 249 Roscoe Pound..called it futile to wait for a statement of absolutes, and recommended practical work on the basis of our present civilization—again an activity entirely legitimate from the relativistic viewpoint. **1964** M. JACOBS *Pattern in Cultural Anthropol.* xii. 297 No anthropologist lacks admiration for northwestern art work, no matter how ridiculously relativistic his dogma. **1979** *Sci. Amer.* Mar. 94/2 It seems that a much more relativistic process is going on in the visual system. The boundary between each target square and its immediate background gives only the relation between the light reflected by each of these areas. **1981** *Times Lit. Suppl.* 13 Feb. 176/4 In *Gulliver's Travels* Swift chose the most 'relativistic' form, the travel book, in order to attack the root of relativism.

2. *Physics.* **a.** Pertaining to or based on the theory of relativity; modified or formulated according to the assumptions or consequences of the theory of relativity.
special relativistic, general relativistic adjs.: based on or taking account of the special theory (only) or the general theory, respectively, of relativity.
1914 L. SILBERSTEIN *Theory of Relativity* iv. 94 It requires, according to the relativistic view itself, some essential, though numerically slight, modifications. **1926** *Physical Rev.* XXVIII. 1070 The relativistic theory of the hydrogen atom is apparently incomplete. **1938** *Ann. Reg. 1937* 355 Heitler and Bhabha..used relativistic quantum mechanics to determine the number of secondary positrons and electrons produced when a fast primary electron passes through matter. **1958** CONDON & ODISHAW *Handbk. Physics* ii. 19 The constancy of v_4 implies a constant ratio between classical time t and relativistic proper time τ. **1970** *Nature* 17 Oct. 273/1 The rectilinear Galilean transformation was discarded by Einstein in favour of the special-relativistic (Lorentz) transformation to a uniformly moving frame. **1972** *Ibid.* 18 Feb. 361/2 The theory of black holes..may perhaps be considered as one of the aspects of general-relativistic physics which is better understood. **1974** G. REECE tr. *Hund's Hist. Quantum Theory* vii. 99 Sommerfeld applied his theory, which took account of the relativistic correction, to the X-ray term.

b. Characterized by or designating circumstances, esp. those involving speeds approaching that of light or large gravitational potentials, in which discrepancies between the predictions of the theory of relativity and of Newtonian mechanics or classical electromagnetism become significant.
1934 *Discovery* Oct. 285/2 He examined the principles of thermodynamics as they apply in a relativistic universe. **1964** *Astrophysical Jrnl.* CXXXIX. 925 It has been argued in the past that the energy of the relativistic particles associated with the Crab cannot be greater than the kinetic energy of the filaments; otherwise the nebula would expand faster than it is observed to do. This argument is only correct, however, if the relativistic particles are trapped within the filaments. **1967** *Ibid.* CL. 1005 To extend these results on neutron and supermassive star models to arbitrarily relativistic stars rotating with arbitrary angular velocity is a problem which..is numerically complicated. **1973** C. W. MISNER et al. *Gravitation* xxiv. 633 The relativistic instability occurs far outside the Schwarzschild radius when the star is very massive...Rotation can stabilize it against relativistic collapse for a while. **1978** *Astrophysical Jrnl.* CCXXIII. 14 Fragmentation of a relativistic shock wave in either the free expansion or the self-similar blast wave solutions probably cannot be avoided.

Hence **relativi·stically** *adv.*
1947 *Physical Rev.* LXXII. 340/1 Relativistically, ν should be replaced by $c\alpha$. **1955** L. D. LANDAU in W. Pauli *Niels Bohr* 52 Perturbation theory has been reconstructed in a relativistically invariant way. **1970** *Nature* 17 Oct. 271/1 To discuss the recoil relativistically we must speak of 4-momentum.

relativitist, var. *RELATIVIST *sb.* 2.
1931 *Sci. Progress* XXV. 632 As the relativitist would point out, only the resultant symmetry of our chemical molecules, inspected in the aggregate, is observable. **1939** *Mind* XLVIII. 62 The relativitist, they tell us, has *discovered* that what we think of as a ruler of fixed length, has in fact different lengths according to its position.

relativity. Add: **2.** The quantitative dependence of observations on the relative motion of the observer and the observed object; that branch of physics which is concerned with the description of space and time allowing for this dependence.
The modern theory of relativity, developed largely by Albert Einstein (1879–1955), is an extension and generalization of the corresponding principles in classical, or Newtonian, mechanics.
The *principle of relativity*, in its restricted form, is the postulate that the laws of nature have the same form in all inertial reference frames; in its more general form, it states that the laws of nature, when expressed in a suitable ('covariant') form, have the same form in all reference frames, whether inertial or not.
The *special theory of relativity* (1905), based on the restricted principle of relativity and the hypothesis of the constancy of the speed of light *in vacuo* as seen by observers in any inertial frames, resulted in a theoretical framework for the unification of space and time in a four-dimensional continuum and for the equivalence of mass and energy, and showed how the uniform relative motion of observers affects their measures of length and time.
The *general theory of relativity* (1915), essentially a theory of gravitation, is based on the general principle of relativity, the postulated equivalence of inertial and gravitational mass, and the assumption that the results of the special theory must be valid in the limiting case of zero gravitational potential; it leads to a new set of equations of motion and the result that space-time is curved by the presence of gravitational fields.
1876 J. C. MAXWELL *Matter & Motion* vi. 84 Our whole progress up to this point may be described as a gradual development of the doctrine of relativity of all physical phenomena. Position we must evidently acknowledge to be relative. *Ibid.* 85 (*heading*) Relativity of force. **1882** J. B. STALLO *Concepts & Theories of Mod. Physics* xii. 204 The same considerations which evince the relativity of motion also attest the relativity of its conceptual elements, space and time. **1905** W. J. G. tr. *Poincaré's Sci. & Hypoth.* v. 76 The state of the bodies and their mutual distances at any moment will solely depend on the state of the same bodies and on their mutual distances at the initial moment, but will in no way depend on the absolute initial position of the system and of [*read* on] its absolute initial orientation. This is what we shall call, for the sake of abbreviation, the law of relativity. [**1905** *Sci. Abstr.* A. VIII. 2277 A. Einstein... The relativity of lengths and times.] **1906** J. W. YOUNG tr. H. Poincaré in *Bull. Amer. Math. Soc.* XII. 243 The principle of relativity, according to which the laws of physical phenomena must be the same for a stationary observer as for one carried along in a uniform motion of translation. *Ibid.* 247 Let us consider the principle of relativity; this principle is not only confirmed by our daily experience,..but it appeals to our common sense with irresistible force. And yet it also is being fiercely attacked. **1912** *Phil. Mag.* XXIII. 375 An acceptance of the Einstein theory of relativity necessitates a revision of the Newtonian system of mechanics. **1916** *Monthly Notices R. Astron. Soc.* LXXVI. 701 These considerations have led Einstein to his postulate of general relativity, which requires the laws of nature to be invariant for *all* transformations of co-ordinates. **1920** R. W. LAWSON tr. *Einstein's Relativity* vii. 20 As a result of an analysis of the physical conceptions of time and space, it became evident that in reality there is not the least incompatibility between the principle of relativity and the law of propagation of light, and that by systematically holding fast to both these laws a logically rigid theory could be arrived at. This theory has been called the special theory of relativity. **1921** *Nature* 1 Dec. 434/2 The result is valid for both the special and the general theory of relativity. **1922** E. P. ADAMS tr. *Einstein's Meaning of Relativity* iii. 68 We shall be true to the principle of relativity in its broadest sense if we give such a form to the laws [of physics] that they are valid in every such four-dimensional system of co-ordinates, that is, if the equations expressing the laws are co-variant with respect to arbitrary transformations. **1928** *Times* 3 Dec. 8/2 The whole point of the theory of relativity is the discovery of invariants, or absolute quantities, the same to all observers, and identical throughout the universe. **1932** W. T. STACE *Theory of Knowl.* xiv. 389 The space-time of modern relativity mechanics. **1959** *Listener* 9 Apr. 631/2 In everyday experience, special relativity gives virtually the same results as Newtonian theory. **1968** *Amer. Jrnl. Physics* XXXVI. 1109/1 Although the principle of relativity is subject to a possible experimental disproof in the future, the importance of the postulational approach is that it freed relativity from electrodynamics as a basis and made special relativity more universal. **1973** L. J. TASSIE *Physics of Elementary Particles* 203 An important result of the theory of special relativity is time dilatation, or the slowing down of moving clocks. **1974** *Encycl. Brit. Macropædia* XV. 584/2 The general theory of relativity derives its origin from the need to extend the new space and time concepts of the special theory of relativity from the domain of electric and magnetic phenomena to all of physics and, particularly, to the theory of gravitation. **1976** M. G. BOWLER *Gravitation & Relativity* p. vii, Einstein's theory of gravitation, general relativity, has been verified at the one per cent level. **1978** *Sci. Amer.* Feb. 131/1 The present understanding of the fundamental laws of nature arose from three principles: special relativity, general relativity and quantum mechanics.

3. The relative grading of posts or salaries, usu. considered within one business (*internal*) or in comparison with others (*external*). Freq. *pl.*
1962 *Rep. Comm. Broadc. 1960* 192 The BBC's policy on the payment of its staff takes careful account of internal and external relativities. In assessing internal relativities, the broad aim is to define the difficulty and responsibility of posts at each level over a very wide range of professions... To maintain external relativities, the Corporation draws comparisons with a suitable range of different employment. **1966** *New Statesman* 21 Jan. 71/1 Union A makes a claim in January, on the grounds that they have fallen behind B and C. When A's claim is agreed, B makes a claim in February, because relativity has been destroyed. **1971** *Nature* 20 Aug. 513/1 The institution pressed for the use of internal relativities to determine salaries. **1974** *Times* 9 Feb. 1/2 The new principles and procedures for adjusting wage relativities, ..since the Government agreed to set up machinery inside the Pay Board to examine major relativity claims.

relativization (relătivəizēⁱ·ʃən). [f. next + -ATION.] **1.** *Physics.* A relativistic treatment of a problem or theorem. *rare.*
1921 H. L. BROSE tr. *Moszkowski's Einstein the Searcher* vii. 162 Now, the conception of time has been entirely revolutionized by Einstein himself... We thus approach a relativization of causality... Something physiological that ultimately..resolves itself into a relativization of time.

2. The action of making relative; the fact or process of being made relative. Freq. in *Philos.* and *Linguistics.*
1942 *Mind* LI. 237 This is not exclusive subdivision, but relativization or canalization. **1945** *Polish Sci. & Learning* vi. 19/1 The relativization of the definability of a sign '*a*' to a set of propositions *X* becomes obvious. **1948** L. SPITZER *Linguistics & Lit. Hist.* 73 His [*sc.* Cervantes'] humor, which admits of many strata..of relativization and dialectics—bears testimony to his high position above the world. **1959** K. R. POPPER *Logic Sci. Discovery* 346, I only learned from Rényi's paper how fertile this relativization could be. **1968** *Language* XLIV. 55 Relativization, Relative reduction and Modifier inversion were set up to handle other constructions. **1977** M. DUMMETT *Elem. Intuitionism* v. 206 The relativization property guarantees that the logical laws which hold good whenever the individual variables are taken as ranging over any admissible domain also hold good when they are confined to some inhabited subdomain which can be characterized by a predicate of the language.

relativize (re·lătivəiz), *v.* [f. RELATIVE *a.* + -IZE.] **1.** *Physics.* To render or treat according to the principles and results of the theory of relativity.
1935 J. DOUGALL tr. *Born's Atomic Physics* iv. 84 Before Einstein, no one ever hesitated to speak of the simultaneous occurrence of two events... Einstein proved that this concept must be 'relativized', since two events may be simultaneous in one frame of reference, but take place at different times in another. **1956** E. H. HUTTEN *Lang. Mod. Physics* iii. 108 If we can make a uniform motion into an accelerated one, with a stroke of the pen so to speak, it means that the concept of force becomes relativised.

2. To render relative; to make something relative to, or dependent on, something else. Freq. in *Philos.* and *Linguistics.*
1937 T. PARSONS *Struct. Soc. Action* xi. 447 His [*sc.* Durkheim's] theory of religion, by associating it with the social type, relativized another great body of phenomena. **1948** L. SPITZER *Linguistics & Lit. Hist.* 81 The pun is a bifocal manner of expression which relaxes and relativizes the firmness with which language usually appears to speaking man. **1966** J. J. KATZ *Philos. Lang.* ii. 14 The philosopher of language..need not restrict his philosophical solutions and claims by relativizing them to the conceptual systems. **1976**

Language LII. 285 Kuhn proposes to relativize the notion of science. **1978** F. BURTON *Politics of Legitimacy* iii. 87 The raid that evening served to relativize the type of criticism that Jimmy was making.

Hence **re·lativized** *ppl. a.* (examples in *Linguistics*).

1972 *Language* XLVIII. 306 This [*sc.* receiving primary stress] should happen, for example, if the relativized NP were the subject of an embedded intransitive sentence. **1977** *Ibid.* LIII. 94 Ross formulates the relativization rule in such a way that it always involves movement of the relativized NP out of the sentence dominating the rest of the relative clause.

relator. Add: **4.** *Linguistics.* A sentence-element (usu. a preposition) serving to relate one phrase to another.

1933 [see *DESCRIPTOR]. **1953** W. J. ENTWISTLE *Aspects of Lang.* v. 157 The *relatum* of a language corresponds to the logical category of substance and finds its pure expression in proper nouns; the *descriptum* corresponds to quantity and has its pure expression in numerals; the *descriptor* with quality and is pure in adverbs; the *relator* with relation and is pure in prepositions. **1965** *Language* XLI. 73 Thus the whole string is a relator-axis phrase of which *on* manifests relator and the rest manifests axis. **1978** *Language* LIV. 353 *Relator* is assigned to constituents that serve to introduce embedded clauses (e.g. *that*), and is thus partially co-extensive with the complementizer of recent TG.

‖ **relatum** (rĭlā·tǒm, -ēⁱ·tǒm). Pl. **-ata.** [a. L. *relātum*, neut. pa. pple of *referre* REFER.] **a.** *Logic.* = RELATE. *sb.* 2. **b.** *Linguistics.* (Brøndal's term for) the substantival member of a prepositional phrase (see *RELATOR 4).

1872 G. GROTE *Aristotle* iii. 101 Habit, disposition, perception, cognition, position, &c., are all *Relata. Ibid.* 102 The *Relatum* and its Correlate seem to be *simul naturâ.* If you suppress either one of the pair, the other vanishes along with it. **1893** W. MINTO *Logic* iii. 118 In mediæval logic the term *Relata* was confined to these perfect cases, but the Category had a wider scope with Aristotle. **1903** B. RUSSELL *Princ. Math.* ii. 24 The class of terms to which some term has the relation *R*..I call the class of *relata.* Thus if *R* be paternity..the relata will be children. **1933** [see *DESCRIPTOR]. **1946** *Language* XXII. 219 The *relatum* is most commonly a noun or other type of substantive expression. **1953** [see *RELATOR 4]. **1974** L. SKLAR *Space, Time, & Spacetime* iii. 167 For temporal and spatiotemporal relata the idealization is that of the instantaneous event.

relaunch, *v.* Add: (Further example.) Also *fig.*

1964 *Yearbk. Astron 1965* 135 The heavier landing vehicle was the penalty to be paid for taking the entire propulsion machinery down on to the lunar surface and re-launching it. **1971** *Daily Tel.* 27 May 1/5 The company was re-launched nearly two years ago... It was originally part of Henry Bowen-Davies' £8m Davies' Investment group which collapsed in 1967. **1980** *Listener* 3 Jan. 6/3 Rupert Murdoch relaunched the *Sun* as a down-market tabloid.

re·launch, *sb.* [f. the vb.] A renewed launch. Freq. *fig.* of a business or commodity.

1970 *Daily Tel.* 2 Mar. 21/6 The re-launch had the desired effect and Vim's share of the market increased from 33 p.c. to 38 p.c. **1979** *Guardian* 14 Nov. 20/1 (Advt.), The relaunch of Times Newspapers Limited signals the return of the most challenging selling opportunities around.

relax, *sb.* Restrict †*Obs.* to sense 2 and add: **1.** (Further examples.)

1853 C. BRONTË *Villette* II. xxiii. 141 That bustle and business to which, till five p.m., there was no relax. **1925** A. S. M. HUTCHINSON *One Increasing Purpose* I. xxii. 137 That..sigh she gave,..and that relax into his arms. **1961** *Times* 2 Nov. 16/2 Miss Brodie herself, who is always arousing her headmistress's suspicions because of her damning of braces and blessing of relaxes.

relax, *v.* Add: **I. 1. b.** *spec.* in *Ent.*

1902 W. J. HOLLAND *Butterfly Bk.* 41 When butterflies or moths have been put up in papers or mounted on pins without having their wings expanded and set it becomes necessary, before setting them, to relax them. **1939** DUNCAN & PICKWELL *World of Insects* xix. 389 Before such stored specimens can be mounted they must be relaxed. **1976** P. W. CRIBB *Lepidopterist's Handbk.* vii. 85, I have just relaxed and set some tortrices without too much trouble.

II. 7. c. Of persons: to become less tense or anxious. Freq. imp., 'stop worrying!', 'calm down!'.

1935 A. J. POLLOCK *Underworld Speaks* 135/2 *You can relax*, the person playing the hand in contract informing his partner that the contract will be made. **1941** *Men Only* July 70 (*caption*) All right, relax. I'm just watching it [*sc.* the baby] for someone! **1954** T. S. ELIOT *Confidential Clerk* I. 18 As you're here, Eggers, I can just relax. **1959** *Woman* 4 Apr. 48/2, I patted his knee. 'Relax, darling. Our problem is soon to be solved.' **1976** C. WOLFF *Older Love* i. 12, I relaxed over a *crème caramel* and was happy.

10. Chiefly *Physics.* To return towards a state of equilibrium.

1959 G. TROUP *Masers* iii. 45 Interactions occur between the lattice vibrations and the molecules, which enable the molecular system to 'relax' to thermal equilibrium. **1972** *Physics Bull.* Aug. 451/3 The electronic spins, initially unpolarized, relax slowly towards their equilibrium polarization which, in the high field applied and at a very low temperature of 0·4 K, is nearly 100%. **1973** *Nature* 24 Aug. 496/1 We have thus assumed that the observed strains result from a single system which relaxed exponentially after the start of the eruption with a time constant of 7·5 d. **1978** *Sci. Amer.* Sept. 124/2 Regular patterns of differential extinction..have occurred as the supersaturated faunas of 13 species of small flightless mammals have relaxed toward the smaller number of species that are appropriate to particular mountaintops.

relaxant, *a.* and *sb.* **A.** *adj.* (Later example.)

1977 *Lancet* 24–31 Dec. 1332/1 It may be that these neurons are involved in mediating relaxant effects of the intestine in response to a food bolus.

B. *sb.* (Later example.)

1977 *Sci. Amer.* May 99/2 One of its active alkaloids is the basis of drugs that are important in modern surgery as muscle relaxants.

relaxation. Add: **6.** *Engin.* and *Math.* A method of solving a set of simultaneous equations (originally *spec.* ones describing the equilibrium of a rigid load-bearing structure) by guessing a solution and successively modifying it to accord with whichever equation or constraint is currently least closely satisfied. Freq. *attrib.*

1935 *Proc. R. Soc.* A. CLI. 60 The method of systematic relaxation... Imagine that one constraint is relaxed, so that one joint is permitted to travel slowly through a specified distance in some specified direction. **1940** R. V. SOUTHWELL *Relaxation Methods in Engin. Sci.* i. 11 The relaxation procedure is a means whereby simultaneous equations may be solved, not exactly, but with steadily increasing approximation. **1957** L. FOX *Two-Point Boundary Problems* iii. 39 In most problems of the type suitable for relaxation the equations can be arranged so that the biggest coefficient in any row lies in the diagonal. **1972** *Physics Bull.* May 273/1 During the war, Southwell and his team had been extending relaxation methods from redundant pin-jointed frameworks to the stress analysis of the continuum.

7. Chiefly *Physics.* The gradual return of a system towards equilibrium; *esp.* the reduction of stress caused by gradual plastic deformation in material held at constant strain. Freq. *attrib.*, as **relaxation time,** the time taken for a system to return to a state of equilibrium; *spec.* (in cases in which the process of return is exponential), the time taken for the deviation from equilibrium to be reduced by a factor *e*.

1867 J. C. MAXWELL in *Phil. Trans. R. Soc.* CLVII. 53 A time T, which may be called the 'time of relaxation' of the elastic force. **1908** J. JEANS *Math. Theory Electricity & Magnetism* x. 349 The time..in which all the charges in the dielectric are reduced to 1/*e* times their original value, is called the 'time of relaxation', being analogous to the corresponding quantity in the Dynamical Theory of Gases. The relaxation-time admits of experimental determination. **1937** *Trans. Amer. Soc. Mech. Engineers* LIX. 451/2 There are many reasons why relaxation tests at constant extension are useful and significant. **1949** *Aircraft Engin.* Jan. 2/1 The field of research offered by the plastic, creep and relaxation properties of metals under general stress systems at high temperatures is yet only partially explored. **1958** *Jrnl. Iron & Steel Inst.* CXC. G3/1 The experiments on relaxation here described based on 10,000 h duration have given some quantitative characteristics for relaxation for 4 types of steel at 410° and 470° C. **1959** G. TROUP *Masers* iii. 35 We shall see that collisions are in fact a form of 'relaxation process' (process tending to restore the system to equilibrium). **1962** CORSON & LORRAIN *Introd. Electromagn. Fields* v. 191 The free charge density ρ therefore decreases exponentially with time at a rate such that after a time..called the relaxation time, it is reduced to 1/*e* or 36·8% of its original value. **1969** C. O. SMITH *Sci. of Engin. Materials* xiii. 367 The relaxation test is usually performed by maintaining total strain (elastic plus plastic) at a constant level and measuring the decrease in load (or stress) as a function of time. **1971** *Nature* 8 Jan. 93/1 Many phenomena, for example, may be assigned their typical relaxation times—the average time for an effect to fade away... Thus, a fit of temper may have a relaxation time of a few minutes, the satiation of hunger by a meal lasts for a few hours. **1972** *Ibid.* 22 Dec. 447/1 Physicists are also interested in such phenomena as the changes in the qualities of the varnish on a Stradivarius violin, these being relaxation phenomena demonstrating both temporal and irreversible properties.

8. Special Comb.: **relaxation oscillator** *Electr.*, a form of oscillator in which the period and resulting waveform are determined by the slow charge and rapid discharge of a resistor–capacitor or inductor–capacitor circuit. See also sense 7 above.

1942 E. WILLIAMS *Thermionic Valve Circuits* v. 128 The simplest relaxation oscillator is perhaps the series connexion of a d.c. supply voltage, a resistance and a condenser, a neon lamp being shunted across the condenser. **1943** *Electronic Engin.* XV. 412 In general the time-base will be derived from a relaxation oscillator producing a 'saw-tooth' waveform. **1966** *McGraw-Hill Encycl. Sci. & Technol.* XI. 438/2 One of the most widely used forms of relaxation oscillator is the astable multivibrator..which generates a rectangular or square wave.

relaxed, *ppl. a.* Add: **3.** esp. (in sense 7 of vb.) informal, leisurely, at ease; unanxious, free from constraint or tension.

1958 *Listener* 19 June 1032/2 All the speakers sounded relaxed and informal. *Ibid.* 14 Aug. 249/2 What struck me most was the leisurely, richly human world—'relaxed' we should call it now, when nobody is relaxed—that it evoked. **1961** *Times* 16 Mar. 15/4 'Relaxed' has taken the place of the outmoded 'bronzed and fit'. **1972** M. WOODHOUSE *Mama Doll* ix. 121 He'll be fine, Bottle. Very relaxed character. **1978** *Times* 23 Apr. 12/4 You want a meal at the right price in a relaxed atmosphere.

relaxedly *adv.* (further examples); **relaxedness** (further examples).

1952 *Scrutiny* XVIII. iv. 275 What we have here, of course, is not relaxedness or distraction. **1957** Relaxedness [see *COMPÈRE *v.*]. **1974** M. Z. LEWIN *Enemies Within* xxxiii. 147, I drove a lot faster and a lot less relaxedly. **1977** *Times* 22 Sept. 8/1 Edward Heath..didn't have anything so relaxedly Edwardian as a confidant.

relaxer. Restrict *rare* to sense in Dict. and add: **2.** One who applies the method of relaxation (sense *6).

1957 L. FOX *Two-Point Boundary Problems* iii. 39 There are many tricks a skilled relaxer can use to accelerate the convergence of the process and generally lighten his work. **1959** A. M. OSTROWSKI in R. E. Langer *Numerical Approximation* 4 One of the fields where this difficulty is felt in particularly high degree is that of relaxation. The practical relaxer has it 'in his fingertips' how to steer the successive relaxations.

relaxin (rĭlæ·ksin). *Physiol.* [f. RELAX *v.* + -IN[1].] An ovarian hormone first found in rodents, in which it relaxes the pelvic ligaments and softens the cervix of the uterus.

1930 H. L. FEVOLD et al. in *Jrnl. Amer. Chem. Soc.* LII. 3341 The only physiological property thus far discovered for this hormone is its action on the pelvic ligaments and for this reason we propose the name 'Relaxin'. **1968** PASSMORE & ROBSON *Compan. Med. Stud.* I. xxxvii. 45/2 The polypeptide hormone, relaxin, is probably also produced by the placenta. **1978** *Amer. Jrnl. Obstetrics & Gynecology* CXXX. 473/1 The role of human relaxin in pregnancy has not been determined but relaxin extracted from human luteal tissue is active in the guinea pig pubic symphysis assay.

relaxing, *vbl. sb.* Add: **2.** *attrib.* in *Ent.*, applied to containers in which dead insects are relaxed, containing a pad soaked with fluid.

1907 *Yesterday's Shopping* (1969) 699/3 Entomologists' requisites..Killing and relaxing boxes. Each..1/6. **1912** H. ROWLAND-BROWN *Butterflies & Moths* I. v 53 The nervures and wing-attachments must be softened to permit of their being rearranged. I have not found that the 'relaxing-boxes' are much good for this purpose with other than recently killed specimens. **1952** E. F. DAGLISH *Name this Insect* p. xiii, After some hours in a relaxing chamber the legs and wings will be as easy to arrange as are those of fresh-killed specimens. **1963** R. L. E. FORD *Pract. Entomol.* 32 Specimens may be left in a relaxing tin for about twenty-four hours when they will be ready to set. **1976** P. W. CRIBB *Lepidopterist's Handbk.* vii. 84 A relaxing box is a clean plastic box with a layer of clean absorbent material at the bottom.

rela·xity. *rare.* [irreg. f. RELAX *v.* + -ITY; cf. LAXITY.] Relaxedness, freedom from restraint or tension; the state of being relaxed.

a **1784** S. JOHNSON *Sermons* (1788) I. xiii. 271 Men have ever been persuaded, that by doing something, to which they think themselves not obliged, they may purchase an exemption from such duties as they find themselves inclined to violate: that they may commute with heaven for a temporal fine, and make rigour atone for relaxity. **1908** *Daily Mail* 30 June 9/5 The great secret of voice production is relaxity.

relay, *sb.* Add: **2 d.** A series of motor vehicles intended to cover a prescribed route (usu. in sequence); an operation involving this.

1942 *R.A.F. Jrnl.* 27 June 6, I chartered a relay of cars which got us to Beirut..up the coast road. **1971** M. TAK *Truck Talk* 129 *Relay*, a procedure commonly used in companies to keep as many trucks as possible moving over the road. **1973** *Amer. Speech 1969* XLIV. 207 *Relay*, driving operation in which the driver takes his unit from one terminal to another, where a new driver takes over to deliver it to the next terminal, and so on. **1975** *Drive* Nov.–Dec. 110/1 The travellers soon continued their journeys—care of AA Relay. *Ibid.* 110/2 Relay's south-east team had to recover a Rolls-Royce..from east London and take it back to ..Chelsea.

e. *Bridge.* In full, *relay bid.* (See quot. 1964.)

1959 T. REESE *Bridge Player's Dict.* 183 The relay method is used in some systems played by European teams. In certain sequences the responder does not try to give a picture of his own hand but makes a series of relay-bids at the lowest level so that he can learn more about his partner's hand. **1961** *Times* 30 Aug. 11/5 If the partner responds the minimum in the suit immediately above the opening bid..his response is either negative (discouraging) or natural (with more than 10 points). In either event it is known as a 'relay' bid and is forcing; it does not indicate a real suit but invites the opener to disclose what values he holds. **1962** *Listener* 27 Sept. 494/2 In this auction North's 1 NT and 2 NT were 'relay bids', just asking partner to describe his hand. **1964** *Official Encycl. Bridge* 452/1 *Relay*, a minimum bid unrelated to the bidder's hand, aimed simply at keeping the bidding open so that the bidder's partner can describe his hand. **1980** *Times* 12 July 7/4 After One Club—One Diamond—One Heart—the usual rebid by responder is One Spade. This is a 'relay' bid, asking opener to clarify his hand.

3. b. In full, *relay race.* A race of runners in sequence; *spec.* one run by teams of four athletes, a baton being passed in each team from one runner to the next. Also (in quot. 1920), each of the four sections of a relay race. Also in other sports, e.g. Swimming, where members of a team perform in sequence. Also *attrib.*

1898 M. SHEARMAN *Athletics* x. 301 So popular has this form of racing become that within the last year a number of athletic meetings have been held at which there were a series of these relay races. **1908** T. A. COOK *Olympic Games* 187 Relay Race 1600 Metres... Teams of four with four reserves. **1908** *Daily Chron.* 18 Apr. 5/6 It looked as if its representatives would carry off the prize for the one mile relay race, in which four runners run one lap, carrying a flag each. At the end of the lap the flag is handed to a relay walker, and in his turn the walker hands the flag to a cyclist who completes the race. **1920** *Isis* 13 Oct. 2/2 Ten yards is allotted each side of the starting line in which to pass the baton to the next competitor, for every relay subsequent to the one which begins the race. **1922** F. W. H. NICHOLAS *Handbk. Athletics for Beginner* (ed. 2) x. 44 Relay 100 yards and relay hurdles may be run up and down. **1927** W. DEEPING *Kitty* xxiv. 310 To him life was like a relay-race: you snatched the baton from the failing hand of the past, and sped ahead without looking back till some other racer took the baton from you. **1929** G. M. BUTLER *Mod. Athletics* ii. 8 Names are taken..and made up into senior and junior relay teams of four each. *Ibid.* 9 Juniors are under no circumstances allowed to compete in the senior relays. **1939** *Encycl. Brit. Bk. of Year* 650/2 Peter Fick lowered the world's record for the 400-metre relay..while Ralph Flanagan swam 400 metres free style in 4 min. 46·2 sec. **1950** *Oxf. Jun. Encycl.* IX. 454/1 There are also two kinds of team relay race: the medley, in which there are exponents of all three styles of swimming; and the free-style, in which all members swim the same stroke. **1952** ARMBRUSTER & MOREHOUSE *Swimming & Diving* (ed. 2) x. 201 The types of relays in swimming are usually of two kinds. *Ibid.* 204 The swimming take-off in relay racing differs from that in back relay racing. **1955** R. BANNISTER *First Four Minutes* ii. 18 He had helped Hungary on two occasions to capture the 4×1,500 metres relay World record. **1958** *Times* 13 Aug. 2/6 The main hopes in this country lie in the men's four by 100 and four by 400 metres relays. **1958** [see *BATON *sb.* 2 b]. **1974** *Country Life* 14 Feb. 292/3 The England women's only gold medal in athletics..came in the 4×400 metres relay. **1976** *Liverpool Echo* 6 Dec. 18/1 Visibility on the course, however, was too poor to permit the senior relay and a three miles race was substituted. **1978** G. WRIGHT *Illustr. Handbk. Sporting Terms* 150/3 *Relays*, events in which teams of swimmers swim in sequence... A relay team usually consists of four swimmers, but occasionally larger numbers are used.

4. a. In mod. use, any electrical device, usu. incorporating an electromagnet, whereby a current or signal in one circuit can open or close another circuit. Also *transf.* (Further examples.)

1907 *Cornhill Mag.* Mar. 363 The difficulty is overcome by using the partly exhausted current to move a special kind of 'switch', or key, called a 'relay'. **1923** E. W. MARCHANT *Radio Telegr. & Teleph.* v. 71 The telephone may be replaced by an ordinary Post Office relay, such as is used for working on the ordinary telegraph line. **1935** MONSETH & ROBINSON *Relay Systems* i. 1 The function of protective relays in modern power systems is to initiate the operation of devices to isolate transmission circuits and apparatus when trouble develops. **1956** G. A. MONTGOMERIE *Digital Calculating Machines* x. 211 For adding numbers, three sets of relays are used, designated as A, B, and C; they are wired together so that, if two numbers are sent respectively to A and B, the sum of the two numbers appears on C. **1968** *Brit. Med. Bull.* XXIV. 200/2 The sensory relay region in the thalamus. **1969** *Times* 16 Jan. 4/7 Relays are instruments used to switch electrical circuits on and off automatically. They usually consist of an electromagnet which, when activated by an electrical signal, opens or closes a switch in another circuit.

b. An installation or satellite which receives, amplifies, and retransmits a radio transmission so that it may be received over a wider area. Freq. *attrib.*

1921 *Wireless World* 10 Dec. 575/1 These men have banded themselves into a relay organisation. They have laid out in definite form certain traffic routes.., and messages..are broadcasted across the country any time of the night... These relay routes enable the transmission of personal messages from coast to coast, and from the Canadian border to the Mexican border. **1923** *Radio Times* 28 Sept. 26/3 The engineers of the British Broadcasting Company will employ a wireless relay across the Thames. **1945** *Wireless World* Oct. 305 (*heading*) Extra-terrestrial relays. Can rocket stations give world-wide radio coverage? **1962** *Rep. Comm. Broadc. 1960* 257 in *Parl. Papers 1961–2* (Cmnd. 1753) IX. 259 The relay companies are prohibited from originating any programmes of their own. **1966** *McGraw-Hill Encycl. Sci. & Technol.* XIII. 469/2 By far the largest number of television circuit miles is provided by microwave radio relay. **1966** *Electronics* 14 Nov. 47 The company has developed an antenna that allows a plane, say flying over North America, to communicate with a relay satellite orbiting about the equator. **1975** D. G. FINK *Electronics Engineers' Handbk.* XXII. 61 The communications satellite is a radio relay, consisting of a receiver and transmitter, plus a command receiver and transmitter, to control the satellite.

c. A radio transmission or programme which has been relayed.

1929 *Radio Times* 8 Nov. 395/3 We were testing all the arrangements for the Schneider Trophy relay, making sure that the loud-speaker system at various points round the oast could pick up our broadcast. **1929** *B.B.C. Yearbk. 1930* 383 Listeners can..expect to find a number of relays of Central European stations included in the British programmes. **1965** *Listener* 25 Nov. 873/2 *Don Carlos* (Third Programme, November 20) was a direct relay. In spite of all the disadvantages—in timing, indifferent quality of reception, and applause—this kind of broadcast has the incalculable quality of excitement and immediacy that no recording or tape can hope to equal.

5. Special Combs.: **relay rack**, a rack or frame on which relays are mounted, usu. used in a telephone exchange; **relay station**, a radio station that serves as a relay; also *fig.*; **relay valve** *Engin.*, a fluid valve in which the main flow is controlled by a diaphragm actuated by a weep derived from the main flow.

1908 *Daily Chron.* 8 Apr. 3/6 Each girl sits in front of a relay rack, fitted with a bewildering number of small holes, each of which represents a subscriber. **1930** [see *RACK *sb.*[2] 5 g]. **1970** *Jrnl. Gen. Psychol.* LXXXII. 58 A desk-type relay rack with two standard rack panels and an enclosed back stood on a table in the experimental room. **1923** *Radio Times* 28 Sept. 2/2 The proposed relay stations.. will have a power of 100 to 150 watts. **1969** *Times* 26 Feb. 8/7 Light..is converted to a train of nervous impulses which are transmitted down the optic nerve to a relay station known as the lateral geniculate body (L.G.B.) and from there to the striate cortex. **1974** *B.B.C. Handbk. 1975* 21/1 Savings on capital expenditure in 1974–5 were achieved through postponement of work on the proposed Caribbean relay station. **1939** R. N. LE FEVRE *Man. Pract. Gas Fitting* xix. 390 The relay valve..is made in a variety of sizes to suit particular gas rates and pipe connections. **1970** MILES & PINKESS *Gas Appliance Control* ii. 41 It is..possible to have a leak in a joint in the weep pipe or in the cover of the relay valve itself which would pass sufficient gas to hold the relay valve open, even if the control were shut. **1977** R. PRITCHARD et al. *Industr. Gas Utilization* ix. 414 Relay valves are used to control gas or air flows using a small actuating valve, which may be a solenoid valve or a thermostat in the weep line.

relay, *v.* Add: **4. a.** *trans.* To pass on or retransmit (telephonic or broadcast signals received from elsewhere); *loosely*, to transmit.

1878 *Telegr. Jrnl.* VI. 274/2 They have finally solved the important problem of *relaying* telephone sounds. **1904** *Marconigram* July 16/2 With a telegraphone in Chicago, one may telephone from New York, have the telegraphone record his message and repeat it over another wire to St. Louis, where another machine relays it to Denver. **1923** *Glasgow Herald* 22 Mar. 9/2 Little progress has so far been made, as the experiments have only recently been commenced, but last night a Birmingham concert was relayed for London with some success. **1923** *Daily Mail* 14 Aug. 5/3 A special orchestral concert which will be relayed to all the broadcasting stations in Britain. **1958** *Radio Times* 14 Feb. 3/3 The sensitive receiving equipment is also used for relaying programmes from the Commonwealth and the U.S.A. **1969** *Times* 16 July 4/1 The television pictures to be relayed back to earth will be taken by a camera fixed on a special attachment. **1974** *B.B.C. Handbk. 1975* 20/2 Prokofiev's opera *War and Peace* was relayed from the New Sydney Opera House in Australia. **1977** *Rep. Comm. Future of Broadcasting* (Cmnd. 6753) iii. 21 We saw a cable company in Toronto relaying programmes on 24 channels: but several of them were relaying the same programme.

b. *transf.* To pass on (a message or information).

1956 A. H. COMPTON *Atomic Quest* ii. 117 These men were thoroughly acquainted with our wartime methods of bomb construction and relayed the techniques to Russia. **1974** *State* (Columbia, S. Carolina) 13 Feb. 5-A/1 President Nixon relayed word through a spokesman Tuesday that he has no plans to visit the Middle East.

Hence **re·layed** *ppl. a.*; **re·laying** *vbl. sb.*

1904 *Marconigram* July 16/1 The steel belt machine will transmit a record..by relaying, to great distances. **1949** *Radio Times* 15 July 6/1 [We] presented an electrophone to our aged father on October 5th, 1908... I have a vivid recollection of..listening to a relayed programme.

relea·rning, *vbl. sb.* [RE- 5 a.] Learning again.

1961 'E. FENWICK' *Friend of Mary Rose* ii. 20 In the new house..he would have an immense amount of relearning to do. **1978** *Dædalus* Fall 33 Nothing is ever learned beyond the need for relearning.

releasable, *a.* Delete *rare* and add later examples.

1936 *Nat. Geogr. Mag.* LXIX. 93/2 Heavy items of apparatus to be carried in releasable form on the outside of the gondola. **1950** *Manch. Guardian* 15 Sept. 7/3 At Church Fenton.., to quote from an Air Ministry News Service message, will be 'a miniature bombing range and miniature aircraft complete with releasable bombs to amuse the children'. **1980** *Nature* 31 Jan. 488/1 The content of LH-RH in the synaptosomal pellet obtained after centrifugation showed a decline with time, indicating depletion of a releasable pool of the neuropeptide.

release, *sb.*[1] Add: **1. c.** *Psychol.* Liberation from emotional or physical tension. Also *attrib.* and in gen. use.

1915 E. B. HOLT *Freudian Wish* i. 20 Just what shall happen depends on the relative strengths of the suppressed wish and of the censor, and on the amount of release which the joke affords as well as on the degree of violence which it does to the censor. **1933** E. & W. MURPHY tr. *Bechterev's Gen. Princ. Hum. Reflexol.* xxv. 272 All processes of release from inhibition are based on the retention—in the centres—of the traces of reflexes. **1934** E. B. STRAUSS tr. *Kretschmer's Text-bk. Med. Psychol.* i. 12 Are they [*sc.* fits] not really a symptom of cortical paralysis (produced by the lesion) in the sense that they result from a release of sub-cortical activities from cortical control? **1936** P. T. YOUNG *Motivation of Behav.* v. 247 Tension and release occur constantly in the trivial events of daily life. **1948** L. KANNER *Child Psychiatry* (ed. 2) xvii. 245 The term 'release therapy' indicates that the ventilation of specifically oriented feelings of hostility, guilt, and anxiety constitutes a main therapeutic facet. **1954** A. H. MASLOW *Motivation & Personality* xi. 187 It is very likely that catharsis, as originally defined by Breuer and Freud, is in essence a more complex variant of release behavior. **1959** *Times* 4 Apr. 7/6 As the American male is said to approach his car as a form of self-expression, so the German sees it as an instrument of release. **1966** *Listener* 4 Aug. 174/1 In some quarters this loss of binding traditions has resulted in the retreat beyond all controls—the anti-culture of 'release'. **1978** M. T. ERICKSON *Child Psychopathology* vi. 117 The therapeutic effect of release therapy is based on the child's acting out or talking about a traumatic event that is the source of the disturbance.

2. d. A written authorization or permission for publication, esp. from an owner of copyright or a person depicted in a photograph.

1965 *Tamarack Rev.* Winter 13 Don't touch anything, and be sure to get a release. **1966** K. GILES *Provenance of Death* i. 6 Publishing your photo in an ad. without a release could be libel. **1970** C. WHITMAN *Death out of Focus* ix. 130 A photographer would be a damned fool to come in here with a print for which he had no release. **1979** R. COX *Auction* vii. 186 The late Herr Schneider bequeathed it [*sc.* a picture] to me and I was given a release by Herbstein as a result.

6. c. *Teleph.* The action of freeing for further use apparatus or circuitry which has been engaged. Freq. *attrib.*

1892 Release key [see sense 6 b in Dict.]. **1919** J. POOLE *Pract. Telephone Handbk.* (ed. 6) xxi. 368 Its armature short-circuits the no-voltage release magnet and the switch arm falls back to its open position. **1921** W. AITKEN *Automatic Telephone Systems* I. 185 The calling receiver may be replaced just before the register is connected and cause a premature release. **1969** S. F. SMITH *Telephony & Telegr. A* ii. 39 If a relay were required to have a high value of release current, it would need as many springs as possible of maximum thickness. **1970** N. N. BISWAS *Princ. Telephony* iii. 80 This alarm circuit becomes a necessity in all exchanges where the release of the entire switching stages is controlled by the calling subscriber.

d. *Phonetics.* The action or manner of relaxing or terminating the obstruction involved in articulating a stop consonant.

1920 in WEBSTER. **1951** Z. S. HARRIS *Methods in Structural Linguistics* 44 In some English dialects perhaps the sequence [tr] (post-dental [t] plus voiceless spirant release), are each composed of smaller segments. **1964** J. C. CATFORD in D. Abercrombie et al. *Daniel Jones* 34 Variations in vocal fold thickness..produce qualitative variations in..the release-sound of glottal stop. **1969** *English Studies* L. 328 This implies that the difference of total duration between [ptk] and [bdg] is very nearly equivalent to the difference of duration of the release stage. **1978** *Amer. Speech 1975* L. 295 In the style of pronunciation favored by barbershoppers, final voiced stops like those in the key words have a release that gives the impression of an indistinct vowel.

e. *Jazz.* A passage of music that serves as a bridge between repetitions of a main melody. Chiefly *U.S.*

1936 L. DOWLING tr. *Panassié's Hot Jazz: Guide to Swing Music* 18 The group of eight measures designated by the letter *b* is called the 'middle part' because it makes the first appearance in the middle of the tune. [*Translator's note*] Also called, quite poetically, 'the release'. **1937** *New Republic* 24 Nov. 69/1 But then the band comes down to the release and Benny holds up one finger and Jess nods. **1946** MEZZROW & WOLFE *Really Blues* (1957) 344 We played a more staccato style on the release. **1949** L. FEATHER *Inside Be-bop* II. 67 In the release there is another beautiful sweeping phrase. **1959** AVAKIAN & PRINCE in M. T. Williams *Art of Jazz* (1960) xvii. 184 Charlie..develops a series of riffs through the first sixteen bars (tension); then, in the eight-bar release, he contrasts this by playing melodic lines characteristically made up mainly of even eighth notes (relaxation), then returns to eight bars of riffs (tension). **1972** A. WILDER *Amer. Popular Song* ii. 56 The conventional *A–A–B–A* structure (main strain: its virtual repetition: a release, almost always new material: and finally, a literal, varied, or extended restatement of the main strain) was used in *Ol' Man River*.

7. The action of releasing information or other material for publication or public showing; the information or material released.

a. (The releasing of) a news item or official statement, usu. to the press. orig. *U.S.*

1907 *N.Y. Even. Post* (semi-weekly ed.) 15 July 4 The report was given to the press associations..labelled 'confidential', with a fixed date for 'release', before which no part of it was to be used. **1927** G. ADE *Let.* 31 May (1973) 120, I will be..up to my eyes in the weekly release grind. **1931** F. L. ALLEN *Only Yesterday* ix. 276 Press agents distributed their canned releases. **1932** *Atlantic Monthly* Mar. 269/1 The press agents..did not pour forth their releases to a..coöperating press. **1957** [see *BACKGROUNDER]. *a* **1974** R. CROSSMAN *Diaries* (1975) I. 343 The release wasn't ready until a few minutes before I had to deliver the speech.

b. The action of making a film available to cinemas or a gramophone record to purchasers; also, the film or record itself.

1912 *Motion Picture Ann.* 25 An Essanay release called 'Sunshine'. **1927** *Daily News* 8 June 4/4 Some of the recent 'releases' show that Hollywood and Germany are being challenged seriously in the matter of production. **1929** '*His Master's Voice' New Records* Mid-June 13 Theme songs from two great American films that are scheduled for release in the autumn. **1932** *New Yorker* 14 May 57/2, I have not seen it [*sc.* a gramophone record] on any official list and it seems to be a special release. **1949** *St. Paul* (Minnesota) *Pioneer-Press* 19 June 11/3 Busiest year on record for total releases is 1921 when American moviegoers had their choice of 854 different features. **1966** *Illustr. London News* 30 July 31/2 Perhaps this could be quietly excised before the film goes out on general release. **1966** *Guardian* 22 Dec. 4/7 In the pop/folk field the best new release is by The Incredible String Band. **1974** *Times* 19 Oct. 9/1 New Releases... Piano Music by Erik Satie. **1977** *Time* 4 July 4 (Advt.), There's a film to watch—a recent release—8 tracks of stereo to listen to, free naturally, and plenty of room to stretch out or stroll about.

8. Special Combs.: **release agent**, a substance which is applied to a surface in order to prevent adhesion to it, esp. in food packaging and concrete construction; **release date**, a date fixed for the release of information or other material (see sense 7 above); **release group**, a group of servicemen due for release from conscripted service; **release note**, a note authorizing the release of (part of) an aircraft as fit for service; now also in extended use.

1960 A. E. BENDER *Dict. Nutrition* 107/2 *Release agents*, substances applied to tinned or enamelled surfaces or plastic films to prevent the food adhering; e.g. fatty acid amides, microcrystalline waxes, petrolatums, starch, methylcellulose. **1965** W. H. TAYLOR *Concrete Technol. & Pract.* vii. 160 An ideal release agent..should produce a clean stripping action with a minimum of surface defects on the hardened concrete. **1974** BRISTON & KATAN *Plastics in Contact with Food* iii. 61 Silicone resins are also used as release agents. The baking industry, for instance, uses silicone resins to coat bread baking pans and hundreds of releases from a single coating of resin have been reported. **1910** *Moving Picture World* 26 Mar. 488/1 (*heading*) Independent release dates. **1932** L. C. DOUGLAS *Forgive us our Trespasses* (1937) xv. 306 He decided not to take another look at the gripping letter until he had done at least one essay. He always tried to keep about three weeks ahead of the release date. **1965** *Amer. N. & Q.* Mar. 105/2 Its fine appendix of 'Serials from 1912 to 1930', showing title, director, cast, release date, releasing company. **1945** *News Chron.* 18 Apr. 2/4 We think it would have been much fairer to lower the release group age, such as all men over 45 in Group One and so on, and let some of the youngsters who have been in so-called deferred jobs have a turn. **1946** *R.A.F. Jrnl.* May 149 W.A.A.F. personnel whose release groups have appeared in an advance promulgation are invited to apply for vacancies. **1930** *Air Ann. Brit. Empire* 234 The firm must issue with every consignment they deliver a release note certifying that all inspection has been carried out. **1963** *Times Rev. Industry* Mar. 51/1 When a motor dealer asked a customer from whom he bought a second-hand Wolseley car to sign a 'release note', which turned out to be a guarantee of a third party's commitments under a hire-purchase agreement, the customer was not liable on the guarantee.

release, *v.*[1] Add: **I. 4. d.** Of a public or military authority: to make available (requisitioned or otherwise withheld items) to the public; to return (land or property) to civilian use.

1917 *Globe* 21 Feb. 4/4 Only this morning a daily paper of some standing remarked that the Government had not 'released' any Colonial mutton..last week. **1945** *Daily Tel.* 27 July 3/3 (*heading*) R.A.F. & Navy to release houses. *Ibid.*, The Admiralty and Air Ministry are to do all they can to alleviate the housing situation by releasing property.

II. 6. a. (Later example with *of*.)

1974 *Petroleum Rev.* XXVIII. 675/3 To release the diver of this chore, remote-controlled systems are being developed.

c. *U.S.* To make (an employee) redundant. *euphem.*

1976 *National Observer* (U.S.) 24 Jan. 1/4 The two most difficult things I ever had to do were, one: tell 23 teachers we were going to release them [etc.]. **1977** *Time* 12 Dec. 54/2 He closed 1,700 stores, released 10,000 employees, borrowed heavily to revamp and enlarge the remaining 1,932 supermarkets.

7. To make available for publication or public showing; to publish (printed matter, recorded material or the like). orig. *U.S.*

1904 *N.Y. Times* 25 July 5 Chairman Cannon's speech and President Roosevelt's response are completed. The latter is in the hands of the press associations, and will be released Wednesday afternoon. **1912** *Motion Picture Ann.* 42 List of Licensed Pictures. Regularly released during the year 1912. **1916** 'B. M. BOWER' *Phantom Herd* v. 71 We've just got to release films the market calls for. **1937** A. THIRKELL *Summer Half* xi. 298 If a film gets to Barchester it means it's been released for simply months. **1957** *Essays & Stud.* X. 5 Among words that incur..reproach are.. *release* (the expression 'to release a film' is denounced by a bishop as 'an abominable Americanism'). **1962** *Sunday Times* (Colour Suppl.) 10 June 7 This is also true of American records, a great many of which are only released because companies have to take them to get some really lucrative artist. **1972** *Daily Tel.* 18 Jan. 9/5 Rehearsals have already started and the record is expected to be released some time in the Autumn. **1980** *Time Out* 21–27 Nov. 49/3 Films considered by their multinational distributors as too 'difficult' to release conventionally.

releaser. Add: **b.** *Dairying.* A device which removes milk from the vessel in which the output of a milking machine accumulates. Freq. *attrib.*

1950 *N.Z. Jrnl. Agric.* Apr. 378/1 Probably the most important part of any milking shed is the releaser room, as it is here that milk or cream can most easily become affected by unsatisfactory conditions. **1950** *Ibid.* Oct. 369 Up-to-date assembly of releaser, cream separator, skimmed-milk pump, and cream cooler. **1967** HARVEY & HILL *Milk* (ed. 4) xiii. 224 Where milk pipe-lines are provided to transmit the milk directly to the dairy, as in parlours, bails or with milk lines in cowsheds, a releaser is required to remove the milk from the system. Sufficient milk accumulates in the releaser jar which operates valves which seal off the vacuum system and allow the milk to be discharged. **1977** D. N. AKAM in Thiel & Dodd *Machine Milking* iii. 82 A design of diaphragm releaser milk pump that is available in the UK is vacuum driven using a pulsator operating at 50 pulsations/min.

c. *Biol.* [tr. G. *auslöser* (K. Lorenz 1935, in *Jrnl. für Ornithol.* LXXXIII. 143).] A sign stimulus (see *SIGN *sb.* 12); restricted by some writers to one that acts between animals of the same species. Freq. *attrib.*

1937 K. LORENZ in *Auk* LIV. 249 All such devices for the issuing of releasing stimuli, I have termed releasers (*Auslöser*), regardless of whether the releasing factor be optical or acoustical, whether an act, a structure or a color. **1953** J. S. HUXLEY *Evol. in Action* iv. 96 The only definite releaser known in man is the pattern made by a mother's smile to her infant. **1953** N. TINBERGEN *Herring Gull's World* xiv. 116 Ritualisation is the result of a secondary evolutionary process which is closely linked to the releaser-function. *Ibid.* xxii. 208 The red patch on the bill seems to be a genuine social releaser. **1962** *Listener* 9 Aug. 207/2 Because animal signal codes are uniform within each species and fixed for long periods, special signal structures may evolve, and these are called releasers. **1971** *Nature* 16 Apr. 432/2 Releaser pheromone effects exist in man, at least in larval forms, and some involve pheromones of other mammals (musk, civetone). **1975** J. ALCOCK *Animal Behavior* vi. 153 The first concept we shall examine is the sign stimulus or releaser, that portion of the total stimulus configuration which acts as the effective cue in releasing a specific behavior pattern. **1980** A. P. BROOKFIELD *Animal Behaviour* vii. 58 Sign stimuli which elicit behaviour in members of the same species are called releasers.

releasing, *vbl. sb.* Add: **2.** Special Comb.: **releasing factor** *Physiol.*, any of several oligopeptides, released from the hypothalamus into the pituitary portal system, which promote the release from the adenohypophysis into the bloodstream of some specific peptidic hormone.

[**1955** *Endocrinology* LVII. 443 Posterior pituitary extracts contain a corticotropin-releasing factor (CRF) that stimulates the release of ACTH from rat anterior pituitary tissue *in vitro*.] **1965** *Ibid.* LXXVII. 609/1 In 1959, Shibusawa *et al.*..claimed to have prepared a thyrotropin releasing factor (TRF) from dog hypothalamic extracts and from urine. **1966** *Brit. Med. Bull.* XXII. 266/2 On this view, various humoral agents (now called releasing factors) are liberated from nerve-endings (of hypothalamic nerve tracts) into the capillaries (primary plexus) of the portal vessels in the median eminence. **1974** M. C. GERALD *Pharmacol.* xxiii. 413 This supreme command post of the endocrine system directs the activity of the anterior pituitary by neurosecretory mediator substances called releasing factors. **1977** *Time* 24 Oct. 42/2 Andrew Schally..isolated identified and synthesized three separate hormones—'releasing factors'—by which the hypothalamus directs the release of key hormones from the pituitary.

relegate, *v.* Add: **2. d.** *Sport.* To reallocate (a team) to a lower division of a league. Cf. *RELEGATION 1 c.

1913 *Times* 28 Apr. 12/5 Norwich County..will..be relegated to the Second Division next season. **1934** *Times* 7 May 4/5 Everton, when they were relegated for the first time in their history, climbed back immediately. **1981** *Times* 6 May 10/3 After a trying beginning, that saw the club relegated to the second division.

relegation. Add: **1. c.** *Sport.* The demotion of a team to a lower division of a league; *spec.* in *Assoc. Football*, the reallocation to a lower division of the Football League of an agreed number of teams scoring the fewest points in a division in the course of a season's play. Also *attrib.*

1924 *Times* 5 May 6/6 Fractions in goal averages decided promotion and relegation. **1928** *Daily Express* 10 Aug. 13/7 Their supporters have recovered from the bitter disappointment felt when relegation became inevitable. **1949** *Times* 9 May 6/5 There was the question about relegation from the Championship. **1951** *Sport* 6–12 Apr. 6/2 Key man in the successful battle now being waged by West Bromwich Albion to steer clear of the First Division relegation zone is Jack Vernon. **1965** [see *INJECT *v.* 2]. **1969** *Listener* 1 May 625/3 On Saturday, more than 250 million people are estimated to have watched the ninth club from the bottom of the table beat a relegation candidate by the odd goal. **1977** *Daily Mirror* 12 Apr. 26/4 We are out of the relegation zone now.

relentment. a. (Later examples.)

1922 JOYCE *Ulysses* 404 The prolongation of labour pains in advanced gravidancy by reason of pressure on the vein, the premature relentment of the amniotic fluid (as exemplified in the actual case) with consequent peril of sepsis to the matrix. **1929** C. E. MONTAGUE *Disenchantment* iv. 65 Great are the forces of decent human relentment after a hearty let-out with the temper.

re-let, *v.* (Earlier example.)

1780 A. YOUNG *Tour in Ireland* I. 53, I found rents in general at 20s. an acre, with much relet at 30s.

re-let (rī·let), *sb.* [f. the vb.] A property that is let again.

1969 *Guardian* 29 Oct. 1/8 A vast increase in the number of 're-lets' among existing corporation houses. **1971** *Daily Tel.* 5 Aug. 10/7 Relets could be made to young people and earn £40 to £50 a week for the landlord instead of perhaps £10. **1976** *Times* 7 Jan. 13 Even allowing for the substantial numbers of relets from the existing stock, the magnitude of the loss of this source of housing in the new communities is evident.

relevance. Add: (Further examples.) Also *spec.* in recent use, pertinency to important current issues (as education to one's later career, etc.); social or vocational relevancy.

1949 *Poetry* (Chicago) Feb. 299 Tate holds that the poem is autonomous, and that the only relevance the subject-ideas have is to each other within the formal meaning of the work itself. **1955** *Bull. Atomic Sci.* Apr. 126/1 Relevance is another one of these non-assessable quantities which circumstances require to be assessed. **1970** *Time* 30 Nov. 40 The impetus came largely from student demands for 'relevance', especially for the overdue admission of more minority-group students. Activism has also done much to curb the old absurdities of trivial research and needless PH.D.s. **1975** *Language for Life* (Dept. Educ. & Sci.) ix. 129 We have heard the case for 'relevance' carried to the point of excluding fantasy or any stories with settings or characters unfamiliar to the pupils from their first-hand experience. **1975** *Times* 12 Feb. 11/7 *Hal* [sc. a novel]—while laudable in its social intentions—is little more than a piecing together of stock responses to the current demand for 'relevance'. **1977** *Chem. in Brit.* Mar. 105/3 It may seem anomalous in these days of 'relevance' philosophy in tertiary education that the average student of chemistry gets little inkling from his teachers..of the vast practical importance of disperse systems in industry. **1978** *New Scientist* 21 Sept. 850/2 'Relevance' in research implies both social efficacy and psychic commitment by the research worker.

relevancy. Add: **1. b.** (Later examples.)

Now less common than *relevance* in general use.

1961 *Jrnl. Physical Chem.* LXV 317/1 We are reporting these investigations..because of their relevancy to problems of the study of apparently simple exchange reactions of chlorine. **1980** *Times Lit. Suppl.* 30 May 609/2 A tendency to confuse relevancy with recency.

2. A relevant remark. (*Nonce use* influenced by IRRELEVANCY.)

1895 'MARK TWAIN' in *N. Amer. Rev.* July 10 Conversations consisted mainly of irrelevancies, with here and there a relevancy, a relevancy with an embarrassed look, as not being able to explain how it got there.

relevant, *a.* Add: **1.** (Later examples.) Cf. *RELEVANCE.

1948 D. CECIL *Two Quiet Lives* II. 140 To learn everything that could possibly be thought relevant to the subject. **1969** *Harper's Mag.* Nov. 86 Either we can commit ourselves to changing the institutions of our society that need to be changed, to make them—to use a term which I hate—'relevant'..or we can sit back and try to defend them. **1970** *N.Y. Times* 1 July 44 Museums should have a more involved or relevant public role. **1976** *Listener* 20 May 627/3 The ultimate sin of the broadcaster is to keep off the air, because of his political or social prejudices, subjects which are relevant and significant. **1978** S. BRADEN *Artists & People* p. xvii, What actually makes a work of art relevant to people? It has been said that relevance is achieved when artists meet the real observations of their public.

relevé (rəlәve). [Fr., lit. 'raised up'.] **1.** = REMOVE *sb.* 2 c.

1825 LADY BLESSINGTON *Jrnl.* Dec. in E. Clay *Lady B. at Naples* (1979) 141 The fragments of *entrées* and *relevés*. **1846** *Jewish Manual, or Pract. Information Jewish & Mod. Cookery* p. xv, *Releves*, or *Removes*, are top and bottom dishes, which replace the soup and fish. **1889** [see *main course* s.v. *MAIN *a.* 11]. **1906** *Mrs. Beeton's Bk. Househ. Managem.* lxii. 1668 *Relevé*.., the remove. A course of a dinner, consisting of large joints of meat, four-footed game, and sometimes joints of fish. **1961** FROUD & TURGEON tr. *Larousse Gastronomique* 805/2 Remove. Relevé—Dish which in French service *relieves* (in the sense that one sentry relieves another) the soup or the fish.

2. *Ballet.* (See quot. 1957.)

1930 CRASKE & BEAUMONT *Theory & Pract. Allegro in Classical Ballet* 66 Execute two *Petits Battements* with a *relevé* and *dégagé*. **1953** *Ballet Ann.* VII. 83 That infinitesimal moment of holding the breath in a *relevé* on point in a held pose. **1957** G. B. L. WILSON *Penguin Dict. Ballet* 227 *Relevé* or *temps relevé*, lit. a lifted step. The raising of the body on half- or full-point or points. **1976** *New Yorker* 29 Mar. 92/3 He has an immobile thick torso, a heaviness in plié and relevé.

rele·vel, *v.* [RE- 5 a.] *trans.* To level again.

1928 *Daily Tel.* 14 Aug. 14/3 Gutters have been filled in, dangerous curb-stones removed, level crossings relevelled. **1975** J. B. HARLEY *O.S. Maps* i. 7 Each area is relevelled in a cyclic system,.. the interval depending on the character of the country. Mountain and moorland areas are relevelled every forty years.

relexification (rīːleksifikēⁱ·ʃən). *Linguistics.* [f. RE- 5 a + Gr. *λέξι-ς* word + -FICATION.] The process of replacing a word or group of words in one language with a corresponding word or group of words from another language, without grammatical adjustment of the items introduced.

1962 W. A. STEWART in F. A. Rice *Stud. Role Second Languages in Asia, Africa, & Lat. Amer.* 46 The vocabulary derived from one source language has been largely replaced ..by a more recent vocabulary derived from another language, while the original grammatical structure is preserved.. This process of relexification seems to be the converse of restructuralization. **1965** *Amer. Speech* XL. 172 William Stewart has hypothesized that this Portuguese-based pidgin was re-lexified to yield the English, Dutch, and French pidgins which are the progenitors of the Creoles. This idea of a re-lexification which left the original syntax almost intact is a very attractive one. **1968** *Word* XXIV. 263 The effect of this process is a kind of continuous and massive 'relexification'. **1971** [see *INITIATOR]. **1972** J. L. DILLARD *Black English* iii. 121 Within the Negro community, the use of Africanisms has been demonstrably larger in the past; allowing for relexification, we can still see a great deal of indirect influence. *Ibid.* 303 Relexification is the replacement of a vocabulary item in a language with a word from another, without a change in the grammar. If I change the sentence I am very tired to I am très tired I have in a sense relexified the English sentence. A 'Latin' sentence like ego amo tu is of course simply a relexification of I love you with Latin words. **1974** R. A. HALL *External Hist. Romance Lang.* 33 According to certain..theories, these two varieties..would have been the predecessors of West African Pidgin Portuguese, from which all other modern pidgins and creoles would have sprung by a process of 'relexification'. **1975** *Language* LI. 685 If all of a group of PC's [*sc.* pidgin or creole languages], such as those usually embraced in relexification hypotheses.., have a common ancestor, then the extension of the use of 'mouth' in that ancestor would account for 'mouth' having the added sense in all those PC's.

relexify (rīle·ksifəi), *v. Linguistics.* [f. as prec. + -FY.] *trans.* To introduce into (a language) vocabulary taken from another language without grammatical adjustment of the items introduced. Hence **rele·xified** *ppl. a.*

1962 W. A. STEWART in F. A. Rice *Stud. Role Second Languages in Asia, Africa, & Lat. Amer.* 46 If a language A can be shown to derive its vocabulary from language B and its grammatical structure from language C, then language A can be both 'restructured B' and 'relexified C' at the same time. *Ibid.*, It is ..possible to consider them all..as relexified forms of some prior language. **1965** *Orbis* XIV. 521 We know that the Philippine creoles were also relexified very rapidly. **1965, 1972** [see prec.]. **1972** J. L. DILLARD *Black English* iii. 122 Hawaiian Pidgin English *pau* (relexified with a Hawaiian word), Melanesian Pidgin English *finish* constitute other relexifications of *cabá*. **1979** *Amer. Speech* LIV. 296 A uniform 'plantation creole'..later 'relexified' into something nearer to the speech of whites.

reliability. Add: **2.** *Statistics.* The extent to which a measurement made repeatedly in identical circumstances will yield concordant results.

1904 *Amer. Jrnl. Psychol.* XV. 238 The reliability with which any system of measurement represents any particular form of intelligence. **1925** F. C. MILLS *Statistical Meth.* xvi. 561 By the study of successive samples, and by the testing of the subordinate elements in a given sample when broken up into significant sub-groups, much more may be learned as to the reliability of a given measure..than by unquestioning acceptance and uncritical employment of the usual mathematical formulas for probable errors. **1938** A. E. WAUGH *Elem. Statistical Meth.* vii. 138 We can increase the reliability of the mean by studying more cases, and..the reliability is greater also when the variation among the original figures is small. **1950** J. P. GUILFORD *Fundamental Statistics in Psychol. & Educ.* (ed. 2) xvii. 473 Tests of differences and correlation coefficients may often prove to be insignificant merely because the measures used were lacking in reliability. **1978** R. J. JESSON *Statistical Survey Techniques* i. 15 In considering reliability we shall be referring to a measure of the closeness of each observation to its own average over repeated trials.

3. *attrib.*, as *reliability engineer, race, test, trial*; **reliability coefficient,** any of various measures of statistical reliability; freq. the coefficient of correlation between two sets of measurements made of the same set of quantities.

1910 C. SPEARMAN in *Brit. Jrnl. Psychol.* III. 281 A very convenient conception is that of the 'reliability coefficient' of any system of measurements for any character. By this is meant the coefficient between one half and the other half of several measurements of the same thing. **1930** *Psychol. Rev.* XXXVII. 140 The reliability coefficient of a variable, *X*, is a special type of correlation coefficient which indicates the degree to which individuals systematically differ from each other in the trait as measured. **1954** *Psychol. Bulletin* LI. 229/1 The several types of reliability coefficient do not answer the same questions and should be carefully distinguished. **1972** *Jrnl. Social Psychol.* LXXXVII. 48 The split-half method was employed and resulted in a reliability coefficient for the instrument of ·83. **1969** *Word Study* Apr. 3/2 The reliability engineers, on the other hand, did not want to avoid taboo words; they were chiefly interested in alarming the program to potential failures. **1977** *Chicago Tribune* 2 Oct. XII. 57/4 (Advt.), Reliability Engineer, to direct and perform component reliability studies, coordinate with system requirements, and function as reliability consultant. **1907** *Strand Mag.* Nov. 491/2 A result extraordinarily interesting should be worked out from this thousand-mile [car] reliability race. **1904** *Technics* Aug. 114 As a 'reliability test', the car was driven from London to Newport (Mon.), a distance of about 160 miles. **1929** *Even. News* 18 Nov. 16/4 [He] crashed on his motor-cycle while taking part in a reliability test on Portsdown-hill. **1902** *Car* 3 Sept. 43/1 The cars entered for the Automobile Club's Reliability Trials which are being held this week began to arrive at the Crystal Palace at a very early hour. **1904** *To-Day* 18 May 58/2 The Automobile Club has arranged to hold a reliability trial for motor boats. **1963** P. DRACKETT *Motor Rallying* i. 9 But the true progenitor of the rally was the reliability trial. **1970** *Which?* July 199/1 We have not done any extended reliability trials on the single samples of television sets we tested.

reliable, *a.* Add: **b.** (Further examples.) Also, a reliable person or animal.

1908 [see *PEACHERINO]. **1910** W. M. RAINE *Bucky O'Connor* (1920) ii. 20, I hate to have you take that gun, though. I meant to run you down with that same old Colt's reliable. **1911** R. D. SAUNDERS *Col. Todhunter* xii. 171 'You never can tell about these old reliables,' said Tom. 'Solomon might take it into his head to get frisky any minute.' **1950** *Western Folklore* Apr. 138 The cowboy's six-shooter speaks a language universally understood. Familiar epithets for the revolver were *equalizer, shootin' iron*,..*Old Reliable*. **1972** *Village Voice* (N.Y.) 1 June 19/3 One of the Governor's old reliables, Assemblyman Robert Kelly, sponsored the bill in the lower house and told everyone how great it was. **1970** E. SNOW *Red China Today* (1976) 33 The 'three-way alliance' of mass organizations, Party 'reliables', and army political work teams which had completed the Party purging.

2. *Statistics.* Yielding concordant results when repeated.

[**1892** *Analyst* XVII. 228 When the Babcock test is made according to the instruction given with the machine, strictly reliable results are obtained.] **1932** *Jrnl. Gen. Physiol.* XVI. 23 Under such conditions it might be expected that volumetric measurements be somewhat less reliable than in the simple case first examined. **1942** J. P. GUILFORD *Fundamental Statistics in Psychol. & Educ.* xiv. 273 By a perfectly reliable test, we mean one that is free from errors of measurement. **1970** D. W. MATHESON et al. *Introd. Exper. Psychol.* ii. 26 A sampling technique is reliable if several samples from the same population yield similar data. *Ibid.* vi. 66 If a test is reliable, a subject will receive approximately the same score each time he takes the test.

relic. Add: **2. c.** An old person. *colloq.*

1869 'MARK TWAIN' in *Buffalo Express* 21 Aug. 1/3, I came upon a noble Son of the Forest sitting under a tree, diligently at work on a bead reticule... I addressed the noble relic as follows. **1902** —— in *Harper's Mag.* Dec. 15/1 'How much of it can you two undertake?' 'All of it!' burst from both ladies at once.. 'You do ring true, you brave old relics!' **1981** B. HEALEY *Last Ferry from Lido* ix. 161 So far as he's concerned the Ca' Silvestro and the old lady are just a pair of ancient relics.

4. c. phr. *relic of barbarism*, a survival or reminder of bad conditions or practices.

1852 *Harper's Mag.* Dec. 126/2 Railing against the church, against society, against institutions, against 'relics of barbarisms'. **1870** J. H. NEWMAN *Grammar of Assent* iv. 75 When Mr. Wilberforce, after succeeding in the slave question, urged the Duke of Wellington to use his great influence in discountenancing duelling, he could only get from him in answer, 'A relic of barbarism, Mr. Wilberforce'. **1919** W. T. GRENFELL *Labrador Doctor* iv. 68 After giving a talk on psychical influence he had the jacket removed as 'a relic of barbarism'. **1921** T. WOLFE *Let.* 2 Sept. (1956) 16 This 'point system' of selecting teachers is a relic of barbarism.

d. *Linguistics.* The survival of an archaic form; an instance of this. (See also *RELICT *sb.* 6.)

1943 *Language* XIX. 257 Nowhere..was there an indication of the genuine vitality of this set of suffixes, which, divested of any specific function, had become mere meaningless relics. **1951** *Amer. Speech* XXVI. 252 The occurrences of *clabbered milk* in the northern counties of the state are probably explained as a sporadic relic. **1962** *Ibid.* XXXVII. 170 In the word *one*, the mid-central vowel is occasionally replaced by /ʊ/—a relic usage evidently related to the pronunciation of *home* as /hʊm/.

3. c. *Biol.* A relict species.

1947 [see *EPIBIOTIC *a.* and *sb.* 1]. **1965** B. E. FREEMAN tr. *Vandel's Biospeleology* vii. 70 *Troglochaetus* would seem to be a marine relic. **1974** *New Phytologist* LXXIII. 974 Thistles, mulleins and foxgloves..appear as the stemless relics of the pachycaul inflorescences.

7. (in sense *4 d) *relic form*; **relic area,** a region noted for the survival of old or otherwise archaic language forms.

1953 *Language Learning* IV. 104 Relic areas, on the other hand, are those whose geographical or cultural isolation, and relative lack of prestige, has caused the retention of older forms or prevented the spread of forms characteristic of these areas. **1962** *Amer. Speech* XXXVII. 171 The regional words used by the Ocracokers are the regional words of the North Carolina coast, especially the relic area which lies around Albemarle Sound. **1972** H. KURATH *Studies Area Linguistics* i. 2 He [*sc.* the area linguist] will reserve judgment and recommend further investigation when the linguistic variants exhibit a complicated and apparently erratic dissemination as in certain transition zones or relic areas. **1933** Relic form [see *hyperform* s.v. *HYPER- IV]. **1951** *Amer. Speech* XXVI. 13 The preservation of relic forms is made possible by geographical or cultural isolation. **1972** M. L. SAMUELS *Linguistic Evolution* vi. 92 The receiving system itself becomes *less* divergent from its neighbour than before, retaining only relic forms from its antecedent.

B. *adj. Geogr., Geol.,* and *Biol.* = *RELICT *a.* 4.

1894 J. GEIKIE *Great Ice Age* (ed. 3) xxxi. 488 In many of the Swedish lakes there occur certain forms of life which appear to be a relic-fauna of the Yoldia Sea. **1926** W. H. TWENHOFEL *Treat. Sedimentation* v. 369 The Salton Sink of California is probably an example of a relic sea which appears to have been severed from the Gulf of California in the building of the Colorado River delta. **1940** *Jrnl. Genetics* XL. 72 At this stage it is usual for some or all of the chromosomes to show 'relic' coils or spirals. These coils are to be regarded as the remains of the spirals of the previous division. **1966** MRS. L. B. JOHNSON *White House Diary* 2 Apr. (1970) 379 He described the 'relic forest' of maple, quaking aspen, Douglas fir, and ponderosa pine with huge trunks. By some strange mystery of nature, they have survived from a much earlier time, when the climate was different here. **1976** H. M. FRENCH *Periglacial Environment* v. 95 The presence of obviously relic pingos..in present-day periglacial environments complicates attempts to identify the conditions for present-day pingo growth. **1978** *Nature* 7 Sept. 19/1 Appropriate physical conditions for the origin of life could exist on the relic regolith grains.

relict, *sb.* Add: **1.** (Further example.)

1884 'MARK TWAIN' *Huck. Finn* xxxvii. 384 Things that was valuable..on account of them being relicts.

3. b. Also *transf.* of a person. (Further example.)

1928 *Daily Express* 3 July 10/2 Our British boards of railway directors are like an ante-room to a museum. They are crowded with relicts of the easy pre-war age for whom the world has never changed.

d. *Biol., Geogr.,* and *Geol.* A relict species, structure, etc.

1905 F. E. CLEMENTS *Res. Methods in Ecol.* 321 *Relict*, a species belonging properly to an earlier type of succession than the one in which it is found. **1950** *Jrnl. Ecol.* XXXVIII. 294 A few relicts of the former open fen are to be seen in the form of scattered plants of *Cirsium palustre*..and *Angelica sylvestris*. **1971** *Nature* 5 Feb. 377/2 Rare plant species are often relicts surviving in restricted ecological niches. The opportunities for these species to spread to other, suitable habitats are minimal. **1977** A. HALLAM *Planet Earth* 17/2 The breccias are revealing to us the relicts of an original lunar crust that formed and was reconstituted several times.

6. *Linguistics.* Used *attrib.* or in *Comb.* to denote language or vocabulary which is a survival of otherwise archaic or old forms. Cf. also *RELIC 4 d, 7.

1934 PRIEBSCH & COLLINSON *German Lang.* vii. 364 Often we find a wedge of linguistic innovation along the rivers and highways with relict-areas preserving ancient forms on the high moors and along the wooded hills. **1947** *Ibid.* (ed. 2) i. 14 The Logudoresian dialect retains certain relict-words with affinities in Basque. **1948** *Trans. Phil. Soc. 1947* 14 It now appears that the original Germanic language of the Low German area was not in any essential matter distinguished from Frisian, but that it was afterwards High Germanized, leaving Frisian as a relict language of its original state. **1963** H. C. DARBY in Brown & Foote *Early English & Norse Stud.* ii. 9 Another example of relict names is found on Dunsmore Heath.

relict, *a.* Restrict † *Obs.* to senses in Dict. and add: **4.** *Geogr., Geol.,* and *Biol.* Surviving from a previous age or in changed circumstances after the extinction or disappearance of related forms or structures.

In origin prob. an *attrib.* use of the sb. rather than a revival of the adj. (cf. quot. 1901).

1898 J. GEIKIE *Earth Sculpture* xvi. 274 The direction, and to a large extent the shape or form of relict mountains, are thus mainly determined by the geological structure. **1901** *Ann. & Mag. Nat. Hist.* VII. 315 Those [animals] remaining in the old place formed a zonally-disposed relict-fauna. **1932** E. W. SINNOTT *Plant Sociology* iv. 63 Besides these characteristic relict species there are others whose fidelity is due to a narrowly specialized adaptation to definite physico-chemical relations of the habitat. **1939** W. H. TWENHOFEL *Princ. Sedimentation* xii. 459 Relict seas are bodies of water that have become separated from the parent body by diastrophic, depositional, or volcanic causes. *Ibid.*, Well-known relict seas are..the Caspian Sea, Lake Nicaragua, and Lake Baikal. **1945** M. J. D. WHITE *Animal Cytol. & Evolution* xiii. 293 [*Saga serrata*] seems to be a 'relict' species, since the localities in which it occurs are very discontinuous and the individual populations of very small size. **1954** W. D. THORNBURY *Princ. Geomorphol.* xvi. 413 Relict features attributable to former existence of periglacial conditions have been described at many places in Europe and North America. **1974** J. D. MILLMAN *Recent Sedimentary Carbonates* I. vii. 221 Coralline algae in continental shelf sediments may be relict but others are modern. **1977** *Birds* Winter 19/1 Fowlmere is a small, relict fen, lying in a hollow of the Gog Magog hills. **1978** *Sci. Amer.* Sept. 111/1 The lobe fins were far less successful as fishes (they survive only as lungfishes and a few relict forms). **1978** T. ROWLEY *Villages in Landscape* ii. 49 Village plans may include relict features of early defensive structures, such as the alignment of Roman town walls.

5. *Astr.* Remaining from the 'big bang'.

1971 *Nature* 3 Sept. 36/2 The discovery in 1965, by Penzias and Wilson, of background radiation which may well be relict radiation from this fireball. **1978** *Sci. Amer.* July 54/3 Encounters between cosmic rays and photons of the relict radiation would severely drain the energy of the cosmic rays above some energy threshold.

relief². Add: **3. a.** (Further examples.) Also, financial assistance afforded to those in need by the state under other legislative provisions.

1921 *Daily Colonist* (Victoria, B.C.) 22 Mar. 1/3 More than $400,000 has now been expended by the city in providing relief, it will be pointed out. **1957** R. HOGGART *Uses of Literacy* ii. 40 At my grandmother's we were not living 'on relief' but, like many around us, we were 'a bit short'. **1965** MRS. L. B. JOHNSON *White House Diary* 12 Aug. (1970) 309 Their world is so narrow, and in their homes—frequently broken homes with one parent or an aged grandparent on relief—the vocabulary is often limited to grunts or profanity. **1966** G. JACKSON *Let.* 3 Mar. in *Soledad Brother* (1971) 95 I've heard men brag about..taking money from black women who are on relief. **1978** S. BRILL *Teamsters* vii. 285 He didn't make a lot... But we never went on relief.

5. b. (Earlier example.)

1709 SWIFT in *Tatler* 10 Sept., Little Parson Dapper, who is the Common Relief to all the lazy Pulpits in Town.

c. (Earlier example.)

1788 W. DYOTT *Diary* 1 Sept. (1907) I. 53 We had ninety dishes, fifty-five the first course and relieves, and thirty-five the second course.

7. Delete *rare* and add: *spec.* remission of income-tax due on a proportion of earned income.

1889 A. CHAPMAN *Income-Tax Grievances & their Remedy* i. 9 Appellants who..prove..that their profits have not been equal to the sum at which they were assessed and have paid duty, are entitled to relief and repayment of tax. **1916** [see *INCOME-TAX]. **1931** *Economist* 28 Feb. 456/2 A resident British holder of 'Kaffirs' is subject to income tax on dividends at the full rate of British tax (4s. 6d. in the £), less Dominion tax relief (at present 2s. 3d., namely, half the

British rate). He is thus liable at the 'reliefed' rate of 2s. 3d. **1969** *Times* 2 May 25 Tax relief can reduce the cost of your investment by up to £16.10.0 per £100 of premium. **1972** *Accountant* 17 Aug. 191/1 The strict ban against relief for part-time directors and employees. **1973** P. O'Donnell *Silver Mistress* iv. 72 If it's a phony charity account..they probably get tax relief. **1977** *Money Which?* Mar. 123/3 If you become entitled to tax relief on a new outgoing or allowance,..tell the taxman straightaway.

9. b. *relief agency, committee, fund* (earlier and later examples), *organization, party, team, work, worker*; **relief road,** a road designed to divert traffic from congested areas; **relief roll** *U.S.*, a list of people receiving state relief; **relief ticket,** a small sum of money given to alleviate hardship; **relief well,** a hole drilled to intersect an oil or gas well in which there is a fire or a blow-out, so as to provide a route for water or mud to stop it.

1951 T. Sterling *House without Door* i. 7 A Jewish relief agency..which trained refugee Jews in manual skills. **1971** Piven & Cloward in M. Edelman *Polit. Lang.* (1977) iii. 53 Relief agencies are..compelled to invent rituals of degradation and to subject their clientele to them. **1842** *Picayune* (New Orleans) 23 Jan. 2/5 The Relief Committee of the Firemen's Charitable Association, will meet..at the Firemen's Insurance Office. **1862** *Times* 14 Apr. 11/4 Proud men..who go before 'relief committees' and submit to be questioned about their wants. **1892** J. C. Harris *On Plantation* 139 Where they lived remote from the relief committees, the families of the soldiers were not so well provided for as they had a right to expect. **1842** S. Bamford *Passages in Life of Radical* II. xxi. 104 He had some money in hand belonging to the relief fund. **1863** *Observer* 26 Apr. 5/4, I cannot..recommend too strongly..to your lady readers' kind consideration, the 'Cracow Ladies' Committee', who are connected with the 'Ladies' Relief Fund Committee' in London. **1914** Relief fund [see *flag-day* s.v. *flag *sb.*[4] 7]. **1952** M. McCarthy *Groves of Academe* (1953) vi. 120 We're not yet relief organisations, you must admit. **1974** *Whig-Standard* (Kingston, Ontario) 11 Jan. 7/1 A..graduate..with many years of experience with relief organizations. **1978** *Internat. Relations Dict.* (U.S. Dept. State Library) 15/2 U.S. agricultural surpluses are donated to 'friendly governments' through non-profit relief organizations. **1933** J. Buchan *Prince of Captivity* i. iii. 85 Now he has gone and lost himself and..they're talking of a relief party. **1940** *Gloss. Highway Engin. Terms* (*B.S.I.*) 9 *Relief road*,..a road to enable through traffic to avoid congested areas or other obstructions to movement. **1959** *Oxford Mag.* 26 Feb. 276/1 A relief road is invented, and it must then be guessed how much of the flow along each existing route will be diverted into it. **1960** *Oxford Mail* 10 Oct. 4/6 The idea of relief roads to link the suburbs with the centre is one that deserves to be considered. **1976** *S. Wales Echo* 27 Nov. 5/7 At present it is planned to join the relief road to Hirwaun Road near Tudor Terrace. **1937** C. Himes *Black on Black* (1973) 127 Remembering suddenly the time the Belle Vernon Milk Company dumped hundreds of gallons of milk into the gutters of Cedar Street when the relief rolls in Cleveland were the highest they'd ever been. **1938** *Sun* (Baltimore) 16 Apr. 8 The President himself has said that road building will 'take very few people off the relief rolls'...Spending should be limited to relief. **1976** *National Observer* (U.S.) 17 Jan. 5/2 Americans who are elderly, blind, disabled, or who have impoverished dependent children—generally, Americans who are on the relief rolls. **1977** M. Edelman *Polit. Lang.* v. 80 Social work counseling..apparently has little or no effect on client satisfaction, behavior, or the size of relief rolls. **1970** *Guardian* 28 Jan. 3/8 Relief teams are racing against the rainy season, due in the Nigerian delta. **1972** *Ibid.* 22 May 10/6 There is a drought at present in the villages... The relief teams have moved in. **1848** *United Irishman* 20 May 224/2 A beautiful and fertile island..became gradually poorer and poorer... Millions of men, who toiled their lives through from morning to night, found at length they had no *rights* but a right to public alms, and had realized, with all their toiling, nothing but the chance of a relief-ticket. **1976** J. O'Connor *Eleventh Commandment* i. 21 He got a bit of beer money and came away laughing; relief tickets, they call them, and worth a couple of quid... The shops that took relief tickets would always overcharge the working class. **1925** A. B. Thompson *Oil-Field Explor. & Devel.* I. vii. 299 On reaching a rich gas sand the Gleason well ran wild at a rate of about 15,000,000 cub. ft. per day... A relief well failed to effect its object, although sunk only 135 ft. away. **1939** D. Hager *Fund. Petroleum Industry* ix. 222 The relief well was deflected so that it reached the burning hole at a depth of 7046 ft. **1975** *Petroleum Rev.* XXIX. 238/3 Just one month after the fire had started, the first relief well commenced injecting sea water. **1979** *Tucson* (Arizona) *Citizen* 3 Oct. 3 A/3 Two relief wells are being drilled at an angle to Ixtoc 1 in an effort to rechannel the gusher to a controlled well. **1879** *Good Words* 495/2 There is another young engineer superintending his dam, a relief work about two miles long. *Ibid.* 566/2 A collector, after having tried to induce some Mhars to go to a famine relief work close by, who refused, looking over a wall saw two of them devouring a dead dog. **1895** Kipling *Day's Work* (1898) 170 They've gone as far as to admit extreme local scarcity, and they've started relief-works in one or two districts. *Ibid.* 202 Then in the evening he pitches in a twenty-page demi-official to me, saying that the people where he is might be 'advantageously employed on relief-work'. **1915** R. Fry *Let.* 28 July (1972) II. 388 I've been a long time in France—went to see the Quaker relief work. **1921** *Daily Colonist* (Victoria, B.C.) 22 Mar. 1/3 At the end of its resources as far as relief work is concerned, the city of Vancouver will urge the Dominion and Provincial Governments to carry a burden which it believes should rightfully be borne by them. **1938** R. D. Finlayson *Brown Man's Burden* 16 They were relief workers and flax-cutters, working hard and making good money. **1973** *Guardian* 9 June 13/4 Latham belongs to that new breed of white man—the relief worker.

relief[3]. Add: **4.** *relief-carving, construction, decoration, panel, -polish* (sb. and vb.), *-polishing, process* (examples); **relief map,** a map that indicates the relief of the land, either by the analogous form of its surface or by a system of colouring, shading contour lines, or the like; **Relief nib** [*Relief*, proprietary name], a manufacturer's name for a special kind of nib.

1892 E. Rowe *Hints on Chip-Carving* 60 In relief-carving the teaching must be individual, and consequently fewer students can be taught by one teacher. **1970** *Oxf. Compan. Art* 960/2 Such sculpture is not properly relief carving (e.g. the figures of gods and giants on the Great Altar of Zeus at Pergamum). **1962** *Times* 28 Feb. 5/1 At the same gallery Mr. Michael Rothenstein shows a small collection of his new relief-constructions. **1960** *Connoisseur's Handbk. Antique Coll.* 236/1 There are various ways of producing relief decoration: by freehand modelling, free-incising or piercing or, more frequently, by pressing soft clay in plaster moulds. **1960** R. G. Haggar *Conc. Encycl. Cont. Pott. & Porc.* 380/1 *Relief decoration*, figures, flowers, and ornamental decoration formed in the mould, or moulded or modelled separately and luted to the ware with slip. **1876** *Nature* 11 May 23/1 Relief-maps and Models illustrating Geological Phenomena all over the world. **1880** 'Mark Twain' *Tramp Abroad* xxxiii. 358 He showed us the whole thing on a relief map. **1934** J. Bygott *Introd. Map Work & Pract. Geogr.* vi. 43 After inspecting even a small-scale relief map of Northern England..we realise that the longest rivers flow from the eastern slopes towards the North Sea. **1971** R. W. Purton *Let's look at Maps & Mapmaking* 16 It is possible to buy relief maps moulded in plastic, on which the physical features are raised as..on a model. [**1908** *Trade Marks Jrnl.* 4 Mar. 347 Relief..Pens..Esterbrook Steel Pen Manufacturing Company..New York..21st November 1907.] **1920** A. Huxley *Limbo* 144 He selected a pen—with a Relief nib he would be able to go on for hours without getting tired—and a large square sheet of writing-paper. **1938** E. Bowen *Death of Heart* II. iii. 214 Today..she made the following purchases... Half a dozen Relief nibs. **1960** *Twentieth Century* Oct. 343 The pen tray filled with compact sheaves of new relief nibs. **1937** *Burlington Mag.* Feb. 59/2 The relief-panels of the Pisa pulpit. **1961** *Times* 21 Dec. 3/3 He makes relief-panels and sculpture from charred wood. **1933** Greaves & Wrighton *Pract. Microsc. Metallogr.* (ed. 2) xiv. 237 Relief polish is obtained..so that micro-constituents are visible under the microscope. **1968** E. Stach in Murchison & Westoll *Coal & Coal-Bearing Strata* i. 4 Nowadays coals are normally relief-polished and then examined under vertically incident light using immersion objectives. **1902** C. Salter tr. *H. F. V. Jüptner's Siderology* II. iii. 121 Relief polishing shows up the hardest constituents, especially cementite, in relief. **1924** Greaves & Wrighton *Pract. Microsc. Metallogr.* vi. 48 Both 'relief polishing' and 'polish attack' may be used to display the microstructure of steels containing cementite. **1889** *Cent. Dict.*, *Relief processes*, those processes in mechanical or 'process' engraving by which are produced plates or blocks with raised lines. **1940** *Chambers's Techn. Dict.* 713/2 *Relief process* (*Photog.*), any colour process using matrices. **1965** Zigrosser & Gaehde *Guide Coll. Orig. Prints* iv. 53 *Relief processes*, a general term that includes woodcuts, wood engravings, linoleum cuts, [etc.].

reliefer[2] (rĭlī·fəɹ). [f. Relief[2] + -er[1].] One who receives state relief (sense *3 a).

1936 *Harper's Mag.* Jan. 203/2 Reliefers don't of course live by themselves and form a compact group with relief as their only topic. **1938** *Sun* (Baltimore) 6 Sept. 8/4 Baltimore streets and alleys could do with a little attention from 'grateful reliefers'. **1947** *Ten Eventful Years* IV. 629/1 *Reliefer*, an unemployed person on federal government relief rolls. **1973** B. Broadfoot *Ten Lost Years* xx. 225 No, we never thought of the poor people. The reliefers.

relieve, *v.* Add: **I. 3. b.** Also *refl.*, to defecate or urinate, and *fig.*

1931 S. Tremayne *Trial A. A. Rouse* 184, I wanted to relieve myself. **1952** Bible (Rev. Standard Version) *I Sam.* xxiv. 3 And he came to the sheepfolds by the way, where there was a cave; and Saul went in to relieve himself. **1956** H. Gold *Man who was not with It* (1965) xii. 99 There's a stomach ache of music..; it churns and stretches, trying to relieve itself. **1960** V. Nabokov *Invitation to Beheading* xiv. 141 The bliss of relieving oneself, which some hold to be on a par with the pleasure of love. **1961** *Encounter* Feb. 25/1 It [*sc.* a kitten] learned to go down into the alley to relieve itself in the dirt there. **1977** *Sunday Times* 30 Jan. 30/3, I urgently wished to be alone to relieve myself (a serious problem in winter orienteering).

5. c. (Later examples.) Also, *euphem.*, to dismiss *from* a position, to deprive *of* membership.

1875 'Mark Twain' in *Atlantic Monthly* June 733/1 He was 'relieved' from duty when the boat got to New Orleans. Somebody expressed surprise at the discharge. **1952** E. O'Neill *Moon for Misbegotten* III. 111 He relieves her of the pitcher and tumblers as she comes down the steps. **1972** *Newsweek* 10 Jan. 11/3 Its present chief..has expelled some 3,000 members (Lascorz was relieved of his membership during a previous clean-up in 1969).

relie·vedly, *adv.* [f. Relieved *ppl. a.* + -ly[2].] In a relieved manner, with relief from anxiety.

1911 R. Brooke *Let.* 22 Dec. (1968) 327, I rather grasp relievedly at them, after I've beaten vain hands in the rosy mists of poets' experiences. **1925** *Glasgow Herald* 1 Aug. 6/3 The country relievedly witnesses the passing of the crisis. **1951** M. Leinster in D. Knight *100 Yrs. Sci. Fiction* (1969) 200 Sometimes he was able to thrust aside..the fact that Jane was dead. Now he grappled relievedly with the question of his sanity or lunacy.

reliever. Add: **1. d.** *N. Amer.* A pitcher who relieves the opening pitcher in a baseball match.

1967 *Boston Herald* 8 May 16/2 Fregosi homered in the fifth..off reliever Bob Humphreys. **1976** *Washington Post* 19 Apr. D1/4 Los Angeles chased reliever Roger Moret in the seventh with a five-run explosion. **1979** *Arizona Daily Star* 5 Aug. C2/2 Craig Swan combined with reliever Neil Allen on an eight-hitter as New York stopped Montreal's five-game winning streak.

relieving, *ppl. a.* Add: **2. a.** *relieving officer* (earlier and later examples).

1836 *Falmouth Pkt.* 23 Sept. 5/2 Application for relief is made to the relieving officer. **1841** *Punch* 23 Oct. 170/2 The family..told me they were literally dying of hunger, and that they had applied to the vestry, who had referred them to the..relieving officer. **1850** C. Kingsley *Alton Locke* II. xiv. 210 In the midst of all the rout, the relieving officer stood impassive, jotting down scraps of information. **1980** G. M. Fraser *Mr American* ix. 167 She has an order for medical attendance from the relieving officer.

relievo[2] (rĭlī·vo). Also **relievio.** [prob. f. Relieve *v.* + *-o[2].] A children's seeking game in which a captured player may be released by another member of his or her side; the call effecting the release.

1888 S. O. Addy *Gloss. Words Sheffield* 296 *Bedlams* or *relievo*, a game played by boys. *Ibid.* 297 If..one of the boys out at field runs through the *den* shouting '*Relievo*', without being caught by the *tenter*, the prisoner is allowed to escape. **1912** J. Stephens *Crock of Gold* v. 39 'It's a nice game,' said the Leprechaun, 'and so is Cap-on-the-back, and ..Relievo, and Leap-frog.' **1913** —— *Here are Ladies* 261 Tip-and-Tig, Horneys and Robbers, Relievo we played. **1969** I. & P. Opie *Children's Games* ii. 110 Names which reflect the rescue element are: 'Release', 'Releaster', 'Relieve-i-o', 'Tig and Relievo', [etc.]. *Ibid.* iv. 172 In Scotland, Wales, and the northern half of England, 'Relievo' is the principal seeking game with two sides. *Ibid.* 173 Commonly it is enough for the 'releaser' to shout 'Relievo' or 'Rallio' or perhaps 'Bish-Bash' as he rushes through the den. **1970** *Daily Colonist* (Victoria, B.C.) 19 Aug. 2/1 Summer streets full of youngsters playing Hoist The Sails, Relievo or Giant Step. **1974** *Amer. Speech 1971* XLVI. 83 Line and running games: crack-the-whip, fly-the-whip, follow-the-leader, leap frog, redman, red rover, rolla-rolla, relievio, [etc.].

relifting, *vbl. sb.* (Further example.)

1904 H. Belloc *Avril* III 105 The repose and the relifting of musical notes.

re·light, *sb. Aeronaut.* [f. the vb.] A re-ignition of a jet engine in flight. Usu. *attrib.*

1945 J. Grierson *Jet Flight* iv. 101 The fuel should be shut off for a minute or so in order to blow surplus fuel out of the engine before the relight. **1955** Mangham & Peace *Jet Engine Man.* vi. 100 The relight button..enables the ignition circuit to be energised without the starter motor. **1976** B. Jackson *Flameout* (1977) II. iv. 69 A thorough examination of the relight systems, every fuel valve, and every fuel feed pipe. **1977** [see *relighting *vbl. sb.*]. **1977** *R.A.F. News* 11–24 May 11/1 Flt Lt Harry Apiafi..suffered a flame out in the Canberra's starboard engine... While attempting a relight, Harry lost the other engine as well.

reli·ghting, *vbl. sb.* [f. Relight *v.* + -ing[1].] The action of the vb.; *spec.* in *Aeronaut.*, the re-ignition of a jet engine in flight.

1955 Mangham & Peace *Jet Engine Man.* v. 98 Relighting is more positive at low engine-windmilling speeds and at lower altitudes. **1960** H. Zeffer *Princ. & Pract. Aircraft Electr. Engin.* xvii. 517 A typical situation in which re-lighting would be necessary is one where a jet engine has been stopped by an accretion of ice entering the air intake. **1965** *Gloss. Mining Terms* (*B.S.I.*) vii. 10 *Re-lighting station*, a place in a mine at which safety lamps can be relighted under controlled conditions. **1977** *R.A.F. Yearbk.* 34/1 The relighting drills cover three contingencies: the 'hot' relight speaks for itself, the unassisted relight involves diving the aircraft to get the engine rpm sufficiently high for a cold relight attempt, and the assisted relight uses the GTS in exactly the same way as starting the engine.

religieuse. Add: Also 8 *erron.* **religieux** (*pl.*).

1. (Earlier and later examples.)

1694 Ld. Perth *Let.* 17 Sept. (1845) 43 Lady Lucy is a most excellent religieuse. **1777** P. Thicknesse *Year's Journey* II. l. 142 This virtuous, and..amiable society of *religieux* [ed. 3, 1789, *religieuses*]. **1959** *Times* 25 July 9/1 They [*sc.* béguinages] are communities of *religieuses* who live in separate houses.

2. (See quot. 1968.)

[**1929** E. J. Kollist *French Pastry, Confectionery & Sweets* iv. 57 Gâteau Religieuse... Set on clean baking-sheet eclairs from pâte à choux paste... In between each eclair decorate with whipped cream.] **1954** C. Turgeon *Tante Marie's French Cakes & Pastries* 50 Little Nuns. *Religieuses*. .. This pastry is perhaps the most popular in all France. **1961** A. Wesker *Kitchen* 11 Pastry called 'Religieuse'. **1968** *Guardian* 17 Feb. 9/8 A Religieuses [*sic*] is a gorgeously opulent edifice of éclairs bound with a mortar of chocolate and cream.

religio-. Add: *religio-ethnic, -historical, -musical, -mystical, -philosophic, -philosophical* (example), *-political, -psychiatric* (also *-psychiatry*), *-sexual.*

1966 J. E. Hofman in J. A. Fishman *Readings Sociol. of Lang.* (1968) 626 Our hypothesis that whenever religio-ethnic concentrations and certain other factors coincide, a situation is created which enhances the ideological climate suitable to retentiveness of the ethnic mother tongue. **1953**

W. R. Trask tr. *Auerbach's Mimesis* i. 17 The reader is at every moment aware of the universal religio-historical perspective which gives the individual stories their general meaning and purpose. **1959** 'F. Newton' *Jazz Scene* iii. 45 'Shouting' sects..have made the most powerful single religio-musical contribution to jazz. **1976** *Listener* 22 July 92/2 George Sand..turned religio-mystical..with a spate of earnest, spiritual books. **1926** Fowler *Mod. Eng. Usage* 393/1 We must take account of religio-philosophic speculations. **1931** *Times Lit. Suppl.* 21 May 408/2 The world-wide religio-philosophical movement known as Theosophy. **1928** *Weekly Dispatch* 3 June 10/5 One of the most remarkable contributions to the religio-political discussion on record. **1979** M. A. Screech *Rabelais* vi. 215 The direct religio-political propaganda. **1964** S. Z. Klausner *Psychiatry & Relig.* i. 1 (heading) Religio-psychiatry: a social institution. *Ibid.*, The religio-psychiatric movement is born through several thousand similar encounters. **1968** *Internat. Encycl. Soc. Sci.* XII. 632/2 Religio-psychiatry is a twentieth-century movement whose participants are concerned with the relation between religious and scientific approaches to mental, emotional, or spiritual healing. **1946** D. C. Peattie *Road of Naturalist* iv. 49 The Poles snarled back a stream of commingled religio-sexual obscenity, to show how dirty they could talk if they pleased.

religion. Add: **4. c.** *religion of nature*: the worship of Nature in place of a more formal system of religious belief.

1902 W. James *Var. Relig. Exper.* iv. 91 In that 'theory of evolution' which..has within the past twenty-five years swept so rapidly over Europe and America, we see the ground laid for a new sort of religion of Nature, which has entirely displaced Christianity from the thought of a large part of our generation. **1961** D. G. James *Matthew Arnold* i. 22 The essay itself is given up chiefly to a warm exposition of her religion of nature.

8. *religion-arousing* adj.; *religion-complex*; *religion-game*.

1957 J. S. Huxley *Relig. without Revelation* (rev. ed.) vii. 174 Potential religion-arousing objects. **1922** *Brit. Jrnl. Psychology* Oct. 117 Such complexes clearly exist in the normal mind with perfectly free access to consciousness, *e.g.* the 'religion complex'. **1961** J. Wilson *Reason & Morals* ii. 120 Thus J. R. Lucas..even puts in a good word for the religion-game.

religionist. Add: (Later examples.) Also, one professionally occupied with religion; a minister or preacher.

1870 O. Logan *Before Footlights & behind Scenes* xl. 603 While clergymen and religionists, as now, stand afar off and denounce the theatre. **1895** *Wales* Aug. 361/2 The antagonism that some classes of religionists have shown to the pastoral care of the church is to be attributed, most frequently, to one of two things. **1939** Wyndham Lewis *Jews* v. 55 The Jews are..the great religionists of the West. **1958** *New Statesman* 6 Sept. 304/3 Lately in the United States *religionist* has taken on a new and definite meaning. When *religionists* are referred to in the current press, it is clear that this term includes anyone who is professionally occupied with religion, of whatever church, movement or status—that is, anyone from Billy Graham to Reinhold Niebuhr. **1966** *Ibid.* 13 May 683/1 Secularists are not demanding what religionists demand and obtain, namely public subsidy for their own propaganda institutions. They deplore all propagandising of children. **1977** *Private Eye* 1 Apr. 8/1 Mr Arthur Blessit..a Los Angeles religionist, was assaulted by a number of similarly moved but differently associated people.

religionless, *a.* Add: **A.** *religionless Christianity* [tr. G. *religionsloses Christentum*], Christianity dissociated from many of the doctrines and practices of conventional religion.

1953 R. H. Fuller tr. *Bonhoeffer's Lett. & Papers from Prison* v. 123 If religion is no more than the garment of Christianity—and even that garment has had very different aspects at different periods—then what is a religionless Christianity? **1963** *Times* 7 May 13/4 Archbishop Heenan is reported in today's Sunday press to have said that Anglican discussions about religionless Christianity are an embarrassment to Roman Catholics who work for Christian unity. **1969** A. Richardson *Dict. Chr. Theol.* 288/2 It is in the light of Barth's denunciation of religion that Bonhoeffer's plea for 'religionless Christianity', by which he meant unpietistic, unchurchy Christianity, should be understood. **1974** *Oxf. Dict. Chr. Ch.* (ed. 2) 187/1 Though writers of the Death of God school have taken up his [*sc.* Bonhoeffer's] idea of religionless Christianity, his teaching represents a search for the beyond in the midst, and a demand for a radical reform of the Church, which in its existing form he thought to have no message for the present day. **1977** *Church Times* 29 Apr. 6/4 Nor is it one of the newer-style jobs in which the intransigent element in Christian faith is dissolved away in..religionless Christianity.

B. as *sb. collect.*, people without religious belief.

1964 *New Statesman* 14 Feb. 254/3 Literature which Arnold was quite right to suggest would come to occupy the importance of religion for the religionless.

religiose, *a.* (Later examples.)

1932 [see *beglamour *v.*]. **1966** I. Jefferies *House-Surgeon* ix. 168 It was only later, when they were improving, that they would complain about their neighbours, or become religiose, or mutter. **1971** *Times Lit. Suppl.* 22 Oct. 1319/2 Donald's parents—the dying, religiose father and steely, moralizing mother—inhabit an area of real, alarming unsavouriness. **1975** J. Nicoll *Dante Gabriel Rossetti* ii. 48 An unhappy love affair with Rossetti's religiose sister Christina.

‖ **religioso** (relidʒiōˑso), *o.* and *sb.* *Mus.* [It., = religious.] **A.** *adv.* As a direction to the performer: in a devotional manner. **B.** *sb.* A devotional effect; a passage to be played devotionally. **C.** *adj.* Having a devotional quality.

1837 J. A. Hamilton *Dict. Mus. Terms* (ed. 4) 58 *Religioso, religiosamente* (Italian), with religious feeling, in a devotional manner. **1876** Stainer & Barrett *Dict. Mus. Terms* 377/1 *Religiosamente, religioso*, in a religious or devotional manner. **1941** W. C. Handy *Father of Blues* v. 63, I was featuring *The Holy City* as a cornet solo and these saxophones contributed wonderfully to the religioso. **1961** *Times* 4 Dec. 14/5 The tremulous, *religioso* registrations with which the organist coloured the recitatives. **1975** *Sunday Times* 14 Dec. 31/1 In the Prologue to 'The Golden Legend'..Sullivan *religioso* sounded no more inspired than the average Mus.D. exercise of a century ago. **1977** *Gramophone* Apr. 1541/2 In the slow movement there is little sense of *religioso* in the bare chordal writing for strings at the start. **1980** *Country Life* 17 Jan. 177 Even more *religioso* than Gounod at times was the Abbé Lizst.

religious, *a.* and *sb.* Add: **A.** *adj.* **3. a.** (Further examples.)

1769 *Account of Society for promoting Relig. Knowl.* 5 The design of this Society being to promote Religious Knowledge among the Poor. **1800** H. More *Let.* 11 Sept. (1925) 177, I knew that every Anti-Abolitionist in the world was..an enemy to religious instruction at home. **1809** M. Waring (*title*) A diary of the religious experience of Mary Waring. **1836** *Introd. Discourse & Lect. Amer. Institute of Instruction 1835* 105 The parent who neglects the religious education of his child might as well suffer him to wander filthy and ragged in the streets. **1850** C. Kingsley *Alton Locke* I. xi. 178 'Schooling hasn't made wages rise, nor preaching neither.' 'But surely..all this religious knowledge ought to give you comfort.' **1858** Geo. Eliot *Scenes Clerical Life* II. 193 It may be that some of Mr. Tryon's hearers had gained a religious vocabulary rather than religious experience. **1872** *Q. Rev.* CXXXII. 534 The people will have to decide at a general election upon this great question of Religious or Secular Education. **1914** G. B. Shaw *Parents & Children* p. c, The last ray of art is being cut off from our schools by the discontinuance of religious education. **1960–61** *Where?* Winter 16/2 *Religious instruction* (*RI*), the only subject which state schools are obliged to teach by law. **1961** *Regulations G.C.E. Examinations* (Univ. London) 22 *Religious Knowledge* Ordinary Level. There will be one paper of $2\frac{1}{2}$ hours. **1968** *Guardian* 28 Nov. 6/3 It is thought that a new attitude in the schools would encourage student teachers to take religious education as a subsidiary subject at colleges of education. **1973** *Listener* 23 Aug. 251/1 To disbelieve in God's existence is..a matter of distrusting the testimony of others or lacking a religious experience oneself.

c. Special collocations. *religious philosophy*: the philosophical study of religion; philosophy that accepts the concept of an omnipotent God; hence *religious philosopher*; *religious psychology*: psychology which accepts that a religious context is basic to man's personality and behaviour.

1840 J. S. Mill in *Westm. Rev.* XXXIII. 297 Of Coleridge as a moral and religious philosopher..there is neither room, nor would it be expedient for us to speak more than generally. *Ibid.* 298 We must be looking for a religious philosophy, and our main hope ought to be that it will be such a one as fulfils the conditions of a philosophy—the very foremost of which is, unrestricted freedom of thought. **1902** W. James *Var. Relig. Exper.* iv. 105 An interpretation of Christ's message which in these very Gifford lectures has been defended by some of your very ablest Scottish religious philosophers. *Ibid.* xviii. 431, I doubt if dispassionate intellectual contemplation of the universe, apart from inner unhappiness and need of deliverance on the one hand and mystical emotion on the other, would ever have resulted in religious philosophies such as we now possess. **1912** R. B. Perry *Pres. Philos. Tendencies* vii. 148 The English school of idealists..has from the outset offered a religious philosophy based on the supremacy of consciousness. **1927** J. S. Huxley *Relig. without Revelation* iv. 120 Those who, through study or profession, are brought into contact with religious psychology. *Ibid.* viii. 290 Thouless, who writes on religious psychology from the standpoint of a psychologist who is also a professing Christian. **1951** E. A. Burtt *Types of Relig. Philos.* (rev. ed.) p. vii, An exposition of the main points of view in religious philosophy. *Ibid.* i. 7 What significant comparisons may we make between the religious psychology of individuals who participate in quite different cultures? **1960** D. A. Lowrie *Rebellious Prophet* xiv. 196 Berdyaev..is inclined to consider him [*sc.* Bulgakov] a religious philosopher rather than a theologian. **1974** B. A. Brody *Philos. of Relig.* p. vii, For centuries, a principal issue in traditional religious philosophy had been whether one could prove the truth or falsity of a variety of fundamental doctrines.

5. Of a horse: **a.** (See quot. 1788.) **b.** *U.S.* 'Having no vicious traits' (D.A.E.).

1788 Grose *Classical Dict. Vulgar Tongue* (ed. 2) sig. Z4ᵛ, *Religious horse*, one much given to prayer, or apt to be down upon his knees. **1869** *Overland Monthly* III. 127 It is amusing to hear one ask of another, when about to purchase a horse: 'Is he religious?'

6. *Comb.*, as *religious-mad, -minded, -sane* adjs.

a **1930** D. H. Lawrence *Apocalypse* (1931) vi. 98 Men were religious-mad: not religious-sane. **1888** C. M. Yonge *Beechcroft at Rockstone* II. xx. 153 Thoroughly religious-minded,..his aspirations had been blighted by his father's death. **1954** A. Seton *Katherine* xxvi. 447 Religious-minded Katherine had never been... This strict penitential garb and talk of pilgrimage were surely some passing derangement.

B. *sb.* **2. b.** Delete † *Obs. rare* and add later examples.

In recent use not a gallicism.

1651 T. Matthew *Life Lady L. Knatchbull* (1931) II. i. 87 Dame Mary Roper..was a much younger Religious. **1922** Joyce *Ulysses* 706 Anal violation by male religious (fully clothed, eyes abject) of female religious (partly clothed, eyes direct). **1939** R. Godden *Black Narcissus* xxx. 273 You've forgotten who you are. You're a religious. A nun. **1948** W. S. Maugham *Catalina* xxix. 189 It behoved Catalina to become a religious. **1980** I. Murdoch *Nuns & Soldiers* i. 56 When she was being converted she was already purposing to be a religious.

religiously, *adv.* Add: **5.** *Comb.*, as *religiously-minded*.

1935 B. Russell *Relig. & Sci.* vi. 144 The sacred history related in the Bible and the elaborate theology of the ancient and mediaeval Church have become less important than formerly to most religiously minded men and women.

reline, *v.*¹, **relining**. *sb. vbl* Add: **a.** (Further examples.)

1921 *Automobile Engineer* XI. 168/1 It is necessary to remove the rear-hubs from their tapers..in order to gain access to the internal brake for relining. **1933** *Radio Times* 14 Apr. 121/2 Have your brakes tested..if they need relining—specify Ferodo... The Ferodo guarantee is tied to the steering wheel of your car when you have the brakes relined with Ferodo. **1976** J. Drummond *Funeral Urn* v. 21 She..asked when she might have the car. He grunted dourly, 'Gotta re-line the brakes.'

b. *spec.* in *Art.* To attach a new backing canvas to (a painting).

1911 M. J. Gunn *Print Restoration & Picture Cleaning* viii. 146 Nothing but re-lining will often save a valuable picture from perishing. **1948** G. L. Stout *Care of Pictures* v. 96 The painting..had been relined at least once. **1957** *Encycl. Brit.* XVII. 68E/2 *Relining*, the procedure of attaching a new or secondary canvas at the back of a canvas support when that fabric has become too weak to serve its purpose or when the ground or paint has become loosened from it. *Ibid.*, If it [*sc.* the painting] has been relined before, the old relining canvas is removed. **1978** *Daily Tel.* 9 Dec. 14/4 He has cleaned, restored or relined over 85 pictures.

reliˑner. [f. Reline *v.*¹ + -er¹.] **1.** A person who provides oil-paintings with fresh linings.

1905 W. H. Hunt *Pre-Raphaelitism* I. 183 The reliner decided that the varnish was neither mastic nor copal. **1911** M. J. Gunn *Print Restoration & Picture Cleaning* viii. 147 In case the services of a picture re-liner and restorer should be needed.

2. Material providing a fresh lining, as for the brakes of a motor vehicle.

1920 *T. Eaton & Co. Catal.* Spring & Summer 395/1 *Tire Reliners* for Ford cars. Made of several layers of heavy tire fabrics. **1945** *Sun* (Baltimore) 8 Nov. 14/3 Motorists could recognize a sound used tire if it had a tread design at least every four inches, no emergency patches on the inside such as boots and reliners, [etc.].

reliquiæ, *pl.* Add: **1.** (Earlier and later examples.) Also, literary remains; unpublished or uncollected writings.

1654 E. Gayton *Pleasant Notes Don Quix.* III. vii. 114 A sort of these Theeves are now redivivous, (the Reliquiæ I believe of Knight-Errantry) who goe by the name of Spirits. **1933** *Times Lit. Suppl.* 2 Nov. 746/2 These reliquiae of Lytton Strachey, collected from periodicals and other sources..belong to all times of his life as a writer. **1948** *Mind* LVII. 517 Scarcely less important..are the Jena manuscripts [of Hegel] published partly by Lasson in 1923 and partly by Hoffmeister in 1931–2. Armed with these *reliquiae* a scholar could approach the making of a commentary with fair confidence.

relish, *sb.*¹ Add: **3. b.** (Earlier and further U.S. examples.) Also *attrib.*

1797 W. Priest *Travels in U.S.A.* (1802) 32 About eight or nine in the morning they breakfast on tea and coffee, attended always with what they call *relishes*, such as salt fish, beef-steaks, sausages, broiled fowls, ham, bacons &c. **1826** J. F. Cooper *Last of Mohicans* I. vi. 72 Glad to eat their venison raw, and without a relish too. Here..we have plenty of salt. **1963** R. I. McDavid *Mencken's Amer. Lang.* iii. 120 *Rolliches*, pickled rolls of meat, are still occasionally made in the Hudson Valley, and sometimes anglicized to *relishes*. **1978** *Chicago* June 221/1 The $4.50 to $7.95 dinners include a relish plate (crisp vegetables, cheddar cheese spread, and scoop of homemade liver pâté).

reˑlished, *ppl. a.* [f. Relish *v.*¹ + -ed¹.] Liked (as food); enjoyed, appreciated.

1901 *Yearbk. U.S. Dept. Agric. 1900* 433 There was an outbreak of seventeen-year cicadas, which afforded an abundant and greatly relished food supply.

reload, *v.* Add: **2. b.** Also, to load (a camera, cassette, etc.) again.

1888 *Judge* Christmas Number 43/1 One Hundred Exposures may be made without 're-loading' the camera. **1897** *Sears, Roebuck Catal.* 473/3 The camera..can be reloaded..[in] any place from which the light is excluded. **1940** *Chambers's Techn. Dict.* 713/2 *Reload*, to remove exposed film and insert unexposed film in a camera or magazine in a dark-room or under light-tight conditions (e.g. in a changing bag). **1977** J. Hedgecoe *Photographer's Handbk.* 45 Instead of buying 35 mm film in cassettes you can purchase a bulk length..and then keep reloading cassettes yourself.

reload (rīˑlōᵘd), *sb.* [f. the vb.] That which serves to reload anything, as a film placed in a camera, etc.

1928 *Daily Express* 14 Dec. 14/6 (Advt.), He can use the rod..Shaving Stick as a reload. **1958** *Newnes Compl. Amat. Photogr.* 75, 35 mm. film is also supplied as daylight-loading or darkroom-loading reloads for cassettes. **1961** *Guardian* 16 Mar. 6 He found..a small Minox pocket camera..and, in a brown paper bag, two Minox reloads. **1976** *Shooting Mag.* Dec. 47/2 Despite the budget price it does not make second-quality reloads. **1977** J. WAINWRIGHT *Nest of Rats* I. vii. 46 A shooter; a thirty-eight Colt 'Agent' revolver... There was a box of re-loads included in the parcel.

reloa·der. [f. RELOAD *v.* + -ER[1].] That which or one who reloads.

1909 *Cent. Dict.* Suppl., *Reloader*,..a self-loading conveyer used to collect and transport coal from a coal-storage yard or pocket and to deliver it to railroad-cars or vessels or to place it in other near-by storage-places. **1973** 'A. HALL' *Tango Briefing* vii. 94 This man's forte was fast use of the automatic reloader... He was using something like a ·44 Magnum. **1976** *Shooting Times & Country Mag.* 18–24 Nov., I would very much appreciate advice from reloaders of home made cartridges. **1976** *Shooting Mag.* Dec. 46/2 No reloaders..should have anything to do with powder of unknown vintage that has been subjected to unknown storage conditions.

reloca·table, *a.* [f. RELOCAT(E *v.* + -ABLE.] That can be relocated.

1872 'MARK TWAIN' *Roughing It* xli. 290 At midnight.. the ledge would be 'relocatable'. **1976** *Milton Keynes Express* 11 June 34/1 (Advt.), Heating Engineer... To initiate sales leads, progress enquiries including those for Intercities Relocatable Boiler House, design systems and negotiate quotations through to acceptance. **1977** *Gloss. Terms Data Processing* (*B.S.I.*) VII. 9/1 *Relocatable program*, a computer program that is in such a form that it may be relocated. **1979** *Personal Computer World* Nov. 69 (Advt.), Relocatable linkable output.

relocate, *v.* For '*U.S.*' read 'orig. *U.S.*' Add: **1. c.** To move to another place; to resettle; to change the location of.

1834 A. LINCOLN et al. in I. D. Tarbell *Early Life A. Lincoln* (1896) xvii. 198 To view and relocate a part of the road..we have made the said relocation on good ground. **1866** *Rep. Indian Affairs* (U.S.) 76 If the Indians could be removed to some remote place equally fertile, and there relocated, it would no doubt be to their advantage. **1908** *Pacific Monthly* Feb. 204/2 The section east of here..has been practically all relocated, in places the new track being miles away from the original location. **1936** *Sun* (Baltimore) 21 July 1/3 Families which could not be supported by a shifting of land to moisture-holding grass production for cattle raising..would be 'relocated'. **1956** H. FOSTER in D. L. Linton *Sheffield* 245 The city does not face what would have been the almost insuperable problem of re-locating its vast heavy industries. **1964** T. W. MCRAE *Impact of Computers on Accounting* i. 23 This was a somewhat laborious business..causing a whole battery of 'words' to be relocated to different addresses. **1970** *Globe & Mail* (Toronto) 25 Sept. B2/8 Each of the three Canadian companies..has been looking at the possibility of relocating their data centres. **1978** *N.Y. Times* 30 Mar. B3/5 Paving the way for the Nestlé Company to relocate its White Plains headquarters on the property.

2. (Earlier and further examples.) Freq. without const.

1841 in WEBSTER. **1851** C. CIST *Cincinnati* 143 [This] determined the company to re-locate on higher ground. **1864** *Congress Globe* 9 Mar. 1018/2 In a larger number of cases these persons having taken homesteads, and again desiring to sell and relocate,..have paid for the lands. **1957** [see *RUNAWAY *sb.* (and *a.*) 7]. **1964** *New Statesman* 3 Apr. 533/2 It offers an enjoyable evening out in Jaguarthreepointfoursville where the hero has relocated from his Scottish tenement by selling cash registers. **1968** 'E. LATHEN' *Stitch in Time* xvi. 134 He was relocating, he explained..because of a sudden desire to specialize in dermatology. **1971** *Daily Mail* 16 Mar. 22/1 (Advt.), Applicants should be prepared to work in our London Office initially, and relocate to new premises in Basingstoke..by 1973. **1978** *New York* 3 Apr. 37/2 The company had to relocate for technical reasons. **1979** *N.Y. Rev. Bks.* 25 Oct. 55/1 (Advt.), Lady author/lecturer who can easily re-locate seeks male counterpart.

relocation. Add: **2.** (Earlier U.S. and later examples.)

1837 A. LINCOLN Let. 5 Aug. in *McClure's* (1896) Mar. 316/1, I also tacked a provision on to a fellow's bill, to authorize the relocation of a road. **1873** *Trans. Illinois Dept. Agric.* X. 371 The court shall appoint three viewers to examine the necessary re-location. **1901** S. E. WHITE *Claim Jumpers* 232 Under the terms of a relocation, we can use the old stakes and 'discovery'. **1948** *Sierra Club Bull.* Dec. 5/1 A general relocation of the road was thereupon planned, including a higher crossing of Yosemite Creek. **1963** C. R. COWELL et al. *Inlays, Crowns, & Bridges* viii. 89 Re-location of the copper ring may be inaccurate in such an elastic material. **1967** *Boston Sunday Globe* 23 Apr. 9/5 A private company has sponsored refugee relocation. **1973** M. MANN (*title*) Workers on the move: the sociology of relocation. **1979** *Navajo Times* (Window Rock, Arizona) 24 May 1/2 He recognized that relocation would be difficult for the Navajos. **1981** J. SUTHERLAND *Bestsellers* i. 29 A move towards bestsellerism..would seem to presage a general relocation of the bestseller.

3. *attrib.*, as *relocation allowance, assistance, cost, director, expense, grant*; **relocation centre** *U.S.*, an internment camp to which persons of Japanese birth or origin were committed during the war of 1939–45.

1958 *Observer* 12 Jan. 18/3 (Advt.), Liberal relocation allowances will be given successful candidates. **1968** *Globe & Mail* (Toronto) 3 Feb. B6/3 (Advt.), Generous relocation allowance. *Ibid.* 17 Feb. B6 (Advt.), Excellent advancement potential and benefits program. Relocation assistance will be offered. **1976** *Star* (Sheffield) 20 Nov. (Advt.), Relocation assistance will be provided. **1943** S. MENEFEE *Assignment: U.S.A.* 68 Hearst reporters got anti-Japanese statements from Mayor Fletcher Bowron and other prominent figures in Los Angeles and played up the Dies Committee's 'exposures' of the relocation centers. **1967** *Economist* 22 Apr. 354/2 In the days just after the bombing of Pearl Harbour, many Americans vented their panic..on the Nisei... The brunt fell most heavily on the large communities on the West Coast... These were evacuated en masse to inland 'relocation centres'. **1970** *Internat. & Compar. Law Q.* 4th Ser. XIX. II. 237 A sparsely populated Coast where relocation costs are nominal. **1963** *Freedomways* Summer 425 A relocation director,..whose job is to help relocate families displaced from areas where new housing is being constructed. **1961** *Times* 27 Jan. 3/3 (Advt.), Relocation expenses guaranteed for selected Engineers. **1977** *Navy News* July 35 (Advt.), Relocation expenses will be considered where appropriate. **1977** *Times Educ. Suppl.* 21 Oct. 52/3 (Advt.), Relocation grants available in approved cases.

relucence, -ency. Restrict † *Obs.* to *relucency* and add later example of *relucence*.

1926 *Spectator* 15 May 849/2 The mystical life..found again and again inspiration and relucence from the poets.

relucent, *a.* (Later *fig.* example.)

1897 F. THOMPSON *New Poems* 33 The relucent song take for thy sacred meeds!

reluctance. 1. b. (Later examples.) Also *attrib.*

1967 KURRELMEYER & MAIS *Electricity & Magnetism* xii. 291 An air gap of 0·1 mm has the same reluctance as 1 m of iron of permeability 10,000. **1968** *New Scientist* 11 Jan. 63/2 The reluctance motor is a synchronous machine; its speed is determined entirely by the frequency of the ac supply. **1977** *Gramophone* Aug. 366/1 The moving-iron (variable reluctance) principle is used with a larger than usual fixed magnet.

relu·ctantism. *rare.* [f. RELUCTANT *a.* + -ISM.] A reluctant state or condition; reluctance.

1906 *Century Mag.* Feb. 552/2 The incisive coldness of Miss Lamb's demeanor..was sufficient to chill..her youthful admirers into a state of objectified reluctantism.

reluctivity. Substitute for def.: The reciprocal of the magnetic permeability. (Later example.)

1917 C. M. SMITH *Electr. & Magn. Measurements* x. 277 Reluctance and its reciprocal permeance are characteristics of the circuit. Reluctivity and permeability are characteristic of the given material.

rem, *a.* Slang abbrev. of REMANDED *ppl. a.*

1887 [see *BUST *sb.*[3] d].

rem (rem), *sb.*[1] Pl. **rem, rems.** [f. initial letters of *roentgen equivalent man.*] Orig., a quantity of ionizing radiation having the same effect on human tissue as one roentgen of X-rays. The dosage in rems is now calculated by multiplying the dosage in rads by the relative biological effectiveness. Cf. *REP[7].

1947 *Nucleonics* Oct. 38/2 The rep and rem units were introduced by Dr. H. M. Parker. *Ibid.* 39/2 Roentgen-equivalent-man (or mammal), rem... One rem is the estimated amount of energy absorbed in tissue which is biologically equivalent in man to 1 r of gamma- or X-rays. By definition: 1 rem = 83/RBE erg/gm tissue. **1957** *Encycl. Brit.* XVI. 591/1 The biological effects of radiation are not solely dependent on the amount of energy released; it is also a question of how highly localized the energy is. Such considerations have led to another unit, the rem, supposed to be that dose of radiation which has the same biological effect as 1 rad of X-radiation. **1958** W. D. CLAUS *Radiation Biol. & Med.* xviii. 431 The dose in rem is obtained by multiplying the physical dose in rads by the RBE appropriate to the situation. **1958** *Observer* 5 Oct. 15/4 The most active watches..could deliver a dose of five rem (units of radioactive dose measurement) within five years. The International Commission on Radiological Protection has recommended that no one should receive an accumulated dose of more than five rem by the age of 30. **1975** *Nature* 27 Mar. 278/2 Fifteen rem is equivalent to 1·5 rad of alpha radiation (since alpha radiation is considered 10 times as carcinogenic as gamma radiation). **1976** *Sci. Amer.* Nov. 31/2 If the fresh fission products from one megaton of fission were spread uniformly over a perfectly flat area of 1,000 square miles, the gamma-ray dose rate one meter above the ground would be about 250 rems per hour after 10 hours.

REM (rem, ā₁ī₁e·m), *sb.*[2] Also **rem.** Abbrev. of *rapid eye movement* (see *RAPID *a.* 2 a). Freq. *attrib.*, designating a distinctive type of sleep that occurs at intervals throughout the night and is characterized by such eye movements, more dreaming and bodily movement, an increased pulse rate, and faster breathing.

1957 DEMENT & KLEITMAN in *Jrnl. Exper. Psychol.* LIII. 340/1 In most of the remaining text the following abbreviations will be used: REM's (rapid eye movements) and NREM's (no rapid eye movements). **1969** *Sunday Times* (Colour Suppl.) 16 Feb. 21/3 Subjects regularly deprived of the opportunity to dream by being woken at the onset of REM periods began to show psychological disturbance after a few nights. **1972** F. R. FREEMON *Sleep Research* i. 4 This second type of sleep, called the rem state, has low voltage EEG activity mixed with bursts of theta waves and frequent conjugate eye movements. **1976** SMYTHIES & CORBETT *Psychiatry* xiv. 265 During REM sleep the brain shows intense metabolic activity. **1977** S. DUNKELL *Sleep Positions* ii. 38 As we continue our journey through the night, the duration of each successive REM phase increases.

remagnetize, *v.* (Earlier example.)

1839 Advt. in G. S. Haight *George Eliot & John Chapman* (1969) 259 Compasses made to order and remagnatized [*sic*].

remain, *v.* Add: **2. c.** *it* (or *that*) *remains to be seen*: it is not yet known or certain.

1796 LD. GLENBERVIE *Diary* 16 Oct. (1928) I. 88 It remains, however, to be seen what will be the ultimate result in the present instance of a struggle as yet perhaps but in its infancy. **1828** *Athenæum* 12 Feb. 103/1 Whether or not the 'Life of Columbus' will restore it, remains yet to be seen. **1859** *Times* 4 Feb. 9/4 That remains to be seen. **1866** MAYNE REID *Headless Horseman* xvi. 88 It remains to be seen how we shall get over it. **1938** H. L. MENCKEN *Let.* 23 Apr. (1961) 427 Whether I'll write anything for publication remains to be seen. **1967** *Listener* 6 July 20/2 How far or how quickly the new government can get anywhere.. remains to be seen. **1976** *Southern Even. Echo* (Southampton) 13 Nov. 3/6 It would remain to be seen to what extent it would be practical or desirable to build houses there.

4. a. Also, with *on*.

1912 J. JOYCE *Let.* 23 Aug. (1966) II. 311 Tomorrow I must pawn my watch and chain in order to remain on a little longer. **1939** H. NICHOLSON *Diary* 11 Apr. (1966) 397 Harold Macmillan is enraged that Chamberlain should remain on.

6. b. Delete † *Obs.*—[1] and add later examples.

1872 HARDY *Under Greenwood Tree* I. I. vi. 78 The tunes they that morning essayed remained with him for years. **1899** 'MARK TWAIN' *Man that corrupted Hadleyburg* in *Harper's Mag.* Dec. 30/2 A remark which he made to me has remained with me to this day, and has at last conquered me. *a* **1927** I. DUNCAN *My Life* (1928) viii. 78 Another, even greater impression, that has remained with me all my life was the 'Rodin Pavillon'. **1977** B. PYM *Quartet in Autumn* vi. 54 She had once noticed an old woman with a lost expression peering through one of the surrounding hedges and that impression had remained with her.

remainder[1]. Add: **3. b.** (Further U.S. examples.)

1872 'MARK TWAIN' *Roughing It* I. 357 There'll be a double-barreled inquest here..and your remainders will go home in a couple of baskets. **1885** —— *Huck. Finn* viii. 62, I was having a good enough time seeing them hunt for my remainders.

5. (Earlier and later examples.) Also *transf.*, an unused portion of goods, unused material; = REMNANT *sb.* 4 b.

1757 *Monthly Rev.* Sept., C. Henderson, Bookseller, under the Royal Exchange, having purchased the remainder of the impression of the following very entertaining book.. proposes to sell them for 4s. only. **1854** *Gowans'* (115 Nassau St., N.Y.) *Catal.* No. 13. 6 Remainders of editions by other publishers. **1865** *N. & Q.* VII. 510/2 (Advt.), 'Remainders' of valuable books, all in new condition, at greatly reduced prices. **1914** J. LEATHAM *Daavit* 69 My dear good old mother bocht a remander fae Johnnie Hitcheon, and took it an' me ti Saunders ti be mizhur't. **1926** C. N. BENNETT *Photogravure* 121 Paper makers, like drapers, have their remnants, though the name for them in the paper making industry is 'remainders'. **1930** J. H. APPEL *Business Biogr. John Wanamaker* viii. 104 'Bargain Room' opened— 'a place where remainders of lots are sold at smaller prices'.

6. *remainder biscuit* (further example); (sense 5) *remainder binding, list, -shop.*

1899 *Sketch* 1 Nov. 62/1 The poor evening paper cannot afford this. It must..be content with the 'remainder biscuit' of the morning's telegrams. **1912** *Chambers's Jrnl.* Dec. 773/2 It is pitiful to see the rows of discarded books in circulating libraries and remainder-shops. **1931** *Times Lit. Suppl.* 10 Sept. 688/2 The unsold sheets of a published book are re-issued with a cancel title or a new preface, or in a remainder binding. **1977** *Gay News* 24 Mar. 21/3, I use anything that's cheap on the remainder list.

7. Special Comb.: **remainder theorem** *Math.*, the theorem that if a polynomial $f(x)$ is divided by $(x-a)$ the remainder will be $f(a)$.

1886 G. CHRYSTAL *Algebra* I. vii. 134 (heading) Results of the application of remainder theorem. **1933** R. W. BRINK *College Algebra* xix. 295 Without performing the divisions, by means of the Remainder Theorem find the remainder after each of the following divisions. **1971** WILLERDING & HOFFMAN *College Algebra* ix. 267 By the Remainder Theorem, the remainder when x^3+7x^2+3x+3 is divided by $x+1$ is 6. As a corollary of the remainder theorem we have the Factor Theorem.

remai·nder, *v.* [f. REMAINDER[1].] *trans.* To dispose of (an unsold part of an edition of a book) at a reduced price; to treat as a remainder (sense 5). Also *transf.* So **remai·ndered** *ppl. a.*, **remai·ndering** *vbl. sb.*

1904 *Heffer & Sons' Catal.* 2 As the History of 'Remaindered' Books would almost prove, it might be said that no Book was really great until it had been 'Remaindered'. **1906** *Times* 17 Nov. 9/3 How many books do we see every year produced by publishers who..'remainder' them at a few pence a copy? **1907** *Times* 25 Mar. 12/1 There is no doubt now that the boycott is not meant to stop remaindering at low prices. **1910** *Library* I. 46 The plays in question were printed in the years with which they are dated and unsold copies..remaindered in 1619. *Ibid.* 49 A nineteen-year-old edition was then being remaindered. **1932** *John o' London's Weekly* 25 June 428 He told me he had bought them when they were remaindered by publishers, at 9d. a copy. **1959** *Daily Tel.* 29 Dec. 6/2 Swift turnover for cash, sometimes of goods specially ordered for the sales, and the 'remaindering' of clothes, carpets, furniture and whatnot which might not otherwise be sold so quickly—or even, where fashion is important, at all. **1968** C. M. VINES *Little Nut-Brown Man* x. 155 He liked his books to be in short supply, thus perhaps appearing better sellers than they were; or he disliked the thought of being remaindered. **1981** *Country Life* 1 Jan. 34/1 Picture-books seem to end up by being sold off cheap as remaindered volumes.

remainer[2]. (Further example.)

1922 JOYCE *Ulysses* 688 How did the centripetal remainer afford egress to the centrifugal departer?

re·make, *sb.* [f. the vb.] **1.** A second formation of a gold-bearing reef. *Austral.*

1865 *Mining Surveyors' Rep.* (Mining Dept., Victoria) Mar. 74 The lode was however very thin, and ran completely out at 70 feet deep, leaving no track. However a party are now prospecting this ground, to discover if a remake of this reef exists.

2. (Also **re-make.**) A remaking of a film or of a script, usually with the rôles played by different actors; an adaptation of the theme of a film.

1936 *Variety* 24 June 4/4 James Melton assigned the lead in Warners' remake of 'Desert Song'. **1940** *Time* 22 Jan. 76/3 The result is not just another remake, for Director Hawks's weird idea was also to remake the sex of his leading character. **1948** *Sunday Pictorial* 18 July 11/4 'If Winter Comes' (Empire) is a re-make of the famous weepie novel. **1952** *Time* 2 June 92/3 *Lovely to Look at* (M-G-M), a re-make of the old Broadway musical *Roberta* (filmed in 1935 with Fred Astaire and Ginger Rogers). **1957** *Observer* 1 Sept. 11/7 The romance is a remake by director Leo McCarey of his 'Love Affair', which seemed a good film when Irene Dunne and Charles Boyer did it twenty years ago. **1960** *Times* 23 Feb. 4/1 A Hollywood company has undertaken a Western remake of Mr. Akira Kurosawa's famous Japanese costume drama. **1977** *New Statesman* 2 Sept. 312/2 The technicolour remake of the talkie remake of some..silent Hollywood goodie.

remand, *sb.* Add: **2.** (Later example.)

1970 G. F. NEWMAN *Sir, You Bastard* i. 35 The door used by remands, down near the witness box.

3. *attrib.*, as *remand prisoner, warrant*; **remand centre,** an institution to which young persons between the ages of 14 and 21 years are remanded to await trial or sentence; since 1967, such an institution for a person of any age; *Canad.*, such an institution for adults; **remand home,** an institution to which young persons between the ages of 8 and 14 years are remanded or are committed for detention.

1948 *Criminal Justice Act* 11 & 12 *Geo. VI* c. 58 s. 48(1)(a) Remand centres, that is to say places for the detention of persons not less than fourteen but under twenty-one years of age who are remanded or committed in custody for trial or sentence. **1967** *Criminal Justice Act Eliz. II.* c. 80 s. 66(1) Notwithstanding that a remand centre is provided under section 43 of the Prison Act 1952 for the detention of persons of or over the age of fourteen but under the age of twenty-one who are remanded or committed in custody for trial or sentence, any person required to be detained in an institution to which the Act applies may be detained in a remand centre for any temporary purpose or for the purpose of providing maintenance and domestic services for that centre. **1970** G. GREER *Female Eunuch* 180 His impudence in courtrooms and remand centres. **1974** *Globe & Mail* (Toronto) 4 Sept. 1/1 The Calgary remand centre—the first in Alberta—is open for business. The centre will house men held in custody between court appearances pending their trials. **1976** *Southern Even. Echo* (Southampton) 10 Nov. 9/2 A Southampton schoolboy was remanded in custody for seven days to Winchester remand centre after the Magistrates decided he was 'unruly'. **1902** *Times* 13 Jan. 9/4 The Children's Committee reported that the three remand homes at Pentonville-road, Harrow-road, and Camberwell-green were opened for the reception of children on January 1. **1933** *Act* 23 & 24 *Geo. V* c. 12 s. 108(2) References in any Act to places of detention provided under Section one hundred and eight of the Children Act, 1908, shall be construed as references to remand homes provided under this Act. **1934** 'J. SPENSER' *Limey breaks In* ii. 21 The policeman who took me to the remand home led me into a restaurant and gave me a good feed before he handed me over. **1963** M. DUGGAN in C. K. Stead *N.Z. Short Stories* (1966) 101, I came in for a couple of remand home stares, bread and water and solitary and take that writ on his eyeballs. **1972** G. SERENY *Case of Mary Bell* I. iii. 46 With her father's agreement, she was taken to stay at Fernwood Remand Home, a Newcastle County Council Children's Home for girls. **1897** Remand prisoner [in Dict., sense 1]. **1977** *Belfast Telegraph* 19 Jan. 4/8 Two visitors to republican prisoners in Crumlin Road jail had been..attacked by loyalist gangs.., a remand prisoner claimed today. **1963** J. N. HARRIS *Weird World Wes Beattie* (1964) i. 12 Wes sits in the Psychiatric Hospital on an attorney general's remand warrant.

remanence. 2. Delete *rare*—[1] and add later examples in *Theol.*

1964 J. STACEY *John Wyclif & Reform* v. 104 The next assertion was a doctrine of Remanence. If annihilation was denied then, in his view, the bread and wine remained bread and wine. **1964** R. H. BAINTON *Hist. Christianity* viii. 238/1 This was not to say..that Christ is not in the sacrament. He is there, in addition to and along with bread and wine, whose substance remains. This doctrine is called remanence. **1974** *Encycl. Brit. Macropædia* XIX. 1051/1 He [*sc.* Wycliffe] sought to replace it [*sc.* the doctrine of transubstantiation] with a doctrine of remanence (remaining).

3. *Physics.* Residual magnetism, *spec.* *RETENTIVITY 1 (but see quot. 1962).

1917 G. D. SHEPARDSON *Telephone Apparatus* IV. 279 When the current has been reduced to zero, there still exists a more or less permanent magnetization such as indicated by *OE*, the power of holding this residual magnetization being sometimes called the 'remanence' of the iron, sometimes expressed as a percentage of the maximum magnetization. **1924** C. R. UNDERHILL *Magnets* xxv. 435 The remanence is the structural flux density of a permanent magnet, sometimes called the residual induction. **1947** *Electronic Engin.* XIX. 379/1 The wire originally used..was a medium carbon steel having a remanence of 6,000/7,000 gauss. **1948** [see *RETENTIVITY]. **1962** M. McCAIG in D. Hadfield *Permanent Magnets & Magnetism* ii. 26 The hysteresis loop of largest area is known as *the* hysteresis loop. The values of remanent magnetism..and coercive force..for this hysteresis loop are known as the remanence and coercivity respectively. This definition of remanence conforms with the usage recommended by the British Standards Institution... In the U.S.A... the same quantity is called residual magnetism, while the word remanence is used to describe the state of an actual magnet after magnetization. Owing to its own self-demagnetizing field such a magnet operates at a point in the top left-hand quadrant of the hysteresis loop. As the British Standard refers to the flux density in such a magnet as 'residual magnetism' there is a complete interchange of meanings of the terms 'remanence' and 'residual magnetism' on the two sides of the Atlantic. **1973** J. G. TWEEDDALE *Materials Technol.* I. iv. 93 When an electromagnetically induced field is changing rapidly, as it might do in a piece of electrical or electronic equipment, it is obvious that a very low remanence is desirable if energy loss and generation of heat is to be avoided. **1976** *Nature* 5 Feb. 381/1 Many of the intrusions have been sampled during our new study and the palaeomagnetism of those possessing stable remanences after a[lternating] f[ield] cleaning is reported here.

remanent, *a.* Restrict 'Now *rare*' to senses in Dict. and add: **4.** *Physics.* Of magnetism: remaining in a substance or specimen after removal of the magnetizing field.

1866 E. ATKINSON tr. *Ganot's Elem. Treat. Physics* (ed. 2) X. v. 678 The iron used for the electromagnet..must be pure, and be made as soft as possible... If this is not the case the bar retains, even after the passage of the current a quantity of magnetism which is called the remanent magnetism. **1912, 1931** [see *RETENTIVITY]. **1939** L. F. BATES *Mod. Magnetism* viii. 258 In general, the remanent magnetism possessed by a ferromagnetic which has been placed in a strong field is sufficient to give satisfactory deflections of a sensitive astatic magnetometer system. **1944** *Proc. IRE* XXXII. 667/2 The remanent flux will go through a series of values corresponding to the sum and difference frequencies between the recording signal and the supersonic signal. **1962** [see *REMANENCE 3]. **1971** I. G. GASS et al. *Understanding Earth* xvi. 237/1 The intensity of this remanent or permanent component of magnetisation in basalts is invariably greater than that induced by the present Earth's field.

‖ **remanié** (rəmani̦e), *a. Geol.* and *Geogr.* [a. F. *remanié*, pa. pple. of *remanier* to rehandle, reshape.] Derived from an older stratum or structure.

[**1866** *Q. Jrnl. Geol. Soc.* XXII. 237 If the Diestien beds be divided into upper sandy ooze and lower muddy ooze, the sections show that where the first has been removed and 'remanié', the resulting Scaldésien beds take the form of 'Crag gris'.] **1870** *Ibid.* XXVI. 72 In this 'remanié' deposit there appears to exist an assemblage of species peculiar to two distinct epochs. **1894** J. GEIKIE *Great Ice Age* (ed. 3) xii. 160 The marine organisms..may indicate an interglacial submergence to the extent of 300 or 400 feet, but on the other hand the deposits in which they occur may be *remoniés*. They may well have been dragged forward by the ice from a lower level. **1913** *Rep. Brit. Assoc. Adv. Sci. 1912* 622 Excavation (some 8 feet deep) in 'rubble-drift' material, mostly *remanié* stuff from the Boulder Clay which caps the hill above. **1957** J. K. CHARLESWORTH *Quaternary Era* I. iv. 87 If the lateral glacier is steep it may fall on a trunk glacier as a remanié glacier. **1964** V. J. CHAPMAN *Coastal Vegetation* vi. 137 If a dune undergoing erosion is stabilized, it represents a moderate remanié form. **1969** BENNISON & WRIGHT *Geol. Hist. Brit. Isles* i. 10 A bed may contain fossils of a previous geological age known as derived or remanié fossils. **1978** *Nature* 16 Nov. 258/2 At Hamilton in western Victoria, a bed of calcareous clay containing phosphatic nodules rests unconformably on limestone and clay of early and middle Miocene age and contains abundant *remanié* foraminifera from both formations.

‖ **remaniement** (rəmanimaṅ). [Fr.: see prec.] A rearrangement, a reconstruction.

1920 *Glasgow Herald* 3 Aug. 5 Much more..needs study in the latest 'remaniement' of the Turkish Ministry... The Grand Vizier..is determined that the new Cabinet shall be composed of moderate men. **1933** E. K. CHAMBERS *Eng. Folk-Play* 87 The play is said to have been given as far back as 1807, but to me it suggests a literary *remaniement.*

remap, re-map (rī-). *U.S.* [RE- 5 a.] = *REDISTRICTING *vbl. sb.* Also *attrib.*

1962 *Nashville Tennessean* 2 Sept. 2-B/1 (*heading*) State remap is still issue. **1962** *Economist* 1 Dec. 908/1 Tennessee has approved a constitutional convention on what is called 're-map'. **1974** *State* (Columbia, S. Carolina) 15 Feb. 4-A/3 The department rejected a bitterly disputed remap plan that would have divided the state into 28 districts drawn to maintain the integrity of county lines.

remargin, *v.* (Later example.)

1952 J. CARTER *ABC for Book-Collectors* 153 When one or more of the three outer margins of a leaf has been restored, it is said to be re-margined.

remark, *v.* Add: **3. a.** Quot. *a* 1704 to read:

1694 LOCKE *Ess. Hum. Und.* (ed. 2) III. ix. 275 It is easie to observe, what has been before remarked, [etc.].

b. Also without *prep.*, to make remarks.

1845 J. RUSKIN *Let.* 17 June in H. I. Shapiro *Ruskin in Italy* (1972) 118 Perhaps..it is an English cheesemonger & his wife, who come in, and remark, as happened to me the other day while I was looking at the gates of Ghiberti.

remarkable, *a.* and *sb.* Add: **A.** *adj.* **1.** Also as quasi-*adv.*

1779 J. WOODFORDE *Diary* 6 Feb. (1924) I. 245 Mr. Ferman and myself went to see a remarkable large Pigg. **1818** W. SEWALL *Diary* 13 Mar. (1930) 39/1 The scholars appeared remarkable well. **1871** E. EGGLESTON *Hoosier Schoolmaster* iv. 39 He uses sech remarkable smart words. **1890** KIPLING *Barrack-Room Ballads* (1892) 8 We aren't no thin red 'eroes.. But single men in barricks, most remarkable like you.

B. *sb.* (Later U.S. example.)

1946 *Richmond* (Va.) *Times-Dispatch* 15 Jan. 10/2 (*heading*) Religious remarkables.

remarque. (Later examples.)

1890 F. G. KITTON *Charles Dickens by Pen & Pencil* I. iv. facing p. 49 Charles Dickens, his wife and her sister—1843... Remarque: Miss Mary Hogarth. **1925** C. MORLEY *Thunder on Left* vii. 80 If they're girls, how mothers hurry to drill and denature those bright dreaming wits. They love them chiefly because they make so pretty a vignette in the margin of their own self-portrait—like a *remarque* in an engraving.

rema·ster (rī-), *v.* Also **re-master.** [RE- 5 a.] *trans.* To make a new master of (a record); to issue (a recording) from a new master: see *MASTER *sb.*[1] 9* a. Hence **rema·stering** *vbl. sb.*

1967 *Punch* 25 Jan. 132/3 Both have been remastered, and only nostalgia entitles you to prefer the original 78s. **1970** *Soviet Weekly* 20 June 4/2 They include speeches which he recorded in the earliest years of Soviet power skilfully remastered and transferred to tape. **1975** *Gramophone* Aug. 322/1 They..will be most grateful to A. C. Griffith for the skill with which the transfer and re-mastering has been carried out. **1977** *Rolling Stone* 19 May 23/1 Jeffreys' best-known song (first released in 1973 as a single on Atlantic and now remastered and included on the new LP).

re·match, *sb.* [RE- 5 a.] A return match.

1941 *Sun* (Baltimore) 10 Apr. 17/1 Abraham Simon, originally the May opponent in a rematch of a 13-round go with the Bomber in Detroit, in June in New York. **1972** J. MOSEDALE *Football* v. 62 They lost the playoff in a rematch with Los Angeles. **1973** *Times* 15 May 14/8 'I didn't hit out enough,' Mrs Court said, depressed over her showing but willing to play a rematch. **1978** *N.Y. Times* 30 Mar. D22/1 He chose to give Muhammad Ali a rematch before taking on Norton.

re:mate·rialize, *v.* [RE- 5 a.] *intr.* To materialize again. Hence **re:materializa·tion**; **re:mate·rialized** *ppl. a.*

1907 W. DE MORGAN *Alice-For-Short* xxvii. 280 It was as nothing to Moses to cease to exist when hunted for, and to re-materialize when convenient. **1921** *Glasgow Herald* 29 Jan. 13/1 The fate of the Manchester Repertory and the failure of the Glasgow one to rematerialise warn us [etc.]. **1928** *Sunday Express* 8 Apr. 5/1 He comes back to each of the characters in the way in which they remember him, and ..because of their glimpses of his rematerialised self, [etc.]. **1956** R. M. LESTER *Towards Hereafter* xiv. 169 Levitation, of course, is often a form of dematerialization and rematerialization. **1959** *Times* 13 Oct. 16/4 Their lot is to be transfixed..sawn in half, dematerialized and rematerialized. **1962** *Punch* 26 Dec. 926/3 It's just a simple matter of Rematerialisation. **1978** *Sci. Amer.* Mar. 54/1 The virtual photon rematerializes into any one of a very large number of possible combinations of new particles.

‖ **remboîtage** (raṅbwatāʒ). [Fr., f. *remboîter* to re-case (a book).] (See quot. 1952.)

1952 J. CARTER *ABC for Book-Collectors* 153 *Remboîtage* means the transferring of a book from its own binding to another more elegant, more nearly contemporary, more appropriate—anyway, more desirable; or, alternatively, the transferring into a superior binding of a text more interesting or more valuable than the one for which it was made. **1968** C. P. BRACKEN *Roman Ring* iv. 27, I defy anyone to detect our remboîtages... Many early books were rebound anyway.

Rembrandt (re·mbrænt). The name of the Dutch painter *Rembrandt* (1606–69) used *absol.* or *attrib.* to designate a Darwin tulip with streaked or variegated flowers.

1902 *Jrnl. R. Hort. Soc.* XXVI. 975 Tulips, Rembrandt... A striped-flowered section raised from the 'Darwin', by MM. Krelage & Son, Haarlem. **1908** *Ibid.* XXXIII. 233 Rembrandts..are broken Darwins, and..often beautifully marked and feathered. **1911** J. WEATHERS *Bulb Bk.* 440/1 What are now known as 'Rembrandt' Tulips are broken or rectified Darwin Tulips. **1929** A. D. HALL *Bk. Tulip* v. 103 The broken forms [of Darwin tulip] are now given a class to themselves and called 'Rembrandts'. **1948** J. C. WISTER *Bulbs for Home Gardens* xi. 122 Rembrandt tulips..are striped varieties, mostly 'rectified' or 'broken' Darwins. **1974** A. HUXLEY *Plant & Planet* xviii. 197 Those tulips called Rembrandts, Bybloems and Bizarres by the fanciers, in which the flowers are streaked or feathered in another colour.

Rembrandtesque, *a.* (Earlier and later examples.)

1863 'OUIDA' *Held in Bondage* I. xi. 242 Look at that little Venus Anadyomene, Arthur, with the fire-light shining on her; quite Rembrandtesque, isn't it? **1934** *Burlington Mag.* May 213/2 The artistic Rembrandtesque pen-and-ink sketches then in vogue. **1952** M. ALLINGHAM *Tiger in Smoke* iii. 55 One of the old naphtha flares..making Rembrandtesque clouds above them. **1976** *Listener* 12 Aug. 174/1 There is not a single illustration from the Book of Job, although one might have expected it to be full of Rembrandtesque motives.

Rembra·ndtian, Rembra·ndtic, *adjs.* = REMBRANDTESQUE *a.*
1863 *Miss Jemima's Swiss Jrnl.* (1963) i. 8 The white mob-caps of the old women having quite a Rembrandtic effect. **1967** *Listener* 16 Feb. 232/1 He uses a swirl of off-white paint to give the face a Rembrandtian nose.

R.E.M.E., REME (ri·mi). Also **Reemy.** [Acronym f. initials of *R*oyal (Corps of) *E*lectrical and *M*echanical *E*ngineers.] A Corps of the British Army, formed on 1 June 1942, which handles the repair and maintenance of military machinery. Also *attrib.*
1942 *Daily Tel.* 1 Sept. 4/4 R.E.M.E.—you may pronounce it 'Reemie'—marks an important step forward in Army organisation and a break with a tradition which goes back to Crécy and Poitiers. **1943** HUNT & PRINGLE *Service Slang* 55 *Reemy*, the Royal Electrical and Mechanical Engineers, formed in 1942 for the repair of Army tanks. **1944** A. JACOB *Traveller's War* xiii. 219 It could not have functioned without R.E.M.E. and the enormous industrial undertaking in the rear which this corps operated. **1965** A. NICOL *Truly Married Woman* 16 He had had an outing.. with Higgins, a REME Lieutenant, to see some ruined, Roman fortifications. **1975** C. MOTT-RADCLYFFE *Foreign Body in Eye* xiii. 209 My son is a corporal in the REME and is working as a fitter in one of the ordnance sheds at Tel-el-Kebir. **1978** R. V. JONES *Most Secret War* xlix. 484 We had two other R.E.M.E. officers, Majors K. G. Dobson and R. A. Fell.

reme:diabi·lity. *rare.* [f. REMEDIABLE *a.*: see -ITY.] = REMEDIABLENESS.
1964 A. O. J. COCKSHUT *Unbelievers* 25 Speculations about the remediability of life..are scattered through his writings.

remedial, *a.* Add: **2.** *Educ.* **a.** Designating or pertaining to special classes, teaching methods, etc., in basic educational skills to help schoolchildren who have not achieved the proficiency necessary for them to be able to learn other subjects with their contemporaries.
1924 E. M. PAULU (*title*) Diagnostic testing and remedial teaching. **1927** *Psychol. Abstr.* I. 217 A group of 29 teachers..took a course in remedial reading... They applied to themselves the remedial techniques about which they were studying. **1942** F. SCHONELL *Backwardness in Basic Subj.* x. 204 If remedial work with backward readers is to be effective, a teacher should have..detailed information from a thorough diagnosis... Remedial methods must have therapeutic as well as pedagogical value. **1975** *Language for Life* (Dept. Educ. & Sci.) xviii. 270 Two groups of children were given remedial education, one in the Remedial Centre and one elsewhere. **1977** *Cork Examiner* 8 June 4/9 The most urgent point here was the need to eliminate overcrowded classes by reducing the pupil–teacher ratio to not more than 35 pupils per teacher and the appointment of more remedial teachers. **1978** *Times Lit. Suppl.* 1 Dec. 1394/2 Caught up in the whole nasty mess is the one other child character in the book, Manjit Mirza, a Sikh girl who shares Ronnie's remedial reading lessons.
b. Of a child: receiving or requiring remedial teaching.
1966 *New Statesman* 22 Apr. 575/2 The youngest, according to her passport, is 11 years old. She looks and acts more like a remedial eight-year-old. **1969** *Word Study* Feb. 1/1, I first became aware that something was amiss, neologically, when I heard a teacher refer to one of her students as 'a remedial reader'. **1975** *Language for Life* (Dept. Educ. & Sci.) xxv. 408 The average weekly time lay between 3 hrs. 12 mins. and 3 hrs. 22 mins. for all except the 12 year old 'Remedial' pupils. **1976** *Cumberland News* 3 Dec. 10/2 And then there was the problem of finding somewhere for the remedial children, who need special teaching.
3. Concerned with or aimed at the overcoming of muscular disabilities or postural defects by means of special exercises.
1925 H. E. STEWART *Physiotherapy* xxii. 321 Faulty postures and weight-bearing..will readily deform one [*sc.* a child] whose tissues are subnormal. It is of vital importance to discover these conditions early and institute proper remedial measures. **1943** O. F. G. SMITH *Rehabilitation, Re-Education & Remedial Exercises* i. 9 When the patient has learnt to use the appliance,..whether a piece of needle-work or a remedial apparatus, some personal responsibility should be put on him to continue the work in his own time. **1951** F. CHARLESWORTH *Chiropodial Orthopædics* viii. 132 Progressive remedial exercises, Faradism and other form[s] of physiotherapy are a necessary adjunct to the treatment. **1974** *Times* 11 Jan. 15/1 This will be discussed..at a meeting with the Councils of the Association of Occupational Therapists, the Chartered Society of Physiotherapy and the Society of Remedial Gymnasts. **1975** ARNHEIM & SINCLAIR *Clumsy Child* vi. 50/2 The most effective remedial program for the clumsy individual is one founded on the principles of psychomotor development.

remediate, *a.* Delete † *Obs.*—¹ and add further *arch.* example.
1906 G. G. COULTON tr. *Pearl* 33 And washed me in blood remediate.

reme·diate, *v.*² [Back-formation from REMEDIATION.] *trans.* To remedy or redress.
1969 *Word Study* Feb. 2/1, I encountered the phrase 'teachers *remediating* speech difficulties' (my italics again). Another patent neologism, I thought, derived obviously from a transitive weak verb *to remediate*, itself a back-formation on the analogy of the often-heard *to orientate* 'back-formed' from the noun *orientation*. **1973** *Black World* Mar. 31 Without supportive services to..remediate their academic deficiencies,..the students experienced an extremely high failure rate the first year. **1976** *Canad. Jrnl. Linguistics* Spring 92 The effect of expansion was to increase the time allowed for segment analysis, thus remediating such falling behind.

remediation. Delete *rare* and add further examples. *Esp.* the giving of remedial teaching or remedial therapy (see *REMEDIAL *a.* 2 a, 3). Freq. *attrib.*
1954 L. J. CRONBACH *Educ. Psychol.* vii. 215 (*heading*) Remediation of emotional difficulties. **1969** *Language* XLV. 599 The report was originally designed to provide descriptive information on which to base linguistic retraining or 'remediation' programs. **1970** H. OSSER in S. Rogers *Children & Lang.* (1975) v. 304 Most research has been concerned with diagnosis of problems rather than with their remediation. **1975** *Language for Life* (Dept. Educ. & Sci.) xvii. 263 The school psychological service has provided a series of in-service training, workshop courses in the assessment and 'remediation' of specific reading difficulties. **1975** ARNHEIM & SINCLAIR *Clumsy Child* vi. 50/1 Because of the inconspicuousness of symptoms and the difficulties inherent in diagnosing clumsiness, delay in remediation has..been the rule rather than the exception. **1978** M. T. ERICKSON *Child Psychopathol.* x. 220 Educational remediation is usually conducted by a teacher who has been trained in a special educational program. *Ibid.*, Most remediation teachers are employed by school systems.

remedy, *sb.* Add: **4.** Also *attrib.*
1920 *Act* 10 *Geo. V* c. 3 § 1(1), As though for the figure '4' in the column relating to the remedy allowance in respect of millesimal fineness there were substituted the figure '5'.

remeet, *v.* Add: **1.** (Further example.)
1953 J. S. HUXLEY *Evolution in Action* iii. 71 A number of forms..which then remet when the ice retreated.
2. *trans.* To meet (a person or thing) again.
1928 *Observer* 24 June 8/6 (Advt.), So tersely..does he tell his tale that within 300 pages we re-meet the classical heroes of three generations. **1970** I. PETITE *Meander to Alaska* I. viii. 77 As usual, in travelling north to Alaska, I had the feeling of remeeting spring.

remember, *v.* Add: **I. 1.** Also *transf.* Cf. *MEMORY *sb.* 1 c, d, 2 d.
1933 *Boys' Mag.* XLVII. 170/1 If two cars pass over the detectors simultaneously then right of way is given to one and the arrival of the other is 'remembered', the right of way being accorded to it as soon as the first is safely through. **1958** *Engineering* 21 Mar. 358/1 Upon playback the machine 'remembers' the original picture without loss of detail. **1980** 'D. RUTHERFORD' *Turbo* ix. 130 They bend on impact instead of breaking but the material remembers its original shape and goes back to it.
4. a. (Later examples, const. *about.*)
1847 G. P. R. JAMES *Whim* III. ix. 164 Remember about the burning of the will. **1891** W. MORRIS *News fr. Nowhere* ix. 67, I *do* remember about that strange piece of baseless folly. **1919** G. B. SHAW *Heartbreak House* I. 9 *Nurse.* Youve actually remembered about the tea! (*To Ellie*) O, miss, he didnt forget you after all!
b. (Further U.S. examples.)
1862 M. D. COLT *Went to Kansas* x. 150, I then remembered of reading of such a practice among Southern ladies. **1903** *Profitable Advertising* Nov. 500 'Do you remember of ever making a purchase as the result of an advertisement?' asked the writer. **1923** B. HECHT *Florentine Dagger* xiii. 224 She remembers dimly, she says, of striking him with a dagger. **1948** *Amer. Speech* XXIII. 237 Of the two or three thousand local [Pennsylvania Dutch] people whose speech the present writer has heard during the past seventeen years, no native has ever said, 'I remember it', but always, 'I remember of it'.
5. b. (Later example.)
1890 C. M. YONGE *Slaves of Sabinus* ii. 22 He remembered him of snow-capped Hermon.
II. 7. a. (Later examples.)
1922 JOYCE *Ulysses* 398 Would to God that foresight had remembered me to take my cloak along! **1935** E. R. EDDISON *Mistress* (1967) xiii. 229 And while he felt about for firm ground then Lessingham again, most courtly and submissive, remembering Derxis of that former passage with Alquemen.

remembering, *vbl. sb.* (Further examples.)
1918 W. STEVENS in *Poetry* (Chicago) May 63 Wait now; have no rememberings of hope, Poor penury. **1969** K. H. PRIBRAM in *Sci. Amer.* Jan. 73 (*title*) The neurophysiology of remembering.

remembrance, *sb.* Add: **7. d.** *Garden of Remembrance* (also with small initials), a garden commemorating the dead, esp. those killed in the world wars of 1914–18 and 1939–45.
1954 J. BETJEMAN *Few Late Chrysanthemums* 46 They'll catch me coming..Across the Garden of Remembrance? No, That would be blasphemy. **1959** *Listener* 22 Jan. 166/1 Here is a statue of Byron... Here are cenotaphs commemorating other philhellenes of several nations... The visit to what is now a garden of remembrance was a profoundly moving experience. **1973** J. ROSSITER *Manipulators* iv. 48 With any luck..I'll find the bastard dead and scattered over a garden of remembrance.

9. a. (Later example.)
1845 C. DICKENS *Let.* 2 Oct. (1977) IV. 396, I send you the claret jug. But for a mistake, you would have received the little remembrance almost immediately after my return from abroad.
10. *attrib.* and *Comb.*, as *remembrance-banquet, wreath*; **Remembrance Day,** the Sunday nearest to 11 Nov., kept in remembrance of those killed in the world wars of 1914–18 and 1939–45, and since 1945 combined with Armistice Day; **Remembrance Service,** a service held on Remembrance Day; **Remembrance Sunday** = *Remembrance Day*; **Remembrancetide,** the period immediately preceding Remembrance Day, considered as if part of the liturgical year.
1930 R. GRAVES *Ten Poems More* 9 A fresh remembrance-banquet to forestall The Knight turned hermit. **1921** *Times* 11 Nov. 12/2 We have received a number of appeals which may be specially associated with 'Remembrance Day'. **1929** *Radio Times* 8 Nov. 440/2 Remembrance Day, Nov. 11. Wear a Flanders Poppy. **1946** [see *Armistice Day*]. **1974** P. MCCUTCHAN *Call for Simon Shard* i. 5 The old soldiers had brought a Remembrance Day wreath. **1964** L. DEIGHTON *Funeral in Berlin* I. 312 You have an invitation. It's the Remembrance Service. **1977** *Belfast Tel.* 14 Feb. 4/6 He would like to tell these people who were sniping at the Legion that its Remembrance services would continue. **1942** C. MILBURN *Diary* 8 Nov. (1979) 157 Remembrance Sunday, and great news today! American troops have landed in North Africa. **1946** *Glasgow Herald* 31 Oct. 4/4 Remembrance Sunday, when Christians gather to remember the young and brave of two generations who died for freedom and the hope of a better world. **1954** R. MACAULAY *Let.* 7 Nov. in *Last Lett. to Friend* (1962) 175 Remembrance Sunday. A poppy on my coat, another on my car. **1977** B. PYM *Quartet in Autumn* v. 42 The only services that drew congregations of any size were Harvest Festival, Remembrance Sunday and the Carol Service at Christmas. **1970** *Sussex Life* Nov. 73/1 Remembrancetide this year will occupy the period November 2–8. **1977** *Daily Tel.* 5 Nov. 14 The 20th century has seen the creation of new commemorative rituals—and those of Remembrancetide are not the only ones. **1977** *Lancs. Life* Nov. 74/3 They have invited..a local boy who served in the RAF..to place the remembrance wreath on their memorial.

remembrancer. Add: **2.** (Further examples.) Also, a memoirist, a chronicler.
1951 [see *CONTINUITY 6]. **1957** *Times* 8 Aug. 8/2 Both [wrote] personal portraits and reminiscences. In both cases Posterity will need to bear in mind that they are not always reliable remembrancers. **1968** G. JONES *Hist. Vikings* IV. ii. 356 Byrhtnoth's brave but..foolhardy stand..found no remembrancer among the victors.

remembrancing, *vbl. sb.* (Further example.)
1952 *Essays in Criticism* II. II. 150 Many religious poems in English had a Latin refrain which gave the recurrent gesture of authority and devotional remembrancing.

remen (re·men). [Ancient Egyptian.] An ancient Egyptian measure of length (see quots.).
1934 F. PETRIE *Measures & Weights* 5 *Remen* (½ of 29·2 in.). The *Remen* doubled was the diagonal of the square cubit, 29·161 [in.]. **1959** *Chambers's Encycl.* IX. 183/1 The Egyptian royal cubit (20·63±0·2 in. or 524±5 mm)... From this cubit was formed the double remen, the length of the diagonal of a square with sides equal to the royal cubit. Thus, the double remen was equal to $\sqrt{2} \times 20{\cdot}63$ in. (29·16 in., 740·66 mm). This was the basis of the ancient Egyptian land measure. **1969** *Listener* 18 Dec. 859/3 The Royal cubit is $\sqrt{2}$ Egyptian remens, i.e. the diagonal of a 1×1 remen square. The 'Megalithic yard' is thus $\sqrt{5}$ remens, or the diagonal of a 2×1 remen rectangle.

remicle (re·mik'l). *Ornith.* [f. L. *rēmi(g-, rēmex* REMEX: see *-cle* s.v. -CULE.] A smaller outermost primary wing feather in some birds.
1887 R. S. WRAY in *Proc. Zool. Soc.* 344 [In the wild-duck's wing] the distal predigital (11) is always small and is designated the remicle. **1924** *Bull. Amer. Museum Nat. Hist.* L. 316 In the three specimens of *Gavia stellata* seen in the flesh the normal number of quills, ten large ones and the remicle, were present. **1964** A. L. THOMSON *New Dict. Birds* 665/2 In most non-passerine species there are—not counting a remicle, if present..—10 primaries in normal individuals.

re·migatory, *a. rare.* [f. L. *rēmigāt-*, ppl. stem of *rēmigāre* to row + -ORY².] Pertaining to or connected with rowing.
1911 J. MUNRO *F. J. Furnivall: a Record* p. xvii, A special providence seems to have guarded over Furnivall on his remigatory excursions.

remi·litarize (rī-), *v.* [RE- 5 a.] *trans.* To re-arm (a country or territory that has earlier been disarmed or demilitarized). So **remilitariza·tion.**
1937 *Nation* 28 Aug. 215/1 Since the remilitarization of the Reich. **1939** WEBSTER Add., *Remilitarize*.., to prepare or equip again with military forces, defenses, etc. **1944** D. THOMSON *French Foreign Policy* (Oxf. Pamphlets World Affairs LXVII) 5 In 1936..Hitler paved the way for all further aggressions by occupying and remilitarizing the left bank of the Rhine. **1969** *Daily Tel.* 5 Feb. 24/6 The explicit intention to re-militarise Sinai and encourage terrorist groups. **1976** *Survey* Summer–Autumn 13 The status quo.. trend in Soviet policy between 1964 and 1973 was obscured by..remilitarization of the stagnant economy.

remind, *v.* Add: **2. a.** Also *absol.*, and with direct speech as obj.

1891 KIPLING *Light that Failed* xiv. 291 It will recall and remind and suggest and tantalise, and in the end drive you mad. **1966** D. F. GALOUYE *Lost Perception* ii. 24 'Manuel sent the last two messages,' Gregson reminded. *Ibid.* iv. 44 Forsythe withdrew from his sightless isolation long enough to remind, 'Next week's Thanksgiving.' **1976** B. FREEMANTLE *November Man* vii. 95 'The details.. indicated criticism of the Soviet Union,' reminded Kodes.

reminding, *ppl. a.* (Earlier example.)

1872 GEO. ELIOT *Middlemarch* II. IV. xxxvii. 271 Even the pale stag seemed to have reminding glances.

remi·nding, *vbl. sb.* [f. REMIND *v.* + -ING[1].] The act of reminding; a reminder.

1836 J. S. MILL *Let.* Feb. in *Wks.* (1963) XII. 294 The things..were not done even after numerous remindings. **1865** —— *Comte* 129 Everything that he can do without the aid of incessant remindings from other thinkers, is merely provisional, and will require a thorough revision.

Remington (re·miŋtən). [The name of Eliphalet *Remington* (1793–1861) and his son Philo (1816–89), gunsmiths of Ilion, New York, the original manufacturers.] A proprietary term for a make of firearms and typewriters.

1865 S. BOWLES *Across Continent* iii. 23 Perhaps he had intuitive knowledge of our brave hearts and our innumerable Colts', Smith and Wessons', Remingtons', Ballards', and double-barreled shot-guns. **1871** W. W. GREENE *Mod. Breech-Loaders* 192 The Remington Rifle...has been extensively used in America, France, Denmark, and Austria. **1888** *Official Gaz.* (U.S. Patent Office) 23 Oct. 350/2 Type-writing machines.—Standard Typewriter Manufacturing Company, New York, N.Y... Used since 1880. 'The word "Remington".' **1895** G. B. SHAW *Let.* 27 Aug. (1965) I. 551, I typewrite on a Bar Lock; but they now all imitate the Remington type so closely that there is no telling. **1895** W. S. CHURCHILL in *Daily Graphic* 27 Dec. 4/3 The rebels, who use Remingtons, fired independently. **1897** *Sears, Roebuck Catal.* 570/2 The Remington Semi-Hammerless Single Barrel Breech Loading Shot Gun... You take no risk in buying the old and reliable Remington. **1906** *Official Gaz.* (U.S. Patent Office) 4 Dec. 1683/1 Remington Arms Company, New York, N.Y... Used ten years. *Remington...* Shotguns, Pistols, Revolvers, and Rifles. **1926** *Trade Marks Jrnl.* 19 May 1177 *Remington...* Typewriters, accounting typewriters and portable typewriters and accessories... Remington Typewriter Company..New York, U.S.A.; manufacturers. **1935** N. MARSH *Enter Murderer* xvi. 193 'Is there a typewriter?' 'There is. A Remington.' **1949** *Lubbock* (Tex.) *Morning Avalanche* 23 Feb. II. 1/1 Among the rare pistols are an 1850 double-barreled dueling pistol.. and a five-shot Remington pistol. **1959** A. K. LANG in *Alfred Hitchcock's Mystery Mag.* Feb. 77/2 The blonde found herself staring down the muzzle of his Remington. **1973** 'A. HALL' *Tango Briefing* ix. 114 A Remington ·410 across his knees..just the one shot. **1975** *Country Life* 9 Oct. 920/4 A link between typewriters and women's emancipation. The first Remingtons were produced in 1873.

reminisce, *v.* Add: **2.** Also with direct speech as obj.

1961 *Dallas Morning News* 10 Sept. VI. 6 'I bought my first dress from him when I was still a struggling young actress,' she reminisces. **1969** A. GLYN *Dragon Variation* viii. 233 'I remember when the whole thing was eighteenth century,' he reminisced. 'Chandeliers, brocades.' **1978** *Daily Tel.* 28 Aug. 3/1 'I remember the teacher asking what we wanted to be,' Signor Santo Del Bon reminisced.

reminiscence. Add: **4.** *Psychol.* An improvement in the memory or performance of something partially learned, occurring after the learning has ceased.

1913 P. B. BALLARD in *Brit. Jrnl. Psychol.* Monograph Suppl. I. II. 17 As obliviscence is a gradual process of deterioration in the capacity to revive past experiences, so is reminiscence a gradual process of improvement in that capacity. *Ibid.* 31 In the case of very young children the interval which secures maximal reminiscence seems to be three days. **1935** *Amer. Jrnl. Psychol.* XLVII. 89 The results of the two experiments..indicate that reminiscence..occurs independently of casual revival or intentional review. **1951** S. S. STEVENS *Handbk. Exper. Psychol.* xvii. 653/1 Although most of the work on reminiscence had used verbal material, the appearance of reminiscence is not restricted to verbal learning. **1978** E. GULIAN et al. in M. M. Gruneberg et al. *Practical Aspects Memory* II. 596 Training sessions following closely together produce no marked improvement in performance and..clear-cut progress shows-up only after a training gap. This finding is akin to the phenomenon of reminiscence, which is described in a wide range of learning studies.

remini·scer. = REMINISCENCER.

1966 *Punch* 30 Nov. 825/1 The revenants and reminiscers: Hearne, Tuckwell, Mozley, Gunning, and the rest—chirpy, inconsequent, lords of anecdote, abbots of unreason.

remini·scing, *vbl. sb.* [f. REMINISC(E *v.* + -ING[1].] The action of the verb REMINISCE.

a **1910** 'MARK TWAIN' *Autobiogr.* (1924) II. 204 A deal of pretty jolly reminiscing was done. **1929** E. W. SPRINGS *Above Bright Blue Sky* 239 She wanted to do a lot of reminiscing, but I cut her short.

remise, *sb.*[2] Add: **4.** A specially planted shelter for partridges. Also *attrib.*

1905 *Kynoch Jrnl.* Jan.–Mar. 45 An instance where this 'remise' system has been carried out most successfully and on a large scale. *Ibid.* 46 When the natural food is exhausted, in hard weather a few handfuls of small corn..are scattered about inside the 'remise', which gives employment to many coveys who are hard pressed for food, and they also serve as a sort of headquarters to which all partridges in the neighbourhood can retire if disturbed. **1939** *Country Life* 11 Feb. p. xxii/2 It is this danger which is also one of the dangers of laying out a partridge *remise* as part of a plantation scheme.

remish (rĭmi·ʃ), slang abbrev. of REMISSION (sense 4 b).

1958 F. NORMAN *Bang to Rights* I. 15 That is if I dont get nicked for nothing and get a few days chokey and a few days remish.

remit, *sb.* Restrict 'Chiefly *Sc.*' to senses in Dict. and add: **3. b.** (rī·mit) *N.Z.* An item submitted for consideration at a conference, etc.

1916 *Maoriland Worker* 12 July 4/7 Messrs. Hutchison and Harper moved that the Order Paper Committee put on a remit dealing with Conscription.—Carried. **1918** *Conf. United Federation of Labor* (N.Z.) 4/1 Mr. B. Martin moved the Auckland District Council remit: 'That capitation to the National Executive from the District Councils under clause 12 be reduced to 3d per member.' **1958** *N.Z. Listener* 5 Sept. 8/2 We might see that New Zealand would put a remit up to the International Board and it would be turned down. **1963** *Manawatu Standard* 9 Apr. 12/9 A Canterbury remit that the Government should appoint a Minister of Road Transport..could not meet with the general approval of the Associated Chambers of Commerce delegates in Rotorua. **1966** G. W. TURNER *Eng. Lang. in Austral. & N.Z.* viii. 174 Policies of influential bodies are a good deal determined by remits from below.

c. A set of instructions, a brief.

1963 *Guardian* 30 May 8/6 The remit given to Sir Gilbert Flemming, who is considering the possibility of the dispersal of Government departments. **1971** *New Scientist* 25 Feb. 407/2 The remit is essentially to produce a scenario of nutritional developments. **1973** M. MACKINTOSH *King & Two Queens* xv. 209 Your self-imposed remit in America was to find out..what he was covering up. **1977** *Undercurrents* June–July 12/3 The answer lies simply in the fact that the DHSS is a bureaucratic department which does not have the remit to support publications other than official government documents.

remitless (rĭmi·tlės), *a. rare.* [f. REMIT *v.* + -LESS.] Without remission; unpardoned; ceaseless.

a **1907** F. THOMPSON *Works* (1913) I. 198 Meek guides and daughters to the blinded heaven In Œdipean, remitless wandering driven.

remittance. Add: **2.** *remittance man* (further examples); also *fig.*

1903 [see *PALOUSER]. **1959** T. S. ELIOT *Elder Statesman* III. 93 Everyone would sneer at the fellow from London, The limey remittance man for whom a job was made. **1969** *Listener* 9 Jun. 42/2 I'd arrived at the end of the line already: the proclaimed remittance man of an obsolete social system. **1975** C. AIRD *Slight Mourning* vii. 69 'Last heard of in the backwoods of Queensland.'.. 'A remittance man, I'll be bound.'

remi·ttence. *rare.* [f. as REMITTENT *a.* + -ENCE; cf. F. *rémittence.*] = REMITTENCY (example in *Path.*).

1901 *Practitioner* Mar. 311 When the paroxysms return in the evening and are prolonged so that the intermission or remittence takes place in the morning, this fever may be easily mistaken for typhoid.

‖ **remittitur** (rĭmi·titʊ̈ɪ). *Law.* [a. L. *remittitur,* third pers. sing. pass. of *remittere* to REMIT.] **1.** The remission of excessive damages awarded to a plaintiff, or a formal statement of this.

1770 G. WILSON *Rep. Cases King's Courts, Westm.* I. 30 The court said plaintiff might take judgment *de melioribus damnis* where several damages are given, or enter a *remittitur.* **1792** B. J. SELLON *Pract. Courts King's Bench* I. xi. 500 Where a verdict was given for a greater sum than the amount of the damages laid in the declaration, the court will suffer amendment to be made by plaintiff, entering a *remittitur* of the *extra* sum. **1848** J. J. S. WHARTON *Law Lexicon* 579/2 *Remittitur damna,* where a jury gives greater damages than a plaintiff has declared for, it may be rectified by entering a *remittitur* for the excess; or, if a plaintiff have signed judgment for the greater sum, the court will give him leave to amend it, by entering a *remittitur* for the excess.

2. The act of sending the transcript of a case back from an appellate to a trial court for record or further work; a formal notice of this.

1794 W. TIDD *Pract. Court King's Bench* II. xli. 718 Where a writ of error determines in the Exchequer Chamber, by abatement or discontinuance, the judgment is not again in this court, till there be a *remittitur* entered. **1796** B. J. SELLON *Pract. Courts King's Bench* II. xx. 526 On the hearing, the lords either affirm or reverse the judgment on which the clerk of the Parliaments draws a *remittitur,* by which the transcript of the record is remanded into the King's Bench, with the affirmance or reversal to be entered of record. **1820** *Tomlins's Law-Dict.* (ed. 3) II. s.v. Remittitur, In cases of appeal, the Record itself, or a transcript thereof, is sent from the Court of *B.R.* to the Exchequer-Chamber, or House of Lords: when judgment is given in the superior Court, or the Writ of Error abates, or is discontinued, the record or transcript is returned (*Remittitur,* sent back), to the Court of *K.B.*, and the entry of this circumstance is termed a *Remittitur.* **1848** J. J. S. WHARTON *Law Lexicon* 579/2 *Remittitur of record,* formerly when a writ of error, in the Exchequer Chamber, abated, or was discontinued, the transcript must have been remitted, and a *remittitur* entered, before a defendant could sue out execution. **1972** *N.Y. Law Jrnl.* 10 Oct. 2/1 Motion to amend the remittitur granted, the return of the remittitur is requested and, when returned, it will be amended.

remix, *v.* Add: Hence **remi·xing** *vbl. sb.*

1956 *Nature* 10 Mar. 490/1 The undiminished fertility of the inbred plants when pollinated by bees promotes rapid remixing of genetic material under favourable conditions. **1975** *McGraw-Hill Yearbk. Sci. & Technol.* 256/1 After extraction, the interaction between the feed stream and the enriched product must be such that isotopic remixing, or scrambling, does not occur.

remnant, *sb.* Add: **2. b.** Also *spec.*, in allusion to Isa. x. 22, a small number of Jews that survives persecution, in whom future hope is vested.

1859 'L.N.R.' *Missing Link* xiii. 171 The Exiled Remnant ..refuse to snuff a candle or poke the fire, but impatiently call, 'Shuboth-guy—Shuboth-guy,' as the stoker passes. **1892** I. ZANGWILL *Childr. Ghetto* II. xv. 16 The rest of the 'remnant' that was met to save Israel looked more commonplace. **1914** J. HASTINGS *Encycl. Relig. & Ethics* VII. 607/2 The function of Judaism is to fulfil the Isaianic ideal of a missionary 'Remnant'. *Ibid.*, Judaism is to be the religion of a Remnant. **1932** C. ROTH *Hist. Marranos* i. 16 It had been only a weak remnant which had accepted baptism as the alternative to death. **1969** *Guardian* 18 Sept. 8/6 (*heading*) Germany's remnant. *Ibid.*, There are only around 30,000 Jews in Germany today, where once there were 600,000. **1972** C. RAPHAEL *Feast of Hist.* i. 32 In the immediate aftermath of the Holocaust, Jewish history.. seemed to offer a message of bleakness... In the Holy Land, the remnant faced enmity and restriction.

d. *Geomorphol.* = *RESIDUAL *sb.* 5.

1893 [see *MONADNOCK]. **1896** *Ann. Rep. State Geologist N.J. 1895* 10 This eastern belt of remnants, which are really outliers of the continuous portion of the Pensauken.., runs through Camden..and Salem counties. **1907** *Amer. Jrnl. Sci.* CLXXIV. 470 At the present time there are remaining only few traces of these old bolson surfaces. Most of these remnants have been preserved only on account of being covered by extensive lava sheets. **1942** [see *BERM 1 b].

6. *attrib.* and *Comb.*

1864 E. G. WHITE *Testimonies* (1871) I. 467 All who have a desire to draw away from God's remnant people..should have the privilege. **1885** —— *Testimony for Church* XXXII. 228 The remnant church will be brought into great trial and distress. **1905** *Westm. Gaz.* 21 Oct. 18/2 'It is not, then, a curious fact,' I said, 'that there should be so many comparatively new books on your remnant stall.' **1905** 'O. HENRY' *Trimmed Lamp* (1907) 115 Did you ever notice me leaning on the remnant counter or peering in the window of the five-and-ten? *a* **1936** KIPLING *Something of Myself* (1937) iii. 75 The *Pioneer* had made as much out of its share in this remnant-traffic as it had paid me in wages. **1972** N. ZNAMIEROWSKI *Rugmaking* 17/1 Remnant counters..are.. excellent sources.

remnantal (re·mnăntăl), *a. Geol.* [f. REMNANT *sb.* + -AL.] Of or pertaining to a remnant.

1907 *Amer. Jrnl. Sci.* CLXXIV. 470 Farther south at Paraje..and at El Paso, the same remnantal levels are noted. **1942** [see *BERM 1 b].

remobiliza·tion. [RE- 5 a.] The action of mobilizing again; a further mobilization.

1919 J. L. GARVIN *Econ. Found. Peace* viii. 152 German workers might then have the sympathy of their class in other lands to a degree making quite impossible the effective re-mobilisation of the Grand Alliance as a debt-collecting agency. **1977** J. L. HARPER *Population Biol. Plants* 392 The demand is met by remobilization of other materials.

remo·bilize, *v.* [RE- 5 a.] *trans.*

1. *Geol.* To make fluid or plastic again.

1954 R. L. PARKER tr. *Niggli's Rocks & Mineral Deposits* xiv. 519 Old deposits may be remobilized in depth and may give rise to solutions that ascend to higher levels. **1965** G. J. WILLIAMS *Econ. Geol. N.Z.* xii. 178/2 Mr Wood's descriptions seem to leave little doubt as to a genetic association of the Moke Creek greenschist and the enclosed copper ore, even though the latter must have been remobilized during metamorphism. **1971** I. G. GASS et al. *Understanding Earth* xxi. 313/1 Continental mountain ranges are..principally composed of original continental crust (in great part remobilized).

2. *Mil.* To recall to active service.

1963 *Times* 26 Feb. 7/7 The prosecutor, M. Gerthoffer, who is a magistrate remobilized with the rank of general, wound up his two-hour final speech.

re·model, *sb. Arch.* [f. the vb.] The act of modelling or constructing a building again; a remodelled building.

1956 *Archit. Rev.* CXX. 119/3 Rethinking is needed on the difference between surface grime on a noble building and a cut-rate remodel which might well show a fundamental lack of architectural conviction or emotive power. **1974** R. C. DENNIS *Conversations with Corpse* ii. 15 A house, French Regency, I think... I imagine it's a remodel. **1978** *Tucson Mag.* Dec. 90/3 In a remodel (existing house) we have to be neater, and work slower.

remonetization. (Earlier U.S. example.)

1877 *Rep. U.S. Monetary Comm. 1876* (44th Congr., 2nd Sess., Senate Rep. No. 703) I. 90 It is not a particular silver coin, the remonetization of which is demanded, but it is the metal silver, in whatever denominations of coin the law may authorize.

remonetize, *v.* (Earlier U.S. example.)
1877 *N.Y. Tribune* 16 Nov. 8/1 They regard the ultimate passage of a bill of some kind, remonetizing silver, as a certainty.

remonstrantly, *adv.* (Earlier example.)
1872 GEO. ELIOT *Middlem.* IV. lxxvi. 240 'But when she saw the good that might come of staying ——' said Dorothea, remonstrantly.

remonstrate, *v.* Now usu. with pronunc. (re·mǫ́nstrēɪt).

remontant, *a.* and *sb.* Add: Also used of strawberry plants bearing fruit for a longer period than usual. (Later examples.)
1923 J. H. MCFARLAND *Rose in Amer.* ii. 21 The Hybrid Perpetual roses are also called Remontant. Both designations are misnomers so far as bloom is concerned. **1965** E. B. LE GRICE *Rose Growing Complete* xii. 170 Single, coarse, once-flowering climbers had, at least a thousand years ago, become many-petalled, or dwarf, or remontant (repeat-flowering). **1968** R. HAY *Gardener's Round* 78 Plant the 'remontant' or perpetual strawberries to have a crop in the autumn. **1969** *Oxf. Bk. Food Plants* 74/2 The perpetuals or remontants are an interesting group [of strawberries], which flower successively during the summer and produce fruit from July till October. **1979** *Guardian* 13 Oct. 15/5 Cover remontant strawberries with cloches.

remo·ralize, *v.* [RE- 5 b.] *trans.* To make moral again; to re-instil with morals. So **remo:raliza·tion.**
1967 *Guardian* 16 Oct. 6/5 Violence and pain still provide an evil satisfaction which the remoralisation of sex has not yet exorcised. **1974** *Daily Tel.* 21 Oct. 6/8 We are able to remoralise whole groups and classes of people, undoing the harm done..by permissiveness in television, in films, on bookstalls. *Ibid.* 21 Oct. 6/8 We shall need intellectual as well as moral courage to grapple with the dilemmas inherent in the remoralisation of public life.

remorse, *sb.* Add: **7.** *remorse-stricken* adj.
1973 M. AMIS *Rachel Papers* 56, I couldn't resist taking a certain fascinated pleasure in his remorse-stricken face.

remo·rtgage, *v.* [RE- 5 a.] *trans.* To mortgage anew; to change the terms of a mortgage on (a property). So **remo·rtgage** *sb.*; **re-mo·rtgaging** *vbl. sb.*
1960 *Farmer & Stockbreeder* 15 Mar. 125/1, I have tried to raise capital by various means, including re-mortgaging, but without success. **1961** BENJAMIN & ATHOLL *How to borrow Money* vii. 77 A practical alternative to offering a second mortgage as the security may be to re-mortgage the house. *Ibid.*, The probability is that you have had the house for a number of years so that if you could effect the re-mortgage, the amount you would have to repay on your present mortgage would be substantially less. *Ibid.* 78 The comparative costs of re-mortgaging and raising a loan on a second mortgage..should be compared. **1976** *Milton Keynes Express* 25 June 33/5 (Advt.), Deposit loans, personal loans, remortgages, second mortgages, business finance. **1977** *S. Wales Echo* 18 Jan. 11/1 (Advt.), Building society re-mortgages and second mortgages arranged. **1978** *Cornish Guardian* 27 Apr. 34/2 (Advt.), Also available—First mortgages, re-mortgages and personal loans for tenants.

remote, *a.* (and *sb.*) and *adv.* Add: **A.** *adj.* **3. f.** Situated, occurring, or performed at a distance (not necessarily great); *remote control*, control of apparatus, etc., at a distance; also (with hyphen) *attrib.*; so *remote-controlled* ppl. adj., *remote-control* vb. trans. and intr. (also *fig.*).
1904 L. ANDREWS *Electricity Control* i. 8 It is probable..that for installations of a few thousand horse-power only, some simple method of mechanical remote control will be generally preferred. **1920** *Wireless World* 7 Aug. 356/1 Pilot's and mechanic's cockpits are not very roomy compartments and therefore it has become standard practice to employ 'remote control', that is to say the main portion of the wireless apparatus..are [*sic*] fitted in one or two boxes which can be suspended in any convenient part of the main fuselage of the machine; these circuits being controlled by a small unit..which may be fitted on the dashboard of the machine. **1933** *Times* 16 May 9/2 A remote control device for the selection of several alternative wireless programmes will soon be made available to the public. **1943** *Gloss. Terms Electr. Engin.* (*B.S.I.*) 84 *Remote-controlled sub-station*, a substation the operation of which is controlled at a distance. **1956** *Nature* 28 Jan. 160/2 The remote-handling device for removal of the collectors containing the enriched product without exposure to air. **1957** *Economist* 9 Nov. 525/2 Because of their radioactivity, none of the materials can be handled normally. All operations are carried out painstakingly by remote control. **1961** G. MILLERSON *Telev. Production* iii. 28 (*caption*) Lens turret,..rotated by rear handle..or remote switching. **1966** P. O'DONNELL *Sabre-Tooth* xv. 203 Two transmitters..were remote-controlled from the H.Q. section. **1967** COX & GROSE *Organization & Handling Bibl. Rec. by Computer* iv. 95 The use of these direct access devices also paves the way for remote-terminal inquiry. **1970** O. DOPPING *Computers & Data Processing* vi. 96 Remote processing of data..normally requires multiprogramming. In remote processing, input and output goes via communication lines. **1970** 'B. MATHER' *Break in Line* xv. 187, I wondered if he were still in Calcutta or was remote-controlling from London. **1970** *New Scientist* 6 Aug. 286/1 The study defines remote-access computing as the use of computers where the main computer installation is at a distance from the user, who employs a terminal device to communicate with the computer over telephone or other links. **1972** *Times* 11 Sept. (Botswana, etc., Suppl.) p. vi/2 (*caption*) Remote sensing, a development of aerial photography, can point to possible indications of mineral deposits. **1973** C. W. GEAR *Introd. Computer Sci.* iv. 162 Many computer systems have low speed input/output devices, called remote terminals, attached to the central computer. **1974** *Harrods Christmas Catal.* 69/1 Remote-control Gantry Crane, battery operated... 28″ high. £8·50. **1977** *Nature* 6 Jan. 34/2 Until this year, the most accurate means of studying the atmospheric pressure at the surface of Mars were provided by remote-sensing from fly-by or orbiting spacecraft. **1978** R. V. JONES *Most Secret War* viii. 68 The German Navy was said to have developed remote-controlled rocket-driven gliders of about three metres span. **1981** *Oxford Jrnl.* 15 May (Advt.), 20″ Colour TV. Remote control. *Ibid.*, 14″ Colour Portable TV with infra-red remote control hand unit.
6. *not the remotest*: also *ellipt.*
1928 D. L. SAYERS *Unpleasantness at Bellona Club* xvii. 205 'Was the quantity marked on the bottle?' 'I haven't the remotest. You'd better ask her.' **1969** E. STEWART *Heads* (1970) 94 'Why do you think he was trailing Father Fields?' 'I haven't the remotest,' Greg said.
B. *sb.* **c.** *U.S. Broadcasting.* An outside broadcast (see quots.). Cf. *NEMO.
1937 *Amer. Speech* XII. 100 A *remote pickup* or simply a *remote* means a program brought from some point other than station studios. **1937**, etc. [see *NEMO]. **1947** *Billboard* 1 Nov. 17 First Remote on War Dead's Arrival... What is believed to be the first video broadcast by a remote unit from a moving object will be essayed tomorrow. **1962** *Sat. Rev.* 1 Sept. 17/2 Accent is not only a low-budget show; it is a 'remote'. A 'remote' shoots on location with video-cruiser facilities, as distinct from a studio show. **1967** *Boston Globe* 30 Mar. 3/1 CBS said in future days Cronkite may be seen in some news remotes while Zenker remains at the desk. **1976** *Listener* 15 July 53/1 'Remotes' are what American television technicians call outside broadcasts.
C. *adv.* In comb. with a pple. forming an adj., = *REMOTELY *adv.* 2 b.
1943, etc. Remote-controlled [see sense A. 3 f above]. **1959** H. BARNES *Oceanogr. & Marine Biol.* iv. 200 Various systems could be devised, some complicated and expensive using remote-indicating compasses, but we have merely mounted an ordinary liquid compass in the field of view of the camera. **1976–7** *Sea Spray* (N.Z.) Dec./Jan. 94 The unit is available either directly mounted to a Borg–Warner marine reverse transmission unit or remote mounted and coupled to engine or reverse gear by a universal joint shaft.

remotely, *adv.* Add: **2. b.** At or from a distance (not necessarily great). Freq. in comb. with a pple. forming an adj.
1957 *Railway Mag.* Nov. 758/2 The remotely-controlled signalbox, normally unstaffed, is retained. **1967** *Jane's Surface Skimmer Systems 1967–68* 122 Take-off (4 hp continuous) for remotely-driven accessory box. **1971** *Physics Bull.* July 395/3 The appropriate parts of the projector are light proof and the shutter is operated remotely so that photographic records may be taken in a lit room. **1973** *BBC Handbk. 1974* 246/2 The network control rooms handle..remotely controlled studios, such as the news studio at Westminster.

remoteness. Add: **b.** A remote region; = REMOTE *sb.* b. *nonce-use.*
1880 'MARK TWAIN' *Tramp Abroad* xxxii. 345 Switzerland, and many other regions which were unvisited and unknown remotenesses a hundred years ago, are in our days a buzzing hive of restless strangers every summer.

remo·tivate, *v.* [RE- 5 a.] *trans.* To motivate anew. Hence **remo·tivating** *vbl. sb.* and *ppl. a.*
1974 *Listener* 28 Feb. 271/1 They try, in a favourite word of probation officers, to 'remotivate' men who have been through the penal system. **1976** *Archivum Linguisticum* VII. 28 Writers tend to be consistent with themselves if not with each other, although rarer forms are probably remotivated on each occasion. **1977** *Spare Rib* Jan. 8/1 Towards the end of my career, interviewers were invited to a Remotivating Lecture with supervisors and regional controllers. **1977** D. MORRIS *Manwatching* 184 (*caption*) Remotivating Actions succeed by replacing a companion's unwanted mood with a new, more attractive mood.

remou: see *REMOUS.

‖ **remoulade** (remulād). *Cookery.* Also **ré-.** [a. F. *rémoulade.*] A French salad dressing (see quots.).
1845 E. ACTON *Mod. Cookery* iv. 135 (*heading*) Remoulade. This differs little from an ordinary salad dressing. **1861** MRS. BEETON *Bk. Househ. Managem.* 241 (*heading*) Remoulade, or French salad-dressing. *Ibid.*, 4 eggs, ½ tablespoonful of made mustard, salt and cayenne to taste, 3 tablespoonfuls of olive-oil, 1 tablespoonful of tarragon or plain vinegar... Green remoulade is made by using tarragon vinegar instead of plain. **1877** E. S. DALLAS *Kettner's Bk. of Table* 376 *Remoulade*..may be..described as a Mayonnaise made with hard-boiled yolks of eggs. **1939** A. SIMON *Conc. Encycl. Gastron.* I. 46/1 *Rémoulade*, a salad dressing consisting of the yolks of hard-boiled eggs, oil and vinegar, salt and pepper. Mustard is sometimes added. **1961** *Listener* 20 Apr. 719/2 There is always a little of it [*sc.* tarragon] in smooth French sauces, such as Béarnaise, tartare, and rémoulade. **1966** N. FREELING *Dresden Green* I. 21 He..stopped at the dairy..for a piece of cheese, celery remoulade salad. **1978** G. VIDAL *Kalki* iii. 79 The preparation of a shrimp remoulade.

re·mould, *sb.* [f. the vb.] A worn tyre on to which a new tread has been moulded. Also *attrib.* Cf. *RETREAD *sb.*
1956 C. WILLCOCK *Death at Flight* iii. 35, I asked the firm's transport department to change both front tyres not three weeks ago. And I told them no remoulds. **1960** *Farmer & Stockbreeder* 29 Mar. 21/1 (Advt.), New and remould tyres on terms! Also the new extra grip remould for town and country use. **1972** *Practical Motorist* Oct. 157/1 A remould uses the carcass of a tyre that has already done a lifetime of service. **1973** *Times* 28 Apr. 4/2 Mr Assender claimed yesterday that £6·50 was a fair price for a 'remould quality' 145-13 tyre. **1976** *Drive* Sept.–Oct. 77/1 *Remould* or *remould quality tyres* should by now have disappeared from the forecourt vocabulary, being replaced by the two official designations.

remount, *sb.* **1. a.** (Earlier example.)
1781 R. F. GREVILLE *Diary* 5 Aug. (1930) 11 This was a favorable opportunity to take a ride, & try a new mare I had lately purchased, & one of a remount, made within a short time of my Appointment.

† **remous** (rəmū·). *Aeronaut. Obs.* Pl. remous (with *erron. sing.* remou). [Fr., = 'eddy, ship's wash'.] (See quot. 1916.)
1911 *Aeroplane* 8 June 8/1 Brooklands has three constant *remous* or eddies, two downward and one upward. *Ibid.*, The only way to get ——'s 'bus into the air is to 'taxi' to the sewage farm *remou* and get pulled off the ground by it! **1914** G. HAMEL *Flying* viii. 167 An attempt has been made, by a well known military pilot, to classify remous as 'rollers', 'half-rollers', and 'wulliwas'. **1915** G. BACON *All about Flying* vi. 106 The little eddies known as 'remous' are more entertaining than annoying. **1916** H. BARBER *Aeroplane Speaks* 140 *Remou*, a local movement or condition of the air which may cause displacement of an aeroplane.

removability. (Earlier examples.)
1789 *Deb. Congress U.S.* 16 June (1834) 464, I am not satisfied that removability shall be acquired only by impeachment. *Ibid.* 6 Aug. (1834) 679 The Senate..insisted on the amendment to the Treasury bill, respecting the removability of the Secretary by the President.

removal. 4. (Further *attrib.* examples.)
1939 M. B. LOWNDES *Let.* 23 Oct. (1971) 183 The removal man..told me some interesting things about the art of moving and storing furniture. **1962** J. G. BENNETT *Witness* xviii. 218 One of the removal men asked him if a sofa was to go 'up the apples'. **1973** *Times* 28 Dec. 16/1 (Advt.), Assistance with removal expenses if necessary. **1974** M. GILBERT *Flash Point* xiii. 115 They wore corduroy trousers and jackets belted at the waist... They looked like removal men. **1979** *Homes & Gardens* June 77/2 They used his pension to buy an old removal van.

removalist (rĭmū·vălist). *Austral.* [f. REMOVAL + -IST.] A person or firm engaged in household or business removals.
1959 S. J. BAKER *Drum* (1960) 139 *Removalist*, a person or firm engaging in the shifting of household or business effects. **1966** —— *Austral. Lang.* (ed. 2) i. 4 There is a good deal of evidence to suggest that..*removalist* (a person or firm engaged in moving furniture, etc.)..is an Australian original. **1971** *Classified Telephone Directory* (Brisbane) Pink Pages 251/1 (Advt.), Approved Government contractor for removals and storage. A. F. Palmer Removalists. **1972** D. WILLIAMSON *Removalists* (1973) 61 A self assured removalist in a dust coat enters. The dustcoat is emblazoned with the emblem 'Aussie Removalists'.

remove, *sb.* Add: **2. c.** (Earlier example.)
1771 B. FRANKLIN in M. Farrand *Benjamin Franklin's Mem.* (1949) 124/1 Every Man at the first Remove, found under his Plate an Order on a Banker.
6. d. *Printing.* The number of sizes by which the type of a footnote or side-note is smaller than that of the text; hence, the note itself.
1890 C. T. JACOBI *Printing* v. 70 Footnotes are nearly always set in type two sizes (or removes, as they are called) smaller than text... Side-notes are frequently put into three or four removes smaller. **1898** J. SOUTHWARD *Mod. Printing* I. xxxvii. 224 The usual type for notes is two or three removes from the text. **1934** V. STEER *Printing Design & Layout* xvi. 293 Footnotes are explanatory notes at the foot of the page usually set in type two removes from the size used for the text. **1960** G. A. GLAISTER *Gloss. Bk.* 345/2 *Removes*, quotations or notes set at the foot of a page and in smaller type than that of the text.

remove, *v.* Add: **I. 1. f.** *Cricket.* Of a bowler or ball: to dismiss (a batsman).
1969 *Wisden's Cricketers' Almanack* 300 Underwood..accounted for Redpath and Walters, each getting an inside edge to the ball that removed him. **1976** *Eastern Even. News* (Norwich) 22 Dec. 14/2 With the fourth ball of his second over Lever removed Venkataraghavan, the ball brushing the batsman's glove before passing through to wicketkeeper Alan Knott. **1977** *Evening Post* (Nottingham) 24 Jan. 16/3 Selvey removed Sivaramakrishnan with his fourth ball.

‖ **remplaçant** (rañplasañ). Also fem. **-e.** [Fr.] One who replaces another; a substitute.
1850 LADY EDDISBURY *Let.* 23 Mar. in N. Mitford *Ladies of Alderley* (1938) 280 At 5 Macaulay sent word he was too ill to come, Ed. could get no remplaçant & so at ¼ to 8, our dinner having dwindled, we sent for Mama. **1880** E. W. HAMILTON *Diary* 23 May (1972) I. 14 The defence of the Government is..that as he [*sc.* Sir B. Frere] is more conversant than any '*remplaçant*' could be with the important question of confederation, he had better be left to carry that through. **1915** W. J. LOCKE *Jaffery* xiii. 177 'We've settled nothing about a remplaçante for Mrs. Considine.'.. 'No one can replace Mrs. Considine.'

‖ **remskoen** (re·mskun). *S. Afr.* Also reimschoon, remschoen, riemschoen, rimschoen; pl. also **-e.** [Afrikaans:—Du.

remschoen, f. *rem* brake + *schoen* SHOE.] = SKID *sb.* 3 a. Also *fig.*

See J. Smuts et al. *Voorloper* (1976) for additional variant forms.

1816 G. BARKER *Diary* 13 Feb. (MS.) in J. Smuts et al. *Voorloper* (1976) 671 My box was set upon the rim-schoen to keep it dry. **1822** W. J. BURCHELL *Trav. Southern Afr.* I. 151 The remschoen (lock-shoe or skid), is a log of wood, generally about eight inches square, and nearly two feet long, having a groove in it to receive the felly of the wheel. **1835** A. STEEDMAN *Wanderings & Adventures in S. Afr.* I. i. ii. 121 On regaining the track, we found the *reimschoon*, or iron slipper, which had fallen from the waggon, lying in the road. **1898** *Cape Argus* 2 Feb. 36, I am pleased to find that my frequent allusion to the backward element in the legislative Council as a *riemschoen party* has gone home. **1912** *East London Dispatch* 2 May 5 Riemschoen Party.—The name applied a few years back to that party in Cape politics which appeared to be averse from progress; the word Riemschoen is applied in other directions with the same meaning, e.g. 'Riemschoen Districts'. **1949** L. G. GREEN *In Land of Afternoon* x. 126 Voortrekker wagons were equipped with wooden axles and the *remskoen* instead of brakes. **1957** *Cape Times* 8 Aug. 9/1 The wagons..with *remskoene* on, slithered down the steep slopes.

‖ **remuage** (rəmuaʒ). *Wine-making.* [Fr., lit. 'moving about'.] The periodic turning or shaking of bottled wine (esp. champagne) to move sediment towards the cork before disgorgement.

1926 P. M. SHAND *Bk. Wine* v. 154 The bottles are now stacked in wooden racks..for the delicate operation of *remuage*. **1935** SCHOONMAKER & MARVEL *Compl. Wine Bk.* i. 34 Here takes place the curious process known as the 'shaking', or *remuage*. **1958** D. MORRIS *French Vineyards* ii. 34 When the *remuage* is finished, the bottles are left in darkness. **1967** A. LICHINE *Encycl. Wines & Spirits* 430/2 *Remuage* (moving around) is a term used in the process of making Champagne. Bottles placed in specially built racks are turned or shaken a little every day for about four months before they are shipped, so that the sediment may move down towards the cork. **1977** T. HEALD *Just Desserts* viii. 187 Along the walls were countless bottles top downwards in racks 'Ready for the *remuage*... Gets the sediment down to the cork.'

‖ **remuda** (rəmū·dă). [Amer. Sp., a. Sp., exchange, replacement.] A herd or collection of saddle-horses kept for remounts.

1892 *Dialect Notes* I. 251 *Remuda*, a 'bunch' of horses, about a score. Usually applied to geldings only. **1903** A. ADAMS *Log of Cowboy* 9 The *remuda*, under Bill Honeyman as horsewrangler, numbered a hundred and forty-two, ten horses to the man. **1907** S. E. WHITE *Arizona Nights* v. 92 In a moment the first of the remuda came into view, trotting forward with the free grace of the unburdened horse. **1924** W. M. RAINE *Troubled Waters* xi. 113 Presently he got up and strolled toward the remuda. **1927** *Blackw. Mag.* Nov. 650/1 In the feeble flare remudas keep on passing. **1955** R. HOBSON *Nothing too Good* vii. 61, I knew this was the horse remuda, the advance guard of the drive. **1972** T. A. BULMAN *Kamloops Cattlemen* ii. 15 They usually brought with them a pretty fair *remuda* of horses.

‖ **remueur** (rəmuœ̄r). *Wine-making.* [Fr., lit. 'mover'.] One who engages in *remuage* (see quots.).

1926 P. M. SHAND *Bk. Wine* v. 154 The *remueur's* task is gradually to work down all the sediment. **1965** O. A. MENDELSOHN *Dict. Drink & Drinking* 279 *Remueur*, the craftsman who daily twists and slightly shakes the bottles containing champagne in the making. **1976** N. ROBERTS *Face of France* xxv. 229 The man who does the tilting and turning [of champagne bottles] is called a *remueur*... He can handle 30,000 bottles a day.

remu·ster, *v.* orig. *Services'.* [RE- 5 a.] *intr.* **a.** with pass. sense. To be assigned to other duties. **b.** for *refl.* To assemble again. Hence **remu·stering** *vbl. sb.*

1942 *R.A.F. Jrnl.* 3 Oct. 13 Because Bill Snooks is unfit for air crew duties, he should be allowed to re-muster to..a sedentary trade. *Ibid.* 14 A.C. 2 So-and-So has certain qualifications which make him suitable for re-mustering or training. **1963** *Times* 5 June 14/1 No. 500 (County of Kent) Squadron, Royal Auxiliary Air Force, disbanded in 1957, will remuster for one day to receive its squadron standard from Lord Avon. **1966** *Punch* 6 July 16 Modern football is a managers' game... Attack is based on the counter which passes the opposing defence before it can remuster after its own attack. **1977** 'J. HERRIOT' *Vet in Spin* (1978) xviii. 166 Normally when an aircrew is grounded he remusters on the ground staff, but yours is a reserved occupation.

remu·tiny, *v.* [RE- 5 a.] *intr.* To mutiny again.

1895 HARDY *Jude* I. iii. 20 He anxiously descended.. trying not to think of..the captain with the bleeding hole in his forehead, and the corpses round him that remutinied every night on board the bewitched ship.

Remy Martin (remi martæ̃n). Also **Rémy Martin.** [Name of the shippers.] The proprietary name of a cognac; a drink of this.

[**1951** T. E. CARLING *Compl. Bk. Drink* v. 42 Principal Cognac Producers..Remy Martin.] **1961** C. WILLOCK *Death in Covert* i. 9 A large shot of Rémy Martin in a balloon glass. **1963** *Official Gaz.* (U.S. Patent Office) 26 Feb. TM 137/1 *Remy Martin* for Cognac. First use 1884. **1965** L. MEYNELL *Double Fault* I. iii. 29 Evelyn Barker had a Rémy Martin in front of her. **1965** P. D. WALL *Trio* 1966) iv. 55 He promptly loaded his briefcase with Pernod and Remy Martin. **1975** D. BLOODWORTH *Clients of Omega* xxv. 242 Sipping his Rémy Martin with its lacing of java. **1976** *Trade Marks Jrnl.* 14 Apr. 783/2 Remy Martin.. Brandy. E. Remy Martin and Co... 29th August, 1973.

remytho·logize, *v.* [RE- 5 b, after *DEMYTHOLOGIZE *v.*] *trans.* To provide with a new mythological system; to reinterpret the elements of (an older mythology) in terms of a newer one. Hence **remythologiza·tion.**

1964 K. G. GRUBB *Layman looks at Church* v. 156 The Bible..has to be 'demythologised' and then remythologised. **1973** R. SLOTKIN *Regeneration through Violence* ii. 36 Both [myth and art] serve as means of ordering and explaining a chaotic and threatening environment. The remythologization of the West began with attempts by French and Spanish Jesuits and English Puritans to order the chaos of the New World. **1974** *Canadian-Amer. Slavic Stud.* VIII. 492 The updating, transformation and 'remythologization' of these legends constituted a form of justification of the validity of their world-view. **1976** H. MONTEFIORE in *Christian Believing* 148, I may expect to 'translate' or 'remythologize' its thought forms and imagery.

Renaissance. Add: Also with small initial.

1. c. (Further examples.)

1842 QUEEN VICTORIA *Jrnl.* 14 Sept. (1980) 37 We..saw the fine greenhouse the Duke has built, all in stone, in the Renaissance style. **1930** R. FRY *Let.* 12 Sept. (1972) II. 650 [Montrésor] has..a very ambitious and rather good Renaissance Gothic church. It's odd what a really good and convenient style that makes—in fact it does Gothic much better with less fuss than Gothic itself. **1963** A. LUBBOCK *Austral. Roundabout* 190 Airy, Renaissance-style stucco arches. **1976** *Early Music* IV. 512/2 (Advt.), Renaissance viols from 16th-century models. **1980** I. MURDOCH *Nuns & Soldiers* i. 40 A programme of Renaissance music.

d. Special Combs. **Renaissance humanism** = HUMANISM 4; **Renaissance man,** one who exhibits the virtues of an idealized man of the Renaissance; also *fig.*

1906 W. H. WOODWARD *Stud. Educ. Renaissance* vii. 128 That the Frenchmen in their King's train should be profoundly impressed with the Renaissance man as they found him declared in Rodrigo Borgia, and his enigmatic son, in Ludovico Sforza or Ercole d'Este, is no cause for wonder. **1948** W. K. FERGUSON *Renaissance in Hist. Thought* iii. 71 Bayle..interpreted Renaissance humanism as an enlightened revolt against barbarism. *Ibid.* v. 128 The discontented rebels against the restrictions of contemporary bourgeois society..took the lead in the idealization of the Renaissance man, combining the cult of genius with that of free, egoistic personality. **1955** P. O. KRISTELLER *Classics & Renaissance Thought* i. 10 Renaissance humanism was not as such a philosophical tendency or system, but rather a cultural and educational program which emphasized and developed an important but limited area of studies. **1970** E. PACE *Saberlegs* (1971) xiv. 132, I knew your father... A fine man. So many-sided. What I believe you would call a Renaissance man. **1975** *Language* LI. 443 Renaissance humanism was responsible for the most successful system of syntactic analysis to be conceived prior to the advent of explicit syntactic theorizing in the 20th century. **1977** *Time* 8 Aug. 32/3 At 50, Hood is the Renaissance man of sailing; he designed, cut the sails and outfitted *Independence*, the first man in history to control every aspect of a 12-tonner from drawing board to helm.

2. a. (Further examples.)

1925, etc. [see *Negro Renaissance* s.v. *NEGRO 7]. **1969** A. COCKBURN in Cockburn & Blackburn *Student Power* 18 The astonishing works of Mao Tse Tung..bear witness to the flowering of the May 4 Movement which..has justly been called the Chinese Renaissance. **1969** *Physics Bull.* June 221/1 The 'renaissance' in optics, one of the oldest disciplines in physics, has been brought about mainly by the advent of the laser. **1973** *Black World* Sept. 95 Arna Bontemps was not of the 'Harlem Renaissance'... His first novel and his poems..appeared just when..the Renaissance flopped. **1975** *Nature* 3 Apr. 391/1 A renaissance occurred in 1969 when Adler proved that bacteria have specific chemoreceptors.

Hence **Renai·ssancer,** one who participates in a renaissance; = next; **Renai·ssancist,** an advocate or student of a renaissance; also *attrib.* or as *adj.*

1895 J. M. FALKNER *Lost Stradivarius* 261 Neo-Platonism ..has enthralled..many minds from Proclus and Julian to Augustine and the Renaissancists. **1899** G. B. SHAW *Let.* 17 Oct. (1972) II. 113 The mosque [of Sulieman]..is a successful attempt to take St Sophia and give it refined grandeur in the spirit of Brunelleschi and the early dignified Renaissancers. **1949** Renaissancer [see *BRAHMSIAN *a.* and *sb.*]. **1973** *Compar. Stud. Soc. & Hist.* XV. 473 That a near-century of scholarship..should fail indeed to validate even the concept of a Renaissance, would appear to have little if any bearing on..the prosperity of the guild of Renaissancists in our time. *Ibid.* 478 In characteristic Renaissancist fashion.

renaissant, *a.* Add: **2.** = RENASCENT *a.*

1972 *Times* 3 Jan. 15 Rapidly rising output and renaissant business confidence and investment are normally a time at which profits rise. **1972** E. LONGFORD *Wellington* II. xxi. 331 This was all very difficult for a renaissant Tory party which meant to win and win soon.

renal, *a.* Add: **2.** *renal dialysis*, dialysis performed artificially as a substitute for normal kidney function; freq. *attrib.* to denote a device to do this; *renal dwarfism, infantilism, osteodystrophy, rickets*, osteodystrophy due to the failure of the kidneys to convert dietary vitamin D to a more active form.

1912 O. MAY in *Univ. Coll. Hosp. Mag.* II. 99 (*heading*) A case of 'renal infantilism'. **1920** H. BARBER in *Lancet* 3 Jan. 18/1 Until some standard text-book gives a full account of this condition it is not easy to select a suitable name; but as the kidney disease not infrequently has a very insidious onset, and many of the cases seek advice for the first time for want of development or bone deformity, some name such as renal dwarfism may be used. **1926** G. V. ASHCROFT in *Jrnl. Bone & Joint Surg.* VIII. 279 Renal rickets is a disease not mentioned in medical text-books. *Ibid.* 288 It is to the association of the typical clinical picture, the typical X-ray picture, and deficient renal function that the term Renal Rickets has been applied. **1929** THURSFIELD & PATERSON *Garrod's Dis. Children* (ed. 2) iii. 123 The primary cause of renal rickets is the inability of the diseased kidneys properly to excrete phosphorus. **1930** *Lancet* 10 May 1002/2 Two conditions associated with bone deformities have been differentiated from late rickets—namely, cœliac rickets and renal rickets. *Ibid.*, Cases of cœliac rickets and renal infantilism only occasionally show rickets. *Ibid.*, Rickets occasionally complicates renal dwarfism. **1943** LIU & CHU in *Med.* XXII. 103 The term 'renal osteodystrophy' seems to be a suitable generic name to include cases of osseous disorder associated with renal insufficiency, while the exact nature of the pathological process in the skeleton is still undetermined. **1957** *Brit. Med. Bull.* XIII. 57/2 The terms 'renal dwarfism', 'renal infantilism' and 'renal rickets', although obviously not invariably applicable, were apt in their original use. **1960** *Jrnl. Amer. Med. Assoc.* 24 Dec. 2124/1 Renal dialysis proved successful in treating previously intractable heart failure. **1962** *Lancet* 2 June 1169/1 More common..is the form associated with renal failure which was at one time called 'renal rickets'..but which is now more elegantly referred to as 'renal osteodystrophy'. **1963** *Ibid.* 5 Jan. 16/1 Renal-dialysis units mostly use complex and powerful artificial kidneys which require experienced surgical, medical, and biochemical supervision. **1974** *Times* 17 Apr. 2/8 If kidneys for transplant were available many people maintained by expensive renal dialysis machines could be given a fuller life and many of the 5,000 who die each year from kidney failure could be saved.

renardite (rĕnā·ɹdəit). *Min.* [a. F. *renardite* (A. Schoep 1928, in *Bull. de la Soc. Française de Min.* LI. 247), f. the name of A. F. *Renard* (1842–1903), of the University of Ghent: see -ITE[1].] A hydrated basic phosphate of lead and uranium, $Pb(UO_2)_4(PO_4)_2(OH)_4.7H_2O$, found as minute, yellow orthorhombic crystals.

1929 *Amer. Mineralogist* XIV. 244 Renardite... Found as minute crystals with quartz, torbernite and clay from the Kasolo Mine, Katanga, Belgian Congo. **1956** [see *DEWINDTITE]. **1971** *Mineral Abstr.* XXII. 267/1 The geological, mineralogical, and metallogenic character of the uraniferous schists of the Salamanca province of western Spain are described... Secondary minerals are represented by gummite,..renardite [etc.].

renascence. **1.** (Later examples.)

1912 E. ST. V. MILLAY in F. Earle *Lyric Yr.* 185 Renascence... O God, I cried, give me new birth, And put me back upon the earth! **1973** *Nature* 20 July 184/3 *The Serengeti Lion*..has greater significance in that it reflects the renascence of animal study in Africa.

rena·tionalization. [RE- 5 b.] The action of removing (a formerly nationalized industry, etc.) from private ownership and bringing it under national control again.

1923 W. P. LIVINGSTONE *Galilee Doctor* IV. ii. 250 It had given them a charter of renationalization. **1957** *Economist* 2 Nov. 437/1 For months the threat of renationalisation kept steel shares subdued and they have been consistent laggards in the market. **1958** *Engineering* 28 Feb. 271/2 Steel leaders are hardening in their opposition to re-nationalisation. **1971** *Guardian* 5 Mar. 13/5 The campaign for 'Renationalisation without compensation'.

rena·tionalize, *v.* [RE- 5 b.] **1.** *absol.* To reinvest with national character.

1927 *Scots Observer* 26 Feb. 15/3 Professor M'Fadyen,.. has given us..a book,..based on his rich experience as a missionary professor in India... The argument that missions denationalise the native is noted, and reasons are given for the contention that missions really renationalise.

2. *trans.* To transfer (a formerly nationalized industry) from private to national ownership again.

1954 *Ann. Reg. 1953* 22 Steel and transport were to be renationalized. **1959** *Daily Tel.* 13 Mar. 19/7 Its proposals not only to renationalise steel and road transport but also to nationalise by one means or another half of British industry. **1980** *Times* 30 Sept. 4/6 The next Labour Government would renationalize..transport activity.

renatura·tion. [RE- 5 a.] The process of restoring the nature or properties of what has been denatured.

1940 *Nature* 31 Aug. 301/1 The reversion of heat denaturation in proteins..has been demonstrated... The present method of renaturation is of interest owing to the well-defined conditions under which the reversion is achieved. **1965** PEACOCKE & DRYSDALE *Molecular Basis Heredity* iv. 37 A quite different approach to this problem has now become available with the discovery that, under carefully chosen conditions, the two strands of DNA of micro-organisms and bacteriophage may be separated and then subsequently reunited to restore the original helical structure and biological activity. This process of 're-naturation' may be followed by centrifugation of DNA. **1978** *Nature* 28 Sept. 352/1 Kunitz demonstrated by enzymatic and physico-chemical methods that renaturation of the inhibitor yielded a product indistinguishable from the original protein.

rena·ture (rĭ-), *v.* [RE- 5 a.] **a.** *trans.* To restore the nature or properties of (what has been denatured).

1946 *Nature* 30 Nov. 768/2 Some fairly close system of supervision by the international authority will be essential to ensure that the denatured material..is not being 're-natured' so as to make it suitable for use in a bomb. **1977** *Sci. Amer.* Apr. 44/2 Stewart found that after cooling and the removal of the detergent the interferon recovered its original biological activity: it was renatured.

b. *intr.* To undergo renaturation.

1965 PEACOCKE & DRYSDALE *Molecular Basis Heredity* iv. 38 Such a close correlation clearly has great potentialities in the assessment of the relationship between micro-organisms but cannot be used for higher plants and animals since their DNA are more heterogeneous and do not 're-nature'. **1973** *Nature* 11 May 55/2 They demonstrated that the centromeric regions..renature the most rapidly after denaturation.

Hence **rena·tured** *ppl. a.*, **rena·turing** *vbl. sb.*; also **rena·turable** *a.*

1955 *Bull. Atomic Sci.* Jan. 12/1 If reconversion of the denatured nuclear explosives is not a protracted process, the threat of seizure, renaturing, and atomic rearmament would remain indefinitely. **1964** G. H. HAGGIS et al. *Introd. Molecular Biol.* xii. 315 Such a renatured DNA regains its biological activity and can be used to transform bacteria. **1970** *Nature* 26 Sept. 1310/1 Renaturable DNA is defined as DNA that after denaturation..rapidly reverts to a duplex when the denaturing conditions are removed.

rench (rentʃ), var. RINSE *v.* (Now chiefly *U.S. dial.*)

1591, etc. [see RINSE *v.* 2 aβ, 4 aβ in Dict.]. *a* **1841** J. GUILD *Jrnl.* in *Proc. Vermont Hist. Soc.* (1937) V. 263 She would..go down to a brook about forty rods and stand in the brook and rench her close. **1859** J. C. HOTTEN *Dict. Slang* 81 *Rench*, vulgar pronunciation of *rinse*. '*Wrench* your mouth out,' said a fashionable dentist one day.—*North.* **1919** H. L. MENCKEN *Amer. Lang.* iii. 91 The Yankees..still clung, in their common speech, to such forms as..rench for rinse,..and the employment of precisely the same forms by thousands of Irish immigrants..gave them a certain support. **1941** E. P. O'DONNELL *Great Big Doorstep* i. 2 How many time I'm gunna tell you..to come and rench out the diaper? **1960** V. WILLIAMS *Walk Egypt* IV. ii. 257 Then you best rench your hands.

rencontre, *sb.* Add: **1. c.** An organized but informal meeting of scientists.

1975 *Chem. in Brit.* XI. 145/1 One approach is to organize small informal meetings—*rencontres*—at which chemists can meet, be educated by (and educate) representatives from the other sciences. **1975** *Physics Bull.* Dec. 515/3 A few months ago the SRC organized a *rencontre* in Aberdeen on 'Combinatorics' which was a get-together for mathematicians, physicists and chemists. **1977** *Chem. in Brit.* XIII. 105 Theoretical research horizons in colloid science formed the theme of a recent *rencontre* sponsored by the Science Research Council.

rendered, *ppl. a.* Add: **2.** Of a brick or stone surface: covered with a render (cf. RENDER *sb.*[2] 5).

1971 *Country Life* 25 Feb. 447 (Advt.), It can be applied to brick, concrete, rendered or roughcast surfaces with equal success. **1973** *Nation Rev.* (Melbourne) 31 Aug. 1450/1 The white rendered, modernised..premises..have been an inconspicuous residential for the past three years. **1978** M. & N. WARD *Home* 90 Stucco-rendered walls.

rendering, *vbl. sb.* **3. c.** (Earlier and later examples.) Also *concr.*

1792 G. CARTWRIGHT *Jrnl. Labrador* I. p. xiii, *Rendering oil*, a sealer's term for melting fat into oil. **1945** *ABC of Cookery* (Ministry of Food) xii. 46 Rendering means melting to extract the fat from surrounding tissues. **1979** N. & I. LYONS *Champagne Blues* 174 We cook the steak in renderings of pork belly.

rendezvous, *sb.* Add: **5. c.** The pre-arranged meeting (and usu. docking) of two or more spacecraft in space; an instance of this.

1959 *ARS Jrnl.* Aug. 592/1 Many proposed space missions will require achieving rendezvous of two bodies in an orbit about a planet. **1962** F. I. ORDWAY et al. *Basic Astronautics* ix. 385 Orbital operations involving rendezvous with satellites or space stations. **1962** *Listener* 29 Nov. 901/2 The vehicle has to be put into a transfer-orbit which will take it from the Earth inward to the orbit of Venus, meeting the planet at a pre-selected rendezvous. **1965** *Times* 16 Dec. 10/1 The Americans achieved the first rendezvous of man in space today. **1969** *Guardian* 22 July 18/3 About ninety minutes after lift-off Eagle began the complex series of manoeuvres leading to rendezvous. **1973** C. SAGAN *Cosmic Connection* xix. 139 Rendezvous and docking maneuvers are reasonably well developed in manned missions even now.

rendezvous, *v.* Add: **1. d.** Of a spacecraft or its crew: to effect a meeting in space, *spec.* to dock with another spacecraft.

1960 *IRE Trans. Aeronaut. & Navig. Electronics* VII. 112/2 The system will eventually rendezvous at R_R. **1966** *Punch* 12 Jan. 68/2 Under bright Uranus We'll rendezvous in space. **1966** *Electronics* 3 Oct. 134, 4 [*sc.* a computer] helped the crew rendezvous and link up with the Agena target on the first orbit. **1969** *Observer* 20 July 7/2 Collins had a difficult time 'space-walking' to an Agena rocket with which they had rendezvoused.

rendezvousing, *vbl. sb.* Add: (Later example.) Also as *ppl. a.*

1965 K. W. GATLAND *Spacecraft & Boosters* II. 90/1 Saint or Satellite Inspector..was intended to provide the capability of rendezvousing with an unidentified satellite orbiting the Earth. **1973** *Daily Colonist* (Victoria, B.C.) 28 Jan. 22/3 Most [clocks] have served rendezvousing couples and time watchers well for many years.

rendingly (re·ndiŋli), *adv.* [f. RENDING *ppl. a.* + -LY[2].] In a rending or heart-breaking manner; painfully.

1926 H. CRANE *Let.* 19 Aug. (1965) 273, I have made up a kind of friendship with that idiot boy... He is rendingly beautiful at times.

rendition. 3. a. For *U.S.* read 'orig. *U.S.*' and add later examples.

1922 JOYCE *Ulysses* 237 Ben Dollard does sing that ballad touchingly. Masterly rendition. **1939** N. MONSARRAT *This is Schoolroom* III. xvii. 385 No account of twentieth-century culture would be complete without reference to the impact of the dance-band world..as well as strange words and phrases like 'rendition'. **1975** *Radio Times* 3 Apr. 17/1 It's comedian Roy Hudd, strumming the strings..with a rendition of 'Auntie Maggie's Remedy'.

b. Visual representation *of* anything.

1959 E. PULGRAM *Introd. Spectrography of Speech* xiii. 89, I chose a sustained sound... The sketch of Fig. 11 is a complete and exact spectrographic rendition of it. **1972** *Sci. Amer.* Nov. 45/2 (Advt.), If you are interested in additional dimensions of photo-optical performance—rendition of corners,..stray-light shielding—this chart..may provide the detailed answer. **1978** *Amateur Photographer* 2 Aug. 109/2 A polarising filter may be used to darken skies without affecting the rendition of foreground detail.

rendu (rañdü), *a.* [Fr., = rendered, delivered.] Of imported goods: designating the price on delivery, including tariffs and delivery costs. Cf. *FRANCO *a.*

1957 CLARK & GOTTFRIED *Dict. Business* 275/2 *Rendu price*, one on imported goods meaning that the price includes the cost of the goods themselves, freight insurance, landing fees, tariffs, and the costs of delivering the goods direct to the buyer's place of business. **1959** E. E. NEMMERS *Dict. Econ.* 254 *Rendu price*, an import *delivered price*. The price of imported goods including all charges for tariff and freight. **1962** [see *FRANCO *a.*].

rendzina (rendzī·nă). *Soil Science.* [a. Russ. *rendzina*, ad. Polish *rędzina*.] A fertile lime-rich soil which occurs typically under grass or open woodland on relatively soft calcareous bedrock (e.g. chalk and some limestones) and has a dark, friable, humus-rich surface layer above a softer pale calcareous layer formed by the breakdown of the underlying rock. Also *attrib.*

1927 C. F. MARBUT tr. *K. D. Glinka's Great Soil Groups of World* 34 The humus carbonate soils such as the Rendzinas ..constitute a good example of the influence of the parent rock on the soil forming process. **1928** C. L. WHITTLES tr. *E. Ramann's Evolution & Classification of Soils* v. 91 Recently under the influence of Russian soil workers the term 'rendzina' has been applied to all soils which have developed from the weathering of calcareous rocks. **1932** G. W. ROBINSON *Soils* xiv. 285 The writer is occupying a debatable position in assigning the chalk soils of England to the rendzina group. **1946** LUTZ & CHANDLER *Forest Soils* xi. 386 Highly calcareous materials frequently give rise to immature soils called rendzinas. **1955** *Proc. Prehistoric Soc.* XXI. 53 Vegetation covering the surface of the loess produced soils due to chemical weathering which can be classified as podsols, chernozems, rendzinas, terra rossas and others. **1971** *Nature* 13 Aug. 453/1 The flora has survived through the post-glacial forest and blanket bog intervals in Teesdale partly on rendzina soils associated with rotted crystalline marble on Widdybank and Cronkley fells. **1973** *Country Life* 29 Nov. 1787/3 *The Rural Landscape of Kent*.. is strictly for the diligent reader who can disentangle rendzinas from stagnogley soils. **1976** *Interim* IV. III. 14 Chalk rendzinas go straight from the A horizon to the C.

renegader (re·nĭgē[i]dəɹ). [f. RENEGADE *sb.* or *v.* + -ER[1].] = RENEGADE *sb.* 2.

1846 J. R. LOWELL in *Boston Courier* 17 June 2 Haint they cut a thunderin' swarth, (Helped by Yankee renegaders).

renegadism. (In Dict. s.v. RENEGADE *sb.*) Also **renegadeism.** (Earlier and later examples.)

1826 B. R. HAYDON *Jrnl.* 25 Feb. in *Autobiogr.* (1853) II. 115 The Academy is certainly modified, but still John Bull never pardons an appearance of renegadeism. **1939** A. J. TOYNBEE *Study of Hist.* VI. 104 The..profanity of Jason.. gave Hellenism such a vogue and Renegadism such an impetus.

renego·tiate, *v.* [RE- 5 a.] *trans.* To negotiate a second or further time. Hence **renego·tiated** *ppl. a.*

1934 in WEBSTER. **1962** *Economist* 16 June 1096/2 The annexes to these agreements, which determine the air services to be operated, are normally re-negotiated every six months. **1969** *Listener* 26 June 894/3 When you propose to renegotiate housing subsidies, this really means higher rents for a lot of people. **1975** *Times* 19 Feb. 2/8 Mr Crosland..is expected to support the argument..when Mr Callaghan..brings back the final renegotiated terms. **1976** *Film & Television Technician* Dec. 1/2 Among the key mechanisms in achieving this, have been the re-negotiated cost of living clauses which the employers have unilaterally abandoned.

renegotia·tion. [RE- 5 a.] A second or further negotiation.

1934 in WEBSTER. **1945** *Britannica Bk. of Year* 771 The renegotiation by the government of original contracts to bring them more in line with actual costs as revealed by experience. **1963** *Ann. Reg. 1962* 274 The renegotiation of the U.S.–Spanish Bases agreement, due for renewal in 1963. **1976** H. WILSON *Governance of Britain* 10 The final Cabinet tally, after the re-negotiations of the terms of entry, was publicly announced to be seventeen in favour, seven against. **1980** *Boston Globe* 30 Mar. 76 Today the 25-year-old..insists on a renegotiation of his contract.

renegue, *v.* Add: Now more commonly with pronunc. (rĭne·g) or (rĭnē[i]·g). Also (*U.S.*) **renig.**

1. (Later examples.)

1914 JOYCE *Dubliners* 163 'There's one of them, anyhow,' said Mr Henchy, 'that didn't renege him.' **1922** —— *Ulysses* 324 We fought for the royal Stuarts that reneged us against the Williamites and they betrayed us.

4. b. (Earlier example, in form *ranague*.)

a **1849** J. KEEGAN *Legends & Poems* (1907) 64 Amn't I to undherstand that..Peggy is goin' to ranague you for Micky Gorman?

c. To change one's mind, to recant; to break one's word; to go back *on* a promise or undertaking or contract; to disappoint expectations. orig. and chiefly *U.S.*

Now the dominant sense, and freq. in spelling *renege*.

1784 A. ELLICOTT *Diary* 24 Nov. in C. V. Mathews *Andrew Ellicott* (1908) i. 27 The Hussey immediately Reniged and reclaimed the Bed. **1866** C. H. SMITH *Bill Arp* 153 When the Secretary read out my name all mixed up with the Republic, I felt I was obleged to renig. **1906** 'O. HENRY' *Four Million* 123 It might brace her up and keep her from reneging on the proposition to skip. **1917** H. FRANCK *Vagabonding down Andes* 32 Hays renigged at the last moment, but I accepted the invitation issued to the 'general public'. **1935** A. SQUIRE *Sing Sing Doctor* ix. 141, I was afraid our man might renege on his contract. **1936** 'N. BLAKE' *Thou Shell of Death* xiii. 236 She turned very calm and quiet... 'I'll never renege. I'll write to Jack... He must come back.' **1946** *Time* 21 Oct. 99/1 The picture begins to renege on its early promise. **1951** A. R. LEWIS *Naval Power & Trade in Mediterranean* v. 150 The naval assault was a success, but Hugh reneged on his side of the bargain. **1962** J. MCCABE *Mr. Laurel & Mr. Hardy* iii. 82 Anderson made a few more films with Stan before he reneged on a contract detail regarding payment. **1968** *Daily Tel.* 13 Dec. 1/2 The Minister is equally annoyed that the National Federation of Building Trade Operatives appears to have reneged on its earlier promise to accept a 1d-an-hour wage cut. **1973** R. LUDLUM *Matlock Paper* v. 43 'You're offering me a chance to renege?' 'Of course. You're under no obligation to us.' **1977** *Time* 7 Mar. 23/1 He was given certain undertakings from other people that they subsequently reneged on. **1981** *Times* 27 Jan. 12/8 Labour's record on immigration has been almost identical to the Conservatives'—it introduced stringent controls and reneged on Britain's commitment to the East African Asians who had United Kingdom passports.

reneguing, *vbl. sb.* (Later example.)

1921 G. B. SHAW *Back to Methuselah* p. lxv, There was no Prime Minister to whom such renagueing or trafficking would ever have occurred.

renewability. (Example.)

1976 *Nature* 27 May 350/2 The renewability of forests is a key point in the book.

renewable, *a.* Add: **2.** Of a source of energy: not depleted by its utilization.

1971 *Sci. Amer.* Sept. 43/2 (*caption*) Continuous, or renewable, energy supply can be divided into two categories: solar and nonsolar. **1972** ROCKS & RUNYON *Energy Crisis* 8 We have already expanded in numbers and living standard far beyond the capacity of our most accessible and renewable energy source [*sc.* flowing water] to sustain us even in the present. **1975** RUEDISILI & FIREBAUGH *Perspectives on Energy* iv. 295 Geothermal, tidal, and wind energy are three ..renewable sources of energy that have been harnessed to a greater or lesser extent. **1978** *Nature* 20 Apr. 661/1 Renewable sources of energy—wind, wave, sun, geothermal heat and the like—are..taken seriously at the United Kingdom Atomic Energy Authority.

B. as *sb.* A renewable source of energy.

1974 *Oceanus* XVII. 20 (heading) Using two renewables. **1980** *Times* 22 Aug. 10/2 The CEGB decision to take the first commercial steps for wind-powered electricity makes it easier..to take renewables seriously.

renewal. Add: **a*.** A planned urban redevelopment. Also in phr. *urban renewal* s.v. *URBAN *a.*

1965 *Economist* 6 Feb. 544/1 For its size Boston is the most renewal-minded city in the country. Mr. Slayton, the federal Urban Renewal Commissioner, recently called its eleven integrated projects..'a laboratory demonstration of renewal techniques'. **1967** *Boston Sunday Herald* 26 Mar. I. 9/6 The BRA leadership is pushing to exempt 'planned unit developments' in renewal areas. **1978** *Jrnl. R. Soc. Arts* CXXVI. 595/2 In urban renewal schemes where roadways and footpaths are altered the lower voltage system usually requires replacement.

b. renewal theory, the branch of probability theory which considers populations of objects which fail and need renewal after randomly distributed intervals.

1940 G. A. D. PREINREICH *Present Status of Renewal Theory* 25 Lotka has a method of mathematically describing renewal theory, using the Hertz method of approximation to the solution. **1958** *Jrnl. R. Statistical Soc.* B. XX. 243

The study of renewal theory has its origins in the discussion of self-renewing aggregates and the non-stochastic treatment of questions of population growth. **1966** S. BEER *Decision & Control* x. 216 Renewal theory concerns itself with strategies for replacing worn out parts, machines, aircraft or anything else that has to be renewed.

reng (reŋ). [ad. Pers. *rang*, Skr. *raṅga* colour, hue.] A colouring, esp. a hair-dye.
1929 REDGROVE & FOAN *Blonde or Brunette?* xi. 73 The leaves, dried and powdered, of *Indigofera argentea*, L. ('reng'), cultivated in Persia, constitute the best form in which to employ indigo. **1934** *S.P.E. Tract* XLI. 16 *Reng* is perhaps now in sufficiently common use by hair-dressers to be accorded a place in the national vocabulary. **1966** J. S. COX *Illustr. Dict. Hairdressing* 79/1 *Henna-Reng*, a hair dye consisting of a combination of Henna and Indigo.

renga (re·ngă). Also **renge, renka.** [Jap., = linked (verse).] A form of Japanese verse established by the 15th century and consisting of a series of half-tanka, contributed by different poets in turn.
See also note s.v. *HAIKU.
1877 W. G. ASTON *Gram. Jap. Written Lang.* (ed. 2) x. 198 *Renka*..is where one person composes part (commonly the second part) of a *tanka*, the remainder being added by some one else. **1890** B. H. CHAMBERLAIN *Things Japanese* 272 A favourite game at these tournaments called *renge*, wherein one person composes the second hemistich of a verse and another person has to provide it with a first hemistich, seems to date from the eleventh century. **1911** —— *Jap. Poetry* IV. 159 This was termed *Renga*, lit. 'linked verses'. **1968** E. MINER *Introd. Jap. Court Poetry* 163 *Renga*... A form dating from about the thirteenth century; several authors would compose a sequence, usually of a hundred sections or stanzas, alternating 5, 7, 5 syllable lines with 7, 7 syllable units, any two of which formed a complete poem.

rengas (re·ŋgas). [Malay.] Any of several East Indian trees of the family Anacardiaceæ, esp. *Gluta renghas*, containing a sap that often produces allergic reactions in those touching it; the wood or sap of this tree. Also *attrib.*
1836 J. LOW *Diss. Soil & Agric. Penang* iv. 200 *Runggas*—a lofty tree, the juice of which is deleterious to the human frame, creating swellings over the whole body. **1935** I. H. BURKILL *Dict. Econ. Products Malay Penin.* I. 1079 Furniture of 'rĕngas' may certainly be used without inconvenience. **1939** A. KEITH *Land below Wind* xiii. 221 One disadvantage of wearing shorts was the long expanse of leg which was left bare, with the result of..patches of *rengas* poisoning from rubbing against the leaves of the *rengas* tree. **1940** E. J. H. CORNER *Wayside Trees of Malaya* I. 116 Most *Rengas*-trees are large and not a few are among the tallest and finest in the forest. **1956** *Nature* 25 Feb. 366/1 The Colonial hardwood, rengas, has been shown to contain two pigments. **1965** R. MCKIE *Company of Animals* xi. 164 Jim..confirms the story of the Rengas tree rash. Some people are allergic to this tree.

renguerra (rengwēə·ră). *Vet. Sci.* Also **renguera.** [S. Amer. Sp. *renguera* limping, lameness, f. *renguear* (Sp. *renquear*) to limp.] = *SWAYBACK 2.
1917 S. H. GAIGER in *Jrnl. Compar. Path. & Therapeutics* XXX. 209 Renguera is a new and hitherto undescribed disease of lambs, occurring in the Peruvian Andes. **1938** *Nature* 5 Mar. 400/1 The resulting lesions of demyelination are anatomically related to those observed in the enzootic paraplegia (renguerra) reported to occur among lambs bred in certain areas in the Peruvian Andes. **1966** A. ROBERTSON *Internat. Encycl. Vet. Med.* II. 698 Synonyms [for copper deficiency]. Enzootic ataxia; swayback;.. renguerra.

renicky-boo: see *RANNYGAZOO.

renierite (rənyēə·rəit). *Min.* [ad. F. *reniérite* (J. F. Vaes 1948, in *Ann. de la Soc. géol. de Belgique* LXXII. B22), f. the name of A. *Renier*, 20th-c. Belgian geologist: see -ITE[1].] A sulphide of copper, germanium, and other metals $(Cu,Fe)_3(Fe,Ge)S_4$, occurring as yellowish tetragonal crystals and granular masses.
1949 *Mineral Mag.* XXVIII. 737 Renierite... Sulphide of Cu, Fe, Ge (7·75 %), Zn, As... Named after Prof. Armand Renier, Director of the Geological Survey of Belgium. Near germanite. **1966** *Mineral Abstr.* XVII. 537/2 Germanium-bearing (250 p.p.m. Ge) sphalerite occurring with galena in mineralized Cambrian limestone and dolomite in..southern Sardinia, is found to contain numerous inclusions of renierite up to 10μ in size.

renig, U.S. var. RENEGUE *v.* in Dict. and Suppl.

renin (rī·nin). *Physiol.* [f. L. *rēnes* kidneys + -IN[1].] † **1.** A substance extracted from animals' kidneys and used in medicine. *Obs.*
1894 G. M. GOULD *Illustr. Dict. Med., Biol. & Allied Sci.* 940/2 Extracts have been prepared from nearly every organ in the animal body;..cerebrin, from the brain,..ossin, from bones, renin, from the kidneys. **1900** DORLAND *Med. Dict.* 565/1 *Renin*, a therapeutic extract prepared from the kidneys of animals.
2. A proteolytic enzyme secreted by and stored in the kidneys, which acts in the blood to convert angiotensinogen (hypertensinogen) to angiotensin (hypertensin). [Coined in this sense as G. *renin* (R. Tigerstedt, in *Compt. Rend. 12me Congrès Internat. de Médecine 1897* (1899) II. II. 29).]
1906 *Lancet* 19 May 1375/2 The pressor substance, to which these workers give the name 'renin', is not dialysable. **1938** *Proc. Soc. Exper. Biol. & Med.* XXXIX. 214 Undialyzed renin (0·2 cc) caused moderate vasoconstriction. *Ibid.* 215 Renin is an enzyme-like substance which is activated by a kinase-like material contained in the protein fraction of plasma and whole blood. **1959** [see *HYPERTENSIN]. **1965** [see *HYPERTENSINOGEN]. **1968** PASSMORE & ROBSON *Compan. Med. Stud.* I. xxxiii. 20/2 Renin is an enzyme which on reaching the blood activates an α_2-globulin called angiotensin formed in the liver, making angiotensin I, a polypeptide containing ten amino acids. Another enzyme converts angiotensin I to angiotensin II by removing two amino acids. This last substance is the most potent pressor agent known. **1977** FREEMAN & DAVIS in J. Genest et al. *Hypertension* vi. 211/1 Renin is synthesized and stored..in the granules of JG [*sc.* juxtaglomerular] cells which are located primarily in the renal afferent arteriole, although these granular cells have also been identified in the efferent arteriolar wall..and in the mesangial cells.

renitence. For † *Obs.* read *rare* and add later example.
1917 C. R. PAYNE tr. *Pfister's Psychoanal. Method* viii. 168 The result of this renitence consists mostly in the continuance of those symptoms of disease which depend on the repression.

renka, var. *RENGA.

renminbi (renminb*i*). Also **jenminpi, renminpi, Renminbi.** [Chinese *rénmínbì*, f. *rénmín* people + *bì* currency.] **a.** The name of the currency introduced in China in 1948. **b.** Occas. used for yuan, the basic unit of this currency.
1957 *Encycl. Brit.* V. 546 B/1 In 1953 the official currency was the jenminpi or People's bank note on the mainland. **1971** [see *JIAO]. **1973** *Times* 21 Mar. (China Trade Suppl.) p. iii/6 The basic unit of renminbi—which is abbreviated to RMB—is the yuan. **1974** *China Reconstructs* July 14/3 The Chinese currency, the Renminbi, is stable. **1975** *Ann. Reg. 1974* 320 More than 60 countries were already using the Chinese renminpi as the trading currency with China. **1979** *Fortune* 21 May 110/2 Its young tellers..eagerly explain to a visitor the tax advantages of converting his money into Chinese renminbi and keeping it in Peking.

renneting (re·nĕtiŋ), *vbl. sb. Cheese-making.* [f. RENNET *sb.*[1] + -ING[1].] The action or process of adding rennet in order to curdle milk. Also *attrib.*
1894 J. OLIVER *Milk, Cheese & Butter* xi. 172 If no other heating than to obtain renneting temperature, this commenced as soon as last milk has arrived. **1917** WALKER-TISDALE & WOODNUTT *Pract. Cheesemaking* xiii. 108 Renneting. Having ripened the milk and regulated it to the renneting temperature, the rennet is added. **1932** R. H. LEITCH *Cheddar Cheese-Making* vii. 41 The standard temperature of renneting Cheddar cheese is 86 degrees Fahrenheit; under average conditions there is no advantage in a higher renneting temperature. **1937** HARVEY & HILL *Milk Products* iv. 200 Renneting is carried out at a temperature of 80°–91° F. **1950** J. G. DAVIS *Dict. Dairying* 100 Renneting. When the correct acidity has been reached rennet is added at the rate of about 1 ml. per gal. of milk... The renneting acidity is one of the crucial points in cheesemaking. **1976** —— *Cheese* III. xxi. 498 There are four crucial stages in cheesemaking. These are the acidity at renneting, the stage of pitching, the point at which the whey is removed from the curd, and the time of milling, salting and putting to press.

reno- (rīno), comb. form of L. *rēnes* kidneys (now more usual than RENI-), as in RENOPERICARDIAL *a.*, *RENOGRAPHY, etc.

renogram (rī·nogræm). *Med.* [f. as next + -GRAM.] A graphical record of the varying radioactivity of a kidney into which a radioactive substance has been injected; also, a radiograph or autoradiograph of a kidney.
1954 P. G. SMITH in M. Campbell *Urol.* I. II. ii. 189 The exposure is made as the last few cc. of the contrast medium are being injected. The needle is immediately withdrawn and a second film is made as rapidly as the cassettes can be changed. This last film is known as a renogram or nephrogram. **1964** C. C. WEBSTER in J. F. Glenn *Diagnostic Urol.* x. 190 (*caption*) The radioisotope renogram and blood clearance tracing are produced with three scintillation probes connected through three rate meters and three recorders. **1974** PASSMORE & ROBSON *Compar. Med. Stud.* III. xxii. 16/1 When hippuran (sodium ortho-iodohippurate) labelled with ^{131}I is given intravenously the substance is secreted rapidly into the proximal tubular fluid. Scintillation counters placed over the kidneys measure the radiation emitted by the isotope and the activity/time curve which is recorded is called the renogram. *Ibid.* 16/2 Patients with unilateral disturbances in renal function show differences in the shape and amplitude of the two renograms.

renography (rīnǫ·grăfi). *Med.* [f. *RENO- + -GRAPHY.] Renal angiography or autoradiography.
1911 *Brit. Med. Jrnl.* 1 Apr. 748 (*heading*) A lecture on renography. **1964** C. C. WEBSTER in J. F. Glenn *Diagnostic Urol.* x. 189 Since its inception in 1955, radioisotope renography has been increasingly utilized for the external measurement of individual kidney function. **1971** *Nature* 17 Sept. p. xi (Advt.), There is an active research programme in renography carried out in conjunction with the renal unit.

Renoiresque (renwāre·sk), *a.* [f. the name of Pierre Auguste *Renoir* (1841–1919), French painter + -ESQUE.] Of, pertaining to, or characteristic of Renoir or his work.
1958 *Listener* 5 June 934/2 He succeeded in creating a Renoiresque atmosphere of the turn of the century. **1961** *Times* 18 Jan. 15/2 In her Renoiresque paintings Morisot lost a little of her freshness. **1971** R. A. CARTER *Manhattan Primitive* xvi. 150 An oddly put-together woman in a.. black scarf top from which her Renoiresque bosom kept emerging.

renominate, *v.* For 'a second term of office' read 'a further term of office' and add later examples.
1927 *New Republic* 21 Sept. 122/2 It declares that Mr. Coolidge must, shall and will be renominated. **1975** J. P. MORGAN *House of Lords & Labour Govt.* vii. 180 They illustrated the possible influence of systems of renominating voting Peers at successive General Elections. **1981** *Times* 28 Apr. 15/2 Devices to make it difficult if not impossible for moderate candidates to be renominated.

reno·rmalizable, *a. Physics.* [f. *RENORMALIZ(E *v.* + -ABLE.] That permits of renormalization.
1955 L. D. LANDAU in W. Pauli *Niels Bohr* 66 This phenomenon, not being renormalizable, cannot be considered within the limits of the theory. **1968** D. LURIÉ *Particles & Fields* vi. 266 Such theories, in which all divergences can be absorbed in the coupling-constant and mass renormalizations and thereby ignored, are known as renormalizable field theories. **1978** *Sci. Amer.* Feb. 132/2 For many years it seemed there was no convincing renormalizable theory of the weak interactions.
So **reno:rmalizabi·lity.**
1955 L. D. LANDAU in W. Pauli *Niels Bohr* 54 This renormalizability of the theory is in reality only approximate. **1975** *Nature* 11 Sept. 95/2 In 1971..a Dutch graduate student, 't Hooft, opened the flood-gates by giving convincing arguments for the renormalisability of a rather special type of Yang–Mills gauge theory.

re:normaliza·tion. *Physics.* [RE- 5 a.] A method used in quantum mechanics of removing unwanted infinities from the solutions of equations by redefining parameters such as the mass and charge of subatomic particles. Freq. *attrib.* Cf. *NORMALIZE *v.* 3 a.
1948 *Physical Rev.* LXXIV. 1430/1 The divergent terms in the line shift problem can be thought to be contained in a renormalization of the mass of a free electron. **1954** W. HEITLER *Quantum Theory of Radiation* (ed. 3) vi. 277 What is observable is the total mass and the total charge of the electron and these include the self-mass and self-charge. Although it is still a major unsolved difficulty of the theory that these quantities turn out to be infinite, they should, whatever their value, be combined with the 'original' mass and charge (i.e. the theoretical mass and charge when no interaction with the radiation field existed at all). For the original plus the self-mass and charge the observed finite values of mass and charge should then be substituted. This procedure will be called the re-normalization of mass and charge. *Ibid.* xxx. 310 This is the relativistic form of the 'renormalization terms'. **1954** *Physical Rev.* XCV. 1329/1 Ever since the overwhelming success of the applications of renormalization technique in quantum electrodynamics, the problem of understanding this renormalization procedure without the use of perturbation methods has been of great interest. **1962** N. R. HANSON in A. B. Pippard et al. *Quanta & Reality* v. 88 Theoreticians..invented a technique to diminish the number of possible solutions into something which practising physicists could manage. The result is a rather arbitrary procedure called 'renormalization'. It rejects as physically unpromising most solutions of any wave equation. **1977** L. STREIT in Price & Chissick *Uncertainty Principle & Foundations of Quantum Mechanics* xviii. 353 Virtually every second calculation of quantum electrodynamics included the process of throwing away an infinite term and interpreting the remainder as the 'correct result'. These procedures were formalized in the renormalization theory of Feynman, Dyson and Schwinger. **1979** *Sci. Amer.* Mar. 67/2 In the 1950's it became apparent that the aims of the renormalization procedure can be achieved by a large family of mathematical transformations; these make up the renormalization group.

reno·rmalize, *v. Physics.* [RE- 5 a.] *trans.* To apply renormalization to.
1955 L. D. LANDAU in W. Pauli *Niels Bohr* 54 The results hereby obtained can be renormalized, that is, if the physical charge of the electron is defined by its interaction with quanta of zero frequency and its mass, as the physical mass of the electron, the undetermined constant Λ disappears from the formulae for the physical effects. **1972** *Sci. Amer.* Nov. 50/1 The second obstacle to a satisfactory theory is that many calculations involving the weak force quickly lead to infinite results. In electromagnetic theory similar divergences are handled by the process called renormalization. Until recently no one could see how to renormalize the divergences presented by the weak force.
So **reno·rmalized** *ppl. a.*, calculated with the use of renormalization.
1954 *Physical Rev.* XCV. 1329/1 A rather unexpected and quite surprising feature is obtained by comparing the renormalized coupling constant with the unrenormalized coupling constant. **1977** M. E. FISHER in U. Landman *Statistical Mechanics & Statistical Methods in Theory & Application* 17 Renormalized field-theoretic perturbation theory.

renosterbos, -bush, varr. *RHENOSTERBOS.

renounceable, *a.* Delete *rare*—¹ and add further examples.

1955 *Times* 8 July 14/2 Renounceable allotment letters and application forms for additional shares have been posted. **1979** *Daily Tel.* 19 Jan. 13/2 A three-for-one capitalisation issue will then produce for Midland 86 million renounceable shares which it can sell free of stamp duty.

renovascular (rīnovæ·sciŭlăɹ), *a. Med.* [f. *RENO- + VASCULAR *a.*] Pertaining to the blood vessels of the kidneys.

1961 *Medicine* XL. 347 (*heading*) Functional characteristics of renovascular hypertension. **1974** PASSMORE & ROBSON *Compan. Med. Stud.* III. xx. 8/1 Neutralization of the activity of angiotensin II by specific angiotensin antibodies does not always prevent or reverse hypertension induced by renovascular means.

renovated, *ppl. a.* Add: *renovated butter* = *process butter* s.v. *PROCESS *sb.* 13.

1899, etc. [see *process butter* s.v. *PROCESS *sb.* 13]. **1906** *Daily Chron.* 13 Sept. 5/2 Mr. Hehner went on to explain the nature of American renovated butter. He said that sometimes butter 'went off', and it was then melted down and the sour milk run off and replaced by pure milk and cream. **1937** HARVEY & HILL *Milk Products* iii. 178 Renovated butter. Butter which has become unfit for human consumption is treated in many countries by a process which is said to render it suitable for such consumption. Such methods, however, are not practised in Great Britain.

renovize (re·novəiz), *v. U.S. rare.* [A blend of RENOV(ATE *v.* + MODERN)IZE *v.*] *trans.* To restore and modernize.

1933 *Daily Progress* (Charlottesville, Va.) 25 Jan. 3/6 A 'renovize Philadelphia' campaign has met marked success in its early stages. **1935** A. P. HERBERT *What a Word!* ii. 53 A North American warrior tells me that she has seen 'to renovise'! **1965** *Amer. Speech* XL. 303 This suffix has been attached to..verbs (*renovize, flavorize*).

‖**renseignement** (rañsẹnʸmañ). [Fr.] (A piece of) information; also, a letter of introduction.

1841 E. EVERETT *Let.* 30 Dec. in Dickens *Lett.* (1974) III. 4/1 At Washington you will be able to get abundance of letters & *renseignement* for every part of the interior. *c* **1863** MRS. GASKELL *Lett.* (1966) 931, I am..sending my courier to you in hopes that you will most kindly give him 'renseignements' on one or two points. **1873** W. JAMES *Let.* 25 May in R. B. Perry *Thought & Char. W. James* (1935) I. xx. 346, I take up the pen today mainly on a matter of business, that is, to get at as early a date as possible certain *renseignements* which may affect my choice of how to spend next winter. **1875** LADY C. SCHREIBER *Jrnl.* 20 Nov. (1911) I. 390 Called on the Consul, saw some fine Oriental dishes at his house, got from him various renseignements. **1921** *Glasgow Herald* 17 May 3/8 Given, however, accurate renseignements, properties of high potential value are to be acquired.

Renshaw¹ (re·nʃǭ). *Tennis.* The name of William Charles *Renshaw* (1861–1904) and his twin brother Ernest (1861–99), used *attrib.* in *Renshaw smash* to denote a kind of fast overhead volley with which they were associated.

[**1882**: see SMASH *sb.*¹ 1 b.] **1883** *Field* 7 July 11/1 Deuce was called in five of the games, and the fifth game was won by four of the 'Renshaw smashes'. **1889** W. M. BROWNLEE *Lawn-Tennis* v. 18 This return very soon was called the Renshaw smash'. **1975** *Oxf. Compan. Sports & Games* 835/1 He took the ball early—the 'Renshaw smash' was celebrated.

Renshaw² (re·nʃǭ). *Physiol.* [Name of Birdsey *Renshaw* (1911–48), U.S. neurologist, who investigated such cells.] *Renshaw cell*: a nerve cell in the spinal cord that is innervated by collaterals from a motor neurone and forms synapses with that and adjacent motor neurones so as to provide an inhibitory feedback path.

1954 J. C. ECCLES et al. in *Jrnl. Physiol.* CXXVI. 533 A detailed study of the interneuronal discharges has established that these interneurones form a specialized group mediating the inhibitory path from motor axons. They may appropriately be given the distinguishing title of 'Renshaw cells'. **1974** M. C. GERALD *Pharmacol.* xv. 277 The Renshaw cells exert an inhibitory influence on the flow of nerve impulses along motor neurons in the spinal cord. **1976** W. R. INGRAM *Rev. Anat. Neurol.* i. 23 Some investigators have questioned the validity of the Renshaw cell concept.

rent, *sb.*¹ Add: **2. b.** *fair rent,* the amount of rent which a tenant may reasonably be expected to pay for the use of specified land or property; *spec.* that officially registered by a Rent Office for a particular tenancy.

1886 *Act* 49 & 50 *Vict.* c. 29 § 6 The landlord or the crofter may apply to the Crofters Commission to fix the fair rent to be paid by such crofter to the landlord for the holding. **1926** *Act* 16 & 17 *Geo. V.* c. 52 § 2 The expression 'full fair rent' in relation to a small holding means the rent which a tenant might reasonably be expected to pay for the holding if let as such and the landlord undertook to bear the cost of structural repairs. **1965** *Act* 13 & 14 *Eliz. II.* c. 75 § 27 In determining..what rent is or would be a fair rent under a regulated tenancy of a dwelling-house regard shall be had,..to the age, character and locality of the dwelling-house and to its state of repair. *a* **1974** R. CROSSMAN *Diaries* (1975) I. 263, I had to deal with all the questions about rateable value and with the fair-rent clauses. **1976** *Southern Even. Echo* (Southampton) 13 Nov. 6/5 The rent officer in determining fair rents can consider under his brief the property and then fix his figure with reference to similar properties.

c. (Later examples.)

Still *Obs.* except in *U.S. dial.* use.

c **1847** J. S. COYNE in M. R. Booth *Eng. Plays of 19th Cent.* (1973) IV. 186 You used not to wear such waistcoats as that when you lived in Fuller's Rents. *a* **1902** S. BUTLER *Way of All Flesh* (1903) lv. 254 A rag and bottle merchant in Birdsey's Rents. **1926** *Dialect Notes* IV. 388 *Rent,*..apartment or rentable house. **1943** [see *rent-hunter* in sense 4 b below].

d. *Pol. Econ.* (See quot. 1817.)

[**1777** J. ANDERSON *Enquiry Nature Corn-Laws* 45 It is not, however, the rent of the land that determines the price of its produce, but it is the price of that produce which determines the rent of the land.] **1815** T. R. MALTHUS *Inquiry Nature & Progress Rent* 1 The rent of land may be defined to be that portion of the value of the whole produce which remains to the owner of the land, after all the outgoings belonging to its cultivation..have been paid, including the profits of the capital employed, estimated according to the usual and ordinary rate of the profits of agricultural stock at the time being. **1817** D. RICARDO *Princ. Pol. Econ.* ii. 49 Rent is that portion of the produce of the earth, which is paid to the landlord for the use of the original and indestructible powers of the soil. **1848** MILL *Pol. Econ.* I. II. xvi. 500 The rent, therefore, which any land will yield, is the excess of its produce, beyond what would be returned to the same capital if employed on the worst land in cultivation. **1884** J. RAE *Contemp. Socialism* ix. 455 No part of Ricardo's theory is more elementary or more unchallenged than this, that the rent of land constitutes no part of the price of bread, and the high rent is not the cause of dear bread, but dear bread the cause of high rent.

e. Money or cash, esp. that acquired by criminal activity or in exchange for homosexual favours; hence *ellipt.* (as quasi-*adj.*), = *rent boy* in sense 4 c below.

1828 W. T. MONCRIEFF *Tom & Jerry* I. 20 Blunt, my dear boy, is..to be able to flash the screens—sport the rhino—shew the needful—post the pony—nap the rent... Money, money, is your universal good. **1925** FRASER & GIBBONS *Soldier & Sailor Words* 242 *Rent,* money: cash. **1936** J. CURTIS *Gilt Kid* xii. 127, I haven't done anything since I've come out of the nick and the old rent's running a bit low. **1967** A. WILSON *No Laughing Matter* III. 306 I've been rent myself once... I just gave what they paid me for. **1977** *Gay News* 24 Mar. 15/3 A word of warning about the Strand Bar in Hope Street... It's rough and some of the people there are rent.

f. *Econ.* The financial advantage or gain regarded as emanating from a particular skill or ability, *spec.* in phr. *rent of ability* (see quot. 1929).

1879 A. MARSHALL *Econ. Industry* II. xii. 144 Rent of rare natural abilities is a specially important element in the incomes of business men. **1905** G. B. SHAW *Irrational Knot* p. xv, There is an important economic factor, first analyzed by an American economist (General Walker), and called rent of ability. **1929** S. E. THOMAS *Elem. Econ.* (ed. 4) xvii. 261 We may say that there is a rent element in both profits and wages, and that this element depends on the natural or acquired gifts of the employer or worker concerned. Where the differential payment is due to differences of ability, it may be suitably and correctly described as a rent of ability. **1930** *Times* 6 May 12/2 The Fabian Society formerly pleaded for the rent of ability, but the plea fell on deaf ears.

4. b. *rent-hunter* (in sense 2 c in Dict. and Suppl.), *-owner, -receiver, -yielding.*

1943 *Boston Herald* 28 July 12/1 A recent..cartoon showed two weary rent-hunters walking past the White House. **1844** MILL *Ess. Pol. Econ.* iii. 89 All which is produced beyond this, whether it be in the hands..of any of the numerous varieties of rent-owners, may be taken for immediate enjoyment. **1943** in E. Blunden *Return to Husbandry* 12 The squire has become an absentee landlord, a mere rent-receiver. **1848** MILL *Pol. Econ.* I. III. v. 565 Selling at a scarcity value..never is, nor has been, nor can be, a permanent condition of any of the great rent-yielding commodities.

c. *rent allowance, assessment, book, contract, control,* (hence *rent-controlled* adj.), *man, office, officer, rebate, restriction, tribunal*; **rent boy** *slang,* a young male homosexual prostitute; **rent car** *U.S.,* a hire-car; **rent party** *U.S.* = *house-rent party* s.v. *HOUSE *sb.*¹ 23; **rent strike,** a refusal to pay rent, usu. by a number of people as a form of protest; **rent table** (see quot. 1952).

1947 *Rep. Assistance Board 1946* iv. 21 The Statutory Regulations provide for the addition of a 'rent allowance' according to the circumstances of each individual case. **1974** COOTE & GILL *Women's Rights* vii. 259 The council gives rent rebates to council tenants and rent allowances to other tenants. **1965** *Act* 13 & 14 *Eliz. II.* c. 75 § 25 There shall be constituted rent assessment committees in accordance with the provisions of Schedule 2 to this Act. **1970** *Internat. & Compar. Law Quarterly* 4th Ser. XIX. II. 208 Generally, the working of the rent assessment committees was commended. **1830** M. EDGEWORTH *Let.* 4 Nov. (1971) 427 The rent to us is to be from his commencement the raised rent. See Rent book. **1973** *Courier & Advertiser* (Dundee) 1 Mar. 6/4, I haven't seen my rent book for three years. **1978** *Lancashire Life* Apr. 67/1 He inspected Aunt Clara's rent-book and asked her for the names of her grocer and butcher. **1969** Rent-boy [see *KEPT *ppl. a.* 1 a]. **1975** *Daily Tel.* 24 July 3/6 Many of the boys became male prostitutes... They became known as 'rent boys'. **1976** DEAKIN & WILLIS *Johnny go Home* iii. 56 Between the ages of fifteen and twenty he had been a rent boy, a boy prostitute living and working in the West End. **1932** W. FAULKNER *Light in August* xv. 338 They went straight to the garage where Salmon keeps his rent car. **1970** *Islander* (Victoria, B.C.) 6 Dec. 7/1 Ben quickly turned his machine into a 'rent' car. 'They call them taxis now,' he explained. **1906** *Chambers's Jrnl.* Jan. 118/1 Evidences of the long-continued disturbance of rent-contracts in Ireland. **1940** W. FAULKNER *Hamlet* I. i. 14 But then I hear tell he always makes his rent contracts later than most. **1931** *Rep. Inter-Departmental Committee Rent Restrictions Acts* (Min. Health) xiv. 46 Some of us, if we had had the task of devising the original system of rent control..would perhaps have proposed the setting up of rent courts. **1965** *Listener* 20 May 727/1 Local authority subsidies, rent control of private rented houses. *a* **1974** R. CROSSMAN *Diaries* (1975) I. 48, I am engaged on rent controls already. **1946** M. B. LOWNDES *Let.* 9 Jan. (1971) 270 Luckily Susan's flat is rent controlled. **1971** B. MALAMUD *Tenants* 6 The building was rent-controlled, and from the District Rent Office..Harry had learned he was a statutory tenant. **1978** I. B. SINGER *Shosha* viii. 152 He had a rent-controlled apartment for which he paid no more than thirty zlotys a month. **1943** L. HUGHES in *Poetry* Sept. 312 The rent man knocked. **1969** *Punch* 1 Jan. 15/1, I do worry about the effect which its long illness is having on its general standing with the butcher, the baker, and the rentman. **1977** COOTE & GILL *Women's Rights* vii. 257 Check the rent register at your local Rent Office. **1965** *New Statesman* 9 Apr. 561/3 Widely publicised rent scales would..make it easier for rent officers. **1973** E. BERCKMAN *Victorian Album* 176 Before we ever took this lease, I went to the Rent Officer. **1976** *Southern Even. Echo* (Southampton) 13 Nov. 6/5 The rent officer in determining fair rents can consider under his brief the property and then fix his figure with reference to similar properties. **1926** C. VAN VECHTEN *Nigger Heaven* ix. 150 There were..the modest rent-parties. **1956** [see *house-party* s.v. *HOUSE *sb.*¹ 23]. **1968** P. OLIVER *Screening Blues* vi. 203 One of the most frequently heard songs in the rent-party repertoire was *The Boy in the Boat.* **1936** G. WILSON *Rent Rebates* 10 There is a not inconsiderable body of opinion which has already expressed itself in favour of the adoption of rent rebate schemes. **1971** *Reader's Digest Family Guide Law* 132/2 To apply for a rent rebate, a tenant must give details of his own income. **1977** *R.A.F. News* 11–24 May 4/6 Some 4,036 soldiers and 59 leading aircraftsmen were on rent rebate. **1921** A. W. BOON *Rent Restriction Act, 1920* 5 The Rent Restriction Act is very intricate and much involved. **1940** *Economist* 5 Oct. 422/2 Profiteers have been threatened with the Rent Restriction Acts. **1952** A. CHRISTIE *Mrs. McGinty's Dead* ii. 17 Under the Rent Restriction Act the landlord couldn't get the old woman out. **1976** *Evening Post* (Nottingham) 17 Dec. 32/8 Rent increases amounting to £2,025..were not included because of the failure to act on the partial lifting of rent restrictions in November, 1973. **1970** *N.Y. Times* 5 Feb. 38/6 The student organization also is lending moral and organizational support to..a widespread local rent strike. **1973** *Freedom* 26 May 1/2 Let the Trade Union movement now show its regard for the value of education by giving..support to student rent-strikes. **1977** *Transatlantic Rev.* LX. 120 In English class he'd go off on a crusade for Food Co-ops and Rent Strikes. **1927** MACQUOID & EDWARDS *Dict. Eng. Furnit.* III. 241 A..type, known as a 'Rent-Table', was introduced about this time [*sc.* 1750]. **1952** J. GLOAG *Short Dict. Furnit.* 387 *Rent Table,* a type of office table made during the second half of the 18th century, with a round or octagonal top, with drawers immediately below. **1961** 'J. WELCOME' *Beware of Midnight* i. 9 The furniture, too, was solid and respectable. There was an octagonal rent table. **1973** V. CANNING *Finger of Saturn* i. 4 He..set his briefcase on the round rent table. **1945** *Daily Herald* 20 Apr. 4/3 Unanimous proposals of the Committee are: The establishment of 198 rent tribunals for England and Wales. **1973** E. BERCKMAN *Victorian Album* 28 It means spending half your life before the Rent Tribunal. **1974** COOTE & GILL *Women's Rights* vii. 256 You may be able to recover the extra amount by going to the Rent Tribunal.

rent, *v.*¹ Add: **2. a.** Also *absol.*

1671 W. BERKELEY in E. D. Neill *Virginia Carolorum* (1886) viii. 335 In Virginia about forty thousand persons.. have come to settle and rent. **1911** M. W. OVINGTON *Half Man* 44 Not only were they unable to rent in neighbourhoods suitable for respectable men and women. **1979** *N.Y. Rev. Bks.* 17 May 6/2 New Yorkers rent. They don't buy.

b. To obtain money from (someone) by criminal means or in exchange for homosexual favours. *slang.*

1898 O. WILDE *Let.* 11 May (1962) 738 Bosie..is devoted to a dreadful little ruffian aged fourteen... Every time he goes home with Bosie he tries to rent him. **1956** C. MACKENZIE *Thin Ice* xiii. 172 'I reckon you thought I was trying to rent Mr. Fortescue, eh?' 'To do what?' I asked in astonishment at such an expression. 'Get money out of him.'

5. (Earlier and later examples.) Also const. *for.* Now chiefly *N. Amer.*

1784 G. WASHINGTON *Diary* 15 Sept. (1925) II. 292 The Plantation on which Mr. Simpson lives rented well—viz. for 500 Bushels of Wheat. **1805** *New-England Palladium* (Boston) 26 July 3/3 Two convenient Tenaments, for small families, that will rent at 12 pr. cent. of what they will be sold for. **1947** *Chicago Daily News* 25 Feb. 1/4 (*caption*) 4-room apartment to rent for $120. **1974** *Whig-Standard* (Kingston, Ontario) 11 Jan. 7/2 The smallest 'bedsitter' apartment in central London rents for about $25 per week.

7. a. Used (with reference to sense 2) in the form *rent-a-* prefixing a noun (usu. with hyphens) to designate the rental of the thing specified, orig. and chiefly a motor vehicle.

Rentacar forms part of a proprietary term in the U.S.

1921 *Chicago Central Business & Office Building Directory* 531/1 *Rent-a-Ford (Inc.)* 1450 S. Michigan av. **1924** *Official Gaz.* (U.S. Patent Office) 19 Feb. 503/1 The Rentacar Company, Toledo, Ohio..Rentacar U-Drive..Automobiles.

Claims use since Aug. 6, 1921. **1935** *Arch. Dermatol. & Syphilol.* XXXII. 78 A man..who owned a 'rent-a-car' business. **1963** *Fortune* Sept. 78 (Advt.), Avis is only No. 2 in rent a cars. So we have to try harder. **1966** J. Gardner *Amber Nine* xi. 161 Martin..was at the wheel of the Rent-a-Car Merc. **1969** 'G. Black' *Cold Jungle* ix. 137 The rentacar Zephyr was still waiting on grass. **1971** *E. Afr. Standard* (Nairobi) 13 Apr. 13/6 Rent-a-train and unit-train operations across North America would siphon more than 4 million tons of cargo from the Seaway. **1972** 'G. Black' *Bitter Tea* (1973) ii. 26 The key to my rentacar was in one of my damp pockets. **1976** *National Observer* (U.S.) 21 Aug. 7/1 Rent-a-horse service is available from a riding school next door. **1977** *Rolling Stone* 19 May 11/2 His is a typical L.A. rent-a-home.

b. In various extended and fanciful uses, as *rent-a-crowd*, *rent-a-mob*, etc., to denote the spontaneous acquisition or instant availability (usu. for some transitory purpose) of the thing specified. Also *transf.* in *concr.* senses.

1961 *Daily Tel.* 21 Dec. 8/6 Dictators!!! When you liberate a territory or mop up a colonialist enclave, are you disappointed and upset to receive only a tepid welcome from the people? Let *rentacrowd* help you! We can supply cheering crowds for all occasions. **1964** C. Driver *Disarmers* x. 233 The phenomenon which Peter Simple of the *Daily Telegraph* cruelly christened 'Rentacrowd': London's instantly available progressive claque ready..to demonstrate on a whole range of causes. **1968** *Guardian* 22 Aug. 8/6 Ali..is the only man in Britain at the moment who can summon up a sizable Rentacrowd fast. **1970** *Peace News* 5 Sept. 7/1 One of the chief rentacops was reportedly bitten in the genitals by one of his own dogs. **1970** *Guardian* 27 Oct. 11/5 The strategy was based upon a tactic which Oxford students called Rentamob..a hard core of rioters who could turn a demonstration into a confrontation. **1972** M. Jones *Life on Dole* i. 11 In Merthyr Tydfil it was the day for the demonstration against unemployment... There are no professional marchers—no Rentacrowd—here. **1976** *Times* 27 Jan. 4/1 Squatters in London are reported to be using children in a 'rent-a-kid' system, as a means of being rehoused. **1977** *New Society* 7 July 15/1 Trouble was caused not by ordinary workers, still less by management, but by Rent-a-picket... 'There's always the Rent-a-crowd element that hangs on to strikes.' **1979** *Daily Tel.* 17 Nov. 2/1 Sir John denied that the trade union movement was contaminated by the 'rent-a-mob' philosophy.

rentability. Delete *rare*—1 and add later examples. *spec.* (see quot. 1964).

1922 W. Schlich *Man. Forestry* (ed. 4) I. ii. 107 These changes should not, in the long run, seriously affect the rentability of the forest industry. **1964** *Financial Times* 3 Mar. 5/2 Rentability is the ratio of an undertaking's profits to its capital. **1976** F. Zweig *New Acquisitive Society* ii. iii. 107 Public enterprise..is also supposed to achieve productivity and rentability.

rental, *sb.* Add: **2. b.** A house, flat, car, etc., let out for rent. Chiefly *N. Amer.*

1952 *Sat. Even. Post* 22 Nov. 25 Sometimes a mob of hoodlums in a rental forced off the road by pursuing police would get tangled up in their own arsenal. **1968** *Globe & Mail* (Toronto) 3 Feb. 3/3 Habitat, Expo's futuristic housing complex, has started a new life as an ordinary rental development. **1970** *New York* 16 Nov. 42/3 They began breaking up the mills and foundries into rentals for small-time manufacturers. **1972** J. Gores *Dead Skip* xi. 76 The house was a rental, and rental properties meant landladies. **1981** *Nordic Skiing* Jan. 47/1 The ski shop carries complete rentals in all sizes and reservations on rental equipment are accepted.

3*. The fact or process of renting (in the sense of Rent *v.*[1] 3).

1915 *Nat. Real Estate Jrnl.* Nov. 332/2 The duty of the agent to owners whose property he has in charge for rental, requires him to make untiring effort to promptly secure desirable tenants. **1928** *Publishers' Weekly* 12 May 1951 The rental of children's books has not so far been well tested out, as only four of the stores replying have collections of children's books. **1977** *Grimsby Even. Tel.* 31 May 11/2 Advt.), The property is on rental.

4. *rental agency, agent, car, house*; **rental library** chiefly *U.S.*, a library at which a charge is made for the loan of books.

1947 S. L. McMichael *How to operate Real Estate Business* xxvii. 221 The rental agency must use considerable tact in fitting tenants into the right locations. **1972** J. Philips *Vanishing Senator* iii. iv. 136 Couldn't you try rental agencies? **1978** R. Ludlum *Holcroft Covenant* xiii. 153 The rental agency was not amused, but Holcroft gave them no choice. **1915** *Nat. Real Estate Jrnl.* Nov. 332/2 (*heading*) Duties of rental agents. **1967** *Boston Sunday Globe* 23 Apr. B43/7 The rental agent is Martin Cerel, Natick realtor. **1979** *N.Y. Rev. Bks.* 17 May 37 (Advt.), Britain's most experienced rental agent is here to give you every assistance with your plans for accommodation. **1962** *Time* 7 Dec. 84/3 Cut-rate rental cars are generally as clean and well-serviced as the big three. **1978** S. Sheldon *Bloodline* xxxiii. 315 It took almost three hours for Max to drive to Lesgets in a Volkswagen, the cheapest rental car he could find. **1953** A. Upfield *Murder must Wait* ix. 85 Rental houses are few.. and the demand for them is heavy. **1928** *Publishers' Weekly* 14 July 169 His basement book-store..is now the home of an unusually successful rental library. **1934** G. Conklin *How to run Rental Library* i. 11 The rental library..is strictly limited to that type of book-renting business which is organized for the purpose of profit. **1946** R. Chandler *Let.* 9 Jan. (1966) 136 The publishers have co-operated in the rental library swindle over a period of years.

rentalsman (re·ntălzmæn). *Canad.* [f. Rental *sb.* by analogy with *Ombudsman.] An official with responsibility for the equitable letting and administration of rented property.

1970 *Deb. & Proc. Legislative Assembly Manitoba* 30 June 3525 In my view, the singularly most unique feature of the proposed amendments is the establishment of the office of Rentalsman. **1971** *Canad. Labour* Mar. 15/3 This rating was based on: a single easy-to-read law, containing a broader statement of tenant rights than the other provinces; appointment of a 'rentalsman' (rental ombudsman); and a public education program on the new legislation. **1974** *Globe & Mail* (Toronto) 13 Apr. 8/2 Ceilings for rent increases..may be breached if the landlord can convince a new Government official called a rentalsman that higher increases are necessary because of costs.

rent-charge. Add: **2.** *attrib.*, as *rent-charge, bank, stock.*

1909 *Daily Chron.* 14 Sept. 5/6 Rent-charge banks were formed to aid the peasants in redeeming these charges. **1869** *Bradshaw's Railway Man.* XXI. 290 The debenture holders having refused to accept the 4½ per cent. rent-charge stock at par. **1909** *Gt. Central Railway Co. Rep.* 6 Aug. 13 The South Yorkshire Rent-Charge Stocks.

‖ **rente** (rant). [Fr.] Stock, esp. government stock; the interest or income accruing from such stock. Cf. Rent *sb.*[1] 3 b.

1873 R. Browning *Red Cotton Night-Cap Country* iii. 185 Lying stretched on straw, The produce of your miserable *rente!* **1920** J. Galsworthy *In Chancery* iii. ix. 283 She had, he knew, but one ambition—to live on her '*rentes*' in Paris. **1926** D. L. Sayers *Clouds of Witness* v. 116 There were substantial dividends from capital invested in French *rentes.* **1927** *Financial Times* 13 July 5/5 French Banks and Rentes hardened, recovering the ground lost recently. **1931** S. Jameson *Richer Dust* xvii. 495, I must find a job... I can't just live on my *rentes.*

rented, *ppl. a.* Add: **3.** *lower-rented.*

1801 Jane Austen *Let.* 3 Jan. (1952) 100 It used to be lower rented than any other house in the row. **1939** M. S. Rice *Working-Class Wives* viii. 195 The shortage will not have been overtaken by 1941 even if the process of 'filtering-up', (i.e. people who can afford to do so vacating the lower-rented houses and moving into unsubsidized higher-rented houses) were steady and complete.

Rentenmark (re·ntənmāɹk). [Ger., f. *renten* securities: see Mark *sb.*[2] in Dict. and Suppl.] A unit of currency introduced in Germany in November 1923 and tied to the nation's industrial and agricultural resources; in 1924 it was replaced by the *reichsmark* (see *Reich).

1923 *Times* 8 Nov. 12/4 The issue of Rentenmarks is to be delayed till it can take place simultaneously throughout the country. **1940** G. Crowther *Outl. Money* i. 19 The Rentenmark note was not itself land, nor was there any method by which the holder of a Rentenmark note could possess himself of the land that was supposed to be behind his note. **1967** T. Stolper tr. *G. Stolper's German Econ.* iv. 91 In the case of the Rentenmark collateral consisted of the 'real-estate debts' of agriculture and of industrial companies. **1974** *Spectator* 21 Dec. 803/1 The Rentenmark was a new unit of currency supposedly backed by the land of the Reich.

renter, *sb.*[1] **4. b.** Delete † *Obs.* and add later examples.

1882 Sweet & Knox *Sk. Texas Siftings* 51 The joyful glee of farming with negro renters 'on the shares'. **1938** *Mississippi* (Fed. Writers' Project) 104 *Renters*, who hire land for a fixed amount to be paid either in crop values or in cash. **1970** J. Blackburn *Land of Promise* viii. 119 He was on his way to see a renter on one of his farms south of town.

6. A male prostitute. *slang.*

1893 O. Wilde *Let.* Mar. (1964) 336, I would sooner be blackmailed by every renter in London, than have you bitter, unjust, hating. **1895** M. Beerbohm *Let.* 3 May (1964) 103 It was horrible leaving the court day after day and having to pass through a knot of renters. **1969** *Jeremy* I. iii. 22/2 *Renter*, male prostitute. **1972** D. Sutton *Lett. R. Fry* I. 5 In many cases 'affairs' were more idealistic than that practised by the 'renters' of Piccadilly.

7. One who organizes the distribution of films to exhibitors.

1908 *Variety* 16 May 11 There are other and larger questions pressing the attention of the exhibitor, renter and manufacturer. **1911** D. S. Hulfish *Cycl. Motion-Pict. Work* II. 112 The film industry is definitely separated into three branches: *manufacturer*, *renter*, and *exhibitor*. The renter owns the picture films. **1920** I. P. Gore in L. Carson '*Stage' Year Bk. 1920* 52 The success which attended the efforts of the exhibitors, renters, and manufacturers, to combat the peril with which they were confronted. **1927** *Melody Maker* Aug. 820/2 The renters could render far more assistance..if they would take more interest in the showing of their films at every cinema where they are booked. **1940** *Economist* 13 July 43/1 To ensure that a minimum number of films are made, renters must produce or acquire one British film.

rentering, *vbl. sb.* Delete † and add later examples. Also *attrib.*

1901 P. N. Hasluck *Tailoring* 21 There are three kinds of absolutely invisible stitches which are used to repair tears... They are stoating, fine-drawing, and rentering. **1921** [see *invisible *a.* 1 f]. **1955** J. E. Liberty *Pract. Tailoring* (ed. 2) iii. 24 Seaming and rentering... this is used in place of stoting when the material does not lend itself to being stoted.

‖ **rentier** (rañti͵e). Also fem. **rentière** (-iˈęr'). [Fr.] One who makes an income from property or investment. Cf. *rente.

1847 in Webster. **1885** *Instructions Clerks Classifying Occupations* (Census Eng. & Wales, 1881) 100 Persons without specified occupations..returned by property, rank, &c... Rentier. **1885** A. Edwardes *Girton Girl* III. xv. 265 We are private citizens—rentières, living on our means. **1921** R. H. Tawney *Acquisitive Society* v. 68 If it [*sc.* a society] is to..avoid the creation of a class of *rentier*, it must not use for current consumption the whole of the wealth annually produced. **1948** A. Huxley *Let.* 25 Jan. (1969) 579 Maria's uncle..is a rentier, living on an unelastic income. **1954** M. Beresford *Lost Villages* ii. vi. 205 Any ex- demesne land which *rentier* lords were prepared..to lease. **1964** T. B. Bottomore *Elites & Society* iii. 45 Pareto's two types of elite..which he also refers to as the 'speculators' and the 'rentiers'. **1969** *Listener* 6 Feb. 173/2 This grumbling, sinisterly superior *rentière* lived opposite Virginia Lodge, Parkwood Hill, the Dales' suburban residence. **1973** 'D. Jordan' *Nile Green* xxxi. 145 It's oil sheiks and Latin American generals and Lebanese rentiers who are going to buy your bonds. **1976** M. Green *Children of Sun* viii. 316 Brian..fulminated against *rentiers* and Money Men..but.. he remained a hedonist and a snob.

renting, *vbl. sb.*[1] Delete *rare* and add: **1.** (Later examples.)

1946 E. O'Neill *Iceman Cometh* p. vii, The renting of rooms on the upper floors, under the Raines-Law loopholes. **1974** *Howard Jrnl.* XIV. 41 Renting to the poor became increasingly unprofitable.

2. *slang.* In the sense of *Rent *v.*[1] 2 b.

1956 C. Mackenzie *Thin Ice* xiv. 183 Mr. Jack Shore has done quite a lot of blackmailing, or in his own elegant phraseology a lot of renting, during his inglorious career. **1963** —— *Life & Times* II. 255 At this date [*sc.* 1899] the cant word among homosexuals for their proclivities was 'so'. That seems to have vanished completely from current cant, though 'renting' for male prostitutes and 'camping' to express the way they attract the soliciting male still survive

3. *attrib.*, as *renting firm, house.*

1920 I. P. Gore in L. Carson '*Stage' Year Bk. 1920* 52 In the same way the big renting firm came to the rescue of its small rival. **1927** *Melody Maker* Aug. 819/2 Every renting house of any standing requires a capable and experienced cinema musician permanently on its staff.

‖ **rentrée** (rañtre). [Fr.] A return, esp. a return home after an annual holiday.

1892 E. Dowson *Let.* 22 Aug. (1967) 240 Many thanks for your note, which I found on my rentrée last week. **1896** Beerbohm in *Yellow Bk.* XI. 20 His *rentrée* into the still silent town strengthened his..resolves. **1913** —— *Fifty Caricatures*, (*caption*) Rentrée of Mr. George Moore into Chelsea. **1961** *Guardian* 22 Sept. 16/1 The Rentrée is the return to the great cities, the beginning of a new school year. **1977** *Times* 30 Aug. 4/1 Life is about to begin again in France... The word of the moment is *la rentrée.*

renunciant, *sb.* (Earlier and later examples.)

1848 T. Arnold *Let.* 2 Jan. (1966) 216 Even now there is a little band of Renunciants scattered over the world. **1931** E. Wilson *Axel's Castle* viii. 257 All were pessimists, renunciants, resignationists, 'tired of the sad hospital' which earth seemed to them.

renversement. Delete † *Obs.* and add later examples. Now *spec.* in *Aeronaut.* (orig. *U.S.*), an aeroplane manœuvre consisting of half-loop effected simultaneously with a half-turn (see also quot. 1956).

1954 W. Faulkner *Fable* 343 The car making the last *renversement* because now it could go no farther. **1956** *U.S. Air Force Dict.* 435/2 *Renversement*,..any airplane maneuver or performance in which the airplane is made to reverse direction, as in a chandelle, Immelmann turn, or wingover. **1966** E. V. Rickenbacker *Rickenbacker* (1968) vi. 106, I immediately put my Spad into a *renversement*—pulled the stick straight back to start a loop and simultaneously rolled it over in a half turn. **1973** *Times* 2 Jan. (Forward into Europe Suppl.) p. xii/6 Perhaps the Henry Moore retrospective..and the Francis Bacon exhibition ..herald a *renversement.*

‖ **renvoi** (rañvwa). *Law.* [Fr., f. *renvoyer* to send back: cf. Renvoy *sb.*] (See quots.)

1897 J. T. B. Sewell tr. Labbé in *Outl. French Law as affecting Brit. Subjects* iv. 69 In order to justify the system which repudiates the doctrine of 'renvoi'..it suffices to define exactly what is the intention of the law which authorizes the foreign law to decide. **1898** *Law Q. Rev.* XIV. 231 An English specialist versed in the problems raised by the conflict of laws may well never have heard the name of the *Renvoi.* **1904** J. P. Bate *Doctrine of Renvoi* iv. 53 The basis of the Renvoi-theory is the doctrine that when a conflict-rule refers a matter to a foreign law, the foreign law is referred to *in its totality.* **1905** J. Westlake *Priv. Internat. Law* (ed. 4) ii. 25 In its substance the subject [*sc.* private international law] has been no less deeply affected by the substitution..of political nationality for domicile as the criterion of personal law, and by the controversy which has consequently sprung up about the doctrine called the *renvoi.* **1935** G. C. Cheshire *Priv. Internat. Law* vi. 133 The second solution is to give a decision on the assumption that the doctrine of *renvoi* is recognized by English law. This famous doctrine, which presupposes that a reference to the law of the domicil means a reference to the whole of that law, may be explained as follows in connexion with our case of X. The English Court, upon referring to the Private International Law of France, finds that it is referred back to English law as being the law f X's nationality. There is a *renvoi* or a remission to English law. **1959** E. Jowitt *Dict. Eng. Law* II. 1525/1 *Renvoi*, a term employed in private international law to denote the sending, or determination, of a matter to or according to the law of a tribunal outside the jurisdiction where the question arose. **1970** *Internat. & Compar. Law Q.* 4th Ser. XIX. i. 36 The generally accepted English view has been that tort cases are outside the scope of the doctrine of *renvoi.*

reoccu·rrence. [Re- 5 a.] A further occurrence; a recurrence.

1817 D. O'Connell *Let.* 24 June (1972) II. 152 There will not be a reoccurrence even of those wretched squabbles.

1964 B. TRNKA in D. Abercrombie et al. *Daniel Jones* 188 The re-occurrence of voiceless consonants in the same morpheme is found more frequently than that of the corresponding voiced consonants.

reorder, *v.* Add: **3. b.** (Later example.)
1967 COX & GROSE *Organization & Handling Bibl. Rec. by Computer* vi. 162 Not all delayed books are going to be re-ordered.

reordered *ppl. a.*, reordering *vbl. sb.* (examples in sense 3 b of vb.).
1938 *New Statesman* 21 May 860/2 Ordered, counter-ordered and reordered machines. **1962** A. BATTERSBY *Guide to Stock Control* v. 42 The boundary between them remains as a mark which indicates the Re-ordering Level (ROL). **1969** *Jane's Freight Containers 1968–69* 416/1 Consistent production rates possible with more frequent re-ordering cycles.

reo·rder, *sb.* [RE- 5 a.] A renewed or repeated order for goods.
1901 *Scotsman* 8 Apr. 9/7 Current trade is confined to small reorders. **1928** *Publishers' Weekly* 9 June 2376 It is not easy on placing advance orders..to get the full value of the suggestions of the clerks, but on the reorders this is simpler. **1977** *Time Out* 21 Jan. 3/3 The chap behind the counter is often the one who chooses the wine he sells and he is there to take your re-orders when you come back.

reo:rganiza·tional, *a.* [f. REORGANIZATION + -AL.] Of or pertaining to reorganization.
1972 *Guardian* 26 Jan. 4/3 Yugoslavia's League of Communists united today behind party reorganisational changes.

reo:rganiza·tionist. [f. REORGANIZATION + -IST.] One who favours (political) reorganization; *spec.* a member of a radical Chinese faction (fl. 1930: see quot. 1975). Also *attrib.* or as *adj.*
1930 *Times* 25 Mar. 23/5 Nanking was faced by a revolt from the so-called 'Reorganisationists', a group mainly consisting of the political leaders of the left who had been excluded from office. **1967** J. ISRAEL in A. Feuerwerker et al. *Approaches to Mod. Chinese Hist.* 292 Many Wuhan figures who cast their lot with Wang Ching-wei (exiled leader of the Reorganizationist faction) argued that the revolution remained 'unfinished'. **1975** I. C. Y. HSÜ *Rise Mod. China* (ed. 2) xxiii. 653 Wang and his left-wing followers were out of office. The latter group retaliated by accusing Chiang of betraying the principles and ideas of Sun, and demanded a reorganization of the KMT in the spirit of the 1924 manifesto—hence their nickname 'The Reorganizationists'.

reorganize, *v.* Also *intr.* for *refl.*
1857 J. HYDE *Mormonism* vii. 183 They completely re-organized in May, 1857. **1972** 'E. LATHEN' *Murder without Icing* i. 14 The time has come for him to reorganize. He will be selling some earlier ventures.
Hence **reo·rganized** *ppl. a.*
1892 'MARK TWAIN' *Amer. Claim.* xiv. 129 The rude impact of the thought of these people upon his reorganized condition of mind. **1929** P. HUGHES *Catholic Question, 1688–1829* III. iii. 283 In the re-organised Catholic Committee, O'Connell had from the first been a force.

reo·rient, *v.* [RE- 5 a.] **1.** *trans.* To re-arrange, give a new orientation or direction to (ideas, etc.); to help (a person) to find his bearings again; to redirect (a thing).
1933 *Times Educ. Suppl.* 25 Feb. 57/4 Russia's children are suffering in the grim struggle; but they are not having to be reborn, to reorient their whole lives. **1939** *Sun* (Baltimore) 25 July 8/7 'Britain has *re-Oriented* her China policy.' I don't know whether that pun was Mr. Byas' own. **1951** G. HUMPHREY *Thinking* ix. 306 Psychic 'scaffolding', 'hypotheses', by which the original *Aufgabe* is reoriented. **1956** A. H. COMPTON *Atomic Quest* 32 His [*sc.* Einstein's] quantum and relativity theories were reorienting physics thought. **1966** D. F. GALOUYE *Lost Perception* vii. 74 'I feel so out of touch,..as though I've stood still for two whole years while everything passed me by.' 'We'll reorient you,' Forsythe assured. **1975** *Nature* 10 July 109/1 On day 123 the satellite was reoriented to allow the four Ariel-V experiments which view along the spin axis to observe Cyg X-1, placing it outside the field of view of this experiment. **1977** D. BENNETT *Jigsaw Man* iv. 71 I'll give you a sort of running commentary,' she said. 'Reorient you.'
2. a. *refl.* To adjust (oneself) *to* something; to come to terms with something; to adopt a new direction or relation.
1937 *Jrnl. Compar. Psychol.* XXIV. 296 The animals did recognize a new situation in the tests... Many took much longer about the first jump in the test trials, and appeared to be re-orienting themselves to the whole environment. **1955** M. LOWRY *Let.* July (1967) 381 What with this eye business I have to revise entirely my method of writing and ..reorient myself to it. **1962** *Lancet* 8 Dec. 1229/2 Some will reorient themselves in their new surroundings in about three weeks, recognising their new ward as their home. **1963** *Economist* 19 Jan. 232/2 If the railways can really re-orient themselves.
b. *intr.* for *refl.*
1960 C. D. SIMAK in *Mag. Fantasy & Science Fiction* June 104 He had to reorient, he knew. He had to come to.. terms..with this situation. **1974** *Nature* 6 Sept. 16/1 The other spectra are so similar to V that Watkins also assigns them to zinc vacancies. But the V[1] centres do not reorient under uniaxial stress. **1977** *Jrnl. Protozool.* XXIV. 29/2 Some conjugating pairs subjected to antiserum treatment separate belatedly, after a partial cortical fusion has occurred and when the conjugants have reoriented into a heteropolar configuration.

reo·rientate, *v.* [RE- 5 a.] **1.** *trans.* = *RE-ORIENT *v.* 1.
1933 *Planning* 6 June 2 The most urgent necessity..for a common and intensive effort by all parties to reorientate their various points of view. **1958** *Times Lit. Suppl.* 21 Nov. 675/1 How does one re-orientate one's philosophy and economic policy? **1959** B. WOOTTON *Soc. Science & Soc. Pathol.* viii. 267 Glueck's object in treating criminality as a disease is to concentrate attention..on the practical problem of how his [*sc.* the offender's] behaviour may be re-orientated. **1981** P. MCCUTCHAN *Shard calls Tune* xv. 163 [He] came to a small town... He knew where he was... He was re-orientated nicely.
2. *refl.* = *REORIENT *v.* 2 a.
1940 *Scrutiny* IX. 196 We may perhaps hope that Scotland will be able to reorientate itself with the end of the epoch that has seen its cultural disintegration. **1959** M. SUMMERTON *Small Wilderness* xiv. 174 Struggling to reorientate myself..I tried to place myself in his shoes. **1979** J. WAINWRIGHT *Duty Elsewhere* xvi. 47 Cooke had reorientated himself a little. He was still dizzy.

reo:rienta·tion. [RE- 5 a.] The action or process of reorienting; a fresh orientation.
1920 *Contemp. Rev.* July 6 There will be needed a great collaboration of wisely directed effort at home, combined with an entire reorientation of attitude and policy on the part of the Allies. **1938** *Burlington Mag.* May 248/2 He seems to minimize the imposition of sartorial forms by commercial dictation, surely more often the cunning contrivance of change for change's profitable sake than the concrete expression of social reorientations. **1942** L. B. NAMIER *Conflicts* 16 Far-seeing statesmen discerned the need of such a reorientation. **1951** R. FIRTH *Elem. Soc. Organization* iii. 110 This is represented..by a re-orientation of resources in goods or labour power. **1967** G. STEINER *Lang. & Silence* 83 Many reorientations, many ways of ordering and choosing are available to scholarship and the imagination. **1977** P. BAELZ *Ethics & Belief* vi. 74 Different religions give different answers to this question, all of them involving both a reorientation of insight and understanding and a new pattern of action.

reovirus (rī·ovəi³rə̆s). *Biol.* [mod.L., f. initial letters of *r*espiratory, *e*nteric, *o*rphan (see *orphan virus* s.v. *ORPHAN *a.* 2) + VIRUS.] Any of a group of related double-stranded RNA viruses that are sometimes associated with disease in animals, including respiratory and enteric infection in man.
1959 A. B. SABIN in *Science* 20 Nov. 1388/1 Studies..have provided the defininitive information required for establishing these strains as members of a new group of viruses, for which I am proposing the name 'reoviruses'. **1970** *Nature* 28 Mar. 1209/1 *Vaccinia* virus and reovirus assemble their mRNA synthesizing enzymes within the mature virion. **1973** R. G. KRUEGER et al. *Introd. Microbiol.* xix. 532/1 Three serological types of reovirus have been identified. The structure of the particles..consists of an RNA core some 40 nm in diameter and an icosahedral capsid 30–50 Å in width. No envelope is present. The 92 capsomeres are closely packed and appear as pentagonal or hexagonal columnar prisms (possibly truncated pyramids) arranged in 5:3:2 symmetry. **1979** *Sci. Amer.* Nov. 65/1 In mice.. reovirus attacks the acinar cells of the pancreas.

reo·xidize, *v.* [RE- 5 b.] **a.** *trans.* To oxidize again.
1940 GLASSTONE *Textbk. Physical Chem.* xii. 1020 The ion, e.g., Ti^{++++}, is first reduced at the cathode, e.g., to Ti^{+++}, which is the active reducing agent; in the process it is re-oxidized to Ti^{++++}, and is again reduced at the cathode and so on. **1957** *Science* 12 Apr. 691/3 Partially reduced ribonuclease..was reoxidized. **1973** *Chem. Soc. Rev.* II. 43 The unwanted epimer can be reoxidized to (78) for recycling.
b. *intr.* To take up oxygen again.
1966 *Economist* 16 Apr. 289/3 The zinc vapour is stripped out of the gases by a spray of molten lead—a vital part of the new process, since it removes the zinc before it can re-oxidise. **1976** *Sci. Amer.* July 78/2 The product of the Purofer process is a briquette that does not reoxidize readily because of its small surface area.

reoxygenate, *v.* Add: Hence **reo:xygena·tion.**
1957 G. E. HUTCHINSON *Treat. Limnol.* I. ix. 593 The full reoxygenation of a very deep lake..presents real difficulties.

rep[1]. Substitute for def: Colloq. abbrev. of REPUTATION. Common in early 18th c.; now chiefly *U.S.* (Later examples.)
1873 J. H. BEADLE *Undevel. West* xix. 367 Of the town proper, a majority of citizens were negroes, with them a few whites of doubtful 'rep', and perhaps a dozen Indians. **1910** E. A. WALCOTT *Open Door* xii. 155 An' me a white man, too, even if me rep. is off color. **1935** 'E. QUEEN' *Spanish Cape Mystery* iii. 68 Got a rep as a bad customer. **1956** 'E. MCBAIN' *Cop Hater* (1958) x. 90 We got a big rep as it is. Ain't nobody in this city who ain't heard of The Grovers. **1978** M. PUZO *Fools Die* iv. 51 He was a legitimate bad guy with an obvious rep in Vegas.

rep[4]. (Further examples.)
1906 [see *CON d]. **1930** E. M. BRENT-DYER *Chalet School & Jo* iv. 57 'There's only rep left, and I've arithmetic and French to write!' protested Cornelia.

rep[5]. Abbrev. of REPRESENTATIVE *sb.*; esp. a sales representative.
1896 T. EYTON *Rugby Football* 10 Joe..has annually played and led the Tauranga reps. against the Auckland teams. **1933** L. G. D. ACLAND in *Press* (Christchurch, N.Z.) 18 Nov. 15/7 *Rep...* Under the arbitration award it is laid down that 'the shearers shall elect a representative', who deals with the employer..whenever any dispute or question arises. **1938** E. AMBLER *Cause for Alarm* ii. 28 No travellers seen except on Tuesdays and Thursdays... Reps.., Tuesdays and Thursdays. **1959** T. GIRTIN *Unnatural Break* xxviii. 101 The local rep of the League of Empire Loyalists got up in the middle and made a protest. **1959** *New Statesman* 19 Dec. 874/1 One young sales rep, whom I met quite early in the month, was already discovering his soul and finding the process painful. **1969** T. LLOYD in R. Blythe *Akenfield* xiv. 218, I am the only member of this club who isn't a farmer's son..or a rep. **1977** *Jrnl. R. Soc. Arts* CXXV. 679/1 We can have three thousand safety reps for a labour force of thirty five thousand. **1979** *Tucson* (Arizona) *Citizen* 20 Sept. 2A/2 The House turned down an amendment by Rep. Eldon Rudd.

rep[6]. Colloq. abbrev. of REPERTORY 3 (occas. of REPERTOIRE); a repertory company or theatre. Freq. *attrib.*
1925 *Amer. Speech* I. 36/2 A rep show is made up of players with a repertoire of plays. **1929** J. B. PRIESTLEY *Good Companions* II. ii. 283 Each member of the troupe prided himself..on having a large répertoire, known always as a 'rep'. **1933** S. O'CASEY *Let.* 24 Sept. (1975) I. 465 A Rep or a Stage Society production. **1948** H. L. MENCKEN *Amer. Lang.* Suppl. II. 690 *Rep company*, a company presenting a répertoire of plays on the road. **1959** *Times* 5 Jan. 12/2 While the productions are out of Oxford we let the theatre to local societies, visiting reps or small-cost tours. **1959** *Manch. Guardian* 30 Jan. 7/1 She has returned to 'weekly rep.', producing for a sound but as yet undistinguished company which must perform potboilers for most of the year. **1971** *Guardian* 27 Sept. 10/1 Faithful and ageing Rep-goers. **1977** R. BARNARD *Death in High C's* ii. 18 You're back with..the same old rep production. **1977** *Radio Times* 12–18 Nov. 15/1 After the war Major Bates joined Worthing rep as stage manager.

† **rep[7].** *Obs.* [f. initial letters of *roentgen equivalent physical.*] A quantity of ionizing radiation that will release the same amount of energy in human tissue as one rad (formerly roentgen) of X-rays. Cf. *REM *sb.*[1]
1947 *Nucleonics* Oct. 38/2 If the energy lost by ionization in the tissues is the same as the energy loss for one roentgen of gamma radiation absorbed in air, the dose is spoken of as one roentgen-equivalent-physical (abbreviated 'rep'). [*Note*] The rep and rem units were introduced by Dr. H. M. Parker. **1955** *Bull. Atomic Sci.* June 211/1 On a conservative estimate, a dose of 200 reps, such as many Hiroshima survivors must have received, would probably have caused each of their offspring to inherit, on the average, at least one mutation produced by the exposure. **1962** F. I. ORDWAY et al. *Basic Astronautics* xii. 494 The rep or roentgen equivalent physical is the unit that equals the ionization produced by other forms of radiation to that of x-rays and gamma-rays. The rep is defined as the amount of particulate radiation that produces an energy absorption of 93 ergs/g in human tissue.

repacification. For *rare*[—1] in Dict. read *rare* and add later example.
1937 *Times* 17 Nov. 17/4 Each costly 'pacification' of Wazirs, Mahsuds, or Mohmands is to be followed by their equally costly repacification at regular and almost predictable intervals.

repacker. (Example.)
1976 *Shell in Industr. Chemicals* (Shell Internat. Petroleum Co.) 5 Group companies sell Teepol to blenders and re-packers.

repaint, *sb.* Add: **1.** (Further examples.)
1901 R. FRY *Let.* 10 Dec. (1972) I. 182, I am at present cutting off the sky with a knife and have found a marvellous landscape underneath, entirely concealed by repaints. **1935** *Burlington Mag.* Nov. 202/1 The picture was..then almost entirely covered with re-paint.
2. (Later examples.) Also *fig.* and *attrib.*
1964 G. MARX *Let.* 27 Oct. (1967) 258, I will be in London in April, doing a repaint job on my old quiz show. **1968** S. JAY *Sleepers can Kill* vii. 74 The car was a black Opel in need of a repaint. **1970** J. WAINWRIGHT *Prynter's Devil* iii. 50 Vac the room first, kiddo. Then start the repaint job.
3. Something repainted, esp. a golf-ball.
1922 WODEHOUSE *Clicking of Cuthbert* i. 16 Why, you are a pearl among women, the queen of your sex... You make the rest look like battered repaints. **1931** M. ALLINGHAM *Look to Lady* xiv. 148 'How's the car business?'..'I sold a lovely repaint in Norward last week... We faked it up lovely—registration book and everything.' **1936** *Sun* (Baltimore) 1 Aug. 817, I should like to know whether they [*sc.* golf balls] are new ones or repaints. **1955** *Times* 23 Aug. 4/4 Repaints cost as much as new balls used to.

repair, *sb.*[2] Add: **3.** *repair bill, kit, -man* (chiefly *U.S.*), *outfit, -ship, -shop* (earlier and later examples), *station, time, work*(*s*).
1908 *Westm. Gaz.* 7 Jan. 4/2 The effects of wear and tear would be reduced to a minimum, and the repair bill..would be kept very low. **1970** *Observer* 1 Feb. 31/6 Ten new pence..now buys a 'Panti-hose and Tights Repair Kit' from Woolworths. **1975** *Times* 28 Aug. 11/8, I do not regard a song and dance as the infallible, all-purpose dramatic repair kit. **1871** W. S. HUNTINGTON *Road-Master's Assistant* ii. 9 It is a common practice for repairmen, when replacing mended iron, to squeeze it in perfectly tight. **1928** *Sat. Even. Post* 4 Feb. 140/1 If your car suffers from any of these common motor ills, take it to your car dealer or repairman. **1958** *Times* 13 Sept. 7/7 Such dilemmas as that of the Los Angeles couple whose T.V. stops one night and the husband must go out and find the repairman. **1976** *Washington Post* 19 Apr. A22/4 The tenants refuse to let repairmen into their apartments. **1908** *Sears, Roebuck Catal.* 517/1 Traveler's big complete repair outfit. **1976** J. R. L. ANDERSON *Redundancy Pay* i. 17 He..bought a pump, repair outfit, and a torch-battery cycle lamp. **1905** *Westm. Gaz.* 16 Nov. 6/2 The King's repair-ship 'Assistance'

was floated off at Tetuan yesterday. **1866** *Harper's Mag.* Sept. 543/1 In the repair-shops of the Columbus and Indianapolis Railroad. **1979** *Jrnl. R. Soc. Arts* July 466/1 Somehow the hospital must contrive to be both repair-shop and home. **1906** *Westm. Gaz.* 27 June 7/3 The mechanic.. hung on to the radiator from the starting-line to the repair-station. **1934** *Discovery* Nov. 326/1 Its main depot and repair station is at Lunghwa near Shanghai. **1962** *Autom. Data Proc.* (*B.S.I.*) 52 *Repair time*, time spent outside the periods allocated to routine maintenance and supplementary maintenance in diagnosing and clearing faults, equipment testing and maintenance. **1962** D. R. Cox *Renewal Theory* vii. 80 Suppose that a machine is subject to stoppages and call the time necessary to restart a stopped machine a repair-time. **1906** *Westm. Gaz.* 22 Aug. 10/1 Important repair work is..being undertaken..at the cathedrals of Winchester, Gloucester, York, and Canterbury. **1907** *Ibid.* 21 Mar. 9/1 With no repair works and with insufficient and sometimes incompetent staff, they ran their omnibuses as many hours as they could anyhow be kept on the road. **1969** *Gloss. Landscape Work* (*B.S.I.*) v. 30 *Repair work*, the treatment of incisions, bruises and other wounds or injuries [in trees etc.].

repairability (rĭpēᵊ:răbi·lĭti). [f. REPAIRABLE *a.* + -ITY: cf. REPARABILITY.] The state or quality of being repairable.

1969 *Jane's Freight Containers 1968–69* 464/1 The ship lines are worried about repairability, particularly in foreign ports.

repairable, *a.* (Further examples.)

1890 [see *ADOPTION 2 d]. **1936** [see *AMENITY 1 a, 3 b]. **1950** [see *DILLY *sb.*[5]]. **1972** *Police Rev.* 10 Nov. 1447/1 There is a reasonable chance that the tyre will be repairable. **1976** *Sci. Amer.* Sept. 73/1 The Shuttle will also provide new capabilities in hauling multiple satellites in a single mission ..performing in-orbit servicing and returning repairable systems.

repai·rableness. [f. REPAIRABLE *a.* + -NESS.] Capacity for being repaired.

1909 *Daily Chron.* 21 Aug. 6/6 The [hosepipe] tyre succumbed to the superior repairableness of the detachable.

repairing, *vbl. sb.*[2] **2.** (Later examples of *repairing lease.*)

1935 E. FARJEON *Nursery in Nineties* 522 The house.. was on a repairing lease, and some hundreds of pounds were demanded if we left at once. **1972** C. DRUMMOND *Death at Bar* ii. 45 The house agent..rubbed his hands at the prospect of getting some free work done on the place for it was not a repairing lease.

repaper, *v.* Add: (Earlier and later examples.) Also *absol.* Hence **repa·pering** *vbl. sb.*

1854 MRS. GASKELL *North & South* (1855) I. vii. 96 The landlord..had relented from his expressed determination not to repaper. **1857** —— *Life Charlotte Brontë* II. xiii. 313 Some re-papering and re-painting in the Parsonage. **1964** L. DEIGHTON *Funeral in Berlin* xxxvi. 207, I scarcely recognized the office. It had been re-papered. **1974** —— *Spy Story* xiv. 134 You said repapering the sitting-room would be for my birthday.

reparation. Add: **5. d.** *pl.* Compensation for war damage owed by the aggressor.

In the *Treaty of Peace* (1919) the English heading of Part VIII is 'Reparation', but the French is 'Réparations'.

1921 *Glasgow Herald* 28 Oct. 11 The mere purchase of foreign securities to meet reparations..simply means the transference of worthless papers from one body of financiers to another. **1931** F. L. ALLEN *Only Yesterday* ii. 24 Lodge.. wanted Germany to be disarmed, saddled with a terrific bill for reparations, and if possible dismembered. **1947** *Sun* (Baltimore) 2 Apr. 10/2 Reparations to Russia must be paid out of current German production. **1976** C. BERMANT *Coming Home* II. v. 184 Israel..partly with the help of German reparations..was experiencing something of an economic miracle.

7. (Further examples in sense 5.)

The sing. and the pl. forms are both found.

1919 J. M. KEYNES *Econ. Conseq. Peace* v. 139 The endless controversy and intrigue between the Allies themselves ..culminated in the presentation to Germany of the Reparation Chapter in its final form. **1919** *Treaty of Peace* VIII. Art. 234 The Reparation Commission shall after May 1, 1921, from time to time, consider the resources and capacity of Germany. **1930** *Economist* 4 Jan. 11/2 The British delegation has left for the Hague to attend the resumed Reparations Conference. **1931** *Times Lit. Suppl.* 24 Sept. 717/3 The impossibility of real Reparations payments. **1968** *Tamarack Rev.* Spring 12 'We have restored Jewish pride.' By taking German reparation money?' **1977** *Time* 10 Jan. 46/1 More than $20 billion of foreign capital has poured in: mostly gifts from Jews abroad, reparations payments from West Germany and U.S. aid.

repartee, *v.* Add: **1.** (Later example.)

1910 G. B. SHAW *Let.* 9 Dec. (1972) II. 957, I spent an hour and a half shouting, bullying..& reparteeing until I was as one in a Turkish bath.

re-parti·tioned, *ppl a.* [RE- 5 a.] That has been partitioned afresh.

1921 N. ANGELL *Fruits of Victory* iii. 100 The new states of repartitioned Europe seem..either unable or unwilling to help their neighbours.

repat (rĭpæ·t), colloq. abbrev. of *REPATRIATE *sb.* (also REPATRIATION). Also *attrib.*

1946 BRICKHILL & NORTON *Escape to Danger* xxii. 197 Typical of the repat. boys was 'Chuck' Lark. **1948** *R.A.F. Rev.* June 5/1 (*heading*) Family camp (for repats). **1968** *Punch* 12 June 854/2 The emotions attendant on leaving had the same admixture as before: the expat and the repat were, after all, the same person. **1974** P. FLOWER *Odd Job* iii. 27 He'd got along on a Repat. pension.

repatriate, *v.* Add: Now also with pronunc. (rĭpæ·t-). **1. b.** *transf.* of money.

1909 *Westm. Gaz.* 6 Aug. 10/4 A definite step is about to be taken to repatriate the United States silver coin which circulates in the Dominion of Canada. **1940** *Economist* 13 Jan. 64/2 A considerable amount of French capital remained in London last September and has for the most part been repatriated over the past four months. **1966** *Wall St. Jrnl.* 14 Nov. 24/4 In addition much of their overseas profits are 'repatriated' thus cutting the balance of payments deficit. **1978** *Whig-Standard* (Kingston, Ont.) 19 Jan. 7/7 Unless the province proposes to seize it [*sc.* the Sun Life Building] as a part of the $400 million to be repatriated to Quebec, it has no legal power to do anything.

c. *Canad.* To devolve or return (legislation) to the constitutional authority of an autonomous country. Cf. *PATRIATE *v.*

1961 *Ann. Reg. 1960* 73 The Federal Government suggested that the British North America Act should be completely repatriated, making it entirely amendable in Canada rather than on application to the British Parliament. **1968** *Globe & Mail* (Toronto) 5 Feb. 8/5 Federal and provincial governments had been unable..to agree on a formula for repatriating and amending the constitution. **1978** *Independencer* (Ottawa) Jan./Feb. 5/1 Any attempt to repatriate our constitution would be divisive and not help National Unity.

repatriated *ppl. a.* (further example).

1966 *Wall St. Jrnl.* 14 Nov. 24/4 Pfizer International's repatriated earnings and exports to affiliates have totaled more than $420 million since 1951.

repatriate (rĭpæ·t-, rĭpēⁱ·triēⁱt), *sb.* [f. the vb.] A repatriated person.

1921 *Glasgow Herald* 15 Nov. 5/3 The majority of these repatriates have the choice of living on totally inadequate means or entering the workhouse. **1945** *Daily Mirror* 27 Sept. 1/4 Seven ships have been named as bringing repatriates home to Britain. **1973** *Times* 17 Nov. 4/8 Mrs Meir, the Prime Minister, and..the Defence Minister, were among those at Lod airport today to give the repatriates a heroes' welcome.

repatriation. Add: Now also with pronunc. (rĭpæ·t-). **1.** (Further *attrib.* examples.)

1945 *Daily Mirror* 27 Sept. 1/4 The last batch of liberated prisoners and internees in Singapore boarded a repatriation ship yesterday. **1951** R. CAMPBELL *Light on Dark Horse* 1 It was through an erroneous repatriation-order that I obtained this last panorama of my early home. **1973** *Bulletin* (Sydney) 25 Aug. 17/3 The Repatriation Commission has amassed a fortune... The Repatriation Act empowers the commissioners to act as guardians of these men's affairs... These pensioners are visited regularly by repatriation officers.

2. *Canad.* Devolution or return of legislation to the constitutional authority of an autonomous country. Also *fig.* Cf. *PATRIATION.

1961 *Ann. Reg. 1960* 73 Justice Minister Fulton proposed a two-stage process beginning with repatriation [of the British North America Act] and followed by the working-out of a method of amendment. **1968** *Globe & Mail* (Toronto) 5 Feb. 8/5 Mr. Pearson was asked..why the federal Government had not discussed repatriation of the constitution from Britain. **1976** *Maclean's Mag.* 17 May 45/2 The arguments for and against the repatriation of the Canadian culture take on a national scope.

repayment. Add: **3.** *Comb.*, as **repayment mortgage** (see quots.).

1965 *Legal Side of buying House* (Consumers' Assoc.) ii. 31 There are two main differences between a fixed mortgage combined with an endowment policy.., and a repayment mortgage. First, the insurance premiums..are eligible for tax relief... Secondly, if the borrower dies before the mortgage is paid off..the endowment assurance policy .. pays all that is due. **1968** B. D. COLEMAN *Money—How to save it, spend it, & make It* iv. 25 This annuity mortgage (also known as a 'repayment' mortgage), ..is simply a mortgage loan on a property to be bought, the principal (or capital borrowed) and interest to be repaid together by means of fixed instalments over a fixed period. **1974** *Listener* 24 Jan. 98/3 A building society prefers its borrowers ..to stick to the simple repayment mortgage: paying back the advance over a period by monthly instalments of capital and interest combined.

repeal, *sb.* Add: **4.** *Comb.*, as **Repeal Warden** *Irish Hist.*, a local official of the Loyal National Repeal Association. Cf. sense 2 b.

1841 D. O'CONNELL in P. S. O'Hegarty *Hist. Ireland under Union* (1952) xiv. 103 The Office of Repeal Warden.. must be purely ministerial. They must not..be considered, as Representatives or Delegates. **1903** M. MACDONAGH *Life Daniel O'Connell* xx. 392 The article further suggested that the Repeal wardens should be instructed in the military uses and abuses of railways. **1966** L. J. MCCAFFREY *Daniel O'Connell & Repeal Year* ii. 70 The most important cogs in the Repeal machinery on the local level were the priests. They organized and participated in Repeal meetings, and they selected the parish Repeal Wardens.

repea·lless, *a. rare.* [f. REPEAL *sb.* + -LESS.] Without any cancellation or repeal; from which nothing is erased.

c **1862** E. DICKINSON *Poems* (1955) I. 318 God can summon every face On his Repealless—List.

repeat, *sb.* Add: **1. c.** In *U.S.* phr. *and repeat*, used to denote the return of a horse or the like back over the distance it has just come. Cf. *RETURN *sb.* 1 g.

1819 *Va. Herald* (Fredericksburg) 19 May 4/5 Second day two miles and repeat, free for all ages. **1856** *Trans. Mich. Agric. Soc.* VII. 276 Trotting horses shall be tested in harness, by going at least one mile and repeat. **1903** A. ADAMS *Log of Cowboy* ix. 131 A race horse can't beat an ox on a hundred miles and repeat to a freight wagon.

d. *Broadcasting.* A repetition of a programme which has already been broadcast.

1937 *Printers' Ink Monthly* May 40/3 *Repeat*, a term denoting the second broadcast of a regular studio program broadcast for those stations not served by the original broadcast due to time differences. **1941** *B.B.C. Gloss. Broadcasting Terms* 28 *Repeat*, repetition (as distinct from reproduction) of a programme which has been broadcast, either live or recorded, on one or more previous occasions. **1959** HALAS & MANVELL *Technique Film Animation* xvi. 144 Animation seemed to be too elaborate a process to undertake for the limited number of repeats possible in the television medium. **1965** *Spectator* 5 Mar. 289/2 In the current fortnight no fewer than twenty-seven of the BBC's programmes are 'repeats'. **1973** *Listener* 6 Dec. 798/2 A true interstice piece was the repeat of E. M. Forster's talk on Crabbe, in the interval of *Death in Venice.* **1976** *Weekend Echo* (Liverpool) 4/5 Dec. 2/3 If B.B.C. and ITV have to put repeats on, why don't they show those that were on 15 to 20 years ago.

5. a. In general *attrib.* (or *adj.*) use, designating a further example or instance of the specified sb.; repeated, occurring again; esp. as *repeat order, performance.*

1888, 1891 [in Dict., sense 4 c]. **1908** A. W. MYERS *Compl. Lawn Tennis Player* xv. 237 'E.R.' comes back in a few minutes for a 'repeat order'. **1935** E. F. BENSON *Lucia's Progress* vii. 206 'Went like hot cakes, ma'am,' said the proprietor, '..and I've just telephoned a repeat order.' **1949** *Radio Times* 15 July 13/4, 9.50 p.m. A repeat performance of *Thaïs* by Massenet. **1961** D. A. BANNERMAN *Birds Brit. Isles* IX. 15 By 10th May all normal clutches have been laid, but repeat-clutches are begun till the last days of May. **1974** J. WAINWRIGHT *Hard Hit* 68 It is a repeat performance of last night; a staring up at the ceiling..a haunting—a remembering. **1978** *Lancashire Life* Nov. 89/1 Postal orders rolled in, followed by repeat orders, together with letters from delighted winners testifying to the efficiency of the pills. **1980** *Times* 6 Sept. 13/5 Last year over half our visitors to London were on repeat visits.

b. Special Combs.: **repeat buying**, the persistent buying of brands with which a shopper is familiar; **repeat fee**, a fee paid to a radio or television artist each time his performance is re-broadcast; **repeat pattern** = sense 4 b; **repeat-sign** *Mus.* = sense 2 d.

1972 A. S. C. EHRENBERG (*title*) Repeat-buying: theory and applications. **1973** *Nature* 3 Aug. 316/1 A longstanding assumption in the theory of repeat buying has now been explained by results on consumers' brand switching behaviour. **1969** *Daily Tel.* 6 Mar. 18 The principle of the repeat-fee for the repeated employment of an artistic work has been established in the entertainment world for more than 50 years. **1975** *Broadcast* 21 July 12/2 Repeat fees had to be avoided. **1959** *Listener* 9 Apr. 629/1 There are even numbers of schools where the bastard activity of hand-painted repeat-pattern-making is still practised. **1967** E. SHORT *Embroidery & Fabric Collage* i. 6 Symmetrical motifs, and repeat patterns, come into their own. **1946** A. L. BACHARACH *Brit. Music of Our Time* iii. 62 *Ostinato* bass-figures..could be indicated by repeat-signs.

repeat, *v.* Add: **I. 1. b.** Used in radio communication, dictation, etc., to emphasize or clarify an important part of the message. Often combined with a negative. Also *transf.*

1938 W. BULLITT Cable 19 Mar. in R. W. Clark *Freud: Man & Cause* (1980) xxiii. 507, I can make available immediately $10,000: but can not (repeat not) be responsible for more. **1943** F. J. BELL *Condition Red* xvi. 259 We are not—— repeat——not——a Jap. **1952** *New Statesman* 24 May 612/2 We must not, repeat not, call *Dragon's Mouth*..a play. **1957** 'J. WYNDHAM' *Midwich Cuckoos* iii. 23 A notification from the R.A.F. was received in Trayne of some unidentified flying object, not, repeat not, a service machine, detected by radar in the Midwich area. **1961** B. PYM *No Fond Return of Love* xi. 104 A notice..which said 'Nobody, repeat *nobody*, is to tamper with the electric heating apparatus in here'. **1973** R. HAYES *Hungarian Game* xxxv. 209 The request was for numbers of people on staff, *repeat*, numbers on staff. **1978** *Guardian Weekly* 8 Oct. 10/2 If— repeat, if—the security forces have been tapping the home telephone of the editor of the Economist.

3. c. With direct speech as obj.: to say or utter again (something that has just been said by oneself or another).

1766 O. GOLDSMITH *Vicar of Wakefield* I. xii. 119 'A groce of green spectacles!' repeated my wife in a faint voice. **1866** C. M. YONGE *Dove in Eagle's Nest* I. ii. 58 'Ah! if the steeple of the Dome Kirk were but finished, I could not mistake it,' said Christina... 'Dome Kirk?' repeated Ermentrude; 'what is that?' **1956** 'C. BLACKSTOCK' *Dewey Death* xii. 278 'He wasn't really bad,' said Barbara... 'Bad!' repeated Mr. Dodds. 'What does that mean?' **1976** H. MACINNES *Agent in Place* xx. 218 'Yes,' Tom repeated, 'he knew he had been tricked.'

II. 6. b. Also, to broadcast (a radio or television programme) again.

1923 *Radio Times* 28 Sept. 12/1 Why is it apparently not thought advisable to repeat the 'Request Nights', which.. are so popular? **1955** *Ibid.* 22 Apr. 28/3 *Music and Movement*..To be repeated on Friday at 9.55 a.m. **1974** *Listener* 29 Aug. 277/3 There could be no better celebration of the art of standing up and holding forth than the late Dr

Bronowski's *The Ascent of Man*, the last episode of which was repeated over the weekend as a tribute.

c. (Later examples.)

1965 *Listener* 10 June 867/2 A certain rugged, irregular shape tends to repeat throughout the picture. **1967** E. Short *Embroidery & Fabric Collage* i. 33 An allover pattern in embroidery differs from one that is printed in that it does not necessarily have to repeat exactly.

d. *Educ.* (orig. *U.S.*). To undertake (a course or period of instruction) again. Cf. *repeater 5 d.

1945 C. V. Good *Dict. Educ.* 342/2 *Repeater*, a pupil who has repeated or is currently repeating the work of a grade or part of a subject at some designated level of difficulty. **1973** *Sun-Herald* (Sydney) 26 Aug. 83/1 A suggestion has come that he should repeat third year as he is so young. **1976** *National Observer* (U.S.) 28 Aug. 6/3 Make them repeat the course, repeat a year, drop a grade in rank, anything short of expulsion. **1977** *Rolling Stone* 5 May 45/3 Mark had to repeat first and second grades.

7. d. (Further examples.)

1954 E. B. White *Let.* 28 July (1976) 398 At my age, Miss T., a writer repeats like an onion. **1981** P. Hansford Johnson *Bonfire* I. vii. 71, I hope these aren't cucumber sandwiches... Cucumber always repeats.

8. b. Also *transf.*

1965 *Listener* 9 Sept. 393/2 It contradicts most cogently the persistent accusation that Strauss repeated himself.

repeatability (rĭpī·tăbi·lĭti). [f. Repeatable *a.* + -ity.] Capacity for being repeated; *spec.* the extent to which consistent results are obtained on repeated measurement (cf. *reproducibility).

1920 *Music & Lett.* Oct. 289 Repeatability is thus in music an element of the beautiful. **1951** G. Humphrey *Thinking* iv. 108 The criterion of repeatability [of experiments] is not fulfilled. **1961** A. Fleur *Hume's Philos. of Belief* 209 The ultimate warrant for accepting these new scientific ideas lies in their implicit open general challenge to falsification and in their implicit open general promise of repeatability. **1965** *Wireless World* July 338/2 The problems of obtaining good stability and repeatability of resistance value. **1972** *Physics Bull.* May 286/1 By using advanced measurement techniques and controlling the loading procedure a short term repeatability of ±1 part in 20 000 (±0·005%) can be achieved. **1976** G. C. Spivak in J. Derrida *Of Grammatology* p. lxxxvi, Denying the uniqueness of words, their substantiality, their transferability, their repeatability, *Of Grammatology* denies the possibility of translation.

repeatable, *a.* Add: *spec.* of a scientific experiment or result.

1935 [see *operation 5 a]. **1949** *Monthly Notices R. Astron. Soc.* CXIII. 396 The reason why so many experiments are approximately repeatable is that we take infinite pains to select them from the others. **1955** R. O. Kapp *Facts & Faith* 45 The precision with which experiments are repeatable does not prove that it is in the nature of matter to behave in an orderly manner but only that it is in the nature of scientists to do so. **1969** *Listener* 6 Mar. 301/1 An American botanist..and his wife..threw up their careers to devote themselves to evolving a repeatable experiment which could incontrovertibly demonstrate ESP. **1977** *Theology* LXXX. 196 We are here neither in the world of sheer unaccountable miracle nor in that of repeatable experiment.

repeater. Add: **3. a.** (Earlier examples.)

1725 C. Mordaunt *Let.* in E. Hamilton *Mordaunts* (1965) vii. 141 It [*sc.* a watch] is a silent Repeator. **1766** H. Brooke *Fool of Quality* I. vii. 290 She did further rob the said right hon. &c. of a large purse of money, his gold repeater, snuff-box, diamond-ring.

b. (Earlier example.)

1782 S. Hood *Let.* 30 Apr. (1895) 135 Sir George..took the Eurydice, Admiral Drake's repeater, to carry his *duplicate* despatches.

d. (Earlier and later examples.) Also in *Teleph.*

1859 T. P. Shaffner *Telegr. Man.* xxxv. 486 If the line be 600 miles long, and the battery arrangements fail to charge it sufficient for telegraphing, it is the practice to operate it by..the application of an apparatus called a repeater. **1923** *Sci. Amer.* Feb. 106/2 The development of the vacuum tube repeaters..put an entirely different aspect on the problems which have confronted the telephone engineer in the past. *Ibid.* 106/3 These repeaters are placed at regular intervals along the line and as the currents become weakened they pick them up, and..deliver back into the line a current many times stronger. **1958** *Times* 1 July 8/3 The idea behind the work now in hand is to make possible the inclusion of submerged repeaters at more frequent intervals along the cable, which would proportionately increase the capacity of the communications system. **1972** *Sci. Amer.* Sept. 102/2 Each repeater used in coaxial cables and each relay station used in microwave links adds some noise, mostly from its input circuits.

e. = *relay *sb.* 4 b. Freq. *attrib.*

1936 *R.C.A. Rev.* I. 26 The modulations are passed on to the distant terminal via the repeater stations. **1940** *Ibid.* V. 36 In order to choose the proper amplifying system it becomes necessary to know the amount of gain to be incorporated in each repeater amplifier. **1946** *Jrnl. Brit. Interplanetary Soc.* VI. 72 Yet three repeater stations circling the Earth could provide a steady, reliable service from Pole to Pole with little more power output than the present London transmitter. **1947** *Proc. IRE* XXXV. 1226/1 In communications systems involving a number of similar repeaters, the distortion permissible in a single repeater is very small. **1959** *Aeroplane* XCVII. 542/1 (*caption*) The 500-lb. repeater satellite proposed by the Space Electronics Corporation. **1965** *New Statesman* 30 Apr. 674/1 Early Bird is an active repeater satellite. That is, it receives signals from powerful ground stations, amplifies them, and re-broadcasts them to the ground. **1972** *Sci. Amer.* Feb. 15/1 Microwaves do not bend with the curvature of the earth, so that for long links it is necessary to use repeaters. **1979** *Ibid.* Jan. 62/3 One example of a 'next generation' circuit that could be built with existing technology is a repeater station in a fiber-optics communication link.

5. For *U.S.* in Dict. read Chiefly *U.S.* **a.** (Earlier and later examples.)

1868 [see *colonist 3]. **1871** *Scribner's Monthly* I. 366 Repeaters changed their coats and hats after every vote. **1904** [see *colonizer 2].

b. (Further examples.) Also, one who repeats an offence; a recidivist.

1899 J. Flynt *Tramping* iv. 386 'Revolver' or 'repeater', is both a tramp and a criminal term for the professional offender, who is continually being brought up for trial. **1938** *Encycl. Brit. Bk. of Yr.* 185/1 These young felons are what prison language describes as 'repeaters', young 'old offenders', who have previously, almost continuously, served prison sentences. **1954** *Daily Mail* 10 Mar. 5/6 As regards the 'repeaters', if a child sees his name in the papers it may well be an incentive..to future wrongdoing. **1965** Mrs. L. B. Johnson *White House Diary* 18 July (1970) 303, I asked Nick about repeaters among young criminals. He used some horrifying figure—I believe it was 70 percent. **1977** *Time* 11 July 35/1 After stronger juvenile laws were enacted and violent repeaters were finally jailed in New Orleans, teen-age homicides declined from 29 in 1973 to five in 1975.

c. Also *gen.*, one who repeats an achievement or success.

1944 *Sun* (Baltimore) 13 Jan. 11/2 Mr. Fetterman and Mr. Huffer..got..certificates for their suggestions. Mr. Fetterman is a repeater. He..isn't sure just how many citations have come from the War Production Board for his ideas.

d. *Educ.* A student who undergoes a course or period of instruction again.

1912 *Jrnl. Educ. Psychol.* June 328, 4640 of the children were 'repeaters'... There is nothing to show whether the per cent. thus promoted consists of repeaters regaining their lost grade or of bright children who were skipping a grade. **1945** [see *repeat *v.* 6 d]. **1976** *National Observer* (U.S.) 6 Nov. 17/3 Repeaters are assigned to schools and remedial classes according to age as well as grade.

e. One who returns repeatedly, esp. to a hotel.

1970 *Globe & Mail* (Toronto) 26 Sept. 31/6 (Advt.), The Bremen probably has the largest number of repeaters on her cruises. **1971** *New Yorker* 4 Dec. 183/2 (Advt.), We're a small hotel... Almost all our guests are repeaters. **1977** *Time* 30 May 21/1 By last week the number of visitors had passed 60,000 (including repeaters), even though news accounts of the 'miracle' cloth have been spotty.

repeatered (rĭpī·təɹd), *a.* *Telegr.* and *Teleph.* [f. Repeater + -ed[2].] Equipped with repeaters.

1932 *Telegraph & Telephone Jrnl.* XVIII. 120/2 The post-war development, as the standard form of trunk line-plant, of repeatered cables which will not carry direct current, drastically limited the progress of further trunk mechanisation. **1964** *Discovery* Oct. 46/1 (*caption*) Repeaters are inserted at intervals along submarine cables to amplify the signal about a million times. A typical trans-oceanic repeatered cable may now carry up to 138 circuits.

repeating, *ppl. a.* Add: **1. f.** Telegr. and Teleph. *repeating coil*, a type of transformer used to transmit a signal from one circuit to another without alteration.

1889 *Telephone* I. 494/2 In connection with one or more of the local circuits on the board are placed repeating coils which terminate in single lines in the local exchanges. **1958** J. R. G. Smith *Elem. Telecomm. Pract.* vi. 105 A repeating coil is a special type of transformer in which the ratio of the windings is equal,..and is used to 'repeat' speech currents from one part of a circuit to another.

4. Of a pattern: repeated or recurring uniformly over a surface.

1959 *Listener* 16 Apr. 679/1 Stuffy repeating patterns, 'folksy' craftwork. **1967** E. Short *Embroidery & Fabric Collage* iii. 74 Initials could be designed as a separate motif or incorporated into a repeating design.

‖ **repêchage** (re-peʃɑ̃ʒ). *Sport* (orig. *Rowing*). Also **repechage.** [a. F. *repêchage*, f. *repêcher* to fish out, rescue; to give an examination candidate a second chance to pass.] An extra contest in which the runners-up in the eliminating contests compete for a place in the final. Also *attrib.*

1928 *Daily Express* 7 Aug. 12 M. Bernasconi, their representative in the single sculls, met Joe Wright..in the repechage—second chance—contests for Saturday's second-round losers. **1948** *Call-Bulletin* (San Francisco) 3 July 5/7 Harvard, upset by Cornell in the first trial heat, got back into the running by the 'repechage' or second-trial system. **1955** *Times* 25 Aug. 2/7 On Friday there will be repechages for teams beaten in the opening heats. **1959** *Times* 20 Apr. 3/1 Those teams knocked out in the first round took part in a *repêchage*. **1976** *Yachts & Yachting* 20 Aug. 375/3 The following day there is a repechage in the same waters. **1978** *Times* 30 June 21/6 The Poles won by virtue of the 'repêchage' principle, which provides for one of the 61 defeated teams to reenter the competition by beating the other defeated teams.

repellant, *a.* and *sb.* Add: **A.** *adj.* **1. c.** = Repellent *a.* 2 b.

1897 *Sears, Roebuck Catal.* 274 [Wrap] made of imported black repellant cloth.

d. = *repellent *a.* 2 d.

1944 *Living off Land* v. 111 Repellant cream should be smeared thoroughly on all parts of the skin which are unprotected by clothing.

B. *sb.* (Further examples in sense of *repellent *sb.* 4.)

1908 *Jrnl. Econ. Entomol.* I. 83 He had tried repellants against the cotton boll weevil, including lemon, cinnamon, tar and clove oil. **1945** *Tee Emm* (Air Ministry) V. 51 Use the shark repellant sparingly. **1958** Moth-repellant [see *moth *sb.*[1] 3]. **1958** *Sunday Times* 20 July 16/5 Simple dressings..and an insect repellant are obvious necessities.

repellent, *a.* and *sb.* Add: **A.** *adj.* **2. d.** Causing certain insects or other animals not to settle or approach.

1971 'G. Black' *Time for Pirates* i. 15 The air reeked from ..mosquito-repellent smudge. **1979** D. Kyle *Green River High* x. 131 We were smothered in repellent cream, but that didn't stop them [*sc.* insects].

B. *sb.* **4.** A substance that causes certain insects or other animals not to settle or approach. Freq. in *Comb.* preceded by the name of the animal, as *insect repellent* (see *insect *sb.* 4 a), etc.

1908 *Jrnl. Econ. Entomol.* I. 81 (*heading*) Experiments with repellents against the corn root-aphis. **1923** *Ibid.* XVI. 222 A very effective repellent for practical use is a mixture of one part furfural to four parts pine tar oil. **1942**, etc. [see *moth *sb.*[1] 3]. **1949** *Consumer Reports* July 311/1, 38 brands of insect repellents. **1950** 'N. Shute' *Town like Alice* 43 If they were to spend another night upon the veranda she must get hold of some mosquito repellent. **1955** *Sci. Amer.* Aug. 76/3 It is neither an attractant nor a repellent to unconditioned salmon, and would have meaning only to those conditioned to it. **1963** 'F. Richards' *First come, First Kill* v. 60, I probably smell to high heaven of insect repellent. **1968** C. Helmericks *Down Wild River North* I. xv. 234 Covering myself..with canvas against the angry insects blown back from the horses' backs, and bathing my hooded face with repellent. **1979** R. Perry *Bishop's Pawn* viii. 144 This left the insects free to concentrate on me and the repellent I was using hadn't matured with age.

repercuss, *v.* Restrict ?*Obs.* to senses in Dict. and add: **3.** [Back-formation from Repercussion.] *intr.* To cause or admit of repercussions (sense *6 a, *fig.*); to have an unwanted or unintended effect; to reflect or rebound *on* something.

1923 [see *extra-organismal* s.v. *extra- 1]. **1969** F. Halliday in Cockburn & Blackburn *Student Power* 323 There are also examples where an initially political campaign by students repercusses back into the campus and detonates an internal revolt within higher education. **1972** *Guardian* 18 Feb. 13/1 The public crucifixion of a mandarin looks likely to repercuss for years. **1975** J. De Bres tr. *Mandel's Late Capitalism* vii. 243 The tendency towards thorough planning and organization within the companies or enterprises of late capitalism necessarily repercusses on the structure of the bourgeois class. **1976** *Daily Tel.* 1 Dec. 3/3 It is a script which the plaintiffs feel cannot do anything but repercuss poorly on their reputation if it is thought that 'King Kong' is associated with that.

repercussion. Add: **6. a.** Also *fig.*, a resulting effect or implication; an unwanted or unintended reverberation. Freq. *pl.*

1906 *Pall Mall Gaz.* 22 Jan. 1 The disasters of Tsardom in the Japanese war have had a repercussion all over Europe. **1935** *Times* 5 July 15/3 The direct effects and indirect repercussions of any projected action. **1948** *Hansard Commons* 26 Jan. 673 All practical measures will be adopted..to minimise repercussions upon other unconvertible European currencies. **1969** T. F. Torrance *Theol. Sci.* ii. 85 The inclusion of that fact in the Reformation doctrine of the Grace of God had immense repercussions. **1978** *Lancashire Life* Oct. 96/1 If the strike could be expected to 'bite' anywhere, with anarchic repercussions, Merseyside was the place.

repercussive, *a.* Add: **4. b.** *fig.* Of an action, decision, etc.: having repercussions (sense *6 a).

1974 *Daily Tel.* 11 May 17/5 He said that because of the decision to go ahead with the tour he was worried about the repercussive effect on British and international sport. **1975** *Financial Times* 27 Oct. 17/4 Britain will in an important sense continue to be 'reliant' on other sources herself, since she cannot escape repercussive consequences in her own industry and economy whenever Western Europe suffers. **1979** *Jrnl. R. Soc. Arts* CXXVII. 554/2 The repercussive effects of pay policy.

reperforator (rĭpɜ̄·ɹfŏrēᶦtəɹ). *Telegr.* [f. Re(ceiving *ppl. a.* + Perforator.] A machine which perforates paper tape in accordance with telegraphically received signals.

1916 *Papers Inst. P.O. Electr. Engin.* No. 59. 22 Parment ..proposes re-perforators at the receiver end for *x* messages, receiving a printed slip simultaneously. **1948** *Annals Computation Lab. Harvard Univ.* XVI. 61 The reperforator and the printer operate on a time division basis. **1973** Goacher & Denny *Teleprinter Handbk.* iii. 10/1 Reperforators are used to store teleprinter signals on punched paper tape so that they may be retransmitted later by means of a suitable tape reader.

repertoire. Add: **b.** *transf.*

1872 E. Braddon *Life in India* vi. 201 A Lascar crossing-sweeper whose native dialect is Bengali or Tamil, and from whose linguistic *répertoire* Oordoo and Hindoo have been wholly omitted. **1959** R. Postgate *Good Food Guide* 211 Latest additions to his marvellous repertoire are Honey Duck..and a poussin stuffed with mushroom butter and herbs, encased in a very thin pastry and baked. **1961** Webster, A small but dependable repertoire of jokes designed to amuse the young—Frank Sullivan. **1965** *Listener* 20 May 753/1 Easily reached from Dublin, New Grange itself, with its rich repertoire of geometric art, is the showpiece of Irish prehistory. **1971** *Nature* 13 Aug. 443/2 The most striking aspects of an animal's behavioural repertoire are often the 'displays' it gives in sexual or aggressive encounters. **1973** *Archivum Linguisticum* IV. 55 The analysis of *repertoires*, namely, what that community knows of and does with the languages concerned.

repertorial (repəɹtōə·riăl), *a.* [f. Repertory + -al.] Of or pertaining to (a) repertory.

1898 J. London *Let.* 6 Dec. (1966) 8 Worth far more than five dollars, at the ordinary repertorial rate of so much per column. **1912** G. B. Shaw *Let.* 1 May in *Lett. to Granville Barker* (1956) 181 To follow a year of Shaw with yet another Shaw is not very repertorial. **1928** *Observer* 1 Apr. 15/3 The producer's laudable desire to deliver Ibsen's humour from the old repertorial gloom was most happily realized in some of the minor parts.

repertorily (re·pəɹtŏrĭli), *adv. rare.* [f. Repertory + -ly[2].] In the manner of repertory.

1928 *Observer* 22 Jan. 13/4 Miss Margot Drake's Ann catches fire in the later phases of the play, but some of the other parts are somewhat repertorily done.

repertory. Add: **3. b.** A type of theatrical presentation in which the plays performed by a company are changed at regular short intervals; repertory theatres collectively.

1896 [see *repertory theatre* below]. **1910** G. B. Shaw *Let.* 30 Apr. in *Lett. to Granville Barker* (1956) 164 Producing a lot of plays merely to ascertain which draws the most money, and running that and dropping the rest is not Propagandist Repertory. **1926** [see *co-star *sb.*]. **1951** *Oxf. Compan. Theatre* 664/2 The pioneer work of all these theatres stimulated an ever-growing interest in Repertory. **1974** *Encycl. Brit. Macropædia* XVIII. 229/1 The change from repertory to the single play and the rise of realistic production also shifted artistic control from the actor to the manager.

c. *ellipt.* for *repertory company.*

1933 P. Godfrey *Back-Stage* ix. 134 The number of small stock companies, calling themselves resident repertories.. continued to consolidate their positions with provincial audiences.

4. *attrib.*, as (sense *3 b) *repertory acting, actor, actress, company, movement, play, player, system, theatre.*

1917 J. Agate *Buzz, Buzz!* ii. 146 It is in this way that Repertory acting gets its revenge. **1951** *Oxf. Compan. Theatre* 664/1 Glasgow audiences became acquainted with Repertory acting and production of a high standard. **1917** J. Agate *Buzz, Buzz!* ii. 145 Let us recall the Repertory actor who, desponding of intellectual success, decided to 'go back to the profession'. **1951** *Oxf. Compan. Theatre* 665/2 John Drinkwater, a Repertory actor and dramatist. **1979** K. O'Hara *Searchers of Dead* vi. 64 Noel was..a sound hard-working repertory actor. **1917** J. Agate *Buzz, Buzz!* ii. 146 The Repertory actress sometimes succeeds in sending you away from the theatre concerned for the character she has been representing. **1977** 'J. le Carré' *Hon. Schoolboy* xiii. 290 She frowned..like a repertory actress doing Forgetfulness. **1909** G. B. Shaw *Let.* 29 Dec. in *Lett. to Granville Barker* (1956) 160, I may shortly doubt whether he will throw himself into the repertory company to be cast for anything you please. **1926** *Scribner's Mag.* Aug. 224/1 Mr. Ames showed what could be done with a first-class repertory company. **1967** *Oxf. Compan. Theatre* (ed. 3) 796/2 There have been many plays, first produced by a repertory company, which have then been transferred to London. **1977** J. Aiken *Last Movement* i. 13 He was..highly experienced; he had been in different repertory companies since the age of sixteen. **1951** *Oxf. Compan. Theatre* 663/2 It is impossible to name any one person as the sponsor of the Repertory Movement in England, but no one can deny that it owes much to the vision and courage of J. T. Grein. **1955** *Radio Times* 22 Apr. 7 The famous Liverpool Playhouse..was founded in 1911 by Miss Horniman, who had started the repertory movement in England. **1974** *Encycl. Brit. Macropædia* XVIII. 231/1 Miss A. E. F. Horniman (pioneer of the British repertory movement). **1903** G. B. Shaw *Let.* 12 Jan. (1972) II. 302 Much Ado.. would come in on tour as a Shakespearean repertory play. **1933** —— in E. J. West *Shaw on Theatre* (1958) 235 All the players in the country, whether they are British Drama League players or Repertory players or regular professional players. *c* **1913** D. McCarthy *Drama* (1940) 60 The repertory system is certainly a means to getting good acting. **1974** *Encycl. Brit. Micropædia* VIII. 514/1 Major English companies using the repertory system include the Royal Shakespeare Theatre in Stratford-on-Avon and London and the National Theatre Company. **1896** W. Archer *Theatrical 'World' of 1895* 390 A repertory theatre, where unbroken runs shall be forbidden by the articles of association. **1897** G. B. Shaw *Our Theatres in Nineties* (1932) III. 273 What we want in order to get the best work is a repertory theatre with alternative casts. **1909** *Times* 9 June 8/6 It may..take a little time for the London public to grow used to the frequent changes of bill which a repertory theatre implies. **1976** E. Dewhurst *After Ball* i. 5 The newly-formed Frensham repertory theatre club had come to the end of its first meeting.

repetend (re·pĭtend), *a. rare.* [ad. L. *repetendus*, gerundive of *repetĕre* to repeat.] That is to be repeated.

1929 R. Bridges *Test. Beauty* iv. 181 Taketh repetend life and exuberant difformity of disorder'd growth.

‖ **répétiteur** (repetitŏr). Also **repetiteur.** [Fr., = tutor, coach.] **a.** One who teaches musicians and singers, esp. opera singers, their parts.

1938 *Oxf. Compan. Mus.* 792/2 *Répétiteur*.., choirmaster of an opera-house. **1941** L. A. G. Strong *John McCormack* iv. 70 Covent Garden in those days was blessed by the possession of a master répétiteur at the piano. **1948** *Penguin Mus. Mag.* June 79 He went to his first post as *répétiteur* at Cologne when he was barely 17. **1961** *Times* 13 July 5/3 A stolid arc of singers gathered round the répétiteur. **1970** *Guardian* 24 Apr. 8/2 The opera-house..needed someone to do three jobs; a *repetiteur* was needed, an oboist and an assistant conductor. **1974** *Courier-Mail* (Brisbane) 3 Aug. 15/10 (Advt.), The Australian Opera has vacancies for experienced repetiteurs. **1977** R. Barnard *Death on High C's* i. 11 Little Mr Pettifer, the repetiteur, was seated at the piano... The cast was bustled into position around him.

b. One who supervises ballet rehearsals, etc.

1952 *Ballet Ann. 1953* 143/1 The Sadler's Wells Ballet... Professor of Dancing and Repetiteur: Harijs Plucis. **1964** W. G. Raffe *Dict. Dance* 416/2 The *répétiteur* is often a private tutor; but in Theatre he is in charge of..the full preparation for the show; he may also be the ballet-master. **1977** *Times* 16 May 8/6 Then to the Royal Ballet..eventually becoming..principal *répétiteur.*

repetition[1]. Add: **6.** *repetition choice, device, phenomenon, rate*; **repetition compound** (see quot.); **repetition compulsion** *Psychoanal.*, a term first used by Freud to describe behaviour that is caused by a more powerful instinct than that of pleasure, whereby a response is repeated regardless of the result; also *transf.*

1934 *Brit. Jrnl. Psychol.* Jan. 254 This difference in repetition choice correlated with a difference in teachers' ratings on the trait of pride. **1957** R. W. Zandvoort *Handbk. Eng. Gram.* ix. i. 286 *Repetition Compounds*.., a type of compound which consists in the repetition of the word constituting its first element: *goody-goody, pretty-pretty.* **1925** A. Strachey tr. *Freud's The Uncanny* in *Coll. Papers* IV. 391 We are able to postulate the principle of a repetition-compulsion in the unconscious mind, based upon instinctual activity and probably inherent in the very nature of the instincts—a principle powerful enough to overrule the pleasure-principle. **1941** L. Trilling in D. Lodge *20th Cent. Lit. Crit.* (1972) 288 [Freud] first makes the assumption that there is indeed in the psychic life a repetition-compulsion which goes beyond the pleasure principle. **1953** A. Koestler in *Encounter* I. ii. 28/2 British foreign policy..and French internal politics..seem to be dictated by this kind of repetition-compulsion. **1961** J. A. C. Brown *Freud* i. 4 This phenomenon, described by Freudians as the repetition compulsion, is met with most frequently clinically ..in the choice of a mate where the same personality type is selected each time. **1974** S. Arieti *Amer. Handbk. Psychiatry* (ed. 2) III. 164/2 In the hyponoic and sometimes.. anoetic qualities of the hypnoid state, the dominance of repetition compulsion becomes apparent. **1941** L. MacNeice *Poetry of W. B. Yeats* 164 The twentieth century suspected most poetic repetition-devices. **1954** A. H. Maslow *Motivation & Personality* xi. 188 (*heading*) Repetition phenomena; persistent, unsuccessful coping; detoxification. **1940** *Chambers's Techn. Dict.* 714/1 *Repetition rate*, the number of times repetition is demanded in a telephone conversation, this being related to the line or transmitter noise, [etc.]. **1948**, etc. [see *pulse repetition rate* s.v. *pulse *sb.*[1] 5]. **1969** *Times* 4 Feb. 13/3 It [*sc.* pulsar NP 0532] has the fastest repetition rate of all known pulsating stars.

repetitional, *a.* (Later example.)

1965 *Eng. Studies* XLVI. 160 It is..harder to ascertain cases of *amphibolia* than repetitional figures or double constructions.

repetitive, *a.* Add: **B.** as *sb.* = *repetition compound* s.v. *repetition[1] 6.

1961 R. B. Long *Sentence & its Parts* xvii. 383 The category of repetitives..includes..a few words with components repeated without change. *Poohpooh, tomtom,*.. and *hushhush* are repetitives of this kind.

repetitor (rĭpe·titŏɹ). [Ger.] A private tutor, esp. in Law, at a German university or college.

1770 *Diary* (MS., Eng. Coll., Rome), Wed 7..in time of Repetition..to y[e] R.C. [Roman College] a little Theological act perform'd by Padre Angeleni one of y[e] Repetitors in y[e] German Colledge. **1886** in Webster. **1895** H. Rashdall *Universities Europe Middle Ages* I. iv. 250 A *Repetitio* in Medicine and Arts [at Bologna]..was, as a rule, not given by the Master himself but by a 'Repetitor', who attended the lecture and then repeated it to the students afterwards and catechized them upon it. **1968** *Listener* 30 May 699/3 The *repetitor*, a lawyer—not a recognised university teacher and often looked at askance by academic lawyers—sets up house in a university town and acts as a kind of 'crammer', compensating for the frequent lack of suitable classes in the legal faculties and other teaching deficiencies.

repha·se, *v.* [Re- 5 a + *phase *v.* 2.] *trans.* To phase again; to readjust the proposed timing of. So **repha·sing** *vbl. sb.*

1957 *Economist* 2 Nov. 423/2 Rather coyly, the Chancellor added his 1958 and 1959 figures together.., remarking only that the revision 'will mean a re-phasing of the nuclear power programme'. **1957** *New Scientist* 7 Nov. 38/2 It is thought necessary to 'rephase' the plan for modernising the railways. **1970** *Daily Tel.* 22 Jan. 21/3 The CEGB may well rephase the programme to avoid 'bunching' and the 'feast and famine' cycle. **1971** *Nature* 19 Feb. 517/2 BP Chemicals International has announced..the rephasing of the construction of a chemical plant at Baglan Bay, South Wales. *a* **1974** R. Crossman *Diaries* (1976) II. 584 Harold [Wilson] and Peter Shore now feel that the whole closure programme over the next eighteen months should be rephased and slowed down.

rephra·se, *v.* [Re- 5 a.] *trans.* To put into different words; to express in an alternative way. Also *absol.* and *fig.* Hence **rephra·sing** *vbl. sb.*

1895 [in Dict. s.v. Re- 5 a]. **1949** M. Mead *Male & Female* viii. 176 The extreme ingenuity with which man has rephrased his own physiology. **1952** M. R. Rinehart *Swimming Pool* xi. 103 Perhaps I'd better rephrase the question. **1953** *Essays in Criticism* III. 109 A good opportunity to rephrase and to say more properly what I had to say. **1961** R. B. Long *Sentence & its Parts* xv. 342 Careful and formal styles..resort to rephrasings that avoid the problem. **1966** Ogilvy & Anderson *Excurs. Number Theory* i. 5 When somebody else comes along and rephrases the question or perhaps asks a new one, a breakthrough results. **1967** Cox & Grose *Organization & Handling Bibl. Rec. by Computer* iv. 98 The second major objective is to develop a man–machine dialoguing capability which will permit real time rephrasing of input queries. **1981** 'J. Ross' *Dark Blue & Dangerous* xiv. 80 I'll rephrase what I said. I *know* that you knew Sergeant Proctor.

replace (rĭplē[i]·s), *a. rare.* [f. the vb.] Designed to replace something that is worn out or is being discarded.

1927 *Daily Tel.* 10 May 4/5 The life of the first tracks was about 2,000 miles... The replace tracks..embody such obvious improvements that they will undoubtedly give a much longer life.

replaceabi·lity. [f. Replaceable *a.*: see *-bility.] The state, property, or condition of being replaceable.

1890 in Webster. **1907** A. W. Pollard *Bks. in House* 37 As to what should be sold and what kept, the one sovereign test is that of replaceability. **1959** P. F. Strawson *Individuals* v. 161 Replaceability by quantifier and variable.

replaceable, *a.* Add: **b.** *absol.* in *Chem.*, denoting those hydrogen atoms in an acid which may be replaced by base.

1895 W. A. Tilden *Introd. Study of Chem. Philos.* (ed. 8) xv. 140 Tartaric acid is a case of similar kind. Its molecular formula cannot be less than $C_4H_6O_6$, on account of the existence of the double tartrates, which prove that the acid contains two replaceable basic hydrogen atoms. **1930** W. R. Anderson *School Cert. Chem.* iv. 47 With sulphuric acid we can get a salt by turning out half the hydrogen present, but this salt still contains replaceable hydrogen. **1962** Parkes & Harrison *Basic Physical & Inorg. Chem.* xv. 202 A normal salt is one in which all the replaceable hydrogen of the acid and the hydroxyl (or oxygen) of the base have reacted to form water.

replacement. Add: **1. b.** *absol.* in *Min.* The dissolution of one mineral and the simultaneous deposition of another in its place. Freq. *attrib.*

1906 *Econ. Geol.* I. 839 As a general term synonymous with 'metasomatism', 'replacement' is preferable to 'substitution'. **1911** *Ibid.* VI. 534 Replacement ore-bodies are generally associated with fissures..capable of conducting solutions from considerable distances. **1928** W. Lindgren *Min. Deposits* (ed. 3) ii. 27 Metallic ores are often formed by replacement. *Ibid.* xxviii. 739 The quartz monzonite contains a great number of replacement veins carrying much tourmaline. **1965** G. J. Williams *Econ. Geol. N.Z.* iii. 23/2 The ore-shoots are typical replacement-bodies of quartz, mullock and pug along narrow shears. **1970** K. C. Jackson *Textbk. Lithol.* iv. 196 Crystal growth, particularly where replacement is important, often results in inclusions of unincorporated minerals in the growing crystal. **1972** M. H. Battey *Mineral. for Students* vi. 160/1 Deposition is also influenced by the nature of the country-rocks. The fluids react with these..to produce replacement deposits in the neighbourhood of the vein fissures.

2. Something which or someone who replaces another.

1894 *Q. Jrnl. Geol. Soc.* L. 383 The hypothesis that the rock is a siliceous replacement of a limestone. **1934** H. G. Wells *Exper. Autobiogr.* I. ii. 62 He..sold little, I think, but jam-pots and preserving jars to the gentlemen's houses round about, and occasional..table glass and replacements. **1944** *Yank* 26 May 3 At the Rapido some replacements couldn't tell the difference between our fire and Jerry's. **1954** W. Faulkner *Fable* 4 The original regiment had been raised in this district... And most of its subsequent replacements had been drawn from this same district. **1973** *Times* 15 Feb. 12/6 There are, however, two significant changes in the list of substitutes (whom rugby officials insist on calling 'replacements' to differentiate between them and the fellows used in other sports for tactical reasons without anyone having gone to hospital).

3. *attrib.* and *Comb.*, as *replacement cost, price, thrust*; **replacement theory** (see quot. 1979); **replacement therapy**, therapy aimed at making up a deficit of a substance normally present in the body.

1928 *Britain's Industrial Future* (Liberal Industr. Inquiry) ii. vi. 67 The capital plant of most..undertakings is relatively small, but the roads are an exception, of which the replacement cost must exceed £1,300,000,000. **1936** J. M. Keynes *Gen. Theory Employment* xi. 135 The price which would just induce a manufacturer newly to produce an additional unit of such assets, *i.e.* what is sometimes called its *replacement cost.* **1963** *Rep. Comm. Inquiry Decimal Curr.* xiv. 141 The true 'replacement cost' is the present value to the user of the future flow of services he could expect from the old machine were it not prematurely replaced. **1977** *Time* 24 Jan.

44/3 Proponents of replacement-cost accounting argue that the machine should be carried on the books at the price of a new machine. **1974** *Terminol. Managem. & Financial Accountancy* (Inst. Cost & Managem. Accountants) 15 *Replacement price*, the price at which material could be purchased, identical to that which is being replaced or revalued. **1957** C. W. CHURCHMAN et al. *Introd. Operations Research* xvii. 482 (*heading*) Relevant costs in replacement theory considerations. **1969** J. ARGENTI *Managem. Techniques* 226 (*heading*) Replacement Theory... Problem... When to replace plant, machinery, etc. **1979** *Gloss. Terms Work Study* (*B.S.I.*) 12 *Replacement theory*, a body of mathematical theory connected with the problems of determining the most economical time to replace or repair a piece of equipment. **1962** H. BURN *Drugs, Med. & Man* xiii. 138 In replacement therapy extracts of glands such as the thyroid gland, the pancreas, the parathyroid gland and the adrenal cortex were prepared from the glands of animals and were given to patients whose own glands were deficient. **1977** *Lancet* 14 May 1048/1 A young woman with von Willebrand disease who asked for a termination of pregnancy and tubal ligation had had..only one bleeding episode in her life requiring replacement therapy. **1971** I. BUTYKAI tr. *Lukovich's Electric Foil Fencing* I. 20 Fencers show a definite preference for angular attacks, replacement thrusts and ripostes.

replacer (rĭplēⁱ·səɹ). [f. REPLACE *v.* + -ER¹.] A person or thing that replaces another; a substitute. Also *attrib.*

1895 in *Funk's Stand. Dict.* **1913** G. B. DIBBLEE *Newspaper* 110 One may perhaps grumble at the rather obvious significance of the new 'replacers'. **1960** *Farmer & Stockbreeder* 9 Feb. 73/1 Early weaning is done at three weeks, the piglets being moved on to a home mixed replacer meal, compounded for £67 10s a ton. **1965** *Language* XLI. 280 The pronominal replacers are marked for low stress.

repla·cive, *a.* and *sb.* [f. REPLACE *v.* + -IVE.] **A.** *adj.* That replaces something else; substitutive; *spec.* in *Linguistics*, of a morph or morpheme.

1948 *Language* XXIV. 440 Morphemes may be classified.. as (1) additive, (2) replacive, (3) additive and replacive, and (4) subtractive. **1949** E. A. NIDA *Morphology* (ed. 2) 72 In English replacive morphemes are abundantly illustrated in the verbs which undergo a change of syllabic in the past-tense. **1965** *Canad. Jrnl. Linguistics* X. 139 It [*sc.* the Giamina language] became extinct not through replacive bilingualism with Spanish or English but with one of the Yokuts languages. **1974** P. H. MATTHEWS *Morphology* vii. 122 *Men*, for example, would be said to consist of the regular allomorph *man* of the morpheme MAN plus a 'replacive morph' ('replace *a* with *e*' or '*a* →*e*') which was assigned as yet another allomorph of PLURAL. **1977** *Word 1972* XXVIII. 193 It seems possible to classify Welsh metanalysis into three main types: *additive, subtractive*, and *replacive*.

B. *sb.* Something which replaces or substitutes for something else; *spec.* in *Linguistics*, a replacive morph or morpheme.

1948 *Language* XXIV. 441 The shift of stress in related nouns and verbs in English..is also a type of replacive. **1949** E. A. NIDA *Morphology* (ed. 2) 55 In the example *feet* as a plural of *foot* we may describe the replacement as /iy←u/. Such morphemes are called 'replacives'. **1954** *Word* X. 224 A 'replacive'..is not by any stretch of the imagination composed of phonemic material. **1962** H. A. GLEASON in Householder & Saporta *Probl. Lexicography* 87 The 'replacive'..quite artificially makes an affix out of a process. **1977** *Word 1972* XXVIII. 203 Complicated series of alterations: some replacives (e.g. *Glama*), but also syncope, assimilation, and so on.

repla·n *v.* [RE- 5 a.] *trans.* To plan again. Hence **repla·nning** *vbl. sb.*

1888 [see RE- 5 a]. **1943** J. S. HUXLEY *TVA* xv. 129 Replanned so as to provide docks and terminals..Guntersville has become transformed. **1946** *Nature* 28 Sept. 438/2 No schemes for reconstructing and replanning London will be satisfactory without drastic adjustments to existing facilities for transport. **1960** *Farmer & Stockbreeder* 22 Mar. 120/3 Farm manager, Frank Stevens, played an important part in replanning the farm. **1976** S. R. SIMPSON *Land Law & Registration* ix. 170 Similar considerations apply to physical planning or replanning and to 'land reform'. **1978** P. BOARDMAN *Worlds of Patrick Geddes* vii. 244 The Viceroy opened a competition with a prize of £500 for the best replanning scheme for the city [*sc.* Dublin].

replantation. Add: **2.** *Med.* Permanent reattachment to the body of a part which has been removed or severed.

1870 [in Dict.]. **1976** *Daily Tel.* 26 Nov. 17/6 One of the first reports of a successful replantation of a hand is published in the current issue of the *Journal of Bone and Joint Surgery*. **1980** *Times* 12 Aug. 11/5 Microsurgical replantation of limbs is carried out throughout the North American continent, Australia and many European countries.

replate, *v.* Add: **2.** *trans.* and *intr.* (See quot. 1961.)

1961 H. B. JACOBSON *Mass Communications Dict.* 283 *Replate*, to recast a page of type to insert an important but late story. **1967** *Punch* 18 Jan. 91/1 This..was replated between editions to alter a reference to the *Guardian's* sales. **1967** M. SHULMAN *Kill 3* I. viii. 54 Since it's a London story, let's hold it till as late as possible. The opposition [newspapers] will have to re-plate if they want to pick it up. **1980** 'L. BLACK' *Eve of Wedding* v. 58 'How late will you stay open?' 'Until about three for fudging. We can replate to about two.'

replay, *v.* Add: **2.** To play (a gramophone record or a tape) again, or to play back; to reproduce (what has been recorded).

1922 *Daily Mail* 18 Nov. 8 Each instrument is fitted with our special 'Repeater' which automatically replays records when desired without the operator's attention. **1962** A. NISBETT *Technique Sound Studio* 241 Tape which is replayed on the same head as was used for recording does not exhibit faults which would be at once apparent if the tape were replayed on most other machines. **1973** *Sci. Amer.* Jan. 117/1 We could replay the recorded sounds at leisure as many times as necessary to make an accurate comparison with the frequencies of our standard disk. **1973** L. COOPER *Tea on Sunday* xi. 93 He recalled the people... So often by running the first interviews through again as if they were a section of a film being replayed he picked up some clue. **1976** DEXTER & MAKINS *Testkill* 140 One of Byron's cover drives, replayed later on TV in slow motion as a textbook stroke. **1977** *Rolling Stone* 19 May 96/2 The Betamax enables you to record (on tape) your favourite TV programs for replaying later.

replay, *sb.* (In Dict. s.v. REPLAY *v.*) Add: Now usu. with pronunc. (rī·plēⁱ). **1.** (Later examples.)

1932 *St. George's Hosp. Gaz.* XXVIII. 25 The re-play took place at Chiswick House, St. Thomas's winning by 7 wickets. **1947** *Sporting Mirror* 7 Nov. p. iii/1 They reached the Junior Cup Final, but after a drawn game at Maidenhead, lost the replay to Reading Albion. **1951** *Sport* 27 Jan.–2 Feb. 4/3 Sunderland were the visitors to St. James' Park in a 6th round replay. **1966** *Listener* 20 Jan. 88/2 The less exhausted players and survivors of replays in the interminable F.A. Cup. **1978** *Morecambe Guardian* 14 Mar. 10/2 In the old days, Chorley were Morecambe's traditional cup rivals and the Shrimps will do well even if they force a replay.

2. The action or an instance of replaying a sound recording, piece of film, etc. Freq. *attrib.*, denoting equipment used for this.

1953 E. S. GARDNER *Case of Green-Eyed Sister* viii. 117 You had insisted on a replay of the tape. **1958** S. ELLIN *Eighth Circle* II. xvii. 132 He put Berrigan's 'I Can't Get Started' on the phonograph and set it for replay. **1962** A. NISBETT *Technique Sound Studio* vii. 130 The facilities for mixing—requiring two replay decks in addition to a mixer and recorder—are generally beyond the scope of the amateur. **1972** *Guardian* 24 Aug. 10/1 It would have been helpful if an echo machine could have produced for the President a replay of his acceptance speech in the same hall four years ago. **1974** *Cleveland* (Ohio) *Plain Dealer* 13 Oct. c. 2/1 The scoreboards will be placed on each side and the instant replay screens at each end. **1975** O. SELA *Bengali Inheritance* xv. 124 Now get the mike connected... He.. pressed the replay tab. **1976** *Daily Tel.* 16 July 3/3 A video-tape machine is to be used by London Transport to run 'replays' of violence at underground stations. **1978** S. BRETT *Amateur Corpse* xv. 137 Gerald spooled through till nearly the end of the tape... The replay button was pressed.

3. *transf.* and *fig.*

1975 P. FUSSELL *Great War* ix. 317 And the economic ruin uncompleted by the Great War was finished by the Second, which necessitated a replay, but much magnified, of immense indebtedness to the United States. **1976** W. H. CANAWAY *Willow-Pattern War* xv. 153, I lay awake..doing an involuntary replay of that horrible dream. **1977** *Time* 30 May 20/2 As Poland approaches the first anniversary of the 1976 riots, an occasion that could invite a replay of last year's protest, the Party Chief is under pressure from Moscow to keep the lid on dissent. **1977** D. ANTHONY *Stud Game* xxiii. 142 Dusty Gordon's party would be a replay of the Hollywood parties Paul Sherwood had dragged me to.

replenishment. Add: **4.** *attrib.*, as *replenishment tanker*.

1963 *Times* 5 Feb. 10/1 The Admiralty had placed an order for three replenishment tankers, to be built on Tyneside. **1976** *Southern Even. Echo* (Southampton) 3 Nov. 2/3 Captain Averill, Master of the RFA replenishment tanker Olwen..was supporting Royal Navy frigates on duty off Iceland.

replete, *a.* **2. a.** (Later U.S. example.)

1973 *N.Y. Law Jrnl.* 5 June 4/4 Statutes are replete with misplaced commas.

replete (rĭplī·t), *sb.* [f. the adj.] Something that is replete; *spec.* an ant which is distended with food.

1908 W. M. WHEELER in *Bull. Amer. Mus. Nat. Hist.* XXIV. 379 In most cases, as McCook has shown, it is the major workers that most readily tend to become repletes. **1923** *Jrnl. Proc. Roy. Soc. W. Austral.* IX. 47 The impulse to develop repletes is probably due to the brief and temporary abundance of liquid food..in arid regions. **1929** *Encycl. Brit.* XX. 885/2 Since ants..have not the art of making receptacles, they [*sc.* honey ants] have adopted the curious method of using the crops of certain workers or soldiers for the purpose of food storage... Individuals thus functioning are termed *repletes*... When hungry the ants stroke the repletes and receive from them droplets of regurgitated honey-dew collected during times of plenty. **1979** *National Geographic* Nov. 630 The swollen worker ants, called repletes, have been fed by other workers until their abdomens are nearly grape size.

reple·vining, *vbl. sb.* [f. REPLEVIN *v.* + -ING¹.] The action of being replevined. (In quot. *fig.*)

a **1953** H. BELLOC *Farewell to Juliet* in *Sonnets & Verse* (1954) 99 One that was pledged, and goes to his Replevining.

replica. Add: **1. b.** (Later examples.) *spec.* in *Linguistics* (see quots. 1956 and 1966). Also *attrib.*

1956 E. HAUGEN in *Publ. Amer. Dial. Soc.* XXVI. 39 The speakers of language B have *borrowed* it from A... The item as pronounced by speakers of A we shall call the *model* and the diffused item as pronounced by speakers of B we shall call the *replica*. **1963** M. FRAYN in Sissons & French *Age of Austerity* xv. 336 The orange-girls, dressed up as replica Nell Gwyns. **1966** R. A. HALL *Pidgin & Creole Languages* i. 5 The European would conclude that it was useless to use 'good language' to the native, and would reply to him in a replica of the latter's incomplete speech.

c. *Mus.* A repeat.

1740 J. GRASSINEAU *Mus. Dict.* 198 *Replica, Reditta*, or *Riditta*, a *repetition*, that is, when one part after a silence repeats or runs over the same notes and intervals, and in fact the same song, which some part had gone over before it, during that silence. **1952** P. A. SCHOLES *Conc. Oxf. Dict. Mus.* 493/1 *Replica* (It.), repeat.

2. *Comb.* **replica method** = *replica technique* below; **replica plate** *Microbiol.*, a plate of culture medium which has been simultaneously inoculated with numerous microbial clones by holding it against a piece of velvet or similar material which has previously had a plate of grown colonies of micro-organisms held against it; so **replica plating**, the technique of making replica plates, usu. with culture media that contain various antibiotics or lack various nutrients, so that unusual clones of micro-organisms can be recognized; **replica technique**, a method of producing a model of an etched metallic surface for subsequent examination in an electron microscope, used when it is impracticable to take a thin slice of the metal.

1941 *Jrnl. Appl. Physics* XII. 695/2 One basic advantage of the replica methods as compared to the direct methods of surface observation with the electron microscope. **1951** V. E. COSSLETT *Pract. Electron Microscopy* ix. 214 Electron microscopy has to be content with the indirect alternative of replica methods, in which an impression is taken from a surface on to a thin film which may then be examined by transmission in the usual way. **1952** J. & E. M. LEDERBERG in *Jrnl. Bacteriol.* LXIII. 399 (*heading*) Replica plating and indirect selection of bacterial mutants. *Ibid.* 400 Replica plating is used to facilitate routine tests involving repetitive inoculations of many isolates on different media. *Ibid.* 401 A single initial plate may be used to imprint more than one fabric if carry-over from one replica plate to another vitiates serial transfer. **1958** *Times* 31 Oct. 10/7 'Replica plating'..enables strains of bacteria resistant to particular antibiotics, for example, streptomycin, to be quickly isolated. This is a simple and beautiful technique, which has proved of extreme value in research. **1970** D. A. HOPWOOD in Norris & Ribbons *Methods in Microbiol.* IIIA. vi. 404 A particularly interesting application of replica plating is in isolating bacterial variants of changed potentiality for sexual reproduction. **1977** *Physiologia Plantarum* XXXIX. 140/2 The cells..then grow with the same arrangement on the replica plate as on the master plate. **1943** *Jrnl. Appl. Physics* XIV. 24/1 The direct replica technique consists in casting a thin film of plastic on the prepared surface. **1955** *Jrnl. Iron & Steel Inst.* CLXXIX. 392/1 A simple two-stage replica technique, using an intermediate dry-stripped Formvar film on to which carbon is evaporated is described. **1966** [see *REPLICATE *v.* 2 b]. **1966** D. G. BRANDON *Mod. Techniques Metallogr.* 50 Surface replica techniques..increase the resolution available to the metallographer by a factor of 100 over that obtainable by optical microscopy but have a much reduced sensitivity to changes in surface tilt.

replicabi·lity. [f. next + -ITY.] The state, property, or condition of being replicable.

1957 *Psychiatry* XX. 80/2 Replicability—six investigators can listen to the same tape, and, within the limits of human error, apply the same analytic categories..and come out with the same transcription. **1971** *Jrnl. Gen. Psychol.* LXXXIV. 304 If that were the case, replicability would depend upon the degree that the important personality variables were adequately sampled. **1972** *Nature* 17 Mar. 99/2 Ascites tumours with high replicability are, felt Dr Steel, toys for the experimentalist. **1978** J. DUNN in Hookway & Pettit *Action & Interpretation* 150 Seeking to render human performance in an idiom in which replicability and inter-observer reliability are at a premium.

replicable, *a.* Restrict † *Obs. rare*⁻¹ to sense in Dict. and add: **2.** That may be repeated experimentally.

1953 J. B. CARROLL *Study Lang.* ii. 34 Reasonably consistent and replicable descriptions of the phonemes of a language. **1973** H. J. EYSENCK *Inequality of Man* iii. 108 Even if we regard the observed slight difference as replicable. **1974** *Encycl. Brit. Macropædia* XIII. 1004/2 Replicable phenomena that can be demonstrated with certainty.

So **re·plicably** *adv.*

1964 CRYSTAL & QUIRK *Prosodic & Paralinguist. Features in Eng.* iv. 50 Shorter pauses than those of unit length appear to be replicably distinctive.

replicase (re·plikēⁱz, -s). *Biochem.* [f. REPLIC(ATE *v.* + *-ASE.] An enzyme which synthesizes a complementary RNA molecule on an RNA template.

1963 SPIEGELMAN & HAYASHI in *Cold Spring Harbor Symp. Quantitative Biol.* XXVIII. 162/1 The RNA-dependent-RNA-polymerase which replicates RNA will be called a replicase. **1971** *New Scientist* 20 May 436/3 In making the complementary RNA the replicase observes a strict one-way system; it moves from the so-called 3′ end of the RNA to the 5′ end. **1973** C. Weissmann et al. in F. T. Kenney et al. *Gene Expression & its Regulation* ii. 20 Viral replicases show a very high template specificity for the homologous, intact viral RNA.., as well as for the complementary minus strand.., to the exclusion of all other, unrelated viral RNAs and most other RNAs examined.

replicate, *sb.* Add: **2.** *Science.* A repetition of an experiment or trial; each of a number of similar parts or procedures which constitute an experiment or trial. Cf. *REPLICATION 4 c.

1929 *Jrnl. Agric. Sci.* XIX. 213 In the earlier quantitative experiments..the precision of the results left much to be desired, since only four replicates could be used. **1953** *New Biol.* XIV. 85 It was decided that ten replicates, each of 50 ears [of wheat], would probably be sufficient to reveal important changes in population from year to year. **1970** *Sci. Jrnl.* May 65/1 Earliness and qualities of the varieties could always be reproduced, even if many replicates were made. **1976** *Jrnl. Heredity* LXVII. 204/2 The germinability from one microscope field..in each drop constituted one replicate. *Ibid.*, Values given represent data from a single pollen sample germinated in replicates as stated.

replicate, *a.* Add: **3.** *Science.* Being a replicate (*REPLICATE *sb.* 2).

1961 *Lancet* 29 July 231/2 Replicate assays (i.e. repeat assays on different days). **1972** *Science* 26 May 914/3 Three to five replicate chemical analyses were made for each major tissue. **1978** *Nature* 3 Aug. 459/1 The Institute of Petroleum method recommends that 24 replicate runs are carried out to obtain reasonable statistics.

replicate, *v.* Add: **2. b.** (Further examples.)

1964 R. D. Heidenreich *Fund. Transmission Electron Microsc.* iii. 71 The intensity distribution bears a close relation to the topography of the surface being replicated. **1966** D. G. Brandon *Mod. Techniques Metallogr.* 47 The original specimen surface may be preserved and the potential resolution of the carbon and silicon monoxide replica techniques still obtained by replicating the surface with a plastic material and then replicating this plastic negative of the surface with carbon or silicon monoxide. **1973** *Sci. Amer.* Jan. 102/1 The simplest method of studying snow crystals is to replicate them by letting them fall into a thin layer of dilute solution of plastic and solvent. The solvent evaporates rapidly, leaving a thin plastic cast of the snow crystal.

c. *Science.* To repeat (an experiment or trial) and obtain a consistent result.

1923 *Biometrika* XV. 283 We may obtain an estimate of what the variability would be if the conditions of any one trial could be replicated in a number of experiments with the same variety. **1969** *Sci. Jrnl.* Dec. 49/2 Beveridge.. replicated Thouless' experimental finding of differential cultural susceptibility to phenomenal regression. **1970** T. Lupton *Managem. & Social Sci.* (ed. 2) iii. 74 The studies have since been replicated with similar groups and different groups. **1973** J. L. Fleiss *Statistical Methods for Rates & Proportions* iii. 26 One often undertakes a study in order to replicate (or refute) another's research findings.

d. *Biol. intr., trans.,* and *refl.* Of genetic material or a living organism: to reproduce or give rise to a copy of (itself).

1957 J. Lederberg in McElroy & Glass *Chem. Basis Heredity* vii. 743 The very interesting statement that the bacterial nucleus apparently does not replicate by a non-dispersive mechanism. **1958** *New Scientist* 10 July 341/1 A characteristic of living matter is its ability to replicate itself. **1960** *New Biol.* XXXI. 20 They [*sc.* the genes] may continue for millions of years exactly replicating their complex structure. **1965** *Listener* 2 Sept. 332/1 It would be fallacious..to suppose that the major code-bearing molecules, the nucleic acids, can..replicate themselves in isolation. **1968** H. Harris *Nucleus & Cytoplasm* i. 7 The other possibility which could account for the persistence of this information in the enucleate cell is that the relevant RNA might be replicated in the cytoplasm. **1969** *Listener* 10 July 34/1 Arthropods survive, replicate, live off their environment. **1972** *Proc. R. Soc.* B. CLXXXI. 29 DNA is replicated at fork-like growing points. **1977** *Sci. Amer.* Nov. 54/3 Attributes by which we identify living things—their capacity to replicate themselves, to repair themselves, to evolve and to adapt. **1979** *Jrnl. R. Soc. Arts* CXXVII. 645/1 The bacterium rapidly divides and replicates.

e. To imitate; to make or be a model or replica of.

1958 *Word* XIV. 365 It is worth considering whether a formalized investigation replicating the game [of 'Twenty Questions'] would not produce a valid and economical description of a vocabulary. **1966** J. J. Katz *Philos. Lang.* iv. 99 Verbal exchanges between the computers replicate the publicly observable phenomena that occur when human speakers communicate in a natural language. **1967** M. Argyle *Psychol. Interpersonal Behaviour* x. 194 Other activities may be used including..setting up groups in cooperation or competition to replicate organizational problems. **1971** *Sci. Amer.* Oct. 53/2 Synthetic melts of lunar composition can replicate the texture seen in the granular moon rocks. **1977** *Times* 19 Nov. 14/4 Striations that could be replicated with modern but not ancient tools. **1979** *Times* 24 Dec. 10/8 The gallery is to have three rooms that replicate rooms at Hutton Castle.

f. To copy exactly.

1970 *Computers & Humanities* IV. 233 The index entries that have been generated in this way, using the computer's ability to replicate strings of characters, are sorted into alphabetic sequence. **1971** *Sci. Amer.* June 88/3 Since binary data are generally consumed within calculation centers, the ability to replicate the data for future manipulations is essential. **1976** *Ibid.* June 63/1 The signal transmitted from the earth is received by the spacecraft's radio system, which faithfully replicates the received phase, increases its frequency by 10 percent and transmits it back to the earth.

replicated *ppl. a.* (further scientific examples); hence also **re·plicating** *vbl. sb.* (usu. *attrib.*) and *ppl. a.*

1926 *Jrnl. Min. Agric.* XXXIII. 506 A replicated experiment provides a valid estimate of error. **1957** F. H. C. Crick in McElroy & Glass *Chem. Basis Heredity* vii. 747 In a replicating structure one expects the bases to pair rather accurately, so that mistakes are rare. **1960** *New Biol.* XXXI. 23 Some persistent change has therefore occurred in the replicating system for proteins. **1961** M. E. Haine *Electron Microscope* x. 245 The replica..has one surface flat and the other following the topography of the replicated surface. *Ibid.*, Replicas were formed in plastic and were limited by the large molecular size of the replicating material. **1971** *Nature* 13 Aug. 502/1 Cellulose acetate replicating tape is used to prepare negative replicas of the etched surfaces. **1976** *National Observer* (U.S.) 17 July 15/3 It appears easy to come up with organic compounds and water. But the big gap is, How often do you get replicating organisms? That, if you will, is the missing link in the origin of life. **1977** *Jrnl. Agric. Sci.* LXXXVIII. 127 (*heading*) Response to family selection based on replicated trials. **1978** *Nature* 20 July 212/2 The combined nicking-closing and negative supercoiling activity of gyrase are presumed to act at some site at or beyond the replicating fork to relieve the positive supercoiling strain which builds up during replication and to aid unwinding.

replication. 4. Restrict † *Obs.* to senses in Dict. and add: **c.** *Science.* Repetition of an experiment or trial so as to test the trustworthiness of its conclusion.

1926 *Jrnl. Min. Agric.* XXXIII. 506 The method adopted is that of replication. **1953** *New Biol.* XIV. 85 More than one sample must always be taken in order to discover the natural variation between individual samples. This is termed 'replication'. **1971** *Jrnl. Gen. Psychol.* LXXXV. 200 The stability of the means can be seen to be high in the replications.

6. (Further examples.)

1951 V. E. Cosslett *Pract. Electron Microscopy* ix. 223 Most materials for replication are initially either too rough or too smooth for the purpose. **1966** D. G. Brandon *Mod. Techniques Metallogr.* 45 A major advance in replication technique was made when Bradley discovered that an evaporated carbon film was virtually structureless and would faithfully follow surface contours down to a limit of resolution of about 20 Å. **1969** *Computer & Humanities* III. 193 Gutenberg's press in mid-fifteenth century made multiple replication of the visual expression of ideas practicable. **1972** *Language* XLVIII. 346 The vocalic sub-hierarchy assigns markedness values exclusively by means of replication, whereas the consonantal sub-hierarchy assigns markedness values by means of complementation *and* replication, depending on the feature specification. **1975** *New Yorker* 3 Mar. 96/3 The real triumph of 'Female Friends' is the gritty replication of the gross texture of everyday life, placed in perspective and made universal.

b. *Biol.* The process by which genetic material or a living organism gives rise to a copy of itself.

1948 *Nature* 5 June 872/2 Replication seems commonly to mark the end of active cell division and the onset of differentiation. **1955** *Sci. Amer.* Oct. 70/1 Sometimes, because of a mistake in some step of the replication process, a daughter cell gets a gene carrying a garbled message; that is, it does not bear precisely the same information as its original counterpart. **1971** D. J. Cove *Genetics* v. 73 (*caption*) M. Meselson and F. W. Stahl's experiment to demonstrate the semi-conservative replication of DNA. **1972** *Proc. R. Soc.* B. CLXXXI. 29 Replication of chromosomal DNA occurs in sections arranged in tandem. **1977** *Sci. Amer.* Dec. 94/2 In viral replication (and microbial replication in general) mutants appear at a frequency of about one in a million particles, depending on the viral strain and the conditions of culture.

replicative, *a.* Add: **2.** *Biol.* Of, pertaining to, or involved in replication.

1960 *New Biol.* XXXI. 130 A hint that some divisions of the plant kingdom have replicative mechanisms that either derange more easily or are more tolerant of novelty than others. **1971** *Sci. Amer.* Aug. 52/1 As has been abundantly demonstrated over the past two decades, DNA is the replicative molecule of the cell. **1975** *Ibid.* May 28/3 We have isolated a structure reflecting that stage: several plus strands of graduated lengths partially bonded to the minus strand on which they are being synthesized; we call such a structure the replicative intermediate. **1976** *Nature* 28 Oct. 731/1 Plasmids can be viewed as primitive bacteriophages that have not yet acquired those specialised functions necessary for a complex replicative cycle.

replicatively, *adv.* (Later example.)

1957 R. K. Merton *Student-Physician* App. C. 304 The second criterion is that results must be *replicatively* consistent.

replicator (re·plikēitǫɹ). [ad. F. *réplicateur* (Jacob & Brenner 1963, in *Compt. Rend.* CCLVI. 298), f. as next + *-eur* -OR.] **1.** *Biol.* A postulated section of nucleic acid at which replication is initiated and away from which it proceeds in one or both directions.

1963 *Cold Spring Harbor Symp. Quantitative Biol.* XXVIII. 331/1 A unit capable of independent replication or replicon would carry two specific determinants... A structural gene controlling the synthesis of a specific initiator... An operator of replication, or replicator, i.e., a specific element of recognition upon which the corresponding initiator would act, allowing the replication of the DNA attached to the replicator. **1969** A. M. Campbell *Episomes* viii. 107 Effectively, the F factor would have taken over the normal replicator function for the major part of the bacterial chromosome. **1973** *Virology* LIV. 270/1 According to the replicon theory, some replication-deficient mutants should be found in the postulated replicator gene. **1978** *Bull. Amer. Acad. Arts & Sci.* Feb. 17 In cases where more than two X chromosomes were present there were multiple late replicators.

2. That which replicates (in any sense).

1964 *Listener* 15 Oct. 575/1 Looking as far into the technological future as I dare, I would like to describe the invention to end all inventions. I call it the replicator; it is simply a duplicating machine. It could make, almost instantly, an exact copy of anything. **1972** *Science* 27 Oct. 359/1 Adult liver..has been described as a 'discontinuous replicator'..that divides at a low 'wear and tear' replacement rate.

replicon (re·plikǫn). *Biol.* [ad. F. *réplicon* (Jacob & Brenner 1963, in *Compt. Rend.* CCLVI. 298), f. *réplic-ation* REPLICATION: see *-ON[1].] **a.** A piece of genetic material which replicates as a unit, beginning at a single site within it.

1963 *Cold Spring Harbor Symp. Quantitative Biol.* XXVIII. 330/2 A genetic element such as an episome or a chromosome (of a bacterium or of a phage) constitutes a unit of replication or replicon. Such a unit can only replicate as a whole... The capacity to behave as a replicon must depend upon the presence and activity of certain specific determinants. In other words, the properties of such units require that they set up specific systems of signals allowing, or preventing, their own replication. **1971** *Jrnl. Molecular Biol.* LVIII. 873 It has been hypothesized that in mammalian cells DNA replication proceeds *via* two replication forks per replicon, which proceed in opposite directions. **1972** *Bacteriol. Rev.* XXXVI. 365/1 The hypothesis was proposed that those DNA molecules that are capable of replication (termed 'replicons') are circular in structure and carry at least two gene loci controlling their replication; at one locus on the replicon is located a regulator gene which produces a diffusible substance (initiator) acting upon the second locus, an operator of replication (replicator), to permit DNA replication to be initiated from that point. **1974** *Nature* 9 Aug. 467/2 Each chromosome contains many tandemly arranged units of replication (replicons), and each replicon is comparable to the whole chromosome of a bacterium or a virus in that its replication is usually bi-directional. **1976** *Ibid.* 29 Jan. 281/1 Each of these components is capable of autonomous replication in certain host strains of bacteria; that is, each is a 'replicon'.

replo·t, *v.* [RE- 5 a.] *trans.* To plot or represent again. So **replo·tter; replo·tting** *vbl. sb.*

1896 *Rep. Board of Ordnance & Fortification* (U.S.) 18 A replotting arm for attachment to the Lewis position-finder. **1897** *Ann. Rep. Chief of Ordnance to Sec. of War 1896* (U.S.) 581 A photograph and description of the Lewis replotter. *Ibid.* 582 With this device it is possible to correctly replot the position of a moving target..at intervals of ten seconds of time without hurry or confusion. **1902** *Encycl. Brit.* XXXI. 367/1 A complete automatic replotter is carried on the table of each instrument, by the use of which the observer can instantly convert the range and direction of the target as read from the instrument into the corresponding range and direction from the gun itself. **1965** Phillips & Williams *Inorg. Chem.* I. xvii. 633 The change in ease of oxidation down the series is brought out by replotting some of the values. **1968** *Economist* 6 July 54/1 If an essential invention occurs out of order, the time-scale has to be revised and the forecast path of advance replotted.

replumb, *v.* Restrict † *Obs.*$^{-0}$ to sense in Dict. and add: **2.** [A separate formation on RE- 5 a.] *trans.* To redo or replace the plumbing in (a building). Chiefly as **replu·mbed** *pa. pple.* Also **replu·mbing** *vbl. sb.*

1909 H. G. Wells *Tono-Bungay* iii. ii. 291 My uncle distinguished himself by the thoroughness with which he did the repainting and replumbing. **1973** *Irish Times* 2 Mar. 26/1 (Advt.), Re-roofed, re-wired and re-plumbed in recent years. **1976** *Newmarket Jrnl.* 16 Dec. 39 (Advt.), These properties have been fully modernised including re-roofing, re-wiring, re-plumbing, etc. **1977** [see *SEE *v.* 22]. **1978** *Morecambe Guardian* 14 Mar. 23/3 (Advt.), The house has been re-wired, replumbed, had a new bathroom installed, etc.

reply, *sb.* Add: **1. d.** *reply-paid* adj. (later examples).

1928 E. Wallace *Double* xviii. 272 It was evidently, from the indicator, a reply-paid message. **1973** *Times* 14 Mar. 4/6 In the present poll this outcome may well have been achieved by the retiring conservators distributing reply-paid proxy forms.

2. b. A pleading by the plaintiff after the delivery of the defence; the final speech of Counsel in a trial.

1837 in Carrington & Payne *Rep. Cases Nisi Prius* VII. 676 The counsel for the prosecution may re-examine the witness, and after the prisoner's counsel has addressed the jury, will be entitled to the reply. **1837** *Rex* v. *Stannard* in *Ibid.* 675 C. Phillips waived his right of reply. **1875** *Act* 38 & 39 *Vict.* c. 77 Sched. 1. § xxiv. 55 A plaintiff shall deliver his reply, if any, within three weeks after the defence or the last of the defences shall have been delivered, unless the time shall be extended by the Court or a Judge. **1898** *Criminal Evidence Act* 61 & 62 *Vict.* c. 36 s. 3 In cases where the right of reply depends upon the question whether evidence has been called for the defence, the fact that the person charged has been called as a witness shall not of itself confer on the prosecution the right of reply. **1961** L. F. Sturge *Basic Rules Supreme Court* xxiii. 62 The position is further confused by the fact that the Rules give the name 'reply' to what the legal profession is accustomed..to call a 'defence to counterclaim'... The modern practice is to head the pleading 'Reply and Defence to Counterclaim' and to head each part respectively 'Reply' (meaning the equivalent of the common law replication) and 'Defence to Counterclaim'. **1964** Ld. Evershed et al. *Atkin's Encycl. Court Forms* (ed. 2) XXXII. 35 Pleadings subsequent to the reply still bear their ancient names: rejoinder, surrejoinder, rebutter and surrebutter, although modern rules do not refer to them by name. **1975** I. H. Jacob *Bullen & Leake's Precedents of Pleadings* (ed. 12) ix. 109 No pleading subsequent to a reply or a defence to counterclaim may be served except with the leave of the court.

4. A signal sent by a transponder in response to interrogation. Also *attrib.*, as *reply pulse.*

1945 [see *interrogate *v.* 4 a]. **1947** L. N. Ridenour *Radar System Engin.* viii. 263 The replies may be made more complicated in a variety of ways for the purpose either of identifying the beacon or of using it as part of an auxiliary communication system. **1963** R. S. H. Boulding *Princ. Radar* (ed. 7) xxii. 471 Measurement of the time from the commencement of the interrogating pulse to the receipt of the beginning of the reply pulse enables the distance between the aircraft and the beacon to be determined. **1965** R. S. Berkowitz *Mod. Radar* I. ii. 12 When the radar interrogates a beacon and receives a reply whose power is fixed by the characteristics of the beacon transmitter, separate calculations are necessary for the out and back paths.

reply, *v.* Add: **I. 1.** (Further *fig.* examples.)

1714 Pope *Rape of Lock* III. 24 The Nymph exulting fills.. the sky; The Walls, the Woods, and long Canals reply. **1785** Cowper *Task* VI. 231 There is in souls a sympathy with sounds... Some chord in unison with what we hear is touched within us, and the heart replies. **1930** R. Campbell *Poems* 9 Clear as a glass the day replies To every feature save her eyes.

3. (Later examples.)

1849 J. L. Campbell *Chief Justices Eng.* II. xxxiii. 401 Lord Mansfield hesitated long about making the right to reply depend upon the giving of evidence by the defendant. **1923** W. G. Russell *Treatise on Crimes* (ed. 8) II. 1835 If the defendant is undefended there is no right to sum up or reply if he calls no witnesses, whether he himself does or does not give evidence: but there is a right to reply if he calls a witness.

repolariza·tion. [Re- 5 b.] A renewed polarization (in the senses of Dict. and Suppl.); the action of repolarizing.

1922 *Public Opinion* 11 Aug. 136/2 What is aimed at is the repolarisation of the individual items of society. **1958** Cranefield & Hoffman in *Jrnl. Gen. Physiol.* XLI. 633 (*title*) Propagated repolarization in heart muscle. **1968** *Economist* 20 July 32/1 It also caused him to predict a repolarisation of South African politics. **1973** *Nature* 9 Feb. 400/1 The immediate consequence of contact of ovum and spermatozoon is an action potential, a depolarization and repolarization including a transient reversal of polarity.

repo·larize, *v.* [Re- 5 b.] *intr.* To polarize again.

1958 J. H. Burn *Lect. Notes Pharmacol.* (ed. 5) 37 Normally a second response can be produced when the intracellular potential has repolarized to only 2/3 of its full resting negativity. **1965** *Math. in Biol. & Med.* (Med. Res. Council) VI. 262 When curve C is reached the only remaining point at which the ionic current is zero is the new value E_r, so that the membrane repolarizes. **1973** *Nature* 9 Feb. 400/2 The eggs then repolarized, somewhat slowly, to the –60 mV typical of the end of phase III. **1980** *Sci. Amer.* May 74/3 In an unmyelinated fiber the entire axonal membrane must depolarize and then repolarize.

repo·lish (rī-), *sb.* [f. the vb.] A renewed polishing.

1905 *Daily Chron.* 9 Sept. 2/6 The floor is waxed and polished, so only needs dusting and a very occasional repolish.

report, *sb.* Add: **2. e.** A teacher's official statement in writing about the work and behaviour of a pupil at a school.

1873 C. M. Yonge *Life J. C. Patteson* I. i. 16 The half-yearly reports often lament his want of zeal and exertion. **1906** R. Brooke *Let.* 1 Apr. (1968) 47 My term's report.. has come in, & is very bad. Result: the family are shocked. **1973** 'M. Innes' *Appleby's Answer* ii. 19 It was a mark I'm simply bound in conscience to put into a pupil's report.

3. e. A statement in which an accusation is made against (a sailor, etc.); the charge itself; esp. in phr. *on report,* on a charge.

1850 H. Melville *White Jacket* II. xxxviii. 246 The names of such offenders shall be put down on the report. **1915** *Recruiter's Bull.* (U.S. Marine Corps., N.Y.) June 17/2, I was in that Corps for fifteen years and never saw a man on report. **1948** Partridge *Dict. Forces' Slang* 154 *In the report,* a colloquial synonym of 'in the *rattle*'. (Navy.) **1963** T. & P. Morris *Pentonville* vi. 126 When an officer observes a prisoner committing an offence he must decide whether or not to place the prisoner on Governor's Report... Reports are heard on every day except Sundays and public holidays. **1969** *Punch* 5 Mar. 350/2 We're just coming up to the conference point with my sergeant, fifteen hundred hours outside Queensway tube. I'll be on report if he catches me exceeding three miles per hour.

f. *weather report*: see Weather *sb.* 6 a in Dict. and Suppl.

8. *attrib.* and *Comb.*, as *report sheet, stage*; **report card,** (*a*) *U.S.*, a document comprising a school report; also *attrib.* and *transf.*; (*b*) *Austral.* (see quot. 1969).

1929 W. Faulkner *Sound & Fury* 223 But to have the school authorities think that I have no control over her, that..I didn't even know she had a report card. **1952** B. Ulanov *Hist. Jazz in Amer.* (1958) xvii. 202 He set up a rating system for bands, based on the report-card letters A to D. **1953** *Manch. Guardian Weekly* 12 Nov. 2/1 The Republicans would be less doleful this morning if they had not seconded so volubly the Democrats' contention that these four elections would constitute 'a report card' on the Eisenhower Administration. **1969** Eagleson & McKie *Terminology Austral. Nat. Football* III. 7 *Report card,* a card on which at the termination of a match, umpires record particulars of any charge(s) they may make against players. **1977** *Time* 22 Aug. 11/3 Carter's early forcefulness..drove six Latin countries..to reject U.S. military assistance rather than agree to prepare 'report cards' for Washington on human rights. **1980** L. St. Clair *Obsessions* xi. 195 Erin's baby bootees, her silver food pusher, her first report card. **1957** C. Smith *Case of Torches* xiv. 189 He wrote it all down... He doodled on his report sheet. **1966** P. O'Donnell *Sabre Tooth* i. 7 His report-sheet shows that he was a good man. **1906** Freeman & Abbott *A.B.C. of Parliamentary Procedure* 74 Reports from Committee of the Whole House. ('Report Stage'.)—When a Bill is committed *pro formâ* to enable the member in charge to introduce numerous amendments..the Bill so amended is reported and recommitted for a future day. **1976** *Liverpool Echo* 6 Dec. 5/8 We expect concessions to be made during the committee and report stages of the Bill.

report, *v.* Add: **I. 2. d.** To say factually. Also with direct speech as object.

1929 M. A. Gill *Underworld Slang* 15/1 Words that can be used in place of..'said'..Reported. **1977** B. Freemantle *Charlie Muffin* iv. 45 'Completely misread the interview,' he reported.

3. a. Also with *back.* Phr. *to report out* (a bill), of a committee of Congress: to return (a bill) to the legislative body for debate.

1883 *Rep. U.S. Bureau Indian Affairs* p. xxiv, The bill as read and referred was reported back by the Senate Committee. **1948** *Sun* (Baltimore) 31 May 8/2 The bill recently was reported out favorably by the House Armed Services Committee. **1965** Mrs. L. B. Johnson *White House Diary* 10 Apr. (1970) 257 The Committee reported out the Civil Rights Bill, quicker and stronger than ever expected. **1976** *N.Y. Rev. Bks.* 15 Apr. 20/3 The Senate Antitrust Subcommittee may well report out a 'vertical divestiture' bill, which will then go before the full Judiciary Committee. **1976** *Daily Tel.* 25 Sept. 10/4 The society..has arranged for its ticket selling committee to meet next Tuesday to report back their ideas to the society. **1979** *Sci. Amer.* July 68/3 The bill was reported out of committee, but when it was pointed out that enforcing such a statute would cost money and that the bill should be referred to the appropriations committee, support waned and the bill did not come to a vote.

II. 5. b. (Later examples.) Also used in less formal contexts of a journalist or broadcaster. Phr. *to report back*: to return with a formal report (*to* one's principal).

1961 *Providence* (Rhode Island) *Jrnl.* 20 July 5 He would study the correct method and report back to the council. **1966** *Rep. Comm. Inquiry Univ. Oxf.* I. 271 An inferior body receives its policy from the superior body and can then be told to do its work and decide within the limits of the policy laid down, only reporting back in cases of real doubt or difficulty. **1968** *Listener* 21 Nov. 667/1 That resolution gave us only 70 hours to report back to the Assembly on the organisation of the force. **1971** *Guardian* 19 Mar. 22/3 The good and bad of compensation: Judy Hillman and Malcolm Stuart report on page six. **1974** *Radio Times* 28 Feb. 35/2 What does a holiday cruise offer you? *Gladys Nicol* reports. *Ibid.* 35/5 The World Tonight: News—Douglas Stuart reporting.

c. Also with *in.*

1969 I. Kemp *Brit. G.I. in Vietnam* viii. 159 'I'm reporting in,' I told him, handing over my orders. **1977** D. Beaty *Excellency* viii. 99 He murmured something about having to report in at the African Airways counter.

reportabi·lity. [f. Reportable *a.*: see -ity.] The quality or state of being reportable.

1960 Bruner & Klein in J. S. Bruner *Beyond Information Given* (1974) vii. 119 The work of Blackwell in America, and of Dixon in England, suggests strongly that the reportability of a stimulus or awareness of a subject depends upon the nature of response alternatives.

reportable, *a.* Add: **2.** That should or must be reported to some authority.

1942 L. D. Kitchin *Road Transport Law* 29/1 No notice need be given..for a test and inspection to be conducted within 48 hours of a 'reportable' accident in which the vehicle has been involved. **1976** *Sci. Amer.* Oct. 28/3 Smallpox was made a reportable disease. **1976** G. Thurston *Coronership* iii. 54 Death in custody in a police station is not, strictly, reportable unless it is unnatural or of unknown cause.

reportage. Add: Also with pronunc. (‖ rəportāʒ). **3.** The describing of events (usu. by an observer); *spec.* the reporting of events for the press or for broadcasting, esp. with reference to its style; an instance of this, a piece of journalistic or factual writing. Also *transf.* and *attrib.*

1891 E. Dowson *Let.* 7 Feb. (1967) 184 Howells..writes in dialect, in Yankee and that's not realism (even Zola doesn't go so far) it's reportage. **1931** *Times Lit. Suppl.* 19 Feb. 129/2 Ludwig's works written before the war, plays, novels, *reportage.* **1938** C. Connolly *Enemies of Promise* xvi. 173 The article has a future, especially in the form of the critical essay..and the skilled 'reportage'. **1942** E. Paul *Narrow St.* xix. 155 What L'Hibou suggested..that Madame Absalom should do with her ears, had best be omitted from this reportage. **1954** Koestler *Invisible Writing* xv. 169 Németh's book was planned as a long psychological novel, Kuncz's book as a straightforward reportage. **1959** L.-H. Liang tr. *Ting Yi's Short Hist. Mod. Chin. Lit.* x. 217 During the early period of the War of Resistance, reportage ..became the most popular of all literary forms among both the writers and the broad reading public. **1961** *Listener* 28 Dec. 1125/3 Where *is* your black-and-white photograph without sun and sparkle?.. A big enough limitation, one would think, to render suspect almost any black and white reportage. **1963** *Movie* Apr. 12/1 The makers of documentary and reportage films. **1965** *Listener* 8 Apr. 535/1 In his fourth sonata..there was too little art (and craft) and too much *reportage.* **1969** *N.Y. Rev. Books* 2 Jan. 28/3 Reportages like his account of a journey through the Sudetenland as the Germans entered. **1978** *Poland* May 52/2 Young people need a confirmation of their knowledge about their own country.., and that..is precisely what they find in a realistic reportage. **1979** *London Rev. Bks.* 25 Oct. 8/4 His study of the Hyde Park orators might have been taken as a masterly piece of reportage.

reportative (rĭpōᵊ·ɹtătiv), *a.* [f. Report *v.* + -ative.] That presents or introduces reported speech.

1973 *New Society* 6 Sept. 580/2 Containing in fact only one four letter word used in a reportative context. **1975** *Language* LI. 804 Normally, a sentence containing the quotative clitic translates with 'one says', 'they say', or 'it is said', i.e. a reportative verb having an unspecified subject.

reportedly, *adv.* (In Dict. s.v. Report *v.*) (Further examples.)

1958 *Times* 28 Nov. 13/6 Some chance remarks reportedly made by Prince Akihito..sent the match-makers searching farther afield. **1959** *Listener* 6 Aug. 199/1 He was..strongly criticized for reportedly kissing an African woman in public. **1972** *New Yorker* 4 Mar. 85/1 What their constituents have said to them since reportedly is not appreciative. **1979** *Time* 2 Apr. 31/1 This probe reportedly is ready to produce indictments against the man that Carter made director of the Office of Management and Budget.

reporter. Add: **1. a.** (Later example.)

1952 P. Edwards in *Shakespeare Survey* V. 35 If the 1609 Quarto of *Pericles* is reconstructed, or 'reported', we should infer, from the suggestion that two hands are at work on the manuscript, that the text was compiled by two 'reporters'.

c. Also (*Sc. Law*), one who receives reports (on juvenile offenders).

1968 *Social Work* (*Scotland*) *Act* c. 49 s. 36(1) For the purpose of arranging children's hearings and for the performance of such other functions in relation to the children's panel or to children's hearings as may be assigned to him by this Part of this Act, a local authority shall, in accordance with the provisions of this section, appoint an officer, whole-time or part-time, to be known as the reporter. **1976** *Howard Jrnl.* XV. 1. 31 The key figure in the new system is the reporter. It is his function to decide, on the basis of reports, whether the child referred to him by the police, social worker or education department is in 'need of compulsory measures of care'.

2. b. (Earlier and later examples.) Also, one who does similar work for other kinds of journal, or for radio or television. Also *reporter-at-large.*

1798 *Deb. Congress U.S.* 21 Mar. (1851) 1289 The House ought to render the reporters as independent..as they could be. **1802** *Monthly Magazine* XIV. 160/1 Two cases have recently occurred within the sphere of the Reporter's observation. **1946** M. McCarthy *Let.* in *Politics* Nov. 367/1 Mr. Hersey..is *The New Yorker's* reporter-at-large. **1968** *Listener* 12 Sept. 322/2 Some of the strikers, including some sports reporters, had proposed a return to work... The radio reporters of *France-Inter* returned ten days later..and TV reporters..agreed to resume work in mid-July.

c. In the titles of newspapers and periodical publications.

1797 (*title*) The reporter, or the general observer. **1853** (*title*) St. Helens newspaper and midweek reporter. **1870** (*title*) Cambridge University reporter. **1956** (*title*) Surrey county reporter. **1961** (*title*) Rating and valuation reporter.

4. *Chem.* In full *reporter group.* A group whose spectroscopic properties are sensitive to its chemical environment and well characterized and which is used as a means of obtaining structural information about a system or molecule in which it occurs.

1970 *Nature* 21 Mar. 1103/1 The method is based on the anisotropy of signals from the nitroxide radical which thus acts as a 'reporter' of molecular motions (for example, whether the spin label is in a region of free or unrestricted movement). **1974** *Sci. Amer.* Mar. 31/1 The method involves attaching a 'reporter' group, usually a nitroxide group that has an unpaired electron, to one of the carbons of a test molecule's fatty-acid tail.

5. *attrib.*, in appositive use, and Comb., as *reporter-director, -material, -photographer, politician, -researcher*; *reporter-like* adj.

1973 C. Bonington *Next Horizon* xx. 276 A complete film team of cameraman, sound-recordist, reporter-director. **1909** C. S. Peirce *Let.* 14 Mar. in R. B. Perry *Tht. & Char. of W. James* (1935) II. 440 So it is reported by my rather reporter-like memory. **1889** 'Mark Twain' *Connecticut Yankee* 108 It was my purpose..to start a newspaper... So I wanted to..be finding out what sort of reporter-material I might be able to rake together. **1978** W. F. Buckley *Stained Glass* ii. 15 One reporter-photographer from *L'Humanité* pressed for admittance. **1894** G. B. Shaw *Let.* 2 Dec. (1965) I. 464 Surely so fine a spirit could have been rescued from the reproach of being..an ignorantly contemptuous reporter-politician? **1976** *Time* 27 Sept. 3/1 More than 70 *Time* correspondents, writers, reporter-researchers and editors set out to assess the South as it is today.

reporterage (rĭpōə·ɹtərėdʒ). [f. REPORTER + -AGE.] = *REPORTAGE 3.
a **1936** KIPLING *Something of Myself* (1937) v. 131 Yet the book was not all reporterage. **1939** JOYCE *Finnegans Wake* (1964) I. 70 Making his reporterage on Der Fall Adams for the Frankofurto Siding.

reporting, *vbl. sb.* Add: **b.** (Further examples.) *reporting company* Canad.: (see quot. 1973).
1886 *Encycl. Brit.* XXI. 842/1 Numerous mechanical reporting machines have been invented. **1973** *Daily Colonist* (Victoria, B.C.) 5 Oct. 9/2 It is a reporting company (new term for what was formerly called a public company) with 5,000 shareholders, mostly in B.C. **1974** *BP Shield Internat.* Oct. 7/3 Prince Philip's masterly handling of the final reporting-back session of the conference.

repo·rtless, *a.* [-LESS.] Unknown, not reported; without repute.
c **1865** E. DICKINSON *Poems* (1955) II. 740 Reportless Subjects, to the Quick Continual addressed—But foreign as the Dialect Of Danes, unto the Rest. *c* **1884** *Ibid.* III. 1120 Still thou art What surgeons call alive—Though slipping—slipping I perceive To thy reportless Grave.

reportorial, *a.* (Earlier U.S. and later examples.)
1858 *82nd Anniv. Amer. Independence* (Boston, Mass.) 6 As far as reportorial observation could extend, the best possible temper prevailed. **1926** [see *DATED *ppl. a.* 3]. **1949** E. B. WHITE *Let.* 20 Nov. (1976) 315 Boyer wrote..some reportorial articles that experienced editors..regarded as thoroughly non-objective. **1955** *Bull. Atomic Sci.* Sept. 249/1 The stifling of routine reportorial inquiry. **1977** M. LIPPER in Bond & McLeod *Newslett. to Newspapers* I. 73 This is especially striking when one keeps in mind..the role of coffeehouses or clubs as forerunners of modern reportorial staffs.

reporto·rially, *adv.* [f. REPORTORIAL *a.* + -LY[2].] In a reportorial manner; as a newspaper reporter.
1862 *N.-Y. Tribune* 22 Apr. 1/4 At headquarters this morning—I mean those of General Heintzelman, to which I am reportorially attached—I found things quiet enough. **1901** *Pop. Sci. Monthly* Feb. 382 Unfortunately, the weather will not let the newspaper alone, and so..the newspaper must keep pegging away at it, editorially and 'reportorially', until the present anomalous state of things is developed. **1972** J. G. VERMANDEL *Last seen in Samarra* xvii. 114 Safer than admitting to firsthand knowledge, but reportorially a flop, as he kept complaining bitterly to Alex. **1981** *Times Lit. Suppl.* 8 May 512/3 Because Wilkinson remains so reportorially self-conscious,..he's unable to comprehend the tramps among whom he lives.

repo·rtship. *rare.* [f. REPORT *sb.* + -SHIP.] An instance of reporting for a newspaper.
1912 G. FRANKAU *One of Us* xiii. 129 It was indeed a triumph of reportship: They gave the artiste's *rôles*, her lap-dog's photo.

repose, *sb.* **5. b.** (Later example.)
1909 *Chambers's Jrnl.* Oct. 664/1 The workmen lost the large conception of their ancestors, the patterns [of carpets] lacked repose.

reposing, *vbl. sb.* (Later *attrib.* example.)
1936 [see *funeral home* s.v. *FUNERAL *sb.* 6].

reposit, *v.* **2.** (Earlier example.)
1800 C. B. BROWN *Arthur Mervyn*, II. iv. 69 The grave was covered, the spade reposited under the shed, and my seat in the kitchen resumed.

reposition, *v.* Delete rare[—1] and add: **a.** (Later examples.)
1959 *Times* 2 Oct. 11/3 Arm rests have been redesigned and repositioned. **1967** COX & GROSE *Organization & Handling Bibl. Rec. by Computer* II. 46 To do so requires that the space left be rapidly and accurately repositioned at the 'exposing' position. **1981** S. BRETT *Situation Tragedy* i. 9 They rearranged their cameras, repositioned their sound-booms.
b. *intr.* To adjust or alter one's position.
1947 A. C. DOUGLAS *Gliding & Soaring* 48 If the tow is to consist of more than two sailplanes the manner in which they shall release or reposition should be decided beforehand. **1977** *Chicago Tribune* 2 Oct. IV. 3/2 The Prisendam will make a second visit in April while repositioning from Singapore to Vancouver.
Hence **reposi·tioned** *ppl. a.*, **reposi·tioning** *vbl. sb.*
1968 P. A. P. MORAN *Introd. Probability Theory* ix. 408 Thus by repositioning there is no restriction in supposing that the distribution of X is confined to the points 0, 1, 2,.., zero being its true left extremity. **1969** *Gloss. Terms Dentistry* (*B.S.I.*) 69 Repositioned flap procedures. (1) Apically repositioned flap operation... (2) Apically displaced flap operation... (3) Laterally repositioned flap operation. **1975** T. ALLBEURY *Special Collection* ix. 60 Air experts had noticed..the repositioned undercarriage members. **1977** *Proc. R. Soc. Med.* LXX. 432/1 No changes in the surgically repositioned bone. **1980** A. COPPEL *Hastings Conspiracy* xxxviii. 230 A major repositioning of large sections of the Soviet Army.

repository, *sb.* **1. c.** (Earlier examples.)
1759 A. MURPHY *Let.* 22 July in D. Garrick *Private Corr.* (1831) I. 101 But yours is Beaver's Repository, and there you must judge whether they [*sc.* the horses] are marketable, or likely to tire before they come to the winning-post. **1767** J. WEDGWOOD *Let.* 23 May (1965) 53, I spent a great part of the day in search of a Room for my repository.

repossess, *v.* Add: (Later examples.) Also *spec.*, to regain possession of or seize (goods being bought by hire-purchase) when a purchaser defaults on his payments.
1964 *Reading Teacher* Dec. 210/2 One might think..of a reading program that would enable the children to investigate more widely on their own the worlds of Robin Hood, the cowboys, the spacemen..when the television is being repaired or repossessed. **1969** *Rolling Stone* 28 June 28/2 The starting point was having their car repossessed in Nashville ten years ago. **1972** *New Society* 12 Oct. 98/3 The record company repossessed the amplifiers and so Bolan, of necessity, switched back to acoustic guitar. **1977** *Field* 13 Jan. 40/1 These committees..are to consider cases where a farmer needs to repossess a cottage for an incoming employee.

reposse·ssed, *ppl. a.* Chiefly *U.S.* [f. prec. + -ED[1].] That has been regained or seized back, esp. by a vendor; second-hand.
1933 *Sun* (Baltimore) 21 Apr. 19/2 (Advt.), Repossessed Car Corp., 31 W. North Ave. **1936** H. L. MENCKEN *Amer. Lang.* (ed. 4) vi. 293 For the former [*sc. second-hand*] the automobile dealers..have substituted *reconditioned, rebuilt, repossessed* and *used.* **1957** O. NASH *You can't get there from Here* 148 When he was knocked down by a repossessed scooter and the Boy Scouts administered Second Aid. **1974** *Sumter* (S. Carolina) *Daily Item* 24 Apr. 14B/5 (Advt.), Save by getting a repossessed home now. **1977** *Times* 12 Dec. 26/9 (Advt.), Sugar daddy offers—repossessed pastel mink coat..lynx collar..£2,000.

repossession. Add: **1.** (Later examples.) Also *spec.*, the recovery of goods being bought by hire-purchase when a purchaser defaults on his payments; legal proceedings to effect this. Also *attrib.*
1938 *Sun* (Baltimore) 26 Feb. 18/1 Some used-car dealers ..employ thugs to beat up customers, if necessary, in repossession activities. **1972** *Mod. Law Rev.* XXXV. I. 24 This balance of power could be achieved if retailers' claims for debt are abolished, leaving repossession or an adverse credit report as the sanctions against non-payment. **1977** *Field* 13 Jan. 40/2 If an occupier refuses an offer of suitable housing, it may provide ground for repossession by the farmer.

repo·st (rī-), *v.*[2] [f. RE- 5 a + POST *v.*[1]] *trans.* To post (a letter, etc.) again.
1963 *Times* 9 Jan. 4/7 Having stolen those postal packets, counsel said, the defendant extracted the passbooks and then reposted them to the building societies. **1977** *Lancs. Life* Nov. 83/3 There were four letters in the box, none of which was addressed to us. Three I re-delivered.., the other I re-posted.
So **repo·stage.**
1855 D. G. ROSSETTI *Let.* 23 Jan. (1965) I. 241, I am asked by William to request from you the re-postage of *Athenaeums* when quite done with.

repo·sting (rī-), *vbl. sb.* [f. RE- 5 a + POSTING *vbl. sb.*[3]] Appointment to a new post.
1970 R. WINGATE *Ismay* vii. 159 In India itself regiments with a century or more's traditions of war, service and comradeship had to be split, inevitably reducing their efficiency during the reposting period to zero. **1972** D. BLOODWORTH *Any Number can Play* xix. 200 Pawkinson-Convoy has been recalled for immediate consultation to London and probable reposting. **1981** J. BINGHAM *Brook* 16 He had applied for a re-posting to Melford.

repoussé. b. (Examples.)
1858 QUEEN VICTORIA *Let.* 1 Apr. in R. Fulford *Dearest Child* (1964) 83 A vase by Veité—silver repoussé, really very fine. **1911** [see *CRUSTA f]. **1977** *Jrnl. R. Soc. Arts* CXXV. 485/1 The part [of the helmet] which covered the forehead is plain, but above it, in *repoussé*, there is an arched ridge round which curly hair is shown.

‖ **repoussoir** (rəpūswār). [Fr., f. *repousser*: see REPOUSSÉ *a.*] An object in the foreground of a painting serving to emphasize the principal figure or scene. Also *transf.* and *fig.*, and *attrib.*
1873 H. JAMES in *Galaxy* Mar. 427 Mr. Casaubon is an excellent invention: as a dusky *repoussoir* to the luminous figure of his wife he could not have been better imagined. **1890** W. JAMES *Princ. Psychol.* II. xxvi. 513 The relative motion felt by the retina is assigned to that one of its components which we look at more in itself and less as a mere repoussoir. **1906** *Westm. Gaz.* 24 Mar. 2/2 A cool, tranquilly pleasing background is degraded to mere dulness in consequence of the gaudy gowns in front of it. Has the word *repoussoir* any meaning to her? **1925** A. HUXLEY *Along Road* III. 169 His exquisitely subtle use of *repoussoirs* and that extraordinary mastery of colour. **1936** *Burlington Mag.* May 208/1 The strong repoussoir character of the trees on the left. **1948** L. SPITZER *Linguistics & Lit. Hist.* v. 235 Since there had to be the Muse..she had to become the *repoussoir*; the personification of the Greek culture which had to be rejected. **1970** T. HILTON *Pre-Raphaelites* v. 150 Brown's..landscapes of the 1850s..shunning the usual devices of *repoussoir* trees and the conventions of aerial perspective. **1974** *Times Lit. Suppl.* 15 Mar. 261/3 The sitter's shoulders sometimes compressed into the narrowing oval of the frame, a *repoussoir* for the all-important face. **1977** 'M. INNES' *Honeybath's Haven* v. 46 The traveller who approaches Hanwell Court by the main drive has the advantage of first viewing the mansion disposed beyond a gigantic *repoussoir* known to art historians as the *Poseidon urging the Sea-Monster to attack Laomedon.*

repper (re·pəɹ). *slang. rare*[—1] [f. REP(UTATION + *-ER[6].] = REPUTATION 4 a.
1910 R. BROOKE *Let.* 7 Nov. (1968) He will find — in his Bed one night: and then she will force him to marry her to save her Repper.

repple depple (re·p'l de:p'l). *U.S. Mil. slang.* Also **reppo depot.** [f. REPL(ACEMENT + DEP(OT modified by reduplication and rhyme.] A replacement depot (see quot. 1945).
1945 *Amer. N. & Q.* Dec. 136/2 *Repple Depple*, overseas replacement depot where soldiers are assembled before sailing back to the United States. **1945** *N.Y. Times Mag.* 9 Dec. 20/3 One of the last phases of the European war's end—the overseas replacement depot or 'repple depple', where Yanks slated for the long voyage home are gathered together... Repple depples, in short, are dreary places. *Ibid.* He talked out of turn to the repple depple Powers-That-Be. **1947** *Amer. Speech* XXII. 216 *Repple Depple* had a less popular form, *Reppo Depot.* A person who never approached the fighting front was a *Reppo Depot Ranger.* **1973** S. ALSOP *Stay of Execution* (1974) III. 283, I suppose in the American army we would have been sent to a Replacement Depot, or Repple Depple. **1978** J. A. MICHENER *Chesapeake* 771 He was sent to Korea, not with a formed unit but to a replacement depot, a repple depple he explained to his parents.

represent, *v.* Add: **9. c.** *Math.* To act as a representation of (a group).
1897 [see *PRIMITIVE *a.* 5 d]. **1971** D. GORENSTEIN in Powell & Higman *Finite Simple Groups* ii. 77 We conclude that $H/O_p(H)$ is faithfully represented as a linear group on the Frattini factor group of $O_p(H)$.

representability. (Examples.)
1879 W. JAMES *Coll. Ess. & Rev.* (1920) 95 The craving for clear representability..leads often to an unwillingness to treat any abstractions whatever as if they were intelligible. **1977** M. COHEN *Sensible Words* i. 14 What these men share is a confidence in the visual representability of meaning.

representation. Add: **2. e.** *Math.* The image of a homomorphism from a given (abstract) group to a group or other structure having some further meaning or significance; such a homomorphism.
1897 W. BURNSIDE *Theory of Groups of Finite Order* ii. 22 As long as we are dealing with the properties of a group *per se*, and not with properties which depend on the form of representation, the group may, if convenient, be replaced by any group which is simply isomorphic with it. **1908** H. HILTON *Introd. Theory of Groups Finite Order* xv. 180 One and the same group of linear substitutions may give rise to two or more representations of G. **1940** D. E. LITTLEWOOD *Theory of Group Characters* iv. 48 To several elements of the group may correspond identical matrices, so that the representation is not simply, but multiply isomorphic with the group. **1949** S. KRAVETZ tr. *Zassenhaus' Theory of Groups* ii. 35 A representation is said to be faithful if the homomorphy induced by the representation is an isomorphy. **1971** D. GORENSTEIN in Powell & Higman *Finite Simple Groups* ii. 76 A faithful, irreducible representation of an abelian group on any vector space is necessarily cyclic. **1974** *Encycl. Brit. Macropædia* I. 752/2 Technically, a representation of a group is a homomorphism of it into another group, most commonly into the group of invertible linear transformations (or matrices) on some linear space. **1980** *Sci. Amer.* May 68/2 The way mathematicians construct a group depends to a large extent on whether the group has a natural representation as the transformations of some geometrical object.

representational, *a.* Add: **b.** *spec.* in *Art.* (See quots. 1961, 1962.)
1923 [see *non-representational* s.v. *NON- 3]. **1934** C. LAMBERT *Music Ho!* II. 115 The repetitions of..[an] underlying curve in an abstract or representational picture have no dramatic content. **1956** R. MACAULAY *Towers of Trebizond* xxii. 256, I could see he [*sc.* an ape] was going to be a painter of the abstract type...I thought Suliman ought to try and be a little representational too. **1959** HALAS & MANVELL *Technique Film Animation* 12 Though there is still..some useful place in normal draughtsmanship and painting for the exactly representational illustration as against a good photograph, there would seem to us to be no argument in favour of an exactly representational animated picture. **1961** M. LEVY *Studio Dict. Art Terms* 96 *Representational art*, that kind of painting or sculpture which tries..to reproduce the physical appearance of objects, persons, or other subjects. As distinct from non-representational art where the interest in surface appearances is of little or no account. **1962** R. G. HAGGAR *Dict. Art Terms* 286/2 *Representational*, describes art in which figures and objects are depicted as they appear to the eye, or as they are known to be, in contradistinction to abstract or non-representational art. **1965** *New Statesman* 9 Apr. 566/2 The academy is now positively soliciting exhibits from Pop artists and abstractionists. However,..there's no cause for alarm. The R[oyal] A[cademy] will continue to show the best of British representational art, but it aims, also, to provide an annual cross-section of everything which is being done by British artists.
representationalism (further examples). So **representa·tionalist** *a.* and *sb.*
1846 J. D. MORELL *Hist. View Philos.* I. ii. 232 The great aim of Reid's philosophy..was..to controvert the

representationalist hypothesis. **1921** A. HUXLEY *Crome Yellow* xii. 115 One could admire representationalism in the Old Masters... But in a modern? **1934** C. LAMBERT *Music Ho!* II. 113 It is all very well to hammer out a theory, however mistaken, that applies to an art functioning in space: it is quite another matter to apply this to an art that functions in time. Most of the modern fallacies about abstraction, literary sentiment, representationalism, romantic contamination, etc. in music are due to ignoring this elementary distinction. **1937** R. I. AARON *John Locke* II. iii. 121 These accounts would have been the same if Locke had never adopted the representationalist position... Though nominally Locke remains representationalist in his explanation of the knowledge we have of our minds, actually he proceeds as if we know ourselves and our operations directly. **1976** *Jrnl. R. Soc. Arts* CXXIV. 567/1 The Brocks were among the last great representationalists, preservers of a world of recognizable human types in clearly defined historical settings. **1978** *N. & Q.* Feb. 91/2 He felt attracted to this best ally of representationalism.

representative, *a.* and *sb.* Add: **A.** *adj.* **1. d.** (Later example.)

1934 A. C. EWING *Idealism* vi. 283 By the term 'representative theory of perception' I mean to cover *any* theory of perception which admits the existence of physical objects in the realist sense but is not a direct theory.

e. *representative fraction:* the ratio of a distance on a map to the distance it represents on the ground. Cf. *R. F.* s.v. *R II. 2 a.

1886 H. D. HUTCHINSON *Mil. Sketching made Easy* i. 2 If the Representative Fraction is marked on a sketch, the scale can be understood, and the sketch can be used, by anyone, even though it be a foreign one. **1969** G. C. DICKINSON *Maps & Air Photographs* vii. 99 Whether written as a fraction or a ratio, this means of expressing the scale is called the representative fraction (R.F. for short) of the map.

2. b. (Later examples.)

1879 GLADSTONE *Gleanings* I. viii. 214 We have, *proh pudor*! found no better method of providing for peace and order in Jamaica..than by the hard and vulgar, even where needful, expedient of abolishing entirely its representative institutions. **1921** H. SAMUEL *Let.* 8 May in M. Gilbert *Winston S. Churchill* (1977) IV. Compan. III. 1461 The very early establishment of representative institutions. **1975** J. PLAMENATZ *K. Marx's Philos. Man* xv. 464 How.. would they [*sc.* the workers] ensure that this system was not as much of a sham as bourgeois representative government was, according to Marx?

B. *sb.* **2. a.** (Earlier and further examples.)

1635 *Essex Inst. Hist. Coll.* (1862) IV. 93/1 By the towne rep[re]sentative, 22 of the 12th moneth. **1787** *Constitution U.S.* i. §2 No person shall be a representative who shall not ..be an inhabitant of that state in which he shall be chosen. **1977** *Time* 18 July 10/3 Young proved himself a sensible and reasonable Representative—and also an independent one. **1979** *Daily Tel.* 8 Jan. 8 Members of Parliament are representatives and not delegates.

b. Also, similar legislative bodies in Australia and New Zealand.

1852 *Act* 15 & 16 *Vict.* c. 72 §32 There shall be within the Colony of New Zealand a General Assembly, to consist of the Governor, a Legislative Council, and House of Representatives. *Ibid.* §40 For the Purpose of constituting the House of Representatives of New Zealand it shall be lawful for the Governor,..to summon and call together a House of Representatives in and for New Zealand. **1891** *National Australasian Convention Debates* 23/1 This Convention [of Sydney, March 1891] approves of the framing of a federal constitution, which shall establish,—1. A parliament, to consist of a senate and a house of representatives. **1930** L. G. D. ACLAND *Early Canterbury Runs* 1st Ser. ii. 27 He was a member of the House of Representatives and of the Provincial Council. **1965** *Austral. Encycl.* VII. 9/1 The Speaker's chair in the House of Representatives is also of interest.

4. a. (Further examples.)

1957 CLARK & GOTTFRIED *Dict. Business & Finance* 299/1 *Representative*, in selling, a salesman, either one employed by the seller or operating as an agent. **1961** P. F. PAYNE *Brit. Commercial Institutions* v. 70 The manufacturer's agent carries out functions similar to those of the wholesaler's representative. **1976** *Gramophone* June 37/3 Raymond Cooke and Robert Cox of KEF demonstrated the excellence of their loudspeakers and there were recitals by record industry representatives.

representativity (re:prĭzentăti·vĭti). [f. REPRESENTATIVE *a.* + -ITY.] Representative character; representativeness.

1901 *N. Amer. Rev.* Apr. 632 By far the most signal instance of Professor Wendell's open-mindedness is his recognition of Mark Twain's..representativity as a Westerner.

representee. Restrict † *Obs.* to senses in Dict. and add: **3.** *Law.* One to whom a representation is made.

1911 G. S. BOWER *Law Actionable Misrepresentation* 1 A representation is a statement made by, or on behalf of, one person (hereinafter called 'the representor') to, or with the intention that it shall come to the notice of, another person (hereinafter called 'the representee'), which relates, by way of affirmation, denial, description, or otherwise, to a matter of fact. **1971** R. A. PERCY *Charlesworth on Negligence* (ed. 5) ii. 34 In *Jones* v. *Still* an honest misrepresentation, even if negligent, was held to give no cause of action, since no duty to take care in making the statement arose because there was no contract, fiduciary relationship or reliance by the representee upon the special skill, knowledge or training possessed by the representor.

representor. Delete † *Obs.* and add: *spec.* in *Law*: one by or on behalf of whom a representation is made.

1911, 1971 [see *REPRESENTEE 3].

repress, *v.*[1] Add: **3. c.** *Psychol.* [tr. G. *verdrängen* (used in this sense by Breuer & Freud 1893, in *Neurol. Centralbl.* XII. 10).] In *Psychoanalysis*, of a patient or person who is the object of study: to keep out of the conscious mind, or suppress into the unconscious (unacceptable memories or desires). Also *absol.*

1909 A. A. BRILL tr. *Freud's Sel. Papers on Hysteria* i. 7 The patient has not reacted to psychic traumas because the nature of the trauma..concerned things which the patient wished to forget and which he therefore intentionally inhibited and repressed from the conscious memory. **1919** M. K. BRADBY *Psycho-Analysis* III. vii. 82 He believes the unconscious to be exclusively composed of contents repressed from the conscious. **1920** *Discovery* Mar. 69/2 The motive for repression is one's personal comfort. One represses to preserve one's peace of mind. **1943** J. S. HUXLEY *Evolutionary Ethics* ii. 15 The impulses whose thwarting generated the guilty hate may themselves become coloured with guilt, or be repressed. **1977** R. A. BARON et al. *Psychol.* x. 337 This unconscious mechanism can begin to create new problems... The individual loses some control over the situation when he represses his awareness of it.

repressed, *ppl. a.* Add: (Later examples in sense of *REPRESS *v.*[1] 3 c.) Also *absol.*

1904 *Psychol. Bull.* I. 357 The theory of Freud, that dreams are disguised realizations of repressed desires. **1919** M. K. BRADBY *Psycho-Analysis* I. iii. 34 It [*sc.* the unconscious] also contains the repressed. **1923** J. S. HUXLEY *Ess. Biologist* v. 187 The publication of Darwin's *Origin of Species* was to them what psycho-analysis is (or may be) to a patient with a repressed complex. **1954** D. RIESMAN *Individualism Reconsidered* (1955) xxii. 336 It was not easy to find convincing evidence for the existence of repressed Oedipal desires in every adult whom he analyzed. **1960** M. SPARK *Bachelors* vi. 81 Repressed homosexuality is a meaningless term because no one can prove it. **1973** J. G. STARKE *Validity of Psycho-Anal.* ii. 14 For psycho-analysts, perhaps the most important component is *repressed* material.

represser. Add: **1.** (Later example in the sense of *REPRESS *v.*[1] 3 c.)

1951 *Jrnl. of Personality* XIX. 472 Repressers..are patients who avoid contact with such emotional material. They are apt to block in the presence of sexual or aggressive stimuli.

2. = *REPRESSOR 2.

1957 [see *REPRESSOR 2]. **1971** *New Scientist* 22 July 182/1 Two classes of DNA-switching molecules are known so far in bacteria, one class acts negatively—repressers—and one acts positively, but indirectly—sigma factors.

repressible, *a.* Restrict *rare*—[0] to sense in Dict. and add: **2.** *Biochem.* That may be inhibited by the action of a repressor; susceptible to the action of a repressor.

1957, 1964 [see *REPRESSOR 2]. **1974** *Nature* 10 May 110/1 The interactions which control repressible and inducible operons in bacteria are now well understood in principle.

repressing (rĭpre·siŋ), *vbl. sb.*[2] Also **re-** (with hyphen). [f. RE- 5 a + PRESSING *vbl. sb.*[1]: cf. *REPRESS *v.*[2]] **1.** A new impression made from an old matrix of a sound recording.

1960 'I. T. Ross' *Murder out of School* iv. 38 Old records.. collectors' items now, that had somehow never come out as well in the long-playing repressings the companies had issued. **1975** *Daily Tel.* 17 Mar. 10/3 If you can only afford one of the three recent issues, it must be 'Chopin 3' of RCA's collection of re-pressings.

2. The action of pressing again.

1967 M. CHANDLER *Ceramics in Mod. World* v. 142 Shaping methods for fireclay bricks include extrusion and wire-cutting (often followed by re-pressing).

repre·ssing, *ppl. a.* [f. REPRESS *v.*[1] + -ING[2].] That represses. So **repre·ssingly** *adv.*

1872 GEO. ELIOT *Middlem.* II. III. xxxii. 152 Solomon put his hand before her repressingly. **1909** A. A. BRILL tr. *Freud's Sel. Papers on Hysteria* vii. 161 What becomes conscious as an obsession and obsessive affect and substitutes the pathogenic memory in the conscious life, are compromise formations between the repressed and the repressing ideas. **1951** *Jrnl. of Personality* XIX. 472 We hypothesized that intellectualizing patients..would show higher accuracy for threatening material than the repressing type of patient. **1975** I. M. BLANCO *Unconscious as Infinite Sets* vi. 82 The unrepressed unconscious of the ego is, in the Freudian conception, the *repressing* aspect of the ego.

repression. Add: **2. c.** *Psychol.* The action, process, or result of suppressing into the unconscious or keeping out of the conscious mind unacceptable memories or desires. Also *attrib.*

1909 A. A. BRILL tr. *Freud's Sel. Papers on Hysteria* iv. 88 If I could now make it probable that the idea became pathogenic in consequence of the exclusion and repression, the chain would seem complete. **1910** S. FREUD in *Amer. Jrnl. Psychol.* XXI. 193, I called this hypothetical process 'repression' (*Verdrängung*), and considered it was proved by the undeniable existence of resistance. *Ibid.*, One of my cases, in which the conditions and the utility of the repression process stand out clearly enough. **1930** R. LEHMANN *Note in Music* VII. 274 Gerald was not free, not calm and balanced: quite the reverse—a tangle of passionate conflicts and repressions. **1939** T. S. ELIOT *Family Reunion* i. 40, I always said his [Lordship Suffered from what they call a kind of repression. **1954** R. F. C. HULL tr. *Jung's Devel. of Personality* in *Coll. Wks.* XVII. iv. 115 No breaking down of repressions can ever destroy true creativeness. **1973** J. G. STARKE *Validity of Psycho-Anal.* ii. 14 In essence, repression is the mental process of rejecting and excluding material from consciousness.

3. *Biochem.* The inhibition of enzyme synthesis by the action of a repressor on an operon.

1957 [see *REPRESSOR 2]. **1959** *Jrnl. Molecular Biol.* I. 176 It now appears to be a general rule, for bacteria, that the formation of sequential enzyme sequences involved in the synthesis of essential metabolites is *inhibited* by their end product. The convenient term 'repression' was coined by Vogel to distinguish this effect from another, equally general, phenomenon: the control of enzyme *activity* by end products of metabolism. **1973** R. G. KRUEGER et al. *Introd. Microbiol.* xv. 437/2 Repression is distinct from feedback inhibition in that the former results in the cessation of enzyme synthesis whereas the latter leads to inactivation of an existing enzyme.

repressive, *a.* (Later examples in sense of *REPRESS *v.*[1] 3 c.)

1921 R. MACAULAY *Dangerous Ages* xii. 234 His phrases drifted over Mrs Hilary's head. '..a deterrent force residing in the ego and preventing us from stepping outside the bounds of propriety..conflict with the progress of human society..inhibitory and repressive power of the censor.' **1944** J. S. HUXLEY *On Living in Revolution* 57 It is much harder to feel strongly about social problems such as malnutrition or unemployment, because the connection with the repressive mechanism is not so automatic. **1968** A. HERON *Towards Quaker View of Sex* i. 7 This still repressive and inhibited outlook towards sex..has brought difficulties to the serious student of human behaviour. **1970** *Nature* 26 Sept. 1371/2 Whose tortured minds are nourished by absurd slogans such as 'creative vandalism' and 'repressive tolerance'.

repressor. Restrict *rare* to sense in Dict. and add: **2.** *Biochem.* A substance which by its action on an operon can inhibit the synthesis of a specific enzyme or set of enzymes.

1957 H. J. VOGEL in McElroy & Glass *Chem. Basis Heredity* ii. 286 In order to facilitate further discussion, the following terminology will be used hereafter: a relative decrease, resulting from the exposure of cells to a given substance, in the rate of synthesis of a particular apoenzyme is termed 'enzyme repression'; the substance thus decelerating enzyme synthesis is a 'represser' ('repressor'); an enzyme-forming system that can be antagonized by a represser is 'repressible'; and, under conditions of repression, the formation of the enzyme is 'repressed'. **1964** G. H. HAGGIS et al. *Introd. Molecular Biol.* x. 273 Either inducible cells contain built-in repressors, which are inactivated by added inducers, or repressible enzyme synthesis depends on intracellular inducers inactivated by external repressors. There is evidence that the first of these alternatives is the correct one. **1971** J. Z. YOUNG *Introd. Study Man* iii. 54 The repressor is produced by a regulator gene. **1973** B. J. WILLIAMS *Evolution & Human Origins* vi. 91/1 Diffusable repressor substances that form complexes with specific operator regions prevent the mRNA transcription.

repressory (rĭpre·sŏri), *a.* [f. REPRESS *v.*[1] + -ORY[2].] Having the qualities of a repressor; designed to repress.

1905 W. J. LOCKE *Morals M. Ordeyne* (1906) xi. 117 But what do I know of the repressory methods employed in seminaries for young ladies? **1954** D. RIESMAN *Individualism Reconsidered* xxii. 347 The repressory forces must draw their energies from the great energy reservoir of the id.

re-pre·ssuring, *vbl. sb.* [f. RE- 5 a + PRESSURE + -ING[1].] The pumping of fluid into an oil well so as to increase or maintain the pressure in the oil-bearing strata, allowing more oil to be extracted.

1929 *Jrnl. Inst. Petroleum Technologists* XV. 430 If a flush field is produced inefficiently and re-pressuring is left until the field is almost commercially exhausted the ultimate yield of the pool must be very considerably less than when properly controlled back-pressures have been used from the beginning and re-pressuring operations commenced in the early life of the field. **1940** *Sun* (Baltimore) 24 Sept. 6/8 An oil field at Walters, Okla., has been revived by a method known as repressuring. **1961** *Economist* 2 Dec. 955/2 This pipeline..will eventually carry..salt water in the opposite direction, to be pumped into the underground structure in order to keep up underground pressure and keep the oil flowing up and out to the coast. This 're-pressuring' project is one of the largest ever undertaken outside the United States.

repre·ssurize, *v.* [RE- 5 a.] *trans.* To pressurize again; to renew pressure in.

1953 *Jrnl. Inst. Electr. Engineers* C. II. 646/2 After completion of the modifications, the system was repressurized, but when the routine 66-kV d.c. 15-min test was applied, failure occurred on two phases. **1962** J. GLENN in *Into Orbit* 41 You have one large handle for repressurizing the cabin with oxygen in case of a bad leak. **1971** *Daily Tel.* 26 July 22/5 He and Irwin will then repressurise their cabin, take off their spacesuits..and then get seven hours rest.

repricing (rĭprəi·siŋ), *vbl. sb.* [RE- 5 a.] The act of changing, usually by increasing, a price.

1959 *Times* 1 June 11/2 If anomalies are to be avoided.. this 'repricing' should be undertaken systematically. **1974** *Daily Colonist* (Victoria, B.C.) 8 Sept. 7/7 There would be re-pricing, probably several times, during the model year.

reprime, *v.*² Add: **b.** *absol.*

1976 *Shooting Mag.* Dec. 65/1 (Advt.), Lee Load-All 12 G... 2nd Station reprimes with a push from inside the shell to prevent concave heads.

reprint, *sb.* Add: **1. b.** *attrib.*

1928 *Publishers' Weekly* 30 June 2603 Bookstores have in a new form a problem that confronted them twenty-five years ago when the reprint fiction began to appear in cloth binding. **1951** A. C. Clarke *Sands of Mars* xi. 135 She immediately sold the second reprint rights of Gibson's latest series. **1951** M. McLuhan *Mech. Bride* (1967) 23/2 The current effort to make almost every reprint cover look lustier than the next has brought them all to a dead level of fleshliness. **1952** E. Mannin *Let.* in *Manch. Guardian Weekly* 16 Oct. 13/1 May I, as an English author who is a victim of the deplorable American publishing habit of farming-out their cheap editions to what are called 'reprint houses', be allowed to point out some important points. **1961** T. Landau *Encycl. Librarianship* (ed. 2) 323/1 *Reprint series*, a number of publications, being reprints, not necessarily related in subject or treatment, issued by a publisher in uniform style and assigned a collective series title. **1964** F. Bowers *Bibliogr. & Textual Crit.* vi. i. 163 The normal reprint transmission of variants is disrupted by the annotator's correction of error. **1981** J. Sutherland *Bestsellers* i. 14 The [American] bookclubs..have in the past been much less reprint affairs than in the UK.

reprint, *v.* Add: **1. a.** Also *absol.*

1934 H. G. Wells *Exper. Autobiogr.* II. ix. 646 Macmillan's, my English publishers, were caught unawares by the demand and had sold out the first edition before they reprinted.

3. *intr.* for *pass.*

1821 R. Southey *Let.* 11 Jan. in *N. & Q.* (1975) Sept. 402/1 Do not bind your set, till I send you some corrections and additions for the first volume, which is now reprinting. **1942** *World Rev.* Apr. 17 In this war he is a Home Guard officer and the author of four training manuals, which, despite the paper shortage, reprint every few months. **1967** *Listener* 12 Jan. 68/3 It will be for these [colour photographs] that *Slowly Down the Ganges* has to reprint. **1980** *Daily Tel.* 21 Aug. 14 The book has sold 10,000 copies since May. It is now reprinting.

reprisal, *sb.* Add: **I. 4. a.** Also *attrib.*, as *reprisal attack, raid.*

c **1945** *Hutchinson's Pict. Hist. War* XII. 157/1 The vicious battering of the industrial and military bases of Germany provoked none of the great so-called 'reprisal' raids which characterised April and May. **1947** R. W. Cooper *Nuremberg Trial* 81 Everything was to be prepared to carry out reprisal attacks on London. **1956** H. Nicolson *Diary* 29 Oct. (1968) 311 Israel has launched against Egypt an attack that seems more serious than a reprisal raid.

reprise, *sb.* Add: Now usu. with pronunc. (rəprī·z).

The renewed influence of Fr. *reprise* is apparent in the modern pronunc. and development of sense 7.

II. 7. d. *transf.* in *Linguistics.* The repetition of a word or word-group occurring in a preceding phrase; a restated element. Also *attrib.* as *reprise construction.*

1950 *Archivum Linguisticum* II. 144 The aim of this article is to establish the frequency with which reprise constructions occur in *Chanson de Roland.* **1955** [see *grammaticalization]. **1959** M. Schlauch *Eng. Lang. in Mod. Times* iv. 99 Reprise constructions (called resumptions by Partridge) in formal discourse employed the appositional pronoun to recall a noun separated from its verb by a long series of interrupting modifiers. **1963** F. T. Visser *Hist. Syntax Eng. Lang.* I. i. 53 Type 'He, Alexander, cwæð.'.. The following 'reprise construction' is remarkable for the subject's being expressed four times. **1971** *Catholic Biblical Q.* XXXIII. 218 This structure makes sense out of *didaskalos* (vs. 10) as a reprise, for, far from ending the preceding unit (as it would as an inclusion), it introduces the theme of vss. 9–15, *Jesus as teacher.*

e. The repetition of a theatrical performance; a restaging or rewriting of a play (esp. for television), a repeated showing of a (piece of) film; a rerun, a replay. Also in extended use, a further performance of any kind; a reconstruction, a repeat.

1953 *Sun* (Baltimore) 9 Oct. 10/2 Mr. Moore came on the screen bubbling over with a joke which he was eager to share with the viewers. It required a reprise from the previous week's performance. **1955** *Times* 20 May 3/4 It is the season for *reprise* at this club theatre. Formerly, in shows of this kind, the menu has included so many delightful dishes of the past served cold by inexpert chefs as to be somewhat gruesomely indigestible. **1961** *Guardian* 1 Feb. 9/4 A polished reprise of his campaign sermons. **1968** *Globe & Mail* (Toronto) 17 Feb. 39 Nancy last night watched a television reprise of her dramatic victory in amazingly fast time in the Olympic giant slalom. **1972** *Publishers' Weekly* 11 Sept. 51/1 The author spins a good tale on the level of a reprise of what life was like for a young girl in a small town 30 years ago. **1977** *Time* 30 May 25/1 Carter headed next to the studios of KNXT-TV for a locally televised reprise of his successful national call-in program.

reprise, *v.* Restrict † *Obs.* (exc. *Arch.*) to senses in Dict. and add: **1. f.** (With pronunc. rəprī·z.) To repeat (a theatrical performance, song, etc.); to restage or rewrite. Cf. *reprise *sb.* 7 e.

1965 *Observer* 5 Dec. 24/3 The theatre rocks as Dolly reprises more times than is artistically justifiable the chorus of this..infectious title-song. **1970** *Ibid.* 29 Nov. 29/1 The song is tearfully reprised off-screen. **1975** *Listener* 5 June 735/1, I decided that..it would be necessary to reprise this scene in a heightened form.

repristinate, *v.* Delete *rare* and add further examples. Hence **repri·stinated** *ppl. a.*

1969 R. H. Bainton *Erasmus of Christendom* (1970) i. 14 The glory of Greece, the grandeur of Rome, the grace of Galilee should repristinate society and revivify the Church. **1970** *Jrnl. Ecumenical Stud.* VII. 804/1 The disavowal of the doctrine..and its displacement by the repristinated authorities of Scripture and Christian experience. **1977** *Theology* LXXX. 200 The power exercised by the remembered and interpreted past has been deliberately conserved and repristinated by methods which have not excluded secular rituals.

repri·vatize, *v.* [Re- 5 b; cf. G. *reprivatisieren.*] *trans.* To make private again; to denationalize. Also *absol.* Hence **reprivatiza·tion.**

1950 Webster Add., Reprivatize v.t. **1959** *Economist* 4 Apr. 53/1 A whole series of political and legal hurdles will have to be taken before the way is clear to denationalise, or reprivatise, in earnest. **1963** *Ibid.* 12 Jan. 136/3 He has promised to continue the work of 'reprivatisation' (denationalisation). **1980** *Evening News Mag.* 18 Jan. 22/1 The ugliest word yet coined by Whitehall is its latest—'reprivatisation', meaning the selling back to private enterprise of parts of nationalised industries. **1980** *Economist* 6 Dec. 18/2 Reprivatisation of the profitable naval yards.

repro (rī·pro). Colloq. abbrev. of Reproduction. **1.** *Printing* and *Photogr.* = Reproduction 1 e. Chiefly *attrib.* in, or *ellipt.* for, *repro proof* = *reproduction proof* s.v. *Reproduction 3.

1946 Melcher & Larrick *Printing & Promotion Handbk.* 247/1 The offset or other printer..should..be encouraged to reject any proofs..of poor quality and ask for better 'repros'. **1948** R. R. Karch *Graphic Arts Procedures* viii. 231 Care must be taken to see that repro proofs are well printed. **1952** R. W. & E. W. Polk *Practice of Printing* (ed. 4) viii. 62 There are two kinds of reproduction proofs (commonly [known as repros) used for the making of plates for letterpress, offset, and gravure. **1967** E. Chambers *Photolitho-Offset* iii. 31 Reproduction proofs on paper can be transferred into same-size negatives... The process..consists in making a repro-proof and covering with a sheet of special film. **1972** *Screw* 12 June 28/4 What's the chance of getting a repro of that shot? **1973** D. A. Spencer *Focal Dict. Photogr. Technol.* 528 Repro pulls can be made on baryta coated paper, or ink-accepting transparent or translucent film. **1977** J. Hedgecoe *Photographer's Handbk.* 17 (*heading*) A repro copy stand.

2. A reproduction or copy, usu. of a piece of furniture (cf. Reproduction 2 a in Dict. and Suppl.). Chiefly *attrib.* or as *adj.* Also *Comb.*

1958 *Spectator* 8 Aug. 193/1 Her Tudorbethan villa, with its Repro-Jaco interior. **1967** *House & Garden* Mar. 79/1 Good traditional design (*not* 'repro') marries brilliantly with good contemporary. **1967** *Sunday Times* 14 May 12/7 The total environment is compromised..by the 'repro' furniture introduced into the flats. **1970** 'D. Halliday' *Dolly & Cookie Bird* ii. 13 We have a workshop of our own for repairs and a bit of repro work. **1973** *Daily Tel.* (Colour Suppl.) 16 Mar. 41/3 You may ask what is the difference between a fake and a 'repro'. **1976** *New Society* 13 May 363/1, I can't imagine..a Rembrandt on the wall opposite, even if it were an unframed repro. **1978** *Morecambe Guardian* 14 Mar. 27/8 (Advt.), Good antique and repro furniture.

reproach, *v.* **2. a.** (Later *absol.* example.)

1961 B. Fergusson *Watery Maze* xv. 364 Like the good soldier he was, he never reproached or repined.

reproachable, *a.* **1.** (Later example.)

1972 *Sunday Tel.* 30 Apr. 14/2 It is here that 'The Green Flag' is reproachable. The history of a rebellion is incomplete if it gives hardly a clue as to the nature and attitudes of the power at which the rebellion was directed.

reprobance. For † *Obs. rare*—¹ in Dict. read '*rare* (only in allusive use of quot. 1604)' and add later example.

1878 Swinburne *Poems & Ballads* 2nd Ser. 213 Like Absalom with locks luxurious, Or like Judas fallen to reprobance.

repro·cess, *v.* [Re- 5 a.] *trans.* To subject (something) to a special process again. So **repro·cessed** *ppl. a.*; **repro·cessing** *vbl. sb.*

1939 *Sun* (Baltimore) 21 Feb. 14/4 'Reprocessed'..should be applied to wool made into a fibrous state for reuse. **1944** *Richmond* (Va.) *Times-Dispatch* 16 Jan. 9/1 A 'reprocessing' routine has been made an important part of the discharge procedure. **1948** *News Chron.* 15 Jan. 2/2 Production can be increased by reprocessing what we used to throw away. **1956** *Nature* 3 Mar. 400/1 The United Kingdom is likely..to re-process the burnt elements from reactors. **1962** E. Godfrey *Retail Selling & Organization* xix. 190 When an item is sold, the punched ticket is returned to the warehouse, where it is re-processed for sales records to be made. **1977** *New Yorker* 9 May 142/2 The Japanese are.. troubled..by our objections to the use of reprocessed nuclear fuel. **1979** *Bull. Amer. Acad. Arts & Sci.* May 44 Participants discussed the time necessary for a nation to convert a reprocessing plant to weapons production and how that time might be lengthened without giving up nuclear energy.

reproduce, *v.* Add: **3. d.** *trans.* To cause to be heard (sound originating elsewhere or on another occasion); also *absol.* Freq. with advbs.

1899 *T. Eaton & Co. Catal.* Spring & Summer 191/1 A graphophone..a perfect machine, reproduces perfectly. **1924** *Radio Times* 19 Dec. 620/1 (Advt.), He can 'pick' up the entertainment being sent out from any British or Continental Station and reproduce it at Loud Speaker strength. **1961** G. A. Briggs *A to Z in Audio* 21 If you can reproduce the bottom note of a double bass properly, you are not doing badly. **1978** *Gramophone* July 272/1 Totally enclosed headphones..can usually reproduce extreme bass frequencies more easily.

reproduced, reproducing *ppl. adjs.* (examples in sense *3 d of vb.).

1941 *B.B.C. Gloss. Broadcasting Terms* 28 *Reproducing desk*, table carrying one or more turn-tables and other equipment for playing gramophone records, disc recordings, or pressings. **1946** *Penguin Music Mag.* Dec. 93 Reproducing instruments are improving as much as recording has improved. **1964** *Listener* 17 Sept. 442/2 Recordings made for the reproducing piano by Josef Lhévinne. **1970** J. Earl *Tuners & Amplifiers* iii. 69 Power so liberated..detracts from the reproduced signals.

reproducer. Add: **2.** (Further examples.) Also, any device for reproducing recorded sound.

1899 *T. Eaton & Co. Catal.* Spring & Summer 191/3 The price of the Universal Graphophone, with a long run clockwork motor recorder, reproducer, hearing, speaking tubes and horn, is $50. **1937** *Jrnl. Soc. Motion Picture Engineers* XXIX. 218 With a high-quality microphone, a high-quality reproducer, and a suitably corrected amplifier, the response curve can be made uniform. **1961** G. A. Briggs *A to Z in Audio* 169 The console includes a tape reproducer with 7½″, 15″ and 30″ speeds. **1978** *Gramophone* Aug. 399/3 The Stanton 681EEE, which continues in production, is already a very fine reproducer.

3. *Computers.* A machine for making copies of punched cards or tape.

1940 W. J. Eckert *Punched Card Methods* ii. 20 The High Speed Reproducer. This machine is used to transfer information from one card to another. **1949** [see *interpreter 5 a]. 1964 F. L. Westwater *Electronic Computers* vi. 100 A machine called a reproducer..automatically reproduces the information in a pack of old cards into new ones. **1970** A. Chandor et al. *Dict. Computers* 291 *Paper tape reproducer*... Also known as a reperforator.

reproducibility (rī:prŏdiū̆sĭbi·lĭti). [f. next + -ity.] The capacity to be produced again; the quality of being reproducible; the extent to which consistent results are obtained when produced repeatedly. Cf. *repeatability.

1936 H. J. Paton *Kant's Metaphysic of Experience* I. xix. 371 Kant assumes that experience presupposes the reproducibility of appearances. **1939** *Jrnl. Amer. Chem. Soc.* LXI 3336/2 The agreement between two such sets of points indicates the reproducibility. **1946** *Nature* 7 Sept. 347/2 In many circuits increased reproducibility of electrical conditions does not indicate an increased reproducibility of light-emitting characteristics. **1953** *Industr. & Engin. Chem.* Feb. 465/1 Within the reproducibility of the data, no effect of change in catalyst quantity or flow rate was noted. **1962** *Listener* 6 Dec. 952/1 This accuracy, and the reproducibility that goes with it, lies at the heart of mass production. **1969** *Physical Rev. Lett.* XXIII. 1402/2 The accuracy obtained for the energy is better than ±0·1% and the reproducibility is about ±0·05%. **1977** J. D. Douglas in Douglas & Johnson *Existential Sociol.* i. 54 This oversimplifies the problem of objectivity by assuming that reproducibility constitutes objectivity and that providing a record of research makes it possible to reproduce results. **1981** *Times Lit. Suppl.* 13 Feb. 169/4 The illustrations to Milton..might suggest that one thing Blake liked about printmaking was the sheer fact of reproducibility, for a surprising proportion of the Milton pictures exist in two or more copies.

reproducible, *a.* Add: (Further examples.)

1949 E. P. Abraham et al. in H. W. Florey et al. *Antibiotics* II. viii. xv. 637 The initial experiments were concerned with finding reproducible conditions for obtaining penicillin. **1972** *Physics Bull.* Jan. 15/1 Atomic clocks now provide a unit of time reproducible to 1 part in 10¹².

Hence **reprodu·cibly** *adv.*

1961 *Jrnl. Physical Chem.* LXV. 317/2 The round cells were reproducibly positioned in the light beam which entered the thermostated mineral oil-bath through a window. **1974** *Nature* 13 Dec. 589/1 A survey of various brain regions of the rat revealed that cell-free fractions from the corpus striatum contained adenyl cyclase which was reproducibly activated by low concentrations of D-LSD.

reproduction. Add: **1. c.** (Earlier example.) Also *attrib.* as *reproduction rate.*

1782 J. Wesley in *Arminian Mag.* Oct. 545 He [*sc.* Buffon] substitutes for the plain word *Generation*, a quaint word of his own, *Reproduction*, in order to level man not only with the beasts that perish, but with nettles or onions **1928**, etc. Reproduction rate [see *gross *a.* 6 a]. **1936** *Discovery* Sept. 298/1 It is the net reproduction rate which measures whether the population is maintaining itself or not.

e. (Earlier and later examples.)

1856 Kay & Johnson *Rep. Cases in Chancery* II. 285 Having regard to the international treaties, the Plaintiff reserves his right of reproduction, which is a sufficiently apt word in this case. **1870** W. A. Copinger *Law of Copyright in Works of Lit.* vi. 101 Copyright may be infringed..by reproduction under an abridged form. **1923** H. Crane *Let.* 21 June (1965) 137 He is offering..$25.00 for the original, and the reproduction rights without any payment. **1967** Karch & Buber *Offset Processes* iv. 71 The cost of reproduction (photographable) proofs..brought about the obvious question.

f. *Econ.* In Marxist theory, the process by which given capital is maintained for further production by the conversion of part of its product into capital; *simple reproduction*, reproduction in which the amount of capital remains constant, any surplus value being consumed; *enlarged, expanded* (etc.) *reproduction*, reproduction in which the amount of capital is increased by conversion of part of the surplus value into additional means of production. Also *attrib.*

1887 MOORE & AVELING tr. *Marx's Capital* II. xxiii. 578 The conditions of production are also those of reproduction. *Ibid.* 579 If this revenue serve the capitalist only as a fund to provide for his consumption..then..simple reproduction will take place. *Ibid.* 582 The value of the capital advanced divided by the surplus-value annually consumed, gives the number of years, or reproduction periods [etc.]. **1939** *Rev. Econ. Stud.* VII. 32 According to Marx's analysis, in the case of enlarged reproduction, if gross investment..is not larger than c_1+c_2..there would be no net accumulation of capital at all. **1955** M. DOBB *Econ. Theory & Socialism* xvi. 266 These examples were designed to show the relations which would need to hold for expanded reproduction (i.e. a process of annual net investment) to take place and continue of its own momentum. **1965** B. PEARCE tr. *Preobrazhensky's New Economics* 62 The consciously adopted economic policy of the State is quite often not a reaction to the difficulties encountered in practice in developing socialist reproduction. **1970** B. BREWSTER tr. *Althusser & Balibar's Reading Capital* III. iii. 266 The analysis of reproduction destroys the appearance..of a 'free' contract between the worker and the capitalist. **1975** *Chinese Econ. Studies* VIII. IV. 79 In the course of reproduction, the scale of operation would not have expanded... This reproduction based on the original scale is called simple reproduction.

g. The process of reproducing sound; the degree of fidelity with which this is done.

1908 *Sears, Roebuck Catal.* 195/2 The Type FH Harvard Disc Talking Machine... Perfectly uniform speed, essential to perfect reproduction, is obtained. **1924** *Radio Times* 19 Dec. 619/2 (Advt.), Sound reproduction that is very near perfection. **1946** *Penguin Music Mag.* Dec. 93 The standard of reproduction with which people appear to be content, even very musical people, is far from satisfactory. **1962** *Times* 5 July 15/4 It would be foolish to assume that sound reproduction has reached a stage of ultimate perfection;.. research is constantly in progress both on ways of improving reproduction from discs and on alternative means of reproduction. **1978** *Gramophone* July 275/1 If headphones are what you want, you will not be disappointed. The reproduction of classical music or pop, piano, voices, orchestra—all are splendid.

2. a. Also, in more recent use, an article of furniture, etc., in a style reproduced from an earlier period. Also *attrib.*

1925 C. CAMP in *Scribner's Mag.* Sept. 318 People who call your best pieces reproductions when you know that they are not. **1925** *Scribner's Mag.* Oct. 15 (Advt.), A reproduction whale-oil lamp which measures 18½ inches to the top of the bulb. **1964** *Times Rev. Industry* Mar. 37/3 Sales [of furniture] are growing (unfortunately, almost entirely of 'reproduction' styles, which do not help our attempts to project an image of a new Britain). **1975** M. KENYON *Mr Big* xx. 190 Some reproduction Chippendale dining-chairs. **1977** *Whitaker's Almanack 1978* 887/1 The footwear industry is based on Florence, reproduction furniture at Cascini and Poggibonsi. **1981** J. B. HILTON *Playground of Death* vi. 71 There were one or two expensive reproduction pieces—a corner cupboard (for drinks) and a Jacobean footstool.

3. Special Combs.: **reproduction constant** or **factor** *Nuclear Physics* = **multiplication constant* or *factor*; **reproduction proof** *Printing*, a printed proof for use as an original for further, photographic, reproduction.

1962 *Newnes Conc. Encycl. Nucl. Energy* 729/1 *Reproduction constant.* This is an alternative, and less-frequently used, name for the multiplication factor..of a reactor. **1945** H. D. SMYTH *Gen. Acct. Devel. Atomic Energy Mil. Purposes* v. 35 The whole success or failure of the uranium project depended on the multiplication factor k, sometimes called the reproduction factor. **1947** *Science* 10 Jan. 28/1 Usually, *k* is called the 'reproduction factor' of the system. A self-sustaining chain reaction evidently is possible only when $k > 1$. **1952** GLASSTONE & EDLUND *Elem. Nucl. Reactor Theory* iv. 79 A multiplication factor or reproduction factor, defined as the ratio of the number of neutrons of any one generation to the number of corresponding neutrons of the immediately preceding generation. **1948** R. R. KARCH *Graphic Arts Procedures* 370/1 (Index), Reproduction proofs. **1949** MELCHER & LARRICK *Printing & Promotion Handbk.* 246/2 Reproduction proofs must be perfect—if anything, more perfect than would be acceptable in finished copy, since every slightest flaw will be duplicated in the whole run. **1967** Reproduction proof [see *REPRO 1].

reproductive (rĭprŏdv·ktiv), *sb. Zool.* [f. the adj.] A reproductive insect.

1934 C. A. KOFOID *Termites* i. 8 The alates become functional reproductives only after they leave the parent colony and, in isolation, start a new one. **1971** E. O. WILSON *Insect Societies* (1972) xix. 370/2 Some of the workers are inseminated and serve as the usual reproductives. **1977** *Nature* 2 June 395/3 At a critical time..approximately one generation time before the season ends, the entire effort is thrown into producing reproductives (queens and males).

reproductory, *a.* For *rare*—⁰ in Dict. read *rare* and add example.

1962 *Sci. Survey* XIX. 289 Reproductory behaviour and its approximate synchronisation depend to a large extent on the action on the central nervous mechanisms of hormones.

repro·file, *v.* [RE- 5 c.] *trans.* To give a new profile to; to reface. So **repro·filed** *ppl. a.*; **repro·filing** *vbl. sb.*

1963 *Times* 24 May (London Underground suppl.) p. xii/5 Wheels where the steel 'tyres' are worn away may be changed for 're-profiling'. *Ibid.*, A worn pair of wheels is readily replaced by a newly reprofiled (or refaced) pair. **1964** J. SUMMERSON *Classical Lang. Archit.* iv. 29 The Mannerist idiom of Vignola whose famous cornice—re-profiled—you will at once recognize.

repro·gram, repro·gramme, *v.* [RE- 5 a.] **1.** *trans.* To program differently; to supply with a new program. Also *transf.* and *fig.*

1963 [implied in REPROGRAMMING *vbl. sb.* below]. **1964** *Ann. Reg. 1963* 390 If any alteration had to be made to the map this could be done simply by re-programming the tape instead of having to redraw the map. **1972** *Listener* 6 July 13/2 A small clockwork mouse..[has] been very fully wound up and pointed in a certain direction, but there doesn't seem to be any means of re-programming it on the way. **1973** *Publishers Weekly* 18 June 9 (Advt.), Shows the hitherto unsuccessful dieter how to 'reprogram' himself for lifetime slimness. **1974** *News & Courier* (Charleston, S. Carolina) 21 Apr. C-10/2 The birds were taken from their nests as babies and were raised as pets. Ben David now is trying to reprogram the birds to fly free and kill to eat and live. **1977** D. RAMSAY *You can't call it Murder* I. 63 He resumed..questions. Bam, bam, bam. As if he were re-programming a computer.

2. To allocate to different spending programmes.

1971 *Hearings Comm. Armed Services, U.S. Senate 92nd Congress 1st Sess.* (S. 939) III. 2093 Fiscal year 1967 Navy funds were reprogramed to match maritime administration funds for program initiation.

So **re·programming** *vbl. sb.*; also **repro·grammable** *a.*

1963 *Rep. Comm. Inquiry Decimal Currency* xiv. 138 in *Parl. Papers 1962–3* (Cmnd. 2145) XI. 195 Ancillary machine costs:..re-programming of computers. **1971** J. Z. YOUNG *Introd. Study Man* xxii. 302 This reprogramming of the read-out of the DNA may serve to bring into play a new complex of enzyme systems. **1974** *Jrnl. Politics* XXXVI. 77 One instrument for executive spending flexibility is 're-programming' of funds within an appropriation. **1978** *Sci. Amer.* Feb. 72/2 Since the machines are reprogrammable, it is feasible to apply them to the assembly of products manufactured in families of models.

reprographer (rĭprǫ·grăfəɹ). [f. as next + -ER¹, as *photographer*, etc.] One who makes facsimile copies of documents.

1967 *Britannica Bk. of Year* 804/1 *Reprography*,.. facsimile reproduction (as by photocopying) of graphic matter (as documents); *reprographer*,..*reprographic, adj.* **1969** S. CUADRA *Ann. Rev. Information Sci.* IV. vi. 178 Old-style reprographers not only mixed their own 'soup', but they also made their own work schedules. **1972** *Libr. Resources* Spring 150 The education of library reprographers is a permanent concern.

reprographic (rĭprŏgræ·fik), *a.* and *sb.* [f. as next + -IC: see -GRAPHIC.] **A.** *adj.* Of or pertaining to reprography.

1961 *Engineering* 17 Nov. 633 Development to improve the efficiency of reprographic services. **1963** *Ibid.* 3 May 606 'Reprographic' has become recognized as the omnibus adjective for the many processes and methods now used to produce copies of documents of all kinds. **1966** *Times* 11 May 17/3 Admel International, of Weybridge, Surrey, a leading maker of what is called reprographic equipment,..is to be sold to an American group. **1973** *Nature* 31 Aug. 535/3 As reprographic technology progresses, interlibrary affiliates grow, and..publishers are likely to find the economic realities of their business approaching prohibitiveness. **1977** *Times* 24 Oct. 3/3 Its [*sc.* HMSO's] empire includes printing presses, binderies, warehouses, bookshops, reprographic units and laboratories.

B. *sb. pl.* (const. as *sing.*) = next.

1967 *Financial Times* 15 Mar. 21/2 The expansion in reprographics has had to call on many branches of technology to cope with the demand for better machines. **1969** *Daily Tel.* (Colour Suppl.) 31 Jan. 13/1 (Advt.), Reprographics: a word coined little over five years ago to describe the means used to reproduce the enormous volumes of drawn, typed and written material which has to be circulated in industry, commerce and government today. **1975** B. J. PERRY in Barr & Line *Ess. Information & Libraries* 119 Information science research is a complex area that requires the application of skills from many different disciplines, including..reprographics. **1980** *Financial Rev.* 5 Mar. 21/4 A 30 per cent drop in world demand for reprographics products.

reprography (rĭprǫ·grăfi). [ad. G. *reprographie*, f. *repro-duktion* REPRODUCTION + *photo-graphie* PHOTOGRAPHY.] The branch of technology concerned with the copying and reproduction of documentary and graphic material.

1961 *Bibliogr., Documentation, Terminol.* I. 105 The term 'reprography' is today used to cover all processes for the photographic reproduction and multicopying of documents. **1962** *Archives* V. 235 *Reprography.* This new and convenient, though not very likeable, word is a collective term for the processes of facsimile reproduction of documents, whether by means of photographic, electronic or other methods. **1963** *Special Libraries* Dec. 646/1 The term 'reprography', coined about ten years ago, is intended to describe all methods of facsimile reproduction of documentary materials with the exception of conventional printing. Although little used in the United States, the term is achieving considerable popularity in Europe. **1967** *Financial Times* 15 Mar. 21/1 The almost unpronounceable word 'reprography' is in. It covers a field with ill-defined boundaries, edging at its simplest into pencil-making and at its most sophisticated into desk-top photosetting. **1977** *Author* Summer 67 Cassettes and other forms of electronic storage are examples of what is becoming known as reprography.

reptation. (Later example.)

1947 R. L. G. IRVING tr. *Casteret's My Caves* iii. 54 Reptation involves an attitude so seldom adopted by the human race that it appears to be the fate allotted to a few inferior creatures.

reptilarium: see *REPTILIARY.

reptile, *sb.*¹ Add: The pronunc. (re·ptəil) is now standard in the U.K. **2.** (Later example.)

1974 WODEHOUSE *Aunts aren't Gentlemen* v. 45 She spoke as follows, her manner and diction similar to those of a sergeant-major addressing recruits. 'What's the matter with you, you poor reptile?'

3. *reptile man* (later example).

1975 J. MCCLURE *Snake* v. 64 The reptile man at the museum..said..that method of preservation had been abandoned.

reptile (re·ptəil), *sb.*² *Math.* Also **rep-tile.** [f. *rep(licating) tile* with a pun on REPTILE *sb.*] A two-dimensional figure of which two or more can be grouped together to form a larger figure having the same shape.

1966 S. W. GOLOMB in *Jrnl. Combinatorial Theory* I. 281 Certain polyominoes are 'rep-tiles', i.e., they can be used to tile enlarged scale models of themselves. **1972** C. S. OGILVY *Tomorrow's Math* (ed. 2) iv. 73 The following are unproven conjectures... Every rep-tile also tiles a parallelogram... A rep-tile with five or more sides cannot be convex. **1977** *Sci. Amer.* Jan. 110/3 Another kind of nonperiodic tiling is obtained by tiles that group together to form larger replicas of themselves. Solomon W. Golomb calls them 'reptiles'.

reptiliary (repti·liări). [f. REPTILE *sb.* + -ARY¹, after *aviary*.] A building or enclosure in which reptiles are kept, as for display. Also **reptila·rium** [-ARIUM]; **repti·llery** [-ERY].

1928 *Daily Tel.* 11 Sept. 14 This is the new open-air reptiliary. **1938** *Times* 30 Apr. 9/4 Before long a reptilarium would be installed at Whipsnade. **1976** *Southern Even. Echo* (Southampton) 10 Nov. 1/4 A reptillery has been in existence at Holiday Hill, near Lyndhurst, for about 15 years. **1978** *Autoworld* No. 68. 23/1 You can visit a wild goat park.., a butterfly reserve,..a reptiliary in the New Forest.

reptilious, *a.* For *rare*—¹ in Dict. read *rare* and add further example.

1936 L. C. DOUGLAS *White Banners* xv. 317 Considering with what reptilious patience she had waited.

reptillery: see *REPTILIARY.

republic, *sb.* (and *a.*) Add: **2. a.** Now also applied loosely to any state which claims this designation.

1947 E. WAUGH *Scott-King's Mod. Europe* 4 Out of it [*sc.* history] emerged the present republic of Neutralia, a typical modern state, governed by a single party, acclaiming a dominant Marshal, supporting a vast ill-paid bureaucracy whose work is tempered and humanised by corruption. **1976** *Whitaker's Almanack 1977* 829/2 Republic of Burundi... Burundi became independent as a Constitutional monarchy but this was overthrown on November 28, 1966. The Constitution and Parliament were also abolished. The President rules through a Cabinet of Ministers and the UPRONA party apparatus. Burundi is a one-Party State.

republican, *a.* and *sb.* Add: **A.** *adj.* **3. a.** (Earlier and later examples in modern sense.)

The Republican party formed in 1854 is now a predominantly conservative party, favouring agricultural, commercial, and financial interests and a limited central government (see M. M. Mathews *Dict. Americanisms*, 1951, and Sperber & Trittschuh *Amer. Polit. Terms*, 1962, for further details of the development of this sense).

1854 A. E. BOVAY *Let.* 26 Feb. in F. Curtis *Republican Party* (1904) I. vi. 177 Urge them..to band together under the name I suggested to you at Lovejoy's Hotel in 1852. I mean the name 'Republican'. **1856** *Porter's Spirit of Times* 4 Oct. 71/1 New Jersey..[was] discovered by the late Republican Convention, in their explorations for a candidate for Vice President. **1905** *Baltimore Amer.* 7 Mar. 4/1 Republican Senators..cannot find desks on the Republican side, as there are more Republicans in the Senate than there are desks for Republican Senators. **1976** *Columbus* (Montana) *News* 1 July 6/3 Charles Eckels attended the Republican Convention in Helena last week as chairman from this District.

b. Used as a distinguishing epithet by political parties outside U.S.

1958 *Listener* 27 Nov. 865/1 One [new French party] is the Republican Centre. **1975** *Financial Times* 31 Oct. 6/8 Mr Ecevit, chairman of the main Opposition, the Republican People's Party (RPP). **1980** S. J. BURKI *Pakistan under Bhutto* ii. 22 The formation of the landlord-dominated Republican Party.

B. *sb.* **2. b.** *transf.* Cf. REPUBLIC *sb.* 3 b.

1816 I. D'ISRAELI *Inquiry Lit. & Polit. Char. James I* 3 His other brothers, the republicans of literature, want a heart to admire the man.

republicanization. (Later example.)

1970 R. A. H. ROBINSON *Orig. Franco's Spain* i. 53 'Republicanisation' of local councils took place on a large scale; possibly this was as much the result of voluntary changes of allegiance..as of arbitrary measures.

republicanly, *adv.* For *rare*—¹ in Dict. read *rare* and add later example.

1837 J. S. MILL *Let.* June in *Works* (1963) XII. 339 Twelve pages on the *immediately present* state of French politics.. written republicanly by Thibaudeau.

Republicrat (rĭpʊ·blĭkræt). *U.S. politics.* Also **Republocrat.** [Blend of REPUBLI(CAN *sb.* 3 + DEMO)CRAT 2.] A member of a political faction that includes both Republicans and Democrats. Also, a conservative Democrat with Republican sympathies.

1940 *Better Eng.* Oct. 55/1 A republocrat, as 'Time' uses it, is a republican or a democrat who will have anyone but Mr. Hoover. **1944** *N.Y. Post* 24 Apr. 19/4 The 'Republicrats', meaning reactionary Democrats in league with the Republicans, want to discredit F.D.R. **1946** *Time* 22 Apr. 11/1 Would you be good enough to give us the names of the 'republocrats' in the House and Senate who have organized for the purpose of defeating President Truman's legislative program? **1949** *Southern Farmer* July 3 All we ask is that the Hindu philosophers tell us how to make the Southern Republicrats climb up a rope and disappear.

Hence **Republicra·tic** *a.*

1944 *New Republic* 19 June 801/1 The Republicratic gang engineering the supposed Southern 'revolt' against the New Deal appears well satisfied with the results of the Mississippi convention.

repudiant (rĭpiū·diănt), *a. rare.* [See REPUDIATE *v.* and -ANT¹.] Characterized by repudiation; = REPUDIATIVE *a.*

1954 W. FAULKNER *Fable* 144 The owner..still..invincibly repudiant.

repudiationist. Add: Also in *gen.* use. Also *attrib.* or as *adj.*

1930 *Times* 11 Nov. 15/4 That is the most effective way in which he can support the Government and repudiate the repudiationists. **1931** *Star* 8 May 16/1 The small Lang 'Repudiationist' rump came to Mr. Scullin's assistance. **1932** *New Statesman* 16 Jan. 53/2 Germany is repudiationist to a man.

repulsion. Add: **3. c.** *Genetics.* The condition of two genes, in an individual heterozygous at each of two linked loci, when the dominant allele of each occurs on the same chromosome as the recessive allele of the other. Opp. *COUPLING *vbl. sb.* 6 e.

[**1908** *Science* 15 May 786/1 When in F_1 the two dominants, femaleness and the *grossulariata* factor coexist, there is a repulsion between them, such that each gamete takes one or other of these two factors, not both. **1911** *Proc. R. Soc.* B. LXXXIV. 3 We were therefore led to recognize—A. A system of partial coupling under which two factors are generally associated. B. A system of complete repulsion (or as we have sometimes called it 'spurious allelomorphism') under which two factors are never associated in the same gamete.] **1926, 1970** [see *COUPLING *vbl. sb.* 6 e]. **1977** MATHER & JINKS *Introd. Biometrical Genetics* viii. 203 The associated distribution will lead to coupling linkage in F_1 and so may be denoted by C, while the dispersed distribution will give repulsion linkage and so may be denoted by R.

5. *attrib.* **repulsion motor** *Electr.*, an a.c. commutator motor for single-phase operation in which current is supplied to the stator only, the armature being short-circuited through the brushes and its current induced from the stator winding.

1904 E. B. RAYMOND *Alternating Current Engin.* iv. 187 The repulsion motor..can be used as an electric brake. **1920** *Whittaker's Electr. Engineer's Pocket-bk.* (ed. 4) 229 The repulsion motor is the simplest and commonest of all a.c. commutator motors. **1972** C. C. BARNES et al. *Electrics* 72/73 148 A repulsion motor has a single-field winding and a wound rotor with a centrifugal device to short-circuit the commutator.

reputational (repiutēⁱ·ʃənăl), *a.* [f. REPUTATION + -AL.] Of or pertaining to reputation.

1921 G. B. SHAW *Let.* 22 Dec. in *B. Shaw & Mrs. Campbell* (1952) 217 It maddens me to see people blundering away.. the reputational chances of their lifetime. **1967** *Listener* 19 Jan. 103/3 [T. F.] Powys is now at the nadir of the twenty-year reputational trough that follows death.

reputed, *ppl. a.* **1.** Delete † *Obs. rare* in Dict. and add: Now used after an adverb, as *internationally reputed*, etc.

Not often found in good sources.

1928 *Daily Express* 8 Aug. 15/3 Dr. Hanslick, the universally reputed professor of musical history. **1969** *Daily Tel.* 4 Aug. 17/6 An internationally reputed geologist.

2. b. *reputed pint, quart*, etc.: (see quot. 1904). Also, the amount of liquid contained by such a measure.

1904 MAKINS & LAMBERT *Licensed Victuallers' Handbk.* (rev. ed.) xiii. 216 Reputed quart means a bottle containing the sixth of a gallon, and a reputed pint a bottle containing the twelfth of a gallon. An Imperial Pint is an eighth part of a gallon. **1935** [see *METHUSELAH 2]. **1959** *Gloss. Terms Packaging* (B.S.I.) 29 The normal bottle of wine should contain ⅙ of a gallon..and is known as a 'reputed quart'... Variants of the above are known as 'mock quarts'..and may be of less capacity.

request, *sb.*¹ Add: **I. 2. b.** *spec.* A letter, etc., asking for a particular record, song, etc., to be played on a radio programme, often accompanied by a personal message; a record played or a song, etc., sung, either over the radio or to a live audience in response to a request.

1928 *Radio Times* 12 Oct. 79/3 The B.B.C. can never promise to comply with requests, for..suitable opportunities may not arise for weeks or even months. **1949** *Ibid.* 15 July 24/3 Listeners' requests played by Sandy Macpherson at the BBC theatre organ. **1966** *Listener* 4 Aug. 181/3 Judging by the requests, the classical and pre-classical composers are out. **1977** *Zigzag* Mar. 8/2 My sister..saw Roy Eldridge..playing requests in a bar.

3. b. (Further example.)

1976 *Daily Tel.* 20 July 2/7 A list should be provided on request.

II. 11. *request item, night, number, programme, session, week*; **requestman** *Naut.*, a seaman who makes a written request to an officer; also *pl.*, applied to the occasion appointed for the presentation of such requests; **request stop,** a stop at which a bus will halt only on request from a passenger or intending passenger.

1923 *Radio Times* 28 Sept. 17/1 Special Request Items. **1972** P. BLACK *Biggest Aspidistra* I. iii. 29 The pluggers kept the initiative by inventing the request item. **1916** 'TAFFRAIL' *Pincher Martin* vii. 116 'Request-men an' defaulters—'shun!' bawled the master-at-arms. **1951** H. HASTINGS *Sea Gulls over Sorrento* in J. C. Trewin *Plays of Year* IV. 75 You'd better write out a request... You know the routine... Requestmen is at 0900 tomorrow morning and not before! **1961** *Times* 27 Feb. 14/6 Shortly after breakfast C.P.O. Coleshill knocked on my cabin door and entered with his list of requestmen and defaulters. **1923** *Radio Times* 28 Sept. 12/1 Why is it apparently not thought advisable to repeat the 'Request Nights', which.. are so popular? **1971** 'D. HALLIDAY' *Dolly & Doctor Bird* iii. 37 The small coloured orchestra..suddenly broke..into a request number for jiving. **1889** *Cent. Dict.*, *Request-program*, a concert program made up of numbers the performance of which has been requested by the audience. **1955** *Radio Times* 22 Apr. 10/2 A request programme of records. **1976** *Times* 4 Aug. 12/3 On the radio, request programmes for 'troopies' in the operational areas aim to keep spirits high. **1959** M. SHADBOLT *New Zealanders* 76 The crackling voice of the request-session announcer. **1943** G. GREENE *Ministry of Fear* IV. i. 223 Buses slid quickly past the Request stops. **1955** O. LANCASTER in *Daily Express* 25 Nov. 1/2 (*caption*) Five years' continuous service without once stopping at a request stop. **1973** *Times* 15 Oct. 17/5 Hiding behind another bus at a request stop so as to avoid seeing the uplifted hand. **1928** *Radio Times* 7 Dec. 649/2 (*heading*) Children's Hour request week... The Fourth Request Week will begin on January 7, 1929.

requester. (Later example.)

1973 *Nature* 13 Apr. 485/2 How many requesters, before writing, saw my paper?

‖ **requeté** (rekete·). *Hist.* Also **Requeté.** [Sp.] A member of a Carlist militia that took the Nationalist side during the Spanish Civil War of 1936–39.

1936 *Times* 26 Aug. 12/4 The troops engaged on the insurgent side have consisted of *requetes*, Navarrese volunteers almost to a man. **1938** *Times Lit. Suppl.* 27 Aug. 558/3 The first, longer and better of the two stories.. describes how a Carlist *requeté* in North Spain deserted his side to secure the reprieve of his father. **1944** WYNDHAM LEWIS *Let.* 5 Jan. (1963) 374, I was glad to learn from Augustus that he had exchanged his requeté uniform for that of the Home Guard. **1957** P. KEMP *Mine were of Trouble* ii. 21 The Requeté movement drew its main strength from the Basque provinces, especially from Navarre. **1979** D. ROBINSON *Eldorado Network* xvii. 129 The Requetés..were a sort of Basque militia... Fought for Franco.

requirant. (Later example.)

1812 in G. E. Cory *Rise of S. Afr.* (1910) I. vii. 213 The R.O. Requirant feels himself obliged to declare that he has not any ground for further action against the defendant.

required, *ppl. a.* Add: **b.** *required reading*, literature which one is required to read for an educational course or which must be read in order to gain an understanding of some subject.

1921 H. J. LASKI in *Holmes–Laski Lett.* (1953) I. 370 They are quite intolerable—pushing little professors full of pedantic details, nosing into the dull routine of unimportant matters, pushing their little quack remedies, interested in getting the wrong books on to lists of required reading. **1930** *Publishers' Weekly* 15 Mar. 1547/1 Some of the important courses in our colleges and universities cannot be taught successfully..because of the lack of a sufficient number of books for required reading. **1954** *N.Y. Times Bk. Rev.* 31 Jan. 1/1 Here is a book that should be required reading for Democrats in 1954. **1962** *Listener* 17 May 873/2 They genuinely stimulate thought and thus become required reading for social critics, amateur and professional. **1976** J. WAINWRIGHT *Walther P.38* 62 The usual sort of stuff which..was 'required reading' for any moderate education.

Hence **requi·redness,** the fact or quality of being required.

1938 W. KÖHLER *Place of Value in World of Facts* ii. 35 At the bottom of all human activities are 'values', the conviction that some things 'ought to be' and others not. Science, however, with its immense interest in mere facts seems to lack all understanding of such 'requiredness'. **1946** C. MORRIS *Signs, Lang. & Behavior* iii. 63 A command such as 'Come here!' may signify with high constancy the requiredness of the response which it prescribes. **1977** A. ECCLESTONE *Staircase for Silence* iv. 78 Péguy spoke often of it as invincible anxiety; while Abraham Heschel called it a sense of requiredness, in the language of the Bible: what is required of me?

requisite, *a.* and *sb.* Add: **A.** *adj.* **b.** *requisite variety*, the variety necessary in a system for it to be able to control another system in which there is variety.

1956 W. R. ASHBY *Introd. Cybernetics* xi. 207 This is the law of Requisite Variety. To put it more picturesquely: only variety in R can force down the variety due to D; only variety can destroy variety. **1966** S. BEER *Decision & Control* xii. 281 But however many interacting sub-systems of preys and predators, big fleas and little fleas, are invoked, it is none the less evident that the balance of animal populations would be grossly upset very rapidly unless the law of requisite variety held in general throughout nature. **1975** R. M. GLORIOSO *Engin. Cybernetics* v. 72 As a minimum requirement, the number of different possible states of the system must equal the number of possible states of the environment, although the proper states of the system must be available as well. Thus, to reduce the variety in the environment, the system must be capable of achieving the 'requisite variety'.

requisitely, *adv.* Delete † *Obs.* and add later example.

1976 *Daily Tel.* (Colour Suppl.) 13 Feb. 29/2 Neither in England nor America could Jack Scalia expect to rise to the top earning bracket until he is over 30 and projects the requisitely aggressive and reliable image.

requisition, *sb.* Add: **5.** *attrib.*, as *requisition form, note, notice, paper, slip.*

1929 T. H. BURNHAM *Engineering Econ.* xv. 206 Tools may only be issued against a requisition form signed by a duly authorized official. **1916** G. FRANKAU *Poetical Wks.* (1923) I. 226 A faked requisition note. **1974** P. GORE-BOOTH *With Great Truth & Respect* 150 We..were alarmed by the appearance of requisition notices on the doors of adjoining houses. **1911** *Daily Colonist* (Victoria, B.C.) 23 Apr. 1/7 Burns said he would start tonight for Los Angeles..Governor Marshall having honored requisition papers. **1938** L. BEMELMANS *Life Class* III. ii. 221 A stack of requisition slips, for the carpentry department, for the painters,..for the printer.

requisitioner (rekwizi·ʃənəɹ). [f. REQUISITION *v.* + -ER¹.] = REQUISITIONIST.

1968 M. GUYBON tr. *Solzhenitsyn's First Circle* lxii. 392 After Christmas they were made to give up half of it for the cities, and the requisitioners were never satisfied.

requisitionize (rekwizi·ʃənəiz), *v. rare.* [f. REQUISITION *sb.* + -IZE.] *trans.* To request or require (one to do something) by written requisition.

1845 J. KEBLE *Let.* 6 Feb. in G. Battiscombe *John Keble* (1963) xiii. 254 If it is thought well to requisitionize the Proctors to veto the affair..you may put my name down to it.

requotation. [RE- 5 a.] A new or revised quotation (of the price of a share).

1964 *Economist* 29 Aug. 848/1 A requotation for their shares. **1973** *Daily Tel.* 14 Feb. 1/6 Pergamon Press..is back in profit and looking for an early requotation on the Stock Exchange.

requote, *v.* Add: Also, to quote a new price for (a share).

1967 *Economist* 27 May 946/4 The shares were requoted after the financial troubles.

re-ra·diate, *v.* Also **reradiate.** [RE- 5 a.] *trans.* To radiate again (what has been absorbed or received). Also *absol.*

1913 F. W. RAYNES *Heating Systems* xv. 184 The arrangement and grouping of the heating surfaces affect the radiant heat transmitted, in that a more or less percentage is rendered ineffective through being simply re-radiated from surface to surface. **1928** *Daily Tel.* 10 Jan. 16 A short-wave receiver of a sensitive type which will not re-radiate, and so interfere with neighbouring receivers. **1942** J. D. STRANATHAN *Particles Mod. Physics.* vi. 255 Electrons of the scattering material are supposed to be set into vibration by the varying electric field. These..are then supposed to re-radiate the energy in all directions. This re-radiated energy represents the scattered X-rays. **1952** *Archit. Rev.* CXI. 18/2 Any type of screen will itself be heated by the sunshine falling upon it, and will re-radiate this heat into the building. **1976** *Sci. Amer.* Sept. 75/3 The earth intercepts a vast amount of solar energy... About 60 percent is reflected without interacting further and most of the remainder is absorbed by the atmosphere or by oceans and landmasses and is promptly reradiated as heat.

Hence **re-ra·diated** *ppl. a.*

1942 [see above]. **1974** HARVEY & BOHLMAN *Stereo F.M. Radio Handbk.* vii. 155 This reradiated signal is picked up by the dipole. **1978** R. V. JONES *Most Secret War* xxi. 175 We could in principle re-radiate this already re-radiated signal back to the aircraft.

re:-radia·tion. [RE- 5 a.] The action of re-radiating; also *concr.*

1881 [in Dict. s.v. RE- 5 a]. **1915** W. H. ECCLES *Wireless Telegr.* 132 The Joulean wastage in the surrounding ground is usually so great that it is well to limit the re-radiation, and to seek rather to transfer the collected energy somewhat rapidly to the detector. **1924** *Times* 17 Jan. 8/5 The first intelligible programmes began to come through in time for successful re-radiation here before the close of the old year. *Ibid.*, A large number of letters have been received..from listeners..commenting on the surprisingly good quality of the re-radiation. **1976** *Nature* 2 Sept. 15/2 Solar radiation is absorbed in ground energy levels of atoms or molecules, producing excitation. Fluorescence or reradiation then follows.

rerail, *v.* Add: (Examples of the simple verb.) Also *fig.*

1895 *Funk's Stand. Dict., Re-rail*.., to put on the track again; to cause to take the rails again, as derailed rolling-stock. **1914** W. de Morgan *Ghost meets Ghost* II. iii. 455 'And where else did you go?' said the Earl, to re-rail the conversation. **1967** G. F. Fiennes *I tried to run Railway* ii. 6, I learned how to re-rail wagons and engines without sending for the crane.

reraise, *v.* Add: (Later example.) Hence **rerai·sing** *vbl. sb.*

1937 *Jrnl. Eng. & Germanic Philol.* XXXVI. 2 The raising (resp. re-raising) of ǣ (< ē) > ē. **1937** *Times* 31 Dec. 12/1 The object of making it impossible for such points of friction to be reraised in future.

re·read, *sb.* [Re- 5 a.] An instance of reading again.

1973 M. Amis *Rachel Papers* 185 Finally, I belaboured one of Gerard Manley Hopkins's sleazier lyrics, implying (a last-minute reread made clear) that it was high time we burned all extant editions of the little fag's poetry. **1977** T. Allbeury *Man with President's Mind* ii. 13 The report got a routine re-read.

re-rea·dable, *a.* [Re- 5 a.] Capable of being re-read; capable of being read about for a second time with pleasure.

1948 F. R. Leavis *Great Tradition* i. 9 His books..have a permanent life as light reading—indefinitely re-readable. **1967** *Punch* 22 Feb. 282/3 He makes the Paris of the 'twenties, Joyce and Fitzgerald re-readable, something of a feat.

re-reader. [Re- 5 a.] One who re-reads.

1957 'O. Edwards' *Talking of Books* 190 It can be argued that all these are specialists or exceptional classes of re-readers. **1965** K. Tillotson *Mid-Victorian Stud.* xxiv. 309 Dickens..is perhaps chiefly a re-reader—going back and back to that shelf of boyhood favourites lovingly enumerated in *David Copperfield.*

re-reco·rd, *v.* Also **rerecord.** [Re- 5 a.] *trans.* To record again. Also *absol.*

1930 *Proc. IRE* XVIII. 1335 Before sound film can be rerecorded a matched print must be made. **1932** *Times Educ. Suppl.* 17 Dec. p. ii/2 The records made by the great tenor..have been re-recorded by the Company. **1955** L. Feather *Encycl. Jazz* 25 He..restored him to the music world by rerecording *Honky Tonk Train Blues.* **1964** *Oceanogr. & Marine Biol.* II. 429 The background characteristics of low speed recordings may be somewhat improved by re-recording at higher speeds. **1977** *New Yorker* 29 Aug. 67/1 The music of long-dead musicians long ago re-recorded for in-flight listening. **1978** W. F. Buckley *Stained Glass* xii. 110 It was recorded and rerecorded that in her youth she had actually studied under Clara Schumann.

Hence **re-reco·rded** *ppl. a.*, **re-reco·rding** *vbl. sb.*

1930 *Proc. IRE* XVIII. 1333 Once it was discovered that re-recording was practical a great many other reasons for its use were discovered. **1962** A. Nisbett *Technique Sound Studio* v. 104 It is now possible to compare the original and re-recorded signals directly. **1975** P. G. Winslow *Death of Angel* ix. 186 It seems to be a re-recording of another tape. **1977** *Gramophone* Aug. 357/2 The incredibly high copying speeds needed to make the exercise economically viable (32 or 64 times normal speed) put severe limits on the re-recorded sound quality.

re-ree·l, *v.* [Re- 5 a.] *trans.* To wind again on to a reel, or from one reel to another. Hence **re-ree·ling** *vbl. sb.*; **re-ree·ler** (see quot. 1964).

1906 R. W. Sindall *Paper Technol.* vi. 75 (*caption*) Double-Drum Reeler. The reels from the paper-machine are re-reeled, slit, and finished off on this machine. **1929** Clapperton & Henderson *Mod. Paper-Making* xvi. 246 (*caption*) Four-drum winder for re-reeling newsprint. **1937** E. J. Labarre *Dict. Paper* 211/1 *Re-reeling machine*, the apparatus on which the web of paper is re-reeled after passing through the operations of tub-sizing..and drying. **1964** *Gloss. Letterpress Rotary Printing Terms (B.S.I.)* 17 *Re-reeler*, an auxiliary unit to rewind the web or webs for subsequent operations. **1967** E. Chambers *Photolitho-Offset* xv. 237 The paper can be either cut into sheets or re-reeled for finishing elsewhere.

re-refine, *v.* Add: (Later examples.) Hence **re-refi·ned** *ppl. a.*; **re-refi·ner**; **re-refi·ning** *vbl. sb.*

1971 *Daily Colonist* (Victoria, B.C.) 10 Feb. 21/5 The re-refined oil sells for 26 cents a quart. **1973** *Sci. Amer.* Feb. 48/3 Today only 100 to 150 million gallons of the 500 million gallons of oil annually drained from the nation's crankcases are re-refined. **1975** *Conservation of Energy* (Shell Internat. Petroleum Co.) 12 Shell companies are examining the most effective means of collecting and re-conditioning used lubricating oils, including re-refining. *Ibid.*, It is possible that 10 per cent of the world demand for lubricants will be met by re-refined oils in the early 1980s. **1977** *Laconia* (New Hampshire) *Evening Citizen* 21 July 5/5 Your car's dirty motor oil might soon be 'rerefined' through an environmentally safe process which will help conserve..crude oil. *Ibid.*, A lot of rerefiners' raw material is being burned as fuel. **1977** *Lubricants Business* (Shell Internat. Petroleum Co.) 8 Re-refining is likely to be primarily attractive in a number of developing countries where savings in foreign exchange could be an important factor.

re-relea·se, *v.* [Re- 5 a.] *trans.* To release (a film, record, etc.) again. So **re-relea·se** *sb.*; **re-relea·sable** *a.*; **re-relea·sed** *ppl. a.*

1948 *Daily Mail* 7 Feb. 2/5 'Mrs. Miniver'..turned up..on 're-release', and lasted only seven days. **1968** *Listener* 26 Sept. 416/2 The Disney product had to be aimed at all ages, it had to be 'endlessly re-releasable'. **1975** *N.Y. Times* 4 Mar. 38/1 The new D. W. Griffith Theater, which has re-released Cocteau's 'Les Enfants Terribles'. **1977** *It* May 28/1 There are the re-released 'Jimmy Weatherspoon and Ben Webster' 'Stitt Palysbird'. **1977** *Guardian Weekly* 28 Aug. 20/1 There are currently 38 Presley albums available in this country..and, with re-releases, he has had 117 singles on sale here.

re-representation. (Later example.)

1932 *Brain* LV. 459 These impulses..may be..passed on to the main part of the lateral nucleus by short inter-nuclear connections where they acquire a re-representation.

re-reveal, *v.* (Earlier example.)

a **1631** Donne *Poems* (1635) 367 Davids Successors, in holy zeale, In formes of joy and art doe re-reveale To us so sweetly and sincerely too, That I must not rejoyce as I would doe.

re-ri·de, *v.* [Re- 5 a.] *trans.* To ride (a route, contest, etc.) again. Hence **re·ride** *sb.*

1884 *Cyclists' Touring Club Monthly Gaz.* Nov. 335/2 Favourable stretches of high-way are ridden and re-ridden with wearying iteration upon safety bicycles, which are 'safe' only in name. **1903** *Daily Chron.* 28 Sept. 8/7 The tie will have to be re-ridden. **1976** *Billings* (Montana) *Gaz.* 17 June 1-h/3 Judges gave one cowboy a fourth reride.

rero·be, *v.* [Re- 5 c.] *trans.* To dress in a fresh robe; to clothe in a robe again. So **rero·bing** *vbl. sb.*

1849 C. Brontë *Shirley* II. v. 126 She immediately took the book from her and, with her own hands, commenced the business of disrobing and rerobing her. **1934** Dylan Thomas *18 Poems* 32 Second Rise of the skeleton and Re-robing of the naked ghost.

re-roll, *v.* (Later examples.) Hence **re-ro·ller,** one who or that which rolls iron or steel again; **re-ro·lled** *ppl. a.*

1931 *Times* 16 Mar. 19/7 The re-rollers are feeling the pinch. **1955** *Times* 14 July 15/3 Difficulties were experienced due to the national shortage of re-rolled steel products. **1963** *Punch* 13 Feb. 242/1 It is one of the largest 're-rollers' in the industry. **1967** Karch & Buber *Offset Processes* viii. 357 Reroll the screens and reassemble them on the pump. **1976** *Woman's Day* (N.Y.) Nov. p. h/1 On lightly floured surface roll out each half 3/16 inch thick. Cut in 3-inch squares (reroll scraps).

re-rou·te, *v.* [Re- 5 a.] *trans.* To set upon a new route; to re-direct. Also *fig.* So **re-rou·t(e)ing** *vbl. sb.*

1929 *Daily Express* 5 Jan. 2/1 Post Office officials..said that it was the first move in a general 're-routing' of mails. **1936** J. Steinbeck *In Dubious Battle* xiii. 203 The police stood, re-routing the traffic. **1961** 'E. Lathen' *Banking on Death* xi. 94 Arthur was on a Chicago–Boston flight which was rerouted to Washington because of the blizzard. **1971** *Daily Tel.* 21 Oct. 14/5 A council is to spend £250 on re-routeing a drainpipe to save an asparagus bed. **1978** S. Herzel in P. Moore *Man, Woman, & Priesthood* viii. 108 Any real understanding of sexuality and spirituality must be re-routed through a new awareness of the metaphoric and personal character of language itself.

re-ro·w, *v.* [Re- 5 a.] *trans.* To row (a race) again. Also *absol.* Hence **re-·row** *sb.*

1892 *Pall Mall Gaz.* 13 June 3/2 The C.U.B.C. had the race re-rowed this morning. **1901** *Daily Chron.* 19 July 8/3 Kingston and London were ordered to re-row. *Ibid.* 12 Aug. 8/2 After a foul and a re-row the Senior Pairs fell to H. U. Gould and C. M. Steele. **1979** *Oxford Mail* 31 May 16/8 Division II (6–10): Subject to rerow 11.45 today.

re-ru·bber, *v.* [Re- 5 c.] *trans.* To provide (a tyre) with a fresh covering of rubber. So **re-ru·bbering** *vbl. sb.*

1908 *Westm. Gaz.* 2 June 4/2 At the end of three months..the first set are sent to be re-rubbered... Re-rubbering [costs] £30. **1923** *Daily Mail* 16 Feb. 5 (Advt.), Tyre re-rubbering and general Tyre repairs. **1973** *Times* 28 Apr. 4/2 A wornout tyre that has been rerubbered with a new tread.

re-run, *sb.* [f. the vb.] **1.** A repeat showing of a motion picture; also, the film itself; also *transf.*, of broadcast or printed material. Also *fig.*

1934 in Webster. **1955** *Times* 28 July 9/7 Film costs rather more than 'live' television, but it has a great advantage for re-run purposes. **1965** *Times Lit. Suppl.* 25 Nov. 1070/4 Re-runs of old silent films. **1968** *Guardian* 22 Mar. 10/6 *Around the World in 80 Days* starts a rerun in 70 millimetre at the Coliseum Cinerama Theatre. **1968** P. Marlowe *Hire me a Hearse* ix. 137 It didn't take very long for Hazard to run the spools through again. In the rerun some of it sounded repetitious. **1971** *Wall St. Jrnl.* 22 July 1/5 Liberty magazine, which was around from 1924 until 1950, makes a comeback with reruns of its old articles. **1978** G. Vidal *Kalki* vi. 151 On the wall opposite the window a row of TV monitors showed us..a rerun of *I love Lucy.* **1979** *Dædalus* Summer 15 The current quarrel..is just the latest rerun of that earlier script.

2. The repeated performance of a computation or computer program. Usu. *attrib.*

1946 J. B. Conant *Man. Operation Automatic Sequence Controlled Calculator* ii. 50 Starting, stopping and rerun instructions. **1958** [see *generator 4 c]. **1980** R. Longbottom *Computer Syst. Reliability* vii. 105 A further category of rerun time is incurred when it is found that previously created files have been lost... The time to restore files is again application dependent.

3. A repeated occurrence or attempt.

1976 H. Wilson *Governance of Britain* iii. 65 A tendency developed in the 1960s for a defeated minister almost automatically to seek for a re-run at Cabinet. **1977** *Daily Tel.* 17 Mar. 1/1 The Left-wing appeared to be in no mood to have a re-run of last year's rebellion, when the Government was defeated by 28 votes.

re-run, *v.* Add: (Further examples.) *spec.* to show (a motion picture) again (also *fig.*); to subject again to an experimental or computational procedure.

1962 'D. Shannon' *Extra Kill* vii. 103 There was a picture Fox made... Last week I saw it's being rerun at a neighborhood house. **1967** E. Chambers *Photolitho-Offset* XV. 239 The product cannot be re-run through the machine. **1971** J. B. Carroll et al. *Word Frequency Bk.* p. xxxvii, The discrepancy was caused by technical problems in making final corrections..in the computer tape... Discrepancies in individual subject categories were so small..that it was not considered worthwhile to rerun the distributions. **1973** *Sci. Amer.* Dec. 45/2 Our entire simulation of the Antennae (with n = 350) could be rerun in less than five minutes on any fast modern computer. **1976** M. Maguire *Scratchproof* viii. 115 Re-run it... Slow down the projection speed. **1976** E. Maclaren *Nature of Belief* ii. 16 You can't re-run a piece of history with different variables the way you can repeat a chemistry experiment without the chlorine. **1977** *Virology* LXXVIII. 207/2 The DNA isolated by this procedure was then rerun in a CsCl density gradient.

Hence **re-run** *ppl. a.*

1929 *Amer. Speech* IV. 386 The term *smoke* is comparatively new..and means an inferior grade of whitish, cloudy alcohol, usually *re-run alky* at that. **1968** A. Diment *Gt. Spy Race* vii. 94 The excuses running through their minds like re-run television shows.

res[1] (rēⁱz). Pl. **res.** [L., = thing.] **1.** orig. in *Law* (see quots. 1851, 1854); hence *gen.*, the condition of something; the matter in hand, the point at issue, the crux.

[**1684** G. Mackenzie *Institutions Law of Scotland* I. ii. 10, I do resolve, first, to lay down what concerns the Persons of whom the *Law* treats: *Secundo*, what concerns the things themselves treated of, such as rights, obligations &c. *Tertio*, the actions whereby these rights are pursued, which answers to the Civilians, *objecta juris, viz. Personae, res, & Actiones.*] **1851** P. Colquhoun *Summary Roman Civil Law* II. 1 *Res*..is used in contradistinction to *persona*... In another and more restricted sense it signifies those objects of rights which are neither *personae, actiones*, nor *facta.* **1854** P. Cumin *Man. Civil Law* 59 *Q.* Define *Res. A.* All physical and metaphysical existences, in which persons may claim a right. **1923** *Law Rep. King's Bench Div.* II. 439 If the res—the thing actually and directly in dispute—has been already adjudicated upon, of course by a competent Court, it cannot be litigated again. **1947** Wodehouse *Full Moon* vi. 126 Do you mind if we get back to the *res.* Time presses. **1949** W. Stevens in *Trans. Connecticut Acad. Arts & Sci.* Dec. 166 The poem is the cry of its occasion, Part of the res itself and not about it. **1966** Wodehouse *Plum Pie* i. 23, I saw that I had better come to the *res* without delay.

2. Used in a number of Latin (*esp.* legal and philos.) phrases, as: **res co·gitans** *Philos.*, the concept of man as that of a thinking being.

[**1641** Descartes *Meditationes* ii. 23 Sed quid igitur sum? res cogitans: quid est hoc? nempe dubitans, intelligens, affirmans, negans, volens, nolens, imaginans quoque, & sentiens.] **1904** J. Iverach *Descartes, Spinoza & New Philos.* iii. 63 It is not possible to take the mind as a thing among other things; a mere *res cogitans* can apprehend nothing but thoughts or ideas. **1962** M. McLuhan *Gutenberg Galaxy* 247 The mental *res cogitans* and the material *res extensa.* **1972** Z. Vendler (*title*) Res cogitans: an essay in rational psychology.

res commu·nis *Law*, common property; something incapable of appropriation.

[*a* **1259** Bracton *De Legibus* (Rolls Ser., 1878) I. 54 Extra patrimonio autem dicuntur res sacræ, et religiosæ, et communes.] **1704** T. Wood *New Institute Imperial or Civil Law* II. i. 65 *Res communes* are those in which no Person has a Property, neither can any one be Master of them, or deprive others of the use of them. **1854** P. Cumin *Man. Civil Law* 65 *Q.* When an island rises in the Sea, who is proprietor?.. *A.* The first occupier: until occupation, no one, it is a *res communis.* **1923** W. S. Holdsworth *Hist. Eng. Law* (rev. ed.) II. III. iii. 273 He [*sc.* Bracton] then discourses upon..res publicæ and res communes. In his treatment of the latter topic there are traces that he had read Azo hastily. **1970** *Internat. & Compar. Law Q.* XIX. 237 It has been suggested that Antarctica has, in fact, become *res communis.*

res exte·nsa *Philos.*, a material thing considered as extended substance.

1940 *Philos. & Phenomenol. Res.* I. 181 This cosmos of meaning and unmeaning into which man is born, this rich structure of all kinds of relationships, is levelled down to the status of *res extensa.* **1962** [see *res cogitans].

res ge·stæ, (an account of) things done, achievements; an account of a person's career; events in the past; in *Law*, the facts of a case, used esp. with reference to evidence that includes spoken words; also in *sing.* **res gesta.**

1616 G. CAREW *Let.* 24 Jan. (1860) 27 In this gazette you may not expect any more than *res gestae.* **1696** W. NICOLSON *Eng. Historical Libr.* I. 213 The like Scruples I have upon me as to some other *Res Gestæ* of this King, which are said to have been written by Robert Bale, sometime Recorder of London. **1794** *Trial of J. H. Tooke* in *T. B. Howell's State Trials* (1818) XXV. 440 That letter your lordships have received, and, I believe, without any objection from this side of the table, probably upon the ground, that as it is an answer to an act which is charged against the prisoner, it is fit to be received as part of the *res gesta* upon the subject. **1815** S. M. PHILLIPPS *Treat. Law of Evidence* I. vii. 202 Hearsay is often admitted in evidence, as part of the *res gestae*; the meaning of which seems to be, that where it is necessary, in the course of a cause, to inquire into the nature of a particular act and the intention of the person who did the act, proof of what the person said at the time of doing it is admissible evidence, for the purpose of shewing its true character. **1930** BURROWS & CAHN *S. L. Phipson's Law of Evidence* vi. 54 Acts, declarations, and incidents which constitute, or accompany and explain, the fact or transaction in issue, are admissible, for or against either party, as forming parts of the *res gesta.* **1936** *Mind* XLV. 518 Signor Gentile..roundly denies any distinction between *res gestae* and *historia rerum gestarum,* maintaining that all history is contemporary history. **1951** S. F. NADEL *Foundations Social Anthropol.* i. 14 Events in the past, which, being as it were closed chapters, *res gestae*, and having had their particular consequences, exemplify more typically the just-so happenings which limit our search for regularities. **1959** A. G. WOODHEAD *Study of Greek Inscriptions* 56 Cross-references concerning offices held or *res gestae* in general. **1969** *N. Dakota Law Rev.* Winter 208 Children talk best in their native habitat. What they say when pressures of emotion and strangeness are absent is more apt to be true, somewhat analogous to *res gestae.*

res i·ntegra *Law* (see quot. 1959); also *transf.*

1754 in F. Vesey *Reports* (1814) I. 11, I confess, if this had been *res integra,* I should doubt, whether the testator's declaration is a proper execution within the fifth clause.. but I find myself bound by such a number of former precedents, that I must give way to their superior weight. **1760** G. GILBERT *Cases in Law & Equity* 250 And if the Matter had been *res integra* and undetermined, he should have held it ill if it had been brought by the other Name. **1834** J. RAM *Science of Legal Judgment* xiv. 126 If the matter were entire.., *res integra,* a new case or point.., it might admit of difficulty. *a* **1873** MILL *Three Ess. Relig.* (1874) 203 The question whether it is so or not is *res integra,* untouched by any of the results of human knowledge and experience. **1959** JOWITT *Dict. Eng. Law* II. 1533/2 *Res integra,* a point governed neither by any decision nor by any rule of law, which must therefore be decided upon principle. **1961** *Times* 15 Feb. 15/3 If the matter were *res integra,* his Lordship saw great force that in 1843 the words 'voluntary contribution' would be understood as intended to cover an annual subscription.

res i·psa lo·quitur *Law,* a principle that the proven occurrence of an accident implies the negligence of the defendant unless he provides another cause; also *transf.* and *attrib.*

1659 H. GRIMSTON tr. *Croke's Reports King James* 508 It is apparent, that the money was lent for Interest, and is more than the Statute permits; Wherefore being usury apparent, the Court shall adjudg it accordingly: And..if the corrupt agreement be not expressed in the verdict, and the matter is apparent to the Court to be usury, there the Jury needs not to shew that it was corruptly, for *res ipsa loquitur.* **1864** in Hurlstone & Coltman *Exchequer Reports* II. 725 There are certain cases of which it may be said res ipsa loquitur, and this seems one of them. **1872** *Wharton's Law-Lexicon* (ed. 5) 846/1 *Res ipsa loquitur* (the thing speaks for itself), a phrase used in actions for injury by negligence where no proof of negligence is required beyond the accident itself, which is such as necessarily to involve negligence. **1908** *Times Law Rep.* XXIV. 551/2 *Res ipsa loquitur* does not mean, as I understand it, that merely because at the end of a journey a horse is found hurt, or somebody is hurt in the streets, the mere fact that he is hurt implies negligence. **1927** LD. HEWART in A. P. Herbert *Misleading Cases* p. v, '*Res ipsa loquitur*', as the man in the street said when a sack of flour, in the best manner of the attic declension, fell upon him from an upper room. **1954** *Cambr. Law Jrnl.* Apr. 132 In *Ybarra* v. *Spangard*..the Californian District Court of Appeal held that the plaintiff might sue all the defendants and recover a joint judgment in a *res ipsa loquitur* situation. **1965** *Mod. Law Rev.* XXVIII. v. 623 When a textbook attains an eighteenth edition surely the maxim *res ipsa loquitur* could hardly boast a better exemplification. **1973** *N.Y. Law Jrnl.* 19 July 12/3 At the new trial plaintiff shall be permitted to produce an expert to establish a case under the doctrine of res ipsa loquitur.

res judica·ta *Law,* a matter that has been adjudicated by a competent court.

[*a* **1259** BRACTON *De Legibus* (Rolls Ser., 1881) IV. 266 Item cadit assisa, si petens petat per assisam quod per judicium amisit, quia cadit assisa propter exceptionem rei judicatæ, & agat si voluerit de falso judicio.] **1693** LD. STAIR *Inst. Law Scotl.* (ed. 2) IV. xl. 675 *Res Judicata* is Relevant, not only being a Decreet between the Pursuer and the Defender; But it is sufficient, if it was between their Predecessors or Authors. **1867** *Wharton's Law-Lexicon* (ed. 4) 830/1 *Res judicata,* a point decided by authority. **1927** C. K. ALLEN *Law in Making* iii. 109 It was a commonplace with the Orators, and especially with Cicero, that the *res iudicata,* or *iudicatum,* was an integral part of the civil law. **1955** *Times* 14 July 11/3 All too often he spoke of *res judicatae* as if they were mere *obiter dicta.* **1972** *Mod. Law Rev.* XXXV. I. 96 The husband's solicitor maintained that the issue of cruelty was *res judicata.*

res non ve·rba, 'things not words'; material fact or concrete action as opposed to mere talk.

1949 E. POUND *Pisan Cantos* lxxxii. 116 And for all that old Ford's conversation was better, Consisting in *res non verba.* **1961** *Times* 26 Apr. 20/2 The strapping muleteer who saves every situation by his guiding principle of *res non verba.*

res nu·llius *Law,* no one's property; strictly, a thing or things that can belong to no one.

[*a* **1259** BRACTON *De Legibus* (Rolls Ser., 1878) I. 60 Res quidem nullius esse dicuntur pluribus modis, natura sive jure naturali, ut feræ bestiæ, volucres, et pisces... Item tempore dicunter res in nullius bonis esse, ut thesaurus.] **1704** T. WOOD *New Inst. Imperial or Civil Law* II. i. 67 *Res nullius* (or things which are not the Goods of any Person or number of Men) are those that are of a *divine* Right. **1833** J. S. MILL in *Jurist* IV. 24 It matters not that the property has now become *res nullius,* and is therefore, properly speaking, our own. **1951** F. SCHULZ *Classical Roman Law* IV. i. 361 Wild animals (game, fishes, birds) were *res nullius* as long as they enjoyed their natural freedom. **1977** *Times Lit. Suppl.* 28 Jan. 110/2 To the South African government, South West Africa had fallen into a state of *res nullius,* and sovereignty was acquired by virtue of her occupation.

res[2] (rez). Abbrev. of RESIDENCE *sb.*[1]

1882 W. WHITMAN *Daybks. & Notebks.* (1978) II. 288 Sam Long 614 Sansom St—res: 3210 Race. **1972** *Guardian* 17 Feb. 11/1 Her own little bijou res in Chelsea. **1972** J. GORES *Dead Skip* x. 68 I've got a res add on Hemovich 5-0-7 Nevada Street.

resaddle, *v.* (Earlier example.)

1856 V. LUSH *Jrnl.* 17 Jan. (1971) 174 Giving them strict injunctions to take care of Rollo I left them to resaddle.

re·sail, *sb.* [f. the vb.] A race sailed again.

1947 *Sun* (Baltimore) 8 Sept. 14/6 In the resail, sailed Saturday, the breeze barely let the racers finish within the time limit. **1970** *Cape Times* 28 Oct. 25/8 Experience has shown that resails of cancelled races are not always successful.

resale. Add: Also with pronunc. (rī·sēⁱl).

2. *attrib.* **a. resale price,** the price at which a commodity is sold again; **resale price maintenance,** the determination by a manufacturer of a minimum price at which his goods may be sold to the consumer or ultimate user.

1919 C. T. MURCHISON *Resale Price Maintenance* x. 159 The rights of a patentee, by conditions of sale, to control the use of his article even after it has passed from him and is in the hands of the vendee, is..unqualifiedly upheld and the *dicta* of the Court are certainly not hostile to the idea of resale price maintenance. **1929** *Congress. Rec.* LXX. 2431 A communication from the chairman of the Federal Trade Commission, transmitting a report of that commission on Resale Price Maintenance. **1936** *Publishers' Weekly* 12 Dec. 2298/2 Compare report of the Federal Trade Commission on resale price maintenance, 70th Cong. 2d Sess. H. Doc. No. 546. **1940** *Economist* 14 Sept. 332/1 Most newspapers were generally in favour of resale-price agreements with boycotting clauses. **1945** *Economica* XII. 228 The trading stamp is primarily the product of resale price maintenance. **1967** *Listener* 27 July 104/3 Price-cutting of chocolate and sweets begins following abolition of resale price maintenance. **1973** *Guardian* 1 June 12/1 Mr Heath..made his reputation at the Board of Trade partly on the abolition of resale price maintenance.

b. In sense 'second-hand'.

1960 *Farmer & Stockbreeder* 29 Mar. (Suppl.) 13/2 Every one of your surplus jute sacks has a good re-sale value. **1967** *Boston Sunday Herald* 26 Mar. I. 38/8 The offices opposite Fisherman's Beach, Swampscott, will specialize in both new and resale homes. **1970** *Globe & Mail* (Toronto) 26 Sept. B2/3 The supply of money is good for conventional mortgages on resale houses. **1975** M. BRADBURY *History Man* iii. 40 It's a very sound residential area.., you'd keep your resale value. **1977** *New Yorker* 24 Oct. 39/2 I'm conducting here a gents' resale business. *Ibid.* 40/3 You were in a gentlemen's resale shop.

resam (resæ·m). [Malay.] A Malaysian tropical fern, *Gleichenia linearis,* which has creeping rhizomes and leathery pinnate leaves. Also *attrib.*

1902 H. N. RIDLEY *Malay Plant Names* 219 Resam. *Gleichenia linearis..* A common fern. **1939** J. D. GIMLETTE *Dict. Malayan Med.* 200/1 *Rĕsam* leaves are used by Malays in making internal and external medicines for fever. **1964** M. E. D. POORE in Wang Gungwu *Malaysia* I. ii. 51 If the frequency of cultivation increases, the land deteriorates seriously..and forest is replaced by unproductive lallang.. or resam (*Gleichenia* spp.).

resanctifica·tion. [RE- 5 a.] A second or further sanctification.

1897 'MARK TWAIN' *Following Equator* xlix. 473 The Fort was built three centuries ago by a Mohammedan Emperor—a resanctification of the place in the interest of *that* religion.

resaw (rī·sǭ), *sb.* [f. RE- 5 a + SAW *sb.*[1] See also RESAWING *vbl. sb.*] **a.** A machine used for the further cutting of sawn wood. **b.** Wood cut by such a machine. Also *attrib.*

1915 *Saw in History* (Henry Disston & Sons) iii. 36 Boards and thin Cants, or Planks, made by the log saw are run through the Resaws and are manufactured into two or more thin boards. **1958** R. H. HORDERN *Woodworking Machinist* I. i. 7 The band mill to achieve the preliminary breaking-down and squaring, and the band or circular resaw to carry out the final resawing. **1971** *Timber Trades Jrnl.* 21 Aug. 38/1 The first band resaw machine to be installed in the district is a Stenner type VHM 36in. *Ibid.* 11 Sept. 43/1 The new production line was so successful that the additional machines were installed. These are a VHS slab resaw followed by an EDS double edger. **1972** J. MINIFIE *Homesteader* viii. 63 Re-saw is a half-inch board with little to recommend it but ductility and ease of handling.

resche·dule, *v.* [RE- 5 a.] *trans.* To replan in accordance with a different timetable; to change the time of (a planned event or activity); *spec.* to arrange a new scheme of repayments of (an international debt).

1966 A. BATTERSBY *Math. in Managem.* viii. 198 It can be ..used to prepare an amended input for re-scheduling the product launch. **1968** *Economist* 17 Feb. 40/1 Requests to reschedule the country's debts for just one more year. **1970** *Daily Tel.* 14 Apr. 5/6 Fords will try to avoid lay-offs by re-scheduling production. **1973** *Times* 14 Dec. 4/5 Programmes will have to be rescheduled, and both ITV and BBC were working on that yesterday. **1977** P. WAY *Super-Celeste* 18 We may be rescheduling the flight. **1978** *N.Y. Times* 30 Mar. A3/3 The United States was prepared to.. reschedule outstanding loans to developing countries. **1980** *Daily Tel.* 3 Sept. 19 The task of rescheduling the Brazilian debt will present international banks with their biggest challenge yet.

Hence **resche·duled** *ppl. a.*, **resche·duling** *vbl. sb.*

1968 S. E. VARNER *Rescheduled School Year* 6 One plan for a rescheduled school year—the all-year school or rotating four-quarter plan—has been discussed. **1973** 'D. JORDAN' *Nile Green* iv. 23 There's this debt rescheduling problem still unsolved... But..we could talk with the [World] Bank and do a joint deal. **1976** P. R. WHITE *Planning for Public Transport* vii. 145 By slight rescheduling of existing runs, a fairly fast direct journey can be provided from the larger village(s)..into the market town.

rescission. 2. (Later examples.)

1931 *Daily Express* 16 Oct. 14/6 Rumours regarding bond interest, caused a sharp rise..in the Four per Cent. Rescission issues. **1964** *Mod. Law Rev.* XXVIII. III. 269 Keeping the contract alive for as long as the employers would tolerate the breach without exercising their right of rescission. **1976** *Evening News* (Newburgh, N.Y.) 12 Sept. 12A/1 The rescission of funds in no way affects the proposed federal prison.

resco·re, *v. Mus.* [RE- 5 a.] *trans.* To score (a piece of music) again. Hence **resco·red** *ppl. a.*; **resco·ring** *vbl. sb.*, the action or an instance of scoring again; a rescored version.

1890 *Daily News* 16 Aug. 5/4 Bizet..once undertook the task of re-scoring Bellini's 'Norma'. *Ibid.* He had thrown the re-scored MS. into the fire. **1926** WHITEMAN & MCBRIDE *Jazz* xi. 227 Most of the rehearsing and discussing and rescoring was done in consultations outside. **1955** G. ABRAHAM in H. Van Thal *Fanfare for E. Newman* 22 Small details and large patches of drastic rescoring alike show Wagner's finer mastery of the orchestra in the 1860s. **1962** *Times* 8 Oct. 16/5 Sir Malcolm Sargent has rescored the music. **1976** *New Yorker* 9 May 129/1 Whether they were played in Arne's own orchestration or in the rescoring by Charles Edward Horn..was not stated. **1981** P. DICKINSON *Seventh Raven* iv. 47 He met this guitarist and rescored the whole bloody thing.

re-scree·n, *v.* [RE- 5 a.] *trans.* To screen again. So **re-scree·ning** *vbl. sb.*

1950 *Hansard Commons* 7 Nov. 770 In view of the replies made yesterday by colleagues of the right hon. Gentleman that the main screening took place in 1943, when circumstances were very different, would he look into the question of whether re-screening, now that circumstances have changed, should be instituted? **1957** MANVELL & HUNTLEY *Film Music* iii. 97 Creating the score by screening and re-screening each sequence where music is required. **1967** E. CHAMBERS *Photolitho-Offset* xi. 160 These Canon optical tone filters..eliminate moiré by diffusing the screen pattern through interference effects during rescreening. **1967** KARCH & BUBER *Offset Processes* ii. 12 Letterpress printed halftones (pictures) in books can often be 'picked up' as line shots, or rescreened for printing by the offset-lithographic process. **1979** *Listener* 29 Nov. 739/1 The Mudd documentary, which CBS will not re-screen, will gradually recede in memory.

rescuable, *a.* Delete *rare* and add later examples. Hence **rescuabi·lity.**

1975 *Sci. Amer.* Dec. 34/2 The transition from Stage I (rescuable) to Stage II (killed) is a first-order, or 'one hit', reaction, whose rate is directly proportional to the amount of colicin. **1976** *Listener* 3 June 693/1 Men had taken the most obvious solace in alcohol, about the only rescuable commodity from many of the ruins. **1979** *Nature* 22 Nov. 382/2 The lack of rescuability of focus-forming activity from transformants caused by MSV DNA fragments remains to be resolved.

rescue, *sb.* Add: **1. b.** *Bridge.* = *rescue bid* in sense 3 c below.

1917 [see *OVERBID *v.* 2 c]. **1932** H. PHILLIPS *One Hundred Contract Bridge Hands* 114 West's double is for 'business'... North does not attempt a 'rescue'.

3. a. *rescue bell, boat, capsule, car, company, co-ordinator, cradle, dinghy, man, mission, operation, party* (further example), *service, ship, squad, station, team, tube, work.*

1939 *Sun* (Baltimore) 26 May 8/6 The rescue bell was plunged down to be attached to one of the aft hatches. **1960** W. O. SHELFORD *Subsunk* vii. 80 *Squalus* sank in an area where there were no appreciable tides to delay the divers or the functioning of the rescue bell. **1941** *Sun* (Baltimore) 12 Aug. 17/2 They had in storage enough Dorchester county white oak to construct keels and frames for all the rescue boats. **1978** *Lochaber News* 31 Mar. 4/6 At the same time the rescue boat from Dochgorroch sped to the scene. **1977** *Sunday Times* 24 Apr. 1/5 We just dropped everything we had in our hands and ran to the rescue capsules, which were closed and lowered down to the sea. **1911** *Chambers's Jrnl.* Nov. 747/2 Half-a-dozen rescue-cars, fitted with life-saving apparatus and carrying a crew of trained men..will be allocated to certain districts. **1975** *Irish Times* 30 May 14/8 Foir Teoranta, the State rescue company, has exercised its right to appoint its nominee. **1973** G. Moffat *Lady with Cool Eye* vi. 70 As rescue co-ordinator..shouldn't you know who's operating in your area? **1977** *N.Z. Herald* 5 Jan. 1-1/1 The fishermen fastened the rope to a bollard and fitted a rescue cradle to run along the rope to the comparative safety of the rocks. **1972** *Police Rev.* 10 Nov. 1444/1 Fluorescent pigments..put to good practical effect in painting rescue dinghies. **1921** *Dict. Occup. Terms* (1927) § 47 *Rescue man*, a member of colliery rescue team, called upon in cases of fire, explosions, etc., in mine to go underground in an attempt to rescue workers. **1940** *New Statesman* 9 Nov. 465/1 The rescue men had blue overalls and white steel helmets. **1977** *R.A.F. News* 11–24 May 2/5 Peter Pitcher rang up his 200th rescue mission when he joined in a flight to pick up three boys from..a mudbank in the Mersey. **1960** *Council Brit. Archaeol. Rep.* x. 41 While excavations as such are excluded from this *Report* it is difficult to omit all reference to the rescue-operations which must follow when attempts to preserve a site have failed. **1975** *Country Life* 3 Apr. 825/1 [Augustus] John himself despised the idea of a 'rescue operation', as he called it, where his reputation was concerned. **1937** *Ann. Reg. 1936* 17 At the same time local authorities were advised to organise rescue parties of six or eight men each for action after air attack. **1976** *Northumberland Gaz.* 26 Nov., Bill Hardcastle opened the rescue service's first harbour fete. **1941** *Sun* (Baltimore) 12 Aug. 17/2 Officials of the Cambridge Shipbuilders, Inc., today pushed plans for eight more rescue ships to be built for the quartermaster. **1944** M. Horton *Let.* 1 Mar. in Schofield & Martyn *Rescue Ships* (1968) viii. 136 The introduction and work of Rescue Ships during phases of the Battle of the Atlantic when the U-boats were on the offensive did a tremendous lot towards maintaining the high morale of the Merchant Navy. **1954** 'M. Cost' *Invitation from Minerva* 176 He headed the Rescue Squad, saw the German shepherd dogs drawn up, the blazing torches. **1973** *N.Y. Law Jrnl.* 2 Aug. 13/5 The defendant.. was taken to the hospital. This was done by a rescue squad. **1979** *Arizona Daily Star* 1 Apr. (Advt. Section) 1/1 Memorials may be made to the Gila County Sheriff's Dept. Rescue Squad. **1908** *Westm. Gaz.* 2 Apr. 7/2 A well-equipped rescue-station and experimental gallery, established by the leading Lancashire coalowners, was opened to-day. **1976** *Cumberland News* 3 Dec. 11/6 Rescue station, Derwentwater Boat Club, Portinscale, Peter Fry Rescue Trust. **1956** M. Stewart *Wildfire at Midnight* ix. 79 The night had been black and wild... Bill Persimmon had telephoned for the local rescue team. **1973** *Guardian* 13 Apr. 24/5 At 11.29, the rescue teams were alerted. **1980** G. Greene *Dr. Fischer* xiii. 88 By the time I reached the ski-lift the rescue team was already on the way up. **1977** *N.Z. Herald* 5 Jan. 1-3/2 The two lifesavers on the helicopter, Mr. M. Lawson and Mr. T. Radonich, jumped into the water with a rescue tube, which was used to fly Mr. Stewart back home. **1946** R. J. C. Atkinson *Field Archaeol.* ii. 67 On rescue-work sites, where the archaeological material is in any case eventually to be destroyed, the question of restoration does not arise. **1962** D. Lessing *Golden Notebk.* iii. 402 The pleasure of recognition, of a bit of rescue-work, so to speak, rescuing the formless into form.

b. *rescue home* (earlier and later examples), *shelter, society, work* (earlier and later examples), *worker* (later example).

1890 W. Booth *In Darkest England* i. vi. 51 The records of our Rescue Homes abound with life-stories..which prove..the existence of numbers of innocent victims. **1927** E. C. Trenholme *Rescue Work* iii. 21 It was through this venture failing that one of them came into a rescue home. **1981** C. Scott *Heavenly Witch* ix. 136 At Nîmes the first rescue home was opened, the start of a chain of rescue homes. **1889** L. Ridding *Woman's League* 12 An Industrial Training Home, Temperance Work, a Rescue Shelter..these various efforts are inspired by the starting of the League. **1869** (*title*) Licensing prostitution; reprinted (with permission) from the Report for 1869 of the Rescue Society, London. **1981** F. K. Prochaska *Women & Philanthropy* vi. 188 The dramatic growth in rescue societies and Magdalene homes. **1884** H. Brown *Is it Nothing to You?* iv. 87 The objects of this society are to promote—(1) Purity among men. (2) A chivalrous respect for womanhood. (3) The preservation of the young from contamination. (4) Rescue work. **1911** G. B. Shaw *Doctor's Dilemma* p. lxxvi, The morbid interest in misery and vice which turns some others to philanthropy and 'rescue work'. **1977** Rowbotham & Weeks *Socialism & New Life* 13 This tendency was reinforced by rescue work and the moral shock with which the middle-class reformers encountered, amidst poverty and overcrowding, the complexities and ambiguities of working-class family patterns. **1930** G. B. Shaw *Wks.* VII. 180 The only logical conclusion apparent is that the White Slave traffickers are in complete control of our picture theatres, and can close them to our Rescue workers as effectively as they can reserve them for advertisements of their own trade.

c. Special Combs., as **rescue archæology,** emergency excavation of archæological sites in the face of projected building or road development; hence **rescue archæologist**; similarly *rescue dig, excavation*; **rescue bid** *Bridge*, a bid made to rescue one's partner from what seems a difficult position, as when his or her bid has been doubled; **rescue breathing,** mouth-to-mouth resuscitation; **rescue circle** *Spiritualism* (see quot. 1961); **rescue mission** *U.S.*, a mission established to help those in need of moral or spiritual rehabilitation; **rescue opera,** an opera, often based on real events, in which the hero or heroine is rescued after great tribulations.

1969 I. N. Hume *Historical Archaeol.* ii. 43 There are no rules that exist specifically to guide rescue archaeologists. **1972** *Rescue News* Autumn 1/1 For some years rescue archaeologists have been worried that the finds from the increasing number of emergency excavations are not receiving proper treatment. [**1966** *Council Brit. Archaeol. Rep.* xvi. 51 The 'rescue' aspect of archaeology has nowadays become particularly important.] **1969** I. N. Hume *Historical Archaeol.* ii. 43 The only recourse is to resort to what is euphemistically known as *rescue archaeology*... Rescue archaeology occurs when time has almost run out. **1978** *Sci. Amer.* Jan. 111 An international campaign of rescue archæology at the ruined city. **1913** F. Irwin *Auction High Lights* 261 The forcing-bids, the doubles and redoubles, the 'rescue'-bids had just this result, that A's hand brought him 604 instead of 299. **1973** *Times* 10 Nov. 10/5 He had been invited to partner a beginner who had no suspicion of the dangers..from uninvited rescue bids. **1961** *Sunday Times* 17 Sept. 4/5 Scandinavian countries have a long lead on Britain in training in 'rescue breathing'. **1968** W. Warwick *Surfriding in N.Z.* 18/2 Attempt rescue breathing as soon as you can reach the victim's face. **1921** A. Conan Doyle *Wanderings of Spiritualist* iv. 93 He has run a rescue circle for the instruction of the lower spirits who are so material that they can be reached more easily by humanity than by the higher angels. **1961** R. Crookall *Supreme Adventure* iii. i. 105 At 'Rescue Circles' where 'earthbound' men (who have shed the Physical Body without being aware of the fact, and whose Soul Body is still enveiled by the vehicle of vitality) are made to realise their condition—that they have 'died'. **1973** *Light* Spring 10 Visitors, or clients, of a rescue circle are more demanding. **1962** *Daily Tel.* 9 July 10/2 'Rescue digs' of this kind have now become one of the principal antiquarian activities of the Ministry of Works. **1957** G. Clark *Archaeol. & Society* (ed. 3) ii. 57 Rescue-excavations, organized in Britain by the Ministry of Works, when known ancient monuments had to be flattened. **1902** S. H. Hadley *Down in Water St.* ii. 39 The first Rescue Mission in the world..was started by Jerry McAuley, October 8, 1872, at 316 Water Street, New York. **1912** P. I. Roberts *Dry Dock of Thousand Wrecks* vi. 93 He has displayed all along the earmarks of a rescue mission worker. **1972** *National Observer* (U.S.) 27 May 7/5 The camp's food.. was below rescue-mission fare. **1943** A. Loewenberg *Ann. Opera 1597–1940* 280 Dalayrac: Léhéman ou La Tour de Newstadt... More successful in Germany where it was one of the favourite 'rescue operas' of that period. **1959** *Listener* 25 June 1128/2 *Les deux Journées* (1800) and *Fidelio* (first version 1805) have a great many features in common: their theme ('rescue opera'), its source in an actual event.

rescue, *v.* Add: **1.** (Later examples.)

1934 G. B. Shaw *Too True to be Good* iii. 95 You were sent out here to rescue my daughter from these dreadful brigands. **1969** I. & P. Opie *Children's Games* iv. 163 Here the seeker is at almost greater disadvantage than in 'Buzz Off', for a hider can rescue a prisoner merely by getting in sight of the den.

3. *spec.* in *Bridge*. Also *absol.*

1921 F. Irwin *Compl. Auction Player* x. 133 It is seldom wise to attempt to 'rescue' your partner from a double. **1958** *Listener* 13 Nov. 805/3 In a match-pointed pairs contest I might consider rescuing to Two Clubs.

rescuee (reskiū,ī·) [f. Rescue *v.* + -ee[1].] One who is rescued.

1950 O. Nash *Family Reunion* (1951) i. 32 In case of fire, no hero he; Merely a humble rescuee. **1954** I. Murdoch *Under Net* xii. 171 The simultaneous sight of so many eligible rescuees was too much for him. **1979** C. Kilian *Icequake* v. 75, I don't feel much like a rescuer just now. Much rather be a rescuee.

rescuing, *vbl. sb.* (Later example.)

1867 A. J. E. Wilson *St. Elmo* viii. 101 If it be Thy will, make her the instrument of rescuing.

research, *sb.*[1] Add: Also with pronunc. (rī·sɜ̄ɹtʃ). **5.** *attrib.* and *Comb.*, as *research assistant, building, bureau, council, degree, department, doctorate, fellow, fellowship, grant, lab, laboratory, library, officer, personnel, post, programme, project, room, scholarship, station, student, unit, vessel, work, worker*; *research-minded* adj.; **research and development,** in an industrial context, work directed on a large scale towards the innovation, introduction, and improvement of products and processes; freq. as *attrib. phr.*; abbrev. *R and D* s.v. *R II. 2 a.

1923 *Industr. & Engin. Chem.* (News ed.) 20 Jan. 10/1 (Advt.), Professorship or assistant professorship in first class college or university desired by chemist, Ph.D., with seven years' experience in university teaching and six years' practical experience in research and development work. **1935** *Chem. & Engin. News* 10 Jan. 15/1 Arthur R. Hitch has resigned from the Ethyl Gasoline Corp. to accept the position of director of research and development with the Nelio-Resin Corp. and the Southern Pine Chemical Co., Jacksonville, Fla. **1946** *Happy Landings* July (verso front cover), It is the latter type of accidents..with which the research and development branches of M.S.A.P. is [*sic*] primarily concerned. **1968** J. Sangster *Touchfeather* xv. 182 Research and development is a notoriously difficult thing to budget for. **1979** *Arizona Daily Star* 5 Aug. B 4/5 The research-and-development costs of a new product, when funded by government, artificially reduce the price of the product. **1914** *Leeds Univ. Tenth Rep., 1912–13* 41 Two Research Assistants in Botany. **1977** D. MacKenzie *Raven & Kamikaze* xi. 128 I've been a senior research assistant for three and a half years. **1934** H. G. Wells *Exper. Autobiogr.* ix. 815 It is the least grandiose and most practicable group of research buildings in the world. **1925** *Scribner's Mag.* Oct. 404/1 The trade-union congress decided to open an 'official' research bureau of its own. **1934** *Amer. Speech* IX. 113/1 *Traffic counts* are made by men from the *research bureau* of a *tourist organization*. **1920** *Brit. Med. Jrnl.* 27 Mar. 447/2 The Committee will come to life again as the Medical Research Council and will act under the direction of a Committee of the Privy Council. **1971** *Nature* 5 Mar. 23/1 Rather more than £100 million are spent through the research councils. **1903** *Encycl. Brit.* XXXV. 788/1 Research degrees. **1960** Eells & Haswell *Academic Degrees* ii. 27 Second in importance as a research degree and much more recent is the Doctor of Education. **1920** M. Beer *Hist. Brit. Socialism* II. xiv. 290 The Fabians have long felt the need for a special research department. **1964** Research department [see *experiment station* s.v. *experiment *sb.* 7]. **1902** *Encycl. Brit.* XXXI. 397/1 The B.Lit. and B.Sc. (founded in 1895, and completed in 1900 by the institution of research doctorates), have attracted graduates from..other countries. **1899** Research fellow [see *fellow *sb.* 7 a]. **1966** *Rep. Comm. Inquiry Univ. Oxf.* II. 387 There are two broad classes of research fellow in the colleges. **1921** *Leeds Univ. Sixteenth Rep., 1919–20* 76 Mr. T. Hanby resigned the Gas Research Fellowship. **1946** [see *grant-in-aid]. **1971** *Daily Tel.* 16 June 10/3 An IBM Research Fellowship has been awarded at Oxford University to Mr. M. R. Topp. **1930** *Univ. Sheffield Ann. Rep., 1929–30* 37 Mrs. May Mellanby..has been appointed a member of the Research Grants' Committee. **1940** H. G. Wells *Babes in Darkling Wood* ii. ii. 150 His income, derived from research grants, scientific writing, a small parcel of investments and gifts from his brother, was precarious. **1949** *Spectator* 18 Nov. 665/1 What the subject really needs..is field-workers and a research grant. **1980** M. Booth *Bad Track* iv. 77 Thank God for research grants. **1973** D. Francis *Slay Ride* xiii. 162 It's a research lab job. **1914** *Leeds Univ. Tenth Rep., 1912–13* 43 A considerable sum of money was raised by public subscription for the establishment of an International Research Laboratory. **1922** *Sci. Amer.* Aug. 100 Long before so-called industrial research laboratories were established in any country, there existed a very thorough international cooperation in scientific research. **1957** C. Smith *Case of Torches* xi. 130 How often do you send reports to the Research Laboratories? **1962** Y. Malkiel in Householder & Saporta *Probl. Lexicogr.* 3 Numerous research-library catalogues make it a point to distinguish between mono-, bi-, tri-lingual and polyglot dictionaries. **1978** *Amer. N. & Q.* XVI. 141/1 During the 1950s a familiar sight at the loading dock of research libraries was the van of Hacker Art Books. **1959** *Times* 27 Apr. (Rubber Industry Suppl.) p. xii/7 Research-minded graduates with high academic qualifications..have excellent opportunities with some of the larger companies. **1971** Halsey & Trow *Brit. Academics* xii. 291 There are more research-minded lecturers than senior lecturers. **1914** *Oxf. Univ. Calendar 1915* 74 Research Officer in Diseases of Trees. **1972** *Classification of Occupations* (Dept. Employment) II. 47/2 Other titles include Research officer (Foreign and Commonwealth office). **1939** R. V. Jones *Most Secret War* (1978) ix. 73 The only method of dealing with the former is direct espionage, or the observation of indiscretions by research personnel concerned. **1972** *Lebende Sprachen* XVII. 47/1 *Research personnel*, Forschungspersonal. **1966** *Rep. Comm. Inquiry Univ. Oxf.* II. 252 Included as full-time are all those with a university and/or college teaching or research post. **1950** *N.Z. Jrnl. Agric.* June 514 (*caption*) The Rukuhia Soil Research Station (Hamilton)..carries out a research programme in soil physics. **1958** *Bull. Amer. Assoc. Petroleum Geologists* XLII. 701 Some years ago the Field Research Laboratory of the Magnolia Petroleum Company began a Recent sediments research program in the Gulf of Mexico. **1977** *Sci. Amer.* Dec. 15/1 He now..carries on a research program in the behavioral ecology of ants. **1949** *Radio Times* 15 July 23/2 Mrs. Proudfoot is engaged on a research project for Nuffield College. **1977** *Canad. Jrnl. Linguistics 1976* XXI. 196 Throughout a good part of his career he has been associated, directly or indirectly, with research projects concerned with the description of corpora of recorded language. **1922** *Leeds Univ. Seventeenth Rep., 1920–21* 75 Honour Students now have the advantage of a separate laboratory, one of the old Research Rooms having been specially equipped for the purpose. **1933** [see *carrel(l b]. **1949** J. Routh in *Granta* (Christmas ed.) 43/2 Then he takes them to the research room where the research workers take down their case histories. **1907** G. B. Shaw *Let.* 21 Mar. (1972) II. 675 Can't you get a research scholarship, and travel for a year or so on that? **1937** *Granta* 3 Feb. 218/2 On graduating he was awarded the Earl of Derby Research Scholarship in History. **1917** *Rep. Fuel Research Board* 10 The Research Station, as planned, will be capable of any extensions which will be required for future researches. **1974** 'E. Ferrars' *Hanged Man's House* v. 42 A lot of scientists in a research station. **1924** *Univ. Sheffield Ann. Rep., 1923–24* 36 There were 8 Post-Graduate Research Students in the Session 1923–24. **1934** H. G. Wells *Exper. Autobiogr.* II. ix. 815 Five hundred..research students from abroad were always to be working there. **1976** R. Barnard *Little Local Murder* x. 129 Why don't you try a research student? **1937** *Whitaker's Almanack* 344/1 Clinical Research Units. **1941** C. Morgan *Empty Room* i. 5 Duckboards stretched across..muddy gravel from the small square Lodge, where, he presumed, Research Unit Seven had their living quarters. *a* **1974** R. Crossman *Diaries* (1976) II. 192 To try to get them a medical school for Warwick University and a motor research unit. **1977** *Guardian* 27 Apr. 6/2 Two research vessels from the Institute of Marine Research at Bergen headed for the area yesterday. **1903** J. B. Tomlinson (*title*) Research work on popular and general subjects. **1935** *Burlington Mag.* Aug. 90/2 Most of the research-work..has already been undertaken. **1950** *Univ. Nottingham Ann. Rep.* 12 The staffing of departments needs to be reviewed in the light of the amount and kind of research required and of the research work in progress. **1917** *Jrnl. Soc. Automotive Engineers* Oct. 262/1 He was an experimental rather than an analytical research worker. **1950** *Univ. Nottingham Ann. Rep.* 12 In many departments the work is seriously hampered simply by lack of space for research workers. **1969** I. & P. Opie *Children's Games* p. vi, The research-worker..blessed with an unending flow of information can be in as embarrassing a position as he whose sources are limited.

research, *v.*[1] Add: Also with pronunc. (rĭ·sɔ̄ːɹtʃ). **1. a.** Delete '*rare* or *Obs.*' and add: Also, to engage in research upon (a subject, a person, etc.).

1942 R. CHANDLER *High Window* (1943) xxxiii. 219 Some I was told, some I researched, some I guessed. **1959** *Encounter* Dec. 32/2 I'll author an article about it after I've researched the matter further. **1965** *New Statesman* 23 Apr. 642/1 Bryan Magee must have worn cosy blinkers when he researched lesbianism for his TV programme. **1971** D. POTTER *Brit. Eliz. Stamps* xv. 180 Collect, study and research your stamps. **1978** S. SHELDON *Bloodline* xiv. 175 She researched the guests, found out their likes and dislikes, what they ate and drank, and what type of entertainment they enjoyed. **1980** *Times* 1 Oct. 1/4 Union leaders..said they wanted time to 'research' the company's case before the next meeting.

b. (Earlier and later examples.) Also const. *in(to), on.*

1781 H. WALPOLE *Let.* 27 Jan. (1858) VII. 505, I know, as Gray would have said, how little I have *researched*, and what slender pretensions are mine. **1935** D. L. SAYERS *Gaudy Night* i. 23, I believe she's researching on the Bacon family. **1958** *Times Lit. Suppl.* 14 Nov. 653/2 The *Savage Affair* is about one Michael Savage..researching into Commonwealth Drama. **1975** *Nature* 6 Nov. 27/3 He is a biochemist who has researched in many areas. **1977** *Navy News* July 12/3 Former lieutenant-commander, John Winton has researched into sea ballads, ships' logs, and sailors' personal writings and reminiscences to produce the latest of his works. **1977** K. O'HARA *Ghost of T. Penry* xv. 142 If you'd ever learn to research properly..you'd know you're always civil.

c. *trans.* To engage upon research for (a book or the like).

1965 *Listener* 4 Mar. 343/3 The book has been thoroughly and conscientiously 'researched', as the Americans say. **1973** *Which?* Dec. 367/1 This continued to research monthly features for sale to the mass-circulation *Daily Mirror.* **1975** *Publishers Weekly* 2 June 49/3 Barbara Villet, ex-*Life* reporter, researched her book in five big New York hospitals.

researchable (rĭsɔ̄·ɹtʃăb'l), *a.* [f. RESEARCH *v.*[1] + -ABLE.] Worthy of being researched; suitable for methodical investigation.

1967 L. VON BERTALANFFY *Robots, Men & Minds* II. 86 There is a wealth of researchable and fascinating problems which..will open new perspectives and bring evolution into the framework of organismic and systems thinking. **1977** A. GIDDENS *Stud. in Social & Polit. Theory* iv. 169 Ordinary language is not therefore just a topic that can be made available for analysis, but is a resource that every sociological or anthropological observer must use to gain access to his 'researchable subject-matter'.

researched, *ppl. a.* Restrict † (*obs.*) to sense in Dict. and add: **2.** That has been subjected to research; that is the result of research.

1956 C. W. MILLS *Power Elite* ii. 33 The old southern aristocracy, in fictional image and in researched fact, is indeed often in a sorry state of decline. **1966** *New Society* 31 Mar. 25/3 This is a thorough, well researched, and authorised biography. **1978** *Jrnl. R. Soc. Arts* CXXVI. 737/2 The project teachers were involved in researched teaching about race relations. That is to say, the majority were either tape-recording their work or teaching with observation by colleagues.

researching, *ppl. a.* (Later examples.)

1930 J. B. PRIESTLEY *Angel Pavement* viii. 393 He wants to come along early next week and bring his researching friend Jiggs or Hoggs or something. **1981** J. SUTHERLAND *Bestsellers* xiii. 145 The most respected researching novelist in Britain is probably Len Deighton.

researchist (rĭsɔ̄·ɹtʃist). [f. RESEARCH *v.*[1] + -IST.] = RESEARCHER.

1923 *Chambers's Jrnl.* Feb. 95/1 In an age when the superstitious seek eagerly for a sign..House of Clays would have disappointed a psychical researchist. **1961** D. ANGUS *Descent of Venus* v. 106 He claims to be a researchist in human relationships.

‖ **réseau** (rezo). Also † 6 *Sc.* **rasour; reseau.** Pl. **-x.** [Fr., = net, web, etc.] **1. a.** A plain net ground used in lace-making.

1578 [in Dict. s.v. RASOUR]. **1578** in F. B. Palliser *Hist. Lace* (1865) xxxiii. 395 Fyve litell vaills of wovin rasour of threde. **1865** F. B. PALLISER *Ibid.* vii. 105 There were two kinds of ground used in Brussels lace, the bride and the réseau. **1911** *Encycl. Brit.* XVI. 41/2 To the period from 1620 to 1670 belongs the development of long continuous scroll patterns with *réseaux* and *brides.* **1953** M. POWYS *Lace & Lace-Making* v. 40 The laces of Louis XVI have a lighter design, finally becoming little more than a border to the Réseau or net grounds on which are sprinkled small sprays. **1959** *Chambers's Encycl.* VIII. 294/1 Later, in the 18th century, Milan lace adopted the *réseaux* made popular in northern Europe. **1975** *Oxf. Compan. Decorative Arts* 524/1 Sometimes the *réseau* was bobbin-made and the threads attached to the open edges of the *toilé*, following the pattern.

b. With qualifying adjective or phrase, as *réseau à l'aiguille* (alegwiy) [Fr. *aiguille*, needle], hand-made net ground; *réseau ordinaire* (ǫɹdinēᵊɹ) [Fr., ordinary], standard machine-made net ground; *réseau rosacé* (rozase) [Fr., rosaceous] a mesh ground with a flower pattern.

1865 F. B. PALLISER *Hist. Lace* vii. 106 Since machine-made net has come into use the 'réseau à l'aiguille' is rarely made, save for royal trousseaux. *Ibid.*, Machinery has now added a third [way of making the réseau], the tulle or Brussels net, 'réseau ordinaire', made of Scotch thread. **1900** E. JACKSON *Hist. Hand-Made Lace* 218 *Réseau Rosacé*, the name given to the réseau ground in Argentan lace. **1911** *Encycl. Brit.* XVI. 41/2 Grounds composed entirely of varieties of *modes* as in the case of the *réseau rosacé*..were sometimes made then [*sc.* about 1700 to 1760]. **1953** M. POWYS *Lace & Lace-Making* iv. 14 The ground is the Réseau Ordinaire and the central filling the Mignon.

2. A network or grid, esp. one superimposed as a reference marking on photographs in astronomy, surveying, etc.

1902 *Nature* 5 June 140/1 The réseau is hinged in front of the plate, its correct register being determined by geometrical contacts. **1906** *Athenæum* 27 Jan. 111/1 Prof. Turner showed specimens of photographic reproductions of *réseaux* for stellar photography made by M. H. Bourget. **1940** C. A. HART *Air Photogr. applied to Surveying* ix. 245 Extreme accuracy of recording on a stereoscopic instrument becomes of value only when there is provided a stable basis of measurement, such as a reseau, a device commonly used in astronomical measurements from photographs. **1963** W. K. KILFORD *Elem. Air Survey* i. 19 A squared réseau is also sometimes engraved on the plate. This will make apparent any distortions of the negative due to non-flatness in the focal plane. **1976** J. B. GARNER et al. *Surveying* xiii. 228 The Principal Point is engraved on this glass, as are a number of small crosses, conventionally at 10mm centres in either direction, all of which are imaged at every exposure. These crosses form a reseau grid and enable the user to determine any subsequent distortion of the film to considerable accuracy.

3. A spy or intelligence network, esp. in the French resistance movement.

1960 G. MARTELLI *Agent Extraordinary* v. 82 This arrangement..enabled him to devote more time..to the running of the *réseau.* **1966** M. R. D. FOOT *SOE in France* ix. 258 Various intelligence réseaux in Paris. **1973** L. SNELLING *Heresy* II. i. 62 These agents made no connection between Graham and the escape *réseau.* **1974** T. ALLBEURY *Snowball* vii. 37 Paul Loussier had been an active member of one of the SOE *réseaux* in Paris when the Resistance was only measured in hundreds.

resect, *v.* Add: **2.** (Further examples.)

1924 R. HOWARD *Surg. Emergencies* iv. 71 The portion of the gut to be resected is brought well out of the wound. **1976** *Nature* 25 Mar. 351/1 Two weeks after the initial operation the correct nerve to the anconeus muscle was crushed, or cut and resected.

3. *Surveying.* To map by resection. **resected** *ppl. a.* (further example).

1888 W. H. RICHARDS *Textbk. Mil. Topogr.* (ed. 2) iv. 38 Having determined stations by intersection, as described, the surveyor may, by reference to them, resect or find the point on his survey which corresponds to his position on the ground. **1913** A. R. HINKS *Maps & Survey* v. 108 Round about the intersected and resected points, the detail is sketched in by eye estimation. **1931** M. HOTINE *Surveying from Air Photographs* vi. 92 The problem is..to resect the position of the perspective centre in space.

resection. Add: **2.** (Further examples, not referring to bone.)

1881 *Amer. Jrnl. Med. Sci.* LXXXII. 263 (*heading*) Resection of about six and a half feet of the small intestine, with recovery. **1926** *Jrnl. Amer. Med. Assoc.* 20 Nov. 1728/2 Prostatic resection is applicable to a large number of cases of prostatic hypertrophy commonly subjected to prostatectomy. **1944** W. W. BABCOCK *Princ. & Pract. Surg.* xxxiii. 650 Avulsion of the entire ganglion has been supplanted by resection or division of the posterior sensory root. **1967** H. S. K. SINGHA *Pocket Surg.* viii. 131 Treatment consists in the resection of all visible tumour together with a wide margin of normal tissue. **1980** *Brit. Med. Jrnl.* 29 Mar. 882/1 Some surgeons can produce primary union of the bowel anastomosis in all but 5–10% of patients..even for anterior resection of the rectum.

3. *Surveying.* The process of determining the position and orientation of a plane table from bearings of points already mapped, prior to mapping surrounding detail in relation to it.

1888 W. H. RICHARDS *Textbk. Mil. Topogr.* (ed. 2) iv. 38 Finding the place by resection with the magnetic needle. **1923** D. CLARK *Plane & Geodetic Surveying* I. 212 Resection is usually confined to small scale work. **1976** M. GILBERT *Night of Twelfth* vii. 86 He demonstrated on the map, 'that brings you into an area roughly here. You can't do an exact resection, of course.'

resectionist (rĭse·kʃənist). *Surg.* [f. prec. + -IST.] One who carries out resection.

1934 *Jrnl. Amer. Med. Assoc.* 24 Feb. 648/1 Transurethral resection..can be done by competent resectionists in more than 95 per cent of obstructions [of the prostate]. **1972** J. P. MITCHELL *Princ. Transurethral Resection & Haemostasis* xxvii. 225 This cumbersome attachment to the normal resectoscope impedes the resectionist.

resectoscope (rĭse·ktŏskōᵘp). *Med.* [f. RESECT *v.* + -O + -SCOPE.] A surgical instrument for transurethral resection.

1926 M. STERN in *Jrnl. Amer. Med. Assoc.* 20 Nov. 1726/2 It has been possible to reduce the problem to a mere cystoscopic procedure by the evolution of a cutting current capable of operating in a water medium, and a cystoscopic instrument for its application. This instrument is provided with a small movable ring or loop of tungsten wire which, when actuated by a suitable current, is capable of removing longitudinal spaghetti-like sections of tissue... Of these instruments I have named..the latter the resectoscope. **1951** M. CAMPBELL *Clin. Pediatric Urology* i. 74 Miniature resectoscopes are now available for transurethral removal of vesical neck obstruction..uretocele or small intravesical growths. **1962** *Lancet* 28 Apr. 914/1, I must admit to a certain amount of fear of producing incontinence in using the resectoscope on the female bladder neck, and prefer to use fulguration first, even if resection is necessary later. **1974** J. D. MAYNARD in R. M. Kirk et al. *Surgery* viii. 180 Provided IVP shows some renal function, treatment [of bladder neck obstruction] consists of posterior bladder neck resection per urethra with a resectoscope.

reseda. Add: **2.** (Earlier and later examples.)

1873 *Young Englishwoman* Mar. 130/1 A costume of réséda-coloured poplinette is composed of a skirt rasterre, and a redingote tunic. *Ibid.* Apr. 182/2 A dress of réséda grosgrain silk. **1927** F. B. YOUNG *Portrait of Clare* 25 She forced herself to dwell upon the vision of the reseda shantung dress designed by Liberty. **1968** E. BRILL *Old Cotswold* v. 85 Its tall spires can sometimes be seen on the banks of newly-widened roads, the pale reseda of its leaves conspicuous among the darker greens of coarser herbage. **1977** *Western Morning News* 30 Aug. 9/2 (Advt.), 1977 BMW 528. Manual. Reseda Green. Sunroof. Tint.

re:sedimenta·tion. *Geol.* [ad. It. *risedimentazione* (C. I. Migliorini 1950, in *Atti Soc. Tosc. di Sci. nat., Mem.* A LVII. 83): see RE- 5 a.] Movement of previously deposited sediment from one location to another by marine currents. So **rese·diment** *v. trans.*; **rese·dimented** *ppl. a.*

1957 *Jrnl. Geol.* LXV. 231/1 Migliorini coined the term 'resedimented rocks' which is not entirely unambiguous but is nevertheless useful as a short way of referring to the deposits of turbidity currents. *Ibid.*, Various types of markings on the sole of the graywackes..explaining them on the basis of resedimentation by turbidity currents. **1973** *Nature* 26 Jan. 267/2 Because most coarse material resedimented from modern stable continental shelves passes down submarine canyons we interpret major occurrences of coarse resedimented material down slope of the Cambro-Ordovician shelf break as evidence of submarine canyon activity. *Ibid.* 268/1 Episodes of resedimentation occurred from soon after the inception of the miogeocline in Lower Cambrian times to the changes in sedimentary polarity..in Middle and Upper Ordovician times. **1978** [see *resuspension* s.v. *RE- 5 a].

reseed, *v.* Add: Also *absol.* (Further examples.) Hence **resee·ded** *ppl. a.*, **resee·ding** *vbl. sb.* (further examples). Also as *sb.*, an area which has been reseeded.

1940 R. G. STAPLEDON *War Food Production Advisory Bull. No. 1* 26 The field was twenty-five acres, of which fifteen were re-seeded. *Ibid.*, The re-seeded portion of the field had the best grass. *Ibid.* 27 By 1938 we considered the area..to be in a sufficiently good condition to plough and re-seed. **1945** 'G. ORWELL' *Animal Farm* viii. 72 The pasture was exhausted and needed re-seeding. **1946** *Nature* 26 Oct. 587/1 Reseeded grassland. **1960** *Farmer & Stockbreeder* 5 Jan. 94/2 During the past 20 years vast acreages of old grassland..have been ploughed and re-seeded on official advice. **1966** *Economist* 24 Sept. 1208/3 Your attack on crofting ignores the remarkable Lewis reseeding schemes. **1970** *Watsonia* VIII. 193 A large area where the *Cerastium* used to grow had been re-seeded. **1973** *Stornoway Gaz.* 2 June 4/3 Maybe you're sleeping soundly o' nights, dreaming of all your frisky lambs and ewes on the surging reseeds. **1981** *Times* 11 Feb. 8/4 The reseeding of rubber plantations in southern Thailand.

rese·gregate, *v.* [RE- 5 a.] *trans.* To segregate again. So **resegrega·tion.**

1923 *Daily Mail* 24 May 6 As travelling facilities improved these races began to resegregate themselves. *Ibid.*, With the upheaval of the war, when..the population was in a state of flux, resegregation probably became more rapid and accentuated. **1954** *Newsweek* 27 Sept. 59/2 (*heading*) Now resegregation. *Ibid.*, In this fashion were Greenbrier County's desegregated schools resegregated. **1970** *Washington Post* 22 Jan. A20/1 'Resegregation' is what may occur when a formerly *de jure* segregated school system complies with the order to desegregate and..people move around in such a way as to 'resegregate' the schools—only on a *de facto* basis this time. **1976** *Time* 27 Sept. 57/3 Another pattern of resegregation occasionally takes place within desegregated schools when students are simply assigned to segregated classes.

resele·ct, *v.* [RE- 5 a.] *trans.* To select again. So **resele·ction.**

1940 F. D. DAVISON *Woman at Mill* I. 83 Lot 32..had been forfeited and was available for re-selection. **1953** *New Biol.* XIV. 47 In Peru a special type [of cotton] of *barbadense* has been acclimatized and reselected. *Ibid.* 58 In Egypt we attempted also a further refinement of purity, and even improvement, by continued reselections of single-plant origin. **1979** *Guardian* 5 July 24/3 The NEC..agreed to put reselection of MPs back on the agenda. **1981** *Observer* 31 May 12/3 One left wing MP..said after last week's National Executive had voted against MP's being reselected unopposed [etc.].

resemblance, *sb.*[1] Add: **1. e.** *Biol.* An evolved similarity in appearance between organisms of different species.

1862 H. W. BATES in *Trans. Linn. Soc.* XXIII. 502 Mimetic analogies..are resemblances in external appearance, shape, and colours between members of widely distinct families. **1902** *Encycl. Brit.* XXVII. 149/2 Mimetic resemblance is far commoner in the female than in the male, a fact readily explicable by selection, as suggested by Wallace. **1912** *Proc. Zool. Soc.* 361 Some of the cases of resemblance [of Blattidæ to Coleoptera] are so detailed and close that it is impossible to regard them as anything but examples of true mimicry. **1931, 1951** [see *MIMICRY 2]. **1968** R. D. MARTIN tr. *Wickler's Mimicry* ii. 22 One of the most astonishing cases of one species resembling another (interspecific resemblance) occurs in a butterfly of the swallowtail family (Papilionidae) in the species *Papilio dardanus*. **1974** *Encycl. Brit. Macropædia* XII. 214/1 In mimicry the animate agent of selection..interacts directly with at least two of the similar forms and is deceived by their similarity... A convergent resemblance, on the other hand, results from the action of similar forces of natural selection..on unrelated organisms, which may be geographically or temporally isolated from each other.

rese·nsitize, *v.* [RE- 5 a.] *trans.* To sensitize again.

1951 M. HYNES *Med. Bacteriol.* (ed. 5) vii. 91 After an interval..antibodies are formed again in sufficient amounts to resensitize the animal. **1967** E. CHAMBERS *Photolitho-Offset* i. 3 If additions are required to the image, it is necessary to 'resensitise' the stone by eliminating from it the insoluble products originating from the gum, which stop penetration by any greasy substance.

resentment. Add: **2. d.** *Social Psychol.* A term introduced by Nietzsche (as G. *ressentiment*) to describe an attitude which arises, often unconsciously, from aggressive feelings frustrated by the sensed inferiority of one's situation or personality and freq. results in some form of self-abasement. Cf. *RESSENTIMENT.

1899 HAUSSMANN & GRAY tr. *Nietzsche's Geneal. Morals* i. 33 The slave-revolt in morality begins by resentment itself becoming creative and giving birth to values—the resentment of such beings, as real reaction, the reaction of deeds, is impossible to, and as nothing but [*sic*] an imaginary vengeance will serve to indemnify. **1911** A. M. LUDOVICI tr. *Nietzsche's Ecce Homo* in *Compl. Wks.* XVII. 20 Freedom from resentment and the understanding of the nature of resentment—who knows how very much..I am indebted to my long illness for these two things. *Ibid.* 21 Nothing on earth consumes a man more quickly than the passion of resentment. **1943** G. A. MORGAN *What Nietzsche Means* vi. 150 At bottom, Nietzsche thinks, resentment is caused by a desire to stun pain. It differs from healthy revenge particularly in that, being impotent to express itself by immediate action, it poisons and consumes within. **1957** H. E. BARNES tr. *Sartre's Being & Nothingness* ii. 47 Others so as to make the Not a part of their very subjectivity, establish their human personality as a perpetual negation. This is the meaning and function of what Scheler calls 'the man of resentment'. **1974** B. F. SKINNER *About Behaviorism* x. 154 The controlling measures used by an authority make it more likely that a person will escape or counter-attack, and relevant conditions may be felt as resentment; at the same time the measures may generate compliant behavior.

resequent (rī·sĭkwĕnt, rĭsī·kwĕnt), *a.* (*sb.*) *Geomorphol.* [f. RE- + *-sequent* in CONSEQUENT, SUBSEQUENT *adjs.*] **a.** Designating, or characterized by the presence of, a stream or streams having a course which follows the dip of strata in the manner of a consequent stream but is stratigraphically at a lower level than the original surface of the underlying geological formation. Hence as *sb.*, a resequent stream.

1906 W. M. DAVIS in *Bull. Amer. Geogr. Soc.* XXXVIII. 608, I suggested a few years ago that streams which, after spontaneous development aside from an original consequent course, come again to follow it, should be called resequent streams. *Ibid.*, In the third stage..a new series of similar streams—lateral resequents—is beginning to be developed on the crown of the then newly-uncovered hard-rock anticlines. **1937** WOOLDRIDGE & MORGAN *Physical Basis Geogr.* xv. 212 A good example is afforded by the Central Weald of Kent and Sussex, where there are many good examples of synclinal valleys for which resequent origin must be deemed probable. **1954** W. D. THORNBURY *Princ. Geomorphol.* v. 114 Resequent valleys drain in the same direction as the original consequent drainage but are at lower topographic levels and have developed with respect to new base levels of erosion. **1970** R. J. SMALL *Study of Landforms* iii. 91 Where inversion of relief has once been achieved, continued erosion can lead to a restoration of the original structure-relief relationship; the synclinal valleys and anticlinal ridges are then, strictly speaking, 'resequent'. *Ibid.*, vii. 235 Synclinal streams may even be 'resequents', which are traditionally regarded as the eventual outcome of drainage development in areas of folded rocks.

b. Of a fault-line scarp or a related feature: having a relief similar to that originally produced by the faulting; freq. *spec.* where such relief results from erosion of an obsequent scarp.

1913 W. M. DAVIS in *Bull. Geol. Soc. Amer.* XXIV. 198 If this change of form is a slope, more or less perfectly graded, descending to the relatively depressed side, it may be called a resequent scarp. **1941** C. A. COTTON *Landscape* xxiii. 265 Fault-line scarps are of two kinds, resequent and obsequent, according as they face in the direction the initial fault-scarp faced on the same line of fault or in the opposite direction. *Ibid.*, Resequent fault-line scarps..are commoner than obsequent. **1970** R. J. SMALL *Study of Landforms* iii. 105 It will be seen that consequent and resequent scarps are very similar, and indeed many would argue that to make a distinction between them is purely academic, on the grounds that it is invariably impossible to decide in actual cases whether or not an obsequent scarp has previously existed along a fault-line (and thus whether the scarp in question is resequent or not).

reserpine (rĭsə̄·ɹpīn). *Pharm.* [ad. G. *reserpin* (J. M. Müller et al. 1952, in *Experientia* VIII. 338), f. initial letter of *RAUWOLFIA + *-e-* + L. *serp-entina* (see below), fem. of *serpentinus* SERPENTINE *a.*: see -INE[5].] A colourless crystalline alkaloid $C_{33}H_{40}N_2O_9$, which is obtained from the roots of several plants of the genus *RAUWOLFIA, notably *R. serpentina*, and is used to treat hypertension and as a sedative.

1952 [see *CHLORPROMAZINE]. **1954** *Jrnl. Amer. Med. Assoc.* 20 Mar. 1040/1 It seems that reserpine reduces the blood pressure by exerting an effect on the central nervous system. **1958** *Observer* 30 Nov. 12/4 New drugs such as chlorpromazine and reserpine make the minds of the mentally ill more accessible. **1966** *New Scientist* 24 Nov. 430/3 Reserpine interferes with the retention, mainly in the hypothalamus.., of a number of amines. **1973** *Sci. Amer.* Sept. 121/1 Once widely used, reserpine has been replaced by the phenothiazines because of the greater frequency of reserpine's serious side effects. **1974** *Times* 20 Sept. 3/7 There seems little doubt that this link between regular use of reserpine and an increased cancer risk is genuine.

Hence **rese·rpinized** *a.*, treated with reserpine; **rese:rpiniza·tion**, the process of, or condition resulting from, treatment with reserpine.

1960 *Federation Proc.* XIX. 266/1 (*heading*) LSD-25 and brain serotonin in reserpinized rat. **1962** *Lancet* 22 Dec. 1330/2 The accumulation and retention of ^{14}C from the blood-glucose in vivo are greatly diminished in the heart of 'reserpinised' rats. **1963** *Federation Proc.* XXII. 364/2 The animal was 5 to 10 times more sensitive to these substances after reserpinization than before. **1973** *Nature* 13 Apr. In the absence of endogenous catecholamines (that is reserpinization) the transient contractile tension response to the ionophore was attenuated, but elevation of resting tension persisted. **1975** *Pediatric Res.* IX. 463 (*heading*) The chronically reserpinized rat as a possible model for cystic fibrosis.

reservable, *a.* (Later example.)

1971 *Daily Tel.* (Colour Suppl.) 29 Oct. 7/1 There were three seat prices—50p, 80p and £1.10. But only the most expensive were reservable in advance.

reservation. Add: **I. 3. b.** (Earlier and later examples.) Also, a tract of land similarly set apart for (*a*) Canadian Indians, (*b*) African Blacks, (*c*) Australian Aborigines.

1789 *Deb. Congress U.S.* 25 May (1834) 41 The reservation,..of six miles square round the fort at Oswego, is within the territory of the State of New York. **1792** *Mass. Hist. Soc. Coll.* (1806) 1st Ser. I. 287 The whole Six Nations live on grounds, called the State Reservations, and are intermediate spaces settled on both sides by white people. **1859** *Native Voice* (Vancouver) (1959) Feb. 5/4 Has the Government of this Island the power to remove the Indians (by purchase) from that piece of outside Victoria Harbour known as the Indian Reservation? **1953** D. CUSHMAN *Stay away, Joe* 22 Won't have anything to do with the Injuns off the reservation. **1957** M. BANTON *W. Afr. City* i. 15 A tangle relating to the ownership of land in the Kru Reservation. **1965** *Austral. Encycl.* I. 88/2 Western Australia maintains 167 native reservations. **1970** *Times* 24 Mar. 6/6 Port Elizabeth is close enough to the Transkei Bantustan (African reservation) to be affected by the complex restrictions designed to stop industry from attracting Africans out of the reservations. **1971** D. HEFFRON *Nice Fire & Some Moonpennies* ii. 18 He told me to remember that when you're off the Reservation, people take you not as an individual but as an Indian. **1973** *Black Panther* 8 Sept. 8/2 The Apaches, originally from Arizona, New Mexico and parts of Mexico, were sent to Florida by the U.S. Army after they refused to remain on a reservation in Arizona.

attrib. (earlier and later examples).

1866 *Rep. Indian Affairs* (U.S.) 100 The reservation Indian is under the protection of the general government. **1946** G. FOREMAN *Last Trek of Indians* 260 Eighty of them came to their agency and enrolled with the reservation Indians. **1977** *Listener* 13 Oct. 462/1 In the 1950s..a whole generation of reds..was squashed... A few of us survivors are kept on like reservation Indians to remind the winners of how tolerant they've become.

c. orig. *U.S.* The action or fact of engaging seats, rooms, places, etc., or of hiring a vehicle, in advance; something reserved in advance. Also *attrib.*

1906 F. LYNDE *Quickening* xiii. 118 That sleeping-car reservation for Thomas Gordon—have you secured it? **1907** *Springfield* (Mass.) *Weekly Republican* 19 Dec. 16 A considerable number of New York and Boston people have made reservations at the Curtis hotel in Lenox for the holiday season. **1925** *Scribner's Mag.* July 32/1 (Advt.), Reservations for 1925–26 should be made as soon as possible to insure entrance. **1935** R. MACAULAY *Personal Pleasures* 18 Do tickets, passports, money, travellers' cheques, packing, reservations, boat trains, inns, crouch and snarl before you like those surly dragons that guard enchanted lands? **1949** *Skyline Trail* (Montreal) Mar. 14/2 It is most important that hikers procure their hotel reservations well in advance. **1968** *Globe & Mail* (Toronto) 17 Feb. 35 (Advt.), For reservations, call or write Atlantic Car & Truck Rental. **1971** *Financial Mail* (Johannesburg) 26 Feb. 656/2 When his travel agent phoned the Cape Town reservation centre about that day's 19.15 flight to Johannesburg, a reservation clerk said: 'We have no idea how many seats are left.' **1977** E. LEONARD *Unknown Man No. 89* xx. 207 Ryan kept going,..past the reservation desk to the foyer.

d. Exemption from military service because of an important civilian occupation. Also *attrib.*, as *reservation age*, etc.

1916 *List of Certified Occupations* (Local Government Board) 4 The *only* ground for making these reservations is that the men protected are engaged on work of national importance. **1940** *Economist* 20 July 73/2 He [*sc.* Ernest Bevin]..is transferring persons to war work by pressure and persuasion rather than by compulsion. An early example of this was the raising of the reservation age in certain industries while postponing the date, so that men below the new age limit could..transfer into war jobs where they would still be reserved. **1941** *Manch. Guardian Weekly* 26 Sept. 194 The test of reservation should be the work a man is actually doing, not his declared occupation. *Ibid.*, The reservation system cannot be said to operate fairly in our present critical state unless its categories are tightened. **1942** *Ann. Reg. 1941* 27 Hitherto all men above the reservation age had been exempted, whether they were actually occupied or not. **1944** *Manpower* (Ministry of Information) 11 Each occupation had its own age of reservation. The more important the job, the lower the age of reservation. The skilled tradesmen in the Armed Forces were drawn from men below the age of reservation in corresponding civilian occupations.

e. = *RESERVE *sb.* 5 e. In full, *central reservation.*

1937 *Memorandum on Lay-Out & Construction of Roads* (Ministry of Transport) 15 Gaps for vehicles in the central reservation should in no case be formed opposite the exits from the minor roads. *Ibid.* 17 The separation of dual carriageways should be effected by a reservation of the greatest width practicable. **1959** *Highway Code* 16 Do not reverse or turn in the carriageway or cross the central reservation. **1972** *Times* 10 June 2/2 Police are to investigate why a new M1 crash barrier near the Toddington service area failed to stop a lorry from crossing the central reservation. **1977** *Oxford Mail* 20 Apr. 1 Oxfordshire's ambulance chief has called for safety barriers down the central reservation of the new Witney Bypass before there is a serious crash.

reservationist (rezəɹvē[i]·ʃənist), *sb.* (and *a.*) *U.S.* [f. RESERVATION + -IST.] One who makes reservations (senses *3 c and 4 a). Also *attrib.* or as *adj.*

1920 *Glasgow Herald* 18 Mar. 9 The reservationist Senators are..too much attached to their limitations and qualifications to abandon them for anything. **1933** W. S. HOLT *Treaties defeated by Senate* x. 296 The reservationists did not constitute a majority. **1978** *N.Y. Times* 30 Mar. B20/1 (Advt.), Reservationist... 2 yrs ticketing exp.

reserve, *sb.* Add: **I. 1. b.** Also, that part of the profit of a joint stock company which is not distributed to shareholders. *hidden reserve*: see *HIDDEN *ppl. a.* 1 d.

1930, etc. [see *HIDDEN *ppl. a.* 1 d]. **1940** *Economist* 25 May 936/1 This has..involved a redefinition of reserves. In former years this item in our figures was a repository for a mixture: reserves provided against specific assets, and other items properly chargeable against profits were combined with 'free reserves' which were, in effect, merely undivided profits. Now the line is more tightly drawn to include the latter and exclude the former. **1974** *Terminol. Managem. & Financial Accountancy* (Inst. Cost & Managem. Accountants) 63 *Reserves*, undistributed or surplus profits. The creation and distribution of certain reserves are affected by company policy and legal considerations, e.g. the provisions of the Memorandum and Articles of Association of the company.

c. The amount of a mineral, or of oil or natural gas, which is known to exist in the ground in a particular region and to be capable of exploitation. Usu. *pl.*

[Cf. quot. 1860 in sense 5.]

1912 M. H. BURNHAM *Mod. Mine Valuation* i. 66 Ore in a developed mine lying below that which the engineer is willing to class as a reserve, and pay for, is 'possible' only. [*Note*] The above table classes as reserves only the ore lying above the deepest level. **1922** *Bull. Amer. Assoc. Petroleum Geologists* VI. 444 Within the last few years the necessity has developed for estimating recoverable reserves on oil and gas properties. **1945** J. A. BROWN in L. M. Fanning *Our Oil Resources* i. 6 In the Maracaibo basin of Venezuela alone there are proved reserves of at least 5 billion barrels of crude oil. **1969** *Australian* 24 Oct. 18/2 Ore reserves fall into four general categories—proven, profitable, possible and indicated. Proven is ore that has been blocked out on four sides; probable is ore that has been opened on two or three sides, while possible ore has been opened on one side only; indicated ore is ore that has been outlined by diamond drilling but which has not been opened by underground work. **1979** *Nature* 26 July 261/1 What the board is actually talking about if it uses the word 'proven' is 'reserves': materials that have been mapped out sufficiently well that they can be the subject of mining by known methods.

d. *spec.* Extra energy; a supply of energy or resilience. Usu. *pl.*

1929 H. CRANE *Let.* c 23 Oct. (1965) 347, I feel quite rested already, but I know that I need a little 'reserve'. **1934** H. G. WELLS *Exper. Autobiogr.* I. vi. 369 Dr. Collins heard of my plight and wrote also. I detected a helpful motive and wrote among other things to assure him that I had 'reserves' for a year or so. **1941** *Lilliput* Mar. 206/1 We had lovely weather all the time. I was so glad. Most children don't feel it, but Jonathan is such a fragile little thing, no reserves at all.

2. c. (Further example.) Also *pl.*, the reserve or second team.

1961 *Daily Express* 14 Jan. 10 Aston Villa assistant manager Dick Taylor..saw 19-year-old Cheung bamboozle Villa reserves. **1976** E. DUNPHY *Diary* in *Only a Game?* v. 147 All you have got to look forward to is Aldershot reserves away next Wednesday. **1976** *Evening Post* (Nottingham) 14 Dec. 18/5 The England reserve, who injured his back against East Midlands last week, is replaced by Nottingham Casuals' Ian Henry. **1977** *Belfast Tel.* 22 Feb. 29/3 He played for the reserves last night and if there is no reaction, he will be in the Thistle first team tonight.

II. 5. b. (Earlier and later examples.) Also as the final element in *Combs.*: see *GAME *sb.* 16 a, *NATIVE *a.* 15, *NATURE *sb.* 15 a.

1805 *Statutes at Large U.S.A.* (1846) VII. 98 The latter [Indian] reserve to be subject to the same laws and regulations as may be established in the circumjacent country. **1832** T. BAILLIE *Acct. Province N. Brunswick* 79 The Richibucto River is also well and thickly settled, to the head of the tide excepting in a large tract reserved for Indians, which reserve is a great drawback on the prosperity of the place. **1852** GODLONTON & IRVING *Kaffir War* III. xvii. 232 They fell upon two Fingo kraals in the 'Reserve'.. and completely destroyed them. **1908** C. MAIR *Through Mackenzie Basin* 57 These reserves are holdings you can select when you please, subject to the approval of the Government. **1911** W. H. KOEBEL *In Maoriland Bush* xix. 253 An occasional small patch of 'reserve' bush throws its long shadow down the steep hillsides. **1928** J. D. TAYLOR *Christianity & Natives of S. Afr.* 6 The Adequacy or Inadequacy of the Existing Native Reserves begins to be recognised as the crux of the Native question. **1953** P. ABRAHAMS *Return to Goli* IV. ii. 106 At the moment the Blacks of the Reserves have only about 10 per cent of the total land area of the Union. **1965** *Austral. Encycl.* I. 88/2 Southern Australia..has allocated a large part..of the western desert in the north-west of the State for aboriginal reserves. **1973** *Black World* June 46/1 Australia, for over 30,000 years a Black man's country, has for the past 200 years been dominated by white western-europeans, and the original inhabitants..have been murdered, poisoned, rounded up and confined on Reserves. **1977** *Belfast Tel.* 22 Feb. 2/7 The two men were working in a reserve containing eight tigers.

d. In textile or pottery decoration: an area which is left the original colour of the material or the colour of the background. Also phr. *in reserve*.

1876 [in Dict., sense 5]. **1910** *Burlington Mag.* XVII. 284/1 [In these early Mohammedan textiles] for the most part the surface is covered by circular reserves in which.. figures..are placed in pairs symmetrically confronted. **1957** K. M. KENYON *Digging up Jericho* v. 79 A design in a dark red slip applied..in a series of diamonds or triangles, often so arranged that the underlying cream slip forms a series of chevrons in reserve. **1971** *Cambr. Anc. Hist.* (ed. 3) I. II. xxiv. 689 The pottery is painted in a brown or blackish paint on a buff to yellow slip. Designs are simple but very distinctive, consisting of horizontal bands with zigzags, triangles, or multiple chevrons, often left 'in reserve'. **1980** *Catal. Fine Chinese Ceramics* (Sotheby, Hong Kong) 166 With reserves of emblems and precious objects alternating with trellis diaper panels around the rim.

e. In full, *central reserve*. A central area separating lanes of a dual carriageway or motorway.

1937 *Sunday Times* 10 Jan., Nearly all the new roads have broad central 'reserves' and broad grass verges on each side. **1968** *Highway Code* 15 When crossing a dual carriageway, treat each half as a separate road. Wait at the central dividing strip (the central reserve) until there is a safe gap in the traffic. **1969** *Times* 21 Apr. 7/1 By-passes, some with dual carriageways and central reserves, present a greater inconvenience.

6. c. (Earlier examples with reference to sales by auction.)

1799 *Times* 1 June 1/1 (Advt.), The beautiful Collection of paintings..now exhibiting, and selling off without reserve. **1805** *Times* 7 Nov. 4/2 The whole of the above are in prime condition, and will be sold without reserve.

d. = **reserve price*.

1854 D. G. ROSSETTI *Let. c* 26 June (1965) I. 203 The rest he put into a sale at Christie's, after taking my advice as to the reserve he ought to put on the Hunt, which I fixed at 500 gs. It reached 300 in real biddings, after which Mac's touters ran it up to 430, trying to revive it, but of course it remains with him. **1911** R. FRY *Let.* 4 Feb. (1972) I. 340 It [*sc.* a picture] was valued by Berenson..at £6,000 but I don't think..that the reserve will be nearly so high as that. **1977** *Irish Press* 29 Sept. 15/5 Fastest trial winner of the day, in 29.87, The Best Band, went to 1,025 guineas, but this was a long way short of the reserve.

IV. 11. a. (Further examples.) Also, pertaining to, designed for, or used by reserves.

1853 MRS. GASKELL *Cranford* xv. 228 Miss Matty would be perplexed as to her duty if she were aware of any little reserve-fund being made for her while the debts of the bank remained unpaid. **1916** 'BOYD CABLE' *Action Front* 125 Men who live month in month out in a narrow territory, bounded on the east by the forward firing line and on the west by..the villages of the reserve billets. **1923** KIPLING *Irish Guards in Gt. War* I. 128 They took over reserve-billets. **1928** [see *DOG-FIGHT 2]. **1959** N. MAILER *Advts. for Myself* (1961) 50 In early 1941 he wrote to his father that he would like to take advantage of his reserve commission to enter the army. **1974** D. KYLE *Raft of Swords* x. 97 In Vancouver..there are a great many British immigrants. Some..are ex-service, still on the reserve list. **1976** *Leicester Advertiser* 26 Nov. 1/4 He was..reserve champion at the East of England [Show]. **1976** M. BUTTERWORTH *Remains to be Seen* iv. 54 His eye was immediately taken by the fuel warning light. He switched to the reserve tank.

b. Special Combs.: **reserve bank,** a central bank holding currency reserves (chiefly *Austral.* and *N.Z.*); **reserve buoyancy,** bouyancy available to a craft in excess of its weight; **reserve cell** *Med.*, a cell whose further differentiation constitutes the renewal of immediately adjacent tissue; freq. *attrib.*; **reserve currency,** a currency widely used in international trade and held in reserves by foreign banks; **reserve price** (see quot. 1957).

1905 C. A. CONANT *Princ. Money & Banking* II. vii. 292 The essential requirement..is an ultimate source of credit which shall be strong enough to inspire confidence in its ability both to redeem its circulating notes and to grant discounts. A central reserve bank, whose credit is unquestionable, is then enabled to meet the demand for credit from private bankers by redistributing the paper in their hands. **1965** *Austral. Encycl.* I. 414/1 At the apex of the structure is the central bank, the Reserve Bank of Australia, which is a government-owned institution established by Act of the Commonwealth Parliament in 1959. **1966** *Encycl. N.Z.* I. 149/2 The extent to which a bank can extend credit which, when used by its customers, will cause it to lose funds to other banks, is determined by the amount of cash it holds at the Reserve Bank and its ability to borrow at the Reserve Bank's discount rate. **1976** *Eastern Even. News* (Norwich) 13 Dec. 1/1 The Reserve Bank in Sydney said the Australian dollar was being revalued by 1.28 per cent. **1904** A. C. HOLMS *Pract. Shipbuilding* vi. 65 Reserve buoyancy may be defined as the lifting power, and is measured by the volume of the hull above the load-line. **1951** D. H. C. BIRT *Sailing Yacht Design* vi. 99 There is no reserve buoyancy forward on heeling to balance that in the after-sections. **1975** W. MUCKLE *Naval Archit. for Marine Engineers* i. 3 It [*sc.* freeboard] provides reserve buoyancy which can enable it to float in the event of damage. **1909** *Amer. Jrnl. Physiol.* XXV. 181 Lymphocytes may be 'reserve cells' kept on hand to immediately combat injury to the tissues. **1930** C. BLOOM in Maximow & Bloom *Textbk. Histol.* xxxiv. 693 Most of the chromophobe cells [of the hypophysis], the so-called chief or principal or reserve cells, have relatively small amounts of cytoplasm. **1940** *Amer. Jrnl. Cancer* XL. 214 (*heading*) Reserve-cell carcinomas. *Ibid.* 216 They appear to be the only epithelial cells in the mucous membrane of the bronchial tree which are concerned with cell division and cell differentiation. It seems reasonable, therefore, to look upon them as the reserve cells from which the ciliated columnar cells and goblet cells are replenished. **1952** *Amer. Jrnl. Obstetr. & Gynecol.* LXIV. 268 Adenomatous hyperplasia and epidermization [in the cervix] seem to be related to activity of a multipotential cell termed the 'reserve cell'. **1975** L. FOULDS *Neoplastic Devel.* II. iii. 111 Convincing photomicrographs of a layer of small cuboidal cells [in cervical epithelium] have been published and these cells have been identified as the basal cells or reserve cells from which the layer of overlying columnar cells is renewed. *Ibid.* 112 Reserve cell hyperplasia without metaplasia consists, as a rule, of not more than five or six layers of cuboidal cells similar to normal reserve cells, covered by an intact layer of columnar cells. **1967** *Listener* 26 Jan. 116/3 Britain, in or out of the Common Market, should maintain sterling as a reserve currency. **1971** *Daily Tel.* 10 May 14/3 The special kind of foreign exchange held in official reserves is called..a *Reserve Currency*. **1978** *Time* 3 July 8/1 The D-mark is being pushed more and more into the role of an international reserve currency. **1919** W. F. & G. D. NOKES *Auctioneer's Man.* (ed. 8) i. 11 A short time before the date of the sale the auctioneer should ascertain the reserve price for the property. **1935** *Chambers's Encycl.* I. 569/1 Where, under the conditions, a sale by auction is subject to a reserve price, no contract is concluded..if the highest bid is lower than the reserve price. **1957** CLARK & GOTTFRIED *University Dict. Business & Finance* 275/2 *Reserve price*, at a public auction, the lowest price which a seller is willing to accept; the price below which he reserves the right to withdraw the goods from sale. **1977** D. CLARK *Gimmel Flask* iv. 74 The vendors..are entirely at the mercy of the ring unless the articles have reserve prices put on them.

reserve, *v.* Add: **6. d.** In pottery decoration, etc.: to leave in the original colour of the material or the colour of the background. Usu. as *pa. pple.*

1875 [see sense 6 in Dict.]. **1885** L. M. SOLON *Art Old Eng. Potter* (ed. 2) iii. 86 A space was reserved between the two ridges, leaving a hollow to be filled in by slips of divers colours. **1908** J. F. BLACKER *ABC of Collecting Old Eng. China* (ed. 2) 41 Rich ground colours were successfully employed... Panels were reserved in white for painting. **1972** *Trans. Oriental Ceramics Soc.* XXXVIII. 123 Round the sides are six small landscapes in panels reserved in red and gilt trellis-diapered ground.

e. To exempt (a person) from military service because he is engaged in an important civilian occupation. Also, to class (a civilian occupation) as high-priority, thereby exempting many of those employed in it from military service.

1915 *Local Govt. Board Circular No. R.4: 1st Suppl.* 1 Mechanics and electricians engaged in the maintenance and repair of tools and machinery, engine men and stokers.. have already been reserved in all trades. **1915**, etc. [implied in **reserved occupation*]. **1922** *Encycl. Brit.* XXXI. 705/2 In a public announcement the list of starred occupations subsequently reserved was set out as follows: [etc.]. **1940** [see *RESERVATION 3 d]. **1941** *Illustrated* 13 Sept. 9/1 Farm workers are reserved at twenty-five, but I knew many of the farm-hands had already joined up. **1950** O. BLAKESTON *Pink Ribbon* ii. 27 Then..along came the war... I was 'reserved' because of my occupation.

13. = BOOK *v.* 4 a, b. Also *absol.*

1935 R. MACAULAY *Personal Pleasures* 20, I never reserve seats in advance, it is quite too much trouble... If a railway ticket does not get me on to a French train, then France is not the land of liberty, equality or fraternity. **1936** G. B. SHAW *Simpleton* II. 70 There are such a lot of priests in the world, Iddy. It would be impossible to reserve seats for them all. **1967** L. DEIGHTON *Expensive Place* iii. 23 What say to La Coupole? It's one of the few places..where we don't have to reserve.

reserved, *ppl. a.* Add: **5. b.** Also *sing.* (Further examples.) Also of seats on a train, etc.

1860 in M. W. Disher *Cowells in Amer.* (1934) 194 Most of the Audience were 'reserved seat' people, and pleasant. **1889** J. HATTON *Reminisc. J. L. Toole* I. i. 19, I glance at the house from the wings, find it crammed, the reserved seats filled with aristocratic and fashionably-dressed people. **1916** G. B. SHAW *Androcles & Lion* Pref. p. xciv, An insane conceit of being the elect of God, with a reserved seat in heaven. **1935** R. MACAULAY *Personal Pleasures* 19 Now for the train;..Second-class... No, nothing else about it matters, and I have no reserved seat. **1980** D. WILLIAMS *Murder for Treasure* v. 50 He too could have travelled in a reserved seat, untroubled, unmolested and delivered on time.

d. In pottery decoration, etc.: left in the original colour of the material or the colour of the background.

1895 in *Funk's Stand. Dict.* **1930** *Discovery* Aug. 255/2 From the fourth level [of the excavations at Ur] came a peculiar form of painted pottery that has been termed 'Reserved slip-ware', the paint being applied to the whole body of the pot and then wiped off at intervals so as to produce a series of striations. **1934** [see *high-lying* s.v. *HIGH *adv.* 10 a]. **1954** M. RICKERT *Painting in Brit.: Middle Ages* 231 *Reserved edges*, spaces left around a painted ornament exposing the vellum of a manuscript page. In Hiberno-Saxon decoration the reserved edges aid in clarifying a complicated pattern of spirals or interlace. **1960** K. M. KENYON *Archaeol. in Holy Land* iii. 62 This slip in turn is partially covered by a red slip, so that the reserved portions of the cream slip form a pattern, usually in some combination of chevrons or triangles. **1977** *Sci. Amer.* Mar. 122/2 (*caption*) Pot *d* carries a 'reserved' design, produced by applying a red slip over an orange underslip.

e. *reserved occupation*, a high-priority civilian occupation, most of those employed in which are exempted from military service.

1915 *Local Govt. Board Circular No. R.2* 2 A list has been prepared..of still further occupations (to be known as 'reserved occupations'), to which, in the public interest, from the point of view of the export trade or for other reasons, it is desirable to extend some measure of protection, either because the persons included in them..are engaged in work which could not be interrupted without serious dislocation or because the industries affected are such that it would be unwise to take more men from them without special investigation. **1940** M. NICHOLSON *How Britain's Resources are Mobilized* 21 A Schedule of Reserved Occupations, designed to ensure that work of national importance should not be endangered through losing too many men to the armed forces. **1944** A. THIRKELL *Headmistress* iv. 79 Her girls wished to go straight into the Forces..while their parents wanted them to..get a job in a reserved occupation. **1960** G. BUTLER *Death lives Next Door* i. 36 Never left England, not me. In a reserved occupation. **1972** M. JONES *Life on Dole* viii. 61 Mining was a reserved occupation, and even young men who wanted to get into uniform found themselves directed to the pits.

reserver[1]. **1.** (Later example.)

1966 *Punch* 7 Dec. 841/2 The room has the great advantage of being changed every day, so that no one except the reserver and his guest know exactly which floor the room is on at any given time.

reservoir, *sb.* **1. b.** Delete † *Obs.* and add later example,

1930 *Daily Express* 6 Oct. 3/7 They were..lying in their bunks... Above them were water reservoirs. The force of the explosion burst the water tanks.

e. A body of porous rock holding a large quantity of oil or natural gas.

1912 E. H. C. CRAIG *Oil-Finding* iii. 47 In the case of calcareous rocks it is probably merely because the limestone affords a porous reservoir that it is found impregnated with oil. **1938** D. HAGER *Pract. Oil Geol.* i. 34 In Mexico the most productive oil reservoirs of the Golden Lane were the reef limestones in the Tamasopa formation. **1951** K. K. LANDES *Petroleum Geol.* iii. 101 The escape of gas to the surface in disproportionate amounts to the oil produced will result in more and more sluggish oil being left behind in the reservoir. **1970** W. G. ROBERTS *Quest for Oil* ii. 16 The first known deposits of mineral oil, or petroleum, were found because they showed themselves as seepages from underground reservoirs. **1980** *Times* 15 May 19/2 British Petroleum has discovered a second, deeper reservoir on its onshore field at Kimmeridge.

2. b. *spec.* in a closed hydraulic system, a tank containing fluid that can be supplied to the system when needed to compensate for small losses. (Further examples.)

1946 W. H. CROUSE *Automotive Mech.* xxv. 550 The master cylinder includes a reservoir or supply tank that contains an additional quantity of brake fluid. **1966** HILLIER & PITTUCK *Fund. Motor Vehicle Technol.* xvi. 418 The flow of fluid from the reservoir to the main chamber is controlled by a compensating valve, which is set to open when the piston is in the fully returned position. **1970** K. BALL *Fiat 600, 600D Autobook* x. 117/2 Normal maintenance of the hydraulic system is confined to checking the level of the brake fluid in the reservoir at regular intervals.

3. c. (Further examples.) Also, a reserve supply of people.

1941 *Illustrated* 13 Sept. 12/2 Inside six months he has raised, clothed, equipped, and put into training on a voluntary basis a reservoir of 200,000 young men as potential air crews for the R.A.F. **1943** W. WILLKIE *One World* x. 131 There exists in the world today a gigantic reservoir of goodwill toward us, the American people. **1973** *Computers & Humanities* VII. 166 Concordances can contribute to linguistic studies as reservoirs of meanings and usages. **1979** *Wichita* (Kansas) *Eagle* 23 May 3C/6 A potential reservoir of additional workers for Wichita manufacturing has been created by McDonnell Corp., which is laying off workers in St. Louis.

d. *Med.* A population which is chronically infested with the causative agent of a disease and can infect other populations. Also *transf.*

1913 [see sense 4 a below]. **1939** C. F. CARTER *Microbiol. & Path.* (ed. 2) xxiv. 253 For the continuous existence of a disease there must be some reservoir of infection. *Ibid.*, The most important reservoirs of infection are human or animal cases or carriers. Plants may be the reservoir of infection in some of the mycoses. **1947** *Ann. Rev. Microbiol.* I. 353. A precise demon- stration of the mechanisms through which the reservoir of the disease functions would constitute a great advance in constructing the biological pattern of influenza. **1965** B. E. FREEMAN tr. *Vandel's Biospeleol.* xv. 246 It would be possible that bats serve as a reservoir of histoplasmosis. **1977** *Sci. Amer.* Mar. 61/2 When no human being harbours the [smallpox] virus, there should remain only one reservoir: the stocks in research and diagnostic laboratories.

3*. ¶ *au reservoir*: see *AU REVOIR.

4. a. (Further examples.)

1884 *Queen* 16 Feb. (Advt.), The 'Victor' reservoir pen can be used with any good fluid ink, and any ordinary nib... Price 3s.6d. **1913** *Trans. Soc. Trop. Med. & Hygiene* VI. 269 The monkey is most probably the normal 'reservoir host' [for *Physaloptera mordens*].

c. Special Combs.: **reservoir engineering,** the study and exploitation of natural oil and gas reservoirs; so **reservoir engineer**; **reservoir rock,** rock (capable of) forming a reservoir for oil or natural gas.

1949 M. MUSKAT *Physical Princ. Oil Production* i. 28 While..the..properties of the reservoir will determine its inherent potentialities as an oil-producing system, there is still much left to the choice of the reservoir engineer with regard to the actual exploitation program to be undertaken. **1973** *Mod. Petroleum Technol.* (Inst. Petroleum) (ed. 4) v. 172 The primary aim of a reservoir engineer is to obtain maximum recovery at minimum cost. **1946** *Petroleum Engineer* Jan. 51/1 The war..has led to a greater realization than ever before of the need for applying the most advanced reservoir engineering principles of production and oil conservation to obtain maximum economic recoveries. **1954** *Mod. Petroleum Technol.* (Inst. Petroleum) (ed. 2) iv. 122 A balanced view of production operations calls for some knowledge of the fundamentals of reservoir engineering as well as of the more purely mechanical methods employed. **1977** *Times* 2 Nov. 3 (Advt.), Reservoir engineering is largely an art... Our job is to get information about..oil-bearing rock..below the sea bed. **1912** E. H. C. CRAIG *Oil-Finding* iii. 46 The relative porosity of strata is one of the determining factors in the movements of oil, and the selection of a reservoir rock. **1951** K. K. LANDES *Petroleum Geol.* vii. 191 Throughout the world, sandstone is by far the most important reservoir rock. **1975** G. ANDERSON *Coring* i. 18 Permeability normally varies from one location to another vertically as well as horizontally in a reservoir rock.

reset, *v.*² Add: **I. 7. a.** To cause (a device) to return to a former state, esp. a condition of readiness.

1919 R. MORDIN *Strowger Automatic Telephone Exchange* iii. 64 When the release magnet armature knocks the double dog out of engagement with the shaft it also, by means of the lever shown, re-sets the side switch. **1931** *Proc. R. Soc.* A. CXXXII. 301 The mechanical relay M_R is used only for extinguishing or resetting thyratron Q. **1977** D. ANTHONY *Stud Game* xxv. 160, I..reset the burglar alarm.

b. *Computers.* To set (a binary cell) to zero; to return (a counting device) *to* a specified value, esp. zero.

1947 *Proc. IRE* Aug. 759/1 The triggered flip-flop is the only one to respond..; as it is reset it gives out a positive pulse. **1956** G. A. MONTGOMERIE *Digital Calculating Machines* iii. 47 If the wheels are left in engagement on the return stroke they are reset to their previous values. **1971** J. H. SMITH *Digital Logic* i. 12 A binary divider is a modified toggle which has only one input. If electrical pulses are applied to this input the unit will 'set'. The second pulse will 'reset' the circuit.

8. To set (hair) again.

1932 E. BOWEN *To North* xii. 120 She..had had, since lunch, her hair shampooed and re-set.

II. 9. a. *intr.* for *refl.* **b.** Of a device: to return to an initial state.

1895 W. J. LOCKE *Gate of Samaria* xvi. 194 She..noticed a look upon Thornton's face,—the after-light, as it were, of a sneer, before the features had time to reset. **1971** *Gloss. Electrotechnical, Power Terms (B.S.I.)* I. iii. 13 A relay resets when it returns to its initial position. **1980** *Sci. Amer.* May 49/1 When both currents are removed, the switched junction automatically resets, closing the loop.

resettable, *a.* Add: (Further examples). Hence **resettabi·lity.**

1971 *Physics Bull.* July 390/1 The smooth tunability and resettability (1:3×10⁴ which is an instrumental limitation) is not understood. **1973** G. J. KING *Newnes Colour T.V. Servicing Man.* I. i. 35/1 Not all models employ a resettable cut-out. **1975** *Gramophone* June 118/2 Resetability [*sic*] of the slider controls could be improved if a cursor line were engraved on the rectangular knob. **1979** *Sci. Amer.* Aug. 131/1 A system of this type can be viewed as a mathematical strongbox with a resettable combination lock.

resettle, *v.* Add: **1. a.** Also without const. Also, to settle again in another place; *spec.* to establish (a homeless or evicted person, etc.) again in a house or community, or (*S. Afr.*) in another area. Cf. *RESETTLEMENT 1 c.

1937 [implied s.v. *RESETTLED *ppl. a.*]. **1951** R. FIRTH *Elem. Social Organiz.* iv. 142 In the olden days in Ireland a working team..was drawn from the community..to re-settle an evicted family. **1965** *Listener* 30 Sept. 482/2 About 1,500 [old people]..require something between forty and fifty days to be resettled back in the community. **1972** *Stand. Encycl. S. Afr.* V. 379/1 A total of 115 000 Bantu from the western areas of Johannesburg and elsewhere were resettled in new homes in new Bantu towns. **1978** C. A. BERRY *Gentleman of Road* ix. 74 You're in a bad state and I'd like to resettle you. **1978** A. BRINK *Rumours of Rain* 105 'How many hundreds and thousands of 'exceptions' do you think there are?' he asked angrily. 'Whole societies uprooted and resettled.' **1981** *Eastern Province Herald* (S. Afr.) 2 June 5/6 This will cause friction between those who are resettled and those who were there before.

rese·ttled *ppl. a.*

1937 *Sun* (Baltimore) 25 May 12/2 Nobody in Washington is able to indicate the means by which resettled farmers and sharecroppers can pay rent on these expensive houses. **1977** *Time* 4 Apr. 21/1 When Sanjay and his elder brother Rajiv visited a community of resettled slumdwellers, they were given a tumultuous welcome. **1981** *Eastern Province Herald* (S. Afr.) 2 June 5/4 The synod..urged the Diocesan Council to create a committee to co-operate with other concerned groups, and resettled people themselves, in planning a strategy to cope with the problems brought about by forced removal.

resettlement. Add: **1. b.** *spec.* The act of resettling demobilized servicemen into civilian life.

1918 *Labour Gaz.* May 175/1 (*heading*) Resettlement of officers and professional men... The report of the Committee appointed to consider the resettlement of officers has been approved by the Minister of Reconstruction. **1920** *Brit. Med. Jrnl.* 4 Sept. 340/1 Many doctors who served long with the forces have found the period following demobilization a time of uncertainty and financial stress. For them 'resettlement' has proved an uphill business. **1922** *Encycl. Brit.* XXX. 821/2 (*heading*) The first two years of resettlement. The success of the preparations which had been made..is indicated by the figures of re-absorption of men demobilized. **1945** *Yorkshire Post* 19 Apr. 3/2 The Minister of Labour has provided several admirably chosen lecturers..to tell Servicemen of the plans made for their release and resettlement when their term of service comes to an end.

c. *S. Afr.* The act of resettling Blacks in their supposed homelands.

In South Africa resettlement involves the enforced removal of Blacks from one area, often followed by a period in temporary resettlement camps, before their removal to the 'homelands'.

1954 *Bantu* Nov. 11 (*caption*) Compare these neat little houses with the unhygienic tin and brick shacks of Sophiatown..and you would understand why the resettlement of the Bantu had become imperative. **1976** A. LEMON *Apartheid* viii. 153 The further resettlement of up to half the existing number of Africans in white areas is being seriously contemplated. **1981** *Observer* 31 May 12/4 About four million have been moved since 1948 and at least another million are marked down for 'resettlement'.

3. *attrib.* and *Comb.*, as *resettlement area, board, camp, centre, grant, office, officer, plan, programme, project, scheme, village.*

1971 *Progress* (Cape Town) May 7/4 The resettlement areas..to which so many African urban people have been endorsed. **1954** *Bantu* Nov. 4 The views expressed in this article are personal and in no way bind the Department or the Natives Resettlement Board. **1973** Resettlement board [see *resettlement programme* below]. **1971** *Progress* (Cape Town) May 7/5 The valiant attempts of the women of these missions and resettlement camps to make some sort of living for themselves and their families. **1972** *Times* 19 Dec. 3/1 There are events planned in all the 14 resettlement camps. **1973** Resettlement centre [see *resettlement programme* below]. **1977** *R.A.F. News* 11–24 May 7/1 Even the resettlement grant does not sweeten the bitter pill. **1945** *Daily Tel.* 17 May 3/3 They would be welcomed at the employment exchanges and the resettlement offices if they had not got a job. **1922** *Encycl. Brit.* XXX. 821/1 A number of officers known as Resettlement Officers were appointed.., whose business was to travel the country and investigate the causes which impeded the turnover from war to peace. **1946** *Lancet* 2 Feb. 177/1 Our resettlement officer almost got the job, but like me he didn't have the Finnish, or the Norwegian, Swedish, or Danish, without which, out there, the execution of big business is apparently impossible. **1974** 'J. LE CARRÉ' *Tinker, Tailor* xxxii. 286 The first person..to visit him was the resettlement officer, talking about a friendly teaching agency. **1945** *Daily Tel.* 17 May 3/3 (*heading*) Mr. Bevin explains resettlement plans. **1973** *Guardian* 16 Apr. 20/1 No more Uganda Asians will be allowed into the resettlement centres. An announcement.. by the Home Office..marks the first stage in the resettlement programme and has the full backing of the Uganda Resettlement Board. **1973** J. HOAGLAND *South Afr.* xi. 299 The Portuguese moved quickly to establish the resettlement program in Mozambique. **1936** *Sun* (Baltimore) 28 Jan. 8/7 The Government's resettlement project at..Reedsville. **1921** W. SHERREN *Rights of Ex-Service Man & Woman* iii. 23 The Civil Liabilities Resettlement Scheme of 1918 was instituted to provide assistance to ex-officers and men who had suffered serious hardship by reason of their military service **1954** *Bantu* Sept. 44 Throughout the ages various Resettlement Schemes have been undertaken similar to the Scheme of the Western Areas of Johannesburg. **1952** *Times* 22 Sept. 5/1 Volunteer teams..after receiving a short course of instruction in spoken Malay..live in the new resettlement villages. **1973** J. HOAGLAND *South Afr.* xi. 299 There were 433,000 Africans living in resettlement villages.

reshape, *v.* (Later examples.)

1916 JOYCE *Portrait of Artist* (1969) 67 The change of fortune which was reshaping the world about him into a vision of squalor and insincerity. **1951** E. E. EVANS-PRITCHARD *Social Anthropol.* v. 86 The theories have been shaped and reshaped by this steady growth of knowledge. **1960** *Farmer & Stockbreeder* 29 Mar. 17/1 British economic policy has had to be reshaped to deal with an adverse trend in the balance of payments.

resha·per (rī-). [f. RESHAPE *v.* + -ER¹.] One who or that which reshapes.

1961 WEBSTER, *Reshaper*, one that reshapes something; *esp.* a worker who does the final blocking of hats. **1964** F. L. WESTWATER *Electronic Computers* iii. 49 The effect of passing through a gate causes a deterioration in the pulse shape. This can be corrected by some non-logical element such as an amplifier or reshaper.

reshaping, *vbl. sb.* (Further examples.)

1951 R. FIRTH *Elem. Social Organiz.* iii. 89 This has been particularly marked with the coming of industrialism, foreshadowing the destruction or radical re-shaping of their social structure. **1964** F. L. WESTWATER *Electronic Computers* iv. 89 The pulse train is fed back into the tube after amplification and re-shaping. **1969** *Gloss. Landscape Work (B.S.I.)* v. 30 *Reshaping*, a pruning operation directed to improving the shape of a tree.

Resh Galuta (rēⁱʃ găl*ū*tā·). Also **Resch Glutha** and with small initials. [Aramaic, lit. 'chief of the exile'.] = *EXILARCH. Also *transf.*

1829 H. H. MILMAN *Hist. Jews* III. xix. 160 Babylon, where, during his days of splendour, the Resch-Glutha fixed his residence. *Ibid.* 162 The Court of the Resch-Glutha is described as equally splendid; in imitation of his Persian master, he had his officers, counsellors, and cupbearers. **1867** C. M. YONGE *Pupils of St. John* x. 159 A stately personage..known as the Resch Glutha, or Chief of the Captivity. **1903** *Jewish Encycl.* V. 293/1 This last story indicates that the resh galuta had by that time become the subject of Mohammedan legend. **1931** C. ROTH *Jewish Bk. of Days* 6 Huna Mari, Prince of the Captivity, executed, 470. This high office (otherwise known as that of Exilarch—*Resh Galutha*) was enjoyed by the secular head of the 'exile' in Babylonia in virtue of his descent from the house of David. **1971** *Encycl. Judaica* VI. 1031/2 During subsequent periods the *nesi'im* of Yemen were referred to as *resh galuta*, although they had no connections with the Babylonian exilarch or the House of David.

reshoot, *v.* (Later examples.)

1900 G. B. SHAW *Let.* 4 Nov. (1972) II. 194 He has.. become too curious to see how their marriage will turn out to reshoot himself more efficiently. **1900** *Law Rep. Appeal Cases* 429 No doubt the action of the current upon the net is calculated more or less to shift the position of it, and so from time to time to make it necessary to gather it up and reshoot it, to restore it to its perpendicular position. **1955** H. KURNITZ *Invasion of Privacy* (1956) xiv. 88 It's a hundred-to-one he'll..reshoot the picture so that not a speck of what you want in it remains. **1956** *Nature* 21 Jan. 120/1 The information can be conveniently stored against the day when better interpretation methods allow one to make the fullest use of the recordings, without having to reshoot in areas which are often exceedingly difficult of access. **1975** R. L. SIMON *Wild Turkey* (1976) xi. 72 *Badass* has had a change in shooting schedule... We're going to have to reshoot two days. **1976** A. DAVIS *Television* 28 Plays were still recorded in sequence... The maxim otherwise was to stop the tape and reshoot only for technical mishaps.

reshoo·ting, *vbl. sb.* [f. prec. + -ING¹.] The action of the verb RESHOOT.

1960 L. COOPER *Certain Compass* 121 There was some re-shooting we could do. **1975** [see *RE-EDIT *v.*, RE-EDITING *vbl. sb.*]. **1978** *Times* 26 Aug. 7/2 We had another preview. The picture was obviously better... He did not think any reshooting was necessary.

Resht (reʃt). The name of a province and town in north-west Iran, used *attrib.* to designate patchwork made there.

1888 A. S. COLE *Descr. Catal. Coll. Tapestry & Embroidery S. Kensington Mus.* 314 Patchwork of cloth of various colours... Resht work. *Persian.* **1923** *Daily Mail* 26 Feb. 15 There is also a kind of Persian patch-work called 'Resht'. It is really an amazingly ingenious mosaic of cloth, only *one* thickness being used, and was generally arranged in four colours—red, green, grey, and white. **1960** H. HAYWARD *Antique Coll.* 237/1 *Resht patchwork*, a type of mosaic patchwork produced at Resht, Persia, during the 18th and 19th cent. for covers and prayer-rugs. The designs are inlaid in coloured felts with outlines and details worked in coloured silks in chain-stitch and couched-work. Inferior examples are often not true patchwork, as the small pieces are applied to the ground and not inlaid.

reshta, var. *RISHTA.

reshuffle, *v.* (Later examples with reference to a redistribution of posts within a cabinet, etc.)

1963 *Ann. Reg. 1962* 117 Chief Akintola proposed to reshuffle the Western Nigeria Development Corporation's management. **1973** A. MANN *Tiara* iii. 18 The London correspondent of *Messaggero* thought the British Cabinet would be reshuffled.

reshuffle, *sb.* Add: (Later examples.) Used *esp.* to denote a redistribution of posts within a government or cabinet, etc.

1922 L. WOOLF *Downhill all Way* (1967) i. 37, I feel that this is no time for a mere reshuffle of the ancient Conservative and Liberal Pack and for entrusting power to one or other of the two parties whose political principles and practice are directly responsible for the disastrous situation in which the country finds itself today. **1931** A. L. ROWSE *Politics & Younger Generation* x. 272 It [*sc.* the Tyrol] should be returned to Austria..at the first reshuffle in Europe. **1940** H. NICOLSON *Diary* 3 Apr. (1967) 65 We get over the telephone the final text of the Government reshuffle. **1947** *New Secondary Education* (Ministry of Educ.) 10 Such reorganisation as could be effected in existing buildings by a 'reshuffle' of the children. **1953** E. SIMON *Past Masters* IV. i. 211 Nothing was ever done about the dry rot... Two rooms are involved... So another grand re-shuffle is at hand. **1955** *Daily Express* 14 Oct. 1/5 (*caption*), I *do* wish the P.M. would make up his mind about the Cabinet reshuffle. **1965** *Listener* 17 June 884/2 A reshuffle in the Fund's liabilities among the various depositors. **1976** *Liverpool Echo* 22 Nov. 17/2 Moore went off injured..and it took them a good quarter of an hour to adjust to the enforced reshuffle. **1978** J. R. L. ANDERSON *Death in Greenhouse* ii. 32 [He] was given his present job at the Foreign Office in the Government re-shuffle..last year.

reshu·ffling, *vbl. sb.* [f. RESHUFFLE *v.* + -ING^1.] The action of the verb RESHUFFLE.

1883 E. W. HAMILTON *Diary* 28 May (1972) II. 440 His having to quit the Government would be a loss in itself, but what is worse it would involve a reshuffling of the cards. **1926** J. S. HUXLEY *Ess. Pop. Sci.* 28 Sexual reproduction means first a reshuffling of the factors, and then a recombination of them in new arrangements. **1934** *Mind* XLIII. 525 The mere repetition and reshuffling of changeless entities to which, according to M. Bergson, we should be condemned if we did not have intuition to tutor us. **1937** *Sun* (Baltimore) 7 Dec. 9/2 The proposed 'reshuffling' of operations and routes of American lines.

reside, *v.*^{1} Add: **2.** (Later *transf.* example.)

1973 C. SAGAN *Cosmic Connection* xiii. 88 Such a solution is liquid at the temperatures and pressures at which the Venus clouds reside.

3. b. (Later example.)

1972 *Incorporated Linguist* XI. 30 The significance of linguistic theorizing resides..in the fact that it provides intellectual training while..introducing the learner to problems of the functioning of linguistic systems.

residence, *sb.*^{1} Add: **1. d.** *Anthrop.* The place in which it is customary for a couple to settle after marriage, according to the prevailing kinship system. Also *attrib.* Cf. *MATRILOCAL *a.*, *NEOLOCAL *a.*, etc.

1865 J. F. MCLENNAN *Primitive Marriage* viii. 154 Teadhloch and cuedichc.., Gaelic names for family, mean the first having a common residence; the second those who eat together. **1889** E. B. TYLOR in *Jrnl. Anthrop. Inst.* XVIII. 247 Now, on looking out from the schedules the adhesions of this avoidance-custom, a relation appears between it and the customs of the world as to residence after marriage. **1924** W. H. RIVERS *Social Organisation* v. 90 The last aspect of father-right and mother-right to be mentioned ..is one with which perhaps I ought to have dealt in the second chapter, namely, the place of residence in case of marriage. **1938** G. A. RIECHARD in F. Boas *Gen. Anthrop.* ix. 421 Among primitives residence is of even greater importance. **1968** JACOBSON & SCHOEPF tr. *Levi-Strauss's Structural Anthrop.* xv. 309 The impact of residence on descent. **1972** E. A. HOEBEL *Anthrop.* (ed. 4) xxi. 427/2 There are, then, five basic varieties of residence. *Ibid.*, It is not a simple..matter as to whether a given household represents one kind of residence pattern or another.

2. b. Used *spec.* with reference to a residential post held by an artist, poet, sculptor, writer, etc., within a community or institution for the purpose of teaching his craft or influencing communal life. Also *transf.* (freq. *joc.*). Cf. also *poet-in-residence* (*POET 1 e).

1954 R. JARRELL *Pictures from Institution* iii. 94 How glad Dr. Rosenbaum was that he was only a Composer in Residence. **1965** *Economist* 30 Oct. 499/2 Its money will also be used..to help symphony orchestras and support artists-in-residence at universities. **1968** MRS. L. B. JOHNSON *White House Diary* 30 Apr. (1970) 667 He [*sc.* Eric Hoffer] said, 'I call myself a conversationalist in residence.' **1970** *Times* 16 Apr. 8/5 No girls throwing smoke in our eyes at last night's Gold Leaf concert..instead a tame composer, a 'composer in residence'... Peter Patterson..is the lucky man commissioned to write pieces. **1972** W. KING *Black Short Story Anthol.* 133 She [*sc.* Alice Walker] is presently writer-in-residence at Tougaloo College, ..Mississippi. **1975** *New Yorker* 5 May 45/3 An artist-in-residence at WNET's Television Laboratory and a consultant on television to the Rockefeller Foundation. **1976** C. BERMANT *Coming Home* I. v. 70 A few weeks later, a Jewish boy was billeted on us... I'm not sure if I welcomed it, for I had begun to enjoy my role as Jew in residence. **1979** *Guardian* 27 June 8/3 (Advt.), Photographer in Residence required... There are no specific teaching commitments but the photographer will be expected to participate in the life of the centre and be available to students and others on an informal basis. **1980** *Early Music Gaz.* Apr. 8 (Advt.), Lessons in solo and ensemble performance are conducted by an artist-in-residence each semester.

5. a. (*of*) *no fixed residence* = (*of*) *no fixed abode* s.v. *ABODE *sb.*^{1} 5. ? *Obs.*

1859 *Times* 1 Feb. 9/5 Robert Murry, 35, and Johanna Murry, 28, described as husband and wife, and travelling ventriloquists of no fixed residence, were charged with attacking and robbing Robert Hobbs on the highway of a purse containing a 5*l.* Bank of England note. **1863** W. HARDMAN *Let.* (1925) ? 24 Aug. 72 His books were curious, inasmuch as the customers had no fixed residences.

e. [tr. Russ. *RESIDENTURA.] A group or organization of intelligence agents in a foreign country.

1969 H. H. COOPER *Cave with Two Exits* i. 69 In Rome he was met by a young man from the Residence... The Resident himself..was extremely secure... His cover was strictly diplomatic.

8. *residence address, permit, time*; **residence city** [tr. G. *residenzstadt*], a seat of a royal or princely court; cf. *RESIDENZ; **residence counsellor** *U.S.*, a psychiatric adviser attached to a residential block in a university; **residence general** [tr. F. *résidence générale*], the official residency of the senior French representative in a French protectorate.

1890 'MARK TWAIN' *Lett. to Publishers* (1967) 264, I do not know your residence-address or Whitford's. **1961** L. MUMFORD *City in Hist.* xiii. 386 The chief new cities built from the sixteenth to the nineteenth century were 'residence cities' for kings and princes, like Versailles, Karlsruhe, and Potsdam. **1973** *Pennsylvania Voice* 10 Oct. 5/1 A residence counselor who has been dealing with a student may feel that he is not properly equipped to help the student resolve his problem. **1955** *Times* 9 May 8/4 The crowd..had tried to break into the residence-general. **1962** *Guardian* 14 Aug. 1/7 Bishop Roseveare was given the letter informing of the cancellation of his residence permit. **1977** *Times* 16 Apr. 12/7 Herr Klee got a job..which clinched his residence permit. **1962** A. BATTERSBY *Guide to Stock Control* viii. 76 With an average stock of 200 tons and annual sales of 1,200 tons, the residence time is 2 months. The more commonly used 'turnover' is 6 times a year, which is the reciprocal of the residence time. **1969** *Gloss. Terms Vacuum Technol.* (*B.S.I.*) 13 *Residence time*, the average time for which a molecule is bound to a surface in a state of sorption. **1977** *Sci. Amer.* May 23/2 The period of time a particular amount of water spends in its cycle is termed its residence time... Deep in the oceans the residence time of a body of water may be more than 1,000 years. **1978** *Nature* 20 July 246/1 The concept of oceanic residence time has been used widely in marine chemistry; element residence times range from 10^8 to < 100 yr, and provide a useful measure of the reactivity of an element in the ocean.

residency. 1. a. Delete † *Obs.* and add later N. Amer. examples. Also *attrib.*

1966 *Publ. Amer. Dial. Soc. 1964* XLII. 35 *Shanty-..Irish*, i.e., those who remain in the lower-class communities near the center of the city (or, irrespective of residency, preserve the social traits of the shanty Irish). **1970** *Daily Colonist* (Victoria, B.C.) 2 Apr. 30/1 The controversial [abortion] measure contains no residency requirement and would allow a pregnancy to be terminated at any time. **1981** *Times* 16 Feb. 15/7 Degrees for people who want to be more effective and secure in their Jobs or Professions... No residency required. (Advt. by an Amer. university.)

c. Of a musician or a band: the state of being permanently or regularly engaged at a club, etc.

1966 *Melody Maker* 7 May 5/3 Colin Smith..has left to take up a residency at London's Georgian Room. **1968** *Ibid.* 30 Nov. 6/1 The Nice..used to have a residency there. **1971** *Ibid.* 4 Sept. 21 She moved back to Chicago and played long residencies there..as a pianist vocalist. **1975** *Evening Herald* (Dublin) 8 May 12/4 (Advt.), *Popular vocalist*..seeks position with musicians..; preference for residency in lounge.

2. a. (Later examples.) Also *transf.* (in sense of RESIDENT *sb.* 2 d) and *attrib.*

1958 L. VAN DER POST *Lost World of Kalahari* v. 90, I spent the evening and night with the Resident and his wife..in the ample Residency. **1971** R. RUSSELL tr. *Ahmad's Shore & Wave* xv. 159, I once met Lord Mountbatten myself in Kashmir at a Residency lunch. **1980** J. HONE *Flowers of Forest* I. 8 The annual reception for the Queen's Birthday at the old British Residency on the Nile.

b. = *RESIDENCE *sb.*^{1} 5 e.

1970 K. BENTON *Sole Agent* xviii. 199 [He is]..supplied by the Soviet Illegal Residency here, in Lisbon, to help Rogov to get rid of the body. **1977** 'J. LE CARRÉ' *Hon. Schoolboy* iii. 53 What did he do up there..his networks blown to smithereens? His foreign residencies, his reptile fund frozen solid by the Treasury—they meant his operational accounts..and not a friend in Whitehall or Washington to call his own? **1981** J. SIMPSON *Moscow Requiem* II. vi. 177 The KGB resident in Riyadh..made his last radio contact with the KGB Residency in Aden.

4. *N. Amer.* The position or station of a resident (*RESIDENT *sb.*^{1} 3); the period during which one holds this position.

1924 *Mod. Hospital* XXIII. 422/1 Residencies should also be offered in general hospitals. **1933** *Southern Med. Jrnl.* XXVI. 773/2, I am not in sympathy with the prolonged residency extending over more than two years. **1949** G. D. WOLF *Physician's Business* (ed. 3) i. 10 A promising young doctor, following a year's internship, could receive an assistant residency for two years. *Ibid.*, The ideal residency is one in which all phases of the specialty are stressed. **1958** F. G. SLAUGHTER *Daybreak* I. i. 9 They were also competing for a residency on the Neurosurgical Service—a vitally important stepping-stone for an ambitious doctor on the last lap of his training. **1975** R. H. RIMMER *Premar Experiments* i. 66 I've got a friend who's an MD... He's doing his residency at Boston City Hospital. **1977** *Washington Post* 24 May 1/2 Georgetown University Medical School and Providence Hospital have announced their joint development of a residency program in..general, or family, practice. **1979** *Sci. Amer.* Oct. 16/3 After an internship and residency at the Hospital of the University of Pennsylvania he was Special Projects Associate in epidemiology at the Mayo Graduate School of Medicine in Rochester, Minn.

resident, *a.* and *sb.*^{1} Add: **A.** *adj.* **2. a.** (Further examples.)

1812 *Laws & Ordinances City of New-York* 202 It shall be the duty of the said resident physician and health commissioner, to meet daily at the health office, from the thirty-first day of May to the first day of October. **1844** [see *grave-trap* s.v. *GRAVE *sb.*^{1} 6]. **1899** SOMERVILLE & 'ROSS' *Some Experiences Irish R.M.* i. 10 You wouldn't meet a Christian out of doors, unless it was..a resident magistrate. **1902** *U.S. Laws & Statutes* (1903) XXXII. I. 694 With the first meeting of the Philippine legislature..there shall be chosen, by the said legislature..two resident commissioners to the United States. **1919** *Bull. Johns Hopkins Hospital* XXX. 191/2 The assistant residents, even those who did not become chief resident physicians, often continued in office for several years. **1931** V. PALMER *Separate Lives* 40 I'm a Resident Magistrate now, you know. One of the biggest stations in the Territory. **1952** GRANVILLE *Dict. Theatrical Terms* 151 *Resident manager*, the manager of the theatre as distinct from the acting manager of a visiting company. He handles all the local business. **1962** PLANO & GREENBERG *Amer. Polit. Dict.* iii. 38 *Resident commissioner*, a delegate elected by the people of a territory to represent them in the House of Representatives. He may speak in the House and serve on committees, but he may not vote... Only Puerto Rico has a resident commissioner. **1963** J. JOESTEN *They call it Intelligence* II. viii. 73 Abel..held the post of 'resident officer'... His job was to recruit and organize local spies. **1974** P. GORE-BOOTH *With Great Truth & Respect* 364 On 16 May 1967, at about 6.00 in the morning, my bedside telephone rang. The Resident Clerk at the Foreign Office said that President Nasser had ordered the United Nations Expeditionary Force to leave the Egyptian frontier with Israel. **1976** *National Observer* (U.S.) 22 May 22/1 The resident correspondent can suggest people to interview. **1977** *Belfast Tel.* 19 Jan. 3/9 The resident band..will be George Chambers and the Apex.

4. Delete † *Obs.* and add later example.

1971 *Nature* 12 Mar. 91/1 The non-polar amino-acids, for example in myoglobin and haemoglobin, are resident in the interior of the protein molecule, out of contact with the aqueous environment.

B. *sb.* **1. a.** Also, a guest staying one or more nights at a hotel or boarding-house.

1956 M. STEWART *Wildfire at Midnight* 103 A little sitting-room beside the residents' lounge. **1969** 'L. BRUCE' *Death with Blue Ribbon* vii. 71 Carolus ordered three doubles. He had stayed in the Residents' Lounge too long.

c. A bird belonging to a species that does not migrate but is found all the year round in a particular area.

1896 KIRKALDY & POLLARD tr. *Boas's Text Bk. Zool.* 465 Woodpeckers..are 'residents', or wander about in a limited locality. **1920** H. F. WITHERBY *Pract. Handbk. Brit. Birds* I. 18 After nesting our residents [*sc.* rooks] are subject to partial and irregular movements—some probably emigrating to Continent. **1978** *Ibis* CXX. 496 In West Africa.. residents and migrants overlap throughout the dry season.

2. b, c, d. These senses now only *Hist.* (Further examples.)

1839 T. J. NEWBOLD *Pol. & Statistical Acct. Straits of Malacca* I. iv. 126 The public property there was estimated ..by the British resident. **1958** [see *RESIDENCY 2 a]. **1965** A. NICOL *Truly Married Woman* 88 Ride to the white man who is Resident. **1971** R. RUSSELL tr. *Ahmad's Shore & Wave* i. 13 The British Resident was confiding to the Finance Minister his distrust of the Prime Minister.

3. *N. Amer.* A medical graduate who has completed an internship and is engaged in specialized practice under supervision in a hospital, usu. as training for independent specialization. Also *attrib.* Cf. *REGISTRAR 3.

1892 *Rep. Johns Hopkins Hospital* III. 21 Dr. William Osler [gave]..Books for Resident's Reading Room. **1914** *Mod. Hospital* II. 30/2 The sixth floor is primarily for residents' quarters. The chief resident will have his study, bed room, and private bath. **1931** E. G. REID *Great Physician* vi. 116 Long term residents took the place of the usual short term internship. His first Resident Physician had under him three assistant residents. **1938** [see *INTERN *sb.*]. **1970** *Globe & Mail* (Toronto) 26 Sept. B8/4 (Advt.), Hospital approved for interne and resident training, nursing school, [etc.]. **1977** 'E. TREVOR' *Theta Syndrome* vi. 85 Never..disturb the senior resident when he's on his rounds, unless the place is on fire.

4. [tr. Russ. *rezidént.*] An intelligence agent (in a foreign country). Cf. also *REZIDENT.

1963 'J. LE CARRÉ' *Spy who came in from Cold* viii. 74 The Resident in a particular country would make a requisition... The Resident could draw it [*sc.* money] himself and hand it to the agent. **1968** A. DIMENT *Bang Bang Birds* v. 63 Of course this Agency has a resident in Stockholm. **1975** *Times* 16 Dec. 7/5 Herr Guillaume soon became a 'resident'—the head of a group of spies.

residenter. Add: **2.** (Further and *transf.* examples.) *old residenter*, a pioneer in the U.S.

1827 *Western Monthly Rev.* I. 70 Hence arose a feud and a collision of authorities between the old and the new 'residenters'. **1880** W. H. PATTERSON *Gloss. Words Antrim & Down* 82 *Residenter, sb.* an old inhabitant. **1898** E. N. WESTCOTT *David Harum* 253, I ain't what ye might call an old residenter. **1921** H. GUTHRIE-SMITH *Tutira* xxii. 212 Such residenters are attracted..by the influx of sparrows, rats, and mice. **1967** *Buchan Observer* 5 Sept. 7 Residenters ..are becoming greatly concerned. **1971** M. TAK *Truck Talk* 130 *Residenter*, any old tractor still used over the road. **1975** *New Yorker* 29 Dec. 36/3 Well, here's an old guy in the audience—an old residenter, that's what they called them—with a long grey beard.

residential, *a.*^{1} **1. a.** Delete 'Now rare or *Obs.*' and add later examples.

1886 *Fortn. Rev.* XXXIX. 24 It [*sc.* a medical college for women] has no residential hall, nor is it desirable perhaps that it should have any. **1910** *Bradshaw's Railway Guide* Apr. 1009 Imperial Hotel. First-class family and residential. **1923** W. J. LOCKE *Moordius & Co.* xxiii. 308 An untidy boarding-house in Torrington Square, Bloomsbury, which called itself a Residential Hotel. **1943** [see *neighbourhood unit* s.v. *NEIGHBOURHOOD 7]. **1960** *Times* 21 Mar. 8/5 Oxford, Cambridge and the other residential universities enjoy special prestige compared with the civic universities. **1963** *Specification & Recommendations for Permanent Residential Caravans* (B.S. 3632) 4 The term 'Permanent residential caravan' means a structure with a wheeled chassis..designed for use as a permanent dwelling..and so constructed as to be movable by towing or other methods of transport. Hereinafter the term 'residential caravan' will be used for brevity. **1969** *Sunday Times* (Colour Suppl.) 9 Nov. 85/4 The residential towers in flat units will next year house only 400 students. **1977** *Times Educ. Suppl.* 21 Oct. 56/2 (Advt.), Required..a head teacher for this newly opening..residential school for maladjusted boys of secondary age. **1981** J. CAREY *John Donne* i. 23 The Inns of Court ..operated like residential clubs or hotels.

b. (Later examples.)

1900 H. A. JONES *Mrs. Dane's Defence* III. 49 My dear Sir Daniel, we live in a residential neighbourhood..and what possible occupation is there..except to discuss scandal. **1922** JOYCE *Ulysses* 647 A phenomenally beautiful tenor voice like that..could easily..procure for its fortunate possessor..an *entrée* into fashionable houses in the best residential quarters. **1981** J. B. HILTON *Playground of Death* iv. 46 Below was the black tumour of a residential area.

2. (Further examples.)

1869 *Bradshaw's Railway Man.* XXI. 298 The moderate advance of rates..did not affect the 'residential' or periodical and season tickets. **1934** WEBSTER, Residential zone. **1952** *Density of Residential Areas* (Ministry of Housing & Local Govt.) 1/1 The term 'residential density'..signifies the degree of closeness with which dwellings, and hence the people occupying them, are arranged in the residential areas of towns and villages. **1961** E. A. POWDRILL *Vocab. Land Planning* v. 97 The residential zone will become an industrial and commercial zone and so creating [*sic*] new problems. **1974** *Drive* Autumn 110/2 Disc parking and residential parking schemes, plus a maze of one-way streets, make life harder for motorists. **1977** *Age* (Melbourne) 18 Jan. 8/3 Parents doing residential adoptions (i.e. going to the country of the child's origin) are approved by the host country.

B. as *sb.* A residential hotel.

1953 K. TENNANT *Joyful Condemned* xxxvi. 351 Margot took down from Stella the address of the residential where she and Dorsie were staying. **1954** J. SYMONS *Narrowing Circle* xxix. 129 She had a connection with the Gongora Residential. **1973** *Nation Rev.* (Melbourne) 31 Aug. 1450/1 The..premises..have been an inconspicuous residential for the past three years.

reside·ntially, *adv.* [f. RESIDENTIAL *a.*[1] + -LY[2].] As a residence; according to residence; with the provision of residential accommodation.

1913 *Chambers's Jrnl.* Jan. 51/2 London contains no single palace residentially associated with our long line of sovereigns. **1922** *Daily Mail* 1 Dec. 8 It is sufficiently developed to be comfortable residentially. **1974** *Sci. Amer.* Sept. 125/1 The American high school has all the requisites of an institution designed to promote mating: single males and females are assembled in substantial and equal numbers, are residentially selected for social homogeneity, [etc.]. **1978** *Daily Tel.* 24 July 13/2 The conference was being held residentially at Lambeth.

‖**residentura** (rezidentūə·ră). Also **rezidentura.** [Russ. *rezidentúra*: cf. *RESIDENT *sb.* 4.] A group or organization of intelligence agents in a foreign country.

1963 A. DULLES *Craft of Intelligence* viii. 102 Within the embassy there would still be intelligence officers, but they would restrict themselves, except in emergencies, to 'clean' operations... This unit the Soviets call the 'legal *residentura*'. Outside the embassy..perhaps in a bookstore or a photography shop...was headquarters of the 'illegal' *residentura*. **1969** A. MARIN *Rise with Wind* i. 8 He wouldn't like to be a Russian *Kaygaybehnik* confronted with Clay... The man was capable of bursting into any accessible *residentura* and slaughtering the comrades. **1977** 'R. ROSTAND' *Killing in Rome* i. 5 Chief of the entire *rezidentura* [in Rome] was the first secretary himself, a KGB colonel. **1979** *Daily Tel.* 15 Oct. 5/2 The deputy chief of the KGB Rezidentura in Tokyo..maintains numerous contacts among the staff and research fellows.

‖**Residenz** (rezide·nts). Also **residenz.** [Ger., lit. 'residence'.] The building in which a German princely court resided before 1918; a town which was the seat of a princely court. Hence **Residenzstadt** (-ʃtat) [G. *stadt* town], the seat of a court.

1840 THACKERAY in *Fraser's Mag.* Aug. 151/2 Twice as many people in the streets as you see at midday in a German *residenz* or an English provincial town. **1848** —— *Van. Fair* lxiii. 570 Troops of people..flock to the Residenz and share in the pleasures of the fair and the festivities there. **1915** F. H. BURNETT *Lost Prince* xxii. 215 But I want to know who lives at the Residenz? **1961** L. MUMFORD *City in Hist.* Note to plate 4. These royal tomb cities were thus the earliest form of permanent Residenzstadt, like Versailles or Karlsruhe. **1965** *Observer* 9 May 40/7 The State apartments in the old Kings' Residenz..are being repainted. **1973** *Country Life* 15 Nov. 1542/1 The two vases in the Residenz in Munich. **1980** *Times* 9 Aug. 8/7 The Residenz, the baroque palace of the Von Schönborns.

residual, *sb.* Add: **1. c.** The difference between an observed or measured value of a quantity and its true, theoretical, or notional value.

1868 J. C. WATSON *Theoret. Astron.* vii. 370 In the case of a limited number of observed values of *x*, the residuals given by comparing the arithmetical mean with the several observations will not..give the true errors. **1872** *Mem. R. Astron. Soc.* XXXIX. 100 The usual treatment of equations, by rendering a minimum the sum of the squares of the residuals, not only assumes equal weights for the observations, but also that positive and negative errors are equally probable. **1906** WRIGHT & HAYFORD *Adjustment of Observations* (ed. 2) ii. 12 The sum of the positive residuals is equal to the sum of the negative residuals. **1923** GLAZEBROOK *Dict. Appl. Physics* III. 647/2 The distribution of 174 residuals in a certain case is shown in Fig. 1. The residuals are the differences between observed and calculated monthly sea levels at three tidal observatories. **1932** *Human Biol.* IV. 478 Departures from the average arm girth and calf girth of children of the given four skeletal dimensions, we have termed residuals and have regarded them as indices of muscular development. **1967** *Oceanogr. & Marine Biol.* V. 12 When the residuals at a port are evaluated at say hourly intervals and then plotted against time, a graphical representation of the variations in the surge component at that port is obtained. **1972** *Nature* 17 Mar. 96/1 A major contribution to understanding of the seismic velocity variation necessarily comes from travel time residuals (these are differences between observed arrival times of P-waves at seismometers and the theoretical arrival time from a standard set of tables).

2. a. (Later examples.)

1967 *Economist* 28 Oct. p. xxxiii/2 According to the recorded items on the balance of payments Sweden should by now be dead broke. The one thing that has kept it afloat is an unexplained positive 'residual' in the balance of payments. **1973** 'E. MCBAIN' *Let's hear It* iii. 42 His first impression was one of total harmony... Her face and figure came as residuals to his brief course in art appreciation.

b. The part of a gravity anomaly or magnetic anomaly that remains after subtraction of the regional. Also *attrib.*

1949 *Geophysics* XIV. 45 Since the density of salt is less than that of the surrounding sediments, its residual is negative. *Ibid.* 516 Residual maps have been used extensively by geophysicists to bring into focus local features which tend to be obscured by the broad features of the field. **1965** KRUMBEIN & GRAYBILL *Introd. Statistical Models in Geol.* xiii. 325 Many residual maps contain geological information of value in exploration for natural resources. **1978** *Nature* 13 July 146/1 After removing the mean values we projected the residuals on to profiles transverse and parallel to the plate motion and averaged the values over 0·5° intervals.

3. Also *transf.*

1899 *Daily News* 24 June 4/1 The casual docker is often a residual—the driftwood of society.

4. A royalty paid to an actor, musician, etc., for a repeat of a play, television commercial, etc.

1966 *Guardian* 14 May 7/1 The 'residuals', or BBC fringe benefits, lie chiefly in adoption by the Transcription Service. **1971** *Daily Tel.* 25 Mar. 21/4 He [*sc.* Frank Sinatra] will continue to receive money from..record royalties, residuals of his television programmes and a share in the profits of his films. **1972** D. RAMSAY *Little Murder Music* 78 'What makes a jingle date such an important affair?.. The money?' 'And how. I could wind up making more in residuals alone.' **1977** *Rolling Stone* 13 Jan. 19/1, I love doing jingles because I get residuals.

5. *Geomorphol.* A portion of rocky or high ground remaining after erosion.

1968 R. W. FAIRBRIDGE *Encycl. Geomorphol.* 587/1 Normal fluvial erosion begins to be established, and eventually, only residuals of limestone..are left standing. **1970** R. J. SMALL *Study of Landforms* v. 162 Above the peneplain, a few isolated hills..would remain. Such residuals were referred to by Davis as 'monadnocks'.

residual, *a.* Add: **2. a.** (Later examples.) *residual legatee* = *residuary legatee* s.v. RESIDUARY *a.* 1 b; also *fig.*; *residual powers* = *residuary powers* s.v. *RESIDUARY *a.* 2 b.

1919 G. B. SHAW in *Irish Statesman* 25 Oct. 428/1 When the enfranchisement of the Dominions began with Canada, the question on which freedom depends: namely, which party is to have residual powers, was hardly raised. Those were early days for democracy; and the residual powers were left technically to England. **1963** *Listener* 21 Feb. 334/1 The Liberals cash in..by claiming to be the residual legatees of the radical tradition. **1967** *Boston Sunday Herald* 30 Apr. III. 10/1 A specially interesting use of this guide's table of 'Life Expectancy' and 'residual values' of textiles is in evaluating garments and other textile items donated to charity. **1969** F. HALLIDAY in Cockburn & Blackburn *Student Power* 296 The dominant 'mainstream' faction.. was labelled as 'Trotskyite', a residual term meaning that the group was Marxist but opposed to the official Japan Communist Party line. **1976** *National Observer* (U.S.) 3 July 8/6 'There shouldn't be any wholesale dumping of what we think are good risks into the residual market,' says the Insurance Information Institute spokesman. **1979** *Jrnl. R. Soc. Arts* Jan. 97/2 Alice was the residual legatee and executrix.

d. Applied to magnetism which is retained after the removal of the magnetizing force or in the absence of a magnetizing current.

1837 *Phil. Mag.* X. 195 If the interrupted keeper be applied to a compound magnet, it will be attracted only with a force equal to the quantity of residual magnetism, which being very small the attraction will be comparatively feeble. **1874** *Tyer's Block Telegraph & Electric Locking Signals* (ed. 5) 14 There is also..an electro-magnet fitted with 'homs' or 'keepers'.., so arranged as to..retain for an indefinite period the residual magnetism produced on the passage of each signal. **1886** [see *RETENTIVENESS 6]. **1902** *Encycl. Brit.* XXX. 430/2 If a bar of hard steel is placed in a strong magnetic field, a certain intensity of magnetization is induced in the bar, but when the strength of the field is afterward reduced to zero, the magnetization does not entirely disappear. That portion which is permanently retained, and which may amount to considerably more than one-half, is called the residual magnetization. **1912,** etc. [see *RETENTIVITY]. **1917,** etc. [see *REMANENCE 3].

e. Applied to the small charge which some capacitors remain capable of delivering after 'discharge'.

1838 FARADAY in *Phil. Trans. R. Soc.* CXXVIII. 24 It is the assumption for a time of this charged state of the glass between the coatings in the Leyden jar, which gives origin to a well-known phenomenon, usually referred to the diffusion of electricity over the uncoated portion of the glass, namely, the residual charge. **1878** *Encycl. Brit.* VIII. 39/2 Kohlrausch called attention to the close analogy between the residual discharge and the 'elastic recovery'..of strained bodies... The instantaneous strain which follows the application of a stress is analogous to the initial charge of the jar, and the gradually increasing strain which follows to the gradual formation of the latent or residual charge. **1921** T. F. WALL *Electr. Engin.* iv. 62 The successive charges after the first discharge are known as residual charges. **1938** H. G. MITCHELL *Textbk. Electr.* iv. 64 The residual discharge of the condenser can easily be explained if we assume that the charge penetrates the glass and cannot all reach the conducting plates when these are connected.

f. *Physical Geogr.* Applied to a deposit or feature formed *in situ* by the weathering of rock, and to a soil largely composed of such material.

1895 *Geogr. Jrnl.* V. 140 Most of the peneplains that I have examined..still possess residual elevations,..evidently to be regarded as unconsumed remnants of the denudation of the former cycle. **1906** E. W. HILGARD *Soils* i. 11 When soils have been formed without removal from the site of the original rock, by simple weathering, they are designated as sedentary, or residual soils. **1933** [see *PENEPLAIN *sb.*]. **1937** WOOLDRIDGE & MORGAN *Physical Basis Geogr.* xi. 150 While its origin has given rise to considerable controversy, all are agreed that it [*sc.* laterite] is essentially a residual deposit. **1944** A. HOLMES *Princ. Physical Geol.* viii. 119 Ultimately the angular block is transformed into an onion-like structure of concentric shells of rusty and thoroughly rotted residual material. **1954** W. D. THORNBURY *Princ. Geomorphol.* iv. 74 Soils were commonly divided into two major groups, residual and transported. Residual soils were classified according to the type of rock from which they were derived. **1972** J. G. CRUICKSHANK *Soil Geogr.* ii. 57 Parent materials may be classified by their mode of formation as follows: 1 Weathered rock in place which produces residual soils.

g. *residual stress*, stress present in an object in the absence of any external load or force.

1931 A. NÁDAI *Plasticity* xxxviii. 259 Stresses of this kind, remaining after partial plastic flow, may be called residual stresses. **1958** *Engineering* 18 Apr. 498/1 The operation of welding gives rise to residual stresses, i.e. stresses which exist independently of the external loading. **1976** LINDBERG & BRATON *Welding & Other Joining Processes* xii. 454 A weldment heated to a temperature at which the yield strength is low..will relieve the residual stresses and increase fatigue life.

residuary, *a.* and *sb.* Add: **A.** *adj.* **1. b.** (Later and *transf.* examples.)

1962 S. E. FINER *Man on Horseback* viii. 123 The Justice party..in a sense was the residuary legatee of the old Democrats. **1967** E. RUDINGER *Wills & Probate* 11 The wife is probably the residuary legatee.

2. b. spec. *residuary powers*, powers remaining with one political group after other powers have been allocated to another group, e.g. as between a federal government and a province.

1919 G. B. SHAW *Let.* in *Irish Statesman* 22 Nov. 536/2 The meaning of residuary powers and the importance of the Australian precedent in their bearing on the Irish national question. **1950** THEIMER & CAMPBELL *Encycl. World Politics* 163/2 In some federations..the powers of the federal government are named in the constitution and all other powers (the residuary powers) belong to the regions.

3. Applied to the Established Church of Scotland after the Disruption in 1843. *Obs.* or *arch.*

1843 *Witness* 19 May 2/7 (*heading*) Residuary Assembly... After the Evangelical Party had left the House [etc.]. **1845** J. BRIGHT in *Hansard Commons* 16 Apr. 882/2 Even in Scotland..there were the Secession Church, the Relief Church, and the Free Church; that which the State upheld being called by the complimentary name of the Residuary Church. **1883** R. CLELAND *Inchbracken* iii. 22 The 'Residuary' Presbytery, as you are pleased to denominate the church of your fathers.

B. *sb.* Also *fig.*

1920 E. GOSSE in *Edin. Rev.* Jan. 47 He was the residuary of his own temperament.

residue. Add: **1. e.** *Sociol.* A term used by Vilfredo Pareto (1848–1923) for fundamental impulses which motivate human conduct, and which are not the product of rational deliberation.

1933 *Harper's Mag.* CLXVII. 573 In each of these two groups of phenomena we have found a constant element, the sentiment out of which both the actions and the explanations rise. The *expression* of such a sentiment is what Pareto calls a 'Residue'. **1935** BONGIORNO & LIVINGSTON tr. *Pareto's Mind & Society* II. vi. 508 It might perhaps be advisable to give word-names to the things we have been calling *a*, *b*, and *c*... Suppose we call the things *a*, *residues*, the things *b*, *derivations*, and the things *c*, *derivatives. Ibid.* 509 Residues correspond to certain instincts in human beings, and for that reason they are usually wanting in definiteness, in exact delimitation. **1935** L. J. HENDERSON *Pareto's Gen. Sociol.* v. 23 Theology and metaphysics and parts of law consist, in great measure, of systematic and extensive derivations from certain very important residues like those involving the words justice, duty, sanctity, and absolute. **1939** F. CREEDY *Human Nature writ Large* xix. 400 Public documents which have won high praise and wide acceptance..owe their acceptability to the fact that their Residues or fundamental assumptions coincide with those of the crowd. **1958** W. STARK *Sociol. of Knowl.* viii. 320 These residues or drives determine all the comings and goings on the stage of life. The 'derivations', or thoughts and beliefs which, objectively speaking, derive from the residues, but which subjectively appear to the people who harbour them as 'their ideas', 'their convictions', 'their philosophies'. **1966** S. E. FINER *V. Pareto: Sociol. Writings* 38 Thus, if you strip from the theory its variable part you are left with a residuum. This is the constant element and Pareto therefore calls it a *residue*.

2. (Later example.)

1967 E. RUDINGER *Wills & Probate* 9 After disposing of specified items and sums of money, you give the remainder—the residue, lawyers call it—to some named person... You could, of course, provide that your residue should be divided..among a number of people.

3. Restrict † *Obs.* to sense in Dict. and add: **b.** *Number Theory.* A remainder left when a given number is divided into some integer; also, a number congruent to a given number modulo a third number; *quadratic, cubic,* etc., *residue,* a remainder left when a given number is divided into the square, cube, etc., of some integer; *residue class,* the class of integers congruent to one another modulo a given number (e.g. 2, 5, 8, 11, etc., are members of a residue class modulo 3).

1860 *Rep. Brit. Assoc. Adv. Sci. 1859* I. 231 The set of numbers 0, 1, 2... P − 1 (or any set of P numbers respectively congruous for the modulus P to those numbers) is termed a complete system of residues for the modulus P. **1899** *Q. Jrnl. Math.* XXX. 363 The same representation of the coefficients also determines the residue when the coefficient is not a multiple of the modulus. **1939** USPENSKY & HEASLET *Elem. Number Theory* vi. 134 Of two numbers congruent for the modulus *m*, each is called a 'residue' of the other modulus *m*. *Ibid.* x. 270 A number *a* is said to be a quadratic residue of another number *m* if the congruence $x^2 = a \pmod{m}$ can be satisfied by some integer *x*. **1948** O. ORE *Number Theory & its Hist.* ix. 214 Since these are the numbers that correspond to the same remainder *r* when divided by *m*, we say that they form a residue class (mod *m*). There are *m* residue classes (mod *m*). **1963** W. W. R. BALL *Math. Recreations & Ess.* (ed. 12) ii. 60 There is an arithmetic of residues, closely analogous to the arithmetic of ordinary numbers. **1966** OGILVY & ANDERSON *Excursions in Number Theory* iv. 43 If we identify every integer, positive, negative, or zero, with its remainder modulo *m*, we thus have all the integers partitioned into congruence classes, or residue classes, modulo *m*. **1977** *Sci. Amer.* July 127/2 Gauss used complex numbers of the form $a + bi$..to formulate and prove a version of the law of quadratic reciprocity for biquadratic residues. The number *k* is said to be a biquadratic residue of another number *m* if *k* is congruent modulo *m* to the fourth power of an integer. Thus the biquadratic residues of 10 are 0, 1, 5 and 6.

c. *Theory of Functions.* (See quots.)

1893 A. R. FORSYTH *Theory of Functions* x. 223 The sum of the residues of a doubly-periodic function relative to a fundamental parallelogram of periods is zero. **1957** T. M. APOSTOL *Math. Analysis* xvi. 524 In many cases it is relatively easy to evaluate the residue at a point without the use of integration. **1959** G. & R. C. JAMES *Math. Dict.* 334/1 If $f(z)$ is an analytic function of the complex variable *z* in the 'deleted' neighbourhood consisting of all *z* satisfying $0 < |z - z_0| < \epsilon$, then the residue of $f(z)$ at z_0 is

$$\frac{1}{2\pi i}\int_C f(z)dz,$$

where *C* is a simple closed rectifiable curve about z_0 in the 'deleted' neighbourhood. The value of the residue is..the coefficient of $(z-z_0)^{-1}$ in the Laurent expansion of $f(z)$ about z_0. **1973** RAUCH & LEBOWITZ *Elliptic Functions, Theta Functions, & Riemann Surfaces* i. 19 A differential of the *first kind* is one whose set of Laurent expansions has no poles. Differentials of the *second kind* have poles but with zero residue at each pole while differentials of the *third kind* allow poles with non-vanishing residues.

5. (Earlier and later examples.) In mod. use applied to any molecule when incorporated without major alteration in a larger one; *esp.* in *Biochem.*, an amino-acid, sugar, or other molecule incorporated in a polymer such as a protein, carbohydrate, etc.

1852 H. WATTS tr. *Gmelin's Hand-bk. Chem.* VII. 76 The compound thus formed by substitution contains therefore the residues of the two compounds united, that is to say, the first compound + the second, *minus* an equal number of H- and O-atoms. *Ibid.* 77 Oxamide..may be regarded as a compound of the two residues, $C^4H^2O^4$ and 2NH. **1886** E. F. SMITH tr. *V. von Richter's Org. Chem.* 30 Ordinarily, radicals are groups containing carbon, while all others, like OH, SH, NH_2, NO_2, are residues or groups. **1903** *Jrnl. Chem. Soc.* LXXXIV. I. 214 The (albumin) molecule may be regarded as made up of 125 groups or residues. **1934** W. R. FEARON *Introd. Biochem.* xv. 231 The test is believed to depend on the hydrolytic unmasking of an aldehyde group in the hexose residue. **1955** H. R. DOWNES *Chem. Living Cells* v. 186 In one sample of lactoglobulin, for example, there were found 20 serine residues, 36 from aspartic acid, and 50 from leucine. **1975** *Nature* 27 Feb. 694/2 Even the smallest protein (say 50 residues) is extremely complicated.

resign, *sb.* For † *Obs.* read *rare* and add earlier and later examples.

1639 CHAPMAN & SHIRLEY *Chabot* v. sig. H3ᵛ, My free Resigne of title, office,..would buy my poore lives safety. **1971** J. V. ALLEN *Cowboy Lore* IV. 159 It was a pistol shot that laid Pete out, It was his last resign.

resign, *v.*¹ Add: **I. 2. c.** Quot. *a* 1704 to read: *c* **1698** LOCKE *Some Thoughts on Conduct of Understanding* (1881) 61 [etc.].

d. Also const. with *inf.*

1898 G. B. SHAW *You never can Tell* II. 265 She smiles in spite of herself, and resigns herself to indulge him a little. *a* **1953** E. O'NEILL *More Stately Mansions* (1964) I. ii. 39 Resign myself to be a grandmother!

II. 5. b. For *U.S.* read 'orig. *U.S.*' and add later examples.

1926 G. B. SHAW *Translations & Tomfooleries* 235 My brothers said I ought to resign from my clubs. **1959** *Chambers's Encycl.* II. 68/1 In 1922 he resigned from office and was raised to the peerage as earl of Balfour. **1973** HOWAT & TAYLOR *Dict. World Hist.* 1619/2 In April 1951 he resigned from the government..in protest against an increase in social service charges. **1980** *Times* 20 Aug. 1/2 Mr A. J. P. Taylor resigned from the British Academy over what he described as a witch hunt by some members to remove Professor Anthony Blunt.

7. (Later Austral. example.)

a **1964** in *Penguin Bk. Austral. Ballads* (1964) 75 'Die or resign, Jack Donahoe!' they [*sc.* police] shouted in their joy.

re-sign, *v.* Add: **b.** *intr.* Of a sportsman, performer, etc.: to sign a contract for a further period. Also *trans.*, to cause (a person) to do this.

1938 C. E. SUTCLIFFE et al. *Story of Football League* iii. 19 The player claimed from the club a sum of £250 which..had been promised him..on re-signing in June. **1951** *People* 3 June 8/3 We are urging players not to re-sign for next season until we have consulted the Ministry. **1976** *Jrnl.* (Newcastle) 26 Nov., Berwick Rangers have re-signed centre-forward Billy Laing..who has been on a month's trial at Shielfield. **1977** *Rolling Stone* 21 Apr. 5/1 (*caption*) The Rolling Stones re-sign with Atlantic.

re-si·gnal (rī-), *v.* [RE- 5 c.] *trans.* To refurnish with railway signals. Hence **re-signalling** *vbl. sb.*

1928 *Observer* 10 June 5/4 (*heading*) Re-signalling London Bridge. **1970** *Railway Mag.* Oct. 577/1 A further stage of the resignalling of the Bristol region..was completed in mid-August.., following which the London–Reading–Bath–Bristol route is now entirely controlled by colour-light signals. **1977** *Modern Railways* Dec. 469/1 However, until the Victoria and Brighton area resignalling projects are completed..the practical scope for a general speed-up of train services is minimal.

resignation. Add: **1. c.** In *Chess.*

1969 A. GLYN *Dragon Variation* ix. 271 One or two of the inexpert protested at the resignation. ('He hasn't been mated, has he? Why does he give up? Why doesn't he play on?')

5. *attrib.*, as *resignation letter, rally, speech.*

a **1974** R. CROSSMAN *Diaries* (1976) II. 713 When the word didn't come he was compelled to write his resignation letter. **1961** *Economist* 2 Dec. 906/1 Democrats are beginning to repudiate their party at public 'resignation rallies'. **1938** H. NICOLSON *Diary* 3 Oct. (1966) 374 It begins by Duff Cooper making his resignation speech.

resigna·tionist. *rare.* [f. RESIGNATION + -IST.] One who follows a philosophy of resignation, a believer in resignationism.

1931 [see *RENUNCIANT *sb.*].

resignee. Restrict ? *Obs.* to sense in Dict. and add: **2.** = RESIGNER.

1761 *Second Let. to Earl of Bxxx* 1 A right honourable resignee. **1973** *Times* 15 May 17/3 The only resignee that Mr Nixon chose to criticize.

resilience. Add: **2.** *spec.* The energy per unit volume absorbed by a material when it is subjected to strain, or the maximum value of this when the elastic limit is not exceeded. (Further examples.)

1908 E. S. ANDREWS *Theory & Design of Structures* i. 27 The work done per unit volume of a material in producing strain is called resilience. **1965** J. A. CORMACK *Definitions Strength of Materials* iii. 67 Show that resilience per cubic inch in direct tension or compression may be expressed in the form $f^2/2E$, where *f* is the intensity of stress induced and *E* is the modulus of elasticity. **1978** B. I. SANDOR *Strength of Materials* iv. 79 The maximum value of the elastic strain energy in a unit volume that has not been permanently deformed is called the modulus of resilience.

resi·liently, *adv.* [f. RESILIENT *a.* + -LY².] In a resilient manner, esp. such that the original position is resumed after bending or other shock.

1946 *Jrnl. Inst. Electr. Engineers* XCIII. IIIA. 330/2 The components were insulated from mechanical shock by mounting them on a tray resiliently supported within the frame. **1977** *BSI News* Oct. 8/3 A straight extension of ISO 2373 for the larger machines is not necessarily possible because of the difficulty of resiliently mounting them.

resilin (re·zilin). *Biol.* [f. L. *resil-ire* to jump back, recoil, RESILE + -IN¹.] An elastic material formed of cross-linked protein chains that is found in the cuticles of many species of insect, notably forming the hinges and ligaments of wings.

1960 *New Scientist* 14 July 104/1 Resilin is a protein of a new kind in which the protein chains are cross-linked by means of bonds of a new sort which are resistant to tryptic digestion. **1960** T. WEIS-FOGH in *Jrnl. Exper. Biol.* XXXVII. 889 The main conclusion is that the characteristic elasticity is caused by a peculiar protein, called resilin, which differs from other structural proteins also in respect of amino acid composition. **1961** BAILEY & WEIS-FOGH in *Biochimica & Biophysica Acta* XLVIII. 453 We therefore propose to name it resilin, derived from the Latin resilire, *i.e.* to spring back (pronounced rez'ilin). (We are indebted to Professor D. S. Robertson, Cambridge, who suggested the name.) **1969** R. F. CHAPMAN *Insects* xxii. 435 Resilin contains various amino acids including two previously unknown ones which provide the links between the protein chains. **1970** *Nature* 26 Dec. 1338/1 Resilin is a significant structural component of the sucking pump in many different insects. **1973** *Sci. Amer.* Nov. 92/3 The flea's leap is powered not by muscle alone but is assisted by the elastic protein resilin.

resilium (rīzi·liŭm). *Conch.* [mod.L., f. as prec. + *-ium*, neut. ending.] The resilient central part of the 'hinge' of a bivalve, which tends to force apart the two valves.

1906 G. BOURNE tr. *Pelseneer's Mollusca* in E. R. Lankester *Treat. Zool.* V. v. 213 The ligament finally becomes external..or internal; in the latter case it is a 'resilium'. **1926** *Proc. Malacol. Soc.* XVII. 44 Nacreous shells.. possess glutinous hinge-joints consisting of conchyolin disposed in a dual fashion as 'resilium'—more or less in the centre of the hinge base—and 'ligament' to the right and left of it. **1962** *Science* 29 June 1121/3 (*heading*) Aragonite in the resilium of oysters. **1973** R. T. ABBOTT *Kingdom of Seashell* 16/1 These valves are brought together by one or two strong adductor muscles and forced ajar by a rubberlike wedge, or resilium, which acts much the same way as a rubber wedge placed in the hinged side of a closing door.

re-silver, *v.* (Earlier and further examples.)

1839 in G. S. Haight *Geo. Eliot & J. Chapman* (1969) 259 Sextants, Quadrants, &c., re-silvered and repaired. **1873** *Young Englishwoman* Jan. 52/1 Whether looking-glasses can be re-silvered... A very good furniture dealer will re-silver this for you. **1973** W. H. HALLAHAN *Ross Forgery* iii. 40 The mirror must have been resilvered not too many years ago.

resin, *sb.* Add: **2*.** Any synthetic material resembling a natural resin; now usu. any of a large and varied class of synthetic organic polymeric materials (solid or liquid) that are thermosetting or thermoplastic (see also quot. 1934) and are used esp. as plastics or their chief ingredients. Freq. with qualifying adj. or sb., esp. *synthetic.*

1883 *Amer. Chem. Jrnl.* V. 338 Concentrated sulphuric acid on a mixture of benzoic aldehyde and resorcin gave a reddish resin. **1909** *Chem. Abstr.* III. 1818 Process of manufacturing synthetic resins as substitutes for shellac, consisting in treating *o*-cresol with formaldehyde in the presence of an acid. **1934** *Chem. Rev.* XV. 123 The resinous plastic field may well be divided into two main divisions dependent upon properties which find reflection in use. (1) The resins, which are melted for flow and cooled for hardening into the finished shape... (2) The resinoids, which in molding are heated for flow and also heated for hardening effect. **1937** *Discovery* Jan. 27/2 A new series of synthetic resins, claimed to be as clear as optical glass and to be..non-shattering,..is being marketed in the United States. **1943**, etc. [see *ION EXCHANGE]. **1951** *Engineering* 20 Apr. 469/3 The setting of synthetic-resin glues by high frequency heating. **1957** *Which?* Autumn 20/2 The actual processing of these fabrics consists of various ways of putting the resin in under heat and pressure. **1970** GAIT & HANCOCK *Plastics & Synthetic Rubbers* iii. 60 Production of phenolic resins is still increasing. **1973** *Materials & Technol.* VI. i. 86 Much imported and all British-made plywood is manufactured with synthetic resin adhesives of one type or other. **1976** *McGraw-Hill Yearbk. Sci. & Technol.* 182/1 Probably the cheapest resin to use for plastic bottles is polystyrene.

3. *resin-based, -bonded, -finished, -scented, -tipped, -treated* adjs.; **resin-weed** (earlier example).

1959 *Times* 3 Mar. 7/7 Resin-based paint. **1940** 'PLASTES' *Plastics in Industry* x. 147 Not only have a number of private houses been built of resin-bonded plywood, but also several garages and petrol stations. **1959** *Engineering* 16 Jan. 86/1 This year there are in evidence still more hulls either moulded or sheathed in resin-bonded glass fibre. **1978** *Lancashire Life* Oct. 125/2 Birchwood ply used for work tops, resin-bonded and waterproofed particle board, steel runners with nylon bearings, [etc.]. **1963** A. J. HALL *Textile Sci.* v. 231 It also has the effect of making the resin-finished fabric tear more easily. **1937** J. BETJEMAN *Continual Dew* 11 Drained dark the pines in resin-scented rain. **1922** JOYCE *Ulysses* 653 A pyre of crosslaid resintipped sticks. **1962** J. T. MARSH *Self-Smoothing Fabrics* i. 5 It was soon observed that the resin-treated fabrics possess certain properties in addition to 'crease-resistance'. **1852** L. B. MACKINNON *Atlantic & Transatlantic Sk.* I. 268, I found that he had spoken the truth, and that the resin grass, or weed, had peculiar leaves which always grew in the same direction.

b. Substitute for def.: *attrib.*, in terms denoting vessels in plants that contain resin secreted by cells lining them, as *resin canal, duct, passage, reservoir.*

1854, etc. [in Dict.]. **1896** W. R. FISHER tr. *Schlich's Man. Forestry* V. 14 Turpentine is chiefly found in the resin-ducts. **1924** W. S. JONES *Timbers* iv. 24 The presence of resin canals in dicotyledonous woods is, as in the case of Conifers, of considerable diagnostic value. *Ibid.* v. 30 Resin ducts are usually absent from the wood of many genera of Conifers. **1938** H. E. DESCH *Timber* ii. 20 Resin canals run vertically in the stem and horizontally in the rays, and are just large enough to be seen with the naked eye. **1967** N. T. MIROV *Genus Pinus* vii. 486 When the pine is wounded, the resin canals are severed. The oleoresin, squeezed from the epithelial cells into the resin canals, may be gathered in receptacles attached below the wound.

resinate, *v.* Add: (Examples.) Also, to impregnate with synthetic resin.

1945 C. S. FORESTER *Commodore* xviii. 198 The Governor had taken advantage of the campaigns in which he had served to study the foods of the different countries. Vienna and Prague had fed him during the Austerlitz campaign; he had drunk resinated wine in the Seven Islands. **1966** *New Scientist* 22 Sept. 667/2 One of the drawbacks in resinating cloth is the tendency to reduce the durability of garments by making fibres more brittle.

resined, *ppl. a.* (In Dict. s.v. RESIN *v.*) Add: **b.** Of wood: from which resin has been extracted or collected.

1926 *Contemp. Rev.* May 640 Resined wood lasts better than wood not resined, or wood from the same tree above the limit of the cuts.

resinification. Add: **2.** A reaction in which a synthetic resin is formed; conversion into a synthetic resin.

1913 *Chem. Abstr.* VII. 1484, H_2O inhibits polymerization and resinification, but favors the production of larger quantities of AcOH and HCO_2H. **1928** *Industr. & Engin. Chem.* Aug. 796/1 If a mixture of phenol and formaldehyde is heated, with or without a catalyst, resinification occurs. *Ibid.*, When a certain degree of resinification is reached, the process is usually interrupted. **1938** *Jrnl. Physical Chem.* XLII. 351 A more active catalyst in the resinification might be expected to increase the number of cross linkages. **1973** *Materials & Technol.* VI. viii. 587 If phenol is added in excess monomethylol phenol..is mainly formed and this, in a secondary condensation or resinification reaction, is converted into polynuclear methylene phenols.

resinify, *v.* In both senses used in connection with synthetic resins. (Further examples.) Also **re·sinified** *ppl. a.*, **re·sinifying** *vbl. sb.*

1920 *Chem. Abstr.* XIV. 3672 The Na salt of the 163° acid completely resinified on illumination in H_2O. **1928** *Industr. & Engin. Chem.* Aug. 798/1 Refractive indices of very highly resinified mixtures. **1933** *Ibid.* June 646/1 Like all resinifying reactions, that which forms vinyl resins is imperfectly understood. **1933** *Chem. Abstr.* XXVII. 4110 The disaggregated mass may be resinified more deeply with CH_2O. **1936** *Trans. Faraday Soc.* XXXII. 388 For the resinifying reactions we refer again to the scheme given earlier. **1963** F. M. DEAN *Naturally Occurring Oxygen Ring Compounds* i. 2 Naturally occurring furans generally resinify in these conditions.

resinized, *ppl. a.* Add: **b.** Containing resin.

1908 W. R. FISHER tr. *Schlich's Man. Forestry* (ed. 2) V. 706 Resinised wood, owing to its easy combustibility, is excellent for kindling purposes, and in mountain districts abroad is still employed for torches.

resinography (rezinǫ·grăfi). [f. RESIN *sb.* + -OGRAPHY.] The study of the morphology, internal structure, and related properties of synthetic resins. Hence **resino·grapher**, one who practises resinography; **resinogra·phic** *a.*, of or pertaining to resinography; **resinogra·phically** *adv.*, by means of resinography.

1946 ROCHOW & GILBERT in J. J. Mattiello *Protective & Decorative Coatings* V. v. 476 Resinography, as the name implies, is the graphic study of resins. The term is proposed by the authors to serve as an analogue of metallography and mineralography. *Ibid.* 484 The resinographer must explain that the effect of magnetite on electrical and other properties should be considered. *Ibid.* 485 Resinographic methods, employing the optical microscope and reflected light, are designed for those large classes of resinous materials which are too opaque for examination by transmitted light. *Ibid.* 503 So much information about the fillers can be gathered quickly from a molding..that Stafford and Williams.. usually briquet a portion of the sample and examine it resinographically. **1949** *Analytical Chem.* XXI. 461/1 A resinographic examination of this type of plastic reveals the number of phases, their mode of association; particle sizes and shapes, and relative reflectivity. **1961** G. L. CLARK *Encycl. Microscopy* 527/1 Demonstration of macromolecular boundaries is the least developed and most difficult part of resinography. **1970** *Encycl. Polymer Sci. & Technol.* XII. 81 Usually there is enough reflectivity in the surface of a resinographic specimen to reveal the topography. **1976** T. G. & E. G. ROCHOW *Resinography* i. 14 Besides information from these four levels of study,..the resinographer must make his own examination and arrive at his own conclusions about the identity and utility of a plastic or fiber.

resinoid, *a.* and *sb.* Add: **B.** *sb.* **2.** A synthetic resin; *spec.* one that is thermosetting, or is not permanently soluble and fusible.

1925 BAEKELAND & BENDER in *Industr. & Engin. Chem.* Mar. 225 The resinous products..are..decidedly infusible. Furthermore, they are insoluble in ordinary solvents and are incomparably stronger and more resistant to chemical and physical agents than the natural resins or the artificial resins of the Novolak type; in order to differentiate them from all these, we feel warranted in designating them more accurately under the name of 'phenol resinoids'. **1934** [see *RESIN *sb.* 2*]. **1935** C. ELLIS *Chem. Synthetic Resins* I. i. 14 The term 'resin' is restricted by some to thermoplastic resins, and the word 'resinoid' is used to designate the heat-hardening resins. **1936** H. W. ROWELL *Technol. Plastics* i. 12 Phenolic and other synthetic resinoids now have an increasing use in the varnish industry. **1949** B. L. DAVIES *Technol. Plastics* xi. 188 The three stages in the polymerization [of phenol with formaldehyde] were first recognized by Baekeland,..all being called resinoids to distinguish them from the permanently soluble, permanently fusible, resins. **1959** *Times* 18 Nov. 12/5 The diamonds produced in the laboratory consist, in effect, of abrasive grit suitable for use in resinoid-bonded grinding wheels.

† **resinophore,** *a.* (*sb.*) *Chem. Obs.* [ad. G. *resinophor* (W. Herzog 1921, in *Österr. Chem.-Zeitung* XXIV. 77): see RESIN *sb.* + -PHORE.] *resinophore group*, a group whose presence in a molecule was considered to be responsible for resinous properties or resin formation. Also *ellipt.* as *sb.*

1922 *Chem. Abstr.* XVI. 1671 The 'resinophore group', formed from ureas capable of being converted into resinous substances, is the complex —N=C=N—. **1935** C. ELLIS *Chem. Synthetic Resins* II. xxv. 562 An investigation of the effect of heat on several mono- and di-arylidene ketones showed that the grouping —CH=CHCO— was responsible for resinification; that is, this group is a 'resinophore'. **1937** R. S. MORRELL et al. *Synthetic Resins & Allied Plastics* xv. 375 Comparison between Herzog and Kreidl's resinophore groups and Standinger's chain theories shows that preference must be given to the latter in any explanation of the causes of resinification.

resinosis (rezinōu·sis). *Forestry.* [f. RESIN *sb.* + -OSIS.] The excessive production of resin (in conifers).

1922 F. DORRANCE tr. *Sorauer's Man. Plant Dis.* I. xvi. 716, I have had the opportunity to observe resinosis as a constitutional disease, i.e. as the manifestation, even in old trees, of a tendency throughout the whole plant body, to form resin excessively. **1968** F. G. BROWNE *Pests & Dis. of Forest Plantation Trees* II. 950 In New Zealand the species [sc. *Pythium undulatum*] is closely associated with a virulent resinosis of the roots, root collars, and stems of *Larix decidua* and *L. leptolepis*.

resinous, *a.* Add: **5.** (Earlier examples.) Now *Obs.*

1742 J. T. DESAGULIERS *Diss. Electr.* 41 The Air being electrical of a vitreous Electricity, and sulphur of a resinous Electricity. **1756** *Phil. Trans. R. Soc.* XLIX. 152 Some writers on electricity have said, that there were two kinds of electrical fire, the one resinous, and the other vitreous.

resist, *sb.* Add: **3. a.** *spec.* Such a composition used to provide protection against the etchant or solvent in photo-engraving, photogravure, or photolithography. (Further examples.)

1886 W. T. WILKINSON *Photo-Engraving on Zinc & Copper* v. 34 When it is judged that the etching has proceeded far enough, the resist of ink and resin is removed by the copious use of turpentine. **1933** T. S. BARBER *Photo-Engraving, Electrotyping & Stereotyping* i. 17 The portions of the bichromated surface which were exposed to light, and already made insoluble, acted as an acid resist. **1960** [see *micro-machining* s.v. *MICRO- 2 a]. **1967** V. STRAUSS *Printing Industry* v. 213 Polyvinyl alcohol..can be dissolved in water and sensitized with bichromates. Such a solution.. can serve as a photomechanical coating resulting in an acid resist. Coating, exposure, and development of polyvinyl alcohol resists do not differ from other resists. But polyvinyl alcohol resists have the advantage that they need not be heated as high as glue-enamel resists in order to make them sufficiently acid-resistant. **1975** FINK & MCKENZIE *Electronics Engineers' Handbk.* VIII. 6 The [semiconductor] wafer surface to be masked is coated with a photosensitive coating known as photoresist, or resist. The masking plate is then..exposed with ultraviolet light... The photomasking step is followed by an etching step. **1978** *Sci. Amer.* Nov. 63/1 The wafer is first coated with an X-ray-sensitive organic polymer called an X-ray resist.

b. *Pottery.* A material (usu. wax-based) which is applied to pottery in order to prevent glaze or lustre from adhering to certain parts and is removed before or during firing. Orig. and freq. *attrib.*

1904 A. HAYDEN *Chats on Eng. China* xii. 231 The.. method, with the design left in white, was produced in handsome and highly artistic styles, and there is a pattern, known as the 'Resist' pattern, which is much sought after. **1910** J. F. BLACKER *ABC of Collecting Old Eng. Pott.* xxiii. 214 The commonest application of silver resist is used on a white or ivory ground. **1933** W. B. HONEY *Eng. Pott. & Porc.* iv. 59 Designs of formal flowers and inscriptions..were also done in darker brown or in 'resist' so as to appear of a lighter colour. **1957** MANKOWITZ & HAGGAR *Encycl. Eng. Pott. & Porc.* 189/2 The decoration is painted upon the glazed surface of the ware in a 'resist', covered with metallic solution and fired, the infusible resist portion firing away during the process leaving a white decoration reserved against a bright metallic background. **1967** M. CHANDLER *Ceramics in Mod. World* iii. 108 (*caption*) The water-soluble resist is washed off before the plates are fired. *a* **1977** *Harrison Mayer Ltd. Catal.* 19/1 Wax resist decoration is very frequently used both under and over a glaze and in combination with stain decoration.

resistance. Add: **1. b.** *passive resistance.* See also as main entry in Suppl.

c. Organized covert opposition to an occupying or ruling power; *spec.* (usu. with def. article and capital initial) in the war of 1939–45, the underground movement formed in France in June 1940 with the object of resisting the authority of the German occupying forces and the Vichy government; any organization of this type with similar ends.

1939 *War Illustr.* 28 Oct. 217/1 Underground resistance to Hitler has been organized amongst the workers in all the big industrial centres of Germany. **1940** *Times* 19 June 6/3 General de Gaulle..broadcast from London a message to the French nation last night. The text of his speech..is as follows:..Whatever happens the flame of French resistance must not and shall not be extinguished. **1946** A. HUXLEY *Let.* 28 Mar. (1969) 541, I was sent a number of French books recently... Novels about the Resistance—half heroism, half unutterable moral squalor. **1959** *Listener* 17 Sept. 454/3 To judge by the atmosphere of this tale the resistance in Denmark must have been a less desperate affair than it was in many parts of Europe. **1967** *Freedomways* VII. 143 The men and women who have been notable in African history—not only the rulers and statesmen, but also the educators and scholars, writers and artists, religious leaders, heroes of resistance. **1976** H. TRACY *Death in Reserve* xxii. 170 In this area, *Sanglier* had been an important man in the Resistance. **1981** *Guardian* 2 June 6/7 In the many rural areas [of Afghanistan] under the control of the resistance and unchallenged by the Russians, the insurgents impose their own curfew.

2. a. (Further examples.)

1953 *Sun* (Baltimore) (B ed.) 9 Sept. 3/4 How germs develop resistance to the drugs. **1968** [see *RESISTANT *a.* 2].

b. *Psycho-anal.* Opposition, freq. unconscious, to allowing memories or desires which have been repressed as unacceptable or disruptive to emerge into the conscious mind.

1905 *Psychol. Bull.* II. 256 Resistance (in the form of indifference, etc.), would greatly delay the inquiry. **1909** A. A. BRILL tr. *Freud's Sel. Papers on Hysteria* vii. 167, I started with the presupposition that..this paranoia must contain unconscious thoughts and repressed reminiscences which have to be brought to consciousness..by overcoming a certain resistance. **1913** E. JONES *Papers on Psycho-Anal.* i. 6 Whenever an individual considers a given process as being too obvious to permit any investigation into its origin, and shows resistance to such an investigation, we are right in suspecting that the actual origin is concealed from him. **1924** J. RIVIERE tr. *Freud's On Psychotherapy* in *Coll. Papers* I. 254 It [*sc.* a technique of suggestion] does not permit us..to recognize the *resistance* with which the patient clings to his disease and thus even fights against his own recovery. **1936** M. M. GREEN tr. *Reik's Surprise & Psycho-Analyst* iv. 52 We have discovered resistance in analysis as the emotional expression of this opposition. **1951** P. M. SYMONDS *Ego & Self* xii. 175 In order to defend the ego against anxiety, resistances are built up against the recognition of these unconscious impulses. **1964** E. KRAPF tr. *Caruso's Existential Psychol.* III. i. 150 Placing the burden of resistance on the patient alone provides a good excuse for one's own incapacity and totalitarian one-sidedness. **1977** C. F. MONTE *Beneath Mask* ii. 53 Resistance to recall is one evidence of motivated forgetting or repression.

c. In *Comb.* with a preceding sb., as *crease resistance*, resistance to creasing, etc.

1932 [see *drug-resistance* s.v. *DRUG *sb.*[1] 3]. **1947** [see *CREASE *sb.*[2] 5]. **1959** *Times* 12 Jan. 11/4 Gives shrink, stretch, and rot-resistance. **1959** [see *flame-resistance* s.v. *FLAME *sb.* 10]. **1966** *Economist* 8 Jan. 113/1 There are now two processes..for giving man-made fibre garments a permanent press. This builds up crease resistance in normal wear. **1973** R. G. KRUEGER et al. *Introd. Microbiol.* xv. 422/1 Transmissible drug resistance was discovered.. around 1960.

3. d. *line*, etc., *of least resistance*: (see quot. 1871); also *fig.*, the easiest method or course of action.

1865 MILL *Auguste Comte* 101 In the play of antagonistic forces, the path it [*sc.* our intelligence] points out is (in scientific phraseology) the direction of least resistance. **1871** G. E. VOYLE *Dict. Artillery Terms* (ed. 2) 185/2 *Line of least resistance*, in blasting or mining, is a line drawn from the centre of the charge perpendicular to the surface of the ground. *Ibid.* 213/1 By taking 1/10 of the cube of the line of least resistance in feet, the proper charge of powder..is given in pounds. **1903** G. B. SHAW *Man & Superman* III. 134 This Life Force says to him 'I have done a thousand wonderful things unconsciously by merely willing to live and following the line of least resistance: now I want to know myself and my destination, and choose my path.' **1908** W. McDOUGALL *Introd. Social Psychol.* vii. 179 He often seems to act, not in the line of least resistance, but in the line of greatest resistance. **1923** W. G. BOULTON *Blasting with High Explosives* xv. 45 L = Line of least resistance in feet... The line of resistance is the shortest distance from the chamber to the surface. **1931** *Economist* 7 Feb. 300/2 This was no doubt the line of least resistance, when money had to be found. **1954** M. SHARP *Gipsy in Parlour* xxiv. 233 He took by nature the line of least resistance. **1967** C. V. BARK *See Living Crocodiles* xi. 184 It is taking the line of least resistance. It saves trouble.

4. a. *spec.* Resistance to an unvarying electric current. (Earlier and later examples.)

1760 J. WESLEY *Desideratum* 17 While the electric fire, which is in all bodies, is left to itself, undisturb'd by any external violence, it is more or less dense... And there is some resistence to every endeavour of altering its density... This resistence is least in metals, minerals, water, quicksilver, animals and vegetables... In these bodies the resistence is greater, when their surface are polish'd. **1767** J. PRIESTLEY *Hist. Electricity* 116 The difference between electric and non electric bodies was owing to the different resistance..to the passage of the electric fluid. **1963** A. F. ABBOTT *Ordinary Level Physics* xxxvii. 479 The resistance of a wire depends on its dimensions and the material from which it is made. **1975** [see *RESISTOR].

6. (sense *1 c) *resistance cell, club, fighter, figure, forces, group, hero, man, movement, network, plan, work, worker*; (sense 4 a) *resistance-capacitance, -capacity* (both used *attrib.*), *-coupling*; *resistance-coupled* adj.; **resistance furnace**, an electric furnace which is heated by passing a current through elements of high resistance; **resistance pyrometer**, a form of resistance thermometer suitable for use at high temperatures; **resistance thermometer**, a temperature-measuring device in which the change in electrical resistance with temperature of a platinum or other metallic wire is measured; **resistance transfer factor** *Biol.*, a plasmid that promotes the transfer from one bacterium to another of a genetic determinant for drug resistance; **resistance welding**, a method of welding in which the heat to cause fusion of the metals is produced by the passage of an electric current through the contact resistance between the two surfaces, these being held together by mechanical pressure.

1942 E. WILLIAMS *Thermionic Valve Circuits* iii. 33 The condenser, C_2, is therefore omitted and the circuit becomes the orthodox Resistance-capacitance Coupling circuit. *Ibid.* 69 Consider the resistance-capacitance coupled circuit. **1962** SIMPSON & RICHARDS *Physical Princ. Junction Transistors* ix. 208 A resistance-capacitance coupled amplifier. **1924** P. J. RISDON *Wireless* xxvii. 221 In the case of resistance or resistance-capacity coupling, instead of an inductance coil, a high resistance is employed for establishing the necessary differences of potential. **1962** SIMPSON & RICHARDS *Physical Princ. Junction Transistors* v. 88 Many audio and low radio-frequency amplifiers, having resistance-capacity coupling between stages. **1972** D. RAMSAY *Little Murder Music* 139, I succeeded in making my way to a resistance cell. **1945** *Sun* (Baltimore) 6 Oct. 2/5 German underground units, composed chiefly of Hitler youth and former prisoners of war, were springing up in all parts of Germany, with some secret 'resistance clubs' reviving the worst of Nazism. **1931** MOYER & WOSTREL *Radio Handbk.* xiii. 684 Resistance-coupled amplifiers. A typical circuit in which the amplifier is connected by the method of resistance coupling. **1962** SIMPSON & RICHARDS *Physical Princ. Junction Transistors* ix. 219 A relatively heavily loaded resistance-coupled stage operating over a reasonably long range of ambient temperature. **1921** J. SCOTT-TAGGART *Thermionic Tubes* vi. 207 A form of coupling between successive valves in an amplifier which has been of considerable use is that known as 'resistance coupling'. **1963** *Listener* 14 Feb. 304/2 He joins up with various bands of multi-racial resistance fighters. **1976** H. TRACY *Death in Reserve* xxii. 172 The local *gendarmerie*, guided by the old Resistance fighters,..covered the flanks. **1958** *Times Lit. Suppl.* 21 Mar. 149/1 The sexual fantasies of various Resistance and non-resistant figures. **1944** Resistance forces [see *E.A.M.* s.v. *E. III]. **1959** *Listener* 16 Apr. 674/3 Fighting between Tibetan resistance forces and the Chinese. **1904** M. MACLEAN *Mod. Electr. Pract.* V. 239 To prevent more or less arcing in what is ostensibly a resistance furnace. **1928** *Jrnl. Iron & Steel Inst.* CXVII. 853 Materials of construction for electric resistance furnaces, and the advantages of the latter over fuel-fired furnaces, are described. **1957** Resistance group [see *COURIER *sb.* 1 b]. **1974** J. THOMSON *Long Revenge* ii. 22 For reasons of security, Mercer wasn't put in direct touch with the local Resistance group. **1975** N. FREELING *What are Bugles blowing For?* vii. 45 Was he a Resistance hero then? **1945** *Daily Herald* 8 May 4/8 The Germans..started shooting at Dutch Resistance men. *Ibid.* 28 May 4/2 Armed forces of the Danish resistance movement have passed a resolution..demanding the arrests [*sic*] of all collaborators. **1953** *Encounter* Nov. 6/2 The rising sales of even the most expensive Japanese garments.. were taken to be a kind of resistance-movement against Western-style attire. **1978** R. V. JONES *Most Secret War* xxiii. 189 It would be some time before the Resistance movements began to operate coherently. **1969** F. HALLIDAY in Cockburn & Blackburn *Student Power* 317 Students also provided the cadres for the various resistance networks.. which channelled arms, funds and information to the FLN. **1944** *Daily Tel.* 15 May 4 Mr. Wareing reveals..the existence of a Resistance plan to seize power. **1899** *Physical Rev.* VIII. 197 The failure of Siemens' resistance pyrometer was simply due to faulty construction. **1920** *Whittaker's Electr. Engineer's Pocket-bk.* (ed. 4) 290 Resistance pyrometers. For exact readings when temperature is steady... Range: minus 200° up to 1000° C. **1959** *Jrnl. Iron & Steel Inst.* CXCIII. 318/3 He then describes the four main types of pyrometer, namely, the optical pyrometer, the resistance pyrometer, the thermocouple, and the radiation pyrometer. **1887** *Phil. Trans. R. Soc.* A. CLXXVIII. 164 In comparing the platinum resistance thermometer with other instruments, it will be seen that it is essentially practical. **1920** *Whittaker's Electr. Engineer's Pocket-bk.* (ed. 4) 286 The Callendar compensated resistance thermometer consists of a pure platinum wire wound on a mica or fireclay frame and connected by stout copper or platinum leads to terminals in the thermometer head. **1959** Resistance thermometer [see *CONDUCTIVITY 2]. **1960** WATANABE & FUKASAWA in *Biochem. & Biophys. Res. Communications* III. 664 Each resistance factor is not a transmissible factor in itself but.. the resistance factors are carried by some transmissible factor... We propose to refer to this factor as 'resistance transfer factor (RTF)' tentatively. **1965** *Times* 26 Feb. 15/3 The resistance transfer factor, like the sex factor, may stimulate conjugation—so that resistance can sweep rapidly through a colony. **1970** PASSMORE & ROBSON *Compan. Med. Stud.* II. xviii. 57/2 Resistance transfer factors represent a world-wide problem which is becoming increasingly serious. **1914** *Proc. Inst. Mech. Engin.* 170 The best, the most controllable and the least likely method of injuring the material, which gave the most uniform satisfactory results, was electric resistance welding. **1927** [see *METALLIC *a.* 1 h]. **1975** BRAM & DOWNS *Manuf. Technol.* ii. 61 Resistance-welding techniques are characterised by the absence of flux or filler. **1959** *Listener* 17 Sept. 454/3 They are engaged in sabotage and resistance work. **1962** L. DEIGHTON *Ipcress File* 221 Grenade was a resistance worker in 1940 when.. every one else in France was rooting for Marshal Pétain. **1974** J. THOMSON *Long Revenge* ii. 23 A suspected French Resistance worker.

resistanceless (rĭzi·stănslės), *a.* [f. RESISTANCE + -LESS.] Marked by a total lack of (electrical) resistance.

1968 *Physics Bull.* Dec. 410/2 The Meissner effect provided an important clue to the understanding of superfluidity, by showing that it was more than resistanceless flow. **1969** [see *EXCITONIC *a.*]. **1978** *Sci. Amer.* Apr. 88/2 Certain properties of the glassy superconductors, such as the transition temperature where resistanceless flow begins, are significantly different from those in crystalline materials.

resistant, *a.* and *sb.* Add: **A.** *adj.* **2.** That is not overcome by some disease or drug. Const. *to.*

1897 MUIR & RITCHIE *Man. Bacteriol.* 291 An animal is shedding into the air..myriads of bacilli which may rapidly spore, and thus arrive at a very resistant stage. **1898** *Yearbk. U.S. Dept. Agric. 1897* 399 The..cross yielded the Golden Clairette, a valuable new sort [of vine], apparently highly resistant to Phylloxera. **1925** *Scribner's Mag.* July 1/1 Genetics has made possible better strains of livestock... Disease is less to be feared because of resistant stocks. **1968** *New Statesman* 5 Jan. 10/3 A germ which normally inhabits the intestines of a cow, for instance, but which normally doesn't harm man, could be rendered resistant, perhaps, to a whole group of antibiotics, and could then escape from the animal, and pass that resistance on to another type of germ which *was* dangerous to man.

3. In *Comb.* with preceding sb.

1902 [see *fire-resistant* adj. s.v. *FIRE *sb.* B. 2]. **1932** [see *drug-resistant* adj. s.v. *DRUG *sb.*[1] 3]. **1936** [see *CREASE *sb.*[2] 5]. **1947** [see *flame-resistant* adj. s.v. *FLAME *sb.* 10]. **1959** *Times* 12 Jan. 11/4 Porous, crush-proof, stress and tear-resistant and washable. **1963** *B.S.I. News* June 8/2 Bad news for burglars was the announcement in May of a BSI specification for thief-resistant locks. **1968** *Times* 12 Oct. 18/8 One of the organisms sometimes responsible for travellers' diarrhoea is now sulphonamide-resistant. **1978** *Cornish Guardian* 27 Apr. 34/6 (Advt.), White Ceiling Tiles all with F.R.A. (Fire Resistant Additive).

B. *sb.* **a.** Delete 'Now *rare*' and add: *spec.* a member of a resistance movement. Cf. *RÉSISTANT.

1944 *Ann. Reg. 1943* 172 To the injury of the United Nations and the French resistants. **1948** W. FORTESCUE *Beauty for Ashes* xxxv. 273 *Mademoiselle*..had been one of the true Resistants, refusing even in the blackest hours of the war to admit even the possibility of defeat, or to allow pessimism among the peasants. **1959** *Sunday Times* 22 Mar. 23/7 A disguised and wounded Hungarian resistant.

‖ **résistant** (resistañ). Also *fem.* **résistante.** [Fr.] A member of the French Resistance (see *RESISTANCE 1 c).

1966 M. R. D. FOOT *SOE in France* vii. 175 Mathilde Carré..proclaimed herself already an ardent résistante. **1967** *Listener* 16 Mar. 370/3 Pierre d'Harcourt was twenty-six when, after Dunkirk, he shed his cavalry uniform to become a pioneer *résistant*. Maybe the cavalry discipline helped to restrain his impetuosity. **1978** *Dædalus* Fall 29 Everyone in France was a 'résistant'.

resister. Add: **1. b.** *spec.* A member of a resistance movement; a resistant. Also with capital initial.

1952 *Chambers's Jrnl.* Feb. 66/2 But all three of them, when they were drunk, believed themselves to have been the most stout-hearted Resisters, members of the Underground. **1959** *Encounter* Aug. 45/1 The treatment accorded to the records of the *Résistance* is especially entertaining... Thousands of Resisters wrote their personal recollections. **1966** M. R. D. FOOT *SOE in France* vi. 129 In Greece and in Yugoslavia SOE sought to back any anti-German bodies of resisters.

resistibility. Add: **1.** (Later example.)

1974 *Times* 4 Feb. 8/2 Irresistibility is simply not borne out by statistics. A survey conducted in 1965 showed not only that 81 per cent of Italian males objected to the closing of licensed brothels but that nearly three quarters made use of prostitutes, which suggests a high degree of resistibility.

resistible, *a.* (Further examples.)

1903 G. B. SHAW *Man & Superman* III. 134 As to your Life Force, which you think irresistible, it is the most resistible thing in the world for a person of any character. **1966** *Listener* 9 Nov. 597/3 The most resistible of the new MPs.. his voice, as usual, half-way between a splutter and a jeer. **1979** *Financial Times* 14 Apr. 21/3 The water babies themselves are frightful infants..given to singing resistible underwater ditties.

resistive, *a.* Add: **2.** *Electr.* Pertaining to, possessing, or resulting from electrical resistance; *spec.* in connection with resistance as a component of impedance (in this sense opp. *REACTIVE *a.* 6 a and b).

1929 *Wireless World* 30 Jan. 116/2 The reactive component in each case is drawn at 90° to the resistive component. **1937** A. V. EASTMAN *Fund. Vacuum Tubes* v. 153 Since power considerations in a voltage amplifier are minor, the output load may be partly reactive instead of resistive. **1947** R. LEE *Electronic Transformers & Circuits* i. 6 With many sine wave electronic transformers, the transformer load is resistive. **1958** *New Scientist* 21 Aug. 658/3 The Stellarator uses resistive heating only in the first stage, to bring the plasma into the million degree region. **1964** R. F. FICCHI *Electr. Interference* 217 Resistive coupling is the association of two or more circuits with one another by means of resistance mutual to the circuits. **1969** L. E. C. HUGHES et al. *Dict. Electronics & Nucleonics* 231/1 Reactive loads are made entirely resistive by adding inductors or capacitors in series or shunt. **1980** *Times* 23 June 18/7 He used the equations for capacitative and resistive loss in electric cables.

resistivity. Add: **1.** Now usu. defined as the resistance of a conductor of unit length and unit cross-sectional area. (Earlier and later examples.)

1885, 1895 [see *-IVITY]. **1943** C. L. BOLTZ *Basic Radio* i. 26 Anyone capable of working out a formula can therefore find the resistance of any conductor by looking up the tables for specific resistance or resistivity. **1962** *Newnes Conc. Encycl. Electr. Engin.* 658/1 Copper of the highest purity has a resistivity lower than that of any other known material except silver. A standard value for the resistivity of annealed copper was established in 1913 by the International Electrotechnical Commission as 0·017 241 Ω per m length and mm² section. **1975** *Country Life* 6 Feb. 331/3 The scientific techniques used by the archaeologists, such as the resistivity meters used to detect areas where the soil is broken up by the tops of mine shafts. **1975** G. ANDERSON *Coring* vii. 121 The porosity of the sand is above 20% and the resistivity ranges from 0.3 ohm-m for saltwater sands to several ohm-meters for oil-saturated sands.

2. Special Combs.: **resistivity surveying,** measurement of the current passing between electrodes embedded in the ground at a series of positions over a given area, in order to identify regions of differing resistivity and hence locate buried structural features; so **resistivity survey,** a set or programme of such measurements.

1927 *Terrestrial Magnetism* XXXII. 49 The Department of Terrestrial Magnetism of the Carnegie Institution of Washington has undertaken a series of resistivity surveys in regions where records of earth-current potential gradient are being obtained. **1952** M. B. DOBRIN *Introd. Geophysical Prospecting* xvi. 298 The interpretation of the actual data obtained in field resistivity surveys is usually a highly empirical and generally unreliable process. **1966** *McGraw-Hill Encycl. Sci. & Technol.* XI. 22/2 Electromagnetic and electrical resistivity surveys are used to locate deposits of metallic sulfides, which, except for sphalerite, are good electrical conductors. **1931** *Engin. & Min. Jrnl.* CXXXI. 325 (*heading*) Earth resistivity surveying. **1953** R. J. C. ATKINSON *Field Archaeol.* (ed. 2) i. 38 Resistivity surveying requires at least two operators, one at the instrument and one to move the electrodes. **1963** *Times* 3 June 6/2 Resistivity surveying has been conducted by Mr. Whybrew, of the Ministry's test branch, and buried features have been detected.

resistor (rĭzi·stəɹ). *Electr.* [f. RESIST *v.* + -OR.] A passive device which impedes the flow of an electric current, used to develop a voltage drop across itself or to limit current flow.

[**1759**: see RESISTER 2]. **1905** *Sci. Amer. Suppl.* 27 May 24586/1 The resistance medium or 'resistor', when solid, usually consists of a core of carbon, coke, or graphite. **1930** *Engineering* 31 Jan. 128/3 A higher-temperature zone heated by non-metallic resistor rods. **1947** R. LEE *Electronic Transformers & Circuits* vi. 181 Tubes may require resistors in the plate and grid leads to damp out parasitic oscillations. **1965** *Wireless World* July 329/2 To monitor this current a 50 Ω resistor is inserted in the earthed lead of the recording head. A 1 kc/s signal source is then injected into the radio input of the recording amplifier and the voltage across the resistor measured with a valve voltmeter or oscilloscope. **1975** FINK & MCKENZIE *Electronics Engineers' Handbk.* vii. 4 Wire-wound resistors usually exhibit an increase in resistance with higher frequencies because of skin effects.

resi·t (rī-), *v.* [RE- 5 a.] *trans.* and *intr.* To sit (an examination) again, usu. after failing at a previous attempt; to retake (an examination), e.g. in order to improve one's grade.

1959 *Chambers's 20th Cent. Dict.* 1380/2 *Resit,..v.i.* to sit an examination again after failing. —— *n.* an opportunity or act of resitting. **1968** *Sunday Times* 30 June 15 So many students resit the engineering examination each year that an eventual pass rate of 80 percent..may occur. **1974** A. FOWLES *Pastime* i. 6 He'd had to re-sit English to get the minimum the library required. **1979** *Jrnl. R. Soc. Arts* Dec. 9/1 The candidates for this session's examination were exclusively restricted to those who had been referred in a previous examination or who were resitting in order to obtain higher grades.

resit (rī·sit), *sb.* [f. the vb.] The act of resitting an examination; also, an examination held specifically to enable candidates to resit. Also *attrib.*

1959 [see *RESIT *v.*]. **1972** D. HASTON *In High Places* ii. 30 For once he'd passed his exams in June and didn't have any resits in September. **1973** *Guardian* 14 June 7/2 Resit school breaks its 11-plus record. Out of 50 pupils..who had to resit their 11-plus examination..31 have passed. **1977** *Belfast Tel.* 19 Jan. 3/4 One wonders how your recent correspondents, who feel that an Eleven-Plus resit is unnecessary, can accept the position arising as a result of the supplementary test which has not been held.

resite (re·zəit), *sb. Chem.* [ad. G. *resit* (H. Lebach 1909, in *Zeitschr. f. angew. Chem.* XXII. 1601), f. L. *rēs-ina* RESIN *sb.* + *-it* -ITE[1].] A name given to the insoluble, infusible resins that are the final products of phenol-aldehyde copolymerizations.

1913 H. LEBACH in *Jrnl. Soc. Chem. Industry* XXXII. 559/2 For the final product, whether it be called Bakelite 'C', Resinite, Condensite, or by some other name, I suggest the name 'Resite'. **1935** C. ELLIS *Chem. Synthetic Resins* I. xiv. 307 Resites (C stage) are branched-chain macromolecules. **1950** *Thorpe's Dict. Appl. Chem.* (ed. 4) X. 24/2 The resin hardens on further heating and becomes insoluble and infusible. This is the 'C' or resite stage and consists of macromolecules with numerous branched and cross-linked chains. **1973** [see *RESITOL].

re-si·te (rī-), *v.* [RE- 5 a.] *trans.* To place on another site; to relocate. Hence **re-si·ting** *vbl. sb.*

1955 *Times* 19 July 9/7 Many argue that the bridge will still be needed even when the tunnel has been built; then the question of re-siting it may arise. **1967** E. CHAMBERS *Photolitho-Offset* viii. 106 These cameras..have facilities for the exact siting of films, plates, transparencies and masks with three-point lay and location pins for accurate re-siting and register of copy. **1969** *Jane's Freight Containers 1968–69* 555/1 They are completely mobile and can be pushed or towed for re-siting. **1976** P. R. WHITE *Planning for Public Transport* x. 213 In so far as population re-sited from existing industrial cities is located in new or expanding towns of about 100 000 population, similar improvements could occur.

resitol (re·zitǫl). *Chem.* [a. G. *resitol* (H. Lebach 1913, in *Chem.-Zeitung* 19 June 734/1), f. *resit* *RESITE *sb.* + *res-ol* *RESOL.] A name given to the rubbery, insoluble resins produced in phenol-aldehyde copolymerizations at a stage intermediate between resol and resite.

1913 H. LEBACH in *Jrnl. Soc. Chem. Industry* XXXII. 559/2 Besides these products, Baekeland distinguishes an intermediate polymerisation product, which he terms 'Bakelite "B"'... This intermediate condensation product I would suggest to call 'Resitol'. **1950** *Thorpe's Dict. Appl. Chem.* (ed. 4) X. 24/2 When heated at temperatures above 100° C. it melts and froths, becoming more viscous and eventually reaching the rubbery stage, the 'B' or resitol stage. **1973** *Materials & Technol.* VI. viii. 588 Phenol resins evolve in three stages, which are connected with the degree of condensation: 1. Resol or A-stage (beginning of condensation): the resin is fluid, soluble, and still contains much water. 2. Resitol or B-stage (continued condensation, slight cross-linking): insoluble, rubbery. 3. Resite or C-stage (final condition of the cured product): infusible and insoluble.

resi·tuate (rī-), *v. N. Amer.* [RE- 5 a.] = RELOCATE *v.* 1 a. Also *refl.*

c **1865** E. DICKINSON *Poems* (1955) II. 734 Bore Death from Passion All His East He—sovreign as the Sun Resituated in the West And the Debate was done. **1974** D. RICHARDS *Coming of Winter* i. 6 He could feel sharp blades of undergrowth so he resituated himself once or twice.

reslash, *v.* Add: Hence **resla·shing** *vbl. sb.*

1970 J. FORD et al. in H. W. Mulligan *African Trypanosomiases* xxvii. 548 He [*sc.* Morris]..checked regeneration by stumping and burning, and not by annual reslashing. **1973** J. J. MCKELVEY *Man against Tsetse* iii. 162 Unpaid community labor, which was recruited under the provisions of the 1937 Sleeping Sickness Ordinance, accomplished almost all of the subsequent slashing and reslashing of regrowth over the years.

reslush (rīslʌ·ʃ), *v. Paper-making.* [RE- 5 b.] *trans.* To convert (dry or semi-dry paper stock) into slush by the addition of water.

1963 *Economist* 11 May 555/2 Drying the pulp for shipping and then 're-slushing' it. **1967** E. CHAMBERS *Photolitho-Offset* xvi. 247 A few mills in this country make pulp from waste paper by 'reslushing'.

resmethrin (re·zmīþrin). [*-ethrin* f. *PYR)ETHRIN.] A synthetic pyrethroid employed as an insecticide in the form of a spray.

1971 *Pesticide Sci.* II. 16/1 (*table*) 5-Benzyl-3-furylmethyl (±)-*cis-trans*-chrysanthemate (Resmethrin). **1971** *Bull. World Health Org.* XLIV. 329/1 Resmethrin was superior to the other synthetic pyrethroids and to the natural pyrethrins against all insects tested. **1975** *Daily Tel.* 25 Oct. 8/2 The answer is to keep a bottle of resmethrin..handy and give any new plants a going over with it.

Resochin (rī·sǫkin). *Pharm.* Also **resochin.** [a. G. *resochin*, f. *reso-rcinol* RESORCINOL + *chin-olin* QUINOLINE.] A proprietary name for *CHLOROQUINE.

1946 *Trans. R. Soc. Trop. Med. & Hygiene* XL. 170 Atebrin, sontochin, resochin and quinine were observed to cause arrest of development and degeneration of ring and amoeboid forms. **1947** [see *CHLOROQUINE]. **1951** *Trade Marks Jrnl.* 12 Dec. 1135/1 *Resochin...* Pharmaceutical preparations. Farbenfabriken Bayer..; Manufacturers and Merchants. **1955** *Official Gaz.* (U.S. Patent Office) 19 July TM 157/1 Farbenfabriken Bayer Aktiengesellschaft, Leverkusen-Bayerwerk, Germany. Filed Dec. 15, 1954. *Resochin.* Applicant claims ownership of German Reg. No. 602,220, dated Nov. 2, 1950. **1958** J. H. BURN *Lect. Notes Pharmacol.* (ed. 5) 105 Chloroquine was also discovered by the Germans as resochin, but was tested and developed in America during the last war. **1970** W. PETERS *Chemotherapy & Drug Resistance in Malaria* i. 5 From the time of its synthesis by Andersag..in 1934, chloroquine, or Resochin as it was first known to the German workers, faced a precarious existence.

resocializa·tion (rī-). *Social Psychol.* [RE- 5 b.] The action or process of (re)inducing conformity to accepted standards of social behaviour. Also *attrib.*

1964 M. ARGYLE *Psychol. & Social Probl.* i. 20 When we come to consider the re-socialization, or indoctrination, of adults, we shall introduce two further principles of learning: cognitive learning and learning by means of emotional arousal. **1970** P. MAYER *Socialization* p. xiii, Major social changes, such as ongoing urbanization or industrialization, involve the resocialization of people of all ages. **1974** M. C. GERALD *Pharmacol.* xii. 232 Some view their program [*sc.* of Alcoholics Anonymous] as a resocialization process attempting to develop individual maturity. **1976** *Guardian* 23 July 15/5 The regular presence of women in the unit, unthinkable in the old isolation system, is seen as an essential part of the resocialisation process by staff and psychiatrists alike. **1977** F. MUSGROVE *Margins of Mind* ix. 196 A period of 'desocialization' may be an important preliminary to the effective resocialization of adults.

reso·ften (rī-), *v.* [RE- 5 b.] To soften again. Hence **reso·ftening** *vbl. sb.*

1611 FLORIO *Worlde of Wordes* 439/3 *Rimollire*,..also to remollifie, to resoften or asswage. **1889** P. N. HASLUCK *Model Engin. Handybk.* 136 By the appearance of the colours we are informed of the temperature of the steel, or in other words, how far, or to what extent the resoftening has progressed. **1894** DUKE OF ARGYLL *Burdens of Belief* 90 Come burnished autumn with thy wealth of flame,..Come leaves with tints too blended for a name, And lakes resoftening lights that come from you. **1963** J. OSBORNE *Dental Mech.* (ed. 5) i. 16 The impression is taken, chilled, the surface resoftened by flaming and the impression reinserted.

resol (re·zǫl). *Chem.* Also **-ole** (-ōᵘl). [a. G. *resol* (H. Lebach 1909, in *Zeitschr. f. angew. Chem.* XXII. 1601), f. L. *rēs-ina* RESIN *sb.* + *-ol* -OL.] A name given to the alcohol-soluble, usu. fluid resins formed as the first stage in phenol-aldehyde copolymerizations and often prepared as precondensates in the manufacture of plastic.

1913 H. LEBACH in *Jrnl. Soc. Chem. Industry* XXXII. 559/2 These initial stages of Bakelite have received various names... Four years ago I proposed to call the whole of this class 'Resoles'. **1933** *Ibid.* LII. 420T/2 Similar *o*-hydroxy-substituted substances are supposed to represent molecules of Bakelite A (resole). **1935** C. ELLIS *Chem. Synthetic Resins* I. xiv. 306 The resols, or initial products of alkaline condensation are mono- or poly-alcohols. **1956** J. N. ANDERSON *Appl. Dental Materials* xxi. 260 The resin is in the 'resole' state and is modified by adding fillers and colouring matter. **1973** *Materials & Technol.* VI. viii. 590 Resols used as starting materials have a very limited storage life owing to the presence of reactive groups.

resole, *v.* Add: **b.** *intr.* To admit of being resoled. *rare.*

1922 *Daily Mail* 24 Nov. 11 (Advt.), You can get 'cheap' shoes which look worse every day you wear them, and won't re-sole once.

resolution. Add: **I. 2. c.** More widely, the act, process, or capability of rendering distinguishable the component parts of an object or closely adjacent optical or photographic images, or of separating measurements of similar magnitude of any quantity in space or time; also, the smallest quantity which is measurable by such a process. (Further examples.)

1902 *Encycl. Brit.* XXXII. 776 A resolving power of 100,000 would suffice for the resolution of the closest lines in the spectrum. **1931** *Proc. R. Soc.* A. CXXXII. 307 The 'resolution' (*i.e.*, the smallest interval of time by which two impulses could be separated and still be separately recorded) of the relay ring..was between 1/100th and 1/200th second. **1935** *Nature* 12 Oct. 592/2 The remarks on numerical aperture may give rise to confusion, as the term 'definition' is used, instead of the correct one, 'resolution'. **1958** *Engineering* 28 Mar. 389/2 The accuracy and resolution of the equipment are both equal to one digit in the fourth significant place. **1962** *Which?* Mar. 70/1 We measured the resolution. This is the ability of the projector to reproduce fine detail. **1968** *Brit. Med. Bull.* XXIV. 255/1 This provides 8-bit resolution for the input samples. **1971** J. Z. YOUNG *Introd. Study Man* ii. 20 As they examine the world more and more minutely with instruments of ever higher resolution they come upon phenomena not previously described. **1972** *Sci. Amer.* July 19/3 A 1,000 kilohertz.. sonar would provide a resolution of 30 centimeters on a target 200 meters away. **1973** *Ibid.* June 47/1 The time resolution of the shutter is about a nanosecond. **1978** *Ibid.* Mar. 144/2 (Advt.), A usable resolution of 0.001° C makes the HP 2804 an excellent choice for measuring minute temperature differences. **1978** *Nature* 18 May p. xviii/1 By means of a selector key the weighing range of 200 g, resolution to 0·01 g, or of 2 kg, resolution to 0·1 g, can be selected.

II. 9. (Earlier example.)

1785 T. PARKINSON *Syst. Mech.* iv. 78 (*heading*) Composition and resolution of forces.

re-solution. Add: Also **resolution.** (Later examples.)

1957 G. E. HUTCHINSON *Treat. Limnol.* I. xi. 708 Evaporation to dryness and resolution liberates some of the previously unreactive iron..in a reactive form. **1966** PHILLIPS & WILLIAMS *Inorg. Chem.* II. xxxii. 524 A second factor controlling the re-solution of the hydroxide in alkali would appear to be the ease of change of coordination number. **1968** R. W. FAIRBRIDGE *Encycl. Geomorphol.* 1051/2 In southern England, many large speleotherms are today being destroyed by drips from the original formative source ('re-solution').

resolvancy (rĭzǫ·lvănsi). *rare.* [f. RESOLVE *v.* + -ANCY.] An outcome or solution.

1930 G. GREENE *Two Witnesses* 84 How utterly grown-up we then become, and the crowded confused days have to be made to clear, have to reach their own resolvancies.

resolve, *v.* Add: **I. 2. d.** (Earlier example.)

1785 T. PARKINSON *Syst. Mech.* iv. 80 One force..may be resolved into any number, either in the same, or different planes, producing the same effect with it.

e. More widely, to distinguish (things of similar magnitude or close together in time). Cf. *RESOLUTION 2 c.

1932 *Proc. R. Soc.* A. CXXXVI. 313 Two particles separated by as little as 1/500th second could be 'resolved' and correctly recorded.

11. a. (Later examples.)

1975 *New Yorker* 17 Nov. 94/2 Bress proposed the questions to be resolved by the jury—whether the subpoenas were properly served on the McSurelys, whether they refused to comply with a lawful command of Congress, and whether their refusal was willful. **1976** *Amer. Speech 1973* XLVIII. 248 Nor can *Atlas* materials resolve Kypriotaki's basic question of lexical or environmental control of initial syllable deletion.

resolvent, *a.* and *sb.* Add: **B.** *sb.* **4.** *Galois resolvent*: see *GALOIS.

resolver. Add: **4.** *Electr.* An electromechanical device which transforms the representation of an electric vector from polar to Cartesian coordinates (see quot. 1956); also, more widely, an electronic device which resolves an input signal into components.

1952 G. A. & T. M. KORN *Electronic Analog Computers* vi. 283 A special rotatable transformer called a resolver. **1956** BERKELEY & WAINWRIGHT *Computers* iii. 101 A special form of transformer known as a resolver..built something like an electric motor... Turning of the rotor varies the coupling between the windings so as to produce the sine and cosine functions. *Ibid.* viii. 353/1 Resolver..a device for resolving a vector into two mutually perpendicular components. **1975** *Daily Tel.* (Colour Suppl.) 24 Oct. 29/1 Many find that they can get a very pleasant 'surround' effect by using a pair of modest rear speakers coupled to a simple unit called a resolver. The Neal resolver, for example, sorts out the signals from a stereo amplifier and passes to the rear loudspeakers the out-of-phase information—the peripheral elements of the sound. **1976** *Sci. Amer.* Feb. 78/1 The addition of servo control calls for feedback from sensors such as potentiometers, encoders and resolvers, which measure the position of each joint.

resolving, *vbl. sb.* Add: **2.** *Comb.* **resolving power**, the capability of an optical or photographic system to separate or distinguish closely adjacent images; also, the similar capability of a radio telescope; **resolving time**, the interval from the start of a counted pulse in a pulse counter to the time when another pulse can be detected and counted separately.

1879 Resolving power [in Dict.]. **1887** *Encycl. Brit.* XXII. 374/1 While the resolving power of a spectroscope with grating..is independent of the wave-length for each order, the resolving power of a spectroscope with prism will vary inversely as the third power of the wave-length. **1955** *Sci. Amer.* Mar. 38/1 The resolving power is measured by the sharpness of the peak; it is usually expressed as the 'half-power beam width', which means the width of the arc along which the antenna receives half or more of the maximum signal power. **1977** J. NARLIKAR *Struct. Universe* iv. 107 Because visual wavelengths are considerably shorter than radio wavelengths.., the optical telescope can achieve a better resolving power with an aperture of a few centimetres than the radio telescope can with an aperture of several metres. **1942** W. B. LEWIS *Electr. Counting* viii. 83 The anode potential rises more rapidly after extinction and the resolving time is reduced. **1948** *Jrnl. Sci. Instruments* XXV. 37/1 The resolving time of the input circuit of the scaler was measured directly by feeding into the scaler pairs of pulses of variable separation. **1963** B. BROWN *Experimental Nucleonics* 175 Due to the short resolving time much higher count rates are possible.

resonance. Add: **1. c.** Substitute for def.: The phenomenon of an oscillating signal (as an electric current or electromagnetic radiation) producing an effect upon an oscillating current of the same frequency; the condition in which a circuit or device produces the largest possible response to an applied oscillating signal, *esp.* when its inductive reactance balances its capacitative reactance. (Earlier and later examples.)

1886 *Electrician* 20 Aug. 296/2 By this to-and-fro reflection, or electrical reverberation or resonance, the amplitude of the received current may be made far greater than the strength of the steady-flow current from the same impressed force. **1897** A. HAY *Princ. Alternate-Current Working* xii. 159 This phenomenon of the neutralisation of an inductance by means of a capacity is generally referred to as electrical resonance. **1920** E. W. STONE *Elem. Radiotelegr.* i. 22 When these two reactances are equal, a state of resonance is said to obtain. **1920** *Whittaker's Electr. Engineer's Pocket-bk.* (ed. 4) 446 Resonance is rarely established with the fundamental frequency of the supply, but is generally due to harmonics. **1943** C. L. BOLTZ *Basic Radio* viii. 129 The phenomenon of a circuit responding most to one frequency is called resonance. **1959** K. HENNEY *Radio Engin. Handbk.* (ed. 5) vi. 46 It was realized that a hollow closed conducting box of arbitrary shape possessed electrical resonance properties similar to the conventional coil and capacitor circuit. **1964** R. F. FICCHI *Electr. Interference* v. 48 Past the point of resonance, the inductive reactance continues to increase and the capacitor is no longer effective as a bypass filter. **1975** D. G. Fink *Electronics Engineers' Handbk.* xv. 30 One type of forced commutation uses resonance to generate an alternation which brings the current in a conducting thyristor to zero.

d. *Physics* and *Chem.* (i) Generally, a condition in which a particle is subjected to an oscillating influence (as an electromagnetic field or another particle) of such a frequency that a transfer of energy occurs or reaches a maximum; an instance of this; an exchange of energy occurring under such conditions.

1895 *Abstr. Physical Papers* (Physical Soc.) I. 355 It is thus impossible that resonance should obtain between the electric waves of Hertz and the molecules of a body, and consequently impossible for an ordinary prism to disperse electric waves. **1902** *Phil. Mag.* III. 396 A new type of light absorption, which it may be possible to refer to the electrical resonance of small metallic particles for waves of light. *Ibid.* IV. 428 The variable nature of the colour..makes it appear improbable that the action is similar to that of aniline dyes; namely, a resonance within the molecule. **1931** *Proc. R. Soc.* A. CXXX. 477 The possibility of the occurrence of line spectra due to a resonance between the α-particle and the nucleus. **1935** *Physical Rev.* XLVII. 751/2 The large cross sections [for neutron scattering] may thus be called a resonance effect, but the 'resonance' is very unsharp. **1959** *Physical Rev. Lett.* II. 427/1 Quite a narrow resonance (half-width ≤ 20 Mev) appears in these cross sections just below this threshold. **1966** Williams & Fleming *Spectrosc. Methods Org. Chem.* iv. 78 Since different protons in an organic molecule have varying electronic environments, the precise value of the magnetic field required to bring any one into resonance at constant frequency will vary slightly from proton to proton. **1970** I. E. McCarthy *Nuclear Reactions* i. 6 The reaction occurred preferentially at four different energies between about 4 MeV and 5·3 MeV. Resonance was said to occur in the α, Al^{27} system at these energies. **1974** *Accounts Chem. Res.* VII. 341/2 The Raman spectra are dominated by the porphyrin vibrational modes which are enhanced by resonance with the allowed electronic transitions in the visible and near-ultraviolet region. **1976** *Sci. Amer.* Jan. 50/2 The method of detection employed is an application of Werner Heisenberg's uncertainty principle and it consists in searching for an enhancement at a particular energy in the probability of interaction between known particles. Such an enhancement is called a resonance.

(ii) *Chem.* = *mesomerism b.

1927 *Sci. Abstr.* A. XXX. 84 (*heading*) The problem of several bodies and resonance in quantum mechanics. [Abstr. of paper by W. Heisenberg in *Ztschr. f. Physik* (1926) XXXIX. 499.] **1931** *Physical Rev.* XXXVII. 489 In some cases there may be several ways of drawing valence bonds in a given compound. In such cases, the real situation is again a combination of the various possibilities, and on account of resonance the energy is lower than it would otherwise be. **1939** L. Pauling *Nature of Chem. Bond* ii. 35 In case that the extreme covalent structure A:B and the extreme ionic structure A^+B^- correspond separately to the same bond energy value, then the two structures will contribute equally to the actual state of the molecule, and the actual bond energy will be greater than the bond energy for either structure alone by an amount equal to the interaction energy of the two structures; that is, resonance between the two structures will stabilize the molecule. *Ibid.* xii. 408 A substance showing resonance between two or more valence-bond structures does not contain molecules with the configuration and properties usually associated with these structures. **1950** N. V. Sidgwick *Chem. Elements* I. 525 From the crystal structure of sodium formate Zachariasen has shown that in the ion there is complete resonance between the two C—O groups. **1968** *Nature* 24 Aug. 801/2 This departure from planarity, by interfering with resonance, was expected to make the molecule so unstable that one hardly expected to find it. **1978** P. W. Atkins *Physical Chem.* xv. 494 These structures are less stable than the Kekulé forms, because the A—D bonds, etc., are long and weak; therefore, although they must be allowed to take part in the resonance they contribute more weakly.

(iii) *spec.* (also *magnetic resonance*) the transition of a particle possessing a magnetic moment between different quantum states in the presence of a magnetic field and electromagnetic radiation of the appropriate frequency; a spectroscopic technique (as *electron spin resonance, nuclear magnetic resonance*, etc.) in which such phenomena are observed.

1938 *Physical Rev.* LIII. 318/2 The experimental procedure is to vary the homogeneous field for some given value of the frequency of the oscillating field until the resonance is observed by a drop in intensity at the detector and a subsequent recovery when the resonance value is passed. **1942** Nuclear magnetic resonance [see *nuclear *a.* 4]. **1952** *Physical Rev.* LXXXVIII. 951/1 We have observed conduction electron spin resonance absorption in fine particles of metallic sodium. **1957** *Endeavour* Oct. 185/1 When atomic nuclei are placed in a constant magnetic field of high intensity and subjected at the same time to a radio-frequency alternating field, a transfer of energy takes place between the high-frequency field and the nucleus. This phenomenon is known as nuclear magnetic resonance. **1965** R. N. Dixon *Spectroscopy & Structure* viii. 182 Electron spin resonance spectrometers usually use fields of the order of 3000 G, and the resonance is then at microwave frequencies of about 9000 Mc/sec. **1967** Atkins & Symons *Struct. Inorg. Radicals* i. 7 Signals can be detected by nuclear magnetic resonance under conditions where lines are too broad to detect by electron spin resonance. **1977** *Nature* 17 Nov. 272/2 The spectrum of the enriched pigment contains one additional resonance at approximately 130·8 p.p.m. downfield from TSP-d_4.

(iv) *spec.* in *Nuclear Physics*, a short-lived particle, or an excited state of a particle, manifested as an increase, at certain well-defined energies, in the probability of interaction of other particles.

1964 *Physical Rev. Lett.* XIII. 64/2 We have searched for a possible spin alignment of the resonance by analyzing the strong decay into $\Xi^*(1530) + \pi$. **1965** *Science* 10 Sept. 1183/2 When the nucleon is exposed to any kind of high-energy beams, it is transformed into short-lived states of higher energy, which are known under various names, such as 'hyperons' or 'resonances'. **1969** *Times* 5 Feb. 13/7 The Xi resonances belong to the heavier class of nuclear particles known as baryons. **1972** G. L. Wick *Elem. Particles* iv. 60 Analyses of particle tracks also helped to reveal numerous short-lived particles called resonances. **1975** *Physics Bull.* Dec. 537/3 Excited states of the nucleons, so called resonances, can be produced by inelastic electron scattering.

e. *Mech.* (i) A condition in which an object or system is subjected to an oscillating force having a frequency close to that of a natural vibration of the object or system; the resulting amplification of the natural vibration.

1899 Franklin & Williamson *Elem. Alternating Currents* v. 59 Mechanical resonance. If a periodic force of given maximum value and given frequency acts upon the body.. the body will be set vibrating at the same frequency as that of the force, and the violence of the motion will be greatest, for the given value of the periodic force, when the frequency of the force is equal to the proper frequency of the body. **1913** *Phil. Mag.* XXVI. 125 If the lower bob is of solid metal ..its damping coefficient will be small and the resonance in consequence probably inconveniently sharp. **1935** J. E. Younger *Struct. Design Metal Airplanes* xv. 272 In the prevention of dangerous structural vibration, the first principle is to avoid resonance. **1952** D. E. Christie *Intermediate College Mech.* xii. 306 In practical engineering it is frequently desirable to keep forced oscillations well away from resonance. **1959** *Listener* 5 Feb. 252/1 Where the lengths of waves and ship are almost equal, we experience severe pitch and heave motions... This 'resonance' can be destroyed in two ways. **1974** *Encycl. Brit. Micropædia* VIII. 525/1 Mechanical resonance..is known to have built up to such large proportions as to be destructive, as in the case of the Tacoma Narrows Bridge.

(ii) Amplification of wave or tidal motion in a body of water when this motion has the same frequency as a natural vibration of the body of water.

1955 P. H. Kuenen *Realms of Water* ii. 37 Lake Baikal.. has..no resonance whatever and the tide is less than one inch. *Ibid.* 42 In the Malay Archipelago..resonances in the separate basins with natural periods of oscillation. **1975** *New Yorker* 12 May 94/2 Certain harbors sometimes have problems with a phenomenon known as resonance, wherein waves that might be, say, two feet high on the outside build up energy within the harbor until waves in there stand ten feet high or higher.

f. *Astr.* The circumstance or phenomenon of the periods of revolution of two bodies about a single primary being, exactly or approximately, in the ratio of two small integers.

1923 *Astron. Jrnl.* XXXV. 70/2 From the mechanical point of view, the chief feature of the motion of an asteroid of the Trojan group is due to resonance. **1928** *Bull. Amer. Math. Soc.* XXXIV. 283 Here the millions of 'stones' or 'rocks' which must constitute those rings revolve round Saturn and resonances are caused by the action of its larger satellites. **1968** R. A. Lyttleton *Mysteries Solar Syst.* vii. 229 The adopted value implied a period of the unknown planet of some 218 years, which is not very different from three times the period of Uranus, namely 84 years. It would be sufficiently near in fact to give a mild resonance, because of the approximate 3:1 ratio. **1979** *Science* 5 Oct. 39/1 Mimas has been implicated because it orbits Saturn in exactly twice the time that any particles happening to orbit within the Cassini division would. This whole-number relationship of orbital periods is called resonance.

g. *fig.* and other *transf.* uses.

1607, etc. [see sense 1 a in Dict.]. **1892** J. Sully *Human Mind* II. xiv. 58 That the corporeal resonance does form an essential ingredient in emotion is abundantly proved by a variety of facts. **1925** J. Laird *Our Minds & Their Bodies* i. 21 It is the commonest thing in the world to say that we are 'not ourselves' when our bodies, so to say, ring differently to us from their normal resonance. **1939** *Scrutiny* VII. 441 In particular, his temperament was painfully out of resonance with his father's. **1956** Day & de la Warr *New Worlds beyond Atom* v. 34 A part of the wave-form emitted by the drug forms a discord with the radiations of the disease while another part of it is in resonance with the organ which is being treated. **1962** E. F. Haden et al. *Resonance-Theory for Linguistics* 48 Resonance in Linguistics is a bond, imagined as a hybrid or a wave, linking two language entities. **1965** J. M. Stephens *Psychol. of Classroom Learning* vii. 176/2 In real life many problems have been solved by this seemingly mysterious, unconscious 'resonance'. **1967** E. H. Lenneberg *Biol. Foundations Lang.* ix. 378 Perhaps a better metaphor still is the concept of resonance... Exposure to adult language behavior has an excitatory effect upon the actualization process much the same way a certain frequency may have..upon a specific resonator; the object begins to vibrate in the presence of the sound. In the case of language onset, the energy required for the resonance is, in a sense, supplied by the individual himself. **1976** *Southern Even. Echo* (Southampton) 16 Nov. 3/5 For much of the piece there is an extra resonance and significance about Gray's otherwise-familiar anti-hero. **1977** A. Sheridan tr. *J. Lacan's Écrits* iii. 86 What is redundant as far as information is concerned is precisely that which does duty as resonance in speech.

2. b. The enhancement of one colour by its proximity to another or others. Cf. *resonant *a.* 2 b.

1933 *Burlington Mag.* Jan. 3/1, I knew that Titian was a master of rich and sumptuous colour. I knew how splendidly he could evoke from his blues and crimsons their fullest and deepest resonance.

3. *resonance frequency, particle, vibration*; **resonance absorption** *Nuclear Physics*, absorption of energy or of a particle under conditions of resonance; *spec.* = next; **resonance capture** *Nuclear Physics*, absorption of a particle by an atomic nucleus which occurs only for certain well-defined values of particle energy; **resonance chamber** = Resonator 2; **resonance energy,** (*a*) an energy value at which resonance occurs; (*b*) *Chem.*, the extent of stabilization of a molecular structure attributed to mesomerism; **resonance fluorescence,** fluorescence in which the light emitted has the same wavelength as that which excites the emission; **resonance hybrid** *Chem.*, a molecular structure which is a mesomeric combination of a number of forms; **resonance radiation,** (the radiation emitted in) resonance fluorescence; **resonance Raman spectrum** [*Raman], a Raman spectrum excited by light having a frequency equal to that of a band in the absorption spectrum of the scattering substance (see quot. 1975[1]); so *resonance Raman effect, spectroscopy*, etc.; **resonance scattering** *Nuclear Physics*, elastic scattering of a particle by an atomic nucleus at an energy of the incident particle for which the scattering cross-section is large compared with that for adjacent values of the energy (cf. *potential scattering* s.v. *potential *sb.* 4 c; **resonance stabilization** *Chem.* = **resonance energy* (*b*).

1945 H. D. Smyth *Gen. Acct. Devel. Atomic Energy Mil. Purposes* iv. 24 The term 'resonance absorption' is used to describe the very strong absorption of neutrons by U-238 when the neutron energies are in certain definite portions of the energy region. **1952** [see sense 1 d (iii) above]. **1961** G. R. Choppin *Exper. Nuclear Chem.* viii. 114 In indium a resonance absorption occurs for neutrons with a kinetic energy of 1·44 ev. **1937** G. Gamow *Struct. Atomic Nuclei* xi. 224 We may have here a case of resonance-capture. **1964** M. Gowing *Britain & Atomic Energy 1939–45* i. 40 Various other ways of reducing the capture of neutrons by resonance capture..were considered. **1919** D. Jones *Outl. Eng. Phonetics* vi. 15 The effect of a resonance chamber in modifying quality of tone may be illustrated experimentally. **1962** A. Nisbett *Technique Sound Studio* iii. 59 The mouth, nose and throat cavities act as resonance chambers for sound coming from the vocal cords. **1931** *Jrnl. Amer. Chem. Soc.* LIII. 1368 The energy of the bond is largely the resonance or interchange energy of two electrons. **1941** in M. Gowing *Britain & Atomic Energy 1939–45* (1964) 430 Neutrons of certain critical, or resonance, energies are strongly absorbed by uranium without causing fission. **1965** Phillips & Williams *Inorg. Chem.* I. iii. 75 The difference between the computed binding energy of a hypothetical structure and that computed using all possible structures, i.e. the actual binding energy of the real molecule, is called the resonance energy. **1925** *Sci. Abstr.* A. XXVIII. 121 In the case of resonance fluorescence the re-emitted line possesses a greater Doppler width than the incident line. **1977** I. M. Campbell *Energy & Atmosphere* viii. 260 (*caption*) Schematic diagram of apparatus for the resonance fluorescence detection of hydroxyl radicals in air. **1921** W. H. Eccles *Continuous Wave Wireless Telegr.* iii. 172 When an external sine force acts upon a vibrator, whether at the resonance frequency or not, it gradually builds up a vibrating motion to a definite final amplitude. **1974** *Encycl. Brit. Macropædia* XIX. 101/2 Wind supplied the power causing the bridge to vibrate at one of its torsional resonance frequencies without sufficient damping. **1939** L. Pauling *Nature Chem. Bond* xii. 407 Each of these tautomers in its normal state is represented..by a resonance hybrid of this structure and others. **1964** N. G. Clark *Mod. Org. Chem.* xxv. 525 The true structure of benzene is..a resonance hybrid, to which the two Kekulé formulae..contribute equally. **1975** *Sci. Amer.* May 43/2 Other resonance particles decay by the 'strong' interaction in about 10^{-23} second. **1905** R. W. Wood in *Phil. Mag.* X. 514 Repeated efforts have been made..to detect a lateral emission of yellow light by sodium vapour when in the act of absorbing sodium light... This seems to be the first case found of the phenomenon, which it may perhaps be well to style resonance radiation, to distinguish it from fluorescence. **1928** [see *quench *v.* 3 d]. **1963** R. W. Ditchburn *Light* (ed. 2) xvii. 661 Sodium absorbs and re-emits as resonance radiation the two well-known yellow lines at wavelengths 5890 Å. and 5896 Å. **1960** tr. Shorygin & Krushinskii in *Soviet Physics Doklady* V. 793 The possibility of observing resonance Raman spectra is limited to a considerable degree by the loss of light due to absorption. **1962** *Pure & Appl. Chem.* IV. 87 The study of the resonance Raman effect can contribute not only to the extension of the technique of Raman spectroscopy, but also to an investigation of the nature of the interaction of light with matter. **1975** *Jrnl. Chem. Soc.: Dalton Trans.* 381/1 When a molecule..is excited with a laser beam whose wavenumber corresponds or closely corresponds with the band maximum of a strongly allowed electronic transition of the molecule, then a rigorous resonance Raman (r.r.) spectrum may be obtained. Such spectra are normally characterised by an enormous increase in the intensity of a totally symmetric fundamental of the molecule together with the appearance of long overtone progressions in this same fundamental. **1975** *Nature* 25 Dec. 770/1 The results of Lewis and Spoonhower using resonance Raman spectroscopy imply the existence of a strong complex between retinal and a tryptophan residue in rhodopsin. **1937** Bethe & Placzek in *Physical Rev.* LI. 462/1 Near resonance, the resonance scattering σ_2 must be added to the potential scattering. **1955** A. E. S. Green *Nuclear Physics* xiii. 456

These deviations are attributed to the interference between the potential and resonance scattering associated with the *l*th partial wave. **1978** *Nature* 26 Oct. 730/1 Resonance scattering of light from a beam of free atoms is an ideal technique for making precise absolute measurements of the shift in wavelength of the light relative to the reference wavelength of the beam atoms. **1939** L. Pauling *Nature Chem. Bond* i. 10 Because the resonating system does not have a structure intermediate between those involved in the resonance, but..a structure which is further changed by the resonance stabilization, I prefer not to use the word 'mesomerism'..for the resonance phenomenon. **1952** [see *oxyanion]. **1978** K. Yates *Hückel Molecular Orbital Theory* iii. 118 In order to evaluate the resonance stabilization of benzene, as represented by the formulation (XI), a comparison should be made with cyclohexatrienes possessing the benzene geometry. **1909** *Westm. Gaz.* 4 Sept. 10/1 If the period of vibration of the two parts is the same 'resonance vibrations' are set up.

resonant, *a.* and *sb.* Add: **A.** *adj.* **1. b.** *Phonet.* Of consonants: liquid or nasal. Cf. the sb. in Dict. and Suppl.

1943 K. L. Pike *Phonetics* vii. 144 The *sonorants* are nonvocoid resonants and comprise the lateral resonant orals and resonant nasals (e.g. [m], [n], and [l]). **1948** W. F. Twaddell in *Language* XXIV. 141 Before the resonant consonants, only /e/, /a/, and /u/ occurred regularly.

2. b. Of colours: emphasizing each other by contrast.

1887 *Portfolio* XVIII. 233/2 His painting has ever become slighter, higher in tone and less full and resonant in colour.

4. a. Involving, exhibiting, or bringing about electrical resonance (Resonance 1 c in Dict. and Suppl.).

1888 *Electrician* 28 Sept. 663/2 Drawing the micrometer terminals so far apart that sparks can only be made to pass by means of resonant action. **1925** Resonant frequency [sense 5 below]. **1938** *Jrnl. Appl. Physics* IX. 654/2 Such a resonator may often be equivalent to a conventional resonant circuit. **1947** R. Lee *Electronic Transformers & Circuits* vii. 192 The heights of resonant peaks and frequency distance between peaks depend upon circuit *Q* and coefficient of coupling *k*. **1959** K. Henney *Radio Engin. Handbk.* (ed. 5) v. 27 Multiple resonance imposes practical limits on the way in which resonant circuits may be combined. **1964** R. F. Ficchi *Electr. Interference* v. 56 The isolation offered by the turns eliminates resonant effects. **1966** *New Scientist* 15 Dec. 627/1 The device, known as a resonant-gate transistor, was developed by a team of scientists in..Pittsburgh.

b. *Physics* and *Chem.* Pertaining to, involving, exhibiting, or taking part in any other kind of resonance.

1934 Resonant frequency [sense 5 below]. **1944** L. F. & M. Fieser *Org. Chem.* xx. 523 Results of the ozonization experiments cited above accord with the concept of two resonant Kekulé forms contributing in an equal extent to the structure. **1960** Dicke & Wittke *Introd. Quantum Mechanics* xvi. 291 When the energy of the incoming particles corresponds to such a state, a resonant condition is said to occur, in which the scattering cross-section is markedly greater than for nonresonant energies. **1965** *Physics Lett.* XIV. 159/1 The enhancement observed [in pion-nucleon interaction] need not necessarily be identified with a resonant state. **1973** *Sci. Amer.* Nov. 125/3 The reason is that one second is about the period at which a 10-inch pendulum vibrates naturally, that is, one second is the frequency of vibration to which the pendulum is resonant. **1976** *Chem. Physics Lett.* XLI. 292/1 The resonant electronic transition is the axial $d_{z^2} \leftarrow d_{z^2}$ transition at 17 450 cm^{-1}.

5. Special collocations: **resonant cavity,** a cavity resonator (see *resonator 3 b); **resonant frequency,** a frequency at which resonance (of any kind) takes place; **resonant scattering** *Nuclear Physics* = *resonance scattering* s.v. *resonance 3.

1945 *Nature* 15 Sept. 323/1 Dr. J. T. Randall applied the resonant-cavity technique to the relatively ineffective magnetron of pre-war days, and made of it a radically new and immensely powerful device which remains the heart of every modern radar equipment. **1955** *Science* 9 Dec. 1132/3 The deuteron beam..then enters the first of two 48-megacycle resonant-cavity accelerator sections. **1925** W. Greenwood *Text-bk. Wireless Telegr. & Teleph.* i. 19 The resonant frequency is..equal to the natural frequency when the damping is negligible. **1934** J. P. Den Hartog *Mech. Vibrations* ii. 52 The forced frequency coincides exactly with the natural frequency... This important phenomenon is known as 'resonance', and the natural frequency is sometimes called also the 'resonant frequency'. **1964** R. F. Ficchi *Electr. Interference* v. 49 The smaller the total inductance, the higher the resonant frequency. **1948** *Physical Rev.* LXXIV. 926/1 The present work was begun with the object of detecting nuclear resonant scattering from Mg^{24} nuclei which are excited by resonant radiation from the radioactive Na^{24} nuclei. **1955** [see *potential scattering* s.v. *potential *sb.* 4 c]. **1963** W. E. Burcham *Nuclear Physics* xiii. 484 From the observed cross-section for the resonant scattering effect, with appropriate account taken of the thermal broadening,..a total width of $(2{\cdot}1 \pm 0{\cdot}4) \times 10^{-5}$ eV for the 412 keV level of ^{198}Hg was found.

B. *sb.* (Further examples.) Also, a liquid consonant.

1948 W. F. Twaddell in *Language* XXIV. 141, /i/ before resonants was at best very rare. **1956** J. Whatmough *Language* 37 Thus we have the class known as resonants (e.g. *l, m*). **1970** B. M. H. Strang *Hist. Eng.* ix. 406 The third sub-system consists of resonants, i.e. sounds which may or may not have syllabic function (thus corresponding to approximants, liquids and nasals in P[resent-day] E[nglish]). **1976** *Archivum Linguisticum* VII. 167 The gemination becomes an additional argument for the reconstruction of laryngeals next to a resonant or *s*.

resonantly *adv.* (further examples).

1971 *Nature* 15 Oct. 469/2 From the observational viewpoint the soft X-ray enhancement..can be interpreted in terms of solar X-rays resonantly scattered in the Earth's atmosphere. **1977** *Gramophone* May 1737/2 Here if anything he is even more resonantly impressive than he was for Klemperer. **1978** *Sci. Amer.* June 124/1 The audio oscillator was tuned to resonantly oscillate the water..so as to cause vibrational standing waves to form on the surface.

resonate, *v.* Add: **1. a.** (Further examples.) Also *fig.*

1946 *Physical Rev.* LXIX. 37 It [*sc.* a resonant cavity] was adjusted to resonate at about 30 mc/sec. **1955** R. S. H. Boulding *Radar Pocket Bk.* vi. 72 An artificial line can be charged from an a.c. supply without a rectifier by making a choke in the charging circuit resonate, at the supply frequency, with the capacitance of the line. **1956** *Jrnl. Chem. Physics* XXIV. 468/1 In NMR spectra nuclei which give signals at the same applied field or resonate with the same Larmor frequency may be considered magnetically equivalent. **1976** *Publishers Weekly* 27 Sept. 80/1 Prose..resonating with the illustrations.

b. *spec.* in *Chem.* To exhibit mesomerism (cf. *resonance 1 d (ii)). Const. *among* or *between* different structures, as if a real physical alternation were occurring.

1933 Pauling & Wheland in *Jrnl. Chem. Physics* I. 369 In the first step the C—C bond breaks and there are formed two phenyl-methyl radicals, which however can resonate between only the structures A and B of Fig. 3. **1957** G. E. Hutchinson *Treat. Limnol.* I. iii. 196 The molecule resonates between the following structures. **1965** G. W. Wheland *Resonance in Org. Chem.* i. 7 Only by exercising the utmost care in the choice of words can one avoid the appearance of implying that the molecules..are oscillating back and forth among the several structures, and hence that these structures must possess real physical significance... The common statements that the hybrid *resonates* among the structures and that the structures *resonate* with one another almost unavoidably give this quite erroneous impression. **1976** *Sci. Amer.* Nov. 59/1 Perhaps the baryon resonates between these configurations, much as the benzene ring resonates between its various possible structures.

2. *trans.* To act as a resonator for; to amplify by resonance.

1904 *Physical Rev.* XVIII. 231 Having the radiating aërial resonating the primary circuit, it is now necessary to have a second primary circuit in tune with the first. **1975** *Sci. Amer.* July 48/2 Signals become convolved when sounds are reverberated or resonated or, in the case of photographs, when images are blurred.

resonating, *ppl. a.* Add: (Further examples). *resonating chamber* = Resonator 2.

1912 *Chem. Abstr.* VI. 3220 An extensive research on the properties and behavior of resonating gas mols. **1933** *Jrnl. Chem. Physics* I. 611 A negative carbon atom, with one unshared and three shared electron pairs, occurs rather often in resonating structures, as in carbon monoxide, [etc.]. **1938** Resonating chamber [see *resonator 2 b]. **1959** E. Pulgram *Introd. Spectrogr. Speech* vii. 55 The resonating tuning fork continues to operate for a while after the struck fork has been stopped. **1968** B. M. H. Strang *Mod. Eng. Structure* (ed. 2) 35 The character of the sound produced can be varied over a considerable range by changing the shape of the resonating chambers. **1974** D. M. Adams *Inorg. Solids* vii. 230 In PbI_2, with its inert pair of *s*-electrons, bonding is via two resonating *p*-electrons. **1974** R. C. Hibbeler *Engin. Mech.* xxii. 958 Resonating vibrations can cause tremendous stress and rapid failure of parts.

resonator. Add: **2. b.** (Further examples.)

1938 *Oxf. Compan. Mus.* 994/2 The frontal sinuses..have apparently considerable value as resonators: it is said that the Australian natives have a great want of resonance in their speech due to the small size of these sinuses. All the resonating chambers or passages mentioned above..are in direct communication with the air which has passed through the vocal cords. **1970** A. C. Gimson *Introd. Pronunc. Eng.* (ed. 2) 11 These cavities [*sc.* pharynx, mouth, nasal cavity] function as the principal *resonators* of the note produced in the larynx. *Ibid.* 19 The way in which the speaker's vibrator and resonators function together.

3. a. Also, any device which displays electrical resonance. (Earlier and later examples.)

1889 *Phil. Mag.* XXVIII. 125 For this proof we must give somewhat different dimensions to our apparatus in order to be able to introduce electric resonators into its interior. **1943** *Proc. IRE* XXXI. 448/1 The simple circuit of Fig. 14(a) is well known as the Hertzian oscillator and is readily recognized as a lumped capacitance associated with a single-turn inductor. At frequencies up to several hundreds of megacycles such a resonator is quite practical.

b. *spec.* (in full *cavity resonator*) a hollow enclosure with conducting walls which is capable of containing electromagnetic fields having particular frequencies of oscillation, and of exchanging electrical energy with them; such devices are used esp. for the amplification or detection of microwaves.

1936 *Proc. IRE* XXIV. 1320 [All of these terminals may act as more or less sharply resonant systems... They may..be thought of as electromagnetic analogues of the Helmholtz resonator.] *Ibid.* 1324 A cylindrical resonator attached to the hollow tube system. **1943** *Ibid.* XXXI. 447/2 The flexibility of the Klystron is seriously limited by the fact that cavity resonators are permanently attached to the grids and thus form an integral part of the tube itself. **1952** Reintjes & Coate *Princ. Radar* (Mass. Inst. Technol. Radar School Staff) (ed. 3) ix. 613 Cavity resonators are hollow metal-walled chambers fitted with devices for admitting and extracting electromagnetic energy. **1956** *Nature* 10 Mar. 470/2 During the past four or five years,..the Radiation Laboratory has concentrated much effort..on the construction of a linear accelerator of the cavity-resonator type. **1966** *McGraw-Hill Encycl. Sci. & Technol.* II. 577/2 Coaxial cavity resonators are often used as wavemeters, particularly for lower than microwave frequencies. **1975** D. G. Fink *Electronics Engineers' Handbk.* ix. 29 In the reflex Klystron a single resonator is used to modulate the beam and extract of energy from it, making the tube simple and easy to tune.

4. An object or system which resonates, in any other sense.

1897 *Abstr. Physical Papers* (Physical Soc.) III. 356 Next a resonator of a perfectly-conducting material is imagined to be introduced. This resonator, while absorbing energy from the incident radiation and radiating it again without loss, will, in general, change the character of the radiation, either in its frequency, the law of its damping, or both. **1914** J. H. Jeans *Rep. Radiation & Quantum Theory* ii. 9 Planck ..supposed that the emission and absorption were accomplished by 'resonators' of perfectly definite periods. **1949** Koestler *Insight & Outlook* p. ix, The theory of memory traces as selective resonator systems suggested in various forms by Jacques Loeb..and others. **1959** E. Pulgram *Introd. Spectrogr. Speech* vii. 55 This effect of sympathetic vibration is called resonance, and the object activated by it is a resonator. **1974** G. Reece tr. *Hund's Hist. Quantum Theory* ii. 24 He [*sc.* Planck] constructed a model for the emission and absorption of radiation at the walls of a black body by assuming the presence of resonators. **1979** *Sci. Amer.* Mar. 81/1 It was soon learned that a particular wavelength could be selected by designing an optical resonator that will allow only the chosen wavelength to pass repeatedly through the amplifying dye cell... The resonator consisted of a partially reflecting glass plate at one end of the laser and a diffraction grating at the other.

resonatory, *a.* For *rare*$^{-1}$ read *rare.* (Further example.)

1961 L. F. Brosnahan *Sounds of Language* i. 2 The process of vocal sound production in language appears on analysis to consist basically of the production of an air-stream, the conversion of some of the kinetic energy of this airstream into acoustic energy in the form of a complex of sound waves, and the subsequent resonatory modulation of that complex.

resorb, *v.* Add: *esp.* in *Physiol.*, to absorb into the circulation (material already in the body, esp. material that has been digested or broken down). (Further examples.)

1901 J. S. Marshall *Princ. & Pract. Operative Dentistry* iv. 76 The absorbent organ secretes..a digestive fluid or soluble ferment which dissolves or digests the dental tissues and alveolar walls, and prepares them to be resorbed. *Ibid.* xxxiv. 509 Bone is resorbed through the action of the osteoclast cells. **1928** Moore & Key tr. *Leriche & Policard's Normal & Path. Physiol. of Bone* iv. 71 If..one brings about increase of circulation, bone in the epiphyses is resorbed to the extent of detaching itself from the investing cartilage and becoming very friable. **1967** M. E. Hale *Biol. Lichens* viii. 118 The acids are not resorbed by the hyphae. **1968** R. D. Martin tr. *Wickler's Mimicry in Plants & Animals* xi. 107 The flea will resorb its eggs if the female host miscarries.

Hence **reso·rbed** *ppl. a.*; **reso·rbing** *ppl. a.*, undergoing resorption; also **reso·rbable** *a.*, that may be resorbed.

1910 J. P. Buckley *Mod. Dental Materia Medica* ii. 315 (*heading*) Resorbed root. **1928** Moore & Key tr. *Leriche & Policard's Normal & Path. Physiol. of Bone* iv. 85 In resorbing callus the cells were hypertrophied. **1967** *Archivum Immunol. et Therapiae Exper.* XV. 809 (*caption*) Section through a resorbable 256 Walker tumor. **1973** *Nature* 9 Mar. 135/2 Seven [voles] were pregnant but four had resorbing embryos. **1976** *Biomed.* XXV. 131/1 Porous resorbable ceramics have been found to be most suitable [as bone substitutes] since they encourage replacement of resorbed ceramic with new bone.

resorbent, *a.* (Later examples.)

1889 *Science* 29 Mar. 232/2 Not until the silicates are developed, and the granitic quartz begins to form, does the resorbent action discontinue. **1962** K. F. Lagler et al. *Ichthyology* viii. 257 When the fish descends..the resorbent capillary network collapses so as to enlarge the area of contact of the gas gland for rapid secretion of gases into the bladder.

resorcinol. Substitute for def.: = Resorcin; a dihydric phenol whose uses include the manufacture of phenol-formaldehyde resins. (Further examples.)

This, rather than *resorcin*, is now the usual name for the substance.

1949 *Thorpe's Dict. Appl. Chem.* (ed. 4) IX. 476/1 Of the dihydric phenols, resorcinol is industrially second to hydroquinone in importance, and is used in considerable amount. **1959** *Times* 27 Apr. (Rubber Industry Suppl.) p. vii/3 In this country all tire cord is impregnated by an aqueous process..using the mixed latices and resorcinol-formaldehyde resin. **1964** N. G. Clark *Mod. Org. Chem.* xxi. 439 The three dihydroxybenzenes are called catechol, resorcinol, and hydroquinone (quinol). **1972** *Materials & Technol.* V. iv. 95 Resorcinol adhesives, with the added advantage of being neutral or nearly so, are superior to all others as adhesives for wood, giving exceptional durability.

resorption. Add: Cf. Resorb *v.* in Dict. and Suppl. (Further examples.)

1889 *Science* 29 Mar. 232/2 While the silicates are crystallizing in a molten mass, if porphyritic quartz is present it undergoes resorption. **1910** Lake & Rastall *Textbk. Geol.* xiii. 232 These phenocrysts have often undergone a certain amount of corrosion, or resorption. **1928** Moore & Key tr.

Leriche & Policard's Normal & Path. Physiol. of Bone iv. 71 When osteoclasts are present there is resorption. **1962** BLAKE & TROTT *Periodontology* viii. 82 In other cases there is resorption of the apices of vital teeth. **1962** K. F. LAGLER et al. *Ichthyology* viii. 247 In many rayfishes..gas resorption is also performed by..the oval organ situated in the posterior portion of the gas bladder. **1974** *Nature* 22 Mar. 343/1 This is accomplished by inhibition of bone resorption, of the tubular reabsorption of calcium, and of the intestinal absorption of calcium.

resorptive, *a.* Delete *rare* and add earlier and later examples.

1886 *Philadelphia Med. Times* XVI. 490/2 The removal of such substances is dependent upon the action of specialized cells, called resorptive or giant cells, and the process is physiological. **1951** *Jrnl. Bone & Joint Surg.* A. XXXIII. 936 All resorptive processes occur principally in relation to calcified matrices and not to osteoid or uncalcified cartilage. **1978** *Sci. Amer.* Feb. 112/3 My own observations of such 'flypaper' trappers as butterworts and sundews suggest that these plants have secretory and resorptive mechanisms that are quite different from the ones likely to operate in pitcher plants.

resort, *sb.* Add: **I. 7.** (Further examples.)

1883 *Harper's Mag.* Sept. 521/1 The bustle of arrival and departure..[animates] the village in the way peculiar to American towns near a 'resort'. **1893** K. D. WIGGIN *Polly Oliver's Problem* (1894) ii. 30 She would become the head of a summer resort, with a billiard-room and a bowling-alley. **1909** 'O. HENRY' *Roads of Destiny* xviii. 294 He was manager at different times of..a dozen hotels and summer resorts, an insurance company, and a district leader's campaign. **1936** [see *holiday resort* s.v. *HOLIDAY 4]. **1976** *Morecambe Guardian* 7 Dec. 14/4 The man behind the proposal described Carnforth as 'a poor little town that could never become a health resort'.

III. 11. *attrib.* and *Comb.*, as (sense 7) *resort city, cottage, estate, hotel, -motel, -motor hotel, railroad station, town*; **resort clothes, -wear,** clothes suitable for wearing at a holiday resort.

1974 *Sumter* (S. Carolina) *Daily Item* 20 Apr. 1A/5 Police mounted a room-by-room sweep of hotels in this resort city. **1978** R. LUDLUM *Holcroft Covenant* viii. 93 In every resort city there was always one major shop that catered to the reading requirements of a specific nationality. **1974** *Country Life* 2 May 1097/2 Their Côte d'Azur collection of women's resort clothes. **1977** N. FREELING *Gadget* i. 24 Bring more than resort clothes... Evening things, feminine. **1971** *Jamaican Weekly Gleaner* 3 Nov. 3/1 A long debate on the merits or otherwise of licensing resort cottages. **1975** *New Yorker* 19 May 115 (Advt.), The Mountain View House is a resort estate with a charm only a century of family ownership can achieve. **1919** E. HOUGH *Sagebrusher* 49 A few passengers from the resort hotel back in the town began to appear. **1977** *Whitaker's Almanack 1978* 778/2 Tourism is the most important industry, with a good choice of resort hotels. **1963** *New Yorker* 1 June 123/1 (Advt.), America's most *funderful* resort-motel. *Ibid.* 8 June 58 (Advt.), America's 3 great new resort-motor hotels. **1928** *Publishers' Weekly* 3 Nov. 1868/1 The..delay involved when a package must change trains in a resort railroad station. **1970** *Southerly* XXX. 124 Occasionally a car hummed along the bitumen..making..for one of the string of resort towns further along the coast. **1972** D. E. WESTLAKE *Cops & Robbers* (1973) xvi. 243 You could always tell a resort town, it ran much heavier to neon. **1965** *Punch* 10 Mar. p. xvi/2, Harvey Nichols's spring collection, which includes Italian and French resort-wear, can be seen on Mar 15. **1975** *Harper's & Queen* June 69 The latest collection of resort wear.

resorter. Add: (Later example.) Also (*U.S.*), one who runs a business in a resort.

1927 *Scribner's Mag.* Apr. 383/2 Take me along on a Southern trip to see what the rich resorters are wearin'? **1978** *Minneapolis Tribune* 4 Apr. 6A/1 The severe reduction of motorized opportunities..would devastate the resorters and outfitters of northeastern Minnesota.

resound, *sb.* (Later example.)

1835 H. EVANS in *Mississippi Valley Hist. Rev.* (1927) XIV. 213 Distinctly..the resound of guns was heard in quick succession.

resound, *v.* Add: **1. a.** Also with *to*.

1861 F. O. MORRIS *Rec. Animal Sagacity & Character* 121 He..lies buried..in those very shrubberies which had so often resounded to his joyous cries.

resounding, *ppl. a.* Add: Also *fig.*

1977 *Guardian Weekly* 4 Sept. 16/1 The Federal Energy Administration..says that in the month ending in mid-August, American oil consumption was up a resounding 8 per cent over the same time last year.

resource. Add: **1. a.** (Later *sing.* examples.)

1965 H. I. ANSOFF *Corporate Strategy* i. 6 A large majority of decisions must be made within the framework of a limited total resource. **1969** *Nature* 20 Dec. 1233/1 Satisfactory land use—that is, one that will provide a sustained yield of a resource—must take full account of the ecology. **1978** *Sci. Amer.* Nov. 82/3 The very best of them, such as W. F. Leopold's classic *Speech Development of a Bilingual Child*, continue to be a rich resource for contemporary investigators.

b. See also *natural resources* s.v. *NATURAL *a.* 6 e.

6. *attrib.* and *Comb.*, as (sense 1 a) *resource allocation, base, limit, zone*; *resource-based, -bound, -intensive, -limited, -poor, -supplying, -wasteful* adjs.; **resource aggregation** (see quot. 1968); **resource centre,** a library or other centre which houses a collection of *learning resources* (*LEARNING *vbl. sb.* 4); such a collection itself; also *attrib.*; **resource industry,** an industry of which the raw materials occur as natural resources; **resource profile** (see quot. 1967); **resource time,** the length of time a resource is required for a specific project.

1967 A. BATTERSBY *Network Analysis* (ed. 2) ix. 144 When Esso Petroleum transferred their accounts to a computer, they recognized 20 categories of clerical staff for resource aggregation. **1968** *Gloss. Terms Project Network Anal.* (*B.S.I.*) 9 *Resource aggregation*, the summation of the requirements of each resource, for each time period, calculated according to a common decision rule. **1964** K. G. LOCKYER *Introd. Critical Path Anal.* viii. 70 The name given by Production Controllers to this aspect of their work is *Loading*; regrettably, new names have been devised by some of the earlier CPA workers, amongst them *Manpower Smoothing*, and *Resource Allocation*. **1965** H. I. ANSOFF *Corporate Strategy* i. 6 A resource-allocation pattern which will offer the best potential for meeting the firm's objectives. **1977** P. JOHNSON *Enemies of Society* vi. 80 Classical economics had dealt with scarcity, value, choice, resource-allocation and efficiency. **1974** *Times* 8 Jan. (Europe Suppl.) p. xvi/5 How do you regard that oil? Is it British or is it European or is it just Shell's? I regard it as part of the resource base. **1967** *Times* 28 Feb. (Canada Suppl.) 32 Resource-based industries..have been characteristic of the economy. **1977** *Bull. Amer. Acad. Arts & Sci.* Oct. 18 Doubts about the continuity of past, present, and future..are expressed in current resource-bound models of growth. **1968** *Globe & Mail* (Toronto) 3 Feb. 47/1 (Advt.), The School has a gymnasium and central library with resource centre. **1971** in T. D. F. Barnard *New Directions in Librarianship* 44 There are new trends towards treating the library as a nexus for resource centre development. **1976** *Ann. Rep. Manpower Services Comm. 1975–76* ii. 20/1 The report therefore recommended that a resource centre should be established so that any organisation wishing to mount industrial relations training could be directed to appropriate sources of advice and teaching material. **1968** *Globe & Mail* (Toronto) 13 Jan. B5/1 Long on resource industry and lean in secondary industry, British Columbia continues to be especially vulnerable to the fluttering of foreign economies and markets. **1970** *Toronto Daily Star* 24 Sept. 1/8 This list..is likely to be lengthened to include some resource industries, pipelines, and possibly steel. **1976** *Conservation News* Sept.–Oct. 20/2 A planned transition to a less resource-intensive economy. **1970** S. L. BARRACLOUGH in I. L. Horowitz *Masses in Lat. Amer.* iv. 132 In many regions there is a sharp resource limit that would permit at most a doubling in the amount of productive land available. **1967** A. BATTERSBY *Network Analysis* (ed. 2) xii. 208 Before running the programme a 'duration limited' run or a 'resource limited' run must be specified. **1977** *Jrnl. R. Soc. Arts* CXXV. 389/1 The processing of many materials could..become energy-limited rather than resource-limited. **1969** *New Scientist* 2 Oct. 18/1 The flow of food and raw materials to the developed nations (almost all of which are resource-poor) will slowly dry up. **1973** *Listener* 20 Dec. 846/2 The resource-poor countries. **1967** A. BATTERSBY *Network Analysis* (ed. 2) ix. 141 Fig. 9.1 is called a 'resource profile' of a project, and it is obtained by 'resource aggregation'. The resources required by each job are specified when its duration is calculated; then when the scheduled starting times have been decided, the requirements are totalled over concurrent jobs for each discrete time period. **1969** R. B. FULLER *Operating Man. Spaceship Earth* ii. 27 They had to control various resource-supplying mines, forests, and lands with which and upon which to build the ships and establish the industries. **1973** *Bulletin* (Sydney) 25 Aug. 50/2 Australia has no idea of proposing the formation of a consortium of resource-supplying countries. **1964** K. G. LOCKYER *Introd. Critical Path Anal.* viii. 72 It is necessary to know the amount of work available—that is, the capacity available. This, too, must be specified in resource-time. **1976** *Carn* Feb. 20/2 It is easy to demonstrate that a resource-wasteful and energy-intensive lifestyle is very damaging to the environment. **1965** *New Statesman* 12 Nov. 732/1 We should select important amenity 'resource zones' such as the Broads and, rather than trying to stop all industrial development in them, get all interested parties to hammer out ways of developing them for all-round use—with recreation taking a high priority.

Also as *v. trans.*, to supply (a person, etc.) with resources; hence **resou·rced** *ppl. a.*; **resou·rcing** *vbl. sb.*

1975 *Listener* 27 Mar. 398/1, I would have gone in for smaller [school] units..resourced from some central agency. **1975** *Library Assoc. Rec.* LXXVII. 258 The policy of the Association..must be against diminished resourcing of libraries. **1975** *Language for Life* (Dept. Educ. & Sci.) ix. 133 These and many other devices ensure that all the non-specialist teachers of English are fully resourced. **1979** *Observer* 23 Sept. 4/8 Social workers have been inadequately trained and inadequately resourced to meet the expectations upon them.

resp (resp), *a. nonce-wd.* Abbrev. of RESPECTABLE *a.* 4 a.

1922 JOYCE *Ulysses* 158 Resp girl (R.C.) wishes to hear of a post in fruit or pork shop.

respect, *sb.* Add: **I. 3. c.** Delete † *Obs.* and add later example.

1904 H. JAMES *Golden Bowl* I. i. 11 She had struck him, in respect to the beautiful world, as one of the beautiful, the most beautiful things.

IV. 16. e. *with* (*all due*) *respect* and varr.: a polite phr. expressing proper deference, freq. used before stating (with some insistence) disagreement with another person's views. Also const. *to*.

1826 M. R. MITFORD *Our Village* II. 207 [My greyhound] is sliding her snake-like head into my hand, at once to invite the caress which she likes so well, and to intimate with all due respect that it is time to go home. **1923** C. MACKENZIE *Parson's Progress* xviii. 257 With all respect to the gentleman at the back of the hall who passed that remark, I tell him that if you think you can do anything with your review.., you're mistaken. **1977** *Belfast Tel.* 28 Feb. 6/4 With respect, I feel that the views expressed by Lord MacDermott are unbalanced from the very isolated position of a judge who, by necessity of office, must lead a somewhat cloistered life. **1977** *Church Times* 22 July 10/1 It is, with the greatest respect to His Grace, very little use to say that the book has 'caused more hubbub than it is worth'. **1978** *Ibid.* 25 Aug. 11/3 With all due respect to your three correspondents, I do not think they have answered M. J. Feaver's question (August 11). **1978** *Times* 13 Mar. 19/4 With great respect, this well-intentioned suggestion seems almost wholly devoid of merit. **1980** J. FOLLETT *Churchill's Gold* II. i. 86 With respect, admiral, we should not be building boats for any other purpose than for sinking enemy shipping.

V. 18. *Comb.*, as *respect-worthy* adj.

1833 [in Dict., sense 16]. **1889** 'MARK TWAIN' *Connecticut Yankee* xiii. 154 They were about all that was useful, or worth saving, or respectworthy. **1915** A. QUILLER-COUCH *Nicky-Nan* xxiii. 296 A neighbours' quarrel, and between folks I know to be so respectworthy. **1973** *Times Lit. Suppl.* 7 Sept. 1024/4 Horatio Parker (who was none the less respect-worthy, never mean or petty).

respectability. Add: **1. a.** Also with a somewhat derogatory implication of affectation or spuriousness.

1907 G. B. SHAW *Major Barbara* III. 281 The seven deadly sins!—Yes, the deadly seven... Food, clothing, firing, rent, taxes, respectability and children. **1969** *Listener* 3 Apr. 443/1 The social cost was high: hypocrisy;..the substitute of 'respectability' (spurious morality) for thought-out morals. Now that couples who aren't ready to support them needn't have children at all, marriage is redundant. **1978** P. BAILEY *Leisure & Class in Victorian England* viii. 178 We approach respectability as a role rather than as an ideology... The myth of substantial working-class respectability.

c. *transf.* Of things.

1903 G. B. SHAW *Man & Superman* p. xxviii, He and I and Mr. Sidney Webb were sowing our political wild oats as a sort of Fabian Three Musketeers, without any prevision of the surprising respectability of the crop that followed. **1976** *Times* 21 May 1/4 The alleged smear campaign against the Liberal Party..gained new respectability yesterday when the Prime Minister confirmed..that attempts were indeed being made to discredit individual members of the Liberal Party.

respectabilize, *v.* Delete *rare* and add further examples.

1933 G. STEIN *Autobiogr. Alice B. Toklas* v. 119 Uhde wished to respectabilise himself and she wanted to come into possession of her inheritance, which she could only do upon marriage. **1940** C. P. SNOW *Strangers & Brothers* xliv. 318 But the café had been respectabilized since then. There were now two floors, and neat waitresses. **1977** *Daily Tel.* 30 Apr. 13/4 Journalists are urged not to 'respectabilize' racist organizations.

respectable, *a.* and *sb.* Add: **A.** *adj.* **4. c.** (Further examples.)

1974 A. PRICE *Other Paths to Glory* I. iv. 41 Make us all a lot of hot, strong coffee while I get myself respectable. **1978** K. ROYCE *Satan Touch* v. 77 Herb Stahm knocked on Ashley's bedroom door. 'It's me, Herb.' 'Come on in. That meant they were respectable.

6. *respectable-tawdry*.

1916 E. POUND *Lustra* 112 A quiet and respectable tawdry trio.

B. *sb.* (Further examples.)

1940 E. GILL *Autobiogr.* vii. 262 With the *young* snobs and the *young* sycophants, the *young* hangers-on of the academies and, above all the young *respectables* there is nothing to be done. **1966** *Guardian* 15 June 9/8 Middle aged respectables here tend to shy away from discussion. **1978** P. G. WINSLOW *Coppergold* 142 You think I'm rotten, don't you?.. You're like Daddy and all the old respectables.

respectfully, *adv.* Add: **b.** *Yours respectfully*: a conventional formula used in the subscription of letters.

1812 'L. IRVING' *Let.* 11 Jan. in C. Mackenzie *My Life & Times* (1963) I. 51 Your early reply through the post office will oblige. Yours respectfully, Leathley Irving. **1859** MRS. GASKELL *Let.* 10 Nov. (1966) 592 Believe me to remain, Yours respectfully E C Gaskell. **1885** R. D. BLACKMAN *Letter-Writer's Vade-Mecum* (ed. 9) 42 In addressing a stranger, the proper salutation is 'Sir',..and the letter may be concluded..'Yours respectfully'. **1907** F. CROCKER *Let.* July in T. H. Baynes *Early Hist. St. Andrew's Church, Oxford* (1973) 14 On behalf of my fellow-workmen I respectfully beg to solicit from you a donation towards the Fund. Yours respectfully. **1960** J. STROUD *Shorn Lamb* v. 56 'Dear mr mall,' it said '..if she says she don't want donald, we will have him, yours respectfully.'

respectively, *adv.* **2.** For † *Obs.* read *rare* and add later example.

1962 *John o' London's* 25 Jan. 82/2 The magistrate is the *Beak* or, less respectively, the *Old Tosser*.

respirate (re·spirēᶦt), *v.* [Back-formation from RESPIRATION.] *trans.* To subject to artificial respiration.

1968 *Exper. Neurol.* XX. 416 The animals were artificially respirated by a Harvard 670 D pump. **1971** *Nature* 28 May 263/2 Trackers were cannulated and the animals were respirated artificially with a Harvard respirator.

respiration. Add: **1. a.** (Further *transf.* example.) *artificial respiration*: see *ARTIFICIAL *a.* 5.

1814 WORDSWORTH *Excursion* VIII. 365 Sails Which.. Pass with the respirations of the tide.

d. *Biochem.* and *Biol.* The biochemical and cellular processes by which absorbed oxygen is combined with carbon in the organism to form carbon dioxide and generate energy; more widely, any metabolic process in which energy is produced by the net transfer of electrons from a substrate to an external oxidant (usu. called *anærobic respiration* when this is not free oxygen); also extended to include energy-producing metabolic processes (fermentations) not involving a separate oxidant.

1856 J. C. MORRIS tr. *Lehmann's Man. Chem. Physiol.* 272 This exchange of oxygen and carbonic acid, which we improperly call respiration, is not confined to any single spot of the organism. **1880** A. GAMGEE *Text-bk. Physiol. Chem. Animal Body* I. ix. 366 The respiration of muscles during contraction. **1900** A. J. EWART tr. *Pfeffer's Physiol. Plants* I. ix. 546 (*heading*) The relationship between aerobic and anaerobic respiration. *Ibid.* 549 The actual anaerobic respiration (or fermentation) continues unchecked. **1908** HALL & DEFREN tr. *Aberhalden's Text-bk. Physiol. Chem.* xviii. 412 It [*sc.* the blood] takes the oxygen from the lungs and gives it up to the tissues. The first gas-exchange is commonly spoken of as external respiration, and the latter as internal respiration. **1929** R. A. GORTNER *Outl. Biochem.* viii. 386 In the dark the respiration of cells is inhibited by carbon monoxide. **1934** A. T. HENRICI *Biol. of Bacteria* xi. 174 Those processes which yield energy for the organism are respiration. *Ibid.* 184 A great many, probably all, microörganisms capable of growing either as strict or facultative anaerobes..may obtain energy by this intermolecular respiration, by a simultaneous oxidation of one compound and reduction of another. **1949** KELLY & HITE *Microbiology* xiv. 175 The phenomenon of 'life without air' has since [Pasteur's time] been explained by the study of anaerobic respiration or fermentation. **1965** G. A. STRAFFORD *Essent. Plant Physiol.* viii. 131 Fermentation is the form of anaerobic respiration carried out by some fungi and bacteria. **1970** AMBROSE & EASTY *Cell Biol.* vi. 183 The pyruvic acid is used for respiration (oxidation of carbon to CO_2) in the mitochondria. **1974** *Nature* 13 Dec. 579/1 The enzymes responsible for the first step in nitrate assimilation and for nitrate respiration are the nitrate reductases, both these processes involving the conversion of nitrate to nitrite.

5. *attrib.*, as *respiration rate.*

1929 R. A. GORTNER *Outl. Biochem.* viii. 242 The sudden rise in respiration rate may be due to the fact that at, or below, 14·75 per cent moisture all, or practically all, of the moisture in the wheat kernel is in the form of bound water. **1970** AMBROSE & EASTY *Cell Biol.* ii. 89 An apparatus originally designed by Warburg can be used to measure respiration rates.

respirator. Add: **2.** Also, a gas mask, or any mask for providing protection against noxious substances in the air. (Further examples.)

1872 *Chem. News* 17 May 239/1 The charcoal respirators invented by me in 1854 are now coming into general use, especially in manufactories and laboratories. *Ibid.*, The respirator is suspended for ten or fifteen minutes over some strong solution of ammonia in a large beaker; in this way the charcoal absorbs a very large amount of ammoniacal gas... The wearer can remain for a considerable time in an atmosphere containing chlorine without suffering any inconvenience. **1915** MRS. BELLOC LOWNDES *Diary* 26 Apr. (1971) 61 The [German] soldiers..had their noses plugged with cotton wool and respirators over their mouths, but even so, 1000 perished by their own gas. **1915** *Sphere* 7 Aug. 146/1 Respirators for the use of the Russian soldiers, who have been again attacked by gas bombs. **1938** *Ann. Reg. 1937* 25 Not a little of the increase was due in reality to military reasons, the Home Office being assigned some £4,000,000 for the provision of respirators and the development of emergency fire brigade services for protecting the civil population in the event of war. **1971** *Brit. Med. Bull.* XXVII. 75/2 The use of..air-fed respirators..could greatly reduce the future incidence of asbestos-related cancers in this work. **1978** CADOGAN & CRAIG *Women & Children First* x. 219 Forbidden to play with his gas mask, he muses bitterly on the 'jolly good times' that should result from unrestricted access to respirators.

3. *Med.* An apparatus for maintaining artificial respiration.

1929 DRINKER & MCKHAN in *Jrnl. Amer. Med. Assoc.* 18 May 1659/2 (*caption*) The mechanical respirator, showing patient ready to be pushed into the tank. **1932, 1938** [see *IRON LUNG 1]. **1966** DUNLOP & ALSTEAD *Textbk. Med. Treatm.* (ed. 10) 941 The action of all positive pressure respirators (or ventilators, as they are more correctly described) is to produce inflation of the lungs at a rate of 14 to 20 cycles per minute, expiration being allowed to occur passively. **1967** SLONIM & CHAPIN *Respiratory Physiol.* iv. 48/2 Drinker-type 'iron lung' respirators are devices built to enclose all the body below the neck. **1977** C. STORR *Tales from Psychiatrist's Couch* xi. 118 His respiratory muscles were working again and he was out of the respirator for large parts of the day.

respiratory, *a.* Add: **2.** Special collocations: *respiratory centre*, a region of the brain which exercises control over respiration; *respiratory pigment*, a protein molecule with a pigmented prosthetic group, involved in the transfer of oxygen or electrons within living systems; *respiratory quotient*, the ratio of the volume of carbon dioxide evolved to that of oxygen consumed; *respiratory syncytial virus*, an RNA virus that causes disease of the respiratory tract; *respiratory therapy* (U.S.), the management of patients receiving artificial respiration or ventilation and of the apparatus involved; so *respiratory therapist*, one trained in this; *respiratory tract*, the passages through which air passes in respiration; *respiratory tree*, a branched system of respiratory passages.

1883 *Encycl. Brit.* XX. 480/1 The respiratory centre must be regarded as the seat of origin of the impulses which cause the muscular movements of inspiration and expiration. **1948** A. BRODAL *Neurol. Anat.* xi. 391 The existence of a respiratory centre is generally admitted in the medulla. **1896** *Q. Jrnl. Microsc. Sci.* XXXIX. 3 A respiratory pigment of a kind unusual in the Chætopoda. **1933** *Biol. Bull.* LXIV. 233 In several of the invertebrates also, respiratory pigments, either hemoglobin or hemerythrin, are found within special cells of the circulating blood or body fluids. **1968** PASSMORE & ROBSON *Compan. Med. Stud.* I. viii. 7/1 Cytochromes. These are respiratory pigments found in all cells. **1890** BILLINGS *Med. Dict.* II. 453/1 *Respiratory quotient*, the relation of the inspired free oxygen to that expired in the form of carbonic acid. **1900** W. S. HALL *Text-bk. Physiol.* iv. 218 The respiratory quotient varies considerably in different *species*, and in the same animal under different conditions. **1968** PASSMORE & ROBSON *Compan. Med. Stud.* I. xxxi. 7/1 Ketosis is associated with a low respiratory quotient (RQ), below 0·75, which reflects a predominance of fat metabolism. **1961** *New Eng. Jrnl. Med.* CCLXIV. 1174/1 The present report presents convincing evidence for the etiologic role of the respiratory syncytial virus in acute respiratory illnesses among children. **1968** *New Scientist* 15 Feb. 368/1 Respiratory syncytial virus (RSV) is now the most dangerous of the respiratory pathogens that affect young children. **1965** P. SAFAR (*title*) Respiratory therapy. **1973** D. A. HOLADAY in Caldwell & Moya *Adv. Respiratory Care & Physiol.* vi. 85 Their duties include..administration of other categories of respiratory therapy to patients in intensive care units, post-anesthesia recovery rooms, and other areas..where continuous ventilators are in use. **1974** TYLER & NETT in T. L. Petty *Intensive & Rehabilitative Respiratory Care* (ed. 2) vi. 79 The patient with acute respiratory failure is being cared for by both nursing and respiratory therapy staffs. *Ibid.* 98 The nurse, respiratory therapist, and, where available, the physical therapist have vital roles in the successful care of any patient from the onset of acute illness throughout the convalescent and rehabilitative phases. **1978** *Detroit Free Press* 16 Apr. (Parade Suppl.) 5/3 Alice Gaul, a former U.S. Navy nurse, and Mary Masal, a respiratory therapist, managed to keep that man alive through the eight-hour flight. **1936** *Discovery* July 206/2 It has not appeared to produce the usual irritative effects of ether on the respiratory tract. **1977** *Chest* LXXI. 346/1 Aerosol topical anesthesia for instrumentation of the respiratory tract was first described in 1949. **1932** BORRADAILE & POTTS *Invertebrata* xviii. 575 Finally there is a short, wide cloaca. Into the latter usually open two long, branched respiratory trees, whose ramifications end in thin-walled ampullae through which water, when pumped in by contractions of the cloaca, passes into the body cavity, carrying oxygen to the coelomic fluid, and so to the organs. **1970** W. H. PARKER *Health & Dis. in Farm Animals* iii. 35 The respiratory tree is an apt phrase used to describe the continuous subdivision of the bronchi.

respire, *v.* Add: **I. 2. d.** To carry out or exhibit the biochemical processes of respiration.

1927 M. BODANSKY *Introd. Physiol. Chem.* viii. 200 A tissue that has been washed until it no longer 'respires' will, upon the addition of glutathione, again take up oxygen and yield carbon dioxide. **1951** M. ABERCROMBIE et al. *Dict. Biol.* 197 Many organisms (or parts of them) respire anaerobically for some time when their supply of oxygen is insufficient for aerobic respiration. **1976** *Sci. Amer.* Feb. 68/2 When the crop is ensiled, the plant cells continue to respire for a period of time and the aerobic bacteria on the plant increase in number.

respirit, *v.* (Further example.)

1929 R. BRIDGES *Testament of Beauty* III. 84 All his Knights cleansed and respirited, reclothed as might be.

respirometer (respirǫ·mĭtəɹ). [f. L. *respirāre* to blow, breathe out + -OMETER.] **1.** *Med.* A device which measures the quantity of air expired, so that the condition of the lungs may be studied; = SPIROMETER.

1889 *Cent. Dict.* 5111/1 *Respirometer*, an instrument which is used to determine the condition of the respiration. **1907** *Arch. Otology* XXXVI. 401 A person afflicted with pulmonary tuberculosis..so weakened by his disease that he can raise the water only six inches in the 'Respirometer'. **1964** BATES & CHRISTIE *Respiratory Function in Disease* ii. 6 For bedside use, the Wright Respirometer, a pocket-sized instrument, is preferable.

2. *Physiol.* A device which measures the rate of consumption of oxygen by a living or organic system.

1915 *Jrnl. Physiol.* XLIX. p. xxiv, (*heading*) A quantitative respirometer. **1923** *Jrnl. Agric. Res.* XXIII. 101 (*heading*) A new and efficient respirometer for seeds and other small objects. **1948** *Jrnl. Exper. Med.* LXXXVII. 177 (*caption*) Details of respirometer chamber to hold twenty eggs. **1969** *Sci. Jrnl.* Nov. 19/2 A simple fully automatic respirometer which measures organic pollution in sewage has been developed.

Hence **respiro·metry**, the measurement of rates of oxygen consumption; **re:spirome·tric** *a.*, by means of or pertaining to the respirometer.

1932 *Jrnl. Gen. Physiol.* XVI. 5 (*heading*) Studies in respirometry. **1960** *Antibiotics Ann.* VII. 563 (*heading*) Respirometric assay of nystatin in animal tissue. **1972** *Ann. Rep. Freshwater Biol. Assoc.* XL. 41 Dr Jones has continued to use respirometric techniques..to study the factors that cause inhibition of bacterial and other biological activity. **1977** A. G. CALLELY et al. *Treatm. Industr. Effluents* xvii. 278 Biological test methods applied to this type of waste include respirometry, aeration flask tests, and continuous treatment tests.

responaut (re·spǫnǭt). [Irreg. f. RESPIRATOR + Gr. ναύτ-ης sailor, after *astronaut*, etc.] A patient dependent upon a mechanical respirator to maintain breathing.

1964 *Sunday Times* 12 Jan. 18/5 The story of the 'responaut' Ann Armstrong as told by Moira Keenan was an enthralling one. **1964** *Med. Officer* 7 Aug. 97/2 A new group of severely disabled people. This group, calling themselves Responauts (because they share similar problems with astronauts and oceanauts in establishing and maintaining communications and vital air supplies) are young people whose lives have been saved through the invention and use of the first artificial organ—an iron lung or mechanical respirator—following a severe attack of respiratory polio. **1965** *Daily Mirror* 30 Dec. 12/2 The Responaut..—a quarterly magazine Ann edits for people like herself who need a breathing machine to keep alive. People the doctors call 'responauts'. **1969** *Guardian* 22 Sept. 7/2 Responauts don't have to be chained to their apparatus in a hospital ward. **1979** *47th Ann. Rep. Pilgrim Trust 1977* 23 The Refresh Trust was formed in 1972..for the purpose of building and equipping a place where a few responauts could safely have a holiday.

respond, *v.* Add: **2. c.** *Bridge.* To make (a bid) in reply to a partner's opening (or subsequent) bid. Cf. *RESPONDER 1 b.

1958 *Listener* 16 Oct. 611/2 East should have responded Two Hearts. **1959** T. REESE *Bridge Player's Dict.* 158 If one diamond were opened and partner responded two clubs, there would not be a sound rebid. **1976** *Times* 1 May 12/6 To partner's opening One Heart it is dangerous to respond Two Clubs.

3. c. (Further examples.)

1876 *Jrnl. Soc. Telegr. Engin.* V. 514 We wish to construct a receiver to respond to a tone made by 128 vibrations per second. **1910** J. ERSKINE-MURRAY *Wireless Telephones* vii. 51 An electric circuit will respond most readily to impulses which come timed to its own natural rate of vibration. **1939** N. DE V. HART *Bridge Players' Bedside Bk.* xii. 57 North responded to the Forcing Two in Diamonds with Two Hearts. **1952** A. GRIMBLE *Pattern of Islands* 233 One or two cases had begun to respond to gynocardate injections. **1954** G. I. M. SWYER *Reproduction & Sex* xv. 203 More of the women..had responded until they were in their fifties or sixties. **1967** M. KENYON *Whole Hog* xx. 195 You could have responded to my three clubs, you could have said something.

‖ **respondeat superior** (respǫ·ndeæt supe·riō͡ɹ), *phr. Law.* [L., 'let the principal answer'.] A maxim embodying the rule of vicarious liability (see quots.).

[**1601** W. FULBECKE *Parallele or Conference Civill Law, Canon Law & Common Law* I. x. f. 76 A plea in Abatement of a writte bee not peremptorie, but a *respondeat vlterius*.] *a* **1634** E. COKE *Fourth Part Inst. Lawes Eng.* (1644) xi. 114 Now it is good to know, how the law commonly called *Respondeat superior*, holdeth in this Court and in other Courts. **1848** W. HARTON *Law Lexicon* 587/2 *Respondeat superior*, (let the superior answer). If a coroner of a county is insufficient, the county, as his superior, shall answer for him. **1903** *Automobile & Carriage Builders' Jrnl.* May 133/2 The maxim *respondeat superior*. **1965** *Mod. Law Rev.* XXVIII. 584 It is trite learning that civil responsibility could in general be imposed *respondeat superior*. **1976** *Billings* (Montana) *Gaz.* 6 July 3-A/2, I have no trouble with the concept of accepting responsibility for one's actions. It's called 'respondeat superior'. That is, the principal is liable for the actions of his agent which are authorized. It was what the Nuremberg trials were all about.

respondent, *sb.* Add: **1. a.** Also in recent use, one who supplies information for a survey. Chiefly *U.S.*

1955 *Bull. Atomic Sci.* 175/2 Almost one-third of the respondents said they were upset by witnessing the casualties. **1961** *Technology* Feb. 34/1 The respondents were not asked how often they had applied each technique, if more than once, since many would probably have no accurate record of this. **1968** *Amer. Jrnl. Public Health* LVIII. 327/1 The questionnaires were unsigned on their return and were thrown into a large pile at the front of the room in such a manner that no one from the military hierarchy could identify the responses of any respondent. **1970** D. GOLDRICH et al. in I. L. Horowitz *Masses in Lat. Amer.* v. 176 The interviewers selected respondents randomly from the household. **1975** *Amer. Speech 1973* XLVIII. 22 Recent behavioral tests..have shown that respondents are capable of identifying informants as black or white from auditory cues only.

4. *Psychol.* The result of, or response to, a specific stimulus (see quot. 1937).

1937 B. F. SKINNER in *Jrnl. Gen. Psychol.* XVI. 274 It is a necessary recognition of the fact that in the unconditioned organism two kinds of behavior may be distinguished. There is, first, the kind of response that is made to specific stimulation... I shall refer to such a reflex as a *respondent* and use the term also as an adjective in referring to the behavior as a whole. **1940** HILGARD & MARQUIS *Conditioning & Learning* iii. 66 Respondents..are movements elicited by recognized stimuli.

respondent, *a.* Add: **3. b.** *Psychol.* Responsive, or that occurs as a reflex, to some specific stimulus; esp. as *respondent conditioning*, the conditioning of an organism to a particular response through the controlled use of a stimulus.

1937 B. F. SKINNER in *Jrnl. Gen. Psychol.* XVI. 274 The distinction between operant and respondent behavior. **1940** HILGARD & MARQUIS *Conditioning & Learning* iii. 72/1 Respondent behavior, like ordinary spinal reflexes, is elicited by specified stimuli. **1966** I. G. SARASON *Personality* iv. 75 The actual role played by reinforcement has been studied intensively in..experimental situations, one involving classical or respondent conditioning. **1974** H. W. BERNARD *Personality* x. 241 Respondent conditioning can also be used as a therapeutic approach.

responder. Add: **1. b.** *Bridge.* The partner of the opening bidder.

1932 *Daily Tel.* 8 Oct. 15/5 The partner of the opening bidder is known as the responder. **1952** I. MACLEOD *Bridge* iv. 49 If the responder raises the opener's suit, it is a quantitative bid only. **1966** *Listener* 13 Jan. 78/2 What happens.. if the responder has only sufficient high card strength to raise One No Trump to Two No Trumps as an invitation to game? **1976** *Times* 1 May 12/7 When there is opposition bidding the responder's duty is to show the strength of his hand.

2. † **a.** An early, electrolytic, form of radio receiver. *Obs.*

1901 *Western Electrician* 27 July 49/1 To the new receiving device its inventors [*sc.* De Forest and Smythe] have applied the name 'responder', a term first suggested by the London Electrician as one suitable for any resistance device sensitive to electric radiations. **1904** *Electr. Rev.* 3 Sept. 330 The principle of this receiver or 'responder', is based upon the fact that the Hertzian oscillations produce sudden electrolytic action in a cell containing certain electrodes and solutions. **1915** W. H. ECCLES *Wireless Telegr.* 246 In one type of electrolytic detector, now merely of historic interest, the processes of electrolysis are employed to form fine threads of metal across the gap or gaps, and these threads are destroyed by the oscillations to be detected. The consequent alteration of resistance is observed by telephone or galvanometer. Of this type is..the 'responder' of de Forest and Smythe.

b. A device which automatically retransmits a pulse or signal on receiving one from an interrogator. Also *responder beacon.*

1945 *Nature* 15 Sept. 323/2 *A* and *B* are pulse-interrogator stations, the aircraft has a responder of constant and accurately known delay-time... 'G-H' and 'Babs'..utilize coded responses sent back by a ground responder-beacon in reply to pulses from an airborne or shipborne interrogator. **1945** *Electronic Engin.* Oct. 735 Vehicles could now carry small questioning transmitters ('interrogators') and obtain replies from 'responder' beacons on land or sea. **1957** *Encycl. Brit.* XVIII. 873Y/1 Beacons of the synchronous sort just described are variously called radar beacons, responder beacons, racons, or transponders, there being no important distinction among these terms. **1966** D. TAYLOR *Introd. Radar & Radar Techniques* iv. 45 A responder beacon..is a 'repeater', in the sense that it would retransmit after a very short time-interval any pulse signal received. **1977** *Offshore Engineer* Aug. 46/2 The remote vehicle's depth, horizontal range, slant range and relative bearing can all be determined by using this single responder in conjunction with Wesmar's new SS400TS sonar tracking system. The responder acts as a transmitter/receiver, receiving electronic signals through an umbilical.

3. *Biol.* and *Med.* An individual, structure, etc., that responds or reacts to some stimulus or treatment.

1963 *Jrnl. Exper. Med.* CXVIII. 954 Responders showed both Arthus and delayed allergic skin reactions to the immunizing conjugates. **1973** *Nature* 30 Nov. 245/1 Cells were classified as either $\beta+$ or $\beta-$ (responders and non-responders to β-adrenergic stimulators) or P+ or P− (responders and non-responders to prostaglandin E_1). **1976** *Lancet* 30 Oct. 928/1 A further analysis was made into responders and nonresponders... The responders were defined as patients in whom the number of ulcers decreased by more than 50% over 2 or more months.

responding, *ppl. a.* (Further examples.)

1921 G. CECIL *Life Ld. Salisbury* II. vi. 219 His action was generally attributed to the decision to call out the Reserves..and Lord Beaconsfield implied as much in his responding speech. **1933** C. VANDYCK *Contract Contracted* 21 As the Playing Trick count is not used until the Trump Suit has been decided upon the Responding Hand is obviously the first one to use it. **1952** I. MACLEOD *Bridge* vi. 73 The responding hand..never assumes, at least until the second trial bid, that the opener is slamming. **1965** in J. Money *Sex Research* 107 Seldom does the responding female directly manipulate the clitoris through an entire sexual response cycle. **1968** R. KYLE *Love Lab.* (1969) xviii. 210 Data on several hundred responding individuals has more scientific validity than data on one.

responsa: see *RESPONSUM.

response. Add: **1. b.** Also *spec.* in *Psychol.* (freq. opposed to *stimulus*), an observable reaction to some specific stimulus or situation; the fact of such reaction.

1908 E. L. THORNDIKE in *Ess. Philos. & Psychol. in Honor W. James* 597 A situation arouses a response which brings an annoying state of affairs. The probability of a similar response in the future is lessened. **1919** J. B. WATSON *Psychol.* i. 16 Having now examined at some length into the general nature of both stimulus and response, we should be prepared to understand the object of a psychological experiment. **1934** H. DAVIS in C. Murchison *Handbk. Gen. Exper. Psychol.* 983 They..constitute an objective response of great value for analyzing the activities of the cortical tissue. **1948** A. C. KINSEY et al. *Sexual Behav. Human Male* v. 159 Evidence of minimal psychic components with good enough physical responses. **1952** FORD & BEACH *Patterns Sexual Behav.* xii. 239 Her capacity for complete response returned. **1957** B. F. SKINNER in Saporta & Bastian *Psycholinguistics* (1961) v. 228/1 Semantic theory is often confined to the relation between response and stimulus which prevails in the verbal operant called the tact. **1965** in J. Money *Sex Research* 101 Three women were able to achieve orgasmic response by breast manipulation alone. **1976** SENTER & DIMOND *Psychol.* vi. 102 Relaxation and anxiety are competing responses. You must behave in one way or the other.

c. The way in which an apparatus responds to a stimulus or range of stimuli.

1911 H. M. HOBART *Dict. Electr. Engin.* II. 630/1 The receiver must be sharply tuned so that the variations of frequency may be sufficient to make an appreciable difference in the strength of its response. **1915** W. H. ECCLES *Wireless Telegr.* 245 Fig. 176 shows the response of the detector (change of *I*) at various values of the intensity of magnetism *I* and the field *H*, for four different magnetic cycles. **1926**, etc. [see *frequency response* s.v. *FREQUENCY 6 a]. **1958** O. R. FRISCH *Nuclear Handbk.* xiv. 16 In designing a scintillation counter the spectrum of the fluorescent radiation must be marked as far as possible with the spectral response of the multiplier. **1961** G. MILLERSON *Television Production* iii. 41 Where the tube's response to red is excessive, this may be held back with an appropriate green or blue filter. **1970** J. EARL *Tuners & Amplifiers* iii. 68 The latest 'quality' amplifiers..boast a power response which is almost as good as the frequency response.

d. *Bridge.* A reply to a partner's opening (or subsequent) bid.

1939 N. DE V. HART *Bridge Players' Bedside Bk.* x. 52 South's response of Six Clubs showed first round control of clubs. **1947** S. HARRIS *Fund. Princ. Contract Bridge* I. iv. 35 It sometimes happens that South is able to make a positive response. **1958** *Listener* 16 Oct. 611/2 West makes her natural response of Three Diamonds. **1967** P. ANDERTON *Play Bridge* iii. 28 The negative response is 2 N.T. in which case the hand will probably be played in 3 H. **1976** *Times* 1 May 12/6 A minimum response can be shown only by a rebid of the suit.

6. *attrib.* and *Comb.*, as *response function, rate*; esp. in *Psychol.*, as *response bias, -movement, pattern, probability, set*; *response-contingent* adj.; **response time** *Electr.*, the time taken for a circuit or measuring device, when subjected to a change in input signal, to change its state by a specified fraction of its total response to that change.

1970 *Jrnl. Gen. Psychol.* LXXXII. 63 These findings appear to be incompatible with the notion that both scales measure 'response bias'. **1958** B. FLANAGAN et al. in Saporta & Bastian *Psycholinguistics* (1961) 415 (*title*) The control of stuttering through response-contingent consequences. **1972** *Sci. Amer.* May 97/1 The results of such analyses produce response functions..which can be plotted to show the mean responses of different species of trees to conditions of temperature, precipitation and prior growth. **1975** D. G. FINK *Electronics Engineers' Handbk.* xxv. 25 The antenna and receiver are configured to match a target signal at a particular angle, delay, and frequency. The radar will respond with reduced gain to targets at other angles, delays, and frequencies. This response function can be expressed as a surface in a four-dimensional coordinate system. **1892** VAN LIEW & BEYER tr. *Ziehen's Introd. Physiol. Psychol.* i. 14 Goltz has termed the automatic movements 'response-movements'. **1936** J. KANTOR *Objective Psychol. of Gram.* xx. 290 For objective psychology, moods are nothing but particular response-patterns or speech-community styles of utterance. **1965** *Brit. Jrnl. Psychol.* LVI. 217 (*heading*) Response patterns and strategies in the dynamics of concept attainment behaviour. **1960** W. N. DEMBER *Psychol. of Perception* (1970) viii. 287 All of the word-recognition experiments can be interpreted in terms of response-probability. **1946** *Jrnl. Amer. Statist. Assoc.* XLI. 522 The number of mail questionnaires and field interviews required to achieve a specified precision will vary with the response rate. **1966** *Rep. Comm. Inquiry Univ. Oxf.* II. 351 The figures for Great Britain are from a survey (with a response rate of 53 per cent.) of those university teachers who responded to the inquiry by the Robbins Committee in 1961–2 (in which the response rate was 86 per cent.). **1970** *Jrnl. Gen. Psychol.* LXXXII. 64 'Response set' is a generalized tendency to be agreeable. **1972** D. P. CAMPBELL in J. N. Butcher *Objective Personality Assessment* vi. 119 Response set, acquiescence and social desirability, are currently popular..even though the data in support of them [as concepts] are will-o'-the-wispy, at best. **1958** R. B. HURLEY *Junction Transistor Electronics* xix. 364 Output response times are reduced by a factor of 2·5. **1970** WILLARDSON & BEER *Semiconductors & Semimetals* V. i. 7 The response time is determined by the rate at which the [infrared detector] element warms and cools. **1975** D. G. FINK *Electronics Engineers' Handbk.* XVII. 49 Performance specifications usually include the response of the system to a step input, measured in terms of response time, rise time, delay time, settling time, and overshoot.

responsibility. Add: **1. a.** (Later examples.)

1973 *Black Panther* 17 Nov. 3/1 The attack was deliberate and appears to be associated with the letter from the 'Symbionese Liberation Army' claiming responsibility. **1974** *Oxford Mail* 26 Oct. 1/4 Four explosions shook New York's business and financial districts within a few minutes today and a self-styled Puerto Rican liberation movement claimed responsibility.

c. Const. *for.*

1903 G. B. SHAW *Man & Superman* I. 17 Mamma knows that she is not strong enough to bear the whole responsibility for me and Rhoda without some help and advice. **1928** E. O'NEILL *Strange Interlude* II. 66 Looks damnably upset... Wants to evade all responsibility for her, I suppose. **1971** G. K. ROBERTS *Dict. Polit. Analysis* 190 The individual responsibility of British ministers for the actions of their civil servants. **1974** *Black Panther* 19 Jan. 3/1 A communique signed by the Symbionese Liberation Army claimed responsibility for the attack. **1975** *Times* 20 Aug. 13/1 Just as one was wondering who would 'claim responsibility' for spoiling the Headingley wicket—Saór Eire, the Women's Liberation Army..—up popped the Campaign to Free George Davis. **1981** M. SPARK *Loitering with Intent* ii. 32, I can't take responsibility for your mother this afternoon.

2. c. A person to whom one is responsible; a person in authority. *Nonce-use.*

1893 E. DOWSON *Let.* c 22 Mar. (1967) 275, I have to let the responsibilities know exactly how many people I have invited.

responsible, *a.* Add: **3. c.** *responsible government*: (see quot. 1910). Also in extended use (esp. under influence of sense 5).

1839 LD. DURHAM *Rep. Affairs Brit. N. Amer.* 142 By creating high prizes in a general and responsible Government, we shall immediately afford the means of pacifying the turbulent ambitions, and of employing in worthy and noble occupations the talents which now are only exerted to foment disorder. **1865** EARL RUSSELL *Essay on Hist. Eng. Govt. & Constitution* p. lxviii, Others said, 'the grant of what is called "responsible government" [in Canada] is a grant of independence. It must be resisted.' **1906** W. S. CHURCHILL in R. S. Churchill *Winston S. Churchill* (1969) II. Compan. I. 506 We are not, of course, confined to any particular form of Responsible Government. **1910** *Colonial Office List* v. i. 633 The colonies possessing responsible government, in which the Crown has only reserved the power of disallowing legislation and the Secretary of State for the Colonies has no control over any public officer except the Governor. **1930** G. B. SHAW *Apple Cart* I. 33 The people have found out long ago that democracy is humbug, and that instead of establishing responsible government it has abolished it. **1957** *Encycl. Brit.* XII. 174/2 The device known as dyarchy, or double government,..was intended to train Indians for responsible government.

5. a. Comb., *responsible-minded* adj.

1960 *Times* 7 Mar. 13/5 Are publishers responsible-minded parents?

responsion. Add: **3.** Responsions was ended by statute in 1960.

responsive, *a.* and *sb.* Add: **A.** *adj.* **1. c.** *Bridge.* Of a double: used to invite a change to an unbid suit in response to a partner's take-out double.

1959 *Listener* 12 Mar. 489/3 His double would be 'responsive'. *Ibid.* 30 July 190/1 The responsive double is a double intended to give information when partner has already made an informatory double. **1964** *Official Encycl. Bridge* 456/2 The minimum strength for a responsive double varies slightly with the level of the auction. **1973** REESE & DORMER *Compl. Bk. Bridge* viii. 120 Responsive doubles are usually played up to the level of three spades.

Responsivist (rĭspǫ·nsivist), *sb.* (and *a.*). *Indian Hist.* [f. RESPONSIVE *a.* + -IST.] One who advocated working within the diarchical administrative system introduced in Indian provinces during British rule. Also *attrib.* or as *adj.*

1927 *Glasgow Herald* 1 Feb. 8 Agitation is afoot in Calcutta against the acceptance by Mr Ghuznavi of one of the two Bengal transferred portfolios with Mr Chakra Varti, the Responsivist leader, as his Hindu colleague. **1927** *Observer* 27 Mar. 11/2 The third general election, held at the end of last year, when the Swarajists, as distinct from the Responsivists, lost ground. **1936** J. NEHRU *Autobiogr.* xlviii. 387, I remember a frequent complaint of my father's that his Responsivist friends had no sense of humour. **1950** L. FISCHER *Life Mahatma Gandhi* xxvii. 234 A dissident group, headed by M. R. Jayakar and N. C. Kelkar, who believed in still more co-operation with the British, but less with the Moslems, split off from the Swarajists and formed the Responsivist party. **1951** D. G. TENDULKAR *Mahatma* II. 307 The Responsivists joined hands with the Independents in Bombay and formed the Indian National Party. **1969** D. DAS *India from Curzon to Nehru & After* xi. 122 The dissidents met at Akola and formed the Responsivist Party. **1970** J. S. SHARMA *India since Advent of British* IV. 271 The Conference of the Responsivists cooperation party which was held at Akola adopted its Manifesto.

responsivity. Delete *rare*—[1] and add further examples.

1901 *Ann. Rep. Board of Regents Smithsonian Inst. 1899–1900* 68 A principle of knowledge which may appropriately be styled the responsivity of mind. **1942** *Amer. Jrnl. Physiol.* CXXXV. 721 Suppression [of cortical response] is a decrease of responsivity of a certain area..caused by previous stimulation of specific cortical regions. **1976** *Lancet* 30 Oct. 953/2 Responsivity to change in America is remarkable.

responsor[2] (rĭspǫ·nsǭɪ). [f. RESPONSE + -OR.] A device that receives and processes the reply from a transponder, being usu. incorporated in the same unit as the interrogator.

1945 *Army & Navy Jrnl.* 18 Aug. 1534/4 *Responsor*, receiver used specifically in IFF system to receive the reply to a challenge. **1947** A. ROBERTS *Radar Beacons* xviii. 388 A simple responsor using a lamp to locate a beacon in range. **1976** P. HONOLD *Secondary Radar* v. 208 *Responsor*, the receiver of responses.

responso·rially, *adv. Eccl.* [f. RESPONSORIAL *a.* + -LY².] In a responsorial manner; with responses.

1901 PROCTER & FRERE *New Hist. Bk. Common Prayer* xi. 406 The Arians..went through the city..to their places of worship, singing responsorially all the way. **1929** E. C. THOMAS *Lay Folks' Hist. Liturgy* II. v. 186 On these occasions the processional chant, or Rogation psalm, was sung responsorially. **1978** P. G. COBB in C. Jones et al. *Study of Liturgy* II. III. v. 186 It is not until the fourth century that there is clear evidence of psalms being sung responsorially.

‖ **responsum** (respǫ·nsŏm). Pl. **responsa.** [L., = answer, response.] **1.** A reply by a rabbi or Talmudic scholar to an inquiry on some matter of Jewish law.

1896 S. SCHECHTER *Studies in Judaism* 1st Ser. xi. 330 The greatest part of the literary activity of the Gaonim consists in their Responsa, in which they gave decisions on ritual questions, or explanations of difficult passages in the Talmud. *Ibid.* 331 The titles borne by the various collections of those Responsa belong to a period later than the author's. **1932** C. ROTH *Hist. Marranos* viii. 201 The responsa of the Levantine rabbis of the period are filled with discussions relating to the position of the Marranos in Jewish law. **1941** G. G. SCHOLEM *Major Trends in Jewish Mysticism* ix. 340 You find Zaddikim who write rabbinical responsa. **1962** B. ABRAHAMS tr. *Life Glückel of Hameln* iii. 66 Good Rabbi Asher..wrote a great responsum in my husband's favour. **1968** *New Scientist* 23 May 385/3 The team is investigating the responsa written by Jewish legal experts in Medieval Spain... A responsum..consists of a judgement usually revolving around a concrete problem in the commercial, social, moral or religious sphere. **1977** *N.Y. Times* 11 Jan. 30/1 Responsa..are fundamental in the evolution of Jewish law. Altogether, there are approximately 500,000 responsa written by 5,000 different authorities.

2. responsa prudentum (prude·ntŏm) *Law* [L., = the answers of the learned], in Roman Civil Law: the opinions and judgements of learned lawyers, variously forming part of this law (cf. Justinian *Inst.* I. ii. § 8). Also *transf.* in modern use.

In cl. Lat. *responsa prudentium* is the usual form, but most of the legal sources cited below have *prudentum* following the example of Blackstone (1765).

1681 LD. STAIR *Institutions Law Scotl.* I. i. 3 And so many times these *responsa prudentium*, have been received with as much Authority, and more heartiness for Laws, than the Dictates of Soveraigns. **1765** BLACKSTONE *Comm. Laws Eng.* I. 80 The *responsa prudentum* or opinions of learned lawyers. **1859** T. C. SANDARS *Institutes Justinian* 13 The *responsa prudentum* came to be enumerated among the direct sources of law. **1877** *Law Rep. Exchequer Division* II. 70 Of course the value of these responsa prudentum is affected by various circumstances. **1883** J. B. MOYLE *Imperatoris Justiniani Institutionum* I. 50 The establishment of the empire brought with it a considerable change in respect of the responsa prudentum.

respray·, *v.* [RE- 5 a.] *trans.* To spray (esp. with paint) again. Hence **respray·ed** *ppl. a.*; **respray·ing** *vbl. sb.* Also **re·spray** *sb.*, the action or fact of spraying again.

1934 *Webster*, Respray, *v.t.* **1959** *Listener* 16 Apr. 657/2 The car had been re-sprayed. **1962** *Law Rep. 1961* 26 July 35 The defendant appealed against so much of the decision as ordered him to pay for the respray. *Ibid.* 40 The defendant should be taken to have injured a motor-car that was already in certain respects (that is, in respect of the need for respraying) injured. **1968** 'D. RUTHERFORD' *Skin for Skin* ii. 16 The engine's nearly perfect but she does need a respray. **1975** G. SEYMOUR *Harry's Game* iii. 46 The stolen and resprayed Cortina. **1976** M. GILBERT *Night of Twelfth* vii. 65 A car which..was resprayed. First with a light grey undercoat, then with a dark grey finish.

Ressaldar: see *RISSALDAR.

‖ **ressentiment** (resa·ntimaṅ). [Ger., a. F. *ressentiment*, f. *ressentir* to RESENT: cf. RESENTIMENT.] = *RESENTMENT 2 d.

1943 G. A. MORGAN *What Nietzsche Means* vi. 151 Nietzsche illustrates the second type, which directs *ressentiment* outward, by anarchists, socialists and communists, who make 'society' to blame for their misery. **1949** R. K. MERTON *Social Theory* iv. 145 We must distinguish it [*sc.* rebellion] from a superficially similar but essentially different type, '*ressentiment*'. Introduced in a special technical sense, by Nietzsche, the concept of *ressentiment* was taken up and developed sociologically by Max Scheler. **1958** F. HEIDER *Psychol. of Interpersonal Relations* xi. 291 For Scheler, as for Nietzsche, '*ressentiment*' is an envy combined with a feeling of impotence to attain the value that another person has. **1968** *Internat. Encycl. Social Sci.* XII. 27/2 Scheler conceives of *ressentiment* as a complex syndrome involving conscious attitudes, feelings, and moral judgments as well as unconscious defenses and wishes. The ressentiment-laden person tends to devaluate authoritative persons and groups. **1975** W. S. SAHAKIAN *Hist. & Syst. Psychol.* i. 31 Nietzsche termed *ressentiment* that form of behaviour arising out of repressed hostility.

rest, *sb.*¹ Add: **I. 3. e.** A year's imprisonment. *Austral. slang* (*rare*).

1882 *Sydney Slang Dict.* 9/2 Dick went pulling down sawney for grub last week, when a cop pinched him. He's gone in the country for a *rest*. **1945** BAKER *Austral. Lang.* vii. 141 Here is a brief glossary of jail sentences: *lag*, three months... *rest*, twelve months [etc.].

f. In colloq. phr. *to give* (something or someone) *a rest*: to stop thinking or talking about.

[**1927** *Amer. Speech* II. 359/1 *Leave that rest a bit..*, let the matter alone for a while. 'Keep quiet, and leave that rest a bit.'] **1931** E. O'NEILL *Hunted* II, in *Mourning becomes Electra* (1932) 137 Give it a rest, Orin! It's over. Give yourself a chance to forget it. **1943** J. B. PRIESTLEY *Daylight on Saturday* xxix. 226 I'm a bit tired of hearing about him today. So let's give him a rest. **1966** R. RENDELL *Vanity dies Hard* ii. 31 Could we give Nesta Drage a rest?.. I was glad when she went away. **1971** —— *One Across* i. 9 'All right Mother,' said Vera. 'Let's give it a rest, shall we?'

II. 12. c. A support or hook for a telephone receiver when not in use, incorporating a switch that is automatically closed when the receiver is lifted.

1889 *Telephone* 15 Feb. 94/2 Improvements in telephone apparatus to be designated as a telephone-receiver rest. **1922** *Telegraph & Telephone Jrnl.* VIII. 97/2 Flash the Switchboard Telephonist into circuit by moving the Receiver rest up and down slowly until she answers. **1948** J. ATKINSON *Telephony* 129/1 The circuit is arranged automatically to switch the lines from the bell circuit to the speaking circuit when the receiver is lifted from its rest or hook. **1961** H. & N. SCHNEIDER *Your Telephone* iii. 26 In the exchange there is a huge electric battery. When you lift your telephone off its rest, a switch inside joins the two wires together.

d. A projecting part of a removable denture that gives it support by lying against a tooth.

1907 H. J. GOSLEE *Princ. & Pract. Crown & Bridgework* (ed. 2) xxv. 465 Providing a rest which will cause the piece to ride largely upon the supporting teeth instead of on the gum tissue. *Ibid.*, An occlusal rest constituting a part of the clasp was early advocated by Dr. W. G. A. Bonwill. **1924** D. D. CAMPBELL *Full Denture Prosthesis* ii. 125 The insertion of occlusion rests or immediate dentures within thirty minutes.. after the teeth have been removed, contributes in a remarkable degree to the patient's confidence. **1942** J. R. SCHWARTZ *Mod. Methods Tooth Replacement* ix. 379 Unfavorable action that may be caused by rests not locked into an inlay occurs when the inclination of the tooth is such that the rest will slip or slide. **1976** TORRES & EHRLICH *Mod. Dental Assisting* xxvii. 815/2 A rest built into an onlay is designed to partially cover a tooth that needs to be built up to the height of the occlusion.

14. a. *rest area, billet, camp* (earlier and later examples), *centre, cure* (earlier and later examples), *day, home, pause, period, stop, therapy*; *rest-giving* adj.; **rest gown,** formerly, a gown used for evening wear at home; **rest room,** (*a*) a room (usu. in a public building) set aside for rest and quiet; (*b*) *U.S.* a lavatory, a W.C.; **rest-tremor** *Path.*, a tremor in a part which is not being voluntarily moved.

1919 W. H. DOWNING *Digger Dial.* 41 *Rest area*, a district to which battalions, on leaving the danger zone, marched by long stages once a year for the purpose of polishing their brass work. *a* **1944** K. DOUGLAS *Alamein to Zem Zem* (1946) 18 Here we halted, having left the heavy squadrons of Shermans and Grants still in our rest area. **1976** G. V. HIGGINS *Judgement D. Hunter* ix. 86 The youth..stopped in a rest area..so that the subject could relieve himself. **1978** W. GARNER *Möbius Trip* ix. 216 In the autoroute rest area at Chennevières..a chauffeured gray Mercedes. **1917** A. G. EMPEY *Over Top* 306 *Rest billets*, shell shattered houses, generally barns, in which Tommy 'rests', when relieved from the firing line. **1925** R. GRAVES *Welchman's Hose* 29 And back in rest-billets The Colonel congratulates 'B' Company on its kits. **1954** W. FAULKNER *Fable* 128 The nine others..had been spending their leaves and furloughs.. among the combat-troop rest-billets. **1889** G. S. MACKENZIE *Let.* 11 Dec. in Ld. Lugard *Diaries* (1959) I. 50 Lay out rest camps and fortified posts at regular intervals. **1919** *Lit. Digest* 29 Mar. 44 A trench-mortar shell hit so close..that I was completely buried and for a moment or two thought I was going to a rest camp (cemetery). **1923** KIPLING *Irish Guards in Gt. War* I. 3 The city became almost a suburb to the vast rest-camps round it. **1971** *Rand Daily Mail* 27 Mar. 23/3 Incidentally, all Natal Parks Board rest camps are fully booked in the Easter holidays. **1940** *Economist* 5 Oct. 422/1 When their roof has gone the family seek refuge, and they find it in temporary rest centres run by the Public Assistance Department of the London County Council. **1976** *Liverpool Echo* 6 Dec. 8/4 Rest centres were made ready on the outskirts of all 'target' areas, like Merseyside, to house the virtual refugees. **1889** *Cent. Dict.*, Rest-cure. **1892** S. HALE *Let.* 28 Apr. (1919) 272 She is at a rest-cure. **1928** BLUNDEN *Undertones of War* 131 Then we went into the trenches..which not long before had been so horrible..but now they..were voted 'a rest-cure sector'. **1959** T. S. ELIOT *Elder Statesman* I. 25 Now's the time to take a long holiday, Let's say a rest cure. **1980** D. ADAMS *Restaurant at End of Universe* ix. 57, I only hope it's gone in for a rest cure... The way it's been living recently it must be on its last elbows. **1911** WEBSTER, Rest day. **1959** *Encounter* Aug. 22/1 People were free to prepare their meals at home on 'rest days'. **1976** J. SNOW *Cricket Rebel* 90, I worked out that we had only one day free from cricket in those last six weeks in Australia apart from the rest days during the Test matches. **1928** BEERBOHM *Lett. to R. Turner* (1964) 270 A solid and..rest-giving figure in the midst of that wild vortex. **1913** MRS. G. DE H. VAIZEY *College Girl* xviii. 257 Margaret herself, in a pink rest-gown curled up in a wicker chair. **1915** *Home Chat* 20 Nov. 326/1 Evening dress..has ceased to exist, its place being taken by smart little demi-toilettes for restaurant and theatre wear, and rest-gowns that are really restful for home wear. **1924** 'J. SUTHERLAND' *Circle of Stars* xxvi. 286 Gathering the folds of her rest-gown about her, Norma went up to the next story. **1925** *Daily Herald* 6 July 6/7 The organization of rest homes, where workers may spend their vacation, is a unique development. **1976** B. BOVA *Multiple Man* (1977) x. 102 Why wouldn't the President simply..cart the old man off to a well-guarded rest home? **1926** *Encycl. Brit.* II. 454/1 An important innovation stressed by the industrial psychologist has been the introduction of short rests, in the middle of a working period, of about 10 or 15 min. duration. These regular breaks are technically known as rest pauses. **1954** J. A. C. BROWN *Social Psychol. of Industry* iii. 71 Two five-minute rest-pauses, morning and afternoon. **1922** *Encycl. Brit.* XXXI. 699/2 In spite of the considerable development of maximum hour regulation in the United States, not much attention has been paid to the question of legal rest periods. **1954** J. A. C. BROWN *Social Psychol. of Industry* iii. 74 The introduction of rest-periods which amounted to two ten-minute breaks in the morning and two in the afternoon. **1981** 'J. ROSS' *Dark Blue & Dangerous* xxii. 123 You will report off duty for a rest period. **1899** *Amer. Jrnl. Sociol.* May 729 Surely it would not be unreasonable to require that suitable rest-rooms be provided for the employés. **1918** A. BENNETT *Pretty Lady* xxvii. 182 Canteens, and rest-rooms, and libraries, and sanitation, and all this damned 'welfare'. **1942** 'M. INNES' *Daffodil Affair* III. 103 His private research block..comprised a library, a museum, rest rooms and living quarters for the subjects. **1955** W. GADDIS *Recognitions* I. iii. 100 If you serve food you gotta have a rest room for ladies as well as men. **1975** *N.Y. Times* 8 Nov. 26/2 The totally unsubstantiated forecasts of effects ranging from the abolition of women's rest rooms to dire financial consequences may well have persuaded many women that it was safer to accept known evils than to risk unknown pitfalls. **1973** *Sunday Bull.* (Philadelphia) 14 Oct. (Parade Suppl.) 16/3 A truck driver napped at a rest stop. **1975** J. GRADY *Shadow of Condor* (1976) xiii. 214 It's another rest stop... Just a picnic table and some trash cans. **1949** *Radio Times* 15 July 24/1 Many people keep their vitality..by regularly practising Rest-therapy. **1925** S. A. K. WILSON in *Lancet* 8 Aug. 270/2 Some cases of disseminated sclerosis..definitely show what I may call a 'rest-tremor' as well as an 'action-tremor'. **1967** *Internat. Jrnl. Neuropharmacol.* VI. 122 There is a great similarity between rest tremor produced by tremorine and rest tremor in human pathology. *Ibid.*, It is likely that rest tremor in human pathology is due to the hyperactivity of these [alpha] cells [of the anterior horn].

c. In sense 8, as **rest energy** *Physics*, the energy inherent in a body by virtue of its possession of rest mass; **rest frame** *Physics*, a frame of reference relative to which a given body is at rest; **rest level** *Hydrology*, the natural level of water in an aquifer or on the ground surface; **rest mass** *Physics*, the mass of a body measured when it is at rest; **rest position** *Dentistry*, the relative position of the jaws when relaxed.

1938 *Forum* Feb. 95/2 From the Lorentz transformation and the assumption of the impulse and energy principle for material particles..the equality of mass and rest-energy is derived. **1962** H. D. BUSH *Atomic & Nuclear Physics* ii. 54 Since the rest mass is m_0, the rest energy is considered to be m_0c^2. **1966** J. WERLE *Relativistic Theory of Reactions* v. 347 We are interested in the scattering angle of particle *d* in a rest frame of particle *b*. **1978** *Nature* 5 Oct. 411/1 The known general absence of Lyman continuum absorption in the rest frame of high redshift QSOs implies that $< 0{\cdot}1$ of the continuum radiation is intercepted by optically thick clouds. **1908** W. COLES-FINCH *Water* xviii. 416 The rest-level in a well or boring is that level to which the water rises upon cessation of pumping. **1956** R. J. C. ATKINSON *Stonehenge* iii. 82 The level at which this pottery and the earliest fragments of bluestone occur is slightly above the rest-level which marks the end of the first phase of rapid silting in the ditch. **1914** L. SILBERSTEIN *Theory of Relativity* vii. 193 The coefficient *m* is called the rest-mass of the particle. **1938** R. W. LAWSON tr. *Hevesy & Paneth's Man. Radioactivity* (ed. 2) iii. 36 We differentiate between the 'rest mass' and the 'translational mass' of β-particles, i.e. the mass of the particle in motion. **1979** *Jrnl. R. Soc. Arts* CXXVII. 577/2 Nuclear fusion can convert 0·7 per cent of the rest mass of the hydrogen core into energy. [**1907** C. R. TURNER *Amer. Textbk. Prosthetic Dentistry* (ed. 3) iv. 243 This position is commonly called 'the resting bite'. **1921** D. GABELL *Prosthetic Dentistry* iv. 76 The closed resting position of the mandible is one of more stable equilibrium than any other, and brings the greatest number of teeth in contact and the jaws closer together.] **1924** T. GOODHUGH *Art of Prosthetic Dentistry* iii. 55 Ask the patient to close, thus registering the proper rest position. **1962** BLAKE & TROTT *Periodontol.* xvi. 163 To bring the mandible into the rest position the patient should be seated comfortably in the chair, the head erect and away from the head rest, with the Frankfort plane horizontal. He is then asked to wet the lips with the tongue, swallow and remain quite still. The mandible should then assume the rest position.

rest, *sb.*² Add: **9.** (Further examples.)

In lawn tennis the usual term is *rally*.

1898 H. F. LAWFORD in W. A. Morgan *'House' on Sport* I. 428, I was told that one rest was eighty-one strokes. **1960** *Times* 18 July 14/4 Warburg..played six strokes in a fine rest. **1975** *Oxf. Compan. Sports & Games* 826/1 During a 'rest' (the real tennis term for a rally), while the player on the hazard side is trying to make a good chase, his opponent on the service side is in a stronger position.

10. *Med.* A small detached part of an organ, surrounded by tissue of another character; esp. as *adrenal rest*, a small displaced part of the adrenal cortex.

1892 R. BOYCE *Textbk. Morbid Histol.* viii. 160 In adult life 'rests' are frequently encountered in the lines of old incisions and punctures and are due to excess of repair tissue. *Ibid.* x. 201 Another class of rests represents vestigial structures. **1898** I. N. KELYNACK *Renal Growths* xiv. 132 Growths arising in adrenal 'rests' appear to be sarcomatous in general characters rather than carcinomatous. **1912** *Q. Jrnl. Med.* V. 157 To present new reasons against the hypothesis that renal hypernephromata are derived from adrenal rests. **1928** J. F. BARNHILL *Nose, Throat & Ear* xi. 157 In sarcoma [of the accessory nasal sinuses] congenital 'rests' in the alveoli of the child..may be assigned as a cause. **1939** T. W. WIDDOWSON *Special or Dental Anat.*

(ed. 6) xii. 300 The epithelial cellular bodies, or rests,..are collections of epithelial cells sometimes seen in the inner portion of the periodontal membrane near to the cementum. **1963** C. L. DEMING in M. F. Campbell *Urology* (ed. 2) II. xxii. 912 Grawitz thought that these tumors came from adrenal rests and termed them hypernephromas.

rest, *v.*[1] Add: **I. 1. c.** orig. *N. Amer.* Of the body of a dead person: to remain at an undertaker's, a chapel, etc., before burial or cremation. (Usu. as pres. pple.)

1967 'CORIOLIS' *Death, Here is Thy Sting* iii. 54 Remains will be resting at the John Doe Funeral Home. **1968** *Globe & Mail* (Toronto) 13 Jan. 37/5 Resting at Bates and Maddocks Funeral Chapel..until 12 noon Monday. **1974** *Almonto* (Ontario) *Gaz.* 4 Apr. 4/3 Predeceased by a brother Harold... Rested at the Kerry Funeral Home. **1976** *Liverpool Echo* 22 Nov. 4/4 Funeral service at Anfield Crematorium... Resting at E. H. Roberts..where flowers may be sent.

2. f. *Theatr.* Of an actor: to be out of work (temporarily), to be unemployed. Also *transf.* (Usu. as pres. pple.)

1890 B. HALL *Turnover Club* 81 It would commend itself particularly to actors 'resting' for the summer. **1912** GALSWORTHY *Pigeon* I. 24 I am an interpreter... At present I am resting. **1923** A. CHRISTIE *Murder on Links* xxii. 250 They're in the provinces, somewhere, I believe—if they're not resting. **1938** G. HEYER *Blunt Instrument* x. 195 A very nice lady. Stage, but she's resting. **1947** J. SYMONS *Man called Jones* 109 She's in this new thing at the Splendid, and I'm resting. That's show business. **1958** *Times* 22 May 12/6 Ten shillings a week..used to go a long way with those who, in actors' parlance, were 'resting'. **1967** *Radio Times* 18 May 21 Except for the occasional coffee-bar job while 'resting', Dinsdale has always managed to earn a living from acting. **1976** R. HILL *Another Death in Venice* I. ii. 33 'Are you on holiday?'..'Resting, to use a theatrical term. Between jobs.'

g. *to rest up*: to recover one's strength by resting. orig. *U.S.*

1895 'MARK TWAIN' in *Harper's Mag.* Aug. 458 The other nquisitor could absent himself and rest up from his fatigues when he got worn out. **1911** H. S. HARRISON *Queed* x. 125 She had been remanded in bed for a day or two to rest up. **1922** Z. GREY *To Last Man* xiii. 284 Get rifle and ammunition, bake bread, and rest up before taking again the trail of the rustlers. **1936** J. CURTIS *Gilt Kid* xiii. 131 The best plan would be to..have something to eat and rest up. **1949** N. STREATFEILD *Painted Garden* xi. 127 She said..she was going to rest-up; I expect that means bed. **1965** M. SHADBOLT *Among Cinders* xxii. 210 Now it was just a place for shooters and trampers to rest up. **1972** J. BLACKBURN *For Fear of Little Men* xi. 116 Adder bites are unpleasant things. .. I advised the fool to rest up a bit longer. **1974** *Times Lit. Suppl.* 1 Feb. 97/1 Attila is resting up in Hungvar, exacting 'hospitality' from the German peoples.

III. 8. a. Also const. *up*. Cf. sense *2 g. Quots. 1975 and 1976 are both *U.S. slang*.

1974 'J. LE CARRÉ' *Tinker, Tailor* xxviii. 241 They're resting you up for a season. **1975** L. DILLS *CB Slanguage Dict.* 50 *Rest 'em up place*, rest area (SE). **1976** LIEBERMAN & RHODES *Compl. CB Handbk.* vi. 157 Hey, we just spotted a smokey at that rest'em up area.

g. *U.S.* To bring the presentation of evidence pertinent to (a law case) to a close voluntarily.

1905 S. W. MITCHELL *Constance Trescot* xiv. 183 All the evidence for the plaintiffs was before the court, and Greyhurst sat down, stating that the plaintiff rested the case. **1950** *Chicago Tribune* 23 Jan. 1/8 Defense attorneys.. elected to rest their case without calling a single witness. **1953** E. S. GARDNER *Case of Hesitant Hostess* xiv. 234 The prosecution objects. The prosecution has rested its case. **1972** *N.Y. Law Jrnl.* 14 Nov. 19/5 Plaintiff had not been cross-examined and certainly had not rested his case.

restart, *sb.* Add: Also stressed *re·start*. Also *attrib.* (Further examples.)

1971 *Computers & Humanities* V. 140 One of the most powerful features of this system is the restart procedure... The restart capability is especially useful under a system which limits the amount of time and records a user can run at any one time. **1977** *Gloss. Terms Data Processing* (*B.S.I.*) VII. 9/2 *Restart condition*, in the execution of a computer program, a condition that can be re-established and that permits a restart of the computer program. *Ibid.*, *Restart point*, a place in a computer program at which its execution may be restarted; in particular, the address of a restart instruction.

restatement. Add: Also in *Mus.* Cf. STATEMENT 1 b.

1944 W. APEL *Harvard Dict. Mus.* 638/2 *Restatement*, same as recapitulation in sonata-form. **1954** *Grove's Dict. Mus.* (ed. 5) III. 440/2 The restatement of the first subject is sufficient indication to the hearer as to what part of the movement he has arrived at. **1959** *Listener* 20 Aug. 297/2 The preparation for the restatement in his first movement is altogether classical in method. **1974** *Encycl. Brit. Macropædia* XVII. 5/2 The first theme is restated in the dominant key. This restatement could appear at first to be the second subject.

resta·ter. [f. RESTATE *v.*[2] + -ER[1].] A person who restates.

1925 G. O'BRIEN *Econ. Effects Reformation* ii. 125 Luther ..regarded Christ and the Apostles as merely the restaters and expositors of the Decalogue.

restaurant. Add: **2.** *attrib.*, as *restaurant car, dinner, -keeper, lunch, manager, meal, proprietor.*

1875 Restaurant car [in Dict.]. **1913** KIPLING *Lett. of Travel* (1920) 220 That terrible restaurant-car dinner in the tunnel. **1967** 'T. WELLS' *What should you know of Dying?* x. 118 He's an elevator man at the Winchenden Arms... He's on the restaurant car. **1899** R. FRY *Let.* Oct. (1972) I. 174 The restaurant dinners all stop at 5.0. **1925** F. SCOTT FITZGERALD *Great Gatsby* iii. 69 A solitary restaurant dinner. **1876** W. WRIGHT *Hist. Big Bonanza* xlviii. 355 Some years ago a restaurant keeper had a number of these customers, who were eating him out of house and home. **1932** H. SIMPSON *Boomerang* vii. 141 The two young men..grinned up at him, and the first, the restaurant-keeper, answered: 'His money is as good as another's.' **1974** 'J. ROSS' *Burning of Billy Toober* ix. 91 Prosser..had had his restaurant lunch sent in on a linen-shrouded tray. **1976** *Liverpool Echo* 6 Dec. 6/6 Restaurant manager Jose Padilla..is always on the look-out for something new for his customers. **1938** *Cook's Continental Time-table* Jan. (Advt.), Comfort to the continent. Right through the winter, Imperial Airways will operate frequent services to Paris,..Full restaurant meals served during flight. **1960** M. SPARK *Bachelors* iii. 43 One can't afford two restaurant meals in one day. **1938** *Sun* (Baltimore) 11 June 9/2 Worley Carrico, middle-aged restaurant proprietor. **1974** *Encycl. Brit. Macropædia* XV. 778/1 The first restaurant proprietor is believed to have been one A. Boulanger, a soup vendor, who opened his business in Paris in 1765.

restauranter (re·stǭrǫ:ntəɹ). *U.S.* [f. RESTAURANT + -ER[1].] = RESTAURATEUR 1.

1887 *Ohio State Jrnl.* 20 July, The headquarters of Mr. Kiesewetter are at Diebold's, an opulent restauranter and general purveyor to the wants of delegates. **1938** *Sun* (Baltimore) 11 June 9/2 (*heading*) Restauranter jailed in fatal shooting.

restauranteur (re:stǭrāntō̄·ɪ). [f. RESTAURANT + *-eur* as in RESTAURATEUR.] = RESTAURATEUR 1.

An erroneous form.

1949 E. HYAMS *Grape Vine in England* viii. 136 The second thinning may be done when the grapes are about the size of those very large and granite-like marrowfat peas which are beloved of English restauranteurs, or used to be. **1958** *Wall St. Jrnl.* 30 Sept. 7/3 Jack Dempsey, one-time heavyweight champion turned restauranteur. **1980** *Guardian Weekly* 20 Jan. 20/3 The growing number of hoteliers and restauranteurs.

re·staurantish, *a. rare.* [-ISH[1].] Resembling a restaurant; suggestive of a restaurant.

1896 A. BEARDSLEY *Let. c* 26 June (1970) 138 I have fallen on my feet here. Two palatial rooms and the additional comfort of being able to feed in a pretty little restaurantish dining-room.

restaurateur. Add: **1.** (Later examples.)

1969 *N.Y. Rev. Bks.* 2 Jan. 16/3 The editor of an intellectual journal has no less claim to being functional than a restaurateur. **1976** *Times* 21 May 4/8 Some had robbed a retired restaurateur of goods and money. **1980** *Amer. Speech* LV. 91 Books of advice to restaurateurs and menu designers suggest the use of foreign languages.

2. (Earlier example.)

1801 C. WILMOT *Let.* 13 Dec. in *Irish Peer* (1920) 13 The 'Palais Royal' is excessively new and entertaining... Libraries, Restaurateurs, Gambling Houses, Coffee Houses.

restauration. Add: **2. d.** (An) alteration or repair intended to restore a building, etc., to something like its original form or use. Cf. RESTORATION 4 b.

1949 E. POUND *Pisan Cantos* lxxx. 86 And I trust they have not destroyed the Old theatre by restaurations, and by late renaissance giribizzi. **1977** *It* May 29/3 Research into restauration of derelict urban or other areas.

restaurative (restǫ·rātiv), *a.*[2] *rare.* [ad. F. *restauratif*: see -IVE.] Having the function of a restaurant; providing restaurant facilities.

1875 in G. J. Holyoake *Hist. Co-operation in Eng.* I. ix. 214 In a short time the restaurative omnibuses will circulate through Paris... These vehicles will contain broth and sauce for the whole city.

rested, *ppl. a.* Add: Also const. *up* (see *REST *v.*[1] 2 g).

1922 E. O'NEILL *Anna Christie* I. 115, I was thinking maybe..he might be willing to stake me to a room and eats till I get rested up. **1929** G. ADE *Let.* 22 May (1973) 141, I am certainly glad to be home after a tedious tour and I am getting all rested up. **1935** M. M. ATWATER *Murder in Midsummer* xxi. 201, I guess we're all rested up. Come along, boys.

resteno·sis. *Med.* [RE-.] A recurrence of stenosis, esp. of a heart valve after surgery to correct it.

1954 *A.M.A. Arch. Internal Med.* XCIV. 777 Other examples of so-called restenosis following commissurotomy have been reported. **1977** *Proc. R. Soc. Med.* LXX. 816/2 Restenosis [of the ear canal] is very common.., especially in those cases where pneumatization is poor and the lateral sinus is abnormally anterior. **1980** *Brit. Med. Jrnl.* 12 Jan. 62/1 Many of these patients will have had a closed mitral valvotomy 10 to 30 years before, and the term 'mitral restenosis' is loosely used to describe the recurrence of their symptoms.

rester[1]. Add: **1.** Also *spec.* an unemployed actor or actress.

1931 R. ALDINGTON *Colonel's Daughter* v. 300 The anteroom of a dramatic agency filled with restless resters.

2. A ledge for placing articles on in front of a balcony in a theatre.

1922 *Rep. Theatres & Music Halls Comm.* in *Minutes Proc. L.C.C., July-Dec. 1921* 158 In order to prevent trays.. being pushed off the resters in the front of balconies at theatres, etc...we have..decided to require..that the rester shall be sloped at, say, an angle of 30 deg.

rest-house. Add: **1. a.** Also, a building with a similar function in Malaysia or Africa. (Further examples.)

1954 [see *NIGERIAN *sb.* and *a.*]. **1964** (*title*) Malaysia: visitors guide. Hotel and rest house directory. **1966** D. FORBES *Heart of Malaya* iii. 43 He..drove to Belinggu and took Abigail to the rest house there. **1972** *Guardian* 22 Sept. 9/1 My night at the Rest House—a hang-over from the colonial days, where Government officials could stay when travelling across country—was interrupted by the distant sound of a gong. **1978** G. GREENE *Human Factor* v. ii. 241 He could even imagine himself in Africa, at some resthouse in the bush.

b. An establishment catering for persons requiring rest and recreation.

1928 GALSWORTHY *Swan Song* III. ii. 231, I feel I should be ever so much more interested if I ran a place of my own in the country—a sort of rest-house that I could make attractive for girls who wanted air and that.

2. *attrib.*, as *rest-house garden, keeper.*

1909 *Athenæum* 24 Apr. 492/1, I dislike the ramshackle rest-house, and its rude indifferent rest-house-keeper. **1973** 'B. MATHER' *Snowline* xv. 183, I withdrew into the resthouse garden again.

resti·mulate, *v.* [RE- 5 a.] *trans.* To stimulate again. Hence **restimula·tion, restimula·tory** *a.* [-ORY[2]].

1796 A. SEWARD *Let.* 11 Dec. (1811) IV. 282 Mr. B. will succeed in his design to re-stimulate the public mind to continue the war. **1822–34** [see RE- 5 a]. **1924** W. B. SELBIE *Psychol. Relig.* iv. 89 What are regarded as influences from the subconscious are due to a restimulation of brain tracts which have been influenced by previous experiences. **1925** T. DREISER *Amer. Trag.* (1926) II. xxxiii. 381 Even his obviously dwindling affection was restimulated by her quite visible need of help. **1962** *Economist* 27 Oct. 332/2 A Keynesian restimulation of internal demand. *Ibid.* 29 Dec. 1256/1 The orthodox thing..may be to take no further restimulatory action..and then to give big tax reliefs in his budget. **1968** *Ibid.* 20 July 18/2 In spurring the re-expansion made possible by a freeing of labour from uneconomic jobs, it will be sensible to rely on tax cuts as the main restimulatory weapon.

resting, *vbl. sb.*[1] Add: **1. c.** *Theatr.* Unemployment; being without an acting job.

1924 G. B. STERN *Tents of Israel* vi. 85 A young singer.. [who] had sold all her things during her long period of enforced 'resting'. **1960** *Times* 28 Sept. 15/1 My theatrical colleagues who are only too familiar with the long periods of 'resting'—which being out of work is so politely called. **1973** J. BURROWS *Like an Evening Gone* i. 12 Though what..she did with herself in the great metropolis, in the frequent intervals of 'resting'—she didn't take typing jobs.

4. a. *resting period.*

1895 *Funk's Stand. Dict.*, Resting period. **1940** *Chambers's Techn. Dict.* 717/2 *Resting period*.., any time in the life of a plant, or plant organ, when no growth or other activity appears to be in progress. **1952** [see *ASPECT *sb.* 14].

b. *resting ground.*

1921 *Daily Colonist* (Victoria, B.C.) 27 Oct. 10/3 Feeding and resting grounds scattered over the country for the use of birds during migration.

c. *resting stage* (Cytology) = *INTERPHASE *sb.* 1.

1896 E. B. WILSON *Cell* ii. 53 There are..some undoubted cases..in which the centrosome remains undivided during the resting stage and only divides as the process of mitosis begins. **1932** [see *INTERPHASE *sb.* 1]. **1957** C. P. SWANSON *Cytol. & Cytogenetics* iii. 48 Cells in interphase, or the resting stage, are characterized by a nucleus that shows little or no definable structure, except for the nucleoli and the prochromosomes.

resting, *ppl. a.* Add: **1. b.** *resting bud*; also in *Cytology*, as *resting* (= interphase) *cell, nucleus*; *Zool.*, **resting egg**, a fertilized egg which can survive the winter or other unfavourable period before hatching.

1895 *Sci. Progress* III. 333 Structural changes in the resting nucleus, which lead up to the formation of the reduced number of chromosomes, and which I have termed collectively the synapsis. **1896** M. HARTOG in *Cambr. Nat. Hist.* II. viii. 200 The fertilised eggs are of the kind termed 'winter' or 'resting' eggs. **1904** *Nature* 24 Nov. 76/2 Figures are given of resting-buds, twigs and their transverse sections [etc.]. **1934** *Biol. Rev.* IX. 160 Among the Cladocera ..the same female may produce both females and males (by parthenogenetic reproduction) and resting eggs (by gametogenetic reproduction). **1953** H. L. EDLIN *Forester's Handbk.* ii. 22 The shoot increases in length only during the annual period of active growth. It grows..by actively dividing cells within the bud at its tip. When autumn comes, this suspends its activity, and becomes a resting bud, protected by bud scales, which remains dormant until the following spring. **1960** L. PICKEN *Organization of Cells* IV. ii. 103 The conflict between the genetic evidence, that the persistence of serial order of discrete genetic units in the linkage groups is of primary importance; and the light microscope evidence, that chromosomes are not visible in the resting nucleus in a majority of cells. **1975** J. B. JENKINS *Genetics* i. 27 In the resting, or interphase, cell the chromosomes are in an uncoiled condition and thus difficult to see. **1976** *Freshwater Biol.* VI. 408/1 Lack of food is probably the most important factor stimulating resting egg production.

c. *Theatr.* Between acting jobs; unemployed.
1958 A. Wilson *Middle Age of Mrs Eliot* II. 143 The rich 'resting' stage stars. **1969** M. Pugh *Last Place Left* xxiii. 178 The waitress..looked like a resting actress who did her resting in daytime. **1971** M. Babson *Cover-up Story* iv. 43 We still had the dubious privilege of representing two 'resting' actors.

3. Restful. *rare.*
1896 A. Beardsley *Let.* 17 Nov. (1970) 205, I wish Mabel could have started from Southampton. I do hope her crossing may be quiet and resting after all her hard work.

restitute, *v.* Add: **3.** *intr.* Genetics. *Cytology.* Of a break in a chromosome or chromatid: to be reversed by restitution (sense *8) of the two broken ends.
1945 *Jrnl. Genetics* XLVII. 13 Some of the breaks which restitute are lethals. **1971** Levitan & Montagu *Textbk. Human Genetics* iii. 135 Nonrearrangement breaks tend to restitute..quite readily.

‖ **restitutio in integrum** (restitiū·tio in inte·grŏm), *sb. phr. Law.* Also **ad integrum.** [L., restoration to the uninjured state, etc.] (See quot. 1909.) Also *transf.*
[*a* **1633** T. Hope *Major Practicks* (1938) II. 207 (*heading*) De Restitutione in Integrum.] **1704** T. Wood *New Institute Imperial or Civil Law* I. ii. 55 A Restitution shall be adjudged in the behalf of the Minor if he is circumvented, tho' the Tutors or Curators were present and consenting, and tho' the Decree was made against the Minor judicially; and this is called *Restitutio in integrum.* **1845** T. Thornton *Notes Cases in Eccles. & Maritime Courts* III. 77 The principle is, that the vessel should be placed *in statu quo* before the collision,—a *restitutio in integrum.* **1902** W. James *Var. Relig. Exper.* vi. 156 When disillusionment has gone as far as this, there is seldom a *restitutio ad integrum.* **1909** *Halsbury's Laws of Eng.* X. 302 The underlying great principle by which the courts are guided in awarding damages is *restitutio in integrum.* By this is meant that the law will endeavour, so far as money can do it, to place the injured person in the same situation as if the contract had been performed, or in the position he occupied before the occurrence of the tort which adversely affects him. **1936** Buckland & McNair *Roman Law & Common Law* xii. 337 An action which had once reached the stage of *litis contestatio* could never be brought again, unless the facts brought the matter within the rather narrow range of cases in which a man could get *restitutio in integrum.* **1975** J. R. Murdoch *Law Estate Agency & Auctions* xiii. 385 Since the principle underlying rescission is '*restitutio in integrum*' it will only be allowed where both parties can be substantially returned to their pre-contractual positions.

restitution. Add: **8.** *Genetics.* The coming together of the two parts of a broken chromosome or chromatid so as to re-form it; also *concr.*, the resulting chromosome or chromatid.
1941 *Cold Spring Harbor Symp. Quantitative Biol.* IX. 154/2 Even at ordinary doses there has been more than one break per gamete, but that break has usually been an invisible, 'restituted' one. How often may this 'restitution' have been imperfect or attended by some local alteration such as a 'gene mutation'? **1945** *Jrnl. Genetics* XLVII. 11 On this view it appears likely that lethals *not* apparently associated with any chromosome change are restitutions. **1980** R. P. Wagner et al. *Introd. Mod. Genetics* x. 273/1 When a chromosome breaks, the two broken ends usually undergo restitution.

9. restitution nucleus *Cytology* [tr. G. *restitutions-kern* (O. Rosenberg 1927, in *Hereditas* VIII. 321)], a cell nucleus having twice the regular chromosome number, formed by an uncompleted mitotic or meiotic cell division.
1927 *Hereditas* VIII. 336 The semiheterotypic meta- and anaphase very often are not completed, but are interrupted by a premature homotypic division, whereby *Restitution-nuclei* are formed. **1950** *Adv. Genetics* III. 197 The zygoid chromosome number is restored through the fusion of two azygoid nuclei, the formation of a restitution nucleus or endomitosis. **1974** *Euphytica* XXIII. 631 The diploid chromosome numbers..may result either from first or second division restitution nuclei of meiosis.

restless, *a.* Add: **2. b.** (Further *Comb.* example.)
1914 'Saki' *When William Came* vi. 101 You must remember that thousands and thousands of the more virile and restless-souled men have emigrated.

3. b. (Further *Comb.* example.)
1889 W. B. Yeats *Wanderings of Oisin* II. 24 Where goes to gaze the restless-footed star Of twilight when he's weary.

re-stock, *v.*[1] Add: Also *absol.*
1906 E. Dyson *Fact'ry 'Ands* iv. 50 Ellis took pity on his emptiness, and Mumps was sent home to re-stock.

restoration. Add: **4. d.** *Dentistry.* Any structure provided to replace dental or oral tissue that has been removed or lost, such as a filling, crown, or bridge.
1934 F. W. Frahm *Princ. & Technics Full Denture Constr.* xxvi. 475 The change from the natural to the artificial teeth is made so easily that the patient becomes accustomed to the supplied restoration in a few hours. **1962** Blake & Trott *Periodontology* xvi. 170 Before the construction of such prosthetic or conservative restorations is begun the occlusion should be studied. **1976** Torres & Ehrlich *Mod. Dental Assisting* xxvi. 802 To seat a restoration the casting is inserted into the tooth or onto the tooth crown.

6. *attrib.* and *Comb.*, as (sense 2 a) *Restoration comedy, drama, dramatist, pamphleteer, wing*; (sense 4 b) *restoration fund.*
1898 G. Saintsbury *Short Hist. Eng. Lit.* VIII. ii. 487 The cloven foot of Restoration comedy—the passionless and malevolent licentiousness of too much thereof. **1910** *Encycl. Brit.* IX. 630/2 Restoration comedy at first followed Jonson. **1925** B. Dobrée *Congreve's Comedies* I. p. xii, The Restoration comedy writers..keep us dancing along to a gay tune. **1955** N. Marsh *Scales of Justice* iii. 53 'Kettle,' Lady Lacklander said... Nurse Kettle did not resent being addressed in this restoration-comedy fashion by Lady Lacklander. **1976** *Amer. N. & Q.* XV. 35/1 In Restoration comedy, reference is often made to the 'canonical hours'. **1898** G. Saintsbury *Short Hist. Eng. Lit.* VIII. ii. 491 The glory..of this Restoration drama was not reached till long after the Restoration itself. **1923** A. Nicoll *Hist. Restoration Drama 1660–1700* i. 3 The study of Restoration drama demands a continual care. **1935** D. L. Sayers *Gaudy Night* iv. 82 Calling people names that poor Miss Lydgate didn't know existed—the worst she knows being Restoration drama. **1977** J. Aiken *Last Movement* vii. 130 I'd cast him as Rochester..or one of those fiends in Restoration Drama. **1912** E. Gosse in *Restoration Plays* p. x, What all the Restoration dramatists suffer from is a tendency to produce common and inadequate poetry. **1923** A. Nicoll *Hist. Restoration Drama 1660–1700* iii. 184 Manners, in the mouths of the Restoration dramatists themselves, meant something quite apart from the modern meaning of the term. **1974** *Encycl. Brit. Macropædia* IV. 113/1 William Congreve, more than any other Restoration dramatist, shaped the English comedy of manners. **1898** G. B. Shaw *Mrs. Warren's Profession* III. 204 Gov'nor's ever so fond of it, because he got up a restoration fund and had it completely rebuilt. **1978** *Lancashire Life* Nov. 140/1 A restoration fund has been launched to restore the decaying 15th century tower of Mitton Church, near Whalley. **1875** Restoration pamphleteer [in Dict., sense 2 a]. **1920** 'O. Douglas' *Penny Plain* xxv. 300 The austere Tudor front, the Restoration wing, the offices built under Queen Anne. **1936** J. Buchan *Island of Sheep* viii. 141 Nothing more modern than the Restoration wing built by Bruce of Kinross.

restorative, *a.* and *sb.* Add: **A.** *adj.* (Examples in *Dentistry.*)
1963 C. R. Cowell et al. *Inlays, Crowns, & Bridges* i. 1 Gold is stronger than other restorative materials and can be used in thin sections without danger of fracture. **1974** *News & Press* (Darlington, S. Carolina) 25 Apr. 17/3 It was first thought that the council might buy a mobile unit and employ a full time dentist who could..do restorative dentistry.

restore, *v.* Add: **3. a.** (Further examples.)
1868 A. J. Munby *Diary* 30 Oct. in D. Hudson *Munby* (1972) 258 The church..is being 'restored', as the phrase is. **1907** G. B. Shaw *Major Barbara* II. 244 He is one of the greatest of our public benefactors. He restored the cathedral at Hakington. **1920** W. B. Yeats *Michael Robartes & Dancer* 24, I, the poet William Yeats, With old mill boards and sea-green slates, And smithy work from the Gort Forge, Restored this tower for my wife George. **1931** J. Betjeman *Mt. Zion* 18 Look up! and how glorious He has restored the roof! **1959** N. Pevsner *Yorkshire: W. Riding* 267 The church was restored in 1876 by Pearson.

d. (See quot. 1955.)
1943 *Amer. Speech* XVIII. 304/1 Restored cereal. **1955** M. Reifer *Dict. New Words* 177/2 *Restore, v.*, to give back to a processed food the nutritive value it originally had.

restorer. Add: **2.** That which restores.
1873, 1893 [see *hair-restorer* s.v. Hair *sb.* 10 in Dict. and Suppl.]. **1911** G. B. Shaw *Doctor's Dilemma* I. 23 Its like a bald-headed man trying to sell a hair restorer.

resto·ringly, *adv.* [-ly[2].] In a restoring manner; restoratively.
1846 J. R. Lowell *Let.* 18 Feb. (1894) I. 115 Falling gently and restoringly as dew on the withered youth-flowers of the oppressor.

restraint, *sb.* Add: **1. c.** Something which restrains or holds in check; esp. *head restraint*, an attachment to the seat of a motor vehicle to prevent the head from jerking back suddenly.
1968 *Wall St. Jrnl.* 5 Aug. 28/4 American Motors Corp. said it will make head restraints standard equipment on all 1969-model cars. **1972** *Times* 28 Nov. 5/6 (Advt.), Both front seats recline, have sockets for optional head restraints. **1973** *Times* 3 July 1/5 Technically, a head rest was purely for comfort, whereas a safety device for protecting the head was termed a head restraint. **1976** *Amer. Speech 1973* XLVIII. 207 There, if he should become violent, he is placed in *restraints* 'straps' in his room. **1980** *Times* 29 Feb. 3 (Advt.), The seats are covered in crushed velour with head restraints at the rear as well as the front.

3. c. *restraint of trade.*
1890 *Statutes at Large U.S.A.* XXVI. 209 Every contract, combination in the form of trust or otherwise, or conspiracy, in restraint of trade or commerce among the several States.. is hereby declared to be illegal. **1913** *Halsbury's Laws of Engl.* XXVII. 532 Under the head of restraint of trade by statute come all those cases in which certain trades have been absolutely forbidden by Parliament. **1933** *Sutton & Shannon on Contracts* xi. 164 A contract in restraint of trade is not contrary to public policy. **1941** *Economist* 5 Apr. 437/2 The greater danger lies in the growing influence of what the common law knows (and used to condemn) as 'agreements in restraint of trade'. **1973** *N.Y. Law Jrnl.* 31 Aug. 1/5 The two-count indictment charged conspiracy in restraint of trade in violation of the Sherman Antitrust Act.

restri·ctable, *a.* [f. Restrict *v.* + -able.] Able to be restricted.
1973 I. Robinson *Survival of English* iii. 82 Economic management is management of human beings, which is just not restrictable to economics.

restricted, *ppl. a.* Add: **b.** In which a speed-limit is operative.
1933 E. Caldwell *God's Little Acre* vii. 107 They passed through the other company towns slowing down in the restricted zones. **1939** *New Statesman* 29 July 196/1 The existing mild supervision of restricted areas is carried out by the so-called 'speed cops'. **1959** *Listener* 2 Apr. 603/1 There are cases where a driver is mistaken about a restricted area.

c. Of documents, information, etc.: for restricted circulation only (see also quot. 1975); not to be revealed to the general public for reasons of national security.
1944 [see *classified *ppl. a.* c]. **1950** [see *clear *v.* 9 c]. **1957** *Ann. Reg. 1956* 345 A new model of the R.A.F.'s only fully supersonic fighter flying in Britain..was taken off the restricted list in August and was demonstrated at the aircraft industry's annual display at Farnborough. **1965** Mrs. L. B. Johnson *White House Diary* 2 Sept. (1970) 313 Then President Truman gave us the tour [of the library], with Max asking all sorts of architectural questions—storage, humidity, traffic routing, vaults for documents that were still restricted. **1972** K. Benton *Spy in Chancery* xv. 180 The Russians always start by asking you to hand over something quite harmless... And then they ask for something that's on the restricted list, but not really secret. **1972** P. Ruell *Red Christmas* ix. 83 What I'm going to tell you is restricted information. That means it's only known to the Prime Minister, [and] security top brass. **1975** *Times* 8 Feb. 2/1 'Restricted' papers ('restricted' is the lowest security classification) had been found on my doormat.

d. *U.S.* Limited to use by non-Jews; denying admission to Jews.
1947 *Cosmopolitan* Jan. 84/2 Is your inn restricted?.. You mean you *do* restrict your guests to Gentiles. **1953** P. Frankau *Winged Horse* I. ix. 41 Draw the slums. Draw the restricted hotels. **1972** W. P. McGivern *Caprifoil* (1973) xii. 204 Anti-Semitism..is not only a matter of restricted clubs and colleges' quotas. **1979** *Listener* 16 Aug. 204/2 'I'm sorry, Mr Marx, but we can't let you use the pool, this country club is restricted.'.. 'Well, my daughter's only half-Jewish, could she go in up to her knees?'

e. *Biol.* Of a virus: unable to reproduce at its normal rate in certain hosts. Of DNA: subject to degradation by a restriction enzyme.
1957 *Virology* III. 500 A certain proportion of the T1 phage produced is now able to multiply on B(P1) or Sh (P1) ('unrestricted phage'). Single-burst experiments.. showed that about 70% of the yielder cells liberate only normal, 'restricted' T1. The other yielder cells produce a mixture of restricted and unrestricted T1. **1965** *Ann. Rev. Microbiol.* XIX. 366 Phage λ variants can be classified with respect to their state of adaptation..by determination of the efficiency of plating (eop) on various hosts... λ·K has an eop of one on K12 and C, i.e., it is accepted, nonrestricted. The same phage λ·K, however, plates only exceptionally on B or on P1-lysogenic strains: it is said to be restricted. *Ibid.* 367 The whole population of restricted DNA molecules.

f. Of a language system: having a limited syntax and lexicon.
1962 B. Bernstein in *Lang. & Speech* V. 32 Two general types of code can be distinguished: *elaborated* and *restricted*... In the case of an elaborated code, the speaker will select from a relatively extensive range of alternatives... In the case of a restricted code the number of these alternatives is often severely limited. **1964** M. A. K. Halliday et al. *Linguistic Sci.* 96 Some registers are extremely restricted in purpose. They thus employ only a limited number of formal items and patterns... Such registers are known as *restricted languages.* **1968** E. W. Gordon in M. Deutsch et al. *Social Class, Race & Psychol. Devel.* xi. 390 Restricted language.. develops as a product of unilateral decision making in the lower-class home. **1971** *Archivum Linguisticum* II. 67 Firth advocated what he called 'partial studies', e.g. the study of newspaper headlines *per se*, in which attention would be drawn to features of the 'restricted language' itself as well as to contrasts between it and other restricted languages. **1975** *Amer. Speech 1973* XLVIII. 35 It has been further suggested that if speakers of a restricted code do not use such conjunctions, their language and probably their logical processes are somehow deficient.

g. Of a person: not allowed to move about freely; confined to a certain area or certain areas.
1971 *Sunday Express* (Johannesburg) 28 Mar. 9/5 'If a restricted person can satisfy me that he can obtain residence overseas and that he has a bona fide intention of not returning to South Africa, I cannot refuse his request for an exit permit,' Mr. Gerdener said. **1971** *Rand Daily Mail* (Johannesburg) 4 Dec. 13/1 Anglican bishops..are accused of defying the Government by wanting to offer help to people banned or restricted under the Terrorism Act. **1972** *Straits Times* (Malaysian ed.) 24 Nov. 21/2 Unemployed, and a restricted resident, Chua Ali Kow, 32, was sentenced to two years' jail.

restrictee (rīstrikti·). [f. Restrict *v.* + -ee[1], after *detainee.*] One whose freedom of movement is restricted, usu. for political reasons.
1959 *Observer* 31 May 6/8 This pay starts in the open camp—no guards, no wire, no warders—at 30s. monthly plus rations. When detainees thus become 'restrictees' they are trade tested and trained for various jobs as clerks or artisans. **1960** *Guardian* 24 Dec. 7/1 The Southern Rhodesian Government must now be keen to release the seven detainees and forty restrictees. **1965** *Spectator* 8 Jan. 35/2 The government can no longer prevent the restrictees from receiving visitors at will and today there is a constant stream on the trains. **1970** *Guardian Weekly* 21 Feb. 6/4

The main legal advantage that restrictees have over detainees is that their term of restriction is defined.

restriction. Add: **1. d.** Deliberate limitation of industrial output.

1888 W. E. NICHOLSON *Gloss. Terms Coal Trade* 71 *Restriction*, an arrangement or understanding among the hewers limiting their day's work to something less than a fair ordinary day's work. **1930** *Economist* 22 Mar. 652/1 At the same time, restriction is being maintained in Oklahoma, while in Texas, although the State Governor views all restriction schemes as a breach of the Anti-Trust laws, a certain amount of voluntary restriction is in force. **1931** *Brit. Jrnl. Psychol.* July 89 Restriction is practised by the non-union worker just as much as it is by the member of a trade union. **1961** *Problems of Progress in Industry* No. 11 p. 11 If their [*sc.* workers'] standards are lower than those considered as reasonable by managers, such behaviour is usually called 'restriction of output'.

4. *Math.* A function $\bar{f}$ whose domain is a subset of a given function *g*, whose codomain is the codomain of *g*, and for which $f(x) = g(x)$ for all *x* in the domain of *f*. Also *restriction mapping*.

1949 SPRINGER & POLLAK *Algebraic Topology* viii. 168 Since f̄ is a restriction of g, we have that the map g̃ of H(A) into H(B) which is reduced by g is exactly the same as the map f̄. **1963** D. BUSHAW *Elem. Gen. Topology* 147 If $f: X \to Y$ and $A \subset X$, the function $fj: A \to Y$, where *j* is the injection map from *A* to *X*, is called the restriction of *f* to *A* and is denoted by $f|A$. **1979** *Proc. London Math. Soc.* XXXVIII. 208 Recall that $D(G,H) = \text{Ker } \rho_H$ where ρ_H: $\text{Der}(G,ZG) \to \text{Der}(H,ZG)$ is the restriction mapping.

5. *Biol.* Limitation of the rate of reproduction of a virus in certain hosts, owing to the destruction of viral DNA by a restriction enzyme.

1962 *Jrnl. Molecular Biol.* V. 47 Host-controlled modification is known to occur in many bacteriophage-host systems and is usually recognized by restriction in the efficiency of plating of the newly modified phage on its former host strain. **1968** *Proc. Nat. Acad. Sci.* LIX. 1305 The complementation studies suggest that restriction activity is conferred by at least two gene functions. **1979** *Nature* 1 Mar. 30/1 Bacteriophage T3 and T7 protect their DNA from restriction by producing, as the earliest detectable phage functions, anti-restriction proteins.

6. Special Comb.: **restriction endonuclease, enzyme** *Biochem.*, an enzyme that divides large molecules of DNA only if there is a specific sequence of several nucleotides (usu. four to six in number).

1977 *Sci. Amer.* Dec. 61/1 An important tool for plus-and-minus sequencing and for molecular biology in general was provided by the discovery several years ago of the enzymes called restriction endonucleases, which cleave large DNA molecules into discrete fragments. **1979** *Nature* 20 Sept. p. v, CP Laboratories Limited have in stock for immediate delivery more than 40 restriction endonucleases. **1965** W. ARBER in *Ann. Rev. Microbiol.* XIX. 368 One might like to assume that a highly specific 'restriction enzyme' only initiates the degradation, for example, by cleavage of DNA, and that these cleavage products are then subject to the action of less specific nucleases. **1977** *Time* 18 Apr. 48/1 Different plasmids, sometimes passed from one bacterium to another, can order up still another kind of chemical weapon, a so-called restriction enzyme, which can sever the DNA of an invading virus, say, at a predetermined point.

restri·ctionism. [f. RESTRICTION + -ISM.] A policy of restricting some practice, institution, etc.

1941 *Economist* 5 Apr. 436/2 It would be a disaster if war-time concentration were to leave any legacy of peacetime restrictionism. **1949** *Hansard Commons* 19 May 631, I do not want to say very much more about this matter of restrictionism, save to say that the body of Captain Ludd has long since mouldered in the grave but his ideas still march on in Britain. **1958** *Economist* 20 Dec. 1066/1 There was a prime example of this restrictionism earlier this week, when employers and building unions in the north together condemned the excellent practice whereby some building workers have entered into voluntary contracts to build some additional houses in certain developing areas after hours. **1968** *Physics Bull.* Nov. 394/2 Restrictionism relates to the absence of true competition due to restrictive trade associations etc. *a* **1974** R. CROSSMAN *Diaries* (1975) I. 34 Office building was an area where, despite my dislike of restrictionism, I might be seriously prepared to think of physical controls to deal with the scandal.

restrictionist. Add: (Earlier and later examples.) Also *attrib.* or as *adj.*

1820 *Niles' Reg.* XVIII. 258/2 We undertake to say that there is not a single *confessed* restrictionist elected throughout the whole territory. **1941** *Economist* 29 Mar. 406/1 The preservation of the margins of, say, August, 1939, as maxima, may simply do the work of monopolists or restrictionists for them. **1951** *Sun* (Baltimore) 19 Mar. 1/2 A powerful bloc of 'restrictionists' is threatening to strike a successful blow at freedom of information in the name of the United Nations. **1962** *Listener* 8 Mar. 400/1 A restrictionist policy which the unions have denounced as the cause of most of the trouble. **1965** *New Statesman* 30 Apr. 673/1 What is needed is..a restrictionist philosophy in the field of reproduction..coupled with an expansionist philosophy in the field of production and distribution of all the other good things of life.

restrictive, *a.* Add: **2.** Also in *Gram.*, esp. of relative clauses.

1878 REED & KELLOGG *Higher Lessons in English* 98 The Adjective Clause, when not restrictive, is set off by the comma. **1895** *Funk's Stand. Dict.* s.v., A restrictive clause. **1924** O. JESPERSEN *Philos. Gram.* viii. 112 In English..only restrictive clauses can be introduced by *that* or without any pronoun. **1957** *Eng. Stud.* XXXVIII. 101 Restrictive clauses..are linked to their antecedents by close syntactic juncture. **1977** *Language* LIII. 70 The pragmatic distinction that Donnellan labeled the 'referential' and 'attributive' uses of definite descriptions is *not* reflected in the mood of restrictive relative clauses.

3. a. (Earlier *Econ.* example.)

1825 J. S. MILL in *Westm. Rev.* Apr. 412 If the landlords would attend a little to these, and some other effects of the restrictive system, we should no longer hear them clamouring..for a protecting duty of 20, 30, or 40 shillings.

b. *spec.* of a covenant.

1882 *Law Rep. Queen's Bench Div.* VIII. 410 With regard to the question of notice, *Tulk v. Moxhay* shews that a restrictive covenant will be enforced, and so do *Cox v. Bishop* and *Wilson v. Hart.* **1911** *Encycl. Brit.* XVI. 157/1 *Restrictive Covenants*:- These may be subdivided into two classes—covenants not to assign or underlet without the lessor's consent..; and covenants in restraint of trade. **1925** *Act* 15 *Geo. V* c. 22 § 10 A covenant or agreement (not being a covenant or agreement made between a lessor and lessee) restrictive of the user of land entered into after the commencement of this Act (in this Act referred to as 'a restrictive covenant'). **1935** *Discovery* Aug. 227/1 A new policy of preserving land by means of restrictive covenants has recently been adopted [by the National Trust], in addition to the older and more expensive method of purchase. **1953** [see *LILY-WHITE *a.* 2]. **1976** *Evening Post* (Nottingham) 15 Dec. 4/4 Mansfield District Council has decided to go ahead with its plan to close the market..despite the failure of their application to the Land Tribunal for the removal of a 100-year-old restrictive covenant on the site. **1979** *Internat. Jrnl. Sociol. of Law* VII. 339 In drafting the contract a planning authority condition that the future occupants do not erect fences has to be translated into a restrictive covenant.

c. *restrictive practice*: an arrangement in industry and trade which restricts or controls competition between firms; an arrangement by a group of workers to limit the output or restrict the entry of new workers: regarded by others as preventing labour or materials from being used in the most efficient way. Hence *restrictive practitioner*.

1928 *Britain's Industr. Future* (Liberal Industr. Inquiry) xiii. 146 The prevalence of these restrictive practices has varied very widely from trade to trade. **1946** *Sun* (Baltimore) 19 Feb. 10/3 The single argument on which all the restrictive practices have rested..was that the demand for housing was so limited that the various factors in the housing field in simple self-protection had to stretch the work out and keep costs high. **1948** *Act* 11 & 12 *Geo. VI* c. 66 § 1 For the purposes of this Act there shall be constituted a Commission, to be called the Monopolies and Restrictive Practices Commission... The Commission shall consist of not less than four nor more than ten members to be appointed by the Board of Trade. **1958** *Spectator* 31 Jan. 133/1 These two trades have been in the forefront as restrictive practitioners. **1964** *Mod. Law Rev.* XXVIII. 337 The House of Lords..handed down an important decision on the question of restrictive practices. **1966** *Economist* 12 Mar. 979/2 Mr Heath would apparently like to hand the supervision of labour relations over to the lawyers, the Tories' favourite restrictive practitioners. **1969** J. ARGENTI *Managem. Techniques* 207 Others blame labour for resisting changes to working methods and manning levels and for perpetuating restrictive practices. **1978** *Jrnl. R. Soc. Arts* CXXVI. 406/2 The moves made by successive Tory Presidents of the Board of Trade in the late '50s and early '60s to curb restrictive practices of various kinds.

restrictiveness. For *rare*⁻¹ in Dict. read *rare* and add later examples.

1978 *Language* LIV. 406 The second desideratum is the goal of restrictiveness: the notion that a theory of language should characterize just the class of possible human languages, and no more. **1980** A. N. WILSON *Healing Art* xviii. 223 Both of them found..emotional restrictiveness necessary.

restrictivist (rĭstri·ktivist), *a.* [f. RESTRICTIVE *a.* + -IST.] Characterized by restriction; limiting.

1966 *New Statesman* 21 Oct. 574/1 Cost-inflation..forces the government to adopt restrictivist policies. **1977** P. JOHNSON *Enemies of Society* viii. 115 Part of the genetic coding of all children is knowledge of the highly restrictivist principles of universal grammar.

restrictor (rĭstri·ktǭɹ). [f. RESTRICT *v.* + -OR.] **1.** One who restricts or advocates restriction.

1825 J. S. MILL in *Westm. Rev.* Apr. 291 It is a proposition which the restrictors themselves do not venture to dispute. **1952** *Chambers's Jrnl.* Apr. 230/1 Restrictive covenants in house or land deeds may be a curse to any buyer... It can happen that covenants are interpreted in a peculiar manner by the restrictors.

2. A device for restricting the flow of a fluid, e.g. by means of a porous medium or an orifice. Freq. *attrib.*

1940 E. MOLLOY *Aeroplane Maintenance & Operation* I. 105 *Restrictor jets*, these..are situated in two recesses opposite the lower edge of the throttle when in the closed position. **1961** R. V. WATTS in D. S. Carton et al. *Rocket Propulsion Technol.* I. 54 By opening the..restrictor, it became possible to set minimum thrust at the required angle. **1966** L. A. H. EASTMAN tr. *G. Schenkel's Plastics Extrusion Technol. & Theory* xiii. 368 The sheet die developed in the U.S.A. for the processing of impact-resistant polystyrene..has a flexible restrictor bar fitted in the upper part of the die, transverse to the flow direction. **1979** *Wear* LIV. 331 The stiffness of hydrostatic [journal] bearings is greatest when valve restrictors are used and decreases progressively with orifice and capillary restrictors.

restrike, *sb.* Add: Also, a reimpression of a print or medal.

1912 *Chambers's Jrnl.* May 327/2 Restrikes of these medals are not uncommon, as it is only within recent years that the Calcutta mint has been prohibited from issuing them. **1965** ZIGROSSER & GAEHDE *Guide to Collecting Orig. Prints* iv. 62 Prints, either late restrikes from the plate or genuine old uncolored impressions, have often been colored by a later hand. **1970** *New Yorker* 20 June 63/2 The reason for this low price..is that the print is a restrike. This means that it was made after the artist's death from the original plate. **1980** *Daily Tel.* 16 Feb. 27/6 In the case of badges, 'restrikes' are a common hazard.

2. *Electr. Engin.* The re-ignition of an arc.

1962 *Newnes Conc. Encycl. Electr. Engin.* 132/2 Suppression of the arc before natural current zero causes severe overvoltages and high frequency multiple restrikes.

restrike, *v.* Add: **b.** *intr. Electr. Engin.* Of an arc: to strike again (STRIKE *v.* 76 a). Also *trans.* (causatively).

1937 [implied in RESTRIKING *vbl. sb.* below]. **1942** A. ARNOLD *Switchgear Pract.* ix. 109 The arc will again restrike. **1955** E. MOLLOY *Electr. Engineer's Ref. Bk.* (ed. 8) vii. 24 It is the rate of rise of the restriking voltage that determines whether or not the arc will restrike. **1962** *Newnes Conc. Encycl. Electr. Engin.* 132/1 To achieve successful interruption [of alternating currents] it is necessary to prevent the arc restriking by separating the contacts to a distance which will withstand the restriking voltage. **1977** R. L. LITTLE *Metalworking Technol.* v. xxiv. 279/1 Restriking an arc... The welder strikes the arc approximately ½ to 1 in. in front of the crater on the side opposite the weld bead.

Hence **restri·king** *vbl. sb.*, *esp.* in *Electr. Engin.*; *restriking voltage*, in a circuit-breaker, the value of the high-frequency voltage surge across the contacts following their separation and the extinction of the subsequent arc between them.

1937 TODD & THOMPSON *Outdoor High Voltage Switchgear* viii. 172 An important factor controlling restriking voltage is the type of machine..supplying the circuit. **1958** J. SHEPHERD et al. *Higher Electr. Engin.* xvi. 405 In oil circuit breakers, where dielectric strengths are normally higher than in air circuit breakers, re-striking may not take place.

restru·cture, *v.* [RE- 5 c.] *trans.* To give a new structure to; to organize into a new pattern; to rebuild, re-arrange. Hence **restru·ctured** *ppl. a.*; **restru·cturer**; **restru·cturing** *vbl. sb.*

1951 K. S. LASHLEY in L. A. Jeffress *Cerebral Mechanisms in Behavior* 119 Some children become very facile at such inversions of words, and re-structure new words without hesitation. **1951** G. HUMPHREY *Thinking* vi. 181 If every response has an element of newness,..why is not restructuring present all the time? **1958** W. J. H. SPROTT *Human Groups* iii. 48 The 'life-space' is constantly changed with 'locomotion', and also with changing awareness, in which case it is often said to be 'restructured'. **1962** *Economist* 22 Sept. 1123/2 The most comprehensive restructuring of international liquidity arrangements since the IMF was founded. **1967** *Observer* 19 Nov. 4/7 Wilson..thought that..his policy of controlled expansion, combined with the 'restructuring' of industry and a better balance between the regions, would in the end do the trick. **1969** *Listener* 17 July 65/3 He [*sc.* the Director-General] did not restructure the radio services of the BBC. **1970** *Times Lit. Suppl.* 23 Apr. 443/2 Lord Robbins is a tough-minded re-structurer. **1976** P. R. WHITE *Planning for Public Transport* x. 208 The question of restructuring private car costs to make them comparable in form is discussed below. **1977** *Belfast Tel.* 22 Feb. 6/2 Proposals for the re-structured council are being studied by the Secretary of State. **1978** W. F. BUCKLEY *Stained Glass* xxii. 212 He spent the first half hour with Overstreet, who pronounced the restructuring of the chapel's trussed roof complete.

‖ **Reststrahlen** (restˌʃtrā·lən), *sb. pl. Physics.* Also as sing. **Reststrahl** and with small initial. [Ger., residual rays, f. *rest* remainder + *strahlen* rays.] Electromagnetic radiation which is selectively reflected from the surface of a crystalline solid when the frequency of the incident radiation is nearly equal to the frequency of vibration of the ions constituting the solid.

1910 *Phil. Mag.* XIX. 761 For the investigation of the extreme infra-red portion of the spectrum the method of 'Reststrahlen' has proved most fruitful. **1942** *Rep. Progr. Physics* VIII. 28 To compare the high-frequency end of the spectrum..with that obtained from other data, e.g. from *Reststrahlen* in the case of ionic crystals. **1965** M. GARBUNY *Optical Physics* v. 285 (*caption*) Filter action of crystallite powders in their reststrahlen region. **1967** *Physical Rev. Lett.* XVIII. 601/2 The sample is opaque in the neighborhood of 23 meV due to *Reststrahl* reflection.

restu·dy, *sb.* [f. the vb.] The act of studying again.

1961 *Newark* (N.J.) *Even. News* 21 Nov. 24/2 (*heading*) N.J. fights restudy of WNTA sale stay. **1962** E. SNOW *Red China Today* (1963) liii. 402, I met a writer less well known than Hsiao Ch'ien, who had completed his 'restudy of the sources of art' in a commune. **1966** *Economist* 22 Jan. 309/1 When the commission sounded the retreat and sent the headache back to the engineers for 're-study', the state engineer suggested drily that the study would take just about a year. **1979** *Nature* 20–27 Dec. 832/1 A restudy of this genus has convinced us that it was based on part of the skull roof of a specialised placoderm.

resty, *a.*[1] **1. a.** (Further examples.)

1920 A. HUXLEY *Leda* 40 The machine is ready to start. The symbolic beasts grow resty, curveting where they stand. **1977** J. AIKEN *Five-Minute Marriage* viii. 126 He guided his horses around the corner... The team appeared to be a trifle fresh and resty.

resty·le, *v.* [RE- 5 a.] *trans.* To style again; to give a new style to. So **resty·led** *ppl. a.*, **resty·ling** *vbl. sb.*

1934 in WEBSTER. **1958** *Listener* 19 June 1006/2 The development of new equipment and the re-styling of the philosophy of design in this new-born industry are a fascinating branch of chemical engineering. **1958** *Times* 22 Oct. 5/5 Details like the front grille and the tail lights have been restyled. **1960** *Farmer & Stockbreeder* 8 Mar. 136/1 Entire pig herd replaced in re-styled buildings. **1965** D. FRANCIS *Odds Against* xx. 249 Her hair had been re-styled... It.. curved in a bouncy curl. **1977** *Lancashire Life* Nov. 153/1 The Granadas have been completely restyled, and now look remarkably like the Audi 100. **1978** 'M. YORKE' *Point of Murder* i. 15 She went..for restyling and emerged bouffant.

resuing (rĭsiū·iŋ), *vbl. sb. Mining.* [Etym. unknown.] A method of stoping in which the rock wall adjacent to a narrow vein is removed before the vein itself, so that the ore can be extracted in a cleaner condition.

1909 H. C. HOOVER *Princ. Mining* x. 101 (*heading*) Resuing. **1910** W. R. CRANE *Ore Mining Methods* ii. 38 Resuing consists in opening up the stopes not in the vein but in the wall-rock, by whatever method of stoping seems best adapted to the existing conditions. *Ibid.* 43 Resuing is applicable to very narrow veins alone, *i.e.*, under 30 inches in width; its chief advantage being that a cleaner grade of ore can be mined than when both vein and walls are broken together. **1973** L. J. THOMAS *Introd. Mining* vi. 188 In some cases narrow veins may be taken by resuing..[which] can be classed as either cut and fill, or as vein mining.

result, *sb.* Add: **3. d.** Usu. *pl.* The final marks, scores, and placings in (*a*) an examination, (*b*) a sports event.

1916 JOYCE *Portrait of Artist* (1969) v. 210 Did you hear the results of the exams? **1937** PARTRIDGE *Dict. Slang* 695/1 *Results*, news of sports results. **1955** *Radio Times* 22 Apr. 42/2 Sport. Today's results and weekend preview. **1968** *Ibid.* 28 Nov. 8/5, 4.55 Racing Results. **1977** *Belfast Tel.* 28 Feb. 9/3 The following are the results of the November exams held by the Institute of Cost and Management accountants.

e. *pl.* Favourable or desired consequences. Also *sing.*, a good or favourable result against an opponent.

1922 E. O'NEILL *Hairy Ape* vii. 73 Take some of those pamphlets with you to distribute aboard ship. They may bring results. **1927** —— *Marco Millions* III. i. 167, I kept my nose to the grindstone every minute... And I got results. **1931** *Punch* 18 May (*caption*) The charming young gold-digger who expected results of an Aberdonian. **1973** E. DUNPHY *Only a Game?* (1977) ii. 52, I think we will get a result at Preston. **1976** *Observer* 21 Nov. 23/1 We needed a result... Perhaps we should have done better than win 1–0.

resultative (rĭzʌ·ltătiv), *a. Gram.* [f. RESULT *sb.* + -ATIVE.] Expressing result. Also *absol.* as *sb.*

1926 H. POUTSMA *Gram. Late Mod. Eng.* II. II. lviii. 545 The attributive past participle mostly has a momentaneous or resultative aspect. **1936** *Jrnl. Eng. & Germanic Philol.* XXXV. 368 The so-called Resultative Perfect requires a somewhat detailed examination. **1957** R. W. ZANDVOORT *Handbk. Eng. Gram.* I. iv. 61 English shares with other languages the use of the *resultative perfect*, which denotes a past action connected, through its result, with the present moment. I've bought a new car. **1963** F. T. VISSER *Hist. Syntax Eng. Lang.* I. iv. 582 Examples of Old English verbs construed with a resultative predicative adjunct are not numerous. **1965** *Language* XLI. 109 In Indic, the perfect, whose function was originally stative,..developed..to a resultative. **1970** J. W. R. LINDEMANN *Old Eng. Preverbal Ge-* I. 4 *Ge-* may convert an intransitive verb into a resultative verb that is transitive. **1977** *Canad. Jrnl. Linguistics* Spring 51 Resultatives..represent a second category where *hə* occurs instead of a resonant plus shwa in reduplicative prefixes.

resume, *v.* Add: **I. 2. b.** Also with direct speech: to go on to say.

1765 H. WALPOLE *Castle of Otranto* i. 16 Yes, I sent for you on a matter of great moment, resumed he. **1789** J. MOORE *Zeluco* I. xxii. 132 'Nay, my good friend,' resumed the Physician, 'it is a matter of indifference to me, what you do or do not believe.' **1850** F. E. SMEDLEY *Frank Fairlegh* xliii. 376 'I have fancied that illness was beginning to sour your temper,' I replied. 'Illness of mind, not body,' he resumed. **1906** *Smart Set* May 9/2 'I guess, friend,' resumed the man with the pipe, 'she's been standin' out here coolin' off for some time, ain't she?' **1922** JOYCE *Ulysses* 620 Mind you, I'm not saying that it's all a pure invention, he resumed. **1976** R. HILL *Another Death in Venice* I. iii. 63 'I'll say this, though,' resumed Wilf, 'I'm worried.'

résumé, *sb.* Add: Also with pronunc. (re-). Also **resume. b.** Chiefly *N. Amer.* = *curriculum vitæ* s.v. *CURRICULUM. Also *fig.*

1961 WEBSTER, *Résumé..specif.*: a brief account of one's education and professional experience. **1968** *Globe & Mail* (Toronto) 17 Feb. 51 If an interview is not convenient at this time, forward your resume, in confidence to Mr. Grossman. **1971** GOLZEN & PLUMBLEY *Changing your Job after 35* viii. 86 The Résumé..will vary considerably with the type and level of job and can be the bare bones of a c.v. or a long, narrative account of your main achievements written up with a special bias. **1973** J. RYDER *Trevayne* (1974) iii. 384 There was an opening. What could look better on a résumé than the White House? **1976** *Glasgow Herald* 26 Nov. 25/1 Please submit detailed resume including personal data, educational background, and work experience. **1979** *Tucson Mag.* Feb. 88/2 She has added several fine credits to her resume since then, including a Washington D.C. debut this year.

resumptive, *a.* and *sb.* Add: **3.** *Gram.* **a.** In Jespersen's terminology: (see quot. 1917). **b.** Indicating resumption of a topic, etc.; having previous reference. So as *sb.* (see quot. 1954).

1917 O. JESPERSEN in *Historisk-Filologiske Meddelelser* I. v. 69 A second class comprises what may be termed *resumptive negation*, the characteristic of which is that after a negative sentence has been completed, something is added in a negative form with the obvious result that the negative effect is heightened. **1954** D. BOLINGER in *Boletín de Filología Universidad de Chile* VIII. 48 Sometimes, for special effects, a presupposed element, even a lengthy one, is repeated though specifically known from the immediate context... We may call such a verbatim or near-verbatim presupposed element a 'resumptive'. *Ibid.* 49 An element which is explicitly resumptive comes after prosodic stress. **1957** *Publ. Amer. Dial. Soc.* XXVIII. 145 A post-accentual resumptive is only a repetition, while a pre-accentual resumptive may be more. **1959** J. C. CATFORD in Quirk & Smith *Teaching of English* (1964) vii. 149, I know of no practical English grammar for foreign learners which describes the use of *oh, ah* or the introductory or resumptive *well.* **1970** M. DAHOOD *Anchor Bible: Psalms III* 337 M[assoretic] T[ext] *'asapperennāh* can be explained as employing the resumptive pronominal suffix. **1975** *Language* LI. 59, I regard Spanish resumptive intonation and beginning position as variant formal means of expressing syntagmatic complexity.

resupply, *v.* Add: Also *absol.*, to take on or acquire a fresh supply.

1977 'J. MCVEAN' *Bloodspoor* xiii. 152 We'll have to resupply. We're mobile and there must be wells. *Ibid.* xviii. 218 They were down to the last few pints but..they'd be able to resupply from one of the tributary streams.

resu·rface, *v.* [RE- 5 a, c.] **1.** *trans.* To provide (a road, etc.) with a fresh surface.

1886 [implied in RESURFACING *vbl. sb.* below]. **1894** *Westm. Gaz.* 23 Apr. 8/3 (Advt.), Old blocks bought up, sold, or resurfaced. **1901** *U.S. Dept. Agric. Yearbk. 1900* 352 When the road was resurfaced with limestone..it became excellent. **1929** *Daily Express* 11 Jan. 2/2 If these minor roads were..strengthened and resurfaced in accordance with modern road practice [etc.]. **1960** *Times* 4 July (Advt. Suppl.) 1/3 Safety razors had not resurfaced the New Man. **1973** 'C. AIRD' *His Burial Too* iii. 31 The Divisional Surveyor decided to resurface the road.

2. *intr.* To come to the surface again. Also *fig.*

1953 P. C. BERG *Dict. New Words in Eng.* 137/1 *Resurface..v.i.*, of a submarine: to come to the surface. **1962** *Times* 3 Apr. 14/6, I would re-surface before the water-splash fell back into the tank. **1968** J. SANGSTER *Foreign Exchange* ii. 57 It was midday when I resurfaced, too late for breakfast. **1971** *Flying* Apr. 73/2, I would resurface to find the airplane starting to turn back. **1973** L. SNELLING *Heresy* II. i. 62 We lose sight of him... Killed by the Gestapo? In an air-raid? In any event he never resurfaced. **1978** J. MCDOWELL in Hookway & Pettit *Action & Interpretation* 151 If it were to be so incorporated, all the difficulties of the relation between behaviour and action categories would presumably resurface.

So **resu·rfacing** *vbl. sb.*

1886 *Cyclist* 4 Aug. 1076/1 The re-surfacing of the Crystal Palace path. **1967** *Antiquaries Jrnl.* XLVII. 271 This structure had been..covered with a plaster surface, perhaps later than the surface of the atrium described above, but present over a sufficiently large area to indicate a general resurfacing. **1978** *Lancashire Life* Mar. 54/3 George's Lane and Belmont Road were selected for resurfacing.

‖ **resurgam** (resɜ̄·ɹgæm). [L.] 'I shall rise again', expressing Christian faith in resurrection at the Last Day. Usu. *transf.* and *fig.*

1662 J. TRAPP *Annotations Old & New Testament* I. 142 Howbeit he had *hope in his death*, and might write *Resurgam* on his grave. **1847** THACKERAY *Van. Fair* (1848) xiv. 126 Arms and Hatchments, Resurgam.—Here is an opportunity for moralizing! **1853** GEO. ELIOT *Let.* 3 Jan. (1954) II. 79 *Now* nothing seems pleasant to me but—*Resurgam.* c **1859** E. DICKINSON *Poems* (1955) I. 56, I slew a worm the other day—A 'Savant' passing by Murmured 'Resurgam'—'Centipede'! 'Oh Lord—how frail are we'! **1929** *Oxf. Poetry* 39 Arise..resurgam..for another day.

resurge, *v.* Add: (Further examples.) Hence also **resu·rged, resu·rging** *ppl. adjs.*

1912 R. BROOKE *Let.* 23 Nov. (1968) 408, I shall be in Cambridge.., dispatching my resurged Dissertation. **1962** G. T. WARWICK in C. Cullingford *Brit. Caving* (ed. 2) v. 184 The clear water from Legalough, which..may resurge at Hanging Rocks. **1965** *New Statesman* 30 Apr. 690/3 That both bomber fleets resurged so mightily in 1944 was due.. to the rapid conversion of the Mustang into a long-range escort. **1976** K. ROYCE *Bustillo* vii. 87 He fought off the resurging need for a drink. **1980** *Times* 1 Nov. 15/3 Mr Manley..leads a rump opposition smaller than that from which Mr Seaga has resurged.

resurgence. Add: **2.** The fissure through which a stream re-emerges at the end of an underground part of its course; the re-emergence of such a stream. [This sense results from the adoption of F. *résurgence* (cf. A. Vandel 1920, in *Bull. de la Soc. zool. de France* XLV. 46).]

1954 W. D. THORNBURY *Princ. Geomorphol.* xiii. 327 The terms rise and resurgence have been applied to the re-appearance of surface waters which have been diverted to underground routes. **1963** D. W. & E. E. HUMPHRIES tr. *Termier's Erosion & Sedimentation* xiv. 303 Sometimes the surface water plunges down into the underground system by way of a sink hole... The river, however, retains its individuality and may return to the surface through a resurgence or spring. **1965** *Geogr. Jrnl.* CXXXI. 37 This subterranean stream maintains a constant flow during all weather conditions, and is joined by a small seepage resurgence and streamlet within a large bedding plane cave.. through which it flows to the main resurgence. **1971** J. N. JENNINGS *Karst* v. 74 A useful distinction can be made between exsurgences fed entirely by seepage waters from the karst and resurgences supplied by the sinking of surface streams.

resurgent, *sb.* and *a.* Add: **A.** *sb.* **2.** = *RESURGENCE 2. Also *attrib.*

1965 B. E. FREEMAN tr. *Vandel's Biospeleol.* i. 12 The outlets of large underground rivers are termed resurgents. **1972** HERAK & STRINGFIELD *Karst* xiii. 435 Resurgent caves..are associated with the uprising of water around the flanks of the Mendips.

B. *adj.* **2.** *Geol.* Applied to steam and other gases which after being absorbed by volcanic magma from groundwater and native rock are subsequently released into the atmosphere.

1908 R. A. DALY in *Amer. Jrnl. Sci.* CLXXVI. 48 These fluids were deposited and buried in the strata. They have been resurrected in their activity. They have 'risen again', both literally and figuratively; they may be called 'resurgent' emanations... All 'resurgent' emanations are of secondary origin. **1917** *Econ. Geol.* XII. 491 'Resurgent' was adapted by the writer..to signify the magmatic emanations of secondary origin, that is, those absorbed from country rock... Von Wolff..extends it to describe also certain pyroclastic deposits... Most authorities on the genesis of ore deposits appear to be opposed to the concept. **1932** F. F. GROUT *Petrogr. & Petrol.* iii. 212 Magmas may acquire gases by assimilating or dissolving..some wall or roof rock that contained gas or water. This is 'resurgent water'.

resurrect, *v.* Add: **1. c.** (Earlier and later examples.)

1852 B. YOUNG *Jrnl. of Discourses* (1854) I. 33/1 We shall not want to look upon our past actions; we shall say..I do not want that to be resurrected, but let it die in the grave. **1904** *Forum* July 132 The..offer made by General Reyes in behalf of the Bogota Government to resurrect and ratify the dead canal treaty. **1942** Z. N. HURSTON in A. Dundes *Mother Wit* (1973) 31/1 They resurrected a joke or two and worried it like a bone.

2. (Further *fig.* example.)

1969 G. M. BROWN *Orkney Tapestry* 52 The ribs of crag and tree Resurrecting with birds.

resurrected, *ppl. a.* Add: **1.** (Earlier example.)

1852 H. B. KIMBALL in B. Young *Jrnl. of Discourses* (1854) I. 355/2 You never will obtain your resurrected bodies, until you bring your spirits into subjection.

2. *Geomorphol.* Of a land form: exposed by erosion after having been covered by deposition.

1925 D. W. JOHNSON *New England–Acadian Shoreline* ii. 27 Resurrected peneplane shorelines appear to be fairly common along the coast of Acadia. **1954** W. D. THORNBURY *Princ. Geomorphol.* ii. 25 Most resurrected features are of local extent and constitute a small portion of the present-day topography. **1970** R. J. SMALL *Study of Landforms* iii. 106 One of the most important types of escarpment associated with faulting is the 'resurrected' or 'exhumed' fault-scarp or fault-line scarp.

resurre·cting, *vbl. sb.* [f. RESURRECT *v.* + -ING[1].] The action of the verb RESURRECT.

1906 P. LOWELL *Mars & its Canals* xii. 130 To call the lunar *maria* seas may..be..only a resurrecting in epitaph what was the truth in its day.

resurrection, *sb.* Add: **II. 5. a.** *resurrection appearance.*

1931 W. TEMPLE *Thoughts on Some Probl. of Day* i. 19 The love revealed in Jesus Christ in His use of divine power..in His Death on the Cross, in His Resurrection-Appearances only to those whose love He had already won. **1977** G. W. H. LAMPE *God as Spirit* vi. 151 Resurrection appearances and empty tomb cannot in themselves furnish first-hand evidence for God's vindication of Jesus.

c. resurrection plant: (*a*) (earlier example); (*b*) (earlier and later examples); (*c*) one of several other plants which stay quiescent during drought and revive when moistened.

(*a*) **1868** A. GRAY *Field, Forest, & Garden Bot.* 374 'Resurrection-Plant'..is a nest-like ball when dry, but when moist it unfolds. (*b*) **1857** G. W. JOHNSON *Cottage Gardeners' Dict.* (ed. 2) 34/2 When it [*sc.* the rose of Jericho] alights in water, or on damp ground, the branches relax and open out, as if its life was renewed; hence its name Resurrection Plant. **1951** *Dict. Gardening* (R. Hort. Soc.) IV. 1753/1 The Rose of Jericho, *Anastatica Hierochuntica*, is sometimes called a resurrection plant. (*c*) **1902** L. H. BAILEY *Cycl. Amer. Hort.* IV. 1507/1 Resurrection plants are great curiosities... The commonest ones are members of the mustard family and the club moss family. **1974** F. N. HOWES *Dict. Useful & Everyday Plants* 217 Resurrection plant.

Several pl[ant]s that appear dead after drought or a dry season but revive again w[ith] rain or moisture have acquired this name.

d. resurrection pie (*transf.* example).

1903 G. B. SHAW *Let.* 11 Sept. (1972) II. 370 We have both got the same job..to strike out a line for the advanced guard that is..neither Manchester resurrection-pie on the one hand nor Protectionist resurrection-pie on the other.

e. resurrection fern, one of several ferns that survive drought, esp. the grey polypody, *Polypodium polypodioides*, of the southern United States.

1909 *Cent. Dict.* Suppl. 467/1 Resurrection-fern..contracts during drouth but revives in moist seasons. **1924** J. A. THOMSON *Sci. Old & New* v. 30 The 'resurrection fern'..curls up its fronds in drought, and uncurls them when the rains return. **1963** B. COBB *Field Guide to Ferns* 56 Even though they wither in a drought they promptly become green again after getting moisture, and are therefore often referred to as Resurrection Ferns.

resuscitable, *a.* Delete *Obs. rare*—¹ and add further examples. Hence **resuscitabi·lity.**

1842 CARLYLE *Let.* 12 Jan. (1904) I. 250 It lies buried under two centuries of quackeries, scepticisms, owleries,—*not* resuscitable. **1908** *Jrnl. Exper. Med.* X. 373 The resuscitability of the animal in such an instance clearly depends on the perfection of the technique employed to resuscitate it. **1919** W. DE MORGAN *Old Madhouse* xvii. 274 Flinder's mill-pool yielded when dredged a resuscitable corpse. **1971** H. PACY *Road Accidents* iii. 73 As with resuscitability, 'life-and-death' decisions are required at the scene of accidents.

resuscitator. Add: **1.** (Further examples.)

1969 J. SECOR *Patient Care in Respiratory Probl.* iv. 165 The nurse's role as a resuscitator in the event of cardiopulmonary arrest has been an issue since the introduction of the procedure. **1977** *Lancet* 1 Jan. 9/1 It may well be that more intelligent parents are better resuscitators.

2. An apparatus used for resuscitation after asphyxia or arrest of respiration.

1929 *Jrnl. Amer. Med. Assoc.* 16 Nov. 1583/1 The E. and J. resuscitator is not a desirable apparatus for use by fire departments. **1938** *Surg., Gynecol. & Obstetr.* LXVI. 721/2 The ideal mechanical contraption for resuscitation is an apparatus which combines an inhalator and a resuscitator. **1943** *Science* 24 Dec. 548/1 The inventors of the pulmotor assumed, and the promoters of 'resuscitators' still claim, that by artificially forcing the lungs and chest through movements like those of breathing, a return of natural respiration should be induced. **1965** H. H. BENDIXEN et al. *Respiratory Care* xii. 122 Artificial ventilation is started by bag and mask. A self-inflating bag or a bellows resuscitator is suitable... A number of mechanical resuscitators are available.

ret, *sb.*¹ (Later examples.)

1949 *Publ. Amer. Dial. Soc.* xi. 62 *Ret, n.* and *v.t.*, a special form of *rot*. The process by which the stalk is prepared for separating the fibre—the rotting of the woody stalk. **1958** *New Biol.* XXVII. 15 In most countries the deseeded flax straw is now retted in warm water in concrete tanks. In the anaerobic ret largely practised in Belgium, the tanks are filled with air-dried straw which is then covered with water at a temperature of 18–27° C.

ret, *sb.*² (See quots.)

1874 HOTTEN *Slang Dict.* (new ed.) 268 *Ret*, an abbreviation of the word *reiteration*, used to denote the forme which, in a printing-office, backs or perfects paper already printed on one side. **1960** G. A. GLAISTER *Gloss. Bk.* 346/1 *Ret*, the second side of a sheet of paper.

ret., abbrev. of RETIRED *ppl. a.* 6. cf. *RETD., RET'D.

a **1912** W. T. ROGERS *Dict. Abbrev.* (1913) 166/1 *Ret.* (gen.), retired;—return. **1973** 'D. SHANNON' *No Holiday for Crime* v. 73 Lieutenant Colonel (ret.) Archer Pound. **1978** R. CONDON *Bandicoot* i. 9 Captain Colin Huntington, R.N. (ret.).

retable. (Later examples.)

1965 C. D. EBY *Siege of Alcázar* (1966) vi. 122 Arab jewels, ceramics, Flemish retables. **1979** *Dædalus* Summer 136 He remembered having noticed at the foot of the retable 'a piece of a host about the size of a small coin'.

retablo. (In Dict. s.v. RETABLE.) Add: (Further examples.) Also, a votive picture displayed in a church.

1906 R. FRY *Let.* 13 Sept. (1972) I. 269 They [*sc.* tombs] are..in the middle of the choir with a huge gold and blue *retablo* behind them. **1930** *Mexican Arts* (Amer. Fed. Arts) 43 A type of Mexican painting that deserves special attention..is the retablo, or votive picture offering. **1939** *Mexican Art & Life* Apr., 'Retablos' in Mexico are little stories of religious character told in pictures and always represent a happening in which great misfortune was threatened but averted through the opportune intervention of some saint invoked by the person in distress. **1950** G. BRENAN *Face of Spain* ii. 55 The whole of one end [of a church] was taken up by a vast gilt retablo, carved and scrolled and ornamented, in the centre of which..stood the miracle-working Virgin. **1965** C. CAUSLEY in *New Statesman* 12 Nov. 738/2 Christ hung down like a hawk-moth caterpillar,..As I walked through the glittering Precinct All the retablos burned like gold. **1976** *Arizona Republic* 16 May N-3/1 There is a companion exhibit of Mexican folk *retablos*, 70 images on tin plates as produced by various Mexican folk artists. **1980** *Times Lit. Suppl.* 9 May 535/3 Peeling, retablo-like posters of high-kicking chorines.

retail, *sb.*¹ (and *a.*). Add: **3.** (Earlier example.)

1851 D. JERROLD *Retired from Business* I. 6 And wholesales don't mix with retails? I think I see.

4. a. (Further examples.) Also *fig.*

1785 *Daily Universal Register* 1 Jan. 3/4 R. Croft, Taylor..at his wholesale and retail warehouse..is now selling ladies' Italian Coats. **1848** MILL *Pol. Econ.* I. III. i. 520 The influence of those causes is ultimately felt in the retail markets. **1898** *Kansas City* (Missouri) *Star* 18 Dec. 2/1 Hatters, garment workers, shoe workers, retail clerks and textile workers. **1926** A. E. TAYLOR *Plato* xv. 379 This enables us to define the sophist again as a retail exporter of the knowledge of goodness.., though we must add that he sometimes retails his merchandise in the home market. **1926** *Times* 6 May 3/3 Coal is not being moved by rail, but retail distribution was being carried on in London yesterday. **1940** G. CROWTHER *Outl. Money* iii. 90 The second value of money which is usually distinguished is the value of money in buying the goods and services which the ordinary family consumes... This second variety can be called the retail value of money, or the cost of living. **1957** *Practical Wireless* XXXIII. 517/2 The British Radio Equipment Manufacturers' Association,..in their monthly retail survey. **1962** *Listener* 13 Sept. 376/2 Every famous jazz composer or retail-chain owner. **1967** G. WILLS in Wills & Yearsley *Handbk. Managem. Technol.* x. 194 *Retail audit*,..continuous research with a panel of retailers to study inventory levels and sales of products over the counter. **1970** *New Society* 5 Mar. 383/3 Retail margins (the difference between the price paid by the shopkeeper and the price paid by the consumer) had previously been gradually rising. **1973** *Times* 25 Apr. 33/5 The brief includes a supermarket of about 40,000 sq ft., other retail units, a night club. **1976** *Daily Tel.* 20 July 1/4 Retail trade showed a slight recovery last month. **1979** *Oil Majors in 1978* (Shell Internat. Petroleum Co.) 7 Gulf suffered reduced sales in Canada but increased them in Europe, partly owing to its acquisition of Mobil's retail outlets in Switzerland.

d. *Comb.*, as **retail price index**, an index of the variation in the prices of retail goods (see *INDEX *sb.* 9 e); **retail price maintenance** = *resale price maintenance* s.v. *RESALE *sb.* 2.

1924 *University Jrnl. Business* June 263 In the construction of retail price and of cost-of-living indexes..significant developments have occurred. **1935** J. H. COVER *Retail Price Behavior* 86 Though it appears that the median may be more satisfactory for a retail price index, the mean is more logical for a cost-of-living index. **1974** *Times* 22 Mar. 17/3 Even by January, the retail price index had climbed half way to that seven per cent trigger point. **1938** S. CHASE *Tyranny of Words* xiv. 175 The new laws for retail price maintenance. **1966** A. BATTERSBY *Math. in Managem.* ix. 232 The appeal to elasticity..has given rise to the fierce arguments about Retail Price Maintenance and the dilemma of those supporters of a competitive economy who attempt to eliminate the effects of free competition.

retailed, *ppl. a.* (Later example.)

1811 JANE AUSTEN *Sense & Sens.* III. xi. 225 It was neither in Elinor's power, nor in her wish, to rouse such feelings in another, by her retailed explanation, as had at first been called forth in herself.

retailing, *vbl. sb.* (Later example.)

1951 in M. MCLUHAN *Mech. Bride* (1967) 36 The specifications required to reach the goals now in sight for businesses of every description—manufacturing, distributing, retailing, servicing!

retain, *v.* Add: **I. 2. b.** (Later example.) *retain-and-transfer* attrib. phr., in *Association Football* (see quot. 1965).

1938 C. E. SUTCLIFFE et al. *Story of Football League* xiii. 120 A result which had completely vindicated the retain and transfer system and declared it to be legal. **1965** *Listener* 1 July 17/1 A 'retain and transfer' system... A player employed by a club could be 'retained' after the expiration of his contract of employment. No other club was then allowed to employ him, although his own club had no obligation to re-employ him. He could also be placed on a 'transfer' list, which signified that his club was willing to transfer him for a specified fee, only a small portion of which went to the player himself. **1974** *Scholarly Publishing* V. 235 The Times New Roman Type..was unacceptable, and consultants had to be retained to redesign it.

4. *absol.* (Later examples.)

1910 E. B. TITCHENER *Textbk. Psychol.* II. 405 The quick learner appears to retain as well as the slow. **1932** *New Yorker* 23 July 17/3 Prior to 1882, even a boy who didn't retain very well could make a kite out of two or three sticks.

retained, *ppl. a.* Add: **2.** (Later examples.) *retained object*, an object of a passive verb; *retained profit* (see quot. 1974).

1934 WEBSTER, Retained object. **1941** FOERSTER & STEADMAN *Writing & Thinking* (rev. ed.) xvi. 153 A verb in the passive voice is transitive only if it has a retained object. **1961** R. B. LONG *Sentence & its Parts* 504 Normal complements of passive-verb-form predicators are sometimes called 'retained objects'. An example is the *time* of *we weren't given time*. **1973** *Country Life* 29 Nov. (Suppl.) 9 (Advt.), Wanted for a retained client A period residence... Price is immaterial. **1974** *Terminol. Managem. & Financial Accountancy* (Inst. Cost and Managem. Accountants) 68 *Retained profits*, profits retained in the business, and not distributed to the owners/shareholders. **1977** *Cleethorpes News* 6 May 32/6 There are unlikely to be any surprises in Grimsby Town's retained list, which is due out today.

retainer¹. Add: **3. a.** (Earlier *transf.* example.)

1778 S. FOOTE *Trip to Calais* III. 78 As you gave me a handsome retainer, I have been in court and open'd the cause.

b. (Further examples.) Also in extended uses. Cf. *retaining fee* s.v. RETAINING *ppl. a.* 2.

1975 O. SELA *Bengali Inheritance* vi. 46 'What are you saying? That we should all..take bribes?' 'We all do,' Chan said. 'We're all on retainers.' The retainer was the monthly share out, the market price for overlooking petty crimes [among Hong Kong police]. **1977** *Guardian* 13 Jan. 20/3 Richards has signed a contract with a Brisbane radio station which gives him a retainer. **1978** S. BRILL *Teamsters* ix. 327 Milano is most probably getting similar retainers from several Teamster locals. **1978** *Lancashire Life* Nov. 76/2 The Clitheroe professional, Peter Geddes, for whom she works as assistant, earning a small retainer in exchange for free lessons, wise advice and a mixture of encouragement and constructive criticism. **1978** M. PUZO *Fools Die* xxvii. 310 Houlinan was Ugo Kellino's personal PR rep with a retainer of fifty grand a year.

retainer². Add: **1. b.** *Dentistry.* A structure cemented to a tooth and connected to a bridge to hold it in place.

1887 S. H. GUILFORD in W. F. Litch *Amer. Syst. Dentistry* II. II. 323 These little fixtures can be used as retainers with perfect success and to the exclusion of a more bulky plate. **1956, 1974** [see *PONTIC *a.*² B]. **1976** TORRES & EHRLICH *Mod. Dental Assisting* xxvi. 797/1 The components of fixed bridgework are the pontics, the retainers and the connectors.

retake (rī·-), *sb.* [f. the vb.] **1. a.** The action of filming a scene, person, or object again; the picture or the scene obtained thus. Also *attrib.*

1918 H. CROY *How Motion Pictures are Made* v. 126 Directly on finishing the scene it is filmed again, the second exposure being called a 'retake'. **1919** H. L. WILSON *Ma Pettengill* ii. 67 Only one little retake, where she's happy over her boy's promotion in the factory. **1930** [see *CAN *sb.*¹ 3 c]. **1938** 'E. QUEEN' *Four of Hearts* iv. 52 Corsi's the most finicky retake artist in pictures. **1941** G. MARX *Let.* 23 June (1967) 27 Here I am on Stage 18 waiting to shoot some retakes. **1960** *Guardian* 12 Dec. 6/2 There's so much to go wrong, the cameras jamming, the lens sticking, and no re-takes [in television]. **1972** D. FRANCIS *Smokescreen* i. 9, I couldn't stand many more retakes of Scene 623... We had retaken it six times.

b. The action of recording music, etc., again.

1962 A. NISBETT *Technique Sound Studio* vi. 115 Music retakes should be recorded as soon as possible after the original. **1963** V. GIELGUD in *Times* 22 Apr. 16/7 A certain perfectionism is possible in tape recording, but I feel that something is wrong if I personally have to go back and do retakes. **1973** 'J. MARKS' *Mick Jagger* (1974) 88 They suggested the use of their own studios for a retake of the same tune.

c. *fig.*

1937 *Sun* (Baltimore) 14 May 21/2 In motion-picture parlance, the Preakness at Pimlico Saturday will be a retake of the Kentucky Derby. **1959** *Punch* 20 May 686/2 She took a quick retake at the title, and..tried to stuff it..inside her blouse.

2. *gen.* The action of taking something a second time.

1939 *Sun* (Baltimore) 17 Feb. 1/8 The purpose of repeating the testimony was to get a record which is to be made public... Senator Sheppard..announced, however, that the re-take of testimony was 'practically concluded'. **1977** C. DEXTER *Silent World N. Quinn* vi. 56 The morning..had been fixed for the 'retake' of the Ordinary-level English Language papers. **1977** *Irish Press* 29 Sept. 18/6 McGhee took the spot-kick, but the 'keeper saved his shot, only to see the referee order a retake because the 'keeper had moved before the ball was kicked.

retake, *v.* Add: **1.** (Later examples in specialized senses.) Cf. *RETAKE *sb.*

1929 H. L. WITWER *Yes Man's Land* xii. 304 This here's no quickie and I can't retake all that stuff and do business. **1972** [see *RETAKE *sb.* 1 a]. **1973** 'D. HALLIDAY' *Dolly & Starry Bird* vi. 82 You have to retake all those pictures this morning. **1977** C. DEXTER *Silent World N. Quinn* vii. 67 She's re-taking a few O-levels.

4. *absol.* To take a second time, take over again.

1962 A. NISBETT *Technique Sound Studio* vi. 115 Discreetly discourage phrases such as 'as I've just said', and retake if they are not clearly editable. **1977** *Horse & Hound* 14 Jan. 43/2 (Advt.), Next intensive one month or week's preparation course for A1 (suitable for those retaking) in April.

retaliant (rĭtæ·liănt), *a. rare.* [ad. late L. *retāliānt-em*, pr. pple. of *retāliāre* to retaliate.] Retaliative.

1925 R. BRIDGES *S.P.E. Tract* XXI. 13 The universal attitude of Englishmen..naturally enough provoked a similar retaliant feeling in America.

retaliator. (Earlier U.S. and later examples.)

1788 W. GORDON *Hist. Independence U.S.A.* IV. 287 A set of vindictive rebels, known by the designation of *Monmouth retaliators*. **1946** G. B. SHAW *Geneva* 25 Women in every generation, look like vindictive retaliators, pugnacious sportsmen, and devout believers.

retama² (rĕtā·mă). Also **ratama.** [Amer. Sp. *retama*.] = *PALO VERDE. Also *attrib.*

1891 J. M. COULTER *Bot. W. Texas* I. 94 *P[arkinsonia] aculeata*..[is] often cultivated for ornament and known as 'retama'. **1903** 'O. HENRY' in *Ainslee's* Dec. 139/2 One December in the Frio country there was a ratama tree in full bloom. **1909** B. MACKENSE *Trees & Shrubs San Antonio* 25 The retama is very elegant and is often planted for ornament. **1926** 'O. HENRY' in *Argosy* Sept. 63/2 How delicious was that morning breeze..fresh and sweet with the breath of the yellow ratama blooms! **1949** *Chicago Tribune* 20 Feb. 30/3 Cedar and mesquite alone are costing Texas ranchers 115 million dollars a year. Add the sage and cactus,..blackjack oak, retama and prickly pear and the toll is terrific.

retard, *sb.* Add: **1.** (Further example.)
1971 *Times* 14 Apr. 14/3 The Government, somewhat in retard of the fact, enacted the..eugenic protection law in 1949.

3. A device in a motor vehicle for retarding the ignition spark.
1932 *Motoring Encycl.* 10/3 The Bosch automatic advance and retard (Fig. 3) is a simple design for a stationary armature type of magneto. **1977** *Hot Car* Oct. 75/3 The old one is capped off still retaining the advance retard.

4. *U.S. slang.* A mentally retarded person.
1970 *Time* 23 Mar. 49 There are..heroin addicts, Air Force and CIA mental retards and Broadway Indians doing a Broadway Snake Dance. **1971** *New Yorker* 16 Jan. 76 The younger son, self-described as 'a hard-core retard', dreams of escaping to the wilds of Oregon to gambol with the bears and squirrels. **1979** *Observer* 21 Oct. 53/5 These are men who have been out of England for years on end... Social retards, they can still hold onto their given obsolete ideas and prejudices about women because of their geographical isolation, and their marooned intellects.

retardance. Delete *Obs. rare* and add: **2.** The action of retarding; also = *RETARDANCY; usu. in *Comb.* with a preceding sb., as *fire, flame retardance.*
1948 *Industr. & Engin. Chem.* Mar. 400/1 Primary emphasis in fire retardance has been directed to coatings or impregnants which will protect a combustible substrate. **1954** *Adv. Chem. Series* IX. 1 Ordinary paints..possess a fair amount of fire retardance..during the first stages of a fire. **1971** *Nature* 4 June 335/1 The introductory chapter includes..smaller sections on the mechanisms of flame retardance..and effective concentrations of retardants.

retardancy (rĭtā·ɹdănsi.) [f. as prec. + -ANCY.] The capability to retard; usu. used in *Comb.* with a preceding sb., as *fire, flame retardancy.*
1947 R. W. LITTLE *Flameproofing Textile Fabrics* v. 172 The dehydration catalysis mechanism of flame retardancy. **1973** KURYLA & PAPA (*title*) Flame retardancy of polymeric materials. *Ibid.* iii. 253 These compounds impart dimensional stability, abrasion resistance, water resistance, and flame retardancy to the backcoated fabric. **1973** *Sci. Amer.* Apr. 13/2 (Advt.), Are you trying to improve fire retardancy of materials or finished products?

retardant, *a.* Delete *rare* and add: Now usu. in *Comb.* with a preceding sb., as **fire-*, **flame-retardant* adjs. (see also RETARDENT *a.*). (Further examples.)
1915 [see *fire-retardant* adj. s.v. *FIRE *sb.* B. 2]. **1947, 1966** [see *flame-retardant* adj. s.v. *FLAME *sb.* 10]. **1971** *Financial Mail* (Johannesburg) 26 Feb. 685/3 Flame-retardant paints. **1973** *Harrod's Xmas Catal.* 59/2 Christmas tree realistically reproduced. Fire retardant. **1976** *Horse & Hound* 3 Dec. 54/1 (Advt.), This specially shaped bed filled with Fire Retardant polystyrene beads takes the ache out of a tired wet dog.

B. *sb.* A substance that reduces or inhibits some phenomenon (usu. specified by a preceding sb., as in prec. sense).
1952 [see *fire-retardant* sb. s.v. *FIRE *sb.* B. 2]. **1959** *New Scientist* 8 Oct. 633/1 By the combined effects of daylength control and a growth retardant, the growth habit of petunia plants can be modified so that the plants flower earlier than usual yet remain compact and bushy. **1971** 'R. MACDONALD' *Underground Man* v. 31 The plane was lost in the smoke.. then climbed out trailing a pastel red cloud of fire retardant. **1975** *Nature* 3 July 4/3 Peel roughness could be controlled by spraying Alar (a growth retardant) on the citrus. **1976** *Shell in Industr. Chemicals* 8 Flame retardants for polyurethane foams.

‖**retardataire** (rətardatęr'), *sb.* and *a.* Chiefly *Art.* [Fr., lit. '(one who is) late in arriving, acting, etc.'.] **A.** *sb.* A work of art executed in the style of an earlier period. **B.** *adj.* Behind the times; characterized by the style of an earlier period.
1903 R. FRY *Let.* 29 June (1972) I. 210, I have assumed that the man whom you called in your notes Lorenzo Bicci is meant for Bicci di Lorenzo. Lorenzo Bicci is much too early, b. 1333 (I'm sure), whereas Bicci di Lorenzo, d. 1452, would just suit this *retardataire.* I am speaking of the Quattrocento *Madonna* with two angels kneeling beneath. **1958** H.-R. HITCHCOCK *Archit.: 19th & 20th Cent.* viii. 148 Only in the design of public monuments..did a pompous and somewhat retardataire eclecticism rule. **1964** *Listener* 19 Mar. 488/2 The greatest Andrea [del Sarto] is *retardataire,* an artist who would have been more at home in the conditions of a quarter of a century earlier. **1966** *Ibid.* 1 Dec. 813/3 English art had always been retardataire. **1973** J. B. TRAPP *Medieval Eng. Lit.* 7 In learning, too, England [by the end of the fifteenth century] was retardataire. **1977** *Times Lit. Suppl.* 14 Jan. 30/4 The *retardataire* appearance of much colonial architecture derives from the poor, often secondhand knowledge of contemporary architectural practice as well as from a conservatism in patrons' tastes.

retardate (rĭtā·ɹdēɪt), *sb.* [ad. L. *retardātus,* pa. pple. of *retardāre* to RETARD.] One who is mentally or educationally retarded; also *attrib.*
1956 *Amer. Jrnl. Mental Deficiency* Jan. 531/1 That promotions to supervisory capacity are within reach of some retardates is demonstrated on Table VI. **1963** N. R. ELLIS *Handbk. Mental Deficiency* v. 159 (*heading*) The role of attention in retardate discrimination learning. *Ibid.* xxi. 669 The achievement of regular-class and special-class retardates in single school systems. **1975** *New Society* 10 July 91/2 Perhaps they would care to visit this hostel for adult retardates..and see the emotionally deviant, socially inadequate, environmentally retarded adolescent. **1976** *Word 1971* XXVII. 521 One might speculate about what skills a reading retardate lacks. **1980** *Brit. Med. Jrnl.* 29 Mar. 930/2 The mentally deficient (call them mentally subnormal, retarded or 'retardates', if you must) have legitimate rights.

retardation. Add: **3. b.** (Earlier example.)
1834 [see *A TEMPO].

4. *Psychol.* Educational progress which is slower than average for the age-group; also, mental backwardness or subnormality in an adult. Cf. *RETARDED *ppl. a.* 1 b.
1907 *Psychol. Clinic* I. 98 The failure of many pupils to be promoted regularly from grade to grade—retardation—has been a subject for..serious consideration. **1914** W. B. DRUMMOND tr. *Binet & Simon's Mentally Defective Children* ii. 16 According to a convention..we regard as defective in intelligence a child who shows a retardation of three years, when he himself is nine years of age or more. **1919** L. M. TERMAN *Measurement of Intelligence* i. 4 We can at least prevent the kind of retardation which involves failure and the repetition of a school grade. **1937** C. L. BURT *Backward Child* iv. 78 Thus, at the age of 10, the borderline for backwardness is a retardation of 1½ years (not, as is so commonly stated, of 2 years), or, in terms of the ratio, 15 per cent. **1963** N. R. ELLIS *Handbk. Mental Deficiency* xxi. 678 Skill areas listed from most to least retardation were reading, arithmetic, writing, and spelling. **1970** HINSIE & CAMPBELL *Psychiatric Dict.* (ed. 4) 666/1 Fashions in labeling this group change almost from year to year; in the 1960's, mental retardation was the favorite appellation, and justifiably so in that it does not imply that inheritance or constitutional defects are always the cause of mental retardation. **1975** BALTHAZAR & STEVENS *Emotionally Disturbed, Mentally Retarded* i. 3 The problems imposed by mental retardation and adaptive behavior.

retarded, *ppl. a.* Add: **1. b.** *Psychol.* Orig., applied to children whose mental or educational progress lags behind that of their contemporaries to a significant degree; later extended to anyone with a measured intelligence less than some value that is itself below the average, esp. when attributed to impaired learning or maturation in childhood and youth. Hence *ellipt.* as *sb.*
1895 G. E. SHUTTLEWORTH *Mentally-Deficient Children* ii. 19 Such children are also described as 'backward', or of 'retarded mental development'—terms corresponding to the 'Enfants arriérés' of French writers..and the 'Tardivi' of the Italians. **1910** J. D. HEILMAN (*title*) A clinical study of one thousand retarded children in the public schools of Camden, New Jersey. **1919** L. M. TERMAN *Measurement of Intelligence* i. 24 (*heading*) The intelligence of retarded children usually overestimated. **1937** C. L. BURT *Backward Child* iv. 79 In the following pages, the word 'retarded' will be used to mean any child whose educational ratio falls below 85 per cent. **1951** H. LOEWY *Retarded Child* (rev. ed.) i. 14 Retarded children can be put into two broad classifications from the teaching point of view: (1) The child with a mental defect. (2) The mentally defective child. **1956** H. MICHAL-SMITH *Mentally Retarded Patient* p. vii, The mentally retarded of all ages are subject to illness as are other people. **1960** TANSLEY & GULLIFORD *Educ. Slow Learning Children* ii. 44 If his reading age is two years below his mental age he is considered retarded and special efforts must be made to get him 'working to capacity'. **1967** BRUSSEL & CANTZLAAR *Chambers's Dict. Psychiatry* 144 A mentally retarded person is one whose intelligence quotient..is below 70. **1973** LA CRUZ & LAVECK (*title*) Human sexuality and the mentally retarded. **1975** BALTHAZAR & STEVENS *Emotionally Disturbed, Mentally Retarded* vi. 87 Critical statements of the value of psychotherapy for the retarded. **1979** *Books & Bookmen* Jan. 43/1 Of those who could be given reliable intelligence tests, thirty-two per cent were defective, with an IQ below fifty, and thirteen per cent were retarded, with an IQ between fifty and seventy. Fifty-five per cent were subnormal or normal, ie, with IQs above seventy.

2. *Physics.* Applied to parameters of an electromagnetic radiation field in which allowance is made for the finite speed of propagation of the radiation, so that the potential due to a distant source is expressed in terms of the state of the source at some time in the past.
1920 *Physical Rev.* XV. 312 (*heading*) Note on the retarded potentials. **1929** MASON & WEAVER *Electromagn. Field* iv. 283, {ρ}, the so-called 'retarded value' of ρ, is given by $\{\rho\} = \rho(x, y, z, t-r/c)$. **1941** C. A. COULSON *Waves* viii. 141 We call $t-r/c$ the retarded time. **1962** CORSON & LORRAIN *Introd. Electromagn. Fields* xiv. 493 The retarded position [z] is less than z by a factor of $1/\{1+(v/c)\}$. **1974** *Encycl. Brit. Macropædia* VI. 660/2 The exact potentials corresponding to a point charge..are not obtained by substituting the total charge for the volume integral indicated in the retarded potentials. The problem arises because of the finite velocity of field propagation, so that the integral of the retarded charge density over space is not in general equal to the total charge. **1975** D. M. COOK *Theory Electromagn. Field* xiv. 402 A potential of this form is referred to as a retarded potential because the potential at time t is determined by the state of the charge at the so-called retarded time t'.

retardee·. *U.S.* [f. RETARD *v.* + -EE.] A mentally retarded person.
1971 *Time* 5 Apr. 38 Almost half are geriatrics cases or mental retardees who receive only custodial care. **1973** *Rehabilitation* Jan.–Mar. 46/2 The Agency was established.. to market..products made by the mentally retarded and thus demonstrate employment possibilities of retardees. **1977** *Monitor* (McAllen, Texas) 28 June 8A/1 A one-day orientation on mental retardation is scheduled Thursday... Parents of retardees and others interested also are invited.

retarder. Add: **a.** (Further examples.)
1971 P. GRESSWELL *Environment* 264 Weed-killers or growth retarders are needed that keep rank growth in check without eliminating all wild flowers. **1980** *Jrnl. R. Soc. Arts* Mar. 175/1 We will find ourselves sooner or later seeking..to break through that asymptote determined by nature's built-in retarders.

b. A substance which slows down a reaction or process.
1878 [in Dict.]. **1946** *Sun* (Baltimore) 7 Oct. 2/5 The meat situation may prolong the housing problem because plaster cannot be made without 'retarder', which is obtained from horn and hoof meal. **1967** MARGERISON & EAST *Introd. Polymer Chem.* iv. 195 Those substances which affect the rate of the polymerization are termed inhibitors or retarders according to whether the rate is reduced to zero or to a finite value. **1974** *Encycl. Brit. Macropædia* IV. 1076/1 The characteristics of concrete often can be improved by including admixtures in the concrete mix. In addition to set-accelerators..there are set-retarders (usually of a sugar base) that are less commonly required.

c. (See quot. 1898.)
1898 W. S. HUTTON *Steam-Boiler Constr.* (ed. 3) vi. 455 The smoke-tubes of multitubular boilers are sometimes fitted with either retarders or radiators, with the object of increasing the efficiency of the heating-surface. A retarder usually consists of a flat strip of sheet-metal twisted spirally, to compel the fuel-gases to travel through the tubes in a spiral-form. **1902** *Rep. Admiralty Comm. Naval Boilers* § 29. 15 The Committee..think it right to state that retarders will be found in many cases to render existing cylindrical boilers more efficient and economical than they are at present. **1903** *Sci. Amer. Suppl.* 24 Jan. 22625/1 The cylindrical boilers should be fitted with retarders in the tubes. **1953** J. N. WILLIAMS *Boiler House Practice* vii. 152 Refractory cores or retarders were employed but with only partial success as the refractory would not stand up to the temperatures which approximated to those of theoretical combustion.

d. *Railways.* An arrangement of rails placed inside and parallel to the running rails in a shunting yard which may be moved sideways so as to act as a brake on the flanges of wagon wheels.
1937 W. G. RAYMOND *Elem. Railroad Engin.* (ed. 5) xiv. 186 The car retarder is a device to control the speed of a moving freight car. **1966** G. F. ALLEN *B.R. after Beeching* viii. 248 Further B.R. applications of this ingenious device may be confined to the outer ends of reception sidings in existing yards already equipped with electronically-controlled, clamp-type retarders, to improve the speed control of shunted wagons after they have left the hump area. **1969** H. R. BROADBENT *Introd. Railway Braking* ii. 11 The retarders used in marshalling yards do not come under the heading of train-operated brakes.

retarding, *ppl. a.* Add: *retarding field, potential.*
1947 F. G. SPREADBURY *Electronics* xviii. 591 In order that no current shall flow it is..necessary to apply a retarding potential, i.e. the anode must be negative with respect to the cathode. **1950** *Jrnl. Physical Soc. Japan* V. 339/1 The assumption that electrons could enter the retarding field (grid-plate space) only a single time. **1953** *Ibid.* VIII. 182 The plate-current distribution in a retarding-field tube of concentric structure. **1963** B. FOZARD *Instrumentation Nucl. Reactors* xi. 138 Such a circuit is provided by a thermionic diode working under what are known as retarding field conditions.

retardive, *a.* (Later example.)
1968 G. JONES *Hist. Vikings* II. i. 66 The retardive effect of high latitude, long winters, severing distance, and a barriered landscape upon the development of the northern kingdoms was considerable.

retd., ret'd, abbrevs. of RETIRED *ppl. a.* 6. Cf. *RET.
1942 PARTRIDGE *Dict. Abbrev.* 83/1 *Ret.*, retired. *Retd.*, returned. (2) A variant of *ret.* **1975** N. LUARD *Travelling Horseman* i. 3 Colonel Stephen Wilmot, US Army (Ret'd), glanced at his watch.

rete. 1. a. Delete † *Obs.* and add later examples.
1905 *Sci. Amer.* 12 Aug. 120/3 Above the planisphere lies the neatly cut out and decorated 'rete' carrying upon its circular interior the constellations of the ecliptic. **1957** *Encycl. Brit.* II. 575/1 Having noted the sun's position for the day in the zodiac circle, rotate the *rete* until the sun's position coincides with a circle on the plate corresponding to the observed altitude. **1974** *Sci. Amer.* May 8/2 This modern descendant of the astrolabe comes packed in a leatherette case with a rete, nine climates, a planet-plotting device and instructions.

2. a. (Further examples.) Also *spec.* in *Zool.*, such a network that supplies the swim bladder of many fishes and releases gas from the circulation for secretion into the bladder so as to increase buoyancy. Also *rete* simply.
1896 [see *red body* s.v. RED *a.* 19 a]. **1897, 1949** [see *GLOMUS 2]. **1961** *Jrnl. Gen. Physiol.* XLIV. 539 The gas gland consists of a cellular layer interposed between the gas gland capillaries emanating from the rete and the lumen of the swim-bladder. **1962** K. F. LAGLER *Ichthyology* viii. 254 In the eel..over 100,000 arterioles and a slightly smaller number of venules give the rete a total surface of over 2 square meters where blood vessels are opposed to one another. **1973** *Sci. Amer.* Feb. 39/3 The tiny vessels intermingle to form slabs of vascular tissue, the *retia,* that lie close to the upper and lower surfaces of the dark muscle...

These *retia* are the heat exchangers that ensure the warmth of the dark muscle. **1974** [see *red gland* s.v. *RED *a.* 19 a].

c. In full *rete testis.* A network of vessels through which spermatozoa pass before leaving the testicle for the epididymis.

1786 W. CRUICKSHANK *Anat. Absorbing Vessels Human Body* II. 140 The absorbents which arise out of the rete testis are exceedingly large. **1821** J. WILSON *Lect. Struct. & Physiol. Male Urinary & Genital Organs* iv. 96 Each of the vessels forming the rete testis sends off a tube, which leaves the body of the testicle and enters the epididymis singly. **1849–52** R. B. TODD *Cycl. Anat. & Physiol.* IV. 977/2 The canals of the rete. **1906** *Practitioner* Nov. 663 Most of these recorded cases [of testicular tumour]..are characterised by *complexity* of growth; and this is explained, I believe, as regards my own, by its origin, which I have traced to the tubules of the rete testis. **1968** PASSMORE & ROBSON *Compan. Med. Stud.* I. xxxvii. 22/1 Each seminiferous tubule is highly coiled... They are looped in such a way that both ends join a series of about thirty short, so-called straight tubules which converge on a network of vessels lying in the mediastinum, the rete testis.

rete·ller. [f. RETELL *v.* + -ER[1].] One who tells or relates anew.

1929 *Cambr. Med. Hist.* VI. xxv. 827 It must be admitted that Chrétien himself does not claim to be an inventor, but rather a re-teller of tales.

retentate (rĭte·ntēit). [f. L. *retent-iō* a holding back (cf. RETENTION) + *-ate*, as in *distillate, filtrate*, etc.] That which fails to pass through a semi-permeable membrane, and so is retained on dialysis.

1959 TURNER & FEINBERG in *Nature* 10 Oct. 1139/1 We propose the term 'retentate' to designate those substances which are retained by semipermeable membranes in the course of dialysis. **1974** *Ibid.* 8 Nov. 176/1 The haemagglutinating activity in galactose..was found in the retentate and could be concentrated quantitatively and washed free of monosaccharide by ultrafiltration. **1977** *Ibid.* 6 Jan. 92/2 Retained molecules (the retentate) remain in the original sample container. Both the retentate and the filtrate fractions can be recovered.

retention. Add: **2. a.** Also *Psychol.*, the ability to retain specific previously learned mental, perceptual, or motor tasks; also *attrib.*, esp. as *retention curve*, the curve on a graph which shows the amount of learning retained over a period of time.

1902 J. M. BALDWIN *Dict. Philos. & Psychol.* II. 470/2 The first [sound] must leave behind it some after-effect which so modifies the second as to determine the judgment. This may also be called retention. **1923** C. S. SPEARMAN *Nature of Intelligence* xix. 304 Those who would trace memory back to retention have more particularly tried to depict it in the guise of associative reproduction. **1940** R. S. WOODWORTH *Psychol.* (ed. 12) x. 337 The retention curve, or 'curve of forgetting', was first obtained by the relearning method... The curve shows a gradual loss of retention with the lapse of time. **1949** POSTMAN & EGAN *Exper. Psychol.* xvi. 381 (*caption*) Retention curve showing the reminiscence phenomenon. **1952** MCGEOCH & IRION *Psychol. Human Learning* (ed. 2) x. 359 In general, the retention of perceptual-motor habits is quite high. **1963** L. J. CRONBACH *Educ. Psychol.* (ed. 2) xi. 350 On a retention test several weeks later they [*sc.* pupils] did better than they had done at the end of the instruction. **1975** G. H. BOWER in W. K. Estes *Handbk. Learning & Cognitive Processes* I. ii. 75 The 'fluctuation' mood of contextual alterations and their effect on retention.

b. (Later example.) Also *attrib.* as *retention rate.*

1972 *N.Y. Times* 3 Nov. 18/4 The retention rates for the addicts referred to the therapeutic communities—which typically hold less than 25 per cent of their patients—are high. **1974** *Amer. Jrnl. Epidemiol.* C. 104/2 In each cohort, the retention rate is similar for the ambulatory patients and for the patients inducted on an inpatient basis. **1977** D. LOURIA in M. M. Glatt *Drug Dependence* iv. 116 Initial efforts were directed to relating retention in a given treatment modality to nine demographic characteristics. *Ibid.*, Retention rates in the six programs studied ranged from over 60 to less than 5 per cent.

c. In Phenomenology, the continued consciousness of or existence in the present of a previous act or event. Cf. *PROTENSION 3 b.

1931 W. R. B. GIBSON tr. *Husserl's Ideas* III. ii. 220 The absolute right of immanent retention, in respect of that in it of which we are conscious as 'still' living and having 'just' happened. **1943** M. FARBER *Found. Phenomenology* xvi. 516 As long as the retention lasts the tone has its own time, it is the same, its duration is the same. **1962** MACQUARRIE & ROBINSON tr. *Heidegger's Being & Time* II. iv. 411 Circumspective making present, however,..is grounded in a *retention* of that context of equipment with which Dasein concerns itself in *awaiting* a possibility. **1966** A. GURWITSCH *Stud. Phenomenol. & Psychol.* vii. 137 The very reality of conscious life, when an act is an enduring one, is a phase of present actuality most intimately connected with a whole continuity of phases retained (in retentions of various degrees). **1974** R. SOKOLOWSKI *Husserlian Meditations* v. 134 The primitive elapsing of the now-consciousness into retention is an 'event' outside time.

3. d. Something that is kept back or retained.

1922 *Daily Mail* 15 Dec. 11 Major Doyle both rode and trained Ilderton, who looked a cheap retention at 100 gs. **1962** *Rep. Comm. Broadcasting 1960* 153 in *Parl. Papers 1961–2* (Cmnd. 1753) IX. 259 Gross licence revenue... Deduct retentions. **1970** P. OLIVER *Savannah Syncopators* 63 There is a frequently expressed opinion that the use of the 'answering' guitar in some blues traditions is a retention from the custom of leader-and-chorus singing.

4. d. (Further example.)

c **1735** *Man of Manners* (ed. 2) 30 We ought to be plain and modest in our Discourse, so as he may take Notice of our Retention.

6. retention money (see quots.).

1911 W. THOMSON *Dict. Banking* 452/2 *Retention money*, money which is retained for a certain time after completion of a contract; e.g. if a contract has been made for £5,000 it may be agreed that 10 per cent. of the money due to the contractor shall be retained till, say, six or twelve months after the completion of the contract. If an assignment of retention money is given as security, notice of the assignment must be given to, and an acknowledgment received from, the person who is liable to pay the money to the contractor. **1974** *Terminol. Managem. & Financial Accountancy* (Inst. Cost and Managem. Accountants) 17 *Retention money*, a sum of money representing an agreed proportion of a price for goods supplied or work completed, such proportion being withheld by the purchaser or contractee for an agreed period of time as security against failure by the supplier or contractor to fulfil his obligations under the terms of the contract.

retentional, *a.* [f. RETENTION + -AL.] Of or pertaining to retention.

1931 [see *PROTENSION 3 b.] **1938** *Mind* XLVII. 517 But even on the 'retentional' interpretation, I am not sure that the doctrine is supported by the introspectible facts. **1966** A. GURWITSCH *Phenomenol. & Psychol.* xii. 305 The source and origin of these modifications is the 'strict present'; the modifications arise from the 'actual now' and are conveyed to the retentional phases.

retentionist. (In Dict. s.v. RETENTION.) Add: **2.** One who advocates the retention of capital (or occas. of corporal) punishment. Used also *attrib.*, esp. of countries which have retained capital punishment.

1956 [see *ABOLITIONIST c]. **1957** *Landfall* (N.Z.) Sept. 248 Those and only those who according to the Retentionists ought to be hanged. **1961** *Spectator* 7 Apr. 464 Retentionists do not..in fact base their desire to retain hanging on a belief that hanging reduces the number of murders. **1972** *Times* 28 Sept. 16/3 Retentionists [of caning] and agnostics can complain that the case for retention is made perfunctorily.

retentiveness. Add: **b.** *Physics.* The capability of retaining a residual magnetic field when a magnetizing field has been removed.

1886 J. HOPKINSON in *Phil. Trans. R. Soc.* CLXXVI. 460 The ordinate OB is what is generally meant by the residual induction after great magnetising force, or the 'retentiveness'. **1902** *Encycl. Brit.* XXX. 430/2 The ratio of the residual magnetization to its previous maximum value measures the retentiveness of the metal. [*Note*] Hopkinson specified the retentiveness by the numerical value of the 'residual induction' (= $4\pi I$). **1924** C. R. UNDERHILL *Magnets* i. 21 The property whereby a magnetic material independently remains a magnet is called retentiveness. **1939** [see *RETENTIVITY].

retentivity. Add: **1.** Now usu. the strength of the magnetic field that remains in a sample after removal of a saturating inducing field. (Further examples.)

1912 BROOKS & POYSER *Magnetism & Electricity* xxv. 414 Retentivity is measured by the 'residual' or 'remanent' magnetism, which persists when the magnetising force is removed. **1924** C. R. UNDERHILL *Magnets* xvi. 291 The retentivity or the residual structural flux density..will be about 9,900 gausses, or about 66 per cent of the induction. **1931** S. R. WILLIAMS *Magnetic Phenomena* i. 52 The property of retaining to a greater or less degree a certain amount of magnetization is called the retentivity of the substance. The terminology of magnetism is rather confusing regarding some of these terms... The consensus of opinion among magneticians at present is to reserve the term *remanent magnetism* for the open-circuit residual magnetism as in the case of a U-shaped permanent magnet with the keeper off. **1939** L. F. BATES *Mod. Magnetism* ii. 58 The specimen is now no longer exposed to a magnetic field, but it still retains a considerable intensity of magnetisation, equal to $Ob/4\pi$, which is termed the retentivity of the material and is a measure of the ability to retain magnetism when not subjected to adverse treatment. Some authorities, e.g. Ewing, term the residual induction *Ob* the retentiveness. **1948** *Electronic Engin.* XX. 351/1 The principal requirements of steels for permanent magnets is that they shall have high remanence (retentivity) and coercive force. **1951** R. M. BOZORTH *Ferromagnetism* xi. 499 In strong fields they [*sc.* the coercive force and the residual induction] approach limiting values called the coercivity and the retentivity, respectively. **1953** J. D. KRAUS *Electromagnetics* v. 239 The retentivity of a substance is the maximum value which the residual flux density can attain. **1966** *McGraw-Hill Encycl. Sci. & Technol.* IV. 489/1 The difference between cores of an electromagnet and a permanent magnet is in the retentivity of the material used.

2. *Psychol.* The capacity or ability to retain learning or to remember.

1909 C. S. MYERS *Exper. Psychol.* xiii. 173 Nor is the superior retentivity of the most distributed readings due to the involuntary revival of the syllables by the subject. **1923** C. S. SPEARMAN *Nature of Intelligence* ix. 132 Our second quantitative principle may be called that of retentivity... It appears not to be restricted to cognition, but to extend to mental processes of almost all sorts. It even governs an immense number of purely physical events. **1938** *Times Lit. Suppl.* 19 Mar. 186/1 These are the laws of mental energy and its constancy, of retentivity. **1961** *Lancet* 12 Aug. 361/2 Spearman held that 'retentivity' was a factor not closely related to general intelligence.

3. *Geol.* The property of rocks and minerals of retaining gases, esp. radiogenic ones.

1960 *Amer. Jrnl. Sci.* CCLVIII. 600 The conditions imposed upon phlogopite..in order that its retentivity be greater than 95 per cent for 10^8 years. **1968** HAMILTON & FARQUHAR *Radiometric Dating for Geologists* i. 19 Chemical alteration which occurs penecontemporaneous with the event to be dated is not pertinent unless it affects the retentivity for argon of the mineral to be dated. *Ibid.* 22 The retentivities vary greatly within a mineral species. **1975** *Nature* 27 Feb. 704/2 The nature of the gas initially present in the heating apparatus markedly influences trace element retentivity at 1,000°C.

rete·xture (rī-), *v.* [RE- 5 a.] *trans.* To treat (material, a garment, etc.) so as to restore firmness to its texture. So **rete·xtured** *ppl. a.*, **rete·xturing** *vbl. sb.*

1953 *Laundries & Laundry Requisites* (ed. 12) 208 (Advt.), Re-texturing agent 'Esdefix' makes garments look newer—last longer. **1960** *Which?* May 110/1 Most dry cleaners..ask whether you want your clothes cleaned in the ordinary way or 'with retexturing'. *Ibid.* 111/1 A panel of 20 people was..asked to see if they could tell the difference between the retextured and other garments. *Ibid.* 111/2 There was no difference in appearance between retextured and simply dry cleaned clothes, but there was an indication that the retexturing process had put something back into the cloth, which might therefore last longer. **1976** B. BALL *Keegan* 9 Selecting a retexturing service for his lousy old jacket. **1977** *Punch* 31 Aug.–6 Sept. 349/1 Lord Kagan has had my raincoats retextured.

retgersite (re·tgəɪzəit). *Min.* [See quot. 1949 and -ITE[1].] A polymorph of nickel sulphate hexahydrate, $NiSO_4.6H_2O$, a secondary mineral occurring as green crusts and tufts.

1949 FRONDEL & PALACHE in *Amer. Mineralogist* XXXIV. 188 A recent survey of the specimens of so-called morenosite in the Harvard collection..proved the natural existence of the tetragonal polymorph of nickel sulfate hexahydrate. The latter substance..is described beyond under the name retgersite. The name is given after the Dutch physical chemist and chemical crystallographer Jan Willem Retgers (1856–1896). **1972** *Mineral. Abstr.* XXIII. 314/1 X-ray powder data..and IR spectra are given for retgersite from sulphide-bearing quartz veins..from Chelmiec, Góry Kaczawskie Mts., Lower Silesia.

rethink, *v.* Add: Now usu. *spec.* with a view to changing intentions or attitudes. **a.** (Further examples.)

1930 E. BULLOUGH tr. E. Gilson in T. F. Burns *Monument to St. Augustine* ix. 292 St. Augustine had but re-thought and deepened, from the point of view of a Christian, the essential elements of Platonism. *a* **1942** B. MALINOWSKI *Sci. Theory of Culture* (1944) iii. 19 At times the thinker does nothing else but to re-think..what the primitive might have or ought to have thought or felt under certain conditions. **1944** J. S. HUXLEY *On Living in Revolution* 18 How can this disintegrating system be reintegrated on a new basis? One way of beginning to rethink our social framework is [etc.]. **1955** *Harper's Mag.* Jan. 12/1 A ranking Administration speaker..said that..the Republican party might 'have to rethink the power and resources policy'. The verb is from the advertising-agency jargon that the Administration has learned to speak so fluently but it is not likely to mean much. **1957** *Times Lit. Suppl.* 6 Dec. 729/2 A summons, in effect, to the younger German historians, which only a few of them have heeded, to rethink the whole of Germany's recent past. **1973** *Daily Tel.* 28 Sept. 7/1 Mrs Thatcher last night promised to rethink methods of awarding grants to married women students. **1977** F. YOUNG in J. Hick *Myth of God Incarnate* ii. 30 In any attempt to rethink christological belief, the primacy of soteriology must be recognized.

b. (Further examples.)

1919 J. L. GARVIN *Econ. Found. Peace* xviii. 439 Not to recognise this and not to re-think accordingly means either not being sincere in support of a real League of Nations or not being competently sincere. **1959** *Times* 16 Oct. 13/4 'Rethink'..has suddenly become modish... It means—it means—. Well... It certainly does not mean to think again, which is not only a rueful but an intransitive process. Think twice, perhaps? Never!.. You think twice before doing something silly; rethinking starts after you have done it. **1975** *Sunday Tel.* 22 June 32/4 (*heading*) Amin rethinks... As one of his conditions for the release of Mr. Hills, the President wants spare parts for Ferret patrol cars.

Hence **rethi·nker**; **rethi·nking** *vbl. sb.* (further examples); **rethou·ght** *ppl. a.*

1919 J. L. GARVIN *Econ. Found. Peace* xviii. 440 The duty of rethinking is not only for some men, but more or less for all men, whatever their previous views. **1944** J. S. HUXLEY *On Living in Revolution* p. vii, Never, I suppose, has the process of re-thinking been so intense as in these past four years. There has been the re-thinking of old problems, the transvaluation of values. **1955** *Times* 25 Aug. 7/4 Much rethinking on the subject of disarmament has been going on in London and Washington. **1959** *Times* 16 Oct. 13/4 Repay, according to the dictionary, means to pay back, re-echo to echo back, regain to gain back; but although the rethinker may, while he is about his business, think back, one has the impression that he is mainly concerned with thinking forward. **1959** *Observer* 18 Oct. 24/7 She was ready with a dash of classless glamour for the new rethought brand image. **1963** *Times* 20 May 7/2 The need for rethinking and reorganization in art education is not questioned. **1971** *Farmer & Stockbreeder* 23 Feb. 25/3 To reverse the fall in the national breeding flock a great deal of rethinking was needed about production methods. **1977** *Meanjin* (Austral.) XXXVI. I. 64 Their language more clearly becomes that of inheritors of the shake-ups and rethinkings of the Fifties and Sixties.

re·think, *sb.* [f. the vb.] An act of rethinking; reappraisal; a product of rethinking.

1958 *Times Lit. Suppl.* 12 Sept. 511/2 Then came Mr. Khrushchev's speech at the Twentieth Party Congress and close behind it the great Communist re-think. **1960** *Design* Feb. 29 The task of orientation towards a mass society required a rethink of..an ideal formula. **1968** *New Scientist* 8 Aug. 293/1 The need for a widespread rethink on attitudes in science education, particularly at university level. **1971** *Guardian* 1 Nov. 8/5 Industry must have a major rethink about the way it uses intelligent, qualified young people. **1976** *Jrnl. R. Soc. Arts* May 285/1 It is more difficult to apply the principles to famous modern buildings which look like a total rethink. **1977** *Listener* 3 Mar. 259/1 The whole area of prisoners' rights is long overdue for rethink.

rethrea·d (rī-), *v.* [Re- 5 a.] *trans.* To thread again. Also *absol.* and *transf.*

1904 *Westm. Gaz.* 16 Feb. 2/1 Should the thread break, it is immediately rethreaded by another device. **1906** *Ibid.* 12 Nov. 2/1 The boat rethreads the line of light. **1932** G. Heyer *Devil's Cub* iii. 35 Mary re-threaded her needle. **1963** *Times* 25 May 9/7 A woman nods in time as she rethreads. **1974** N. Freeling *Dressing of Diamond* 173 Just rethread and set it on automatic record. **1974** M. Babson *Stalking Lamb* iii. 28 The needle needed rethreading. She had come to the end of the length of silk.

retia, pl. Rete in Dict. and Suppl.

retiary, *a.* Add: **2. b.** Using a net to catch Lepidoptera.

1967 V. Nabokov *Speak, Memory* vi. 131 America has shown even more of this morbid interest in my retiary activities.

‖ **reticella** (retitʃe·lă). [It., dim. of *rete* net: see Rete.] A lace-like fabric produced esp. in Venice in the 15th, 16th, and 17th centuries. Also used *attrib.* to designate the type of geometric pattern characteristic of this fabric. Cf. next.

1865 F. B. Palliser *Hist. Lace* iv. 58 One Francesca Bulgarini also instructed the schools [at Siena] in the making of lace of every kind, especially the Venetian reticella. **1900** E. Jackson *Hist. Hand-Made Lace* 194 Reticellas, or Greek Point laces, were made chiefly from 1480 to 1620, the designs being always of the stiff geometrical type. **1932** D. C. Minter *Mod. Needlecraft* 54/2 Reticella is a style of work based on cut or drawn threads. **1960** B. Snook *Eng. Hist. Embroidery* 50 White work is much heavier in style in the late 16th and early 17th centuries... Drawn threadwork fillings and reticella motifs are combined in highly conventional leaves and flowers. **1977** Fleming & Honour *Penguin Dict. Decorative Arts* 658/1 *Reticella*, a decorative fabric made, like cutwork and drawn work, from panels of woven lines but with less use of the textile threads and much more free needlework.

‖ **reticello** (retitʃe·lo). [It., f. as prec.] **1. a.** As pl. **reticelli.** A network of fine glass threads embedded in some Venetian glass. **b.** Glass formed with this type of decoration. Also *reticello glass*.

[**1858** A. W. Franks *Vitreous Art* in J. B. Waring *Art Treasures of U.K.* 9 (*heading*) Lace and reticulated glass... The reticulated glass (*vasi a reticelli*) is a variety of the lace.] **1899** R. Glazier *Man. Historic Ornament* 95 The Venetians used with equal skill all the old methods of glass-making..*reticelli*, a network of white lines enclosing at the intersection a bubble of air. **1907** E. Dillon *Glass* xiii. 206 When two series of..rods are arranged to cross one another at an angle, we get a reticulated pattern, and within the *reticelli* thus formed a bubble of air may be caught up. **1926** W. Buckley *European Glass* 39 An example of 'Reticelli', or in German, 'Netz-glas'. **1977** Fleming & Honour *Penguin Dict. Decorative Arts* 658/2 *Reticello glass*, glass decorated with a mesh of opaque white threads beneath the surface. *Ibid.* 822/2 During the C16 they..began to make *reticello* or filigree glass.

2. = prec.

1953 M. Powys *Lace & Lace-Making* iii. 5 Soon the worker built up the lace decoration by throwing threads across these wide-open spaces in either direction, forming geometrical patterns and weaving in and out or button-holing over the threads that bridge the gap, Reticello.

reticle. Add: **3.** A disc or the like with a pattern of opaque and transparent portions which can be rotated in the path of a beam of light or other radiation so as to modulate it.

1959 *Proc. IRE* XLVII. 1566/2 The particular space-filtering properties associated with typical picket fence, checkerboard, and star reticles, as they operate in square or circular field stops, are shown in Figs. 5 and 6. **1961** *Jrnl. Optical Soc. Amer.* LI. 1011/1 In the detection of infrared radiation, it is common practice to interrupt the incident beam periodically to produce an alternating signal for electronic processing. The means used to accomplish this is usually a multisectored spinning aperture called a reticle. **1966** L. M. Biberman *Reticles in Electro-Optical Devices* iii. 30 A simple reticle providing 'two-level' phase modulation is shown... If a small image is focused upon such a rotating reticle, the reticle can provide an indication of the radial position of that image by means of the phase information in the pulses of transmitted radiation.

reticular, *a.* Add: **1. a.** *spec.* (i) *reticular tissue*, tissue of the reticuloendothelial system which helps to form the framework of lymphatic tissue, bone marrow, and the tissue of the spleen and liver.

1848 *Quain's Elem. Anat.* (ed. 5) I. p. cxiii, The substance known by the names of 'cellular', 'areolar', 'filamentous', and 'reticular' tissue. **1892** H. E. Clark *Wilson's Anatomist's Vade Mecum* (ed. 11) I. 16 Reticular tissue is found in all lymphatic glands, in the pharynx and tonsils, the solitary and agminate glands of the intestine, the thymus gland, and in the spleen... From its presence in lymphatic glands it has been named 'adenoid' and 'lymphoid' tissue. **1941** *Lancet* 11 Jan. 46/1 The relationship of the angioid proliferations to the reticular tissue is..complex.

(ii) Applied to a diffuse network of intermingled nerve fibres and nerve cell bodies in parts of the brain stem, one of the functions of which is to mediate changes in the degree of wakefulness.

1887 G. D. Thane *Ellis's Demonstr. Anat.* (ed. 10) ii. 197 In the dorsal portion of the medulla oblongata..the longitudinal fibres derived from the anterior and lateral columns of the cord..give rise to a structure that is known as the reticular formation of the medulla. **1949** Moruzzi & Magoun in *Electroencephalogr. & Clin. Neurophysiol.* I. 455/1 The following account..explores the relations of this reticular activating system to the arousal reaction to natural stimuli. **1962** A. Huxley *Island* xi. 171 Animal experiments indicated that it affected the reticular system. **1968** Passmore & Robson *Compan. Med. Stud.* I. xxiv. 20/1 It seems that consciousness is determined by the activity of the reticular formation and many anaesthetics act particularly upon it. **1975** D. & I. Jordan tr. M. Zimmermann in R. F. Schmidt *Fund. Neurophysiol.* vii. 221 There is a constant 'activating' afferent flow from the reticular system to the cerebrum that controls the state of consciousness. Therefore, the term 'reticular activating system' is used to denote this functional property of the Formatio reticularis.

(iii) *reticular cell*, a fibroblast or other unspecialized cell, esp. a phagocytic cell that helps to form the framework of the reticuloendothelial system and plays an essential role in blood formation; cf. *reticulum cell* s.v. *reticulum 5.

1925 Strong & Elwyn *Bailey's Text-bk. Histol.* (ed. 7) iv. 75 Others maintain that the delicate fibers run in the peripheral cytoplasm (ectoplasm) of the reticular cells. **1927** *Amer. Jrnl. Path.* III. 523 Study of the so-called reticular cells of the spleen, lymph nodes and other organs show [*sic*] that they possess fibroglia fibrils and that they, therefore, are fibroblasts. *Ibid.* 525 There are no reticular cells other than fibroblasts. **1938** H. M. Carleton *Schafer's Essent. Histol.* (ed. 14) 48 The granular leucocytes, lymphocytes and monocytes are all derived from a columnar stem-cell called by Sabin the reticular cell. **1938** *Jrnl. Path. & Bacteriol.* XLVII. 461 The term 'reticular cell' was first introduced by Ribbert (1889) in describing the cells of lymphoid tissue to distinguish between the 'endothelial cells' of the lymph sinuses and the reticular cells proper. **1970** T. S. & C. R. Leeson *Histology* (ed. 2) vi. 105/1 Reticular cells may give rise to free macrophages, to early precursors of erythrocytes and leukocytes, and perhaps to other cell types. **1975** *Jrnl. Path.* CXVII. 119 The term reticular cell should be reserved for the dendritic reticular cell of Nossal *et al.* *Ibid.* 121 *Reticular cell*, a phrase with so many meanings as to be meaningless.

4. Of or pertaining to the reticulum of a ruminant.

1923 G. H. Wooldridge *Encycl. Vet. Med., Surg. & Obstetrics* II. 1025/1 This operation [*sc.* rumenotomy]..is sometimes performed for exploratory purposes in obscure cases of ruminal, reticular, or omasal indigestion. **1966** Dalling & Robertson *Internat. Encycl. Vet. Med.* V. 2633 The reticular contents are liquid and offer no resistance to a thorough examination.

reticulate, *a.* Add: **a.** (Further examples.)

1965 A. Holmes *Princ. Physical Geol.* (ed. 2) 1279/2 (Index), Reticulate (trellised) drainage. **1968** R. W. Fairbridge *Encycl. Geomorphol.* 90/1 A stream or river bed is said to have a braided pattern when the deeper channels form a lacy or reticulate network of divergent and convergent members. *Ibid.* 961/2 (*caption*) Braided pattern ('reticulate drainage') in semiarid environment.

b. *spec.* in *Bot.*, as an epithet of one kind of thickening of the walls of xylem elements.

1873 F. H. Hooker tr. *Le Maout & Decaisne's Gen. Syst. Bot.* 116 Cells may either be homogeneous, or punctate, or rayed, or reticulate, or spiral. **1907** W. C. Stevens *Plant Anat.* vii. 109 The tracheids are elongated cells especially adapted to be water carriers by numerous thin places in the walls in the form of bordered pits or associated with spiral, annular, or reticulate thickenings. **1976** Bell & Coombe tr. *Strasburger's Textbk. Bot.* (rev. ed.) II. ii. 304 Now begins the more extensive differentiation, particularly of the cell wall... The wall becomes thickened, usually by a process of opposition. In the conducting elements, for example, annular, spiral or reticulate thickenings are formed, and lignification sets in.

reticulate, *v.* **1.** Add: Also *fig.*

1971 *Nature* 17 Dec. 394/1 The central device employed in network thermodynamics is the conceptual separation of 'reversible' and 'irreversible' processes. That is, we mentally reticulate the system into subsystems, each of which either stores energy reversibly or dissipates energy without storage.

reticulated, *ppl. a.* Add: **1. c.** *spec.* of porcelain, etc. Cf. *pierced *ppl. a.* c.

1881 Audsley & Bowes *Keramic Art of Japan* 143 There are several specimens of pierced, or what is termed reticulated, porcelain. **1908** J. F. Blacker *Chats on Oriental China* xiii. 152 There is a white biscuit class, very rare, often having two walls or divisions, of which the outer one only is biscuit, reticulated or pierced with a fine network or trellis of various patterns, through which the interior wall can be seen. **1970** [see *pierced *ppl. a.* c]. **1974** Savage & Newman *Illustr. Dict. Ceramics* 245 (*caption*) Teapot with reticulated outer wall and handle with moulded terminals, creamware, Leeds, c. 1785. **1980** *Catal. Fine Chinese Ceramics* (Sotheby, Hong Kong) 166 Reserved on a reticulated florette and *wan* diaper-ground infilled in green.

reticulation. Add: **a.** *spec.* in *Photogr.*, (the formation of) a network of wrinkles or cracks in a photographic emulsion.

1888 H. C. Jones *Introd. Sci. & Pract. Photogr.* xix. 239 Concerning the reticulation of gelatine films, increase of the bichromate tends to produce grain. **1929** R. H. Goodsall *Beginner's Guide to Photogr.* vi. 36 The removal of a negative from a comparatively warm bath of developer to a cold fixing solution..may cause 'frilling' or reticulation, *i.e.* curious wavy marks in the gelatine. **1967** V. Strauss *Printing Industry* v. 269/2 It seems that the tonal qualities of collotype prints result from the interaction of two related items. One is generally called reticulation; the other is varying ink receptivity. **1977** J. Hedgecoe *Photographer's Handbk.* 241 Modern films have built-in resistance to reticulation.

b. ? *Austral.* and *N.Z.* A network of pipes used in irrigation and water supply. Also *transf.* (see quot. 1977).

1936 *Jrnl. R. Soc. W. Austral.* XXII. p. xxi, The Government has helped very materially in the following ways to meet the increased demand for water:—1. By reticulation from the Mundaring–Kalgoorlie pipe-line... 2. By 'District Water Supplies', *i.e.*, reticulation from rock-catchments. **1937** *Discovery* June 186/2 Twenty miles of 12-inch pipe have been laid from the dam to the mines; the dam and reticulation lines cost £150,000. **1977** *N.Z. Herald* 8 Jan. 2–10/4 (Advt.), We require..two plumbers with experience in commercial work. The contract involves complete reticulation of bedroom wings in conjunction with building renovations.

reticule. 2. (Earlier example.)

1801 C. Wilmot *Let.* 13 Dec. in *Irish Peer* (1920) 21 'Reticules'..are a species of little Workbag worn by the Ladies, containing snuff-boxes, Billet-doux, Purses, Handkerchiefs, Fans, Prayer-Books, Bon-Bons, Visiting tickets.

reticulin (rĭti·kiŭlin). *Histology.* [a. G. *reticulin* (M. Siegfried 1892, in *Ber. ü. die Verh. d. K. Sächs. Ges. der Wissensch. zu Leipzig* (Math.-Phys. Cl.) XLIV. 306): cf. next and -in[1].] A structural protein with an affinity for silver stains that is present in healing wounds and forms a fine network in the lymph nodes, spleen, and liver; now regarded as a form of collagen.

1899 *Jrnl. Physiol.* XXIV. p. x, The fibres of reticular or retiform tissue are anatomically continuous with, and histologically identical with, the white fibres of connective tissue. According to Siegfried they are however chemically different, for they yield not only gelatin, but also a new substance he has named reticulin. **1902** *Ibid.* XXVIII. 321 Miss Tebb believes that reticulin is collagen, which has been changed by alcohol and ether. **1930** *Amer. Jrnl. Path.* VI. 631 In successful preparations, reticulin stains black while collagen bundles stain yellow, thereby fortifying Mall's conclusion that reticulin..is a substance different from collagen. **1947** *Ann. Rev. Microbiol.* I. 133 Following up an observation..that incubation with *Cl[ostridium] welchii* Type A filtrates causes rapid disintegration of muscle, and that this is due..to destruction of the reticulin scaffolding, Oakley *et al.*..have confirmed the presence of a collagenase enzyme in such filtrates. **1973** Law & Oliver *Gloss. Histopath. Terms* 118 *Reticular fibres.* These elements of connective tissue are often loosely referred to as 'reticulin' which perhaps more accurately should be confined to the constituent protein. A long-standing controversy still rages over their relationship with collagen fibres; although reticular fibres possess a strong argyrophilia and collagen fibres do not..examination under the electron microscope shows no basic structural dissimilarity. **1974** R. M. Kirk et al. *Surgery* ii. 30 Phagocytes attached to reticulin fibrils line sinusoids in the lymph nodes, liver, spleen, bone marrow, and certain endocrine glands such as the anterior pituitary, adrenal and thymus glands.

reticulitis (rĭtikiŭlǝi·tis). *Vet. Sci.* [f. Reticul(um + -itis.] Inflammation of the reticulum of a ruminant.

1905 Moussu & Dollar *Dis. Cattle, Sheep, Goats & Swine* v. 186 Rumenitis or reticulitis may..follow the ingestion of irritant foods or plants. **1970** A. R. Jennings *Animal Path.* v. 91 A common cause of reticulitis is the penetration of the reticular wall by a sharp foreign object.

reticulocyte (rĭti·kiŭloˌsǝit). *Med.* [f. Reticulo- + -cyte.] **a.** A red blood cell which has lost its nucleus but is not yet mature, characterized by a granular or reticulated appearance when suitably stained.

1922 E. B. Krumbhaar in *Jrnl. Lab. & Clin. Med.* VIII. 11 The presence of reticulated or 'skeined' erythrocytes..in the peripheral blood..has..in the last decade..assumed clinical importance as an index of the activity of blood formation. I would suggest..that when the normal percentage of these cells in the peripheral blood is exceeded, the condition be designated 'reticulosis'... The word 'reticulocyte' might similarly be substituted for 'reticulated erythrocytes'. **1956** *Nature* 28 Jan. 190/1 Although reticulocytes have practically their full complement of haemoglobin, evidence from amino-acid incorporation studies suggests that these cells, unlike mature erythrocytes, still have protein-synthesizing capacity. **1968** H. Harris *Nucleus & Cytoplasm* i. 12 The mammalian reticulocyte continues to synthesize haemoglobin for some days after elimination of the cell nucleus.

b. *attrib.*, as *reticulocyte level*; **reticulocyte count,** the proportion or concentration of reticulocytes in the blood.

1922 E. B. Krumbhaar in *Jrnl. Lab. & Clin. Med.* VIII. 14 The temporary rise in the reticulocyte count immediately after transfusions were begun was found in another dog, and considered by us as probably due to bone marrow irritation. **1961** *Lancet* 26 Aug. 490/1 The reticulocyte and platelet counts were 3·6 % and 228,000 per c. mm. respectively. **1980** *Brit. Med. Jrnl.* 29 Mar. 892/1 Thirty patients receiving haemodialysis..showed significant increases ($p < 0{\cdot}001$).. in reticulocyte count. **1946** *Nature* 2 Nov. 627/1 All the rabbits used in these experiments showed a normal reticulocyte level of 1·0–2·0 per cent.

reticulocytosis (rĭti:kiŭlosəitōᵘ·sis). *Med.* [f. prec. + -OSIS.] The presence in the blood of abnormally many reticulocytes.

1926 in R. J. E. SCOTT *Gould's Med. Dict.* 1110/1. **1929** *Arch. Internal Med.* XLIV. 502 (*heading*) Reticulocytosis produced by liver extract. **1956** *Nature* 28 Jan. 190/2 Preparations of rabbit blood containing 70–90 per cent reticulocytes, obtained following reticulocytosis induced by phenylhydrazine. **1977** *Jrnl. Clin. Invest.* LIX. 639/2 Patients with reticulocytosis..did not have increased denatured hemoglobin. **1980** *Brit. Med. Jrnl.* 29 Mar. 893/2 The delayed onset of reticulocytosis after the beginning of cytolysis suggests that hepatocyte regeneration rather than hepatocyte destruction was the stage when this erythropoietin secretion occurred.

reti:culoendothe·lial, *a. Med.* Also with hyphen. [ad. G. *retikulo-endothelial*: cf. RETICULO- and *endothelial* adj. s.v. ENDO-.] Of, pertaining to, or designating a diverse system of tissues and cells characterized by their phagocytic ability and now known to be involved in the immune response.

The circulating monocytes of the blood are now usu. included, but formerly were excluded by some authors.

1924 *Physiol. Rev.* IV. 548 In various experimental conditions..the whole reticulo-endothelial system, all the histiocytes in the body and chiefly in the abdominal organs and in the bone marrow are entering a phase of functional stimulation. **1929** *Lancet* 5 Oct. 711/1 The distribution of reticulo-endothelial cells might be determined by the injection into animals of various dye substances which were taken up by the cells. **1947** *Ann. Rev. Microbiol.* I. 291 Until recently it was generally held that antibody formation is the function of the 'reticuloendothelial system' i.e., phagocytic tissue cells. **1974** R. M. KIRK et al. *Surgery* ii. 7 Reticuloendothelial rather than bloodborne cells participate. **1977** *Proc. R. Soc. Med.* LXX. 523/1 From this sort of information we can derive circumstantial evidence in favour of impaired reticuloendothelial function in patients with liver disease.

reticuloendotheliosis (rĭti:kiŭlo,endopīli-ōᵘ·sis). *Med.* Also with hyphen. [ad. G. *reticuloendotheliose* (O. Ewald 1924, in *Deutsch. Arch. f. klin. Med.* CXLII. 227): see prec. and -OSIS.] Hyperplasia of some part of the reticuloendothelial system.

1926 *Q. Cumulative Index Current Med. Lit.* XII. 591/1 Reticulo-endothelial reaction or 'reticulo-endotheliosis' (leukemia form?). **1933** *Jrnl. Path. & Bacteriol.* XXXVII. 327 The other group of cases (in which sinus reticulum is affected) is represented by monocyte leukaemia, and by certain of the cases described as systematic aleukaemic reticuloendotheliosis. **1958** R. W. RAVEN *Cancer* II. xxiv. 452 The word reticuloendotheliosis was originally used, by analogy with myelosis and lymphadenosis, to describe a systematized proliferation of 'reticuloendothelial cells', of which the monocytes are representatives in the circulating blood. Both leukaemic and aleukaemic forms of reticuloendotheliosis were recognized. **1978** *Nature* 20 July 269/2 'Pool' sensitisation of T cells from patients with hairy cell leukaemia (leukaemic reticuloendotheliosis) gives rise to CTL [*sc.* cytotoxic T lymphocytes] that lyse autologous leukaemia cells but not autologous normal lymphocytes.

reti:culosarco·ma. *Path.* [ad. F. *réticulosarcome* (C. Oberling 1928, in *Bull. de l'Assoc. Française pour l'Étude du Cancer* XVII. 279): see RETICULO- and SARCOMA.] A sarcoma arising from the reticuloendothelial system.

1938 *Jrnl. Path. & Bacteriol.* XLVII. 473 The idea of grouping all the neoplastic conditions of reticular tissue under the generic term reticulosarcoma. **1953** *Brit. Jrnl. Surg.* XLI. 75 (*heading*) Multiple reticulosarcoma of the duodenum and jejunum. *Ibid.* 76/2 Description and classification of reticulosarcomata. **1958** R. W. RAVEN *Cancer* II. xxiv. 452 In 1928 Oberling introduced the name reticulosarcoma as a generic term for all neoplasms of the LRS [*sc.* lymphoreticular system]: since then varieties such as lymphocytic and lymphoblastic reticulosarcomas..and sundry more disputable cytological types have been listed. **1974** R. M. KIRK et al. *Surgery* ii. 31 If the growth contains a large number of reticulin fibres, as revealed by special staining methods, the growth is called a reticulosarcoma.

reticulosis (rĭtikiŭlōᵘ·sis). *Med.* Pl. **-oses** (-ōᵘ·sīz). [ad. G. *retikulose* (E. Letterer 1924, in *Frankfurter Zeitschr. f. Path.* XX. 392): see RETICULO- and -OSIS.] Proliferative disease of reticuloendothelial cells.

Quot. 1922 s.v. *RETICULOCYTE a illustrates a different sense.

1932 B. D. PULLINGER in *Rose Res. on Lymphadenoma* 134 The term 'reticulo-endotheliosis' is not applicable to any member of the group. The term 'reticulose' or 'reticulosis' (Letterer) is more suitable. **1958** R. W. RAVEN *Cancer* II. xxiv. 453 The term *reticulosis* was first used in 1924, when Letterer described his original case of what is now often known as Letterer–Siwe disease: he interpreted the case as a variety of 'aleukaemia', which he named..*aleukämische Retikulose bzw. Retikuloendotheliose*... In 1934, Letterer stated that the term reticulosis should be used..only in relation to a systematized proliferation of reticulum cells, in which these cells did *not* proceed to form..fibres. **1977** *Proc. R. Soc. Med.* LXX. 46/2 The subject of the symposium held on the second afternoon was The Reticuloses; it dealt with management of the leukaemias in children and adults, and of Hodgkin's disease and the non-Hodgkin lymphomas.

reticulum. Add: **4. a.** *Histology.* Retiform tissue forming part of the reticuloendothelial system.

1870 H. POWER tr. *Stricker's Man. Human & Compar. Histol.* I. ii. 65 A remarkable form of connective tissue occurs in the supporting and investing reticulum of the glands of the lymphatic system and allied organs in connection with their blood capillaries, and around the fasciculi of fibrillar connective tissue. *Ibid.* 66 In the fresh condition, the reticulum is soft and easily torn. **1896** *Johns Hopkins Hosp. Rep.* I. 171 A tissue practically identical with reticulum is widely distributed throughout the body. *Ibid.* 202 Since they [*sc.* liver fibrils] seem to be identical with the reticulum of lymphatic glands, spleen and mucous membrane, I shall retain for them the name reticulum. **1964** *Jrnl. Exper. Med.* CXX. 1083 The most interesting feature.. of this reticulum web in primary follicles is its possible importance in the induction of immune responses. *Ibid.* 1084 A fine web of phagocytic reticulum in primary follicles was found to be responsible for antigen localization.

b. *Cytology.* The firmer parts of the cytoplasm; *Obs.* except in *endoplasmic reticulum*, a complex and often extensive system of membrane in the cytoplasm of a cell, containing RNA and involved in protein synthesis.

1891 *Quain's Elem. Anat.* (ed. 10) I. 173 (*caption*) Protoplasm, showing a reticulum of plastin. *Ibid.*, In most cells.. it is found that a differentiation of the protoplasm has occurred in such a manner that a part of it appears under high powers of the microscope in the form of a network or spongework... The network is known as the reticulum or spongioplasm. **1896** [see *ENCHYLEMA]. **1948** PORTER & THOMPSON in *Jrnl. Exper. Med.* LXXXVIII. 24 b (*caption*) The relatively large mitochondria lie amidst strands of the endoplasmic reticulum. **1953** *Ibid.* XCVII. 736 This component is absent from the thinner (ectoplasmic) margins of the cell and appears instead to occupy the central or endoplasmic portions of the cytoplasm. From its location and form it has come to be referred to as the endoplasmic reticulum and by this name it has been noted in previous reports. **1974** M. C. GERALD *Pharmacol.* iii. 52 The endoplasmic reticulum, when viewed under an electron microscope, resembles a thin tubular network. **1976** *Sci. Amer.* Mar. 27/1 There were striking changes in the ultrastructure of the liver cell: the mitochondria..were enlarged and distorted, and the smooth membranes of the endoplasmic reticulum, the site of enzymes associated with the metabolism of alcohol and other substances, proliferated.

c. *Histology.* = *RETICULIN.

1927 *Amer. Jrnl. Path.* III. 524 Reticulum as a chemically distinct intercellular substance does not exist; it is collagen in separated form, rendered prominent by the silver stain. **1941** *Cancer Res.* I. 234/1 By using a method which differentiates collagen from reticulum, we have found that, as age advances, there is a transformation of the latter into the former in the endometrium.

5. Special Comb.: **reticulum cell**, variously used to denote cells of the reticuloendothelial system; cf. *reticular cell* s.v. *RETICULAR *a.* 1 a(iii); [the sense is due to Ribbert, who used G. *reticulumzell* (*Beitr. zu path. Anat. u. zu allg. Path.* (1889) VI. 206)].

1912 E. A. SCHÄFER *Textbk. Microsc. Anat.* 400 The ramified cells which cover the reticular tissue of the lymph-sinus often contain a considerable number of pigment-granules, especially in the medulla of the gland. These reticulum-cells are phagocytic. **1939** COOPER & JONES *Human Histol.* iv. 44 There is no obvious matrix, and the unhampered connective tissue or reticulum cells possess active phagocytic properties. **1975** *Jrnl. Path.* CXVII. 119 The terms reticular cell and reticulum cell are widely and variously used to describe cells in lymph-nodes. It has been suggested..that the term reticulum cell should be applied to cells in lymph-nodes which are not readily described as macrophages, lymphocytes, fibroblasts, endothelial cells or leukocytes and that the term reticular cell should be reserved for the dendritic reticular cell of Nossal et al. *Ibid.* 121 *Reticulum cell*, heterogeneous group of cells some of which bind antigen, some of which synthesise DNA, some of which may be macrophage precursors. *Ibid.*, The term 'reticulum' cell appears a useful omnibus word to describe all the mesenchymal cells of the lymphoreticular tissue which cannot at present be clearly categorised. Clearly as more is learned about these cells, fewer cells will fall within the category 'reticulum cell'. *Ibid.* 122 The popliteal lymph nodes showed macrophages, fibroblasts, endothelial cells and a heterogeneous group of cells here described as reticulum cells.

retie, *v.* Add: Also *absol.*

1954 A. G. L. HELLYER *Encycl. Garden Work* 106/2 If there is any doubt on this point, do not disturb the scion but retie at once.

retimber, *v.* Add: Also, to reforest.

1924 J. A. HAMMERTON *Countries of World* III. 1928/1 The state..is responsible for the systematic retimbering of the Alps in the upper valley of the Durance.

retinaculum. Add: **2. c.** In collembolans, a fused pair of appendages which hold back the furcula before releasing it for a spring.

1923 H. M. LEFROY *Man. Entomol.* 15 A curious appendage, the so-called 'catch' or retinaculum,..holds the furca in place when not in use. **1939** H. WOMERSLEY *Primitive Insects S. Austral.* 81 When the retinaculum releases the spring, the latter strikes the ground, forcing the insect to leap a considerable distance. **1969** R. F. CHAPMAN *Insects* xiv. 264 The appendages of the third and fourth segments of the abdomen of many Collembola form the retinaculum and the furca which are used in locomotion.

retinal, *a.* Add: Hence **re·tinally** *adv.*, with respect to or by means of the retina.

1970 *Jrnl. Gen. Psychol.* LXXXII. 228 The results clearly indicate that retinally disorienting novel outline shapes from training to test does not lead to recognition disturbances. **1974** *Sci. Amer.* Jan. 79/1 Tilted-head subjects recognized the environmentally upright (but retinally tilted) figures about as well as the upright observers did. **1980** *Ibid.* Jan. 92/3 In normal three-dimensional viewing it is quite irrelevant whether or not a baseboard is retinally collinear with a molding.

retinal (re·tinæl), *sb. Biochem.* [f. RETIN(A + *-AL².] = *RETINENE; usu. *spec.* vitamin A_1 aldehyde. Also **retina·ldehyde** in the same sense.

1944 MORTON & GOODWIN in *Nature* 1 Apr. 406/1 The elegance and accuracy of Wald's work on retinal extracts makes us hesitate to suggest that the term *retinene* is inappropriate. Unfortunately, it suggests a retinal carotenoid... Perhaps *retinaldehyde* is more appropriate than retinal. **1960** *Jrnl. Amer. Chem. Soc.* LXXXII. 5581/1 The pure substance hitherto known as retinene shall be designated retinal. **1963** *Nature* 30 Mar. 1279/1 In accordance with recent recommendations of the Committee on Nomenclature of the International Union of Pure and Applied Chemistry, we shall use hereafter the following terminology: for vitamin A, 'retinol'; for vitamin A aldehyde (retinene), 'retinal' or 'retinaldehyde'; for vitamin A acid, 'retinoic acid'. **1968** A. WHITE et al. *Princ. Biochem.* (ed. 4) xl. 902 Upon bleaching, rhodopsin dissociates to yield the protein, opsin, and a carotenoid, retinal (formerly retinene or vitamin A_1-aldehyde). **1969** *Nature* 1 Feb. 432/1 Retinaldehyde forms a Schiff base with an aliphatic amino-group on opsin. **1976** *Sci. Amer.* June 42/2 Retinal, complexed with various proteins, or opsins, is the chromophore of all visual pigments in animals.

retinene (re·tinīn). *Biochem.* [f. RETIN(A + -ENE.] Either of two closely related yellow carotenoids, the aldehydes of vitamins A_1 and A_2 respectively (*spec.* that of the former), which occur esp. in the retina combined with opsin as rhodopsin; (sometimes followed by distinguishing numeral). Now more usu. known as *retinal*.

1934 G. WALD in *Nature* 14 July 65/1 In the retinas of dark adapted animals, no xanthophyll and only a trace of vitamin A occurs. Instead their chloroform extracts contain a third carotenoid with novel properties. I have named this substance retinene. **1950** *Sci. News* XV. 17 Kühne found, when visual purple is acted on by light, that a new substance is formed which he called visual yellow. The latter has now been shown to be closely related to, if not identical with, the aldehyde of vitamin A_1, called retinene-1. **1956** *Nature* 28 Jan. 176/1 In the retina, the retinene formed by bleaching rhodopsin ordinarily is reduced to vitamin A. **1970** *Ibid.* 22 Aug. 778/1 Vision..is triggered by isomerization of the carotenoid, retinene.

retinitis. Add: **b.** *retinitis pigmentosa* [mod.L.: fem. of *pigmentōsus*, f. *pigment-um* pigment + *-ōsus*: see -OSE¹], a chronic, hereditary form of retinitis characterized by the occurrence of black pigment in the retina and leading gradually to blindness.

1861 *Amer. Med. Monthly & N.Y. Rev.* XV. 183 Let us hope that there may soon be found a remedy for retinitis pigmentosa. **1865** *Ophthalmic Rev.* I. 47 The occurrence of pigment in the retina.., on account of its marked character in the case of the Spanish Marquis Ariani, was called morbus Arianus, an appellation which has, since Donders's pathological and anatomical researches, become changed into that of retinitis pigmentosa. **1910** *Encycl. Brit.* X. 98/1 Where the connective tissue elements are primarily affected [by retinal inflammation], the condition is a slow one, similar to sclerosis of the central nervous system. The gradual blindness which this causes is due to compression of the retinal nerve elements by the connective tissue hyperplasia, which is always associated with characteristic changes in the disposition of the retinal pigment. This retinal sclerosis is consequently generally known as retinitis pigmentosa, a disease to which there is a hereditary predisposition. **1925** *Amer. Jrnl. Ophthalm.* VIII. 375/1 Since the eye changes are so constantly associated with bodily defects, hereditary, congenital and acquired, the nervous system may be the primary seat of the affection of which retinitis pigmentosa is only the ocular expression. **1952** C. P. BLACKER *Eugenics* x. 242 Retinitis pigmentosa, a serious disease of the eye which has been much studied, may be determined by at least five separate genes of which only one is clinically distinguishable from the rest. **1969** *Listener* 16 Jan. 66/1 One serious congenital abnormality—a form of blindness manifest in adults, *retinitis pigmentosa*—the early symptoms of which are likely to appear after a man is married and had children, who will then continue to carry the gene.

retino- (re·tinŏ-), comb. form of RETINA, used in terms in *Med.*, as **re:tinoblasto·ma** (pl. -omata) [see BLASTO-, *-OMA], a malignant, familial tumour of the retina occurring chiefly in young children; **retino-ce·rebral** *a.*, of or pertaining to the retina and the brain; **re:tinochoroi·dal** *a.*, pertaining to the retina and to the choroid; **re:tinochoroidi·tis** = *CHOROIDO-RETINITIS; **retino·pathy** [*-PATHY 2], non-inflammatory disease of the retina;

so **retinopa·thic** *a.*; **retino-te·ctal** *a.*, of or pertaining to the retina and the optic tectum; **retinoto·pic** *a.* [Gr. τοπικ-ός of or pertaining to place], (of a projection on the optic tectum) that preserves the spatial relations of the sensory receptors of the retina. Also RETINOSCOPY.

1924 *Trans. Amer. Ophthalm. Soc.* XXII. 26 We therefore recommend that the term glioma of the retina be not used, except temporarily as a synonym or explanation to one of the following, which may more properly be applied to this condition: Neuro-epithelioma..; Retino-blastoma, proposed by Mallory; or Retino-cytoma. **1940** S. DUKE-ELDER *Text-bk. Ophthalm.* III. xxxvi. 2832 Retino-blastomata.. are common, forming the great majority of retinal 'gliomata'. **1966** WRIGHT & SYMMERS *Systemic Path.* II. xl. 1637/1 A retinoblastoma is a highly malignant tumour that arises in the pars optica of the retina. It usually appears during the first two years of life. **1976** *Path. Ann.* XI. 319 Exfoliated cells of medulloblastoma, neuroblastoma, and retinoblastoma are characterized by nuclear molding and clustering of adjacent cells. **1891** Retino-cerebral [see *FATIGUE *sb.* 1 c]. **1930** *Jrnl. Physiol.* LXIX. 433 An interaction is occurring between the retino-cerebral apparatuses of the two eyes. **1962** H. C. WESTON *Sight, Light & Work* (ed. 2) v. 168 The 'overpowering' of the retino-cerebral or visual sensory system does not occasion the painful feeling experienced when we are dazzled. **1895** *Arch. Ophthalm.* XXIV. 334 (*heading*) Three unusual cases of retino-choroidal degeneration. **1971** *Jrnl. Amer. Vet. Med. Assoc.* CLVIII. 740 (*heading*) Retinal and retinochoroidal lesions in early neuropathic canine distemper. **1881** G. SIGERSON tr. *J. M. Charcot's Lect. Dis. Nerv. System* II. iii. 41 The lesion of the optic nerve which sometimes supervenes in glycosuria and syphilitic retino-choroiditis. **1975** *Ann. Ophthalm.* VII. 853/1 Toxoplasmosis is an important cause of focal exudative retinochoroiditis. **1933** *Amer. Jrnl. Ophthalm.* XVI. 612/1 From 1856..until the present, the question of a retinopathic entity due to diabetes has remained unsettled. **1976** *Lancet* 30 Oct. 961/2 The mean prolactin concentration in retinopathic patients was 11 : 5 ng/ml. **1932** *Amer. Jrnl. Med. Sci.* CLXXXII. 137 Retinal arteriosclerosis in association with hemorrhages and sharply defined white patches, so-called arteriosclerotic retinopathy. **1939** M. L. HINE *May & Worth's Man. Dis. Eye* (ed. 8) xviii. 288 To distinguish the non-inflammatory affections from the inflammatory, the now-accepted term 'retinopathy'..has been adopted. **1966** WRIGHT & SYMMERS *Systemic Path.* II. xl. 1629/2 Formerly, it was supposed that the variety of ophthalmoscopical appearances associated with the vascular retinopathies merely represented different phases of the same disease: now, however, it is generally recognized that.. three distinct forms can be differentiated—(i) arteriosclerotic retinopathy, (ii) hypertensive retinopathy, and (iii) diabetic retinopathy. **1978** *Jrnl. R. Soc. Med.* LXXI. 636/1 The impression is that encephalopathy and retinopathy are particularly related to the severity and rate of rise of blood pressure. **1962** *Nature* 1 Dec. 898/2 (*heading*) Retinotectal connexions after retinal regeneration. **1977** *Ibid.* 6 Jan. 52/1 The topography of the retino-tectal projection onto the optic tectum was found to be similar in the bullfrog and leopard frog. **1961** *Jrnl. Physiol.* CLVII. 27P In sixteen frogs the normal retinotopic projection on the optic tectum had been restored after optic nerve regeneration. **1979** *Nature* 12 Apr. 623/1 If these exchanges were cumulative, it is arguable that any nascent retinotopic order should become scrambled before axons reach the brain.

retinoid (re·tinoid), *sb. Biochem.* [f. *RETIN(OL[2] + -OID.] Any substance displaying vitamin A activity.

1976 M. B. SPORN et al. in *Federation Proc.* XXXV. 1332/1 Natural forms of vitamin A and synthetic analogs of vitamin A; this entire set of molecules, both natural and synthetic, we shall call retinoids, in a manner analogous to the naming of carotenoids or steroids. **1976** *Lancet* 27 Nov. 1174/1 The value of using the synthetic retinoids in the treatment of these dermatoses lies not only in the excellent therapeutic response but also in the comparative lack of toxicity. **1980** *Nature* 17 Apr. 626/1 Retinoids reduce the saturation density and/or growth rate of many normal and tumorigenic cell lines.

retinol[1]. Add: Now *Obs.*

retinol[2] (re·tinǫl). *Biochem.* [f. RETIN(A + -OL.] Either of vitamins A_1 and A_2 (*spec.* the former), which are yellow carotenoid alcohols of formulæ $C_{20}H_{30}O$ and $C_{20}H_{28}O$ respectively; (sometimes followed by distinguishing numeral).

1960 *Jrnl. Amer. Chem. Soc.* LXXXII. 5581/1 The pure substance hitherto known as vitamin A_1 or axerophthol shall be designated retinol. **1968** A. WHITE et al. *Princ. Biochem.* (ed. 4) l. 1048 Vitamin A activity in mammals is exhibited by α-, β-, and γ-carotenes, by retinol and retinol$_2$.. and by a few other carotenoids. **1976** *Nature* 4 Mar. 49/2 Vitamin A (retinol) is a nutrient essential for vision, growth, reproduction and proper differentiation of epithelial tissue.

Also **retino·ic** *a.*, in *retinoic acid*, the carboxylic acid obtained from retinol by oxidation; hence **retino·ate**, the anion of this; **re·tinyl** *attrib.*, denoting esters of retinol; **retiny·lidene**, [*-IDENE], the group in which form retinal exists in rhodopsin, i.e. a side chain linked to opsin by a double bond formed in a condensation reaction between the aldehyde group of retinal and an amino group of the opsin.

1960 *Jrnl. Amer. Chem. Soc.* LXXXII. 5581/1 The pure substance hitherto known as vitamin A acid shall be designated retinoic acid. **1968** A. WHITE et al. *Princ. Biochem.* (ed. 4) l. 1049 Retinyl esters, the form present in ingested liver and fish-liver oils, are hydrolyzed in the intestine. *Ibid.*, Retinoic acid..readily replaces retinol in the rat diet. **1969** *Nature* 1 Feb. 435/1 There could perhaps be a direct interaction between the charged quanidinium ion and the molecular orbitals of the retinyledene [*sic*] chromophore. **1970** R. W. MCGILVERY *Biochem.* xxvi. 645 Since it won't save vision, it is apparent that retinoate is not readily reduced to retinal. *Ibid.*, Polar bear livers..contain as much as 30 micromoles of retinyl esters per gram—a 20-year supply for a human in each pound. **1973** *Nature* 16 Nov. 166/2 The only action of light in vision is the photoisomerisation of the 11-*cis* retinylidene (derived from vitamin A aldehyde) prosthetic or chromophoric group of rhodopsin, from the 11-*cis* to the all-*trans* configuration. **1976** *Ibid.* 4 Mar. 49/2 Some retinol is oxidised to retinoic acid (vitamin A acid) *in vivo*, but if an animal is provided with retinoic acid in place of dietary retinol, it can only partially substitute for the missing retinol.

retinula. Add: Also anglicized as **retinule** (re·tiniūl). [Coined in Ger. by H. Grenacher in *Untersuchungen über das Arthropoden-Auge* (1877) ii. 17.] Also *attrib.* (*appositively*). (Further examples.)

1924 *Glasgow Herald* 31 May 4/2 The insect's compound eye..has its numerous lenses and retinules each wrapped up in a black mantle. **1978** *Nature* 29 June 772/1 The *Drosophila* compound eye consists of about 700 ommatidia, each containing six peripheral and two central retinula cells (photoreceptors).

retinyl: see s.v. *RETINOL[2].

re-ti·p, *v.* [RE- 5 c.] To supply with a new tip. Hence **reti·pping**, *vbl. sb.*

1839 URE *Dict. Arts* 853 He had rendered entirely unserviceable 126 punches or borers, besides 26 others which had been re-tipped with steel. **1947** J. STEINBECK *Wayward Bus* i. 4 People stopped bringing..their ploughs for retipping.

retiracy. 1. (Earlier examples.)

1829 *Virginia Lit. Museum* 30 Dec. 460/1 *Retiracy*, 'solitude'. **1839** C. M. KIRKLAND *New Home* xi. 64 The important matter of supper being in some sort concluded, preparations were made for '*retiracy*'.

retiral. Now chiefly *Sc.* **1.** Delete *rare* and add further examples.

1964 J. D. MACKIE *Hist. Scotl.* ii. 22 The retiral which followed the departure of Agricola. **1976** *Scotsman* 24 Dec. 13/1 (Advt.), Retiral collection in aid of children's homes.

2. (Further examples.)

1939 *Daily Tel.* 18 Dec. 12/5 (Advt.), Owing retiral of Foreman Pattern Maker..a vacancy occurs for a first-class Man with organising ability. **1965** J. POTTER *Death in Office* i. 10 You will recall my telling you of a verbal agreement between the late Chairman and myself that my retiral should be at my own discretion. **1973** *Stirling Observer* 25 July 11/6 A special retiral presentation is being made by the chairman. **1978** *Lochaber News* 31 Mar. 14/1 (Advt.), Young person required for civil engineering stores to fill vacancy due to retiral.

retire, *v.* Add: **I. 1. f.** Chiefly *Cricket.* (Earlier and later examples.) Also *to retire hurt*, of a batsman: to leave the field because of injury suffered at the crease; also *fig.*

1851 W. CLARKE in W. Bolland *Cricket Notes* 128 You must..make the man play out... Perhaps before that is the case, you will have caused him to retire. **1863** *Lillywhite's Cricket Scores* III. 62 Wansell..was given out unfairly, and refused to retire. **1867** *Ball Players' Chron.* 6 June 2/1 His run, however, was the only one scored, as the next three strikers retired in succession. **1877** *Wisden's Cricketers' Almanack* 223 (*heading*) Lancashire v. Nottinghamshire. *Ibid.* 224 Nottinghamshire... F. Wyld, retired (*hurt*). **1892** *Ibid.* 209 Mr. E. C. Streatfield (Pembroke), not out 6—retired hurt. **1901** H. BLEACKLEY *Tales of Stumps* iv. 105 Amidst.. loud applause, he retired with thirty-eight runs to his credit. **1906** E. DYSON *Fact'ry 'Ands* xvii. 233 It..batted 'er in ther basket with 28lb. iv grey sugar paper done up tough, 'n' she retired 'urt. **1925** A. CHRISTIE *Secret of Chimneys* xv. 141 Poor little Michael didn't get it [*sc.* a disappointing answer] as straight from the shoulder as he might have done. But he retired hurt all the same. **1961** F. H. BURGESS *Dict. Sailing* 170 *Retire*, withdraw from a race. **1977** *Arab Times* 3 Dec. 9/6 Kurian had to retire hurt after scoring 11 runs.

III. 11. a. Now also in *gen.* use.

1961 M. SPARK *Prime of Miss Jean Brodie* iii. 71 She had been retired before time. **1980** *Times* 19 Feb. 1/1 One idea being strongly canvassed is that Sir Charles Villiers, British Steel's chairman, should be retired early.

b. (Earlier and later examples.)

1881 'MARK TWAIN' *Prince & Pauper* (1882) xix. 244 He was so awkward at this service that she retired him from it. **1974** *Sci. Amer.* Dec. 139/1 This material served for about a year before I retired it. **1980** D. FRANCIS *Reflex* viii. 91 It's his last season... I'll have to retire him [*sc.* a racehorse].

c. *U.S. Baseball.* To cause (a batter or team) to retire; to put out.

1874 *Chicago Inter Ocean* 6 July 9/1 Schafer was retired on a fly caught by Meyerle in left field. **1889** N. F. PFEFFER *Scientific Ball* 33 Runners move up every time the ball is pitched;..the clever baseman will be guided by the action of the man he wants to retire. **1917** C. MATHEWSON *Second Base Sloan* 180 The first batsman was retired on an easy toss from Chase to Jim. **1949** *News-Herald* (Marshfield, Wisconsin) 19 July 9/4 Nowitzke gobbled up Bauer's grounder and threw him out to retire the side. **1972** *N.Y. Times* 4 June v. 1/7 Lyle retired the first 11 batters and wound up allowing just three singles.

retiree (rĭtəiᵊrī·). *U.S.* [f. RETIRE *v.* + -EE[1].] One who has retired from a business or occupation; a pensioner.

1945 W. PEGLER in *Times-Herald* (Washington) 3 Oct. 9/1 How many amputees were there, General Bradley wanted to know, resorting to a ghastly form that has given us, also, trainees, discharges, and retirees. **1962** *Economist* 29 Dec. 1278/1 The 'retirees', people of modest means drawn from all parts of the United States. **1967** MRS. L. B. JOHNSON *White House Diary* 10 May (1970) 516 One of the retirees of the ILGWU..came up to me with a big bouquet of yellow roses. **1972** C. WESTON *Poor, Poor Ophelia* xvii. 102 The couple..were..retirees for whom living on a sailboat was apparently a life's dream. **1975** 'G. BLACK' *Big Wind* ii. 24 The retiree kept spraying my face with fury as he told me. **1979** *Tucson* (Arizona) *Citizen* 3 Oct. 18A/4 Waves of retirees have headed for country parts of Missouri.

retirement. Add: **6.** *attrib.* and *Comb.*, as (sense 2 b) *retirement age, city, community, home, pension, pensioner.*

1919 *Rep. Departmental Comm. Old Age Pensions* App. 157 in *Parl. Papers* (Cmd. 411) XXVII. 299 Your retirement age seems very low. **1976** A. WHITE *Long Silence* xix. 164 The driver, one of the colonel's men, long past retirement age. **1964** V. BARTLETT *Tuscan Retreat* i. 24 'Retirement cities' such as are growing up in the United States..lived in only by old people. **1976** *National Observer* (U.S.) 14 Feb. 9/1 Many elderly people trying to find a retirement community have heard stories of developments going broke. **1979** *Tucson* (Arizona) *Citizen* 20 Sept. 8C/1 At least 60 persons have put down deposits to buy security for their old age in the form of 'life contracts' with a proposed retirement community here. **1968** *Globe & Mail* (Toronto) 13 Feb. 31/4 (Advt.), Small retirement home, 2 bedrooms, 3 piece bath. **1977** E. AMBLER *Send no more Roses* x. 248 Buy that nice retirement home you've always dreamed of owning. **1942** W. BEVERIDGE *Soc. Insurance & Allied Services* III. 96 The pensions proposed in the Plan for Social Security are retirement pensions, not old age pensions. **1973** *Times* 13 Jan. 19/7 Basic retirement pensions are a flat amount..per week. *a* **1974** R. CROSSMAN *Diaries* (1976) II. 644 Should the exemptions be for retirement pensioners or for people over sixty-five?

retirer. (Later example.)

1978 *Oxf. Diocesan Mag.* July 5/3 The main problem of retirement has to be faced by the retirer himself.

retiring, *vbl. sb.* **2. b.** (Examples of *retiring age.*)

1919 *Rep. Departmental Comm. Old Age Pensions* App. 153/1 in *Parl. Papers* (Cmd. 411) XXVII. 299 The retiring age in this case is 50, but, providing the consent of the company is obtained, members are not bound to retire at that age. **1945** 'G. ORWELL' *Animal Farm* iii. 26 There was a stormy debate over the correct retiring age for each class of animal. **1973** G. GREENE *Honorary Consul* v. v. 329 If you were in the Service you would have passed the retiring age quite a while ago.

retoo·l, *v.* [RE- 5 a, c.] *trans.* **1.** To rework or shape again with a tool.

1866 [in Dict. s.v. RE- 5 a].

2. To furnish (a factory, etc.) with fresh tools; to provide new manufacturing equipment for.

1940 *Economist* 5 Oct. 432/2 In case of a change in the design or type of equipment to be produced, the manufacturer must be given ample time to plan its production and if necessary to re-tool his works. **1951** CUNNINGHAM & SHERMAN *Production of Motor Vehicles* iii. 76 It will be necessary to retool many existing machines already in the shop. *Ibid.*, To retool means to provide new jigs, fixtures, clamping devices, cutting tools..and other implementation that makes machines and machine tools effective for a particular operation. **1963** *Economist* 10 Aug. 510/2 The scheduled shut-downs this month to retool for the new 1964 models. **1976** LD. HOME *Way Wind Blows* iv. 58, I agreed with him that a home-based market was necessary if we were to re-tool our factories for export.

Hence **retoo·ling** *vbl. sb.*

1942 *Sun* (Baltimore) 8 Jan. 14/1 The publication goes on to say that 'retooling'..is not the only problem. **1951** G. MARX *Let.* 23 Jan. (1967) 34 Between retooling for the war effort and dueling with Wald and Krasna, I presume you are a fairly busy man. **1962** E. SNOW *Red China Today* (1963) xxvii. 204 Plant in considerable confusion due to expansion and retooling. **1977** G. V. HIGGINS *Dreamland* xii. 146 Vulcan Forge Limited..[had] been a bit slow in retooling to resume production for its prewar markets.

retort, *sb.*[1] Add: **2. b.** *retort courteous*: in allusion to quot. 1600 in sense 2 a. Also *retort discourteous.*

1908 [see *OAR *sb.* 5 a]. **1928** A. HUXLEY *Point Counter Point* iv. 64 The question..fairly invited the retort discourteous. **1977** H. L. MCGUFFIE in Bond & McLeod *Newslett. to Newspapers* III. 197 The quarrel in print..ranged all the way from the Retort Courteous to the Lie Direct.

retort, *sb.*[2] Add: **5.** *retort furnace.*

1879 *Encycl. Brit.* X. 91/2 Retort furnaces are commonly fired or heated with a portion of the coke which forms one of the bye-products of the gas manufacture. **1958** A. D. MERRIMAN *Dict. Metallurgy* 287/1 *Retort furnace*, a metallurgical furnace consisting of a fire-chamber, and frequently regenerative chambers, in which the retorts are placed for containing the materials for treatment. *Ibid.*, Cast-iron retorts are sometimes used in the retort furnace for treatment of mercury ores.

retort, *v.*[1] **I. 3. c.** (Earlier example.)

1811 JANE AUSTEN *Sense & Sens.* III. i. 26 Marianne was going to retort, but she..forbore.

retort, *v.*[2] Substitute for def.: To heat in a retort in order to separate or purify substances. (Earlier and later examples.)

1850 N. KINGSLEY *Diary* 26 May (1914) 123 A warm [day;] the boys retorted the last weeks work. **1924** *Jrnl. Inst. Petroleum Technol.* X. 537 That refinery is supplied.. with the crude oil and ammoniacal liquor derived from the shale retorted there. **1948** *Rep. Progr. Appl. Chem.* XXXIII. 40 The raw shale is retorted at four crude oil works and the crude products are refined at Pumpherston. **1964** J. E. RANSOM *Range Guide to Mines & Minerals* iv. 58 There is a 200-ounce limit on the possession of retort sponge gold obtained by retorting the gold–mercury amalgam.

retortive, *a.* Add: **3.** Also, characterized by retorts.

1949 G. B. SHAW in *Strand Mag.* July 20/2 A trumpery farce may win an uproarious success by its retortive back-chat.

retouch, *sb.* Add: **2.** *Archæol.* Secondary trimming or shaping applied to a stone implement at some period after initial manufacture; an instance of this.

[**1921** M. C. BURKITT *Prehist.* iv. 65 Having blocked out the implement in the rough it had then to be finished with what is known as secondary working or trimming (French, *retouche*).] **1926** D. A. E. GARROD *Upper Palæolithic Age in Britain* i. 38 The tang is well worked, with a steep retouch along both sides and enough of the upper part is left to give an idea of the form. **1932** *Jrnl. R. Anthrop. Inst.* LXII. 261 A fair proportion of lunates and other microliths showed a peculiar retouch which was found on three or four specimens, only at Shukba. **1957** V. G. CHILDE *Dawn European Civilization* (ed. 6) xi. 211 The technique of bifacial retouch on flint flakes and blades is more likely to have reached the north from the south-east than from the south-west. **1964** H. HODGES *Artifacts* vii. 103 The initial roughing out of a stone tool is usually referred to as *primary flaking*, while any later working..is called *secondary flaking* or *retouch*. **1977** *Antiquaries Jrnl.* LVII. 212 *Flint scraper*:..limited fine steep marginal retouch.

retouching, *vbl. sb.* Add: **3.** *retouching desk* (example), *varnish*.

1889 E. J. WALL *Dict. Photogr.* 163 Some sort of retouching desk is needed. **1895** *Montgomery Ward Catal.* Spring–Summer 253/2 French Retouching Varnish, for oil or water color paintings. **1934** H. HILER *Notes Technique Painting* iii. 166 Retouching varnish is a quick-drying varnish used to bring out..parts of the picture which have gone flat or 'dead' in drying.

retract, *v.*[1] Add: **1. e.** *Phonetics.* To pronounce (a sound) with the tongue drawn back.

[**1889** A. J. ELLIS *Early Eng. Pronunc.* v. 17 In D 6, 7, the tongue is often merely retracted.] **1890** H. SWEET *Primer of Phonetics* 73 The first element of the diphthong in *high* is retracted towards ɑ̟. **1970** M. SWANTON *Dream of Rood* 33 CGmc. *a* fronted to early OE *æ* and retracted instead of broken before an *l* or *l*-group.

retract, *v.*[2] Add: † **1. c.** *Chess.* In a chess problem: to take back or unmake (a move). *Obs.*

1871 *Dubuque Chess Jrnl.* 12 White retracts his last move and mates in 1 move. **1881** F. C. COLLINS *Sel. Chess Probl.* 111 Retract White's last move, then White to play, and Mate in One move. **1890** B. G. LAWS *Two-Move Chess Probl.* iii. 16 Retract White's move by replacing White knight at K4, and Black pawn at QB4, then play P × P, *en passant*, discovering mate. **1907** [see *RETRACTOR 4].

retracting *vbl. sb.*[2] (later example).

1874 T. M. BROWN *Bk. Chess Probl.* 20 The *Dubuque Chess Journal* Tourney..for 'retracting' problems.

retractable, *a.* Add: **3. a.** (Later examples.)

1920 *Flight* XII. 96/2 As a result of the unfortunate accident..Messrs. Vickers, Ltd., were unable to show their 'Viking' flying boat with retractable land undercarriage. **1933** *Jrnl. R. Aeronaut. Soc.* XXXVII. 446 Modern U.S.A. commercial aircraft attain higher speeds by clean design and use of retractable carriages. **1936** *Ibid.* XL. 715 Armament (defensive):..1 machine gun 12·7 calibre in retractable turret firing rear; [etc.]. **1968** MILLER & SAWERS *Techn. Devel. Mod. Aviation* III. ii. 54 One can find designs as early as Penaud's in 1871 that were well streamlined and incorporated a retractable undercarriage (first used by du Temple in 1858 on an airplane that did not fly).

b. Applied to an object which admits the retraction of a component part.

1961 *Lebende Sprachen* VI. 103/2 Retractable ball-point pen. **1962** A. NISBETT *Technique Sound Studio* ii. 39 Retractable ball-point pens can be a menace—people will fiddle with them, and produce a sharp, unidentified click every ten or fifteen seconds.

retracted, *ppl. a.* Add: **b.** *Phonetics.* Of a sound: pronounced with the tongue drawn back.

1874 A. J. ELLIS *Early Eng. Pronunc.* IV. 1105/1 As he pronounced this *s* to me, it sounded like a retracted (‚s) with a rattle of moisture. **1908** H. SWEET *Sounds of Eng.* 37 Quite distinct from the fully retracted back vowels. **1975** *Language* LI. 282 Less easy to pin down are the retracted sibilants.

retractile, *a.*[1] Add: **a.** *spec.* in *Med.*, applied to a testis in the inguinal region that can readily be manipulated into the scrotum or vice versa.

1938 SPENCE & SCOWEN in *Lancet* 29 Oct. 983/2 We have used the following terms:—(1) Retractile testes.. (2) Retained testes. **1968** TURNER & BLOODWORTH in J. M. B. Bloodworth *Endocrine Path.* xiii. 438/1 This has probably been due, in large part, to the failure of many observers to distinguish between the retractile testis and the true cryptorchid testis. **1977** *Lancet* 24–31 Dec. 1361/1 The 2 other boys, 1 aged 10 years with small inguinal testes and the other aged 13½ years with one impalpable and one retractile testis, showed no improvement.

retractile, *a.*[2] For *rare*—[1] read *rare* and add further example.

1920 H. G. WELLS *Outl. Hist.* xxix. 327/2 Hadrian, his successor, was of a cautious and retractile disposition.

retraction. Add: **4. e.** *Phonetics.* The drawing back of the tongue in the articulation of speech sounds; articulation thus effected.

1890 H. SWEET *Primer of Spoken Eng.* 4 Each of the vowels formed by the different combinations of retraction and height is either *narrow* or *wide*. **1895** R. MORRIS *Hist. Outl. Eng. Accidence* (ed. 2) ii. 18 We distinguish three horizontal positions, or degrees of retraction of the tongue. **1927** *Year's Work Eng. Stud.* 1925 40 The third point deals chiefly with the phenomena of secondary retraction. **1977** *Archivum Linguisticum* VIII. 76 The only major objection to it must be that there are no other cases in Old English of non-velarized *l* preventing fronting or causing retraction.

retractive, *a.* and *sb.* Add: **A.** *adj.* † **3.** Of a chess problem: involving the retracting of a move or moves. *Obs.*

1890 J. RAYNER *Chess Probl.* 9 A retractive problem is one in which some move..has to be retracted, and then mate or sui-mate in a given number of moves. **1890** B. G. LAWS *Two-Move Chess Probl.* 16 These are called 'Retractive' problems.

retractor. Add: **4.** *Chess.* (See quot. 1907.)

1902 *Brit. Chess Mag.* 455 Two-move retractors. **1907** S. S. BLACKBURN *Terms & Themes Chess Probl.* 33 Retractors. Problems wherein the conditions require that the last move of one, or both, of the players shall be retracted, and that, when this is done, the problem shall be solved according to the usual conditions. **1937** T. R. DAWSON *Caissa's Wild Roses in Clusters* 14/1 A simple changed-mate retractor theme.

retrai·n, *v.* [RE- 5 a.] *trans.* To train again; *spec.* to teach (a skilled or trained person) a new skill. Also **retrai·ning** *vbl. sb.*

1934 in WEBSTER. **1937** *Jrnl. Compar. Psychol.* XXIV. 290 On the re-training trials of the following day, this behavior persisted. **1964** MRS. L. B. JOHNSON *White House Diary* 11 Jan. (1970) 39 He had been out of work for two years and then he heard about the retraining program. **1977** P. STREVENS *New Orientations in Teaching of Eng.* p. vii, Helping to train and re-train teachers. **1977** *Whitaker's Almanack* 1978 980/1 Under the rules of the Fund the Commission can assist in training and retraining schemes by reimbursing 50 per cent. of the cost financed by a public authority.

‖ **retraite** (rətrẹt). Also erron. **rétraite.** [Fr.: a mod. re-borrowing of *retraite* (see RETRAIT *sb.*[1]).] **1.** = RETRAIT *sb.*[1] 3 b. Also *en retraite*, in retirement or seclusion.

1860 MRS. GASKELL *Let.* 27 Aug. (1966) 631, I quite understand the wisdom of French ladies going into rétraite. **1958** L. DURRELL *Mountolive* v. 102 Pombal is doing all this legitimately. He is on local leave. I am *en retraite*.

2. *Mil.* = RETRAIT *sb.*[1] 2.

1883 *Standard* 21 Sept. 3/1 A grand dinner..was followed by the performance of a *retraite* by the combined bands of the Eleventh Army Corps.

retranscri·be, *v.* [RE- 5 a.] *trans.* To transcribe again. So **retranscri·ption.**

1805 Retranscription [in Dict. s.v. RE- 5 a]. **1810** D. WORDSWORTH *Let.* 28 Feb. in W. Knight *Mem. Coleorton* (1887) II. 112 He [*sc.* Coleridge] has written a whole *Friend* more than once in two days. They are never re-transcribed, and he generally has dictated to Miss Hutchinson, who takes the words down from his mouth. **1841** I. D'ISRAELI *Amenities of Lit.* I. 175 Anthony Wood indignantly re-transcribed the whole of his English copy, and left the fair volumes to the care of the university. **1965** *Canad. Jrnl. Linguistics* Spring 85 Most forms are quoted from that source but are retranscribed. **1977** *Word* 1972 XXVIII. 256 The forms which Alonso has cited are not minimal pairs and should be retranscribed as follows.

retransfer, *sb.* Add: **2.** *Printing.* An impression taken from a lithographic image using special ink and paper for the purpose of transferring it to another lithographic surface.

1946 A. KIRK in H. Whetton *Pract. Printing & Binding* xviii. 207 Imperfect retransfers should be scrapped immediately. Good retransfers can be placed face down on a clean sheet. **1965** ZIGROSSER & GAEHDE *Guide Coll. Orig. Prints* iii. 30 If the facts..are known, the authenticity might be questionable, since the artist did not actually work on each retransfer of the original master image. **1967** E. CHAMBERS *Photolitho-Offset* xvii. 259 Before retransferring from litho plates or stones, a thin layer of retransfer ink should be applied with a nap roller to the image.

retranslate, *v.* **1.** (Earlier example.)

1860 G. H. LEWES *Let.* c 10 July in *Geo. Eliot Lett.* (1954) III. 319 There are paragraphs which read like a translation from a language into which one cannot *re*translate them.

retransportation. (Earlier example.)

c **1751** S. RICHARDSON *Let.* (1804) VI. 61 How I missed you, on my re-transportation!

retravirus (re·trăvəiᵊrɒs). *Biol.* [mod. L., f. initial letters of *re*verse *tra*nscriptase (see *TRANSCRIPTASE) + VIRUS.] = *RETROVIRUS.

[**1974** *Intervirol.* IV. 202 Retraviridae are enveloped virions about 100 nm in diameter... They contain about 1.5% of 60–70S RNA... Some species that have been examined also contain a small amount of DNA... All viruses in the family contain antigenically specific reverse transcriptase (RNA-dependent DNA polymerase).] **1977** *Virology* LXXIX. 239 Xenotropic type C retraviruses were isolated from cell-free uterine extracts of normal adult NIH Swiss mice.

re·tread, *sb.* Chiefly *U.S.*, *Austral.*, and *N.Z.* [f. the vb.] **1.** A tyre supplied with a fresh tread; = *REMOULD *sb.*

1914 *Auto-Motor Jrnl.* 4 Apr. 423 So exact is the work.. that a retread is scarcely distinguishable from an original. **1921** *Daily Colonist* (Victoria, B.C.) 10 Apr. 10/6 Always carry a 'retread' as a spare. Don't throw away your old casings until you have had them retreaded at least once. **1943** *Sun* (Baltimore) 4 Feb. 7/2 Retread is new rubber over the same area as recap, but all the way down to the cord fabric. **1968** *Wanganui* (N.Z.) *Chron.* 15 Nov. 10/6 (Advt.), Insist on safe shoulder retreads. **1973** A. COOKE *Amer.* 12, I found myself rediscovering—on re-tread tires at the compulsory thirty-five miles an hour—the whole American landscape. **1976** *Drive* Sept.–Oct. 77/1 A retread is a reprocessed tyre made from a secondhand carcass welded to new tread rubber. **1977** *Bulletin* (Sydney) 22 Jan. 58/3 (Advt.), Because Bandag retreads run longer, you'll spend less time and labour changing worn tyres.

2. *transf.* and *fig.* **a.** *Mil. slang.* A retired soldier recalled for (temporary) service, a 'dug-out'. Also in extended use, esp. of retrained persons.

1941 *Salt* 22 Dec. 36/2 Characteristically the Australians call a small reconnaissance tank a 'dingo', and a 1914–1918 soldier enlisted a second time a 'retread'. **1945** BAKER *Austral. Lang.* II. viii. 152 A soldier of the 1914–18 war who has joined up again is a *retread*. **1948** *Amer. Legion Mag.* Oct. 26 Retreads will reune: Retreads, men who served in both World Wars..will hold their first reunion..at Miami. **1953** *Economist* 17 Oct. 178/2 The pro-Eisenhower *Chicago Daily News* called his appointees 'Governor Stratton's team of Republican retreads'. **1962** *Listener* 16 Aug. 232/2 They also have shorter courses for older men, known rather depressingly as 're-tread' courses. **1965** C. KOCH *Casual Company* I. i. 7 I've got retreads, and chickens bloated with fever, but they turn to at reveille. **1977** D. BEATY *Excellency* ii. 21 A diplomat with thirty years experience..not the retread given a job with other unwanted Civil Servants.

b. Of things.

1964 *Lebende Sprachen* IX. 35/3 Mr Kennedy's plans are retreads of older projects. **1976** *Times Lit. Suppl.* 1 Oct. 1232/1 An all-too-familiar exegesis that has nothing new to say about Eliot.., a critical retread representing the kind of discussion that came in the 1930s. **1979** *Arizona Daily Star* 22 July (Parade Suppl.) 8/3 It is hard to imagine that we shall face another 10 years of the same romantic nostalgia and retread pop culture as was dished out by the '70's.

retrea·d, *v.* [RE- 5 c.] *trans.* **1.** To furnish (a tyre) with a fresh tread.

1908 *Daily Report* 7 Feb. 11/4 (Advt.), 10–12 h.p. Wolseley, in excellent condition, front pneumatics, just been retreaded. **1912** *Motor Manual* (ed. 14) iii. 107 It is possible, in most cases, to have them retreaded by the makers.

2. *fig.* To retrain (a person) or provide with fresh employment, esp. after initial retirement. *U.S. slang.*

1963 *Lafayette Alumnus* Apr. 22/1 'Retreaded'..indicated that upon retirement, De Kay, Furness [etc.]..gave their learning, experience, and wisdom a capping. **1966** *Wall St. Jrnl.* 2 Dec. 1/4 To 'retread' many retired nurses and other skilled professionals through refresher courses.

Hence **retrea·der**; **retrea·ded** *ppl. a.*, **retrea·ding** *vbl. sb.*

1914 *Auto-Motor Jrnl.* 4 Apr. 423 During the retreading.. it is very often found that the casing requires strengthening. **1921** *Dict. Occup. Terms* (1927) § 608 *Tyre retreader*, attaches new treads to worn tyre covers. **1937** *Sci. Amer.* Dec. 347/1 Retreading..involves nothing more nor less than replacing with new live rubber the tread which has become worn smooth under the abrasive action of the road. **1951** U. V. TROUBRIDGE tr. *Guareschi's Little World of Don Camillo* 207 The explosion had..been caused..by one of the retreaded tyres of the lorry. **1964** G. MITCHELL *Death of Delft Blue* xxi. 228 Look over their used cars and retreaded tyres. **1976** *Globe & Mail* (Toronto) 3 July 6/1 A retreaded provincial politician who was fired from the Davis Cabinet. **1977** *Financial Times* 4 June 5/3 The retreading industry would welcome it, because casings are their raw material.

retreat, *sb.* **3. d.** Delete *rare* and add later examples.

1914 W. B. WRIGHT *Quaternary Ice Age* vii. 155 They are named by Penck retreat-stadia ('Rückzugsstadien'), but it is considered probable that they were formed at the ends of periods of readvance. **1954** W. D. THORNBURY *Princ. Geomorphol.* viii. 201 The factors influencing the retreat of slopes are far more complex than is generally realized. **1963** R. A. DALY *Changing World of Ice Age* i. 21 (*caption*) Two principal moraines of retreat in Finland. **1970** R. J. SMALL *Study of Landforms* xi. 388 If the ice is affected by episodes of retreat, separated by stillstands, a number of smaller, sub-parallel ridges ('recessional' or 'stadial' moraines) will be formed.

10. *Comb.*, as *retreat house.*
1920 J. F. Briscoe in *Rep. First Anglo-Catholic Congress* 182 There ought to be a retreat-house in every diocese. **1958** *Church Times* 14 Feb. 10/3 With its membership growing, part of the accommodation in the retreat house has had to be taken to house the brethren. **1979** *Country Life* 6 Dec. 2188/3 Rydal Hall..was leased to the diocese of Carlisle..as a retreat house and conference centre.

retreatal, *a.* (rĭtrī·tăl). [f. Retreat *v.* + -al.] Of or pertaining to the contraction and retreat of ice sheets and glaciers.
1896 *Amer. Geologist* XVIII. 156 The stages of retreatal deposits ending in Greenwich cove illustrate the shrinkage and final disappearance of a tongue of the ice. *Ibid.* 160 (*heading*) Retreatal formations on the central and eastern shores of the bay. **1937** *Geogr. Jrnl.* XC. 233 Most of this erosion occurred during the maximum stage of glaciation and very little during the retreatal stages. **1937** Wooldridge & Morgan *Physical Basis of Geogr.* xxii. 378 Retreatal stages of the ice in the valleys are marked by 'stadial moraines'. **1968** R. W. Fairbridge *Encycl. Geomorphol.* 327/1 Bergdahl (1963) has recently published a series of studies on the Närke plain where estuarine clays from the Baltic progressively overlap closely spaced ridges of retreatal moraines, each winter season being marked by another ridge, at 170–280 meter intervals.

retreating, *ppl. a.* **1.** (Further examples.)
1961 M. Levy *Studio Dict. Art Terms* 97 *Retreating colour*, a colour, such as blue, which in a painting appears to retreat into the distance. **1962** *Punch* 25 Apr. 655/2 'Retreating defence'—the rapid funnelling back and massing of defenders inside the penalty area. **1977** *Daily Express* 29 Mar. 32/4 The 'reserves' had an extra couple of players, in the form of the England coaching staff, to thicken a retreating defence still further.

retreatism (rĭtrī·tiz'm). [f. Retreat *sb.* + -ism.] **1.** A policy of retreat; advocacy of (military) withdrawal.
1951 *Times* 24 Feb. 7/3 General Eisenhower returned to Europe this week bringing assurance that his country has rejected the 'retreatism' advocated by Mr. Herbert Hoover and supported by Senator Taft. **1976** J. Rowan *Ordinary Ecstasy* ii. 25 If we see everything as perfect as it is, we may be inclined to quietism and retreatism in political terms.
2. *Sociol.* A state of passive withdrawal from society induced by a sense of inability to attain its norms or to offer resistance to them.
1957 R. K. Merton *Social Theory* (rev. ed.) iv. 153 Retreatism..is an expedient which arises from continued failure to near the goal by legitimate measures and from an inability to use the illegitimate route because of internalized prohibitions. **1963** T. & P. Morris *Pentonville* vii. 173 Retreatism in prison is comparatively rare, and can be identified with either an extreme manifestation of institutional neurosis..or with various stages of mental illness. **1969** in Lindzey & Aronson *Handbk. Social Psychol.* (ed. 2) IV. xxxiii. 352 With warfare no longer possible, there is a great deal of retreatism and social withdrawal. **1970** *New Society* 31 Dec. 1158/2 Thus, men like Roy..would still maintain that the only rational solution was retreatism.

retreatist (rĭtrī·tist), *sb.* (and *a.*) [f. as prec. + -ist.] **1.** One who advocates a policy of retreat; a supporter of (military) withdrawal.
a **1925** Curzon *Leaves from Viceroy's Notebk.* (1926) iii. 142 The Retreatists would not have these proposals at any price. **1951** *Times* 20 Feb. 4/5 Mr. Wherry and others like him.. now dislike being called isolationists, but have been called 'retreatists' instead.
2. *Sociol.* One who has succumbed to retreatism (sense 2).
1957 R. K. Merton *Social Theory* (rev. ed.) v. 189 Retreatists are even more reluctant to enter into new social relations with others than are those described as 'alienated'. **1960** Cloward & Ohlin *Delinquency & Opportunity* i. 21 These terms..do not necessarily reflect the attitudes of members of the subcultures. Thus the term 'retreatist' does not necessarily reflect the attitude of the 'cat'. **1963** T. & P. Morris *Pentonville* vii. 173 The retreatist rejects both goals and means.
3. *attrib.* or as *adj.*
1957 R. K. Merton *Social Theory* (rev. ed.) v. 187 The retreatist pattern consists of the substantial abandoning both of the once-esteemed cultural goals and of institutionalized practices directed toward those goals. **1973** *Sociol. Rev.* XXI. 419 The attitudes and values of people whom they call retreatist, and the immediate conditions under which the response occurs.

retreative (rĭtrī·tiv), *a.* [f. Retreat *sb.* or *v.* + -ive.] Pertaining to or suggestive of retreat; tending to withdraw.
1899 B. Tarkington *Gentleman from Indiana* xix. 376 As they neared the brick house Harkless made out, through the trees, a retreative flutter of skirts on the porch. **1977** *Times Lit. Suppl.* 25 Mar. 332/3 A melancholic, self-retreative, self-distrustful constitution.

re-treatment. (Earlier example.)
1867 J. A. Phillips *Mining & Metallurgy Gold & Silver* x. 216 (*heading*) Re-treatment of first tailings.

retribalization (rĭtrəi:bǎləizē[1]·ʃən). [f. next.] The process of making or becoming retribalized.
1964 M. McLuhan *Understanding Media* ii. xxxii. 344 Today we appear to be poised between two ages—one of detribalization and one of retribalization. **1967** *Listener* 20 July 75/1 What Marshall McLuhan calls the tendency to retribalization in the multi-sensual experiences enjoyed by young people. **1970** *Internat. & Compar. Law Q.* XIX. i. 152 The general retribalisation designs of the present régime.

retribalize (rĭtrəi·bǎləiz), *v.* [f. Re- + Tribal *a.* + -ize. Cf. *detribalize *v.*] *trans.* To restore (a person or society) to a tribal state; to encourage the tribal instincts and habits of. So **retri·balized** *ppl. a.*; **retri·balizing** *vbl. sb.*
1963 *Economist* 7 Sept. 805/2 A sprinkling of retribalised black statelets. **1964** M. McLuhan *Understanding Media* ii. xxiii. 229 It was easy for the retribalized Nazi to feel superior to the American consumer. *Ibid.* xxiv. 236 We have begun retribalizing with the same painful groping with which a preliterate society begins to read and write. *Ibid.* xxx. 304 The power of radio to retribalize mankind, its almost instant reversal of individualism into collectivism, Fascist or Marxist, has gone unnoticed. **1967** *Guardian* 9 Sept. 6/3 The effect of television as such is to retribalise and deliteratise mankind. **1969** A. Cohen *Custom & Politics in Urban Africa* i. 29 As the migrant becomes more settled, by being drawn into active participation in the social life of the Quarter—economically, politically, morally, and ritually—he becomes increasingly more '*retribalized*'.

retribute, *v.* **2.** (Later example.)
1933 W. H. W. Sabine *Guido & Girls* xi. 130 Those foul thoughts that lately have been mine, Thus justly retributed by the laws..that are divine.

retribution. 1. b. (Later example.)
1850 Thackeray *Pendennis* I. xxxvii. 355 She thought his retribution of the hundred pounds an act of angelic virtue.

retri·butivist, *sb.* (and *a.*) [f. retributive *a.* + -ist.] A believer in retributive justice. Also *attrib.* or as *adj.*
1939 *Mind* XLVIII. 157 Retributivists have been pushed into holding that pain *ipso facto* represses the worse self and frees the better, when this is contrary to the vast majority of observed cases. **1968** *Economist* 13 July 48/2 The current fashion..is to take it for granted that certain doctrines, such as the retributivist, are so discredited as to merit nothing but the most perfunctory and hostile attention. **1969** *Listener* 17 July 87/3 Why should we punish criminals? 'To ensure that they get their deserts,' says the Retributivist. *Ibid.* 88/1 Most of us have our retributivist moments ('Are you suggesting that Eichmann should have gone *scot free*?').

retri·ck, *v. rare.* [Re- 5 a.] *trans.* Of a heavenly light: to cause (a beam) to shine again. Also in fig. phr. *to retrick one's beams,* to restore one's mood; to regain one's happiness, shrug off despair.
Always with reference to Milton's line in *Lycidas*.
[**1637** Milton *Lycidas* in *Poems* (1968) 253 The day-star.. tricks his beams, and with new spangled ore, Flames in the forehead of the morning sky.] **1833** [implied in Retricked *ppl. a.*]. **1863** Trollope *Small House at Allington* (1864) II. iii. 28 We have retricked our beams in our own ways, and our lives have not been desolate. **1880** —— *Duke's Children* III. xxiv. 286 It is so that a man is stricken down... But it is given to him to retrick his beams.

retrievable, *a.* (Further examples.)
1967 *Times Rev. Industry* Oct. 84/1 Formalized techniques or procedures..for continuously carrying intelligence into retrievable form. **1974** C. Taylor *Fieldwork in Medieval Archaeol.* i. 18 The information..needs to be sorted and assembled in some form of retrievable system.

retrieval. Add: **1. b.** *spec.* = *information retrieval* s.v. *information 8. Freq. *attrib.*
1958 *Bull. Canad. Libr. Assoc.* Apr. 193/1 One of the reasons which makes these machines fundamentally uneconomical at present is that the frequency of demand for exactly the same mechanical retrieval process in reference work is rarely sufficient to justify the large initial cost of coding and mechanizing all that a machine incapable of judgment needs, to perform the process. **1966** *Jrnl. Amer. Med. Assoc.* 13 June 950/1 This technique allows medical narrative and numerical data to be collected efficiently in a form acceptable as computer input for subsequent storage, analysis, and retrieval. **1968** *Globe & Mail* (Toronto) 3 Feb. b7/5 The computer's instant retrieval mechanism can make available, within 24 hours, any information contained in major Canadian collective labor agreements. **1972** *Bookseller* 4 Mar. 1463/3 It is highly important..that new systems of cataloguing and retrieval shall be built into the new library. **1974** W. Garner *Big enough Wreath* xi. 138 How many men did you say you had on your..tapes?.. All tucked away in your retrieval system. **1979** J. E. Rowley *Mechanised In-House Information Syst.* i. 26 Retrieval keys, such as indexing terms are stored adjacent to the records to which they relate.

retrieve, *sb.* Add: **3. c.** A controlled exercise for a gun-dog simulating the retrieval of game; the object retrieved.
1932 L. Sprake *Art of Dog Training* v. 94 The pupil is taken to the regular training ground, and one or two retrieves of the usual dummy commence the proceedings. **1937** E. B. Moffit *Elias Vail trains Gun Dogs* ix. 134 Gallery critics at field trials are puzzled at the difficulty that many handlers experience in getting a dog to go out far enough to a retrieve. **1953** E. Stonex *Golden Retriever Handbk.* ix. 108 He must bring it right up to you—never let him run round you in circles with his retrieve. **1963** M. Brander *Gundogs* iv. 37 Only the very earliest retrieves of all should be made with the dummy or plaything thrown in full view in the open, so that the pup is encouraged to run in after it at once. **1976** *Field* 2 Sept. 474/1 He now performs the basic five retrieves as advocated by Maurice Hopper without any histrionics. **1979** *Country Life* 26 July 220/1 The gundog area has..a timed retrieve competition (the scurry).
d. *U.S. Sport.* The act of intercepting or otherwise regaining possession of the ball.
1961 in Webster. **1974** *State* (Columbia, S. Carolina) 15 Feb. 3-b/1 Barron is averaging 19.3 points a game and has been getting 11.5 retrieves per contest.

retrieve, *v.* Add: **I. 2. d.** To obtain again (stored information).
1962 *Communications Assoc. Computing Machinery* V. 12/2 Some kind of indexing scheme that can retrieve records ..within a short period of time. **1968** *Brit. Med. Bull.* XXIV. 195/1 By means of electronic pulses the data would be placed inside the computer system,..and be available for analysis at a future date as well as being able to be retrieved on demand. **1971** *Nature* 19 Mar. 155/2 Many short notes and letters contain the first 'rush' announcement of extremely important results—just what a current-awareness service should aim to retrieve. **1975** J. B. Harley *O.S. Maps* p. xiv, In the process of retrieving information the Survey's Librarian..has conjured otherwise elusive papers into my hands.

retrieveless, *a.* (Further example.)
c **1871** E. Dickinson *Poems* (1955) III. 836 Till some retrieveless Night Our Vigilance at waste The Garden gets the only shot That never could be traced.

retriever. Add: **1. b.** (Earlier example.)
1830 M. R. Mitford *Our Village* IV. 110 His noble Newfoundland dog, (a retriever is the sporting word).
2. (Later example.)
1977 *Tennis World* Sept. 17/3 'Baseliners', 'retrievers and 'counter-punchers' are players who stay back from the net.

retrieverish (rĭtrī·vəriʃ), *a.* [f. Retriever + -ish[1].] Resembling or suggestive of a retriever.
1909 H. G. Wells *Tono-Bungay* iii. ii. 243 There were two or three fox-terriers, a retrieverish mongrel, and an old, bloody-eyed, and very evil-smelling St. Bernard.

retrieving, *vbl. sb.* (Further examples.)
1962 *Communications Assoc. Computing Machinery* V. 11 (*heading*) Information structures for processing and retrieving.
attrib. **1972** J. S. Hall *Sayings from Old Smoky* 3 A computer-like retrieving process.

retrim, *v.* (Examples of *absol.* use.)
1966 D. Francis *Flying Finish* xviii. 217, I put on full flap, maximum drag..retrimmed..felt the plane get slower and heavier. **1977** 'O. Jacks' *Autumn Heroes* v. 71 You drag 'em out, boss, while I re-trim.

retro-. Add: **3. a. retroana·lysis** *Chess*, analysis of a position so as to reconstruct the moves of the game leading to that position; also *transf.*; so **retroanaly·tical** *a.*; **retrocognition,** (*b*) *Psychol.*, paranormal cognition of events in someone or something else's past; **retrodispla·cement,** displacement rearwards; **re·trofocus** *a. Photogr.*, designating an optical system in which the distance of the rear surface from the image of an object at infinity exceeds the focal length, usu. achieved by placing a diverging group of lenses before a converging group.
[**1933** H. Phillips *Week-End Problems Bk.* 182 Profound and puzzling retrograde analysis is needed to prove the legality of the key-move.] **1937** T. R. Dawson *Caissa's Wild Roses in Clusters* 13/1 Trio of retro-analyses. **1979** *Sci. Amer.* Dec. 20/2 Most chess problems deal with the future, such as how can White move and mate in three. Smullyan's problems belong to a field known as retrograde analysis (retro analysis for short), in which it is necessary to reconstruct the past. **1980** *Daily Tel.* 21 Apr. 13/7 Retro-analysis is..the root of much scientific thinking. It is as useful to the astronomer pondering the creating of the universe by observing space as it appears *now* as it is to the detective who solves a murder by deducing the series of events that led to the crime. **1966** *New Statesman* 10 June 858/3 It contains a good many highly complicated 'retro-analytical' problems. **1980** *Daily Tel.* 21 Apr. 13/7 The chess-board here is being used only as a tool for an exercise in retro-analytical deduction. **1962** C. D. Broad *Lect. Psychical Res.* 402 What I will call 'states of *direct* but not ostensibly *recollective retro-cognition*'. **1969** J. J. Macintosh in Macintosh & Coval *Business of Reason* 154 In the absence of a body there is no way of distinguishing between veridical memories and what might be called accurate retro-cognition. **1973** *Daily Tel.* (Colour suppl.) 30 Nov. 27/4 *Retrocognition*, as precognition, but of past events. **1903** *Med. Rec.* (N.Y.) 27 June 434/2 (*heading*) The treatment by anterior vaginal section of retrodisplacement of the uterus, complicated by adhesions. **1972** *Biol. Abstr.* LIII. 3376/2 Physical exertion of women employed in mechanical coal dressing does not affect the incidence of.. retrodisplacement of the uterus. **1965** *Focal Encycl. Photogr.* (rev. ed.) II. 1293/2 Retrofocus lenses are almost invariably of the inverted telephoto type. **1977** J. Hedgecoe *Photographer's Handbk.* 323 In wide-angle, retro-focus constructions the back focus is much greater than the focal length which allows room for mirrors etc. within the camera construction. **1979** *Amat. Photographer* Feb. 95/2 The normal simple calculations for finding the effective f/number when engaged in close-up work with extension tubes or bellows do not always give the right answers when using a telephoto or retrofocus lens.
b. *retro-cæcal, -cardiac, -duodenal, -peritoneal, -pubic, -uterine* (earlier example);

retro-bu·lbar, situated or occurring behind the eyeball.

[**1866** A. VON GRAEFE in *Archiv für Ophthalm.* II. 147 Als solche erscheint mir die Annahme einer retrobulbären Neuritis.] **1879** *Archiv für Ophthalm.* VIII. 328 (*heading*) Three cases of retrobulbar, pulsating, vascular tumor. **1879** E. NETTLESHIP *Student's Guide Dis. Eye* II. xvii. 225 Neuritis behind the eye (retro-bulbar neuritis). **1961** *Lancet* 29 Apr. 908/2 Retrobulbar neuritis is a rare, though well-recognised complication of addisonian pernicious anæmia. **1964** S. DUKE-ELDER *Parsons' Dis. Eye* (ed. 14) 568 Retro-bulbar injections should be preceded by an injection of procaine. **1903** *Amer. Med.* V. 836/1 Case I. Retrocecal gangrenous appendicitis. **1961** *Lancet* 23 Sept. 671/2 *Staph[ylococcus] aureus*..was isolated from..the retrocæcal abscess. **1901** *Ibid.* 12 Jan. 118/2 This clear zone is somewhat triangular in shape. Dr. Mignon proposes to call it the retro-cardiac triangle. **1908** *Practitioner* Dec. 863 The 'retro-cardiac triangle', seen when the patient is in the lateral oblique position. This triangle is bounded by the heart in front, the spine behind, and the diaphragm below. *Ibid.* 827, I am inclined to think that transduodenal or retro-duodenal operations for this condition should be avoidable. **1893** *Trans. Path. Soc.* XLIV. 69 The case is..an example of what Astley Cooper termed the mesenteric variety of retro-peritoneal hernia. **1977** *Lancet* 28 May 1133/1 Retroperitoneal hæmorrhage occurred in 5 patients. **1967** TAYLOR & COTTON *Short Textbk. Surg.* xxvi. 397 Retropubic Prostatectomy. The prostate is approached.. via a suprapubic incision through the cave of Retzius, the potential space between the back of the pubis and the bladder... A drain is inserted into the retropubic space. **1851** *Monthly Jrnl. Med. Sci.* XIII. 278 (*heading*) Retro-uterine sanguineous tumours.

c. Terms in *Astronautics* relating to retro-rockets and their use, as *retro-ignition*, *-impulse*, *-manœuvre*, *-propulsion*, *-system*, *-thrust*.

1967 *New Scientist* 21 Sept. 595/1 Retro-ignition was delayed for 12·5 seconds, coming at 150 000 feet instead of the normal 274 000 feet. **1961** H. H. KOELLE *Handbk. Astronaut. Engin.* xxv. 29 The instantaneous retro impulses applied tangentially to the trajectory. **1976** *Sci. Amer.* June 7/3 In the Viking missions..the retromaneuver ..that will put the spacecraft in orbit around Mars will be based on commands sent from the earth at least a day earlier. *Ibid.* 59/1 Those commands will cause the spacecraft's retro-propulsion system to fire for 43 minutes, subtracting enough velocity to place the spacecraft in an elliptical orbit around Mars. **1962** S. CARPENTER in *Into Orbit* 56 The retro-system is rigged so that the rockets will not fire..unless the capsule is in the correct attitude. **1962** RILEY & SAILOR *Space Syst. Engin.* iv. 86 The retro-thrust is directed at such an angle as to provide a desired range. Increases in retro-velocities result in small range angles.

retro (re·tro), *sb.* [Short for *RETRO-ROCKET.] = *RETRO-ROCKET b.

1961 *New Scientist* 21 Sept. 719/3 Whether because of the timing of the order, or the impulse of the retros, or drift of the wind.., the robot cosmonaut got away from its shepherds on the sea and fell into the water seventy miles from the nearest waiting ship. **1962** S. CARPENTER in *Into Orbit* 56 The pilot must..have the capsule pointed exactly right when the retros fire. **1966** *Word Study* Dec. 1/2 Commander Alan B. Shepard, whose flight lasted only fifteen minutes, was precise and terse: 'Disarm.' 'Auto retro jettison circuit.'

retroaction. Add: **4. b.** *Psychol.* The effect of later learning on the memory of what was learnt previously. Also *attrib.*

1949 POSTMAN & EGAN *Exper. Psychol.* xvi. 378 Maximum retroaction occurs when original and interpolated learning are approximately equal in strength. **1953** C. E. OSGOOD *Methods & Theory in Exper. Psychol.* xiii. 562 The fact that so-called 'rest' control groups show loss in retention has already been noted in connection with the logic of transfer and retroaction experiments. **1971** L. POSTMAN in J. W. Kling et al. *Woodworth & Schlosberg's Exper. Psychol.* xxi. 1110/2 The treatment corresponds to the rest condition in experiments on retroaction.

retroactive *a.* Add: **1. a.** (Later examples.) Also with *to.*

1952 *Sun* (Baltimore) 22 Mar. 6/4 A handsome wage increase..allows 12.5 cents an hour immediately and retroactive to January 1. **1978** J. PAXTON *Dict. Europ. Econ. Community* (rev. ed.) 49 The United Kingdom..informed the Council of Ministers on 27 March that a subsidy would be granted on sugar and made retroactive to 1 Feb. **1979** *Arizona Daily Star* 5 Aug. c8/4 Placed Paul Hartzell, pitcher, on the 21-day disabled list, retroactive to last Thursday.

c. *retroactive infinitive* (Gram.), an active infinitive that has a preceding noun as its object.

1946 O. JESPERSEN *Mod. Eng. Gram.* V. xv. 233 Retroactive infinitives are found in connexion with the adverbs *yet* and *still*:..Rome and Naples—even Florence are yet to see (= we have not yet seen; *are yet to be seen* would mean 'can still be seen').

4. *Psychol.* That affects the remembering of what has been previously learned; esp. as *retroactive inhibition*, the inhibiting effect on recall that can be produced by attention given to new material after the original learning. Cf. *INHIBITION 4, *PROACTIVE *a.*

1909 C. S. MYERS *Exper. Psychol.* xiii. 163 This 'retroactive inhibition' is yet another cause of the greater difficulty in learning longer than shorter studies. *Ibid.* 166 Similar experiments have been conducted with the object of proving retro-active, i.e. backward association. **1909** *Psychol. Monogr.* X. IV. 138 With G. retroactive inhibition was obvious. Each series was remembered fairly well until the next was given. **1915** *Ibid.* XIX. IV. (*title*) A study of retroactive inhibition. **1938** *Brit. Jrnl. Psychol.* Jan. 244 It could be argued that retroactive inhibition might influence the result by preventing the possibility of such recall. **1948** E. R. HILGARD *Theories of Learning* vi. 162 The natural conjecture on the assumption of continuous variation is that the amount of retroactive inhibition would increase gradually as dissimilarity was increased. **1963** COFER & MUSGRAVE *Verbal Behav. & Learning* 7 Many facts of acquisition are consistent with either formulation, but..others, especially the facts of proactive and retroactive interference, are not. **1965** J. M. STEPHENS *Psychol. of Classroom Learning* viii. 203 Your experience with the second task would work back to strengthen the rather tentative earlier association. This backward-working process is called retroactive facilitation. **1966** J. M. BROWN et al. *Appl. Psychol.* 36 A common explanation for this loss of retention is that newly learned material inhibits that previously learned. A technical term for this is retroactive inhibition. **1975** G. H. BOWER in W. K. Estes *Handbk. Learning & Cognitive Processes* I. ii. 75 An inherent restriction on retrieval times would then produce the observable phenomena of retroactive interference.

retrodi·ction. [f. RETRO- + DICTION, after PREDICTION *sb.*] The explanation or interpretation of past actions or events inferred from the laws that are assumed to have governed them. Cf. *POSTDICTION.

1895 J. M. ROBERTSON *Buckle & his Critics* x. 311 Let us first put a little order in our conception of prediction and 'retrodiction' as they indisputably take place in the settled sciences. *Ibid.* 316 The same reasoning applies to errors of interpretation, of what we have called 'retrodiction'. **1939** *Mind* XLVIII. 421 L-propositions are plainly useless save in so far as they assist prediction—or retro-diction—as to particular matters of fact. **1940** *Philosophy* XV. 22 It may be what Mr Ryle calls a *retrodiction*, as when I infer from marks seen in the snow that a cat has passed that way. **1956** J. N. FINDLAY in H. D. Lewis *Contemp. Brit. Philos.* 185 Prediction and retrodiction alike depend on the presence in our world of what have been called 'world-lines'. **1960** I. BERLIN in W. H. Dray *Philos. Analysis & Hist.* (1966) 13 In the case of an historical study, retrodiction—filling in gaps in the past for which no direct testimony exists with the aid of extrapolation performed according to relevant rules or laws. **1975** J. W. CORNMAN *Perception, Common Sense & Sci.* viii. 302 The argument based on retrodiction might prompt another reply, namely, that the supposed fact of retrodiction violates Heisenberg's uncertainty principle. *Ibid.* 303 Epistemic and causal indeterminacy limit prediction but not retrodiction.

Hence (as a back-formation) **retrodi·ct** *v. trans.* and *absol.*, to infer by retrodiction (cf. *POSTDICT *v.*); **retrodi·cting** *vbl. sb.* Also **retrodi·ctable, retrodi·ctive** *adjs.*, **retrodi·ctively** *adv.*

1932 H. H. PRICE *Perception* vii. 201 Any perceptual act is bound to be among other things a prediction,..and in the same way it must be 'retrodictive' as well. **1949** G. RYLE *Concept of Mind* v. 124 They are inference-tickets, which license us to predict, retrodict, explain and modify these actions, reactions and states. **1951** W. H. WALSH *Introd. Philos. Hist.* ii. 41 It has been said that whilst it is certainly not the business of historians to predict the future, it is very much their business to 'retrodict' the past. **1952** *Mind* LXI. 225 Attempts to predict or retrodict when no grounds for rational belief are obtainable. **1956** E. H. HUTTEN *Lang. Mod. Physics* vi. 222 We now interpret 'causality' as meaning that there can be formulated a universal sentence which ..allows us to derive a singular, descriptive, predictive or retrodictive, sentence. **1959** J. BLISH *Clash of Cymbals* v. 104 Time in our experience is not retrodictable. *Ibid.* 105 Can we write a convergent retrodictive equation? **1966** C. G. HEMPEL *Philos. Nat. Sci.* vi. 72 The theory was used by Halley..to identify it retrodictively with comets whose appearances had been recorded on six previous occasions. **1975** J. W. CORNMAN *Perception, Common Sense & Sci.* viii. 303 Is there any reason to think that retrodicting the position and momentum of an entity more precisely than stated by the uncertainty principle violates the principle? **1976** *Times Lit. Suppl.* 27 Aug. 1057/4 What a historical model is meant to do: not to allow us to predict or retrodict..but to provide insight into and explanations of historical events.

retroduction. Delete *rare*—⁰ and add later examples. *spec.* in *Philos.*, a type of logical reasoning that develops from some commonly accepted proposition until reasons are found that may alter the acceptance or understanding of the original proposition (see quot. *a* 1914). Also *transf.*

1786 J. PINKERTON *Anc. Scotish Poems* I. p. xxxiii, The poor man [*sc.* Walter Goodall] was writing a *retroduction* to Fordun. *a* **1914** C. S. PEIRCE *Coll. Papers* (1931) I. 28 There are in science three fundamentally different kinds of reasoning, Deduction.., Induction..and Retroduction (Aristotle's ἀπαγωγή, but misunderstood because of corrupt text, and as misunderstood usually translated *abduction*). *Ibid.* 29 Retroduction is the provisional adoption of a hypothesis, because every possible consequence of it is capable of experimental verification, so that the persevering application of the same method may be expected to reveal its disagreement with facts. **1939** *Mind* XLVIII. 378 In discussing 'the leap of the mind from data to hypothesis' he makes no reference to C. S. Peirce's *Retroduction*. **1958** N. R. HANSON *Patterns of Discovery* 217 Retroductions do not always lead to syntheses like those of Newton, Clerk Maxwell, Einstein and Dirac. They sometimes show the first chink in the old armour. **1965** P. CAWS *Philos. of Sci.* xxxii. 243 This is the essential ingredient in what Peirce called retroduction, the intuitive jump from observed facts to hypotheses about them. **1976** C. SELLTIZ et al. *Res. Methods Social Relations* (ed. 3) ii. 32 In the process of determining explanations for observed events, social scientists often reason *from* conclusions to reasons *for* conclusions. We call this inference process *retroduction*, in contrast with deduction and induction. In retroduction, we try to think of plausible reasons why some event could have occurred in an attempt to construct an explanation of why the event did occur.

Also **retrodu·ctive** *a.*, pertaining to or characterized by retroduction; **retrodu·ctively** *adv.*

a **1914** C. S. PEIRCE *Coll. Papers* (1932) II. 491 Induction ..is manifestly adequate, with the aid of retroduction and of deductions from retroductive suggestions, to discovering any regularity. **1958** N. R. HANSON *Patterns of Discovery* iv. 86 *H* cannot be retroductively inferred until its content is present in 2. **1974** P. ACHINSTEIN in F. Suppe *Struct. Sci. Theories* 357 Retroductive or explanatory reasoning..is reasoning falling under the logic of discovery, whereas deductive reasoning from established theories is reasoning falling under the logic of justification. **1976** C. SELLTIZ et al. *Res. Methods Social Relations* (ed. 3) ii. 32 An example of retroductive reasoning appears in a study of the decline in trust in the national government during the last decade.

re·tro-engine. *Astronautics.* Also as one word. [f. RETRO- + ENGINE *sb.*] = *RETRO-ROCKET b.

1967 *Britannica Bk. of Year* 804/1 *Retro-engine*, retro-rocket. **1971** *New Scientist* 6 May 305 Each Mariner.. carries to Mars..about 1000 lbs of fuel for the 14-minute retroengine burn needed to slow it to the requisite orbital speed. **1977** *Sci. Amer.* Nov. 52/1 With the help of its retroengines and parachute it dropped to the surface of Mars.

retro-fire (re·trofəiᵊɹ), *v.* Also **retrofire.** [f. RETRO- + FIRE *v.*¹] *trans.* To ignite or fire (a retro-rocket); to fire a rocket engine so as to give (a spacecraft) backward thrust. Also *absol.*

1961 *Ann. Rev. Med.* XII. 315 Periodically, a very lightweight disposable capsule may be retro-fired in such a way that the capsule together with all unwanted materials will be incinerated on re-entering the atmosphere. **1969** [see *free return* s.v. *FREE *a.* D. 2]. **1969** *Guardian* 14 Mar. 1/8 At 5 31 (BST) over Hawaii, Scott retrofired the main service propulsion engine..and Apollo 9 began its long arching descent.

retro-fire (re·trofəiᵊɹ), *sb.* Also **retrofire.** [f. RETRO- + FIRE *sb.*] The process or action of burning a retro-rocket. Also *attrib.*

1962 J. GLENN in *Into Orbit* 42 The clock is pre-set on the ground according to a timing for retro-fire which we have computed before the mission. **1962** *Flight Internat.* LXXXI. 263/1 Kauai Island acquires the spacecraft,..and checks the retro-fire clock for possible change if Mercury control so advises. Point Arguello..gives back-up command to the spacecraft after the clock initiates retro-fire. **1967** *New Scientist* 16 Nov. 424/2 It is not impossible to visualize a carefully controlled descent, the only limitations being the weight of propellants needed for continuous retro-fire. **1974** *Encycl. Brit. Macropædia* XVII. 369/2 Below the Command Module is the Service Module. It..contains the propulsion system for midcourse corrections, retrofire to achieve lunar orbit, and thrust to return from lunar orbit into Earth trajectory.

So **re·tro-fi:ring** *vbl. sb.*

1962 J. GLENN in *Into Orbit* 41 You superintend the retro-firing sequence from here with toggle switches. **1968** *Guardian* 24 Dec. 1/3, 3 21 p.m.: second retrofiring to bring spacecraft into a circular orbit 69 miles above the moon's surface. **1971** *Ibid.* 1 July 1/5 In order to carry out the descent to earth..retro-firing took place at 01.35.

retrofit (re·trofit), *sb.* orig. *U.S.* Also with hyphen. [f. RETRO(ACTIVE *a.* + RE)FIT *sb.*] A modification made to a product, esp. an aircraft, to incorporate changes made in later products of the same type or model.

1956 in W. A. HEFLIN *U.S. Air Force Dict.* 441/1. **1962** *Flight Internat.* LXXXI. 292/1 Fig. 2 is a plot of the ratios of revenue lost versus maintenance and first costs for retro-fitted and 'designed-in' equipment. It points out.. that the economic cut-off point for retrofit is near the 100ft ceiling, ¼ mile point. **1963** T. PYNCHON *V.* x. 286 An injury of the sexual organs could still be simulated by an attachable moulage, but then this blocked the cooling vent... A new retrofit, however, eliminated this difficulty, which was felt to be a basic design deficiency. **1967** *Times Rev. Industry* May 55/3 It is some indication of Avimo's position that it has been involved in three major retro-fits for aircraft—that is, the instruments already installed in the aircraft have been taken out and Avimo's put in instead. **1978** *Solar Energy* (Shell Internat. Petroleum Co.) 5 Thus the markets and products are likely to split into 'new' products incorporated, for example, into roof structures of new buildings, and 'retrofit' applications for existing housing stock.

retrofit (re·trofit), *v.* orig. *U.S.* Also with hyphen. [f. prec.] *trans.* To subject to a retrofit; to modify so as to incorporate changes made in later products of the same type or model. Also *absol.*

1956 in W. A. HEFLIN *U.S. Air Force Dict.* 441/1. **1971** *Sci. Amer.* June 2 The..passenger entertainment and service system..is now in service in the first class sections of a Boeing 747 which American Airlines retrofitted. **1973** *Guardian* 18 Jan. 4/4 American aircraft manufacturers are now researching a modification, known as 'retro-fitting' their engines to make them a good deal quieter... But Concorde ..cannot be retrofitted except at extreme cost. **1975** *Daily Colonist* (Victoria, B.C.) 3 May 14/4 You can't retrofit... That is, an existing furnace—coal or oil-fired—cannot feasibly be replaced with a solar system. **1979** *Nature* 5 Apr. p. xiii/1 The B305W can be supplied either as a module for retro-fitting to an existing pumping system or can be supplied installed as an integral package with the Ion Tech B500 high vacuum pumping system.

Hence **re·trofitted** *ppl. a.*, **re·trofitting** *vbl. sb.*

1960 *Aeroplane* XCIX. 145/2 Lately I've been collecting examples of dreadful Americanese. Such as unitized, retrofitted, heat treat, destruct button, [etc.]. **1962** [see *RETROFIT *sb.*]. **1975** *Times Lit. Suppl.* 23 May 563/1 The 'retrofitting' of jet aircraft to make them quieter. **1975** *Nature* 30 Oct. 727/1 New models and retrofitted older planes were, even in 1972, achieving 6 dB reductions on the figures quoted for their noisier brothers. **1977** *Blair & Ketchum's Country Jrnl.* (Brattleboro, Vermont) May 33/2 The Mount Washington hung on by virtue of its convention facilities, its retrofitted bathrooms and sprinkler system.

retroflex, *a.* Add: **2.** *Phonetics.* Pronounced with the tongue curled back; cacuminal.

1915 [see *CACUMINAL *a.*]. **1932** D. JONES *Outl. Eng. Phonetics* (ed. 3) xxv. 199 Retroflex sounds (also called 'cerebral', 'cacuminal' or 'inverted' sounds) are those in the formation of which the tip of the tongue is curled upwards towards the hard palate. **1942** *Amer. Speech: Reprints & Monogr.* No. 4. 41 This sound is generally clearly retroflex in the Great Smokies, as in most American speech. It is heard in such words as the following: Birch, bird, birth, Burchfield, burn. **1964** B. HONIKMAN in D. Abercrombie et al. *Daniel Jones* 78 The frequent retroflex consonants in the languages of India and Pakistan are produced with the tongue curled back. **1973** J. C. WELLS *Jamaican Pronunc. in London* 128 Dentals, alveolars, retroflex sounds, and palato-alveolars. **1977** *Publ. Amer. Dial. Soc.* 1974 LXI/LXII. 36 Again, the retroflex mid-central vowel comes from different speakers.

re·troflex, *v.* [Back-formation from RETROFLEXED *a.*] *trans.* and *intr.* To turn or fold back. So **re·troflexing** *ppl. a.*

1898 H. C. PORTER tr. *Strasburger's Text-bk. Bot.* 396 The male branches give rise..to spherical stalked antheridia, which open at the apices by means of retroflexing valves. **1934** WEBSTER, *Retroflex*, v.i., to turn or bend backward. **1954** S. DUKE-ELDER *Parsons' Dis. Eye* (ed. 12) xxiii. 405 A large corneal section is made as for cataract.., the cornea retroflexed by traction on the suture, and a triangular piece of iris more deliberately excised.

retroflexed, *a.* Add: **2.** *Phonetics.* = *RETROFLEX *a.* 2.

1932 D. JONES *Outl. Eng. Phonetics* (ed. 3) xxv. 200 Retroflexed vowels may be represented in phonetic transcription. **1950** —— *Phoneme* p. xiii, ɪ fricative tongue-tip r; also the corresponding frictionless continuant, and a retroflexed variety of this. **1973** *Amer. Speech* 1969 XLIV. 263 The study consequently proposed to measure the degree to which the Midland dialect, in the form of heavily retroflexed postvocalic /r/, appears in Austin.

retroflexion. Add: **2.** *Phonetics.* Articulation of a sound with the tongue curled back.

1932 D. JONES *Outl. Eng. Phonetics* (ed. 3) ii. 11 In many parts..the effect of the *r* appears as a modification known as 'retroflexion' or 'inversion' of the preceding vowel. **1954** *Bull. School Oriental & Afr. Stud.* XVI. 558 It is well known as a feature of Sanskrit 'internal sandhi' that the coarticulation of retroflexion with constriction has more extensive syntagmatic implications than its coarticulation with occlusion. **1964** R. H. ROBINS *Gen. Linguistics* iii. 98 All vowel sounds may be characterized by retroflexion... This retroflexion is one of the characteristics of what is loosely called in Britain 'an American accent'. **1973** *Amer. Speech* 1969 XLIV. 263 A careful study of this feature was therefore planned and conducted to determine the degree of retroflexion of /r/.

retrogradation. Add: **3. b.** *Physical Geogr.* The landward retreat of a beach or coastline caused by wave-erosion.

1922 C. A. COTTON *Geomorphol. N.Z.* I. xxviii. 391 This process is termed progradation (as contrasted with retrogradation, the cutting-back of a coast by marine erosion). **1937** WOOLDRIDGE & MORGAN *Physical Basis of Geogr.* xxi. 332 Retrogradation comprises not only beach recession but the general recession of the coastline under wave-attack. **1954** W. D. THORNBURY *Princ. Geomorphol.* xvii. 442 Retrogradation of a shore line may go on so rapidly that small streams are unable to keep pace in downcutting with the rate of sea-cliff recession. As a result, these streams enter the sea from hanging valleys. **1968** R. W. FAIRBRIDGE *Encycl. Geomorphol.* 941/2 During retrogradation, a wide belt of beach ridges with their overlying dunes..may be rapidly removed.

retrograde, *a.* and *sb.* Add: **A.** *adj.* **3. e.** *Petrol.* Of a metamorphic change: resulting from a decrease in temperature or pressure. Opp. *PROGRADE *a.* 1.

1932 A. HARKER *Metamorphism* xx. 342 The changes which befall metamorphosed rocks subsequently to the culmination of metamorphism..are of the nature of degradation... This class of changes includes what Becke has styled 'diaphthoresis', implying ruin or corruption; but this rather cumbrous term has not been very widely adopted. It will be more convenient to speak of retrograde metamorphism. **1971** I. G. GASS et al. *Understanding Earth* i. 34/1 The metamorphism of many igneous rocks involves the replacement of a very high-temperature original mineral assemblage by a metamorphic assemblage at a lower temperature. This type of change, though not strictly referred to as retrograde since the starting material is not a metamorphic rock, nevertheless has all the essential characters of retrograde metamorphism. **1980** *Nature* 29 May 320/2 The Alpine uplift was accompanied by widespread retrograde metamorphism.

6. (Later examples.) Also *in retrograde* adv. phr.

1954 W. FAULKNER *Fable* 5 For another instant, the cavalry held. And even then, it did not break. It just began to move in retrograde while still facing forward. **1959** A. G. WOODHEAD *Study of Greek Inscriptions* iii. 24 The assorted sherds of early date..show writing in both directions, but the majority of fragments..have their messages written retrograde. **1980** *Early Music* Jan. 111/2 Its slow movement incorporates the melody 'God Save the King', played first retrograde, later in inversion and finally in its normal form.

7. Of amnesia: pertaining to incidents preceding the causal event.

1935 *Lancet* 5 Oct. 763/1 The duration of this retrograde amnesia. **1960** *Jrnl. Compar. & Physiol. Psychol.* LIII. 524/1 Retrograde amnesia induced by electroconvulsive shock..or other trauma. **1969** *Times* 14 Apr. 6/8 Concussion, anaesthesia..and dosage with various drugs, are all known to impair the memory of the immediate past, a phenomenon known as retrograde amnesia. **1979** 'S. WOODS' *This Fatal Writ* 150 'He remembered too much..everything..up to and including the blow on the head. And you know..that's just not possible.' 'Retrograde amnesia.'

retrograde, *v.* Add: **1. b.** To cause to move backward.

1910 *Jrnl. Geol.* XVIII. 165 Headlands are cut back, or retrograded.

retrograding, *vbl. sb.* and *ppl. a.* (Further examples.)

1910 *Jrnl. Geol.* XVIII. 166 The retrograding of the shore ..due to active wave erosion. **1919** D. W. JOHNSON *Shore Processes & Shoreline Devel.* vi. 295 The phenomenon of a shifting fulcrum between a retrograding cliff and a prograding beach plain. **1968** R. W. FAIRBRIDGE *Encycl. Geomorphol.* 941/2 The retrograding shore line may cut back at an angle to previously formed ridges.

retrogressive, *a.* and *sb.* Add: **A.** *adj.* **3. c.** *Petrol.* = *RETROGRADE *a.* 3 e.

1931 *Amer. Jrnl. Sci.* CCXXI. 8 No one criterion is a safe basis for the determination of retrogressive metamorphism. **1948** *Mem. Geol. Soc. Amer.* XXX. 299 Retrogressive metamorphism, or diaphthoresis, is the mineralogical adjustment of relatively high-grade metamorphic rocks to temperatures lower than those of their initial metamorphism. The process is thus a special case of polymetamorphism (repeated metamorphism).

retrolental (retro,le·ntăl), *a. Path.* [f. RETRO- + L. *lent-*, *lens* lentil (see LENS) + -AL.] Situated or occurring behind the lens of the eye; *retrolental fibroplasia*, a disease caused by administration of high concentrations of oxygen to (esp. premature) infants, characterized by proliferation of retrolental tissue and sometimes leading to blindness.

1942 T. L. TERRY in *Trans. Amer. Ophthalm. Soc.* XL. 262 Considerable thought has been given to the selection of an appropriate term for this disease condition. Early in the study..the term 'retrolental fibroplasia' was suggested by Dr. Harry K. Messenger. **1963** H. L. BIRGE in A. Sorsby *Mod. Ophthalm.* II. i. 6 (*heading*) Retinopathy of prematurity (retrolental fibroplasia). *Ibid.*, Retrolental fibroplasia is a primary retinal disease of non-inflammatory origin resulting from disordered retinal vascularization. **1975** *Daily Colonist* (Victoria, B.C.) 2 June 2/6 Born prematurely, he was blinded by retrolental fibroplasia, an eye disease brought on by the extra oxygen needed to keep him alive soon after birth.

retroreflective, *a.* (In Dict. s.v. RETRO- 3 a.) Add: **2.** Also **retro-reflective.** Having or being the property of a retro-reflector.

1960 *Guide Civil Land Aerodrome Lighting* (*B.S.I.*) 40 In the case of taxiways which have occasional use, retroreflective markers along the edges may be found to provide adequate guidance. **1961** *Space Res.* II. 287 Search light illumination of a retro-reflective satellite. **1970** *Sci. Amer.* Mar. 41/2 A billiard ball sent..into the corner of the table will, after two bounces, return along a path parallel to its incident direction. In the case of light three reflecting surfaces, all at right angles to one another, form a corner with the same retroreflective property.

re·tro-reflector. Also **retroreflector.** [f. RETRO- + REFLECTOR.] A device which reflects light back along the incident path, irrespective of its angle of incidence.

1961 *Space Res.* II. 290 A satellite carrying a radio beacon and an optical retro-reflector. **1969** *Daily Tel.* 21 July 17/3 The device which may foretell earthquakes is the laser ranging retro-reflector. It simply reflects..narrow beams of laser light sent up to it from earth. **1976** *Sci. Amer.* Feb. 51/1 The first is the lunar laser-ranging experiment, in which pulses of laser light are beamed through a telescope on the earth at one of the retroreflectors placed on the moon by the Apollo astronauts.

re·tro-rocket. [f. RETRO- + ROCKET *sb.*[3]] † **a.** (See quot.) *Obs.*

1948 W. LEY *Rockets & Space Travel* 347 *Retro-rocket*, anti-submarine weapon fired from planes backward with velocity matching plane speed so that the weapon fell vertically... Retro-rockets sank the last 'probable' German submarine in the war, on April 30, 1945.

b. *Astronautics.* An auxiliary rocket on a spacecraft that points in the forward direction, so as to provide thrust opposing forward motion when fired.

1957 *Times* 9 Nov. 6/6 To bring the satellite safely down from its orbit would require the use of what he called 'retro-rockets' to slow its speed. **1958** *New Statesman* 18 Oct. 512/1 It consisted of a three-stage rocket, plus a retro-rocket... The third stage was intended to circle the moon.. but it had attached a fourth stage—the retro-rocket—designed to discharge in the opposite direction and thus act as a brake. **1962** J. GLENN in *Into Orbit* 37 The engineers worked out three different ways of firing the small retro-rockets which would start us back towards the earth. **1963** *Guardian* 8 Apr. 1/3 It [*sc.* Lunik 4] will use retro-rockets to effect a soft landing on the lunar surface. **1974** *Encycl. Brit. Macropædia* XVII. 359/2 In the case of a spacecraft whose mission is to land softly on the Moon, on approach trajectory the attitude-control subsystem will rotate the spacecraft so that its retrorocket and landing radar are pointed toward the lunar surface.

retrospective, *a.* (and *sb.*) Add: **1. b.** Of an exhibition, programme of music, or the like: showing the development of the work produced, usu. by one artist, over a period. Freq. *ellipt.* as *sb.* (often const. *of* to introduce what is being exhibited).

1919 R. FRY *Let.* 22 Feb. (1972) II. 447 It's really a good show: a retrospective exhibition of Dudley..arranged all round the walls of the big room. **1931** —— *Let.* 3 Mar. (1972) II. 654 I've been having a retrospective show (forty years of work). **1932** [see *RAYOGRAPH]. **1954** *Burlington Mag.* XCVI. 162/1 A retrospective exhibition..provides a much-needed opportunity to review Pasmore's..development.. from a Euston Road 'impressionism',..up to his most constructivist reliefs. **1964** *Listener* 5 Mar. 400/2 Once again the Marlborough has scooped all its rivals with a retrospective of the greatest of all the German Expressionists. **1969** *Vogue* Nov. 30/2 A true treasure at the Guggenheim, Constantin Brancusi—a complete retrospective of his work. **1972** *Village Voice* (N.Y.) 1 June 59/2 The Museum of Modern Art has been running a Will Rogers Retrospective. **1973** *Radio Times* 18 Jan. 49/1 As a prelude to tomorrow evening's major retrospective of music by Luciano Berio, Misha Donat introduces a work which represents a turning-point in his career. **1975** *Times Lit. Suppl.* 11 July 759/5 It is five years since Bill Brandt's retrospective of 125 photographs was shown at the Hayward Gallery. **1979** *Daily Tel.* 31 Dec. 12 The National Film Theatre gave him [*sc.* Alfred Hitchcock] a major retrospective. **1980** *Times* 8 Jan. 9/8 The retrospective does throw in a bonus in the shape of a room of very early work before..Dali became appreciably Dali.

re:trospecti·vity. *rare.* [f. RETROSPECTIVE *a.* + -ITY.] = RETROSPECTIVENESS.

1920 *Glasgow Herald* 23 Feb. 11/2 The adoption of the principle of the non-retrospectivity of financial law.

retrospectus (retrospe·ktŏs). [a. L. *retrospectus*, pa. pple. of *retrospicere* to look back, or f. RETRO- + *-spectus* after CONSPECTUS, PROSPECTUS.] A retrospective review or summary.

1964 *Listener* 15 Oct. 603/1 Mr. Brooke's conspectus (or retrospectus) of the impact of the second world war on British writers. **1971** *Guardian* 22 May 9/3 The Nonesuch [Press]..has a Retrospectus rather than a Backlist.

‖ **retroussage** (rətrusāʒ). [Fr., f. *retrousser* to turn up, tie up.] In etching: (see quots.).

1959 P. & L. MURRAY *Dict. Art & Artists* 271 Retroussage is a term used in etching to describe the action of passing a ball of muslin lightly over an inked plate with the intention of dragging some of the ink out of the lines and smearing it across the plate. **1965** ZIGROSSER & GAEHDE *Guide to Collecting Orig. Prints* iv. 45 For etchings a little ink is often left on the plate, giving the print a slight tone instead of a dead white, and with a cloth the ink is drawn up slightly out of the lines in an operation known as *retroussage*.

retroussé, *a.* Add: (Earlier and further examples.) Also *ellipt.* as *sb.*

1802 C. WILMOT *Let.* 25 Apr. in *Irish Peer* (1920) 57 General MacDonald..is tall, and thin, the nez retroussé and his eyes round and solemn. **1871** *Young Englishwoman* July 393/2 The Gabrielle dress..falling with puff or *retroussé* of any kind at the back, is very graceful in outline. **1885** [see *oyster-plant* s.v. *OYSTER 5 d]. **1930** *Daily Express* 6 Oct. 5/4 Whereas Yvonne's is retroussé, Jane's nose is—well, it's *not* snub. **1967** J. R. & P. H. NAPIER *Handbk. Living Primates* I. 16 In the gelada baboons..the face is moderately prognathic..but the nose is short and retroussé.

retrovirus (re·trovəiᵊrŏs). *Biol.* [mod. L., f. initial letters of *re*verse *tr*anscriptase (see *TRANSCRIPTASE) + -O + VIRUS.] An RNA virus of the family Retroviridæ, characterized by oncogenicity and the possession of reverse transcriptase. Cf. *RETRAVIRUS.

[**1976** *Virology* LXXI. 375 Family Retroviridae (RNA tumor virus group formerly genus *Leukovirus*).] **1977** *Nature* 8 Sept. 105/2 The successful transfection of a retrovirus by DNA extracted from infected cells was first achieved by Hill and Hillova. **1978** *Ibid.* 9 Feb. 543/1 There has been increasing interest in the isolation of mammalian retroviruses and their evolutionary relatedness to different species.

Hence **re·troviral** *a.*

1979 *Nature* 29 Mar. 420/1 Our results could also be seen as evidence of a marked propensity of retroviral DNA to undergo genetic gymnastics, including deletion.

retsina (retsī·nă). Also **retzina, rezina.** [ad. mod.Gr. ρετσίνα, f. ρετσίνι resin, f. Gr. ῥητίνη pine resin (cf. L. *resina*).] A Greek resinated wine.

1940 H. J. GROSSMAN *Guide Wines, Spirits, Beers* xvi. 160 Present-day Greeks still prefer a resinated to a natural wine... These wines are available in the United States. They are labeled *Retsina*. **1952** W. PLOMER *Museum Pieces* xiii. 113 We drink retsina under the pine-trees. **1960** L. DURRELL *Clea* I. i. 20 The promised farewell dinner of lamb on the spit and gold *rezina* wine. **1966** [see *MOUSSAKA]. **1973** 'D. JORDAN' *Nile Green* xxxii. 154 We went down on to the quay to eat fish and drink retsina. **1977** *New Yorker* 6 June 31/3 The three boys' choirs participating in the Berlioz presented him with a jeroboam of retsina.

re·tting, *ppl. a.* [f. RET *v.*² + -ING².] That rets or rots.

1930 *Discovery* Dec. 408/1 The clean flax fibre obtained from the harvested flax straw is a silky lustrous material of a pale cream colour, not susceptible to the attack of retting bacteria. **1978** *Sci. Amer.* Aug. 75/3 The seeds then sink to the bottom of the retting liquid, and the residue is removed by flotation and screening.

retune, *v.* Add: **b.** To rephrase (the words of a song, etc.).

1959 I. & P. OPIE *Lore & Lang. Schoolch.* vii. 107 In no great space of time the schoolchild ditty, When I was young and had no sense I bought a fiddle for eighteen pence,..was re-tuned in her honour: Lottie Collins, she had no sense, She bought a piano for eighteen pence.

c. To tune (electronic equipment) to a different frequency. Also *absol.*

1962 SIMPSON & RICHARDS *Physical Princ. Junction Transistors* xiv. 357 It is desirable to retune the input and output circuits to satisfy this condition. **1970** R. HILL *Clubbable Woman* vii. 204 Jenny's portable radio began to play..brass-band music. This faded..but then returned louder than before as though the set had been re-tuned. **1977** *Sci. Amer.* June 77/2 He need only retune his receiver to a slightly lower frequency. **1978** *Daily Tel.* 27 Nov. 13/6 Does the BBC realise that the surest way to make you either switch off or re-tune is to make you unsure about what is actually going out?

d. To alter the tuning of (an engine).

1974 P. CAVE *Mama* (new ed.) ii. 10 He was the unofficial repairman of the London Angels, the guy who could take a beaten-up old engine and retune it until it could fly.

Hence **retu·ning** *vbl. sb.*

1909 M. GREENWOOD in L. Hill *Further Adv. Physiol.* 410 'Retuning' with orange, red and green both act like orange itself in inducing a negative image. **1960** *Practical Wireless* XXXVI. 390/1 It provides a substantially constant power gain over the whole of the band 1·5Mc/s to 24Mc/s and therefore needs no retuning when the working frequency is changed. **1976** D. MUNROW *Instruments Middle Ages & Renaissance* ix. 77/4 Mattheson's complaint that a lutenist spent most of his life tuning rather than actually playing reflects the inconvenient necessity of regular re-tunings, which upset the stability of the instrument.

retu·rfing, *vbl. sb.* [f. RETURF *v.* + -ING¹.] The action or fact of covering with new turf.

1974 *Listener* 24 Jan. 119/1 She directed the returfing of a lawn overnight to please her husband. **1978** *Nature* 7 Sept. 51/2 The ground levels within the stones of Stonehenge have been altered during the last 25 yr by re-turfing, by the laying of gravel in 1963 and by its replacement with turf in 1978.

return, *sb.* Add: **I. 1. a.** *spec.* in *Theol.* = *PAROUSIA.

1914 J. F. SILVER (*title*) The Lord's return seen in history and in Scripture as premillennial and imminent. **1931** W. MONTGOMERY tr. *A. Schweitzer's Mysticism of Paul* vi. 111 Since a time-interval has been interposed between the Resurrection and Return, the Resurrection of Jesus has become an independent event. **1970** J. L. HOULDEN *Paul's Lett. from Prison* 107 *Saviour*: Paul's only use of this as a title for Christ. It refers to him in his role at his final return. **1977** G. W. H. LAMPE *God as Spirit* vi. 171 We can, perhaps, retain the idea of a visible *parousia*: not in the impossible sense of a personal return of Jesus from a heavenly throne, but in the form of the consummation of God's creation of mankind.

c. (Further examples.) Also as adj. phr.

1837 DICKENS *Let.* 22 Feb. (1965) I. 237 The best plan therefore, will be for you to write me *by return*. **1889** E. DOWSON *Let.* 18 Feb. (1967) 37 Tell me..by return of post if possible what will have happened when I am next to resume the story. **1905** JOYCE *Let.* ?18 Aug. (1966) II. 105, I send you by this post *A Painful Case* which you are to copy and send back by *return of post*. **1949** N. MITFORD *Love in Cold Climate* I. ii. 20 She always answered letters by return of post. **1957** *Practical Wireless* XXXIII. 509/1 A by-return service of all types and sizes. **1981** J. STUBBS *Ironmaster* i. 21 They say now that we shall have letters 'by return of Post', meaning that we write today and receive a reply..the day after tomorrow.

e. (Later examples.) Also *attrib.* (passing into *adj.*), and in *day-return* (= *day-ticket* s.v. DAY *sb.* 24).

1905 E. M. FORSTER *Where Angels fear to Tread* vi. 164 It was an irritable couple who took tickets to Monteriano. 'Singles or returns?' said he. *a* **1911** D. G. PHILLIPS *Susan Lenox* (1917) I. viii. 126 He had the return half of his own ticket. **1924** D. MOORE *Fen's First Term* ix. 93 'Third single, please.' 'Return?' inquired the clerk. **1931** D. L. SAYERS *Five Red Herrings* iii. 41 He had taken a first-class return to Glasgow. **1952** 'J. TEY' *Singing Sands* iv. 63 'So he had a return ticket.' 'Yes. The return half was in his wallet.' **1973** D. LANG *Freaks* 41, I went down there for a visit on a cheap day-return. **1975** 'A. YORK' *Dark Passage* (1976) vii. 88 I'll be back tomorrow, I should think. But make the return half of the ticket open, will you? **1977** S. BRETT *Star Trap* xv. 167 The man didn't stop to buy a ticket. He must have a return.

g. *and return*, and back again.

1887 C. B. GEORGE *Forty Years on Rail* v. 88 The train.. ran from Waukegan to Chicago and return every day.

h. *return to nature*, the abandonment of urban life in favour of rustic simplicity.

1902 CHESTERTON *Twelve Types* 142 Some think that the return to nature consists in drinking no wine; some think that it consists in drinking a great deal more than is good for them. **1908** E. J. BANFIELD *Confessions of Beachcomber* I. ii. 54 The conviction that the career of the Beachcomber, the closest possible 'return to Nature' now popularly advocated, has charms none other possesses. *c* **1914** WYNDHAM LEWIS *Let.* (1963) 65, I might devote two or three words..to scouring the 'banal' nakedness of various 'Return to Nature' shits. **1978** *Times* 3 Oct. 14/3 This is not a plea for the simple life, a return to nature, or a general rising against the machines.

2. b. See also HAPPY *a.* 3 in Dict. and Suppl.

II. 6. a. Also *pl.* (See quot. 1963.) *Canad.*

1809 A. HENRY *Trav. & Adventures Canad.* I. iv. 40 Here, the returns, in furs, are collected, and embarked for Montréal. **1843** R. CAMPBELL *Jrnl.* 10 June in C. Wilson *Campbell of Yukon* (1970) viii. 68 As soon as the river opened, Whitford left with a boat & crew and the returns for Fort Simpson. **1908** C. MAIR *Through Mackenzie Basin* 183 There was still much work to be done in the way of transport of outfit and returns between Anderson and Fort Good Hope. **1963** G. S. MCTAVISH *Behind Palisades* xx. 84 'Returns'..was the generic name for furs, and all trade results which were returned to the Old Country in exchange. **1971** *Alberta Hist. Rev.* Autumn 9 During the next few years he..visited the posts and carried the returns down-river to St. Louis.

b. *return on capital*, gain, profit, or income earned by capital (see also quot. 1970).

Various other phrases, e.g. *return for capital*, *return to capital*, and *return to invested capital* were used from the late nineteenth century onward.

1938 W. L. CRUM in *Harvard Business Rev.* XVI. 336 The return on invested capital is one of the most significant.. among possible measures of corporate performance. No entirely satisfactory determination of the average rate of return on invested capital..can be made, but data accumulated over recent years..enable us to prepare a fairly close estimate. **1962** A. BATTERSBY *Guide to Stock Control* x. 94 'Return on capital' has been used in this book as a concise description of the cost of holding stocks, for two principal reasons—it is often the predominant cost and the most readily variable. **1969** J. ARGENTI *Managem. Techniques* 102 Confusion over the term 'Return on Capital' is considerable since this can have either the traditional meaning or the DCF meaning and there is no fixed relationship between these two figures. **1970** M. GREENER *Penguin Dict. Commerce* 285 *Return on capital*, a rather nebulous phrase. In the terminology of investment analysis and accounting it means the profit earned by *capital*... In company accounts return on capital is often the ratio that the profit bears to the total *equity* funds or shareholders' funds employed... The phrase 'return on capital' is frequently used when what is really meant is *dividend yield* or *earnings yield*.

III. 9. c. *spec.* in *Cricket*, a summary of bowling figures at the end of play.

1976 J. SNOW *Cricket Rebel* 44 My return read nought for 117. **1977** J. LAKER *One-Day Cricket* 137 Bob White.. must have surprised many Londoners with a number of fine returns since he left Lords.

11. e. *ellipt.* In various sports: a return match.

1958 F. C. AVIS *Boxing Reference Dict.* 111 *Return*, a second contest with a boxer whom one has previously fought. **1964** *Guardian* 2 Mar. 7/6 Or we might arrange for a monkey's (monkey's paw—draw) so that we can have a return. **1977** *Daily Express* 29 Mar. 32/4 England..could only score four in the return at Highbury.

12. c. (Later examples.)

1974 *Country Life* 24 Jan. 152/3 West should have led the Heart Nine, to ask for a Diamond return. **1978** *Times* 22 July 9/4 East led his ♠7, in order to..invite a spade return for a ruff.

e. (Earlier and later examples.)

1833 J. NYREN *Young Cricketer's Tutor* 70 He had..such a rapid return..that I have seen many put out..in a single run. **1906** A. E. KNIGHT *Compl. Cricketer* iv. 143 Inaccurate and wild returns not merely give away runs, they contribute to general slovenliness and slackness. **1972** J. MOSEDALE *Football* x. 139 McElhenny embellished the performance with 52 yards on two kickoff returns, 32 on the punt returns.

15. a. (Further examples.)

1892 I. ZANGWILL *Childr. Ghetto* III. 53 He let himself fall backwards, impinging noiselessly upon a heap of 'returns' of number one. **1902** *Chambers's Jrnl.* Feb. 114/1 The bags of tea, known as 'returns' which the samplers who come to the warehouse bring from the establishments they represent. **1934** T. WOOD *Cobbers* xi. 132 'Any returns?' says the waitress, challengingly. **1971** *Publishers' Weekly* 20 Dec. 16/1 The average rate of returns (unsold books) in the industry as a whole is about 50%. **1977** *Private Eye* 13 May 6/3 As the evening's performance was a charity gala, there would be no cheap seats available. Returns were few and would start at £3.

b. = *RECOVERY 5 f.

1909 *Brit. Birds* II. 364 The returns for a species so much shot as the Woodcock are shown to be scarcely more than 5 per cent. **1959** *Jrnl. du Conseil* XXV. 58 Haddock tagging..has shown that returns may come from the position of liberation after a very long period of freedom, or from a long way off after a comparatively short time. **1975** *Trans. Illinois State Acad. Sci.* LXVIII. III. 282 Band returns from quail released September or earlier indicated a general dispersal of 0·3–0·5 miles from the release site.

IV. 16. a. *return chaise* (earlier example), *flight, load, mail, omnibus, post, ship*; **return address,** the address to which a postal item is to be returned in case of non-delivery; **return date** *U.S. Law*, the date on which a specified person is required to appear in court; **return envelope** *U.S.*, an addressed envelope enclosed with a letter for the recipient's reply; **return fare,** the fare for a return-ticket.

1928 *Publishers' Weekly* 30 June 2605 All envelopes must carry the name and return address of the sender in the upper left hand corner. **1798** G. THOMPSON *Sentimental Tour* 20 Falling in with a return-chaise, I agreed with the driver for a cast—So far, for so much. **1972** *N.Y. Law Jrnl.* 24 Oct. 18/7 A subpoena without a specific return date and a specific place of attendance is invalid. **1973** *Ibid.* 31 Aug. 1/1 There is a substantial probability that he will not appear in court on the return date. **1886** 'MARK TWAIN' *Lett. to Publishers* (1967) 205 Enclose a stamped and printed return-envelop. **1974** *Spartanburg* (S. Carolina) *Herald* 19 Apr. A4/8 So send for my booklet 'How to Prevent Platonic Marriage', enclosing a long stamped return envelope, plus 25 cents. **1976** *Eastern Even. News* (Norwich) 22 Dec. 7/3 The clerk..should..see if it was possible to reintroduce the reduced rate return fare in off peak hours. **1979** *Homes & Gardens* June 26/4 The return air fare to Nice is a cracking £180. **1966** M. WOODHOUSE *Tree Frog* x. 74 I've booked my return flight. **1976** *New Yorker* 15 Nov. 83/1 The European booking agent who had arranged for the Belgrade and London appearances paid for their return flight. **1913** JONES & WYATT *Motor Traction for Business Purposes* 15 This matter of light mileage naturally brings us to the question of return loads. **1977** 'D. RUTHERFORD' *Return Load* i. 25 We have a job for you... A return load. **1864** *Harper's Mag.* Jan. 205/2 Miss Amber answered the letter by return mail. **1975** P. FUSSELL *Gt. War & Mod. Memory* ii. 67 Geoffrey Keynes specialized in receiving antiquarian booksellers' catalogs and buying books by return mail. **1860** A. J. MUNBY *Diary* 21 Feb. in D. Hudson *Munby* (1972) 51 Waiting for the return omnibus, I discovered some pretty Gothic schools, new, on the green. **1885** *List of Subscribers, Classified* (United Telephone Co.) (ed. 6) 226 (Advt.), Estimates per return post. **1912** W. OWEN *Let.* ?14 Nov. (1967) 168, I flatly disobeyed your Return-Post command. **1929** M. DE LA ROCHE *Whiteoaks* ix. 137 Alayne wrote by return post. **1977** *Private Eye* 13 May 22/2 Send small sample of urine and £3 for reliable and strictly confidential results by first class return post. *c* **1700** EVELYN *Diary* an. 1680 (1955) IV. 212, I went to visite a French Stranger,..who having been thrice at the *East Indias, Persia* & other remote Countries, came hither in our returne ships from those parts.

b. *return current* (further example), *flow.*

1957 G. E. HUTCHINSON *Treat. Limnol.* I. v. 268 We have a wind drift at the surface almost along the direction of the wind, and a region near the bottom of current flowing against the wind, the so-called return current. **1964** *Economist* 23 May 837/3 The only possible source is 'return-flow' from irrigation.

c. *return conductor.*

1847 *Phil. Mag.* XXX. 194 The earth has been made to act the part of the return conductor.

e. return room, a mezzanine room at the turn of a flight of stairs.

1914 JOYCE *Dubliners* 82 He glanced up and saw Jack regarding him from the door of the return-room. **1922** —— *Ulysses* 296 The other boot which he had been looking for was at present under the commode in the return room. **1927** ST. JOHN ERVINE *Wayward Man* I. ii. 35 The return-room at the top of the first flight of stairs could be converted into a kitchen.

17. *return crease* (earlier and later examples).

1775 *New Articles Game of Cricket* 2 The Bowling-Crease must be parallel with the Stumps, Three Feet in Length, with a Return-Crease. **1902** [see *CALL *v.* 4 m]. **1948** *Sporting Mirror* 21 May 6/1 Three creases are marked out at each end of a cricket pitch—the bowling crease, return crease and popping crease. **1963** *Times* 23 Apr. 4/7 He [*sc.* an umpire] is required..to see whether the bowler is no-balling on the return crease. **1976** J. SNOW *Cricket Rebel* 99 Stackpole's bat was outside the return crease at the time the wicket was broken.

19. *return entertaining, leg, match* (later examples; also *fig.*), *thanks, tie.*

1899 'MARK TWAIN' in *Forum* (N.Y.) Mar. 29 You can judge..what sort of return-entertaining she has done. **1973** *Times* 31 Oct. 10/5 After Soviet objections to playing the return leg in the Santiago stadium..Fifa..sent a delegation to investigate. **1891** W. G. GRACE *Cricket* iv. 108 The return match, at Lord's..was more encouraging to us. **1915** J. BUCHAN *Thirty-Nine Steps* i. 18 This is the return match for the *pogroms*. The Jew is everywhere. **1929** *Evening News* 18 Nov. 16/6 In a return ice hockey match yesterday Berlin beat London by four goals to two. **1971** *Nature* 23 July 213/1 This follows..a conference in Washington a month ago... A 'return match' meeting to clinch the project is scheduled for Madrid for early August. **1973** *Times* 21 Mar. 9/6 The suspense of the medical report and the outcome of the return match. **1977** *Times* 8 Dec. 17/4 Contrary to my prematch forecast and your diarists' ex post account, I did not win: nor has a return match been played or planned. **1907** *Yesterday's Shopping* (1969) 361/1 'Return thanks' cards... Return thanks for kind enquiries and sympathy. **1972** *V.A.T.: Scope & Coverage* (H.M. Customs) 33 Postcards..acceptance cards; 'thank-you' or 'return-thanks' cards. **1972** G. GREEN *Great Moments in Sport: Soccer* xi. 108 The return tie was played at Maine Road.

return, *v.* Add: **1. 4. b.** *to return to nature*: to abandon urban life in favour of rustic simplicity. Cf. *RETURN *sb.* 1 h.

1902 G. K. CHESTERTON *Twelve Types* 141 This attempt to re-establish communication with the elemental, or, as it is sometimes more roughly and fallaciously expressed, to return to nature.

III. 16. d. *Cricket.* Of a bowler: to achieve (bowling figures) in an innings or other session of play.

1969 *Times* 29 July 9/2 The best bowling figures..were returned by Bore. **1976** J. Snow *Cricket Rebel* 112 Sussex.. were rolled over for 104, Warwickshire left-arm spinner Jim Allan returning career-best figures of five for 11. **1977** J. Laker *One-Day Cricket* 69 Gilmour returned the staggering figures of 12–6–14–6.

returnabi·lity. [f. Returnable *a.* + -ity.] The fact or condition of being returnable; capacity to return or be returned.

1920 in Webster. **1973** *Daily Tel.* (Colour Suppl.) 23 Mar. 13/1 The main problem was one of 'returnability'. 'The British Government has to be sure some country will receive you when your visa for England has expired.' **1973** *Times* 29 Oct. 15/8 A device could be used..which the customer would..associate with returnability. The use of the device would clearly indicate..that the package is the property of the supplier. **1981** *Times* 19 Jan. 3/6 The commission's proposed directive on beverage containers..is now expected to appear without any of the references to mandatory recycling or returnability contained in earlier drafts.

returnable, *a.* **1. b.** (Later examples.)

1972 *V.A.T.: Gen. Guide* (H.M. Customs) 34 Containers (returnable). **1973** *Sat. Rev. Society* (U.S.) May 70/3 Buy returnable bottles..participate in your local recycling program when you must use nonreturnable containers. **1981** *Country Life* 7 May 1228/1 The price of a returnable bottle is shared by many users.

returned, *ppl. a.* Add: **2. b.** Designating a discharged serviceman who has returned home from a war. *Canad., Austral.,* and *N.Z.*

1915 *Eye Opener* (Calgary, Alberta) 11 Dec. 2/3 An army of returned soldiers..who have been away fighting for the Empire are not going to..allow themselves to be told what is right and what is wrong by a bunch of stay-at-home aldermen or freak legislators. **1921** *Daily Colonist* (Victoria, B.C.) 24 Mar. 1/4 A body of 600 returned men today marched to the city hall and demanded..that no returned men be refused relief by the city council. **1930** W. K. Hancock *Australia* xiii. 274 The only notable non-political body in Australia (excluding the churches) is the Returned Soldiers' League. **1947** E. A. McCourt *Music at Close* I. vi. 65 Latimer stopped..to pick up..a returned man living on a settlement grant. *a* **1948** L. G. D. Acland *Early Canterbury Runs* (1951) xi. 314 After the 1914–18 War the Government resumed the Old Man Range country..and settled a returned soldier on it. **1950** *N.Z. Jrnl. Agric.* Jan. 26/2 Ten 10-acre sections have been allocated to returned servicemen. **1961** P. White *Riders in Chariot* viii. 236 You cannot tell me..that a home is not a home, with so many going roofless, and so many returned men.

3. *returned empty* (example in lit. sense, and later *transf.* examples).

1946 P. Bottome *Lifeline* xv. 137 A milk lorry..goes from here taking returned empties, and bringing back milk at dawn. **1961** B. Fergusson *Watery Maze* ix. 220 Several of these [ships] were veterans both of Ironclad and Torch, which meant that they had already spent months in unprofitable voyaging as returned empties, so to speak. **1977** C. Allen *Raj* i. 23/2 Early in the nineteenth century.. unmarried women were regularly shipped out..to meet the demand for wives... Those who returned without husbands or fiancés were known as 'Returned Empties'.

returnee·. orig. *U.S.* [f. Return *v.* + -ee[1].] One who returns or is returned from abroad to his native land, *esp.* from war service or exile. Also *attrib.* and *transf.*

1944 *Newsweek* 17 July 62 The biography of a returnee fits into a regular pattern. **1945** *Christian Sci. Monitor* 17 Mar. 10/2 (*caption*) A launch filled with returnees and their wives sets out on exploration tour of the coves. **1955** *Sci. News Let.* 27 Aug. 142/3 They suggest a brainwashing in reverse as treatment for returnees showing symptoms of mental sickness. **1969** *Daily Tel.* 27 Dec. 5/2 The Communists counted 54 dead, nine taken prisoner and 31 'returnees' during the truce period. A 'returnee' is a Viet Cong guerilla who surrenders peacefully to the South Vietnamese Government, thereby securing all citizen's privileges. **1974** W. Hunt *North of 53 Degrees* x. 60 The Klondike gold had escaped the grasp of these returnees. **1977** *Guardian Weekly* 18 Sept. 15/3 They want to go back to Russia... Would-be Soviet returnees. **1981** *Times* 22 Jan. 8/3 The former hostages, already inelegantly dubbed 'returnees'.

return-ticket. Add: (Earlier and later examples.) Also *fig.*

c **1847** J. S. Coyne in M. R. Booth *Eng. Plays of 19th Cent.* (1973) IV. 195 There's poor Mary White gone..to that bourne from whence no traveller gets a return ticket. **1850** Thackeray *Pendennis* II. xxxv. 339 (*heading*) Chapter xxxv. Shows how Arthur had better have taken a return-ticket. **1922** [see *come-back *sb.*[2] 2]. **1946** *Happy Landings* July 8/3 If you take your parachute into the air you have a certain return ticket, and one that, should you need to use it, will bring you safely down to earth. **1977** *Times* 15 June 16/2 The cautious person travels from capitalism to socialism with a return ticket.

re-type, *v.* Add: Now usu. as one word without hyphen. **2.** (Further examples.)

Now the usual sense.

1898 H. G. Wells *Let.* 1 Jan. in *G. Gissing & H. G. Wells* (1961) 70 Parts I have reshaped, rewritten and retyped time after time. **1952** S. Kauffmann *Tightrope* iv. 58 Rose retyped Russell's memo for him in the usual five copies. **1961** 'E. Lathen' *Banking on Death* xiii. 105 The letter had to be retyped. **1976** H. MacInnes *Agent in Place* xiii. 136 Typed, retyped, torn up. The discarded pages filled the waste-basket. **1979** *Amer. N. & Q.* Apr. 126/1 Faulkner entrusted the job to Phil Stone, who in turn gave the typescript to his secretary, Grace Hudson, to retype.

Hence **rety·ped** *ppl. a.*, **rety·ping** *vbl. sb.* Also **re·type** *sb.*, a retyped copy.

1930 D. L. Sayers *Strong Poison* xiv. 183 She..threw it into the waste-paper basket together with the re-type which she had begun. **1943** J. Reith *Diary* 4 May (1975) vi. 303 The vice-controller had my retyped memo today. **1967** Karch & Buber *Offset Processes* iv. 74 The IBM Selectric Composer..allows automatic justification of the right-hand margin with a retyping. **1979** *Amer. N. & Q.* Apr. 126/1 William Faulkner sent the newly revised and retyped text to Liveright.

retzian (re·tsiǎn). *Min.* [f. the name of Anders Jahan *Retzius* (1742–1821), Swedish naturalist.] A basic arsenate of manganese, calcium and rare earth elements, known as dark brown orthorhombic crystals from Sweden.

1895 H. Sjögren in *Bull. Geol. Inst. Univ. Upsala* II. 54 (*heading*) Retzian, a new arseniate from the Mossgrufva, Nordmark. *Ibid.* 59 The crystals of retzian are prismatic. **1921** *Bull. U.S. Geol. Survey* No. 679. 126 Retzian..strongly pleochroic. **1967** *Amer. Mineralogist* LII. 1610 The crystal structure of retzian is an interesting sheet structure.

retzina, var. *retsina.

Reub, Rube (rūb), abbrevs. *Reuben 1. Also *attrib.* Cf. *hey, Rube!* s.v. *hey *int.*

1896 Ade *Artie* i. 8 If I had time I'd go over to that church and make a lot o' them Reubs look like thirty-cent pieces. **1899** 'J Flynt' *Tramping with Tramps* 396 *Rube*, a 'hoosier', or 'farmer'. **1904** [see *bark *v.*[1] 2 b]. **1915** *Dialect Notes* IV. 200 *Reub, rube*, local name for rustic... 'On the Fourth of July the Reubs all come to town.' **1919** [see *kike]. **1927** *Scots Observer* 26 Feb. 3/4 They know a Rube when they see him, or a guy, or a crook, or a bonehead. **1937** *Lit. Digest* 3 Apr. 21/3 Child labor laws..have forced children [of circus people] into schools for a certain number of months a year. This contact with 'rubes' and 'townies' has given rise to new interests. **1946** E. O'Neill *Iceman Cometh* iv. 253 The boys tell me the rubes are wasting all their money buying food and times never was so hard. **1949** F. Sargeson *I saw it in my Dream* 218 Mr Anderson said Cedric was just a rube. **1953** W. Moore *Bring Jubilee* ii. 20 Rube, huh? Much money you got?.. O.K., Reuben. Come along. **1956** W. R. Bird *Off-Trail in Nova Scotia* iii. 69 Don't try to talk down to someone you meet in those places no matter if they look like rubes for ten to one they've seen more of the world than you have. **1970** R. Price *Gt. Roob Revolution* 5 The word 'rube' (from Reuben) was originally used by carnival people to identify the farmers, yokels, and assorted rural types. **1973** J. Gores *Final Notice* xxiv. 158 The rube who wanders into the pool hall and loses a few games... Then the bets get bigger and he..starts clearing tables. **1975** *New Yorker* 29 Dec. 36/3 We had one girl who did a good rube act. **1976** *Time* 20 Dec. 17/1 They were an unsolemn pair, the young man who likes his rube image and the impeccably dressed man who looked more like a smooth character actor than a politician of enormous influence.

Reuben (rū·bən). *U.S.* and *Canad. colloq.*

1. The personal name *Reuben* applied to suggest the conventionally conceived figure of a farmer or rustic; a country bumpkin.

1804 in S. Larkin *Nightingale* 284 But she, tho' conscious of his worth, Had chose a youth more rare; a rustic Reuben was his name. **1890** B. Hall *Turnover Club* iv. 49, I overheard one of a knot of Reubens standing on a corner. **1901** (*song-title*) The wedding of the Reuben and the maid. *Ibid.*, You've heard about the Reuben and the time he came to town. **1905** 'H. McHugh' *You can search Me* 60 I've a couple of new card tricks..that will leave the Reubens gasping for air. **1911** H. Quick *Yellowstone Nights* xii. 313, I took a basket of eggs an went in among 'em, feelin' like a animal trainer in a circus parade as the Reubens gathered around the train. **1953** [see prec.].

2. In full, *Reuben sandwich.* A large sandwich containing cheese, meat, and sauerkraut, usu. made with rye bread and served hot.

Not obviously connected with sense 1.

1956 *Institutions* Oct. 44/2 'The Reuben'..is a grilled 3 decker sandwich of heroic proportions. Three slices of russian rye bread generously spread with thousand island dressing contain swiss cheese and corned beef slices interlaced with sauerkraut. **1967** *N.Y. Times* 10 Oct. 50 The Reuben sandwich..has become wildly popular in most areas of the United States. **1970** *Favorite Recipes of Lutheran Ladies* 15 Reuben Sandwich... Spread 6 slices bread with dressing, top with cheese, 1 tablespoon sauerkraut and corned beef. **1976** in K. M. Thomas *Winning Sandwiches for Menu Makers* 2/2 The recipes in this book represent the best of twenty years of sandwich competition, starting with the champion of the first contest in 1956, the now ubiquitous 'Reuben'.

reune (rīˌyū·n), *v. U.S. colloq.* [Back-formation from Reunion.] *intr.* To hold a reunion.

1901 *Princeton Alumni Weekly* 8 June 774/1 As the secretary of a class which has 'reuned' frequently..I wish to direct your attention to a breach of etiquette. **1929** *Amer. Speech* V. 175 Several years ago the late E. K. Graham, then president of the University of North Carolina, in speaking of class reunions, used somewhat facetiously the word *reune* instead of the locution *have a reunion*. It seems that the word has stuck. **1929** E. W. Springs *Above Bright Blue Sky* 237 She had seen in the paper where the 14th was going to reune at the banquet. **1948** *Amer. Legion Mag.* Oct. 26/1 (*heading*) Retreads Will Reune. **1949** Mencken in Kirby & Woolf *Philologica* 316 The embryologist of speech discerns several processes in the making of such novelties [*sc.* new verbs]. Some are simply nouns unchanged, e.g., *to contact*.. others are back-formations from nouns, e.g., *to locate, to enthuse, to reune.*

reunification. Add: (Further examples.) Hence **reunifica·tionist,** a supporter or advocate of reunification.

1955 *Times* 14 July 8/5 No policy is acceptable to Germany which does not have for its aim the reunification of the country in peace and freedom, and at the earliest possible moment. **1959** *Daily Tel.* 9 Apr. 10/3 Plans for control and inspection, and for a ceiling for forces, would be accepted only if progress towards German reunification went with them. **1967** *Listener* 6 July 20/2 For him [*sc.* Dr. Adenauer] German reunification was a necessary pre-condition of détente. **1970** W. Johnson *Cameroon Federation* v. 105 What incensed the reunificationists most, however, was the belief that the Territory had not received its just due even from the government of Nigeria. **1976** *Survey* Winter 18 One can imagine the Japanese reaction to the reunification of Korea under communist leadership.

reunify, *v.* (Later examples.)

1955 *Times* 8 July 8/3 The Assembly endorsed the main conclusions of M. de Menthon's report, which formed the basis of the debate—the need to establish a real system of security, to reunify Germany by means of free elections, and to construct a united Europe. *Ibid.* 13 July 6/4 French reactions to the suggestions, made in a recent leading article in *The Times*, that Germany might be reunified on the basis of a demilitarized eastern zone, are not *prima facie* favourable.

reunion. 3. (Later *attrib.* examples.)

1929 E. W. Springs *Above Bright Blue Sky* 233 Are you going to the Aviators' Reunion Dinner to-night to celebrate the anniversary of the Armistice? **1952** M. Allingham *Tiger in Smoke* xv. 218 He was due to give an impersonation of his old officer at a reunion dinner. **1976** *Laurel* (Montana) *Outlook* 9 June 12/4 A two-hour program is being planned by a reunion committee and will be held from 2 to 4 p.m. in the Laurel Senior High School gymnasium.

re-up (rī·ˌʌp), *v. U.S. Services' slang.* [f. Re- 5 a + Up *v.*: see quots. 1930, 1942.] *intr.* To re-enlist. Also as *sb.*, one who re-enlists. Hence **re-u·pping** *vbl. sb.*

1906 *Soldier Slang* in C. M'Govern *Sarjint Larry an' Frinds, Re-up*, to re-enlist. **1913** [see *hitch *sb.* 8]. **1930** W. H. Waldron *Old Sergeant's Conferences* vii. 122 To 'Re-up' is to reenlist on the day following discharge... The 'Up' refers to holding up his hand to receive the oath of enlistment. **1942** E. Colby *Army Talk* 174 When enlisting and being sworn in, a man is said to 'hold up his right hand' for three years. So when he does it after being discharged, he 're-ups'. **1955** *Air Force Times* (U.S.) (Eastern ed.) 31 Dec. 13/1 Despite the surprising success of the re-up efforts, the problem of getting qualified replacements for the still critical 'hardcore' skills remains. **1958** *Ibid.* 2 Aug. 1/4 (*heading*) Re-Upping Quickly Pays Off. **1970** *Times* 28 May 7/7 The person they are likely to meet is the recruiting officer with his 're-up' quota to fill. **1972** J. Gores *Dead Skip* xi. 75 If he'd re-upped when his two years in the army were finished, he'd have been a sergeant by now. **1974** *Black Panther* 9 Feb. 22/1, I was told to talk to a recruiter on base about re-enlisting... He told me that if I re-up for the four-year reserve commitment he would fix it up so that I had a job waiting for me.

reupho·lster (rī-), *v.* [Re- 5 c.] *trans.* To upholster anew. So **reupho·lstery.**

1935 *Amer. Speech* X. 154/2 Entire [car] bodies rebuilt, reupholstered. **1943** F. Thompson *Candleford Green* vii. 116 The easy chair had been carried away to be re-upholstered. **1976** R. Rendell *Demon in my View* ii. 22 The sofa and the two armchairs had been re-upholstered. **1977** *Time* 4 July 6/3 Mortified French officials rushed the vehicle back to its manufacturer, where men on the assembly line worked frantically on reupholstery..and a new paint job. **1978** *N.Y. Times* 30 Mar. C13/3 (Advt.), Upholstery & reupholstery workroom. **1978** *P.O. Telephone Directory, Preston Area: Yellow Pages* 357 (Advt.), Specialists in upholstery & re-upholstery.

reusable (rīyū·zăb'l), *a.* [f. Re-use *v.* + -able.] Capable of being re-used; suitable for a second or further use.

1959 *Sears, Roebuck Catal.* Spring & Summer 835/1 Paper plates..With re-usable plastic bag. **1962** *Guardian* 5 Dec. 6/3 Paper place mats..disposable, but certainly reusable several times. **1967** *Times Rev. Industry* Feb. 39/1 (Advt.), Dictamite takes a whole hour's dictation on one tiny reusable tape cartridge. **1970** *New Scientist* 26 Feb. 407/1 Those contractors who have plans for the airframe or engines of the reusable shuttle must submit them to NASA. **1971** *Engineering* Apr. 59/2 Some strippable coatings are reusable. **1975** *Nature* 17 Jan. 149/2 Out of the other end, or rather ends, come several potentially valuable by-products. Three grades of reuseable paper, two already pronounced as suitable for board making by commercial board mills, one suitable for high grade fuel.

Hence **reusabi·lity.**

1970 *Sci. Jrnl.* Aug. 32/2 'Reusability'—the introduction of launch vehicles and spacecraft that can be flown to space, returned and used again. **1973** *Daily Tel.* 24 Jan. 19 (Advt.), It had to meet rigid specifications. Uniform size and shape, chemical content, heat resistance, ventilation, reusability.

reu·sage (rī-). [Re- 5 a.] A second or further usage.

1956 *Discovery* July 230/2 Earlier examples of reusage of bricks by Saxon builders are numerous.

‖ **réussi** (reˌusi), *a.* Also fem. **réussie.** [Fr.] Fine, excellent, successful.

1948 F. R. Leavis *Great Tradition* ii. 37 Adam [Bede], we know, is a tribute to her father; but he is also the Ideal Craftsman, embodying the Dignity of Labour. He too is *réussi*. **1953** 'N. Blake' *Dreadful Hollow* vi. 75 She drew out of its wrappings an elaborate construction of shells enclosed by a glass dome. 'He must have made it himself. You see? It's a sort of mausoleum. Rather weird and *réussi*, isn't it?' **1958** B. Nichols *Sweet & Twenties* iii. 48 Here, I thought, is a woman who is completely *réussie*.

Reuter (roi·təɹ). The name of Baron Paul Julius von *Reuter* (1816–99), founder of a telegraphic and pigeon post bureau in Aachen in 1849, used *attrib.* and in the possessive to denote (the activities of) a news agency named after him, whose London headquarters were established in 1851. Also (in form **Reuters**) used *absol.*

[**1859** *Times* 31 Oct. 6/5 The following telegrams have been received at Mr. Reuter's office.] **1860** *Times* 1 Oct. 7/1 (*heading*) Reuter's Telegrams. **1913** Kipling *Lett. of Travel* (1920) 222 No newspapers come aboard, only clipped Reuter telegrams. **1964** M. McLuhan *Understanding Media* ii. xxiv. 235 A Reuters dispatch for December 13, 1962, reported from Tokyo. **1967** *Listener* 28 Dec. 860/1 In the early days of BBC news when they were terrified of infringing the rights of newspapers they used to read out the Reuter tapes. **1969** *Observer* 5 Oct. 1/2 Reuter correspondent Anthony Grey was a free man in Peking tonight after being held hostage by the Chinese for 26 lonely months. **1977** *New Yorker* 3 Oct. 98/2 My guide..would be an Englishman.. John Peet, who had covered Germany for Reuters, the British news agency. **1980** M. Lutyens *Edwin Lutyens* xv. 232 Every morning Roderick's special Reuter messenger boy brought me a letter from him.

reutiliza·tion (rī-). [Re- 5 a.] A second or further utilization.

1936 *Discovery* July 230/2 Virtually all English brickcraft originated by the reutilisation of Roman bricks in mediaeval buildings. **1957** *New Biol.* XXIII. 81 The induced enzyme therefore appeared to be synthesized from amino acids present in the free amino acid pool and not by partial breakdown of other cell proteins, followed by the reutilization of the peptide moieties produced.

reu·tilize (rī-), *v.* [Re- 5 a.] *trans.* To utilize again. Hence **reu·tilized** *ppl. a.*

1889 *Lancet* 21 Sept. 585/2 After the white cells have lived their life and done their work, portions of their worn-out carcases may be reutilised in the body as nutriment. **1964** D. Nichols in *Oceanogr. & Marine Biol.* II. 408 Cornil, Mosinger and Calen (1935 a, b) were of the opinion that the matter eliminated by some amoebocytes in the epithelium was re-utilized by others. **1972** *Biblical Theol. Bull.* Feb. 30 Some of these reutilized traditional materials deserve a separate mention, namely the various formulas of prayer.

Rev., abbrev. of Reverend *a.* and *sb.* 2 c, d.

In U.S. usage freq. without preceding article.

1721 D. Wilkins *Leges Anglo-Saxonicæ* (list of subscribers), The Rev. Mr. Henry Briggs of Loose in Kent, [etc.]. **1785,** etc. [see Reverend *a.* and *sb.* 2 c]. **1876** W. Whitman *Daybks. & Notebks.* (1978) I. 37 Rev. R. P. Graves. **1884** [see Chasuble 1]. **1917** *Congress. Rec.* (Daily ed.) 14 Dec. 294/2 Rev. Joseph Burt Webster to be chaplain with rank from October 5, 1917. **1939** *Time* 27 Nov. 50/3 (*heading*) Mr. for Rev. **1943** R. Llewellyn *None but Lonely Heart* xxi. 118 Reverend Ernest Mott. Oxford, he is. Followed 'em on His bike as far as Hammersmith Bridge every year since '98. Ain't you, Rev, boy? **1969** C. Burke *God is Beautiful, Man* (1970) 74 The Revs. in the church got cut in on it too. **1972** J. Maryland in T. Kochman *Rappin' & Stylin' Out* 213 Say, Rev., tell them 'bout the little white lady. **1973** *Philadelphia Inquirer* (Today Suppl.) 7 Oct. 14/3 Rev. Velasquez recalls that before the first trial he heard Tony's defense attorney say [etc.]. **1978** *Listener* 9 Mar. 296/3 Religious broadcasting is not a job for a good man... Even the radio Revs and their staff are always set apart from other departments.

rev (rev), *sb.* Also **rev.** (with point). Abbrev. of Revolution *sb.* 4 c.

1901 *Catal. Mech. Engin. Coll.* (Victoria & Albert Mus.) I. 35 The example has 3 in. cylinders, with 4 in. stroke, and is intended to run at 300 revs. per min. **1918** *Chambers's Jrnl.* May 301/1 The revs dropped off. **1932** S. C. H. Davis *Motor Racing* vi. 87 The car went well, held its revs. with something in hand. **1942** *Tee Emm* (Air Ministry) II. 87 The revs. of the engine..can be controlled by the pilot in one of two ways. **1966** R. Maxwell in T. Wisdom *High-Performance Driving* v. 44, I stayed in each gear to maximum revs for best acceleration on the short, so-called straights. **1969** *Listener* 22 May 734/1, I admit to having enjoyed recently Kagel's *Improvisation Ajoutée* for organ.. at 45 r.p.m. In retrospect I am convinced that those extra 11⅔ revs per minute tightened up the form of this fascinating work to a slight but ideal degree. **1972** *Daily Tel.* 25 Feb. 2/7 As I got round the bend onto the main road I felt the revs begin to build up. When this happened I changed up a gear.

2. *Comb.* **rev-counter** (and varr.), † **rev-meter,** an instrument that measures and displays the rate of rotation, esp. of an engine, or the number of rotations.

1917 *Blackw. Mag.* May 803/2 The rev.-counter showed that the number of revolutions per minute had fallen off appreciably. **1948** M. Laski *Tory Heaven* iv. 58 The car.. had a searchlight and a wireless mast and outside gears and a rev counter. **1967** E. Chambers *Photolitho-Offset* viii. 103 It is possible to compute mathematically the required settings which are..mechanically applied in different ways. For example,..by using a rev-counter and vernier dials attached and synchronised with the movements of the lens board and copyboard carriages. **1976** *Glasgow Herald* 26 Nov. 19/5 The speedometer and rev. counter are..right in front of the driver. **1917** E. C. Middleton *Way of Air* vii. 49 The pilot is able to distinguish his instruments..the altimeter, which records the height, 'revmeter' which indicates the speed of the engine and the compass.

rev (rev), *v.* Pa. t. **revved,** pres. pple. **revving.** [f. the sb.] **1.** *trans.* To cause (an internal-combustion engine) to run quickly, esp. before bringing it into use; to speed *up*. Freq. *absol.* Also *fig.*

1920 *Blackw. Mag.* Oct. 449/1 A British Fighter whose pilot was revving up his 250-horse-power Rolls Royce Falcon. **1922** Joyce *Ulysses* 420 O get, rev on a gradient one in nine. **1934** [see *idle *v.* 4 a]. **1942** *Sat. Even. Post* 5 Sept. 22/1 Jimmy revved up and the engine burst into a deep-throated roar. **1944** A. Thirkell *Headmistress* i. 28 'Rev. her up, Copper.' The ginger-haired bicyclist..roared away up the street. **1956** *Sun* (Baltimore) 24 Apr. 21/1 Bill Hartack revved up his already torrid riding pace here today by winning four races out of seven tries to push his total victory for the year to 94. **1966** J. Betjeman *High & Low* 50 Loving relations Rev in the car park, changing gear at the bend. **1968** Mrs. L. B. Johnson *White House Diary* 31 Mar. (1970) 644 Lyndon came in with that jaunty step that I've seen him rev up under the most intense tension. **1973** A. Hunter *Gently French* iii. 23 The mech gently revved it, bringing in the supercharger. **1977** *Time* 13 June 47/2 He and a cousin revved up the company, branched into trucking and started hauling coal. **1978** J. Irving *World according to Garp* xii. 234 He revved his engine as if he were clearing his throat.

2. *intr.* Of an internal-combustion engine: to run (quickly), esp. with the clutch disengaged. Also said of the vehicle. Freq. with *up*.

1923 *Daily Mail* 9 Mar. 12 This little engine..cheats the taxation authorities by its long stroke and its capacity for 'revving' fast without vibration. **1930** *Times* 29 Mar. 17/6 (Advt.), The oil..is specially refined for the fast-revving engines of to-day. **1951** 'J. Wyndham' *Day of Triffids* i. 9 The released cross-traffic would rev. and roar as it started up the incline. **1955** G. Greene *Quiet American* ii. ii. 111 All round me I could hear the cars of the soldiers and the diplomats revving up: the party was over for another year. **1960** J. Betjeman *Summoned by Bells* vii. 73 There's a Frazer–Nash. Gosh, what an engine! Did you hear her rev? **1965** *Motor* 17 July 8/1 The Anglia revs faster at any given speed in top. **1973** J. Pattinson *Search Warrant* vi. 90 He heard a motor engine revving up, dying away, revving again.

Hence **re·vved-up** *a.* (in quots., *fig.*); **re·vving** *ppl. a.* and *vbl. sb.*

1931 E. M. Brent-Dyer *Chalet School & Jo* xxi. 261 I'm so revved up,..I simply *can't* rest. Please, may I go for a walk instead? **1972** J. Aiken *Butterfly Picnic* vi. 107 My mind seemed revved up to operate at twice its normal pace. **1976** J. Carroll *Madonna Red* v. (1977) 174 The rush of his revved-up thinking. **1978** M. Harrison in *Islands* (N.Z.) Aug. 86, I didn't dream of standing by the revving plane, the wires of the fences caught the whisper of the landing-lights. **1979** K. Conlon *Move in Game* iii. 32 The man who drove his scarlet MG with much revving of the engine.

revaloriza·tion (rī-). [Re- 5 a.] The action or process of establishing a fresh price or value for something; revaluation. So **reva·lorize** *v. trans.*

1926 *Glasgow Herald* 6 Aug. 8 A preliminary revalorisation [of the franc] through a restoration of confidence should first be attempted. **1928** *Britain's Industr. Future* (Liberal Industr. Inquiry) v. xxviii. 410 The desire to 'revalorise' the currency (i.e. to raise its exchange value) before 'stabilising' it. This process of revalorisation..is infallibly accompanied..by severe trade depression. **1928** *Daily Tel.* 27 Mar. 14/3 The leading banks..replied that they would not advance a pfennig until the war debts had been revalorised and admitted. **1962** *Listener* 12 Apr. 624/2 If we are to have ministerial meetings they need not always be at the level of Heads of Government. Foreign Ministers must be revalorized. **1977** *Times* 27 Apr. 23/5 Mr Healey gets beta plus for revalorizing personal reliefs to counter about one year's fiscal drag. **1979** *Daily Tel.* 4 Apr. 10 These increases give effect to the re-valorisation of personal allowances provided for by Section 22 of the Finance Act 1977. **1979** *Maledicta* III. 71 In their attempts to enshrine and revalorize their own blackness and that of their intended audience, these poets of cultural nationalism frequently seem to assume [etc.].

reva·luate (rī-), *v.* [Back-formation f. Revaluation.] *trans.* To reassess, form a new valuation of. Also *absol.* Hence **reva·luating** *ppl. a.*

1949 Wellek & Warren *Theory of Lit.* iv. 34 The practicing critic..will revaluate the past. **1965** 'A. Burgess' in *Listener* 18 Feb. 275/1 'Another revaluation of Joyce would make one scream.' By the waters of Marylebone I sat down and wept, wondering whether to sink my revaluating galleys. **1977** *Times* 5 July 5/4 Even if a firm offer is made, however, both the British and French Governments will undoubtedly demand time to revaluate their respective commitments.

revaluation. Add: **a.** *spec.* in literary criticism.

1936 F. R. Leavis (*title*) Revaluation. **1976** *UCT Stud. in English* (Univ. Cape Town) Oct. 1 After the critical revaluations of the past twenty years, Wallace Stevens can no longer be thought of as an eccentric. **1978** *Times Lit. Suppl.* 1 Dec. 1393/2 What he is doing is practising the classic American trick of hurling effete European vice out of the window and then lugging it back through the door, wearing a coonskin cap and called Revaluation.

b. A second or further valuation of the financial or monetary worth of something, *spec.* a revision (usu. an increase) of the official value of a currency in relation to gold or another currency.

1925 *Times* 22 Sept. 22/6 The German Embassy has issued the following information regarding the German Law of Revaluation:—Mortgages, land and annuity debts..will on principle be revalued at 25 per cent. of their gold value. **1946** *Times* 13 July 7/1 Revaluation will tend to neutralize the impact [of disparity with U.S. prices] on the Swedish economy. **1955** *Times* 27 June 9/3 No ratepayer can properly gauge the effect of revaluation until he knows what rate his local authority intends to levy in the new dispensation. **1962** *Ann. Reg. 1961* 465 Sterling was under pressure as a result of general uncertainty following the revaluations of the Deutschemark and Dutch guilder. **1968** *Guardian* 20 Nov. 12/2 Revaluation means increasing the value of a currency in terms of other currencies. **1971** *Daily Tel.* 10 May 1/1 Dr Schmidt, president of the National Bank [of Austria] said losses to the reserves caused by the revaluation amounted to 1,500 million schillings. **1978** *Financial Times* 30 Jan. 2/6 The half per cent revaluation of the Dirham against the dollar..brought it into line with the currencies of Bahrain and Qatar.

revalue, *v.* Add: (Earlier and later examples.) *spec.* To adjust (usu. increase) the value of (a currency) in relation to gold or another currency.

1592 H. Wotton *Let.* in *Reliquiæ Wottonianæ* (1685) 668 The Sum should be revalued. **1925** [see *revaluation b]. **1946** *Times* 13 July 7/1 (*heading*), Swedish Krona Revalued. **1962** *Ann. Reg. 1961* 245 On 5 March the Deutschemark was revalued upwards by 4·75 per cent. **1968** *Guardian* 16 Nov. 1/2 The French..have been putting strong pressure on the Germans..to revalue. This would..make German exports less competitive. **1978** *Financial Times* 30 Jan. 2/5 The Bahrain dinar was revalued by 2 per cent against the U.S. dollar at the opening of business in Bahrain on Saturday.

revamp, *v.* Add: (Further examples.) Also, to rewrite in a new form; to renovate, remake, devise anew; to revise. Hence **revamped** *ppl. a.*; **revamping** *vbl. sb.* (further examples).

1850 D. G. Mitchell *Lorgnette* I. 141 Even the soberer subjects of History, he told me, must be re-vamped in some tasty way. **1878** 'Mark Twain' in *Atlantic Monthly* May 617/2 He had to keep on procuring magazine acceptances and then revamping the manuscripts to make them presentable. **1931** Ford & Crowther *Moving Forward* xi. 164 We decided to revamp our entire industry from top to bottom. **1934** J. A. & A. Lomax *Amer. Ballads & Folk Songs* i. 37 Sanders then changed the words 'Jimmie Jones' to 'Casey Jones'. Later it was picked up by some traveling vaudevillians and revamped to make the popularly known song, 'Casey Jones'. **1941** W. C. Handy *Father of Blues* xii. 169 The revamped outfit was acting strangely, whispering behind their hands. **1945** Nelson & Wright *Tomorrow's House* vii. 79 This is just the living-room function slightly revamped. **1947** *Sun* (Baltimore) 22 Dec. 2/1 Eastern and western states will revamp their foreign policies in the light of the situation in Germany. **1950** *Manch. Guardian Weekly* 7 Dec. 3 The British did some rapid discreet revamping of their agenda. **1956** W. H. Whyte *Organization Man* (1957) 99 Several of the technical schools have been revamping their curriculums. **1960** O. Skilbeck *ABC of Film & TV* 108 *Re-vamp*, to use an existing set for further shooting by altering it and adapting its practicals for another sequence. **1961** *Harper's Bazaar* Dec. 60 Brilliant revamping of the famous Helena Rubinstein flat in Paris. **1965** *Listener* 16 Dec. 984/2 Over the past three years they [*sc.* the East Germans] have done a lot of revamping, and are introducing what they rather ponderously call 'the new system of planning and guiding the national economy'. **1968** *Observer* 29 Dec. 32/3 On Wednesday, *Punch* appears revamped and under new editorship. **1979** *Jrnl. R. Soc. Arts* CXXVII. 122/1 The new or revamped public schools did not set out to equip their pupils to lead great industrial enterprises.

revamp *sb.* (later examples).

1943 *Yank* 10 Feb. 8 If a plane comes in badly shot up and has to go to basic engineering for a revamp, two crew members will go with her and personally inspect everything that's done. **1973** *Scotsman* 12 Jan. 3/1 Rockware Glass, the £16 million container group, are planning a major revamp of their factories. **1979** *Now!* 21–7 Sept. 59/3 The Navy IQ test was introduced in 1942, and given a 'revamp' in 1977.

‖**revanchard** (rəvaṅʃāɹ), *a.* [Fr.] = *revanchist *a.*

1961 *Washington Post* 28 Aug. A-8/4 Placed before the fact..of a separate state which..immediately started to acquire a belligerent revanchard character, the population of East Germany in their turn created another German state. **1964** *Listener* 1 Oct. 523/2 In the eighteen-eighties, thanks partly to Boulanger, it was the Right [in France] which became militantly *revanchard*, and by the turn of the century it was denouncing the Left for being socialist, pacifist, semitic, and *dreyfusard*.

‖**revanche** (rəvaṅʃ). [Fr.] Requital, revenge; the giving of like for like. *spec.* A nation's policy of securing the return of lost territory.

1858 Queen Victoria *Let.* 22 June in R. Fulford *Dearest Child* (1964) 117 She never allows a word to be said against Leopold who in revanche is much kinder to her than he was. **1870** G. Meredith *Let.* 9 Oct. (1970) I. 427 You greatmindedly took my criticism, and I long for the *revanche* of giving praise. **1889** M. S. Van de Velde *Cosmopolitan Recoll.* I. v. 162 He [*sc.* Prince Gortchakoff] has on his record the fate of Sleswig and of Denmark; Sadowa, the *revanche* of Sebastopol. **1894** G. du Maurier *Trilby* III. viii. 157 When they come back from *La Revanche*, may Madame Cantharidi ..welcome the returning heroes. **1895** M. Corelli *Sorrows of Satan* X. 108 Meanwhile I was surrounded by the rest of the men, all of them repeating the Viscount's suggestion of a 'revanche'. **1914** G. B. Shaw in *New Statesman* 14 Nov. (Suppl.) 20/1 France had given up hope of her Alsace–Lorraine *revanche*. **1919** J. M. Keynes *Econ. Consequences* *of Peace* (1920) iii. 32 Each guarantee that was taken, by increasing irritation and thus the probability of a subsequent *Revanche* by Germany, made necessary yet further provisions to crush. **1930** H. G. WELLS *Autocracy of Mr. Parham* IV. ii. 285 An unhoped for *revanche* offered itself plainly and clearly to the German people. **1934** B. RUSSELL *Freedom & Organization 1814–1914* xxxii. 495 He [*sc.* the Kaiser] caused England to join France and Russia, thereby encouraging Germany's enemies everywhere, awaking in France renewed hope of the *revanche*. **1939** A. J. TOYNBEE *Study of Hist.* IV. 118 The Justinianean *revanche*, in the sixth century, against the Vandals and the Ostrogoths. *a* **1943** R. G. COLLINGWOOD *Idea of Hist.* (1946) 169 History is regarded not only as a possible and legitimate form of knowledge but as the only genuine knowledge that exists or can exist. But this *revanche* not only fails in doing justice to natural science, it also misunderstands history. **1958** *Listener* 10 July 57/1 In 1914..France wanted Revanche.

revanchist (revɒ·nʃist), *sb.* and *a.* [f. prec. + -IST: cf. Fr. *revanchiste* (also used).] **A.** *sb.* One who seeks reprisal or revenge; *spec.* one who seeks to avenge the defeat of Germany in the war of 1939–45. **B.** *adj.* Also **revanchi·stic.** Pertaining to or characterized by a policy of reprisal or revenge.

1926 *Scots Observer* 13 Nov. 19/1 A Germany contented, satisfied, and prosperous would pay her debt and achieve a bloodless but a complete victory. It is France's policy that the sores be kept open even if they give a handle to Monarchist revanchists. **1953** *Ann. Reg. 1952* 195 The creation in Western Germany of hired forces of *revanchistes* under the command of Hitlerite generals. **1954** *Times* 5 Mar. 6/4 'Then their real aims will be revealed as well as their aggressive, revanchist calculations,' Mr. Molotov added... The Soviet Foreign Minister said the Adenauer Government was now 'the mainstay of the west German revanchists who want to clear the road to the resurgence of German militarism'. **1955** *N.Y. Times* 10 May 28/1 Far from being an instrument of either 'American aggressors' or 'German revanchists' (as Soviet propaganda would picture it), the North Atlantic alliance is entirely a defensive organization. **1959** *Times* 30 Mar. 5/4 Austria had undertaken to prohibit all Fascist and 'revanchist' organizations, and to wipe out all remaining traces of the Nazis. **1960** *Guardian* 25 Oct. 7/2 Revanchist speeches were being made..on the borders of Czechoslovakia. **1961** *Evening Bull.* (Philadelphia) 24 Aug. 1/8 Air corridors were set aside for the three Western Powers to insure the needs of their military garrisons, and not for subversive and revanchist (revenge-seeking) purposes. **1961** *Times Lit. Suppl.* 17 Nov. 815/4 Between the wars the Hungarians were only revisionists. No one labelled them as revenge-seekers and the communists had surely not yet invented that bastard word 'revanchist'. **1965** *New Statesman* 19 Mar. 432/1, I asked a prominent East German lawyer why, rather than sneer about 'revanchists', they did not support this attempt to convict Nazi criminals. **1965** *Listener* 16 Dec. 983/2 East German propaganda would say it [*sc.* living in West Germany] meant living under 'a state-monopolistic revanchistic militarist regime'. **1967** *Ibid.* 3 Aug. 155/3 When journalists and scholars..label Israeli revanchistes 'Jewish fascists', it's apparent that such tastelessness is even less bearable in non-fiction. **1968** *Daily Tel.* 1 Nov. 34/3 The statement referred also to the 'revanchist and expansionist forces in control in Bonn'. **1973** *Guardian* 19 Oct. 14/6 Not terrorists but revanchist states were the greater threat [to Israel]. **1976** T. ALLBEURY *Only Good German* xiii. 94 A sabotage team operating against the Warsaw Pact countries..supported by the CIA and West German revanchists. **1977** *Time* 7 Feb. 15/3 O'Brien supports a referendum to amend the Irish constitution to remove its revanchist claim on Ulster.

Hence **reva·nchism**, a policy of seeking reprisal or revenge.

1954 *Times* 5 Mar. 6/4 (*heading*) Mr. Molotov on German 'Revanchism'. **1957** *Wall Street Jrnl.* 6 Dec. 6/5 The struggle against West German militarism and revanchism (seeking for revenge), which are now threatening peace, is a vital task facing the peace-loving forces of the German people and all the nations of Europe. **1959** *Listener* 3 Sept. 344/2 The aim of this offer is to take the edge off accusations of revanchism. **1960** *Guardian* 7 Dec. 32/6 Developments in Germany do not go unscanned for signs of militarism and revanchism. **1971** *Listener* 7 Jan. 5/2 If imperialist aggression and German revanchism cease to be credible threats, what grounds are there for maintaining Soviet garrisons in satellite countries? **1974** *Times* 19 Feb. (European Defence Suppl.) p. ii/7 There is a body of opinion which holds that the Russians are looking more in the direction of the Bundeswehr, prompted by an undying fear of German revanchism.

Revd., abbrev. of REVEREND *a.* and *sb.* 2 c.

1693 W. KENNETT in W. Somner *Treat. Roman Ports & Forts* 1 The Life of Mr. Somner. To the Rev[d]. Mr. James Brome. **1811** SHELLEY *Let.* 17 Feb. (1964) I. 52 If any letter comes directed to the Revd. Charles Meyton, it is mine. **1926** FOWLER *Mod. Eng. Usage* 502/1 *Reverend* is abbreviated *Revd* or now usually *Rev.* **1971** C. COLVIN *M. Edgeworth's Lett. from Eng.* p. xxxvi, The Revd. Daniel Augustus Beaufort.., father-in-law of R. L. Edgeworth.

revealing, *ppl. a.* (Later example.)

1927 BELLOC *Hist. Eng.* II. 210 The second rebellion against Henry II was a longer and much more revealing thing than the first.

revealingly *adv.* (further example).

1973 *Nature* 30 Mar. 306/2 There is the case of Graham Young..who, having been 'cured' at Broadmoor..of enjoying poisoning people, had an unfortunate relapse and poisoned several more. Revealingly, his last bout of evil.. was not attributed to mental disease: this time he was sent to prison.

revegetate, *v.* Add: **2.** *trans.* To produce the growth of new vegetation on (disturbed or barren ground). Of a plant: to colonize anew.

1955 *Sci. Amer.* June 50/3 Revegetating the area with plants more drought-resistant than the native flora and fertilizing the land are two of the most helpful measures. **1963** D. W. & E. E. HUMPHRIES tr. *Termier's Erosion & Sedimentation* i. 20 The tropical jungles spread out north and south, revegetating the sands and 'fixing' the dunes. **1971** *Nature* 4 June 287/1 Practical techniques were developed for revegetating bare, industrially derelict land near Swansea. **1975** *Sci. Amer.* Dec. 27/2 Halogeton, a toxic weed, is among the first and most tenacious plants to revegetate disturbed desert land. **1976** *Nature* 26 Aug. 733/2 All their contracts with coal suppliers contain a clause requiring that strip mined lands be restored and revegetated.

Hence **reve·getated** *ppl. a.*; **revegetation** (further examples).

1974 *Nature* 15 Feb. 428/1 Revegetation of toxic spoil from industrial processes. **1974** *Environmental Conservation* I. 60/1 Natural revegetation proceeds very slowly in arctic areas. **1976** *Billings* (Montana) *Gaz.* 2 July, Hodder's research involves comparing cattle weight gains on re-vegetated spoils that have been heavily fertilized to gains on unfertilized native range.

reveille. The pronunc. is now usu. (rivæ·li).

‖ **réveillon** (reveᵉiyoṅ). [Fr.] A night-time feast or celebration, orig. one that took place after midnight on Christmas morning. Also *attrib.*

1803 E. WYNNE *Diary* 25 Dec. (1940) III. iv. 98 Xmas Day. Sunday. We had midnight Prayers and a Reveillon. **1894** G. DU MAURIER *Trilby* I. III. 240 The whole Quartier seemed alive with the *réveillon*. **1932** H. NICOLSON *Diary* 1 Jan. (1966) 104 He had spent *réveillon* at the Fabre–Luces and had been kept up..till 8 am. **1965** M. WALLENSTEIN *Merlin's Forest* xx. 205 A man was hanging out a large decorated menu for the Christmas Eve *réveillon*. **1967** C. DURRELL tr. *Oliver's French at Table* ii. 69 Pope Julius I decreed that Christmas should be celebrated on 25 December, this providing an excuse for what soon became the traditional *réveillon*—an enormous midnight feast. **1967** *Guardian* 30 Dec. 7/8 French housewives..on Christmas Eve were hosts or guests at the traditional Réveillon supper. On New Year's Eve there is a Réveillon supper all over again. **1971** *Ibid.* 9 Dec. 11/5 A few loose segments [of garlic] to perfume the new year *Reveillon* soup. **1976** *Newmarket Jrnl.* 16 Dec., Called Reveillon, their elaborate suppers and festivities often continue until the early hours.

Revelation. Add: **4*.** A proprietary name for a make of leather goods, used esp. to denote an expanding suitcase.

1923 *Trade Marks Jrnl.* 2 May 876 Revelation...Bags, trunks, suitcases, attaché cases, card cases, cigar and cigarette cases, wallets and similar containers, all being goods made of leather or principally of leather... Jigger, Limited, ..London,..; merchants. **1935** G. GREENE *Basement Room* 115 Grains of rice..fell on to his Revelation suitcase. **1938** D. DU MAURIER *Rebecca* vi. 60 My Revelation suit-case and the stout hold-all. **1964** J. GARDNER *Liquidator* i. 15 The battered multi-labelled tan Revelation stood packed. **1967** 'F. CLIFFORD' *All Men are Lonely Now* I. iv. 62 He had brought a Revelation from the flat and now he packed the twenty-five folders into it. **1975** *Listener* 9 Jan. 48/1 If one has a folding cycle, one can wrap it up..in a Revelation suitcase.

revelationism (revĕlēi·ʃəniz'm). [f. REVELATION + -ISM.] The fact or process of making a revelation; advocacy of or belief in revelation.

1949 E. L. MASCALL *Existence & Analogy* vii. 175 The theistic issue is..immediately raised..by a..discussion of.. the extreme 'revelationism' of Kierkegaard, Barth, Brunner and their disciples, and the Thomist *analogia entis*.

revelator. Add: **1.** (Earlier and later examples.)

1801 *Massachusetts Spy* 20 May 1/2 They shall have their part (saith John the Revelator) in the lake which burneth. **1840** *Latter-Day Saints Millenial Star* June 28/1 The prophet Daniel and the revelator John. **1980** *Times Lit. Suppl.* 25 July 842/3 Lawrence's rhapsodies on John the Revelator's horses.

2. A name given to the president of the Church of Jesus Christ of Latter-day Saints.

1867 W. H. DIXON *New Amer.* II. ii. 12 The Mormon will put his trust in Joseph, as a natural seer and revelator. **1895** *Denver Times* 5 Mar. 8/2 Joseph Smith, the son of the martyr Joseph Smith, is now prophet, seer and revelator. **1974** *Time* 7 Jan. 59/3 Lee was one of the youngest men ever to become 'prophet, seer, and revelator' of the Mormons.

revenant[2]. Add: Also fem. **revenante. 1.** (Earlier and later examples.) Also *attrib.*, as *adj.*, and *fig.*

1827 T. J. DIBDIN *Reminisc.* I. vi. 110 She will however frequently make her appearance in this narrative, not as a *revenante*, but prior to the period of her final departure. **1909** R. BROOKE *Let.* 16 Apr. (1968) 166 It looks a little like Second Childhood, doesn't it? I think it is merely the first, revenant. **1910** J. C. LAWSON *Mod. Greek Folklore & Anc. Greek Relig.* 407 If the devil in possession of the corpse chose to agitate it and drive it out of the grave, the dead demoniac was at once a *revenant*. **1942** 'M. INNES' *Daffodil Affair* III. iii. 91 The papers were full of strange elysiums, cigar-and-whisky empyreans, *revenants* who reported lawn-tennis tournaments on the pavements of paradise. **1955** [see *COME-BACK *sb.*[2] 3]. **1958** *Times* 24 Nov. 12/2 Leonard Salzedo has written the concerto for this *revenant* among solo instruments. **1968** T. KINSELLA *Nightwalker* 11 A revenant, A rain-worn, delicate Stone shape. **1969** P. ANDERSON in Cockburn & Blackburn *Student Power* 257 In the closed space of Gombrich's preoccupations, the psychology which was once exorcized is a revenant which necessarily returns to rule. **1970** R. LOWELL *Notebk.* 179 (*title*) Revenants. **1972** *Daily Tel.* (Colour Suppl.) 12 May 61/1 In Eastern Europe..thousands of villagers still believe in the malignity of the *revenant* dead.

revenge, *sb.* Add: **7.** *attrib.*, as *revenge-killing, play, seeker, tragedy.*

1975 O. SELA *Bengali Inheritance* xvii. 147 That war was long over... A revenge killing after all this time was absurd. **1967** Revenge play [see *NOIA]. **1980** *Dædalus* Spring 133 He made *Hamlet* out of the tired revenge play tradition. **1961** *Guardian* 25 Nov. 1/4 It was essential..to 'tie the hands of West German militarists and revenge-seekers'. **1957** N. FRYE *Anat. Crit.* 209 The revenge-tragedy is a simple tragic structure. **1977** S. SCHOENBAUM *William Shakespeare* x. 154 Chettle..is remembered, if at all, for his revenge tragedy of *Hoffman*.

‖ **revenons à nos moutons** (rəvənoṅz a no mutoṅ), *phr.* [Fr., lit. 'let us return to our sheep', with allusion to the confused court scene in the Old French *Farce de Maistre Pierre Pathelin* (*c* 1470).] 'Let us return to the subject': an exhortation to cease digressing.

[**1617** J. CHAMBERLAIN *Let.* 22 Feb. in T. Birch *Court & Times James I* (1848) I.459 But, *pour retourner à nos moutons*, this feasting begins to grow to an excessive rate.] **1822** *Blackw. Mag.* May 610 *North.* On proceeds..Byron..the immoral, irreligious, and unpatriotic tendency of too many of his productions... *Omnes* (sing). Very good song, Very well sung, Jolly companions every one... *North. Revenons a nos moutons*! Childe Harold. **1839** THACKERAY in *Fraser's Mag.* Aug. 228/2 But, *revenons à nos moutons*, let us return to that sweet lamb, Master Thomas. **1850** —— *Pendennis* I. xxxvii. 364 That brings me back to my point—revenons à nos moutons. Yes, begad! revenons à nos moutons. *c* **1909** D. H. LAWRENCE *Collier's Friday Night* (1934) II. 48 *Ernest.* I'll bet the dear boy enjoys that blush. *Beatrice.* Ra-ther! (*Artlessly revenant à son mouton.*) And he'll have the rose and all, to rejoice the cockles of his heart this time. **1926** J. S. HUXLEY *Ess. Pop.Sci.* 27 But *revenons à nos moutons*—to our chromosomes. **1932** A. CHRISTIE *Peril at End House* ii. 37 *Revenons à nos moutons*... I implore you to be serious. **1966** 'H. CARMICHAEL' *Suicide Clause* xi. 124 You didn't come here to listen to irrelevant chatter. So, *revenons à nos moutons*. **1972** *Country Life* 9 Nov. 1243/2 *Revenons à nos moutons*. As soon as I saw my cards, the earlier hand flashed through my mind.

‖ **reventa** (reve·nta). [Sp., = resale.] (See quot. 1932.)

1932 E. HEMINGWAY *Death in Afternoon* iv. 40 The reventa are ticket brokers who take over all or most of the unsubscribed tickets from the bull ring management and sell them at a twenty per cent increase over their face value. **1960** *Times* 14 Nov. 16/7 If you want the best seats in Spain only the *reventa* has them.

revenue. Add: **6. c.** (Earlier example.)

1883 ZEIGLER & GROSSCUP *Heart of Alleghanies* 257 My pards mout tak' ye fer a revenoo, an' let a hole thro' ye.

7. a. *revenue account, act* (earlier example), *agent, boat, cutter* (earlier example), *department, expenditure, man* (further example), *stamp, tariff.*

1869 *Bradshaw's Railway Manual* XXI. 392 Confusion between capital and revenue accounts..has led to the undue increase of capital. **1970** R. W. WALLIS *Accounting* x. 142 If the local authority charges similar fares and has similar expenses to those of the private undertaking, it too will make a profit or 'revenue account surplus'. *Ibid.* 147 The public authority 'provision for debt redemption' or 'loans redeemed' accounts tend to be equivalent to the 'depreciation provision' account..provided the revenue account is charged with an amount approximating to the amount of depreciation of the asset concerned. **1791** G. WASHINGTON *Diary* 4 June (1925) IV. 196 The discontents which it was supposed the last Revenue Act..would create subside as fast as the law is explained. **1864** *Statutes at Large U.S.A.* XIII. 224 Revenue agents..[shall] aid in the prevention, detection, and punishment of frauds upon the internal revenue. **1943** *Chicago Daily News* 24 Dec. 6/1 We would hate to be a revenue agent with that gal up in the cove. **1846** *Knickerbocker* XXVIII. 244 The revenue-boat from the *guardacosta* came on board before our sails were furled. **1790** *Deb. Congress U.S.* (1834) 1st Congress 2nd Sess., App. 2277 The officers of the revenue cutters herein-after mentioned. *Ibid.* 2 July (1834) 1003, I likewise nominate the following persons to fill offices in the Revenue Department of the United States. **1964** S. BRITTAN *Treasury under Tories* iv. 101 The Inland Revenue and Customs and Excise (jointly known as 'the Revenue Departments'). **1961** WEBSTER, Revenue expenditure. **1968** JOHANNSEN & ROBERTSON *Managem. Gloss.* 116 *Revenue expenditure*, expenditures of cash which are undertaken to maintain asset values (e.g. repairs) or to obtain current revenue (e.g. raw material purchases, factory payroll). **1970** R. W. WALLIS *Accounting* x. 140 [In central government accounting] the distinction between capital and revenue expenditure is not recognized. **1979** *Daily Tel.* 6 Apr. 10/6 After deducting more than £3 million earmarked for capital projects, the council's new grant represents a rise in its revenue expenditure of about 19 per cent. **1895** *Century Mag.* July 378/2 I'm always skeered o' the revenue men bein' about. **1870** J. K. MEDBERY *Men & Mysteries Wall St.* 52 The acknowledgements are covered with revenue stamps. **1820** *Deb. Congress U.S.* 24 Apr. (1855) 1966 They enacted a treasury tariff, a revenue tariff, without the least regard to the situation of the country. **1887** *Courier-Jrnl.* (Louisville, Kentucky) 19 Feb. 4/1 They are the identical arguments which the Courier-Journal has been pounding into the understanding of the people in its fight for a revenue tariff.

b. *revenue-earner; revenue-paying, -sharing, -yielding.*

1963 *Times* 23 Mar. 11/1 Sport in general is a major revenue-earner. **1910** J. LONDON *Let.* 9 Aug. (1966) 317 The idea that a judge of rectitude should..try a case between a non-resident like me and a revenue-paying, vote-swinging tenant like Muldowney. **1971** *New Yorker* 10 July 43 Brock's dominant theme was much the same as what President Nixon would later call 'revenue sharing'—that government had to be returned to local control by way of sending the taxpayers' money back to the states, counties, cities, and towns. **1973** *Black Panther* 17 Mar. A/3 Even the facade of Revenue Sharing as the promise of a 'new lease on life' for American cities is fast becoming a sad joke. **1976** *National Observer* (U.S.) 2 Oct. 10/1 Boston's Housing Improvement Program, an apparently successful effort to use Federal revenue-sharing money to upgrade city neighborhoods and preserve existing housing. **1898** E. HOWARD *To-morrow* v. 53 A considerable outlay would be incurred in respect of markets, water supply, lighting, tramways, and other revenue-yielding undertakings.

revenuer (re·vĕniuːəɹ). *U.S.* [f. REVENUE + -ER[1].] A revenue agent.

1880 *Daily Inter-Ocean* (Chicago) 1 June 12/1 His wife and daughter discharged their conjugal and filial duty by.. watching from their home for the approach of the 'Revenyors'. **1895** 'C. E. CRADDOCK' *Mystery of Witch-Face Mountain* 15 The 'revenuers'..never rode alone. **1941** *Charlottesville* (Va.) *Daily Progress* 16 Aug. 1/5 The sharp rise in sugar and grain prices, coupled with the increased efforts of the 'revenooers' to ferret out the distilling outfits in the mountains have made it too perilous for most of the old-timers. **1949** *Américas* Aug. 10/1 The 'revenoo-ers' slowed the production of illegal whiskey. **1955** W. FAULKNER *Fable* 173 The sheriff..and the city strangers in their city hats and neckties and shoes, smelling, stinking of excise officers, revenuers. **1963** *Times* 19 Mar. 10/7 The 'revenuer' keeps track of large sales of sugar. **1974** W. GARNER *Big enough Wreath* x. 131 Moonshiner, made his own likker..scared stiff of being caught by the revenuers. **1974** *New Yorker* 3 June 43/2 Jon tried to persuade Anne and Ruth to take their bathing suits off... 'Listen, as long as we're back up here where the revenooers can't get at us, we might as well have a good time.'

reverb (rĭvɜ̄·ɹb), *sb.* Colloq. abbrev. of *REVERBERATION 1 c.

1961 in WEBSTER. **1968** *Blues Unlimited* Dec. 10 Muddy's new album Electric Mud is a morass of feedback,..reverb and every other trick. **1971** *Melody Maker* 13 Nov. 36/4 The features are the same as the bass amp, but with twice the channels, plus reverb and tremolo. **1976** BOOT & THOMAS *Jamaica* 34/1 They had about as much sheet reverb as the human body can stand.

So **reve·rbed** *a.*, adapted to produce a reverberating sound.

1977 *Rolling Stone* 30 June 102/2 Edmunds' treatment of Crudup-cum-Presley's 'My Baby Left Me'..captures the Sun sound from its string bass to its reverbed rhythm guitar.

reverberant, *a.* Add: Hence **reve·rberantly** *adv.*, in a reverberant manner.

1961 in WEBSTER. **1976** *Gramophone* Oct. 644/1 He is made to stand out too reverberantly against the street-vendors' cries in Act 2. **1977** *Rolling Stone* 24 Mar., We've come to expect strong personalities in female C&W singers. Dolly Parton is the buxom, reverberantly mature earth mother.

reverberation. Add: **1. c.** *spec.* Temporary persistence or prolongation of sound without perceptible distinct echoes, produced either by repeated reflection from nearby surfaces or artificially. (Further examples.)

1828 E. HOLMES *Ramble among Musicians of Germany* 194 The effect of an excellent orchestra is heightened by the structure of this edifice, which admits of a fine echo and reverberation. **1905** E. ATKINSON tr. *Ganot's Nat. Philos.* (ed. 10) IV. i. 203 When a person is speaking in a large empty room, the reverberation from the walls and ceiling produces a confused effect. **1948** P. M. MORSE *Vibration & Sound* (ed. 2) xxxii. 387 If the room is used chiefly for music, we can allow more reverberation without detriment. **1962** A. NISBETT *Technique Sound Studio* xi. 188 'Echo' is something of a misnomer for a studio technique which serves to extend reverberation without (it is hoped) introducing any actual echoes. *Ibid.* 191 Reverberation is added by an echo chamber. **1975** G. J. KING *Audio Handbk.* i. 22 It is the aim of hi-fi reproduction..to reproduce the whole of the original, including the reverberation, which should not be unduly modified by the listening room.

3. c. *Plumbing.* = WATER-HAMMER 2.

1967 *Gloss. Sanitation Terms* (*B.S.I.*) 63 *Reverberation*, a hammering sound caused by violent surges of pressure in water pipes. **1972** J. HASTINGS *Plumber's Compan.* 168 The working plumber is unlikely to use 'reverberation' or even 'concussion' when speaking of water hammer.

5. *attrib.*, as **reverberation chamber,** a room specially designed to reflect sounds produced within it; **reverberation time** *Acoustics*, the time taken, after cessation of production of a steady sound, for the average sound intensity at a given frequency in a room or enclosure to die away, *spec.* to decrease by 60 decibels.

1932 P. E. SABINE *Acoustics & Archit.* vi. 120 With a source of sound whose acoustic output can be varied in measured amounts the absorbing power of the reverberation chamber both in its standard condition and with the absorbent material present can be determined directly. **1966** *McGraw-Hill Encycl. Sci. & Technol.* I. 665/2 Two types of rooms especially constructed for research and development are..the random diffusion or reverberation chamber and the anechoic room. **1969** Reverberation chamber [see *SABIN]. **1927** I. B. CRANDALL *Theory of Vibrating Syst. & Sound* v. 203 We define *T*, the reverberation time of the given enclosure as the time required for the energy density to sink from one prescribed level to another. *Ibid.* 211 A new concept of reverberation time more nearly in accordance with the actual conditions under which concert rooms are used. **1932** [see *ACOUSTICAL *a.* b]. **1952** *Sci. News* XXIII. 83 Recent concert hall designs have included large quantities of polished wood as a surface finish in an endeavour to prevent the reverberation-time falling away at high frequencies. **1975** G. J. KING *Audio Handbk.* i. 22 For the reproduction of music the reverberation time should not be too large otherwise the 'definition' will be impaired owing to the commencement of a new component of sound before those preceding have died away.

‖ **reverdie** (rəvęrdi). [Fr.] In medieval French lyric poetry: a song which celebrates the re-appearance of spring.

1933 R. TUVE *Seasons & Months* i. 13 This description.. includes the same details as the opening stanza of a Middle English spring song or an Old French *reverdie*. **1976** *Scottish Rev.* Spring 19 In a song, 'The Dark Days are By', in March 1940, he uses the simplest and barest of words to convey the mood of a traditional *reverdie*.

reverend, *a.* and *sb.* Add: **2. b.** Also *absol.*, as a form of address.

1964 *Church of Eng. Newspaper* 11 Dec. 17/3 When I received the letter addressing me as 'Dear Reverend' I was so pleased..that I determined to subscribe to the journal. **1967** C. ARMSTRONG in *Ellery Queen's Mystery Mag.* July 11/1 What you'd better do, Reverend, is go over to the motel and rest. **1974** J. WAINWRIGHT *Hard Hit* 8 'I dunno you, reverend. I think you're making some sorta...' 'Mistake?'

c. (Later examples.) Pl. *reverends*. Use without *the* is again current.

1939 R. E. WOLSELEY in *Ken* 9 Mar. 62/3 Ten devices.. invented by southern journalists to avoid using 'Mr.', 'Mrs.', and 'Miss', in front of the names of Negroes are: Mademoiselle Madame Professor Doctor Reverend [etc.]. **1961** R. B. LONG *Sentence & its Parts* x. 230 There is a feeling that these [honorific modifiers] should be preceded by the article *the* and followed by given names and family names together, as in *the Reverend George Brewster*; but there is also a marked tendency to treat *reverend* exactly as the noun honorifics are treated, as in *Reverend Brewster will preach at the eleven-o'clock service*. **1973** *Publishers' Weekly* 7 May 61/2 (Advt.), The Reverends Rudolf Harvey and Lawrence Burke.

d. (Further examples of *sing.*)

1859 O. L. JACKSON *Colonel's Diary* (1922) ii. 8, I..heard a very good sermon—from a Reverend from Pittsburgh. **1943** G. GREENE *Ministry of Fear* III. ii. 191 That [car], sir—that's the reverend's... We thought it only right to let the vicar know. **1971** *Language* XLVII. 30 Whether or not the notorious Reverend or his students sat up nights inventing such errors, attested errors reveal the same kind of metathesis. **1976** J. MCNEISH *Glass Zoo* vii. 71 Funny, that cloak of yours. I know a Reverend in Leeds got about like that.

reverie, *v.* Add: (Later example.) Also *trans.*, to contemplate or recall with relish or enjoyment.

1961 B. MALAMUD *New Life* 315 He reveried accomplishment..foresaw an effective if..short career. **1980** P. VAN GREENAWAY *Dissident* viii. 168 He reveried on.

reversal, *sb.* Add: **4.** *Photogr.* The process by which a positive image is produced on exposed photographic material without an intervening negative stage. Freq. *attrib.* (see sense *5).

1878 *Proc. R. Soc.* XXVII. 292 When the strength of the permanganate, or hydroxyl, was correct a reversed image of the least refrangible end of the spectrum was obtained,.. the reversal taking place somewhere near D, extending into the ultra-red. **1890** HURTER & DRIFFIELD in *Jrnl. Soc. Chem. Industry* 31 May 464/1 We accordingly distinguish four different periods of exposures... The last portion of the curve we term the period of 'reversal'. *Ibid.* 464/2 This period we have named the period of reversal because within this period happens that peculiar phenomenon, the transformation of the negative into the positive, the 'solarisation', 'reversal', &c. **1907** SHEPPARD & MEES *Invest. Theory Photogr. Process* II. vi. 212 Various forms of reversal in the photographic process are known, not all of equal interest or importance. **1927** C. B. NEBLETTE *Photogr.* viii. 205 No photographic process is, strictly speaking, free from the effects of reversal. **1969** *Focal Encycl. Photogr.* 1294/1 The positive image produced by reversal is..intrinsically finer in grain than the negative from which it is derived.

5. *attrib.* and *Comb.* (chiefly in sense *4), as *reversal method, paper, stock, transparency*; **reversal film,** film that gives a positive image directly when it is processed; **reversal process** *sb.* = sense 4 above; so **reversal-processed** *ppl. a.*, **reversal processing** *vbl. sb.*; also **reversal-process** *v. trans.*; **reversal speed** *Aeronaut.*, the air speed above which the effect of a control surface is reversed, and at which it is nullified, by the aerodynamic effect of the elastic distortion of the aircraft caused by operation of the surface.

1931 J. H. REYNER *Cine-Photogr. for Amateurs* i. 10 Reversal film..will make excellent positives from under exposed film. **1962** *Which?* May 131/1 There are two types of colour film on the market—reversal film, which produces 'positive' transparencies (slides).., and negative film. **1970** *Amateur Photographer* 11 Mar. 60/3 While positive film is comparatively cheap and good results are possible,.. results cannot be nearly as pleasing as those obtained with conventional black-and-white reversal film. **1938** G. H. SEWELL *Amateur Film-Making* ii. 13 It is also possible by applying different solutions [to an exposed film] to 'fix' the film, i.e. dissolve away the silver and leave the salts, and if this is done, the residue of silver salts can then be exposed to light and developed, and it will be found that a positive image will result. That is known as the 'reversal' method. **1969** M. J. LANGFORD *Adv. Photogr.* xvi. 360 Using reversal paper to print direct from positive transparencies. **1920** W. GAMBLE *Photogr.* xi. 80 Development is as usual, and there is no reversal process as in the case of the Autochrome. **1944** T. A. LONGMORE *Med. Photogr.* 363 Development is carried out by the reversal process in order to produce a positive image to satisfy the requirements of the additive colour process. **1955** *Jrnl. Photogr. Sci.* III. 129/1 Deep-etch plates and most bi-metal processes require positives to produce a positive image by a reversal process during platemaking. **1973** Reversal-process *v.* [see *reversal processing* vbl. sb. below]. **1977** J. HEDGECOE *Photographer's Handbk.* 73 The paper prints must be reversal processed using 8 or 9 stages similar to Ektachrome processing. **1964** L. A. MANNHEIM tr. *Croy's Camera Copying & Reproduction* 150 Reversal-processed prints are liable to yield uneven image densities. **1938** D. A. SPENCER *Colour Photogr.* x. 143 The correct exposure is normally that which will leave the highest highlight just transparent after reversal processing. **1973** W. THOMAS *SPSE Handbk. Photogr. Sci. & Engin.* ix. 547 Films designed for reversal processing are available, and some black-and-white negative films can be reversal-processed. **1947** *Jrnl. R. Aeronaut. Soc.* LI. 5/2 For a stiff enough wing there will theoretically be one reversal speed in the subsonic range and two in the supersonic. **1966** *McGraw-Hill Encycl. Sci. & Technol.* I. 90/2 Elastic distortion of an airplane increases rapidly as its speed increases toward the divergence speed and reversal speed. **1969** J. ELLIOT *Duel* III. ii. 233 She went to..learn the mysteries of negatives and reversal stock. **1967** *Economist* 7 Jan. 67/3 Ciba's new process for making colour prints from reversal transparencies.

reverse, *sb.* Add: **1. b.** Also, in *Contract Bridge*, a rebid in a suit of higher rank than that which one has previously bid.

1936 E. CULBERTSON *Contract Bridge Complete* xi. 128 The bid of a higher ranking suit by a player who has bid one of lower rank is called a 'Reverse'. **1939** N. DE V. HART *Bridge Players' Bedside Bk.* 132 Logically..an exception occurs when the partner forces the original bidder to reverse. In that case, the reverse may not indicate additional values. **1951** I. MACLEOD *Bridge* ii. 23 The reverse primarily shows, or ought to show, the shape and not the strength of the holding. **1964** FREY & TRUSCOTT *Bridge Player's Dict.* 420/2 *Reverse*, an unforced rebid at the level of two or more, in a higher-ranking suit than that bid originally; a type of strength-showing bid... The English definition of a reverse by the opener is slightly wider in scope: a bid of a third suit in an uncontested auction which prevents responder returning to the original suit at the level of two... This allows for..a *high reverse*.

6. e. (See sense *12 a.)

12. a. Reverse gear; hence *in reverse*. Also *transf.*

1882 *Engineering* 10 Mar. 219/3 Locomotives having unbalanced slide valves are handled with the greatest ease by means of this steam reverse. **1900** W. W. BEAUMONT *Motor Vehicles & Motors* xiv. 246 The gear speeds with normal speed of motor are for 3½, 10 and 20 miles per hour, with reverse at 4 miles per hour. **1920** R. T. NICHOLSON *Bk. of Ford Van* x. 44 Use your reverse as a brake, in addition to the foot brake and the slow speed. **1925** B. GARBUTT *Bk. of Austin 12* v. 29 You can imagine what would happen if, thinking you were going into..third speed, you really got into reverse in mistake. **1925** F. SCOTT FITZGERALD *Great Gatsby* iii. 67 'Back out,' he suggested... 'Put her in reverse.' **1937** *New Motoring Encycl.* 664/1 The ability to drive a car in reverse accurately and smoothly is essential to correct driving technique. **1958** *Spectator* 22 Aug. 245/1, I started to go into reverse immediately. I backed out of the dining-room. **1973** G. MOFFAT *Lady with Cool Eye* viii. 84 The car..was in neutral instead of bottom or reverse. **1976** *S. Wales Echo* 27 Nov. 5/7 He pleaded not guilty to..using a motor vehicle with a reversing light on when he was not travelling in reverse.

b. The name of the position of the gear lever or selector corresponding to reverse gear.

1963 [see *PARK *sb.* 5 c]. **1965** PRIESTLEY & WISDOM *Good Driving* v. 42 *Park* or *Reverse* must not be selected whilst the car is moving. **1970** F. LEIGH *Bk. of Renault R16* ii. 8 On 1965–67 cars the reverse is found inwards down by second gear. **1974** D. FRANCIS *Knock Down* xv. 191 The driver was shifting the gears from reverse to forward.

reverse, *a.* and *adv.* Add: **1. d.** *reverse fault* (Geol.), a fault in which the relative downward movement occurred in the strata situated on the underside of the fault plane (cf. *NORMAL *a.* 2 d).

1878 [see *NORMAL *a.* 2 d]. **1889** *Amer. Jrnl. Sci.* XXXVIII. 259 The explanation of the reverse faults seems obvious enough. They occur, as we have already said, mostly in strongly folded regions. Such folds can only be produced by lateral pressure. **1962** READ & WATSON *Introd. Geol.* I. viii. 481 Reverse faults are those in which the hanging-wall rocks moved up the dip of the fault-plane relative to the rocks of the foot-wall. *Ibid.* 482 There is much more justification for referring to reverse faults, which involved a shortening of the crust, as compressional faults. **1976** S. JUDSON et al. *Physical Geol.* vii. 152/2 In a reverse fault, the least principal stress is vertical.

e. *reverse angle*: (*a*) *Cinemat.* and *Television.* The opposite angle from which the subject was seen in the preceding shot; freq. *attrib.*; also *reverse shot.* (*b*) *Squash.* Used with reference to a stroke played on to the side wall of the court opposite to the server; usu. *attrib.*

1934 WEBSTER, *Reverse shot*, reverse-angle shot. **1939** B. C. KIESLING *Talking Pictures* 318 *Reverse shot*, the photograph of a scene from the opposite direction from which it was originally taken. **1948** [see *LENGTH *sb.* 10 b]. **1952** L. ANDERSON *Making a Film* 267 Shot in two set-ups: first from the foot of the bed, then (for Penny's entrance) on the reverse angle, over Anselmo's shoulder. **1961** G. Millerson *Technique Television Production* 244 (*caption*) Location can be lost through reverse-angle cutting. **1968** *Squash Rackets* ('Know the Game' Ser.) 39/1 The reverse angle stroke is one played on to the opposite side wall. **1976** *Listener* 26 Feb. 230/3 The journalists were most patient with our retakes and reverse angles.

f. *reverse Polish*: see *Polish *a.* d.

g. *Contract Bridge. reverse bid* = *reverse *sb.* 1 b.

1939 N. de V. Hart *Bridge Players' Bedside Bk.* 132 A reverse bid logically shows considerable strength when it is made in such a way that the partner cannot put the bidder back to his first-bid suit without raising the bidding to a higher level than that at which the bidder could himself have returned to the suit. **1963** *Listener* 10 Jan. 102/3 He lacks the general strength for a 'reverse' bid of Two Hearts.

5. a. (Later examples.) *reverse dictionary*: a dictionary in which the words are arranged so that, read backwards, they are in alphabetical order; *reverse discrimination* = *positive discrimination* s.v. *positive *a.* 15; *reverse pass* (see quots. 1960, 1978).

1921 E. de Lissa in E. H. D. Sewell *Rugby Football up to Date* xv. 264 We are going to practise all the summer together to see if we can't bring off some of that 'reverse' passing, during next season. **1937** E. K. O'Brien in *Bridge World* Aug. 27 (*heading*) The reverse signal. **1951** *Sport* 7–13 Jan. 8/4 Ormondroyd..took a reverse-pass in fine style and went through the opposition like a bullet. **1954** *Newsweek* 26 Apr. 57 To help Scrabble fans, cross-word puzzle addicts, and other persons troubled for a word ending in 'X', 'Y' or 'Z', a 'reverse' dictionary has been compiled at the University of Massachusetts. **1954** *N.Y. Times* 30 May 34/5 Fisk officials cite her case as being possibly an example of 'reverse integration', a phrase enunciated in the light of the recent Supreme Court decision prohibiting segregation in the public schools. There are two others at Fisk who offer comparable examples. They are white students in the undergraduate school. **1959** *Listener* 27 Aug. 334/3 Of various other signalling methods, mainly continental, the one most interesting to note is the 'reverse peter', credited to the Austrian expert K. Schneider. **1960** E. S. & W. J. Higham *High Speed Rugby* i. 18 *The reverse pass.* This is a pass which is used to reverse the direction of the passing movement. As the ball is passed out to a player, he passes it back in again. **1961** *Times* 16 Jan. 3/5 Dodds was only inches wide with a reverse-stick shot. **1962** Y. Malkiel in Householder & Saporta *Probl. Lexicogr.* 17 Students of suffixes have derived considerable benefit from rhyming dictionaries and from their close congeners, the 'reverse' (*rückläufig*) dictionaries. **1962** T. Masters *Surfing made Easy* 65 *Reverse pullout*, kicking out with the body turning in the opposite direction. **1969** *Guardian* 11 Oct. 8/6 The Hunt report on Northern Ireland..sets its face firmly against the allocation of reserved places for Roman Catholics within the police—'reverse discrimination' it calls it. **1971** M. Lehnert (*title*) Reverse dictionary of present-day English. **1973** *Computers & Humanities* Mar. 221 There is a reverse concordance..and a key-word-in-context.. index. **1976** *National Observer* (U.S.) 27 Nov. 3/1 If the Court rejects the concept of reverse discrimination, numerous educational and business programs across the country that give preferential treatment to minorities and women would be continued and probably expanded. **1978** *Sunday Times* (Colour Suppl.) 28 May 34/3 *Reverse pass*, when a player runs in one direction then passes in the other [in football].

b. *spec.* with reference to engines and vehicles; *reverse* (*idler*) *gear*, a gear wheel or mechanism which enables a vehicle or vessel to travel in reverse without reversing the rotation of its engine; also *fig.*; *reverse lever*, a lever by means of which the reverse gear of an engine may be brought into use; *reverse thrust*, thrust used to retard the forward motion of an aircraft, rocket, etc.; the condition of providing this; freq. *attrib.*

1882 *Engineering* 10 Mar. 219/3 An indicator R is..located upon the same pin as the reverse lever. **1900** G. D. Hiscox *Horseless Vehicles, Automobiles, Motor Cycles* xii. 242 Three speeds forward and a reverse slow speed. **1907** F. Strickland *Man. Petrol Motors & Motor Cars* xiii. 179 If the countershaft is driven faster than the engine, the reverse pinion would have to be driven very much faster. **1907** R. B. Whitman *Motor-Car Princ.* viii. 121 When the car is going forward, the square shaft and countershaft revolve in opposite directions; but when the reverse gear is introduced between them, the square shaft is revolved in the same direction as the counter-shaft, reversing the rotation of the driving wheels. **1907** W. F. M. Goss *Locomotive Performance* v. 105 An attempt is made to operate a locomotive with the reverse-lever in its extreme forward position at high speed. **1923** *Rep. Internat. Air Congr.* 594 (*caption*) The effect of reverse thrust on the gliding angle of the airplane. **1931** F. L. Allen *Only Yesterday* i. 7 He must remember to brake with the reverse pedal, or the low-speed pedal. **1933** *Discovery* July 221/1 The pilot has only to move the throttle and reverse lever, there being one position for forward and one for reverse. **1936** E. A. Phillipson *Steam Locomotive Design* x. 330 One of the most successful power reverse gears..is that operated by compressed air. **1947** *Shell Aviation News* No. 112. 22/1 The reduction of landing run by means of reverse-thrust braking will probably prove a very desirable feature for large aircraft. **1955** W. H. Crouse *Automotive Transmissions & Power Trains* i. 17 The reverse idler gear is always in mesh with the small gear on the end of the countershaft. **1959** *Listener* 26 Feb. 372/1 The October Moon probe carried eight small vernier rockets and one rather larger reverse-thrust rocket in addition to its main power plant. **1973** W. McCarthy *Detail* iii. 204 David..tried to accustom himself to the British car. He found the reverse gear and slowly backed out. **1976** B. Jackson *Flameout* (1977) i. 20 The catastrophe resulting from one of the engines being in reverse thrust at takeoff. **1979** *Guardian* 7 July 9/4 In the present era, everything has gone into reverse gear. New building is postponed, new hospitals..cannot open.

c. *reverse osmosis* (Physical Chem.), the process by which water or another medium tends to flow across a membrane in the direction opposite to that for natural osmosis when subjected to a hydrostatic pressure greater than the osmotic pressure.

1955 *Ann. Rep. Saline Water Comm. 1954* (U.S. Dept. Interior) i. 10 Development of membranes and procedures for demineralization of saline water by reverse-osmosis methods are provided for in several contracts. **1970** *New Scientist* 14 May 337/3 Laboratory experiments have shown that cheddar cheese whey can be concentrated five-fold by reverse osmosis, or separated into a high-protein product. **1977** *Hongkong Standard* 14 Apr. 9/6 Other processes, notably reverse osmosis (whereby pure water is forced through membranes under pressure, leaving salts behind) show great longterm promise, but at present are suitable only for small plants or for purifying brackish water rather than sea-water.

d. *reverse transcriptase*: see *transcriptase.

5*. *reverse charge*: used *attrib.* to designate a telephone call for which the charge has been reversed (see *reverse *v.* 9 d).

1932 *Telegr. & Teleph. Jrnl.* XVIII. 118/1 Possible new types of service, such as..'reverse charge' calls. **1978** L. Heren *Growing up on The Times* i. 23, I..dialled the overseas operator and placed the reverse-charge call.

6. *adv.* **b.** *Comb.* with *ppl. adjs.*, as *reverse-acting, -applied, -biased.*

1957 E. B. Jones *Instrument Technol.* III. 117 Increase of the output pressure from the controller will cause the valve to close and so reduce the flow through the valve. Such a valve is described as 'reverse acting'. **1962** Simpson & Richards *Physical Princ. Junction Transistors* iv. 54 This condition applies to an even greater extent for reverse-applied voltages when the current flowing through the device is very small. *Ibid.* v. 75 The high resistance of the reverse-biased collector junction. **1975** D. G Fink *Electronics Engineers' Handbk.* vii. 32 When a *pn* junction is reverse-biased, the free electrons in the *n*-type material are attracted toward the positive terminal of the power supply and away from the junction.

reverse, *v.*[1] Add: **I. 8. a.** Also *refl.*

1944 *Sun* (Baltimore) 5 Apr. 10/2 The court has reversed itself, to be sure, but the reversal does not surely involve any real change in American attitudes on deeply controversial questions. **1978** *Guardian Weekly* 7 May 15/5 President Carter..has reversed himself, and now backs legislation to buy 225,000 tons. **1979** *Publishing News* 29 June 6/4 It..was turned down by the Literary Guild and *Reader's Digest*... A short time later, both book clubs reversed themselves and *Hotel* went on to spend a year on the best seller lists.

9. c. To put (a motor vehicle) into reverse gear; to drive (a motor vehicle) backwards. Also *absol.*

1902 W. Robinson *Gas & Petroleum Engines* (ed. 2) xvii. 782 The vehicle is reversed by a hand lever which moves sliding sleeves bolted to the bevel wheels of the reversing gear. **1902** *Motor-Car World* III. 106/2 When it is required to reverse, the car can instantly be driven forward again, without it being necessary to replace the reversing gear into its usual position. **1913** G. B. Shaw *Let.* 17 Sept. in *B. Shaw & Mrs. Campbell* (1952) 148, I..had to drive right up it..reversing at impossible hairpin corners. **1932** F. J. Camm *Bk. Motors* xiv. 127 It is dangerous and discourteous.. to reverse unless you know that all is clear. **1939** J. Harrison *Motor-Cars To-day* ix. 111 When one wishes to reverse the car the bottom-speed wheel is moved towards the rear of the gearbox. **1941** L. D. Kitchin *Road Transport Law* 28/2 A vehicle must not be reversed for a greater distance or time than may be requisite for the safety or reasonable convenience of the occupants of that vehicle or of other traffic on the road. **1959** E. H. Clements *High Tension* viii. 134 His young step-cousin began to reverse her car. **1966** 'A. Hall' *9th Directive* xx. 187 He told the chauffeur to reverse the Lincoln. *a* **1976** A. Christie *Autobiogr.* (1977) vii. ii. 332, I don't think I can really reverse at all... The car never seems to go where I think it's going. **1977** D. MacKenzie *Raven & Kamikaze* iv. 49 Raven reversed and killed the motor.

d. Phr. *to reverse the charges*, to make the recipient of a telephone call responsible for paying for the call.

1927 *Sat. Even. Post* 30 Apr. 30/2 'Let's Call Up Sam and Tell Him What We think of Him.' 'Magnifique! And Don't Forget to Reverse ze Charges.' **1951** 'E. Crispin' *Long Divorce* xiv. 172 If you want to go on talking we must reverse the charges. **1972** 'W. Haggard' *Protectors* iii. 38 Phone me at once... Reverse the charges.

II. 10. b. (Earlier U.S. and later examples.)

1864 M. B. Chesnut *Diary* 6 July (1949) 418 A lame man can't reverse—as they call it in waltzing. **1912** V. B. Carter *Diary* 25 May in *Winston Churchill* (1965) xviii. 254 As he [*sc.* Ld. Fisher] never reverses I reel giddily in his arms and lurch against his heart of oak.

13. *Contract Bridge.* To rebid in a suit of higher rank than that which one has previously bid.

1939 N. de V. Hart *Bridge Players' Bedside Bk.* 132 An exception occurs when the partner forces the original bidder to reverse. In that case, the reverse may not indicate additional values. **1959** *Listener* 29 Jan. 229/1 He has already shown five hearts, inasmuch as he bid that suit and then reversed in spades.

reversed, *ppl. a.* Add: **b.** *reversed fault* = *reverse fault* s.v. *reverse *a.* and *adv.* d; *reversed-polarity Grammar*, used attributively of a complex interrogative construction in which positive and negative appear in each of two parts (e.g. *this is good, isn't it?*, and *this isn't any good, is it?*).

1876 Reversed fault [in Dict.]. **1882** A. H. Green *Geol.* xi. 492 The hade or slope is almost always towards the downthrow side: exceptions to this rule are called 'reversed faults'. **1929** M. H. Haddock *Disrupted Strata* iii. 36 In the common type of fault,..the striking angle θ will give a normal fault when obtuse and backthrust is present, or when acute and forethrust is present; the reversal of these remarks holds for reversed faults on the same fault plane. **1969** Bennison & Wright *Geol. Hist. Brit. Isles* x. 251 The Dent Line, a complex structure which has the effect of a reversed fault. **1957** D. L. Bolinger in *Publ. Amer. Dial. Soc.* xxviii. 113 The speaker courteously anticipates a possibly negative answer. This is perhaps related to the original sense of reversed-polarity conduciveness. **1975** *Language* LI. 26 What is the relation between constant polarity tags and reversed-polarity tags?.. The tags below both have reversed polarity:..a. Caterpillars have legs, don't they? b. Caterpillars don't have legs, do they?

reverser. Add: **1. b.** A control used to bring about reversal of the direction of motion of a vehicle; *esp.* a switch which changes the connections of electric traction motors to this end.

1905 Ashe & Keiley *Electric Railways* vi. 111 The function of the reverser..is to perform the proper connections of armature and field terminals, depending upon whether a forward or a backward motion of the car is desired. **1927** R. E. Dickinson *Electric Trains* iv. 62 The Reverser in multiple unit controls is usually in the form of a rocking arm carrying the contacts and making electrical connection with suitable fingers for reversing the direction of motion of a group of two motors. **1972** *Railway World* Oct. 449 Grif altered the regulator setting from time to time, but had no reverser with which to contend.

c. = *thrust reverser* s.v. *thrust *sb.* 7.

1967 D. P. Davies *Handling Big Jets* iv. 59 With a reverser efficiency of 50 % the net change will be from 1,000 lbs. forwards to 500 lb. reverse.

Reversi. **2.** (Later examples.)

1963 I. Gandy *Staying with Aunts* iii. 62 Another favourite game..was Reversi... Someone found the opportunity to change a whole row of counters to their own colour. **1976** *Time* 27 Dec. 2/3 The 'new' Japanese game Othello bears a remarkable resemblance to an English board game called Reversi.

reversible, *a.* and *sb.* For **b** read **B** and add:

A. *adj.* **1. a.** (Further examples.)

1899 *T. Eaton & Co. Catal.* Spring & Summer 116/1 Men's reversible coats, made of napa tan leather, lined with heavy drab corduroy. **1910** F. Yeigh *Through Heart of Canada* ii. 36 The famous reversible falls of the St. John River..are best viewed from the suspension bridge. **1921** A. W. Graban *Textbk. Geol.* I. xvii. 525 A reversible fall is produced, facing inward when the ocean is highest and outward when it is lowest. **1926** *Daily Colonist* (Victoria, B.C.) 9 Jan. 18/1 (Advt.), Reversible Rugs, shown in Oriental designs and colorings. They are made of hard-wearing jute and have the appearance of wool rugs. **1957** *Encycl. Brit.* XXIII. 459/1 Reversible fabrics may have..two series of differently coloured welts or warps to one of the other series, in which event they may be similarly figured on both sides by causing the threads of the double series to change places. **1974** *Times* 14 Apr. 7/2 The coats and capes ..are all reversible with soft knitted mohair on the outside and a sort of super deluxe dishcloth knitting inside.

b. Of a propeller: capable of providing reverse thrust, usu. by reversal of the pitch of the blades while the direction of rotation remains unchanged. So *reversible-pitch* attrib. phr.

1907 H. Chatley *Problem of Flight* vii. 86 Reversal of motion can be obtained by the use of change speed gearing, which is altered for the backward motion, so that its torque is reversed... Reversible wings to the helices can also be used for this purpose, but the rigidity would probably be impaired. **1922** *Flight* XIV. 657/2 An airscrew..has been produced by..one of the first airscrew making firms in America... It comprises a system of special blades, and a mechanism for varying the pitch of same..but the airscrew is reversible as well. **1923** *Rep. Internat. Air. Congr.* 588 This propeller is reversible as well as adjustable, and can be used as a brake in landing on rough terrain. **1930** F. E. Weick *Aircraft Propeller Design* xi. 188 The effectiveness of the reversible-pitch propeller as an air-brake..has been experimented with by both the Army and the Navy. **1935** J. W. Anderson *Diesel Engines* xv. 347 On reversible propellers the blades are twisted by suitable mechanism to give the proper angle for the desired direction of motion of the boat. **1951** P. Du Cane *High-Speed Small Craft* xi. 131 Variable (controllable) reversible-pitch propellers have so far been fitted in relatively few experimental craft built in Great Britain. **1965** C. N. Van Deventer *Introd. Gen. Aeronaut.* viii. 197/2 Towards the end of WW II the final refinement to propellers was perfected with the reversible pitch propeller. **1967** *Jane's Surface Skimmer Syst. 1967–68* 12/1 A 230 hp flat-six aero-engine drives a reversible-airscrew for propulsion.

2. *Physics* and *Chem.* **a.** *Thermodynamics.* Of a change or process: that is capable of reversal, completely and in detail; strictly, applicable to an ideal change in which the system is in equilibrium at all times. Also applied to a system undergoing such changes.

1856 *Phil. Mag.* XI. 216 The temperatures of two bodies are proportional to the quantities of heat respectively taken in and given out in localities at one temperature and at the other, respectively, by a material system subjected to a complete cycle of perfectly reversible thermo-dynamic operations, and not allowed to part with or take in heat at any other temperature. **1878** [in Dict., sense 1 a]. **1922** GLAZEBROOK *Dict. Appl. Physics* I. 929/1 The expansions and compressions and the transfers of heat that occur in a real engine are never strictly reversible, some of them indeed are far from being reversible. **1950** W. J. MOORE *Physical Chem.* i. 22 Reversible processes are never realizable in actuality since they must be carried out infinitely slowly. **1958** CONDON & ODISHAW *Handbk. Physics* v. 5/1 All reversible engines working between the same two heat reservoirs must have the same efficiency. **1963** A. E. J. HAYES *Appl. Thermodynamics* v. 53 When a fluid undergoes a reversible process it passes through a series of equilibrium states, i.e. states in which the fluid properties are uniform throughout. The term reversible does not merely imply ability to operate in the reverse direction, but also that the process must be able to retrace its path through the same sequence of equilibrium states. **1978** P. W. ATKINS *Physical Chem.* ii. 62 In thermodynamics a reversible change is one that can be reversed by an infinitesimal modification of a variable.

b. Applied to chemical reactions which in normal circumstances also take place in the opposite direction, and hence yield an equilibrium mixture of reactants and products.

1885 *Jrnl. Chem. Soc.* XLVIII. I. 117 Reversible chemical changes are thus brought into the class of reciprocal phenomena. **1899** J. MCCRAE tr. *A. Reychler's Outl. Physical Chem.* 241 The reversible reaction $BaSO_4 + K_2CO_3 \leftrightarrows K_2SO_4 + BaCO_3$. **1912** J. W. MELLOR *Mod. Inorg. Chem.* vi. 99 Opposing reactions are also called incomplete or reversible reactions in contradistinction to irreversible or complete reactions typified by the action of zinc on sulphuric acid, where the reaction is completed in one direction and is not opposed by a counter reaction. **1950** N. V. SIDGWICK *Chem. Elements* II. 1213 These acids..are formed by the action of water on the elementary halogen, which leads..to a reversible hydrolysis of the type $X_2 + H_2O \rightleftharpoons HX + HOX$. **1972** R. A. JACKSON *Mechanism* iv. 85 When aliphatic fluorides are dissolved in antimony pentafluoride, a reversible reaction leads to the formation of carbonium ions.

c. Applied to an electrochemical cell in which the chemical reaction can be reversed by the application of a sufficiently large opposing e.m.f.; hence to quantities measured under, or pertaining to, conditions in which the e.m.f. of the cell is balanced by an applied e.m.f. and no current is flowing.

1895 C. S. PALMER tr. *Nernst's Theoret. Chem.* IV. vi. 599 Strictly speaking, all reversible batteries can be used as accumulators. **1936** R. W. GURNEY *Ions in Solution* viii. 90 Under these circumstances it is found that the processes in each half-cell..are now simply taking place in the reverse direction. Such a cell is called a reversible cell—meaning reversible both in its mechanism and in the thermodynamic sense. **1957** G. E. HUTCHINSON *Treat. Limnol.* I. xi. 693 It is usual to term the actual potential measured the irreversible oxygen potential, while the theoretical value calculated may be termed the reversible oxygen potential. **1977** N. J. SELLEY *Exper. Approach to Electrochem.* iv. 63 The value of the applied p.d. for which the current is zero is the 'reversible cell potential'..for the back reaction. **1978** P. W. ATKINS *Physical Chem.* xii. 346 A cell that is not truly reversible will respond to a small imbalance by supplying appreciable currents in one direction or the other, and it may be very difficult to detect its true balance point.

d. *Physical Chem.* Of a colloid or colloidal system: capable of being changed from a gelatinous state into a sol by a reversal of the treatment which turns the sol into a gel or gelatinous precipitate. Of a change of state: characterized by this property.

1899 *Jrnl. Physiol.* XXIV. 175 (*heading*) Heat-reversible colloidal mixtures. **1915** [see *IRREVERSIBLE *a.* 3]. **1930** *Engineering* 4 July 6/2 The power of absorption [of clay] being due to its containing a large proportion of matter in a state of fine division, forming a 'non-rigid reversible gel'.. composed of colloidal matter. **1955** J. OSBORNE *Dental Mech.* (ed. 4) i. 18 The cooling process is relatively slow, since all reversible hydrocolloids are bad conductors of heat. **1970** *Encycl. Polymer Sci. & Technol.* IV. 27 To redissolve reversible colloids, none of those drastic measures are required which are so characteristic of irreversible colloids.

B. *sb.* Also, a garment faced on both sides, so that it may be worn with either outside.

1863 *Cornh. Mag.* Jan. 89 The housebreakers' wives and children, maybe, take their turn during the day: at night, the men themselves watch. On such occasions they often wear 'reversibles', or coats which may be worn inside out; one side being of a bright, the other of a dark colour. **1905** *Eng. Dial. Dict.* V. 93/1 *Reversible*, a double cloth with a face, *gen.* made of better quality than the back. w. Yks. **1964** *McCall's Sewing* ii. 31/2 *Reversible*, fabric that has been finished so that either side may be used or a garment finished so that it may be turned and worn on either side.

reve·rsibly, *adv.* [f. REVERSIBL(E *a.* + -LY[2].] In a reversible manner.

1889 in *Cent. Dict.* **1944** [see *ACTIN].

reversing, *vbl. sb.* Add: **b.** *spec.* The action of driving a motor vehicle backwards.

1900 W. W. BEAUMONT *Motor Vehicles & Motors* xiv. 246 The gearing..is for three speeds and reversing. *Ibid.* xxxi. 539 No reversing gear is provided, the reversing being effected by spur gearing. **1929** J. B. PRIESTLEY *Good Companions* I. ii. 67 Miss Trant discovered once again the terrors and dangers of reversing. **1959** *Motor Manual* (ed. 36) vi. 182 Reversing at night can be somewhat difficult.

2. Special Combs.: **reversing lamp, reversing light**, a light at the rear of a motor vehicle for illumination and to warn that the vehicle is reversing.

1960 R. IRESON *Penguin Car Handbk.* 125 Reversing lamps giving a white light to the rear are standard fittings on some higher priced cars. **1954** *Motor Manual* (ed. 35) xii. 250 A separate switch is provided to control the reversing light, and in some cases this is of normal type under the driver's direct control, but in others it is operated by the movement of the gear lever into the reverse position. **1968** *Radio Times* 28 Nov. 43/1 Not all cars have reversing lights fitted as standard. **1976** [see *REVERSE *sb.* 12 a].

reversing, *ppl. a.* Add: **1. a.** (Earlier example.) *reversing propeller*, a reversible propeller (see *REVERSIBLE *a.* 1 b).

1804 M. LEWIS in *Orig. Jrnls. Lewis & Clark Expedition* (1904) VI. 230 The reversing telescope when employed as the eye-piece gave me a more full..image. *a* **1817** JANE AUSTEN *Northanger Abbey* (1818) II. xv. 320 No unworthy retraction.., no reversing decree of unjustifiable anger, could shake his fidelity. **1907** F. STRICKLAND *Man. Petrol Motors & Motor Cars* x. 151 In the small sizes [of marine motor] this is done by having either a reversing propeller or a reversing gear worked with clutches, the engine being always kept running. **1935** J. W. ANDERSON *Diesel Engines* xv. 347 Small marine engines of 100 or 150 hp. are universally non-reversible. They usually run on the governor and reversing is obtained through reversing propellers in the very small sizes or reverse gears. **1973** D. WRIGHT *Marine Engines & Boating Mech.* xiii. 184 A variable pitch and reversing propeller which will transmit and absorb ¾ hp per 100 rev/min giving..7½ hp at 1,000 rev/min.

b. *reversing layer* or *stratum*. Substitute for def.: A region of the solar atmosphere above the photosphere, formerly thought to be responsible for bringing about reversal of emission lines in the solar spectrum to absorption lines. Now *rare*. (Later examples.)

1926 H. N. RUSSELL et al. *Astron.* I. vii. 196 The reversing layer, extending to a height of a few hundred miles above the photosphere and composed of the vapors of many of the familiar terrestrial elements. This merges gradually into the chromosphere. **1955** *Sci. Amer.* Sept. 194/2 The sun is entirely gaseous... From the outside in, the outer layers are the corona, the chromosphere, the reversing layer and the photosphere. **1974** *Encycl. Brit. Micropædia* II. 908/3 The lower chromosphere was formerly called the reversing layer because it was thought responsible for producing the dark lines of the solar spectrum that appear reversed against the bright continuous spectrum; actually the weak dark lines and bright continuum can be produced in essentially the same regions... The term reversing layer is now seldom used.

3. Special collocations: *reversing falls*, a waterfall or rapid in a narrow sea inlet in which the water flows in opposite directions when the tide is coming in and going out, because of the constricting effect of the narrow inlet; *reversing gear, lever* = *reverse gear, lever* s.v. *REVERSE *a.* and *adv.* 5 b; *reversing mill*, a rolling mill used in sheet metal production in which the metal is passed backwards and forwards between the same pair of rolls, which can have their direction of rotation reversed; *reversing thermometer*, a mercury-in-glass thermometer, normally used to obtain the temperature at depth in the ocean, which can be inverted at a depth and then retains its reading until its orientation is restored.

1910 W. O. RAYMOND *River Saint John* i. 3 Among the topographical features worthy of note are the remarkable 'reversing falls' at its mouth. **1961** E. WAHL *This Land* iv. 271 As the tide continues to rise the water begins to flow upstream and soon it is tumbling over the rock ledges in the opposite direction. This oddity of nature, called the Reversing Falls, has been a great tourist attraction for many years. **1974** *Encycl. Brit. Macropædia* VII. 780/2 The tide range is magnified by the narrowness and shape of the bay, a rise of 46 feet (14 metres) being common in Chigneto Bay and 53 feet (16 metres) in Minas Basin... The rising tide produces a 'reversing falls' at the mouth of the Saint John River. **1867** *Engineering* 29 Mar. 300 (*heading*) Screw reversing gear for locomotive engines. **1904** T. H. WHITE *Petrol Motors & Motor Cars* II. 108 When applied to an automobile, it is usual to make the reversing gear of a similar design to the slow-speed forward gear. **1972** S. H. HENSHALL *Medium & High Speed Diesel Engines for Marine Use* xv. 269 A single uni-directional engine with oil operated reversing gear could easily be combined on one lever on the bridge. **1887** *Engineering* 7 Oct. 393/1 A locomotive having an ordinary reversing lever to operate the links. **1925** *Marine Oil-Engine Handbk.* (ed. 6) ix. 76 The shaft (B) and with it the clutch (D) can be moved endways by the reversing lever through the usual double flange and collar. **1888** *Lockwood's Dict. Mech. Engin.* 285 Reversing mill. **1909** *Jrnl. Iron & Steel Inst.* LXXX. 15 The capital cost of an electrically driven reversing-mill is greater than that of a steam-driven mill. **1932** *Iron & Coal Trades Rev.* CXXV. 730/1 Our representative had an opportunity of inspecting an 18,000-h.p. (peak) reversing-mill motor... The motor is intended to drive a 3-stand reversing mill. **1967** A. H. COTTRELL *Introd. Metall.* xxii. 439 The first rough rolling of such an ingot is done in a cogging mill between large cast iron rolls. This is usually a two-high reversing mill. **1912** MURRAY & HJORT *Depths of Ocean* v. 217 In 1878 Negretti and Zambra of London constructed a reversing thermometer, which has played a prominent part in physical oceanography. **1928** RUSSELL & YONGE *Seas* xii. 260 A 'reversing thermometer' is used, that is one in which there is an S-shaped bend, so that if it be suddenly turned upside down the thread of mercury is broken and a permanent record of the temperature is obtained. The thermometer on reaching the required depth is reversed by means of a weight which slides down the wire and releases a spring catch. **1963** G. L. PICKARD *Descriptive Physical Oceanogr.* vi. 89 After corrections..the reversing thermometer yields the temperature to an accuracy of about +0·02 C°.

reversion[1]. Add: **III. 8.** *attrib.*, as *reversion clause, duty*.

1933 P. GODFREY *Back-Stage* vi. 74 He should have a reversion clause in his contract, so that if in any year his play is not performed a certain number of times the rights will revert to him. **1909** *Westm. Gaz.* 28 May 8/1 Clause 7 deals with reversion duty. **1959** JOWITT *Dict. Eng. Law* II. 1554/1 *Reversion duty*, a duty formerly payable under the Finance (1909–10) Act, 1910, in certain cases on the determination of leases more than twenty-one years.

reversion[2]. For *rare*—[1] read *rare* and add: **b.** A drawing based upon an earlier sketch.

1848 D. G. ROSSETTI *Let.* Sept. (1965) I. 44 His last design is a re-version from Retzsch's outline of the same subject.

reversionary, *a.* (and *sb.*). Add: **2.** *spec.* in *reversionary bonus*, an increase in the amount of an insurance policy payable at the maturation of the policy or the death of the person insured.

1898 [see HM s.v. *H III.]. **1930** *Economist* 29 Mar. 702/2 The reversionary bonus for 'with profits' policies has been maintained at the rate to which it was raised. **1969** *Times* 30 Apr. 26 In the United Kingdom the rate of reversionary bonus for Ordinary branch assurances has been increased by 2s. per cent.

reversis. Add: **a.** (Earlier and later examples.)

1796 (*title*) Rules of Reversis, as played in the Fashionable Circles. By a Gentleman. **1977** *Jrnl. Playing-Card Soc.* May 23 Reversis is historically important as the earliest known negative complex trick-taking game.

b. (Later example.)

1977 *Jrnl. Playing-Card Soc.* May 28 To make reversis a player must win all eleven tricks.

revert, *sb.* Add: **2.** (Later and *transf.* examples.)

1927 LD. BRAYE *Fewness of my Days* 159 A palace of antiquities, not only for the archæologist but also..for a Revert to the ancient faith. **1960** *Times Lit. Suppl.* 24 June 401/1 Professor Empson is anti-modern. Not a mere revert, of course,..he makes respectful acknowledgment to the views of Blake and Shelley.

revert, *v.* Add: **II. 8. c.** To cause to return *to* a former condition or practice.

1973 *Nature* 2 Mar. 16/1 It is possible to produce a crystalline area (memory state), to measure the change in optical transmission (read out), and to revert the same area to the amorphous state (erase). **1975** *Daily Tel.* 1 Aug. 2/5 Left-wingers in the Amalgamated Union of Engineering Workers tried to revert the union to its previous system of electing officials at branch meetings. **1977** *Evening Post* (Nottingham) 24 Jan. 2/7 The suggestion to revert a central site to agricultural use seems both practical and sensible.

revertant, *a.* Restrict *Her. rare*—[0] to sense in Dict. and add: **2.** *Biol.* Having reverted to the normal phenotype though of mutant or abnormal ancestry.

1955 *Genetics* XL. 893 Both revertant (adenine-independent, non-purple) and non-revertant (adenineless, purple) components could be separated by conidial platings. **1970** *Nature* 5 Dec. 908/1 Revertant cells selected from this line exhibit many of the properties of untransformed cells.. although they retain the SV40 genome. **1981** *New Scientist* 18 June 744/2 *E. coli* is so 'weak' that it can easily mutate back to its ordinary cousin... These 'revertant mutants' quickly take over.

B. *sb.* *Biol.* A revertant cell, organism, or strain.

1955 *Genetics* XL. 893 Tests of a number of these purple revertants revealed..that they were heterocaryons. **1971** *Nature* 25 June 488/1 By applying selection pressures to cultures of transformed malignant cells it is possible to select so-called revertants—cells which behave in culture as if they were normal. **1974** *Ibid.* 11 Oct. 483/1 Clones obtained on NFM-histidine were either prototrophic or revertants which grew on histidine as sole nitrogen source.

revertose (rĭvɔ̄·ɹtōᵘz). *Chem.* [f. REVERT *v.* + -OSE[2].] A substance obtained by the action of maltase on glucose, now regarded as a mixture of sugars.

1903 A. C. HILL in *Jrnl. Chem. Soc.* LXXXIII. 580 The larger portion..has optical and reducing properties between those of maltose and of glucose. It consists mainly of a biose..which I have called revertose. **1938, 1965** [see *GALLISIN].

revet (rīve·t), *v.*[2] [RE- 5 a.] *trans.* To 'vet' again; to recheck, to re-examine. Hence **reve·tting** *vbl. sb.*

1963 *Times* 26 Apr. 18/4 He asked whether Vassall had been vetted as necessary for his special post, and was told that he would be revetted before he went. This 'revetting' consisted simply of a check of his name against security service records to ascertain whether they contained any information about him indicating that he held subversive beliefs. **1973** *Times Lit. Suppl.* 26 Jan. 96/4 Pictorial evidence..and..sculptural evidence..revetted by a wide choice of floor mosaics. **1979** P. HARCOURT *Sleep of Spies* I. ii. 34 Everyone's being re-vetted, of course... They're doing some re-vetting there too.

review, *sb.* Add: **I. 3.** (Earlier *attrib.* examples.)

1740 *Life & Adv. Mrs. Christian Davies* 500 He allowed me exclusive of all others to sell beer in the Deer Park on a review day. **1781** R. F. GREVILLE *Diary* 4 Aug. (1930) 9 We came on Ashford Common where the Blues were drawn up in Review Order.

5. d. Also *attrib.*

1965 *New Statesman* 19 Mar. 430/1 Only on one point does he reject the BMA case—he insists that the Review Body must work out the new pay-levels. **1968** *Panorama* (Austral.) May 2/4 They sat in 'review board' to use an advertising agency term. They were briefed on the new type of meal which the management had in mind. **1971** D. BAGLEY *Freedom Trap* ii. 53 'You have been classified as a high risk... If you weren't so stupid you could get yourself out of this jam.' 'Out of this nick?' 'I'm afraid not... But the Review Board would look upon you very kindly if you co-operated with us.' **1977** *Belfast Tel.* 22 Feb. 12/1 The Industrial Relations (Northern Ireland) Order 1976 became law. It implements recommendations of the Review Body on Industrial Relations which reported in 1974.

7. a. Also, of music, drama, etc.

1929 [see *GAG *sb.*[1] 3 c]. **1967** J. PHILIP et al. *Best of Granta* I. 18 Jazz features regularly in the record reviews.

c. (Later examples.) *review article*, an article that is a review; *review copy*, a copy of a new book sent for review to a periodical, writer, etc.

1836 J. S. MILL in *London & Westm. Rev.* Apr. 17 The attention cannot sustain itself on any serious subject, even for the space of a review-article. **1855** BAGEHOT *Coll. Wks.* (1965) I. 310 In truth review-writing but exemplifies the casual character of modern literature. *Ibid.* 312 The review-like essay and the essay-like review fill a large space. **1858** CARLYLE *Fredk. Gt.* I. I. i. 16 The British Writer..images to himself a royal Dick Turpin, of the kind known in Review-Articles. **1903** G. B. SHAW *Let.* 15 July (1972) II. 338 To whom do you propose to send review copies? **1906** A. BENNETT *Let.* 27 Feb. (1966) 69, I sent him a list of review-quotes but I have seen no result. **1907** F. M. FORD *Let.* ? Sept. (1965) 26, I had proposed to run to a column a week at, say, your ordinary review rates. **1933** LEAVIS & THOMPSON *Culture & Environment* 44 Examine the review pages of a Sunday newspaper. **1937** H. NICOLSON *Diary* 11 July (1966) 307 Read my review books and spend a peaceful afternoon. **1965** *New Statesman* 19 Mar. 455/1 Judgments of this kind are proper to the review-article of modern length. **1966** C. MACKENZIE *My Life & Times* V. 243, I asked..if we might count on review records coming regularly from H.M.V. **1976** *Guardian* 17 Apr. 11/6 Scarcely a day goes by without review copies reaching this office of books..on growing potato crops on the windowsills of Chelsea. **1978** *Amer. N. & Q.* XVI. 162/2 The front endsheets..are upside down in one review copy. **1979** *London Rev. Bks.* 25 Oct. 2/2 Any squeeze on review space squeezes fiction first.

review, *v.* Add: **7.** Also, to write criticism of (music, drama, etc.).

1873 LYTTON *Kenelm Chillingly* II. IV. iv. 232 By the way, when we come by-and-by to review the exhibition at Burlington House, there is one painter whom we must try our best to crush. **1976** *Gramophone* Feb. 1404/3 The Denon PMA-500 amplifier has been a real pleasure to review.

reviewability (rĭviū·ăbi·lĭti). [f. REVIEWABLE *a.* + -ITY.] The quality or state of being judicially reviewable.

1975 *Columbia Law Rev.* LXXV. 132 Ultimate determinations as to the reviewability of particular decisions may take into account the nature of the agency's functions and the impact of review on its effectiveness and other legislative policies.

reviewable, *a.* Add: *spec.*, subject to judicial review.

1883 *Nation* (N.Y.) 20 Dec. 501/2 The proceedings in any criminal trial are reviewable by the full bench, whenever the judge who presides at the trial certifies that any point raised at it is doubtful. **1964** *Mod. Law Rev.* XXVII. 331 Nor can a decision reviewable on habeas corpus be considered a nullity which could be disregarded when attacked collaterally. **1974** *Sci. Amer.* June 22/1 We held that adequacy of treatment is reviewable in court.

reviewery (rĭviū·əri). *rare.* [f. REVIEW *sb.* + -ERY.] The genre of the review; reviews considered collectively.

? **1876** R. L. STEVENSON *Lett.* (1911) I. 215, I was not a hundred miles from being miserably drowned, to the.. permanent impoverishment of British Essayism and Reviewery.

reviewing, *vbl. sb.* **1.** (Later *attrib.* examples.)

1951 M. MCLUHAN *Mech. Bride* (1967) 10/2 The editors stand at mock attention on the reviewing platform, thumb on nose. **1964** *Mod. Law Rev.* XXVII. 331 Inferior courts and tribunals are at the mercy of the court's reviewing power. **1977** *Time* 4 Apr. 53/1 At his Inaugural parade, Jimmy Carter's reviewing stand was warmed by a specially constructed solar heating unit.

‖**revirement** (rəvirmaṅ). [Fr., f. *revirer*: see REVIRE *v.*[2]] An alteration of one's plans; a complete change of attitude or opinion.

1913 W. S. CHURCHILL *Let.* 18 Dec. in *World Crisis 1911–14* (1923) viii. 173 If on a general *revirement* of Naval Policy the Cabinet decide to reduce the quota, it would be indispensable that a new exponent should be chosen. **1975** *Government & Opposition* X. 276 Contradictions are caused not so much by economic fluctuations—but rather by political *revirements*.

revise, *sb.* Add: **2. b.** (Earlier and later examples.)

1844 DICKENS *Let.* 29 June (1977) IV. 153 Mr. Dickens will be glad if Mr. Newby will send a complete revise of the whole book..to Mr. Overs for his attentive perusal. **1875** A. THACKERAY *Let.* in H. Ritchie *Lett. A. T. Ritchie* (1924) viii. 163 Mr. Payn writes sternly for the revise for my story and I must not write any more now. **1970** W. GARNER *Puppet-Masters* xxxvi. 259 Here's the revise. We had it retyped with the new ending.

3. (Later *attrib.* example.)

1972 H. EVANS *Newsman's English* i. 8 The copy is normally passed to a third executive, the 'revise editor'. On American dailies he is a 'slot man'.

revise, *v.* Add: **3. b.** (Later example.)

1939 N. MARSH *Overture to Death* v. 57 Then he gave himself four minutes to revise the conversation he had planned to have with Dinah.

c. To go over (a subject already learnt) in preparation for an examination. Also *absol.*

1946 'B. TRUSCOT' *First Year at University* v. 66 Assuming the examination to be in May or June,..[the Easter] vacation should..be devoted to revision, and the work to be revised must be systematically divided up among the time available. **1977** C. DEXTER *Silent World N. Quinn* xii. 109 You revise, I suppose?..I mustn't keep you from your revising.

revising, *vbl. sb.* (Later example.)

1969 C. FREMLIN *Possession* xvii. 137 Janice said what about her revising?.. How could she ever get through her Mocks next term? **1977** [see *REVISE *v.* 3 c].

revising, *ppl. a.* (Earlier example.)

1757 RICHARDSON *Let.* 19 Nov. (1964) 337 Your Ladiship's Correspondence & mine, will be ye safer, because of its length, & for its being only in our own Hands; & if it has yr. Ladiship's revising Eye, will be of ye less consequence.

revision. Add: **1.** Also *spec.*, the action of going over a subject that has already been learnt, esp. in preparation for an examination.

1916 A. HUXLEY *Let.* 1 May (1969) 98, I am busy with revision, doing papers for my tutor under examination conditions. **1937** CORBETT & EICHELE (*title*) Classified revision exercises in German. **1979** *Observer* 29 July 21/1, I thought the end of school term might be a good occasion for a little revision.

revisionism (rĭvi·ʒəniz'm). *Politics.* [f. REVISION + -ISM.] **1.** A policy first put forward in the 1890s by Edward Bernstein (1850–1932) advocating the introduction of socialism through evolution rather than revolution, in opposition to the orthodox view of Marxists; hence a term of abuse used within the communist world for an interpretation of Marxism which is felt to threaten the canonical policy.

1903 *Social-Democrat* VII. 84 (*heading*) Revisionism in Germany. **1909** E. C. HARVEY tr. *Bernstein's Evolutionary Socialism* p. xxii, Subsequently the views put forward in the book have received the bye-name of Revisionism. **1934** P. & I. PETROFF *Secret of Hitler's Victory* iii. 40 In the social democratic ranks extreme revisionism predominated. **1947** *Partisan Rev.* XIV. 396 Is it permissible, is it orthodoxy or revisionism, for a Marxist to take any significant ideas from the prevailing fashion of the 'neo-Kantian' revival? **1958** *Times* 4 Aug. 7/2 It is not only over Yugoslav 'revisionism' that China has lately taken a distinctive and uncompromising attitude. **1959** M. S. LEVIN tr. *Lenin's Against Revisionism* 122 The ideological struggle waged by revolutionary Marxism against revisionism at the end of the nineteenth century is but the prelude to the great revolutionary battles of the proletariat. **1962** *Listener* 8 Mar. 404/2 Russian Khrushchevian revisionism. **1965** *New Statesman* 18 June 945/2 China was going to fight Soviet revisionism to the bitter end. **1969** A. G. FRANK *Latin Amer.* (1970) xiv. 221 There exists no dual society in the world today and all attempts to find one are attempts to justify and/or cover up imperialism and revisionism. **1975** J. DE BRES tr. *Mandel's Late Capitalism* xvi. 517 Cheprakov's revisionism is here unequivocally spelt out.

2. A term used for a revised attitude to some previously accepted political situation, doctrine, or point of view; *concr.*, the name of the policy adopted by a right-wing Zionist group, active during the formative period of the State of Israel; mostly *U.S.*, a movement to revise the accepted versions of American history, esp. those relating to foreign affairs since the war of 1939–45.

1921 *Glasgow Herald* 4 Apr. 10 The British Foreign Office has got over its momentary lapse into revisionism. **1932** *Palestine Post* 25 Dec. 6/2 The leader of the Revisionism, Jabotinsky. **1939** G. F. HUDSON *Turkey, Greece & E. Mediterranean* (1940) 28 Turkey, Greece, Rumania, and Jugoslavia therefore left out Bulgaria, and concluded between themselves a pact of mutual guarantee, the foundation of the so-called Balkan Entente (9 Feb. 1934). This was in effect an alliance against Bulgarian revisionism, just as the Little Entente was an alliance against Hungarian revisionism. **1940** *Economist* 6 Apr. 606/2 The Near Eastern States offer a happy hunting-ground to the roving ambition of predatory Great Powers. Once again, it is a question of revisionism *versus* the *status quo*. **1949** KOESTLER *Promise & Fulfilment* III. 302 The conflict between Revisionism and official Zionism was mainly one of character and temperament. **1953** J. A. LUKACS *Great Powers & E. Europe* p. viii, The somewhat vague concept of historical revisionism is applicable only when there is an abundance of well-documented historical writing which, because of its unilateral emphasis or perspective, needs to be counterbalanced. *Ibid.* III. 282 Ribbentrop..termed the Russian attitude [over Finland] as 'reasonable', stemming from an aim of 'modest revisionism'. **1959** *Encounter* Sept. 64/2 A humanistic revisionism can be secured only by revising the claims of science itself. **1960** S. G. EVANS *Short Hist. Bulgaria* v. 175 The extent of German economic penetration and the degree of national chauvinism in the ruling class, leading to a clamant revisionism, plus the fact that Hitler appeared to be winning, made it certain that they would turn the way they did. **1965** *New Statesman* 1 Oct. 486/2 One linguistic difference between American and British historians lies in the frequency with which they use the word 'revisionism'. It is common currency in Transatlantic seminars and journals, but hardly ever heard in this country. *Ibid.*, 'Revisionism' goes on all the time because of disagreement about the moral and political significance of what happened. **1973** in R. Staar *Yearbk. on Internat. Communist Affairs* 80 The fact that the work was not condemned or suppressed, but indeed approved..by Georgian authorities, until Moscow intervened, indicated that historiographical 'revisionism' was rife in the republic. **1977** *Time* 15 Aug. 26/1 Revisionism is starting on Johnson as it has started on other Presidents.

revisionist, *sb.* and *a.* Add: **A.** *sb.* **1.** (Later examples in senses of *REVISIONISM.)

1909 [see *OPPORTUNIST 1 a]. **1915** L. B. BOUDIN *Theoret. Syst. K. Marx* i. 11 What they [*sc.* critics] claim is that they [*sc.* Marx's theories] were based on insufficient data, and that our present knowledge requires the revision of some of his tenets or the supplementing of them by some qualifying truths... Hence, the name *Revisionists*, under which most of the newer Marx-critics are known, and the term *Revisionism* applied to their writings and teachings. **1927** H. E. FOSDICK *Pilgrimage to Palestine* (1928) xii. 288 Some [Zionists] are revisionists, trying to force Britain's hand and compel aggressive action towards making Jews the dominant political power. **1930** *Time & Tide* 6 Sept. 1125/2 Professor Barnes is what is known as a 'revisionist', in other words, an exponent of historical views on this subject, almost completely reversing those dominant in England and America eleven years ago. **1949** R. K. MERTON *Social Theory* 115 The fallacious premise..found also in the writings of such Freudian revisionists as Fromm, that the structure of society primarily restrains the free expression of man's fixed native impulses. **1957** *Observer* 27 Oct. 6/2 The purge will be used to root out..the 'revisionists' who evince a negative attitude towards the Soviet Union. **1962** *Daily Tel.* 17 Nov. 16/3 The article is an important move in the Moscow–Peking dispute. It accused the 'revisionists' of retreating from the decisions taken jointly in Moscow. **1966** C. POTOK *Chosen* (1967) xiii. 226 Every shade of Zionist thought was represented..from the Revisionists, who supported the Irgun, to the Neturai Karta, the Guardians of the City..Jerusalem. **1973** P. HOLLANDER *Soviet & Amer. Society* i. 13 The revisionists simply cannot believe that if American foreign policy was wrong (criminal, bankrupt, or irresponsible) in regard to Vietnam, it could have been otherwise in different historical situations, especially if Communism was at issue. **1976** *Times* 9 June 16/2 It is not easy to strengthen contacts with Yugoslavian communists while keeping Spanish and French 'revisionists' at arm's length.

B. *adj.* That advocates or supports revision; pertaining to revisionism or revisionists.

1866, 1888 [in Dict., sense 1 *attrib.*] **1903** *Social-Democrat* VII. 97 Thus, the so-called democratising of industry through the company makes for the Social Revolution, and renders Revisionist Socialism impossible. **1925** *Zionist Rev.* IX. 48/1 The Radical and the Revisionist Opposition. **1934** *Sun* (Baltimore) 16 Oct. 10/3 The 'revisionist' historian of the war has transferred the responsibility for that great tragedy from the shoulders of the German military autocracy to those of M. Poincaré. **1949** KOESTLER *Promise of Fulfilment* II. 259 A Revisionist doctor makes his living on Revisionist patients, goes to Revisionist cafés and frequents only Revisionist circles. **1961** *Listener* 30 Nov. 905/2 Much fruitful thinking is now going on within the framework of revisionist Marxism about the kind of relation which exists between basis and superstructure. **1969** *Amer. N. & Q.* Oct. 31/2 It is 'revisionist' history in the finest sense, a wholly new interpretation of the sources. **1971** *Human World* Nov. 18 In Chinese polemics of the same period, it was discernible that the primary object of Peking's venom was the 'revisionist social imperialism' of the 'new Tsars'. **1974** *Times* 18 Feb. 7/2 Their local Communist Party committees should carry out reforms aimed at preventing the growth of 'revisionist' tendencies. **1977** *Time* 30 May 4/3 The recent cluster of 'revisionist' books on Nazism, which would soften the frightening teachings of this maniacal movement.

revisit, *v.* Add: **2.** Also *fig.* (cf. sense 1). Always in pa. pple.

1971 *Language* XLVII. 503 (*heading*) The phoneme revisited. **1975** I. ROBINSON *New Grammarians' Funeral* ix. 169 (*heading*) 'The science of language' revisited. **1976** *Lingua* XL. 321 (*heading*) The *-ing* form revisited. **1977** *Language* LIII. 277 (*heading*) Conversational postulates revisited.

revitalization. Add: Also *attrib.*, as *revitalization movement.*

1956 A. F. C. WALLACE in *Amer. Anthropol.* LVIII. 265 A revitalization movement is defined as a deliberate, organized, conscious effort by members of a society to construct a more satisfying culture. **1970** R. D. ABRAHAMS *Positively Black* vi. 151 Perhaps the most important feature of resemblance between revitalization movements and the present separatist position is that both turn on the idea of social and cultural polarization within a pluralistic situation.

revival. Add: **1. b.** Also, the act of resuming a series of broadcast programmes.

1955 *Times* 13 May 16/1 The B.B.C. had left the door open... The minimum gap before such a revival would be six months. **1976** in *Amer. Speech* (1978) LIII. 58 We retain the right to edit our material which includes excessive emotionalism or statements which could be detrimental to S[tar] T[rek] fandom or revival.

3. b. (Earlier and later *attrib.* examples.)

1831 J. J. STRANG *Jrnl.* 31 July in M. M. Quaife *Kingdom of St. James* (1930) 195 The revival meeting lasted a fortnight or more. **1891** *Atlantic Monthly* June 813/2 The old slaves are loath to give up the hysteric emotionalism of revival preaching. **1956** R. MACAULAY *Towers of Trebizond* (1957) ix. 88 Then there had been the Billy Graham mission, which had passed through the other day, hired a room in the municipal buildings, and held a revival service through an interpreter. **1969** C. BURKE *God is Beautiful, Man* (1970) 98 One day there was a guy named Peter in a revival tent on an empty lot. **1976** *Times* 13 Feb. 7/5 In 1876 he [*sc.* William Booth] set up as music publisher with Revival Music, a collection of hymns and gospel songs used by the Christian Mission, as his army was known until 1878.

revivalist. Add: **3.** *attrib.* or as *adj.*

1875 [in Dict., sense 2]. **1956** M. STEARNS *Story of Jazz* (1957) iii. 30 The ceremonies became famous for their revivalist power and frenzy. **1965** G. MELLY *Owning Up* xi. 128 Revivalist jazz was based on the Negro jazz of the 'twenties.

revive, *v.* Add: **II. 9. c.** Also *intr.* for *pass.* Also in modern use, to resume (a series of broadcast programmes).

1912 G. B. SHAW *Let.* 13 Feb. in *Lett. to Granville Barker* (1956) 179 The play [sc. *Hamlet*] revives sensationally every 15 years or so. **1955** *Times* 13 May 16/1 The B.B.C. had left the door open when its run ended. It would be too soon for Hughie Green to 'raise his eyebrows' in September, 1949, because he had not been told that it would be revived. **1977** *Times Lit. Suppl.* 25 Feb. 200/2 The plays..do not in my view revive successfully today.

revivication. Add: Now *rare.* (Further example.)

1929 V. WOOLF *Let.* 11 May (1978) IV. 56 Last night we had a terrific revivication; the resurrection day was nothing to it.

revoker. Delete *rare* and add further examples.

1904 *Bridge & Progressive Bridge* 13 The penalty for a revoke is the addition of three tricks to the score of the opposing side, or the deduction of three tricks from the Revoker's score at the option of the opposing side. **1922** E. F. BENSON *Miss Mapp* xi. 261 This way of taking a revoke was new to Tilling, for the right thing was for the revoker's partner to sulk and be sarcastic for at least twenty minutes.

‖ **revolera** (revolē·ră). *Bullfighting.* [Sp.] A movement in which the cape is fluttered above the matador's head (see also quot. 1957).

1957 A. MACNAB *Bulls of Iberia* vi. 60 At times, good matadors prefer to finish off their series of passes in a gentler way with a *larga*,..in the form the *revolera* in which the cape swirls above the man's head... The term *revolera* is often loosely used for *serpentina* and *vice versa.* **1967** [see *MARIPOSA].

‖ **révolté** (revǫlte). fem. **révoltée;** also unaccented and *erron.* **revolté.** [Fr.] One who revolts; a rebel or iconoclast; a nonconformist.

1890 E. DOWSON *Let. c* 11 June (1967) 153 The *révolté*. .I conceive as a violent & rather venomous person. **1910** G. B. SHAW in *Nation* 24 Dec. 544/1 Mary Fitton is quite modern, an *amoureuse* and a *révoltée*. **1934** R. CAMPBELL *Broken Record* 21, I have never been a *révolté*. **1938** *Sat. Rev. Lit.* (U.S.) 19 Nov. 4/3 The book is worth reading for those few chapters dealing with the association of those young revoltees. **1963** 'HAN SUYIN' *Four Faces* 219 The British have always had the genius of stimulating revoltees. **1978** *Dædalus* Fall 98 Now they felt more competent to question the assumptions of the public school avant-garde revolté.

revo·ltingness. [f. REVOLTING *ppl. a.* + -NESS.] The state or quality of being disgusting; repulsiveness.

1749 J. CLELAND *Mem. Woman of Pleasure* II. 5 The revoltingness of gross, rank, and vulgar expressions. **1907** G. MURRAY *Rise Gk. Epic* v. 122 Homer has cut out these stories for their revoltingness. **1957** WODEHOUSE *Over Seventy* xvi. 153 He..smiled a smile of just the right degree of revoltingness.

revoltive (rĭvǫ·ltiv), *a. rare*—[1] [f. REVOLT *sb.*[1] + -IVE.] Characterized by revulsion; = REVOLTED *ppl. a.* 3.

1954 W. FAULKNER *Fable* 241 A wounded man..was stared at with the same aghast distasteful revoltive pity and shock and outrage as a man in an epileptic seizure at high noon on a busy downtown corner.

revolute, *v.*[2] (Further examples.)

1921 [see *BOLSH *v.*]. **1937** *Aeroplane* 16 June 744/2 Many of the supporters of the Red agitators are merely using Moscow money to ginger up their own Unions, without any intention of revoluting.

revolution, *sb.* Add: Now usu. with pronunc. (revŏlū·ʃən). **III. 6. c.** *Geol.* A major mountain-building episode, esp. one extending over a whole continent or occurring at the close of a geological era.

1802 J. PLAYFAIR *Illustrations Huttonian Theory* 2 The earth has been the theatre of many great revolutions, and.. nothing on its surface has been exempted from their effects. To trace the series of these revolutions, to explain their causes,..is the proper object of a Theory of the Earth. **1845** C. LYELL *Trav. N. Amer.* I. iv. 99 The physical revolutions of the territory at present under consideration. **1863** J. D. DANA *Man. Geol.* III. iv. 403 After the long ages of comparative quiet, when the successive Palaeozoic formations were in slow progress, and finally the rock-foundation of the continent east of the Rocky Mountains was nearly completed, a change of great magnitude began, which involved the Appalachian region with the continental border adjoining, and well merits the title of Appalachian revolution. **1915** C. SCHUCHERT in Pirsson & Schuchert *Text-bk. Geol.* II. xli. 749 During the Appalachian Revolution much of eastern North America was again thrown into pronounced folds, faulted and widely thrust to the west and northwest. **1932** L. C. SNIDER *Earth Hist.* iii. 66 Environments of living things change very rapidly during such episodes, and as a result the faunas and floras before a revolution are quite different from those after it. **1978** W. L. STOKES et al. *Introd. Geol.* xvi. 379/2 There were no strong interactions between plates during the Cambrian Period, but there were extensive collisions during the Middle Ordovician to Devonian (Caledonian Revolution).

d. *the green revolution*, a great increase in the production of cereal crops in developing countries consequent on the introduction of high-yield varieties and the application of scientific methods to agriculture.

1970 *Financial Times* 23 Mar. 10/5 The primary factor behind the recovery has been the growth of agricultural output... Of course, the so-called Green Revolution is still very patchy. **1972** *Guardian* 30 Dec. 12/3 The green revolution took place only in wheat, not the coarse grains, pulses, and rice which the poor prefer. **1976** *Sci. Amer.* Sept. 31/1 The 'green revolution' of the late 1960's represented a significant improvement in grain-crop productivity, primarily in parts of Asia and Latin America. **1977** *Jrnl. R. Soc. Arts* CXXV. 226/1 The Green Revolution, in which new high yielding, short strawed varieties of wheat and rice were introduced into Third World countries.

7. c. In the Marxist doctrine of social evolution, the class struggle between the bourgeoisie and the proletariat leading in time to the downfall of capitalism and to its replacement by communism; also *continuing, continuous, uninterrupted revolution*, designating the concept of permanent revolution (cf. *PERMANENT *a.* 1 d).

1850 H. MACFARLANE tr. *Marx & Engels's Communist Manifesto* in *Red Republican* 16 Nov. 171/3 We have followed the more or less concealed civil war pervading existing society, to the point where it must break forth in an open revolution, and where the Proletarians arrive at the supremacy of their own class through the violent fall of the Bourgeoisie. **1920** B. RUSSELL *Pract. & Theory Communism* ii. 32 The Third International is an organization which exists to promote the class-war and to hasten the advent of revolution everywhere. **1937** E. H. CARR *Internat. Relations* iii. 73 The duty of every good Communist was to spread throughout the world the same revolution which had been successful in Russia. **1964** GOULD & KOLB *Dict. Social Sci.* 602/2 According to this [Marxist] view, great political and social revolutions are the instruments of the 'inevitable' progress of mankind towards a society in which freedom, self-government, social harmony, and equality will dominate. **1969** S. R. SCHRAM *Pol. Thought Mao Tse-tung* (rev. ed.) iii. 203 The basic idea, that of a bourgeois-democratic revolution under the hegemony of the proletariat, was to be further developed by Mao Tse-tung. **1975** *Chinese Econ. Stud.* VIII. IV. 9 Lin Piao's, and other similar swindlers' advocacy of this fallacy was to vainly attempt to use the productivity-first viewpoint as a weapon to oppose the continuing revolution. **1975** J. PLAMENATZ *K. Marx's Philos. of Man* i. 26 There is still talk of 'revolution' as something that the 'contradictions' of capitalism or of 'bourgeois society' will bring about, but there is much more uncertainty as to who the makers of the revolution will be. **1977** 'S. LEYS' *Chinese Shadows* (1978) viii. 169 The discrimination..between 'permanent revolution' (a Trotskyist heresy) and 'continuous revolution' (a genial and creative development brought to Marxist thought by Mao Tse-tung). **1978** *Fontana Dict. Mod. Thought* 464/2 Lenin.. thought that the revolution would pass first through the 'bourgeois' and then through the 'socialist' stage in his scheme of 'uninterrupted' revolution.

11. *Russian Hist.* The revolutionary activity of different factions in Russia during 1917 which resulted in the overthrow of the existing regime and the establishment of a socialist state, the Union of Soviet Socialist Republics. Cf. *Russian Revolution* s.v. *RUSSIAN *a.* 2 d*.

1917 *Times* 13 Nov. 6/2 The Bolsheviks have dropped their offensive attitude, considering themselves now in the position of organizers of the defence of the Revolution against the armies of Kerensky, Korniloff, and Kaledin. **1932** R. H. B. LOCKHART *Mem. Brit. Agent* IV. iii. 221 A Russian of good family, who long before the revolution had sacrificed a fortune for his Socialist convictions. **1948** B. D. WOLFE *Three who made Revol.* i. 38 The two decades of Russian history from the Revolutions of 1917 to the purges of 1937. **1959** P. WILES tr. *Schakovskoy's Privilege was Mine* x. 107 Another young relative, born after the Revolution, became emotionally involved with a Soviet intellectual. **1978** J. MOLYNEUX *Marxism & Party* iii. 58 During the rise of the revolution, the Mensheviks were in large part swept along by events.

12. *attrib.*, as *revolution counter* (= *rev-counter* s.v. *REV *sb.* 2), *indicator*. See also sense 8 b in Dict.

1961 WEBSTER, Revolution counter. **1962** *Which? Car Suppl.* Oct. 139/1 Loud rattle from revolution counter cable. **1922** Revolution indicator [see *air sextant* s.v. *AIR *sb.*[1] B. III. 6].

revolutionary, *a.* and *sb.* Add: **1. a.** (Further examples.) Also *Comb.*

1919 G. B. SHAW *Heartbreak House* p. ix, Heartbreak House was quite familiar with revolutionary ideas on paper. **1930** [see *ORGIASTICAL *a.*]. **1937** 'C. CAUDWELL' v. 94 *Illusion & Reality* Revolutionary-puritan ideals of liberty. **1941** KOESTLER *Scum* 19 They had an explanation ready for every occasion... They called it 'revolutionary dialectics'. **1959** *Encounter* XIII. 78 Even after the revolutionary-existentialist mood in Poland faded. **1960** [see *LUFTMENSCH, LUFTMENSH]. **1970** W. KLATT in D. J. Dwyer *China Now* (1974) xviii. 345 In 1967 and 1968 Chinese Press and radio reports revealed population data of a more serious type. These emanated from the Revolutionary Committees in China's chief administrative regions. **1975** C. P. MACKERRAS *Chinese Theatre in Mod. Times* x. 177 The well known Szechwanese Opera actress Ch'en Shu-fang..performed in a modern revolutionary opera in May 1971. **1977** *Undercurrents* June–July 10/1 Capitalism has developed (even if the revolutionary left's response to it has not).

Hence **revolutiona·rily** *adv.*

1864 R. COBDEN *Let.* 3 May in J. Morley *Life R. Cobden* (1881) II. xviii. 448 It was feared..that if he went to the provinces he might be talking too revolutionarily. **1927** *Daily Express* 11 Feb. 1/1 Lisbon is traversed from north to south by wide avenues—splendid places for those who are revolutionarily inclined. **1956** W. S. CHURCHILL *Hist. Eng.-Speaking Peoples* I. II. vi. 181 He [*sc.* Richard I] made new and revolutionarily heavy demands for taxation. **1971** *Frendz* 21 May 8/2 Revolutionarily aware people can't be fooled by these kinds of people.

revolutioneering, *vbl. sb.* Add: Also, agitation for revolution. *rare.*

1941 *World-Telegram* (N.Y.) 8 Jan. 23/2 We had trouble with the Muscovites before and..made them promise..to leave off revolutioneering in our midst.

revolutionism. (Earlier and later examples.)

1841 C. FOX *Jrnl.* 20 Apr. (1972) 105 He [*sc.* John Sterling]..thinks 'The Misanthrope' his [*sc.* Molière's] best, and considers that all the din and stir of French Revolutionism is prefigured in it. **1959** C. OGBURN *Marauders* (1960) ii. 48 Equally he liked to inveigh against the English, for whom his animus seemed to compound Midwestern isolationism, an early American revolutionism, and an unexpected outcropping of Scottish nationalism. **1976** M. J. LASKY *Utopia & Revolution* (1977) v. 225 Before the emergence of a clear, simple concept of linear progress, both utopianism and revolutionism took their turns on the wheel of fortune.

revolutionizing, *vbl. sb.* and *ppl. a.* (Earlier examples.)

1799 J. MORSE *Sermon Exhibiting Present Dangers* 17 The Clergy have been among the first victims to that sanguinary revolutionizing spirit which now convulses the world. **1854** GEO. ELIOT tr. *Feuerbach's Essence of Christianity* vii. 77 Words possess a revolutionizing force; words govern mankind.

revolutionology (revŏlūʃənǫ·lŏdʒi). [f. REVOLUTION *sb.* + -OLOGY.] The science or study of revolution.

1905 D. M. WALLACE *Russia* II. xxxv. 325 Such are a few characteristic extracts from a document which might fairly be called a treatise on revolutionology. **1932** *Sunday Times* 26 June 11/3 Trotsky is trying to work up a theory and science of revolutions, a sort of Revolutionology.

revolve, *sb.* **3. b.** A revolving stage. In full, *revolve stage*.

1938 *Times* 25 Aug. 8/4 A new electric revolve has been installed in place of the winch-controlled one. **1959** *Punch* 20 May 688/3 It is a big stage... In the middle is a revolve that goes round as easily as a bicycle wheel. **1972** T. STOPPARD *Jumpers* 11 The National Theatre production was mounted on a revolve stage. **1975** *Country Life* 26 June 1689/2 A revolve has been added to the stage which, thanks to hydraulic machinery, can assume any shape the director pleases. **1980** *Daily Tel.* 29 Aug. 10/5 The technical difficulties bedevil the scenery hoists and drum revolve. *Ibid.*, The revolve had given the contractors and the board endless difficulties.

revolver. Add: **1. b.** *revolver grip, pistol, range, shooting, shot* (earlier example), *target*; *revolver-like* adj.

1971 I. BUTYKAI tr. *Lukovich's Electric Foil Fencing* I. 20 Most foilists seem to prefer the revolver grip. **1925** T. DREISER *Amer. Tragedy* (1926) II. III. xix. 228 His voice..as opposed to Mason's revolver-like 'Excused!' **1866** J. MACGREGOR *Thousand Miles in Rob Roy Canoe* ii. 35 So my friend capped his revolver-pistol, and I acted as a pointer dog. ? **1891** W. S. CHURCHILL *Let.* in R. S. Churchill *Winston S. Churchill* (1967) I. Compan. I. v. 262, I went to the 'Revolver Range' & shot 12 shots with a full sized weapon. **1918** W. OWEN *Let.* 21 June (1967) 559 Today [I] have been Revolver Shooting. *a* **1861** T. WINTHROP *John Brent* (1862) xix. 208 They were close to us, within easy revolver shot. **1918** W. OWEN *Let.* 24 June (1967) 560 The hideous faces of the Advancing Revolver Targets I fired at last week.

revo·lvered *a.*, provided with a revolver or revolvers.

1901 *Pall Mall Gaz.* 6 Mar. 1 The revolvered footman..is not quite so grotesque as the revolvered Protestant lecturer.

1922 *Blackw. Mag.* Jan. 123/1 Whom should he see but his American friend the casket king, still picturesque and revolvered, on his way to the station bar. **1963** [see *LEATHER-JACKET 5].

revolving, *ppl. a.* Add: **c.** (Further examples.) Also *spec.* of an article of furniture or other simple mechanical construction, as *revolving door*, etc.

1866 GEO. ELIOT *Let.* 4 Aug. (1956) IV. 294 Col. Hamley's volume..lies now on my revolving desk as one of the books I mean first to read. **1883** *Heal & Son Catal.: Bedsteads & Furnit.* 185/3 Mahogany, Walnut, or Oak Revolving Chair. **1892** G. MEREDITH *Let.* 25 Sept. (1970) II. 1101 Will..says that he and his Daisy had thoughts of a revolving book-case. **1907** *St. Nicholas* Oct. 1104/2 It was his stated duty to attend one of the big revolving doors that opened upon the main street. **1912** G. B. SHAW *Let.* 27 Oct. in *B. Shaw & Mrs. Campbell* (1952) 51 Revolving stages present no difficulty... They are made in Germany. **1936** A. THIRKELL *August Folly* vi. 175 We put the white wine in the revolving bookcase. **1966** J. GLOAG *Social Hist. Furnit. Design* vii. 185 A late eighteenth century revolving bookcase in three tiers on a pillar and claw base. **1974** 'E. LATHEN' *Sweet & Low* ii. 23 Appeals for..a revolving stage at the repertory theater. **1977** *New Yorker* 9 May 35/1 They were not completely comfortable with escalators and revolving doors. **1980** L. LEWIS *Private Life of Country House* ii. 19 A revolving bookcase which must not be twirled round at speed because the books fell out.

d. *Econ.* Applied to credit, etc., available in return for smaller regular repayments (see also quot. 1919). *revolving fund*, a fund that is continually replenished as it is drawn upon.

1919 W. THOMSON *Dict. Banking* (ed. 2) 564/2 *Revolving credit*, a credit opened with a bank by an importer in order to enable an exporter to obtain payment for goods when ready for shipment. **1928** *Britain's Industr. Future* (Liberal Industr. Inquiry) II. ix. 101 The Local Loans Fund is a revolving fund vested in the National Debt Commissioners. **1962** *Economist* 16 June 1116/2 A 'revolving fund' is to aid the export industries. **1970** *Washington Post* 30 Sept. B13/4 (Advt.), Let Sears clean all your draperies—expert cleaning, prompt service! Charge it on your Sears revolving charge. **1972** *Daily Tel.* 15 Mar. 17 Midland Bank yesterday became the first of the big clearing banks to introduce a permanently revolving credit scheme for private customers. **1977** *Time* 28 Feb. 40/2 A department store, for example, must inform buyers that the interest charge of 1½ % a month on the unpaid balance in a revolving-credit account amounts to 18 % a year. **1980** *Jrnl. R. Soc. Arts* Apr. 303/2 *The Architectural Heritage Fund* describes the work of this revolving fund which makes low interest loans to building preservation trusts.

Revudeville (rĭvi*ū*·dəvil). [f. *REVU(E + VAU)DEVILLE.] A form of variety entertainment presented at the Windmill Theatre, London, between 1932 and 1964. Also *transf.*

1932 *Times* 3 Feb. 12/7 (Advt.), Windmill Theatre Revudeville 8.30. **1932** *Times* 4 Feb. 10/2 'Revudeville.'.. The Windmill Theatre turned last night from talking films to variety and *revue* turns. **1937** *Daily Express* 6 Feb. 15/1 Eric Barker, who holds forth at the Windmill Theatre, where they've just passed five years of non-stop revudeville. **1937** *Evening News* 19 Jan. 5/3 (*heading*) 'A Day at the B.B.C.'.. Skit in Revudeville. **1966** J. R. TAYLOR *Penguin Dict. Theatre* 228 Another phenomenon deserving of mention is *Revudeville* at the Windmill Theatre, a form of continuous variety show with comedy and nudes which ran in various editions from the 1930s... It closed in 1964.

revue (rĭvi*ū*·). [a. F. *revue* REVIEW *sb.*] **1.** A theatrical entertainment presenting a review (usu. satirical) of current events, plays, etc.; now also an elaborate musical show consisting of numerous unrelated scenes. Also without art., the genre of such entertainments.

1872 J. R. PLANCHÉ *Recoll.* I. iv. 73 My theatrical labours in the year 1825 terminated with the production at the Adelphi..of a one-act piece on the 12th December, entitled 'Success; or a Hit if you like it', which I only mention because it was the first attempt in this country to introduce that class of entertainment so popular in Paris called 'Revue'. **1879** —— *Extravaganzas* III. 311 It is, in fact, 'a dramatic political allegory'. A *Revue*, not of theatrical and other popular novelties..but of the State of Europe at a critical period. *Ibid.* IV. 89 Jokes upon passing events..in a *Revue*..are, of course, indispensable. **1893** *Times* 27 Nov. 7/4 *Under the Clock* has been described as a *revue* of the sort which is popular in the French theatres towards the close of the year. **1899** *Times* 4 Apr. 5/2 It looks as if musical farces were declining in popularity when a specimen of this class of piece has to be called a *revue* and announced as an 'entirely new form of entertainment'. The *revue*..has never had the same favour here that it enjoys in Paris. **1908** M. BEERBOHM in *Sat. Rev.* 18 Jan. 74/1 The attempts to popularise in London something like the Parisian 'revue' have been such dismal failures. **1913** *Punch* 9 July 41/3 The report that Mr. Lloyd George will shortly appear in a Revue at the National Liberal Club. **1920** A. G. GARDINER *Leaves in Wind* 71 One of those dismal things called revues, that are neither comedies nor farces, nor anything but shambling, hugger-mugger contraptions into which you fling anything that comes handy. **1923** R. NEVILL *World of Fashion 1837–1922* xii. 269 Anything like a real *revue* is impossible in modern London... Any allusion to current politics such as are made in Parisian revues is at once denounced as being in bad taste. **1967** *Oxf. Compan. Theatre* (ed. 3) 798/1 During the Second World War the vogue for revue continued... Revue became a feature of the little theatres..but it was not until the advent in London of *Beyond the Fringe*,..which was seen in Edinburgh on 10 May, 1961, that satire entered the field. **1972** *Daily Tel.* 22 Nov. 15 The new revue at the Cambridge, 'Behind the Fridge', stars Peter Cooke, Dudley Moore, and no one else. **1981** *Country Life* 12 Feb. 409/4 Noël Coward's..*This Year of Grace*..was a revue and not a book or a play.

2. *fig.*

1899 A. E. W. MASON *Miranda of Balcony* iii. 35 After he had fallen asleep, a curtain was raised upon a fantastic *revue* of the past week. **1934** T. S. ELIOT *Elizabethan Ess.* 167 The romantic comedy is a skilful concoction of inconsistent emotion, a revue of emotion... It consists in an internal incoherence of feelings, a concatenation of emotions.

3. *attrib.* and *Comb.*

1919 B. TARKINGTON *Let.* 30 Mar. in *On Plays* (1959) 10 What is really most valuable in it is the revelation, by an intimate, of the modern 'Revue' girl. **1933** M. ALLINGHAM *Sweet Danger* xvi. 197 She washed and changed with the speed of a revue star. **1933** P. GODFREY *Back-Stage* xiv. 174 The attempt to attract the smart, sophisticated section of the post-War public into patronizing the revue theatres. **1963** *New Yorker* 15 June 7 Ronny Graham's revue-eyed view of life..sometimes gets bug-eyed. **1975** *Listener* 9 Jan. 57/1 With all the resources of splendid new theatres..we..[are] dragging up old revue skits.

Hence **revue·tte** *nonce-wd.*, a short revue; **revue·-ish** *a.*, characteristic of a revue; **revu·ist**, a writer of revues.

1927 *Observer* 25 Sept. 11/1 Alfred Savoir, in collaboration with Rip, the revuist, has written 'Comme le temps passe'. **1930** *Daily Express* 6 Oct. 5/3 Jane Renouardt in Rip's revuette gives a marvellous initation of Yvonne Printemps. **1969** *Listener* 20 Feb. 251/1 The authors of *Your Own Thing* can't handle this bold stuff... This is a revue-ish comment on rock music.

revusical (rĭvi*ū*·zikăl). orig. and chiefly *U.S. slang.* [f. *REVU(E + MU)SICAL *sb.*] A theatrical entertainment that combines elements of the revue and musical.

1931 *Amer. Speech* VII. 45 *Torso tossers* dance in *revusicals* which might even turn out *floperoos*. **1935** A. C. BAUGH *Hist. Eng. Lang.* x. 378 Often such coinages [of portmanteau words] are formed with a playful or humorous intent... *Paradoxology, alcoholiday, anecdotage, revusical, yellowcution*, and the like, often reveal flashes of wit. **1936** *Daily Mirror* (N.Y.) 22 Apr. 10/4 Harriet Hoctor's class in 'The Ziegfeld Follies', the revusical. **1941** *Amer Speech* XVI. 16/1 Pardon Us Please, 'presenting thirty-five stars in person', advertises itself in newspapers as a *Revusical*. **1967** *New Idea* (Austral.) 23 Feb. 6/4 John McKellar's invention, a revusical, opening in Sydney..called Hail Gloria Fitzpatrick. The Phillip Theatre..coined the word revusical to describe a show that will cover every facet of theatre work.

revved, revving: see *REV *v.*

reward, *sb.*[1] Add: **II. 4. a. reward book**, a book given as a prize at school.

1820 [in Dict.]. **1865** C. M. YONGE *Clever Woman of Family* I. iii. 82 A summary pawning of all poor Lovedy's reward books. **1977** W. FEAVER *When We were Young* 92/1 The cheap, spongy paper of reward books and annuals.

e. In phr. *to go* (*pass*, etc.) *to one's reward*, to die (and go to heaven). Also in ironic use. orig. *U.S.*

1883 'MARK TWAIN' *Life on Mississippi* li. 503 He went to his reward, whatever it was, two years ago. **1896** J. CURTIN tr. *Sienkiewicz's Quo Vadis* lxx. 521, He went to his reward like a conqueror. **1942** E. PAUL *Narrow St.* xxiii. 202 Vladimir de Pachmann..has recently died. I wept..when I read that the grand old poet of the piano..had gone to his reward at the age of eighty-five. **1949** G. DAVENPORT *Family Fortunes* III. iv. 266 It was lucky for Mrs. Wilkens, Lou Belle thought, that her grandfather Aaron Toler had passed to his reward. **1975** D. LODGE *Changing Places* ii. 49 His beloved parent had passed to her reward from this very bed. **1977** D. WILLIAMS *Treasure by Degrees* ii. 19 When the old baggage was finally called to her reward..his own temporal benefit would be substantial.

f. *Psychol.* A recompense for a response which reinforces specific learning or behaviour. Freq. *attrib.*, esp. as *reward cell, centre, system*, with reference to areas of the brain in or near the hypothalamus which, when stimulated, reward the organism with sensations of pleasure. Cf. *PUNISHMENT 1 b.

1907 R. M. YERKES *Dancing Mouse* vii. 100 In connection with the discussion of motives, it is an important fact that forms of reward are far harder to find than forms of punishment. **1912** *Jrnl. Animal Behavior* II. 50 It seems evident from this experiment that a combination of punishment and reward-motives is more effective in bringing about visual discrimination in the rat than is either punishment or reward used alone. **1929** *Brit. Jrnl. Psychol.* Oct. 173 Some experiments on the influence of the amount of food given as a reward on the rate at which young chickens learn. **1952** E. L. & R. E. HARTLEY *Fund. Social Psychol.* ix. 274 Without reinforcement or reward, no connection will be established between response and motivation. **1956** *Sci. Amer.* Oct. 108/3 At this point we assumed that the stimulus must provoke curiosity; we did not yet think of it as a reward. *Ibid.* 116/3 The main question..is to determine how the excited 'reward' cells act upon the specific sensory-motor systems. **1964** M. ARGYLE *Psychol. & Social Probl.* ii. 26 A most interesting series of attempts to demonstrate the acquisition of drives by reward learning has been carried out with monkeys. **1974** M. C. GERALD *Pharmacol.* x. 186 Drugs capable of causing the release of norepinephrine,.. are able to increase the rate of self-stimulation when electrodes are placed in the reward center. *Ibid.*, The reward system is located in the medial forebrain bundle. **1977** E. L. DECI in VON H. Gilmer & Deci *Industrial & Organizational Psychol.* (ed. 4) viii. 208 Intrinsic rewards are ones which a person administers to himself or herself.

rewa·rdingness. [f. REWARDING *ppl. a.* + -NESS.] The quality or state of being rewarding.

1951 *Mind* LX. 124 The subject of modal logic is of course extremely difficult. These are two illustrations of the dangers of any sort of intuitive approach to it even in Aristotle, and at the same time of its rewardingness for anyone who forgoes that approach. **1972** M. ARGYLE *Social Psychol. of Work* iv. 60 Rewardingness may be an important part of this general ability—rewarding people are both more popular and influential. **1978** A. RYAN in Hookway & Pettit *Action & Interpretation* 66 If we want to know why someone does what he does, we must look to the goals he is seeking, and to his beliefs about their rewardingness to himself.

rewa-rewa. Also **riwa-riwa.** Substitute for first part of def.: A tall broadleaved forest tree, *Knightia excelsa*, of the family Proteaceæ, native to New Zealand and bearing long, narrow, toothed leaves and racemes of tomentose red-brown flowers followed by woody pods. (Earlier and later examples.)

1831 G. BENNETT in *London Med. Gaz.* 5 Nov. 150/1 *Knightea excelsa*... This tree is abundant in the New Zealand forests, and is named Riwa-riwa by the natives. **1838** J. S. POLACK *N.Z.* II. 396 The *Rewá rewá*..is a handsome grained wood, very serviceable to the builder and joiner... It grows to the height of sixty feet. **1966** *Encycl. N.Z.* III. 70/1 The rewarewa..grows to heights of up to 90 ft.

rewash, *v.* Add: Hence **rewa·shed** *ppl. a.*

1908 *Sears, Roebuck Catal.* 170/1 Inner tubes..made..of the very best quality of Upper River Para rewashed rubber. **1965** G. J. WILLIAMS *Econ. Geol. N.Z.* vii. 69/2 Detrital gold was mined in the Preservation Inlet area from rewashed glacial debris.

reweave, *v.* Add: (*absol.* example.) Hence **rewea·ving** *vbl. sb.*

1929 *Oxford Poetry* 6 These worn and tangled threads of day reweave Like memory's or music's threads. **1963** *Economist* 2 Feb. 392/2 It is this reweaving of America with Europe that General de Gaulle is now challenging. **1964** *McCall's Sewing* xv. 265 (*heading*) Reweaving/Invisible Patching. *Ibid.*, You can only use threads ravelled from the fabric for reweaving.

rewhisper, *v.* (Earlier example.)

1754 RICHARDSON *Grandison* I. xxxvii. 271 I'll be hang'd if Miss Byron thinks so, re-whisper'd she.

re-wind, *v.* Add: (Further examples.) Also, to wind back. Also *absol.*

1967 H. HARRISON *Technicolor Time Machine* xii. 118 'Reel is almost empty on the back projection.'.. 'Rewind it then.' **1972** D. E. WESTLAKE *Bank Shot* iv. 23 He pushed the stop button on the cassette recorder, rewound, and played it back. **1977** D. BAGLEY *Enemy* ix. 65, I switched off the recorder and rewound the tape. **1977** J. HEDGECOE *Photographer's Handbk.* 12 After taking the last picture you disengage the film wind mechanism and rewind the exposed film into its cassette. **1980** C. FITZGIBBON *Rat Report* iii. 57 He re-wound the tape and played it over several times.

rewinding *vbl. sb.* (examples of *attrib.* use).

1930 *Daily Express* 6 Sept. 2/1 Fire broke out in the rewinding room of the Rialto Cinema..yesterday. **1958** *Newnes' Compl. Amat. Photogr.* 71 Nothing is more infuriating than to lose exposed film through a difficult rewinding system.

re·wind, *sb.* [f. the vb.] **1.** A mechanism for winding film, tape, or the like backwards.

1938 G. H. SEWELL *Amateur Film-Making* v. 52 A rewind..consists essentially of two uprights each bearing a spindle, and one or both of them having a geared drive so that a spool of film placed on one can be wound off on to the other. **1958** *Newnes' Compl. Amat. Photogr.* 71 If possible, the rewind should be tested with an old film. **1973** C. BONINGTON *Next Horizon* xiii. 196, I got half a dozen pictures of him as I manipulated the rewind and trigger with frozen fingers.

2. The action or process of winding paper, recording tape, etc., backwards.

1964 *Gloss. Letterpress Rotary Printing Terms* (*B.S.I.*) 6 *Rewind*, the procedure for taking several butt ends of paper and winding them into a reel for use in the press. **1965** *Wireless World* July 34/1 (Advt.), Tape lifted during rewind from all heads or in contact with play-back head only if required. **1970** O. DOPPING *Computers & Data Processing* xv. 236 In using long magnetic tape files comprising many reels of tape, the time for rewind and exchange of reels can become appreciable.

3. *attrib.*

1931 J. H. REYNER *Cine-Photogr. for Amateurs* x. 122 The film is then placed on the re-wind apparatus. **1964** *Gloss. Letterpress Rotary Printing Terms* (*B.S.I.*) 6 *Rewind join*, the adhesion between the butt ends of two webs which are wound into a reel in the printing works. **1972** Rewind starter [see *recoil starter* s.v. *RECOIL *sb.* 4 b]. **1972** F. DURBRIDGE *Bat out of Hell* v. 182 He operated the rewind switch, took the tape back to zero. **1974** *News & Courier* (Charleston, S. Carolina) 19 Apr. (Wickes Lumber Advt. Suppl.) 8 Efficient and safe with a 3.5 h.p. Briggs & Stratton rewind-start engine. **1978** *SLR Camera* Nov. 69/1 The film speed setting is adjusted by the rotation of a collar surrounding the rewind knob.

rewi·re, *v.* [RE- 5 c.] **1.** *trans.* To provide with new wires, esp. for conducting electricity.

1903 *Motoring Ann.* 295 In cases of trouble from short circuits or broken wires, there is no remedy but to re-wire the car. **1910** *Installation News* IV. 64/2 They have decided to rewire the whole building. **1973** E. BERCKMAN *Victorian Album* 25 Would you object if we rewired the whole flat? **1981** *Times* 4 Mar. 23/3 The electrician who re-wires houses at the weekend.

2. To transmit (a telegraphic message) again. *rare*.

1907 *Westm. Gaz.* 2 Dec. 13/1 News..is telegraphed to Madrid, to be forthwith re-'wired' to the capitals.

Hence **rewi·ring** *vbl. sb.*; also **rewi·reable** *a.*

1930 A. BENNETT *Imperial Palace* lxxii. 616 Obviously a lot of re-wiring would have to be done. **1934** WEBSTER, Rewirable. **1976** *BSI News* Nov. 16/1 Three-pin rewireable or non-rewireable plugs will be available for the connection of Class I equipment (i.e. equipment requiring earthing). **1977** *Lancashire Life* Nov. 75/2 The amount raised will be put..to pay for some much needed re-wiring in the Institute.

re·wire, *sb.* [f. the vb.] A rewiring.

1934 in WEBSTER. **1976** *Star* (Sheffield) 20 Nov. (Advt.), House rewires by qualified electrician.

reword, *v.* **3.** (Earlier example.)

1882 G. M. HOPKINS *Note-bks. & Papers* (1937) 431, I.. had to leave out or reword all passages speaking of God's kingdom as falling.

rework, *v.* Add: **1. b.** *spec.* in *Geol.* Of a natural agent: to alter, esp. to remove and redeposit (rock or the like).

1870 C. F. HARTT *Thayer Exped.: Sci. Results Journey Brazil* xix. 573 Where the surface of the rock..had been covered by a thick layer of loose material, the glacier reworked this loose material, and when it disappeared left it as a paste. **1939** P. D. TRASK *Recent Marine Sediments* III. 202 The tidal mud is reworked as rapidly as it is deposited. **1962** READ & WATSON *Introd. Geol.* I. vii. 381 Loose pyroclastic accumulations are always liable to be reworked by wind, streams and other surface-agents and may then be redeposited along with appropriate kinds of sedimentary rocks. **1964** *Oceanogr. & Marine Biol.* II. 122 Mud-feeding animals play a significant part in re-working the sediment even on the floor of the abyssal parts of the ocean. **1977** *Sci. Amer.* Mar. 94/3 One extreme hypothesis is that most if not all of it [*sc.* continental crust] was made early in the course of the earth's chemical differentiation and that ever since then it has been reworked, that is, heated, melted, recrystallized and deformed.

2. To change the variety of (a plant) by grafting.

1942 *Jrnl. Pomol.* XIX. 194 When reworking apple trees liable to attack by silver leaf after grafting, it is important to retain as much of the head of the tree as possible. **1950** *N.Z. Jrnl. Agric.* June 538/2 Auckland growers decided to rework thousands of Delicious trees to other varieties.

Hence **rewo·rked** *ppl. a.*; **rewo·rker,** one who works (something) again, *spec.* a reviser or redactor; **reworking** *vbl. sb.* (further examples).

1886 T. S. HUNT *Mineral Physiol. & Physiogr.* vii. 275 The layer of ground and 'reworked' decayed material resting on the gneiss, found by Hartt in Brazil. **1939** P. D. TRASK *Recent Marine Sediments* III. 197 This type of bedding indicates frequent reworking of the sediments under the influence of currents of varying strength and direction. *Ibid.* 201 In these areas the sediments are reworked deposits, not new ones. **1955** J. G. DAVIS *Dict. Dairying* (ed. 2) 157 Reworking of butter invariably increases the count and also increases the size of the water globules. **1970** J. R. L. ALLEN *Physical Processes of Sedimentation* iv. 140 The beds preserved have properties denoting extensive sediment reworking. **1972** G. JONES *Kings, Beasts, & Heroes* II. i. 66 The story-tellers of the *Mabinogion* are to a high degree reworkers of old material, borrowers from an often remote antiquity. **1977** *Early Music* Oct. 581/1, I think it is a pity that the models of the two known reworkings are not identified more clearly. **1979** *Dædalus* Summer 94 The reader is not simply beckoned to catch an unwonted glimpse of the diverse states of a subtly reworked self-portrait.

rewrite, *v.* Add: **2. a.** Also *refl.*

1928 *Manch. Guardian Weekly* 5 Oct. 265/2 The events of the last four years in which the history of 1906 to 1914 was rewriting itself.

c. *Linguistics.* To write (an analysis of a phrase or sentence structure) in a different form, usu. by expansion. Also *absol.*

1955 N. CHOMSKY *Logical Struct. Linguistic Theory* vi. 235 We can produce derivations from this linear grammar by applying the conversions S_i (interpreted as the instruction 'rewrite X_i as Y_i') in sequence. **1957** —— *Syntactic Structures* v. 40 These rules can be dropped if we rewrite ..so that either *C* or *M*, but not both, can be selected. **1970** *Canad. Jrnl. Linguistics* XV. 95 Many contemporary linguists describe their data in terms of a system of rules which state that one string of symbols is to be rewritten as another string of symbols. *Ibid.* 97 We know that rule 1 must be the first rule executed because S is the initial symbol and rule 1 is the only rule that rewrites S. **1972** *Archivum Linguisticum* III. 14 A lexical redundancy rule could also be used to rewrite the semantic feature as a syntactic one.

Hence **rewri·ter,** one who revises or rewrites; **rewriting** *vbl. sb.* (earlier examples); also *attrib.*, as **rewriting rule** *Linguistics*, a rule that governs the rewriting of a structural analysis.

1838 J. S. MILL *Let.* 19 Oct. in M. FAWCETT *Life Sir W. Molesworth* (1901) x. 204 This winter..will see me through the whole of it except the rewriting. **1854** C. M. YONGE *Heartsease* I. II. xii. 309 She has..given me some re-writing to do. **1912** *Collier's* 28 Sept. 17/2 By all the earmarks it was a 'three head' to be laconically telephoned into a 'rewriter' who would dutifully chronicle the event in 100 words. **1934** BLUNDEN *Choice or Chance* 51 Rewriters, novelists and mirth-provokers. **1965** N. CHOMSKY *Aspects of Theory of Syntax* ii. 66 The natural mechanism for generating Phrase-markers..is a system of *rewriting rules*. A rewriting rule is a rule of the form..$A \rightarrow Z/X - Y$ where *X* and *Y* are (possibly null) strings of symbols, *A* is a single category symbol, and *Z* is a nonnull string of symbols. **1970** *Language* XLVI. 261 These PS rules generate the structure-sensitive $a^nb\ a^n$ quite simply with one non-terminal category and two rewriting rules.

rewrite (rī·rəit), *sb.* [f. the vb.] **1. a.** orig. *U.S. slang.* The act of revising a text; a revised text. (Chiefly in journalistic and publishing use.)

1926 E. B. WHITE *Let.* Sept. (1976) 75 Carl..gravitated naturally down to Mr. Hearst's American and got a job on rewrite. **1933** PARTRIDGE *Slang To-day & Yesterday* iii. 181 *To vet* a book is to revise it, whether for the author or for his publisher; if the work entailed amounts to a virtual re-writing, the resulting typescript or manuscript is a *re-write*. **1938** E. POUND *Let.* 22 Apr. (1971) 307 How *much* revision do you propose to make in the proofs?.. We're not out for collaboration and rewrite à la E.P. **1952** *Scrutiny* June 3/3 Dryden states the case nicely in the *Preface* to his rewrite of Shakespeare's *Antony and Cleopatra*. **1960** *News Chron.* 23 Feb. 6/3 Belting out a rewrite of a wobbly third act. **1972** H. EVANS *Newsman's English* ix. 191 Mix both techniques—rewrite the lead into the story but edit the rest of it on copy... Or you can move nearer to a full-scale rewrite. **1976** G. MCDONALD *Confess, Fletch* (1977) xxv. 121, I haven't got the rewrite man I need... The guy I've got on rewrite now is a kid.

b. *attrib.* and *Comb.*, esp. as **rewrite man,** one employed to rewrite newspaper copy for publication; also *transf.*

1901 *Munsey's Mag.* Nov. 222/1 Much of the copy that reaches the big newspaper offices is passed over to the 'rewrite man'. **1912** G. M. HYDE *Newspaper Reporting* ix. 125 The terms 'rewrite story' and 'follow-up, or follow, story', are names which newspaper men apply to the rehashed or revised versions of other news stories. **1935** *Amer. Mercury* July 379/2, I have yet to discover an instance of real literary talent being brought to the surface by back-breaking chores on the rewrite desk. **1949** 'G. ORWELL' *Nineteen Eighty-Four* II. iii. 131 She could describe the whole process of composing a novel, from the general directive issued by the Planning Committee down to the final touching-up by the Rewrite Squad. **1955** H. ROTH *Sleeper* xv. 126 She seemed..capable, especially of rewrite, and good rewrite people are hard to find. **1960** R. ST. JOHN *Foreign Correspondent* i. 12, I had been a rewrite man in Camden, New Jersey. **1973** *Times* 2 Mar. 14/4 He is..the GLC's chief strategic planner and 'rewrite man' on planning policy. **1977** *Detroit Free Press* 11 Dec. 3-B/3 He phoned the story in over a vodka and orange juice. 'It ain't much,' he told the rewrite man.

2. *Linguistics*. The act or process of writing an analysis of a phrase or sentence structure in a different form, usu. by expansion. Freq. *attrib.* and *Comb.*, esp. as **rewrite rule** = *rewriting rule* s.v. *REWRITING *vbl. sb.*

1960 R. B. LEES *Gram. Engl. Nominalizations* i. 2 The rewrite rules, which permit the conversion of given strings of symbols into more expanded strings. **1964** E. BACH *Introd. Transformational Gram.* ii. 17 In the grammar above the items to the left and right of the 'rewrite' arrow are strings of symbols. **1967** *Word* XXIII. 289 The equivalence of the different classes manifesting identical functions *is* implicit in the rewrite-rule formulations. **1971** *Amer. Speech 1968* XLIII. 132 If the universals generally posited by linguists for human language can be formulated as a set of re-write rules whose elements are unordered by nature, then the relatedness between languages is determinable. **1977** *Trans. Philol. Soc. 1975* 79 Many individual verbs will no doubt need extra specifications in terms of 'context-sensitive rewrite rules'.

rex[2]. Delete ‖ and *rare* and add: **1. b.** (With capital initial.) Used, during the reign of a king, esp. in law reports, to designate the prosecution in criminal proceedings. Cf. *REGINA.

1657 *Reports of Edward Bulstrode* I. 96 *Dominus Rex*, and Sir William Fitzwilliams against Ives. **1717** W. SALKELD *Reports of Cases Court of King's Bench* 324 Rex *versus* Bear. **1792** W. BOSCAWEN *Treat. Convictions on Penal Statutes* 48 This was one of the points in the case of *Rex v. Hall*, last cited. **1848** E. W. COX *Reports of Cases in Crim. Law* II. 423 *Rex* v. *Webb* is no authority for that distinction. **1976** *Law Reports Queen's Bench Div.* 373 Rex v. Bishop of Lincoln (1637).

2. A rabbit or mouse belonging to a variety so called, distinguished by a genetic mutation in which the guard hairs are reduced and wavy or completely lacking, giving the fur a soft, plushy texture; also, the characteristic mutation itself. Also *attrib.*

1929 *Jrnl. Heredity* XX. 192 Rex rabbits produce only rex offspring when bred with each other. **1935** *Nature* 14 Sept. 434/2 During the years 1927–29..a new class of rabbit, namely the 'Rex', with fur like the mole..was imported from France and Germany. **1939** *Ibid.* 23 Sept. 557/1 The rex mouse has a coat somewhat similar to that of the same character in the rabbit... Rex is an autosomal dominant to normal. **1956** C. AUERBACH *Genetics in Atomic Age* iv. 16 The Rex rabbit..has a mole-like fur. **1977** *West Briton* 25 Aug. 34/2 (Advt.), Rabbits: Breeding pairs and young. Rex, dwarf, English and Dutch.

3. A cat belonging to the breed so called, developed in Cornwall and Devon during the 1950s and 1960s, and distinguished by short curly or wavy fur. Also *attrib.*

1960 *News Chron.* 28 July 6/3 There's going to be a Rex kitten. This is the curly-coated kitten—a new breed which experimental breeders are trying to establish. **1965** *Observer* (Colour Suppl.) 31 Jan. 4/3 A new sort of highly exclusive curly-coated cat called a Rex. **1972** M. BABSON *Murder on Show* x. 125 The Devon Rex and the Cornish Rex. Strange, friendly, fantasy creatures, with curly astrakhan coats and great butterfly ears. **1977** D. S. RICHARDS *Handbk. Pedigree Cat Breeding* vii. 107 No rex cats should be mixed with other breeds.

Rexine (re·ksīn). Also **rexine.** The proprietary name of a kind of imitation leather used in upholstery, book-binding, etc. Also *attrib.* and *Comb.*

1911 COUTTS & STEPHEN *Man. Libr. Bookbinding* iv. 56 There are several textile fabrics, known as Rexine..and Pegamoid, etc., produced as substitutes for leather. **1915** *Trade Marks Jrnl.* 18 Aug. 860 Rexine... Artificial leather and goods manufactured wholly or principally thereof.. British Leather Cloth Manufacturing Co., Limited,..Hyde, near Manchester; leather cloth manufacturers. **1922** [see *PEGAMOID]. **1930** *Daily Tel.* 5 Apr. 21/3 (Advt.), Sale... Three-piece suites in hide, rexine and fabrics, [etc.]. **1946** T. H. WHITE *Mistress Masham's Repose* xix. 158 She carried a Rexine shopping bag. **1960** *Practical Wireless* XXXVI. 287/1 (Advt.), This contemporary cabinet in two-tone grey rexine is ideal for the modern home. **1963** J. CLEMENTS *Bookbinding* ix. 78 Rexine and some imitation cloths need to be cleaned with methylated spirit..before tooling. **1971** R. P. JHABVALA *Experience of India* 140 Their drawingroom was furnished with a blue rexine-covered sofa-set. **1975** E. BURDETT *Craft of Bookbinding* viii. 361 Leathercloth..was the original waterproof cloth first made at the turn of the century, one of the best known being 'Rexine', with a surface consisting of several coatings of nitro-cellulose. **1977** *Transatlantic Rev.* LX. 161 In the dining room, never used, there was a square table with six rexine-seated chairs around it.

Rexism (re·ksiz'm). [f. L. (*Christus*) *Rex*, (Christ) the King: see -ISM.] A right-wing Roman Catholic political movement established in 1935 in Belgium. So **Re·xist** *sb.* and *a.*

1936 *Times* 23 May 13/5 The Liberals represent the 'Rexists' as disguised Catholics. At all events, in spite of an entrance fee used for propaganda, the 'Rexist' meetings have drawn the biggest crowds. *Ibid.* 26 Oct. 13/3 M. Vandervelde, the Minister for Public Health, to-day addressed the Socialist Congress in Brussels on the attitude of the Socialist Party towards recent events, internal and external. His remarks on the relative merits of Rexism and Communism were loudly cheered by the Congress. **1937** 'E. B. ASHTON' *Fascist* viii. 245 M. Degrelle's 'Rexists'. **1954** B. & R. NORTH tr. *Duverger's Pol. Parties* II. ii. 313 The violent surge of Rexism in Belgium in 1936 followed by just as violent a decline. **1966** 'HAN SUYIN' *Mortal Flower* xvi. 344 Degrelle (who had organized the Rexists, something like the Nazi Brownshirts). **1971** M. LYON *Belgium* v. 70 In 1935 a twenty-nine-year-old ex-student of Louvain University named Léon Degrelle started a Belgian movement in favour of his own brand of authoritarianism flavoured with Christianity, which he called Rexism from the name Christus Rex (Christ the King).

Reye (rəi, rē^i). *Path.* [The name of Ralph Douglas Kenneth *Reye* (1912–78), Australian pædiatrician, who with others first described the syndrome in 1963 (*Lancet* 12 Oct. 749–52).] *Reye's* (or *Reye*) *syndrome*: an often fatal metabolic disease of young children.

1965 *Amer. Jrnl. Dis. Children* CX. 95/1 The possible occurrence of the Reye syndrome in the United States. **1969** *Ibid.* CXVII. 721/1 Thirty-three cases of Reye's syndrome (acute encephalopathy with fatty infiltration of the viscera). **1976** *Nature* 20 May 184/1 A number of children, mostly from areas that have been heavily sprayed in the past, have died from Reye's syndrome, a condition first described in 1963 following the US Air Force's aerial defoliation in Vietnam and Thailand. The disease causes increased susceptibility to viral infection, and it is the spray dispersal emulsifiers which are suspect; the sprays used are Fenitrothion and Phospamidon. **1977** *Daily Colonist* (Victoria, B.C.) 17 Dec. 12/1 There is no connection between the chemical Fenitrothion and the sometimes fatal children's disease called Reye's syndrome.

Reynolds (re·nǒldz). *Physics.* The name of Osborne *Reynolds* (1842–1912), Irish engineer and physicist, used *attrib.* (and in the possessive as *Reynolds'*, occas. *erron.* as *Reynold's*) to designate quantities discovered and concepts used by him, as **Reynolds number,** a dimensionless number used in fluid mechanics as a criterion to determine whether fluid flow past a body or in a duct is steady or turbulent, evaluated as $lv\rho/\nu$, where l is a characteristic length of the system, v is a typical speed, ρ is the mass-density, and ν is the kinematic viscosity of the fluid; *magnetic Reynolds number*, a number analogous in formation to the Reynolds number, used to describe the dynamic behaviour of a magnetized plasma; **Reynolds stress,** the net rate of transfer of momentum across a surface in a fluid resulting from turbulence in the fluid.

1910 *Sci. Abstr.* A. XIII. 406 The flow..is conditioned by the so-called Reynolds' number. **1930** DOUGALL & DEANS tr. *Ewald's Physics of Solids & Fluids* vi. 273 This number, which gives the ratio of the forces of inertia and the forces of viscosity, is called Reynolds' number, in honour of Osborne Reynolds, the discoverer of this law of similarity. **1952** *Ark. f. Fysik* V. 322 The non-dimensional ratios are analogous to Reynolds' number in ordinary hydrodynamics. In magneto-hydrodynamics there are many numbers of this kind entering in different combinations in different cases. **1958**, etc. [see *NUSSELT]. **1962** W. B. THOMPSON *Introd. Plasma Physics* iv. 50 These conditions may be combined to give the condition for typical magneto-hydrodynamic behaviour... This condition was derived by Lundquist (1952) who called *M* the magnetic Reynold's number. **1974** *Encycl. Brit. Macropædia* XIV. 507/2 When the magnetic Reynolds number is much greater than one, resistance effects can be ignored and the magnetic lines of force are said to be frozen to (or to move with) the plasma. **1975** *Sci. Amer.* Nov. 83/1 In a large hummingbird.. the mean value of the Reynolds number for the flow past oscillating wings is 15,000; in a large wasp..it is 4,000; in the small fruit fly *Drosophila*..it is 200, and in the tiny parasitic wasp *Encarsia fomosa*..it is less than 20. **1977** J. L. HARPER *Population Biol. of Plants* ii. 42 The flight Reynolds numbers for spores, pollen and the tiny dust seeds such as those of *Monotropa* and many orchids are usually so small that movement in air is dominated by viscous forces. **1943** *Q. Appl. Math.* I. 11 A new set of equations is obtained which differs from the first only in the presence of additional terms added to the mean values of the stresses due to viscosity. These additional terms are called the Reynolds stresses or eddy stresses. **1947** HUNSAKER & RIGHTMIRE *Engin. Appl. Fluid Mech.* viii. 137 This fictitious [shear] stress is called either the turbulent shear stress..or the Reynolds stress, after Osborne Reynolds, who first pointed out the existence of turbulent momentum transfers. **1964** *Oceanogr. & Marine Biol.* II. 17 They concluded that the portion of the spectrum which they had measured contributed only about $\frac{1}{8}$ of the total turbulent energy and that the spectrum for $k > 0{\cdot}02\ cm^{-1}$ could not make a major contribution to the Reynolds stresses.

rézbányite (re·zbānyəit). *Min.* Also **rezbanyite**, (sense 1) **retz-**. [f. *Rézbánya*, name of a village in Hungary (now Băiţa in Romania): see -ITE[1].] † **1.** (See quots.) *Obs.* [ad. G. *rezbanyit* (R. Hermann 1858, in *Jrnl. f. prakt. Chem.* LXXV. 450).]

1868 J. D. DANA *Syst. Min.* (ed. 5) 100 Retzbanyite... A lead-gray ore of bismuth. **1896** A. H. CHESTER *Dict. Names Minerals* 231 *Retzbanyite*, an obs. name for an impure var. of cosalite.

2. An orthorhombic lead and copper bismuth sulphide found as light grey masses. [ad. G. *rezbanyit* (A. Frenzel 1883, in *Mineral. und petrogr. Mittheil.* V. 178).]

1884 *Jrnl. Chem. Soc.* XLVI. 266 From the analyses, the formula of rezbanyite is calculated to be $4PbS,5Bi_2S_3$. **1968** *Mineral. Abstr.* XIX. 18/1 In the Fe–Cu deposits of l'Adrar Taliouine [Algeria], in addition to pyrite and chalcopyrite the rare minerals..rézbányite..and tetrahedrite occur.

‖ **rez-de-chaussée** (redəʃose). [Fr.] The ground floor of a building.

1802 C. WILMOT *Let.* 6 Oct. in *Irish Peer* (1920) 99 Its rez de chaussee is open'd by 60 arches through which one enters into the Amphitheatre. **1837** J. F. COOPER *Recoll. Europe* II. x. 245 Besides the *rez de chaussée*, which is but little above the ground, there are two good stories all round the building. **1842** BARHAM *Ingol. Leg.* 2nd Ser. 262 The *rez-de-chaussée*,—as some call the ground floor. **1871** C. SCHREIBER *Jrnl.* 3 June (1952) 124 All open spaces and cellars under the *rez-de-chaussée* of the houses. **1959** M. S. BRIGGS *Everyman's Conc. Encycl. Archit.* 272 *Rez-de-Chaussée* (Fr., literally 'level with the ground'), hence, the ground floor or ground storey of a building.

‖ **rézel, rezel** (rezel), **rézeuil** (rezöy), arch. varr. *RÉSEAU 1.

1865 F. B. PALLISER *Hist. Lace* ii. 17 This plain netted ground was called réseau, rézel, rézeuil. *Ibid.* 19 Teachers of the art soon caused the various patterns to be reproduced in..samplars.., and young ladies worked at them diligently, as a proof of their competency in the arts of cutwork, lacis, and rézeuil. **1900** E. JACKSON *Hist. Hand-Made Lace* 218 *Réseau*, (1) Identical with Rezel and Rezeuil.

re-ze·ro (rī-), *v.* [f. RE- 5 a + *ZERO *v.*] *intr.* and *trans.* To return to a zero position.

1971 *Amateur Photographer* 13 Jan. 51/2 This operates only when the camera is loaded and automatically re-zeros when the film cartridge is removed. **1978** *Nature* 17 Aug. 675/2 A further advantage is that the instrument can be re-zeroed simply by opening a valve which connects the two arms of the instrument allowing the pressure to equalise.

‖ **rezident** (rezide·nt). Pl. **rezidenty.** [Russ., in same sense.] = *RESIDENT *sb.* 4.

1968 W. GARNER *Deep, Deep Freeze* xii. 132 The London *rezidenty*: 'illegal' agents who are members of Soviet *rezidentsii* in foreign countries. **1969** J. FREDMAN *Fourth Agency* vi. 47 Appointed 1st Secretary Soviet Embassy, Washington. This post believed to be official 'Rezident' for direction of all illegals under G.R.U. tutelage in U.S.A.

‖ **rezidentsia** (rezide·ntsiă). Pl. **rezidentsii.** [Russ., in same sense.] = *RESIDENTURA.

1968 W. GARNER *Deep, Deep Freeze* xi. 130 A *rezidentsia* is a network of Soviet 'deep-cover' agents working in a foreign country. Its members..are known as Illegals. *Ibid.*, One country may have several independent and unrelated *rezidentsii*.

rezidentura, var. *RESIDENTURA. **rezina,** var. *RETSINA.

rezo·ne (rī-), *v.* [RE- 5 a.] *trans.* To assign (land, property, or people) to a new zone. Hence **rezo·ned** *ppl. a.*, **rezo·ning** *vbl. sb.*

1951 *Southern Reporter* 2nd Ser. LIII. 720 Chapter 17833..does not empower the Board of Adjustment to zone or rezone land located within Dade County but outside the boundaries of its municipalities. *Ibid.*, The action of the Board of Adjustment,..'was, in legal effect, the rezoning of said land by said Adjustment Board and is wholly void for want of jurisdiction in said Adjustment Board so to do.' **1961** *Guardian* 16 Jan. 6/3 On the opening of a new school our 8-year-old son was re-zoned to the new school. **1964** *Daily Tel.* 24 Jan. 23/7 (*heading*) Rezoned acres for houses. *Ibid.*, To curb office development London County Council is considering rezoning more than 54 acres, some already approved for offices. **1966** 'D. SHANNON' *With Vengeance* iii. 39 It had been a realtors' meeting: something to do with..a re-zoning matter. **1974** *Union* (S. Carolina) *Daily Times* 24 Apr. 1/3 The city council denied the request to rezone B-1 business districts to include the operation of retail liquor stores. **1976** *Time* 27 Sept. 55/2 In 1970 a rezoning brought black and white kids together in some school districts. **1978** *N.Y. Times* 30 Mar. B3/5 The Town Board in Harrison, N.Y., has voted unanimously to rezone 131 acres of land.

Rgveda, Rgvedic, varr. RIG-VEDA, *RIG-VEDIC *a.* (*sb.*)

1886–7 *Trans. Philol. Soc.* 658 Professor Max Müller says, on the metrical laws of the Rg Veda, 'The object of the Prātiçākhya is to register all the facts which possess a phonetic interest'. **1953** *Ibid.* *1952* 125 In the Ṛgveda..the paradigms of *devī* and *vṛkīḥ* are essentially distinct. **1962** J. GONDA (*title*) The aspectual function of the Rgvedic present and aorist. **1971** *Archivum Linguisticum* II. 112 Circumstances have changed since the admirable study by Gonda on the present and aorist aspects of the Rgveda. **1974** *Encycl. Brit. Macropædia* IX. 440/2 The Ṛgveda, Atharvaveda, and Sāmaveda are purely metrical texts mainly used by priests in their ritual. *Ibid.* 442/2 Ṛgvedic has forms with affixes *ya* and *tva* functioning as future passive participles.

rhababe, var. *REBAB. **rhabd:** see *RHABDUS 2.

rhabditid (ræ·bditid), *a.* and *sb.* *Zool.* [f. RHABDIT(IS + -ID[3].] **A.** *adj.* Belonging to the family Rhabditidæ of nematodes or the order or suborder Rhabditida (or Rhabditata) containing it, the members of which are characterized by a rhabditiform œsophagus. **B.** *sb.* A rhabditid nematode.

1930 E. C. FAUST *Human Helminthol.* 607/1 (Index), Rhabditid larvæ. **1933** *Jrnl. Washington Acad. Sci.* XXIII. 513 Male:..tail not extending beyond bursa; caudal papillae arranged as in the peloderan group of rhabditids. **1951** L. H. HYMAN *Invertebrates* III. xiii. 292 Rhabditid juveniles have repeatedly been found in terrestrial snails. **1962** J. D. SMYTH *Introd. Animal Parasitol.* xxv. 284 Subclass II. Phasmidia (= Secernentea)...Sub-order 3. Rhabditata (Rhabditids). Small transparent meromyarian worms. **1964** *Nematologica* X. 343 (*heading*) A xenic cultivation of two species of rhabditid nematodes on a commercial medium. **1980** *Parasitol.* LXXXI. II. p. lvii, Live rhabditid larvae were found contaminating the microfilarial cultures.

Rhabditis. Add: Also **rhabditis.** [Coined in Fr. by F. Dujardin in *Hist. nat. des Helminthes* (1845) 239.] Substitute for def.: A nematode worm of the genus so called (family Rhabditidæ), the members of which are found in soil, water, and decaying organic matter and in the larval stage are facultative parasites of mammals. (Further examples.)

1906 P. FALCKE tr. *Braun's Animal Parasites of Man* 276 In the papules [on a boy's skin] the observer found one or more rhabditis. **1967** P. A. MEGLITSCH *Invertebr. Zool.* viii. 278 (*caption*) Anatomy of *Rhabditis*, a typical nematode. **1971** A. F. BIRD *Structure of Nematodes* x. 235 Mapes..was unable to detect breakdown of food in the posterior bulb of *Rhabditis* and concluded that the principal role of the bulb flaps was a valvular rather than a crushing one.

b. *Comb.*, as **Rhabditis-form**, a form (of a nematode worm) characterized by a rhabditiform œsophagus; **Rhabditis-like** *a.* = RHABDITIFORM *a.* in Dict. and Suppl.

1886 W. E. HOYLE tr. *Leuckart's Parasites of Man* 96 Such is the case with..*Rhabdonema* (*Ascaris*) *nigrovenosum* .., whose *Rhabditis*-form, living in the excrement of frogs, differs very little from the animals related to it. **1897** PARKER & HASWELL *Text-bk. Zool.* I. vi. 287 The embryos [of the Nematode *Ascaris nigrovenosa*] pass from the lungs into the enteric canal of the host, are expelled with its fæces, and develop in water into a sexual Nematode, called the *Rhabditis*-form, in which the sexes are separate. **1906** P. FALCKE tr. *Braun's Animal Parasites of Man* 276 It must have belonged to the rhabditis-like larva of a Nematode.

rhabditiform (also **rhabdiform**) *a.*, also *spec.* having or being a short, thick œsophagus with a bulb at the proximal end and another medially, as in the free-living, non-parasitic larval stages of certain nematodes; (further examples).

1924 *Jrnl. Helminthol.* II. 58 The latter [*sc.* the œsophagus of *Rhabdias fuscovenosa*] has completely lost its rhabditiform shape and is now very narrow for the greater part of its length. **1951** L. H. HYMAN *Invertebrates* III. xiii. 304 The developing eggs pass into the host's buccal cavity and thence are swallowed into the digestive tract where they hatch into rhabdiform young, so called because of the rhabditoid form of their pharynx. **1969** A. M. DUNN *Vet. Helminthol.* I. 10/2 The oesophagus [in Nematoda]..differs in form according to the higher taxon to which the worm belongs... It may be filariform..; rhabditiform, with anterior and posterior swellings, in many free-living and plant-parasitic adult nematodes and..in the free pre-infective stages of the strongylates; bulb-shaped, [etc.]. **1973** T. C. CHENG *Gen. Parasitol.* xvii. 607/1 After molting, rhabditiform larvae become filariform larvae.

rhabditoid (ræ·bditoid), *a.* and *sb.* *Zool.* [f. RHABDIT(IS + -OID.] **A.** *adj.* **a.** = RHABDITIFORM *a.* in Dict. and Suppl. **b.** Belonging to the superfamily Rhabditoidea of nematodes. **B.** *sb.* A rhabditoid nematode.

1886 W. E. HOYLE tr. *Leuckart's Parasites of Man* 97 (*caption*) Rhabditoid form of *Rhabdonema* (*Ascaris*) *nigrovenosum*. **1932** BORRADAILE & POTTS *Invertebrata* viii. 221 The classical life history of *Ancyclostoma*... First larval form (rhabditoid) with a buccal cavity like *Rhabditis*. **1951** [see *RHABDIFORM *a.*]. **1961** E. R. & G. A. NOBLE *Parasitol.* xv. 719 Members of all four rhabditoid families occur in intimate relationship with soil-dwelling insects. **1962** J. D. SMYTH *Introd. Animal Parasitol.* xxv. 292 [Sub-order] Rhabditata. Usually possess the 'rhabditoid' type of pharynx. **1973** T. C. CHENG *Gen. Parasitol.* xvii. 593/1 In rhabditoids..the buccal capsule is divided into three sections.

rhabdo-. Add: **rhabdomere** (further examples); hence **rhabdome·ric** *a.*; **rhabdomyo·lysis** *Path.*, the pathological lysis of skeletal muscle; **rha:bdomyosarco·ma** *Path.*, a malignant neoplasm of skeletal muscle (malignant rhabdomyoma), or (but see quots. 1958, 1976) of embryonic tissue; **rha·bdosome,** † **-soma** *Palæont.* [Gr. σῶμα body], a colony of conjoined graptolites; **rha·bdovirus** *Biol.*, any of the group of RNA viruses that includes the rabies virus.

1932 BORRADAILE & POTTS *Invertebrata* x. 274 In the midst of each retinula is a vertical rod, known as the rhabdom, secreted by the cells of the sheaf in vertical sections which, when they are distinct, are known as rhabdomeres. **1974** *Nature* 29 Mar. 380/3 In the worker honey bee, ..eight photoreceptor cells..each contribute a wedge of microvilli (termed a rhabdomere). **1969** *Ibid.* 9 Aug. 641/1 No noticeable swelling of the rhabdomeric microvilli was observed during exposure to ultraviolet light. **1976** *Ibid.* 12 Aug. 626/2 The ultrastructure of invertebrate rhabdomeric visual cells have been studied. **1956** D. H. BOWDEN et al. in *Medicine* XXXV. 351 Biochemical and histological data have been obtained in three children with paroxysmal myohaemoglobinuria. These findings indicate that the recurrent symptom complex is the result of a pathological process in which striated muscle suddenly undergoes lysis. As a more satisfactory description of the disease, we propose that the condition be renamed acute recurrent rhabdomyolysis. **1963** *Amer. Jrnl. Med.* XXXIV. 554/1 Idiopathic recurrent rhabdomyolysis with myoglobinuria is a syndrome characterized by acute skeletal muscle weakness and pain associated with the passage of urine that is darkly pigmented owing to myoglobin. **1976** *Lancet* 18 Dec. 1343/1 Rhabdomyolysis is usually caused by serious muscle trauma (crush injuries), electric shock, arterial occlusion, or toxins (drugs, sea-snake bite). **1898** T. N. KELYNACK *Renal Growths* xi. 104 (*caption*) Rhabdo-myo-sarcoma of left kidney. **1940** PACK & ANGLEM in H. W. Dargeon *Cancer in Childhood* 95 The recurrent rhabdomyosarcomas, the diffusely invasive sarcomas of striated muscle and those which are so deeply adherent that a local excision is not feasible, are best treated by amputation. **1958** *Trans. Ophthalm. Soc.* LXXVIII. 96 The exact cytological classification may eventually prove to be important from the prognostic and therapeutic point of view, so that the term rhabdomyosarcoma should not be applied unless striations have been demonstrated unequivocally. **1974** J. R. WILBUR et al. in *Neoplasia of Head & Neck* 281 Rhabdomyosarcoma is the most common soft tissue sarcoma in children. **1976** *Proc. R. Soc. Med.* LXIX. 897/1 It has been suggested (Ashton 1958) that all such tumours should be regarded as embryonal sarcomas because of their origin from undifferentiated foci of mesenchymal cells, and that the term 'rhabdomyosarcoma' should be applied only when there is evidence of longitudinal and cross-striations in the tumour cells, an indication perhaps of some degree of differentiation. **1893** *Lunds Univ. Årsskrift* XXIX. XII. 1, I have prepared.. a series of longitudinal and transverse sections through the rhabdosoma of several species. **1910** *Encycl. Brit.* XII. 366/2 It is the general practice of palæontologists to regard each graptolite polypary (rhabdosome) developed from a single sicula as an individual of the highest order. **1935** TWENHOFEL & SHROCK *Invertebr. Paleontol.* iv. 90 The *Dendroidea* include graptolites with fan-shaped rhabdosomes composed of branches or stems joined together into a trellis-like framework by means of transverse bars. **1966** *McGraw-Hill Encycl. Sci. & Technol.* VI. 259/2 The Ordovician graptoloids have been subdivided into a large number of genera, based mainly on the branching and form of rhabdosome. [**1965** *Ann. Inst. Pasteur* CIX. 633 The viruses possessing RNA, helical symmetry and a naked nucleocapsid, the order of *Rhabdovirales* is subdivided into two suborders according to the rigidity or flexibility of the virion.] **1966** *Progress Med. Virol.* VIII. 404 Rhabdovirus group. This group was recently proposed to include members whose structure is rod-shaped but is more like a bullet, flat at one end and rounded at the other. **1976** *Jrnl. Gen. Virol.* XXXII. 369 Rhabdoviruses infecting plant and vertebrate cells differ in their morphology.

rhabdom. (Further example).

1977 *Sci. Amer.* July 108/2 A compound eye is made up of ommatidia: tiny individual eyes that point in different directions. Each ommatidium consists of a lens that focuses light on several receptor cells sharing the common light-sensitive organ known as a rhabdom.

rhabdomancer. (Later examples.)

1944 S. PUTNAM tr. *E. da Cunha's Rebellion in Backlands* v. 237 Skilled rhabdomancers capable of indicating with their mysterious wands the exact spot where a stream of water might be found. **1971** *Daily Tel.* 17 Aug. 8/1 Their predictions have no more validity..than the predictions of crystal-gazers, rhabdomancers, oömancers and observers of the flights of birds. **1976** *Worcester* (Mass.) *Telegram* 10 Sept. 7/1 This one is for *Rhabdomancers*. Among the other things dowsers are called [are] water witches, water diviners, water finders.

rhabdomancy. (Later example.)

1976 *Worcester* (Mass.) *Telegram* 10 Sept. 7/1 The formal term for dowsing is *rhabdomancy*. In Arkansas—but probably not in Danville, Vt.—..it is also known as witch-wiggling.

Rhabdopleura (ræbdǫplū̆ə·ră). *Zool.* [mod. L., f. RHABDO- + Gr. πλευρά rib, side.] A member of the genus of protochordates so called, belonging to the class Pterobranchia and having two tentacle-bearing arms.

[**1869** G. J. ALLMAN in *Q. Jrnl. Microsc. Sci.* IX. 58 The remarkable polyzoon for which the genus *Rhabdopleura* has been constituted is eminently distinguished by the presence within its cœnœcium of a rigid chitinous rod.] **1885** *Encycl. Brit.* XIX. 435/1 The dwelling of Rhabdopleura is a branched system of annulated tubes of a delicate membranous consistency, each tube corresponding to a single polypide. **1955** [see *CEPHALODISCUS].

rhabdus. Add: **2.** Also anglicized as **rhabd** (ræbd).

1940 [see *DIACTINE *a.*].

rhachi(o)-: see also *RACHI-, RACHIO- and related main entries in Suppl.

Rhætian, *a.* and *sb.* Add: Also **Ræetian.** Substitute for def.: **A.** *sb.* **a.** A native or inhabitant of Rhætia or the Rhætian Alps in eastern Switzerland. **b.** The name of either of two languages (*a*) = RHÆTO-ROMANIC *sb.*; (*b*) = *RHÆTIC *sb.* (Earlier and further examples.)

1600 HOLLAND tr. *Livy's Romane Hist.* v. 202 And doubtlesse, the nations about the Alpes, especially the Rhetians, had their beginning thus. **1607** TOPSELL *Four-f. Beasts* 33 The Italians call a Badger Tasso, the Rhetians, Tasch. *Ibid.* 40 The herbe Wolfbanie..is poison to Foxes..as the Alpine Rhætians affirme. **1867** *Chambers's Encycl.* IX. 246/1 A third Teutonic people, the Goths, entered the country of the Rhætians, which nearly corresponded with the Grisons. **1933** L. BLOOMFIELD *Language* iv. 64 The inscriptions in ancient Rhaetian show this language to have been an off-shoot of Etruscan. **1939** L. H. GRAY *Foundations of Lang.* xii. 384 The Raetian of Italy has also been regarded as akin [to Etruscan]. **1970** *Times Lit. Suppl.* 8 Jan. 40/2 The five national tongues—French, Spanish, Portuguese, Italian and Rumanian—and..their five regional varieties—Occitanian or Provençal..Catalan..Dalmatian..Romansch or Rhaetian (now strictly West Rhaetian, for that alone has evolved a recognized written language), and Sardinian. **1972** W. B. LOCKWOOD *Panorama Indo-European Lang.* iii. 23 The sphere of Latin..embraced the Alpine area, where it replaced Rhaetian, a language of unknown affinities attested in a handful of inscriptions.

B. *adj.* **1.** Of or pertaining to Rhætia or the Rhætian Alps.

1618 H. WOTTON *Let.* in L. P. Smith *Life & Lett. Sir H. Wotton* (1907) II. 149 At the next general assembly of the Rhætian communities. **1880–1** [in Dict.]. **1888** *Encycl. Brit.* XXIV. 45/2 Bormio and Valtellina were annexed..in 1815 (despite the remonstrances of the Rhætian leagues) to the kingdom of Lombardo-Venetia.

2. *Geol.* Of, pertaining to, or designating the highest (youngest) of the three stages constituting the Upper Triassic in Europe. Also *absol.*

1955 G. G. WOODFORD tr. *Gignoux's Stratigraphic Geol.* vii. 324 This Swabian facies of the Rhaetian is found everywhere in Europe outside of the Alpine domain. **1959** WELLS & KIRKALDY *Outl. Hist. Geol.* (ed. 4) xv. 232 Ammonite specialists..recognise a Rhaetian Stage as the topmost stage of the Triassic System. **1966** D. T. DONOVAN *Stratigraphy* viii. 178 In 1864 E. Renevier proposed the Rhaetian Stage for the Rhaetic Formation. *Ibid.*, It is difficult to decide whether the Rhaetian fauna as a whole is more like that of the Trias or the Lias. **1969** *Proc. Geol. Soc.* Aug. 154 The use of *Rhaetian*, not Rhaetic, as the name for the latest Triassic age/standard stage is supported. It has been agreed (by the Stratigraphy Committee) to retire the word 'Rhaetic'.

Rhætic, *a.* Add: Also (as *sb.*), the epoch during which the strata were deposited. (Further examples.)

The Rhætic beds lie between the Keuper series of the Upper Triassic and the Liassic of the Lower Jurassic. They have been assigned variously to the Triassic and (esp. in Britain) to the Jurassic, and also to form a separate system between the two; they are now regarded as forming a series of the Triassic.

1904 [see *NON-SEQUENCE]. **1909** [see *OPHIOLITIC *a.*]. **1948** R. L. SHERLOCK *Permo-Triassic Formations* II. 244 Since most of the vulcanism took place in the Rhaetic, which we regard as Jurassic, it need not be described here, but the fact has an important bearing on the correlation of Gondwana Strata. **1963** [see next]. **1969** BENNISON & WRIGHT *Geol. Hist. Brit. Isles* xii. 279 The Rhaetic Beds, not exceeding 100 feet thick..,are important as a datum of reference at the top of the Triassic and can be presumed to be approximately contemporaneous throughout the outcrop. **1971** B. W. SPARKS *Rocks & Relief* x. 334 In the Alps of eastern Switzerland, ammonites found in the Rhaetic are more closely related to Triassic than to Jurassic forms. **1980** *Daily Tel.* 7 Apr. 8/8 Derived fossils from the Avon gravels are also among the gift with vertebrate remains from the Rhaetic Bone Bed at Aust Cliff including 34 teeth of the lung fish.

B. *sb.* Also **Ræetic.** An ancient language of the Rhætian Alps and the area to the south of them. Also as *adj.*

1933 J. WHATMOUGH in R. S. Conway et al. *Prae-Italic Dial. Italy* II. 4 Arrian (*Tact.* 44) distinguishes explicitly between Raetic spoken by the Raeti, and Keltic spoken by the Kelts, as late as the time of Hadrian. **1939** L. H. GRAY *Foundations of Lang.* xi. 332 It is generally agreed that it [*sc.* Illyrian]..was connected with at least two ancient Italic dialects: Venetic..and Messapic..and to these we may perhaps add Raetic, with some sixty fragments. **1948** D. DIRINGER *Alphabet* II. ix. 501 The Raetic and other Alpine alphabets. **1952** *Archivum Linguisticum* IV. 87 Rhetic and Pyrenean scholars. **1974** R. A. HALL *External Hist. Romance Langs.* iii. 51 Among those [pre-Italic dialects of Italy] commonly considered to be Indo-European..are..Rhaetic, in the Alps north of present-day Venetia, Lombardy, and Piedmont, and perhaps in the Po valley before the coming of the Etruscans..and of the Gauls. **1977** *Canad. Jrnl. Linguistics* Spring 31 The Early Italic dialects of Celtic, Ligurian, Lepontic, Raetic, and Venetic.

Rhæ:to-Etru·scan. [f. *Rhæto-* (see RHÆTO-ROMANIC *a.* and *sb.*) + ETRUSCAN *a.* and *sb.*] A hypothetical ancient language group.

1939 E. PROKOSCH *Compar. Gmc. Gram.* 55 Celtic, Finnic, Rhaeto-Etruscan.

Rhæ:to-Lia·ssic, *a.* *Geol.* [f. as prec. + LIASSIC *a.*] Of or pertaining to the Rhætic and Liassic series or the geological epochs during which they were deposited. Also **Rhæ:tic-Lia·ssic** *a.*

1963 D. W. & E. E. HUMPHRIES tr. *Termier's Erosion & Sedimentation* xviii. 357 The Rhaetic-Liassic Basin of Northwest Scania, Sweden, which is of paralic type, has been partly supplied by rivers, and partly by the sea. It provides an example of rhythmic sedimentation comprising at least twelve cycles in the Rhaetic and the Hettangian. **1965** *Senckenbergiana Lethaea* XLVI. 127 (*heading*) Rhaeto-Liassic plant microfossils from the Leigh Creek coal measures, South Australia. **1970** B. E. BALME in B. Kummel *Stratigraphic Boundary Probl.* 387/1 Species of *Falcisporites* ..are typically Triassic in Australia and are especially abundant in coals and other sediments of Middle to Late Triassic, and Rhaeto-Liassic age.

Rhæ:to-Ro·man, *a.* and *sb.* Also **Rhe-.** [Back-formation on RHÆTO-ROMANIC *a.* and *sb.* after *Roman.*] **A.** *adj.* = RHÆTO-ROMANIC *a.* **B.** *sb.* A speaker of Rhæto-Romanic.

1931 *Times Educ. Suppl.* 15 Aug. 320/4 The University of Geneva is creating a professorship in rheto-roman languages. **1933** C. D. BUCK *Compar. Gram. Gk. & Lat.* 29 The Rhaeto-Roman dialects in parts of present Switzerland and northeastern Italy are a series of numerous dialects which cannot be reckoned as either French or Italian dialects, and of which some are used locally as written languages, as Romansh, Upper and Lower Engadine, Ladin, Friulian. **1942** K. W. DEUTSCH in J. A. Fishman *Readings Sociol. of Lang.* (1968) 601 Rheto-Romans found their ancient language introduced on a basis of full equality into the administration of Switzerland.

Rhaeto-Romance. Also **Rae-.** (In Dict. s.v. RHÆTO-ROMANIC *a.* and *sb.*) (Earlier and later examples.)

Now the more usual term.

1877 [see *LADIN]. **1934** WEBSTER, Rhaeto-Romance languages. **1937** J. ORR tr. *Iordan's Introd. Romance Linguistics* i. 11 The dialects of the Rheto-Romance area. **1941** M. E. MAXFIELD in *Studies in Romance Lang. & Lit.* (Univ. N. Carolina) II. 1 (*title*) Raeto-Romance bibliography. **1952** *Archivum Linguisticum* IV. 87 Rheto-Romance *agör*. **1969** G. PRICE *Present Position Minority Lang. W. Europe* 9 Romansh—otherwise known as Raeto-Romance; it is no part of our concern to discuss whether or not the various Romansh dialects of the Swiss canton of the Grisons (Graubünden), the non-Italian Romance dialects of the Dolomite valleys (known as Ladin) and Friulan (spoken in north-east Italy) are rightly considered to be forms of the same language. **1976** *Language* LII. 703 Rohlfs' latest publication..represents an excellent introduction to the history of Rhaeto-Romance. **1977** C. F. & F. M. VOEGELIN *Classification & Index World's Lang.* 298 Rhaeto-Romance = Raeto-Romance = Rheto-Romance = Ladin = Rhaetian.

Rhages (rā·dʒiz). The name of a city in Persia (now Rayy in Iran, near Tehran), used *attrib.* to designate a type of pottery made there from the eleventh to the thirteenth centuries, characterized by polychrome enamelling.

1909 G. C. PIER *Pottery of Near East* v. 81 The Rhages lustre ware is well illustrated by the superb vase. **1925** B. RACKHAM tr. *E. Hannover's Pott. & Porc.* I. ii. 65 The greatest possible caution is..required in the case of the most expensive of all the Rhages wares, those with a wealth of figures and colours in the decoration. **1935** A. CHRISTIE *Death in Clouds* xi. 117 There was a good deal of Rhages ware and other Persian pottery. **1957** *Encycl. Brit.* XVIII. 371/2 The designs on this Rhages enamelled ware are pencilled with miniature-like fineness recalling..the beautiful workmanship in the manuscript illuminations of the early 13th century. **1974** SAVAGE & NEWMAN *Illustr. Dict. Ceramics* 240 Rayy (*Rhages*) ware, a type of Persian pottery made at Rayy, near Teheran, *c.* 1037–1256. The body is medium-hard and coarse. Many pieces have a blue ground, and the backs of some dishes have a deep-blue glaze.

rhamnose (ræ·mnōᵘz). *Chem.* [a. G. *rhamnose* (Raýman & Kruis 1887: see *Chem. Centralblatt* (1888) XIX. 6): see RHAMNUS and -OSE[2].] A methyl pentose sugar with reducing properties which occurs widely in nature, esp. combined as glycosides in berries of the buckthorn and other shrubs of the genus *Rhamnus.*

1888 *Jrnl. Chem. Soc.* LIV. 667 As the analogy of the sugar $C_6H_{12}O_5$ to the dextrose series is brought into prominence, the authors propose to call it *rhamnose*, because it also appears to be identical with the sugar obtained by Liebermann from Rhamnus. **1888, 1890** [in Dict. s.v. RHAMNETIN]. **1931** E. C. MILLER *Plant Physiol.* viii. 408 Rhamnose, $CH_3C_5H_9O_5$, is a pentose in which one atom of hydrogen has been replaced by a methyl group. **1970** R. W. MCGILVERY *Biochem.* xxiv. 585 Glycoproteins commonly contain residues of L-fucose..and some have residues of L-rhamnose (6-deoxy-L-mannose)... The mammalian nucleotide carrier of rhamnose is not known for certain.

Hence **rha·mnoside,** a glycoside in which rhamnose is the sugar.

1904 *Jrnl. Chem. Soc.* LXXXVI. I. 681 Rhamnosides. **1907** *Chem. Abstr.* I. 83 Violaquercetrin of *Viola tricolor* is identical with rhamnoside of buckwheat. **1959** *New Biol.* XXIX. 35 A substance having some characteristics of a sugar and provisionally called a 'rhamnoside', has been found in water from the Gulf of Mexico in concentrations of up to 50 milligrams per litre.

rhamphotheca (ræmfoþī·kă). *Ornith.* [mod. L. (J. C. W. Illiger *Prodromus Systematis Mammalium et Avium* (1811) 150), f. Gr. ῥάμφος beak + θήκη sheath.] The modified integument, usu. horny but in some birds leathery, that covers the jaws and forms the bill.

1870 BAIRD & COOPER *Ornithol.* I. 567 *Ramphotheca* [indexed as *rhamphotheca*], the horny covering, or sheath of the jaws. **1890** [see *gnathotheca* s.v. *GNATHO-]. **1972** P. STETTENHEIM in D. S. Farner et al. *Avian Biol.* II. i. 45 In ptarmigans (*Lagopus* spp.) and certain other grouse (*Tetrao* spp.), the rhamphotheca is shed intact after the breeding season.

rhapidosome (ræ·pidosōᵘm). *Microbiology.* [f. Gr. ῥαπίς, ῥαπιδ- rod + -O + *-SOME[4].] A small rod-shaped body, frequent in bacteria of certain species.

1963 R. A. LEWIN in *Nature* 6 Apr. 104/1 It is proposed that for the present these rod-shaped particles be called 'rhapidosomes'. **1967** *Jrnl. Bacteriol.* XCIV. 1755/1 It is not likely that the rhapidosomes of *Pseudomonas*, *Proteus*, and *Photobacterium* are either phage or parts of phage since similar structures have been seen in every strain examined. *Ibid.* 1755/2 The function of these rhapidosomes is unknown, but..they may be involved as anchorage for the nucleoplasm and may serve as an axis around which rotation occurs during replication. **1972** *Nature* 24 Mar. 144/3 Rhapidosomes are in essence two overlapping hollow cylinders... The two components are made of distinct protein subunits and there is no nucleic acid associated with the rhapidosome. **1977** *Canad. Jrnl. Microbiol.* XXIII. 1604/1 Rhapidosomes resemble bacteriophage tails.., but are often found alone, with no phage heads, coats, or other phage-like appendages.

rhapsodizing, *ppl. a.* (Earlier example.)

1814 JANE AUSTEN *Mansf. Park* II. iv. 76 You will think me rhapsodizing.

rha·psody, *v.* [f. the sb.] **1.** = RHAPSODIZE *v.* 2.

1822 *Blackw. Mag.* Aug. 231/2 A conclusion, in which Sidney heartily joined, rhapsodying—'O Paris, fatal was the hour!' [etc.].

2. = RHAPSODIZE *v.* 3.

1899 *Westm. Gaz.* 13 June 2/3 Miss Jane H. Oakley..rhapsodies this morning on 'Our Guns'. **1909** W. J. LOCKE *Septimus* xxi. 321 His face beamed as it had beamed in the days when he had rhapsodied over the vision of an earth one scab to be healed by Sypher's Cure.

rhasophore, var. *RASOPHORE.

rhe (rē¹). *Physics.* [ad. Gr. ῥέ-ος stream.] A unit of dynamic fluidity, defined variously as the reciprocal poise or the reciprocal centipoise (see quots.); also, a unit of kinematic fluidity, equal to the reciprocal centistokes.

1928 BINGHAM & THOMPSON in *Jrnl. Amer. Chem. Soc.* L. 2879 The fluidity at 20° of a saturated solution of copper was 63·9 rhes. [*Note*] Reciprocal *poises*. **1933** *Physics* IV. 207/2 All the alcohols have a positive association as expected, and it is appreciably higher at a fluidity of 10 rhes than at 50 rhes. *Ibid.* 388 (*caption*) Fluidity data of organic compounds in rhes at regular intervals of temperature. **1958** *Van Nostrand's Sci. Encycl.* (ed. 3) 1417/2 *Rhe*, the absolute unit by which fluidity is measured or expressed. It is the reciprocal centipoise. **1961** *Handbk. Chem. & Physics* (ed. 43) 3151 *Fluidity*, the reciprocal of viscosity. The cgs unit is the rhe, the reciprocal of the poise. **1974** *McGraw-Hill Dict. Sci. & Techn. Terms* 1261/1 *Rhe.* 1. A unit of dynamical fluidity, equal to the dynamical fluidity of a fluid whose dynamic viscosity is 1 centipoise. 2. A unit of kinematic fluidity, equal to the kinematic fluidity of a fluid whose kinematic viscosity is 1 centistoke [*sic*].

Rhea, Rea (rī·ă). Jocular aphetic form of DIARRHŒA, GONORRHŒA, etc.

1935 M. B. CAREY *Mademoiselle from Armentieres* II. 65 Oh, the Rea sisters came to Brest, Parlez-vous, Leucor, Gonor and all the rest. **1971** *Coming, Dear!* 29 And now that famous rendition of *I got it bad and that ain't good* by the famous Rhea sisters Pya, Dia and Gonna.

rhe(e)bok, -buck. (Further examples.)

1834 A. SMITH *Jrnl.* 14 Nov. (1939) I. 137 Saw the common rheebok. **1839** W. C. HARRIS *Wild Sports S. Afr.* 384 *Redunca Capreolus.* The Rhee Buck. Rhee-bok of the Cape Colonists. **1862** J. S. DOBIE *Jrnl.* 10 Sept. in *S. Afr. Jrnl.* (1945) 23 Saw both oribi and rhebuck, the former very pretty animals. **1889** H. A. BRYDEN *Kloof & Kerroo* xvi. 297 The Voal or Grey Rhebock..is..plentiful on most of the mountain ranges. **1910** J. BUCHAN *Prester John* xiv. 230 There were droves of smaller game—rhebok and springbok and duikers. **1950** *Cape Argus* 17 July 4/4 Two dainty rhebuck stood and gazed at us. **1958** L. VAN DER POST *Lost World of Kalahari* v. 91 Barely fifty feet from me five rhee-buck got up from their warm beds behind a ledge of rock. **1959** *Encounter* Sept. 53 These mountains of up-pointed spears Hold eland, oribi and rhebok.

rheid (rī·id), *sb.* and *a.* [f. Gr. ῥέ-ειν to flow + *-id*, after *liquid.*] **A.** *sb.* A substance which undergoes viscous flow when at a temperature below its melting point.

1954 S. W. CAREY in *Jrnl. Geol. Soc. Australia* I. 70 The substance deforms as a fluid. In order to distinguish it from a liquid (seeing that it is below its melting point)..such a substance is here named a rheid. **1963** TURNER & WEISS *Struct. Anal. Metamorphic Tectonites* viii. 321 We still have no knowledge of the threshold conditions beyond which rocks such as granite and schist..can be regarded as rheids.

B. *adj.* Characteristic of a rheid; that is a rheid.

1954 *Jrnl. Geol. Soc. Australia* I. 83 There are..numbers of empirical observations of solid intrusion of serpentine by rheid flow. **1962** L. C. KING *Morphol. Earth* iv. 123 The long period over which the Jura folding has been accomplished, from Oligocene to late-Pliocene time, favours the idea of slow, rheid creep in the basement. **1965** A. HOLMES *Princ. Physical Geol.* (ed. 2) ix. 204 While ice or any other solid body in a rheid state is slowly flowing, the deformation stress may temporarily increase to a point where the material is compelled to fracture, if only momentarily. **1972** J. G. DENNIS *Structural Geol.* v. 102 A material is rheid by virtue of the time of observation. Rocks are not rheid in a quarry operation, but they are so during geological deformation.

Hence **rhei·dity**, the phenomenon of rheid behaviour; also, a measure of the rheid behaviour of a substance, equal to the time required for the viscous deformation to become one thousand times as great as the elastic deformation.

1954 S. W. CAREY in *Jrnl. Geol. Soc. Australia* I. 70 Duration..to allow the viscous term to become a thousand times as great as the elastic term... This may be adopted arbitrarily as the threshold of wholly fluid behaviour and will be referred to as the rheidity of the substance for the given conditions. **1965** A. HOLMES *Princ. Physical Geol.* (ed. 2) x. 238 The rheidity of salt is..about 10^8 to 10^9 seconds..i.e. between 3 and 30 years. *Ibid.* xi. 282 Fifty years ago little or nothing was known of the phenomena of rheidity and diapirism.

Rheingold (rəi·ngōᵘld). [Ger., lit. 'gold of the Rhine', name of an opera by Wagner.] An express train that runs between Amsterdam and Basle, along the course of the Rhine. Also *attrib.*

1935 C. WINCHESTER *Railway Wonders of World* I. 492/3 The 'Rheingold' express is one of the most famous of European Pullman trains. It runs between the Hook of Holland and Basle. *Ibid.* 583/1 The 'Rheingold' is among the..most comfortable trains on the Continent. **1955** H. NICOLSON *Diary* 25 Jan. (1968) 274 It is cold and dark when the steamer reaches Rotterdam... The Rheingold express is hot and comfortable. **1968** R. SAWKINS *Snow along Border* ii. 6 You can catch the Rheingold—it's a marvellous train, one of the Trans-Europe expresses. **1969** *Sat. Rev.* (U.S.) 4 Jan. 48/2 To make a railroad voyage in like style today, an American must journey overseas. In Germany he rides the *Rheingold*; in France, the *Mistral.* **1973** *Guardian* 17 Mar. 14/5 The 'Rheingold' from Basle to Amsterdam..has a vista-dome observation car.

rhema: see *RHEME.

rhematic, *a.* Add: **2.** Of or pertaining to a *RHEME.

1959 J. FIRBAS in *Brno Studies in English* I. 39 The thematic elements are less important..than the rhematic elements. **1969** K. H. WAGNER *Generative Gram. Studies Old Eng. Lang.* i. 49 Although there can be no definite proof, it is to be assumed that the rhematic constituent carries the primary stress. **1977** J. LYONS *Semantics* II. xii. 507 There is a very high correlation..between occupying initial position and being thematic, rather than rhematic.

rhe·matize, *v. Linguistics.* [f. *RHEMAT(IC *a.* + -IZE.] *trans.* To advance (a non-verbal term) to the status of a separate rheme. Hence **rhematiza·tion**; **rhe·matizing** *ppl. a.*

1959 J. FIRBAS in *Brno Studies in English* I. 43 Rhematic elements..communicatively strengthen basically thematic positions if they occur in them; they..'dynamize' them, rendering them transitional or 'rhematizing' them. *Ibid.* 51 Sentences that contain special rhematizing means of FSP [Functional Sentence Perspective]. **1969** K. H. WAGNER *Generative Gram. Studies Old Eng. Lang.* i. 49 The rheme is placed immediately before the verb just in case there is a non-verbal constituent which can undergo rhematization. *Ibid.* 50 Generally speaking only previously mentioned constituents can be thematized, and only non-mentioned ones can be rhematized.

rheme (rīm). *Logic* and *Linguistics.* Also **rhema.** Pl. **rhemas, -ata** (*rare*), **rhemes.** [ad. Gr. ῥῆμα, -ατος that which is said, word, saying.] That part of a proposition or sentence which expresses a single idea. Specialized use in current linguistics: that part of a sentence giving new information about the theme. Cf. *MONORHEME, *RHETIC *a.*

1892 C. S. PEIRCE in *Open Court* VI. 3417/1 A rhema is closely analogous to a chemical atom or radicle with unsaturated bonds. A non-relative rhema is like a univalent radicle; it has but one unsaturated bond. A relative rhema is like a multivalent radicle. *Ibid.*, Two non-relative rhemas being joined give a complete proposition. *Ibid.* 3417/2 It follows that if we find three distinct and irreducible forms of rhemata, the ideas of these should be the three elementary conceptions of metaphysics. **1897** J. P. POSTGATE in *Fortn. Rev.* Sept. 428, I propose..to call the expression of a single idea or notion a *rheme* from ῥῆμα, 'a thing said' and to distinguish the expressions of qualifications and connections of such *rhemes* by calling them *epirrhemes* though, as a general term, *rheme* may serve for both. *c* **1903** C. S. PEIRCE in *Coll. Papers* (1932) II. II. ii. 144 A *Rheme* is a sign which, for its Interpretant, is a Sign of qualitative Possibility, that is, is understood as representing such and such a kind of possible Object. **1955** [see *PHEME]. **1959** J. FIRBAS in *Brno Studies in English* I. 39 Those sentence elements which convey something that is known, or may be inferred, from the verbal or from the situational context..are to be regarded as the communicative basis, as the theme of the sentence. On the other hand, those sentence elements which convey the new piece of information are to be regarded as the communicative nucleus, as the rheme of the sentence. **1972** J. VACHEK in V. Fried *Prague Sch. Linguistics* i. 19 The other part, now usually called the rheme, contains the essential information transmitted by the given sentence-utterance and so substantially enriches the listener's knowledge. **1976** *Archivum Linguisticum* VII. 130 He points out that the distinction between old and new information has been recognized as the dichotomy of 'theme' and 'rheme' in the Prague school of linguistics, and under the terms 'topic' and 'comment' in recent times. **1976** GEACH & KENNY *Prior's Doctrine of Propositions & Terms* 88 Predicates thus conceived as propositions with their subjects left out he called 'rhemes', from the Greek for 'verb'. More often he excepts proper names and especially demonstrative pronouns, i.e. the kinds of 'terms' which may fill the blanks in 'rhemes' but which are not 'rhemes' themselves.

† **Rhénan** (renaṅ), *a. Geol. Obs.* Also **Rhenan(e).** [a. F. *Rhénan* Rhenish, ad. L. *Rhēnanus*, f. *Rhēnus*, the river Rhine.] The name given by A. Dumont (*Bull. de l'Acad. R. de Belg.* (1848) XV. 684) to an independent *terrain* ('system') of the Palaeozoic found in the Rhineland (see quot. 1853[1]), identified by later writers with the Lower Devonian or the Siegenian and Emsian stages; of or pertaining to that series or those stages. Also *absol.*

1853 *Q. Jrnl. Geol. Soc.* IX. 24 [The *Terrain Rhénan* of M. Dumont comprises three divisions, of which the lowest or *Système gedinnien* appears to belong to the top of the Silurian system. The two upper divisions, called *Ahrien* and *Coblenzien*, which are consequently intermediate between the Old Red Sandstone and the Silurian system, have not yet been recognized in England.] *Ibid.* 25 The red sandstones are not naturally the base of the Eifel series, but rather the top of the Rhenane series. *Ibid.*, The 'Gedinnian system' must be entirely separated from the Rhenane series, with which..it has no organic remains in common. **1895** J. D. DANA *Man. Geol.* (ed. 4) 626 The Lower, Middle, and Upper divisions [of the Devonian] are named (1) the Rhénan, (2) the Eifelian, and (3) the Famennian. *Ibid.* 627 In the Eifel, the three divisions, the Rhénan, Eifelian and Famennian are well developed. **1931** GREGORY & BARRETT *Gen. Stratigraphy* 250 (*table*) Rhenan.

rhenate (rī·nēⁱt). *Chem.* [f. *RHEN(IUM + -ATE[4].] A salt of the anion ReO_4^{-2}. So **rhe·nic acid,** H_2ReO_4, the parent acid of these salts, which is unstable and is known only in solution.

1929 *Chem. Abstr.* XXIII. 1833 A soln. of black ReO_2 in dil. HNO_3 gives a yellow-red coloration, yellow with NaOH, from which $Ca(OH)_2$ or $Ba(OH)_2$ ppts. bright yellow salts, rhenates, stable only in alk. soln. **1932** J. W. MELLOR *Comprehensive Treat. Inorg. Chem.* XII. lxv. 478 The yellow product in all these cases is either an acidic soln. of rhenic acid, H_2ReO_4, or a salt of that acid, namely the rhenates, $R^1_2ReO_4$. **1950** N. V. SIDGWICK *Chem. Elements* II. 1292 Rhenium trioxide is formally the anhydride of rhenic acid H_2ReO_4, the salts of which can be obtained in solution. **1962** J. E. FERGUSSON et al. in B. W. Gonser *Rhenium* 38 Of the complex compounds of Re^{VI}, the green rhenate $BaReO_4$ has been prepared as mixed crystals with $BaSO_4$. **1973** R. D. PEACOCK in J. C. Bailar et al. *Comprehensive Inorg. Chem.* xxxix. 940 Concentrated alkali induces dismutation to perrhenate and dioxide, so that it is not possible to prepare rhenates(VI) in aqueous solution—alkali fusion in the absence of air is necessary.

Rhenish, *a.* and *sb.* Add: **A.** *adj.* **1. a.** Also, in Archæology, used to designate a type of pottery made in the Rhineland in the Roman period.

1954 M. WHEELER *Rome beyond Imperial Frontiers* (1955) I. iv. 48 One was a black-glazed Rhenish beaker of familiar late type. **1955** I. A. RICHMOND *Roman Brit.* iv. 177 Production of Samian ware was brought to an end by the invasion of Gaul in the later third century... The gap was filled by..an increasing volume of imports of Rhenish glass-ware and Rhenish glazed pottery decorated with white slip. *Ibid.* 179 Rhenish pottery..comprises jugs, beakers, and vases. The fabric is thin, with a highly-polished dark colour coating, usually ornamented in simple running scrolls or medallions in white slip. **1957** *Archaeologia Æliana* XXXV. 187 (*heading*) Narrow-mouthed beakers in Rhenish ware. **1964** G. WEBSTER *Romano-British Coarse Pottery* (Council for Brit. Archaeol. Research Rep. No. 6) 7 *Rhenish ware*, pottery from the Rhineland imported into Britain during the late second century and later.

2. *Rhenish wine* (later example).

1972 *Guardian* 30 Nov. 15/4 Of the rich Rhenish wines, the Alsatian Traminer and Gewurztraminer are becoming popular.

3. *Rhenish stoneware*, stoneware manufactured in the Rhineland, usually salt-glazed.

1925 B. RACKHAM tr. *E. Hannover's Pott. & Porc.* I. iii. 197 The manufacture of stoneware [in Germany] was confined to certain districts; its centre was for centuries the Rhineland from Coblenz to Cologne. Its present designation 'Rhenish stoneware' is, however, of comparatively recent date. **1974** SAVAGE & NEWMAN *Illustr. Dict. Ceramics* 245 *Rhenish stoneware*, saltglazed stoneware made in the Rhineland from the latter part of the Middle Ages, but principally in the 16th and 17th centuries, at a number of centres, the largest of which was Cologne. It was exported in great quantities at the time, and imitated extensively in the 19th century. It is especially noted for relief work.

4. *Rhenish fan*, a fan-shaped bundle of isoglosses in the Rhine valley, separating Low from High German.

1933 L. BLOOMFIELD *Language* xix. 343 Some forty kilometers east of the Rhine the isoglosses of the great bundle that separates Low German and High German begin to separate and spread out northwestward and southwestward, so as to form what has been called the 'Rhenish fan'. **1961** R. E. KELLER *German Dialects* 249 The Rhenish Fan..was seen as the result of a linguistic thrust from south to north along the River Rhine. **1977** *Word 1972* XXVIII. 233 The 'Rhenish fan' has its counterpart in the isoglottic bundles separating North and South Wales.

B. *sb.* (Later examples.)

1922 JOYCE *Ulysses* 331 What say you, good masters, to..a medlar tansy and a flagon of old Rhenish? **1970** M. KELLY *Spinifex* i. 24 Letting the chilled Rhenish dissolve a hard, nervy lump inside.

rhenium (rī·niŏm). *Chem.* [mod.L., coined in Ger. (W. Noddack et al. 1925, in *Sitzungsber. d. Preuss. Akad. d. Wissensch.* 409), f. *Rhēn-us*, L. form of the name of the river Rhine: see -IUM.] A very dense, refractory, rare metallic element belonging to the manganese group, resembling platinum in appearance, and obtained in small quantities from molybdenite ores. Symbol Re; atomic number 75.

1925 [see *MASURIUM]. **1938** R. W. LAWSON tr. *Hevesy & Paneth's Man. Radioactivity* (ed. 2) xvi. 160 In the case of the element 75 (rhenium), the regularities in the periodic classification..allowed definite predictions on the chemical nature of the missing substance to be made, so that the element could be looked for with success. **1950** N. V. SIDGWICK *Chem. Elements* II. 1291 Such sulphides as molybdenite (MoS_2) may contain as much as 1, and in two cases as much as 10 and 21 parts of rhenium per million. **1961** *New Scientist* 30 Nov. 557/3 The resistance to corrosion offered by rhenium metal has for long been appreciated by industry and its special properties have frequently been put to good use. **1963** I. L. FINAR *Org. Chem.* (ed. 4) I. xii. 276 Both rhenium heptaselenide and heptasulphide are good catalysts for hydrogenation. **1971** *World Petroleum* June 193/1 This catalyst, containing platinum and rhenium, exhibited such exceptional stability characteristics that it was possible to employ it at substantially lower operating pressures, so that marked increases in yields of motor fuel of a given octane rating, of hydrogen and of aromatics were obtainable. **1973** R. D. PEACOCK in J. C. Bailar et al. *Comprehensive Inorg. Chem.* III. xxxix. 905 Rhenium, the dvi-manganese of Mendeléev, and the least abundant of the natural chemical elements, was the last..to be identified by conventional chemical methods. *Ibid.* 938 Rhenium forms three anhydrous oxides: the dioxide, the trioxide and the heptaoxide.

rhenosterbos(ch), -bush (renǫ·stəɹbǫs, -bǫʃ, -buʃ). *S. Afr.* Also **renosterbos, -bush, rhinoster bos(ch), bush.** [Afrikaans, f. *renoster* rhinoceros + *bos* bush.] A shrub with greyish foliage, *Elytropappus rhinocerotis*, belonging to the family Compositæ, native to South Africa, and bearing small scale-like leaves and clusters of small purple flowers; = *rhinoceros-bush* s.v. RHINOCEROS 3 in Dict. and Suppl.

1812 A. PLUMPTRE tr. *Lichtenstein's Trav. S. Afr.* I. 73 We found here in abundance a plant which..the colonists call..*rhinosterbosjes*, because, they say, that in the time when the rhinoceros was an inhabitant of the country, it used to feed very much upon this plant. **1822** W. J. BURCHELL *Trav. Interior S. Afr.* I. 101 A neat pale bushy shrub, of the height of three or four feet, called Rhinoster bosch (Rhinoceros bush). **1850** R. GRAY *Jrnl.* 19 Dec. (1851) 199 More dreary than usual, with its unbroken monotonous rhinoster bush. **1896** R. WALLACE *Farming Industries Cape Colony* 81 The rhenoster bush has spread more widely and more quickly than exotic plants generally do. **1939** *Nature* 11 Mar. 412/2 The 'rhenosterbush'..represents the most arid kind of sclerophyll. **1948** *Cape Times* 6 Feb. 14/5 The rhenosterbos could be subdued by burning. *Ibid.* 22 Sept. 9/6 The stunted renoster bush has already appeared. **1955** V. M. FITZROY *Dark Bright Land* 55 Papa means to clear the lower slope of a grey scrub they call rhenoster bush. **1966** E. PALMER *Plains of Camdeboo* xvii. 277 Tea made of the leaves of the rhenoster or rhinoceros bush to cure their indigestion. This low grey bush..sprawls over many of our Karoo mountains. **1973** Y. BURGESS *Life to Live* 113 You can try some wildeals or renosterbos in a little brandy to make you strong.

rheo-. Add: **rheˈobase** *Physiol.* [ad. F. *rhéobase* (L. Lapicque 1909, in *Compt. Rend. Soc. de Biol.* LXVII. 283), f. *base* BASE *sb.*[1]], the minimum electrical stimulus which, applied continuously, can excite a nerve or muscle; cf. *CHRONAXIE, CHRONAXY; hence **rheobaˑsic** *a.*; **rhe:ogonioˑmeter** *Physics*, a form of goniometer which can be used to measure shearing stresses in Newtonian and non-Newtonian fluids; hence **rhe:ogonioˑmetry**; **rheˑogram** *Physics*, any diagram exhibiting experimental results pertaining to rheology (see quots.); **rheomoˑrphism** *Geol.* [ad. G. *rheomorphose* (H. G. Backlund 1937, in *Bull. Geol. Inst. Univ. Uppsala* XXVII. 234), f. Gr. μορφ-ή form], the process by which a rock becomes mobile and partially or completely fused, usu. the result of heating by the addition of extraneous magmatic material; so **rheomoˑrphic** *a.*; **rheˑophil(e)** *a. Zool.* [-PHIL, -PHILE], tending to seek or inhabit an environment of flowing water; also as *sb.*, such an organism; hence **rheophiˑlic, rheoˑphilous** (also stressed *-phiˑlous*) *adjs.*; **rheophoˑbic** *a. Zool.* [-PHOBIC], tending to avoid or not to inhabit an environment of flowing water; so **rheˑophobe**, such an organism; **rheˑophyte** *Bot.* [-PHYTE], a plant that is confined to flowing water; hence **rheophyˑtic** *a.*; **rheˑoreceptor** *Zool.*, a sensory receptor that is sensitive to the flow of the surrounding water; hence **rheˑoreceptive** *a.*

1924 *Nature* 22 Mar. 427/1 The rheobase is the intensity in volts of a constant current closed instantaneously which will just excite if continued indefinitely. **1944** *Electronic Engin.* XVII. 27/2 In measuring chronaxie a current value is found which, when caused to flow for infinite time, will produce a minimal contraction in the muscle under observation. (For this purpose any period in excess of one second can be referred to as infinity.) This current value is called the Rheobase. **1952** *Ibid.* XXIV. 334/1 The ratio of this current to the rheobase depends on the rate of accommodation of the nerve. **1965** S. OCHS *Elements Neurophysiol.* ii. 21 A utilization or utilized time also occurs during the..shorter times of excitation found when using stimulating pulses stronger than rheobase. **1976** *Exper. Neurol.* L. 71 The C-fibers had a rheobase of 0·033 mA and a utilization time of 7·80 msec. **1942** *Chem. Abstr.* XXXVI. 6636 With faradization the rheobasic effect was decreased, the chronaxia increased. **1944** *Electronic Engin.* XVII. 27 Chronaxie is defined as that period of time for which a current, having twice the rheobasic value, must flow in order to produce the same minimal contraction. **1965** S. OCHS *Elements Neurophysiol.* ii. 20 When a rheobasic current is used, the nerve actually becomes excited a short time after the onset of the step pulse current. **1946** *Nature* 2 Nov. 614/2 The practical application of the Weissenberg rheogoniometer. **1949** K. WEISSENBERG in *Princ. Rheol. Measurement* (Brit. Rheologists' Club) iii. 39 It has therefore become necessary to design a new instrument, termed Rheogoniometer, which measures the macroscopically observable forces and displacements in a sufficiently comprehensive manner. **1974** [see *RHEOMETRIC *a.*]. **1974** *Physics Bull.* Jan. 20/2 These theories..led to the design of..the 'rheogoniometer' which allowed for the first time the movements and forces in flowing fluids to be measured as functions of time and in all three dimensions in space. **1976** *Nature* 5 Feb. 389/1 Rheogoniometry seems to measure T_s as accurately as previous methods. **1933** SCHOFIELD & BLAIR in *Proc. R. Soc.* A. CXXXIX. 558 A study was made of the rate of elongation of cylinders of unyeasted dough hung vertically by their upper ends and allowed to extend under the action of gravity... It has been found convenient to mark on the dough cylinders a series of fine parallel lines accurately spaced 1 mm. apart. The marks were made by successive turns of a fine wire wrapped round a frame, which are wetted with enamel, the marks remaining wet long enough to be subsequently printed off on to a strip of duplicator paper... The print (which may be called a rheogram) is available for whatever analysis appears suitable. **1941** J. STANLEY in *Industr. & Engin. Chem.* (Anal. Ed.) June 404/2 These facts are secured from the rheograms. **1944** G. W. S. BLAIR *Surv. Gen. & Appl. Rheol.* x. 123 Stanley..used the word 'rheogram' to describe a rate-of-shear stress curve. This is confusing, since such flow curves are quite different from the charts so described by Schofield and Scott Blair. **1974** P. L. MOORE et al. *Drilling Practices Manual* vi. 224 One procedure suggested by Forbes includes construction of a regular rheogram chart of shear stress versus shear rate. **1937** *Proc. Geologists' Assoc.* XLVIII. 275 The quartz-felspar intergrowths of the rheomorphic veins are less perfectly micropegmatitic. **1954** *Amer. Jrnl. Sci.* CCLII. 602 The term 'rheomorphic' in accordance with its derivation means 'flow form'. It was introduced by Backlund (1937) to describe the flowage of rocks where there is no evidence to show that the rocks concerned were melted and capable of liquid flow. **1962** E. A. VINCENT tr. *Rittmann's Volcanoes* vi. 199 Migmatitic granites thus frequently show very well marked rheomorphic structures on solidification. **1937** *Proc. Geologists' Assoc.* XLVIII. 260 These are clearly cases of rheomorphism. [*Note*] Backlund has introduced the term *rheomorphism* for the process whereby a pre-existing rock becomes partially or completely mobilised or fused as a result of the introduction of migrating materials (in great or small amount) with concomitant rise of temperature. **1964** L. U. DE SITTER *Struct. Geol.* (ed. 2) xxix. 402 In some of these pockets of recrystallized nonoriented rock the random orientation of gneissic or schistose inclusions or xenoliths proves that this disturbance can develop into flow. This phenomenon has been called 'rheomorphism'. **1934** WEBSTER, Rheophile, -phil *adj.* **1964** *Oceanogr. & Marine Biol.* II. 417 It appears as though *A. chiajei* is a slow-growing sediment feeder..whereas *A. filiformis* is a more rheophile suspension feeder with rapid growth. **1965** B. E. FREEMAN tr. *Vandel's Biospeleol.* xvii. 294 *Gammarus* are stream animals and are essentially rheophiles. **1974** *Nature* 8 Feb. 395/1 Rheophobic species may co-exist with the rheophiles. **1963** L. BIRKETT tr. *Nikolsky's Ecol. of Fishes* I. 76 Rheophilic fishes are also at the same time oxyphilic, i.e. they require plenty of oxygen. **1979** Rheophilic [see *rheophobic* adj. below]. **1951** L. H. HYMAN *Invertebrates* II. x. 192 Some turbellarians are rheophilous, i.e., limited to flowing water. **1965** B. E. FREEMAN tr. *Vandel's Biospeleol.* xxiv. 391 According to Poulson (1961) *Amblyopsis spelaeus* is rheophilous. *Ibid.* xvii. 294 *Niphargus orcinus virei* is a 'rheophobe'. **1979** E. N. K. CLARKSON *Invertebr. Palaeont. & Evol.* ix. 220/2 Some rheophobes live in deeper waters, so that a fair amount of detrital material has accumulated by the time it reaches them. **1965** B. E. FREEMAN tr. *Vandel's Biospeleol.* xxiv. 395 The fish, *Typhlichthys subterraneus*, is probably rheophobic. **1974** Rheophobic [see *rheophile* adj. above]. **1979** E. N. K. CLARKSON *Invertebr. Palaeont. & Evol.* ix. 220/2 Rheophobic crinoids live in current-free waters though most deep water crinoids are rheophilic. **1932** *Bull. Jard. Bot. Buitenzorg* 3rd Ser. XII. 201, I draw the attention towards the remarkable fact that the leaves of *Neonauclea rheophila* and *Nauclea angustifolia* agree entirely with those of other well-known rheophytes. **1950** *Flora Malesiana* I. iv. p. lvii, Rheophytes are plants restricted to riverbeds. **1981** C. G. G. J. VAN STEENIS (*title*) Rheophytes of the world. **1975** T. C. WHITMORE *Trop. Rain-Forests Far East* 187 *Garcinia cataractalis*, a rheophytic shrub with narrow willow-like stenophyllous leaves and crimson fruits. **1951** L. H. HYMAN *Invertebrates* II. x. 93 Rheoreceptive cells have been identified in *Mesostoma* and *Bothromesostoma*. **1948** *Nature* 25 Dec. 1000/2 Rheoreceptors [in Tunicata]: margins of the siphons—not only do the siphons bend to face a water-current, but also bend upwards against gravity. **1971** J. D. CARTHY in J. E. Smith et al. *Invertebr. Panorama* x. 220 (*caption*) A section through the head of the flatworm *Mesostoma* to show four of the eight rheoreceptors, the two groups of chemoreceptors and four tactile receptors.

rheological (rī,ǒlǫˑdʒikăl), *a. Physics.* [f. as next + -ICAL.] Of or pertaining to the deformation and flow properties of matter.

1930 *Jrnl. Rheol.* I. 509 (*heading*) Teaching rheological technique. **1946** *Nature* 10 Aug. 199/2 With non-Newtonian liquids their peculiar rheological properties can be demonstrated by this method. **1956** *Sci. News* XL. 66 The rheological properties of clay dispersions are of particular importance in the ceramic and petroleum industries. **1959** *Times* 8 Jan. 2/6 (Advt.), The British Food Manufacturing Industries Research Association has vacancies for research staff to conduct investigations into..the rheological behaviour of chocolate, particularly at low rates of shear. **1974** *Sci. Amer.* Dec. 88/3 Solidification proceeds from spheroidal growth centers. The rheological (flow) properties of this structure are quite different from those of the dendritic structure.

Hence **rheoloˑgically** *adv.*

1945 *Jrnl. Appl. Physics* XVI. 338/2 The asphalt industry has also been rationalized, rheologically speaking. **1963** *New Scientist* 22 Aug. 382/1 We may say that modern rheology began with J. L. M. Poiseuille's investigations of the flow of blood. He.., in 1842, published his law governing the flow through capillaries of rheologically simple liquids. **1973** *Nature* 14 Sept. 78/2 In a rheologically young planet, we expect that quakes will occur whenever the total elastic energy in a certain region exceeds some critical value.

rheologist (ri,ǫˑlŏdʒist). *Physics.* [f. next + -IST.] One who studies or is expert in rheology.

1931 *Jrnl. Rheol.* II. 108 This number contains an index to the literature which should be useful to all rheologists. **1947** *Nature* 11 Jan. 70/1 The gap between the colloidal chemist and the physicist is being bridged by the rheologist. **1959** *Times* 5 Mar. 2/3 (Advt.), Dough rheologist. An experimental officer..to assist in rheological studies in a laboratory fully equipped with..dough testing machines. **1963** *New Scientist* 22 Aug. 382/1 A fundamental task of the experimental rheologist is to measure viscosity and other flow problems.

rheology (ri,ǫˑlŏdʒi). *Physics.* [f. RHEO- + -LOGY.] **a.** The study of the deformation and flow of matter, esp. the non-Newtonian flow of liquids and the plastic flow of solids. **b.** The rheological properties *of* a substance.

1929 *Jrnl. Rheol.* I (*title-page*), Journal of Rheology published by the Society of Rheology. **1930** *Ibid.* I. 508 A large number of words have been suggested and John R. Crawford, late Professor of Latin at Lafayette College, inclined to the belief that 'rheology' is the most appropriate designation. **1947** *Nature* 11 Jan. 71/1 The rheology of suspensions is fundamentally dependent on the dispersion coefficient of the medium. **1968** B. S. MASSEY *Mechanics of Fluids* i. 23 The fluids with which engineers most often have to deal are Newtonian, that is, their viscosity is not dependent on either the rate of shear or its duration; and the term 'mechanics of fluids' generally refers only to Newtonian fluids (the study of non-Newtonian liquids is termed 'rheology'). **1968** M. PYKE *Food & Society* ix. 130 The firmness or toughness of foodstuffs is also a relevant measure of their quality; rheology is the branch of science which has been developed to measure and describe such characteristics. **1978** *Nature* 30 Mar. 478/2 During his eight years at M.I.T., Goetze and his associates became one of the world's leading groups in the study of the rheology of rocks.

rheometer. Add: **1.** (Earlier example.)

1839 *Ann. Electr., Magn. & Chem.* IV. 70 On this plan my Reometer (an instrument described in Gehler's Phil. Dictionary, new edition, vol. vi, sec. 3, p. 2494) is constructed and brought into action.

2. b. Any instrument for measuring the rheological properties of matter, esp. one which measures the viscous stress of a fluid.

1945 *Jrnl. Appl. Physics* XVI. 338 A modified Bingham-type rheometer. **1950** *Jrnl. Sci. Instruments* XXVII. 209 (*heading*) A continuous-shear rheometer for measuring total stress in rubber-like materials. **1967** CONDON & ODISHAW *Handbk. Physics* (ed. 2) III. iii. 48/1 Rheological properties are determined quantitatively in rheometers (plastometers), for which the viscometers are the prototype, either with their absolute value or relatively to the magnitude of the same property in a standard material. **1971** *Nature* 5 Nov. 50/1 The slime was diluted to various concentrations with clean water from the natural environment and then tested in a portable rheometer.

rheometric *a.* (earlier and further examples); **rheometry** (further example).

1843 C. WHEATSTONE in *Phil. Trans. R. Soc.* CXXXIII. 309 The voltaic element which I have employed in most of my rheometric researches. **1967** CONDON & ODISHAW *Handbk. Physics* (ed. 2) III. iii. 48/1 (*heading*) Rheometry. **1972** *Physics Bull.* Feb. 85/1 It has developed a rheometric device for measuring the reaction between oil, water and detergent, based on the rheometer at the School of Pharmacy at London University. **1974** *Nature* 22 Mar. 328/1 In order to characterize the rheological behaviour of the aqueous sugar solution, an extensive series of tests was done with a rheometric mechanical spectrometer and with a Weissenberg Rheogoniometer.

rheopexy (rīˑŏpeksi). *Physical Chem.* [f. RHEO- + *-PEXY.] The property, possessed by some sols, of undergoing accelerated gelation when subjected to gentle mechanical agitation. Cf. *THIXOTROPY. So **rheopeˑctic** *a.*

1935 FREUNDLICH & JULIUSBURGER in *Trans. Faraday Soc.* XXXI. 921 It is too cumbrous to say 'thixotropic sols which can be solidified by orienting the particles'. Graham used the word 'pectous'..for sols which have turned to a jelly. We therefore propose to call a thixotropic sol, which may be solidified by gentle movement, 'rheopectic', and the phenomenon itself 'rheopexy'. **1958** *U.S. Patent 2,846,394* 1/1 The grease is a rheopectic lubricant composition which essentially comprises an oleaginous base thickened with..a lithium soap of a hydroxy stearic acid. **1963** *New Scientist* 22 Aug. 384/1 The viscosity in the return part of the programme is greater than the viscosity at the same rate of shear in the upward part. This behaviour is called rheopexy. **1967** *Ibid.* 20 July 143/2 The technique is to add to the fuel a high-molecular-weight polymer..which converts the fuel into a 'rheopectic gel'... Such a fluid undergoes a large change in viscosity and volatility when subjected to shear forces above a certain level. **1978** C. J. GEANKOPLIS *Transport Processes & Unit Operations* ii. 105 In design procedures for thixotropic and rheopectic fluids for steady flow in pipes, the limiting flow-property values at a constant rate of shear are sometimes used.

rheostat. Add: Also, a resistor whose resistance can be varied by mechanical means, esp. a variable wire-wound resistor used for controlling large currents. (Further examples.)

1920 *Whittaker's Electr. Engineer's Pocket-bk.* (ed. 4) 561 In one form of rheostat, the grids are formed of rectangular wire in one continuous length. **1960** *Practical Wireless* XXXVI. 373/1 (Advt.), Variable rheostats, heavy duty slider resistor rated at 25 amps. **1972** P. MARKS *Collector's Choice* i. 26 All the lights and rheostats. **1974** *Encycl. Brit. Micropædia* VIII. 548/2 The rheostat can adjust generator characteristics, dim lights, and start or control the speed of motors... A special type of rheostat is the potentiometer.

Hence **rheˑostatted** *a.*, fitted with or controlled by a rheostat.

1978 J. UPDIKE *Coup* (1979) v. 211 The symbolic riband of gold on his forehead took glitter from the rheostatted spotlight.

rheostatic, *a.* Add: **b.** *rheostatic brake*, a form of brake used in vehicles driven by electric traction motors, in which the motors are made to act as generators, the power so generated being dissipated in the starting rheostats; so *rheostatic braking*.

1920 *Whittaker's Electr. Engineer's Pocket-bk.* (ed. 4) 563 Brakes for tramcars may be classified as follows:..(2) Electric rheostatic brakes, in which the car motors are converted into generators and are loaded on rheostats, the brake being applied and regulated from the controller. **1931** R. A. BISHOP *Electr. Trolley Bus* v. 118 The rheostatic brake so adjusted as not to overstress the transmission. *Ibid.* 192 (Index), Rheostatic braking. **1954** A. T. DOVER *Electr. Traction* (ed. 3) viii. 130 For rheostatic braking either of the schemes..are employed. **1971** *Mod. Railways* May 197/2 As train speed is reduced and the rheostatic brake fades, proportional air brake is automatically re-established on the locomotive.

rheotaxis (ri,otæˑksis). *Zool.* [a. G. *rheotaxis* (C. Herbst 1894, in *Biol. Centralbl.* XIV. 694): see RHEO- and TAXIS.] The orientation or movement of an animal (or, formerly, a plant) in response to a current of water

1900 in B. D. JACKSON *Gloss. Bot. Terms* 318/1. **1903** *Amer. Naturalist* XXXVII. 201 The ear is held to be an organ directly concerned with the reactions of a fish to a current of water (rheotaxis). **1906** A. J. Ewart tr. *Pfeffer's Physiol. Plants* III. iv. 356 Roth..could detect no rheotaxis in *Euglena viridis*. **1951** L. H. Hyman *Invertebrates* II. x. 213 Planarians that habitually live in flowing water usually exhibit a positive rheotaxis, for obviously without such a reaction they could not maintain themselves in their habitat. **1970** *Nature* 24 Oct. 375/1 It is generally accepted that spermatozoa constrained to move in a fine tube swim preferentially upstream (they exhibit positive rheotaxis) when a current is established in the tube.

Hence **rheota·ctic** *a.*, exhibiting or pertaining to rheotaxis; **rheota·ctically** *adv.*

1900 B. D. Jackson *Gloss. Bot. Terms* 318/1 Rheotactic. **1903** *Science* 3 Apr. 531/1 They are..rheotactic, thigmotactic and phototactic in the highest degree. **1954** G. L. Clarke *Elem. Ecol.* ii. 57 The rheotactic reactions of most stream fish is such that they swim against the current and thus maintain their position in the stream. **1973** *Netherlands Jrnl. Sea Res.* VII. 180 No significant difference can be seen between the effect of bottom or surface currents on the rheotactic behaviour of the starfish. **1975** F. Creutzberg in O. Kinne *Marine Ecol.* II. ii. viii. 599 *Palaemon serratus* and *P. xiphias* did not respond rheotactically in the experimental current channel.

rheotropism (rĭ,ǫ·trǒpiz'm, rĭ,otrōu·piz'm). *Zool.* and *Bot.* [ad. G. *rheotropismus* (B. Jönsson 1883, in *Ber. d. deutsch. bot. Ges.* I. 521): see Rheo- and Tropism.] The orientation or movement of an animal or plant in response to a current of water.

1887 H. E. F. Garnsey tr. *A. de Bary's Compar. Morphol. & Biol. Fungi* ix. 449 Rheotropism. If a stream of water is made to flow slowly through a moistened porous substratum, ..the plasmodia which are vegetating on the moist surface wander in the direction of the stream. **1898** [see *chemotropism]. **1965** B. E. Freeman tr. *Vandel's Biospeleol.* xxiv. 391 Gammarids show a very strong positive reaction towards running water and swim energetically against it... The name positive rheotropism has been given to this reaction.

So **rheotropic** (-trǫ·pik, -trōu·pik) *a.*, exhibiting or pertaining to rheotropism.

1897 *Ann. Bot.* XI. 182 It [*sc.* the plasmodium] moved with the current, i.e. became negatively rheotropic. **1920** A. Arber *Water Plants* xxii. 282 Stems responded to the stimulus by their own activity and might thus be called positively rheotropic. **1931** G. K. Noble *Biol. Amphibia* xiv. 346 Steinmann..has reinvestigated the problem in tadpoles and newts and would attribute the rheotropic response to compensatory reflexes initiated by the labyrinth. **1968** F. R. H. Jones *Fish Migration* xii. 269 He studied the rheotropic responses of elvers in a circular flume.

rhesus. Add: [a. specific name of *Macacus rhesus*, formerly *Simia rhesus* (J. B. Audebert *Histoire naturelle des Singes* (1799) II. 5).] **1.** Also *rhesus macaque*. For *Macacus rhesus* substitute *Macaca mulatta*. (Earlier and later examples.)

1827 E. Griffith et al. tr. *Cuvier's Animal Kingdom* I. 289 The pig-tailed baboon, or Rhesus of Audebert, is the short-tailed Macaque of Buffon. **1906** E. Ingersoll *Life Animals: Mammals* 30 The widespread little yellowish Bengal or rhesus monkey..abounds in northern India. **1932** S. Zuckerman *Social Life Monkeys* vi. 88 More has been written about the reproductive mechanisms of the Rhesus macaque than about those of all the other primates together. **1948** *Psychol. Abstr.* XXII. 381/2 Large numbers of rhesus monkeys living in a semi-natural environment are shown with special emphasis on social interactions. **1967** J. R. & P. H. Napier *Handbk. Living Primates* III. 375 In spite of Fooden's proposition..that the crab-eating macaque, *M. fascicularis*, and the rhesus macaque, *M. mulatta*, should be considered conspecific, they are here retained as separate species. **1976** *Amer. Jrnl. Vet. Res.* XXXVII. 969/1 Rhesus macaques have been selected most for studying radiation sickness. **1978** D. Symons in E. O. Smith *Social Play in Primates* 209 Long term studies of free ranging rhesus monkeys indicate that the ranks of females and immature males are determined by the political milieu into which they are born.

2. *Med.* Used *attrib.* and in *Comb.* with reference to a major blood group consisting of three principal antigens to which naturally occurring antibodies are rare, and which are important because hæmolytic disease of the newborn is usually the result of antibodies produced in the blood of a rhesus-negative mother in response to the rhesus-positive blood of the fetus; (so called from being first discovered in the rhesus monkey); as *rhesus agglutinogen, antibody, antigen, incompatibility, system*; **rhesus baby**, an infant suffering from hæmolytic disease of the newborn owing to incompatibility between its own rhesus-positive blood and its mother's rhesus-negative blood; **rhesus factor**, any or all of the rhesus antigens, esp. the most important one; **rhesus-negative** *a.*, lacking the most important and common rhesus antigen, and therefore able to produce antibodies to it; so **rhesus-positive** *a.*, having this antigen.

1941 *Amer. Jrnl. Obstetr. & Gynecol.* XLII. 925 In the great majority of the cases the blood factor involved has been shown to be either identical with or related to the Rh (Rhesus) agglutinogen first described by Landsteiner and Wiener with the aid of rabbit sera prepared by injection of Rhesus blood. **1945** *Nature* 5 May 542/1 (*heading*) The new rhesus antibody. **1973** *Nursing Times* 24 May 668/2 Particular attention was paid to blood tests for Rhesus antibodies. **1947** G. F. Roberts *Rhesus Factor* i. 5 The rhesus antigen, being foreign to the recipient, provoked the formation of an antibody which would agglutinate rhesus positive red cells. **1950** *Sci. News* XV. 121 On the left is part of the surface of the red cell bearing a configuration which is responsible for the specificity of the rhesus antigen. **1967** *Spectator* 8 Dec. 706/1 A new serum to save rhesus babies was developed in Britain. **1968** *Sci. Amer.* Nov. 49/2 Among the 850,000 births each year in Britain,..the number of 'rhesus' babies is probably not more than about 5,000. **1942** *Jrnl. Amer. Med. Assoc.* 7 Mar. 843/1 Statistical data on the Rh (Rhesus) factor. **1958** *Listener* 17 July 87/1 In 1939 Levine..found a fourth system [of blood-groups], which has been named the Rhesus factor. **1969** *Times* 6 May 12/5 Incompatibility arises between the mother and her fœtus when the latter alone carries the Rhesus blood group factor. **1947** G. F. Roberts *Rhesus Factor* v. 32 The question of rhesus incompatibility must..be considered in terms of C, D and E. **1971** H. & M. Brant *Dict. Pregnancy, Childbirth & Contraception* 204 Rhesus incompatibility does not..cause any defect in development of the baby such as a hole in the heart or the blue baby condition. **1943** *Brit. Med. Jrnl.* 4 Sept. 293/2 Treat these infants by transfusion with rhesus-negative blood, free of agglutinins and thus test out the recommendation that rhesus-negative blood would produce better results than rhesus-positive blood. **1950** *Sci. News* XV. 126 The rhesus negative characteristic is almost unknown in the Far East. **1961** P. Mason *Common Sense about Race* I. iii. 52 In Britain five persons out of six are classed as Rhesus positive in the Rhesus blood-group system, while one in six is Rhesus negative. **1971** J. Z. Young *Introd. Study Man* xl. 587 In the majority of pregnancies Rhesus-negative women do not..become immunised by a Rhesus-positive foetus. **1943**, etc. Rhesus-positive [see *rhesus-negative* above]. **1958** *Listener* 17 July 87/1 The Rhesus system has been of service not only in making the medical profession to some extent genotype-conscious but in demonstrating the genetic complexity of the regions of the germ-plasm responsible for blood-group polymorphisms. **1974** P. Svendsen *Introd. Animal Physiol.* x. 113 About twenty different blood group systems are known in man. Of these the ABO and the rhesus systems are the most important.

rhetic (rī·tik), *a.* [f. Gr. ῥητ-ός stated + -ic.] Designating or pertaining to an utterance that has the property of meaning (in its elements of sense and reference), as distinct from its identity as sound and words. Hence **rhe·tically** *adv.* Cf. *rheme.

1955 J. L. Austin *How to do Things with Words* (1962) vii. 93 To say anything is..to perform the act of using that pheme or its constituents with a certain more or less definite 'sense' and a more or less definite 'reference' (which together are equivalent to 'meaning'). This act we may call a 'rhetic' act. *Ibid.* viii. 97 When different phemes are used with the same sense and reference, we might speak of rhetically equivalent acts. **1969** W. Cerf in K. T. Fann *Symposium on J. L. Austin* IV. 356 The suspicion arises that the phonetic act, the phatic act and the rhetic act are not subclasses, but parts of the locutionary act. **1971** M. Furberg *Saying & Meaning* (ed. 2) ii. 57 Reports of someone's words in indirect speech are reports of his rhetic act.

rhetoric, *sb.*[1] Add: **1. e.** Literary prose composition, esp. as a school exercise.

1828 R. Whateley *Elements Rhetoric* 4 Some writers have spoken of Rhetoric as the Art of Composition, universally; or, with the exclusion of Poetry alone, as embracing all Prose-composition. **1944** H. J. C. Grierson *Rhetoric & Eng. Composition* p. iii, Of University teaching in English I had enjoyed just fifty lectures at Aberdeen, of which twenty-five were devoted to Rhetoric or, as Rhetoric had come to mean under Dr. Alexander Bain and his successor William Minto, English Composition. **1953** T. S. Eliot *Amer. Lit. & Amer. Lang.* 5, I am happy to remember that in those days English composition was still called Rhetoric. **1972** *Lebende Sprachen* XVII. 35/2 *US* rhetoric—*BE/US* literary composition.

2. c. Delete † *Obs.* and add later examples.

1942 W. Stevens *Parts of World* 143 Midsummer love and softest silences, Weather of night creatures, whistling all day, too, And echoing rhetorics more than our own. **1949** Koestler *Promise & Fulfilment* II. v. 274 It was a disappointing speech—emotional rhetorics without a constructive programme. **1976** *Sunday Times* (Lagos) 3 Oct. 10/4 We cannot decide on the fundamental values and goals that will bind the present and future generations on the basis of vague ideas, irrelevant foreign slogans and rhetorics.

e. (*b*) (later examples); (*c*) of artistic style or technique.

1941 W. H. Auden in *Southern Rev.* VI. 729 Around them boomed the rhetoric of time. **1963** R. I. McDavid *Mencken's Amer. Lang.* 339 Among the neo-Aristotelian critics *rhetoric* is a current fashionable synonym for technique... The *Rhetoric* of Fiction. **1964** J. Summerson *Classical Lang. Archit.* iv. 33 Well, there are three buildings which, I believe, demonstrate..the 'rhetoric' of the Baroque. **1976** *Howard Jrnl.* XV. I. 52 The rhetoric of treatment will have to be replaced by the reality of treatment.

rhetorically, *adv.* Add: **a.** (Further examples.) Also in *Comb.*

1904 B. Russell in *Mind* XIII. 522 We may imagine a rhetorically minded soldier in battle saying to himself: 'To advance is to die, to retreat is dishonour; better death than dishonour.' **1927** E. O'Neill *Lazarus Laughed* IV. 177 He laughs with a wild triumphant madness and again rhetorically. *a* **1974** R. Crossman *Diaries* (1975) I. 210 By means of a conscious rhetorically- and demagogically-forced row with the Opposition I won back both their respect and my popularity among my own party. **1976** *Nature* 13 May 92/1 The choice between guns and butter was rhetorically offered by Goebbels to the German public.

rhetorician. Add: Also 8 **returrition. 3.** (Earlier and later examples.)

1676 in *Cath. Rec. Soc. Publ.* (1972) LXIII. 60 Rhetoricians. Jo. Brockholes. Jo. Townly. **1716** N. Blundell *Diary* 3 May (1952) ix. 164 Mr Carroll being to leave, gave his schoolfellows the Returritions a treat. **1773** H. T. Blount *Diary* 17 Apr. in *Cath. Rec. Soc. Publ.* (1972) LXIII. 354 Master John Bradshaw, Rhetorician, left the College, and returned to England. **1809** [see *philosopher 1 c].

rhetoricize (retǫ·risəiz), *v.* [f. Rhetoric *sb.*[1] + -ize.] **a.** *intr.* = Rhetorize *v.* **b.** *trans.* (Chiefly in *ppl. a.*) To characterize with rhetoric; to make rhetorical. Also *fig.* Hence **rheto:riciza·tion**, the act or process of rhetoricizing.

1676 R. Meggott *Sermon on St. Paul's Day* 10 But we (as he very melancholily rhetoriciseth) are naked, impotent, and shiftless. **1932** C. S. Lewis in *Essays & Stud.* XVII. 62 A detailed study of the *Book of Troilus* would reveal this 'rhetoricization', if I may coin an ugly word, as the common quality of many of Chaucer's additions. **1934** T. Wood *Cobbers* xviii. 235 This youngster was born with a golden tongue in its mouth and was fed on rhetoricized milk. **1965** *New Statesman* 22 Oct. 604/1 All excellently put—though a tendency to rhetoricise is already apparent in the plea for 'the real impenetrable human person'. **1972** G. S. Fraser in Cox & Dyson *20th-Cent. Mind* II. xi. 395 The moral stance is strong just because, unlike Lawrence's changing and always dramatized or rhetoricized moral stances, it is not assertive.

rheumatic, *a.* and *sb.* Add: **A.** *adj.* **3. b.** Also *fig.*

1934 E. Sitwell *Aspects Mod. Poetry* i. 14 The cramped and rheumatic eight-syllable lines..are not suitable to his themes. **1958** J. Press *Chequer'd Shade* i. 14 It is obscure, less because of its vocabulary than because the entire movement of the syntax is rheumatic and muscle-bound.

4. b. *rheumatic fever* (later example).

1974 Passmore & Robson *Compan. Med. Stud.* III. xvi. 51/2 Rheumatic fever is an immunological disorder developing after an infection by a group A β-haemolytic streptococcus. Its major clinical features are fever, polyarthritis, carditis, chorea, erythema nodosum and annulare, and subcutaneous nodules.

d. Pertaining to rheumatism.

1886 H. Baumann *Londinismen* 155/2 *Rheumatic dodge*, List einer Bettler-klasse, welche Rheumatismus erheuchelt. **1976** *Lancet* 27 Nov. 1202/2 The hospital's closure was strenuously opposed by the consultant rheumatologists to whom it was obvious that to halve the number of beds in the regional centre would gravely impair the rheumatic service.

B. *sb.* **1.** Also *sing.*

1918 V. Woolf *Diary* 16 July (1977) I. 169 He is a ridiculous figure precisely like the false Mandrill, especially now that he's bent with the rheumatic, & can only creep and crawl.

rheumatism. 2. (Further examples.)

1910, 1915 [see *fibrositis]. **1966** Wright & Symmers *Systemic Path.* I. iii. 113/2 The focal lesions of acute rheumatism are usually found in close relationship to arteries.

rheumatoid, *a.* Add: (Further examples.) Also, of or pertaining to rheumatoid arthritis; *rheumatoid factor*, any of a group of substances in the blood which are present in increased amounts in persons with rheumatoid arthritis.

1949 R. M. Pike et al. in *Jrnl. Immunol.* LXIII. 447 The property of agglutinating sensitized sheep cells to a marked degree appears to be associated almost exclusively with the serum in rheumatoid arthritis. The phenomenon is due to a factor which is present in the serum-globulins and its effect is not diminished on storage for considerable periods. Until this factor is more completely characterized, it may be conveniently termed the 'rheumatoid factor'. **1950** *Sci. News* XV. 134 The adrenal cortex may play an important role in the pathogenesis of rheumatic and rheumatoid conditions in man. **1956** *Proc. Soc. Exper. Biol. & Med.* XCII. 198/2 Sensitized cells which were strongly agglutinated by the rheumatoid serum. **1957** *Proc. R. Soc. Med.* L. 47 The appearance in the serum of rheumatoid arthritics of a factor similar to those induced in the rabbit sera..suggests that it, too, is an antibody to the non-specific groups of immune γ-globulin. **1957** *Ann. Rheumatic Dis.* XVI. 448/1 The term 'rheumatoid factor' (R.F.) has been applied to the substance or substances in the serum of most individuals having rheumatoid arthritis which combines with immune globulins or substances closely associated with immune globulins. **1970** Passmore & Robson *Compan. Med. Stud.* II. xxx. 9/2 This mode of origin was suggested for rheumatoid arthritis; in this disease numerous features..combine to support the idea that this is a 'disorder of the immunological mechanism' or even an autoimmune disease... Today there is more support for the alternative hypothesis that rheumatoid arthritis..may be caused by an exogenous agent like a virus or bacterium. **1980** *Sci. Amer.* July 42/2 Among the commonest autoantibodies in man are 'rheumatoid factors', a group of antibodies directed against gamma globulin.

rheumatology (rūmătǫ·lǒdʒi). [f. Rheumat(ism + -ology.] The study of rheumatism and rheumatic diseases.

1949 J. L. Hollander *Comroe's Arthritis* (ed. 4) i. 15 Rheumatology is the study of the Rheumatic Diseases, including arthritis, rheumatic fever, fibrositis, neuralgia, myositis, bursitis, gout, and other conditions producing somatic pain, stiffness and soreness. **1957** *Times* 20 Dec. 7/2 The Senate of London University have instituted a chair of rheumatology to be tenable at the Postgraduate Medical School, Hammersmith. **1973** *Daily Colonist* (Victoria, B.C.) 8 June 27/1 Dr. C. S. Man, a Taiwanese physician completing his post-graduate training in rheumatology and physical medicine in Canada. **1976** *Lancet* 25 Dec. 1419/1 He performed much fundamental research in rheumatology and was responsible for the first controlled trial of gold therapy in rheumatoid arthritis.

Hence **rheumato·logist**, a specialist or expert in rheumatology.

1949 W. Graham in J. L. Hollander *Comroe's Arthritis* (ed. 4) vii. 115 It is becoming more and more the conviction of rheumatologists that patients with arthritis respond best to treatment in a fully integrated rheumatism center. **1971** *Daily Tel.* 22 Mar. 3/7 The situation was noticed by a consultant rheumatologist who takes a clinic once a month at the cottage hospital. Every time he comes he has to deal with a fair number of cases of gout. **1977** *Lancet* 9 Apr. 793/1 The use of immuno-suppressive drugs to treat bulbous dermatoses was prompted by results obtained by rheumatologists treating autoimmune connective tissue diseases.

rhexia. In etym. insert after 'Linnæus': *Corollarium Generum Plantarum* (1737) 7. Substitute for def.: A perennial herb of the genus so called, belonging to the family Melastomaceæ, native to eastern North America and bearing white or purple flowers; also called meadow beauty or deer grass. (Earlier and later examples.)

1819 A. Rees *Cyclopædia* XXX. s.v., The species cultivated are; the Virginian rhexia. .and the Maryland rhexia. **1824** H. E. Lloyd tr. *Spix & Martius's Travels in Brazil* II. iv. ii. 213 Large rhexias (*quaresima*) covered with purple flowers adorned the hill. **1887** *Cent. Mag.* July 327 Parts of New England have already a midsummer flower nearly as brilliant. .in meadow beauty, or rhexia. **1951** *Dict. Gardening* (R. Hort. Soc.) IV. 1757/2 Rhexias do best in a bed of peat but may be grown in pots.

rhexigenous (reksi·dʒėnəs), *a. Bot.* [f. Gr. ῥῆξις breaking (see next) + *-genous.] Of an intercellular space in plant tissue: formed by the spontaneous mechanical rupture of cells. Hence **rhexi·genously** *adv.*, **rhexi·geny.**

1940 *Chambers's Techn. Dict.* 722/1 Rhexigenous. **1957** *Bot. Rev.* XXIII. 304 Rhexigenous lacunae would appear to be quite common in fleshy fungi, while lysigenous and schizogenous ones are more often found in higher, green plants. **1965** K. Esau *Plant Anat.* (ed. 2) viii. 188 Other large air spaces may arise lysigenously or rhexigenously. *Ibid.* xvii. 487 Large spaces may also result from a more or less extensive breakdown of cells by processes of lysigeny or rhexigeny. **1965** Bell & Coombe tr. *Strasburger's Textbk. Bot.* 103 (*caption*) Intercellular canal produced by the rupture of the annularly thickened tracheids of the protoxylem and the surrounding parenchyma (i.e. rhexigenously). **1978** *Acta Amazonica* VII. 484/2 Rhexigenous lacunae are present both in the petiole and midrib of the leaf blade.

rhexis (re·ksis). Also 5 **rixis.** [mod.L., ad. Gr. ῥῆξις, f. ῥηγνύναι to break.] † **1.** *Med.* Outpouring of blood through the ruptured wall of a blood vessel. *Obs.*

a **1425** Rixis [see Secondary *a.* 2 a]. **1684** tr. *Blancard's Physical Dict.*, *Rhexis*, the same that [*sic*] *Rhegma*. **1881** A. Flint *Treat. Princ. & Practice Med.* (ed. 5) i. i. 27 When the extravasation is through the ruptured wall of a vessel, it is called hemorrhage by rhexis. **1899** Allbutt *Syst. Med.* VI. 244 It cannot be doubted that the red corpuscles escape by diapedesis not by rhexis. **1914** T. W. Widdowson *Notes on Dental Surg. & Path.* iv. 53 In some acute inflammations the capillary walls may give way, resulting in an extravasation of blood (rhexis) into the surrounding tissue.

2. *Biol.* The fragmentation of a cell or cellular component.

1930 Maximow & Bloom *Text-bk. Histol.* iii. 66 In the granular leukocytes the nucleus may undergo fragmentation into separate parts (rhexis) or shrinkage (pyknosis). **1965** N. F. Rodman et al. in Sasahara & Stein *Pulmonary Embolic Dis.* 35 Platelet rhexis begins with disintegration of the central-most alpha granulomeres and is evidenced by an electron-lucent zone containing disintegrating alpha granulomeres. **1968** J. A. Serra *Mod. Genetics* III. xx. 130 To be efficient the polyploidizing chemicals must not cause rhexis or fragmentation of the chromosomes.

rhinarium. Add: **b.** (Further examples.)

1947 J. Stevenson-Hamilton *Wild Life S. Afr.* xiv. 102 The grey rhebuck. .has woolly fur, a large rhinarium, and no gland patches under the ears. **1976** *Nature* 29 Jan. 339/1 These [*sc.* resemblances between *Tarsius* and the anthropoids] include the absence of a rhinarium, a retinal structure similar to the anthropoid fovea.

Hence **rhina·rial** *a.*

1929 F. W. Jones *Man's Place among Mammals* xiv. 86 The details of rhinarial structure. **1955** W. C. O. Hill *Primates* II. 3 Shortening of the face. .is partly due to reduction in the size of the nasal apparatus, including under this head not only the olfactory organs but also the rhinarial complex.

Rhine[3]. Add: **b. Rhine daughter, maiden** [tr. G. *Rheintochter*], each of three water maidens, guardians of the Rheingold in Wagner's cycle of operas *Der Ring des Nibelungen* (1853–74); also used allusively of the fair blonde physique with which they are usu. portrayed.

1897 W. A. Ellis *Richard Wagner's Prose Works* VI. 108 The 'Rhine-daughters' were played by Frl. Lilli and Marie Lehmann and Frl. Lammert. **1899** G. Bell *Let.* 16 Aug. (1927) I. 51 We saw all the properties, and all the mechanism of the Rhine maidens. **1911** G. B. Shaw *Shewing-Up of Blanco Posnet* 356 From the Rhine maidens in Wagner's Trilogy, and the bathers in the second act of Les Huguenots, to the ballets of water nymphs in our Christmas pantomimes and at our variety theatres, the sound hygienic propaganda of the bath, and the charm of the undraped human figure, are exploited without offence on the stage to an extent never dreamt of by any novelist. **1922** T. S. Eliot *Waste Land* 59 The Song of the (three) Thames-daughters begins here... V. *Götterdämmerung*, III, i: the Rhinedaughters. **1940** W. Faulkner *Hamlet* iv. i. 276 To those below what Brunhilde, what Rhinemaiden on what spurious river-rock of papier mâché. **1950** A. Wilson *Such Darling Dodos* 82 With her enormous height and ample frame, her flaxen hair and bovine eyes, she was like a head prefect in the role of a Rhine maiden. **1965** V. Canning *Whip Hand* xiii. 148 The blond Siegfried type. .and Katerina and Lottie, a couple of hand-picked Rhine-maidens. **1972** J. Symons *Players & Game* xviii. 136 Her hair is fine as that of a Rhine maiden.

rhinegrave. Add: **2.** [through F. *rhingrave*.] = *petticoat breeches* s.v. Petticoat *sb.* (*a.*) 9.

1885 H. A. Dillon *Fairholt's Costume in Eng.* (ed. 3) II. 349 *Ringrave* or *Rhingrave*, full breeches, with bunches of ribands at the knee. Molière, in the 'Bourgeois Gentilhomme', mentions them. **1934** *Times Lit. Suppl.* 25 Oct. 728/2 The word 'skirt' can then be kept for the rhinegrave or petticoat breeches of the Restoration. **1960** C. W. Cunnington et al. *Dict. Eng. Costume* 162/2 *Rhinegraves*,. . immensely wide in the leg and pleated or gathered on to a waistband, falling like a divided skirt to the knees or just above.

Rhinelander (rəi·nlændəɹ). [f. Rhineland + -er[1]: cf. G. *Rheinländer*.] **1.** A native or inhabitant of the Rhineland.

1858 H. Mayhew *Upper Rhine* ii. 51 Chickens cost from 6*d.* to 1*s.* each. .though it must not be imagined that for this price the birds are anything like our own in quality, it being the custom of the Rhinelanders to fatten no animal for food. **1861** *Times* 7 Oct. 6/3 What have the pious Belgians or the warm-hearted Rhinelanders. .done in defence of the Pope's authority? **1866** J. Bryce *Holy Rom. Emp.* (ed. 2) xvii. 338 The fall in a.d. 1477 of the great principality. .was seen with pleasure by the Rhinelanders. **1902** G. Meredith *Let.* ? 3 Mar. (1970) III. 1427 He is a descendant of those indomitable Lower Rhinelanders, who gave such trouble to the Romans. **1928** *Daily Tel.* 27 Mar. 14/2 A parallel case. . is the veto placed by the Coblenz High Commission on the singing by the Rhinelanders of the 'Wacht am Rhein'. **1977** 'R. West' *Celebration* 528 'From Frankfurt!' exclaimed my mother happily. 'You are a Rhinelander!'

2. (Freq. in G. form *Rheinländer*.) A variety of German polka.

1887 A. Zorn in P. J. S. Richardson *Social Dance of Nineteenth Cent. in England* (1960) ix. 102 In the year 1850 there appeared in all parts of Europe the 'Schottische', a round dance which had, as early as 1844, been executed in Bavaria under the name 'Rheinlaender', and in the Rhenish countries it was known as the 'Bavarian Polka'. **1912** A. Huxley *Let.* 13 May (1969) 41 There was a gingerbeer and other beer stall and a dancing floor where about fifty peasants in weird Hessian costume were dancing what I learnt was a Rhinelander, which looks like a mixture between a polka and a two-step. **1938** B. Schönberg tr. *Sachs's World Hist. of Dance* vii. 436 The *Rheinländer* or the Bavarian *polka*, in contrast to the *galop*, is a slow polka. **1953** J. Lawson *Europ. Folk Dance* xii. 116 Another polka-like step is called the *Rheinländer* and has an attractive zig-zag pattern.

rhinencephalon. Add: (Earlier and further examples.)

1846 R. Owen *Hunterian Lect.* II. viii. 184 The 'rhinencephalon' consists of two lobes of grey matter, which receive the prolongations of chiefly white fibres from the prosencephalon and its crura. **1890**, etc. [see *pallium 3 d]. **1901** *Jrnl. Anat. & Physiol.* XXXV. 438 After Turner's memoir of 1890, the old term 'rhinencephalon' attained a much greater vogue. *Ibid.* 441 The German Anatomical Nomenclature Commission adopted the teaching of His in this matter in its entirety, and called his 'lobus olfactorius' the 'rhinencephalon', under the mistaken idea that it represented the region so-called by Turner. **1908, 1921** [see *archipallium]. **1978** C. Reid *Primer Human Neuroanat.* xv. 141 The rhinencephalon refers to the olfactory part of the brain and the use of this term at the present state of knowledge is fraught with difficulties.

rhinencephalic *a.* (earlier and later examples).

1846 R. Owen *Hunterian Lect.* II. viii. 181 A few of the medullary fibres. .are continued forwards and outwards, as 'rhinencephalic crura'. **1956** *Sci. Amer.* Oct. 108/2 The test was performed on the animal with the electrode in the rhinencephalic nerve.

rhinestone. Add: **b.** (Earlier and later examples.) Also *fig.* and *attrib.* Hence **rhi·nestoned** *a.*, decorated with rhinestones.

1888 A. Randall-Diehl *Two Thousand Words* 179 *Rhinestone*, a stone which may be made to resemble the diamond. 'Rhinstones [*sic*] as well as paste, are taking the place of diamonds off as well as on the stage.' **1931** W. Faulkner *Sanctuary* xxviii. 283 The hat bore a rhinestone ornament. **1961** Webster, Rhinestoned adj. **1967** 'La Meri' *Spanish Dancing* (ed. 2) vii. 96 Rhinestones covered boleros, *queso* hats and shoe-heels in a blinding flash. **1975** *New Yorker* 20 Oct. 154/1 This is an exasperating book... It has far too many rhinestones. **1976** L. St. Clair *Fortune in Death* xiii. 126 Blonde showgirls. .in plumed headdresses and rhinestoned G-strings. **1977** *Time* 29 Aug. 24/2 The music got slicker and often sillier, turned from rock toward rhinestone country and spangled gospel. **1981** *Times* 7 July 11/1 The intricate rhinestone and bead embroidery.

rhinion (rəi·ni,ɒn). *Anat.* [a. G. *rhinion* (A. von Török 1888, in *Monthly Internat. Jrnl. Anat. & Physiol.* V. 281), f. Gr. ῥῖν-ός, ῥίς nose: see *-ion[2].] The foremost point at which the two nasal bones meet.

1904 W. L. H. Duckworth *Morphol. & Anthrop.* x. 229 *Rhinion*, the most prominent point at which the nasal bones touch each other. **1937** *Amer. Jrnl. Physical Anthrop.* XXII. 486 *Rhinion*, the lower end of the internasal suture. **1968** H. de Villiers *Skull of S. African Negro* ix. 127 Nasion may be inset and thus lie at a greater or lesser distance from a line joining glabella to rhinion. *Ibid.* 128 Even moderately curved profiles ending abruptly at rhinion (category 1) or recurving slightly before rhinion (category 2) occur most commonly in the South African Negro.

rhino[2]. Add: **1.** (Further example.) Also *attrib.* and *fig.*

1890 F. D. Lugard *Diary* 22 Feb. (1959) I. ii. 111 Fresher rhino tracks, and elephant spoor everywhere. **1938** J. S. Huxley in *Times* 17 Aug. 11/5 Has not the time come when we can discard our etymological prejudices, accept the usage of the ordinary man, and frankly use 'rhinos'? **1973** M. Amis *Rachel Papers* 27 When I awoke that morning the bedroom was a rhino pen. **1979** *Monitor* (McAllen, Texas) 15 July 8E/5 Three of the surviving rhino species are Asian and two are native to Africa.

2. Special Combs.: **rhino beetle, bird, horn** = *rhinoceros beetle*, etc., s.v. Rhinoceros 3 in Dict. and Suppl.

1958 J. Slimming *Temiar Jungle* i. 14 The bundle contained a large rhino beetle, still alive but half suffocated. **1951** R. Campbell *Light on Dark Horse* x. 131 The various types of rhino-birds and tick-birds. .give warning to the game on whose parasites they feed. **1957** —— *Portugal* v. 87, I came across mermaids on the Rufigi River while trading in poached rhino-horns. **1974** O. Manning *Rain Forest* i. iv. 62 You could find his name on the dockets of some pretty strange things. .Rhino horn, cantharides. **1979** *Monitor* (McAllen, Texas) 15 July 8E/5 Rhino horn has long been valued as an aphrodisiac by the oriental cultures.

rhino-. Add: **rhi:nolaryngi·tis** (see quot. 1900); **rhi:nolaryngo·logy** the study and pathology of the nose and larynx; hence **rhi:nolaryngolo·gic** *a.*; **rhi:nolaryngo·logist,** an expert or specialist in rhinolaryngology; **rhi:nopharyngi·tis,** inflammation of the nose and pharynx; **rhi:nopneumoni·tis** *Vet. Sci.*, any of three similar contagious diseases of horses, caused by herpes viruses and characterized by rhinitis; **rhinotheca,** for 'beak' read 'upper jaw'; [coined by J. C. W. Illiger in *Prodromus Systematis Mammalium et Avium* (1811) 150]; **rhino:trachei·tis** *Vet. Sci.*, a respiratory disease of cattle; also, a similar disease of cats.

1900 Dorland *Med. Dict.* 571/2 *Rhinolaryngitis*, inflammation of the mucous membrane of the nose and larynx. **1959** B. Wootton *Social Sci. & Social Path.* iv. 139 The incidence of, and the death rate from, rhinolaryngitis and infantile diarrhoea are abnormally high. **1933** *Jrnl. Amer. Med. Assoc.* 14 Oct. 1248/2 American physicians who studied in Vienna without having visited Professor Hajek's rhinolaryngologic clinic. **1938** Rhino-laryngologist [see *leprosarium]. **1959** *Jrnl. Laryngology & Otology* LXXIII. 65 Chordomata occur in the domain of the Rhino-laryngologist much more than anywhere else. **1900** Dorland *Med. Dict.* 571/2 Rhinolaryngology. **1905** *Amer. Jrnl. Med. Sci.* CXXX. 733 (*heading*) Local anæsthetics in rhino-laryngology. **1933** *Jrnl. Amer. Med. Assoc.* 18 Mar. 852/2 (*heading*) Substitute for cocaine and procaine in rhino-laryngology. **1896** *Amer. Yearbk. Surg.* 850 (*heading*) Neurasthenia due to ear-diseases and to rhinopharyngitides. **1951** M. Hynes *Med. Bacteriol.* (ed. 5) xi. 177 The meningococcus is spread from carrier to carrier by air-borne infection and settles in the nasopharynx, sometimes giving rise to rhinopharyngitis but usually causing no symptoms. **1957** E. R. Doll et al. in *Cornell Vet.* XLVII. 37 The most constant and severe lesions in the equine fetus also are in the respiratory tract. Uncomplicated natural infection by the virus causes a febrile reaction accompanied principally by a rhinitis. Accordingly, rhinopneumonitis, which embraces the nasal catarrh and pulmonary lesions, is designated as the name for the disease. **1978** *Jrnl. R. Soc. Med.* LXXI. 660 Foals aborted as a result of rhinopneumonitis. .are also of expected normal weight and size. **1955** *Jrnl. Amer. Vet. Med. Assoc.* CXXVI. 463 (*heading*) Infectious necrotic rhinotracheitis of cattle. *Ibid.* 463/1 At first this condition was referred to simply as a virus disease... For the last two years it has been called necrotic rhinotracheitis or, for brevity, just 'necrotic rhinitis'. **1970** Jubb & Kennedy *Path. Domestic Animals* (ed. 2) iii. 166/2 Feline viral rhinotracheitis was undoubtedly the principal infection in 'cat distemper' or 'cat flu', etc., until Crandall and Maurer gave it pathological distinction. **1977** *Lancet* 13 Aug. 356/1 Hereford cattle may be susceptible to the carcinogenic action of an ocular herpesvirus (e.g., bovine rhinotracheitis virus) that has been inactivated by exposure to ultraviolet radiation.

rhinocerine, *a.* Add: **2.** Characteristic of or resembling a rhinoceros.

1958 *Listener* 16 Jan. 102/1 The white rhino, a shy dozy animal who likes to. .lie in the mud and dream deep rhinocerine dreams. **1977** J. McClure *Sunday Hangman* iv. 34 The rhinocerine person of Sergeant Cecil Arnot.

rhinoceros. Add: **1. b.** (Earlier examples.)
1613 MARSTON *Insatiate Countess* I. sig.A4ᵛ, Mountebancke with thy Pedanticall action, Rimatrix, Buglors, Rhimocers [*sic*]. **1869** T. TAYLOR *Our Amer. Cousin* II. 29 There's that damned rhinoceros again.

3. *rhinoceros-run*; *rhinoceros-black, -like* adjs.; **rhinoceros auklet,** a puffin of the north Pacific, *Cerorhinca monocerata* (= *rhinoceros auk*); **rhinoceros bird,** (*b*) (earlier and later examples); **rhinoceros bush,** also = *RHENOSTERBOS; (earlier and later examples); **rhinoceros puff-adder,** for def. read: = **rhinoceros viper*; **rhinoceros viper,** a venomous West African snake, *Bitis nasicornis*.
1887 R. RIDGWAY *Man. N. Amer. Birds* 12 Rhinoceros auklet. **1976** *Islander* (Victoria, B.C.) 19 Sept. 13/1 Common Murres and Rhinoceros Auklets were in abundance. **1822** J. CAMPBELL *Travels S. Africa: Narr. Second Journey* I. xxiv. 282 There is a brown bird, about the size of a thrush, called the rhinoceros' bird, from its perching upon those animals and picking off the brush-lice which fix on him. **1947** J. STEVENSON-HAMILTON *Wild Life S. Afr.* v. 47 The black rhinoceros..is often accompanied by rhinoceros birds (*Buphaga*), which give the alarm on the approach of enemies. **1925** E. SITWELL *Troy Park* 82 Rhinoceros-black (a flowing sea!). **1731** G. MEDLEY tr. *Kolb's Pres. State Cape Good-Hope* II. 104 The Delight of his [*sc.* the rhinoceros's] Tooth is a Shrub, not much unlike the Juniper... The Cape-Europeans call it the Rhinoceros-Bush. **1839** W. C. HARRIS *Wild Sports S. Afr.* 30 Barely sufficient quantity of fuel, from a shrub called the rhinoceros bush, could be obtained. **1915** E. R. LANKESTER *Diversions of Naturalist* xxviii. 260 The skulls and whole skeletons of great rhinoceros-like animals..are dug up in early tertiary sands. **1909** *Chambers's Jrnl.* Sept. 568/2 Elephant-tracks and rhinoceros-runs pierced the jungle here and there. **1910** R. L. DITMARS *Reptiles of World* IV. 327 The Rhinoceros Viper is..the most beautifully coloured of all poisonous snakes. **1965** R. & D. MORRIS *Men & Snakes* i. 16 The rhinoceros viper has a snout appendage of large pointed scales which looks like an erect horn.

rhinocerotid (raɪnɒsĕrǫ·tid). *Zool.* [f. mod.L. family name *Rhinocerotidæ*: see RHINOCEROS and -ID³.] A fossil mammal of the family Rhinocerotidæ.
1969 *Nature* 1 Feb. 452/1 Both forested and riverine environments are suggested by the Nagri tragulids, anthracotheres, rhinocerotids and dinotheres. **1976** *Ibid.* 5 Aug. 464/1 The existence of two rhinocerotids has been established by the discovery of skulls of both *Ceratotherium* and *Diceros*.

rhinophyma (raɪnofaɪ·mă). *Med.* Pl. **rhinophymata, -phymas.** [mod.L. (coined in Ger. by H. von Hebra 1881, in *Vierteljahresschrift f. Dermatol.* VIII. 603), f. Gr. ῥῑν-ός, ῥίς nose + L. *phȳma* swelling, tumour (ad. Gr. φῦμα growth, tumour).] Chronic enlargement and reddening of the nose with hypertrophy of its sebaceous glands.
1882 *London Med. Rec.* IX. 69/1 (*heading*) Hebra.—On rhinophyma. **1915** *Lancet* 18 Sept. 643/2 Rhinophymata give rise to much mental distress and worry, and a desire to shun all society on account of the unsightly appearance produced by their presence. **1920** *Jrnl. Amer. Med. Assoc.* 22 May 1450/1 Operative removal of rhinophymas has not offered much encouragement to surgeons. **1947** G. D. WOLF *Ear, Nose & Throat* xx. 407 Rhinophyma is the advanced and terminal stage of acne rosacea of the nose. **1973** *Sci. Amer.* Sept. 4/2 *An Old Man and His Grandson*, painted by Domenico Ghirlandaio late in the 15th century... The old man apparently suffers from rhinophyma, a condition in which the nose becomes knobby and enlarged as a result of rosacea, a chronic disease involving overactivity of the sebaceous glands. Usually the nose is also reddened, because small blood vessels become dilated.

rhinoplasty. (Earlier and later examples.)
1842 T. D. MÜTTER *Recent Improvem. Surg.* 33 Adopting the phraseology of Zeis, I include under the expression *plastic surgery*, all the specific terms..such as rhinoplasty when the nose is made, cheiloplasty when the lips, [etc.]. **1978** *Detroit Free Press* 16 Apr. (Detroit Suppl.) 14/4 If the same surgeon does a rhinoplasty he'll probably be paid $800 to $1,200.

rhinosporidiosis (raɪ:nospŏridi,ōᵘ·sis). *Path.* [f. mod.L. *Rhinosporidi-um*, name of a genus of fungi (Minchin & Fantham 1905, in *Q. Jrnl. Microsc. Sci.* XLIX. 521: see RHINO- and SPORIDIUM) + -OSIS.] Chronic infection of mucous membrane and rarely of skin by the fungus *Rhinosporidium seeberi*.
1923 ASHWORTH & TURNER in *Edin. Med. Jrnl.* XXX. 337 (*heading*) A case of rhinosporidiosis. **1935** *Indian Med. Gaz.* LXX. 76/1 Reports of rhinosporidiosis in females are rare. **1965** *New Scientist* 22 Apr. 243/3 Rhinosporidiosis is a widespread disease causing obstructive growths in the nasal passages of bathers and divers in southern Asia and S. America.

Also **rhinospori·dial** *a.*, pertaining to or caused by rhinosporidiosis.
1923 *Trans. R. Soc. Edin.* LIII. 332 The three series of Rhinosporidium, which I have studied..agree so closely with one another and with the examples described by Minchin and Fantham as *Rhinosporidium kinealyi*..that they obviously belong to the same species, and the other Rhinosporidial nasal polypi recorded in natives of India and Ceylon are also no doubt due to this species. **1954** R. D. G. P. SIMONS *Med. Mycol.* xxxiv. 369 Rhinosporidia granuloma has been found in many countries.

rhinoster bos(ch), bush, varr. *RHENOSTERBOS(CH), -BUSH.

rhinovirus (raɪ·novaɪᵊrŏs). *Biol.* [mod.L., f. RHINO- + VIRUS.] Any of a group of picornaviruses including those which cause some forms of the common cold.
1961 C. H. ANDREWES in *Yale Jrnl. Biol. Med.* XXXIV. 201 It was reported that some rather different viruses had been cultivated from colds in adults and that these had strong claims to be the agents which were being sought. These newly discovered agents, for which the name Rhinovirus is proposed, are the subject of this paper. **1970** *Daily Tel.* 1 Dec. 5/3 Symptomless rhinovirus infections occur. In addition, rhinoviruses and rhinovirus colds are most prevalent in the spring when sudden changes in temperature most commonly occur. The rhinoviruses are responsible for most colds. **1974** *Nature* 27 Sept. 276/1 Picornaviruses can be divided by physiochemical methods into five subgroups: enteroviruses (for example polio, swine vesicular disease), cardioviruses (such as EMC, Maus Elberfeld (ME)), foot and mouth disease viruses (FMDV) and human and equine rhinoviruses. **1978** G. A. SHEEHAN *Running & Being* x. 140 We become infected with one of the numerous rhinoviruses.

rhipidistian (ripidi·stiăn), *sb.* and *a.* [f. mod.L. *Rhipidistia* (E. D. Cope 1887, in *Amer. Naturalist* XXI. 1017), f. Gr. ῥιπίς, ῥιπιδ- fan + ἱστία pl. of ἱστίον sail + -AN.] **A.** *sb.* A fossil fish belonging to the superorder Rhipidistia, which includes primitive crossopterygian fishes with paired fins that may have muscular lobes. **B.** *adj.* Of or pertaining to a fish of this kind or the group as a whole.
1916 *Mem. & Proc. Manch. Lit. & Philos. Soc.* LX. II. 23 Extensive fusions may have taken place between the bones of the head of Rhipidistians. **1931** J. R. NORMAN *Hist. Fishes* xvii. 358 One of the earliest members of the order is the interesting *Dipterus*, found in the Old Red Sandstone of Scotland along with the early Rhipidistians and Palaeoniscids. **1964** *Bull. Mus. Compar. Zool. Harvard* CXXXI. 313 (*heading*) The comparative anatomy of the snout in rhipidistian fishes. *Ibid.* 331 The etmoid endocranium has been described in the following rhipidistian genera: *Ectosteorhachis*.., *Eusthenopteron* [etc.]. **1978** *Sci. Amer.* Sept. 111/1 The earliest amphibians arose from a primitive group of lobe fins (the rhipidistians), and so all four-footed vertebrates (tetrapods) and their descendants also evolved from this vanished fish stock. **1979** *Nature* 18 Jan. 176/2 The mutual relations of salmon (an actinopterygian), lungfish (a dipnoan) and cow (a mammal, a class which can be traced back to rhipidistian crossopterygians by way of reptiles and amphibians) are certainly worthy of serious consideration.

rhipiphorid (ripi·fǫrid), *sb.* and *a.* *Ent.* Also **Rhip-.** [f. mod.L. family name *Rhipiphoridæ*, f. generic name *Rhipiphorus* (L. Bosc 1792, in *Jrnl. d'Hist. Nat.* II. 293, as *Ripiphorus*), f. Gr. ῥιπίς fan + mod.L. *-phorus* (see -PHOROUS): see -ID³.] **A.** *sb.* A beetle of the group Rhipiphoridæ, larvæ of which are endoparasites in insects, esp. wasps. **B.** *adj.* Of, pertaining to, or designating a beetle of this group.
1899 D. SHARP *Insects* II. v. 267 The elytra are, in several Rhipiphorids,..reduced to a very small size, and the wings are not folded. **1909** *Cent. Dict.* Suppl., *Rhipiphorid* adj. **1957** *Ann. Entom. Soc. Amer.* L. 96/1 The importance of genitalic structure in rhipiphorid taxonomy. **1968** R. H. ARNETT *Beetles U.S.* 635 Hymenopteran larvae attacked by rhipiphorids generally complete their development up to pupation before they are killed. **1973** EVANS & EBERHARD *Wasps* vi. 236 (*caption*) *Macrosiagon flavipenne*, a rhipiphorid beetle that is a parasite of *Bembix* wasps.

rhipsalis (ripsēⁱ·lis). *Bot.* Also **Rhipsalis.** Pl. **rhipsalides** (ripsæ·lidīz), **rhipsalises.** [mod.L. (J. Gaertner *De Fructibus & Seminibus Plantarum* (1788) I. 137), f. Gr. ῥίψ wickerwork, mat + L. *-ālis* (see -AL).] Any cactus of the genus so called, which is the only one to occur naturally in the Old World and comprises plants with branching stems, many of which are epiphytes with hanging branches; cf. *mistletoe cactus* s.v. *MISTLETOE 3.
1831 *Curtis's Bot. Mag.* LVIII. 3080 (*heading*) Rhipsalis Cassytha. Naked Rhipsalis. **1837** *Mag. Zool. & Bot.* I. 469 The fruit of Rhipsalis has been considered to possess a different structure from that of all other Cacteæ. **1884** L. CASTLE *Cactaceous Plants* 72 The chief distinguishing characters relied upon being the position of the flowers—namely, at the points of the branches, instead of being produced at the sides as in the other Rhipsalises. **1944** S. PUTNAM tr. *E. da Cunha's Rebellion in Backlands* i. 35 The sinuous rhipsalides, twining like green vipers through the tree branches. **1962** *Amateur Gardening* 24 Feb. 2/1 Several genera are epiphytes, growing..on the..branches of trees.. [including] the various species of mistletoe cactus, rhipsalis.

rhitidome, var. RHYTIDOME in Dict. and Suppl.

rhizina. Substitute for def.: A root-like structure on the underside of a lichen, consisting of one or several rhizoids. (Further examples.)
rhizine is the usual form of the word.
1914 M. DRUMMOND tr. *Haberlandt's Physiol. Plant Anat.* v. 260 Among lichens the lower side of the thallus produces numbers of rhizoidal hyphae, which..act as root-hairs. In certain species they are united to form stout strands, the so-called rhizines. **1938** G. M. SMITH *Cryptogamic Bot.* I. xv. 515 A rhizine may consist of a single simple to branched hypha or of a number of parallel hyphae that lie closely applied to one another. **1977** *Nature* 6 Jan. 46/1 In contrast to lichens and mosses, whose rhizines and rhizoids serve mainly for attachment, trees have root systems which transport sulphate upward.

rhizo-. Add: **rhizo·tomy** *Surg.*, section of a spinal nerve root.
1911 *Brit. Med. Jrnl.* 2 Sept. 523/2 Dorsal rhizotomy failed to give permanent and complete relief [from pain]. **1955** NAFFZIGER & ADAMS in A. B. Baker *Clin. Neurol.* III. xxviii. 1445 The conversion of a spastic into a flaccid paraplegia by anterior rhizotomy is now well established. **1977** *Lancet* 17 Sept. 594/2 Before the advent of drug treatment for spasticity, the only remedy lay in irreversible operations such as tenotomies and rhizotomies.

rhizobium (raɪzōᵘ·biŏm). Also **Rhizobium.** Pl. **-ia.** [mod.L. (coined in Ger. by B. Frank 1889, in *Ber. d. deutsch. bot. Ges.* VIII. 338), f. RHIZO- + Gr. βίος life.] A bacterium of the genus so called, which comprises heterotrophic aerobic individuals that form root nodules on leguminous plants and fix atmospheric nitrogen symbiotically with the plants.
1921 R. E. BUCHANAN *Agric. & Industr. Bacteriol.* iii. 32 Rhizobium.—These organisms are minute rods, motile when young, by means of flagellata. **1947** *Endeavour* VI. 130 When the seed of a legume develops in a soil containing *Rhizobia* the latter are attracted to the region of the developing root hairs. **1966** *McGraw-Hill Encycl. Sci. & Technol.* XI. 546/2 The treatment of leguminous seeds with bulk preparations of effective rhizobia is widely practiced.. for the purpose of..improving the yield and quality of leguminous plants. **1972** A. H. GIBSON in Leigh & Noble *Plants for Sheep in Austral.* xi. 103 Considerable attention has been given to the development of techniques for estimating numbers of rhizobia in the soil. **1973** [see *NODULATE *v.* a].

Hence **rhizo·bial** *a.*, of or pertaining to rhizobia; **rhizo·bially** *adv.*
1957 *Times* 2 Dec. (Agric. Suppl.) p. vi/5 Both were inoculated with a peat-bound rhizobial culture and the fortuitous treading of the grazing animal was the only way in which the seeds could be covered. **1971** *Nature* 16 July 175/1 The degree of rhizobial invasion after transfer of the cultured soybean root cells is related to the growth factor additions to the MS medium. **1977** *Whitaker's Almanack 1978* 1030/1 Much of the recent work has been concentrated on showing that the selection of the right legume with the appropriate rhizobial species depends on the lectin existing in the legume. **1977** J. L. HARPER *Population Biol. Plants* xi. 365 Small amounts of ¹⁵N, a stable isotope, had been applied to the soil so that the nitrogen available to both species in the soil could be distinguished from the rhizobially fixed nitrogen which was unlabelled.

Rhizoctonia (raɪzǫktōᵘ·niă). [mod.L. (A. P. de Candolle *Flore française* (1815) VI. 110), f. RHIZO- + Gr. κτόν-ος murder + -IA¹.] A fungus of the form-genus so called, which comprises sterile fungi some of which cause disease in plants; also, a fungus formerly placed in this genus but reassigned following the discovery of a sexual state. Freq. *attrib.*
1897 W. G. SMITH tr. *K. F. von Tubeuf's Diseases of Plants* II. i. 201 The spores open by a longitudinal slit, and a germ-tube emerging from each end branches into a mycelium which soon takes on the form of a rhizoctonia-strand. **1916** *Bull. Illinois Agric. Exper. Station* No. 189. 376 There are recognized in America two species of truly parasitic Rhizoctonias. **1927** *Ann. Appl. Biol.* XIV. 290 (*heading*) Rhizoctonia 'foot-rot' of the tomato. **1937** F. D. HEALD *Introd. Plant Path.* xi. 226 The damping-off by Rhizoctonia is..serious in both garden and field. **1953** F. T. BROOKS *Plant Diseases* (ed. 2) xv. 299 Other fungi producing small sclerotia also attack cereals and grasses, notably *Sclerotium rhizodes* Auersw., now considered to be a Rhizoctonia. **1965** BELL & COOMBE tr. *Strasburger's Textbk. Bot.* 506 *Corticium solani* causes the *Rhizoctonia*-disease (a root rot) of potatoes. **1977** J. L. HARPER *Population Biol. Plants* vi. 174 Density-dependent mortality is well known in forest nurseries where it is usually associated with pathogenic activity (e.g. Gibson (1956) showed that *Rhizoctonia* was responsible for killing a higher proportion of seedlings in overcrowded plots).

rhizoid, *sb.* Substitute for def.: A delicate root-like structure on the underside of many lower plants. (Further examples.)
1914 M. DRUMMOND tr. *Haberlandt's Physiol. Plant Anat.* v. 226 The trichomes in question..are endowed with the properties of typical root-hairs, but in addition possess many of the capacities of roots; in particular, rhizoids agree with roots in being sensitive to the influence of light, gravity and moisture, whereas genuine root-hairs are quite free from these forms of irritability. **1952** J. CLEGG *Freshwater Life* iv. 88 Stoneworts have no roots in the strict botanical sense, but root-like structures, or rhizoids, penetrate the mud and serve to anchor the plants. **1965** BELL & COOMBE tr. *Strasburger's Textbk. Bot.* 70 Roots are lacking in the Bryophyta, but in their place most possess delicate rhizoids. **1977** [see *RHIZINE].

rhizomic (rəizōᵘ·mik), *a. Bot. rare.* [f. RHIZOM(E + -IC.] Pertaining to or of the nature of a rhizome.

1902 *Nature* 21 Aug. 399/2 The examination of rhizomic material of the unique fern *Matonia pectinata.*

rhizoplane (rəi·zoplēⁱn). *Ecol.* [f. RHIZO- + PLANE *sb.*³] (See quot. 1949.)

1949 F. E. CLARK in *Adv. Agronomy* I. 246 It would be more logical to speak of this microflora in terms of the root surfaces than in terms of the soil adjacent to the roots of plants. This goal can be obtained by the use of the term, *rhizoplane.* The rhizoplane is defined as the external surfaces of plant roots together with any closely adhering particles of soil or debris. **1961** *Canad. Jrnl. Bot.* XXXIX. 175 Infestation of the roots of tomato seedlings with naturally occurring rhizoplane fungi. **1975** *Sydowia Ann. Mycol.* XXVII. 312 *(heading)* Fungi isolated from rhizosphere, rhizoplane and soil.

rhizoplast (rəi·zoplɑst). *Microbiology.* [f. RHIZO- + -PLAST.] A fibrous structure running from the nucleus of a protozoan to a blepharoplast (kinetosome).

1915 I. MCCULLOCH in *Univ. Calif. Publ. Zool.* XVI. 3 In the central part of the hyaline body there is a large vesicular nucleus connected directly with the extranuclear organelles, the rhizoplast, 'kinetonucleus', flagellum, basal granule and the 'axostyle'. *Ibid.* 5 The rhizoplast is a faint line connecting the 'kinetonucleus' with the nucleus. **1947** *Ann. Rev. Microbiol.* I. 8 In the Polymastigina the anteriorly placed blepharoplast is the center of organization. From it originate the flagella, the rhizoplasts, the axostyles, [etc.]. **1976** EDINGTON & GILLES *Path. in Tropics* (ed. 2) ii. 55 The eccentric spherical nucleus is about 1 μm in diameter and the rod-shaped rhizoplast may or may not be detectable.

rhizopod². Add: **2.** *Zool.* Usu. in L. form **rhizopodium** (pl. **-podia**). In Protozoa, a pseudopodium that branches and anastomoses to form a network.

1931 R. R. KUDO *Handbk. Protozool.* ii. 26 Rhizopodia. These are branching (reticulopodia) or anastomosing (myxopodia) temporary cytoplasmic projections. **1940** L. H. HYMAN *Invertebrates* I. iii. 119 Thread-like pseudopodia that branch and anastomose into networks are termed reticulopods or rhizopods. **1958** G. A. KERKUT *Borradaile & Potts's Invertebrata* (ed. 3) ii. 17 Granules may often be seen to stream up and down the axopodia and rhizopodia. **1972** M. S. GARDINER *Biol. Invertebrates* vi. 177/2 The rhizopodia of Foraminifera are characteristically filamentous and branching, with anastomoses of the branches forming a network.

Rhizopus (rəi·zopʊs). [mod.L. (C. G. Ehrenberg 1820, in *Nova Acta Physico-Med. Acad. Cæsareæ Leopoldino-Carolinæ Naturæ Curiosorum* X. 198), f. RHIZO- + *-pus* (f. Gr. πούς foot), in allusion to the form of its rhizoids.] A fungus of the genus so called (class Zygomycetes), the members of which are saprobic and include the bread-mould fungus and many that cause disease (*Rhizopus rot*) in fruit and vegetables.

1887 H. E. F. GARNSEY tr. *A. de Bary's Compar. Morphol. & Biol. Fungi* v. 153 Branched gonidiophores..rise in a curve into the air from well-fed mycelia in a similar manner to the stolons of Rhizopus. **1912** *Jrnl. South-Eastern Agric. College, Wye* XXI. 387 On November 28th neither 4 nor 5 showed signs of the *Rhizopus* rot and as other fungi began to appear the experiment was not continued. **1927** GWYNNE-VAUGHAN & BARNES *Struct. & Devel. Fungi* 320 For rough cultures of *Mucor* and *Rhizopus* it is only necessary to scatter a little dust upon a slab of moist bread. **1953** F. T. BROOKS *Plant Dis.* (ed. 2) viii. 115 The chief factors in preventing Rhizopus rot are temperature and humidity. **1957** [see *MUCORMYCOSIS]. **1969** G. N. AGRIOS *Plant Path.* ix. 260 Attempts have..been made to control *Rhizopus* rots by irradiating the fruit with gamma radiation. **1975** *Mycologia* LXVII. 394 Another problem was the luxuriant, tall, spreading growth of certain molds, such as *Rhizopus*, which obscure all other fungi.

rhizosphere (rəi·zosfiᵊɹ). *Bot.* [ad. G. *rhizosphäre* (L. Hiltner 1904, in *Arbeiten der deutsch. Landwirtschaftsges.* XCVIII. 69): see RHIZO- and SPHERE *sb.*] The sphere of chemical and bacteriological influence of the roots of a plant.

1929 R. L. STARKEY in *Soil Sci.* XXVII. 319 The plants withdraw considerable amounts of substances (principally inorganic) from the rhizosphere.., and eventually introduce large amounts of organic matter to the soil in the form of their dead tissues. **1956** *Nature* 4 Feb. 221/1 A small epiphytic fern..common not only on trunks and branches, but also having a tendency to settle on leaves, to which it attaches itself by spreading roots and root hairs... Fungi living in the rhizosphere of the fern infect the tree-support and cause the die-back of the branches. **1972** J. G. CRUICKSHANK *Soil Geogr.* vi. 175 At all sites, plant roots have a rhizosphere, created by their excreted organic solutions and maintained by vast numbers of organisms. **1976** *Jrnl. R. Soc. Arts* CXXIV. 583/2 In some tropical species there is an association of nitrogen-fixing bacteria in the rhizosphere (not actually in the root itself, in nodules, but around the root) which are believed to exchange nitrogen and carbohydrates with the plant.

rho (rōᵘ). [Gr. ῥῶ.] **1.** The seventeenth letter of the Greek alphabet, Ρ, ρ.

*c*1400 MANDEVILLE *Trav.* (MS. Cotton Titus C. xvi, fol. 9ᵛ), An Abc of anoþer manere A. B. C. Δ...o.breuis. pi. cophe. ro. summa. tau. [etc.]. **1611** [see *CHI-RHO]. **1746** T. NUGENT tr. *De Port Royal's New Method of Learning Gk. Tongue* I. I. ii. 3 The Greeks have 24 letters, whose Figure, Name, and Power are as followeth:..Rho..Sigma..Tau. **1883** I. TAYLOR *Alphabet* II. vii. 106 Even before the transmission of the alphabet to Italy the primitive Greek *rho*.. which at Thera is hardly distinguishable from *delta*, began to be differentiated by a short tail. **1965** J. W. WENHAM *Elements N.T. Gk.* i. 18 The alphabet... Rhō.

2. *Statistics.* Used to represent a coefficient of correlation calculated from the ranks of the data and answering to the product-moment coefficient.

[**1910** C. SPEARMAN in *Brit. Jrnl. Psychol.* III. 287 He [*sc.* K. Pearson] has worked out the relation between the coefficients of ranks..and those of measurements, assuming Gaussian distribution. It is $r = 2\sin(\pi\rho/6)$, where ρ denotes the coefficient for ranks.] **1940** R. S. WOODWORTH *Psychol.* (ed. 12) iii. 89 'Rho' is a measure of correlation, known as the rank-difference measure. **1949** Q. MCNEMAR *Psychol. Statistics* vi. 98 Rho is not as consistent from sample to sample as *r*, does not possess the mathematical advantages inherent in *r*, and therefore has merit only when the observations involve ranks, i.e. are not measures. **1970** *Jrnl. Gen. Psychol.* LXXXIII. 209 These two rankings were then correlated by use of Spearman's rho. **1978** *Maledicta* II. 55 The computed rho of 0·7006 indicates that there is a high degree of systematic ordering between male and female rest room graffiti.

3. *Physics.* In full *rho meson.* A meson with zero hypercharge, unit isospin, unit spin, and negative parity that has a mass of about 770 MeV (1506 times that of the electron) and on decaying usu. produces two pions. Freq. represented by ρ.

1961 S. BERGIA et al. in *Physical Rev. Lett.* VI. 370/1 The possibility of detecting experimentally the $T = 0$ unstable particle (which we shall denote by ρ) is discussed. **1970** *New Scientist* 16 Apr. 105/2 The rho meson is produced in this case from high energy photons incident on the complex nuclei. The rho is scattered in the nucleus before decaying. **1973** L. J. TASSIE *Physics of Elementary Particles* x. 115 In subsequent experiments, the ρ^+ has also been observed. **1977** S. WEINBERG *First Three Minutes* vii. 141 Rho mesons behave as if they consist of a quark and an antiquark.

rhochrematics (rōᵘkrēmæ·tiks), *sb. pl.* [f. Gr. ῥοή or ῥόος stream, flow + χρηματ-, χρῆμα thing (in pl., goods) + -IC 2.] The science of the flow of materials and products from their sources to their final disposal. Hence **rhochremati·cian**, one who studies or makes use of this science.

1960 *(title)* Rhochrematics, a scientific approach to the management of material flows. **1960** *Aeroplane* XCIX. 495/1 The object of this discussion of 'rhochrematics' (a word which you won't find in your dictionary) was to show that the interaction among the separate functions of material flow and distribution and manufacturing costs must be studied and co-ordinated in order to arrive at an accurate product cost. **1962** *Flight Internat.* LXXXI. 322/1 To be 'with' air freight you must be able to throw away words like rhochrematics, inventory management, regional warehousing, etc. **1977** *Containerisation Internat.* June 59/2 As for the Rhochrematicians, if the container had not existed, they would have had to invent it.

rhodamine (rōᵘ·dămīn). *Chem.* Also **Rhodamine.** [ad. G. *rhodamin* (see E. Weingärtner 1887, in *Chem.-Zeitung* 25 Dec. 1620): see RHODO- and AMINE.] Any of a class of synthetic xanthene dyestuffs, chiefly reds, which are obtained by condensation of phthalic anhydride with *m*-aminophenols.

1888 *Jrnl. Soc. Chem. Industry* 31 May 386/2 The Badische Anilin u. Soda Fabrik have introduced a new colour Rhodamine. **1892** *Ibid.* 30 Apr. 345/2 Certain benzylated *m*-amidophenol derivatives can be condensed with phthalic anhydride to yield new basic rhodamine dyestuffs. **1903** C. SALTER tr. *G. von Georgievics' Chem. Dyestuffs* 199 On eliminating alkyl groups from Rhodamine by heating along with acids, the products obtained are..Rhodamines of a yellower tinge, *e.g.*, Rhodamine G (triethylrhodamine). **1947** C. L. BIRD *Theory & Pract. of Wool Dyeing* iv. 53 Rhodamine B is widely used, in spite of its very moderate fastness to light, on account of its brilliant shade, level dyeing properties, fastness to washing and sulphur stoving, and cheapness. **1968** E. N. ABRAHART *Dyes & Intermediates* x. 226 The use of Rhodamine B as a food colour has been discontinued for a number of years on account of its suspected carcinogenic nature. **1973** *Physics Bull.* July 419/3 The successful operation of the cw rhodamine 6G dye laser. **1976** *Sci. Amer.* Feb. 133/2 My method of detecting the location of colorless components of the sample is to stain them with a water-soluble dye such as rhodamine B.

rhodanizing (rōᵘ·dănəiziŋ). *Chem.* [f. RHOD(IUM² + -AN + -IZE + -ING¹.] (See quot. 1971.)

1936 *Discovery* July 218/1 The recently-discovered 'rhodanising' process for rendering silver untarnishable by the use of rhodium, is comparatively simple to operate, and can be applied to old as well as new silver. **1971** T. C. COLLOCOTT *Dict. Sci. & Technol.* 1007/1 *Rhodanizing*, the process of electroplating with rhodium, especially on silver, to prevent tarnishing.

rhodanthe (rodæ·nþi). [mod.L. (J. Lindley 1835, in *Edwards's Bot. Reg.* XX. 1703), f. Gr. ῥόδον rose + ἄνθος flower.] An annual herb, *Helipterum* (formerly *Rhodanthe*) *manglesii*, belonging to the family Compositæ, native to Australia, and bearing pink everlasting flowers.

1835 J. LINDLEY in *Edwards's Bot. Reg.* XX. 1703 *(heading)* Captain Mangles's Rhodanthe. **1927** *Jrnl. R. Hort. Soc.* LII. 271 They [*sc.* everlasting flowers] were represented in the trial by three stocks of Acroclinium, three of Rhodanthe, [etc.]. **1959** *Times* 17 Jan. 9/5 Helichrysums, acrocliniums, rhodanthes; all annuals and easy to raise in a greenhouse or warmed frame. **1962** [see *HELIPTERUM].

Rhode Island (rōᵘd əi·lănd). The name of an eastern state of the United States, used *attrib.* or *absol.* to designate plants or animals associated with the region, as **Rhode Island bent** = RED-TOP 2 (in Dict. and Suppl.); **Rhode Island greening**, a variety of green-skinned apple, or the tree producing it; **Rhode Island Red**, a domestic fowl belonging to the breed so called, distinguished by brownish-red plumage; **Rhode Island White**, a chicken belonging to a variety of the Rhode Island Red, having white plumage.

1790 S. DEANE *New-Eng. Farmer* 123/1 The Rhode Island bent, as it is called, or red top grass, will do with less drying than some other grasses. **1899** *U.S. Dept. Agric. Yearbk. 1898* 494 Creeping bent..and Rhode Island bent..are much prized for lawns. **1929** J. W. BEWS *World's Grasses* v. 198 The former [sc. *Agrostis tenuis*] is known as 'Rhode Island Bent'. **1795** J. JAY *Let.* 12 Dec. in *Columbia Library Columns* (1970) May 43 Ten are of a kind called Rhode Island Greenings. **1817** W. COXE *View Cultivation Fruit Trees* 129 Jersey, or Rhode-Island Greening. Sometimes called the Burlington Greening. **1884** E. P. ROE *Nature's Serial Story* 400 Those umbrella-shaped trees are Rhode Island greenings. **1896** *Country Gentleman* (Albany, N.Y.) 26 Nov. 911/2 The Rhode Island Red is a breed of fowls which is exciting considerable interest. **1902** *Outing* Apr. 64/2 The Rhode Island Red has originated in this country. A certain Mr. William Tripp, then of Little Compton, in the State of Rhode Island, bought from a neighbour..a rose-combed Brown Leghorn cockerel to cross upon his flock of buff Malay hens. **1931** E. CALDWELL *Amer. Earth* 76 We lived on a small farm and had..a flock of Rhode Island Red chickens. **1937** Rhode Island Red [see *KERRY²]. **1977** J. HODGINS *Invention of World* (1978) iii. 51 A dozen Rhode Island Reds Anna looked after for their eggs. **1926** *Bull. U.S. Dept. Agric.* No. 1506. 9 The Rhode Island White..is identical with the Rose-Comb Rhode Island Red, except that the plumage should be pure white. **1949** F. B. HUTT *Genetics of Fowl* 16 Color is the sole difference between the Rhode Island Whites and Rhode Island Reds.

Rhodes (rōᵘdz). [The name of Cecil John *Rhodes* (1853–1902), British financier and imperialist.] **1.** Applied *attrib.* to scholarships awarded annually since 1902 to students from the U.S., the British Commonwealth, South Africa, and Germany, for study at the University of Oxford; also to the scholars who receive these awards.

1902 G. CALDERON *Adventures Downy V. Green* xvi. 97 He had done three years at Harvard, and had come up with a Rhodes scholarship to Oxford. *Ibid.* 101 This is Mr. Cheney, Rhodes Scholar of Pusey. **1905** G. B. SHAW *Let.* 7 Oct. (1972) II. 566 Handsome of me not to make you a Rhodes scholar, by the way. **1909** K. PEARSON *Probl. Pract. Eugenics* 32 Cecil Rhodes..determined that the Rhodes scholars should be selected for ability, physique and character combined. **1911** M. BEERBOHM *Zuleika Dobson* viii. 129 The American Rhodes Scholars..are a noble, rather than a comfortable, element in the social life of the University. **1914** C. MACKENZIE *Sinister St.* II. III. ix. 688 Do you really think these Rhodes Scholars from America and Australia and Germany are going to affect us? **1934** C. STEAD *Seven Poor Men of Sydney* vi. 186 Handley, the Rhodes Scholar,..had shoulders like an ox. **1949** *Cavalier Daily* (Univ. Virginia) 22 Oct. 1/2 Robert D. Roller and Tiffany Williams, Jr. have been selected as the University's eligible candidates for this year's Rhodes Scholarship. **1955** [see *ROCK *v.*¹ 5 d]. **1965** *Austral. Encycl.* VII. 415/1 Rhodes Scholars cannot reasonably be expected, in all cases, to be paragons of intellect, literary and scholastic attainments, sporting ability, moral force, public spirit and leadership. **1973** E. PACE *Any War will Do* (1974) II. 102 Nobody out here is exactly Rhodes Scholar material. **1977** *Oxf. Univ. Gaz.* 3 June 850/1 The generosity of the Rhodes Trustees enables Lady Margaret Hall to invite applications for a Rhodes Visiting Fellowship for Women tenable at the college for two years starting in October 1978 or January 1979.

2. Rhodes (or **Rhodes'**) **grass**, a perennial grass, *Chloris gayana*, native to Africa and widely cultivated elsewhere as a pasture grass.

1915 R. MARLOTH *Flora S. Afr.* IV. 20 In some districts *Chloris gayana* (Rhodes' grass) and *Phalaris coerulescens*.. have also been found very valuable. **1929** J. W. BEWS *World's Grasses* v. 179 'Rhodes grass', a native of Africa,..is cultivated in the S.W. States of N. America, in Hawaii, and in Australia. **1940** F. D. DAVISON *Woman at Mill* 1. 87 The settlers were felling scrub..burning it off and sowing it to rhodes-grass..making fine grass paddocks. **1962** *New Scientist* 1 Mar. 487/3 Since the beginning of the century, when it was introduced into Australia from its native home in Africa, Rhodes grass (*Chloris gayana*) has become the dominant pasture species. **1977** J. L. HARPER *Population Biol. Plants* xi. 364 Hill examined the nitrogen relations of *Chloris gayana* (Rhodes grass).

Rhodesian (rōᵘdɪ·ʃiăn, -ʒăn), *a.* and *sb.* [f. (sense A. 1) the name of C. J. *Rhodes* (see *Rhodes) + -ian; (other senses) *Rhodesia* (see note) + -an.

Rhodesia (so called in the late nineteenth century after Cecil Rhodes) was orig. the name of a large British territory in southern Africa comprising North-Eastern and North-Western (later Northern) Rhodesia, and Southern Rhodesia. Northern Rhodesia became known on independence (1964) as Zambia, and Southern Rhodesia (then Rhodesia) became Zimbabwe on independence (1980).]

A. *adj.* † **1.** With pronunc. (rōᵘ·dziăn). Of or pertaining to C. J. Rhodes. *Obs.*

1891 *Review of Reviews* Jan. 8/2 He maintains that the Portuguese..are most objectionable people, whose elimination from South Africa is one of the planks of the Rhodesian platform. **1893** *Work & Workers* Nov. 450/2 Lo Bengula's forces, bent on revenge, are slowly moving towards the Rhodesian settlements. **1897** [see *Krugerism].

2. Of, pertaining to, or belonging to Rhodesia.

1895 *Rhodesian Mining & Finance Co. Ltd. Prospectus* 5 (*heading*) Form of Application for Shares. To the Directors of the Rhodesian Mining & Finance Company, Limited. **1899** M. M. Verney *Mem.* IV. vii. 258 He might be in the 'moral meridian' of Rhodesian politics to-day. **1902** *Encycl. Brit.* XXXII. 232/1 In November 1897 the Rhodesian Railway..had reached Bulawayo. **1935** *Discovery* Nov. 315/2 Here is an argument that should be retained in the mind of the exploiters of the countryside, whether Rhodesian, American, or even British. **1956** *African Affairs* LV. 70 MacDonald..commanded a Rhodesian battalion in the second world war. **1974** *Standard Encycl. S. Afr.* X. 141/2 In the Second World War it was decided to use the Rhodesian military potential in a somewhat different fashion. Rhodesian youths..made good officers, especially in colonial units. **1977** *Whitaker's Almanack 1978* 596/2 The Rhodesian prime minister (Mr Ian Smith) announced major relaxations in the racial laws.

3. Special collocations. **a.** Palæont. *Rhodesian man*, a fossil hominid usually considered to be an early type of *Homo sapiens*, known from remains found at Broken Hill, Northern Rhodesia, in 1921; *Rhodesian skull*, the skull of Rhodesian man.

1921 A. S. Woodward in *Nature* 17 Nov. 372/2 The newly discovered Rhodesian man may therefore revive the idea that Neanderthal man is truly an ancestor of *Homo sapiens*. **1937** *Jrnl. R. Anthrop. Inst.* LXVIII. 51 *Javanthropus* appears to be more primitive than the European Neandertal man and has quite a resemblance to the Rhodesian Man. **1946** F. E. Zeuner *Dating Past* ix. 296 Another undated Neandertaloid is the Rhodesian Skull. **1952** *Proc. Prehist. Soc.* XVIII. 125 This fossil [*sc.* the Florisbad skull] is now generally accepted as being a specialised type not much older than Rhodesian man. **1973** B. J. Williams *Evol. & Human Origins* xi. 185/1 The Saldanha skull provided another specimen almost identical to that of Rhodesian Man. *Ibid.*, The Rhodesian skull differs in minor features from the classic Neandertal of Europe. **1978** *Sci. Amer.* Sept. 150/2 Rhodesian man..a form no longer considered a distinct species.

b. *Rhodesian* (*tick*) *fever*, *redwater*, *sleeping sickness* = *East Coast fever* s.v. *east D. 1 b.

1904 Rhodesian redwater, tick fever [see *east D. 1 b]. **1904** *Jrnl. Trop. Med.* VII. 322/1 We are dealing with true Texas fever and not the atypical South African or Rhodesian fever. **1962** Gordon & Lavoipierre *Entomol.* xxix. 184 The chief vector of Rhodesian sleeping sickness..is *G*[*lossina*] *morsitans*.

c. *Rhodesian lion dog* or *ridgeback*, a large, short-coated, light brown dog belonging to the breed so called, distinguished by a ridge of hair along the middle of the back, growing in the opposite direction to the rest of the coat.

1930 *Observer* 9 Feb. 13/2 Such rarities as..Rhodesian lion dogs, distinguished by the ridge of hair running along the back the reverse way of the rest of the coat. **1937** *Our Dogs* 10 Dec. 886/2 The belief that the Rhodesian Ridgeback is the direct result of crossing the old Cuban Bloodhound with the Hottentot Hunting Dog arose a considerable time ago. **1948** C. L. B. Hubbard *Dogs in Britain* xxi. 373 The Rhodesian Ridgeback obtains its name from this crest of hair which is present in all true specimens of the breed. *Ibid.* 375 It [*sc.* the Rhodesian Ridgeback] was for some years known in Britain as the Rhodesian Lion Dog. **1955** J. Packer *Valley of Vines* iv. 44 Their house stood empty save for the Native boy, Elias, and two Rhodesian ridgebacks. **1979** A. Price *Tomorrow's Ghost* xi. 182, I think we ought to have dogs... A pair of Rhodesian Ridgebacks—'Lion Dogs'.

B. *sb.* **1.** A native or inhabitant of Rhodesia. (Until independence usu. specifically a white inhabitant of Rhodesia.)

1897 *Rhodesia* 27 Nov. 62/2 To avow that the average Rhodesian is any better than other frail humanity would be untrue; but they are no worse. **1901** G. Grey in *Geogr. Jrnl.* XVIII. 64 No one could fail to be impressed by the magnificence of the mighty river, much less a Rhodesian. **1936** *Jrnl. R. African Soc.* XXXV. 47 It is well..that the present generation of Rhodesians should be occasionally reminded that their prosperous condition has not been attained without much endurance. **1956** *African Affairs* LV. 70 The attitude of most Rhodesians may be said to be that, although they see in advancement of the African a possible limitation of their own privileges, they would not wish that progress to be curbed. **1977** *Time* 8 Aug. 26/2, I [*sc.* Ian Smith] have the backing of the majority of Rhodesians. I believe Rhodesians are prepared to move, but not in the direction of a sellout.

† **2.** *pl. Stock Exchange.* The shares of Rhodesian mining companies. *Obs.*

1901 [see *Kaffir Circus* s.v. *Kaffir 4]. **1936** *Economist* 28 Mar. 726/1 Rhodesians also failed to share in the improvement in the Kaffir department, and prices tended to sag.

† **3.** A Rhodes Scholar. *Obs.*

Perhaps better regarded as formed on *Rhodes with pronunc. (rōᵘ·dziăn).

1903 *'Varsity* 3 Mar. 209 Herds of cattle..infest the streets on market-days... However, we may look for an improvement..when the stock whips of the Rhodesians have become common weapons. **1905** *Athenæum* 16 Dec. 837/2 The Rhodesians are well spread out amongst the Colleges. Of the present year Christ Church takes 7; Balliol and Oriel, 5;..and the other Colleges 3 or less.

rhodesite (rōᵘ·dzəit). [f. the name of Cecil *Rhodes* (see *Rhodes) + -ite[1].] **1.** (With capital initial.) An admirer or supporter of Rhodes or his policies. *rare.*

1897 [see *Krugerism]. **1900** *Oldham Chron.* 15 Dec. 5/3 Sir Alfred Milner has displayed a singular lack of judgment. The High Commissioner has added one more to the many evidences on record of how completely he has been captured by the [Jameson] Raidites and Rhodesites.

2. *Min.* A hydrous silicate of calcium, sodium, and potassium, $(Ca,Na_2,K_2)_8Si_{16}O_{40}\cdot 11H_2O$, found as fibrous white orthorhombic crystals.

1957 E. D. Mountain in *Mineral. Mag.* XXXI. 607 A small specimen at first thought to be natrolite has proved to be a new mineral, for which the name rhodesite is proposed. **1969** *Amer. Mineralogist* LIV. 251 Rhodesite occurs as aggregates of radiating white, silky fibers associated with magadiite and trioctahedral montmorillonite in an altered silicic lava.

Rhodian, *a.* and *sb.* Add: **A.** *adj.* **c.** Designating a rhetorical style characteristic of the ancient Rhodian school of oratory; also, of the school itself.

1852 Disraeli *Ld. George Bentinck* xii. 203 The debate was opened by a dashing speech from Mr. McCarthy, worthy of the historical society in the most fervent hour of its Rhodian eloquence. **1876** —— in *Hansard Commons* 11 Aug. 1138 After the Rhodian eloquence to which we have just listened, it is rather difficult for the House to see clearly the point which is before it. **1954** H. Caplan in *Cicero's Ad Herennium* 193 The Rhodian school opposed the overloud delivery of the Asiatic orators. **1969** R. A. Lanham *Handlist Rhet. Terms* 90 *Rhodian style*, the middle style between Atticism and Asiatismus.

d. Designating a style of pottery characterized by brilliant red pigment, formerly thought to derive from Rhodes. Properly, a variety of later Isnik ware.

1899 R. Glazier *Man. Hist. Ornament* 80 In the Rhodian Ware..the purple is replaced by a fine opaque red of great body, called Rhodian red, produced from Armenian bole. **1900** F. Litchfield *Pott. & Porc.* vii. 244 We can readily recognise as a distinct class of decorative ware what is now known as Rhodian. **1957** [see *Isnik]. **1977** *Jrnl. R. Soc. Arts* CXXV. 482/2 A large Bichrome V ware crater, decorated on both sides between the handles with animals in what is certainly a perfect imitation of the Rhodian style of the seventh century BC.

rhodie, var. *rhody.

rhodinol (rōᵘ·dinǫl). *Chem.* [a. G. *rhodinol* (U. Eckart 1891, in *Arch. d. Pharm.* CCXXIX. 364), f. Gr. ῥόδιν-ος of or from roses (f. ῥόδον rose): see -ol.] An open-chain terpenoid primary alcohol, $C_{10}H_{20}O$, which is a red liquid first isolated from rose oil, and now known to be a mixture of two isomeric forms and to be identical with citronellol except in respect of the relative proportions of the isomers.

1892 *Jrnl. Chem. Soc.* LXII. i. 203 The author proposes the name rhodinol for the compound. **1894** *Ibid.* LXVI. i. 141 When oil of pelargonium is subjected to careful fractional distillation under reduced pressure, it yields rhodinol, ..identical..with the rhodinol obtained from oil of roses. **1929** [see *menthone]. **1953** D. H. R. Barton in E. H. Rodd *Chem. Carbon Compounds* IIb. xii. 496 The question of the constitution of citronellol and rhodinol is still a matter of controversy. **1956** I. L. Finar *Org. Chem.* II. viii. 265 Rhodinol is identical with citronellol, but the proportions of the two forms are different from those which occur in citronellol; the identity of citronellol and rhodinol is shown by the products of ozonolysis. **1959** P. de Mayo *Mono- & Sesquiterpenoids* i. 40 Rhodinol, isolated from rose oil, was for a long time considered to be distinct from citronellol, but it would appear that pure rhodinol and pure citronellol are identical.

Hence **rho·dinal** [a. G. *rhodinal* (op. cit., p. 373): see *-al[2]], the aldehyde, $C_{10}H_{18}O$, which is obtained by oxidation of rhodinol and is an analogous mixture of isomers resembling citronellal.

1900 *Jrnl. Chem. Soc.* LXXVIII. i. 452 Analyses are quoted in further proof of the isomeric change of rhodinal into menthone. **1929** [see *hydroxycitronellal* s.v. *hydroxy- 3]. **1951** A. W. Johnson et al. in E. H. Rodd *Chem. Carbon Compounds* Ia. viii. 504 Citronellal and its isomer rhodinal are olefinic aldehydes. **1956** I. L. Finar *Org. Chem.* II. viii. 265 A detailed study of rhodinal has shown that this compound is identical with citronellal, but consists of a mixture of the two forms in different proportions.

rhodium[2]. Add: **b.** *rhodium plating, -plated* adj. (hence *rhodium-plate* vb. trans.).

1962 L. S. Sasieni *Optical Dispensing* i. 4 A very satisfactory alternative way of producing a frame with a white finish is to rhodium-plate a yellow gold filled frame. *Ibid.* vii. 170 A rhodium-plated or gold-filled supra. **1971** *Flying* Apr. 112/3 (Advt.), Pilots Sunglasses. Air Force style rhodium plated adjustable metal frame. **1978** *Neiman-Marcus Christmas Bk.* 29 The glitter of rectangular cut crystals, hand-set in rhodium-plated 2″ bar pins. **1950** *Thorpe's Dict. Appl. Chem.* (ed. 4) X. 539/1 Rhodium plating baths have come into extensive use during the past 20 years for producing a non-tarnishing finish on silverware and on electrical-contact materials. **1962** L. S. Sasieni *Optical Dispensing* i. 23 The effect of a white gold filled frame is often produced by rhodium-plating.

rhodo (rōᵘ·do). Colloq. abbrev. of Rhododendron 2. Cf. *rhody.

1920 *Punch* 19 May 399/2 *Jack's* passion for abbreviation ('rhodos' for rhododendrons) being the only ground of quarrel. **1939** *N. & Q.* CLXXVI. 412/1 *Narciss...* This is a common abbreviation among gardeners, florists, and others, like 'Chrysanths', 'Rhodos', and other curtailments of long botanical names. **1976** *Country Life* 5 Feb. 305/2 Budding rhodos and camellias could still be nipped.

rhodo-. Add: † **rho·dophane** [*-phane* after *diaphane*] = *rhodopsin; **rhodophycean** (-fəi·siăn) *a. Bot.* [ad. mod.L. *Rhodophyceæ*, f. Gr. φῦκος seaweed], of or pertaining to the class Rhodophyceæ, which comprises the red algæ and is coextensive with the division Rhodophyta; **rho·dophyte** *sb. Bot.* [ad. mod.L. *Rhodophyta*: see -phyte], a member of the division Rhodophyta, which comprises the red algæ and is coextensive with the class Rhodophyceæ; *a.*, of or pertaining to this division; **rho·doplast** *Bot.* [a. G. *rhodoplast* (A. F. W. Schimper 1885, in *Jahrb. f. wissensch. Bot.* XVI. 40): see -plast], a chromoplast containing a red pigment, phycoerythrin, found in red algæ.

1878–9 W. C. Ayres tr. W. Kühne in *Jrnl. Physiol.* I. 115 We have found it expedient to wash with slightly warmed alcohol, which though it removes a little Rhodophane, as we may call the third pigment, takes up without failure the last remains of xanthophane. **1951** Rhodophane [see *lipochrome* s.v. *lipo-]. **1935** J. E. Tilden *Algae* iii. 27 A long time must have elapsed between the Cyanophycean and Rhodophycean periods, in which the blue-green and the red algae in turn constituted the dominant flora of the sea. **1938** G. M. Smith *Cryptogamic Bot.* I. viii. 295 The gradual increase in temperature of surface waters as one passes from polar to tropical regions is correlated with a change in composition of the rhodophycean element in the flora. **1964** *Amer. Jrnl. Bot.* LI. 580/1 Rhodophycean algae which have similar external form..do not have a comparable internal organization. **1967** *Virginia Jrnl. Sci.* XVIII. 110 (*heading*) *Porphyridium sordidum* Geitler in America, with comments on the distribution of other North American rhodophytes. **1974** R. Y. Stanier in Carlile & Skehel *Evolution in Microbial World* 223 Both in terms of nucleo-cytoplasmic structure and in terms of the overall composition of their pigment systems, rhodophytes and cryptophytes show many differences. **1976** *Nature* 22 Jan. 176/3 Knoll and Barghoorn's observations..counsel caution in interpreting the Bitter Springs fossil biota as containing *bona fide* remains of chlorophyte or rhodophyte algae. **1886** *Jrnl. R. Microsc. Soc.* 640 For the chromoplasts of the Phæophyceæ the author proposes the term phæoplasts; for those of the Florideæ rhodoplasts. **1932** R. E. Torrey *Gen. Bot.* x. 184 In the brown and red algæ the pigment is brown or red and the plastids are called respectively phæoplasts and rhodoplasts. **1965** Bell & Coombe tr. *Strasburger's Textbk. Bot.* iii. 466 The Rhodophyceae are usually red or violet, rarely dark purple or reddish-brown. Almost without exception the cells have a single nucleus and contain numerous simple chromatophores or rhodoplasts..in which chlorophyll..and the associated carotinoids in the lamellae of the plastids are masked by a red, strongly fluorescent, water-soluble pigment, phycoerythrin.

Rhodoid (rōᵘ·doid). Also **Rhodoïd, rhodoid.** [a. F. *Rhodoïd*, f. L. *Rhod*(*anus* the River Rhône + *-oïd*(*e* -oid.] A proprietary name for an incombustible thermoplastic derived from cellulose acetate.

1918 *Trade Marks Jrnl.* 5 June 590 *Rhodoid...* Celluloid in sheets, rods, tubes and similar forms. Société Chimique des usines du Rhone (anciennement Gilliard, P. Monnet et Cartier).., France; manufacturers.—18 Dec. 1917. **1934** *Archit. Rev.* LXXV. 20/2 The sparkling black rhodoid covers of this book. **1934** *Times Lit. Suppl.* 8 Feb. 93/1 Bound in black 'Rhodoid', a non-inflammable celluloid, the book opens easily. **1937** *Discovery* Jan. 25/2 The accompanying illustration of one of the artist's oil pictures on rhodoid. **1952** *Chem. Abstr.* XLVI. 2868 Studies on the effect of the base on crystn. of Au films were extended to: KCl,..Rhodoid, Plexiglas, and glass... It [*sc.* the resistivity] is higher on Rhodoid and Plexiglas than on glass. **1957** *Official Gaz.* (U.S. Patent Office) 14 May TM 49/2 *Rhodoïd...* For raw or partly prepared plastic material and particularly plastic material having a cellulose acetate base in the form of powder, blocks, rods, sheets, leaves, plates, and plaques.

rhodologist (rōᵘdǫ·lŏdʒist). [f. Gr. ῥόδον rose + -ologist.] One who studies roses, esp. the taxonomic relationships of the members of the genus *Rosa*.

1911 *Jrnl. Bot.* XLIX. 298 Several important works on Scandinavian roses have been put forth by the distinguished

Swedish rhodologist, Dr. S. Almquist. **1920** *New Phytol.* XIX. 156 *R*[*osa*] *hibernica*..is now regarded by all rhodologists as a hybrid. **1924** A. H. Wolley-Dod *Roses of Britain* 3 Continental rhodologists have expressed the opinion that the genus reaches its greatest degree of complication in Britain.

rhodopsin (rodǫ·psin). *Biochem.* [a. G. *rhodopsin* (Ewald & Kühne 1878, in *Untersuchungen aus d. physiol. Inst. d. Univ. Heidelberg* I. 181), f. *rhod-o* Rhodo- + Gr. ὄψ-ις sight, vision + *-in* -in[1].] The brilliant purplish-red light-sensitive pigment found in the retina of man and most other animal species, which consists of a protein (opsin) bonded to a prosthetic group (retinal) which is ultimately liberated by the action of light in the photochemical process of vision; = *visual purple* s.v. *visual *a.* and *sb.*

1886 [in Dict. s.v. Rhodo-]. **1937** *Nature* 12 June 1018/1 In every detail so far examined, the porphyropsin system faithfully reproduces the behaviour of the rhodopsin system, but with quite different components. **1959** S. Duke-Elder *Parsons' Dis. Eye* (ed. 13) iii. 26 Rhodopsin is a chromoprotein, the molecule of which consists of a reactive part, a chromophore, responsible for the preferential absorption of light, attached to a protein which acts essentially as a support. **1967** *New Scientist* 9 Feb. 330/2 Rhodopsin, the pigment of the retinal cones, has its absorption maximum at a wavelength of 5550 angstroms. **1968** M. Pyke *Food & Society* vii. 93 One of the chemical functions of vitamin A is known to be the re-conversion of the retinal pigment, rhodopsin [*printed* rhodospin], which becomes bleached in bright light, to its receptive state as visual purple. **1976** *Sci. Amer.* July 108/1 In all animals, invertebrates and vertebrates alike, the visual pigment rhodopsin is present in the photoreceptor membrane of the visual cells.

rhodora (rodō^ə·ră). [mod.L. (Linnæus *Species Plantarum* (ed. 2, 1763) 561), a. L. *rhodōra* the plant *Filipendula ulmaria*, f. Gr. ῥόδον rose.] A deciduous shrub, *Rhododendron canadense*, formerly the only species of the genus so called, belonging to the family Ericaceæ, native to north-eastern North America, and bearing rose-purple or white flowers early in spring. Also *attrib.*

1786 J. Abercrombie *Gard. Daily Assistant* 32/2 *Rhodora* or Canada rosebay. **1838** [see *kalmia]. *c* **1859** E. Dickinson *Poems* (1955) I. 101 The Crocus stirs her lids—Rhodora's cheek is crimson. **1869** J. G. Fuller *Uncle John's Flower Gatherers* 59 The Azaleas..are beautiful cousins of the Rhodora. **1942** W. R. van Dersal *Ornamental Amer. Shrubs* vi. 84 Valued for its early, bright rose-purple flowers and rich in its associations is the Rhodora, *Rhododendron canadense.* **1951** E. Graham *My Window looks down East* xx. 176 The lavender-pink Rhodora is in bloom. **1958** G. A. Petrides *Field Guide Trees & Shrubs* 363 Rhodora Azalea... A low shrub with blunt-tipped somewhat hairy leaves.

rhodusite (rō^u·dŭsəit). *Min.* [ad. G. *rhodusit* (H. von Foullon 1891, in *Sitzungsber. d. k. Akad. d. Wissensch.* (Math.-Nat. Classe) C. 176), f. *Rhodus* L. name of the Mediterranean island Rhodes: see -ite[1].] A fibrous variety of riebeckite in which some of the iron is replaced by magnesium.

1894 *Jrnl. Chem. Soc.* LXVI. ii. 461 He [*sc.* von Foullon] describes an asbestos-like variety of glaucophane... For this he proposes the name of rhodusite. **1965** E. W. Heinrich *Microsc. Identification of Minerals* x. 271 There are.. varieties of riebeckite (rhodusite) in which Mg replaces Fe^{2+} to a variable ex tent.

rhody (rō^u·di). *colloq.* Also 9 **roddy; rhodie.** [f. Rhod(odendron + -y[6].] = Rhododendron 2. Cf. *rhodo.

1851 H. Mayhew *London Labour* I. 133/2 I've bought roddies, as I calls them (rhododendrons), at 4s. a dozen. **1937** Partridge *Dict. Slang* 696/1 *Rhody, -ie,* a rhododendron: 'nursery' and familiar coll.: C. 20. **1943** C. S. Churchill *Let.* 17 May in M. Soames *Clementine Churchill* (1979) xxii. 336 Your favourite rhodie was in full bloom. **1951** W. Sansom *Face of Innocence* viii. 106 Among the rhodies a polishing and a stoking were abroad. **1973** *Country Life* 25 Jan. 231/3 I'm overrun by..*Rhododendron ponticum*... The pontic rhodie is drear indeed.

rhombencephalon (rǫ:mbense·fălǫn). *Anat.* [a. G. *rhombencephalon*: see Rhombo-, Encephalon.] The hind-brain, comprising the metencephalon together with the myelencephalon.

1897 C. L. Dana *Textbk. Nerv. Dis.* (ed. 4) i. 3 The posterior vesicle develops into the rhombencephalon or posterior brain. **1900** A. Hill tr. *H. Obersteiner's Anat. Central Nerv. Syst.* (ed. 2) ii. 48 His has divided the brain somewhat differently; into (1) Rhombencephalon, which includes the after-brain, hind-brain, and isthmus..(2) Mesencephalon..(3) Prosencephalon. **1934** R. R. Grinker *Neurol.* i. 12 Division of the rhombencephalon into metencephalon (cerebellum), and myelencephalon (medulla). **1962** *Gray's Anat.* (ed. 33) 976 The rhombencephalon comprises the medulla oblongata, pons and cerebellum; its cavity is the fourth ventricle. **1966** *McGraw-Hill Encycl. Sci. & Technol.* IX. 58/2 In dorsal view the ventricle of the myelencephalon, together with the metencephalon, has a rhomboid appearance, which is why this brain section is sometimes called the rhombencephalon.

Hence **rho:mbencepha·lic** *a.*

1954 Penfield & Jasper *Epilepsy & Functional Anat. of Human Brain* vii. 285 (*heading*) Cerebellar vertigo (rhombencephalic).

rhombic, *a.* Add: **1.** *spec.* applied to a radio aerial with a horizontal rhombic shape. Also *ellipt.* as *sb.*

1935 *Proc. IRE* XXIII. 24 The structure was descriptively termed the 'diamond-shaped' antenna.., but it has since become known as the 'rhombic' antenna and will be so designated here... Checking measurements were made on small-scale rhombic antennas operating at correspondingly short wavelengths. **1950** K. Henney *Radio Engin. Handbk.* (ed. 4) xiv. 653 When two rhombics are used in broadside as a single system, one common support can be used without balance problems, when fed symmetrically. **1968** *Radio Communication Handbk.* (ed. 4) xiii. 62/1 The average gain of a rhombic is 3db greater than that of a *V* aerial with the same legs and this is to be expected because the rhombic is twice as large. *Ibid.* 62/2 The design of *V* and rhombic aerials is quite flexible and both types will work over a 2 : 1 frequency range. **1975** D. G. Fink *Electronics Engineers' Handbk.* xxii. 64 The rhombic antenna is in wide use.

rhombiferan (rǫmbi·fĕrăn), *a.* and *sb.* *Palæont.* Also **Rhombiferan.** [f. as Rhombifer + -an.] **A.** *adj.* Of or pertaining to a group of cystoid echinoderms whose calyx plates are penetrated by groups of tubes forming a rhombic pattern. **B.** *sb.* A rhombiferan echinoderm.

1920 H. L. Hawkins *Invertebr. Palæont.* ii. iii. 160 Late forms of Rhombiferan Cystids, and perhaps of Amphoridea, have been reported from the Devonian, but they are inconspicuous. **1962** D. Nichols *Echinoderms* xi. 136 A section of a pore-rhomb..shows that in some rhombiferans the depressions between the pores of each pair were deep grooves. **1966** *McGraw-Hill Encycl. Sci. & Technol.* IV. 366/1 (*caption*) Rhombiferan cystoid (*Echinoencrinus,* Ordovician), showing pore rhomb and anus on side of calyx. **1978** *Jrnl. Paleont.* LII. 717/2 The elongate, cylindrical stems of *Caryocrinites ornatus*..resemble those of many crinoids and differ from the short conical stalks typical of rhombiferans.

rhombochasm (rǫ·mbokæz'm). *Geol.* [f. Rhombo- + Gr. χάσμ-α yawning hollow.] (See quot. 1958.)

1958 S. W. Carey in *Continental Drift* (Geol. Dept., Univ. of Tasmania, Hobart) 192 Rhombochasm..will be used for a parallel-sided gap in the sialic crust occupied by simatic crust, and interpreted as a dilatation. **1976** *Nature* 15 Apr. 590/1 Figure 3 *a* shows a rhombochasm, like the Gulf of California, forming behind the arc and marginal basin fragment.

rhomboclase (rǫ·mboklē^iz, -s). *Min.* [ad. Hungarian *rhomboklas* (J. S. Krenner 1891, in *Magyar tudományos Akad. Értes.* II. 96), f. *rhombo-* Rhombo- + Gr. κλάσ-ις breaking, cleavage (cf. Orthoclase).] A hydrated ferric acid sulphate, $HFe(SO_4)_2 \cdot 4H_2O$, found as colourless or pale-coloured thin tabular crystals.

1910 *Mineral. Mag.* XV. 429 (*heading*) Rhomboclase. **1938** *Amer. Mineralogist* XXIII. 742 Rhomboclase occurs at Alcaparrosa, near Cerritos Bayos [N. Chile], intimately associated with szomolnokite and roemerite. **1968** I. Kostov *Mineralogy* 499 Rhomboclase is orthorhombic-dipyramidal, occurring as colourless to white or greenish thin tabular crystals with perfect {001} cleavage.

rhombogen. Add: [ad. F. *rhombogène* (E. van Beneden 1876, in *Bull. de l'Acad. R. de Belgique* XLI. 1195).] (Earlier and later examples.)

1883 [see *infusorigen]. **1899, 1972** [see *nematogen* s.v. *nemato-].

Rhone (rō^un). Also **Rhône.** The name of a river which runs from Switzerland, through southeastern France, to the Mediterranean Sea, used *attrib.* and *absol.* to designate wines made from grapes growing in the Rhone valley (esp. between Lyons and Avignon).

[**1833** C. Redding *Hist. Mod. Wines* v. 124 The red wines Glun, Châteaubourg, Soyons, Tournon, St. Jean de Musois, Vion, and others, are Rhone flavoured wines.] **1852** E. Twisleton *Let.* 9 Oct. (1928) iv. 56, I have now fallen peaceably into liking Bordeaux, Burgundy, and the Rhone wines in all their variety. **1935** A. E. Housman *Let.* 21 Sept. (1971) 376 There are also many good restaurants and some excellent Rhone wine. **1963** L. Charteris *Saint in Sun* (1964) 184 You and I..can wash down our *cailles* with a red Rhône. **1965** A. Sichel *Penguin Bk. Wines* iii. 165 The general name 'Rhône wines' can be misleading, since some, grown in the *département* of the Rhône, belong to other appellations, and some wines with the appellation 'Rhone' come from the valley of the Rhône in other *départements.* **1976** *Times* 3 Apr. 13/4 The curious white Rhônes that are made from the Viognier grape.

rhoorkee, var. *Roorkee.

Rhoosian (rū·ʃ^iăn), *sb.* and *a.* Also **Rooshan, Rooshian, Roosian.** Joc. var. of Russian *sb.* and *a.*

1843 [see *Prooshan *a.* and *sb.*]. **1864** *Daily Tel.* 26 July 5/3, I never did 'room' with a Rooshian before, and I'd like to know them stript. **1878** W. S. Gilbert *H.M.S. Pinafore* ii. 28 For he might have been a Roosian, A French, or Turk, or Proosian, Or perhaps Itali-an! **1898** J. D. Brayshaw *Slum Silhouettes* 151 I'm off to the Cattle Market to buy one o' those little Rooshian ponies. **1914** W. de la Mare in *Sat. Westm. Gaz.* 22 Aug. 2/3 With Dreadnoughts here, two kinds of French, the Rooshans at your heel. **1940** E. Pound *Cantos* lix. 86 And the rhoosians (Orosians) served a sort of lunch To the chinese ambassadors. **1974** F. Selwyn *Cracksman on Velvet* ii. 70 The Rhoosians couldn't stop him at Inkerman and nor will you.

rhopalic, *a.* Add: (Further examples.) Also as *sb.*

1943 J. T. Shipley *Dict. World Lit.* 482/1 *Rhopalic verse,* ..wedge verse, in which each word is one syllable longer than the preceding one. Occasionally, of a stanza in which each line is a foot longer than the preceding line, as Crashaw's *Wishes to His Supposed Mistress.* **1956** [see *epanaleptic* adj. s.v. *epana-]. **1975** W. R. Espy *Almanac of Words at Play* p. xxii, *Rhopalic,* a snowballing line or passage in which each successive word has one more syllable (or letter) than the last.

rhopalium (rō^upē^i·liŏm). *Zool.* Pl. **-ia.** [mod.L., f. Gr. ῥόπαλον club.] Each of a number of marginal sense-organs in some jellyfish. Hence **rhopa·lial** *a.*

1888 Rolleston & Jackson *Forms Animal Life* (ed. 2) 782 These tentacles shorten, and their basal portions are converted into the sensory bodies or rhopalia of the Medusa. **1979** *Nature* 13 Sept. 141/2 Swimming in scyphozoans is under control of rhopalial pacemakers. *Ibid.,* Jellyfish stopped swimming when we removed the rhopalia. *Ibid.,* Motor impulses originating in the rhopalium and conducted into the subumbrellar nerve-net were recorded.

rhopheocytosis (rō^ufī:osəitō^u·sis). *Biol.* [ad. F. *rhophéocytose* (Policard & Bessis 1958, in *Compt. Rend.* CCXLVI. 3196), f. Gr. ῥοφεῖν to gulp down: cf. Phagocytosis and *pinocytosis.] The process whereby a cell absorbs material into small vacuoles without first sending out projections.

1962 *Blood* XIX. 645 The cell does not extend any veils as is characteristic of micropinocytosis, but appears to 'aspirate' the external material. This process, therefore, appeared to deserve a special designation, and coined [*sic*] for it the term 'rhopheocytosis'. **1964** D. W. Allen in Bishop & Surgenor *Red Blood Cell* viii. 324 The authors assume that the ferritin is transferred from reticulum cell to erythroblast by a form of micropinocytosis which the authors call 'rhopheocytosis'. **1974** *Nature* 15 Feb. 462/1 A dense and continuous dark labelling was seen in contact with the membrane of all normoblasts, surrounding the whole perimeter of the cell, including rhopheocytosis invaginations.

rhotacism. Add: Also as mod.L. **rhotaci·smus.**

1897 *Syd. Soc. Lex.,* Rhotacismus. **1959** 'A. Burgess' *Beds in East* ii. 49 'But I'm hungwy.' A pathetic little-girl's rhotacismus. **1977** *Times Lit. Suppl.* 11 Feb. 147/3 The privileged families, productive of good shots with..pronounced rhotacismus, are still there to help kill pheasants.

rhotacization (rō^u:tăsəizē^i·ʃən). *Philol.* [f. Rhotacize *v.* + -ation.] **a.** = Rhotacism 2. **b.** = *r-colouring* s.v. *R I. 1 c.

1973 J. M. Anderson *Struct. Aspects Lang. Change* vi. 119 (*heading*) Rhotacization. **1975** *Amer. Speech 1973* XLVIII. 111 The symbol [ɜ] is used for the stressed mid-central vowel whether with or without rhotacization.

rhotacize, *v.* Add: **2.** *trans.* To convert (a sound, esp. *s*) into *r.*

1965 *Language* XLI. 64 The prothesis rule must apply before *b* is deleted and..*b* must be deleted before the *s* can be rhotacized. **1977** *Ibid.* LIII. 51 The traditional form **esom* was rhotacized into **erom.*

Hence **rho·tacized** *ppl. a.*; **rho·tacizing** *ppl. a.* and *vbl. sb.*

1887 Rhotacizing *ppl. a.* [in Dict.]. **1893** J. Clark *Man. Linguistics* vii. 181 Wherever, medially, in Italic, an *s* between two vowels followed an unaccented syllable, the final result gave *z* in the non-rhotacising dialects, such as Oscan, and *r* (through *z*) in the rhotacising dialects, such as Latin and Umbrian. **1976** *Language* LII. 342 The nasal vowel would be found in a completely oral environment—and thus subject to denasalization, giving the standard examples of rhotacized forms. **1977** *Ibid.* LIII. 53 The form **som* was not sensitive to rhotacism, even when placed after a word ending in a vowel.., because the word boundary suspended the rhotacizing effect.

rho-theta (rō^u‚þī·tă). [The Greek letters ρ (*rho*) and θ (*theta*), used symbolically in radar to denote distance and bearing respectively.] Used *attrib.* to denote radar navigational systems in which the position of aircraft is measured as range and bearing from a single ground station. Also *absol.,* denoting a position measurement.

1957 *Electronics* 1 June 156 (*heading*) Vortac beacons for rho-theta navigation. **1961** *Engineering* 7 Apr. 479/3 Any type of fix designation, fix identifier, longitude-latitude, relative direction, or rho-theta is accepted by the direct processing routine. **1975** D. G. Fink *Electronics Engineers' Handbk.* xxv. 94 In ICAO practice, the DME is nearly always associated with a VOR, the two systems forming the basis for a rho-theta area navigation system.

Rhovyl (rō^{u}·vil). Also **rhovyl.** A proprietary name for a type of polyvinyl chloride fibre.

1949 *Official Gaz.* (U.S. Patent Office) 7 June 45/1 Société Rhovyl, Paris, France... *Rhovyl*... For threads and yarns containing filaments of polyvinyl chloride. **1949** *Trade Marks Jrnl.* 21 Dec. 1148/2 *Rhovyl*... All goods included in Class 23. Société Anonyme Rhovyl..21, Rue Jean-Goujon, Paris, France; manufacturers. **1963** A. J. Hall *Student's Textbk. Textile Sci.* ii. 97 Since Rhovyl fibres are very inert chemically and are not inflammable..they can be used in the production of fabrics having industrial rather than textile uses. **1972** *Guardian* 31 Oct. 11/5 Underwear; Heavy-weight tights in nylon or rhovyl or wool/Helanca.

rhubarb. Add: **3*. a.** The word 'rhubarb' as repeated by actors to give the impression of murmurous hubbub or conversation. Hence allusively.

1934 A. P. Herbert *Holy Deadlock* 194 The chorus excitedly rushed about and muttered 'Rhubarb!' **1952** *Radio Times* 17 Oct. 11/3 The unemployed actors had a wonderful time. We'd huddle together in a corner and repeat 'Rhubarb, rhubarb, rhubarb' or 'My fiddle, my fiddle, my fiddle'—and it sounded like a big scene from some mammoth production. **1958** *Observer* 7 Dec. 18/5 Actors, who shout 'rhubarb—rhubarb—rhubarb' to give the impression of a distant riot. **1960** J. Betjeman *Summoned by Bells* ix. 105 And in the next-door room is heard the tramp And 'rhubarb, rhubarb' as the crowd rehearse A one-act play in verse. **1972** P. Dickinson *Lizard in Cup* xi. 174 The conversation..was meaningless; they might just as well have been muttering 'rhubarb, rhubarb'. **1976** *Gramophone* June 71/2, I wondered if the chorus would have made a better effect had the words been less clearly articulated (like actors in a crowd scene muttering 'rhubarb').

b. *Mil. slang.* A low-level flight for opportune strafing.

1943 *Time* 22 Mar. 51/1 When a fighter pilot flies low over France, strafing whatever he finds—trains, troops, airdromes—he is 'on a rhubarb'. **1945** C. H. Ward-Jackson *Piece of Cake* (ed. 2) 51 *Rhubarb*.., a ground-strafing, go-for-anything-you-see worthwhile sortie. **1956** J. E. Johnson *Wing Leader* vi. 79 We began to carry out low-level flights over France. These operations were known by the code name *Rhubarb*. *Ibid.* 80 Usually our *Rhubarb* efforts yielded little more than a staff car. *Ibid.*, I loathed those *Rhubarbs* with a deep, dark hatred.

c. *U.S. slang.* A heated dispute, a row; *spec.* a disturbance or argument on the field of play at a sporting (orig. *Baseball*) event.

1943 *N.Y. Herald Tribune* 13 July 22/3 Mr 'Red' Barber,..who has been announcing the games of the Brooklyn Dodgers, has used the term 'rhubarb' to describe an argument, or a mix-up, on the field of play. **1947** *Time* 22 Sept. 70/1 Next inning, at the plate, there was a face-to-face exchange of hot words..—the kind of rough passage that fans appreciatively call a 'rhubarb'. **1949** *Richmond* (Va.) *Times-Dispatch* 17 Jan. 3/2 The citizen waiting for a streetcar yesterday was of several minds about the 'rhubarb' between the Virginia Transit Company and its drivers. **1950** *Sun* (Baltimore) 20 June 21/2 Such talk is not publicized for obvious reasons. But this has reached type, and one of those so-called 'rhubarbs' is in the pot stewing away. **1959** *Washington Post* 11 Feb. c5/1 Among those who had bets on Dorothy's Best in Monday's false start rhubarb,..most were back to racing's cold war. **1973** *Times* 15 Aug. 7/3 'Rhubarbs', the name used for noisy arguments that break out on the field, started when a Yankee batter, after missing a Perry special, yelled 'spitter' at him. **1975** F. Kennedy *Alberta was my Beat* xii. 147 It was at the Montreal Stampede that the big 'rhubarb' occurred, involving..Canada's top bucking horse rider. **1976** *National Observer* (U.S.) 3 July 15/3 To be conned? Now that always starts a rhubarb, and in this week's hand it started when a defender fell for a *pseudo* end-play.

d. *slang.* Nonsense, worthless stuff.

1963 *Radio Times* 3 Oct. 17/1 Dig this Rhubarb..a new kind of television entertainment... Which (we hope) will prove that there is no shortage of writers for television so long as you are not particular about whether they are still alive or not. **1976** *Telegraph* (Brisbane) 6 July 12/2 They gave me some rhubarb about violating the firework zone. **1977** *Times Lit. Suppl.* 3 June 673/1 Peking opera..employed..a huge repertoire consisting almost entirely of rhubarb. **1979** *Times* 22 Feb. 5/7 We should look at the individual... Whether he or she went to the right school..that's rhubarb.

4. a. *attrib.* and *Comb.*, as (senses 1–3) *rhubarb crumble, fritters, jam, juice, powder* (earlier example), *pudding, tart* (earlier example); (sense *3* a) *rhubarb noise*; **rhubarb disease** = *crown rot* s.v. *CROWN *sb.* 35.

1958 Rhubarb crumble [see *crumble *sb.* 2 b]. **1976** *Cumberland & Westmorland Herald* 1 Aug. 1/6 For their sweet course, pupils could make a choice from fresh fruit..hot mince pies and custard and rhubarb crumble and custard. **1924** Rhubarb disease [see *crown rot* s.v. *crown *sb.* 35]. **1855** E. Acton *Mod. Cookery* (rev. ed.) xix. 383 (*heading*) Rhubarb fritters. **1861** Mrs. Beeton *Bk. Househ. Managem.* 797 (*heading*) Rhubarb jam. **1873** *Young Englishwoman* Nov. 571/1 A receipt for making rhubarb jam. The rhubarb must..be well boiled with..preserving sugar and..bitter almonds. **1977** K. O'Hara *Ghost of T. Penry* viii. 67 Harriet ate a lot of bread-and-butter with the rhubarb jam. *c* **1863** T. Taylor in M. R. Booth *Eng. Plays of 19th Cent.* (1969) II. 84, You will make it champagne?.. None of your home-brewed; I buy my rhubarb-juice at the greengrocer's. **1971** *Guardian* 15 Feb. 6/5 His father-in-law drinks rhubarb juice by the glassful. **1958** D. Wallace *Forty Years On* v. 63 There was an uproar. From the general rhubarb noise the Dean could be heard. **1977** *Gramophone* Aug. 340/1 There is almost no theatrical production, sound-effects or 'rhubarb' noises. **1784** J. Woodforde *Diary* 9 Mar. (1926) II. 121 Mr. Thorne left..a Rhubarb Powder to take to Morrow. **1861** Mrs. Beeton *Bk. Househ. Managem.* 672 (*heading*) Boiled rhubarb pudding. **1946** *Farmhouse Fare* (Farmers Weekly) 135 Rhubarb pudding..flour..dates..syrup..milk..cocoa..margarine..rhubarb... Bake in hot oven. **1793** J. Woodforde *Diary* 11 May (1929) IV. 28 We had for Dinner to day, hashed Calfs Head..& a Rhubarb Tart.

rhu·barb, *v. slang* (orig. *Theatr.*). [f. the sb.] *intr.* Of an actor: to repeat 'rhubarb' (*rhubarb 3* a); to mumble indistinctly in order to represent the noise of a crowd. Freq. *transf.* in gen. use. Also redupl. Occas. *trans.* with direct speech as obj.

1958 *Spectator* 11 July 47/1 'Hear, hear,' they rhubarb-rhubarbed. **1965** *Observer* 20 June 25/5 The barons, mildly rhubarbing in some awkwardly symmetrical pieces of stage grouping, rightly suspect the King of double-dealing. **1966** I. Jefferies *House-Surgeon* iv. 79 We rhubarbed till he had gone. **1967** D. Skirrow *I was following this Girl* xxxv. 210, I listened hard and rhubarbed my way through, trying to make any sort of sense of what I was hearing. **1976** *Daily Tel.* 21 Sept. 11/2 Livia faced the Roman mob, all seven of them, rhubarbing at the Palace back door. 'You wait,' she cried imperiously, 'until my husband gets home!'

So **rhu·barber**, an actor who repeats 'rhubarb'; also *transf.*; **rhu·barbing** *vbl. sb.* and *ppl. a.*

1953 A. McQueen *Let.* 31 Aug. in Partridge *Dict. Slang Suppl.* (1961) 1247/2 When a few actors gathered backstage and represented 'noise without' made by a mob, they intoned the sonorous word 'rhubarb'. The action was called 'rhubarbing', the actors 'rhubarbers'. **1965** *New Statesman* 20 Aug. 266/2 A floodlit market place at night with hucksters arriving to tempt the rhubarbers. **1970** *Times* 27 Feb. 13/5 The few attempts at pageantry generally come to grief against painted backdrops, watched by a handful of rhubarbing commoners. **1978** *Daily Tel.* 10 May 36/6 Mr Jenkin showed himself to be a formidable rhubarber in his own right. He nodded and moved his lips with the utmost vigour.

rhumba, var. *rumba *sb.* and *v.*

rhumbaba, var. *rum baba* s.v. *baba^2.

rhumbatron (rʊ·mbătrǫn). *Electronics.* [Irreg. f. Gr. ῥύμβ-ος, ῥόμβ- whirling motion (f. ῥομβεῖν to turn around) + *-tron.] A cavity in which bunching of an electron beam is produced by an applied radio-frequency field, or conversely a pulsed beam produces a radio-frequency voltage across a gap in the cavity.

1939 R. H. & S. F. Varian in *Jrnl. Appl. Physics* X. 322/1 The resonant properties of practically closed metal vessels... In our laboratory, these have been called 'rhumbatrons', from the Greek word 'rhumba', meaning rhythmic oscillation. **1939** *Jrnl. R. Aeronaut. Soc.* XLIII. 388 A beam of electrons representing a constant current is sent through two metal containers acting as resonators and known as Rhumbatrons. In the first Rhumbatron is an oscillating electric field, parallel to the stream and of such strength as to change the speeds of the electrons by appreciable fraction...In the second Rhumbatron..a considerable fraction of the power of the arriving electron bunches is converted into power of high frequency oscillations. **1947** *Electronic Engin.* XIX. 149/1 Examination of the 'rhumbatron' type of circuit used by the Varians introduces us to an interesting new phenomenon..the existence of an isolated electric field within each rhumbatron, in spite of the fact that the whole of the exterior of each rhumbatron and the drift-tube itself are constantly at r.f. earth potential. **1968** *Radio Communication Handbk.* (ed. 4) ii. 23/1 A klystron is a valve containing an electron gun..from which a narrow beam of electrons is..focused through small apertures across which one or more oscillatory circuits are connected; these circuits are in the form of hollow toroidal chambers known as rhumbatrons.

rhydectomy, var. *rhytidectomy.

rhyme, *sb.* Add: **4.** (senses 2 and 3) *rhyme-analogy, -compulsion, -form, -type, -word* (further examples); *rhyme-like* adj.; **rhyme scheme,** the ordered patterning of end-rhymes in metrical composition; **rhyme sheet,** a broadsheet containing verses for display.

1930 A. W. Aron in *Curme Vol. Linguistic Studies* 19 By *rhyme-analogy* we mean the associational process by which the gender of a word is influenced by other words with similar suffixes or other similar endings. **1923** R. Graves *Feather Bed* 17 Sacred Carnivals trundle through my mind, With Rhyme-compulsion mottoing each waggon. **1927** W. E. Collinson *Contemp. Eng.* 7 Rhyme-forms which have aroused H. G. Wells' anger, like *roly-poly*. **1934** Rhyme-form [see *letter-name* s.v. *letter *sb.*^{1} 7 a]. **1957** N. Frye *Sound & Poetry* 125 Having rejected formal rhyme, he by no means avoids subdued rhymelike effects. *a* **1931** E. Pound *Make it New* (1934) vii. 400 Where both Rossetti and I went off the rails was in taking an English sonnet as the equivalent for a sonnet in Italian. I don't mean in overlooking the mild difference in the rhyme scheme. **1962** W. Nowottny *Lang. Poets Use* viii. 192 This..is very emphatically signalled as some kind of new departure by a change in the rhyme-scheme. **1981** J. Brabazon *Dorothy L. Sayers* iii. 27 Her mind constantly absorbed in..a language, a rhyme-scheme, an astronomical phenomenon. **1920** (*title*) Rhyme sheet (Poetry Bookshop). **1943** N. Marsh *Colour Scheme* i. 16 The archly-reproachful rhyme-sheets in bathrooms and lavatories. **1968** D. Hopkinson *Incense-Tree* ii. 22 On the walls of our nursery, my mother had pinned rhyme sheets published by the Poetry Bookshop. **1945** C. L. Wrenn in *Slavonic & East Europ. Rev.* XXIII. 123 Both have sought..to preserve alike the rhythm and the rhyme-types of their originals. **1943** —— in *Trans. Philol. Soc.* 32 A glance at the apparatus, for instance, of any well-edited Middle English text will show how a study of the orthography of the rhyme-words in a poem..may point the way to an original reading. **1960** A. Clarke *Horse-Eaters* 27 The nasal syllable in Houyhnhnm Brings rhyme-word.

rhyme, *v.* Add: **3. d.** *U.S. Blacks.* Const. *up.* To improvise (a blues composition).

1968 P. Oliver *Screening Blues* 16 Blues singers pride themselves on their ability to 'rhyme up a song' but they do not consider this an essential requirement of their music. **1968** *Blues Unlimited* Sept. 13, I rhymed up a song and called it 'The Auction Day blues'.

rhymelet (rəi·mlėt). [f. Rhyme *sb.* + -let.] A short piece of rhyme or poetry.

c **1870** M. Collins in F. Collins *Lett. & Friendships* (1877) I. v. 66, I meant to say your rhymelets smell More of the country than Pall Mall. **1917** J. Adams *Student's Guide* 76 Many of us..have been grateful to the author of certain flagrant rhymelets.

rhyming, *vbl. sb.* Add: **b. rhyming dictionary** (earlier and later examples); **rhyming slang,** a variety of (orig. Cockney) slang in which a word is replaced by a phrase which rhymes with it (see quot. 1933); also *rhyming slang(st)er*.

1775 J. Walker *Dict. Eng. Lang.* p. v, A rhyming dictionary in a living language, for the purposes of poetry, seems no very unnatural or useless production. *a* **1846** B. R. Haydon *Autobiogr.* (1927) i. 4, I remember him with his rhyming dictionary, composing his verses and scanning with his fingers. **1964** 'E. McBain' *Ax* x. 191 I'd like to buy a rhyming dictionary... I promised somebody I'd find a rhyme. [*c* **1850** in R. Pearsall *Worm in Bud* (1969) i. ii. 49 The new style of cadgers' cant..is done all on the rhyming principle.] **1859** Hotten *Dict. Slang* 134 The cant, which has nothing to do with that spoken by the costermongers, is known in Seven Dials and elsewhere as the Rhyming Slang, or the substitution of words and sentences which rhyme with other words intended to be kept secret. *Ibid.* 135, I learn that the rhyming slang was introduced about twelve or fifteen years ago. **1911** J. W. Horsley *I Remember* xi. 252 The more modern rhyming slang..invented and chiefly used by costermongers, to whom 'daisy roots' is a substitute for the word boots. **1933** 'G. Orwell' *Down & Out in Paris & London* xxxii. 238 Twenty-five or thirty years ago..the 'rhyming slang' was all the rage in London. In the 'rhyming slang' everything was named by something rhyming with it—a 'hit or miss' for a kiss, 'plates of meat' for feet, etc. **1973** B. Aylwin *Loads of Cockney Cobblers* p. vi, Of course the Cockney—a born linguist—will adapt his rhyming slang specifically *for* the Common Market. **1977** *Listener* 5 May 588/3 Any speaker of Anglo-American knows that 'bread' as a synonym for 'money' is the work of those dreary cockney rhyming-slangers. 'Bread and honey', money. **1948** Partridge *Dict. Forces' Slang* 155 Before the First World War, it was in common use in the Forces, even in Scottish regiments, such was the influence of the Cockney, who is the expert rhyming slangster.

rhy·mingly, *adv.* [f. Rhyming *ppl. a.* + -ly^2.] In a rhyming manner.

1880 Ruskin in *19th Cent.* Aug. 198 The necessity..of completing the nomenclature rhythmically and rhymingly.

rhymsterette (rəi:mstəre·t). *nonce-wd.* [f. Rhymester + -ette.] A female rhymer; an inferior poetess.

1957 V. Nabokov *Pnin* vii. 180 A fair sample of her production is the kind of stuff that émigré rhymsterettes wrote after Akhmatova: lackadaisical little lyrics.

rhynchocœle, *a.* and *sb.* For **a, b** read **A, B** and add: **B.** *sb.* **2.** *Zool.* Also **-cœl,** † **-cœlum.** A body cavity in nemertean worms that contains the introverted proboscis.

1902 *Encycl. Brit.* XXXI. 121 (*caption*) Rhynchocœl. *Ibid.*, The cavity into which the proboscis is retracted, the rhynchocœlum, is formed by a split which appears in the mesoblast surrounding the epiblastic pit. **1932** Borradaile & Potts *Invertebrata* vii. 205 When the muscles of the proboscis sheath contract and press upon the fluid in the rhynchocoel the proboscis is everted. **1972** M. S. Gardiner *Biol. Invertebrates* ii. 51/1 Except for this rhynchocoele, the body is solid in the sense that the digestive tract and other organs are surrounded by parenchyma cells.

Hence **rhynchocœ·lic** *a.*, of or pertaining to the rhynchocœle.

1902 *Encycl. Brit.* XXXI. 121 (*caption*) Rhynchocoelic blood-vessel.

rhynchodæum (riŋkodī·ɒm). *Zool.* Pl. **-æa** (-ī·ă). [mod.L. *rhynchodæum* (coined in Ger. by A. Oswald 1893, in *Vierteljahrsschr. der Naturf. Gesell. in Zürich* XXXVIII. 347), f. Gr. ῥύγχ-ος snout + ὁδαῖον, neut. of ὁδαῖος that is on or by the way (f. ὁδός way).] The cavity anterior to and partially containing the proboscis of certain invertebrates, esp. ribbon-worms of the phylum Nemertea and gastropods of the genus *Buccinum*. Hence **rhynchodæ·al** *a.*

1894 *Jrnl. R. Microsc. Soc.* 328 Oswald proposes to call the space between the introvert or proboscis [of certain gastropods] and its sheath the rhynchodæum, its anterior opening the rhynchostome, the opening at the apex of the proboscis the pharyngostome, and the oral aperture proper, where ectoderm joins the endoderm, the gastrostome. **1912** *Mem. Liverpool Marine Biol. Comm.* XX. 30 The cavity (part of the external world) between the proboscis and its sheath..is known as the Rhynchodaeum, and the opening of the latter, or the false mouth, is the Rhynchostome. **1963** R. D. BARNES *Invertebr. Zool.* viii. 119/2 The lumen of the rhynchodaeum is continuous with that of the proboscis proper. **1972** R. GIBSON *Nemerteans* i. 38 The proboscis pore opens immediately into the rhynchodaeum, a rather short tubular chamber that in many pelagic hoplonemerteans is very short. *Ibid.*, Rhynchodaeal musculature, if present, is usually weak and predominantly composed of circular fibres. **1975** *Zeitschr. f. Morphol. der Tiere* LXXX. 67 In *O[enopota] levidensis* the rhynchodaeal walls have a series of annular folds, whose musculature appears to allow dilation and contraction. The dilation could enlarge the rhynchodaeal space, conceivably of assistance in prey capture and engulfment.

rhynchokinesis (riŋkŏkəinī·sis, -kĭn-). *Zool.* [ad. G. *rhynchokinetik* (H. Hofer 1949, in *Acta Zool.* XXX. 213), f. Gr. ῥύγχο-ς beak, snout + κινητικ-ός moving: see KINETIC *a.* (*sb.*) and *KINESIS.] A process, found in some birds and lizards, by which the upper bill or jaw may be raised relative to the cranium by extensive bending of nasal and premaxillary bones.

1963 W. J. BOCK in C. G. Sibley *Proc. XIII Internat. Ornithol. Congr.* I. 46 Hofer showed that rhynchokinesis is correlated with a schizorhinal nostril. **1964** *Jrnl. Morphol.* CXIV. 15/1 Some birds have a form of kinesis that cannot be easily assigned to either prokinesis or rhynchokinesis. **1964, 1973** [see *PROKINESIS]. **1974** P. J. K. BURTON *Feeding & Feeding Apparatus in Waders* II. 33 Two principal modifications are found in present day birds. These are prokinesis, in which the upper jaw moves about a pivot formed by a narrow strip of flexible bone at the fronto-nasal hinge; and rhynchokinesis, in which bending occurs over a wider zone, some distance along the bill. Rhynchokinesis involves a change in bill shape.

So **rhynchokinetic** (-kəine·tik) *a.*

1960 [see *PROKINETIC *a.*]. **1964** *Jrnl. Morphol.* CXIV. 14/1 The rhynchokinetic skull is characterized by a region of bending located somewhere along the dorsal bar of the upper jaw. **1974** P. J. K. BURTON *Feeding & Feeding Apparatus in Waders* II. 33 It is..convenient to distinguish between moderately rhynchokinetic species in which bending occurs along the whole length of the upper jaw anterior to the internasal septum, and highly rhynchokinetic species in which reinforcement of the dorsal bar anterior to the nasal partition has moved the zone of bending much further forward.

rhynchonellid (riŋkone·lid). *Zool.* and *Palæont.* [ad. mod.L. family name *Rhynchonellidæ*, f. generic name *Rhynchonella* (G. Fischer von Waldheim 1809, in *Notice des Fossiles du Gouvernement de Moscou* 35), f. *rhynchon-* (irreg. f. Gr. ῥύγχος snout) + *-ella*, dim. suffix (see -EL²): see -ID³.] An articulate brachiopod of the family Rhynchonellidæ, whose members are found as both fossils and living animals.

1913 C. R. EASTMAN tr. *Zittel's Text-bk. Zool.* (ed. 2) I. v. 399 Few Rhynchonellids agree with the genotype, which is *Rhynchonella loxia* Fischer..from the Upper Jura of Russia. **1920** A. M. DAVIES *Introd. Palæont.* i. 37 Young specimens of this group are the best on which to study the deltidial plates.., which in so many rhynchonellids become obscured by the curvature of the beaks. **1936** *Geogr. Jrnl.* LXXXVII. 431 Other fossils include cephalopods, gastropods, rhynchonellids and crinoid stems. **1970** R. M. BLACK *Elements Palaeont.* xi. 158 A number of different stocks of brachiopods survived into the Mesozoic... The most commonly occurring forms..are rhynchonellids and terebratulids. The rhynchonellids are in general less important after the Jurassic.

Rhynchosporium (riŋkospō³·riɒm). Also rhyncho-. [mod.L. (E. Heinsen 1900, in *Jahrb. d. Hamburg. Wissensch. Anstalten* (3 Beiheft) XVIII. 43), f. Gr. ῥύγχο-ς snout + σπορ-ά sowing + L. *-ium*, neut. of *-ius*, adj. suffix.] A fungus of the genus so called, members of which cause leaf blotch in cereals and other grasses; also, the disease caused by this fungus. Also *attrib.*

1920 *Phytopathology* X. 54 (*heading*) Evidence of disease resistance in barley to attacks of Rhynchosporium. **1937** *Jrnl. Agric. Res.* LV. 175 (*heading*) *Rhynchosporium* scald of barley, rye and other grasses. *Ibid.* 180 In the early stages of the development of *Rhynchosporium* in the host tissue the mycelium is wholly subcuticular. **1967** *Punch* 26 July 140/3 Then there is Vulcan—an interesting new six-row winter barley, which, it is thought, will eventually be granted rights. It has, in effect, double resistance, being almost immune to Mildew and the dreaded Rhynchosporium. **1971** *Country Life* 7 Oct. 936/1 Another important fungoid disease..is rhynchosporium..which makes black blotches on the leaves of barley.

rhynchostome (ri·ŋkostōᵘm). *Zool.* [ad. G. *rhynchostom* (A. Oswald 1893, in *Vierteljahrsschr. der Naturf. Gesell. in Zürich* XXXVIII. 347), f. Gr. ῥύγχος snout + στόμα mouth.] The anterior opening of the rhynchodæum in proboscis-bearing gastropods.

1894, 1912 [see *RHYNCHODÆUM]. **1975** *Zeitschr. f. Morphol. der Tiere* LXXX. 71 The prey could be engulfed by the rhynchostome and rhynchodaeal sphincter functioning as gripping organs and working in ratchet fashion to pass the prey in.

rhynchotal (riŋkōᵘ·tăl), *a.* *Ent.* [f. as RHYNCHOTOUS *a.* + -AL.] = RHYNCHOTOUS *a.*

1903 *Nature* 23 Oct. 616/1 Additions to the rhynchotal fauna of Central America.

rhyodacite (rəiˌŏdēⁱ·səit). *Geol.* [f. RHYO(LITE + DACITE.] A type of extrusive volcanic rock having a porphyritic texture and intermediate in composition between rhyolite and dacite.

1913 A. N. WINCHELL in *Jrnl. Geol.* XXI. 214 The volcanic equivalent of granodiorite, which may be appropriately called rhyodacite, forms another intermediate group between the alkalcic and the alkaline rocks. **1932** A. JOHANNSEN *Descriptive Petrogr. Igneous Rocks* II. 356 Rhyodacites are the extrusive equivalents of granodiorites. They are rocks of porphyritic habit, usually white, yellowish, reddish, or grayish in colour, and showing phenocrysts of quartz, plagioclase, and some ferromagnesian constituent, in a microcrystalline, cryptocrystalline, or glassy groundmass. **1970** MACDONALD & ABBOTT *Volcanoes in Sea* vii. 143/2 The rhyodacite of Mauna Kuwale, in the Waianae Valley on Oahu, appears to be an unusual, extreme type derived by differentiation of the tholeiitic basalt magma in the same way that trachyte is derived from alkalic basalt. **1977** A. HALLAM *Planet Earth* 164/1 Most provinces of rhyolitic volcanics contain substantial amounts of rhyodacite as well as true rhyolite.

rhyolite. Add: In mod. use, a type of acidic extrusive volcanic rock, usu. pale in colour and porphyritic in texture, having phenocrysts esp. of quartz or potassium-feldspar in a fine-grained or glassy groundmass which commonly shows flow structure. (Earlier and later examples.) [First as G. *rhyolith* (not *-lit*) (*Jahrb. d. K. K. Geol. Reichs-Anstalt* (Wien) (1860) XI. 156).]

1868 *Mem. Calif. Acad. Sci.* I. 50 The name 'rhyolite' was proposed, early in 1860, for certain rocks frequently occurring on the southern slope of the Carpathians. **1932** A. JOHANNSEN *Descriptive Petrogr. Igneous Rocks* II. 268 Most rhyolites are light in colour: white, yellow, brown, or pink, but yellowish green and even deep red rocks are found. **1944** A. HOLMES *Princ. Physical Geol.* xx. 455 During the late Pleistocene there were paroxysmal eruptions of rhyolite-tuffs, followed later by flows of rhyolite. **1955** *Sci. News Let.* 9 July 20/2 The ancient implements are made chiefly of slate and shale but some are of jasper, quartz and rhyolite porphyry (rock of lava origin). **1971** I. G. GASS et al. *Understanding Earth* i. 22/1 The rock types granite, diorite and gabbro are all coarse-grained and usually found in intrusions. They are matched compositionally by fine-grained rocks, respectively rhyolite, andesite and basalt, which are characteristically found as surface lava flows (extrusions). **1977** A. HALLAM *Planet Earth* 164/1 Rhyolite eruptions are characteristic of areas of active mountain-building such as island arcs (e.g., Sumatra, Japan, West Indies), and mountain chains such as the Andes.

Rhyssa (ri·să). *Ent.* [mod.L. (I. L. C. Gravenhorst *Ichneumonologia Europæa* (1829) III. 260), f. Gr. ῥυσ(σ)ός shrivelled, wrinkled.] An ichneumon of the genus so called, the members of which prey upon the larvæ of wood-boring insects, esp. in conifers, and are usu. black with white face and markings.

1908 C. MORLEY *Ichneumons Gt. Brit.* III. 26 *Rhyssae* are found flying in pine woods, where the larvae of Sirices attack the solid timber. **1931** *Discovery* Dec. 386/1 As a popular study of the woodwasp and its major parasite, Rhyssa, the film is in its essentials admirable. **1969** R. F. CHAPMAN *Insects* xxx. 629 The parasite *Rhyssa* (Hymenoptera) is able to detect the larva of its host *Sirex* (Hymenoptera) through several inches of wood as a result of olfactory stimulation.

rhythm, *sb.* Add: The pronunc. (ri·ð'm) is now standard. **II. 5. c.** *ellipt.* A rhythm instrument or musician (also *sing.* for *pl.*); a rhythm section. orig. *U.S.*

1938 D. BAKER *Young Man with Horn* iii. 145 Every fourth dance..turned out to be a trumpet solo by Rick Martin, flanked by some rhythm. **1947** R. DE TOLEDANO *Frontiers of Jazz* 68 The instrumental blend and precision of each section—reed, brass, rhythm. **1956** M. STEARNS *Story of Jazz* (1957) xv. 170 The standard number of musicians in a dance band was nine: two trumpets, two saxes, one trombone, and four rhythm (banjo, piano, drums, and tuba). **1970** *New Yorker* 23 May 80/3 Sy Oliver..is holding a retrospective of his work..with the help of a nine-piece group that includes two trumpets,..and three rhythms.

8. *Geol.* and *Physical Geogr.* Regularity in the way something is repeated in space; also, a feature that is repeated at regular intervals of space.

1914 C. B. CRAMPTON *Geol. of Caithness* ix. 89 Sedimentary rhythm in marine deposits usually depends on the principle of the development of calcareous and terrigenous strata from opposite directions to overlap one another. **1924** *Proc. Yorks. Geol. Soc.* XX. 125 There is a rhythm in the succession of the beds, occasionally interrupted, but always discernible. **1937** *Bull. Geol. Soc. Amer.* XLVIII. 1935 Many mud-sand rhythms include strata too thick for seasonal accumulation. **1951** *Geol. Mag.* LXXXVIII. 166 The major rhythmic units attain a thickness of 100 or so feet but minor or partial rhythms also occur suggesting small changes in the intensity of the flow movement. **1976** P. D. KOMAR *Beach Processes & Sedimentation* x. 278 For many reported occurrences it is not possible to determine whether crescentic bars or some other shoreline rhythm are being described.

9. a. *attrib.* and *Comb.*, as (sense 1) † *rhythm prose*; (sense 4) *rhythm-foot, -word*; *rhythm-deaf, -drunk* adjs.; (sense 5) *rhythm-accent, dancer, group, musician, -pattern, singing*; **rhythm and blues** orig. *U.S.*, blues music with a strong rhythm; **rhythm club** *Hist.*, a club which specialized in the presentation of jazz; **rhythm guitar,** a guitar upon which the chord sequences of a melody are played; so *rhythm guitarist*; **rhythm instrument,** an instrument that constitutes part of the rhythm section of a musical band; **rhythm man,** one who plays a rhythm instrument; **rhythm section,** that part of a musical (orig. jazz) band whose main function is to supply the rhythm, often consisting of a piano, double-bass, and drums, sometimes with a guitar or other instruments.

1948 *Penguin Music Mag.* Oct. 36 For instance, Russian composers rely on rhythm-accent for their effect more than on harmony or melody. **1949** *Billboard* 25 June 30/2 Records listed are rhythm and blues records that sold best in stores according to the Billboard's special weekly survey. **1955** A. J. MCCARTHY *Jazzbook 1955* 84 Rhythm and blues is a Negro music and it was already in full flower when the jazz fans became aware of its existence. The actual musical content of the average rhythm and blues record is very limited. **1960** *Melody Maker* 31 Dec. 5/2 When we got to 'The Preacher', they both objected violently. 'No, no, no, no! We can't record that! That's rhythm and blues!' **1967** J. WILSON in L. Deighton *London Dossier* 25 The Stones.. had their first central London club engagement at the old Marquee. Rhythm 'n Blues in England began there with the late Cyril Davis, who died a few years ago. **1977** MCKNIGHT & TOBLER *Bob Marley* 10 Unlike soul, jazz or rhythm and blues, reggae remains the inviolable preserve of black musicians. **1933** *Melody Maker* 2 Dec. 2/1 (*heading*) All the rhythm clubs doing well. **1959** 'F. NEWTON' *Jazz Scene* xiii. 246 The student will observe the absence of Rhythm Clubs in Hampstead, Kensington or Chelsea. **1963** *Listener* 14 Mar. 458/1 People of my generation had to rely on their gramophones and the rhythm clubs to carry them through this period of deprivation. **1942** Rhythm dancer [see *JITTERBUG *sb.* 2]. **1926** FOWLER *Mod. Eng. Usage* 505/2 This writer has produced a single sentence seventeen lines long without a single slip in grammar. That so expert a syntactician should be rhythm-deaf is amazing. **1916** W. B. YEATS *Reveries over Childhood* 194 Verse spoken by a man almost rhythm-drunk at some moment of intensity. **1883** G. M. HOPKINS 7 Nov. *Let.* (1956) 329 Music is..the very place where the difference of time-feet and rhythm-feet recognised in Greek poetry is still in force. **1959** G. FREEMAN *Jack would be Gentleman* vi. 129 'Give us a song first.'.. 'Okay; but you'll have to do without the rhythm group.' **1973** *Guitar* Sept. 5/2 Plenty of familiar faces in the band:.. Charlie McCracken (ex-Taste, bass) and Spencer on rhythm and slide guitar. **1977** MCKNIGHT & TOBLER *Bob Marley* vi. 79 The instrumental chores of the band were shared like this: Marley—vocals, rhythm guitar; Family Man—bass. **1967** *Listener* 21 Dec. 802/1 If you encounter a little riot of colour ambling along Charing Cross Road,..it is the rhythm guitarist of The Who. **1977** *Zigzag* Mar. 17/5 Bill Cheatham ..switched from being their roadie to their rhythm guitarist. **1927** *Melody Maker* Sept. 926/3 The bass, being a rhythm instrument, must conform to the rhythm set by the rhythm section. **1952** B. ULANOV *Hist. Jazz in Amer.* (1958) vi. 51 The rhythm instruments—drums, bass, and guitar—made up the engine that powered the jazz machine: their function was to keep the syncopated beat going in regular almost inflexible alternations of weak and strong accents. **1949** L. FEATHER *Inside Be-Bop* III. 96 Seldom takes solos, but fine rhythm man. **1952** B. ULANOV *Hist. Jazz in Amer.* vi. 66 St. Cyr is the redoubtable rhythm man who kept such a fine beat going for Jelly Roll Morton's Red Hot Peppers and Louis Armstrong's Hot Five and Seven. **1977** *Rolling Stone* 19 May 83/1 Problems related to studio overdubbing (not Benson, but rhythm musicians). **1946** R. BLESH *Shining Trumpets* i. 18 Rhythm-pattern of dancers' feet. **1970** Rhythm pattern [see *RHYTHMIC *a.* 1 a]. **1599** Rhythm prose [in Dict., sense 1 a]. **1927** Rhythm section [see *rhythm instrument* above]. **1938** D. BAKER *Young Man with Horn* iii. 117 Rick.. started setting chairs together..in threes: reed section, brass section, rhythm section. **1955** A. MORGAN in A. J. McCarthy *Jazzbook 1955* 18 With a coloured front line.. and a mixed white and coloured rhythm section (Dodo Marmorosa, Barney Kessell, Red Callender and Don Lamond) these recordings are amongst the best examples of the use of a guitar in a bop rhythm section. **1977** *Times* 15 Nov. 17/6 An enthusiastic rhythm section whose drummer.. sometimes allowed his effervescence to occlude his marvellous sense of swing. **1934** S. R. NELSON *All about Jazz* iv. 73 Whiteman..started the fashion for organized rhythm singing with the Rhythm Boys. **1977** *Belfast Tel.* 22 Feb. 8/2 The American group's breed of close harmony and tight rhythm singing. *c* **1874** G. M. HOPKINS *Jrnls. & Papers* (1959) 279 In Greek the scanning is by..rhythmic beat, that is beat belonging only to the rhythm-words, not to the sense-words.

b. Used *attrib.* with reference to the periodic variation of fertility in women, esp. in **rhythm method,** a method of birth control depending upon continence during the period of ovulation.

[**1920** W. M. GALLICHAN *Critical Age of Woman* iii. 52 (*heading*) The sexual rhythm in women.] **1934** *New Republic* 5 Sept. 98/2 The rhythm theory of fertility and sterility in women was briefly explained to the Committee.

1940 N. E. HIMES *Pract. Birth-Control Meth.* viii. 125 Most authorities..believe the rhythm method unreliable. *Ibid.* 126 If a Catholic woman will not use a scientific method, it is perhaps better that she use the rhythm method than none at all. **1955** P. S. HENSHAW *Adaptive Human Fertility* xi. 208 Couples who wish to use the rhythm method for preventing conception have been advised to avoid coitus during the period of the nineteenth through the ninth day before the beginning of the next expected menstrual period. **1961** *Guardian* 3 Mar. 13/3 Even those most hostile to the use of contraceptives are in favour of the rhythm method. **1971** *Sunday Mirror* 25 July 11 We follow the rhythm system. But we don't use it to avoid procreation. We use it to *have* children. That's the way it was meant to be. **1972** *Human World* May 23 You use the rhythm method not just by having intercourse now, but by not having it next week, say.

rhythmal (ri·ðmăl), *a. rare.* [f. RHYTHM *sb.* + -AL.] = RHYTHMICAL *a.* 3.

1908 HARDY *Dynasts* III. I. vi. 346 Whose emissaries knock at every door, In rhythmal rote.

rhythmic, *a.* and *sb.* Add: **A.** *adj.* **1. a.** Also appositively, as *rhythmic-melodic* adj.

1946 R. BLESH *Shining Trumpets* ii. 36 The..principle of free rhythmic-melodic improvisation. **1970** P. OLIVER *Savannah Syncopators* 55 Repeated rhythm patterns and rhythmic-melodic patterns..such as are characteristic of boogie-woogie and blues piano.

3. *Geol.* and *Physical Geogr.* Exhibiting or characterized by a spatial rhythm or periodicity.

1914 C. B. CRAMPTON et al. *Geol. of Caithness* ix. 89 In the Helman Head Beds the rhythmic sequence is confined to continental, alluvial, and lacustrine deposits. **1960** TURNER & VERHOOGEN *Igneous & Metamorphic Petrol.* (ed. 2) xi. 292 Gravitational settling of heavy dark minerals within the layer of mush carpeting the floor..is thought to be responsible for the rhythmic layering so widely prevalent in the lower levels. **1976** P. D. KOMAR *Beach Processes & Sedimentation* x. 265 Attempts at classifying rhythmic shoreline features generally stress their spacings. Beach cusps are considered to have smaller spacings.., while sand waves.. and giant cusps have larger spacings.

rhythmicity (riðmi·siti). [f. RHYTHMIC *a.* + -ITY.] Rhythmical quality or character; the capacity for maintaining a rhythm.

1901 *Buck's Handbk. Med. Sci.* (ed. 2) III. 109/2 The pulse rate presents more or less regular and extensive variations in the course of a day... They are hardly the expression of an inherent rhythmicity. **1910** *Heart* I. 217 The ventricles are freed of the influence of their pace-maker, and their rate of beat is consequently slow until the dormant rhythmicity becomes fully awakened. **1944** *Mind* LIII. 271 Variability in size, number, direction, space, distance and rhythmicity is probably the most important characteristic in the primitive visual field. **1969** *Nature* 23 Aug. 782/1 Cutting the nerves..which connect the corpora cardiaca to the sub-oesophageal ganglion..caused a gradual loss of rhythmicity in otherwise intact cockroaches. **1971** CHIN-WU KIM *Survey Linguistic Sci.* 63 It definitely has a tendency to maintain iambic rhythmicity.

rhythmicize (ri·ðmisəiz), *v. rare.* [f. RHYTHMIC *a.* + -IZE.] *trans.* To make (a song) rhythmical; to endow with rhythm. Hence **rhy:thmiciza·tion.**

1907 R. BOUGHTON *Bach* iii. 47 We must have before us the melody of Luther's noble hymn, rhythmicized according to Bach. **1979** *Early Music* Apr. 283/1 It is true that we felt at liberty to experiment with rhythmicization and other aspects of performance style.

rhythmite (ri·ðməit). *Geol.* [ad. G. *rhythmit* (B. Sander 1936, in *Mineral. und petrogr. Mitt.* XLVIII. 190) f. *rhythm(us* RHYTHM *sb.* + *-it* -ITE[1].] Each of the repeated units in a sedimentary formation exhibiting a rhythmic structure; *spec.* a varve.

1946 *Prof. Paper U.S. Geol. Survey* No. 212. 30/2 The word 'rhythmite', used by Sander for the individual units of rhythmic beds, will be adopted here as a brief term to designate the couplet of distinct sedimentary types of rock, or the graded sequence of sediments, that form a unit bed or lamina in rhythmically bedded deposits. **1951** E. B. KNOPF tr. *Sander's Contributions to Study of Depositional Fabrics* 135 We have the same need for names to denote rocks of this sort (possibly rhythmites) as we had for tectonites and similar names. [*Translator's note*] It has been suggested by A. Knopf that 'laminites' might be a better term than 'rhythmites' in order to avoid the positive implication of perfect periodicity in the recurrence of laminae. **1969** BENNISON & WRIGHT *Geol. Hist. Brit. Isles* xvi. 361 In lake deposits counting of seasonally banded deposits, varves (or rhythmites)..can be used for dating such sediments up to 10,000 years old. **1976** *Nature* 18 Mar. 235/1 The rhythmites make up a regular series of plane beds with only occasional discontinuities caused by local penecontemporaneous erosion and minor faulting.

rhythmize, *v.* Delete *rare* in Dict. and add: (Further example.) Also *absol.*, to establish a steady rhythm.

1933 *Brit. Jrnl. Psychol.* Jan. 263 In some simple factory tasks it seems impossible not to rhythmize. **1946** *Scrutiny* Dec. 94 A number of impressions that would otherwise be merely a sequence can, if rhythmized, be perceived as an organized whole.

Hence **rhy·thmiza·tion; rhy·thmized** *ppl. a.*; **rhy·thmizing** *vbl. sb.*

1901 E. B. TITCHENER *Exper. Psychol.* I. II. x. 339 The object of this experiment is to bring out the fact of subjective rhythmisation, or (as it is also termed) subjective accentuation. **1933** *Brit. Jrnl. Psychol.* Jan. 263 The rhythmized impressions are differentiated according to their position within the rhythm unit. *Ibid.*, In typewriting,.. individual differences in rhythmizing are far more marked. **1946** *Scrutiny* Dec. 94 The experience of rhythm is..an active process, the process of rhythmization. **1955** G. ABRAHAM in H. Van Thal *Fanfare for E. Newman* 21 Similarly rhythmised string chords replace the 'scrub' tremolo.

rhytidectomy (rəitide·ktǫmi). *Surg.* Also in contracted form **rhydectomy.** [f. Gr. ῥυτιδ-, ῥυτίς wrinkle + *-ECTOMY.] The surgical removal of wrinkles, esp. from the face.

1931 R. J. E. SCOTT *Gould's Med. Dict.* (ed. 3) 1217/1 Rhytidectomy. **1939** S. FOMON *Surg. of Injury & Plastic Repair* xix. 1348 (*caption*) Ehrenfeld rhydectomy. **1954** ZUBEK & SOLBERG *Human Devel.* v. 106 Once character lines are fully developed, the only recourse is rhytidectomy—that is, plastic surgery through which wrinkles are removed by traction on the skin—and even such drastic measures are only temporary. **1960** S. FOMON *Cosmetic Surg.* viii. 455/2 The benefits that accrue from a facial rhydectomy are manifold. **1971** *Daily Colonist* (Victoria, B.C.) 15 Aug. 29/4 The face lift or rhytidectomy takes care of sagging jowls and heavy expression lines—seldom the fine ones. **1977** *Chicago Tribune Mag.* 2 Oct. 23/1 Whereas the price of a complete rhytidectomy (face-lift) in the United States..averages between $2,500 and $5,000..Lotter's maximum charge is $2,500.

rhytidome. Add: Also (*rare*) **rhitidome.** Substitute for def.: The outer part of the bark of a woody plant, composed of layers of dead phloem and cork. (Further examples.)

1896 W. R. FISHER *Schlich's Man. Forestry* V. 486 The Turkey-oak is used here and there in Austria for the production of bark, but on account of its forming, at an early age, a deeply-cracked rhitidome, or dead bark..it is of little value. **1925** EAMES & MACDANIELS *Introd. Plant Anat.* ix. 215 Hypodermal layers..may be combined with periderm..to form rhytidome, as in *Dracaena.* **1953** K. ESAU *Plant Anat.* xiv. 332 In some rhytidomes parenchyma and soft cork cells predominate; others contain large amounts of fibers. **1976** *Flora* CLXV. B. 326 Rhytidome composition.. is considered also to be important for fungal bark infections.

‖ **ri** (ri). Pl. **ri.** [Jap.] **1.** A traditional Japanese unit of length equal to 36 *cho*; in modern use equivalent to approximately 2·44 miles (3·93 kilometres).

1845 *Encycl. Metrop.* XX. 486/2, 1 long ri = 3 standard miles nearly. 1 short ri = 2 ditto ditto. **1874** *Trans. Asiatic Soc. Japan 1873–4* 33 After a somewhat disagreeable walk of 3 *ri* Kusatsu is reached. **1876** H. W. BATES *Illustr. Trav.* 248/1 The *ri* is little short of two and a half miles. **1890** B. H. CHAMBERLAIN *Things Japanese* 352 Tokyo.. covers an immense area, popularly estimated at four *ri* in every direction, in other words, a hundred square miles. **1897** *Japan Times* 10 Apr. 3/4 How many *ri* of the inundated tracts of land along the rivers could possibly be polluted by the poisonous matter from the mine? **1964** *Japan* (Unesco) (rev. ed.) 847 *Ri* (36 chō), 3·92727 kilometre, 2·44033 miles.

2. In Japan (in ancient times) and Korea, the smallest subdivision of rural administration.

1959 R. K. BEARDSLEY et al. *Village Japan* iii. 40 We have already mentioned the division of old Kibi into provinces (*kuni*). These were further divided into districts (*kōri*, later *gun*), and still further into villages (*gō*, today 'mura') and hamlets (*ri*). **1966** J. W. HALL *Govt. & Local Power in Japan, 500 to 1700* iii. 82 Groups of fifty or fewer *ko* formed the administrative village, called *ri*. *Ibid.* 83 In 715 the name *ri* was abandoned, and the fifty-*ko* units were renamed *gō*. These newly named administrative villages were then divided into two or three smaller units to which the term *ri* was applied... For some reason the *ri* was discontinued as a unit of official organization in 740. **1971** *Korean Folklore & Classics* III. 7 Mr. Kwak lived in Sa Dong Ri. **1972** P. M. BARTZ *South Korea* 54/1 A *myon* may be divided into one or more *ri*... It is usually translated into English as 'village', but a *ri* does not *ipso facto* contain a village. It is merely the smallest area of rural subdivision.

ria. Delete ‖ and substitute for def.: **1.** A long narrow inlet of the sea formed by the partial submergence of an unglaciated river valley. [Adopted as a technical term in Ger. by F. von Richthofen *Führer für Forschungsreisende* (1886) ix. 309.]

The wider use represented by quots. 1899, 1915 has not been generally adopted.

1899 *Proc. Amer. Acad. Arts & Sci.* XXXIV. 220 The term *ria*, from the Spanish, may be advantageously used to cover all types of subaerially carved troughs, including von Richthofen's fjord, ria, dalmatian, and limian types. **1915** *Ann. Assoc. Amer. Geographers* V. 82 The Spanish word, ria, introduced into German by Richthofen, and now widely adopted, means any broad or estuarine river mouth, and not necessarily an embayment produced by the partial submergence of an open valley in a mountainous coast, in the sense that Richthofen originally proposed. **1939** *Geogr. Jrnl.* XCIII. 235 Many of the rivers enter the heads of rias which extend many miles inland. **1946** L. D. STAMP *Britain's Struct. & Scenery* v. 49 The best example of a coastline of drowned valleys or ria coast is the south-west of Ireland. Soundings show that the floor of the ria..slopes steadily seawards and there is no 'lip' as there is in the case of a glaciated valley. **1974** *Encycl. Brit. Micropædia* IX. 560/2 Generally occurring along a rugged coast perpendicular to a mountain chain, many rias were formed by the rise in sea level after the melting of the vast continental glaciers. **1977** MILLWARD & ROBINSON *Landscape of Brit.* 46 In the South-West Peninsula, the deeply set valleys give rise to long branching arms of the sea known as 'rias'.

2. *attrib.*, as *ria shoreline*; **ria coast** (also † **rias coast,** after G. *riasküste* (von Richthofen, loc. cit.)), a coast marked by numerous rias.

1902 *Encycl. Brit.* XXVIII. 623/1 A further subdivision depends on the character of the inter-relation of land and sea along the shore producing such types as a fjord-coast, ria-coast, or lagoon-coast. **1924** tr. *Wegener's Orig. Continents & Oceans* 53 These strongly planed-down chains.. stretch..westwards so as to form a wild jagged type of coast (the so-called rias-coast) in south-western Ireland and Brittany. **1946** [see above]. **1977** A. HALLAM *Planet Earth* 94 For example, drowned river valleys of the ria coasts, such as those of southwest Ireland, can be differentiated from glacially eroded drowned coasts. **1919** D. W. JOHNSON *Shore Processes & Shoreline Devel.* iv. 173 Shorelines formed by the partial submergence of a land mass dissected by normal river valleys, which may be called ria shorelines, after the ria coast of northwestern Spain..; thus used, the term ria is not restricted to the narrow meaning assigned to it by von Richthofen.

rial, *sb.*[1] Restrict 'Now only *Hist.*' to senses in Dict. and add: **5.** Also **riyal. a.** The monetary unit of Iran, introduced in 1930 and equal to one hundred dinars.

1932 A. T. WILSON *Persia* x. 278 The Gold Standard Act [of 28 Mar. 1930] establishes as the legal unit of currency the gold rial, to be represented in coinage by the *pahlevi* of 20 rials and the half pahlevi of 10 rials. **1936** *Encycl. Islam* III. 1162/3 The modern Persian riyāl is a money of account: originally (1930) 20 riyāls = £1 stg. but by the system finally adopted in 1933, 100 dinārs = 1 riyāl = 1 pahlavi = £1 stg. **1948** D. N. WILBER *Iran* 213 The rial is also popularly referred to as the kran. **1953** A. SMITH *Blind White Fish in Persia* vii. 115 Eggs, 11 rials; mast, 4 rials; grapes, 18 rials. **1972** *Times* 20 Oct. 9/4 Smuggled opium is sold in Iran at a price below the 17·5 rials (about 10p) a gram the Government charges registered addicts. **1973** E. HYAMS *Final Agenda* v. 61 'Can I have that map?' 'Forty-five *rials*, sir.' **1976** R. MOORE *Dubai* i. 6 Fitz removed a thousand-rial note, about fifteen dollars, and placed it in the envelope.

b. The monetary unit of Saudi Arabia.

1939 H. ST. J. B. PHILBY *Sheba's Daughters* ii. 21 It is perhaps sufficient to mention that the camels hired by him for our use cost no more than 15 Riyals (about £1 sterling) apiece for a journey that occupied two and a half months. **1951** *Chambers's Jrnl.* Nov. 689/2 In the 19th century the dollar was banned in the Ottoman Empire, including Egypt, and became obsolete in Tunis and Algeria. Rather later, Ibn Saud of Arabia substituted, not without difficulty, his own rials for it. **1964** *Ann. Reg. 1963* 308 The sum of 244 million riyals was allocated to provide free education for everyone. **1970** *Times* 3 Apr. (Arab League Suppl.) p. x/5 The Government has already spent more than 4,000m. rials in five years developing communications. **1977** *Arab Times* 13 Dec. 4/5 Recently Shahwa found at Ahmad Al Jaben Street a bag containing KD 1,300 and Saudi Rial 2,594 and an expensive watch.

c. Any of various monetary units of other countries of the Middle East (see quots.).

1959 *Statesman's Year-bk.* 1383 The monetary unit is the Sudanese pound (£S), divided into 10 Riyals. **1968** *Listener* 4 Jan. 7/1 A guerrilla attack on the outskirts of Sanaa for a few Yemeni riyals. **1970** *Whitaker's Almanack 1971* 917/2 Oman... On May 7, 1970, a new currency was brought into circulation. The main unit is the *Rial Saidi* = £1. Each *rial* is divided into 1,000 new *Baiza*. **1972** *Times* 15 May (Qatar Suppl.) p. iv/6 Banknotes of one, five, 10, 25, 50 and 100 Riyals. **1977** *Times* 18 Feb. (Banking Suppl.) p. v/5 In ..1976 the Qatari rial joined the Bahrain dinar and the United Arab Emirates dirham in the travellers' reciprocity scheme.

rialto. Add: (Earlier examples.) Also *fig.*

1596 SHAKES. *Merch. V.* I. iii. 108 Signior Anthonio, many a time and oft In the Ryalto you haue rated me About my monies and my vsances. **1611** CORYAT *Crudities* 169 The Rialto which is at the farther end of the bridge as you come from S[t]. *Marks*, is a most stately building, being the Exchange of Venice, where the Venetian Gentlemen and the Merchants doe meete twice a day, betwixt eleuen and twelue of the clocke in the morning, and betwixt fiue and sixe of the clocke in the afternoone. **1869** S. R. HOLE *Bk. about Roses* i. 11 There the poor Rose-trees stand..in the spring a *rialto*, *rendezvous*, common-room, and tap for all the riff-raff of the insect world.

riata. Add: Also **reata.** (Earlier and later examples.) Also in Comb., as *riata-man.*

1846 *Californian* 12 Sept. 1/1 A riata (rope) was made fast to the broken bone and the jaw dragged out. **1853** *Harper's Mag.* Aug. 308/2 Each mule being secured by a long *reata*..was permitted to graze until sunset. **1924** F. R. BECHDOLT *Tales of Old-Timers* 103 They had failed to take into account..a skill with the reata. **1934** *Amer. Ballads & Folk Songs* 409 Old Sandy Bob was a riata-man. **1948** F. BLAKE *Johnny Christmas* I. 41 Johnny loosened the horse-hair knots, then..took down his rawhide riata. **1964** F. O'ROURKE *Mule for Marquesa* 126 He sliced rope lengths from the reatas tied to the saddles. **1970** *Arizona Highways* Oct. 48/1 Now Buster Jig was a *riata* man, With his gut-line coiled up neat.

rib, *sb.*[1] Add: **I. 1. d.** A joke; a teasing or joking remark. Chiefly *U.S.*

1929 J. P. MCEVOY *Hollywood Girl* iii. 39 Of course it was just a rib to see him, as the only thing I know about newspapers is that they smell fresh. **1952** *Herald-Tribune* (N.Y.) 25 Jan. 18/3 Wilt said, 'He is a parasite.' Maybe this was a rib. **1958** J. WAIN *Contenders* 8 The mere idea of Robert as a schoolmaster is, of course, a screaming rib. **1964** 'E. QUEEN' in *Cavalier* Aug. 15/2 'Dad, is this a rib?' 'I wish I could joke about it.'

e. Slang phr. *to get into* (someone's) *ribs*: to borrow or otherwise obtain money from (someone). (Only in Wodehouse.)

1939 WODEHOUSE *Uncle Fred in Springtime* iii. 47 Leave it to me. I will get into his ribs for you. **1951** —— *Old Reliable* xviii. 200 It was..the worst possible moment anyone could have selected to approach him with the idea of getting into his ribs for twenty thousand dollars. *a* **1975** —— *Sunset at Blandings* (1977) viii. 59 Did he discover that Jeff was the son of the man who got into his ribs for that substantial sum, there would be no question of engaging him as his secretary.

III. 11. e. *Aeronaut.* A structural member in an aerofoil, positioned more or less fore-and-aft and serving to define the contour of the aerofoil and sometimes also as part of the load-bearing structure.

1888 [see *PROPELLER 3 c]. **1919** H. SHAW *Text-bk. Aeronaut.* ix. 109 The chief function of the ribs is to give the wing its correct shape, while they also serve as compression members between the two spars, and as a framework for the attachment of the fabric. **1941** N. H. ANDERSON *Aircraft Layout & Detail Design* ii. 24 The term 'skewed rib' is applied to a rib that is bent inboard or outboard along its line of intersection on a spar. **1965** C. N. VAN DEVENTER *Introd. Gen. Aeronaut.* vii. 141/2 The ribs are secured to the spars, and since they are curved they give the wing its familiar aerodynamic shape when it is covered with a 'skin' of aluminium alloy. **1966** D. STINTON *Anat. Aeroplane* xi. 206 Ribs may be built up like frames, be light as formers, or be made like bulkheads.

IV. 13. a. *rib-chop, -end, -steak*; **rib-cage**, the chamber formed by the ribs and their connecting tissues, which contains the lungs, heart, etc.; also *fig.*; **rib-eye** *N. Amer.*, a cut (cf. *EYE *sb.*[1] 16 e) of meat that lies along the outer side of the rib (of beef-cattle); usu. *attrib.*, as *rib-eye muscle, steak.*

1909 *Daily Chron.* 9 July 9/4 By any outward pressure about the waist, the diaphragm is hampered in its movement, and breathing becomes costal; that is, a woman then breathes only within her chest or rib-cage. **1932** W. FAULKNER *Light in August* x. 212 Feeling..his white chest arch deeper and deeper within his ribcage. **1959** *Times* 17 Aug. 10/6 The builder showed me some of the points of a racing pigeon... The full rib-cage inside which the heart and lungs generated the energy for sustained flight. **1978** J. IRVING *World according to Garp* i. 25 There were two waist gunners tucked into the rib cage of the plane. **1936** Rib chop [see *BEST *a.* 5]. **1979** *Lore & Lang.* Jan. 29 Rib chops. **1851** H. MELVILLE *Moby Dick* II. xxxix. 259 So did this old whale leave his aged bulk, and now and then partly turning over on his cumbrous rib-ends, expose..the unnatural stump of his starboard fin. **1979** *Lore & Lang.* Jan. 27 Rib end of sirloin. **1926** *Nat. Provisioner* 3 Feb. 10/1 Roast-ready rib is prepared..starting at a fixed point determined by measuring off 3 in. from extreme outer tip of rib-eye muscle at 12th rib. **1943** P. T. ZIEGLER *Meat we Eat* xvi. 251 The quartering is done by inserting the knife at the desired spot below the rib eye muscle. *Ibid.* 255 A recent practice is to cut out the rib eye of the better grades of ribs and serve them as *club steak.* **1966** A. HAWKINS *Steak Book* (end-paper), Club steak. Country Club steak. Delmonico steak. Ribeye steak. **1974** *Greenville* (S. Carolina) *News Piedmont* 20 Apr. 5/1 (Advt.); 4 oz. Ribeye steak... 59c. **1978** *Chicago* June 229/1 Recommended: the special rib-eye steak and the Lithuanian roast duck. **1922** JOYCE *Ulysses* 659 On the middle shelf..a small dish containing a slice of fresh rib-steak. **1976** *Columbus* (Montana) *News* (Joliet Suppl.) 27 May 3/4 (Advt.), Rib steak..lb. $1.69.

b. rib-bender (earlier and later examples); **rib-digger**, a person given to light-hearted banter; so **rib-digging** *ppl. a.*; **rib-tickler**, that which amuses; a joke or aphorism; hence **rib-tickling** *ppl. a.*

1861 H. RHYS *Theatr. Trip through Canada & U.S.* xii. 108 He was licked in five minutes by as many of Morrissey's rib-benders. **1901** G. B. SHAW *Admirable Bashville* II. 311 My calling hath appointed me to pangs. This is a rib-bender; but I can bear it. **1929** Rib-digger [see *BACK-SLAPPING *ppl. a.* and *vbl. sb.*]. **1925** H. J. LASKI *Let.* 28 Apr. in *Holmes–Laski Lett.* (1953) I. 737 In a very different genus, *Love* by the Countess von Arnim which seemed to me devilish clever, with a sly rib-digging quality not unworthy of Jane Austen. **1933** P. GODFREY *Back-Stage* vii. 98 By the introduction of 'stage business'..the skilled comedian can transform very thin stuff into a real 'rib-tickler'. **1963** *Times Lit. Suppl.* 24 May 379/2 He does include some real rib-ticklers. **1976** M. MILLAR *Ask for me Tomorrow* viii. 66 'Isn't that a funny idea?' 'A real rib-tickler.' **1936** J. L. HODSON *Our Two Englands* vi. 108 This centre for providing violent or exquisite or rib-tickling emotions has a Fun-house resembling a super-modern factory. **1977** *It* June 26/4 Your old pal has written this rib-tickling tale specially for jubilee freaks all.

14. b. *rib-knit, -weave.*

1968 J. IRONSIDE *Fashion Alphabet* 247 A rib knit (i.e. purl and plain) fabric is much more elastic than a plain knit. **1973** *Guardian* 10 Apr. 13/2 Cape faced with chunky ribknit. **1964** *McCall's Sewing* iv. 51/2 The Rib Weave which has ribbed or corded effects in either the warp or filling direction is another variation of the plain weave. **1968** J. IRONSIDE *Fashion Alphabet* 261 *Rib weave*: the ribbed effect is obtained by using thicker or doubled yarn in one direction.

c. *rib-cloud*; **rib-joint** *U.S. slang*, a brothel; **rib-randing** *Basketry* (see quot. 1953); also (as back-formation) *rib-rand* vb. trans.; **rib-roll** *sb.*, a farm roller with a ribbed or hooped surface; hence as *vb. trans.*; **rib-stall**, a set of wall-bars for physical exercises.

1868 G. M. HOPKINS *Jrnls. & Papers* (1959) 170 At sunset featherbed sky with a fluffy and jointed rib-cloud. **1943** M. SHULMAN *Barefoot Boy with Cheek* xx. 192 One night Scott became involved in a fracas in a Minneapolis rib joint. **1965** C. COLTER in A. Chapman *New Black Voices* (1972) 70 Forty-third Street,..the street of rib joints and taverns. **1975** *Amer. Speech 1969* XLIV. 91 The great majority represent middle-class restaurants. There are a few exceptions: a few drugstores, 'rib joints', snack bars, and a couple of 'soul food' places in the black ghetto. **1912** T. OKEY *Introd. Art of Basket-Making* ix. 92 *Rib-randing*..is used..where it is desirable to break the monotony of a deep space of simple randing. **1953** A. G. KNOCK *Willow Basket-Work* (ed. 5) 17 *Rib-Randing.* This is produced by carrying the randing rod in front of two stakes instead of one, as in ordinary randing. **1959** D. WRIGHT *Baskets & Basketry* ii. 36 *Rib-randing*..must be worked over a number of stakes not divisible by three. The close weave is useful on lids. *Ibid.* iv. 125 Rib-rand the ball..finishing with a round of pairing. **1969** G. E. EVANS *Farm & Village* 176 *Rib-roll*, land roller with corrugated surface. **1971** *Arable Farmer* Feb. 29/2 The crop is not rib rolled until the peas have chitted and are just coming through. **1908** *Mosquito* Dec. 2 The heart of the Games' Mistress still yearns after some more ribstalls, a Norwegian ladder, and a bench for remedial work.

rib, *v.*[1] Add: **4. b.** To discredit; to incriminate. *U.S. slang. rare.*

1926 *Clues* Nov. 162/1 *Rib*, to frame up. **1929** HOSTETTER & BEESLEY *It's a Racket!* 236 *Rib*, to talk about anyone, to talk slander about anyone. **1935** *Amer. Speech* X. 52/2 To rib (to discredit).

c. To annoy or threaten; to put pressure on (someone). *U.S. slang. rare.*

1929 D. HAMMETT *Red Harvest* iv. 49 If Max Thaler means anything to you, you ought to pass him the word that Noonan's trying to rib him.

d. To fool or dupe; to tease; to make fun of (someone or something). *slang* (orig. *U.S.*). Also *absol.*

1930 *Amer. Mercury* Dec. 457/2 *Rib, v.*, to beguile. 'We rib the sap that it's McCoy and he goes for it.' **1934** J. O'HARA *Appointment in Samarra* (1935) 98 Mr. Robert Hermann is in his best form, ribbing me about last night. **1938** *New York Panorama* xi. 262 Armstrong..could take a pop tune and reinterpret it, often *ribbing* (satirizing) it. **1941** K. TENNANT *Battlers* xiii. 143 The busker pricked up his ears when he heard the merry-go-round owner 'ribbing' Fosdick on the number of lodgers he was taking in nightly. **1942** *Sun* (Baltimore) 2 Feb. 8/4 I've been here about a year and every once in a while I get 'ribbed' about Baltimore. **1955** L. P. HARTLEY *Perfect Woman* viii. 78 When the chaps rib her she doesn't quite know how to act up. **1958** J. WAIN *Contenders* 30 Baxter just thought I was ribbing him. **1960** 'N. SHUTE' *Trustee from Toolroom* 294 Quit ribbing, Sol. **1967** H. STOREY in *Coast to Coast 1965–6* 203 One of the neighbours had ribbed him about 'being on the bottle'. **1972** M. WILLIAMS *Inside Number 10* xii. 303 Jim Callaghan has always been very charming to me, though I won't say that once I began to work for Harold I was not often ribbed and left with the odd, slightly acid remark ringing in my ears. **1976** *Times Lit. Suppl.* 31 Dec. 1640/3 [Ben] Jonson was ribbed on more than one occasion for daring to put forth his collected works even before he could have been called middle-aged.

Ribaga (rĭba·gă). *Ent.* The name of Constantino *Ribaga* (*fl.* 1897–1929), Italian zoologist, used *attrib.*, in the possessive, and with *of* to designate a pouch on the abdomen of female insects, chiefly of the family Cimicidæ, into which spermatozoa are deposited by the male during copulation.

Orig. restricted in application to a part of the organ now so called (see quot. 1920).

1920 F. W. CRAGG in *Indian Jrnl. Med. Res.* VIII. 46 Its only attachment is to the ventral wall of the abdomen, by means of a structure to be described as the organ of Ribaga. *Ibid.* 51 Berlese considered that these granules are waste products, produced during the digestion of the spermatozoa, and excreted through the organ of Ribaga. **1957** RICHARDS & DAVIES *Imms's Textbk. Entomol.* (ed. 9) I. 189 In the Cimicidae and in *Xylocoris* the sperms are deposited in Ribaga's organ..and from there pass through the haemocoele to the ovaries. **1970** *Entomol. Abstr.* II. 38/1, 5829 ♀ C[imex] lectularius from a variety of sources showed 185 specimens with an abnormality of the Ribaga organ.

riband, *sb.* Add: **5. b.** *riband-back* adj.

1955 R. FASTNEDGE *Eng. Furnit. Styles* vii. 166 Chippendale had good reason for satisfaction. The riband-back chair..notably expressed the style of his *Director* period. **1960** H. HAYWARD *Antique Coll.* 238/1 '*Ribband-back' chair*, a mahogany chair, the splat carved in the form of knotted ribbons and bows in a manner highly expressive of rococo taste.

c. riband cane, var. *ribbon cane* s.v. *RIBBON *sb.* 10 c.

ribbed, *ppl. a.* **2. b.** (Earlier examples.)

1756 in *Essex Inst. Hist. Coll.* (1907) XLIII. 277 Smith wore when he went away..blue ribb'd Stockings. **1782** in *Ibid.* (1859) I. 13/1 A patton [*sc.* pattern] of White Ribed Stuff for a Wescoat & Briches.

ribbing, *vbl. sb.* Add: **1. b.** (The action of) teasing or joking at another's expense (see *RIB *v.*[1] 4 d). *slang* (orig. *U.S.*).

1935 WODEHOUSE *Luck of Bodkins* xxiv. 301, I was just kidding. Sure! Ribbing, we call it over here. **1935** *Sun* (Baltimore) 9 Mar. 6/2 A dozen fat rainbow trout were in the [swimming] pool—another case of Hollywood 'ribbing'. **1939** I. BAIRD *Waste Heritage* xv. 192 There was a brief outbreak of good-natured ribbing. **1951** *Sport* 30 Mar.–5 Apr. 3/2 Stan had to contend with a good deal of ribbing from his team-mates. **1956** C. P. SNOW *Homecomings* 139 Orthodox opinions, collective gibes, a bit of ribbing—that was enough to keep them zestful. **1968** *Globe & Mail Mag.* (Toronto) 13 Jan. 12/3 Unlike..rustic yokels..they can even take a ribbing. **1976** M. & G. GORDON *Ordeal* (1977) iii. 15 He was..the only man at the party to wear a tie. He took a ribbing about that.

2. (Further examples in *Knitting.*)

1948 'P. WENTWORTH' *Traveller Returns* xxi. 134 She had begun Johnny's second stocking and almost finished the ribbing at the top. **1958** C. FREMLIN *Hours before Dawn* xxi. 173 Her niece..was frowning dreadfully over the spacing of the button holes in the front ribbing. **1962** 'E. PETERS' *Funeral of Figaro* iii. 69 Two inches of neat ribbing stood stiff on the bright blue plastic needles. **1973** D. BIGGS *Knitting for Fun* 41/2 If you can knit a square you can make this gay poncho... Join corners of neck ribbing.

ribbok (ri·bǫk), var. REEBOK.

1947 H. C. BOSMAN *Mafeking Road* xii. 67 He remembered having had that same feeling once before when he had shot a ribbok. **1953** *Cape Argus* 25 Apr. 8/4 The animals include ribbok, grysbok,..and one blue wildebeest. **1966** E. PALMER *Plains of Camdeboo* vii. 124 'The skull is ribbok,' he said, 'and that's the tibia of a buffalo.'

ribbon, *sb.* Add: **I. 2.** Also *pl.*, prizes or decorations awarded to the winners of a competition or show; chiefly in phr. *in the ribbons*, among the prize-winners. Also *fig.*

1932 *New Yorker* 23 July 42/3 He [*sc.* a horse] went off like the stock market on Saturdays and wasn't in the ribbons. **1974** *News & Press* (Darlington, S. Carolina) 25 Apr. 11/1 Bobby Gurley's efforts in the 50-yd. dash and softball throw won first-place ribbons. **1977** *Horse & Hound* 10 June 24/2 (*caption*) Julia Watts on her Song of the Sea,..again in the ribbons among the hacks at the Hertfordshire Show.

5. d. Also *spec.* a strip of land, esp. a path or road.

1923 *Times* 26 May 7/4 Pedestrians should not walk in the road..but should keep to the footpaths or ribbons on the Downs specially prepared for them. **1948** 'J. TEY' *Franchise Affair* ix. 90 The London–Larborough road was a black straight ribbon in the sunshine. **1958** *Spectator* 6 June 721/3 The factories are in other parts of the borough, along the ribbon of Western Avenue. **1966** *Guardian* 10 Aug. 14/2 The consultants put great emphasis on the need for landscaping and the creation of ribbons of open spaces in and around Warrington. **1976** M. MAGUIRE *Scratchproof* xii. 182 Staring out at the ribbon of road ahead.

e. A long, narrow strip of thin impregnated fabric or coated plastic wound on a spool, used as the inking agent in a typewriter or printer (in earlier use, a similar strip used in hand-stamping devices). Also *attrib.*

a **1877** KNIGHT *Dict. Mech.* III. 1936/2 Ribbons for hand-stamps are tapes saturated with an oily pigment. **1883** J. G. PETRIE *Man. Type-Writer* 16 For ordinary writing a black ribbon is best. *Ibid.*, Ribbons will last a long time if they are taken care of. **1907** *Yesterday's Shopping* (1969) 357/2 The..Typewriter Desk..has drawers for holding Carbon, Ribbons, Stationery. **1951** A. C. CLARKE *Sands of Mars* iv. 33, I should have warned you to use a black ribbon. Contrast isn't so good with blue. **1962** *Which?* Dec. 358/2 All the models had automatic ribbon reverse. **1976** N. MEYER *West End Horror* viii. 77 Address typewritten—on a Remington in need of a new ribbon.

f. *ellipt.* = *ribbon microphone* (sense 9 c below).

1937 *Printers' Ink Monthly* May 40/3 *Ribbon*, a velocity microphone. **1962** A. NISBETT *Technique Sound Studio* ii. 44 The two microphones can be so placed that the only move necessary to get from one to the other is a slight turn. The ribbon will have a smooth, realistic quality.

II. 9. a. *ribbon-manufacturer* (earlier and later examples), *threader.*

1799 *Times* 1 June 2/1 The Bill for Regulating the Wages of Ribbon Manufacturers, in Coventry. **1883** M. BLIND *George Eliot* iii. 26 Mr. Bray was a wealthy ribbon manufacturer. **1973** M. LASKI *Geo. Eliot* 23 Mr Pears was a ribbon manufacturer. **1931** Ribbon threader [see *MUSHROOM *sb.* 3 e]. **1969** E. H. PINTO *Treen* 318 The ribbon threader, a round-ended, tapering rod, nearly 1 ft. long, with a large eye at the narrow end, was once a commonplace implement.

c. *ribbon-knit, shop, work*; **ribbon cartridge**, (*a*) a pick-up cartridge that works on the same principle as the ribbon microphone; (*b*) a cartridge containing a spooled typewriter ribbon for easy and clean insertion into and removal from a typewriter; **ribbon chute** = *ribbon parachute* below; **ribbon clerk** *U.S. slang* (see quot. 1953); also fig.; **ribbon-copy** *U.S.*, the top copy of a (typed) letter or document; **ribbon microphone** or (*colloq.*) **mike**, a microphone whose electrical output results from the motion of a thin metal ribbon mounted between the poles of a permanent magnet; **ribbon parachute**, a parachute having a canopy consisting of an arrangement of closely spaced tapes.

1975 G. J. KING *Audio Handbk.* viii. 172 Instead of a coil of wire a single conductor in the form of a 'ribbon' may be used, the result being a ribbon cartridge. **1977** *New York Rev. Bks.* 12 May 17/2 (Advt.), The Lexikon portables use Ribbon Cartridges that snap in. **1946** *Sun* (Baltimore) 18 July 13/2 The parachute itself is of revolutionary design. Known as a 'ribbon chute' it is composed of 150 individual ribbons approximately two inches wide. **1927** E. POUND *Let.* 29 Dec. (1971) 215 Am I expected to respect either myself or anyone else because some graduated ribbon-clerk offers me 75 bucks for writing blah in a false-pearl and undies monthly? **1953** Berrey & Van den Bark *Amer. Thes. Slang* (1954) §563/1 Stock Market... *Ribbon clerks, lambs*, amateur, small-fry traders who take occasional flings in the market. **1977** *Time* 11 Apr. 24/1 Flying has become so routine that the notably pragmatic insurance companies charge pilots no more for policies than they do ribbon clerks. **1968** R. Lockridge *Plate of Red Herrings* xi. 147 Always they send us carbons... They send the ribbon copies to book publishers. **1976** M. Millar *Ask for me Tomorrow* 28, I can type this letter up for you... How many copies do you need?.. You'll want to give her the ribbon copy. **1969** C. Armstrong *Seven Seats to Moon* xii. 109 Her hands kept busy with a ribbon-knit costume she had been working on for weeks. **1974** *Country Life* 3/10 Jan. 54/2 Wool bouclé suits, ribbon knits and embroidered sweaters. **1931** *Jrnl. Acoustical Soc. Amer.* III. 59 The ribbon microphone consists of a lightly corrugated metallic ribbon suspended in a magnetic field and freely accessible to air vibrating from both sides. **1944** *Electronic Engin.* XVI. 328/3 A simple detector for supersonics in the region of 20 kc/s can be made from an old ribbon microphone. **1975** G. J. King *Audio Handbk.* ix. 200 The ribbon microphone..tends to respond to the particle velocity of a sound wave. **1957** *Practical Wireless* XXXIII. 714/2 Most ribbon mikes have a transformer built in at the bottom of the case. **1948** *Jrnl. Brit. Interplanetary Soc.* VII. 95 The containers were lowered successfully for the first time by ribbon parachutes. **1956** W. A. Heflin *U.S. Air Force Dict.* 442/2 *Ribbon parachute*, a type of parachute consisting of numbers of ribbons held in place by equally-spaced tapes, with spacing between the ribbons to give the required porosity. The ribbon parachute was developed in Germany and used during WW II. **1699** M. Lister *Journey to Paris* 176 Many of the great Ribban Shops remove out of the Palais hither. **1857** Geo. Eliot in *Blackw. Mag.* July 62/1 The Dissent..had let off half its chapel area as a ribbon-shop. **1856** O. Jones *Gram. Ornament* xv. 3 Various patterns, mostly geometrical, consisting of interlaced ribbon-work,..and strange monstrous animals and birds. **1960** H. Hayward *Antique Coll.* 238/2 *Ribbon work*, embroidery in fine, narrow silk ribbons often combined with chenille thread and aerophane.

10. a. *ribbon bed, decoration, flame, handle, ornament, pattern, road; ribbon-back(ed)* adj.; **ribbon-building** = next; **ribbon development** [*development 3 d], the building of houses in a single line along a main road, usu. one leading out of a town or village; hence **ribbon-developed** *a.*

1920 *Burlington Mag.* Oct. 195/1 Thomas Chippendale is usually credited with being the originator of the ribbon-back chair. *Ibid.* 196/1 Nearly all the known variations of the ribbon-back have the ball-and-claw foot in addition. **1980** *Times* 2 June 4/7 A set of six ribbon-back Chippendale chairs. **1966** A. W. Lewis *Gloss. Woodworking Terms* 14 Ribbon-backed chairs with cabriole legs are a typical feature [of the Chippendale period]. **1969** *Sears Catal.* Spring/Summer 26 Cardigan Sweater... Matching color buttons on a ribbon-backed border. **1879** C. M. Yonge *Magnum Bonum* III. xxxi. 642 Cutting scarlet geraniums in the ribbon beds. **1928** *Daily Express* 27 Sept. 10/6 Ribbon-building should be abolished. **1935** D. L. Sayers *Gaudy Night* xiv. 299, I was born there, and I shall be sorry if I live to see the land sold for ribbon-building. **1939** V. G. Childe *Dawn European Civilization* (ed. 3) ii. 16 Punctured ribbon decoration and pedestalled goblets have analogies also in the Balkans. **1931** A. L. Rowse *Politics & Younger Generation* viii. 199 New colonies of semi-detached villas, and..ribbon-developed roads. **1927** *Garden Cities & Town Planning* XVII. 172/2 The writers are well aware of the disadvantages of 'ribbon' development. **1929** *Times* 19 Jan. 8/1 Your condemnation of ribbon development building along arterial roads is especially applicable to the new arterial Reigate to Dorking road. **1934** J. B. Priestley *Eng. Journey* x. 336 We passed through several villages that looked hardly more than slums that had been scattered along the road. This odd ribbon development is fairly common in colliery areas. **1954** M. Beresford *Lost Villages* viii. 275 With ribbon-development, petrol-stations and roadhouses it may find itself no longer the deserted village. **1979** J. E. Morpurgo *Allen Lane* iv. 138 The desert of ribbon development and light industrial estates..had been allowed to sprawl all over Middlesex. **1958** *Chambers's Techn. Dict.* Add. 1010/1 *Ribbon-flame burner*, a tubular gas-burner on which a ribbon of flame is produced by means of alternating corrugated and plain steel strips inserted in a milled slot, thus forming honeycombed flame ports, or by the tube being drilled with lines of very fine holes in close formation. **1973** *Times* 30 July 11/2 The cooker embodies another step forward in technology—a ribbon flame instead of the old jets, inherently more stable and less likely to blow out in a draught. **1957** V. G. Childe *Dawn European Civilization* (ed. 6) ii. 17 The vases may be provided with..flanged ribbon handles. **1972** *Trans. Oriental Ceramics Soc.* XXXVIII. 54 A grey earthenware tripod vessel, three-lobed, with a ribbon handle. **1941** *Oxoniensia* VI. 32 There were a fair number of vaulting ribs found *passim* at the east end of both aisles... A few ribs were found decorated with ribbon ornament. **1940** *Burlington Mag.* Dec. 180/2 The traditional Anglo-Saxon Ribbon Pattern themes. **1954** M. Rickert *Painting in Brit.: Middle Ages* 231 *Ribbon pattern*, sometimes used to describe plait work or strap work; any flat ribbon-like ornament. **1956** G. Taylor *Silver* ii. 24 During the ninth and tenth centuries Scandinavian influence was strong.. mostly characterized by asymmetrical ribbon patterns and animal forms. **1929** *Times* 29 Aug. 13/6 (*heading*) Park ways and ribbon roads. **1934** T. S. Eliot *Rock* i. 21 And now you live dispersed on ribbon roads, And no man knows or cares who is his neighbour. **1969** *Daily Tel.* 18 Jan. 9 A ribbon-road framed with cream-painted filling stations..and bright blue and white bus signs every few miles.

b. ribbon figure, grain, a striped pattern of grain seen in some quarter-sawn hardwoods (see quots.).

1940 Brown & Panshin *Commercial Timbers U.S.* x. 242 The quarter-sawn surface of interlocked-grain wood exhibits a characteristic striped or ribbon figure. **1964** P. Koch *Wood Machining Processes* ii. 16 The interlocked and alternately inclined grain, which forms a ribbon figure, presents a machining problem. **1934** *Archit. Rev.* LXXVI. 64/3 Very handsomely figured timber is exported... Material possessing 'ram's horn' figure, is also met with, and 'stripe' or 'ribbon-grain' is relatively common. **1948** *New Biol.* IV. 87 Mahogany is also best converted in this way [*sc.* by quarter-sawing], in this case to show the 'ribbon-grain' figure due to the inclination of the fibres to the vertical axis differing in successive growth rings; this results in differential light reflection from the boards comparable to that shown by a freshly rolled lawn.

c. ribbon (also † **rib(b)and**) **cane,** a variety of sugar cane whose mature stalks have red or purplish longitudinal stripes.

1811 G. Mathison *Notes Jamaica* 65 The riband or striped cane is no longer cultivated by judicious planters. **1833** B. Silliman *Man. Sugar Cane* 10 The varieties of Cane cultivated in the United States, are the Creole,..the Ribbon Cane [etc.]. **1834** *Visit to Texas* x. 92 The ribband cane requires to be planted every three years. **1929** L. F. Carr *America Challenged* 252 Some extra fine ribbon-cane molasses. **1938** M. K. Rawlings *Yearling* xviii. 215 The red ribbon cane had made a fair stand. **1961** F. G. Cassidy *Jamaica Talk* xvi. 350 Ribbon and stripe or striped cane..is still being grown.

ribbon, *v.* Add: **3.** Of a road, track, etc.: to continue in the manner of a ribbon; to stretch *out* like a ribbon. Also *transf.* Hence **ri·bboning** *vbl. sb.* and *ppl. a.*

1926 J. B. Ames *Valley of Missing Men* iv. 29 The trail ribboned endlessly through a rough, hill country that seemed utterly deserted. **1926** *Hutchinson's Best Story Mag.* Nov. 88/2 He led it [*sc.* a horse] silently down to the river bank, where the great white road ribbons out eastward to the sea. **1959** *Observer* 30 Aug. 7/1 The same ferro-concrete and glass blocks are going up in Zürich and in New Delhi, accompanied..by the same ribboning-out of metropolis into suburbia. **1968** R. V. Beste *Repeat Instructions* xix. 197 The Bestyet Fish Saloon was frying and a queue of customers ribboned out through the door on to the pavement. **1969** 'J. Morris' *Fever Grass* xxi. 185 The road ribboned in three lazy twists. **1976** H. Tracy *Death in Reserve* xxi. 168 He drove back..looking at the ribboning road with unblinking bright eyes.

ribbonism. (Earlier example.)

1828 Anglesey *Let.* 31 Mar. in R. Peel *Mem.* (1856) I. 34 Ribbonism is extending.

ribby, *a.* **1.** Delete *rare*—[1] and add later examples. Also *fig.*, suggestive of or resembling ribs.

1851 H. Melville *Moby Dick* II. xv. 129 In bony, ribby regions of the earth. **1924** C. E. Montague *Right Place* ix. 122 All sorts of ribby ridges and intercostal hollows dropping down from that spine to the water-line on each side. **1934** T. Wood *Cobbers* viii. 101 The homesteads, iron roofed and set about with ribby water-butts. **1970** *Daily Tel.* 7 May 17/1 The fortunes of Courtaulds were founded in Victorian times on black crêpe,..a ribby material widows and mourners wore. **1977** 'H. Osborne' *White Poppy* xv. 118 The horses..were miserable creatures, ribby and pathetic.

2. *slang.* Dirty, shabby; seedy, run-down; unpleasant, nasty.

1936 J. Curtis *Gilt Kid* 33 Nearby was a little café... Ribby kind of a gaff, but I might as well go in. **1976** P. Alexander *Death of Thin-Skinned Animal* xx. 207 She lived at the ribby end of Maida Vale. **1977** M. Russell *Dial Death* I. iv. 28 'How are—things?' 'Ribby'.

ribible. (Further examples in *poet.* use.)

a **1770** Chatterton *Poems* (1777) 3 The swote ribible dynning yn the dell. **1928** Blunden *Retreat* 19 And Chatterton's ribibles dinned in the dell.

ribitol (rəi·bitǫl, ri·bitǫl). *Chem.* [f. *rib(ose + *-itol.] A colourless crystalline pentahydric alcohol, $HOCH_2{\cdot}(CHOH)_3{\cdot}CH_2OH$, which is obtained by reduction of ribose and occurs in the leaves of pheasant's eye, *Adonis vernalis*; also known as *adonitol*.

1946 *Adv. Carbohydrate Chem.* II. 117 Upon recrystallization from ethanol the melting point and mixed melting point with an authentic sample of ribitol was 101·5–102°. **1948** *Jrnl. Amer. Chem. Soc.* LXX. 2809/1 All of the acetates of the pentitols have been described in crystalline form save that of ribitol (synonym, adonitol). **1954** [see *pentitol]. **1968** A. White et al. *Princ. Biochem.* (ed. 4) xli. 913 When ribitol is present, the sugar substituent appears always to be linked to the 2-position of this alditol. **1970** R. W. McGilvery *Biochem.* x. 188 Ribitol is the alcohol corresponding to ribose rather than the sugar itself, so riboflavin is not a nucleoside.

Hence **ri·bityl** [-yl], the univalent radical derived from ribitol by the loss of a terminal hydroxyl group.

1946 *Jrnl. Org. Chem.* XI. 83 Hydrogenation of these triacyl arylamine ribosides yields triacyl ribityl amines. **1970** R. W. McGilvery *Biochem.* x. 189 The ribityl group is a part of the flavin, not something extra.

riblet. (Further examples.)

1949 M. Mead *Male & Female* xviii. 375 In ancient Samoa, the women made lovely bark-cloth, pressing out the fluctuating, beautifully soft lines against mats on which the pattern was sewed in coconut-leaf riblets. **1962** *Aeroplane* 23 Aug. 24/3 To this metal structure are attached the glass-fibre leading- and trailing-edge units. The former is in one piece from tip to engine nacelle and contains 11 glass-fibre riblets. **1975** *Nature* 16 Oct. 577/2 It [*sc.* a fossil bivalve of genus *Neoschizodus*] is closely related to the widely distributed *N. laevigatus* (Ziethen) of Lower to Middle Triassic age, but differs in having a radial riblet on the posterior area, and in possessing striations on some teeth.

ribo- (rəi·bo). *Biochem.* Comb. form of *ribose: **ri:bohomopo·lymer** [*homopolymer* s.v. *homo-], a polymer of any one of the ribonucleosides; **ribonu·clease** [*nuclease], any enzyme which catalyses the hydrolysis of RNA into oligonucleotides and smaller molecules; **ri:bonucleopro·tein** [*nucleoprotein], a combination of a protein with RNA; **ribonu·cleoside,** a nucleoside containing ribose; **ribonu·cleotide,** a nucleotide containing ribose. Also *riboflavin, *ribonucleic *a.*

1971 *Nature* 23 July 254/1 It seems probable that both the ribohomopolymers and the natural ribonucleic acids do catalyse a reaction *in vitro*. **1975** *Ibid.* 25 Sept. 327/2 Enzymatic activities for synthesising four ribohomopolymers, including poly(G), have been found in rat liver, and all are stimulated by RNA. **1938** Dubos & Thompson in *Jrnl. Biol. Chem.* CXXIV. 502 The ribonuclease used in the following experiments was extracted from a commercial preparation of dried pancreatin. **1946** *Nature* 27 July 129/2 Many enzymes are not specific as to substrate; but ribonuclease, a depolymerase, is highly specific for ribonucleic acid. **1971** J. Z. Young *Introd. Study Man* xxvi. 372 Haldane noted that ribonuclease is the smallest known enzyme, containing 124 amino-acid residues. **1940** *Science* 18 Oct. 361/1 The virus of equine encephalomyelitis (Eastern strain) is a complex of high molecular weight consisting of phospholipids, cholesterol, fatty acid and ribonucleoprotein. **1968** A. White et al. *Princ. Biochem.* (ed. 4) ix. 204 Since that time, many additional plant viruses have been isolated as crystalline substances, and they are all ribonucleoproteins. **1974** D. & M. Webster *Compar. Vertebr. Morphol.* ix. 182 The perikaryon [of a neuron] contains..the same organelles found in most cells. However, it has a far greater concentration of densely folded, rough endoplasmic reticulum (ribonucleoprotein). **1931** Levene & Bass *Nucleic Acids* vi. 129 A fifth ribonucleoside was discovered by Benedict and his coworkers. **1968** A. White et al. *Princ. Biochem.* (ed. 4) xxix. 667 Synthesis of RNA occurs only when all four ribonucleoside triphosphates are present. **1929** *Jrnl. Biol. Chem.* LXXXI. 215 There occur in nature ribonucleotides of two types. **1959** *Ibid.* CCXXXIV. 2351/1 Studies designed to elucidate the mechanism by which ribonucleotides are converted into deoxynucleotides in extracts of *Escherichia coli*. **1970** R. W. McGilvery *Biochem.* xx. 473 The deoxyguanosine and deoxyadenosine nucleotides required for synthesis of DNA are formed by reduction of the corresponding ribonucleotides.

riboflavin (rəiboflē[i]·vin). *Biochem.* Also **-ine.** [a. G. *riboflavin* (P. Karrer et al. 1935, in *Helv. Chim. Acta* XVIII. 429): see *ribo- and *flavin 2.] Vitamin B_2; a yellow pigment that is a flavin having a ribityl side-chain and is present in many foods (esp. milk, liver, and green vegetables), deficiency of which leads to poor growth and deterioration of the skin.

1935 *Brit. Chem. Abstr.* A. 1286/2 Synthetic *d*-riboflavin.. has a growth-promoting power equal to that of the purest samples of natural lactoflavin, with which it appears in other respects to be identical. **1945** [see *aneurin, -ine]. **1954** *New Biol.* XVII. 117 In rats, riboflavin deficiency produces cleft palate and shortening of the limbs. **1967** M. Kenyon *Whole Hog* xvi. 166 Thirty grams of niacin and about ten each of pantothenic acid and riboflavin. **1970** R. W. McGilvery *Biochem.* xxvii. 676 Riboflavin not only occurs in most foods but is also synthesized by the intestinal flora. As a result, a primary deficiency of riboflavin is very rare.

ribonucleic (rəiboniū·klī,ik, -niuklī·ik, -ē[i]·ik), *a.* *Biochem.* [f. *ribo- + *nucleic *a.*] *ribonucleic acid*: a generic term for any of the nucleic acids yielding ribose on hydrolysis; they occur chiefly in the cytoplasm of cells, where they direct the synthesis of proteins, and in some viruses, where they also store the genetic information. Abbrev. RNA.

1931 Levene & Bass *Nucleic Acids* ix. 299 Yeast nucleic acid..is the most readily available starting material for chemical work on ribonucleic acids. **1944** *Ann. Reg. 1943* 354 Ribonucleic acids..were found to be widely distributed in high concentrations in mammalian tissues. **1958** *Times* 26 Sept. 15/2 This slightly damaged ribonucleic acid may be the key to the action of interferon. **1967** *Daily Tel.* 8 June 14/6 High concentration in the brain of a chemical known as ribonucleic acid greatly increases the capacity for learning. **1971** J. Z. Young *Introd. Study Man* xi. 147 Nerve cells are characterized by a larger amount of ribonucleic acid in their cytoplasm.

ribose (rəi·bō[u]z, -s). *Biochem.* [a. G. *ribose*, f. *rib-onsäure* (both E. Fischer 1891, in *Ber. d. Deut. Chem. Ges.* XXIV. 4215), f. *ribon* (formed arbitrarily by rearrangement of some of the letters of *arabinose*, name of the related sugar from which Fischer prepared ribose) + *säure* acid: see -ose[2].] **1.** An aldopentose sugar, the lævorotatory (d-) isomer of which occurs widely in nature as a constituent of many nucleosides and several vitamins and enzymes.

1892 *Jrnl. Chem. Soc.* LXII. I. 439 The precipitate..contains the chief portion of the ribose. **1927** [see *pentose]. **1937** *Nature* 30 Oct. 745/2 Phosphopyridine nucleotides.. consist of a pyridine derivative, namely, nicotine acid amide, adenine, two molecules of a sugar, ribose, together with..phosphoric acid. **1938** *Thorpe's Dict. Appl. Chem.* (ed. 4) II. 287/1 Ribose is also a component of lactoflavin. **1948** W. W. PIGMAN *Chem. of Carbohydrates* iii. 104 The universal occurrence of D-ribose in all living cells should make this sugar of the greatest interest to biochemists and biologists. **1960** *New Biol.* XXXI. 40 Another type of nucleic acid containing a different sugar, ribose, and named ribonucleic acid or RNA. **1970** AMBROSE & EASTY *Cell Biol.* vii. 247 The pentose sugar ribose is formed from glucose by an oxidative pathway known as the hexose monophosphate shunt.

2. *attrib.* or as prefix = *RIBO-; **ribose nucleic, ribosenu·cleic acid** = **ribonucleic acid*; also *ribose nucleoprotein, nucleotide*, etc.

1920 *Jrnl. Biol. Chem.* XLIII. 329 Referring only to the ribose nucleotides, the observations are as follows. **1929** *Ibid.* LXXXI. 712 The sugar was obtained in the same manner as in the case of the ribose nucleoside. **1942** *Ibid.* CXLIV. 589, 5 to 6 per cent of the virus is a ribosenucleic acid. **1943** *Nature* 11 Dec. 693/1 Ribose nucleic acid is not restricted to plant tissues. **1944** *Ibid.* 10 June 711/2 The chloroplasts..contain plasmonucleoproteins (ribose nucleoproteins). **1957** *New Biol.* XXIII. 84 Ribonuclease, an enzyme that destroys ribose nucleic acid. **1960** *Ibid.* XXXI. 16 A different kind of nucleic acid (RNA, ribosenucleic acid, which differs from DNA in having a slightly different pentose sugar). *Ibid.* 17 RNA is found in living material closely combined with protein, as ribosenucleoprotein.

ribosome (rəi·bosōᵘm). *Cytology.* [f. *RIBO-(NUCLEIC *a.* + *-SOME⁴.] Each of the particles of ribonucleic acid and associated proteins found in the cytoplasm of living cells, which bind to messenger RNA and synthesize polypeptides.

1958 R. B. ROBERTS *Microsomal Particles & Protein Synthesis* p. viii, To some of the participants, microsomes mean the ribonucleoprotein particles of the microsomal fraction contaminated by other protein and lipid material; to others, the microsomes consist of protein and lipid contaminated by particles. The phrase 'microsomal particles' does not seem adequate, and 'ribonucleoprotein particles of the microsome fraction' is much too awkward. During the meeting the word 'ribosome' was suggested... The present confusion would be eliminated if 'ribosome' were adopted to designate ribonucleoprotein particles in the size range 20 to 100 S. **1961** *Times* 18 Aug. 12/4 Protein synthesis seems in fact to be localized in small bodies, known as ribosomes. **1967** *New Scientist* 28 Sept. 661/1 The ribosomes of mitochondria are probably of the 70*S* (bacterial) variety. **1974** M. C. GERALD *Pharmacol.* iii. 52 Some of the reticulum appears 'rough', because of the presence of dense bodies termed ribosomes.

Hence **ribos·mal** *a.*, of or pertaining to a ribosome; *ribosomal RNA*, the RNA of a ribosome.

1960 *Jrnl. Molecular Biol.* II. 109 It appears likely..that ribosomal protein, like histone.., consists largely of α-helical protein. **1961** *Nature* 13 May 581/2 It was thought most likely that ribosomal RNA was genetically specific. **1970** AMBROSE & EASTY *Cell Biol.* iii. 114 It now seems that one of the chief metabolic functions of the nucleolus is the synthesis of ribosomal RNA, and possibly even the formation of complete ribosomal particles..from RNA and ribosomal proteins.

ribosyl (rəi·bosəil, -il). *Biochem.* [f. *RIBOS(E + -YL.] A univalent radical derived from ribose by loss of a hydroxyl group.

1947 *Jrnl. Biol. Chem.* CLXXI. 377 The preparation from the deacylated free nucleosides with a 5 to 10 per cent excess of chlorine, as described for the synthesis of 1-D-ribosyl-5-chlorouracil, is undoubtedly the method of choice. **1957** *Biochem. Jrnl.* LXV. 609 (*heading*) Enzymatic transfer of the ribosyl group from inosine to adenine. **1970** R. W. MCGILVERY *Biochem.* xx. 465 The rate of the reaction is probably always limited by the supply of the ribosyl compound.

ribuck, var. *RYEBUCK.

ribulose (rəi·biŭlōᵘz, -s). *Biochem.* [f. *RIB(OSE + *-ULOSE².] A ketopentose sugar which in the form of phosphate esters is an important intermediate in carbohydrate metabolism and photosynthesis.

1936 *Jrnl. Biol. Chem.* CXV. 731 The formation of *d*- and *l*-ribulose from *d*- and *l*-arabinose respectively has been demonstrated. *Ibid.* 747 Five portions (75 gm. each) of *l*-arabinose, treated with pyridine.., gave a total of some 100 gm. of crude ribulose. **1959** I. L. FINAR *Org. Chem.* (ed. 3) I. xviii. 433 Two monosaccharides, ribulose and sedoheptulose, play an essential part in the photosynthesis of carbohydrates. **1959** A. WHITE et al. *Princ. Biochem.* (ed. 2) xviii. 417 Were all the 3-phosphoglyceric acid converted to hexose by reversal of glycolysis,..no ribulose diphosphate would be available to serve as acceptor for CO_2 in subsequent fixation reactions. **1976** *Nature* 27 May 344/2 It is easy to formulate schemes for the synthesis of 2′-amino-2′-deoxyribose from ribose or ribulose and ammonia..but we have been unable to obtain appreciable yields of the amino sugars in this way.

ribwork. (Earlier example.)

1848 E. BRYANT *What I saw in California* xxi. 271 These *rancherias* consist of a number of huts constructed of a rib-work or frame of small poles.

Ricard (ri·kaɪ). [Name of the manufacturers.] The proprietary name of an aniseed-flavoured aperitif; a drink of this.

1965 *Trade Marks Jrnl.* 21 July 977/1 Ricard... Aperitif wines containing aniseed for sale in England, Scotland and Wales. Ricard (a Société anonyme organised under the laws of France),..Paris, France; distillers and merchants. **1967** G. GREENE *May we borrow your Husband?* 11, I sat with a Ricard on the terrace. **1970** T. KENRICK *Only Good Body* 8 Sit down at your table, order a Ricard. **1971** *Guardian* 22 May 7/4 The local aperitif is Ricard, a dry *pastis* taken with plenty of ice and water which makes it change colour in much the same manner as Dettol. **1976** 'A. YORK' *Dark Passage* i. 6 Harrington..ordered a Ricard and another beer.

ricasso (rĭka·so). [It.] The part of the blade of a sword that is next to the hilt.

1884 R. F. BURTON *Bk. of Sword* vii. 125 In the Italian foil, which preserves the plate, the section of the blade between that and the grip is called the *Ricasso*. **1885** E. CASTLE *Schools & Masters of Fence* xv. 235 We have adopted the French word pas d'âne, and we may as well likewise, for want of a better, adopt the Italian word 'ricasso', used to designate that part of the blade between the cup guard and the quillons of the Italian foils and duelling swords. **1948** *Proc. Prehist. Soc.* XIV. 155 Only those swords with parallel-sided blades, ogival tips and deep rectangular ricassos have been included. **1959** G. SAVAGE *Antique Collector's Handbk.* 23 Swords are often decorated in a variety of ways... A common place for decoration is the *ricasso*—the flat, rectangular part of the blade immediately below the hilt. **1970** F. WILKINSON *Edged Weapons* iii. 38/2 The use of the *ricasso* to obtain a better grip on the sword had led to the introduction of loops, rings and bars attached to the hilt. **1978** N. K. SANDARS *Sea Peoples* 100 In neither area did the parallel-edged flange-hilted sword develop a leaf-edged blade for strong cutting action, nor a milled ricasso at the grip.

Ricci (rī·tʃi). *Math.* [Name of C. G. *Ricci* (1853–1925), Italian mathematician.] *Ricci tensor*: a symmetric second-order tensor obtained by contracting the Riemann–Christoffel tensor.

1923 VEBLEN & THOMAS in *Trans. Amer. Math. Soc.* XXV. 554 This we shall call the Ricci tensor because it reduces to the tensor studied by Ricci for the case of the Riemann geometry. **1926** L. P. EISENHART *Riemannian Geom.* i. 22 The Ricci tensor..was first considered by Ricci who gave it a geometrical interpretation in case g_{ij} is the fundamental tensor of a Riemann space. **1967** CONDON & ODISHAW *Handbk. Physics* (ed. 2) II. vi. 50/1 The vanishing of the Ricci tensor does not imply the vanishing of the Riemann-Christoffel tensor and consequently does not insure the Minkowski character of Einstein space–time in the large. **1974** *Nature* 5 Apr. 472/1 The precise mathematical quantity which describes the curvature of space–time is known as the Ricci tensor R_{jk}, which is a 4 × 4 array of numbers defined at each point of space–time.

rice, *sb.*¹ **4.** Delete † *Obs.* and add later examples.

1895 R. MARSDEN *Cotton Weaving* viii. 272 The hanks are placed upon light, collapsible hexagon reels termed rices. **1953** A. JOBSON *Househ. & Country Crafts* xi. 124 The winder worked in conjunction with a wrap wheel, or an adjustable wool winder, which was a stand to which were attached rices or runners. **1957** SIMPSON & WEIR *Weaver's Craft* (ed. 8) viii. 94 It is a great saving of time if a 'rice' or 'swift' is available, in which case the wool may be taken directly from the skeins to the warping board.

5. rice creel, a frame for holding rices (sense 4).

1895 R. MARSDEN *Cotton Weaving* viii. 272 They are very light, and easily revolve with the pull of the thread. This is termed the rice creel.

rice, *sb.*² **4. a.** Substitute for def.: In full, *wild rice*. An aquatic North American grass, *Zizania aquatica*, or its seeds. (Earlier and later examples.)

1775 A. HENRY *Trav. & Adventures Canada* (1901) 242 The women brought me a further and very valuable present, of twenty bags of rice. **1950** *Chicago Tribune* 18 Mar. 10/3 New rice will stir in the lake's dark bed.

5. a. *rice ball, bran, brandy, bun, cracker, -flake, flour* (further examples), *gin, meal* (earlier example), *mould, noodle, oil, polish, pudding* (earlier and later examples), *-salad, -slop, soup, spirit*.

1850 *New England Farmer* II. 322/1 Rice Balls.—Pour upon half a pound of rice three pints of boiling milk [etc.]. **1974** G. JENKINS *Bridge of Magpies* ix. 141 His contribution consisted of some rice balls and bright sticky sweets. **1909** *Cent. Dict. Suppl.*, Rice-bran. **1970** SIMON & HOWE *Dict. Gastron.* 327/1 Rice bran is the first major by-product removed from the rice kernel during the milling process. **1937** M. COVARRUBIAS *Island of Bali* v. 109 *Arak*, distilled rice brandy. **1971** R. PURVIS *Treasure Hunting in Brit. Columbia* ix. 114 Old rice-brandy flasks are considered..rare collectors' items. **1889** J. WHITEHEAD *Steward's Handbk.* 420/1 Ground Rice Buns. **1963** A. L. SIMON *Guide Good Food & Wines* 222/1 Rice Buns. **1970** J. KIRKUP *Japan behind Fan* 3 Peppery rice crackers wrapped in seaweed. **1973** *Sunday Bull.* (Philadelphia) 7 Oct. (Parade Suppl.) 28/3 Fredericks is a six-meals-a-day man, and so paused two hours after breakfast for an ounce of Gruyere cheese, some brown rice crackers and a glass of milk. **1947** J. STEINBECK *Wayward Bus* i. 5 Boxes of cornflakes, riceflakes, grapenuts, and other tortured cereals. **1970** SIMON & HOWE *Dict. Gastron.* 327/1 There are rice flakes..that may be eaten cold. **1878** *Amer. Home Cook Bk.* 15 Mix the rice-flour smoothly with the water. **1959** A. K. LANG in H. Q. Masur *Murder most Foul* (1973) 71 His pushers would..cut the strong brown heroin with lactose or rice flour. **1971** *Fashion Panorama* (Ceylon) Apr.–June 30 The pounding of rice flour continued. **1969** *Listener* 12 June 814/1 The village chief himself asked us to a dinner of dried deer and shrimp crackers, chicken and lettuce, sweet potato and duck and rice gin. **1789** G. WHITE *Selborne* II. lviii. 280 The dogs..are fed for the table with rice-meal and other farinaceous food. **1906** *Mrs. Beeton's Bk. Househ. Managem.* 1044 (*heading*) Whole rice mould. **1922** 'R. CROMPTON' *More William* ii. 31 Rice-mould! Every single day. I *hate* it, don't you? **1965** H. BURKE *Chinese Cooking for Pleasure* 17/2 Rice noodles with prawn and chicken. **1980** *Times* 6 Dec. 11/3 Chicken.. and rice noodle Army-style as a change from rice. **1970** SIMON & HOWE *Dict. Gastron.* 327/1 Rice oil is the oil extracted from rice bran and polish. **1972** *Guardian* 25 Sept. 1/6 Rice oil—a widely used foodstuff. **1909** *Cent. Dict. Suppl.*, Rice-polish. **1970** SIMON & HOWE *Dict. Gastron.* 327/1 Rice polish is the final layers removed from the rice kernel during the polishing process. **1709** W. KING *Useful Trans. in Philos.* III. 53 Of these I shall discourse at large, when I treat of butter'd Wheat,..Rice-Pudding, and Oat-cakes. **1948** *Good Housek. Cookery Bk.* 427 *Fruit Rice Pudding.* As for Rice Pudding, adding a cupful of seeded raisins..to the milk and rice. **1966** F. SHAW et al. *Lern Yerself Scouse* 75 *Yer cudden knock de skin off a rice puddn*, you are a weakling. **1973** 'I. DRUMMOND' *Jaws of Watchdog* ix. 122 Melons were sliced into, prawns shelled, rice-salads scooped out. **1922** JOYCE *Ulysses* 391 She queasy for a bowl of riceslop. **1747** H. GLASSE *Art of Cookery* ix. 78 A Rice Soop. **1797** J. WOODFORDE *Diary* 8 May (1931) V. 34 We had for Dinner, some Rice Soup..rost Beef &c. **1827** M. WILMOT *Jrnl.* 27 Aug. in *More Lett.* (1935) 297 The supper for all begun with a cup of rice soup, which was handed round to each. **1909** J. JOYCE *Let.* 20 Dec. (1966) II. 277, I would like roast beef[,] rice-soup, [etc.]. **1963** A. L. SIMON *Guide Good Food & Wines* 220/2 Rice Soup. **1967** O. WYND *Walk Softly* i. 9 Crack a couple of bottles of rice spirit over two bows on the same day. **1978** *Nagel's Encycl.-Guide: China* 1447 Rice spirit, known as yellow wine, is drunk warm, from little china bowls.

b. *rice-clearing, -country* (later example), *-flat, lake, paddy, plantation* (earlier and later examples), *swamp* (earlier and later examples), *terrace*.

1895 CONRAD *Almayer's Folly* vi. 116 Finding shelter under that man's roof in the modest rice-clearing. **1975** *Country Life* 2 Jan. 9/2 Georgia [USA] proved good rice country. **1882** *Trans. Asiatic Soc. Japan* X. 44 The river, after making a bend round some rice flats, turns in and sweeps right under the high bank. **1905** 'L. HOPE' *Indian Love* 57 The velvet rice-flats lie so emerald green. **1820** J. D. DOTY *Let.* 27 Sept. in *Wisconsin Hist. Coll.* (1876) VII. 199 The Indians around Sandy Lake, in the month of September, repair to Rice Lake to gather their rice. **1831** J. M. PECK *Guide for Emigrants* 14 A third [boat] may start from the rice lakes at the head of the Mississippi. **1870** J. W. MCCLUNG *Minnesota* 235 It is finely watered by Rum River passing out of Mille Lac through numerous small marshy rice lakes. **1933** N. WALN *House of Exile* i. 18 Rice paddies roughened by dead stubble. **1945** *Newsweek* 24 Sept. 50 Calling themselves members of 'The Rice Paddy Navy', American naval personnel—disguised as Chinese—set up more than fifty weather stations in unoccupied China. **1977** J. CLEARY *High Road to China* v. 186 The road that ran through the rice paddies. **1787** in *Documentary Hist. Amer. Industr. Society* (1910) I. vii. 323 Great Encouragement will be given to an Overseer of a sober industrious Character, to manage a Rice and Lumber Plantation, about Thirty Miles from Charles-Town. **1957** P. WORSLEY *Trumpet shall Sound* iv. 81 Another cult-leader..was interested in government schemes for establishing rice-plantations. **1975** *Guardian* 2 Jan. 38/1 In Colonial days each [estate] was a prosperous rice plantation. **1731** *Pennsylvania Gaz.* 29 Apr.–6 May 2/2 These Rice Swamps are flat low Grounds, by the Sides of Rivers or Runs. **1957** M. BANTON *W. Afr. City* i. 21 The first clearing of rice swamps in the Scarcies involved much arduous and dangerous work. **1952** *Oxf. Jun. Encycl.* VI. 378/1 (*caption*) Rice terraces in Bali, Indonesia. **1973** D. MAY *Laughter in Djakarta* iii. 52 They were driving right past the rice terraces... Women were..thinning out the young rice on several of the terraces.

c. *rice-barn, -crater, -crop* (later examples), *cultivation, diet, husk, kernel, kettle, -measure, -port, -pot, sack, shoot*; *rice-white* adj.

1901 *Chambers's Jrnl.* Aug. 538/1 Nearer the water a few small houses..and a higher two-storied rice-barn. **1926** T. E. LAWRENCE *Seven Pillars* (1935) IV. xlvi. 266 Two raised each smaller cauldron and tilted it, letting the liquid splash down upon the meal till the rice-crater was full, and the loose grains at the edge swam in the abundance. **1965** 'LAUCHMONEN' *Old Thom's Harvest* ii. 24 We aint gwine get no water to plant ricecrop. **1973** 'B. MATHER' *Snowline* iii. 34 A tidal wave in the Bay of Bengal last year that.. ruined the rice crop. **1841** M. EDGEWORTH *Let.* 14 Mar. (1971) 584 Entertaining accounts by master of agricultural-different processes in different parts of the world—Rice cultivation—Irrigation—India. **1960** I. A. STANTON *Dict. for Med. Secretaries* 44/2 *Rice diet*, a diet consisting of rice, sugar, fruit and fruit juice. **1965** H. BURKE *Chinese Cooking for Pleasure* 12/2 Chinese pickled eggs..[are] bought ready to eat. One simply cracks and removes their outer casing of rice husks and clay. **1975** *Country Life* 16 Jan. 153/3 A pillow of rice-husks. **1970** SIMON & HOWE *Dict. Gastron.* 326/1 The edible rice kernel is found in a hard shell-like hull surrounded by several layers of bran. **1895** CONRAD *Almayer's Folly* v. 86 The fire was burning in the cooking shed, with the rice kettle swinging over it. **1936** *Burlington Mag.* Jan. 40/2 The great Imperial rice-measure from the Metropolitan Museum. **1903** CONRAD *Typhoon* i. 6 Outlandish names of lumber-ports, of rice-ports, of cotton-ports. **1862** MRS. MASON *Civilizing Mountain Men* I. ii. 24 Holding in his hand a wicker rice-pot, which shone in the dimness like a great bowl of gold. **1895** CONRAD *Almayer's Folly* iv. 81 He eyed..the aged statesman sitting..by his domestic rice-pot. **1978** L. DEE tr. *Hsia Chih-Yen's Coldest Winter in Peking* vii. 133 They took these scraps, even the burnt crusts in the rice pots, and made them into 'nutrition supplements'. **1970** 'D. HALLIDAY' *Dolly & Cookie Bird* iii. 33 You all meet over the trolleys with your long-grain rice sacks at the mainline Cash & Carry. **1895** CONRAD *Almayer's Folly* xi. 216 In the middle of a shadowless square of moonlight, shining on a smooth and level expanse of young rice-shoots, a little shelter-hut perched on high posts,..seemed very small. **1966** 'A. Hall' *9th Directive* xxv. 229 The flooded earth where the tender rice-shoots stood. **1973** 'B. Mather' *Snowline* xiv. 167 Village women.. were dibbling rice shoots into the monsoon-flooded paddy. **1871** G. M. Hopkins *Jrnls. & Papers* (1959) 216 In returning the sky in the west was in a great wide winged or shelved rack of rice-white fine pelleted fretting.

6. a. *rice-cooker, -farmer, -husker, -planter* (earlier and later examples).

1974 *Daily News* (Tanzania) 27 Sept. 8/4 (Advt.), Complete Akai stereo system,..rice-cooker, crockery, cutlery, imported suits. **1977** *South China Morning Post* (Hong Kong) 22 July 1/5 My daughter was taking a broken rice-cooker to a repair shop. **1961** *Nat. Geogr. Mag.* Aug. 242/1 Practically all the people of Laos,..about two million of them—are rice farmers. **1977** P. Theroux *Consul's File* 127 The Malay rice-farmers met and decided to bring their problem to a *bomoh*—a medicine-man. **1901** Kipling *Kim* iv. 106 They could hear the old lady's tongue clack as steadily as a rice-husker. **1775** *Amer. Husbandry* I. 66 It concerns only those who have dealings with London, these are the tobacco and rice planters. **1838** J. J. Audubon *Ornith. Biogr.* IV. 318 In South Carolina the Golden-eye is abundant during winter, when it at times frequents the reserves of the rice-planters. **1949** C. S. Murray *This our Land* iv. 74 With favorable prices, and slave labor comparatively cheap, quite a few rice planters piled up large fortunes.

b. *rice-dressing, -growing* (further examples), *-planting.*

1901 *Chambers's Jrnl.* Feb. 125/1 An English firm.. erected a rice-dressing mill on the shores of the Caspian. **1946** *Nature* 5 Oct. 462/1 A rice-growing village neither very rich nor very poor. **1972** *Country Life* 28 Dec. 1796/2 Rice growing is another highly photogenic occupation. **1852** W. G. Simms *Sword & Distaff* xxx. 210 It's lucky I do know something of rice planting. **1903** 'P. Pennington' *Woman Rice Planter* (1913) i. 1 You have asked me to tell of my rice-planting experience. **1962** E. Snow *Red China Today* (1963) xxviii. 212 Of numerous rice-planting machines invented by peasants the most popular is operated by two people. **1965** 'Lauchmonen' *Old Thom's Harvest* i. 8 He.. dream about them blasted ricefields and riceplanting.

7. rice and peas = *peas and rice* s.v. *pea[1] 1 d; **rice bowl,** (*a*) a dish out of which rice is eaten; (*b*) an area in which abundant quantities of rice are grown; also *attrib.*; **rice-Christian,** substitute for def.: one, esp. an Asian, who adopts Christianity for material benefits; (further examples); **rice crispies** = *Rice Krispies* below; also *sing.*; **rice-convert** = *rice-Christian* above; **rice-grain,** (*a*) *pl.* (in Dict.); (*b*) used *attrib.* to describe a type of decoration on porcelain in which perforations are made and allowed to fill with melted glaze; **Rice Krispies,** proprietary name of a breakfast cereal made from rice; **rice powder,** a face powder with a pulverized rice base; hence *rice-powdered* adj.; **rice-shell** (earlier example); **rice-stitch,** (*b*) a type of cross-stitch (see quots.); **rice table, tafel** = *rijsttafel.

1947 E. N. Burke *Stories told by Uncle Newton* II. 8 Some people call the midday meal 'lunch' but we always called it dinner on Sundays. As usual it consisted of a half moon of rice and peas; a few blocks of yams, [etc.]. **1958** B. Hamilton *Too Much of Water* iv. 74 He swore that all three must come to a real Barbadian breakfast..at Fair Hope. 'Maan,' he said, 'I give you flying fish an' pepper-pot, an' pudding and souse, an' rice and peas.' **1969** *Daily Tel.* 11 Jan. 14/1 To bring tears to ex-patriate Jamaican eyes just mention..rice an' peas. **1922** W. S. Maugham *On Chinese Screen* li. 206 The coolie's rice bowl has its rough but not inelegant adornment. **1943** *Sun* (Baltimore) 10 June 12/2 Hunan and Hupeh, 'rice bowl' provinces of East Central China. **1950** P. Bottome *Under Skin* xx. 166 On my tray there was a little porcelain bowl... She said, 'This is my rice bowl—my mother gave us each one.' **1950** *Times* 25 Apr. 7/2 In Cambodia and Laos, and even in Cochin-China, important as a rice-bowl area, the situation is better. **1969** *Commerce* (Bombay) 26 July 153/1 Agrarian unrest..has been a hardy annual for more than two decades now in Thanjavur district—Tamil Nadu's 'rice bowl' which has 1·4 million acres under paddy cultivation. **1972** 'M. Hebden' *Killer for Chairman* i. iv. 52 She moved an empty rice bowl on the table. **1975** *Times* 4 Mar. 1/6 According to reports from Cambodia, once the rice bowl of Indo-China, civilian deaths from starvation are increasing. **1979** *Times of India* 17 Aug. 14/3 Waters in Kuttanad, the rice bowl of Kerala, have been severely polluted by massive application of pesticides in paddy fields. **1883** *Encycl. Brit.* XVI. 518/1 The Propagation Society is now proclaiming the gospel in nearly six hundred and fifty villages in the Tinnevelly district, amongst not merely food-seeking 'rice Christians' but those who have had the courage to face severe persecution for joining the Christian church. **1941** A. J. Cronin *Keys of Kingdom* (1942) iv. vii. 179 The wisdom of Father Chisholm's determination to have no rice-Christians in his flock was now apparent. **1959** P. Fleming *Siege at Peking* iii. 40 The missions, whose less spiritually minded adherents were known as 'rice-Christians', thus tended to become centres of privilege. **1973** *Listener* 31 May 721/2 'Rice Christians', people who were outcasts in China..willing to come into the hands of the Church and the reformers. **1956** 'C. Blackstock' *Dewey Death* ii. 36 The fourteen-year-old at the breakfast table..can devour the Black Mass with her rice crispies. **1963** *Guardian* 5 Oct. 5/6 The mouse..eats a Rice Crispy like a sandwich. **1977** P. B. & J. S. Medawar *Life Sci.* i. 14 The sound—as of innumerable mice eating Rice Crispies—that sometimes accompanies long-distance telephone calls. **1926** T. E. Lawrence *Seven Pillars* (1935) ix. xcix. 548 We wanted no rice-converts. Persistently we did refuse to let our abundant and famous gold bring over those not spiritually convinced. **1910** *Encycl. Brit.* V. 746/1 Sometimes the perforations are left clear, but in the rice-grain pattern the incisions are generally filled up with the melted glaze so that they become like so many windows in the walls of the piece. **1960** H. Hayward *Antique Coll.* 238/2 '*Rice-grain' decoration,* a decoration used on Chinese porcelain in which small perforations in the body are filled with transparent glaze; a technique adopted from Persian pottery, popular during the 18th cent. **1971** L. A. Boger *Dict. World Pott. & Porc.* 285/2 The rice grain pattern is characteristic of the Ch'ien Lung period, 1736–1795. **1974** Savage & Newman *Illustr. Dict. Ceramics* 139 (*caption*) Persian pottery bowl with rice-grain piercing, 17th century. **1936** *Trade Marks Jrnl.* 30 Sept. 1212/1 Kellogg's Rice Krispies... A food made of rice, for human consumption. Kellogg Company of Great Britain Limited,..London,.. merchants. **1961** *Esquire* Aug. 57 She'd..pour the milk over the Rice Krispies, to wake up the fellow. **1967** *Trade Marks Jrnl.* 24 May 685/1 Rice Krispies... Cereal preparations principally of rice, being breakfast foods. Kellogg Company of Great Britain Limited,..Manchester; manufacturers. **1971** R. K. Smith *Ransom* (1972) i. 22 A bowl of Rice Krispies with sliced bananas. **1975** *New Yorker* 7 July 32/1 Harry prepared his breakfast in the kitchen—Rice Krispies with skimmed milk, and Sanka sweetened with saccharin. **1874** M. T. Nash tr. *Cazenave's Female Beauty* i. 28 Various means are proposed as protection against them [*sc.* alterations produced by tan and sunburn]... That which I prefer most is a little pure rice powder. **1892** C. Campbell tr. *Baroness Staffe's Lady's Dressing-Room* iii. 335 If you buy your rice-powder, be careful not to choose it perfumed with orris-root. **1934** M. Verni *Mod. Beauty Culture* xlii. 416 A simple and useful face powder is made in the following way—2 oz. of pure rice powder. 2 dr. of french chalk. ½ dr. of oxide of zinc. **1972** R. Corson *Fashions in Makeup* xv. 355 Rice powder and powdered arrowroot starch were commonly used to remove shine from the skin. **1922** Joyce *Ulysses* 523 As they are now, so will you be, wigged, singed,..ricepowdered. **1955** T. Sterling *Evil of Day* iii. 33 Mrs. Sheridan's rice-powdered hand made a familiar gesture. **1838** J. J. Audubon *Ornith. Biogr.* IV. 33 Those beautiful shells, which, on account of their resemblance to grains of rice, are commonly named rice-shells. **1934** M. Thomas *Dict. Embroidery Stitches* 169 *Rice stitch*.., a Canvas Stitch usually worked in a thick thread for the large crosses and a fine thread for the smaller stitches. **1960** G. Lewis *Handbk. Crafts* 87 Rice stitch has as its foundation a large cross, with the two arms double the size of the simple cross stitch, and when it has been made 4 short stitches are worked across all four corners of the main cross. **1976** P. Clabburn *Needleworker's Dict.* 227/1 *Rice stitch*.., variation of cross stitch much used in modern canvas work and needlepoint. **1909** Webster, Rice table. **1926** A. Huxley *Jesting Pilate* ii. 184 The only truly Rabelaisian feature of Javanese diet is the Rice Table. **1943** D. Welch *Maiden Voy.* xiv. 114 Mr MacDonald decreed we should have rice tafel.

rice, *v. Cookery.* [f. Rice[2].] *trans.* To press (food) through a coarse sieve to produce granular shapes. So **riced** *ppl. a.*, **ri·cing** *vbl. sb.*

1923 J. Conrad *Handbk. Cookery* 16 If the potatoes are not to be used at once..it is a good idea either to rice them in a ricer or to mash them. **1926** I. C. Smith *Blue Bk. Cookery* xxiii. 331 Riced Potatoes. Boil the potatoes. While still hot, press them through a potato-ricer. **1933** *Sun* (Baltimore) 27 Feb. 3/7 Boiled stuffed capon, with riced potatoes, cauliflower, [etc.]. **1947** M. Given *Mod. Encycl. Cooking* II. 1502 Put hot, freshly boiled, peeled potatoes into a ricer... Rice the potatoes directly into a hot serving dish. **1957** M. McCarthy *Memories Catholic Girlhood* 224 A salad.. sprinkled with riced egg yolk. **1966** *Vogue* Nov. 148/2 Mashed, riced, boiled or baked potatoes. **1969** R. & D. De Sola *Dict. Cooking* 191/2 *Ricer*, utensil for ricing cooked vegetables and fruits by forcing them through a perforated container.

rice-bird. 3. Substitute for def.: *U.S.* One of several small birds found in rice-fields, esp. the bobolink, *Dolichonyx oryzivorus.* (Earlier and later examples.)

1731 M. Catesby *Nat. Hist. Carolina* I. 14 The Rice-bird ..[is] esteemed in Carolina the greatest delicacy of all other Birds. **1957** O. Breland *Animal Friends & Foes* ii. 70 Robins, meadowlarks, bobolinks, and even flickers were often served in restaurants as 'rice birds'. **1958** S. A. Grau *Hard Blue Sky* 17 A yellow and black ricebird whizzed over his head.

rice grass (in Dict. s.v. Rice[2] 7). **a.** Either of two grasses of the genus *Leersia, L. oryzoides* (= Cut-grass) and *L. hexandra,* which are tall perennial grasses having rhizomatous roots and growing in wet ground.

1857 C. Johnson *Grasses Gt. Brit.* 4 *Leersia oryzoides.* Rice Grass... First noticed as a native of Britain in September 1844..at Henfield, Sussex. **1889** [in Dict. s.v. Rice[2] 7]. **1973** Tothill & Hacker *Grasses S.E. Queensland* i. 17 The coastal region provides conditions for numerous freshwater streams, ponds, bogs, etc... Common grasses of these sites are water couch.., common reed.., swamp rice grass (*Leersia hexandra*).

b. *Austral.* and *N.Z.* In full *meadow rice grass.* A perennial grass, *Microlæna stipoides,* that grows in tufts from creeping rhizomes in semi-shaded ground. Also called *weeping grass.*

1889 [in Dict. s.v. Rice[2] 7]. **1973** Atkinson & Bell in G. R. Williams *Nat. Hist. N.Z.* xv. 375/1 On Macauley Island..a combination of fire..and goats..had by 1966 reduced the vegetation to a short grassland dominated by rice grass, *Microlaena stipoides*, [etc.].

c. A grass of the genus *Spartina,* esp. *S. townsendii,* a tall, rhizomatous, perennial grass that grows on salt marshes and estuaries and has useful soil-binding properties. Also called *cord grass, marsh grass.*

The event referred to in quot. 1907[1] is said to have occurred in 1870.

1907 *1st Rep. R. Comm. Coast Erosion* 367/2 in *Parl. Papers* (Cd. 3683) XXXIV. 1 Many years ago a ship from the River Plate is said to have come in with a kind of rice grass. It was quite accidental: it came over in a wheat cargo. It sprang up near Southampton. These little plants, which are estuarine plants from Argentina, gradually spread out over Southampton Water, and the whole of Southampton Water from Carlshot Castle right up to Redbridge is entirely covered with what some people call 'Sea Rice' and others 'Rice Grass'. **1907** *Bull. Misc. Information R. Bot. Gardens, Kew* 196 In response to a letter asking whether any light could be thrown on the name 'rice-grass', which has now for the first time been quoted in connection with *Spartina*, the vernacular name hitherto given being 'cord-grass', Lord Montagu of Beaulieu, writes on May 2, 1907,:—'Mr. Rankin..told me he thought the plant growing on my foreshore was *Spartina stricta*, and not the *alterniflora.* He seemed to be quite aware of the term "rice-grass"... Personally I have never heard this word.' **1917** *Chambers's Jrnl.* Mar. 207/1 One of these schemes relates to a certain form of seaweed, locally known as rice-grass, which is rapidly covering Poole Harbour. **1944** J. S. Huxley *On living in Revolution* 72 During the last half-century a new type of rice-grass appeared in Western Europe, and has been so successful that the Dutch have used it to reclaim land from the sea. **1961** M. Ashby *Plant Ecol.* x. 193 Wherever the vigorous rice-grass..is present it replaces most of the stages in the succession.., and may form almost a pure stand from pioneer mud-binding to the high marsh, which can be used for grazing.

d. *Austral.* and *N.Z.* Any of various grasses of the genus *Tetrarrhena* (see quots.).

1930 A. J. Ewart *Flora of Victoria* 137 *T[etrarrhena] accuminata* R. Br., Pointed Rice Grass. Stems long and slender. *Ibid.* 138 *T. distichophylla* R. Br., Hairy Rice Grass. A tufted, branched perennial grass, creeping at the base, ascending to a height of 1 foot or more. **1962** N. C. W. Beadle et al. *Handbk. Vascular Plants Sydney District & Blue Mts.* 529 *Tetrarrhena*... Wiry Rice Grass. **1962** J. H. Willis *Handbk. Plants Victoria* I. 91 *T. juncea*... Forest Wire Grass (Wiry Rice Grass, Tangle Grass.) **1973** Tothill & Hacker *Grasses S.E. Queensland* iii. 261 *Tetrarrhena* sp. Wiry Rice Grass. A scrambling, wiry, but fairly slender perennial.

e. *U.S.* In full *Indian rice grass.* A perennial grass, *Oryzopsis hymenoides,* growing in clumps in semi-arid regions of the western U.S.

1935 A. S. Hitchcock *Man. Grasses U.S.* 415 Nearly all the species are highly palatable to stock, but are usually not in sufficient abundance to be of importance, except *O. hymenoides* (Indian ricegrass), which..furnishes much feed. **1968** F. W. Gould *Grass Systematics* v. 195 *Oryzopsis hymenoides* (Roem. & Schult.) Ricker, Indian ricegrass.., is an important forage species.

f. *U.S.* In full *pinyon rice grass.* A perennial grass, *Piptochætium fimbriatum,* with stiffly erect stems and leaves that is common in open pine forests in the mountains of northern Mexico and the southwestern U.S.

1951 Kearney & Peebles *Arizona Flora* 115 (*heading*) *Piptochaetium.* Pinyon rice grass. **1973** R. H. Wauer *Birds of Big Bend National Park* 26 Grasses that include Pinyon Ricegrass.

ricer (rəi·səɹ). *Cookery.* [f. *rice *v.* + -er[1].] A utensil for ricing food.

1896 *Columbus* (Ohio) *Dispatch* 21 Nov. 11 Cook one quart of blanched chestnuts in boiling stock till tender, press them through a ricer [etc.]. **1936** *Sears Catal.* 655/1 Potato Ricer Removable heavy retinned seamless bowl... 26c. **1963** M. McCarthy *Group* xiv. 325 Girls today were.. opening a tin of baby food, instead of..pressing beef in the ricer for beef juice. **1969** [see *rice *v.*]. **1970** Simon & Howe *Dict. Gastron.* 327/2 The ricer is usually built in the shape of a metal basket with a snugly fitting metal plunger which exerts pressure on the vegetables within as they are pushed through.

‖ **ricercar, ricercare** (ritʃɛrkā·r, -kā·re). *Mus.* Pl. ricercare, ricercares, ricercari, ricercars. [It., f. *ricercare* to search out.] Any of a variety of musical forms, characteristically in a fugue style, found between the 16th and 18th centuries (see quots.). Cf. Research *sb.*[1] 4.

1789 C. Burney *Gen. Hist. Music* III. ii. 176 Short instructions for composing masses, motets, psalms, madrigals, and *ricercari*. *Ibid.*, This term [sc. *ricercari*], which implied any work of fancy, and original invention, was succeeded by *fantasia*, as *fantasia* was by *sonata*. **1881** Grove *Dict. Mus.* III. 126/2 *Ricercare* or *Ricercata*.., an Italian term of the 17th century, signifying a fugue of the closest and most learned description. Frescobaldi's Ricercari (1615), which are copied out in one of Dr. Burney's note-books.., are full of augmentations, diminutions, inversions, and other contrivances. **1944** W. Apel *Harvard Dict. Mus.* 643/1 These ricercares could be sung. *Ibid.* 644/1 In the later literature for the lute..the lute ricercar more and more approaches the style of the imitative ricercar. **1945** *Musical Q.* XXXI. 459 These works..fall into three types: the one monothematic ricercare, a few ricercari with one main subject..and the commonest type—the polythematic ricercari. **1947** A. Einstein *Mus. Romantic Era* xvii. 294 The 'schools' of the ricercar, whether called fugue as in Germany, *tiento* as in Spain, or fancy as in England, were different, but the spirit and form were the same. **1954** *Grove's Dict. Mus.* (ed. 5) VII. 154/2 The distinction which has been drawn between the *ricercare* as a more learned and the *fantasia* as a more fanciful variety is not really supported by the facts. **1959** *Collins Mus. Encycl.* 547/2 Contrapuntal ricercars were written for instrumental ensembles in the 16th cent. **1961** I. HORSLEY in *Acta Musicologica* XXXIII. 29 (*title*) The solo ricercar in diminution manuals: new light on early wind and string techniques. **1961** *Times* 9 Sept. 11/3 The three-part ricercare for solo harpsichord starts the work. **1968** *New Oxf. Hist. Music* IV. xi. 557 The *ricercari* and fantasias up to the end of the sixteenth century all preserve the principal features of the motet. **1969** *Daily Tel.* 25 Jan. 12 Palestrina wrote few madrigals, and the ricercare are his only known purely instrumental compositions. **1976** D. MUNROW *Instruments Middle Ages & Renaissance* 72/1 Like keyboard instruments, the strings developed a vast solo repertory with their own idiomatic forms of the prelude, ricercar, and *tastar de corde*. **1977** *Folio* Winter 30 It seems very possible that the keyboard ricercare could be held up as the one and only time that J. S. Bach actually wrote with the piano rather than the harpsichord, clavichord or organ in mind. **1980** *Early Music* Apr. 248/1 The first-named turn out to be descendants of the lute preludes so described two centuries before, not ricercars in the fugal sense at all.

‖ **ricercata** (ritʃərkā·tă). *Mus.* Pl. ricercate. [It., pa. pple. (fem.) of *ricercare* to search out.] = *RICERCAR, RICERCARE.

The more usual term is now *ricercar(e*.

1740 J. GRASSINEAU *Mus. Dict.* 198 *Research*, or *Ricercata*, a kind of prelude or voluntary play'd on an Organ, Harpsichord, Theorbo, etc., wherein the composer seems to look out or search for strains and touches of harmony, which he is to use in the regular piece to be play'd afterwards. **1819** REES *Cycl.* XXX, *Ricercata*, a research, a flourish, a prelude, an impromptu, a voluntary. **1881** [see *RICERCAR, RICERCARE]. **1958** A. JACOBS *New Dict. Mus.* 310 Ricercata. **1977** *Early Music* July 415/1 Practising Virgiliano's ricercate without slurs..will also encourage properly relaxed double tonguing.

rice-water. Add: **1.** (Earlier example.)

1789 G. PARKER *Life's Painter* iv. 31 Genuine Hollands, or right Jamaica, qualified with rice-water, spirited lemons, and a proper dash of fragrant oranges.

2. (Earlier example.)

1833 *Lancet* 12 Oct. 116/2 The rice-water evacuations which notoriously result from the disease.

rich, *a.*, *adv.*, and *sb.* Add: **I. 7. d.** (Later examples.)

1936 N. COWARD *To-night at 8.30* II. 40 Me, grumble! I like that, I'm sure. That's rich, that is. **1977** J. ANDERSON *Appearance of Evil* i. 6 'You have experienced a spontaneous demonstration of disapproval..at your last recital.' 'Spontaneous! That's rich.'

8. d. Of the mixture in an internal-combustion engine: containing an amount of fuel greater than that required for complete combustion.

1915 G. A. BURLS *Aero Engines* vi. 106 The rich mixture is diluted by additional air supplied through the light adjustable spring-loaded automatic air-valve. **1917** WODEHOUSE *Uneasy Money* x. 117 Your chauffeur, having examined the carburettor, turns to you and explains the phenomenon in these words: 'The mixture is too rich.' **1920** R. B. WHITMAN *Tractor Princ.* iv. 55 The most serious result of a rich mixture..is in the production of carbon, and the carbonization of the engine. **1971** P. J. McMAHON *Aircraft Propulsion* vi. 196 During an acceleration..the fuel/air ratio will already be richer than for normal steady running.

II. *adv.* and *Comb.* **9. b.** (Later example.)

1864 G. M. HOPKINS *Poems* (1967) 15 From easy runnels the rich-piecèd land I water with my foot.

c. (Later example.)

1925 BLUNDEN *Eng. Poems* 93 Rich-tongued anew The foreign birds are come.

10. b. (Later examples.)

1922 JOYCE *Ulysses* 726 Those richlooking..drinks those stagedoor johnnies drink with the opera hats. **1930** E. WAUGH *Vile Bodies* x. 195 A really good story my second day on the paper. This ought to do me good with the Excess—*very* rich-making.

10*. In reduplicated form.

a **1725** E. TAYLOR *Dialogue between Justice & Mercy* in *Poet. Wks.* (1939) 40, I to him will hold out in my hand The golden scepter of my Rich-Rich Grace. **1963** P. H. JOHNSON *Night & Silence* x. 58 Living with the rich-rich suited him right now. **1974** 'J. MELVILLE' *Nun's Castle* viii. 176 Ted probably was rich. Not superlatively rich (rich rich as the slang goes) but solidly, comfortably endowed. **1977** *South China Morning Post* (Hong Kong) 13 Apr. 14/3 Karl Lagerfeld always puts together a mouth-watering collection for Chloe (aiming towards those rich-rich women who buy from Valentino).

III. *absol.* or as *sb.* **11. a.** Also in phr. *the rich get richer* (*and the poor get poorer*).

1921 KAHN & EGAN *Ain't we got Fun* (*song*) 5 There's nothing surer The rich get rich and the poor get children. **1936** C. SANDBURG *People, Yes* 164 The rich get richer and the poor get children. The rich have baby napkins, the poor have diapers. **1972** *Times* 8 May 14/1 It is the old story of the rich getting richer and the poor getting poorer, this time by courtesy of Dr Borlaug's miracle grains. **1973** *Black Panther* 31 Mar. C/1 County underassessment too, perpetuates the 'rich get richer' cycle in Oakland.

12. Also in phr. *new rich*: cf. *NEW *a.* 8 d.

1909 *Daily Chron.* 3 Nov. 3/5 It is concerned with the intrusion of Saul Dene, a 'new rich', into a Yorkshire country set.

rich, *v.*[1] Restrict † *Obs.* to sense 2 in Dict. and add: **1.** (Later examples.)

1912 J. MASEFIELD *Widow in Bye Street* 86 Sunwarm gorses rich the air with scent. **1925** E. O'NEILL *Desire under Elms* I. iv. 50 Blood an' bone an' sweat—rotted away—fertilizin' ye—richin' yer soul—prime manure, by God, that's what I been t' ye! **1955** E. POUND *Classic Anthol.* II. 126 Falls snow, fine sleet Plus drizzle and soak Riching, by mulch, full favour the grain Of all our folk.

Richard. Restrict † *Obs. rare* to sense in Dict. and add: **2.** [More formal equivalent of *DICK *sb.*[6]] A detective.

1914 JACKSON & HELLYER *Vocab. Criminal Slang* 70 *Richard, noun.* General currency. A detective. Derived from the process of nicknaming, but in reverse of the usual custom. Thus from the term '*detective*', 'dick' was suggested and hence '*Richard*' was derived. Or, following the corruption of the English 'Robert' to 'Bob' and 'Bobby', the American parallel was suggested. **1952** in Wentworth & Flexner *Dict. Amer. Slang* (1960) 426/2 Mickey Spillane, who turns out epics about a private richard named Mike Hammer. **1964** H. KANE *Snatch an Eye* xxiv. 147 The richard tails his own client... If the private detective shows up, it means that the client did not shake him. **1967** E. McGIRR *Hearse with Horses* i. 7 Private eye, poor Richard, or shamus. **1974** —— *Murderous Journey* 12 A surprisingly high proportion of well-to-do murderers hire private richards to delve into the demise of the victim.

3. [Shortening of *Richard the Third*, rhyming slang for *BIRD *sb.* 1 d.] A girl, woman.

1950 P. TEMPEST *Lag's Lexicon* 180 *Richard.* A girl. The girl friend. **1960** 'A. BURGESS' *Doctor is Sick* xiv. 107 Judged by some of vem glamorous richards on ve telly. **1964** *Listener* 31 Dec. 1053/1 What Richard's gonna look at them in them 'airy outfits and them big boots. **1970** G. F. NEWMAN *Sir, You Bastard* viii. 232, I was just sleeping at this Richard's place during the day... I didn't know she was brassing.

4. Prefixed to another word, so as to form a name or nickname, or used in a phrase with specific sense: **poor Richard** (see quot. 1970); **Richard Roe** *Law*, the name formerly given to a fictitious defendant in actions of ejectment; *U.S.*, also an unidentified defendant in criminal proceedings; **Richard's himself again** (orig. in quot. 1700) (see quot. 1911).

1700 CIBBER *Richard III* v. 52 Conscience avant; Richard's himself again. Hark! the shrill Trumpet sounds, to Horse: away! My Soul's in Arms, and eager for the Fray. **1768**, etc. [see *John Doe* s.v. JOHN 4]. **1779** 'R. SAUNDERS' *Poor Richard's Prophesy* 4, I have frequently heard one or other of my adages repeated, with, as *poor Richard says*, at the end on't. **1870** *Brewer's Dict. Phr. & Fable* 747/1 *Richard Roe*, a mere nominal defendant in actions of ejectment. The name used to be coupled with *John Doe*, but these airy nothings are no longer the lawyer's tools. **1911** *Conc. Oxf. Dict.* s.v. *Richard*,..*Poor R.'s sayings*, maxims from almanacs issued by Benjamin Franklin with *Poor R.* as pseudonym; *R.'s himself again*.., said by or of person recovered from despondency, fear, illness, &c. **1928**, **1957** [see *John Doe* s.v. *JOHN 4]. **1970** *Brewer's Dict. Phr. & Fable* (rev. ed.) 851/1 *Poor Richard*, the assumed name of Benjamin Franklin in a series of *almanacs* from 1732 to 1757. They contained maxims and precepts on temperance, economy, cleanliness, chastity, and other virtues; and several ended with the words 'as poor Richard says'.

richardia (ritʃā·ɹdiă). [mod.L. (C. Kunth 1818, in *Mém. Mus. Hist. Nat. Paris* IV. 433), f. the name of Louis Claude Marie *Richard* (1754–1821), French botanist + -IA[1].] = *CALLA 2.

1859 *Curtis's Bot. Mag.* LXXXV. 5140 (*heading*) Spotted-leaved Richardia. **1914** W. F. ROWLES *Garden under Glass* vi. 100 Any good potting soil will suit Richardias. **1951** [see *CALLA 2].

Richardson[1] (ri·tʃăɹdsə̆n). The name of Sir John *Richardson* (1787–1865), Scottish naturalist and explorer, used *attrib.* or in the possessive in the names of birds or other animals first collected by him or named in his honour, as **Richardson('s) (ground) squirrel**, a spermophile, *Citellus richardsoni*, found in central North America; cf. *picket-pin gopher* s.v. *PICKET *sb.*[1] 7; **Richardson('s) grouse**, the North American spruce grouse, *Canachites canadensis*; **Richardson's jager** = *Richardson's skua*; **Richardson's owl**, the Arctic owl, *Ægolius funerea richardsoni*; **Richardson's skua**, the Arctic skua, *Stercorarius parasiticus*.

1831 W. SWAINSON in R. Jameson *Wilson & Bonaparte's Amer. Ornithol.* IV. 334 The next species in size and importance is Richardson's grouse (*Tetrao Richardsonii*), so named in honour of Dr. Richardson, the distinguished traveller. *Ibid.* 354 Richardson's jager, whole plumage, brown. **1835** L. JENYNS *Man. Brit. Vertebr. Animals* 282 Richardson's Skua. **1856** J. CASSIN *Illustr. Birds Amer.* 185 Richardson's Owl... The largest of this genus. **1868** *Amer. Naturalist* II. 529 Richardson's squirrel. **1896** R. RIDGWAY *Man. N. Amer. Birds* (ed. 2) 260 Northern North America; south, in winter, to northern border of United States.. Richardson's Owl. **1897** R. B. SHARPE in A. H. Miles *Conc. Knowl. Nat. Hist.* 264 Richardson's skua..nests in the Orkneys and Shetland Isles, as well as in some of the Hebrides and on the north-west of Scotland. **1901** *Daily Colonist* (Victoria, B.C.) 30 Oct. 1/6 The Richardson grouse, or fool hen, a smaller species..abound everywhere at lower levels. **1927** *Daily Express* 30 Nov. 9/5 At Regent's Park.. a 'Richardson's Owl'. **1940** E. T. SETON *Trail of Artist-Naturalist* 189 The Richardson or yellow ground squirrel.. nests in colonies like those of the prairie dog. **1947** R. T. PETERSON *Field Guide to Birds* (ed. 2) 137 The facial discs of Richardson's Owl are framed with black. **1963** D. A. BANNERMAN *Birds Brit. Isles* XII. 17 As a summer visitor to nest in the British Isles, Richardson's skua is much more numerous and more widely spread than the very local great skua.

Richardson[2] (ri·tʃăɹdsə̆n). *Electronics.* [Name of Sir Owen W. *Richardson* (1879–1959), English physicist.] *Richardson('s) equation*: an equation giving the maximum current density of electrons emitted by a hot metal surface in terms of its temperature and work function. Also called *Richardson–Dushman equation* [Saul *Dushman* (1883–1954), U.S. physicist].

1925 [see *OUTGASSING *vbl. sb.*]. **1939** H. J. REICH *Theory & Appl. Electron Tubes* ii. 17 Richardson's equation holds only for the saturation current. **1950** P. G. ANDRES *Surv. Mod. Electronics* ii. 41 At the turn of the century O. W. Richardson, using the analogy of evaporation at the surface of a liquid, developed an equation for electron emission. Later S. Dushman modified Richardson's equation. **1958** *Chambers's Techn. Dict.* 1010/1 Richardson-Dushmann equation. **1967** CONDON & ODISHAW *Handbk. Physics* (ed. 2) VIII. vi. 77/1 (*heading*) Statistical derivation of the Richardson equation. **1975** D. G. FINK *Electronics Engineers' Handbk.* I. 32 If the electrons are removed from the emitting surface as rapidly as they are released, the emission is temperature-limited and the density of current of emitted electrons obeys the Richardson-Dushman equation $J = (1-R)A_0T^2\epsilon^{-\phi/kT}$. *Ibid.* XXVII. 12 If $Vc < \phi_e$,..the saturation current density j_s is as given by Richardson's equation.

Richardson[3] (ri·tʃăɹdsə̆n). *Physics.* The name of Lewis Fry *Richardson* (1881–1953), English physicist, used *attrib.* and in the possessive to designate quantities and concepts discovered by him, as **Richardson('s) criterion**, a criterion, depending on the value of the Richardson number, used to determine whether flow in a stratified fluid will be turbulent or laminar; **Richardson('s) number**, a dimensionless number given, essentially, by the ratio of the fluid density gradient to the square of the velocity gradient.

1934 D. BRUNT *Physical & Dynamic Meteorol.* xiii. 255 Richardson's criterion agrees with that given by Prandtl except for a factor ½. **1948** *Jrnl. Marine Res.* VII. 280 One type of nondimensional number, the Richardson number.. $r = gE/(V')^2$. **1956** *Nature* 3 Mar. 435/2 A regime of effectively free convection of heat begins to operate in the surface layers of the atmosphere at a negative Richardson number as low as 0·02 or 0·03. *Ibid.*, This transforms the Rayleigh criterion into a Richardson criterion. **1957** G. E. HUTCHINSON *Treat. Limnol.* I. v. 255 Richardson's number. **1964** *Oceanogr. & Marine Biol.* II. 19 If, as is usually the case in the ocean, the density of the water increases with depth, stability effects will tend to reduce the intensity of the turbulence... The stability effect is usually considered in terms of the Richardson number. **1974** *Encycl. Brit. Micropædia* VIII. 570/1 The Richardson number, or one of several variants, is of practical importance in weather forecasting and in investigating density and turbidity currents in oceans, lakes, and reservoirs.

Richardsonian, *a.* and *sb.* Add: **A.** *adj.* (Earlier and later examples.)

1786 A. SEWARD *Let.* 29 Mar. (1811) I. 135 Miss Reeves' reply to my Stricture on her Richardsonian absurdity, is at once weak and artful. **1844** THACKERAY in *Fraser's Mag.* XXIX. 709/1 It is entirely unnatural, theatrical, of the Davidgian, nay, Richardsonian drama. **1930** A. BIRRELL *Et Cetera* ix. 161 Doddridge's love affairs are narrated by him at Richardsonian length. **1952** *Essays in Crit.* II. 388 Fielding ridiculed the Richardsonian use of the present tense in *Shamela.* **1975** M. BUTLER *J. Austen & War of Ideas* xiii. 295 She [*sc.* Jane Austen] is the Fielding of her period, reacting against the Richardsonian individualism of the sentimental genre.

B. *sb.* (Later examples.)

1892 A. BIRRELL *Res Judicatæ* i. 32 The great Napoleon was a true Richardsonian. **1932** J. M. S. TOMPKINS *Pop. Novel in England 1770–1800* iv. 120 Such arrant Richardsonians as..the inevitable book-sellers' hacks.

Richard's pipit (ri·tʃăɹdz). [tr. F. *pipi Richard* (L. J. P. Vieillot in *Nouveau Dict. d'Hist. Nat.* (1818) XXVI. 491), named after Monsieur *Richard*, an amateur ornithologist of Lunéville, who first made it known.] A large pipit, *Anthus novæseelandiæ* (which includes the former *A. richardi*), found in large areas of the Palæarctic region.

1833 P. J. SELBY *Illustr. Brit. Ornith.* (ed. 2) I. 264 (*heading*) Richard's pipit. **1870** *Zoologist* V. 1984 Richard's Pipit... Some of them are doing well in confinement. **1921** *Ibis* III. 653 La Touche..appears to recognize this southern Chinese race of Richard's Pipit. **1953** D. A. BANNERMAN *Birds Brit. Isles* II. 51 Richard's pipit has been found over a hundred times in the British Isles since the first established record in 1812 when one was netted near London. **1971** *Country Life* 9 Sept. 616/2 It is the Scarborough bird-watchers who have made Filey Brigg famous..seeking for and identifying rare visitors..such as Richard's pipit.

Richebourg (riʃbūr). Name of a wine-growing district of the Côte de Nuits, France, used to designate the red wine produced there.

1833 C. Redding *Hist. Mod. Wines* v. 97 Further on is the Vosnes... The most celebrated of these wines are the Romanée St. Vivant.., Romanée-Conti, Richebourg, and la Tache. **1878** G. Meredith *Lett.* (1970) II. 559 Hockheimer or dry, still, red Bouzy, Richebourg and your friend to wash all down. **1926** [see *Melba]. **1932** E. Hemingway *Death in Afternoon* i. 11 A liver that will not allow me to drink Richebourg, Corton, or Chambertin. **1973** H. McCloy *Change of Heart* v. 49 What would you like with the *tournedos*? Richebourg?

Richelieu (riʃ·lyö). [Of obscure origin. Possibly the name of Cardinal *Richelieu* (1585–1642).] Used *attrib.* to designate a form of cut-work in which the spaces are connected by picoted bars, used in clothing and household accessories.

1880 *Myra's Jrnl. Dress & Fashion* Sept. 437/2 (*heading*) Edging in Richelieu guipure... The scallop..is worked in the same way, and the material cut away underneath. **1882** [see Strasburg]. **1895** *Montgomery Ward Catal.* 301/2 Ladies' Extra Fine Lisle Thread Hose, Richelieu ribbed. **1923** *Daily Mail* 26 June 15 Another lovely set is in Richelieu embroidery on linen edged with Point de Venise. **1967** E. Short *Embroidery & Fabric Collage* ii. 39 Another type of white work used for accessories and children's clothes was Richelieu work, an elaborate form of cut work. **1975** P. Clabburn *Needleworker's Dict.* 227/1 *Richelieu embroidery*, type of whitework where, as in Renaissance embroidery, the design is outlined in buttonhole stitch, the fabric cut away, and the spaces joined with bars or brides. The difference between the two types is that here the joining bars are decorated with picots.

richellite (riʃe·ləit). *Min.* [a. F. *richellite* (Césaro and Despret 1883, in *Ann. de la Soc. géol. de Belgique* X. 36), f. *Richelle*, name of a locality near Visé in Belgium, where it was discovered; see -ite[1].] A hydrated basic phosphate of calcium and ferric iron, usu. also containing fluorine, which occurs as amorphous reddish- or yellowish-brown masses.

1884 *Jrnl. Chem. Soc.* XLVI. 1102 (*heading*) Richellite, a new mineral species. **1935** J. W. Mellor *Comprehensive Treat. Inorg. & Theoret. Chem.* XIV. lxvi. 412 G. Cesaro and G. Desprez [*sic*] described a mineral from Richelle, Belgium, which they called richellite. The analysis corresponds with calcium ferric fluophosphate, although G. Cesaro gave $8Fe(PO_4).Fe_2OF_2.(OH)_2.36H_2O$ for the formula. **1963** *Amer. Mineralogist* XLVIII. 300 Richellite, a calcium-iron hydrated phosphate, appears to be virtually amorphous.

ri·chening, *ppl. a. rare.* [f. Richen *v.* + -ing[2].] That is becoming richer.

1930 *G. K.'s Weekly* 26 July 316/2 Each generation of mankind may be said to inherit an ever-richening treasure of synthetic wisdom from the total past.

Richi, obs. var. Rishi in Dict. and Suppl.

richish, *a.* For *rare*—[1] read *rare* and add further example.

1955 Priestley & Hawkes *Journey down Rainbow* xii. 179 Yet another poet (wisely married to a richish wife).

Richter (ri·χʸtəɹ). *Geophysics.* The name of Charles Francis *Richter* (b. 1900), American seismologist, used *attrib.* with reference to a logarithmic scale he devised for expressing the magnitude of an earthquake (see quot. 1935 s.v. *magnitude 2 c) as calculated from the oscillations of a seismograph trace, and ranging from negative values for micro-earthquakes to about 8·9 for the most catastrophic.

1938 L. D. Leet *Pract. Seismol. & Seismic Prospecting* ix. 304 Since the Richter magnitude scale is logarithmic in amplitudes, doubling the magnitude gives a scale logarithmic in energies and log E = log E_0+2 M where M is the magnitude on the Richter scale. **1957** *Bull. Seismological Soc. Amer.* XLVII. 287 'Magnitude' refers to an estimate of the Richter magnitude by the Seismological laboratory at Pasadena. **1969** R. L. Wiegel *Earthquake Engin.* (1970) ix. 169 Richter has correlated Modified Mercalli intensity with the earthquake's Richter magnitude as follows. **1971** [see *magnitude 2 c]. **1976** *National Observer* (U.S.) 8 May 19/3 It is when the magnitude starts reaching 5.5 on the Richter Scale and higher that destruction is wrought. **1977** A. Hallam *Planet Earth* 63/3 In general, the larger events—those with Richter magnitudes greater than 5 or 6—do not occur in regions of plate creation but are associated only with the more violent process of plate underthrusting.

b. *fig.*

1967 *Boston Sunday Herald* 7 May (Show Guide) 17/1 This novel about the Nation's Capital in the period from Pearl Harbor to Senator McCarthy falls somewhere between the sententiousness of Allen Drury and the political astuteness of Anthony Trollope—say about 4 on a Richter scale that measures the quakes of getting and holding office. **1975** *New Yorker* 6 Oct. 140/2 We correspondents who remained in the city tried to assess the rumours as best we could on a sort of Richter scale of our own: if we heard enough reports from different sources about a particular occurrence, we figured that the story was true and gave it a high rating. **1977** H. Greene *FSO-1* xix. 171 In an arm of government as seismologically sensitive as the Foreign Service, the news..was a shock on the level of six or seven on the diplomatic Richter scale.

richterite (ri·χʸtërəit). *Min.* [ad. G. *richterit* (A. Breithaupt 1865, in *Berg- und Hüttenmännische Zeitung* XXIV. 364), f. the name of H. Theodor *Richter* (1824–98), German metallurgical chemist: see -ite[1].] **a.** A manganiferous mineral of the amphibole group, $(Na,K)_2(Mg,Mn,Ca)_6Si_8O_{22}(OH)_2$, found as elongated brown, yellow or rose-red monoclinic crystals. **b.** The end member of the series of amphiboles containing this, which lacks manganese and has the ideal formula $Na_2CaMg_5Si_8O_{22}(OH)_2$.

1868 J. D. Dana *Syst. Mineral.* (ed. 5) 215 The Richterite of Breith[aupt]..is near schefferite in composition. **1946** *Chem. Abstr.* XL. 7089 Richterite is found to form a special type of Mg-rich amphiboles distinguished by the replacement of Ca by Na (K) as compared with tremolite. **1965** E. W. Heinrich *Microsc. Identification of Minerals* x. 273 Richterite,..a rare manganiferous amphibole, is closely allied to soda tremolite. **1978** *Mineral. Mag.* XLII. 543 [Report on Nomenclature of Amphiboles as approved by International Mineralogical Association.] Sodic-calcic Amphiboles. This group is defined as monoclinic amphiboles in which $(Ca+Na)_B \geq 1·34$ and $0·67 < Na_B < 1·34$... End Members: Richterite [etc.].

Richter's hernia (ri·χʸtəɹz). *Med.* [Named after August Gottlieb *Richter* (1742–1812), German surgeon, who described the condition in *Abhandlung von den Brüchen* (1778) ch. xxiv.] A hernia which does not involve the whole width of the gut, so that the lumen remains open.

1887 F. Treves in *Medico-Chirurg. Trans.* LII. 153, I would venture to suggest the title 'Richter's hernia'..to make still more clear the lines that should separate this hernia from that known as Littre's, and partly because with Richter must rest the main credit of establishing the individuality of this lesion. **1929** *Amer. Jrnl. Surg.* VII. 864/1 A strangulation of part only of the circumference of the intestinal wall is a Richter's hernia. *Ibid.* 864/2 One should be suspicious of a Richter's hernia when the present illness was ushered in by the incarceration of a long-standing hernia, and where the illness persists. **1974** R. M. Kirk et al. *Surgery* vii. 139 Part of the bowel wall may be strangulated, leaving the lumen unobstructed, in Richter's hernia.

ri·cing[2]. [f. Rice[2].] (See quot. 1937.)

1937 E. J. Labarre *Dict. Paper* 201/1 *Ricing*, a term applied, chiefly in esparto mills, to the mottled or grainy look-through due to 'crowding' or crushing..; in Scotland also referred to as 'rawny' (Sc. rawns, the roe of fish). It is generally used when the paper shows characteristic small knots due to the stuff being too wet beaten, and having too much rubbing in the machine chests. **1963** R. R. A. Higham *Handbk. Papermaking* ii. 42 This type of beater [*sc.* Taylor beater] is suitable for short-fibred stock such as esparto, where only light treatment is called for and which at the same time tends to prevent *ricing* of the fibres, produced by excess whipping of stock.

rick, *sb.*[1] Add: **2. a.** *rick-builder, -building, -burner* (earlier example), *-burning* (later example), *-lifter, -shifter.*

1905 *Eng. Dial. Dict.* V. 96/2 *Rick-builder*, a man who builds ricks. **1936** *Discovery* Nov. 363/2 The old lacemakers and the hurdle maker, the shepherd and the rick builder, the last being an artist in hay,..inhabit the old-world village. **1960** *Farmer & Stockbreeder* 23 Feb. 55/3 Many of us are so steeped in the old rick-building tradition of 'keeping the middle up' that we still do it with silage. **1844** *Punch* VII. 17 (*caption*) The home of the rick-burner. **1939** D. Cecil *Young Melbourne* viii. 206 The riotings and rick-burnings..roused his fear of revolution. **1910** *Encycl. Brit.* XIII. 108/2 Various forms of rick-lifters are in use, the characteristic feature of which is a tipping platform on wheels to which a horse is attached between shafts. **1924** *Glasgow Herald* 24 Dec. 6/7 Skiffs have been transported across the island on rick-lifters to augment the temporary fishing fleet. **1957** E. E. Evans *Irish Folk Ways* xii. 155 Carried at last to the haggard or rick-shifters or slipes..the hay is built into small circular stacks (pikes).

rick, *sb.*[4] *slang.* [Origin unknown.] = *gee *sb.* 3. Also *attrib.* or as *adj.*, fictitious, sham.

1928 [see *gee *sb.*[3]]. **1934** P. Allingham *Cheapjack* vii. 63 On..occasions the worker has a rick, that is to say, a confederate planted in the crowd, whom he could always choose as the first bidder. **1967** *Sunday Tel.* 7 May 5/5 If you are standing near a bookie's joint, undecided, and a merchant dashes in and places a bet, such as 'Seventy pounds to forty. On top', don't take a blind bit of notice. It's a rick bet... It don't even go in the book. Its sole object is to push or goad you into making your bet.

rick, 'rick (rik), abbrev. Rickshaw, ricksha.

1889 Kipling in *Pioneer Mail* 16 June 743/1 All the sahibs hailed 'rick-shaws—they call them '*ricks* here [*sc.* in Hong Kong]. **1962** *Coast to Coast 1961–62* 82 Hell, wouldn't they sit up? the blokes at the tuck shop, the twits in Leaving. Wouldn't credit it, his going for a Jap sheila in a bloody rick.

rick, *v.*[1] (Later N. Amer. examples.)

1914 *Dialect Notes* IV. 78 *Rick up, v. phr.*, to pile up (brush). **1951** H. E. Giles *Harbin's Ridge* xi. 102 When I got there Faleecy John was ricking up cook wood in the corner of the yard. I pitched in to help. I like to rick wood. **1962** M. E. Murie *Two in Far North* I. ii. 23 Thank heaven for the nine cords of good spruce wood ricked up in the back yard.

rickardite (ri·kāɹdəit). *Min.* [f. the name of Thomas A. *Rickard* (1864–1953), U.S. mining engineer + -ite[1].] A tetragonal telluride of copper found as brittle, metallic, purplish-red masses in a number of copper mines in Colorado and elsewhere.

1903 W. E. Ford in *Amer. Jrnl. Sci.* CLXV. 69 Rickardite occurs at Vulcan, Col., in the Good Hope mine... Rickardite itself occurs in small lens-shaped masses, generally rather intimately associated with native tellurium. **1943** R. D. George *Minerals & Rocks* viii. 223 Weissite, Cu_5Te_3..occurs associated with rickardite. **1949** *Amer. Mineralogist* XXXIV. 442 Rickardite is a mineral of striking and unmistakable appearance. **1963** *Structure Rep.* 1956 XX. 101 Cu_7Te_5 is rickardite, and was formerly described as $Cu_{4-x}Te_2$.

ricker. For *Naut.* read orig. *Naut.* and add later examples in various *spec.* senses.

1905 W. B. *Where White Man Treads* 20 Posts..driven into the ground at such an angle over the fire that when the rickers, on which the birds were hung, were laid into them, the fat dripping from the upper tier missed the one below. **1940** *Chambers's Techn. Dict.* 724/2 *Rickers*, round timber of less than 2½ in. diameter in the middle. **1958** *N.Z. Timber Jrnl.* May 56/2 *Ricker*: (a) A long pole or sapling used for handling floating timber at the docks. (b) A kauri tree in the pole stage, N.Z.

ri·cket, *sb.*[2] *Criminals' slang.* [Origin unknown.] A blunder, mistake.

1958 F. Norman *Bang to Rights* I. 36 If you are chopping all day..you must at some time make a ricket and chop your hand. **1963** *Oxford Mail* 23 Aug. 1/6 You obviously know a lot. I have made a ricket (mistake) somewhere.

ri·cket, *v. rare.* [Back-formation from Rickety *a.*] *intr.* To move in a rickety manner; to lurch.

1897 T. De Leon *Bachelor's Box* v. 44 Van muttered to himself, as the cab rocked and ricketed down the street. **1955** L. A. G. Strong *Deliverance* ii. 65 One of the back legs of his chair was short, so that..it ricketed to and fro.

ricketic (rike·tik), *a. Med.* [f. Ricket+ -ic.] = Rickety *a.* 1, 3.

1972 *Lancet* 20 May 1113/2 A biochemist friend..is campaigning for the use of 'ricketic' as the proper adjective for rickets. **1973** *Nature* 28 Sept. 180/2 Both parent compounds have long been known to possess similar anti-ricketic activity in man.

ricketiness. (In Dict. s.v. Ricketily *adv.*) (Earlier example.)

1867 G. M. Hopkins *Further Lett.* (1956) 48 The more frankly you confess the 'ricketiness' of yr. position, do you see, the less excuse you have yourself for staying in it?

rickets. Add: Also 7 **rackets, rekets. 1.** (Earlier and further examples.) Now known to be a vitamin D deficiency disease.

1634 *Parish Clerks' Company Bill of Mortality* (Guildhall Libr. MS. *St.424.9*), Diseases and Casualties this year.. Rickets 14. **1653** J. Bulwer *Anthropometamorphosis* xx. 332 This new disease, commonly called the Rickets, or more properly the Rackets. **1661** J. Bird *Ostenta Carolina* 53 The Disease is not exprest by a word of the singular number *reket*, but plurally *rekets*. *Ibid.*, The calling of it, as we do, *rekets* pronouncing of it as if it were written with (*i*) in the first syllable, there is little difference in the sound whether it be written with (*e*) or (*i*). **1883** *Medico-Chirurg. Trans.* LXVI. 204 The characteristic symptoms of the so-called acute rickets..are not due to rickets at all but are truly scorbutic. **1919** *Lancet* 15 Mar. 408/2 An examination of the results obtained suggests that rickets is a deficiency disease which develops in consequence of the absence of some accessory food factor or factors. **1974** Passmore & Robson *Compan. Med. Stud.* III. xxiv. 20/1 Rickets..is caused by deficiency of vitamin D, due to a combination of a dietary lack and inadequate exposure to sunlight, necessary for the synthesis of the vitamin in the skin. In the absence of vitamin D the absorption of calcium from the gut is impaired and there is a disturbance of calcium and phosphorus metabolism.

rickettsia (rike·tsiă). Also **Rickettsia.** Pl. **-iæ, ias.** [mod.L. *Rickettsia* (coined in Ger. as the name of a genus by H. da Rocha-Lima 1916, in *Berliner klin. Wochenschr.* 22 May 567/2), f. the name of H. T. *Ricketts* (1871–1910), U.S. pathologist, who first described such organisms in 1909 (*Jrnl. Amer. Med. Assoc.* 30 Jan. 379–80) and died of typhus contracted as a result of his research on them: see -ia[1].] Any of a group of very small rod-shaped or coccoid micro-organisms that are mostly intracellular parasites in vertebrates and include the causative agents of several febrile diseases in man. Freq. *attrib.*

1919 *Jrnl. Med. Res.* XLI. 87 The name 'Rickettsia' has been applied by da Rocha-Lima to minute bacillary forms found by Hegler and von Prowazek in typhus fever, and regarded as identical with bodies described by Ricketts in Mexican typhus. **1922** Hiss & Zinsser *Textbk. Bacteriol.* (ed. 5) xlviii. 944 Rickettsia-like microorganisms may be present in lice fed upon healthy people... It is not at all conclusively definite that the Rickettsia bodies are micro-organisms. **1935** *Discovery* Dec. 375/2 Very significant is the distinction between the various infection-chains of the different forms of Rickettsia disease. **1947** *Ann. Rev. Microbiol.* I. 337 This preparation contains rickettsiae and tissue particles in suspension. **1951** WHITBY & HYNES *Med. Bacteriol.* (ed. 5) 360 The rickettsiæ are primarily intestinal parasites of arthropod blood-sucking insects..but some half-dozen species have become adapted to invade the animal body and cause disease. **1969** *Times* 3 June 6/2 The trachoma agent is one of a group of tiny organisms called the Rickettsias. **1976** *National Observer* (U.S.) 21 Aug. 8/4 The disease is caused by micro-organisms called rickettsiae, which resemble very small bacteria but, like a virus, grow only in susceptible cells. **1976** A. L. SMITH *Microbiol. & Path.* (ed. 11) xxvii. 271/2 The rickettsias of the genus *Rochalimaea* can be cultured in host cell-free media. **1979** *Sci. Amer.* Oct. 88/2 Although..we had isolated the causative agent of Legionnaires' disease, for several weeks we did not know whether the organism was a rickettsia or a bacterium.

Hence **ricke·ttsial** *a.*, of, pertaining to, or caused by rickettsiæ.

1940 W. H. HOLMES *Bacillary & Rickettsial Infections* V. 76 They discovered that trench fever is a true rickettsial disease transmitted by the body louse. **1947** *Ann. Rev. Microbiol.* I. 338 A method for the preparation of rickettsial antigens from yolk sacs without the use of ether has also been developed. **1977** *Time* 31 Jan. 36/2 The discovery was made not by a man who hunts ordinary bacteria, but by a specialist in leprosy and rickettsial diseases like typhus and spotted fever.

rickettsialpox (rike·tsiălpǫks). Also **rickettsial pox.** [f. *RICKETTSIAL *a.* + POX *sb.*] A mild rickettsial disease transmitted by mites.

1946 R. J. HUEBNER et al. in *Public Health Rep.* LXI. 1605 Because of a clinical resemblance to chickenpox and because the organism isolated from one patient has the morphological and cultural characteristics of rickettsiae, the name 'rickettsialpox' is proposed. **1955** *Sci. News Let.* 11 June 373/2 New diseases, Q fever and rickettsialpox, have appeared and some old ones, polio, Coxsackie virus infections, and infectious hepatitis, or jaundice, have increased in the period covered by Dr. Dauer's report. **1970** *New Scientist* 27 Aug. 407/2 Mice probably play a greater part than rats in the transmission of..rickettsial pox (which closely resembles chickenpox).

rickety, *a.* Add: **3. b.** *rickety rosary*, a line of swellings on either side of the chest, reminiscent of strings of beads and symptomatic of rickets.

[**1887** VICKERY & KNAPP tr. *Strümpell's Text-bk. Med.* 868 There is a swelling at the junction of the cartilages with the ribs, which can be felt and seen through the skin, and produces what is called the 'rosary of rickets'.] **1907** G. F. STILL in W. Osler *Mod. Med.* I. xxxiii. 876 The most frequent [osseous] manifestation [of rickets] is the so-called 'rickety rosary', or beading of the ribs, a thickening at the costo-chondral junction which in a thin child can be seen and in others easily felt. **1970** W. H. PARKER *Health & Dis. in Farm Animals* i. 7 In a pup or child suffering from rickets they can actually be seen because of the enlargement of the joints which occur with this disease, giving rise to the grim phrase 'a rickety rosary'. **1974** PASSMORE & ROBSON *Compan. Med. Stud.* III. xxiv. 21/2 In the chest an early sign [of rickets] is bleeding of the costochondral junctions. This is called rickety rosary as the beads extend in chain fashion down both sides of the thorax.

ri·ckety-ra·ckety, *a.* [redupl. f. RICKETY *a.*] Unsteady; shaky; tottering.

1895 *Punch* 21 Sept. 135 (*caption*) We're a rare old—fair old—rickety, rackety crew. **1931** J. R. MACDONALD in *Times* 5 Nov. 14/4 The whole world has got into what we in this corner of it would call a ricketty-racketty state. **1976** D. HEFFRON *Crusty Crossed* v. 39 We were given some rickety-rackety set of train coaches with old wooden bench seats.

rickey (ri·ki). orig. *U.S.* Also **Rickey, ricky.** [prob. f. the surname *Rickey*.] An iced drink consisting of gin, whiskey, or the like, mixed with lime or lemon juice and carbonated water. Freq. with defining word prefixed, esp. *gin rickey*.

1895 G. J. KAPPELER *Mod. Amer. Drinks* 97 *Brandy rickey.* In a thin medium-sized glass put one lump of ice, the juice of half a lime, one jigger brandy, fill the glass with siphon carbonic water; drink while effervescent. *Ibid.*, Canadian rickey. *Ibid.*, Gin rickey. **1906** *Mrs. Beeton's Bk. Househ. Managem.* xlix. 1511 *Gin rickey. Ingredients.*—1 wineglassful of gin, 1 dessertspoonful of lemon or lime-juice, seltzer water, ice... *Note.*—Any other spirit may be used..and would..give its name to the compound. **1908** 'O. HENRY' *Gentle Grafter* i. 13 Why, in Bryan's second campaign,..they used to give me three gin rickeys and I'd speak two hours longer than Billy himself could on the silver question. **1925** F. SCOTT FITZGERALD *Great Gatsby* vii. 140 Tom came back, preceding four gin rickeys. **1928** [see *GIMLET *sb.*[1] 1 c]. **1930** G. R. BROWN *Washington* xi. 369 In course of time, the 'rickey' came to be referred to as the 'gin rickey', whereas it had always been a 'whiskey rickey'. **1945** P. CHEYNEY *I'll say she Does!* iii. 72 The lyin' woman is like a gin ricky without any gin. **1975** M. AMIS *Dead Babies* xiii. 67 By 12.30, Giles had consumed five gin-rickies, four gin-and-tonics, three gin-and-its, two gin-and-bitters, and one gin. **1975** *Washington Post* 27 Jan. A 19/1 A certain Col. Joseph Rickey used to frequent a drinking place in E Street known as Shoomaker's... The original Rickey, a la Shoo's, consisted of Bourbon, soda and lime juice. In time gin was substituted for the Bourbon and..[the Colonel's] name was forever attached.

rickle, *sb.*[2] Add: Also *Anglo-Ir.* **1. a.** (Later examples.)

1922 J. BUCHAN *Huntingtower* iii. 57 Huntingtower was the auld rickle o' stanes at the sea-end. **1934** E. LINKLATER *Magnus Merriman* 197 There was a smug trim smooth little minister..and a rickle of rural inanity behind. **1963** *Field Archaeol.* (Ordnance Survey) (ed. 4) 53 A careful search will often show associated hut sites and even field boundaries in the form of long rickles of stones.

2. (Later example.)

1871 G. M. HOPKINS *Jrnls. & Papers* (1959) 213 [Lancs.] Roberts says the first grass from the scythe is the *swathe*, then comes the *strow* (tedding), then *rowing*, then the foot-cocks, then *breaking*, then the *hubrows*, which are gathered into *hubs*, then sometimes another break and *turning*, then *rickles*, the biggest of all the cocks, which are run together into *placks*, the shapeless heaps from which the hay is carted.

3. (Earlier and later examples.)

1700 *Black Bk. Kincardineshire* (1843) 130 He hid the said web among a rickle of truffs. **1957** E. E. EVANS *Irish Folk Ways* xiv. 184 The peats are turned and built into larger and larger piles, turn-foots, castles, rickles, lumps and clamps. **1979** *Country Life* 27 Sept. 964/1 Turf..will be built into..piles with varying names such as rickles, castles, lumps and clamps.

rick-rack: see *RIC RAC, RICK-RACK.

rickshaw, ricksha. (Later *attrib.* examples.)

1915 G. FRANKAU *Tid'apa* ii. 10 'Come here. Come up here, dear,' they cry To the drunkly-waving seaman as his rickshaw-wheels roll by. **1923** D. H. LAWRENCE *Birds, Beasts & Flowers* 173 The rickshaw boys begin to understand. **1933** M. LOWRY *Ultramarine* iii. 144 The rickshaw-wallah ran away with us, his sandals padding. **1951** R. CAMPBELL *Light on Dark Horse* ii. 34 Zulu Rickshaw-pullers ..emptied quarts of heady 'tchwala'. **1969** *Observer* 29 Oct. 29/2 A posse of rickshaw-cycles and cyclists come tearing round the corner. **1973** *Country Life* 1 Nov. 1322/2, I found myself face to face with a hundred rickshaw-tricycle boys. **1977** 'S. LEYS' *Chinese Shadows* (1978) iii. 108 His father, a rickshaw 'boy', always beaten up by capitalists, was covered with welts and scars. **1977** *N.Y. Rev. Bks.* 14 Apr. 3/2 They were privileged to support servants and dealers, Chinese teachers.., horse boys, amahs, cooks, guides, ricksha men. **1978** *Chinese Lit.* XII. 13 He decides to become a rickshaw-puller, the lowest of the low.

ri·cky, *a.* *rare.* [f. RICK *sb.*[2] + -Y[1].] = RICKETY *a.* 2 c.

1922 D. H. LAWRENCE *Aaron's Rod* viii. 87 A maudlin crying to be loved, which makes your knees all go ricky.

ricky, var. *RICKEY.

ricky-tick (ri:ki͵ti·k), *sb.* and *a.* *slang* (chiefly *U.S.*). [Imitative.] **A.** *sb.* An even, repetitive, or monotonous rhythm, as in early jazz; old-fashioned 'straight' jazz or ragtime. **B.** *adj.* Of musical rhythm or tempo: even, repetitive, monotonous; of music: trite, old-fashioned, 'corny'. Also *transf.* and as *adv.* Cf. *RINKY-DINK *sb.* and *a.*, *RINKY-TINK *a.*

1938 *Brit. Empire Mod. Eng. Illustr. Dict.* 1257/1 Ricky-tick (*Am.*): Old-fashioned jazz. **1942** BERREY & VAN DEN BARK *Amer. Thes. Slang* § 578/31 Of tempo and tone... *clubhouse, hotel, rickty-tick* [*Index*, ricky-tick], gently softly. *Ibid.* § 579/2 'Straight jazz.' (Old-fashioned jazz, which reproduces the score faithfully, as distinguished from 'swing'.)..*ricky-tick. Ibid.* § 579/14 Outmoded; non-'swing', *ricky-tick.* **1958** *Gramophone* Dec. 328/2 A rather ricky-tick rhythm. **1967** *Time* 22 Sept. 61/1 It sizzles with musical montage, tricky electronics and sleight-of-hand lyrics that range between 1920s ricky-tick and 1960s raga. **1968** *N.Y. Times* 5 Feb. 29/1 To the ricky-tick of Guy Lombardo's 'I don't want to get well, I'm in love with a beautiful nurse', three maimed Army veterans fumble through a dance routine. **1968** *New Yorker* 18 May 6/2 A big red fire engine, peanut shells on the floor, and ricky-tick banjo music summon up the plinking eighteen-nineties, or whatever. **1969** *N.Y. Rev. Bks.* 21 Aug. 8/3 The rickytick, ingroup details sprinkled through the text. **1970** *Atlantic Monthly* June 104/1 Ricky-tick Conductor jointed like a walking-stick Insect, with silver glasses, silver punch, And silver seat in his sere serge. **1970** *Wall St. Jrnl.* 15 June 1/1 The critics..have dismissed the Welk brand of music as hopelessly square, bland ricky-tick rhythms aimed at a fading generation.

Hence **ri:cky-ti·cky** *a.* = *RICKY-TICK *a.*

1952 B. ULANOV *Hist. Jazz in Amer.* xiv. 157 They rejected his ricky-ticky beat with distaste. **1970** *Time* 12 Jan. 44/1 White music has always been very ricky-ticky, steppity-step, plunkety-plunk-banjo. **1976** *Times Lit. Suppl.* 23 Apr. 486/2 Weill's errant and loudly stated bass-line throwing up the odd chord that violently subverts the triteness of the ricky-ticky melody.

ricochee (ri·kǒʃi), repr. colloq. pronunc. of RICOCHET *sb.*

1903 KIPLING *Five Nations* 188 An' waits till the sights come on. For 'Im an' 'Er an' a hit (Direct or ricochee).

ricochet, *sb.* Add: **2. b.** *ricochet mound*; **ricochet word** (see quots.).

1902 *Kynoch Jrnl.* Apr.–May 80/2 At various points we have placed ricochet mounds, the first of which will catch any low or accidentally fired shot. **1881** *Brewer's Dict. Phr. & Fable* (ed. 12) 742/2 Reduplicated or Ricochet words, of intensifying force. Chit-chat, click-clack. **1967** W. & M. MORRIS *Dict. Word & Phr. Origins* II. 228 His hobby is collecting what he calls 'Siamese-twin words'..from *argy-bargy* to *zoot suit.* The word experts call these 'reduplicated words' or, in lighter moments, '*ricochet words*'.

ricochet, *v.* **2.** (Earlier example.)

1758 J. AMHERST *Jrnl. Siege of Louisbourg* in *Gentl. Mag.* XXVIII. 387/2 [Guns] to ricochet the works and the town.

‖ **ricordo** (rīko·rdo). Pl. **ricordi.** [It., lit. 'memory'.] A token of remembrance, souvenir; in *Art*, a copy made by a painter of a composition by another painter.

1926 *Contemp. Rev.* Dec. 770 Such is the little Play acted in Azusa, and for me a beautiful last *ricordo* of a place I had learned to love. **1974** *Times Lit. Suppl.* 25 Jan. 73/5 This much disputed, and admittedly unusual, drawing may in fact be Rembrandt's 'ricordo' of a composition by another, earlier, artist. **1975** *Ibid.* 21 Mar. 300/3 The authors have analysed La Tour's paintings one by one, paying attention to, and discussing, even the poorest and most miserable copies or *ricordi* of his compositions.

‖ **ricotta** (rīkǫ·tă). [It.: see RICOCT.] A kind of Italian cottage cheese. Also attrib. in *ricotta cheese*.

1877 *Encycl. Brit.* VI. 772/2, 524,700 lb of 'ricotta', a fresh common cheese made after the butter and cream have been for the most part removed from the milk. **1923** [see *milky-sapped* s.v. *MILKY *a.* 5]. **1966** T. PYNCHON *Crying of Lot 49* i. 10 Her trip to the market..to buy ricotta and listen to the Muzak. **1971** *Sunday Times* (Colour Suppl.) 28 Mar. 39/1 *Ricotta*... Made of ewe's milk (or rather the whey left over from making Pecorino) it is soft, unsalted and short-lived. Ricotta is particularly popular in Rome..where it is eaten with salt and black pepper or with sugar and cinnamon. Used extensively in Italian cookery... It is also the basis of two popular puddings. **1978** *Chicago* June 231/1 For dessert, try casatelli, delicate ravioli like dumplings filled with ricotta and sprinkled with cinnamon and sugar. **1981** *Times* 9 Apr. 9/7 Fritters of soft ricotta cheese... For Easter ricotta fritters are flavoured with grappa.

ric-rac, rick-rack (ri·kræk). *Fashion.* Also as one word. [Origin unknown: perh. reduplicated form of RACK *v.*[3] or RICK *v.*[2]] A decorative zigzag braid used as a trimming for garments. Also *attrib.*

1884 I. M. RITTENHOUSE *Jrnl.* 25 Aug. in R. L. Stout *Maud* (1939) 326 Splendid sempstress—clothes nearly all done—Rickrack and feather-edge on the moon. **1911** C. HARRIS *Eve's Second Husband* 279 A wife who wore rick-rack braid on her petticoats. **1926** *Daily Colonist* (Victoria, B.C.) 7 Jan. 11/1 (Advt.), House Dresses..trimmed with attractive colored chintz and rick-rack braid. **1941** *Amer. Speech* XVI. 99 A *wee-waisted* model may have alliterative *ric-rac-rows.* **1956** J. POTTS *Diehard* i. 5 Rick-rack trimming around the collar and long sleeves. **1960** *Harper's Bazaar* Apr. 76 Loosely sashed sheath..trimmed with black ric-rac. **1972** *Vogue* Feb. 51/1 White cotton piqué decorated here by waves of ricrac. **1974** *Sumter* (S. Carolina) *Daily Item* 24 Apr. (Belk Stroman Advts. Suppl.) 13 'Our Miss B' flare skirt, shirt-look bodice with white collar or ric-rac. **1976** *Daily Tel.* 29 Oct. 17/3 Yves St Laurent..resolutely translated autumn's long wool peasant skirts into spring's long cotton ones. He threw rick-rack and red curtain bobbles on them.

Hence **ri·c-rac, ri·ck-rack** *v. trans.*

1972 *Vogue* Feb. 46/2 *Poppy dress*..pinked and ric-racked. **1974** *State* (Columbia, S. Carolina) 3 & 4 Mar. G12 (*caption*) A green tablecloth rickracked with pink, blue and lemon completes the look.

rictus. Add: **2. a.** (Later examples.) Also *transf.* and *fig.*

1912 R. B. C. GRAHAM *Charity* 12 A skin like parchment, which gave her face, when worked upon by a slight rictus in the nose she suffered from, a look, as of a horse about to kick. **1957** L. DURRELL *Justine* II. 107 This ghastly *rictus* gouged out in his taut cheeks. *a* **1963** S. PLATH *Crossing Water* (1971) 21 Under the eyes of the stars and the moon's rictus He [*sc.* an insomniac] suffers his desert pillow. **1969** *Listener* 2 Jan. 27/3 To the comedians I like I find I go more than half-way. I find myself sitting with a rictus of amused incredulity and surprise. **1974** R. ADAMS *Shardik* xlix. 397 A child with a continuous twitching of the head gazed up wide-eyed, his mouth gaping in a kind of rictus of startled alarm. **1977** 'M. INNES' *Honeybath's Haven* iv. 38 The muscular effort required..had the effect of contorting his features into a ferocious *rictus*.

rid, *v.* Add: **I. 1. c.** (Later dial. and U.S. examples.)

1891 HARDY *Tess* III. lii. 199 Are you house-ridding today? **1919** T. K. HOLMES *Man from Tall Timber* xii. 144 I'll rid up the place and get our dinner. **1939** F. THOMPSON *Lark Rise* vi. 104 Fireplaces were 'ridded up', and tables and floors were scrubbed.

riddance. Add: **5. b.** (Further examples.) Also in phr. *good riddance of* (or *to*) *bad rubbish*.

1847 DICKENS *Dombey* (1848) xliv. 438 A good riddance of bad rubbish!.. Get along with you, or I'll have you carried out! **1863** [in Dict.]. **1924** M. IRWIN *Still she wished for Company* xviii. 220 If all they say downstairs is true..it's good riddance to bad foreign rubbish. **1928** S. SASSOON *Mem. Fox-Hunting Man* VIII. ii. 287 It may well be wondered how the Hunt had survived the despotism of the old-world grandee, with whom previous Masters had been obliged to cooperate (as 'best Master we've ever had' while they reigned, and 'good riddance of bad rubbish' when they resigned). **1975** *Times* 4 July 5/3 The American War of Independence..can be seen, as George III consoled himself by looking at it, as good riddance to bad rubbish. **1977** H. FAST *Immigrants* II. 110 A dead Chinese was good riddance to bad rubbish.

ridden, *ppl. a.* **2.** (Later example.)

1976 *Leicester Advertiser* 26 Nov., Best ridden Dartmoor awards have been anonymously donated at the NPS and Bath and West shows, and there is also the Allendale Award for the most versatile pony under saddle—for ridden classes have for a long time been a poor relation in all pony breed classes.

riddle, *sb.*[1] Add: **4.** *riddle-rid* adj.

1918 W. DE LA MARE *Motley* 44 Old and alone, sit we, caged, riddle-rid men.

5. *riddle-ballad, -book* (earlier example), *-game, -song*; **riddle canon** (see quot. 1889).

1816 JANE AUSTEN *Emma* I. x. 176 There go you and your riddle-book one of these days. **1889** *Cent. Dict.* s.v. *canon*[1], *Enigmatical canon,..riddle canon,* in old music, a canon in which one part was written out in full and the number of parts was given; the remaining parts were to be written out by the student in accordance with the requirements of an enigmatical inscription written upon the music. **1934** WEBSTER, Riddle ballad. **1950** M. J. C. HODGART *Ballads* i. 14 The 'riddle' ballads are at the beginning of Child's collection... The basic theme of these is that of a mortal outwitting a supernatural being by quickness of wit, and of the magic power of the Word expounded in riddles. **1954** J. R. R. TOLKIEN *Fellowship of Ring* 21 Gollum challenged Bilbo to the Riddle-game. **1965** M. SPARK *Mandelbaum Gate* ii. 32 She heard the familiar lilt of the riddle song, 'One Kid', from the lips of her lolling cousins.

riddle, *sb.*[2] Add: **4. riddle-board, -land** (see quots.).

1818 *Massachusetts Spy* 14 Oct. 4/3 'And what..is riddle land?' That which is of so open and loose a texture as to let the rain falling on it pass through it. **1969** E. H. PINTO *Treen* 141 Riddleboards were formerly used in the North of England and Scotland for making oatcake or oatbread.

riddle, *v.*[1] **2. c.** (Later example.)

1941 T. S. ELIOT *Dry Salvages* v. 14 Release omens By sortilege, or tea leaves, riddle the inevitable With playing cards.

riddle, *v.*[2] Add: **2. a.** (Earlier *fig.* and later examples.)

1872 'MARK TWAIN' *Curious Dream* 87, I dosed him with bad jokes, and riddled him with good ones. **1916** 'BOYD CABLE' *Action Front* 209 You machine-gunners riddling holes in a target or a row of posts.

b. (Later *fig.* example.)

1928 *Daily Mail* 3 Aug. 16/7 London is riddled through and through with receivers of textile goods.

riddle-bread, -cake. (Later examples.) Also *U.S. dial.*

1915 *Dialect Notes* IV. 240 *Riddle cakes,* griddle cakes. **1969** E. H. PINTO *Treen* 141 In Scotland and North-east England, oatbread was often known as haver or riddle cake and in North-west England as haverbread or riddlebread.

riddled, *ppl. a.*[1] For *rare*—[1] read *rare* and add later example.

1918 G. FRANKAU *One of Them* x. 76 '*À vous le plein, Madame.*' Keen brains unravel The riddled sum. '*Deux louis — soizante-dix* [sic].'

riddler[1]**.** (Later example.)

1978 *Jrnl. Lancs. Dialect Soc.* XXVII. 24 The earliest recorded English riddles, in which the riddler looks at familiar objects in an unfamiliar light.

riddling, *vbl. sb.*[1] (Later *attrib.* example.)

1969 G. M. BROWN *Orkney Tapestry* 60 Into the riddling region where gods and men negotiated only an elite could trespass—men who had made a long study of the black arts.

ride, *sb.*[1] Add: **1. a, b.** (Earlier example.) Also esp. in colloq. phr. *to have* (or *give*) *a rough* (*easy*, etc.) *ride*.

1759 J. WESLEY *Jrnl.* 13 Aug. (1764) 74 Monday, 13. I took a little ride to Croydon. **1969** S. HYLAND *Top Bloody Secret* ii. 234 Judging by what he said on the phone, he won't give you an easy ride. **1969** *Times* 11 July 8/8 The new 'town managers' seem to be having a rough ride in London. **1974** *Times* 5 Nov. 15/1 President Giscard d'Estaing has had a fairly quiet ride until now. **1976** *Eastern Even. News* (Norwich) 9 Dec. 10/4 It seems to me that he is being given an unnecessarily rough ride. **1978** *Times* 17 Jan. 19/5 Union officials..met the new Leyland chief... He was given a rough ride.

f. *to take for a ride* and varr. (orig. *U.S.*): (*a*) *colloq.* to tease; to mislead deliberately, to hoax, to cheat; (*b*) *slang* to take on a car journey with the intention of murdering or kidnapping.

(*a*) **1925** *Dialect Notes* V. 344 *Take for a ride,* jolly; josh. **1929** J. P. MCEVOY *Hollywood Girl* vii. 109 What was the name of that girl he was crazy about?.. Dugan. But Jack isn't bragging about it. She certainly took him for a ride. **1931** E. LINKLATER *Juan in Amer.* IV. ii. 283 'Do you mean that?' asked Mr. Adelaide nervously. 'Nonsense,' said Mr. Boles. 'He's taking you for a ride.' **1956** A. WILSON *Anglo-Saxon Att.* II. i. 203 But for Vin, there were winks and the tongue stuck in the cheek, the wide boy who wasn't to be taken for a ride by anyone. **1962** *John o' London's* 25 Jan. 94/3 A young American teacher who goes to Persia and gets taken for quite a few rides. **1973** 'D. JORDAN' *Nile Green* ix. 43 She said, quickly, '..Are you an expert?'.. I said, 'Not at all... You could take me for a ride any day you chose.' **1976** J. I. M. STEWART *Memorial Service* xvi. 271 The provost had taken me on a ride to Otby in more senses than one.

(*b*) **1927** *Vanity Fair* (N.Y.) Nov. 132/3 'Taking him for a ride' is underworld for enticing a person to death. **1929** *Sun* (Baltimore) 15 Mar. 2/6 Possibility that Joseph Drell, wealthy cigar store owner, may have been 'taken for a ride' by underworld enemies, tonight was engaging the attention of detectives investigating his kidnapping. **1931** F. L. ALLEN *Only Yesterday* x. 261 Another favourite method was to take the victim 'for a ride': in other words, to lure him into a supposedly friendly car, shoot him at leisure, [etc.]. **1933** WODEHOUSE *Heavy Weather* i. 12 Perhaps some Duke who doesn't want to see himself in the 'Peers I Have Been Thrown Out Of Public Houses With' chapter has been threatening to take him for a ride. **1935** 'J. GUTHRIE' *Little Country* ix. 166 When they shoot a man [in America] they call it sending him for a ride. **1941** *Strand Mag.* Aug. 332/1 You're not only being taken for a sail, Mrs. de Courcy, but also for a ride. Your passage-money back to Singapore is just five thousand pounds. **1944** E. S. GARDNER *D.A. calls Turn* vii. 64 These persons whispered that some day Carr would mysteriously disappear, and no one would ever know whether he had quietly faded into voluntary oblivion or had been 'taken for a ride'. **1979** T. BARLING *Olympic Sleeper* ix. 103 Not Costas driving... They must be dumping the cab. Or taking Costas for a ride.

g. *slang.* An act of sexual intercourse. Cf. RIDE *v.* 3 and 16.

1937 PARTRIDGE *Dict. Slang* 696/2 *Ride,*..an act of coïtion. **1977** J. B. HILTON *Dead-Nettle* xviii. 155 I'd slipped in once or twice while Frank was out. She deserved a slow ride in-between times with that big old oaf. **1981** 'J. STURROCK' *Suicide most Foul* i. 25 He reckons to have a ride on her..even if he has to marry her to get it.

h. *for the ride*: for fun; as an observer only. *colloq.*

1960 WENTWORTH & FLEXNER *Dict. Amer. Slang* 427/1 *Ride, go along for the,* to join in passively, usually for the fun of it, without making an active contribution. **1963** 'J. MELVILLE' *Burning is Substitute for Loving* ii. 41 Everyone went to the supermarket for the ride. It was fun. **1968** *Economist* 12 Oct. 99/1 The pension funds could keep buying equities for the ride. **1971** M. BABSON *Cover-up Story* xi. 122 They're a little nervous about getting a courtroom full of fans just along for the ride. **1977** J. WAINWRIGHT *Nest of Rats* II. iv. 167, I wouldn't know—I am along strictly for the ride.

i. *spec.* in *Surfing*.

1968 *Surfer Mag.* Jan. 48/2 I'd try and get long rides. **1971** *Times* 9 Aug. 5/2 You compulsively turn and start paddling your board out to sea for 'just one more ride'. **1975** *Oxf. Compan. Sports & Games* 1005/2 For a straight-wave ride, the surfer stands with flexed joints in a relaxed stance with one foot either side of the lateral and longitudinal centre line.

4. a. (Further examples.)

1949 'J. TEY' *Brat Farrar* xiv. 123 He's a lovely ride. And he can jump anything you can see the sky over. **1963** A. DUGGAN *Story of Crusades* iv. 39 The warhorse was usually a stallion, which made it a nuisance in camp and an uncomfortable ride. **1977** *Horse & Hound* 10 June 36/1 (Advt.), Brown gelding... A great ride, would be ideal for Master.

b. A motor vehicle. *N. Amer. slang.*

1930 *Amer. Speech* VI. 134 *Ride,* n., automobile. **1972** C. MILNER *Black Players* v. 136 With his unspectacular conservative suits and modest 'ride' (a Toyota station wagon).

c. A roundabout or other device on which one rides at an amusement park or fair. Chiefly *U.S.*

1934 in WEBSTER. **1953** *Amer. Speech* XXVIII. 117 *Kiddie rides, n.,* general term for the merry-go-round and other rides which attract children's patronage. **1966** T. PYNCHON *Crying of Lot 49* v. 121 Down at the city beach, long after the pizza stands and rides had closed, she walked unmolested. **1968** D. BRAITHWAITE *Fairground Archit.* 103 In 1927 Joseph and Robert Lusse of Philadelphia produced an accomplished design. Since that time, 'Dodg'ems' have been the most consistently popular ride on the fairground. **1977** H. FAST *Immigrants* II. 138 He'd go on all the rides with me.

5. b. *Jazz slang.* A swinging rhythm; also, an improvised passage in such a rhythm.

1936 *Delineator* Nov. 49/2 *Ride,* easy-going rhythm. **1952** B. ULANOV *Hist. Jazz. in Amer.* (1958) xi. 122 In that famous record he gave the chords of the tonic and the dominant a noisy ride. **1956** E. HUNTER *Second Ending* I. 75 You give him all the hot rides. **1970** P. OLIVER *Savannah Syncopators* 37 The 'ride' of a New Orleans jazz band, the 'slow and easy' slow-drag of a country blues band, have no counterpart in the forceful thrust of the multilineal drum rhythms. **1973** J. WAINWRIGHT *Pride of Pigs* 175 The washboard player tapped the off-beats..lifting the rhythm and giving it ride.

6. a. The characteristic motion of a motor vehicle or other means of transport in respect of passenger comfort, smoothness, etc.

1937 [see *ride-control* below]. **1947** [see *ride comfort* below]. **1962** *Which? Car Suppl.* Oct. 126/2 The Sunbeam Rapier's ride was choppy. **1974** *Country Life* 21 Feb. 378/3 The ride is very comfortable, with normal road shocks eliminated before reaching the occupants. **1980** *Times* 29 Feb. 23 Ride is on the firm side, but acceptably so, and the same can be said of the seats.

b. The quality of a horse's gait when being ridden.

1955 H. SMITH *Horseman through Six Reigns* xix. 189 Most of the Irish hunters are shown fairly green... Their ride can either improve or deteriorate..after two or three years in England. **1955** *Times* 10 June 4/2 Mr. Deptford's grey Valeta..stood second, and Miss Wainwright's chestnut Lovely Boy third. With hacks nearly everything is in the ride.

7. *attrib.* and *Comb.*, as (sense 1 a) *ride-sharing*; (sense *1 f) *ride job, killing*; (sense 2 a) *ride-gate, -path, -side*; (sense *5 b) *ride solo, tempo*; (sense *6 a) *ride characteristic, comfort, control, height, luxury*; **ride cymbal,** a cymbal used by jazz drummers for keeping up a continuous rhythm (opp. to a *crash cymbal* used mainly for single 'crashes').

1961 *Which? Reports on Cars* 14 *Ride characteristics* for driver and passenger are assessed subjectively and, where possible, measured by instruments. **1947** Ride comfort [see *gust effect* s.v. *GUST *sb.*[1] 3]. **1977** *Lancashire Life* Mar. 118/3, I..was impressed with its ride comfort over rough mountain roads. **1937** *Times* 13 Apr. (Brit. Motor Suppl.) p. xxxviii/2 The chassis specification includes a 21-h.p. 6-cylinder engine..; ride-control hydraulic shock-absorbers front and rear. **1956** M. STEARNS *Story of Jazz* (1957) xviii. 234 Clarke made the single right-hand 'ride' or 'top' or 'front' cymbal the rhythmic center. **1965** *Crescendo* Oct. 10/1 The ride cymbal with snare/bass drum independence.. is a free lesson for any student of jazz drumming. **1977** *New Yorker* 9 May 51/1 He had a ride cymbal, and he played it.. four beats to the bar. **1919** J. MASEFIELD *Reynard* I. 53 A jam of horses in the spinney, Close to the ride-gate. **1971** *E. Afr. Standard* (Nairobi) 10 Apr. 8/6 Suspension is fully independent all round, incorporating automatic ride-height control. **1978** *Hot Car* June 91/2 The ride-height of cars used for towing caravans and trailers. **1955** *People* (Austral.) 5 Oct. 5/2 No policeman would have to risk being mistaken for a mobster doing a gangland ride job. **1935** A. J. POLLOCK *Underworld Speaks* 96/2 *Ride killing,* when assassins take the victim for a ride in an automobile and slay him. **1979** *Jrnl. R. Soc. Arts* Dec. 38/2, I shall always remember the impression of ride luxury when we first interconnected that Alvis. **1892** B. POTTER *Jrnl.* 25 Oct. (1966) 293 There were rights-of-way, ridepaths over the hills, notably by the Spittal. **1973** *Sunday Bull.* (Philadelphia) 7 Oct. (Parade Suppl.) 14/3 The Minnesota Highway Department has set up a state employees' ride-sharing operation. **1977** *Chicago Tribune* 2 Oct. XIII. 3/2 For a considerable number of motorists polled, it would take $2 gasoline to push them into sacrificing pleasure driving or switching to..ride-sharing to get to their jobs. **1943** J. W. DAY *Farming Adventure* xvii. 187 For two miles we rode through half-grown timber, the ride-sides choked with thistles, blue- and red-headed, tangled with long grasses and tall flowering weeds. **1949** *Ebony* June 41 When Willie plays a ride solo, he is better received than anyone else in the band. **1940** *Swing* Jan. 25 The other side is *Bugle Call Rag* at ride tempo.

ride, *v.* Add: **I. 1. d.** *to ride for a fall* (earlier and later examples).

1884 E. W. HAMILTON *Diary* 16 Jan. (1972) II. 544 He [*sc.* Goschen] believes that C. [*sc.* Chamberlain] is 'riding for a fall' and has doubts as to his loyalty towards Mr. G. **1904** G. B. SHAW *Let.* 31 Dec. (1972) II. 479, I conclude that on turning it over you have concluded that you had better ride for a fall than face the economies that would be needed to allow the shop to clear itself. **1951** J. D. SALINGER *Catcher in Rye* xxiv. 242, I have a feeling that you're riding for some kind of a terrible, terrible fall. **1963** *Review & Herald* 31 Jan. 7/3 People who spread their physical favors around over all the available members of the opposite sex are riding for a fall in the realm of final, lasting happiness with any one person.

h. *to ride herd on* (rarely, *over*): to guard and control (a herd of cattle) by riding on its perimeter; also *transf.*, to keep guard over, be in charge of, keep in check; to boss, subject to discipline. *N. Amer.*

1897 A. H. LEWIS *Wolfville* xviii. 235 The way them pore darkened drunkards rides herd on each other..is as good as sermons. **1902** —— *Wolfville Nights* xviii. 266 I'm romancin' leesurly along the street when I encounters a party who's ridin' herd on one of these yere telescopes. **1906** H. GREEN *At Actors' Boarding House* 367 Buck was riding herd on all the Dutch ovens in camp, filled with baking bannocks. **1940** *Variety* 3 Apr. 39 The name bands are come on for the record jockeys who ride herd over not only Decca records but all the others. **1944** *Sun* (Baltimore) 17 Nov. 8/6 Her mother-in-law..and a cousin of her husband..arrived in Albany to-day to ride herd on the Dewey small fry. **1955** R. P. HOBSON *Nothing too Good for Cowboy* vi. 51 Some of the horses would be night horses for riding herd on the cattle. **1973** *Whig-Standard* (Kingston, Ontario) 11 Aug. 7/1, I was riding herd on a hundred head of beeves. **1977** 'E. McBAIN' *Long Time no See* xi. 172 Two men who should be taking care of people getting robbed or mugged, go to waste our time instead riding herd on a bunch of street hoodlums.

i. *Jazz slang.* To play with an easy or easily flowing rhythm.

1929 T. WALLER (record title) Ridin' but walkin'. **1933** *Melody Maker* 23 Dec. 7/1 Ellington..never played the sort of music to cause Sonny Green to 'ride' in the Sidney-Mansie manner. **1938** *Metronome* Feb. 25 When they ride, you can't help getting a lift. **1977** J. WAINWRIGHT *Do Nothin'* xi. 184 When Ellington opens on an eight-bar piano intro..you know that..when the full outfit starts leaning back and riding, you are going to be lifted cloud-high.

j. —— *rides again*: someone or something makes a reappearance, usu. under different or unexpected circumstances or in modified form.

1939 (*film title*) Destry rides again. **1941** *Pleasures of Publishing* (Columbia Univ. Press) 3 Feb., Our good friend Helen Bower of the Detroit *Free Press* sends us a circular which..is headed, 'Blackstone Rides Again', and is an announcement for a new edition of Blackstone's Commentaries. **1961** C. WILLOCK *Death in Covert* xii. 203 One headline said: *Regency Rakes Ride Again.* **1972** J. WAINWRIGHT *Requiem for Loser* iv. 72 The publisher said: 'A sequel?'.. He [*sc.* the author] said: 'What d'you think we should call it? *Drover Rides Again,* or *Son of Drover?*' **1977** I. SHAW *Beggarman, Thief* III. iv. 240 Willie Abbott rides again.

k. *to ride work*: to exercise a racehorse.

1950 *Landfall* IV. 19 Gordon, did you know I ride work now in the mornings? **1959** M. GEE in C. K. Stead *N.Z. Short Stories* (1966) 271 He'd ridden work on the horse and knew her well. **1979** D. FRANCIS *Whip Hand* vi. 74 A work jockey is a lad who rides work on the gallops. *Ibid.* xiv. 174 My girl assistant says she saw you riding work on the Heath.

l. *spec.* in *Surfing*.

1963 *Observer* 13 Oct. 15/4 Riding a wave gives me a feeling of control. I know when I'm riding well and when I'm not. **1975** *Oxf. Compan. Sports & Games* 1005/2 A surfer who prefers to ride with his right foot forward is called a 'goofy footer'.

m. *to ride shotgun*: to travel as an (armed) guard in the seat next to the driver of a vehicle. Hence *transf.* and *fig.*, to act as a protector; to ride in the passenger seat of a motor vehicle. Chiefly *U.S.*

1963 B. S. JOHNSON *Travelling People* v. 107 And if you want anyone to ride shotgun for you, just you let Henry know. **1966** *National Observer* (U.S.) 26 Dec. 1/2 The gunships 'ride shotgun' on the highly vulnerable, more lightly armed transports. **1971** M. TAK *Truck Talk* 131 *Ride shotgun*, to ride in the passenger seat of the tractor. **1972** *National Observer* (U.S.) 27 May 1/1 Bob Earle was riding shotgun when suddenly my car skidded hard, its rear whipping out to the right. **1972** J. WAMBAUGH *Blue Knight* (1973) xv. 284 On nightwatch it's comforting sometimes to have someone riding shotgun or walking beside you. **1976** *Wymondham & Attleborough Express* 3 Dec. 2 He offered to ride shotgun for me. **1980** *Times* 21 Jan. 5/2 It was quite by chance that *The Times* found itself riding shotgun for the Red Army.

6. c. (Further examples.)

1931 *Daily Express* 21 Sept. 15/4 The course rode dead, and was not in favour of weight-carrying. **1974** *Country Life* 3 Oct. 925/3 While there were refusals in plenty, most of them due to rider-failure, the course rode well.

d. Of a motor vehicle: to admit of being driven, in respect of passenger comfort, etc. Cf. *RIDE *sb.*[1] 6 a.

1973 *Milestones* Winter 27/3 The car rode quite well, handling bad surfaces with aplomb.

II. 9. c. To pursue a course without intervention; to rest without further elaboration; to pass without comment; chiefly in phr. *to let* (something) *ride*, to leave alone; to allow to take its natural course.

1921 S. FORD *Inez & Trilby May* iii. 52 If I'd been brought up in a pawn shop I might describe 'em better, but, being no gem expert, I'll have to let it ride at that. **1933** H. L. ICKES *Diary* 14 Nov. (1953) I. 121, I was assured through Marx that the thing would be allowed to ride. **1938** 'R. HYDE' *Nor Years Condemn* 171 Ah, let her ride and see what happens. **1944** R. CHANDLER *Lady in Lake* xi. 63 'Kind of smelly work, to my notion.' I let that ride. **1959** H. HOLT *Wreath for Lady* xi. 68 'We'll let it ride like that for the present,' said the detective. **1961** J. WADE *Back to Life* vi. 56, I let it ride. I couldn't be bothered to reply. **1975** J. SYMONS *Three Pipe Problem* xvi. 158 You think you can just let it ride?

10. a. Also *fig.*

1956 B. HOLIDAY *Lady sings Blues* (1973) viii. 76, I knew that night I had the future of the whole band riding on me. **1964** G. B. SCHALLER *Year of Gorilla* (1965) iv. 87 They had tried to raise pigs and failed, and their luck now rode on a crop of turnips. **1972** *Village Voice* (N.Y.) 1 June 70/4 Basically, however, the election will ride on Lowenstein. **1976** *National Observer* (U.S.) 25 Sept. 10/2 A lot was riding on grapes, but the quality of the white wine made from the postwar harvest was poor.

11. b. (Further examples.)

1890 *Dialect Notes* I. 19 Your collar rides up behind. **1922** JOYCE *Ulysses* 528 The scanty, daringly short skirt, riding up at the knee to show a peep of white pantelette, is a potent weapon. **1951** *Sunday Times* 28 Oct. 11/4 'Ski pyjamas' with deeply-ribbed ankles and wrist-bands that won't ride up. **1971** *Guardian* 24 Aug. 9/1 The pantie..holds the blouse from riding up.

III. 14. c. (Later *transf.* examples.)

1974 *State* (Columbia, S. Carolina) 3 Mar. 1-D/3 Clemson pulled ahead midway the second half and rode the fine play of Terrell Suit to a 71-58 triumph over Georgia Tech. **1976** *Southern Even. Echo* (Southampton) 15 Nov. 13/2 Vinazzani appeared to ride a tackle from Earles and then fall over his own feet.

IV. 15. c. *to ride a hobby*: to pursue a favourite occupation or subject to an excessive degree. Cf. HOBBY *sb.*[1] 5.

1823, 1874 [see HOBBY *sb.*[1] 5]. **1875** *N. Amer. Rev.* CXX. 189 He must of course be naturally of a rather attitudinizing turn, fond of brooding and spouting and riding a theological hobby. **1876** J. FERGUSSON *Hist. Indian & Eastern Archit.* VI. ii. 425 It may look like riding a hobby to death, but I cannot help suspecting a wooden origin for it.

d. *to ride* (*the*) *gain* (Broadcasting): to reduce or increase the gain when the input signal becomes too large or too small, in order to keep the output within the limits of succeeding equipment. *colloq.*

1937 *Printers' Ink Monthly* May 40/3 *Ride gain*, to compress the volume range of a program electrically in order to transmit it over lines and equipment within proper limits. **1962** A. NISBETT *Technique Sound Studio* v. 100 Overmodulation on music must be avoided not by 'riding the gain' but by careful preparation—gradually pulling back on the gain control for half a minute or so before the peak is due.

e. *to ride the clutch*: in driving a motor vehicle, to keep one's foot too long on the clutch pedal, depressing it slightly.

1965 PRIESTLEY & WISDOM *Good Driving* iii. 30 The second common fault is 'riding the clutch'. **1968** *Practical Motorist* Feb. 622/4 Unless you are moving off, changing gear, or braking keep your foot away from the clutch pedal. 'Riding' the clutch is the fastest possible way of wearing out the friction lining.

16. (Later examples.)

1922 JOYCE *Ulysses* 762 That blackguard-looking fellow with the fine eyes peeling a switch attack me in the dark and ride me up against the wall without a word. **1978** S. ALLAN *Inside Job* iii. 41 She mounted him and rode him.. until they climaxed together.

17. c. To annoy, worry, rile. *colloq.* (orig. *U.S.*).

1918 H. C. WITWER *From Baseball to Boches* 359 Well, Joe, the mob begins to ride me. **1926** S. LEWIS *Mantrap* viii. 92, I guess I *have* been riding you pretty hard... I'm sorry. **1938** G. HEYER *Blunt Instrument* viii. 155 They won't arrest you. You needn't let that bugbear ride you. **1940** R. CHANDLER *Farewell, my Lovely* iii. 22 Go ahead and ride me. Everybody else does. **1948** F. BROWN *Murder can be Fun* (1951) vii. 104 Dineen didn't like that so he rode Jerry every chance he had. **1959** 'J. R. MACDONALD' *Galton Case* (1960) xvii. 140 Don't let it ride you. You're a willing man, but you can't take on responsibility for all the trouble in the world. **1973** N. GRAHAM *Murder in Dark Room* x. 65 'It's still murder.' 'That's what's riding me,' he said. 'I feel I almost had a hand in it.'

18. c. *spec.* in *Surfing*. Also *fig.*

1953 'S. RATTRAY' *Bishop in Check* 101 One-half per cent of them play tennis—or swim, or surf-ride. **1968** W. WARWICK *Surfriding in N.Z.* 2 The Duke..caught a wave and rode it until a short distance from the shore. **1969** *Times* 14 Apr. 6/7 Powerful enough to accelerate atomic particles, the particles 'riding' on the waves and gaining energy from them. **1970** *Studies in English* (Univ. Cape Town) I. 26 Most surfers leave the wave before they reach the soup, as it is tricky to ride. **1975** *Oxf. Compan. Sports & Games* 1005/1 A surfer can ride the wave in a straight line..to the beach or, by weight transference, turn his board to the right or left.

d. To travel in or on (a train, public transport vehicle, etc.), to be a passenger on. Chiefly *U.S.* Also in various phrases, chiefly connected with tramp life, as *to ride the blind*(*s*) [*BLIND *sb.* 10], to travel on a blind baggage car without paying one's fare; *to ride* (*the*) *cushions*, to travel luxuriously; to travel as a paying passenger; *to ride the rails*, to travel by rail (esp. without a ticket); *to ride the rods* [*ROD *sb.*[1] 9 g], to travel on a bar underneath a railway carriage or wagon.

1906, etc. [see below]. **1926** J. BLACK *You can't Win* vii. 80 'Let's ride the passenger trains,' I said. **1934** D. RUNYON in *Collier's* 3 Mar. 9/1 He is a great hand for riding the tubs back and forth between here and Europe. **1941** B. SCHULBERG *What makes Sammy Run?* vi. 122 He spent three weeks riding the street cars and the buses and trying to get by the studio reception desks. **1962** A. SHEPARD in *Into Orbit* 95, I honestly never felt that I would be the first man to ride the Mercury capsule. **1964** MRS. L. B. JOHNSON *White House Diary* 11 Sept. (1970) 195 They said they would be delighted to ride the train with me through North Carolina. **1972** *Publishers' Weekly* 24 Jan. 25 Bill is too young to remember when you could ride the subway for a nickel. **1978** *Detroit Free Press* 16 Apr. 1A/2 Willie Ramsey leaves his house on the west side of Detroit and rides buses for nearly two hours to reach his factory job.

1906 *Dialect Notes* III. 153 *Ride* (*the*) *blind*, *v. phr.*, to steal a ride on a blind baggage car or on a railway train. 'I've spent all my money; I'll have to *ride the blind back*.' **1950** A. LOMAX *Mr. Jelly Roll* 172, I..was ashamed to wire for money. So I decided to hobo..and, when the train pulled out the Denver station, I was riding the blinds.

1918 *Dialect Notes* V. 29 *To ride the cushions*, vb. phr... to travel first class. **1924** 'DIGIT' *Confessions 20th Cent. Hobo* 12 *Ride the cushions*, travel by passenger train in the orthodox manner. **1929** H. W. ODUM in A. Dundes *Mother Wit* (1973) 195 Thought I would ride cushions till my money give out. **1946** MEZZROW & WOLFE *Really Blues* i. 17 Riding the cushions on my way home made me think of another train ride I once took. **1972** *Amer. Speech 1968* XLIII. 289 *Ride the cushions*, to deadhead.

1946 MEZZROW & WOLFE *Really Blues* i. 17 We hit Cape Girardeau, Mo., dirty from riding the rails. **1977** *It* June 4/4 According to the Railways Act of 1889, Section 538.., it is an offence to ride the rails 'without having previously paid the proper fare'.

1907 J. LONDON *Road* 24 The tramp, snugly ensconced inside the truck, with the four wheels and all the framework around him, has the 'cinch' on the crew—or so he thinks, until someday he rides the rods on a bad road. **1925** G. H. MULLIN *Adventures of Scholar-Tramp* xi. 157 He wanted to get into Philly late that very afternoon. That would probably mean riding the rods of a fast mail on the Pennsylvania, he said, adding the casual hope that we would have no trouble finding rods fit to ride. **1935** J. T. FARRELL *Studs Lonigan* III. xvi. 377 Or maybe lose a leg or get killed under a train, or freeze to death riding the rods in winter. **1946** MEZZROW & WOLFE *Really Blues* i. 5 He spent years.. digging the riffs the wheels were knocking out when he rode the rods.

e. *to ride the lightning*: to suffer execution on the electric chair. *U.S. slang.*

1935 *Jrnl. Abnormal Psychol.* XXX. 364 *Ride the lightning*, to be electrocuted. **1965** *Daily Progress* (Charlottesville, Va.) 22 Mar., He pleaded for an opportunity to 'ride the lightning' of the electric chair. **1968** *Sunday Truth* (Brisbane) 15 Sept. 10/3 Four hours before I was 'to ride the lightning' in the chair a man came to the jail and confessed.

20. d. *transf.* To lead (a person) *off* a subject or away from a desired end; to side-track.

1908 A. CHAMBERLAIN *Politics from Inside* 128 We got several of our discussions in before them and 'rode them off', to use a racing phrase. **1928** 'SAPPER' *Female of Species* x. 161 Look here, Peter—we've got to try and ride them off.

21. a. *to ride on a rail* (earlier and later examples).

1837 HAWTHORNE *Twice-Told Tales* 161 The millmen.. [hesitated whether to] ride him on a rail, or refresh him with an ablution at the town-pump. **1843** DICKENS *Mart. Chuz.* (1844) xxi. 267 'If I can realise your meaning, ride me on a rail!' returned the General. **1854** S. SMITH *'Way Down East* x. 251 Others..proposed..giving him a good coat of tar-and-feathers and riding him out of town on a rail. **1929** E. LINKLATER *Poet's Pub.* xxiii. 253, I was ridden on a rail..in nothing but a torn shirt. **1949** *Sat. Even. Post* 2 July 67/1, I feel somewhat like the man who was being ridden out of town on a rail.

e. To bring *in* or introduce (a cinematographic picture) with an accompaniment of music.

1927 *Observer* 17 Apr. 3/3 The orchestral prelude is usually quite elaborate, and the picture is what is called 'ridden in'.

rideable, *a.* Add: **3.** Suitable for being hunted on horseback. *rare.*

1910 *Blackw. Mag.* Apr. 557/1 We were a long time before we found a rideable pig.

Rideal–Walker (ridī:l wǭ·kəɹ). [f. the names of Samuel *Rideal* (1863–1929) and J. T. Ainslie *Walker* (1868–1930), English chemists, who described the test in 1903 (*Jrnl. R. Sanitary Inst.* XXIV. 424).] *Rideal–Walker method* or *test*, a procedure for determining the germicidal efficiencies of disinfectants relative to phenol as a standard; hence *Rideal–Walker coefficient*, a measure of germicidal efficiency obtained by this method.

1907 *Jrnl. R. Sanitary Inst.* XXVIII. 379 He wished to draw attention to a few points..in connection with the practical details of the Rideal-Walker method of standardisation of disinfectants. **1919** *Jrnl. State Med.* XXVII. 62 The Rideal-Walker test..is difficult in execution on account of the attempt to include in one test all the variable factors. **1940** *Thorpe's Dict. Appl. Chem.* (ed. 4) IV. 32/1 The Rideal-Walker coefficient is obtained by dividing that dilution of the disinfectant which shows life in 2½ and 5 minutes, but no life thereafter, by that dilution of carbolic acid..which shows life in 2½ and 5 minutes, but no life thereafter. **1965** TURK & PORTER *Short Textbk. Microbiol.* v. 27 The Rideal-Walker coefficient was at one time widely used as a measure of the potency of an antiseptic. **1971** H. CHICK et al. *War on Dis.* ix. 89 The errors in the Rideal-Walker test were avoided by the modifications introduced in the Chick-Martin technique.

rided, *a.* (Further example.)

1938 J. W. DAY *Dog in Sport* v. 73 The bracken on his downland slopes was rided into broad squares.

rideman. Restrict † *Obs.* to sense in Dict. and add: Also **ride man, ride-man. 2.** *U.S. slang.* An operator of a roundabout or similar device at an amusement park or fair.

1926 *Amer. Mercury* Dec. 464/2 Every reader along Broadway knows that 'Lemon Stands Don't Interest Ride Men' means that poor-paying amusement parks fail to attract operators of roller-coasters, chute-the-chutes and carousels. **1942** BERREY & VAN DEN BARK *Amer. Thes. Slang* § 524/9 *Ride man*, a roller-coaster operator.

3. *Jazz slang.* A musician who improvises in a pronounced rhythm (see also quot. 1970). *U.S.*

1935 *Vanity Fair* (N.Y.) Nov. 38/2 *Ride-men* is the term applied to the improvisers of these licks. **1942** BERREY & VAN DEN BARK *Amer. Thes. Slang* § 576/4 *'Swing' musician*, ..rideman. **1945** *Band Leaders & Record Rev.* Mar. 20 Within a horn blast of Hollywood and Vine, the crossroads of Glamour-town, can be found many lairs of the hepcats—haunts of gates and ride men. **1970** C. MAJOR *Dict. Afro-Amer. Slang* 97 *Ride man*,..in jazz, the leading soloist, who establishes the pace.

ride-off, rideoff (rəi·dǫf). [f. RIDE *v.* + OFF *adv.*, after **play-off*, etc.] In a competitive event involving horsemanship: a round or phase of competition to resolve a tie or determine qualifiers for a later stage.

1973 *Country Life* 19 July 148/2 Mrs Lorna Johnstone winning on El Farruco, the horse with whom she reached the ride-off in the Olympic dressage. **1976** *Billings* (Montana) *Gaz.* 17 June 1-H/3 About 300 riders..qualified at regional rideoffs nationwide.

ride-on (rəi·dₗǫn), *a.* [f. RIDE *v.* + ON *prep.*] Of a power-driven lawn mower, etc.: on which the operator rides.

1969 *Times* 13 Dec. p. vii/5 He would more than recoup the cost of a 24 in. ride-on type of motor mower. **1972** *Country Life* 23 Mar. 703/3 A number of ride-on rotaries are also available. **1977** *Sunday Tel.* (Colour Suppl.) 5 June 11 (Advt.), The Simplicity range of ride-on tractors is the most competitive of its kind on the market.

rideout. Restrict † *Obs.*—[1] to sense in Dict. and add: **2.** *Jazz slang.* Also **ride-out.** A final chorus. Also *attrib.*

1939 *Metronome* May 19 *Pussy Willow* has a great ride-out. **1946** R. BLESH *Shining Trumpets* xii. 286 The Hot Seven's..ride-out ensemble sounds like a free-blowing parade band. **1952** B. ULANOV *Hist. Jazz in Amer.* vi. 52 Whether they are playing a solo.., or pushing a ride-out chorus to its obstreperous end, their harmonic thinking is vertical. **1962** *Jazz Monthly* Oct. 24 *Folk Forms* is reduced to a short bass solo, a short drum solo and a ride-out. **1977** *New Yorker* 8 Aug. 68/2 'On the Other Side of the Tracks'.. has an ebullient and remarkable rideout section.

rider. Add: **I. 2. e.** A passenger, esp. one using public transport. Now chiefly *U.S.*

1886 H. BAUMANN *Londinismen* 156/1 *Rider*.., Droschkenkutscher-Slang: Passagier, Fahrgast. **1930** [see *JOB *sb.*[2] 4 f].

1966 *Economist* 26 Feb. 798/1 The bankrupt suburban railway services in the East..want to get out of the money-losing passenger business entirely, letting their hundreds of thousands of daily riders fend for themselves as best they can. **1972** J. GORES *Dead Skip* (1973) xiii. 89 Kearny opened the rider's door for her: the tall blonde slid in. **1977** *New Yorker* 1 Aug. 28/1 Over the decade 1965 to 1975, the city's transit system, according to the Temporary Commission, lost twenty per cent of its riders.

f. *easy rider*: see *EASY *a.* 14 c.

g. *spec.* in *Surfing.*

1963 *Observer* 13 Oct. 15/4 The wave traps and dumps the rider, burying him for half a minute or longer. **1968** W. WARWICK *Surfriding in N.Z.* 13/1 Quite often a rider can be so locked in on a fast breaking wave that an ordinary pullout is impossible. **1975** *Oxf. Compan. Sports & Games* 1005/1 The belly-board rider slots in by paddling ahead of the oncoming wave.

6. b. Short for *circuit-rider* s.v. *CIRCUIT *sb.* 10.

1884 'C. E. CRADDOCK' *In Tennessee Mts.* I. 15 The rider says ther's some holp in prayer. *Ibid.* III. 143 All them Peels, the whole lay-out, war gone down ter the Settlemint ter hear the rider preach.

II. 14*. *Ophthalm.* Each of a set of linear opacities extending radially outward from the main opacity in some kinds of cataract.

1892 A. DUANE tr. *Fuchs's Text-bk. Ophthalm.* viii. 371 The riders on the periphery of the lamellar cataract originate from the fact that a second layer, peripherally situated with regard to the first, is beginning to become opaque, doing so first only at isolated spots corresponding to the equator of this first layer... These partial opacities embrace the equator of the inner opacity in front and behind; they ride upon it, as it were, whence the name riders. **1937** E. WOLFF *Dis. Eye* vi. 65 When viewed with the ophthalmoscope mirror..the disc and riders appear black or grey, and the clear lens around shows the normal red reflex. **1964** S. DUKE-ELDER *Parsons' Dis. Eye* (ed. 14) xix. 266 The opacity is usually sharply demarcated and the area of the lens within and around the opaque zone is clear, although linear opacities like spokes of a wheel (called riders) may run outwards towards the equator.

ri·der, *v. U.S.* [f. the sb.] *trans.* To strengthen (a fence) with riders.

1760 G. WASHINGTON *Diary* 15 Apr. (1925) I. 155 Good part of my new fencing that was not Riderd was leveld. **1787** *Ibid.* 27 Apr. III. 208 Women staking and ridering fence of the said field. **1858** J. A. WARDER *Hedges & Evergreens* 151 In Delaware..worm-fences, not ridered, were to be five feet high.

ridered, *a.* Add: **2.** (Earlier and later examples.) Also, of a building: having a ridered fence (*rare*). Cf. STAKE *sb.*[1] 2 c.

1852 *Trans. Mich. Agric. Soc.* III. 333 The staked and ridered domicil. **1855** *Chicago Weekly Times* 17 May 3/5 A whirlwind..scattered in every direction a strong 'staked and ridered fence'. **1885** 'C. E. CRADDOCK' *Prophet Gt. Smoky Mts.* xii. 231 The corn that Dordain had ploughed on the steep slope was high, and waved above the staked and ridered fence. **1946** G. FOREMAN *Last Trek of Indians* 169 All their farms were inclosed with good rail fences sufficiently high to secure their crops, many of them 'staked and ridered'.

ridership. Restrict *rare* to sense in Dict. and add: **2.** orig. *N. Amer.* The number of passengers (using a particular form of public transport). Also *attrib.*

1972 W. G. DAVIS *Urban Transportation Policy for Ontario* 5 This emphasis on the needs of the passenger and the improvement of service has enlarged ridership considerably. **1975** *Nature* 20 Feb. 580/2 This move has already been reflected in increased public transport 'ridership' figures in most communities. **1979** *Monitor* (McAllen, Texas) 9 July 8B/8 Allegheny [Airlines] operates no DC-10's, so it has picked up part of the ridership while those planes are grounded. **1981** *Daily Tel.* 7 Mar. 18 Costs are more or less fixed whatever the level of ridership and the only way of improving revenue is to attract more off-peak passengers.

ridge, *sb.*[1] Add: **4. a.** (Examples referring to submarine features.)

1944 A. HOLMES *Princ. Physical Geol.* xv. 319 In the shallower depths, over sub-tropical and tropical submarine banks and ridges, the shells of pteropods become abundant. **1954** W. D. THORNBURY *Princ. Geomorphol.* xviii. 462 Off the coast of California..there is a series of submarine basins and ridges similar in origin to the faulted structures landward from them. **1961**, etc. [see *MID-OCEAN *a.* b, *MID-OCEANIC *a.*]. **1977** A. HALLAM *Planet Earth* 99/3 Topographic forms can greatly influence currents, which may for example be..diverted round large hills and ridges.

c. For def. read: an elongated region of high barometric pressure. (Further examples.)

1914 *Seaman's Handbk. Meteorol.* (Meteorol. Office) vii. 81 An area of considerably higher barometric pressure.., either as a ridge..or in the more extensive form of an anticyclonic system. **1968** G. M. B. DOBSON *Exploring Atmosphere* (ed. 2) vi. 136 Troughs and ridges tend to circulate round the pole from west to east, but the general westerly wind at these heights has a much greater speed, and the air actually flows through these troughs and ridges. As the air blows into a low pressure trough it descends, while as it approaches a ridge it ascends. **1977** *Hongkong Standard* 14 Apr. 16/2 A ridge of high pressure covers the northern part of the south China Sea.

5. a. *transf.* (Later examples.)

1815 WORDSWORTH *Spanish Guerillas* in *Poems* II. 255 They have learnt to open and to close The ridges of grim War. **1895** W. B. YEATS *Death of Cuhoollin* in *Poems* 203 My father dwells among the sea-worn bands, And breaks the ridge of battle with his hands.

Comb. (Further examples.)

1919 J. MASEFIELD *Reynard* 51 Meadows ridge-and-furrow ploughed. **1958** *New Biol.* XXVI. 40 This is particularly well shown in grasslands in which there are marked variations in the height of the water table, such as the characteristic ridge and furrow grasslands of Britain. **1967** *Listener* 6 July 10/3 The head gardener to the Duke of Devonshire, Joseph Paxton, then invented ridge and furrow roofing, without rafters. **1974** C. TAYLOR *Fieldwork in Medieval Archaeol.* iii. 57 The ridge and furrow ends on a well-marked terrace which was both a trackway through the fields and a headland on which the plough was turned.

6. d. One of the many raised lines on the skin that are esp. noticeable on the fingers and palms of the hand and the sole of the foot.

1842 *Penny Cycl.* XXII. 86/2 Each such ridge shows on its summit a little furrow dotted with minute apertures. **1866** *Chambers's Encycl.* VIII. 756/1 The cross grooves that intersect the ridges and papillæ on the hands and feet. **1892** F. GALTON *Finger Prints* i. 1 Let no one despise the ridges on account of their smallness, for they are in some respects the most important of all anthropological data. **1920** E. WALLACE *Daffodil Mystery* xxviii. 220 Compare them!.. Line for line, ridge for ridge,..it is Milburgh's thumb-print. **1940** R. MORRISH *Police & Crime-Detection* x. 89 The ridges ('papillary' ridges as they are called) are formed by the mouths of the ducts of the sweat-glands. **1966** T. S. & C. R. LEESON *Histology* xiii. 250/1 Ridges are absent on the forehead, external ear, perineum, and scrotum. **1980** A. SILVERSTEIN *Human Anat. & Physiol.* vii. 97/2 The patterns of grooves and ridges we see are in the epidermis, but they do not originate there. They are produced by variations of folds and ridges in the underlying dermis.

7. a. *ridge-cap* (later example), *rope*; *ridge-roofed* adj.

1975 *Whig-Standard* (Kingston, Ontario) 4 Sept. 23/6 [Her] specialty is to make ridge cap shakes which are joined and overlapped alternately to make a leak-proof seal for the roof ridge. **1963** H. N. SAVORY in Foster & Alcock *Culture & Environment* iii. 34 A small rectangular, ridge-roofed house. **1933** Ridge rope [see *A TENT].

b*. In sense 4, as *ridge crest, prairie* (U.S.), *road* (U.S.), *system, -top, walk.*

1963 L. F. CHITTY in Foster & Alcock *Culture & Environment* vii. 179 From Onibury, the general trend of the way is clear, but its actual line is partly problematical: there is no longer an extended ridge-crest to give it definition. **1971** I. G. GASS et al. *Understanding Earth* xxi. 303/1 This relationship..poses the question of whether these volcanoes in the flanking basins originated on ridge crests and remained active while they were carried away upon the spreading sea-floor. **1977** A. HALLAM *Planet Earth* 97/3 The mean depth below the water surface of the world's ridge crests is 2700 m (8775 ft). **1882** *Econ. Geol. Illinois* II. 73 The prairies are..of two classes—those that are a little elevated and rather level near the lower course of the streams, and more elevated and rolling prairies on the higher ridges. The latter are the so-called 'ridge prairies'. **1817** *N. Amer. Rev.* IV. 185, I have returned by the ridge road. **1871** *Harper's Mag.* Dec. 46/2 These 'ridge-roads'.. form a system of ready-made highways. **1961** Ridge system [see *MID-OCEAN *a.* b]. **1971** I. G. GASS et al. *Understanding Earth* xxi. 302/2 Such volcanoes are mostly found along the ridge systems, particularly in the Atlantic. **1877** Ridge-top [in Dict., sense 7 c]. **1977** G. SCOTT *Hot Pursuit* viii. 74 The ground began to climb..and we were on a ridge-top... The mountain ranges stretched away. **1940** W. A. POUCHER *Lakeland through Lens* 43 Their proximity to the Buttermere Valley makes the western end of these ridges equally approachable, and incidentally very fine ridge walks either way. **1976** *Lancs. Even. Post* 7 Dec. 8/4 The switchback skyline of the Troutbeck fells..provides one of the best ridge walks in eastern Lakeland.

c. *ridge-bank, -chain, -line* (later example, in sense *6 d); (sense *6 d) *ridge characteristics, -count, system*; also *ridge-hop* vb.

1945 C. MANN in B. James *Austral. Short Stories* (1963) 72 The house they had on the ridge-bank was near the middle of the river bend. **1968** J. ARNOLD *Shell Bk. Country Crafts* 164 This..left the wagoner free to throw the ridge-chain over the back-pad. **1954** F. CHERRILL *Cherrill of Yard* vii. 75 The incriminating impressions of the ridge characteristics of a fragment of his palm. **1970** P. LAURIE *Scotland Yard* ix. 200 These ridge-counts go in as well. **1976** Ridge-count [see **phenylthiocarbamide*]. **1973** C. BONINGTON *Next Horizon* xviii. 247 The twin-engined Fokker Friendship ridge-hops over the tree-covered tentacles of the great peaks. **1940** R. MORRISH *Police & Crime-Detection* x. 91 Ridge-lines on the print may represent furrows which have become filled with blood on the finger. **1954** F. CHERRILL *Cherrill of Yard* vii. 69 The patterns on the ends of the fingers are simply a culmination of the ridge system which covers the whole of the palmar surface of the hands.

8. ridgeback = *Rhodesian ridgeback* s.v. *RHODESIAN *a.* 3 c; **ridge barrow** *Archæol.* [BARROW *sb.*[1] 3], a type of long, earthen grave-mound; **ridge cucumber,** a cucumber of a variety suitable for growing outside in a temperate climate, freq. grown on ridges of soil (cf. RIDGE *sb.*[1] 5 c); **ridge runner** *U.S. slang*, a southern mountain farmer, a hill-billy; also in Blacks' use, any white person; **ridge tent** (see quot. 1963); **ridgewise** *adv.*, in the manner of a ridge.

1937 *Our Dogs* 10 Dec. 886/3 The ridge in the breed..is present in practically every Ridgeback puppy. **1945** L. G. GREEN *Where Men Still Dream* 167 The finest type of Bushman hunting dog, a light brown ridgeback mongrel with dark stripes and a trace of the greyhound in its appearance, is now verging on extinction. **1977** P. C. VENTER *Soweto* 51 A ridgeback yawned and got up from the polished door step. **1951** *Field Archæol.* (Ordnance Survey Prof. Papers No. 13) (ed. 3) 15 The whole affair, which belonged to Neolithic times, was..interpreted as an eccentric form of long barrow to which the term 'ridge barrow' has been applied. **1963** *Ibid.* (ed. 4) 28 A variant of the earthen long barrow which seems to be confined at present to Dorset is the so-called 'ridge-barrow' which was found during the excavation of Maiden Castle near Dorchester. **1851** Ridge cucumber [in Dict., s.v. RIDGE *v.* 4 a]. **1933** H. H. THOMAS *Pop. Encycl. Gardening* 257/2 The plants must be grown out in a greenhouse or frame, with the exception of the Ridge Cucumber and the Gherkin, which can be grown out of doors in summer. **1962** *Listener* 25 Oct. 698/1, 2 small ridge cucumbers. **1933** *Amer. Speech* VIII. III. 31/1 *Ridge runner*, originally an Arkansas, rather than a Kentucky, hill billy. Any uncouth, stupid fellow. **1947** A. M. TROUT *Greetings from Old Kentucky* 9 While strolling through the woods one day with my friend, Bill Curry, a ridge runner from London, in Laurel County, we came upon a large bunch of hogs. **1966** *Publ. Amer. Dial. Soc.* 1964 XLII. 31 The most characteristic feature of Negro terms for Caucasian is the tendency to expand particularized designations for Caucasians to include all members of the race, e.g., terms for poor Southerners:..*ridgerunner* [etc.]. **1913** J. F. M. H. STONE *Caravanning & Camping-Out* xiv. 125 The tent I have the most liking for..is the type known as 'ridge tent', 'patrol tent', or 'emigrant tent'. **1926** E. E. REYNOLDS *Camping for All* iii. 13 Stanley..states that one of these double-roof ridge tents withstood three hundred days of rain. **1963** *Camping* ('Know the Game' Series) 3/2 *Ridge Tents.* These have long sides to the roof supported by upright poles at each end... A ridge tent with roof running down to the ground is called an A-tent. **1977** *Grimsby Even. Tel.* 5 May 3/6 (Advt.), Wanted, small ridge tent with fly-sheet. **1725** Ridge-wise [in Dict., sense 7 b]. **1743** W. ELLIS *Mod. Husbandman* Nov. vii. 316 They..cover the Turneps and Foss with Earth, Ridge-wise. **1902** J. BUCHAN *No-Man's-Land* i. 5 A sort of plateau, benty and rock-strewn, running ridge-wise above a chain of little peaty lochs.

ridge, *sb.*[2] For † *Obs.* read '*Obs.* exc. *U.S.*' and add: (Later example.) Also, any metal coin.

1931 *Writer's Digest* Oct. 29 *Ridge*, a gold coin of any denomination. **1935** *Amer. Speech* X. 13/2 *Chink*, metal money; loose change. (Obs.) Modern *ridge, coin.* **1955** *Publ. Amer. Dial. Soc.* XXIV. 78 Pockets were actually picked for metal coins—*ridge* or *smash.*

ridge (ridʒ), *a. Austral. slang.* [f. RIDGE *sb.*[2]] Good, all right, genuine.

1938 PARTRIDGE *Dict. Slang* (ed. 2) 1026/2 *Ridge*, adj., good; valuable: Australian. **1953** K. TENNANT *Joyful Condemned* i. 4 'It's ridge, Hec,' she assured him. 'He won't come here again.' **1971** D. IRELAND *Unknown Industrial Prisoner* vii. 130, I convinced her the whole thing was ridge!

ridgeling. (Further example.)

1974 E. C. STACEY *Peace Country Heritage* ii. 103 Reddon studied the occurrence of ridglings in boars and sought to determine if it was a hereditary trait, which it proved to be.

ridge-pole. Add: **2.** (Earlier example.) Also *fig.*

1814 *Niles' Weekly Reg.* V. 322/2 At the time I left the boat the waters were about midway on the roofs of the houses generally, and quite to the ridge poles of several. **1955** E. POUND *Classic Anthol.* III. 184 High, pine-covered peak full of echos, Proud ridge-pole of Heaven.

ridger. Add: **1.** (Earlier example.)

1733 W. ELLIS *Chiltern & Vale Farming* 322 Two Ropes or Chains..are held by the Ridger of the Cart-saddle.

2. (Further examples.)

1947 T. HENNELL *Countryman at Work* 70 The 'free ends' of the thatch (where the building ends vertically, and the thatch cannot be continued round the corners) must be made up to the proper thickness with long rods or ridgers, which are first bent upwards to a right angle, pinned in the edges of thatch, finally bent again and pinned down across it. **1977** *Grimsby Even. Tel.* 5 May 3/6 (Advt.), BMB Iron Horse, in perfect working order, with two pair of wheels,.. plough, drag, skerry, potato lifter and ridger.

ridgey-dite (riːdʒi dəi·t), *a. Austral. rhyming slang.* [After *RIDGY-DIDGE *a.*] All right; = *RIDGE *a.*

1953 K. TENNANT *Joyful Condemned* xxx. 295 He'd tell you himself I'm ridgey-dite. I worked for him.

ridgie-didge, var. *RIDGY-DIDGE *a.*

Ridgway (ri·dʒwēi). The name of the *Ridgway* family, used *attrib.* and *absol.* to designate pottery and porcelain produced from 1792 by the brothers George (*c* 1758–1823) and Job Ridgway (1759–1814), or by their descendants.

1911 J. F. BLACKER *Nineteenth-Cent. Eng. Ceramic Art* ix. 207 To say that there will be little old Ridgway ware and china amongst future collections is to assume that fashion will never fail in its pursuit of fine specimens. That is probably true; useful articles stand in another class, and though there is fine old Ridgway it is not easy to get. **1960** H. HAYWARD *Antique Coll.* 239/1 Ridgway earthenware & porcelain. **1972** G. A. GODDEN *Illustr. Guide Ridgway Porcelains* ii. 10 It is extremely unlikely that we shall ever be able to identify positively the eighteenth-century Ridgway earthenwares. *Ibid.* 14 The Ridgway porcelain dessert and tea-wares do not at this pre-1830 period bear any factory trade-mark. **1974** *Encycl. Brit. Micropædia* VIII. 577/3 (*caption*) Ridgway porcelain inkpot, a caricature of Job Ridgway's wife..*c* 1810.

ridgy-didge (ri:dʒidi·dʒ), *a. Austral. slang.* Also **ridgie-didge, ridgy-dig, rigi-dig.** [Elaboration of *ridgy*, f. *RIDGE *a.* + -Y[6], -IE.] = *RIDGE *a.*

1953 BAKER *Australia Speaks* 102 *Ridgy-didge* or *ridgy-dig*.., honest, genuine, okay. **1953** R. BRADDON in I. Bevan *Sunburnt Country* 130 The phrase is used invariably either as a simple question 'Ridgy Didge?' or as an unequivocal assurance: 'Ridgy Didge!' **1963** L. GLASSOP *Rats in New Guinea* xii. 153 'It's ridgie-didge,' said Eddie. 'Spit me death.' **1968** *Courier-Mail* (Brisbane) 27 July 11 Strike me handsome! What a fair dinkum, dinki-di, rigi-dig, bonzer, curl-the-mo, nob of cods these O'Grady blokes are, mate! **1976** *Sunday Sun* (Brisbane) 1 Aug. (Fun Holiday Guide) 1/1 Just to prove I'm ridgie-didge, I talked to my friends at Sunday Sun.

ridiculosity. (Further examples.)

1773 J. HOADLY *Let.* 16 Nov. in D. Garrick *Private Corr.* (1831) I. 583 You seem now to give into Dr Goldsmith's ridiculosity in opposition to all sentimentality. **1960** C. ACHEBE *No Longer at Ease* xii. 119 Pat said it was all silly and ridiculous. She actually used the word *ridiculosity*, which made Obi smile internally.

ridiculous, *a.* Add: **1. c.** *slang.* Outstanding, excellent.

1959 *Jazz* Summer 209 His technique is ridiculous! **1960** D. CERULLI et al. *Jazz Word* 95 To a jazzman..*ridiculous* is wonderful. **1968** *Scottish Daily Mail* 3 Jan. 6 Superlatives ..gradually increased with the years into 'out-of-sight', 'ridiculous' and 'unbelievable'.

2. b. *adv.* Also *colloq.* (Further examples.)

1834 C. F. HOFFMAN *Winter in West* (1835) I. 270 Those Indians behaved most *ridiculous*. They dashed children's brains against the door-posts. **1976** *Daily Mirror* 11 Mar. 24/2 Don't talk ridiculous!

riding, *sb.* Add: **1.** (This ceased to be an official designation after Local Government reorganization outside Greater London on 1 Apr. 1974.)

2. b. *spec.* An administrative or electoral district in Canada. Also *transf.*

1792 in *Rep. Bureau Archives Ontario* (1906) IV. 180 The said county of Glengarry, bounded as afore said, shall be divided into two ridings. **1853** *Elora* (Ontario) *Backwoodsman* 21 Apr. 2/5 When I do seek the votes of the electors of the north riding, I shall fearlessly submit my qualifications and character to the judgment of all who can cast aside their personal feelings and look only to the public good. **1867** [in Dict.]. **1890** *Grip* (Toronto) 29 Mar. 213/1 In that riding the New Party had only 50 pledged members, but pulled nearly 800 votes. **1921** [see *BÂTONNIER]. **1957** *Maclean's Mag.* 6 July 36/2 At one time Spadina regularly returned J. B. Salsberg as an LPP member to the Provincial Legislature, a habit that inspired a waggish reporter to tag it the 'Little Red Riding'. **1970** D. WATERFIELD *Continental Waterboy* ii. 10 H. W. Herridge, C.C.F. member for West Kootenay, our M.P., gave a talk at Nakusp, warning of the considerable changes that might be expected in the economics of his riding. **1975** *Times Lit. Suppl.* 10 Oct. 1189/3 A communist member once sat briefly in parliament for a Montreal riding. **1978** *Toronto Star* 26 Feb. A4/3 The allegations are directed against Georges Marchais, 58, France's outspoken Communist leader who is standing for re-election by the 80,000 voters in the Kremlin riding of Val-de-Marne.

riding, *vbl. sb.* Add: **I. 1. e.** Provoking, teasing, annoying. *U.S. colloq.*

1927 *Amer. Speech* Dec. 167/2 *Riding*, being sarcastic. **1930** D. HAMMETT *Maltese Falcon* xviii. 220 The boy said: 'You bastard, get up and shoot it out if you've got the guts. I've taken all the riding from you I'm going to take.'

II. 5. a. *riding-blanket, -boot* (later examples), *-breeks, cap* (later example), *costume, gauntlet, hat* (later examples), *mac.*

1935 H. L. DAVIS *Honey in Horn* xi. 165 She pulled her riding-blanket down on her bare shoulders with a temperish jerk. **1851** HAWTHORNE *House of Seven Gables* i. 18 With such a tramp of his ponderous riding-boots as might of itself have been audible in the remotest of the seven gables, he advanced to the door. **1952** E. O'NEILL *Moon for Misbegotten* I. 56 He is dressed in..immaculately polished English riding boots with spurs. **1980** G. M. FRASER *Mr American* xxvi. 533 A field officer in Sam Browne, red tabs, and gleaming riding boots. **1916** W. OWEN *Let.* 10 Feb. (1967) 380 Brown has riding-breeks. **1976** *Alyn & Deeside Observer* 10 Dec. 21/6 (Advt.), Riding macs, riding caps with new collapsible peaks, hunting bowlers. Bargain price. **1944** A. CLARKE *Viscount of Blarney* 42 A Gallant in eighteenth-century riding costume appears at doorway. **1855** F. DUBERLY *Let.* 29 Jan. in E. E. P. Tisdall *Mrs. Duberly's Campaigns* (1963) iv. 124, 6 pairs of doeskin riding gauntlets, 7½. **1782** J. WOODFORDE *Diary* 24 Apr. (1926) II. 19 For a riding Hat for Nancy..pd. 1. 13. 6. **1811** JANE AUSTEN *Let.* 18 Apr. (1932) II. 69, I must have a straw hat, of the riding hat shape. **1978** 'F. PARRISH' *Sting of Honeybee* iv. 51 The other old lady..fitted them out with riding hats, and helped them on to small, fat, elderly ponies. **1961** M. KELLY *Spoilt Kill* II. 91 She was..wearing an old riding mac. **1974** L. DEIGHTON *Spy Story* xvi. 163 A figure in a dirty white riding mac.

b. *riding-quirt.*

1951 R. CAMPBELL *Light on Dark Horse* xxiii. 337 The dried penis of a bull which we carry in those parts in place of a riding-quirt.

c. *riding boat, carriage* (earlier example), *chair* (later example), *horse* (earlier and later examples), *-pony, stallion*; also of machinery on which the operator rides (cf. *RIDE-ON *a.*), as *riding mower, plough.*

1908 G. SANGER *70 Yrs. Showman* xvi. 57 My father was able to add 'riding' or 'over and over' boats, as they were called, to his peep-show and roundabouts. **1785** T. JEFFERSON *Notes Virginia* VIII. 158, 5,126 wheels of riding carriages. **1971** *Country Life* 11 Mar. 528/2 It is impossible to judge how many of these chamber horses, also called dandy horses and riding chairs, were made. **1641** *Rec. Early Hist. Boston* (1877) II. 61 Its ordered that all dry cattle shall be driven of the necke, and not be suffered to abide there, except Riding horses. **1714** *Essex Inst. Hist. Coll.* (1883) XX. 179 Voated that the Neck of Land..be granted and reserved for the use of the Town of Salem for a pasture for Milch Cows and Rideing Horses. **1940** W. FAULKNER *Hamlet* IV. i. 255 The tethered wagons and riding horses and mules. **1977** *Horse & Hound* 10 June 5/3 Our present efforts to breed riding horses. **1969** *Sears Catal.* Spring/Summer 5 A compact yet powerful Riding Mower that's truly easy to start. **1976** *Billings* (Montana) *Gaz.* 17 June 6-F/1 (Advt.), Bolens 5 HP riding mower. **1911** *Encycl. Brit.* XXI. 851/2 The '*sulky*' or *riding plough* is little known in the United Kingdom. **1960** DAVIES & VAUGHAN *Beyond Old Bone Trail* xi. 74 We bought..a riding plough—the 'walking' model was right out of date. **1954** J. R. R. TOLKIEN *Fellowship of Ring* I. xi. 190 The two or three riding-ponies. **1940** W. FAULKNER *Hamlet* I. i. 15 Colonel John Sartoris his self shot Ab for trying to steal his claybank riding stallion during the war.

d. *riding code, instructor, lesson, mistress, -muscle, tournament*; **riding ballad** (earlier example).

1800 W. SCOTT *Let.* 18 Oct. (1932) I. 105, I do not mean entirely to limit my collection to the Riding Ballads, as they are called in our country, those namely which relate to Border feuds and forays. **1971** *Riding for Recreation* (Brit. Horse Soc.) ii. 3/1 The British Horse Society in consultation with other organisations has compiled a Riding Code. **1946** M. C. SELF *Horseman's Encycl.* 342 The proper choice of a riding instructor is of utmost importance. **1977** N. MARSH *Last Ditch* iii. 63 A riding instructor or some such in the army. **1886** F. H. BURNETT *Little Lord Fauntleroy* viii. 159 Fauntleroy took his first riding lesson. **1975** J. MCCLURE *Snake* viii. 110 Business so bad..and yet his kid goes to riding lessons. **1895** *Funk's Stand. Dict.*, Riding mistress. **1926** GALSWORTHY *Silver Spoon* III. vii. 275 A riding mistress was teaching a small boy to trot. **1914** D. H. LAWRENCE *Prussian Officer* 2 His orderly, having to rub him down, admired the amazing riding-muscles of his loins. **1934** *Sun* (Baltimore) 15 Aug. 9/3 The amateur riding tournament today. **1941** *Ibid.* 20 Aug. 11/7 The mountain folk..also will have their wood-chopping and sawing contests, riding tournament and rifle shoot.

ridley (ri·dli). [Etym. unknown.] Either of two species of marine turtle, *Lepidochelys kempii* of the Atlantic or *L. olivacea* of the Pacific and Indian Oceans.

1942 A. F. CARR in *Proc. New England Zool. Club* XXI. 8, I believe that a change in the non-technical designation of *kempii* is indicated. Some time ago..Stewart Springer.. told me of a species of sea turtle, known locally as the 'ridley', which was recognized as distinct by the natives of the Keys. *Ibid.* 9 Henceforth I shall use ridley. **1952** —— *Handbk. Turtles* 402 A ridley will die, apparently of rage and frustration, if placed on its carapace out of water. **1966** R. C. STEBBINS *Field Guide Western Reptiles & Amphibians* 89 Pacific ridley... A relatively small sea turtle with uniformly olive-colored heart-shaped carapace... More a bottom dweller than other marine turtles. **1974** *Encycl. Brit. Micropædia* IX. 12/2 The Atlantic ridley is widely known as the 'bastard turtle', the name stemming from the mistaken belief that it is the offspring of a green turtle and a loggerhead. **1980** *Economist* 16 Aug. 26/1 The Kemp's ridley is being wiped out.

ridotto, *sb.* (Earlier *attrib.* example.)

1826 M. KELLY *Reminisc.* I. 204 The ridotto rooms, where the masquerades took place, were in the palace.

riebeckite (rī·bekait). *Min.* [ad. G. *riebeckit* (A. Sauer 1888, in *Zeitschr. d. Deut. geol. Ges.* XL. 138), f. the name of Emil *Riebeck* (d. 1885), German explorer: see -ITE[1].] A mineral of the monoclinic amphibole group, $Na_2Fe^{2+}{}_3Fe^{3+}{}_2Si_8O_{22}(OH)_2$, found as dark blue or black prismatic crystals and often containing magnesium.

1889 *Jrnl. Chem. Soc.* LVI. 109 This hornblende, named riebeckite, has the same composition as arfvedsonite, and is the analogue of ägirin of the augite series. **1941** *Proc. Prehist. Soc.* VII. 65 This hornblende..recalls the habit and mode of occurrence of riebeckite in the paisanites. **1965** G. J. WILLIAMS *Econ. Geol. N.Z.* ix. 141/1 It should not pass unnoticed that the Taipo Valley thorite occurrence also contains rutile..and that the presence of riebeckite suggests an alkali environment. **1977** A. HALLAM *Planet Earth* 136/2 Riebeckite is a member of the amphibole group.

Riedel (rī·dĕl). *Med.* The name of B. M. K. L. *Riedel* (1846–1916), German physician, used in the possessive to designate (*a*) an unusually long lobe of the liver; (*b*) a rare condition of uncertain status in which the thyroid gland is largely replaced by dense fibrous tissue.

1905 KINNICUTT & POTTER tr. *Sahli's Diagnostic Methods* 311 (*caption*) Riedel's projection of the liver in cholelithiasis. **1932** *Practitioners Libr. Med. & Surg.* I. vi. 567 Riedel's lobe is an occasional linguiform process of liver substance projecting caudally from the caudal border of the right lobe. If detectable by palpation or percussion it may be mistaken for an enlarged gallbladder; of course the two may coexist. **1978** *Jrnl. R. Soc. Med.* LXXI. 200 The homogeneous echogenic mass of the lower border of the liver is either a Riedel's lobe, if of the same echogenicity as the liver; or a tumour, if of differing echogenicity.

1917 H. FRENCH *Index Differential Diagnosis Main Symptoms* (ed. 2) 158 Progressive and extreme fibrosis of the organ such as is seen in ligneous thyroiditis, or Riedel's disease. **1966** WRIGHT & SYMMERS *Systemic Path.* II. 1111/2 (*heading*) Riedel's thyroiditis... This disorder, formerly known as Riedel's struma, 'woody thyroid', or invasive fibrous thyroiditis, is not unanimously accepted as a distinct disease entity. Up to twenty years ago the term was widely used synonymously with Hashimoto's disease.

‖ **riegel** (rī·gĕl). *Physical Geogr.* Also **Riegel.** Pl. **riegels, riegeln.** [Ger., a. MHG. *rigel* crossbar for fastening, OHG *rigil* bar; see RAIL *sb.*[2]] A low, transverse ridge of resistant bedrock on the floor of a glacial valley; = *rock bar* s.v. *ROCK *sb.*[1] 9 a.

1910 *Geogr. Jrnl.* XXXV. 284 Where a barrier of more resistant rock has hemmed in a portion of the valley (*Riegel*), narrow picturesque gorges have been cut. **1916** G. TAYLOR *With Scott* iii. 136 Leaving the glacier and the upper lake, I proceeded east to the Riegel... This bar across a great glacial gorge was paralleled by many in the Swiss Alps... In my opinion this bar (or riegel), and the more important one we discovered..are relics of 'steps' in the original topography. **1954** W. D. THORNBURY *Princ. Geomorphol.* xv. 370 Steps..have been attributed to the effects of varying rock hardness, the idea being that risers and associated riegels mark hard rock 'bars' across a glacial trough. **1957** G. E. HUTCHINSON *Treat. Limnol.* I. i. 71 The basins are divided by transverse ridges, presumably *Riegeln* or rock bars. **1968** R. W. FAIRBRIDGE *Encycl. Geomorphol.* 745/1 Partly worn-down cross-valley bars of resistant rock ('riegels') remain, impounding lakes, though these have commonly been drained by rivers that have cut gorges through the riegels since the melting of the glaciers.

‖ **riel** (rī·əl). [Khmer.] The basic monetary unit of Kampuchea, equal to 100 sen.

1956 *Whitaker's Almanack 1957* 886/1 The official rate of exchange (1956) was 97.7 *riels* = £1. **1964** *New Statesman* 17 Jan. 79/1 The black market value of the pound sterling rose to 300 riel after the quarrel with America. **1977** 'J. LE CARRÉ' *Hon. Schoolboy* xv. 341 Going rate is three million riels to the Minister... Less if you pay gold.

riem. Add: Also with pronunc. (rim). (Earlier and later examples.)

1822 W. J. BURCHELL *Trav. S. Afr.* I. 151 The *riem* (or halter), is a leathern thong about twelve feet in length, with a noose at one end, by which it is fixed round the ox's horns. **1840** [see *BRAY *v.*[4]]. **1932** C. FULLER *Louis Trigardt's Trek* 100 We loosened the *riem* on one hind wheel. **1952** *Cape Argus* 15 Nov. 7/9 She then tied a riem around my neck and hit me with a leather belt. **1966** E. PALMER *Plains of Camdeboo* x. 184 Finally he tied a riem round the ant-bear's hindquarters.

Riemann (rī·mæn). *Math.* The name of G. F. Bernhard *Riemann* (1826–66), German mathematician, used *attrib.* and in the possessive to designate various concepts of his, as **Riemann geometry,** Riemannian geometry; **Riemann('s) hypothesis,** the hypothesis (unproved by 1981) that all the zeros of the Riemann zeta function, except those on the real line, have a real part equal to ½; **Riemann integral,** a definite integral obtained by subdividing the interval of integration, multiplying the width of each subdivision by the greatest or the least value of the integrand within it, summing the products so obtained, and taking the limit of the sum as the width of the subdivisions tends to zero; so **Riemann integrable** *adj. phr.*, **Riemann integration; Riemann('s) surface,** a surface which covers a plane more than once, and so could be used to plot a function that is not single-valued; **Riemann tensor,** the Riemann–Christoffel tensor; **Riemann zeta** (or ζ) **function,** an analytic function ζ of the complex variable *s*, equal almost everywhere to $\{1^{-s}+2^{-s}+3^{-s}+\ldots\}$.

1922 *Proc. Nat. Acad. Sci.* VIII. 23 The functions λg_{ij} satisfy (2.4) and give a Riemann geometry. **1974** R. M. PIRSIG *Zen & Art of Motorcycle Maintenance* (1976) III. xxii. 257 He turned to the question, Is Euclidian geometry true or is Riemann geometry true? He answered, The question has no meaning. **1924** *Proc. Cambr. Philos. Soc.* XXII. 296 We assume Riemann's hypothesis. *Ibid.*, We assume the truth of the Riemann hypothesis. **1959** *Listener* 23 Apr. 715/2 This conjecture, now known as the Riemann hypothesis, has never been either proved or disproved. **1957** K. S. MILLER *Advanced Real Calculus* iv. 49 If $\bar{I} = \underline{I}$ we shall say that $f(x)$ is Riemann integrable or simply integrable on $[a,b]$ and write $I = \int_a^b f(x)dx$. **1972** A. G. HOWSON *Handbk. Terms Algebra & Anal.* xxvii. 136 If *f* is bounded on *I* then it is Riemann integrable..on *I* if and only if it is continuous almost everywhere..on *I*. **1914** *Proc. London Math. Soc.* XIII. 133 Corresponding to Riemann's extension of the notion of an integrable function, we now have a certain class of functions which may be said to possess a 'Riemann' integral with respect to the monotone increasing function $g(x)$, that is to say a function such that the summation..has a unique and finite limit, however the points *x* are chosen in their corresponding intervals, and however those intervals are constructed, provided only the length of the greatest of them approaches zero as $n \to \infty$. **1970** S. KOTZ tr. *Pesin's Classical & Mod. Integration*

Theories vii. 112 The Riemann integral can be defined in two ways: by the Riemann process as the limit of Riemann's sums and by the Darboux process as the common value of the lower and upper integrals. **1939** I. S. Sokolnikoff *Advanced Calculus* iv. 99 It seems desirable to begin the study of Riemann integration by presenting a reasonably careful definition of the definite integral based on the intuitive concept of the area under the curve. **1893** A. R. Forsyth *Theory Functions Complex Variable* xv. 336 The region, in which the variable *z* exists, no longer consists of a single plane but of a number of planes.., often called sheets... The aggregate of all the sheets is a surface, often called a Riemann's Surface. **1893** Harkness & Morley *Treat. Theory Functions* vi. 205 We shall show how to form a Riemann surface in some simple special cases. **1932** A. Huxley *Brave New World* iv. 73 Two thousand Beta-Minus mixed doubles were playing Riemann-surface tennis. **1974** *Encycl. Brit. Macropædia* I. 726/2 A compact Riemann surface is homeomorphic to the (topological) surface obtained from a sphere by cutting *g* pairs of holes in it and attaching to each pair of holes a handle. **1922** *Proc. Nat. Acad. Sci.* VIII. 24 Where $R_{pq,rs}$ is the Riemann tensor of the first kind. **1957** *Physical Rev.* CV. 1089/1 It is the Riemann tensor which characterizes the presence of radiation. Physically, this is because the Riemann tensor describes the variations in the gravitational field from event to event in space-time. **1973** Hawking & Ellis *Large Scale Structure of Space–Time* ii. 42 Having split the Riemann tensor into a part represented by the Ricci tensor and a part represented by the Weyl tensor, one can use the Bianchi identities..to obtain differential relations between the Ricci tensor and the Weyl tensor. **1899** *Messenger of Math.* XXIX. 114 If $\zeta(s, a, \omega)$ be the extended Riemann ζ function. **1931** *Q. Jrnl. Math.* II. 161 The theory of the Riemann zeta-function. **1966** Ogilvy & Anderson *Excursions in Number Theory* iii. 35 We needed a value of the Riemann Zeta-function, the technical name for the series that converged to $\pi^2/6$.

Riemann–Christoffel (rīːmænˌkri·stǫ̈fĕl). *Math.* [f. prec. + the name of E. B. *Christoffel* (1829–1900), German mathematician.] Used to designate a tensor of the fourth order whose components are functions of a covariant co-ordinate system and the corresponding contravariant system, and which occurs in the mathematical description of curved space-time.

1918 A. S. Eddington *Rep. Relativity Theory of Gravitation* iii. 40 The required equations of the law of gravitation must, therefore, include the vanishing of the Riemann–Christoffel tensor as a special case. **1956** G. C. McVittie *Gen. Relativity & Cosmol.* ii. 30 In relativity theory applications of the tensor calculus a very important part is played by a symmetrical tensor of rank two, called the Ricci tensor, which is obtained by contraction from the Riemann–Christoffel tensor. **1974** *Encycl. Brit. Micropædia* VIII. 580/2 The Riemannian curvature is obtained by first contracting the Riemann–Christoffel curvature tensor, applying it to two vectors spanning the subspace in question, and then dividing by the area of the parallelogram formed from the vectors.

Riemannian (rīmæ·niăn), *a. Math.* [f. as prec. + -ian.] Used to designate a non-Euclidean geometry which is everywhere positively curved, and various associated concepts.

1920 A. S. Eddington *Space, Time & Gravitation* xii. 183 The world became non-Euclidean; a new geometry called Riemannian geometry was adopted. **1923** *Ann. Math.* XXIV. 367 A generalization of Levi-Civita's concept of infinitesimal parallelism in a Riemannian manifold. **1926** L. P. Eisenhart *Riemannian Geom.* ii. 35 The metric defined..is called the Riemannian metric and a geometry based upon such a metric is called a Riemannian geometry. Also we say that the space whose geometry is based upon such a metric is called a Riemannian space. **1965** H. Eves *Survey of Geom.* II. xiv. 341 One can describe Riemannian geometry as the mathematical study, couched in geometrical terminology, of an arbitrary quadratic differential form. **1974** *Encycl. Brit. Micropædia* VIII. 580/2 In Riemannian geometry, a straight line of finite length can be extended continuously without bounds, but all straight lines are of the same length.

‖ **riempie** (ri·mpi). *S. Afr.* Also **riempje.** Var *rheimpy* s.v. Rheim. Freq. used for the seats of chairs or stools. Also *attrib.* and in *Comb.* Cf. Rimpi in Dict. and Suppl.

1913 D. Fairbridge *That which hath Been* xx. 229 Heavy teak chairs with *riempje* seats were ranged round the wainscot with mathematical precision. **1920** R. Y. Stormberg *Mrs. Pieter de Bruyn* xxiii. 76 Ouma du Preez on the riempje settee devoutly clasped her cotton-mittened hands. **1937** S. Cloete *Turning Wheels* vi. 100 While dozing in her wide riempie-bottomed chair, she had seen one girl and two men leave the camp. **1938** E. A. Walker *Great Trek* 41 A couple of deal tables and *riempie* chairs and stools..as seats along the stoep. **1939** 'D. Rame' *Wine of Good Hope* I. iv. 44 Even Lowell, perched on a little riempie stool beside Grim..smiled at the torrent of high-pitched abuse. **1943** 'B. Knight' *Covenant* (1944) i. 34 Jannion saw her mother hook her foot under the top of the *riempie*-strung stool. **1949** M. Masson *Narrowing Lust* xix. 180 Calmly she seated herself on a stool of riempje. **1953** M. Murray *Fire-Raisers* x. 101 He saw that Sarel was lying on the riempje sofa, his feet on one arm. **1971** *Cape Times* 13 Feb. 21/3 (Advt.), 2 riempie seated chairs.

‖ **riempiestoel** (ri·mpistuːl). *S. Afr.* Also **riempies-stoel.** [Afrikaans, f. prec. + *stoel* stool.] A *riempie*-seated chair or stool.

1933 W. MacDonald *Romance of Golden Rand* 72 Louw Geldenhuys, sitting on a *riempiestoel* in the little office. **1953** U. Krige *Dream & Desert* i. 75 Marta, sitting on her *riempiestoel* in front of the door leading to the kitchen. **1963** H. C. Bosman *Unto Dust* 122 A newly-appointed veldkornet, looking important, seated on a riempies-stoel.

riemschoen, var. *remskoen.

Riesling (rī·sliŋ, -zliŋ; *also* rəi·zliŋ). [Ger.] The name of a variety of vine and grape widely grown in Germany, Austria, Alsace, and elsewhere; the dry white wine produced from this grape. Also *attrib.*

1833 C. Redding *Mod. Wines* V. 168 The white wines are ranked in quality as follows: Riesling, muscadine, Kléber, or Klebner, and common. Riesling wine is distinguished by a particular bouquet, by strength, and durability. **1888** *Encycl. Brit.* XXIV. 609/1 The grape from which it [*sc.* Sercial] is produced is of the Riesling variety. *Ibid.* 611/1 Amongst the leading descriptions of vine plants in German vineyards the Riesling stands out pre-eminent. **1902** E. R. Emerson *Story of Vine* vii. 127 The Steinberg is a hill about three miles from the Rhine... Only Riesling vines are grown, but several grades of wine are made. **1954** P. Highsmith *Blunderer* (1956) ii. 18 Walter ordered a broiled fish and a bottle of Riesling. **1959** *Times* 21 Sept. 13/3 *Johannisberg*.., as it is made from the *riesling* grape, has some of the fuller fruitiness of German wines. **1961** *New Statesman* 15 Dec. 921 (Advt.), *Riesling*. Per crate of 12 at 7/9 each. **1977** *Time* 21 Nov. 59/1 Riesling, the small yellow grape from which come the classic wines of Moselle, Alsace and the Rhine. **1980** D. Bloodworth *Trapdoor* x. 56 A chilled bottle of Jugoslav Riesling.

Rifa'ee, var. *Rufai.

rifampicin (rĭfæ·mpisin). *Pharm.* [f. *rifam(y)cin with inserted *pi-* f. *piperazine.] A reddish-brown crystalline powder, a member of the rifamycin group of antibiotics, which is used to treat a wide range of diseases, esp. pulmonary tuberculosis.

1966 N. Maggi et al. in *Chemotherapia* XI. 285 The hydrazone..3-(4-methyl-piperazinyl-iminomethyl)-rifamycin SV, named by us 'rifampicin'. **1969** *Times* 12 May 16/3 The antibiotic called rifampicin could interfere with the production of R.N.A. molecules. **1970** *Nature* 25 July 382/1 Rifampicin has also been found to be active against some viruses. **1975** *Sci. Amer.* Mar. 126/2 The fast-acting antibiotic rifampicin, found in a soil organism..in 1957, was proved against leprosy in the 1960's. **1980** *Brit. Med. Jrnl.* 29 Mar. 900/2 In three [families] rifampicin had been given to contacts and family members because the initial presentation of the child suggested meningococcal disease.

rifampin (rĭfæ·mpin). *Pharm.* [f. as *rifampicin.] The equivalent in the U.S. Pharmacopeia of *rifampicin.

1968 *Antimicrobial Agents & Chemotherapy* 519/1 The in vitro and in vivo activity of rifampin against gram-positive bacteria. **1972** *Evening Telegram* (St. John's, Newfoundland) 27 June 4/8 The great danger in rifampin is that tuberculosis bacteria, which cause the disease, can readily become resistant to the drug. **1978** *Pediatr. Res.* XII. 491 Haemophilus influenzae type b infection in a day care center: eradication of carrier state by rifampin.

rifamycin (rĭfăməi·sin). *Pharm.* orig. **rifomycin.** [Prob. f. It. *rifo-rmare* to reform + *-mycin.] Any of a class of natural and semi-synthetic antibiotics of which the first examples were isolated from the fungus *Streptomyces mediterranei*.

1959 P. Sensi et al. in *Farmaco* (Ed. Sci.) XIV. 146 The antibiotic, named by us rifomycin, shows a high activity against gram-positive bacteria and mycobacteria. **1960** *Antibiotics Ann. 1959–1960* 262 Rifomycin has been isolated in our laboratories from the fermentation broths of a strain of *Streptomyces mediterranei*. **1963** *Antibiotics & Chemotherapy* XI. 61 The Rifamycins constitute a group of antibiotics, produced by a new Streptomyces. **1970** *New Scientist* 24 Dec. 546/1 Rifamycin B *per se* is not active against bacteria but slowly degrades in aqueous solution to yield an active product, rifamycin SV. **1976** *Lancet* 11 Dec. 1304/2 The rifamycin antibiotics have been used in the treatment of leprosy since 1963.

riff, *sb.*[3] (Later example.)

1952 M. Tripp *Faith is Windsock* iv. 67, I believe I am right in diagnosing his dog's trouble as riff. This is invariably picked up in damp places and frequently appears in the clefts between the toes.

Riff (rif), *sb.*[6] and *a.* Also **Rif.** [f. *Rîf*, the name of a district in Morocco.] **A.** *sb.* A Berber of the Rîf district of Morocco. **B.** *adj.* Of or belonging to the Riffs.

1923 *Contemp. Rev.* Nov. 616 Representatives of the Riffs now demand the formal recognition of the Riff republic. **1925** *Glasgow Herald* 6 July 9/2 Several Riff attacks in the neighbourhood of the River Liben have been repulsed. **1926** *Chambers's Jrnl.* Mar. 158/1 Hussein was a good Riff, and the killing lust was upon him. **1964** C. Mackenzie *Life & Times* III. 76 There might be other Riffs about with rifles who would shoot us in the hope of plunder.

riff, *sb.*[7] [Abbrev. of Riffle *sb.*] **1.** A simple musical phrase repeated over and over, often with a strong or syncopated rhythm, and freq. used as background to a solo improvisation. Also *attrib.* and in *Comb.*

1935 [see *dig *v.* 6 c]. **1940** [see *backing *vbl. sb.* 7 b]. **1946** R. Blesh *Shining Trumpets* xii. 277 Henderson.. established the current trend of riff-swing. **1951** *Landfall* V. 286 She never could manage riff rhythms or any jazz rhythms. **1955** *Jazzbook 1955* 8 When played with the passion and abandon of a great orchestra like Basie's the riff is an exciting revelation; as a trick phrase in the hands of a mediocre band it becomes the most banal of musical devices. **1962** J. Baldwin *Another Country* I. i. 16 They might swap stories of..gigs they'd played, riffs they remembered. *Ibid.* 20 He..beat a riff with his fingers. **1972** *Blues & Jazz* Sept. 11/3 The saxes come in with an unoriginal but beautifully swinging riff when Fats makes his vocal entry. **1976** A. Murray *Stomping Blues* v. 60 The actual mood of the performance..is determined by the up-tempo beat plus the riff-style call-and-response choruses. **1976** *Zigzag* Apr. 28/1 The band shine best when they are tackling unison riffs and counter riffs with customary ease. **1978** *Oxford Times* 31 Mar. 19/1 The harmonica introduction is unforgettable and the tune has a very catchy backing riff. **1980** M. Booth *Bad Track* iii. 68 The sax cut in with Mel's violin scrawking against the drums and the low riff of the electronic piano.

2. In extended use: a repeated phrase, idea, or situation.

1970 *New Yorker* 14 Nov. 166/2 He has an opportunity for some lovely comic riffs. **1972** *Times Lit. Suppl.* 29 Dec. 1570/4 These schizoid riffs are not the half-hearted impersonations of madness..but characterizations which exhibit the mania and pain of true suffering. **1974** *Black World* Dec. 52/2 There are some new riffs played out in this novel, riffs which are significant when measured against Baldwin's earlier novels. **1976** *Times Lit. Suppl.* 19 Mar. 318/4 Mr Morphet has not sufficiently discussed Hodgkin's community of ideas with painters of his generation, for he uses riffs, as it were, from many of his contemporaries.

riff, *sb.*[8] = *riffle *sb.* 3 b.

1960 *20th Cent.* Mar. 256 The most cursory riff through the..daily and weekly press.

riff, *v.*[1] Restrict † *Obs.* to sense in Dict. and add: **2.** With *through* = *riffle *v.* 3 c.

1956 W. H. Whyte *Organization Man* (1957) xxv. 347 Riff through these maps quickly, and in the few seconds.. you can see in crude animation the fissures begin to widen.

riff, *v.*[2] [f. *riff *sb.*[7]] *intr.* To play riffs in popular music. Also *fig.* (in context *trans.*). Hence **ri·ffing** *ppl. a.*

1955 *Jazzbook 1955* 8 Few things were more satisfying than Jimmy Rushing shouting the blues with the band riffing away behind him. **1959** C. MacInnes *Absolute Beginners* 158 He said life was a junction: the junction, he said, of composite opposites (he liked that group, and riffed it several times). **1966** *Melody Maker* 7 May 13/1 The Faces storm into this new one with powerful guitar, and riffing organ. **1968** *Blues Unlimited* Sept. 23 Horns coming in to riff nicely after the build-up. **1977** *Gramophone* Sept. 525/2 What comes across most forcefully is the band's ability to riff fearlessly and hypnotically.

Riffian (ri·fiăn), *sb.* and *a.* Also **Rifian.** [f. *Riff *sb.*[6] and *a.* + -ian.] = *Riff *sb.*[6] and *a.*

1867 'Mark Twain' *Innoc. Abroad* (1869) viii. 77 There are stalwart Bedouins of the desert here, and stately Moors ..and Jews, whose fathers fled hither centuries..ago; and swarthy Riffians from the mountains. **1899** A. E. W. Mason *Miranda of Balcony* ii. 23 A Riffian sauntered by..a great coarse tail of hair swinging between his shoulders. **1909** *Westm. Gaz.* 13 Aug. 5/4 The guns are now trained against the town, and are evidently being handled by Riffian merchants familiar with the main buildings. **1924** *Glasgow Herald* 30 July 13 The Riffians planned to surprise the convoy sent to Xauen. **1931** *Times Lit. Suppl.* 10 Dec. 1008/4 A plot is being hatched for the organization of a fresh Riffian rebellion against the French in Morocco. **1965** C. D. Eby *Siege of Alcázar* (1966) 21 The Riffian tribes of Spanish Morocco. **1977** P. Raymond *Matter of Assassination* viii. 88 The Hamitic accent of Rifian Berber.

ri·ffing, *vbl. sb.* [f. *riff *v.*[2] + -ing[1].] The action or fact of playing riffs.

1936 *Harper's Mag.* Apr. 570/2 'Jamming', 'cat-time', 'swing', 'riffing', 'getting off', 'going to town', 'ragging', 'gut-bucketing', and all the rest are names for the *hot* performance, which is the heart and soul of jazz. **1949** L. Feather *Inside Be-bop* vi. 42 Jo Stafford's arrangement of *The Gentleman is a Dope* began with four bars of unmistakably bop riffing. **1958** G. Boatfield in P. Gammond *Decca Bk. of Jazz* xxiv. 310 These are extraordinary and unique tracks, with Dodds making soaring and at times agonizing music against the sombre riffing of the brassmen. **1976** A. Murray *Stomping Blues* vii. 104 The process of riffing (from the verb, *to riff*) refers not only to making riff phrases..but also to improvisation in general.

riffle, *sb.* Add: **I. 3. a.** Also *riffle-shuffle.*

1970 K. Roos *What did Hattie See?* xi. 105 He gave the deck a riffle shuffle, carefully not disturbing the four bottom cards. **1972** *Sci. Amer.* July 104/1 With your back still turned, ask him to cut the deck several times, then give it one thorough riffle-shuffle.

b. A quick skim or leafing through (of pages of a book, papers, etc.).

1960 *Guardian* 28 Oct. 6/4, I skimmed the book in a first riffle. **1967** *Adv. Inorg. Chem. & Radiochem.* X. 373 A fast riffle through the thallium volume of Gmelin's *Handbuch*.. uncovers the following mixed valence compounds. **1979** J. Gardner *Nostradamus Traitor* vii. 22 Just a riffle through the books.

II. For *U.S.* read 'orig. and chiefly *U.S.*' **4. a.** Also *Canad.* (Earlier and later examples.)

1785 R. Butler *Jrnl.* in *Olden Time* (1847) Oct. 440 Met riffles, all very shallow, struck with the barge several times. **1948** *Sat. Even. Post* 23 Oct. 36/2 In the lingo of our Rogue River guides, a riffle is anything between a foaming cataract and white-water rapids heavily sprinkled with boulders.

1962 M. E. MURIE *Two in Far North* II. vi. 153 In the course of the morning we fought our way over six riffles. **1976** *Nature* 5 Aug. 483/1 Other research workers have noted that the spacing of riffles in straight and meandering channels is between five and seven channel widths and that skew shoals in flumes have been found to be 6.5 channel widths apart. **1980** *Birds* Summer 22/2 Dipper and common sandpiper are associated with rapid flowing, relatively well aerated water with riffles (shallow sections)—features generally only found on upland rivers.

b. *to make the riffle*: to succeed in crossing a rapid; hence *fig.*, to be successful in an attempt or undertaking.

1853 F. A. BUCK *Let.* 31 Dec. in *Yankee Trader in Gold Rush* (1930) 130 'Madam La Marquise'..built a splendid saloon, opened and flourished for about two months but couldn't make the riffle. **1873** 'MARK TWAIN' & WARNER *Gilded Age* xxxi. 279 There's old Balaam, was in the Interior—..he's made the riffle on the Injun; great Injun pacificator and land-dealer. **1887** [see sense 4 a in Dict.]. **1911** R. D. SAUNDERS *Col. Todhunter* i. 19, I aint got no business doin' that, but I'll try if I can make the riffle. **1950** *Daily Ardmoreite* (Ardmore, Okla.) 14 Feb. 8/1 [The] Rexroat girls [were] doing their best trying to win first in the basketball tournament but they couldn't quite make the riffle.

c. A ripple or ruffle.

1938 M. K. RAWLINGS *Yearling* x. 92 A slight breath of air rippled across the marsh and the water rippled under it... 'Jest enough of a riffle,' Penny said, 'and the moon jest right.' **1960** J. STROUD *Shorn Lamb* ii. 17, I had one sensational glimpse of a long white leg and a riffle of white underwear. **1975** *New Yorker* 27 Oct. 111/3 We stood and listened to the silence—to the voices of birds, to the stir of a breeze in the trees, to the riffle of moving water.

5. a, b. More widely, a transverse bar or channel, usu. one of a series, for breaking a flow of fluid or sorting or separating a stream of particles. (Earlier and later examples.)

1850 N. KINGSLEY *Diary* 7 May (1914) 120 Finished the riffles to the machine to day. **1915** *Trans. Amer. Inst. Mining Engineers* LI. 405 During the past three years there has been developed at Morenci a new type or arrangement of riffles. **1939** A. M. GAUDIN *Princ. Mineral Dressing* xiii. 298 Riffles are of great importance to tabling. They are responsible for the increased capacity of riffled decks over smooth ones. **1951** KIRK & OTHMER *Encycl. Chem. Technol.* VII. 307 A sluice is essentially an inclined trough or launder, the bottom of which is provided with transverse strips or riffles, with variable spacing. **1955** H. R. COX *Gas Turbine Princ. & Pract.* xviii. 9 The primary air and fuel stream is divided on leaving the pump by a simple riffle arrangement. **1964** F. CHICHESTER *Lonely Sea & Sky* v. 48 We shovelled the gravel into long boxes with 'riffles', small pieces of wood across them, which stopped the heavy gold when the pay dirt was washed through the box by the river. **1968** COULSON & RICHARDSON *Chem. Engin.* (ed. 2) II. xvii. 691 A series of slats, or riffles as they are termed, about ½ in. in height... The large particles and the less dense material are carried downwards, and the remainder is carried parallel to the riffles.

riffle, *v.* Restrict *rare* to senses 1–2 c and add: **2. d.** *U.S.* To ruffle in a slight or rippling manner. Also *fig.*

1901 S. E. WHITE in *Century Mag.* LXII. 466/1 The breeze and the sun played with the prairie grasses, the breeze riffling them over. **1926** *Ladies' Home Jrnl.* Nov. 228 Even the wail of music from the Palace of Dance barely riffled his preoccupation. **1977** D. HARSENT *Dreams of Dead* 24 A wind riffling the orchard.

3. a. (Later examples.)

1939 *Reader's Digest* May 29/1 Pick up and riffle a deck of cards. All you see is a blur of card ends. **1973** 'J. ASHFORD' *Double Run* iv. 30 Comyns collected up the cards and riffled them into a pack with slow and deliberate movements.

b. To flick through (papers, books, etc.); to thumb (a block of paper, a book, etc.), releasing the leaves in (usu. rapid) succession.

1922 H. TITUS *Timber* viii. 77 He riffled the pages slowly. **1938** R. FRANKEN *Gold Pennies* xv. 159 Mrs. Miller glanced at the opening paragraph, and then riffled the pages tentatively. **1948** *Electronic Engin.* XX. 367/3 The material to be counted must be riffled so that a step-like edge is presented, though the riffling need not be perfect. **1957** T. STURGEON in D. Knight *100 Yrs. Sci. Fiction* (1969) 125 Slim lifted the paper out of the box, ..riffled a thumbful of the sheets at the top. **1958** J. BALDWIN in *Mademoiselle* Mar. 149/1 He quickly riffled some papers on his desk, putting on a business air as rakishly as she had seen him put on his hat. **1977** G. DURRELL *Golden Bats & Pink Pigeons* iv. 87 He took my passport and riffled it..like an expert card sharper.

c. *intr.* To thumb or leaf *through*. Also *transf.* and *fig.*

1931 *Sun* (Baltimore) 19 Feb. 10/7 Yesterday, while riffling through a new book of memories and character sketches,..I saw it said that Mr. Bertrand Russell..reads detective fiction. **1959** *Times* 5 Nov. 14/6 A blonde girl.. propped a music-stand in front of her, and riffled through a script. **1960** V. NABOKOV *Invitation to Beheading* vi. 64 The draught riffled through the papers on the table. *Ibid.* vii. 74 He produced..a thick batch of home snapshots of the smallest size. Riffling through them as through a deck of cards, he began placing them one by one on the table. **1962** *Listener* 22 Nov. 845/2, I was riffling through these morbid thoughts. **1967** *Boston Sunday Globe* 23 Apr. B41/5 Riffling through a few recent editions of morning and evening Globes and New York, Washington, and Philadelphia newspapers we come across lines that read: Mortgage cut near [etc.]. **1979** A. HAILEY *Overload* I. x. 60 At his desk he riffled through the messages.

riffled (ri·f'ld), *a.* [f. RIFFLE *sb.* + -ED².] Provided with riffles.

1915 *Trans. Amer. Inst. Mining Engineers* LI. 416 The effect of the uniform feed and water distribution over this completely riffled table is to produce uniform velocities in the water. **1927** *Chambers's Jrnl.* Feb. 109/2 In action the human dry-blower shovels some sand on to the top perforated riffled sheet: and then he shakes the entire machine. **1951** KIRK & OTHMER *Encycl. Chem. Technol.* VII. 310 The modern bumping table is a deck concentrator of the riffled or strake type. **1968** COULSON & RICHARDSON *Chem. Engin.* (ed. 2) II. xvii. 691 Riffled tables can be used for separating materials down to about 300-mesh in size, provided that the difference in the densities is large.

riffler². Restrict *dial.* to sense in Dict. and add: **2.** A trough or sluice containing one or more upright boards to divide or retard the flow through it.

1850 N. KINGSLEY *Diary* 17 May (1914) 122 Stoped down to day and made a panning trough to pour quicksilver from the riffler into. **1924** E. C. TUCKER et al. *Manuf. Pulp & Paper* IV. vi. 24 Rifflers, or sand traps, are wood troughs through which the stock flows from the regulating box to the screens. *Ibid.* 25 The riffler is divided into two runs by the central dividing board. **1963** R. R. A. HIGHAM *Handbk. Papermaking* ii. 67 With rifflers and sand tables the stock is passed at approximately 0·5% consistency along narrow channels in the base of which are felt-covered boards which are set at right angles to the flow of stock.

riffling (ri·fliŋ), *vbl. sb.* [f. RIFFLE *sb.* and *v.* + -ING¹.] **1.** An arrangement or system of riffles (sense 5).

1915 *Trans. Amer. Inst. Mining Engineers* LI. 408 It was found impossible with this system of riffling to handle successfully the range of sizes..coming from the jigs. **1951** KIRK & OTHMER *Encycl. Chem. Technol.* VII. 307 There are endless variations of riffling.

2. The action of RIFFLE *v.* 3.

1948 [see *RIFFLE *v.* 3 b]. **1964** A. WYKES *Gambling* i. 15 A quick riffling through the replies..confirmed my suspicion.

riffling (ri·fliŋ), *ppl. a.* [f. RIFFLE *v.* + -ING².] Of water: moving in riffles; agitated.

1754 J. PREBLE in *New-England Hist. & Geneal. Reg.* (1868) XXII. 408 The navigation to Norridgewalk is considerably difficult by the reason of the rapidity of the stream, and riffling falls. **1911** J. F. WILSON *Land Claimers* ix. 123 She..heaved her catch up out of the grip of the riffling water.

riff-raffy (ri·fˌræfi), *a.* [f. RIFF-RAFF + -Y¹.] Having the character of riff-raff; disreputable.

1928 D. H. LAWRENCE *Lady Chatterley* 309 She was lost, lost utterly in this world of riff-raffy expensive people. **1962** *New Yorker* 10 Mar. 29/2 Brunswick..kept improving the tone of bowling alleys..hiring architects and decorators to make sure the places wouldn't look riff-raffy.

riffy (ri·fi), *a.* *Jazz.* [f. *RIFF *sb.*⁷ + -Y¹.] Full of riffs; repetitive.

1952 B. ULANOV *Hist. Jazz in Amer.* xvi. 194 Artie recorded some small band jazz, riffy but fresh. **1964** *Listener* 27 Aug. 319/3 Lyttleton played the sort of music (riffy swing) he first achieved fame eschewing. **1976** *Gramophone* June 101/3, I didn't go too much on *Mop mop*, which got a bit 'riffy'.

Rifian, var. *RIFFIAN *sb.* and *a.*

rifle, *sb.*³ Add: **1. b.** *rifle-calibre, cannon, -grooved, -pistol.*

1940 *War Illustr.* 5 Jan. 554/2 The armament is believed to consist of two shell-firing guns as well as four rifle-calibre machine-guns. **1861** E. COWELL *Jrnl.* 14 May in M. W. Disher *Cowells in Amer.* (1934) 347 The steamer, Pawnee was moored in front of the city, yesterday, with her guns (rifle cannon) and mortars so commanding it. **1977** 'J. GASH' *Judas Pair* ii. 27 [Duelling pistols] should have walnut stocks, and usually be rifle-grooved. **1883** 'MARK TWAIN' *Life on Mississippi* 317, I arose and drew an elegant rifle pistol on him.

2. a. (Earlier examples.)

1770 G. WASHINGTON *Diary* 5 Mar. (1925) I. 368 By John Jost for my Rifle in full £6.10. **1772** D. TAITT *Jrnl.* 5 Apr. in N. D. Mereness *Trav. Amer. Colonies* (1916) 537 Others took the Cock off his rifle and Sixteen Carrots of Tobacco.

b. (Earlier and later examples.)

1843 W. C. MACREADY *Diary* 18 Sept. (1912) II. 222 He came back to introduce Mr Webster of the Rifles to me. **1952** E. WAUGH *Men at Arms* I. ii. 77, I got seconded to the African Rifles. **1971** S. HILL *Strange Meeting* iii. 200 The Rifles were still advancing.

3. a. *rifle-butt* (hence occas. as *v. trans.*), *-oil, -rag, -sight, -thong.*

1968 *Listener* 27 June 826/3 But strip away the abstract terminology and watch tough heavily-armoured cops beating up boys and girls with rifle-butts, and the spectacle becomes embarrassing. **1977** *Rolling Stone* 16 June 36/1 There's just this part of him that's seven feet tall, big as a house, and wants to rifle-butt everybody around. **1923** KIPLING *Irish Guards in Gt. War* I. 46 It is very hard to get any sort of rifle-oil. **1933** F. RICHARDS *Old Soldiers never Die* 43 We had..no rifle-oil or rifle-rag to clean our rifles with. *a* **1914** in *Penguin Bk. Austral. Ballads* (1964) 221 They had sought him over their rifle-sights. **1932** AUDEN *Orators* III. 112 That rifle-sight you're designing: is it ready yet? **1917** W. OWEN *Coll. Poems* (1963) 39 Knit in the webbing of the rifle-thong.

b. *rifle-gallery, -match.*

1880 E. LEATHES *Actor Abroad* xiv. 165 Beneath the building, scooped out of the cliff, are a bowling-alley and a rifle-gallery. **1880** 'MARK TWAIN' *Tramp Abroad* 626 No information about prize fights.., rifle-matches, or other sporting matters.

c. *rifle artillery, battalion, company* (earlier example), *corps* (earlier example).

1861 LD. PALMERSTON *Let.* 30 Dec. in Ld. Cowley *Paris Embassy during Second Empire* (1928) xi. 234 They still attack in columns which would be blown to pieces by the French rifle artillery long before they could come into contact with their opponents. **1775** *Jrnls. Continental Congress U.S.* (1905) III. 305 To John Biddle,..Commissary of the riffle Battalion. *Ibid.* (1905) II. 250 The expences incurred for raising and arming the riffle companies. **1777** J. THACHER *Military Jrnl.* (1823) 121 The gallant Colonel Morgan, at the head of his famous rifle corps..commenced the action.

d. *rifle-shooting* (later example), *twirling.*

1974 *Ridge Citizen* (Johnston, S. Carolina) 18 Apr. 1/6 Her special training while in school consists of several years of rifle twirling while a member of the Thurmond Color Guard. **1981** E. NORTH *Dames* xiv. 268 There was a rifle range nearby and Major Frimley taught rifle shooting to the girls.

e. rifle-coat = *rifle-frock*; **rifle-frock** (earlier examples); **rifle-grenade,** a grenade discharged from a rifle; **rifle microphone** (or *colloq.* **mike**) *U.S.* = *gun microphone* s.v. *GUN *sb.* 15; **riflescope** *U.S.*, a telescopic rifle sight.

1877 *Rep. Indian Affairs* (U.S.) 5 The coats to be in shape like the old fringed rifle-coat or blouse. **1782** J. TRUMBULL *M'Fingal* IV. 78 While rifle-frocks sent Gen'rals cap'ring. **1811** *Niles' Weekly Reg.* I. 45/2 In this valuable class of cotton goods are included rifle-frocks. **1915** Rifle grenade [see *drain-pipe* s.v. *DRAIN *sb.* 5]. **1928** C. F. S. GAMBLE *Story of N. Sea Air Station* v. 87 It was also intended that the Marten Hale rifle-grenade should be issued for use from aircraft. **1962** A. NISBETT *Technique Sound Studio* 255 *Gun microphone* (Am.: *Rifle Microphone*), moving coil microphone with a battery of tubes of different lengths leading out along the axis. **1974** *Some Technical Terms & Slang* (Granada Television), *Rifle mike*, a specialised form of microphone used in filming. **1978** *Broadcast* 17 July 9/3 He..feels better off handing in his rifle mike. **1961** WEBSTER, Riflescope. **1978** *Detroit Free Press* 5 Mar. c 9/4 (Advt.), A spring sale... All riflescopes..¼ off.

rifle, *v.*¹ Add: **1. e.** *intr.* To make a vigorous search *through*.

1966 D. F. GALOUYE *Lost Perception* xiv. 147 He turned to see Weldon Radcliff sitting at a polished desk and rifling through a file holder. **1977** *Woman & Home* Nov. 154/2 Grace started to rifle through the contents of her bag. **1978** *Vogue* Feb. 88/2 Visitors from all over the world rifle through the tweeds and tartans.

rifle, *v.*³ Add: **2. b.** *transf.* To hit or kick (a ball) hard and straight. Hence **ri·fling** *ppl. a.*²

1948 [see *OVERRUN *v.* 10 a]. **1973** *Times* 13 Apr. 13/3 In the end it was the low rifling backhand drive from Gomozkov that defeated him. **1975** *New Yorker* 7 Apr. 91/1 The pivot play, in which the ball was rifled in to the center positioned at the foul line with his back to the basket. **1977** *Daily Mirror* 16 Mar. 30/5 Referee James Brimmell stepped in to save the 22-year-old Scot after the challenger had pinned him on the ropes for fully a minute, rifling in a furious stream of punches. **1978** *Guardian* 27 Feb. 16/4 Robson.. seized on a rebound..and joyfully rifled the equaliser past Shilton.

rifle-gun. For Now *arch.* read Now *arch.* exc. *U.S. dial.* and add *U.S. dial.* examples. Also *attrib.*

1913 H. KEPHART *Our Southern Highlanders* xiii. 286 Everywhere in the mountains we hear of biscuit-bread,.. rifle-gun, rock-clift, [etc.]. **1949** 'J. NELSON' *Backwoods Teacher* x. 105 A generation was growing up which..knew only by hearsay..of 'rifle-gun' (a proper distinction from shotgun) balls run in molds on the 'chimley hurth'. **1951** L. CRAIG *Singing Hills* 13 Mr. Givens and his son had taken their rifle-guns and their dog and had gone off hunting.

rifle range. 2. (Earlier and later examples.)

1862 *St. Andrews Gaz.* 3 Oct. 3/4 At the rifle range, the corps was divided into two squads, the one party firing against the other. **1978** J. IRVING *World according to Garp* xii. 236 We would not allow an outdoor rifle range in the suburbs!

riflery (rəi·f'lˌri). Chiefly *U.S.* [f. RIFLE *sb.*³ + -RY.] Rifles collectively; firing from rifles; shooting with rifles. Also *attrib.*

1846 R. B. SAGE *Scenes Rocky Mts.* xxiv. 198 A volley of riflery was discharged among the promiscuous throng, with fatal effect. **1869** *Punch* 27 Mar. 119/1 Once before Shakespeare's Cliff reverberated with the roar of riflery. **1962** *Transylvania Times* (Brevard, N. Carolina) 9 Aug. 5/4 The 1962 Riflery season at Camp Illahee went off with a 'bang' as 196 girls started their National Rifle Association qualifications. **1976** *National Observer* (U.S.) 17 Apr. 13/5 (Advt.), Counselor instruction in..riflery, hiking, arts and crafts.

rifle-shot. Add: **1.** (Earlier examples.)

1803 A. ELLICOTT *Jrnl.* 249 We anchored about rifle shot from the sloop. **1816** *Niles' Reg.* IX. Suppl. 190/2 The schooner now thought it prudent to claw off, and had just escaped out of rifle shot.

3. (Earlier examples.)

1837 W. IRVING *Capt. Bonneville* I. viii. 160 There were the remains of the rude fortress in the swamp, shattered by rifle shot. **1846** R. B. SAGE *Scenes Rocky Mts.* xvii. 145 The sharp crack of a rifle-shot.

rift, *sb.*² Add: **2. f.** *Quarrying* (chiefly *U.S.*). Any of a series of parallel planes along which (normally igneous) rock may most easily be split, freq. distinct from the natural bedding planes. Also, the property by which such rocks tend to split most easily in one direction.

1886 T. S. Hunt *Min. Physiol. & Physiogr.* vii. 274 A phenomenon..apparently due to superficial alternations of temperature on certain crystalline rocks, which have resulted in establishing in them..a series of rifts or divisional planes parallel to the present surface, which are well known to quarrymen. **1907** *Bull. U.S. Geol. Survey* No. 113. 27 Another peculiarity of rift is that the angle of its inclination may at some places be modified by gravity. **1912** H. Ries *Building Stones & Clay-Products* iii. 96 The rift is an obscure foliation, either vertical (or nearly so) or horizontal, along which the granite splits more readily than in any other direction. **1934** O. Bowles *Stone Industries* vii. 81 In quarrying, a good rift assists greatly as it facilitates bed lifting where open bed planes are absent. *Ibid.*, Rift is due chiefly to orientation of grains. **1937** *Mem. Geol. Soc. Amer.* V. 19 The term, rift, denotes the peculiar property of granitic rocks to split relatively easily in a direction other than the 'bedding' (which is parallel to the earth's surface). **1960** O. Bowles in J. L. Gillson et al. *Industr. Min. & Rocks* (ed. 3) xv. 327/1 [Paving stones] are shaped by hand processes involving expert knowledge of the 'rift' and 'run' directions of easy splitting.

g. A large fault running parallel to the major regional relief, esp. one bounding a rift valley; also, a rift valley.

1921 E. J. Wayland in *Geogr. Jrnl.* LVIII. 345 The term 'Western Rift' is used in this paper to denote that part of the Great Rift Valley system which forms the western boundary of Uganda... The two terms 'Eastern Rift' and 'Western Rift' are here introduced for the sake of convenience; they are not proposed as geographical names, or intended for other than local use. **1924** J. G. A. Skerl tr. *Wegener's Orig. Continents & Oceans* xi. 166 The East African rift-valleys form the most beautiful example of such rifts. **1936** B. Willis *E. Afr. Plateaus* 55 The great San Andreas rift of California, 500 miles long, is a fault. **1957** G. E. Hutchinson *Treat. Limnol.* I. i. 12 There has been some uptilting all around the margins of the plateau bounded by the Albert–Edward–Tanganyika system of rifts. **1970** *Kenya Farmer* Feb. 12/3 Looking at the rainfall figures for 1969 in the Lower Rift we see that..only a few lucky farmers got enough rain to begin planting.

4. *rift basin, fault, faulting, -system, tectonics*; **rift block** *Physical Geogr.*, a horst or a graben; **rift saw** (see quot. 1958); **rift sawing** *vbl. sb.* = *quarter sawing* vbl. sb. s.v. *QUARTER *sb.* 30; so **rift-sawn** *ppl. a.*; **rift valley,** substitute for def.: a large, elongated valley with steep walls formed by the relative depression of a block of the earth's surface and bounded by nearly parallel faults or fault-zones; cf. *GRABEN; (further examples); **Rift Valley fever,** a disease of animals of the Rift Valley of East Africa which can affect humans as a mild fever and is caused by an arborvirus.

1978 *Nature* 13 July 133/1 For most ancient rift basins, it is very difficult to demonstrate whether rifting was preceded or accompanied by doming. **1929** D. Johnson in *Compt. Rend. 15th Internat. Geol. Congr.* II. 361, I shall consider only four major types of blocks included between bounding faults:..II. Rift blocks; or those relatively raised or lowered between normal faults. **1944** A. Holmes *Princ. Physical Geol.* xix. 439 The boundary faults are then regarded as steep upthrusts and the rift blocks as wedges (widening in depth) held down by pressure from the upriding sides. **1954** W. D. Thornbury *Princ. Geomorphol.* x. 266 The relatively raised blocks are commonly called horsts and the lowered blocks grabens, when they are the direct effects of faulting. Johnson (1929) preferred the name rift blocks for them, but there are objections to its use because rift is often applied to earthquake rifts.., along which movement has been largely horizontal. Johnson would call an uplifted block a rift block mountain or horst and a lowered block a rift block basin or graben. **1977** A. Hallam *Planet Earth* 78/3 Although the Cenozoic phases of rift faulting are well documented, geological mapping in older rocks has shown that the rift faults frequently coincide with ancient tectonic dislocations. **1909** Webster, Rift saw. **1958** *N.Z. Timber Jrnl.* May 56/2 *Rift saw*, a special type of circular saw, usually with inserted teeth, for converting slabbed logs into flooring strips. **1909** Webster, Rift sawing. **1920** F. T. Hill *Pract. Aeroplane Construction* iv. 97 Rift sawing..is to be preferred [for aircraft work]. **1968** F. Hilton *Craft Technol. for Carpenters & Joiners* i. 17 (*heading*) Quarter or rift sawing. **1920** F. T. Hill *Pract. Aeroplane Construction* iv. 98 Rift-sawn spruce can now be obtained in this country. **1965** W. H. Brown *Introd. to Seasoning Timber* ii. 20 The boards so cut [*sc.* in radial plane] are known as quarter sawn, edge grain, or rift sawn. **1972** M. Verney *Boat Repairs & Conversions* v. 93 All pine timber used for decking needs to be rift-sawn. **1908** *Geogr. Jrnl.* XXXI. 217 (*heading*) The East African rift-system. **1978** *Nature* 13 July 133/1 The East Greenland Triassic–Jurassic rift seems to be part of a three-armed rift system where the two other arms are represented by a little known basin along the coast of Southeast Greenland, and by parts of the northern North Sea graben complex. **1976** *Ibid.* 9 Sept. 119/1 Rift tectonics are amply demonstrated by lateral inconsistence and temporal heterogeneity in Upper Palaeozoic and Mesozoic stratigraphy. **1946** L. D. Stamp *Britain's Structure & Scenery* xxiii. 228 The area is structurally a rift valley let down between parallel faults but is not otherwise a valley in the ordinarily accepted meaning of the word. **1954** W. D. Thornbury *Princ. Geomorphol.* xix. 508 The volcanoes along the African rift valleys and the Rhine graben, as well as the *puys* of central France, display a..linear arrangement. **1968** R. W. Fairbridge *Encycl. Geomorphol.* 947/2 Detailed surveys of rift valleys in Africa, the Middle East and elsewhere show that idealized symmetric graben profiles are rarely seen, that the opposite sides are frequently asymmetric, and that there is often only a single fault. **1976** K. Thackeray *Crownbird* ii. 33 He found himself looking at the sides of the rift valley, recognizing different strata. **1931** Daubney & Hudson in *Jrnl. Path. & Bacteriol.* XXXIV. 578 We have proposed the name *Rift Valley fever* as a popular alternative to our first suggestion *enzootic hepatitis*, which was originally applied to the disease in sheep. The latter is hardly a suitable name for the human disease, since we have as yet no evidence that the liver is involved in man. **1962** Gordon & Lavoipierre *Entomol. for Students of Med.* xix. 121 The demonstration in 1949 that a species of *Eretmapodites* (*E. chrysogaster*) was capable of acting as a vector of Rift Valley fever under natural conditions, has increased the interest of the epidemiologist in this group of mosquitoes. **1978** *Nature* 26 Jan. 308/2 Rift Valley fever or enzootic hepatitis is a severe viral infection which primarily affects sheep and cattle causing many deaths in pregnant and newborn animals. The disease occurs naturally only in Africa and by 1912 it was recognised in the Rift Valley in Kenya.

rift, *sb.*[4] **1.** (Earlier and later examples.)

1727 in *Documents Colonial Hist. New-York* (1855) V. 826 The French..have no way but to come up from Montreal to the Lake against a Violent Stream, all full of Rifts and Falls and Shallows. **1845** J. F. Cooper *Chainbearer* II. vi. 80 The most that can be done with it [*sc.* the lumber]..will be to float it down to the next rift. **1879** *Scribner's Monthly* Nov. 21/1 In one hanging rift close by the bank..I took at five casts fifteen fish.

rift, *v.*[1] **1. a.** (Later examples.)

a **1861** T. Winthrop *John Brent* (1862) xix. 209 A little pathway in the sage-bushes suddenly opened before me, as a lane rifts in the press of hurrying legions 'mid the crush of a city thoroughfare. **1898** H. S. Canfield *Maid of Frontier* 75 The mass of vapor overhead rifted for a moment. **1979** *Nature* 22 Nov. 378/2 The block rifted from mainland South-east Asia and met with the northwards drifting Australian continent during the Neo-gene.

ri·fting, *vbl. sb.*[2] [f. Rift *v.*[1] + -ing[1].]

1. Chiefly *U.S.* **a.** *Quarrying.* The occurrence or development of rifts in rock. Cf. *RIFT *sb.*[2] 2 f.

1889 *9th Ann. Rep. U.S. Geol. Survey* 602 (*heading*) Rifting of the quarried rocks. **1891** *Amer. Jrnl. Sci.* CXLI. 269 Rifting is..dependent upon the thousands of minute dislocations which occur in every cubic inch of rock. **1937** *Mem. Geol. Soc. Amer.* V. 20 Rifting in granites has been known for a long time.

b. The action of splitting mica into thick sheets.

1939 G. A. Roush *Strategic Min. Supplies* xii. 345 The books [of mica] are first split into slabs about $\frac{1}{8}$ inch thick (rifting). **1954** S. J. Johnstone *Minerals for Chem. & Allied Industries* 331 The preparation of mica for the market usually involves..rifting into sheets sufficiently thin to be cut by hand with a blade. **1960** S. A. Montague in J. L. Gillson et al. *Industr. Min. & Rocks* (ed. 3) xxvii. 559/1 The operations of rough splitting and trimming mica are termed 'rifting' or 'sheeting'.

2. *Physical Geogr.* The process of severing of areas of the earth's crust into distinct blocks or plates by formation of rifts. Cf. *RIFT *sb.*[2] 2 g.

1924 J. G. A. Skerl tr. *Wegener's Orig. Continents & Oceans* xi. 166 Folding and rifting are only different effects of one and the same process. **1969** *Times* 20 May 12/7 Major rifting of the Earth's surface. **1969** *Nature* 11 Oct. 140/1 Although rifting was completed during the Lower Cretaceous, significant continental drift did not occur until the Lower Turonian. **1978** *Ibid.* 13 July 127/1 The eruptions were accompanied by extensive rifting..which led to formation of the Sveinagjá graben.

fig. **1975** W. Safire *Before the Fall* x. iv. 667 There was no rift..between the President and his national security adviser. There was plenty of rifting going on between Henry and the White House staff.

riftless, *a.* (Earlier example.)

1797 *Spirit of Farmers' Museum* (1801) 71 From the gnarl'd oak..To the green vine, which twines its riftless sides.

rig, *sb.*[6] Add: **1.** Also [infl. by Da. *rig*, Norw., Sw. *rigg*], = Rigging (*vbl.*) *sb.*[2] 2.

1888 L. A. Smith *Music of Waters* 222 Out in Pamerent in Holland, There lay a brig so old; Worn out was her hull, And worn out was her rig. **1889** *Musical Times* 1 July 394/2 On page 222 she uses the word 'rig' as 'rigging', whereas even a landsman knows the difference. **1903** *Rudder* Feb. 52/1 Mr. Crowninshield has changed the overhangs slightly..and has put on a slightly larger rig. **1934** *Yachting Monthly* LVI. 463/1 The weight and center of gravity of the rig must be considered.

2. (Earlier examples.) *rig of the day* (Naut.), the uniform to be worn on any particular day.

1843 T. C. Haliburton *Attaché* I. xii. 218 Congregations are rigged out in their..bran new clothes, silks, satins.., and all sorts of rigs. **1853** 'P. Paxton' *Stray Yankee in Texas* xxvii. 267 Here was a rig for a July day in Texas, with the thermometer at 105° in the shade! **1914** [see *NUMBER *sb.* 5 c]. **1948** Partridge *Dict. Forces' Slang* 155 *The rig-of-the-day*. The dress that is to be worn for the day is 'piped' with 'Hands to breakfast and clean; rig-of-the-day, number—whatever it is'. **1961** F. H. Burgess *Dict. Sailing* 154 *Out of the rig of the day*, incorrectly dressed.

3. Delete *U.S.* and add: **a.** (Further examples.) *spec.* = *oil rig* s.v. *OIL *sb.*[1] 6 e.

1885 *Encycl. Brit.* XVIII. 716/2 When the location of a well has been determined, a derrick or 'rig' is built, which consists of the derrick itself and a small house for an engine. **1946** E. Hodgins *Mr. Blandings builds his Dream House* I. vi. 89 Mr Blandings' well was being drilled... The rig's motor roared and stank. **1957** *Economist* 21 Dec. 1080/3 During 1958 test wells will be drilled in the Benin area in Western Nigeria..; five rigs are now drilling. **1974** E. Ambler *Dr. Frigo* I. 46 It's not the same as ordinary off-shore drilling. The rigs have to be different. **1975** *Daily Tel.* 24 May 11/4 Some gas production rigs built up to 10 years ago for the southern North Sea had designs which underestimated the full vigour of the waves.

b. orig. and chiefly *N. Amer.* (Earlier and later examples.) Also, any vehicle; *spec.* a lorry, a truck.

1831 A. Stoddard *Diary* 30 Nov. in *Michigan Hist. Mag.* (1927) XI. 472 Breakfast swallowed we stepped into our next rig, which was a lumber wagon. **1872** 'Mark Twain' *Roughing It* xlvi. 325 I've heard tell of carriages all my life... I mean to have the nobbiest rig that's going. **1931** H. F. Pringle *Theodore Roosevelt* I. i. 4 A rig had been..summoned from a near-by stable. **1938** *Amer. Speech* XIII. 307 *Rig*, also a designation for any bus. **1938** *Commercial Car Jrnl.* June 60/3 *Rig*, a truck. **1942** Berrey & Van den Bark *Amer. Thes. Slang* § 766/2 (*Bus, taxicab, truck.*)..oilcan, rig, tub. **1957** J. Kerouac *On Road* (1958) 16 A great big tough truckdriver..got his rig under way. **1963** *Amer. Speech* XXXVIII. 45 Rig.., a tractor and semitrailer; sometimes just a tractor. **1969** *Publ. Amer. Dial. Soc.* LII. 35 *Rig*, any truck on the fire fighting force. 'Back the rig in.' **1970** J. H. Gray *Boy from Winnipeg* 63 The [fire brigade] horses were kept in box stalls behind the rigs which were all parked facing the street. **1972** J. Minifie *Homesteader* x. 85 When the last rig had pulled out my father went down to the barn. **1974** *Times* 11 Feb. 6/7 Mr Nixon came on the air..to urge the drivers to get their 'big rigs' back on the road. **1976** *Daily Tel.* (Colour Suppl.) 16 July 10/1 No CBer ever drives. He cooks or pushes a rig. **1976** L. Deighton *Twinkle, Twinkle Little Spy* xxiii. 225 The gargantuan trailer-trucks rolled south to Timbuktu in convoy, enough drivers in each rig to eat and sleep in relays. **1977** *Hot Car* Oct. 76/2 Pulled into Steeple Claydon early Sunday morning and looked out across nearly 250 vans, trucks, rods and rigs.

c. Any apparatus or device.

1868 *Rep. Iowa Agric. Soc. 1867* 174, I consider the Victor mill & Cook's evaporator the best rig for making sirup profitably from cane. **1950** *Engineering* 10 Mar. 265/2 Regrinding is extremely simple; the drill steel is placed on a rig and the tip is ground either by a pedestal grinder or by a hand grinder. **1973** *Sci. Amer.* Nov. 1/3 (Advt.), Before a new seat enters production, its suspension must survive 300,000 load changes on a vibrating rig. **1977** *Amer. Speech 1975* L. 65 *Rig n*, hypodermic needle used to inject drugs into a vein. 'A rusty rig will give you hepatitis.' **1979** *Sci. Amer.* Dec. 52/1 Intravenous infusion, which is normally done in a hospital with an elaborate rig involving bottles of fluid, connecting tubes and cannulas.

d. An amateur's radio transmitter and receiver; also, a telegraph, a radar set, or the like.

1942 Berrey & Van den Bark *Amer. Thes. Slang* § 810/2 *Telegraph*, ethegraph, kid, Old Betsy, rig, she. **1960** *Daily Progress* (Charlottesville, Va.) 29 Sept. 39/3 Hams have their own slang terms. 'Rig' is what they call their sending and receiving equipment and 'shack' is the name of the room or structure housing their sets. **1966** M. Woodhouse *Tree Frog* xxi. 155 This [radar] rig is operational two per cent of the time. **1976** A. Hope *Hi-Fi Handbk.* 10 After the purchase of a house and a car, an impressive hi-fi rig may well be the next most expensive item ever bought by a householder. **1977** *Rolling Stone* 30 June 118/4 But by the time you added a booster amplifier, and perhaps a separate cassette unit—not to mention a CB rig—you ended up with no leg room. **1978** *Observer* 18 June 4/2 The normal range of a regular watt rig is between five and ten miles.

e. The penis. *coarse slang.*

1964 *Amer. Folk Music Occasional* I. 12 There is a certain latitude in the approach to Negro blues where women are sweet food..and sex is hard, virile labor (I got a big tall rig, it drills way down deep). **1973** M. Amis *Rachel Papers* 92 All weekend I cried,..thought of ways of committing suicide,..considered lopping off my rig with a razor-blade.

4. *attrib.*, as (sense 3 a) *rig crew, medic* (colloq.), *operator.*

1972 L. M. Harris *Introd. Deepwater Floating Drilling Operations* xviii. 191 The shortage of personnel is not limited only to rig crews. **1977** *Observer* 24 Apr. 1/6 The rig crew was about to install a safety valve on the top of a production pipe. **1977** *Lancet* 8 Oct. 751/1 Resuscitation during this period is the responsibility of a sick-bay attendant ('rig medic') or, if life-supporting measures are required in a pressure chamber, of a suitably trained diver. **1975** *Offshore* Aug. 51/1 A rig operator, on the average, will call on the divers two or three times a month for inspection, repairs or retrieval of lost equipment.

rig (rig), *sb.*[7] *dial.* Also **rigg.** [Perh. f. Wrig *v.*, as the fish is remarkable for the way it twists itself round the line on which it is caught.] The tope, *Galeorhinus galeus*, a shallow-water shark found in the eastern Atlantic and in the Mediterranean; in quot. 1963 = *HUSS *sb.*

[**1547** *Act 1 Edw. VI* vii. m. 5 pisces regał, viz' sturgions balenas catas porpec' delphinos regges graspes. **1549** *Act 3 Edw. VI* ii. m. 40 pisces regał videlt sturgiones balenas cetas porpec' delphinos rigges graspes.] *c* **1700** in *Newnes Encycl. Angling* (1963) 90/2 Royal fish, viz. sturgeons, grampuses, whales, porpoises, dolphins, riggs and graspes, and generally whatsoever other fish having in themselves great and immense size or fat. **1887** Parish & Shaw *Dict. Kentish Dial.* 128 *Rig*, the common tope. *Galeus vulgaris*.—Folkestone. **1927** *Glasgow Herald* 7 Sept. 12/7 On the south-east coasts of England a species of small shark, known locally as 'rigg', is caught on strong lines baited with mackerel. **1963** [see *HUSS *sb.*].

rig, *v.*[2] Add: **1. d.** (See quot. 1956.)

1909 *Aero Man.* 104 By rigging diagonal wires across top and bottom and across both sides, the entire frame of the glider will be rendered quite rigid. **1916** *Aëronaut. Jrnl.* XX. p. ii (Advt.), Steel wire strands & cords of galvanised or plated steel wire (for rigging aircraft). **1956** W. A. Heflin *U.S. Air Force Dict.* 443/1 *Rig.* 1. To assemble, adjust, and align the major components of an *aircraft*; *specif.*, to assemble and align the airfoils or other surfaces of an *aircraft*. 2. To fit out an *aircraft* with control cables, bracing cables, pulleys, turnbuckles, and the like. **1978** *Sci. Amer.* Nov. 135/1 The Wrights also flew the machine as a glider, experimenting by rigging it with a dihedral angle.

rig, *v.*⁶ Add: **1. b.** To take to task; to rag or tease. *U.S.*

1892 *Dialect Notes* I. 231 *Rig*, to tell a joke on. 'He rigged him good.' **1899** A. H. QUINN *Pennsylvania Stories* 100, I rigged him about it once and he said he'd reform.

2. (Further examples.)

1933 *Lit. Digest* 1 July 40/3 'It's in the bag' is an expression..to designate that prize-fights or horse-races have been rigged. **1935** *Sun* (Baltimore) 30 Oct. 1/2 The way the 'election' was rigged made an opposing farmer seem a sap. **1955** *Times* 23 June 10/2 Mr. J. McShane..claimed that that meeting had been 'rigged' and that rank and file London dockers would not resume work on Monday. **1966** *Wall St. Jrnl.* 25 July 1 'Top 40' record lists that allegedly are rigged by gifts of free records by the carload. **1967** W. SOYINKA *Kongi's Harvest* 72, I did my best to rig the results in favour of the state co-operatives.

3. *to rig the market*, also *fig.*

1978 A. RYAN in Hookway & Pettit *Action & Interpretation* 76 The only question at issue here is whether we should treat his account of social interaction as a story about how we rig the market, or as a story about how we engage in putting on a good show.

riga² (ri·gă). [Hausa.] A man's loose-fitting robe, worn in West Africa.

1923 *Daily Mail* 14 June 7 The two Sudanese hunters.. saw London... Wearing long white cloaks, or rigas,..they began a search for Captain Buchanan. **1928** *Daily Express* 6 Oct. 9 There appears on the verandah steps a dignified Mohammedan in flowing 'riga'. **1932** J. CARY *Aissa Saved* liii. 287 God, in a white riga and a new indigo turban. **1973** J. J. MCKELVEY *Man against Tsetse* iii. 171 A flowing yellow *riga* Nigerian style over a brown business suit. **1977** P. NEWMAN et al. *Mod. Hausa–Eng. Dict.* 100/1 The *riga*, worn over a shirt and trousers, is the standard attire in much of West Africa.

rigaree (rigărī·), *a.* Also **rig-a-ree**. *Glass-Blowing.* [Perh. ad. It. *rigare*: see next.] Applied to a pattern of raised bands upon a glass vessel, or the method of producing such bands.

1923 H. J. POWELL *Glass-Making in Eng.* iii. 22 (*caption*) Base of tumbler, showing rig-a-ree decoration. *Ibid.* 44 *Rigaree marks*, parallel lines on a raised band, tear or collar of glass, produced by ridges on the edge of a small metal wheel. **1946** W. B. HONEY *Victoria & Albert Mus. Glass* i. 8 Softened glass is readily drawn out into threads, and these may be wound upon ('trailed') and attached to a vessel and melted in to give a more or less smooth surface; such threads may be drawn together with tools into a network or be impressed with a patterned wheel, making the so-called 'rigaree' trail. **1960** H. HAYWARD *Antique Coll.* 240/1 *Rigaree trail*, a process of glass-blowing in which applied threads of glass are attached to a vessel. **1965** [see *PASSGLAS].

‖ **rigatoni** (rigatōᵘ·ni), *sb. pl.* (Also used as *sing.*) [It. f. *rigato* pa. pple. of *rigare* to draw a line, to make fluting.] Short hollow tubes of pasta in fluted form; a dish of this pasta.

1930 H. BURKE *Cookery Bk.* 100 'Rigattoni' is the Italian name for a special kind of macaroni which comes in short thick tubes. **1958** *Catal. County Stores, Taunton* June 17 *Naples Macaroni*... Cut—Millenghe, Rigatoni, Cannelloni—a lb. ½. **1962** *Punch* 25 July 129/1 *Capellini*,..*rigatoni*, *tagliatini*, noodles and a hundred other traditional shapes [of pasta]. **1967** A. BAILEY in L. Deighton *London Dossier* 56 A plate of really excellent spaghetti, rigatoni, tagliatelli or ravioli. **1976** *Times* 10 July 10/7 Home-made cannelloni or rigatoni with mussels, are other first courses worth trying.

‖ **rigaudon** (rigodoṅ). [Fr., of obscure origin: see RIGADOON *sb.*] = RIGADOON *sb.*

1706 [see note in small type below RIGADOON *sb.*]. **1923** E. SITWELL *Bucolic Comedies* 26 Dancing with angels all in a round, Hornpipe and rigaudon on the Fair's ground. **1938** *Oxf. Compan. Mus.* 801/2 The rigaudon was gay and lively until its promotion from the village green to the aristocratic ball-room and the court, when it took on dignity. **1959** *Collins Mus. Encycl.* 549/2 *Rigaudon*.., a Provençal dance in lively 2/2 time which was adopted into the suite and into the ballet of French opera in the late 17th cent. **1970** W. APEL *Harvard Dict. Mus.* (ed. 2) 734/1 The *rigaudon* also occurs in the suites of modern composers (Grieg, *From Holberg's Time*; Ravel, *le Tombeau de Couperin*). **1979** *Early Music* Jan. 40/1 The French use this (2-)metre in various dances such as..rigaudons, gavottes, rondeaus, [etc.].

rigescent, *a.* Delete *Bot.* and add examples.

1966 *Punch* 20 July (Advt. facing p. 107), The tough, rigescent and unyielding bar of iron is heated to the required temperature. **1974** *Nature* 5 Apr. 512/1 Sodium dodecyl sulphate..left an intact rigescent integument inside which was the intact starch sheath.

rigged, *ppl. a.*¹ Add: **3.** Fitted *up*, esp. as an expedient or makeshift.

1932 C. ISHERWOOD *Memorial* I. iii. 36 The rigged-up stage was backed by sackcloth curtains.

4. Fixed *up*, equipped.

1935 A. J. POLLOCK *Underworld Speaks* 97/2 *Rigged up*, all ready with auto, tools, pistol, machine gun, etc., for a criminal job.

rigger¹. Add: **1. b.** One who attends to the rigging of aircraft.

1912 *Flight* 20 Apr. 348/2 N.C.O.'s and air mechanics will be required as engine drivers, fitters,..riggers, &c. **1920** [see *RIGGING (*vbl.*) *sb.*² 1 b]. **1930** *Daily Express* 6 Oct. 2/5 Norcott, A. W. J., aged twenty-nine, rigger... No previous flying experience before joining R 101 in October 1929. **1942** *R.A.F. Jrnl.* 30 May 30 By what, then, is the R.A.F. kept in the air?.. Perhaps by the riggers..or the Observer Corps?

4. (Earlier and further examples.)

1893 [see *IN-RIGGER]. **1935** L. LUARD *Conquering Seas* i. 9 They drove those full riggers in the good old days.

6. a. One who works on an oil rig (orig., on a rotary one). **b.** One who is employed in the construction of oil rigs.

1949 *Amer. Speech* XXIV. 35 From this conflict emerged the titles..*rigger*..and *swivel neck* for rotary drillers. **1974** *BP Shield Internat.* Oct. 8/3 Highlands Fabricators created their own skilled local workforce..by training 610 former farm workers..as welders, riggers and fabricators. **1977** *Offshore Engineer* May 10/2 (Advt.), Manpower—experienced Fitters, Riggers and Welders.

rigger³ (ri·gəɹ). *Austral.* and *N.Z. slang.* [Origin unknown.] (See quot. 1941.)

1941 BAKER *Dict. Austral. Slang* 60 *Rigger*, a quart bottle of beer, esp. a quart of draught beer in a square-faced gin bottle. **1943** F. SARGESON in *Penguin New Writing* XVII. 66 I'd meet him every day, and I'd always bring a couple of riggers.

rigging, (*vbl.*) *sb.*² Add: **1. b.** The work of adjusting the wires, control surfaces, etc., of an aircraft.

1914 *Flight* 3 July 700/2 The list of lectures..are as follow..Rigging, and Training of Riggers. **1920** G. C. BAILEY *Compl. Airman* xxii. 173 Rigging is the art of erecting the machine and so adjusting the various surfaces, controls, etc., that it is in a fit condition for flying. The upkeep of the machine is also part of the rigger's work. **1937** *Discovery* Sept. 293/1 A very elementary account of the rigging and truing-up of an aircraft. **1941** NORCROSS & QUINN *Aviat. Mechanic* viii. 345 (*caption*) Cadet class in rigging at Randolph Field, Tex. A biplane involves all the fundamentals of rigging.

2. *to climb the rigging*: to become angry, lose one's temper. *Naval slang.*

1916 'TAFFRAIL' *Carry On!* 27 To get angry is to 'get dizzy' or 'climb the rigging'.

b. The system of ropes and wires used to support the structure of and distribute the load of an airship or aircraft.

1843 *Mechanics' Mag.* 8 Apr. 276/1 The direct resistance of the car, masts, and rigging, in the construction of aerial vehicles, will..probably put a limit to their velocity not much exceeding 24 to 30 miles per hour. **1900** J. M. BACON *By Land & Sky* i. 12 The balloon on rising fouled a big elm, and for a moment remained caught high up among the boughs. Then it tore off a large branch entangled in the rigging. **1919** H. SHAW *Text-bk. Aeronaut.* xvii. 198 In the Parseval type [of airship], the car is suspended from a large elliptical rigging band just below the centre of the envelope. **1969** *Gloss. Aeronaut. & Astronaut. Terms* (*B.S.I.*) VII. 6 *Rigging*, the system of wires or cords and their attachments, by which the dead weight, or the main cable tension, is distributed over the hull or envelope. **1977** D. BEATY *Excellency* i. 7 The weekends he'd spent.. servicing Cirrus engines and checking the rigging of Austers in return for free flying lessons.

c. In full *rigging lines*. In a parachute, the system of cords which join the canopy to the harness.

1929 *Aeronautics* (H.M.S.O.) 109 The rigging is so parcelled that it is pulled out gradually, the part already released remaining taut and straight, the whole of the rigging emerging before the commencement of the withdrawal of the body. **1935** C. G. BURGE *Encycl. Aviation* 489 *Rigging Lines*, the cords which transmit the load from the harness (or life lines) to the body of the parachute. **1952** *Chambers's Jrnl.* May 262/2 A bad exit can cause the rigging-lines to tangle and prevent the 'chute from opening. **1958** *Listener* 7 Aug. 202/2 There were casualties..due to tangling of the rigging lines, or faulty exit. **1972** *Daily Tel.* 16 May 3 The Prince of Wales was turned upside down when his feet caught in the rigging lines of his parachute as he hurtled seawards from 1,200ft during his controversial jump from an RAF plane.

ri·gging, (*vbl.*) *sb.*³ [f. RIG *v.*⁶ + -ING¹.] The action of the verb RIG⁶; trickery, swindling; ragging or teasing; manipulation of prices; electoral fraud.

1839, etc. [see THIMBLERIG *v.*]. **1912** H. CROLY *Marcus A. Hanna* 460 He was constantly on the lookout for a chance to joke about the peccadilloes of his friends. There were few of them who escaped this kind of rigging. **1932** *Sun* (Baltimore) 27 Apr. 15/7 His general chronicle of stock-price 'rigging'. **1946** *Ibid.* 27 Dec. 1/8 One of the sharpest breaks came in New York and Chicago wholesale butter markets... Much of the mystery surrounding the break in New York, where charges of 'rigging' had been heard, was removed. **1959**, **1961** [see *ballot-rigging* s.v. *BALLOT *sb.*¹ 4]. **1980** G. M. FRASER *Mr American* xxii. 430 It isn't rigging, you see. You couldn't rig a British judge and jury nowadays.

riggish, *a.* Add: Occas. in wider (i.e. non-dialectal) use. (Later examples.)

1963 T. PYNCHON *V.* i. 15 Which after forty-five years was nothing for any riggish Pappy Hod to be finding out. **1973** *Daily Tel.* 25 Apr. 15/3 Both have a sweetness that disinfects Wycherley's basic cynicism, whose spirit is admirably personified by Frances Cuka's unashamedly riggish Lady Fidget.

Riggs (rigz). *Path.* [Name of John Mankey Riggs (1810–85), U.S. dentist, who described the condition in 1876 (*Pennsylvania Jrnl. Dental Sci.* III. 99–104).] *Riggs'(s)* (also erron. *Rigg's*) *disease*: a disease of the tissues adjacent to the teeth, characterized by suppuration and inflammation of the gums.

1877 *Dental Cosmos* XIX. 70 What do I know about Riggs's disease (so-called).—How does it happen that this title has come into existence? *Ibid.* 185 The trouble which has come to be called Riggs's disease has not hitherto responded to..treatment. **1887** C. S. TOMES *Syst. Dental Surg.* (ed. 3) 695 The discharge, which is a prominent symptom in the more acute cases, suggested the name pyorrhoea alveolaris, which has passed into general currency, while the warm advocacy of a particular form of treatment, and the consequent attention drawn to its advocate in connection with the disease, has led to the frequent use of the term Riggs's disease. **1900** 'MARK TWAIN' in *McClure's Mag.* Jan. 290 If you don't know what Riggs's Disease of the Teeth is, the dentist will tell you. **1923** K. H. THOMA *Teeth, Diet & Health* vi. 78 Other names for pyorrhea are Rigg's disease, receding gums, and pericementoclasia, the latter being the latest scientific term.

right, *sb.*¹ Add: **II. 9. b.** (Further examples.) *right-to-life* adj. phr., designating persons, etc., opposed to the abortion of the unborn fœtus or concerned with this issue; hence **right-to-lifer**.

1916 G. B. SHAW *Androcles & Lion* p. lxx, We must begin by holding the right to an income as sacred and equal, just as we now begin by holding the right to life as sacred and equal. **1972** *Times* 22 Jan. 18/7 English law does not yet recognize a right to privacy. **1973** A. E. WILKERSON *Rights of Children* 312 It is doubtful that in the right-to-life controversy the rights of the unborn child will be inviolate. **1973** *Austral. Humanist* XXVI. 1/1 The victory of the Roman Catholic-dominated Right to Life Association over the McKenzie–Lamb private members Bill to provide abortions on request..will be seen by social historians of the future as pyrrhic. **1977** *Time* 25 July 2/3 If the Government provided its citizens with alternative birth control methods (free of charge), there would be fewer abortions. Even the right-to-lifers would like that.

c. (Further examples.) *right-to-work*, phr. used *attrib.* with reference to a worker's right not to be required to join a trade union. *U.S.*

1958 *Economist* 15 Nov. 599/2 So far the only change that Mr Meany has committed himself to seek is one to remove the provision which allows the states to adopt 'right-to-work' laws. These are laws forbidding employers and unions to enter into contracts that require workers to join the union within a specified period. **1967** *Harper's Mag.* Mar. 8 You might have then seen the virtue of the right-to-work policy... What would have been gained..if you sanctioned a system by which this honest and qualified ex-con were compelled to join a union against his will as the price of holding his new-found job? **1976** *Globe & Mail* (Toronto) 22 Mar. 6/1 In 1967 the great bulk of federal civil servants were given the right to strike. **1979** *Tucson Mag.* Mar. 31/3 Both [cities] are situated in a right-to-work state.

f. In *pl.* A title or authority to perform, publish, film, or televise a particular work, event, etc. *serial rights*: see SERIAL *adj.* b in Dict. and Suppl.

1890 KIPLING *Let.* in C. E. Carrington *Rudyard Kipling* (1955) vii. 162 Harper & Co. bought the serial rights for American and paid me. **1913**, etc. [see *film rights* s.v. *FILM sb. 7 c]. **1935** *Discovery* Sept. 277/1 The cost of the televising rights for the fight would have to be such as to compensate for the loss of cinema rights. **1939** D. L. SAYERS *In Teeth of Evidence* 208 There were the touring rights..and film rights..and probably radio rights. **1953** [see *ASTRONOMICAL *a.* 1 b]. **1959** *Bookseller* 17 Jan. 124/1 American publishers..claim..that the financial rewards of book-publishing come not from mere publishing but from the sale of film, paperback, serial and other rights. **1974** I. PARSONS in A. Briggs *Ess. Hist. of Publishing* 49 Richardson had made binding agreements with a succession of Dublin booksellers under which he was to receive certain sums in return for exclusive rights. **1981** *Bookseller* 27 June 2226/1 We've sold the US and UK rights in books on the South Island of New Zealand. **1981** M. SPARK *Loitering with Intent* xii. 220 The Triad [Press] sold the American rights, the paperback rights, the film rights, and most of the foreign rights.

g. *rights issue*. An issue of shares offered at a special price by a company to its existing shareholders. Also *ellipt.*

1955 *Times* 20 Aug. 11/2 The Commercial Bank of Australia's 'rights' issue of 2,105,868 Ordinary shares of 10s. (Australian currency) at 15s. each has been over-subscribed without recourse to the underwriters. **1960** *Economist* 8 Oct. 187/1 Successive mergers..reduced its proportionate holding. So, too, did the rights issues of ordinary shares, for as an American investor Bendix could not subscribe for the new shares but had to sell its rights. **1968** *Sun* 25 Oct. 10/5 With last night's price for the ordinary 18s. 9d., the 'rights' are worth a little over 2d. per share, which is not very much. **1970** *Money Which?* Mar. 61/2 Under a rights issue, a company in which you already own shares offers you the chance to buy new shares at a special price. **1976** *Birmingham Post* 16 Dec. 9/5 Lazards are to discuss the intricate and difficult problems of the conflicting timing of its offer for Dunford and Elliott and Dunford's rights issue with the takeover Panel. **1981** *Times* 24 Apr. 15/4 Rowntree Mackintosh..is to raise £42m after expenses from shareholders with a rights issue... Terms of the issue are one new ordinary share at 160p for every four held.

10. b. (Further examples of phr. *in one's own right*.) Now freq. used in general senses, without reference to a particular title or claim.

1863 *Times* 11 Mar. 5/2 The Crown Princess of Prussia ..has always been popular in her own right. **1939** G. B. SHAW *In Good King Charles's Golden Days* I. 47 When I am King—as I shall be, in my own right, and not by the leave of any Protestant parliamentary gang. **1965** *Listener* 2 Sept. 331/1, I shall try to say something of the fundamental problems of science which are of the deepest significance in their own right. **1966** *Ibid.* 20 Oct. 560/1 It is a pity that Tvardovsky is so little known in the west. He is a very perceptive critic, and a considerable poet in his own right. **1971** *Guardian* 12 Nov. 9/4 The Domaine de la Rayre..is a wine of character..in its own right. **1978** I. B. SINGER *Shosha* iii. 50 He has a nasty wife and estranged children who are rich in their own right.

IV. 17. d. (Earlier and later examples.) Usu. applied to any political group holding conservative principles.

1825 *Ann. Reg. 1824* 152/1 M. de la Bourdonnaye (leader of the extreme right). **1830** *Ann. Reg. 1829* 157/2 All the new ministers belonged to the extreme right. **1848** MRS. GASKELL *Let.* 2 Nov. (1966) 60, I never can ascertain what I am in politics; and veer about from extreme Right,—no, I don't think I ever go as far as the extreme Left. **1940** W. TEMPLE *Thoughts in War-Time* iii. 24 The Right tends to have a fuller sense of historical continuity than the Left. **1954** KOESTLER *Invisible Writing* xxxvi. 385 The trial of the so-called 'Anti-Soviet Block of Rights and Trotskyists' took place in Moscow. **1955** *Times* 23 May 11/7 There is much division among the delegates of free countries on how to deal with the Left and Right dictatorship delegations. **1960** O. MANNING *Great Fortune* xviii. 220 We did nothing to establish a liberal policy that could save the country from either extremity—Left or Right. **1969** A. G. FRANK *Latin Amer.* xix. 316 The current wave of government repression against the Left need not mean a permanent move to the Right. **1974** J. WHITE tr. *Poulantzas's Fascism & Dictatorship* IV. 224 In the struggle against the Left Opposition..the Comintern took a turn to the 'right'.

e. In various sports, the right side or wing of the field of play; a player occupying this position (cf. *RIGHT WING 2).

1867 *Ball Players' Chron.* 8 Aug. 6/3 The nine will be as follows:..Peters, right. **1892** *College Index* (Auburn, Alabama) Nov. 27 Mr. G. O. Shackleford, the Athens left guard, who gave our right so much trouble at the match game in Atlanta last February has entered college here. **1934** in B. James *England v Scotland* (1969) 152 Attack after attack on the English goal. Superb work by that sprite of a player, Cook, on the extreme right. **1949** *Telephone-Reg.* (McMinnville, Oregon) 4 Aug. 2/1 Jimmy 'Whiskers' Beard then drove both in with a single to right.

18. c. (Further examples.)

1898 [see *LAND *v.* 2 e]. **1930** *Daily Express* 6 Oct. 11/5 The blow with which he dropped Compere for the full count was a right to the jaw. **1937** C. HIMES *Black on Black* (1973) 130 He'd go out fast with the garrote in his left hand, throw a hard right at the bastard's face. **1972** J. MOSEDALE *Football* iv. 49 Bob Snyder..threw a roundhouse right that knocked Matheson out the door.

d. A shot fired at game with the right barrel of a double-barrelled shotgun; a bird or beast hit by such a shot. Cf. RIGHT AND LEFT, RIGHT-AND-LEFT *sb.* 2.

1893, etc. [see *LEFT *sb.* 4].

e. *Surfing.* The (use of the) right foot.

1968 *Surfer Mag.* Jan. 73/1 Eamonn Matthews..caught some nice rights. **1970** *Surf '70* (N.Z.) 44/2 There were good lefts and occasional rights with Ted Spencer carving turns people thought were impossible.

f. A right-hand turn. *U.S.*

1961 WEBSTER, s.v., Take the right at the fork. **1969** D. E. WESTLAKE *Up your Banners* v. 35 The light turned green and she made a right. **1977** R. E. HARRINGTON *Quintain* vi. 49 A blue Rover had made a right off a side street to pull in ahead of the cab. **1981** G. V. HIGGINS *Rat on Fire* xiii. 96 Leo Proctor took a right in Dorchester Avenue and drove the van south.

V. 21. *Comb.* **right-left** *attrib. phr.*, of or between right and left.

1968 M. S. LIVINGSTON *Particle Physics* vii. 132 The parity conservation expresses this symmetry between events in the real world and their mirror images, this right-left symmetry of form. **1970** S. ROKKAN *Citizens, Elections, Parties* x. 335 He sees in this circumstance a possible explanation for the absence of a clear-cut tradition of right-left polarization in the United States. **1978** *Science* 24 Feb. 852 (*heading*) Right-left asymmetries in the brain.

right, *a.* Add: **I. 3. a.** *right triangle*, a right-angled triangle.

1903 J. MCMAHON *Elem. Geom.* i. 62 In a right triangle the side opposite the right angle is called the hypotenuse. **1970** J. R. BYRNE *Mod. Elem. Geom.* v. 153 Suppose that we had a 'Book of Standard Right Triangles' for angles from measure 1 to 89°.

II. 7. e. *that's right*, used to express affirmation or agreement; *is that right?* phr. inviting confirmation of a statement or proposal; *to get* (something) *right*, to be accurate or correct (in a certain matter), to have (something) clear in one's mind.

1905 *N.Y. Even. Post* 7 Apr. 2 The President's address was frequently interrupted with applause and cries of 'That's right'. **1922** 'K. MANSFIELD' *Voyage* in *Garden Party* 186 'And you've got your cabin tickets safe?' 'Yes, dear.'.. Grandma felt for them inside her glove and showed him the tips. 'That's right.' **1925** A. CHRISTIE *Secret of Chimneys* x. 96 'You recognized the body as that of one of your guests?' 'That's right, inspector.' **1930** G. B. SHAW *Apple Cart* I. 12, I say to them 'You are supreme: exercise your power.' They say, 'That's right: tell us what to do'; and I tell them. **1932** *N. & Q.* June 415/2 We not are even simple-minded enough to say 'yes'; we prefer to say 'That's right'. **1933** *Punch* 16 Aug. 195 (*caption*) *Tourist* (*after two miles of it*). 'Look here, Alfonso, let's get this right. Have you adopted us or have we adopted you?' **1938** G. GREENE *Brighton Rock* VII. vii. 335 'So he was at your school.' 'That's right.' **1951** C. P. SNOW *Masters* III. xxxvii. 301, I expect Eliot has got everything he said right. **1958** *Spectator* 4 July 26/2 He *does* contrast the Spencers and the Churchills (Sir Winston is a Churchill not a Spencer, or have I got it right?). **1976** L. DEIGHTON *Twinkle, twinkle, Little Spy* x. 99 'They would take it real bad.' 'Is that right,' said Mann.

8. c. *right sort, stuff*: an alcoholic drink. *slang.*

1820 J. H. REYNOLDS *Fancy* 110 *Right sort*, gin. **1927** WODEHOUSE *Meet Mr Mulliner* vi. 198 A sharp spasm had reminded him how much of the right stuff he had in him at that moment.

d. Of persons and things: regarded with approval; socially acceptable; potentially influential.

1842, 1883 [see SORT *sb.*[2] 11 b]. **1900** H. JAMES *Little Tour in France* (ed. 2) vii. 76 The middle of the eighteenth century..was surely, in France at least, the age of good society, the period when the 'right people' made every haste to be born in time. **1901** J. VAIZEY *About Peggy Saville* x. 76 Travelling is good fun if you..provide yourself with introductions to the right people. **1928** KIPLING *Bk. of Words* xi. 86 It may be a snobbish way of putting it, but a man should know 'the right people' in the great world of books. **1931** S. JAMESON *Richer Dust* xv. 445 She went regularly to their houses, and with them to the right restaurants. **1936** A. CHRISTIE *Murder in Mesopotamia* xx. 178 She's young and she's crude, but she's the right sort. **1946** G. MILLAR *Horned Pigeon* i. 6 All of these officers were 'the right sort'. Which meant that their parents had all had sufficient money to send them to the more expensive schools. **1956** I. BROMIGE *Enchanted Garden* I. iii. 28 The importance of knowing the right people, of being seen with the right people. **1963** L. PETERS *Tarakian* vii. 98 Firth..had been to one of the 'right' schools, and one of the 'right' universities, and.. belonged to one or two of the 'right' clubs. **1973** 'D. HALLIDAY' *Dolly & Starry Bird* xi. 161 He had been to all the right schools and belonged to all the right clubs. **1981** J. CAREY *John Donne* ii. 77 Goodyer knew the right people... He mingled with the dispensers of power and lobbied them on Donne's behalf.

e. *Criminals' slang.* Reliable, trustworthy (from the criminal's point of view); friendly or sympathetic to criminals. Freq. in phr. *right guy*. Also *right croaker*, a doctor who will treat criminals without informing the police, or give prescriptions for drugs.

1856 in G. L. Chesterton *Revelations of Prison Life* I. ix. 137 They [*sc.* the swell mobsmen] frequent those public-houses the landlords of which they know to be what they term right (*i.e.* a thief's friend). **1886** A. PINKERTON *Thirty Years a Detective* 324 You will find him game, a good workman an a ded rite man. **1891** J. BENT *Criminal Life* 272 Will you go and tell Dutch Doll to come up to try and get me right twirl (good warder). **1891** 'F. W. CAREW' *No.* 747 i. 4 Warder—who, when accessible to a bribe, is termed a 'right-screw'. **1906** H. GREEN *At Actors' Boarding House* 61 Sammy explained that..the remainder had dwindled rapidly, what with treating the gang and being a right guy generally. **1911** [see *BOOB *sb.* 1]. **1914** JACKSON & HELLYER *Vocab. Criminal Slang* 70 *Right*,..sympathetic in a criminal sense; fixed; squared. **1926** [see *IN AND IN *adv.* b]. **1929** W. R. BURNETT *Little Caesar* I. i. 8 Some day he'll turn yellow. Hear what I say. He's not right. **1929** HOSTETTER & BEESLEY *It's a Racket!* vii. 93 To him [*sc.* the racketeer], a physician or surgeon is only a 'croaker', a 'right croaker' if he is the sort who will treat a fugitive criminal's wounds or injuries without notifying the police. **1938** J. PHELAN *Lifer* viii. 70 'Friend of yours?' inquired Mansell. 'Sure. Mine and Art's and Bill Weldon and—and anyone that's *right*.' **1951** *Evening Sun* (Baltimore) 27 Mar. 4/1 He [*sc.* a dope addict] may have found he could acquire prescriptions..from a doctor who had his price... (The doctor was a 'right croaker'). **1953** W. BURROUGHS *Junkie* vii. 71 When I told Gains what the hotel clerk said to me and how lucky we were he happened to be a right guy, he said, 'We've got to pack in. We can't last with this crowd.' **1969** *Publ. Amer. Dial. Soc.* LI. 23 We shall use this vocabulary..to indicate how both races equally—but separately—participate in such aspects of a common 'inmate culture' as those of *right guys* and *stoolpigeons*.

10. d. (Earlier example with reference to a person's age.)

1777 P. THICKNESSE *Year's Journey* II. 228 Get it [*sc.* information] from a French officer, or a priest, provided they are on the *wrong* side of forty... Avoid all acquaintance with either, on the *right* side of thirty.

13. b. (Further examples.) Now chiefly *Austral.* and *N.Z. colloq.* (influenced by *all right*: see sense 15 c below). Also *right as rain* (see sense 15 a below).

1873 C. M. YONGE *Pillars of House* IV. xlvii. 320 With the shout 'As right as a trivet', Charles Audley the younger ..rode on. **1909** BEERBOHM *Yet Again* 229 He looked,..'fit as a fiddle', or 'right as rain'. **1914** W. W. JACOBS *Night Watches* I. 14 'It was done in the collision,' said Mr. Scutts... 'I was as right as rain before then.' **1959** *Listener* 15 Jan. 115/2, I gave him a drink..and he was right. **1960** G. SANDERS *Mem. Professional Cad* I. iii. 35 It had severed some ligaments or what-not that caused him to have a slight limp afterwards, but apart from that he was as right as rain. **1963** A. LUBBOCK *Austral. Roundabout* 48 She poked her head out and cried: 'Are yer right?' I answered that I was far from right. **1944** P. W. COWAN in *Coast to Coast 1943* 166 He gave Mac the lantern. 'Think you'll be all right?' Anything you want?' 'I'll be right,' Mac said. **1967** N. FREELING *Strike Out* 30 'Was there anything wrong with the horse?' 'Not a thing... Horse was right as rain.' **1977** J. AIKEN *Last Movement* ii. 48 He will be right as rain,.. don't you worry. **1980** J. MELVILLE *Chrysanthemum Chain* 169 He'll surface as right as ninepence in due course.

e. Colloq. phr. *I'm all right, Jack*: see *JACK *sb.*[1] 3 c.

f. *to see* (someone) *right*, to look after (someone), to protect (that person's) interests.

1974 D. FRANCIS *Knock Down* xii. 147 Get me ten good two-year-olds and I'll see you right. **1975** *Times* 4 Jan. 12/6 No one's ever come to me before a fight and said 'Do this or do that and we'll see you right.'

14. b. (Further examples.)

1856 C. M. YONGE *Daisy Chain* II. xvi. 515 'I must be away from it all.'.. 'Forgetting your*self*,' said Ethel. 'Right. I want to have no leisure to think about myself,' said Norman. **1877** A. J. MUNBY *Diary* 23 Jan. in D. Hudson *Munby* (1972) 386 'I think I should go lengthwise down the boards,' said Massa, gravely. 'Right!' said the servant. **1883** H. SMART *At Fault* xviii. 213 Everybody will come to you; they will say Mr. Marlinson knows all about it. And you can reply, 'Right you are, I do... But..my lips are sealed.' **1912** E. R. BURROUGHS in *All-Story Mag.* Oct. 246/2 'If the mutineers are victorious our one slim hope lies in not having attempted to thwart or antagonize them.' 'Right you are, Alice. We'll keep in the middle of the road.' **1923** D. H. LAWRENCE *Kangaroo* xiv. 310 The same good-humoured, right-you-are approach from everybody to everybody. 'Right-you-are! Right-O!' Somers had been told so many hundreds of times, Right-he-was, Right-O!, that he almost had dropped into the way of it. **1935** 'L. FORD' *Burn Forever* xiii. 120 'I reckon you'd jes' as soon drive him over yonder to th' Crossroads? Hit ain't but a little piece.' 'Right,' Ben said... He opened the car door and turned back. **1970** R. GADNEY *Drawn Blanc* iv. 28 'Have you ever thought of working for the Foreign Service?' 'The British one?' 'Right.'

c. *too right* (*Austral.* and *N.Z. colloq.*), expressing agreement or approval.

1919 W. H. DOWNING *Digger Dial.* 51 *Two eyes right* or *too right*, certainly. **1926** K. S. PRICHARD *Working Bullocks* iv. 41 'That's to say you're as big a fool fruit-growing as Bill Graeme is catching wild horses.' Wally Burke's eyes took the fire-light as he smiled. 'Too right,' he said. **1936** *Punch* 22 Apr. 456/2 For she is crumbling, the poor old boat... 'Take care you don't put the brush through her.' 'Too right,' as the girls of Melbourne used to say. 'Too painfully right.' **1943** D. STEWART *Ned Kelly* I. i. 23 Devine's still in the lock-up?.. Too right he is. **1963** D. BALLANTYNE in C. K. Stead *N.Z. Short Stories* (1966) 162 'Dad, you're not going out at this time of night, are you?' my mother said. 'Too right I am,' Grandad said. **1977** *Zigzag* Aug. 31/1 Something better change—too right mate!

d. Phr. *how right you are* (and variants) used to express strong agreement or affirmation.

1927 H. T. LOWE-PORTER tr. *Mann's Magic Mountain* iv. 183 He saw how right Joachim had been in saying that it was hard to get acquainted here. **1935** D. L. SAYERS *Gaudy Night* viii. 167 'She's awfully kind. But I'm always having to be grateful... It makes me want to bite.' 'How right you are,' said Harriet. **1942** E. WAUGH *Put out More Flags* ii. 98 'I expect they thought that if we had time we should try and stop them coming.' 'How right they were.' **1957** M. KENNEDY *Heroes of Clone* I. i. 8 'Don't say exclusive when you mean expensive.'.. 'How right you are!' **1967** O. NORTON *Now lying Dead* i. 1 Not that anything they decided could embarrass the police, as the coroner gently pointed out. And how right he was. **1970** G. BUTLER *Coffin from Past* xiv. 147 'I always said I'd move away from here... I never liked the district.'.. 'How right you were,' he said.

e. Appended as an interrogative to the end of a statement, inviting agreement or approval, = *am I right?* orig. *U.S.*

1961 'E. FENWICK' *Friend of Mary Rose* (1962) x. 126, I gave her fifty dollars..fifty bucks, that's not raisins, right? **1968** *New Yorker* 4 May 49 We'll always groove with one another, right? **1969** 'P. KAVANAGH' *Such Men are Dangerous* i. 27 He was just doing his job, right? **1971** *Melody Maker* 13 Nov. 36/6 You're getting paid, right? Let's have a little co-operation around here. **1977** *Time* 26 Sept. 43/2, I was living alone on the West Side, in a one-room apartment with the bathroom out in the hallway and the bathtub in the kitchen, right? **1981** G. V. HIGGINS *Rat on Fire* xxvi. 159 You been here before, right? You can probably read the sign.

15. a. Colloq. phr. *right as rain* (see also sense 13 b above).

1894 W. RAYMOND *Love & Quiet Life* x. 108 ''Tes so right as rain, Zir,' zes I. **1894** SOMERVILLE & 'ROSS' *Real Charlotte* II. xx. 78 If only this infernal Fitzpatrick girl would have stayed with her cads in Dublin everything would have been as right as rain. **1908** A. S. M. HUTCHINSON *Once aboard Lugger* VI. vi. 332 We'll pull through right as rain. **1929** W. P. RIDGE *Affect. Regards* 110 If your husband hadn't put a spoke in, it would have been as right as rain. **1930** G. B. SHAW *Apple Cart* I. 15 *Proteus.* How did you get on with the King? *Boanerges.* Right as rain, Joe. You leave the king to me. **1973** *Times* 15 Dec. 7/5, I wished to renew my membership in the club. He licked his lips with relish as he lifted my familiar card from his file cabinet. 'Right as rain, sir.'

c. (Further examples.) Also in predicative use, in the sense 'satisfactory, acceptable', and as *adj. phr.* (see *ALL RIGHT 2). *all right by* or *with* (someone): acceptable to (that person).

1898 G. B. SHAW *Candida* II. 124 It will be all right: he will forgive me. **1914** —— *Fanny's First Play* III. 198 Is your aunt all right? **1939** R. CHANDLER *Let.* 19 Feb. (1966) 195 *The Big Sleep* is very unequally written. There are scenes that are all right. **1950** W. HAMMOND *Cricketers' School* i. 20 That was all right by Jim! **1958** *Listener* 20 Nov. 835/1 If ever he wants to use what I'm going to say, it's perfectly all right with me. **1959** *Ibid.* 22 Jan. 153/1 Joe said: 'That's all right by me.' **1962** L. DEIGHTON *Ipcress File* iii. 25 'You want a meal?' 'Yes,' I said quickly. 'That's all right, then, sit down.'

d. *she's* (or *she'll be*) *right*: all is well, that is fine. *Austral.* and *N.Z. colloq.*

1947 D. M. DAVIN *For Rest of our Lives* xvi. 81 She'll be right as soon as we get back with the boys again. **1950** *N.Z. Listener* 3 Mar. 12 'She's right!' Miss Cooper said, with a good Pig Islander's inflexion. **1958** *Ibid.* 9 May 6/4 'They'll be very upset to think that they couldn't have met you gentlemen here, but I'll convey your regards to them, and thank you very much.' Ike said, 'She's right, ma'am, she's right.' **1959** *Times* 27 June 7/7 He calls in the appropriate tradesman, who fixes the thing so that it works again, but not very well. He protests and is told: 'She'll be right.' **1961** B. CRUMP *Hang on a Minute* 33 Thanks for the beer, added Jack. She's right, said the barman. Hope you get the job. **1974** A. BUZO *Coralie Lansdowne says No* 65 'There's more in the car. I'll go and get it.' 'Do you want a wheel-barrow?' 'She'll be right.'

III. 17. e. As an intensifying word in derogatory and ironical contexts. Phr. *a right one*: a fool; an extremely stupid or awkward person.

1960 *Daily Tel.* 21 Jan. 15/7 Two young soldiers of the R.A.S.C. were described as 'right mugs' in written plans that apparently referred..to Pte. John Terence Bush's attempted escape. **1962** L. DEIGHTON *Ipcress File* xxx. 190 We'd been a couple of right ninnies. Followed all the way! **1965** *Oxford Mail* 17 Nov. 11/5 Mr. Weir said that when student teacher Ian Brodie first broached his dream of a monster sandwich he thought: 'I've got a right one 'ere.' **1968** B. TURNER *Sex Trap* xiv. 131 'I got a right one today,' she said. 'Thought I'd had them all, you know, but this one wanted me to hold his John Thomas.' **1973** *Observer* 14 Jan. 1/4 'The Government did not know that there was no settlement in writing, and how could an order apply to something which did not exist,' he said. 'The Government made a right mess of it.' **1976** *Southern Even. Echo* (Southampton) 13 Nov. 9/4 He said the Conservative party would inherit a 'right old mess'. **1978** I. MURDOCH *Sea* 104 'You look a right clown,' I said.

18. b. *Math.* Used to denote an entity whose definition involves a pair of elements in a conventionally defined order (see quots.).

[**1905** *Trans. Amer. Math. Soc.* VI. 203 So that 6× and the right-hand distributive law fail. **1933** *Ann. Math.* XXXIV. 483 When $F(x) = D_1(x)D_2(x)$ we shall call $D_2(x)$ a right-hand and $D_1(x)$ a left-hand divisor of $F(x)$.] **1937** [see *IDEAL *a.* and *sb.* B. 3]. **1938** F. D. MURNAGHAN *Theory of Group Representations* iv. 91 The set Hs^{-1} (which consists of the inverses of the elements of the left coset *sH*) has no element in common with *H*. We term it the right coset of *H* determined by s^{-1}. **1962** CURTIS & REINER *Representation Theory Finite Groups* ii. 50 The group *M* is called a right R-module if there is a product *mr* defined such that $mr \in M$ and $(m_1+m_2)r = m_1r+m_2r$, $m(r_1+r_2) = mr_1+mr_2$, $m(r_1r_2) = (mr_1)r_2$, $m.1 = m$, for all $r \in R$, $m \in M$... The right regular module R_R is defined similarly, and its submodules are the right ideals of *R*. *Ibid.* viii. 395 Let *S* be a subset of *A*... The right annihilator $r(S)$ is given by $r(S) = \{a \in A: Sa = 0\}$. **1971** E. C. DADE in Powell & Higman *Finite Simple Groups* viii. 280 We regard the *R*-endomorphisms as right operators on *M*. **1972** A. G. HOWSON *Handbk. Terms Algebra & Anal.* v. 28 Similarly, we can form the set of all elements of the form *zx*, where $z \in S$ and, denoting this by *Sx*, refer to it as a right coset of *S*. *Ibid.*, There is no universal convention regarding which set of cosets should be termed 'right' and which 'left'.

21. Special collocations in sport: *right back, centre, corner, end, forward, guard, half.* Also *right field* (Baseball): the part of the outfield to the right of the batter as he faces the pitcher; also, a fielder in this position; *right fielder*: a fielder in the right field. See also *RIGHT WING 2, *RIGHT-WINGER (*b*).

1897 *Encycl. Sport* I. 419/2 The right back and the right half-back look after the opposing left wing forwards. **1956** *Granta* 18 Feb. 5/1, I had a very easy game at right back. **1951** *Sport* 6–12 Apr. 18/4 It was only justice when their right-centre Hunt opened their account with a try. **1969** EAGLESON & MCKIE *Terminol. Austral. Nat. Football* III. 9 *Right centre*, the player occupying the right centre position in a team. **1955** R. SMITH *Doyle's Lifetime in Hurling* iv. 34 Harney roving down to the right corner angled a grand point. **1975** *Irish Independent* 27 May 12/1 Kilkenny will be without..right corner back Fan Larkin and right corner forward Mick Brennan in next Sunday's Wembley [hurling] tournament. **1896** CAMP & DELAND *Football* 344 Instructions to Right End... You should help the right tackle block his man. **1970** *Washington Post* 30 Sept. D3/5 Brown, the 6-foot-5, 265-pound defensive right end, charged through Baltimore's offensive line. **1974** *Cleveland* (Ohio) *Plain Dealer* 13 Oct. C.12/7 The Jackets locked up the game with 10 : 09 remaining as quarterback Jim Tressel jaunted around right end for a 16-yard touchdown. **1857** *Spirit of Times* 29 Aug. 404/3 Enterprise Club. Maxfield, catcher;.. Davis, right field; Knight, second base. **1867** [see *left field* s.v. *LEFT *a.* 3 c]. **1949** *Marshfield* (Wisconsin) *News-Herald* 19 July 9/4 Corbett hit a change of pace pitch on a line into right field for the second Tomahawk hit. **1970** *Globe & Mail* (Toronto) 25 Sept. 31/3 With one out, Bob Robertson lined a double down the rightfield Line. **1974** *Evening Herald* (Rock Hill, S. Carolina) 18 Apr. 6/3 Mike Williams then unloaded a triple down the rightfield line . . . Roberson and Williams came around to score on a Mussman balk. **1867** *Ball Players' Chron.* 25 July 1/4 The right fielder was active at times, once making a very handsome stop. **1889** 'MARK TWAIN' *Connecticut Yankee* xlii. 533 What a handy right-fielder he was! **1912** C. MATHEWSON *Pitching in a Pinch* 27 Kane, the little rightfielder on the Cincinnati club, was the first man up. **1957** [see *left fielder* s.v. *LEFT *a.* 3 c]. **1977** *Time* 12 Dec. 57/1 In 1927, with Leftfielder Meusel hitting .337, Centerfielder Earle Combs .356 and Rightfielder Babe Ruth .356 plus 60 home runs, the Yankees had what many students of the game consider the best outfield in baseball history. **1911** P. H. DAVIS *Football* xviii. 446 *Yale*... Right Guard, R. C. Tripp, '06. **1970** *Washington Post* 30 Sept. D1/3 Right guard Vince Promuto was trying to loosen up a bruised knee and rookie Paul Laaveg of Iowa filled in for him. **1905** P. WALKER *How to play Assoc. Football* 36 In this and following diagrams.. L.B., R.H...represent respectively..left-back, right-half. **1928** in B. James *England v Scotland* (1969) vi. 134 Right-half Edwards worked hard and at times effectively. **1947** *Sporting Mirror* 7 Nov. 9/1 Tunstall, United forward, raced after a long pass from his right half. **1951** *Sport* 7–13 Jan. 13/4 Perseverance has repaid Billy Stroud, right-half-back of Newport County. **1969** EAGLESON & MCKIE *Terminol. Austral. Nat. Football* III. 10 *Right half forward*, the player occupying the right half-forward position in a team. **1975** *Irish Times* 24 May 3/1 Their right-half forward, Francis Loughnane, a man who..has won many games for the county.

IV. 22. a. Conservative, reactionary; applied *spec.* to (members or supporters of) that part of a political party or grouping especially noted for its conservatism (see RIGHT *sb.* 17 d in Dict. and Suppl.); *right of centre* [CENTRE *sb.* 15]: tending to hold conservative political views.

The use originates with the seating positions of the 1789 French National Assembly: see quot. 1837 and the note in Dict. s.v. CENTRE *sb.* 15.

1794 tr. *C. Desmoulins's Hist. Brissotins* 40 La Source, the least corrupted of those who voted with the left, and dined with the right side of the Convention, but whose pride was excited against Robespierre. **1829** *Ann. Reg. 1828* 162/2 The result of this election proved that..the union—scarcely a natural union—of a fraction of the extreme right or royalist side, with the whole of the left, or liberal side, which, at the general election had driven him from office, was still continued to keep him out. **1837** CARLYLE *French Revol.* I. vi. 307 There is a Right Side (Coté Droit), a Left Side (Coté Gauche); sitting on M. le President's right hand, or on his left: the Coté Droit conservative; the Coté Gauche destructive. **1933** *Labour Monthly* July 419 In order to defend 'democracy' it is necessary to maintain a Left Cartel Government in office so as to defeat the menace of a Right Bloc Government. **1938** D. M. PICKLES *French Polit. Scene* iii. 60 A group labelled 'Democratic' is invariably Right, as (with one exception) are all groups labelled 'Republican'. **1958** P. JOHNSON in N. Mackenzie *Conviction* 207, I had a job on..a glossy Paris magazine. It was vaguely right-of-centre, superficially progressive. **1962** *Listener* 18 Jan. 115/1 The party has in fact swung round so fast that some worthy stalwarts who think of themselves as right-of-centre are still surprised suddenly to find themselves stranded way out on the left of the official party line. **1964** GOULD & KOLB *Dict. Social Sci.* 383/2 The term *right* is most commonly (though not exclusively) used as a pejorative term, by those who believe themselves to be on the left. **1973** R. E. M. IRVING *Christian Democracy in France* viii. 260 Although boosted by extreme right votes, the CD did even worse than the Centre in 1962. **1974** T. ALLBEURY *Snowball* xiii. 69 A right-of-centre Trades Union delegate and a Midlands MP passed notes. **1976** *National Observer* (U.S.) 28 Aug. 13/2 They survive by being cleaner than clean, righter than right, and purging everybody else except their own carefully selected proteges. **1977** *Times* 18 Feb. 12/4 Constituency pressure against a number of right-of-centre MPs..has undermined the party's position in the country. **1978** *Times* 26 July 15/4 We were dazzled..whether we were politically right, left or centre.

b. *right deviationism*: in a Communist party or society, (advocacy of) departure or divergence from orthodox principles or policies towards more conservative principles. So *right deviationist*, an advocate or proponent of such principles.

1930 [see *DEVIATION 3 e]. **1957** R. N. C. HUNT *Guide to Communist Jargon* xxix. 103 The Party and its leaders..will be accused of that form of opportunism which goes by the name of right-deviationism. **1958** G. M. CARTER *Politics of Inequality* ii. 61 In September, 1931, Bunting, W. H. Andrews, Solly Sachs and other prominent Communists were expelled from the Party for 'right deviationism'. **1958** P. KEMP *No Colours or Crest* vii. 141 This attitude branded him as a Right deviationist in the eyes of his fellow Communists.

V. 23. *Comb.* **a.** Parasynthetic, as *right-eyed, -footed, -twisted.* **b.** *right-counter, -cross*; **right bower**, the jack of trumps in Euchre; also *fig.*; **right-to-left** *attrib. phr.*, designating movement from the right to the left.

1839 *Spirit of Times* 24 Aug. 294/2 The *right* and *left bower* in the game of *Euchre.* **1863** in *Ann. Army of Cumberland* 501 Smith..said he would..furnish him with a letter of introduction to his 'right bower' in Nashville. The right bower proved to be Dr. Hudson. **1872** G. P. BURNHAM *Mem. U.S. Secret Service* p. vii, *Right bower*, the second-best card in *euchre*; next to the white 'joker'. **1946** MOREHEAD & MOTT-SMITH *Penguin Hoyle* 29 The second-highest is the jack of the trump suit, called the *right bower*. *a* **1964** H. P. TRITTON in *Penguin Bk. Austral. Ballads* (1964) 228 Gently turn the sheep around so the right bower couldn't see. **1950** J. DEMPSEY *Championship Fighting* 10 He landed a right-counter to the head. **1965** G. MCINNES *Road to Gundagai* iii. 52, I..followed it up with a..right-cross with the school cap. **1904** *Science* 8 Apr. 592/1 If right-eyed, the engineer can see the track and signals better from the right side of the boiler than from the left. *Ibid.* 593/2 It may be better for the oculist to leave a person right-eyed rather than to give such lenses as suddenly compel left-eyedness. **1932** *Amer. Jrnl. Ophthalm.* XV. 321/1 Most right handed people are right eyed. **1934** *Times Lit. Suppl.* 4 Jan. 4/2 All the animals that set themselves to grip their prey, are right-footed. **1960** V. JENKINS *Lions Down Under* 174 He came up into an orthodox right-to-left threequarter movement. **1964** E. A. NIDA *Toward Sci. Transl.* vi. 136 In many instances a very long sentence, even though having right-to-left attribution and with several potential terminal points, must be broken up into smaller segments to avoid formal overloading of the communication. **1969** *Listener* 24 July 119/3 Clark acknowledges the assistance of Carlo Pedretti, with his unrivalled knowledge of Leonardo's hand (especially of that maddening right-to-left script). **1934** *Times Lit. Suppl.* 4 Jan. 4/2 A right-twisted shell lies conveniently for the waves breaking upon it so that they may press it more closely to the rock. **1934** 'H. MACDIARMID' *Stony Limits* 120 A right-twisted shell lies apt for the waves..to press it more closely to the rock.

right, *adv.* Add: **2. a.** (Further examples of *right along.*) Also in sense 'all along' (chiefly *U.S.*).

1880 'MARK TWAIN' *Tramp Abroad* xlii. 497 We tore right along, over rocks, rubbish, gullies, open fields. **1965** *Listener* 21 Oct. 608/1 Is the American Government prepared to take up this kind of initiative..? *Harriman.* Yes, we have been doing that right along.

3. b. (*b*) (Further examples of *right off*; also used *absol.*)

1931 [see *LEVEL *v.*[1] 8]. **1952** M. LOWRY *Let.* 11 Jan. (1967) 285 Also, right off, I want to thank yourself..most sincerely for the superlative Christmas present. **1976** *National Observer* (U.S.) 14 Aug. 8/1 Right off, I'm overwhelmed by the vegetables inside: mounds of crimson, vine-ripened tomatoes [etc.].

(*c*) (Further examples of *right away.*)

1903 G. B. SHAW *Man & Superman* IV. 151 *Violet.* Go away until I have finished speaking to your father. *Hector.* No, Violet: I mean to have this thing out, right away. **1909** R. E. KNOWLES *Attic Guest* ix. 121, I told him one day how Charlie was still urging me to consent that it should be soon, right away soon. **1942** *Short Guide Gt. Brit.* (U.S. War Dept.) 5 You will find out right away that England is a small country. **1957** *Practical Wireless* XXXIII. 727/2 (Advt.), Post this off right away. **1978** D. QUINN *Fear of God* 121 'It's very important—see what you can turn up.' 'Right away,' Helen said.

c. For *U.S.* read orig. *U.S.* and add further examples.

1955 'J. CHRISTOPHER' *Year of Comet* iii. 108 Find yourself a drink. I'll be right up. **1969** R. WILLIAMS in D. Knight *100 Yrs. Sci. Fiction* 286 A few minutes later, however, Pete Martens in Appliances called me up... 'Thank you, Pete,' I said. 'I'll be right down.' **1972** 'T. COE' *Don't lie to Me* vii. 70 'We're all set, Dan.' He looked at her in surprise, as though he'd never seen her before, and then said, 'Fine, be right with you.'

6. a. *right now, then* (further examples). Now also in sense 'immediately', 'without delay' (chiefly *U.S.*).

1932 KIPLING *Limits & Renewals* 84 Mackworth: 'Swear you will. At once.' Haylock: 'I swear I will. Right now.' Me (and it's not my fault that I love English): 'None of your Transatlantic slang here. Say "at once".' **1948** 'N. SHUTE' *No Highway* iv. 82 He's not the only passenger that's in a nervous state right now. **1953** *Manch. Guardian Weekly* 19 Mar. 7 There never was a time when respect for law and legal process was more important to our people than right now. **1957** *New Yorker* 2 Nov. 68/3 Explaining that she had to go back to the hotel herself right then to get dressed.. she returned to the car. **1959** C. FREMLIN *Uncle Paul* iii. 30 *I'll* find her a hotel. Right now. **1959** *Listener* 19 Nov. 895/1, I hardly think readers will be reaching it off the shelves a quarter of a century hence as eagerly as, right now, I am reaching for *The Small Years.* **1975** R. L. SIMON *Wild Turkey* (1976) i. 2 We'd better start right now.

7. a. *right on!* Used as an expression of enthusiastic agreement, approval, or encouragement. Also as *attrib. phr. U.S. slang.*

Freq. in Black English in the U.S.

1925 in Odum & Johnson *Negro & his Songs* vii. 202 Railroad Bill was a mighty sport, Shot all buttons off high sheriff's coat Den hollered, 'Right on, Desperado Bill!' **1968** B. SEALE in *Ramparts* 20 Oct. 32/1, I said, 'Right on.' I was right behind him. This brother..knew what to do, when to do and how to do it. **1970** *New Yorker* 20 June 50/2 Miss Williams said, 'You have not adequately answered those questions,' and sat down, to cheers, whistles, and a cry of 'Right on!'—conceivably the first time the chairman had ever heard the phrase live. **1970** *Melody Maker* 12 Sept. 34 'Only in a capitalist society could art be turned to profit.' 'Right on.' **1970** *Time* 19 Oct. 45 In Boston, Homans is known as a 'right-on lawyer'—he defends blacks, war protesters and poor people. **1971** J. KILLENS in A. Chapman *New Black Voices* (1972) 59 But now, on with the story. And Black Blessings to you all. Right on. **1972** *Listener* 27 Jan. 123/2 A whole albumful of 'right on' soul music. **1973** *Black World* May 32/2 If Marx were alive he could see his way clear to say to this observation, 'Right on, Brother!' **1974** K. MILLETT *Flying* II. 198 Right on, Vita, so you must have waged your woman's war for years. **1976** *Spare Rib* Oct. 32/1, I had just read *Sappho Was a Right-On Woman* by Sidney Abbott and Barbara Love. **1979** *Daily Tel.* 3 Sept. 4/1 A correspondent remarked: 'You don't portray any crisis feeling.' The President replied: 'Right on.'

b. (Later example of *right there.*)

1948 AUDEN *Age of Anxiety* v. 116 He'll be right there With His Eye upon me.

9. a. (Further examples.)

1891 W. B. YEATS *Let.* Apr. (1954) 167 The 'proofs' of the Blake book are coming in... The illustrations look right well. **1954** *Manch. Guardian Weekly* 5 Aug. 12/3 Sometimes ..there is a fight. If the incident takes place in a public-house it is often worse. 'It's broken bottles right fast; and, brother, I get out.' **1981** P. MALLORY *Killing Matter* ix. 97 Cale was doing right well for himself.

b. (Further examples.) Now chiefly *U.S. right smart*: see SMART *a.* 7 b in Dict. and Suppl.

1869 'MARK TWAIN' *Innoc. Abr.* 134, I did not feel right comfortable for some time afterward. **1881** —— *Prince & Pauper* iii. 40 They were waved aside with a right royal gesture. **1884** C. H. SMITH *Bill Arp's Scrap Bk.* vi. 75 Go get me a switch, right straight. **1936** M. MITCHELL *Gone with Wind* xlii. 755 Miz Wilkes is right sensible, for a woman.

1952 *Manch. Guardian Weekly* 20 Mar. 4/3 Yes, sir, as far as this state's concerned, he looks right nice where he is. **1977** *Washington Post* 7 Sept. c5/2 It turned out that some of them were women who would like to be in my place—who hate me and would like to see me gone. I slipped into a right unpopular place when I married George Wallace.

13. c. (Further examples of *all right.*) Now usu. in weakened senses, 'indeed', 'certainly'.

1911 *Maclean's Mag.* Mar. 96/2 He's a high flier, all right. **1915** J. Buchan *39 Steps* iv. 81 It was no question of preventing a war. That was coming, as sure as Christmas... Karolides was going to be the occasion. He was booked all right, and was to hand in his checks on June 14th. **1930** J. B. Priestley *Angel Pavement* v. 249 Yes, I saw you all right. You looked very annoyed, too. **1933** M. Lowry *Ultramarine* vi. 245 Boy, but it was hot all right. **1943** *Illustr. London News* 9 Jan. 30/1 Coffee was being burnt in Brazil because there were not enough purchasers for it in Europe. But this was solely because the people of Europe lacked the currency with which to buy it. They wanted the coffee all right. **1944** B. Hutchison *Hollow Men* viii. 107 I'm afraid, all right.

15. b. *right, left, and centre*: everywhere; in all directions.

1956 H. & M. Williams *Plaintiff in Pretty Hat* ii. 61 Pontificating..and expressing your damned opinions and judgements right, left and centre as if you're Solomon in all his glory? **1958** *Times* 19 Sept. 6/7 Mr. Eric Longsworth.. suggested that the duty of the committee should be to take action whenever a theatre was threatened, lobbying 'right, left, and centre' local and national bodies. **1963** [see *bundobust]. **1967** 'G. North' *Sgt. Cluff & Day of Reckoning* x. 91 Do any of us want Barker asking folk questions, right, left, and centre? **1970** J. Porter *Rather Common sort of Crime* x. 115 A boy like Rodney..couldn't possibly be earning enough money to go around buying whisky right, left and centre? **1977** *Times* 25 Jan. 5/7 People are doing it [*sc.* committing suicide] right, left and centre all the time. There is nothing to it nowadays.

16. a. *right-hearted, -justified* (sense 15).

1848 J. R. Lowell *Fable for Critics* 41 All honour and praise to the right-hearted bard Who was true to The Voice when such service was hard. **1908** M. & J. Findlater *Crossriggs* xlvii. 346 Alex gave it the reverent attention that details of the kind will always command from right-hearted people. **1970** *Computers & Humanities* IV. 167 References were to be right-justified.

b. *right-acting, -feeling* (examples), *-judging, -seeing*; **right-reading,** such as can be read without first being reversed by a mirror.

1973 E. Bullins *Theme is Blackness* 160 If I was a right-actin' sister I wouldn't go into this, you understand..but you know I ain't right-actin'. **1869** Mill *Subj. Women* iv. 149 Among right-feeling and well-bred people, the inequality is kept as much as possible out of sight. **1883** 'Mark Twain' *Life on Mississippi* 432 Any right-feeling reptile would do that. **1868** Mill *Let.* 9 June (1910) II. 113 The detestation of the right-judging among his fellow-creatures. **1955** J. Ashworth *Operation & Mech. of Linotype & Intertype* II. xxxiii. 329 The film magazine is a holder containing the film and a mechanism for advancing it between lines... Production models will be able to produce either wrong- or right-reading positives as desired. **1967** Karch & Buber *Offset Processes* iv. 87 Images can be right reading or wrong (as seen in a mirror) reading to suit the process used in offset-lithography. **1855** Bagehot *Coll. Wks.* (1965) I. 284 A particularly rational and right-seeing man.

c. Delete † and add: *right-justify* [back-formation from *right-justified* in sense *16 a].

1970 *Computers & Humanities* IV. 169 The point at which the line is to be padded with blanks to right-justify the reference. **1980** Glass & 'De Nim' *Second Coming* 58 He could right justify and multiple column per page and footnote with only a little more work.

right about, *sb., adv.* (and *a.*). Add: **A.** *sb.* **3.** A change of mind; the adoption of an opinion or policy contrary to that previously held.

1936 O. Nash in *Bad Parents' Garden of Verse* 59 You ask, and properly ask, no doubt, Whence this astonishing right-about? **1956** *Sun* (Baltimore) 28 Sept. 12/2 The resolution completes the policy rightabout which the American comrades..began after Khruschev denounced Stalin and Stalinism.

right and left, right-and-left, *adv.* (*v.*), *a.*, and *sb.* Add: **A.** *adv.* **1. b.** (Earlier and later examples.) Also, from every quarter; indiscriminately.

1839 F. Hastings *Let.* 8 Mar. in R. B. Martin *Enter Rumour* 51, I wished you to know the truth..and you are welcome to tell it right and left. **1863** Mrs. Gaskell in *All Year Round* VIII. 560/1 Mr. Wilkins has written everywhere, right and left. **1873** 'Mark Twain' *Gilded Age* 319 You still begin to squander a fortune right and left. **1876** C. Schreiber *Jrnl.* 26 July (1911) I. 472 Froeschel, of Hamburg, was there buying right and left. **1884** G. Meredith *Let.* 13 May (1970) II. 735, I am now rejecting kind invitations right and left, for I see I shall not be released before the first or second week of next month. **1912** T. Dreiser *Financier* xxx. 341 The stocks had been unloaded freely right and left. **1927** J. N. McIlwraith *Kinsmen at War* xix. 194 Stephen struggled and slashed right and left. **1962** P. Gregory *Like Tigress at Bay* xiv. 142 Rudy was there now, smirking, bowing to the customers, giving orders right and left.

C. *sb.* **2.** Also *transf.* and *fig.*

1935 A. P. Herbert *What a Word!* vii. 221 This is the best right-and-left I have found. Issue is a 'conclusion' in one sentence and 'question' in the next. **1978** R. V. Jones *Most Secret War* xli. 390, I felt that we had achieved one of the best 'right and lefts' of all time by picking out the 14th and 15th Companies.

right angle. Add: *right-angle fold* (Printing), a fold at right angles to a previous fold; so *right-angle folding*.

1931 H. Jahn *Hand Composition* xvi. 264 Models..which operate at high speed on both parallel and right-angle fold work. **1946** A. Monkman in H. Whetton *Pract. Printing & Binding* v. 59 Machines are available to fold large and small sheets and for parallel or right-angle folding. **1956** H. Williamson *Methods of Book Design* xix. 312 Some machines are equipped with turn-tables, so that..successive parallel folds can be converted at will into right-angle folds. **1972** A. G. Martin *Finishing Processes in Printing* ii. 19 When a number of single sheets are collectively folded once, the technique is known as 'lump folding'. This method is used for make-up of account-book sections and no right-angle folds are employed.

right-branching, *a. Linguistics.* [Right *adv.*] Of a grammatical construction, etc.: having the majority of its constituents on the right of its tree diagram. Also as *vbl. sb.*

1961 N. Chomsky in *Proc. Symposia Appl. Math.* XII. 13 From the fact that memory is finite, the fact that a sentence is heard or spoken from 'left-to-right'.., or the fact that the rules of a generative grammar..may be partially ordered, nothing whatsoever can be concluded about left- and right-branching in P-markers. *Ibid.* 14 We would predict that a hearer..would tend to treat right-branching units..as successive and disjointed, rather than integrated segments, on first hearing. **1965** —— *Aspects of Theory of Syntax* i. 13 Right-branching structures are those with the opposite property [to left-branching], for example,..[this is [the cat that caught [the rat that stole the cheese]]]. **1965** [see *left-branching *a.*]. **1978** *Language* LIV. 84 In English, sentential complement constructions are right-branching.

righteous, *a., adv.*, and *sb.* Add: **2*.** *U.S. slang.* Fine, excellent; of good quality. Freq. in collocations (see quots.), esp. *righteous moss* [see *moss *sb.*[1] 5 e], hair of good texture or characteristic of a white person.

Freq. in Black English in the U.S.

1942 Z. N. Hurston in *Amer. Mercury* July. 84 It [*sc.* his hair] looked just like that righteous moss, and had so many waves you got seasick from looking. **1944** C. Calloway *Hepsters Dict., Righteous,* splendid, okay. Ex., 'That was a righteous queen I dug you with last black.' **1944** D. Burley in A. Dundes *Mother Wit* (1973) 212 *Righteous,* pleasing to the senses, glorious, pretty, beautiful, mighty. **1945** L. Shelly *Jive Talk Dict.* 31/2 *Righteous riff,* interesting conversation. **1946** Mezzrow & Wolfe *Really Blues* (1957) 377 *Righteous bush,* marihuana. **1963** T. Pynchon *V.* x. 281 'She's up there' Matilda said, with a smile for everybody, even musicians with a headful of righteous moss, who were making money and drove sports cars. **1967** [see *lame *sb.*[2] 2]. **1968–70** *Current Slang* (Univ. S. Dakota) III–IV. 103 *Righteous egg, n.* a good guy. **1970** C. Major *Dict. Afro-Amer. Slang* 97 *Righteous Moss,* white folks' hair. **1976** *Daily Mirror* 2 Apr. 20/2 *Righteous,* can mean same as dread; also good or excellent.

righter[2]. Add: Also in *equal righter*, an advocate of equal rights for women.

1896 *Truth* 22 Oct. 1029/2 Some ladies—evidently Equal Righters—reproach me with having last week devoted far more space to the Czar than to his consort.

right hand. Add: **4.** *right-hand drive*, a steering system in a motor vehicle in which the steering wheel and other controls are fitted on the right side instead of on the left. Also *attrib.* So *right-hand driving* vbl. sb.

1912 *Horseless Age* 21 Feb. 375/2 In right hand drive cars it [*sc.* the steering column] is located directly in front of the right hand front passenger. **1936** M. Kennedy *Together & Apart* iii. 178 'But don't you,' she asked, 'find the right-hand driving rather confusing?' 'I don't mind it. But in Sweden it's left-hand.' **1940** R. Chandler *Farewell, my Lovely* viii. 55 The car had a right-hand drive. **1956** [see *left hand 3]. **1965** *Listener* 10 June 878/2 The two latest French saloons, the Renault 16 and the Peugeot 204, did not appear at Silverstone last Wednesday because right-hand drive versions are not yet available. **1969** J. Leasor *They don't make them like that any More* vi. 185, I thought that all Mercedes exported to England before the war had right-hand drive? **1974** A. Price *Other Paths to Glory* ii. viii. 208 Got 'GB' in the back..the Jag had that—that's English. An' right-hand drive—that's English too.

right-handed, *a.* (*adv.*) **6.** Delete *rare* and add further examples as *adv.*

1910 *Blackw. Mag.* July 24/1 A single stag has swung right-handed. **1929** *Morning Post* 30 Dec. 13/1 He [*sc.* a fox] ..left at the Toft end going straight..over the railway, leaving Kingston village right-handed. **1936** P. Fleming *News from Tartary* 194 We turned right-handed and slanted down to the foothills. **1976** *Horse & Hound* 3 Dec. 22/2 He ran right-handed over Clawson Lodge, Clawson Hill Farm.. where he tried the earths.

right-hander. Add: **2.** (Further examples.)

1968 *Listener* 19 Sept. 357/1 If to right-handers this heart-cry sounds wildly exaggerated, it can only be because they are unaware of the inconvenience..they perpetually inflict on those of us who live the half-life of the submerged left. **1972** *Sci. Amer.* Apr. 83/3 It is an interesting fact that right-handers with a strong family history of left-handedness show better speech recovery than people without left-handed inheritance. **1978** *Amer. Speech* LIII. 285 Stone tools surviving from that epoch were mainly chipped by right-handers.

3. A bend to the right in a road, track, etc.

1970 J. Miles *Expert Driving Police Way* xv. 139 On a right-hand bend I usually do not dip so early, as the lights are pointing away from oncoming traffic, but on certain right-handers I find it an advantage to have my lights dipped. **1973** 'J. Ashford' *Double Run* xiv. 113 The first right-hander with slightly banked curve was dead ahead.

right-ho, var. *righto *int.*

rightie, var. *righty. **rightie-ho,** var. *righty-ho *int.*

rightism (rəi·tiz'm). Also with capital initial. [f. Right *sb.*[1] 17 d + -ism.] The political view or principles of 'the right'.

1939 H. G. Wells *Holy Terror* ii. i. 101 The formulae of the gangsters varied from extreme leftism to extreme rightism. *Ibid.* iii. ii. 270 Two great systems of ideas faced each other in the world, 'Leftism' and 'Rightism'. **1940** W. Stevens *Let.* 12 Jan. (1967) 351 There are a lot of things that the workers are doing that I do not believe in... I think this explains my rightism. **1951** Koestler *Age of Longing* i. 27, I take it for granted that one must fight in self-defence... I merely wish to point out that this has nothing to do with..leftism, rightism, capitalism, and socialism or any other idea or ism. **1959** B. & R. North tr. *M. Duverger's Pol. Parties* (ed. 2) ii. ii. 346 The 'rightism' of governmental alliances is consequently opposed to the leftism of public opinion. **1960** *Times Lit. Suppl.* 22 Apr. 260/3 The anti-rightism which Mr. Clark saw was the tail-end of the campaign against the intellectuals begun in 1957. **1961** *Spectator* 20 Oct. 535/2 Some comparisons and conclusions may now be drawn as a basis for gauging the strength and prospects of American rightism. **1966** *Punch* 28 Dec. 971/1 He has set down the worst excesses of radical rightism of the past two hundred years. **1974** *Time Out* 27 Sept. 23/1 Walker's own naivete, not content with equating criticism of the Kremlin line with rightism, extends to a total misunderstanding of political activity.

rightist (rəi·tist), *sb.* and *a.* Also with capital initial. [f. as prec. + -ist.] **A.** *sb.* A member or adherent of 'the right' in politics.

1937 *Times* 22 Sept. 8/2 The assassinations of the past six years [in Japan] were due to the discontent of younger officers and Rightists with depression or threats of depression. **1945** C. Burney *Dungeon Democracy* iii. 70 He was, in Austrian politics, known to be a Rightist and a Catholic. **1958** *Times Lit. Suppl.* 26 Sept. 546/4 The Chinese intellectual of to-day, pilloried as a 'bourgeois rightist' might well feel that the old cycle is at work once again. **1959** *Listener* 10 Sept. 379/1 There have been a good many people, so-called rightists, who thought that the authorities were trying to drive the country [*sc.* China] rather too fast. **1960** G. Mikes *How to be Inimitable* 53 The Labour Party has a few real leftists and the Tories a few real rightists (and vice versa). **1965** *New Statesman* 2 July 18/2 You are told that President Clark Kerr has created the myth that there are people worse than himself—rightists baying in the legislature. **1970** [see *law *sb.*[1] 3 a]. **1974** J. Mitchell *Death & Bright Water* v. 45 Greek fighting Greek, Right against Left... By that time Michael was a rightist too.

B. *adj.* Of, pertaining to, or characteristic of 'the right' in politics; tending to conservatism.

1938 *Time* 30 May 34/3 By daybreak enraged Rightist students found their university had been taken over by the United Socialist Youth of Mexico. **1940** C. S. Lewis *Let.* 17 Jan. (1966) 176 You will presently see both a Leftist and a Rightist pseudo-theology developing. **1957** *Economist* 28 Sept. 1032/1 In Hongkong the continuing reiteration of official reports from the Chinese Communist press of unrest, crime, 'rightist' plotting, food black-marketing and counter-revolutionary activity..gives an impression of smouldering crisis or impending explosion. **1959** B. & R. North tr. *M. Duverger's Pol. Parties* (ed. 2) ii. ii. 347 Within the Third Force the influence of the M.R.P. continually declined between 1947 and 1951, to the advantage of the Radicals and the Right wing, in accordance with the 'rightist' trend of alliances. **1966** *Listener* 3 Nov. 660/3 He identified himself wholeheartedly with the 'moderate' and 'rightist' aspects of Stalinism. **1969** F. Halliday in Cockburn & Blackburn *Student Power* 309 It was decided..to reactivate an old system whereby rightist students were formed into 'University Defence Groups'. **1970** R. A. H. Robinson *Origins Franco's Spain* ii. 67 The exception in the two Rightist minorities was Royo Villanova. **1974** *Times* 4 Nov. 14/6 The [Durham University] debating society is regarded as a Rightist organization. **1974** T. P. Whitney tr. *Solzhenitsyn's Gulag Archipelago* I. i. ii. 52 The nonexistent 'rightist opposition' would come later. **1977** *Time* 3 Jan. 9/1 In the Middle East, Syrian President Hafez Assad gained new stature by forcibly bringing to a halt the civil war in Lebanon involving rightist Christians, left-wing Moslems, and their Palestinian allies.

rightly, *adv.* Add: **3. d.** Phr. *I don't rightly know*, expressing reserve: 'I am not sure.'

1861 T. Hughes *Tom Brown at Oxf.* III. iii. 48, I don't rightly know, sir. **1954** R. Bissell *High Water* viii. 93, I spose so, but I don't rightly know.

right-minded, *a.* Add: **1.** (Further examples.) Also *transf.*

1933 *Granta* 19 Apr. 358/1 These appointments have been virtually closed to Jews, Socialists, and indeed any but right-minded nationalists for many years. **1961** *Times* 28 Dec. 11/4 For those who enjoy books set in Oxford, there were at least two detective stories, a right-minded farce by Mr. Dacre Balsdon [etc.].

rightmost (rəi·tmōust), *a.* [f. Right *a.* + -most.] Situated or occurring farthest to the right. Also *absol.*

1963 *New Yorker* 15 June 28/2 The three casement windows on my left (the rightmost of which is missing a hook latch). **1964** *IBM Systems Jrnl.* III. 125 Decimal digits.. appear in fields of variable length..and are accompanied by a sign in the rightmost four bits of the low-order byte. **1971** *Language* XLVII. 263 All the cases discussed involve the movement or deletion of verbal objects rather than subjects. The reason is that since the NSR [nuclear stress rule] assigns primary stress to the rightmost element, only cases in which the underlying rightmost element has been affected by transformations can provide crucial evidence. **1973** [see *PACKED *ppl. a.*[1] 1 c]. **1978** *Language* LIV. 411 Complex NP Shift applies in 9, where the complex NP does not substitute for the rightmost constituent in S.

rightness. Add: **5.** (Earlier example.)
1884 [see *BILATERALITY].

righto (rəi·tō^u), *int.* Also **right-ho, right-o, right-oh.** [f. RIGHT *a.* + H)O *int.*[1] 5.] An exclamation expressing agreement with or acquiescence in an opinion, proposal, etc., or compliance with a request. Also as *sb.*, an acceptable person, and as *v. intr.*, to acquiesce, agree. Cf. *RIGHTY-HO *int.*
1896 E. TURNER *Little Larrikin* i. 12 'Hurry up now and be a good kid.' 'Right-O!' said Lol cheerfully. **1899** *Punch* 7 June 274/3 *Dear Clarence*, —Yours to hand. Righto! Announcement sent to *Morning Post.* Thine, *Mabel.* **1902** C. J. C. HYNE *Mr. Horrocks, Purser* 52 Do it how you like, only anyway do it. 'Right-O,' said the fourth officer. **1905** *Pall Mall Mag.* Oct. 456/2 'We will leave Mrs Bergman's name out of the question.' 'Right oh', assented Leonard. **1912** *Collier's* 26 Oct. 16/3 'Right-oh,' said the young man. **1915** T. BURKE *Nights in Town* 191 Righto, laddie, righto. I get you. **1916** 'BOYD CABLE' *Action Front* 134 'Then if the shells pitch too near we can slip the cable and run for it.' 'Right-oh!' said the captain. **1920** WODEHOUSE *Damsel in Distress* viii. 110 'Give this note to Lady Maud.' 'Right-ho.' **1921** GALSWORTHY *To Let* I. v. 53 Stable secret! Righto! **1922** JOYCE *Ulysses* 420 We two, she said, will seek the kids where shady Mary is. Righto, any old time. **1924** F. M. FORD *Some do Not* I. ii. 44 On Monday I shall telegraph: 'Righto' and nothing else. **1930** [see *GO *v.* 58 d]. **1930** KIPLING *Limits & Renewals* (1932) 267 We'll expect her at nine, then... Righto! **1936** WODEHOUSE *Laughing Gas* iv. 41, I had met her when she was taking a holiday at Cannes. We became chummy. I asked her to marry me. She right-hoed. So far, so good. **1937** G. FRANKAU *More of Us* xi. 120 Thought she like that? He wouldn't put it past her. Righto. Then let her learn which was the master. **1949** N. MARSH *Swing, Brother, Swing* ix. 212, I never say 'right-ho'. He'll think I'm demented. **1952** WODEHOUSE *Pigs have Wings* ii. 56 All set. She right-hoed like a lamb. **1974** J. THOMSON *Long Revenge* ix. 106 'You're Mr Finch..?' Finch replied that he was and Ken replied, 'Right-oh.'

right of way. Add: **1. a.** (Further example.)
1925 A. J. TOYNBEE in *Survey Internat. Affairs 1920–23* 41 The part played by the League in the problems of the right of way through the Kiel Canal..is noticed in Part III.

b. The right to build and operate a railway line on land belonging to another; the land on which a railway line is built. *U.S.*
1839 *Jrnl. Indiana Ho. Representatives 1838* 23 Sess. 101 Mr. Blair introduced bill no. 32, to grant the right of way to Illinois. **1883** *Rep. Indian Affairs* (U.S.) p. xxii, I had the honor to submit to the Department..the draft of a bill.. to grant a right of way to the Carson and Colorado Railroad Company. **1902** S. E. WHITE *Blazed Trail* 407 On either side of the right-of-way lay mystery in the shape of thickets. **1919** T. K. HOLMES *Man from Tall Timber* xxix. 365 The right-of-way of the railroad was not wide enough to halt the conflagration in any case. **1931** H. F. PRINGLE *Theodore Roosevelt* I. viii. 94 The locomotives of the Northern Pacific were still a novelty to those who lived along the right of way. **1949** *Boston Sunday Globe* 1 May (Fiction Mag.) 13/5 My suggestion is that you put some guards out there patrolling the right-of-way.

2. (Earlier example.)
1805 *Times* 7 Nov. 4/1 In passing through the inclosures belonging to the Defendant, he arrived at a gate which was fastened, and, considering it a public way, he forced the lock... [He] wrote... I always considered it a public right of way.

3. a. The legal right of a pedestrian or user of a (motor) vehicle to proceed with precedence over other vehicles and road-users at a particular point where their paths cross or converge. Also of sea-traffic.
1913 *Evidence Sel. Comm. Motor Traffic* I. 343/2 in *Parl. Papers* VIII. 93 One of the objections raised here by other witnesses to it was that vehicles going along the main thoroughfares would not slow up at all for the side streets if they thought they had the right of way? **1920** *Statutes of Manitoba* 10 Geo. V. c. 81 s. 10 p. 268 When a person operating a motor vehicle meets another person operating a motor vehicle or driving any draft animal at a crossroad or intersection of roads or streets, the person to the right hand of the other shall have the right-of-way. **1925** *Motor* 29 Dec. 1100/1 The existing rule of the road being 'keep to the left', surely so long as a driver can drive on the left of the centre of the road he has right of way. **1934** *Glasgow Herald* 16 Apr. 11/5 There must be crossing-places where the pedestrians' right of way is inviolable and the motorist must pass over at his peril. **1954** *Highway Code* ii. 6 Give way to pedestrians on uncontrolled zebra crossings. They have the right of way. **1954** *Lloyd's List Law Rep.* I. 144/2 That does not, of course, mean to say that the up-coming ship has anything in the nature of an absolute right of way, because, as has been frequently laid down, there must be some give and take between the two vessels. **1958** *U.S. & Canad. Aviation Reports* 453 As a seaplane was coming down to a lake for a landing..another seaplane started its take-off run..its pontoons damaged the wing and rudder as it passed over. *Held*: The take-off airplane pilot was solely at fault for failing to yield right-of-way to the descending seaplane. **1975** *N.Y. Times* 31 Oct. 38/2 Syvester Lachut was cited by a Castle Shannon patrolman for failing to yield the right-of-way at a street crossing.

b. *transf.* in *Sport.*
1963 *Amer. Speech* XXXVIII. 204 Reference is made to.. *trail hogs* who do not give the *right of way* to slower skiers. **1967** J. SEVERSON *Great Surfing* Gloss., *Right of way*, the surfer who is already on the wave and riding has the right of way and others coming into the wave should respect this right.

4. *attrib.*, as (in sense *1 b) **right-of-way man**, one who surveys a right of way for a railway.
1891 *Harper's Mag.* Nov. 886/2 The first men to follow the engineers..are 'the right-of-way men'. **1904** F. LYNDE *Grafters* xxviii. 361 Our right-of-way man has just sent a telegram to all agents.

right-thinking, *a.* [RIGHT *adv.* 16 b.] Thinking rightly; holding sound or acceptable views. Also *transf.* Hence **right-thinker** *sb.*
1829, 1850 [see RIGHT *adv.* 16 b]. **1890** KIPLING in *Pioneer Mail* (Allahabad) 19 Mar. 394/1 And verily it is not a good thing to live in the East for any length of time. Your ideas grow to clash with those held by every right-thinking white man. **1920** A. HUXLEY *Limbo* 137 Jacobsen himself rarely volunteered a remark about the war; it was taken for granted that he thought about it in the same way as all other right-thinking folk. **1922** S. LEWIS *Babbitt* iii. 34 It was the very best of water-coolers, up-to-date, scientific, and right-thinking. **1930** E. RICE *Voyage to Purilia* xix. 293 Was marriage..regarded by all right-thinking Purilians as the summit of happiness? **1931** A. HUXLEY *Music at Night* 172 Granted the preliminary assumption that concupiscence is wicked, right-thinkers are justified in specially discriminating against the representations of this sin... Among the right-thinking the doctrine of the inherent wickedness of concupiscence is still held with an extraordinary intensity. **1934** B. RUSSELL *Freedom & Organization 1814–1914* xxviii. 394 The area must not be in Asia or Africa; this was clear to all right-thinking people. **1939** *Ann. Reg. 1938* I. 12 Lord Snell..gave eloquent expression to the grief and indignation felt by all right-thinking men at what was happening in Austria. **1961** *Times* 11 July 12/6 Now no right-thinking suburbanite would be seen on his lawn without wearing Bermudas. **1961** *Times Lit. Suppl.* 1 Dec. 861/2 *Midcentury* is one prolonged grouse..about those 'right-thinkers' dedicated to 'the word with the welfare label'. **1974** 'J. LE CARRÉ' *Tinker, Tailor* xxxviii. 335 He ought to censure him on behalf of right-thinking men.

right-turn. [f. RIGHT *a.* + TURN *sb.*] A movement to the right, *spec.* one made by a motor vehicle from one road to another. Also *attrib.* and as *v. intr.* So **right-turning** *ppl. a.*
1960 *Guardian* 24 June 20/4 Much of the present congestion in the area is due to right-turning traffic. **1967** *Gloss. Highway Engin. Terms* (*B.S.I.*) 11 *Right-turn lane*, an auxiliary deceleration and waiting lane constructed between an overtaking lane and a central reserve or traffic island so that vehicles approaching a junction can slow down and wait clear of other traffic. **1968** *Highway Code* 17 When it is safe, give a right turn signal and..take up position just left of the middle of the road, or in the space marked for right-turning traffic. **1972** *Guardian* 26 June 1 The ring system has been evolved to do away with the conflicts of right-turning traffic. **1973** J. GORES *Final Notice* xvi. 102 They *should* right-turn toward the freeway on-ramp.

rightward, *adv.* and *a.* Add: **B.** *adj.* **a.** (Further examples.) Also in political sense (see RIGHT *sb.*[1] 17 d in Dict. and Suppl.).
1941 'G. ORWELL' in *Partisan Rev.* July–Aug. 319 The recent rightward swing means that we are being regimented by wealthy men and aristocrats rather than by representatives of the common people. **1972** *Sci. Amer.* July 86/3 Usually a reader sees a page of text and moves his eyes over it, ordinarily in a rightward and downward direction. **1977** *Times* 4 Oct. 14/1 A rightward trend towards the centre on the part of M. Mitterand.

b. *rightward welding* (see quots.).
1941 A. C. DAVIES *Sci. & Pract. Welding* iii. 146 Rightward welding..was introduced some years ago to compete with electric arc welding in the welding of plate over $\frac{3}{16}$ in. thick... In this method the weld progresses along the seam from left to right, the rod following the blowpipe. **1967** M. D. JACKSON *Welding* iv. 203 There are two methods of making downhand welds with the oxy-acetylene process and these are generally known as leftward welding or rightward welding, the terms being descriptive of the direction of welding. **1975** BRAM & DOWNS *Manuf. Technol.* ii. 48 In rightward welding the flame is directed towards the completed part of the joint and welding proceeds from left to right.

rightwards *adv.* (later examples, in political sense).
1968 *Listener* 7 Nov. 610/3 The novelist Kingsley Amis is regarded, by himself among others, as having moved 'rightwards' with the years. **1971** P. WORSTHORNE *Socialist Myth* iii. 33 Any Labour Government has to lean over Rightwards to avoid being suspected of lack of patriotism.

right wing. [f. RIGHT *a.* + WING *sb.*] **1.** *Mil.* See RIGHT *a.* 18, WING *sb.* 7 a.

2. In football and similar games: the position of a player on the right side of the centre(s); a player occupying this position; the part of the field in which the right wing normally plays. Cf. WING *sb.* 7 b.
1882 in Charles-Edwards & Richardson *They saw it Happen* (1958) 299 Of the Rovers forwards the right wing pair first became prominent. **1900** in B. James *England v Scotland* (1969) iii. 72 For England, Crabtree was cleverly holding the Scottish right wing in check and showing grand form. **1901** *Encycl. Sport* II. 419/2 The left back and left half-back attend to the opposing right wing forwards. **1947** *Sporting Mirror* 7 Nov. 3/2 Appearing in their league side on the right wing and, later, at centre forward he became very popular with the Shepherds Bush spectators. **1969** EAGLESON & MCKIE *Terminol. Austral. Nat. Football* III. 10 *Right wing*, a variant for right centre. **1974** *Observer* 1 Sept. 18/3 Hall improvised brilliantly up and down Liverpool's right wing interpassing with Heighway.

3. That section of a political party, assembly, or other body most tending to hold conservative or reactionary views (see RIGHT *sb.*[1] 17 d in Dict. and Suppl.). Freq. (with hyphen) *attrib.* or as *adj.*
1905 W. JAMES *Meaning of Truth* (1909) v. 124 If the formula ever became canonical, it would certainly develop both right-wing and left-wing interpreters. **1927** U. SINCLAIR *Oil!* xiv. 348 Jacob Menzies had been clubbed almost insensible on the picket-line. Jacob was the 'right wing' brother..who had been earning his education by pressing students' pants. **1928** E. & C. PAUL tr. *Stalin's Leninism* 322 Is our Party..making any concessions to the right-wing deviation of the Communist International? **1933** *Labour Monthly* Apr. 237 We are not yet at the point where the right wing advocates dictatorship of the proletariat. **1937** 'G. ORWELL' *Road to Wigan Pier* xii. 243 The thinking person, by intellect usually left-wing but by temperament often right-wing, hovers at the gate of the Socialist fold. **1940** W. TEMPLE *Thoughts in War-Time* iii. 23 The Right Wing tends to emphasise..the distinction between the Government and the community and apply to the Government the ethics of trusteeship. **1941** J. S. HUXLEY *Uniqueness of Man* ii. 80 It is not eugenics but right-wing politics if we merely talk of favouring the breeding of the upper classes of our present social system at the expense of the lower. **1955** *Times* 7 July 8/4 The right-wing monarchists and neo-Fascists [in Italy] are expected to 'wait and see'. **1957** *Economist* 26 Oct. 299/2 President Castillo's strong-arm methods steered the country between communism and right-wing nationalism. **1958** M. ARGYLE *Relig. Behaviour* viii. 83 It seems likely that Catholics have an intrinsically right-wing attitude. *Ibid.*, Protestants support right-wing parties, Jews support the left and have radical attitudes. **1964** *Ann. Reg. 1963* 5 The job of foreign affairs spokesman went to Mr Patrick Gordon Walker..and the remainder of the 'shadow' portfolios were distributed among other right-wing personalities. **1973** M. AMIS *Rachel Papers* 57 Had he poked a switchblade into an enlightened student (for Norman was passionately right-wing)? **1974** J. WHITE tr. *Poulantzas's Fascism & Dictatorship* iii. 126 The Liberal Party itself was in an increasing state of decomposition, with Salandra's right wing now dominant. **1981** *Times* 15 June 2/7 A new right-wing pressure group publication circulating among moderates.

Hence **right-winger,** (*a*) a member of a political right wing; (*b*) in *Football*, a player on the right wing. Also **right-wingery, right-wingism; right-wingy** *a.*
1928 E. & C. PAUL tr. *Stalin's Leninism* 322 They hesitate between embracing the tenets of Leninism and throwing in their lot with the right-wingers. **1929** Right-winger [see *cross-pass* s.v. *CROSS- B.] **1937** WYNDHAM LEWIS *Blasting & Bombardiering* 306 Mr. Douglas Jerrold stands out from the hardboiled crowd: he is the brains of the Right. I think he is the Sotelo of English right-wingery. **1951** *Sport* 16–22 Mar. 13/3 In 20-year-old Brian Siddall..Stoke appear to have found a right-winger of unbounded promise. **1960** *News Chron.* 1 July 4/3 The back-bench Right-wingers want a strong-man Chancellor. **1962** *Tuscaloosa* (Alabama) *News* 12 Feb. 4/6 A meeting of the American Jewish Congress which had been discussing right-wingism in the USA. **1973** D. KYLE *Suvarov Affair* iv. 36 'Why do I represent the Russians?' he would ask. 'Because they want me to. Though why they pick a right-winger like me I can't imagine.' **1973** *Scotsman* 13 Feb. 1/1 Almost all students, including moderates and Right-wingers, are convinced that they must not go on, and that serious disturbances will result if they do. **1977** *Listener* 13 Jan. 60/4 Some people have thought that your heroes are rather snooty and right-wingy and so forth. **1978** *Listener* 13 July 59/4 An..irrational right-wingism, which eschews all 19th-century liberalism.

ri·ghtwise, *adv.* [f. RIGHT *a.* + WISE *sb.*[1] II.] In a right-hand direction.
1908 HARDY *Dynasts* III. II. ii. 369 Henceforward, masses of the foe Withdraw, and, firing as they go, Pass rightwise from the cockpit out of sight.

righty (rəi·ti). Also **rightie.** [-Y[6].] **1.** *U.S.* A right-handed person; *spec.* in *Baseball*, a right-handed pitcher; a batter who stands on the left side of the plate and swings the bat from right to left. Also quasi-*adv.*
1949 *Sun* (Baltimore) 3 June 18/7 Pie—a rightie..compiled an all-time average of 300-plus against all kinds of pitching. **1963** R. I. MCDAVID *Mencken's Amer. Lang.* 564 In baseball, switch hitters speak of their relative prowess batting *lefty* and *righty.* **1974** *Anderson* (S. Carolina) *Independent* 18 Apr. 8c/4 Smith, a righty with an assortment of pitches, struck out 15 Mets and yielded only three walks as he overpowered the visitors. **1975** *New Yorker* 15 Sept. 27/3 The Sox put in..Cleveland, a righty who hadn't seen action in sixteen days. *Ibid.* 22 Sept. 102/3 He never hit righty in a game.

2. A right-winger in politics. Also *transf.* and *attrib.*
1967 *Listener* 10 Aug. 164/1 'The lefties are almost completely in control of the nation's communications.'.. The righties have, then, a case. *Ibid.* 164/3 He might just as easily be a militant atheist or Trotskyite as a rightie.

1969 *Time* 31 Oct. 53 England's thin red line of intellectual royalists is being overrun by 'progressive' reformers who deliberately sabotage old-fashioned academic virtues... The Manchester Guardian called them a 'tightly knit bunch of righties'. **1970** *Guardian* 19 Nov. 9/4 This sounds a bit like his Righty chum, Bernard Levin, but not like any Lefty I know. **1976** *Sunday Tel.* 29 Aug. 14/4 This ecclesiastical equivalent of Enoch Powell has done and said much more than demand the old Latin Mass, and this is where the majority of Catholics part company from the Rightie of Trent. **1978** *Spectator* 21 Oct. 17/2 Such rightie code-phrases as 'the need for discipline in our schools'.

righty-ho (rəi·tihōᵘ), *int.* Also **rightie-ho, righty-oh**, etc. [f. RIGHT *a.* + -Y⁶ + HO *int.*¹ 5.] = *RIGHTO *int.*

1927 D. L. SAYERS *Unnatural Death* xv. 170 'You will remember who you are, won't you?' 'Righty-ho.' **1938** [see *AUNTIE, AUNTY b]. **1942** A. CHRISTIE *Body in Library* v. 51 She said she had a headache..so I said righty ho, and that was that. **1945** E. WAUGH *Brideshead Revisited* 13 For Christ's sake don't say 'rightyoh'. **1959** T. B. MORRIS *Death among Orchids* xix. 170 Righty-ho, darling! That's the lot for now. **1960** B. COBB *Don't lie to Police* iii. 43 Oh, righty-oh. Come right in. **1960** I. CROSS *Backward Sex* 65 O.K. kid and righty ho old top. **1973** J. PORTER *It's Murder with Dover* ii. 20 'I should make it now, Prissy.'.. 'Rightie-ho!' Lady Priscilla set off..for the kitchen.

rigid, *a.* and *sb.* Add: **A.** *adj.* **1. a.** (Further *Comb.* example.)

1932 W. FAULKNER *Light in August* vii. 140 He walked stiffly past her, rigidfaced.

c. *spec.* of an airship: belonging to the type whose shape is maintained by a framework and not (chiefly) by the pressure of gas in the envelope.

[**1902** *Encycl. Brit.* XXV. 101/2 He [*sc.* Count Zeppelin] has gained an advantage by attaching his propellers to the balloon,..but this requires a rigid framework and a great increase of weight.] **1909** A. BERGET *Conquest of Air* ii. 26 There is obviously another way..; it is to make the balloon rigid. **1910** C. C. TURNER *Aerial Navig. To-day* iv. 62 One of the most famous airships of the rigid type was Zeppelin No. 4. **1930** *Daily Express* 6 Oct. 2/4 He..was engaged on research into problems connected with rigid airship construction. **1977** *It* June 16 And so began the era of the rigid airship. **1980** *Nature* 20 Mar. 288/1 In retrospect, this was the most successful rigid airship designed in this country but the Air Staff decided that they had no use for it and it flew for the last time on 20 September 1921.

d. Phr. *to bore, scare*, etc., (someone) *rigid*: to be excessively boring, frightening, etc. *colloq.*

1943 [see *BIND *v.* 22]. **1952** M. TRIPP *Faith is Windsock* xiii. 200 Dick's bloody unruffled ways and his bloody reasonable talk bind me rigid. **1970** O. NORTON *Dead on Prediction* vii. 136 *You* shook him rigid, producing that photograph of her. He was afraid he'd be suspected. **1972** K. CAMPBELL *Thunder on Sunday* 58 It's no tourist place, I assure you... You'd be bored rigid. **1976** R. BARNARD *Little Local Murder* viii. 102 They'll have made the connection: anonymous letters—murder. And..they'll be scared rigid.

3. b. (Further examples.) Also of personality, and of traits and mental processes. Cf. *RIGIDITY 2 b.

1949 *Jrnl. Personality* XVII. 322 A man with rigid delusions may readily bring his delusions in and out of conscious processes. **1960** M. ROKEACH *Open & Closed Mind* ix. 183 Rigid thinking should be expected to lead to difficulties in thinking analytically. **1964** GOULD & KOLB *Dict. Social Sci.* 494/1 Personalities which are highly integrated may be spoken of as 'rigid'. **1972** *Jrnl. Social Psychol.* LXXXVII. 66 Of the three tests used, only the inventory gave meaningful differences, with Communists and Fascists being more rigid than normals. **1972** A. STORR *Dynamics of Creation* viii. 92 The obsessional [personality] is controlled, inhibited, and rigid in his ideas.

5. b. *Logic.* (See quots.)

1972 S. A. KRIPKE in Davidson & Harman *Semantics of Natural Lang.* 269 Let's use some terms quasi-technically. Let's call something a *rigid designator* if in any possible world it designates the same object, a *non rigid* or *accidental designator* if that is not the case. **1975** N. RESCHER *Theory of Possibility* iv. 86 A *rigid designator*—i.e., one that inevitably specifies precisely the same individual in the context of *every* possible world. (This concept coincides pretty much with what is traditionally referred to..as a 'logically proper name' for an individual.) **1976** *Times Lit. Suppl.* 12 Nov. 1434/3 Ruth Marcus's suggested criterion for rigidity of predicates; that *F* is rigid if necessarily anything that is *F* is necessarily *F*.

B. *sb.* **2.** A rigid airship. Cf. sense 1 c of the adj.

1919 *Sphere* 19 July 54/1 Reports to the Admiralty.. urging them to build rigids without delay. **1920** *Glasgow Herald* 3 Dec. 5 The lecturer said that after comparing non-rigids, semi-rigids, and rigids it was obvious that it would be the rigid airships which would be developed for commercial work. **1928** *Daily Tel.* 12 June 17/2 The Mayfly, the first naval rigid, was being built. **1963** A. SMITH *Throw out Two Hands* ii. 31 Lighter-than-air flying suddenly took on a sterner aspect with the development of the dirigible... The word blimp comes from this period for, so the generally accepted story goes, the dirigibles were classified into A—rigid and B—limp. Be that as it may, the rigids were the most exciting.

rigidification (ridʒi:dĭfikēⁱ·ʃən). [f. RIGIDIFY *v.*: see -FICATION.] The action of making or becoming rigid. Also *fig.*

1947 *Sun* (Baltimore) 31 Oct. 10/2 Would not the proposed rigidification of the whole approach..offer hazards of its own? **1965** *Jrnl. Immunol.* XCIV. 130/1 Rigidification of a portion of a normally motile cell membrane may lead to its rupture. **1973** B. R. WILSON *Magic & Millennium* xii. 384 An over-institutionalization, a rigidification, not only of religious practices, beliefs, and procedures, but also of the entire pattern of life of a new community. **1980** P. GREENHALGH *Pompey* i. 208 Cato's faction displayed that inflexibility of purpose which reacts to increasing isolation by rigidification rather than relaxation.

rigidify, *v.* Delete *rare* and add: **a.** (Further examples.)

1920 A. S. EDDINGTON *Space, Time & Gravitation* ii. 39 If a substantial aether analogous to a material ocean exists, it must rigidify, as it were, a definite space. **1942** *Nature* 14 Nov. 564/1 If we conceptually rigidify such a system into a definite formal scheme, we can think of it as a set of alternative canalized paths. **1961** B. R. WILSON *Sects & Society* 1 The sect..seeks itself to rigidify a pattern of behaviour. **1973** P. EVANS *Bodyguard Man* ii. 23 Rigor mortis had already begun to rigidify the cells.

b. (Further examples.)

1979 *Nature* 16 Aug. 538/3 The slightly enhanced 'mobility' of the substrate binding area is intriguing, in particular, if it were to be found that these segments 'rigidify' on substrate binding. **1981** *Times Lit. Suppl.* 20 Feb. 202/1 Now he [*sc.* A. Goehr] is assumed, as a Cambridge professor, to be rigidifying in the academy.

Hence **rigi·dified** *ppl. a.* (chiefly in *pred.* use); **rigi·difier.**

1912 J. GALSWORTHY in *Daily Mail* 27 May 4/4 Which of us does not know the deflecting power of trusteeship, rigidified, as it is, by law? **1956** J. S. BRUNER et al. *Study of Thinking* v. 128 One could begin either way—adopting either a part or a whole hypothesis—and arrive at the same conclusion provided one did not become rigidified before the process of proof was completed. **1968** *Listener* 21 Mar. 365/2 In literature, some artists are naturally rigidifiers and others naturally moulders. **1977** T. BERGER *Who is Teddy Villanova?* i. 6, I am, with expanded chest and rigidified tendons, just..five feet ten.

rigi-dig, var. *RIDGY-DIDGE *a.*

rigidity. Add: **1. b.** *modulus of rigidity* (also *rigidity modulus*).

1877 *Encycl. Brit.* VII. 805/2 The 'modulus of rigidity' of an isotropic solid is the amount of tangential stress divided by the deformation it produces. **1930** *Engineering* 11 Apr. 465/2 In this problem, accurate values of the bulk modulus..and the rigidity modulus..were required. **1966** *McGraw-Hill Encycl. Sci. & Technol.* IV. 419/2 The shear or rigidity modulus..measures the resistance of the material to change in shape without change in volume.

2. b. *Psychol.* Inflexibility and unadaptability in a person's outlook and responses.

1943 K. F. WALKER et al. in *Character & Personality* XII. 35 This additional source of interference might well be called *disposition-rigidity*, and consists of the influence of an habitual activity on a less well-established activity. **1946** P. M. SYMONDS *Dynamics Human Adjustm.* vii. 171 Forms of personal rigidity either in gesture or posture..or thoughts again represent methods of defense against active impulses and hence anxiety. **1949** *Jrnl. Personality* XVII. 321 We hope to demonstrate experimentally what principal forms of rigidity exist. **1960** M. ROKEACH *Open & Closed Mind* ix. 184 High rigidity should lead to difficulties in the analytic phase of thinking. **1973** D. L. SCHAEFFER tr. *Cohen's Patterns of Personality Judgment* iv. 277 These findings would lead us to anticipate positive correlations between judgmental variance and both the neuroticism and the rigidity scores on the personality questionnaire.

rigidize (ri·dʒidəiz), *v.* [f. RIGID *a.* + -IZE.] *trans.* To make rigid. Chiefly as **ri·gidized** *ppl. a.*; also **ri·gidizing** *vbl. sb.*

1948 *Rev. Sci. Instruments* XIX. 725/2 The case of the.. meter is made of rigidized metal. *Ibid.* Rigidizing, or texturing, of the sheet from which the case is formed contributes greater impact strength..than could be provided by plain metal. **1961** *Aeroplane* CI. 379/1 Both are made in 'rigidized' stainless steel to enable them to withstand the severe handling to which this type of equipment is subjected. **1962** *Flight Internat.* LXXXI. 104/1 The 'rigidizing' is accomplished mechanically by stretching the aluminium foil beyond its elastic limit when the structure is fully inflated. **1964** *New Scientist* 23 Jan. 201/1 A balloon that was supposed to become 'rigidised' by the stretching of its plastic skin as it inflated. **1977** *Film & Television Technician* Mar. 10/1 (Advt.), Reward! £200 for information leading to the recovery of a rigidised case containing spare parts for Steenbeck Editing Machines.

rigmarole, *sb.* (and *a.*). Add: **1. c.** *transf.* A succession of tiresome duties; a lengthy procedure; a fuss, a 'palaver'.

1955 *Times* 24 June 12/5 The Government set up..the whole rigmarole of scheduling, listing, and building preservation orders. **1965** M. SPARK *Mandelbaum Gate* I. vi. 178 The whole rigmarole about the film unit visiting Qumran was plainly an occasion for citing the case of the producer. **1977** *Grimsby Even. Tel.* 14 May 10/5 The Wakefield Trophy series is a good way to introduce lads or girls in the area to cycle racing without having to go to the expense and rigmarole of training.

rigmarole *v.* (further example).

1922 JOYCE *Ulysses* 756 O beau pays de la Touraine that I never even sang once explaining and rigmaroling about religion and persecution.

rigmo. Also **rig-mo.** A slang shortening of *rigor mortis* (s.v. RIGOR 2).

1966 *New Statesman* 8 Apr. 512/3 'The foot curls a bit, you know,' confides Liberace as a coffin-salesman, 'when rigmo sets in.' **1975** *Observer* 6 Jan. 17/2 Embalmers' aids like the Natural Expression Former (a plastic device which, inserted into the mouth after rig-mo—as we call it in the trade—sets in, can produce a seraphic smile on the deceased face).

rigol, *sb.* Restrict '*Obs.* exc. *dial.*' to senses in Dict. and add: **1.** (Later examples with reference or allusion to SHAKES. 2 *Hen. IV* IV. v. 36.)

1733 L. THEOBALD *Wks. Shakes.* III. 517 Hence a Rigolet, or Rigol, may, I presume, stand in English for a Circle, any Thing round. **1826** HAZLITT *Plain Speaker* II. ix. 263 Here love's golden rigol bound his brows. **1883** G. MACDONALD *Princess & Curdie* xix. 145 His crown..lay in front of him, his long, thin old hands folded round the rigol, and the ends of his beard straying among the lovely stones.

2. c. *Sailing.* (See quots.)

1961 F. H. BURGESS *Dict. Sailing* 172 *Rigol*, the outboard semicircular gutterway over a porthole. **1976** *Oxf. Compan. Ships & Sea* 711/2 *Rigol*, a curved, semicircular steel strip riveted to a ship's side over a scuttle with the object of deflecting any water which runs down the side of the ship and preventing it from entering the scuttle when it is open.

‖ **rigolette** (rigolet). *Obs. U.S.* [Fr., f. the name of a character in *Mystères de Paris* (1842–3) by Marie-Joseph ('Eugène') Sue.] A variety of woollen head-scarf worn by women.

1863 L. M. ALCOTT in *Commonwealth* 29 May 1/3 All night hovering like a massive cherubim in a red rigolette over the slumbering sons of man. **1866** 'E. FOXTON' *Herman* I. ii. 40 At last his sister appeared, in her blue evening cloak and *rigolette*, with the flowers in her hair peeping out between its strings of tiny pearl balls. **1867** *Student & Schoolmate* Mar. 90 Kitty wore a Rob Roy cloak and a dainty white hood, called in those days a rigolette (though how the fashion-maker spelt the word I don't know).

rigor. Add: **2. b.** *fig.*

1929 W. FAULKNER *Sanctuary* (1981) v. 59 A tradition.. in the throes of its own rigor-mortis. **1934** C. LAMBERT *Music Ho!* II. 131 *Socrate*..has something of the rigor mortis always associated with overtheorized music. **1977** *Rolling Stone* 16 June 39/2 He showed up at the producer's black-tie party, an occasion to normally give him rigor mortis.

rigoristic (rigǒri·stik), *a.* [f. RIGORIST + -IC.] Of, pertaining to, or characteristic of a rigorist; austere, stringent.

1907 W. JAMES *Pragmatism* iv. 160 Pluralism..has no need of this dogmatic rigoristic temper. **1934** *Times Lit. Suppl.* 7 June 398/2 Carlyle's failure to impose his narrow, rigoristic, moralistic, joyless Annandale view of the world upon the world, added an element of tragedy to his deeply tragic sense of life. **1955** L. ROSENFELD in W. Pauli *Niels Bohr* 92 One might well regard any rigoristic conception of this problem as superfluous.

‖ **Rigsdag** (ri·gzdag). [Da., f. gen. of *rige* realm + *dag* DAY; cf. *REICHSTAG, *RIKSDAG.] The name of the Parliament of Denmark, formerly comprising two Houses, the Landsting and the Folketing.

In 1953 the upper chamber and the name Rigsdag were abolished. The remaining single chamber is called the Folketing.

[**1645** J. HOWELL *Lett.* VI. i. 1 He was at Rensburgh..at a Richsdagh an Assembly that corresponds our Parliament.] **1883** *Students' Encycl.* II. 368/1 D[enmark] is governed by a hereditary monarchy, and by a National Assembly or *Rigsdag*. **1938** J. H. S. BIRCH *Denmark in Hist.* xx. 337 The Constitution provided for two Assemblies, the Folketing and the Landsting. The Rigsdag, which comprised the two Assemblies and was to meet annually, exercised jointly with the King legislative power and the right of imposing taxes. **1956** W. L. SHIRER *Challenge of Scandinavia* iv. 278 There was a national election on April 21, 1953, for the Lower House (Folketing) of the Rigsdag. **1972** S. OAKLEY *Story of Denmark* xiii. 178 The new ministry put forward a very liberal project, largely the work of Lehmann and Monrad, which envisaged a *Rigsdag* of two houses, both elected by universal male suffrage.

‖ **Rigsmaal** (ri·gzmǭl). Also **rigsmaal.** [Da., f. as prec. + *mål* (formerly *maal*) language; cf. *RIKSMÅL.] = *DANO-NORWEGIAN *sb.* Cf. *LANDSMÅL.

1902 *Encycl. Brit.* XXXI. 275/1 The close of 1899 and the beginning of 1900 were occupied by a discussion, which drowned all other interests, and in which every Norwegian author took part, as to the adoption of the *landsmaal*, or composite dialect of the peasants, as the national language in place of the *rigsmaal* or Dano-Norwegian. **1932** W. L. GRAFF *Lang.* 387 A form of Danish with Norwegian peculiarities ('rigsmaal') was adopted as the official and literary language [of Norway]. **1959** A. C. BAUGH *Hist. Eng. Lang.* (ed. 2) 36 This regeneration of the national speech has not succeeded in displacing Dano-Norwegian (*Rigsmaal*).

Rig-vedic (rig,vē·dik), *a.* (*sb.*) Also **Rig Vedic, Rigvedic.** [f. RIG-VEDA + -IC; cf. *RGVEDIC *a.* (*sb.*).] Of or pertaining to the Rig-veda. Also as *sb.*, Rig-vedic Sanskrit.

1881 *Encycl. Brit.* XII. 781/1 The conquest of the vast new tracts thus included seems not to have commenced till the close of the Rig-Vedic era. **1895** E. W. HOPKINS

Relig. India iii. 74 The end of the Rig Vedic period. **1923** H. D. GRISWOLD *Relig. of Rigveda* ii. 28 The primary source for the Rigvedic age is, of course, the *Rigveda*. **1968** *Language* XLIV. 8 The dual and the present indicate that the full grade (whether developed in common or separately in Rigvedic and Avestan) is secondary. **1975** *Language* LI. 115 The most intriguing bit of evidence presented in EIP involves glide formation and glide vocalization in Rigvedic Sanskrit.

rijsttafel (rəi·stāfĕl). Also **reistafel, rijstafel.** [Du., f. *rijst* RICE[2] + *tafel* TABLE *sb.*] A South-East Asian rice dish (see quots.).

1889 S. J. HICKSON *Naturalist in N. Celebes* ix. 224 As an article of food these small prawns are much prized by the natives, and the Dutchman is very glad to add the *kleine garnalen* to his list of comestibles at the *rijsttafel*. **1932** W. S. MAUGHAM *Narrow Corner* xvi. 124 *Reistafel* was served. They piled their plates with rice and curry, fried eggs, bananas and a dozen strange concoctions. **1933** L. DEELEY *Internat. Cookery* 12 Travellers to the Far East all know the famous Rijstafel, to be met on board and ashore, from Ceylon to Shanghai. To describe every dish served is almost impossible. It includes curried fish, rabbit, chicken, served with rice and the famous Kroepoek Oedang which is a special kind of dried shrimp. **1937** C. CONNOLLY in L. Russell *Press Gang!* 89 Some stewards from the P. & O. worked away at the punkahs, or at distributing reistafel and planters' punch. **1962** P. HELM *Death has Thousand Entrances* iv. 86 The meal, an Indonesian rijsttafel, was over. **1965** B. SWEET-ESCOTT *Baker St. Irregular* viii. 243 The problem was discussed by us with the Dutch over many a *reistafel* in Colombo. **1969** *Daily Tel.* 14 Jan. 15/7 The rijsttafel, served in a multitude of dishes, is delicious—with rare strange spices, sometimes hot, but always delicate and more subtle than much Chinese food. **1977** J. DIDION *Bk. Common Prayer* II. ii. 65 She knew the Indonesian couple who did the rijsttafel.

‖ **rikka** (ri·ka). Also **rikkwa.** [Jap., lit. standing flowers.] A traditional form of Japanese flower-arrangement.

1889 J. CONDER *Theory Jap. Flower Arrangem.* (1935) 25 The use of many different kinds of flowers in one composition though followed in the earlier styles of *Rikkwa* and *Shin-no-hana* is opposed to the principles of the purer styles. **1914** M. AVERILL *Jap. Flower Arrangem.* i. 28 Rikkwa and Nageire are the two branches into which Ike-bana has been divided. **1934** A. KOEHN *Art Jap. Flower Arrangem.* xvii. 131 A huge well-shaped Pine branch or Bamboo spray formed the centre of these 'rikkwa' designs. **1965** W. SWAAN *Jap. Lantern* iv. 49 There are two main styles [of ikebana]: the formal *rikka* arrangements used to decorate the altars of Buddhist temples..and the *nageire* or 'thrown-in' style. **1976** *San Antonio* (Texas) *Express* 14 Oct. 3-G/1 *Rikka* is the oldest established form [of flower arrangement], dating back five centuries. It is a complex style with 11 main branches presenting a stylized representation of the landscape of Buddhist paradise.

‖ **Riksdag** (ri·ksdag). Also **riksdag.** [Sw., f. gen. of *rike* realm + *dag* DAY; cf. *RIGSDAG.] The name of the Swedish Parliament.

Since 1971 a one-chamber Parliament.

1887 *Encycl. Brit.* XXII. 743/1 The riksdag meets every year on January 15, and consists of two houses. **1893** W. W. THOMAS *Sweden & Swedes* xvii. 217 The Riksdag, or Diet, of Sweden is opened with great pomp and ceremony... Both houses of the Riksdag leave the parliament building and come to the palace to have their sessions opened by the King. **1955** *Ann. Reg. 1954* 234 These elections had, possibly, important effects on the Riksdag elections. **1976** S. LLOYD *Mr Speaker, Sir* iii. 93 The Speaker..cannot adopt the Swedish practice under which, when the votes are equal, the Talsmand of the Riksdag has to draw lots.

‖ **Riksmål** (ri·ksmǫl). Also **riks-, -maal.** [Norw., f. gen. of *rike* realm + *mål* language; cf. *RIGSMAAL.] = *DANO-NORWEGIAN *sb.* Cf. *LANDSMÅL.

The usual term now for this language is *Bokmål*.

1926 *Encycl. Brit.* II. 1090/1 Simultaneously with this lyric flourishing in the *riksmaal*, no adequate revival has taken place in the *landsmaal*. **1939** L. H. GRAY *Foundations of Lang.* 346 Norwegian died out as a literary language in the Middle Ages, when it gave place to Danish, which, under the appellation of *Riksmaal*, served as the standard speech until the nineteenth century and, indeed, still so functions to a considerable extent. The *Riksmaal* is now yielding place to a truly national *Landsmaal*, based upon indigenous Norwegian dialects. **1952, 1966** [see *NYNORSK]. **1972** W. B. LOCKWOOD *Panorama Indo-Europ. Lang.* 125 *Landsmål* 'National Language'..in 1885 won official recognition beside Dano-Norwegian, now known as *Riksmål* 'Language of the Realm'.

rile, *v.* Add: **2. a.** Also const. *up*.

1857 J. G. HOLLAND *Bay-Path* iii. 32 It only raises the devil in me, and riles me all up. **1872** W. A. HICKMAN *Brigham's Destroying Angel* iii. 72 Some of the boys began to get terribly riled up. **1929** W. FAULKNER *Sound & Fury* 67 'Getting Quentin all riled up,' Dilsey said. 'Why can't you keep him away from her.' **1966** T. PYNCHON *Crying of Lot 49* iii. 68 Calculating this ought to rile up public opinion some.

riled *ppl. a.* (further example); also **riled-up.**

1856 S. SMITH in *National Intelligencer* 26 Jan. 3/1, I found the President..looking kind of riled and very resolute. **1978** G. A. SHEEHAN *Running & Being* x. 137 If we go to bed mad we are likely to wake up with a riled-up stomach.

Riley (rəi·li). orig. *U.S.* Also **Reilly.** [A common Irish surname.] In colloq. phr. *the life of Riley*, a comfortable, enjoyable, and carefree existence.

The phrase is freq. said to owe its origin to one of a number of late nineteenth-century songs (as, for example, in W. & M. Morris, *Dict. Word & Phr. Origins* (1962) 215, and S. J. Raff in *Amer. Speech* (1976) LI. 944 ff.) but has not been traced earlier than the song of 1919, which gave it currency.

1919 H. PEASE *My Name is Kelly* (song) 3 Faith and my name is Kelly Michael Kelly, But I'm living the life of Reilly just the same. **1923** E. RICE *Adding Machine* VI. 85 This is the life of Riley all right. **1936** H. MILLER *Black Spring* 142 The old man's leading the life of Reilly. **1949** J. B. PRIESTLEY *Delight* 7 The life of Reilly, which some people imagine me to lead, has been further away than a fading dream. **1960** *20th Cent.* May 387 The executive is..living the life of Riley by tax evasion and expense account. **1965** J. PORTER *Dover Two* vi. 70 The native cunning which had enabled him to live the life of Riley with no visible means of support..failed him dismally now. **1978** *Daily Tel.* 8 Feb. 6/7 It is simply not true that we don't pay tax and are living the life of Riley.

rill, *sb.*[1] Add: **1. a.** *spec.* A small trickle of water formed temporarily in soil or sand after rain or tidal ebb.

1883 T. C. CHAMBERLIN *Geol. Wisconsin* I. 43 Rills, especially those following outgoing tides furrow the sand or mud, particularly in flowing over a pebble, shell or other obstruction. Such grooves where preserved constitute rill marks. **1908** *Jrnl. Geol.* XVI. 748 The word 'rill' will be used to indicate such a streamlet in an overloaded condition, that is previous to the degree of concentration necessary to cut a gully. **1925** *Water-Supply Papers U.S. Geol. Survey* No. 499. 96 As the supply of débris is small these rills are not fully loaded and are effective eroding agents. **1939** *U.S. Dept. Agric. Yearbk. 1938* 1167 Frequently in sheet erosion the eroding surface consists of numerous very small rills. **1966** *McGraw-Hill Encycl. Sci. & Technol.* XII. 430/2 All traces of the rills are removed after the land is tilled. **1968** R. W. FAIRBRIDGE *Encycl. Geomorphol.* 1102/1 In calm weather, the backwash of the returning water [on a beach] has little energy, creating a diamond pattern of small rills. **1975** R. V. RUHE *Geomorphol.* vi. 108/1 During intense runoff, a divide between two rills is broken by caving, by undercutting by a deeper rill, or by overflow.

c. *rill action, channel, -cutting, erosion, -mark* (further example), *wash*; *rill-threaded* adj.

1960 B. W. SPARKS *Geomorphol.* iv. 69 In the wet season the middle section of the slope may be under the influence of concentrated rill action. **1962** L. C. KING *Morphol. of Earth* v. 137 Following the cutting of a steep hillside by rill and gully action.., surface water requires to be discharged across a relatively flat terrain to an adjacent stream channel. *Ibid.* 138 The water..may be insufficient to form sheets and then passes across the pediment in rills only. Where this occurs frequently, pediments are scored by rill channels. **1968** R. W. FAIRBRIDGE *Encycl. Geomorphol.* 819/2 Frequently the cutting of rill channels and gully heads is by far the most active process operating upon the steeper slopes. **1925** *Water-Supply Papers U.S. Geol. Survey* No. 499. 96 Rill cutting at the foot of mountain slopes. **1962** L. C. KING *Morphol. of Earth* v. 138 The zone of laminar flow..is often elided, and rill-cutting and gullying appear extensively upon many pediments. **1939** *U.S. Dept. Agric. Yearbk. 1938* 1167 *Rill [erosion]*,.. accelerated erosion by water which produces small channels that can be obliterated by tillage. **1966** *McGraw-Hill Encycl. Sci. & Technol.* XII 431/1 *(caption)* Rill erosion showing how water has followed the old corn rows. **1963** D. W. & E. E. HUMPHRIES tr. *Termier's Erosion & Sedimentation* x. 211 Tidal currents which occur during the retreat of the sea from a beach form a pattern of fine channels, particularly where the water is retarded by obstacles, pebbles or shells. These channels or rill-marks formed on the surface of moist, soft sand can be preserved by fossilization. **1933** R. CAMPBELL *Flowering Reeds* 28 The shimmering beams of a morning that sinewed The lowlands with silver, and trawled to the plains, Rill-threaded, the sweep of its glittering seines. **1908** *Jrnl. Geol.* XVI. 751 *(heading)* Hypothesis of rill-wash applied to the St. Louis region. **1937** *Bull. Geol. Soc. Amer.* XLVIII. 343 The interstream areas..are today being lowered chiefly by tributary streams and rill wash. **1972** A. YOUNG *Slopes* vii. 62 Surface flow may be divided into sheetwash, where the ground is entirely or largely covered by a moving layer of water, and rillwash, when the water flows mainly as micro-channels.

3. (Earlier and later examples.)

1876 E. NELSON *Moon* iii. 71 There is one class of formations..which, from their unknown nature, cannot well be classified. These are the rills or clefts. **1954** *Proc. Nat. Acad. Sci.* XL. 1103 The rills are cracks in the surface, about 1″ (2 km.) in width and narrower, occurring almost anywhere on the moon. **1963** A. N. STRAHLER *Earth Sci.* v. 83/2 Rills may be on the order of a mile wide and as long as 150 miles.

4. *Phonetics.* [ad. Da. *rille* (O. Jespersen *Fonetik*, 1899).] Used *attrib.* to designate a fricative produced by forcing air through a groove-like aperture between the tongue and the roof of the mouth (see quots.).

1912 E. PROKOSCH in *Amer. Jrnl. Philol.* XXXIII. 197 Spirants of these places of articulation can be formed in two ways: either, the surface of the tongue is convex, so that the breath passes through a narrow slit, as with *þ, χ*; or, the tongue forms a more or less distinct rill in its median line, as with *s, sh*. The former may be called slit sounds, the latter rill sounds. **1918** A. W. ARON in C. F. Hockett *Leonard Bloomfield Anthol.* (1970) 56 They are synonymous with what we call in Jespersen's terminology 'rill spirants', namely unvoiced *s*, voiced *z*, and the sibilants in *shall* and *azure*. **1958** C. F. HOCKETT *Course in Mod. Linguistics* viii. 72 Both English /sz/ and English /θð/ are normally apico-alveolar, but the former are *rill* spirants, the latter *slit* spirants.

rille. (Further examples.)

1957 *New Scientist* 7 Nov. 16 Criss-crossing the lunar surface there are alignments of mountains, valleys and trench-like formations called rilles. **1971** *Daily Colonist* (Victoria, B.C.) 25 July 2/3 A gorge called Hadley Rille cuts an 80-mile long 1,200-feet-deep gash across the..face of the moon. **1977** A. HALLAM *Planet Earth* 15/3 These features, known as rilles, are shallow, often sinuous, valleys that cut across the maria.

rilled (rild), *a.* [f. RILL *sb.*[1], RILLE + -ED[2].] Marked by or possessing rills or rilles; having narrow grooves.

1924 R. NEWSTEAD *Guide to the Study of Tsetse-Flies* 24 Wings with the membrane slightly rilled. **1935** O. DAVIES *Roman Mines in Europe* i. 39 In prehistoric times ore was pounded with rilled hammers. **1957** N. K. SANDARS *Bronze Age Cultures in France* iii. 130 Rilled [G. *gerillt*] ware pots are of various shapes... Rilled decoration appears quite suddenly in France with graves and bronzes. **1970** R. E. HORTON in G. H. Drury *Rivers & River Terraces* v. 154 In the latter case..a rilled surface may not develop. **1974** *Nature* 12 Apr. 573/2 The two large craters Oppenheimer and Schrödinger were also rilled. Small rilled craters are again found within larger flat-floored craters.

rillett(e)s. Add: The form ‖ **rillettes** (riyet) is now usual. (Earlier and later examples.) Also **rillettes de Tours,** a finely-minced pork pâté from the Tours region of France.

1889 J. WHITEHEAD *Steward's Handbk.* IV. 420/1 *Rillettes de Tours*, cold cakes of meat of the head-cheese order. At the Paris ham fairs the rillette makers build up fancy pyramids of small rillettes and decorate them. **1894** G. DU MAURIER *Trilby* I. III. 238 Tongues, hams, *rillettes de Tours*..for the supper. **1931** A. DE CROZE *What to eat & drink in France* xix. 160 *Rillettes de Tours* (same preparations as for 'Rillons', but the dices of meat are chopped and warmed again before being potted). **1960** E. DAVID *French Provincial Cooking* 215 Another speciality..was the pâté made largely with *grattons*, the little browned scraps which are the residue after the pork fat has been melted down, and which were also the original ingredient of the renowned *rillettes de Tours*. **1973** *Times* 26 May 12/5 One local resident..writes, properly conscience-stricken, in praise of its [*sc.* a restaurant's] rillettes and ratatouille.

rilling (ri·liŋ), *sb.*[2] *Archæol.* [f. RILL *sb.*[1] + -ING[1].] Pottery decoration or marking of a rilled nature. Cf. *RILLED *a.*

1940 C. F. C. HAWKES *Prehist. Found. Europe* iv. 98 There are straight or curving bands of rilling. **1957** N. K. SANDARS *Bronze Age Cultures in France* iii. 130 The rilling is close-set, lightly drawn with a blunt implement on the moist clay, leaving a noticeable ridge between the rills. **1964** H. HODGES *Artifacts* i. 29 The presence on the inner and outer surfaces of pottery of fine horizontal grooves and ridges, called *rilling*, caused by the coarser particles in the clay body and irregularities of the potter's hands, is commonly held to be a certain indication that pottery was wheel-thrown.

rilling, *vbl. sb.* Delete † and add: **1.** (Later examples.)

1975 R. V. RUHE *Geomorphol.* vi. 107/2 Rilling, a more effective erosion agent than sheet wash.., is a dominant process in hillslope reduction. **1978** W. W. EMMETT in M. J. Kirkby *Hillslope Hydrol.* v. 171 Rilling is generally considered to be evidence of more accelerated erosion than sheet erosion.

2. Flow in rills.

1929 R. BRIDGES *Testament of Beauty* I. 12 Valleys vocal with angelic rilling of rocky streams.

Rilsan (ri·lsæn). Also **rilsan.** [Invented word: *ri-* f. F. *ricin* castor-oil plant (see RICINUS).] A proprietary name (orig. used in France) for a kind of nylon used esp. as a fibre.

1951 R. DUMON in *Rev. Gén. Caoutchouc* XXVIII. 348 Rilsan, a new plastic of the polyamide type..made out of castor oil, may be spun in order to get textile threads. **1952** *Sun* (Baltimore) (B ed.) 28 Feb. 4/3 Two plants to produce rilsan already have been built and a third is under construction. **1956** *Official Gaz.* (U.S. Patent Office) 27 Mar. TM 185/1 Rilsan Corporation, Boston, Mass. Filed May 17, 1955. *Rilsan*... For synthetic yarns. Use since July 27, 1953. **1963** *Trade Marks Jrnl.* 2 Oct. 1393/2 Rilsan... All goods included in Class 22 made of plastics. Organico.., Paris... Manufacturers. **1963** A. J. HALL *Textile Sci.* ii. 84 Rilsan fabrics can be permanently pleated under appropriate high temperature heat-setting conditions. **1969** —— *Stand. Handbk. Textiles* (ed. 7) i. 60 At present Rilsan fibres are used in articles such as brushes.

rim, *sb.*[1] Add: **1. b.** (Further examples of a drum.)

1934 [see *rim-shot*, sense 6 below]. **1976** *New Yorker* 8 Mar. 108/3 He would hit the snare directly, or hit the snare-head and the rim (a rim shot).

d. *pl. spec.* that part of the frame of a pair of spectacles which surrounds the lens.

1865 DICKENS *Mut. Fr.* II. III. vi. 48 Mr Wegg, in fitting on his spectacles, opened his eyes wide, over their rims, and tapped the side of his nose. **1903** G. B. SHAW *Man & Superman* IV. 147 He pauses quietly to take out and put on his spectacles, which have gold rims. **1923** A. HUXLEY *Antic Hay* x. 156 For semi-evening dress, shell rims with gold ear-pieces—and gold nose-bridge. **1937** J. SQUIRE *Honeysuckle & Bee* i. 24 They certainly wouldn't swallow my yarn at a 'Spike' if I turned up in tortoiseshell rims.

3. c. *U.S. slang.* The outer edge of the semi-circular or horseshoe-shaped desk at which a newspaper's sub-editors work.

1923 W. G. Bleyer *Newspaper Writing & Editing* (rev. ed.) i. 10 The copy-desk is semicircular in form, and the head copy-reader sits in the 'slot', or inside of the desk, while the copy-readers occupy places around the outside, or 'rim'. **1933** Garst & Bernstein *Headlines & Deadlines* ii. 26 The copy desk usually is semicircular or horseshoe-shaped.. The copy editors sit 'on the rim'. **1976** *National Observer* (U.S.) 2 Oct. 4/2 At 9:05 p.m., Crimson President Jim Kramer hurries over to the rim, where Managing Editor Margaret Shapiro is marking copy.

4. d. *ellipt.* = *rim-rock*, sense 6 in Dict. and Suppl. *N. Amer.*

1869 J. Anderson *Rough but Honest Miner* in *Sawney's Lett.* (ed. 2), He hammers at the rock, Believin' it's a rim, When ten to ane 'tis naething But his fancy's whim. **1946** *Notes Placer-Mining* (Brit. Columbia Dept. Mines Bull. No. 21) 21 The first shallow diggings gave way to.. sniping operations along the rims or on weathered bed-rock. **1976** *Billings* (Montana) *Gaz.* 4 July 8-D/4 (Advt.), Between the rims, comfortable, pleasant and quiet 2 and 3 bedroom duplex.

6. rim band, a driving belt or rope passing around a rim wheel; **rim-brake** (earlier and later examples); **rim drive,** a method of driving a gramophone turntable by means of frictional contact between the motor shaft and the inner rim of the turntable, often with an intermediate wheel between the two; so **rim-driven** *a.*; **rim-fire** (examples in latter sense); **rim light** *Photogr.* and *Cinemat.*, a lamp placed behind the subject in order to produce the appearance of a halo of light; also, the light produced by a lamp in such a position; so **rim lighting; rim man** *U.S. slang*, a newspaper sub-editor (cf. sense 3 c above); **rim-rack** *v. trans. U.S. dial.* (chiefly *Naut.*), to injure or damage (something) (see also quot. 1929); also *fig.*; hence **rim-racked; rim-rock,** for *U.S.* read *N. Amer.* and add: earlier and later examples; hence as *v. trans.*, to drive (sheep) over a cliff (see quot. 1944); also **rim-rocker,** (*a*) one who rim-rocks sheep; (*b*) (see quot. 1968); **rim-shot,** a drum-stroke in which the stick strikes the rim and the head of the drum simultaneously; **rimstone** *Geol.*, a thin layer of calcite deposited round the rim of an overflowing basin or in an evaporating pool of water, characteristic of karst topography; **rim wheel,** substitute for def.: on a spinning mule, a large pulley which transmits drive to the spindles and serves as a fly-wheel; (later examples).

1890 J. Nasmith *Mod. Cotton Spinning Machinery* xi. 184 Over this the endless cord or band driving the spindles is passed—being known as the 'rim band'. **1970** H. Catling *Spinning Mule* ix. 163 Minders naturally spared neither trouble nor expense to keep their rim bands in the best possible condition. **1896** A. Sharp *Bicycles & Tricycles* xxxii. 528 Tyre and Rim Brakes.—The brake is usually applied to the tyre of the front wheel. **1917** *Cycling Man.* 18 Rim brakes are the most common in use. **1974** *Listener* 14 Feb. 212/2 The effectiveness of rim brakes is reduced..in wet weather. **1961** E. N. Bradley *Records & Gramophone Equipment* iii. 69 Wow could also occur as a result of damage to the turntable rim (in a rim-drive system). **1962** A. Nisbett *Technique Sound Studio* viii. 147 Quick-start techniques fall into two categories, depending on the type of drive employed by the turntable. (i) Rim drive. **1976** A. Hope *Hi-Fi Handbk.* iv. 43 In an idler wheel or rim drive design the motor drives a sequence of rollers... Belt drive tends to be quieter, and more expensive, than rim drive. **1956** G. Slot *Hi-Fi from Microphone to Ear* vii. 67 The rim of the turntable (if it is rim-driven) [must be] perfectly circular. **1900–1901** *Kynoch Jrnl.* Dec.–Jan. 41/2 The first real rifle I possessed was an antiquated rim-fire rook rifle. **1977** D. Seaman *Committee* 14 Sedgwick assembled the ·22 Marlin rimfire repeater. **1940** W. Nurnberg *Lighting for Photogr.* iv. 105 The greatest luminosity in a rim-light picture is obviously always the main light produced by the basic illumination. **1948** —— *Lighting for Portraiture* ii. 84 A combination of basic cross lighting..supplemented by a rim light on the near side, is bad. **1961** P. Snow *Electronic Flashlight Photogr.* xiv. 115 We are already using two backlights for 'rim-light' effects on the subject. **1977** J. Hedgecoe *Photographer's Handbk.* 94 Generally it is advisable to reveal some detail in the rest of the face by using frontal light. This should be soft, shadowless and less intense than the rim light. **1940** W. Nurnberg *Lighting for Photogr.* iii. 61 If we now move the light source horizontally we obtain side-lighting, and when continuing this movement rim-lighting. **1971** *Listener* 11 Nov. 671/2 The Fonda film has everything:..minimal rim-lighting, fancy focus-pulls. **1933** R. M. Neal *Newspaper Desk Work* ii. 7 Copyreaders..are designated as 'rim men'. **1970** R. K. Kent *Lang. Journalism* 113 Rim men are the copy-readers who sit at the rim to do their work. **1914** *Dialect Notes* IV. 78 *Rimrack*, to injure, damage. **1929** F. C. Bowen *Sea Slang* 112 *Rim-Rack, to*, to strain or damage a vessel, particularly by driving her too hard in a sea. Very frequently used on the Grand Banks. **1952** *Amer. Legion Mag.* July 5/2, I am going to tell you right now my husband is not joining the American Legion another year if you keep up this rim-racking the Administration. **1957** *Maine Coast Fisherman* July 21/1 If nets have been rimracked it means working on deck under flood repairing nets and gear. **1974** J. Dowell *Look-Off Bear* 32 Faded denim workshirt, rim-racked old felt hat..and calf-high lumberman's rubbers. **1860** H. Greeley *Overland Journey* 350 It is one of the arts of the miner to know just where to tunnel through the 'rim rock' so as to strike what was the bottom of the lake. **1942** Berrey & Van den Bark *Amer. Thes. Slang.* §917/9 *Rimrock*, to drive sheep over a precipice. **1944** R. F. Adams *Western Words* 128/2 *Rim rockin' sheep*, running sheep over a cliff to destruction. This was often done during the wars between the cattle and the sheep factions. **1949** *World-Herald Mag.* (Omaha, Nebraska) 18 Sept. 18/5 Cattle raisers destroyed the flocks [of sheep] by clubbing, shooting, dynamiting,..poisoning, and stampeding them over cliffs—a practice sometimes called rim-rocking. **1958** 'W. Henry' *Seven Men at Mimbres Springs* ix. 101 They're..crawling the rimrock to smell out what took Major Mobry off so suddenlike. **1976** *Billings* (Montana) *Gaz.* 27 June 5-D/8 (Advt.), Canyon setting surrounded by the rimrocks, nestled in Spring Valley. **1934** *Nat. Geogr. Mag.* Feb. 213/2 My first companion, John Mullens, of Homestead, a 'rim-rocker'.. steered me through in six days. **1950** *Amer. Speech* XXV. 305 The term *rimrockers* goes back to the days of the cattle-sheep wars. **1968** R. F. Adams *Western Words* (rev. ed.) 251/2 *Rim rocker*, a cowboy's name for a horse agile enough to climb steep hills and travel over rocks and rough country. **1934** E. Little *Mod. Rhythmic Drumming* 25 A characteristic feature of rhythmic drumming is the rim-shot. This is the effect obtained by striking the snare drum head and the edge of the counter hoop simultaneously. **1968** *Crescendo* May 30/3 Bellson's rhythm is tremendous. His sympathetic fills, from 'cute' rimshots to make-'em-'ave-it roar-ups kicking the phrases are worth the price of the record alone. **1977** J. Wainwright *Do Nothin'* viii. 133 The right stick is used for the fireworks: for the rimshots, for the off-beats, for the roll-work. **1930** W. M. Davis in *Bull. Geol. Soc. Amer.* XLI. 485 Rimstone has been added to the list to name calcareous deposits formed around the rims of overflowing basins. **1968** R. W. Fairbridge *Encycl. Geomorphol.* 1051/1 Rimstone dams greater than 40 feet in height are known while micro-forms only a few millimetres high abound on stalagmites and flowstone. **1971** *Islander* (Victoria, B.C.) 24 Jan. 5/3 Rimstones are the layers of calcite left by receding pools. **1894** J. Lister *Cotton Manuf.* vi. 54 The main shaft drives the spindle by the rim wheel. **1950** J. W. Radcliffe *Woollen & Worsted Yarn Manuf.* xxv. 351 (*caption*) Fast and loose pulleys, rim wheels for driving spindles, and the backing-off friction.

rim, *sb.*⁴ (Earlier example.)

1817 G. Barker *Diary* 15 May in *Voorloper* (1976) 674 Oxen rims were also cut.

rim, *v.*¹ Add: **2.** *intr.* Of a steel ingot: to form an outer skin of relatively pure steel. Also *trans.* (causatively).

1958 A. D. Merriman *Dict. Metallurgy* 290/2 Steels which contain not more than 0·15% C can be made to 'rim'. **1967** A. H. Cottrell *Introd. Metallurgy* xi. 138 Only low-carbon steels contain enough oxygen to rim satisfactorily. **1974** *Encycl. Brit. Macropædia* XVII. 651/2 Plain carbon steels containing between 0·04 and 0·25 percent carbon can be rimmed successfully.

rim, *v.*³ [Perh. var. of Ream *v.*³ in Dict. and Suppl.; cf. Rim *v.*¹ and *rimmer³.]

1. a. *intr.* (See quot. 1923.) *U.S. dial.* **b.** *trans.* (See quot. 1972.) *coarse slang* (orig. *U.S.*).

1923 *Dialect Notes* V. 219 *Rim*, v., to be desirous of sexual intercourse, wanting to be bred. Said especially of sows. **1959** W. Burroughs *Naked Lunch* 90 'Darling, I want to rim you,' she whispers... 'All right. I'll go wash my ass.' 'No, I'll wash it.' **1972** B. Rodgers *Queens' Vernacular* 172 *Rim*, 1. To lick or suck anus. 2. to lubricate the anus with saliva, usually as a prelude to fucking. 'Tense? Try getting rimmed.' **1975** M. Amis *Dead Babies* xv. 74 Skip'd rim a snake so long as someone held its head.

2. *N. Amer. slang.* To cheat, to swindle (a person). Cf. *ream *v.*³ 4.

1945 V. J. Monteleone *Criminal Slang* 84 *Rim*,..to cheat; to swindle: to defraud. **1973** D. Hughes *Along Side Road* vii. 54 Ten bucks? For that old thing? I'd be rimming you, Charles.

‖ **rimaye** (rimāy). [Fr., f. L. *rīma* fissure + F. *-aye*, collective suffix.] = *bergschrund.

1920 H. Raeburn *Mountaineering Art* viii. 107 At the foot of the snow-slope, just where it eases into the glacier, runs a long chasm in the ice, the *bergschrund*, *randkluft*, or *rimaye*. **1949** A. Roch *Climbs of my Youth* xiv. 118 Taking to a couloir of easy broken rock, we soon reached the rimaye, where one last rappel had to be placed. **1957** E. A. Wrangham *Sel. Climbs Range Mont Blanc* iii. 67 Go up the Dôme glacier,..to the rimaye below the Col des Aiguilles. **1974** G. Sutton tr. *Mazeaud's Naked before Mountain* i. 22 Slide he did, but into the rimaye, and we had to look for him and pull him out. *Ibid.*, The rimaye..is the large crevasse formed around the head of a glacier where it detaches itself from the mountain.

Rimbaldian (rimbæ·ldiăn), *a.* Also (ræ̃mbō·diăn) **Rimbaudian**; ‖ **Rimbaldien, Rimbaudien.** [ad. F. *Rimbaldien*, f. the name of Arthur *Rimbaud* (1854–91), French poet + *-ien* -ian.] Of, pertaining to, or characteristic of Rimbaud or his poetry.

1924 R. Macaulay *Orphan Island* xxii. 296 A hundred birds unballed themselves and sang... 'Very Rimbaudien,' said Charles dizzily. **1952** *Essays in Crit.* II. 21 Her capacity for dissatisfaction..might have led to Rimbaldian adventures or Baudelairean visions. **1957** L. Varèse in *Rimbaud's Illuminations* p. xiv, The cardinal tenet of the *Rimbaldien* cult has been that *Une Saison en Enfer* was the nineteen-year-old boy's farewell to literature, his *mea culpa*. **1965** R. G. Cohn *Toward Poems of Mallarmé* 5 *Le Sonneur* indicates he [*sc.* Mallarmé] could have trodden further along the earthy Rimbaldian path. **1976** *Listener* 25 Nov. 691/3 The roared Rimbaudian lyrics of Peter Hammill. **1978** *Amer. Poetry Rev.* Nov./Dec. 30/1 Alcohol is the means but it is really fate at work—something a little Faustian, a little Coleridgian or Rimbaldian.

rimbellisher (rimbe·lĭʃəɹ). [f. Rim *sb.*¹ + Em)bellisher.] An ornamental chromium-plated rim placed round the wheel-hub of a motor vehicle; a wheel-trim. (No longer current.)

1949 *Motor* 10 Aug. 2 We announce the 'Rimbellisher' as an important addition to the already extensive range of ACE roadwheel disc equipment. This handsome accessory is a superimposed chromium rim which adds the finishing touch and makes wheel cleaning easier. **1955** *Times* 14 June 10/1 The wheels are fitted with rimbellishers as standard equipment. **1958** *Times* 12 Dec. 1/5 (Advt.), Jaguar 3·4 litre Saloon..fitted with overdrive, radio, rimbellishers, wing mirrors.

Rimbochay, Rimboché, obs. varr. *rinpoche.

‖ **rimbombo** (rimbǫ·mbo). *rare*⁻¹. [It.; cf. Rimbomb *v.*] A booming roar; a resounding or reverberation.

1873 Geo. Eliot *Let.* 20 June (1956) V. 422 Shallow undiscriminating scorn, made to seem profound by a 'rimbombo' of rhetoric (like the singing into big jars to make demon-music in an opera).

rime, *sb.*¹ Add: **2.** ‖ **e.** *rime couée* = *tailed rime* s.v. Tailed *a.* 1 d.

c **1330** [see Couwee *a.*]. **1775** T. Tyrwhitt *Canterbury Tales of Chaucer* IV. 72 Though Robert of Brunne in his Prologue professes not to attempt these elegancies of composition, yet he has intermixed several passages in Rime Couwée. **1893** [see Tailed *a.* 1 d]. **1935** *Essays & Stud.* XX. 97 The rime couée or romance stanza of six lines (double eight and six). **1945** E. K. Chambers *Eng. Lit. at Close of Middle Ages* i. 25 The metre of the Chester plays..is a Romance metre of the type known as *rime couée* or tail-rhyme.

‖ **f.** *rime riche* = *rich rhyme* s.v. Rich *a.* 7 c.

[**1903** H. J. Chaytor *Compan. French Verse* iv. 23 Rimes are also distinguished as rich and sufficient (riche, suffisante).] **1904** Brandin & Hartog *Bk. French Prosody* iv. 53 Victor Hugo uses the *rime riche* more than any of his predecessors. **1930** A. Huxley *Vulgarity in Lit.* 35 When Laforgue wrote of that '*roi de Thulé, Immaculé*' his *rime riche* was entirely above suspicion. **1961** A. Clarke *Later Poems* 92 With the exception of the sonnet and the little experiment in *rime riche*, these pieces came to me quite unexpectedly.

5. *rime-making.*

1935 C. S. Lewis in *Lysistrata* May 22 Rude rime-making wrongs her beauty, Whose breasts and brow.. Bewitch the worlds.

rime, *sb.*² Add: In scientific use now distinguished from hoar-frost (see *hoar-frost). (Further examples.)

1895 [see *hoar-frost]. **1912** W. de la Mare *Listeners* 23 At midnight 'neath a maze of stars I flame with glittering rime. **1921** A. E. M. Geddes *Meteorol.* vi. 182 Hoar frost must not be confused with rime, which is an accumulation of frozen moisture on trees, &c., and is formed only during fog. **1947** *Jrnl. R. Aeronaut. Soc.* LI. 274/1 With a smaller rate of catch of water, at a lower temperature of the air, the water will freeze in the area of catch producing ice which has a porous structure, and a mat surface. This type is known as rime ice. **1978** *Sci. Amer.* Apr. 144/3 When the saturation is higher than 140 percent, the growth of crystals is so rapid that rime (an amorphous deposit of frozen droplets) grows on the crystals and destroys their optical faces.

Comb. **1891** Kipling *Barrack-Room Ballads* (1892) 204 It's North you may run to the rime-ringed sun. **1910** W. de la Mare *Three Mulla-Mulgars* iii. 46 The rime-laden branches of the trees.

rime, *v.*¹ **3.** (Later examples.)

1915 *Encycl. Relig. & Ethics* VIII. 258/1 'Riming people to death—a practice used by the *filid* as well as by the druids—was connected with the power of the spoken word. **1969** J. Wainwright *Big Tickle* 166 He'll rime you—you lousy git—he'll rime you to ribbons.

rime, *v.*² Add: (Further examples.) In scientific use now restricted to mean: to cover with rime (see *rime *sb.*²). Also *intr.*, to become rimed.

1907 N. Munro *Daft Days* xxxii. 266 Oh, London, London!.. The multitudinous monuments rimed by years. **1966** *Jrnl. Faculty Sci. Hokkaidō Univ.* 7th Ser. II. 331 In Japan, most of snow crystals are more or less rimed. Therefore the grade of riming is very important. **1973** *Sci. Amer.* Jan. 105/1 When a crystal rimes, material is added mostly on its underside, thus increasing its weight without greatly increasing its air resistance. *Ibid.*, The more a crystal is rimed, the faster it rimes. **1978** *Nature* 24 Aug. 791/2 (*caption*) Ice fragments collected downwind of an ice-coated sphere riming at −7°C.

Hence ri·ming *vbl. sb.*²

1966 [see above]. **1969** *Jrnl. Atmospheric Sci.* XXVI. 138/1 This apparent multiplication of ice crystals may be associated with the process of riming of the crystals. **1973** *Sci. Amer.* Jan. 105/1 When a snow crystal evolves within a cloud of supercooled water drops, it can grow not only by stealing vapor from around the drops but also by actually colliding with individual drops. The process is called riming, and it is an important complication in all types of snowflakes and snow crystals. **1978** *Nature* 24 Aug. 791/1 (*heading*) A possible mechanism of ice splinter production during riming.

rimed, *ppl. a.*[2] Delete *rare*—[1] and add further examples. Cf. *RIME *sb.*[2]

1954 U. NAKAYA *Snow Crystals* ii. 87 Snow crystals with numerous water droplets attached are very frequently observed in our climate... This type is better called a rimed crystal. **1973** *Nature* 26 Oct. 451/2 Mossop *et al.* report small ice crystals..but always in association with rimed ice pellets. **1975** *Ibid.* 22 May 317/1 Unrimed and lightly rimed planar and spatial crystals were sampled.

rime-frost. For ? *Obs.* read *rare* and add later examples.

1904 in *Eng. Dial. Dict.* **1957** BLUNDEN *Poems of Many Years* 298 Their poor limbs shook With the wind's or the rimefrost's blue stroke.

rimer, *sb.*[2] Add: Now *rare.* Also (*U.S.*) rimmer (ri·məɹ). (Further examples.)

1865 J. H. A. BONE *Petroleum & Petroleum Wells* 22 But the hole must be as nearly round as possible, and therefore the tools are taken out, and a 'rimmer', or 'reamer', sent down, which cuts down the irregularities of the hole. **1894** W. J. LINEHAM *Text-bk. Mech. Engin.* vi. 209 Round holes are cleaned by the Parallel Rimer..and taper holes by means of a Taper Rimer. **1907** *Yesterday's Shopping* (1969) 701/2 Rimers, square or half round.

rimland (ri·mlænd). [f. RIM *sb.*[1] + LAND *sb.*] A peripheral area of land of political or strategic significance.

1944 N. J. SPYKMAN *Geogr. of Peace* iv. 38/1 The central continental plain can continue to be called the heartland but..it is..to be equated with the political extent of the Union of Soviet Socialist Republics. Beyond the mountain barrier, the coastland region..may..be referred to as the rimland, a name which defines its character accurately. *Ibid.* 43/2 In the three great world wars of the nineteenth and twentieth centuries,..the British and Russian empires have lined up together against an intervening rimland power as led by Napoleon, Wilhelm II, and Hitler. **1973** J. C. PLANO et al. *Polit. Sci. Dict.* 331 *Rimland theory*, the theory that emphasizes the rimlands of Europe, the Middle East, Africa, South Asia, and the Far East as the keys to the security of the United States. **1979** *Daily Tel.* 23 June 17/3 Commanders of the small forces of Western Europe are extremely disturbed by the strong hold the Soviet Union and its satellites have acquired in what are dubbed 'the rimlands' of the world's greatest concentration of crude oil in the Persian Gulf.

rimless, *a.* Delete *rare* and add further examples of the word used of spectacles.

1908 *Sears, Roebuck & Co. Catal.* 187/2 Rimless spectacles are the very latest and most stylish spectacles made. **1923** A. HUXLEY *Antic Hay* x. 156 And for full dress, gold-mounted rimless pince-nez are refinement itself. **1934** J. B. PRIESTLEY *Eng. Journey* i. 5 He had a sharp nose, a neat moustache, rimless eyeglasses. **1953** K. TENNANT *Joyful Condemned* xviii. 162 The magistrate looked over the top of his rimless glasses. **1977** D. JAMES *Spy at Evening* vii. 38 He..balanced a pair of rimless spectacles on the tip of his nose.

rimmed, *a.* Add: **3.** *rimmed steel* = *rimming steel* s.v. *RIMMING (*ppl.*) *a.*

1926 *Iron Age* CXVII. 1778 (*heading*) Rimmed steel and how it is made. **1926** *Jrnl. Iron & Steel Inst.* CXIV. 579 The particular physical features of an ingot of good rimmed steel are a solid outer skin and certain gas-holes. **1959** *Ibid.* CXCI. 231 A statistical investigation into the existence of a functional relationship between tapping slag iron and carbon and manganese losses in rimmed steels. **1963** W. H. DENNIS *Metallurgy of Ferrous Metals* xiii. 199 Rimmed steels possess a high degree of cleanliness.

rimmer[3]. U.S. var. RIMER *sb.*[2] in Dict. and Suppl.

rimming, (*ppl.*) *a.* [f. RIM *sb.*[1] or *v.*[1]] *rimming steel*: a low-carbon steel in which deoxidation has been controlled and limited to produce ingots having an outer rim or skin relatively free from carbon and impurities.

1926 *Iron Age* CXVII. 1778 Rimming steel is also called by some 'open steel', because the top of the ingot does not freeze over as rimming in proceeds, but the central metal continues fluid and in active motion for some minutes after teeming. **1930** *Engineering* 14 Mar. 357/2 Exceptions are metals such as steel of the 'rimming' type, from which very large quantities of gas are rapidly evolved during solidification. **1956** J. DEARDEN *Iron & Steel To-Day* (ed. 2) ix. 148 Low carbon steel which has been only partially killed is known as 'rimming steel' because of the rim of almost pure iron which forms the outer portion of the ingot. **1967** A. H. COTTRELL *Introd. Metallurgy* xi. 138 The alternative is to prevent the metal from shrinking by allowing a small amount of CO to form as bubbles, when it freezes. This is done in rimming steels. These are low-carbon (< 0·15 per cent C) steels usually used for sheet steel pressings.

‖ **rimon** (rimō·n). Pl. rim(m)onim. [Heb., lit. pomegranate.] A pomegranate-shaped ornament for a Jewish Law-scroll. Cf. POMEGRANATE 2.

[**1845** J. KITTO *Cycl. Bibl. Lit.* II. 635/1 Rimmon..is mentioned in numerous places in the Old Testament, and is universally acknowledged to denote the Pomegranate-tree and fruit... We find frequent mention of it as an ornament..in the temple.] **1946** *Hebrew Union Coll. Ann.* XIX. 363 Three Torah scrolls,..in vertical positions, are visible, dressed in beautiful mantles and crowned with golden *Rimmonim.* **1962** 'E. MCBAIN' *Empty Hours* 112 'I was putting the *rimonim* back onto the handles of the scroll.' 'Putting the what, sir?' Carella asked. 'Listen to the big Talmudic scholar,' Meyer said, grinning. 'Doesn't even know what *rimonim* are. They're those decorative silver covers, Steve, shaped like pomegranates.' **1976** Y. L. BIALER *Jewish Life* 188 *Rimon*, an adornment for the *sefer Torah. Ibid.* 189 *Rimonim* are made of gold, silver, crystal,..shaped like upright crowns, arched towers, [etc.].

rimpi. Add: Also rimpey, rimpje. (Further examples.)

1887 A. A. ANDERSON *25 Yrs in Waggon* I. xii. 280 A rope of beads of sufficient length to go round the loins twice and fastened in front with a piece of rimpey. **1914** KIPLING in *Geogr. Jrnl.* XLIII. 372 The smell of home-made rimpje on a Dutch farm at the other side of the world.

Rimpoche, var. *RINPOCHE.

rim-schoen, var. *REMSKOEN.

‖ **rin** (rin). [Jap.] A Japanese monetary unit, equal to $\frac{1}{10}$ sen; also, a coin of this value. Also *collect.* as *pl.*

1875 [see YEN]. **1875** [see SEN]. **1891** A. M. BACON *Japanese Girls & Women* vi. 160 There is something picturesque about these sen and rin. **1931** *Economist* 2 May 947/1 [Japanese] savings banks followed suit..reducing the rate [on deposits] by 1 rin per diem or 0·365 per cent per annum. **1962** R. A. G. CARSON *Coins* 548 The bronze sen and 5 rin pieces of this reign had as obverse type the kiri-flower crest which had appeared on the gold obans and kobans of the shogunate.

‖ **rinceau** (rænso). *Art.* Also 8 **rainçeau.** [Fr., in the same sense.] (See quot. 1962.)

1778 R. & J. ADAM *Works in Archit.* I. 5 We..have added grace and beauty to the whole, by a mixture of grotesque (E) stucco, and painted ornaments, together with the flowing rainçeau (F) with its fanciful figures and winding foliage. **1917** A. D. F. HAMLIN *Hist. Ornament* vii. 98 The *rinceau*..which is a combination of the S-line, the spiral, the vine-motive and the acanthus leaf, was developed during the Alexandrian age into an ornament which has contributed a most important element into the splendor of Roman, mediæval and modern art. **1941** *Burlington Mag.* July 25/1 There is an eagle at each corner with *rinceaux*, and above are half-compartments with garlands. **1962** R. G. HAGGAR *Dict. Art Terms* 290/2 *Rinceau*, an elaborate foliated spiral or scroll pattern.

rind, *sb.*[1] Add: **1. d.** *Bot.* A hard outer layer on a fungus.

1887 H. E. F. GARNSEY tr. *A. de Bary's Compar. Morphol. & Biol. Fungi* iii. 58 In other forms the rind is distinguished from the medulla by gelatinous cell-walls, as in the pileus and stipe of Agaricus (Mycena) vulgaris. **1927** GWYNNE-VAUGHAN & BARNES *Struct. & Devel. Fungi* 1 The hyphae..may give rise to root-like strands known as rhizomorphs, or to a compact resting body, the sclerotium, the outer cells of which are modified to form a rind, protecting the inner regions from desiccation. **1951** J. A. MACDONALD *Introd. Mycol.* ii. 14 In a few cases the mycelial cord is surrounded with a dark rind similar to that which surrounds a sclerotium. **1974** *Canad. Jrnl. Bot.* LII. 1128/2 About 5½ days after inoculation, a definite organization of mycelia to form the rind was observed.

4. (Further examples in *Anat.*)

1950 [see *ADRENAL *a.*]. **1974** *Nature* 4 Oct. 428/2 The ganglia have a cell rind formed by nerve cell perikarya.

6. c. *slang.* Impudence, effrontery, 'cheek'. Cf. *CRUST *sb.* 7 b.

1903 A. M. BINSTEAD *Pitcher in Paradise* iii. 79 With that preface they had the immortal rind to pull out a fifth document for me to sign, guaranteeing them the starting-price as returned nightly in *The Evening Standard.* **1915** WODEHOUSE *Something Fresh* v. 154 You have the immortal rind to suppose that I will stand being nagged and bullied. **1977** *Times Lit. Suppl.* 1 July 791/1 *The Björn Borg Story* (I'm glad they didn't have the rind to use the word 'Life').

7. rind grafting, grafting in which the scion is inserted between the bark and the wood of a stump; = *crown-grafting* s.v. CROWN *sb.* 35; so **rind graft.**

1947 R. J. GARNER *Grafter's Handbk.* viii. 181 Unlike the oblique cleft the rind graft must be tied firmly with soft string. **1956** *Dict. Gardening* (R. Hort. Soc.) (ed. 2) II. 918/1 All those [branches and spurs] left are grafted by whip-and-tongue or rind-grafts according to size. **1726** R. BRADLEY *Improvements Planting & Gardening* (ed. 5) 558 The first Sort of Graffing which I shall mention, is that Sort which we call Whip Graffing, or Rind Graffing. **1881** *Encycl. Brit.* XII. 236/2 Crown-grafting or rind-grafting..is preferable to cleft-grafting, inasmuch as it leaves no open spaces in the wood. **1882** [in Dict.]. **1969** *E. Afr. Agric. & Forestry Jrnl.* XXXV. 144/2 An attempt was made to try 'rind grafting' on the species at breast height..under field conditions.

rind, *v.*[1] Add: **b.** To rub or remove skin from (a person or animal) or from (an item of food, *esp.* bacon: see sense 5 of the *sb.*).

1893 *Eng. Illustr. Mag.* Sept. 872/1 Tom Walker used to rub his bleeding fingers in the dust after being rinded by David Harris. **1962** *Sunday Times* 14 Jan. 30/3 Rind the bacon rashers and peel the bananas.

rinforzando (rinfǫɹtsæ·ndo). *Mus.* [It., gerund of *rinforzare* to strengthen.] A sudden stress or crescendo made on a short phrase; a direction to make this. Also *fig.*

1801 BUSBY *Dict. Mus. Rinforzando*, the same as *Forzando.* **1812** [see CRESCENDO 1 a]. **1858** GEO. ELIOT *Scenes Clerical Life* I. 48 Mr. Spratt was boxing the boys' ears with a constant *rinforzando.* **1944** W. J. FINN *Conductor raises his Baton* (1946) iv. 132 *Rinforzando* is only akin to *sforzando* but is often treated as a *subito* by conductors. The term *rinforzando* is not found in many modern scores. **1965** E. KAHN *Conducting* v. 58 *Rinf.* or *rfz* (rinforzando) indicate an emphasis on a short phrase.

ring, *sb.*[1] Add: **I. 1. e.** Phr. *to get the ring*, to become engaged to be married (usu. said of a woman).

1914 JOYCE *Dubliners* 122 Lizzie Fleming said Maria was sure to get the ring and..Maria had to laugh and say she didn't want any ring or man either. **1951** in M. McLuhan *Mech. Bride* (1967) 95 The girls who get the rings. **1979** D. COOK *Winter Doves* II. iii. 64 Got the ring yet, Walter? Has she proposed to you yet?

3. g. = *curtain ring* s.v. CURTAIN *sb.*[1] 8.

1814 JANE AUSTEN *Mansf. Park* I. xv. 296 The curtain will be a good job... We shall be able to send back some dozens of the rings. **1847** C. BRONTË *Jane Eyre* II. i. 2 A woman..sewing rings to new curtains. **1926–7** *Army & Navy Stores Catal.* 1106/1 Rod for curtains... Plain Ball Ends... Rings, per dozen (½ in. larger than pole).

h. A metal or plastic band placed round the leg of a bird, usu. when a nestling, so that it may be uniquely identified when caught on a later occasion; a *leg-ring* (see *LEG *sb.* 17 a); also, a similar marker placed on a limb of a bat.

1907 *Brit. Birds* I. 58 The plan of marking birds by an aluminium ring round the leg has often been tried, but never in a really systematic fashion... To place rings on the legs of young birds just before they fledge would not be a great difficulty. **1909** *Ibid.* III. 5 We have had prepared a number of rings, of which we will send a supply..to any reader of the Magazine who will undertake to mark birds. **1925** TURNER & GURNEY *Bk. about Birds* vii. 71 Much has been discovered about the movements of birds by fixing small numbered rings on the legs of young birds in the nest. **1958** *Listener* 30 Oct. 684/1 The 'ring' is generally a thin strip of aluminium, shaped like the letter 'C' and is marked with a number and some sort of address. On a bird, it is clamped round the leg; but a bat's leg is too delicate for this, so the ring is put round the fore-arm. **1973** *Guardian* 5 Feb. 11/5 The British Bird Fancy Council..is now introducing a system of coded rings..and encouraging breeders to keep full records.

i. A bottomless vessel used in *ring culture.*

1962 H. G. W. FOGG *Chrysanthemum Growing* ix. 62 The roots in the rings will not need any watering between feeds. **1964** *Times Lit. Suppl.* 21 May 442/2 Much of the early work on ring culture, a system of growing plants in bottomless pots or 'rings', was carried out at the Lenton Research Station under the direction of the author [*sc.* A. W. Billitt]. Ring culture has become now firmly established both as a commercial and amateur method of growing chrysanthemums, carnations and tomatoes. **1976** *Observer* (Colour Suppl.) 9 May 12/2 The best way to grow tomatoes is by 'ring culture'. The soil in the greenhouse..is replaced with aggregate, such as clinker, and the tomatoes planted in rings, or bottomless pots.

4. b. *pl.* A competitive game in which rings are thrown on to hooks.

1906 B. KENNEDY *Wander Pict.* 245 Over yonder on the [inn] wall is the target with hooks at which they play the game of rings. They stand off and pitch rubber rings on to the hooks.

II. 7. f. *slang.* The anus. Phr. *to spew one's ring* (and similar phrases), to vomit violently.

1949 PARTRIDGE *Dict. Slang* (ed. 3) 1154/1 *Ring*,.. anus (also *ring-piece*): low: late C. 19–20. **1952** T. A. G. HUNGERFORD *Ridge & River* 130 'I'd get shot in the ring, that's what I'd get,' said Wallace. **1965** R. STOW *Merry-go-Round in Sea* 174, I bet I would have booted him in the ring if he hadn't run. **1966** K. AMIS *Anti-Death League* I. 32 Then the technique is to slip him a glass of Scotch or whatever he's hooked on about half a minute before the emetine makes him spew his ring. **1971** B. W. ALDISS *Soldier Erect* 105, I can't take this sodding shitting Wog beer... Makes me spew my ring every time! **1978** R. BUSBY *Garvey's Code* iii. 28 We just left the husband and he's bringing his ring up.

8. a. (Earlier and later examples of *rings round* (or *under*) *the eyes.*)

1850 THACKERAY *Pendennis* II. vii. 70 The rings round his eyes were of the colour of bistre. **1856** C. M. YONGE *Daisy Chain* II. xii. 472 He looked very wan, with the dark rings round his eyes, a deeper purple than ever. **1902** A. BENNETT *Anna of Five Towns* x. 258 It's a shame to send you home with those rings round your eyes. **1911** O. ONIONS *Widdershins* 270 The bistred rings that weeks of nursing had put under her dark eyes. **1973** R. THOMAS *If you can't be Good* xiii. 111, I thought there were some new lines in his face. I wasn't imagining the dark rings under his eyes. **1981** T. HEALD *Murder at Moose Jaw* xi. 133 There were dark rings under her eyes and her face was pinched.

e. A gold-coloured band worn on the sleeve to designate rank in the armed services. Also *transf.*

1942 *R.A.F. Jrnl.* 13 June 32 They were all of superior rank to myself... My solitary ring did not allow me to voice my suspicions. **1943** HUNT & PRINGLE *Service Slang* 55 *Rings*, abbreviated reference to an Officer's rank, denoted in the Navy and R.A.F. by the number of rings on his sleeve. **1950** 'D. DIVINE' *King of Fassarai* xv. 116 Bull's got more rings than I have. Why shouldn't he have his headaches too? **1952** M. TRIPP *Faith is Windsock* i. 14 Now that Bergen has got his ring there doesn't seem so much point in staying N.C.O. with the others. **1953** 'N. SHUTE' *In Wet* v. 164 Go into the R.A.F. and try to make a go of it, and get the rings because you've earned them, not because you're heir to the Throne. **1970** D. FRANCIS *Rat Race* iv. 55 No such thing was possible in one of his aircraft, he had told me stiffly, and I could take my four gold rings away... I hadn't worn my captain's jacket for nearly two years. **1976** 'A. HALL' *Kobra Manifesto* xvi. 218 The pilot stood there, a tall mahogany-faced type with four gold rings on his sleeve.

9. i. (Earlier and later examples.)

1835 A. SMITH *Diary* 27 July (1940) II. 131 The old ring-kop was speaking... This ring-kop was the person in charge of the party... None of the others had rings. **1866** [see *head-ring* s.v. *HEAD *sb.* 66]. **1925** D. KIDD *Essential Kaffir* 33 Only married men are allowed to wear this ring. **1952** [see *head-ring* s.v. *HEAD *sb.* 66].

III. 10. d. *Chem.* A number of atoms bonded together to form a closed chain.

1869 *Jrnl. Chem. Soc.* XXII. 361 The hydrocarbon benzole is of so much interest from its derivatives, that it has attracted a good deal of attention, and to explain its molecular constitution, the six atoms of carbon have been represented as arranged in a ring. **1889** G. M'GOWAN tr. *Bernthsen's Text-bk. Org. Chem.* 461 Phthalic acid or its derivatives ensue on the breaking up of the compound, not only from one but from both of the six-cornered rings. **1927** N. V. SIDGWICK *Electronic Theory of Valency* xiv. 251 Only a very few chelate rings of more than six atoms have been observed. **1950** *Thorpe's Dict. Appl. Chem.* (ed. 4) X. 339/1 Treatment of pyrrole with hydroxylamine causes a smooth opening of the ring. **1964** N. G. CLARK *Mod. Org. Chem.* ii. 21 Pyridine..has a structure very similar to that of benzene; the six-membered ring, however, contains a trivalent nitrogen atom. **1974** D. M. ADAMS *Inorg. Solids* vi. 183 Sulphur has quite a complex allotropy: the thermodynamically stable form consists of S_8 crown-shaped rings in close-packed layers.

e. *Cytology.* A chromosome, group of chromosomes, or part of a chromosome in the form of a loop, without free ends.

1929 *Jrnl. Genetics* XXI. 44 A single ring of four may be formed at diakinesis, the other chromosomes assorting themselves in separate pairs. **1949** DARLINGTON & MATHER *Elem. Genetics* vi. 129 From the exchange system of pairing a ring of four, chain of four, two chains of two, or a chain of three with a univalent, can arise at metaphase. *Ibid.* xii. 263 *Oenothera lamarckiana*, whose chromosomes normally form a ring of 12 and one pair. **1962** *Lancet* 29 Dec. 1384/1 Monosomic chromosomes may be subject to hazards in meiosis—from autosynapsis, leading to centric and acentric rings and fragments, to centric aberrations leading to iso-chromosomes.

11. a. (Further examples.) *spec.* a combination of dealers, contractors, or the like, who cooperate in buying or selling at agreed price-levels, in order to increase their profits. Also *attrib.*

1870 W. W. FOWLER *Ten Years in Wall St.* i. 28 The bulls often unite to raise the value of particular stocks, and form those combinations known in the 'Street' as 'cliques', 'rings' or 'pools',—terms nearly synonymous. **1909** [see *CONFERENCE 4 e]. **1929** *Times* 31 Oct. 14/4 In order to safeguard the home consumer against exploitation by the producers' 'rings', which the coal-marketing schemes will establish, the Government will set up in every district a special committee to keep a watch on prices. **1936** *Sun* (Baltimore) 2 Dec. 3/1 In addition Thorp advocates.. more stringent regulations of auction and sales rings. **1949** J. SYMONS *Bland Beginning* 22 That's Foskiss. Buys everything for the ring. Doesn't give the small men a chance. **1955** *Times* 13 May 9/1 Wellington City Council, which recently protested strongly against the submission of equal tenders by a number of British firms, has now decided to accept a tender for electric cable which is £3,000 below the 'ring price'. **1961** R. GODDEN *China Court* VII. 274 She comes back from sale after sale... She gets to know their 'tricks' as she calls them, a childish word for the ring. **1964** [see *MONOPSONY]. **1968** R. H. R. SMITHIES *Shoplifter* viii. 175 The Ring..was an organization of English dealers who attempted to take over the entire antiques business—rigging auctions, intimidating retailers, fixing prices. **1968** *Sunday Times* 10 Nov. 1/2 Ring dealing is when dealers agree not to force the price up by bidding against each other at an auction. **1971** *Nature* 6 Aug. 365/1 The overt reason for the anti-trust laws is to prevent the formation of cartels and similar price-fixing rings. **1972** 'M. DELVING' *Shadow of Himself* ii. 24 'I don't doubt there'll be a ring,' he added, bitterly... He was referring to the system by which several dealers agree to let one of their number bid for all, thus cutting down the competition and squeezing out opposition.

c. An organization or network of people engaged in espionage.

1943 D. POWELL *Time to be Born* vi. 128 He had no secret mission to investigate the spy rings and unmask the Nazi agents. **1961** R. SETH *Anat. Spying* iii. 45 In a very short time counter-espionage knew the names and whereabouts of all twenty-six members of the ring. **1972** A. MORICE *Murder on French Leave* viii. 104 The cinema had been the meeting-place with another operator in the spy ring. **1981** R. AIRTH *Once a Spy* xii. 139 When Franklyn's ring broke up..I went back to work for Bonn.

11*. *Math.* [a. G. *ring*, used in this sense.] A set of elements with two binary operations ('addition' and 'multiplication') which is a group under addition and closed under multiplication, and with the property that multiplication is distributive over addition and associative.

Some writers also require a ring to have an identity element for multiplication.

1935 *Ann. Math.* XXXVI. 406 It is only in integrally closed rings like in the theory of algebraic numbers that the decomposition theorems naturally take on a multiplicative form. **1967** [see *FIELD THEORY]. **1968** D. G. NORTHCOTT *Lessons on Rings, Modules & Multiplicities* i. 1 From this point onwards, when we speak of a ring it is to be understood that we always mean a ring with an identity element. **1971** J. H. CONWAY in Powell & Higman *Finite Simple Groups* vii. 244 The ring of 24×24 matrices.

IV. 13. a. Phr. *to keep* (or *hold*) *the ring*, to be an onlooker at a fight; to stand by while others quarrel. Chiefly *fig.*

1829 P. EGAN *Boxiana* 2nd Ser. II. 678 At least 500 Irishmen, armed *à la shilelah*, kept the ring. **1905** *Spectator* 21 Jan. 79/1 There is a cynicism which nothing but conscious impotence could excuse in the thought of 'keeping a ring' while the Bulgarians of the Principality..are drawn into a life-and-death struggle with the Turks. **1924** GALSWORTHY *White Monkey* I. vii. 54 Keep clear and keep the ring!.. Good friendly terms with..all the outlying countries that we can get at by sea. And let the others dree their weirds. **1928** *Britain's Industr. Future* (Liberal Industr. Inquiry) III. xv. 166 There are still many people who hold that the State ought not to meddle with industry,..but should confine itself to holding the ring while the disputants fight out their differences. **1970** *Times* 8 Apr. 1 Is there a limit to the amount of time that the Army can reasonably be expected to stay here [*sc.* in Ulster] holding the ring, if the humans involved here are not going to solve their own problems? **1970** *Atlantic Monthly* Nov. 6 Does the phrase 'Asians helping Asians', or, as critics put it, 'Asians fighting Asians', mean that the United States will provide everything but the front-line manpower, or that it will step back and help hold the ring, or that it will become a mere spectator? **1978** *Jrnl. R. Soc. Arts* CXXVI. 400/1 Its [*sc.* Government's] task in the economic field is to hold the ring between the many popular pressures, frequently irreconcilable, which assert themselves.

b. (Earlier examples.)

1775 G. SELWYN *Let.* 8 Dec. in *15th Rep. R. Comm. Hist. Manuscripts* App. VI. 306 in *Parl. Papers 1897* (C. 8551) LI. 1 The devil a bit will he ever part with, but by putting it into the Ring, where he is nicked, and the money gone. **1822** *Sporting Mag.* X. 4/2 Mr. Bayzand was well known in the ring as a betting man. *Ibid.* 192/2 He never opened his mouth in the ring *under five hundred*. **1845** DISRAELI *Sibyl* I. I. ii. 12 'Will any one do anything about Hybiscus?' sang out a gentleman in the ring at Epsom.

d. A prison-yard; a fence or wall surrounding this.

1898 O. WILDE *Ballad of Reading Gaol* 7 And I and all the souls in pain, Who tramped the other ring. **1900** 'ODYSSEUS' *Turkey in Europe* i. 28 They [*sc.* the Avars] were celebrated for their 'rings', enormous circular fences with which they surrounded the prisoners and plunder they had taken.

e. *Austral.* (See quot. 1941.)

1941 BAKER *Dict. Austral. Slang* 60 *Ring*, the scene of operations of a two-up school or the school itself. **1948** [see *DOUBLE-HEADER e].

14. a. Also *ring-around.*

1907 JOYCE *Chamber Music* p. ix, Winds of May, that dance on the sea, Dancing a ring-around in glee From furrow to furrow.

d. (Further examples.) Also with *make*, and in extended uses.

1907 WODEHOUSE *White Feather* viii. 88 Dexter's had taken thirty points off the School House just after half-time. 'Mopped them up,' said the terse and epigrammatic Painter. 'Made rings round them.' **1917** 'CONTACT' *Airman's Outings* 139 Snatches of familiar flying-talk..made rings round the Hun. *c* **1928** T. E. LAWRENCE *Lett.* (1938) 572 It riles me unbearably to lose my scalp to a lot of fellows round whom I can make rings. **1939** *War Illustr.* 4 Nov. 252/1 We saw a large black aeroplane travelling at a high speed. It was being pursued by two British fighters and they made rings round it. **1947** *Sporting Mirror* 7 Nov. 10/3 The return of Dodds revitalised the Everton attack which ran rings round Sheffield United. **1950** 'S. RANSOME' *Deadly Miss Ashley* iii. 39, I can't help feeling we're having rings run around us. **1961** E. WAUGH *Unconditional Surrender* III. iv. 292 Tito has..gone to join the Russians... Our chaps are rather annoyed about it... I bet Winston is. I told you he'd make rings round the old boy. **1973** 'D. JORDAN' *Nile Green* xxxiv. 167 The deal's been bust... The Russians ran rings round us. **1980** *Times Lit. Suppl.* 27 June 724/2 Balfour was an undeniable flop and Joseph Chamberlain made rings round him.

V. 15. a. *ring-bearer, -bright, -finder, -game, -having, -lore, -plait.*

1932 W. FAULKNER *Light in August* xi. 237 He was twelve then, and they wanted him to be the ringbearer. **1954** J. R. R. TOLKIEN *Fellowship of Ring* II. viii. 393 'And you, Ring-bearer,' she said, turning to Frodo. **1976** *Laurel* (Montana) *Outlook* 30 June 3/5 Gary Martin of Laurel, brother of the groom, was ring bearer. **1949** BLUNDEN *After Bombing* 14 A child's eye drooped, so gleamed the ring-bright shell. **1954** J. R. R. TOLKIEN *Fellowship of Ring* II. i. 237 And you are the heir of Bilbo, the Ring-finder. **1886** *Lippincott's Monthly Mag.* Mar. 239 The ring-games, or 'carols', are great favorites, as they were among the English court ladies. **1916** A. S. NEILL *Dominie Dismissed* vii. 98 The ring games down at the school there nearly all deal with love and matrimony. **1972** *Times* 7 Aug. (Jamaica Suppl.) p. ii/4 She has recorded Kumina music, ring games and Pocomania meetings. **1912** E. POUND *Ripostes* 27 He hath not heart for harping, nor in ring-having Nor winsomeness to wife. **1890** W. JONES *Finger-Ring Lore* p. vii, In thus contributing to the extension of knowledge, the subject of ring-lore has a close affinity to that of numismatics, but it possesses the supreme advantage of appealing to our sympathies and affections. **1954** J. R. R. TOLKIEN *Fellowship of Ring* II. ii. 57 All that he would reveal to us of his ring-lore. **1908** W. G. COLLINGWOOD *Scandinavian Brit.* 245 The ornament with ring-plaits.. cannot be earlier than the tenth century.

c. *ringwise* adj.

1944 *Sun* (Baltimore) 29 Mar. 15/2 Salica, ringwise and cunning, was unwilling to trade punches. **1958** F. C. AVIS *Boxing Ref. Dict.* 95 *Ringwise*, gifted in ring tactics.

e. *Chem.* In sense 10 d, as *ring-closure, -compound, -formation, -opening, -structure*, etc.

1946 *Nature* 28 Dec. 930/1 The problem of effecting ring-closure through the meta- and para-positions of the benzene nucleus. **1964** N. G. CLARK *Mod. Org. Chem.* xv. 294 On heating..these compounds readily undergo ring-closure through loss of a molecule of ethanol. **1932** *Discovery* Aug. 246/1 The changes during the coalification process proceed only to a half-way stage between the most stable kind of carbon chain compound, and the most stable kind of ring compound. **1961** *New Scientist* 16 Mar. 668/1 Almost any organic compound gets decomposed in time, even stable ring compounds like phenol, naphthalene and toluene. **1913** J. B. COHEN *Org. Chem. Adv. Students* II. ii. 111 Nearly all the above reactions may become intramolecular if the necessary grouping is present, and in such cases ring formation follows. **1967** MARGERISON & EAST *Introd. Polymer Chem.* iii. 129 These formulations of the reactions of difunctional monomers have ignored the possibility of ring formation. **1959** Ring-opening [see *DECARBOXYLATE *v.*]. **1967** MARGERISON & EAST *Introd. Polymer Chem.* v. 261 Other ring-opening polymerizations in this class include the conversion of caprolactam to nylon 6. **1930** *Engineering* 18 Apr. 525/2 These investigations indicated that the cellulose molecule had a ring structure.

16. *ring-base, -brooch, -ditch, -foot, -gasket, -handle, -hook, -scissors, -weight.*

1957 V. G. CHILDE *Dawn European Civilization* (ed. 6) v. 60 Ring bases and genuine handles betoken an unusual degree of sophistication. **1960** T. BURTON-BROWN *Early Mediterranean Migrations* i. 27 The comparative frequency of ring-bases in the red-polished..wares..is a detail of some significance. **1883** C. T. GATTY *Catal. Mediæval & Later Antiquities Mayer Museum* 37 *Ring brooch*, in silver; inscribed on one side, in niello work, +AVE: MARIA: GRACIA: PLENA: D, and on the other +AGLA+NO. A+S: BLASIV. **1931** J. EVANS *Eng. Posies & Posy Rings* p. xii, Such inscriptions were commonly engraved in the thirteenth and fourteenth centuries on the ring-brooches that were used to fasten the dress at the neck. **1977** *Antiquaries Jrnl.* LVII. 457/1 Note on the significance of the Londesborough ring brooch. **1936** *Oxoniensia* I. 8 In the following pages some account is given of the investigation of barrows and ring-ditches in the Oxford area. **1954** S. PIGGOTT *Neolithic Cultures* ii. 32 These cultures are sometimes associated with causewayed ring-ditches of a funerary or ceremonial nature. **1927** PEAKE & FLEURE *Priests & Kings* x. 162 Deep cups have been found with rounded bottoms, also bottles with lugs instead of handles and sometimes with hollow ring-feet. **1980** *Catal. Fine Chinese Ceramics* (Sotheby, Hong Kong) 76 The well-finished ring foot decorated with incised key-fret. **1972** L. M. HARRIS *Introd. Deepwater Floating Drilling Operations* ix. 93 An AX ring gasket provides a metal-to-metal seal between the connector and the wellhead. **1936** *Burlington Mag.* July 26/1 The pair of..candlesticks with ring-handles has the Britannia standard marks with the date-letter for 1736–37. **1972** *Trans. Oriental Ceramics Soc.* XXXVIII. 58 A grey earthenware jar and cover, with ring-handle masks in relief. **1913** J. MASEFIELD *Daffodil Fields* 72 Its open door, With old wrought bridle ring-hooks at each flank. **1961** *B.S.I. News* Nov. 25 (*title*) Dimensions of ring-hook automatic hitch. **1908** *Practitioner* June 769 Later Mr. Jessop introduced his 'ring-scissors', which made this piecemeal removal of the gland an easier matter. **1922** JOYCE *Ulysses* 665 Though ringweight lifting had been beyond his strength..he had excelled in his stable and protracted execution of the half lever movement on the parallel bars.

18. a. ring armature *Electr.*, an armature having a ring winding; **ring beam,** a ring-shaped beam of yarn; **ring binder,** a loose-leaf binder having clasps that pass through holes in the paper and can be closed to form rings; similarly **ring binding; ring book,** a notebook having the form of a **ring binder*; **ring-building** *Archæol.*, the forming of vessels by adding successive layers of ring-shaped pieces of clay; hence **ring-built** *a.*; **ring circuit,** (*a*) *Electronics* = *ring counter* below; (*b*) *Electr.*, a wiring arrangement for power distribution in domestic or similar premises in which sockets and fixed appliances are connected to a single loop of cable which starts from and returns to a fuse-box; **ring complex** *Geol.*, an association of igneous intrusions arranged in an arcuate or ring-like plan; **ring counter** *Electronics*, a counting circuit consisting of a number of flip-flops or other bistable devices wired in a closed loop; **ring-craft** (further examples); also *transf.* of other sports; **ring culture,** the technique of growing plants in a bottomless cylinder containing nutrients and resting on an inert bed through which water is provided; **ring current,** (*a*) *Geophysics*, a belt of charged particles which orbit the earth, trapped by the magnetic field in its ionosphere; (*b*) *Chem.*, a circulation of electrons in an annular molecular orbital (e.g. in aromatic molecules) under the influence of a magnetic field; **ring dike, dyke** *Geol.*, a dike that is arcuate or roughly circular in plan, formed by upwelling of magma along ring fractures following cauldron subsidence of a circular block; **ring flash** *Photogr.*, a circular electronic flash tube that fits round the camera lens to give shadowless lighting of a subject near the lens; **ring-fort** *Archæol.*, a fort or other position defended by ringed entrenchments; **ring fracture** *Geol.* [tr. G. *kreisbrüche*], a conical or nearly cylindrical fault associated with cauldron subsidence; **ring gland** *Zool.*, a gland in dipteran larvæ which secretes ecdysone; **ring-junction**, a road junction at which traffic is channelled in two directions round a central island, entering and leaving by smaller islands; **ring-keeper**, (*b*) (examples); **ring-kop** *S. Afr.* [Afrikaans *kop* head], an African tribesman or warrior entitled to wear a head-ring (see Head *sb.* 66 in Dict. and Suppl.); **ring-lock** (examples); **ring main**, (*a*) an electric main that starts from and returns to a particular power station or sub-station, so that each consumer has an alternative path for supply in the event of a failure; also = *ring circuit* (*b*) above; (*b*) *Plumbing*, an arrangement of pipes forming a closed loop into which steam, water, or sewage may be fed and whose points of draw-off are supplied by flow from two directions; **ring modulator** *Electronics*, a circuit that incorporates a closed loop of four diodes and can be used for balanced mixing and modulation of signals; **ring oiling**, a method of automatic lubrication of bearings in which a ring rests upon and turns with the journal and also dips into a reservoir containing the lubricant; so **ring-oiled** *ppl. a.*; **ring oiler**; **ring-opener**, a seal on a tin container which is broken by pulling a ring attached to it; **ring-play** *U.S.*, a circular dance movement accompanied by song; **ring-pored, -porous** *adjs. Forestry*, applied to woods in which the large pores produced in spring form partial or complete rings; cf. *diffuse-porous* adj. s.v. *diffuse *a.* 2 f; hence **ring porosity, -porousness**; **ring-pull** *a.*, designating a tin container fitted with a **ring-opener*; **ring-rope**, (*b*) usu. *pl.*, = Rope *sb.*[1] 2 c; **ring rot** [tr. G. *bakterienringfäule* (A. Spieckermann 1914, in *Landwirtsch. Jahrb.* XLVI v. 660)], a bacterial disease of the potato, affecting the tubers, caused by *Corynebacterium sepedonicum*; **ring scaler** *Electronics* = *ring counter* above; **ring-seat** = *ringside seat* s.v. *ringside b; **ring shake** *Forestry*, a partial or complete separation of two or more consecutive growth rings in a tree; = Cup-shake; so **ring-shaken** *a.*; **ring-shout** *U.S.*, a religious dance consisting of loud singing and circular movement; **ring-sight** *Mil.* (see quot. 1973); **ring spanner**, a spanner in which the jaws are in the form of a ring with internal serrations, which fit completely around the nut and put pressure on all its faces; **ringspot, ring spot**, (*a*) any of several plant diseases characterized by annular spots or marks on the leaves; (*b*) an annular mark on a plant or animal; so **ring-spotted** *a.*; **ring-toss** (earlier examples); **ring velvet**, velvet so fine that a width of it can be drawn through a ring; **ring-watch** (see quot. 1962); **ring winding** *Electr.*, a form of armature winding in which each turn of the winding passes through the centre of the hollow armature core (cf. *Gramme[2]); **ring-work**, (*a*) (later examples); **ring-worm** *U.S. slang* (see quot. 1929); **ring-yarn**, yarn produced by ring-spinning.

1893 Ring armature [see *Gramme[2]]. **1974** *Encycl. Brit. Macropædia* VI. 610/1 The ring armature..enormously improved the efficiency of early electric generators. **1924** *Times Trade & Engin. Suppl.* 29 Nov. 247/1 Ring beams are now worse off in margin by 1d. per lb. compared with a month or six weeks ago. **1929** A. J. Vaughan *Mod. Bookbinding* II. 136 *The ring binders.* These employ rings which may be opened or closed, the paper being pierced with round holes. **1977** *New Yorker* 27 June 30/1 Forced into proximity as we were by ledgers, ring binders, and jars of mucilage. **1977** P. D. James *Death of Expert Witness* II. v. 80 A quarto-sized loose-leaf notebook with a ring binding. **1923** H. A. Maddox *Dict. Stationery Terms* 67 *Ring books*, loose-leaf books arranged on the principle of split or hinged rings, which by a finger lever motion open to receive the leaves punched to fit the rings. **1942** H. A. Maddox *Dict. Stationery* 94 Ring book. **1965** P. Wylie *They both were Naked* I. iv. 149 My second address was neatly arranged in a ring-book. **1957** V. G. Childe *Dawn European Civilization* (ed. 6) xi. 204 From Sweden to Siberia..all pots were manufactured by the same technique of ring-building. **1964** H. Hodges *Artifacts* i. 26 *Ring-building*... The walls of the vessel are formed by the addition of sausage-shaped rolls of clay of various lengths. **1963** E. M. Jope in Foster & Alcock *Culture & Environment* xiii. 337 In the tenth to twelfth centuries, the distinctive bar-lip style of pottery, flat-based and coil- or ring-built, rooted firmly in the simplest techniques of prehistoric pottery-making. **1964** H. Hodges *Artifacts* i. 29 Much early pottery that has been described as wheel-thrown was probably initially ring-built and only finally given its form on a rotating wheel. **1931** *Proc. R. Soc.* A. CXXXII. 306 The simplified 'chain' arrangement of thyratrons, from which the more useful 'ring' circuits..were developed. **1946** *Rev. Sci. Instruments* XVII. 185/2 The two pentodes of each trigger pair form opposite partners in the ring circuit. **1961** B. Pym *No Fond Return of Love* xxiv. 236 Her loud clear tones were addressed to the London Electricity Board, and the conversation seemed to be about power plugs and something called a 'ring circuit'. **1962** N. D. Watts in G. A. T. Burdett *Automatic Control Handbk.* xviii. 10 Fig. 11 shows a ring circuit in which the primer electrodes are omitted for simplicity. **1963** *Times* 6 May (Electric Power Suppl.) p. vii/3 Complete interchangeability at multiple points throughout the house is achieved by the 'ring circuit'. **1974** A. Douglas *Noah's Ark Murders* viii. 75, I thought lighting these days was on ring circuits—surely one burned-out fuse shouldn't mean total failure? **1916** E. B. Bailey et al. *Geol. Ben Nevis & Glen Coe* viii. 109 The fault serves as the inner boundary of the ring-complex known as the Fault-Intrusion. **1965** A. Holmes *Princ. Physical Geol.* (ed. 2) xi. 261 Intrusions in the form of concentric arcs or rings are of two distinct types, forming ring complexes such as are exceptionally well developed around the Tertiary volcanic centres of NW Britain. **1976** *Nature* 23 Sept. 307/1 The duration of about 5 Myr for the igneous activities in this ring complex is especially informative in terms of the formation of one complete ring complex. **1942** W. B. Lewis *Electr. Counting* viii. 90 A thyratron ring counter which could have any number of thyratrons arranged in a ring with an arc in one of them. **1969** J. J. Sparkes *Transistor Switching* viii. 195 If the outputs of the last flip-flop..are connected back to the inputs of the first flip-flop then a Ring Counter is formed. **1971** J. H. Smith *Digital Logic* vi. 121 Ring counters, which were used for many years using gas filled trigger valves, will give a count related to the number of stages. If there are *n* stages the counter will count to *2n*. **1900** A. Conan Doyle *Green Flag* iv. 125 A hard veteran, full of cool valour and ring-craft, could give ten or fifteen years and a beating to most striplings. **1922** Joyce *Ulysses* 313 Handicapped as he was by lack of poundage, Dublin's pet lamb made up for it by superlative skill in ringcraft. **1957** A. MacNab *Bulls of Iberia* xii. 136 As for the *lidia*, the general ringcraft, he [*sc.* Belmonte] admits he knew nothing of it and cared less. **1976** *Daily Record* (Glasgow) 29 Nov., Len Harvey, one of the greatest exponents of ringcraft British boxing has produced, died at his London home yesterday. **1961** *Amateur Gardening* 4 Nov. Suppl. 42/2 Ring culture. In recent years the growing of certain plants, chiefly tomatoes, in bottomless containers has come into vogue. **1962** H. G. W. Fogg *Chrysanthemum Growing* ix. 60 Ring culture, a term which was, I believe, first used as a result of experiments, at Tilgate Horticultural Research Station. **1964, 1976** [see sense 3 i above]. [**1933** *Terrestrial Magn.* XVIII. 82 Whether the latter [current] will close upon itself so as to become an isolated current-ring.] **1941** *Ibid.* XLVI. 1 In our theory of geomagnetic storms, we attribute the main phase to a hypothetical electric ring-current. **1956** *Proc. R. Soc.* A. CCXXXVI. 522 To find the effect of the ring current on the proton resonance line we have to average over orientations. **1962** F. I. Ordway et al. *Basic Astronautics* iv. 164 The ring current system probably consists of low energy particles and is able to effectively disturb the terrestrial magnetic field... It is estimated that a current flow of 1,000,000 amp exists. **1966** Williams & Fleming *Spectrosc. Methods Org. Chem.* iv. 88 Protons attached to systems which can sustain a ring current suffer a paramagnetic shift relative to olefinic protons of isolated double bonds. **1976** *Jrnl. Geophysical Res.* LXXXI. 2701/1 The decay of the proton ring current by charge exchange loss. **1915** *Summary of Progr. Geol. Survey 1914* The Loch Bà felsite is the most perfect example of a ring-boss, or ring-dyke, anywhere known. **1931** *Amer. Jrnl. Sci.* CCXXII. 145 The ring-dike is found between the granite frame and the volcanics of the mountains wherever bed rock is exposed. **1976** *Nature* 23 Sept. 307/1 The 7·6 ± 0·2 Myr isochron..combines various samples from the three inner distinct ring dykes..made up of alkaline granites and quartz syenites. **1969** L. Gaunt *Commonsense Photogr.* xiii. 218 There are special ring flash units which fit round the lens and give even, almost shadow-free lighting. **1975** G. Skoglund *Colour in your Camera* (ed. 6) 144 Shadowless 'multi-directed' lighting, can be produced by a piece of equipment known as a 'ring-flash'. **1978** *SLR Camera* Aug. 45/2 To my knowledge it is the only 100mm lens which has a built-in ring flash that will continuously focus from 1/15 down to life size. **1935** *Discovery* Apr. 102/1 Ring-forts of earth or stone represent one of the most common kinds of monuments of antiquity throughout Ireland. **1937** *Proc. Prehist. Soc.* III. 407 It is hardly justifiable to class ring-forts as fortified sites; they were ordinary farmsteads with a natural measure of protection, and assumed the character of a fortified settlement only if the site was very large. **1960** S. Cruden *Scottish Abbeys* 21 The massive circular stone wall of the 'ring-fort', of late Iron Age or Dark Age date. **1976** *Country Life* 6 May 1163/1 Ring forts..are common all over Ireland. **1919** *Geol. Mag.* LVI. 469 In some ways the most interesting feature of Old Iceland is the ring-fracture system (*Kreisbrüche*) of the north-west peninsula. **1924** E. B. Bailey et al. *Tertiary & Post-Tertiary Geol. Mull, Loch Aline, & Oban* i. 7 It was in Iceland that the word *ring-fracture* (*Kreisbrüche*) was introduced by Thoroddsen. **1965** A. Holmes *Princ. Physical Geol.* (ed. 2) xi. 261 The ring dyke..represents the case where the weight of the keystone..has produced the ring fractures within which subsidence—often referred to as cauldron subsidence—has taken place. **1937** E. Hadorn in *Proc. Nat. Acad. Sci.* XXIII. 481 Since it has been shown that the ring has a glandular function, the term 'ring-gland' may be used so long as no homology to other structures in other insects has been established. *Ibid.* 484 Puparium-formation can be accelerated by transplantation of a normal ring-gland to lethal larvae. **1978** *Molecular & Gen. Genetics* CLXIV. 79/2 The ring gland donors were at the late larval stage by which ecdysone production was likely to have begun. **1972** *Guardian* 26 June 1/3 In this new ring junction traffic turning right goes between the island in the centre and the off-side mini-roundabout. **1973** *Daily Tel.* 3 Aug. 17/1 The experimental 'ring junction' to ease traffic congestion at the Plough roundabout..may be made permanent by winter. **1912** *Chambers's Jrnl.* June 394/1 He organized a body of 'ring-keepers' to preserve order as far as possible. **1922** Joyce *Ulysses* 510 The virgins..burst through the ring-keepers and the ropes and mob him with open arms. **1835** Ring-kop [see sense 9 i above]. **1910** J. Buchan *Prester John* viii. 149 In such a man one would have looked for a *ring-kop*, but instead he had a mass of hair..long and curled like some popular musician. **1935** *Brit. S. Afr. Ann.* 35 Our principal native warrior, an old 'ringkop', promptly took up his quarters in a friendly tree. **1856** G. Price *Treat. Fire & Thief-Proof Depositories & Locks & Keys* xiv. 205 Two centuries ago the puzzle-lock attracted far more attention than any other... The chief among them are *ring-locks*. **1868** A. C. Hobbs *Constr. Locks* iii. 17 According to the kind of handle employed, it [*sc.* the room-lock] may be a knob lock or a ring lock. **1965** G. McInnes *Road to Gundagai* ix. 137, I..ambled gently down the drive toward the ringlock gate. **1892** J. A. Fleming *Alternate Current Transformer* II. ii. 207 (*caption*) The Metropolitan Company's system of ring mains. **1901** F. B. Crocker *Electric Lighting* II. 505 (Index), Ring mains. **1904** *Electr. World & Engineer* 27 Feb. 396/2 The four batteries of boilers constituting each section of the boiler plant are interconnected by a 10-in. main and a 4-in. auxiliary line, both in the form of a ring main... With the location of the valves adopted in the event of rupture of any section of a ring main the trouble may be localised by shutting off the disabled section, the remaining half of the main being kept in service. **1930** *Engineering* 17 Jan. 92/1 In the near future it would probably be necessary to connect these lines by ring mains. **1945** *Jrnl. R. Aeronaut. Soc.* XLIX. 529/1 It is avoided in the larger warships by the spread of the ring main (all below armour) which is admitted as not feasible in aircraft. **1959** Goodin & Downing *Domestic Sanitation* iv. 97 The use of ring mains tends to reduce the size of pipes which must be used and are [*sic*] of great value in maintaining supplies when bursts occur. **1962** *Which?* Mar. 82/1 You will also need a convenient electric power point. Having a new one installed—especially in an older house where there is no ring main—may mean a lot of new wiring. **1962** *Newnes Conc. Encycl. Electr. Engin.* 202 Ring mains offer the possibility of a firm supply at all times, but the cost of the complicated protective gear.. makes such schemes justifiable only in cases where no loss of supply can be tolerated. **1976** G. Moffat *Short Time to Live* vi. 53 He'd..modernise the place: put in a ring main, dig drains, build a septic tank. **1938** *Nippon Electr. Commun. Engin.* Apr. 118/2 Although there are many considerations when it comes to the connecting method of rectifiers in the various carrier suppressed modulators, one of the most effective is that of the so-called Ring modulator. **1974** Harvey & Bohlman *Stereo F. M. Radio Handbk.* ii. 17 Another way of generating sidebands without the carrier appearing in the output is to employ a ring modulator. **1974** *Down Beat* 18 July 42/2 The ring modulator adds both upper and lower sidebands of sound to the original tone. These modulated outputs will be the sum of and the difference between the frequencies of the original tone and an internal sine wave or external source. **1920** J. R. Battle *Handbk. Industr. Oil Engin.* vii. 421 There have been cases where hot running, ring-oiled bearings have been made to run cool. **1930** *Engineering* 11 July 39/3 The outer end of the crankshaft is supported by a ring-oiled outboard bearing and pedestal. **1968** J. J. O'Connor *Stand. Handbk. Lubric. Engin.* xxxv. 11 Lead babbitt.. is frequently used as the bearing material for ring-oiled motors. **1962** G. A. T. Burdett *Automatic Control Handbk.* xii. 11 Ring oiler. **1970** B. Pugh *Pract. Lubric.* viii. 164 Small [steam] turbines usually have the simplest arrangements for bearing lubrication, i.e. ring oilers or standard type lubricators. **1972** R. C. Gunther *Lubrication* xi. 304 Ring oiler consists of a free metal ring that rides on the journal and carries oil from a reservoir located below the bearing. **1904** *Electr. Rev.* 10 Sept. 410 The journal bearings are of the ring-oiling, self-aligning type. **1920** T. C. Thomsen *Pract. Lubric.* ix. 158 Ring oiling is employed largely on modern high-speed shafting bearings. **1974** P. Cave *Mama* (new ed.) vii 46 Mama took a can of beer which was thrust towards her and ripped off the ring opener. **1975** G. V. Higgins *City on Hill* iii. 74 He.. brought out two cans of beer... They stripped off the ring openers and drank. **1977** H. Innes *Big Footprints* II. iii. 187 Abe snapped the ring-opener of his [beer] can..and drank. **1935** *Bull. Folk-Song Soc. Northeast* ix. 11 The movement, with upraised hands, is not dissimilar to that in certain types of *ring-play*. **1942** L. Parrish *Slave Songs Georgia Sea Islands* iv. 99 This ring-play varies in action wherever I see it done... The tune, however, always remains the same. **1972** R. D. Abrahams in T. Kochman *Rappin' & Stylin' Out* 222 The numerous songs, ring-play, and verbal routines in Tobagonian Bongo (wake), as performed by adults in the community. **1909** P. T. Maw *Pract. Forestry* viii. 164 The so-called 'ring-pored' trees—Oak, Ash, Elm, Spanish Chestnut, and Acacia. **1978** A. Bernatzky *Tree Ecol. & Preservation* iv. 53 *Fraxinus*, *Castanea*, *Quercus*, and *Robinia* are ring-pored. **1940** *Bot. Gaz.* CII. 115 Ring porosity is restricted to..the North Temperate zone. **1950** Metcalfe & Chalk *Anat. Dicotyledons* I. p. xlvii, Ring-porousness, or the development of a marked zone of larger vessels at the beginning of a growth ring, appears to be accompanied by an increase in the length of the complete vessels in the pore zone. **1902** F. Roth *First Bk. Forestry* III. 222 The ring-porous woods, like oak, ash, chestnut. **1928** [see *diffuse *a.* 2 f]. **1956** F. W. Jane *Struct. Wood* xi. 250 Very approximately,..the timber of a ring porous hardwood possesses maximum strength when its growth rings number between 6 and 10 to the inch. **1968** G. Tsoumis *Wood as Raw Material* ii. 14 Growth rings are generally more distinct in ring-porous than in diffuse-porous woods. **1970** *Times* 16 Feb. (Food in Britain Suppl.) p. iii/3 Easy opening devices are undergoing considerable development—and ring-pull and zip-top cans are already available. **1973** 'D. Halliday' *Dolly & Starry Bird* vii. 89 Poor Jacko, who treated birds and ring-pull cans as one problem. **1922** Joyce *Ulysses* 313 The Santry boy was declared victor to the frenzied cheers of the public who broke through the ringropes and fairly mobbed him with delight. **1942** J. Masefield *Generation Risen* 30 The seconds' faces Watch through the ring-ropes. **1920** E. F. Smith *Introd. Bacterial Dis. Plants* iv. i. 474 Spieckermann's ring rot of Potato. **1946** *Sun* (Baltimore) 30 May 7/5 Even though potatoes 'look nice' they may harbor the dangerous ring-rot disease. **1974** Z. Király et al. *Methods Plant Path.* viii. 180 (*caption*) Processed plant extract of a ring-rot infected tuber. **1960** *Gloss. Atomic Terms* (U.K. Atomic Energy Authority) 46 Ring scaler. **1963** B. Fozard *Instrumentation Nucl. Reactors* viii. 79 If the scheme of Fig. 8.4 is extended to form a ring scaler, all the indicating cathodes may be connected together. **1920** Ring-seat [see *goods *sb. pl.* 2 b]. **1929** Wodehouse *Mr. Mulliner Speaking* iv. 134 The sportsman in him whispered that he was missing something good, for ring-seats to view which many men would have paid large sums. **1905** *Sci. Amer. Suppl.* 25 Mar. 24433/1 Ringshake..consists in a partial or entire separation of two consecutive annual rings, and appears on a cross section as one or more splits running concentrically around the log. **1938** H. E. Desch *Timber* xi. 133 Serious splits are often called 'shakes'... These are of several types, *e.g.*, ring-shake where the separation follows a growth ring, star-shake where the ruptures radiate outward from the pith. **1968** J. Arnold *Shell Bk. Country Crafts* 84 They used to 'split the heart'..as this obviated what were known as 'ring-shakes'. **1851** J. Brown *Forester* (ed. 2) ii. 199, I have seldom seen one [chestnut] which had arrived at the age of fifty or sixty years, which was not ring shaken in the heart-wood. **1931** R. W. Gordon in A. T. Smythe et al. *Carolina Low Country* 199 One of the simplest forms [of shouts], known as the 'ring shout', is apparently widespread. In this, the shouters form a circle and proceed around and around in a sort of slow processional, facing always in one direction. **1942** L. Parrish *Slave Songs Georgia Sea Islands* iii. 54 Shouting appears to be of two types: Along the coast of Georgia and South Carolina the most popular form is the ring-shout. **1970** P. Oliver *Savannah Syncopators* 56 A 'ring-shout'—a shuffling dance in counter-clockwise direction performed by a circle of worshippers which gradually intensified in tempo and collective excitement. **1940** N. Monks *Squadrons Up!* viii. 213 The circular (ring) sight for his eight machine-guns. **1942** *Tee Emm* (Air Ministry) II. 133 Before he had judged range with his ring sight, now he had to estimate without it. **1973** J. Quick *Dict. Weapons* 374/2 *Ring sight*, a sight, especially a gunsight, in the shape of a ring or concentric rings, through which aim is taken and range is estimated. **1930** *Buck & Hickman Ltd. Gen. Catal. Tools & Supplies* 285 Ring spanners. **1970** K. Ball *Fiat 600, 600D Autobook* x. 121/2 (*caption*) Adjusting brake shoe cams. Movement of the ring spanner..on the adjusting nut. **1973** J. Leasor *Host of Extras* ix. 166, I unlocked the..tool box..and took out a roll of ring spanners. [**1906** M. C. Cooke *Fungoid Pests Cultivated Plants* 50 The ringed brown spot (*Septoria Chrysanthemi*)..has apparently been confined to Italy.] **1923** Salmon & Wormald in *Jrnl. Min. Agric.* XXX. 148 The diseased areas on the leaf first appear as brown spots... As the spots reach a diameter of ⅛ in. or so, the central dead portions drop out, leaving the characteristic perforations... The name 'ring-spot' disease appears suitable to designate this form of injury which strikes the eye of the grower as he walks over the field. **1927** *Phytopathology* XVII. 325 (*caption*) Ringspots in an early stage of development with margins of alternating zones of chlorotic and normal tissue. **1939** *Jrnl. Pomol.* XVII. 27 Ring Spot, the common name accepted in this country for the disease [of lettuces] caused by the fungus mentioned [sc. *Marssonina Panattoniana*], has been widespread in temperate regions from an early date. **1964** *Phytopathology* LIV. 702/1 No ringspot virus was detected in uninoculated primary leaves through the sixteenth day. **1971** *Country Life* 18 Feb. 381/1 Ringspot, Mottle and Vein Mottle are only three of the viruses afflicting carnations. **1974** *Ibid.* 28 Nov. 1648/1 In Scotland..members of this race [*sc.* large heath butterflies] differ from English specimens in having fewer ring-spots on the under-surface of the wings. **1980** *Daily Tel.* 16 Jan. 8/3 There are some Cornish cauliflower types which have not been available for about 30 years which we think were resistant to a disease called ringspot. **1961** R. W. Butcher *Brit. Flora* II. 762 Leaves broad, lanceolate, grey-green, ring-spotted, flat and broadened from the base. **1871** *Sports & Games* July 121 A new Game, *ring toss*,..affords an attractive out-door sport, and furnishes a degree and kind of physical exercise that improves and develops the general health and strength. **1874** *St. Nicholas* Jan. 171/2 There are many other games to be found in the shops.. such as 'Ring-toss', 'Magic Hoops', and 'Parlor Croquet'. **1927** *Times* 20 Oct. 17/4 The bride..wore a picture gown of white ring velvet. **1931** *Daily Tel.* 21 May 6/3 A green satin beauté gown..lined with green ring velvet. **1932** G. Greene *Stamboul Train* ii. ii. 99 Could you get me five yards of ring velvet? **1952** C. W. Cunnington *Eng. Women's Clothing* vii. 232 Evening gown in mulberry ring velvet. **1939** F. Scott Fitzgerald *Let.* Mar. (1964) 53 As it is a lavish gesture it should be a simple present..on the other angle from a ring-watch. **1962** E. Bruton *Dict. Clocks & Watches* 147 *Ring watch*, a watch mounted in a finger ring. **1892** S. P. Thompson *Dynamo-Electr. Machinery* (ed. 4) xii. 309 (*caption*) Development of ring winding for 4-pole machine. **1893** [see *drum-winding* s.v. *drum *sb.*[1] 13]. **1922** A. H. Avery *Dynamo Design & Constr.* ix. 122 The winding is electrically continuous, and progresses steadily forward round the armature just as with the ring winding. **1963** L. F. Chitty in Foster & Alcock *Culture & Environment* vii. 177 A ringwork beside the Knighton road may be medieval. **1975** J. G. Evans *Environment Early Man Brit. Isles* vii. 164 Earthworks such as motte-and-bailey castles and ring-works preserve a buried soil and ditch sequence which can be used to extract environmental evidence. **1929** Hostetter & Beesley *It's a Racket!* 236 *Ringworm*, one who is a regular attendant upon prize fights and boxing matches. **1930** *Forum* Dec. 373/2 Many of these words..are employed daily in our own sports pages. Even the most casual American *ringworm* will recognize these: *knob, mugg, the one-two punch,* [etc.]. **1954** *Sun* (Baltimore) 30 Mar. 18/7 'Ring worms', as some are in the habit of referring to fight fans, have a hot one coming up Friday night when Kid Gavilan takes a shot at Bobo Olson and his middleweight title. **1892** J. Nasmith *Students' Cotton Spinning* ix. 348 A method of winding ring yarn on a cylindrical surface. **1909** *Westm. Gaz.* 13 Aug. 8/4 A determined effort is being made by cotton-spinners in Lancashire who produce ring yarn to form an association to keep up prices.

b. ringbarker *Austral.*, a stick-insect, *Podacanthus wilkinsoni,* which in swarms devours the leaves of eucalypts; **ring-billed** († **mew**) **gull**, a New World gull, *Larus delawarensis*; **ring-eye,** (*b*) (examples); = *silver-eye* s.v. Silver *sb.* and *a.* 21 c; cf. *white-eye* s.v. White *a.* 12 e; **ring perch** (examples); = *ringed perch* s.v. Ringed *ppl. a.* 5.

1935 K. C. McKeown *Insect Wonders Austral.* xviii. 149 Another fine stick-insect is found in the Walcha district, where it is popularly known as the 'Ringbarker', because of the dying brown appearance of the trees after the insects have stripped them of their foliage. **1965** *Austral. Encycl.* VIII. 295/2 Most phasmids are solitary in habit. One of the few gregarious forms, the ringbarker (*Podacanthus wilkinsoni*), sometimes appears in countless numbers in various districts of New South Wales, where it defoliates the eucalypts. **1831** Ring-billed mew-gull [in Dict., sense 17]. **1834** T. Nuttall *Man. Ornithol. U.S. & Canada* II. 300 Ring-billed Mew Gull... Sp. Charact.—Commissure of the stout ringed bill rather longer than the tarsus. **1844** J. E. DeKay *Zool. N.Y.* II. 309 The Common gull.., although called the Ring-billed Gull in the books, has received no other popular name than Brown Winter Gull. **1917** T. G. Pearson *Birds of Amer.* I. 47/1 The California and Ring-billed Gulls generally nest together in big colonies on the inland lakes. **1975** *Behaviour* LII. 143 Parent Ring-Billed Gulls are able to recognize their own chicks after about 7 to 9 days posthatching. **1951** J. Frame *Lagoon* 47 She was big and warm and knew about cats and little ring-eyes. **1953** *Landfall* VII. 21 They caught a blackbird and two ring-eyes. **1877** C. Hallock *Sportsman's Gazetteer* 272 Yellow Perch; or Ring Perch.—*Perca flavescens*. **1947** J. H. Brown *Outdoors Unlimited* 233 'Ring' perch, or yellow perch as they are more widely called, offer the earliest fishing in this part of the country.

ring, *sb.*[2] Add: **2. c.** (Later *transf.* examples.)

1957 G. Ryle in C. A. Mace *Brit. Philos. in Mid-Cent.* 264 The word 'analysis' has..a good laboratory or Scotland Yard ring about it. **1973** *Times Lit. Suppl.* 21 Sept. 1091/3 The 'special relationship' with Japan, using a phrase which will have an ironic and melancholy ring in British ears.

d. *Electronics.* A sequence of damped oscillations at the resonant frequency of a circuit; an individual oscillation in such a sequence.

1949 *Electronic Engin.* XXI. 207/3 Thus the deliberate introduction of a ring into the response can be a means of improving the sharpness of the transition edges of the observed picture. **1971** J. Earl *How to choose & use Pickups & Loudspeakers* iii. 87 (*caption*) This pulsed-tone shows only slight 'ringing'... An insufficiently low value load could incite worse rings than this. **1975** G. J. King *Audio Handbk.* ii. 43 No amplifier worthy of the hi-fi label should exhibit rings or overshoot into a load of pure resistance. *Ibid.* v. 122 Since the ring is very quickly damped, giving virtually an overshoot effect, this sort of performance is perfectly acceptable.

3. c. orig. with *up.* A call on a telephone. Also, each of a series of ringing sounds produced by a telephone receiving a call; *to give* (someone) *a ring*, to call by telephone. Cf. *Ring *v.*[2] 10 b.

1900 [see *hullo *int.*]. **1910** *Daily Chron.* 26 Feb. 6/2 It is only that most modern of human summonings, a telephone 'ring up'. **1930** J. B. Priestley *Angel Pavement* iv. 157 I'll just give the City Transport a ring to see if they've heard anything about that lot we sent to Norwich. **1934** T. E. Lawrence *Let.* 14 Sept. (1938) 819 Give me a ring at Hythe and let us meet. **1948** [see *central *sb.*]. **1951** T. Sterling *House without Door* x. 109 The telephone rang... It went on ringing... She listened, anticipating each ring to the second. c **1952** A. Huxley *Lett.* (1969) 660 If you ever come into town, why don't you give me a ring? **1960** [see *book *sb.* 4 d]. **1963** V. Nabokov *Gift* ii. 137 There's no guarantee the room is not already disposed of, but still I would advise you to give her a ring. **1973** 'M. Underwood' *Reward for Defector* vi. 44 Give me a ring later this evening and let me know. **1976** H. Nielsen *Brink of Murder* i. 9 He dialled his own number... Kevin.. answered on the fourth ring.

d. Phr. *the dead ring* (*of*): see quot. 1916. Cf. *Ringer[2] 5. *Austral.* and *N.Z. slang.*

Possibly belongs under some other sense of the noun.

1916 C. J. Dennis *Songs of Sentimental Bloke* 124 *The dead ring*: a remarkable likeness. **1948** D. W. Ballantyne *Cunninghams* i. xv. 81 They [*sc.* the sons] were the dead ring of Gil. **1951** —— in *Landfall* V. 166 A fine little chap. Dead ring of his old man, eh?

5. *ring-in*: a fraudulent substitution; the action of 'ringing in' (see Ring *v.*[2] 13 b). *Austral. slang.*

[**1924** *Truth* (Sydney) 27 Apr. 6 *Ring in*, false.] **1941** Baker *Dict. Austral. Slang* 60 *Ring-in*, a horse or dog that is fraudulently entered in a contest under an assumed name and/or disguised. **1969** C. Drummond *Odds on Death* vii. 152 The elderly book-makers..were his hosts... Past losses were debated... 'A ring-in after all these years,' had said a ruined giant of a man disgustedly. **1971** *Telegraph* (Brisbane) 26 June 5/1 All these are checked against the dog, and the chances of a 'ring-in' are completely eliminated.

ring, *v.*[1] Add: **1. d.** (Earlier and later examples.) Also *S. Afr.*

1868 [implied in *ringing *vbl. sb.*[1] 4]. **1890** 'R. Boldrewood' *Colonial Reformer* II. xviii. 111 A desultory entry into the receiving yard then takes place... The 'ragers' observing this movement keep wildly and excitedly 'ringing', like a first class Maëlstrom. **1928** 'Brent of Bin Bin' *Up Country* x. 172 'Well, are you going to stay?' 'Can't, thank you. Our mob was ringing a bit when I left.' **1941** I. L. Idriess *Great Boomerang* vii. 56 The cattle began to ring, the centre beasts edged outwards, then turned inward and began to sniff, to paw the earth. **1947** J. Stevenson-Hamilton *Wild Life S. Afr.* x. 72 The [buffalo] herds ring to protect themselves against marauders in much the same way as the herds of domestic cattle do. **1959** H. P. Tritton *Time means Tucker* 71 When they [*sc.* cattle] drift the only thing that can be done is try to turn them and get them circling, or ringing as the drover terms it.

6. c. To put a numbered ring on the leg of (a bird) so that it may be identified subsequently; to treat (a bat) similarly.

1908 *Brit. Birds* I. 327 A large number of birds of various species are ringed each year at Rossitten on the Baltic. **1925** Turner & Gurney *Bk. about Birds* vii. 72 When he escaped from the Sudan long after, he was able to tell those who ringed the bird that it had been found in Omdurman. **1958** *Listener* 30 Oct. 684/2 We have now ringed nearly 3,000 bats. **1971** *Daily Tel.* 22 June 8/4 A tufted duck, ringed in Essex two years ago by the British Trust for Ornithology, has been found in West Pakistan, where it was shot by a hunter in Rawalpindi. **1978** P. Conder *RSPB Guide to Birdwatching* 102 Many ringers, particularly those working on a population of a particular area, ring nestlings.

11. *Austral. slang.* To beat (a shedful of men) at sheep-shearing. Also *transf.* Cf. Ringer[1] 5 a in Dict. and Suppl.

1895 A. B. Paterson *Man from Snowy River* (1896) 136 The man that 'rung' the Tubbo shed is not the ringer here, That stripling from the Cooma side can teach him how to shear. **1899** 'S. Rudd' *On our Selection* 84 He shore..at Welltown, and rung the shed by half a sheep. **1905** in A. B. Paterson *Old Bush Songs* 27 And once I rung Cudjingie shed, and blued it in a week. **1957** D. Niland *Call me when Cross turns Over* v. 132 He would take on anything, wheat-lumping, tree-felling, shearing—always ringing the shed—droving, anything at all that suited him. **1967** *Telegraph* (Brisbane) 25 Mar. 2/5 To 'ring the shed' a shearer's cook has to earn more money than the top shearer.

12. To draw a circle round (something printed) so as to focus attention on it.

1970 R. K. Kent *Lang. Journalism* 113 *Ring*, to draw a circle around; encircle, as to signify various directions in copy editing. **1981** *Times* 23 June 2/2 She [*sc.* the Prime Minister] has probably already ringed a date in the autumn of 1983 for the election.

ring, *v.*[2] Add: **B. I. 1. d.** Of an electric circuit or a solid body: to undergo damped oscillation at its resonant frequency.

1952 G. C. Smith in Molloy & Poole *Television Engineers' Servicing Man.* 12 The flyback 'overshoots' and 'rings', but it is frequently damped out by a capacitor and a resistance in series across the coils. **1973** *Newnes Colour Television Servicing Manual* I. ii. 56/2 The amplified signal delivered from its collector causes T1 to 'ring'. **1975** *Nature* 24 Jan. 233/1 It has been widely accepted..that a [nuclear] test fired while the Earth was ringing from a really major earthquake..would be impossible to detect.

2. d. Of a telephone (bell): to produce the ringing sound which indicates that there is a caller on the line (Line *sb.*[2] 1 e).

1924 J. Reith *Broadcast over Britain* iii. v. 168 If people are moving about the room, or the telephone rings..the [radio] play has simply no chance. **1951** M. Kennedy *Lucy Carmichael* i. iv. 27 The telephone rang at intervals all the evening. **1979** T. Wiseman *Game of Secrets* iv. 48 He spent an hour getting himself reconnected, and after that he waited for the telephone to ring.

II. 6. a. (Later examples with reference to the summoning of servants.)

1856 Dickens *Dorrit* (1857) i. x. 81 'I must refer you,' returned Mr. Barnacle, ringing the bell, 'to the Department.' **1914** L. Woolf *Wise Virgins* ii. 31 They [*sc.* servants] won't stay because you ring the bell for them while they're at dinner!

d. *to ring the bell*: to win recognition; to be a complete success (see also *Bell *sb.*[1] 7 c).

1915 *Munsey's Mag.* Apr. 561/2, I am reading your 'Barry Newton' yarn. It scores a bulls' eye, it rings the bell, it brings a coconut to earth. **1925** E. Wallace *Strange Countess* x. 93 'You've certainly rung the bell this time, Lois.' 'It seems too good to be true, doesn't it?' **1945** *Daily Mirror* 15 Aug. 3/3 Leeds Corporation has fifty 'retired' trams to sell... They think a tram would 'ring the bell' as a home, week-end bungalow, or greenhouse. **1976** *Church Times* 30 July 7/5 The wise sight-seer knows that, however alert and receptive he is, even the treasures of Florence aren't going to ring the bell every time.

e. *to ring a bell* (colloq.): see *Bell *sb.*[1] 7 d.

7. a. (Further examples.) Also *spec.* to summon or send *for* a servant or required object by this means.

1847 E. Brontë *Wuthering Heights* I. x. 202 Why not have Mrs. Dean up to finish her tale?.. I'll ring: she'll be delighted to find me capable of talking cheerfully. **1864** H. Cullwick *Diary* June in D. Hudson *Munby* (1972) 195 Me by myself in that kitchen..ready to do any thing for 'em whenever they rang for me. **1926** D. L. Sayers *Clouds of Witness* ii. 49 Ring for anything you want. **1980** N. Marsh *Photo-Finish* vii. 188 Alleyn..put his thumb on the bell.. and Marco came in... He said: 'You rang, sir?'

10. a. (Later *fig.* examples.) *to ring in*, also, to include, take into consideration; to bring (someone) into an operation, activity, etc.

1900 Ade *Fables in Slang* 74 The Pew-Holders didn't even admit..that the Preacher had rung in some New Ones [*sc.* names]. 1922 D. H. Lawrence *England, my England* 45 The clanging pain in his head rang out the rest of his consciousness. 1925 T. Dreiser *Amer. Tragedy* II. III. xvi. 202 She can't be kept out of the case... We'll have to ring her in, I'm afraid. 1954 Wodehouse *Jeeves & Feudal Spirit* viii. 72 I've got the whole family here... I only wanted Trotter, but Mrs. T. and Percy rang themselves in. 1973 *New Yorker* 17 Feb. 88/2 With that one stroke, the union could ring in a lot of public figures. 1974 *Publishers Weekly* 30 Dec. 90/1 Mr. Brooke is summoned from far away Lima, and an old suitor of Philippa's, Lord Tancred, is rung in to help.

b. *spec.* to call (someone) by telephone. Freq. with *up*. Also *absol.*, and with *round* (= to call a succession of people by telephone), *through*.

1880 *Punch* 17 July 13/2 For you upon them both may frown, And say that you are shocked, or May knock the Secretary down, And then ring up the Doctor. 1882 T. D. Lockwood *Pract. Information for Telephonists* 130 Ask the office operator to ring up the complaining person and await results. 1889 [in Dict.]. 1906 S. Ford *Shorty McCabe* vi. 150 He was goin' to ring up the police reserves. 1913 G. B. Shaw *Let.* 14 July in *B. Shaw & Mrs. Campbell* (1952) 132, I shall ring up tomorrow in spite of my dread of being unwelcome. I rang a second time today; but the answer was buzz, buzz. 1930 J. B. Priestley *Angel Pavement* viii. 398 He rang me up last night, at home, to say he'd just arrived and would be down this morning. 1934 T. E. Lawrence *Let.* 14 Sept. (1938) 819 It lies on my conscience that you so often ring up vainly. 1934 N. Marsh *Man lay Dead* xii. 207 I'll ring through at about one o'clock. 1940 H. G. Wells *Babes in Darkling Wood* II. i. 134 There were one or two people he might ring up, but probably they would be holiday-making now and out of town. 1948 'N. Shute' *No Highway* vi. 169 While I was down there, Miss Learoyd rang through. 1955 *Times* 22 July 10/6 Two young friends rang me up rather excitedly the other evening and asked me if I would go round and give them my advice. 1958 L. A. G. Strong *Treason in Egg* vii. 127 You'd better ring the police. 1960 J. Stroud *Shorn Lamb* xv. 170 If he does [turn up], I'll ring round for a hostel. 1969 *Listener* 6 Feb. 187/1 When Jelly Roll Morton..played his compositions to the Harlem team, eyebrows were raised no further than the pejorative 'don't ring *us*' level. 1974 A. Morice *Killing with Kindness* ii. 14 He was going to ring round in the morning and fix up for us all to go and see them. 1974 *Times* 7 Feb. 14/6 By ringing and writing to every MP, Service and the bill's sponsors have so far secured 74 pledges to be present. 1977 'M. Underwood' *Murder with Malice* x. 91 'Thanks for ringing, sir. I appreciate it.'.. Nick dropped the receiver back. 1980 A. Auswaks *Trick of Diamonds* iii. 80 'Don't ring us, we'll ring you,' grunted Bob Jones sarcastically. 1981 J. Wainwright *All on Summer's Day* 66 Ring round the other divisions. I want some C.I.D. men.

c. (Earlier and later examples.) Also *fig.* and *intr.* for passive (with the curtain as subject).

1772 D. Garrick *Peep behind Curtain* II. i. 30 Pray be so good as to ring down the curtain, that we may rehearse in form. 1807 *Monthly Mirror* Aug. 133 The prompter rings the lofty curtain down. 1913 F. H. Burnett *T. Tembarom* xv. 186 'Now,' he said, 'we can ring up for the first act.' She filled the teapot. 1916 S. Kaye-Smith *John Galsworthy* 63 Thus the curtain rings down on Irene Forsyte, crushed under the heel of prosperity. 1950 H. F. Maltby (*title*) Ring up the curtain.

d. *to ring off* (earlier and further examples). Now more usu., to discontinue a telephone conversation by replacing the receiver, = *hang up* s.v. *Hang *v.* 28 a. Also *fig.*

1882 T. D. Lockwood *Pract. Information for Telephonists* 85 Frequently an annunciator between two circuits when connected to allow the subscriber, if he please, to ring off. 1899 *Electrician* 1 Dec. 181/2 Ringing off is avoided, as this is performed automatically by replacing the receiver on the hook. 1900 [see Phone *sb.*[2] and *v.*]. 1906 A. Bennett *Whom God hath Joined* iv. 158 He rang off, curtly, without another word. 1920 R. Macaulay *Potterism* III. i. 104 You mustn't ring off yet, indeed you mustn't. Hold on while I tell daddy. 1935 *Punch* 21 Aug. 223/1 'I'm coming round to wring your wretched little neck!' shouted Mr. Applestalk as he rang off. 1938 E. Bowen *Death of Heart* III. i. 328 'So then you rang off?' 'No, he did. It was his tea-time, no doubt.' 1967 M. Kenyon *Whole Hog* i. 12 I'll ring him anyway... 'Bye now—Yes, I'm going to *ring off*. 1973 S. Dobyns *Man of Little Evils* xii. 127 The operator came back on the line. 'I'm afraid your party has rung off.'

fig. 1895 *Inlander* Dec. 114 *Ring off*, stop talking. 1906 E. Dyson *Fact'ry 'Ands* vi. 71 'Shut up! D'yeh 'ear?.. Arr-r-r ring off, cant yeh!' The girl..opened a startled eye. 1938 F. M. Ford *Let.* 26 Nov. (1965) 305, I will ring off. Let us know from time to time how things go with you. 1940 F. Sargeson *Man & his Wife* 34 Wouldn't you like to stay out here for good? Fred said. Ring off, Ken said. I got a bite.

e. *to ring back*, to reply to (a previous caller) by telephone. Also *absol.* and as *sb.*

Quots. 1971 and 1972 represent technical senses in Telephony.

1942 N. Balchin *Darkness falls from Air* iii. 57, I hung up. 'Pearce is going to ring you back,' I said. 1944 H. McCloy *Panic* 118 This is Jim, testing. I'm going to hang up and then I want you to ring me back. 1960 I. Jefferies *Dignity & Purity* xi. 181 I'll ring you back Gobbo. Couple of minutes. 1969 P. N. Walker *Carnaby & Conspirators* vii. 68 'Make a check on Henry Pritchard too, sir.'.. 'Will do. Will you ring me back?' 1971 *Gloss. Electrotechnical, Power Terms* (*B.S.I.*) III. ii. 28 *Ring-back signal*, a backward signal to recall a calling subscriber held by the operator. 1972 *Sci. Amer.* Sept. 120/1 When the path is found, the signal-distributor sends electrical signals to ring the telephone of the called subscriber and sends ringback tones to the caller. 1974 M. Birmingham *You can help Me* iii. 47 There was one caller from a public call-box who..didn't ring back. 1977 W. Marshall *Thin Air* i. 11 He said quickly, 'I'll ring you back.'

f. *to ring in*, to report by telephone. Also *trans.*, to transmit (a verbal message) by telephone.

1949 N. Marsh *Swing, Brother, Swing* xi. 254 I'll ring in then and get something to eat. 1956 *New Statesman* 18 Aug. 180/3 We had to think about finding a telephone booth from which to ring in a preliminary story. 1964 M. Banton *Policeman in Community* iii. 83 The beat officer has to 'ring in' to headquarters every hour from automatic boxes mounted on standards at the kerbside. 1971 B. Graham *Spy Trap* i. 7 He..drove to the secondary rendezvous point. .. Maybe Hannifin had rung in. 1975 *Listener* 16 Oct. 505/1 People ring in, wanting help.

11. c. *to ring up*: to make a record of; *spec.* to record (a sale) on a cash register or similar device. Also fig.

1937 J. T. Farrell *Fellow Countrymen* 180 He paid Kitty fifteen cents, which she rang up. 1939 *Sun* (Baltimore) 18 Jan. 5/5 Asked if the ship's speeds in any of its previous trips through the canal had been 'rung up', Leonard Nieberline, first officer, answered in the negative. 1948 C. Himes *Black on Black* (1973) 267. When she stopped at the cash register across from him to ring up a sale he said, 'Baby, I really love you.' 1956 A. Huxley *Adonis & Alphabet* 167 Energies which, if canalized and directed, can be made to do useful work and ring up handsome profits. 1957 *Economist* 21 Dec. 1051/1 Last Saturday, when the strike was crumbling, the shops stayed open until nine; many rang up record sales. 1962 *Times* 15 Mar. 9/7 The items in connexion with which he was accused did not appear upon the cash receipt slip. The cashier must have omitted to ring these up. 1968 [see *Driver 2 b]. 1970 *Daily Tel.* 14 Nov. 15/3 One technique is to bully the check-out girl and get her sufficiently confused to miss the fact that half the goods have been pushed through without having been rung up. 1976 'E. McBain' *Guns* vii. 148 The cashier rings up the check, money comes tumbling down the cash register chute.

13. a. *spec.* to effect a fraudulent change in the identity of a motor vehicle.

1967 N. Lucas *CID* vi. 80 The two cars are..rebuilt into one 'bastard' car... The process is known as 'ringing' cars. 1971 *Drive* Summer 22/1 Like any commercial venture, the business of car ringing—changing a vehicle's identity—has to be cost-effective. 1977 A. Hunter *Gently Instrumental* ii. 19 The Parry brothers..copped three apiece for ringing cars.

ring-a-ring (ri·ŋări·ŋ). Also ringaring, etc. [Fanciful extension of Ring *sb.*[1]] A circle or circular movement. *Ring-a-ring o' roses* (and variants), a game played by children holding hands in a circle (also *transf.*).

1881 K. Greenaway *Mother Goose* 48 Ring-a-ring-a-roses, A pocket full of posies. 1922 Joyce *Ulysses* 506 I'm a tiny tiny thing Ever flying in the spring Round and round a ringaring. 1927 W. E. Collinson *Contemp. Eng.* 11, I can be brief in mentioning the various games we played during childhood. I will mention..ring a ring o' roses. 1945 C. S. Forester *Commodore* xxiii. 259 The Governor..tried to dance a sort of ring-a-ring-of-roses with the two Englishmen. 1953 A. Clarke *Moment Next to Nothing* II. 32 He was near that oak, speaking of Marravaun—A ring-a-ring o' birds around him. 1957 J. Masters *Far, Far the Mountain Peak* i. 5 Why don't I suggest a game of ring-a-ring-a-roses, or kiss-in-the-ring? 1963 *Times* 30 May 4/2 England now were playing arrogant football and stroking the ball from man to man as though they were playing ring-a-ring-o'roses. 1972 G. Green *Great Moments in Sport: Soccer* ii. 38 While the opposition was being enticed into these closely woven webs of ring-a-roses, two..of the front runners would be streaking ahead into the unguarded places. 1974 *Times* 1 Apr. 1/8 Strong men blenched and broke into a sweat of embarrassment when made to dance 'Ring-a-ring o' roses' in public outside Guildhall.

ring-bark, *v.* Add: **a.** Also, to remove a narrow or incomplete ring in order to check rapid growth. (Further examples.) **ring-barking** *vbl. sb.* (further examples).

1938 C. P. Ackers *Pract. Brit. Forestry* vi. 215 This is the time to ring-bark and let these rough poles, after they have done their job, topple over as branchless rotten logs. *Ibid.* xi. 341 Partial ring barking is practised in some orchards so as to check the sap of the tree and so induce more free fruiting. 1961 *Observer* 18 June 35/5 Successfully greedy roots can mean fruitless apples and pears, and 'ring barking' is the remedy. 1975 H. F. Heady *Rangeland Managem.* iv. 57 Ring-barking by voles killed as much as 84 percent of the *Artemisia tridentata* in some Montana stands.

ring-bolt. For *Naut.* read 'orig. *Naut.*' and add further examples.

1840 *Crockett Almanac 1841* 19 A ring bolt in the barn floor. 1958 L. Durrell *Balthazar* iv. 90 Firm as a figure held by ringbolts. 1968 E. R. Buckler *Ox Bells & Fireflies* xv. 215 He just grabbed the sonofabitch by the scruff o' the neck and lifted him about two feet offa the floor—and, by God, by the time he was through with him, he brought him to the ringbolt and don't you think he didn't. 1974 R. Adams *Shardik* xxvi. 210 The tie-bars..were secured by chains to ring-bolts set..in the walls and floor.

ring-dance. (Further examples.)

1910 [see *Polska]. 1933 E. K. Chambers *Eng. Folk-Play* 202 There is a general resemblance between Sword Dances proper and..Ring, Hoop, or Garland Dances. 1946 R. Blesh *Shining Trumpets* v. 98 He had the work-songs, the spiritual, the ring-dance. 1960 Auden *Homage to Clio* 28 Rustics in a ring-dance pantomime.

ringed, *ppl. a.* Add: **2. c.** Of a bird: bearing a ring or rings on one or both legs.

1908 *Brit. Birds* I. 298 Should anyone come across any of Herr Mortensen's ringed birds at any time, it is hoped they will send the ring, foot, and data of capture either to him or to me. 1948 *Ibid.* XLI 233 Recoveries of ringed Mallard are in the vast majority of cases obtained from birds shot. 1978 P. Conder *RSPB Guide to Birdwatching* 104 The table of longevity shows that ringed birds are able to survive to a good age.

5. ringed carpet, a pale grey moth, *Cleora cinctaria*, with dark patches on the forewings; **ringed penguin**, the chinstrap penguin, *Pygoscelis antarctica*.

1866 Ringed carpet [see Carpet *sb.* 4]. 1896 J. W. Tutt *Brit. Moths* xi. 300 The Ringed Carpet..is abundant at Lyndhurst in May and early June, on the dwarf firs among the heather. 1948 W. J. Stokoe *Caterpillars Brit. Moths* II. 197 The Ringed Carpet... The New Forest in Hampshire is said to be the district *par excellence* for this species. 1919 Ringed penguin [see *Adélie]. 1964 A. L. Thomson *New Dict. Birds* 611/1 The Chinstrap (or Ringed) Penguin..is most abundant in the Antarctic Peninsula.

Ringelmann (ri·ŋĕlmæn). [Of uncertain attribution; perh. the name of Maximilien *Ringelmann* (1861–1931), French scientist.] Used *attrib.* and †in the possessive with reference to a means of estimating the darkness and density of smoke by visual comparison with a chart bearing different shades of grey (formed by lines ruled with different spacings on a white card); as *Ringelmann card, chart, scale.*

1898 S. B. Donkin *Heat Efficiency of Steam Boilers* ix. 184 Ringelmann's smoke scale.—Professor Ringelmann has conceived the idea of representing different intensities of smoke, from light through grey to black, not by small sample tints, which are apt to be misleading, but by an arrangement of lines on white paper, drawn in a particular way. 1905 W. Nicholson *Smoke Abatement* vii. 144 Copies of the Ringelmann Smoke Scales..are obtainable. 1923 H. G. Clinch *Smoke Inspector's Handbk.* vii. 74 (*heading*) Measurement of smoke—Ringelmann's shade cards. 1954 [see *dark smoke* s.v. *Dark *a.* 13 c]. 1958 *New Scientist* 5 June 101/1 Discharge of smoke darker than Shade 2 on the Ringelmann chart..for a total of more than ten minutes within eight hours is forbidden. 1962 *B.S.I. News* May 20 The B.S.I. has..undertaken..the preparation of standard Ringelmann charts and the measurement of solids emitted from chimneys.

ringer[1]**.** Add: **5. a.** (Earlier and later examples.) Also *N.Z.*

1871 'R. Boldrewood' in *Cornh. Mag.* XXIII. 85 The 'Ringer', or fastest shearer of the whole assembly. 1888 —— *Robbery under Arms* I. ix. 110 Jim..was trying to shear sheep and sheep with the 'ringer' of the shed. 1910 C. E. W. Bean *On Wool Track* 196 The man who shears most sheep is the 'ringer'. 1927 M. M. Bennett *Christison* xxii. 193 With the new shearing machines a hundred sheep a day were shorn easily, while ringers scored over two hundred. 1934 T. Wood *Cobbers* 196 He can shear a hundred a day: a hundred and twenty, a hundred and fifty; two hundred—even three hundred and twenty, at times, if he is a Ringer—that is the quickest of the team. 1952 J. Cleary *Sundowners* iii. 138 By the end of the day he wanted to be the 'ringer' shearer. 1963 N. Hilliard *Piece of Land* 90 The ringer of the Maori shearing gang that year had been Keko. 1965 *N.Z. Listener* 26 Feb. 15/2 In shed shearing the position of 'Ringer' is sought after and competition among shearers has always been keen.

b. An expert. *Austral. slang.*

1918 C. J. Dennis *Digger Smith* 112 *Ringer*, expert. 1923 'B. L. Standish' *Lego Lamb, Southpaw* iii. 26 'That guy's a ringer,' declared Shultz. *c* 1926 'Mixer' *Transport Workers' Song Bk.* 24 For I'm classed among the 'ringers', And from others stand apart. 1943 *Amer. Speech* XVIII. 256 With Americans a *ringer* is a double; here [*sc.* in Australia] he is an expert. 1965 *Telegraph* (Brisbane) 5 July 8 Ringer (the best—old shearing-shed term later adopted by townies).

6. One who rings birds.

1909 *Brit. Birds* III. 5 Any finder of a ring so marked should realise that communication with the 'ringer' is intended. 1946 *Ibid.* XXXIX. 260 The ringer probably keeps a sharper look-out for dead birds than the ordinary person. 1966 *Punch* 14 Dec. 897/3 Ringers try to recapture each bird in colonies of sea birds for an annual ring check, and quite often they catch the same bird each year for six years or more in their gardens. 1978 P. Conder *RSPB Guide to Birdwatching* 103 In the early days when there were few ringers, most of the birds were recovered dead but as more ringers took part in the scheme..so the numbers of live recoveries increased.

7. *Austral.* A stockman; a station hand.

1909 J. X. A. Cameron *Spell of Bush* (1910) 48 Dam-sinkers, fencers, scrub-cutters, ringers, and other men doing contract work in the vicinity. 1942 C. Barrett *On Wallaby* i. 14 'Jim the Ringer' came in every month for 'a bender'. 1953 'N. Shute' *In Wet* x. 348 His camp consisted of..a humpy shelter made of gum tree boughs for his white ringer, Phil Fleming. 1954 B. Miles *Stars my Blanket* xxiii. 204 The stockman—or 'ringer' as he is called—rides into the yard with a lasso and 'rings' his bullock in true wild-west style. 1964 *Sunday Mail Mag.* (Brisbane)

27 Sept. 3/1 A ringer..is a Queensland stockman who holds his cattle during a muster by 'ringing' them on horseback. **1977** *Telegraph* (Brisbane) 12 Jan. 3/1 The pub, local waterhole for stockmen, ringers and station hands.

8. *colloq.* An officer in an air force; a member of an air-crew. Also with preceding numeral, indicating rank.

The use is derived from the rings indicating rank worn on the sleeve of an officer.

1943 C. H. Ward-Jackson *Piece of Cake* 51 Pilot Officer is a 'Half-ringer', and Squadron Leader a 'Two and a half ringer'. **1945** Baker *Austral. Lang.* 163 *Ringer*, an officer. **1976** 'A. Hall' *Kobra Manifesto* v. 65 One of the air-crew, a two-ringer.

ringer[2]. Add: **4.** *U.S. slang.* A horse or other competitor fraudulently substituted for another in a race or other sporting activity; one who engages in a fraud of this kind.

1890 *Stock Grower & Farmer* 9 Aug. 8/2 At the same time 'Andy Croker' is the most notorious 'ringer' on the turf. **1914** 'High Jinks, Jr.' *Choice Slang* 17 *Ringer*, a name applied to a man or horse dishonestly entered in an event with others far below his class and a class in which he could not be entered legitimately. **1928** Foy & Harlow *Clowning through Life* 188 We had scarcely made the match when we were given a secret tip that Bennett was a 'ringer'. **1935** A. J. Pollock *Underworld Speaks* 98/1 *Ringer*, a race horse who has been substituted under the name of another horse in a race. **1938** M. Lane *Edgar Wallace* iii. v. 304 He was an attractive young man, known in his own profession as 'Ringer' Barrie for his ability to ring the changes of disguise on race-horses. **1944** *Fortune* Sept. 140/2 The chance that 'ringers'—good horses masquerading as poor ones under assumed names—can be sneaked into races. **1958** *Sun* (Baltimore) 15 Aug. 20/2 Evidence.. tends to show that it was not a horse called Bye Bye Will that won that race but a 'ringer'. **1966** *Listener* 27 Oct. 613/3 He rode third in a regimental steeplechase: the winning horse was later found to be a ringer. **1973** B. Broadfoot *Ten Lost Years* xxi. 240 Some teams used to bring in ringers, a Yankee, or a guy from the East. **1980** *Times* 11 Mar. 6 The Crown claimed that the horse had been switched and that the winner was in fact a 'ringer', a more successful stablemate called Cobblers March.

5. *to be a (dead) ringer for* (or *of*): to resemble closely; to be an exact counterpart of. *slang* (orig. *U.S.*).

1891 *Sporting Times* (N.Y.) 4 July 10/4 Homan is a 'dead-ringer' for Anson. **1900** Ade *More Fables* 162 Bob.. was a Ringer for a United States Senator, all except the White Coat. **1903** 'O. Henry' in *Ainslee's* Mar. 129/2 The man was a ringer for the pictures of the fat Weary Willie in the funny papers. **1916** J. Buchan *Greenmantle* xiii. 174 Now you're in these pretty clothes you're the dead ringer of the brightest kind of American engineer. **1946** *New Yorker* 16 Mar. 22/1 The Nissen hut..which were [*sic*] dead ringers for the council lodges the Iroquois Indians used to build. **1954** Wodehouse in *Encounter* Nov. 43/2 We also felt like minor infusoria at the bottom of a well. 'Wodehouse,' I remember saying to myself more than once, 'Alter your appearance very slightly, and you would be a ringer for a waterbeetle.' **1959** *Punch* 21 Oct. 251/1 He [*sc.* a shark] has life pretty easy and apart from the gill-rakers is a ringer for Patrick Joseph. **1960** B. Keaton *My Wonderful World of Slapstick* 122 Going through the casting book we found a man and woman who were dead ringers for the Belgian rulers. **1970** 'T. Coe' *Wax Apple* xii. 89 Doctor Fredric Cameron..was an almost dead ringer for J. Roger Urbermann. **1973** C. Sagan *Cosmic Connection* xiii. 92 There is little doubt that the average person's view of Hell—sizzling, choking, sulfurous, and red—is a dead ringer for the surface of Venus.

6. *U.S. slang.* An outsider or intruder; an imposter, *spec.* one who attaches himself to a political or other group to which he does not belong.

1896 Ade *Artie* xi. 100 About a dozen ringers followed us in and stood around rubberin'. **1904** *N.Y. Tribune* 18 Oct. 1 The members of the Manhattan & Democratic clubs occupied front seats. The press seats were largely occupied by ringers. *Ibid.* 8 Nov. 3 The Democratic leaders to-day started to send a lot of alleged 'ringers' across the line into West Virginia to vote to-morrow. **1926** *Clues* Nov. 162/1 *Ringer*, one who butts in on another's racket. **1928** *Manch. Guardian Weekly* 26 Oct. 335/2 Perhaps seventy-five were really newspaper men and women, the others being what the American language calls 'ringers', 'gate-crashers', or 'dead-heads'. **1940** Wodehouse *Eggs, Beans & Crumpets* 59 Too often, when you introduce a ringer into a gaggle of Pekes, there ensues a scrap like New Year's Eve in Madrid. **1963** S. Greer *Metropolitics* v. 104 We have omitted the 'ringer'; none of our respondents claimed to recognize the spurious name. **1965** M. Bradbury *Stepping Westward* vii. 357 This is quite a party. I'm going to feel a real ringer. **1978** *Detroit Free Press* 2 Apr. (Detroit Suppl.) 8/1 Inside the lobby of the dilapidated building, Blow Dry scans the inhabitants, hoping..that no one will spot her as the ringer. **1981** C. R. Lajeunesse *Dead Man Running* xi. 35 A ringer for you will be leaving your place, same car, same registration.

7. *slang.* A false registration plate attached to a stolen motor vehicle; a thief who uses these.

1962 *New Statesman* 21 Dec. 899/1 The driver stays with the car regardless, and the car is equipped with ringers (false number-plates). **1964** E. Parr *Grafters All* ii. 25 The car is now driven to a hideaway, where ringers (false number-plates) are substituted. **1970** P. Laurie *Scotland Yard* iii. 69 All the ringer has to do is buy a [car] key, come along as innocent as pie, open the door and drive off to wherever he does his ringing. **1971** *Drive* Summer 21/2 When the professionals—the car 'ringers'—get to work, the profit on a skilfully doctored vehicle can be more than £500. **1971** *Road Ahead* (Brisbane) Sept. 18 In Britain, 'ringers' produce very special cars. 'Ringers' are experts in modifying stolen cars, giving them a new identity.

8. *ringer-up.* A person making a telephone call; = *caller *sb.* 1 f. Cf. *ring *v.*[2] 10 b.

1963 N. Marsh *Dead Water* (1964) v. 117 The ringer-up was Miss Cost. **1968** P. Dickinson *Skin Deep* v. 104, I don't take on casual ringers-up. **1970** Y. Carter *Mr. Campion's Falcon* xxii. 161 The lunatic fringe—the compulsive ringers-up.

Ringer[3] (ri·ŋəɹ). *Biol.* The name of Sydney *Ringer* (1834–1910), English physician, used *attrib.*, *absol.*, and in the possessive to denote physiological saline solutions of a type which he introduced and which usu. contain (in addition to sodium chloride) salts of potassium and calcium.

1893 *Jrnl. Physiol.* XIV. 200 Ringer's solution kept the heart beating vigorously for more than thirty hours. **1913** *Rep. Brit. Assoc. Adv. Sci. 1912* 660 A heart perfused with a Ringer solution without lime stops much earlier than when perfused with a Ringer solution without lime and without potassium. **1915** *Jrnl. Physiol.* L. 138 Isotonic Ringer or sodium chloride is not an indifferent fluid. **1932** W. Burridge *Excitability* xxi. 173 We..washed out the muscle with saline or Ringer. **1956** *Nature* 18 Feb. 340/1 Ringer solution was injected through the catheter into the sinus in order to show that no larger anastomoses still existed between the sinus and other veins. **1964** W. G. Smith *Allergy & Tissue Metabolism* ii. 19 Schacter has demonstrated that Ringer perfused rabbit tissues release histamine in anaphylaxis. **1967** K. M. Smith *Insect Virol.* v. 105 The sucrose is then removed by dialysis in a cellophane bag immersed in cold Ringer's solution. **1975** *Nature* 10 Jan. 99/2 When the Ringer was made sufficiently hypertonic so that twitch movement was essentially eliminated, the second component propagated throughout the fibre.

Comb. **1958** [see *centrifugation]. **1977** *Proc. R. Soc. Med.* LXX. 160/1 His blood pressure fell from 130/80 mm Hg before anaesthesia to 50 mm Hg during the operation, despite rapid injection of 2 litres of Ringer-lactate solution.

Ringerike (ri·ŋərikə). The name of a district centred on Honefoss north of Oslo in Norway used *attrib.* (after H. Shetelig *Norske Aarsberetning* (1909), 96–107) to designate a style of late Viking art, characterized by abundant use of plant motifs as ornament.

1924 A. F. Major tr. *J. Brøndsted's Early Eng. Ornament* iii. 293 Shetelig has more recently dealt with these rune-stones; he christens them after the reddish sandstone, which is quarried at Ringerike in the south of Norway, the 'Ringerike Group' and their plant ornament the 'Ringerike style'. **1936** A. W. Clapham *Romanesque Archit.* viii. 193 The decoration also includes a free use of interlacement, chevron-ornament, and a foliage of Ringerike or late Viking type. **1937** E. V. Gordon tr. *Shetelig & Falk's Scandinavian Archæol.* xvii. 303 In the Ringerike style the ancient animal ornament was thrust firmly into the background. **1952** D. T. Rice *Eng. Art 871–1100* v. 127 The new manner is known as the Ringerike style, and it is distinguished by the employment of a characteristic leaf ornament. **1970** Foote & Wilson *Viking Achievement* ix. 307 The style was directly succeeded by the Ringerike style, which first appeared early in the first quarter of the eleventh century. *Ibid.* 310 Ringerike elements were still appearing on Irish objects in the 1120s. **1973** *Times* 1 Nov. 4/5 A unique discovery is a wooden panel with decoration in the Ringerike style of the twelfth-century, with an animal design. **1976** D. Verey *Cotswold Churches* ii. 18 At Bibury, the capital..on the north [of the chancel arch] is in Ringerike style. Many motifs are Scandinavian.

ring-fence, *sb.* Add: **b.** (Later *fig.* examples.)

1950 *Times* 8 Feb. 6/3 The decline is understood to be due mostly to the removal of the 'ring-fence' round the industry, that is, the provision of the Control of Engagement Order requiring miners to stay in coal-mining employment. **1965** *Economist* 6 Nov. 623/2 Imports into ECSC have not been held out by the tariff 'ring fence' erected after the last recession.

ring-fence, *v.* Add: (Further examples.) Also *fig.*

1903 R. Fry *Let.* 30 Jan. (1972) I. 203 B.B. should not have it said that he is capable of political scheming to ring-fence Italian art. **1974** *Northern Times* (Golspie, Sutherland) 2 Aug. 3/4 The proposal to ringfence Embo village was not acceptable for grant purposes.

ringhals (ri·ŋhals). Also **rinkhals.** [ad. Afrikaans *rinkhals*, f. *ring* ring + *hals* neck.] A large venomous spitting cobra, *Hemachatus hæmachatus*, of the family Elapidæ, found in southern Africa, and distinguished by a white ring or two across the neck of an otherwise brown or black skin. Also *attrib.*

1793 tr. *C. P. Thunberg's Trav. Europe, Afr. & Asia* I. 208 A colonist had been bitten in the foot some time before by a serpent of the species called Ringhals (or Ringneck). **1835** J. W. D. Moodie *Ten Years S. Afr.* I. xv. 316 The puff-adder, the ring-hals, and the berg-adder, are very poisonous and very numerous. **1864** T. Baines *Explor. S.-W. Afr.* xiv. 449, I think the species is called 'ring hals' (or ringed throat) in the Colony. **1906** *Westm. Gaz.* 16 Jan. 4/1 A Spurred Chameleon, a small Monitor, and a couple of Ring-hals snakes. **1925** *Other Lands* July 44/2 They pointed to the half-open door, where she saw uncoiling itself a large ringhals. **1931**, etc. [see *cobra]. **1939** S. Cloete *Watch for Dawn* v. 62 With the bite of a mamba or a ringhals the heart sometimes beat even after life had gone. **1947** *Cape Argus* 29 Nov. (Mag. Section) 1/3 Cobras, like the ringhals and indeed all other snakes make for cover when they feel the approach of some intruder. **1956** A. G. McRae *Hill called Grazing* vi. 47 The six-foot-long Rinkhals cobra, reared above its coils, hood flattened and tiny, evil head weaving. **1972** L. van der Post *Story like Wind* ix. 292 She..saw, sitting upright on its tail, black as ebony and shining as with oil, a seven-foot rinkhals cobra.

ringie (ri·ŋi). *Austral. slang.* [f. Ring *sb.*[1] + -ie.] The keeper of the ring in a game of *two-up.

1941 Baker *Dict. Austral. Slang.* 65 *Ringie*, the keeper of a two-up school. **1949** *Strand Mag.* Dec. 100/1 The ringie takes care of operations inside the ring of side betters which gathers round the two protagonists. **1951** F. Hardy *Power without Glory* 323 Red Ted was 'Ringie'. He supervised the game in the ring itself, seeing that the pennies were spun fairly, and calling the results.

ringing, *vbl. sb.*[1] Add: **1. a.** Also, the putting of a numbered ring on a bird or a bat. (Further examples.)

1910 *British Birds* III. p. iii, There is every indication that facts of the utmost interest and importance will be brought to light by the ringing of birds. **1953** Lockley & Russell *Bird-Ringing* i. 5 It was in 1899 that Herr Christian C. Mortensen laid the foundations of scientific bird-ringing when he placed his first aluminium rings, stamped with numbers, on the legs of young starlings. **1958** *Listener* 30 Oct. 684/2 For our first attempt at bat-ringing..my wife and I and a friend climbed up into the roof of a barn.. where we knew there was a colony of bats. **1978** P. Conder *RSPB Guide to Birdwatching* 101 The Protection of Birds Act 1967, prohibits ringing except under licence issued by the Nature Conservancy Council through the British Trust for Ornithology.

4. The action of cattle in forming a ring. Cf. Ring *v.*[1] 1 d in Dict. and Suppl.

1868 C. W. Browne *Overlanding in Australia* 77 After an hour's amusement of this sort, they stop of their own accord. This evolution is termed 'ringing'. **1941** Baker *Dict. Austral. Slang* 60 *Ringing*, the milling of cattle.

ringing, *vbl. sb.*[2] Add: **1. c.** *ringing-up*, in senses 10 b, c of the verb.

1835 Dickens *Sk. Boz* (1836) 1st Ser. II. 205 Let us take a peep 'behind' previous to the ringing up. **1924** Galsworthy *White Monkey* iii. xiv. 316 He..closeted himself in the telephone booth... Ringing-up was quicker. **1949** N. Mitford *Love in Cold Climate* i. v. 51 This ringing-up of Paris seemed to me a most dashing extravagance. Aunt Sadie..only made trunk calls in times of crisis.

2. b. *Electronics.* The phenomenon of transient damped oscillation occurring in a circuit at its resonant frequency as a result of a sudden change in voltage level; also, in *Television*, the occurrence on the screen of black lines to the right of a white object, caused by transient oscillation in the video amplifier of the receiver.

1949 *Electronic Engin.* XXI. 207/2 If the attenuation of the high frequencies takes place too suddenly (i.e. sharp cut-off) then we get ringing. **1953** H. A. Chinn *Television Broadcasting* xvi. 640 A spurious peak or a sharp cutoff in the response-frequency characteristic..discloses itself in the resulting picture display as..repetitions of the original signal. This manifestation of 'ringing' of the video circuits can be detected by observation of vertical lines in the picture. **1961** *Times* 20 Nov. (Television Suppl.) p. xii/1 Gross defects are obvious to any viewer either by poor contrast, lack of definition, 'ringing', or unwanted interference. **1969** J. J. Sparkes *Transistor Switching* iv. 113 In practice the inductance in the emitter wire through which the drive current has to flow is likely to limit switching speed or cause 'ringing' in the output voltage. **1978** *Gramophone* Jan. 1336/2 There is no suggestion of overshoot or ringing, showing that the amplifier is extremely stable and has a good damping factor.

4. ringing tone *Teleph.*, the sound produced in a caller's telephone to indicate that connection has been made to another telephone and it is ringing.

1924 W. Aitken *Automatic Telephone Syst.* III. lvi. 272 A portion of the ringing current also passes over the upper condenser,..and the caller receives the ringing tone. **1943** G. Greene *Ministry of Fear* i. v. 80 He dialled the number... He was almost afraid to hear the ringing tone. **1970** T. Lewis *Jack's Return Home* 181 The ringing tone only went once before someone lifted the receiver.

ringle-ji·ngle, *v.* *nonce-wd.* [f. Ringle *v.*[2] + Jingle *v.*] *intr.* To write in verse.

1913 G. B. Shaw *Let.* 7 Feb. in *B. Shaw & Mrs. Campbell* (1952) 83, I never have to think of how to say anything in prose... Yet, when I want frightfully to ringle-jingle with words they wont come that way.

ring-master. Add: (Further examples.) Also as *v. trans.*

1943 C. H. Ward-Jackson *Piece of Cake* 51 *Ringmaster*, squadron commander. **1952** L. Bell *Inside Fight Game* iv. 73 A match maker can be, and often is, the promoter of a boxing show. His license also permits him to officiate as ringmaster. **1958** F. C. Avis *Boxing Ref. Dict.* 95 *Ringmaster*, the official in charge of the arrangements at a boxing venue. **1964** *New Statesman* 17 Apr. 616/1 To bring off this effect, *Caligula* needs producing as a kind of play-within-itself: a fantastic circus of cruelty ring-mastered by Caligula for a circle of witnesses as sane as he is. **1969** P. West *Words for Deaf Daughter* iii. 72 Speeding up, you ringmaster him [*sc.* a budgerigar] through his full repertoire of forward rolls and swift, thudding vaults.

1972 *N.Y. Times* 4 June v. 9/6 James Fallon, the manager, and C. L. (Honey) Craven, the ringmaster, both expressed their pleasure with the new surface. 'The new ring makes things much easier for the rider,' said Fallon.

Hence **ri·ngmastership**, the art or status of a ringmaster; also *fig.*

1966 *Economist* 22 Oct. 378/2 That they did not do so during last week's conference was due in considerable measure to some masterly ringmastership on the part of the party chairman, Sir Dan Mason. **1969** *Daily Tel.* 6 Oct. 15/7 Most circuses get by without script-writers but this one had five, doubling up as clowns performing what they had written under the ringmastership of Ian McNaughton.

ring-neck, *sb.* Add: **1. a.** Also, a ring-necked pheasant, etc.

1921, 1965 [see *MONGOLIAN *a.* 4].

ring-net, *sb.* Add: **2. b.** A form of long seine-net which is supported at the ends by separate boats, one of which moves in a circular path towards the other in order to trap the fish within the net, used esp. in the Scottish fishing grounds to catch herring.

1949 MITCHISON & MACINTOSH *Men & Herring* 21 A ring net is about a hundred fathoms long and twenty fathoms deep and mostly set so that the back rope with the corks is almost on the top of the water. **1950** P. F. ANSON *Scots Fisherfolk* vii. 80 Ring-nets have always been the favourite gear employed on the Firth of Clyde and Loch Fyne. **1969** D. B. THOMSON *Seine Net* vii. 131 Most of these [boats] are dual-purpose seine net and ring-net boats... They have a low rail and large fish hold hatch to suit the ring net operation. **1978** M. GRAY *Fishing Industries of Scotland, 1790–1914* vi. 122 With fish from ring-net boats the transports could be in Glasgow by early in the day although the supply from the drift-net boats, slower to unload, would not arrive till later in the day.

So (in sense *2 b) **ri·ng-net** *v. trans.*; hence **ri·ng-netter**, a fishing boat intended for use with ring-nets; **ri·ng-netting** *vbl. sb.*

1936 *Discovery* Dec. 388/1 Scottish West Coast fishermen in Loch Fyne..were engaged in ring-netting herring. **1952** G. MAXWELL *Harpoon at Venture* ii. 47 The Mansons.. brought the first new ring-netter to Mallaig after the war. **1960** WILLIAMSON & BOYD *St. Kilda Summer* i. 23 Cunningham had sent his ring-netter, *A' Mhaighdean Hearrach*, to take us off. **1969** D. B. THOMSON *Seine Net* vii. 131 The mast is stepped so it can be lowered when the vessel is engaged in ring netting. **1978** M. GRAY *Fishing Industries of Scotland, 1790–1914* vi. 120 In the 1830s the drift-net fishermen found, or felt, themselves threatened by a rival body—the fishermen who adopted the technique variously described as 'trawl-', 'seine-' or 'ring-netting'. As a description, 'ring-netting' is probably the most accurate term. In this new form of fishing..two boats operated together, holding the different ends of a net some 150 yards in length; the net was cast as one boat moved from a starting-point near its partner, to form a wide circle as it returned to the original point, and the haul was completed by gradually constricting the circle till the fish were in a concentrated mass ready to be hauled aboard. *Ibid.* 121 It was possible..for ring-netters also to carry drift-nets which they would shoot on occasion.

ringocandy. *nonce-wd.* [? f. RINGO var. ERYNGO or RING *sb.*[1] + *o'* (= of) + CANDY *sb.*[1]] Some kind of confection.

1922 JOYCE *Ulysses* 199 Hot herringpies, green mugs of sack, honeysauces, sugar of roses, marchpane, gooseberried pigeons, ringocandies.

ri·ng-road. [f. RING *sb.*[1] + ROAD *sb.*] A by-pass road encircling a town or urban area.

1928 *Daily Express* 27 Aug. 8/6 London has no form, no symmetry. I suggest that we could give her this by cutting a broad ring-road through the old nineteenth century suburbs. **1933** L. P. ABERCROMBIE *Town & Country Planning* iv. 144 The external Ring road has been frequently made to avoid the destructive widening of an old village. **1942** *Country Life* 9 Oct. 692/3 Among recommendations are..removal of markets from the central areas to positions on the ring road. **1943** FORSHAW & ABERCROMBIE *County of London Plan* iv. 53 We are strongly of the opinion that a relatively fast traffic ring-road is essential. **1952** *Ann. Reg. 1951* 402 The system of arterial ring-roads was abandoned, largely on grounds of cost. **1956** *Sun* (Baltimore) 17 July 12/2 Mr. McVoy establishes a priority system in which the first need is the ring road around the inner city. **1963** *Times* 22 Feb. 5/2 A ring road will surround the new centre and a recently built open market is to be doubled. **1971** *Country Life* 3 June 1377/1, I knew a priest in Tirana who fought the City Council over a plan to drive a ring-road through his church. **1981** B. HINES *Looks & Smiles* 31 They..caught a bus out to the Ring Road where a Trading Estate was being developed.

ringrou·ndabout, *v. nonce-wd.* [RING *v.*[1]] *trans.* To surround.

1922 JOYCE *Ulysses* 189 The faithful hermetists..ringroundabout him.

ringside (ri·ŋsəid). Also **ring side, ring-side.** [f. RING *sb.*[1] + SIDE *sb.*[1]] **a.** The area immediately surrounding a boxing ring or other sports arena; more generally, the area which accommodates spectators; the scene of a sporting activity. Also *transf.*

1866, 1896 [in Dict. s.v. RING *sb.*[1] 15 c]. **1926** [see *BARRERA]. **1930** [see *HOOK-UP]. **1956** B. HOLIDAY *Lady sings Blues* (1973) xix. 159 There at the ring-side was Mrs. Helen Hironimus, the Alderson warden. **1965** *Universe* 15 Oct. 12/4 (*heading*) My conversations at the ringside. **1976** [see *OPENING *ppl. a.* 1 b].

b. *attrib.* and *Comb.*, as *ringside judge*, *table*; **ringside seat**, a seat immediately adjacent to a boxing contest or other sporting activity; also *transf.* and *fig.*

1976 *Scotsman* 15 Dec., The ringside judges may score it a clear victory for Kohl, leader of the Christian Democrats. **1932** *Daily Express* 20 Sept. 19/5, I trust my health will be good when he makes his debut. I want to be in a ringside seat. **1934** WODEHOUSE *Right Ho, Jeeves* xvii. 212 From the fact that he spoke as if he had a hot potato in his mouth without getting the raspberry from the lads in the ringside seats, I deduced that he must be the head master. **1940** *War Illustr.* 19 Jan. 638/3 From our 'ringside' seats in the air, we saw a spectacle which made us heartily glad it was not our duty to attack a British warship! **1947** G. GREENE *19 Stories* 75 Like a bull he was on show, sitting there mournfully in the plaza with his dog, a magnificent spectacle for which we all had ring-side seats. **1975** V. CANNING *Kingsford Mark* viii. 140 Carlo found the rifle... Unseen, he would have a ringside seat. **1929** D. RUNYON in *Cosmopolitan* July 59/1, I see Waldo Winchester, the scribe, sitting at a ringside table all by himself.

Hence **ri·ngsider**, one who occupies a position at a ringside; a spectator.

1898 A. M. BINSTEAD *Pink 'Un & Pelican* iv. 87 Old Jack Baldock, always the noisiest of ringsiders, was howling at the Fulham lad. **1954** C. L. B. HUBBARD *Compl. Dog Breeders' Man.* 202 A woman exhibitor can handle her dog well, feel comfortable, and please the ringsiders..by wearing a simple but practical outfit. **1960** *Times* 28 Sept. 16/6 With money at stake among some ringsiders, not everyone was thinking calmly. **1976** J. SNOW *Cricket Rebel* 113 He spooned a simple catch from a stroke ringsiders described as a 'protective jab'.

ringster. Add: **1.** (Earlier and later examples.)

1875 *Chicago Tribune* 15 Dec. 4/1 The support secured for Mayor Cobb was sufficient..to defeat the unholy alliance of ringsters and politicians by which Boardman's nomination was first obtained. **1908** *Nation* 16 Apr. 344/3 Hereafter the word [grafter] cannot be lightly used as a synonym for any malefactor at the head of a corporation, or any political ringster.

2. *U.S.* A member of a price-ring. Cf. *RING *sb.*[1] 11 a.

1878 *Congress. Rec.* 20 Mar. 1915/1 As the honest contractor will not go into a business where he has to evade the law, the ringster has it all his own way. **1879** *Harper's Mag.* Oct. 717 The inopportune arrival of several cargoes of Texan beef broke the ring and ruined the ringsters. **1904** I. M. TARBELL *Hist. Standard Oil Co.* I. 107 'Deserters', 'ringsters', 'monopolists' were the terms applied.

3. A boxer.

1926 G. CARPENTIER *Art of Boxing* 5 Some 'ringsters'—I use this word in a particular sense, as you will see—have severely battered countenances after a career of a few years as pugilists. **1965** *Eng. Stud.* XLVI. 465 A boxer, among scores of other appellations, may be..a *ringster*.

ringtail, ring-tail. Add: **3. a.** (Later examples.)

1873 'VANDERDECKEN' *Yachts & Yachting* 185 A racing cutter will be fitted with four gaff-topsails, viz., a jib-headed or ring-tail topsail that is set without a yard. **1901** S. H. KING *Dog-Watches* 59 The Victoria, had a throat and peak mainsail instead of the mutton-leg mainsail and ringtail gaff topsail of the Excelsior. **1934** [see *JAMIE GREEN].

4. (Written **ring tail.**) A dog's tail which is curled so as to form nearly a complete circle.

1872 'IDSTONE' *Dog* x. 87 The tail should be of a moderate length,..not curved over the back, not carried low, nor curved at the end like what in Bulldogs is called a 'ring tail'. **1961** J. LANNING *Great Danes* viii. 73 Ring tails are a hereditary fault and were common at one time.

5. *U.S. slang.* A worthless person, a hobo.

1926 *Amer. Speech* I. 652/2 *Ring-tail*, a Hobo who is carrying a 'grouch'. **1931** 'D. STIFF' *Milk & Honey Route* 205 He [*sc.* an unpopular fellow] is also a *ring tail*. Such hobos are often under suspicion. **1935** A. J. POLLOCK *Underworld Speaks* 98/1 *Ring tail*, an ignorant, loud mouthed, vulgar person. **1947** *Amer. Speech* XXII. 214 In the Pacific Theater..the sobriquets applied to the Japanese were particularly hateful, as *ringtails, yellow bastards*, and a host of unprintables.

6. *Austral. slang.* (See quots.)

1941 BAKER *Dict. Austral. Slang* 60 *Ringtail*, a coward. **1943** *Amer. Speech* XVIII. 256 With Americans a *ringtail* is a grouchy person; with Australians he is a coward.

7. *attrib.*, as *ringtail roarer, snorter*, etc., = RING-TAILED *a.* 4 in Dict. and Suppl.

1832 J. K. PAULDING *Westward Ho!* I. xiv. 124, I got tired of making fun of the ringtail roarer. **1859** *Oregon Argus* 10 Dec. 1/1 Here lies James D. Porter, Who lived as he hadn't orter, But as a Methodist exhorter Was a regular ring-tail snorter. **1862** J. R. LOWELL *Biglow Papers* 2nd Ser. 25 My eldes' boy's so took up, wut with the Ringtail Rangers An' settin' in the Jestice-Court for welcomin' o' strangers.

ring-tailed, *a.* Add: **3.** (Further example.) Cf. *RINGTAIL, RING-TAIL 4.

1894 R. B. LEE *Hist. & Descr. Mod. Dogs* (*Non-Sporting Division*) ix. 239 The tail should be..not curved upwards at the end, called 'ring tailed'.

4. *ring-tailed roarer* (earlier and later examples applied to persons). Also in other fanciful collocations, applied to persons and things, as *ring-tailed snorter, squealer*, etc.

1830 *Painesville* (Ohio) *Tel.* 15 June 1/5 *Ringtailed Roarers*, a most violent fellow, a Crockett. **1836** *Crockett's Yaller Flower Almanac* 9, I am a raal ringtailed roarer. **1837** R. M. BIRD *Nick of Woods* I. iii. 56 Stranger, my name's Ralph Stackpole, and I'm a ring-tailed squealer! **1944** B. A. BOTKIN *Treas. Amer. Folklore* i. 175 The ring-tailed roarer is a comic version of the frontiersman who wrestles single-handed with the wilderness. **1947** *Chicago Tribune* 2 Nov. IV. 9/2 The 'ring-tailed Roarers' of the pioneer days shout their raucous delight, unsubtle, earthy, outlandish, direct. **1950** *Ithaca* (N.Y.) *Jrnl.* 1 Aug. 6/2 You'll have to hand it to this..secretary of agriculture... He's a ring-tailed snorter. **1972** J. MOSHER *Adultery* IV. xxiii. 190 Listen to that wind coming up, would you? She's a ring-tailed snorter.

ring-wall. Add: Also **ringwall, ring wall.**

1. a. (Later examples.) Also *fig.*

1944 *Cape Times* 25 Oct., In trade they did not want the ring-wall of the British Empire round them. **1950** H. L. LORIMER *Homer & Monuments* i. 27 A ring-wall of slabs was erected round the graves on the new level. **1963** L. F. CHITTY in Foster & Alcock *Culture & Environment* vii. 175 When its site was first 'bull-dozed' in 1947, the ruins of a broad ring-wall were revealed, constructed of local tilestones. **1970** I. PETITE *Meander to Alaska* II. xi. 111 He was in the process of repairing the foundation [of a house] with a concrete ring wall.

b. A roughly circular eminence surrounding a crater or mare on the moon or a similar formation on the earth, freq. of volcanic origin.

1950 W. LEY *Conquest of Space* 86 Copernicus is probably the most beautiful of all lunar craters. Its ringwall is 12,000 feet high at the highest point; its diameter is 56 miles. **1962** E. A. VINCENT tr. *Rittmann's Volcanoes* iii. 122 Ring-walls (ramparts) with outflows of lava are common. **1966** *Earth-Sci. Rev.* I. 231 The continents [on the Moon] are very mountainous and the mountains and lesser eminences generally form parts of the 'ringwalls' of maria and craters. **1968** R. W. FAIRBRIDGE *Encycl. Geomorphol.* 682/2 The island [*sc.* Makatea] rises on all sides from very deep water with a fringing reef.., bounded in the inner side by an abrupt or overhanging cliff of ancient coral limestone... To the inside again, there is a second cliff.., and a second rocky terrace. Within this ring-wall is a moat-like depression.

ringway (ri·ŋwē[i]). [f. RING *sb.*[1] + WAY *sb.*[1]] A circular system of major roads round a town or urban area.

1969 *Daily Tel.* 16 Apr. 17/6 The council's plans for ringways were absolutely essential if London was to remain a major world city. **1970** [see *ORBITAL *a.* 3]. **1971** *New Scientist* 8 July 102/2 Terence Bendison describes the traffic-swept gulf between Shepherds Bush and Holland Park, where part of the inner ringway has been imposed on streets and houses. **1973** R. BUSBY *Pattern of Violence* vi. 96 The familiar streets..down the east ringway to the Queen's underpass.

ri·ngwise, *adv.* [f. RING *sb.*[1] + WISE *sb.*[1] II.] In the form of a ring or rings; so as to produce a ring-shape.

1889 *Lancet* 3 Aug. 244/1 Their foreheads are tattooed ringwise, with singularly shaped cuttings in the skin. **1915** E. R. LANKESTER *Diversions of Naturalist* 101 Backbone-pieces and the body muscles attached ring-wise to them. **1922** JOYCE *Ulysses* 62 Pepper. He sprinkled it through his fingers, ringwise, from the chipped eggcup.

ringy, *a.*[1] Add: Also **ringey. 2.** *N. Amer. slang.* Irritable, contentious, angry.

1932 *South of Market Tribune* (San Francisco) 23 Dec. 22 Nothing will make the boss more ringey. **1934** M. C. BOATRIGHT *Tall Tales from Texas* 30 He's a good-natured bird and don't git ringy about it. **1942** BERREY & VAN DEN BARK *Amer. Thes. Slang* § 284/6 *Ill-tempered*..ringy. **1955** R. P. HOBSON *Nothing too Good for Cowboy* xviii. 187 To take some of the snoose out of the ringy Batnuni bunch [of cattle]. **1962** [see *ONERY, ONNERY, O'N'RY]. **1977** *N.Y. Times* 11 Jan. 20/1 He thought Miss Longet had been 'ringy' the day she shot and killed Mr. Sabich.

rink, *sb.*[2] Add: **2. b.** (Later examples.)

1968 *Globe & Mail* (Toronto) 3 Feb. 35/5 Webb, whose rink is composed of Jean Dye, Bill and Helen Ferguson, scored 39 points for its three wins. **1976** *S. Wales Echo* 26 Nov., The only Merthyr rink which returned a winning card was that skipped by Noel Tippett.

3. c. *N. Amer.* A frozen surface on which ice hockey is played. Also, a hall or stadium containing this.

1896 *Times* (Niagara-on-the-Lake, Ont.) 27 Feb. 1/4 The Niagaras..know just how to toss the puck around from one end of the rink to the other in order to score. **1945** W. H. PUGSLEY *Saints, Sinners & Ordinary Seamen* 90 In the early months of the war..ratings lived in a converted hockey rink. **1953** *Canad. Geogr. Jrnl.* XLVI 138/2 The children maintain their own open air hockey rink on the ice. **1974** *Plain Dealer* (Cleveland, Ohio) 26 Oct. 5-D/1 The Elysium had been a little rink which could accommodate almost 2,000.

4. A measured strip of bowling-green on which a match is played. Also, the players allotted to a rink.

1864 W. W. MITCHELL *Man. Bowl-Playing* 21 When..any number of players, not exceeding eight, form sides and commence a game, they make what is called a rink. *Ibid.*, The space or division of the Green is also commonly called a rink. **1897** *Encycl. Sport* I. 129/2 *Rink*, (1) a narrow section of a bowling-green, some twenty feet in breadth taken by one party for their game. (2) All the players upon the two sides. (Both terms are more common in Scotland than England.)

1906 *Canadian Mag.* Sept. 475/2 Like curling.., [bowling] permits of an adjournment occasionally in order that..the opposing rinks may 'join' each other and have 'something'. **1975** *Oxf. Compan. Sports & Games* 94/2 The green is divided by boundaries of fine string into six 'rinks' the length of the green and 19 to 21 ft. (5.8–6.4 m.) wide. **1976** *Laws of Game* (Eng. Bowling Assoc.) (ed. 3) 4 The green shall be divided into spaces called rinks, each not more than 19 feet nor less than 18 feet wide.

5. *attrib.* and *Comb.*, as *rink boot, -side*; **rink rat** *N. Amer.*, a youth who seeks casual work at an ice-hockey rink in return for free admission, etc. (see also quot. 1945); **rink string**, a length of string which marks the boundary of a rink on a bowling-green.

c **1885** in M. Johnson *Amer. Advertising* (1960), Childs's Cash Shoe Store. 'Ladies' rink boots' a specialty. **1945** L. Shelly *Jive Talk Dict.* 31 *Rink rat*, skating rink enthusiast. **1965** *Victoria* (B.C.) *Daily Times* 20 July 10/6, I was a rink rat at the Forum. **1970** J. H. Gray *Boy from Winnipeg* 51 Two Fort Rouge schoolboys from the Kennedy rink rats eventually made good as professionals. **1916** A. Bridle *Sons of Canada* 26 The genial boss..sits in his fur-lined greatcoat at the rinkside. **1972** 'E. Lathen' *Murder without Icing* (1973) ii. 17 He was at rinkside. On the ice, the New York Huskies were having a workout. **1960** R. Williams *Border Country* iv. 113 Harry went up to the bowling green to..set out the rink-strings and the mats.

rink, *v.* Add: (Earlier and later examples.) Also *trans.* (in quot. *fig.*).

1877 H. Sidgwick in A. & E. M. Sidgwick *Henry Sidgwick* (1907) v. 326, I 'rinked' or 'runk' (I do not know how the verb is conjugated)... It is not half as amusing as real skating. **1909** 'W. N. P. Barbellion' *Jrnl.* 25 Dec. (1919) 24, I..idly scan magazines in the Library and occasionally rink—with palpitation of the heart as a consequence. **1946** R. Campbell *Talking Bronco* 25 The zephyr from the blue nevadas, Stirruped with kestrels, smoothly rinking The level wave where halcyons drowse.

rinker (ri·ŋkəɹ). *dial. rare.* [f. *rink*, dial. var. Ring *sb.*[1] + -er[1]: cf. *ring* a circle into which marbles are thrown (*Sc. Nat. Dict.*) and Ringer[1] 1.] A marble (see quot.[1]); a game of marbles.

1910 A. Bennett *Clayhanger* i. i. 6 They were not the paltry marble of today, plaything of infants, but the majestic 'rinker', black with white spots, the king of marbles in an era when whole populations practised the game. *Ibid.* 9 The open gates of a manufactory disclosed six men playing the noble game of rinkers on a smooth patch of ground... They were celebrated marble-players, and..they shot the rinkers from their stubby thumbs with a cannon-like force and precision.

rinkite (ri·ŋkəit). *Min.* [ad. Sw. *rinkit* (J. Lorenzen 1884, in *Öfversigt af k. vetensk. Förh.* 111), f. the name of Henrik Johannes *Rink* (1819–93), Danish geologist and explorer: see -ite[1].] A silicate mineral similar to (or identical with) mosandrite, found as reddish- or yellowish-brown crystals from Greenland.

1886 *Jrnl. Chem. Soc.* L. 676 Rinkite. **1887** *Mineral. Mag.* VII. 234 Fluorite is fairly abundant, and also two of the rarer minerals—laavenite and rinkite. **1937** *Mineral. Abstr.* VI. 179 Rinkite from Greenland gave sp. gr. 3.458 and an orthorhombic cell..containing two molecules $[SiO_4]_2[(Ti, Ce)F]\ Ca_2Na$. **1971** *Ann. Rep. Delegates Sci. Area Univ. Oxford 1970* 131 Accessions... Rinkite..from south-west Greenland. **1971** *Acta Crystallogr.* B. XXVII. 1277 Rinkite, $(Ti,Nb,Al,Zr)(Na,Ca)_3(Ca,Ce)_4(Si_2O_7)_2(O,F)_4$ approximately, is a silicate crystallizing in the monoclinic system.

rinktum (ri·ŋktəm). *rare. Southern U.S. dial.* alteration of Rectum.

1929 W. Faulkner *Sound & Fury* 86 You know what I'll do. I'll skin your rinktum.

rinky-dink (ri·ŋkidiŋk), *sb.* and *a. slang* (chiefly *U.S.*). Also **rinkey-dink, rinkydink, rinky-dinky.** [Orig. unknown: cf. *ricky-tick *sb.* and *a.*]

A. *sb.* Something that is worn out or antiquated; a worthless object. *spec.* a cheap place of entertainment. Also in phr. *to give* (someone) *the rinky-dink* and varr., to cheat or swindle (someone).

1912 A. H. Lewis *Apaches N.Y.* xii. 265 They was lyin'.. an' givin' each other th' rinkey-dink in th' old days same as now. **1922** J. A. Dunn *Man Trap* i. 8 Jimmy abhorred mining corporations with a lot of stockholders and a few of those liable at any moment to hand you the rinky-dink and freeze you out by due process of legal indifference toward small-fry claimants. **1942** *Harper's Bazaar* July 21/2 Don't give me the rinkydink. **1951** *Atlantic Monthly* Mar. 80/1, I think of Sweet Mama Stringbean as she was called when she played the Rinky-dinks for $25 a week. **1956** S. Longstreet *Real Jazz* 147 *Rinky-dink* is broken-down stuff. **1969** *New Yorker* 1 Nov. 6/2 *Red Garter*..eighteen-nineties rinky-dink, complete with fire engine, but the banjo band is above average. **1977** *Amer. Speech 1975* L. 65 *Rinky-dink* ..*n*, something that is cheap or worn out. 'His car is a real rinky-dink.'

B. *adj.* Worthless, worn out, trivial; old-fashioned, outmoded.

1913 *Wells Fargo Messenger* I. 105/3 She did not care to ruin her life as a Sunday supplement feature to some rinky-dinky foreign count. **1942** Berrey & Van den Bark *Amer. Thes. Slang* § 675/12 Baseball... *Rinky-dink ball*, inferior playing. **1946** Mezzrow & Wolfe *Really Blues* vii. 87 My struggle-buggy was getting to look like a rinky-dink old tin can on wheels. **1951** E. Waters *His Eye is on Sparrow* vi. 77 Of all those rinky-dink dumps I played, nothing was worse than the Monogram Theatre in Chicago. **1973** *Globe & Mail* (Toronto) 24 Sept. 5/3 He thinks it hasn't been legalized only because of 'rinkydink politics' but he decries other aspects of the drug scene and says he thinks he's kept some of his young patients from getting involved. **1979** *Fortune* 15 Jan. 5 Facet [was]..a rinky-dink outfit with no real resources and not much to offer.

rinky-tink (ri·ŋkitiŋk), *a. slang* (chiefly *U.S.*). [Imitative: cf. prec. and Tink *int.* and *sb.*] Designating a jazz or ragtime piano on which simple, repetitive tunes are played; tinkling, jangling. Cf. *ricky-tick *a.*

1962 E. Lucia *Klondike Kate* ii. 34 A rinky-tink piano or a scratchy gramophone had its intoxicating effect upon her. **1974** *News & Courier* (Charleston, S. Carolina) 25 Apr. 5-a/1 Scott Joplin played his toe-tappers on a rinky-tink piano. **1975** J. Gores *Hammett* (1976) i. 12 A rinky-tink piano was bashing out 'Ja-Da'.

Rinne (ri·nə). *Med.* Also (*erron.*) **Rinné.** The name of Heinrich Adolf *Rinne* (1819–68), German otologist, who described a form of the test in 1855 (*Vierteljahrschr. f. d. prakt. Heilkunde* XLV. 72), used in the possessive, *attrib.*, and *absol.* to designate a diagnostic test for deafness (see quot. 1883).

1883 tr. *Politzer's Text-Bk. Dis. Ear* 693 Rinne's experiment..consists in setting a tuning-fork..on the vertex or on the mastoid process, and allowing it to vibrate till the note is no longer heard; the prongs of the fork are then brought close to the ear, and in normal circumstances the tone will be heard again (positive experiment). **1899** G. Bacon *Man. Otology* ii. 81 Rinné's test... If heard again, which is the case in the normal ear, this is called the positive Rinné test. **1902** tr. *Brühl & Politzer's Atlas & Epitomy Otol.* 87 Positive result of Rinne's experiment, or positive Rinne. **1959** H. A. Newby *Audiol.* iv. 61 If the patient replies affirmatively, the result of the test is said to be a Rinné negative... A Rinné test on a normal ear will yield a positive result. **1974** Passmore & Robson *Compan. Med. Stud.* III. xxxii. 3/2 In conductive deafness, bone conduction is better heard than air conduction and Rinne's test is negative.

rinneite (ri·nə,əit). *Min.* [a. G. *rinneit* (H. E. Boeke 1908, in *Chem. Zeitung* XXXII. 1228), f. the name of Friedrich *Rinne* (1863–1933), German mineralogist: see -ite[1].] A rhombohedral chloride of iron, potassium, and sodium, $K_3FeNaCl_6$, which is known as colourless, pale rose, violet, or yellow granular masses from saline deposits, and can be prepared artificially.

1909 *Jrnl. Chem. Soc.* XCVII. ii. 153 Rinneite... An anhydrous mineral..has been found in considerable quantities at the Nordhäusen Works. **1953** *Q. Jrnl. Geol. Soc.* CVIII. 289 At Rockhead the marl is much richer in rinneite and carnallite than at the other boreholes. Several coarse, colourless to yellow, rinneite inclusions..were found. **1970** *Rocks & Minerals* XLV. 376/1 Rinneite has been reported as a secondary mineral in the salt mine at Winnfield Dome.

‖**Rinpoche** (ri·npǫtʃe). Also **Rimpoche,** etc. [Tibetan, lit. 'precious (jewel)'.] An honorific title given to a chief priest among Tibetan Buddhists. Cf. *panchen.

1774 G. Bogle *Narr. Mission to Tibet* (1876) iii. 26 A tower, about five or six stories high,..is appropriated to Lama-Rimboché. **1784** S. Turner *Let.* 2 Mar. in *Acct. of Embassy to Court of Teshoo Lama in Tibet* (1800) iii. 364 The death of Gesub Rimbochay, offered a new prospect of opening..communication. **1800,** etc. [see *panchen.] **1863** tr. *E. Schlagintweit's Buddhism in Tibet* xii. 153 The *Panchen Rinpoche* is considered to be an incarnation of Chenresi's celestial father, Amitābha. **1882** *Encycl. Brit.* XIV. 23/1 The Dalai Lāma..is actually called the *Gyalpo Rinpotshe*, 'the glorious king',—his companion being content with the title *Pantshen Rinpotshe*, 'the glorious teacher'. **1889** M. Monier-Williams *Buddhism* xi. 284 The other Grand Lāma who resides in the monastery of Tashi Lunpo.. has the Tibetan title of Panchen Rinpoche (Pañ-ćen Rin-po-će), 'the great Paṇḍit Jewel'. **1929** D. Macdonald *Land of Lama* ii. 43 This cleric..was now allowed to assume the incarnation of Buddha Amitabha, with the title of *Panchen Rimpoche* or 'Precious Gem of Learning'. **1980** D. Hart-Davis *Heights of Rimring* xvi. 174 Access to the monastery could be gained only by means of a contraption which the *rinpoches*, the lamas, let down on a rope.

rinse, *sb.* Add: **2. c.** A solution (or cream) which temporarily tints or conditions the hair. Also, an application of this.

1928 *Daily Mail* 25 July 3/6 Though the price of Icilma Shampoos remains at 3d., each packet now contains a wonderful Toning Rinse suitable for every shade of hair, which removes *all trace of lather*, and leaves the hair in a state of exquisite burnished beauty. **1942** M. Dickens *One Pair of Feet* ix. 189, I think I shall go and have a platinum rinse next payday. **1944** M. Laski *Love on Supertax* x. 93, I think I'll have a blue rinse to-day. **1948** M. Sturges-Jones *In Wedlock Wake* 137 Why don't you try a blond rinse?.. It wouldn't make you look bleached. **1949** N. Mitford *Love in Cold Climate* 221 A blue rinse for her grey hair. **1958** J. Cannan *And be a Villain* vii. 155 Age must be disguised, hushed up with dyes and rinses. **1959** *Spectator* 24 Sept. 394/3 Women..with bitter-sweet smiles and blue-rinse bobs. **1962** D. Lessing *Golden Notebk.* iii. 345 'I did try a rinse,' he remarked, 'but the grey shows through.' **1977** B. Pym *Quartet in Autumn* i. 2 Letty knew that there were white hairs interspersed with the brown and that most people would have had a brightening 'rinse' anyway.

3. In *Comb.*, as **rinse-aid** (see quot. 1963).

1963 *Which?* 6 Feb. 50/1 Five [dishwashing] machines.. supplied rinse aids. These are liquids added to the final rinse water to make it flow more easily and prevent it from remaining as drops on the surface. **1970** *Ibid.* Oct. 294/1 Some detergents—or rinse aids—leave a white deposit on everything.

rinse, *v.* Add: **4. c.** Const. *out*. Also *absol.*

1953 [see *drip-dry *v.*]. **1976** M. Millar *Ask for Me Tomorrow* (1977) xvi. 132 You're not helpless. Can't you rinse out your own socks?

d. To treat (hair) with a rinse. Cf. *rinse *sb.* 2 c. Also *absol.*

1959 N. Lofts *Heaven in your Hand* 125 His mother, of course, used make-up too, and had her hair 'rinsed' and waved. **1962** J. Braine *Life at Top* xiii. 170 Tom was..very proud of his mane of white hair... There were some people in Dufton who said that he blue rinsed it a little. **1971** M. Kelly *25th Hour* i. 53 Louise's hair seemed to go an elegant grey all at once (she rinses a bit of course).

Rinyo-Clacton (ri·nyo,klæ·ktən), *a. Archæol.* [f. the place-names *Rinyo*, Orkney + *Clacton*, Essex.] Of, pertaining to, or designating the culture represented by Late Neolithic grooved ware first discovered at Rinyo and Clacton.

1954 S. Piggott *Neolithic Cultures Brit. Isles* x. 280 *The Rinyo-Clacton culture.* Defined originally by 'Grooved ware'..the culture has a curious distribution, mainly concentrated in two separate areas, one in south-east England and the other in the Orkneys, though intermediate sites are now being discovered. **1963** E. S. Wood *Collins Field Guide Archaeol.* ii. ii. 105 The northern branch of the Rinyo-Clacton culture..have left in Orkney remains from which a fairly complete picture of their economy can be built up: at Skara Brae and at Rinyo are groups of squarish stone huts. **1967** *Antiquaries Jrnl.* XLVII. 182 Rustication as a decorative motif can occur on three styles of British Late Neolithic pottery—on Beakers, Fengate Ware, and Grooved or Rinyo-Clacton ware. **1970** Bray & Trump *Dict. Archæol.* 256/1 To the Late Neolithic belong the highly decorated wares of Peterborough and Rinyo-Clacton styles.

rio, var. *ryo.

Rioja (rio·ha). Also **rioja.** [The name of a district of northern Spain.] A wine produced in this district.

1907 *Yesterday's Shopping* (1969) 96/1 *Claret*..Rioja (Spanish), per dozen flagons 21/9. **1920** G. Saintsbury *Notes on Cellar-bk.* ii. 18 Other light Spanish wines of this class (of the Riojas, etc., we may speak separately) are excellent. *Ibid.* vi. 89 White Rioja (a capital beverage liquor). **1926** E. Hemingway *Sun also Rises* xix. 257 We had roast young suckling pig and drank *rioja alta*. **1934** R. Macaulay *Going Abroad* xxiii. 182 Wicker flasks of rioja. **1951** R. Postgate *Plain Man's Guide to Wine* vii. 108 Of table wines which a foreigner may be offered, Rioja ('J' pronounced as 'H') is..a full, strong wine produced in the north, mostly red and with a heavy plush-like flavour. **1965** G. Household *Olura* 157 Allarte's capacity for red Rioja, anchovies and bread was astonishing. **1973** *Country Life* 26 Apr. 1162/1 Rioja..comes from the north of the country, about 100 miles south of the western Pyrenees. *Ibid.* 1162/3 There is both red and white Rioja..and the red is certainly the more distinguished.

riometer (ri,ǫ·mitəɹ, rəi·ǫmitəɹ). *Geophysics.* [f. the initial letters of *r*elative *i*onospheric *o*pacity + -meter.] An instrument which permits continuous measurement of the absorption of cosmic radio waves by the ionosphere.

1959 Little & Leinbach in *Proc. IRE* XLVII. 315/2 Thirteen of the commercially built units, now called 'riometers' (Relative Ionospheric Opacity Meters) are currently in use... The riometer is a self-balancing receiving system in which a local noise source is continuously made equal to the noise power from the antenna. **1968** G. M. B. Dobson *Explor. Atmos.* (ed. 2) viii. 151 An entirely different method which is now being much used is to measure the intensity of cosmic radio waves which are constantly reaching the earth from the galaxy. These radio waves will be absorbed as they come down through the D region, so that low intensity of cosmic radio waves received at the ground means strong absorption by the D region. These instruments are generally known as riometers. **1972** *Nature* 28 Jan. 215/1 Ground based observations using a 27 MHz riometer and an H magnetometer indicated almost quiet ionospheric conditions. **1980** *Ibid.* 17 Jan. 278/2 The Siple riometer operates at 30 MHz and has a response time of 0.25 s to increases or decreases in signal intensity.

‖**rione** (*rio·ne*). Pl. **rioni.** [It.] A district or administrative division of Rome. Cf. Region 5.

1927 *Daily Express* 23 Nov. 12 Nine new fountains have been inaugurated in Rome, each corresponding to a rione, or section of the city. **1936** G. F.-H. & J. Berkeley *Italy in Making* II. vii. 115 The orders were sent out to the heads of each of the rioni (fourteen in number) in Rome. Each head of a rione sent his orders to his capi-squadra (heads of squadrons). **1965** C. Hibbert *Garibaldi & his Enemies* i. iv. 50 In every *rione* deputies were appointed to take command of the citizens when the bells of the Capitol and Montecitorio summoned them to arms. **1979** *Jrnl. R. Soc. Arts* Nov. 775/1 The triangular shed..is a new social centre meant to revive and support a local form of civic organization, the *rione*, an alternative to the centralized bureaucracy, church and *municipio*.

riot, *sb.* Add: **2. d.** (Further examples.)
1969 *Morning Star* 9 July 4/3 The trees are flourishing better than ever, and the borders have been a riot of colour. **1974** 'S. WOODS' *Done to Death* 184 The garden was a riot of colour.

4. c. *to read the Riot Act* (also with small initials): in *transf.* use, to announce or declare that (unruly) action or conduct must cease; to reprimand or caution sternly.
The Riot Act was repealed in 1973.
1819 W. BRADFORD *Let.* 17 Dec. in M. Wilmot *More Lett.* (1935) 39 She has just run out to read the riot act in the Nursery. **1842** C. FOX *Jrnl.* 18 Apr. (1972) 123 Sydney Smith said, 'Lady Holland is not one woman, but a multitude; just read the Riot Act and you'll presently see them disperse!' **1906** J. LONDON *Let.* 20 Oct. (1966) 211 You might have found out, before you read me the riot act. **1946** D. HAMSON *We fell among Greeks* xvii. 187, I met the E.D.E.S. envoys and read them the riot act, so to speak. **1976** P. HILL *Hunters* x. 131 Read her the riot act, tell her to be a good girl and take her home.

d. *colloq.* (orig. *Theatr.*). Something extremely successful or amusing; *spec.* an uproariously successful performance or show, a 'smash hit'. Also of persons.
1909 P. G. WILLIAMS in *Sat. Even. Post* 5 June 17/2 *A riot*, great success. **1919** F. HURST *Humoresque* 195 If you think that is a riot..you wait until you see the way they're going to eat me up in the court scene. **1929** J. B. PRIESTLEY *Good Companions* II. i. 249 There isn't a more promising little show anywhere... It could have been an absolute riot. **1933** N. STREATFEILD *Tops & Bottoms* xxii. 287 He was a riot. **1936** P. QUENTIN *Puzzle for Fools* xxvi. 253 He'd be a riot in a mental hospital. **1943** J. B. PRIESTLEY *Daylight on Saturday* xv. 101 These shows—they're a riot. **1959** E. H. CLEMENTS *High Tension* viii. 134 Get that word-perfect.. and you'll be a riot tomorrow. **1976** J. SNOW *Cricket Rebel* 110 His rendering of 'Barnacle Bill the Sailor' was a riot and became his party piece.

e. In full, *riot sale.* A sale. *U.S. slang.*
1952 *N.Y. Post* 26 Sept. 73/1 (Advt.), Auto 'riot' sale. **1969** *Punch* 5 Feb. 193/1 Some of New York's stores are having a shoe riot.

5. *attrib.* and *Comb.* **a.** General attrib. uses (sense 4), as *riot area, call, control, zone*; **b.** designating equipment worn or carried (esp. by peace-keeping forces) in a riot, as *riot equipment, gear, gun, helmet, shield, stick*; also (parasynthetically) *riot-helmeted* adj.; also of persons or vehicles equipped to quell riots, as *riot police, squad, tank, van, wagon*; **c.** in instrumental, etc., uses, as *riot-battered, -prone, -ripe, -scarred, -torn* adjs.; **d. riot gas**, an irritant gas fired in capsules into a mob to quell rioting, tear-gas.
1973 *Freedom* 2 June 3/1 No one who lives in the riot areas of Belfast needs any reminders of what violence can look like. **1976** *Daily Times* (Lagos) 27 Aug. 9/2 Unofficial reports said 20 bodies were found in the riot battered township on Wednesday. **1905** *N.Y. Even. Post* 7 Nov. 2 Charges of illegal voting resulted in a disturbance which police were unable to subdue, and a riot call was sent in. **1964** KIRK & OTHMER *Encycl. Chem. Technol.* (ed. 2) IV. 877 In the last few years, an agent, CS, has been developed for riot control. **1974** *North Myrtle Beach* (S. Carolina) *Times* 17 Apr. 1/5 The riot control unit then had to make its way to Hillside Drive and make a similar sweep to quell trouble spots on that street. **1955** H. KURNITZ *Invasion of Privacy* (1956) xii. 79 The old man is handing out riot equipment and orders are shoot to kill. **1968** *Punch* 4 Dec. 804/1 Jelly-crazed five-year-olds can now be quietened with a discreet blast of MACE lavender-perfumed riot gas. **1969** *Guardian* 22 Jan. 1/3 A powerful fragmentation grenade which will scatter CS riot gas among demonstrators is being developed by the Ministry of Technology. **1978** *N.Y. Times* 30 Mar. A5/6 Thousands of policemen..in riot gear. **1930** *Morning Post* 9 Apr. 11 Detectives in motor-cars equipped with 'riot guns' toured through the districts where violence was anticipated. **1976** 'B. SHELBY' *Great Pebble Affair* 49 Officer Hodgson with his riot gun. **1969** S. GREENLEE *Spook who sat by Door* xiii. 112 Watching the police in riot helmets and the angry faces of the crowd. **1973** 'S. HARVESTER' *Corner of Playground* III. v. 212 Tight-lipped young officers, whites of eyes gleaming under rim of riot-helmet. **1970** *Daily Tel.* 18 Apr. 5/3 Three young women were wounded by shotgun pellets when 200 riot-helmeted, sheriff's deputies dispersed a crowd of about 700 smashing windows at a bank. **1958** *Daily Sketch* 2 June 2/5 Riot police armed with rifles, machine-guns and tear-gas tensed for an attack by Communist demonstrators. **1977** *Times* 18 Feb. 7/5 Riot police took control of Rome University tonight after using tear gas to disperse angry left-wing students. **1967** *Economist* 7 Oct. 45/2 Property-owners in riot-scarred (and riot-prone) neighbourhoods. **1968** *Ibid.* 20 July 40/3 Many state capitals are now humming with reports of 'mass' cancellations by insurers of policies covering property in riot-prone areas. **1910** KIPLING *Rewards & Fairies* 103 Tom Dunch an' some of his kidney was drinkin' themselves riot-ripe. **1965** *Jet* 16 Sept. 50 Martin Luther King, Jr. was forced to invoke the name of Elijah Muhammed to gain a hearing in the riot-scarred community of Watts. **1967** Riot-scarred [see *riot-prone* above]. **1967** *Economist* 7 Jan. 31/1 (*caption*) Calcutta police behind riot shields. **1968** *Guardian* 21 Oct. 18/7 Mr Callaghan has issued no instructions to the Commissioner of the Metropolitan Police,..about the use of tear gas, water cannon, riot shields, troops, or other weapons familiar to demonstrators in Paris. **1978** *Peace News* 25 Aug. 4/1 The police included a large contingent of the Special Patrol Group with riot shields. **1981** *Daily Tel.* 3 Mar. 2/1 Police, some with riot shields and crowbars, stormed the building. **1948** *New Yorker* 1 May 75/1 A trio of jeeps, bringing the *celere*, or riot squad. **1955** *Times* 25 Aug. 9/2 The requirements for this are good intelligence arrangements and a mobile riot squad such as the strategic reserve in Cyprus will provide. **1977** *New Yorker* 24 Oct. 132/3 The prison's three riot squads..officially called..correctional emergency-response teams. **1930** J. DOS PASSOS *42nd Parallel* v. 404 He'd been halfstunned by a riotstick. **1972** R. PERRY *Fall Guy* i. 28 The police arrived..with their riot sticks in evidence..lead-weighted batons. **1978** D. FRANCIS *Trial Run* xi. 156 They were armed..with riot sticks. Nasty hard things like baseball bats, swinging from a loop of leather round the wrist. **1966** L. COHEN *Beautiful Losers* I. 134 It is not enough that she and Prince Philip will be greeted by police cordons, riot tanks, and the proud backs of hostile crowds. **1969** C. HIMES *Black on Black* (1973) 286 The riot tank didn't know where to look for him. **1968** *Economist* 12 Oct. 3/2 The..riot-torn country of Northern Ireland. **1976** *Ulverston* (Cumbria) *News* 3 Dec. (Suppl.) p. i/3 *Shoot!*..Containing articles by well-known footballers, the 'lowdown' on the riot-torn 1975 European Cup Final. **1981** *Yorks. Post* 9 July 1/3 Prince Charles wants to help youngsters in Liverpool's riot-torn Toxteth area. **1973** J. DRUMMOND *Bang! Bang! You're Dead!* xxxiv. 116 There were extra police on duty, and several riot vans under the trees. **1976** J. MCCLURE *Rogue Eagle* xiv. 234 There were a couple of riot vans double-parked outside. **1969** *Guardian* 5 Aug. 1/7 Finally riot wagons were moved in to block the oblique junction. **1973** *Black Panther* 28 July 3/2 Police arrived in buses and riot wagons. **1975** R. H. RIMMER *Premar Experiments* (1976) i. 56 According to my informant, Bren and Merle were living in a rundown tenement house in the 'riot zone'.

riot, *v.* Add: **II. 6. b.** To engage in a riot or violent disturbance.
1755 JOHNSON, *To Riot*..4. To raise a sedition or uproar. *a* **1832**, etc. [implied in RIOTING *vbl. sb.* 2]. **1981** W. EBERSOHN *Divide the Night* v. 71 When they [*sc.* blacks] rioted they did it with greater anger here [*sc.* in Johannesburg] than anywhere else. **1981** *Yorks. Post* 9 July 4/5 As thoroughly decent a group of people as you would wish to meet, they did not riot in the streets.

7. *Hunting.* = *to run riot* s.v. RIOT *sb.* 3 a. Also const. *after, on.*
1954 J. I. LLOYD *Beagling* 143 *Riot*, to hunt anything other than their legitimate quarry. **1971** *Country Life* 7 Oct. 897/1 Hounds will riot more readily after roe deer than any other species. **1976** *Horse & Hound* 3 Dec. 38/1 A great deal of time would be spent, however, correcting the pack rioting on Scotch sheep.

rioty (rəi·əti), *a. nonce-wd.* [f. RIOT *sb.* + -Y[1].] Riotous; noisy, rackety.
1819 KEATS *Let.* 20 Sept. (1958) II. 206 Bless the child, how rioty she is!

rip, *sb.*[4] **3.** (Earlier and further examples.) Also *U.S.*, esp. in *Music.* Also *transf.*, a burst (of laughter).
1855 *Knickerbocker* XLV. 129 List to the rip and the roar of the song. **1867** 'T. LACKLAND' *Homespun* II. 271 Sometimes he could not help giving a rip of laughter that drew the eyes of the whole school round to him in an instant. **1933** *Metronome* Mar. 34 The rip is produced by short and quick glissando up to the tone, attacked sforzando and cut off quickly. **1961** A. BERKMAN *Singers' Gloss. Show Business* 75 *Rip*, an effect in which the entire band plays a fast glissando up to a heavily accented note to emphasize or punctuate a violent action or thought.

4. *U.S. police slang.* (See quots.)
1939 *Fortune* July 101/3 An inspector's lieutenant.. found the patrolman lounging with his gloves off, smoking a cigarette. Probable penalty: one day's 'rip' (fine of a day's pay). **1958** *N.Y. Times Mag.* 16 Mar. 88/3 Rip—A fine imposed for infraction of police regulations: e.g., 'I got a five-day rip' (fined five days' pay).

5. *attrib.* **rip cord**, (*a*) *Aeronaut.* = **ripping cord*; (*b*) *Aeronaut.*, a cord which holds a parachute pack closed and which, when pulled, opens the pack and allows the parachute to unfold and inflate; (*c*) *fig.*; **rip line, panel, valve** *Aeronaut.* = *ripping line, panel, valve* s.v. *RIPPING *vbl. sb.* 2 b.
1909 V. LOUGHEED *Vehicles of Air* 108 Practically a valve is the 'rip cord', by means of which a seam running along the side of a balloon can be laid open. **1911** *Sci. Amer.* 25 Mar. 300/1 In case of accident the aviator, by pulling a rip cord, can open the parachute. **1925** [see *pilot chute* s.v. *PILOT *sb.* 6]. **1946** W. F. BURBIDGE *From Balloon to Bomber* 40 In 1908, an American parachutist, invented a 'free parachute'... The parachute was packed into a container worn on the airman's chest and released by a whale-bone spring operated by a rip-cord. **1969** *Daily Colonist* (Victoria, B.C.) 7 Feb. 36/1 'Then you'd better put on a parachute if you're afraid,' Beachel said. 'How does the chute work?' Till asked. 'Where is the rip-cord?' **1974** [see *ripping line* s.v. *RIPPING *vbl. sb.* 2 b]. **1975** 'D. JORDAN' *Black Account* I. xix. 100 He was big..and wide but ripcord lean. **1981** W. WINWARD *Ball Bearing Run* ix. 111 It would be necessary to fall clear of the bomber stream before pulling the rip-cord. **1963** A. SMITH *Throw out Two Hands* viii. 95 Above it [*sc.* the basket of a balloon].. were the valve line (for gentle release of gas) and the rip line (for a total release of gas). **1933** *Sun* (Baltimore) 22 Nov. 2/7 Rather than take a chance on crossing the bay with his diminishing gas, he pulled the rip panel and down they came. **1963** A. SMITH *Throw out Two Hands* v. 63 You lose the rope. Then you pull it again, and this time you can feel it jerking open the rip panel. **1978** A. WELCH *Bk. of Airsports* v. 81/1 For this purpose a rip panel is built into the balloon near the top and is kept closed with either a parachute rip or Velcro. **1907** *Jrnl. Soc. Arts* 19 Apr. 602/2 By means of the rip valve they were able to come down pleasantly and easily.

rip, *sb.*[5] Add: **1. b.** *ellipt.* = **rip current.*
1941 *Jrnl. Geol.* XLIX. 338 The term 'rip' might also be used as an abbreviation, which removes the unfortunate tidal connotation of the popular term 'rip tide'. **1968** R. W. FAIRBRIDGE *Encycl. Geomorphol.* 950/2 The width of the central 'trunk' of the rip can be quite narrow, perhaps only a few tens of feet, but the effect of the current can sometimes be detected up to a mile or more from the shore. **1968** W. WARWICK *Surfriding in N.Z.* 20/2 Remember to dive beneath broken waves and do not swim against rips, they will only take you a short distance out to sea before fading out. **1977** *Herald* (Melbourne) 17 Jan. 6/9 He was helping to rescue four people caught in a rip when the accident happened.

2. (Earlier and later examples). Chiefly *U.S.*
a **1828** in B. JAMES *Jrnl.* (1896) II. 195 We passed several very dangerous places, which they there [on the Kennebec R.] termed 'rips', which was [*sic*] a confused number of rocks and large stones in the direct way we were obliged to pass, and which generally had a fall of some few feet. **1839** E. HOLMES *Explor. Aroostook River* 7 The existing obstacles which present themselves to the present navigation of this river, are, the 'rips', which are occasioned principally by loose boulders of rock. **1941** B. A. WILLIAMS *Strange Woman* III. i. 128 After that we'd skin 'em [*sc.* scurry ducks] out and tie a string to 'em and let 'em hang in rips of the quickest water we could find. **1977** *New Yorker* 9 May 106/3 A couple of tributaries came into the river,..and they deepened the pools and improved the rips.

3. Special Comb.: **rip current**, an intermittent, strong, narrow current on or near the surface of the sea, flowing directly out from the shore and acting to remove water which has been brought to the shore by waves and wind; **rip tide**, (*a*) = **rip current*; (*b*) = sense 1; (*c*) *fig.*
1936 F. P. SHEPARD in *Science* 21 Aug. 181/2 The name 'rip tide' is certainly not appropriate, since the current described has nothing to do with the tide... The name 'rip current' is suggested, since it is close to the other name and describes the way in which the current rips through the oncoming breakers. **1941** *Jrnl. Geol.* XLIX. 339 The chief seaward return of water moved in by the waves seems to be in the form of rip currents. **1957** G. E. HUTCHINSON *Treat. Limnol.* I. v. 358 The usual pattern..is the development of longshore currents which return to the free water at particular points..as rip currents. **1973** *Daily Tel.* 15 Aug. 6/3 He believed a rip current may have been responsible for carrying the 20 bathers out to sea. **1862** Rip tide [in Dict., sense 1]. **1931** *Daily Progress* (Charlottesville, Va.) 26 Aug. 1/2 Surf bathing as a means of avoiding the heat was made unattractive to many because of the possibility of the recurrence of dangerous 'rip tides'. **1936** [see **rip current*]. *a* **1963** S. PLATH *Ariel* (1965) 45 Your stooges..Riding the rip tide to the nearest point of departure. **1970** I. PETITE *Meander to Alaska* I. v. 47 Riptides, eddies,..complicate a cruiser's traffic patterns. **1973** *Sunday Bull.* (Philadelphia) 14 Oct. (Parade Suppl.) 14/4 Probably the toughest rescue I had was a Mexican family unfamiliar with the riptides. They wandered out about 400 yards into the surf, then started yelling. **1976** *New Yorker* 22 Mar. 106/2 Their echoings of Futurism and Expressionism—for example, the riptides of black diagonals in Dove's 'Field of Grain Seen from Train'. **1977** *Time* 28 Mar. 45/3 In Colombia, surging coffee revenues have been accompanied by a riptide of 26% inflation. **1978** J. A. KNAUSS *Introd. Physical. Oceanogr.* x. 219 Rip tides can be dangerous to the unwary swimmer.

rip, *sb.*[6] Add: **2. a.** (Later examples in the milder sense.)
1918 GALSWORTHY *Five Tales* 77 My grandfather lived to be a hundred; my father ninety-six—both of them rips. **1935** S. DESMOND *Afr. Log* ii. 264 A humble repentant sinner—once perhaps 'a bit of a rip'—but very appealing. **1951** *Chambers's Jrnl.* Nov. 656/2 Would you believe it, the old rip had a flutter in Norland Deeps himself?

b. (Further examples.)
1893 G. B. SHAW *Let.* 4 Sept. (1965) I. 404 The mother a most deplorable old rip. **1910** P. W. JOYCE *English as we speak it in Ireland* xiii. 313 *Rip*, a coarse ill-conditioned woman with a bad tongue.

rip, *v.*[2] Add: **I. 1. a.** (Further examples.)
1861 *Once a Week* 10 Aug. 180/1 The joy of ripping out the middle stump of a good batter surpasses even that of wiping a man's eye at an overhead cock-pheasant. **1977** P. HILL *Fanatics* 33 They've ripped out the phone.

b. *slang.* To steal.
1904 'No. 1500' *Life in Sing Sing* 252/1 *Rip*, to steal with impunity. **1970** *Time* 22 June 52/3 For extra, unanticipated personal needs, he 'rips off'—or steals... Some of those who take jobs in department stores or markets steal what they can... Some who work in restaurants or drugstores let their friends in to eat or rip what they need. **1976** *Telegraph* (Brisbane) 20 Apr. 1/3 They believe some have ripped millions of dollars from Medibank since it began. **1977** *Guardian* 23 June 3/4 (Advt.), While the fluff saps the mark, the dip rips the wad.

c. *Baseball.* To score (a hit) in a vigorous manner.
1970 *Washington Post* 30 Sept. D2/5 Renko ripped his run-scoring hit in the second. **1974** *Anderson* (S. Carolina) *Independent* 19 Apr. 5B/4 Designated-hitter Duke Sims.. ripped a run-scoring double over first base.

d. Of a competitor or team: to defeat overwhelmingly. *U.S.*
1974 *State* (Columbia, S. Carolina) 3 Mar. 1-D/6 South Carolina..ripped the Cougars, 104–86, behind a sparkling 37-point performance by Alex English. **1976** *Springfield* (Mass.) *Daily News* 22 Apr. 40/4 Three runaways featured action in the Bi-County League. St. Mary's romped over Westfield Voke, 16–3; Gateway ripped Belchertown, 12–1; Smith School blitzed Holyoke Trade, 12–0. **1978** *Detroit Free Press* 2 Apr. 5E/11 (*heading*) Borg rips Smith, gains WCT finals.

2. a. (Later examples.) Also with *through.*
1930 [*BEST *a.* 7 b]. **1973** 'J. PATRICK' *Glasgow Gang Observed* iii. 30 He had..fifty-nine stitches on the side of his face; he had been 'ripped' only a few weeks ago. **1976**

Honolulu Star-Bull. 21 Dec. H-6/1 Meanwhile, the Davis Cup nations are ripped by political squabbling.

e. To open or release, or to deflate, by the use of a rip cord. Also *absol.*

1902 J. ALEXANDER *Conquest of Air* iii. 54 There was an arrangement for ripping the cover when ready to descend. *Ibid.* 55 They immediately ripped the balloon and commenced their descent. **1907** G. BACON *Record of Aeronaut* xiv. 263 Mr. Spencer was in favour of ripping open the valve. **1920** G. C. BAILEY *Compl. Airman* xxxi. 242 The ripping panel is a specially sewn section of the fabric, a cord lead to which enables the balloonist to rip it at will. **1963** A. SMITH *Throw out Two Hands* xxi. 219, I..remember fumbling for the rip-panel cord... Had I ripped?

3. a. Also *fig.*

1976 *National Observer* (U.S.) 14 Aug. 12/1 What rips you up is the craziness... I felt like, well, since I loved them both, they should love each other. They don't.

d. *Cricket.* Of a ball: to hit (a stump or stumps) on delivery at speed, so as to knock it (or them) back or out of the ground. Also with bowler as subj.

1832 P. EGAN *Bk. Sports* 348/2 She [*sc.* the ball]..Ripp'd up the *off* and *centre*! **1887** F. GALE *Game of Cricket* xiv. 244 Nothing would be better for cricket itself than for a young unknown cricketer..to rip up the wickets of some of the county cracks.

4*. *Austral. slang.* To annoy intensely; usu. in phr. *wouldn't it rip you*, used as an expression of exasperation.

1941 *Argus* (Melbourne) *Week-End Mag.* 15 Nov. 1/3 Another universal favourite is still the famous 'Wouldn't it —!' Never given the final words (the completed sentence has several variations on 'Wouldn't it rock you!' or 'Wouldn't it rip you!') the explanation depends upon inflexion as to whether it conveys disgust, amazement, or pleasure. **1944** L. GLASSOP *We were Rats* xiii. 74 'I can't do it,' he said again. 'There are no partitions between the places... It's disgusting..'. Everyone gaped at him. 'What's wrong with this galah?' asked somebody and another said, 'Well wouldn't it rip you? What do you expect him to throw?' *Ibid.* xxviii. 162, I had the idea that if you joined the A.I.F. you had to fight in the front line. I know now how many men it takes to keep one in those trenches. Do you know our divisions have even got a mobile laundry, decontamination unit and mobile bath unit? Wouldn't it rip you?

4. to rip off.** *slang* (orig. *U.S.*). Cf. also *RIP-OFF *sb.* (i) To steal; to embezzle.

1967 *Trans-Action* Apr. 7 The hustler 'burns' people for money, but he also 'rips off' goods for money; he thieves, and petty thieving is always a familiar hustle. **1971** *It* 4–18 Nov. 3/5 An analysis of 800 documents ripped off from the Pennsylvania FBI office. **1972** *National Observer* (U.S.) 27 May 12/2 Bank robbery? It's only Establishment money that's being ripped off. **1974** *Black Panther* 16 Mar. 6/2 Spiro got caught ripping off tax money. **1977** *New Yorker* 9 May 34/2 First he owned an Atala, but it got ripped off, so he bought a Peugeot. **1981** A. CROSS *Death in Faculty* viii. 90 Soldiers are always ripping things off, from their own outfit, from the enemy, everything.

(ii) To exploit financially; to cheat or defraud; to rob; to deceive.

1971 *Frendz* 21 May 16/4 The young people are well aware that they are being ripped off by these parasites, and, quite naturally, think that the visiting musicians are on the side of the promoters. **1973** *Black World* Jan. 33/1 Individuals within the group felt that there were too many instances of their singly being 'ripped off' and exploited as Black artists. **1973** *N.Y. Law Jrnl.* 2 Aug. 13/5 He, Harris, and Sydnor had 'ripped' off patrons and the owner of the bar. **1974** S. ELLIN *Stronghold* 55 Experimental group therapy sessions which we all attended..partly because ripping off the amiable idiot who conducted them was better than another game of checkers. **1976** *Kingston* (Ontario) *Whig-Standard* 19 Jan. 19/3 Mrs. Baird and Mrs. LaMarche were in complete agreement as to who were the worst offenders at ripping the consumer off: Television and auto repairs. **1976** *Observer* 22 Feb. 6/3 Many women think all garages consider they can 'rip off' women drivers. **1977** *Spare Rib* July 35/2 A police guard formed in front of Mothercare in Oxford St—afraid we'd attack it for the way it rips off motherhood. **1978** *Detroit Free Post* 5 Mar. A 23/1 Sid Luft's 14-year-old lawsuit charging that his late wife Judy Garland was ripped off..by Hollywood executive David Begelman. **1981** *Times* 23 Apr. 4/8 Martin was not ripping me off.

(iii) To have sexual intercourse with; *esp.*, to rape.

1971 *Black Scholar* Sept. 32/1 If she had been any other broad he would have ripped her off..that night. **1973** *Black World* Sept. 53, I done shot dope, been to jail, swilled wine, ripped off sisters, passed bad checks. **1974** *Guidelines to Volunteer Services* (N.Y. State Dept. Correctional Services) 42 *Rip off*, rape, pull a job.

(iv) To burgle, to steal from (a store, etc.).

1972 'E. MCBAIN' *Sadie when she Died* iii. 30 Q. Why did you go into the apartment? A. To rip it off. Q. To burglarize it? A. Yes. **1973** *Black World* Jan. 54/2 They were ripping off a furniture store in a few hours. **1977** *Rolling Stone* 24 Mar., Not when young blacks have ripped off bookstores across the country to get illegally what the lack of a job prevents them from getting legally.

(v) To copy; to plagiarize.

1975 *Radio Times* 12–18 July 9/4 Just about everyone (including the Immaculate Jean-Luc Godard) ripped off Dick Lester's cool style. **1977** *Undercurrents* June–July 11/4 I've never yet refused a request to reproduce anything of mine but I've lost count of the times I've been ripped off. **1978** *Sci. Amer.* June 26/1 Two books, one an instruction manual for a geometrical instrument.., the other a witty polemic against a Padovan student who had sought to rip off that very instruction book!

II. 7. a. (Examples of the simple use.) *let her rip* (earlier and later examples); *to let* (someone or something) *rip*: to allow (that person or thing) to go, to continue unchecked, etc.; *to let rip*: to let fly, to let oneself go.

1853 *Daily Morning Herald* (St. Louis) 19 Jan. (Th.), We've got 'em on the hip, Letter Rip! Letter Rip! **1863** *Harper's Mag.* Oct. 716/1 We cannot raise a tip To pay our board and laundry bill, And have to 'let 'em rip'. **1869** H. PHILLIPS *Jrnl.* 14 Dec. (typescript) 203 All hands tailing sheep let them rip at night. **1881** A. BATHGATE *Waitaruna* ix. 139 Most of the [diggers], when they found I would not buy, would throw their picks down and say if I would not buy them I could take them or let them rip as I pleased. **1888** 'R. BOLDREWOOD' *Robbery under Arms* II. xiii. 211 He rips over to Daly's mob, borrows a horse, saddle, and bridle, and leads him straight down to our camp. **1894** F. A. BARKLY *Among Boers & Basutos* (ed. 2) xiv. 186, I galloped round the Kopje with my police and half-a-dozen volunteers..and we 'letrip' to use the Africander expression. **1909** C. OWEN *Philip Loveluck* xii. 175, I can rub along somehow ..by letting the pressing rip. **1915** WODEHOUSE *Psmith Journalist* xxv. 203 And now..let her rip. What can I do for you? **1916** 'BOYD CABLE' *Action Front* 255 A shell cracked overhead, and the shrapnel ripped down along the trench behind them. **1926** GALSWORTHY *Silver Spoon* III. iv. 246 Alec would know where he was when it was over, and so would she!.. Let it rip! **1930** A. BENNETT *Imperial Palace* ix. 45 He let them rip..because he enjoyed the grand spectacle of their passion. **1947** H. READ *Grass Roots of Art* iii. 71 We cannot..oppose the machine. We must let it rip, and with confidence. **1965** *Listener* 22 July 140/1 Should one try to make the action clear and comprehensible..or let rip with the poetry? **1966** *Ibid.* 17 Nov. 718/3 What would you do about all these many wage increases... Would you let them all rip? **1971** C. BONINGTON *Annapurna South Face* viii. 95 Almost as soon as I had let rip, however, I realized the injustice of my complaint. **1977** MCKNIGHT & TOBLER *Bob Marley* x. 134 The other view, which was expressed by the minority, was 'let her rip!'. **1977** *Sounds* 9 July 8/1 A frantic 'live' sounding version of The Stones' 'The Last Time' which rips along grandly, seven minutes and forty-four seconds of unadulterated pure fire. **1978** *Dumfries Courier* 20 Oct. 28/1 The present difficult decisions..will be thrust into insignificance if inflation lets rip again.

c. *to rip and tear*: to rage, to rave; to go raging *about*.

1873 'MARK TWAIN' & WARNER *Gilded Age* xxvii. 249 A man wants rest, a man wants peace—a man don't want to rip and tear around *all* the time. **1884** 'MARK TWAIN' *Huck. Finn* xxi. 207 It was perfectly lovely the way he would rip and tear. **1886** BAUMANN *Londinismen* 157/1 Ripping and tearing about. **1917** *Dialect Notes* IV. 342 *Rip and tear*, to rave.

d. In quasi-adverbial use.

1884 [see SOCKDOLAGER 3].

III. 9. *Comb.* as **rip-and-read**, used *attrib.* to designate material supplied by teletype which is read on radio or television; also of an organization supplying such material; **rip-and-tear** *U.S.*, used *attrib.* to designate crude and violent methods in crime; also *transf.*; cf. sense 7c above; **rip-off**, used *attrib.* to designate an opening device that has to be torn off; **rip-stop**, used *attrib.* and *absol.* of nylon clothing or equipment woven so that a tear will not spread; **rip track** *N. Amer.*, a section of railway line used as a site for repairs to carriages.

1973 *New Journalist* (Austral.) July–Aug. 6 The 'rip-and-read' news service of Sydney's labour [radio] station, 2KY. **1974** HAWKEY & BINGHAM *Wild Card* ii. 26 The newscaster was reading..rip-and-read copy—a story that had just come up on an agency teletype machine that the news editor rated too big to hold while it was rewritten. **1937** E. H. SUTHERLAND *Professional Thief* 241 *Rip-and-tear*, adj., without caution; same as 'raw-jaw', or 'murder grift'. **1955** D. W. MAURER in *Publ. Amer. Dial. Soc.* xxiv. 93 They do not constitute the upper echelons of the profession. They are also known as *clout and lam mobs*, *hijackers*, or *rip and tear mobs*. **1965** G. JACKSON *Let.* 12 Mar. in *Soledad Brother* (1971) 66 Understand though that you do not live in the real rip-and-tear world. **1973** *Nation Rev.* (Melbourne) 31 Aug. 1436/6 The knife edged ripoff tag on the top of some cans. **1971** C. BONINGTON *Annapurna South Face* App. B. 249, 2-man [tent], in ripstop nylon. **1976** *National Observer* (U.S.) 14 Feb. 9/3 (Advt.), Prime Duck Down socks... Covered with blue ripstop nylon. **1978** *Sci. Amer.* Feb. 158/3 Other covering materials include sailcloth..and nylon rip-stop. **1960** *Glossaria Interpretum: Chemins de Fer* 1882 Voie de réparations,..Repair track, rip track *Am.* **1973** *Amer. Speech 1969* XLIV. 246 Various parts of the yard have names..such as *riptrack* (a long section of track—possibly several tracks if the yard is large—which is used for car repair).

ripe, *a.* (*sb.*[3] and *adv.*). Add: **2. a.** Also, *ripe peeler* (PEELER[1] 2 b).

1952 *Sun* (Baltimore) (B ed.) 23 June 12/5 Language peculiar only to soft-crabbing... *Ripe peeler*—Has the same characteristics as the 'green peeler' but is more advanced in the shedding process.

b. (Later example.)

1949 G. DAVENPORT *Family Fortunes* I. iv. 54, I swear, Martha, if I'd of met you when you was still ripe, I'd have left Hattie's mother, kids and all, to follow you clear to California, I would.

3. a. (Later example.) Also *absol.*

1930 WODEHOUSE *Very Good, Jeeves!* iv. 102 Having got me in sporting mood with a bottle of the ripest.

b. (Later examples.)

1810 E. WEETON *Let.* 25 Feb. (1969) I. 240, I have had another boil on my face... I neither lanced, nor poulticed it, but when ripe, let the matter out with a needle. **1909** *Dialect Notes* III. 363 *Ripe*, said of a boil when it is ready to be lanced.

d. (See quot. 1949.)

1949 A. R. DANIEL *Bakers' Dict.*, *Ripe dough*, technical term for a dough ready for scaling having received a period of fermentation sufficiently protracted to enable the gluten to reach its most extensible condition. **1962** *Listener* 22 Mar. 511/1 There is a stage in breadmaking when the dough is said to be 'ripe'.

8*. In various slang senses. **a.** Drunk (cf. sense 7 d in Dict.). **b.** Fine, excellent; thoroughgoing (also used ironically); hence, beyond reasonable bounds, excessive. **c.** Angry.

1823 'J. BEE' *Slang* 149 *Ripe*—drunk. First cousin to mellow. **1923** WODEHOUSE *Inimitable Jeeves* ix. 89, I liked the place, and was having quite a ripe time there. **1925** *Flynn's* 14 Mar. 281/1 *Ripe*, drunk. **1932** A. J. WORRALL *Eng. Idioms* 33 He was shooting at cats with darts. I told him it was a bit ripe and asked him to stop. **1948** PARTRIDGE *Dict. Forces' Slang* 156 *Ripe*, complete, thoroughgoing. Usually allied with 'bastard'. **1959** I. & P. OPIE *Lore & Lang. Schoolch.* iii. 53 They come down like a ton of bricks on people who tell a stale joke. 'Do you know where Smudger takes his girl?' gags the would-be comic, 'He takes her behind a bush because it's very *privet*.' Whereupon the 'ripe one' is complimented: 'Oh lor, last time I heard that the tears rolled down my bib.' **1964** *Australasian Post* 21 May 13 Even a ripe shiner isn't just a black eye to the man in the white coat. It is a peri-optic ecchymosis. **1966** R. JEFFRIES *Death in Coverts* iii. 93 We all joked about it and Bill got really ripe. No sense of humour. **1967** R. CAMPBELL in *Coast to Coast 1965–66* 20 Jack'll be ripe pickings by the time that old buzzard comes around from the police station to close the pub. **1969** 'J. FRASER' *Cock-pit of Roses* xvi. 127 'What the bloody hell are you playing at?' 'That's ripe considering you just near broke my arm!'

10. a. *ripe-aged, -bearded, -meated.*

1922 JOYCE *Ulysses* 59 Slapping a palm on a ripemeated hindquarter. **1934** WEBSTER, *Ripe-aged.* **1944** E. SITWELL *Green Song* 11 We heard in the dawn the first ripe-bearded fire Of wheat. **1952** C. DAY LEWIS tr. *Virgil's Aeneid* v. 95 Ripe-aged Acestes.

ripely, *adv.* **3.** (Later examples.)

1939 JOYCE *Finnegans Wake* (1964) 474 His locks of a lucan tinge, quickrich, ripely rippling. **1973** *Daily Tel.* 13 Aug. 12/3 Stravinsky's 'Firebird'... Ozawa encourages a ripely romantic performance.

ripener. Add: **3.** A device in which honey is allowed to stand until it is fit to be put in jars.

[**1883** *Brit. Bee Jrnl.* XI. 209/2 The above simple arrangement..will combine that of a honey-extractor and a honey-ripener in one compact piece of apparatus.] **1905** *Instruction in Bee-Keeping* (Dept. Agric. & Techn. Instruction for Ireland) 20 The ripener..is a tinned iron cylinder about 19 inches in depth by about 8½ inches in diameter, and fitted with a treacle tap at the base. **1930** W. HERROD-HEMPSALL *Bee-Keeping* I. ix. 525 The ripener was so named because at one time both the unsealed and sealed honey used to be extracted together, it was then run into the ripener and allowed to stand for some time in a warm room. **1971** *Country Life* 18 Nov. 1347/1 The ripener, into which the extracted honey is put, so that air bubbles may escape in due time, was so heavy that it was all both of us could do to lift it.

ripening, *vbl. sb.* Add: **3.** In various industrial processes, applied to a stage in which a material is left to stand until desired properties are attained; *spec.* in rayon manufacture (see quot. 1957).

1919 *Jrnl. Soc. Chem. Industry* 31 Oct. 373T/1 There result, upon application of partial hydration ('ripening'), esters of high viscosity and great strength, suppleness, and wearing qualities. **1932** *Discovery* Sept. 289/1 After ripening has been completed the soluble salts are removed. **1937** *Ibid.* Aug. 247/1 The actual process is a long one.., the polymerisation process alone occupying from 90 to 120 hours, after which a 'ripening' process for the synthetic rubber of three to eight days is necessary. **1950** R. W. MONCRIEFF *Man-Made Fibres* viii. 96 Ripening is an essential part of the viscose process; 'young' viscose cannot be spun satisfactorily. **1957** *Textile Terms & Definitions* (Textile Inst.) (ed. 3) 82 *Ripening*,..(1) A process in the production of cellulose acetate consisting of the splitting off of some of the acetic acid and most of the combined catalyst present in the primary cellulose acetate. (2) A process in the manufacture of viscose rayon in which the viscose is matured prior to spinning. The rate of ripening is controlled by the time and temperature at which the spinning fluid is maintained. The process is sometimes called maturing or ageing. **1973** *Materials & Technol.* VI. iv. 307 This 'ripening'..results in a solution which will later give easier coagulation, and it is allowed to proceed until a required amount of hydrolysis has taken place.

4. *attrib.*, as *ripening-time.*

1910 W. DE LA MARE *Three Mulla-Mulgars* i. 7 The great Ukka-tree, which he had climbed at ripening-time.

ripicolous, *a.* (Examples.)

1906 J. B. SMITH *Explanation Terms Entomol.* 117 Ripicolous: dwelling on river banks: riparian. **1965** B. E. FREEMAN tr. *Vandel's Biospeleol.* xiii. 196 The Bembiinae are essentially ripicolous.

ripienist. (Later examples.)

1935 P. A. SCHOLES *Radio Times Music Handbk.* 18 A 'full' body of strings and a smaller body of two or three solo string players—the 'ripienists' and the 'concertinists', as we may call them. **1944** W. APEL *Harvard Dict. Mus.* 646/2 *Ripienista* (Ripienist) is an orchestral player.

ripieno, *a.* and *sb.* Add: Also **ripiano.** **1. a.** (Further examples.)

1740 J. GRASSINEAU *Mus. Dict.* 203 *Ripiano*, or *Ripiéno*, signifies *full*, and is used in pieces of music in parts, to distinguish those parts that play now and then to fill up, from those that play throughout the piece. **1933** *Radio Times* 14 Apr. 82/3 Miners, cotton spinners and the like who get a real kick from the ripiano cornet and the bombardon. **1954** *Grove's Dict. Mus.* (ed. 5), I. 914/1 In Britain the instrumentation ultimately became as follows for the purpose of contests: 1 Soprano Cornet in E♭.. 1 Repiano Cornet in B♭. [*Note*] 'Repiano' is a spelling peculiar to the brass band. *Ibid.* 914/2 Nowadays only one [*sc.* flugelhorn] is used, playng a separate part or combining with the repiano cornet. **1962** [see *CONCERTINO 2]. **1978** *Daily Tel.* 13 Mar. 11/1 The Choir—with the youthful ripieno Chorus—responded with clear tone and vitality.

b. Occas. with It. pl. **ripieni.** (Earlier and later examples.) Also *collect.*, the group of accompanying instruments that form the main orchestral body in a concerto, as distinct from the concertino (*CONCERTINO 2).

1740 J. GRASSINEAU *Mus. Dict.* 203 There are.. two kinds of *Ripiénos*, one whereof plays the part of the little chorus exactly... The other sort is much better, because they play a different part. **1930** *Radio Times Dict. Mus. Terms* 50 *Ripieno*, the instruments which form the accompaniment, as opposed to those which have solo parts. **1935** P. A. SCHOLES *Radio Times Music Handbk.* 18 In the Concerto Grosso.. the idea is.. that *two bodies* of instruments are.. responding to one another antiphonally... The larger body is called *Ripieno*.., and the smaller one '*Concertino*'. **1944** W. APEL *Harvard Dict. Mus.* 646/2 'Ripieni' indicates the full orchestra.., as distinguished from the soloists... The term 'senza ripieni', however, is not identical with 'orchestra silent', but calls for the leading members only of the orchestra, i.e., for a smaller ensemble used for the accompaniment of the soloists. **1960** *Times* 2 Nov. 16/6 A *ripieno* of six players (five strings and harpsichord). **1961** [see *CONCERTINO 2]. **1976** *Gramophone* Dec. 1028/3 The balance and interplay between voices and ripieno are two of the several outstandingly successful features of the present performances.

riplet: see *RIPPLET.

rip-off (ri·pǫf), *sb. slang* (orig. *U.S.*). Also **rip off, ripoff.** [f. *to rip off* s.v. *RIP *v.*[2] 4**.]
1. One who steals, a thief.

1970 *Manch. Guardian Weekly* 2 May 16/4 'Who do you have on Haight Street today?' he [*sc.* a San Francisco drug peddler] said disgustedly... 'You have burn artists (fraudulent dope peddlers), rip-offs (thieves), and snitchers (police spies).' **1971** *Rolling Stone* 24 June 8/3, I call them rip-offs, and they are, nothing but pirates and vultures.

2. A fraud, a swindle; a racket; an instance of exploitation, esp. financial.

1970 *Melody Maker* 12 Sept. 29 *Rip off*, capitalist exploitation. **1970** *Time* 21 Dec. 4/1 This is what, in contemporary parlance, is called a rip-off. **1971** *It* 9–23 Sept. 12 Fun Caterers of Battersea.. had the main catering concession (the biggest rip-off there.) **1973** *Houston* (Texas) *Chron.* 21 Oct. 7/3 Dunlop said the increased spring markups had been 'inflationary', a polite word in the context for 'ripoff'. **1974** *Sunday Sun* (Brisbane) 28 July 24/2 The great snackbar rip-off that had city workers weeping into their salad rolls. **1975** *N.Y. Times* 14 Apr. 30/4 A five-day week, with ten paid holidays, plus a ten-week paid vacation yearly. Such a contract is a 'rip-off'. **1977** *Time* 4 July 21/1 They [*sc.* French soldiers and civil servants] get rich and Djibouti gets nothing. That's not enlightened colonialism. It's a bloody rip-off. **1980** *Times* 31 May 2/3 Britain's 41 motorway service areas.. have attracted such accolades as 'poor', 'appalling' and 'a rip-off'.

3. An imitation or plagiarism, usu. one made in order to exploit public taste.

1971 *Newsweek* 18 Oct. 38/3 Most of the architecture is Inspired Bastard, most of the historical re-creations are Shameless Ripoff. **1974** *Publishers Weekly* 4 Mar. 72/2 This kaleidoscopic fantasy, a ripoff on everything from spy novels to the Oedipus complex. **1976** *Time* (Canada) 19 Jan. 16/3 Flynt runs three Hustler Clubs in Ohio, tacky rip-offs of the Playboy Clubs, offering expensive drinks and leggy 'hostesses'. **1977** *Private Eye* 1 Apr. 4/1 *Blue Belle* [*sc.* a film], yet another of the seemingly endless *Emmanuelle* rip-offs. **1980** *Jewish Chron.* 29 Feb. 30/2 We were treated to a kaleidoscopic mess of fifties rip-offs, sixties platitudes and seventies mistakes; shirtwaisters, minis, halter-necks, op art, sloppy joes, bermudas and, latest ubiquity, the flying suit.

4. a. *attrib.* passing into *adj.*

1971 *National Times* (Austral.) 15–20 Feb. 1/3 In Sydney comics and books have been appearing from the 'rip-off' press—the underground printers and publishers who are printing editions of banned books sneaked singly through Customs. **1973** *Nation Rev.* (Melbourne) 24–30 Aug. 1399/6 The poor unfortunate buyer getting lumbered.. with the cost of the device (at ripoff prices). **1973** *National Observer* (U.S.) 6 Oct. 23/3 The 'rip-off' blues, the blues that musicians get when they write songs that make other people rich and leave them poor as before. **1975** *Time* 12 May 17/1 The rip-off capital of the world [*sc.* Saigon]. **1976** *New Yorker* 5 Apr. 31/2 Cargo leaving New York for places like South America is often a kind of object lesson in rip-off economics. **1976** *Times* 11 June 8/1 The trade in old books is an incongruous mixture of fine art almost beyond price and the rascally hustle and rip-off hugger-mugger of a flea market.

b. *Comb.*, as **rip-off artist, merchant**, one who carries out a rip-off; a thief, fraud, or racketeer.

1971 *Friendz* 21 May 11/2 Rip-off artists are only occasionally armed or violent; more usual is.. the traditional conman. **1971** J. MANDELKAU *Buttons* xiii. 149 From now on my club was going to have nought to do with the Alternative society and its rip-off merchants. **1974** *Amer. Speech* 1970 XLV. 210 Bring your own food. There won't be any ripoff merchants there. **1977** *It* May 5/2, I am not suggesting that the Pink Floyd are rip-off artists, but it is undeniable that much contemporary music is a response to alienation. **1977** C. MCFADDEN *Serial* xxxix. 84/2 He checked out the chain lock that secured his Motobecane against rip-off artists.

Ripolin (ripolæn). [Fr.] The proprietary name of a make of paint.

[**1889** *Trade Marks Jrnl.* 25 Dec. 1/1 Ripolin 92,910. Chemical substances used in manufactures or philosophical research, and anti-corrosives... 2nd October 1889.] **1907** *Yesterday's Shopping* (1969) 157/1 Ripolin enamel. White, black, sulphur, [etc.]. Tin... 1/0. **1922** C. K. S. MONCRIEFF tr. *Proust's Swann's Way* II. 29 My room in the Grand Hôtel de la Plage.. the walls of which, washed with ripolin, contained.. a finer air. **1934** A. HUXLEY *Beyond Mexique Bay* 32 We prefer the lighter woods, we prefer metal and glass and ripolin.

riposte, *v.* **2.** (Later examples.)

1898 J. M. COBBAN *Angel of Covenant* xiii. 147 'Had I not taken pains with the foolish old man,' riposted Maudlin, blushing high, 'we should yet be sitting at mumchance.' **1958** *Observer* 6 Dec. 864/1 The western powers might logically riposte by offering to discuss a free and neutral status.. for all Berlin. **1972** *Daily Tel.* 27 May 12 'But I'm David Broome,' says the show jumper. 'I don't care if you are Basil Brush,' ripostes the sergeant-major. **1977** T. HEALD *Just Desserts* 191 'But what do we have to show for it?' 'We have unlimited access to the former Scoff network,' riposted Bognor.

ripped (ript), *ppl. a.* (and *pa. pple.*). [f. RIP *v.*[2] + -ED[1].] **1.** *dial.* Cut, slit.

1823 E. MOOR *Suffolk Words & Phr.* 129 *Fleeches.* The portions into which a tree or piece of timber is cut by the saw, in its first position over the saw-pit... When turned and *ripp'd* or *rippen'd*, that is, cut into smaller portions, such portions are called *Scantlins*, in Suffolk and.. elsewhere. **1880.** J. H. MAXWELL *Sheep-Marks* 15 Topped on both ears, ripped on near.

2. With *up.* **a.** Angry. **b.** Torn up.

1941 *Amer. Speech* XVI. 190 *Ripped up*, angry. **1973** 'E. MCBAIN' *Hail to Chief* i. 3 The ripped-up sections of planking.

3. (As *pa. pple.*) Under the influence of a drug. *U.S. slang.*

1971 *Rolling Stone* 24 June 16/1 It comes on so fast all with one toke. By the third you're ripped to the gills for several hours. **1973** D. LANG *Freaks* 17 Oh, wow, boy, are you ripped! **1975** C. JAMES *Fate of Felicity Fark* vi. 55 On he gabbled as if ripped on Speed. **1981** *Listener* 1 Jan. 23/3 The story is of a threatened pop singer who, though he gets ripped at need, is really very moral.

4. *slang.* With *off.* Of a person: robbed; exploited; of a thing: stolen.

1971 *New Yorker* 22 May 40 (*title*) Ripped off. **1975** *Maclean's Mag.* Sept. 8/2, I can 'hate men' but many of them are in the same spot as I am: co-opted, ripped-off and mad. **1976** SCOTT & KOSKI *Walk-In* iv. 23 The garages where you can buy hot tires and ripped-off hub caps.

ripper. Add: **1. a.** (Further examples.)

1909 *Daily Chron.* 20 Aug. 1/1 The theory most generally entertained is that the canister.. was left in a coal train in the mine by a ripper or ripper's assistant... **1967** *Gloss. Mining Terms* (*B.S.I.*) VIII. 22 *Ripper*, a man who rips. **1979** B. HINES *Price of Coal* 31 Sid and the other rippers stayed on the paddy until it reached the end of the track.

b. A criminal who rips the bodies of his victims; *spec.* = *Jack the Ripper* s.v.* JACK *sb.*[1] 36. Also *transf.* and *Comb.* Hence (*nonce-wds.*) **rippero·logist**, a student of the crimes of Jack the Ripper; **rippero·logy.**

1890, etc. [see *Jack the Ripper* s.v. *JACK *sb.*[1] 36]. **1909** J. R. WARE *Passing Eng.* 209/2 *Ripper*, daring murderer of women. **1935** *Amer. Speech* X. 20/1 *Ripper.* 1. A degenerate who molests, rapes, or mutilates women in parks or other secluded spots; probably from Jack the Ripper. 2. A shrewd or lucky fellow who 'gets away with murder'. **1970** C. MAJOR *Dict. Afro-Amer. Slang* 98 *Ripper*, one who has a reputation for cutting others with a knife. **1974** A. DOUGLAS *Noah's Ark Murders* iv. 40 The series of Ripper-like murders that had all but ended his own life. **1974** G. MOFFAT *Corpse Road* iii. 41 'The Ripper stopped at six [murders].' 'Perhaps this one won't stop.' **1975** D. RUMBELOW *Compl. Jack the Ripper* 5 To.. 'Ripperologists' everywhere—not forgetting *Jack* who brought us all together. **1977** *Guardian Weekly* 27 Feb. 20/3 This file-work gives a little more definition to the blurred (and in places bizarrely touched-up) picture of the dark side of late-Victorian high life that has been emerging during our seventies, mostly through the addition of new bits of information to that arcane old science known as Ripperology. **1979** W. J. FISHMAN *Streets of E. London* 102/2 It is still debated whether Turner was the first victim [of Jack the Ripper]. Some 'Ripperologists' suggest that Polly Nichols was the first. **1979** *Guardian* 1 June 4/1 The 'Yorkshire Ripper'.. has murdered 11 women in less than four years. **1981** *Yorks. Post* 8 July 7/1, I don't want people to cash in on what the Ripper did to my daughter.

2. a. (*c*) *Criminals' slang.* A tool for opening safes, etc.

1889 FARMER *Americanisms* 460/1 *Ripper* or *Mason Ripper*, (1) a new and ingenious implement of burglary, used in opening safes or vaults with iron surfaces. **1925** *Flynn's* 14 Mar. 281/1 *Ripper*, a can-opener (a burglar's tool). **1963** R. I. MCDAVID *Mencken's Amer. Lang.* 717 The use of *stew* is declining, modern *heavy gees* preferring to use a *stick*, *ripper* or *can opener* on laminated safes.

b. An implement that is attached to a tractor to break up concrete or hard soil.

1955 'N. SHUTE' *Requiem for Wren* i. 20 This war [against the rabbits] went on continuously with tractor-drawn rippers to destroy the warrens. **1963** OGLESBY & HEWES *Highway Engin.* (ed. 2) xiv. 476 In recent years large rippers mounted on huge crawler tractors.. have been used successfully to break up loose or fractured rock. **1976** *Billings* (Montana) *Gaz.* 2 July 11-c/8 (Advt.), Power Tilt Straight dozer with Ateco swinging swank ripper. **1979** *Arizona Daily Star* 5 Aug. (Advt. Section) 9/2 Teeth for backhoes, loaders, ripper points, corner bits, cutting edges for all makes.

3. a. (Earlier and later examples.) Also, of a person, *spec.* an attractive young woman. In recent use, chiefly *Austral. slang.* Also *attrib.*

1838 *Bell's Life* 26 Aug. 4/1 One of Mr. Mynn's best balls, technically a 'ripper', took the top of the middle stump. **1846** *Swell's Night Guide* 40 In conjunction with the above is Miss Emma Watling, a regular ripper. **1848** [see *CREEPER 10**]. **1848** J. MITCHELL in *Amer. Speech* (1935) X. 41/1 *Ripper.* anything very large of its kind. [A Nantucketism.] **1905** *Pall Mall Mag.* July 111/1 He had found her a ripper as to looks. **1935** AUDEN & ISHERWOOD *Dog beneath Skin* I. ii. 37 What do you think of her? Isn't she a ripper? **1951** E. LAMBERT *Twenty Thousand Thieves* x. 182. 'Good letter, Chips?' A gurgle. 'It's a ripper!' **1969** A. O'TOOLE *Racing Game* xviii. 200 'Not a bad run,' I observed... 'A ripper,' Badger agreed. **1970** *Sunday Truth* (Brisbane) 10 May 64 If I'm ever asked what Australia is like, I'll say, 'She's a bloody ripper, mate!' **1973** *Australian* 7 July 16, I love this ripper country. **1976** *Courier-Mail* (Brisbane) 13 Mar. 19/11 Nagle has a fine ear for Australian dialect. The books' a 'ripper', as his characters might say.

4. *U.S. Pol.* (See quot. 1937.) Also *attrib.*

1895 *Columbus* (Ohio) *Dispatch* 1 Apr. 4/2 The Merryman ripper bill looks very much as if the Republicans of this city were going to the legislature for offices. **1937** J. R. SCHULTZ in *Amer. Speech* XII. 319 The word 'ripper' is commonly used in Pennsylvania political parlance to describe a bill that abolishes an office or commission of state or city. Such an act is said usually to have as its purpose the elimination of an officer or member of a commission who is unfriendly to the party in power.

5. *Sc.* A simple fishing tackle consisting of 'a line having attached to it a heavy metal bar fitted with hooks' (*S.N.D.*).

1925 *Glasgow Herald* 17 Aug. 7 He.. caught a 20 lb. ling with a ripper. *c* **1930** in *Scot. Nat. Dict.* (1968) VII. 455/3, I vrocht aa efterneen at the ripper, bit I hid nae luck. **1946** *Aberdeen Press & Jrnl.* 2 July, The primitive method of fishing with dandy lines, consisting of ripper and hooks.

ripping, *vbl. sb.* Add: **1. a.** (Later examples.)

1900 in FARMER *Public School Word-bk.* 167. **1911** R. NEVILL *Floreat Etona* vii. 224 In the days when such a close connection existed between Eton and King's, a Colleger leaving to go to Cambridge used to go through the old form known as 'Ripping'... The two folds of the Colleger's serge gown were sewn together in front, and the Provost 'ripped' them asunder. **1973** 'J. PATRICK' *Glasgow Gang Observed* iv. 41 The case for the defence collapsed.. when Big Dick boasted.. that the attack was 'the biggest rippin' Ah've done'. **1979** *Jrnl. R. Soc. Arts* Jan. 93/1, I was very interested in your ideas about shifting the rippings from the coal face and spreading it into the sea.

2. b. *Aeronaut.* Used *attrib.* with reference to a strip of fabric sown into and forming part of the skin of a balloon and to the cord which, when pulled, tears this strip away to bring about rapid deflation, as *ripping cord, line, panel, rope, valve.*

1907 *Strand Mag.* Feb. 149/1 The utility of the ripping-cord was brought home to me.. in a recent ascent. **1908** A. HILDEBRANDT *Airships Past & Present* xvi. 184 The ripping-cord was the invention of the American aeronaut, Wise, in 1844; Godard introduced it in France in 1855. **1910** Ripping cord [see *ripping panel* below]. **1907** *Strand Mag.* Feb. 151/2 Faure.. is the first aeronaut who had the courage to experiment with the ripping-line in mid air. Till he made his first attempt about two years ago, all balloonists thought that to pull the ripping-line anywhere but on the ground meant suicide. **1974** *Oxford Jun. Encycl.* (rev. ed.) IV. 35/2 Among other important equipment is the ripping-line or rip-cord, which is painted red so that it shall not be pulled in mistake for the valve line. **1908** A. HILDEBRANDT *Airships Past & Present* xvi. 184 The ripping-panel is placed on that side of the covering to which the guide-rope is attached. **1910** C. C. TURNER *Aerial Navigation* iii. 45 On coming within a few yards of the ground he pulls the ripping panel open, the cord from which comes down through a hole near the neck of the balloon. In some balloons,.. the ripping cord passes through the neck. **1919** H. SHAW *Text-bk. Aeronaut.* xvii. 195 For emergency cases a 'ripping panel' is fitted, for use when a quick descent is necessary. **192·** *Encycl. Brit.* XXX. 89/1 One complete series of balloons came down with unexpected suddenness, all being deflated by the rupture of their ripping panels. On examination, it was found that moisture had condensed on the ripping ropes and frozen there, until each cord was about as thick as a man's forearm. **1907** G. BACON *Record of Aeronaut* xiv. 255 Aeronautical experts.. advised.. that, as the balloon might have to remain inflated for a long while before starting, one of large size should be employed, and a 'solid' or 'ripping' valve substituted for the usual 'Butterfly' variety. **1912** C. B. HAYWARD *Pract. Aeronaut.* 51 The usual 'ripping valve' is also provided in the form of a narrow strip of balloon fabric glued over a long cut in the envelope.

ripping, *ppl. a.* Add: **1.** (Further *fig.* examples.)

1896 G. F. NORTHALL *Warwickshire Word-bk.* 192 *Ripping, adj.* Sharp, cutting, as applied to cold weather; e.g. 'a ripping frost'. Midlands. **1932** H. J. MASSINGHAM *World without End* 297 Words like.. 'ripping' or 'sniping', the adjectives of a very sharp frost.. are playlets in themselves. **1978** J. WAMBAUGH *Black Marble* x. 237, I have a ripping headache.

2. a. Also advb., and as a complement. (Further examples.) *Obsolescent.*

1846 *Swell's Night Guide* 74 One calls for the 'lanciers'; another, the 'caledonians'; when the Boshman, ripping innocent of either..strikes up the college hornpipe. **1894** 'A. HOPE' *Dolly Dialogues* ix. 51 She did look ripping in that white frock. **1898** [see *KNOCK-OUT *sb.* 4]. **1911** D. H. LAWRENCE *White Peacock* II. ii. 229 She was very fine and frank and unconventional—ripping, I thought her. **1921** [see *DUG-UP *a.*] **1921** H. WILLIAMSON *Beautiful Years* 137 Jack was excited about his friend going to school with him. 'I say, how ripping, man!' he cried. **1944** [see *DECENT *a.* 5 b]. **1978** PALIN & JONES (*title*) Ripping yarns.

† **b.** Very fast or rapid. *Obs.*

1826 [in Dict., sense 2]. **1828** *Bell's Life* 27 July 4/1 The ripping bowling of the Captain. **1846** W. DENISON *Cricket: Sk. Players* 22 Mr. Osbaldeston, and Brown of Brighton, afterwards launched forth as 'fast ripping bowlers'. **1868** H. WOODRUFF *Trotting Horse* xi. 116 There is no occasion for the ripping spurts which intervene in the other training. **1877** *London Society* June 537/1 Hinkly's bowling was ripping indeed.

ri·ppingness. *Obsolescent.* [f. RIPPING *ppl. a.* + -NESS.] Splendid quality; excellence.

1910 A. BENNETT *Clayhanger* IV. xii. 566 'She's a ripping woman.'.. His preoccupation with the rippingness of Mrs. Chris Hamson. **1927** C. E. MONTAGUE *Right off Map* xviii. 174 It's the doing the thing that..makes you half drunk with the rippingness of it.

rippit, var. RIPPET. *Sc.* and *U.S. dial.*

1851 W. ANDERSON *Rhymes* 195 Sic a rage an' a rippit I seldom hae seen. **1870** J. C. DUVAL *Adventures Big-Foot Wallace* xlii. 270 At last the manager threw his hat among 'em and called out, 'Stampede all', and the 'rippit' commenced. **1887** [see RIPPET]. **1913** H. KEPHART *Our Southern Highlanders* xiii. 294 If they quarrel, it is a ruction, a rippit, a jower, or an up-scuddle—so be it there are no fatalities which would amount to a real fray. **1913** J. SERVICE *Memorables* 67 Some dreidfu' nicht rippit there had been amang the cairters. **1928** M. CHAPMAN *Happy Mountain* 313 Degrees of feeling among unfriendly neighbors... *A rippit*, fight with fists. **1958** *Huntly Express* 19 Dec. 6 For fear ony rippits brook out at the dance.

ripple, *sb.*³ Add: **1. a.** (Later examples.)

1941 L. D. BALDWIN *Keelboat Age* 71 The breaking of the water over the bars and chains was known to the boatmen as ripples, or riffles. **1964** F. O'ROURKE *Mule for Marquesa* ii. 50 'How do we cross?'..'Quicksand to the right. You move out the bar, angle downstream to that big ripple, then straight on across.'

2. a. *spec.* in *Physics*, a wave on the surface of a fluid the restoring force for which is provided by surface tension rather than by gravity, and which consequently has a wavelength shorter than that corresponding to the minimum speed of propagation.

1871 W. THOMSON in *Phil. Mag.* XLII. 374 The 'Capillary waves'..referred to by Russell are what I, in ignorance of his observations.., had called 'ripples'. **1887** *Amer. Jrnl. Math.* IX. 67 Sir W. Thomson proposes to distinguish by the name of ripples those waves whose length is less than the above critical value of λ [wavelength]. **1938** L. M. MILNE-THOMSON *Theoret. Hydrodynamics* xiv. 377 Ripples are waves on [*ed.* 2: in] whose propagation capillarity plays the predominating part. **1966** *McGraw-Hill Encycl. Sci. & Technol.* XIV. 417/1 Ripples generated by wind at the interface between air and water on oceans and lakes are of importance to the friction of air flowing over water, and to the reflection and scattering of electromagnetic and sound waves.

b. (Further examples.)

1968 J. WINEARLS *Mod. Dance* (ed. 2) ii. 38 Raising and lowering can follow each other in uninterrupted snake-like ripples. **1972** *Courier-Mail* (Brisbane) 3 July 2/6 Laurence (Lord) Olivier, on every official opening night at the Old Vic, was reserving front-blocks of seats, 'the Ripples' for students whose natural reaction might..introduce 'ripples' to break down the first-night social-or-coterie stuffiness. **1977** *Design Engin.* July 19/3 High number of commutator segments giving very smooth operation (low torque ripple) over a speed range from zero to several thousand rev/min. **1979** *Time* 2 Apr. 20/3 As Finland bottomed out of recession, pre-election polls showed a ripple to the right.

d. A name for an ice cream manufactured with an admixture of coloured syrup that gives it a rippled appearance.

Registered as a proprietary name in the U.S.

1939 *Ice Cream Trade Jrnl.* Nov. 19 (Advt.), Fudge ripple ice cream. *Ibid.*, This delicious fudge syrup is incorporated in your own vanilla ice cream as you fill the can from a batch freezer or incorporated in your vanilla ice cream by a special fudge ripple attachment as it flows from your continuous freezer. **1942** *Official Gaz.* (U.S. Patent Office) 16 June 511/1 Gerald G. Balch, doing business as Balch Flavor Co., Pittsburgh, Pa... Ripple... For ice cream and flavoring concentrate for use in the manufacture of variegated type of ice cream and for use in the manufacture of a flavoring adapted to be applied on or to ice cream, sold in bulk. Claims use since Oct. 23, 1939. **1973** HYDE & ROTHWELL *Ice Cream* vii. 141 (*caption*) Diagram of Hoyer ripple machine. **1976** *Milton Keynes Express* 25 June 10 (Advt.), Ice Cream... Raspberry Ripple, 4 litre £1.10. **1977** 'J. BELL' *Such Nice Client* xvi. 156 A pork pie..and an ice ripple from the freezer..brought her back into fighting shape. **1981** *Times* 2 May 7/4 Dessert..angel food cake, blueberry cheese cake, fudge, ripple ice cream.

3. Also *fig.*, a rumour.

1977 N. ADAM *Triplehip Cracksman* vii. 71 There's a ripple he's walking a bit heavy these days.

4. (Earlier and later examples.)

1853 *Alta California* (San Francisco) 31 May 2/1 Repeated instances have come to our knowledge when the amount of gold saved has been doubled by a little alteration or improvement made in the ripple-box. **1902** *Chambers's Jrnl.* Mar. 176/1 This process consists of passing the sand through an arrangement of inclined sieves, which by reason of 'ripples' or bars of wood fastened transversely across their surfaces, discard all light material that cannot pass the various meshes. **1938** D. FORBES *My Life in S. Afr.* vi. 87 One had to keep the earth moving all the time. If it once settled to the bottom of the box it formed a solid mass, and did not settle into what are called the ripples on the bottom of the box made to catch the gold.

5. *Electr.* Small periodic variations in voltage superposed on a direct voltage or on an alternating voltage of lower frequency. Freq. *attrib.*

1920 *Whittaker's Electr. Engineer's Pocket-bk.* (ed. 4) 152 When the rotor is slotted, as in turbo-alternators with cylindrical rotors, a ripple is induced in the conductor-pressure. **1928** *Observer* 17 June 26/3 Manufacturers should publish a curve of inductance against direct current component, measured at ripple frequency. **1947** R. LEE *Electronic Transformers & Circuits* iii. 66 Reactors are used in electronic power equipment to smooth out ripple voltage in d-c supplies, so they carry direct current in the coils. **1967** *Electronics* 6 Mar. 308/2 Quadrature rejection is 40 db minimum, while ripple is 0·5% peak-to-peak of full scale output. **1972** *Physics Bull.* Aug. 491/2 An automatically adjusting transformer ensures high stability; ripple is 1 mV peak to peak.

6. Applied to a method of firing or discharging in succession or at intervals.

1944 *Shorter Oxf. Eng. Dict.* (ed. 3) Add., *Ripple*.., applied to a method of firing torpedoes in succession. **1951** *Life* 18 June 54/3 (*caption*) Using six rocket launchers with 24 tubes each, the platoon in a matter of seconds blasted Red positions with 144 rounds—a barrage which rocketmen call a 'ripple'. **1968** *Daily Express* 12 Feb. 2/5 *Ripple*, an attacker's technique of sending off his missiles in waves, so that a defender fires his defensive missiles at the first waves and has nothing left to deflect the final blow.

7. *attrib.* and *Comb.*, as *ripple burnish*, (poet.) *-dripple*, *ware*; *ripple black, fresh, -warped* adjs.; **ripple (pony) cloth**, cloth having a rippled appearance; also *attrib.*; **ripple control** *Electr.*, a method of performing simple control operations, such as switching of street lights, by superposition of a high-frequency switching signal on the mains supply; **ripple(-through) counter** *Electronics*, a type of binary counter consisting of a number of bistable circuits wired in cascade, so that each changes its state only after all the preceding ones have changed state; **ripple effect**, the continuous and spreading results of an event or action; **ripple-fired** *adj.* [cf. sense 6 above], (of missiles) fired in rapid succession or at intervals; so **ripple-firing** *a.*; **ripple-flaking** *Archæol.*, a method of flaking flint; so **ripple-flaked** *a.*; **ripple sole**, a kind of rubber sole having thick ripple-shaped ridges; hence **ripple-soled** *ppl. a.*; **ripple stitch**, a drawn fabric stitch (see also sense 2 in Dict.).

1965 *Wireless World* Aug. 28 (Advt.), Dial escutcheon measures 6" long by 4⅛" wide, finished ripple black. **1964** H. HODGES *Artifacts* i. 31 The effect of this ripple burnish can be highly decorative. **1922** Ripplecloth [see *house-jacket* s.v. *HOUSE *sb.*[1] 19]. **1930** *Daily Express* 6 Oct. 5/2 (Advt.), Pure wool ripple cloth, for cosy dressing gowns. **1957** M. B. PICKEN *Fashion Dict.* 276/1 *Ripple cloth*, woolen dress fabric with long silky hairs on right side. Also called *zibeline*. **1977** B. PYM *Quartet in Autumn* xvi. 139 Her old blue ripple-cloth dressing gown. **1938** *Jrnl. Inst. Electr. Engin.* LXXXIII. 827/1 The fullest advantage can only be taken of the ripple control principle if a central ripple transmitter ..can be designed to cover the entire network fed at high tension from that point. **1952** J. M. WALDRAM *Street Lighting* xx. 381 A ripple control system operating about 500 lamps in an urban area, pre-war. **1974** *Times* 4 Feb. 16/6 It seems..opportune to raise again the..question of ripple control. For the uninitiated, it is a means of transmitting coded signals from a central control point over the existing mains network to operate switching contactors at any point in the network, e.g., domestic consumers' premises. **1967** *Electronics* 6 Mar. 160/1 It cannot be used in ripple counters or other circuits requiring the toggle function. **1973** *Sci. Amer.* May 110/3 Combinations of flip-flops and NAND gates interconnected as described are known as ripple counters. The reason is that input pulses 'ripple' through the string of flip-flops sequentially, each device triggering the next one in the series. **1916** BLUNDEN *Harbingers* 49 The ripple-dripple of the brooks. **1966** *Wall St. Jrnl.* 14 Feb. 10/3 Price-boosting already is producing a 'ripple effect' in which companies pass on increased costs in higher price tags on their own products. **1973** *Times* 20 Dec. 12/4 Industrial expansion is now halted by the three day week, not to say by the ripple effect of the public expenditure cuts. **1977** *Detroit Free Press* 11 Dec. 7-B/4 The ripple effect from the 'Star Wars' film has taken on tidal wave proportions. **1954** *Sun* (Baltimore) (B ed.) 25 June 10/3 Proximity-fused bombs or photo flash bombs..high explosive rockets, ripple fired rockets, smoke rockets and guided missiles. **1949** A. R. WEYL *Guided Missiles* 31 Control of the launching manœuvre can be electric, for example, by closing a circuit which ignites a propelling charge, or electronic. The former is preferred for small missiles, with 'ripple-firing' control for the multiple and successive launching of A.A. missiles. **1960** *Oxf. Univ. Gaz.* 4 Mar. 805/2 A fine ripple-flaked flint knife with gold leaf attached to the blunt end. **1899** Ripple-flaking [in Dict., sense 2 b]. **1921** *Chambers's Jrnl.* 5 Feb. 145/1 Brierly Stretton and I were..discussing the intensive examination of ripple-flaking. **1944** BLUNDEN *Shells by Stream* 44 While some freed fountain of delight Played beauty ripple-fresh and bright. **1952** C. W. CUNNINGTON *Eng. Women's Clothing* 296 *Ripple pony cloth*..Resembles a finely ribbed miroir velvet with a bright finish. **1963** N. MARSH *Dead Water* (1964) viii. 201 Gentleman's country shoes, size nine-and-a-half ripple soles. **1970** *Globe & Mail* (Toronto) 26 Sept. 52/2 (Advt.), Women's Slippers... Some ripple rubber soles. **1977** C. MCFADDEN *Serial* xli. 88/2 Kate had already gone springing off in her ripple-sole Famolares. **1977** *Austral. Furnishing Buyers Guide* Spring/Summer 58/4 With heels, steel tips, crepe and ripple soled shoes, carpets are getting much more wear and tear. **1933** K. S. LOFTHOUSE *Compl. Guide Drawn Fabric* 22 *Ripple stitch*... Worked from right to left... Three pairs are worked with six threads between. **1971** J. H. SMITH *Digital Logic* vi. 103 In the asynchronous counter..the trigger input of each binary is from the preceding output... This mode of operation gives an inherent delay in the ripple-through counter. **1931** Ripple ware [see *BADARIAN *a.*]. **1962** V. NABOKOV *Pale Fire* 143 The ripple-warped reflection of a ledge that jutted high above his present position.

ripple, *v.*³ **1. b.** (Later *transf.* and *fig.* examples.)

1924 R. CAMPBELL *Flaming Terrapin* iii. 45 In spangled pride A python ripples from his shrivelled hide. **1929** D. H. LAWRENCE *Pansies* 39 We ripple with life through the days.

d. To pass quickly *through* each of a series in turn.

1967 *Electronics* 6 Mar. 47/3 It will ripple through a truth table in maybe 100 microseconds,..moving through all possible logic combinations. **1973** *Sci. Amer.* May 110/3 Input pulses 'ripple' through the string of flip-flops sequentially, each device triggering the next one in the series.

2. a. (Further examples.)

1922 T. S. ELIOT *Waste Land* iii. 36 The brisk swell Rippled both shores. **1974** *Sat. Rev. World* (U.S.) 2 Nov. 32/3 The lake..was rippled by a sailboat.

c. (Later example.) Also, to let *out* or utter with a rippling sound.

1901 A. E. W. MASON *Clementina* xiii. 155 The girl reading it drew a breath and rippled out a laugh of gladness. **1913** C. MACKENZIE *Sinister St.* I. II. x. 313 'Why, you silly old thing..,' rippled Stella.

rippled, *ppl. a.* **a.** (Later examples.)

1903 H. G. WELLS *War in Air* v. 154 A rippled veil of still, thin sunlit cirrus. **1927** PEAKE & FLEURE *Peasants & Potters* vii. 100 Plain, incised, and rippled ware. **1930** R. CAMPBELL *Poems* 2 The rippled silver of her breasts. **1950** FRANSDEN & NELSON *Ice Cream* xvii. 177 Rippled ice cream: as the plain vanilla ice cream is drawn from the freezer into the package, specially prepared syrups..are added by means of a special nozzle so as to produce a marbled effect.

ri·ppleless, *a.* [-LESS.] Without causing ripples, unmarked by ripples.

1923 J. S. HUXLEY *Ess. Biologist* iii. 113 The Crested Grebe... Its brilliant white belly, protective grey-brown back, rippleless and effortless diving, [etc.]. **1941** STEINBECK & RICKETTS *Sea of Cortez* xiv. 131 The lagoon [was] rippleless.

ripplet. (Earlier example in form *riplet*.)

1820 SHELLEY *Orpheus* in *Compl. Poet. Wks.* (1904) 699 Each riplet makes A many-sided mirror for the sun.

rippling, *vbl. sb.*³ Add: **2.** (Earlier and later examples.)

1745 W. POTE *Jrnl. Captivity French & Indian War* (1896) 55 This Day was foul weather the Greatest part of the Day, and likewise verey bad Paddling, on account of Ripplings and falls. **1832** W. D. WILLIAMSON *Hist. Maine* I. 57 Here are ripplings, to avoid which, a canal was cut twenty rods in length.

rip-rap, *sb.* Add: **1. b.** (Later examples.) Also, the sound of fireworks detonating. Also *transf.*

1909 HALL CAINE *White Prophet* I. i. 8 Once more the words rang like a rip-rap down the line. **1930** *Sea Breezes* Dec. 72 The glare and rip-rap of the fireworks ashore..told that the Old Year 1882 had expired. **1942** *Sun* (Baltimore) 13 Mar. 13/3 Sea-coast guns on Fort Wool, known to civilians as the Rip Raps, will be fired Saturday between 9 A.M. and noon. **1974** *Country Life* 28 Nov. 1682 A firework party..rockets sped into the sky..followed by.. sparklers and even 'rip-raps' round our feet.

c. (See quot.)

1959 I. & P. OPIE *Lore & Lang. Schoolch.* xviii. 381 There are more than sixty established names for the pursuit of illegally knocking at doors... *Rip Rap*. Derby.

3. For *U.S.* read orig. *U.S.* and add: More widely, loose stone used for revetments, embankments, or the like; also, a structure made of this. (Earlier and further examples.)

[**1822** *Niles' Reg.* 15 June 252/1 The expense of getting stone, and delivering it at the Rip Raps and Point Comfort.] **1833** H. BARNARD *Let.* 4 Mar. in *Maryland Hist. Mag.* (1918) XIII. 314 We passed in our way..Old Point Comfort, upon which you know Fortress Monroe is situated—the ripraps directly opposite, which two will effectually secure the Bay. **1838** J. CHILDS *Western Railroad* (1839) 25 To guard the embankments by rip-rap walls. **1880** *News & Press* (Cimarron, New Mexico) 9 Sept. 3/3 It is the intention of the company to raise the grade of the approaches on both sides, protecting the exposed surfaces by what is technically known as 'rip rap', a kind of loose rock work. **1892** *Outing* July 254/1 At the worst places ripraps of brush and stones have been built to confine the river to its bed. **1926** *Daily Colonist* (Victoria, B.C.) 11 July 36/3 It was necessary to blast out a way at the cliffside, with occasional banks of rip-rap, and stretches of trestle. **1931** *Sun* (Baltimore) 1 Sept. 9/6 A railroad section foreman, blasting for rip rap stone, found the first sample of the ore in western Pike county [Arkansas]. **1975** *Offshore* Aug. 36/2 After placement the base was grouted into position and a wall of rip-rap placed right round the base to protect it against scour. **1976** *Billings* (Montana) *Gaz.* 16 June 7-A/2 The time required to obtain a riprap permit for Montana rivers and streams.

rip-rap *v.*, **rip-rapping** *vbl. sb.* (Further examples.)
1884 *Harper's Mag.* Sept. 504/1 Cliff ledges..[are] connected one terrace above by the other, by..a natural rip-rapping of fallen fragments. **1897** M. B. KER in E. L. Wilson et al. *Mountain Climbing* vi. 286 We riprapped the bottom of the slope to prevent slipping down the hill. **1904** *Dialect Notes* II. 420 Highland Avenue is rip-rapped on one side. **1938** *Sun* (Baltimore) 8 Nov. 5/3 Another [project] is for rip-rapping the river bank. **1943** B. A. DE VOTO *Year of Decision* 332 They had to..pry boulders out of their course, riprap swamp patches, sometimes bridge brooks that could not be crossed otherwise. **1976** *Columbus* (Montana) *News* 27 May 8/3 The resolution was signed for the riprapping of property by the Absarokee lagoon.

‖ **ripresa** (riprē·sa). *Mus.* [It.] A repeat; a refrain (see quot. 1947).
1740 J. GRASSINEAU *Mus. Dict.* 204 *Ripresa.* See *Repeat.* **1876** STAINER & BARRETT *Dict. Mus. Terms* 379/2 *Ripresa*... (1) A reprise or burden. (2) A repeat. **1947** E. BLOM *Everyman's Dict. Mus.* 501/1 *Ripresa*,..a refrain, especially in the 14th–15th cent. It. ballata and frottola. **1977** *Early Music* July 326/2 The ballata consists of a refrain or ripresa of one to four poetic lines, followed by two piedi..and a volta.

ri·pripple *v.*, nonce semi-reduplication of RIPPLE *v.*³
1922 JOYCE *Ulysses* 85 He saw his trunk and limbs riprippled over.

ri·p-roaring, riproaring, *a.* orig. *U.S.* [Cf. RIPROARIOUS *a.*] Full of vigour, spirit, or excellence; first-rate; boisterous; full-blooded.
1834 W. A. CARUTHERS *Kentuckian in N.Y.* I. 62 There was a rip-roaring sight of slight o' hand and tumbling work there. **1845** J. J. HOOPER *Some Adventures Simon Suggs* x. 127 And I seed the biggest, longest, rip-roarenest, blackest, scaliest..allegator. **1884** E. W. NYE *Baled Hay* 231 He thought..Kirke was there..to give Laramie the grandest, riproaringest tempest of mirth that she had ever experienced. **1905** *Dialect Notes* III. 64 We had a rip-roaring time. **1906** *N.Y. Even. Post* (Sat. Suppl.) 8 Sept. 1 When he was called upon to address the conference he got a rip-roaring welcome. **1923** *Daily Mail* 28 Feb. 10 (Advt.), It's a rip-roaring, red-blooded yarn that no man or woman will be able to read unmoved. **1948** *Sunday Pictorial* 18 July 11/3 A rip-roaring performance by Oscar Homolka. **1950** C. FRY *Venus Observed* II. ii. 70 Well, here's a rip-roaring gauntlet to be run By a couple of God's children. **1958** *Times* 3 Nov. 3/1 It was a match in which little skill was shown, but for all that a rip-roaring, babel-like affair of incessant movement and high good spirits. **1979** *Guardian* 14 Apr. 9/7 Rip-roaring commercial [film] successes.
Hence **ri:p-roa·ringly** *adv.*
1951 *Sport* 27 Jan.–2 Feb. 12/2 Their young side..is having a rip-roaringly successful cup season.

riproarious, *a.* For *U.S.* read orig. *U.S.* (Earlier and later examples.)
1830 *N.Y. Constellation* 11 Sept. 2/5 The English traveller had put up at a little log tavern on the banks of the Savannah, where the *riproarious* conduct took place. **1840** *Congress Globe* 2 Apr. 376/1 Here and there a gentleman from both political parties, who had been drawn out by curiosity to witness their riproarious proceedings [at the Whig 'powwows']. **1948** R. W. CHAPMAN *Lexicography* 6 The *Dictionary of American English*..stopped at 1900, before the trickle of that rip-roarious idiom became a flood. **1975** J. I. M. STEWART *Gaudy* iii. 57 It was one of those rare books which, while enjoying riproarious popular success, at the same time owns sufficient intrinsic merit to achieve among the critical a kind of classic status straight away.

riproa·riously, *adv.* [f. RIPROARIOUS *a.* + -LY².] In a riproarious or boisterous manner.
1834 D. CROCKETT *Narr. Life* xi. 78 The next day it rained rip-roriously.

ri·psnorter. orig. *U.S.* Also **rip-snorter.** [f. RIP *v.*² + SNORTER¹ 2: cf. RIPROARIOUS *a.*] Someone or something exceptionally remarkable in appearance, quality, strength, or the like; *spec.* a storm, a gale. Cf. SNORTER¹ 2 b.
1840 *Crockett Almanac* 20/1 Of all the ripsnorters I ever tutched upon, thar never war one that could pull her boat alongside of Grace Peabody. **1885** *Santa Fé Weekly New Mexican* 20 Aug. 2/6 Any galoot who wants the Ripsnorter for a year can have it left at his bar-room on payment of three red chips in advance. **1889** K. MUNROE *Dory Mates* (1890) vi. 84 Boys, we are in for a regular 'rip-snorter'. I never saw a nastier night. **1924** R. CLEMENTS *Gipsy of Horn* v. 87 It came on to blow in a way that the packet-rats called a 'rip-snorter'. **1931** A. J. CRONIN *Hatter's Castle* II. ix. 368 Did you see that shot of mine, cocky?.. It was a—a regular nor'easter—a pickled ripsnorter. **1941** BAKER *Dict. Austral. Slang* 60 *Ripsnorter*, something particularly good. An amusing or eccentric person. **1951** *New Yorker* 3 Mar. 28/1 The villain is a real ripsnorter. **1972** *Last Whole Earth Catalog* (Portola Inst.) 445/3 This is Gurney Norman the author speaking, bringing you the end of this folk tale, and it's a rip-snorter.

ri·psnorting, *a.* orig. *U.S.* Also **rip-snorting.** [f. prec.] = *RIP-ROARING, RIPROARING *a.*
1846 *Yale Lit. Mag.* June 336 What a rip-snorting red head you have got! **1904** *Topeka* (Kansas) *Capital* 2 June 4 It is now stated that Bryan will make a rip-snorting speech at the St. Louis convention. **1926** *Spectator* 10 July 44/1 It's a ripsnorting, red-blooded show—a wow. **1926** [see *HOTSY-TOTSY *a.*]. **1956** N. COWARD *South Sea Bubble* I. i. 12 You're a rip-snorting old careerist, darling. **1959** *Daily Mail* 17 Feb. 4/5 The Count Basie riff-number *Alright, Okay, You Win*, with ripsnorting backing. **1976** P. HENISSART *Winter Quarry* xxvii. 276 These ripsnorting professional anti-communists. **1978** *Detroit Free Press* 14 Apr. 15B/4 A ripsnorting cockroach race, with the men on their hands and knees, urging their bugs down makeshift lanes.
Hence (as a back-formation) **ri·psnort** *v.*, to go boisterously, to rollick; **ri:psno·rtingly** *adv.*
1974 *Publishers Weekly* 24 June 59/2 It's a definitive book, ripsnortingly adult. **1975** C. A. HADDAD *Moroccan* vii. 83 'Come to Daddy,' I said..she clambered on my back and together we ripsnorted our way to Ilanit. **1979** 'A. HAILEY' *Overload* II. x. 159 Water which promptly became high-pressure steam and ripsnorted to a separate superheater section.

Ripuarian, *a.* and *sb.* Add: **A.** *adj.* **3.** Designating a northern dialect of Middle Franconian German.
1910 *Encycl. Brit.* XI. 779/2 The boundary-line between Low and High German..may roughly be indicated by the..place-names, on the understanding..that the Ripuarian dialect..is to be classed with High German. **1934** PRIEBSCH & COLLINSON *German Lang.* II. vii. 323 Within Middle Franconian the Ripuarian dialect..keeps unshifted *rp.*
B. *sb.* **2.** The name of a dialect of Middle Franconian German.
1910 *Encycl. Brit.* XI. 780/1 Middle Franconian.., which ..represents a kind of transition dialect to Low German, is itself divided into (α) Ripuarian or Low Rhenish with Cologne and Aachen..as centres, and (β) Moselle Franconian with Trier..as principal town. **1934** PRIEBSCH & COLLINSON *German Lang.* II. i. 88 In Ripuarian—the Northern dialect of Middle Franconian—the unshifted form *ūp* (up) 'auf' is found. **1939** L. H. GRAY *Foundations of Lang.* xi. 349 Middle Franconian appears in two sub-forms: *Ripuarian* in the north, and *Moselle* in the south. **1961** R. E. KELLER *German Dial.* vii. 249 Luxemburgish appears ..as a relic area..separated..from Ripuarian by the *Dorp/Dorf* isogloss in the north. **1970** CHAMBERS & WILKIE *Short Hist. German Lang.* iii. 21 Middle Franconian, divided into Ripuarian (in the Cologne area) and Moselle Franconian.

Rip Van Winkle (rip væn wi·ŋk'l). The name of a character in Washington Irving's *Sketch Book* (1819–20), a good-for-nothing who falls asleep for twenty years, applied: **a.** *transf.* to a person unfamiliar with prevailing conditions.
1833 *Advocate* (Shelbyville, Kentucky) 28 Sept. 2/4 Wm. C. Preston, of South Carolina, in one of his furious tirades, applied to the State of North Carolina, the somewhat degrading epithet of 'the Rip Van Winkle of the South'. **1852** DICKENS *Bleak Ho.* (1853) ii. 5 Both the world of fashion and the Court of Chancery are things of precedent and usage; over-sleeping Rip Van Winkles, who have played at strange games through a deal of thundery weather. **1892** G. B. SHAW *Fabian Soc.* 20 There are some Rip Van Winkles in our movement who are only now waking up. **1939** C. DAY LEWIS *Child of Misfortune* III. i. 262 A Rip Van Winkle's self-pity would seize him. **1945** R. HARGREAVES *Enemy at Gate* 187 That somewhat shop-soiled military Rip van Winkle, Giuseppe Garibaldi. **1974** H. McCLOY *Sleepwalker* ii. 17 What was she? A girl Rip Van Winkle who had been asleep since 1940?
b. *attrib.* to something characteristic of or resembling Rip Van Winkle or (an aspect of) his experience.
1849 *Picayune* (New Orleans) 21 July 1/6 A person absent for three weeks, on returning, almost fancies that he has been taking a Rip Van Winkle slumber. **1893** I. ZANGWILL *Ghetto Tragedies* 133 Is it possible that I can get into touch again with my youth..after a sort of Rip Van Winkle sleep? **1959** *Times* 6 May 15/7 Time, in Česky Krummau, seems to have stopped about the year 1800. In this Rip-van-Winkle atmosphere, we were taken to the tiny castle chapel, where there is a baroque organ in which every single pipe is in its original state. **1977** W. H. S. SMITH *Young Man's Country* iii. 93 On the wall, as if to convince me that I was not in a Rip Van Winkle dream, was a list of S.D.O.s.
So **Rip Van Wi·nkleish** *a.*, characteristic of or resembling Rip Van Winkle, ignorant of present conditions; hence **Rip Van Wi·nkledom,** (*a*) the Catskill Mountains in the state of New York, the site of Rip Van Winkle's sleep; (*b*) a state of prolonged sleep; **Rip Van Wi·nkleism,** an outmoded custom or opinion.
1829 *Mechanic's Press* (Utica, N.Y.) 5 Dec. 28/1 His Rip Van Winkleish habits asked no more than to pursue 'the even tenor of their way'. **1842** C. M. KIRKLAND *Forest Life* II. 228 [Reading an old-fashioned book] was counted among my Rip-Van-Winkle-isms. **1852** *Harper's Mag.* Aug. 420/2 A Pilgrim from the backwoods..had just been awakened from a Rip-Van-Winkleish existence of a quarter of a century by the steam-whistle of the Erie Railroad. **1888** G. B. SHAW *Let.* 9 Feb. (1965) I. 185 He persists in his 18th century Rip-van-Winkleism. **1892** *Outing* Apr. 48 (*title*) A cyclist's visit to Rip Van Winkledom. *Ibid.* 50/2 We are already in the confines of Rip Van Winkledom. **1911** BEERBOHM *Lett. to R. Turner* (1964) 195 It made me feel very Rip-Van-Winkleish to find no Alfred Douglas. **1956** M. LOWRY *Let.* 13 Nov. (1967) 391 She..has also for the latter part of this time been mostly asleep... She emerged from this Ripvanwinkledom, feeling and sounding better than she has in ten years.

Riquewihr (rī·kvīᵊɹ). The name of a town in Alsace, applied to white wines produced there.
1947 T. E. CARLING *Wine-Wise* vi. 34 The latter [*sc.* Gentil, Riesling and Traminer] are usually sold under the name of the grape, coupled with that of the village—as Riesling-Riquewihr, and Traminer-Ribeauvillé, etc. **1951** E. PAUL *Springtime in Paris* x. 184 Was it Chablis, Pouilly or Riquewihr with the oysters? **1963** I. FLEMING *On H.M. Secret Service* xxiv. 264 You are just in time for some good Strasbourg sausage and a passable Riquewihr. **1974** C. WILSON *Bk. of Booze* iii. 124 Alsace wines..are usually sold under the name of the grape—Riesling, Traminer, Sylvaner, etc.—and sometimes the town—Riquewihr being perhaps the best known.

riroriro (rī·rorīro). [Maori.] Also (with hyphen) **riro-riro.** The New Zealand grey warbler, *Gerygone igata*, a small wren-like bird belonging to the subfamily Malurinæ of the family Muscicapidæ.
1835 W. YATE *Acct. N.Z.* (ed. 2) ii. 58 *Riroriro*, a very small brown bird, with white feathers under the wings and tail. **1860** [see *FAN-TAIL *sb.* 3]. **1884** M. A. MARTIN *Our Maoris* viii. 125 There is a little bird called Riro-riro in New Zealand from its note. **1939** D. CRESSWELL *Present without Leave* 32 The riro-riro..has a small wistful song. **1955** W. R. B. OLIVER *N.Z. Birds* (ed. 2) 477/1 Mention of the Riroriro occurs in many stories, songs and proverbs of the Maori.

‖ **ris de veau** (rīdəvō). Also erron. 9 **riz de veau.** [Fr.] A dish of sweetbread of veal. Freq. in *Comb.* Also *fig.*
1820 M. EDGEWORTH *Let.* 4 June (1979) 144, I give you one dinner by which you may judge all the rest—Bouilli de boeuf—..ris de veau piqué—maquereau, [etc.]. **1861** MRS. BEETON *Bk. Househ. Managem.* 909 *Entrées.* Riz de Veau aux Tomates. **1877** E. S. DALLAS *Kettner's Bk. of Table* 452 *Roasted Sweetbreads.* This is what the French set down as the *Ris de veau à l'Anglaise.* **1927** N. WAINWRIGHT tr. *Dekobra's Madonna of Sleeping Cars* xiv. 187 There are no great men except the inventors and the developers of science. All the rest amount to more or less *ris de veau* surrounding an Adam's apple. **1938** L. MACNEICE *I crossed Minch* vii. 101 I'll have a little ris de veau, I think. **1964** L. DEIGHTON *Funeral in Berlin* xxiii. 126 There is *entrecôte* or *ris de veau.* **1975** R. STOUT *Family Affair* viii. 188 Sweetbreads poached in white wine, dipped in crumbs and eggs, sautéed, and doused with almonds in brown butter... They call it *ris de veau amandine.*

rise, *sb.* Add: **I. 4. c.** *Cricket.* The upward movement of a ball after pitching.
1851 J. PYCROFT *Cricket Field* viii. 165 Slow balls can be pitched nearer to the bat, affording a shorter sight of the rise. **1897** P. NORMAN *West Kent Cricket Club* 40 There was always a good spin on his ball, and he could..give it that 'abrupt rise', as it has somewhere been called, which is so fatal to many a good batsman.
d. *Theatr.* The raising of the curtain at the beginning of a scene. In phr. *at rise*, whereby the playwright introduces the description of the opening situation.
1905 [see *curtain-rise* s.v. *CURTAIN *sb.* 8]. **1933** S. KINGSLEY *Men in White* II. i. 77 Three months later... At rise: Mr Houghton, short, stodgy, aggressive..the economist, has just finished reading a report. **1961** BOWMAN & BALL *Theatre Lang.* 17 *At rise*, at the moment when the rising curtain first discloses a scene; said often of the relative positions of actors at such a moment. *Ibid.* 301 *Rise*,..the going up of a curtain (also as the *curtain rise* or the *rising*). **1962** [see *curtain-fall* s.v. *CURTAIN *sb.* 8].
e. *slang.* = ERECTION 4. Usu. in phr. *to get a rise.*
1949 PARTRIDGE *Dict. Slang* (ed. 3) 1154/2 *Rise, get a*, to experience an erection. **1973** M. AMIS *Rachel Papers* 55 'Have you fucked Sue?.. What was it like?'.. 'It was okay, except I couldn't get a proper rise.'
6. c. Also of other precious metals and stones.
1940 I. L. IDRIESS *Lightning Ridge* xv. 99 Andy sank five hundred shafts, toiled for years and years, and never made a rise.
d. *slang.* A fit of anger.
1877 'ETON BOY' *Day of my Life* i. 11, I told him for his good; he needn't get in such a rise about it. **1895** H. W. NEVINSON *Neighbours of Ours* i. 21 Mrs. Sullivan was in a fair rise about it, sayin' as 'e'd took us all in.
8. For *Obs.*—¹ read *Obs.* and add later examples.
1848 D. COX *Let.* 29 July in F. G. Roe *David Cox* (1924) ii. 59 It was expect[ed] there would be a rise among the Irish. **1853** DICKENS *Child's Hist. Eng.* in *Househ. Words* 17 Sept. 71/1 He had some wild hope of gaining the Irish people over to his side by favoring a rise among them.
II. 9. b. A long, broad, gently sloping elevation rising from the sea bed, esp. that at the edge of a continental shelf.
1903 *Geogr. Jrnl.* XXII. 193 The *elevation* is either entirely surrounded by depressions or is a prolongation of the continental border. The *rise* is an elevation which rises gradually with an angle of only a few minutes of arc, irrespective of whether it is wide or narrow... Rises carry the chief features of suboceanic relief, so that if the ocean floor was changed into dry land they would act as the main watersheds. **1954** W. D. THORNBURY *Princ. Geomorphol.* xviii. 477 A good example of a rise or swell is that in the Pacific Ocean known as the Hawaiian swell or rise. It is a comparatively gentle rise some 600 miles wide and about 1900 miles long. **1974** *Nature* 30 Aug. 694/2 States like Argentina, Australia, Canada..will prefer to go beyond 200 miles to the outer edge of the continental rise if this is larger than 200 miles.
III. 14. Also in *Phonetics.* Cf. *rise-fall* below.
1911 *Encycl. Brit.* XXI. 465/2 A high rise, which begins high, and consequently can only rise a little higher, expresses simple question, while..a low rise..expresses

various degrees of surprise or indignation. **1932** [see *fall-rise* s.v. *FALL *sb.*[1] 29]. **1965** *Language* XLI. 210 This scale maintained its neatness only when the nuclear exponent was a simple 'fall' or 'rise'. When the nucleus was 'fall-rise', 'rise-fall', or 'fall-plus-rise', two phenomena were observed.

15. b. Delete *colloq.* and add further examples.

1915 W. S. MAUGHAM *Of Human Bondage* cvii. 564 If they were not worth a rise it was better to sack them at once. **1921** [see *RAISE *sb.*[1] 5 c]. **1957** E. H. SHEPARD *Drawn from Memory* vii. 131 She..said that her 'intended' was going to receive a rise and work on the passenger trains. **1978** *Verbatim* Sept. 12/1 The influence of British usage in America is more and more evident: *The New York Times*, 1 April 1978, in referring to the increased settlement for transit workers in New York City, called it a '6% Rise'.

c. For '(See quot.)' read: *the rise of* (an amount or period of time), more than, above (that quantity); *and the rise*, and more. (Earlier and later examples.) Now *rare*. Cf. RISING *pr. pple.* 3.

1834 in J. S. Bassett *Southern Plantation Overseer* (1925) 66, I muste plante the rise of a hundred aceres in coten. **1839** *Southern Lit. Messenger* V. 379/1 It is the rise of a week since I last shifted. **1845** J. J. HOOPER *Some Adventures Simon Suggs* xii. 141 Bill..has been ded the rise of twenty year. **1858** in N. E. Eliason *Tarheel Talk* (1956) 290 At Mr Collins thar has bin de rise of A hundred down with the measles. **1905** 'O. HENRY' in *Everybody's Mag.* Dec. 820/1, I will undertake for to say that I've seen the rise of $50,000 at a time in that tin grub box that my adopted father calls his safe.

IV. 20. *Comb.*, as *rise-and-fall* adj.; **rise-fall** *Phonetics*, a rise and subsequent fall of pitch compressed into one syllable (cf. *fall-rise* s.v. *FALL *sb.*[1] 29); also *attrib.*; **rise time** *Electronics*, the time required for a pulse to rise from 10% to 90% of its steady value.

1926 *Gloss. Terms Electr. Engin.* (Brit. Engin. Stand. Assoc.) 159 *Rise-and-fall pendant*, a pendant the height of which can be regulated by means of a pulley and counter-weight or similar device. **1950** *Engineering* 21 July 59/2 Sellers include a 'rise and fall clause' in their contracts. **1974** tr. *Wertheim's Evolution & Revolution* i. 64 Oswald Spengler ..elaborated the rise-and-fall concept as a world-wide cyclical movement from which no human civilization could escape. **1977** *Grimsby Even. Tel.* 14 May 6/5 (Advt.), 3-phase saw bench with rise and fall table, £80. **1964** CRYSTAL & QUIRK *Syst. Prosodic & Paralinguistic Features in Eng.* iv. 50 Such nuclei are of the following seven types: fall, rise, level, fall-rise, rise-fall, fall-plus-rise, and rise-plus-fall. **1966** G. N. LEECH, *Eng. in Advertising* v. 49 The..advertisement ..contains three examples of the rise-fall tone... A contour line above each example indicates the position of the rise-fall. **1973** *Archivum Linguisticum* IV. 25 In paratone I..the 'low rise-fall'..is likely to be followed by the 'wide fall'. **1947** *Rev. Sci. Instruments* XVIII. 643/1 To obtain best possible rise times for the pulses, care is required in laying out the components. **1952** *Proc. IRE* XL. 962/1 Because of limited bandwidth, the pulse takes a certain length of time to build up its amplitude, i.e., it requires a certain 'rise time'. **1969** J. J. SPARKES *Transistor Switching* i. 22 The turn-on time is divided into two parts, the delay time..and the rise time. **1975** G. J. KING *Audio Handbk.* ii. 41 Extended high-frequency response is..required to ensure that the rise time of the amplifier is not less than that of transient-type programme signal components.

rise, *v.* Add: **B. I. 1. h.** *Welsh dial.* Of a funeral party: to depart from the home of the deceased or bereaved before the interment.

1959 *Western Mail* (Cardiff) 18 Feb. 3/1 The funeral on Friday, Feb. 20, rising at 3 p.m., for interment at Gwaelod-y-Brithdir Cemetery. **1976** *Ibid.* 8 Jan. 10/2 The funeral..will be rising at 2 p.m. for New Bethel Chapel, from her daughter's residence.

3. c. In *imp.* phr. *rise and shine*, a command to wake up and leave one's bed. orig. *Armed Forces'*.

1916 *Recruiters' Bull.* (U.S. Marine Corps) Apr. 11/2 He rapped at the door and in stentorian tones cried, 'Rise and shine... Wiggle a toe.' **1917** KIPLING *Diversity of Creatures* 237 A high sun over Asia shouting: 'Rise and shine!' **1927** P. RILEY *Mem. Blue-Jacket* 89 Hands were called at 5:30 a.m., the bo'sun's mates going around the deck shouting 'All hands, rise and shine.' **1946** J. IRVING *Royal Navalese* 146 *Rise and shine!*, the boatswains' mates' call to The Hands to roust them out in the morning. **1953** G. BELL *Black Marigolds* xix. 189 Wakey, wakey, rise and shine, or have you fainted? **1973** H. NIELSEN *Severed Key* x. 105 'Rise and shine, lovebirds!' he shouted. 'The honeymoon is over!'

II. 14. b. (Further *fig.* examples.)

1932 E. M. BRENT-DYER *Chalet Girls in Camp* xii. 193 'I *said* it to make Juliet rise—and she hasn't risen!' cried Jo. **1966** *Listener* 6 Oct. 507/2, I should perhaps apologise for having risen to the bait of Mr Wilkinson's provocative letter. **1974** 'J. LE CARRÉ' *Tinker, Tailor* i. 17 He knew they were teasing him but he was unable not to rise.

III. 15. b. *to rise to the occasion* (further examples).

1889 E. DOWSON *Let.* 12 Apr. (1967) 66 Limehouse won't produce a dinner but if you can stand it 'possibly my old Sonia's larder may rise'—not 'to the occasion' but to a scratch tea. **1906** G. B. SHAW *Let.* 7 May (1972) II. 622 The tenor..rose to the occasion and was bully. **1922** H. CRANE *Let.* 7 Dec. (1965) 107 This parodist and facile assessor could so gracefully rise to the occasion of a new attitude. **1952** M. LASKI *Village* ii. 38 Sheila had risen splendidly to the occasion and offered..to wash up. **1975** *Harper's & Queen* May 138/2, I told my parents... It would be a mistake to say they were enthusiastic, but they *do* rise to the occasion.

V. 29. b. *U.S.* To exceed in number or amount.

1838 'B. SMITH' *Motley Bk.* 177 Brother George counted the strokes of his arm upon the cushion, and he thinks he rose a hundred in the course of the sermon. **1877** S. O. JEWETT *Deephaven* 133, I like well enough to see a hog that'll weigh six hundred,..but for my eatin' give me one that'll just rise three.

riser. Add: **II. 7. b.** *Geomorphol.* The steeply sloping part of each of the step-like parts of a glacial stairway or similar landform.

1930 F. E. MATTHES *Geol. Hist. Yosemite Valley* 95/2 All the other steps in the upper Merced Canyon have risers and sills composed of very sparingly jointed or wholly massive rock. *Ibid.* 98/1 These steps..have conspicuously sheer, smooth fronts, or risers. **1954** W. D. THORNBURY *Princ. Geomorphol.* xv. 369 Each step [in a glacial stairway] typically has three component parts: a riser, a riegel, and a tread. **1974** *Encycl. Brit. Macropædia* XIX. 641/1 The establishment of runoff after wastage of the ice has occurred will lead to a series of waterfalls or cascades at the site of each riser in the stairway. **1975** C. TAYLOR *Fields in Eng. Landscape* iv. 90 The most characteristic features of strip lynchets are usually their steep risers, sometimes of considerable height.

9. (Further examples.)

1950 *Times Rev. Industry* Sept. 16/2 (Advt.), Risers act as reservoirs of molten metal to compensate for liquid shrinkage. **1967** A. H. COTTRELL *Introd. Metallurgy* xiii. 184 The metal is poured into a sand mould through a gate, down a sprue and along a runner. A riser has also to be provided, leading upwards from the top of the casting, to provide a pool of molten metal to feed the casting as it freezes and shrinks. **1973** J. G. TWEEDDALE *Materials Technol.* II. ii. 36 Risers are vertical channels rising to the top of the mould, which help to control flow by trapping slag and in which the rise of metal in the mould and the progress of solidification can be followed.

10. (Earlier examples.)

1821 J. FERGUSSON *Brit. Pat. No. 4594.* 18 Oct., In the process of printing from stereotype plates the plates are put upon and fastened to certain materials or apparatus called by different names, such as blocks, matrix plates, risers, &c., which are made either of iron, brass, type metal, ..gypsum, wood [etc.]. **1841** W. SAVAGE *Dict. Art of Printing* 702 *Risers*, the material upon which stereotype plates are fixed, in order to be printed.

12. a. = *rising main* (b) s.v. *RISING *ppl. a.* 6; **riser diagram**, a diagram of the risers in a building.

1898 *Engin. Rec.* 26 Nov. 566/1 The grouping of risers has been made..so that the average current demand on each pair of lighting bars will be about equal. **1924** T. CROFT *Conduit Wiring* iii. 68 (*caption*) Riser diagram of conduit wiring in a hotel building. **1930** MOYER & WOSTREL *Industr. Electr. & Wiring* v. 146 Wires and cables serving as main risers or feeders in buildings of fire-resistive construction, may be run bare..under special conditions. **1967** G. A. T. BURDETT *Electr. Installations* 36 Especially suitable for short runs and for individual risers from a main distribution board on the ground floor.

b. A vertical pipe for the upward flow of a fluid; *spec.* (*a*) one carrying water or steam from one floor to another in a central heating system; (*b*) one extending from an offshore drilling or production platform to the sea-bed, through which drilling may be done or oil or gas may flow. Also *riser pipe(line)*.

1908 A. G. KING *Pract. Steam & Hot Water Heating* xi. 111 The riser or risers..rise directly to the top floor or attic ..and here branch in the several directions necessary to feed the various drop risers supplying the radiators. **1941** *Nature* 15 Mar. 315/1 The tall 'risers', that is, vertical 5-in pipes which convey the water up to the projector nozzles, are spaced throughout the plantation as required. **1961** *B.S.I. News* Nov. 17/1 The code will recommend the installation of fire lifts and internal fire mains or 'risers' to assist firemen in applying water to a fire as early as possible. **1969** T. STANLEY *More Small Bore Heating* ii. 77/3 The pipework is being run under..the first floor with drops and risers to radiators on the ground floor. **1972** L. M. HARRIS *Introd. Deepwater Floating Drilling Operations* xii. 133 Selection of the riser-pipe steel is critical for a long-life, trouble-free operation. **1975** *Offshore Progress: Technol. & Costs* (Shell Internat. Petroleum Co.) 6 As the rig rises and falls with the heaving surface of the sea, the riser must be held in vertical tension in order to prevent it from buckling. **1977** *New Yorker* 9 May 38/1 Behind the riser pipe in the bathroom Puttermesser kept weeks' worth of Sunday *Times* crossword puzzles.

13. *Cricket.* A ball that rises sharply on pitching.

1955 *Times* 5 July 4/4 Shackleton could not draw away quickly enough from a riser from James and was acrobatically caught in the slips.

14. = *lift-web* s.v. *LIFT *sb.*[2] 18.

1927 C. A. LINDBERGH *We—Pilot & Plane* viii. 140, I left the ship head first and was falling in this position when the risers whipped me around into an upright position and the chute opened. **1975** tr. *Melchior's Sleeper Agent* (1976) iii. 230 When the [parachute] canopy is fully open you will swing under it... You will check the oscillation by tugging on the two risers in the direction of your swing... He grabbed hold of two of the webbed risers. **1976** L. SANDERS *Hamlet Warning* (1977) xxix. 277 He pulled the ring, saw the silk deploy... He fought the risers, stopping his oscillation.

rishi. Add: Also 8 **Richi.** (Earlier and later examples.)

1766 J. CLELAND *Way to Things by Words* 91 The language of the antient *Richi*, or of the *Vedams*, is often hardly intelligible, even by the most skilful, who know only the Sanscort, fixed by the grammars. **1916** [see *JNANA]. **1934** A. D. WALEY *Way & its Power* App. ii. 114, I see no reason to doubt that the 'holy mountain-men' (*shêng-hsien*) described by *Lieh Tzŭ* are Indian *rishi*... It is at least a possibility that some knowledge of the *yoga*-technique which these rishi used had also drifted into China. **1939** *Antiquity* XIII. 15 The Aryan rishis sang their Vedic hymns. **1971** *Shankar's Weekly* (Delhi) 11 Apr. 22/2 Mythological stories of irate Rishis hurling curses at trespassers came to mind and every moment one feared our Rishi's wrath.

rishon (ri·ʃɒn). *Particle Physics.* [a. Heb. *ri'šôn* first, primary; cf. *-ON[1].] A hypothetical particle postulated as a constituent of quarks and leptons.

1979 H. HARARI in *Physics Lett.* LXXXVIB. 84/2 The most economical set of building blocks consists of two $J = 1/2$ objects: one charged ($Q = 1/3$) and one neutral...We denote the charged particle by T and the neutral one by V. We name these particles 'rishons'. [*Note*] 'Rishon' means first, primary (in Hebrew). **1979** *New Scientist* 5 July 22/3 The charged leptons can consist of the three charged rishons (TTT) and the neutrinos of three neutral rishons (VVV), but the fractionally-charged quarks are made up of different combinations such as TTV or VVT. **1981** *Sunday Times* 1 Mar. 15/2 The latest theory reduces all the matter in the universe to just two kinds of basic particles. Its originator—Haim Harari of the Weizmann Institute in Israel—has named the particles *rishons*, from the Hebrew for primary.

‖ **rishta** (riʃta·). Also **rishtu, reshta.** [Tadzhik.] A local name in part of the Soviet Union for the guinea-worm (*Dracunculus medinensis*), a common parasite of man and other mammals, and the disease which it produces.

1834 A. BURNES *Trav. Bokhara* II. 180 Among the diseases of Bokhara, the most distressing is the guinea-worm, or Dracunculus, here called 'rishtu': it is confined to the city. The inhabitants believe that the disease arises from drinking the water of the cisterns in summer, when they become fetid and infested with animalculæ. **1885** H. LANSDELL *Russ. Central Asia* II. liii. 146 What I had seen and been warned of in Samarkand, made me specially fearful of the *rishta*, a well-known disease in Bokhara. **1923** *Chambers's Jrnl.* July 472/2 The barber-surgeon trying to operate on a young man for 'rishta', that troublesome parasite which burrows into the skin. **1966** E. SCHUYLER *Turkistan* iv. 82 The Sarts are not only attacked by the usual maladies.. but they have besides two or three which are peculiar to the country... One of these is the *reshta*, or 'Guinea-worm'.

rising, *vbl. sb.* Add: **II. 8.** Also const. *up*.

1942 W. S. CHURCHILL *End of Beginning* (1943) 145 People very often fall by the very means which they have used and built their hopes upon for their rising-up!

11. b. (Further U.S. examples.)

1834 W. SEWALL *Diary* 7 Dec. (1930) 160/1 Laid up with a bad rising on my hand. **1867** A. D. RICHARDSON *Beyond Mississippi* xi. 133 He spoke of a swelling upon his knee as a 'rising'. **1938** M. K. RAWLINGS *Yearling* xix. 236 None of us ain't got risin's. **1949** T. CAPOTE *Other Voices* v. 104, I had me a rising on my butt big as a baseball. **1972** E. WIGGINTON *Foxfire Bk.* 244 Scrape the white of an Irish potato and place the scrapings on the bump. Bind them on with a clean cloth. This will draw the risin' (boil) to a head.

15. a. Also *Comb.*, as *(salt-)rising bread* (N. Amer.).

1865 MRS. STOWE *House & Home Papers* 236 Salt-rising bread. **1882** G. M. BARBOUR *Florida* iii. 56 The feast of hog, hominy, beef..and likely a few villainous compounds of flour, cheapest brown sugar, or sirup, and called *cake* or 'risin'-bread'. **1933** *Sun* (Baltimore) 3 Feb. 10/7 The Western correspondent..is talking about a foodstuff that resembles salt-rising bread..about as much as lady fingers resemble Russian black bread... Only a slight quantity of corn meal is used in the preparation of salt-rising bread. **1960** J. J. ROWLANDS *Spindrift* 172 The meat..was flanked by plates of moist and closely knit salt-rising bread. **1973** L. RUSSELL *Everyday Life Colonial Canada* viii. 96 'Salt-rising' bread was made without benefit of yeast.

rising, *ppl. a.* Add: **4. c.** (Further examples.) Also, characterized by increase in vocal stress or a rise in pitch. Also *Comb.*, as *rising-falling*.

1881 G. M. HOPKINS *Lett. to R. Bridges* (1955) 40, I call *rising rhythm* that in which the slack comes first, as in iambs and anapests, *falling* that in which the stress comes first, as in trochees and dactyls. **1894** H. SWEET *Anglo-Saxon Reader* (ed. 7) p. xciv, There is a tendency to combine different types in a line, the falling types A and D being most frequent in I, while in II the rising types B and C are preferred. **1931** G. NOËL-ARMFIELD *Gen. Phonetics* (ed. 4) xiii. 69 These [signs] may be combined to showing falling-rising, rising-falling, and so forth. **1955** *Archivum Linguisticum* VII. 155 The Greek circumflex is not, essentially, a rising-falling accent. **1964** R. H. ROBINS *Gen. Linguistics* 111 Tones may..rise or fall, or rise and fall, or fall and rise (rising, falling, rising-falling, falling-rising tones, respectively), and be distinguished by the actual direction in which the pitch moves. **1973** *Archivum Linguisticum* IV. 19 Typical sequences of tones..in which a final falling tone is preceded by a rising tone.

6. rising damp, moisture absorbed from the ground into a wall; **rising diphthong** *Phonetics*, a diphthong in which the final vowel is more prominent; **rising main**, (*b*) an electricity main passing from one floor of a building to another; **rising sun**: see SUN *sb.* 2 a.

1956 W. A. G. BRADMAN *Taking Care of Your Home* iv. 61 Rising damp..is invariably characterized by a line of dampness appearing above the skirtings. **1975** *Times* 30

Oct. 6/5 The walls had been sodden with rising damp for years. **1888** H. Sweet *Hist. Eng. Sounds* (ed. 2) 9 A 'rising'..diphthong. **1892** J. Wright *Primer Gothic Lang.* viii. 43 A diphthong may be defined as the combination of a sonantal with a consonantal vowel. And it is called a falling or rising diphthong according as the stress is upon the first or second element. **1960** P. H. Reaney *Orig. Eng. Place-Names* 45 In Devon, OE *ēa* frequently became a rising diphthong in ME and survives with initial *y*: Yalland, Yelland. **1940** *Chambers's Techn. Dict.* 727/2 *Rising mains*, in an electrical installation, a mains circuit which runs from one floor of a building to another. **1967** G. A. T. Burdett *Electr. Installations* 37 Where conditions allow there are advantages in using purpose-made rising mains.

rising, *pr. pple.* Add: **3. a.** (Earlier example.)

1837 W. Jenkins *Ohio Gazetteer* 64 It enjoys a yearly income of rising $4,500.

risk, *sb.* Add: **1. d.** *at* (or † *in*) *risk, at high* (etc.) *risk*: in danger, subject to hazard. Also as *adj.* (See also sense *2 c.)

1901 'L. Malet' *Counsel of Perfection* xi. 243 Whether the capital owned by his better nature was not in risk of being exhausted—whether the drafts made on it might not eventually be dishonoured. **1965** *New Statesman* 10 Dec. 951/2 (Advt.), The appointment should be of interest to those who are prepared to assist in training child care officers and actively supervising casework of 'at risk' families. **1966** *Listener* 10 Feb. 199/1 It is necessary to know both the number of legitimate children born to women in this age-group and the number of married women at risk. **1972** *Daily Tel.* 5 May 6/8 Eight thousand historic churches in England are at risk through damage and decay. **1973** *Sci. Amer.* July 20/2 Women who were at high risk of bearing retarded infants. **1977** *National Trust* Spring 9/1 Soon nearly half our elms will be dead and the remainder all at risk. **1977** *Lancet* 23 July 203/1 The baby was considered to be at high risk.

e. A person who is considered a liability or danger; one who is exposed to hazard. (Freq. with qualifying word.)

1948 [see *clearance 5 c]. **1954** *Manch. Guardian Weekly* 22 Apr. 3/1 A loyalty risk is a man whose paramount allegiance to the United States is in doubt. A security risk is one who may be consciously the most adamant patriot but whose judgment or tactlessness may cause him to make decisions or disclose information that could harm the national security. **1961** *Lancet* 12 Aug. 328/2 That patients classified as 'poor risks' according to Russek's criteria..show a higher mortality-rate is no cause for wonder. **1976** W. Greatorex *Crossover* 32 He was frozen out... He was treated as a security risk..but it didn't bother him.

2. a. Also (freq. without article), the chance that is accepted in economic enterprise and considered the source of (an entrepreneur's) profit. *all risks*: see *all *a.* E. 13. Cf. *uncertainty.

1776 Adam Smith *Wealth of Nations* I. i. x. 136 The ordinary rate of profit always rises more or less with the risk. **1848** Mill *Pol. Econ.* I. ii. xv. 479 The difference between the interest and the gross profit remunerates the exertions and risks of the undertaker. **1921** F. H. Knight *Risk, Uncertainty, & Profit* ii. 41 The doctrine that profit is to be explained exclusively in terms of risk has been vigorously upheld. **1944** A. Cairncross *Introd. Econ.* vi. 76 The more fickle the demand, either from one season to another, or from year to year, the stronger will be the tendency to spread risks and steady production by diversifying output. **1977** B. Benjamin *Gen. Insurance* xi. 271 The mathematics of risk theory and of model building do not at present cover these kinds of business risks other than by incorporating past investment experience.

c. *Law.* In phr. *at* (one's, etc.) *risk*, of merchandise, etc.: at the liability of a stated party. Also of persons, liable to repay loss or damage.

1798 [in Dict., sense 2 a.] **1887** *Law Rep. Queen's Bench Div.* XVIII. 65 The expression 'at ship's risk' cannot be strictly correct, because the ship has no risk. **1970** *New Society* 5 Feb. 209/1 He therefore should be at risk where the car causes damage.

3. *attrib.* and *Comb.*, as *risk aversion, -bearing, category, factor, level, management, -taker, -taking*; *risk-free* adj.; **risk analysis,** the systematic investigation and forecasting of risks in business and commerce; similarly **risk–benefit analysis; risk capital,** money that is put up for speculative business investment; **risk money,** (*b*) = *risk capital* above; **risk profile,** a forecast of the probable range of hazards in an enterprise; **risk-rate,** a rate of interest related to a degree of hazard in an enterprise.

1964 *Harvard Business Rev.* Jan.–Feb. 95 (*heading*) Risk analysis in capital investment. **1977** R. E. Megill *Introd. Risk Analysis* xv. 173 In the search for new oil and gas fields, risk analysis takes the judgments of explorationists and engineers and translates them into the language of probability. Risk analysis, thus, helps a manager make reasonable decisions. **1964** W. S. Vickrey *Metastatics & Macroecon.* v. 88 The differential between long- and short-term interest rates thus requires both liquidity preference and risk aversion to sustain it. **1972** *Accountant* 21 Sept. 349/2 Any application of probability theories to decision-making must have regard to the susceptibilities of the decision-maker, his own attitudes and those of his corporation —in particular, their 'risk aversion factor'. **1931** *Economist* 21 Nov. 957/1 The establishment of confidence, which would make possible a reduction of the premium on risk-bearing. **1958** *Times Lit. Suppl.* 25 July 426/4 In discussing the reward of risk-bearing the author refers to the special information that some may have and to the riches of others, thus finding that 'risk-taking surpluses' accrue. **1975** *Physics Bull.* May 203/2 One fears that until recently no such risk-benefit analysis would have been attempted. **1976** *Conservation News* Nov.–Dec. 3/1 On risk/benefit analysis, where many people hold that value judgements are involved, common ground seems impossible to find. **1948** *Sun* (Baltimore) 7 Apr. 19/1 He contended that newly saved risk capital in 1946 and 1947 supplied only $700,000,000 of the $50,500,000,000 of new money required by American industry. **1962** *Economist* 19 May 693/1 'Incentives' have not been dulled and 'risk capital' has not dried up. **1976** F. Zweig *New Acquisitive Society* i. vii. 69 The old acquisitiveness provided long-term risk-capital for industrial development. **1973** *Sci. Amer.* Sept. 65/1 Women were assigned to one of four risk categories. **1971** *Brit. Med. Bull.* XXVII. 23/2 Does the prevalence of individual risk factors..differ between soft-water and hard-water areas? **1950** *Mind* LIX. 126 The 'reactionaries' are those who believe that scientific enquiries can proceed from risk-free observational records immune from statistical tests. **1980** *Sci. Amer.* Mar. 33/3 People do not seek a risk-free society, but they do find it hard to manage risks that are not fully understood. **1962** A. Battersby *Guide to Stock Control* iii. 28 We already have two possible figures... Why are these figures different from each other? Because they correspond to different *risk levels.* **1970** *New Scientist* 15 Jan. 93/2 The risk-level of the former can be detected at interview. **1963** Mehr & Hedges (*title*) Risk management in the business enterprise. **1978** *Financial Rev.* (Austral.) 27 July 25/3 Risk Management, whatever you call it, is part and parcel of a big Insurance Broker's business. **1944** H. A. Wallace *Century of Common Man* xiv. 70 A business man ought to be able to get his 'risk money' back before he has to pay too much in the way of taxation. **1969** *Daily Tel.* 29 Dec. 12/2 The oilmen are also aware that if the Gas Council is pushed further into exploration the Government will have to provide 'risk money' on a large scale. **1969** J. Argenti *Managem. Techniques* 233 When the forecast is made, an estimate of the probability of the range of errors is also made and this is used to calculate the 'risk profile' of the project. **1928** *Britain's Industr. Future* (Liberal Industr. Inquiry) iii. xvi. 187 Capital will not be forthcoming for any enterprise unless it can expect (*a*) a normal rate of interest..and (*b*) in addition to that a 'risk-rate' corresponding to the chance of loss in the particular business; and this risk-rate must vary according to the conditions of every industry and of every concern. **1944** R. Lehmann *Ballad & Source* iii. 148 That is just a phrase the petty-cautious use against the fiery ones, the risk-takers. **1957** A. C. L. Day *Outl. Monetary Econ.* xxxviii. 491 Willing risk-takers (e.g. settlers in new countries). **1979** *N.Y. Rev. Bks.* 25 Oct. 49/2 McCagg's attempt is evidently to reconcile the sober wartime Stalin..with the postwar risk-taker. **1921** F. H. Knight *Risk, Uncertainty, & Profit* ii. 46 If risk were exclusively of the nature of a known chance or mathematical probability, there could be no reward in risk-taking. **1936** J. M. Keynes *Gen. Theory Employment* xxiv. 372 Diminishing unduly the motive towards risk-taking. **1948** *Sun* (Baltimore) 7 Apr. 19/1 Mr. Hooper..explained that eager risk taking by individual investors is essential to the smooth operation of the free enterprise system. **1975** 'E. Lathen' *By Hook or by Crook* xiv. 132 'He's always taken big chances.'.. 'That's the risk-taking his children are alarmed about.'

riskiness. Add: **2.** The quality of being *risqué*. Cf. Risky *a.* 3.

1877 *Argus* (Melbourne) 5 Dec. 6/1 Mr. Albery..has so far brought it [*sc.* a play] to the level of English requirements that we have it now with its original humour, but freed from its accompanying riskiness. **1938** H. Granville-Barker *Quality* 5 What rule would he [*sc.* Gilbert Murray] make for distinguishing a play written to exploit the mere riskiness of a subject and such a one as Ibsen's *Ghosts*.

risky, *a.* Add: **1. b.** *Social Psychol.* Phr. *risky shift*: in decision-making, the shift of opinion towards an option involving greater risk that may take place when responsibility for the decision rests with a group rather than an individual.

1964 M. Wallach et al. in *Jrnl. Abnormal & Social Psychol.* LXVIII. 272/1 Group responsibility in the presence of group decision lead to a strong risky shift. **1967** Kogan & Wallach in *New Directions in Psychol.* III. 240 Risky shifts took place with high regularity for groups of both sexes. **1972** M. Argyle *Social Psychol. of Work* vi. 133 Whatever its causes the risky shift is clearly a source of unwise decisions in groups. **1978** Lamm & Myers in *Adv. in Exper. Social Psychol.* XI. 149 Some researchers have used a rating scale (degree of preference for the risky vs. the cautious course of action). By and large, risky shift is obtained on items which elicit risky individual responses.

Risley (ri·zli). The name of Richard *Risley* Carlisle (d. 1874), U.S. gymnast and circus performer, used *attrib.* (and *absol.*) to designate an act in which a supine acrobat juggles another with his feet, as *Risley act, business,* etc. Also *transf.*

[**1843** *N.Y. Herald* 4 May 2/2 One of the chief attractions ..was Prof. Risley and his boy. **1846** *Illustr. London News* 7 Feb. 101/1 The very clever performances of Mr. Risley and his two sons continue to be nightly received with loudest acclamations.] **1861** H. Mayhew *London Labour* III. 94/2 (*heading*) The Street Risley. *Ibid.*, There is but one person in London who goes about the street doing what is termed 'The Risley performance'. *Ibid.* 97/1 We've been continuing ever since at this Risley business. I lay down on a carpet, and throw then summersets from feet to feet. *Ibid.* 98/1 I've done the Risley in the streets of London. **1901** *Cassell's Mag.* Sept. 389/1 (*caption*) A Risley Pose. *Ibid.* 389/2 There will be a day when a Japanese is an underman and a young Westerner a top-mounter, or *vice versâ*; and we shall see a brilliant show of Risley act or juggling. **1912** M. B. Leavitt *50 Yrs. Theatr. Managem.* xxv. 381 The second European 'hit' was made by Risley and his two sons, presenting the tossing and tumbling of the youngsters, to this day called the 'Risley Act'. **1931** *Amer. Mercury* Nov. 353/2 *Risley act*, one in which three acrobats lie on their backs and toss a fourth from one to the other. **1938** N. Streatfeild *Circus is Coming* vii. 117 He told them about the first Risley who had the idea of juggling with a real boy. Of how the idea caught on, and that kind of performance was always known as a 'Risley act'. **1957** J. & A. Durant *Pict. Hist. Amer. Circus* ii. 20 The 'Risley Act' (balancing with the feet while lying on the back) was performed by the Aztecs.

‖ **risoluto** (rizǫlū·to), *a.* and *adv.* *Mus.* [It.] † **A.** *adj.* (See quots.) Cf. Resolved *ppl. a.* 7. *Obs.*

1740 J. Grassineau *Mus. Dict.* 19 *Canone partito*, or *risoluto*,..is when all the parts of a perpetual fugue are writ either in partitions, or different lines, or in separate parts, with the proper pauses that each is to observe, and therein differs from *Canone Chiuso*. *Ibid.* 204 *Risoluto*, resolved: thus we say a syncoped discord is *resolved*.

B. *adv.* With resolution or emphasis. (Used as a direction on a musical score.)

1837 J. A. Hamilton *Dict. Mus. Terms* (ed. 4), *Risoluto* (Italian), with boldness and resolution. **1876** Stainer & Barrett *Dict. Mus. Terms* 379/2 *Risoluto*,..with resolution. **1976** *Gramophone* Feb. 1337/3 Harrell enters with a confidence and firmness that may contradict the overall marking *quasi improvisando*, but which faithfully reflects the more specific *risoluto*.

Risorgimento (risǭːɹdʒime·nto). Also **risorgimento.** [It., = renewal, renaissance.] **1.** The movement which led to the unification of Italy as an independent state with its capital at Rome in 1870.

1889 J. A. R. Marriott *Makers Mod. Italy* ii. 38 In 1847 Cavour, in conjunction with Santa Rosa, Cesare Balbo, and others, founded a new journal, named the *Risorgimento*, for the purpose of disseminating constitutional ideas of government. **1902** *Encycl. Brit.* XXIX. 628/2 Few dates in modern European history equal in significance that of 20th September 1870, when the Italian troops under General Cadorna took possession of Rome in the name of the Italian nation, and completed at one stroke..the work of the Risorgimento. **1902** G. Meredith *Let.* 15 Apr. (1970) III. 1436 Mazzini.. never wavered in the faith he had that their sacrifices would lead to the Risorgimento. **1905** Mrs. H. Ward *Marriage of W. Ashe* iv. xviii. 363 He had sat late with his hosts,—men prominent in the Risorgimento, and in the politics of the new Kingdom,—discussing the latest intricacies of the Roman situation and the prospects of Italian finance. **1910** W. H. Griffin *Life Robert Browning* x. 158 The events of the *risorgimento*. **1933** *N. & Q.* 4 Mar. 161/2 The Risorgimento was..kept free from that violence of popular fury.. which touches both the French and the Russian re-making of the nation with a sort of devilishness. **1937** A. Huxley *Ends & Means* x. 155 Before the Risorgimento the Austrians governed Italy by means of gendarmes, spies and *agents provocateurs*. **1955** *Times* 6 June 8/7 Count Alessandro Casati, one of Italy's elder statesmen and a true representative of the Italian liberal tradition of the Risorgimento, died on Saturday night. **1957** *Sunday Times* 8 Dec. 7/6 The Risorgimento heroes. **1961** *Listener* 19 Oct. 611/1 The partisan movement [in Italy] and the second Risorgimento which followed. **1977** *New Yorker* 2 May 101/1 Prosperity united Italy in ways the *risorgimento* never had.

2. *transf.* A revitalization or renewal of activity in any sphere.

1957 R. Chase in *Partisan Rev.* Summer 369 The poetic *risorgimento* of Ezra Pound and his group. **1959** *Listener* 17 Dec. 1062/2 This has been more than an economic and industrial *risorgimento*. **1978** Ld. Birkenhead *R. Kipling* xv. 215 The lethargy and frivolity of his own countrymen, upon whom he now turned..his indignation in a passionate but vain attempt to inspire a *risorgimento*.

risorius (ris-, rizōᵊ·riŭs). *Anat.* [ellipt. for mod.L. *musculus risorius* (J. D. Santorini *Observationes Anatomicæ* (1724) i. 33), f. L. *musculus* muscle + *risor* laugher (f. *ridēre* to laugh) + *-ius*, adj. suffix.] A muscle of facial expression running from the parotid fascia to the corner of the mouth, variable in form and sometimes lacking.

1829 J. & C. Bell *Anat. & Physiol. Human Body* (ed. 7) I. 279 [The Platysma myoides] terminates on the face and jaw. Some of its fibres, mounting over the bone of the jaw, are inserted near the depressor anguli oris; and others, a little higher on the face, are called *risorius santorini*. **1867** W. Sharpey et al. *Quain's Elem. Anat.* (ed. 7) I. 176 The risorius or smiling muscle (Santorini), consisting of some very thin fasciculi,..joins the orbicularis and depressor anguli oris at the angle of the mouth. **1902** D. J. Cunningham *Text-Bk. Anat.* 377 The risorius is a thin flat muscle which forms partly a continuation of the platysma myoides on the face, partly a separate muscle, with an origin from the masseteric fascia. **1936** A. Huxley *Eyeless in Gaza* xviii. 233 The whole mechanism of the excruciating grimace, the upward and outward pull of the zygomaticus major, the sideways tug of the risorius. **1961** L. F. Brosnahan *Sounds of Language* iv. 80 This suggests again a cline in gene frequency, the decrease in the mean height running in the same direction through the African-European-Asiatic population as the increase in the frequency of the occurrence of the risorius muscle in the face.

risotto. Delete ‖ and add: Now usu. with pronunc. (rizǫ·to). (Earlier and later examples.) Also *Comb.*

1855 E. ACTON *Mod. Cookery* (rev. ed.) xxxii. 615 (*heading*) Risotto à la Milanaise. 1950 E. LINKLATER *Mr. Byculla* vi. 68 A Risotto Bolognese for one and threepence. 1960 *Housewife* May 91/1 My deep freeze usually contains..a risotto or two. 1981 E. DEWHURST *Trio in Three Flats* iii. 19 Cathy's asked me to supper..risotto and a complicated salad.

‖ **risqué** (ri·ske, ri·ske), *a.* Also **risque.** [Fr., pa. pple. of *risquer* RISK *v.*] = RISKY *a.* 3.

1867 'OUIDA' *Under Two Flags* II. iv. 121 She..sang..the most wicked and *risqué* of her slang songs. *Ibid.* viii. 207 It was..too simple, too little *risqué*. A child might do it. 1894 A. BEARDSLEY *Let.* c 3 Jan. (1970) 61 Our idea [in starting *The Yellow Book*] is that many brilliant story painters and picture writers cannot get their best stuff accepted in the conventional magazine, either because they are not topical or perhaps a little risqué. 1899 J. LONDON *Let.* 30 Mar. (1966) 26 Our magazines are so goody-goody, that I wonder they would permit a thing as risque and as good as that. 1913 E. POUND *Let.* 30 Mar. (1971) 18 Again to your note: 'Risqué.' Now really!!! Do you apply that term to all nude statuary? I admit the verse 'To Another Man on his Wife' might deserve it, but you're not including that. Surely you don't regard the Elizabethans as 'risqué'? 1924 *Brit. Weekly* 18 Dec. 301/3 In remote corners others are reading *risqué* novels with a sex interest. 1952 *Scrutiny* XVIII. 317 Not infrequently Mr. Auden seems to be trying to atone for this by indulging in slightly *risqués* side-glances. 1962 V. CONNAUGHT *Secret Heart of Princess Alexandra* i. 15 She enjoys a good joke, even if it is a little risqué, provided it is well told. 1975 *Country Life* 25 Dec. 1804/1 Directors were turning out sophisticated, risqué social comedies.

Riss (ris). *Geol.* The name of a tributary of the Isar in Austria and Germany, adopted by A. Penck (in Penck & Brückner *Die Alpen im Eiszeitalter* (1909) I. I. 110) and used *attrib.* to designate the third (penultimate) Pleistocene glaciation in the Alps, and in conjunction with *WÜRM to designate the following interglacial period. Also *absol.*

1910 *Zeitschr. f. Gletscherkunde* IV. 244 The interval between the Riss and the Würm.., the Riss–Würm interglacial stage. *Ibid.*, The moderate erosion..which the Riss drift has experienced. 1927 [see *MOUSTERIAN, MOUSTERIAN *a.* and *sb.*]. 1931 *Discovery* Sept. 282/2 The fluvio-lacustrine deposits, rich in volcanic elements, of the Tiber Valley, which Roman geologists hold to be contemporary with the warm interglacial period intervening between the Riss and the Würm glaciations of the European Ice Age. 1944 A. HOLMES *Princ. Physical Geol.* xii. 247 The depth reached by weathering during Riss-Würm time is found to be about three times that achieved on similar but later deposits exposed during post-Würm time. Since the latter is about 25,000 years, it follows that the Riss-Würm interval cannot have been less than 75,000 years. 1968 R. W. FAIRBRIDGE *Encycl. Geomorphol.* 335/1 There appears to be unanimity that during the Last Interglacial (Riss-Würm or Sangamon) there were sea-levels of the order of 7·5 meters..and 3·5 meters..higher than the present. 1971 *Nature* 22 Jan. 253/2 It is now recognized that the species *Homo sapiens* is of at least Riss age. 1974 *Sci. Amer.* June 96/1 The next to last major advance, known to scholars as the Penultimate Glacial (Riss II in the Alpine sequence), marked the end of the Middle Pleistocene some 125,000 years ago.

rissaldar (risāldā·ɹ). *Indian.* Also **risal(a)dar** and with capital initial. [Hind. *risāldār, risālādār*, f. Pers. *risāla* troop of horse.] Now the more usual form of RESSALDAR. Also *Comb.*, as *rissaldar-major*.

1842 W. MILES tr. *Meer Hussein Ali Khan Kirmani's Hist. Hydur Naik* xxiii. 327 The Nawaub now gave orders to the Risaladárs of the regular and irregular infantry, to encircle the fort, and then commence the attack with their artillery and musketry. 1848 J. H. STOCQUELER *Oriental Interpreter* 198/1 *Rissaldar*, an officer of the Irregular India cavalry, whose rank corresponds with that of a captain of a troop. 1851 J. B. FRASER *Mil. Mem. Lieut.-Col. J. Skinner* I. ix. 274 The rissaldars finding so much money in their hands, began to quarrel about the division of it. 1927 Rissaldar-major [see *en grande tenue* s.v. *EN *prep.*] 1951 J. MASTERS *Nightrunners of Bengal* 337/2 There were three grades of Native Officers..: infantry—subadar-major, subadar, jemadar; cavalry—rissaldar-major, rissaldar, jemadar. 1964 A. SWINSON *Six Minutes to Sunset* ii. 30 A Risaldar-Major with the impressive name of Khan Bahardur Fazal Dad Khan turned up. 1981 V. POWELL *Flora Annie Steel* xiii. 109 Roshan has risen to the rank of *rissaldar* (Indian officer).

Risso (ri·so). The name of Giovanni Antonio *Risso* (1777–1845), Italian naturalist, used in the possessive in **Risso's dolphin** to designate the grampus, *Grampus griseus*, first described as *Delphinus rissoanus* by A. G. Desmarest in 1822 (*Mammalogie* II. 579).

1871 *Proc. Zool. Soc.* 506 Prof. Flower, F.R.S., read a paper on the so-called Risso's Dolphin. 1924 [see *CAA'ING WHALE]. 1927 *Daily Express* 5 Sept. 2/5 Pelorus Jack, the famous white Risso's dolphin, which for years has piloted ships into Wellington Harbour, New Zealand,..is missing. 1960 G. MAXWELL *Ring of Bright Water* v. 62 Contrary to information contained in the majority of text-books, in which Risso's dolphin is described as a rarity, it is in fact the commonest of all the lesser whales to visit the Hebrides in summer. 1971 M. & R. MOFFETT *Dolphins* 18 The grampus, or Risso's dolphin, lives far out at sea.

ristocetin (ristosī·tin). *Pharm.* [Arbitrarily formed; *-cetin* f. *ACTINOMY)CET(ES + -IN[1].] An antibiotic substance (now known to be a mixture) obtained from the actinomycete *Nocardia lurida* and formerly used to treat staphylococcal infections.

1957 W. E. GRUNDY et al. in *Antibiotics Ann.* 1956–7 687 A new antibiotic that has been given the generic name ristocetin was isolated from the fermentation beer of an actinomycete. 1960 M. E. FLOREY *Clin. Appl. Antibiotics* IV. iii. 77 Isolated from the fermentation liquor of an unidentified actinomycete called by the authors *Nocardia lurida* and obtained from soil at Colorado Springs, ristocetin gives promise of being of value in the treatment of staphylococcal and other infections. 1968 J. H. BURN *Lect. Notes Pharmacol.* (ed. 9) 111 Vancomycin and ristocetin do not appear to induce the emergence of resistant staphylococci. 1980 *Brit. Med. Jrnl.* 18 Oct. 1039/1 The coagulation studies were diagnostic of Glanzmann's thrombasthenia with diminished platelet aggregation in response to ristocetin.

‖ **ristorante** (ristōra·nte). [It.] An Italian restaurant in Italy or elsewhere.

1925 W. J. LOCKE *Great Pandolfo* iv. 40 Washer-up in a relative's *Ristorante* in a mildewed corner of Soho. 1967 *Observer* 24 Sept. 31/5 Stopping at the first *ristorante* for a drink. 1968 R. SAWKINS *Snow along Border* xviii. 148 The Villa Messina was near a *ristorante* called 'Sud-Est'. 1973 'S. HARVESTER' *Corner of Playground* II. iv. 102 A table outside a *ristorante* on a Rome side-street. 1981 'M. YORKE' *Hand of Death* xii. 102 The Ristorante Sorrento was in a narrow street that led to Fletcham Abbey from the market square.

† **rit** (rit), *sb.*[2] Slang. abbrev. of RITUALIST 2. *Obs.*

1878 *Oxf. Times* 23 Mar. 8/1 *On dit* that five notoriously ritualistic undergraduates were received into the Church of Rome... Most of these young gentlemen have distinguished themselves in Oxford as Roaring Rits. 1898 A. CAVALIER *Let.* in C. Mackenzie *My Life & Times* (1963) II. 243 My mater calls me a 'dirty Rit'. 'So we've got a Rit in the house, have we.' 1909 J. R. WARE *Passing Eng.* 209/2 *Rit*,.. a ritualistic clergyman.

rit, *sb.*[3] *dial.* [Shortened form of RITLING: see RECKLING.] The smallest and weakest pig of a litter; a ritling. Also *transf.* of a person.

1885 R. HOLLAND *Gloss. County of Chester* (1886) 288 *Rit*.., the smallest pig of a litter. Also applied to a puny child. 1940 *Manch. Guardian Weekly* 15 Mar. 216 We gave special food to the rit of one brood (the little one known in other parts [than Cheshire] as the runt or reckling, and by other names). 1962 ORTON & HALLIDAY *Survey Eng. Dial.* I. I. 279 Q[uestion] What do you call the smallest and weakest pig of the litter?.. La[ncashire]..ɹɪt. 1969 ORTON & BARRY *Ibid.* II. I. 288 Ch[eshire] ɹɪt... St[affordshire].. ɹɪt.

rit., *sb.*[4] *Mus.* Abbrev. of *RITARDANDO.

1886 [see *A TEMPO]. 1959 *Collins Mus. Encycl.* 552/1 *Ritardando*,..commonly abbreviated *rit.*

Ritalin (ri·tălin). *Pharm.* Also **ritalin.** A proprietary name (orig. used in Switzerland) for the drug methylphenidate hydrochloride, a central nervous system stimulant related to amphetamine; methyl-α-phenyl-α-piperid-2-ylacetate hydrochloride, $C_{14}H_{19}NO_2 \cdot HCl$.

The appearance of the word in trade-mark literature predated the introduction of the drug by a number of years.

1949 *Trade Marks Jrnl.* 1 June 477/1 *Ritalin*... Pharmaceutical preparations for use in the treatment of the nervous system. CIBA Limited..manufacturers and merchants.—28th May 1948. 1949 *Official Gaz.* (U.S. Patent Office) 16 Aug. 594/2 CIBA Limited, Basel, Switzerland. Filed July 9, 1948. *Ritalin.* Applicant claims ownership of Swiss Registration No. 107,093, dated Mar. 28, 1944. 1954 *Chem. Abstr.* XLVIII. 8945 Ritalin..has a psychomotor excitatory effect, producing psychic stimulation and a coördinated increase in motility in exptl. animals. 1955 *Ann. N.Y. Acad. Sci.* LXI. 101 This new drug, phenidylate—phenyl-(α-piperidyl)-acetic acid methyl ester (Ritalin)—is a synthetic preparation which could be described as a psycho-analeptic, a mental and physical stimulator which..seems to counterbalance the reserpine-depressing activity. 1970 *Daily Tel.* 30 June 3/1 The United States Food and Drug Administration has urged doctors to exercise extreme caution in prescribing Ritalin because of the danger of addiction. *Ibid.* 3 Dec. 13 More than 200 youngsters regularly visited his surgery and home and were given National Health Service prescriptions for the 'soft' drugs drynamyl, ritalin and mandrax. 1976 H. FERGUSON *Confessions Long Distance Acid Head* 7 Apart from cannabis, I have used barbiturates,..procaine, ritalin, even apomorphine once.

‖ **ritardando** (ritaɹdæ·ndo). *Mus.* Pl. **ritardandi, -os.** [It., pr. pple. of *ritardare* to slow down.] A musical direction indicating a gradual reduction of speed; as *sb.* = RETARDATION 3 b; a passage where this occurs.

1811 BUSBY *Dict. Mus.* (ed. 3) Ritardando. (Ital.) An expression implying a slackening of the time. c 1865 E. DICKINSON *Poems* (1955) II. 724 Dying at my music!.. Hold me till the Octave's run! Quick! Burst the Windows! Ritardando! 1889, etc. [see *ACCELERANDO]. 1893, etc. [see *ALLARGANDO]. 1958 *Times* 22 Nov. 9/3 He is inclined to begin his ritornelli faster than is comfortable to the soloists and at the end to draw out an absurd *ritardando*. 1966 *Listener* 25 Aug. 286/1 This constant variation can be heard on many levels; in the brilliant interplay of pure unmixed tone-colours, in the fluctuations of tempo between fast and slow, accelerando and ritardando, and, in particular, in the rhythm. 1978 *Jrnl. R. Soc. Arts* CXXVI. 356/1 There must always be a reason and purpose for these slight accelerandos and ritardandos which we call rubato.

rite. Add: **1. a.** *the last rites* = *the last sacraments* s.v. *SACRAMENT *sb.* 2 e; *rite A, B*: the two classes of Eucharistic rite in the Church of England's *Alternative Service Book 1980*, distinguished by being in present-day English and traditional liturgical English, respectively.

[1786 BURNS *Poems Sc. Dial.* 190 The last, sad, mournful rites bestow!] 1922 C. KERR *Cecil Marchioness of Lothian* xv. 228 Dr Talbot said Mass in her room and she was given the last rites of the Church. 1927 *Times* 11 July 14/4 Canon Breen, the local parish priest, was hurriedly brought and administered the last rites. 1961 P. J. HEPBURNE-SCOTT tr. J. C. Didier (*title*) The last rites. 1975 *Times* 8 Nov. 1/7 The cardinal..received the sacrament of the sick (previously called 'last rites'). 1977 *Belfast Tel.* 27 Jan. 9/5 Their call is being backed up by local priest, the Rev. Peter Burns, who gave Mr. Moyna the Last Rites. 1980 *Daily Tel.* 24 Oct. 3/1 (*heading*) Queen [to be] at new Synod Rite A service. *Ibid.*, The form of service will be Rite A from the new Alternative Service Book... The service is a revision of that known hitherto as Series 3. 1980 *Alternative Service Bk.* 1980 5 The Order for Holy Communion Rite A. *Ibid.* 6 The Order for Holy Communion Rite B. 1980 *Alternative Service Bk.* 1980: *Commentary* 74 The main further change made from Series 3 to Rite A is the separation of the commemoration of the departed from the summary sentences commending all the worshippers to God. 1980 *Times Lit. Suppl.* 14 Nov. 1281/2 Even the Lord's Prayer is now on sale in three versions—that of the Book of Common Prayer..; that of Rite A *et passim* and that of Rite B *et passim*.

d. *pl.* Used as a journalistic term for any ceremony (*U.S.*).

1950 *Richmond* (Va.) *Times-Dispatch* 1 Apr. 1/2 (*heading*) Airport rites set for 2 p.m. today at Byrd. Planes, personalities will mark ceremony. 1957 *Sun* (Baltimore) 21 Jan. B-1/6 (*heading*) Rites at White House performed before 80. Press is barred from ceremony in East Room.

e. Anthrop. *rite of intensification*: a rite marking a special event affecting a social group and tending towards strengthening the bonds uniting its members; usu. *pl.*; *rite of passage* = *RITE DE PASSAGE.

1909 *Folk-Lore* XX. 510 What M. van Gennep has here done is to enforce his contention by considering..a number of the sequences of rites to which he has given the title of Rites of Passage. 1947 CHAPPLE & COON *Princ. Anthropol.* xxi. 507 A Rite of Intensification..restores equilibrium for the group after a disturbance affecting all or most of its members. 1959 W. GOLDSCHMIDT *Understanding Human Society* v. 178 Rituals involving the whole community, called rites of intensification, re-enforce the initiate's sense of belonging and serve to strengthen group ties. 1960 VIZEDOM & CAFFEE *Van Gennep's Rites of Passage* p. vii, Passage might more appropriately have been translated as 'transition', but in deference to van Gennep and general usage of the term 'rites of passage', this form of the translation has been preserved. *Ibid.* p. ix, Ceremonies which accompany and assure the changes of the year, season, or month are rites of passage. 1970 P. SPENCER in P. Mayer *Socialization* 148 The second type, performed when misbehaviour was expected from the moran and when their corporate unity and morale were low, were rites of intensification pure and simple. 1971 K. THOMAS *Relig. & Decline of Magic* iii. 57 The subsequent raising of the age at which children are expected to undergo it [*sc.* confirmation] to fourteen or so has given it a more pronounced role as a rite of passage marking the arrival of 'social' puberty. 1978 W. A. HAVILAND *Cultural Anthropol.* (ed. 2) xiii. 346/1 Rites of intensification..are particularly common among horticultural and agricultural people, with their planting, first fruit, and harvest ceremonies. 1978 *Times Educ. Suppl.* 13 Jan. 15/1 The transition from fifth-year courses to A level involves a rite of passage to 'real' history 1978 *Chatelaine* Dec. 17/1 And hockey is not just a sport. It's a rite of passage.

‖ **rite de passage** (rit də pasāʒ). *Anthrop.* Pl. **rites de passage.** [Fr., lit. 'rite of passage', a term coined by Arnold van Gennep: see quot. 1909.] Any of the rites of separation, transition, and incorporation that mark an individual's social existence from birth to death as he passes from one stage of life to another; ritual that marks the end of one phase and the start of another. Cf. *RITE 1 e.

[1909 A. VAN GENNEP (*title*) Les rites de passage.] 1911 *Man* XI. 30 Should we be right in including many of the cases of *rites de passage* in a general category of rites de *première fois*? 1934 R. BENEDICT *Patterns of Culture* ii. 25 In order to understand puberty institutions, we do not most need analyses of the necessary nature of *rites de passage*. 1949 G. BATESON in M. Fortes *Social Structure* 45 A poor man was about to undergo one of the important and expensive *rites de passage* which are necessary for persons as they approach the top of the Council hierarchy. 1957 M. BANTON *W. Afr. City* xi. 210 Both native and Aku *rites de passage* appear to have been influenced by Creole practices. 1964 W. MCCORD in I. L. Horowitz *New Sociol.* xxv. 435 Most..practiced traditional *rites de passage*. 1972 M. ARGYLE *Social Psychol. of Work* iv. 67 The transition to a new job involves some degree of re-socialization, and the shift is sometimes assisted by a public ceremony..known to sociologists as a rite de passage. 1977 *Times* 22 Mar. 12/2 The [Newfoundland] seal hunt is..a necessary *rite de passage* for all young men.

‖ **ritenuto** (ritenū·to), *a.*, *adv.*, and *sb.* *Mus.* [It., pa. pple. of *ritenere*, f. L. *retinēre* to hold back.] **A.** *adj.* and *adv.* Of musical movement: restrained, held back in tempo. Used adverbially as a direction indicating immediate reduction of speed. **B.** *sb.* (*pl.* **ritenuti** or **ritenutos**). A phrase or passage thus indicated.

1828 BUSBY *Mus. Manual* 148 Ritenuto. (Ital.) Movements to which this term is prefixed, are to be performed in a gentle, delicate, and restrained manner. **1888** L. A. SMITH *Music of Waters* 15 Chorus. *Ritenuto molto.* Low-lands, Low-lands, Hur-rah, my John! **1952** *Conc. Oxf. Dict. Mus.* 500/2 *Ritenuto*, 'Held back', i.e. 'Slower' (immediately, not gradually as with *Ritardando* and *Rallentando*; but it may be that some composers have not observed this distinction). **1955** G. ABRAHAM in H. Van Thal *Fanfare for E. Newman* 14 A boisterous tutti fortissimo ending by ten quiet bars, *un poco ritenuto.* **1955** [see *DIMINUENDO]. **1959** *Times* 12 Jan. 12/6 Their Bach was of the sewing-machine school, their Brahms full of ugly *ritenuti.* **1975** *Daily Tel.* 4 Feb. 11/1, I must protest against end ritenutos that came as an anti-climax in a good many of the variations. **1976** *Guardian* 13 Apr. 10/5 He plays strongly and straightforwardly; the rubatos and ritenutos are there.

rithe. (Further examples.)

1925 A. MOORE *Last Days of Mast & Sail* vii. 216 [The Bosham boats] are most dangerous-looking and would not live long in a seaway, but in the channels and rithes of Chichester Harbour the water is generally smooth and they continue in use generation after generation. **1931** BELLOC *Cranmer* ii. 21 There stood on the Eastern edge of the town of Cambridge, just beyond the King's Ditch, as it was called (a runnel of water, the Long Rithe, which drained that flooded land and led from a mill above), a little place already known in this year, 1503, as 'Jesus' College.

ritodrine (ri·todrīn). *Pharm.* [Invented word.] A sympathomimetic agent used esp. as a uterine relaxant in cases of premature labour, when it is administered as an intravenous infusion of the hydrochloride; 2-*p*-hydroxyphenethylamino-1-*p*-hydroxyphenyl-propanol, $C_{17}H_{21}NO_3$.

1971 *Amer. Jrnl. Obstetr. & Gynecol.* CX. 111/1 Ritodrine hydrochloride, previously identified as Du-21220, is a sympathomimetic amine with beta-adrenergic–inhibitory properties. **1977** *Lancet* 8 Oct. 777/2 In Britain two [drugs] have been licensed for use as agents which inhibit labour—namely, salbutamol and ritodrine.

ritornello. Add: Also *fig.*

1977 *Times Lit. Suppl.* 1 July 796/4 The Marxist theme is a ritornello appearing at the end of each chapter rather than at the conclusion of the book. **1978** *Ibid.* 13 Oct. 1153/3 What is the correlation between schools and literacy?.. The irrelevance of schools is a persistent *ritornello* here.

Ritschlian (ri·tʃliăn), *a.* and *sb.* [f. the name of Albrecht *Ritschl*, German theologian (1822–89).] **A.** *adj.* Of or pertaining to Ritschl or his doctrines. **B.** *sb.* A follower of Ritschl or a student of Ritschlianism.

1891 *Chambers's Encycl.* VIII. 733/2 The distinguishing feature of the Ritschlian theology is perhaps the eminence it gives to the practical, ethical, social side of Christianity. *Ibid.* 734/1 The Ritschlians now form a large and important school in Germany. **1938** *Times Lit. Suppl.* 30 Apr. p. x/2 For a generation past the influence of the Ritschlian tradition has been far more potent in Scottish theology. **1952** *Hibbert Jrnl.* 1951 L. 12 The Ritschlian contempt for 'speculative Theism'. *Ibid.* 15 The *Fourth Gospel*, with such New Testament epistles as *Romans* or *Ephesians*, neglected if not deliberately excluded by Ritschlians in favour of the Synoptists' parables of a 'Kingdom of God' to be established here and now. **1957** *Oxf. Dict. Chr. Ch.* 1168/2 The so-called 'Ritschlian School' was characterized by its stress on ethics and on the 'community', and by its repudiation of metaphysics and religious experience. **1970** *Evangelical Q.* XLII. 95 The last four words tend to nullify the import of the preceding, which as such is the usual Ritschlian explanation; the doctrine of the subjective origin of the thing. *Ibid.* 99 The Ritschlians were, therefore, strongly opposed to the separation which had been made in traditional theology between the person and work of Christ.

Hence **Ri·tschlianism**, the theological or philosophical doctrines of Ritschl.

1892 J. ORR in *Thinker* Aug. 148 Ritschlianism has a metaphysic, and a specially dangerous one. **1917** BARTLET & CARLYLE *Christianity in Hist.* v. v. 596 Ritschlianism and Catholic Modernism are the most marked movements in this direction. **1969** D. L. MUELLER *Introd. Theol. A. Ritschl* iii. 105 This idea so crucial for comprehending Ritschl's conception of faith became a kind of watchword of later Ritschlianism. **1970** *Evangelical Q.* XLII. 97 All possibility of speaking of an absolute nature in the Deity as the ground of His historical manifestations is in Ritschlianism swept aside.

Ritsu (ri·tsu), *sb.* Also **Risshu** (ri·ʃu). [f. Jap. *ritsu* law, moral law.] A Buddhist sect of the early Tang period, introduced in the 8th century to Japan where it flourished, concerned primarily with the study of monastic discipline and ordination rites.

[**1727** J. G. SCHEUCHZER tr. *Kæmpfer's Hist. Japan* I. II. v. 199 In the 1850 streets of this city, there were 1050 of the *Ten Dai's* religion,..9912 of *Rit.*] **1880** E. J. REED *Japan* I. iv. 91 The Ritsu, introduced by the Chinese priest Kanshin, under the empress Koken. **1917** A. K. REISCHAUER *Stud. Jap. Buddhism* iii. 86 Last of these older sects to reach Japan was the Ritsu (Vinaya Sect), introduced in 754, though it would seem that its doctrines..were among the first teachings to be introduced into Japan. **1931** G. B. SANSOM *Japan* II. vi. 121 The Ritsu sect did not trouble much about doctrinal questions, but paid special attention to discipline and correct spiritual succession. **1935** C. ELIOT *Jap. Buddhism* viii. 232 After the establishment of this new Kaidan, the Risshū seems to have declined though it somewhat revived in the twelfth century.

ritter, var. *RUTTER².

Ritter's disease (ri·təɹz). *Med.* [Named after Gottfried *Ritter* von Rittershain (1820–83), Bohemian physician, who first described it as a distinct entity in 1878 (*Central-Zeitung f. Kinderheilkunde* II. 3–23).] A sometimes fatal form of dermatitis affecting newborn infants.

1888 *Amer. Jrnl. Med. Sci.* XCV. 11 The pemphigus simplex acutus, like Ritter's disease, belongs to the first weeks of life, but appears earlier, sometimes in the first few days after birth. **1931** B. WILLIAMSON *Handbk. Dis. Children* xvii. 143 Pemphigus neonatorum (Ritter's disease) ..occasionally is luetic in origin, but more often it is a septic infection associated with unclean midwifery. **1966** *Amer. Jrnl. Dis. Children* CXI. 391/2 The exact etiology of Ritter's disease has never been finally established, many investigators having reported an association with staphylococcal infection.

ritual, *a.* and *sb.* Add: **A.** *adj.* **1.** *spec.* in *Archæol.*, applied to objects or constructions.

1901 A. J. EVANS *Mycenaean Tree & Pillar Cult* 9 At the foot of the handle of axe, namely, appears in each case that distinctive piece of Mycenaean ritual furniture..described as 'the horns of consecration'. **1934** *Burlington Mag.* Mar. 139/1 Other ritual bronzes said to have been found with the *kuang*. **1941** *Antiquity* XV. 142 (*title*) A datable 'ritual barrow' in Glamorganshire. **1951** *Field Archæol.* (Ordnance Survey Prof. Papers No. 13) (ed. 3) 42 Another curious type of site about which our knowledge is imperfect is the so-called 'ritual' well, or Belgic burial shaft. **1954** S. PIGGOTT *Neolithic Cultures* ii. 56 It is possible that some of the 'ritual holes' frequently recorded from near the burials in the Wessex barrows may have been post-holes, but the majority seem to have served some other unexplained purpose connected with the funerary rites. **1963** W. F. GRIMES in Foster & Alcock *Culture & Environment* v. 105 No doubt in due course something like 'sacred circle' or 'ritual circle' frankly avowing ideas about their use will become permissible for a majority of them. **1975** P. WARREN *Aegean Civilization* ii. 43 The individual who made the so-called Harvester Vase..created a masterpiece. Here are 27 figures marching around a ritual vase a few inches high.

2. *ritual murder*, murder carried out as a rite; also *fig.* and *attrib.*; similarly *ritual killing*.

1896 [in Dict.]. **1936** C. DAY LEWIS *We're not going to do Nothing* 14 Organised mass-murder—as apart from ritual-killings, blood-feuds and the like—can admit of only one satisfactory explanation. **1950** M. HAY *Foot of Pride* v. 119 In Germany, the ritual-murder legend was the chief..excuse for a series of riots all over the country which threatened the Jews with complete extermination. **1962** L. DEIGHTON *Ipcress File* i. 9 The man..was now using knife and fork to commit ritual murder on a cream pastry. **1964** M. SUTHER et al. tr. *Maritain's Moral Philos.* 142 (*heading*) The ritual murder of Realities that are elevated to the skies. **1966** *New Statesman* 15 July 78/3 The sudden revival in Russia of the ritual-murder myth after half a century of anti-religious mass education. **1972** J. MCCLURE *Caterpillar Cop* ii. 24 Back marked by long cuts... Those wounds suggest a ritual killing.

3. In extended and trivial use: pertaining to or constituting a social or psychological ritual (see sense B. 2 below); used, occurring, etc., as a social convention or habit.

1947 *Atlantic Monthly* July 114/2 Many political speeches ..are delivered in a language which is above people's heads and is in fact a 'ritual survival' from an age in which electors were few and literate. **1953** H. S. SULLIVAN *Interpersonal Theory of Psychiatry* xviii. 307 All these ritual avoidances and preoccupations give one a feeling that one is making some sense in an important area of living. Actually one is not making any sense at all, because one is completely inaccessible to any data. **1972** W. LABOV *Language in Inner City* viii. 305 Those who have some knowledge of urban ghetto culture will recognize Rel's remark *Your mother's a duck* as a ritual insult. **1975** R. COLLINS *Conflict Sociol.* iii. 115 We can tell the difference by the increase in ritual elements as the talk becomes more sociable, the orienting gestures are toward each other rather than toward the topic. **1977** B. PYM *Quartet in Autumn* i. 5 He offered her the bag of jelly babies, but this was only a ritual gesture and he knew that she would refuse. *Ibid.* v. 40 Most of the inhabitants of the village were retired married couples with the ritual grandchildren.

B. *sb.* **2. a.** (Later examples.) Now freq. in *sing.* Also in extended and trivial uses.

1906 J. G. FRAZER *Adonis, Attis, Osiris* 325 When the Bechuanas are about to found a new town, they observe an elaborate ritual. **1911** BEERBOHM *Zuleika D.* iii. 29 He cared for his wardrobe and his toilet-table..merely as..a ritual in which to express and realise, his own idolatry. **1914** J. S. HUXLEY in *Proc. Zool. Soc.* I. 506 We must now go on to consider a very different question... I mean the gradual change of a useful action into a symbol and then into a ritual. **1958** J. O'CONOR *Iron Harp* in J. C. Trewin *Plays of Year* XVI. 179 He's had no lunch... Ah, now, that won't do. A man should never miss the ritual of a good meal. **1975** R. COLLINS *Conflict Sociol.* iii. 97 All that animal language lacks in comparison to human rituals, is a symbolic significance or *naming* quality... We usually assume that animal rituals are innate but that human rituals are learned. **1975** L. LEE *I can't stay Long* (1977) 203 The ritual of bargaining was long and elaborate.

b. *spec.* in *Psychol.* A series of actions compulsively performed under certain circumstances, the non-performance of which results in tension and anxiety.

1932 M. GABAIN tr. *Piaget's Moral Judgment of Child* iv. 359 The rituals attached to eating, going to bed, etc., show the hold which habit has over his [*sc.* the child's] nature. **1946** O. FENICHEL *Psychoanal. Theory of Neuroses* xiv. 268 Touching rituals replace taboos; washing compulsions, fears of dirt; social rituals, social fears. **1956** H. S. LIPPMAN *Treatm. Child in Emotional Conflict* ix. 113 The diagnosis of obsessional neurosis in a child depends primarily on the presence of ceremonials or rituals which he cannot control. **1968** L. EIDELBERG *Encycl. Psychoanal.* 382/2 Although similar in pathogenesis, it is useful to distinguish between rituals and other obsessive-compulsive manifestations. **1972** A. STORR *Dynamics of Creation* viii. 98 The ritual had started originally as an attempt to purge himself of the guilt surrounding masturbation.

3. (Later examples.)

1923 J. S. HUXLEY in *Jrnl. Linnean Soc.* XXXV. 255 The effect as of tension, of emotional ritual, so familiar to all those who have watched birds during courtship, is marked. **1947** CHAPPLE & COON *Princ. Anthropol.* xix. 481 This question of the conditioned nature of symbols is a basic requisite to the understanding of the whole subject of ritual. **1961** L. THOMPSON *Toward Sci. of Mankind* xi. 182 Hopi ritual may be viewed as a complex, but logical and ordered, whole, which expresses symbolically the Hopi conception of the universe, the law, and the life process. **1969** in Halpert & Story *Christmas Mumming in Newfoundland* 112 'Ritual' here is broadly defined as largely symbolic activity, aimed towards controlling social relations. **1971** L. NEAL in A. Gayle *Black Aesthetic* 285 Like all good ritual, its purpose is to make the audience stronger, more sensitive to the historical realities that have shaped our lives and the lives of our ancestors.

Comb.

1868 J. G. WHITTIER in *Atlantic Monthly* Feb. 221 Nor ritual-bound nor templeward Walks the free spirit of the Lord! **1930** D. H. LAWRENCE *A Propos Lady Chatterley* 36 The strange priest-controlled, ritual-fulfilled condition of the earlier Egyptians. **1937** M. COVARRUBIAS *Island of Bali* viii. 216 The ritual-magic dances characteristic of primitive peoples.

‖ **ritualia** (rituē^i^·liă). *nonce-wd.* [L., pl. of *rituāle* relating to rites or ceremonies.] Objects used in or connected with religious rites and ceremonies.

1931 *Times Lit. Suppl.* 5 Nov. 864/2 The records of this synagogue may contain papers of great interest, and its *ritualia* certainly include objects of considerable beauty.

ritualism. Add: **1.** (Later examples.)

1935 B. MALINOWSKI *Found. Faith & Morals* i. 6 It is rather the recognition of his practical and intellectual limitations, and not the illusion of the 'omnipotence of thought', which leads man into ritualism. **1952** GERTH & MARTINDALE tr. *Weber's Anc. Judaism* xiii. 336 Prophecy together with traditional ritualism of Israel, brought forth the elements that gave to Jewry its pariah place in the world. **1975** M. DOUGLAS *Implicit Meanings* v. 79 So the tension between ritualism of established authority and enthusiasm from the outlying borders of society, the dynamic of reform in European history, must have its counterpart in the unwritten history of any primitive tribe.

2. *Sociol.* (See quot. 1957.)

1949 R. K. MERTON *Social Theory* iv. 141 The socialization patterns of the lower middle class thus promote the very character structure most predisposed toward ritualism. **1955** P. M. BLAU *Dynamics of Bureaucracy* xii. 193 Three variations of displacement of goals were observed, all of which differed from ritualism. **1957** R. K. MERTON *Social Theory* (rev. ed.) v. 184 Ritualism refers to a pattern of response in which culturally defined aspirations are abandoned while 'one continues to abide almost compulsively by institutional norms'. **1961** O. J. HARVEY et al. *Conceptual Syst.* ii. 43 (*heading*) Concreteness disposes toward ritualism. **1963** T. & P. MORRIS *Pentonville* vii. 172 Two kinds of ritualism may be distinguished—the *ritualism of identification* and the *ritualism of dependency.* **1974** H. R. BOBBITT et al. *Organizational Behav.* iii. 61 Ritualism appeared to result more from lack of security in important social relationships ..than from overidentification with rules or strong habituation.

ritualist. Add: **2.** *spec.* in *Anthrop.* In a tribal society, one who performs a ritual.

1969 M. DOUGLAS *Natural Symbols* ii. 35 The primitive ritualist, in his ascribed social system, expresses cosmic orientations and moral directives in condensed symbols. **1974** B. & R. HILL *Spirit in Stone* iii. 35 A man whom we will call the ritualist and several assistants are fishing for salmon with a reef net. *Ibid.*, The ritualist carefully hands the children the fish he has caught. **1977** L. J. BEAN in Fogelson & Adams *Anthropol. of Power* 123 Individuals may ..obtain it [*sc.* power] by inheriting or purchasing ritual equipment, and the knowledge that goes with it, from a shaman and/or ritualist.

3. Someone whose behaviour is characterized by ritualism (esp. in sense *2). Also *attrib.*

1949 R. K. MERTON *Social Theory* iv. 140 The syndrome of the social ritualist is both familiar and instructive. **1957** *Ibid.* (rev. ed.) v. 185 Situations patterned by the social structure which invite the ritualist response of overconformity to normative expectations. **1963** T. & P. MORRIS *Pentonville* vii. 172 The ritualist has largely rejected the socially approved goals altogether, and fallen back upon punctilious conformity. **1969** M. DOUGLAS *Natural Symbols* i. 2 The ritualist becomes one who performs external gestures which imply commitment to a particular set of values, but he is inwardly withdrawn, dried out and uncommitted.

ritualistic, *a.* Add: (Later examples.) Also, characteristic of ritual actions or behaviour.

1949 R. K. MERTON *Social Theory* iv. 140 The ritualistic type of adaptation can be readily identified. **1952** GERTH & MARTINDALE tr. *Weber's Anc. Judaism* xiii. 336 In Israel, originally, ritualistic segregation from strangers was totally absent. **1962** I. Sarnoff *Personality Dynamics & Devel.* xii. 350 An individual may be led to develop ritualistic acts symbolizing both aspects of his conflict. **1971** P. Greenacre *Emotional Growth* I. xi. 169 The nature of the early shattering experience could sometimes be deciphered from the ritualistic behavior accompanying the use of the fetish. **1973** *Black World* June 4/1 One of the most salient characteristics of the New Black Theater..is its ritualistic aspect. By ritualistic, I mean the strong presence of *symbols, characterizations, themes* and *language styles* which are frequently repeated from play to play. **1977** *Lancashire Life* Nov. 136/3 Very many people..do not attend church because they are bored by ritualistic services.

rituality. Restrict † *Obs.* to sense 1 in Dict. and add: **2.** (Later example.) *rare.*

1974 *Times* 16 Apr. 7/6 What Solzhenitsyn writes about ideological rituality, about the harmful waste of millions of people's time and efforts on this chatter that inculcates twaddle and hypocrisy, is indisputable.

ritualization (ritiuălǝizēi·ʃǝn). [f. Ritualiz(e *v.* + -ation.] **1.** *Zool.* The evolutionary process by which an action or behaviour pattern in an animal loses its ostensible function and changes into an effective social signal for other members of the species.

[**1914** J. S. Huxley in *Proc. Zool. Soc.* I. 506 A very different question..is also well brought out in the pairing-habits of the Great Crested Grebe: I mean the gradual change of a useful action into a symbol and then into a ritual. **1923** —— in *Jrnl. Linnean Soc.* (*Zool.*) XXXV. 278 The 'ritual' use of non-sexual actions during courtship.] **1942** N. Tinbergen in *Bibliotheca Biotheoretica* I. 90 Substitute movements often have signal functions, and, doubtless in connection with these functions, may be extremely ritualised, so that they become unrecognisable when no comparative study is made. The degree of ritualisation actually reached is impressively illustrated by Lorenz' careful study of the epigamic movements of Anatinas. **1952** —— in *Q. Rev. Biol.* XXVII. 23/2 This new function [of releasing responses in other individuals] must have started a new evolutionary development during which the displacement activities became increasingly better adapted to it. This evolutionary displacement I have called 'ritualization', following Huxley (1923). **1965** *New Scientist* 17 June 768/2 The chief survival value of ritualization is obviously in the recanalization or the discharging of aggression. **1966** W. H. Thorpe in Thorpe & Zangwill *Current Probl. Animal Behaviour* ii. 94 In the process of ritualisation, certain elements are exaggerated whilst other elements tend to disappear entirely. **1974** *Nature* 3 May 8/3 Another feature of mutual courtship [in birds] is the extent of ritualisation; but this also applies to many male unilateral displays where the sexes have different plumage.

2. *Psychol.* The formalization of certain actions that serve to express a particular emotion or state of mind which is either innate or acquired as part of a social code.

1932 M. Gabain tr. *Piaget's Moral Judgment of Child* i. 42 This phenomenon..is the counterpart of that sort of ritualization of behaviour which can be observed in any baby before it can speak or have experienced any specifically moral adult pressure. **1934** Gesell & Thompson *Infant Behav.* iii. 190 Ritualization is a reinstatement of the situation, a method of defining and perhaps improving new abilities; but it is itself a general ability, an intrinsic product of growth. **1951** J. Holloway *Lang. & Intelligence* x. 189 The systematization of language is exactly parallel to the ritualization of behaviour. **1961** C. & W. M. S. Russell *Human Behav.* ii. 93 Ritualization serves to make the movement provide simple key stimuli, by simplifying it and exaggerating it. **1970** E. Klinghammer tr. *Eibl-Eibesfeldt's Ethology* vi. 101 The cultural ritualizations of man follow the pattern of phylogenetic ritualization. **1978** E. Erikson *Toys & Reasons* ii. 69, I will chart only one use of playfulness throughout life which has received little attention, namely what I call ritualization in everyday life.

3. The action of forming a social or religious ritual.

1952 Gerth & Martindale tr. *Weber's Anc. Judaism* xiii. 353 This ritualization of dietary habits made commensalism very difficult. **1952** T. Parsons *Social System* 414 The particularism, traditionalism, and 'ritualization' of traditional Chinese society. **1962** M. Gluckman *Ess. Ritual of Social Relations* 24, I propose to use the phrase 'ritualization of social relationships'—and for brevity 'ritualization'—to define this tendency... I can only plead that my readers should..take 'ritualization' as referring to a stylized ceremonial. **1966** *Phil. Trans. R. Soc.* B. CCLI. 413 If we consider the ritual of coronation from the point of view of its manifest subject matter, we describe it as the ritualization of eminent office. **1978** J. D. Crichton in C. Jones et al. *Study of Liturgy* i. 5 One of the most constant features of human history is the ritualization of the great events of human life, birth, marriage, and death.

ritualize, *v.* Add: **2.** (Further examples.)

1967 V. W. Turner *Forest of Symbols* iv. 94 A number of critical moments of transition which all societies ritualize and publicly mark. **1975** M. Douglas *Implicit Meanings* ix. 142 To provide such detailed analyses of life crises, afflictions and of how the Ndembu ritualise them, creates thorny problems of interpretation. **1979** *Dædalus* Summer 130 Strong emotion can be ritualized.

3. *Zool.* To cause (an action or behaviour pattern) to become ritualized.

1961 *Centennial Rev. Arts & Sc.* Fall 406 Because the pattern [of behaviour] was empirically determined..one is never quite certain which behaviour elements are effective, and the whole pattern becomes ritualized. **1965** *New Scientist* 17 June 768/1 Animals tend to ritualize their aggression, rearing up, roaring, showing their teeth, or erecting their ruffs,..in such a way that an adversary recognizes the intention and reacts accordingly. **1968** R. F. Ewer *Ethology of Mammals* viii. 192 In the spotted hyaena, smelling of the ano-genital region has been ritualised into a greeting ceremony which is regularly performed when members of a group meet. **1972** *Sci. Amer.* Sept. 59/1 Birds intending to fly..typically crouch, raise their tail and spread their wings slightly just before taking off. Many species have ritualized these movements into effective signals... The signals serve to coordinate the movement of flock members, and also may warn of approaching predators.

ritualized, *ppl. a.* Add: (Further examples.)

1932 M. Gabain tr. *Piaget's Moral Judgment of Child* i. 16 The child handles the marbles at the dictation of his desires and motor habits. This leads to the formation of more or less ritualized schemas. **1976** R. M. Keesing *Cultural Anthropol.* xvii. 369/1 Ritualized combat on the traditional 'battlefield' gives a vivid picture of one side of tribal warfare. **1978** E. Erikson *Toys & Reasons* ii. 73 Any ontogenetic reconstruction of the relation of play to politics would have to begin with the meaning of ritualized interplay for the development of the individual ego.

2. *Zool.* Of an animal's action or behaviour pattern: not having its ostensible function but serving as a signal to other members of the species.

Some of the examples are better interpreted as *pa. pple.*

1942 [see *ritualization 1]. **1964** G. B. Schaller *Year of Gorilla* (1965) ix. 239 Natural selection may act on such displacement activities by enhancing their effectiveness as communicatory signals; they may become stereotyped and be incorporated into a definite display—they become ritualised. The fact that the gorilla often places a leaf between its lips suggests that this curious gesture may be a ritualised act of displacement feeding. **1966** K. Z. Lorenz *On Aggression* xiv. 241 All the culturally evolved norms of 'fair fighting', from primitive chivalry to the Geneva Convention, are functionally analogous to phylogenetically ritualized combat in animals. **1971** *Nature* 18 June 469/1 The rutting conflicts of most species [of cervid] are largely ritualized, antlers serving the function of display more than as jousting weapons. **1978** D. Symons in E. O. Smith *Social Play in Primates* 208 Because fighting entails serious risk, ritualized signals have evolved by which animals communicate aggressive intent and, thereby, avoid fighting.

ritually, *adv.* (Further examples.)

1914 J. S. Huxley in *Proc. Zool. Soc.* I. 506 The Grebe is interesting as showing all three stages of the process at one time—the passive attitude employed sometimes directly, sometimes symbolically, and sometimes ritually. **1966** K. Z. Lorenz *On Aggression* v. 48 In our European common shelduck for example, the whole process..contains no ritually fixed parts. **1972** T. R. Williams *Introd. Socialization* viii. 183 Some American Indian cultures such as the Hopi and Zuni, ritually observe puberty for one or for both sexes. **1978** G. Wainwright in C. Jones et al. *Study of Liturgy* ii. i. 37 Ritually, a novel feature of the Protestant worship was the giving of independent value to hymns in the structure of the service.

Ritz, *sb.* (*a.*) [The name of the Swiss-born hotelier César *Ritz* (1850–1918), given to his luxury hotels in Paris, London, New York, and elsewhere.] **a.** Used allusively of a large and luxurious hotel, *esp.* in negative phrases. Also *attrib.* and as *adj.*

1910 R. Fry *Lett.* (1972) I. 336, I will not pretend that my cuisine rivals the Ritz. **1922** F. Scott Fitzgerald (*title*) The diamond as big as the Ritz. **1926** E. Hemingway *Sun also Rises* xix. 238 We drove in to Biarritz and left the car outside a very Ritz place. **1928** W. S. Maugham *Ashenden* vi. 93 They came to a tavern in a blind alley, noisome and evil... 'It's not the Ritz,' he said, 'but at this hour of the night it's only in a place like this that we stand a chance of getting something to eat.' **1942** M. Dickens *One Pair of Feet* vii. 111 A phrase that often sprang, unvoiced, to my lips, was 'This ain't the ruddy Ritz'. **1960** R. Kirkbride *Innocent Abroad* xii. 87 Lousy as the room was, I was damn' glad to have it... 'It isn't the Ritz,' I said. 'But we got nowhere else to go.' **1973** W. H. Canaway *Harry doing Good* i. i. 14 The outhouse..was warm and fusty..but..for fifty pence who would expect the Ritz? **1978** *Vogue* Feb. 8/2 Creating charming country house suites with prints, quilting, Roman blinds, pretty colours, real Ritz comfort.

b. Colloq. phr. *to put on the ritz*, to assume an air of superiority. *U.S.*

1926 R. Lardner in *Hearst's Internat.* Jan. 33/2 If you mention some really worth while novel like, say, 'Black Oxen', they think you're trying to put on the Ritz. **1929** I. Berlin *Puttin' on the Ritz* (song) 3 If you're blue and you don't know what to do Why don't you go where Harlem sits Puttin' On The Ritz. **1945** L. Saxon et al. *Gumbo Ya-Ya* i. 11 You had to put on the ritz downtown, which some of the gals didn't like. **1980** H. Luce *In Midst of Death* iii. 34 We'll have to decide how long we can go on putting on the Ritz in this house. Personally, I'd much rather live in a cottage.

ritz, *v. U.S. colloq.* [f. prec.] *trans.* To behave haughtily towards (someone); to snub. (See also quot. 1962.) Also *refl.*, to give oneself airs.

1911 G. Ade in *Chicago Daily News* 16 Sept. 28/2 They went abroad and began to Ritz themselves. **1924** H. C. Witwer in *Cosmopolitan* Nov. 42/2 We graciously presented Bertha with permission to bring him up to dinner at our flat one night, and he Ritzed and four-flushed us all till me and Hazel had to either dash out into the great outdoors or else give this big blah a sofa pillow shower! **1939** R. Chandler *Big Sleep* iii. 30 You sent for me. I don't mind your ritzing me. **1941** [see *high-hat *v.*]. **1962** S. Strand *Marketing Dict.* 636 *Ritzed it*, in the fashion field, adding glamour to a fabric or dress so that it will have public appeal. One way would be to advertise it in a class magazine. **1978** *Vogue* Feb. 8/2 (*heading*) Ritzing the Ritz.

Ri·tzian, *a.* [f. as prec. + -ian.] Worthy or typical of the Ritz.

1908 F. Hopwood *Let.* 11 Jan. in R. S. Churchill *Winston S. Churchill* (1969) II. Compan. ii. 742 A banquet of Ritzian splendour. **1918** G. Frankau in *Poetical Wks.* (1923) II. 179 Veil from these eyes their last too vivid canto:—Those Ritzian chambers on the Place Vendôme. **1940** 'Gun Buster' *Return via Dunkirk* ii. vii. 142 Veal cutlets, tinned peas, cheddar cheese and vin rouge awaited me at the Command Post. In the circumstances, a Ritzian repast.

ritzily, ritziness: see *ritzy *a.*

ritzy (ri·tsi), *a. colloq.* (orig. *U.S.*). Also Ritzy. [f. *Ritz *sb.* + -y[1].] **a.** (In a complimentary sense.) Having class, poise, or polish; smart, stylish, glamorous, 'classy'. **b.** (In a derogatory sense.) Of persons: haughty, pretentious, ostentatious; of things: flashy, pretentious-looking.

1920 Wodehouse *Jill the Reckless* (1922) xvi. 240 The Duchess, abandoning that aristocratic manner criticized by some of her colleagues as 'up-stage' and by others as 'Ritz-y', [etc.]. **1923** *Variety* 15 Nov. 19/2 The upstaginess and ritzy attitude of the movie stars has become a matter of common talk. **1926** S. Lewis *Mantrap* i. 20 Now there's some real Ritzy dancing-pumps... Had 'em done specially. **1930** E. Wallace *White Face* v. 49 She's got the only respectable apartment... All Ritzy. **1932** S. Gibbons *Cold Comfort Farm* xvii. 237, I want a new Gary Cooper..only more ritzy. Someone who can look good in a tuxedo. **1938** E. Bowen *Death of Heart* ii. iv. 243 Friend of your sister-in-law?.. He'll be a bit ritzy for us, then, won't he? **1943** *Archit. Rev.* XCIII. 80/4 There is no disguising the vulgarity of his Tokio hotel, the ritzy streamlining of his Johnson house, the mere ugliness of the Jones house of 1929. **1947** *People* 22 June 5/1 That glamour gal of British trains, the ritzy, resplendent Golden Arrow. **1949** 'G. Orwell' *Let.* 5 Sept. in B. Crick *G. Orwell* (1980) xvii. 399, I feel ghastly and can't write much, but we had a wonderful journey down yesterday in the most ritzy ambulance you can imagine. **1951** M. McLuhan *Mech. Bride* (1967) 80/2 'Ritzy dames' who are provided with custom-built allure. **1958** *Woman's Own* 10 Sept. 33/1 For that ritzy touch, get octopus or ham in champagne. **1959** W. D. Pereira *North Flight* iv. 54 You should see 's eldest kid... Bone idle. Goes to one of them ritzy schools, but it won't 'elp 'im none. **1963** *Observer* 1 Dec. 8/3 A stunning report, with its ritzy format and private jokes. **1970** R. Freeth *Lighting* iv. 32/2 If you want to be really 'Ritzy' install a filament reflector bulb as well over the cooker and sink. **1976** *Evening Advertiser* (Swindon) 31 Dec. 10/7 When I buy skin-food it's the product I'm interested in, not a ritzy bottle to decorate the dressing table. **1979** *Daily Tel.* 4 June 17/4 (Advt.), It looks most glamorous..for lounging in a ritzy beachside cafe.

Hence **ri·tzily** *adv.*, **ri·tziness.**

1928 *Motion Picture Classic* Jan. 27 They whirl ritzily out to Beverly Hills. **1929** M. Lief *Hangover* 234 'Oh that?' she said sort of ritzily, 'why, that's only her filling-station!' **1965** *Harper's Bazaar* Nov. 70 Lids can now be coated ritzily and memorably with Max Factor's Iridescent Gold shadow. **1967** N. Tomalin in L. Deighton *London Dossier* 285 Neighbourhoods of unbelievably stuffy ritzyness. **1970** 'O. John' *Diamond Dress* xiii. 145 The smooth, spacious ritziness of this large store.

‖ **riva** (ri·va). [It.] In Italy, a river-bank, sea-shore, or quay; *spec.* the *Riva degli Schiavoni* in Venice.

1880 F. J. Sitwell tr. *Yriarte's Venice* p. xii, The Riva and its Denizens. **1888** H. James *Aspern Papers* I. i. 13 The old palace..overlooked a..canal, which had a narrow *riva* or convenient footway on either side. **1909** J. Joyce *Let.* 7 Sept. (1966) II. 249, I long to see the lights twinkling along the *riva* as the train passes Miramar. **1928** Beerbohm *Variety of Things* 186 As I passed along that Riva, I would try to imagine Venice as she was. **1965** H. Honour *Compan. Guide to Venice* v. 77 The Fondamenta dell'Arsenale leads down to the *Riva degli Schiavoni*... To your left the Riva sweeps up to the public gardens.

rivalrous, *a.* Add: **2.** Given to rivalry; acting as a rival. orig. *U.S.*

1920 in Webster. **1961** F. H. Allport in Webster, s.v., Ascendant, expansive, and rivalrous students. **1963** *Observer* 21 Apr. 29/4 In the three- to six-year-old stage boys become rivalrous with their fathers, girls with their mothers. **1965** *Amer. N. & Q.* Sept. 14/2 A rivalrous and divided Italy had little more to offer. **1972** M. Mead *Blackberry Winter* (1973) vi. 70 Sisters, while they are growing up, tend to be very rivalrous and as young mothers they are given to continual rivalrous comparisons of their several children. **1980** *N.Y. Times* 28 Oct. C1/1 Even geographical separation cannot sever their closeness or quell their rivalrous strivings.

rivalry. Add: **1. b.** *Psychol.* Lack of fusion of the visual fields presented separately but simultaneously to each eye when these are sufficiently different, there being instead an alternation of perceived images.

1878 A. Gamgee tr. *L. Hermann's Elem. Human Physiol.* (ed. 2) x. 427 (*heading*) Rivalry of the fields of vision. **1950** K. N. Ogle *Res. Binocular Vision* vi. 61 Depending on the particular characteristics of the image patterns falling on the retinas of the two eyes, fusion will be complete or partial, or as an antithesis of fusion, the patterns may actually exhibit a rivalry or resistance to fusion. **1974** L. Kaufman *Sight & Mind* viii. 306 Even when the inner square is seen floating above the background lines in the stereoscope, all the lines are in a constant state of binocular rivalry.

rived, *ppl. a.* (Later examples.)

1853 *Trans. Mich. Agric. Soc.* IV. 156 Either the rived or sawed bolt may be used. **1887** *Century Mag.* Apr. 901/1 The earliest houses of worship in America belonged to the make-shift order of architecture,—four walls of..rived clapboards with earth filled in between.

‖ **rive gauche** (rīv gōʃ). [Fr.] = *left bank* s.v. *LEFT *a.* 3.

1862 MRS. GASKELL *Jrnl.* Feb. in *Fraser's Mag.* (1864) Apr. 435/1 We went to-day along the Boulevard Sévastopol, Rive Gauche, to pay a call. **1894** G. DU MAURIER *Trilby* I. II. 51 Then back again to the quays on the *rive gauche* by the Pont Neuf. **1928** R. HALL *Well of Loneliness* xxxi. 289 Of course you'll have to live on this side, the Rive Gauche is the only possible Paris. **1948** A. WAUGH *Unclouded Summer* ii. 16 It was his belief that the Americans who were creating an *emigré Rive gauche* colony had sold their birthright. **1959** *Listener* 28 May 941/2 All those romantic stories..which have been going the rounds of the *rive gauche* ever since. **1977** *Times* 19 Feb. 9/1 Those whose shelves are filled with rarities, generally secured for 'next to nothing' on the Rive Gauche.

rivelling, *ppl. a.* (Later example.)

1878 G. M. HOPKINS *Poems* (1967) 74 But his eye no cliff, no coast or Mark makes in the rivelling snowstorm.

river, *sb.*[1] Add: **I. 1. f.** *Printing.* (See quot. 1948.) Also *river of white.*

1898 G. B. SHAW *Let.* 5 Jan. in *Ellen Terry & Shaw* (1931) 287 Oh those proofs, those proofs! Imagine..sticking in words to make the printing look decent—to get the rivers of white out of it! **1927** —— *Let.* 7 Mar. in *To Young Actress* (1960) 114 They avoided white patches and rivers in the rich black block of letterpress. **1929** *S. P. E. Tract* XXXIII. 437 In careful book-printing the possibility of manipulating spaces is limited, because evenness is desirable, and rivers of white on the page must be avoided. **1948** M. E. SKILLIN et al. *Words into Type* 546 *River,* a streak of white space in printed matter caused by the spaces between words in several lines happening to fall one almost below another. **1967** *Guardian* 13 Oct. 5/3 Morison holding up a book, inspecting the printed page for rivers of white caused by bad printing.

g. The finest grade of diamond. Cf. *river stone* in sense 4d below and WATER *sb.* 20.

1934 in WEBSTER. **1946** G. STIMPSON *Bk. about Thousand Things* 267 *River* and *extra river* are now used to denote diamonds of the finer qualities. **1965** J. Y. DICKINSON *Bk. of Diamonds* viii. 219 *River,*..the finest color grade in diamonds; an extraordinarily transparent stone may be called 'an extra river stone'. **1973** *Times* 25 Aug. 17/3 The (more or less) accepted English classes run thus in descending order: (1) finest fine white or river *alias* blue-white.

3*. Phrases. **a.** *to sell down the river*: to sell (a troublesome slave) to the owner of a sugar-cane plantation on the lower Mississippi, where conditions were harsher than in the northern slave States; hence *fig.*, to deliver (one) over to slavery (*rare*); to let down, betray. *colloq.* (orig. *U.S.*).

1851 MRS. STOWE in *National Era* 14 Aug. 1/2 I've had one or two of these fellers, and I jest sold 'em down river. **1894** 'MARK TWAIN' *Pudd'nhead Wilson* ix. 113 Ole Marse Driscoll 'll sell you down de river. **1927** WODEHOUSE *Small Bachelor* i. 21 When Sigsbee Waddington married for the second time, he to all intents and purposes sold himself down the river. **1941** AUDEN *New Year Let.* II. 44 'I'll fix you something for your liver'; And thus he sells us down the river. **1943** K. TENNANT *Ride on Stranger* ix. 98 'Perhaps we could persuade Mrs. Brewster to abandon that part of the pageant?' 'Oh don't!.. She'd like to sell me down the river as it is, cheap.' **1955** E. POUND *Section: Rock-Drill* (1957) lxxxvi. 24 England not yet sold for the Suez—That would have been 20 years later, or was it '74? At any rate, sold down the river, passed over Parliament. **1958** HAYWARD & HARARI tr. *Pasternak's Dr. Zhivago* vi. 155 It's my considered opinion, Yurochka, we've been sold down the river. **1976** *Southern Even. Echo* (Southampton) 16 Nov. 3/3 Some aspects of Britain's education system needed to be put right but 'we should not sell it down the river' Education Secretary Mrs. Shirley Williams said last night.

b. *up the river*: (orig.) to Sing Sing prison, situated up the Hudson River from the city of New York; hence *fig.*, to or in prison. *colloq.* (orig. *U.S.*).

1891 in H. Campbell *Darkness & Daylight* (1892) ii. 75 Lager-beer had come up since I went up the river. **1905** C. H. DAY *Actress & Clerk* v. 53, I didn't go up the river for several stretches for nothing, I didn't. I've got a record. **1946** *Chicago Daily News* 5 Mar. 8/3, I done it. Send me up the river. Give me the hot seat. **1951** WODEHOUSE *Old Reliable* i. 18 A member of the jury which three years before had sent him up the river for what the Press of New York was unanimous in describing as a well-earned sentence. **1963** J. N. HARRIS *Weird World Wes Beattie* (1964) iii. 24 But I *still* want to talk to Mrs. Leduc and find out why she sent the boy up the river.

c. *down the river*, used in various senses, as: into slavery (cf. sense 3* a above); finished, past, over and done with; to prison (cf. sense 3* b above). *colloq.* (orig. *U.S.*).

1893 'MARK TWAIN' in *Century Mag.* Dec. 238/1 Percy Driscoll slept well the night he saved his house-minions from going down the river. **1930** J. B. PRIESTLEY *Angel Pavement* ii. 80 And up to eighteen months ago, I'd have told you that Claridge and Molton was one of the soundest concerns in the business. And look at 'em now. Properly in Queer Street. Absolutely down the river. **1931** *Sun* (Baltimore) 31 Jan. 1/5 True enough, I used to hustle a little beer in the old days —but that's all down the river. **1939** 'E. QUEEN' in *Blue Bk. Mag.* Oct. 18/1 'Mike's car's gone down the river.' 'I thought the champion was wealthy,' said Mr. Queen. 'Not any more.' **1974** *Times* 31 Jan. 4/5 He had overheard Miss Jones threatening Mr Dee 'to send him down the river for life'.

II. 4. a. *river-bridge, -coast* (later example), *flat* (earlier and later examples), *-front, -glade* (earlier and later examples), *-grove, hill, -island* (later examples), *-isle, -lane, -marsh, -meadow, road, -shore* (earlier example), *state, terrace* (later example), *town, -trail, -walk* (later examples).

1915 E. POUND *Cathay* 20, I had to be off to So, far away over the waters, You back to your river-bridge. **1940** W. FAULKNER *Hamlet* I. iii. 77 His destination was not far: a little under a mile to the river bridge, a little more than a mile beyond it. **1960** R. CAMPBELL tr. *A. Rimbaud's Drunken Boat* in *Coll. Poems* III. 17, I felt no more the guidance of my tow-men As I came down by listless river-coasts. *a* **1816** B. HAWKINS *Sk. Creek Country* (1848) 47 On the right side, off from the river flats, the land is waving. **1977** *Weekly Times* (Melbourne) 19 Jan. 62 (Advt.), A very scenic property rising from irrigated river flats to undulating and hilly terrain, with magnificent outlook. **1855** *Chicago Weekly Times* 16 Jan. 1/1 To lease for a term of years. 200 feet river front, ready docked. **1978** J. A. MICHENER *Chesapeake* 237 He had been discussing her with young men of the region, offering them..even a stretch of river-front, if they would marry his eldest daughter. **1848** B. SMITH in *Rep. to authorize Draining of Ever Glades* (U.S. Congress Comm. Publ. Lands) 19 The name Ever Glades is doubtless of English gift, and probably was originally 'River Glades'. **1957** BLUNDEN *Poems of Many Years* 284 You see Old Night Begin to shade the river-glade. **1930** —— *Poems* 290 The secret paths of river-groves. **1793** J. FILSON in G. Imlay *Topogr. Descr. W. Terr. N. Amer.* (ed. 2) II. 118 After passing the Miami River hills..the country in places is broken. **1948** *Clarke County Democrat* (Grove Hill, Alabama) 29 Apr. 4/2 The river hill, while not yet quite subdued, is nothing like the formidable barrier that it once was. **1913** J. LONDON *Valley of Moon* xvii. 479, I wouldn't trade a square mile of this kind of country for the whole Sacramento Valley, with the river islands thrown in and Middle River for good measure. **1939** AUDEN & ISHERWOOD *Journey to War* i. 31 The British Consulate is in the foreign concession, on the river-island of Shameen. **1900** J. A. JOYCE in *Fortn. Rev.* Apr. 577 Through the trees can be seen the town harbour, and the fjord,..as it stretches past headland and river-isle out to the sea. **1947** C. S. LEWIS in *Punch* 21 May 434/1 He held at the finish but a small river-isle. **1968** G. JONES *Hist. Vikings* III. iii. 224 The river-lanes of France and the Low Countries. **1978** C. TOMLINSON *Shaft* 43 They..narrow out into A now-smooth riverlane. **1930** E. POUND *XXX Cantos* vi. 24 By river-marsh, by galleried church-porch. *c* **1847** THOREAU in J. L. Shanley *Making of Walden* (1957) 198 Men who frequent the river meadows and solitary ponds in the horizon-connecting links between towns. **1912** P. S. ALLEN *Let.* 11 Apr. (1939) 101 We even found fritillaries growing..flowers which we have hitherto always associated with the moisture of Thames' river-meadows. **1776** G. WASHINGTON *Let.* 27 Dec. in *Boston Gaz.* (1777) 20 Jan. 2/1, I formed my detachment into two divisions, one to march up the lower or river road, the other by the upper or Pennington road. **1829** J. MACTAGGART *Three Yrs. Canada* II. 202 When the snow falls deep, before the ice has had time to freeze to any considerable thickness, the *river roads* remain dangerous all the season. **1955** E. A. COLLARD *Canad. Yesterdays* 302 Some experienced travellers on the river-roads even carried 'choke-ropes'. **1770** G. WASHINGTON *Tour to Ohio* in *Olden Time* (1846) I. 423 At the lower end of the Long Reach..is a large bottom, but low, and covered with beach near the river shore. **1845** *Southern Lit. Messenger* XI. 578/1 There, too, should be present..all the river States, to deliberate upon the present condition of those great arteries of commerce among them. **1976** *Daily Times* (Lagos) 4 Sept. 2/2 Divisional administration in the River state has been abolished with immediate effect. **1969** BENNISON & WRIGHT *Geol. Hist. Brit. Isles* VI. xvi. 366 River terraces..are remnants of former floodplains dissected by the rejuvenation of rivers consequent upon uplift. *a* **1850** G. G. FOSTER *New York Naked* (*c* 1855) vii. 74 Here he fell in, accidentally, with a rich banker and capitalist, from one of the river towns. **1938** H. ASBURY *Sucker's Progress* ix. 212 When they came ashore they demanded women and whisky, and the river towns provided both in great abundance. **1977** B. F. CHAMBERLIN in Bond & McLeod *Newslett. to Newspapers* IV. 248 The legislature had been established as the 'supreme power' of the Commonwealth in an agreement among the early Seventeenth-Century river towns. **1902** S. E. WHITE *Blazed Trail* III. xxx. 211 The little procession..took its way up the river-trail. **1923** L. Y. ERSKINE *River Trail* viii. 58 In the morning Geoffrian..set out for the river trail. **1914** KIPLING in *Nash's & Pall Mall Mag.* Nov. 181/1 A river front, a narrow terraced river-walk in front of semi-oriental houses. **1976** *State Jrnl.* (Lansing, Michigan) 11 July B-7/1 Ducks are a long-time attraction to visitors... Now residents can enjoy them while strolling along the new 'Riverwalk'.

b. *river-bend, -edge, -line, mouth* (earlier example), *ravine, -reach* (earlier example), *-system* (later examples).

1898 W. H. OGILVIE *Fair Girls & Gray Horses* 33 By stock-routes brown and burnt and bare, by flood-wrapped river-bends, They've hunted them from gate to gate—the drover has no friends! **1972** R. G. KAZMANN *Mod. Hydrol.* (ed. 2) iv. 115 On the Mississippi River..a number of river-bend cutoffs have been constructed. **1883** 'MARK TWAIN' *Life on Mississippi* xxii. 256 St. Louis is a great city; but the river-edge of it seems dead. **1945** *Finito! Po Valley Campaign* (15th Army Group) 7 Behind these riverlines were the machine gun nests. **1958** N. LEVINE *Canada made Me* v. 127 Old bits of dead grass, like tufts of hair, stuck out of the mud. Near the riverline the snow had not melted. **1979** R. COX *Auction* ii. 41 'The Yanks must be going flat out,' said Horst. 'Thank God we're not defending that riverline.' **1790** J. BACKUS *Diary* 6 Dec. in W. W. Backus *Geneal. Mem. Backus Family* (1889) 93 Came down to the river mouth of a large run. **1788** J. MAY *Jrnl. & Lett.* (1873) 75 We contemplated in our plans a grand bridge over the river ravine. **1879** *Encycl. Brit.* X. 276/2 The river-ravine likewise crept backward, but at a more rapid rate. **1849** THOREAU *Week Concord Riv.* 370 There is a pleasant tract on the bank of the Concord, which I have in mind;..the open wood, the river-reach. **1879** *Encycl. Brit.* X. 272/1 In a vast river system like that of the Mississippi, the area of drainage is..extensive. **1962** H. R. LOYN *Anglo-Saxon Eng.* i. 9 For the main part the river-systems drain west in this area.

c. *river-craft* (earlier and later examples), *steamboat, steamer, traffic.*

1837 DE QUINCEY in *Blackw. Mag.* July 94/1 From the want of bridges, or sufficient river craft for transporting so vast a body of men. **1963** *Times* 18 May 16/5 (*caption*) Various kinds of rivercraft on the Yangtze Kiang in China. **1979** A. MORICE *Murder in Outline* xiv. 115 A boatyard belonging to..an old-established family firm, who hired out river craft. **1857** M. H. STACEY *Jrnl.* 24 May in *Uncle Sam's Camels* (1929) II. 28 What an immense difference we find between the quiet Sundays at home and the bustling ones on board these river steamboats. **1902** CONRAD *Youth* 67, I was going to take charge of a two-penny-halfpenny river-steamboat with a penny whistle attached! **1833** E. T. COKE *Subaltern's Furlough* v. 70 The American river steamers are noble vessels. **1903** JOYCE *Let.* 8 Feb. (1966) II. 26, I..came back to Paris in one of the little river-steamers. **1936** *Discovery* Dec. 379/2 The ordinary river-steamer services. **1879** *Rep. Comm. Navig. River Thames* p. xxx in *Parl. Papers 1878–79* (C. 2338) XLI. 245 As to the hour at which the ordinary river traffic or daylight excursions should end, there is more difference of opinion. **1968** W. WARWICK *Surfriding in N.Z.* 40/3 Dangerous currents and river traffic.

d. *river board, -crossing, -cult, -damp* (later example), *-debris, -dream, -fancy, -flow, -glimpse, -link, lot, -mist, police, trip, -voyage, week*; **river blindness,** (blindness due to) onchocerciasis; **river capture** *Physical Geogr.*, the natural diversion of the headwaters of one stream into the channel of another, freq. resulting from rapid headward erosion of the latter stream; **river engineering,** the branch of civil engineering concerned with the improvement and control of rivers; **river gravel,** gravel that was formed on the bed of a river; **river ooze, River Ouse,** rhyming slang for 'booze'; **river-pay** (later example); **river stone,** a diamond found during river-digging.

1955 *Times* 8 July 9/7 Some types of blindness are more intractable. Such, for example, is the notorious 'river blindness' of the Gold Coast, where in the northern territories there are estimated to be 40,000 blind people. **1972** *Daily Tel.* 22 Nov. 4/4 One French project is to eradicate 'river blindness', an insect-born disease which has ravaged and depopulated the valleys of the Volta rivers. **1975** *Sci. Amer.* Oct. 53/2 There are villages in tropical Africa and Central America where as many as 15 per cent of the people are blind. They are victims of 'river blindness', a frequent complication of the parasitic disease onchocerciasis which.. has recently been recognized as a major public-health problem throughout the tropical world. **1948** *Act.* 11 & 12 *Geo. VI* c. 32 § 1 The Ministers shall..by order establish boards (to be known as 'river boards') for the areas so defined, who shall have the functions conferred on or transferred to them by or under the following provisions of this Act, being functions relating to land drainage, fisheries and river pollution and certain other functions relating to rivers, streams and inland waters. **1963** *Times* 23 Jan. 6/3 The information they had gathered in the past fortnight from river boards throughout the country made it seem likely that when the thaw came it would reveal an urgent need for many land drainage and flood control schemes. **1901** *Geogr. Jrnl.* XVIII. 227 Examples taken from various parts of Italy of alteration in the direction of valleys due to river-capture, etc. **1937** WOOLDRIDGE & MORGAN *Physical Basis Geogr.* xv. 211 The river-captures of the first cycle will still be legible in the pattern of the drainage, but there will now be no direct evidence of the former continuity of consequent drainage lines. **1960** B. W. SPARKS *Geomorphol.* vi. 112 The type of river capture described is largely explained by differences in rock resistance, but another factor becomes of importance in areas of permeable rocks: the possibility of underground diversion preceding and aiding surface capture. **1977** A. HALLAM *Planet Earth* 76/1 Possible signs of river capture that can often be detected in the landscape include windgaps and elbows of capture, incision of the capturing stream below the capture, and the evident misfit nature of the beheaded stream. *a* **1951** E. HILL in Murdoch & Drake-Brockman *Austral. Short Stories* (1951) 292 The blacks ran with him for four or five miles, as far as the river-crossing. **1965** AUDEN *About House* (1966) 29 Shrines where a subarctic fire-cult could meet and marry A river-cult from torrid Greece. **1963** *Landfall* Mar. 23 River-damp softened her hair: her skin smelled of soap. **1951** R. CAMPBELL *Light on Dark Horse* 121 The ridge of river-debris after the flood, ran along the base of these strandlooper-dunes. **1936** AUDEN *Look, Stranger!* 15 Whose river-dreams long hid the size And vigours of the sea. [**1882** L. F. VERNON-HARCOURT *Rivers & Canals* I. p. v, In preparing a course of lectures on 'River and Canal Engineering'..it appeared to me that a book might be useful.] **1886** *Encycl. Brit.* XX. 571/2 River Engineering. The improvement of rivers may be considered under two aspects, [etc.]. **1966** *McGraw-Hill Encycl. Sci. & Technol.* XI. 585/1 Technical knowledge is inadequate to explain fully the relationship between stream form and valley slope, but it is necessary in river engineering to recognize it. **1934** BLUNDEN *Mind's Eye* III. 170 Spenser, in his *Faerie Queene*..marries the Medway to the Thames with a great display of river-fancy. **1960** *Times* 25 July 11/6 A rise in river-flow. **1964** *Oceanogr. & Marine Biol.* II. 34 When they have a sufficiently high sediment concentration to give a density of the riverflow exceeding that of the salt water, rivers entering the ocean may similarly sometimes continue as underflows. **1875** 'MARK TWAIN' in *Atlantic Monthly* Jan. 70/1 The 'point' above the town, and the 'point' below, bounding the river-glimpse and turning it into a sort of sea. **1874** *Q. Jrnl. Geol. Soc.* XXX. 229 A careful examination of this very interesting deposit convinces me that we have here preserved portions of an old river-gravel. **1975** J. G. EVANS *Environment Early Man Brit. Isles* iii. 61 River gravel is a major economic concern. It is used extensively for road and building foundations.. It is also much needed as land for building on. *a* **1862** THOREAU *Maine Woods* (1864) 251 The Allegash..here consists principally of a chain of large and stagnant lakes, whose thoroughfares, or river-links, have been made nearly equally stagnant by damming. **1704** *Public Rec. Colony of Connecticut* (1868) IV. 493 Part of a lot called the River lot, purchased of the said Nathan[ll] Holt. **1968** E. RUSSENHOLT *Heart of Continent* II. v. 76 Families already living along the Assiniboine, exercise 'squatter's rights', and lay claim to the newly-surveyed River Lots. **1926** KIPLING *Debits & Credits* 233 And the river-mist runs silver round their knees! **1931** BROPHY & PARTRIDGE *Songs & Slang 1914–1918* (ed. 3) 350 *River Ouse*, a booze, a drink(ing). **1962** R. COOK *Crust on its Uppers* ix. 76 The place still bulging with smoke and river ooze. **1825** G. F. LYON *Brief Narr. Unsuccessful Attempt to reach Repulse Bay* 2 On the 16th Commissioner Cunningham arrived from Chatham, and the ship's company received their river pay, with three months' advance. **1800** P. COLQUHOUN *Treat. Commerce & Police River Thames* i. 22 The nature of the several articles of Trade and Manufacture..cannot fail to produce a conviction of the indispensable necessity of a well-planned and energetic System of *River-Police*; to regulate and control the economy of so vast a machine, and to protect such an astonishing mass and variety of Property. **1974** *Times* 15 Apr. 2/1 It sank before river police could note its registration marks. **1887** J. MACKENZIE *Austral Africa* II. IV. iv. 87 The 'river stones', as they are called, are usually more valuable than those found in 'dry diggings' or mines. **1904** L. J. SPENCER tr. *Bauer's Precious Stones* I. II. 186 The higher quality of the river stones as compared with those from the dry diggings does not militate against the truth of this theory as to their origin. **1898** J. S. WEBB in *Century Mag.* Mar. 672 (*title*) The river trip to the Klondike. **1912** W. OWEN *Let.* 23 June (1967) 142 Mrs. Lott's River Trip is to be next Tuesday. **1954** J. R. R. TOLKIEN *Fellowship of Ring* 400, I hoped the river-voyage would beat him, but he is too clever a waterman. **1932** D. H. LAWRENCE *Last Poems* 30 Come then!.. In a week! The ancient river week, the old one.

e. *river-bailiff, family, Indian, pilot, pirate, -thief* (earlier and later examples); *river-rat* (earlier and later examples); **River Brethren** *pl.*, members of a Christian sect originating (*c* 1770) among settlers on the Susquehanna river, characterized esp. by the performance of baptisms only in rivers; **river hog, pig** *N. Amer. slang* = RIVER-DRIVER.

1905 W. OWEN *Let.* 7 Aug. (1967) 25 He was fishing this morning when a river bailiff came up. **1854** J. BELCHER *Relig. Denominations U.S.* 919 Others were organized into a body called, *The River Brethren*, partly from the locality in which they were first found, near the Susquehanna, and Conestoga, and chiefly from their baptisms being celebrated only in rivers. **1951** H. E. GILES *Harbin's Ridge* xxiii. 202 And they baptized different, too. Face forward in the water, three times. In the early days, back in Pennsylvania, they'd been named the River Brethren on account of it, I'd heard. **1937** A. HUXLEY *Let.* 15 Dec. (1969) 429 This last is an appendage on one of the numerous vast estates of what are called 'The River Families', who have been living here in a feudal sort of way, in some cases, for two or more centuries. **1902** S. E. WHITE *Blazed Trail* lvi. 384 And now we've gone and bust, just because that infernal river-hog had to fall off a boom. **1964** *Outdoorsman* (Campbellford, Ontario) Dec. 1/2 One may see a visitor with a misty look in his eye; an old blacksmith, top loader, barn boss, teamster, cookie or river hog who has returned to a fleeting glimpse of an era long gone by. **1680** W. HUBBARD *Gen. Hist. New Eng.* in *Mass. Hist. Soc. Coll.* (1815) 2nd Ser. V. 33 The River Indians, such who had seated themselves in seuerall commodious plantations up higher upon Connecticutt river. **1785** T. JEFFERSON *Notes Virginia* 388 The Mohawks carried on a furious war down the Hudson against the Mohiccons and river indians. **1907** F. W. HODGE *Handbk. Amer. Indians* I. 786/2 Mahican ('wolf'). An Algonquian tribe that occupied both banks of the upper Hudson r... To the Dutch they were known as River Indians. **1921** *Dialect Notes* V. 113 *Riverpig*,..a lumberman who follows the drive in low water and dislodges logs from bars, mud, etc. **1947** *Sat. Even. Post* 8 Mar. 20/1 River pigs bristled all around him, men who hadn't seen a town or a saloon for nine months. **1883** *Harper's Mag.* Oct. 799/2 Mr. Clemens..in his character, first, as an apprentice to the occupation of a river pilot. *c* **1849** 'N. BUNTLINE' *B'hoys of N.Y.* iv. 30 Alvorado began to see how well his friend and rival River Pirate was situated. **1962** S. E. FINER *Man on Horseback* xii. 230 The force of river pirates known as the Binh Xuyen. **1883** J. GREENWOOD *Tag, Rag, & Co.* 35 With enough of 'river rats' to occupy my thoughts during my overland journey home, I paid my old waterman his due. **1905** *Bull. U.S. Forest Service* LXI. 44 *River rat*, a log driver whose work is chiefly on the river; contrasted with Laker. **1976** *Kingston* (Ontario) *Whig-Standard* 4 June 28/1 Tom Harrison, a 'river rat' since 16, has purchased the Gananoque Water Taxi. **1853** DICKENS *Down with Tide* in *Househ. Words* VI. 481/2 River thieves can always get rid of stolen property..by dropping it overboard. **1882** J. D. MCCABE *New York* xxxiv. 518 Another dangerous class of criminals are the river thieves, or 'River Pirates'.

f. *river-crosser, -inspector.*

1936 M. FRANKLIN *All that Swagger* xviii. 167 He saddled the river-crosser—a tall old grey. **1875** 'MARK TWAIN' in *Atlantic Monthly* Feb. 221/2 We had a fine company of these river-inspectors along, this trip.

g. *river-borne, -caught, -cut, -encircled, -fed, -formed* (later example), *-rounded*; also with pres. pples., as *river-winding*.

1928 *Daily Tel.* 4 Dec. 12/4 Splitting the market into two, for river-borne and rail-borne supplies respectively. **1924** A. J. SMALL *Frozen Gold* xii. 248 Others sat round the braziers and held great slabs of river-caught salmon against the red-hot grids. **1957** G. E. HUTCHINSON *Treat. Limnol.* I. i. 81 Other authors have believed the lakes to occupy river-cut valleys. **1951** River-encircled [see *mountain-cresting* adj. s.v. *MOUNTAIN 7 b]. **1913** E. F. BENSON *Thorley Weir* i. 21 A strip of river-fed grasses and herbs of the waterside. **1977** A. HALLAM *Planet Earth* 50 Glacial erosion modifies river-formed valleys into U-shapes. **1879** G. M. HOPKINS *Poems* (1967) 79 Cuckoo-echoing, bell-swarmèd, lark-charmèd, rook-racked, river-rounded. **1951** S. SPENDER *World within World* ii. 39, I used to go for long walks and bicycle rides into the hilly, tree-scattered, river-winding countryside.

h. With adjs., as *river-dark, -thick, -wise.*

1925 E. SITWELL *Troy Park* 100 She swims across the river-dark vast floors. **1924** —— *Sleeping Beauty* xv. 53 How river-thick flow your fleeced locks. **1934** WEBSTER *Riverwise*, adj. **1940** *Sun* (Baltimore) 22 Apr. 3/6 River-wise city officials..expressed belief the inundation would prove more annoying than damaging.

5. *river-bird, -fly*; **river bass**, substitute for def.: one of several freshwater fishes of the family Centrarchidæ, esp. the black bass, *Micropterus salmoides*; (earlier and later examples); **river chub** (earlier example); **river herring** (earlier and later examples); also, formerly, the mooneye, *Hiodon tergisus*; **river pearl**, a pearl from a freshwater mussel, esp. *Margaritifera margaritifera*; **river trout** (earlier examples).

1857 *Spirit of Times* 11 Apr. 86/2 The Oswego (sometimes known as the 'river bass') is the heavier fish, often attaining to eight pounds weight. **1890** W. D. HOWELLS *Boy's Town* 30 There were men who were reputed to catch at will, as it were, silvercats and river bass. **1910** W. DE LA MARE *Three Mulla-Mulgars* iv. 52 They heard the trump-billed river-birds calling their secrets one to another. **1882** River chub [see *horny-head* s.v. *HORNY *a.* (*sb.*) 7]. **1958** J. CAREW *Black Midas* vi. 128 A river fly 'lighted on the tip of Belle's nose. **1842** J. E. DEKAY *Zool. N.Y.* IV. 266 [The river mooneye] is known under the popular names of Herring, River Herring, and Toothed Herring. **1977** *Hongkong Standard* 12 Apr. 2/8 Officials of the National Marine Fishery Services found illegal amounts of river herring in the trawler's hold 240 miles southeast of Boston. **1885** *Encycl. Brit.* XVIII. 447/2 River-pearls are produced by the fresh-water mussels inhabiting the mountain-streams of temperate climates in the northern hemisphere. **1963** P. MOYES *Murder à la Mode* iii. 55 Get me lots of gold bracelets and some river pearls. **1975** *Times* 6 Mar. 5/1 The borders..are adorned with sapphires, rubies, emeralds, and river pearls. **1834** *Chambers's Edin. Jrnl.* 6 Dec. 357/3 Fish (we speak of river trout) spawn seldom in such [slow, muddy] waters. **1867** *Harper's Mag.* Dec. 48/1 He has already achieved unequalled success in breeding river-trout.

6. *river-cress, palm, willow*; **river birch** (examples); **river (red) gum**, substitute for def.: the most widespread of the red gum-trees, *Eucalyptus camaldulensis*; cf. *RED GUM[2] 2; (later examples); **river white gum**, a gum-tree, *E. andreana*, with smooth white bark; (earlier and later examples).

1853 W. DARLINGTON *Flora Cestrica* (ed. 3) 275 Black Betula. Black Birch. Red Birch. River Birch. **1884** C. S. SARGENT *Rep. Forests N. Amer.* 161 Red Birch. River Birch... Used in the manufacture of furniture. **1969** T. H. EVERETT *Living Trees of World* xiii. 104/1 The river birch grows in lowlands from Massachusetts to Florida. **1953** A. CLARKE *Moment Next to Nothing* I. i. 18 I've little to offer a guest... But it is yours, a round of bread, a pick Of river-cress and goat-cheese. **1911** C. E. W. BEAN '*Dreadnought' of Darling* ii. 17 A single line of railway runs straight out into the back country..and stops within sight of the river gums. **1963** W. E. HARNEY *To Ayers Rock & Beyond* iii. 29 The gaunt river-gums..grow along the bank and bed of this one-time mighty river. **1964** D. VARADAY *Gara-Yaka* ix. 74 In the lush valleys among the rock forts..there stand magnificent River Palms. **1930** A. J. EWART *Flora Victoria* 821 River Red Gum. A fairly tall tree, up to 80 or 150 feet high, with a greyish-white bark shedding in thin leaves or flakes. **1973** G. M. CHIPPENDALE *Eucalypts W. Austral. Goldfields* 183/2 The river red gum is the most widespread eucalypt in Australia. **1884** A. NILSON *Timber Trees New South Wales* 58 River White Gum.—Trunk smooth and nearly white. **1961** PENFOLD & WILLIS *Eucalypts* xii. 249 The tree [sc. *E. andreana*] is known as 'White Top', or 'River White Gum', and occurs fairly plentifully on the river banks and mountain ranges of eastern New South Wales. **1963** M. SHADBOLT *Summer Fires & Winter Country* 233 In summer we swam down under the river-willows.

river, *v.* Add: **2.** *intr.* To follow a river-like course.

1921 A. CLARKE *Sword of West* 23 Far below me lay A deep green valley rivering through grey mist.

river-bottom. (Earlier examples.)

1752 C. GIST *Jrnl.* 20 Feb. (1893) 75 Then continued our course..the last 5 [miles] thro the river bottoms, which were a mile wide and very rich. **1793** G. IMLAY *Topogr. Descr. W. Terr. N. Amer.* (ed. 2) 411 At the edge of the wood lands, and before your descend [*sic*] into the river bottoms, one of the most charming prospects..displays itself.

ri·ver-di:gging. orig. *U.S.* [f. RIVER *sb.*[1] + DIGGING *vbl. sb.*] **a.** *pl.* Gold or diamond diggings in the neighbourhood of a river or stream, or in a dried-up river-bed. **b.** The action of digging at such a place. Hence **river-digger.** Cf. DIGGING *vbl. sb.* 4.

1851 D. B. WOODS *Sixteen Months at Gold Diggings* i. 13 The 'river diggings' include the bars and auriferous portions of the channels of the tributaries of the Sacramento and San Joaquin, during their passage through the foot-hills. **1862** [see *dry diggings* s.v. *DRY *a.* C. 3]. **1881** E. E. FREWER tr. *Holub's Seven Yrs. S. Afr.* I. iii. 60 The settlement at the river-diggings sprang up with a rapidity as marvellous as those of California. **1904** L. J. SPENCER tr. *Bauer's Precious Stones* I. II. 185 The amalgamation of the 'dry diggings' to form the De Beers Consolidated Mines, has had the effect of increasing the number of river diggers. **1920** F. C. CORNELL *Glamour of Prospecting* i. 10 A modicum of genuine men of past experience—principally ex-'river-diggers'—men whose small capital was running away like water for bare necessities in this miserable dust-hole of creation. **1947** L. HASTINGS *Dragons are Extra* i. 10 Dabbling in river-digging for diamonds. **1947** *E. Afr. Ann. 1946–7* 122/1 The 'river diggings' of South Africa where workings extend.. along present or ancient river beds.

river-driver. For *U.S.* read *N. Amer.* and add later examples. Hence **ri·ver-drive**, a drive of logs down a river; **ri·ver-driving**, the action of driving logs down a river.

1854 F. J. BULLARD *Now-a-Days* 65 River drivin' is the pootiest part of loggin', I think. **1908** S. E. WHITE *Riverman* v. 50 How does river-driving strike you? **1920** *Rod & Gun in Canada* Nov. 646/1 We were enjoying the sights we saw along the line: the lakes, rivers, the river-drives. **1937** C. M. WILSON *Aroostook* 105 The 'river-drives' were the consummation of turning out the timber. **1963** *Canada Month* Nov. 22/1 The lumber trade furnished employment for thousands of lumber jacks, river drivers, and sailors. **1972** [see *pick-pole* s.v. *PICK *sb.*[1] 8]. **1974** D. SEARS *Lark in Clear Air* ii. 27 He..got a job as boss on a river-drive. *Ibid.* xiv. 178 Tommy bought a new pair of river-driving boots.

riverine, *a.* and *sb.* Add: **A.** *adj.* **2.** Also, resembling a river.

1884 E. JENKINS *Week of Passion* II. iv. 156 His face,.. deeply rutted, here and there, with expressive valleys and riverine lines of wrinkle.

rivering (ri·vəriŋ), *ppl. a. nonce-wd.* [Cf. RIVER *v.* in Dict. and Suppl.] Flowing in river form.

1939 JOYCE *Finnegans Wake* (1964) I. 216 Beside the rivering waters of, hitherandthithering waters of. Night!

riverrun[1] (ri·vəɪˌrʌn). *nonce-wd.* [Cf. RUN *sb.*[1] 29 a.] The course which a river shapes and follows through the landscape.

1939 JOYCE *Finnegans Wake* (1964) I. 3 Riverrun, past Eve and Adam's, from swerve of shore to bend of bay, brings us by a commodius vicus of recirculation back to Howth Castle and Environs.

river runner. *N. Amer.* [f. RIVER *sb.*[1] + RUNNER.] **a.** One who drives a river-vessel. **b.** One who engages in the leisure activity of running, or travelling down, a river in a small craft (as a rubber dinghy, etc.). Hence **river run**[2], **river running.**

1913 O. A. ROTHERT *Hist. Muhlenberg Co.* xxxi. 393 The coal barges were taken up and down the river by men known as 'river runners'. **1962** *Nat. Geographic* Apr. 561/1 (*caption*) River runners stop for a swim in the Little Colorado's Blue. **1965** MRS. L. B. JOHNSON *White House Diary* 28 Oct. (1970) 330 I'll never be satisfied after having been down the Snake River until I've become a river runner. **1968** *Sunset* Mar. 34/2 On your first river-running excursion..you'll..welcome all the advice you can get. *Ibid.* (*heading*) What to take on a River Run. **1974** C. F. MARTIN *Sierra Whitewater* 8 The drive from San Francisco Bay to good river runs is thus about an hour shorter than the drive to good skiing. **1976** *National Observer* (U.S.) 24 Jan. 12/2 River running in an inner-tube, skeet shooting, and trout fishing are speedily arranged at minimal cost.

riverscape (ri·vəɪskēɪp). [f. RIVER *sb.*[1] + SCAPE *sb.*[3]; formed in imitation of LANDSCAPE.] **1.** A picturesque view or prospect of a river.

1903 C. S. SMITH *Barbizon Days* 17 Moret has noble turreted gateways and Grez a church more picturesque than that of Montigny, riverscapes more alluring, and a ruined château. **1927** H. V. MORTON *In Search of England* xii. 213 All the beauty and peace of the Warwickshire countryside have been packed into one riverscape. **1966** *New Statesman* 25 Nov. 793/1 Nobody listened to his proposal to replace Rennie's Waterloo Bridge with a tunnel to save spoiling a fine riverscape.

2. A painting of a river or riverside scene.

1930 *Time & Tide* 9 May 606 Mr. Lamorna Birch and Sir H. Hughes Stanton show very capable riverscapes. **1964** N. FREELING *Double-Barrel* iii. 91 The arrangement opposite: a wholly bluey-greeny Monet riverscape over a little writing table. **1975** *Gramophone* Dec. 1065/1 The record is very well produced with a fine autumnal riverscape by Monet on the front.

riverside. Add: **b.** *riverside bathing, sand, village.*

1760 G. WASHINGTON *Diary* 14 Apr. (1925) I. 153 Has 2 Pecks of sd. Earth and 1 of Riverside Sand. **1914** W. OWEN *Let.* 1 June (1967) 257 They went to visit some friends who lived in a riverside village. **1946** *Nature* 31 Aug. 290/1 At the age of fourteen, he contracted severe rheumatic trouble, as a result of river-side bathing.

riverward, *adv.* and *a.* Add: **B.** *adj.* (Later example.)

1966 D. VARADAY *Gara-Yaka's Domain* xi. 121 In the riverward spoor a few drops of blood showed up.

ri·verwise, *adv.* [f. RIVER *sb.*[1] + WISE *sb.*[1]] In the manner of a river; in relation to a river.

1927 JOYCE *Lett.* (1966) III. 164 She has grown—riverwise—since the night you heard her under the sign of Ursa Minor. **1946** R. GRAVES *Poems 1938–45* 20 They carry Time looped so river-wise about their house There's no way in by history's road To name or number them. **1946** R. BLESH *Shining Trumpets* vii. 151 The French laid out the city, eleven squares riverwise and six squares deep.

rivery, *a.* Delete *rare* and † *Obs.*—[1] and add: **1.** (Later examples.)

1916 A. HUXLEY *Burning Wheel* 13 Lorelei, Combing the silken mystery, The glaucous gold of her rivery tresses. **1977** *Rolling Stone* 19 May 86/3 'The Wheel' is more Western bop than swing, a brilliant, rivery thing that makes it easy to understand why Charlie Parker liked jamming with Ray Price's band.

2. (Later examples.)

1889 W. B. YEATS *Wanderings of Oisin* 78 From rolling valley and rivery glen, With horsemen hurrying near and far, I drew at evening my mailed men. **1973** P. LIVELY *Ghost of Thomas Kempe* ii. 17 Green, rivery, elm-scattered Oxfordshire.

Rivesaltes (rivsalt). The name of a town near Perpignan in southern France, used *attrib.* and *absol.* of a sweet wine produced there.

1824 A. HENDERSON *Hist. Anc. & Mod. Wines* II. ii. 178 At Salces..a white wine is grown, which..is thought to resemble Tokay; but, in point of richness, it is inferior to the Rivesaltes. **1836** C. REDDING *Mod. Wines* (ed. 2) v. 131 The quantity of Rivesaltes muscadine made is about sixty-five hogsheads per annum. *c* **1870** in H. W. Allen *No. 3 St. James's St.* (1950) 185/1 Rivesaltes, pints—42/-. **1920** [see *JURANÇON]. **1971** A. DURKAN *Vendange* ix. 85 A speciality from this district are the dessert wines called Vin Doux Naturel... The best-known names are Banyuls, Muscat de Frontignan, Muscat de Lunel, Rivesaltes, Maury and Grand Roussillon.

rivet, *sb.*[1] Add: **1. e.** *pl.* Money, coins. *slang.*

1846 *Swell's Night Guide* 130/1 *Rivets*, money. **1848** *Sinks of London laid Open* 121 *Rivits*, money. **1937** 'J. CURTIS' *You're in Racket* xviii. 190 'So you got a bit of rivets to speculate?' 'I ain't said so. All I said as I could put up a bit.'

2. *rivet bar, head, hearth, tail*; **rivet gun,** a hand-held tool for inserting rivets.

1890 D. K. CLARK *Steam Engine* I. 657 The diameter of the ⅝-inch rivet-bars was reduced to ·03 inch. **1950** *Nat. Geogr. Mag.* Sept. 297 (*caption*) Chattering rivet guns attach the door to a barrel section of a Constellation. **1902** *Encycl. Brit.* XXXII. 597 The riveters also work in squads, ..with sometimes a catcher, *i.e.*, a boy to pass on the heated rivets when the distance from the rivet-hearth is great. **1978** *Jrnl. R. Soc. Arts* CXXVI. 690/2 On long-term creep tests at operating temperatures, it was found that the rivet heads and tails cracked.

riveter. Add: **2.** (Further examples.) (See also quot. 1963.)

1928 [see *BOATSWAIN 3]. **1963** JONES & SCHUBERT *Engin. Encycl.* (ed. 3) 1068 'Riveting machines', according to common usage, differ from 'riveters' in that the riveting operation with a machine is effected by a succession of blows or by a compressive rotating action, whereas a riveter merely subjects the rivet to compression.

riveting, *ppl. a.* (In Dict. s.v. RIVET *v.*) (Further examples.)

1854 *Rambler* Feb. 198 Riveting as were these narratives when we first read them..those who now read them for the first time are generally disappointed. **1967** N. MARSH *Death at Dolphin* v. 129 Her smart friends..said things like: 'Absolutely riveting' and 'Loved your play'. **1975** *Evening Standard* 24 June 20/1 Landladies..are far more genned up on local history and things to do (plus some riveting gossip) than the managers of more impressive emporia. **1979** E. H. GOMBRICH *Sense of Order* x. 271 'Some 2500 years ago'—Kurz sums up his riveting article—'a Greek artist conceived the strange idea of putting a movable ring into the mouth of a lion.'

ri·vetingly, *adv.* [f. RIVETING *ppl. a.*] In a riveting manner.

1971 *Guardian* 21 June 11/1 'Yesterday's Men' was an extreme example: it provided rivettingly viewable entertainment. **1973** *Daily Tel.* 22 Nov. 10/3 His animation of wartime London is uncannily detailed, rivetingly atmospheric.

Riviera (rivyēᵊ·rä). Also **riviera.** [It., lit. 'coast, shore'.] **1.** The name of the Italian sea-board about Genoa, applied also to the Mediterranean coast from Marseilles in France to La Spezia in Italy, a fashionable winter resort in the 19th century and more recently popular for summer holidays; usu. with *the.* Also *attrib.* Cf. RIVER *sb.*[1] 3.

[**1632**: see ROOT *sb.*[1] 4 c]. **1766** J. NORTHALL *Trav. through Italy* VI. ii. 471 The dominions of this State consist of the countries extending along the sea-coast, on both sides, from the city of Genoa, which are called the eastern and western Rivieras. This word in Italian signifies a strand. **1797** *Encycl. Brit.* VII. 426/2 The people of Genoa revolted..and reduced a great part of the Riviera. **1852** DICKENS in *Keepsake* 120 He had hired an old place on the Riviera, at an easy distance from my city, Genoa. **1863** GEO. ELIOT *Let.* Oct. (1956) IV. 111, I shall imagine you winding along the Riviera, and then settling in sight of beautiful things. **1892** I. ZANGWILL *Childr. Ghetto* II. II. i. 270, I had better take a hansom to the Riviera at once. **1909** C. F. G. MASTERMAN *Condition of England* ii. 57 In Biarritz, Pau, Dinard—he might have said in the whole *côte d'azur* of the Riviera—'the English have conquered us,' he declares **1939** S. DE MADARIAGA *Christopher Columbus* iii. 25 Eating and drinking..in that Genoese riviera so sunny and full of the joy of existence. **1941** KOESTLER *Scum of Earth* 28 There was an elderly Riviera-Englishman on the platform. **1978** *Times* 18 Mar. 11/1 The Riviera or Cote d'Azur has a special affinity with the English who apart from the Romans were its first holidaymakers.

2. *transf.* Applied to other coastal regions considered to resemble the Mediterranean Riviera. Also with *a* and *pl.*, and *attrib.*

1891 M. F. SWEETSER *King's Handbk. U.S.* 175 The old convents and churches..and the yachting in the adjacent waters, furnish a great variety of interest for visitors to the American Riviera. **1904** *Railway Mag.* Sept. 258 'The Riviera Express' is the title chosen by Mr. J. C. Inglis, the General Manager of the Great Western Railway, as the most apposite name for the Plymouth–Paddington non-stop express. **1910** *Bradshaw's Railway Guide* Apr. 1126 Lyme Regis, Dorset. Hotel Alexandra... The only hotel in its own grounds in the English Riviera. **1911** HEATH & HASLEHURST (*title*) The Cornish Riviera. **1922** WODEHOUSE *Girl on Boat* xvii. 307 'Why not Cornwall?' said Sam. 'The Riviera of England!' **1951** W. SANSOM *Face of Innocence* iii. 36 He did not know the rivieras, I knew them well. **1974** *Sat. Rev. World* (U.S.) 19 Oct. 43/1 Every properly equipped nation must have a Riviera.

Rivieran (rivyēᵊ·răn), *a. rare.* [f. prec. + -AN.] Of, pertaining to, or characteristic of the Riviera.

1897 A. BEARDSLEY *Let.* 1 Apr. (1970) 290, I have been getting into quite a glow over a packet of Rivieran photographs. **1909** *Westm. Gaz.* 21 Sept. 4/2 'The climate,' she writes, 'is of quite Rivieran mildness during the winter months.'

rivière. Add: **1.** (Earlier and later examples.)

1879 M. E. BRADDON *Vixen* I. xvi. 304 The special presents which stood out..were—a *rivière* of diamonds.., a pair of priceless crackle jars, a Sèvres dinner-service of the old *bleu-du-roi*. **1958** M. KELLY *Christmas Egg* II. 61 Rivière—what was that?—of large brilliant diamonds, with ear-rings en suite, silver.

2. *needlework.* A row of open-work.

a **1855** C. BRONTË *Professor* (1857) II. xviii. 9 A 'rivière', or open-work hem round a cambric handkerchief. **1886** in A. Adburgham *Shops & Shopping* (1964) xviii. 209 In Blonde de Seville, it [*sc.* a lace fichu] falls into cascades and rivières.

riwa-riwa, var. *REWA-REWA.

rix-dollar. Add: **2.** A unit of currency introduced into certain former colonies, as by the Dutch in Cape Province and the English in Ceylon. (See also quot. 1962.)

1785 G. FORSTER tr. *Sparrman's Voy. Cape Good Hope* I. 19 Board and lodging are paid for here as at the Cape, from one rix-dollar to one and a half a day. **1790** E. HELME tr. *Le Vaillant's Trav. Afr.* I. ii. 21 While I was there [*sc.* at Capetown] butchers meat was very cheap; I have seen thirteen pounds of mutton bought for an escalin; (elevenpence English) an ox for 12 or 15 rix dollars; (at six shillings and nine-pence English, the rix dollar) ten quarters of corn for 14 or 15 Rix-dollars, and other things in proportion. **1827** G. THOMPSON *Trav. & Adventures Southern Afr.* I. I. iv. 79 He provides a salary of 400 rix-dollars to encourage a day-school for females. **1836** *Penny Cycl.* VI. 453/2 In the district of Putlam they were faced boldly in the open forest, and ensnared singly, for a reward varying according to the size and description of animal, from 11 to 352 rix-dollars. **1866** J. LEYLAND *Adventures Far Interior S. Afr.* III. 233 The charge for crossing in the barge was fifteen shillings, or ten rix dollars. **1900** A. H. KEANE *Boer States* p. xviii, *Rixdollar*, a coin current in the Cape in colonial times. **1962** R. A. G. CARSON *Coins* 533 The Dutch monetary system of a rix-dollar or rijksdaalder of 48 stuiver was continued [in Cape Province] by the British in the early nineteenth century.

riyal: see *RIAL *sb.*[1] 5. **riyo,** var. *RYO.

riza (rī·ză). [Russ., f. OSlav. *riza* garment.] A metal shield or plaque framing the painted face and other features of a Russian icon, and engraved with the lines of the completed picture.

1927 E. H. MINNS tr. *Kondakov's Russ. Icon* ii. 37 As long ago as the fourteenth century, under Greek influence, the Russians began to cover..the figures with plates of silver showing in more or less relief the outlines and folds of the clothes and vestments: such a plate is called a *riza*, properly speaking a garment, especially a chasuble:.. The parts of the figures left unclothed, faces, hands, and the like, all the flesh tints, show through holes in the *riza.* **1931** P. ROMANOV tr. *Zarine's Three Pairs of Silk Stockings* ii. 9 One hall was full of pictures... Another was covered with ikons with old rizas of pearl. **1963** T. T. RICE *Russian Icons* 25 It became usual to encase an icon in a costly metal cover or *riza*, in which openings were cut to show the essential sections of the painting. **1970** *Guardian* 1 Apr. 16/5 Sometimes elaborate silverwork was added, covering much of the surface and leaving only the faces and figures visible. This metalwork, the riza, was occasionally ornamented with precious or semi-precious stones. **1978** *Daily Tel.* 24 Aug. 12/5 Among the collection is a 17th century icon of the Virgin of Kazan, with embossed silver-gilt riza..dating from the end of the 19th century.

rizalite (rizā·ləit). *Geol.* [f. *Rizal*, the name of a province of central Luzon in the Philippines (named after Dr. José *Rizal* (1861–96), Philippine patriot) + -ITE[1].] Any tektite of the type characteristically found in the neighbourhood of Manila.

1928 H. O. BEYER *Philippine Tektites* (1961) I. 21 Since.. our Luzon material cannot be properly classed as either Billitonite or Australite..I am proposing the name *rizalite* as a temporary designation for it. **1937** *Mineral. Abstr.* VI. 403 A popular account is given of the tektites ('rizalites'), mostly from Rizal province, which are spherical or cylindrical. **1940** *Pop. Astron.* XLVIII. 44 Rizalites (pitted spheroids, ovals, and cylindrical forms being most characteristic). *Ibid.* 45 The most typical Rizalites occur only in Luzon, although a few similar, pitted specimens are known from Borneo and Java.

r-less: see R I. 1 c.

RNA. *Biochem.* Also (*rare*) **R.N.A. 1.** Abbrev. of *ribonucleic acid.

See also *messenger RNA, *ribosomal RNA, *transfer RNA.

1948 *Jrnl. Biol. Chem.* CLXXV. 989 Protein, phospholipides, and ribonucleic acid (RNA) are lost from the liver. **1959** *Sunday Times* 14 June 24/3 RNA carries the genetic information in the small viruses only, while DNA does this in all other organisms. **1968** H. HARRIS *Nucleus & Cytoplasm* iii. 57 No precise mechanism for this RNA-mediated regulation [of genetic activity] has yet been put forward. **1968** *Times* 19 Oct. 4/8 Further decipherment of the genetic code depended on synthesizing artificial RNAs containing all 64 possible triplet combinations. **1969** R. B. FULLER *Operating Man. Spaceship Earth* iv. 52 The genes and the R.N.A. and D.N.A. and other fundamental principles governing the fundamental design controls of life systems. **1977** *Nature* 27 Oct. 834/1 Enzymatic rather than chemical methods were used to degrade the RNA.

2. Special Combs. **a. RNA virus,** a virus in which the genetic material is RNA.

1963 *Nature* 17 Aug. 664/1 The use of specific inhibitors has led to the conclusion that the replication of small RNA viruses is not dependent on the integrity of host DNA. **1975** *Ibid.* 23 Oct. 634/3 Many RNA viruses are involved in animal cancers and it is believed that some human cancers may be caused in the same way.

b. In names of enzymes acting on RNA, as *RNA polymerase, replicase, synthetase.*

1962 *Biochem. & Biophysical Res. Communications* VII. 30 The stimulation by the phage DNA is dependent on the addition of purified RNA polymerase with polymerase-poor fractions. **1973** R. G. KRUEGER et al. *Introd. Microbiol.* xi. 331/1 RNA polymerase is a complex enzyme whose affinity for different promoters..depends upon protein factors which are not tightly bound to the core enzyme. **1965** *Biochem. & Biophysical Res. Communications* XVIII. 283 (*heading*) Isolation of turnip yellow mosaic virus RNA replicase. **1969** *New Scientist* 18 Dec. 590/1 These small spherical viruses contain RNA, which functions directly as messenger, coding for three proteins, coat protein, 'maturation factor' and RNA replicase. **1962** F. H. BERGMANN in *Methods in Enzymol.* V. 708 Since the term 'amino acid-activating enzyme' thus represents only a partial description of the catalytic activity of such enzymes, the term 'amino acyl RNA synthetase' is more appropriate. **1968** *Times* 29 Oct. 7/4 The third [gene] specifies an enzyme, called RNA synthetase, which produces copies of the RNA strand.

RNase (ārenē¹·z). *Biochem.* Also **RNAase** (ārenē¹·ē¹z). [f. *RN(A + *-ASE.] = *ribonuclease* s.v. *RIBO-.

1957 *Jrnl. Biochem.* XLIV. 761 This RNase was inhibited by various metal ions. **1961** *Biochimica & Biophysica Acta* XLVII. 145 When yeast protoplasts are incubated with RNase, protein synthesis is inhibited. **1961** *Ibid.* LI. 190 The gel-filtration method is recommended as a suitable method to obtain the highly active fraction from RNAase I core. **1968** A. WHITE et al. *Princ. Biochem.* (ed. 4) xii. 258 The histidine residues of RNase are uniquely reactive with iodoacetate or bromoacetate at pH 5·5. **1977** *Nature* 22/29 Dec. 760/2 The ability of cassava latent virus nucleic acid to infect *N*[*icotiana*] *clevelandii* was destroyed by DNase but not RNase.

roach, *sb.*[1] Add: **2. b.** *roach fisherman, swim*; **roach pole,** a type of rod used in fishing for roach.

1974 *Country Life* 30 May 1333/2, I didn't have much success as a roach fisherman. **1897** *Encycl. Sport* I. 24/2 On the Thames, the bank-angler commonly uses a long bamboo roach-pole and tight line. **1944** 'N. SHUTE' *Pastoral* i. 3 With his long greenheart roach-pole, his bag of ground bait, and his gentles. **1971** *Country Life* 16 Dec. 1730/4, I believe the Lea roach-pole anglers were then regarded as supreme masters of that particular art. **1902** *Chambers's Jrnl.* Nov. 699/1, I was preparing to fish a not unpromising roach-swim, and was trying the depth.

roach, *sb.*[3] Add: [App. a *transf.* use of ROACH *sb.*[1]] **1.** (Further *transf.* example.) Cf. *roach-back(ed)* s.v. ROACH *sb.*[1] 2 a.

1955 W. W. DENLINGER *Compl. Boston* I. 105 Many Boston terriers with level backs will show roach on a cold day.

2. a. *U.S.* A roll of hair brushed upwards and back from the face; a topknot (see quot. 1959[2]). Also *attrib.*, as *roach cut.*

1881 J. C. HARRIS in *Century Mag.* June 244/2 Den he take en walk upter de little Gal, Brer Rabbit did, en pull he roach, en bow, en scrape he foot, en talk mighty nice en slick. **1929** W. FAULKNER *Sound & Fury* 177 A man with a fierce roach of iron grey hair. **1959** E. TUNIS *Indians* 47/2 Most of the head was plucked or singed bare for a roach cut; only a strip of hair was left from front to back. *Ibid.* 48/1 The most usual ceremonial headdress in the East was the artificial roach.

b. *attrib.* in sense of *ROACHED *a.* 2.

1781 *R. Georgia Gaz.* 8 Mar. 4/2 (Advt.), A Black Horse, about 13 and an half hands high, half roach main [etc.]. **1835** J. T. Irving *Indian Sk.* II. 4 She was mounted upon a little wall-eyed, cream-coloured pony, with a roach mane and a bobtail.

roach, *sb.*[4] Add: Chiefly *U.S.* **1.** (Further examples.)

1942 E. Paul *Narrow St.* x. 75 Her failure to get results kept her hopping like a roach in a skillet. **1950** *Harlem Q.* Fall–Winter 21 A fat roach sluggishly made its way ceilingwards. **1976** *National Observer* (U.S.) 29 May 15A/3 The Postal Service is the kind of problem most members think shouldn't exist. It's like roaches in the kitchen.

2. *slang.* A policeman.

1932 *Evening Sun* (Baltimore) 9 Dec. 31/5 *Roach*, policeman. **1968** *Word Study* Dec. 5/1 Not only is a policeman a *bull*; he may also be a *roach*.

3. *slang.* The butt of a cigarette, *spec.* a marijuana cigarette. (Perh. a different word.)

1938 *New Yorker* 12 Mar. 47/2 A pinched-off smoke, or stub, is a roach. **1953** W. Burroughs *Junkie* ii. 29 'Would you like to get high?' Mary asked. 'There may be a roach around here somewhere.' **1966** T. Pynchon *Crying of Lot 49* iii. 64 Holding up the glowing roaches of their cigarettes..to spell out alternate S's and O's. **1971** *It* 2–16 June 2/1 Freaks from several other pads saved all our roaches for a week and posted them to Det. Sgt. Boothe who is the chief of Bournemouth drug squad. **1972** M. J. Bosse *Incident at Naha* i. 46, I..took out my pot pouch and cigarette paper... I..rolled myself a joint... I had finished the roach down to my fingernails.

4. *attrib.* and *Comb.*, as (sense 1) *roach killer, poison, -powder*; *roach-crawling* adj.; (sense *3) *roach holder*; **roach clip** = *roach holder* above.

1968–70 *Current Slang* (Univ. S. Dakota) III–IV. 103 *Roach clip*, a small metal clip used to smoke marijuana, resembling a paper-clip or tweezers. **1979** *Christian Science Monitor* (Eastern ed.) 21 Nov. B1/1 Clearly visible through the shop's windows are..'roach clips' for holding the butt of a marijuana cigarette. **1964** S. Leaks in J. H. Clarke *Harlem* 23 *Harlem*, a dingy-dirty cluster of roach crawling rat-infested brownstones and tenement flats. **1967** *Evening Standard* 26 June 7/3 In Haight-Ashbury [in San Francisco] there are now over 30 psychedelic boutiques..selling at inflated prices such items as..roach holders (cigarette holders specially designed for reefer smoking). **1973** *Sunday Express* (Trinidad & Tobago) 8 Apr. 13/2 I'm on the floor, surrounded by pots and pans etc. shaking the can of roach killer. **1975** *New Yorker* 23 June 29/2 St. Vincent's emergency room is one of my favorite emergency rooms in the whole world. I know it well, from the time..my daughter ate the roach poison. **1930** J. Dos Passos *42nd Parallel* 60 A smell of ham and coffee and roachpowder. **1931** E. Pound *Let.* 6 Oct. (1971) 236 In reply to yr. last: I am not interested in roach-powder but if the janitors and swabbers can't keep the place clean, I take it *somebody* has got to provide insecticide or even squash the individual cockroach.

roach, *v.* Add: **2. a.** (Earlier example.)

1818 *Missouri Gaz.* 25 Dec. 4/5 His mane has been divided..and that part that laid on the left side, cut off as if to roach him.

b. Of persons: to brush or cut (the hair) in a roach. Also with *up*.

1833 *Sk. & Eccentr. D. Crockett* ii. 38 His hair was roached, and he wore an air of much dignity. **1853** J. G. Baldwin *Flush Times Alabama* 108 His hair was roached up, and stood as erect and upright as his body. **1900** Ade *More Fables* 62 He would go to School with his face scrubbed to a shiny pink and his Hair roached up on one side. **1919** H. L. Wilson *Ma Pettengill* iii. 84 She was..a kind of a slaty blonde with bobbed hair—she'd been roached fore and aft. **1932** L. C. Douglas *Forgive us our Trespasses* (1937) iv. 79 His hair roached high to show he had an intellectual forehead. **1950** L. Hughes *Simple speaks his Mind* xvi. 86 Her head was all done fresh and shining with a hair-rocker roached up high in front.

roached, *a.* For *U.S.* in Dict. read 'Chiefly *U.S.*' and add: **1.** (Earlier and later examples.) Also *Comb.*, as *roached-backed* adj.

1776 *New England Chron.* 25 Jan. 3/3 (Advt.), Strayed or stolen..a sorrel horse..roach'd back, 3 white feet, [etc.]. **1844** E. C. Watmough *Scribblings & Sk.* (ed. 2) 176, The two [horses] with roatched backs, and ears glued to their necks, were scrambling. **1894** 'Mark Twain' in *St. Nicholas* Feb. 355/1 Roached-backed ones that he said was hyenas. **1945** C. L. B. Hubbard *Observer's Bk. Dogs* 56 Body [of Dandie Dinmont terrier] low-to-ground, roached-backed. **1955** W. W. Denlinger *Compl. Boston* I. 172 For a dog with a naturally roached spine, nothing can be done. **1979** T. Gray *Chihuahua* (ed. 5) vii. 98 Another fault, a slightly roached back, will often level out by the time the puppy is three-parts grown.

2. Of hair (on a horse or person): brushed or cut in a roach. Hence, having hair dressed in this way. Also *roached-up*.

1790 *Augusta* (Georgia) *Chron.* 13 Mar. 3/1 A Bay Horse, roached mane and a small switched tail. **1836** *Southern Lit. Messenger* II. 303/1 The..fat, impudent pony, with roached main and bobtail. **1856** P. Cartwright *Autobiogr.* xii. 141 This young man had a mighty bushy roached head of hair. **1891** *Appeal-Avalanche* (Memphis) 26 Apr. 7/2 Strayed... one dark bay colt, roached mane and end of tail cut off. **1944** Duncan & Nickols *M. Graham* 91 There were twenty-seven big, little, and middlin'-sized boys and girls, giggling and whispering about the master's roached, curly red hair. **1949** 'J. Nelson' *Backwoods Teacher* 268 If she wants to go 'round lookin' like an old roached-up mule, *we* don't care.

roaching, *vbl. sb.*[2] *U.S.* [f. Roach *v.* + -ing[1].] The action of brushing or cutting the hair in a roach. Also, the process or fact of this.

a **1883** G. W. Bagby *Sel. Misc. Writings* (1885) II. 27 You see it [*sc.* his individuality] in the tie of his cravat, the cut of his coat,..the roaching of his hair. **1903** *N.Y. Even. Post* 24 Oct. (Saturday Suppl.) 2/1 When brought to market he [*sc.* the mule] undergoes the process of 'roaching', which consists of removing all the hair of poor quality and scanty growth.

roachy (rōu·tʃi), *a.* *U.S.* [f. Roach *sb.*[4] + -y[1].] Infested with cockroaches; resembling cockroaches (see also quot. 1900).

1900 *Dialect Notes* II. 54 *Roachy, adj.*, pertaining to poor work or preparation. **1937** F. Scott Fitzgerald *Let.* 8 Oct. (1964) 19 You are right that romantic things really happen in roachy kitchens and back yards. **1979** P. L. G. Bateman *Household Pests* II. 93 They contaminate more than they consume, polluting everything with a foul 'roachy' odour which is persistent.

road, *sb.* Add: **I. 4. b.** (Later example.)

1978 *Lancashire Life* July 63/1 He took young Sam down the pit and showed him the seam, eighteen inches high, which he had to work in a road about six feet wide.

c. For *U.S.* read 'Chiefly *U.S.*' and add further examples.

1898 H. E. Hamblen *Gen. Manager's Story* 68, I was passed along from one road to another, my transportation costing me nothing. **1921** *Daily Colonist* (Victoria, B.C.) 11 Mar. 2/3 The railway official quoted said he could not state whether the Canadian roads would follow the lead of the United States roads in cutting wages. **1932** *Atlantic Monthly* Mar. 318/2 Those railways..were once so prosperous that men..thought the roads would own the country unless curbed. **1942** *R.A.F. Jrnl.* 3 Oct. 3 (*caption*) Blast area with damage to roads and wagons, and a group of derailed wagons. **1950** O. S. Nock *Brit. Locomotives* 4 The regulator opening was varied a little to suit the rise and fall of the road. **1963** *Wall St. Jrnl.* 24 Jan. 29/3 The road..operates in Guatemala and El Salvador. **1967** *Listener* 6 Apr. 461/2 At Edenbridge sidings they..told us to stand in number three road to get our breakfast.

e. *spec.* with qualifying word, a common trade-route (now freq. for illicit goods).

1931, etc. [see *silk-road*, s.v. *silk *sb.* 10 a]. **1977** *Listener* 1 Dec. 733/1 The lost city of Zufar, the port which marked the beginning of the incense road, where ships unloaded spices from Asia for the classical Roman world. **1977** H. Osborne *White Poppy* xliii. 272 The gendarmes would be..watching..the opium roads.

5. a. *on the road*: also *spec.* of a person travelling as (*a*) a salesman, (*b*) a tramp; (earlier and later examples in sense 'on tour'). Also *N. Amer.*, = *away *adv.* 11 (cf. sense 9d below).

1860 Dickens *Uncomm. Trav.* in *All Year Round* 28 Jan. 321/1, I am both a town traveller and a country traveller, and am always on the road. **1870** O. Logan *Before Footlights* xxviii. 367 The organ of the circus people..gives many curious details of circus-life Behind the Scenes, and 'on the road'. **1897** *Forum* Feb. 735 It is the man who wilfully and knowingly makes a business of crime..that I have found in largest numbers 'on the road'. **1907** J. London *Road* 194 As a sample of life on The Road, I make the following quotation from my diary. **1908** A. Bennett *Old Wives' Tale* I. iv. 70 He was a traveller for the most renowned and gigantic of all Manchester wholesale firms... He had been on the road for Birkinshaws for several years. **1920** Wodehouse *Jill the Reckless* (1922) xiv. 210 You've got to stick around with this show after it opens on the road. **1931** M. Allingham *Police at Funeral* xxi. 277, I know a 'busy' when I see one. I 'aven't been on the road for thirty years without gettin' inside once or twice. **1937** 'G. Orwell' *Road to Wigan Pier* ix. 182, I would find out about tramps..and then, when I..knew the ropes well enough, I would go on the road myself. **1956** B. Holiday *Lady sings Blues* (1973) i. 2 When he went on the road with that band it was the beginning of the end of our life as a family. **1967** J. B. Priestley *It's an Old Country* xv. 162 He was drinking hard, always a dam' silly thing to do on the road, except with a few old customers. **1968** *Globe & Mail* (Toronto) 15 Jan. 17/6 A team with the experienced potential of the defending cup champions is letting its fans down badly when it wins only four of 19 games on the road. **1977** *Daily Express* 29 Mar. 20/2 We start touring America in May, move on to Europe and England by September, and we are taking the 70 musicians on the road.

f. In extended uses based on *all roads lead to Rome* (*Rome 1 b (*d*)).

1917 E. Thomas in *Ann. New Poetry* 55 Now all roads lead to France. **1942** E. Paul *Narrow St.* xxiii. 209 All roads lead straight to me, as you have so often remarked. **1974** D. G. Compton, *Continuous Katherine Mortenhoe* vi. 165 'Where to now?'..I gestured widely... 'All roads lead out of town.'

g. *one for the road*: see *one *numeral a.* 1 d. Also with other numerals.

1955 J. P. Donleavy *Ginger Man* (1957) xix. 184 'You've had a few.' 'Five for the road. Never let it be said that I took to the highway or even byway without fuel for me little heart.'

6. c. (Further examples.)

The expression stems from a saying attributed to Euclid by Proclus (*Comm. on Euclid* Prol.): μὴ εἶναι βασιλικὴν ἀτραπὸν ἐπὶ γεωμετρίαν there is no royal short cut to geometry.

1857 Trollope *Barchester T.* II. i. 2 There is no royal road to learning; no short cut to the acquirement of any valuable art. **1918** A. S. Eddington *Rep. Relativity Theory Gravitation* ii. 27 Some readers will find the next two chapters difficult,..but I doubt if there is any royal road to relativity. **1954** 'N. Shute' *Slide Rule* vii. 158 There is no royal road to risk capital, no tap that can be turned on. **1966** P. Green tr. *Escarpit's Novel Computer* xiv. 173, I had to obtain that last official stamp of approval which could open up the royal road towards an easy and fruitful career. **1971** *Daily Tel.* 19 Apr. 23 The royal road for the research scientist in industry is signposted by positive answers to some critical questions: [etc.].

g. *capitalist road* [tr. Chinese *zīběn zhǔyì dàolù*], esp. during the Cultural Revolution in China, an observable tendency to adopt political ideals and practices leading towards capitalism. Cf. *roader[1] 7.

1966 *Peking Rev.* 12 Aug. 8/2 The main target of the present movement is those within the Party who are in authority and are taking the capitalist road. **1966** *N.Y. Times* 11 Dec. 3/3 Peking newspapers..attacked Hsia Yen, a playwright and former Deputy Minister of Cultural Affairs, as one of those in authority in the Communist party who had taken 'the capitalist road'. **1971** W. F. Dorrill in T. W. Robinson *Cultural Revol. in China* ii. 72 Numerous accusations were raised against the 'handful' in authority in the Party who were following the 'capitalist road'. **1973** T. R. Tregear *Chinese* iii. 58 The reliance on the profit motive and bonuses—Economism and 'taking the capitalist road', as he [*sc.* Mao] dubbed it. **1978** *China Reconstructs* Nov. 2/2 Anyone who pushed production or technical research was labeled as taking the capitalist road and ignoring politics.

7. b. (U.S. and Austral. examples.)

1826 A. Royall *Sk. Hist., Life, & Manners U.S.* 58 Put them cheers, (chairs) out of the road. **1924** E. O'Neill *Desire under Elms* III. i, in *Compl. Wks.* II. 200 Git out o' my road! Give me room! I'll show ye dancin'. **1943** K. Tennant *Ride on Stranger* xxiv. 269 Yes, I was cowardly enough to wait until you were out of the road. **1953** *Amer. Speech* XXVIII. 253 You are in the road... Get out of my road.

8. d. *any road, anyroad* = Anyway *adv.* and *conj.* 3. (Chiefly *north. dial.*)

1896 F. M. T. Palgrave *Hetton-le-Hole Words* 38 'Any road' (anyhow). **1932** P. MacDonald *Rope to Spare* xi. 156 Anyroad, sir, to cut a long story brief, I gets down to the mill-'ouse. **1964** O. E. Middleton *Walk on Beach* ii. 28 And how is the arm today, anyroad? **1968** M. Woodhouse *Rock Baby* vii. 67 We knew we'd have to expect one or two failures... Any road, we crossed it off. **1976** 'J. Charlton' *Remington Set* i. 5 Any road, what's it to you?

II. 9. a. *road-car* (further examples), *engine, tanker, -wagon* (earlier and later examples).

1906 *Chambers's Jrnl.* 24 Feb. 205/2 In appearance it is a very different thing from the road-car which may perhaps be regarded as its parent. **1955** A. Budrys in D. Knight *100 Yrs. Sci. Fiction* (1969) 251 Just before he reached the Boonesboro town line, he saw the locked and weathered cottage standing for sale... He had pulled his roadcar up to a gentle stop, swung sideways in his seat, and looked at it. **1976** *Times* 20 Mar. 14/6 Many off-track activities including a concours d'elegance of classic road cars. **1875** *Encycl. Brit.* I. 323/2 (*heading*) Road-Engines. **1886** *Walla Walla* (Washington) *Union* 24 Nov. 3/4 The 'hog' will haul nine loaded cars up the heavy Alto grade, while the ordinary road engine had a hard tussel to haul four or five. **1925** S. O'Casey *Let.* 11 Sept. (1975) I. 147 A lumbering road-engine, with its monstrous, monotonous rumble. **1971** J. Terrell *Bunkhouse Papers* xii. 155 A road engine purring over beyond the depot, waiting to hook on to the Limited. **1968** *Guardian* 1 Oct. 5/2 Road tanker drivers..are protesting against the proposal..to install a tachograph in lorries. **1979** *Jrnl. R. Soc. Arts* CXXVII. 406/2 Oil..would be taken by road tanker to Furzebrook. **1743** W. Ellis *Mod. Husbandman* June iv. 37, I sent thirty-four Bushels at one Time..by a common Road Waggon. **1880** Hardy *Trumpet-Major* II. xvi. 14 This gentleman..suggested that Bob should wait till three or four that afternoon, when the road-waggon would arrive. **1968** J. Arnold *Shell Bk. Country Crafts* 150 Road-wagons could not be run during the months of winter.

b. *road-bank* (earlier example), *-bed* (further examples), *-bend, -cut, -cutting, -dust* (earlier example), *frontage, island, -rail, sign, -stone* (further examples), *stud, surface*.

1863 B. Taylor *Hannah Thurston* III. ii. 54 As they drove homewards through the cool evening air, through..the golden-rods on the road-banks. **1902** *Chambers's Jrnl.* Jan. 61/1 In order that the oiling may be confined to the road-bed only, the rails are kept free from spraying by guards on the sprinkling-car. **1938** L. Mumford *Culture of Cities* 316 Small wonder that the Nile and the Euphrates ..were the roadbeds of their civilization. **1979** *Arizona Daily Star* 5 Aug. I. 3/1 In addition to some rocky roadbeds and a pretty rotten record for staying on schedule, it is true that there are a number of well-aged cars. **1911** J. Masefield *Jim Davis* iii. 36 The watcher at the road-bend came running back. **1978** *Nature* 8 June 459/1, I have collected unweathered samples from new exposures in quarries and roadcuts in the type area. **1936** *Discovery* Jan. 21/2 The Aculeate Hymenoptera, many of which take advantage of banks in road-cuttings and well-trodden paths, all made by man. **1854** Dickens *Hard T.* II. vi. 195 So strange to have the road-dust on his feet instead of the coal-grit. **1942** *London Replanned* 5/2 Better building sites on important road frontages. **1976** *Evening Post* (Nottingham) 15 Dec. 15/4 (Advt.), Pleasant semi-detached house with half an acre of land. Road frontage 39′ 6″. **1932** L. Golding *Magnolia St.* III. iii. 511 She..took up her stand just off the pavement... Tram-drivers, chauffeurs, cyclists..accepted her as part of the landscape, like a road-island. **1903** J. Masefield *Cargoes* in *Broad Sheet* No. 17, With a cargo of Tyne coal, Road-rails, pig-lead. **1904** *Car* VII. 240/2 Road signs... The conference held..to consider the desirability of uniformity of action with regard to signs and notice boards. **1914** *Autocar* XXXIII. 574/2 Owing to the fact that the mutilation of road signs by sportsmen and others has caused considerable confusion..the California State Automobile Association is reported to have lately placed a bull's eye target on each post. **1949** N. Marsh *Swing, Brother, Swing* ix. 211 There's one thing.. that's sticking out of this mess like a road-sign and I can't read it. **1976** P. Lively *Stitch in Time* i. 3 Maria saw this place announce itself with a road-sign. Lyme Regis. She had been studying road-signs throughout the journey. **1886** *Encycl. Brit.* XX. 583/2 The qualities required in a good road stone are hardness, toughness, and ability to resist the action of the weather. **1958** [see *aggregate *ppl. a.* and *sb.* B 5]. **1970** *Railway Mag.* Oct. 577/2 The roadstone is transferred to road vehicles for transport to the motorway site. **1935** *Economist* 11 May 1112/1 Several rather special branches of the local steel industry have experienced some increase of activity.., notably armaments, aircraft steel..and stainless steel road studs. **1959** E. K. Wenlock *Kitchin's Road Transport Law* (ed. 12) 112/2 No vehicle, except a solo bicycle.., may stop on a road between the road studs and the crossing. **1886** *Encycl. Brit.* XX. 583/1 The road surface should have just enough convexity to throw the wet off freely. **1976** 'J. Ross' *I know what it's like to Die* xxiv. 151 Seeing the road surface slipping sideways as he toppled.

c. *road accident, atlas, casualty, construction, death, expenses, haulage, junction, kill, maintenance, manners, map, -march, marching, -marker, -meet, -meeting, -name, noise, project, race, -railway, rumble, safety, signing, space, speed, system, toll* (later examples), *-tour, traffic, transport, -web, wheel.*

1935 'Owner-Driver' (*title*) Road accidents and speed limits. **1976** P. Driscoll *Barboza Credentials* I. i. 16 A policeman..had seen the bodies of enough road-accident victims to know what to expect. **1905** (*title*) Pratt's road atlas of England and Wales for motorists. **1963** *Which?* July 196/1 When maps are bound together in book form, they are called road atlases. **1971** *Guardian* 7 July 1 The Minister for Transport..announced..new measures designed to reduce road casualties. **1961** *Suspense* Mar. 119 One of his officers found him a job with a road construction company. **1977** *Borneo Bull.* 7 May 17/1 (Advt.), Sakai..of Japan have been making road construction machines since 1918. **1936** A. Christie *ABC Murders* xvii. 124 There are, what is it—about 120—road deaths every week? **1966** *Listener* 22 Sept. 412/1 The natural life of man..may still be short for many of us in organized society today, if road deaths continue at their present rate. **1839** Dickens *Let.* 1 Mar. (1965) I. 515 The money for the coach-fares and road expences will be paid by you and Mitton. **1938** *Act* 1 & 2 *Geo. VI* c. 44 §1 For the purpose of regulating the remuneration of workers employed upon road haulage work..there shall be established by the Minister of Labour..a board..to be called the Road Haulage Central Wages Board. **1977** 'D. Rutherford' *Return Load* ii. 30 The road haulage world was a friendly one. **1936** *Discovery* Oct. 317/2 The first busy road junction in the country to be equipped with invisible ray apparatus, to enable pedestrians to cross the roads in safety. **1972** R. & R. Wright *Cariboo Mileposts* 40 They [*sc.* magpies]..usually feed on carrion or road-kills. **1976** *Islander* (Victoria, B.C.) 28 Mar. 7/2 Road kills have taken a few sheep of breeding age annually. **1961** *Atlanta Constitution* 6 Mar. 4 It [*sc.* DeKalb's budget] includes..increased expenditures for essential services such as..sanitation and road maintenance. **1942** *Ann. Reg. 1941* 98 A serious deterioration of road-manners. **1963** Bird & Hutton-Stott *Veteran Motor Car* 159 The result may be a hybrid but it is undeniably magnificent with better-than-100 m.p.h. performance and perfect road manners. **1883** *Wheelman* (Boston, Mass.) I. 315 The preparation of road maps and posting of guide-boards are to be important features in next season's work. **1959** *Times* 25 June 12/6 My best aid was a road-map, which showed all dry sandy areas in Holland. **1972** 'H. Buckmaster' *Walking Trip* 112 She..stopped at a magazine kiosk and..bought a road map of Scotland. **1960** *Times* 17 Sept. 7/7 A steelband may have any number of instrumentalists, from the basic four up to a 'carnival road-march side' of over 100. **1977** *R.A.F. News* 8–21 June 7/1 Although very little is heard of road marching in the UK..on the Continent it is almost a national pastime. **1970** J. McN. Dodgson *Place-Names of Cheshire* I. 166 ME *clywe, cle(o)we*..might be used here..to denote a mound serving as a landmark and road-marker on the wild moors. **1976** *Billings* (Montana) *Gaz.* 20 June 1-B/4 Mocabee said Ferguson's motorcycle struck a road marker. **1924** J. Masefield *Sard Harker* III. 114 The tracks at the road-meet led away to the left. **1954** J. R. R. Tolkien *Fellowship of Ring* 18 As still passed to and fro through that ancient road-meeting. **1914** *Sat. Even. Post* 4 Apr. 12/1 Beside the monakers or road names of a hundred hoboes were scratched such messages as: 'Beware of dog'. **1965** *Eng. Stud.* XLVI. 266 The variant..can be confirmed from the Windsor road-name. **1970** J. McN. Dodgson *Place-Names of Cheshire* I. 49 The road-name *Lymestrete.* **1963** *Times* 4 June 7/7 Above 65–70 m.p.h...road noise was high. **1973** *Times* 24 May 35/1 The engine is remarkably quiet and there is almost no road or wind noise. **1976** *Southern Even. Echo* (Southampton) 18 Nov. 32/5 Six Filipinos working on a road project in the southern island of Mindanao were killed in an ambush. *a* **1904** W. J. Fisher *Let.* in S. Weintraub *London Yankees* vi. 201, I am anxious to do nothing to discourage motoring, and I do not at all object to this road race. **1926** E. Hemingway *Sun also Rises* xix. 247 Organizing the road races had made him know France... All spring and all summer and all fall he spent on the road with bicycle road-racers. **1954** *Sun* (Baltimore) 24 Nov. 17/2 The world's longest road-race test of car stamina and driving skill. **1976** *Cumberland News* 3 Dec. 19/3 The Border mens' team came home in eleventh position in the Brampton to Carlisle ten mile road-race. **1960** E. Bowen *Time in Rome* i. 18 Hilarious buses, electric road-railways zooming into the hills. **1952** *Jrnl. Accoustical Soc. Amer.* XXIV. 661/1 In playback of a monaural recording of road rumble through a speaker, the observer can assign a direction to the source. **1976** *Honolulu Star-Bull.* 21 Dec. F-1/1 Undercoating insulates you from hot roads, reduces road rumble, and protects against stone chip damage. **1920** *Sci. Amer.* 6 Nov. 467 Automobile Signals for Danger Spots... New illustrations of old ideas for street comfort and road safety. **1937** M. Borden *Black Virgin* i. 4 Road-safety instruction for school children. **1977** C. Watson *One Man's Meat* x. 95 The chief constable..muttered 'Good gracious me, road safety committee.' **1968** *Autocar* 14 Mar. 24/1 British road signing is often the best in Europe. **1979** *Internat. Jrnl. Sociol. of Law* Feb. 68 There are various ways by which the police could prevent and control traffic disorders and road accidents:..proper and adequate road-signing, [etc.]. **1911** *Encycl. Brit.* XXIII. 393/1 The remainder of the road space is formed as an earthen track. **1975** *Times* 14 Mar. (Small Car Suppl.) p. ii/3 If you took 3 ft off the average car, you would have another six million feet of road space [in London]. **1964** L. Deighton *Funeral in Berlin* xxiv. 135 It's a good road... There was no need to burn up any road-speed records. **1977** 'E. Trevor' *Theta Syndrome* vi. 83 The TR-2 had collided with another vehicle..at a much higher road speed. **1845** *Chambers's Edin. Jrnl.* 19 Apr. 242/1 The whole road system of Great Britain..is..the most awkward and absurd institution on the face of the earth. **1904** W. M. Ramsay *Lett. Seven Churches* xxix. 416 Laodicea was a knot on the road-system. **1932** F. L. Wright *Autobiogr.* III. 321 The United States everywhere already affords increasingly great road-systems. **1976** G. Seymour *Glory Boys* i. 7 The maps..showed..the road system of northern France. **1966** B. Castle in *Highway Code* 1 The road toll is a tragic waste—a waste of lives, a squandering of resources. **1977** *Borneo Bull.* 7 May 36/1 Razali's death pushed the road toll to 17. **1920** Wodehouse *Jill the Reckless* (1922) xviii. 269, I sold it half-way through the road-tour. **1864** *Great Western Mag.* Jan. 36 Some idea of the startling effect which it had upon the road traffic may be formed from the fact that the Commissioners of the Metropolitan Roads.. ceased to light the roads near Kensington. **1909** *Chambers's Jrnl.* June 340/1 A successful attempt was made to conduct road-traffic without the use of animal-power. **1977** *Whitaker's Almanack 1978* 140/1 Lighting-up Times, ..under the Road Traffic Act, 1956, are from half an hour after sunset to half an hour before sunrise. **1913** H. E. Wimperis (*title*) The principles of the application of power to road transport. **1969** *Jane's Freight Containers 1968–69* 231/1 Road-transport-weigh-bridge at the entrance of the Uberseehafen. **1925** W. Deeping *Sorrell & Son* vi. 58 Then take the road-web for the ordinary tourist. London some hundred miles. Salisbury thirty or so. **1939** H. Hodge *Cab, Sir?* 266 The meter records the fare..switching from miles to minutes automatically as soon as the road-wheels stop turning. **1975** *Country Life* 2 Jan. 32/3 Sports road wheels with radial-ply tyres.

d. N. Amer. *attrib.* or as *adj.* with reference to sporting fixtures played away from home, as *road game, trip,* etc. Cf. *on the road* above (sense 5a) and *away *adv.* 11.

1961 *Newsweek* 14 Aug. 44/3 He broadened teammates' minds by reading sensitive passages aloud during road trips. **1961** *Dallas Morning News* 10 Oct. II. 3 The Texans have two more road games—at Buffalo and Houston—before they play for the old folks again. **1968** *Globe & Mail* (Toronto) 13 Jan. 42/5 The Leafs..have won only four of 19 road games. **1973** *Weekend Mag.* (Montreal) 27 Jan. 12/2 Working with ropes and on stools in stretching exercises in hotels on long road trips. **1976** *Billings* (Montana) *Gaz.* 5 July 1-C/3 Hoff also said the Mustangs two road victories at Lethbridge helped settle the club down and give it some confidence. **1979** *Arizona Daily Star* 1 Apr. C2/4 On the road games, Bill wanted the home team to take the court first because he loved to come out and kick them off the end of the court he wanted.

10. a. *road board, -contractor, haulier, -master* (earlier and later examples), *-party* (earlier and later examples), *scout.*

1865 *Geelong* (Austral.) *Advertiser* 27 Feb. 123/8 (*heading*) Meredith Road Board. **1915** *Political Q.* May 180 The Road Board..has restricted the grants to completing advances promised before the war. **1885** *List of Subscribers, Classified* (United Telephone Co.) (ed. 6) 74 (*heading*) Contractors—road and sewer. **1936** *Discovery* Feb. 55/1 The diversion of the roadway..did not suit the plans of the road-contractors. **1937** *Daily Tel.* 16 Feb. 7/2 (*heading*) Road hauliers win test case. **1977** *Modern Railways* Dec. 473/1 Rail movement cannot yet match the norm of around 60,000 miles a year which properly run road hauliers get from their vehicles. **1825** *Kingston* (Ontario) *Chron.* 7 Jan. 3/3 Bulls and Oxen to run at large—Fences 5 feet high. Road Masters to be Judges of Fences. **1856** *N.Y. Herald* 12 Jan. 1/4 James Flood is road master of his section; any obstruction being on the track it is the duty of the flagman to exhibit his red flag. **1905** Kipling *Actions & Reactions* (1909) 21 On my uncle's farm, in Connecticut. He was what they call road-master there. **1966** *Kingston* (Ontario) *Whig-Standard* 1 Sept. 3/2 The roadmaster came down on his track speeder and gave us a fatherly talking to. **1840** Road party [see *iron gang* s.v. *iron *sb.*[1] 12]. **1945** Baker *Austral. Lang.* ix. 182 Heavy boots were called *road party boots.* **1931** *Star* 8 May 16/1 While being chased by a road scout on a motor-cycle..a car collided with a lamp post.

b. *road-repairer, -upper, -user* (further examples).

1921 *Dict. Occup. Terms* (1927) §44 *Road repairer*;.. keeps roadways in repair below ground; [etc.]. **1932** Auden *Orators* II. 49 Acting suspiciously as road-repairers. **1928** *Daily Express* 12 June 3/4 The 'road-uppers' are busy in London again. **1922** *Daily Mail* 25 May 4/4 Always show..courtesy to all other road users. **1959** *Radio Times* 23 Oct. 3/1 Certain categories of road-users are barred..; these include pedal cyclists, invalid carriages and 'L' drivers. **1976** *Oadby & Wigston* (Leics.) *Advertiser* 26 Nov. 6/5 As an ordinary citizen and road user he said he had been concerned enough about the road to see the police and Harborough District Council about it.

11. a. *road-building, -burning, -hugging, -patching, -pricing, -surfacing.*

1910 W. James in *McClure's Mag.* Aug. 467/2 To coal and iron mines,..to road-building and tunnel-making,.. would our gilded youths be drafted off. **1980** *Times* 29 Feb. 18 Civil engineers claim £200m debt backlog on road-building contracts. **1931** T. E. Lawrence *Let.* 11 Mar. (1938) 716 After that some road-burning [i.e. fast travelling on the roads], I hope. **1963** *Times* 29 Jan. 3/7 The lightness of steering and smooth road-hugging feel of the..suspension give the car..a steady gait. **1977** *Custom Car* Nov. 70/1 (Advt.), An incredibly wide tyre for road-hugging traction-action! **1974** *Evening Herald* (Rock Hill, S. Carolina) 18 Apr. 4/1 These costs—for paving, road-patching materials, garbage containers, county employe salaries, all keep climbing each year. **1964** *Punch* 17 June 878/3 A panel research statement on 'road pricing'. **1976** P. R. White *Planning for Public Transport* x. 210 If road pricing were introduced in urban areas to indicate scarcity of road space, then some reduction in national fuel-tax rates would be appropriate. **1912** Kipling *Diversity of Creatures* (1917) 10 The sputter and crackle of road-surfacing machines. **1959** *Chambers's Encycl.* XI. 725/1 Many other methods of road surfacing have been experimented with.

b. *road-shy.*

1914 'Saki' *Beasts & Super-Beasts* 32 He [*sc.* a horse] was not really road-shy, but there were one or two objects of dislike that brought on sudden attacks of what Toby called the swerving sickness.

c. With ppl. adjs., as *road-hauled, -killed, -stained.*

1969 *Jane's Freight Containers 1968–69* 2/2 European road-hauled transport. **1980** *Topeka* (Kansas) *Capital* 23 Feb., I once unsuspectingly ate and enjoyed a turkey vulture (which my funloving host passed off as a road-killed wild turkey). **1964** F. Warner *Early Poems* 67 Gathering her road-stained dress She lay within a rock recess.

12. road allowance *Canada*, (*a*) a strip of land retained by government authorities for the construction of a road; (*b*) an area at either side of a road which remains a public right-of-way; **road apples** *pl. N. Amer. slang*, horse droppings; **road band,** a touring group of musicians; **road-borne** *a.* (further examples); **road-bound** *a.*, dependent on roads; restricted to using roads; **road brand** *N. Amer.*, a temporary brand given to cattle in transit; hence as *vb. trans.*; **road breaker,** (*a*) one employed to break up the road surface prior to repair, etc.; (*b*) a mechanical tool used for this; **road bridge,** a bridge that carries a road; **road company** *U.S.*, a travelling theatrical company; **road control,** a station for checking travellers' credentials, etc.; a group of people making such checks; **road-craft,** (*a*) knowledge of or skill in matters pertaining to the use of the road; road sense; (*b*) *collect.* = **road traffic*; **road crew,** the group of 'roadies' which accompanies a touring band of musicians; **road drill,** (*a*) a mechanical drill used for breaking up road surfaces; (*b*) the routine for crossing a road safely; **road driver** *U.S.*, (*a*) one who drives animals on the road; (*b*) a long-distance lorry-driver; **road-farer,** one who travels by road; also **road-faring** *sb.* and *a.*; **road-ferry,** a ferry serving a road; **road fund,** a fund, esp. that established by the Roads Act of 1920, to meet provisions for roads; **road hand** (earlier U.S. example); **road-head,** (*a*) *Mining*, the part of a roadway between the last support and the face; so **road-heading,** mining at a road-head; (*b*) = *road-end*; **road hockey** *Canada*, a type of hockey played in the road; **road-holding,** the ability of a car to retain its stability; **road-house,** also, any roadside establishment providing refreshment or entertainment; (further examples); **road hunter,** a hound which is adept at following a scent on the road; so **road-hunting** *a.*; **road kid** *slang*, a boy tramp or hobo; **road life,** the life of those who are 'on the road'; **road manager,** an organizer of tour details and supervisor of equipment, etc., for musicians 'on the road'; **road-mark,** (*a*) a road sign (in quot. *fig.*); (*b*) *U.S.* = **road brand*; **road-mobile** *a.*, suitable for transporting by road; **road oil** *N. Amer.*, oil sprinkled on the roads to lay dust; **road patrol,** (*a*) a person or group of people patrolling the roads; (*b*) *Canada*, a machine used in the maintenance of unpaved roads; **road racer,** (*a*) a vehicle used in road-racing; (*b*) a contestant in a road race; **road–rail,** used *attrib.* with the sense 'suitable for use on both road and railway', or 'accommodating a road and a railway'; **road-railer,** a goods vehicle that can run on both road and rail (see quot. 1964); a container which can be transported by both road and rail; cf. *Ro-

RAILER; **road rash** *slang*, grazing caused by falling from a skateboard; **road roller,** a heavy mechanical roller used for flattening road surfaces; **road-runner** (earlier and later examples); **road-running** *vbl. sb.*, running on the roads for sport or exercise; also as *ppl. a.*; **road sense,** capacity for intelligent handling of vehicles or coping with traffic on the road; **road show,** a show given by touring actors or musicians, usu. with the minimum of equipment and preparation; also *transf.* and *attrib.*; hence as *vb. intr.*; **road sweeper,** (*a*) a person who sweeps roads; (*b*) a device for sweeping roads; **road train,** a large lorry pulling one or more trailers; **road tunnel,** a tunnel through which a road passes.

1844 *Niagara* (Ontario) *Chron.* 29 May 2/2 A bill was introduced..entitled 'An act to close up the Road Allowance between Lots Nos. 42 and 43..in the township of Cayuga'. **1947** E. A. McCOURT *Music at Close* 43 He..rode west along the road-allowance until he reached a part of the country which was new to him. **1958** J. G. MACGREGOR *North-West of 16* ii. 27 He carefully stepped off this distance, which was the 'road allowance', and came to another great spruce at the exact corner of his land. **1973** *Kingston* (Ontario) *Whig-Standard* 14 Mar. 3/1 In the 1783 survey of the lakefront townships, the provision had been made for a 60-foot road allowance across the front. **1942** BERREY & VAN DEN BARK *Amer. Thes. Slang* § 124/2 *Road apples*, horse dung. **1951** M. SPILLANE *One Lonely Night* v. 112 Smart? Sure, just like road apples that happen behind horses. **1970** J. H. GRAY *Boy from Winnipeg* 53 The best pucks were always those supplied by passing horses, 'road apples' we called them. **1937** *Amer. Speech* XII. 48/1 *Road band*, a traveling unit. **1976** *Casper* (Wyoming) *Star-Tribune* 29 June 17/6 (Advt.), Wanted: vocalist for road band. **1977** *Zigzag* Mar. 2/1 Those guys had been my road band anyway. **1914** KIPLING *Years Between* (1919) 78 That I may sing of Crowd or King or road-borne company. **1973** *Daily Tel.* 10 Aug. 14 In 1971 road-borne freight amounted to 52,000 million ton-miles. **1937** L. HART *Europe in Arms* x. 120 The limitations of the large road-bound coaches or lorries which compose such bus columns were made manifest. **1941** *Washington Post* 4 Sept. 12/5 Members of both divisions pointed today to powerful motor vehicles roadbound because of continuous rains. **1874** J. G. McCOY *Hist. Sk. Cattle Trade* i. 7 The slight brand put on the stock at that time [when the herd is started to market over the trail] is called a road brand, in contradistinction to the ranch brand, which is usually put on the animal when young. **1933** J. V. ALLEN *Cowboy Lore* ii. 44 When cattle were driven to market, it was easy for them to get mixed up with others, and this accounts for the *road brand*, used for rapid identification. **1955** W. FOSTER-HARRIS *Look of Old West* viii. 229 Unless a trail herd was under one brand, which ordinarily it wasn't, it was customary to road-brand the animals—that is, give them an extra insignia to identify them on their journey. **1928** *Daily Mail* 31 July 13/3 One side of Kensington-road..is also in the hands of the road-breakers. **1967** *Gloss. Highway Engin. Terms* (*B.S.I.*) 39 *Road breaker*, a power driven tool for breaking up road pavements by impact. **1976** *Southern Even. Echo* (Southampton) 6 Nov. (Advt. Suppl.) 8/5 Road breakers, angle and straight girders, rock drills. **1819** *Massachusetts Spy* 3 Nov. 2/3 A salute was fired from a road-bridge by a detachment..of artillery. **1870** E. G. E. WARD *Jrnl.* 13 Sept. in D. P. Carew *Many Years, Many Girls* (1967) i. 16 He had heard the Road bridge blown up, and feared the railway would follow, and that I might not get out of Paris! **1935** *Discovery* Oct. 300/2 The new road-bridge over the Severn. **1976** *Liverpool Echo* 7 Dec. 17/5 The swim is downstream of the new road bridge over the River Dee at Eccleston. **1900** *Everybody's Mag.* II. 583/2 In the years of association which I have had..with 'road companies' I have become familiar with the types. **1959** W. FAULKNER *Mansion* ix. 205 The old road-company drammer reversed in gender: the frantic child clinging this time to the prospective groom's coattail. **1977** *New Yorker* 3 Oct. 129/1 The carryings-on of Gavino's mother, a road-company Anna Magnani in an Italian version of 'Sons and Lovers'. **1946** R. CAPELL *Simiomata* ii. 69 Evert himself drove him through the German road-controls to..the east coast of Attica. **1966** M. R. D. FOOT *SOE in France* x. 326 They were arrested by a road control that for once searched the greengrocer's lorry they were hidden in. **1868** T. WRIGHT *Great Unwashed* 265 The old tramp..has a beneficial knowledge of what may be called road-craft. **1897** 'H. S. MERRIMAN' *In Kedar's Tents* xii. 130 Conyngham learnt much of that road-craft which had raised Concepçion Vara to such a proud eminence among the rascals of Andalusia. **1917** 'CONTACT' *Airman's Outings* 9 Mirrors of polished steel, as used on the handlebars of motor-cycles, to give warning of roadcraft at the rear. **1934** WEBSTER, *Roadcraft*.., skill or dexterity in driving on a road. **1963** *Times* 19 Feb. 11/3 What is wanted is a more radical reform in the driving test calculated to lift the standard of roadcraft as quickly as possible to the much higher level demanded by the scrum of the modern highway. **1974** *Country Life* 17 Oct. 1108 Apart from the roadcraft side, the mechanical side can pay dividends if one learns to use the car sympathetically. **1976** *Evening Post* (Nottingham) 15 Dec. 5/6 The threat is thought to follow Stewart's visit to Newcastle two years ago, when there was an incident at a city nightclub involving some of his road crew. **1977** *Sounds* 9 July 19/2 We've got the best road crew we could find. **1934** S. SPENDER *Poems* (ed. 2) 41 At corners of day Road drills explore new areas of pain. **1973** *Scottish Sunday Express* 5 Aug. 4/2 Clever dog to obey the road drill! **1976** 'J. FRASER' *Who steals my Name?* viii. 99 You've got the road drills outside *your* office... I can't hear myself think. **1897** *Boston Morning Jrnl.* 4 Jan. 5/6 The half-mile track is convenient of access to road drivers from the city. *Ibid.*, The road driver frequently drives his own horse a trial mile. **1929** *Sat. Even. Post* 16 Nov. 41/3 R is for Road Driver, the name long-distance haulers give the lad that knows his cucumbers. **1973** *Amer. Speech 1969* XLIV. 207 *Road driver*, driver who drives long distances. **1923** *Daily Mail* 22 May 4 Hotels,..which set out to cater efficiently for the growing army of roadfarers. **1961** *Times* 6 Sept. 13/4 There has even been a proposal to collar 'roadfarer' for drivers of private motor cars. **1915** R. WELLBYE (*title*) The roadfaring handbook to inexpensive motor touring. **1925** *Chambers's Jrnl.* June 379/2 She would probably not average over 2 m.p.h., which seems almost incredible to a different section of the road-faring fraternity. **1920** *Act* 10 & 11 *Geo. V* c. 72 Sched. 1, The definition of 'roads' shall be extended so as to include road-ferries and footways. **1793** *Jrnl. House of Keys* (I.O.M.) 18 Dec. (MS.), Several matters, which I would mention as worthy your Serious and frequent Consideration...1st. The Road Fund. **1845** *Chambers's Edin. Jrnl.* 19 Apr. 242/1 The whole together along with 69 steelyards, or cast-weighing machines, having cost the road fund not less than L. 10,000. **1920** *Act* 10 & 11 *Geo. V* c. 72 §3 There shall be established for the purposes of this Act,..a fund to be called the Road Fund. **1975** M. SIMPSON *Chrome Connection* vi. 143 Could I see your road fund licence, sir? **1873** J. E. LESTER *Atlantic to Pacific* v. 28 At this station ..we shall see the 'John Chinamen' as road-hands. **1883** W. S. GRESLEY *Gloss. Coal-Mining* 205 *Road-head* (S[cottish]), see *Gate-end*. **1934** *Webster*, *Roadhead*, the end of a road (*dial.*). **1950** E. MASON *Pract. Coal Mining* I. viii. 121 (*caption*) Arrangement at the roadhead of a double unit face. **1958** J. C. F. STATHAM *Coal Mining Pract.* IV. iv. 244 About 30 per cent. of fatal and serious non-fatal accidents from falls occur at roadheads, i.e. the short length of roadway within 10 yd. of the working face. **1958** A. J. TOYNBEE *East to West* xlviii. 144 We rounded a corner and saw our car waiting for us at the road-head. **1976** *Nature* 12 Aug. 532/3, I..walked..back to the road-head. **1969** *New Scientist* 27 Feb. 444/1 These four tunnels are being driven by the four roadheading machines. *Ibid.*, This method reduces the manpower needed for road-heading by about half. **1965** *Kingston* (Ontario) *Whig-Standard* 28 Dec. 24 (*caption*) Road hockey was back in style Monday as these youngsters proved in a rough game played in Portsmouth during the afternoon. **1976** *Ibid.* 13 Feb. 22/1 A nearby road hockey game played with the numerous readily available road apples. **1932** *New Yorker* 14 May 32/2 Great attention has been devoted to suspension and road-holding. **1959** G. FREEMAN *Jack would be Gentleman* iii. 50 Sports cars are..better than the average family saloon—steering, road-holding, everything that adds up to real safety. **1975** *Times* 14 Mar. (Small Car Suppl.) p. ii/9 The Mini's greatest asset is probably its road-holding. **1936** O. LANCASTER *Progress at Pelvis Bay* 63 Many..who..motor down..by way of the new Flushbrook By-pass, must be familiar with the..'Hearts Are Trumps' roadhouse. **1944** 'N. SHUTE' *Pastoral* i. 8 In peace-time it had been something of a road-house, with a snack-bar. **1957** J. BRAINE *Room at Top* x. 92 Four months in Warley had given me a fixed taste for either the roadhouse or the authentic country pub. **1972** D. ANTHONY *Blood on Harvest Moon* ii. 18 Across the highway was a roadhouse where, according to the sign, you could dine, dance, and drink. **1897** *Encycl. Sport* I. 560/1 The only thing he [*sc.* the huntsman] *can* do is to..try every gateway and likely-looking spot where she [*sc.* the hare] may have turned off or lain down, but it is a mere matter of luck unless he has the real road hunter. **1977** *Horse & Hound* 14 Jan. 20/1 In the old days they [*sc.* foxes] probably ran the roads much more because they were quieter. The minor roads were not even tarmacked, with the result that you had your 'road hunting hounds' much more frequently. **1970** J. LONDON *Road* 173 A boy on the Road..is never a gay-cat; he is a road-kid or a 'punk'. **1937** 'D. BOYLE' *Keeping in Trouble* iii. 38 He was a 'road-kid', that is to say he found his company, within the great confederation of tramps, with youngsters of his own age or less. **1902** *N.Y. Times Mag.* 28 Dec. 12/1 A comedian who has seen so much of the unlovely side of 'road' life that he might well be the writer of tragedies. **1956** B. HOLIDAY *Lady sings Blues* viii. 93 He always wanted me to ride up with him.. and sometimes Benny, our road manager. **1978** *Detroit Free Press* 16 Apr. 23A/3 Police..accused the road manager, who wasn't identified, of giving alcohol to a 14-year-old and an 18-year-old girl. **1879** G. M. HOPKINS *Lett. to R. Bridges* (1955) 77 The island was so Marian that the very Milky Way we made a roadmark to that person's shrine. **1881** *Lippincott's Mag.* XXVII. 570/1 Every animal, besides the regular brand of the owner, has his tail bobbed and a 'road-mark' put upon him during the drive. **1908** MURRAY & MILLER *Round-Up* 268 Having cut out the stock for the drive, a road mark, a supplementary brand for identification, is burned into the hides. **1922** *Encycl. Brit.* XXX. 249/1 The French guns up to the 6 in., and howitzers up to the 9.45 in. inclusive will be road-mobile... All heavier natures will be on railway mountings. **1921** *Daily Colonist* (Victoria, B.C.) 8 Apr. 6/3 The Saanich works committee last night authorized the purchase of $7,000 worth of road oil and one hundred tons of asphalt. **1976** *Billings* (Montana) *Gaz.* 1 July 1-c/3 Finally, the commission approved the purchase of 25,000 gallons of road oil from the state. **1899** KIPLING *Stalky & Co.* 252, I engineering myself..into command of a road-patrol—no shovellin', only marching up and down. **1958** *Cut Knife* (Saskatchewan) *Grinder* 3 Apr. 1/6 In the Rural Municipality of Cut Knife, the burgesses were asked to vote upon Bylaw 12 authorizing the Council to purchase a new road patrol. **1963** *Times* 8 Jan. 11/1 Their road patrols say that many motorists are unaware that a dry cloth, or some paper handkerchiefs used to soak up the condensation or melted snow thrown over the sparking plugs, leads and distributor, could often save them from being stranded. **1970** *R.A.C. Guide & Handbk.* 39 Road Patrols..equipped with vans, are on daily duty. **1908** H. G. WELLS *War in Air* i. 14 Even a road-racer, geared to a hundred and twenty, failed to satisfy him. **1954** *Sun* (Baltimore) 24 Nov. 17/2 (*heading*) Road racers top 3 marks. **1976** *Norwich Mercury* 19 Nov. 12/1 For road racers and scramblers the financial drain is even worse. **1927** *Times* 20 Dec. 11/3 The 'road-rail' truck represents in a modified form the upper part of a railway wagon which can be exchanged between road and rail vehicles. **1963** *Times* 8 June 14/3 Two-day talks between British and French Government officials on whether there should be a Channel rail bridge or a road-rail tunnel ended in London yesterday. **1977** *Modern Railways* Dec. 494/1 The works include..the rebuilding of 20 stations to create fully-equipped road-rail interchanges. **1960** *London Midland Region Staff News* (Brit. Railways) Feb./Mar., The Roadrailer..is similar in appearance to the normal tractor drawn semi-trailer seen on the roads. It differs in two respects, however. At the rear, there is a special device which retracts the road wheels and lowers a pair of rail wheels. At the front, a special coupling fits into the rear end of another similar trailer. **1964** *Economist* 15 Aug. 663/3 British Railways' latest ploy to attract traffic from the roads involves..freight wagons which ride the rails for most of the journey and then take to the roads as trailers to deliver goods directly to the customers' doorstep. British Roadrailer Services is being set up as a joint company by British Railways and the Transport Holding Company to develop the use of these roadrailers. **1965** *Ibid.* 26 June 1559/2 The lorry people might make use of liner trains, or better, the new 'roadrailers' (of which they own half with the railways), for convenient loads of odd packages on the longer runs. **1976** *Daily Tel.* (Colour Suppl.) 30 July 10/3 It is hard on both rider and wardrobe. Young skateboarders proudly show off their 'road rashes'. **1978** *Skatcat's Quiz Bk.* (R. Soc. Prevention of Accidents) 5 'Road rash' isn't clever. As well as hurting for over a week, bad grazes or cuts are the signs of bad skateboarding. **1886** *Encycl. Brit.* XX. 583/1 In Great Britain horse-rollers have to a great extent been superseded by steam road rollers. **1971** *Daily Nation* (Nairobi) 10 Apr. 25/2 Tenders are invited for one three-wheel road roller. **1856** *Hutching's Mag.* Nov. 201/2 The Road-Runner is seldom seen in trees, unless pursued very closely. **1930** R. MACAULAY *Staying with Relations* xix. 275 Not a thing to look at, on this so-called road, only cactus and chaparral and road-runners and those darned flowering aloes. **1972** G. DURRELL *Catch me a Colobus* ix. 188 A Road-runner—a strange little bird with a crest and a long tail and enormous flat feet. **1908** A. SHRUBB *Running* x. 66 Of all forms of pedestrianism..there can be nothing superior to cross-country running... Track or road running is apt to grow monotonous, however exciting it may be; but there is nothing monotonous in an open country run. **1934** V. WOOLF *Writer's Diary* (1953) 216, I cannot without more labour than my roadrunning mind can compass describe the queer impression of sunny impersonality. **1962** LYDIARD & GILMOUR *Run to Top* viii. 68 Ordinary tennis shoes..don't cushion against the constant jarring of road running which can damage leg joints. **1976** *Cumberland News* 26 Nov., Go into the road running strongholds. **1923** *Daily Mail* 10 Aug. 6/3 The good driver uses care instinctively because he has the imagination or 'road-sense' which tells him instantly what he can and what he cannot do. **1947** J. DEAN *Murder Most Foul* v. 98 Before the war the B.B.C. conceived the..idea of engaging racing drivers to give broadcasts on 'road sense'. **1975** 'M. YORKE' *Small Hours* ii. 20 She was..bad at parking..though her road sense was good. **1908** *Variety* 16 May 1 De Dio, a foreigner,..has been engaged by Martin Beck for his Orpheum Road show next season. **1939** J. B. PRIESTLEY *Let People Sing* xiv. 412 I'm booking acts for a road-show. **1942** BERREY & VAN DEN BARK *Amer. Thes. Slang* § 596/2 *Go on tour*,..road-show. **1959** *Time* 28 Sept. 32/3 Road-showing in Cole Porter's *Can-Can* in Toronto, the French singer-comedienne..had to negotiate a ramp leading out of the tent-theater. **1961** *Wall St. Jrnl.* 8 Nov. 3/2 The Kennedy Administration opened its road show to inform citizens across the country what's going on in Washington. **1976** J. McCLURE *Rogue Eagle* ii. 28 The sprained ankle which forced her to drop out of an American roadshow. **1977** *Time* 25 Apr. 52/1 Some were impressed more by the viewpoint espoused in the road-show tactics of Phyllis Schlafly, an Alton, Ill., housewife and an active Republican. **1909** Road-sweeper [used in def. of ROADER[1] 4]. **1937** *Times British Motor Number* 13 Apr. p. xxxviii/2 The Karrier road sweeper..is also popular abroad. **1939** G. B. SHAW *Geneva* i. 16 The president and parliament are elected by adult suffrage every two years. So are all the judges and all the officials, even the road sweepers. **1973** *Times* 18 June 3/2 Teachers at a local school have been parking outside and thereby frustrating the mechanical road sweeper. **1959** Road train [see *pedal-radio* s.v. *PEDAL *sb.* 7]. **1964** L. DEIGHTON *Funeral in Berlin* xxxi. 164 One of those heavy trucks with two trailers that they call 'road trains'. **1977** 'D. RUTHERFORD' *Return Load* i. 12 The driver of the Scania road train drew level with the cab of the British vehicle. **1939** *Encycl. Brit. Bk. of Year* 684/1 A project of a new road tunnel through the St. Gothard. **1976** J. LUND *Ultimate* x. 91 The long road tunnels through the mountain got them there quickly.

roadability (rōᵘdăbi·lĭti). [f. ROAD *sb.* + ABILITY.] Suitability for being driven on the road; roadworthiness; road-holding ability.

1925 C. MORLEY *Safety Pins* 116 When the car has a 126-inch wheelbase, it makes it very easy riding and gives it charming 'roadability'. **1928** *Sunday Dispatch* 16 Sept. 5 (Advt.), Wider track, lower centre of gravity, improved roadability. **1973** *Sci. Amer.* Dec. 2/1 (Advt.), Put these characteristics of engine performance and roadability together, and it's not surprising that BMW owners will tell you no other car comes close for combining brilliant responsiveness with precise control.

roadable (rōᵘ·dăb'l), *a.* [f. ROAD *sb.* + -ABLE; see prec.] Suited to being driven on roads.

1929 *Bookman* (N.Y.) May 301/1 Motor car advertising of the past decade has brought forth the remarkable word 'roadability'... A car that has 'roadability' is, presumably, 'roadable'; that is, it can be roaded—whatever that might mean. **1935** A. P. HERBERT *What a Word!* ii. 51 What sort of a car, I wonder, is a car which is not 'roadable'? **1972** *Daily Tel.* 22 Nov. 4/5 A 'roadable' aircraft has been shown at the Detroit Motor Show... It can be driven on the road or flown from an area smaller than a football field.

roadblock (rōᵘ·dblǫk). Also **road block, road-block.** [f. ROAD *sb.* 4 + BLOCK *sb.* 19 a.] **a.** A barrier or obstruction on a road, usu. one set up by the army or police.

1940 *Hutchinson's Pict. Hist. War* 7 Aug.–1 Oct. 4 Demonstrations of how to build road-blocks, how to deal with tanks,..how to deal with refugees on the road, are all part of the Home Guard training. **1943** *Ann. Reg. 1942* 63 The road blocks for obstructing tanks were also found to be much more formidable than had been anticipated. **1954** X. FIELDING *Hide & Seek* v. 67 Pedestrians..were often searched by the sentries manning the road-blocks. **1958** 'A. GILBERT' *Death against Clock* xii. 167 When you put up your road blocks, then I have to take the diversion. **1971** *Daily Tel.* 23 July 1/5 A soldier fired at a car which broke through a roadblock, hitting the back window. **1977** *Centuryan* (Office Cleaning Services) Christmas 15/4 They had not gone far before they came to a roadblock caused by an accident. **1978** *N.Y. Times* 30 Mar. A5/2 The complex is now guarded by 14,000 riot policemen who man roadblocks and monitor highway traffic from camouflaged roadside positions.

b. *fig.*

1945 *Tuscaloosa* (Alabama) *News* 19 June 4/5 The French general is probably the only remaining road block to Communism in France. **1952** *Sun* (Baltimore) 29 Feb. 19/3 This bill has been subjected to roadblock after roadblock by those attempting to delay its passage during these closing days of 1952 General Assembly session. **1957** *Economist* 7 Sept. 770/1 In every direction the logic of the Korean economy runs headlong into a political roadblock. **1963** J. MITFORD *Amer. Way of Death* v. 177 An English contributor to the American *Professional Embalmer* describes some of the roadblocks he has encountered. **1977** MILLER & SWIFT *Words & Women* v. 71 Nowhere are the semantic roadblocks to sexual equality more apparent—or significant—than in the language of the dominant organized religions.

Hence as *v. trans.*

1954 in WEBSTER Add. **1955** *Newsweek* 10 Jan. 20/1 The debate that followed roadblocked Mr. Eisenhower's legislative program for weeks. **1965** *Canad. Jrnl. Linguistics* X. 153 The analysis of texts, opening the way to ethnographic and historical studies that otherwise would still be roadblocked. **1972** *Listener* 10 Feb. 167/2 The Army road-blocked Newry.

road-book. Add: **1.** Also *transf.*

1931 *Times Lit. Suppl.* 29 Jan. 80/2 The civil aviation section [of *Jane's All the World's Aircraft*] continues to act as a world-wide aviation 'road-book'.

2. Also *spec.*, a log-book kept by the driver of a commercial vehicle.

1939 'N. BLAKE' *Smiler with Knife* xvii. 246 You sign my road-book, cock, or I'm not opening this van.

roadeo (rōᵘ·di͵o). *U.S.* [f. ROAD *sb.*, after RODEO.] A gathering of lorry drivers for competitive events in and exhibitions of driving skill.

1948 *Sun* (Baltimore) 23 Aug. 11/1 To be eligible to enter the roadeo drivers must have completed one year of no-accident driving for the same employer. **1952** *N.Y. Times* 12 Oct. II. 18/2 The American Trucking Associations, Inc., was holding its annual Roadeo, a competition for champion, professional truckdrivers. *Ibid.* 18/2 The Roadeo course is a hard test of man's ability at the wheel. **1955** *Amer. Speech* XXX. 150 The roadeo or competition of truck drivers is now a familiar institution. **1971** M. TAK *Truck Talk* 131 *Roadeo*, the National Truck Roadeo, an exhibition and competition of driving skills in various classifications of motor vehicles for expert truckers.

roader¹. Add: **6.** *Taxi-drivers' slang.* A long-distance taxi fare or journey.

1939 H. HODGE *Cab, Sir?* ii. 28 It may be a long job—a 'roader' as we call it—out to Richmond or Highgate. **1978** *London-Wide Radio Taxis* (Licensed Taxi Drivers Assoc. Ltd.) [Publicity leaflet] p. iii/2 Roaders are an everyday event on radio. Put yourselves into the shoes of a director of a company who requires a taxi for a long distance haul. Does he go out into the street and hail a cab or send his secretary to find one? Of course he doesn't. He rings for a cab.

7. *capitalist roader* [tr. Chinese *zǒuzīpài*, short for *zǒu zīběn zhǔyì dàolù dāngquánpài*], esp. during the Cultural Revolution in China, a term for Party officials, e.g. the secretary of a provincial Party committee or the chairman of a people's commune, who were alleged to have capitalist tendencies. Cf. *capitalist road* s.v. *ROAD *sb.* 6 g.

Used of people of various views who are out of favour with the Chinese leadership.

1967 *Economist* 7 Oct. 26/1 The unsurprising absence of Liu Shao-chi, Teng Hsiao-ping and their fellow 'capitalist-roaders' brings the politburo membership down from the 24 who were elected in the first flush of the cultural revolution in August 1966 to the 15 who are still appearing today. **1970** E. SNOW *Red China Today* (rev. ed.) xlix. 389 Lau Shaw himself committed suicide in 1966 when he was attacked by Red Guards as a 'revisionist' and 'capitalist roader'. **1973** R. TAYLOR *Educ. & Univ. Enrolment Policies in China, 1949–1971* 15 The so-called capitalist-roaders refused to admit any of them on the grounds that worker-peasant children were not of high enough scholastic calibre. **1976** *Financial Times* 24 Nov. 6/1 The official Hsinhua news agency, writing about Mme. Mao and the so-called 'gang of four' or the 'new capitalist roaders', was saying that she was a 'big careerist' who 'prostrated herself in admiration before Western bourgeois things'. **1978** HUA KUO-FENG in *Peking Rev.* 10 Mar. 11/1 The 'gang of four'..openly dished up a counter-revolutionary political programme equating veteran cadres with 'democrats' and 'democrats' with 'capitalist-roaders' and agitated for rounding up 'capitalist-roaders' at all levels from the central down to the local.

road hog, *sb.* (See ROAD *sb.* 12.)

1891 *Outing* Dec. 238/2 The 'road hog' curses him and the wayside brute calls out the dog. **1898** [see ROAD *sb.* 12]. **1909** *Q. Rev.* Jan. 143 The habitually reckless motorist..commonly known as the 'road-hog'. **1925** *Public Opinion* 14 Aug. 151/3 Road-hogs who run down pedestrians. **1932** D. L. SAYERS *Have his Carcase* ii. 29 A fast saloon car..overtook them... 'The beastly road-hog!' said Mr Perkins. **1970** 'D. HALLIDAY' *Dolly & Cookie Bird* iv. 52 You're a road-hog... What do you drive at home? **1972** K. BONFIGLIOLI *Don't point that Thing at Me* xiv. 122 'Lost my temper... Bloody road-hog.' 'He might easily have done us a mischief,' I agreed.

Hence **roa·d-hog** *v. intr.*, to be or act like a road hog; so **roa·d-hogging** *vbl. sb.* and *ppl. a.* Also **roa·d-hoggery,** behaviour characteristic of a road hog; **roa·d-hoggish** *a.*, having the driving habits of a road hog; hence **roa·d-hoggishness; roa·d-hoggism,** a road-hoggish act.

1914 'I. HAY' *Knight on Wheels* xviii. 174, I wouldn't go road-hogging if I were you... Road-hogging is rotten bad form. **1923** *Daily Mail* 28 May 5 In four days, without road-hogging, we have covered 646 miles of Britain. **1926** *Glasgow Herald* 12 July 6/3 The perfect Sunday—to hide at home while the rest of the world road-hogged it out of town. **1927** *Scots Observer* 16 July 10/4 Avoiding excess of speed and other road-hoggisms. **1928** *Daily Express* 24 Apr. 10/2 The road-hogging motor-coach. **1930** *Time & Tide* 7 Feb. 172 No motorist, however road-hoggish he may be, deliberately slays a child or any other person. **1933** A. MORRIS *Digging in South-west* 80 Road-hogging is one of the most anti-social characteristics in the world. **1963** *Guardian* 21 Jan. 6/3 Chief vice of bad drivers.—Men: Sheer selfishness and road-hoggery. **1965** *Punch* 28 July 138/3 The film started with the customary pop music and some sinister hints of teenage drug-taking, road-hoggishness, violence and debauchery. *Ibid.* 20 Oct. 569/2 Some road-hoggery was due to the imperfect construction of the motor car. **1974** D. FRANCIS *Knock Down* xiv. 174 Letting loose that road-hogging two-year-old.

roadie (rōᵘ·di), *sb.* Also **roady.** [f. ROAD *sb.* + -Y⁶, -IE.] = **road manager*; an assistant employed by a touring musical band whose duties include the erection and maintenance of equipment. Hence as *v. intr.*

1969 FABIAN & BYRNE *Groupie* ix. 72 Bill, the roadie, buys me a drink. **1972** *Daily Tel.* (Colour Suppl.) 17 Nov. 26/3 Each individual musician has his own personal roady who is an expert in the instrument that his governor plays. **1976** *New Musical Express* 17 Apr. 24/5 Even allowing for roadies and so on, aren't there far too many people being supported by far too few? **1976** *Star* (Sheffield) 20 Nov., The author once roadied for the band. **1980** *Times Lit. Suppl.* 28 Mar. 365 He even gets paid as a roadie on tour.

roading, *vbl. sb.*¹ Add: **2. b.** *concr.* A road surface. *rare.*

1857 J. E. RITCHIE *Night Side of London* 5 The cost of this paved roading was 14 millions.

roadman. Add: **2.** A person using the roads for any purpose. An itinerant canvasser or seller of goods, a travelling salesman; a tramp or vagrant; a road-racer.

1906 S. E. SPARLING *Introd. Business Organiz.* 206 Another method of direct selling is found in the system of canvassers and road-men sent out by factories. **1912** A. S. M. HUTCHINSON *Happy Warrior* v. vi. 318 There cried to them 'Away! away!' all the instinct that, since first law came on the land, has bade roadmen, gipsies, outlaws, take immediate flight from trouble. **1949** A. MILLER *Death of Salesman* II. 80 You're a road man, Willy... We've only got a half-dozen salesmen on the floor here. **1951** *Sport* 27 Apr.–3 May 11/4 Sutherland..is a sprinter turned roadman, and it was in a sprint finish that he won his Empiad title in New Zealand. **1955** *Publ. Amer. Dial. Soc.* XXIV. 84 One can discern two different kinds of thief..: the *road man* is the more venturesome, the more restless. **1962** J. D. MACDONALD *Key to Suite* (1968) ii. 16 Once in Atlanta..one of Federal's road men..goosed the wife of the executive vice-president. **1976** *Star* (Sheffield) 29 Oct. 27/1 The Horseshoe climb..is noted as a 'roadman's' course where riders such as Waugh can beat the hill specialists at their own game.

roadmanship (rōᵘ·dmănʃip). [f. prec. + -SHIP.] Ability to drive on the roads; skill in using the roads.

1953 P. C. BERG *Dict. New Words* 137/2 *Roadmanship*, skill in using public roads; e.g. the Highway Code tells you the principles of good roadmanship. (Perhaps after horsemanship.) **1958** *Archit. Rev.* CXXIII. 300/2 Skill in driving and roadmanship, allied with the glamour of the superior vehicle, enable the ordinary person to express his innate sense of craftsmanship. **1959** *Economist* 16 May 9/2 An Israeli can give the impression that no other country has ever suffered from juvenile delinquency or bad roadmanship. **1973** *Daily Tel.* (Colour Suppl.) 7 Dec. 25/2 Drivers with high standards of car control and roadmanship.

† **roadometer** (rōᵘdǫ·mĭtəɹ). *Obs.* [f. ROAD *sb.* + -OMETER.] **a.** A device for measuring distance travelled. **b.** (See quot. 1926.)

1848 W. CLAYTON *Latter-day Saints' Emigrants' Guide* 3 The distances from point to point are shown as near as a *Roadometer* can measure. **1859** B. D. WILLIAMS *Let.* 9 May in L. R. Hafen *Overland Routes to Gold Fields* 238 The road..from Leavenworth city to Denver city, is 689 miles in length by the roadometer. **1926** *Glasgow Herald* 14 Oct. 6 There is a considerable range of motor car attachments, including a roadometer which automatically indicates the position of the car on the road by a scale which shows the camber.

roadscape (rōᵘ·dskēⁱp). [ROAD *sb.*] A view or prospect of a road; a picture of a road. Also, landscaping of a road.

1942 BERREY & VAN DEN BARK *Amer. Thes. Slang* § 137/4 *Roadscape*, a view of a road. **1959** *Archit. Rev.* CXXV. 245/3 In turning over pictures of German autobahnen, so competent in detail, it comes almost as a relief to find a piece of roadscape that doesn't work,—an example of how not to do it (the only one in this article). **1968** *Radio Times* 28 Nov. 21/1 Roadscape with rusting rails... The second of four talks on Los Angeles.

roadside. 2. (Further *attrib.* examples.)

1925 F. SCOTT FITZGERALD *Great Gatsby* v. 98 Light, which fell unreal on the shrubbery and made thin elongating glints upon the roadside wires. **1939** JOYCE *Finnegans Wake* (1964) I. 31 The roadside tree the lady Holmpatrick planted. **1936** *Discovery* Apr. 125/1 A pair of roadside thieves in Nevada. **1949** *Sun* (Baltimore) 14 July 8/2 The Pennsylvania Highway Department is receiving appreciative comment from the motorists on its roadside rests. **1961** *A.A. Handbk.* 12 A.A. Roadside Telephone Boxes are placed at carefully selected points along main roads. **1976** *Deeside Advertiser* 9 Dec. 24/3 His companion was thrown against roadside signs.

roadster. Add: **2. a.** (Further *attrib.* example.)

1974 *Greenville* (S. Carolina) *News* 23 Apr. 11/2 Thursday's performances have two Roadster pony classes.

b. (Further *attrib.* example.)

1922 [see *basket-car* s.v. *BASKET *sb.* B. 1 b].

c. *U.S.* A light carriage.

1892 *Hist. Rev. Industr. & Commerc. Growth York County* 68 The former [repository and office] carries a fine line of..everything in light and heavy work from the most substantial farm truck to the lightest finished roadster. **1901** *Dialect Notes* II. 146, I went to a farmer near and hired a young horse and a roadster.

d. orig. *U.S.* A type of motor car, esp. an open two-seater. Also *attrib.*

1908 *Sci. Amer.* 8 Feb. 104 Cadillac... Model G—Roadster, $2000. **1922** H. TITUS *Timber* xxix. 255 Rowe stood..a long interval,..watching her roadster disappear into the jack pines. **1928** F. N. HART *Bellamy Trial* ii. 30 We drove out from New York in my roadster. **1938** G. GREENE *Brighton Rock* VI. ii. 249 Where did you bring a swell blonde to if not the Cosmopolitan,..driving over the down in a scarlet roadster. **1948** W. SANSOM *South* 122 Round the narrow corner of old grey walls nosed the chromium grill, the long bonnet, and then all the pale gleaming length of a torpedo-shaped roadster. **1962** *Punch* 17 Oct. 560/2 Drag entries come in a profusion of classes: dragsters, modified roadsters, roadsters, [etc.]. **1973** D. LEES *Rape of Quiet Town* ii. 33 It was lucky I left my purse in your roadster. **1977** *Custom Car* Nov. 5/4 As for handicap racing in the Roadster and Production classes, the spectators seem to enjoy watching it.

3. b. For *U.S.* read 'orig. *U.S.*' and add earlier and later examples.

1890 N. P. LANGFORD *Vigilante Days* II. vi. 92 Henry Plummer was chief of the band;..Cyrus Skinner, fence, spy, and roadster. **1925** G. H. MULLIN *Adventures Scholar Tramp* iv. 56 The roadsters, or hobos who travel, are seldom without smoking or chewing tobacco. **1970** *Oxf. Mail* 27 Apr. 1/3 When we first saw the man we thought nothing about it. Roadsters are a common sight in these parts. **1974** 'J. ROSS' *Burning of Billy Toober* iv. 35 The body was probably that of a roadster using the shed to sleep in.

roa·d test. [ROAD *sb.*] A test of the performance of a vehicle on the road. Hence (usu. with hyphen) as *v. trans.*, to test (a vehicle) on the road; also *transf.* and *fig.*; so **roa·d-tester; roa·d-testing** *vbl. sb.*

1906 S. KRAUSZ *ABC of Motoring* 134 This completes the chassis, and..the automobile is ready for examination and road test. **1921** *Dict. Occup. Terms* (1927) 115/2 *Tester, car;..road tester (motor)*; drives finished chassis to test it under road conditions. **1937** *Times British Motor Number* 13 Apr. p. xxiii/2 It is the practice of Vauxhall Motors to road test every Vauxhall car and Bedford truck which is made. *Ibid.*, A certain proportion of the cars still undergo extended road tests. **1946** *Time* 29 July 80 This 60-ft. aluminium–magnesium bus was road-tested in California last week. **1949** *Life* 4 Apr. 129/1 In the U.S. many of the best brains go into business and the public secures their services only after they have been seasoned and road-tested on this severe and impartial proving ground. **1953** *Sun* (Baltimore) 10 July 4/6 Road tests are planned at the Army's Aberdeen (Md.) Proving Ground. **1961** *Times* 14 Feb. 17/2 We cannot feel sorry that these cars are coming off the road. We road-test the best of them and 50 to 60 per cent are definitely death traps. **1968** *Guardian* 10 Sept. 3/7 Maiden voyagers on the Cunarder QE2 will have..to road-test the ship. **1971** *Daily Tel.* 16 July 7 (Advt.), Howard Hunt is a road-tester. Every XJ6 is roadtested twice. **1977** *Custom Car* Nov. 80/2 (Advt.), Koni road testing is real tough, and includes a full international rally and racing programme.

roadwork. Also road work, road-work. [ROAD *sb.*] **1.** Work done in building or repairing roads. Also *pl.*, repairs to roads.

1869 *Bradshaw's Railway Manual* XXI. 100 To effect a diversion of road and other works. **1895** *Funk's Stand. Dict.* s.v. *road, n., road-work, n.*, labor expended in making or repairing roads. **1951** R. FIRTH *Elem. Social Organiz.* iii. 118 There is one frame of organization.. which regards a farm as a place for a man and his family ..to use as a base from which to operate..in getting cash from road-work. **1958** J. G. MACGREGOR *North-West of 16* vii. 95 Up to this time all roadwork had been voluntary and consisted of a settler doing enough along the road each way from his place to remove the trees that fell across it. **1965** F. SARGESON *Mem. Peon* ii. 21 His regular hours of road-work labour. **1966** D. FRANCIS *Flying Finish* x. 126 The horsebox drivers..had to make a detour because of roadworks.

2. (See ROAD *sb.* 12.)

3. The work of an itinerant thief. *Criminals' slang.*

1925 H. LEVERAGE in *Flynn's* 14 Mar. 281/1 *Road work*,..pocket picking, etc., done while traveling. **1955** *Publ. Amer. Dial. Soc.* xxiv. 84 Because of the stresses and strains of road work, he [*sc.* the road man] is usually a sharp, alert thief.

4. Work done on the roads, esp. exercise and training by athletes, sportsmen, etc.

1903 SOMERVILLE & 'ROSS' *All on Irish Shore* 159 The five couple and Carnage were..on a scent that was a real comfort to them after nearly five miserable months of kennels and road-work. **1928** *Funk's Stand. Dict.* s.v. *road, n., road-work, n.*, exercise taken on a road, as by athletes in training. **1950** J. DEMPSEY *Championship Fighting* xxiv. 183 *Roadwork* means running on the road. **1964** D. FRANCIS *Nerve* xvi. 190 A..little used secondary road..served only two farms and one private house, and because of its quietness it was a regular route for the Axminster horses on roadwork days. **1969** G. E. EVANS *Farm & Village* x. 113 The most trouble we had with Suffolks on road-work was *splinters* and *side-bone*. **1971** A. BURGESS *MF* vi. 69 They trotted along, as in road-work, in their orange-and-cream jerseys. **1977** *Time* 25 July 39/2 He was doing roadwork and punching bags in preparation for his role in Martin Scorsese's *Raging Bull*, a film about Fighter Jake La Motta.

roa·dworthiness. [f. ROADWORTHY *a.* + -NESS.] Roadworthy character; reliability on the road.

1923 *Daily Mail* 6 Aug. 4/4 One object was to demonstrate the roadworthiness or otherwise of these..family cars. **1928** *Daily Tel.* 16 Oct. 17 The low centre of gravity gives to the new Humber a road-worthiness unequalled. **1955** *Times* 1 July 6/6 The Government have dropped the proposals for compulsory tests of vehicles for road-worthiness. **1980** N. FREELING *Castang's City* xvi. 105 Polish those boots, boy, and examine them for road-worthiness.

roady, var. *ROADIE.

roaf, var. *ROUF.

roak. Add: *roke* is the usual form. (Further examples.)

1914 [see *LAP *sb.*[3] 2 e]. **1923** GLAZEBROOK *Dict. Appl. Physics* V. 363/2 Rokes are formed from ingot cracks, blowholes at or near the surface, and certain kinds of surface defect of the ingot, and in the case of rolled bar they are usually radial when examined on a cross-section. **1945** GREAVES & WRIGHTON *Pract. Microsc. Metallogr.* x. 173 Rokes..consist of fissures..with their surfaces separated by a thin film of scale or other impurity. **1951** G. R. BASHFORTH *Manuf. Iron & Steel* II. x. 320 Subcutaneous blowholes, occurring very near the skin of the ingot, may become oxidized during reheating, resulting in the formation of 'roaks' and seams in the finished bars or blooms. **1967** A. K. OSBORNE *Encycl. Iron & Steel Industry* (ed. 2) 354/2 Rokes. (Roaks.) **1974** P. WRIGHT *Lang. Brit. Industry* xix. 184 Ingot defects have various names, for instance the *roke*, into which a surface blowhole rolls out.

roam, *v.* Add: **4.** *trans.* To cause (the eyes) to look over a scene. *rare.*

1900 J. BLOUNDELLE-BURTON *Seafarers* xii. 118 As he spoke he roamed his eye around the tranquil, glassy sea.

roan, *a.* and *sb.*[1] Add: **A.** *adj.* **b.** *Hippotragus equinus.* (Earlier and further examples.)

1839 W. C. HARRIS *Wild Sports S. Africa* xxii. 194 We descended into a valley, bent upon the destruction of a roan antelope. **1970** *Daily Nation* (Nairobi) 16 Jan. 13/1 Going south along the lake is the Lambwe Valley Game Reserve, small and still undeveloped, but possessing the rare Roan Antelope.

B. *sb.*[1] **1. c.** (Further examples.)

1958 L. VAN DER POST *Lost World of Kalahari* vi. 111 It's unbelievable! They're there in thousands! Zebra, wildebeest, roan! **1978** *Times* 23 Nov. 13/9 Extensive softwood planting in the [Kenyan] plains is displacing much of its game, such as roan and sable.

3. A fashion shade: cf. sense A. c.

1960 [see *GRÈGE *a.* and *sb.*].

roar, *sb.*[1] Add: **2. b.** *to go with a roar*, to make uninterrupted progress or be a conspicuous success. *colloq.*

1845 DICKENS *Let.* 6 Aug. (1977) IV. 347 It was a most prodigious success; and went, with a roar, all through. **1903** G. B. SHAW *Let.* 12 June (1972) II. 331 'The Admirable Bashville'..went with a roar from beginning to end. **1907** *Punch* 1 May 308/2 Everything went with a roar.

roar, *v.* Add: **1. c.** (Earlier examples.)

1815 B. WYNNE *Diary* 28 July (1940) III. xii. 378 The Girls, who *roared* the whole way, laughing at the odd vehicle. **1828** T. CREEVEY *Let.* 3 Mar. in J. Gore *Creevey's Life & Times* (1934) xii. 260 Brougham's letter is..in folly and insanity by no means inferior to his former effusions. We both *roared* at it.

3. e. To travel on a vehicle which is making a loud noise; to motor rapidly. Also *fig.*

1923 *Motor Cycling* 26 Sept. 658/3 Marsden roared through on his last lap. **1951** *Amer. Speech* XXVI. 230/2 Wesleyan roars to victory. **1958** B. NICHOLS *Sweet & Twenties* x. 128 They were all roaring off to Ascot. **1963** *New Yorker* 15 June 58 George Rotan..roared back to win eleven of the next twelve. **1970** P. LAURIE *Scotland Yard* iii. 69 The one getting in slams the door and roars off, nearly running my mate over. **1973** *Times* 22 Jan. 9/8 The closest he came to betraying anxiety last evening was when he suddenly started roaring ahead.

4. c. Const. *up*. To abuse, to reprimand. *slang* (chiefly *Austral.*).

1919 W. H. DOWNING *Digger Dial.* 42 *Roar up*, upbraid; abuse. **1925** FRASER & GIBBONS *Soldier & Sailor Words* 244 *Roar up*, to abuse. **1944** W. E. HARNEY *Taboo* (ed. 2) 63, I roared him up, but it was no good. **1947** N. LINDSAY *Halfway to Anywhere* 69 Bill was able to roar him up, anyway, for having the blinkin' cheek to come shoving his nose into Bill's affairs. **1962** [see *ROARING FORTIES 2].

roarer[1]. Add: **1. a.** (Further example.)

1903 W. S. BLUNT *Seven Golden Odes* 33 Fled to the land of the lions, roarers importunate.

4. (Earlier example.)

1827 *Massachusetts Spy* 10 Jan. 1/4 The Albany beau.. drinks brandy and talks politics, swears at the servants, and quarrels with his landlord and is in fact what he styles himself, 'a real roarer'.

5. *U.S.* An oil-well from which the oil pours rapidly and noisily.

a **1885** B. J. CREW *Pract. Treat. Petroleum* (1887) vii. 227 We have no right, perhaps, to expect a continuance of the 'roarers', or 'gushers' as they are termed.

roaring, *ppl. a.* Add: **4.** (Further examples.) *roaring days* (Austral.), the time of the Australian gold-rush; also *transf.*, hey-day; *the roaring twenties*, the third decade of the twentieth century (with reference to the post-war buoyancy of that period).

1897 H. LAWSON *Coll. Verse* (1967) I. 339 But these seem dull and slow to me compared with Roaring Days. **1921** M. E. FULLERTON *Bark House Days* (1931) xiv. 144 We loved the stories of the 'roaring fifties'. **1930** *Sat. Rev.* 15 Mar. 328/1 The giants of the roaring 'twenties ought to be able to achieve glory of some sort in half as many years. **1936** 'W. HATFIELD' *Australia through Wind Screen* 53 In its roaring days 'The Duchess' was better than many a goldmine. **1973** *Times* 2 Mar. 14/2 The theme [of the ball] will be the roaring twenties. **1978** *Dædalus* Fall 30 For those belonging to the classes of the immediate post-World War I period, the massacre of the young officers..meant that countless positions..had become vacant in all spheres of society; this led to an ephemeral but marked shift to a more youthful establishment; hence, the Roaring Twenties.

7. (Earlier and later examples.)

1755 C. CHARKE *Life* 153 But was..fully convinced, that I should carry on a roaring Trade. **1976** *Milton Keynes Express* 25 June 7/2 These attractions did a roaring trade round the perimeter of the sports hall.

8. Also as a general intensive: full-blooded, whole-hearted; unqualified, out-and-out.

1963 D. LESSING *A Man & Two Women* 302 If you are going to make love, what does it matter who with? Why shouldn't she simply walk into the street, pick up a man and have a roaring sexual affair with him? **1965** *Listener* 18 Nov. 806/1 Psychiatric treatment has not proved a roaring success. **1970** MRS. L. B. JOHNSON *White House Diary* p. xiv, I feel..a deep, roaring faith in and love for this country.

roaring forties. **1.** See FORTY *a.* and *sb.* B. 4. Now usu. restricted to those parts of the oceans between latitudes 40° and 50° south, where strong westerly winds blow; occas. also applied to the winds themselves.

1883, 1893 [see FORTY *a.* and *sb.* B. 4]. **1906** W. MARRIOTT *Hints to Meteorol. Observers* (ed. 6) 68/1 *Roaring forties*, the regions between lat. 40° and 50°S., where the 'brave West winds' blow. **1924** R. CLEMENTS *Gipsy of Horn* vii. 126 Right 'roaring forties' weather came down on us with a swoop. **1953** A. A. MILLER *Climatology* (ed. 8) xi. 199 In the southern hemisphere the disturbance of the planetary winds is much less; 'Roaring Forties' and the 'Brave West Winds' blow all the year round with considerable force. **1966** F. CHICHESTER in *Sunday Times* 30 Oct. 3/6 Twice I have entered the Roaring Forties and been driven out by gales and squalls.

2. *fig.* **a.** The fifth decade of life. **b.** *Naut. slang.* (See quot. 1948.)

1867 *Harper's Mag.* Sept. 509/2 A very pretty woman, whose bark of life had not as yet drifted into the 'roaring forties'. **1930** H. K. PASMA *Close-Hauled* II. 211, I am in my roaring forties now. **1948** PARTRIDGE *Dict. Forces' Slang* 156 *Roaring forties*, Lieutenant Commanders between 40 and 50 years of age. **1962** GRANVILLE *Dict. Sailors' Slang* 96/2 *Roaring forties*, rough seas in 40–50 degrees south latitude, hence, a slang name for certain taut-handed lieut-commanders in their forties, who are always roaring up the hands.

roaringly, *adv.* (In Dict. s.v. ROARING *ppl. a.*) (Further examples.)

1947 DYLAN THOMAS *Let.* 1 Mar. (1966) 298, I was roaringly well, then, some minutes after, a little mewling ruin. **1980** *Daily Tel.* 21 July 10/3 This festival built its name in the 'fifties under Jean Vilar's direction, with Gérard Philipe as star, by staging French classics with a zest and a roaringly romantic appeal to basic theatrical values which gave birth to the rightly named Théâtre National Populaire.

roast, *sb.* Add: **4.** Also, an instance of this. (Further examples.) (See also quot. 1900.) Now chiefly *N. Amer.*

1900 *Dialect Notes* II. 54 *Roast, n.* 1. Unfair treatment, as hard marking in a course. 2. A partial decision, as from an umpire. 3. A severe criticism. 4. A reproof. **1903** *Booklovers Mag.* Dec. 663/1 This national love for a good 'roast', this spirit of mockery, this national habit of joking, is the one great thing about us that foreigners can't understand. **1976** *Globe & Mail* (Toronto) 16 Feb. 16/1 (*caption*) It was billed as a roast to mark Mr. Sniderman's 25th year in the music business, but in reality it was a heart-warming evening because the roasters had only kind words for this beloved couple, who've done so much for Canada.

roast, *v.* Add: **4. b.** (Earlier and later examples.) Also, to criticize, to denounce.

1710 *Let. to Noble Lord occasion'd by Proc. against Dr. Henry Sacheverell* 16 As for Dr. Sacheverell, nothing will serve some of 'em but Roasting him; using the Expression of a Furious Zealot against him, who is since Dead. **1890** in Barrère & Leland *Dict. Slang* II. 183/1 Another letter received from one W. T. Nelson, of Cleveland, severely roasts both. **1895** W. C. GORE in *Inlander* Dec. 114 *Roast, v.* 1. To censure. 2. To ridicule. **1905** 'H. MCHUGH' *You can search Me* iii. 50 If he were to roast our Skinski it might hurt our business. **1912** J. SANDILANDS *Western Canad. Dict., Roast*, to expose, to abuse, to rate, to tell a person off. A roasting, a severe rating or castigation in a speech. **1920** WODEHOUSE *Jill the Reckless* (1922) xviii. 267 I've an idea..that the critics will roast it. **1966** *Listener* 27 Oct. 613/3 Their methods caused a scandal and they were roasted in the press by Labouchère. **1976** F. TRUEMAN *Ball of Fire* ii. 39 They made me twelfth man and I was roasted for falling asleep in a deck-chair during play. **1977** *Times* 28 Oct. 8/5 During the evening the Prince was 'roasted' by Martin—a friendly American custom of insulting a person as a sign of favour.

roast beef. Add: **b.** *roast-beef-of-old-England-man, sandwich*; **roast beef coat** = *roast beef dress.*

1818 'A. BURTON' *Adventures J. Newcome* II. 117 His ship-washed linen out he laid, And roast beef coat in smart parade. **1831** M. EDGEWORTH *Let.* 29 Mar. (1971) 507 Her husband is one of the thin dried old race of true hunter and shooter men and roast beef of old England-men. **1967** 'D. SHANNON' *Chance to Kill* (1968) xiii. 189, I even remember what she had... It was the hot roast-beef sandwich. **1971** D. ENEFER *Screaming Orchid* xii. 103, I had stopped..for roast beef sandwiches and bitter beer.

roasting, *vbl. sb.* Add: **1. b.** (Further examples.)

1895 *Wales* May 222/1 Your father will make short work of giving you a roasting. **1900** 'FLYNT' & 'WALTON' *Powers that Prey* 122 Nettie was emboldened to continue her 'roasting'. **1942** J. B. PRIESTLEY in *R.A.F. Jrnl.* 3 Oct. 2, I..have taken and dished out uproarious insults. .. My friendly hosts have been anxious about the way in which I would take this elaborate 'roasting'. **1963** *Times* 25 Feb. 3/6 The crowd, which cheered wildly all the time for the popular Mormon elder from neighbouring Utah, gave Tiger a 'roasting' several times and they booed lustily when the decision was announced as a draw. **1977** *Time* 28 Mar. 8/3 In their exchanges with the Russians, members of the U.S. delegation anticipate a bit of a roasting.

2. a. *roasting device, fork, kitchen, machine, tin.*

1923 H. CRANE *Let.* 5 Dec. (1965) 159 The ten pound bird was put into a wonderful roasting machine... You put the bird on a long spit that had a crank and catches... You must have seen one of these roasting devices. **1950** W. BIRD *Nova Scotia* ii. 37 On the wall are such items as an otter head, and feet,..and brass roasting forks. **1960** E. DAVID *French Provincial Cookery* 66 A shallow rectangular baking or roasting tin. **1965** E. TUNIS *Colonial Craftsmen* vi. 67 Sometime near the beginning of the eighteenth century, perhaps earlier, somebody invented the 'roasting kitchen', a reflecting oven built as an arch-topped box on legs, with one open side to face the fire.

rob, *v.* Add: **1. a.** (Further *transf.* and *fig.* examples.)

1926 *Publishers' Weekly* 19 June 1966/1 You may improve your golf game... Why not get rid of that disconcerting slice which robs your drive? **1948** R. M. AYRES *Missing Tide* i. 44 The food's quite good, and they don't rob you, anyway.

d. *Association Football.* To deprive (an opposing player) of the ball.

1882 *Blackburn Times* 1 Apr. 6/3 Goodhart started the ball from the centre, but he was instantly robbed by Strachan. **1970** *Times* 30 Sept. 15/4 Novak held on too long in midfield and was robbed by Graham. **1976** *Morecambe Guardian* 7 Dec. 8/2 Towers and Thomas forced the defence into some confusion when a backpass went astray. Finch had to move quickly to rob Thomas who was charging through.

5. (Further examples.)

1919 G. B. SHAW *Heartbreak House* II. 77, I should rob all the money back from Mangan. **1939** JOYCE *Finnegans Wake* (1964) III. 453 Robbing leaves out of my taletold book. **1953** [see *robber trench* s.v. *ROBBER 2 b]. **1977** *Irish Press* 29 Sept. 5/5 Vincent Walker..was found guilty of robbing the sum of £8,798.

robber. Add: **2. a.** *robber-book, -haunt.*

1884 'MARK TWAIN' *Huck. Finn* ii. 13 The rest [of the oath] was out of pirate books, and robber books. **1937** J. W. DAY *Sporting Adventure* 91 The magpies will go off to their robber-haunts in lonely carrs of willows down on the marshes.

b. robber baron [BARON 1], a feudal lord who engaged in plundering; also *transf.*, *spec.* [*BARON 2 b] in *U.S.*, a financial or industrial magnate of the late nineteenth century who behaved with ruthless and irresponsible acquisitiveness; also *attrib.*; **robber trench** *Archæol.*, a trench representing the foundations of a wall, the stones of which have been partially or entirely removed.

1878 C. F. ADAMS *Railroads* 145 The commissioner has not hesitated to give his opinion of the foreign owner as a 'robber baron'. **1882** C. SCHURZ in *Boston Herald Suppl.* 30 June 1/3 It will not be surprising at all to see some day a movement set on foot to put an end to the operations of the modern robber barons, who, by corporate rascality, supplemented with tricks of the stock exchange, manage to plunder at will not only their fellow-gamblers, but the innocent bona fide investors in corporate enterprises. **1930** J. S. HUXLEY *Bird-Watching* ii. 32 Predaceous glaucous gulls, the robber barons of the Arctic bird-world. **1934** M. JOSEPHSON (*title*) The robber barons. **1949** *Jrnl. Econ. Hist.* Nov. 187 In studying the so-called 'robber barons', Destler was impelled to consider also a few early 'career men'. **1957** *Times Lit. Suppl.* 8 Nov. 670/3 Next she builds up an immensely lucrative cosmetic business, backed by a robber-baron tycoon named Jim Seymour. **1962** J. BRAINE *Life at Top* x. 131 A robber baron of the Middle Ages. **1976** M. J. LASKY *Utopia & Revolution* (1977) ii. 74 Bakunin joined the call for a crusade of destruction, and he, too, became a robber baron in a holy cause. **1979** *Time* 2 Apr. 45/1 For years psychiatrists have also been regarded as medicine's robber barons. **1953** R. J. C. ATKINSON *Field Archaeol.* (ed. 2) ii. 72 On many Roman and later sites where ancient buildings have once stood, the stone will have been partially or completely robbed from the walls and foundations for re-use elsewhere. In such cases the walls can be traced only as 'robber-trenches'. **1967** *Antiquaries Jrnl.* XLVII. 196 The outer edge of the wall and robber trenches has been found along most of the edge of the north aisle and around the west end. **1978** *Ibid.* LVIII. 106 A late Roman beaded and corrugated pin similar to one found at Lydney was found in robber trenches of the medieval cloister.

c. *robber gull*; **robber-fly** (earlier and later examples).

1871 *Amer. Naturalist* IV. 686 A robber-fly..burrows in the sand. **1970** *Age* (Melbourne) 22 June, Another [family] comprising the predatory robber-flies. **1946** J. W. DAY *Harvest Adventure* vi. 86 The big robber gull dropped like a sack of wheat, without a kick, at seventy yards.

Hence **ro·bberish** [-ISH[1]], *a.*, suggestive of robbers; **ro·bberism** [-ISM], control by or the business of robbers; robbery; **ro·bberling** [-LING[1]], a little or puny robber.

1855 SWINBURNE *Let.* 4 Aug. (1959) I. 6, I longed for you all to be there,..for it [*sc.* a cave] was admirably robberish. **1913** D. H. LAWRENCE *Love Poems & Others* 8 Under the glistening cherries... Three dead birds lie: Pale-breasted throstles and a blackbird, robberlings Stained with red dye. **1921** *Glasgow Herald* 18 Jan. 6 Communism in Russia is robberism.

robbery. Add: **3.** *fig.* An excessive financial demand; a proposal which wholly or chiefly benefits the proposer; an outrageous injustice; esp. in *daylight robbery*, *highway robbery* (s.v. *HIGHWAY 4).

c **1863** T. TAYLOR *Ticket-of-Leave Man* I. 10 *Dalton*: I won't go higher than fifteen bob for a fiver. *Moss*... Only fifteen—it's robbery. **1874** E. P. ROE *Barriers burned Away* v. 38 'I want five dollars out of you before you take that trunk off.' 'Why, this is sheer robbery,' exclaimed Dennis. **1886**, etc. [see *highway robbery* s.v. *HIGHWAY 4]. **1949** D. M. DAVIN *Roads from Home* I. i. 8 'I can never afford it,' said his sister. 'It's daylight robbery.' **1976** *Springfield* (Mass.) *Daily News* 23 Apr. 39/1 Though the Celtics are well known for their game-long verbal abuse of officials, Wednesday night they got away with robbery. **1977** *Times* 28 Feb. 8/5 It was, in fact, a bit of daylight robbery. As Jimmy Andrews, the disappointed Cardiff manager, said later: 'Everton had all the big names and the luck.'

robbo (rǫ·bo). *Austral. local slang.* [f. the name *Rob*(*inson* (see quot. 1897) + *-O[2].] A horse and trap; a sulky; a poor horse; the driver of a horse and trap. Also, anything or anyone not up to standard, and in other extended uses.

1897 *Bulletin* (Sydney) 23 Jan. 11/3 In answer to a correspondent's question as to the derivation of 'robbo' (Sydney slang for the vehicle ordinarily called a 'sulky') 'J.P.' writes as follows..:—'Four Bob Robbo'—four shillings Robinson. Robinson, who lived in the classic suburb of Waterloo, Sydney.., came into a bit of money and bought a horse and trap. The money was spent, and Robinson tired of feeding the horse, which got poor; so he then sometimes let out the horse and trap (both somewhat worse for wear) for 4s. per half-day. There was a run on the cheap hire, and Rob. bought two other horses and traps, which he let out at the same price. A neighbouring livery-stable keeper and his employés resented Rob's cutting-down prices; and, when any of the rival's equipages passed, used to cry out, in derision, 'Four Bob Robbo!' The cry was taken up by the kids, and has now become a Waterloo classic. *Ibid.*, 'Robbo' has in an extensive Sydney circle come to mean anything unsatisfactory. For instance, a girl enters a jeweller's shop with: 'Watcher been givin' us? Look at the clasp of this 'ere bracelet I bought of yer last week. It's gone bung already. It's a fair robbo.' *Ibid.*, Also 'robbo' has come to mean amateur. **1906** A. J. TOMPKINS *With Swag & Billy* 51 Right out of the haunts of the motor, the bike and the Robbo. **1939** K. TENNANT *Foveaux* IV. v. 430 There was old Bert Robinson... 'E kept a livery stable down at the Foot. I s'pose you've 'eard of the Four-bob Robbos, then? The chaps used to go an' hire a cart for four bob and take it round loaded with vegetables. The kids used to call after 'em, 'Four Bob Robbo, Four Bob Robbo.' Old Bob Noblett, 'e's an old man now, but I can remember when Bob Noblett was a four-bob robbo. **1956** *Collins New Eng. Dict.* (Austral. & N.Z. Suppl.) 1279/2 *Robbo, Four-Bob-Robbo*, a horse and sulky... Now used only for a decrepit horse.

robe, *sb.*[1] Add: **1. c.** A dressing-gown. See also *bath robe* s.v. *BATH *sb.*[1] VI.

1854 DICKENS *Hard T.* II. viii. 223 She arose, put on a loose robe, and went out of her room in the dark. **1931** J. B. FAGAN *Improper Duchess* I. 25, I puta on my silk robe, I go down to his rooms. **1938** M. ALLINGHAM *Fashion in Shrouds* vi. 73 'Robe's' the new name for dressing-gown. **1945** 'L. LEWIS' *Birthday Murder* (1951) x. 152 She..put on the white terry-cloth robe. **1955** T. STERLING *Evil of Day* xiii. 134 A man in a robe and slippers. **1957** F. & R. LOCKRIDGE *Practise to Deceive* (1959) xiii. 181 Susan wore a white towelling robe. **1966** *Wall St. Jrnl.* 7 Jan. 2/2 Penney officials noted heavy sales in women's robes and sleepwear. **1970** G. F. NEWMAN *Sir, You Bastard* viii. 246 Tying his robe, he stepped out and along to the kitchen. **1976** *New Yorker* 26 Jan. 50/3 At lunch, Mrs Fox, still in pajamas, slippers, and robe, nearly drops a tray on Mrs Tompkins' head.

7. *robe-cloak, -coat.*

1908 G. B. SHAW *Lett. to Granville Barker* (1956) 139, I have persuaded her to be discovered next time in a robe-cloak. **1746** in R. Chambers *Traditions of Edinburgh* (1846) 47 No misses in skirts and jackets, robe-coats, nor stay-bodied gowns, to be allowed to dance in country-dances. **1911** C. MACKENZIE *Passionate Elopement* xviii. 170 Swansdown misses..put into corsets almost as soon as they were out of robe-coats. **1964** *New Shetlander* No. 70. 27 She wuir a hap, rob cott an bratt.

robe (rōub), *sb.*[2] Also **'robe.** Abbrev. of WARDROBE.

1935 *Spectator* 7 June 972/1 Mr. Toop, a wholesale furniture-maker in the Curtain Road with whom I once had dealings, introduced me to some pretty examples of what grammarians, I believe, call aphaeresis. 'If you want a 'Board,' he would say, 'I'd choose wawnut every time: but when it comes to a 'Robe, there's nothing to touch m'yogany.' **1969** *Sydney Morning Herald* 24 May 43/9 (Advt.), Built-in robes. **1974** T. R. DENNIS in J. Burnett *Useful Toil* III. 354, I did a bedroom suite for £21; it had a six-foot robe..dressing-table and tall-boy and bed to match. **1977** *Evening Gaz.* (Middlesbrough) 11 Jan. 11/7 (Advt.), Two double bedrooms, one with fitted unit and 'robe.

robe, *v.* Add: **1.** Also, to apparel (oneself) in a dressing-gown.

1969 *New Yorker* 31 May 32/1 If I am resolute, I will arise and robe myself.

‖ **robe de nuit** (rōb dǝ nwī). [Fr.] A night-dress.

1855 TROLLOPE *Warden* ii. 21 He has exchanged..those shining black habiliments for his accustomed *robe de nuit*. **1897** G. STEVENS *Let.* 2 Nov. in *Lett. W. Stevens* (1967) 16 Your Mother is making up some sort of..a Robe-de-Nuit something to cover your abused anatomy as you wander ..to the toilet. **1911** E. M. CLOWES *On Wallaby* v. 119 A lady whose husband had seen another lady going to the bath in her *robe de nuit* alone. **1968** J. IRONSIDE *Fashion Alphabet* 71 *Robe de Nuit*, nightdress.

‖ **robe de style** (rōb dǝ stīl). [Fr., lit. 'robe of style'.] (See quot. 1969.) Also *fig.* and *attrib.*

1928 [see *eau-de-Nil* s.v. *EAU]. **1931** *Times Lit. Suppl.* 25 June p. i/4 Dignincont's..etchings and Coulouma's clear setting in Baskerville lend an expensive *robe de style* to a novel which seems more at home in a yellow jacket. **1963** *Times* 24 Jan. 12/4 John Cavanagh's bridal model, a soft vision in white chiffon, cut on *robe de style* lines, with chiffon veil falling from a flowered chignon, has given rise to much speculation whether this studied simplicity will be reflected in the gown that Princess Alexandra will choose for her wedding. **1969** R. T. WILCOX *Dict. Costume* (1970) 293/1 *Robe de style*, the twentieth century infanta style, an evening fashion for which Lanvin of Paris became famous; its vogue was in the nineteen twenties and thirties. It had a tight bodice with a bouffant skirt, ankle or floor length.

Robert. Add: **3.** (Further examples.)

1899 'J. FLYNT' *Tramping with Tramps* II. 231 But look out for the Robert and the Dee (the policeman and the detective). **1929** T. L. DAVIDSON *Murder in Laboratory* xiv. 108, I stopped and asked a Robert the time. **1968** J. LOCK *Lady Policeman* iv. 34 Believe it or not PCs are still occasionally wished, 'Good morning, Robert!'

5. *Robert sauce, Sauce Robert*: see SAUCE *sb.* 1 in Dict. and Suppl.

6. *Naut. slang.* A spell off duty; a sleep, a 'nap'.

1935 'L. LUARD' *Conquering Seas* xii. 140 I'll get head down for a proper robert.

Robertian (rǫ̆bǝ·ɹtiăn), *a.* [f. prec. + -IAN.] Of or pertaining to Robert the Strong (*d.* 866), count of Anjou and of Blois, or his descendants, who became kings of France. Also as *sb.*, a follower or successor of Robert the Strong.

1903 D. C. MUNRO *Hist. Middle Ages* vii. 66 Charles the Simple..had little power, and the kingdom was wrested from him in 923 by a member of the Robertian house. **1942** STRAYER & MUNRO *Middle Ages* vi. 147 Otto had the advantage of being the brother-in-law both of the Carolingian king and of the head of the rival Robertian family. **1957** *Encycl. Brit.* IX. 589 Henceforth there ensued a long duel between the Robertians and the Carolingians in which three times the Robertians were chosen and might have taken the crown.

Robertine (rǫ·bǝɹtīn, -ǝin), *sb.* and *a.* [f. as prec. + -INE[1].] **A.** *sb.* A follower of Robert of Melun (d. 1167), English-born scholastic theologian.

1846 T. WRIGHT *Biogr. Brit. Lit.: Anglo-Norman Period* IV. 201 His disciples formed a sect which was long known by the name of Robertines. **1906** W. H. SCHOFIELD *Eng. Lit. to Chaucer* ii. 52 At Mont St. Geneviève the 'Robertines' long continued to discuss their leader's great work..the *Summa Theologiae*, which above all gave warrant for his repute as a metaphysician.

B. *adj.* = *ROBERTIAN *a.*

1938 Z. N. BROOKE *Hist. Europe* iv. 96 The ambition of the Robertine house dictated the fortunes of the French kingdom in the tenth century.

Hence **Roberti·nian** *sb.*, a follower or successor of Robert the Strong.

1910 *Encycl. Brit.* X. 813/1 The struggle against the Robertinians went on relentlessly. *Ibid.* 813/2 There was a kind of *entente cordiale* between the Carolingians and the Robertinians and Otto.

Robertonian (rǫ:bǝɹtōu·niăn). [f. as prec. + *-onian* as in *Caledonian, Patagonian,* etc.] A follower of Robert the Strong (see *ROBERTIAN *a.*).

1936 H. A. L. FISHER *Hist. Europe* I. xvii. 208 Robert the Strong, Count of Paris, fought for ten years against the Northmen... The Robertonians were as distinguished for caution as for courage.

Robertsonian (rǫ:bǝɹtsōu·niăn), *a. Cytology.* [f. the name of William R. B. *Robertson* (1881–1941), U.S. biologist, who first described such translocations in 1916 (*Jrnl. Morphol.* XXVII. 220) + -IAN.] Applied to the formation of a metacentric chromosome from two heterologous acrocentric chromosomes by the fusion of their centromeres or by a translocation with the loss of a small fragment; and to karyotypic changes brought about by this process.

1954 M. J. D. WHITE *Animal Cytol. & Evol.* (ed. 2) x. 192 In certain groups such as the Acrididae, 'Robertsonian' rearrangements or whole-arm transpositions account for a large part of the obvious differences in caryotypes. **1955** *Nature* 2 Apr. 601/1 The wide variation in the mitotic numbers must be attributed to Robertsonian changes. **1960** *Jrnl. Nat. Cancer Inst.* XXIV. 1187 A large mediocentric chromosome and a heterochromatic minute were formed, apparently at the expense of two acrocentric chromosomes, providing a classic example of a Robertsonian relationship, manifesting itself within the neoplastic cell population of a transplantable tumor. **1973** *Nature* 3 Aug. 262/1 The most common chromosomal changes seen in vertebrate evolution are Robertsonian fusions which create one metacentric from two acrocentrics and inversions which, if pericentric in nature, change the position of a centromere. **1974** *Ibid.* 10 May 164/1 These consisted of thirty-eight Robertsonian translocations, forty-seven reciprocal translocations and nine pericentric inversions.

Robertson's law (rǫ·bǝɹtsǝnz). *Cytology.* [f. as prec. + LAW *sb.*[1]] The law that states that the number of chromosome arms of a population or species tends to remain constant, although the number of chromosomes may vary. Cf. prec.

1945 M. J. D. WHITE *Animal Cytol. & Evol.* viii. 170 In certain groups 'Robertson's law' explains many of the more obvious changes in chromosome shape. **1956** *Jrnl. Morphol.* XCIX. 265 Well-documented instances of chromosomal phylogeny conforming to Robertson's law have been reported from several groups of animals.

Robespierrist (rōu·bspiēǝrist), *sb.* and *a.* [f. the name of *Robespierre* (see below) + -IST.] **A.** *sb.* A follower of Maximilien François Marie Isidore de Robespierre (1758–94), one of the leaders in the French revolution; a Jacobin (sense 2). **B.** *adj.* Associated with, or adhering to, Robespierre.

1834 [see *ORLEANIST]. **1904** J. R. M. MACDONALD in *Cambr. Mod. Hist.* (1907) VIII. xii. 338 The Commune, whose conception of the ultimate ends of the *coup d'état* differed *toto cœlo* from those of both Dantonists and Robespierrists. **1929** L. R. GOTTSCHALK *Era of French Revol.* I. III. iii. 263 (*heading*) The Robespierrists destroyed. **1937** *Downside Rev.* Oct. 519 It is certain that the laws [of Ventôse] contributed to the fall of the

Robespierrists. *Ibid.*, The majority of the Committee were unsympathetic and obstructive, which increased the tension between them and the Robespierrist minority. **1975** G. RUDÉ *Robespierre* 9 It marks a welcome addition to Robespierrist studies. *Ibid.* 43 While the Jacobins and the Convention—even the Robespierrists among them—were prepared to tolerate controls and State-direction of the nation's economy merely as exceptional and temporary measures, [etc.].

robiboo, var. *RUBBABOO.

robin[1]. Add: **II. 3.** (Earlier and later examples.) For *U.S.* read *N. Amer.*

1703 S. SEWALL *Diary* 16 Mar. (1879) II. 75 The Robbins cheerfully utter their Notes this morn. **1944** S. BELLOW *Dangling Man* 172 A few large birds, robins and grackles, appeared in the trees. **1966** *Vancouver Province* 19 Nov. 1/5 The robin had been sitting in a mountain ash tree in his front yard.

4. b. *blue robin*, add: *Sialia sialis*; (earlier example).

1844 J. E. DEKAY *Zool. N.Y.* II. 65 The Bluebird, or Blue Robin as it is called in the western counties.

c. robin-chat, one of several African thrush-like birds belonging to the genus *Cossypha* of the family Turdidæ.

1901 A. C. STARK *Birds S. Afr.* II. 209 (*heading*) Noisy Robin-Chat. **1931** *Discovery* May 138/2 The robin chat.. is smart in appearance, with..blue shoulder patches and bright orange-rufous underparts. **1960** *Times* 29 Sept. (Nigeria Suppl.) p. xxi/7 The colourful white-headed robin chat, that richest and most versatile of Nigerian songsters.

5. *robin-anthem*; **robin's egg** (further examples); usu., **robin's egg blue; robin-snow** (earlier example in a more general sense).

1853 THOREAU *Jrnl.* 11–12 Jan. in *Writings* (1906) x. 462 He says that the most snow we have had this winter (it has not been more than one inch deep) has been only a 'robin snow' as it is called, *i.e.* a snow which does not drive off the robins. **1881** Robin's-egg blue [see *PEACOCK *sb.* 4*]. **1887** M. E. WILKINS *Humble Romance* 15 A dress-pattern of robin's-egg blue silk. **1910** *Busy Man's Mag.* Dec. 65/1 On either side were swift hills mottled with green and gold, ahead a curdle of snow-capped mountains, above a sky of robin's-egg blue. **1933** N. WALN *House of Exile* I. iii. 43 Two lovely robin's-egg-blue bowls and two pairs of ivory chopsticks. **1951** E. PAUL *Springtime in Paris* v. 91 Cloud battalions retreating, and stragglers streaked with red—geranium, salmon, vermilion, magenta. Between them, their complements of robin's egg, turquoise, and faint bottle green. **1951** AUDEN *Nones* (1952) 15 A robin with no Christian name ran through The Robin-Anthem which was all it knew. **1970** R. LOWELL *Notebk.* 27 The boys.. Crawling the swimming pool's robin's-egg sky. **1978** M. PUZO *Fools Die* xi. 118, I gave up all thoughts of buying a Cadillac and settled for the robin's-egg blue Dodge.

III. 6. a. (Later example.)

1913 D. H. LAWRENCE in *New Statesman* 16 Aug. 595/2 We called the purple primroses 'robins', for no reason, unless that they bloomed in winter.

7. b. (Earlier example.)

1853 J. RICHARDSON *Let.* 24 May in N. E. Eliason *Tarheel Talk* (1956) 290 We caught 19 brim & robbins.

robing, *vbl. sb.* Add: **4.** *robing-table*.

1927 T. WILDER *Bridge San Luis Rey* ii. 19, I slipped into the sacristy, climbed the robing-table..and walked in.

Robin Hood, *sb.* Add: **1.** (Further examples of allusive use.) Also, more widely, any person who acts irregularly for the benefit of the poor.

1931 J. BUCHAN *Blanket of Dark* v. 96 This Catti.. robbed especially rich men..but spared the Church and the poor—a shabby Robin Hood. **1948** G. V. GALWEY *Lift & Drop* iv. 70 Strip cartoons relating the adventures of Hugh Stinton the Robin Hood of private enquiry agents. **1967** *Listener* 30 Mar. 421/2 The challenge of an Asian-style Robin Hood telling the poor that they will be fattened with good food for which the rich and corrupt..will be forced to pay. **1973** P. B. AUSTIN tr. *Sjöwall & Wahlöö's Locked Room* xxiv. 203 She thought of him as a Robin Hood who stole from the rich to give to the poor. **1976** *Oadby & Wigston* (Leics.) *Advertiser* 26 Nov. 2/4 The plot involves five main characters, all budding Robbin Hoods who realise there is money in fur coats. **1978** M. PUZO *Fools Die* xi. 119, I still had a little bit of the Robin Hood in me.

attrib. and *Comb.* (Further examples.)

1951 KOESTLER *Age of Longing* II. iii. 235 Pierre.. practised a kind of Robin Hood democracy. **1963** A. LUBBOCK *Austral. Roundabout* 161 The bushrangers also had a number of allies..for their Robin Hood attitude to their victims. **1975** *Times* 18 Apr. 4/7 A home loan fraud with a Robin Hood quality..to obtain mortgages for Asian immigrant families. **1977** *It* May 29/3 Ideally these would be assessed on a Robin Hood basis.

5. Robin Hood's barn, used as the type of an out-of-the-way place; esp. in phr. (*a*)*round Robin Hood's barn*, by a circuitous route (lit. and fig.).

a **1854** J. F. KELLEY *Humors of Falconbridge* (1856) 220 The way some folks have of going round 'Robin Hood's barn' to come at a thing. **1878** *N. & Q.* 22 June 486/2 'Where have you been today?' 'All round Robin Hood's barn! I have been all about the country, first here and then there.' **1913** E. M. WRIGHT *Rustic Speech* xi. 189 To go round by Robin Hood's barn (Cmb. w. Midl.) is to go a roundabout way, to go the farthest way. **1928** S. LEWIS *Man who knew Coolidge* 17 When it came to *talking*, why say, he wandered all round Robin Hood's barn! **1934** E. M. RHODES *Beyond Desert* 201 Wagon-road goes all around Robin Hood's barn to get to my place. **1951** H. WOUK *Caine Mutiny* xxxix. 464, I have gone all the way around Robin Hood's barn to arrive at the old platitudes, which I guess is the process of growing up. **1977** *Time* 31 Jan. 1/3 Your article on birth control goes around Robin Hood's barn for an answer to the birth control problem.

6. Used *attrib.* and *absol.* to designate a type of high-crowned hat with the brim turned up at the back and down at the front, trimmed with a feather.

1894 C. G. HARPER *Revolted Woman* ii. 43 Rational Dress..is only Bloomerism with a difference... A 'Robin Hood' hat, even as in the bygone years, crowns this confection. **1939** R. CHANDLER *Big Sleep* xi. 79 Her black hair was glossy under a brown Robin Hood hat. **1944** A. THIRKELL *Headmistress* x. 220 What interested him was her hat; a kind of Robin Hood hat of green felt with a long quill stuck jauntily through the crown. **1960** *News Chron.* 11 Apr. 8/4 Gone are the heavy-looking trilbies... In their place have come the delta and the Robin Hood. **1966** 'A. YORK' *Eliminator* iv. 66 Wilde..dressed in flannel bags and a sports coat, added an old Robin Hood. **1975** W. HILLICK *Bracknell's Law* 36, I was accosted by a little old woman in black: black coat, black stockings, black hat—and all a throwback to the forties, with the hat of the Robin Hood type.

Hence **Robin-Hoo·dish** *a.*, characteristic of a Robin Hood; beneficent to or benefiting the poor.

1974 *Listener* 18 July 86/3 The morally respectable, Robin-Hoodish bank robbery.

Robinocracy (rǫbinǫ·krăsi). [f. the name *Robin* (ROBIN[1]) + -OCRACY.] The régime of Sir Robert Walpole (1676–1745), the predominant figure in British politics between 1721 and 1742; the clique led by Walpole; the period of Walpole's supremacy.

1727 *Craftsman* 22 July 71 This week was publish'd Robin's Panegyrick on Himself and his Friends at Westminster; modestly proving that they were all very honest Fellows and deserving Patriots; with a full Confutation of the charge of Bribery and Corruption Offered to the consideration of the Freeholders; Citizens, Burgesses and Freemen of Great-Britain. *Populus me sibilat, at mihi plaudo.* Hor. Printed for S.B. W.W. and T.W. Printers to the Robinocracy. *a* **1902** ACTON *Lect. Mod. Hist.* (1906) xvi. 274 After the fall of Walpole it was observed..that the country felt itself superior to the government. This was the natural result of the time known as the Robinocracy; not because he devised liberal measures, but because he was careful to be neither wiser nor more liberal than the public. **1974** J. B. OWEN *Eighteenth Cent.* i. 23 On 19 April 1722 Sunderland died of pleurisy, and the way was open for Walpole to assert his supremacy. The Robinocracy had begun. **1977** W. A. SPECK *Stability & Strife* x. 222 Bolingbroke could be highly persuasive and his essays were the most substantial contemporary critiques of the Robinocracy.

robin redbreast. Add: **1. d.** *U.S.* = ROBIN *sb.*[1] 3 in Dict. and Suppl.

1696 S. SEWALL *Diary* 4 Jan. (1878) I. 242 Some say they saw a Robin-Redbrest to-day. **1865** *Atlantic Monthly* May 517/1 Shortly after Robin-Redbreast.. [arrives] the Golden-Winged Woodpecker. **1949** *Hobbies* Oct. 155/1 Robin Redbreast—most familiar of North American birds—has thrived as man's close neighbor.

robinre·dbreasted, *a. nonce-wd.* [f. ROBIN REDBREAST + -ED[2].] Clad in a red waistcoat.

1922 JOYCE *Ulysses* 465 Tom Rochford, robinredbreasted, in cap and breeches.

Robinsonade (rǫ:binsənē̆i·d, ‖ -ādə). Also **Robinsonnade** and with lower-case initial. Pl. **Robinsonades, ‖ -aden.** [ad. G. *Robinsonade* (coined by J. G. Schnabel, *Die Insel Felsenburg* (1731), Preface): see next and -ADE.] A novel with a subject similar to that of *Robinson Crusoe*; a story about shipwreck on a desert island.

1847 *Blackw. Mag.* Sept. 330/2 These outcasts from civilisation, the adventures of most of whom would furnish abundant materials for a Robinsonade. **1941** P. B. GOVE *Imaginary Voy. Prose Fiction* p. ix, The late Hermann Ullrich, whose knowledge of the influence of *Robinson Crusoe* has probably never been equaled, put on the title page of his bibliography of robinsonades in 1898 'Teil I'. *Ibid.* I. v. 125 Imitations of *Robinson* have been known usually as *Robinsonaden* or *robinsonades* (only rarely as robinsoniads), and similar works published before 1719 as *prerobinsonades*. **1967** B. W. ALDERSON tr. *B. Hürlimann's Three Centuries Children's Bks. in Europe* xvii. 252 Robinsonnades, like history, geography, and travel books, have always had a big attraction for the Swiss. **1974** *Encycl. Brit. Micropædia* VIII. 618/3 *Robinsonade*, novel written in imitation of *Robinson Crusoe*.. dealing with the problem of the castaway's survival on a desert island. **1978** D. WAGGONER *Hills of Faraway* 16 The Robinsonade is, of course, named for *Robinson Crusoe*, and is the story of a castaway—a voyage cut short—in an isolated setting, which the author can use to describe his ideas of the basic elements separating man from beast.

Robinson Crusoe (rǫ·binsən krū·so). The name of the eponymous hero of Daniel Defoe's fictional narrative (1719), who survives shipwreck on a desert island, used allusively. Also *attrib.* and (rare) *ellipt.* as *Robinson*. Cf. *CRUSOE. So **Ro·binson Cru·soe** *v. trans.*, to maroon on a desert island; **Ro·binson Cru·soic** *a.*

1768 *London Mag.* Oct. 543/1, I am of late from a sprightly fellow become a peevish mal-content; and am as unhappy among the people of England, as if some misadventure had Robinson-crusoed me, by throwing me into a desert-isle..where I could have nothing but seals and wild goats for my companions. **1849** L. HUNT *Bk. for Corner* I. 14 There are Robinson Crusoes in the moral as well as physical world..;—men, cast on desert islands of thought and speculation; without companionship; without worldly resources; forced to arm and clothe themselves out of the remains of shipwrecked hopes, and to make a home for their solitary hearts in the nooks and corners of imagination and reading. **1856** E. K. KANE *Arctic Explorations* I. xxvi. 348 A host of expedients were to be resorted to, and much Robinson Crusoe labor ahead. **1878** TROLLOPE *How 'Mastiffs' went to Iceland* ii. 6 Though the life of a Robinson Crusoe or a few Robinson Crusoes may be very picturesque, humanity will always desire to restore a Robinson Crusoe back to the community of the world. **1919** G. B. SHAW *Matter with Ireland* (1962) 213 His Robinson Crusoic independence of his neighbors. **1930** R. CAMPBELL *Adamastor* 30 Of all the ocean-gods and mages The last surviving Robinson. **1941** L. MACNEICE *Poetry W. B. Yeats* x. 218 Eliot..in *After Strange Gods* has grouped Lawrence and Yeats..as writers who have suffered from the lack of an established religion and a traditional moral code and who have invented for these things Robinson Crusoe substitutes. **1974** H. MACINNES *Climb to Lost World* iv. 53 The army compound..had a Robinson Crusoe atmosphere with the palm and pau pau trees. **1979** 'G. BLACK' *Night Run from Java* viii. 76 One [island] where I could Robinson Crusoe the marine accident victims.

robinsonite (rǫ·binsənəit). *Min.* [f. the name of S. C. *Robinson* (b. 1911), Canadian geologist + -ITE[1].] A bluish or grey lead antimony sulphide occurring as slender prismatic crystals and fibrous or compact masses.

1952 L. G. BERRY et al. in *Amer. Mineralogist* XXXVII. 438 The powder pattern obtained by Professor Peacock was found to be identical with one of several unidentified patterns obtained by Dr. S. C. Robinson at Queen's University during his investigation of the synthesis of lead antimony sulphides... The name robinsonite is given to this new mineral in honor of Dr. Robinson, whose synthesis made its identification possible. *Ibid.*, Robinsonite occurs as a primary mineral with pyrite, sphalerite, stibnite, and boulangerite in small pieces in oxidized ore bodies at the Red Bird mercury mine, Pershing County, Nevada. **1973** *Canad. Mineralogist* XII. 199/1 The Pb-Sb-S system..has been examined..between 300 and 700°C. Five phases have been synthesized: Phase I ($3PbS{:}Sb_2S_3$) stable between 642 and 605°C; boulangerite ($5PbS{:}2Sb_2S_3$) stable below 638°C; Phase II ($3PbS{:}Sb_2S_3$) stable between 603 and 405°C; robinsonite ($6PbS{:}5Sb_2S_3$) stable between 582° and 318°C; zinckenite ($PbS{:}Sb_2S_3$) stable below 545°C. *Ibid.* 205/2 Preservation of robinsonite, which appears to break down below 318°C, as a mineral is a perplexing problem; natural robinsonite may be stabilized by small amounts of impurities.

robomb (rōu·bǫm). *temporary.* [f. *ROB(OT + BOMB *sb.*] = **robot bomb*, **flying bomb*.

1944 *Saturday Night* (Toronto) 22 July 17 (*heading*) Germany's robombs another case of 'too little and too late'. **1945** H. S. ZIM *Rockets & Jets* xix. 266 Like the V-I robomb it must be given a high initial speed before the engine begins to operate.

robot (rōu·bǫt). [Czech, f. *robota* forced labour; used by Karel Čapek (1890–1938) in his play *R.U.R.* ('Rossum's Universal Robots') (1920).] **1. a.** One of the mechanical men and women in Čapek's play; hence, a machine (sometimes resembling a human being in appearance) designed to function in place of a living agent, esp. one which carries out a variety of tasks automatically or with a minimum of external impulse.

1923 P. SELVER tr. *Čapek's R.U.R.* 28 You see..the Robots have no interest in life. They have no enjoyments. **1923** *Times* 9 June 10/5 If Almighty God had populated the world with Robots, legislation of this sort might have been reasonable. **1928** *Daily News & Westm. Gaz.* 20 Apr. 11/4 The latest..Rotary Press, a veritable Robot in the complicated work it performs night after night without hitch. **1937** *Spectator* 23 Apr. 758/1 Men who will go to their doom with the unswerving directness of robots. **1942,** etc. [see *ROBOTIC *sb.* 1]. **1945** *Sun* (Baltimore) 9 Feb. 6–O/2 A robot, which never forgets, will do the job. **1958** [see *ANDROID]. **1969** I. & P. OPIE *Children's Games* xii. 340 'They pretend to be robots gone mad,' reports a headmaster. **1976** *Sci. Amer.* Feb. 77 (*caption*) Spot-welding robots..are used in assembling the underbodies of Chevrolet Novas. **1979** *Daily Tel.* 7 Nov. 6/8 The British Robot Association believes between 6,000 and 7,000 robots were in use world-wide in industry last year. **1980** *Times* 1 July 19/5 A *real* robot is programmable; it can be programmed to perform different, and changing tasks. In 1978 Japan put 1,100 playback or programmable robots into its factories.

b. A person whose work or activities are entirely mechanical; an automaton.

1923 *Westm. Gaz.* 22 June 7/5 Mr. G. Bernard Shaw defined Robots as persons all of whose activities were imposed on them. **1926** C. E. M. JOAD *Babbitt Warren* 82 Robots live by standardization. **1929** C. CONNOLLY *Let.* in *Romantic Friendship* (1975) 325 America is..a great youthful boisterous robot. **1943** J. B. PRIESTLEY *Daylight on Saturday* ix. 55, I thought it would be better having a fairly intelligent..girl instead of one of these little office robots. **1977** G. W. H. LAMPE *God as Spirit* ii. 51 The person who is 'seized' by the Spirit is thought of as a passive object, temporarily reduced to the status of a robot.

c. Chiefly *S. Afr.* An automatic traffic-signal.

1931 *Even. Standard* 5 Aug. 2/1 (*heading*) Traffic 'Robots' in the City. **1939** *Forum* (Johannesburg) 4 Feb. 35/1 The Daily Dispatch, East London, is critical of a proposal to fix robots in the town's streets. **1948** H. V. MORTON *In Search of S. Afr.* 17 Another word used in South Africa, but long discontinued in England, is robot for traffic lights. **1958** *Johannesburg Star* 16 Dec. 6/7 Johannesburg drivers..want to turn right or left while pedestrians, with the robot in their favour, are crossing. **1969** A. FUGARD *Boesman & Lena* II. 38 When the robot said 'Go' there at Berry's Corner I was nearly *bang in my broek*. **1974** *Eastern Province Herald* 2 Oct. 9 Vandals removed the lamps from seven traffic robots and the flashing head from a warning pole.

d. A robot bomb. *temporary*.

1944 *Daily Tel.* 11 July 1/5 Many of the robots launched against England on Sunday night finished up in the sea. **1944** J. LEES-MILNE *Prophesying Peace* (1977) 86 From here Jamesy saw his first robot.

2. *attrib.* and *Comb.*, as *robot army, astronaut, -brain, clerk, -land, -maker, masses,* (*petrol*) *station, -pilot, satellite, system, type, -worker; robot-controlled, -like* (also *adv.*), *-run* adjs.; **robot bomb** = *flying bomb* s.v. *FLYING *vbl. sb.* 3; **robot plane,** (*a*) = *queen bee* s.v. *QUEEN *sb.* 13; (*b*) = **robot bomb*; **robot roost,** a place for the storage of robot bombs; **robot teacher,** an electronic teaching aid; **robot train,** a robot-controlled underground train.

1927 *Morning Post* 20 Aug. 9 (*heading*) Robot army 'gassed'. **1961** *Daily Tel.* 14 Sept. 1/4 Technicians at Cape Canaveral, Florida, successfully sent a Project Mercury space capsule carrying a robot astronaut and recovered it from the Atlantic. **1944** *Sun* (Baltimore) 20 June 9/1 Most military authorities here are generally agreed that the robot bomb or plane is of..little military value. **1944** *N.Y. Times* 25 June 4E/1 (*heading*) Germans' robot bomb is a potential menace. **1945** G. MILLAR *Maquis* xiv. 292 A false report that a certain factory there was making parts for the robot bombs that the Germans had begun to send to London. **1951** KOESTLER *Age of Longing* I. viii. 140 The ancient Neanderthaler with a modern robot-brain. **1954** *Britannica Bk. of Year* 637/2 *Radar-Brain*, a device used to guide supersonic missiles from the ground, and *Robot-Brain*, a similar apparatus built into the missile. **1928** *Daily Express* 8 June 3/2 A new automatic selling machine, described as the 'Robot clerk', which will say 'Thank you' and give change, will replace the present automatic machines. **1964** *Ann. Reg. 1963* 394 London transport had also developed a robot-controlled underground train. **1960** KOESTLER *Lotus & Robot* II. vi. 173 The robotland reflected in the mirror makes us shudder. **1927** *N.Y. Times* 7 Mar. 16 An iron Robotlike woman Rotwang had made previously. **1928** *Daily Express* 11 Aug. 3/7 The romance of past centuries and robot-like drama of modern times meet at Sandwich. **1972** T. MCHUGH *Time of Buffalo* xi. 132 Among the most widespread was the Pawnee myth of the robotlike buffalo skull that pursued and devoured people. *Ibid.* 133 Marching robotlike after the coyote, the skull eventually devoured him. **1976** B. BOVA *Multiple Man* (1977) xiv. 147 That same robot-like Oriental butler served us steaks. **1946** J. T. SHIPLEY in W. S. Knickerbocker *20th Cent. Eng.* 131 Despite robot-makers..human nature changes, if at all, but slowly. **1946** J. S. HUXLEY *Unesco* ii. 43 The robot masses and class-types of ancient Mesopotamia and Egypt. **1972** *Times* 9 Nov. 35/1 (*heading*) Robot petrol stations. *Ibid.*, The two trends now being combined to produce what BP..calls robot stations, namely self-service and automatic money acceptance. **1930** *Aberdeen Press & Jrnl.* 31 Mar. 7/3 One of these robot-pilots has been fitted to a big twin-engined Supermarine Napier flying boat. **1951** A. Y. BRAMBLE *Air-Plane Flight* xv. 247 Automatic control or 'robot-pilot' is really a piece of control mechanism rather than an instrument as generally understood. **1935** Robot plane [see **queen bee*]. **1944** J. LEES-MILNE *Prophesying Peace* (1977) 84 Dame Una made stately preparations to dive under the table at the first sound of a robot plane. **1944** *Sun* (Baltimore) 20 June 1/3 United States heavy bombers struck twice today at the robot roost around Pas de Calais. **1958** I. ASIMOV *Naked Sun* i. 11 Fear of open spaces that barred them from the robot-run farming and mining areas of their own planet. **1958** C. C. ADAMS *Space Flight* 142 A manned satellite will be a formidable project... Unlike the robot satellite, it cannot be built in the laboratory and then installed in or on a rocket for delivery to orbit. **1976** *Sci. Amer.* Feb. 77 (*heading*) Robot systems. **1961** *Daily Tel.* 5 Sept. 21/5 Two robot teachers were on show in the Psychology Section. One, like a portable television set, had nine black knobs and a red button on the front. The pupil presses the black knobs to give his answer and the red button to obtain the correct solution. **1963** *Ibid.* 9 Apr. 17/4 (*heading*) Robot train tested with passengers. **1959** H. BARNES *Oceanogr. & Marine Biol.* 177 It is convenient to mount a Robot-type camera in a water-tight case, usually fastened to a pole. **1935** H. G. WELLS *Things to Come* 13 All the balderdash..about 'robot workers' and ultra skyscrapers, etc., etc., should be cleared out of your minds.

Hence **robotee·r,** an expert in the making of robots; **robote·sque** *a.*, resembling or suggestive of a robot; **robo·tian** *a.*, of or belonging to a robot or robots; **ro·botism,** mechanical behaviour or character; **robo·tnik** [*-NIK], a person behaving with mindless obedience to authority; **ro·botry,** the condition or behaviour of robots; **ro·boty** *a.*, robot-like.

1924 *Observer* 6 Jan. 12/2 When we reach the gloomy depths of 'commercial English'—..we are dealing with a mere thing of use, the very pith and genius of Robotry. **1927** *Daily Express* 30 Aug. 3/4 The Girl in the Lift must on some occasions drop her magnificent Robotry. *Ibid.* 5 Sept. 9/1 There are times when they seem to be purely robotesque, automata driven by impulses of destruction beyond their control. **1928** *Ibid.* 17 Mar. 4/2 A few have their wooden craniums transfixed by bodkins, and some have Robotian hooks instead of hands. **1928** *Observer* 29 Jan. 9/3 (*heading*) The robotism of architecture. **1933** E. E. CUMMINGS *eimi* 3 Horridly roboty child smothered by ferocious Blau, swinging a ditto balloon at end of wire. **1944** C. L. MOORE in *Astounding Sci. Fiction* Dec. 155/2 The impression of robotism was what she meant to convey. **1946** *Amer. Jrnl. Psychol.* LIX. 190, I wish to define the rôle of robotism in psychology, to show what sense there is in talking about robots. **1955** *Times* 27 July 9 It might be a pretty compliment to the brothers Capek ..if we called this new way of life robotry. **1960** *Times Lit. Suppl.* 16 Sept. 593/2 Too much law, and too centralized authority in all things breeds a society of automata, robotniks and helots. **1970** A. TOFFLER *Future Shock* ix. 180 Despite setbacks and difficulties, the roboteers are moving forward.

robotic (robǫ·tik), *a.* and *sb.* [f. *ROBOT + -IC.] **A.** *adj.* Of or pertaining to robots; characteristic of or resembling a robot.

1941 I. ASIMOV in *Astounding Sci. Fiction* May 50 You'd cut your own nose off before you'd let me get the credit for solving robotic telepathy. **1946** *Amer. Jrnl. Psychol.* LIX. 192, I believe that robotic thinking helps precision of psychological thought. **1947** I. ASIMOV in 'E. Crispin' *Best SF Two* (1956) 111 The mathematical interpretation of verbal reactions of robots is one of the more intricate branches of robotic analysis. **1959** *Archit. Rev.* CXXV. 212/3 His line is bold, his colour is bright but lifeless, and his figuration is decoratively robotic. **1963** *New Worlds Sci. Fiction* Apr. 52 Johnston wouldn't have been..surprised to find out that more than half of the city's population was robotic, no matter how cleverly they were disguised. **1973** M. AMIS *Rachel Papers* 49, I said in a robotic voice: 'Christ I'm sorry about that I had no idea it was your party and I wondered whether you might possibly let me make it up to you.' **1976** L. DEIGHTON *Twinkle, Twinkle Little Spy* viii. 84 The kind of dispassionate robotic bastard that communism breeds.

B. *sb.* **1.** *pl.* The art or science of the design, construction, operation, and application of robots and the like; the study of robots; *laws of robotics*, a set of rules devised to govern the actions of robots, enunciated in the science fiction stories of Isaac Asimov (see quot. 1968[1]).

At first a science-fiction term but now more generally used of automatic processes in industry.

1941 I. ASIMOV in *Astounding Sci. Fiction* May 53 There's irony in three of the greatest experts in robotics in the world falling into the same elementary trap, isn't there? **1942** —— in *Ibid.* Mar. 100/1 Let's start with the three fundamental rules of Robotics—the three rules that are built most deeply into a robot's positronic brain. **1957** —— *Naked Sun* (1958) i. 21 The robot showed no adverse response. It couldn't, of course. Its responses were limited and controlled by the Laws of Robotics. **1968** —— in *Sci. Jrnl.* Oct. 116/2 Eventually, I formulated these safeguards in the shape of 'The Three Laws of Robotics'. 1. A robot may not injure a human being or, through inaction, allow a human being to come to harm. 2. A robot must obey the orders given it by human beings, except where such orders would conflict with the First Law. 3. A robot must protect its own existence, except where such protection would conflict with the First or Second Law. **1968** *Times* 1 Nov. 23/2 Significant technological advances in the field of 'robotics'—the use of robots in the field of industrial automation—were announced today. **1974** G. BUTLER *Coffin for Canary* viii. 100 Perhaps we are robots. Robots acting out the last Law of Robotics...To tend towards the human. **1978** *Observer* (Colour Suppl.) 22 Oct. 15/2 In dealing with the many aspects of robotics—historical, philosophical, mythical, actual and projected—Jasia Reichardt defends the machine against some of our more excessive fears about this artificial image of ourselves. **1979** *Topic* (Imperial Coll., London) 22 Jan. 9/1 Support is planned for..new computer applications (e.g. industrial robotics).

2. *sing.* A robot. *rare*.

1951 C. SIMAK *Time & Again* (1956) v. 20 The robotic clicked and chuckled. It moved a pawn... A human simply can't beat a robotic expert. **1981** *Times* 10 Mar. 4/1 Will he consider direct grants for the purchase of such robotics?

So **robo·tical** *a.*; **robo·tically** *adv.*; **robo·ticist,** an expert in making and operating robots; **robo·ticized** *a.*, robotized.

1940 I. ASIMOV in *Super Sci. Stories* Sept. 70/2 Johnson is an expert Roboticist. **1942** —— in *Amazing Stories* Feb. 227/1 Austin Wilde, Robotical Engineer, turned to Sam Tobe and said, 'Did you get anything out of the robot?' **1947** —— in 'E. Crispin' *Best SF Two* (1956) 127 The government cruiser was making ready to carry the two roboticists back to Earth. **1957** —— *Naked Sun* iii. 35 A thoroughly roboticized economy. **1960** M. SCRIVEN in S. Hook *Dimensions of Mind* xiii. 120 The roboticist in his task of duplicating the brain functions of higher vertebrates. **1972** *Internat. Jrnl. Man-Machine Stud.* IV. 444 The most obvious computer solution would be to simple search serially through each region to find which was the largest. For a roboticist using a serial computer, that may well be the best approach. **1976** K. BONFIGLIOLI *Something Nasty in Woodshed* v. 53 Sam got up in a robotical sort of way. **1979** C. THOMAS *Snow Falcon* 24 Asked to rehearse once more lines he knew by heart... Robotically, he began.

robotize (rōᵘ·bǒtəiz) *v.* [f. *ROBOT + -IZE.] *trans.* **a.** = *AUTOMATE *v.* 1. **b.** *fig.* To render mechanical or lifeless, to cause to act as if lacking will or consciousness. So **ro·botized** *ppl. a.*; also **robotiza·tion.**

1927 C. M. GRIEVE *Albyn* 46 Dostoevsky's mistake was to imagine that Russia alone could prevent the robotization of Europe. **1927** *Daily Express* 7 Nov. 10/2 Lacking a skilled class of artisans, it is only by Robotising industry that she can hope to fight her way back to prosperity. **1928** *Ibid.* 20 Apr. 13/3 Sir William Joynson-Hicks..protested that he had not seen any sign during the last few months that the House [of Commons] had become robotised. **1928** *Observer* 15 Jan. 11/2 These robotised people..are only employed and allowed to exist because no one has yet been sufficiently energetic to invent a machine to replace them. **1930** *Ibid.* 16 Feb. 17/6 He adds..that in machine mass production lies the foundation of the evil, saying: 'We must not robotise America.' **1952** B. WOLFE *Limbo* xv. 236 Even when I was a kid the big plants had been pretty completely robotized. **1967** L. VON BERTALANFFY *Robots, Men & Minds* II. 64 The robotization of the human individual. **1969** *N.Y. Rev. Bks.* 2 Jan. 13/4 The masses, through state victory chants, book burning,..robotized phalanxes of soldiers, devour their enemies. **1975** *New Yorker* 21 Apr. 24/2 Katharine Ross plays the young New Yorker who moves to Stepford and discovers that the wives have been robotized by their husbands. **1976** *Sci. Amer.* Feb. 77/1 During the 1930's and 1940's petroleum refineries and petrochemical plants were extensively 'robotized' by inserting rather simple analogue control instruments in the feedback loops that regulated the pressure, temperature and flow rates in distillation columns, catalytic crackers and other equipment designed to process continuously flowing materials.

robotology (rōᵘbǫtǫ·lǒdʒi). [f. *ROBOT + -OLOGY.] The study of robots; robotics. So **roboto·logist.**

1946 *Amer. Jrnl. Psychol.* LIX. 190 The second robot is beginning the progress in his world which, if generalized, would make him into a scientist,..or at least a robotologist. *Ibid.* 192 When the physiological picture is complete it will be found that physiology is not necessarily identical with robotology. **1970** A. TOFFLER *Future Shock* (1971) ix. 210 In a quite different field of robotology there is progress, too. Technicians at Disneyland have created extremely life-like computer-controlled humanoids capable of moving their arms and legs, grimacing, smiling, [etc.]. **1972** *Computers & Humanities* VI. 135 Such a theory will..be part of a general performance theory, certain aspects of which are..covered in what one might call 'general robotology'..such as questions pertaining to the interaction between robot and man.

robotomorphic (ro:bǫtomǭ·ɹfik), *a.* [f. *ROBOT + *-omorphic*, after ANTHROPOMORPHIC *a.*] Designating or pertaining to a view of man as a robot or an automaton.

1969 KOESTLER in Koestler & Smythies *Beyond Reductionism* 2 The common target of these 'holy discontents'..seems to be what von Bertalanffy called the robotomorphic view of man. **1970** *Times* 17 Dec. 15/4 You say I overestimate the dangers of the Robotomorphic or Ratomorphic view. **1974** *Nature* 30 Aug. 765/1 The 'rōbotomorphic' mechanistic view of man implied in behaviouristic psychology.

Rob Roy. Add: **1.** Also *ellipt.*

1938 J. BETJEMAN *Oxf. Univ. Chest* v. 97 At the ferry you board a punt or canoe or rob roy and paddle down the stream of the Cherwell. **1976** *Country Life* 8 Apr. 870 The Rob Roys were essentially all-purpose canoes.

2. A cocktail made of Scotch whisky and vermouth.

1960 'P. QUENTIN' *Green-Eyed Monster* i. 5 The two of them were..drinking Rob Roys. **1962** H. KANE *Killer's Kiss* xi. 75 'A drink, Mr. Chambers?' 'Double Rob Roy, not too sweet.' **1975** M. H. CLARK *Where are Children?* vi. 44 Jonathan's favorite drink—a Rob Roy with a twist.

robust, *a.* Add: **1. d.** (Further examples.) Also *Anthrop.* Opp. *gracile*.

1964 B. S. KRAUS *Basis Human Evol.* vii. 224 Those [individuals] of Swartkrans and Kromdraai were considerably taller and more robust, perhaps attaining the stature and weight of modern Man. **1977** *Times Educ. Suppl.* 21 Oct. 11/2 The first gracile australopithicene to be found was the skull that Dart found at Sterkfontein half a century ago, but more recently robust hominids have also been identified at the South African sites.

4. Applied to a statistical test that yields approximately correct results despite the falsity of certain of the assumptions on which it is based; also, to a calculation, process, or result if the result is largely independent of certain aspects of the input.

1955 BOX & ANDERSEN in *Jrnl. R. Statistical Soc.* B. XVII. 1 To fulfil the needs of the experimenter, statistical criteria should (1) be sensitive to change in the specific factors tested, (2) be insensitive to changes, of a magnitude likely to occur in practice, in extraneous factors. A test which satisfies the first requirement is said to be powerful and we shall typify a test which satisfies the second by calling it 'robust'. **1966** S. BEER *Decision & Control* x. 232 What is important is the recognition of common features in the set of outcomes; these are the inductive inferences which may be classed as forecasts. We say that the system is robust in respect to a particular set of outcomes. **1972** *Jrnl. Social Psychol.* LXXXVIII. 204 The tests are robust regarding the assumptions of normality and equality of variances, but only when sample sizes are equal. **1978** *Nature* 16 Nov. 264/1 The ANOVA assumes equality of variances, a condition not satisfied here, however the test is robust to small deviations in homoscedasticity. **1979** *Sci. Amer.* Apr. 69/2 This conclusion, they point out, 'is robust, in that we have derived it from the global geochemical distribution of uranium, and we have also derived it from the U.S. uranium-mining history and from a wide variety of subsets of the U.S. uranium-mining history'.

robusta (robʊ·stă). [fem. of L. *rōbusta* Robust, specific (now varietal) epithet (L. Linden *Catal. Plantes économiques de l'Horticole coloniale* (1900) 64).] An evergreen variety of coffee, *Coffea canephora* var. *robusta*, native to Africa and widely cultivated elsewhere for its heavy crops of small beans; also, the beans produced by a tree of this kind. Also *attrib.*

1909 *Philippine Agric. Rev.* II. 590 A new variety of coffee known as 'robusta'..was discovered some years ago growing wild on the estates in Africa. *Ibid.*, The robusta coffee planted in east Java yields after three years. **1922** [see *Arabica]. **1944** *Empire Jrnl. Exper. Agric.* XII. 191 Robusta coffee..grows wild in many of the wetter forests of Uganda. **1959** [see *Arabica]. **1961** F. L. Wellman *Coffee* v. 81 The most common variety is named Robusta, and this type has large, dark-green leaves... Trees of the Robusta variety tend to have a flattened top. **1976** *Times* 7 May 22/5 Fears of a shortage ..sent robusta coffee prices to new all-time highs on the London markets. *Ibid.*, Shortages will increase the demand for African robustas.

robusticity. For *rare* read 'Chiefly *Anthrop.* and *Zool.*' (Further examples.)

1946 F. E. Zeuner *Dating Past* ix. 299 They show nothing of the robusticity and exuberance of bodily growth of Crô-Magnon Man, whose contemporaries they were. **1959** *Chambers's Encycl.* I. 460/2 Other features than size, e.g. shape and robusticity, are expressed in anthropometry by indices. **1971** *Nature* 5 Feb. 407/1 In overall size and robusticity the fossil closely resembles the pygmy chimpanzee.

robustness. Add further examples in senses 1 d and *4 of the adj.

1953 G. E. P. Box in *Biometrika* XL. 318 This remarkable property of 'robustness' to non-normality which these tests for comparing means possess, and without which they would be much less appropriate to the needs of the experimenter, is not necessarily shared by other statistical tests. **1973** J. Buettner-Janusch *Physical Anthropol.* viii. 240 [Modern man] may walk bipedally. Among the specializations that permit this are the shape of the arch and the position and robustness of the big toe. **1974** Adby & Dempster *Introd. Optimization Methods* iv. 78 A concept both more vague and much more difficult to ensure is termed robustness. A robust algorithm is one which in practice usually yields the global minimum or a good local minimum of any function of even a large number of variables from a poor initial approximation.

roc. *β.* (Further examples.)

1924 *Nature* 19 Apr. 564/2 Purely fabulous species, such as the phœnix and the rukh, are likewise dealt with. **1974** *Encycl. Brit. Micropædia* VIII. 619/2 The Kublai Khan inquired..about the *rukh* and was brought what was claimed to be a *rukh*'s feather, which may really have been a frond of the *Raphia* palm.

‖ **rocaille** (rokāʸ). Also **rocail** and with capital initial. [a. F. *rocaille* rock-work, rococo.] An artistic or architectural style of decoration characterized by ornate rock- and shell-work; a rococo style. Also *attrib.* or as *adj.*

1856 M. Digby Wyatt in O. Jones *Grammar of Ornament* I. xix. 109 The twisted and foliated scrolls and shells ..grew into the 'rocaille' and grotto-work of [baroque]..; degenerating at last into..'Chinoiserie'. **1905** *Scribner's Mag.* July 47 Rocaille differs from our rockwork in that it does not attempt to imitate the natural formation of rocks, but rather seeks to create architectural forms by combinations of pebbles and shells, such as conventionalized figures of sea-gods, and dolphins. **1936** *Burlington Mag.* Oct. 187/1 Louis XVI, who did not care for the 'rocaille' style like his grandfather. **1944** J. Lees-Milne *Prophesying Peace* (1977) 69 A cliff-like structure hung with reliefs, and encrusted with shells, sea urchins and rocaille ornaments. **1958** *Listener* 2 Oct. 530/1 The staggering rocaille on Bena Lulua figures. **1960** *Times* 14 Jan. 14/5 Sauceboats of 1737 having shell shaped bowls or *rocaille* bases. **1975** J. Gores *Hammett* (1976) xi. 82 The ornate rocaille pier glass. **1979** E. H. Gombrich *Sense of Order* vii. 189 To what extent can Riegl's method be used for the explanation and analysis of the Rocaille? Are these playful shells..just another metamorphosis of the acanthus?

‖ **rocambolesque** (rǫkæ:mbǫle·sk), *a.* [a. F. *rocambolesque* fantastic, f. *Rocambole* the name of a character in the novels of Ponson du Terrail (1829–71), French author, the subject of improbable and fantastic adventures + -esque.] Of or resembling Rocambole (see etym.); incredible, fantastic.

1949 Koestler *Promise & Fulfilment* I. viii. 91 It was the first anti-British terror act of the Irgun and it displayed already all the features of rocambolesque etiquette. **1960** B. Marshall *Divided Lady* I. xxi. 75 How amused the General would have been by this rocambolesque religiosity. **1976** *New Society* 13 May 370/3 An exemplary surrealistic life..which included a *rocambolesque* episode.. in which he kidnapped his Bulgarian mistress from her husband.

‖ **roche,** *sb.*[2] Delete entry: see *roche moutonnée.

Roche (rōᵘʃ). *Astron.* The name of Edouard Albert *Roche* (1820–83), French mathematician, used *attrib.* and in the possessive to denote concepts arising out of his work, as **Roche('s) limit,** (*a*) the closest distance to which a self-gravitating body (strictly a fluid body: see quot. 1900) can approach a more massive body without being pulled apart by the gravitational field of the latter body; (*b*) the smallest continuous equipotential surface (having the form of two lobes meeting at a point) which can exist around both members of a system of two gravitating bodies, *spec.* a binary star system; **Roche lobe,** either of the two volumes of space (meeting at a point) that are bounded by Roche's limit (*b*) in a binary system; **Roche zone,** the region of space within Roche's limit (sense (*a*)).

1889 G. H. Darwin in *Harper's Mag.* June 73/1 The distance of..2·44 of a planet's radius I call Roche's limit for that planet. **1900** *Astrophysical Jrnl.* XI. 122 In the derivation of Roche's limit the assumption was made that the satellite was a perfectly homogeneous incompressible fluid, and that its rotation and revolution were performed in the same period. **1930** R. H. Baker *Astron.* v. 212 All parts of Saturn's rings lie within Roche's limit. **1959** Z. Kopal *Close Binary Syst.* iii. 133 Such configurations represent the largest closed equipotentials capable of containing the whole mass of the respective components, and will hereafter be referred to as their Roche limits. **1969** *Times* 10 July 12/8 If the moon had ever come within a critical distance of earth, known as the Roche limit, the tidal forces raised by the earth would have disrupted it. **1972** W. Strohmeier *Variable Stars* vii. 182 Expansion of the components in close binaries towards their Roche limits, in a time scale of 10^6 years, can also give rise to an exchange between the rotational and orbital momenta. **1974** *Sci. Amer.* Feb. 53/1 Only a body with more than gravitational cohesion can withstand the tidal effects within Roche's limit. [**1960** *Astrophysical Jrnl.* CXXXII. 149 (*caption*) The radii of the Roche-limit lobes for a mass ratio of unity.] **1969** *Ibid.* CLVIII. 571 Morton concluded that on such a time scale the contact component would be stable, shrinking within the Roche lobe after initial mass loss. **1975** *Sci. Amer.* Mar. 30/3 In the evolution of a typical binary, as soon as one of the components expands to a volume larger than that of its Roche lobe the matter outside the lobe will begin to flow toward the companion star. **1971** I. G. Gass et al. *Understanding Earth* vii. 112/2 What would happen if the Moon were to enter the Roche zone? **1978** *New Scientist* 23 Nov. 607/2 One or more former moons of Uranus spiralled into the planet's Roche zone where they broke up because of tidal forces, producing the parent fragments of the rings.

rochea (rōᵘ·ʃiă). [mod.L. (A. P. de Candolle *Plantarum Historia Succulentarum* (1803?) 103), f. the name of François de la *Roche* (d. 1813), French botanist + -a 2.] A succulent plant of the genus so called, belonging to the family Crassulaceæ, native to South Africa, and bearing leathery leaves and clusters of white, pink, or red flowers.

1932 A. J. Macself *Amateur's Greenhouse* xi. 253 Hybrid Kalosanthes or Rocheas in white, rose, etc., are similar in habit. **1955** V. Higgins tr. *Bertrand's Indoor Plants* 84 Rochea... For some years now the florists have offered this attractive plant on Mother's Day. **1979** A. Huxley *Reader's Digest Success with House Plants* 340/3 Rocheas are small shrubs grown primarily for their clusters of flowers.

‖ **roche moutonnée** (roʃ mutone). *Physical Geogr.* [Fr., f. *roche* rock, Roche *sb.*[1] + *moutonnée* Moutonnée.] A bare rock outcrop which has been shaped by glacial erosion, characteristically smoothed and rounded by abrasion but often also displaying one side (the 'downstream' side) which is rougher and steeper because of plucking. Hence **ro:che mouto·nnéed** *a.*, abounding in *roches moutonnées.*

De Saussure (see quot. 1786), to whom the term is frequently attributed, applied the adj. *moutonnée* to small rounded hillocks (usu. covered with vegetation) which suggested, *en masse*, a fleece or a wig of a style termed *moutonnée*. These features do not correspond to the meaning of *roches moutonnées* which later became accepted, and were not associated by de Saussure with glaciers. (See also s.v. in *Gloss. Geol.* (Amer. Geol. Inst., 1972) 613.)

[**1786** H.-B. de Saussure *Voyages dans Alpes* II. xlviii. 512–3 Plus loin, derriere le village de *Juviana* ou *Envionne* on voit des rochers qui ont une forme que je nomme *moutonnée*... Les montagnes que je désigne par cette expression sont composées d'un assemblage de têtes arrondies, couvertes quelquefois de bois, mais plus souvent d'herbes, ou tout au plus de broussailles. Ces rondeurs contigues & répétées forment en grand l'effet d'une toison bien fournie, ou de ces perruques que l'on nomme aussi *moutonnées*.] **1843** J. D. Forbes *Trav. through Alps* iii. 53 The surface of rock..is even and rounded, often dome-shaped or spheroidal, showing the structure of the rock in section... Such surfaces were called Roches Moutonnées by De Saussure. **1862** *Q. Jrnl. Geol. Soc.* XVIII. 187 For many miles in the Alb Valley, both above and below St. Blasien, *roches moutonnées* stand like islands through the alluvium. **1865**, etc. [see Roche *sb.*[2]]. **1905** *Bull. Geol. Soc. Amer.* XVI. 51 The northern slopes..have been considerably smoothed by ice action... The whole surface is rochemoutonnéed, especially on the north, where nearly all rocks are absolutely fresh. **1935** *Discovery* Mar. 79/2 Dome-like rocks are exposed which in appearance recall the ice-formed *roches moutonnées*. **1957** J. K. Charlesworth *Quaternary Era* I. xi. 251 De Saussure gave the name roche moutonnée to the distinctive, rounded forms which abound in glaciated terrain (he himself failed to associate them with ice) and give the effect of a thick fleece or the wavy wigs styled *moutonnées* in his day (they were slicked down with mutton tallow). **1977** A. Hallam *Planet Earth* 86/3 Many valleys are very deeply incised, with U-shaped cross-profiles and floors composed of smoothed, striated and streamlined rock hummocks (called roches moutonnées).

Rōchū, var. *Rōjū.

rock, *sb.*[1] Add: **I. 1. b.** For '*U.S.* and *Austr.*' read 'orig. *U.S.*', and add: Also freq., a stone used as a projectile. (Further examples.)

1890 Barrère & Leland *Dict. Slang* II. 183/2 *Rocks* (American), small stones or pebbles... The term is used in some parts of England. **1939** J. Stuart in *Esquire* May 55/1, I pull a round rock from my pocket. I let th' rock go. I holler: 'Rocks! Watch out!' **1968** *New Society* 29 Aug. 304/1 It is now frequent for British newspapers to record that during some riot or disturbance the crowd has thrown 'rocks' (= 'stones'). **1969** *West Australian* 5 July 1/1 Several policemen fell to the ground after they were hit with rocks. **1976** *Billings* (Montana) *Gaz.* 17 June 1-F/5 Ambulance services were suspended when mobs hurled rocks at the vehicles, injuring drivers. **1979** *Observer* 16 Sept. 1/1 The Belfast house of Mr Gerry Fitt, Social Democratic and Labour MP for East Belfast, was besieged by about 200 youths armed with rocks yesterday.

d. *Canad.* = Curling-stone.

1911 R. E. Knowles *Singer of Kootenay* 296 Every man of them held his breath as the flying rock came to the port. **1963** *Times* 25 Feb. (Canada Suppl.) p. xvi/1 The Scots melted cannon balls to fashion their 'rocks' and played the game on the frozen St. Lawrence river and ponds in the area. It is interesting that rocks made of iron were still being used in parts of Ontario and Quebec as late as 20 years ago. **1974** *Globe & Mail* (Toronto) 20 Feb. 33/7 Dr. Will McTavish of Winnipeg and Ralph Smith of Noranda excelled at getting their draws into the centre of the house and knocking out opposition rocks.

2. d. *on the rocks*: also (esp. of a marriage, etc.), on the point of dissolution; finished.

1958 E. Wilson in *N.Y. Post* 1 June 2/3 [Roberto Rossellini's] headlined romance with Sonali Das Gupta is now reported on the rocks. **1975** *Globe & Mail* (Toronto) 12 Sept. 12/6 Simply adding more ice to a marriage that's already on the rocks won't save the partnership, the Law Reform Commission of Canada says in a paper on divorce.

e. (Earlier and later examples.) Also *spec.* a dollar. In phr. *a pocketful of rocks*, a large amount of money.

1840 *Picayune* (New Orleans) 31 July 2/2 He was just on the eve of leaving town with his 'pockets full of rocks'. **1846** in D. Corcoran *Pickings from New Orleans Picayune* 143 Here I am in town without a rock in my pocket. **1847** J. S. Robb *Streaks of Squatter Life* 165 If I had a 'pocket full of *rocks*', you should share them. **1858** J. R. Lowell *Poet. Wks.* II. 284 A pocket-full of rocks 'twould take To build a house of free-stone. **1905** *Dialect Notes* III. 17 *Rocks*, dollars. **1942** Z. N. Hurston in A. Dundes *Mother Wit* (1973) 224/1, I don't bet, but I'll doubt you. Five rocks! **1949** *Cavalier Daily* (Univ. of Va.) 22 Oct. 4/1 They got a campaign goin' around here to try to stick us students six rocks just to go..and listen to some old bag yell her fool head off.

f. *slang* (orig. *U.S.*). A precious stone, *spec.* a diamond. Cf. *rock-diamond* (sense 6 d) in Dict.

1908 H. Green *Maison de Shine* 83 'So that's his new wife, eh?' said Goldie later. 'Did you pipe the rocks she had on?' **1926** J. Black *You can't Win* xiii. 178 I'll unharness these 'rocks'. **1929** [see *loogan]. **1936** J. Curtis *Gilt Kid* v. 57 Some of the women present, he saw, were wearing goodish rocks. **1953** 'S. Ransome' *Drag Dark* (1954) vi. 60 Goodlee wrote his check..then walked out with the rock. **1968** A. Diment *Bang Bang Birds* vii. 106 He..listened to my vague replies like my advice was worth its weight in sparkling rocks. **1973** 'I. Drummond' *Jaws of Watchdog* i. 12 'We will see some of the most beautiful jewellery in the world... The emeralds.'.. 'Personally,' said Jenny, 'I call it vulgar, having all those rocks on a yacht.'

g. In *U.S.* colloq. phr. *between a rock and a hard place*: without a satisfactory alternative, in difficulty (see also quot. 1921).

1921 *Dialect Notes* V. 113 *To be between a rock and a hard place*,..to be bankrupt. Common in Arizona in recent panics; sporadic in California. **1959** L. Roberts *Up Cutshin & Down Greasy* v. 82 That was one time dad was between a rock and a hard place. **1963** D. Ogilvy *Confessions Advertising Man* xi. 160 As a private person, I would gladly pay for the privilege of watching it without commercial interruptions. Morally, I find myself between the rock and the hard place. **1976** T. Wolfe *Mauve Gloves & Madmen* 37 The dive brings you down so low, you are now down into the skeet range of that insidiously well-aimed flak! This, as they say, puts you between a rock and a hard place.

h. Usu. *pl.* An ice-cube or crushed ice for use in a drink. In phr. *on the rocks*, (of a spirituous liquor) served with ice. *slang* (orig. *U.S.*).

1946 *Amer. Speech* XXI. 35 *Rocks*, ice. **1948** F. Brown *Murder can be Fun* (1951) iii. 44 A slug or two of rock and rye won't hurt you. **1949** *Life* 14 Nov. 63 Ordering a Scotch on the rocks at the bar. **1952** N. Spain in C. Asquith *Second Ghost Bk.* 36, I..went in and fixed myself a Scotch on rocks, neat. **1955** J. B. Priestley *Journey down Rainbow* 220 They all drank a lot of whisky-on-the-rocks. **1959** 'J. Christopher' *Scent of White Poppies* vi. 82 Rocks in your Scotch, Cam? I can get some from the fridge. **1966** *Listener* 20 Oct. 573/2 For some reason, no one knows quite why, Americans insist on having ice, or 'rocks' as they call it, always in easy reach. **1978** R. Ludlum *Holcroft Covenant* iii. 39 That was scotch on the rocks, wasn't it?

i. pl. *slang.* The testicles; = Stone *sb.* 11a. In coarse phr. *to get one's rocks off*, to achieve sexual satisfaction, to ejaculate; also, in weakened sense, to obtain enjoyment.

1948 *Amer. Speech* XXIII. 249/1 *Get your rocks off*, an expression used to denote extreme enjoyment. **1961** *Ibid.* XXXVI. 150 Expressions using *rocks* and *stones* to mean testes are at least as old as the Renaissance, but in the mouths of today's teen-agers, *hot rocks* seems to imply only a warm romantic interest by a teen-ager of either sex in one of the opposite gender. **1971** *Frendz* 5 Aug. 22/2 Get yer rocks off Seymour. OK. But there are limits. Surely. **1972** *Show* Sept. 55/2 Unrelenting sequences of unsympathetic characters getting their rocks off. **1975** J. Braine *Pious Agent* vi. 23 I'd get a swift kick in the rocks. **1975** G. V. Higgins *City on Hill* vii. 195 I've been reduced to dressing up in order to get my rocks off. **1978** *Chicago* June 90/3 This is a good film for getting your rocks off, but not the sort you will remember much about two weeks later. **1978** J. Irving *World according to Garp* xi. 205, I don't get my rocks off by humiliating myself, you know.

j. *U.S. Baseball slang.* An error. In phr. *to pull a rock*, to make a mistake.

1939 E. J. Nichols *Hist. Dict. Baseball Terminol.* (thesis, Pa. State College) 57 *Pull a rock*, see 'boner'. *Ibid.* 9 *Boner*, an error in judgment. **1951** *Birmingham* (Alabama) *News* 31 July 16/3 How does a guy who has been labeled 'the perfect player' feel after pulling his first 'rock' in a long and brilliant baseball career? **1952** *Philadelphia Even. Bull.* 4 Oct. 13/2 Who deserved the rap for the 'rock' that cost the Yankees yesterday's World Series game? **1955** *Daily Progress* (Charlottesville, Va.) 5 May 10/7 'Luckily, it didn't hurt us but I pulled a rock.' Durocher then went on to explain his 'rock', which didn't prevent the Giants from winning. .. 'Good strategy, my foot,' mocked Durocher after the game. 'It was a real rock.' **1956** *Sun* (Baltimore) 26 Apr. B 25/3 Bill changed his mind and lifted Rhodes out of the lineup... The criticism was that he had 'pulled a rock'.

3. g. Mineral ore. *U.S.*

1830 *Workingman's Gaz.* (Woodstock, Vermont) 28 Oct. 38/1 The surface is almost covered with rock, all which contains gold..which is obtained by breaking or pounding the rock. **1896** C. H. Shinn *Story of Mine* 78 The quartz prospector..only pans out a few ounces of powdered rock. **1902** O. Wister *Virginian* xv. 172 Are they taking much mineral out? Have yu' seen any of the rock? **1948** *Los Angeles Times* 12 Jan. II. 8/3 (*heading*) Ruby mine runs into rich rock.

5. a. Delete *U.S.* and add later example.

1977 *Grimsby Even. Tel.* 5 May 18/2 Principal sorts were: Cod 1,712 kits, haddock 1,059,..rocks 23, skate 58,..monk 16.

II. 6. a. *rock-arch, -barrier, -bluff, -chamber, -chimney, -cliff, -crust, -drift, -flat, -floor, -fortress, -hill, ledge, -point, -pool* (further examples), *-rampart, -shelter* (further examples), *-shrine, -stack, -terrace, -wall.*

1936 H. Nicolson *Let.* 28 Sept. (1966) 274 The precipices,..the rock-arches..roared back at us. **1940** C. Day Lewis tr. *Virgil's Georgics* iv. 90 Proteus shelters within behind a huge rock-barrier. **1886** A. Winchell *Walks & Talks in Geol. Field* 53 We have seen..the rock-bluffs bounding..the basins of the great lakes. **1954** J. R. R. Tolkien *Fellowship of Ring* 217 There was a cave or rock-chamber behind. *Ibid.* 401 There were many birds about the cliffs and the rock-chimneys. **1972** *Shooting Times & Country Mag.* 1 July 17/3 A rock 'chimney' up which I was none too happy in ascending. **1952** S. Spender *Learning Laughter* 9 From the ship we saw houses on a green shelf above a rock-cliff. *a* **1963** C. S. Lewis *Poems* (1964) 45 Down far under his rock-crust. **1951** W. de la Mare *Winged Chariot* 16 Sweet salt-tanged air, birds, rock-drift. **1959** Blunden *Hong Kong House* 2 It was no garden—so adust, red-dry the rock-drift soil was. **1967** *Oceanogr. & Marine Biol.* V. 483 In the most subtropical areas,..the fauna living between the algae covering these rock-flats may be greatly impoverished. **1905** *Jrnl. Geol.* XIII. 393 The desert plain may be reduced to a lower level than that of the deepest initial basin; and then a rock-floor,..unrelated to normal baselevel, will prevail throughout. **1946** F. E. Zeuner *Dating Past* vii. 223 Resting on an irregular rock-floor at about 7·5 metres above low sea-level, a beach conglomerate is found. **1934** W. S. Churchill *Marlborough* II. xv. 331 Coblenz..stands opposite the majestic rock-fortress of Ehrenbreitstein. **1946** R. Campbell *Talking Bronco* 41 Rock-fortress of your sex and gender! *a* **1862** Thoreau *Maine Woods* (1864) 262 Being struck with the perfect parallelism of these singular rock-hills,..I took out my compass. **1963** D. W. & E. E. Humphries tr. *Termier's Erosion & Sedimentation* xiii. 260 This type of coastal cornice, or rock ledge, is thus a phenomenon of marine abrasion. **1849** D. G. Rossetti *Let.* 18 Oct. (1965) I. 74 One rock-point standing buffeted alone, vexed at its base with a foul beast unknown. **1948** L. MacNeice *Holes in Sky* 31 Foam-quoits on rock-points. **1907** E. Gosse *Father & Son* vi. 156 The antiquity of these rock-pools..used to occupy my Father's fancy. **1955** V. Palmer in B. James *Austral. Short Stories* (1963) 32 He stared into rock-pools. **1924** R. Campbell *Flaming Terrapin* vi. 94 The brink of the abyss, Where into space the sharp rock-rampart drops. **1927** Peake & Fleure *Hunters & Artists* 40 A small rock-shelter, now quarried away. **1971** *World Archaeol.* III. 147 Puntutjarpa is a minor sacred site about 150 ft west of the rockshelter. **1933** *Burlington Mag.* June 290/2 A small seated Buddha-image,..cut out of a rock-shrine at Yiin-Kang. **1969** *Tanzania Notes & Rec.* July 3 The great rock-shrine of Tita, in southern Turu near Puma, is in the eyes of the Turu themselves less powerful than similar shrines in the mountains of Sandawe country and in Isanzu. **1969** G. M. Brown *Orkney Tapestry* i. 17 There among them, standing out to sea a little, is the rock-stack called The Old Man of Hoy. **1892** *Bull. Geol. Soc. Amer.* III. 65 Raised marine deposits with an arctic fauna occur over the latest moraines in Scandinavia... Bravais, half a century ago came to the conclusion that two elevated rock-terraces in northern Norway examined by him are not horizontal but descend toward the north. **1968** R. W. Fairbridge *Encycl. Geomorphol.* 1184/2 [River] terraces may be cut into the solid rock or consist of a rock bench veneered with a comparatively small thickness of alluvium (rock terrace). **1904** W. M. Ramsay *Lett. Seven Churches* xxv. 360 At times an oblique crack develops in the rock-wall. **1954** J. R. R. Tolkien *Two Towers* 73 At the far end the rock-wall was sheer.

b. *rock art, -carving* (examples), *-drawing* (examples), *-engraving, -painting, -picture.*

1959 J. D. Clark *Prehist. S. Afr.* ix. 248 The rock art tells us little for certain about marriage customs. **1974** B. & R. Hill *Spirit in Stone* 11 With very few exceptions most rock art sites are located near villages. **1907** H. M. Chadwick *Origin Eng. Nation* xii. 306 The rock-carvings at Tegneby. **1950** H. L. Lorimer *Homes & Monuments* vi. 354 The well-known rock-carving of Ivriz on which a King appears before the god of vegetation. **1938** H. A. Winkler *Rock-Drawings of Southern Upper Egypt* I. 26 The discovery of rock-drawings showing boats of a type foreign to Egypt. **1977** H. Innes *Big Footprints* I. i. 33 The location of the rock drawings. **1920** H. G. Wells *Outl. Hist.* I. xvii. 126/1 From rock engravings we may deduce the theory that the desert was crossed from oasis to oasis. **1959** J. D. Clark *Prehist. S. Afr.* ii. 29 The first European in Rhodesia to see rock engravings was probably Thomas Leask who saw those near Wankie in 1869 when on a hunting trip to the Zambezi. **1908** *Encycl. Relig. & Ethics* I. 822/2 The rock-paintings..are either stencilled..or painted in outline. **1977** *Times* 23 Apr. 14/1, I read of a Bushman woman wearing a circle of beads..'exactly like that of her ancient prototype' in an early rock painting. **1939** *Man* No. 119. 178/2 On one of the stalactite pillars..was found a big round stone with.. traces of red paint on its surface, as used in the rock-pictures. **1952** V. G. Childe *New Light Most Anc. East* (ed. 4) ii. 17 The rock-pictures..demonstrate the survival of the 'Rhodesian fauna'.

c. *rock-movement, porosity, -type.*

1907 *Bull. Geol. Survey N.Z.* No. 3. 95 Differential rock-movement is recorded by the well-slickensided faces and the plastic finely comminuted rock-material occurring in the plane of contact. **1946** *Nature* 6 July 31/1 G. A. Maximovich.., after making a compilation of several thousands of determination[s] of rock-porosity,..has calculated the average porosities of different types of rocks. *Ibid.* 3 Aug. 172/1 The commonest rock-type [on Heard Island] is trachybasalt.

d. *rock-cut, -cutting, -land, -top, -vine, -wilderness.*

1873 J. H. Beadle *Undevel. West* 139 A long rock-cut. **1965** G. McInnes *Road to Gundagai* ix. 134 Each rattling rock-cut, each looping embankment and low trestle bridge carried us further into an unbelievable land. **1873** 'Mark Twain' & Warner *Gilded Age* 420 There is Newark,..then marshes, then long rock cuttings, devoted to the advertisements of patent medicines. **1891** M. E. Ryan *Pagan of Alleghanies* 96 The rest of that rock-land is going to break away sometime. **1946** W. de la Mare *Traveller* 17 He..had wakened to the rock-land. **1960** *Wall St. Jrnl.* 30 Nov. 7/3 The technique of 'rockland' farming was developed a few years ago in south Florida... Growers use the rockland in preference to more fertile soil partly because..rocklands are on higher ground and are less subject to flooding. **1927** D. H. Lawrence *Mornings in Mexico* 135 High on a narrow rock-top. **1927** Joyce *Pomes Penyeach*, Gold-brown upon the sated flood The rockvine clusters lift and sway. **1927** D. H. Lawrence *Mornings in Mexico* 162 The great, hollow, rock-wilderness space of that part of Arizona.

7. a. *rock-crushing, -infesting, -loving* (earlier example), *-rolling.*

1966 A. Battersby *Math. in Managem.* i. 16 This rock-crushing argument may bell be used to suppress a bright boy. **1940** A. H. Gardiner *Theory of Proper Names* i. 7 The rock-infesting monsters. **1847** Emerson *Poems* 230 A wild-rose, or rock-loving columbine, Salve my worst wounds. **1957** R. Campbell *Coll. Poems* II. 106 But now the longed-for sound, As of rock-rolling torrents underground, Approaches.

b. *rock-climbing* (further examples), *-folding, -painting.*

1923 G. D. Abraham *First Steps to Climbing* iv. 45 It is a well-considered opinion that rock climbing is the most important branch of mountaineering. **1977** *Times* 19 Jan. 14/1 Wasdale Head proclaims itself as the birthplace of rock climbing. **1965** G. J. Williams *Econ. Geol. N.Z.* iii. 20/1 It is very clear that there is a general parallelism between rock-folding and the trend of the lodes. **1965** R. & D. Morris *Men & Snakes* i. 17 Australia is the only continent where rock painting is still practised regularly today.

c. *rock beater, climber* (further examples), *-hopper, -hunter, -painter.*

1935 *Discovery* July 203/2 The rock is..crushed in rock beaters. **1940** F. Smythe *Adventures of Mountaineer* vii. 75, I knew my companion to be a magnificent rock climber, as agile and as active as a cat. **1977** *R.A.F. News* 27 Apr.–10 May 20/6 St Athan's mountain rescue team.. were asked to help rescue a rock climber who had fallen in the Brecon Beacons. **1959** S. J. Baker *Drum* 140 *Rock-hopper*, a person who fishes from rocks on a sea-coast. **1969** *Man* (Austral.) Mar. 12/2 Many rock-hoppers are experienced rock climbers, of a breed who, for sport, crawl like flies over the granite. **1971** R. Purvis *Treasure Hunting in Brit. Columbia* ii. 47 The first rockhunter to emerge in the early stone age wasn't interested in the beauty or gem quality of stones. **1919** H. G. Wells *Outl. Hist.* xii. 77/2 The simplicity, directness, and detachment of a later Palæolithic rock-painter appeal more to modern sympathies than does the state of mind of these Neolithic men. **1961** L. van der Post *Heart of Hunter* 9, I gave a brief account of the tragic extermination of this little hunter and rock-painter by the Black and the White invaders of his ancient country.

8. a. *rock-born, -bound* (further examples), *-bred* (further examples), *-bristled, -cut* (further examples), *-girt* (earlier example), *-guarded, -living, -nurtured, -perched, -rooted* (further examples), *-staked.*

1849 J. R. Lowell in *National Anti-Slavery Standard* 23 Aug. 50/6 Taghkanic's rockborn child Dares gloriously the dangerous leap. **1913** W. B. Yeats in *Brit. Rev.* Apr. 89, I have kept my faith though faith was tried To that rock-born, rock-wandering foot. **1937** De la Mare & Jones *This year: Next Year* 12/2 The lovely sirens sing.. in their rock-bound solitude. **1978** *Amer. Poetry Rev.* Nov./Dec. 20/3 Along the stormy, rockbound Ligurian coast. **1920** W. B. Yeats in *Dial* Nov. 462 She seemed to have grown clean and sweet Like any rock-bred, sea borne bird. **1941** L. B. Lyon *Tomorrow is Revealing* 22 Encounter The rock-bred wolf or risk the valley road. **1847** J. R. Lowell *Summer Storm* in *Poems* 2nd Ser. 66 Like the toothless sea mumbling A rock-bristled shore. **1933** *Burlington Mag.* Nov. 237/1 The paintings in the rock-cut Chapels of Cappadocia. **1979** *London Rev. Bks.* 25 Oct. 14/2 (Advt.), Two hundred years ago.. Buddhist rock-cut shrines, the mosques of Moslems,..were all but unknown to Europeans. **1845** E. A. Poe in *Graham's Mag.* Dec. 251/1 No billow breaking into foam Upon the rock-girt shore of Time. **1929** C. E. Robinson *Hist. Greece* vi. 63 One great advantage indeed the Attic folk possessed in the admirable rock-guarded harbours adjacent to their capital. **1923** D. H. Lawrence *Birds, Beasts & Flowers* 41 A rock-living, sweet-fleshed sea-anemone. **1913** W. B. Yeats in *Brit. Rev.* Apr. 87 Rock-nurtured Aoife took a pin. **1913** W. de la Mare *Peacock Pie* 64, I long to watch the sea-mew wheel Back to her rock-perched mate. **1890** *Congress. Rec.* 7 June 5802/1, Every rock-rooted advocate of the gold standard is in favor of [this provision]. **1930** W. B. Yeats *Wild Apples* 1 Unsheltered by steading, Rock-rooted and grown, A great tree of Erin, It stands up alone. **1894** Kipling *Seven Seas* (1896) 131 Thou hast not toiled at the fishing..Nor worked the war-boats outward through the rush of the rock-staked seas.

b. *rock-arched, -browed, -chested, -floored, -walled, -wombed* (later example).

1833 J. G. Whittier *Poet. Wks.* (1898) 559/2 Through rock-arched Winooski the salmon leaps free. **1944** Blunden *Shells by Stream* 19 Above the rock-browed shag-haired weir. **1939** Dylan Thomas *Map of Love* 4 If the dead starve, their stomachs turn to tumble An upright man in the antipodes Or spray-based and rock-chested sea. **1905** W. M. Davis in *Jrnl. Geol.* XIII. 388 The initial relief will be extinguished even under the slow processes of desert erosion, and there will appear instead large, rock-floored plains sloping toward large waste-floored plains. **1879** J. G. Whittier *Poet. Wks.* (1898) 257/1 Church that..Saw within the rock-walled bay Treville's lilied pennons play. **1954** W. Faulkner *Fable* 260 The rock-wombed powder magazines under the Gates of Hercules.

c. *rock-footed, -hard, -solid, -steady, -still, -white*; also *rock-blackness.*

1968 R. P. Warren *Incarnations* (1970) 11 The moon, eastward and over The ridge and rock-blackness, rears. **1911** Beerbohm *Zuleika D.* xxii. 317 Sole and splendid survivor he stood, rock-footed, before her. **1935** 'L. Luard' *Conquering Seas* v. 69 Plenty of rock-hard, shelf cod. **1978** S. Sheldon *Bloodline* xxii. 250 The man was fully aroused now, rock-hard. **1972** *Ulster* (Sunday Times Insight Team) xvi. 273 They had seen their support in the area—once rock-solid—steadily and severely eroded. **1976** A. Price *War Game* I. ix. 175 He'll never sit for this seat... It's rock-solid Conservative. **1928** *Outlook* 26 May 650/1 Consols were rock-steady at 112. **1976** J. Wainwright *Who goes Next?* 151 The killer held the rifle rock-steady. **1976** J. B. Hilton *Gamekeeper's Gallows* ii. 20 He cocked his eye up to the pressure-dial. The needle was rock still, not even trembling. **1916** Blunden *Pastorals* 21 Through the bindweed's rock-white mesh.

9. a. rock bar *Physical Geogr.* = *riegel; **rock biscuit** (earlier example); **rock bit** *Oil Industry*, a drilling bit for use in hard formations; **rock bolt** *Mining*, a tensioned rod passing through a bed of rock and anchoring it to the body of rock behind; so **rock bolting**, the practice or technique of using rock bolts; **rock-bottom**, substitute for def.: bed-rock; also *fig.*, the fundamental or lowest possible level, nadir (see also quot. 1866); also *attrib.* or as *adj.*, lowest possible, unbeatable (of prices, etc.); fundamental, firmly grounded, honest, sound; (earlier and later examples); **rock-bun** (earlier example); **rock cake** (earlier example); **rock candy** (earlier and later examples); also in *Big Rock Candy Mountain(s)*, a song about a mythical earthly paradise, used allusively in sense 'utopia'; **rock climb**, the ascent of a rock-face; also as *v. intr.*; **rock coal** *U.S.*, anthracite; **rock creep,** the creep (*CREEP *sb.* 7a) of rock, boulders, etc.; **rock-crusher,** (*a*) a machine used to break down rocks; (*b*) *fig.* in *Bridge*, a superlative hand; also *attrib.*; **rock-dust** *N. Amer.*, pulverized stone used to prevent explosions in coal mines; so **rock-dusting** *vbl. sb.*; hence **rock-dust** *v. trans.*, to treat (a mine) with pulverized stone; **rock-duster** (see quot. 1975); **rock-face,** a vertical expanse of natural rock; also *transf.* and *fig.*; also **rock-faced** *a.*; **rockfall,** the descent of loose rocks; a mass of fallen rock; **rock fan** *Physical Geogr.*, an eroded rock surface similar in shape to an alluvial fan, with a convex profile in transverse section; **rock fence** chiefly *Southern U.S.*, a stone wall; **rock-fill** *Engin.*, large rock fragments used to form the bulk of the material of a dam; freq. *attrib.*; **rock-flour,** substitute for def.: finely powdered rock, esp. that formed as a result of glacial erosion; (further examples); **rock-garden** (later example); so **rock-gardener; rock glacier,** a large mass of rock debris, in some cases mingled with ice, which moves gradually downhill in the manner of a glacier; **rock gong** *Archæol.* (see quots.); **rock happy** *U.S. Mil. slang*, mentally disturbed through serving too long on a (Pacific) island; **rock-hog,** a labourer engaged in tunnelling through rock; **rock hole,** (*a*) a tunnel; (*b*) *Austral.*, a natural depression in a rock that catches water; **rock hound** *colloq.* (orig. *U.S.*), (*a*) a geologist; (*b*) an amateur mineralogist; hence **rock-hounding** *vbl. sb.*, the hobby or activity of an amateur mineralogist; **rock-house,** (*a*) a house built of stone or quarried rock; (*b*) a shady place under overhanging rocks providing a suitable habitat for ferns; **rock mechanics,** the branch of science and engineering concerned with the mechanical properties and behaviour of rock; **rock of ages** *Rhyming slang*, wages; **rock-peg** *Mountaineering*, a nail-like device hammered into rock to assist climbing; **rock phosphate,** a sedimentary rock containing phosphates in high proportion; phosphorite; **rock pile** *U.S. slang*, (*a*) a heap of stones; (*b*) a jail or prison, in allusion to the convict's task of breaking stones; also *transf.* and *fig.*; **rock pitch** *Mountaineering*, an expanse of rock between belay points; **rock piton** *Mountaineering*, a piton used to assist climbing of rock; **rock river** = *rock glacier* above; **rock scorpion** (earlier and later examples); **rock-slide** orig. *U.S.*, a slippage of rock; a rough mass of rock that has subsided thus; also *fig.*; **rocksman** *Sc.* = ROCKMAN 1; **rock stream** = *rock glacier* above; **rock sugar** (later example); **rock waste,** fragments of rock produced by weathering; **rock well,** an oil well drilled through superficial deposits of clay, sand, or the like into underlying rock; **rock wool,** a material such as limestone, slag, or the like, made into the form of a fine, matted fibre, esp. for use in thermal insulation or soundproofing.

1912 W. H. HOBBS *Earth Features* xxvi. 377 When the backward grades upon the valley floor are especially steep, the rock step becomes a rock bar, or riegel, of which nearly every Alpine valley has its example. **1954, 1957** [see *RIEGEL]. **1963** D. W. & E. E. HUMPHRIES tr. *Termier's Erosion & Sedimentation* v. 121 Special characteristics such as cirques..and rock bars can always be recognized. **1861** MRS. BEETON *Bk. Househ. Managem.* 852 (*heading*) Rock biscuits. **1920** *Engin. & Mining Jrnl.* 7 Feb. 404/1 The invention and development of rotary rock bits lagged behind the introduction and successful application of the rotary method of drilling. **1974** R. D. GRACE in P. L. Moore et al. *Drilling Practices Man.* iv. 66 Rock bits should be economical in the shale. **1955** L. A. PANEK in *Rep. Investigations U.S. Bureau of Mines* (1956) No. 5154. 1 The practice of roof bolting or rock bolting to stabilize rock surrounding underground excavations has increased..within a few years. **1957** *Q. Colorado School of Mines* July 235 Because of their increasingly extensive use in non-coal mines, we prefer to call these devices 'rock' rather than 'roof' bolts and will refer to them as such. **1973** L. J. THOMAS *Introd. Mining* viii. 310 Rock bolts, sometimes called roof bolts, are the first line of defence in many mining and civil engineering applications. [**1856** 'OLD COLONIST' *How to Farm & Settle in Austral.* 56 This lowest bottom, 'the rock' as it is emphatically termed, in reference to its character as a bar to further digging for gold.] **1866** *Oregon State Jrnl.* 24 Nov. 2/2 A sound democrat, or 'rock bottom', never shrinks from the requirements of his master. **1890** in Barrère & Leland *Dict. Slang* II. 183/1 Other freight wars, covering much less territory than the present, have gone to rock bottom before any attempt has been made to restore rates. **1902** W. N. HARBEN *Abner Daniel* 273 See here, I've got a rock-bottom proposal to make to your people. **1904** —— *Georgians* 200 Now cool off, an' let's git down to rock-bottom. **1923** D. L. SAYERS *Whose Body?* vii. 167 There aren't many men who wouldn't be nice—to her, and even then, if they aren't rock-bottom she can see through them. **1930** *Sat. Even. Post* 26 July 14/1 'Pay you?.. How much, Angelo?' 'The rock bottom is half a million.' **1935** H. EDIB *Clown & his Daughter* xlv. 258 By the time she had touched the rock-bottom of misery she had also reached a decision. **1955** D. DAVIE *Articulate Energy* vii. 69 We are sobered and shocked when the mood reaches rock-bottom. **1977** *Belfast Tel.* 19 Jan. 7/8 Builders engaged in this work were rapidly reaching 'rock bottom'. **1980** *Daily Tel.* 16 Jan. 23/4 In this way, the service can be offered at rock-bottom prices. **1889** J. WHITEHEAD *Steward's Handbk.* IV. 420/2 *Rock buns*, rough rocky looking cakes made of ¾ lb. each butter, sugar and currants, [etc.]. **1868** M. JEWRY *Warne's Model Cookery* 613/1 *Rock cakes*,..butter..flour..sugar..lemon..eggs..brandy. **1723** J. NOTT *Cook's & Confectioner's Dict.* sig. U6, *To candy Nutmegs*... Pour your Candy to them,..set them in a warm Place for about three Weeks, and they will be of a Rock Candy. **1906** M. P. W. LOCKE (*song-title*) Big Rock Candy Mountains. *Ibid.*, Come to the Big Rock Candy Mountains, And I'll show you the bees and the cigarette trees And the soda water fountains. **1930** G. MILBURN *Hobo's Hornbk.* 61 To homeguards 'The Big Rock Candy Mountains' may appear a nonsense song, but to all pied pipers in on the know it is an amusing exaggeration of the ghost stories used [by jockers] in recruiting kids. *Ibid.*, Said the bum to the son, 'O, will you come To the Big Rock Candy Mountains.' **1949** C. HIMES *Black on Black* (1973) 278 He set up all the boys in the neighbourhood to peanut brittle and icecream and rock candy. **1961** *Life Treas. Amer. Folklore* 294 The Hobo Special climbs Big Rock Candy Mountain. **1975** *Daily Colonist* (Victoria, B.C.) 16 Apr. 4/4 The goal is their 20th century version of the big rock candy mountain. **1895** W. M. CONWAY *Alps from End to End* 402/2 (Index), Rock Climbs, Where to find. **1929** F. S. SMYTHE *Climbs & Ski Runs* iii. 14 My first rock climb was the Little Gully. **1934** WEBSTER, Rock climb *v.* **1960** *Guardian* 11 July 1/4 He had intended to rock-climb with a companion. **1976** G. MOFFAT *Over Sea to Death* v. 52 She would be even happier were she to reach the top by way of a rock climb. **1858** *Southern Lit. Messenger* XXVI. 189/2 Ef thar had bin..a fier-plais instid uv a great to burn rock cole, the thing would uv bin kumpleat. **1913** O. A. ROTHERT *Hist. Muhlenberg County* 389 The early blacksmiths called this fuel 'rock coal', thus distinguishing it from charcoal. **1938** C. F. S. SHARPE *Landslides* iii. 31 Rock-creep.—It is sometimes observed that although creeping masses of rock have moved many feet their original relation to the bedrock can still be recognized. **1960** [see *CREEP *sb.* 7a]. **1968** R. W. FAIRBRIDGE *Encycl. Geomorphol.* 275/2 Such movement of rock debris induced by gravity as talus creep, rock creep, and debris slides all transport rock fragments to lower elevations. **1897** Rock-crusher [see sense 7c in Dict.]. **1952** I. MACLEOD *Bridge* iv. 39 The Two Club bid..has the double advantage of freeing the other bids of Two of a suit for specialized use, and coping with the rockcrusher hands which do not qualify for a Strong Two opening. **1965** *Times* 9 Jan. 9/7 Her bidding was cautious to a degree, requiring a positive rock crusher for anything above the level of one. **1973** *Country Life* 24 May 1503/1 A first-class collection of hands... 5 [Clubs]..shows a rock-crusher, asking partner to choose the suit. **1938** *Richmond* (Va.) *Times-Dispatch* 7 Nov. 6/2 Sprinkling of the rock-dust through the mines allays the highly explosive coal dust. *Ibid.*, The Bureau of Mines has a new argument in support of its plea that all coal mines be rock-dusted to prevent explosions. **1947** *Sun* (Baltimore) 27 Mar. 1/2 Reports of the State Inspection said the mine was 'not adequately rock-dusted'. **1977** *Transatlantic Rev.* LX. 80 Inside, [there is] the rockdust rumble of grinding teeth, molar on molar. **1975** *Publ. Amer. Dial. Soc. 1973* LIX. 48 *Rock duster*,..1, a mechanical blower, often caterpillar track or train wheel mounted, which forces rock dust against the dangerously dusty areas of the mine... 2, a worker in charge of distributing rock dust throughout the mine, by hand or machine. **1926** *Daily Colonist* (Victoria, B.C.) 20 July 12/4 By rock dusting is meant the spreading of incombustible dust throughout a mine in sufficient amount to cool and extinguish the flame of an incipient explosion. **1932** *Durant* (Okla.) *Daily Democrat* 10 Mar. 4/5 By rock dusting, a practice made mandatory by the 1929 legislature, this coal dust is mixed with an equal amount of rock dust, the latter lowering the ignition point of the mixture. **1938** *Richmond* (Va.) *Times-Dispatch* 7 Nov. 6/2 Rock-dusting also is advocated as a means of increasing visibility in the mines and preventing minor accidents. **1855** Rock-face [see sense 6a in Dict.]. **1931** C. DAY LEWIS *Coll. Poems* (1935) 76 As one who wanders into old workings Dazed by the noonday, desiring coolness, Has found retreat barred by fall of rockface. **1940** *Chambers's Techn. Dict.* 728/2 *Rockface*, (*Masonry*) the form of face given to a building-stone which has been quarry-faced. **1968** *Amer. Speech 1967* XLII. 295 *Rock-face stone*,..slabs of stone sawed on the top and bottom surface (up to five surfaces), which are then placed in a machine exerting pressure and cracking the stone. This leaves a pleasing rough surface toward the outside. **1972** *Times* 29 Nov. 28/8 (Advt.), The..appeal is to the younger person who really wants a vital and interesting job as a change agent at the 'rock face'. **1944** K. LEVIS in Murdoch & Drake-Brockman *Austral. Short Stories* (1951) 427 The men were separated in bunches cut off by rock-faced water-beds. **1970** H. BRAUN *Parish Churches* xviii. 216 The face of the stone is left 'rock-faced' and not worked at all except along its margins. **1930** *Times Educ. Suppl.* 24 May p. i/2 Crossing the débris of a huge rockfall which apparently came down recently. **1967** M. J. COE *Ecol. Alpine Zone Mt. Kenya* 87 The Tarn..is enclosed at its lower edge by the rock fall. **1971** *World Archaeol.* III. 150 The rockfall layers at Puntutjarpa were of considerable archaeological interest. **1900** W. M. DAVIS in *Bull. Geol. Soc. Amer.* XI. 210 Near the base of the mountain front nearly all of the ravines broaden and their floors become distinctly convex, thus imitating the form well known in alluvial fans, though rarely matched in an eroded surface of solid rock. These convex floors will be called rock fans. **1932** *Amer. Jrnl. Sci.* CCXXIII. 392 The alluvial fan is the expression of that form where deposition alone has occurred, or where considerable deposition has accompanied erosion of bedrock. The 'rock fan'..is the same form..where erosion has exceeded deposition. *Ibid.* 393 Rock fans must be carved by streams, and cannot be produced by simple weathering back of the mountain front. **1968** R. W. FAIRBRIDGE *Encycl. Geomorphol.* 965/1 The rock fans described range in area from several acres when steep, 20–26°, to one or more square miles when gentle, ½–7°. **1970** R. J. SMALL *Study of Landforms* ix. 310 The existence of rock fans.. has been disputed by many geomorphologists, who have claimed that such fans are in reality no more than the alluvial fans that they are supposed to resemble so closely. **1896** *Dial. Notes* I. 423 *Rock fence*, a stone wall. **1949** H. KURATH *Word Geogr. Eastern U.S.* 31/2 For a fence built of loose stone the North Midland uses *stone fence* as against the Northern *stone wall* and the Southern *rock fence*. **1974** *Amer. Speech 1971* XLVI. 60 *Rock fence* appears in southern Illinois (a South Midland settlement area) as expected. **1911** *Sci. Amer.* 17 June 592 (*caption*) Characteristic rockfill across a creek. **1960** *Times* 7 Mar. 8/3 It is hoped..to save the Temples from inundation by means of an earth and rock-fill dam. **1969** E. W. MORSE *Fur Trade Canoe Routes* II. v. 55 The dam and its rockfill now obscure the upper portion of the portage. **1976** *National Observer* (U.S.) 19 June 4/1 The Interior Department's Bureau of Reclamation has been building dams, including 250 out of rock-fill and earth. **1937** *Geogr. Jrnl.* LXXXIX. 43 Great angular blocks of rock are embedded in a jumble of fragments from the size of dust upwards, it is, in fact, a loose breccia of large pieces associated with smaller ones grading down to the finest rock-flour. **1963** G. L. PICKARD *Descriptive Physical Oceanogr.* iii. 23 In fjords fed by rivers from glaciers, the surface low-salinity layer may be a milky white from the finely divided 'rock flour'. **1975** J. G. EVANS *Environment Early Man Brit. Isles* ii. 44 A prerequisite of the formation of wind-blown deposits is a dry land surface from which frost-shattered rock flour can be whipped up and transported. **1962** R. PAGE *Education of Gardener* viii. 231 By the end of the nineteenth century rock-gardens had become a lasting feature of British gardens. **1942** E. WAUGH *Put out More Flags* iii. 172 The word 'Colonel' for Basil had connoted an elderly rock-gardener. **1905** W. CROSS *Silverton Folio* (U.S. Geol. Survey. Geol. Atlas of U.S. No. 120) 25/2 All the accumulations..just described impress one with the sense of motion.. So noticeable was this that in the field they were spoken of as 'rock-glaciers' and upon the map receive the name 'rock streams'. **1910** S. R. CAPPS in *Jrnl. Geol.* XVIII. 360 The special agents of degradation with which I wish to deal at present..I have called rock glaciers... In material the rock glaciers are composed of angular talus. **1954** W. D. THORNBURY *Princ. Geomorphol.* iv. 85 Kesseli concluded that the rock glaciers of the Sierra Nevada were essentially fossil glaciers. **1968** R. W. FAIRBRIDGE *Encycl. Geomorphol.* 711/1 If the surface of the ice is densely covered with blocks, one may speak of a rock glacier, but, in North America, 'rock glacier' does not necessarily involve ice. **1955** B. E. B. FAGG in *3rd Pan-Afr. Congr. Prehist.* (1957) xlvii. 310 Very extensive exploration of the granite hills revealed the existence of large numbers of these hammered rocks, which I think can best be described as rock gongs. They consist of huge natural spalls or exfoliations of rock which happen to rest or be wedged in a position favourable to the production of musical notes. **1959** *S. Afr. Archaeol. Bull.* XIV. 112/2 Rock gongs should be described as 'ringing rocks' or 'sounding stones'. **1961** K. P. WACHSMANN in A. Baines *Mus. Instruments through Ages* i. 30 Recent studies have revealed many instances of slabs of rock being used as if they were drums. These 'rock gongs', as their discoverers called them, occur in Africa north of the equator, in Europe, and in Asia. **1945** *Yank* 15 June 2/2 The set routine can drive a man nuts wherever he is... Out here [*sc.* the Marianas] the expression is rock happy... In the Pacific there is no escape from places like Kwajalein. **1946** *Richmond* (Va.) *Times-Dispatch* 9 May 12/1 GI's..were growing rock happy from too long internment on a coral island. **1909** *Chambers's Jrnl.* Dec. 828/2 The rock-hogs had not proceeded far before they pierced a large pocket. **1954** V. LYSENKO *Yellow Boots* 190 They spoke of dynamite and flying rock responsible for the death of many a 'rock-hog'. **1895** M. PEMBERTON *Impregnable City* II. xiv. 285 Darkness of the rock-hole. **1936** I. L. IDRIESS *Cattle King* iv. 30 He learned probabilities and signs by means of which waterholes may be located in apparently dry creeks, and in rock-holes in valley or gorge. **1944** *Living off Land* iii. 50 Locating water in the form of soaks, springs and rock-holes. **1922** *Daily Ardmoreite* (Ardmore, Okla.) 10 Jan. 6/2 (*heading*) Interesting tale of work in Africa told by Texas rock hound. **1940** *Fortune* Mar. 83 Drillers consider themselves a superior breed, look with scorn upon 'rockhounds' (geologists), 'chemicos,' pipemen, roughnecks, etc. **1949** *Natural Hist.* LVIII. 220/1 There are numerous semiprecious stones to interest the 'rock hound'. **1962** E. LUCIA *Klondike Kate* viii. 175 Kate was central Oregon's first serious rock hound, of which there are thousands today. **1970** *Nature* 4 Apr. 45/2 Its bias is naturally towards the United States, where 'rock hounds' and geological societies are much more common than in the United Kingdom. **1979** *N.Y. Times Mag.* 30 Sept. 88/2 (Advt.), Exclusive metal ratchet device permits shovel to be locked into any position... A necessity, too, for sportsmen,..fishermen, hikers, rockhounds. **1949** *Desert Mag.* June 31/1 In all my rockhounding I have never seen sand fly so fast. **1973** *Daily Tel.* 25 Aug. 16/1 The objects of his search might be coins, lost jewellery, Victorian ceramics, or if he feels like a change a spot of rockhounding—searching for semi-precious stones—or gold-panning in Scotland. **1976** *Globe & Mail* (Toronto) 3 July 35 (*heading*) Go rockhounding or trail riding, for everything goes in Ontario. **1818** E. P. FORDHAM *Jrnl.* 26 Jan. in *Personal Narr.*

Trav. (1906) 154 They had a strong rock house among the hills. **1883** E. A. Smith *Rep. Geol. Survey Alabama 1881–82* 438 Underneath the overhanging cliffs, or 'rock houses', as they are termed, grow abundantly some of our rarest and most beautiful ferns. **1889** *Harper's Mag.* Dec. 120/1 Thet thar rock house o' his'n, which he hev quayried the rock an' put up hisse'f, I 'low it's the beatenes' house in creation. **1901** C. Mohr *Plant Life Alabama* 17 The..fern, *Trichomanes petersii*,..with others like it hidden in the dark recesses of rocky defiles and the so-called 'rock houses'. **1948** E. N. Dick *Dixie Frontier* 26 Along the rivers in certain places the rocks projected out over the banks. Hunters and early settlers sometimes lived in the shelter of these for months. They were known as rock houses. **1956** *Q. Colorado School of Mines* LI. iii. (*title-page*) Symposium on rock mechanics. Papers and discussion from the first annual symposium on rock mechanics. **1966** *McGraw-Hill Encycl. Sci. & Technol.* XI. 599/2 An understanding of rock mechanics is essential to elucidate the processes which mold the face of the earth. **1977** A. Hallam *Planet Earth* 104/2 The engineering geologist works with experts in the related fields of soil mechanics and rock mechanics. **1937** Partridge *Dict. Slang* 702/2 *Rock of ages*, wages. **1974** P. Wright *Lang. Brit. Industry* x. 89 If there's no *rock of ages* (wages), there may well be a *bull an' cow* (row). **1971** C. Bonington *Annapurna South Face* x. 118 He put in a couple of ice-screws, then, having run out of these, hammered in ordinary rock-pegs, which are much shorter than ice-screws and not nearly as secure. **1868** *Chem. News* 13 Nov. 238/2 (*heading*) Rock phosphates. **1900** [see *phosphatizing* vbl. sb. s.v. *phosphatize *v.*]. **1936** [see *phosphate 1 b]. **1949** *Thorpe's Dict. Appl. Chem.* (ed. 4) IX. 482 Sedimentary rock phosphate, or phosphorite, occurs in two forms: in thick beds, usually of high phosphatic content; and in layers of nodules, commonly of lower phosphatic grade. **1965** G. J. Williams *Econ. Geol. N.Z.* xvi. 250/2 Free went on to suggest the possibility of fusing rock-phosphate with greensands and dolomite to give a mixed fertilizer. **1888** *Congress. Rec.* 1 May 3571/1 If this were a police court, the Senator from Indiana would be sent to the rock-pile for being drunk and disorderly. **1927** K. Eubank *Horse & Buggy Days* 127 We were..given 30 days on the rock pile or the privilege of leaving town on the first rattler out, which took us into Memphis. **1945** *Seafarers' Log* 13 Apr. 6/3 Had one of the Bull Line rock piles [*i.e.* a ship on board which work is hard] in. **1945** L. Shelly *Jive Talk Dict.* 16/2 *Rockpile*, a very tall building. **1947** *Sat. Even. Post* 23 Oct. 132/3 Everybody was dead-pan and silent. But disciplined—like convicts on a rock pile. **1949** W. Stevens *Let.* 12 Dec. (1967) 659 We call the office the rockpile, yet so large a rockpile is a good deal more than that. **1970** C. Major *Dict. Afro-Amer. Slang* 98 *Rock pile*, any tall building. **1929** Rock pitch [see *ice-ridge* s.v. *ice *sb.* 7 b]. **1955** [see *etrier]. **1934** *Canad. Alpine Jrnl.* XXII. 128 These analogs of rock pitons..have now definitely passed their test for usefulness. **1972** D. Haston *In High Places* i. 12 It should be noted that ice overhangs can be tackled on ice-pitons in the same way as rock overhangs on rock-pitons. **1920** *Natural Hist.* XX. 172/1 In rate of flow these rock rivers are probably slower than the ice rivers, or glaciers. **1954** W. D. Thornbury *Princ. Geomorphol.* iv. 85 Striking examples of rock glaciers, rock streams, or rock rivers have been described..in the Sierra Nevada of California. **1818** 'A. Burton' *Adventures J. Newcome* iv. 239 Fagged he was in every limb, And the Rock Scorpions laughed at him. **1916** 'Taffrail' *Pincher Martin* viii. 145 They arrived at Gibraltar, where the ships went alongside the Mole..to take in coal. But here..the fuel was carried on board in small baskets on the backs of nondescript, garlic-scented aliens known as 'rock scorpions'. **1976** *Daily Colonist* (Victoria, B.C.) 10 June 4/1 The 29,000 Gibraltarians—affectionately known to generations of British seafarers as Rockscorpions—have been eyeing Madrid hopefully. **1851** H. Melville *Moby Dick* II. xiv. 123 Some mossy rock-slide from the Patagonian cliffs. **1921** *Daily Colonist* (Victoria, B.C.) 29 Mar. 13/5 Owing to a big rockslide west of Terrace, B.C., the G.T.P. passenger train from Prince Rupert is now twenty-four hours late. **1959** R. Campbell *I would do It Again* xviii. 127 We took saddle horses across the flat as far as the mountain slope, which was covered by a rockslide. **1970** R. Lowell *Notebk.* 203 Is it my imagination or..Pound's Cantos lost in the rockslide of history? **1971** *Islander* (Victoria, B.C.) 13 June 2/4 The pica and ground squirrel may be seen around the rock slides on the edge of the meadow. **1980** *Beautiful Brit. Columbia* Summer 33 The main trail to Eva Lake..across rock slides. **1852** W. Macgillivray *Hist. Brit. Birds* V. 434 The dexterity of these rocksmen is truly astonishing. **1905** Rock stream [see *rock glacier* above]. **1909** *Prof. Papers U.S. Geol. Survey* No. 67. 31 The name 'rock stream', which has been found a convenient descriptive term, was suggested by the peculiar streamlike appearance of the deposits, which look as if they had moved down the cirques or valleys after the manner of glaciers. **1964** W. C. Putnam *Geol.* x. 238/1 (*caption*) A rock stream or rock glacier is composed of frost- and ice-shattered rock filled with interstitial ice which slowly moves downslope. **1970** R. J. Small *Study of Landforms* x. 333 Fossil rock streams exist in many temperate lands today. **1889** J. Whitehead *Steward's Handbk.* iv. 420/2 *Rock sugar*,..candy rock work used to build up ornamental pieces of confectionery and to sell as sponge candy. **1907** *Bull. Geol. Soc. Amer.* XVIII. 358 If the moist epoch last long, the mountains of arid countries, such as Persia,..must lose their naked character and become well shrouded with rock waste. **1946** F. E. Zeuner *Dating Past* vii. 220 This cave, the Grotta Gualtari..was completely sealed by rock-waste. **1865** A. Gesner *Pract. Treat. Coal, Petroleum, & Other Distilled Oils* (ed. 2) ii. 40 The rock wells, as they are termed, are those deeper borings which resemble those of Pennsylvania. **1867** *Ure's Dict. Arts* (ed. 6) III. 404 The rock-wells are of two characters, namely, 'pumping' and 'flowing'. **1928** E. R. Powell *U.S. Pat.* 1,656,828 2/1 It is to be understood that so-called rock wool is made directly from the rock which contains only the slight trace of sulphur; while so-called mineral wool is made from the slag which contains the higher percentages of sulphur. **1936** [see *plasterboard]. **1959** *House & Garden* Dec.–Jan. 57 The outer walls of the house are constructed of two brick skins with a cavity between filled with rock wool for insulation. **1975** G. J. King *Audio Handbk.* vi. 136 A material..which possesses a high value of acoustical absorbitivity; some commonly used materials being rockwool..and polyurethane foam.

b. rock borer, for 'the family *Petricolidæ*' substitute 'the superfamily Saxicavacea'; (later examples); **rock chuck,** the North American yellow-bellied marmot, *Marmota flaviventris*; **rock crab** (earlier example); **rock goat** (earlier and later examples); **rock hyrax** = *rock rabbit* (*a*), *dassie 1; **rock lizard,** an African or Australian dragon lizard belonging to the family Agamidæ; (see also sense 9 a in Dict.); **rock lobster,** esp. the marine crayfish, *Palinurus vulgaris*; (later examples); **rock python,** one of several large snakes of the family Boidæ, esp. the African *Python sebæ*; **rock rabbit,** substitute for def.: a hyrax belonging to the genus *Procavia* or *Dendrohyrax*, esp. the African *P. capensis*; (earlier and later examples); (*b*) = *pika; **rock rat,** (*c*) a South American rodent, *Aconæmys fuscus*; (*d*) an Australian thick-tailed rat belonging to the genus *Zyzomys*; **rock scorpion,** a southern African scorpion, *Hadogenes lawrencei*; (see also sense 9 a); **rock worm,** add def.: a marine polychæte worm belonging to the family Eunicidæ; (later examples).

1928 Russell & Yonge *Seas* vi. 148 The largest and most efficient rock borers are bivalve Molluscs. **1971** *Oxf. Bk. Invertebr.* 86/1 *Hiatella* is a rock-borer (if the rock is soft enough). **1913** *Outing* Jan. 451 (*caption*) Not a wood-chuck, but a 'rockchuck'. **1947** B. A. De Voto *Across Wide Missouri* 162 Robes..were made from..beaver,..wolf, or even rockchuck. **1968** *National Observer* (U.S.) 22 July 6/5 Bones of such small mammals as the rock chuck, rock squirrel, northern pocket gopher, and pygmy rabbit, were found in the Altithermal strata. **1837** J. L. Williams *Territory of Florida* 105 The Rock Crab is common on the Atlantic coast. **1607** Topsell *Foure-f. Beasts* 244 (*heading*) The Helvetian Alpian wilde or Rocke-Goat. **1820** J. Campbell *Trav. S. Afr.* I. ii. 29 The rock-goat..had found its way to a place, which no human foot had ever yet trod. **1954** G. Durrell *Bafut Beagles* iii. 59 'Rock hyrax.'.. 'Yes. How you de call um for Bafut?' 'Here we call um N'eer.' **1966** C. Sweeney *Scurrying Bush* iii. 36 Although the rock hyrax is only about sixteen inches long and weighs little more than eight pounds when adult, it is not an animal to trifle with. **1937** *Discovery* May 137/2 The Rock Lizard can be met with all over the [Nullarbor] plains. **1947** J. Stevenson-Hamilton *Wild Life S. Afr.* xxxv. 318 There are nine species of so-called Rock Lizards (*Agama*) known as koggelmannetjies in South Africa. **1928** Russell & Yonge *Seas* xiv. 316 The handsome Spiny or Rock Lobster or Crawfish..differs from the lobster in its larger size. **1953** *Sun* (Baltimore) 9 Sept. 10/7 The name of the South African crawfish was changed by law to 'rock lobster'. **1961** [see *crawfish *sb.* 1 b]. **1969** *N.Z. News* 17 Dec. 5/3 Under the [new] regulations crayfish are referred to as rock lobster. The change is necessary to promote the labelling of crayfish as rock lobster in marketing in overseas countries. **1974** *Times* 9 Dec. 12/4 A notice outside advertised baby rock lobster tails with two veg. **1910** R. L. Ditmars *Reptiles of World* iv. 227 Another big serpent is the African Rock Python. **1934** A. Russell *Tramp-Royal in Wild Austral.* xxxviii. 251 We rode almost on top of a rock python one day... He was ten feet long. **1965** R. & D. Morris *Men & Snakes* i. 16 Bushmen will eat snakes when available and especially prize the large rock python. **1840** B. Shaw *Memorials S. Afr.* xii. 147 There were numerous traces of rock rabbits. **1846** [see *dassy]. **1878** J. H. Beadle *Western Wilds* 457 The rock rabbits..ran from covert to covert with a peculiar low moaning cry. **1927** A. Philip *Painted Cliff* 69 Rock-rabbits shrilled, darting amongst the rubble. **1931, 1952** [see *dassie 1]. **1962** *Field, Horse & Rodeo* (Calgary) Nov. 15/3 The Pika (or Rock Rabbit) spends most of the daylight hours cutting and gathering vegetation. **1972** J. McClure *Caterpillar Cop* iv. 46 Danny was going up and down those stairs like a rock rabbit. **1976** T. Walker *Spatsizi* vii. 68 A rock rabbit had been busy storing dried leaves and grasses for winter. **1964** E. P. Walker et al. *Mammals of World* II. 1045/2 Rock rats are active beneath the snow in winter. **1970** W. D. L. Ride *Guide Native Mammals Austral.* ix. 148 Adults of these rock-rats are easily recognized because they have thick tails. **1971** L. H. Matthews *Life Mammals* II. vii. 216 The rock rat, *Aconæmys fuscus*, the only species of the genus, with short, hairy, but untufted tail is about the size of a common rat. **1976** *Nature* 24 June 639/2 Many surveys produce novelties; animals considered very rare or extinct are discovered in some numbers (for example..the rock rat, *Zyzomys woodwardi*). **1789** W. Paterson *Narr. Four Journeys Country of Hottentots* 165 The Black, or Rock Scorpion, is nearly as venomous as any of the serpent tribe. **1973** *Stand. Encycl. S. Afr.* IX. 544/2 The rock-scorpion, *Hadogenes*, is extraordinarily flattened, being adapted for living in narrow fissures between rocks. **1963** R. P. Dales *Annelids* 14 Some relatives of the eunicid rockworms..are surprisingly like earthworms. **1971** *Oxf. Bk. Invertebr.* 98 The eunicids (rock worms and palolos) form a large and varied family of rock-dwellers and mud-burrowers.

c. rock duck, add: *Histrionicus histrionicus*; (later example); **rock sandpiper,** substitute for def.: the purple sandpiper, *Erolia maritima*, or a similar bird, *E. ptilocnemis*, of the Pacific coast of North America; (later examples); **rock snipe** (earlier and later examples); **rock wren,** substitute for 'see quots.': (*a*) one of several wrens belonging to the genus *Salpinctes*, found in parts of western North America; (*b*) a New Zealand wren, *Xenicus gilviventris*; (earlier and later examples).

1965 E. Richardson *Living Island* 185 The handsomest duck I have seen..the male harlequin or rock-duck. **1903** E. Coues *Key to N. Amer. Birds* (ed. 5) II. 817 Feather-leg Sandpipers. Rock Sandpipers. **1961** R. T. Peterson *Field Guide Western Birds* (ed. 2) 112 Rock Sandpiper... In winter, very similar to Purple Sandpiper of Atlantic. **1835** J. J. Audubon *Ornith. Biogr.* III. 558 Their marked predilection for rocky shores has caused them to be named 'Rock Snipes' by the gunners of our eastern coast. **1917** T. G. Pearson *Birds Amer.* I. 232 Purple Sandpiper... Other Names.—Rock Sandpiper; Rock Snipe. **1858** S. F. Baird *Birds Pacific Railway Routes* 357 Rock Wren... High central plains through the Rocky mountains. **1869** [see **cactus wren*]. **1946** D. C. Peattie *Road of Naturalist* iii. 39 The rock wrens and the canyon wrens..watered the air with rapture. **1966** R. A. Falla et al. *Field Guide Birds N.Z.* 194 Rock Wren... Habitat is distinctive, mainly open screes, moraines and fell-fields of mountains above the bushline. **1973** R. D. Symons *Where Wagon Led* I. v. 77 All around us rose the bubbling songs of the rock wrens.

d. rock beauty, substitute for def.: a small, dark brown and yellow, Caribbean reef fish, *Holacanthus tricolor*; (examples); **rock eel,** (*b*) = **rock salmon* (*c*); **rock salmon,** (*c*) a commercial name for the catfish, *Anarhichas lupus*, or a dogfish, *Scyliorhinus stellaris* or *S. caniculus*; cf. *huss; **rock skipper,** a small marine fish belonging to the family Gobiidæ, able to survive out of water for a limited time; **rock sole,** a flatfish, *Lepidopsetta bilineata*, found in the Pacific Ocean off the western coast of North America; **rock sturgeon,** add to def.: *Acipenser fulvescens*; (examples).

1892 T. D. A. Cockerell in *Bull. Inst. Jamaica* I. 9/1 Rock Beauty. Head, anterior part of the trunk, caudal and margins of the soft dorsal and anal fins yellow: the remainder brownish-black. **1959** R. P. L. Straughan *Salt-Water Aquarium in Home* iv. 85 Rock Beauties..need plenty of aeration. **1965** Mrs. L. B. Johnson *White House Diary* 3 June (1970) 281 Rock beauties, yellow about half-way back and yellow tails, and the rest of them brown. **1977** D. J. Coffey *Encycl. Aquarium Fish* 141/1 Rock Beauty... From the Caribbean, this yellow fish has a black patch that expands with age. **1969** A. Wheeler *Fishes Brit. Isles & N.-W. Europe* 46/1 The dogfish..is sold as rock eel and rock salmon. **1931** J. R. Norman *Hist. Fishes* xix. 385 It has been found convenient to market this perfectly wholesome fish [*sc.* cat-fish] under a more pleasing name, and..it is sold as 'Rock Salmon'. **1957** R. Campbell *Portugal* iv. 65 In the [London] fried-fish shops..'rock salmon'..is the trade name for shark. **1958** *Times* 18 July 7/1 Rock salmon is in fact usually catfish. **1963** [see *huss *sb.*]. **1969** A. Wheeler *Fishes Brit. Isles & N.-W. Europe* 452/2 It [*sc.* the catfish] is sold with the related species under the names rock salmon and rockfish. **1977** *Times* 8 Feb. 9/4 Rock salmon has had its name changed..by the trades description act, and is now called Huss. **1905** D. S. Jordan *Guide to Study of Fishes* II. xxix. 510 The rock-skippers..are herbivorous, with serrated teeth set loosely in their jaws. These live in rock-pools of the tropics and leap from rock to rock. **1966** C. Sweeney *Scurrying Bush* xi. 154 There are perhaps a hundred or more kinds of rock skippers in tropical oceans, all able to shuffle and wriggle along on spray-soaked rocks. The kind that I found was as goggle-eyed as any and..resembled a small seal with a frog's head, the flipper-like pectoral fins supporting the front of the body. **1965** A. J. McClane *Stand. Fishing Encycl.* 730/2 Rock sole are only occasionally taken by hook and line. **1971** *Islander* (Victoria, B.C.) 21 Mar. 2/3, I have taken in recent years..rock sole and sand sole. **1877** C. Hallock *Sportsman's Gazetteer* I. 329 Rock Sturgeon.—*Acipenser rubicundus*. This is the sturgeon of the great lakes. **1961** E. S. Herald *Living Fishes of World* 67/2 The eastern American lake or rock sturgeon has been known to reach a weight of 300 pounds.

e. rock beauty, also called *Petrocallis pyrenaica*; (examples); **rock chestnut-oak** (examples); **rock elm,** substitute for def.: one of several North American elms, esp. *Ulmus thomasii* or its timber; (earlier and later examples); **rock maple,** substitute for def.: the sugar maple, *Acer saccharum*, or its timber; (earlier and later examples); **rock melon** = Cantaloup; **rock oak** (earlier and later examples); **rock tripe** (earlier and later examples).

1870 W. Robinson *Alpine Flowers for Eng. Gardens* ii. 272 *Petrocallis Pyrenaica*—Beauty of the Rocks... A 'rock beauty!' as everybody must confess who sees its fresh light-green tufts, not more than an inch high, and cushioned snugly amidst the broken rocks. **1930** H. Correvon *Rock Garden & Alpine Plants* xii. 249 *D*[*raba*] (*Petrocallis*) *pyrenaica*. Rock Beauty. **1964** A. N. Griffith *Collins Guide to Alpines* 205 This very small genus [sc. *Petrocallis*] provides us with one charming little plant which well deserves its name of Rock Beauty. **1810** F. A. Michaux *Hist. Arbres Forestiers de l'Amérique Septentrionale* I. 23 Rock chestnut oak..seul nom donné à cette espèce dans les Etats de New-York et de Vermont. **1832** D. J. Browne *Sylva Amer.* 285 The rock chestnut oak is sometimes 3 feet in diameter, and more than 60 feet high. **1897** G. B. Sudworth *Nomencl. Arborescent Flora U.S.* 156 Chestnut Oak..[also called] Rock Chestnut Oak. **1830** *Trans. Lit. & Hist. Soc. Quebec* III. 84 The timber of this variety..is known by the name of Rock Elm. **1955** *Bush News* (Port Arthur, Ontario) Feb. 3/5 Southern Ontario..is sending..rock elm timbers to Britain. **1972** *Handbk. Hardwoods* (Forest Prod. Res. Lab.) (ed. 2) 73 Rock elm may be distinguished from other commercial elms by the small size and sparse distribution of its early wood pores. **1775** S. THAYER *Jrnl.* 30 Sept. in *Rhode Island Hist. Soc. Coll.* (1867) VI. 4 The timber [is] large and of various kinds, such as Pine, Oak, Hemlock and Rock Maple. **1949** 'J. NELSON' *Backwoods Teacher* xxvi. 265 Hi Slocum..had tapped a few rock maples he knew about—though this is not really maple syrup country. **1977** *New Yorker* 27 June 30/3, I..fell over a rock-maple chair and skinned my knee. **1980** *Early Music Gaz.* July 12/1 (Advt.), Made of impregnated rock maple and finished in dark color. **1871** V. LUSH *Jrnl.* 16 Mar. (1975) 105 Blanche bought 8 fine rock melons for 4/o... Blanche has reduced 6 of them into jam. **1882** [see *pie-melon]. **1929** [see *CANTALOUP]. **1972** J. S. GUNN in G. W. Turner *Good Austral. Eng.* iii. 60 Is there any difference at all between..rock melon/cantaloup and many other pairs? **1699** *Public Rec. Colony Connecticut* (1868) IV. 304 Running eastward three hundred rod to a rock-oak tree markt. **1949** COLLINGWOOD & BRUSH *Knowing your Trees* 224 Sometimes this tree is called rock oak or mountain oak because it grows on high, rocky slopes. **1854** MAYNE REID *Young Voyageurs* 384 Rock-tripe..was a black, hard crumply substance that nearly covered the surface of the rock, and was evidently of a vegetable nature. **1907** *St. Nicholas* July 847/1 'Rock-tripe', another lichen, has been eaten in the arctic regions in times of famine. **1952** F. MOWAT *People of Deer* 37 Sometimes she scrabbled through the drifts on hilltops and found..a handfull of rock-tripe, a kind of moss.

rock, *sb.*[3] Add: **1. b.** Phr. *rock of eye* = *rack of (the) eye* s.v. RACK *sb.*[1] 4f.

1890 BARRÈRE & LELAND *Dict. Slang* II. 183/2 *Rock of eye and rule of thumb* (tailors), refers to doing anything which requires scientific treatment by guesswork. **1957** N. SQUIRE *Theory of Bidding* xiii. 216 Honour-tricks will be counted at their normal value as in the Table of Honour-tricks, but with additions found by rock-of-eye.

2. orig. *U.S.* **a.** Musical rhythm characterized by a strong beat.

1946 MEZZROW & WOLFE *Really Blues* vii. 90 The Cotton Pickers..came on with a steady rock that was really groovy. **1952** H. SINCLAIR *Music out of Dixie* vi. 245 He played eight bars of a new introduction he had thought up and..[said] 'I want that steady rock.' **1952** R. A. WATERMAN in S. Tax *Acculturation in Americas* 217 Musical terms like 'rock' and 'swing' express ideas of rhythm foreign to European folk tradition, and stem from African concepts. **1970** P. OLIVER *Savannah Syncopators* 36 Jazz developed a different kind of rhythmic feeling with a lifting movement between adjacent beats which the jazz musician identifies as 'rock' or 'swing'.

b. = *ROCK AND ROLL. Now freq. used to encompass most modern popular music with a rocking or swinging beat. Also the last element in *Combs.*, as *acid rock, folk rock,* etc.; see *hard rock* (*c*) s.v. *HARD *a.* 22a, *PUNK ROCK, *raga rock* s.v. *RAGA 2.

1957 *Beat* Sept. 7/1 'It's the answer to Rock,' said one and all... But a new sound package of diluted Rock, Hill-Billy tunes and ersatz Blues assails our ears. **1959** *Daily Mail* 17 Feb. 4/4 *Yellow Dog Blues* played in basic style by Joe Darensbourg's band..unexpectedly popped up among the rock. **1960** M. SPARK *Ballad of Peckham Rye* (1964) iv. 58 Findlater's rooms were not given to rowdy rock but concentrated instead upon a more cultivated jive, cha-cha, and variants. **1963** J. T. STORY *Something for Nothing* v. 166 'It's only folk singing,' Albert told him. 'Well, it makes a change from all this old rock,' said Sid. **1965** *Time* 17 Sept. 102/2 Folk rock owes its origins to Bob Dylan, 24, folk music's most celebrated contemporary composer. **1968** *National Observer* (U.S.) 3 Nov. 24 It has been clear for some time that 'rock' is getting longer, more sophisticated, more ambitious, restless with chordal limitations and the three-minute format. **1969** *Britannica Bk. of Year* (U.S.) 799/1 *Acid rock*, rock 'n' roll songs whose titles or lyrics make cryptic reference to drugs. **1969** *Rolling Stone* 28 June 38/4 (Advt.), Two guitarists needed immediately... Booked for TV show in a few mos. Have material, underground & acidrock. **1972** *Saturday Night* (Toronto) Sept. 42/2 Like light shows, psychedelic posters and acid rock, it seems to have emerged first in California. **1976** *New Statesman* 17 Dec. 884/1 The whole of rock..had grown away from its roots, absorbing the influences of poetry, folk and protest music, and in the Sixties becoming central to the internal communications of a whole generation.

c. *attrib.* and *Comb.*, as *rock album, artist, band, beat, club, critic, criticism, culture, fan, festival, group, guitarist, history, idiom, lyric, movement, movie, music, musical, musician, number, opera, press, record, show, singer, singing, song, star, thing*; also *rock-dominated, -tinged* adjs.

1979 *Yale Alumni Mag.* Apr. 30/3 Many sociable Soviets turned out to be dealers on the thriving Soviet black market..interested primarily in acquiring American blue jeans.., rock albums, dollars, or chewing gum. **1973** *Black World* Nov. 45/2 Many rock and soul artists have retained their interest in..gospel music. **1968** *Listener* 13 June 774/1 There was a rock band that whooped it up all the louder, to drown the inevitable news. **1978** G. VIDAL *Kalki* vi. 154 A rock band deafened us. **1969** *Listener* 20 Feb. 251/1 They..claim to have brought 'the rock beat, the *now* sound, to the American Musical Theatre'. **1972** *Jazz & Blues* Sept. 4/2 A slashing rock beat. **1965** M. MORSE *Unattached* v. 177 A 'rock' club was started for younger teenagers. **1977** *Rolling Stone* 13 Jan. 8/3 If rock critics recognize and understand this as a problem, why don't they do something about it? **1977** *N.Y. Rev. Bks.* 14 Apr. 40/4 Mark Miller's 'review'..of recent rock criticism seriously distorts its subject. **1967** *Economist* 8 Apr. 144/1 This is politics fashioned for the young: 'the rock culture', it is being called. **1977** *Rolling Stone* 24 Mar., His full-blown, upper-register style is ingeniously contrasted with Walden's simple, melodic, rock-dominated charts. **1961** *Times* 12 Aug. 7/6 More intelligent than the majority of 'rock' fans. **1968** *Rolling Stone* 12 Oct. 1/3 'The best freaking scene ever,' said one musician. The Sky River Rock Festival and Lighter Than Air Show was not dampened by the rain that fell over Labor Day weekend. **1971** M. SMITH *Gypsy in Amber* xix. 144 I've never seen a rock festival. **1967** *Listener* 14 Sept. 350/2 Rock groups..concentrated on achieving the authentic and personal expression. **1977** *It* May 10/1 Perhaps there are also rock groups who would be prepared to perform at benefit concerts. **1977** *Gay News* 24 Mar. 28/2 His cohorts perform well too especially Ray Russell, even if he is inclined to go in for circular solos, just like a rock guitarist. **1976** *New Statesman* 17 Dec. 884/2 It is this concern with rock history which distinguishes them from others who have called for a return to the basic virtues of good ole rock-'n'roll. **1976** *Gramophone* Dec. 952/2 The Amazing Rhythm Aces, a band from Tennessee..successfully combine country, rockabilly, swing and nostalgia into the rock idiom. **1976** *Listener* 18 Nov. 645/2 Most rock lyrics are straight melodramas. **1975** *Ibid.* 18 Sept. 370/2 The rock movement saw our present crisis coming and died of shock. **1971** *It* 4–18 Nov. 19/1 The financial success of cheap rock movies. **1967** *Listener* 23 Nov. 681/3 Is there an analogy between films and rock music? **1978** *Hi-Fi News* Sept. 7 Popular and rock music benefit from this performance. **1969** L. ROXON *Rock Encycl.* 420 By the end of 1968, in spite of all the talk about rock and the new music, the big rock musical had still to be done. **1977** F. WELDON in *Winter's Tales 23* 192 Brian offers..Hugo a part in a new rock musical going on in the West End. **1968** *Listener* 4 July 18/1 Rock musicians can now sing anything that can be said by traditional forms of creative expression, and more besides. **1969** L. ROXON *Rock Encycl.* 42 There is not a rock musician working today who has not consciously or unconsciously borrowed from his [*sc.* Chuck Berry's] sound. **1957** *Sat. Rev.* (U.S.) 5 Oct. 6 You feel it in a beat—in jazz—real cool jazz or a good gutty rock number. **1969** *Newsweek* 9 June 95 It was almost inevitable that the British group The Who should write the first rock opera. **1979** *Newsday* 31 Dec. 26 Francis Coppola's dazzlingly beautiful, nightmarish Vietnam combat adventure, staged like a psychedelic rock opera, is a provocative drama flawed by a murky ending. **1977** *Zigzag* Aug. 6/2 He's one of the only rock press geezers worth reading. **1977** *Chainsaw* Sept./Oct. 7/1 The national weekly rock press do have articles on new-wave groups. **1971** B. MALAMUD *Tenants* 45 They danced to some rock records Willie had brought along in a paper bag. **1960** *New Left Rev.* May–June 33/1 He met Mr. Parnes at a Liverpool rock show. **1959** *Punch* 10 June 788/2 Richard, like most rock singers, dances from the knees in a style borrowed from African warriors. **1973** J. JONES *Touch of Danger* xxvii. 164, I met this boy and dropped out with him. He wanted to be a rock singer. **1977** *Rolling Stone* 30 June 25/1 One good reason Elliman wants to remain with Clapton is that his band serves as a fine outlet for her rock singing. **1960** *Times* 26 Feb. 16/4 This song conforms to the pattern of the teenagers' acceptance to-day. It is a rock song with a rock gimmick. **1976** *New Yorker* 17 May 125/2 A rock star with a limp feather boa draped around her shoulders. **1978** G. VIDAL *Kalki* vi. 153 Deafening was what H.V.W. would call the din from the rock stars' dressing rooms where electric guitars whined. **1959** C. MACINNES *Absolute Beginners* 56 The days when the Rock thing first broke. **1977** *Rolling Stone* 7 Apr. 26/2 His first solo album, *Solid*, a fine mixture of love ballads with jazz- and rock-tinged soul, has been selling short of hit status.

rock, *v.*[1] Add: **5. c.** *colloq.* (orig. *U.S.*). To cause to move with musical rhythm, esp. with the beat of *ROCK *sb.*[3] 2b. Occas. (esp. in early use) with sexual connotations (see also sense *7b).

1922 T. SMITH in Godrich & Dixon *Blues & Gospel Records 1902–1942* (1969) 648 (*song-title*) My man rocks me (with one steady roll). **1938** C. CALLOWAY *Hi de Ho* in R. S. Gold *Jazz Lexicon* (1964) 256 *Rock me*, send me, kill me, move me with rhythm. **1939** W. HOBSON *Amer. Jazz Music* (1940) iii. 54 Albert Ammons's *Boogie Woogie Stomp*.., in jazz slang, might be said to 'rock the joint'. *Ibid.* iv. 87 Simple jazz-rhythmic phrases..may be blasted out by players with enough lip and lung strength in a way that will 'rock' the crowd. **1951** DAVIS & HUNTER *Rock Little Baby* (song) 3 Some girls like men who are big and strong, You'll be my man, Just as long as you Rock little daddy, Work little daddy, Rock little daddy, Rock me all night long. **1956** B. HOLIDAY *Lady sings Blues* (1973) xi. 103 We used to rock that joint. **1961** *Jazz Notes* Feb.–Mar. 39, I don't remember anyone who could 'rock' a Kenilworth audience before! **1972** *Even. Telegram* (St. John's, Newfoundland) 24 June 10/4 Joan Morrissey and a group known as The Commanders Showband were 'really rockin' 'er' at the Staff Club. **1977** *Rolling Stone* 7 Apr. 3/2 (Advt.), Boston, man. They really rock and roll. They rocked the place apart.

d. *fig.* To distress, perturb, upset; to surprise, startle, dumbfound. *to rock the boat*: see *BOAT *sb.* 1d. *colloq.*

1940 E. POUND *Cantos* lii. 11 Gold brokers made profit Rocked the exchange against gold. **1941** *Argus Weekend Mag.* (Melbourne) 15 Nov. 1/3 Another universal favourite [in Australia] is still the famous 'Wouldn't it ——!' Never given the final words (the completed sentence has several variants on 'Wouldn't it rock you!' or 'Wouldn't it rip you!'), the exclamation depends upon inflexion as to whether it conveys disgust, amazement, or pleasure. **1947** N. MARSH *Final Curtain* ix. 139 Has Troy seen about the Will?... It'll rock them considerably. **1951** *Sun* (Baltimore) 9 June B1/1 His diplomatic phrasing wrapped the punch in polite words, but Grady was nonetheless rocked. **1955** 'N. SHUTE' *Requiem for Wren* vii. 197 It turned out you were a Rhodes scholar, which rocked her a bit. **1960** *Sunday Express* 24 July 1/3 It is not only from the Opposition that Mr. Macmillan can expect criticism. His decision will rock the Tory Party too. **1966** [see *OFF-BROADWAY *sb.*]. **1981** *Observer* 22 Mar. 7 (*heading*) New sex scandals rock Washington.

6. d. (Further example.)

1937 I. BAIRD *John* ix. 103 Tiber rocked back on his heels.

e. *to rock along*, to continue in typical fashion. *U.S. colloq.*

1906 J. W. CARR in *Dial. Notes* III. 153 *Rock along*, to continue unsettled... 'So the matter rocked along and nothing was done.' **1946** *Sun* (Baltimore) 10 Oct. 2/1 The creation of a new board or administrator..would permit the program to rock along much as it is now. **1972** J. S. HALL *Sayings from Old Smoky* 115 *Rockin' along*, going along as usual. 'Everything is rockin' along just like when Lena was here.'

f. In Mountaineering: to work one's way *up* a chimney by a rocking movement.

1920 G. W. YOUNG *Mountain Craft* 168 The body is kept upright in the middle on the spring of the bent knees and supported by the pressure of the hands, placed like the feet one against each wall. In this fashion we can 'rock' up satisfactorily.

7. a. Of popular music: to possess a rocking rhythm (see *ROCKING *ppl. a.* 1c); to exhibit the characteristics of rock music.

1938 *Metronome* July 21 *Harry James' Lullaby in Rhythm* really rocks. **1946** R. BLESH *Shining Trumpets* xiii. 309 The music..jumps rather than rocks. **1977** *Rolling Stone* 24 Mar., Waters has written six new tunes for the album, marking the end of a long dry spell, but his standards and one old Willie Dixon tune rock the hardest.

b. To perform, or dance vigorously and in an improvised way to, popular music with a strong beat (*ROCK *sb.*[3] 2a); hence, to play or dance to rock music (*ROCK *sb.*[3] 2b), to rock and roll. Occas. (esp. in early use) with sexual connotations (see sense *5c).

[**1934**: see *ROCK AND ROLL.] **1948** MOORE & REIG (*song-title*) We're gonna rock. **1951** DAVIS & HUNTER (*song-title*) Rock little baby. **1953** FREEDMAN & DE KNIGHT (*song-title*) We're gonna rock around the clock. **1956** *Look* 26 June 45 Elvis Presley. The hottest thing rockin', sings throbbing lyrics that sound almost unintelligible. *c* **1956** 'L. SLIM' *Rooster Blues* in P. Oliver *Screening Blues* (1968) vi. 193 We got to rock tonight baby, yes, we got to rock tonight. **1974** *Down Beat* 18 July 38/2 The band now isn't together enough to play all that... I mean they try to rock and they don't. **1977** *Time* 1 Aug. 16/2 In a Salisbury discothèque last week..'troopies' (soldiers) and their birds were rocking to a song about the country's bad news.

c. *to rock out*, to enjoy oneself enthusiastically, *esp.* by playing or dancing to rock music. Also as *attrib. phr. colloq.* (chiefly *U.S.*).

1968 *Surfer Mag.* Jan. 47/3 Maria likes rock-out dancing and surfing. **1972** B. RODGERS *Queens' Vernacular* 173 *Rock out*,..to enjoy oneself to the fullest. **1977** *Rolling Stone* 5 May 74/3 Even on the Stones' 'Happy', Lofgren changes the rock-out showpiece of hero Keith into a more subdued and funky shuffle. **1977** C. MCFADDEN *Serial* (1978) lii. 110/2 Kate..went to find the Reverend Thurston on the dance floor, where he was rocking out with Marlene.

rock, *v.*[2] Add: **2.** (Earlier example.)

1836 *Public Ledger* (Philadelphia) 30 Aug. 1/4 Rock him! rock him! cried the boys, rock him round the corner... The wearer was 'rocked' till he turned his cloak inside out.

3. *W. Country dial.* To remove the calcareous deposit or 'fur' from the inside of (a kettle).

1880 HARDY *Trumpet-Major* II. i. 4 The broken clock-line was mended, the kettles rocked, the creeper nailed up, and a new handle put to the warming-pan. **1905** in *Eng. Dial. Dict.* V. 138/1 Kettle wants rocking.

ro·ckabi:lly. orig. *U.S.* Also **rock-a-billy.** [Blend of *ROCK (AND ROLL and *HILL)-BILLY.]

1. A type of popular music, originating in the southeastern U.S., combining elements of rock and roll and hill-billy music. Also *attrib.*

1956 *Billboard* 8 Dec. 22/3 Johnny Burnette is on hand to inject a touch of rockabilly in 'Lonesome Train'. **1957** *Variety* 23 Oct. 18/1 [The film] 'Rockabilly Baby' will hit a responsive chord among teenagers. **1959** *Times* 9 Nov. 9/6 Rockabilly and hula hoops came and went. **1962** *Globe & Mail* (Toronto) 19 Nov. 6/6, I suggest that as a public service the rock-a-billy radio stations join together to present an informative, unsponsored, prime time, two-hour program. **1971** R. A. CARTER *Manhattan Primitive* (1972) xx. 190 A drummer, a guitarist, and a trumpet player pounded out rockabilly. **1976** *Time* 27 Sept. 90/3 Honky-tonk songs..came out of Texas in the late 1930s and early '40s. Elvis and Jerry Lee Lewis adapted the style to rock 'n' roll in the '50s. Sometimes called rockabilly, it celebrates booze, gambling, fighting, steppin' out, temptation and, like all country music, love. **1980** *Daily Mirror* 10 Apr. 12/2 Rockabilly is Eighties style. Special shops are opening to cater for the revived demand.

2. A person who performs this music.

1958 *Britannica Bk. of Year* 519/2 *Rockabilly*, a word ingeniously compounded from the expressions *Rock 'n' roll* and *Hillbilly*, and meaning a country singer. **1968** *Rolling Stone* 25 May 1/3 They called Elvis the 'rockabilly'. **1969** B. C. MALONE *Country Music U.S.A.* 246 A hybrid specimen developed: an individual who possessed characteristics of both the rock-and-roll and country singer, the rockabilly.

ro·ckaboo:gie. Also **rock-a-boogie.** [Blend of *ROCK (AND ROLL and *BOOGIE(-WOOGIE.] A type of popular music, combining elements of rock and roll and boogie-woogie. Also *attrib.*

1956 B. DARNELL et al. (*song-title*) Rock-a-boogie baby. *Ibid.*, He's got a little rattle He shakes around, I don't know where that rhythm he ever found, Oh he's a Rock-a-boogie Baby, Rock-a-boogie Baby of mine. **1956** BENSON & JONES (*song-title*) Rock-a-boogie swing. *Ibid.*, You can see the kids a-dancin', Hear the music ring, It's a brand new beat, It's the rock-a-boogie swing... You got-ta rock. You got-ta roll. **1975** *Listener* 25 Dec. 889/2 That noted rockaboogie guide, the *Daily Express.* **1977** *Zigzag* Apr. 14/2 We were more refined, tasteful if you like, as opposed to the old good time rock-a-boogie.

rock-a-bye (rǫ·kăbəi), *v.* Also **rock-a-by.** [f. ROCK *v.*[1] + *bye* (see BYE-BYE[1]).] *imp. phr. rock-a-bye, baby*: a traditional phrase (esp. in a nursery rhyme) to induce an infant to fall asleep, used as an accompaniment to the rocking of a cradle. Also with joc. var. (see quot. 1954). Cf. HUSHABY *int.*

1805 *Songs for Nursery* 36 Rock-a-bye, baby, thy cradle is green, Father's a nobleman, mother's a queen. **1812** *Mother's Gift* 5 Rocka-by baby bunting, My father's gone a hunting. *c* **1820** in I. & P. Opie *Oxf. Dict. Nursery Rhymes* (1951) 58 Rock a bye baby—puss is a lady..So hush a bye babe lie still. **1954** DYLAN THOMAS *Under Milk Wood* 81 Rockabye, grandpa, in the tree top..When the bough breaks the cradle will fall, Down will come grandpa, whiskers and all. **1975** *101 Favourite Nursery Rhymes* 58 Rock-a-bye, baby, on the tree top, When the wind blows the cradle will rock; When the bough breaks the cradle will fall, Down will come baby, cradle and all.

rock and roll. Also **rock-and-roll, rock 'n' roll.** [f. vbl. phr. *to rock and roll*: see ROCK *v.*[1] and ROLL *v.*[2] in Dict. and Suppl.] **1.** A type of popular dance-music characterized by a heavy beat and simple melodies, often with elements of the 'blues'. Cf. *rhythm and blues* s.v. *RHYTHM *sb.* 9a.

[**1934** S. CLARKE (*song-title*) Rock and roll. **1951** DAVIS & HUNTER *Rock Little Baby* (song) 1 Rock little daddy, Work little daddy, Rock little daddy, Send me with a rock and roll. **1954** *Billboard* 27 Nov. 29 (Advt.), Rockin' rollin' rhythmic! Ella Mae Morse with Big Dave and his orchestra.] *Ibid.* 25 Dec. 18/4 Alan Freed..will sponsor his first 'Rock and Roll Jubilee Ball' at the St. Nicolas Arena here on January 14 and 15. **1955** *N.Y. Times* 26 Mar. 17 According to William E. Kelsey Jr., a business man who has organized such parties, 'Rock 'n Roll' is less to blame for the situation than are the alcoholic beverages taken straight by boys and girls from 16 to 19 years old. **1956** *Observer* 30 Dec. 8/8 What else happened in 1956? Elvis Presley happened. So did Rock 'n' Roll. **1957** D. HAGUE in S. Traill *Concerning Jazz* 113 The only blot on the ledger of good productive jazz is that monstrosity at first referred to as 'Rhythm and Blues' and now more popularly called 'Rock and Roll'. **1959** *Times* 27 June 7/3 'Rock 'n' Roll' was so closely followed by Skiffle that the uninitiated were apt to confuse the two. **1962** *Listener* 1 Nov. 703/2 The bulletins last night kept breaking into the rock-'n'-roll. **1968** A. LIPSON *Russian Course* 1 Hooliganism is defined [in the Soviet Union] as 'behavior exhibiting disrespect for the social order'. Includes: scoffing at authority, playing rock and roll, wearing loud clothes, as well as rowdyism and petty criminal acts. **1969** N. COHN *AWopBopaLooBop* (1970) i. 15 In 1951, a DJ called Alan Freed launched a series of rhythm reviews at the Cleveland Arena... These shows featured coloured acts but were aimed at predominantly white audiences and, to avoid what he called 'the racial stigma of the old classification', Freed dropped the term R&B and invented the phrase Rock'n'Roll instead. **1974** A. SHAW *Rockin' '50s* xii. 106 In a liner note for an End album *Alan Freed's Top 15*, Freed claimed that he began using the term 'rock and roll' in 1951. **1977** *Rolling Stone* 21 Apr. 74/1 You know her life was saved by rock and roll. **1977** *Zigzag* Aug. 5/1 Y'see I write about punk and you just want to read about something that'll scare your mum, I'm sure that elsewhere someone will let ya know it IS only rock'n'roll.

2. A dance to this music.

1958 [see *CHARLESTON]. **1958** *Times Lit. Suppl.* 21 Nov. p. xxxii/5 Alex Moore leads beginners of any age through the mysteries of ballroom dancing, from the waltz..to the Mambo and 'Rock 'n' Roll (Jive)'. **1960** *Master Detective* July 83/2 Rock and Roll, that's what I'm good at. I got a terrific collection of platters.

3. *attrib.*, as *rock and roll ball, band, craze, dance, dancer, group, lyric, music, number, party, record, revivalism, revivalist, riot, road show, singer, song, star, station, stuff, tune.*

1954 *Billboard* 25 Dec. 18 (*heading*) Freed to sponsor 'Rock & Roll' ball. **1972** *Guardian* 28 June 16/1 It [*sc.* the Rolling Stones] is the raunchiest, flashiest, most exciting rock 'n' roll band in existence. **1980** *Oxford Times* 1 Feb. 23/3 On tracks like 'Rock Music' they seem to want to be a hard rock 'n' roll band. **1977** *Times* 18 Apr. (Gramophone Suppl.) p. iv/3 By the 1950s..popular music was to make another revolution for the record business... The rock'n'roll craze symbolized in the figure of Elvis Presley. **1955** *Life* 2 May 19, I am a teen-ager and I see no future in the rock 'n roll dance craze. **1966** A. YOUNG in *Spero* I. ii. 21 New things he'd worked out on drums for a Rock & Roll dance. **1957** E. PAUL *That Crazy Amer. Music* 243 The contemporary crop of rock and roll dancers include the young folks near the head or toward the foot of each class. **1968** *Crescendo* Feb. 16/3 This is a rock and roll group! **1955** *Life* 2 May 19, I think you need a teen-ager's view on rock 'n roll lyrics. **1956** *Look* 26 June 47 A record spins, and the boys and girls react to rock 'n' roll lyrics with laughter, not involvement. **1956** *Newsweek* 23 Apr. 32 Rock-and-roll music, he [*sc.* Asa Carter] said, 'is the basic, heavy-beat music of Negroes. It appeals to the base in man, brings out animalism and vulgarity.' **1958** *Publ. Amer. Dial. Soc.* xxx. 39 Now that that age group [*sc.* teenagers] is concerned with 'rock and roll' music, the jazz audience still remains composed..of young people of college age. **1955** *Life* 18 Apr. 168/2 *Cash Box*..challenged anybody to find smut in the top rock 'n roll numbers. **1969** *Listener* 3 Apr. 470/3 He can get them swinging with a rock-and-roll number. **1955** *N.Y. Times* 26 Mar. 17/3 A month ago Mr. Kelsey organized a 'Rock'n Roll' party for 2,000 at an armory here. **1957** *Gramophone Popular Record Catal.* III. 157 Rock and roll party. **1955** *Life* 18 Apr. 168 But parents and police were startled by other rock 'n roll records' words which were frequently suggestive and occasionally lewd. **1974** *Guardian* 27 Mar. 12/6 Bill Haley's return to London for yet another bout of rock and roll revivalism. **1972** *Jazz & Blues* Sept. 5/1 The Rock 'N' Roll revivalists. **1958** *Punch* 19 Nov. 665/1 If in the fullness of time it sparks off a rock-'n'-roll riot in Hamburg or Tokyo they receive the news with a grunt. **1977** *Sounds* 1 Jan 2/4 The Glitter Band will no longer back him up and the old rock 'n' roll road show has been wound up. **1956** *Look* 26 June 42 Lillian Briggs is a rock 'n' roll singer who also plays at the trombone. **1964** *Amer. Folk Music Occasional* I. 16, I think a lot of Rock and Roll singers and blue singers, they really have the feeling exactly as we about gospel. **1955** *Life* 18 Apr. 168 *Variety*..cranked out indignant stories about 'leerics' in the rock 'n roll or rhythm and blues songs. *Ibid.* (*caption*) Contingent of bounding dance fans at Easter show in Brooklyn's Paramount Theater greet roster of rock 'n roll stars performing latest songs on stage. **1972** J. L. DILLARD *Black English* vi. 261 A title from one of the rock and roll star's songs. **1973** E. BULLINS *Theme is Blackness* 46 Steve fumbles with the radio dial and finds a rock 'n' roll station. **1957** *New Yorker* 26 Oct. 35/2, I do enjoy a good opera production...I don't enjoy this rock-'n'-roll stuff. **1972** D. HASTON *In High Places* iii. 45 Robin..was whistling a rock-'n-roll tune.

Hence as *v. intr.* (freq. considered as comprising two separate verbal units for the purpose of forming derivatives, etc.: see also *ROCKING *vbl. sb.*[1] 4), to play or dance to rock-and-roll music; **rock and roller**; **rock and rolling** *vbl. sb.* and *ppl. a.*

[**1951** DAVIS & HUNTER *Rock Little Baby* (song) 1 Rock little baby, Rock and roll, Rock me in rhythm, Satisfy my soul.] **1956** *Time* (Overseas/Atlantic ed.) 18 June 37 Pop Record Maker Mitch Miller, no rock 'n' roller, sums up for the defense: 'You can't call any music immoral.' **1956** *Time* 24 Sept. 48 *My Boy Elvis*..is a real rock 'n' roller. **1956** *N.Y. Times Mag.* 4 Nov. 44/3 (*heading*) Europe rocks 'n' rolls. **1957** *Economist* 21 Sept. 946 (Advt.), Fibreglass..baffles the chatter of rock-'n-rollers—and keeps the place warm as neatly as it keeps the peace. **1957** *Observer* 15 Dec. 7/4 Gay shirts for the boys who skiffle and rock 'n' roll are equally hard to discover. **1958** H. MAXWELL *Railway Mag. Miscellany* 6 We can..for an hour or so Rock and Roll to a more thunderous and more significant beat than that which passes for Music with us today. **1959** A. WESKER *Roots* I. 19 There's nothing wrong with rock 'n rolling, only God preserve me from the girl that can do nothing else! **1960** *News Chron.* 29 Mar. 3/2 Rock 'n' roller Cliff Richard. **1960** P. HASTINGS *Sandals for my Feet* I. vi. 61 Those rock and rolling Romeos. **1966** *Listener* 20 Oct. 568/1 There were already a dozen or so young people rocking and rolling wildly to some vintage discs of Elvis Presley. **1976** *Weekend Echo* (Liverpool) 4/5 Dec. 1/2 A concert by veteran rock-and-roller Bill Haley. **1977** [see *ROCK *v.*[1] 5c]. **1977** *Sounds* 9 July 18/1 Silly really that the American rock 'n' rolling public..should take Starz to its heart so readily.

Rockaway. Substitute for etym.: [f. the place name of *Rockaway*, New Jersey.] and add: (Earlier and later examples.) Also *attrib.*

1845 M. M. NOAH *Gleanings from Gathered Harvest* 174, I keep a little Rockaway wagon. **1846** *Spirit of Times* 9 May 121/1 The price of a 'Rockaway' carriage which will carry eight persons depends very much on its finish. **1944** T. D. CLARK *Pills, Petticoats & Plows* 292 Everywhere carriage makers turned out fancy..'cutunders', 'rockaways',..and 'heavy duties'. **1948** J. D. RITTENHOUSE *Amer. Horse-Drawn Vehicles* 19 Rockaway or depot wagon.

rockbridgeite (rǫ·kbridʒəit). *Min.* [f. the name of *Rockbridge* County, Virginia, where the first specimens were recognized + -ITE[1].] A basic phosphate of iron and manganese which is found as dark green or black masses and crusts (turning brown in air owing to oxidation) in limonite and pegmatite deposits.

1949 C. FRONDEL in *Amer. Mineralogist* XXXIV. 513 The specific name dufrenite is here re-defined to apply to a particular member of the dufrenite-complex, and the new name rockbridgeite is proposed for another common member of this complex. **1951** C. PALACHE et al. *Dana's Syst. Min.* (ed. 7) II. 868 Rockbridgeite occurs in the United States in a limonite deposit on South Mountain near Midvale, Rockbridge County, Virginia. **1970** *Amer. Mineralogist* LV. 166 A remarkable occurrence at Fodderstack Mountain, Montgomery Co., Arkansas, shows fibrous masses of rockbridgeite with mammillary surfaces and color banding.

rockburst (rǫ·kbɒ̄ɹst). Also **rock burst.** [f. ROCK *sb.*[1] + BURST *sb.*] A sudden, violent rupture or collapse of highly stressed rock in a mine.

1928 *Daily Mail* 3 Aug. 18/1 The rockburst at a depth of nearly 5,000ft. in the City Deep mine that has..caused the deaths of two Europeans and eleven natives, is described as one of the biggest pressure bursts experienced on the Rand goldfield. **1942** *Mine & Quarry Engin.* VII. 233/1 One of the major problems of mining at depth lies in the occurrence of rockbursts. **1946** C. B. JEPPE *Gold Mining on Witwatersrand* I. x. 790 'Pressure bursts' or 'rock bursts'..major effects of excessive differential stresses. **1967** *New Scientist* 14 Dec. 678/1 The success of US and Soviet workers in predicting rockbursts underground. **1978** *Mining Equipment Internat.* June 17/1 Rockbursts currently account for about 80% of South African underground mine fatalities.

Rockefeller (rǫ·kəfelə). The name of John D. *Rockefeller* (1839–1937), Amer. financier and philanthropist, used as the type of an immensely rich man. Also *attrib.* Hence **Ro:ckefelle·rian** *a.*, designating that which only a rich man could afford.

1938 I. GOLDBERG *Wonder of Words* vii. 136 Anciently, men looked up to Crœsus..as a man of immense wealth... Thousands of years later men still say, 'He is a Rockefeller,' or 'He is a Rothschild.' **1939** 'F. O'BRIEN' *At Swim-Two-Birds* i. 63, I rejoined..that I..was no Rockefeller, thus utilizing a figure of speech to convey the poverty of my circumstances. **1941** B. SCHULBERG *What makes Sammy Run?* i. 14 I'm not exactly Rockefeller, but I'm always good for a little touch. **1975** P. LORRAINE *Ask Rattlesnake* I. v. 88 'You don't remember anything?.. But, James, you could be—' 'A Rockefeller?' **1976** *National Observer* (U.S.) 24 Apr. 14/2 The daily rates are Rockefellerian,.. beginning at about $183 for two in high season from Dec. 20 through April 21. **1976** R. CONDON *Whisper of Axe* I. xiii. 77 Nobody, not even the Rockefeller boys, can shake up the cash for a hunnert keyes [of heroin]. **1979** *N.Y. Times Mag.* 30 Sept. 14/4 That uncle, whom I still think of as a Mellon, a Rockefeller,..would collapse in awe of my annual grocery bill today.

rocker[1]. Add: **1. c.** A popular song that rocks (see *ROCK *v.*[1] 5c and 7a); a rock song.

1954 *Billboard* 6 Nov. 52/4 The deep-voiced chanter hands the rocker a good performance... The boys bow on the label with a so-so reading of a new rocker here. **1970** *New Yorker* 12 Dec. 187/1 'One More Weekend', a honky-tonk rocker..is about getting away. **1974** *Guardian* 22 Mar. 14/5 'Raised on Robbery' is a successful all-out rocker (with witty but still bleak lyrics). **1977** *Sounds* 1 Jan. 4/2 The songs they write alternate between brittle rockers, melodramatic movies and clever pop songs.

d. One who performs, dances to, or enjoys rock music (see *ROCK *sb.*[3] 2b); *spec.* a teenager or young adult of a type characterized by liking rock and roll, typically wearing long hair and a leather jacket, and riding a motorcycle (freq. contrasted with *MOD *sb.*[3]). Also *transf.*

1963 [see *MOD *sb.*[3] and *a.*]. **1963** *Economist* 28 Dec. 1332/2 Teenagers want..motor bikes and leather jackets to show that they are 'rockers'. **1964** *Spectator* 17 Apr. 503/1 Brighton cancelled its proposed 'beat festival' next month on hearing that the Mods and Rockers were coming in force. **1965** *New Statesman* 19 Nov. 801/1 A couple of literary Rockers rang up anonymously: 'We'll bomb the gallery if [Ezra] Pound turns up.' **1966** C. MACKENZIE *Paper Lives* iv. 54, I cannot think that *Romeo and Juliet* is made more accessible to the imagination of young people by making the Capulets what I believe are called Mods and the Montagues what I believe are called Rockers. **1972** *Listener* 10 Aug. 187/2 Chuck Berry is the rocker's rocker and the real man. **1973** J. WAINWRIGHT *Pride of Pigs* 82 He was..a nineteen-year-old who had once identified himself as a greaser and, before that, as a Rocker, but who now led a provincial chapter of Hell's Angels. **1977** *Time* 3 Jan. 56/2 The debuting Barbra brings a hostile rocker audience to their feet with the wonder of her funkiness.

2. c. (Further examples.)

1923 WODEHOUSE *Inimitable Jeeves* viii. 78 The Duke is off his rocker. **1932** E. WAUGH *Black Mischief* v. 195 It's going to be awkward for us if the Emperor goes off his rocker. **1943** 'C. DICKSON' *She died a Lady* vii. 58 We're wondering if there was anybody who cared enough about Mrs. Wainright to go off his rocker and kill both of 'em when she fell for somebody else. **1953** 'M. INNES' *Christmas at Candleshoe* xxi. 221 'His behaviour is certainly very aberrant. Would it, one wonders, be occasioned by a sudden abnegation of the ratiocinative faculty?' 'Off his rocker—eh?' **1961** [see *FLIP *sb.*[2] 5]. **1976** T. SHARPE *Wilt* xiv. 144 'To put the record straight, what I said was that some of them were...' 'Off their rockers?' suggested the reporter.

4. b. For *U.S.* read 'orig. *U.S.*' and add earlier and later examples.

1852 in Mrs. Stowe *Key to Uncle Tom's Cabin* (1853) 136/1 Will be sold,..Hairseat Chairs, Sofas and Rockers. **1855** S. ROBINSON *Jrnl.* 18 Nov. in *Kansas* (1856) viii. 98 [He was] seated in the nice large rocker drawn up before [the fire]. **1905** *Delineator* May 829/1 The Windsor rockers are not so common as the side chairs. **1911** *Daily Colonist* (Victoria, B.C.) 30 Apr. 4/5 (Advt.), Bedroom suites in white enamel..rockers, in white enamel to match. **1978** *Lancashire Life* Apr. 42/3 Ah sit theer i' mi rocker, Just startin' to nod off.

c. (Earlier examples.)

1830 *Boston Transcript* 15 Dec. 2/3 The surface mines, which are of very inferior importance, require no other labour than that necessary in washing the earth in *rockers*, or large inclined troughs with mercury. **1833** H.

BARNARD *Let.* 18 Apr. in *Maryland Hist. Mag.* (1918) XIII. 346 The top soil is removed—then the gravel is washed, by being thrown into what is called a rocker, or cradle, which is in fact a little more than a large cradle. **1852** [see *LONG TOM 2].

f. A tanning vat in which hides are rocked to and fro on a pivoted frame. Freq. *attrib.*

1885 C. T. DAVIS *Manuf. Leather* xviii. 353 Another form of handler in use is known as the rocker handler, and it consists of a frame constructed of wood, and hung by pivots in the centre of the top of the vat so as to give a dipping movement of 7 or 8 in. to each end of the frame. **1897** *Ibid* (ed. 2) xxiv. 382 The hides are next suspended in 'rockers'... They remain in the 'rockers' from seven to ten days. **1969** T. C. THORSTENSEN *Pract. Leather Technol.* v. 69 The hides are tied and hung in rocker racks and tanned by the vegetable tanning process. Prior to vegetable tanning, the hides in the lime condition are put in rockers containing deliming and bating materials.

g. A rock-shaft, rocker arm, or any similar rocking device forming part of a mechanism; *esp.* (*a*) a device for controlling the positions of brushes in a dynamo, and (*b*) a rocker arm in an internal-combustion engine.

1888 S. P. THOMPSON *Dynamo-Electric Machinery* (ed. 3) iii. 63 The rockers which support the brush-holders should admit of sufficient angular displacement being given to the brushes. **1893** R. GRIMSHAW *Locomotive Catechism* 178 Lengthen the rocker, so as to lower the entire motion. **1915** G. A. BURLS *Aero Engines* vi. 108 When the 'plus' part of the cam comes into contact with the roller the upper end of the rocker U is pushed upwards and the lower-end depressed, thus opening the valve. **1921** *Motor Electr. Manual* iii. 50 A magneto that has been standing out of use..is very liable to have a sticking rocker. **1928** *Evening News* 18 Aug. 1/3 Gallop then had to go into the pits with rocker trouble. **1935** T. E. LAWRENCE *Lett.* (1938) 855 The front rocker ran dry... So we pulled down the rocker assembly, and found more bits of Harry M's. string in the rocker-fulcrum pipe! **1961** *Carbon Brushes & Electr. Machines* xiv. 221 The correct location of the brush rocker is usually indicated by the machine constructor by a pair of marks, one on the rocker and one on the frame of the machine. **1970** K. BALL *Fiat 600, 600D Autobk.* i. 9/1 The design is conventional, incorporating..overhead valves operated by pushrods through rockers. **1975** F. PORGES *Design of Electr. Services for Buildings* i. 3 The switch opens when the bottom of the rocker is pressed and shuts when the top is pressed.

5. b. (Earlier example.)

1854 B. F. TAYLOR *Jan. & June* II. 155 The boys sha'n't skate? Who grudges them the 'rockers'?

c. *Ice-skating.* = *rocking turn* s.v. *ROCKING *vbl. sb.*[1] 3.

1892, 1902 [see *COUNTER *sb.*[4] 6]. **1936** *Sun* (Baltimore) 15 Feb. 13/2 There are 72 different school figures the skater must learn... Counters, rockers, brackets, loops, threes. **1973** *Times* 7 Feb. 15/8 He looked ill at ease on the first figure, the forward outside rocker.

d. 'One of the curved stripes under the three chevrons that indicate the grade of a sergeant (as in the U.S. Army and Marine Corps)' (Webster 1961). Also *transf.*, any similar badge bearing a slogan or device.

1944 *Yank* 6 Oct. 15/1 'Woddya want, fellah?' said the sergeant. He was thin for a top kick and his blouse was much too big. The bottom rocker reached down to his elbow. **1948** *Christian Sci. Monitor* (Mag. Sect.) 6 Nov. 8/1 Sergeant second class—three stripes, two 'rockers'—has been changed to sergeant first class. **1967** E. E. KERRIGAN *Amer. Badges & Insignia* i. 27 Next come first, second, and third grade sergeants, which were separated into both line and staff grades. The arcs, or 'rockers', indicated line grade, and straight lines below indicated grade. **1971** J. MANDELKAU *Buttons* vii. 81 The patch consisted of the top rocker—three inches wide, red on white—*Hell's Angels.* The bottom rocker said, *England* and between them I carried the small death's head. **1976** *New Yorker* 15 Mar. 102/2 Wetsel, a staff sergeant (E-6) with three stripes and one rocker, arrived in the company.

e. The upward curve on a surfboard.

1963 *Surfing Yearbk.* 43/1 *Rocker*, the slight upward slope in a surfboard. **1968** W. WARWICK *Surfriding in N.Z.* 3/2 The nose, was rounded with a slight uplift or rocker. **1970** *Studies in Eng.* (Univ. of Cape Town) I. 27 Less familiar words include *rocker*, or *banana*, which indicates the curvature of the surfboard along its length.

6. For *attrib.* in Dict. read '*attrib.* and *Comb.*' and add: (also in sense 2 b) *rocker bearing, box, gear, shaft* (earlier and further examples), *sieve, tailing*; *rocker-less* adj.; **rocker arm,** a rocking lever in an engine; *esp.* one in an internal-combustion engine which serves to work a valve and is operated by a push-rod from the camshaft; **rocker(-bottom) foot** *Med.*, a foot with the sole curved downwards; **rocker panel,** in a motor vehicle, a panel forming part of the bodywork below the level of the passenger door; **rocker switch,** an electrical switch having a mechanism incorporating a spring-loaded rocker.

1860 CLARK & COLBURN *Rec. Pract. Locomotive Engine* 67/1 The block..is carried upon the upper end of an arm, attached to, and vibrating upon the lower end of the rocker-arm. **1874** *Railroad Gaz.* 9 May 170/2 This block is attached to the lower rocker-arm by a pin, *c*, which works freely in the block. **1928** *Evening News* 18 Aug. 1/3 Baron d'Erlanger's Lagonda broke a valve rocker arm, and had to retire. **1970** K. BALL *Fiat 600, 600D Autobk.* i. 12/2 Take off cylinder head cover, rocker arm and shaft assembly. **1930** *Engineering* 30 May 696/3 The Aintree end [of the bridge] was treated..by means of four 100-ton jacks, and fixed rocker bearings weighing 5 tons each were placed in position. **1975** *New Yorker* 17 Feb. 26/2 He [*sc.* a robot] has rocker bearings for hands, shock absorbers for forearms,..hubcaps for shoulders. **1950** *Jrnl. Bone & Joint Surg.* XXXIIA. 344 Sonnenburg saw 688 cases of congenital club-foot, 42 cases of flat-foot, and 15 cases of congenital convex pes valgus or 'rocker-bottom' foot... In two of the cases club-foot was present originally; due to mistreatment, rocker-foot developed. **1956** *Clin. Orthopaedics* VIII. 94/2 If applied properly to give pressure under the cuboid, the packed felt will prevent the disastrous deformity of rocker foot. **1977** N. E. SHAW in *Bone & Joint Dis.* (Brit. Med. Assoc.) 114 (*caption*) Calcaneus is in equinus and is tucked up behind ankle joint. Rocker-bottom deformity has developed. **1892** J. G. A. MEYER *Mod. Locomotive Constr.* 199 The lifting-shaft bearing and rocker-box..are bolted to the front splice. **1965** *Motor* 17 July 3/2 Condensation in the rocker box of his B.M.C. 1100. **1902** F. J. A. MATTHEWS *Electr. Motor Installations* iii. 51 No rocker-gear is fitted to the machine, so that it is impossible..to alter the position of the brushes. **1950** NEWTON & STEEDS *Motor Vehicle* (ed. 4) vi. 118 (*caption*) Rocker gear of refined design for overhead camshaft. **1922** D. H. LAWRENCE *Aaron's Rod* i. 9 A baby was cooing in a rocker-less wicker cradle. **1921** C. W. TERRY *Pract. Motor Body Building* xxxviii. 255 A standard pattern taxi-cab with recessed rocker panels at the back. **1952** T. A. WOHLFEIL et al. *Automobile Body Reconditioning* vii. 88/1 Rocker panels are boxlike sections consisting of inner and outer panels welded to the edge of the floor pan. **1978** *N.Y. Times* 29 Mar. A25/4 (Advt.), Porsche '77... Sport wheel, fogs, alloys, rocker panel. **1842** R. & G. L. SCHUYLER in *Q. Papers Engin.* (1844) I. IV. 2 The valves..are of our own contrivance, and peculiar to this ship; they are worked by a separate eccentric and rocker shaft, which is set as to follow the motion of the steam valve. **1939** *Automobile Engineer* XXIX. 300/2 Rubber gland packing effectively seals the rocker shaft against leakage. **1950** *Engineering* 4 Aug. 104/1 A number of parts such as valves and valve gear..rocker shaft components, and bearings, are interchangeable with the six- and eight-cylinder engines. **1869** *Overland Monthly* III. 301/2 The united crash of pebbles on hundreds of quickly agitated rocker sieves, sounded in his ear like the roar of a cotton factory. **1884** *Bull. U.S. Nat. Museum* No. 27. 575 Cradle or Rocker Sieve, for washing the contents of the dredges. **1964** *Electr. Engineer's Ref. Bk.* (ed. 11) xxx. 79 (*heading*) Rocker switch. **1971** *Daily Tel.* 24 Nov. 11/4 The facia has been tidied up and rocker switches provided. **1975** F. PORGES *Design of Electr. Services for Buildings* i. 3 The advantages of the rocker switch are that it is easier to operate and that it is almost impossible to hold half open, even deliberately. **1906** C. DE L. CANFIELD *Diary of Forty-Niner* ii. 18 Worked out the claim and before I moved the Tom, tried some of the rocker tailings.

rockeried (rǫ·kərid), *a.* [f. ROCKERY + -ED[2].] Furnished with a rockery or rockeries.

1966 J. BETJEMAN *High & Low* 67 But strew the roads with tin signs 'Keep Left', 'M4', 'Keep Out!' Command, instruction, warning, Repetitive adorning The rockeried roundabout.

rocket, *sb.*[3] Add: **1. b.** In proverbial phr. *to rise like a rocket and fall like a stick* (cf. STICK *sb.*[1] 4 h) and varr., describing a sudden, meteoric rise and subsequent fall, as of fortune, etc.

1792 T. PAINE *Let. to Addressers* 4 As he [*sc.* Burke] rose like a rocket, he fell like the stick. **1838** R. H. BARHAM *Let.* 7 Mar. (1870) II. vii. 48 Poor man, he has gone up like a rocket and is coming down like the stick. **1909** *Brit. Weekly* 7 Jan. 405/3 We know the talk about a man going up like a rocket and coming down like a stick... It is generally the man's own fault. **1922** JOYCE *Ulysses* 364 My fireworks. Up like a rocket, down like a stick. **1950** G. B. SHAW *Farfetched Fables* 83 Political adventurers and 'tin Jesuses' rose like rockets to dictatorships and fell to earth like sticks.

c. Any elongated device or craft (as a flying bomb, a missile, a spacecraft) in which a rocket engine is the means of propulsion.

1919 R. H. GODDARD *Method of reaching Extreme Altitudes* (Smithsonian Misc. Coll. LXXI. No. 2) 1 The problem was to determine the minimum initial mass of an ideal rocket necessary, in order that on continuous loss of mass, a final mass of one pound would remain, at any desired altitude. **1920** *Photo Play* 7 Sept. 1/1 The theory of a Professor Goddard that a rocket could be sent to the moon. *Ibid.*, The propulsive power of the rocket..is derived from a series of multiple charges. **1929** *Amazing Stories* May 151 In the meantime, Dr. Mueller busied himself with making the rocket shipshape, for in spite of every precaution the supplies were in chaos. **1944** *Times* 11 Nov. 2/1 For the last few weeks the enemy has been using his new weapon, the long-range rocket, and a number have landed at widely scattered points in this country. **1949** W. LEY *Conquest of Space* (1950) i. 21 The rocket is a mile high and the spectators realize that there is still a deafening sound beating upon their ears. **1964** *Yearbk. Astron. 1965* 160 The rocket plummeted down near Guericke in the Mare Nubium, within a few miles of its intended position. **1970** N. ARMSTRONG et al. *First on Moon* iv. 76 At the time of Apollo 11 there was no doubt that the Saturn V was the most powerful operational rocket on earth. **1977** *Whitaker's Almanack 1978* 595/1 Mozambique troops fired rockets into the centre of Rhodesia's border city of Umtali but damage was stated to be minimal.

d. In full *rocket engine* or *motor.* An engine operating on the principle of the pyrotechnic rocket, providing thrust by the same method as a jet engine but without depending on the surrounding air for combustion (see also quot. 1971).

1919 R. H. GODDARD *Method of reaching Extreme Altitudes* (Smithsonian Misc. Coll. LXXI. No. 2) 6 By application of the above principles, it is possible to convert the rocket from a very inefficient heat engine into the most efficient heat engine that ever has been devised. **1929** *Sci. Wonder Q.* Fall 7 Prof. Hermann Oberth, a German of Mediarch, and Prof. Robert H. Goddard, an American of Worcester, Massachusetts..have solved it, though..only theoretically, by means of the rocket motor. **1931** *Jrnl. R. Aeronaut. Soc.* XXXV. 34 The fuel loading for rocket engines is a different matter from that of an engine of the explosion type. **1939** *Astounding Sci. Fiction* May 61/1 Each man in the crew tensed himself, gathering his abdominal muscles to resist the enormous acceleration developed by the launching catapult and the ship's own rockets acting in conjunction. **1960** C. H. GIBBS-SMITH *Aeroplane* xv. 122 The Messerschmitt Me 163 *Komet* fighter..had swept-back wings, a Walter liquid-fuel rocket motor, and a speed of 590 m.p.h. **1965** W. R. CORLISS *Space Probes & Planetary Exploration* x. 204 Because they will be used for delicate maneuvers, the on-board rockets have to be precisely controlled not only in thrust level but also in thrust duration and direction. **1971** P. J. MCMAHON *Aircraft Propulsion* x. 294 The convention of speaking of liquid fuel rocket *engines* but of solid fuel rocket *motors* is established in Britain. **1972** *Guinness Bk. Records* 128/2 The car was powered by a liquid natural gas/hydrogen peroxide rocket engine delivering 22,000 lb. s.t. maximum and thus theoretically capable of 900 m.p.h. **1977** *Engin. Materials & Design* Aug. 25/1 In rocket motors extremely high temperatures are developed (up to 3500°C). **1977** I. RIDPATH *Signs of Life* viii. 153 In its simplest form, the nuclear rocket uses as a propellant liquid hydrogen, which is heated to a gas by the reactor and expelled at high speed.

e. *off one's rocket*, mad. Cf. ROCKER[1] 2c. *slang.*

1925 FRASER & GIBBONS *Soldier & Sailor Words* 244 *Rocket, off one's*, mad. **1959** I. & P. OPIE *Lore & Lang. Schoolch.* x. 179 He is cracked, he's cuckoo... He's off his rocket ('Off your rocket' is a development of 'off your rocker').

f. A severe reprimand. Freq. *to give* (or *get*) *a rocket. slang* (orig. *Mil.*).

1941 *New Statesman* 30 Aug. 218/3 [War-time slang.] *To stop a rocket*, receive a reprimand. **1942** E. WAUGH *Put out More Flags* ii. 153 The C.O. led Captain Brown away. 'He's getting a rocket,' said the anti-tank man. *a* **1944** K. DOUGLAS *Alamein to Zem Zem* (1946) xii. 77, I contended [*sic*] myself with giving him a rocket, and told them to hurry up and mend the tank. **1949** 'N. BLAKE' *Head of Traveller* III. xiv. 231 Your Superintendent gave me a rocket yesterday about 'harbouring her', as he put it. **1957** I. MURDOCH *Sandcastle* vii. 104 Demoyte had pondered the outrage..made a mental note to give Mor a rocket when he next saw him,..and felt immensely better. **1961** A. WILSON *Old Men at Zoo* i. 36 If Beard's to blame, then he should get the rocket. **1975** J. I. M. STEWART *Young Pattullo* vii. 155 Fish was sent to the Provost and given a rocket.

3. *rocket aeroplane, age, airplane, base, battalion, boat* (earlier and later examples), *engineer, flight, flyer* (later examples), *flying, frame* (earlier example), *fuel, installation, jet, pilot, projectile, propellant, propulsion, research, scientist*; *rocket-launching* vbl. sb. and ppl. adj., *-shooting* vbl. sb.; *rocket-assisted, -boosted, -borne, -carrying, -driven, -firing, -like* (later example), *-powered, -propelled, -tracking* adjs.; **rocket astronomy,** the branch of astronomy in which measurements are made by instruments carried by rockets above the atmosphere; **rocket-bomb,** (*a*) (see quot. 1895); (*b*) = *flying bomb* s.v. *FLYING *vbl. sb.* 3; (see also quot. 1973); **rocket car,** a car powered by a rocket engine; **rocket chamber,** the combustion chamber of a rocket engine; **rocket gun,** a gun firing rockets; **rocket launcher,** a device or structure for launching rockets; **rocket-man,** (*a*) a soldier responsible for firing rockets (? *obs.*); (*b*) *colloq.* an astronaut; **rocket net** *sb.*, a net having small rockets attached, which is laid on the ground and then propelled so as to envelope a group of feeding birds for ringing; hence **rocket-net** *v. trans.*, to trap in this way; **rocket netting** *vbl. sb.*; **rocket pad,** a launching pad for a rocket; **rocket plane,** (*a*) an aircraft powered by a rocket motor; (*b*) an aeroplane armed with rockets; **rocket projector** = *rocket launcher* above; **rocket range,** (*a*) a rocket-launching range (cf. *RANGE *sb.*[1] 11c); (*b*) the area within range of a rocket; **rocket-rattling** *vbl. sb.* and *ppl. a. colloq.*, threatening with the military use of rockets or nuclear weapons (after *sabre-rattling* s.v. *SABRE *sb.* 4a); **rocket ship,** (*a*) a spaceship powered by rockets; (*b*) a warship armed with rockets; **rocket sled:** see *SLED *sb.*[1] 2b; **rocket tube,** (*a*) a tube out of which a rocket is fired; † (*b*) a rocket motor.

1932 H. NICOLSON *Public Faces* I. 16 With this explosion chamber the problem of the rocket aeroplane was finally solved. **1959** *Globe & Mail* (Toronto) 15 July 1/3 Scout laws created in the horse and buggy days don't always fit into today's rocket age. **1959** *Listener* 10 Dec. 1024/1 The strange and striking contrasts that must exist between the buildings of the Victorian and Edwardian periods and those that will be put up in the Rocket Age. **1928** *Sci. Amer.* Sept. 260/1 (heading) Can there be a Rocket Airplane? **1929** *Amazing Stories* May 148 The series of experiments were given their first impetus by the German rocket airplanes, successfully designed for the Berlin-to-New York air service. **1941** *Flight* 23 Jan. p. b/1 It may be expected that rocket-assisted take-off can be made more effective if not very efficient. **1950** *Sci. News* XV. 82 Rocket assisted take-offs by heavy bombers are quite common. **1959** *Economist* 17 Jan. 221/1 The RAT (rocket-assisted torpedo), a complicated but highly praised anti-submarine device. **1960** *McGraw-Hill Encycl. Sci. & Technol.* XI. 600/2 Rocket astronomy, first used in 1945 in the United States with German V-2 rockets, has been especially fruitful in studies of solar phenomena. **1971** *New Scientist* 18 Mar. 636/2 The emphasis is on the more modern approach which has grown up over the past 10 years as balloon and rocket astronomy have aided observations. **1954** M. Caidin *Worlds in Space* 177 In the opinion of many, the combination of the moon-launched rocket with an atomic bomb war head merited a thorough investigation of the value of the lunar rocket base. **1958** *New Statesman* 4 Jan. 1/1 The government seems determined to go ahead and establish American rocket-bases in Britain. **1976** *New Yorker* 15 Mar. 79/1 He explained that Intelligence had come to suspect that a North Vietnamese Army rocket-battalion/command group had moved into the Song Quan Valley. *c* **1829** D. Jerrold in M. R. Booth *Eng. Plays of 19th Cent.* (1969) I. 168 I'd fight yard-arm to yard-arm for you.., or fight in a rocket boat. **1948** W. Ley *Rockets & Space Travel* 197 They..were massed on the decks of special 'rocketboats', rack after rack of self-propelled projectiles, fired electrically from below deck... One such rocket boat could, in the space of a few minutes, throw as much steel and high explosive as the turrets of three battleships. **1895** *Funk's Stand Dict.*, *Rocket-bomb*, a harpoon-rocket. **1943** Mrs. Belloc Lowndes *Let.* 20 Dec. (1971) 247 A good many people believe the rocket-bomb is coming, but a famous airman laughed at the idea of its being a real danger to London. **1949** 'G. Orwell' *Nineteen Eighty-Four* I. viii. 85 'Steamer' was a nickname which..the proles applied to rocket bombs. **1973** J. Quick *Dict. Weapons & Mil. Terms* 375/3 *Rocket bomb*, an aerial bomb equipped with a rocket to give it added velocity and penetrating power after being dropped from an aircraft. **1958** *Technology* Mar. 25/1 Scientists and the services have hurried into print with space plans.., among them rocket-boosted.. engines to fire a payload to the moon. **1962** W. B. Thompson *Introd. Plasma Physics* i. 4 Recently, rocket- and satellite-borne counters have detected belts of energetic radiation..high above the earth's atmosphere. **1971** *Sci. Amer.* July 74/2 X-ray observations with rocket-borne instruments have shown that the remnant of Tycho's nova is also a strong source of X rays. **1930** *Times Educ. Suppl.* 25 Oct. p. iv/1 The rocket-car experiments of the late Herr Max Valier. **1976** *Star* (Sheffield) 30 Nov. 12/9 Gabelich strapped himself into a rocket car named Blue Flame and covered two measured miles..at an average speed of 630 mph. **1961** *Guardian* 25 Oct. 11/2 Rocket-carrying submarines. **1936** *Smithsonian Misc. Coll.* XCV. No. 3. 2 In these experiments it was shown that a rocket chamber and nozzle, since termed a 'rocket motor', could use liquid oxygen together with a liquid fuel, and could exert a lifting force without danger of explosion. **1939** *Astounding Sci. Fiction* May 59/1 Injecting excess charges of fuel into the rocket chambers. **1928** Rocket-driven [see *rocket-propelled* below]. **1978** R. V. Jones *Most Secret War* viii. 68 The German Navy was said to have developed remote-controlled rocket-driven gliders of about three metres span and three metres long. **1951** *Jrnl. R. Aeronaut. Soc.* LV. 92/1 Rocket propellants must have certain undesirable features, and it is the task of the rocket engineer to minimise the consequences of these. **1970** H. Trevelyan *Middle East in Revolution* 149 The Iraqi Air Force.. attacked the rebel headquarters with rocket-firing aircraft. **1978** R. V. Jones *Most Secret War* xliii. 403 The attack took place on 16th March with rocket-firing Typhoons of No. 198 Squadron. **1930** H. Chatley *Princ. Rocket Propulsion* 3 This is the basis of the dreams of rocket flight to the moon. **1934** H. G. Wells *Exper. Autobiogr.* I. vi. 328 They did not so much climb to success; they were rather caught by success and blown sky high... Only one item in this rocket flight is significant here. **1959** *Times Lit. Suppl.* 20 Mar. 167/2 The book is, in the main, a really excellent elementary account of rocket flight and space travel. **1927** *Amazing Stories* Nov. 725 Many schemes have been proposed for space flying, and some of the more recent ones, notably the Goddard Rocket Flyer, seem to come closest toward a strictly scientific solution of the problem. **1939** *Ibid.* Sept. 112 She had attached herself to him, demanding that he teach her how to pilot a rocket flier. **1929** *Sci. Wonder Q.* Fall 7 While writing the story, the author has had the collaboration of practically all the German scientists who have of late come into prominence in their researches into not only rocket flying, but space flying and astro-physics. **1931** *Wonder Stories* Jan. 900 We have succeeded in securing near Berlin a suitable rocket flying field, a large field on which the starting supports for the different rockets were set up. **1835** J. E. Alexander *Sketches in Portugal* v. 126 Saldanha's artillery consisted of four 5½-inch howitzers, six 9-pounders, six of 6, two of 3, and three rocket frames. **1931** *Amazing Stories* Dec. 804 A battleship has destroyed Albertville, Ontario, site of the Canadian rocketfuel factory and magazine. **1937** *Discovery* Sept. 277/2 Equipping this type of aeroplane with rocket engines, complete with rocket fuel. **1977** *Time* 18 July 35/3 It is known as phencyclidine hydrochloride, but youngsters on this latest and fastest-spreading high know it as 'angel dust', 'rocket fuel' and 'goon'. **1884** *Bull U.S. Nat. Museum* No. 27. 281 The rocket-gun..throws a large rocket and explosive lance weighing eighteen or twenty pounds, which acts in the capacity of a harpoon and bomb, and is used mainly in coast whaling. **1935** *Jrnl. R. Aeronaut. Soc.* XXXIX. 410 The main characteristic of..rocket guns..is the increase of their efficiency when the ratio of weight of the rocket..to the weight of the charge decreases. **1944** *Jane's All World's Aircraft* p. iii/2 The rocket-guns with which some..fighters were equipped.. enabled them to attack. **1959** E. H. Clements *High Tension* ii. 33 The Hebridean rocket-installations. **1944** *Aviation* Jan. 149/3 The mass of a rocket jet can be readily varied by feeding more or less fuel..into the rocket motor. **1944** Rocket launcher [see *launcher 2]. **1977** *N.Y. Rev. Bks.* 23 June 3/2 He learned to slaughter people with rifles and knives and explosives or to blast them to pieces with rocket launchers. **1956** A. H. Compton *Atomic Quest* 223 The great installations along the coast..turned out to be rocket launching platforms. **1968** *Times* 16 Dec. 7/3 The systematic recording of disturbances like these could be used to provide remote observers with information about rocket launchings. **1973** D. Kyle *Raft of Swords* (1974) iii. 19 Our force of rocket-launching submarines came into service. **1952** S. Spender *Learning Laughter* 38 There was a screen of cypress trees with the column of one palm tree in their midst, bursting rocket-like at the apex. **1821** G. R. Gleig *Narr. Campaigns Brit. Army* xix. 270 Attached to this corps of infantry, were a party of rocket-men, and two light three-pounder guns. **1938** *Sci. Amer.* May 270 (*heading*) Number one rocket man. **1964** *Galaxy Mag.* Oct. 181/1, I was a Rocketman 3/c on the Moon, guarding the Aristarchus base against invaders from outer space. **1972** *Melody Maker* 20 May 16/2 Elton John remains..a writer (with Bernie Taupin) of songs of lasting merit... The success of his beautiful 'Rocket Man' single proves that he has survived all the flack. **1948** *Severn Wildfowl Trust Ann. Rep.* 43 Although this report is primarily concerned with the activities of the Trust during the year 1947, it seems that such an important development as the first attempt with the Trust's new rocket nets for ringing the wild geese should be included although it took place early in 1948. **1952** *Blackw. Mag.* Feb. 106/1 When they want to tell t'other from which, they rocket-net them and paint their sterns. **1954** *Brit. Birds* XLVII. 316 By rocket nets, it has been possible to make an intensive study of the population of the Pinkfoot. **1973** *Wildfowl* XXIV. 164/2 A lot of effort went into attempting to rocket net Barnacle Geese. **1979** *Ibid.* XXX. 165/2 A single catch of 372 Barnacle Geese at Caerlaverock in October (one of the largest catches made with rocket nets) provided much valuable data. **1953** *Severn Wildfowl Trust 5th Ann Rep.* 22 The rocket-netting technique has undergone considerable modification during the four years since the first experiments were made. **1969** *Wildfowl* XX. 86/1 The Wildfowl Trust's rocket-netting programme had concentrated on the Pink-footed Goose since this proved the easiest to trap in the large numbers needed. **1965** *Time* 23 July 36 For those pictures, JPL's boss..and his crew had sweated out Mariner's launch from a Cape Kennedy rocket pad. **1977** *Jersey Even. Post* 26 July 14/3 It was vandalized by the German rocket-pad crews. **1949** R. A. Heinlein *Red Planet* i. 6, I still think I'd like to be a rocket pilot. **1958** C. C. Adams *Space Flight* p. vii, There have been space books for children—our present space cadets and future rocket pilots. **1928** *Pop. Mechanics* Nov. 718/2 Valier has calculated that a rocket plane could be shot from Berlin to New York in ninety-three minutes. **1929** *Mech. Engin.* Nov. 865/1 The rocket plane with its possibility of moving at speeds..would seem to be the answer to the problem of quick transportation. **1932** A. Huxley *Brave New World* iv. 70 The deeper drone of the rocket-planes hastening, invisible, through the bright sky five or six miles overhead. **1945** *Daily Tel.* 7 Aug. 1/6 R.A.F. shattered panzer counter-attack in Normandy. Rocket planes knocked out 35 tanks. **1949** *Ann. Reg. 1948* iv. 416 Earlier in the year (in May) it was reported from America that the rocket-plane Bell XS-1 had been flown faster than sound. **1965** W. R. Corliss *Space Probes & Planetary Exploration* x. 209 Rocket planes and helicopters are possible prime movers for unmanned landers, but surface locomotion is much more likely. **1936** *Pop. Science* May 16/2 An experimental rocket-powered glider..carried the cargo to its intended destination. **1948** *Electronics* June 93/1 Rocket-powered engines of one particular type employ two kinds of fuel. **1959** *Daily Tel.* 23 Feb. 11/6 This year two test pilots are expected to make the first flights in the rocket-powered North American X-15. **1943** *Fortune* June 92/2 A strange gun called the bazooka that fires a rocket projectile. **1944** T. N. Dalton *Jet Propulsion* 44 The Encyclopaedia Britannica says that rocket projectiles were used by the Chinese. **1945** L. E. O. Charlton *R.A.F. & U.S.A.A.F. July 1943—Sept. 1944* 292 (*caption*) Thunderbolt showing rocket projectors fitted to one of its wings. **1961** B. Fergusson *Watery Maze* ix. 235 The mass of rocket projectors pointing into the air from an LCT 2. **1932** *Bull. Amer. Interplanetary Soc.* Feb. 8 How best can we utilize each of these as a rocket propellent? **1944** C. P. Lent *Rocket Res.* 67/1 After using the rocket propellants the flying weight is only 1780 Kg and during the period of ascent the total weight averages less than 2000 Kg. **1928** *Sci. Amer.* Sept. 260/1 The recent German experiments with rocket propelled cars and gliders have attracted much attention, and it is now asked whether rocket-driven airplanes are not possible, navigating at fantastic speeds. **1951** *Mind* LX. 119 We have the idea now of a rocket-propelled missile capable of flying from Moscow to New York. **1978** R. V. Jones *Most Secret War* xxxix. 371, I already knew of two liquids used by the Germans in the rocket-propelled glider bombs they had been using against our ships. **1928** *Explosives Engineer* VI. 457 (*heading*) Motoring by rocket propulsion. **1929** *Sci. Wonder Stories* Aug. 265 Aeronautical authorities have stated recently that the future development of the airplane will be along the lines of rocket-propulsion. **1942** *Aeronautics* Aug. 49/2 The greatest reason against rocket propulsion of aeroplanes is the question of oxygen, its weight and storage in an aeroplane. **1963** *Listener* 23 May 866/1 Even before Verne's death the idea of using rocket propulsion for space-travel had been put forward by..Konstantin Eduardovich Tsiolkovskii. **1948** *Hansard Commons* 15 Mar. 1805 We have joint research stations; for instance, the one about which there has been considerable publicity, the rocket range in Australia. **1971** 'D. Halliday' *Dolly & Doctor Bird* ii. 24 The tracking of moonshots and other missiles from the American rocket range is done by the electronic brains in these stations. **1976** *New Yorker* 15 Mar. 79/1 A..command group had moved into the Song Quan Valley, ten miles to the west and almost within rocket range of the division headquarters. **1960** *News Chron.* 21 July 4/5 The..retaliation threats, the rocket-rattling over Cuba. **1961** *Sunday Express* 29 Jan. 1/4 President Kennedy has put a sharp curb on rocket-rattling, anti-Russian speeches. **1969** *Guardian* 31 Mar. 10/1 Rocket-rattling by any large Power over a weaker neighbour is deplorable. **1937** *Discovery* Sept. 269/1 Fundamental problems of rocket research. **1977** *Whitaker's Almanack 1978* 165/1 The progress of rocket research during the last war led to the development by the Germans in 1944 of the V.2 rocket. **1952** *Sun* (Baltimore) 5 Sept. 2/6 Take it from the rocket scientists who expect to fly to Mars some day—flying saucers are not space ships from another planet. **1959** *Listener* 5 Mar. 410/1 Rocket-scientists are not unaware of this. **1927** *Literary Digest* 25 June 20/1 He [*sc.* Max Valier] is even now building a rocket-ship. **1928** *Amazing Stories* Aug. 427 Not to mention the rocketships that might be in the air. **1936** *Forum & Century* July 38/2 But the question of whether rocket ships will ever reach the planets can be even approximately answered only when intensive research has been carried on over many years. **1951** W. Ley *Rockets, Missiles & Space Travel* p. viii (*caption*) One of the Navy's 'rocket ships' bombarding Peleliu Island on the same morning that was D-Day in Europe. **1969** *New Yorker* 12 Apr. 53/1 Anybody on earth with a pair of binoculars can see that setting a rocket ship down there would be a tricky operation. **1981** *Daily Tel.* 15 Apr. 1 The American space shuttle landed on a dry lake bed in California's Mojave Desert yesterday to complete the maiden flight of the first re-usable rocketship. **1925** R. Graves *Welchman's Hose* 35 And watched the nightly rocket-shooting, varied With red and green, and livened with gun-fire. **1971** 'D. Halliday' *Dolly & Doctor Bird* ii. 24 There are four main rocket-tracking stations in the Bahamas. **1881** W. D. Hay *300 Years Hence* iv. 70 The largest [projectiles] requiring apparatus like the old rocket-tubes and howitzers, and dealing certain death to every living thing within a mile of the place of explosion. **1898** D. Beatty *Diary* 8 Apr. in W. S. Chalmers *Life & Lett. David, Earl Beatty* (1951) ii. 33, I with the Rocket tube first occupied a position on the left of the Artillery. **1932** *Flight* XXIV. 1023/1 The rocket tube or rocket motor, as it is called in Germany..is filled with powder of special composition.

rocket, *v.* Add: **1. a.** (Later examples.)

1967 [see *napalm *v.*]. **1973** *Houston* (Texas) *Chron.* 21 Oct. 1/1 The 22-year-old officer, whose tank had been rocketed, said the Egyptian soldiers..threw what they apparently thought was his body out of the ditch. **1978** *Guardian Weekly* 12 Feb. 6/1 Six vessels..are rocketing besieging guerrilla forces around the port of Massawa.

b. To propel (someone) at speed, as by a rocket; to send by rocket. Also *fig.*

1837 J. Cottle *Killcrop* in *Early Recoll.* II. 316 From yon tall rock I'll hurl him to perdition... I'll rocket him. **1958** *Listener* 16 Oct. 603/2 Probably he [*sc.* an astronaut] will come down in a large sphere..because the retardation he will experience in this way will expose him to no worse strains than those he suffers in any case as he is rocketed upwards. **1959** *Times* 11 June 3/6 A boundary rocketed his score to a dozen. **1966** I. Asimov *Fantastic Voyage* i. 10 We would pile him into an X-52 and rocket him through inner space.

c. To reprimand severely. Cf. *rocket *sb.*[3] 1f. *slang* (orig. *Mil.*).

1948 Partridge *Dict. Forces' Slang* 156 He rocketed me like hell. **1971** J. Wainwright *Dig Grave* 96 The assistant chief constable was still rocketing Sergeant Sykes.

2. c. In general use: to move like a rocket, to speed; (of prices, etc.) to increase substantially, to soar. Also const. with advbs.

1881 *Baily's Mag.* Oct. 37 He played too forward and a little too quick to a very quick, straight ball, and she 'rocketted' between the wickets. **1924** W. J. Locke *Coming of Amos* xxiv. 312 A flash of lightning rocketed across the black gap of the open window. **1924** H. G. Wells *Exper. Autobiogr.* I. v. 219 The more brilliant investigators rocket off into mathematical pyrotechnics and return to common speech with statements that are.. nonsensical. **1937** J. Betjeman *Coll. Poems* (1958) 44 The heart of Thomas Hardy flew out of Stinsford churchyard... It rocketed over the elm trees. **1947** *Evening News* 5 Nov. 1/5 A hectic day's trading..sent the shares rocketing on Monday from 13s. 3d. to 23s. 9d. **1952** Dylan Thomas *Coll. Poems* 132 Up through the lubber crust of Wales I rocketed to astonish The flashing needle rock of squatters. **1957** *Economist* 2 Nov. 375 Manufacturer's exports rocket 23 times in 7 years! **1972** D. Haston *In High Places* ii. 29 The rope rocketed out. This was really high-quality ice climbing in action. **1976** *Times* 17 Mar. 2/8 Mr Benn rocketed to prominence as a potential future party leader..in the early 1970s. **1979** *Jrnl. R. Soc. Arts* CXXVII. 431/2 It goes along relatively steadily till 1972, then rockets up and comes back down and has just rocketed up again.

rocketeer. Delete *rare*⁻¹ and add: **1.** (Further examples.)

1945 F. H. M. Lloyd *Hurricane* i. 12 Fighter, night-fighter, fighter-bomber, tank-buster, 'rocketeer', ship-fighter, merchant-ship protector...in thirty different forms and on thirty-seven different fronts, the Hurricane went into action. **1974** D. Seaman *Bomb that could Lip-Read* ix. 70 The flash..won't affect the man firing the rocket-launcher... I want every rocketeer to fire his two rounds.

2. One who experiments or works with rockets; a rocket expert or enthusiast.

1929 *Review of Reviews* Sept. 91 (*heading*) The new race of rocketeers. **1935** *Jrnl. Brit. Interplanetary Soc.* Oct. 13 *Rocketeer*, one who experiments with rockets. **1953** J. N. Leonard *Flight into Space* 25 One philosophical rocketeer pointed to the fact that man's body stands midway in size between the atoms it contains and the great galaxies that float beyond the stars. **1957** P. Moore *Sci.*

& Fiction 18 Lucian's seamen are the logical ancestors of the rocketeers and space-cadets of to-day. **1960** *New Statesman* 2 Jan. 7/3 While the rocketeers burst into space, the advances that touched the man in the street were mostly of the kind of wide-screen movies and stereophonic records. **1971** *Nature* 23 Apr. 494/2 The group of astronomers at the University of Leicester, who have been among the most successful X-ray rocketeers, are still producing valuable data. **1972** *Sci. Amer.* Dec. 118/3 Model rocketeers fly light reflyable rockets they make themselves or from kits.

rocketee·ring, *vbl. sb.* [f. prec. + -ING[1].] = *ROCKETRY.

1932 D. LASSER *Conquest of Space* vii. 116 The support of a financier of world-wide experience, and of men of science..comes as a revelation to those who viewed the field of 'rocketeering' as a visionary dream. **1938** *Forum* Feb. 96/2 Rocketeering may, in some distant future, take us to the moon or elsewhere in space. **1962** *Times Lit. Suppl.* 2 Feb. 68/5 The race is therefore on, for a greater prize..than any that can be won by rocketeering.

rocketer. Add: † **b.** *Cricket.* = SKYER. *Obs.*

1886 *Cricket* 25 Feb. 18/1 A good man..is the man to go for a 'pocketer' [*sic*] between the wickets. *Ibid.* 25 Mar. 35/2 In my last letter of course 'Pocketer' ought to read 'Rocketer'. **1887** F. GALE *Game of Cricket* iv. 70 He hit [the ball] too quick, and instead of going out of the field, as it might have done, it went up a tremendous rocketer. **1900** *Badminton Mag.* Oct. 380 The great smiter..hit a ball very high straight to the young blacksmith... But for some reason—whether he was thinking too much of the style of the thing, or was unused to rocketers—..the ball fell with a hollow clank on the top of his head.

ro·cketing, *ppl. a.* (Further examples.)

1952 DYLAN THOMAS *Coll. Poems* 172 He..prays, Who knows the rocketing wind will blow The bones out of the hills. **1959** *Economist* 25 Apr. 318/2 Behind the increase in imports there is cited a 'rocketing' increase in Dutch production. **1964** M. ARGYLE *Psychol. & Social Probl.* xvi. 199 We are astounded however by the rocketing crime rate, [etc.]. **1970** *Daily Tel.* 8 May 17 Doctors, headmasters and health educationists are disturbed by the rocketing numbers of young smokers.

ro·cketing, *vbl. sb.* [f. ROCKET *v.* + -ING[1].] The action or practice of the vb. in various senses.

1928 P. F. NOWLAN in *Amazing Stories* Aug. 427 The favorite American method of propulsion was known as 'rocketing'. **1972** *Guardian* 4 May 15/8 Rocketing of Saigon, plus ground probes near the capital, could shake the politicians..out of their current isolation. **1975** *Church Times* 14 Mar. 1/5 Rocketing and shelling of the airfield was going on as the plane left.

rocketry (rǫ·kėtri). [f. ROCKET *sb.*[3] + -RY.] The science or use of rockets and rocket propulsion. Also *fig.*

1930 G. E. PENDRAY in *Bull. Amer. Interplanetary Soc.* Nov.–Dec. 4 The practical work of getting a liquid-fuel rocket actually into the air was a contribution of America's, as were the three most fundamental achievements of modern rocketry. **1934** *Jrnl. Brit. Interplanetary Soc.* I. 1. 3 There you have the nucleus of the British movement in rocketry. **1934** *Astronautics* Mar. 7 'Rocketry' itself is a coined word, first suggested at a meeting of the American Interplanetary Society in 1930 and since widely adopted. **1943** C. S. LEWIS *Perelandra* vi. 91 He was a man obsessed with the idea which is.. circulating all over our planet in obscure works of 'scientifiction', in little Interplanetary Societies and Rocketry Clubs. **1951** 'J. WYNDHAM' *Day of Triffids* ii. 30 Sustained research in rocketry had at last succeeded in attaining one of its objectives. It had sent up a missile which stayed up. **1957** *Times* 10 Oct. 10/1 The American programme..called for the launching of small test spheres this year..to check rocketry instrumentation. **1958** *Sunday Times* 14 Sept. 7/4 His [*sc.* Thomas Wolfe's] absurd rocketry about great America, decadent Europe and so on. **1962** F. I. ORDWAY et al. *Basic Astronautics* ii. 21 A scientific analysis of rocketry applied to high altitude meteorological research. **1968** A. DIMENT *Bang Bang Birds* v. 70 A collection of scientists..who weren't quite bright enough to get into the rocketry racket. **1977** *Daily Tel.* 28 July 1/6 The small spaceport at Kagoshima ..looked more like a station for amateur rocketry than a serious rival to Cape Canaveral.

rocketsonde (rǫ·kėtsǫnd). Also **rocket-sonde, rocket sonde.** [f. ROCKET *sb.*[3] + *-sonde*, after *RADIOSONDE.] A package of meteorological or other scientific instruments which is carried aloft by a rocket, released in the upper atmosphere, and floats down by parachute, transmitting measurements automatically by radio.

1949 E. DURAND in G. P. Kuiper *Atmospheres Earth & Planets* iv. 134 (*heading*) Rocket sonde research at the Naval Research Laboratory. **1951** *Jrnl. Brit. Interplanetary Soc.* X. 18 Direct measurements have been made by means of rocket-sondes to altitudes of over 100 miles. **1963** *Proc. 1st Internat. Symp. Rocket & Satellite Meteorol.* 23 The rocketsonde, at the present time, measures the temperature only; the wind is determined by radar tracking of the metallized parachute. **1969** MCINTOSH & THOM *Essent. Meteorol.* vii. 112 Above the ceiling of balloons, information is provided by rocket sonde or by satellite. **1976** *Nature* 13 May 124/1 The phase of the annual oscillation in the zonal winds at 82 km is consistent with the phase of this oscillation in the lower mesosphere determined from rocketsonde data.

rock-fish. Add: **1.** Also = *rock salmon* (*c*) s.v. *ROCK *sb.*[1] 9d. (Earlier and later examples.)

1598 FLORIO *Worlde of Wordes* 279/1 Piota,..a kind of rock fish. **1969** [see *rock-salmon* s.v. *ROCK *sb.*[1] 9 d].

3. = *KLIPFISH 1.

1731, 1806 [see *KLIPFISH 1].

rockfoil (rǫ·kfoil). [f. ROCK *sb.*[1] + FOIL *sb.*[1]] = SAXIFRAGE.

1879 RUSKIN *Proserpina* I. viii. 160 Their names..can be pleasantly said..in this order..Roof-foil, Rock-foil, Primrose. **1887** G. NICHOLSON *Illustr. Dict. Gardening* III. 311/1 Rockfoil. A name, suggested by Ruskin, for the genus *Saxifraga*. **1914** IRVING & MALBY *Saxifrages* i. 1 There is no other genus of rock plants that is so extensive as that of the Rockfoils. **1963** R. D. MEIKLE *Garden Flowers* 159 (*heading*) Saxifrage, Rockfoil.

rockie, var. *ROCKY *sb.*

rocking, *vbl. sb.*[1] Add: **2. b.** The action of using a rocker (*ROCKER[1] 4 c) in gold-mining.

1850 J. W. AUDUBON *Western Jrnl.* (1906) 202 The men began 'rocking' yesterday, one cradle, and get about a dollar an hour. **1859** *Brit. Colonist* (Victoria, B.C.) 3 Apr. 2/1 The lowest sum named by any miner as the product of a day's rocking is three to five dollars. **1896** C. H. SHINN *Story of Mine* 42 We started to rocking with my water.

3. rocking-turn, a movement or figure in skating (see quot.). Cf. *ROCKER[1] 5 c.

1869 VANDERVELL & WITHAM *Syst. Figure-Skating* 219 After having exhausted the Q, I began to consider the feasibility of making the change direct from the inside forwards to inside backwards and *vice versâ*..by the employment of a kind of turn, for which..I can find no more simple..name than the 'Rocking Turn'.

4. The action or practice of playing or dancing to popular music with a strong beat and rocking rhythm, *esp.* rock and roll.

1948 R. BROWN (*song-title*) Good rockin' tonight. **1956** *Newsweek* 18 June 42/3 (*heading*) Rocking and rolling. **1974** *Down Beat* 18 July 38/2 The lyricism is as fervent as ever, but the rocking isn't... I don't mean..that the band ought to be rocking.

rocking, *ppl. a.* Add: **1. b.** *Prosody.* Designating a metre in which each foot consists of a stressed syllable standing between two unstressed syllables.

c **1883** G. M. HOPKINS *Poems* (1918) Pref. 1 If the stress is between two slacks there will be Rocking Feet and Rhythms. **1932** F. R. LEAVIS *New Bearings in Engl. Poetry* v. 167 Rocking Feet and Outriders will help no one to read his [*sc.* Hopkins's] verse. **1957** B. DEUTSCH *Poetry Handbk.* (1958) 130 When the stress falls between two unstressed syllables, as in this line of Swinburne's 'Far oút to the shállows and stráits of the fúture, by roúgh ways or pleásant', the rhythm is a rocking one. **1965** A. F. SCOTT *Current Lit. Terms* 249 When the metrical stress falls between two unstressed syllables, the rhythm is called rocking.

c. Of popular music: characterized by a strong beat and rocking rhythm (cf. *ROCK *sb.*[3] 2); that is performed in the style of rock music.

1949 *Billboard* 3 Dec. 108/2 Combo drives thru a rocking riffer, with a punching bary sax leading the way. **1954** *Ibid.* 13 Nov. 98 Another spirited rhythmic side in which the lead singer soars out wild and free over the rocking beat provided by the rest of the group. **1959** G. AVAKIAN in M. T. Williams *Art of Jazz* (1960) ix. 88 One of the fastest rocking blues ever made. **1968** *Melody Maker* 30 Nov. 6/6 A rocking version of B. B. King's 'Sweet Sixteen'. **1976** *Leicester Trader* 24 Nov. 4/7 One rocking track called Winnebago even reminds me of..the opening track from Argent's second album.

rocking-chair. Add: **1.** (Earlier Amer. example.)

1766 in *Hobbies* (1949) Sept. 50/2 1st Mo. 1766, to a rocking Chair for andrew hunter 3/.

2. Used *attrib.* to designate something considered as being conducted or obtained at home, without first-hand experience of normal difficulties; spec. *rocking-chair money*, unemployment benefit. Cf. *ARM-CHAIR, ARMCHAIR. Chiefly *U.S.*

1933 *Sun* (Baltimore) 27 Feb. 6/3 A question which delights every sewing circle and rocking-chair parade in the country. **1944** *Amer. Speech* XIX. 156/2 *Rockin' chair money*, unemployment compensation. **1946** *Richmond* (Va.) *Times-Dispatch* 16 Jan. 5/2 An increase in 'rocking chair money' for the State's unemployed. **1959** *Globe & Mail* (Toronto) 22 Apr. 7/1 The somewhat less sophisticated people of the Maritimes have a happier name for Unemployment Insurance... 'Rockin' Chair Money'. **1962** *Daily Tel.* 10 Sept. 10/2 A third U2 incident over Communist territory..will renew groans at the President's rocking-chair diplomacy.

Rockingham (rǫ·kiŋăm). The title of Charles Watson-Wentworth, second Marquis of *Rockingham* (1730–82), applied *attrib.* to earthenware, china, a variety of glaze, etc., produced on his estate at the Old Works, Swinton, Yorks., from *c* 1745 to 1842. Also applied loosely to similar products. Now usu. designating pieces of a tea-service. Also *ellipt.*

[**1832** G. RICHARDSON in *Cabinet Cycl.* No. 26. 22 At the Rockingham works, which have been so named in compliment to their early patron, the celebrated marquess of Rockingham, porcelain is now produced which vies successfully in every kind of excellence with that of older English establishments.] **1857** J. MARRYAT *Hist. Pott. & Porc.* (ed. 2) xii. 291 They [*sc.* the works] also manufactured the brown or chocolate-coloured ware, which obtained the name of 'Rockingham ware'. **1863** W. CHAFFERS *Marks Pott. & Porc.* 134 A sort of brown or chocolate-coloured ware, made in the beginning of the present Century, obtained the name of Rockingham ware. **1869** C. SCHREIBER *Jrnl.* 4 Nov. (1911) I. 60, 3 Rockingham cups and saucers and 3 plates. **1870** *Ibid.* 11 Feb. (1911) I. 66 A few good bits of Chelsea,..one of Rockingham (very good). **1881** C. C. HARRISON *Woman's Handiwork* II. 110 The temperature at which Rockingham ware is fired is suitable for this [underglaze] work. **1900** F. LITCHFIELD *Pott. & Porc.* vii. 94 The ware is highly glazed, some of it being not unlike the brown Rockingham ware. **1935** G. GREENE *England made Me* ii. 57 The Minister stood above his Rockingham china. **1957** MANKOWITZ & HAGGAR *Conc. Encycl. Eng. Pott. & Porc.* 194/1 '*Rockingham*' *glaze*, a lustrous, purple-brown lead glaze (stained with manganese) made at the Rockingham factory, Swinton, early nineteenth century, and in Staffordshire. **1960** R. COLLIER *House called Memory* xii. 171 Croquet on the lawn at four o'clock with the Rockingham tea-service as background. **1963** *Times* 23 Feb. 11/7 There were many bone china potters in Staffordshire making cottages: their productions, without any justification, are classed arbitrarily as Rockingham and thus acquire the market value of that establishment's brilliant reputation. The flowers on Rockingham cottages are usually less disproportionately large than those ornamenting cottages made elsewhere. **1965** [see *DAVENPORT[2]]. **1973** L. COOPER *Tea on Sunday* 11 The dark blue and gold Rockingham cup.

rocking-horse. Add: (Earlier and later examples.) Also *fig.*

1724 in *N. & Q.* (1942) 7 Feb. 76/1 Rocking Horse. William Bird, turner, just without Newgate. **1922** JOYCE *Ulysses* 495 Result of the rockinghorse races. **1936** F. R. LEAVIS *Revaluation* iv. 112 Prior takes happily to those anapaestic, rocking-horse rhythms. **1964** D. VARADAY *Gara-Yaka* vii. 64 Then she bounded back in rocking-horse cheetah gait.

Rockite. Add: Now only *Hist.* (Further example.) Also **Ro·ckism.**

1830 *Times* 6 Nov. 3/6 There is little doubt that distress and desperation form the mystery, and that a kind of English *Rockism* is in operation. **1848** MILL *Pol. Econ.* I. II. ix. 375 Rockism and Whiteboyism are the determination of a people, who have nothing that can be called theirs but a daily meal.., not to submit to being deprived of that for other people's convenience. **1949** C. GRAVES *Ireland Revisited* viii. 101 The Rockites, hidden among the cliffs and intending to trap the Bantry party, revealed their presence.

rockless, *a.* (Later example.)

1977 *Lancashire Life* Nov. 82/1 What, on its almost rockless coast, has the County Palatine got?

rock-like, *a.* Substitute for def.: Resembling a rock; possessing the qualities of rock; hard or firm as rock. (Further examples in *fig.* use.)

1959 P. BULL *I know Face* ii. 29 This line had to be delivered in a steady rock-like voice. **1963** *Times* 5 June 16/3 His endearing character with its rocklike qualities won him innumerable friends from many generations. **1975** R. BARCLAY *Ernest Bevin & Foreign Office* iv. 79 Just as he himself had always been rock-like in his loyalty to Churchill, so from now on he remained absolutely firm in his support of Attlee.

rock 'n' roll: see *ROCK AND ROLL.

rockoon[2] (rǫkū·n). [Blend of ROCK(ET *sb.*[3] and BALL)OON *sb.*[1]] A rocket fired from a balloon; a balloon carrying a rocket to be fired in the upper atmosphere.

1953 *Sci. News Let.* 8 Aug. 89/2 The balloon-rocket technique, commonly referred to as Balloon Assisted Take-Off or Rockoon, was developed by Dr. James A. Van Allen, head of the State University of Iowa physics department. **1955** *Sun* (Baltimore) (B ed.) 23 Nov. 14/6 The release of rockoons will be synchronized with similar releases in the Northern Hemisphere. **1959** *New Scientist* 20 Aug. 244/2 Analysis of magnetic measurements by balloon-borne rockets (rockoons)..has revealed a second 'electrojet' current..around the Earth. **1963** A. MACLEAN *Ice Station Zebra* iv. 59 Drift Stations habitually carried rockets..and radio-sondes and rockoons. The sondes were radio-carrying balloons..: the rockoons, radio rockets fired from balloons.

rock-ribbed, *a.* Add: **2.** *fig.* Resolute, uncompromising, staunch; esp. of political allegiance. orig. *U.S.*

1887 *Courier-Jrnl.* (Louisville, Kentucky) 3 May 4/4 Mr. Straus is a rock-ribbed Democrat. **1911** H. S. HARRISON *Queed* 292 Various feelings had gradually stiffened an early general approval into a rock-ribbed resolve. **1925** T. DREISER *Amer. Trag.* (1926) I. I. xvi. 122 Clyde always struck her as one who was not any too.. rock-ribbed morally or mentally. **1950** *Manch. Guardian* 20 Feb. 6/6 The dyed-in-the-wool Democrat can be fanatical in devotion to his party's creed and traditions. So can the rock-ribbed Republican. **1961** *Economist* 28 Oct. 341/2 He is a man of such rock-ribbed integrity. **1969** *Daily Tel.* 11 Oct. 12 A Massachusetts seat that has always been held by rockribbed Republicans. **1976** *Pub-*

lishers Weekly 16 Apr. 88/1 Goldwater, rockribbed in his sincerity, speaks for many Americans currently disenchanted with Washington's government-by-bureaucracy.

rock-rose. Add: **4.** *N. Amer.* The bitter root, *Lewisia rediviva*, a small perennial herb belonging to the family Portulacaceæ, native to western North America, and bearing solitary pink or white flowers.

1906 *Contrib. U.S. Nat. Herbarium* XI. 49 The rock-rose or bitterroot..occurs abundantly in crevices of 'scab', making a brave show with its beautiful rose-colored flowers. **1963** *Beaver* Autumn 53/1 The rolling hills, cactus and rock roses..flooded the dry land with character and colour. **1973** R. D. SYMONS *Where Wagon Led* I. v. 77 We should find some rock roses here.

5. An aggregate of tabular crystals of a mineral suggestive of the petals of a rose; = *ROSE *sb.* 16e, *ROSETTE *sb.* 5e.

1933 *Amer. Mineralogist* XVIII. 261 The barite occurs as sand barites or barite rosettes (locally called 'rock roses') and barite accretions. **1962** W. A. DEER et al. *Rock-Forming Minerals* V. 193 Concretions of barytes in sandstone sometimes take the form of rosettes known as 'sand barites', 'rock roses' or 'desert roses'. **1977** A. HALLAM *Planet Earth* 85 (*caption*) Desert roses (or rock roses) display one of the more unusual modes of occurrence of evaporitic minerals... Found..only in arid areas, these clusters of platy crystals are typically of barite or gypsum.

rock-staff². Substitute for entry:
rock-staff². *E. Anglian dial.* [ROCK *sb.*²]. A distaff. Also *fig.*, a superstition; a fancy, crotchet; esp. in phr. *an old woman's rock-staff.*

1765 *Compl. Maltster & Brewer* p. xxiii, The notion of pease bloom, and weeds being up in the water, is but a meer old woman's rockstaff. *a* **1825** R. FORBY *Vocab. E. Anglia* (1830) II. 279 *Rock-staff*,..a distaff; from which..the wool *was* spun 'by twirling a ball below'... 'An old woman's *rockstaff*,' is a contemptuous expression for a silly superstitious fancy. **1867** *N. & Q.* 3rd Ser. XI. 215 She is so full of her old woman's rock-staffs. **1895** P. H. EMERSON *Birds, Beasts, & Fishes Norfolk Broad-land* II. xix. 396 There is a curious rockstaff in the marshlands that a viper's slough will draw thorns from your flesh.

rocksteady (rǫ·kste:di). Also **rock-steady, rock steady.** [f. *ROCK *sb.*³ 2 + STEADY *a.* 4.] A style of popular music, originating in Jamaica, characterized by slow tempo and stressed off-beat. Also, a dance to such music. Also *attrib.* Cf. *REGGAE.

1969 *Observer* 12 Jan. 3/8 West Indian teenagers..nowadays..danced to music called 'rocksteady'. *Ibid.* 23 Nov. 25/8 Aspiring Kingston..dancing the Reggae, Jamaica's successor to the Ska and the Rocksteady. **1971** A. SALKEY in *One Love* 7 We have been quick to recognise the excellence and the appeal in the musical alternative of the..*Rock Steady* and *Reggae.* **1971** *Daily Tel.* (Colour Suppl.) 30 July 7/4 As ska, rocksteady or blue-beat, music like this has been around in Britain for more than a decade, hidden amidst the West Indian subculture in London, Birmingham and elsewhere. **1973** *Telegraph-Jrnl.* (St. John, New Brunswick) 28 July 5/2 A West Indian rock-steady band was playing. **1977** MCKNIGHT & TOBLER *Bob Marley* iii. 41 Ska mutated into 'rock steady'... Rock steady was slower in tempo than ska—again to assist the singers in their unenviable task of shouting louder than the volcanic eruptions produced by a bass player with..amplification... Rock steady is further distinguished from ska by the extra syncopation involved. *Ibid.* vi. 72 It was 1968 and Johnny Nash, a black American singer..had achieved several hits with rock steady type songs. **1980** *Melody Maker* 19 Jan. 25/4 Saxa played with some of the early rock-steady acts that toured Britain, like Desmond Dekker and Laurel Aitken.

rock-water. (Later example.)

1948 F. BLAKE *Johnny Christmas* I. 40 Yet in this utter lack of sound, except for the sputter of flames and the musical seep of rock-water, Johnny came alert, strangely, as if awakened by a thin cry of warning.

Rockwell (rǫ·kwel). The name of Stanley P. *Rockwell*, 20th-cent. U.S. metallurgist, used *attrib.* with reference to a hardness test which he introduced, in which the depth of penetration of the material (usu. a metal) by a steel ball or a diamond cone is measured under specified conditions; hence also used to denote values of relative hardness determined by such methods.

1920 *Foundry Trade Jrnl.* XXII. 778/2 A new hardness testing apparatus, called the Rockwell hardness tester, is now available. **1922** S. P. ROCKWELL in *Trans. Amer Soc. Steel Treating* II. 1013 The Rockwell hardness tester is at present made in three sizes. **1922** *Chem. Abstr.* XVI. 3296 Formulas..are given for conversion from the Rockwell value to the Brinell value. **1930** *Engineering* 19 Sept. 358/1 Rockwell hardness measurements and X-ray diffraction patterns had shown that lattice distortion could be accompanied by appreciable softening. **1945** A. T. BIRKBY *Phenolic Plastics* v. 56 The V.P.N. and Rockwell 'C' test equivalents of this are 700–750 and 58–60 respectively. **1976** *Islander* (Victoria, B.C.) 16 May 15/3 Get a blade with a Rockwell hardness factor of 57 to 59... Steel less than Rockwell 57–59 is too soft and won't hold a cutting edge.

rocky, *a.*¹ Add: **1. b.** (Earlier example.) *Rocky Mountain Indian* (earlier example); **Rocky Mountain bee plant,** an annual herb, *Cleome serrulata*, belonging to the family Capparidaceæ and bearing racemes of pink flowers; **Rocky Mountain canary,** a burro or jack-ass; **Rocky Mountain feathers,** wood shavings; **Rocky Mountain (spotted) fever,** a sometimes fatal rickettsial disease transmitted by ticks; **Rocky Mountain goat,** the North American mountain goat, *Oreamnos americanus*; = MAZAME 2, *mountain goat* s.v. MOUNTAIN 9c in Dict. and Suppl.; **Rocky Mountain grasshopper** = **Rocky Mountain locust*; **Rocky Mountain iris,** a blue-flowered iris, *Iris missouriensis*, found in south-western North America; **Rocky Mountain juniper,** a small conifer, *Juniperus scopulorum*, found in the south-western United States; **Rocky Mountain locust,** a migratory North American grasshopper, *Melanoplus spretus*; **Rocky Mountain oyster,** lamb's fry; **Rocky Mountain sheep,** the bighorn sheep, *Ovis canadensis*; = *big-horn* s.v. BIG *a.* B. 2 in Dict. and Suppl.; **Rocky Mountain spotted fever** = **Rocky Mountain fever*; **Rocky Mountain spotted (fever) tick,** a brown or grey tick, *Dermacentor andersoni*, found in parts of western North America, where it is the vector of Rocky Mountain fever; **Rocky Mountain wood tick** = prec.

1802 in *Med. Repository 1803* 238 In the fall of 1800 I was on an excursion, on horseback, through the plains that are situated between the Sascatchievan and Missis-sourie Rivers, along the rocky mountains.

attrib. **1900** B. B. SMYTH *Plants & Flowers of Kansas* i. 14 Such temperatures..are generally supposed to be destructive to plant life; but the following plants live through them and continue to thrive: Pincushion cactus, prickly pear,..Rocky Mountain bee plant. **1939** *Nat. Geogr. Mag.* Aug. 227/2 Bees are attracted in such great numbers to the nectar secreted abundantly by these dainty blossoms..that the species is often called 'Rocky Mountain bee plant'. **1963** J. J. CRAIGHEAD et al. *Field Guide Rocky Mt. Wildflowers* 69 Rocky Mountain Bee-plant..is a much-branched annual 2–5 ft. tall. **1905** *Outing* Apr. 47/2 His varied outfit he packs on the back of the 'Rocky Mountain canary'. **1929** *Amer. Speech* V. 147 The burro or jackass of the early days is still called a *Rocky Mountain canary*, because of its tuneful voice. **1962** *Maclean's Mag.* 18 July 44/2, I started a fire with a handful of 'Rocky Mountain feathers'—dry shavings—made that morning before we left our previous camp. **1886** *Buck's Handbk. Med. Sci.* III. 85/2 The 'Rocky Mountain Fever', so called by practitioners on the slope of that great mountain chain, exhibits frequent divergences from the true clinical features of typhoid fever, and may show a continued remittent type, but the pathology observed in not a few of these cases links them to typhoid fever. **1917** *Indian Med. Gaz.* LII. 16/1 Most observers place the incubation of the Rocky Mountain fever at three to seven days. **1939** *Brit. Encycl. Med. Pract.* XII. 340 The other types [of tick-borne typhus] can be most easily understood by considering the respects in which they differ from Rocky Mountain fever. **1842** J. E. DEKAY *Zool. N.Y.* I. 112 Rocky Mountain Goat..larger than the common goat. **1884–5** [see GOAT 1 b]. **1901** *Daily Colonist* (Victoria, B.C.) 11 Oct. 1/6 The Rocky Mountain goat captured..last spring..is to be sent to the London Zoo this week. **1949** *Canad. Alpine Jrnl.* May 55 We had seen elk, moose, Rocky Mountain goats, and bighorn. **1909** WEBSTER 944/1 The allied migratory Rocky Mountain grasshopper..sometimes travels in vast hordes in the region west of the Mississippi. **1966** DAVIDSON & PEAIRS *Insect Pests* (ed. 6) viii. 129 The Rocky Mountain grasshopper is considered the most important migratory species in the United States and Canada. **1806** P. WAKEFIELD *Excursions N. Amer.* xliii. 380 We saw some straggling parties of Rocky Mountain Indians. **1880** T. MEEHAN *Native Flowers & Ferns U.S.* 2nd Ser. I. 103 As it is the only species of *Iris* found there the common name of 'Rocky Mountain Iris' has suggested itself to us. **1963** J. J. CRAIGHEAD *Field Guide Rocky Mt. Wildflowers* 34 Rocky Mountain Iris..usually bears from 1 to 4 variegated violet-blue flowers. **1898** G. B. SUDWORTH *Check List Forest Trees U.S.* 35 *Juniperus scopulorum* Sargent. Rocky Mountain Juniper. **1949** COLLINGWOOD & BRUSH *Knowing your Trees* 135 The twigs of the Rocky Mountain juniper..are four-sided, with leaves arranged alternately in pairs. **1972** L. HANCOCK *There's a Seal in my Sleeping Bag* viii. 182 Old dried whitened Rocky Mountain juniper trees sprout the artistic bulky stick nests of the double-crested cormorants. **1878** *Rep. Comm. Agric. 1877* (U.S. Dept. Agric.) 264 The Rocky Mountain Locust, or Grasshopper of the West. **1930** S. HENRY *Conquering our Great Amer. Plains* 319 Coming home late one afternoon for supper I stepped back surprised to see what became known as Rocky Mountain locusts covering the side of the house. **1972** V. A. LITTLE *Gen. & Applied Entomol.* (ed. 3) vii. 94 Although the Rocky Mountain locust is found throughout most of the United States, it is considered a pest of importance only in the Great Plains region. **1889** J. WHITEHEAD *Steward's Handbk.* IV. 420/2 *Rocky Mountain oysters*, Lambs' fries. **1940** C. L. BROWN et al. *Amer. Cooks* 71 (*heading*) Fried lamb's fries, or Rocky Mountain oysters. **1804, 1818** Rocky Mountain sheep [in Dict.]. **1904** [see *ARGAL]. **1936** D. MCCOWAN *Animals Canad. Rockies* v. 45 Rocky Mountain sheep..are almost entirely guided by what we call instinct. **1977** D. ANTHONY *Stud Game* xxviii. 188 They hunted Rocky Mountain sheep with bow-and-arrow. You have to be good to do that. [**1903** Rocky Mountain spotted fever: see *spotted fever* s.v. *SPOTTED *a.* and *ppl. a.* 3 a.] **1905** *U.S. Hygienic Lab. Bull.* XX. 8 Rocky Mountain 'spotted fever' is reported for Idaho, Montana, Nevada, Oregon, Wyoming, ?Washington State, and possibly Utah and Alaska. **1906** *Jrnl. Amer. Med. Assoc.* 7 July 33/1, I arrived in Missoula, Montana, April 21, 1906, equipped for the bacteriologic and hematologic study of the so-called Rocky Mountain spotted fever. **1947** *Ann. Rev. Microbiol.* I. 346 The fatality rate in Rocky Mountain spotted fever is greatly influenced by age. **1974** *Greenville* (S. Carolina) *News* 23 Apr. 3/2 The little ticks that carry Rocky Mountain spotted fever didn't have to find a warm spot under a log this winter. **1937** *Jrnl. Econ. Entomol.* XXX. 52 The first, known popularly as the Rocky Mountain spotted fever tick, or Rocky Mountain wood tick, is our most versatile species as a disease vector. **1976** *Islander* (Victoria, B.C.) 7 June 14/2 The most serious type of infection, called tick fever, is transmitted by the Rocky Mountain spotted tick. **1937** Rocky Mountain wood tick [see **Rocky Mountain spotted fever tick*]. **1951** METCALF & FLINT *Destructive & Useful Insects* (ed. 3) xxiii. 983 The Rocky Mountain wood tick is the most important tick in the United States. **1976** *National Observer* (U.S.) 21 Aug. 8/4 The Rocky Mountain wood tick carries the illness in the West.

c. (Earlier examples.)

1827 J. SMITH *Let.* 12 July in *Dict. Americanisms* (1951) II. 1409/2, I allude to the country of the Great Salt Lake, West of the Rockies. *a* **1861** T. WINTHROP *John Brent* (1862) vi. 60 At the foot of those bare, bulky mounds of mountain by which the Wasatch range tones off into the great plains between it and the Rockys, we overtook the Salt Lake mail.

Hence **ro·ckily** *adv.*

1972 D. HASTON *In High Places* ix. 100 Almost an ideal mountain panorama. Fitzroy, Poincenot and satellites rockily bounding the right, rounding off towards Pere Giorgio at the head of the valley. **1981** *Times Lit. Suppl.* 6 Feb. 147/5 The difficulties of absorbing women into a group so rockily traditional as the police.

rocky, *a.*² Add: **a.** (Earlier and later examples.) Also, in recent use, tipsy, drunken.

1737 *Pennsylvania Gaz.* 6–13 Jan. 2 He's Rocky, Raddled,..Lost his Rudder. **1912** A. BENNETT *Matador of Five Towns* 157 'What's up with that wheel?' 'It's rocky, that's what that wheel is.' **1938** 'N. SHUTE' *Ruined City* x. 204 The whole thing was a pretty rocky deal. **1941** *Direction* IV. v. 15/2 Stack had been..gettin leapin drunk... One morning in April, 1906, after he had had a rocky night and had a headache built for a hippopotamus he was out..to cool the burnin thirst in his throat. **1947** *Partisan Rev.* XIV. 493, I was drinking scotch on an empty stomach, and beginning to feel a trifle rocky myself. **1951** A. BARON *Rosie Hogarth* I. vi. 62 A chap always felt a bit rocky after he'd shown what he was made of. **1977** D. BEATY *Excellency* vii. 90 The régime's rocky. The future of the country's uncertain.

b. For *slang* read *colloq.* and add to def.: Now usu. in sense 'difficult, hard'. (Earlier and later examples.)

Some cases may be equally well interpreted as examples of a *fig.* use of ROCKY *a.*¹ 1 a.

1873 J. MILLER *Life amongst Modocs* 71 We may have a rocky time down there, my boy. **1960** B. KEATON *My Wonderful World of Slapstick* 13, I am by no means overlooking the rough and rocky years I've lived through. **1976** E. DUNPHY *Only a Game?* iii. 90, I had played well in the first half at Swindon when things were rocky.

c. *colloq.* In poor health; ill, unwell.

The sense in quot. 1792 is unclear; it may be ROCKY *a.*¹ 2 b.

1792 F. BURNEY *Let.* 28 Jan. (1972) I. 106 A former Patient is often alarmed..but she is very *Rocky*..& she will be glad when the alarm passes over. **1926** E. HEMINGWAY *Sun also Rises* I. vii. 56 What's the matter, darling? Do you feel rocky? **1929** M. DE LA ROCHE *Whiteoaks* iii. 56 Is Wake feeling rocky to-night? **1932** G. GREENE *Stamboul Train* II. i. 62, I guess you're a bit rocky. You haven't escaped from anywhere, have you? **1954** G. DURRELL *Bafut Beagles* viii. 151 'Made you feel a bit rocky?' inquired the doctor cheerfully, feeling my pulse.

ro·cky, *sb.* *Naval slang.* Also **rockie.** [f. ROCKY *a.*²] (See quots.) Also *attrib.* or as *adj.*

1919 W. LANG *Sea Lawyer's Log* 29, I have seen an officer who presides directly over our naval destinies fix the eye of a basilisk upon a luckless 'rockie' who incautiously spoke of a parade. **1927** 'GIRALDUS' *Musings of Merry Matloe* (ed. 2) 186 *Rocky*, a Royal Naval or Fleet Reserve man. Also a R.N. Reserve officer who once was more commonly known as a 'Cargo Shifter'. **1929** F. C. BOWEN *Sea Slang* 112 *Rockies*, R.N.V.R. ratings training in H.M. ships in peace time and very highly valued as worked ratings. Before the War it was also applied to R.N.R. ratings, seldom since. **1948** PARTRIDGE *Dict. Forces' Slang* 156 *Rockies*, officers of the Naval Reserves. **1957** KERR & GRANVILLE *Royal Naval Volunteer Reserve* vi. 91 The active-service men labelled them [*sc.* RNVR ratings] a 'rocky' lot—'rocky' being an oblique reference to unstable sea-legs and the waved tapes in their blue jean collars.

rococo, *a.* and *sb.* Add: **A.** *adj.* **1.** (Further examples.)

1870 M. ARNOLD in *Pall Mall Gaz.* 29 Nov. 3/2 We heard the honest German soldiers *Hoch-ing*, hurrahing, and God-blessing in their true-hearted but somewhat *rococo* manner. **1902** H. L. WILSON *Spenders* ix. 92 She is rather a beauty, you'll find;..a bit rococo in manner, I suspect.

2. a. (Earlier and later examples.) Also of interior decoration.

1841 C'TESS BLESSINGTON *Idler in France* I. i. 21 The whole [of the terraces near La Tour-Magne at Nîmes] offering a curious mixture of military and *rococo* taste.

1918 *Heal & Son Catal.: Cottage Furnit.* 1 The 'new art' overmantel smothered in rococo photograph frames. **1967** N. FREELING *Strike Out* 40 Presentation silver..in every conceivable pattern from curliest rococo to bleakest Swedish. **1972** *Country Life* 7 Dec. 1574/1 All these rooms have delicate rococo plaster ceilings picked out in pale pastel shades. **1980** *Early Music* Apr. 173/2 The organ sonatas of C. P. E. Bach from the 1750s are a good match for the rococo organ in Midwolda (1772).

transf. (Further examples.)
1931 *N. & Q.* 15 Aug. 109/2 It is further planned to give Goethe plays and rococo concerts on an open-air stage. **1938** W. S. MAUGHAM *Summing Up* 28 Dryden flourished at a happy moment... He was the first of the rococo artists. **1941** *Jazz Information* Nov. 21/2 James P. [Johnson] made his first player piano rolls..as a 'race' feature alongside the rococo but immensely popular efforts of Phil Ohman. **1955** *Times* 21 July 7/7 Stravinsky's choice of a more or less definite rococo pastiche is a highly appropriate musical idiom. **1959** *Listener* 26 Nov. 952/1 Haydn's symphonic music began as rococo entertainment. **1967** G. STEINER *Lang. & Silence* 28 This would..lead one to ask whether..the rococo virtuosity of Salinger is arguing an absurdly diminished and enervating view of human existence. **1970** *Oxf. Compan. Art* 987/1 The painter to whom the epithet 'Rococo' has most often been loosely applied is, perhaps, Watteau, and in his rejection of the *grand sujet* and his fanciful and curvacious rhythms he does..fit into the movement.

b. *Embroidery.* (See quots.)
1882 CAULFIELD & SAWARD *Dict. Needlework* 426/1 Rococo Embroidery is used for table borders, fire screens, and cushion covers, and is made with écru linen foundations, ornamented with filoselles. **1934** M. THOMAS *Dict. Embroidery Stitches* 171 *Rococco stitch*,..must be worked on a very wide-meshed canvas of even weave and the little groups or bundles of stitches are set in alternate squares, leaving the others open and rather 'pulled' in effect. **1960** G. LEWIS *Handbk. Crafts* 38 Frequently these two are the only stitches used to the neglect of the many others which would greatly enrich many pieces of work, such as.. French stitch..and Rococo stitch. **1960** B. SNOOK *Eng. Hist. Embroidery* 82 Rococo stitch is particularly effective. *Ibid.* 98 Designs of flowers, bouquets, ferns, ribbons and tassels..were either in varied silk stitchery on satin, or in tent stitch on canvas if enclosed in a rococo border.

B. *sb.* **1.** (Further examples.)
1935 W. S. MAUGHAM *Don Fernando* x. 224 Decoration ..degenerated with time to the frivolous ornament of rococo. **1947** A. EINSTEIN *Mus. Romantic Era* iii. 20 The 18th-century stylistic period that preceded the Empire, the Rococo, had been a last tremulous echo of the grandeur of the Baroque. **1954** [see *BAROQUE *a.* (*sb.*)]. **1965** *Listener* 3 June 830/1 The drawing in nearly all Monticelli's pictures is reminiscent of the rococo.

rococoCity. (Further example.)
1916 A. HUXLEY *Let.* 29 Dec. (1969) 118 My monocle is very grandiose, but gives me rather a Greco-Roman air of rococòcity.

rod, *sb.*[1] Add: **I. 5. b.** (Further examples.)
1935 B. PERRY *And gladly Teach* viii. 181 After showing me how often he had been 'high rod' on his stretch of the river, he would 'O.K.' all of my estimates with a smile. **1975** *Oxf. Univ. Gaz.* 16 Jan. 428/1 (Advt.), Prospective rods may apply for descriptive booklet.

c. Used in association with GUN *sb.* to designate the twin pursuits of fishing and shooting.
1840 J. WILSON (*title*) The rod and the gun, being two treatises on angling and shooting. *c* **1860** in A. Adburgham *Shops & Shopping* (1964) vii. 74 Their [*sc.* the fabrics'] close imitation of the colour of the natural objects surrounding the *Sportsman* have rendered them an absolute necessity for the pursuits of the rod or gun. **1912** E. D. CUMING (*title*) With rod and gun. **1966** *Times* 28 Feb. (Canada Suppl.) p. ii, Canada is a..catch-your-limit rod-and-gun of a country.

d. *transf.* The right to fish a length of river.
1932 G. CORNWALLIS-WEST *Edwardians go Fishing* v. 60 A friend of mine was invited to fish..on one of the upper reaches of the Test owned by Colonel Sneyd, who had kept a rod himself but had let two other rods to men who had little if any knowledge of the art of dry fly fishing. **1958** *Angling Times* 28 Feb. 11/3 The Board offers 14 rods to let during the 1958 season for its fishery on the River Piddle. **1970** *Daily Tel.* 9 Nov. 8/6 Fishing fees range from £250 to £400 a rod annually.

III. 9. a. *spec.* = *control rod* s.v. *CONTROL *sb.* 5; also (in full *fuel rod*), a long, slender piece of fuel for a nuclear reactor.
1956 *Ann. Rev. Nucl. Sci.* VI. 329 The fuel loading consists of roughly five tons of natural UO_2 or uranium metal as round rods clad with Zircaloy. *Ibid.* 334 Two automatic regulating rods ordinarily hold the power level within 3 per cent of the desired value. **1959** C. HODDER-WILLIAMS *Chain Reaction* ix. 113 Did he leave it so late that the 'X holes' had warped out of alignment and the rods wouldn't drop? **1964** *Jrnl. Brit. Nucl. Energy Soc.* III. 298/1 By utilizing a high energy, high strain rate deformation process, the fuel rod is not only completely encapsulated but..the can wall is pressurized into the anti-rachetting grooves. **1975** J. R. LAMARSH *Introd. Nucl. Engin.* vii. 262 The ordinary movement of the rods in most power reactors is controlled..by an on-line computer. **1979** K. FOLLETT *Triple* iv. 77 The reactor has three thousand fuel channels, each channel containing eight fuel rods.

d. One of the elongated light-sensitive cells in the retina responsible primarily for vision in poor light. Cf. CONE *sb.*[1] 10.
1866 [in Dict., sense 9 b]. **1905** A. FLINT *Handbk. Physiol.* xxvi. 658 The rods are regular cylinders, their length corresponding to the thickness of the layer, terminating above in truncated extremities, and below in points which probably are continuous with the filaments of connection with the nerve-cells. **1937** CARLSON & JOHNSON *Machinery of Body* xi. 447 At the point where the optic nerve enters the retina there are no rods and cones. **1958** BROCKLEHURST & WARD *Gen. School Biol.* xiv. 185 Rods are more numerous near the periphery of the retina, and cones..near its centre.

e. *slang.* The penis; the erect member.
1902 in FARMER & HENLEY *Slang* s.v. Penis. **1934** E. POUND *Eleven New Cantos* xxxix. 46 His rod hath made god in my belly. **1960** A. WEST *Trend is Up* x. 454 'I want you to love me and cherish me all the days of my life.' 'You want the rod, you silly bitch, you fouled-up boarding-house bitch,' he said, 'that's what you want.' **1975** B. MEGGS *Matter of Paradise* VI. iii. 142 He was seventeen..rod cocked and aimed at every passing female object.

f. *slang* (chiefly *U.S.*). A gun; a pistol or revolver.
1903 H. HAPGOOD *Autobiogr. of Thief* xii. 289 The dago dropped the smoke-wagon and the bartender threatened to put him in prison for pulling a rod on respectable people. **1926** J. BLACK *You can't Win* xi. 145, I think I shall put a small 'rod' in my coat pocket hereafter. **1929** D. RUNYON in *Hearst's Internat.* Oct. 201/1 Dave the Dude takes personal charge of Wild William and removes a rod from his pants pocket. **1934** A. MERRITT *Burn Witch Burn!* v. 65 'Pass your rods, Paul.' Without a word the chauffeur dipped into his pockets and handed him a pair of automatics. **1942** WODEHOUSE *Money in Bank* (1946) xxv. 224 If I've got to stick up an eat-'em-alive baby like her with nothing but a finger in my pocket, I want an extra cut... Either I have a rod, or it's seventy-five–twenty-five. **1953** K. TENNANT *Joyful Condemned* iv. 34 What's wrong with *you*, waving that rod about like a bloody half-wit. **1965** [see *BETSY]. **1978** J. CARROLL *Mortal Friends* II. iv. 179, I ain't getting my ass blown off because you're stupid. You won't get near Zorelli with a rod anyways.

g. *N. Amer. slang.* The draw-rod of a railway carriage or truck. Cf. *RIDE *v.* 18d.
1904 *Outing* July 486/2 Thousands of miles in the United States and Canada he has wandered on rods and blind baggages. **1924** J. TULLY *Beggars of Life* 56, I beat it through De Kalb last night on the rods of a mannerfest meat train. **1931** 'D. STIFF' *Milk & Honey Route* 192 We beat it on the run... Some rode the rods on passengers, While some blew out on freights. **1959** *Punch* 17 June 799/2 One does not picture train-robbers lurking at the top of the bank, nor even hoboes riding the rods.

h. *slang* (chiefly *U.S.*). = *HOT ROD.
1945 [see *HOT ROD]. **1948** *Hot Rod Mag.* July 4/3 With Carson upholstery And all the fine gear Of a more beautiful rod You never will hear. **1957** J. KEROUAC *On Road* I. xii. 79 A burly blond kid in a souped-up rod. **1972** J. GORES *Dead Skip* vii. 45 A two-bit Mission District auto and accessory dealer who specialized in old cars for conversion to dune buggies, drag cars, rods, and the like. **1978** *Hot Car* June 91/1 With just a beach buggy to his credit at that stage, Brian saw some US rods in Chicago and planned to build himself a C Cab on his return to this country.

IV. 11. b. *rod-bender*; *rod-case* (earlier and later examples), *licence*, *-ring*, *-stand*.
1956 *People* 13 May 12/6 He reckons that morning and evening are the best times for rod-benders, using bread flake and paste, on a 16- or 18-hook, for roach. **1976** *S. Wales Echo* 26 Nov., Steve..thought he had hooked a good cod when he struck into a real rod-bender at The Leys. **1852** C. M. YONGE *Two Guardians* i. 2 His numerous equipments, consisting of a long rod-case, a fishing-basket and landing-net. **1918** KIPLING in *Story-Teller* Dec. 221/2 'Did you? Good!' he replied heartily over the rod-case on his shoulders. **1969** *Sears, Roebuck & Co. Catal.* Spring–Summer 713/1 Ted Williams Rod Case... Foam-lined compartments at both ends for reels, accessories. **1976** *Eastern Daily Press* (Norwich) 19 Nov. 21/4 The proposed new charges..will be in addition to, and completely separate from, the rod licence charge. **1885** J. W. MARTIN *Float Fishing & Spinning* (ed. 2) 181/2 Rod-rings. **1972** *Shooting Times & Country Mag.* 1 July 12/1 Take care to ensure that the line can still run through the rod rings. **1902** *Chambers's Jrnl.* July 425/1 Any trout-rod, even after a brief life spent in such a manner, might have accepted its pensioner peg on the rod-stand.

c. In sense *9d as *rod cell, pigment, vision*; *rod-free* adj.
1940 *Chambers's Techn. Dict.* 728/2 Rod-cell. **1970** AMBROSE & EASTY *Cell Biol.* i. 26 In the complex light-sensitive rod cells of the vertebrate retina the membrane and fibre structure of cilia have been modified to receive light and convert it into an electrochemical stimulus. **1915** J. H. PARSONS *Introd. Study of Colour Vision* III. 204 Beyond the rod-free central area the cones diminish continuously in number. **1921** E. B. TITCHENER *Text-bk. Psychol.* xxii. 89 Animals whose eyes lack this rod-pigment—fowls, pigeons—are strictly diurnal in their habits. *Ibid.*, Whether the visual purple is essentially concerned in rod-vision. **1921** R. S. WOODWORTH *Psychol.* (1922) x. 226 Dim-light vision, or twilight vision as it is sometimes called, is rod vision and not cone vision.

12. rod puppet, a puppet operated and supported by rods; **rod-rider** *U.S.*, one who rides the rods (see sense 9 g above); hence **rod-riding** *ppl. a.*
1930 *Puppetry* I. 64 Stick or Rod Puppets. **1949** P. MCPHARLIN *Puppet Theatre in Amer.* xx. 347 Rod-puppets have stirred up interest for their novelty and adaptability. **1960** *Guardian* 19 Oct. 9/5 The Chinese theatre, with its impressive traditional rod puppets. **1976** *Jrnl. R. Soc. Arts* Apr. 254/1 A larger form of glove puppet can be produced by placing the figure on a rod; this is called a rod puppet. **1952** L. HUGHES *Laughing to keep from Crying* 60 The rod-riders got off nowhere near the station. **1967** B. J. BANFILL *Pioneer Nurse* iv. 43 Many readers may not have heard about the Rod Riders, who formed a part of history in opening the west. During the 'Awful Thirties', this name was given to wandering embittered men. *Ibid.* 44 Rod Riders..planned to steal rides on trains. **1953** W. BURROUGHS *Junkie* x. 95 This type cop could just as well be an oldtime rod-riding thug.

rod, *v.* Add: **4.** *trans.* To push a rod through (a drain or pipe) in order to clear it. Hence **ro·ddable** *a.*, capable of being rodded.
1924 E. G. BLAKE *Plumbing* I. xvii. 149 A manhole should be provided at each alteration of the direction of the drain, and at intervals of not more than from 80 yds. to 100 yds. in all straight runs. This will enable any obstruction to be cleared by rodding the drain. **1949** ESCRITT & RICH *Work of Sanitary Engineer* (ed. 2) xxii. 275 The disconnecting trap..is provided with a rodding arm which permits the outgoing line of pipe to be rodded. *Ibid.* xxiv. 283 The outlet should..be arranged so that it is easily roddable. **1971** B. LINDEN *Home Owner's Maintenance Guide* ii. 28 The drain pipes will probably have to be rodded to clear the blockage.

5. *intr.* Const. *up.* To arm oneself with a gun or guns. Cf. *ROD *sb.*[1] 9f. *U.S. slang.*
1929 [implied in *RODDED *ppl. a.* 4]. **1935** N. ERSINE *Underworld & Prison Slang* 63 *Rod up* and we'll blow. **1950** *Harper's Mag.* Feb. 75/2 They do not rod up, or arm themselves.

6. *trans.* To 'soup *up*' or convert (a car) into a hot rod. Cf. *ROD *sb.*[1] 9h. *U.S. slang.*
1972 J. GORES *Dead Skip* v. 32 A young man with an old car (hence, probably rodding it up, hence, probably, a car-lover).

rodded, *ppl. a.* Add: **4.** Const. *up.* Armed with a gun or guns. Cf. *ROD *v.* 5. *U.S. slang.*
1929 D. RUNYON in *Hearst's Internat.* Oct. 201/1 None of the guests are supposed to come rodded up, this being strictly a social matter. **1930** *Flynn's* 12 Apr. 402/2, I was rodded up an' I could 'a' give him the works..but it wasn't worth it. **1938** D. RUNYON *Furthermore* ix. 171 It is very much against the law for guys to go around rodded up this way in New York City.

rodden: see *RODHAM.

rodder (rǫ·dəɹ). *slang* (chiefly *U.S.*). [f. ROD *sb.*[1]] = *hot rodder* s.v. *HOT ROD; one who converts cars into hot rods. Cf. *ROD *sb.*[1] 9h.
1949 *Hot Rod Mag.* Feb. 18/2 The rod news is rather short this month. I guess the California rodders now know why we keep our cars parked in the winter months. **1953** BERREY & VAN DEN BARK *Amer. Thes. Slang* (1954) § 81a/2 *'Hot rod' owner*,..hot rodder, rod jockey, rodder. **1972** *World of Wild Wheels* (Custom Car) 58/1 When the British rodder glances through American Street Rod magazines he is faced with 99 per cent American cars. **1977** *Hot Car* Oct. 15/2 Brighter news for the rodder is another kit available from G. A. Stanley Palmer Ltd.

rodding, (*vbl.*) *sb.*[1] Add: **2. b.** The action of *ROD *v.* 4.
a **1890** [in Dict., sense 2]. **1945** W. J. WOOLGAR *Pract. Plumber & Sanitary Engin.* 313/1 Rodding eyes are useful at changes of direction and at the top end of a long branch drain. **1953** L. B. ESCRITT *Building Sanitation* (ed. 3) viii. 94 A light manhole cover is provided in a central position to facilitate rodding. **1973** *BSI News* Apr. 5 (*caption*) Members of the code drafting committee..watch a demonstration of rodding to remove blockages in drainage pipes.

4. *Geol.* A linear structure in metamorphic rocks characterized by the arrangement of grains of a constituent mineral, esp. quartz, in parallel rods. Also *rodding structure*.
1907 B. N. PEACH et al. *Geol. Structure of N.-W. Highlands of Scotland* (Mem. Geol. Survey) xii. 211 In the exposures of these dykes, which happen to cross the direction of rodding almost at right angles, no plane-foliation is observable. **1923** *Q. Jrnl. Geol. Soc.* LXXIX. 439 In the hornblende-schists there is actual rodding or elongation of the crystals. **1953** *Proc. Geologists' Assoc.* LXIV. 119 Rodding is developed from quartz that has been introduced into, or has segregated in, the rocks. **1970** K. C. JACKSON *Textbk. Lithology* vii. 426 Associated with the larger-scale folding may be the segregation of more mobile constituents such as quartz, resulting in a small-scale rodding structure.

roddon: see *RODHAM.

roddy, obs. var. *RHODY.

rode, *sb.*[2] For *U.S.* read *N. Amer.* and add further examples.
1792 G. CARTWRIGHT *Jrnl.* I. p. xiii, *Rode*, a small tow-line, of four inches and an half; made use of by shallops, by way of a cable. **1950** R. MOORE *Candlemas Bay* I. 45 His anchor and rode were stowed down under the stern. **1963** J. T. ROWLAND *North to Adventure* x. 147 With both hooks down and a long scope of rode she should be able to ride out anything.

rode, *v.*[2] Add: Hence **ro·ding** *vbl. sb.* (freq. *attrib.*) and *ppl. a.*
1888 [in Dict.]. **1927** E. SANDARS *Bird Bk. for Pocket* 156 Cock's nuptial display ('Roding'),..plumage fluffed out and uttering call. **1955** *Times* 10 May 12/5 These two sounds, so useful as an aid to seeing woodcock, are constantly uttered during its 'roding' flights, which start at sunset, are continued for perhaps an hour, and are resumed at dawn. **1973** *Ibis* CXV. 135 Many workers have described the roding behaviour of the Woodcock and speculated on its biological meaning.

rodent, *a.* and *sb.* Add: **B.** *sb.* **2.** *attrib.* and *Comb.*, as *rodent controller, officer, operative, operator*; *rodent-carried, infested, -like, proof* adjs.; **rodent-run** *Ornith.*, a run made by some birds when disturbed in which they resemble a running rodent.

1959 *New Biol.* XXIX. 96 A rodent-carried bacterium caused the Black Death. **1970** *Daily Tel.* 14 May 2/8 A senior rodent controller..was yesterday presented with the British Empire Medal for his 18 years' work destroying rats. **1979** *Dædalus* Summer 137 They all confirm that the chapel was rodent infested. **1978** P. PORTER *Cost of Seriousness* 3 Just as at seven the teeth stick out which Later slope in, rodent-like. **1944** *Liverpool Echo* 31 Jan. 2/2 Westminster City Council's rat-catcher is in future to be called Rodent Officer. **1973** in *Fremdsprachen* (1976) XX. 212/1 Fourteen visits from a rodent officer..had not stemmed the infestation. **1944** *Sunday Times* 5 Nov. 6/2 When it comes to official jargon, can you beat turning our old friend the rat-catcher into a 'Rodent Operative'? **1972** *Daily Tel.* 1 May 3/4 The Ministry also advises people to consult their local authority's rodent operative on the best way of applying whatever measures they decide on. **1979** J. GARDNER *Nostradamus Traitor* ii. 248 'Are you a rat-catcher, Mr. Kruger?'..'They are called rodent operatives nowadays.' **1946** *Word Study* May 2/2 Euphemisms..*rodent operator* for *rat-catcher*. **1972** C. DRUMMOND *Death at Bar* vii. 179 The lunatic..is now a traveller for a firm of rodent operators. **1977** *Field* 13 Jan. 68/1 (Advt.), It's horse sense to buy your food storage bins direct from the manufacturer. A quality product. Rodent proof. **1950** *Ibis* XCII. 28 We observed that a husky dog would immediately chase the Purple Sandpiper that made a 'rodent-run' and would be completely fooled. **1961** D. A. BANNERMAN *Birds Brit. Isles* X. 197 Birds of this northern race [of golden plover] will sit until almost trodden upon, and then shuffle away looking much like a teal in the process, though some would prefer—without too much regard for the truth—to speak of its 'rodent-run'. **1976** VAN TYNE & BERGER *Fund. Ornith.* (ed. 2) iv. 209 The 'rodent-run' display..has been reported for a number of shorebirds.., for some tundra species, and for the Green-Tailed Towhee.

rodentian, *a.* For *rare*—¹ read *rare* and substitute for def.: Of, pertaining to, or consisting of rodents.

1974 *Amer. N. & Q.* XIII. 25/1 The latent comedy in Chaucer's further gathering of words with obvious rodentian associations.

rodenticide (rǫde·ntisəid). [f. RODENT *sb.* + -CIDE I, after *insecticide*, etc.] A poison used to kill rodents.

1938 *Bull. Calif. Dept. Agric.* XXVII. 172 This material ..might serve both as a rodenticide and an insecticide. **1961** *Times* 18 July 6/6 The use of toxic chemicals is governed by a voluntary notification scheme agreed between the Government departments and the industrial association concerned, covering insecticides, fungicides, herbicides and rodenticides. **1975** *Nature* 24 Jan. 275/2 Field populations of common rats..resistant to anticoagulant rodenticides..have appeared in Scotland, Denmark, [etc.].

Hence **rodentici·dal** *a.*, of or pertaining to a rodenticide; poisonous to rodents.

1939 *Jrnl. Amer. Vet. Med. Assoc.* XCV. 486/1 Human poisoning has resulted from..accidental ingestion of the metal used for entomological and rodenticidal purposes. **1979** P. L. G. BATEMAN *Household Pests* i. 25 Pest control chemicals are selected for their insecticidal or rodenticidal efficiency.

rodeo. Delete ||, for *Amer.* read 'orig. *U.S.*', and add: Now also with pronunc. (rōᵘ·di,o). **3. a.** A public exhibition of skill, often in the form of a competition, in the riding of unbroken horses, the roping of calves, wrestling with steers, etc.

1914 B. M. BOWER *Flying U Ranch* 16 They have them rodeos on a Sunday, mostly, and they invite everybody to it, like it was a picnic. **1925** *Annual Rodeo Program* (Tucson, Arizona) 3 We extend a cordial invitation to you to come to Tucson for our Annual Rodeo. **1938** D. COOLIDGE *Arizona Cowboys* ii. 27 The round-up had just begun. They call it *rodéo*, in Spanish, but the cactus cowboys pronounced it rodér. The contest riders of today have given it another twist and call it ró-deo. **1940** *Arizona* (Arizona Work Projects Administration Writers' Project) 72 That distinctively western entertainment, the rodeo, was originally an exhibition of cowboy skill in the regular activities of cattle ranch and range. But today it is largely commercialized and many of its features are of the circus type, remote from the cowpuncher's everyday life. **1950** *Manch. Guardian Weekly* 5 Oct. 6/2 Madison Square Garden is presently dedicated to Gene Autry and the annual rodeo. **1976** *Columbus* (Montana) *News* 27 May 1/4 One of those injured was a prime mover and instigator of this rodeo, Ed Miller, who is currently in St. Vincent's with a broken leg.

b. *transf.* A similar exhibition of competitive skill in the riding of motor-cycles, fishing, etc.; also used more generally of other types of competition. Also *fig.* Cf. *ROADEO.

1927 *My Oklahoma* July 23/1 Oklahoma is going to have a state-wide baby rodeo next year. **1928** *Daily Express* 7 May 15/3 On Wednesday..a motor-cycle rodeo in the afternoon will be followed by a carnival procession through the town. **1940** *Sun* (Baltimore) 11 Sept. 1/7 Nazi bombers smashed at London with increasing violence early today in their fourth consecutive dusk-to-dawn rodeo of destruction. **1949** *Daily Progress* (Charlottesville, Va.) 22 Aug. 9/1 Entries for the fishing rodeo for youngsters here must be in by Thursday.

4. *attrib.* and *Comb.*, as *rodeo circuit, clown, cowboy, ground, parade, queen, rider, riding* (*sb.* and *a.*).

1961 M. S. ROBERTSON *Rodeo* 101/1 The California Rodeo..is one of the Big Four, the rodeos whose pioneering and consistent greatness bridged the years from the inception of the 'cowboy tournaments' to the modern rodeo circuit. **1980** *Country Life* 13 Nov. 1819/1 He..started bronc riding in the rodeos...Demobbed, he returned to the rodeo circuit. **1927** *Progressive Arizona* IV. ii. 7 The arena presents a scene of animation with the judges, time-keepers, contestants, performers, event clerks, and Jolly, 'the funniest rodeo clown of them all' milling about. **1941** L. B. CHAFFIN *Sons of West* xv. 222 This trick, in almost every identical move, is practiced by modern rodeo clowns of today. **1958** E. H. PEPLOW *Hist. Arizona* II. xx. 405 The competitive life of a rodeo cowboy is shorter than that of an athlete in almost any other sport. **1892** Rodeo ground [in Dict., sense 1]. **1979** *Tucson Mag.* Apr. 68/3 Admission is charged for this event at the rodeo grounds. **1941** *La Fiesta de los Vaqueros Program* (Tucson, Arizona) 9 Tucson and its guests spend two hours..standing on each other's toes in order to see the rodeo parade. **1976** *Billings* (Montana) *Gaz.* 10 June 1-A/5 In Hardin, activities include a weeklong carnival beginning Monday followed by a rodeo Friday and a rodeo parade at noon Sunday. **1945** *Pueblo* (Colorado) *Star-Jrnl.* 3 June 7/3 Nine girls at the Pueblo ordnance depot will don cowboy hats, bright shirts, and jeans to vie for the honor of rodeo queen. **1975** R. HOBAN *Turtle Diary* xxv. 115 She'd..been a rodeo rider, done roller derbies, wrestled, had three husbands and all kinds of troubles. **1979** 'G. BLACK' *Night Run from Java* i. 7 A rodeo rider thrown by a bronco. **1974** *Times* 7 Jan. 8/3 We did hunter trials, show jumping, rodeo riding, and so on. **1976** *Evening Standard* 29 Dec., The Hard Breed. Rodeo-riding Cain slain by younger brother.

Hence **rode·o** *v. intr.*, to compete in a rodeo. Also **rode·oer**; **rode·oing** *vbl. sb.* (All also with stress on first syllable.)

1959 *Rodeo Sports News* 1 Nov. 2/1 I've wondered.. what the contestants do when they quit rodeoing. *Ibid.* 15 Nov. 2/4 A cowboy who would rather hunt than rodeo —we've got everything in the northwest! **1970** *Ibid.* 15 Nov. 2/2 A top bull rider who rodeoed up through the mid-sixties stopped by and said hello the other day. **1976** *Oregonian* (Portland, Oregon) 14 June C3/2 Because it is not a sport sanctioned by the National Collegiate Athletic Association, rodeoers are free to compete in professional rodeo while they are still on the college circuit. **1977** *New Yorker* 6 June 74/2 They loved making cowhands of their frisky little girls—they took them riding and roping and rodeoing.

rodgersia (rǫdʒə̄·ziă). Also **Rodgersia.** [mod.L. (A. Gray 1859, in *Mem. Amer. Acad.* New Ser. VI. 389), f. the name of John *Rodgers* (1812–82), American admiral + -IA¹.] A large perennial herb of the genus so called, belonging to the family Saxifragaceæ, native to eastern Asia, and bearing compound leaves and terminal panicles of small white flowers.

[**1902** *Gardeners' Chron.* 23 Aug. 131/2 At present in the rock garden at Kew there is in flower, for the first time in Europe, a new species of Rodgersia.] **1908** R. FARRER *Alpines & Bog-Plants* ix. 185 Of foliage plants for the lake-side..there is nothing to surpass the Rodgersias. **1962** *Amateur Gardening* 24 Mar. 4/2 Among foliage plants for the waterside there are none to surpass the rodgersias. **1976** *Country Life* 6 May 1172/3 There is a wealth of plants..including hardy plants such as gunneras, rodgersias, hostas and hellebores.

rodham (rǫ·dăm). *E. Anglia.* Also **rodden, roddon.** [Of obscure formation (see note below).] A raised bank in the Fen district of East Anglia, consisting of the bed and levees of a dry river-course which have been raised above the level of the adjacent land by deposition of silt, usu. by the incoming tide, and by compaction and lowering of the adjacent peat soil; occas. used to signify only a levee bounding such a river-course.

The spelling *roddon* was adopted and popularized by G. Fowler (see quot. 1932), whilst the older form in -(*h*)*am* remains dominant in local use. Any connection with *roddin* (cf. E.D.D. and ROD *sb.*²) is unlikely.

[**1857** T. WRIGHT *Dict. Obsolete & Provincial Engl.* II. 806 *Roddam*, a bed of sand resting on the clay beneath the peat, in the fens of Cambridgeshire.] **1932** G. FOWLER in *Geogr. Jrnl.* LXXIX. 210 There are numerous raised banks of laminated silt or shell maul meandering through the Fens. Neither historians nor geologists appear to have noticed them... Fen dwellers however have noted these banks but generally without realizing their origin. They call them *roddons*. This word appears to be allied to *roddin* or *rodden*, which Wright in his 'English Dialect Dictionary'..gives as meaning a narrow road, path or sheep track. I spell the word *roddon* as it sounds; and I prefer it as a spelling to *rodham*, as used in the name Rodham Farm, as the latter appears corrupted in the second syllable. **1945** B. E. DORMAN *Story of Ely* i. 3 These raised river beds are known as roddens... One fine example..can be seen..alongside..the road from Littleport to Shippea Hill. The few houses along this road are nearly all built on the rodden, for it provides a firmer foundation than peat. **1957** A. K. ASTBURY *Black Fens* v. 26 Levees formed as parallel ridges one on either side of the main channel... Where subsequent cultivation has been long and constant the two levees may tend to merge into one general bank of silt... But all such levees, whether separate or merged, are in the black fens known as rodhams. *Ibid.* 27 Fowler..used the form roddon—influenced by the fact that in the north of England the word roddin or rodden means a narrow road... But although later writers have adopted Fowler's spelling, the fact remains that fenmen themselves call these things rodhams. **1957** G. E. HUTCHINSON *Treat. Limnol.* I. i. 119 The tidal water from this shallow arm of the sea, the southward continuation of the modern Wash, was evidently very turbid and deposited levees at the sides of the channels, known as roddons, along which it ran. **1963** E. S. WOOD *Collins Field Guide to Archaeol.* II. 199 Silt Banks, otherwise known as roddons, or rodhams, are caused by tidal action depositing silt up slow rivers. **1971** *Norfolk Fair* Feb. 36/3 Old extinct watercourses can be traced by the rodhams of silt and the slades of chalky material. **1974** J. R. RAVENSDALE *Liable to Floods* i. 21 Gordon Fowler..noticed a roddon in the north-east corner of Cottenham parish.

Rodinesque (rodæne·sk), *a.* [f. the name of Auguste *Rodin* (1840–1917), French Romantic School sculptor + -ESQUE.] Of, pertaining to, or reminiscent of Rodin or his work, marked by masterly realism and love of movement.

1905 G. B. SHAW *Let.* 13 Mar. (1972) II. 521 It is a bad case of helpless genius in the first blaze of youth; and the drawings are queer and Rodinesque enough to be presentable at this particular moment. **1934** *Sunday Times* 11 Feb. 6/1 Mr. O'Casey's eye-appeal is the old business of Rodinesque, Volga-Boatmannish stage-grouping. **1934** F. SCOTT FITZGERALD *Tender is Night* I. iv, As if the features..had been molded with a Rodinesque intention. **1962** *Times* 14 Feb. 15/1 Little Rodinesque bronze figures..are on show in the front gallery.

rodingite (rōᵘ·diŋəit). *Petrogr.* [f. the name of the River *Roding*, S. of Nelson, New Zealand + -ITE¹.] A crystalline rock consisting of diallage and grossularite (or hydrogrossularite), often with prehnite and chlorite, and typically found in or adjacent to serpentinite masses, having been formed by the calcium metasomatism of basic or ultrabasic igneous rocks.

1911 J. M. BELL et al. in *Bull. N.Z. Geol. Survey* No. 12. 31 Dykes of a coarse-grained gabbro-like rock penetrate the serpentines in many places... The writers have applied to the rock the name 'rodingite', owing to the typical exposure occurring on the River Roding. **1954** *Mineral. Mag.* XXX. 525 (*heading*) Rodingite from the Girvan–Ballantrae complex, Ayrshire. **1976** *Neues Jahrb. für Mineral.* (*Monatshefte*) 188 The rodingites described here show an absolute prevalence of garnet, which has a variable composition ranging from an almost pure grossularite..to an intermediate member of the grossularite-andradite series.

Hence **rodingi·tic** *a.*; also **ro·dingitized** *ppl. a.*, converted into rodingite; **ro·dingiti:zing** *ppl. a.*, **ro:dingitiza·tion.**

1953 *Jrnl. Faculty of Sci., Hokkaido Univ.* 4th Ser. VIII. 419 (*heading*) On the rodingitic rocks within the serpentinite masses of Hokkaido. **1971** *Canad. Jrnl. Earth Sci.* VIII. 642/2 This subdivision..improved the permeability for rodingitizing fluids. *Ibid.* 643/1 (*caption*) Serpentinized and partially rodingitized peridotite. *Ibid.* 644/1 Development of garnets, hydrogarnets (hibschite), in a process somewhat similar to rodingitization. **1975** *Contrib. Mineral. & Petrol.* XLIX. 233 The latter described rodingitic material in their study of serpentinized ultramafic rocks dredged from the Mid-Atlantic Ridge at 45°N. *Ibid.*, Partially rodingitized olivine gabbros were also found. *Ibid.* 253 The rodingitization of the gabbroids and the serpentinization of the ultramafics appear to be two concomitant and complementary metasomatic processes.

rodman. Add: **2.** (Earlier and later examples.) Chiefly *U.S.*

1853 A. W. WHIPPLE in *Rep. Explorations for Railroad to Pacific Ocean* (U.S. War Dept.) (1856) I. i. 5 The chainmen and rodmen being ignorant of their duties, little more than teaching them could this day be accomplished. **1972** *Publishers' Weekly* 7 Aug. 48/2 In Chicago in 1925, when he was a rodman with a Cook County surveying crew.

3. *slang.* One who handles a gun; a gunman. Cf. *ROD *sb.*¹ 9f.

1924 G. C. HENDERSON *Keys to Crookdom* 396 Assaulter, rough guy, hard bird, rod man, rod toter. **1931** *Amer. Speech* VII. 113 He used to be a rodman on the convoy, but he didn't have the guts for that job. **1940** W. R. BURNETT *High Sierra* i. 12 We need a rodman... You're it. *a* **1953** DYLAN THOMAS *Quite Early one Morning* (1954) 39 A raid by the vice-squad on a clip-joint for retired rod-men. **1962** *John o' London's* 4 Oct. 325/2 Robert is victim number two of this assassination, the only witness who could identify the rod-man.

rodney. Add: **3.** [Perh. a different word.] A small fishing boat or punt. *Canad.*

1895 *Christmas Rev.* (Newfoundland) 18 Jim Leary, whose handiwork, whether displayed in the construction of baitskiff, smack, skiff, punt or rodney, was always superior to what any other man in the settlement could turn out. *c* **1900** in *Regional Lang. Stud.—Newfoundland* (1978) VIII. 24 *Rodney*, small, single crosshand[ed] punt. **1908** N. DUNCAN *Every Man for Himself* ix. 260 'Launch that rodney,' Wull directed, 'an' put me on shore.' **1923** *Sunday at Home* Dec. 153/1 The punt..was one of the small, light type of boat called a 'rodney', and it was used mainly for shooting about the harbour, or on sealing trips. **1931** J. R. SMALLWOOD *New Newfoundland* 266 Often he'd take us to sail in his rodney, Out over the water. **1966** A. R. SCAMMELL *My Newfoundland* 36 Sid, go over to Blanchard's and keep an eye on what they're doing. Take the rodney.

Rodriguan (rǫdrī·găn), *a.* and *sb.* [f. *Rodrigues* (see below) + -AN.] **A.** *adj.* Of, pertaining to, or characteristic of the island of Rodrigues, a dependency of Mauritius in the western Indian Ocean, or its people. **B.** *sb.* A native or inhabitant of Rodrigues.

1973 *Times* 5 Mar. (Mauritius Suppl.) p. v/1 The islanders are very Rodriguan-minded. *Ibid.*, An elected island council..would give Rodriguans a chance to put their views. **1974** *Islander* (Victoria, B.C.) 25 Aug. 2/4 We found the Rodriguans interesting. **1977** G. DURRELL *Golden Bats & Pink Pigeons* iv. 86 A large, chocolate-coloured Rodriguan in a handsome, khaki uniform.

roe[1]. Add: **2. roe ring,** a track worn by roe deer running in circles prior to mating; **roe-stalking,** the hunting of roe-deer on foot; so **roe-stalker.**

1951 H. TEGNER *Roe Deer* iii. 27 (*caption*) Shape of roe rings: small circles denote small trees or bushes as axes around which roe form these runs. **1960** M. BURTON *Wild Animals* 128 A feature of the rutting season [of roe deer] which has attracted a good deal of attention in recent years has to do with the use of 'roe rings', in which a form of courtship takes place. **1974** F. HOLMES *Following Roe* i. 10 Roe rings, well-trodden runs in the shape of a circle or a figure-of-eight, are evidence of roe residence if they have been recently used. **1927** EDWARDS & WALLACE *Hunting & Stalking Deer* xlii. 237, I have never yet met a roe-stalker who did not love the roe. **1906** J. G. MILLAIS *Mammals Gt. Brit. & Ireland* III. 178 There are of course hundreds of estates in the North where Roe-stalking is not possible. **1973** *Country Life* 26 July 254/3 A week's roe-stalking in Britain is..one of the most sought-after privileges among European devotees.

roe[3]. Substitute for etym. 'Perh. a transf. use of ROE[2]' and add further examples.

1920 A. L. HOWARD *Man. Timbers of World* 144 *Mahogany, Cuba*... Many of the logs are beautifully figured or marked with wavy and curly grain, which is variously termed splash mottle, roe and mottle, fiddle-back, plum, snail, blister and cross-bar. **1938** B. J. RENDLE *Commerc. Mahoganies* 5 Mahogany is remarkably stable and does not shrink and swell so much as most woods. Irregularities of the grain produce a variety of figure—fiddleback, blister, stripe or roe, curl, mottle, etc. **1952** J. GLOAG *Short Dict. Furnit.* 396 *Roe*, a name given to the regular appearance of dark figures and spots in figured mahogany, which give a mottled effect, like a fish roe. A form of roe figure occurs in flowered, or East Indian, satinwood. **1968** *Canad. Antiques Coll.* Aug. 24/2 *Roe figure*, this is alternate bands of twisted grain which produce stripes parallel to the length of the tree. When viewed in certain lights from either end the light and dark stripes are reversed.

rœblingite (rǝ̄·bliŋǝit). *Min.* [f. the name of W. A. *Rœbling* (1837–1926), U.S. civil engineer + -ITE[1].] A rare, monoclinic, basic sulphate-silicate of lead, calcium, and other elements, occurring as compact white masses of minute crystals.

1897 PENFIELD & FOOTE in *Amer. Jrnl. Sci.* CLIII. 415 At the request of Mr. Nason the authors take pleasure in naming this mineral roeblingite in honor of the celebrated engineer, Mr. W. A. Rœbling of Trenton, N.J. **1966** *Amer. Mineralogist* LI. 507 Only a tentative formula, $(Pb_4S_4O_{16})R_{16}Si_{12}O_{44}H_{20}$, where R = Ca, Mn, Sr, Na, and K,..can be assigned to roeblingite.

Roedean (rōᵘ·dīn). The name of an independent public school for girls (founded 1885) in the borough of Brighton, applied (usu. *attrib.*) to refined speech or behaviour in (young) women, such as is popularly associated with the girls of this school. (Freq. in derogatory use.)

1948 C. DAY LEWIS *Otterbury Incident* 83 Now don't go all Roedean with me, beautiful. **1958** J. CANNAN *And be a Villain* iv. 94 Dropping the high clear Roedean voice she affected and speaking naturally. **1963** M. FRAYN in Sissons & French *Age of Austerity* 336 The orange-girls.. articulating 'Come, gentle people, buy', in sub-Roedean accents. **1969** S. HYLAND *Top Bloody Secret* ii. 114 The switchboard girl spoke English in the best Roedean manner. **1972** J. ROSSITER *Rope for General Dietz* iii. 31 Her accent was a creamy 1969-vintage Roedean. **1977** F. BRANSTON *Up & Coming Man* x. 95 A Roedean accent which could have flayed the skin off a waiter.

Roederer (rō̆·dǝrǝɹ). Also **Rœderer.** The proprietary name of a champagne produced by the firm of Roederer in Rheims.

1872 B. JERROLD *London* vii. 68 The would-be aristocrat flashing his silver mug of foaming Rœderer in the eyes of the Vulgar. **1876** *Trade Marks Jrnl.* 15 Nov. 803/1 Theophile Roederer & Co. Reims. Maison fondée en 1864. ..Gustave Bousigues, dit Bley, of and on behalf of the firm of Theophile Roederer and Co., Reims, France; champagne wine merchants... Champagne wine. **1907** [see *MUMM]. **1920** G. SAINTSBURY *Notes on Cellar-bk.* v. 74, I had some good wines of it—Pommery and Krug and Roederer among them. **1974** H. R. F. KEATING *Underside* xvi. 156 There was Roederer to drink, a small case of it packed in ice.

‖ **roemer** (rō̆·mǝɹ). [a. Du. *roemer*, G. *römer*; cf. RUMMER.] A type of decorated German or Dutch wine-glass with a knobbed or 'prunted' stem.

1897 A. HARTSHORNE *Old Eng. Glasses* 47 Germans were making roemers in the Low Countries before the middle of the seventeenth century, and there also the quaint vessel had a long course, being the glass *par excellence*, with its delicate shades of blue, yellow, or green, that the painters never tired of painting. **1926** W. BUCKLEY *European Glass* 55 Particular mention should be made of the 'roemer', a form that is usually acknowledged not only to be the most beautiful product of the German industry but one of the most beautiful forms that has been made in glass in any country. **1942** [see *PASSGLAS]. **1972** *Country Life* 23 Mar. 700/2 No one who is familiar with German and Dutch glass..can fail to notice ..the prunts on the stems of the popular wine glass of those days—the roemer.

roemerite (rǝ̄·mǝrǝit). *Min.* Also **römerite.** [ad. G. *römerit* (J. Grailich 1858, in *Sitzungsber. d. K. Akad. d. Wissensch. in Wien* XXVIII. 272), f. the name of Friedrich Adolph *Römer* (1809–69), German geologist: see -ITE[1].] A hydrated sulphate of ferrous and ferric iron, often containing zinc, which occurs as rust-brown to yellow triclinic crystals, usu. as an oxidation product of pyrite.

1877 E. S. DANA *Text-bk. Mineral.* III. 373 Alum and Halotrichite Groups. Here belong: Tschermigite, ammonium alum. Kalinite, potassium alum... Also Roemerite, and Voltaite. **1903** *Jrnl. Chem. Soc.* LXXXIV. II. 555 Römerite was prepared by allowing a mixture of powdered ferrous sulphate and acid ferric sulphate to remain in contact with moist air for several months. **1927** *Amer. Mineralogist* XII. 282 Chemically, roemerite is a double sulphate of ferrous and ferric iron, the ferrous iron of which may sometimes be replaced by zinc and magnesium, and the ferric iron by aluminum. **1970** *Ibid.* LV. 78 Roemerite is generally the result of an oxidation of iron sulfides.

Roentgen, roentgen (rö·ntχyĕn; now usu. anglicized, as rɒ·ntyĕn; also rǝ̄-nt-, rǫ-nt-; -gĕn, -ʒĕn). Also **Röntgen, röntgen.** [The name of Wilhelm Conrad *Röntgen* (1845–1923), German physicist, who discovered X-rays in 1895 (*Sitzungsber. d. Phys.-Med. Ges. z. Würzburg* 132).] **1.** *attrib.* († or in the possessive), as *Roentgen rays*, X-rays. Hence *Roentgen photograph, therapy*, etc. Occas. written as a prefix (cf. *ROENTGEN-, ROENTGENO-). Now chiefly *U.S.*

1896 [in Dict. s.v. RÖNTGEN]. **1896** *Lancet* 1 Feb. 326/2 Do Roentgen's rays possess germicidal properties? *Ibid.* 22 Feb. 477/1 Two preliminary short exposures to Roentgen rays indicated that the metal..was probably embedded among the bones of the wrist. **1910** *Arch. Roentgen Ray* XV. 85 In Roentgentherapy the filter has brought the treatment of hypertrichosis once more into the domain of practical politics. **1911** *Encycl. Brit.* XXIII. 695/1 The radiation..from tin is as penetrating as that given out by a fairly efficient Röntgen tube. *Ibid.*, The incidence of Röntgen rays on matter causes the matter to emit cathodic rays. **1933** U. V. PORTMANN in O. Glasser *Sci. of Radiol.* xii. 221 In the beginning of roentgen therapy only skin diseases and some superficial malignant conditions were treated. **1940** H. K. PANCOAST et al. (*title*) The head and neck in roentgen diagnosis. *Ibid.* xi. 773 The chest should always be included as a part of any roentgen examination of the neck, particularly in infants and young children. **1953** A. J. DELARIO *Roentgen, Radium & Radioisotope Therapy* iii. 17 Because roentgen rays have such short wave-lengths, they cannot be diffracted by various diffraction gratings, as can visible light. **1956** L. A. HADLEY *Spine* iv. 95 By this method it is possible to furnish roentgen evidence of ligamentous or soft tissue injury. **1959** W. T. MOSS *Therapeutic Radiol.* ii. 35 With few exceptions all roentgentherapy techniques, by necessity, entail skin irradiation. **1959** W. T. MURPHY *Radiation Therapy* xxxvi. 770 Roentgen sickness is not frequently seen after pelvic irradiation. **1972** H. L. KUNDEL in E. J. Potchen *Current Concepts in Radiol.* I. i. 1 (*heading*) Factors limiting roentgen interpretation—physical and psychologic. **1978** S. SHELDON *Bloodline* ii. 33 A Roentgen desk in the library.

2. (Usu. in the form **roentgen.**) In full **roentgen unit.** The unit of exposure to X or gamma radiation, equal to the quantity of radiation that gives rise to ions carrying a total charge of 2·58 coulombs (regardless of sign) per kilogramme of air. Abbrev. *r.* [Proposed (in Fr.) by I. Solomon 1921, in *Arch. d'Électr. méd. expér. & clin.* XXIX. 362.]

The precise definition of this unit has been altered several times. Cf. *REM *sb.*[1], *REP[7].

1922 [see *R II. 4]. **1932** *Radiology* XVIII. 95/2 At the second International Congress of Radiology in 1928..the measurement of air ionization was accepted as the basis of international dosage measurement and a definition was given of the unit of dosage designating a roentgen unit and written in abbreviated form as 'r'. **1938** R. W. LAWSON tr. *Hevesy & Paneth's Man. Radioactivity* (ed. 2) xxiv. 258 The maximum daily dosage of γ-rays that a human being can tolerate without apparent harm is 0·1 röntgen unit. **1950** *Radiology* LV. 744/1 As our exciting energies increased, we were placed in a position of having continually to modify the definition of the roentgen in order to cope with the new properties of the higher-energy radiations. Because of this situation, minor modifications in the definition of the roentgen were made in 1931, 1934 and 1937. **1955** *Bull. Atomic Scientists* Sept. 257/2 It is known that radiation dosages in the levels of 400 roentgen units..are lethal to about half the individuals exposed. **1956** *Brit. Jrnl. Radiol.* XXIX. 355/2 The radiation dose in röntgens within any volume element is determined by the number and energy of the photons passing through that element during the exposure, irrespective of the local distribution of matter. *Ibid.* 356/1 Difficulties have only arisen when we have tried to make the röntgen do service for a unit of absorbed dose. **1959** *Listener* 26 Nov. 929/2 The fall-out from testing bombs gives a thirty-year dose of ·1 roentgen. ..The dose from natural radiation is about 3–5 roentgens. **1970** PASSMORE & ROBSON *Compan. Med. Stud.* II. xxxiii. 4/2 The same exposure (in roentgens) may result in different absorbed doses (in rads) in different tissues. **1977** [see *PROTOCOL *sb.* 3].

Hence † **Roe·ntgenized** *ppl.a.*, subjected to the action of X-rays; also † **Roe·ntgenize** *v. trans.* (*rare*: in quot. *fig.*); † **Roe:ntgeniza·tion.**

1897 *Phil. Mag.* XLIII. 243 The effect can in no way be due to conduction through the Röntgenized air. **1899** Röntgenized [see RÖNTGENIZE *v.*]. **1907** *Med. Rec.* (N.Y.) 9 Nov. 760/2 In the use of radium, if enclosed in aluminium or mica receptacles, we utilize the beta or cathode ray. This we cannot do in Roentgenisation. **1909** E. REICH *Nights with Gods* 17 It [*sc.* jealousy] has Röntgenised the most hidden interiors. **1920** *Arch. Radiol. & Electrotherapy* XXIV. 270/1 Röntgenisation of the lymphatic glands should always supplement radium therapy.

roentgen-, roentgeno-. Chiefly *U.S.* Also **röntgen(o)-.** Comb. forms of *ROENTGEN, as in **roentgenky·mogram** [ad. G. *röntgenkymogramm* (Gött & Rosenthal 1912, in *München med. Wochenschr.* 17 Sept. 2033)], a recording made with a kymograph (sense *2); **roentgenky·mograph** = *KYMOGRAPH 2; **roe:ntgenkymogra·phic** *a.*, of, pertaining to, or involving the roentgenkymograph; hence **roe:ntgenkymogra·phically** *adv.*; **roe:ntgenkymo·graphy** [ad. G. *röntgenkymographie* (Gött & Rosenthal 1912, loc. cit.)], the process or technique of using a kymograph (sense *2); kymography; **roe·ntgenogram,** an X-ray photograph; cf. RADIOGRAPH *sb.* 2 in Dict. and Suppl.; **roe·ntgenograph** *sb.* = prec.; also as *v. trans.*, to take an X-ray picture of (an organ, etc.); = *RADIOGRAPH *v.*; **roentgenogra·phic** *a.*, pertaining to or involving roentgenography; hence **roentgenogra·phically** *adv.*; **roentgeno·graphy,** radiography carried out by means of X-rays; **roentgenolo·gic, -lo·gical** *adjs.*, of, pertaining to, or involving roentgenology; hence **roentgenolo·gically** *adv.*; **roentgeno·logist,** one who practises roentgenology; **roentgeno·logy,** † (*a*) (see quot. 1905); (*b*) (the field of science concerned with) the medical use of X-rays, esp. as a diagnostic tool; cf. *RADIOLOGY; **roe·ntgenoscope** *sb.* = *FLUOROSCOPE; hence as *v. trans.*, to examine by means of a fluoroscope; **roentgenosco·pic** *a.*, fluoroscopic; hence **roentgenosco·pically** *adv.*; **roentgeno·scopy,** fluoroscopy; **roentgenothe·rapy,** radiotherapy carried out by means of X-rays.

1913 *Arch. Roentgen Ray* XVII. 379 (*caption*) Roentgenkymogram of the left ventricle. **1930** *Arch. Internal Med.* XLV. 63 The slit in the lead sheet was placed over this point and the roentgen-kymogram taken. **1942** A. M. MASTER *Electrocardiogram* (ed. 2) 226 The character of the ventricular pulsations, as seen..in the roentgenkymogram, may..lead to the suspicion of cardiac aneurysm. **1913** *Jrnl. Amer. Med. Assoc.* 4 Apr. 1127/2 (*heading*) Analysis of electrocardiogram by means of the Roentgenkymograph. **1968** LUISADA & SAINANI *Primer of Cardiac Diagnosis* xviii. 117 The waves revealed by the electrokymograph are similar to those of the roentgenkymograph. **1930** *Arch. Internal Med.* XLV. 71 Variability of stroke volume was surmised because of..the different shape of the roentgen-kymographic curves produced by ventricular systole. **1970** G. H. ALEXANDER *Heart* i. 10/2 The roentgenkymographic studies of the heart which have been done at St. Francis by the author since 1957. **1940** *Amer. Heart Jrnl.* XIX. 462 Characteristic abnormalities in left ventricular pulsation as recorded roentgenkymographically in 200 cases of myocardial infarction. **1913** *Arch. Roentgen Ray* XVII. 378 (*heading*) Roentgenkymography: a roentgenographic method of demonstrating the movement of the heart. **1971** *Amer. Jrnl. Roentgenol.* CXI. 868/1 The authors have studied by analytic roentgen kymography the pulsations of the thoracic aorta in 5 patients. **1904** F. P. FOSTER *Appleton's Med. Dict.* 1707/1 *Röntgenogram*, a Röntgen ray picture. **1907** *Med. Rec.* (N.Y.) 10 Aug. 246/1 He remembered a case where a Roentgenogram demonstrated an object in the right ureter, and a diagnosis of a stone was made; but on incision no stone was found. **1977** *Jrnl. Bone & Joint Surg.* LIX. 575/1 The fracture was demonstrated.. by a roentgenogram of the carpal tunnel. **1905** *Jrnl. Amer. Med. Assoc.* 23 Dec. 1971/1 The film is then inserted, held in place by an assistant or the patient himself, the point of pressure being..on the particular tooth to be Roentgenographed. **1909** *Cent. Dict.* Suppl., *Roentgenograph*,..a radiograph; a Röntgenogram. **1940** *Amer. Jrnl. Roentgenol.* XLIV. 944/1 The side of a bone cavity opposite the focus is to be roentgenographed. **1965** *Ibid.* XCV. 135/1

When roentgenographed, the involved areas show widened diploic space and radial striation of bone spicules. **1977** *Environmental Res.* XIII. 47 Serial roentgenographs of histologically confirmed massive fibrotic lesions in 14 deceased gold miners were retrospectively studied. **1909** *Amer. Jrnl. Med. Sci.* CXXXVII. 377 (*heading*) A Röntgenographic study of peristalsis. **1961** R. D. BAKER *Essent. Path.* ix. 169 It is the calcification in the primary tuberculous complex which makes possible the recognition of the condition by roentgenographic study. **1977** *Amer. Jrnl. Med.* LXII. 366/2 Eight of the 14 atypical cases were diagnostic problems because of atypical roentgenographic and clinical features. **1909** *Amer. Jrnl. Med. Sci.* CXXXVII. 420 The width of the apices of the lungs has not yet been sufficiently studied roentgenographically to find employment diagnostically. **1965** *Arch. Internal Med.* CXV. 580/2 Her hands were normal and roentgenographically both hands and feet were normal. **1905** *Nature* 27 July 301/1 Among the results of the recent Röntgen congress at Berlin has been the authoritative adoption by a special committee of the following terminology:—Röntgenology = the study of Röntgen rays, Röntgenoscopy = observation by Röntgen rays, Röntgenography = photography by the rays... Röntgenotherapy and the verb to Röntgenise in their obvious meanings. **1958** *Optima* Sept. 130/2 The double platinum salts, such as platinum lithium cyanide or platinum thorium cyanide, are brilliantly fluoroscopic, and are used in roentgenography and fluoroscopy. **1912** *Amer. Jrnl. Med. Sci.* CXLIII. 754 (*heading*) A Röntgenologic study of spastic obstipation. **1967** *Amer. Jrnl. Roentgenol.* CI. 457/2 (*caption*) Roentgenologic signs of hypertrophic pyloric muscle in a 66 year old man. **1911** *Arch. Roentgen Ray* XV. 328, I propose to give my impressions from the Roentgenological point of view. **1925** S. LEWIS *Martin Arrowsmith* xxv. 292 The clinic did, perhaps, give overmany roentgenological examinations to socially dislocated women who needed children and floor-scrubbing more than pretty little skiagraphs. **1977** *Surgery* LXXXII. 848 (*heading*) An aggressive roentgenological and surgical approach to acute mesenteric ischemia. **1915** *Amer. Jrnl. Roentgenol.* II. 795/1 The cases to be examined roentgenologically are selected from those which have gastric symptoms. **1968** JACKMAN & BEAHRS *Tumors of Large Bowel* iv. 50 This method enabled them to find additional polyps, other than those detected roentgenologically. **1905** *Jrnl. Amer. Med. Assoc.* 23 Dec. 1971/1 Permit me to make a few remarks about the technic employed, which, I think, will be of value to every Roentgenologist. **1961** R. D. BAKER *Essent. Path.* xix. 533 Granules of calcium often form in the pineal after puberty and are helpful in locating the midline of the brain for the roentgenologist. **1905** Roentgenology [see *roentgenography* above]. **1914** *Jrnl. Amer. Med. Assoc.* 22 Aug. 651/2 The utility of some insight into Roentgen procedures on the part of the general practitioner does not nullify the advantages of specialization in roentgenology. **1977** *Surg., Gynecol. & Obstetr.* CXLIV. 563/2 Conventional roentgenology confirmed the presence of a tumor at the gastroesophageal junction. **1923** *Amer. Jrnl. Roentgenol.* X. 722 (*heading*) A plea for the use of the roentgenoscope in the diagnosis of urinary calculi. **1924** *Ibid.* XI. 93/2 With most..types of the tilt-table roentgenoscope, it will be necessary to remove the screen ordinarily used. **1926** *Jrnl. Amer. Med. Assoc.* 19 June 1904/2 An arrangement should be made by which the patient can be roentgenoscoped at right angles without change of position. **1955** *Amer. Jrnl. Roentgenol.* LXXIV. 812/1 Anyone who has roentgenoscoped an infant's chest realizes that an infant can squeeze virtually all the macroscopic air out of his lungs..with crying. **1909** *Amer. Jrnl. Med. Sci.* CXXXVII. 418 When both apices are equally or only slightly darkened, I have grown cautious with röntgenoscopic diagnosis. **1965** *Biol. Abstr.* XLVI. 8241/2 (*heading*) Roentgenoscopic investigation of oil-bearing seeds. **1909** *Amer. Jrnl. Med. Sci.* CXXXVII. 420 The process, röntgenoscopically at least, slowly advances, and after weeks is recognized as tuberculosis. **1945** *Amer. Jrnl. Roentgenol.* LIII. 608/1 The alimentary canal as observed roentgenoscopically. **1904** F. P. FOSTER *Appleton's Med. Dict.* 1707/1 *Röntgenoscopy*, examination with the aid of the Röntgen rays. **1914** *Jrnl. Amer. Med. Assoc.* 21 Nov. 1828/1 Roentgenoscopy has proved that ossification may ..occur in the epiglottis. **1971** *Biol. Abstr.* LII. 5081/1 The essential methods of roentgenological examination ..are roentgenoscopy and roentgenography. **1903** *Med. Rec.* (N.Y.) 31 Jan. 168/2 Extravagant promises will discredit the new and delicate field of Röntgenotherapy. **1925** *Jrnl. Amer. Med. Assoc.* 28 Feb. 671/1 Roentgenotherapy effects a complete disappearance of palpable lymph nodes and reduces the spleen to its normal size. **1960** *Biol. Abstr.* XXXV. 4048/1 Giving 2–3 drops each of validol..on sugar to patients with carcinoma of various sites (50) after a session of roentgenotherapy..usually eased the general reaction to the irradiation.

roe·ntgenite. *Min.* Also **röntgenite.** [f. *ROENTGEN, ROENTGEN + -ITE[1].] A rhombohedral fluorocarbonate of cerium, lanthanum, and calcium, $Ca_2(Ce,La)_3(CO_3)_5F_3$, found as small yellow or brown crystals in association with other rare-earth minerals at Narsarsuk, Greenland.

1953 G. DONNAY in *Amer. Mineralogist* XXXVIII. 868 (*heading*) Roentgenite, $3CeFCO_3.2CaCO_3$, a new mineral from Greenland. **1966** Z. LERMAN tr. *K. A. Vlasow's Geochem. & Mineral. of Rare Elements* II. VIII. 272 Röntgenite $Ce_3Ca_2(CO_3)_5F_3$. Identity established by Donnay in 1953 during X-ray analysis of rare-earth fluocarbonate specimens from Greenland. **1975** *Amer. Mineralogist* LX. 351 Intimate syntaxy between parisite, synchisite, roentgenite, and bastnaesite was..observed even on a very fine scale.

roepperite (rə̄·pərait). *Min.* [f. the name of William T. *Roepper* (1810–80), German-born U.S. mineralogist + -ITE[1].] A black mineral of the olivine group containing iron, manganese, and zinc.

The name *röpperit* (G.) was also proposed in 1872 by A. Kenngott (in *Neues Jahrb. f. Mineral.* 188) for a species of manganiferous dolomite described by Roepper.

1872 G. J. BRUSH in *Dana's Syst. Min.* (ed. 5) App. I. 13 Roepperite. Iron, manganese, zinc, chrysolite... Roepperite, *G. J. Brush.* **1875** E. S. DANA *Ibid.* App. II. 49 Kenngott..has proposed to give the name rœpperite to the manganese dolomite, analysed by Rœpper... Almost simultaneously..Brush gave the name rœpperite to the new chrysolite of Rœpper, and there is no question but that this name should be received. **1961** *Amer. Mineralogist* XLVI. 549 Roepperite is black... It has been described as a variety of tephroite containing notably high amounts of FeO and ZnO. **1972** *Ibid.* LVII. 977 The infrared spectrum of the zincian olivine roepperite..is comparable to those of Fe-Mn olivines and bears no resemblances to the spectrum of willemite containing tetrahedral Zn^{2+}.

roesslerite (rə̄·slĕrəit). *Min.* Also **rösslerite.** [ad. G. *rösslerit* (R. Blum 1861, in *Jahresber. der Wetterauischen Ges. für die ges. Naturkunde* 33), f. the name of Carl *Rössler*, 19th-c. German scientist: see -ITE[1].] A hydrated acid arsenate of magenesium, $MgHAsO_4.7H_2O$, which occurs as small colourless plates forming an oxidized crust on some arsenical deposits, and has been prepared artificially.

1868 J. D. DANA *Syst. Min.* (ed. 5) 556 A mineral in monoclinic crystals occurs at Joachimsthal and Kremnitz. ..which is probably rœsslerite. **1903** *Jrnl. Chem. Soc.* LXXXIV. II. 656 Crystals..of the arsenic compound, $(NH_4)MgAsO_4,6H_2O$, isomorphous with struvite were obtained, and at the same time crystals of rösslerite $(MgHAsO_4,7H_2O)$. **1951** C. PALACHE et al. *Dana's Syst. Min.* (ed. 7) II. 712 Artificial roesslerite is precipitated together with $MgNH_4AsO_4.6H_2O$..from an acid solution of disodium arsenate and ammonium sulfate by a solution of magnesium sulfate. **1973** *Acta Crystallographica* B. XXIX. 287/1 Roesslerite is biaxial negative.

‖ **roesti** (rö̆·sti). Also **rosti, rösti.** [Swiss Ger.] A Swiss style of fried potatoes. (Variously taken as *sing.* and *pl.*)

1952 H. SUTTON *Footloose in Switzerland* ii. 55 The most typical dish of Zurich is something known as *g'schnetzeltes*... It comes served with noodles or roesti, which are home fries. **1953** *New Horizons* (Pan Amer. World Airways) (new ed.) 122/1 Each region [of Switzerland] has its specialties: *Fondue* and *Raclette*..in the French section..sausages, roasts and fried potatoes (*Rösti*) in the German section. **1961** P. CANNON *Eating European* 223 The Swiss *Rosti*, which is close to being their national home dish, is made with cooked potatoes. **1961** N.. S. HAZELTON *Continental Flavor* 304 *Roesti* is really a version of home-fried potatoes, and certainly the best. **1973** M. WALDO *Compl. Round-World Cookbk.* 145 Fried Potatoes... Rösti.

rog (rǫdʒ), *int.* Abbrev. of *ROGER[2] 6.

1955 R. J. SCHWARTZ *Compl. Dict. Abbrev.* 155/3 *Rog*, roger. **1969** *Guardian* 21 July 1/3 Back came the single syllable answer from the spacecraft... 'Rog.' **1970** N. ARMSTRONG et al. *First on Moon* xiv. 354 'You're cleared for landing.'.. 'Rog. Gear is down and locked.'

Rogallo (rogæ·lo). Also **rogallo.** The name of Francis M. *Rogallo*, 20th-c. U.S. engineer, used *attrib.* and *absol.* to designate a light, flexible, triangular wing deployed by means of tension lines or rigid tubes and used on spacecraft and for hang-gliding.

1961 Rogallo wing [see *PARAGLIDER]. **1968** *McGraw-Hill Encycl. Space* i. 127 The tanks..are specially arranged to accommodate the housing of the recovery wing. The latter, known by the names of Paraglider, Flex-wing or Rogallo Wing (from the name of its inventor, Francis M. Rogallo, director of the large wind-tunnel at NASA's Langley Research Center) is a flexible wing which is deployed in flight and enables the rocket to glide. **1974** *Observer* (Colour Suppl.) 7 Apr. 68/1 The rogallo, a triangular kite-shape wing made of aluminium tubing with a nylon sail. **1974** *Sci. Amer.* Dec. 138/1 Most sky surfers first learn to fly on a Rogallo kite. **1978** A. WELCH *Bk. of Airsports* i. 9/2 They come in an increasing variety of shapes and sizes, ranging from the basic rogallo for club and school use to almost aeroplane planform hang gliders.

rogan (rōᵘ·găn). *Canad.* Also 8 **roggan,** 9 **roggin.** [ad. Canad. Fr. (*h*)*ouragan*, f. Algonkian (see W. S. Avis *Dict. Canadianisms*).] A water-tight container made of birch-bark.

1743 J. ISHAM in *Publ. Hudson's Bay Rec. Soc.* (1949) XII. 188 A Roggan. Slawee. **1791** P. FIDLER *Jrnl.* 10 Nov. in *Publ. Champlain Soc.* (1934) XXI. 523 We are obliged to roast all & make water by immersing red hot stones into a roggan of Snow. **1820** J. CLOUSTON *Jrnl.* 10 July in K. G. Davies *Northern Quebec & Labrador Jrnls. & Corr. 1819–35* (1963) 57 He had a wooden roggin which would hold about five gallons. **1894** *Outing* Nov. 127/1, I saw..the 'rogans', or water-tight vessels of birch-bark, beautifully stitched with roots, and trimmed around the opening with colored porcupine-quills. **1922** *Beaver* June 7/1 Ornamented work baskets, plain baskets or 'rogans', for holding fish, game, berries, or canoe pitch are also made of the bark. **1968** E. S. RUSSENHOLT *Heart of Continent* I. i. 1 These hunters heat stones in their open fires; and drop them into birch bark rogans filled with water and meat—until the water boils and cooks the meat.

Roger[2]. Add: **3. a.** (Further examples.)

Quot. 1653 in Dict. seems to be a ghost.

1720 D'URFEY *Pills* VI. 201 Here's a Health to the Queen, let's Bumpers take in hand, And may Prince G——'s Roger grow stiff again and stand. *c* **1800** BURNS in *Merry Muses of Caledonia* (1959) 147 Bonie lassie, braw lassie, Will ye hae a soger? Then she took up her duddie sark, An' he shot in his Roger. *c* **1863** 'PHILO CUNNUS' *Festival of Passions* II. 25 With my right hand, I grasped my flaming Roger.

6. Also with small initial. As *int.* Used to represent the letter *r* (= received) in radio transmission (see quot. 1947). Also *transf.* in general use, an expression of affirmation.

1941 *Amer. Speech* XVI. 168/1 *Roger!* Expression used instead of *okay* or *right.* (Air Corps). **1943** *Signal Training (All Arms): Signal Procedure* I. 9 *Roger*, used to mean 'message received'. **1945** *Sun* (Baltimore) 25 Jan. 9 Sometimes a voice called, 'Flak.' Once I heard one pilot say, 'Are you hit?' The reply was, 'Roger, I am hit. Going home.' **1947** *Amer. Speech* XXII. 110 In radio procedure the letter R, or *roger*, possesses the code designations 'received', or 'I have received your message', when signalled by the station addressed... Nevertheless, since radio operators or pilots signalling *roger* are receipting for a message, it has also come to mean unofficially 'O.K.' or 'I understand'. **1954** J. MASTERS *Bhowani Junction* xix. 170, I heard the duty officer on the R/T: 'Dogfish Six speaking... Roger, over.' **1960** *Sunday Express* 18 Sept. 1/3 If he wanted to speak to you he would ask you to go in. Roger? **1963** D. IRVING *Destruction of Dresden* III. ii. 132 'Tell the aircraft in top height band to come down below the medium cloud.' 'Roger.' **1971** D. HASTON in C. Bonington *Annapurna South Face* xvii. 210 At first it had been a chore to use them [*sc.* radios] and the jargon of Roger, Over, etcetera, had seemed artificial, but sitting in the specific loneliness of Camp VI it was a good feeling to communicate with others.

roger (rǫ·dʒəɹ), *v.*[1] *slang.* Also **rodger.** [f. ROGER[2].] *trans.* To copulate with (a woman); to have sexual intercourse with. Also *absol.* Hence **ro·gering** *vbl. sb.* and *ppl. a.*

1711 W. BYRD *Secret Diary* 26 Dec. (1941) 459, I rogered my wife. *c* **1750** A. ROBERTSON *Poems* 98 Dear sweet Mr. Wright..Go rodger to-night Your Wife, for ye want her. **1763** BOSWELL *Jrnl.* 4 June in *London Jrnl.* (1950) 273, I picked up a little profligate wretch and gave her sixpence... 'Should not a half-pay officer r-g-r for sixpence?' **1771** [see RAGMATICAL *a.*]. **1870** *Cythera's Hymnal* 81 He rogered the National School. **1884** tr. *Abishag* in *Old Man Young Again* (1898) I. 36, I gave Mrs. P—. a really good rogering, and sent her to sleep perfectly contented. **1919** E. POUND *Sel. Lett.* (1971) 150 If I were, however, a professor of Latin in Chicago, I should probably have to resign on divulging the fact that Propertius occasionally copulavit, i.e. rogered the lady to whom he was not legally wedded. **1931** E. WAUGH *Diary* 14 Jan. (1976) 347 He got very drunk and brought a sluttish girl back to the house. He woke me up later in night to tell me he had rogered her and her mama too. **1942** E. PAUL *Narrow St.* xvi. 116 When Rudolph Valentino died... 'Hey, American,' yelled Madame Absalom... 'What did that *type* have that other men have not? He must have rogered half the women in your country?' **1953** *Landfall* Sept. 179 You black-mouth, you night bird, you rogering swine. **1953** DYLAN THOMAS *Let.* 22 June (1966) 409, I..sulked all morning over my warm beer as they..rolled rodgering down. **1961** A. WILSON *Old Men at Zoo* i. 54 I'm not at all sure about the Empress Theodora. I fancy she was rogered by an ape more than once in her circus acts. **1967** D. PINNER *Ritual* xvii. 167 He singed the rogering labourers...It took minutes before fornication subsided. **1972** 'R. GORDON' *Doctor on Brain* xxiii. 168 'Who is the father of the child?' 'The man who rodgered her, of course.' **1976** K. BONFIGLIOLI *Something Nasty in Woodshed* iii. 32 You won't catch him... The bloke who rogered Mrs Breakspear.

roger (rǫ·dʒəɹ), *v.*[2] *U.S.* [f. *ROGER[2] 6.] *trans.* To acknowledge (a message, etc.) as received.

1962 J. GLENN in *Into Orbit* 195 Both of these readings were within limits and I rogered the message. **1977** J. WAMBAUGH *Black Marble* (1978) vi. 83 'We just got a call,' he said. 'Roger it, please.'

Roger de Coverley. (Earlier examples with *Sir* and in abbreviated form.)

1804 H. WYNNE *Diary* 19 Dec. (1940) III. v. 147 We danced Sir Roger de Coverly. **1875** L. TROUBRIDGE *Life amongst Troubridges* (1966) x. 101, I danced every dance except Sir Roger, at the end.

Rogerene (rǫ·dʒərīn). *U.S.* [f. the name *Rogers* (see below) + *-ene* as in NAZARENE *a.* and *sb.*] A member of a small religious sect founded by John *Rogers* (1648–1721) in Connecticut, opposed to some of the formal practices of churches and participation in military service. Also *attrib.* in *Rogerene Quaker.*

1754 J. HEMPSTEAD *Diary* 17 Mar. in *Coll. New London Co. Hist. Soc.* (1901) I, A Company of the Rogerens..held their meeting after our meeting was over. **1820** *Niles' Reg.* 22 July 366/1 A contagious disorder is now raging among the sect known by the name of Rogereen Quakers in Grotan. **1865** *Harper's Mag.* May 812/2 In the year 1720 a sect arose in New London, Connecticut, called, from their leader, 'Rogerenes'. **1865** *Massachusetts Hist. Soc. Coll.* VII. 584 John, the third son of James Rogers, of New London, and the founder of the sect of Rogerenes, of whom a small number still remain in that vicinity. **1931** *Times Lit. Suppl.* 6 Aug. 602/3 The Shakers, the Christadelphians and the Rogerenes are other sects. **1943** *New England Q.* Mar. 3 On a wooded hill above Mystic,

Connecticut, live the remnants of a little-known religious sect called the Rogerenes, or sometimes Rogerene Quakers.

Roget (rǫ·ʒēi). The name of Peter Mark *Roget* (1779–1869), English physician and philologist, used *absol.* with reference to his *Thesaurus of English Words and Phrases*, a catalogue of synonyms first published in 1852. Also in *Comb.*

1940 *Times* 19 Apr. 7/4 To journalists and other writers, weary of racking their brains or raking the well-thumbed pages of Roget in search of alternatives, the word 'Quisling' is a gift from the gods. **1955** E. Blishen *Roaring Boys* III. 152 Charles was like some oral Roget, uttering long lists of horrid synonyms. **1962** L. Deighton *Ipcress File* xiii. 75 A few books remained on the shelves, a *Roget*, a business directory..and a *Chambers's Dictionary*. **1970** D. L. Emblen *P. M. Roget* xv. 276 Again and again, letters to *The Times* and other papers call upon other writers..to consult their 'Roget' before making such execrable use of the language. **1973** M. Amis *Rachel Papers* 113 So ended my short, derivative, *Roget*-roughaged essay, complete with stage-directions.

‖ **rognon** (rǫnʸoṅ). [Fr.] **1.** Chiefly *pl.* In Gastronomy, (a dish of) kidneys. Also *attrib.* and *Comb.*

1828 Lytton *Pelham* I. xii. 79 What cook *can* possibly respect men who..eat *rognons* at dinner instead of at breakfast. *c* **1864** S. O. Beeton in N. Spain *Mrs. Beeton* (1948) II. vi. 212 Everybody had just well breakfasted upon cotelletes, omelettes, Rognons. **1877** C. Reade *Woman-Hater* I. v. 97 After the *rognons à la brochette*, and a bottle of champagne, he let out. **1923** A. Huxley *Antic Hay* iv. 61 'And where are my *rognons sautés*?' he shouted at the waiter. **1967** A. Wilson *No Laughing Matter* iii. 337 She..cooked specially for him as she had not done for ages, rognons Bercy and omelette confiture. **1972** *Guardian* 11 Mar. 15/3 [The] Brasserie du Nord..is noted..for its *saucisson* and *rognon* dishes. **1979** *Times* 15 Dec. 6/6 My mother followed the sun... She lay down.. darkening like *rognons* on a spit.

2. *Mountaineering.* A rounded outcrop of rock or stones surrounded by a glacier or an ice-field.

1935 S. Spencer *Mountaineering* 364 *Rognon*, rounded rock in the centre of a glacier. **1957** R. G. Collomb *Dict. Mountaineering* 127 In Victorian days some *rognons* were used as sleeping places.., e.g. the Stöckje on the Scheonbuhl [*sic*] glacier near Zermatt. **1958** *Jrnl. Glaciology* III. 264 On the upper parts of the Glaciar Universidad there had been little change. After 1945 the surface sank slightly around a *rognon* (rounded nunatak) at 3930 m. **1963** *Oxford Mountaineering* 11 At the top of the rognon the snow steepened and we had to traverse up and round to the foot of the..couloir which leads on to the face. **1973** C. Bonington *Next Horizon* xxi. 279 Our way lay across the glacier and up a rognon, a sort of island of rocks round which the glacier flowed on either side.

rogue, *sb.* Add: **2. d.** *rogue and villain*: rhyming slang for 'shilling'.

1859 Hotten *Dict. Slang* 145 *Rogue and villain*, a shillin,—common pronunciation of shilling. **1877** J. W. Horsley *Jottings from Jail* i. 3 Come, cows and kisses, put the battle of the Nile on your Barnet Fair, and a rogue and villain in your sky-rocket. **1965** *Australasian Post* 4 Mar. 46 *Shilling*... Sometimes known in rhyming slang as a 'rogue and villain'. **1973** B. Aylwin *Load of Cockney Cobblers* xiv. 62 *Rogue & villain*, shilling.

5. a. Also *fig.* (*attrib.* or as *adj.* in quots.).

1963 *Times Lit. Suppl.* 18 Jan. 44/3 His role is that of the *advocatus diaboli* rather than the rogue elephant. **1978** K. Gregory *First Cuckoo* 21 The nation's rogue elephants rampage, shattering complacency and compelling many to an agonizing reappraisal.

b. Also *fig.*

1926 J. Masefield *Odtaa* x. 171 He roused up as a big, elderly rogue-bull of a man..came in. **1939** G. Household (*title*) Rogue male. **1977** N. Adam *Triplehip Cracksman* v. 56 I wasn't sure I liked myself..rogue male acting instinctively, obeying the territorial imperative.

6*. *attrib.* or as *adj.* in general use, denoting: **a.** An inexplicably aberrant result or phenomenon; an extra or misplaced item in a list, table, etc.

1952 *Analyst* LXXVII. 171 With the exception of one rogue result, the present estimates are as concordant as can reasonably be expected. **1964** C. Dent *Quantity Surveying by Computer* iii. 30 A device enabling you to switch the machine to manual and continue using it as an ordinary typewriter is very useful if, for instance, you wish to insert a 'spot' item, or other 'rogue' item in the bill of quantities, at the last moment. **1972** *Physics Bull.* Oct. 611/1 The tables have been well produced and very few errors were detected. In the body of the table, only one rogue point was noticed. **1979** *Personal Computer World* Nov. 73/2 When the program detects the rogue value, this is an indication that the input list is complete and further processing can continue.

b. Something that is inexplicably faulty or defective.

1962 *Daily Tel.* 18 Jan. 12/7 Manufacturers are aware that 'rogue' and sub-standard cars are sold to the public. **1965** *New Statesman* 30 Apr. 695/2 A group of American bombers..go rogue through a mechanical foul-up. **1971** *Atom* Apr. 99/1 Such differences are readily detectable and allow experimental fuel elements to be checked for rogue fuel pellets. **1974** *Guardian* 14 Mar. 9/2 His counsel ..told Mr Justice Phillips... 'You are familiar with the expression 'rogue car'. Well, this was rather like a rogue house.'

c. That which lacks appropriate control; something which is irresponsible or undisciplined.

1964 *Daily Tel.* 22 Feb. 14/6 Frequent complaints were made about a very small number of 'rogue' firms which belonged to neither the Association of British Travel Agents nor the Travel Trade Association. **1972** *Accountant* 19 Oct. 496/1 How is the ordinary man in the street to tell whether it has been calculated on the 'fair' basis as laid down by the legislation, or the unfair basis which will no doubt be perpetrated by a considerable number of rogue traders? **1979** *Daily Tel.* 4 Apr. 3 A housewife's game of patience came to an abrupt end when a 20-ton 'rogue' mechanical shovel begun crunching its way through the walls of her semi-detached home. **1981** *New Scientist* 29 Jan. 278/3 (*caption*) Gamma-ray bursts may come from collisions between rogue asteroids and neutron stars.

7. *rogue-word*; *rogue-eyed* adj.

1867 Meredith *Vittoria* I. ix. 133 She had, in tripping down the Piazza with her rogue-eyed cousin from Milan, looked away [etc.]. **1922** Joyce *Ulysses* 48 Roguewords, tough nuggets patter in their pockets.

8. **rogue's gallery**: also **rogues' gallery**; (earlier and later examples); also *transf.* and *fig.*

1859 *Amer. Jrnl. Photogr.* II. 75 The Rogues' Gallery is located at the police head quarters... The photographer is a regularly appointed policeman. **1904** [see *Pink *sb.*⁵]. **1945** 'E. Queen' (*title*) Rogues' gallery. **1955** *Publ. Amer. Dial. Soc.* xxiv. 41 His [*sc.* a pickpocket's] face appears more frequently than any other type of criminal in 'rogue's galleries' and police files. **1959** *Listener* 26 Nov. 946/1 Mr. Klein's second collection of arch-deceivers, his new rogues' gallery, is fascinating. **1973** 'I. Drummond' *Jaws of Watchdog* x. 133 His face was not recognised in the rogues' gallery, nor did his description tally with any known criminal. **1977** McKnight & Tobler *Bob Marley* 10 Bob Dylan, Arthur Lee, Keith Richard, Bob Marley—the rogue's gallery of rebel input that forms the hard stuff at the centre of rock.

rogue, *v.* Add: **4.** Also, to take *out* (inferior plants) from a crop. (Further examples.)

1965 *Sunday Mail Mag.* (Brisbane) 26 Sept. 15 Sometimes we speak of 'rogueing' a crop, which means taking out the plants which aren't typical of the variety or which have become diseased. **1967** *Sunday Times* 19 Feb. 31/4 Small flowered plants should be rogued out or not allowed to seed. **1978** *Country Life* 20 July 184/3 White foxgloves..once established will seed themselves. If you keep roguing out any coloured throwbacks they could become a permanent feature.

roguer (rōᵘ·gəɹ). [f. Rogue *v.* + -er¹.] A person employed to identify and eliminate inferior plants in a crop, esp. of potatoes.

1945 T. Whitehead et al. *Potato in Health & Dis.* (ed. 2) vii. 77 The roguer should remove or mark all plants which in any character differ substantially from the variety under consideration. **1960** *Times* 29 July 12/6 The roguer's job is to sample the crop for wrong varieties or disease. **1967** A. E. Cox *Potato* vii. 157 The roguers working in pairs—one marking plants and the other lifting and carrying them off—should deal with only two drills at a time.

roguing, *vbl. sb.* **3.** (Later examples.)

1968 *Punch* 18 Sept. 410/3 Any plants not true to type are removed by systematic 'roguing', which may account for a further ton per acre. **1978** Hide & Lapwood in P. M. Harris *Potato Crop* xi. 432 Roguing (negative selection) and later multiplication from disease-free plants (positive selection) were used to improve the health of seed.

Rohilla (rōᵘhi·lă), *sb.* and *a.* Also † **Rohella, Rohila.** [Pashto 'inhabitant of Roh', f. place-name *Rōh*, a district of Afghanistan: see also quot. 1885.] **A.** *sb.* A member of a people of Afghan origin inhabiting the Bareilly district of Northern India. **B.** *adj.* Of or pertaining to this people.

1773 W. Hastings *Diary* 21 Aug. (1948) 6 The Vizier added that the Abdallee maintained a Correspondence with the Rohellas. *Ibid.*, Money..due to the said Nabob by virtue of any engagement between him and the Rohilla chiefs. **1786** Burke *Wks.* (1868) IV. 221 That the said Warren Hastings..did, in September, 1773, enter into a private engagement with the said Nabob of Oude..to furnish him..with a body of troops for the declared purpose of 'thoroughly extirpating the nation of the Rohillas'. **1829** J. Tod *Rajast'han* I. xxv. 672 The fragments were..placed in position to receive the flesh-pots of the sons of Ishmaël, the mercenary Rohilla Afghan. **1885** G. C. Whitworth *Anglo-Indian Dict.* 269/2 *Rohillā*. [Pashṭo, from *roh*, a mountain.] The name of a highland clan of Paṭhāns who early in the eighteenth century took possession of the district, now called after them, Rohilkhand. **1892** Kipling *Barrack-Room Ballads* 104 We drove the black Rohillas back. **1921** G. A. Grierson *Linguistic Survey of India* X. 9 After the death of Aurangzēb, in 1707, the dissensions among the Hindūs of Bareilly enabled 'Alī Muḥammed K͟hān, the leader of the Rōhilā Paṭhāns, to obtain possession of the country which is now called, after the name of the tribe, Rohilkhand... It is hardly necessary to point out the connexion between Rōh and Rōhilā. The latter word means literally an inhabitant of the Rōh. **1960** J. S. Watson *Reign of George III* xii. 309 These Afghan soldiers of fortune, called the Rohillas, were suspected of co-operation with the Marathas. **1971** R. Russell tr. *Ahmad's Shore & Wave* vi. 52 Some Rohillas had recently been arrested and charged with a series of burglaries and armed robberies.

‖ **rohrflöte** (rō·rflō̆tə). *Mus.* Also **rohr flute**; *pl.* **-n.** [G., f. *rohr* tube + *flöte* flue-stop.] An organ stop having its pipes partly closed, the stopper at the top of each pipe being pierced by a thin tube.

1773 C. Burney *Present State of Mus. Germany* II. 305 Catalogue of stops in the Great Organ at Haarlem built by Müller 1738... 5. *Roer fluit*, 8 ft. with a funnel or small pipe upon the top. Eng. equivalent, Diap. half stopt. **1855** [see *gedackt, gedact]. **1898** Stainer & Barrett *Dict. Mus. Terms* 387/2 Rohrflöte, (Ger.) Reed-flute. An organ stop consisting of closed pipes, the tone of which is slightly reedy in quality, but very sweet. **1911** W. & T. Lewis *Mod. Organ Building* v. 93 Many stops.. occupy an intermediate position between two classes; as, for instance, a Rohr Flute. This stop is made to produce an upper harmonic which renders its timbre rather flutey in character, but at the same time, the fundamental tone is sufficiently obvious to link it with a Stopped Diapason. **1938** *Oxf. Compan. Mus.* 668/1 *Rohrflöte* or *Rohr Flute* (literally 'Reed Flute', but 'reed' here means a tube), of metal stopped pipes, with a slender tube through the stopper (hence the name). **1959** *Collins Mus. Encycl.* 554/1 *Rohrflöte*,..an organ stop of the flue type. The pipe is stopped at one end, but the stopper is pierced by a hole, in which is inserted a metal tube or chimney. **1966** P. Williams *European Organ 1450–1850* vii. 238 Organ-builders evidently brought with them new stops like *Rohrflöten*.

roibek, var. *rooibekkie. **roibok,** var. *rooibok.

‖ **roi fainéant** (rwa fe̜neaṅ). [Fr., lit. 'sluggard king': see Fainéant *sb.* and *a.*] One of the later Merovingian kings of France, whose power was merely nominal. Also *transf.* and *fig.*

1879 *Encycl. Brit.* IX. 530/2 Children were kings in both Austrasia and Neustria; we reach the days of the 'do-naught' princes, the *rois fainéants*, and of the struggle between the mayors of Austrasia and Neustria. **1898** L. Sergeant *Franks* xiv. 199 Dagobert's death.. marked the beginning of a series of Merovingian *rois fainéants*. **1929** W. R. Inge *Assessments & Anticipations* ii. 35, I have acquiesced in the undignified rôle of a *roi fainéant*. **1935** *Chambers's Encycl.* IV. 810/1 Charles Martel, *maire du palais* to the 'Rois Fainéants', defeated Arab invaders at Poitiers. **1966** *Economist* 1 Jan. 23/1 The launching of the Sputnik in 1957, in the reign of the *roi fainéant*, President Eisenhower, seemed to justify Khrushchevian boasts that America's days of..supremacy were numbered. **1975** J. H. M. Salmon *Society in Crisis: France in 16th Cent.* viii. 193 The last years of Charles IX were those of a *roi fainéant*. The king ordered a new offensive against the Protestants of the south and La Noue in the west, but there were no resources to finance his armies.

roil, *v.*³ Add: **2.** (Later example.)

1907 *Springfield* (Mass.) *Weekly Republ.* 17 Jan. 6 The publication of such a work naturally roiled the publishers of Webster's international dictionary.

3. *intr.* To move in a confused or turbulent manner; to billow.

1939 W. Faulkner *Wild Palms* 26 As something recognisable roils momentarily into view from beneath stagnant and opaque water, then sinks again. **1963** T. Pynchon *V.* i. 22 Engine exhaust roiled in clouds around him. **1964** D. F. Galouye *Counterfeit World* xiii. 113 The waters roiled with the restless presence of thousands of—. **1977** *Time* 6 June 46/2 Strange currents flow for years in the deeps of the American society, then for reasons unclear suddenly roil to the surface.

Hence **roi·ling** *ppl. a.*

1967 C. O. Skinner *Madame Sarah* viii. 171 Sarah glanced down at the roiling flood water. **1976** U. Curtiss *Birthday Gift* xiv. 132 One thing stood clearly out of the whole roiling mess.

roiled, *ppl. a.* For 'of the passions' read 'esp. of the passions' and add further *fig.* examples. Also with *up*.

1929 *Sun* (Baltimore) 12 June 1/1 It will be seen when the Senator gets roiled he can go the paces with the next one among the friends of the people. **1939** J. Steinbeck *Grapes of Wrath* x. 123 Your Pa's pa, he quoted Scripture all the time. He got it all roiled up, too. **1975** in W. Viereck *Lexikalische Ergebnisse des Lowman-Survey* I. iv. 279 If he lost his temper, you say he got... roiled.

roily, *a.* Add: *roily oil*, petroleum containing much emulsified water. Hence **roi·liness.**

1912 *Mem. Geol. Surv. India* XL. 121 [The well] being shut down at first on account of the 'roiliness' or emulsification of the oil. *Ibid.*, Two wells; one of these was a 'dry hole', but the other flowed during the first 24 hours 18,000 gallons of an emulsion of oil and water known in America as roily oil. **1915** Redwood & Eastlake *Petroleum Technol. Pocket-bk.* iv. 214 On recommencing pumping the well gave nothing but 'roily oil' for more than a month. **1920** E. H. C. Craig *Oil-Finding* (ed. 2) iii. 71 In a porous rock...oil and water may be inextricably intermingled... Such a rock struck in a well will probably yield 'roily oil', an emulsion very difficult to separate into its constituents, oil and water.

roineck, var. *rooinek.

‖ **roi soleil** (rwa sǫle̜y). [Fr., lit. 'sun king'.] A title commonly used to designate Louis XIV of France, derived from a heraldic device used by him; applied *transf.* to any similarly pre-eminent individual, ruler, or divinity. Also *attrib.*

1890 G. BIRDWOOD *Rep. Misc. Old Rec. India Office* 222 The earliest coins minted by the English in India were of copper, stamped with a figure of an irradiated *lingam*, the phallic 'Roi Soleil'. **1943** E. M. W. TILLYARD *Elizabethan World Picture* vii. 83 The *roi soleil* is indeed one of the most persistent of all Elizabethan commonplaces. **1958** *Spectator* 6 June 721/2 Her rule is no longer the *roi-soleil* variety. **1961** *Listener* 31 Aug. 319/2 Popular books on Picasso in which the artistic *roi soleil* of the post-war years is still pictured as on some barricade or other. **1966** *Guardian* 31 Dec. 5/3 Cecil Harmsworth King, the *roi soleil* of Long Acre. **1978** *Times* 27 May 7/1 The palmy days of the Roi Soleil.

‖ **Rōjū** (rō·dʒū). Also **Rōchū, rōjiu, rōjū,** etc. [Jap.] The senior councillors or ministers of state in Japan under the Tokugawa government (1603–1867).

1874 F. O. ADAMS *Hist. Japan* I. I. x. 71 The successors of Jyéyasŭ..were mostly *fainéants*, as were their almost hereditary ministers, the rōjiu. **1893** F. BRINKLEY tr. *Hist. Empire Japan* viii. 329 In the event of the Shogun himself taking the field, he had to be accompanied by all the feudal barons, the Ministers of State (*Rochu*) becoming generals and the *Wakatoshiyori* holding chief command over the bannerets. **1912** E. LEE tr. *Saito's Hist. Japan* 147 The board of the 5 Rōchū, the treasurers... controlled the imperial court officials and Daimiō. *a* **1922** J. MURDOCH *Hist. Japan* (1926) III. i. 4 These five constituted the Great Council, which was presently to become known as the Rōjū. **1970** J. W. HALL *Japan* x. 175 The *Rōjū* were given authority over matters of national scope. **1974** *Encycl. Brit. Macropædia* X. 71/2 By reorganizations in 1633–42 the executive..was almost completed, as represented by the offices of senior councillors (rojū), [etc.].

roky (rōᵘ·ki), *a.*[2] *Founding.* [f. *roke*, var. ROAK (in Dict. and Suppl.) + -Y[1].] Possessing or characterized by rokes.

1932 E. GREGORY *Metallurgy* ii. 58 Some of these cracks may escape detection in the forge, and unsound roky billets are thus produced. **1940** SIMONS & GREGORY *Steel Manuf.* xix. 141 It is not uncommon for these cracks to be unnoticed in advance of forging or rolling, and they then elongate and 'open-out', producing 'roky' billets.

rolag (rōᵘ·læg). *Spinning.* [a. Gael. *rolag*, dim. of *rola* a roll.] A roll of carded wool ready for spinning.

1932 SIMPSON & WEIR *Weaver's Craft* v. 30 The wool is now lifted lightly on the right-hand card, and placed on the back of the left, where it is rolled between the two card backs into a neat roll, or 'rolag'. **1964** H. HODGES *Artifacts* ix. 128 The roll of carded or combed fibres, the *rolag* or *sliver*, may be wound round a second rod. **1977** Y. DEUTCH *Weaving & Spinning* 129 The wool must first be teased and carded to separate the fibres and prepared for spinning by forming a roll of wool or rolag. *Ibid.*, Before spinning you will need to prepare by hand about 45 cm (18 in) of woollen thread from a rolag.

Rolandic (rolæ·ndik), *a. Anat.* Also **rolandic.** [f. next + -IC.] Used to designate various features of the central nervous system associated with Rolando (see next), as (*a*) the motor region or area of the cerebral cortex; (*b*) the fissure or sulcus of Rolando; (*c*) the angle at which the fissure of Rolando meets the median plane of the brain.

1881 C. G. COMEGYS tr. *J. M. Charcot's Lect. Dis. Spinal Cord* v. 49 We have enclosed within these pyramidal lines, what is known as the Rolandic region of the cerebral cortex, and which represents..a region endowed with special physiological properties. **1883** W. B. HADDEN tr. *J. M. Charcot's Lect. Localisation of Cerebral & Spinal Dis.* v. 193 The central, median, or, if you will so term them, the Rolandic convolutions. **1890** *Jrnl. Anat. & Physiol.* XXV. 3 In most hemispheres a small variable tertiary furrow may be detected below the lower end of the Rolandic fissure. *Ibid.* 19 By the 'Rolandic angle' I mean the angle which is formed by the meeting of the upper end of the sulcus with the mesial plane. **1908** H. E. SANTEE *Anat. Brain & Spinal Cord* (ed. 4) iii. 56 The average Rolandic angle is 71° 7′. **1910** G. G. DAVIS *Appl. Anat.* 36 The Rolandic area embraces the ascending frontal, or precentral, and posterior portion of the three frontal convolutions, the former being in front of the fissure of Rolando, or central fissure. **1921** TILNEY & RILEY *Form & Functions Central Nerv. Syst.* xxxvi. 643 The entire length of the Rolandic fissure is 8 cm. *Ibid.*, The *gyrus Rolandicus*... extended the entire length of the two Rolandic fissures. **1962** M. C. H. DODGSON *Growing Brain* vii. 55 The determination of Cunningham's Rolandic Index may be useful in doubtful instances. **1972** M. L. BARR *Human Nerv. Syst.* xiii. 207 The rolandic sulcus indents the superior border of the hemisphere about 1 cm behind the midpoint between the frontal and occipital poles. **1974** L. F. SIES *Aphasia Theory & Therapy* i. 54 The third area..is located within the mid-saggital fissure, just anterior to the Rolandic motor foot area.

Rolando (rolæ·ndo). *Anat.* The name of Luigi *Rolando* (1773–1831), Italian anatomist, used with *of* and *attrib.* to designate: **a.** A fissure or sulcus of the brain separating the frontal lobe from the parietal lobe, described by him in 1825 (*Mem. d. R. Accad. d. Sci. di Torino* XXIX. 163). [tr. F. *sillon de Rolando* (F. Leuret 1839, in *Anat. Comparée du Syst. Nerv.* (1839–57) I. vi. 398).]

1839–47 R. B. TODD *Cycl. Anat. & Physiol.* III. 696/2 Two superior convolutions are met with above the fissure of Sylvius, between which is placed..the fissure of Rolando. **1861** *Proc. Zool. Soc.* 248 Fig. 1 was drawn from an almost fresh brain, fig. 2 represents a brain which had been for several months in spirit. The roundness of outline of the latter as compared with the former, and the more transverse direction of the fissure of Rolando, are very remarkable. **1890** *Jrnl. Anat. & Physiol.* XXV. 139 It is a question if the fissure of Rolando is present in any other brains than those of Apes and Man. **1921** TILNEY & RILEY *Form & Functions Central Nerv. Syst.* xxxvi. 643 The fissure of Rolando has been found interrupted near its middle in the brains of several distinguished men. **1974** *Encycl. Brit. Macropædia* XII. 982/2 The two major grooves on the lateral surface of the brain are the lateral fissure (fissure of Sylvius), which starts at the base of the brain and extends upward and backward on the lateral surface, and the central sulcus (sulcus of Rolando), which runs from the middle of the dorsal border of the hemisphere downward almost to the lateral fissure.

b. The translucent gelatinous substance which fills the ends of the posterior grey horns of the spinal medulla.

1853 BUSK & HUXLEY tr. *A. Kölliker's Man. Human Histol.* I. 408 The posterior, longer and thinner [horns].. at the free edge are invested with a more transparent layer, containing a preponderance of smaller nerve-cells —the substantia gelatinosa of Rolando. **1872** H. POWER tr. J. Gerlach in S. Stricker *Man. Human & Compar. Histol.* II. xxx. 361 The posterior cornua are divisible into two portions,..an anterior and a posterior, which last, owing to its peculiar translucency when examined with the naked eye, has long been known as the substantia gelatinosa of Rolando. **1929** HEWER & SANDES *Introd. Study Nerv. Syst.* vi. 20 Fibres..giving off collaterals arborising round cells of the substantia gelatinosa of Rolando. **1976** *Expr. Brain Res.* XXVI. 77 Peripheral neurotomy..induced a series of peculiar, *sui generis* alterations, both in the Rolando substance and in the dorsal column.

rôle. Delete ‖ and add: Now usu. spelt **role.**

1. a. For 'Chiefly *fig.*' read 'freq. *fig.*' and add: Also *spec.*, a part in a play, opera, film, or broadcast drama; = PART *sb.* 9. See also *title-rôle* s.v. TITLE *sb.* 11.

1886, 1900 [see *title-role* s.v. TITLE *sb.* 11]. **1912** M. B. LEAVITT *50 Yrs. Theatr. Managem.* xiv. 184 Jennie Winston, an Australian, was likewise famous as a male impersonator and was also a favorite in leading operatic rôles. **1937** D. FROHMAN *Encore* xv. 199 In the course of his subsequent long career on the stage, he included in his repertoire more than a hundred and thirty difficult rôles. **1973** R. ROUD in P. Noble *Favorite Movies* x. 103 In *Citizen Kane*..Welles does indeed play a role in his film. **1980** D. GARFIELD *Player's Place* iv. 157 Studio actors have been found wanting in the performance of 'classical' roles.

For *transf.* read: **b.** The typical or characteristic function performed by someone or something; freq. in phr. *to play a role.* (Later examples.)

1944 J. S. HUXLEY *On Living in Revolution* 73 He [*sc.* Darwin] was aware that isolation might play a role in the production of new species. **1957** E. LEHRMAN tr. *N. A. Gorchakov's Theatre in Soviet Russia* v. 108 Did the Communist Party have any ideas of its own about the role of the theater before the Revolution of October, 1917? **1963** J. & E. NEWSON *Patterns of Infant Care* i. 21 One of the maternal grandmother's chief roles..is being steadily taken over by the doctor, the midwife and the health visitor. **1973** A. R. PREST in Crick & Robson *Taxation Policy* ix. 129 A more recent study does seem to suggest a more positive role for these devices. **1981** *Newsweek* 4 May 74/3 The so-called hypothalamic-pituitary axis is the master-control center for hormones throughout the body and also plays an important role in emotions.

2. *Social Psychol.* The behaviour that an individual feels it appropriate to assume in adapting to any form of social interaction; the behaviour considered appropriate to the interaction demanded by a particular kind of work or social position.

1913 G. H. MEAD in *Jrnl. Philos.* X. 377 This response to the social conduct of the self may be in the rôle of another—we present his arguments in imagination and do it with his intonations and gestures... In this way we play the rôles of all our group; indeed, it is only in so far as we do this that they become part of our social environment. **1936** R. LINTON *Study of Man* viii. 114 Every individual has a series of rôles deriving from the various patterns in which he participates and at the same time *a rôle*, general, which represents the sum total of these rôles. **1949** R. K. MERTON *Social Theory* iii. 110 A conception basic to sociology holds that individuals have multiple social roles and tend to organize their behavior in terms of the structurally defined expectations assigned to each role. **1950** T. M. NEWCOMB *Social Psychol.* viii. 280 A position has no meaning without its accompanying role. **1961** E. GOFFMAN *Encounters* 85 In sociology there are few concepts more commonly used than 'role', few that are accorded more importance, and few that waver so much when looked at closely. **1967** M. ARGYLE *Psychol. Interpersonal Behaviour* iv. 73 By a 'role' is meant a pattern of behaviour which is shared by most occupants of a position, and which comes to be expected of them. The role usually includes a series of distinct relationships with people in other positions. **1977** R. HOLLAND *Self & Social Context* v. 82 There is no attempt to explore the possibility that psychologists' and sociologists' own roles may influence their definitions and uses of the concept of role.

3. An expression, usu. in the form of a symbol or series of symbols, of the function or signification of a term appearing in an index or thesaurus, used esp. as a means of indicating its possible relevance to other terms with which it may be associated. Usu. *attrib.*, as *role indicator, operator.*

1961 *Amer. Documentation* XII. 98 (*heading*) Notes on the use of roles and links in coordinate indexing. **1963** *Aslib Proc.* XV. 297 With 'roles' each keyword is classified by function. **1970** A. CHANDOR et al. *Dict. Computers* 332 *Role indicator*, a code associated with a keyword to identify it as a noun, verb, or adjective, etc. **1976** *Program* X. 18 *Prevulcanization* is stripped to *prevulcanis* (a) to *prevulcan* (a) to *vulcan* (da): the letters within parentheses indicate the role indicator. **1977** A. C. FOSKETT *Subject Approach to Information* (ed. 3) vi. 81 One of the rules used by Coates is that when we have a *thing* defined by the *material* of which it is made, the thing precedes the material, which is introduced by the role operator. **1979** J. E. ROWLEY *Mechanised In-House Information Syst.* I. 46 Roles or role indicators are appended to an index term at the indexing stage to indicate the use of the term in that context.

4. *attrib.* and *Comb.* (sense 2), as *role absorption, -assumption, -creating, -differentiation, -expectation, -structure, -structuring, theory, theorist; role-assuming, -determined, -determining* adjs.; **role conflict,** the difficulties encountered when one role makes conflicting demands on an individual or when an individual has several roles whose demands are conflicting; **role distance,** detachment from one's role; also (with hyphen) as *vb.*; **role model,** someone who, in the performance of a role, is taken as a model by others; **role-play,** the performance of a role, esp. the deliberate rehearsal or acting of a particular role, freq. used as a technique in training or psychotherapy; so **role-play** *v. intr.* and *trans.*, **role-player, role-playing** *vbl. sb.*; **role relation, relationship** (see quot. 1957); **role reversal,** the assumption of a role which is the reverse of that normally performed; **role-set** (see quot. 1957); **role-taking,** the imaginary assumption, leading to understanding, of another's role; hence (as back-formation) **role-take** *v. intr.*

1937 J. L. MORENO in *Sociometry* I. 51 The weaker the role absorption by the ego, the more often can the ego soliloquize. **1932** *Amer. Jrnl. Sociol.* XXXVII. 378 Our habitual self, or character, is, however, a natural precipitate of this rôle-assuming vocation. *Ibid.*, The technique here involved is that of 'rôle-assumption'. **1957** *Brit. Jrnl. Sociol.* VIII. 108 Theories of the middle range.., for example, of reference groups and social mobility, of communication, role-conflict and the formation of social norms. **1964** M. ARGYLE *Psychol. & Social Probl.* xiv. 169 People are often exposed to role-conflicts, usually between the demands of different roles, such as how much time to devote to the job or family, sometimes to complexities in the position, as in the case of the military chaplain. **1977** M. EDELMAN *Polit. Lang.* iv. 75 The professional and the public official whose function it is to 'help' the inadequate,..is..eager to play his or her role, equipped with a built-in reason to discount or re-interpret qualms, role conflicts, and disturbing facts. **1943** Role-creating [see **role-playing*]. **1956** C. W. MILLS *Power Elite* i. 25 Some elite men *are*..typically role-determined, but others are at times role-determining. **1968** B. MAYO *Moral Agent* in *R. Inst. Philos. Lect.* I. iii. 63 This cannot possibly be the sense of 'personal' which is contrasted with 'role determined', for his actions certainly are decided by..his role. **1967** C. MARGERISON in Wills & Yearsley *Handbk. Managem. Technol.* 18 The owner-managers of the nineteenth century were largely role-determining actors—they were able to control their factories and affairs very much in the manner that they wished. **1955** P. E. SLATER in A. P. Hare et al. *Small Groups* 499 What is the relationship of personality factors to role differentiation? Are there factors which predispose an individual to assume a particular role? **1972** M. ARGYLE *Social Psychol. of Work* viii. 180 Role-differentiation appears in small social groups, as division of labour appeared in the earliest human communities. **1961** E. GOFFMAN *Encounters* 93 This 'effectively' expressed pointed separateness between the individual and his putative role I shall call *role distance*... The individual is actually denying not the role but the virtual self that is implied in the role. **1972** M. L. SAMUELS *Linguistic Evol.* (1975) vii. 146 R. B. Le Page suggests to me that in England there would be good reasons for the aristocracy of the late fourteenth and early fifteenth centuries to adopt affected forms of speech as a means of 'role-distancing' from the lower classes, from whom they had hitherto been differentiated by speaking French. **1978** A. RYAN in Hookway & Pettit *Action & Interpretation* 68 The question whether the crucial element in the dramaturgical picture is that cluster of insights which goes under the general heading of 'role distance'. **1979** *Internat. Jrnl. Sociol. of Law* VII. 289 Not that the average performer seems conscious of any evidence on his part of role-distance; on the contrary, such ritual commitment furnishes the core of his identity. **1951** PARSONS & SHILS *Toward Gen. Theory of Action* iv. 190 Role-expectations are patterns of evaluation. **1969** in Halpert & Story *Christmas Mumming in Newfoundland* 142 Cat Harbour..is normally characterized by rather rigid and formal role expectations. **1957** W. THIELENS in R. K. Merton *Student-Physician* II. 138 By the time students enter law or medical school, those whose decisions were made earliest are most likely to have a role model. **1977** *N.Y. Times Mag.* 26 June 10/2 If the teacher was a 'role model', parents were obviously unaware of it. **1961** R. J. CORSINI et al. *Roleplaying in Business & Industry* i. 9 If they stopped now and then and discussed, evaluated, and practiced alternative ways of reacting, they roleplayed. **1964** M. ARGYLE *Psychol. & Social Probl.* x. 133 Students role-play some of the situations they will meet on the job. **1970** *Peace News* 2 Oct. 3/4 During a strategy game, a situation may arise which is so interesting that the group may want to roleplay it. When the roleplay is over, people can return to the strategy game. **1979** *Lore & Lang.* Jan. 4 Dylan (5:3) is taking part in a 'spiderman' role-play, and another participant tries to drag him away. **1943** J. L. MORENO in *Sociometry* VI. 438 Role-player is a literary translation of the German word 'Rollenspieler' which I have used. **1978** *Dædalus* Summer 137 He [*sc.* the bourgeois] is the man who, when dealing with others, thinks only of himself, and, in his understanding of himself, thinks only of others. He is a role-player. **1980** *Times Lit. Suppl.* 31 Oct. 1221/3 The hero of Anne Tyler's new novel, Morgan Gower, is an inveterate role-player. **1943** J. L. MORENO in *Sociometry* VI. 438 It may be useful to differentiate between *role-taking*..—*role-playing*—which permits the individual some degree of freedom—and *role-creating*. **1951** *Amer. Sociol. Rev.* XVI. 181/2 In *role-playing* one does not pretend anything. A policeman arresting a person is..performing or *playing* a role expected of one holding the position of public protector. **1960** W. H. WHYTE *Organization Man* v. 56 The role of slugger—not just a role-playing role, either—was assigned in advance. **1980** *Times Lit. Suppl.* 23 May 575/5 Role-playing is perhaps the true subject of the modern novel. **1940** *Sociometry* III. 20 The pattern of rôle relations around an individual as their focus, is called his cultural atom. **1950** T. M. NEWCOMB *Social Psychol.* xiii. 453 These four kinds of role relationships call for quite different sets of activities on his part. **1957** E. BOTT *Family & Social Network* i. 3 A *role-relationship* is defined as those aspects of a relationship that consist of reciprocal role expectations of each person concerning the other. **1977** R. HOLLAND *Self & Social Context* v. 97 The person with a strong ego can integrate experience of his past role-relationships and put it to the use of role-performance. **1951** *Occupational Psychol.* XXV. 65 The method of role-reversal is designed to change the cognitive structure of disputants so that their social perception changes from divergence to convergence. **1967** M. ARGYLE *Psychol. Interpersonal Behaviour* x. 188 Role-reversal: here a trainee takes the reverse of the role he would take in real life, e.g. a foreman takes the role of a shop-steward. **1975** W. A. HAVILAND *Cultural Anthropol.* xiii. 319/2 During the installation rites of a chief among the Ndembu.., a different type of role reversal is manifest; the chief must sit in silent humility while he is reviled.. by anyone who feels so inclined. **1957** R. K. MERTON in *Brit. Jrnl. Sociol.* VIII. 110 Unlike Linton, I begin with the premise that each social status involves not a single associated role, but an array of roles. This basic feature of social structure can be registered by the..term, role-set... By role-set I mean that complement of role-relationships in which persons are involved by virtue of occupying a particular social status. **1968** P. K. BOCK in J. A. Fishman *Readings Sociol. of Lang.* 215 Radically different behavioral expectations *are* attached to the role of 'teacher' in connection with various members of the corresponding role-set. **1977** WARREN & PONSE in Douglas & Johnson *Existential Sociol.* x. 274 Instead, they have been concerned with social roles, role sets, and so on. **1940** *Sociometry* III. 21 This often produces a typical conflict in the rôle-structures of two marriage partners. **1978** A. RYAN in Hookway & Pettit *Action & Interpretation* 67 The sociologist may, perhaps, rest content with giving a structural description of a society's role structure. **1967** D. COOPER *Psychiatry & Antipsychiatry* v. 84 There seemed an obvious need for a separate unit with less ritual and less rigid role-structuring. **1972** *Jrnl. Social Psychol.* Dec. 247 The ability to role-take accurately, or empathize, is the ability to see, feel, respond, and understand as if one were the other person. **1934** G. H. MEAD *Mind, Self & Society* IV. 254 The immediate effect of such rôle-taking lies in the control which the individual is able to exercise over his own response. **1951** *Amer. Sociol. Rev.* XVI. 180/2 The term role-taking meant, for Mead, a strictly mental or cognitive or empathic activity, not overt behavior or conduct. **1964** M. ARGYLE *Psychol. & Social Probl.* x. 136 It [*sc.* indoctrination induced by Chinese 'thought reform'] can perhaps best be described as a piece of ego-involved role-taking, produced by extreme coercion, together with the temporary adoption of a new frame of reference. **1972** *Jrnl. Social Psychol.* Dec. 247 Role taking refers to the imaginative reconstruction by ego of alter's role. **1954** G. LINDZEY *Handbk. Social Psychol.* I. 238/1 More than any other single group, the role theorists have developed and used the conception of the self as an intervening variable. **1977** R. HOLLAND *Self & Social Context* v. 91 Up to this point I have dealt with the *structural* role theorists represented in Coser and Rosenberg's book of readings. **1954** G. LINDZEY *Handbk. Social Psychol.* I. 238/1 The trend in role theory is in the study of the interactions of self and role as coordinates and not as parallels. **1972** W. C. COE *Challenges of Personal Adjustment* viii. 215 Role theory bridges the gap between the constructs of sociology and of psychology.

Hence **role** *v. trans.*, to provide (a term) with a role indicator; **ro·ling** *vbl. sb.*

1976 *Program* X. 14 (*heading*) A minicomputer retrieval system with automatic root finding and roling facilities. *Ibid.* 24 The presence of the connective merely ensures that the first word in the multi-word phrase is roled and stored.

roleo (rōu·lio). *U.S.* Also **rolleo.** [f. ROLL *v.*[2] + ROD)EO.] (See quot. 1942.) Also *attrib.*

1933 *Nat. Geographic* Feb. 166 (*caption*) A floating log affords precarious footing; yet this expert woodsman.. rides it standing... Contests in this sport are a part of the 'Rolleo' celebration held annually. **1942** BERREY & VAN DEN BARK *Amer. Thes. Slang* §513 *Rolleo*,..a log-rolling contest. **1948** *Chicago Tribune* 6 July 1. 1/4 The others learned that the roleo is like a rodeo—except that instead of riding ornery bronchos, the contestants ride on floating logs that spin so fast the water churns up like a lawn sprinkler. **1949** *Boston Globe Mag.* 9 Oct. 8/1, I only wish your dad could see you roll at the Roleo. **1954** *Ocean Press* 24 Aug. 7/3 Running first won the world's championship at a 'roleo' in 1942 and has held the title ever since. **1956** *Sun* (Baltimore) 29 June 11/1 Lawrence Bergeron,..president of the National Roleo Association, drowned today while competing in the 'old-timer' finals of the world championship log-rolling championships.

Rolex (rōu·leks). The proprietary name of a make of watch. Also *attrib.*

1912 *Trade Marks Jrnl.* 14 Aug. 1242 'Rolex'... Watches. Wilsdorf & Davis,..London,..; watch manufacturers. **1957** J. BRAINE *Room at Top* iv. 40 A young man with sleek black hair, a shiny red face and a gold Rolex Oyster. **1970** W. WAGER *Sledgehammer* (1971) xvi. 99 He glanced down at the face of his gold Rolex. **1973** J. ROSSITER *Manipulators* xiv. 138 The watch on his wrist [was] an upper-bracket Rolex. **1977** B. FREEMANTLE *Charlie Muffin* xvii. 170 He looked at the heavy Rolex watch that had been part of the élite snobbism of the Green Berets in Vietnam.

Rolf (rǫlf). Also **rolf.** The name of Ida P. *Rolf* (1897–1979), U.S. physiotherapist, used *attrib.* to designate her technique of deep massage (also known as 'structural integration') aimed at reducing muscular, and consequently psychic, tension. Hence as *v. trans.* Also **Rolfed** (rǫlft) *ppl. a.*; **Ro·lfer,** a practitioner of this technique; **Ro·lfing** *vbl. sb.*, the Rolf technique.

1958 D. LAWSON-WOOD *Psycho-Logics & Posture* 11 The author is a fully qualified and registered masseur and physiotherapist, and is engaged..in further intensive study and research in the Rolf Technique. **1970** *Psychol. Today* IV. 58/1 Rolf and the older rolf practitioners recognize the importance of this emotional component. *Ibid.* 88/3 In the case of the rolfed subjects there was no training. **1971** W. C. SCHUTZ *Here comes Everybody* 176 One man has been Rolfed many times and one area of difficulty is a rounded back. **1972** G. DOWNING *Massage Bk.* 155 The pain..stops immediately when the Rolfer's hand is taken away. **1972** *New Yorker* 21 Oct. 34/2 Everyone under twenty-five discussed Rolfing... Rolfing is a system of deep massage that stretches and rearranges the tissue surrounding the muscles. **1977** *N.Y. Times* (City ed.) 15 July C. 22/2 We already spend far too much time practicing artificial modes of sociability, such as group encounters, sensitivity training, 'T' groups, Rolfing and the like. **1979** *Brit. Med. Jrnl.* 24 Mar. 796/2 There are also those..who heal with rolfing, shiatsu, polarity treatment, aeriontherapy, or psionic medicine.

roll, *sb.*[1] Add: **II. 6. e.** A quantity of bills or notes rolled together; hence, the money a person possesses. *U.S.* and *Austral.* Also phr. *a roll Jack Rice couldn't jump over*, a large quantity of money (*Austral. slang*).

1846 *Dollar Newspaper* (Philadelphia) 22 Apr. 4/6 He also had a roll which he said contained $600. **1904** *N.Y. Times* 16 May 5 It was as easy to be separated from one's 'roll' at a shell game there a quarter of a century ago as it was ten years ago. **1907** 'O. HENRY' *Trimmed Lamp* 171 He drew out his 'roll' and slapped five tens upon the bar. **1912** J. SANDILANDS *Western Canad. Dict.*, *Roll*, or *Wad*, a person's present supply of dollar bills or paper money. Roll him is to rob him of his money. **1919** H. L. WILSON *Ma Pettengill* ii. 62 [He] asked her how big her roll was, saying that he lived out there and it cost something to make a home. *a* **1925** [see *CUT *v.* 56 q]. **1926** J. BLACK *You can't Win* iv. 35 No Missouri dip would take his roll, extract two fifty dollar bills, and put the rest back in his pocket. **1945** BAKER *Austral. Lang.* v. 107 A man.. may even be fortunate enough to have a roll Jack Rice couldn't jump over. Jack Rice was a racehorse noted for his performances over hurdles. **1954** T. RONAN *Vision Splendid* II. 119 'I've got a roll Jack Rice couldn't jump over.' Marty produced one of those wads of currency Mr. Tappingham had seen only in the cruder American films and started peeling off ten-pound notes. **1960** 'N. CULOTTA' *Cop this Lot* v. 82 Man walks around with a roll in 'is kick Jack Rice couldn' jump over, an' 'e's not worth a zac.

f. A quantity of photographic or cinematographic film supplied rolled up; a spool of film.

1890 [see sense 13 c]. **1925** *Kodak Mag.* July 109 It is quite a good idea to develop just one or two rolls, to make sure that you are giving correct exposures. **1960** O. SKILBECK *ABC of Film & TV Working Terms* 110 Some Magazines hold..only two hundred feet of Stock and the Rolls are smaller than normal. **1973** C. MCCARRY *Miernik Dossier* (1974) 147 I'm sending you a roll of snaps to keep for me... You can have them developed. **1976** K. THACKERAY *Crownbird* v. 82 Priest was loading a roll of Tri-X into a black Nikon.

g. *spec.* = *music roll* (*b*) s.v. *MUSIC *sb.* 12d.

1902 *Encycl. Brit.* XXXI. 767/1 The use of the perforated roll acts by means of the ingenious and indeed faultless application of pneumatic leverage to the ordinary piano. **1906, 1913** [see **music roll*]. **1921** A. HUXLEY *Crome Yellow* x. 94 The music stopped... He.. turned to the cabinet where the rolls were kept. He trod off the old roll and trod on the new. **1926,** etc. [see **piano roll*]. **1928** *Melody Maker* Feb. 161/3 Holding back the licenses of the 'Mechanical' reproductions on records and rolls. **1956** S. LONGSTREET *Real Jazz* 129 James P. Johnson was a great man on the rolls. Till 1920 he punched a lot of rolls. After that he recorded sides. **1972** *Jazz & Blues* Oct. 6/3 Changing the playing speed of the roll does not alter the pitch. **1977** *Times* 25 June 26/9 (Advt.), Pianola piano..100 rolls..£700.

h. A rolled-up quantity of a prohibited drug.

1962 'K. ORVIS' *Damned & Destroyed* v. 36 Loaded. Full of heroin. Carrying a roll, too. **1976** *Whig-Standard* (Kingston, Ontario) 21 Jan. 45/3 Bruce denied any knowledge of the roll, claiming his suitcase had been left unopened in the motel.

10. c. An item of food (other than bread) that is rolled up or doubled over before being cooked; chiefly with defining words, as *fig-*, *meat*, *potato roll*. See also *jelly roll* s.v. *JELLY *sb.*[1] 4, *pancake roll* s.v. *PANCAKE *sb.* 3, *sausage roll* s.v. SAUSAGE 4d, *Swiss roll* s.v. SWISS *a.* 2.

1845 E. ACTON *Mod. Cookery* xvi. 420 Excellent meat rolls. Pound..veal, chicken, or turkey... Form it into small rolls..fold them in good puff-paste, and bake them. **1922** JOYCE *Ulysses* 25 A bag of figrolls lay snugly in Armstrong's satchel. *a* **1944** K. DOUGLAS *Alamein to Zem Zem* (1946) 62 Meat roll and excellent ersatz coffee graced our menu. **1950** *Mrs. Beeton's Bk. Househ. Managem.* 1181 *Potato rolls*... Cut the potatoes into small pieces... Roll out the paste to the thickness of ⅛ of an inch, cut in rounds or squares 4 inches across, fill each with the vegetables, fold it over like a turnover, and bake.

11. b. (Examples of *hollow roll*.)

1904 GOODCHILD & TWENEY *Technol. & Sci. Dict.* 288/2 *Hollow roll*, a lead roll made by bending over the edges of sheet lead, and so forming a tube. **1960** *B.S.I. News* May 23 Guidance on the use of lead sheet used as a covering for roofs... Design methods for both the wood-roll and hollow-roll systems.

12*. *Geol.* An ore body in sedimentary rock that has a C- or S-shaped vertical cross-section cutting across strata. Freq. *attrib.*

1942 *Bull. U.S. Geol. Survey* No. 936. 363 The vanadium-bearing hydrous mica is..in part concentrated..in thin zones that cut across bedding. As the zones..are curved or wavy, they are called rolls by the miners. **1955** *Prof. Papers U.S. Geol. Survey* No. 300. 239/1 Similarities between roll ore bodies and the more prevalent tabular ore bodies in sedimentary rocks of the Colorado Plateau. *Ibid.* 239/2 In cross section, rolls commonly show C, S, and 'socket' shapes.., but in plan are linear. **1976** R. I. RACKLEY in K. H. Wolf *Hand-bk. Strata-Bound & Stratiform Ore Deposits* VII. iii. 116 The uranium 'roll' has long been known to uranium producers.

13. a. *roll film*, *-shutter*, *tobacco* (later examples).

1895 *Montgomery Ward Catal.* Spring & Summer 217/1, 1 Roll Film, for 25 exposures—.20 1 Box of 5 Rolls of Film (for 25 exposures each) 1.00. **1902** *Encycl. Brit.* XXXI. 690/2 In many ways the most convenient and compact hand cameras are those made specially for use with the roll-film cartridges in many different sizes. **1933** *Discovery* Feb. 59/2 Roll films are used, each roll containing one hundred exposures. **1951** YARSLEY & KITCHEN in H. M. Langton *Synthetic Resins* (ed. 3) ii. 116 The bulk of the many millions of feet of cine film used throughout the world to-day is still celluloid, and 3½ mil celluloid is the base for amateur roll film. **1977** J. HEDGECOE *Photographer's Handbk.* 10 By the 1890s George Eastman's rollfilm camera allowed many pictures to be taken at one loading. **1911** *Chambers's Jrnl.* Feb. 141/2 At the kerb end the front is provided with a roll-shutter. **1922** Rollshutter [see *DOWN-COMING *ppl. a.*]. **1913** I. COWIE *Company of Adventurers* 311 Accordingly Whitford placed on the dressed buffalo skin which they had placed on the ground before them, two pint measures of tea and a yard of thick Canadian roll tobacco. **1929** MOBERLY & CAMERON *When Fur was King* 35 One and a half feet of Canadian roll tobacco sold for one..made-beaver.

c. *roll-end*; *roll-munching* adj.

1970 *Toronto Daily Star* 24 Sept. 27/1 (Advt.), Roll ends at cost. **1976** *Bridgwater Mercury* 21 Dec. 5/1 (Advt.), Room-size remnants. We must clear dozens of roll-ends to make room for new stocks. **1970** G. F. NEWMAN *Sir, You Bastard* viii. 210 The bar was packed with fat roll-munching office workers.

III. 17. *roll-produced* adj.; **roll feed,** a feed mechanism supplying paper, strip metal, etc., by means of rollers; so **roll-feeding** *vbl. sb.*; **roll-fed** *ppl. a.*; **roll-forming** *vbl. sb.*, cold forming of metal by repeated passing between rollers; so **roll-form** *v. trans.*; **roll-formed** *ppl. a.*; **roll mark,** a mark produced on sheet metal in flattening it with an imperfect set of rollers.

1967 KARCH & BUBER *Offset Processes* ii. 31 *Flexographic*. This process involves the use of rotary (web or roll fed) printing from rubber plates. **1968** *Gloss. Terms Mechanized & Hand Sheet Metal Work* (*B.S.I.*) 19 *Roll feed*, a feed mechanism that imparts continuous or intermittent motion to strip by means of rollers in contact with both surfaces. **1967** V. STRAUSS *Printing Industry* vi. 362/2 Roll feeding was originally developed for the production of metropolitan newspapers by relief printing. *Ibid.* 363/1 Designers of roll-feeding machinery have devised a number of different roll-feeding methods. **1949** *Tool Engineers Handbk.* (Amer. Soc. Tool Engineers) 989 Most sheet and strip metals can be successfully roll-formed. **1958** *Times Rev. Industry* June 20/1 The cylindrical body sections are made from two plates, roll-formed cold to shape and welded together. **1971** *Engineering* Apr. 59/1 Some permanent plastic coatings..will endure the metal to which they are applied being drawn, roll-formed, bent, and pressed, without cracks developing or the coating peeling. **1949** *Tool Engineers Handbk.* (Amer. Soc. Tool Engineers) 989 Generally speaking, the sharpest corner practicable to maintain on a roll-formed section would be one having an outside radius equal to the metal thickness. **1977** *Engin. Materials & Design* Aug. 50/3 Because the rivets are roll-formed, they are straighter than extruded rivets. **1932** E. V. CRANE *Plastic Working of Metals* v. 91 Bending Operations.—Bar-folders, brakes, drawbenches, roll-forming machines and bending dies in presses share the field. **1954** J. F. YOUNG *Materials & Processes* (ed. 2) xix. 805 Roll forming consists of passing strip stock between sets of shaped driven rollers. **1967** S. KALPAKJIAN *Mech. Processing of Materials* vi. 202 A further development of roll forming is the production of welded tubing, starting with a flat strip. **1923** GLAZEBROOK *Dict. Appl. Physics* V. 364/1 The effect of alternate heating and cooling is to cause small cracks in the surface of the rolls, which lead to slight ridges, or 'roll marks'. **1962** G. R. BASHFORTH *Manuf. Iron & Steel* (ed. 2) IV. iv. 138 Sections are liable to develop certain defects, such as.. 'roll marks' due to defective or badly worn rolls. **1952** J. B. OLDHAM *Eng. Blind-Stamped Bindings* i. 4 The use of a roll-produced decoration.

roll, *sb.*[2] Add: **1. b.** In *go and have a roll*: go away, 'get lost'. *slang.*

1941 BAKER *Dict. Austral. Slang* 34 *Have a roll!, go and,* go to the devil! **1959** I. & P. OPIE *Lore & Lang. Schoolch.* x. 192 Juvenile language is well stocked..with expressions inviting a person's departure, for instance:..go and have a roll.

c. Esp. in phr. *to have a roll on* and varr.: to have a conceited bearing, to give oneself airs. *Eng. Public School slang.*

1881 C. E. PASCOE *Everyday Life in our Public Schools* 160 Anything approaching 'swagger' is severely rebuked; there is no more objectionable quality than that understood by the expression, 'He's got such a horrid roll on'. **1908** D. COKE *House Prefect* i. 11 Brereton, they decided, had a bit of a roll on. **1913** A. LUNN *Harrovians* iii. 53 Ewen was an ugly lout, and was beginning to put on roll...after the game, his tendency to 'put on roll' was duly checked in the approved fashion.

d. (An act of) rotation of a vehicle or craft about an axis parallel to its direction of motion.

In the case of ships the movement consists of a partial rotation, immediately reversed, caused by wind or waves; with aircraft it is either a similar unintended movement or a deliberate manœuvre consisting of a complete turn through 360°; with motor vehicles and helicopters it is a tipping (outwards and inwards respectively) in cornering.

1862 W. FROUDE *Rolling of Ships* 75 All ships having the same 'periodic time', or period of natural roll, when artificially put in motion in still water, will go through the same series of movements. **1907** J. MASEFIELD *Tarpaulin Muster* xvi. 161 At the last of her rolls there comes a clattering of tins, as the galley gear and whack pots slither across to leeward, followed by cursing seamen. **1912** *Techn. Rep. Advisory Comm. Aeronaut. 1911–12* 102 The pendulum movement from side to side..misleads the pilot into operating his wing flaps to recover the vertical position of his body. By this he may aggravate the roll. **1918** W. G. MCMINNIES *Pract. Flying* x. 194 The roll, which consists of making the machine loop sideways and continue in the same direction as it was travelling before the manœuvre, is done with the engine on or off. **1920** *Nature* 11 Mar. 47/2 For use on board ship the compass must be mounted..so that the rolls..shall have but small effect on the compass. **1942** N. MACMILLAN *How to pilot Aeroplane* xv. 100 The full roll, the half roll, and the double half roll can all be made on the glide or during a zoom as well as on the level. **1945** J. M. LABBERTON *Marine Engineers' Handbk.* ix. 1389 The maximum velocity will occur at the vertical position and diminish to zero at the extremities of the roll... The maximum dynamic effect will occur at the maximum angle of roll. **1953** M. RAUSCHER *Introd. Aeronaut. Dynamics* 660/2 (Index), Roll or Bank, angle of. **1957** J. SHAPIRO *Helicopter* iii. 52 The sideways attitude of the helicopter against the horizon is known as its 'roll'. A more frequently used term for the same condition is 'bank'. **1961** *Times* 28 Mar. 4/6 There is a good deal of roll when cornering fast. **1967, 1974** [see *PITCH *sb.*[2] 2b]. **1974** *Physics Bull.* Jan. 11/1 The six component wind tunnel balance..will be able to measure three forces (lift, drag and side force) and three moments (pitch, yaw and roll) on any aircraft model it supports. **1978** *Lancashire Life* Apr. 141/1 The Fiat 132-2000 rides very well indeed on all kinds of road surface and corners capably with a minimum of roll.

e. *Gymnastics.* An exercise in which the body is rolled into a tuck position and turned in a forward or backward circle.

1898 F. GRAF et al. *Hints to Gymnasts* III. 176 Before attempting any kind of..rolls..or handstands, the pupil should have mastered thoroughly all kinds of straight arm swinging exercises. **1920,** etc. [see *neck-roll* s.v. *NECK *sb.*[1] 16]. **1935** *Encycl. Sports* 331/1 When half the roll has been accomplished the hands are changed from behind the head to a position in front, so that the body is then pivoted on the inside of the arms. **1955** *Simple Gymnastics* ('Know the Game' Series) (ed. 2) 25 *Forward Roll* —Bend forward and take the weight of the body on the hands. Tuck the head well under and roll with the knees on the chest. **1956** KUNZLE & THOMAS *Freestanding* ii. 32 From a forward roll to stand, to a cartwheel sideways down the same line as the roll.

f. A throw (at dice).

1926 G. ADE *Let.* 26 Oct. (1973) 114 This kind of party [*sc.* a 'Monte Carlo' party] is the wildest and most hilarious thing you ever heard. Before we got through Sunday evening the crap shooters were rolling for a hundred thousand a roll. **1966** O. NORTON *School of Liars* iv. 62 Ben rattled the dice-box. 'Now..we'll have a quick roll before Hank the Bank comes, and I think Scott's in the chair.' **1969** R. C. BELL *Board & Table Games* II. v. 91 The first caster throws all five dice on his first roll. **1974** *Times* 20 Feb. 19/2 We are still schooling craps on this and we think we can make it on the next roll.

g. *colloq.* An act of sexual intercourse. *a roll in the hay*: see *HAY *sb.*[1] 3.

1942 BERREY & VAN DEN BARK *Amer. Thes. Slang* § 362/1 *Copulation,*..roll. **1962** P. GREEN tr. *S. de Beauvoir's Prime of Life* I. ii. 80, I had several unpleasant incidents with truck drivers, not to mention a commercial traveler who wanted me to have a roll with him in the ditch, and left me flat in the middle of the road when I refused. **1976** P. FERRIS *Detective* viii. 146 It involves State Security. Your Rosemary has been having a roll with a Cabinet Minister.

3. b. *Phonetics.* = TRILL *sb.*[2] 3. Cf. ROLL *v.*[2] 4c, *ROLLED *ppl. a.* 4.

1950 D. JONES *Pronunc. of Eng.* (ed. 3) I. 95 Another variety of the 'burr' is a uvular fricative sound (without roll)... One may also hear a uvular roll with accompanying friction. **1973** J. D. O'CONNOR *Phonetics* ii. 47 Rolls consist of several rapidly repeated closures and openings of the air passage, as in the rolled *r*-sounds of Scottish or Italian... [The] uvular roll is common in Dutch for *r* and may be heard in French and German too—the sound is reminiscent of a gargling noise.

8. *attrib.* and *Comb.*, as *roll angle, plane*; **roll axis,** the axis about which a vehicle or craft rolls; **roll bar,** an overhead metal bar to protect the occupants of a motor vehicle in the event of its overturning; **roll cage,** in a motor vehicle, a centre box section designed to protect the occupants if the vehicle overturns; also *attrib.*; **roll cast** *Angling,* (see quot. 1960[1]); hence as *vb. trans.* and *intr.*; *roll-casting* vbl. sb.; **roll rate,** the angular velocity of a vehicle or craft about its roll axis.

1961 *Which? Reports on Cars* 14 Published reports so far have been based on subjective assessment of roll angle. **1970** *Motoring Which?* July 99/2 All three had low roll angles. **1950** NEWTON & STEEDS *Motor Vehicle* (ed. 4) xxxi. 566 The roll axis for a car having axles at front and back will be some distance above ground level while that having independent suspensions at front and back will have a roll axis lying at ground level. **1962** Roll axis [see *pitch axis* s.v. *PITCH *sb.*[2] 26]. **1954** *Amer. Speech* XXIX. 101 *Roll bar, n.,* a curved bar welded or bolted to the frame rails extending upward in back of the driver's seat to protect him in case he 'flips' over. **1957** *Life* 29 Apr. 133 In sanctioned meets cars must have roll bars over driver's seat. **1969** H. NIELSEN *Darkest Hour* xiii. 143 Goddard.. went over the embankment... The car has a roll bar, but you can see what happened. The door sprung open and he went out of it head first. **1979** *Tucson Mag.* Mar. 25/1 A removable forward hardtop and a convertible softtop rear window are separated by a Targa-style rollbar. **1972** *Sci. Amer.* Apr. 9/3 (Advt.), And 'roll cage' construction. The kind that soon, by law, may be required on all cars. **1973** *Times* 18 Oct. 35/3 The body comprises a one-piece glass-fibre outer shell on a steel monocoque centre section, with built-in rollcage. **1976** *Good Motoring* May 12/1 The roll-cage passenger compartment and anti-intrusion bars in the doors to help in side impacts. **1934** R. KELLY *Fishing* 9 (*heading*) The Roll Cast. This cast is used where trees and brush overhang the banks of the stream. **1947** R. BERGMAN *With Fly, Plug & Bait* II. vi. 113 A skillful and long roll cast is essential. *Ibid.,* When roll casting I grease my line carefully. *Ibid.,* My torpedo head tapered line also has rather a stiff finish and roll-casts well. **1960** EDWARDS & TURNER *Angler's Cast* x. 101 The Spey cast..is the simplest roll cast. *Ibid.* 105 If the angler is fishing the left bank of the river, with obstructions behind him, his only method of getting the line out is to roll cast. **1960** C. WILLOCK *Anglers' Encycl.* 158/2 *Roll-cast,* a fly cast in which the line is picked off the water without being thrown behind. **1972** *Trout & Salmon* June 58/3 Then make a roll-cast, but instead of roll-casting the line on to the water, roll it into the air. **1947** R. BERGMAN *With Fly, Plug & Bait* II. vi. 113, I have a special level line with a rather stiff finish which is especially fine for roll casting. **1960** EDWARDS & TURNER *Angler's Cast* x. 101 The average angler..thinks nothing of roll casting, with constant changes of direction, for half-a-day on his own trout stream. **1971** *Aeronaut. Jrnl.* LXXV. 295/2 Some selected type of manoeuvre, such as pitch attitude, or pitch rate, or normal acceleration, and corresponding quantities in the roll plane. **1961** W. R. KOLK *Mod. Flight Dynamics* viii. 146 An airplane's ability to roll is properly a characteristic of its maneuverability, but is also a cornerstone of its flying qualities by reason of the unstable pitch-yaw resonance encountered at roll rates exceeding the natural frequencies in either pitch or yaw. **1975** G. H. SAUNDERS *Dynamics of Helicopter Flight* v. 178 When the roll rate builds up to the point where the damping moment equals the control moment, no further increase in roll rate is achieved.

roll, *v.*[2] Add: **I. 1. a.** *to roll the bones,* to play dice. *U.S. slang.*

1929 H. W. ODUM in *Amer. Mercury* Sept. 49/2 So we sets 'round in circle an' starts rollin' them bones. *Ibid.* 58/1 Gonna roll them bones. Gonna git some money an' play bad. **1945** L. SAXON et al. *Gumbo Ya-Ya* vii. 127 Today in the colored sections of the city there are always circles of men 'rollin' the bones' playing *Indian* Dice, which is any game of Craps unsupervised by a syndicate and without a player for the 'house'.

e. Also *trans.* To bowl (a game making a specified score, a number of strikes). *U.S.*

1974 *Cleveland* (Ohio) *Plain Dealer* 13 Oct. c.8/3 Marge Dimario, bowling in the Top Ten League at Ambassador Brookpark Lanes, rolled a 275 game. **1979** *Arizona Daily Star* 1 Apr. c2/6 Earl Anthony..rolled nine strikes in the championship match yesterday.

f. Computers. *to roll out,* (*a*) (see quots. 1954, 1962[1]); (*b*) to transfer (data held in a main memory) to an auxiliary store when a program of greater priority requires the former; similarly *to roll in* (in two senses).

1954 *Computers & Automation* Dec. 20/2 *Roll out,* to read out of a register or counter by the following process: add to the digits in each column simultaneously; do this 10 times (for decimal numbers); when the result in each column changes from 9 to 0, issue a signal. **1962** *Gloss. Terms Automatic Data Processing* (*B.S.I.*) 86 *Roll out* (*to*), for a counter which counts modulo *n*, to read its content by causing it to count a sequence of *n* pulses, determining at what stage in the sequence the content passes through zero. *Ibid.* 87 *Roll in* (*to*), to increase the content of a counter by causing it to count a sequence of pulses. **1969** P. B. JORDAIN *Condensed Computer Encycl.* 435 When main memory is released by any program, or a task terminates and its space becomes available, a task that had been rolled out can be rolled in and restarted. **1970** O. DOPPING *Computers & Data Processing* ix. 123 The programs are..often stored in secondary memories, and the necessary program parts are rolled in to the primary storage when needed. When another program needs the memory space, some program parts may have to be rolled out to secondary storage again.

2. a. (Earlier and later U.S. *fig.* examples.)

1859 *La Crosse* (Wisconsin) *Union* 24 Oct. 2 He ought.. to pitch in and help roll up a big majority for Randall. **1900** *Congress. Rec.* 23 Jan. 1103/2 They answered them by rolling up a plurality of 5,665 votes for the member from Utah out of a total of 67,805. **1951** *Sun* (Baltimore) 19 June 7/3 In the state elections of Lower Saxony..the SRP rolled up nearly 400,000 votes. **1976** *Billings* (Montana) *Gaz.* 4 July 11-A/1 The powerful PRI has always rolled up massive victories in every election during the past half century.

5. f. To rob (esp. someone drunk, drugged or sleeping). *slang.*

1873 A. S. EVANS *À la California* xii. 298 When one of these fellows makes a raise by 'rolling a drunk' (i.e., taking the valuables from the pockets of a drunken man on the sidewalk), he will take a single bed at 37½ cents. **1892** C. C. JENKYNS *Hard Life in Colonies* 165 To 'roll drunks' was to frequent drinking saloons, to follow any man who left drunk, roll him into the gutter and rob him. **1912** [see *ROLL *sb.*[1] 6 e]. **1923** A. PRICE *Dreams* 3 My money, I kept in my cutter shoes, And I wasn't rolled the endurin' trip, So the whole ten days I hit the booze, With a downhill haul, and I let her rip. **1935** *Sun* (Baltimore) 2 July 1/1 We decided to get him drunk in his room the next night..and roll him. **1939** R. CHANDLER *Big Sleep* xx. 167 Here we are with a guy who..has fifteen grand in his pants... Somebody rolls him for it and rolls him too hard, so they have to take him out in the desert and plant him among the cactuses. **1949** *Life* 24 Oct. 23 She heard her new friends kidding about rolling guys. **1955** W. GADDIS *Recognitions* III. v. 940 She paid all the bills at the George Sank and gave him a terrific time for a couple of days and then rolled him. **1958** G. GREENE *Our Man in Havana* v. v. 245 In some of these places they try to roll you. **1960** *Times* 21 Sept. 3/7 We walked through a few back streets and Lutt suggested 'rolling' (robbing) someone. **1962** E. LUCIA *Klondike Kate* iv. 107 The dames seldom rolled the miners or slipped them a Mickey. **1968** *Globe & Mail Mag.* (Toronto) 13 Jan. 7/4 If a hustler is not himself homosexual,..he is called 'trade'. Rough trade refers to hustlers who are liable to beat up or roll the homosexual, either after or instead of sexual relations. **1974** in W. R. Hunt *North of 53 Degrees* vii. 42 If you don't get drunk, you don't get rolled. **1978** *Courier-Mail* (Brisbane) 22 Apr. 10/4 He had given much thought before sentencing two aboriginal women.. for 'rolling' a man in a hotel.

g. To start moving; *spec.* (esp. in command *roll 'em*) to start (cameras) filming. *slang.*

1939 J. DELL *Nobody ordered Wolves* iv. 51 Someone shouted, 'Roll 'em,' and, someone else, 'Quiet there.' **1949** R. CHANDLER *Little Sister* xix. 131 He went back beside the camera. The assistant shouted 'roll 'em' and the scene went through. **1959** *Elizabethan* June 26/1 The director call out 'Action' to the actors, then 'Roll 'em' and the cameraman starts the camera. **1973** J. DRUMMOND *Bang! Bang! You're Dead!* xxxi. 107 We may need the trucks at any time... I'll phone if I want you to roll 'em. **1977** *Rolling Stone* 21 Apr. 63/6 'Roll 'em'! crackled over the radio.

h. *fig.* To reduce, cut *back* (esp. prices). *U.S.*

1943 *Funk & Wagnalls New Stand. Encycl. Yearbk. 1942* 81/1 In many instances, wholesale or manufacturers' prices were 'rolled back' to an earlier date. **1943** *Sun* (Baltimore) 29 May 1/3 We are, therefore, confronted with the choice of rolling back the cost of living..or permitting an adjustment of wages and other income in line with the increase in the cost of living. **1944** *Ann. Reg. 1943* I. 287 Four 'pressure groups'..decisively vetoed the President's plan to 'roll back' farm prices to the level of the previous September. **1951** *Manch. Guardian Weekly* 15 Mar. 10/4 The Tampa *Tribune* in Florida..prominently reported,..the Government's promise to roll back meat prices. **1972** *Daily Tel.* 25 Apr. 4/7 From first reports, he thought perhaps 10 per cent. of America's large businesses would be required to 'roll back' prices because of excessive profits. **1975** *Washington Post* 26 Dec. A 22/1 The focus of this..bill is its attempt to roll back oil prices. **1977** *Time* 25 July 5/2 Fully 1.15 million workers were jobless in June... Unless the Giscard regime can roll back that figure, it could become a lethal weapon in the hands of the left.

i. *Econ.* With *over.* To finance the repayment of (maturing stock, or the debt it represents) by the issue of new stock.

1957 *Jrnl. Finance* Mar. 52 Since the success of a refunding offer is measured in terms of the percentage of the maturing obligation which is 'rolled over' into the new issue, it is required that the Treasury tailor its terms to the needs of the market. **1959** *Wall St. Jrnl.* 27 Jan. 17/3 Government bond dealers said that they expect the Treasury to announce late this week its plans for refunding nearly $15 billion of Federal debt maturing next month. How the Treasury will roll over these securities is anybody's guess. **1973** *Daily Tel.* 15 Sept. 23/3 Existing maturities are normally 'rolled over' (refinanced on their redemption date by the issue of further bonds at whatever the going rate of interest happens to be), thus giving the municipal treasurer a virtually perpetual access to the money market. **1976** *Economist* 16 Oct. 105/2 Even without any increase in interest rates since early April, 1976, the cost of servicing the national debt was bound to increase..from the need to roll over £2.8 billion of gilt-edged stock due to mature during the year.

8. a. *spec.* To make (a cigarette) by rolling paper round loose tobacco. Freq. in phr. *to roll one's own*: to make one's own cigarettes; also *fig.* Hence *roll-your-own* attrib. and ellipt.

1885 DICKENS *Dorrit* (1857) I. i. 6 He was now rolling his tobacco into cigarettes by the aid of little squares of paper. **1892** H. G. PARKER *Pierre & his People* 128 He slowly rolled a cigarette. **1893** [in Dict.]. **1903** A. BENNETT *Leonora* iii. 69 He had extraordinary aptitudes for drawing corks..and rolling cigarettes. **1930** *Amer. Speech* VI. 92 The following expressions belong to colloquialisms and slang, including movie and radio neologisms... *Rolls its own.* [Etc.]. **1932** J. D. CARR *Poison in Jest* xi. 157 He produced papers and tobacco... 'Good American,' he announced. 'I roll my own.' **1934** WEBSTER, *Roll one's own*,..to do things without outside aid. **1936** L. HELLMAN *Days to Come* I. 18 He has started to roll a cigarette. Quickly Julie offers him a box from the table. **1940** *Amer. Speech* XV. 335/2 Cigarettes..may be *home-made, rolls*, or *roll-your-owns*. **1941** *N.Y. Times* 25 July 14/5 'Ghosting' is routine in public papers in the United States, and has been since our history began... Mr. Roosevelt proved again today that he can roll his own whenever he has the time and the inclination. **1952** *Arena* (N.Z.) XXXI. 2 But then Charlie would have rolled himself one, and looked up at the hills and pretended he didn't hear. **1960** J. MCNAMEE *Florencia Bay* 59 Looks sixty. Thin face. Dark. Looks a little Indian but not our kind of Indian. Rolls his own. **1975** R. L. SIMON *Wild Turkey* (1976) xx. 149, I..took out some papers and started to roll a joint. **1977** *Daily Mirror* 30 Mar., Roll-your-own cigarette tobacco will also go up—but pipe tobacco and cigars escape. **1980** *Forest Products News* (Wellington, N.Z.) XVII. I. 6 He had come straight out of the bush with his roll-your-own.

fig. (Further examples of phr. 'rolled into one'.)

1879 T. HARDY *Let.* 26 Mar. (1978) I. 64 It is possible that he & the ancestor of your relative were two different persons who were in India at the same time, & so got rolled into one. **1907** G. B. SHAW *Major Barbara* 167 My methods..would be no use if I were Voltaire, Rousseau, Bentham, Mill, Dickens, Carlyle, Ruskin, George, Butler, and Morris all rolled into one. **1951** M. MCLUHAN *Mech. Bride* (1967) 135/2 He is the Supreme Court and human fate rolled into one. **1978** *N. & Q.* Feb. 94/1 Social and political historian, literary critic and man of the theatre rolled into one.

b. *fig.* (Further examples.)

1906 KIPLING *Puck of Pook's Hill* 221 Then the Winged Hats began to roll us up from each end of the wall. **1949** *Sun* (Baltimore) 25 Nov. 1/3 Capture of these critical defenses..placed the Americans in position to roll up the whole Yamashita defense front. **1963** 'J. LE CARRÉ' *Spy who came in from Cold* iii. 24 He had made a mistake in Berlin, and..his network had been rolled up.

10. c. To make or form by passing a material between rollers.

1967 A. H. COTTRELL *Introd. Metall.* xxii. 442 This principle has been particularly developed in Rohn and Sendzimir mills for rolling thin foil. **1972** *Daily Tel.* 14 Apr. 21/2 This hid a 6 p.c. rise for the billets and nil rise for the reinforcing bars which are rolled from them.

10*. *to roll off*, to cause (the frequency response of audio apparatus) to decrease smoothly at the end of its range; also *to roll in* or *on*, to cause a similar increase. Cf. sense 24 below.

1970 J. EARL *Tuners & Amplifiers* v. 105 The receiver must incorporate a network which rolls the treble response off at the same rate as the transmitter rolls it on. **1975** *Hi-Fi Answers* Feb. 69/3 In a three-way speaker you've got to get the mid-range to cover the whole of the speech band all in one go,..and you've got to get it down to at least two octaves below the frequency at which you want to roll it in. **1975** G. J. KING *Audio Handbk.* ii. 38 Some designers prefer deliberately to roll-off the bass around 30 Hz. **1976** *Gramophone* Aug. 359/3 It also rolls off the curve sharply from 12·5 Hz to 6 Hz.

II. 11. c. Also (gen.), to start moving. (Further examples.) Also *transf.* and *fig.*

1944 L. LARIAR *Man with Lumpy Nose* viii. 75 'Do me a favor and go home and write it!' McEmons stood over the reporter menacingly. 'Get rolling!' The reporter shuffled out of the room. **1952** S. KAUFFMANN *Philanderer* (1953) iv. 61 'Let's roll, dreamer', said Perry. **1956** A. H. COMPTON *Atomic Quest* i. 55 To help get the atomic program rolling. **1959** I. JEFFERIES *Thirteen Days* viii. 108, I..waved the drivers on. As they rolled I gave them one last treat..by taking my hat off. **1965** *New Statesman* 14 May 753/1 The private train is ready to roll. **1970** W. SMITH *Gold Mine* xii. 31 Wake up. Time to roll. **1977** *Observer* 3 Apr. 11/3 The PanAm captain then shouted: 'The bastard's not been given permission to roll. We're on the runway. We're on the runway.'

d. Of the foot: to slip on or upon an object.

1878 R. L. STEVENSON in *Temple Bar* LII. 55 His foot rolled upon a pebble. **1904** L. TRACY *King of Diamonds* ix. 123 Philip..almost fell too, for his left foot rolled on the constable's staff.

e. *roll on* ——: expressing a wish that time may pass quickly until a particular event; may (something) come soon.

1885 M. DAVITT *Leaves from Prison Diary* I. 150 'A burst in the City. Copped while boning the swag. 7 Stretch, 1869. Roll on 1876. Cheer up, pals.' Another—'Hook, 7 ys. Roll on time.' **1917** F. T. NETTLEINGHAME *Tommy's Tunes* 21 When this ruddy war is over, Oh! how happy we shall be!.. Roll on, when we go on furlough; Roll on, when we go on leave. **1936** J. CURTIS *Gilt Kid* ii. 19 'Well,' said the Gilt Kid, 'this is a whole lot better than making scrubbing brushes back in the old Monastery Garden.' 'Yes, and saying to yourself, "Roll on Cocoa".' **1958** M. K. JOSEPH *I'll soldier no More* xiii. 237 'What's your new gaffer like, Tom?' 'Like a barber's cat... I should worry—roll on my ticket.' **1962** *Sunday Express* 21 Jan. 15/5 Roll on the mid-twentieth century Venus. And the best of synthetic luck to her. **1970** M. TRIPP *Man without Friends* i. 15 He wakes at seven..saying 'Roll on my retirement.' **1978** K. AMIS *Jake's Thing* x. 98 Roll on wrist-watch television.

f. To taxi in an aircraft. *Obs.* exc. *Hist.*

1910 *Flight* 24 Sept. 776/1 Messrs B. H. Barrington Kennett.., A. Aitken, and St. Croix Johnstone..are 'rolling' whenever the weather is suitable. **1915** KIPLING *Diversity of Creatures* (1917) 423 Wynn..had finished 'rolling'..and had gone on from a 'taxi' to a machine more or less his own. **1961** C. B. SMITH *Testing Time* iii. 48 It was still quite an event to leave the ground, and many would-be fliers spent their whole time 'rolling' (as taxying was then called).

g. *heads will roll* and varr.: there will be executions; also *fig.*, some will be ousted from power or position; also in extended and weakened uses.

1930 *Daily Herald* 26 Sept. 1/1 Giving evidence, Hitler declared..'If our movement is victorious there will be a revolutionary tribunal which will punish the crimes of November 1918. Then decapitated heads will roll in the sand.' **1940** *Time* 5 Aug. 22/1 Echoes of 'Heads will roll' Hitlerism were heard from Paris to Marseille. **1961** *Time* 1 Dec. 77/3 A.M.C. made it clear, too, that more heads would roll if the workers still failed to get the message. **1963** A. HOWARD in Sissons & French *Age of Austerity* 17 Mr Macmillan's head rolled at Stockton-on-Tees at 10.25 a.m. **1966** P. O'DONNELL *Sabre-Tooth* xvi. 225 'Suppose this improbable thing happens?'..'Then no doubt my head will roll.' **1972** *National Observer* (U.S.) 27 May 7/2 President Nixon decreed 'heads will roll' if 'petty bureaucrats' hinder Jaffe's war on narcotics. **1978** *Rugby World* Apr. 45/1 Wales lost, and heads rolled.

h. Of a movie camera or cameraman, etc.: to be in action; to start filming.

1938 'E. QUEEN' *Four of Hearts* iv. 53 'Then it's okay to shoot the works now, Butch?'.. 'We're rolling, Sam.' **1938** F. SCOTT FITZGERALD *Let.* 18 Apr. (1964) 28 It may come right at the crucial point of this picture (due to roll in June, but perhaps not starting till the fifteenth). **1958** *Punch* 17 Sept. 382/3, I can imagine the whole cast falling about with hysterical laughter the moment the cameras stop rolling. **1971** D. E. WESTLAKE *I gave at the Office* (1972) 178 'Okay, Jay,' Joe finally said, from behind the camera and lights and sound equipment. 'Let her roll.' **1978** G. VIDAL *Kalki* iii. 75 A man with a clapboard stood between the camera and the door. 'Start rolling,' said the director.

12. b. *to roll up*. (Earlier and later examples.) Also, to arrive; to appear on the scene.

1861 *Goulburn* (New South Wales) *Herald* 18 Sept. 2/2 It is not by accident that flags are unfurled with mottoes upon them, as 'roll up', 'no Chinese'. **1920** G. BELL *Let.* 24 Oct. (1927) II. xix. 567 When the Mayor of Bagdad rolled up at 9 or the Naqib sent his son Saiyid Mahmud I was obliged to 'endosser' dressing-gown and go out to see them. **1929** 'SAPPER' in *Legion Bk.* 214 The man hasn't rolled up yet, but he won't be long. **1955** W. GADDIS *Recognitions* III. v. 863 The sight of a soiled limousine parked up the street..clouded his face with the memory of the girls from the American Embassy in Madrid who had rolled up the day before. **1968** M. WOODHOUSE *Rock Baby* xxiv. 232 They had to wait for me to roll up because I had the D.F. set, which meant I was the only one who could pin it down precisely. **1976** J. WAINWRIGHT *Who goes Next?* 161 A townie. A bit overdressed..he once rolled up in a velvet jacket. **1977** *Water Sport* (Austral.) Jan. 56/2 So please roll up and bring some of your friends.

e. *to roll along* = sense 12 b in Dict. and Suppl.

1928 A. WAUGH *Last Chukka* 82 She entertains whoever there may be that chooses to roll along.

16. c. (Later examples.)

1978 *Chicago* June 124/2 With money rolling in from the rest of the family empire..he began buying, parcel by parcel, the farmland around his family's estate. **1979** D. LOWDEN *Boudapesti 3* ii. 16 No, it's not money... We were quite well off... It was rolling in.

18. a. Also of motor vehicles. *rolling in the aisles*: see *AISLE 5 b.

1954 *Amer. Speech* XXIX. 101 *Roll, v.i.*, to overturn. **1968** *Sun* 12 Nov. 8/4 While the world sleeps, they [*sc.* rally drivers] 'yump' and 'wrong slot' and sometimes have the misfortune to 'roll'. **1976** *Billings* (Montana) *Gaz.* 1 July 2-A/4 The patrol said American Horse's vehicle rolled three times after the collision.

e. *to roll out*: to get out of bed, to get up. *U.S. colloq.*

1884 W. SHEPHERD *Prairie Experiences* 237 The cook's voice shouts 'Roll out'... Before you have time to dress.. it is 'Breakfast!' **1930** L. HUGHES *Not without Laughter* xv. 183 When his mother rolled out at six o'clock to go to work, he woke up again. **1942** Z. N. HURSTON in A. Dundes *Mother Wit* (1973) 223/1 All you did by rolling out early was to stir your stomach up. **1963** *Amer. Speech* XXXVIII. 271 The term *roll out* means 'to get out of bed in the morning'.

19. a. Hence *rolling-in-money* absol. as *sb.*

1960 AUDEN *Homage to Clio* 74 The rolling-in-money, The screamingly-funny.

21. a. Also with *down.*

1898 *Forest & Stream* 19 Feb. 156/2 Before the wind reached us the schooner rolled down at such an angle that her crew commenced to shorten sail. **1916** F. W. WALLACE *Shack Locker* (1922) 166 She rolled down an' came up with a dory a-hangin' on her fore-cross-trees.

e. Of an aeroplane: to turn about its longitudinal axis.

1909 'AERO-AMATEUR' *Flying* ix. 55 If the wings of a soaring, or gliding machine are curved upwards in the form of a bow the machine certainly has a tendency to travel in a straight line, but will have also a tendency to roll badly. **1918** J. M. GRIDER *War Birds* (1927) 69 He was looping and rolling between the church spires. **1976** *Times* 17 July 12/3 The Pitts, a small and exceptionally manoeuvrable biplane..can roll through more than 360° in a second.

f. *to roll with the punches* (and varr.), of a boxer: to move the body away from the opponent's blows in order to lessen their impact; *fig.*, to adapt oneself to difficult circumstances, take troubles in one's stride.

[**1941** F. GILMORE *Push Yourself* iv. 27 In boxing it is called 'rolling the punch' when a boxer, not having time to avoid being hit, deliberately moves with the punch when it hits him.] **1951** J. J. WALSH *Boxing Simplified* viii. 32 In an actual bout he will not have so much time to roll with the blow. **1956** H. KURNITZ *Invasion of Privacy* ii. 15 He had mastered the trick of rolling with the punches, rendering himself invisible when a crisis darkened the neighbouring skies. **1963** J. CROSBY *With Love & Loathing* 48 Madison Avenue rolls with the blow; it watches carefully which direction the cookie crumbles. **1979** *Now!* 21–27 Sept. 74/1 It would be possible to roll with such punches were it not for the fact that the 1980 election season has already begun and a seemingly invincible Democratic contender has suddenly launched himself into the fight.

24. *to roll off*, (of audio apparatus) to exhibit a response decreasing smoothly to zero with increasing signal frequency; so *to roll in*, to exhibit a response increasing similarly from zero. Cf. sense *10*.

1959 *Consumer Reports* Sept. 452/2 The newer *Jansen* [tweeter] also rolled off slightly in the extreme high-frequencies. **1962** A. NISBETT *Technique Sound Studio* 253 The simplest form of filter (one resistor and one condenser) rolls off at 6 dB/octave above or below a certain frequency. **1970** J. EARL *Tuners & Amplifiers* i. 25 Many [loudspeaker] systems employ two units, one.. going from about 30 or 40Hz and rolling-off due to the action of the crossover around 1 or 2 kHz and the other for treble rolling-in at about 1 or 2 kHz and responding up to 16 kHz or higher. *Ibid.* iii. 69 The majority of amplifiers have in-built high-pass filtering, rolling off around the 20 to 30Hz mark. **1976** *Gramophone* July 235/1 Further tonal correction is provided by push-buttons, to provide separate filters rolling off at 7 and 10kHz respectively.

ro·ll-around, *a.* [f. *to roll around.*] That can be moved around on wheels or castors.

1973 *Sunday Bull.* (Philadelphia) 7 Oct. (Parade Suppl.) F12 (Advt.), The GE Countertop Oven is versatile in other ways, too. You can use it on a roll-around cart, or build it in. **1976** *Amer. Speech 1974* XLIX. 116 *Roll-around wet bar*, portable counter equipped with a sink.

ro·ll-away, *a.* Also **rollaway.** [f. *to roll away.*] That may be removed on wheels or castors. Also *absol.* as *sb.*, a roll-away bed.

1938 *Sun* (Baltimore) 13 Oct. 11/3 Mr. Latham invented the 'roll-away' stage over the footlights which is used in many motion-picture houses. **1941–2** *Sears, Roebuck Catal.* 689/4 Odora Roll-Away Chest... 4 easy-rolling ball bearing casters. *Ibid.* 1274/7 (Index), Roll-a-way Chests 689 Roll-a-way Cots 904C. **1958** *Daily Progress* (Charlottesville, Va.) 4 June 14/2 Cots and roll-aways donated by townspeople after a radio appeal. **1960** *Farmer & Stockbreeder* 29 Mar. 119/1 There are no litter problems, eggs are laid in rollaway nests, the floor area per bird is only 1 sq ft. **1960** *Washington Post* 27 Nov. E3 Three rollaway beds and a cot are stacked during the day on the back porch. **1966** A. CAVANAUGH *Children are Gone* II. iii. 30 A musty old building... Three rooms with a rollaway bed, which she and two other girls had taken turns occupying. **1969** *Islander* (Victoria, B.C.) 16 Nov. 2/2 The charming young hostess..offered to get a roll-away cot for me. **1971** A. A. MICHELE *You don't have to Ache* ix. 188 Frequently the 'rollaways' that motels keep for the use of children are harder and better for your back than the regular bed mattress. **1974** *Country Life* 21 Nov. 1580/2 You get another big double bed down-stairs and a roll-away bunk.

roll back, roll-back, rollback. [f. *to roll back.*]

1. The action or fact of rolling backwards.

1937 *Times British Motor Number* 13 Apr. p. xxii/4 More than one method is available for automatically preventing roll back on an incline. **1949** SHURR & YOCOM *Mod. Dance* v. 181 The swift roll-back carries body weight onto the shoulders. **1978** *Daily Tel.* 4 Mar. 1/8 They died as nine Gnats swept across the airfield to practise a 'roll back'—a manoeuvre performed by the Red Arrows for several years without incident.

2. [*ROLL *v.*² 5 h.] *U.S.* A reduction or decrease; *spec.*, a return (of commodity prices, etc.) to a lower level. Also *attrib.*

1942 *Time* 11 May 80 OPA have denied their [*sc.* retailers'] plea for a 'roll-back' of ceiling dates that would recognize the lag between rising wholesale and retail prices. **1943** *Funk & Wagnalls New Stand. Encycl. Year Bk. 1942* 373/1 For Price Roll Back and Price Squeezes, see *Business Review* under *Commodity Prices*. **1943** *Sun* (Baltimore) 19 May 7 Promised 'roll backs' on cabbage and lettuce will still leave prices of these foods, at the farm, three times as high as they were a year ago. *Ibid.* 1 July 14/3 Congress had been equally unkind to his eager plan to detour around the thornier difficulties of farm-price control by a rollback food-subsidy scheme. **1945** *Richmond* (Va.) *News Leader* 20 Aug. 10 The OPA is standing pat on its prediction of a clothing price rollback—eventually. **1959** *Time* 27 Apr. 15/2 The cold war's boundaries in 1959 were much as they had been in 1953—the rollback had been in men's minds, not real estate. **1972** *Fortune* Jan. 101/1 Even the 3.9 percent price increase the company posted for its 1972 models last July, before the price freeze forced a rollback, would have recovered only 65 percent of the unit cost increases anticipated for the current model year. **1973** *Black Panther* 21 Apr. 2/2 This decision provides a legal basis to begin a roll-back of that power. **1974** *Financial Times* 15 Aug. 17/6 We do need the 'roll back' which ex-President Nixon promised but (predictably) did not deliver. **1976** *Lebende Sprachen* XXI. 153/2 The pilot noticed an inflight engine roll back from 90 to 80% rpm.

roll-call. Add: **1.** (Earlier examples.) Also (*U.S.*), a calling over of a list of members of a legislative or similar body in order to ascertain how each wishes to vote on a particular measure.

1775 *Essex Inst. Hist. Coll.* (1912) XLVIII. 61 This morning we went to rol col & then got our Brefust. **1777** *Ibid.* (1877) XIII. 118 Ordered that the Hour for Roll Call be altered to Nine o'clock in the morning. **1899** [in Dict., attrib.]. **1902** *Ann. Rep. Amer. Hist. Assoc. 1901* I. 323 Except for the provision in the constitution there would have been no roll call on these votes. **1947** *Economist* 27 Dec. 1047/1 The sponsors of ERP avoided a roll-call on the first vote in order to take one on the agreed Bill. **1955** *Times* 4 Aug. 6/7 In foreign policy the President secured bipartisan support on nearly every occasion; in 32 Senate roll-calls the Democratic majority failed to agree with the Republican majority only once. **1972** *Computer & Humanities* VI. 184 The data are placed on cards with one record holding the yea..or nay..votes of one congressman on every roll-call.

attrib. *roll-call analysis, vote* (further examples).

1950 *N.Y. Times* 20 Apr. 1/6 The Senate adopted today, by a roll-call vote of 66 to 0, a resolution directing the Secretary of the Navy to confer appropriate posthumous decorations on the crew of the Privateer that presumably was shot down..over the Baltic sea. **1963** *Midwest Jrnl. Polit. Sci.* VII. 156 (*heading*) A second look at the validity of roll-call analysis. **1970** *Computers & Humanities* V. 8 Several embarked on similar scalogram excursions into roll-call analysis of collegial bodies, both with and without computers. **1970** *Internat. & Compar. Law Q.* XIX. 1. 68 On a vote by show of hands, the required two-thirds majority was not obtained, but a second (roll-call) vote was taken, and the retention of the reference..was confirmed. **1979** *Tucson* (Arizona) *Citizen* 20 Sept. 2A/4 Rep. Robert Bauman, R-Md., said the House voted against the bill because it came on a roll call vote, which puts each member on record as either supporting or opposing the measure to which the pay raise was attached.

ro·ll-call, *v.* [f. the sb.] *trans.* To call the roll for (a group or body of persons). Also *fig.*

1928 *Daily Express* 19 Mar. 12/2 The German officers were counted or 'roll-called' in their rooms to save them the trouble of having to assemble or fall in with the other prisoners. **1962** V. Nabokov *Pale Fire* 55 But who can teach the thoughts we should roll-call When morning finds us marching to the wall?

roll-collar. Delete '(Now *rolled collar*)' and add: (Later examples.) Also *attrib.*

1907 E. P. Oppenheim *Secret* ii. 15 He wore..a made-up white tie, with the ends tucked in under a roll collar. **1922** Joyce *Ulysses* 72 Stylish kind of coat with that roll collar. **1929** *Even. News* 18 Nov. 6/5 (Advt.), Below we show the D. B. Chester with long roll collar. **1963** *Times* 23 Jan. 12/4 The ubiquitous, exquisitely soft, reversible woollens were used for perfectly tailored, gently precise coats with tiny roll-collars. **1973** S. B. Jackman *Guns covered with Flowers* vi. 98 He dressed quickly—pants, T-shirt, roll-collar shirt, dark slacks.

ro·ll down, roll-down. [f. *to roll down.*] A game in which balls are rolled down a board into numbered holes, slots, or the like; a table or stall where this is played. Also *attrib.*

1926 *Variety* 29 Dec. 7/4 The outdoor show game with its 'rag front',..'roll downs', [etc.]. **1942** Berrey & Van den Bark *Amer. Thes. Slang* § 626/21 *Roll-down*, a gambling device using small balls rolling down between pins to holes in the bottom of the table. **1943** K. Tennant *Ride on Stranger* vii. 61 But the Roll-Down Table was not doing too badly despite the rain... The players could shelter while they rolled the billiard balls down the green felt into shallow cups.

rolled, *ppl. a.* Add: **1. a.** (Further examples.) Also with sbs. used *attrib.*

1819 M. Edgeworth *Let* ?10 Mar. (1971) 181 All the fashionable trimmings are of that rolled sort of flounces. **1866** Geo. Eliot *Felix Holt* III. xlvi. 221 The grandeur of barbaric forms—when rolled collars were not yet conceived. **1928** *Daily Mail* 3 Aug. 10/4 Members of the audience looked twice before they could..appreciate the fact that she had rolled stockings. **1962** L. Deighton *Ipcress File* xxv. 164 The British man..put on his rolled brim hat. **1967** G. Watkins in *Coast to Coast 1965–66* 208 The blue texture of his rolled-neck sweater was filled with sand. **1976** F. Warner *Killing Time* 1. vi. 18 Snowy my trainer turned up..in his green rolled-neck sweater. **1977** S. Brett *Star Trap* xi. 125 Dinner jacket, but not the old double-breasted or now-dated rolled-lapel style. **1978** D. Devine *Sunk without Trace* 6 The rolled umbrella was part of his stock-in-trade and was no index to the weather.

b. *rolled-up* (further examples); also *rolled-down.*

1891 Hardy *Tess* II. xxiv. 35 Dairyman Crick kept his shirt-sleeves permanently rolled up past his elbows. **1916** Joyce *Portrait of Artist* i. 47 He looked at Athy's rolled-up sleeves and knuckly inky hands. **1961** 'E. Lathen' *Banking on Death* (1962) xviii. 145 Stan Michaels, clad in a blue work shirt with rolled-up sleeves. **1968** M. Woodhouse *Rock Baby* xvii. 160 She leaned against my rolled-up sleeping-bag. **1972** J. Gores *Dead Skip* (1973) vii. 43 The air coming in through the rolled-down window..was wet and heavy. **1977** J. Aiken *Last Movement* xi. 234 If he'd had a rolled-up Piero [*sc.* a painting] with him it would have been different.

3. a. (Earlier example.)

1789 *Deb. Congress U.S.* 17 Apr. (1834) 167 It was agreed to lay an impost of seven and a half per cent..on..slit or rolled iron.

b. *rolled gold* (further examples).

1975 *Country Life* 20 Mar. 747/1 Rolled gold ballpoint pen. **1980** M. Booth *Bad Track* x. 182 He watched her..light her cigarettes with a thin ladies' lighter of rolled gold.

c. *rolled oats*: oats which have been husked and crushed.

1888 L. Hargis *Graded Cook Bk.* 514 Tuesday. Breakfast. Rolled Oats. **1921** *Daily Colonist* (Victoria, B.C.) 29 Oct. 8/1 (Advt.), Robin Hood Rolled Oats, large drum 24¢. **1960** A. E. Bender *Dict. Nutrition* 87/2 Rolled oats—crushed by rolling and partially pre-cooked. **1974** *Encycl. Brit. Micropædia* VII. 458/2 Rolled oats, flattened kernels with the hulls removed, are used mostly for oatmeal.

d. *rolled asphalt* (see quots.).

1938 B. H. Knight *Mod. Road Construction* v. 56 Rolled asphalt is a mixture of sand and broken stone, slag or clinker bound together with asphaltic bitumen and laid hot. **1977** *Bitumen* (Shell Internat. Petroleum Co.) 4 Rolled asphalt contains a large proportion of sand, a relatively small amount of stones, and about equal proportions of medium-hard bitumen and filler. It provides a durable surface often lasting over 20 years, and is widely used in the United Kingdom for surfacing heavy-duty roads.

4. *Phonetics.* Articulated with a trill.

1909 D. Jones *Pronunc. Eng.* 25 There are no infallible rules for learning to pronounce the rolled *r*. **1935** [see *apical *a.* 2]. **1962** A. C. Gimson *Introd. Pronunc. Eng.* viii. 205 Any strongly rolled [r] sound, whether lingual or uvular, is not acceptable in RP. **1967** J. D. O'Connor *Better Eng. Pronunc.* iii. 78 Sometimes they [*sc.* foreign learners] use a *rolled* sound in which the tip of the tongue flaps very quickly several times against the alveolar ridge..or the uvula taps against the back of the tongue in a similar way.

Rollei (rǫ·ləi, -li), proprietary abbrev. *Rolleiflex.

1950 *Trade Marks Jrnl.* 26 July 687/1 *Rollei*... Photographic, cinematographic and optical apparatus and instruments. Franke and Heidecke... Braunschweig, Germany. **1972** M. Woodhouse *Mama Doll* viii. 91 Sean-baby jumped down..cranking the handle of a Rollei. **1976** T. Allbeury *Only Good German* ii. 10 'How did you sell it?' 'On the black market, got a Leica and a Rollei.'

Rolleiflex (rǫ·ləifleks, -lifl-). [Proprietary name.] A make of camera.

1930 *Trade Marks Jrnl.* 8 Jan. 44/2 *Rolleiflex*... Photographic cameras, optical instruments, optical lanterns and slides, kinematograph apparatus, stereoscopes and magnifying glasses, all being goods included in Class 8. Franke and Heidecke... Braunschweig, Germany. **1959** C. MacInnes *Absolute Beginners* 20 Around my neck hung my Rolleiflex.

rolleo, var. *roleo.

roller, *sb.*[1] Add: **I. 1. b.** A rubber-covered cylinder used for reducing one's weight.

1930 *London Mercury* Feb. 323 She makes the roller earn its keep, I can tell you! **1975** G. Howell *In Vogue* 55/2 The serpentine slimness was an essential... You bought rubber rollers with studs all over them.

3. c. A type of exercise wheel (see quot.).

1970 *Which?* Sept. 288/1 Once you got fit with skipping ropes and chest expanders... Now it is..rollers. Maybe you haven't seen one yet. It consists of a wheel about six inches in diameter, and a handle on each side. You kneel down, grasp the handles, roll forwards, and then roll back to the kneeling position.

5. b. A cylindrical device used for applying paint, wallpaper, etc., to a flat surface.

1955 *N.Y. Times* 12 June II. 16/6 Self-feeding rollers should be emptied, and the inside cleaned with whatever solvent is indicated for the kind of paint used. **1959** *Listener* 12 Feb. 311/1, I am often asked whether it is better to use a brush or a roller for painting. **1975** *Times* 28 Aug. 5/1 Embossed wallpapers..can be..applied in different manners (by roller, or by sponge..are just two of them).

III. 15. b. A low rising or undulation on land. *U.S.*

1849 N. Kingsley *Diary* 29 Nov. (1914) 88 The land on the left rises in rollers from 10 to 50 feet and the soil appears rich.

16. b. *U.S. slang.* A policeman.

1964 *N.Y. Times Mag.* 23 Aug. 62/3 *Rollers*, police. **1967** 'I. Slim' in T. Kochman *Rappin' & stylin' Out* (1972) 388 The rollers cruised by in a squad car. **1973** C. & R. Milner *Black Players* v. 108 Look, for a roller (policeman) to come to this door—he's insane, he's gotta be a nut.

17. b. *Holy Roller* (earlier and later examples). Also *attrib.* and as *Roller.*

1842 *Southern Q. Rev.* (New Orleans) I. 400 It is a new species of religion, which sprang up..contemporaneously with the enthusiasm of the 'Holy Rollers'. **1927** M. de la Roche *Jalna* v. 65 You'd make a good Methodist of the Holy Roller variety. **1928** *Amer. Mercury* Oct. 182/1 To the true Roller every word in his theological vocabulary..and every moral experience, no matter how trivial, is a symbol of forces whose presence inspires him to delirium. **1958** M. Argyle *Relig. Behaviour* iv. 34 The Baptists and other Evangelical groups were rather similar in 1850 to the Pentecostalists of today, and there are signs that the present Holy Rollers are becoming assimilated. **1961** C. McCullers *Clock without Hands* x. 198 A part-time preacher who was able to make his Holy Roller congregation talk in strange tongues. **1969** *New Yorker* 14 June 78/2 They sound like fire-and-brimstone preachers in Holy Roller churches.

c. In baseball, a ball that rolls along the ground after being hit by the batter.

1880 *Chicago Inter-Ocean* 15 May 7/1 Flint sent a roller to Crane, and he touched the first batter on the way to second. **1949** *Fargo* (N. Dakota) *Forum* 23 July 8/8 Corcoran's roller, on which there was an error, enabled Erickson to count, making it 3 to 2. **1973** *Tucson* (Arizona) *Daily Citizen* 22 Aug. 57/6 Walslewski mishandled a slow roller by Burney. **1976** *Billings* (Montana) *Gaz.* 16 June 1-c/3 Martin beat out a slow roller over second base.

d. Formerly, a machine used in the early stages of a pilot's training (see quots.).

1917 J. R. McConnell *Flying for France* iv. 143 First of all, the [flying] student is put on what is called a roller. It is a low-powered machine with very small wings. It is strongly built to stand the rough wear it gets, and no matter how much one might try it could not leave the ground. **1929** *Papers Mich. Acad. Sci., Arts & Lett.* X. 319/1 *Roller*.., an aviators' training machine which ran along the ground. Just about ready to fly, but which could not quite rise.

IV. 18. d. A thief; one who steals from drunken persons; a prostitute, esp. one who robs her customers. Cf. *jack-roller* s.v. *Jack *sb.*[1] 33a. Chiefly *N. Amer. slang.*

1915 *N.Y. World Mag.* 9 May 14/3 *Roller*, a pickpocket. **1935** *Amer. Speech* X. 14/1 *Creeper*, a prostitute who robs inebriated patrons. Modern *roller*. **1935** L. Bogan in P. Oliver *Screening Blues* (1968) vi. 230 I'm just a stomp-down roller and I like to strut my stuff. **1948** [see *lush *sb.*[2] 2]. **1973** *Daily Colonist* (Victoria, B.C.) 17 May 24/2 In addition to warning the public that rollers have been operating, the spokesman asked persons who are robbed to notify police.

19. Delete † *Obs.*⁻¹ and add: Also *sing.* Now usu. a metal or plastic cylinder round which the hair is rolled. (Earlier and later examples.)

1795 tr. *C. P. Moritz's Trav.* 87 In the morning, it is usual to walk out in a sort of negligée [*sic*]..your hair not dressed, but merely rolled up in rollers, and in a frock and boots. **1881** *Queen* 12 Mar. (Advt.), The Parisian leather roller, for curling the fringe, 1s. the dozen. **1940** C. McCullers *Heart is Lonely Hunter* 1. iii. 32 Her hair was done up in steel rollers. **1941–2** *Sears, Roebuck Catal.* 637/3 *Bob Roller*, a real aid in achieving the smooth, neat appearance of a well-groomed pompadour hair-do! Catches up all loose ends—..invisible when in hair. Makes neat, low rolls at the nape of your neck. *Ibid.* 637/4 *Hair Rollers.* Use these rayon and lastex tube rollettes to make those puffy, pompadour rolls at the front and the sides of your new hair-do. **1959** *Woman* 2 May 4/4 How do I keep my bouffant hair style looking just set? The secret lies in my home-made rollers—big, fat ones made from cotton wool wrapped round with paper hankies. **1960** *Sunday Express* 24 July 12/5 He was winding some of my hair on to a roller. Mr. Roger is my hairdresser. **1971** *New Scientist* 19 Aug. 401/2 The inamorata ..with hair in rollers, or hanging rat-tailed from the bath. **1977** P. Carter *Under Goliath* iii. 17 The women in pink rollers nattered on the doorsteps.

20*. A control in an aircraft for regulating roll.

1959 Hopkin & Thomas in *Jrnl. R. Aeronaut. Soc.* LXIII. 572/2 *Roller, pitcher, yawer* may well find general acceptance. **1961** *Shell Aviation News* Dec. 4/1 Instead of a stick,..we ought to have a motivator, or perhaps three motivators, namely a roller, a pitcher, and a yawer.

V. 22. a. *roller-belt, -head, machine, shelf.*

1967 E. Chambers *Photolitho-Offset* ix. 127 A positive roller-belt transport system is provided accepting any film base from 0·002 to 0·075 in. thick without the use of leaders, hangers, clips, etc. **1967** M. Chandler *Ceramics in Mod. World* ii. 68 A rotating jigger-tool or roller-head, which completes the shaping of the back. **1950** *Chambers's Encycl.* II. 788/1 In all printing processes, whether they use blocks, roller machines or silk screens it is important to make use of special devices or expedients to ensure that the successive colour applications 'register' exactly. **1960** *Farmer & Stockbreeder* 22 Mar. (Suppl.) 8/2 The cost of running a mains-driven mower like the Ladybird roller-machine..works out at about 1d per hour. **1958** T. Landau *Encycl. Librarianship* 273/1 *Roller shelves*, large shelves for storing folios, etc., which rest on a series of small rollers. **1976** *Gloss. Documentation Terms* (*B.S.I.*)

57 *Roller shelves*, large shelves which rest on a series of rollers, designed for storing folios and other large volumes. Sometimes the volumes rest directly on the rollers.

b. *roller-blind* (later examples), *caption, door, reefing, shade, shutter*.

1909 *Chambers's Jrnl.* Nov. 767/1 Also the hideous, cumbersome, expensive concomitant, the roller-blind? **1956** *Railway Mag.* Nov. 735/1 A large inward-opening aluminium door on which is mounted the roller-blind route indicator. **1973** *Times* 23 Mar. 13/5 In theory a roller-blind is a simple thing to make. **1960** D. WILSON in *Television Playwright* 259 We move in towards the painted Dove on the fuselage and hold for the roller caption. **1976** *Star* (Sheffield) 26 Nov., The man walked up to the lorry.. pushed up the roller door and walked off with two cartons of..cigarettes. **1924** *Trans. Newcomen Soc. 1922–3* III. 47 John Bywater (No. 2782 of 1804) patented a roller reefing gear in which a hit-and-miss arrangement allowed the sweeps to be reefed or unreefed from inside the mill. **1945** *Archit. Rev.* XCVIII. 72/2 A further step forward was the invention, by Captain Stephen Hooper in 1789, of the 'roller reefing sail'. **1962** *Listener* 11 Jan. 85/3 Water-skiing with roaring speed-boats, and roller-reefing gear on yachts. **1976** *Yachts & Yachting* 20 Aug. 385/3 (Advt.), Proctor alloy spars, roller reefing, spinnaker and jib winches. **1961** WEBSTER, Roller shade. **1962** *Amer. Speech* XXXVII. 173 The typically Southern coast expressions *lightwood*..for 'kindling wood', and *curtain* for 'roller shade'. **1937** *Times British Motor Number* 13 Apr. p. vi/3 There are more roller shutters for vans instead of hinged doors, which are apt to swing out. **1938** *Archit. Rev.* LXXXIII. 81 Access to the window is by means of a roller shutter. **1978** *Cornish Guardian* 27 Apr. 5/3 (Advt.), Roller shutter garage doors.

23. b. *roller-drying, levelling, painting, printing*; also *roller-dry, -paint, -print* vbs.; *roller-dried, -driven* adjs.

1939 *Jrnl. Dairy Res.* X. 202 Roller-dried milk cannot be reconstituted so completely as spray-dried milk. **1962** J. T. MARSH *Self-Smoothing Fabrics* xi. 174 In general, festoon chambers were very commonly employed until after World War II, when roller-driven machines became more popular, particularly those with independent drive for each roller. **1932** *Bull. Hannah Dairy Res. Inst.* No. 3. 123 This milk was roller-dried. **1950** J. G. DAVIS *Dict. Dairying* 486 Whey from cheese or acid casein manufacture can be successfully roller dried after neutralisation with calcium hydroxide. **1932** *Bull. Hannah Dairy Res. Inst.* No. 3. 119 Broadly speaking, the successful commercial processes [for the manufacture of milk powder] may be reduced to three main types:—(1) Roller-drying, (2) Spray-drying, (3) Dough-drying. **1939** *Jrnl. Dairy Res.* X. 202 The great heat to which milk is exposed in roller drying. **1933** *Jrnl. Iron & Steel Inst.* CXXVII. 593 In order to eliminate these strains, the sheets are generally passed through roller levelling machines just prior to the stamping operation. **1973** J. G. TWEEDDALE *Materials Technol.* II. iv. 97 Roller-levelling is a means for producing a reasonably-straight flat product from a long prismatic shape. The principle involves 'snaking' the section through a series of offset rolls which bend the section plastically, alternately in opposite directions. Starting first with a fairly severe bend and then with progressively less severe bends until the section is almost perfectly straight... The alternate bending irons out kinks and plastic flow difference left in the material from previous operations. **1960** *Times* 12 Dec. 15/3 Having roller-painted all her rooms herself. **1959** *House & Garden* July 94/3 Roller painting, with all its attendant perils of upsetting the paint tray. **1959** *Manch. Guardian* 2 July 4/1 All London bus tickets were roller-printed by the conductors. **1911** *Encycl. Brit.* XXVI. 696/2 In its simplest form the roller-printing machine consists of a strong cast iron cylinder mounted in adjustable bearings capable of sliding up and down slots in the sides of the rigid iron framework. **1936** [see *hand block* s.v. *HAND *sb.* 63]. **1963** A. J. HALL *Textile Sci.* iv. 203 Roller printing is the most convenient and satisfactory method of printing long 'runs' of a multi-coloured pattern on fabric. **1975** *Oxf. Compan. Decorative Arts* 281/1 Copper-plate printing replaced block printing in 1781 and roller printing followed shortly after.

c. Parasynthetic, as *roller-bearinged* adj.

1922 *Encycl. Brit.* XXX. 36/2 Connecting-rods of rotary and radial engines consist usually of one master-rod, ball or roller-bearinged [etc.].

24. roller arena, a roller-skating rink; **roller bearing,** a bearing in which the journal is free to rotate round a ring of metal rollers; **roller bit** *Oil Industry*, a drilling bit in which the cutting teeth are on rotating conical or circular cutters; **roller box,** a box containing rollers; *spec.* (*a*) one containing drawing-rolls in a cotton-spinning machine; (*b*) (see quot. 1967); **roller-cloth** = *roller-towel*; **roller coaster,** substitute for def.: a kind of switch-back railway at an amusement park; (further examples); also *transf.*, *fig.*, and *attrib.*; hence as *v. intr.*; *roller-coasting* (further examples); hence (as back-formation) *roller-coast* vb. trans. and intr.; **roller-coat** *v. trans.*, to apply with a roller (sense *5 b); **roller derby, Roller Derby,** a name for a type of speed-skating competition on roller-skates, now one with specified periods during which skaters can physically assist their own team members and impede opponents; such a competition; **roller drier,** an apparatus in which milk is dried on the surface of one or more heated rollers, in the manufacture of milk powder; **roller hearth furnace** (see quot. 1970); **roller hockey,** a type of hockey played on roller-skates; = next; **roller polo** = *rink polo* s.v. POLO 2; **roller print,** (*a*) a fabric with a design produced by roller-printing; (*b*) a roller for printing or impressing a design; **roller steady** *Engin.* [STEADY *sb.* 2 b], a device which grips between rollers the article being turned on a lathe; **roller-towel** (earlier and later examples); **roller-towelling,** a type of cloth used for roller-towels; **roller tube** *Biol.*, a tube which is continually rotated so as to moisten with nutrient solution the cells or tissue being grown in it; freq. *attrib.*; **roller-type** *a.*, of a kind that has the form or movement of a roller.

1971 *Islander* (Victoria, B.C.) 18 July 11/1 A large assemblage was at the roller arena to see the sights. **1857** J. B. PASCAL *Brit. Pat. 465* 4 Figure 3 is an elevation of the roller bearing of the axis. **1884, 1886** [in Dict., sense 22 a]. **1915** V. W. PAGÉ *Model T Ford Car* iii. 117 The differential mechanism and the wheel end of the axle utilize roller bearings. **1958** *Times Rev. Industry* Aug. 32/1 The spindle..runs in pre-loaded taper roller bearings. **1970** B. PUGH *Pract. Lubrication* v. 45 An advantage of.. roller bearings in preference to sleeve bearings is that they require the minimum of maintenance. **1918** *Oil Weekly* 27 July 25 (Advt.), Caddo bits will make more hole in hard rock for any given amount of money, than any other roller bit on the market. **1924** L. C. UREN *Textbk. Petroleum Production Engin.* vi. 152 The Reed roller bit.. is equipped with eight disc-shaped cutters having teeth milled around their circumference and mounted in a massive steel frame. **1966** *McGraw-Hill Encycl. Sci. & Technol.* II. 295/2 Penetration is by rotation of drill bits of two types: (1) roller bits, which have rolling cutters with projecting hard teeth; and (2) drag bits, with fixed chisel-type hard cutting edges. **1888** C. T. JACOBI *Printers' Vocab.* 113 *Roller box*, the receptacle in which rollers are kept to protect them from dust, etc. **1902** T. THORNLEY *Cotton Combing Machines* iii. 85 In times past a good deal of trouble has arisen in connection with the quadrant and roller box system. **1950** A. W. JUDGE *Centre, Capstan & Automatic Lathes* II. v. 204 Fig. 242 shows a roller box tool..in operation on a turret automatic. **1967** J. L. & G. H. F. NAYLER *Dict. Mech. Engin.* 299 *Roller box*, a cutting tool-holder used on capstan lathes and automatic lathes. The box holds a cutting tool and two rollers positioned so that part of the reaction force from the cutting tool is taken by the rollers, thus preventing distortion of the work. **1975** BRAM & DOWNS *Manuf. Technol.* v. 135 Various methods are used to set up the roller box, the one chosen depending on whether or not the work has been previously machined. **1862** 'G. HAMILTON' *Country Living* 11, I become acquainted.. with the *modus operandi* of 'roller-cloths'. **1877** E. S. WARD *Story of Avis* 224 A roller-cloth would do, dear. **1973** *Nation Rev.* (Melbourne) 31 Aug. 1465/1 It is a ritual that defies time..and the giant forces that roller-coast us at increasing velocity to some eerie destination. **1978** *Chatelaine* (Canada) Dec. 14/2 Canada's rates of inflation and cost of living are roller-coasting. **1903** *Boston Transcript* 7 Oct. 16 The cable cars run over routes that would shame a Coney Island roller coaster. **1931** [see *JITTER *sb.* 1]. **1945** J. STEINBECK *Cannery Row* xvi. 100 Phyllis Mae had broken her leg getting out of the roller coaster. **1949** *Sun* (Baltimore) 1 July 28/5 Maryland found herself saddled with a system of 'roller coaster' roads. **1957** N. FRYE *Sound & Poetry* p. xx, Speeded-up metrical rhythms, such as Swinburne's roller-coaster anapests, are unmusical. **1961** *John o' London's* 6 July 21/1 The ever-accelerating roller-coaster of science. **1962** WODEHOUSE *Service with Smile* vii. 116 Her emotions were somewhat similar to those of a nervous passenger on a roller coaster at an amusement park who when it is too late to get off feels the contraption gathering speed beneath him. **1965** L. R. HUBBARD *Scientology Abridged Dict.* 26 A person 'roller coasters', i.e., gets better, then worse, etc., only when connected to a Suppressive Person or Group, and in order to cease roller coastering must receive processing intended to handle such. **1967** A. WEST in *Coast to Coast 1965–66* 214 They entered [the restaurant] through an underwater tunnel that began just next to the roller-coaster ticket office. **1968** *Surfer Mag.* Jan. 53/2 Martinson attempts a roller coaster down an Arpoador wave. **1969** *Observer* 3 Aug. 35/1 He may 'rollercoaster', bursting through a breaking wave, turning and bouncing down through the foam. **1970** *Studies in English* (Univ. Cape Town) I. 27 Yet another kind of wave is the rollercoaster... A rollercoaster wave is one that does not break continuously from one end to the other, but breaks in sections all along its length, thus offering the surfer a tricky, 'up and down' ride. **1971** G. G. LUCE *Body Time* v. 170 A physician who knew his patient's time print, the shape of his temperature and activity-rest cycle, and who knew where his patient was on this daily roller coaster, might have much less trouble interpreting the results of clinic tests. **1975** *New Yorker* 21 Apr. 36/1 She lost John—left him the way popcorn flies out of the bag on the roller coaster. **1977** *Time* 24 Jan. 14/2 Private sterling deposits have fluctuated little, while official deposits have roller-coastered. **1960** R. W. MARKS *Dymaxion World of B. Fuller* 27/2 Ducks, however, are anatomically unfitted for such aerial roller coasting. **1968** W. WARWICK *Surfriding in N.Z.* p. iv, *Roller coasting*, one way of dropping and climbing on a wave. **1961** WEBSTER, Roller-coat *vt.* **1971** *Engineering* Apr. 61/2 Protectalac..can be brushed, sprayed, roller or curtain coated. **1976** *Broadcast* 29 Mar. 8/3 An epoxy/polyurethane material..was then roller-coated on to the.. floor space. [**1935** *Chicago Tribune* 13 Aug. 19/6 A 3000 mile roller skating derby will open at noon today when 50 skaters begin the long grind inside the main hall of the Coliseum.] **1936** *N.Y. Times* 11 Sept. 34/4 The Roller Derby, first of the kind to be seen in New York, and in which fourteen teams of skaters composed of men and girls are entered, got well under way at the Hippodrome last night... The derby is a mythical race from Salt Lake City to New York. **1945** *Life* 21 May 81/1 The Chicago Coliseum fairly whistled with roller skates. The occasion was the tenth annual Roller Derby. **1972** *Guardian* 17 Feb. 10/1 A documentary study of a young man..trying to become a Roller Derby star..practising an amalgam of speed-skating and all-in wrestling. **1975** R. HOBAN *Turtle Diary* xxv. 115 She was American... She'd..been a rodeo rider, done roller derbies, wrestled. **1979** *Tucson Mag.* Apr. 38/1 However, if you didn't know Tucson is the only city in America where roller derby is played on radials. **1932** *Bull. Hannah Dairy Res. Inst.* No. 4. 61 The powder obtained from the standard roller drier is not a high class product. **1963** A. W. FARRALL *Engin. for Dairy & Food Products* xiv. 410 The drum dryer, often called roller dryer. **1958** *Engineering* 11 Apr. 472/2 The mesh-belt type of furnace is satisfactory for strip of relatively low melting point material such as copper, but roller-hearth or walking beam furnaces may be required for..iron or nickel. **1970** *Gloss. Industr. Furnace Terms* (*B.S.I.*) 15 *Roller hearth furnace*, a furnace in which the charge is carried forward on driven alloy steel or refractory rollers. **1926** *Daily Colonist* (Victoria, B.C.) 9 Jan. 12/4 Roller Hockey League entries close today. **1975** *Oxf. Compan. Sports & Games* 845/1 The roller hockey stick is similar in shape to a field hockey stick but flat on both sides of the blade. **1895** *Spalding's Official Roller Polo Guide for 1896* 5 New England is now the only section in which roller polo rages. **1968** J. IRONSIDE *Fashion Alphabet* 246 *Roller print:* the colours for the design are applied directly to the cloth. **1969** E. H. PINTO *Treen* 100 Butter prints are of five distinct types and many patterns and sizes. The types are..(5) roller prints. **1920** J. G. HORNER *Turret Lathe Practice* ii. 20 Roller steadies were found essential at the time that attempts were being made to utilise the high-speed steel to the greatest advantage in turret practice. **1964** S. CRAWFORD *Basic Engin. Processes* v. 140 Many jobs require a special form on their end face... This can readily be produced with a roller steady ending tool which consists of two hardened-steel rollers which contact the finished diameter of the work and are closely followed by a form tool which produces the desired shape on the end of the component. **1975** BRAM & DOWNS *Manuf. Technol.* v. 135 The roller-steady turning tool-holder has two rollers incorporated into the design. **1845** *Knickerbocker* XXV. 444 Beside the window was the linen roller-towel. **1980** D. WILLIAMS *Murder for Treasure* v. 46 A copious length of roller towel unhitched from its cabinet. **1881** C. C. HARRISON *Woman's Handiwork* i. 48 Among other washing fabrics used in art needlework are *crash, roller-towelling, bamboo-cloth*, [etc.]. **1932** D. C. MINTER *Mod. Needlecraft* 246/2 Roller towelling or Russian crash or zephyr. **1933** *Amer. Jrnl. Cancer* XVII. 753 With the roller tube method these cells can be allowed to re-implant themselves in another portion of the tube. **1936** *Ibid.* XXVII. 49 Roller tubes of different types have been used with good results. **1947** *Anat. Rec.* XCIX. 157 We cultured the hearts of 10-day-old chick embryos and grew them in test tubes in a roller-tube apparatus. **1964** M. HYNES *Med. Bacteriol.* (ed. 8) xxiv. 353 An analogy to solid bacterial media was first provided by the roller-tube technique of tissue culture. Fragments of tissue are embedded in plasma clot in the tube, and continually moistened with culture medium by rotating the tube. Sheets of cells grow out from the tissue inoculum. **1960** *Farmer & Stockbreeder* 1 Mar. 72/1 For moving, the washer is mounted on roller-type wheels. **1964** S. CRAWFORD *Basic Engin. Processes* xiv. 304 Similar in general principle to the above, but having roller-type anvils.

roller-board. Add: **2.** [ROLLER *sb.*[1] 7.] A board on rollers.

1958 J. KEROUAC *On Road* I. x. 58 Dean was frightfully waked up by the legless man on the rollerboard. **1963** *Lebende Sprachen* VIII. 106/3 *Roller-board*.., Rollbrett zur Reparatur unter dem Wagen.

roller-coaster: see ROLLER *sb.*[1] 24 in Dict. and Suppl.

roller-skate. Add: **1.** (Earlier example.)

1863 *Rep. Comm. Patents 1861* (U.S.) I. 280 A roller skate provided with two rows of tubular adjustable rollers.

2. A vehicle considered to resemble a roller-skate, spec. (*a*) a tank; (*b*) a small car. *slang.*

1941 *Reader's Digest* Feb. 92 The boys of Britain's R.A.F. have developed a language all their own...'roller skates' are tanks. **1961** PARTRIDGE *Dict. Slang* Suppl. 1127/2 *Roller skate*, a small, light waggon. **1976** LIEBERMAN & RHODES *Compl. CB Handbk.* vi. 135 *Rollerskate*, a small or foreign car.

ro·ller-skate, *v.* [f. the sb.] *intr.* To use roller-skates; to travel on roller-skates. Also *fig.*

1928 *Daily Tel.* 7 Feb. 4/7 Splendid and Partner can roller-skate as agilely on one table as Barrie Oliver can dance on another. **1935** W. FORTESCUE *Perfume from Provence* 93 What more amusing than to watch the pompous Monsieur Jeannot slip on a piece of banana skin and skid into a heap of oranges, some of which scatter under the stalls and are swiftly prigged by alert urchins, while other marketers roller-skate on the remainder? **1942** BERREY & VAN DEN BARK *Amer. Thes. Slang* § 728/4 *Drive fast*,..roller-skate. **1967** in Cox & Grose *Organiz. Bibliogr. Rec. by Computer* VII. 185 The National Employee Index..was referred to constantly—so much so that the messengers had to roller-skate through the file to gain access to it. **1973** *Times* 12 Nov. 18/6 Indeed children were roller-skating all over the place. **1977** J. CLEARY *High Road to China* vii. 226 The last event in the programme... A roller-skating race... Can you roller-skate?

roller-skating. Add: Also *attrib.*

1884 *N.Y. Weekly Tribune* 13 Aug. 4/3 Down at the roller skating rink having an awfully good time. **1888** *Boston Jrnl.* 4 Oct. 2/4 The roller-skating craze..has died out in this section. **1910** *Cycling* 2 Mar. 202 (*caption*) The roller-skating craze in Germany—a lady's race. **1949** *Time* 18 Apr. 25/1 The village board..should wake up, give the kids a roller-skating rink. **1977** [see *ROLLER-SKATE *v.*].

ro·ller-ski, *sb.* [f. as ROLLER-SKATE *sb.*: see SKI *sb.*] A kind of ski, about three feet in length, fitted with small wheels like those on a roller-skate, and used for skiing on roads, etc. Hence as *v. intr.*; also **ro·ller-ski:er, ro·ller-ski:ing** *vbl. sb.*

1978 *Skiing* Spring 58/1 Roller skiing has become *de rigueur* for dedicated cross-country skiers because..'it's the closest thing to skiing you can get without snow'. *Ibid.*, Tim roller-skis about 1,500 km..between seasons. *Ibid.*, Roller skis don't have brakes. **1979** *Capital Times* (Madison, Wisconsin) 23 Nov. 45/1 That enthusiast was using rollerskis, a training tool champion skiers have employed for years to maintain form. *Ibid.*, Every championship cross-country skier relies on so many meters of rollerskiing during the off-season. *Ibid.* 45/2 One of the most avid rollerskiers around is Madison Police Chief David Couper. *Ibid.* 45/3 How did Koch keep his top form over the summer? He rollerskied.

rollicking, *vbl. sb.* Add: **2.** Also **rollocking.** A severe reprimand. *colloq.*

1938 F. D. SHARPE *Sharpe of Flying Squad* 332 *A rollicking*, a telling off. ('He gave the copper a real rollicking.') **1958** M. K. JOSEPH *I'll soldier no More* ii. 54 Someone's dropped a clanger. Someone's going to get a rollocking. **1970** G. F. NEWMAN *Sir, You Bastard* vi. 174 You were on the cards for one hell of a rollicking. **1973** *Observer* 18 Nov. 37/5 The unknown Fourth Division manager who gave his forward line a fearful rollicking.

rollicking, *ppl. a.* **a.** (Earlier example.)

1811 in E. Mathews *Mem. C. Mathews* (1838) II. viii. 148 Some of the 'rollicking fellows' (as they call themselves) who perform in that Court.

rollicky, *a.* Add: (Earlier example.) See also quot. 1942.

1881 W. S. GILBERT *Patience* (*c* 1891) I. 7 A smack of Lord Waterford, reckless and rollicky—Swagger of Roderick, heading his clan. **1942** BERREY & VAN DEN BARK *Amer. Thes. Slang* § 278/20 *Hilarious*,..rollicky.

rolling, *vbl. sb.*[2] Add: **I. 1. b.** Short for LOG-ROLLING. *U.S.*

1819 [see **rolling bee*]. **1848** in H. Howe *Hist. Coll. Ohio* 358 Many times were we called from six to eight miles to assist at a rolling or raising, and cheerfully lent our assistance to the task. **1922** D. T. HERNDON *Centennial Hist. Arkansas* I. 209 The trees were felled, cut, or burned into lengths so that they could be handled, and then the neighbors were invited to the 'rolling'.

c. *slang.* Robbing. Cf. *ROLL *v.*[2] 5f.

1939 C. R. COOPER *Designs in Scarlet* i. 21 The 'rolling' or robbing of a man with whom they had been in company, on their alleged promise of sexual intercourse. **1948** *Sun* (Baltimore) 5 Jan. 9/5 Some of the more heavily doped victims of the fraulein 'rolling' racket have met the dawn clad in nothing more substantial than a pair of shorts. **1969** *Jeremy* I. III. 24/1 'Rolling' occurs most often in the lavatories of cinemas. **1973** *Times* 3 Apr. 14/7 Tony Bogle, a youth worker with Law's association, said: 'Mugging has been with us a long time. When the skinheads used to do it, they called it rolling.'

d. With *back*: see *ROLL *v.*[2] 5h.

1944 *Ann. Reg. 1943* 287 [An] organisation..strongly in favour of subsidies and the 'rolling back' of prices. **1979** *Daily Tel.* 2 Nov. 1 Stronger control of the economy and a rolling back of Socialist extravagance.

3. b. *rolling up* (Printing), preparing a lithographic plate for printing (see quots.).

1937 *Discovery* Oct. 300/1 Rolling up follows. The stone is kept damp, and the ink roller passed over it and the design charged with ink. **1967** E. CHAMBERS *Photo-litho-Offset* xvii. 260 The transferred image requires strengthening before printing and the non-printing areas require fully desensitising to guarantee clean printing in the white areas. This operation in plate preparation is termed 'rolling up'. **1968** *Canad. Antiques Collector* June 6/2 The [lithographic] stone having been coated with 'etch' is left for 24 to 48 hours and then the original drawing is completely removed (washed out) and the crayons, inks, etc. replaced by the special printing inks required in the process. This stage is called 'rolling up' and is accomplished with a hand-made leather covered roller.

II. 4. d. *Surfing.* With *over.* (See quots.)

1962 T. MASTERS *Surfing Made Easy* 65 *Rolling over*, rolling beneath the board to get past larger broken waves. **1965** J. POLLARD *Surfrider* ii. 20 For the big ones start 'rolling over'. This is done by dropping underneath your board and hanging on by the 'rails', the sides, when a wave has broken and the white water is coming towards you.

5. b. = *MAKING *vbl. sb.*[1] 8b. Also, a hand-rolled cigarette. *N. Amer. colloq.*

1913 *Collier's* 1 Feb. 28 Forty 'rollings' in each 5 cent muslin sack [of tobacco]. **1940** *Amer. Speech* XV. 213/1 The day before payday, the camp's 'smoking' has become scarce and 'rollings' or 'makings' are at a premium. **1956** H. S. M. KEMP *Northern Trader* 89 The tobacco was medium cut, suitable for pipe or the 'rollings'. **1965** *Sun* (Vancouver) 31 Dec. 27/1 (*heading*) 'Rollings' are safer... Dr. E. R. Threthewie..said..that home-made cigarettes burn at a lower temperature..[which] reduces the amount of cancer-producing substances produced. **1973** B. BROADFOOT *Ten Lost Years* xix. 216 Enough money for rollings. You know, roll your own tobacco.

6. b. A turning movement of an aeroplane or motor vehicle about the direction of motion.

1911 G. H. BRYAN *Stability in Aviation* ix. 166 Devices such as fins or bent-up planes..may cause serious rolling when the aeroplane is suddenly struck by a side wind. **1922** *Encycl. Brit.* XXX. 18/1 French pilots again pointed the way in the art of 'rolling', a manoeuvre in which the aeroplane is rolled about its longitudinal axis. **1930** *Morning Post* 21 July 4/4 Sideway or rolling occurs at right angles to the propeller shaft. **1974** H. ASHLEY *Engin. Anal. Flight Vehicles* i. 4 Rolling is accomplished by ailerons and/or spoilers, placed near each wing tip and deflected in an antisymmetrical manner.

III. 9. a. *rolling action, axis, drag, instability, motion, movement, oscillation, stability*; (sense *1 b) *rolling bee*; **rolling chamber,** a compartment for water-ballast extending across the beam of a ship; **rolling moment,** the moment acting on an aircraft about its longitudinal axis; **rolling paper** *U.S.* (usu. *pl.*), paper for making hand-rolled (esp. marijuana) cigarettes.

1915 A. FAGE *Aeroplane* v. 68 We ignored the rolling action due to the difference between the relative wind speeds of the wings. **1953** *New Biol.* XIV. 66 Stability can be related to any of the three axes—the rolling axis (parallel to its direction of flight), the yawing axis.., and the pitching axis. **1819** W. KEYES *Jrnl.* 21 May in *Wisconsin Mag. Hist.* (1920) III. 463 Attended a rolling bee this morning. **1900** *Geogr. Jrnl.* Jan. 34 The ship has a rolling chamber to keep her steady. **1976** *National Observer* (U.S.) 25 Sept. 17/1 'A lot of the problem is overcoming rolling drag,' he says, a problem compounded because the aerobike's pedals are connected only to its propeller and not to its wheels. **1921** *Rep. & Mem. Aeronaut. Res. Comm.* No. 745. 6 If, whenever one wing goes down due to a 'bump',..the wing tends to go down further, the motion shows 'rolling instability'. **1950** *Gloss. Aeronaut. Terms* (*B.S.I.*) 1. 22 *Rolling instability*, the instability whereby the motion of the aircraft takes up an increasing oscillation after a rolling disturbance and does not settle down to a horizontal position. **1914** *Techn. Rep. Advisory Comm. Aeronaut. 1912–13* 117 Measurements of ..rolling moment, for varying angles of yaw. **1939** L. BAIRSTOW *Appl. Aerodynamics* (ed. 2) iv. 188 Since L denotes rolling moment and *p* the angular velocity of roll. **1974** H. ASHLEY *Engin. Anal. Flight Vehicles* i. 4 At high speeds, rolling moment may be exerted simply by differential rotation of two all-movable horizontal stabilizers. **1923** *Rep. & Mem. Aeronaut. Res. Comm.* No. 846. 1 It was found necessary..to augment considerably the damping of the rolling motion. **1912** *Techn. Rep. Advisory Comm. Aeronaut. 1911–12* 103 The one claim that is made for the 'lower centre of gravity aeroplane' is that, although it rolls, the rolling movement is a steady one. **1958** D. PIGGOTT *Gliding* iii. 16 The ailerons control rolling or banking movements about the longitudinal axis. **1915** A. FAGE *Aeroplane* vi. 86 If the moments of inertia of the machine about the longitudinal and normal axes be small, the yawing and rolling oscillations will be rapid. **1971** *Aeronaut. Jrnl.* LXXV. 297/2 The ability of an aircraft to maintain the desired direction of motion depends mostly on the roll response to aileron, the steadiness of the motion being influenced by the dutch-roll mode, which is a combined yawing and rolling oscillation. **1977** *Rolling Stone* 5 May 81/4 (Advt.), Includes rolling papers and free legal-highs catalogue. **1979** *Christian Science Monitor* (Eastern ed.) 21 Nov. B2/2 The sale of rolling papers at supermarkets and the open sale of drug paraphernalia at head shops tend to signal children that the drug culture must be okay. **1921** *Rep. & Mem. Aeronaut. Res. Comm.* No. 745. 6 In still air, the test for rolling instability would be given by a jerk on the ailerons sufficient to depress one wing. If, after subsequent return of the control column the aeroplane tends to resume an even keel, there is 'rolling stability'. **1938** *Aircraft Engin.* Jan. 15/1 The effect on rolling stability of lowering the flaps..is quite small.

rolling, *ppl. a.* Add: **1. e.** Also, renewable; subject to periodic review; responsive to changing conditions.

1959 *Daily Tel.* 8 July 10/3 Western policy, particularly as foreseen by Mr. Macmillan and Mr. Selwyn Lloyd, can be expressed as 'rolling negotiations'. **1960** *Guardian* 27 Oct. 1/5 His successful efforts to secure a three-year rolling programme for major [road] improvements. **1962** *Listener* 10 May 796/2 Nor is rolling planning, by which long-term targets are modified each year in the light of changing circumstances, any answer. **1971** *Guardian* 31 Mar. 13/6 The new rolling three year contract which gives the Authority an opportunity to warn a company to do better. **1972** *Times* 14 Sept. 18/5 The Post Office..has a five-year rolling programme (meaning that it is regularly reviewed) to spend £3,000 m on overall improvements and developments. **1978** *Broadcast* 9 Jan. 17/2 We disagree with their suggestion that the present system of rolling contracts be replaced by fixed term contracts. **1981** *Listener* 26 Feb. 290/3 Radio London..cannot compete with LBC as a news station offering a 'rolling' format —regular bulletins linked by expanded news items..and local information.

f. Staggered, rotating; esp. of strikes, power-cuts, etc., that take place in different places in succession. orig. *U.S.*

1961 WEBSTER s.v. Rolling *adj.*, The economy was going through a rolling adjustment in which first one industry and then another was affected. **1969** *Age* (Melbourne) 24 May 3/8 The secretary of the Trades Hall Council..condemned threats of further rolling strikes. **1974** *Ebony* Feb. 36/1 If this phase fails, we will have no choice except to turn to mandatory cutbacks, and then perhaps rolling blackouts. **1979** 'A. HAILEY' *Overload* IV. xi. 351 'If we do have a serious oil shortage, almost certainly there will be rolling blackouts. You know what those are?'.. 'I think so. It means electric power will be off in different places for hours at a time.'

5. (Later examples.)

1903 G. B. SHAW *Man & Superman* III. 71 Rolling slopes of brown with olive trees instead of apple trees in the cultivated patches. **1914** CHESTERTON *Flying Inn* xxi. 252 Before the Roman came to Rye or out to Severn strode, The rolling English drunkard made the rolling English road. **1949** *Boston Sunday Globe* 1 May (Fiction Mag.) 3/2 This was rolling prairie with mottes of timber and brush thickets. **1977** *Time* 14 Mar. 48/2 (Advt.), The majestic mountain views of Trinchera Peak and Mount Blanca..stand as silent sentinels protecting the rolling foothills.

6. a. *rolling croquet, cultivator, ground, hitch* (earlier and later examples), *library, refinery* (slang), *road, table* (see quots.); **rolling boil** *Cookery*, a continuous rapid boil; **rolling lift bridge,** a type of bascule bridge (see quot. 1930).

1969 *Daily Tel.* (Colour Suppl.) 5 Sept. 31 Heat fermented barley mash..to a 'rolling boil' in a portable boiler above the stove. **1972** K. LO *Chinese Food* I. 20 This soup is then brought to a rolling boil. **1877** *Encycl. Brit.* VI. 609/2 *Rolling croquet*, in which the balls are sent together in nearly the same line, is made by trailing the mallet after the balls as soon as the stroke or tap is made. **1975** *N.Z. Jrnl. Agric.* Sept. 18/1 (Advt.), Yet the fact remains that the Lilliston-Lehman rolling cultivator continues along in a class by itself. **1883** W. H. PARKER *Recoll. Naval Officer* iii. 22 On the third day toward sunset we succeeded in anchoring on the 'rolling ground' just outside the harbour [of Rio de Janeiro], and the most dangerous anchorage we could have selected. **1959** *Internat. Hydrogr. Bull.* VIII. 241 Subsequently when anchored in other offshore rolling grounds on the New Zealand coasts, *Lachlan*'s ship's company comforted themselves with the memory that this was not so bad as the Zephyr. **1769** W. FALCONER *Universal Dict. Marine* s.v. hitch, A rolling-hitch. **1883** *Man. Seamanship for Boys' Training Ships R. Navy* (Admiralty) (1886) 87 Q. What is a rolling-hitch used for..? A. Bending a small rope to a large one, putting a tail jigger on a backstay. **1976** *Oxf. Compan. Ships & Sea* 719/2 A rolling hitch properly tied will never slip. **1920** R. FROST *Let.* 19 Sept. (1972) 94, I ran into the rolling library at Manchester Vt and had a good talk with Miss Frank who seemed to have been getting experience as well as selling books. **1930** F. J. TAYLOR *Mod. Bridge Constr.* viii. 124 Of the two types of bascule bridge, it may be well to deal with the Rolling Lift or Scherzer type first. The motion of this type of bridge is similar to that of a rocking chair as it rolls back at the same time as the end rises... The majority of rolling lift bridges at the present day are of the single-leaf class. **1933** *Discovery* Apr. 129/2 The scheme must..provide for rail and road cross-river traffic by means of viaducts and rolling lift bridges. **1975** L. DILLS *CB Slanguage Dict.* 51 *Rolling refinery*, truck hauling gas or oil (SW). **1976** PERKOWSKI & STRAL *Joy of CB* 174 *Rolling refinery*, a truck hauling gasoline or oil. **1969** 'D. RUTHERFORD' *Gilt-Edged Cockpit* vii. 117 Its tests on the 'rolling road' completed..the driver had taken it up to Silverstone. **1970** *Daily Tel.* 11 Feb. 14/5 A full diagnostic centre, including such refinements as a 'rolling road', to give engine and brake tests under simulated high speeds, involves considerable investment. **1971** *Timber Trades Jrnl.* 14 Aug. 71 (Advt.), Stenner VB 42in rolling table log bandsaw machine, 20ft tables, VG type feed gear, with all electrics and control gear.

rolling (rōᵘliŋ), *pr. pple. colloq.* [f. ROLL *v.*[2] 19.] Short for *rolling in money, wealth,* etc.

1905 H. A. VACHELL *Hill* ix. 186 He's going to marry a girl who is simply rolling. **1921** G. O'DONOVAN *Vocations* xiii. 193, I wish the dear nuns would share some of their poverty with us. They must be rolling. **1922** C. SIDGWICK *Victorian* xxi. 163 He isn't a bad old thing at all and he's simply rolling. **1936** R. LEHMANN *Weather in Streets* III. 352, I ought to get quite a decent screw—these film people are rolling. **1967** E. LEMARCHAND *Death of Old Girl* iii. 31 She was rolling, and insisted on making him a decent allowance. **1976** *Listener* 6 May 574/4 Cyril at the forge, who started out shoeing plough-oxen for shillings, but who is now rolling due to horse-trials at Badminton and polo at Cirencester.

rollio (rǫ·lio), var. ROULEAU 3.

1816 *Ackermann's Repository* Oct. 241/1 The trimming is a rich rollio of intermingled gauze and satin at the bottom of the dress. **1960** C. W. CUNNINGTON et al. *Dict. Eng. Costume* 183/1 *Rollio*.., a trimming of material rolled into a very narrow tubular shape.

rollmops (rōᵘ·lmǫps). [Ger.] A rolled fillet of herring, flavoured with sliced onions, spices, etc., and pickled in brine.

Sometimes erroneously treated as a plural.

1912 G. FRANKAU *One of Us* 30 *Rollmops* is here, and *Hackfleisch*, *Speck* and *Huhn*. **1926** E. HEMINGWAY *Torrents of Spring* xii. 107 We lunched on rollmops. **1951** *Good Housek. Home Encycl.* 637/1 Rollmops are usually packed in brine. **1964** *Listener* 21 May 850/1 For the soused herring *à la crème* you will need: 8 roll-mop herrings [etc.]. **1973** L. HEREN *Growing up Poor in London* iii. 62 She would also buy roll-mops and soft cheese. **1975** *Courier-Mail* (Brisbane) 27 Sept. 15/7 He used to love her rollmops—fish things on skewers.

ro·ll-neck, *a.* [ROLL *sb.*[1] 13.] Having a roll-collar. Hence as *sb.*, a garment, usu. a sweater, with a roll-collar. So **ro·ll-necked** *a.*

1942 N. BALCHIN *Darkness falls from Air* vii. 127 The inspector was wearing a roll-necked Jaeger pull-over. **1948** *Melody Maker* 28 Feb. 4/3 The young chap..wore a blue roll-neck sweater. **1955** 'D. CORY' *Phoenix Sings* v. 89 A big fellow in a rollneck pullover. **1968** *Daily Mirror* 20 Aug. 9/1 And I got a couple of bright flowery roll-neck tops which will also go with the slacks. **1968** *Guardian* 19 Sept. 8/3 John Cranko came on stage after the première of his latest ballet in a white silk roll-neck. **1970** T. LEWIS *Jack's Return Home* 148 He had on a white silk rollneck and a bright red cardigan. **1977** *Time Out* 17–23 June 80/1 (Advt.), Former male model—but more the jeans and rollneck type.

rollock (rǫ·lək). *slang.* [Alteration of BALLOCK, *BOLLOCK.] **a.** *pl.* As *int.* = *BOLLOCK 3. **b.** Comb., *rollock naked* adj. = **ballock-naked* adj.

1961 'B. WELLS' *Day Earth caught Fire* ii. 31 'Rollocks!' said Maguire and his voice was deliberately gruff to hide his embarrassment. **1962** A. WESKER *Chips with Everything* I. i. 11 Even if you're stark rollock naked, you'll all spring to attention.

rollocking, var. *ROLLICKING *vbl. sb.* 2.

rolloff, roll-off (rō^{u}·lǫf). [f. *to roll off.*] **1.** *Ten-Pin Bowling.* A game to resolve a tie or determine the qualifier for a later round of competition.

1947 *Richmond* (Va.) *News-Leader* 2 May 22 (*heading*) Scher wins Major Men's Pin Championship after rolloff. **1975** *Cleveland* (Ohio) *Plain Dealer* 6 Apr. 7-c/3 When they bowl in the rolloffs each contestant will be presented a Brunswick bowling bag as the prize for gaining the finals. **1976** *Eastern Even. News* (Norwich) 27 Aug., He won the roll-off competition with an eight game total of 1474 for a tournament average of 185. **1979** *Arizona Daily Star* 22 July c2/4 He won in the two-frame roll-off.

2. The smooth fall of response with frequency of a piece of audio equipment or the like at an end of its range. Cf. *ROLL *v.*^{2} 10* and 24.

1950 *Audio Engin.* Aug. 28/2 It is due to irregularities in the groove walls, and if heard through a flat system, sounds smooth or satiny, corresponding to initially white (flat spectrum) noise with perhaps some roll-off of the highs. **1956** *IRE Trans. Audio* IV. 35/2 To obtain the smooth transition between the woofer and tweeter, the two units should be designed to complement each other, both as to level balance and for obtaining the required rolloff in the low-frequency unit at the crossover frequency. **1959** KUH & PEDERSON *Princ. Circuit Synthesis* xiii. 212 In practice, the roll-off of the magnitude of the transfer function of an *m*-derived delay line is primarily due to the dissipation of the inductances. **1975** G. J. KING *Audio Handbk.* ii. 39 From the practical point of view, it is commonly necessary to introduce infrabass roll-off at least to attenuate rumble and other infrasonic noises which are often present on the programme signal.

3. First throw at dice.

1966 O. NORTON *School of Liars* vi. 94 [We] flipped for roll-off. Wally's ace took the box.

roll-on (rō^{u}·lǫn), *sb.* and *a.* [f. *to roll on.*] **A.** *sb.* **a.** Also *pl.* A type of elasticated corset designed to be stepped into and rolled up on to the body. **b.** A deodorant, etc., applied by means of a rolling stopper at the mouth of the container.

a. 1941 *Amer. Speech* XVI. 96 Do you like these *Roll-ons?* **1945** *Richmond* (Va.) *Times-Dispatch* 29 Mar. 3/2 A start could be made by changing the corsets—reminiscent of cumbersome bone and lacing styles—and attracting young women with the idea of..roll-ons. **1960** M. CECIL *Something in Common* 40 Holding the base of her roll-ons firmly, she wriggled inside them optimistically. **1963** *Times* 7 June 8/1 He was searched and underneath a woman's roll-on was found to have 28 bars of gold weighing 61lb. in a belt. **1972** *Times* 26 June 13/5, I..found myself in a bedroom in which was a very surprised lady struggling into her roll-on.

b. 1960 *Which?* Feb. 35/2 Body mist, the only roll-on to contain hexachlorophane, weakened nylon and viscose rayon.

B. *adj.* That rolls on; involving rolling on.

1950 B. PYM *Some Tame Gazelle* i. 9 She liked her clothes to fit tightly and always wore an elastic roll-on corset. **1960** *Which?* Feb. 35/1 Most of those who commented preferred the roll-on method to either spray or stick. **1962** *Fuller Brush Products* Feb. 2/2 'Roll-On' anti-perspirant and deodorant. **1975** N. FREELING *What are Bugles blowing For?* xx. 118 Her mind was furnished with moisture cream and roll-on deodorants. **1981** *Radio Times* 16–22 May 26/2 (Advt.), Two-way stretch roll-on girdle.

ro·ll-on, ro·ll-off. [f. *to roll on, to roll off.*] Used *attrib.* with reference to a method of transportation of vehicles by ship in which they are simply driven on to the vessel at the beginning of the voyage and off it at the end. Cf. *lift-on, lift-off* s.v. *LIFT *v.* 14.

1955 *Sun* (Baltimore) 3 Nov. 10/2 At Palm Beach, he said, two major facilities of immediate value and interest are available to roll-on, roll-off shippers. **1958** *Engineering* 21 Mar. 354/3 Improvements are being made, including.. the introduction of special containers, palletisation and of roll-on/roll-off methods. **1963** *Times Rev. Industry* Dec. 31 Collect a combined load from a number of British factories. Utilize the rollon-rolloff ferry services and deliver the goods direct to the continental buyer without using any expensive foreign warehouse space. **1967** *Sunday Times* 1 Jan. 24/6 Car-carrying liners with roll-on, roll-off facilities. **1969** *Guardian* 23 July 16/8 A ferry terminal for roll-on, roll-off passenger traffic. **1970** *Times* 2 June (Container Suppl.) p. ii/2 By the mid-1970s it is estimated that about 160 ocean-going purpose-built cellular container ships and roll-on roll-off ships with container capacity will be operating on the world's trade routes. **1972** *Guardian* 14 Aug. 20/2 Plans for a roll-on, roll-off ferry to Shetland from Aberdeen. **1976** *Southern Even. Echo* (Southampton) 16 Nov. 1/5 Dockers have threatened to close Portsmouth Docks in a move to stop Brittany Ferries from opening a freight service. They argue that yet another roll-on roll-off service would affect the jobs of dockers at ports like Poole.

ro·ll-out. Also **rollout.** [f. *to roll out.*] **1.** An act of moving or wheeling out; *spec.* the official rolling out of a new aeroplane or spacecraft. Also *attrib.*

1957 *Britannica Bk. of Year* 512/1 *Rollout,* the rolling of an aeroplane from the production line. **1967** *Economist* 16 Dec. 1158/2 The roll-out ceremony and the preparations now being made for Concorde's first flight not only mark the half-way stage in the aircraft's development, but also the point at which costs begin to rise really sharply. **1973** *Nature* 9 Feb. 360/2 The landing of Luna-21 and roll-out of Lunokhod-2 into the Mare Serenitatis area ..is already being hailed by the Soviet press as a precursor of cooperation in space between the United States and the USSR. **1976** *Daily Tel.* 18 Sept. 15 A milestone in the development of the next era of space travel was reached yesterday with the roll-out of America's first shuttle spacecraft.

2. The part of a landing during which an aircraft travels along the runway losing speed.

1959 *IRE Trans. Aeronaut. & Navig. Electronics* VI. 59/1 The objective..was to develop a full instrument-landing system which included touchdown and rollout. *Ibid.* 69/2 The roll out was accomplished by using the large hand-brake lever to keep the directional gyro centered until a full stop was completed. **1964** *Sci. Amer.* Mar. 33/1 If landings in Category III are adopted, however, the approach, flare decrab, touchdown and possibly rollout will be performed automatically. **1970** *Graphic* 12 Nov. 3 Two weeks following the first multiple flame-out, that same plane was loaded with 128 passengers headed for Mexico City. It landed safely. But no sooner was it on the ground—still on rollout—than all four engines quit again!

3. *Amer. Football.* A play in which a quarterback moves away from his protective blockers before attempting to pass. Also *attrib.*

1959 *Washington Post* 8 Nov. c6/4 A series of quarter-back roll-outs. **1969** *Eugene* (Oregon) *Register-Guard* 3 Dec. 2D/1 The Spartans would run what looked like a rollout and then fire the ball from one side of the field to the other. **1970** *Globe & Mail* (Toronto) 28 Sept. 18/7 A rollout quarterback, with outstanding running ability, Gabler has had difficulty connecting with receivers. **1977** *Chicago Tribune* 2 Oct. III. 4/3 We switched from our regular 5-2 defense into a 4-3 in the second half to try to keep their quarterback from getting around the corner on rollouts. **1969** D. TALLMAN *Directory of Football Defences* iii. 58 The roll-out pass is identical to the sprint-out, except that the quarterback, when clearing from the center will execute a roll-out or reverse-pivot technique.

ro·ll-over. orig. *U.S.* Also **rollover, roll over.** [f. *to roll over.*] **1.** An overturning, a turning upside down; a complete revolution.

1945 *Richmond* (Va.) *Times-Dispatch* 19 Mar. 2/4 (*heading*) Yank describes B-29 roll over in Osaka raid. **1950** *Dance Mag.* Dec. 35/2 Her 'dance' included back-bends, cartwheels, splits and 'four successive rollovers'. **1955** *Sun* (Baltimore) 19 July 17/6 Crash rollovers, head on collisions and T-bone crashes. **1962** *Amer. Speech* XXXVII. 272 All sorts of strapping and cushioning devices to insure survival of the driver in case of a high-speed collision or roll-over. *c* **1973** J. CHOLERTON *Adv. Acrobatic Tricks & Dances* (Assoc. Amer. Tap Dancing) 11 Two backward rollovers, two nip-ups (to left), to centre. **1973** *Sci. Amer.* Feb. 80/1 Although frontal collisions are the most frequent accidents, side collisions and roll-overs are by far the most dangerous. **1977** *Time* 24 Jan. 2/3 (Advt.), The ESV's have proved their life-saving value in head-on and rear-end collisions, side-swipes and roll-overs.

2. *Econ.* Extension or transfer of a debt or other financial relationship; *spec.* reinvestment of money realized on the maturing of stocks, bonds, etc.; an issue of stocks or bonds replacing one which matures.

1958 *Fortnightly Rev.* (Anderson & Strudwick, Richmond, Va.) 27 June 4 *Roll-over,* a stock or bond issue which takes the place of one that is maturing (and into which the money realized on the maturing issue may be put). **1958** *Washington Post* 6 Nov. A18/1 We have..a roll-over, something in the order of $23 billion worth of short-term notes, I think four times, certainly three. **1972** *Times* 27 June (Tokyo Suppl.) p. v/4 The Japanese phrase 'circular-buying' covers the roll-over of speculative funds from one sector to another. **1976** *National Observer* (U.S.) 22 May 9/5 (Advt.), If you've been buying notes, bills or certificates of deposit for yourself or your organization, you'll find it's a lot easier to buy Dreyfus Liquid Assets. There's no paperwork, no worrying about maturity dates, roll-overs, safe-keeping or delivery—and there's no sales charge.

3. *attrib.* and *Comb.,* as (sense 1) *roll-over accident, bar, protection;* (sense 2) *roll-over contract, contribution, credit, facility, provision, relief.*

1970 *Motoring Which?* July 107/2 Door release buttons stuck out a little—might allow doors to open in a roll-over accident. **1970** *Daily Tel.* 15 June 6/5 Roll-over bars have long been standard fittings on open racing cars. **1973** P. EINZIG *Roll-Over Credits* xv. 102 At the time of writing there is a complete lack of standardisation in the terms of roll-over contracts. **1976** *National Observer* (U.S.) 3 July 9/1 In such a situation the transfer of funds is treated as a 'roll-over contribution'. **1973** P. EINZIG *Roll-Over Credits* i. 3 One of the most important changes has been the evolution..of the system of roll-over credits—medium term credits with variable interest rates which are adjusted at fixed intervals to changes in the current market rates for short-term credits. **1975** *Daily Tel.* (Colour Suppl.) 25 July 30/3 If a creditor will only lend his money at short-term, but a debtor cannot hope to pay his debts for a long time, he is offered what is called a 'rollover facility'—a debt which is nominally short-term, but is automatically relent when it falls due for payment. **1972** *Times* 28 Dec. 21/1 Meeting all the foreseeable regulations on crash and roll-over protection. **1974** *Daily Tel.* 27 Apr. 21/2 Some developers had been hoping that the 'roll over' provisions would have been extended to the new tax. **1973** *Scotsman* 12 Jan. 6/2 Changes in capital gains tax should give either tapering relief on gifts or, if this is rejected, roll-over relief provisions on gifts. **1976** *Incorporated Linguist* XV. 72/2 The 'roll-over relief' where the gain on the disposal of an asset is transferred into the asset which replaces it, so that although the [capital gains] tax is payable, it is so only on the disposal of the final asset (eg on retirement). **1977** D. W. HEALEY in *Times* 30 Mar. 4/8, I propose an improved rollover relief for what is often called 'domestication', that is the transfer of an overseas branch to a separate non-resident company.

rolloway, var. *ROLOWAY.

Rolls (rō^{u}lz), colloq. abbrev. *ROLLS-ROYCE. Also *attrib.* and *fig.*

1928 E. WALLACE *Double* i. 9 Dick knew the gentleman very well by name; indeed, he had recognised his big yellow Rolls standing outside the hotel. **1932** AUDEN *Orators* III. 101 In Rolls or on bicycle they bolt for mama. *a* **1963** 'BEACHCOMBER' *Best of Beachcomber* (1963) ix. 102 She has a Rolls body and a Balham mind. **1965** *New Statesman* 14 May 753/3 He is essentially a working.. journalist who sees the paper 'off the stone' in the composing room every night before driving by Rolls to his Greenwich home. **1977** C. MCCULLOUGH *Thorn Birds* x. 224 Do you think Bob might let me borrow the old Rolls, if not the new one?

Rolls-Royce (rō^{u}lz roi·s). [Name of the manufacturing company.] **1.** A Rolls-Royce motor car.

1908 *Trade Marks Jrnl.* 26 Feb. 300 *Rolls Royce...* Motor cars and chassis included in this class. Rolls Royce, Limited, Cooke Street, Hulme, Manchester; Motor car manufacturers. **1915** 'I. HAY' *First Hundred Thousand* xiii. 173 Not long ago he was..driving a Rolls-Royce for a Duke. **1932** D. H. LAWRENCE *Last Poems* 256 Do you hear my Rolls Royce purr, as it glides away? **1936** J. B. PRIESTLEY *Walk in City* i. 5 So he popped into a long black Rolls-Royce. **1958** [see *BISH]. **1975** *Sunday Times* 16 Nov. 44/3 The electric oven..had a dark glass front like a pop star's Rolls-Royce.

2. *fig.* **a.** Any product considered to be of the highest quality.

1916 W. A. ROBSON *Aircraft in War & Peace* xi. 161 None of the different machines made for these specialised purposes..will compare with the best pleasure aeroplane, the Rolls-Royce of the air. **1923** A. BENNETT *Things that have interested Me* II. 107 The Row was flanked by processions of nun-like nursemaids pushing single prams and double prams—the Rolls-Royces of the pram-world. **1957** A. MACNAB *Bulls of Iberia* ii. 28 The famous Murubes of old. Principal herd·of main-line Vistahermosa. The 'Rolls-Royce' of taurine breeds. **1974** *Daily Mail* 24 Aug. 12/6 A lustrous Isphahan—the finest are the Rolls-Royces of rugs—size 6ft. by 4ft. might take two women two years to complete, and the value would be £1,800. **1977** *New Yorker* 19 Sept. 92/2 There was a nine-foot Bechstein—which many people feel is the Rolls-Royce of pianos—but when she opened the lid she found a mouse inside, eating the felt.

b. *attrib.* passing into *adj.*

1951 H. HASTINGS *Seagulls over Sorrento* in *Plays of Year 1950* IV. I. 45 Wot the 'ell's a bloke like 'im with a Rolls Royce accent..want to get mixed up in this mob for? **1960** *Sunday Express* 6 Nov. 16/6 Stanley Baker's rugged style has put him up in the Rolls-Royce class of actors. **1961** PARTRIDGE *Dict. Slang* Suppl. 1251/2 A bit Rolls Royce in his ideas. **1974** *Daily Tel.* 7 June 16 Vintage port—the Rolls-Royce end of the trade—accounts for only about one per cent. of port production. **1977** *Times* 23 Dec. 14/1 Norman Royce..disclaimed any pretensions to a 'Rolls-Royce performance', as a speaker.

Hence (*nonce-wds.*) **Rolls-Roy·ced** *a.* travelled in a Rolls-Royce; **Rolls-Roy·celess** *a.*, without a Rolls-Royce, devoid of Rolls-Royces; **Rolls-Roy·cey** *a.*, suggestive of a Rolls Royce; exceedingly wealthy.

1918 G. FRANKAU *One of Them* iii. 29 And the shrill cycle-bell's first tintillations Resounded from the dawning to the dark In a Rolls-Royceless, Peter Pan-less Park. *Ibid.* xxi. 162 For scarce a score of Rolls-Royced miles away..Miss Parker sat. **1926** D. H. LAWRENCE *Let.* 7 July (1932) 664 He was very nice; and apparently rich, too rich: Rolls-Roycey.

roll stone. *U.S.* A stone rounded by friction or attrition on a beach or in the bed of a river.

1845 J. C. FRÉMONT *Rep. Exploring Expedition* 124 A swift current, over a bed composed entirely of boulders or roll stones. **1872** *Rep. Vermont Board Agric.* I. 688 A fine specimen of gold from a rollstone he found, while digging a well.

roll-top, *a.* and *sb.* Add: **A.** *adj.* **1.** (Earlier and later examples.)

1887 *Trial H. K. Goodwin* (Massachusetts Supreme Judicial Court) 15 That shows the position of the roll-top desk which was in the front office. **1923** R. Herrick *Homely Lilla* xi. 173 A young woman looked up from the roll-top desk where she was running over a typed list of names. **1933** H. Nicolson *Jrnl.* 27 Jan. (1980) I. 47 Two brown-wood roll-top desks are pushed against the wall. **1977** C. McCullough *Thorn Birds* vii. 130 The roll-top desk stood alongside one of the big windows.

2. Applied to other items having a roll-over top or a top with a rolled shape.

1977 *Wandsworth Borough News* 7 Oct. 22/1 (Advt.), Kitchen/breakfast room..with Ascot sink water heater, solid fuel boiler, built-in larder, glazed china cupboard and small roll-top bath. **1977** *Time* 19 Dec. 43/1 A trendy new kitchen..may..include a Fasar range,..chopping-block islands with separate vegetable sinks, a rolltop condiment 'garage', [etc.].

B. *sb.* **1.** A roll-top desk.

1895 in *Funk's Stand. Dict.* **1912** W. Owen *Let.* 23 Mar. (1967) 125, I have suffered in being informed that the 'Roll Top' is sold. **1932** E. Bowen *To North* xii. 115 It was a relief not having her sprawling to telephone over Emmeline's roll top. **1980** *Family Handyman* Sept. 28/1 He'd priced rolltops in a downtown department store and knew he'd cut the cost in half.

2. The flexible top of a roll-top desk.

1913 in Webster. **1978** M. Kenyon *Deep Pocket* viii. 91 Peckover sat at the desk, slid the roll-top up.

roll-up, *sb.* Add: **1. b.** Also applied to salad, cooked food, etc., that is rolled up to form (part of) a dish. *U.S.*

1949 *New Yorker* 19 Nov. 94/3 Lunch box salad roll-ups. Roll up individual servings of finely shredded vegetable salad or coleslaw in a cabbage or lettuce leaf, fasten with a toothpick, [etc.]. **1952** *Sun* (Baltimore) 17 Jan. (B ed.) 12/1 (*heading*) Apple-ham rollups. **1977** *Chicago Tribune* 2 Oct. xi. 3/1 Place 2 tablespoons of mixture on each slice of roast beef; roll up. Place green beans on bottom of buttered shallow 10-by-6-by-2-inch casserole. Top with roll-ups.

c. (Earlier example.)

1831 M. Edgeworth *Let.* 6 May (1971) 536 A dressing-case—leather-roll-up which he preferred to a box.

d. A hand-rolled cigarette. *slang* (orig. *Prisoners'*).

1950 P. Tempest *Lag's Lexicon* 181 A 'good' roll-up is one that has a reasonable amount of tobacco in it. **1958** F. Norman *Bang to Rights* 55 A real snout, not even a roll up. **1963** T. Parker *Unknown Citizen* i. 23 The cigarette..was tasteless after the strong roll-ups in prison. **1967** *Daily Tel.* 21 Feb. 15/7 They smoked what one girl described as a 'roll-up', a loosely-rolled cigarette containing hemp. **1977** *New Society* 6 Oct. 24/2 An old man with one leg coughed in an agonising manner as he inhaled a very thin and slightly sad looking roll-up.

B. *adj.* That can be rolled up; suitable for rolling up; made by rolling up.

1908 *Sears, Roebuck Catal.* 97/1 Two roll-up straps. **1923** *Daily Mail* 12 Feb. 2 (Advt.), Roll-up felts at half price. **1939–40** [see *fold *v.*¹ 1 e]. **1948** *Sunday Pictorial* 29 Aug. 6/4 A prisoner will do anything for tobacco. He will sell his dinner for two thin 'roll-up' cigarettes which have less tobacco in them than there is in a respectable cigarette-end. **1964** *McCall's Sewing* 168/1 The true roll-up sleeve..must be made of fabric with no right and wrong side. **1966** J. Gardner *Amber Nine* x. 148 Back down the cat-walk to the main roll-up garage-type door. **1974** *Camping & Caravanning* Sept. 12/3 The awning has a nylon zip arched 'stable door' type doorway and a complete roll-up front.

roll-uppable (rōᵘlʌ·păb'l), *a.* *nonce-wd.* [f. *to roll up*, Roll *v.*² 8b + -able.] Able to be rolled up, suitable for rolling up.

1961 T. Hughes *Meet my Folks!* 33 Or the roll-uppable rubber ladder.

rolly, *a.* Add: Also *Comb.*, as *rolly-eyed* adj.

1965 G. McInnes *Road to Gundagai* xi. 197 Another..known to us as 'The Rolly-Eyed Duke'.

Rolly (rǫ·li). Representation of a popular pronunc. of *Rollei.

1961 Partridge *Dict. Slang* Suppl. 1251/2 *Rolly*, a Rolliecord or Rollieflex [*sic*] camera. **1971** 'A. Hall' *Warsaw Document* xxi. 271 Let everyone know you're the press, take plenty of Rollies. **1973** K. Benton *Craig & Jaguar* iii. 28 There was nothing of value..only his Rolly, and that was broken.

roloway. Also **rolloway.** Delete † *Obs.* Substitute for etym. and def.: [a. the specific name of *Simia roloway* (J. C. D. von Schreber *Säugthiere* (1774) I. 186), prob. f. the animal's native name in Ghana.] A large black and white guenon, *Cercopithecus diana roloway*, found in parts of tropical West Africa and distinguished from the Diana monkey by a longer, white beard. Also *attrib.* (Later examples.)

1894 R. Lydekker *Royal Nat. Hist.* I. iv. 102 The real name of the diana monkey in its native districts is said to be Roloway on the Gold Coast. **1910** W. P. Westell *Bk. Animal Kingdom: Mammals* ix. 163 The Roloway Monkey is often mistaken for the handsome Diana, to which it is very similar. **1966** W. C. O. Hill *Primates* VI. 531 This form has been much confused with the preceding; many authors.. having treated the Roloway as the Diana. **1966** R. & D. Morris *Men & Apes* viii. 234 Diana and rolloway monkeys have been considerably reduced in numbers.

rolwagen (rōᵘ·lwægən). Also **rollwagon, rolwaggon, row-waggon,** etc. [a. Du. *rolwagen*, lit. 'roll-wagon'.] A kind of Chinese cylindrical porcelain vase, or a Dutch imitation of this (see quot. 1960).

1675 [see Roll-wagon]. **1761** H. Walpole *Let.* 13 June (1928) II. 119 Don't trouble yourself about Delft—nay, I am now afraid you should get any, lest you should pack it up in an old china jar, and really find a meaning for that strange auctioneers word, a *rowwaggon.* **1786** *Catal. Portland Museum* 19 A 2-handled jar, and 2 row waggons. **1895** Rimbault & Clinch *Soho & its Associations* ii. 35, 1 pair of blew china rowlwaggons. **1954** T. Volker *Porcelain & E. India Co.* v. 20 Two carrack flasks, one broken, 15, two small *rolwagens. Ibid* [Note] *Rolwagen* is a name still in use in the porcelain trade in Holland, denoting a cylindrical vase, usually with a flat lip. **1957** *Apollo* June 251/1 'Rollwaggon' (or however you care to spell it) is still used of the cylindrical-bodied vases of the type frequently found in Transitional and K'ang Hsi blue-and-white. **1960** R. G. Haggar *Conc. Encycl. Continental Pott. & Porc.* 383/2 *Rol-wagens*, corrupted in English to *row-waggons, roll-wagons*, the name given to cylindrical vases found in K'ang Hsi blue-and-white.

roly-poly, *sb.*, *a.*, and *adv.* **5.** *attrib.* For 1848 quot. substitute:

1841 Thackeray *Gt. Hoggarty Diamond* (1849) xii. 168 You said I make the best rolly-polly puddings in the world.

Rom. Add: Also pl. **Rom.**

1910 *Encycl. Brit.* XII 38/1 Only those who starting from the ancient Byzantine empire have travelled westwards..call themselves by the name of Rom. **1973** *Guardian* 26 Mar. 7/1 The continued historical prejudice against the Rom—as the gipsies call themselves. **1976** *Sci. Amer.* Jan. 131/2 The Rom always try to cooperate.

b. *attrib.*

1973 *Guardian* 26 Mar. 7/2 The non-conforming way of life of the Rom people seems to attract increasing intolerance. **1976** *Sci. Amer.* Jan. 131/2 The Rom families that are studied here..spent almost half of their time away from home, travelling.

rom., abbrev. of Roman *sb.*¹ 4, used esp. as a proof-correctors' mark.

1824 J. Johnson *Typographia* II. 216 Rom. **1902** A. E. Housman *Let.* 30 Nov. (1971) 62 It ought to stand upright, not to slant (I have written 'rom.' in the margin). **1954** T. W. Chaundy et al. *Printing of Math.* ii. 53 Italic is restored to normal (i.e. roman) type by 'rom.' in the margin. **1973** S. Beale *Collins's Authors' & Printers' Dict.* (ed. 11) 379/1 *Rom.*, roman type.

Romagnol, Romagnole (rōᵘmănʸǫ·l, -ōᵘ·l), *sb.* and *a.* Also in It. form **Romagnolo** (fem. **-ola**, pl. **-oli**). [ad. It. *Romagnolo*, f. *Romagna* (see below).] **A.** *sb.* A native or inhabitant of the Romagna, a district of northern Italy (now part of the region of Emilia-Romagna). **B.** *adj.* Of or pertaining to the Romagna or its inhabitants.

1821 Byron *Don Juan* iv. 118 Juan's companion was a Romagnole. **1841** *Penny Cycl.* XX. 70/2 The Romagnoli are lively and quick, but they have the character of being hasty and violent. **1860** E. B. Browning *Napoleon III in Italy* in *Poems before Congress* 11 Piedmontese, Neapolitan, Lombard, Tuscan, Romagnole, Each man's body having a soul. **1901** M. Carmichael *In Tuscany* iii. 115 A hot-headed Romagnol, Alfonso Cerquetti,..had the hardihood to publish a pamphlet pointing out errors in the new Vocabolario of the Academy. **1926** *Contemp. Rev.* Mar. 297 General Pangalos might imitate the ancient Roman, rather than the modern Romagnole Dictator,..and retire to his Eleusinian farm. **1934** E. Pound *Eleven New Cantos* xxxv. 25 The Romagnols wd. come here to Mantua. **1966** S. Mann *Collecting Playing Cards* i. 31 The Romagnole pack resembles the Piacentine in many ways. **1973** M. West *Salamander* i. 42 Ask that fellow over there, the street-cleaner, what he is. He will answer, 'I am a Sard, a Calabrese, a Neapolitan, a Romagnolo.' **1975** *Times Lit. Suppl.* 31 Oct. 1311/1 Even the title *Amarcord*, Romagnolo dialect for 'I remember', hints..at the identity of the director and the subject of the memories.

So **Roma·gnan** [-an] *a.*; **Romagne·se** [-ese] *sb.* and *a.*

1845 *Encycl. Metrop.* XII. 385/2 Demoralization has never, perhaps, sunk human nature lower than we find it among the Romagnese [*c* 1500]. **1931** M. Yeo *St. Francis Xavier* vi. 62 Fogs from the Romagnan marshes enveloped the city. **1933** *Times Lit. Suppl.* 8 June 385/3 Already in Dante's 'Purgatorio' a Romagnese gentleman laments the days when 'ladies and knights,..toils and ease, inspired love and courtesy'. **1972** *Sansoni-Harrap Stand. Italian & Eng. Dict.* I. ii. 1120/2 Romagnese dialect.

romaine (romē̆·n). [a. Fr. fem. of *romain* Roman.] **1.** *U.S.* = Cos. Also *attrib.*

[**1885** W. Miller tr. *Vilmorin-Andrieux's Veget. Garden* 309 The Paris market gardeners grow, under the name of *Romaine Plate*, a variety which appears to be intermediate between the Green and the Gray Paris Cos Lettuces.] **1907** H. W. Wiley *Foods & their Adulteration* VI. 284 Among the varieties which are most highly prized for this purpose [*sc.* salad] are the cabbage lettuce and the variety known as Romaine. *Ibid.*, The Romaine lettuce is more highly prized by most connoisseurs. **1942** E. Paul *Narrow St.* vi. 50 Cabbages, cauliflowers,..potatoes, lettuce, romaine, *chicorée* and other salad leaves. **1966** T. Pynchon *Crying of Lot 49* i. 11 The..garlicking of a bread, tearing up of romaine leaves. **1972** *New Yorker* 22 July 22/2 Fifteen romaine lettuces for four-fifty. **1978** *N.Y. Times* 30 Mar. c7/1 Cos or romaine..grows upright and forms tight sheaths of rich green leaves.

2. Any of various crêpe fabrics. *romaine crêpe* (see quot. 1968 and cf. quots. 1923 s.v. *crêpe). Also *attrib.*

1922 *Glasgow Herald* 26 Apr. 10 The bride..wore a gown of white romaine. *Ibid.*, The two bridesmaids..wore white crepe romaine dresses. **1932** *Daily Tel.* 25 Apr. (Advt.), Coat of wool romaine. **1932** *Daily Express* 25 June 9/5 Lady Haslam..was in love-in-a-mist romaine armure. **1939** M. B. Picken *Lang. Fashion* 122/1 *Romaine*, sheer silk fabric in basket weave, made of fine yarns, having smooth surface and slightly more body than triple sheer. **1952** C. W. Cunnington *Eng. Women's Clothing* 296 *Romaine*.., a lining fabric of French make, in warp satin weave. A sheer silk fabric in basket weave. Also 'a light woollen with dull surface and flat square weave'. **1957** M. B. Picken *Fashion Dict.* 277/1 *Romaine crep*, heavy sheer crepe. **1968** J. Ironside *Fashion Alphabet* 223 *Romaine crêpe*, a heavy, semi-sheer crêpe usually in a dull finish rayon, sometimes silk, made to resemble wool crêpe.

‖ **romaji** (rōᵘ·madʒi). Also **romazi**, and with capital initial. [Jap., f. *roma* Roman + *ji* letter(s).] A system of Romanized spelling for the Japanese language.

[**1888** B. H. Chamberlain *Handbk. Colloq. Japanese* i. 9 There is a party in favour of the adoption of the Roman alphabet. Its organ, the '*Rōmaji Zasshi*', gives articles..romanised according to a simple phonetic system.] **1903** R. Lange *Text-bk. Colloq. Japanese* p. xviii, *Romaji* is designed to represent phonetically the standard pronunciation of the present day. **1935** *Amer. Speech* X. 274/2 Several movements for Romaji, Japanese written phonetically in Roman letters, are under way. [**1939** *Jrnl. Amer. Oriental Soc.* LIX. 99 The Japanese had long ago worked out a diaphonic spelling called *Nipponsiki* (Japanese-Style) *no Rômazi* and propagated it in competition with the reigning bastard English-Italian system named after Hepburn.] *Ibid.* 102 The present use of rōmazi during an extended period is a hindrance rather than a help in the mastery of Japanese as it is normally written. **1950** D. Jones *Phoneme* 102 The name of the mountain which used to be written Fuji in the old Rōmaji system is now written Huzi. *Ibid.* 105 In the new Rōmazi orthography hi and si are distinguished. **1966** P. S. Buck *People of Japan* (1968) x. 130 The Japanese have to master *romaji*, Japanese spelled in Roman letters.

‖ **Romalis** (romā·lis). [Sp.] A Spanish gypsy dance (see quots.). Also, the music of this dance.

1841 Borrow *Zincali* I. vi. 317 Chicharona danced the Romalis (Gypsy dance) before her. **1846** [see *ole¹]. **1889** L. A. Smith *Through Romany Songland* 54 The famous Romalis, the dance which Tiberius may have seen, and which no one but a gipsy dances in Spain. It is danced to the ancient Oriental music of hand-clapping, and to an old religious Eastern tune, low and melancholy, diatonic, not chromatic, and full of sudden pauses which are strange and startling. It is sung in unison, and has a chorus in which every one joins. **1967** 'La Meri' *Spanish Dancing* (ed. 2) v. 74 This Romalis is part of a wedding ceremonial. The melody is Eastern; diatonic, low, melancholy and with sudden breathtaking pauses. Some..even identify it with the dance which Salome did before Herod.

Roman, *sb.*¹ Add: **I. 1. c.** (Further examples.)

1950 T. Williams *Roman Spring of Mrs. Stone* i. 34 Patience, said the Contessa. Rome was not built in a day! I am a Roman, said Paolo, but I am not Rome. **1967** C. Seton-Watson *Italy from Liberalism to Fascism* ix. 334 He was an intelligent man, but vain and irresolute, with a Roman's liking for *combinazioni.*

3. c. The dialect of the modern Romans.

1598 [see *Neapolitan *sb.* d]. **1642** J. Howell *Instructions Forreine Trav.* xi. 138 There is in Italy the Toscan, the Roman, the Venetian, the Neapolitan,..and others..and all these have severall Dialects and Idiomes of Speech. **1973** *Daily Tel.* (Colour Suppl.) 22 Feb. 65/3 She..spoke such a flowery Roman that I wondered if this wasn't a sort of cultural or social dust thrown into one's eyes.

5. b. A Roman hyacinth.

1925 *Glasgow Herald* 26 Aug. 8/7 Early Romans are in, but at a very high price. **1934** 'E. M. Delafield' *Provincial Lady in Amer.* 126 Early Romans should certainly be well above ground now.

II. 6. (Further examples.)

1936 S. Dark *Manning* iii. 101 Tory Romans were henceforth allowed to wear primroses in their buttonholes on the anniversary of the death of Benjamin Disraeli. **1956** R. Macaulay *Towers of Trebizond* xxii. 255, I decided that it should stick to Anglican churches, eschewing both Knox and the Romans. **1962** V. J. K. Brook *Life Abp. Parker* xix. 343 He had constantly to entertain those given into his charge by the Council—Romans or others—that he might reason with them. **1965** M. Spark *Mandelbaum Gate* ii. 45 Latest bulletin from the Holy Romans..they'll take at least another month to decide. **1975** Byfield & Tedeschi *Solemn High Murder* (1976) i. 2 The Romans might have a nice large new..church right in town..but the little Anglican wooden shack..had wine.

roman, *sb.*³ *S. Afr.* Also **roo(i)man.** [Afrikaans, f. *rooi* red + *man* man.] **1.** A marine fish, *Chrysoblephus laticeps*, belonging to the family Sparidæ and having reddish skin. Also *attrib.*

1790 E. HELME tr. *Le Vaillant's Trav. Afr.* I. ii. 22 Among those [fish] in greatest estimation, they distinguish the *rooman*, a red fish [etc.]. **1801** [see STEENBRASS]. **1804** R. PERCIVAL *Acct. Cape of Good Hope* 43 The most common is the Roman fish... It is of a deep rose colour and of the perch kind. **1893** [see *KINGKLIP]. **1957** S. SCHOEMAN *Strike!* iii. 32 It is universally known as 'roman', although some anglers and fishermen call it 'rooi roman' (red roman). **1971** *Cape Argus* 14 May 14 John Hughes shot a roman of 4,1 kg—which is equal to the South African spearfishing record.

2. A large nocturnal sun-spider belonging to the order Solifuga (or Solpuga) and having a sandy-coloured body.

1905 F. PURCELL in Flint & Gilchrist *Sci. in S. Afr.* III. iii. 178 The large nocturnal..species of *Solpuga*..are variously known by the name of Romans, Jagd-spinnekoppen (Hunting Spiders) or Haar-sheerders (Hair cutters). **1966** E. PALMER *Plains of Camdeboo* xiv. 233 On the farm we know..the nocturnal species [of spiders] as Rooimans or Red Men, and of these latter I can neither think nor speak except in capitals.

‖ **roman** (romaṅ), *sb.*[4] [Fr.: see ROMAUNT *sb.* and *a.*] A romance; a novel. Esp. in phrases: **roman à clef**, a novel in which actual persons are introduced under fictitious names; **roman à thèse**, a novel that seeks to further a viewpoint or expound a theory; **roman d'aventure** = ROMANCE *sb.* 2; **roman de geste** = **chanson de geste*; **roman expérimental**, a realistic novel based upon deterministic theories of human nature of an alleged scientific character; also *fig.*; **roman fleuve**, a sequence of self-contained novels; **roman noir**, a Gothic novel, a shocker, a thriller; **roman policier**, a story of police detection.

1765 [see ROMAUNT *sb.* and *a.* 1]. **1868** Roman de geste [see *CHANSON 2]. **1884** W. JAMES *Will to Believe* (1897) 173 Like the friends of M. Zola, we pique ourselves on our 'scientific' and 'analytic' character, and prefer to be cynical, and call the world a 'roman expérimental' on an infinite scale. **1889** E. DOWSON *Let.* 5 May (1967) 75 We.. may..evolve a brilliant *roman*. **1893** H. JAMES *Let.* 23 Jan. in P. Gunn *Vernon Lee* (1964) x. 138 Her books of fiction are a tissue of personalities of this hideous roman-à-clef kind. **1905** Roman d'aventure [see *LAI[1]]. **1913** G. TURQUET-MILNES *Influence of Baudelaire* v. v. 250 In his [*sc.* Arthur Machen's] works we again meet the distrust of nature from the documentary point of view—the distrust of 'Romans à Clef'. **1928** A. CHRISTIE *Mystery of Blue Train* x. 81, I see, Madame, that you have a *roman policier*. **1931** *Times Lit. Suppl.* 26 Feb. 151/4 The 'Radcliffian' novel, or *roman noir*, as the French call it. *Ibid.* 31 Dec. 1054/4 The study aims at giving a detailed analysis of the German criticism of Zola's Rougon-Macquart cycle and his theory of the *roman expérimental*. **1934** WEBSTER, Roman à thèse. **1936** *Times Lit. Suppl.* 15 Feb. 121/3 Those great *romans-fleuves* whose unnumbered volumes have no other purpose than to show us to ourselves as we appear. **1940** H. G. WELLS *Babes in Darkling Wood* 5 They pass at last..into more or less honest fact telling, into 'historical reconstruction', the *roman à clef*, biography, history and autobiography. **1954** K. TILLOTSON *Novels of Eighteen-Forties* I. 3 The *roman à thèse* is already establishing itself. **1955** *Times* 4 Aug. 10/3 *The Typewriter* is not great Cocteau, but it is fine melodramatic fare and strangely compelling emotionally. It has wit and good dialogue, but this is essentially a tragedy set in the frame of a *roman policier* and the answer to the mystery remains unanswered and unguessable until the very last scene. **1957** *Encycl. Brit.* I. 945/1 The inter-influence of French and English literature can be studied in the Breton romances and the *romans d'aventure* even better than in the epic poetry of the period. **1959** *Listener* 3 Dec. 1007/3 The re-creation of the medieval *roman*..in *The Story of Reynard*. **1965** *Ibid.* 27 May 799/1 *David in Silence*..is also in its way a *roman à thèse*. **1965** *Observer* 5 Sept. 21/5 The film is a *roman policier*. **1966** J. CARTER in Glover & Greene *Victorian Detective Fiction* p. xiv, The early *roman policier* writers. **1971** J. POPE-HENNESSY *A. Trollope* xvii. 364 We might claim..that *An Eye for an Eye* initiated the series of Trollope's *romans noirs*. **1972** V. GIELGUD *Black Sambo Affair* xxvii. 208 A fine collection of *romans policiers*. **1974** *Bookseller* 15 June 2696/3 He [*sc.* Anthony Powell] obviously feels reasonably protective towards the maestro of the *roman fleuve*. **1977** *New Yorker* 24 Oct. 184/2 A roman à clef whose skeleton key would seem to be the unsavory case of Alice Crimmins and her two murdered children. **1978** *Times Lit. Suppl.* 1 Dec. 1405/5 Success takes him to Hollywood, and there you feel a roman à clef, based on Puzo's profitable frustrations in movieland, is intended.

Roman, *a.*[1] Add: **I. 3.** Also *Comb.*, as *Roman-looking* adj.

1869 'MARK TWAIN' *Innoc. Abr.* xlviii. 505 We came to a..Roman-looking ruin.

4. a. spec. *Roman father*, a dominating head of a family.

1750 W. WHITEHEAD *Roman Father* v. ii. 74 Has not a Roman father power to take The lives of all his children? **1906** KIPLING *Puck of Pook's Hill* 148 There can't be much of the Roman Father about you! **1922** T. E. LAWRENCE *Let.* 26 Aug. (1938) 361 Perhaps I'm playing the Roman father trick, and it's not as bad as I think. **1940** H. G. WELLS *Babes in Darkling Wood* I. iv. 89 My Roman father! The Cadi of Clarges Street! **1962** *Listener* 25 Oct. 694/1 Dr Borosdin, the almost Roman father. **1977** P. G. WINSLOW *Ditch Hill Murder* II. 153 Richard had taken to playing the Roman father to Lerida.

d. *Roman holiday*, an occasion on which entertainment or profit is derived from injury or death; a scene of suffering considered as an object of amusement; a pitiable spectacle.

Orig. a holiday for a gladiatorial combat: see quot. 1818 s.v. HOLIDAY *sb.* 2.

1886 'S. COOLIDGE' *What Katy did Next* ix. 223 (*heading*) A Roman holiday. **1931** R. FERGUSON *Brontës went to Woolworth's* xxv. 220 There. I've made a Roman holiday of my dear little acquaintance, and I only hope I'm right. **1951** G. GREENE *Lost Childhood* 47 The critics..were perhaps influenced by horror at the Roman holiday. **1957** 'H. CARMICHAEL' *Put out that Star* x. 103 All you people ever think about is how you can turn any damn' thing at all into money: anything to make a Roman holiday. **1966** P. O'DONNELL *Sabre-Tooth* xv. 205 She had watched impassively, caring nothing for the man's death but loathing the Roman-holiday manner of it. **1967** A. WILSON *No Laughing Matter* III. 329 Was this what Picasso's wonderful Guernica stood for, this Roman holiday? **1972** A. HUNTER *Vivienne* x. 131 A Roman holiday was in the making, and the number of reporters had risen to five.

5. c. *Roman uncial* = SEMI-UNCIAL *a.* (*sb.*)

1897 [see *half-uncial* s.v. *HALF- II. n]. **1906** E. JOHNSTON *Writing & Illuminating* i. 38 Roman uncials were fully developed by the fourth century.

8. Also, *Roman-Doric*, *-Dutch* (later examples).

1928 R. NEVILL *Romantic London* ii. 39 The lower order is Roman-Doric. **1957** LD. HAILEY *Afr. Survey 1956* xxii. 1520 In South Africa ownership of the land is, in accordance with the principles of Roman-Dutch law, held to comprise all values in the land including mineral rights. **1964** J. SUMMERSON *Classical Lang. Archit.* 49/1 The Greek order has no base, nor is a base prescribed by Vitruvius, though in practice the Roman Doric always has a base, the Greek never. **1972** *Mod. Law Rev.* XXXV. 1. 46 There is no warrant in Roman-Dutch law for a discretion as wide as that enunciated by the Appellate Division.

II. 10. *Roman fever* [transf. use of 13c], a fondness for the Church of Rome, a desire to be converted to Rome.

1877 O. WILDE *Lett.* (1962) 45 Poor Dunskie: I know he looks on me as a renegade; still I have suffered very much for my Roman fever in mind and *pocket* and happiness. *a* **1884** M. PATTISON *Mem.* (1885) vi. 226 The daughter had got the Roman fever in her veins. **1929** S. LESLIE *Anglo-Catholic* xii. 171 Edward..assured him he had not left the Anglican Church, though the Anglican Church, he thought, had probably left him. The Canon only said, 'For Roman fever there is no cure and for Rome there is no leechdom.' **1952** R. MACAULAY *Let.* 12 Jan. (1961) 248, I am glad Dom Gregory Rees thinks 'Roman fever' abated; I don't notice it myself, anyhow among the laity.

III. 13. d. Applied to a bidding system in Bridge orig. used by certain Italian players, or to various conventions and signals within this system.

1959 BELLADONNA & AVARELLI *Roman Club Syst. Distrib. Bidding* 2 In this fashion the person who is already playing bridge can learn one phase of the Roman Club expertly before going on to the next formula. **1959** REESE & DORMER *Bridge Player's Dict.* 190 *Roman system*... Opening bids of one diamond, one heart, and one spade, show a genuine suit and are forcing for one round. **1964** *Listener* 21 May 851/1 'Roman leads'..is a method whereby the lower of two touching honours, rather than the higher, is the normal lead. **1970** S. HUGHES *Art of Coarse Bridge* iv. 93 Patiently South explained that the Roman Club..meant that he had either a minimum balanced hand or a very strong one. **1975** *Times* 27 Sept. 10/7 Opening bids with double meanings which we now associate with the Roman and other artificial systems.

IV. 14. b. *Roman chamomile* (earlier example).

1815 F. P. CHAUMETON *Flore Médicale* II. 123 *Latin* Anthemis nobilis... *Anglais* Chamomile; Roman Chamomile; Sweet-scented chamomile.

15. b. (Earlier example.)

1607 TOPSELL *Foure-f. Beasts* 655 The hornes..are so lively expressed by Pliny... They are..long, about two Roman feet and three palmes... They are in breadth where they ioyne to the head, three Roman fingers and a half.

16. c. (Further examples.) = *PARKER'S CEMENT.

1889, 1917 [see *PARKER'S CEMENT]. **1919** A. T. BASSETT *S. Barnabas', Oxford* vi. 67 Some amusement was caused at the time by a box bearing the words 'Roman Cement', in large letters, being delivered at the Church for use in the connection with repairs to the campanile. **1970** H. BRAUN *Parish Churches* xix. 223 Roman cement is difficult to procure, but an admixture of lime with the Portland cement will help to improve the colour to some small extent. **1977** *Sci. Amer.* July 82/2 The high quality of Roman cements, which is evident in the number and solidity of the Roman structures still standing, was due in large measure to the added discovery that lime mixed with reactive siliceous material (in the form of crushed tiles or volcanic ash) gave a cement that developed superior strength and water resistance. 'Roman cement' made in this way enjoyed wide prestige and retained its popularity with little improvement or development until the end of the 18th century.

f. *Roman ring* = *flying ring* s.v. *FLYING *ppl. a.* 3.

1911 *Daily Colonist* (Victoria, B.C.) 26 Apr. 5/4 They [*sc.* vaudeville athletes] begin by drawing their body from the floor on Roman rings with snail-like slowness. **1965** F. SARGESON *Mem. Peon* vi. 165 The creak of parallel bars and Roman rings.

17. *Roman sandal*, *satin* (further examples), *scarf*; **Roman bath** = **Roman tub*; **Roman tub** *U.S.*, a large sunken bathtub.

1855 E. TWISLETON *Let.* 6 Apr. (1928) xiv. 266 Mrs. Carlyle was sumptuous, in a black velvet and Roman scarf. **1914** C. MACKENZIE *Sinister St.* II. III. iv. 559 Stella.. was rushing from window to window, trying patterns of chintz and damask and Roman satin. **1934** WEBSTER, Roman sandal. **1939** M. B. PICKEN *Lang. Fashion* 130/2 *Roman sandal*, sandal with front composed entirely of straps, equally spaced. **1961** *Harper's Bazaar* Feb. 69 The splendid Roman striped satin of a Heppelwhite chair. **1971** *Sunday Nation* (Nairobi) 11 Apr. 20/1 (Advt.), Boots, Roman Sandals. **1972** *Fortune* Jan. 140c (Advt.), You'll have a cocktail lounge and restaurant on the premises. An outside elevator joining the opulent pool deck area and the beach. A Roman tub in your master bath. **1976** *Bathroom Ideas* 58/2 Blue, blue is this Roman bath set apart from the rest of the room. **1979** *Arizona Daily Star* 5 Aug. (Advt. Section) 16/9 Features formal dining, atrium, 2-way fireplace, roman tub in master bedroom.

Romanaccio (romanā·tʃio). [It.] A modern dialect spoken in the city of Rome.

1963 *Guardian* 6 June 11/2 Cardinal Agagianian.. speaks 11 languages including Romanaccio (Roman cockney). **1973** M. WEST *Salamander* ii. 163 A stable-boy laughed and I flew at him, clawing and punching and screaming in Romanaccio.

Roman candle. [ROMAN *a.*[1]]

1. See ROMAN *a.*[1] 16d.

2. A parachute jump on which the parachute fails to open; a parachute which fails to open. Also (in full *Roman candle landing*) an unsatisfactory landing by an aircraft. *slang.*

1943 HUNT & PRINGLE *Service Slang* 56 *Roman candles*. 'When a parachute simply fails to open. (Of course, on landing, you dash to the stores and get another.)' **1943** C. H. WARD-JACKSON *Piece of Cake* 52 *Roman candle landing*, a bad landing. **1952** *Chambers's Jrnl.* May 261/2 It is not so very long ago since parachute-jumping was a stunt indulged in by steel-nerved men of boundless courage performing in air circuses. In those days, the sight of some hapless individual streaming to earth with a 'Roman candle' (an undeveloped 'chute) was not exceptional. **1959** *Chambers's 20th Cent. Dict.* Add. 1389/1 *Roman candle*, a bad landing by aeroplane: a landing by parachute when the parachute fails to open.—v.i. to make such a landing. **1961** E. WAUGH *Unconditional Surrender* II. v. 141 The first thing the commandant asked when I reported Crouchback's accident. 'A Roman Candle?' he asked. **1976** A. WHITE *Long Silence* vii. 59, I experienced the sense of relief that says, 'This time, no roman candle!'

3. A Roman Catholic. *slang.*

1941 G. KERSH *They die with their Boots Clean* II. 57 There's services for C. of E-ers and Roman Candles. **1959** I. & P. OPIE *Lore & Lang. Schoolch.* xvi. 344 In Staines, Catholics are 'Roman Candles', and R.C. children call the Protestants 'Old Proddy Dogs'. **1974** P. HAINES *Tea at Gunter's* ii. 18 She said: 'I've noticed you lots—you're a Roman candle, aren't you?' 'What?'..'*R.C.*, silly.'

Hence **Roman-ca·ndle** *v. intr.*, to make a parachute jump with a parachute that fails to open.

1959 [see sense 2 above]. **1975** tr. *Melchior's Sleeper Agent* (1976) III. 230 *He had roman-candled!* The chute had not opened! He was plunging toward oblivion.

Ro·man Catholi·city. [f. ROMAN CATHOLIC *sb.* and *a.* + -ITY.] Roman Catholicism.

1806 M. B. PEMBRIDGE *R.C. Church Vindicated* i. 40 These edifices still bear the external signature of Roman Catholicity. **1965** E. O'BRIEN *August is Wicked Month* xvii. 218 'It's your Roman Catholicity,' he said.

Romance, *sb.* and *a.* Add: **I. 1.** *Comb.* (Earlier and later examples.)

1882 E. A. FREEMAN *Lect. Amer. Audiences* I. v. 155 Did not the Norman Conquest..bring with it a settlement of strangers, of Romance-speaking strangers, enough to destroy all pretence on the part of the English nation to pure Teutonic descent? **1964** Romance-based [see *Latin-based* s.v. *LATIN *sb.* 5]. **1964** E. PALMER tr. *Martinet's Elem. Gen. Linguistics* v. 150 The Romance-speaking clerks of the eighteenth century..used.. variously a local Romance language and another language, Latin.

II. 3. b. (Earlier example.)

1816 [see *HISTORICAL *a.* 3].

5. a, b. *spec.* (also with pronunc. rōᵘ·mæns) a love affair; idealistic character or quality in a love affair; a love story; that class of literature which consists of love stories.

1916 G. B. SHAW *Overruled* 81, I felt my youth slipping away without ever having had a romance in my life; for marriage is all very well; but it isnt romance. Theres nothing wrong in it, you see. **1921** MENCKEN *Amer. Lang.* (rev. ed.) vii. 209 The chief movement in American.. would seem to be toward throwing the accent upon the first syllable... I might add..*defect, excess, address, magazine, decoy* and *romance*. **1922** JOYCE *Ulysses* 280 Chorusgirl's romance. Letters read out for breach of promise. **1936** 'G. ORWELL' *Keep Aspidistra Flying* x. 264 When a customer demanded a book of this category or that,.. 'Sex' or 'Crime' or 'Wild West' or 'Romance' (always with the accent on the *o*), Gordon was ready with expert advice. **1939** N. MONSARRAT *This is Schoolroom* xvii. 385 The dance-band world..has given us a new pronunciation—'bokay' for bouquet, 'rómance' thus accented. **1942** T. RATTIGAN *Flare Path* I. 26 He was on a week's leave, and we were married before he went back to his Squadron. What the papers would call a whirlwind wartime romance. **1951** in M. McLuhan *Mech. Bride* (1967) 24/2 She loved him with another woman's body.. one of the tensest, most passionate romances you have ever experienced. **1954** [see *FANTASY, PHANTASY *sb.* 4 f]. **1960** *Times* 28 Sept. 15/4 Harry, undaunted by a succession of parties at which he has done nothing whatever, always attends in the hope of finding romance. **1966** C. MACKENZIE *My Life & Times* V. 193 The cinema audience wants rómance. We must give them rómance. **1971** J. FLEMING *Grim Death & Barrow Boys* vii. 87 It's the end of ro-mance, is marriage.

7. a. *romance-writer* (further example); *romance-reading* (later example), *-weaving, -writing* (further examples); *romance-wards adv.*

1876 *Westm. Rev.* XLIX. 361 The novelist proper studies to represent his little world as the great world is; whereas the romance-writer..builds an ideal world. **1887** *Contemp. Rev.* LI. 172 Really good romance writing is the most difficult art practised by the sons of men. **1904** 'MARK TWAIN' in *Harper's Weekly* 10 Dec. 11/1 There was no romance-reading that night. **1904** W. H. HUDSON *Green Mansions* 2 Let us hope that now, at last, the romance-weaving will come to an end. **1920** R. MACAULAY *Potterism* vi. iii. 228 He was also leaning romancewards and departing from the realm of pure truth. **1979** *N. & Q.* Feb. 90/2 Hanning tends to brush aside these technical difficulties of romance-writing.

b. *romance-like* adj.

1971 K. MILLETT *Sexual Politics* (1972) I. i. 5 That Ida has dressed herself in a collapsible bathrobe and silk stockings is not only accommodating but almost romance-like.

8. *romance-literature, thriller.*

1905 *N. Amer. Rev.* CLXXX. 5 You have made the American home..beautiful with your..noble romance-literature. **1961** *Times Lit. Suppl.* 8 Dec. 2/1 The growing success of the romance-thriller, where the basic plot of virgin-marries-older-man is sharpened..by often well-devised and dramatic villainy. **1975** *Listener* 20 Nov. 685/1 The many competent women writers of 'romance thrillers'.

romance, *v.* Add: **5.** *trans.* To have a romance or affair with, to court.

1942 BERREY & VAN DEN BARK *Amer. Thes. Slang.* § 354/4 *Court,*.. race, romance, run with, run *or* chase after, rush. **1956** B. HOLIDAY *Lady sings Blues* (1973) vi. 59, I was accused of romancing everyone in the band. **1970** M. BUTTERWORTH *Vanishing Act* xi. 125 A good-looking chap..could do a bit of counter-jumping and romance the lady customers..if he had the cheek. **1976** T. GIFFORD *Cavanaugh Quest* v. 79 They were working on my kind of music... I'd romanced Anne to old stuff like that and we'd made love to Claude Thornhill recordings. **1980** N. DEMPSTER in *Daily Mail* 10 Apr. 19/3 He has been romancing Antonia for a year.

‖ **romancé** (romaňse), *ppl. a.* Fem. **romancée.** [Fr., f. *romancer* (see ROMANCE *v.*).] Fictionalized, rendered in the form of a novel; *spec.* of a biography.

The fem. *romancée* is used in quot. 1962 because of Fr. *la biographie.*

1938 *Times Lit. Suppl.* 10 Sept. p. v/2 Signor Falta carefully avoids whatever may appear *romancé.* **1962** *Times* 5 July 17/4 The result is a solid, readable biography, slightly *romancée.*

romancing, *vbl. sb.* Add: Also occas. with pronunc. (rōᵘmænsiŋ).

1879 G. MEREDITH *Egoist* II. vii. 156 Oh! Mrs. Montague, that is what the country people call roemancing...

roma·ncingly, *adv. rare.* [f. ROMANCING *ppl. a.* + -LY².] In a romancing manner.

1908 H. JAMES *Spoils of Poynton* p. xii, By just so much would the muse of 'dialogue', most usurping influence of all the romancingly invoked, be routed without ceremony.

Romanée (romane). The name of a vineyard in the commune of Vosne-Romanée in the Côte d'Or department of France used *absol.* to designate the red wine produced there. Also, **Romanée-Conti, Romanée St. Vivant,** similar wines of this commune.

1833 [see *MUSIGNY]. **1845** *Encycl. Metrop.* XXV. 1279/1 The Romanée St. Vivant comes from a vineyard called by that name, at a monastery so styled, where it was brought to perfection by the sons of the church. It is little, if any thing, inferior to Romanée–Cônti. **1858** THACKERAY *Virginians* I. xxix. 226 He..could distinguish between Clos Vougeot and Romanée with remarkable skill. **1904** A. BENNETT *Great Man* xvi. 174 He had gathered..that the greatest of all burgundies was Romanée-Conti. **1920** G. SAINTSBURY *Notes on Cellar-bk.* iv. 55 A Romanée of '87 which was good. **1936** BENTLEY & ALLEN *Trent's Own Case* xii. 143 The Romanée St. Vivant 1904 which was to follow the Meursault. **1976** G. MOFFAT *Over Sea to Death* xv. 175 Maynard.. ordered a second bottle of Romanée-Conti.

Romanesco (rōᵘmăne·sko), *a.* and *sb.* [It.] (Of or pertaining to) a modern dialect spoken in the city of Rome.

1967 P. E. H. DURSTON *Mortissimo* (1968) xvi. 135 The Romanesco accent had been perfect. **1973** M. WEST *Salamander* i. 56, I had friends there: Castiglione, who used to be a great locksmith.., Giuffredi, the poet, who wrote satires in Romanesco which nobody read any more.

romanesque, *a.* (and *sb.*) Add: **4.** Romantic. ? *Obs.*

1799 MALTHUS *Diary* 24 June (1966) 87 He spoke of him [*sc.* Gustavus III] as..a little too romanesque and bizarre. **1850** C. M. YONGE *Kenneth* xx. 237, 'I know he thinks your point of honour rather romanesque,' said Effie, in her French-English. **1869** K. H. DIGBY *Little Low Bushes* 260 All fair things, lovely,..wild, or romanesque.

Romani: see ROMANY³ *sb.* and *a.*

1899 F. H. GROOME *Gypsy Folk-Tales* p. lxxx, *Bakht,* the Rómani word for 'luck' or 'fortune'. **1972** *Guardian* 28 Nov. 14/3 The Gipsy Council is..printing readers..in Romani and English. **1973** *New Society* 6 Dec. 595/1 Joint general secretary of the World Romani Congress. **1976** *Word 1971* XXVII. 357 Romani-English is distinctive because it has developed largely within a closed community.

Romanian, *a.*¹ (Earlier example.)

1841 BORROW *Zincali* II. III. ii. 104 The curiosity of some learned individuals..induced them to collect many words of the Romanian language, as spoken in Germany, Hungary, and England.

Romanian (romōᵘ·niăn), *sb.* and *a.*³ [f. *România,* f. the native name *Român*: see ROUMAN *sb.* and *a.*, and -AN, -IAN. This is now the officially preferred form: cf. ROUMANIAN *sb.* and *a.*, *RUMANIAN *sb.* and *a.*]

A. *sb.* **1.** A native or inhabitant of Romania (now the Socialist Republic of Romania); = ROUMANIAN *sb.* 1, *RUMANIAN *sb.* 1.

1956 S. FISCHER-GALATI *Romania* I. i. 2 One [theory], proposed by the Romanians, is that most of the inhabitants 'took to the mountains' of Transylvania. **1967** P. LATHAM *Romania* IV. 216 The Romanian from ancient times has embellished his surroundings with painting, carving, pottery and weaving. **1969** W. FORWOOD *Romanian Invitation* i. 18 Of their wines, Romanians are rightly boastful. **1971** O. MANNING *Romanian Short Stories* p. viii, The more the Romanians change, the more they are themselves. **1973** *Ann. Reg. 1972* 123 Possibly the replacement of Ulbricht by Honecker and the normalization of relations betwen the two Germanies made the move more acceptable to the Romanians. **1974** *Encycl. Brit. Macropædia* XV. 1053/2 The widespread rich folk costumes and the ancient folklore of Romanians.. provide a reminder of the country's long traditions.

2. The language of Romania, a Romance language which has been exposed to many foreign, esp. Slavonic and Greek, influences; = ROUMANIAN *sb.* 2, *RUMANIAN *sb.* 2.

1954 PEI & GAYNOR *Dict. Linguistics* 187 *Romanian,* a Romance language, the national tongue of Romania, and the native language of approximately 15,000,000 people. **1956** S. FISCHER-GALATI *Romania* I. i. 2 The Balkan Kutso-Vlach people speak a language akin to Romanian. **1969** W. FORWOOD *Romanian Invitation* ii. 25 The name Bucharest,..in Romanian București, evokes the..days of leisurely railway journey across the Ruritanian map of Europe. **1972** M. L. SAMUELS *Linguistic Evol.* vi. 95 Romanian, Bulgarian and Albanian..share a number of features. **1974** K. KATZNER *Lang. of World* (1977) II. 95 Rumanian, more correctly spelled Romanian, is, as its name suggests, one of the Romance languages. **1976** 'D. FLETCHER' *Don't whistle 'Macbeth'* 48 None of us spoke Romanian.

B. *adj.* Of or pertaining to Romania, its inhabitants, or their language; = ROUMANIAN *a.*, *RUMANIAN *a.*

1956 S. FISCHER-GALATI *Romania* I. i. 2 The Romanian nation was formed through the union of the Romans and the native population. **1967** P. LATHAM *Romania* I. 18 The Romanian Black Sea coast faces east. **1969** W. FORWOOD *Romanian Invitation* i. 17 The pleasures of the Romanian kitchen are very special. **1971** O. MANNING *Romanian Short Stories* p. ix, Romanian music is either gypsy music or peasant music. **1973** *Ann. Reg. 1972* 122 It was a relatively inward-looking year for the Romanian Communist Government and its leader. **1976** P. CLABBURN *Needleworker's Dict.* 228/1 Romanian stitch has one cross at a slight angle, romanian couching has several crosses at the same angle. **1979** *Records & Recording* Aug. 61/2 The distinguished Romanian soprano sings the part quite beautifully.

Romanichal: see *ROMANY³ 3 b.

Romanicist (romæ·nĭsist). [f. ROMANIC *a.* (*sb.*) + -IST.] A student of Romance (sense 1); a scholar versed in Romance languages or literature.

1930 K. MALONE in *Studies in Honor of H. Collitz* 328 *Romanicist*..seems to be the only word that fits the case [of the Romance philologist]. **1937** J. ORR tr. *Iordan's Introd. Romance Linguistics* iv. 279 Ferdinand de Saussure..was an Indo-Europeanist, not a Romanicist. **1957** *Archivum Linguisticum* IX. 90 From the Romanicist's viewpoint.

‖ **romanità** (romanitā·). Also with capital initial. [It., f. next.] **a.** = next. **b.** The spirit or influence of the central Roman authorities of the Roman Catholic Church; acceptance of papal policy.

1927 *Observer* 19 June 13/1 He [*sc.* Machiavelli] was too great a realist for his intellect to suffer imprisonment by humanist admiration for Rome, or, as we call it today, *romanità.* **1963** *Economist* 7 Dec. 1007/2 The assertion of collegial status for the bishops has been advanced jointly with a demand that the Curia should be internationalised... Yet internationalisation by itself is secondary. Indeed, it might sharpen the existing reasons for complaint: foreigners have been known to succumb to *Romanita*; they lack the engaging and emollient Italian supposition that laws are, on the whole, unlikely to be obeyed.

‖ **romanitas** (romā·nitas, romæ·nitās). Also with capital initial. [late L.] The spirit or ideals of ancient Rome; Romanism.

1947 *Horizon* Feb. 84 The *romanitas* upon which Europe was founded. **1961** *Listener* 16 Nov. 814/1 The natural pride in *Romanitas* which has passed into his [*sc.* Pope Leo I's] thinking from secular tradition. **1975** *Times Lit. Suppl.* 25 Apr. 464/4 Amid the decline and fall of a civilization to which he owed both his religion and his *romanitas,* St Augustine inscribed..the charter of an enduring Christian culture. **1977** *History* LXII. 174 One would wish to know..the extent to which there remained a concept of *romanitas* in Celtic Britain.

romanization. 4. (Further examples.)

1925 C. H. BREWITT-TAYLOR *San Kuo* I. p. ii, The Wade system of romanisation, in which the vowels are Italian, has been used. **1934** *Bull. Inst. Hist. & Philol. Acad. Sinica* IV, IV. 387 The French system of romanization of Chinese. **1961** *Amer. Speech* XXXVI. III. 177 Chang Ker Chiu gives both characters and the romanization ₒ*in*—'*yan* for 'craving for tobacco or opium'. **1963** [see *PINYIN]. **1973** *Lancet* 14 July 78/1 Even this difficulty is compounded by the fact that there are about a dozen systems of romanization (e.g., the same point may be described as Ho-ku, He-gu, or Ro-Kou). **1975** *Daily Colonist* (Victoria, B.C.) 22 Aug. 5/1 China is preparing to move into..romanization of the written Chinese language.

Ro·manness. [-NESS.] The quality of being influenced by Rome or by Roman Catholicism.

1959 *Catholic Times* 20 Mar. 5/4 His theory that the Welsh were profoundly conscious of their Roman-ness.

Roman-nosed, *a.* Add: (Further example.) Hence **Ro·man-nosedness** (*nonce*).

1912 J. S. HUXLEY *Individual in Animal Kingdom* iii. 80 In all Metazoa there is, before and during the sexual process, a shuffling and recombination of the chromosomes of the nucleus—those bodies which taken together appear to determine the characteristics of the offspring, or at least those which mark it off from others of the same species,—whether it shall be tall or short, fair or dark, chubby or lanky, tip-tilted or Roman-nosed. **1912** D. H. LAWRENCE *Let.* 24 Dec. (1932) 87 If it's destined to have a snub nose, it's sheer waste of time to harass the poor brat into Roman-nosedness.

Romano (romā·no). [It., = Roman.] In full *Romano cheese.* A strong-tasting hard cheese, orig. made in Italy.

1908 DOANE & LAWSON *Varieties of Cheese* 39 The Formaggio Pecorini are the sheep's-milk cheeses made in Italy... The most common cheese of this sort is the one designated Cacio Pecorino Romano, or merely Romano. *Ibid.*, In making Romano cheese the milk is heated to 100° F. and coagulated by rennet in fifteen minutes. **1918** J. L. SAMMIS *Decker's Cheese Making* (ed. 6) xxx. 218 *Romano.* This is usually made from skim milk [in America]. **1949** N. STANDEN *Art of Cheese Cooking* 30 Romano, in Italy, used to be made from sheep's milk which gave it a pungent flavor. In this country, though, it's made from cow's milk and is correspondingly milder. **1955** R. C. BROWN *Compl. Bk. Cheeses* iii. 26 Romano is not as expensive as Parmesan. **1966** MARQUIS & HASKELL *Cheese Bk.* II. 64 The black-rinded and..grainy-looking Romano..is much stronger than Parmesan. **1976** N. THORNBURG *Cutter & Bone* viii. 199, I have..some ridiculously expensive Romano cheese compliments of George.

Romano-. Add: Now usu. with pronunc. (romā·no). Also, *Romano-British* (earlier and later examples), *-Briton, -canonical, -cosmopolitan, -Egyptian, -Germanic* (later example), *-Hellenistic, -Saxon, -Visigothic.*

1847 J. Y. AKERMAN (*title*) An archaeological index to remains of antiquities of the Celtic, Romano-British and Anglo-Saxon periods. **1963** *Times* 21 Feb. 5/7 Caerwent was the only fully developed Romano-British town in Wales. **1975** J. G. EVANS *Environment Early Man Brit. Isles* vi. 157 There was some colonization by the Belgae and Romano-British people of areas not previously taken up. **1896** A. H. KEANE *Ethnol.* II. xiv. 398 The Teutons merged everywhere in diverse proportions with the Romano-Britons. **1956** AUDEN *Old Man's Road,* So thought (I think) the last Romano-Briton. **1909** WEBSTER, Romano-canonical. **1974** A. WATSON *Legal Transplants* vii. 45 Some Roman law was creeping in primarily as a result of the acceptance of rules of romano-canonical procedure. **1923** R. G. COLLINGWOOD *Roman Britain* iii. 68 Houses..never losing their Celtic stamp or becoming Romano-cosmopolitan instead of Romano-British. **1934** WEBSTER, Romano-Egyptian. **1964** W. L. GOODMAN *Hist. Woodworking Tools* 33 Most of the adzes..appear to be of a similar pattern to the Romano-Egyptian adze described earlier. **1980** *Jrnl. R. Soc. Arts* July 534/2 In the Romano-Germanic tomb of a little girl, was found a decorated goose egg. **1972** D. DAKIN *Unification of Greece* i. 5 Many Byzantines began to see themselves not as heirs to the Romano-Hellenistic traditions of the West but as the successors of ancient Hellas. **1956** J. N. L. MYRES in D. B. Harden *Dark-Age Brit.* 16 (*heading*) Romano-Saxon pottery. **1970** J. L. SHNEIDMAN *Rise of Aragonese-Catalan Empire* I. v. 154 In the city of Urgel..during the period of Arab domination the bishop had..governed the city under the Romano-Visigothic law called the *Fuero Juzgo.*

Romanowsky (rōᵘmǣnǫ·fski). *Histology.* Also **-ofsky, -ovski, -ovsky.** The name of Dmitriy Leonidovitch *Romanowsky* (1861–1921), Russian physician, used *attrib.*, in *Comb.*, and in the possessive to designate a stain and staining technique devised by him, and a class of derived stains and techniques, used for the detection of parasites in blood.

1903 *Brit. Med. Jrnl.* 30 May 1253/1, I was struck by the curious appearance..of small round or oval bodies... On staining them by Romanowsky's method, they were found to possess a quantity of chromatin, of a very definite and regular shape, which clearly differentiated them from blood plates or possible nuclear detritus. *Ibid.* 28 Nov. 1401/1 The deep red of the Romanowsky-stained chromatin of the bodies is represented by black in the drawings. **1906** *Boston Med. & Surg. Jrnl.* CLIV. 643/1 A staining fluid, devised by me for use in the staining of blood films according to the method of Leishman, which gives the so-called Romanofsky polychrome staining. **1930** [see *ORTHOCHROMATIC *a.* 2]. **1947** *Ann. Rev. Microbiol.* I. 48 They compared their findings made in this way with parallel studies employing the ordinary technics of smears stained with Romanowsky's stain. **1960** E. GURR *Encycl. Microsc. Stains* i. 267 The azurs 1, A, B and C, and methylene violet..are present in varying degrees in the Romanowsky type of stains. The latter consists of methylene blue and its oxidation products in combination with eosin. **1970** J. C. SWARTZWELDER et al. in J. E. Blair et al. *Man. Clin. Microbiol.* xlix. 440/1 Stained with Giemsa or some other Romanowski dye. **1978** *Nature* 22 June 595/1 The cytoplasm stains a pale blue with Romanovsky stains, and the single nucleus..a reddish-purple.

Romansh, *sb.* and *a.* Add: Also *α.* **Romantsch.** *β.* **Rumansch.** (Further examples.) Also used of other Rhæto-Romance dialects and of this group of dialects as a whole.

1946 *Archit. Rev.* C. 58/1 It is for us a matter of course that the Alemanic part of the country would speak German, the French Swiss part French,..and the Rhaetian districts Romansch, that, for instance, the Grisons, which comprise districts speaking German, Italian and Romansch, should publish their decrees in all three languages. **1969** *Language* XLV. 185 To counter Italian nationalist claims, Romansh was officially established as the fourth national language of Switzerland in 1939. **1970** *Times Lit. Suppl.* 8 Jan. 40/2 He is fully conversant with the five national tongues—French, Spanish, Portuguese, Italian and Rumanian—and with their five regional varieties—Occitanian or Provencal.. Catalan..Dalmatian..Rumansch or Rhaetian (now strictly West Rhaetian, for that alone has evolved a recognized written language), and Sardinian. **1971** *Language* XLVII. 797 (*heading*) Targets and paradigmatic borrowing in Romantsch.

b. (Further examples.)

In quot. 1920 referring to an ethnic group.

1880 [see *LADIN]. **1920** *Q. Rev.* Apr. 443 Its population is not of German, but of Allemanic race, the only exception being that part which is of Romantsch origin. **1969** [see *RHÆTO-ROMANCE].

romantic, *a.* and *sb.* Add: **A.** *adj.* **1. c.** Of a work of modern literature, etc.: having romance as its subject; treating of a love affair.

1960 R. REES *For Love or Money* ii. 30 The doctrine of D. H. Lawrence's *Fantasia of the Unconscious*: that sexual passion, unrelated to the religious impulse..leads to sterility and death—as in *Anna Karenina*, in *Carmen*, and in the greater part of European 'romantic' literature. **1977** B. PYM *Quartet in Autumn* i. 3 Unable to find what she needed in 'romantic' novels, Letty had turned to biographies of which there was no dearth. **1981** S. RADLEY *Chief Inspector's Daughter* i. 15, I get depressed because I write romantic fiction instead of straight novels.

4. b. (Earlier and further examples.) Also of ballet (see quot. 1957). Also, of, pertaining to, or characteristic of romanticism in literature, etc.

1812 H. C. ROBINSON *Jrnl.* 19 May in E. J. Morley *Henry Crabb Robinson on Bks.* (1938) I. 84 We proceeded to Coleridge's first lecture... He spoke of religion, the spirit of chivalry,.. and a classification of poetry into ancient and romantic. **1813** *Edin. Rev.* Oct. 206 The poetry of the Spanish peninsula seems to have been more romantic and less subject to classical bondage than that of any other part of Europe. **1814** W. TAYLOR in *Monthly Rev.* Apr. 364 The eleventh [chapter] divides European poetry into two schools, the classical, and the romantic. **1833** W. MAGINN in *Fraser's Mag.* VIII. 64 'The noticeable man [*sc.* Coleridge] with large grey eyes'—the worthy old Platonist—the founder of the romantic school of poetry. **1908** P. E. MORE *Shelburne Ess.* 5th Ser. 119 Like Friedrich Schlegel, he indulges in the romantic irony of smiling down upon himself and walking through life like a *Doppelgänger*. **1928** [see *CLASSICAL *a.* 6 d]. **1930** W. EMPSON *Seven Types of Ambiguity* i. 27 Before the Romantic Revival the possibilities of not growing up had never been exploited so far as to become a subject for popular anxiety. **1937** D. BUSH *Mythology & Romantic Trad. in Eng. Poetry* p. xiii, The effect of both the romantic and the industrial movements was to make the artist, if not an anti-social figure, at any rate an isolated one. **1938** *Oxf. Compan. Mus.* 810/1 By the 'Romantic School' in music is meant the group of active spirits in that movement which began in Germany with Weber (born 1786)... Or it can be carried back as far as Schubert (born 1797) and Beethoven (born 1770). **1951** F. KERMODE *Romantic Image* vii. 132 The next step forward in Romantic aesthetic depended upon a new theory of language. **1957** G. B. L. WILSON *Penguin Dict. Ballet* 230 *Romantic ballet*, used, somewhat narrowly, to describe the ballets produced during the period of the Romantic revival in literature in the early nineteenth century, or roughly from 1830–1850, taking as their theme the odyssey of mortal man in love with some female spirit of the air or water or with some maiden risen from her tomb... The dividing line is a slender one, i.e. in the romantic ballet the accent is on colour or mood rather than form and design which is predominant in the classical ballet. **1959** F. GADAN et al. *Dict. Mod. Ballet* 329/1 Several other great Romantic dancers appeared as La Sylphide. **1960** BECKSON & GANZ *Reader's Guide Lit. Terms* (1961) 108 Romantic irony occurs when a writer builds up a serious emotional tone and then deliberately breaks it and laughs at his own solemnity. **1977** J. A. CUDDON *Dict. Lit. Terms* 573 *Romantic revival*, a term loosely applied to a movement in European literature (and other arts) during the last quarter of the 18th c. and the first twenty or thirty years of the 19th c.

5. (Further examples.)

The examples given here, illustrating the collocation of the adjective with *love, lover, friendship*, and the like, provide evidence of the emergence of its common present-day use to convey the idealistic character or quality of a love affair. Cf. *ROMANCE *sb.* 5 a, b.

1728 F. HUTCHESON *Ess. Passions* I. iv. 94 A Romantick Lover has..no Notion of Life without his Mistress, all Virtue and Merit are summed up in his inviolable Fidelity. **1754** R. BERENGER in *World* 4 July 474, I know several unmarried ladies, who in all probability had been ..good wives and..mothers, if their imaginations had not been early perverted with the chimerical ideas of romantic love,..upon which principle, a footman may as well be the hero as his master. **1769** J. USHER *Clio* (ed. 2) 82 Innocent and virtuous love..inspires us with heroic sentiments,..a contempt of life, a boldness for enterprize, chastity, and purity of sentiment... People whose breasts are dulled with vice, or stupified by nature, call this passion romantic love; but when it was the mode, it was the diagnostic of a virtuous age. **1778** S. TIGHE *Let.* 2 Apr. in G. H. Bell *Hamwood Papers* (1930) 27 There were no gentlemen concerned, nor does it appear to be anything more than a scheme of Romantic Friendship. **1806** BYRON *Fugitive Pieces* 23 And friendships were form'd, too romantic to last. **1858** LYTTON *What will he do with It?* (1859) III. VII. xiv. 135 (*heading*) Romantic Love pathologically regarded by Frank Vance and Alban Morley. **1866** C. M. YONGE *Dove in Eagle's Nest* II. ii. 41 Good substantial wedded affection was not lacking, but romantic love was thought an unnecessary preliminary, and found a vent in extravagant adoration not always in reputable quarters. **1942** T. BAILEY *Pink Camellia* vii. 50 The lovemaking was of the purely romantic kind, for Cecily would have no other. **1945** *New Statesman* 23 June 408/3 The book opens with a tale of romantic friendship at Oxford in the years following the first great war. **1966** *Listener* 7 Apr. 509/3 Nowadays, however, educated young West Africans have discovered the alleged virtues of romantic love. They stress the idea of marriage being a true union of husband and wife as well as an economic partnership. Love will be the most important thing when they marry. **1971** E. MAVOR *Ladies of Llangollen* v. 96 The strange ambivalence of the pre-Freudian romantic friendships. **1975** J. PLAMENATZ *Karl Marx's Philos. of Man* xiv. 400 The idea of romantic love has flourished in the same kind of society as the small family. Indeed, this family is quite often seen as the creature of romantic love: it is set up by a man and a woman who come to love one another and who choose each other as life partners. **1978** *Morecambe Guardian* 14 Mar. 17/2 Partnerships flourish. A romantic attachment is possible, but do not take it too seriously.

B. *sb.* **2.** (Earlier and further examples.) Also, a composer of romantic music.

1827 CARLYLE in C. E. Norton *Two Notebks. of T. Carlyle* (1898) 111 Grossi..has written a new Epic... Grossi is a Romantic. **1927** R. H. WILENSKI *Mod. Movement in Art* 30 Nineteenth-century romantics deliberately left out all the features which the admirers of classical painting were accustomed to regard as indispensable to art. **1932** W. B. YEATS *Words for Music* 11 We were the last romantics, chose for theme Traditional sanctity and loveliness. **1933** A. DAVIDSON tr. *Praz's Romantic Agony* 4 The thirst for the infinite..animates the lines of the Romantics. **1938** *Oxf. Compan. Mus.* 113/1 Despite their sheer musical beauty, his [*sc.* Brahms's] compositions are strongly charged with what may be called an extra-musical emotion; hence the classification of their composer as a romantic. **1960** A. O. LOVEJOY in M. H. Abrams *Eng. Romantic Poets* 15 To be unsophisticated, to revert to the mental state of 'simple Indian swains', was the least of the ambitions of a German Romantic... The greatness of Shakespeare, in the eyes of *these* Romantics, lay in his Universalität. **1961** C. CLUTTON in A. Baines *Mus. Instruments* ii. 66 The [organ] works of Liszt and Franck,..and of such late romantics as Reger, Jongen, and Elgar, rely upon a very large instrument. **1966** H. G. SCHENK *Mind of European Romantics* i. 6 Rationalism was attacked by the Romantics not on the grounds that the intellectual results yielded by it were false, but rather on the grounds that they were inadequate. **1977** *Times* 18 Oct. 24/9 White tuxedos are occasionally supplied to shipboard romantics.

roma·ntic, *v.* [f. the adj.] *trans.* = ROMANTICIZE *v.* 1. Also with *up*.

1969 G. LYALL *Venus with Pistol* xxii. 137 It was a fairly flat scene of somewhere in Venice, a bit romanticked up. **1972** *Guardian* 8 June 2/1 'Elizabeth R' starts a new run if you like your history romanticked.

roma·nticalism. *rare.* [f. ROMANTICAL *a.* + -ISM.] = ROMANTICALITY.

1922 W. J. LOCKE *Tale of Triona* xiii. 142 She..was driven by she knew not what idiot romanticalism into the grey worries of wifehood and motherhood.

romantically, *adv.* Add: **3.** *Comb.*, as *romantically-minded* adj.

1952 'M. COST' *Hour Awaits* 227 It appears that this Professor..is romantically minded. **1965** HOUSE & STOREY *Lett. C. Dickens* I. p. xxi, The kind suggested here by the romantically-minded Kate.

romanticism. 3. (Earlier and further examples.)

1823 *New Monthly Mag.* IX. 175/2 The French Academy ..has determined never to receive within its bosom any one polluted by the dramatic heresy of romanticism. **1830** [see *CLASSICISM 1]. **1934** C. LAMBERT *Music Ho!* II. 118 A title like the *Pathetic Symphony* is looked on as an example of decadent romanticism. **1937** D. BUSH *Mythol. & Romantic Trad. in Eng. Poetry* xii. 398 In various ways and for various reasons the broad deep stream of romanticism had run thin. **1941** P. H. LANG *Music in Western Civilization* xv. 746 In Beethoven classicism became romantic, and in Schubert romanticism became classic. **1957** F. KERMODE *Romantic Image* viii. 145 Romanticism is just the new disease at the stage of mania. **1960** A. O. LOVEJOY in M. H. Abrams *Eng. Romantic Poets* 5 The offspring with which Romanticism is credited are as strangely assorted as its attributes and its ancestors. **1978** *Times Lit. Suppl.* 25 Aug. 944/5 This..biography has its interest..as a portrait of a very unhappy man whom Romanticism destroyed.

romanticist. Add: **1.** (Earlier example.) Also in music.

1827 CARLYLE in *Edin. Rev.* XLVI. 325 Their grand controversy, so hotly urged, between the Classicists and Romanticists..shows us sufficiently what spirit is at work in that long stagnant literature. **1883** GROVE *Dict. Mus.* III. 152/2 We cannot acquit the younger romanticists of the charge of an excessive realism. **1938** *Oxf. Compan. Mus.* 810/1 It is..sometimes considered that the classical element..in the work of those two [*sc.* Schubert and Beethoven] was strong enough to rank them as the last of the Classicists rather than as the first of the Romanticists. **1941** P. H. LANG *Music in Western Civilization* xv. 746 If Weber, Chopin, and Schumann are accepted as full-blooded romanticists, we..cannot enrol the composer of the *Unfinished Symphony*..in their company. **1970** W. APEL *Harvard Dict. Mus.* (ed. 2) 738/1 These traits need not imply that nonromantic music lacks emotional appeal. Nor does it mean that the romanticists were not form-conscious.

romanticize, *v.* Add: Hence **roma:nticiza·tion; roma·nticizing** *vbl. sb.*

1899 *Speaker* 14 Apr. 424/2 Enlivened by champagne and some grotesque romanticising on the part of the amorous Duchess. **1935** *Mind* XLIV. 95 His [*sc.* Nietzsche's] 'Dionysus philosophy' is a typically Germanic brutalisation, exaggeration, romanticisation of something borrowed. **1968** G. ASHE *Quest for Arthur's Britain* i. 28 Leland's romanticisation of Henry VIII was elaborately transferred to Elizabeth by Edmund Spenser.

roma·nticky, *a. rare.* [f. ROMANTIC *a.* + -Y[1].] Of a romantic character.

1912 D. H. LAWRENCE *Let.* ?5 Nov. (1962) I. 154, I want to read something romanticky—feel like it.

romanticness. (Later example.)

1968 H. KONINGSBERGER *Revolutionary* v. 13 The romanticness of..tears shed by women in Turgenev.

Romantsch, var. ROMANSH *sb.* and *a.* in Dict. and Suppl.

Romany[3]. Add: **3. b.** Special Combs., as **Romany chal, Romanichal** [CHAL], a (male) gypsy; **Romany chi** (tʃəi) [Romany *chai* girl], a gypsy girl; **Romany rye** [*RYE *sb.*[3]], a man, not a gypsy, who associates with gypsies.

1843 BORROW *Zincali* (ed. 2) I. 32 Those were brave times for the Rommany chals. **1851** [see GORGIO]. **1953** J. DE B. LEVY *As Gypsies Wander* i. 38 His pleasure was extreme when he first heard that non-Gypsy people had written poems in praise of *Romanichals*. **1960** G. E. C. WEBB *Gypsies* i. 19 Whoever heard of a *gorgio* coming up to a *Romanichal* and greeting him with words of the old language? **1857** Romany chi [see GORGIO]. **1876** [see CHAL]. **1933** K. BERCOVICI (*title*) The Romany chai. **1851** BORROW *Lavengro* II. xxvi. 236 Here the Gypsy gemman bee, With his Roman jib and his rome and dree—Rome and dree, rum and dry Rally round the Rommany Rye. **1857** —— *Romany Rye* II. ix. 113 'I'll bet a crown,' said the jockey, 'that you be the young chap what certain folks call "The Romany Rye".' **1915** F. CUTTRISS *Romany Life* xi. 242 He introduced me as a Romany Rye. **1929** K. BERCOVICI *Story of Gypsies* x. 231 What is most astounding..is the mention made of the natives of England of good families who were found in the company of these Gypsies... Who could they be, these gentlemen, these first Romany ryes? **1973** *Cassell's Encycl. World Lit.* (rev. ed.) I. 489/1 The Gypsy Lore Society in Liverpool, which was founded by the American Romany Rye Charles Godfrey Leland.

romanza. Restrict † *Obs.* to sense in Dict. and add: ‖ **2.** *Mus.* [a. It., Sp. *romanza*.] Pronunc. (roma·nză); in Sp. contexts also (romā·nþă). A romantic song or melody; a lyrical piece of music; = ROMANCE *sb.* 4 b.

1834 *Chambers's Edin. Jrnl.* III. 110/2 Another youth.. begins singing a Spanish romanza. **1938** *Oxf Compan. Mus.* 810/2 *Romanza*.., a song or song-like instrumental composition. **1970** J. BLADES *Percussion Instruments* x. 196 Alexander Goehr scores for the lion's roar in his *Romanza for 'cello and orchestra* (1968). **1975** *New Yorker* 16 June 97/3 Then the romanza begins.

‖ **romanze** (roma·ntsə). *Mus.* Pl. **romanzen.** [Ger., = romance.] A composition of a tender or lyrical character; *spec.* a slow, romantic instrumental piece or movement. Cf. prec. and ROMANCE *sb.* 4 b.

1883 GROVE *Dict Mus.* III. 147/2 The Romanze in Mozart's D minor PF. Concerto differs..from the slow movements of his other Concertos in the extremely tender and delicate character of its expression. **1947** A. EINSTEIN *Mus. Romantic Era* xi. 130 It joins together five movements—Introduction, Allegro, Romanze, Scherzo, and Finale—into an uninterrupted whole. **1970** W. APEL *Harvard Dict. Mus.* (ed. 2) 736/2 The German *Romanze* is primarily an instrumental composition of a lyrical character. *Ibid.*, Vocal *Romanzen* occur mostly in operas.

Romary (rōᵘ·māri). [f. the name of the manufacturer.] The proprietary name of a brand of biscuits.

1926–7 *Army & Navy Stores Catal.* 8/2 Biscuits.. Romary Ginger Nuts. **1929** *Trade Marks Jrnl.* 4 Dec. 2029 Romary's... Biscuits. A. Romary & Company, Limited,..Tunbridge Wells, Kent; manufacturers. **1934** E. BOWEN *Cat Jumps* 192 The Romary biscuits. **1977** P. HARCOURT *At High Risk* I. viii. 101 His secretary.. placed beside me a plate of Romary biscuits.

Romayne, obs. f. ROMAN. For 'obs.' read 'obs. exc. as applied to carving, etc. with a motif of heads in medallions'. Pronunc. (romē̆i·n). (Later examples.)

1904 P. MACQUOID *Hist. Eng. Furnit.* iii. 50 Chair.. decorated..with medallioned heads surmounted by conventional ornament in the Italian manner, and which in this century obtained the name 'Romayne Work'. **1955** R. FASTNEDGE *Eng. Furnit. Styles* 287 *Romayne carving*, decorative *motifs* taking the form of small profile heads in medallions, introduced in the early sixteenth century. **1961** *Times* 2 Dec. 11/7 Small objects, carved with Romayne heads. **1969** E. H. PINTO *Treen* 196/1 The first two snuff boxes of this type, carved with 'Romayne heads'..were very worn and I thought that they were genuinely mid or late 16th-century. **1975** *Oxf. Compan. Decorative Arts* 672/2 *Romayne work*, contemporary term for a decorative motif consisting of small profile-heads in medallions carved on furniture and panelling. This form of decoration was introduced into England from Italy in the time of Henry VIII and was often combined with Tudor roses and traditional Gothic tracery or linenfold.

romazi, var. *ROMAJI.

Romberg (rǫ·mbɜ̄ɪg). *Med.* The name of Moritz Heinrich *Romberg* (1795–1873), German physician, used in the possessive, *attrib.*, and *absol.* to designate (*a*) the test of requiring a patient to stand with feet together and eyes closed, and (*b*) the sign or symptom, diagnostic of ataxia, shown by a patient who then sways or falls (described by Romberg in *Lehrb. d. Nervenkrankheiten des Menschen* (1846) I. 795).

1885 *Jrnl. Nervous & Mental Dis.* XII. 354 'Romberg's symptom'—*i.e.* inability to stand with the eyes shut and the feet together—is not always present. *Ibid.* 355 'The Romberg symptom'. **1932** *Practitioners Libr. Med. & Surg.* II. xxiii. 809 The Romberg test for static ataxia is carried out by having the patient stand with heels and toes together with open eyes and then with closed eyes. The tendency to sway appreciably with the eyes shut constitutes a positive Romberg. **1961** *Lancet* 9 Sept. 569/1 Both legs were slightly weak, and Romberg's sign was positive. **1977** *Ibid.* 10 Dec. 1228/2 Neurological examination revealed a vertical gaze palsy,..and a tendency to fall backwards on Romberg's test.

Rome, *sb.* Add: **1. b.**

(*a*) (Earlier and later examples.)

1545 R. TAVERNER tr. *Erasmus's Adages* sig. D 1ᵛ Ye may use this prouerbe when ye wyll signyfye that one daye..is not ynoughe for..acheuynge..a greate matter ..Rome was not buylt in one daye. **1822** SCOTT *Fortunes of Nigel* II. x. 237 Rome was not built in a day—you cannot become used to your court-suit in a month's time. **1849** C. BRONTË *Shirley* I. v. 123 'As Rome,' it was suggested, 'had not been built in a day, so neither had mademoiselle Gérard Moore's education been completed in a week.' **1873** 'F. FERN' *Memorial Vol.* 347 Rome wasn't built in a day;—cooks can't be manufactured in a minute. **1901** S. LANE-POOLE *Sir H. Parkes* xvii. 316 The Japanese..went too fast and fell into grave commercial, monetary, and administrative troubles. Neither Rome nor New Japan could be built in a day. **1941** P. CHEYNEY *Trap for Bellamy* iv. 58 Bellamy said: 'Life is what you make it. Rome wasn't built in a day.' **1950** T. WILLIAMS *Roman Spring of Mrs. Stone* I. 34 Patience, said the Contessa. Rome was not built in a day!

(*b*) (Later examples.)

1976 N. THORNBURG *Cutter & Bone* i. 22 'When in Rome,' he said finally, shuddering. **1977** *Rolling Stone* 21 Apr. 73/3 He had a point—when in Rome and all that—but it was a point he was not exactly loath to make.

(*d*) *c* **1380** CHAUCER *Troilus & Criseyde* (1894) II. 36 For every wight which that to Rome went, Halt nat o path, or alwey o manere. *c* **1391** —— *Astrolabe* (1872) Prol. 29 Ryht as diuerse pathes leden diuerse folk the rihte wey to Rome. **1806** R. THOMSON tr. *La Fontaine's Fables* IV. XII. xxiv. 110 Three pious men, having one end in view, Their way to heaven with equal zeal pursue.— Three diff'rent roads the three concurrents chose, All roads alike conduct to Rome...—So those Thought they might part, and yet get on secure. **1861** C. READE *Cloister & Hearth* I. xxiv. 270 All roads take to Rome. **1872** W. BLACK *Strange Adv. Phaeton* vi. 111 'Surely the road to Oxford is easy to find.' 'It is,' I say to her. 'For you know all roads lead to Rome, and they say that Oxford is half-way to Rome—*argal*—.' But knowing what effect this reference to her theological sympathies was likely to have on Tita, I thought it prudent to send the horses on. **1911** J. A. THOMSON *Introd. Sci.* iii. 63 All roads lead to Rome, and he must be a bold man who will declare any of Nature's beckonings to be unworthy of attention. **1912** J. S. HUXLEY *Individual in Animal Kingdom* vi. 154 All roads lead to Rome: and even animal individuality throws a ray on human problems.

3. c. Special Comb.: **Rome-Berlin axis** [*AXIS¹ 4 b], the association formed in 1936 between Fascist Italy and National Socialist Germany.

1936 [see *AXIS¹ 4 b]. **1938** E. AMBLER *Cause for Alarm* viii. 128 The Rome-Berlin axis is one of the most effective principles of European power-politics that has ever been stated. **1939** 'G. ORWELL' *Coming up for Air* III. i. 182 Rubber truncheons, Rome-Berlin axis, Popular Front. **1976** S. HYNES *Auden Generation* vii. 193, 1936 is the peripeteia, the point where the action turned:..the Rome-Berlin Axis was formed [etc.].

roméite (rōᵘ·meˌəit). *Min.* Also **romeite.** [f. ROME(INE + -ITE¹.] An antimonate of calcium, $Ca_2Sb_2O_7$ (usu. also containing other elements esp. iron or titanium), which occurs as yellow or yellow-brown octahedral crystals. Formerly known as *roméine.*

[**1850** J. D. DANA *Syst. Min.* (ed. 3) 416 (*heading*) Romeine, *Damour*,..Romeit.] **1868** *Ibid.* (ed. 5) 547 Romeite was found by B. de Lom at St. Marcel in Piedmont. **1916** *Bull. U.S. Geol. Survey* No. 610. 96 The Brazilian so-called atopite is..identical with the romeite from Italy. **1953** *Mineral Mag.* XXX. 101 The definition of stibiconite..includes the mineral roméite, which has long been recognized as a calcium antimonate. **1968** I. KOSTOV *Mineral.* II. 265 Roméite and hydrocervantite.. have adsorbed water.

Romeo (rōᵘ·mio). [Name of the hero of Shakespeare's tragedy *Romeo and Juliet.*]

1. A lover, a passionate admirer; a seducer, a habitual pursuer of women. Also *attrib.*

1766 C. ANSTEY *New Bath Guide* ix. 59 May I oft my Romeo meet, Oft enjoy his Converse sweet. **1867** TROLLOPE *Claverings* I. iii. 35 He has come out so strong in the Romeo line... We shall have him under your bedroom window with a guitar. **1917** E. O'NEILL *Long Voyage Home* in *Smart Set* Oct. 56/2 *Driscoll*..Shut up, ye Rooshan baboon! A foine Romeo you'd make in your condishun. **1942** *Sun* (Baltimore) 26 Mar. 10/2, I think from the way I so often see his eyes cast far up and around through the open spaces that he is also playing a bit of Romeo. **1974** G. MITCHELL *Javelin for Jonah* iii. 48 Henry..locked up the mansion to keep out any prospective Romeos who might fancy a visit to the women students' rooms. **1976** *Leicester Chron.* 26 Nov. 2/4 He's known as the studio's resident Romeo, with a social life and a string of girlfriends which must be exhausting rather than exhilarating.

2. (With small initial.) Also *romeo slipper.* A type of high slipper, now only for men, usu. made of felt and with elasticated gores. *U.S.*

1895 *Montgomery Ward Catal.* Spring & Summer 514/2 Men's leather sole Romeo... This slipper is made of one piece of black felt. *Ibid.* 514/3 Ladies' Romeo... Made of toilet felt, fur trimmed. **1898** *Morse & Rogers Money Saver* Oct. 17 (Advt.), Men's romeo slippers. Don't be out of slippers. Romeos are becoming more and more popular. **1924** E. FERBER *Show Boat* i. 5 Peeping..around this, the baffled eye could just glimpse oddments and elegancies such as..a pair of scuffed tan kid bedroom slippers (men's) of the sort known as romeos. **1952** R. BISSELL *Monongahela* xix. 205 While sitting on the bunk pulling on your romeos you wonder what side of the family this madness comes from that makes you live like this.

3. *Romeo and Juliet*: Anglicization of Sp. *Romeo y Julieta*, the proprietary name of a Havana cigar. (Also semi-Anglicized as *Romeo and Julieta, Romeo y Juliet.*) Also *attrib.*

1904 *Trade Marks Jrnl.* 7 Sept. 1105 Romeo y Julieta... Tobacco, cigars, cigarettes and snuff. Rodriguez Argüelles & Co.,..Havana, Cuba; cigar manufacturers. **1907** *Yesterday's Shopping* (1969) 64/2 *Havana cigars...* 'Romeo and Julieta'. **1945** A. HUXLEY *Time must have a Stop* v. 51 His Uncle Eustace lighted the massive Romeo and Juliet. **1957** J. OSBORNE *Entertainer* II. 43 Gave me a box of Romeo and Juliet cigars. **1966** *Guardian* 19 Mar. 6/6 The host had his mouth full of Romeo y Juliet cigar. *Ibid.* 12 Oct. 5/5 One could always finish with a cigar; say Romeo y Julieta, coronas, 660s the hundred, 5½ inches long.

romer (rōᵘ·məɹ). Also **Romer.** [Named after Carrol *Romer* (1883–1951), British barrister, who invented it.] A small piece of plastic or card with scales along two edges meeting at a right angle, or (if transparent) bearing a grid, used for measuring the map reference of a point within the grid printed on a map.

1933 *Geogr. Jrnl.* LXXXII. 47 This Romer, as it was called after the gentleman who invented it. **1943** F. F. CROSSLEY *Map Reading* iii. 15 In order to facilitate the estimation of the last figure of the reference it is useful to construct a Romer... The sides of the Romer are subdivided into tenths. **1960** S. TURNER *Rallying* 38 The cross-roads might thus be given as 25401464. For plotting of this accuracy a romer is necessary. **1963** P. DRACKETT *Motor Rallying* iii. 41 Lining up the Romer so that one straight edge of the rectangle is in line with 386 and the straight edge meeting it is in line with 443, the point of bisection gives the place referred to. **1969** G. C. DICKINSON *Maps & Air Photographs* viii. 114 Of course a different romer is needed for each scale. **1975** J. B. HARLEY *O.S. Maps* ii. 24 A point..can be indicated still more closely by estimating the tenths of the appropriate grid square either by eye or by means of a romer.

römerite, var. *ROEMERITE.

Romeward, *adv.* and *a.* Add: **3. b.** Directed towards or facing the city of Rome.

1850 J. MILEY *Hist. Papal States* I. 6 Not less so on the Adriatic side of the Apennines than on the Romeward side. **1979** *London Rev. Bks.* 25 Oct. 5/3 Salim's flight to London can be compared..to the Romeward journey in Virgil.

Ro·mewardness. [-NESS.] Tendency towards Roman Catholicism.

1901 *Daily Chron.* 27 Aug. 5/1 The young Duchess was forgiven by her relatives for her Romewardness.

Romish, *a.* **3.** For † *Obs.* read *arch.* (Further examples.)

1816 T. J. HOWELL *Stranger in Shrewsbury* 182 During its subjection to the Romish yoke, this country formed part of the province of Flavia Cæsariensis. **1917** W. OWEN *Let.* 14 Feb. (1967) 435 Do you need a Brooch? I saw an Egyptian one, rather huge,..and an Assyrian. No they wouldn't do since you no longer wear your Ancient British frocks. All the others in this town are either Romish, or nondescript.

‖ **rommelpot** (rǫ·məlpǫt). Also **rommel pot, rommel-pot.** [Du., = rumble pot.] **a.** A type of drum used in southern Africa (see quot. 1840). **b.** A type of drum used in the Low Countries (see quots. 1964, 1976).

1840 B. SHAW *Memorials S. Afr.* iii. 44 The rommel pot is a bamboo over which a piece of skin is tightly stretched, and is used as a drum at their [*sc.* the Namaquas'] dances. **1881** *Encycl. Brit.* XII. 311/1 The 'rommel-pot' was a kind of drum. **1964** S. MARCUSE *Mus. Instruments* 446/2 *Rommelpot*.., Dutch and Flemish friction drum with friction stick, made of an earthenware pot sometimes containing water, closed at the top by an animal bladder. The friction stick penetrates the center of the bladder and is rotated or pushed up and down. **1970** J. BLADES *Percussion Instruments* x. 196 In Flanders the rommelpot is particularly associated with Christmas. **1976** D. MUNROW *Instruments Middle Ages & Renaissance* v. 34/1 The rommelpot..is a type of friction drum... The action required is not scraping the stick to and fro but rubbing it gently with moistened fingers.

Romney (Marsh) (rɒ·mni, rǫ·mni māɹʃ). The name of an area of rich grazing land on the coast of Kent, used *absol.* and *attrib.* to designate a stocky, long-woolled sheep of the breed so called.

1837 W. YOUATT *Sheep* vii. 239 In some parts of the east of the county a polled breed of middle size, a cross between the Romney Marsh and the South Down, is found. **1861** I. BEETON *Bk. Househ. Managem.* 327 (*caption*) Romney-Marsh Ewe. *Ibid.*, The Romney Marsh..is a highly useful..variety..of the English domestic sheep. **1891**, **1894** [see *KENT *sb.*³]. **1922** V. SACKVILLE-WEST *Heir* iv. 42 It's like sheep..Oxfordshire don't do on Romney Marsh, and Romney Marsh don't do in Oxfordshire. **1923** [see *LEICESTER]. **1926** *Daily Colonist* (Victoria, B.C.) 16 Jan. 15/5 Two handsome Romney rams, proud and bellicose,..were landed today. **1950** *N.Z. Jrnl. Agric.* Jan. 15/3 The Romney sheep was by then [*sc.* about 1890] the dominant breed. **1957** [see *KENT *sb.*³]. **1974** T. ALLBEURY *Snowball* xiv. 72 It's been said that Romney Marsh sheep are bred only for survival. **1976** *Leicester Advertiser* 26 Nov. 11/5 The Animal Breeding Research Organisation is importing four hairy Romney rams from New Zealand. **1978** *Jrnl. R. Soc. Arts* CXXVI. 590/2 Factors limiting lamb production in New Zealand Romneys.

romp, *sb.* Add: **2. b.** Phr. *in a romp*, with the greatest ease.

1901 J. RALPH *War's Brighter Side* xv. 249 One said to me, as he pointed at Maghersfontain Kopje, 'Set a brewery upon top of that and my regiment will take the place in a romp.' **1904** 'O. HENRY' in *Everybody's Mag.* Feb. 192/1 Rompiro will win in a romp... We'll carry the country by 10,000.

3. *attrib.*, as *romp-suit* = *ROMPER 2.

1961 W. SANSOM *Last Hours of Sandra Lee* iv. 70 A fresh-faced girl in a romp-suit.

romp, *v.* Add: **2. a.** Also *transf.*

1928 *Sunday Express* 22 July 1/1 The child of 1928 simply romps through papers which were 'teasers' for the child of 1914. **1951** *People* 17 June 2 Petula Clark, who romps away with her first grown-up part with all-star honours. **1960** *Times* 16 May 19/1 He and Davies romped to a 5–1 lead. **1964** *Amer. Folk Music Occasional* I. 40 Those..lists of Broadway..romp up past the million mark in a few months. **1968** J. SANGSTER *Touchfeather* ii. 8, I romped through the training, passing out eventually with the highest marks anyone could remember. **1976** *Southwest Times Record* (Fort Smith, Arkansas) 20 Sept. 1 B/1 The Dallas Cowboys overcame a rash of early errors and romped to a 24–6 National Football League victory over the New Orleans Saints.

b. Also *transf.* (Earlier and later examples.)

1881 E. W. HAMILTON *Diary* 28 Oct. (1972) I. 178 The Liberal candidate, though a Roman Catholic and not supposed to be a good candidate, simply 'romped in'. **1910** A. BENNETT *Clayhanger* III. xvii. 444 A demy poster ..to inform the public that the true friend of the public was 'romping in'. **1927** *Observer* 18 Sept. 17/2 It is a bad blow to official Labour that Mr. Larkin should have romped home in north Dublin. **1950** *Sport* 22–28 Sept. 4/1 On Saturday the Forest 'stiffs' romped home to a 5–1 victory over Halifax. **1974** *Times* 2 Mar. 4/7 Mr Thorpe..romped home in his own constituency while Liberals elsewhere were generally less successful. **1977** *West Briton* 25 Aug. 18/1 Troon were handsome winners on Saturday when, facing a Hayle score of 200 for seven, they romped home by seven wickets.

romper. Add: **2.** Usu. *pl.* Also *romper suit.* A one-piece garment for a child to wear at play; a casual one-piece garment worn esp. by young women. (See also quots. 1941, 1943.)

1909 *Dialect Notes* III. 364 *Rompers, n. pl.* A one-piece garment for children to play in. **1915** R. W. LARDNER *Bib Ballads* 3 Hark! A voice from the easy chair: 'He hasn't a romper that's fit to wear.' **1922** *Moving Picture Stories* 23 June 24/1 The dainty bit of femininity, by the way, wore a suit of gingham rompers. **1922** *Westm. Gaz.* 20 Oct. 9 (Advt.), An attractive romper suit for a small child is made of white washing material. **1928** L. NORTH *Parasites* 18 Many of them wore sweaters that would have put Joseph's coat to shame. And very long, very baggy knickers, Hollywood rompers. **1941** *Amer. Speech* XVI. 186/2 [British Army slang] *Rompers*, battle dress. **1943** 'T. DUDLEY-GORDON' *Coastal Command* 85 Sipping hot coffee as he took off his rompers (combined parachute harness and Mae West life-jacket) he told us of his first night raid. **1964** C. WILLOCK *Enormous Zoo* vii. 128 He wore his one-piece romper suit and his three-foot-wide straw hat. **1970** *Women's Wear Daily* 23 Nov. 31/2 We see little rompers..as a possible replacement. **1974** A. GODDARD *Vienna Pursuit* II. 77 A toddler in pale blue rompers.

rompish, *a.* (Earlier and later examples.)

1709 W. KING *Useful Trans. in Philos.* I. 37 The Dance was something Rompish. **1977** *Listener* 5 May 592/1 *Albert Herring* is altogether an awkward, disconcerting affair—so rompish on the surface.

romulea (rǫmiū·liă).. Also **Romulea.** [mod. L. (J. F. Maratti *Plantarum Romuleæ et Saturniæ in Agro Romano* (1772) 13), f. *Romul-us*, name of the mythical founder of Rome.] A small bulbous plant of the genus so called, belonging to the family Iridaceæ, native to coastal regions of southern Europe and South Africa, and bearing yellow, red, or purple flowers resembling a crocus.

1876 J. G. BAKER in *Jrnl. Bot.* XIV. 236 There are specimens in the herbaria either of Kew or the British Museum, with the exception of three of the *Romuleæ*. **1887** *Gardeners' Chron.* 5 Feb. 184/2 The hardier section of Romuleas belonging to the Mediterranean regions are also worthy our attention. **1909** R. FARRER *In Yorkshire Garden* viii. 148, I was quite terrified at the aspect of the Romulea clumps that my kind Cornish friend sent me the other day, so wild, so long and wiry-haired was their aspect. **1928** R. MACAULAY *Keeping up Appearances* ii. 14 Back from the beach stretched grassy slopes, purple and pink with romulea and silene. **1964** A. N. GRIFFITH *Collins Guide to Alpines* 243 Other romuleas, including the less hardy species from S. Africa, will be found described in detail.

‖ **rondavel** (rǫndā·vel). *S. Afr.* Also † **rondabel, ronddawel.** [a. Afrikaans *rondavel.*] A round tribal hut of primitive construction, usu. with a thatched, conical roof. Also *transf.*, a similar simple building used esp. as a holiday cottage; also as an outbuilding on a farm, etc.

1891 J. WIDDICOMBE *Fourteen Yrs. in Basutoland* 84 Mr. Charles Bell had very kindly engaged a Mosuto..to build us a round hut, or *rondavel*, as the whites usually call it. **1900** A. H. KEANE *Boer States* p. xviii, Rondabel, ronddawel, a round hut..; is now an outhouse detached from the dwelling, and used as a kitchen. **1904** A. WILMOT *Life & Times Sir R. Southey* iii. 69 At present the Landdrost lies in a 'Rondavel' of reeds and mud. **1910** J. BUCHAN *Prester John* iii. 53 There were some twenty native huts, higher up the slope, which the Dutch call *rondavels.* **1924** *Chambers's Jrnl.* Jan. 53/1 At the scene of operations rondavels have been constructed to accommodate the workers. **1936** 'THE IDLER' *Rolling Home* xxxi. 385 It consisted of a dozen rondavels grouped round a central thatched dining-room...A rondavel is a circular room built of brick or mud with a door and windows and is roofed with stout thatch. **1951** R. CAMPBELL *Light on Dark Horse* ii. 51 Even our Governor-Generals sleep, in the hot weather, in thatched rondavels walled with a mixture of cow-dung and mud. **1958** M. SPARK *Go-Away Bird* 102 She had used to squat with old Makata..outside his large rondavel. **1965** *Spectator* 8 Jan. 35/3, I slept in one of the rondavels..vacated for me for the occasion. There are twenty of these—tin huts twenty feet in diameter and partitioned to form two tiny semi-circular rooms. **1973** G. DURRELL *Beasts in my Belfry* vi. 121 The [bears'] dens, which were scattered among the bramble bushes that filled the enclosure, were beehive-like rondavels of stone covered with earth and turf. **1976** *Vogue* Jan. 114/3 Antigua..the Anchorage Hotel.. accommodation units, ranging from rondavels to air-conditioned rooms with patios.

‖ **rond de cuir** (roṅ də küir). [Fr., lit. 'circle of leather'.] A round leather cushion, commonly used on office chairs in France; hence *transf.*, a bureaucrat.

[**1893** G. COURTELINE (*title*) Messieurs les Ronds-de-Cuir.] **1915** W. J. LOCKE *Jaffery* viii. 101 Do you think a leather seat for that hard wooden chair—what the French call a *rond-de-cuir*—would very greatly impair the poor fellow's imagination? **1938** *Times Lit. Suppl.* 28 May 368/3 Into the next twelve years he crowded all his life's work, his volumes of stories and novels..his good-bye to a *rond de cuir.* **1963** I. FLEMING *On H.M. Secret Service* xxiv. 259, I am just a pilot. I am not a 'rond de cuir', a chairborne flyer. **1969** *Punch* 5 Mar. 363/2 The island in this Octave is Barra, where he is in charge of the Home Guard and conducts a running fight on its behalf with the *ronds de cuir* of Whitehall. **1975** *Listener* 4 Sept. 314/4 How many *ronds-de-cuir* in peripheral *mairies*.. must have lived through Robespierre!

‖ **rond de jambe** (roṅ də ʒaṁb). *Ballet.* Pl. **rond(s) de jambes, ronds de jambe.** [Fr., lit. 'circle of the leg'.] A circular movement of the leg in dancing. Freq. in *Comb.* (see quots.).

1828 R. BARTON tr. *Blasis's Code of Terpsichore* II. 101 Suppose it is the left leg that stands on the ground whilst the right, in the second position, is prepared for the movement, make it describe a semicircle backwards, which brings your legs to the first position, and then continue on the sweep till it completes the whole circle, ending at the place from whence it started. This is what we technically term *ronds-de-jambe.* *Ibid.* 102 The practice of *grands et petits battemens*, the *rond-de-jambes* on the ground and in the air,..&c. **1889** G. B. SHAW in *Star* 4 Oct. 2/4 The *entrechats, battements, ronds de jambes, arabesques, élévations*, and what's-his-names of the art of theatrical dancing. **1922** BEAUMONT & IDZIKOWSKI *Man. Classical Theatr. Dancing* II. i. 34 *Ronds de Jambe à Terre* serve to enable you to turn your leg well outwards. *Ibid.* 53 The celebrated dancers Gardel and Vestris are credited with the invention of the *rond de jambe en l'air.* **1930** CRASKE & BEAUMONT *Theory & Pract. Allegro in Classical Ballet* II. 70 Execute a *Double Rond de Jambe en dedans, sauté*, that is:- Spring upwards off the *right* foot. While the body is in the air—Execute with the *left* foot a *Double Rond de Jambe en l'air en dedans.* **1975** *New Yorker* 26 May 91/1 His passé leg in a multiple pirouette sweeps through rond de jambe en l'air into the opening battement of a series of grands jetés en tournant.

ronde. Restrict *Typog.* to sense in Dict. and add: **2.** A round dance; a dance in which the participants move in a circle or ring.

[**1931** G. L. NUTE *Voyageur* 41 The call for *la ronde* was issued. This dance was another customary part of the journey, and it was entered into heartily despite the moralizing tone of the verses.] **1950** MARCEL-DUBOIS & ANDRAL *Dances of France* I. 21 In the Bourbonnais a peasant wedding is the great occasion for traditional Rondes, ring dances, by all the guests after the banquet. One such Ronde is..round a fire. **1974** *Islander* (Victoria, B.C.) 30 June 16/3 Wives and daughters of the traders joined in, and Warre partook of a Canadian ronde, a dance in which, he wrote, 'your admiration of your partner is expressed by kissing her openly as often as she will permit'. **1977** *Early Music* July 431/3 There are no descriptions of dances specifically called 'Ronde'. The name implies a round dance and rhythmically they fit either a Branle..or an Almaine.

3. A round or course of talk, activity, etc.; a treadmill. Cf. *ROUND *sb.*[1] 13c.

1957 *Economist* 19 Oct. 196/1 The subject has been completely submerged in the economic discussions which dominate the current *ronde.* **1977** *Times Lit. Suppl.* 1 Apr. 401/4 Heinz already represented the first step away from what was ultimately unbearable about the homosexual *ronde.*

rondelier (rǫndĕliə·ɹ). *nonce-wd.* [f. RONDEL + -IER.] A poet who composes rondels.

1878 G. M. HOPKINS *Lett. to R. Bridges* (1955) 49, I am very glad to hear the Rondeliers have come to see the beauty of your poetry.

‖ **rondeña** (rǫnde·nyă). [Sp.] A variety of song or dance native to Ronda in Andalusia.

1883 GROVE *Dict. Mus.* III. 599/2 Songs and dances often derive their names from the provinces or towns in which they are indigenous; thus *rondeña* from Ronda. **1954** *Ibid.* (ed. 5) III. 372 Most forms [of Andalusian song]..have four lines of eight syllables, and these include forms such as *granadinas, rondeñas*,..descended directly or indirectly from the *fandango.* **1967** 'LA MERI' *Spanish Dancing* (ed. 2) vi. 82 The Rondeñas originated as a lover's serenade under the window of his sweetheart, as did the Tarantos of the Levant.

‖ **rondeur** (roṅdör). [Fr.] *pl.* Roundness, rounded forms or lines; *spec.* the curves of the female body.

1938 H. G. WELLS *Apropos of Dolores* iii. 113 A vast majolica plaque insisting upon the Rape of the Sabines, but always recalling to my mind, I don't know why—the rondeurs I suppose—that bustling cheese market at Alkmaar. **1966** *Guardian* 5 Aug. 8/4 These wide coats and dresses..will be able to take our rondeurs in their swing.

rondine (rǫ·ndīn), *a. nonce-wd.* [f. F. *rond* ROUND + -INE[4], after *blondine.*] Made round, rounded.

1923 E. SITWELL *Bucolic Comedies* 70 Fat blondine pearls Rondine curls Seem.

‖ **rond-point** (roṅˌpwaṅ). [Fr., f. *rond* ROUND + *point* centre.] **a.** In a garden: a circular space or centre whence paths radiate. **b.** In a town or city: a circus or roundabout where roads converge.

1884 H. JAMES in *Atlantic Monthly* May 631/2 A *jardin français*..with little blue-green perspectives and alleys and *rond-points.* **1903** A. H. BEAVAN *Tube, Train, Tram, & Car* x. 120 Sloane Street, where anyone approaching town by way of Kensington, meets the first of the numerous metropolitan 'rond-points'. *Ibid.* 121 A few doors from the 'rond-point' in Brompton Road. **1948** *Archit. Rev.* CIII. 158/2 Foremost in his mind he must have had such questions as where to place his rond-points and their radiating streets, and how to co-ordinate and integrate the various units of the plan. **1964** *Shell Gardens Bk.* 169 *Rond-Point*, a circular space or clearing from which avenues and alleys diverge or upon which they converge and from which one may get vistas of various parts of a garden or park. **1967** C. HUSSEY *Eng. Gardens & Landscapes 1700–1750* v. 41 The enclosing shrubberies were threaded by walks, straight for the most part but irregularly aligned, connecting sundry *rond-points* and mounds, to debouch at unexpected angles into the glade.

Roneo (rōᵘ·nio), *sb.* Also **roneo.** [f. the initial letters of ROTARY *a.* and *Neostyle* (see quot. 1901 below).] The proprietary name of various kinds of office equipment, esp. a duplicating machine. Freq. *attrib.* and *Comb.*

1901 *Trade Marks Jrnl.* 27 Nov. 1182 Roneo... Paper.., stationery and bookbinding. Neostyle Manufacturing Company, Limited. **1914** D. FRASER *Winning a Primitive People* III. xxvi. 272 A native clerk is there.. turning on the Roneo hundreds of copies of some circular to the teachers. **1919** *Trade Marks Jrnl.* 13 Aug. 1138 Roneo... Type printing machines, type setting machines, and embossing machines. Roneo, Limited,.. London. **1920** *Glasgow Herald* 3 Dec. 10 The staff of typists and Roneo operators required is very numerous and well paid. **1926** *Socialist Rev.* June 10 No printed newspapers (a few roneo bulletins), no trains. **1934** *Times Lit. Suppl.* 8 Mar. 162/3 *Roneo.*—As one must have it, why not have the derivation—Rotary Neostyle? **1941** E. R. EDDISON *Fish Dinner* xiii. 229 I'll go on for a bit: get my covering memorandum into shape... You've got the annexes all off the roneo now, have you? **1947** *Trade Marks Jrnl.* 5 Mar. 120/1 Roneo... Duplicating apparatus, duplicating machines..Roneo Limited,.. Romford, Essex, and.. London,..; manufacturers and merchants. **1950** *Official Gaz.* (U.S. Patent Office) 12 Dec. 377/1 *Roneo.* Applicant claims ownership of British Registration No. 241,483 dated Oct. 23, 1901, and United States Registration No. 182,682. For duplicating machines and their parts, duplicating apparatus and their parts. **1958** S. HYLAND *Who goes Hang?* xxxi. 136 The complexities of the Roneo strip-index on which he was working. **1973** J. WAINWRIGHT *High-Class Kill* 119 An official statement; typed-out, Roneo-copied. **1977** *Gay News* 24 Mar. 22/4 One available in bookstores is Alain Huet's *Agence Tasse*, a roneotyped newssheet.

Hence as *v. trans.*, to copy or reproduce with a Roneo duplicating machine (usu. *pass.* with pa. pple. *roneo'd*); **ro·neo'd** (also **roneo(-)ed**) *ppl. a.*, **ro·neo-ing** *vbl. sb.*

1921 *Spectator* 7 May 584/1, I have had the memorandum 'Roneo'd' for circulation among near acquaintances. **1926** *Contemp. Rev.* June 682 Newspapers were reappearing in weird type-written or roneo-ed form. **1928** *Bull. Internat. Fed. League of Nations Societies* May–June 5 Among the documents which have been translated, roneoed and distributed by the Secretariat may be cited the following important Memoranda. **1934** *Planning* I. xxiii. 8 In addition to this broadsheet a roneoed bulletin goes round fortnightly to the hundred working members telling them what each group is doing. **1935** *Punch* 6 Mar. 262/2 He said he liked the little poem and was having some copies 'roneo'd'. **1940** W. S. CHURCHILL *Second World War* (1949) II. 631 The officials concerned in roneo-ing the various circulations. **1956** *Eng. Stud.* XXXVII. 146 The preface to the present (roneo'd, not printed) book. **1966** *Listener* 23 June 915/1 They studied the roneoed exam papers. **1974** D. SEAMAN *Bomb that could Lip-Read* xv. 144 Back would come a roneoed letter.

Rong (roŋ), *sb.* and *a.* [Native name.] = *LEPCHA *sb.* and *a.*

1840 A. CAMPBELL in *Jrnl. Asiatic Soc. Bengal* IX. I. 379 The real Lepcha, or Rong proper, has no tradition whatever..connected with the advent of his tribe into this part of the world. **1854** J. D. HOOKER *Himalayan Jrnls.* I. v. 127 They, or at least some of their tribes, call themselves Rong, and Arratt, and their country Dijong. **1876** G. B. MAINWARING *Gram. Róng (Lepcha) Lang.* p. vii, The proper name of the Lepchas, as they call themselves, is—Róng. *Ibid.* I. 1 The Róng (Lepcha) Alphabet may be divided into two parts. **1909** G. A. GRIERSON *Linguistic Survey of India* III. I. 233 The Lepchas are considered as the oldest inhabitants of Sikkim... They call themselves Róng... The number of speakers of Róng in Sikkim and Darjeeling were..estimated. *Ibid.*, Róng literature comprises Buddhistic and other religious books. **1938** G. GORER *Himalayan Village* i. 35 The Lepchas do not call themselves Lepchas; they call themselves *Rong.*

rongeur (roṅʒö·ɹ). *Surg.* [a. F. *rongeur* gnawing, a rodent, f. *ronger* to gnaw.] A strong surgical forceps with a biting action, used for removing small pieces from bone. Also *rongeur forceps.*

a **1884** KNIGHT *Dict. Mech.* Suppl. 764/1 Post's rongeur is specifically for the mastoid bone. **1888** *Buck's Handbk. Med. Sci.* VI. 176/2 The gnawing, or rongeur, forceps are necessary for the removal of the edges of bone and of diseased parts not otherwise accessible. **1908** J. W. SLUSS *Emergency Surg.* II. iv. 401 Provide, besides the ordinary instruments, Rongeur forceps, a mallet and chisel, or a trephine. *Ibid.* 405 The dura is now exposed, and if the opening..needs to be enlarged, the dura should be detached from the edge of the bone and the chisel or rongeur employed. **1927** J. B. MACALPINE *Cystoscopy* xi. 160 The cystoscopic rongeur..may be used to break up stones which are very soft and friable. **1938** D. MUNRO *Cranio-Cerebral Injuries* vii. 90 At least 1 large and 1 small biting rongeur. **1966** G. L. HOWE *Minor Oral Surg.* xi. 221 The ease and speed..are due to the use of the side-cutting rongeurs (alveolotomy shears).

‖**ronggeng** (rǫ·ŋgeŋ). [Malay.] **a.** A dancing-girl in Malaysia. **b.** A form of Malaysian popular dancing, often accompanied by singing.

1817 T. S. RAFFLES *Hist. Java* vii. 342 The common dancing girls of the country..are called *rông'geng*, and are generally of easy virtue... The *róng'gengs* accompany the dance with singing. **1849** ONG-TAE-HAE *Glance at Interior of China* 57 Native actresses are called ronggengs ..they flourish a paper fan, sing native songs, and perform savage dances. **1910** R. J. WILKINSON *Papers on Malay Subjects: Life & Customs* III. 28 A *ronggeng* sings and acts. **1927** R. J. H. SIDNEY *In Brit. Malaya Today* xxiv. 281 We were treated to a pukkah Malay *ronggeng*. **1966** G. BLACK *You want to die, Johnny?* vi. 112 We got radio Binton, with *ronggeng* music. **1972** M. SHEPPARD *Taman Indera* 89 The most popular of these [dances] was called *Ronggeng*—a word which now means a professional dancing girl who dances and sings. **1976** LD. HOME *Way Wind Blows* vii. 116 Tunku Abdul Rahman..taught me —or rather tried to teach me—the ronggeng, the Malaysian dance in which the male, as far as I could see, plays a subordinate role to the female with hilarious results.

rongo-rongo (rǫ·ŋgo͵rǫ·ŋgo). *Archæol.* [Native name.] Hieroglyphic signs or script found on wooden tablets on Easter Island, a Chilean dependency in the eastern Pacific Ocean; the art of incising these. Also *attrib.* and *ellipt.*

1919 K. ROUTLEDGE *Mystery of Easter Island* xvi. 243 The tablets, known as 'kohău-rongo-rongo', were an integral part of life on the island. *Ibid.* 244 Every clan had professors in the art who were known as rongo-rongo men ('tangata-rongo-rongo'). *Ibid.* 249 Kaara was servant to the Ariki, and had been taught rongo-rongo by him. ..The matters with which..the rongo-rongo would deal, such as genealogies, lists of ariki, or the wanderings of the people. **1947** D. DIRINGER *Alphabet* viii. 137 The script *rongo-rongo* was the monopoly of organized teachers; every clan had its own 'writing professors', that is, experts in the art who were known as *tangata-rongo-rongo*, 'rongo-rongo-men'. *Ibid.*, A less elaborate kind of rongo-rongo was called *tau*. **1957** M. BULLOCK tr. *Métraux's Easter Island* xii. 188 The spear carried by the leader..recalls the staff sometimes borne by the Easter Island *rongorongo*. *Ibid.*, The name given to these [hieroglyphic] tablets, *kohau rongorongo*. **1958** T. HEYERDAHL *Aku-Aku* vi. 164 The cave contained every possible thing except *rongo-rongo*.

‖**ronin** (rōᵘ·nin). Also with capital initial. [Jap.] In feudal Japan, a lordless wandering samurai; an outlaw. Also *transf.* in recent use, a Japanese student who has failed and is permitted to retake a university (entrance) examination.

1871 A. B. MITFORD *Tales of Old Japan* I. 4 The word *Rônin*..is used to designate persons of gentle blood, entitled to bear arms, who have become separated from their feudal lords. *Ibid.* 18 Then the Rônins lost patience. **1876** W. E. GRIFFIS *Mikado's Empire* I. xxvii. 278 When too deeply in debt, or having committed a crime, they left their homes and the service of their masters, and roamed at large. Such men were called *rōnins*, or 'wave-men'. **1899** KIPLING *From Sea to Sea* I. xxi. 415 And now let us go to the tomb of the Forty-Seven Ronins. **1947** R. BENEDICT *Chrysanthemum & Sword* vii. 138 The huge invincible *ronin* (a lordless samurai who lives by his own wits), the hero Benkei. **1967** D. & E. T. RIESMAN *Conversations in Japan* 17 Many had been *ronin* (the name given those who try again and again over a period of years to pass the exams), and finally when they made it were exhausted. **1970** *Observer* (Colour Suppl.) 8 Feb. 32/2 High school students who fail the university exam and are waiting to try again are called *ronin*, a reference to the landless samurai of old Japan which clearly describes their unhappy displaced position in a chronically status-sensitive society. **1974** *Encycl. Brit. Micropædia* VIII. 663/1 *Ronin*, in Japan, masterless samurai (warrior aristocrats) of the Kamakura (1192–1333) and Tokugawa (1603–1867) periods who were often vagrant and disruptive and sometimes actively rebellious.

ronk (rǫŋk), *a. dial.* [var. RANK *a.*] Unmanageable, refractory, unruly; depraved, libidinous; cunning. Hence **ro·nkness.**

1877–1905 in *Eng. Dial. Dict.* **1908** E. M. SNEYD-KYNNERSLEY *H.M.I.* xvii. 191 'Well, sir, he is not a bad sort of boy, but he is—er—er—' I broke in to his relief: 'His mother says he is *ronk*.' The master jumped at it: 'That's exactly what he is, sir: he's ronk.' *Ibid.*, 192 Choir-boys have an established reputation for ronkness. **1972** *Times* 31 Oct. 14/7 'Ronk' means what the yokels of London would describe as 'randy'.

Ronson (rǫ·nsən). The proprietary name of a brand of cigarette lighter. Also *attrib.*

1929 *Trade Marks Jrnl.* 11 Sept. 1516/1 Ronson... Pyrophoric lighters. The Ronson Art Metal Company, Limited. **1957** C. MACINNES *City of Spades* I. vii. 44, I..held out my Ronson...when, hey presto! the lighter was flicked from my hand. **1961** C. WILLOCK *Death in Covert* xi. 199 Mr Goss took his Ronson lighter from his pocket and flicked it into flame. **1972** O. SELA *Bearer Plot* ii. 18, I leaned forward with my Ronson. The flame whooshed up.

Röntgen. Add: see *ROENTGEN (now the more usual spelling).

röntgenite, var. *ROENTGENITE.

Ronuk (rǫ·nɒk), *sb.* Also **ronuk.** The proprietary name of a make of polish; *spec.* a brand of floor polish. Hence as *v. trans.*, to polish with Ronuk. Also **ro·nuked** *ppl. a.*; **ro·nuker,** one who uses Ronuk.

1896 *Trade Marks Jrnl.* 8 Apr. 325 Ronuk... Polishing preparations. Thomas Mottley Fowler and Thomas Horace Fowler, trading as T. M. Fowler,.. Brighton; manufacturers. **1912** *Daily Chron.* 5 Mar. 4/5 'Ronuk' imparts a brilliant polish. *a* **1913** 'BARON CORVO' *Desire & Pursuit of Whole* (1934) i. 3 The profane vulgar who want..brown boots properly ronuked, and linen stiffly starched. **1916** *Yorkshire Post* 29 June 10/3 In one hall three or four shovel-fuls of dirt are taken up by the ronukers as against one in any other hall, and twice as long is taken to ronuk this hall than any other hall, and three times the amount of ronuk is needed. **1918** KIPLING in *Story-Teller* Dec. 227/1 You'll often find half a dozen Brethren..polishing and ronuking and sweeping everything they can get at. **1927** W. E. COLLINSON *Contemp. Eng.* 66 One curious development of some nouns is their power to form verbs: to zog a stain off (with a scouring powder), to ronuk [*rɔnʌk*] a floor (polish). **1929** *Trade Marks Jrnl.* 6 Mar. 404/2 Ronuk... Floor polish. Ronuk, Limited,.. Portslade,.. London,.. Manchester; and.. Cape Town, South Africa. **1955** N. BALCHIN *Fall of Sparrow* ii. 62 He was a big, bulky man, completely bald, and it was believed that the house matron polished his head every day with Ronuk.

'roo, roo *sb.*² (rū). *Austral. colloq.* [Shortened form of *kangaroo.*] **a.** = KANGAROO *sb.* 1.

1904 'S. RUDD' *Sandy's Selection* 11 Dead 'roos were common enough, but seldom was a live one thrown in Sandy's way. [**1926**: see *KANGA².] **1933** *Bulletin* (Sydney) 30 Aug. 21/3 The whites have a kindly feeling for the 'roo. **1945** *Coast to Coast 1944* 80 First time he's seen a blasted roo. **1966** *Southerly* XXVI. 110 Possums and roos to trap. **1977** *Caravan World* (Austral.) Jan. 59/1 The river had brought emus and 'roos close to the road. **1979** *Daily Tel.* 23 Aug. 11/7 The baby roo tries to get herself adopted by other animals but they prove to be unsatisfactory means of transport.

b. *attrib.* and *Comb.*, as *roo bus, meat, shooter, steak*; **roo-bar** (see quot.); **'roo rat** = KANGAROO-RAT 1.

1976 *Car Facts & Feats* (ed. 2) III. 158 (*caption*) The cage in front of the head lamps is affectionately known as a 'roo-bar'. **1968** K. WEATHERLY *Roo Shooter* 12 The roo bus swept round a corner, into full view about twenty yards away; the shooter hit the brakes, depressed the clutch and grabbed the ·22 all in the same instant. **1977** *Weekly Times* (Melbourne) 19 Jan. 33/5 Not bad this 'ere veal. Not a touch on roo meat though. **1947** I. L. IDRIESS *Isles of Despair* xxxii. 212 Hungrily she.. satisfied her craving for land flesh. Kangaroo, wallaby.. flying fox, 'roo rat, porcupine. **1980** *Age* (Melbourne) 1 Apr. 11/1 The national controversy between conservationists and those who want to increase the commercial exploitation of the kangaroo, notably the professional 'roo shooters and the farmers, [etc.]. **1926** K. S. PRICHARD *Working Bullocks* 21 When he had cooked and eaten the piece of 'roo steak he had been carrying.

Hence **roo** *v.*² *intr.*, to hunt kangaroos.

1932 K. S. PRICHARD *Kiss on Lips* 82 Rooin' this week, Colonel?... Cripes, that's something like!

roocoocoo (rūkūkū·), *v.* Also **roocooroo** (rūkūrū·). [Imitative.] *intr.* Of a pigeon or a dove: to coo.

1922 JOYCE *Ulysses* 225 The..porch..where pigeons roocoocooed. **1960** C. DAY LEWIS *Buried Day* ii. 31 The roo-coo-rooing of doves.

rood, *sb.* Add: **6. Rood-fair** (further examples).

1931 J. BUCHAN *Blanket of Dark* 86 Old John Naps was at the Rood Fair on Barton Heath. **1957** *Dumfries & Galloway Standard* 26 Jan. 3/2 The 'Reed' Fair, as we pronounced it in our Dumfries dialect—'Reed' was a corruption of Rude or Rood or Cross.

roode bec etc. (varr. of words of Afrikaans origin normally spelt *rooi-*): see *ROOIBEKKIE etc.

roof, *sb.* Add: **1. a.** (Later examples of pl. *rooves.*)

1903 *Dialect Notes* II. 352 *Roof, n. pl.* rooves. Common plural in Mass. **1938** C. HIMES *Black on Black* (1973) 165 W'en de panic cum an' de Lawd tek yo' food an' yo' clothes an' de rooves off'n yo' haids, den laff. **1939** [see *council (housing) estate* s.v. *COUNCIL 17].

c. Also (not usu. *poet.*), a home, a household; a dwelling-place.

1853 C. BRONTË *Villette* I. iii. 29 The evening, by restoring Graham to the maternal roof (his days were passed at school), brought us an accession of animation. **1922** D. L. SAYERS *Let.* 18 Dec. in J. Brabazon *Dorothy L. Sayers* (1981) ix. 96 He simply has not a red cent or a roof. **1979** J. RATHBONE *Euro-Killers* iii. 34 She had been happy to give them a free roof until they got work.

e. In phrases (chiefly *colloq.*). (*a*) *to raise* (or *lift*) *the roof*: to create an uproar, to make a resounding noise; (*b*) *the roof falls in*: something disastrous occurs, everything goes wrong; (*c*) *come off the roof*: don't put on airs; (*d*) *to hit the roof* = *to hit the ceiling* (*CEILING *vbl. sb.* 5b); (*e*) *to go through the roof*: to become very angry (see also sense *2a).

(*a*) **1860** M. J. HOLMES *Cousin Maude* 57 Ole master'll raise de ruff, case he put 'em away to sell. **1894** 'MARK TWAIN' in *Century Mag.* June 233/1 She was here to watch the trial now, and was going to lift up just one 'hooraw' over it... 'When dat verdic' comes, I's gwine to lif' dat *roof*, now, I *tell* you.' **1905** *Eng. Dial. Dict.* V. 147/2 *Oxf.* Do be quiet, or you'll raise the roof (G.O.). **1922** WODEHOUSE *Girl on Boat* xvi. 253, I couldn't get within ten feet of that dog without its lifting the roof off. **1959** *Times* 19 Jan. 3/3 A good song to raise the roof. **1972** J. W. THOMPSON in W. King *Black Short Story Anthol.* 255 She flew from the kitchen like a startled sparrow, her hands perched nervously upon her hips—all set to raise the roof!

(*b*) **1866** D. BOUCICAULT *Flying Scud* in Nicoll & Cloak *Forbidden Fruit & Other Plays* (1940) 172 She undertook with all her veight to sit upon my knee. Fourteen stun six, I thought the roof had fell in. **1958** J. MORGAN *Expense Account* ii. 26 And it all worked out exactly right—up to the moment he walked into his office. Then the roof fell in. **1976** H. MACINNES *Agent in Place* xvii. 191 Georges said, 'I think the roof just fell in.' Tony had no reply. For once he was quite speechless.

(*c*) **1895** W. P. RIDGE *Minor Dialogues* ix. 86 She took up such a 'igh and mighty attitude..so I says to her, I says, 'Come off the roof.'

(*d*) **1925** FRASER & GIBBONS *Soldier & Sailor Words* 245 *Roof, to hit the*, to get into a temper. **1928** J. P. MCEVOY *Show Girl* ix. 133 Milton gave me a couple of drinks early in the evening out of his flask and Jimmy hit the roof. **1971** V. CANNING *Firecrest* x. 149 The P.M. and his cabinet..would hit the roof if they knew half of the things that went on.

(*e*) **1958** *Spectator* 25 July 133/1 Would it have hurt if someone had done it to you before? You'd have gone through the roof? **1975** J. SYMONS *Three Pipe Problem* xviii. 179 The company are simply wild. They have gone through the roof.

2. a. Also, = *CEILING *vbl. sb.* 6d. *to go through the roof* (and varr.), of bids, prices, sales, etc.: to surpass the expected limit, to reach extreme heights.

1939 *Richmond* (Va.) *Times-Dispatch* 16 Aug. 17/8 Spokesmen for the shellers contended that since the price pegging program put a 'roof' on the price they must pay for peanuts they were entitled to a 'floor' against possible losses from 'innocent' over-buying. **1946** E. HODGINS *Mr. Blandings builds his Dream House* viii. 118 The Knapp sales curves were going through the roof. **1947** *Forum* (Johannesburg) 24 May 15/3 The Labour Party continues to snipe at the Government for refusing to take the roof off the maize price. **1962** *Listener* 28 June 1113/2 (Advt.), Starting salary from £11.10.0 per week to £12.16.0 per week according to qualifications, rising to roof of £14.2.0 per week. **1965** *New Statesman* 16 July 101/4 (Advt.), Starting salary £2,185–£2,445 according to relevant experience and qualifications rising to a roof of £2,835. **1972** *Times* 24 Oct. 10/3 Only a few special treasures were bid through the roof. **1973** *Times* 30 Oct. 19/6 On lots that were rare and undamaged they [*sc.* prices] went through the roof.

c. (Later examples.) Also, *spec.* in *Mountaineering* (see quot. 1963²).

1963 A. GREENBANK *Instructions in Rock Climbing* ix. 98 On the lip of an overhang which has no footholds immediately below... You jockey one boot up the rock, pressing on the flat face, then throw a knee over the edge of the 'roof'. *Ibid.* 151 *Roof*, the underside of an overhang. **1972** D. HASTON *In High Places* viii. 94 After an easy first pitch there was a series of overlapping roofs leading to a big ledge, followed by a line of cracks and chimneys to the top. **1976** *Newmarket Jrnl.* 16 Dec., Left-back Mickey Fordham latched on to a pass from Eley to fire home a third into the roof of the net.

d. Also (*Austral.*), the stratum lying immediately over material that contains opal.

1931 M. S. BUCHANAN *Prospecting for Opal in Australia* 8 Almost all the sheet of potch containing opal lies within two ft. from the roof. **1960** *People* (Broadway, New South Wales) 27 Apr. 51 Pipe opal..is mostly found in soft, white clay between one and six inches below the overlying sandstone 'roof'.

e. A high mountain range or plateau; the highest part (*of* a region); *the roof of the world* [tr. Wakhani *bam-i-dunya*], orig. applied to the Pamirs, later also to Tibet or the Himalayas.

1842 *Chinese Repository* XI. 143 The Wakhanis name this plain Bam-i-Duniah, or 'Roof of the World', and it would indeed appear to be the highest table-land in Asia. **1876** T. E. GORDON (*title*) The roof of the world, being the narrative of a journey over the high plateau of Tibet to the Russian frontier and the Oxus sources on Pamir. *Ibid.* ix. 121 We were now about to cross the famous 'Bam-i-dunya', 'The Roof of the World', under which name the elevated region of the hitherto comparatively unknown Pamir tracts had long appeared in our maps. **1889** G. N. CURZON *Russia in Central Asia* v. 144 Descending from the hidden 'Roof of the world', its waters tell of forgotten peoples and whisper secrets of unknown lands. **1902** D. G. HOGARTH *Nearer East* 31 The course of this ridge in the Anatolian roof..determines the parting of all the waters. **1953** J. MASTERS *Lotus & Wind* xix. 235 Few travellers used this route that arched over the roof of the world to link India with Chinese Sinkiang. **1956** G. N. PATTERSON *God's Fool* i. 13, I sat there in that remote valley in Tibet where no white man had ever been, fifteen thousand feet above sea-level on the roof of the world. **1959** *Listener* 15 Jan. 140/3 If you want to give yourself a test of stamina and skill in map reading you can walk the Roof of Wales. **1968** N. Tranter *Cable from Kabul* ii. 29 Look—this area's called the Roof of the World. It's no place for aircraft. **1973** *Guardian* 20 Oct. 13/3 Identification of Church and State in Tibetan Buddhism dates from the 1640s. But the *feel* of an independent way of life on the battlemented roof of Asia is immensely older. **1979** *Yale Alumni Mag.* Apr. 2/3 (Advt.), Snow-capped peaks of the Himalayas along the roof of the world.

f. *Aeronaut.* = *ceiling *vbl. sb.* 6 b. ? *Obs.*
1917 [see *ceiling *vbl. sb.* 6 b]. **1940** *S. P. E. Tract* lv. 193 *Roof* is the zenith of a plane's ascent.

6. a. (Later examples.)
1926 Maines & Grant *Wise-Crack Dict.* 7/1 *Dropping one's roof*, losing one's hat. **1949** R. M. Howe *H. Gross's Criminal Investigation* (ed. 4) viii. 162 *Titfa, roof, bonnet or tile*, hat.

c. An umbrella. ? *Obs.*
1844 E. Hall *Diary* in O. A. Sherrard *Two Victorian Girls* (1966) xi. 106 [A] family roof [umbrella] and a great blanket shawl.

7. a. Also, *roof-board, -capping, comb, -deck, -decking, -glass, -outlet, -pane, -ridge* (earlier and later examples), *-roller, -screen, -shelter, -slab, -space* (later examples), *-terrace, -thatch, -thatching, -truss* (later example).
1848 O. S. Fowler *Home for All* (1851) 90 Since the roof boards cross these rafters, so as to form an arch the other way, surely no greater solidity or strength can be required. **1940** *Chambers's Techn. Dict.* 730/1 *Roof boards*, boards laid on a roof to provide a foundation and an undercovering to the covering materials proper, such as slates, tiles, etc. **1968** O. S. Nock *Railway Enthusiast's Encycl.* 246 (*caption*) G.W.R.: an early example of dining-car service, with rather flamboyant roof-boards, c. 1900. **1977** *36 Home Handyman Projects* (Austral. Home Jrnl.) 74/1 Roof capping is usually put on with cement. After a few years of sun, wind and rain the cement cracks and falls out. **1908** *Encycl. Relig. & Ethics* I. 687/1 On the roof was a roof comb—one of the most distinguishing features of Maya architecture. **1971** *Country Life* 4 Nov. 1219/2 A three-room temple surmounted by an enormous stone roof-comb originally carved with an impressive seated figure. **1947** *Archit. Rev.* CII. 117 The whole of the area on which this house is built is utilized for outdoor functions; above the living-room-kitchen part is an open roof-deck, below the bedrooms a car-port. **1979** *Arizona Daily Star* 5 Aug. (Advt. Section) 20/1 The roof deck affords fantastic views. **1960** *Farmer & Stockbreeder* 16 Feb. (Suppl.) 40/1 When used as the roof-decking to your new buildings or as a suspended ceiling to your existing ones, Stramit keeps temperatures constant. **1978** C. Tomlinson *Shaft* 39 Leaves might fall On to the roof-glass. **1967** *Gloss. Sanitation Terms (B.S.I.)* 41 *Roof outlet*, a rainwater fitting, normally provided with a grating, for building into a flat roof to receive rainwater for discharge into a rainwater pipe. **1922** Joyce *Ulysses* 265 Roll of Bensoulbenjamin rolled to the quivery loveshivery roofpanes. **1874** B. F. Taylor *World on Wheels* 218 There is singing everywhere:.. from the second rail of the fence, a gust of melody; from the roof-ridge, a solo. **1917** Conrad *Shadow-Line* ii. 79 Here and there in the distance, above the crowded mob of low, brown roof ridges, towered great piles of masonry. **1936** *Discovery* Aug. 251/2 A roof roller [excavated at Tell Duwein, near Jerusalem] was identical in form with that in use today in Palestine. **1971** *Gloss. Terms Fire (B.S.I.)* ii. 7 *Roof screen*, a vertical screen fitted internally to the roof of a building to divide the roof into bays, so that smoke and hot gases from a fire are contained within the bay of origin. **1928** D. H. Lawrence *Lady Chatterley* x. 145 Only one or two [chicks]..still dibbed about in the dryness under the straw roof-shelter. **1963** *Gloss. Gen. Building Terms (B.S.I.)* 20 *Roof slab*, a slab forming the continuous loadbearing structure of a roof and spanning between supports. **1960** *Farmer & Stockbreeder* 16 Feb. 49/2 (Advt.) Agrecon buildings give..a maximum roof-space. **1970** J. Earl *Tuners & Amplifiers* i. 12 A simple indoor or roofspace aerial would be suitable for the reception of local stations. **1937** *Archit. Rev.* LXXXII. 119 (*caption*) The roof-terrace is paved with 'Paropa' patent slabs. **1912** 'Q.' *Hocken & Hunken* xix. 239 With a rampant climber such as Rosa Devoniensis it is advisable to cut out each autumn, and clean remove some of the old wood; and this is no easy job when early neglect has allowed the plant to riot up and over the roof-thatch. **1968** J. Arnold *Shell Bk. Country Crafts* 329 Hazel rods have many other uses, such as for salmon-traps on the Severn.. and pegs for roof-thatching. **1964** W. L. Goodman *Hist. Woodworking Tools* 197 It may be, however, that the original French word *fermoir* has something to do with the *ferme* or roof-truss.

8. a. *roof-walker; roof-levelling* adj.
1863 G. M. Hopkins *Let.* 4 May (1956) 78 Leaving a candle burning, which I thought would keep the roof-walker in..suspense. **1920** W. B. Yeats *Michael Robartes & Dancer* 20 And one bare hill Whereby the haystack and roof-levelling wind..can be stayed.

c. Locative, instrumental, etc., as *roof-clustered, -mired, -rent, -wrecked* adjs.; *roofward(s)* adv.
a **1879** W. Howitt in M. Howitt *Autobiogr.* (1889) I. vii. 227 Clouds of smoke..burst from the windows and streamed up roofwards. **1880** 'Mark Twain' *Tramp Abroad* xix. 171 A hill..with..its..roof-clustered cap of architecture. **1922** Hardy *Late Lyrics & Earlier* 283 The bower we shrined to Tennyson, Gentlemen, Is roof-wrecked. **1932** Auden in *Rev. Eng. Stud.* (1978) Aug. 302 A sleepy liftboy swirled us roofward. **1933** C. Day Lewis *Magnetic Mountain* 50 Yet passing derelict mills and barns roof-rent. **1955** A. Clarke *Later Poems* (1961) 48 A cage-bird came among sparrows..Plucked, roof-mired, all in mad bits.

9. roof bolt *Mining*, a tensioned rod anchoring the roof of a working to the strata above; so **roof bolting** *vbl. sb.*, the practice of using roof bolts; **roof-brain,** the cerebral cortex; **roof-climb** *v. intr.*, to climb over the roofs of buildings; so *roof-climber, roof-climbing* vbl. sb.; **roof-drip,** a drip or dripping of water from a roof; **roof-garden** (*a*) (earlier and further examples); freq. applied to a place for eating or entertainment situated on the roof of a building; also *attrib.*; (*b*) (see quot. 1932); **roof-jack,** (*a*) *Canad.*, a pole supporting the roof of a tent; (*b*) *Canad.*, a smoke vent of a chimney; (*c*) *U.S.*, a support for a house painter engaged in painting a roof; **roof-man** = *gutter-man* (*c*) s.v. *gutter *sb.*[1] 8; **roof organization** [tr. G. *dachsorganisation*], a parent organization; **roof pendant** *Geol.*, a mass of country rock projecting downwards into an intrusive body such as a batholith; **roof-rack,** a framework upon the roof of a motor vehicle to which luggage is attached; **roof-rail** (see quots.); **roof rat,** *Rattus rattus alexandrinus*, a climbing rat which has a brownish back and greyish underparts; (examples); **roof-scraper** (see quot.); **roof-spotter,** an observer posted at the top of a building to give warning of hostile aircraft; so **roof-spotting; roof-top** (in Dict., sense 7 a), used *attrib.* of something situated on top of a building; **roof-watcher** = **roof-spotter*; **roof-water,** rain-water collected from or falling from the roof of a building.
1955 *Trans. Inst. Mining Engineers* CXIV. 849 Roof bolts cannot be used to replace normal supports at the face, but they have been used to advantage to bolt weak immediate beds together or to stronger beds above. **1973** L. J. Thomas *Introd. Mining* vii. 276 It is unwise to rely on roof bolts to hold up the roof bar and the lip of the entry. **1954** *Jrnl. Chem., Metall. & Mining Soc. S. Afr.* LIV 285/1 It was necessary to resort to roof and side bolting and pig netting in order to protect the personnel. **1958** I. C. F. Statham *Coal Mining Pract.* II. ii. 144 An inversion of roof bolting, so-called floor bolting, in which bolts are inserted in holes drilled into the floor has proved successful in reducing floor lift. **1940** C. S. Sherrington *Man on his Nature* vii. 222 Observation indicates rather a roof-brain which overseers subordinate mechanisms. **1960** *20th Cent.* Dec. 549 At the beck and call of those more primitive regions..the roof-brain wakes or sleeps. **1951** 'M. Innes' *Operation Pax* vi. vi. 286 If you roof-climb,.. then you just can't..sit in libraries too. **1932** *Daily Mirror* 28 May 6/4 An appeal to undergraduate roof-climbers is made in the 'Cambridge Review'. **1932** G. Greene *Stamboul Train* iii. i. 123 He intended to do no more roof-climbing that night. **1970** R. Lowell *Notebk.* 238 Thud of roofdrip. **1893** M. Holley *Samantha at World's Fair* 286 Why, the very elevator you rode up to the ruff garden on wuz made by a woman. **1895** *N.Y. Dramatic News* 6 July 2/1 The growth of the roof garden idea has undoubtedly tended toward the obliteration of the regular forms of theatrical amusement during the heated term. **1911** *Chambers's Jrnl.* Feb. 113/1 Thus the director..has an opportunity to go to any part of the hotel, from the kitchen to the roof-garden, if he wants to look into matters. **1932** *Santa Fe Mag.* Jan. 34/1 A mallet type or a helper engine on a mountain job is a *sacred ox* or a *roof garden.* **1959** P. Oliver in M. T. Williams *Art of Jazz* (1960) xii. 110 The musicians and singers who had recently enjoyed a booming success at the..dance-halls and roof-gardens, were now finding themselves 'laid off'. **1958** J. G. MacGregor *North-West of 16* iii. 42 Beside the roof-jack it [*sc.* some animal] lay all night, and there..was a bulge it made in the roof of the tent. **1970** R. & J. Paterson *Cranberry Portage* xiv. 88 Cranberry settlement squatted beneath a shifting smoke blanket, upheld by blue-grey columns spinning upwards from a hundred galvanized roof jacks. **1975** *Amer. Speech 1969* XLIV. 23 *Roofjack, n.* 1. A 12′ to 14′ plank with cleats affixed to shingles or embedded into roof material and which supports the painter; it serves as a platform from which steeply pitched roofs are painted. 2. A platform made for the pitch of a roof, flexible and made of wood; it is raised level against the pitch of the roof and thus allows the roof to be worked. **1921** Roof-man [see *gutter-man* s.v. *gutter *sb.*[1] 8]. **1948** W. R. Benét *Reader's Encycl.* 541/2 s.v. *Institute of France*, It is a roof organization and embraces these five academies. **1906** R. A. Daly in *Bull. Geol. Soc. Amer.* XVII. 336 The whole forms a huge irregular block of roof rock almost completely surrounded and probably underlain by..granite. Such a block, once a downwardly projecting part of a roof in stock or batholith, may be named a 'roof pendant'; it is analogous to the pendant of Gothic architecture. **1934** C. R. Longwell et al. *Outl. Physical Geol.* ix. 173 Batholith: partly uncovered by erosion; P and P′ are masses of invaded country rock projecting deeply downward into the batholith. They are termed roof-pendants. **1961** *Amer. Mineralogist* XLVI. 249 Erosion has lowered the surface to the point where only patches of the metamorphics have been preserved, embedded in a matrix of the quartz diorite as roof pendants or 'curtains'. **1960** *News Chron.* 29 Apr. 10/5 Anyone..can..have his car fitted with..a roof-rack. **1976** P. Cave *High Flying Birds* i. 13 Just load the kites on to my roof-rack, drive down to the nearest Channel ferry service and go looking for the perfect hill. **1930** *Motor Body Building* LI. 105/1 'Coachwork Nomenclature' *Front roof rail*, the cross bar joining the front ends of the cant rail. *Rear roof rail*, the cross bar at the back of the top of the body joining the rear ends of the cant rail. **1969** *Jane's Freight Containers 1968–69* 18/3 6. Freight container components... 6.8. *Roof rails*, longitudinal structural member situated at the top edge on either side of the freight container. **1882** D. C. Beard *Amer. Boys Handy Bk.* xxiii. 210 The roof rat in the Southern States came originally from Egypt. **1926** *Genetics* XI. 456 The roof rat..is common in the southern states, especially along the seaboard. **1957** O. Breland *Animal Friends & Foes* i. 17 The two most important kinds of house rats are the brown, or Norwegian, rat and the black, or roof, rat. **1971** *New Scientist* 15 Apr. 178/2 The term 'rat' could refer to..the black rat..and its colour varieties such as the roof rat. **1909** J. R. Ware *Passing Eng.* 210/2 *Roof scrapers (Theatrical)*, gallery boys—especially those standing behind the highest row of seats—and therefore nearer the roof. **1940** *Manch. Guardian Weekly* 18 Oct. 288 If we are appointed roof-spotters to our office, then we must have sharp eyes, good ears, shrewd judgment, and a knowledge of aeroplane types. *Ibid.* 1 Nov. 322 The reports to the Ministry show that the roof-spotting system is welcomed by the workers. *Ibid.*, In the aggregate many thousands of man-hours have been saved by efficient roof-spotting. **1935** *Discovery* Apr. 94/2 He was cautious as to the advent of roof-top landings and city aerodromes. **1961** Conyn & Marten *Bali Ballet Murder* xxi. 220 One of those roof-top nightclubs [in New York]. **1963** *House & Garden* May 55/2 A rooftop garden in the Palazzo Wolkov. **1972** F. Forsyth *Odessa File* i. 9 The underground car park..200 yards from the house where he had his roof-top flat. **1979** *Tucson Mag.* Apr. 65 Distinguished by its..rooftop solar collectors, the system has 621 square feet of flat plate collectors. **1941** Roof-watcher [*see* *Jim Crow[2]]. **1879** *Harper's Mag.* June 134/1 During storms the roof water increases this action. **1910** W. De Morgan *Affair of Dishonour* iv. 55 To him who drinks no water, roof-water and well-water are welcome alike.

roof, *v.* Add: **2. a.** (Further examples.) Also with a person as object and with *over*.
a **1820** Blake *Jerusalem* xix, in *Compl. Writings* (1972) 642 And Los was roof'd in from Eternity in Albion's Cliffs. **1891** E. Arnold *Light of World* 10 The impartial skies Roof one race in. **1935** A. J. Cronin *Stars look Down* i. xxii. 211 The inrush had roofed in the Swelly: for fifty yards a barrier of water blocked the ropeway. **1972** R. Adams *Watership Down* ix. 36 Far around.. stood the orderly rows of beans,..roofing them over.

roofage. (Later *transf.* example.)
1950 M. Peake *Gormenghast* xviii. 108 A posse of professors in a whirl of gowns and a shuffling roofage of mortar-boards.

roofed, *ppl. a.* **1.** (Later examples.)
1909 C. F. G. Masterman *Condition of England* viii. 254 The roofed-in labyrinthine airless ant-heaps of Mr. Wells's nightmare. **1923** D. H. Lawrence *Birds, Beasts & Flowers* 27 All your ponderous roofed-in erection of right and wrong. **1931** [see *breeze-way, breezeway]. **1934** L. B. Lyon *White Hare* 11 The roofed glade's a sieve That lets drip through sweet water. **1946** F. Sargeson *That Summer* 107 We all went under a little roofed-in part. **1976** 'G. Black' *Moon for Killers* vi. 83 A roofed-over area that looked almost big enough to be a bus depot.

roofer. Add: **2.** A hat. *slang.* Cf. Roof *sb.* 6 a.
1859 G. W. Matsell *Vocabulum* 74 *Roofer*, a hat. **1941** Baker *Dict. Austral. Slang* 61 *Roofer*, a hat.
3. = *Collins[1]. In full, *hospitable roofer.* Also *attrib.*, as *roofer letter.*
1914 *Sphere* 7 Mar 312/3, I learn from *The Evening News* that that which some call..a 'roofer'—that is to say, a letter of thanks for hospitality—is also known as a Collins. **1935** F. M. Ford *Let.* 27 Sept. (1965) 243 They [*sc.* references] will at least serve as a hospitable-roofer. **1937** G. Frankau *More of Us* vii. 75 That bashful Hebe, too, received fair tip..Sophie, red roses and a roofer letter, With 'kind regards to her young ladyship', And, 'hoping the old boy's catarrh is better'. **1971** C. Williams-Ellis *Architect Errant* vii. 103, I felt that I really ought to write to the owner, Lord Townshend, at least some sort of a roofer or an apology. *Ibid.* xv. 217 In my roofer letter to Vita, I, of course, paid due homage to her so passionately loved Knole.

roofing, (*vbl.*) *sb.* Add: **1. b.** *roofing felt.*
1894 *Country Gentlemen's Catal.* 269 *Roofing felt.*—The best known weather-resisting material yet introduced for roofing purposes. **1929** *Morning Post* 2 Oct. 6/5 These industries include electrical engineering, paint and varnish making, roofing-felts,..and the manufacture of linoleum. **1954** *Paper Terminol.* (Spalding & Hodge, Ltd.) 51 *Roofing felt*, a very porous, soft and thick paper made from low-grade materials and used as a base for impregnation with bitumen, tar, etc.

roofless, *a.* Add: **3.** Applied to poker played with no limit to the raise.
1912 R. W. Service *Rhymes of Rolling Stone* (1913) 104 Your trouble was a roofless game of poker now and then.

roof light. Also **roof-light, rooflight.** [Roof *sb.*] **1. a.** A flashing warning light that projects upwards from the roof of a motor vehicle. **b.** A small interior light attached to the underside of the roof of a motor vehicle.
1958 'Castle' & 'Hailey' *Flight into Danger* viii. 107 At the turn-off..a police cruiser stood..its roof-light blinking a constant warning. **1961** *Times* 11 July 3/6 Coathooks, rooflights, clocks, and mirrors. **1970** A. Ross *Manchester Thing* 58 The automatic roof light gave me a quick glimpse of two men, then the driver reached up to switch it off. **1977** *Daily Tel.* 13 Jan. 17/1 An RAF helicopter crew..were guided up a valley in thick fog and darkness by the roof-light of a Land-Rover.

2. A panel in or on the roof of a building or vehicle made of a material which admits light.

1961 *Engineering* 27 Oct. 552 A new series of rooflights have been designed. **1967** *Gloss. Caravan Terms (B.S.I.)* 2 *Rooflight*, for the purpose of expressing rooflight dimensions for catalogues, the roof aperture through which light and air pass. **1978** A. Fenton *Island Blackhouse* 18 All other windows..are fixed roof lights in the thickness of the thatch.

roo·fline, roof-line. [Roof *sb.* 7 a.] **1.** The outline or silhouette of a roof or a collection of roofs.

1857 C. Vaux *Villas & Cottages* 54 Some degree of picturesqueness can always be obtained by the treatment of the roof-lines. **1886** [see Roof *sb.* 7 a]. **1936** W. Faulkner *Absalom, Absalom!* ix. 366 It loomed, bulked, square and enormous, with jagged half-toppled chimneys, its roofline sagging a little. **1955** E. Bowen *World of Love* i. 9 The long low roofline framed by too much sky. **1976** 'Trevanian' *Main* i. 14 Above the roofline, defused city-light glows in the damp, sooty air.

2. The outline of the roof of a car, usu. as seen in side elevation.

1967 [see *notch-back* s.v. *notch sb. 6]. **1971** *Daily Tel.* 20 Oct. 7/2 The styling competition winner is the Cirrus, a dart-shaped 2+2 GT car with a roofline only 49in high.

roofscape (rū·fskēip). [f. Roof *sb.* + Scape *sb.*[3]] A scene or view of roofs.

1928 *Observer* 22 July 9/3 It appears I do not mention certain roofs and arcades that Mr. Gwynn has seen. Let me inform Mr. Gwynn that every week..I pass twenty wonderful roofscapes which are probably quite unknown to Mr. Gwynn. **1949** *Archit. Rev.* CV. 277/2 (*caption*) Roofscape: a view from the roof of almost any St. John's Wood house reveals at once the factor which contributes most to the character of the place—trees. **1954** L. P. Hartley *White Wand* 23 From my bedroom windows I enjoyed a roofscape. Domes and towers gave it grandeur and formal beauty, but what chiefly fascinated me was the roofs themselves. **1965** N. Freeling *Criminal Conversation* II. iv. 112 He was high..and possessed several roof- and streetscapes. **1975** C. N. Manlove *Mod. Fantasy* vi. 215 The actual shape and relief of Sark are throughout close to what we are told of those of Gormenghast, with its long wings, its broken tower and its huge flat roofscapes.

Also **roo·fscaping** *vbl. sb.* [after *landscaping *vbl. sb.*], (see quot. 1967).

1962 *Spectator* 30 Mar. 426 One characteristic of roofscaping has all but vanished over the past decade or so—that of building rose-covered archways or pergolas. **1967** *Britannica Bk. of Year* (U.S.) 804/2 *Roofscaping*, the landscaping of rooftops (as of apartment houses and office buildings).

roof-tile. Delete ? *Obs.* and add: In mod. use, a tile used as a roofing material; a roofing tile. Also *fig.* (Later examples.)

1793 J. Woodforde *Diary* 3 Mar. (1929) IV. 12 It blowed off many Tiles from the old part of the House, some Roof Tiles. **1936** *Discovery* May 142/2 The dangerous sprinkling of snow over the 'roof tile' slabs [of Mount Everest]. **1940** 'Gun Buster' *Return via Dunkirk* I. i. 11 The house was its old self even to the last brick, the last roof-tile. **1957** *Jrnl. Geol.* LXV. 239/1 The deeply trenched roof-tile shapes of figure 8 and the delicate fern-frond pattern..shown in figure 9 are two of several different shapes exposed in a single quarry of that area.

So **roof tiler.**

1921 *Dict. Occup. Terms* (1927) § 570 Roof tiler. **1973** *Times* 16 Oct. 4/8 Mr Walsh, aged 24, a roof tiler. **1976** *Star* (Sheffield) 29 Nov. 10/2 (Advt.), Roof tiler required in the very near future.

roof-tree. Add: Also **rooftree. 1.** (Later examples.) Also *fig.*

1923 T. S. Eliot *Waste Land* v. 23 Only a cock stood on the roof-tree. **1950** D. Gascoyne *Vagrant* 38 Entangled in the thicket of World Roof-Tree's dense leaves. **1955** E. Pound *Classic Anthol.* III. 184 High, pine-covered peak full of echos, Proud ridge-pole of Heaven, roof-tree Whence descended the whirl of spirits. **1969** *New Scientist* 13 Mar. 554/1 An enormous rooftree 558ft long has just been inched up from ground level to serve as the chief single member of the new hangar which is being built by BOAC.

rooi-aas (roi·ās). *S. Afr.* [Afrikaans, f. *rooi* red + *aas* bait.] = *red-bait.

1895, 1905 [see *red-bait]. **1913** W. Thompson *Sea Fisheries Cape Colony* ii. 48 Eastwards of Cape Point the place of this crustacean is filled by red-bait (*rooi-as*). **1930** [see *red-bait].

rooibaadjie (roi·baiki, -baikyi). *S. Afr.* Also **Roed Vatje, rooiba(a)tje, -baaitje.** [Afrikaans, f. *rooi* red + *baadjie* jacket.] **1.** A British regular soldier, a redcoat. Now chiefly *Hist.*

1848 H. Ward *Five Yrs. in Kaffirland* I. v. 164 And how Umhala would laugh at the *Roed Vatjes*! **1858** [see sense 2]. **1885** J. Nixon *Compl. Story Transvaal* x. 183 First of all the officers, regular and irregular, should be fired at, and then the men with the puggarees round their hats (that is, the volunteers); and as for the rovi-baatjes [*sic*] (red-backs, i.e. regulars), it didn't matter about them—they would be sure to run when their officers were killed. *Ibid.* xi. 202 The moment the Boers rushed out to attack, after they saw their friends coming down the hill-side, the 'bastards' naturally took to flight, and sixty of his [*sc.* the Boer commandant's] men followed them, and thereupon the 'rooibatjes' fled also. **1897** E. Glanville *Tales from Veld* xxvi. 200 Sonny, them *rooibaaitjes* can fight, but they're foolish. **1941** S. Cloete *Hill of Doves* (1942) viii. 116 Why, our men were soldiers, veterans of wars, when these Rooibaadjies were but children. **1971** *Daily Dispatch* (East London, Cape Province) 18 Dec. 9 A young British rooibaadjie lurched towards him from the shadows!

2. A red larval form of the South African brown locust, *Locustana pardalina.*

1858 H. Calderwood *Caffres & Caffre Missions* xii. 157 The youngest locusts..are then partly red and partly black... Sometimes they are called *roibatjes*—that is, red-coats, in allusion to the soldiers. **1875** C. B. Bisset *Sport & War in Afr.* 170 You see the very earth become alive with diminutive insects,.. increasing in size and becoming the colour of the brightest red. At this stage they are called the Rooi baatyes or red soldiers. **1902** *Trans. S. Afr. Philos. Soc.* XI. p. xlv, The young of the migratory one [*sc.* a locust]..are so gaily coloured as to have earned for them the local name of '*rooi-batjes*', or redcoats. **1972** *Stand. Encycl. S. Afr.* VII. 21/1 Young crowded hoppers would develop into typical phase *gregaria* 'rooibaadjies'.

rooibekkie (roi·beki). *S. Afr.* Also **roibek, rood(e)bec, -bekje, rooibe(c)k(ie), rooibekje.** [Afrikaans, f. *rooi* red + *bek* beak + *-ie* dim. suff.] Either of two birds with red beaks, the waxbill, *Estrilda astrild*, or the pin-tailed whydah, *Vidua macroura.*

1793 tr. *C. P. Thunberg's Trav. Europe, Afr., & Asia* I. 312 The *Loxia Astrild*, on account of its red beak, was called Rood-beckje, or *Red-beak*, and was found in great numbers in the farmers gardens. **1822** W. J. Burchell *Trav. Interior S. Afr.* I. xii. 266 The *Roode-bekje* (Red beak), a small finch,.. is a very common bird. **1861** Lady Duff Gordon *Let.* 10 Dec. in *Lett. from Cape* (1921) 60, I will try to bring home some cages of birds—Cape canaries and 'roode bekjes' (red bills), darling little things. **1868** J. Chapman *Trav. Interior S. Afr.* II. i. 17 We shot and skinned some birds, among which was a long-tailed finch (king rooi bekkie). **1890** A. Martin *Home Life on Ostrich Farm.* i. 18 Another soft-voiced little singer is the *rooibeck*, or red-beak. **1899** R. B. & J. D. S. Woodward *Natal Birds* 66 This bird [*sc.* the pin-tailed widow bird] derives its name from its pretty wax-like red bill, which resembles that of the estrilda, and in common with them it is called *roibek*. **1900** A. C. Stark *Birds S. Afr.* I. 98 Common Waxbill..'Roodebec'..and 'Rooibeckie' of Dutch Colonists. **1913** [see *king *sb.* 7 a]. **1936** E. L. Gill *First Guide S. Afr. Birds* 32 Pin-tailed Widow-bird, King Rooibekkie,..is also parasitic; the eggs are laid in nests of the common Rooibekkie. **1952** *Cape Times* 15 Jan. 9/8 Farmers are demanding the extermination of the common rooibekkie, or waxbill. **1963** S. Cloete *Rags of Glory* 548 The rooibekkies were still chattering in the trees.

rooibok (roi·bǫk). *S. Afr.* Also **roibok, roodebok, rooibuck, rooye bok.** [Afrikaans, f. *rooi* red + *bok* buck.] = *impala.

1824 W. J. Burchell *Trav. Interior S. Afr.* II. xi. 215 One [antelope] is called *Paala* (Parla) by the Bichuanas, and is known by the name of *Roodebok* (Redbuck). **1835** A. Smith *Diary* 27 Aug. (1940) II. 182 They had much difficulty in getting them to..carry the flesh of a rooye bok. **1866** T. Leask *Diary* 12 May (1954) 44 Saw some rooibok, but felt too done up to go after them. **1875** [see *impala]. **1896** H. A. Bryden *Tales S. Afr.* 65 Smallfield ..had shot a good rooibok. **1926** *Glasgow Herald* 31 Aug. 2/6 He had got a rooibuck (or impala) ram. **1932** Fuller & Fouche *Louis Trigardt's Trek* vi. 65 He told..about a *rooibok* and two geese they had shot. **1947** [see *impala]. **1968** L. G. Green *Full Many a Glorious Morning* 189 Palapye Road, named by an extinct tribe after the rooibok, was once the site of the 'post office tree'.

rooibos (roi·bǫs). *S. Afr.* Also **rooibosch, rooibostee.** [Afrikaans, f. *rooi* red + *bos* bush.]

1. An evergreen South African shrub of the genus *Aspalathus* (formerly *Borbonia*), belonging to the family Leguminosæ, and cultivated for its leaves which are used to make a kind of tea; also, the beverage made from the leaves. Also *attrib.*

1911 *S. Afr. Jrnl. Sci.* VII. 374 The author described.. a *Borbonia*, the source of Cape 'rooibos' tea. **1932** Watt & Breyer-Brandwijk *Medicinal & Poisonous Plants S. Afr.* 70 *Borbonia pinifolia* Marl.,..Rooibostee..and *Borbonia cordata*..are also used as teas. **1946** [see *bush tea* s.v. *bush *sb.*[1] 11]. **1948** *Cape Argus* 18 Dec. 7/9 Dr. Pieter le Fras Nortier..established a flourishing rooibos industry. **1949** L. G. Green *In Land of Afternoon* iii. 52 Bush tea is..an entirely different plant—a legume. You hear it called rooibos. *Ibid.* 53 The ants of the district collect rooibos seeds and store them underground. **1951** *Cape Times* 17 Oct. 2/6 Mr. Riordan was..a well-known rooibosch tea farmer. **1977** *Daily Tel.* 5 Mar. 18 Rooibosch is almost entirely free from tannin and contains no caffein.

2. A shrub or small tree, *Combretum apiculatum*, belonging to the family Combretaceæ, native to central and southern Africa, and bearing red or yellow foliage in winter, and spikes of scented yellow flowers.

1932 Watt & Breyer-Brandwijk *Medicinal & Poisonous Plants S. Afr.* 128 The Zulus regard *Combretum erythrophyllum* Sond., Bush willow,..Rooibos,..as poisonous. **1972** Palmer & Pitman *Trees S. Afr.* III. 1633 The rooibos is a valuable fodder tree.

rooi-els (roi·els). *S. Afr.* Also **rood(e) els, elze.** [Afrikaans, f. *rooi* red + *els* alder.] An evergreen tree, *Cunonia capensis*, belonging to the family Cunoniaceæ, native to southern Africa, and bearing compound leaves and racemes of fragrant cream flowers; also, the reddish wood of this tree. Cf. *red alder, red els* s.v. Red *a.* 17 d in Dict. and Suppl.

1801 J. Barrow *Acct. Trav. Interior S. Afr.* I. v. 339 Roode els..stands water well. **1822** W. J. Burchell *Trav. Interior S. Afr.* I. vii. 143 Its colonial name is *Rood Elze* (Red Alder), although the tree has not..the least resemblance to the Alder of Europe. **1948** *Cape Times* 5 Aug. 8/7 If trees must be planted, let them rather be the ..rooi els and other local forest trees. **1972** Palmer & Pitman *Trees S. Afr.* I. 665 The rooi-els grows in moist mountain forests.

rooigras (roi·χras). *S. Afr.* Also **rooigrass.** [Afrikaans, f. *rooi* red + *gras* grass.] A southern African grass, *Themeda triandra*, which goes a reddish colour in winter. Also *attrib.*

1889 H. A. Bryden *Kloof & Karroo* iv. 88 Much of the lower parts of these hills is clothed with rooi-grass. **1907** T. R. Sim *Forests & Forest Flora Cape of Good Hope* iv. 37 The rushes have given place to rooi-grass. **1929** J. W. Bews *World's Grasses* vi. 253 'Rooi gras'..is a valuable forage grass. **1950** *Cape Times* 30 Oct. 9/6 A. C. Erasmus scattered the first *rooigras* seeds in the..bare land recently cleared. **1966** C. A. W. Guggisberg *S.O.S. Rhino* iv. 92 The dominant grass throughout the..range of the southern white rhino is *Themeda triandra*, which stands quite high and is popularly known as 'rooigrass'. **1972** *Stand. Encycl. S. Afr.* V. 320/2 A large number of species, e.g. Guinea grass.., rooigras.., the finger-grasses ..are important pasture grasses.

rooihout (roi·hǭᵘt). *S. Afr.* Also **roodehout, roye-houtt.** [Afrikaans, f. *rooi* red + *hout* wood.] One of several trees with reddish wood, esp. the Cape plane, *Ochna arborea*, or its wood. Also *attrib.*

1790 E. Helme tr. *Le Vaillant's Trav. Afr.* II. xiv. 288 Another tree, called *Roye-houtt*, (red wood) so named from its deep red colour, grows very thick. **1896** E. Clairmonte *Africander* i. 2 A flock of long-tailed house birds..would dash past to settle in a *rooihout* tree. **1907** T. R. Sim *Forests & Forest Flora Cape of Good Hope* xiv. 163 Cape Plane..Roodehout. **1973** *Eastern Province Herald* (Port Elizabeth) 28 May 13/2 No self-respecting woodcutter would have the handle of his axe made from any timber other than 'rooihout' (Cape plane) a reddish close grained wood.

rooikat (roi·kat). *S. Afr.* Also **roode-kat.** [Afrikaans, f. *rooi* red + *kat* cat.] = Caracal.

1785 G. Forster tr. *Sparrman's Voy. Cape of Good Hope* I. 150 Another kind of cat, as it is called, or the *roode-kat*, is..supposed to possess a great medicinal power in its skin. **1880** J. Nixon *Life among Boers* vi. 142 There is another kind, known as the rooiket, whose skin is highly prized for making karrosses. **1939** S. Cloete *Watch for Dawn* v. 70, I am as slim as a rooikat and this is my country. **1948** *Cape Times* 4 Dec. (Mag. Section) 3/4 A lithe red shape trotting through the bush ahead.. was my first sight of the African lynx or rooikat. **1966** E. Palmer *Plains of Camdeboo* ix. facing p. 160 (*caption*) The brilliant coloured lynx or rookat—rich red with jet-black ear tufts.

rooikrans (roi·krans). *S. Afr.* Also **rooi-kran(t)z.** [Afrikaans, f. *rooi* red + *krans* wreath, in allusion to the red aril of the seed.] A yellow-flowered shrub, *Acacia cyclops*, of the family Leguminosæ, native to Western Australia, and naturalized in southern Africa, where it is also called the golden willow. Also *attrib.*

1917 R. Marloth *Flora S. Afr. Suppl.: Common Names* 71 Rooikrans... From Australia..one of the Golden willows. **1920** *S. Afr. Smallholders' & Fruit Growers' Year Bk. 1920–1921* 175 Rooikrantz—A shrubby wattle useful for firewood. **1950** [see *Port Jackson willow* s.v. *Port Jackson]. **1953** *Cape Times* 9 July 14/2 Silver trees are being choked by young self-seeded cluster pines and rooikrans. **1957** *Cape Times Mag.* 20 July 10/4 He wielded the chopper as easily as a man—severing the tough branches of the rooikrantz trees. *Ibid.* 10/6 On the outskirts of the rooikranz trees they began to dig.

rooiman, var. *roman *sb.*[3]

rooinek (roi·nek). *S. Afr.* Also **roineck** and with capital initial. *Pl.* **rooineks, rooinekke.** [Afrikaans, f. *rooi* red + *nek* neck.] A term applied by Afrikaans-speaking South Africans to the British or to English-speaking South Africans.

1890 'S. Erasmus' *Prinsloo of Prinsloosdorp* ii. 14 One morning he was on the market with his waggon when two men—English Rooineks—came and said: 'Piet, do you want to make £15?' **1896** H. A. Bryden *Tales S. Afr.* 210 Cornelis would open up, and yarn to me in a way that, until you know him well, the Boer seldom manifests to the *rooi-nek*. **1900** *Captain* III. 121/1 *Rooinek* scout. **1900** Kipling in *Daily Express* 13 June 4/5 And you will see how we can shoot rooineks. **1921** *Chambers's Jrnl.* Jan. 32/1, I was thinking of the efforts that that infernal rooinek (red-neck) of a son of yours is making to deprive me of my only child. **1937** C. R. Prance *Tante Rebella's Saga* 47 A rascally Irish 'rooinek' whose real name had been Pat Murphy till he changed it to Piet van der Merwe when he turned Afrikander. **1947** H. C. Bosman *Mafeking*

Road 117 But of course no rooinek can make a living out of farming, unless they send him money every month from England. **1962** [see *LIMEY a]. **1963** S. CLOETE *Rags of Glory* xxxix. 316 The Englishmen were sunburned, red as lobsters. They did not go brown like the Boers. That's why we call them rooineks—rednecks—Renata thought. **1969** VISCT. BUCKMASTER *Roundabout* xviii. 279 An English taxi-driver told me that he had lived for twenty years in Cape Town, only still to be called 'A bloody roineck', the name given to our troops in the Boer war. **1972** *Daily Dispatch* (East London, S. Afr.) 2 Feb. 6 Nasty little racist jibes, which we South Africans have been listening to for the past 10 years, about Van der Merwe and the Rooinekke and 'a bantu'. **1975** 'D. JORDAN' *Black Account* v. 32 The Afrikaner industrialists ..had emerged since 1948 to challenge the English *rooineks* and their dominance of South African finance.

rooirhebok (roirē·bǫk). *S. Afr.* Also **roode, rooye rheebok.** [Afrikaans, f. *rooi* red + *RHE(E)BOK.] The mountain reedbuck, *Redunca fulvorufula.* Also *attrib.*

1835 A. SMITH *Diary* 11 July (1940) II. 107 During this season the male and female of the rooye rheebok are generally apart. **1835** A. STEEDMAN *Wanderings S. Afr.* I. II. iv. 176 We observed, at some little distance, several antelopes of the description called *roode-rheebok*, which were running up the mountain. **1850** [see RHEEBOC]. **1904** [see NAGOR]. **1912** J. STEVENSON-HAMILTON *Animal Life Afr.* x. 157 Rooi rhebok favour the lower slopes of hills. **1957** *Cape Argus* 13 July 7/5, I have seen a rooirhebok ewe battling to save her kid from an eagle.

rook, *sb.*[1] Add: **4. a.** *rook-babble, -roost, -scarer; rook-scaring* vbl. sb.; *rook-crowded, -delighting, -racked, -routed* adjs.

1948 C. DAY LEWIS *Poems 1943–47* 21 The rook-babble of bathers. **1964** *Listener* 24 Dec. 1009/2 Goal-posts, a public-house, a rook-crowded birch. **1914** W. B. YEATS *Responsibilities* 37 Suddenly I saw the cold and rook-delighting Heaven. **1879** G. M. HOPKINS *Poems* (1967) 79 Lark-charmèd, rook-racked, river-rounded. **1937** J. W. DAY *Sporting Adventure* 88 The great rook-roosts of winter, the annual nightly gatherings of thousands of these birds, are breaking up. **1923** BLUNDEN *To Nature* 46 In the rook-routed vale. **1910** Rook-scarer [used in Dict. in def. of *roof-starver*]. **1946** J. W. DAY *Harvest Adventure* xvi. 266 A rat-catcher is a Pest Control Officer and a rook-scarer a Corvine Operator! **1895** 'ROSEMARY' *Under Chilterns* i. 20 The poor child ain't fit for sech work as that there rewk-scarin' this weather. **1910** [used in Dict. in def. of *roof-starving*]. **1969** G. E. EVANS *Farm & Village* v. 55 Some called it *bird-keeping* or *bird-tending*—keeping the birds off the newly sown land—while others referred to it simply as *rook-scaring.*

b. rook-drive, an expedition to shoot rooks; **rook rifle** (further examples); **rook-worm,** add: esp. the larva of the cockchafer, *Melolontha melolontha*; (later examples).

1969 R. BLYTHE *Akenfield* 20 'Did you kill men, Davie?' 'I got several'—the same answer to a question on how he did on a rook-drive. **1900** E. GLYN *Visits of Elizabeth* 50 She amused herself..by shooting at rabbits..with a rook rifle. **1907** [see *EJECTOR 2]. **1921** 'K. MANSFIELD' *Let.* 3 Feb. (1977) 215 My grandpa said a man could travel all over the world with a clean pair of socks and a rook rifle. **1972** *Shooting Times & Country Mag.* 4 Mar. 11/1 Somehow we got hold of a .300 rook rifle cartridge. **1976** *Ibid.* 16–22 Dec. 46/4 (Advt.), Holland and Holland .410 converted rook rifle, £70. **1959** E. F. LINSSEN *Beetles Brit. Isles* II. 124 The larvae of the Cockchafer—sometimes called by farmers White Grubs or Rookworms—are exceedingly destructive. **1973** J. M. CHINERY *Field Guide Insects Brit. & N. Europe* 303 It is said that rooks are particularly fond of both adult and larval cockchafers and the larvae are often called rookworms.

rook (ruk), *sb.*[4] U.S. shortening of *ROOKIE.

1905 *Bluejacket* Mar. 190/1 The sailors there said we were 'rooks'. **1927** *Amer. Speech* II. 278/1 *Rook*,.. novice. **1935** *Our Army* (U.S.) June 12 A life-long profession from club-footed 'Rook' to Top Soak. **1941** G. KERSH *They die with their Boots Clean* II. 85 This here Spencer drops weight...millions of stones that rook lost. **1942** *Yank* 23 Sept. 17 In the horse cavalry, recruits do not complain as loudly about kitchen police as do the rooks in other branches.

rook, *v.*[1] **1.** (Further examples.)

1938 *Sun* (Baltimore) 11 Oct. 24/2 There have been numerous complaints that the growers have been 'rooked'. **1969** *Listener* 10 Apr. 482/3 Because we had been rooked at the door, none of us ever thought of boycotting the desk where another seated veteran..was selling post-cards. **1977** *Capital Times* (Madison, Wisconsin) 27 Jan. 10/3 The Federal Trade Commission thinks that a lot of people have been rooked by these buying clubs.

rookery. Add: **2. a.** (Earlier example.)

1832 A. EARLE *Narr. of Residence on Tristan d'Acunha* 357 We visited what they call a 'penguin rookery'.

b. (Earlier and later examples.)

1832 B. MORRELL *Four Voyages* p. xxiv, The word *rookery*..has been applied by all our South Sea navigators to the breeding encampments of various oceanic animals, such as seal, penguins, &c. **1846** *McLean Papers* 22 Dec. 42 (typescript), A boat goes out in search of a 'rookery' as they term the collected seals on any spot. **1932** S. ZUCKERMAN *Social Life Monkeys & Apes* v. 69 Bull seals fight each other..for territory in the rookery or mating ground. **1972** L. HANCOCK *There's a Seal in my Sleeping Bag* vii. 145 The rocky shores of Triangle Island itself are used by the Steller sea-lions as hauling-out grounds, while those of the large islets immediately off the main island are breeding grounds and rookeries.

3. (Earlier and later examples.)

1792 G. GALLOWAY *Poems on Various Subjects* 74 Then I begin my follies to repent, With naked elbows and a coat thread bare... So for to hide my God I need no bags, While like to rookry dogs I'm cloth'd with rags. **1971** *Daily Tel.* 2 Dec. 6/4 The artisans, a potent radical force, were very different from the a-political desperate starvelings of the London rookeries. **1973** *N.Y. Law Jrnl.* 4 Sept. 5/3 Look at the city's unrepairable slums housing miserably over a million people... These rookeries are beyond repair. **1976** M. BUTTERWORTH *Festival!* vii. 106 Arnold..lay in a crude shelter..in the heart of a close-packed slum of some of the worst habitations at the festival; a rookery so vile that it had been totally rejected by all the rest.

4. (Earlier and later examples.)

c **1820** *Oh, What a Row!* (song) People toiling, roasting, boiling, bless us! such a rookery. **1925** *Dialect Notes* V. 340 *Rookery*, confusion, ruckus. **1942** BERREY & VAN DEN BARK *Amer. Thes. Slang* § 5/1 *Disorder n.*,..riz-raz, rookery, [etc.].

rookie (ru·ki). *slang.* Also **rookey, rooky.** [Origin uncertain; perh. corruption of RECRUIT *sb.*] **1.** A raw recruit, *spec.* (*a*) an army or police recruit; (*b*) a novice at a sport, etc., esp. a first-year player in a particular team (chiefly *N. Amer.*).

1892 KIPLING *Barrack-Room Ballads* 68 So 'ark an' 'eed, you rookies, which is always grumblin' sore. **1893** [in Dict. s.v. ROOKY *sb.*]. **1900** I. L. REEVES *Bamboo Tales* 100 One of his men, a green 'rookie'. **1909** R. A. WATSON *Happy Hawkins* 142 'Why, you blame rookie,' sez I, 'You don't really think I was mad do you?' **1913** *Chicago Record-Herald* 1 Mar. 12/2 Cal tried out Lefty Delano, a New Brunswick southpaw rookie. **1913** H. A. FRANCK *Zone Policeman 88* ix. 275 From the lieutenant to the newest uniformless 'rookie' every member of the police was swarming in and out of the building. **1918** I. CRUMP *Conscript 2989* 6 Oh, you rookey. **1929** *Daily Express* 15 Jan. 9/7 In 1915..he was a member of the Baltimore baseball team as a gawky 'rookie'. **1930** *Punch* 16 Apr. 443/1 The keen young rooky, just fresh from his public school. **1939** *Airman's Gaz.* Dec., Who was the Rookie here who thought..Blanco was a Spanish General. **1956** 'E. MCBAIN' *Cop Hater* (1958) ix. 81 A squad car driven by a young rookie. **1961** F. H. BURGESS *Dict. Sailing* 173 *Rooky*, a brand new hand. **1966** *Time* 8 July 60/3 The new enlarged S. & S. will be in a more powerful position to bid for blockbusting authors, whose contracts have been escalating as rapidly as those of prize pro football rookies. **1975** *Listener* 16 Jan. 66/2 [He] flew with Hunt to Hong Kong, as a police rookie. **1976** *Billings* (Montana) *Gaz.* 16 June 5-c/1 Rookies Chris Evert..and Rod Laver..headed the list of players named Tuesday to the World Team Tennis Western Division All-Star team. **1979** *Tucson* (Arizona) *Citizen* 20 Sept. 1D/1 He was rookie of the year on the Professional Golfers Association tour in 1965.

2. *attrib.* passing into *adj.*

1930 E. H. LAVINE *Third Degree* (1931) 102 The shooting of 'rookie' Patrolman James A. Broderick. **1944** *Chicago Daily News* 21 Oct. 11/1 They expressed themselves..as willing to trade..for the rookie outfielder. **1954** L. ARMSTRONG *Satchmo* 37 They gave me the rooky greeting saying, 'Welcome, Newcomer'. **1963** *Listener* 4 Apr. 585/1 To the eye of the rookie policeman they were as unobtrusive as the pavement stones. **1968** [see *CHARLEY-HORSE, CHARLEY HORSE]. **1972** M. WILLIAMS *Inside Number 10* xii. 322, I recall the times he was censorious with us about security and times when he treated us like the latest members of an awkward squad in a rookie army. **1974** *Spartanburg* (S. Carolina) *Herald* 18 Apr. C1/7 The Dallas Cowboys lost a fifth player to the World Football League Wednesday when rookie tight end John Kelsey of Missouri signed with the Honolulu Hawaiians. **1977** *Daily Mirror* 30 Mar., Rookie police constable Paul Weaver, 19, saved a 74-year-old widow from her blazing home. **1977** D. L. ALTHEIDE in Douglas & Johnson *Existential Sociol.* iv. 137 Rookie reporters..learn the ropes and eventually become bored with the questions of newcomers. **1980** *Washington Star* 18 July A6/3 Reagan's nomination is the penultimate step in a steady 12-year drive to the White House that began with a feeble tentative pass at the office in 1968 when he was derided as a Grade B Hollywood movie actor and a rookie right-wing fringe governor of California.

rooking, *vbl. sb.*[1] (Later examples.)

1936 *Sat. Even. Post* 19 Dec. 11/1 What else could we do but quit? Mel wasn't treatin' you square. Can you deny it? I won't speak for myself, though I was gettin' a fancy rookin', too, singin' and all. **1955** *Sun* (Baltimore) 10 Sept. 6/4 They submit to a rooking involving thousands of dollars.

rooking, *ppl. a.* (Later example.)

1934 DYLAN THOMAS *18 Poems* 20 A rooking girl who stole me for her side.

rookus (ru·kəs), var. *RUCKUS.

1893 H. A. SHANDS *Some Peculiarities of Speech in Mississippi* 53 *Rookus*, a word signifying a quarrel or row. **1902** 'O. HENRY' in *Ainslee's Mag.* Mar. 130/1 He talks all spraddled out..'bout the rookuses he's been in. He claims to have saw the elephant and hearn the owl. **1924** W. M. RAINE *Troubled Waters* vi. 60 Course there'll be a rookus between him and Joe Tait.

b. rookus-juice *U.S. slang*, liquor.

1929 *Amer. Speech* IV. 385 Such terms as *rookus juice, third rail*,..and *bust-head* are evidently references to the potency or the effect of the liquor designated. **1942** BERREY & VAN DEN BARK *Amer. Thes. Slang* §99/1 *Liquor*..rinse, rookus-juice, [etc.]. **1951** *Western Folklore* X. 80 Give me a shot of:..rookus juice.

rooky, *sb.* Substitute for entry:
rooky, var. *ROOKIE.

room, *sb.*[1] Add: **I. 2. a.** Also in phr. *room at the top.*

1900 W. JAMES *Let.* 2 Apr. (1920) II. 121 Verily there is room at the top. S— seems to be the only Britisher worth thinking of. **1914** A. BENNETT *Price of Love* vii. 143 The Imperial had set out to be the most gorgeous cinema in the Five Towns; and it simply was. Its advertisements read: 'There is always room at the top.' **1929** *Times* 11 Jan. 13/4 When successful men give schoolboys their prizes they generally throw in a little advice. They recommend industry, neatness, punctuality, and other virtues, but they also dwell on the saying that there is always room at the top. **1933** W. S. MAUGHAM *Sheppey* III. 89 You have to be pretty smart with all the competition there is nowadays... There's always room at the top. **1947** 'G. ORWELL' *Eng. People* 22 The masses..know it is not true that 'there's plenty of room at the top'. **1957** J. BRAINE *Room at Top* xxviii. 230 You're the sort of young man we want. There's always room at the top. **1960** *20th Cent.* July 79 Academically speaking, the room at the top in sociology is lessening. **1980** *Times* 14 Jan. 5/5 In that last crisis, McEnroe suddenly looked young and vulnerable and Borg's tennis told him bluntly that, for the time being, there was no room at the top.

b. *no room to swing a cat in* and varr.: see SWING *v.*[1] 7 a.

II. 6. c. (Earlier and later examples.) Cf. *fishing-room* s.v. FISHING *vbl. sb.*[1] 5 b in Dict. and Suppl.

1620 R. WHITBOURNE *Discourse & Discovery of New-found-land* 30 [They] doe cut downe many of the best trees they can finde, to build their stages and roomes..; hewing..and destroying many others that grow within a mile of the Sea, where they use to fish. **1937** P. K. DEVINE *Folk-Lore Newfoundland* (Gloss.), *Room*, a fishing premises: stage, flakes and store. **1948** *Canad. Geogr. Jrnl.* Mar. 110/1 Fishing off Labrador is carried on by fishermen who leave Newfoundland in May or June and reside at 'rooms' (buildings used by the fishermen) on various parts of the Labrador coast until the close of the season. **1954** F. BRIFFETT *Story of Newfoundland & Labrador* 32 A man's fishing property—flakes, stages and stores—was known as his room. **1963** J. T. ROWLAND *North to Adventure* iv. 54 Most of the schooner men had permanent stations, or 'rooms',..with storehouses and fish stages. **1975** *Canad. Antiques Collector* Mar.–Apr. 10/2 Of a crew of 40, there would be 24 to man eight small boats and 16 to work on the room.

8. a. Also *spec.* (chiefly *pl.*) a room or rooms for public gatherings, an assembly room, auction room, gambling room, etc.; at Lloyd's of London, the area where insurance business is carried out.

1766 C. ANSTEY *New Bath Guide* vii. 45 The Captain is come, And so kind as to go with us all to the Room. *Ibid.* viii. 48 (*heading*) Mr. B-n-r-d goes to the Rooms. His opinion of Gaming. **1771** SMOLLETT *Humph. Cl.* I. 115 In the forenoon, they crawl out to the Rooms or the coffee-house. **1779** F. BURNEY *Diary* Oct. (1842) I. 254 In the evening we all went to the rooms. The rooms, as they are called, consisted, for this evening, of only one apartment, as there was not company enough to make more necessary. **1822** W. HAZLITT in *New Monthly Mag.* IV. 112 An old gentleman..who looked as if he had played many a rubber at the Bath rooms. **1876** GEO. ELIOT *Dan. Der.* I. II. xv. 291 They moved off together to saunter through the rooms, Sir Hugo saying as they entered the large *saal*—'Did you play much at Baden, Grandcourt?' **1904** A. E. W. MASON *Truants* xxiii. 217 She..bought a visitor's list at the kiosk in front of the rooms. **1928** A. CHRISTIE *Mystery of Blue Train* xxvii. 214 He found [him] in the Rooms, jauntily placing the minimum stake on the even numbers. **1931** *N. & Q.* 29 Aug. 155/2 Book auctions.—May I voice a long overdue protest against the pernicious and iniquitous custom prevailing in the 'Rooms' of doing up parcels of books with string. **1933** D. C. PEEL *Life's Enchanted Cup* x. 121 The Rooms were so crowded that I could not get near enough to play at my chosen table. **1946** G. STIMPSON *Bk. about Thousand Things* 51 This bell, which hangs in a clock-topped tower in 'Lloyd's Rooms' was salvaged from the frigate Lutine. **1962** H. O. BEECHENO *Introd. Business Stud.* xvi. 153 He [*sc.* the broker] will then take this in to 'the Room' at Lloyd's and approach one or more leading underwriters. **1972** [see *OLD BOY].

10. a. *room air, -fellow, maid, number, paper, rent* (earlier and later examples), *ticket; room-keeper* (later example); *room-breaking* vbl. sb.; **room clerk,** in a hotel, guest-house, etc., a clerk who assigns rooms to patrons; **room divider:** see *DIVIDER 9; **room service,** the provision of food or drink for a hotel guest in his room, or the department providing this; **room temperature,** the temperature of a, or the, room, esp. that which is comfortable for occupants, conventionally taken as about 20°C; also *attrib.* and *fig.*; **room-to-room** *attrib.*, (of a telephone) connecting rooms within the same building.

1957 *Encycl. Brit.* XI. 353/1 Louis Savot..developed for the Louvre a fireplace in which room air was drawn through passages under the hearth and behind the fire grate. **1975** *New Yorker* 22 Dec. 78/3 He decided to discontinue Berger's oxygen therapy. He wanted him breathing room air again. **1951** S. SPENDER *World within World* 36 After the room-breaking episode the attitude of my fellow freshmen towards me altered. **1916** W. A. DU PUY *Uncle Sam, Detective* 49 The room clerk had suggested that it was the custom of the hotel that guests without baggage should pay in advance. **1978** S. SHELDON *Bloodline* xxxiii. 315 Before Max left Chamonix, he stopped at the desk of the Kleine Scheidegg hotel and talked to the room clerk. **1930** R. MACAULAY *Staying with*

Relations ix. 122 Snakes might be her companions, wild cats her room-fellows, but she..abandoned herself to these. **1922** JOYCE *Ulysses* 304 The meal should be divided..among the members of the sick and indigent roomkeepers' association. **1955** A. ROSS *Australia 55* xv. 212 The room-maid says the world will end, not with an atom bomb, but with a flood. **1976** *Evening Standard* 14 June 26/3 (Advt.), Room maids, m/f, required by London Penta Hotel. **1959** A. CHRISTIE *Cat among Pigeons* iv. 54 Must have given me the wrong room number. **1968** 'M. CARROLL' *Dead Trouble* ii. 22 The receptionist..asked what room number. **1976** H. NIELSEN *Brink of Murder* xii. 94 Send up a fifth of Buchanan's. .. You know my room number. **1870** P. FITZGERALD in *All Year Round* V. 112/1 The decorations of the Jericho Theatre are rather of a homely cast, room paper garnished with bead mouldings. **1973** *Canad. Antiques Collector* Jan.–Feb. 20/1 A few scattered stories of the early elegance of room paper survive. **1818** *N. Amer. Rev.* Mar. 427 The room rent and wood are estimated upon the condition that two students live in a College room. **1851** C. CIST *Sk. Cincinnati in 1851* 65 The annual term bill for room-rent..and incidental expenses is ten dollars. **1942** *Amer. Mercury* July 90 That meant..maybe room rent and a reefer or two. **1930** A. BENNETT *Imperial Palace* vii. 32 The head floors-waiter did not conceal his belief that the room-service was the basis of prosperity. **1935** WODEHOUSE *Luck of Bodkins* xxiv. 311 If you go to that phone and call Room Service, you can get all the champagne you want. **1949** O. NASH *Versus* 99 (*title*) Mrs. Purvis dreads room service. **1965** I. FLEMING *Man with Golden Gun* vii. 94 Order what you want from Room Service. **1971** R. THOMAS *Backup Men* xviii. 156 The room service waiter..brought the hamburgers and coffee. **1974** P. GORE-BOOTH *With Great Truth & Respect* 155 The only way I found of getting any relaxation at all was to be extravagant and have 'room service' breakfast. **1978** *Time* 3 July 47/2 Half-eaten room-service sandwiches. **1924** J. G. A. SKERL tr. *Wegener's Orig. Continents & Oceans* 128 They can prove that the earth is about two or three times as rigid at room-temperature as steel. **1945** R. T. ROLFE *Dict. Metallogr.* 4 It may consist..of a period of standing at room temperature. **1959** J. BRAINE *Vodi* xiv. 193 Of course the red wine should be at room temperature. **1962** SIMPSON & RICHARDS *Physical Princ. Junction Transistors* ix. 211 The effect of these two factors is to make it desirable to place the operating point at a lower point than would be decided by room-temperature conditions. **1974** *Times* 13 Nov. 12/5 Put the mixture..overnight in the refrigerator. Allow to come up to room temperature again before baking. **1976** I. LEVIN *Boys from Brazil* v. 143 He wasn't accorded a warm or even room-temperature welcome. **1977** *Nature* 17 Feb. 660/2 The bK_{590} intermediate..has a lifetime of 2 μs at room temperature. **1905** A. BENNETT *Tales of Five Towns* II. 264 She pushed his room-ticket across the page of the big book. **1938** Room-to-room [see *BUZZ *sb.*[1] 1 d].

b. *room-sealed* ppl. adj.

1963 *B.S.I. News* May 15/2 B.S. 3561 refers to fan-assisted air heaters,..and room-sealed heaters, giving requirements for their construction and performance. **1967** *Gloss. Terms Gas Industry (B.S.I.)* 78 *Room-sealed appliance*, an appliance which, when in operation, has the combustion air inlet and the combustion products outlet isolated from the room in which the appliance is installed.

III. 13. d. (Further example.)

1861 *Macm. Mag.* Dec. 141/2 Missis would still keep going on with her parties and company, o' rum o' minding her farm and dairy.

room, *adv.* For *Obs.* read *arch.* or *dial.* and add: **2.** (Later example.)

1969 G. M. BROWN *Orkney Tapestry* 134 Guidman, go to your bacon And cut us doon a daggon Cut it lucky, cut it room, Look 'at you dunno cut your toom.

3. a. (Later example.)

1902 J. M. BARRIE *Little White Bird* xv. 163 He was drifted towards the far shore, where are black shadows he knew not the dangers of, but suspected them, and so.. went roomer of the shadows until he caught a favouring wind.

room, *v.*[2] **2.** For *U.S.* read 'chiefly U.S.' and add: **a.** (Further examples.) Also *to room it*.

1912 F. M. HUEFFER *Panel* I. i. 19 She and me were on the old North Circuit. Roomed it and ate off the same old herring together. **1937** *Observer* 22 Aug. 7/2 He dressed like a hobo, hitch-hiked from San Francisco to Los Angeles, and roomed on the town's Main Street as a plain British seaman. **1969** L. MICHAELS *Going Places* 167 Slotsky helped him with chemistry and French—Finn's reason for rooming with him in the first place. **1973** *Time* 25 June 11/1 John..roomed with Barry Goldwater Jr., who now is his neighbor. **1977** *Western Mail* (Cardiff) 5 Mar. (Rugby Suppl.) 4/2 It was on that tour that I developed a close friendship with many of the Welsh players... TGR and JPR I roomed with on many occasions, waiting on them hand and foot. **1979** *Yale Alumni Mag.* Apr. (Suppl.) CN12/1 Charlie, with whom I roomed, stayed through freshman year.

b. (Earlier example.)

1860 *Blackw. Mag.* Jan. 112/2 A miserable public house, where I was 'roomed', or in other words, put into the same room with, a rising medical practitioner.

rooman, var. *ROMAN *sb.*[3]

roomer, *sb.* For *U.S.* read 'orig. *U.S.*' and add: **1.** (Earlier and later examples.)

1871 L. H. BAGG *4 Years at Yale* 46 *Roomer*, a word used by landladies to designate a lodger or occupant of a room who takes his meals elsewhere. **1905** 'O. HENRY' in *N.Y. World Mag.* 20 Aug. 4/2 There was rejoicing among the gentlemen roomers whenever Miss Leeson had time to sit on the steps. **1912** J. SANDILANDS *Western Canad. Dict.*, *Roomer*, a lodger who has living accommodation in a house and gets his food elsewhere. **1919** *Studies* VIII. 304 There is no 'board' provided, but simply a room... A 'roomer' has all the perfect liberty of a latchkey... She can entertain what visitors she likes in her own room. **1939** *Sun* (Baltimore) 6 Jan. 1/2 Held with Joseph Malone, 27, as a material witness was Elizabeth Gelula, 23,..a third-floor roomer. **1959** M. CHAMBERLIN *Dear Friends & Darling Romans* v. 50 There were, besides me, two other roomers in the apartment. *a* **1968** M. RICHLER in R. Weaver *Canad. Short Stories* (1968) 2nd Ser. 151 'Meet your new roomer,' Mervyn said. **1973** *Kingston* (Ontario) *Whig-Standard* 5 Mar. 28 (Advt.), Roomers, $15 weekly with kitchen facilities. **1976** *National Observer* (U.S.) 25 Sept. 8/2 A roomer who had been helping to install some additional bathrooms was heating wax on a hot plate in his room.

2. With a numeral prefixed: a house with that number of rooms, as *six-roomer*.

1853 DICKENS *Bleak Ho.* lxiv. 612 'It's a six roomer, exclusive of kitchens,' said Mr. Guppy, 'and in the opinion of my friends, a commodious tenement.' **1972** *Daily Tel.* 8 Mar. 22 Some high figures for Chelsea houses—£29,000 for a six-roomer in First Street.

roome·tte. *N. Amer.* [f. ROOM *sb.*[1] + -ETTE.] A small sleeping-compartment on a train; also, a small bedroom for letting. Also *attrib.*

1938 *Sun* (Baltimore) 14 June 20/2 The roomettes are small, completely inclosed rooms with accommodations for one traveler. Washstands fold into the walls after use. **1945** *Sci. Amer.* Mar. 170 Two-Story Pullmans—..the cost margin is reduced to a narrower point in the new duplex roomette car... Each roomette has individual control of heat, light, and air conditioning. **1957** *New Yorker* 26 Oct. 68/3 Seated in his roomette, he opened the paper nervously. **1960** *Times* 19 Jan. 16/5 Travellers seeking rest between planes will rent roomettes, containing bed and bath, by the hour. **1971** *Guardian* 15 Sept. 11/1 Wandering from my roomette to the observation car as Canadian National transported me through the Rockies. **1974** *News & Courier* (Charleston, S. Carolina) 17 Feb. 1-A/8 The 9:40 arrives at 9:55 and everyone piles on—except me. My reserved 'roomette' is gone because a car was taken off the train somewhere between Jacksonville and Savannah. **1976** *Billings* (Montana) *Gaz.* 30 June 5-D/6 (Advt.), Chalet Roomette, private bath, refrigerator, washing facilities, $75 + dep. **1980** *Times* 4 Feb. 12/5, I was in a single sleeper, which Amtrak [*sc.* an American railway corporation] call a 'roomette'—probably the ugliest composite word ever invented. **1980** *Daily Tel.* 7 Nov. 15/1 He settled into his cramped, double-glazed Australian train cabin ('Roomette' in Strine).

roo·mie, *sb. U.S. colloq.* Also **roomy.** [f. ROOM *sb.*[1] + -IE.] A room-mate.

1918 *Sat. Even. Post* 6 July 5/3, I wouldn't make no holler at that if they had of left us pick our own roomys. **1945** *Richmond* (Va.) *Times-Dispatch* 26 July 14/7 Shortstop Skeeter Newsome, 'Inky's' roomie on the road, went home because of illness in his family. **1967** 'E. QUEEN' *Face to Face* xvi. 76 The Temple girl is given an alibi by her roomie. **1973** J. WAMBAUGH *Blue Knight* viii. 122, I called Craz my old roomie because..twenty years ago, I moved into this big house with him. **1976** 'B. SHELBY' *Great Pebble Affair* 77 One of the screws came and rattled the bars on my cage. 'Hey... We finally got you a roomie.'

roo·ming, *vbl. sb.* [f. ROOM *v.*[2]] **1. a.** The letting of rooms to lodgers. **b.** The occupying or sharing of rooms. Chiefly *attrib.* See also ROOMING-HOUSE in Dict. and Suppl.

1959 *Listener* 11 June 1012/1 Houses that are now usually converted into rooming apartments of inconvenient character. **1967** *Economist* 21 Oct. 264/2 The crowded rooming areas of central London. **1968** *Globe & Mail* (Toronto) 3 Feb. 41/1 (Advt.), Large family home 8 rooms huge kitchen 2 washrooms garage, walk-out basement to backyard. Perfect area for rooming. **1970** *Cape Times* 28 Oct. 20/2 (Advt.), Fine 7-roomed residence. Excellent rooming proposition. Fully furnished. **1977** *Rolling Stone* 5 May 50/1, I already have the rooming list.

2. rooming-in orig. *U.S.* (see quot. 1947); also *transf.* (see quot. 1978) and *attrib.*

1946 *Mod. Hospital* Dec. 44/2 Three Detroit hospitals.. have been..experimenting in certain selected cases with a 'rooming-in' plan which permits the mother to have her baby at her bedside. **1947** JACKSON & THOMS in *Connecticut State Med. Jrnl.* XI. 175/1 Rooming-in is a term applied to that form of hospitalization where mother and newborn baby room together and in which the mother takes as much care of the baby as possible. **1950** *N.Y. Times* 30 Dec. 16/2 About 75 per cent of expectant mothers who plan to have their babies at Grace-New Haven Community Hospital..now are requesting the rooming-in plan whereby they may keep their babies with them instead of having them cared for in the hospital nursery... Rooming-in is preferred by more women with higher education and by women with husbands in upper occupational classifications. **1960** F. W. GOODRICH *Maternity* vii. 103 Most ideal rooming-in set-ups make some provision for the baby to be returned to the nursery when the mother so desires. **1965** *Nursing Times* 5 Feb. 182/1 The siting of a nursery far distant from the wards added to the difficulties of the staff in spite of the fact that rooming-in was practised. **1974** G. B. LIPKIN *Psychosocial Aspects of Maternal-Child Nursing* x. 56/1 The nurses in the rooming-in unit stress their function as instructors in child care. **1978** *Who's Who* 1934/1 A 'Rooming-In' hospital for mother nursing of infants and small children with congenital defects requiring plastic surgery.

rooming-house. For *U.S.* read orig. *U.S.* and add further examples.

1909 *Washington Times* 2 Mar. 1 Hundreds of persons who never slept in any but first-class hotels when away from home will tonight get their rest in rooming houses. **1911** *Daily Colonist* (Victoria, B.C.) 1 Apr. 13/1 (Advt.), 14 roomed house, just overhauled, repainted and in first class condition. One of the best rooming house propositions in the city. **1923** E. F. WYATT *Invis. Gods* III. ii. 105 Fairfax Avenue was now a nondescript street of rooming houses, apartments and carpet-cleaning establishments. **1932** *New Yorker* 9 Apr. 36/2 Miss Cedarholm..succeeded ..to the ownership of the brick dwelling at 338 Schermerhorn Street. This she continued to operate as a rooming-house. **1957** V. NABOKOV *Pnin* iii. 64 There had been—in yet another rooming house—a still cozier bedroom-study. **1958** 'N. SHUTE' *Rainbow & Rose* iii. 76 Ma went there for the movies, and then when her contract ended she kept a rooming house. **1961** *Daily Tel.* 25 Mar. 16/5 The body of a woman.., was found by police officers last night in a rooming house in Lorenzo Street, King's Cross. **1973** *Sun-Herald* (Sydney) 26 Aug. 3/3 Police said another grandchild witnessed the stabbings in a rooming house. **1976** *Billings* (Montana) *Gaz.* 7 July 10-A/6 She moved to Washington D.C., where she was a proprietor of a rooming house for 20 years.

roomless, *a.* (Later example.)

1971 *Daily Tel.* 27 Sept. 6 (*heading*) Sleeping bags and camp beds for roomless students.

room-mate. For *U.S.* read orig. *U.S.* and add earlier and further examples.

1789 W. DUNLAP *Father* IV. 42 We were room mates at Halifax. **1873** C. M. YONGE *Pillars of House* III. xxx. 170 The room and the room-mate that had seemed so disgusting to home-bred Felix. **1912** A. BRAZIL *New Girl at St. Chad's* i. 19 One of my room-mates snored atrociously. **1923** *Jrnl. Exper. Psychol.* VI. 436 She admitted having sold..clothing taken from her roommate. **1949** A. HUXLEY *Let.* 11 May (1969) 598 It would be very unwise to try to pay back two thousand in the first year—particularly at the price of having a room mate. **1951** *Sport* 27 Apr.–3 May 8/3 Stan and Jack are fellow-Geordies who were England room-mates last summer. **1954** W. K. HANCOCK *Country & Calling* ii. 66 My room-mate, Percy Dicker, is now my brother-in-law and a man of renown in the Wangaratta district of Victoria. **1975** D. LODGE *Changing Places* ii. 101 His roommate freaked out on LSD. **1978** H. WOUK *War & Remembrance* xxviii. 287 The third roommate, the squadron exec, was writing in the ready room.

roomy, var. *ROOMIE.

roorback. Substitute for etym. [The name of the fictitious author Baron von *Roorback* (see quot. 1864)] and add: Also **roarback.** (Earlier and later examples.)

[**1844** *Republican Sentinel* (Richmond, Va.) 4 Oct. 3/3 The rapid succession of events in the 'Roorback' line, has satisfied us, that the whole matter is a *quiz* or a *forgery*.] **1855** I. C. PRAY *Mem. J. G. Bennett* 368 Among the efforts made to defeat the election of Mr. Polk was one to which allusion is frequently made in political discussion, politicians speaking of a political lie as a 'Roorback'. **1870** L. BAUGH *To Voters of Washington County* (broadside), Beware of 'Roarbacks' on the eve of the election. **1913** A. B. REEVE *Poisoned Pen* xii. 367 Billy McLoughlin knows how to make the best use of such a roorback on the eve of an election. **1947** *Chicago Daily News* 27 Mar. 6/1 The roorback stage of the closing days of the campaign broke wide open today with appeals to racial and religious prejudice coming to the surface in many sections of the city. **1963** R. I. MCDAVID *Mencken's Amer. Lang.* 180 Since the exposure of the fraud actually helped Polk, it is sometimes spelled *roarback*.

Roorkee (rūᵊ·ɹkī). Also **Roorkhee, rhoorkee, Roorkie.** The name of a town, northeast of Delhi, in Uttar Pradesh, India, used *attrib.* in **roorkee chair,** a type of collapsible chair, with wooden frame and canvas back and seat, originally produced there; also *ellipt.*; **roorkee work,** a kind of canvas work associated with Roorkee.

1905 *Army & Navy Co-op. Soc. Rules & Price List* 15 Mar. 261/2 Roorkhee folding chair. Each 18/9 (Supply uncertain) Do. do., English make, of ash throughout, better finished. Each 21/6. **1907** *Yesterday's Shopping* (1969) 281/2 Roorkhee Folding Chair. English make, of ash throughout, well finished... Do., in green canvas with back... An improved form of Roorkee chair, it having a leg rest. **1936** J. CARY *Afr. Witch* viii. 158 Four chairs, including the Resident's well-known *rhoorkee*, taller than the rest, were empty. **1937** G. FRANKAU *More of Us* xiv. 147 Splendid sank Circe to a canvas throne Of rhoorkee work. **1953** J. MASTERS *Lotus & Wind* v. 69 There was no furniture left except a folding table and a Roorkie chair on which the colonel sat. **1973** 'B. MATHER' *Snowline* xvi. 189, I lay back in a long Roorkhee chair. **1975** C. ALLEN *Plain Tales from Raj* v. 65 Perhaps some Roorkee chairs, made of canvas stretched on wood.

Roosevelt (rōᵘ·z(ə)velt, rū·-). The name of Theodore *Roosevelt* (1858–1919), President of the United States 1901–9, used *attrib.* or in the possessive in **Roosevelt('s) elk, wapiti** to designate a large, dark-coloured elk, *Cervus canadensis roosevelti*, found in coastal forests of north-western North America, and named in his honour by C. H. Merriam in 1897 (*Proc. Biol. Soc. Washington* XI. 271).

1897 *Proc. Biol. Soc. Washington* XI. 272 Roosevelt's Wapiti... Size large; head and legs black (probably only in winter pelage); skull and antlers massive. **1902** STONE

& CRAM *Amer. Animals* 34 Roosevelt's Elk... Larger and darker coloured, with heavier horns. **1923** *Outing* Apr. 3/1 The Olympic peninsula..contains vast, unmapped forests..teeming with the lordly Roosevelt elk. **1975** *Islander* (Victoria, B.C.) 26 Jan. 16/4 The Olympic, or Roosevelt elk, are common in Olympic Park.

Rooseveltian (rōᵘ·z(ə)veltiăn, rū·-), *a.* [f. the family name *Roosevelt* + -IAN]. Of, pertaining to, or characteristic of Theodore Roosevelt (see prec.), or Franklin Delano Roosevelt (1882–1945), President of the U.S. 1933–45, or the Roosevelt family in general. Hence **Roo·seveltism.**

1908 *Sci. Amer.* 25 Jan. 59/3 In this advanced twentieth century we had fondly hoped that the 'nature faker' at least was a product of the Rooseveltian age of literature. **1909** *Weekly Ardmoreite* (Ardmore, Okla.) 24 Feb. 8/1 Quarantine lifts Mar. 4... Get rid of Rooseveltism. **1915** *Fatherland* (N.Y.) 20 Dec. 346 We do not believe that the German Americans will have to choose between the devil of Rooseveltism and the deep sea of Wilson. **1923** A. HUXLEY *On Margin* 164 In true Rooseveltian style, he admired energy for its own sake. **1940** *Economist* 16 Nov. 601/2 He can make the official policy of the United States Government more completely Rooseveltian than it has been. **1948** *Chicago Tribune* 1 Feb. I. 37/3 It is a typical example of Rooseveltian democracy where charity is invited where it is not needed. **1953** *News* (Lynchburg, Va.) 6 May 6/1 That is not Rooseveltism. It is not New Dealism... It is good old-time Jeffersonian democracy. **1953** R. NIEBUHR *Christian Realism & Polit. Probl.* (1954) v. 59 The *status quo*, until the Rooseveltian era, permitted a degree of non-interference by the state.. which must make America a paradise for all true devotees of *laissez-faire*. **1965** *Economist* 16 Jan. 221/2 The profile ..bears a distinctly Rooseveltian chin. **1974** *Listener* 31 Jan. 148/1, I recall being the only child in my class who did not come from the Rooseveltian atmosphere of the homes of the Thirties. **1977** *National Observer* (U.S.) 22 Jan. 17/1 And Eleanor was an accomplished smiler in her own right, adding weight to the theory that smiling was a major Rooseveltian impulse. **1979** *N.Y. Rev. Bks.* 17 May 30/4 Schaller thus finds in early 1941, long before Pearl Harbor, the origin of the Rooseveltian program which wound up five years later in General Marshall's unavailing postwar mediation.

rooseveltite (rōᵘ·z(ə)veltəit, rū·-). *Min.* [ad. Sp. *rooseveltita* (R. Herzenberg 1946, in *Bol. Técnico* (Facultad Nacional Ingeniería, Univ. Técnica, Oruro, Bolivia) No. 1. 10), f. the name of Franklin D. *Roosevelt* (see prec.): see -ITE[1].] An arsenate of bismuth, $BiAsO_4$, which is found as a white or grey crust in veinlets of wood-tin in Bolivia and Argentina.

1947 *Amer. Mineralogist* XXXII. 372 (*heading*) Rooseveltite. **1949** *Mineral. Abstr.* X. 9 It is named rooseveltite, and is perhaps isomorphous with pucherite. **1972** *Tschermaks Mineral. und Petrogr. Mitt.* XVII. 65 Rooseveltite occurs in the weathering zone of the San Francisco de los Andes and Cerro Negro de la Aquadita mines, located in the San Juan Province, Argentina.

Rooshan, Rooshian, Roosian, varr. *RHOOSIAN *sb.* and *a.*

Roosky (ru·ski), var. *RUSKY *a.* and *sb.*[2] in Dict. and Suppl.

roost, *sb.*[1] Add: **1. c.** (Later example.) Also without const.

1966 D. LACK *Population Stud. Birds* ix. 156 At night they assemble in immense roosts, often in thorns.

d. (Earlier and later examples.)

1818 *London Guide* p. xii, *Roost*, bed. *Ibid.* 225 Coming from roost one morning,..I met old acquaintance, B—e, in Barbican. **1930** R. CAMPBELL *Adamastor* 72, I.. Who now am but a roost for empty words. **1944** [see *robot roost* s.v. *ROBOT 2]. **1946** MEZZROW & WOLFE *Really Blues* xii. 219, I know I'm gonna call some hogs soon as I hit my roost.

e. *to rule the roost*, now the more usual form of *to rule the roast* s.v. ROAST *sb.* 1 b.

1769 in *William & Mary Coll. Q. Mag.* (1908) Jan. 175 They say she rules the Roost, it is a pity, I like her Husband vastly. **1828** A. N. ROYALL *Black Bk.* II. 315 These priests will rule the roost. **1893** *Boston Jrnl.* 20 Apr. 5/3 England rules the roost. Her ships at Hampton Roads admittedly the finest. **1926** FOWLER *Mod. Eng. Usage* 509/1 *Rule the roast* (*roost*). The OED gives no countenance to *roost*, it does not even recognize that the phrase ever takes that form; but most unliterary persons say *roost* & not *roast*; I have just inquired of three such, & have been informed that they never heard of *rule the roast*, & that the reference is to a cock keeping his hens in order. **1931** R. CAMPBELL *Georgiad* ii. 29 The great Tu Quoque rules the golden roost. **1938** A. CHRISTIE *Appointment with Death* v. 37 Her husband thought a lot of her and adopted her judgment on almost every point. He was an invalid for some years before he died, and she practically ruled the roost. **1955** 'A. GILBERT' *Is she Dead Too?* vi. 114 'Miss Bannerman was very jealous, and she didn't care for children or animals.' 'Then she could have found herself some other lodgings. You'd scarcely let her rule your roost.' **1963** *New Yorker* 15 June 16/3 The London underworld, where Peter Sellers rules the roost. **1974** S. ELLIN *Stronghold* (1975) 36 My grandfather..ruled the roost, and he was a firm ruler for all his mild manner.

rooster. Add: **1. a.** (Earlier and further examples.)

1772 A. G. WINSLOW *Diary* 14 Mar. (1894) 45 Their other dish..contain'd a number of roast fowls—half a dozen, we suppose, & all roosters at this season no doubt. **1806** *Balance* (Hudson, N.Y.) 22 July 227 (Th.), The New York Rooster—may he continue to crow! **1870** J. H. B. NOWLAND *Early Reminisc. Indianapolis* 149 It was during this canvass [in 1840] that Tom gave to the Democratic party their emblem, which they have claimed ever since, the chicken cock, or rooster. **1922** JOYCE *Ulysses* 646 Chalk a circle for a rooster. **1923** E. W. BENJAMIN *Marketing Poultry Products* iv. 120 Cock, or Rooster.—These are the mature males. **1951** M. A. JULL *Successful Poultry Managem.* (ed. 2) xi. 348 A cock or old rooster is a mature male chicken with coarse skin, toughened and darkened meat.

b. (Earlier and further examples.)

1785 GROSE *Dict. Vulgar T.*, *Queer rooster*, an informer that pretends to be sleeping, and thereby overhears the conversation of theives in night cellars. **1821** P. EGAN *Life in London* II. v. 276 Roosters and the 'peep-o'-day boys' were out on a prowl for a spree. **1840** *Log Cabin* 5 Sept. 3/2 *Chapman*, the great Rooster of the Loco-Foco party,..was formerly one of the editers [*sic*] of an Infidel paper, the Boston Investigator. **1855** *N. Amer. Rev.* CXLI. 434 The toughest set of roosters that ever shook the dust of any town. **1883** *Bird o' Freedom* 7 Mar. 3/1 Whether the returned member be a rooster or not time will tell. **1923** R. D. PAINE *Comrades of Rolling Ocean* xiv. 252 What was that rooster's name?

c. *U.S.* A wild violet as used in a children's game.

1884 *Harper's Mag.* June 94/1 Purple violets..were slaughtered by hundreds, for the projecting spur under the curved stem at the base of the flower enabled the boys to hook them together and 'fight roosters', as they termed it. **1946** C. RICHTER *Fields* 231 In April they played Hens and Roosters, yoking their wild white and blue violets to see which would get its head pulled off.

d. A bird that is roosting or about to roost.

1949 *Brit. Birds* XLII. 323 The more leisured flight of the roosters [*sc.* starlings] was in contrast to the steady procession of the migrants.

3. rooster comb *U.S.* = **rooster head*; **rooster('s) head** *U.S.*, the American cowslip, *Dodecatheon meadia*, or a wild violet of the genus *Viola*; also *attrib.*; **rooster tail** *N. Amer.*, the curved plume of water thrown up by a speedboat or surfboard.

1964 MRS L. B. JOHNSON *White House Diary* 21 May (1970) 142 One little girl..offered me a bunch of red and yellow wildflowers—'snake tongue' and 'rooster comb'. **1894** *Jrnl. Amer. Folk-Lore* VII. 94 *Dodecatheon Meadia*, var., shooting stars, roosters' heads. **1934** H. VINES *This Green Thicket World* 171 One not thicketed might have felt sorry for the blue daisies, white daisies, roosterheads. **1947** *Atlantic Monthly* July 41/2 Spring not only brought tadpoles but..big bunches of rooster-head violets that the children picked in the woods. **1953** *Marine Digest* 19 Sept. 29/1 She was boxed in on the first turn by Gale and the two Such Crusts and their combined rooster tails just about sank her. **1956** *Sun* (Baltimore) 26 Oct. 34/5 It ruled..that it was 'highly probable' the wake or fall of water from the 'rooster tail' of the boat travelling at high speed had caused the damage. **1963** *Pix* 28 Sept. 62/4 *Rooster-tail*, wake of a board. **1976** *Telegraph-Jrnl.* (St. John, New Brunswick) 7 Aug. 3/3 The small craft skim the river at incredible speeds. Their giant rooster tails sometimes reach a height of 90 feet.

Hence **roo·sterish** *a.*

1898 'MARK TWAIN' in *Harper's Mag.* Mar. 536/2 He stands vast and conspicuous..self-satisfied and roosterish.

roosting, *vbl. sb.*[1] Add: **2. a.** *roosting area, behaviour, habit, site, -stick, -time* (later examples), *-tree* (earlier example).

1976 T. SOPER *Everyday Birds* v. 59 When birds reach the vicinity of the roosting area there will often be a spectacular flying display. **1953** *Brit. Jrnl. Animal Behaviour* I. 91 (*heading*) The winter roosting and awakening behaviour of captive Great Tits. **1964** A. L. THOMSON *New Dict. Birds* 709/1 Roosting behaviour varies from species to species, and to some extent within a species. **1976** H. M. DOBINSON *Bird Count* ix. 150 (*heading*) Roosting habits of our most common species. **1953** *Brit. Jrnl. Animal Behaviour* I. 91/2 Aggressive behaviour over roosting sites was seen on a few evenings. **1927** W. DE LA MARE *Told Again* 287 The hens on their roosting-sticks. **1743** W. ELLIS *Mod. Husbandman* July xvi. 77, I..took the Hen and her Young at Roosting Time. **1825** C. WATERTON *Wanderings in S. Amer.* 119 All the Toucanets feed on the same trees... You will find it has only been a dinner party, which breaks up and disperses towards roosting time. **1953** *Brit. Jrnl. Animal Behaviour* I. 91/1 In England the changes in the roosting times [of Great Tits] are similar to those in the north but less marked. **1834** J. J. AUDUBON *Ornith. Biogr.* II. 41 These roosting-trees of the Buzzards are generally in deep swamps, and mostly in high dead cypress trees.

root, *sb.*[1] Add: **I. 1. d.** In phr. *on* (*its*) *own roots*, used to describe a plant whose tissues all developed from the same embryo; not grafted or budded.

[**1822** J. C. LOUDON *Encycl. Gardening* II. 436 The scion is a part of the living vegetable, which, united or inserted in a stock or other vegetable of the same nature, identifies with it, and grows there as on its natural stem and roots.] **1869** S. R. HOLE *Bk. about Roses* viii. 112 The two trees ..are on their own roots, but the Rose thrives stoutly on the Brier and the Manetti, budded and grafted, wherever roses grow. **1914** H. H. THOMAS *Gardening for Amateurs* 696/1 Plants may grow rampantly on their own roots to the material disadvantage of any useful products. **1944** KAINS & MCQUESTEN *Propagation of Plants* (rev. ed.) xiv. 334 Why do not nurserymen sell us plants on their own roots? The answer is that in no other way [than grafting] can fruit trees true to name be propagated so rapidly. **1968** *Horticultural Abstr.* XXXVIII. 630/2 Gialla Precoce Morettini on its own roots flowered earlier on a sandy soil than on a clay soil.

3. c. *U.S. dial.* A spell effected by the supposedly magical properties of certain roots. Cf. *root doctor, worker*, sense 22 below.

1935 Z. N. HURSTON *Mules & Men* 340 Nearly all of the conjure doctors practice 'roots'. **1962** *Jrnl. Amer. Folklore* LXXV. 313 Local synonyms for the spell are 'curse', 'trick', 'fix', 'conjure', 'root', and 'hoodoo'.

4. a. (Later examples used of hair.)

1940 W. FAULKNER *Hamlet* III. ii. 198 The bleached hair darkening again at the roots since it had been a year now since there had been any money to buy more dye. **1970** G. F. NEWMAN *Sir, You Bastard* viii. 213 Brown roots growing through her split blonde hair.

c. (Further examples.)

1910 *Aëronaut. Jrnl.* XIV. 115 The angle of incidence of each wing gradually decreases from the root to the tip. **1948** H. CONSTANT *Gas Turbines* v. 77 The blades stall at the root and tip. **1978** D. KÜCHEMANN *Aerodynamic Design of Aircraft* vi. 429 The upwash generated by that part of the body ahead of the root of the gross wing should also be close to that generated by the portion of the gross wing ahead of the root and should again be small.

d. *slang.* The penis.

1846 *Swell's Night Guide* 119/1 *Flash*, to sport, to expose, he flashed his root. **1902** FARMER & HENLEY *Dict. Slang* V. 289/2. **1970** K. MILLETT *Sexual Politics* III. vii. 329 It measures intelligence as 'masculinity of mind', condemns mediocre authors for 'dead-stick prose', praises good writers for setting 'virile example' and notes that since 'style is root' (penis), the best writing naturally requires 'huge loins'.

5. b. The bottom of the groove of a screw thread.

1892 *Screws & Screw-Making* (Britannia Co., Colchester) iii. 39 The diameter at the root of the thread. **1920** F. J. CAMM *Screw Cutting* i. 6 In some instances American screws are measured at the bottom of the thread B; this portion is often called the root. **1964** S. CRAWFORD *Basic Engin. Processes* (1969) xiv. 299 The root is the bottom portion of the groove between the flanking surfaces of the thread.

II. 11. d. *pl.* Established ties with a locality or region; one's social, cultural, or ethnic origins or 'background'. Also in colloq. phr. *to put down roots*, to become established in a place, to settle down.

1921 R. MACAULAY *Dangerous Ages* iv. 82 The..infinitely loved Barry, who was going to give her roots. **1949** G. B. SHAW *Buoyant Billions* II. 21 Plenty of money and no roots. No traditions. **1969** A. G. THOMAS in L. Durrell *Spirit of Place* 117 On three occasions, when he has bought a house and put down roots, the whole collection has been posted out to him. **1977** *Gay News* 7–20 Apr. 10/4 In Scots and Welsh schools children are taught about their national roots, culture and history. **1977** P. THEROUX *Consul's File* 184 Is it possible to put down roots here?.. The Chinese won't, the Tamils can't, the Malays pretend they have them.

III. 14. a. (Further examples.)

1876 *Rep. Brit. Assoc. Adv. Sci. 1875* II. 13 (*heading*) Theorems on the *n*th roots of unity. **1941** COURANT & ROBBINS *What is Math.?* ii. 100 The complex cube roots of 1..are the roots of the equation $x^2 + x + 1 = 0$. **1966** *Math. Rev.* XXXI. 29/1 If α is an algebraic integer, $\alpha \neq 0$, α not a root of unity, then at least one of the conjugates of α has absolute value greater than 1.

c. A unique node or vertex of a graph from which every other node can be reached. Also *root node*.

1857 A. CAYLEY in *Phil. Mag.* XIII. 172 The inspection of these figures will show at once what is meant by the term in question, and by the terms *root, branches*,..and *knots* (which may be either the root itself, or proper knots, or the extremities of the free branches). **1881** *Amer. Jrnl. Math.* IV 266 In a tree of N knots, selecting any knot at pleasure as a root, the tree may be regarded as springing from this root, and it is then called a root-tree. **1965** *Proc. Cambr. Philos. Soc.* LXI. 499 A tree is a connected topological graph without circuits. The vertices will also be called nodes or individuals. There is often one distinguished node called..the root. **1973** C. W. GEAR *Introd. Computer Sci.* vii. 282 Formally, a tree is a set of nodes connected by branches such that there is one and only one way of going from one node to another via branch connections, and which has a distinguished node called the root node. **1973** S. EVEN *Algorithmic Combinatorics* vi. 109 A vertex *v* is called a root..of the graph if every vertex of the graph is reachable from *v*. **1976** E. MINIEKA tr. *Berge's Graphs & Hypergraphs* (ed. 2) iii. 32 A graph does not always have a root. **1977** *Sci. Amer.* Apr. 70/1 The location of the first key to be examined in a binary tree is traditionally known as the root; in the 31-word example the root is 16.

d. *digital root*: the digit obtained when all the digits of a number are added and the process is repeated on successive results until the outcome is a single digit.

1956 G. A. MONTGOMERIE *Digital Calculating Machines* vii. 140 One such check number is the 'digital root' obtained by adding all the digits of the number. **1973** *Sci. Amer.* Dec. 120/1 One way to do it makes use of the old accountant's trick for checking addition by digital roots.

16*. Miscellaneous senses of uncertain affinity. Cf. *ROOT *v.*[1] 9.

a. *slang.* (orig. *Schoolboys'*). A forceful kick. Also **root about** (see quot. 1900).

1900 Farmer *Public School Word-Bk.* 169 *Root-about..* (The Leys), promiscuous football practice. **1934** N. Scanlan *Winds of Heaven* 46 Matt gave him 'a root in the gear' and told him not to talk like a stable boy. **1961** in Webster, Caught him a great root with his boot on the backside.

b. *Austral. coarse slang.* An act of sexual intercourse. Also, a (female) sexual partner.

1959 in R. Chamberlain *Stuart Affair* (1973) xi. 111 Did you have a root? **1961** F. Hardy *Hard Way* iii. 77 The conversation led inevitably to women. Our shabby criminal struck a match revealing..a sign scrawled on the wall: 'Best American root—ring such and such a number.' **1969** *Private Eye* 4 July 14/3, I hear tell these *artists* in London don't exactly have to chase the odd *root.* **1973** A. Buzo *Rooted* I. 43 Hey, do you remember the time he got pissed out of his mind and fronted up to this old duck and asked her for a root? **1974** P. Kenna *Hard God* I. 33 Have you ever gone all the way with a girl?.. You know what I mean. Have you ever had a real root? **1976** D. Ireland *Glass Canoe* 147 Johnny Bickel..thought she'd be an easy root and began to take notice of her.

IV. 17. a. *root-bud* (later example), *-system, -thread, -tip, -zone.*

1977 J. L. Harper *Population Biol. of Plants* 290 Both sexes spread clonally by means of root buds. **1902** *Encycl. Brit.* XXV. 439/1 The presence of a feeble absorptive root-system and an extended surface of the shoot for transpiration and transudation are the outstanding points [of hydrophytes]. **1969** P. Thrower *Every Day Gardening* iv. 85/2 Budding is really a form of grafting and enables the grower to unite a garden rose with a root system or 'stock' obtained from a wild or vigorous rose. **1954** J. R. R. Tolkien *Fellowship of Ring* I. vii. 141 His grey thirsty spirit drew power out of the earth and spread like fine root-threads in the ground. **1954** —— *Two Towers* 66 Something between root-tip and leaf-tip. **1967** L. Picken *Organization of Cells* iv. 127 In the presence of low concentrations of phenolic compounds growing root tips also showed a temporarily increased frequency of fragmentation [of chromosomes]. **1953** J. Ramsbottom *Mushrooms & Toadstools* xviii. 206 The microflora is greater in the region of actively growing roots than in the soil generally: this is perhaps particularly true of bacteria, but also holds for fungi. This root-zone of increased population is known as a rhizosphere.

b. *root-canopy.*

1930 Blunden *Poems* 318 Thus the sacred well Is passed, and now the far root-canopy Issues its people, swift and slippery.

c. *root-forming, -room, -sort; root-eaten, -filled, -fringed, -pale, -weary* adjs.

1915 *Proc. Soc. Antiquaries London* XXVII. 149, I have often picked up on the surface of the camp pieces of old root-eaten human bones. **1918** *Atlantic Monthly* CXXII. 122 The Place d'Etoile was perhaps first adumbrated by wild boars concentrating on a root-filled marsh. **1946** *Nature* 19 Oct. 555/1 The root-forming capacity of penicillins G and X almost certainly resided in these substances themselves. **1944** Blunden *Shells by Stream* 5 Upon the root-fringed dais. **1960** S. Plath *Colossus* 63 Root-pale her meagre frame. *c* **1887** G. M. Hopkins *Poems* (1967) 103, I do advise You, jaded, let be; call off thoughts awhile Elsewhere; leave comfort root-room. **1977** *Interim* IV. iv. 4 Strips of unripened green, retarded from maturity by the moisture and greater root-room in the ditch's silts below. **1960** T. Hughes *Lupercal* 33 Worm-sort, root-sort, going where it is profitable. **1931** A. Huxley *Cicadas* 51 Never a tortured flower Shudders, root-weary, on the verge of flight.

18. *root-cellar* (later examples), *-crop* (later examples), *-cutting board, -field, -puller, -pulper, vegetable* (later examples); *root-loving, -pulping* adjs.

1872 Root-cellar [see *grain-box* s.v. *Grain *sb.*[1] 18 a]. **1965** E. L. Myles *Emperor of Peace River* II. ii. 184 After that we collected the potatoes and put them in the root cellar. **1901** L. H. Bailey *Princ. Vegetable-Gardening* ix. 271 Root crops require a cool season and a deep soil. **1969** *Oxf. Bk. Food Plants* 172 (*heading*) Crucifer and composite root crops. **1969** E. H. Pinto *Treen* 95 The introduction and gradual increase throughout the 18th century, in the growing of root crops for animal winter feed, led to the importance of the well worn root cutting board. **1932** Blunden *Fall in, Ghosts* 9 The crucifix surmounting the steps of granite in the middle of the rootfields. **1977** F. Parrish *Fire in Barley* ii. 18 Dan heard the bloodhounds..race across the root field towards the farm. **1947** C. S. Lewis in *Punch* 1 Oct. 324/1 Fruit-loving, root-loving gods. **1856** *Trans. Mich. Agric. Soc.* VII. 54 D. O. & W. S. Penfield, Detroit, one iron root puller. **1952** S. Selvon *Brighter Sun* ix. 161 With a root-puller attached the tractor would move up to a tree and the arms would reach down into the earth and wrest the tree out. **1940** *Chambers's Techn. Dict.* 730/1 *Root pulper,* a machine comprising a rotating steel disc furnished with cutters, to which roots that have been cleared of soil are fed. **1978** *Morecambe Guardian* 14 Mar. 22/3 (Advt.), Bale Sledge, Buck Rake, Root Pulper. **1910** *Chambers's Jrnl.* Mar. 207/2 The electricity furnished by this means serves to light the house.., and drives a chaff-cutter, a circular saw, and a root-pulping machine. **1957** P. Worsley *Trumpet shall Sound* 15 The people live by cultivating..root-vegetables. **1976** *Southern Even. Echo* (Southampton) 1 Nov. 4/3 The sandy soil there, he reckons, suits root vegetables just fine.

19. *root-treatment; root-filling, -planing, -rising; root-filled* adj.

1963 C. R. Cowell et al. *Inlays, Crowns, & Bridges* viii. 84 A post-retained crown is commonly indicated for a root-filled anterior tooth the natural crown of which has become discoloured. **1977** *Proc. R. Soc. Med.* LXX. 439/1 Teeth root-filled or crowned before operation were excluded from these results. **1963** C. R. Cowell et al. *Inlays, Crowns, & Bridges* viii. 85 The root filling should be well condensed **1969** *Gloss. Terms Dentistry* (*B.S.I.*) 23 *Root filling,* the permanent filling and sealing of the root canal of a tooth to avoid the accumulation within the root canal of fluids or micro-organisms. **1962** Blake & Trott *Periodontology* x. 105 For pockets under 3mm, only removal of calculus and root planing and polishing are necessary. **1922** D. H. Lawrence in *Poetry* XXI. 65 Until your veiled head almost touches backward To the root-rising of your erected tail. **1927** W. E. Collinson *Contemp. Eng.* 60 If a tooth is decaying or hollow we have it stopped or filled..or we have root-treatment (sterilization and withdrawal of nerve).

20. *root-cause, -conception* (further example), *-confusion, -divergence,* etc. (Now passing into adj.)

1915 E. Carpenter *Healing of Nations* i. 12 One might be on safer ground by trying to get at the root-causes of this war. **1977** J. Wainwright *Day of Peppercorn Kill* 191 He didn't trust us, Dick—that's the root cause. **1934** *Downside Rev.* LII. 223 As to the second root-conception of Cistercianism, the mere enunciation of an opinion..cannot be allowed. **1940** W. Empson *Gathering Storm* 25 The mind..now less easily decides On a good root-confusion to amass Much safety from irrelevant despair. **1927** Auden & Day-Lewis *Oxf. Poetry* p. vi, The logical conflict, between the denotatory and connotatory sense of words, which is the root-divergence of classic and romantic. **1933** E. Partridge *Words, Words, Words!* I. 88 The root-idea of blood as something vivid or distressing or both still colours the use of the adjective. **1923** D. H. Lawrence *Kangaroo* vii. 141 Hardly sympathy at all, but an ancient sort of root-knowledge. **1960** *Spectator* 7 Oct. 518/2 Mr. Kimche is arguing against the consistent record, and against the very root-logic of Zionism. **1933** H. Read *Art Now* I. 47 This brings us down to the root-problem of aesthetics. **1957** M. Swan *Brit. Guiana* iv. 68 It is one of the root problems of the country. **1924** R. Hichens *After Verdict* III. xiv. 491, I hated her Then because I loved you. That was the root reason. *a* **1957** R. Campbell tr. A. de Campos in *Coll. Poems* (1960) III. 138 Which, once constructed, announce themselves As Real-Things, Spirit-Things, or Entities of the Stone-Soul, Made ours at certain moments by root-sensations. **1976** S. Hynes *Auden Generation* ii. 56 As the decade moved on, these images took on heavier symbolic meanings..but the root-sense of the images remained the same.

21. b. (Further examples.) *root-accent, -class, determinative, -element, -enlargement, -expansion, form, -language, -morpheme, -noun, -play, -stem, stress, -syllable* (later examples), *-word* (later examples); *root-accented, -final, -initial, -forming, stressed* adjs.

1935 G. K. Zipf *Psycho-Biol. of Lang.* 133 The explanation offered by Jespersen for extensive root-accent. **1975** *Language* LI. 140 The more commonly occurring root-accented forms *trắmane, dắmane, dhắrmane, bhắrmane.* **1879** W. D. Whitney *Sanskrit Gram.* ix. 208 The root-class [of verbs]..its present-stem is coincident with the root itself. **1965** G. Y. Shevelov *Prehist. of Slavic* xxiv. 367 It is to be assumed that in these words the varying consonants had not been originally a part of the root but were the so-called root determinatives, a kind of suffixes whose function is no longer discoverable. **1935** G. K. Zipf *Psycho-Biol. of Lang.* 145 When the accent.. was not on the endings, it was always on the stem-formative (suffix or infix) and not on the root-element. **1976** *Archivum Linguisticum* VII. 63 The discrepancy between the consonants..is easily accounted for by the assumption of different root-enlargements. **1895** P. Giles *Short Man. Compar. Philol.* xxv. 370 The details of the theory of root-expansion are..as yet too little worked out. **1965** H. M. Hoenigswald in W. Winter *Evidence for Laryngeals* 93 Such extra-Indoiranian etymologies as have been advanced with any promise mostly involve root-final position for the voiceless aspirates. **1973** *Trans. Philol. Soc. 1971* 68 *sil-* is not a permissible Indo-European root form. **1933** L. Bloomfield *Language* 275 Even our root-forming morphemes..have some flexibility. **1956** *Language* XXXII. 453 The root-initial verb aspect markers are most aptly described in terms of simulfixation. **1972** *Ibid.* XLVIII. 477 The alternations in the non-nasal prefixes are conditioned by the voicing of the root-initial consonant. **1885** *Encycl. Brit.* XVIII. 774/1 A Chinese monosyllable or an Egyptian or Polynesian dissyllable is radical, unless there can be demonstrated in some part of it a formative value; and a language wholly composed of such words is a root-language. **1935** G. K. Zipf *Psycho-Biol. of Lang.* 177 The total magnitude of complexity of the root-morpheme *fac,* a typical example, was diminished. **1950** *Lingua* II. 241 He makes only a few isolated remarks about the morphemes that occur most frequently, i.e. the root-morphemes. **1972** *Language* XLVIII. 477 Such a proto-initial is very poorly attested by the comparative data in root-morphemes. **1879** W. D. Whitney *Sanskrit Gram.* xiii. 314 The root-noun used as infinitive has the same form, and the same accent,..as in its other uses. **1962** C. Watkins *Indo-European Origins of Celtic Verb* I. 185 The verbal root **med-* being identical with the athematic root noun **med-.* **1970** M. Dahood *Psalms* III. 109 The rootplay evident in *yilbᵉšu* and *boštām*..is of a piece with the wordplays that wryly characterize many biblical and Canaanite laments. **1879** W. D. Whitney *Sanskrit Gram.* v. 129 Root-stems, having in them no demonstrable element added to a root. **1979** T. Burrow *Problem of Schwa in Sanskrit* 66 The root stem *nās-* f. 'nostril, nose' inflects with long vowel in the only strong case which occurs in the Veda. **1965** G. Y. Shevelov *Prehist. of Slavic* iv. 68 In all these cases the Li[thuanian] F[alling]P[itch] type has root stress. *Ibid.* 69 Analogy with the root stressed instr[umental] and loc[ative] pl[ural]. **1900** H. Sweet *Hist. Lang.* vi. 103 The place of the accent [in Aryan] was not restricted by any considerations of quantity or distance from the end of the word,..nor was it restricted to the root-syllable of a word, as was afterwards the tendency in the Germanic language. **1972** *Language* XLVIII. 477 Arranging the words in the alphabetical order of their root-syllables. **1918** R. Bridges in G. M. Hopkins *Poems* 100 Passages where, in a jungle of root-words, emphasis seems to oust euphony. **1954** H. Read *Anarchy & Order* 196 The root-word *vir* [in *virtue*] has the implication of masculinity.

22. root-aorist *Philol.,* in certain Indo-European languages, an aorist formed by adding personal endings directly to the root-syllable of the verb; **root-ball,** (*a*) = Nigger-head 1 a in Dict. and Suppl.; (*b*) the mass formed by the roots of a plant and the soil between and around them; hence **root-balled** *a.*; **root beer** (earlier and later examples); **root-bound** *a.*, † (*a*) bound or held by roots; (*b*) = Pot-bound *a.*; also *fig.*; †**root bread** *U.S.*, the bulbs of *Camassia quamash* (cf. Camas, Quamash), formerly baked and eaten in western North America; **root canal,** the pulp-filled cavity within the root of a tooth; **root cutter,** (*a*) an implement for cutting edible roots; (*b*) one for cutting tree roots underground; **root cutting,** a cutting taken from the root of a plant; **root digger,** (*b*) (earlier and later examples); **root doctor** *U.S. dial.*, one who treats ailments by means of roots, a herb-doctor; also = *root worker* below; **root gall** (see quot. 1902); **root-graft** *sb.*, (*a*) a graft of a scion on to a root; (*b*) a naturally occurring graft between the roots of neighbouring trees; hence **root-graft** *v. trans.*, to graft by means of a root-graft; **root-grafted** *ppl. a.*, **root-grafting** *vbl. sb.*; **root-knot,** a disease of many crop and other plants, caused by infestation of the roots with the nematode *Heterodera marioni* producing characteristic swellings or nodules; freq. *attrib.*; **root-mean-square** *Physics,* a mean calculated as the square root of the arithmetic mean of the squares of a set of values; freq. *attrib.*; **root nodule,** a swelling on a root of a legume or other higher plant containing symbiotic micro-organisms which fix nitrogen; **root pressure** *Bot.* [tr. G. *wurzelkraft* (J. von Sachs *Handb. der Exper.-Physiol. der Pflanzen* (1865) IV. vii. 199)], the hydrostatic pressure generated in the roots of a plant, which helps the sap to rise in the xylem; **root rot,** a disease of plants, attacking the roots; **roots reggae,** a style of reggae music considered as an expression of the black Jamaicans' cultural identity; **root swell(ing),** an outgrowth of a tree above a root, forming a natural buttress; † **root tubercle** = *root nodule* above; **root worker** *U.S. dial.*, one who uses roots to work spells, a conjurer (cf. sense 3 c above); so **root work.**

1879 W. D. Whitney *Sanskrit Gram.* xi. 276 Imperative forms of the root-aorist are not rare in the early language. **1955** H. G. Lunt *Old Church Slavonic Gram.* iv. 89 The most wide-spread type of the older aorists was the so-called 'root-aorist', attested by over 650 examples with some 27 verbs. **1976** *Archivum Linguisticum* VII. 62 In Oscan-Umbrian *-e-* is the sign of a secondary thematization of the Indo-European root-aorist. **1930** *Sat. Even. Post* 13 Dec. 11/2 Bogs of black muck dotted with devilish, rotating root-balls that throw a man waist-deep. **1956** X. Field *Housewife Bk. House Plants* I. 31 If the outside of the root ball is a network of roots re-potting is called for. **1973** J. L. Faust *Bk. House Plants* 37 If the root ball of the plant is very tightly packed and hard, it can be squeezed a bit to break it apart. **1966** *Gloss. Landscape Work* (*B.S.I.*) iv. 19 *Root-balled,* with roots contained within a well-defined mass of soil (in practice usually wrapped with protective material). **1843** *Knickerbocker* XXII. 85 Let..the temperance halls and the root-beer perambulatories make answer. **1921** [see *Coca-Cola]. **1974** E. Brawley *Rap* II. xix. 250 Sucking on his root beer freeze through a red plastic straw. **1634** Root-bound [in Dict., sense 17 c]. **1885** R. T. Cooke *Root-Bound* 11 My plants do blossom well.. and I don't know why unless it is because they are root-bound. *Ibid.* 12 It's good for folks and flowers too to be root-bound..sometimes; especially, if we want to bring forth good fruit. **1946** *Nature* 23 Nov. 762/2 Further experiments show the importance of..the feeding of root-bound plants with a balanced fertilizer prior to transplanting. **1976** *S. Wales Echo* 27 Nov. 4/1 He informed the schoolmaster that finding a square root meant looking for limp leaves in seedlings or pot plants, this condition being caused by them being root-bound in box or pot. **1805** W. Clark in *Orig. Jrnls. Lewis & Clark Expedition* (1905) III. 85 Traded for some root Bread & skins to make shirts. **1806** J. Ordway in Lewis & Ordway *Jrnls. Western Explor.* (1916) 352 We bought a little dark couloured root bread which is not good but will Support nature. *c* **1840** D. Thompson *Narr. Explorations W. Amer. 1784–1812* (1916) II. iv. 413 An old Man made a short speech, and made a present of two cakes of root bread (not moss). **1893** *Dental Rec.* XIII. 523 (*heading*) Filling root canals with coal wadding. **1923** *Ibid.* XLIII. 269 The root-canals afford excellent hold for posts. *Ibid.* 682 The first requisite for root-canal filling is the complete sterilisation of the root-canal and tubuli. **1978** S. Sheldon *Bloodline* xli. 356 A dental bill for root-canal work for Charles Martel. **1807** Root cutter [in Dict., sense 18].

a **1877** KNIGHT *Dict. Mech.* II. 1975/2 To bring the roots to a convenient size for the stock and to remove the danger of choking, root-cutters were introduced. **1943** J. STUART *Taps for Private Tussie* xxii. 226 You could follow the mule behind a locust-beamed plow with a sharp root cutter in it and hear the roots pop. **1969** E. H. PINTO *Treen* 18 Root Cutters. The traditional type illustrated..with pivoted knife at one end, was made in a considerable range of hardwoods.., and was used generally..by apothecaries. **1954** A. G. L. HELLYER *Encycl. Garden Work* 68/2 As a rule root cuttings are taken while the plant is dormant, which means generally, in winter. **1969** P. THROWER *Every Day Gardening* v. 108/1 Propagation by root cuttings is the best way of increasing many thick-rooted perennials like verbascums, Oriental poppies, phlox, anchusa and *Limonium latifolium*. **1831** W. GORDON *Let.* 3 Oct. in A. H. Abel *Chardon's Jrnl. at Fort Clark* (1932) 346 Many of these [Snake Indians] go by the name which signifies Root digger, because they live by digging roots. **1837** W. IRVING *Capt. Bonneville* II. xii. 204 These are of that branch of the great Snake tribe called Shoshokoes, or Root Diggers, from their subsisting, in a great measure, on the roots of the earth. **1947** B. A. DE VOTO *Across Wide Missouri* 432 'Root-digger'..describes all the tribes, most of them superior tribes, that lived in localities where there were staple crops of edible roots and bulbs. **1821** J. HOWISON *Sk. Upper Canada* xii. 195 'Oh!' said the woman, 'if I had but the *root* doctor that used to attend our family at Connecticut; he was a dreadful *skeelful* man.' **1890** *N.Y. Age* 19 Apr. 1/1 Carmier was what people call down here a root doctor... He only rode around the county..and made his living curing the sick and selling his medicine. **1900** *Jrnl. Amer. Folklore* XIII. 228 People git conjur from the root-doctors and one root-doctor often works against another, the one that has the most power does the work. **1934** [see *MOJO[1]]. **1962** *Jrnl. Amer. Folklore* LXXV. 315 She finally went to a root doctor and was informed that her husband and three women had placed a spell upon her. **1902** L. H. BAILEY *Cycl. Amer. Hort.* IV. 1545/2 The term root-gall is usually applied to the abnormal enlargement of roots due to insects and other animal organisms. **1933** *Jrnl. R. Hort. Soc.* LVIII. 233 The absence of detailed information regarding the infective stage of the root-gall nematode and its life history has been remedied. **1977** J. L. HARPER *Population Biol. Plants* xvi. 484 (*caption*) *Biorrhiza pallida* forms root galls and meristem galls on the oak at different seasons. **1824** J. C. LOUDON *Encycl. Gardening* (ed. 2) II. 396 Such root-grafts grow with uncommon vigour. **1900** L. H. BAILEY *Cycl. Amer. Hort.* II. 661/2 In the West apples at least are usually root-grafted. **1951** F. J. CHITTENDEN *Dict. Gardening* II. 919/2 Rhododendrons..are..frequently root-grafted, using roots of common species of their genus as stocks. **1956** *New Biol.* XX. 101 There is evidence that the fungus can infect trees only through wounds that penetrate the bark. The disease spreads locally by means of natural root grafts. **1900** L. H. BAILEY *Cycl. Amer. Hort.* II. 663/2 In the East..budded apple trees are preferable to root-grafted trees. **1942** KAINS & MCQUESTEN *Propagation of Plants* (rev. ed.) xii. 294 Ten Walldow root-grafted trees were all dead but one limb on one tree. **1707**, *c* **1820** Root grafting [see sense 17 a in Dict.]. **1886** G. NICHOLSON *Illustr. Dict. Gardening* II. 91/2 Plants largely propagated by Root-grafting are Bignonias, Clematis, Hollyhocks, and Wistarias. **1977** J. L. HARPER *Population Biol. of Plants* 235 It is doubtful whether any careful search has ever been made to detect the extent of root grafting in other communities of herbs. **1889** *Bull. U.S. Dept. Agric. Div. Entomol.* No. 20 (*title*) The root-knot disease of the peach, orange, and other plants in Florida, due to the work of Anguillula. *Ibid.*, 9, I..can find no mention of the root-knot..prior to the year 1857. That year Hon. P. J. Berckmans..found this disease prevalent. *Ibid.*, In 1876 I found the root-knot prevalent over Florida, and learned from old residents that as far back as 1805 it had been known. **1912** E. W. SWANTON *Brit. Plant-Galls* viii. 107 Miss Ormerod first reported the occurrence of this pest, known as the 'root-knot' eelworm, in Britain. **1954** *New Biol.* XVI. 113 The Root Knot Eelworm..is a tropical or sub-tropical species which in Britain infests the soil of heated glasshouses... Its host-range includes almost all the decorative plants grown in conservatories. **1976** *Daily Times* (Lagos) 8 June 2/2 The workshop is discussing Integrated Crop Protection System with emphasis on root-knot diseases affecting economic crops. **1895** *Electrician* 27 Sept. 721/1 A short time ago Dr. Fleming published a new and ingenious method of plotting wave forms with polar co-ordinates, and of directly obtaining therefrom the root mean-square value. **1927** S. H. LONG *Navigational Wireless* i. 7 Thus the effective value I equals the square root of the mean value of the squares of all the instantaneous values. This is often called the root-mean-square value, or R.M.S. value or virtual value. **1956** A. A. TOWNSEND *Struct. Turbulent Shear Flow* iii. 51 The rate of increase of the decay scale is proportional to the root-mean-square turbulent velocity. **1978** *Nature* 9 Mar. 143/2 We note here that sound pressures as well as displacement are expressed as root-mean-squares. [**1899** J. B. FARMER *Botany* ix. 44 Plants which have not these nodules on their roots are unable to utilize the free atmospheric nitrogen.] **1907** F. CAVERS *Plant Biol.* iii. 119 The root-nodules of leguminous plants contain a micro-organism which fixes free atmospheric nitrogen. **1949** A. NELSON *Introd. Bot.* xxv. 391 The root nodule, so typical of this bacterial association with a legume, commences when the bacterium enters the root hair of the legume. **1976** BELL & COOMBE tr. *Strasburger's Textbk. Bot.* (rev. ed.) 293 In the root nodules of alder, *Hippophae*, *Eleagnus*, and also probably of *Myrica* and *Casuarina*, the organisms concerned are symbiotic actinomycetes, also capable of fixing atmospheric nitrogen. **1875** BENNETT & DYER tr. *Sachs's Text-bk. Bot.* III. i. 600 (*caption*) Apparatus for observing the force with which water escapes under root-pressure from the transverse section of a stem. **1896** *Phil. Trans. R. Soc.* B. CLXXXVI. 572 An important function of root-pressure, *i.e.*, to dissolve up and clear out the gaseous contents of such conduits as are occupied by bubbles. **1931** E. C. MILLER *Plant Physiol.* iv. 168 Under conditions of low transpiration or in the spring before the leaves are unfolded, water is forced into the conducting vessels of the root and up through the stem under pressures varying from a fraction of an atmosphere to several atmospheres. This pressure is evidenced by the bleeding of cut vines and branches of certain species of plants and is apparently connected with the exudation of water from the leaves of plants, which occurs under certain conditions. This pressure, which is set up in the fibrovascular bundles of the stem and root due to the water which is being forced in them is known as 'root pressure'. **1976** *Sci. Amer.* May 104/3 Although Hales had discovered the existence of root pressure, he concluded that the roots are not solely responsible for the pressure of the sap in the branches. **1883** Root rot [in Dict., sense 17 a]. **1933** *Jrnl. R. Hort. Soc.* LVIII. 280 The occurrence of root-rot of Sweet Peas ..is described as one of the causes possibly associated with the streak disease of Sweet Peas. **1978** EVANS & KUMM *Woman's Own Pot Plant Doctor* 21/1 The commonest reason for all house plants dying off is root rot. **1977** MCKNIGHT & TOBLER *Bob Marley* x. 127 What reaches our ears is no longer roots reggae. **1978** *Oxford Times* (City ed.) 24 Feb. 15 This is a good example of roots reggae complete with chunky rhythm and 'dub' echoes. **1932** *Sun* (Baltimore) 6 Sept. 6/11 The famous Wye oak..is reported to be 27 feet 8 inches in circumference four and a half feet above ground, but the measurement taken at this point is said to include large root swells. **1902** *Forestry Q.* I. 56 The influence of the enlarged base of the bole (root-swelling) is appreciable at the breast-high point, and gives the stem a neiloid form. **1954** W. E. HILEY *Woodland Managem.* ix. 134 By girthing at 6 feet instead of 5 feet it may be possible to get away from the root swelling which usually occurs at the base of a large tree and often gives rise to inaccurate estimating. **1887** H. MARSHALL-WARD in *Phil. Trans. R. Soc.* B. CLXXVIII. 539 The first close investigation of these root-tubercles (as they may be shortly termed) is due to Woronin. **1894** *Knowledge* 1 Mar. 68/1 (*heading*) The root-tubercles of peas, beans, and vetches. **1897** W. G. SMITH tr. *Tubeuf's Dis. Plants* ix. 101 First-year alders without tubercles do not thrive in soil free from nitrogen..; when, however, provided with root-tubercles they assimilate nitrogen. **1967** D. C. TINLING in *Psychosomatic Med.* XXIX. 483 (*heading*) Voodoo, root work, and medicine. **1970** M. WALKER *Prophets for New Day* 29, I run down to Sis Areny's And told her what I seen 'Root-worker's out to git me What you reckon that there mean?'

root, *v.*[1] Add: **II. 3. b.** *Austral. slang.* (See quot. 1959.)

The placing of this sense is uncertain; it may be, or be apprehended as, a *fig.* use of sense 9 b below.

1945 BAKER *Austral. Lang.* viii. 152 The authentic digger form is *Wouldn't it root you!* A regimental paper 'Wiry' (1941) took its name from the first letters of the words in this phrase. **1951** D. STIVENS *Jimmy Brockett* 244 'It looks as though we're rooted, smacker,' I told Herb. **1959** BAKER *Drum* II. 140 *Root*,..to outwit, baffle, exhaust, utterly confound (someone). Whence, *to be rooted*, to be exhausted or confounded; *get rooted!* Go to blazes! **1961** M. CALTHORPE *Dyehouse* (1962) xl. 186 'He can get rooted, for all I care,' Collins said bitterly. **1973** *Telegraph* (Brisbane) 15 Nov. 3/1 Mr. Whitlam later admitted having said in an aside: 'It is what he put in his guts that rooted him.' **1974** J. POWERS *Last of Knucklemen* III. ii. 93 'What the hell's goin' *on* here?' 'The Hun's rooted—that's what!' 'Done like a dinner!'

3*. To cause (a cutting) to grow roots.

1824 J. C. LOUDON *Encycl. Gardening* (ed. 2) II. 400 All plants which are difficult to root..will be found in the first instance..to throw out roots only, from the ring of herbaceous matter. **1884** D. T. FISH *Pop. Gardening* I. 212/1 One strong argument in favour of rooting roses at that season [*sc.* spring] consists in the fact that they have all the summer before them to grow into plants. **1925** W. WATSON *Gardener's Assistant* VI. 82/1 We root a Cactus by drying it in the sun. **1969** P. THROWER *Every Day Gardening* iii. 45/1 Cuttings which have been rooted under mist, or in a heated propagator, must be hardened off..before planting them in the open ground.

4. c. (Further examples.)

1941 *Sun* (Baltimore) 25 Nov. 14/3 The trouble into which he intervened roots in a controversy over whether welding is a separate 'art' or not. **1955** E. POUND *Section: Rock-Drill* lxxxix. 56 The Civil War rooted in tariff.

III. 9. Miscellaneous senses of uncertain affinity. (Perh. properly developments of *v.*[2])

a. *trans.* and *intr.* To kick, esp. in the backside. *slang* (chiefly *Schoolboys'*).

1890 BARRÈRE & LELAND *Dict. Slang* II. 186/1 *Root, to* (schools and London), to give one a kick behind. **1914** 'I. HAY' *Lighter Side School Life* ii. 52 We rooted Sowerby afterwards for grinning. **1934** *Bulletin* (Sydney) 31 Jan. 32/2 Give the horse that can root a bit to the horse-breaker or the head stockman is the general rule, or, better still, to the blacks. **1946** B. MARSHALL *George Brown's Schooldays* xxxvii. 145 Rooting them [*sc.* new pupils] up the backside is the only way of dealing with them.

b. *Austral. coarse slang. trans.* (usu. with a male subject). To copulate with; *intr.*, to copulate, to engage in sexual intercourse. Also in phr. *to root like a rattlesnake*, to copulate vigorously.

1958 R. M. STUART in R. Chamberlain *Stuart Affair* (1973) ii. 12, I took her bathers off. Then I raped her. She was hard to root. **1966** P. WHITE *Solid Mandala* 185 We'll root together so good you'll shoot out the other side of Christmas. **1969** *Private Eye* 1 Aug. 14 The Pope's a Jew if that jam tart doesn't root like a rattlesnake. **1974** K. COOK *Bloodhouse* 110 We found this bloody little poofter down on the beach fiddling with a bird... Couldn't even root her.

root, *v.*[2] Add: **1. c.** (Further examples.) Also const. *about, around.* Now also *colloq.*

1904 in *Eng. Dial. Dict.* V. 151/2 They like to rute about the house. **1916** JOYCE *Portrait of Artist* v. 203 He allowed his mother to..root into the folds of his ears. **1920** R. MACAULAY *Potterism* I. ii. 20 Watching Tane's.. hand with its short square fingers rooting in the sand for shells. **1943** V. PALMER in *Coast to Coast 1942* 29 Charlie rooted about in the nose of the dinghy drawn up above the tide. **1977** C. ROCKS *Winter's Tales 23* 132, I rooted around till I found the kettle.

d. For *U.S. slang* in Dict. read *colloq.* (orig. *U.S. slang*) and substitute for def.: To cheer *for* a (baseball, etc.) team. Also *transf.*, to be active *for* a person or thing by giving support, encouragement, or applause. Also without const. (Earlier and later examples.)

1889 *N.Y. Semi-Weekly Tribune* 5 Nov. 5/4 Murphy has done little but 'root' for the Giants this year. **1895** J. S. WOOD *Yale Yarns* 152 We rooted hard, too, and did a lot of shouting and yelling. **1922** S. LEWIS *Babbitt* v. 66 Zilla keeps rooting for a nice expensive vacation. **1943** *Crisis* July 201/3 The papers of Los Angeles crowed... They rooted and cheered. **1951** *Sport* 30 Mar.–5 Apr. 3/1 If the rules of the tournament made it possible for Stan to be transferred to Newcastle tomorrow, then the whole country would be rooting for the 'Magpies' on April 28th. **1951** in M. McLuhan *Mech. Bride* (1967) 8/1 He rooted fiercely for the underdog, perhaps because he was so much the underdog himself. **1959** N. MAILER *Advts. for Myself* (1961) 400 If he dares not to castrate his hatred of society..then I would have to root for him because he may have been born to write a great novel. **1967** *Boston Sunday Herald Mag.* 9 Apr. 4/3 You'll find it becomes a whole different game from just sitting in your armchair, rooting blindly. **1971** A. BURGESS *MF* xii. 140 A popcorn-eating audience roots for two youths fighting a huge engulfing python. **1976** A. MILLER *Inside Outside* vii. 81, I..wound up in front of the Visiting Committee with the Governor rooting for me.

e. *root hog or die*, used of or addressed to persons, implying the necessity of labour or exertion to maintain life or prosperity. Also as *attrib. phr. N. Amer.*

1834 D. CROCKETT *Narr. Life* viii. 60 We therefore determined to go on the old saying, root hog or die. **1843** *Amer. Pioneer* II. 419 This letter exhibits his as well as my own case in that day; for it was 'root hog or die', and hard times have come back again! **1879** A. W. TOURGÉE *Fool's Errand* xxv. 150 The 'root-hog-or-die' policy. **1904** *N.Y. Even. Post* 20 Aug. 4 'The school and college', explained plains President Eliot, 'cannot use the method of Nature—root, hog, or die.' **1931** J. T. ADAMS *Epic of Amer.* i. 37 At the beginning of most settlements it was 'root, hog, or die' for all. **1976** *Globe & Mail* (Toronto) 9 June 41/6 Many of that generation, however, no longer put up with that root-hog-or-die kind of motivation.

rootage. Add: **3.** A system of roots; a root-stock.

1895 in *Funk's Stand. Dict.* **1927** H. E. FOSDICK *Pilgrimage to Palestine* 60 The very rootage from which came Aaron's rod that budded..the solemn monks still show to the visitor.

rooted, *ppl. a.* Add: **1. a.** (Further examples.) *spec.* Having been made to grow roots.

1852 G. W. JOHNSON *Cottage Gardener's Dict.* 304/2 A rooted cutting is not a new plant, it is only an extension of the parent. **1969** P. THROWER *Every Day Gardening* viii. 196/2 Give the rooted cuttings as much light as possible to prevent them from becoming drawn.

rooter[1]. Add: **1. b.** A machine for loosening the surface of the ground.

1950 *N.Z. Jrnl. Agric.* Oct. 333/2 At first a small rooter was used which was designed for scarifying pavements and roads and which could be drawn by a 40 h.p. tractor. **1965** G. J. WILLIAMS *Econ. Geol. N.Z.* Plate xxxix, This very pure calcareous material is soft enough to be excavated by rooters, and in consequence can be produced at low cost.

rooter[2]. **2.** For *rare* in Dict. read '*colloq.* (chiefly *U.S.*)' and substitute for def.: One who cheers or 'roots' for a (baseball, etc.) team. Also *transf.*, one who supports or encourages another; a warm advocate, a partisan. (Earlier and later examples.)

1890 *N.Y. Press* 8 July 6/1 At this juncture the New York rooters began to 'pull' for the home team, but the effort was useless, not a man..succeeded in reaching first base. **1901** *Daily Colonist* (Victoria, B.C.) 31 Oct. 4/3 'What makes him look so very white?' inquired the fairy maid. 'He's had the starch knocked out of him,' the woolly rooter said. **1931** L. STEFFENS *Autobiogr.* II. III. xxxiii. 593 They..don't ask about, they don't hear of, the always existing few quiet students with concealed gifts in the rooters at a football game. **1939** G. ADE *Let.* 7 July (1973) 212, I attended the [1912 Republican] convention as a spectator and also as a rooter for Theodore Roosevelt. **1952** *Manch. Guardian Weekly* 12 June 3/3 General of the Army Eisenhower..came..to hold his first political press conference before the New York reporters... There was also present a motley and vociferous band of rooters. **1959** *Times Lit. Suppl.* 6 Nov. p. xix/1 The exclusive audience that goes to Twickenham or Lord's is replaced by millions of rooters. **1963** D. OGILVY *Confessions Advert. Man* i. 14 This will give us 49,700 rooters for Ogilvy, Benson and Mather. **1978** *N.Y. Times* 29 Mar. B 5/1 The Wildcats' coach..had walked back into the stands to embrace his family and shake hands with some rooters with blue and white buttons.

rootfast, *a.* (Later *poet.* example.)

1953 C. DAY LEWIS *Italian Visit* iii. 36 A character root-fast Like a man's in the deposit of all his acts.

root-house. **2.** (Earlier and later examples.) **1790** *Pennsylvanian Packet* 30 Mar. 4/2 On the premises are..two arched stone root-houses. **1961** W. O. MITCHELL *Jake & Kid* 28 'Bin a real fine summer fer vegetables,' he said then. 'Too bad yer ma don't have no root house.' **1970** *Islander* (Victoria, B.C.) 22 Nov. 13/2 Into the root house went the potatoes, carrots and other root vegetables.

rootiness. Add: Also *fig.* Cf. RACINESS. **1937** G. M. YOUNG *Daylight & Champaign* 193 Here is exactly the harshness and rootiness, the integrity and objectivity that our poetry needed.

rooting, *vbl. sb.*[1] Add: **1. b.** *rooting medium.* **1935** A. F. HORT *Garden Variety* IV. 229 The rooting medium is about six inches of ordinary builders' sand.

5. *coarse slang.* Of a male: the action or process of copulating. (Now chiefly *Austral.*: cf. *ROOT *v.*[1] 9 b.) **1922** JOYCE *Ulysses* 754 All the poking and rooting and ploughing he had up in me. **1970** G. GREER *Female Eunuch* 41 All the vulgar linguistic emphasis is placed upon the *poking* element; *fucking, screwing, rooting, shagging* are all acts performed upon the passive female.

rooting, *vbl. sb.*[2] Add: **2.** *slang* (chiefly *U.S.*). Cheering, encouraging, or otherwise supporting. Also in *Comb.*, as *rooting interest.* Cf. ROOT *v.*[2] 1 d. **1937** D. RUNYON in *Collier's* 21 Aug. 32/4 No talking and no rooting from the spectators is permitted. **1971** L. KOPPETT *N.Y. Times Guide Spectator Sports* viii. 155 There is the team element as a rooting interest. **1977** *Time* 25 July 51/2 *One on One* is a picture that..transcends its humble conception and develops what movie people used to call a 'rooting interest' in its characters.

rooting, *ppl. a.*[2] Add: **2.** In redupl. Comb., as **rootin' tootin'**, (*a*) *dial. rare*, inquisitive, meddlesome; (*b*) *slang* (chiefly *N. Amer.*), noisy, rumbustious, boisterous; rip-roaring, lively. Cf. *ROOTY-TOOT. **1875** NODAL & MILNER *Gloss. Lancs. Dial.* 228 He's a *rootin'* tootin' sort of a chap. **1924** L. B. KOZLOWSKI in *Catal. Copyright Entries* (U.S. Copyright Off.) III. 5698 (*song-title*) Roottin-toottin-Lou; from Kalamazoo. **1937** *Film Daily* 1 May 4/3 (*heading*) Gene Autry in Rootin' Tootin' Rhythm. **1948** *Sun* (Baltimore) 7 Jan. 13/1 Basketball games today have developed into rootin', tootin' contests, with more of the emphasis on the tootin'. **1949** *N.Y. Times Bk. Rev.* 27 Mar. 32 'Smoke up the Valley' is actually a rootin'-tootin' romance of blazing six-shooters and gore. **1963** *New Statesman* 24 May 786/3, I also..expressed mild surprise about a rootin' tootin' night club that advertised 'Girls! Girls! Girls!'

rootle, *v.* Add: **1.** Also const. *about, round.* (Further examples.) **1917** KIPLING *Diversity of Creatures* 261 There's a tin of cocoa in my study somewhere... Rootle round till you find it. **1929** V. WOOLF *Room of One's Own* i. 14 The chapel itself was marsh too, where the grasses waved and the swine rootled. **1936** A. CHRISTIE *Cards on Table* ix. 85 I'll leave you my keys and..you can rootle to your heart's content. **1943** *Theology* xlvi. 159 It is coming to be seen that he [*sc.* Nietzsche] rootled about in the subsoil of the modern mind to the profit of few things so much as the Christian Faith. **1959** *Elizabethan* Apr. 10/2 We rootled among the debris for something to eat. **1964** P. WHITE *Burnt Ones* 203 On the way, as she rootled after the lovely little lighter, I was relieved to see her bag was still stuffed with notes. **1977** *Zigzag* Apr. 43/3 He rootled about under the stairs and found an unopened Christmas present bottle of Glenfiddich.

2. (Further examples.) Also *transf.* **1945** D. REES *Cambridge Murders* xiii. 135 He set one or two members of his staff to rootle out the past histories of all the people whose names had been mentioned. **1955** M. BANKS *Commando Climber* x. 189 Their [*sc.* the reindeers'] disappearance has been attributed to a late autumn thaw..which covered their winter pasture with a crust of ice that prevented them rootling out their fodder. **1978** *New Scientist* 20 July 171/2 Pigs which rootle out the eggs and eat the vulnerable young.

rootless, *a.* Add: **1. b.** (Further examples.) **1934** A. WOOLLCOTT *While Rome Burns* 93 Those rootless widows who wear buttoned shoes. **1977** R. BARNARD *Blood Brotherhood* viii. 79 Rootless young men, without families.

rootlessness (further examples); also roo·tlessly *adv.* **1927** E. BOWEN *Hotel* xiv. 167, I haven't had time for a feeling of rootlessness. **1929** A. HUXLEY *Do what you Will* 157 Nature-worship is..so refined, so rootlessly high-class. **1958** *Times Lit. Suppl.* 3 Jan. 4/4 Mr Mellers characterizes the nineteenth century Russian Westernizers' music as 'rootlessly European' and believes that Stravinsky has merely made this rootlessness symbolic of the modern artist in general. **1978** P. MOORE *Man, Woman, & Priesthood* i. 4 In an age of rootlessness which is searching for significant tradition, we have much to offer if we have the courage to dig deep enough. **1980** *Church Times* 1 Aug. 2/4 Drinking problems are, more often than not, connected with other social problems such as homelessness and rootlessness.

root-stock. Add: **3.** A stock on to which another variety has been grafted or budded. **1933** H. H. THOMAS *Pop. Encycl. Gardening* 392/1 The shoot of the required variety is united with a suitable rootstock or with a branch of an established tree of the same kind. **1954** A. G. L. HELLYER *Encycl. Garden Work* 208/2 An apple may be described as grafted upon paradise rootstock. **1969** P. THROWER *Every Day Gardening* iv. 84/2, I keep a close lookout throughout the season for suckers growing from the roots below the union of the rose and the rootstock.

rooty, *sb.* Add: Also **rootey. a.** (Further examples.) Cf. *ROTI[2]. **1900** KIPLING in J. Ralph *War's Brighter Side* (1901) xv. 253 And the 'umble loaf of 'rootey' Costs a tanner, or a bob. **1900** 'M. THYME' in *Ibid.* xx. 316 Bully beef and rooty, and Something's give me a pain. **1957** [see *JILDI]. **1959** *Listener* 5 Mar. 406/1 Eight ounces of 'rooty'—that is bread.

b. rooty gong (*GONG[2] 2 a), a medal formerly awarded to members of the British Army in India (see quots.). **1925** FRASER & GIBBONS *Soldier & Sailor Words* 245 *Rooty gong*, long service Medal. **1936** F. RICHARDS *Old-Soldier Sahib* vi. 108 The Good Conduct medal or 'Rooty Gong'..was so called because it was a regular ration-issue, like bread or meat or boots. **1948** PARTRIDGE *Dict. Forces' Slang* 157 *Rooty gong*,..*Rooti* is the Indian Army word for bread, the implication being that the wearer has eaten a tremendous aggregate of Service loaves and therefore deserves it.

rooty, *a.* Add: Also, belonging to or suggestive of roots. **1905** E. F. BENSON *Image in Sand* xviii. 292 The warm wind bore with it..the good, moist, rooty smell of the dusky heather.

rooty-toot (rū·ti,tūt). *slang* (chiefly *U.S.*). Also **root-a-toot**, etc. [A redupl. form, ult. of echoic origin, usu. representing the sound of a trumpet; cf. *rootin' tootin'* s.v. *ROOTING *ppl. a.*[2] and TOOT *v.*[2]] Something noisy, riotous, or lively; *spec.* an early style of jazz music. Also as *adj.* and (in various nonce-uses) *vb. intr.* **1887** T. DARLINGTON *Folk-Speech of S. Cheshire* 319 There was a *rooty-tooty* at Cholmondeley last Setterday, an' everybody from raïnd about went bu' mey. **1907** G. B. SHAW in *Neolith* Nov. 9 The trumpet angel..root-a-tooted at the sky. **1931** O. NASH *Hard Lines* 24 Oh rooti-ti-toot for Smoot of Ut. **1936** *Amer. Mercury* XXXVIII. p. x/2 *Rooty-toot*,..razz-ma-tazz. **1937** G. FRANKAU *More of Us* iii. 38 So Izzy Cohen (y sus Boys) root-tooting Moved Innocent to choric rhapsody. **1938** *Brit. Empire Mod. Eng. Illustr. Dict.* 1257/2 *Rooty-toot* (Am.), old-fashioned jazz. **1951** W. MORUM *Gabriel* I. iii. 39 He knew hambone and joanna meant trombone and piano, But what could be a rooty-toot, a gobstick, skins and skeletons? **1976** *Listener* 29 July 120/3 It's all done to the most cheerful, rooty-tooty music imaginable. **1977** *Time Out* 28 Jan.–3 Feb. 17/3 Ma, some of them songs are rooty-toot-toot but the whole damn show is as real as George Wallace fairy and as sassy as a pile of rocking horse sheet.

rope, *sb.*[1] Add: **I. 2. c.** (Earlier and later examples.) Phr. *on the ropes*: see quot. 1958; also *fig.* Also, the ropes marking the boundary of a cricket ground. **1829** P. EGAN *Boxiana* 2nd Ser. II. 158 Lenney found himself hanging on the ropes, where he was milled down. **1888** R. H. LYTTELTON in Steel & Lyttleton *Cricket* xvi. 439 There is a strong cord running all round the ground, every decently hard hit is certain to reach the ropes if the ball once passes the fieldsman. **1892** *Sporting Life* 31 May 3/4 Among his hits were three drives over the ropes for 6. **1901** G. B. SHAW *Admirable Bashville* II. i. 302 The Australian Champion and his challenger..fought to a finish... The bold Ned Skene revisited the ropes to hold the battle for his quondam novice. **1904** A. A. MILNE in *Punch* 18 May 358/1 Time was I cared for cricket,..Cutting a ball to the ropes for four. **1924** 'W. FABIAN' *Sailors' Wives* xv. 175 You've got him on the ropes. They tell me he shows signs of matrimony. **1958** F. C. AVIS *Boxing Reference Dict.* 78 *On the ropes*, said of a boxer who is forced back on to the ropes by his opponent, or is lying helpless on them. **1971** *Times* 27 Sept. 9/8 Griffith was defenceless against the ropes and his own corner as Monzon unleashed a string of straight rights and lefts. **1972** *Times* 16 May (Wall Street Suppl.) p. iv/2 A good section of the industry was on the ropes and there were times when I wondered if it would survive. **1976** J. SNOW *Cricket Rebel* 168 (*caption*) Ray Illingworth hooks..in the England v West Indies Test at the Oval, 1973. The ball, arrowed, is on its way to the ropes. **1977** J. LAKER *One-Day Cricket* 88 Three further perfectly timed shots had cleared the boundary ropes. **1977** *New Yorker* 25 July 70/3 Miss Wade was on the ropes several times in the first set, but she stayed in there and managed to win it, 7-5. **1980** *Tablet* 26 Jan. 81/3 There is talk that the Kennedy campaign is not just 'on the ropes', but that it is plain dead.

f. *transf.* A type of lodging-house (see quot. 1836). **1836** DICKENS *Pickw.* (1837) xvi. 160 The twopenny rope..is just a cheap lodgin'house, vere the beds is twopence a night... They has two ropes, 'bout six foot apart, and three from the floor, which goes right down the room; and the beds are made of slips of coarse sacking, stretched across 'em... At six o'clock every mornin', they lets go the ropes at one end, and down falls all the lodgers. **1973** L. HEREN *Growing up Poor in London* i. 10 One of the ropes, or lodging houses, was home for Indian pedlars... The rope was next to a pub.

g. A skipping-rope. Cf. *to jump rope* s.v. *JUMP *v.* I f. **1874** R. L. STEVENSON in *Portfolio* V. 116 A mistress of the art of skipping..the rope passed over her black head and under her scarlet-stockinged legs with a precision and regularity that was like machinery. **1927** C. V. GODDARD in *Word Lore* II. 128 Never leave the rope empty Go to church on Ash Wednesday. **1959** I. & P. OPIE *Lore & Lang. Schoolch.* xii. 239 People from the surrounding villages bring great lengths of clothes-line with them, and skip ten and even fifteen abreast in each rope. **1978** J. IRVING *World According to Garp* vii. 133 Jumping rope for half an hour in a corner of the gymnasium.

h. *Mountaineering.* A climbing-rope. So *transf.*, a group of climbers, *esp.* one that is roped together. Also *attrib.* and *fig.* **1892** C. T. DENT *Mountaineering* ii. 71 There is no part of the Alpine equipment for those who intend to go above the snow line..more important than the rope. **1919** G. D. ABRAHAM *On Alpine Heights & Brit. Crags* i. 10 The legs of both were steadied by the second climber, who secured the rope around a projecting knob of rock. **1935** R. L. G. IRVING *Romance of Mountaineering* vii. 114 Tom de Lépiney runs out fifty metres of rope in crossing, held by the rope from as high as possible. **1935** D. PILLEY *Climbing Days* iv. 84 And for those who did not lead, but still desired to take the share of responsibility which falls to any genuine member of a *rope*, a climb would help. **1941** C. KIRKUS *Let's go Climbing* iii. 46 When a rope travelling south meets a rope travelling west the result is apt to be rather like a Maypole dance. **1955** M. BANKS *Commando Climber* v. 89 Lower down we passed under some tottering, unstable-looking séracs, in company with an Italian and a French rope. **1965** A. BLACKSHAW *Mountaineering* vii. 195 A wet rope should not be left coiled, as this will delay drying and encourage deterioration. **1968** P. CREW *Encycl. Dict. Mountaineering* 100/2 In artificial climbing rope management can become very complicated. **1972** D. HASTON *In High Places* iv. 52 We reckoned on teaming up two ropes of two, Eley with me and Geoff with Dennis English. **1979** D. CLARK *Dread & Water* ii. 33 It's up to you and your pals on the same rope to make your own decisions as the need crops up.

i. A rope suspended vertically in a gymnasium for climbing and other exercises. **1903** *Handbk. Physical Training* (Admiralty) I. 30 For rope climbing the class will be formed up about 4 paces from the ropes. **1940** MCCLOW & ANDERSON *Play Gymnastics* 87 Small boys who are free in the gymnasium show a great interest in equipment upon which they can climb or from which they can hang. They never seem to tire of swinging on the ropes. **1965** D. R. CASADY et al. *Handbk. Physical Fitness Activities* xii. 96/2 When climbing the rope, one must climb down as well as up.

3. (Later examples.) So *transf.*, capital punishment. Also in phr. *to take a rope*, to hang oneself. **1934** H. N. ROSE *Thes. Slang* 18/1 Jim got a rope this morning. **1935** A. J. POLLOCK *Underworld Speaks* 98/2 *Rope*, hanging. **1935** J. HARGAN *Gloss. Prison Lang.* 7 *Rope, take a*, to hang oneself, to commit suicide. **1950** H. E. GOLDIN *Dict. Amer. Underworld Lingo* 180/2 *Rope*, capital punishment by hanging; (loosely) capital punishment by any means. **1976** *Leicester Mercury* 14 Oct. 4/4 The complete disregard for law and order which is so prevalent today is the direct result of the policies of himself and most members of the Labour Government which resulted in the cane being abolished for disobedient schoolboys, the birch for thugs and the rope for murderers.

4. b. *to come to the end of one's rope*, (*b*) to come to the end of one's resources, to be at the end of one's tether. So *at the end of one's rope*, etc. **1931** F. L. ALLEN *Only Yesterday* ii. 32 Physically the President was almost at the end of his rope. **1943** M. CARPENTER *Experiment Perilous* 214 I've come, I think, to the end of my rope. **1954** N. COWARD *Future Indefinite* v. vi. 321 What I had been dreading for a long time happened. I collapsed finally and knew that I had come to the end of my rope. **1971** *Ink* 12 June 7/4 On Monday, 24 May, the Mans strikers—now at the end of their rope financially—voted to accept the compromise proposals. **1977** *Transatlantic Rev.* LX. 79 Judy was at the end of her rope.

c. (Further examples.) Also *to show one, understand, the ropes.* **1850** 'J. TIMON' *Sketch* 18 Aug. in *Opera Goer* (1852) II. 186 The belle of two weeks standing, who has 'learned the ropes'. **1854** *Congress. Globe* 33rd Congress I Sess. App. 893/2 They are familiar with all the dodges of the season, understand the ropes about town [etc.]. **1860** T. C. HALIBURTON *Season-Ticket* viii. 226 Tell me..about Canada, and show me the ropes. *a* **1911** D. G. PHILLIPS *Susan Lenox* (1917) II. ii. 20 I'll show you the ropes... You'll find the job dead easy. **1937** 'G. ORWELL' *Road to Wigan Pier* ix. 182, I would find out about tramps and how you got in touch with them..and then, when I..knew the ropes well enough, I would go on the road myself. **1949** E. WAUGH *Loved One* 133 Mr Schultz had found a young man to take Dennis's place and Dennis was spending his last week at the Happier Hunting Ground in showing him the ropes. **1973** G. GREENE *Honorary Consul* I. i. 26 Fortnum knew the local ropes. He saved the Ambassador a lot of trouble. **1976** J. I. M. STEWART *Young Pattullo* ii. 43, I was being made aware..that I didn't quite know the ropes.

e. *to pull the ropes*, to direct or influence events. ? *Obs.* **1876** W. G. NASH *Century of Gossip* iv. 70, I cum purty near..tellin' 'em that Elton wouldn't pull a rope for him, if he got the nominashun. **1900** G. N. BOOTHBY *Maker of Nations* i. 19 You *do* require to know the ropes. And what is more, you require to be very careful how you pull those ropes when you are familiar with them.

f. *money for old rope*: see *MONEY *sb.* 6 h.

II. 5. c. (See quot. 1950.) Also *attrib.*, as *rope silk*. **1880** L. HIGGIN *Handbk. Embroidery* i. 4 'Embroidery', or Bobbin Silk..is manufactured in what is technically called 'rope', that is, with about twelve strands in each thread. When not 'rope' silk, it is in single strands, and is then called 'fine' silk. **1910** *Art Needlework* 2/2 Arden's 'Hazel' Embroidery No. 3... As thick as (and closely resembling) those silks called 'Rope' and 'Cable', it can be used for merely outlining with long and short stitch. **1950** *Mercury Dict. Textile Terms* 430/1 *Rope silk*, an embroidery silk thread consisting of singles doubled into threads and these doubles again doubled to form a strong thread.

d. *U.S. slang.* A cigar.

1934 H. McLellan in *Detective Fiction Weekly* 10 Nov. 29/2 He jerked a cigar out of her mouth... 'It burns my stomach to see a dame smoking a rope'. **1940** *Amer. Speech* XV. 335/2 A cigar is *rope*. **1960** Wentworth & Flexner *Dict. Amer. Slang* 433/2 *Rope*, a cigar... Occasional use in comic papers and by would-be wits. **1978** H. Wouk *War & Remembrance* vii. 66 Carter Aster was smoking a long brown Havana tonight. That meant his spirits were high; otherwise he consumed vile gray Philippine ropes.

e. *Anthrop.* A system of descent or inheritance in which the link is formed from father or mother to the children of the opposite sex (see quot. 1935).

1935 M. Mead *Sex & Temperament* x. 176 Instead..of organizing people into patrilineal groups or matrilineal groups..the Mundugumor have a form of organization that they call a *rope*. A rope is composed of a man, his daughters, his daughters' sons, his daughters' sons' daughters; or if the count is begun from a woman..her sons, her sons' daughters..[etc.]. **1953** A. K. C. Ottaway *Educ. & Society* ii. 25 Inheritance [among Mundugumor] passes from father to daughter, and then to her son. This is known as a 'rope'. **1968** *Internat. Encycl. Social Sci.* VIII. 405/2 Men may be linked cross-sexually to their mothers, and women to their fathers, to produce the alternating or cross-sexual system of the 'rope'. **1976** H. Reading *Dict. Social Sci.* 181 *Rope*, descent group resulting from alternating descent.

f. *slang.* Marijuana.

1944 D. Burley in A. Dundes *Mother Wit* (1973) 211 Marijuana-Weed—..*rope*. **1945** L. Shelly *Jive Talk Dict.* 16/2 *Rope*... Marijuana cigarette. **1972** [see *muggle[2]].

g. *Astr.* A group of magnetic lines of force twisted together.

1961 H. W. Babcock in *Astrophysical Jrnl.* CXXXIII. 577 The fluid shear will be affected by the increased magnetic viscosity of local field concentrations, and these will be twisted into more or less discrete flux strands or 'ropes'... The flux ropes may be visualized as roller bearings. **1977** *Nature* 21 Apr. 686/1 More than 90% of the total magnetic flux, outside pores and sunspots, that emerges from the sun is confined to ropes that are only a few hundred kilometres across.

6. b. (Earlier and later examples.)

1617 T. Roe *Jrnl.* 6 Oct. in Purchas *Pilgrimes* (1625) I. iv. xvi. 571, I told him I had a rich Pearle, and some other ropes faire. **1931** *Amer. Speech* VII. 113 Get this rope to the fence before we fall for receiving. **1966** A. Loos *Girl like I* vii. 145 Gaby Deslys..wore 'ropes' of pearls, as they were then called.

7. b. A bacterial condition of bread and the like in which it may be drawn into strands.

Cf. quot. 1850 s.v. Ropiness.

1899 J. Blandy *Baker's Guide* (ed. 4) iii. 169 (*heading*) Rope in cakes. **1921** W. & W. C. Jago *Technol. Bread-Making* xvii. 345 During hot weather bread is liable to an outbreak of the disease called 'rope'. *Ibid.*, Modern writers agree in ascribing rope to bacterial activity. **1972** *Sci. Amer.* Mar. 18/1 Baked goods, for example, go stale rapidly. Once made, they are often exposed to mold spores that become active in warm weather or high humidity. In bread the spores produce a condition called 'rope'.

III. 8. a. *rope bed, bedstead, -bit, -bridge* (later examples; also *fig.*), *sling, sole, tow.*

1925 H. Crane *Let.* 17 June (1965) 208 A lot of wonderful old rope beds and furniture came right along with it. **1972** E. Wigginton *Foxfire Bk.* 140 The rope bed was once the only bed to be found in this area. **1971** *Canad. Antiques Collector* Sept.–Oct. 15/1 Another early..bed is the low poster rope bedstead. **1940** C. Day Lewis tr. *Virgil's Georgics* iii. 61 Try a rope-bit In his mouth now and then. **1923** Rope-bridge [see *jhula]. **1961** L. van der Post *Heart of Hunter* 10, I was possibly the only person who could start this kind of interpretation; who could be this kind of improvised little ropebridge over the deep abyss between the modern man and the first person of Africa. **1965** A. Nicol *Truly Married Woman* 39 It used to take them about an hour to make a detour to cross..on the swinging rope bridge. **1901** Merwin & Webster *Calumet 'K'* i. 5 'Slack away!' he called to the engineers, and he cast off the rope sling. **1957** Clark & Pyatt *Mountaineering in Brit.* xvi. 239 Rope-slings were used thus as early as 1931. **1971** C. Bonington *Annapurna South Face* xi. 127 Standing in a rope sling, suspended from a peg, he was able to reach up to another crack above the overhang and hammer in a further peg, clipped in another sling and pulled himself up. **1894** *T. Eaton & Co. Catal.* Spring & Summer 31/1 White canvas bathing shoes, rope soles. **1964** Rope sole [see *mess-boy* s.v. *mess *sb.* 7]. **1965** *Economist* 25 Dec. 1416/3 In the [U.S.] National Forests there are 199 developed winter sports sites equipped with 164 chair lifts..312 rope tows and 48 ski jumps. **1968** *Globe & Mail* (Toronto) 13 Jan. 35/7 London's Ski Club with seven rope tows. **1978** W. F. Buckley *Stained Glass* xv. 147 He found it irresponsible that his thoughts should turn to skiing, which he longed to attempt in the lofty Alps after several winters of rope tows in Vermont during hectic weekends away from Yale.

b. *rope-boy, -knout, skipping, socket.*

1952 *Landfall* Sept. 206 Ropeboys just standing can feel cocky pride in shouting. **1970** *Guardian* 26 Nov. 13/2 A rope boy, in climbing diction, is a second man who spends patient hours securely belayed as he holds or pays out the rope for a leader. *a* **1918** W. Owen *Mental Cases* in *Poems* (1920) 8 Thus their hands are plucking at each other; Picking at the rope-knouts of their scourging. **1969** R. D. Abrahams *Jump-Rope Rhymes* p. xv, Rope skipping..with men..is now part of the training program for some athletic activity..rather than a game. **1889** *Cent. Dict.*, Rope-socket. **1935** *Discovery* Apr. 118/2 Actual drilling is done by a 'string' of tools... At the top of the string is the connecting rope socket, which permits the tools to turn freely, ensuring a round hole.

d. *rope-climbing, spinning* (later examples).

1903 [see sense 2 i above]. **1965** D. R. Casady et al. *Handbk. Physical Fitness Activities* xii. 96/2 Rope climbing promotes the development of a strong grip. **1926** *Daily Colonist* (Victoria, B.C.) 17 July 10/2 Mr. Ash..had plenty of thrills among the Mexican bandits and cattle thieves, during which time he became expert with the revolver, the lasso, and rope spinning. **1969** G. E. Evans *Farm & Village* xi. 126 This saddler's shop, with 'a rope-spinning ground' behind it was sold by auction in July 1875 at the Lion Inn, Debenham. **1975** F. Kennedy *Alberta was my Beat* viii. 92 Guy Weadick ..when he found that he could not successfully ride outlaw horses, turned to rope spinning.

e. *rope-soled, -swung.*

1920 *Blackw. Mag.* Apr. 507/2 He was dressed quaintly in well-washed dungarees,..a gaudy waist-cloth, rope-soled shoes [etc.]. **1955** M. Allingham *Beckoning Lady* iii. 39 She was wearing a bright blue dress..and rope-soled shoes. **1973** G. Mitchell *Murder of Busy Lizzie* iv. 47 She pulled on a pair of rope-soled shoes. **1957** A. Clarke *Too Great a Vine* 23 Rope-swung victims ring that bell.

9. rope border (esp. in *Basketry*), a border resembling the twisted strands of rope; **rope-boring,** the boring of wells with a drill suspended and worked by means of a rope; **rope brown,** a type of strong brown paper orig. made from old rope; **rope burn,** a burn caused by the friction of a rope; hence as *v. trans.*; **rope embroidery silk** = sense 5 c above; **rope horse,** a horse ridden by one roping an animal; **rope race,** the compartment or passage through which a driving-rope passes; **rope rider** (see quot.); **rope-sight,** in bell-ringing, facility in judging when to pull a rope, from the position and movement of others; **rope silk:** see sense 5 c above; **rope stitch** (earlier and later examples); **rope-trick,** restrict † to sense in Dict. and add: (*b*) a juggling trick or sleight-of-hand involving a rope or ropes; freq. in *Indian rope-trick*; also *fig.*; **rope-walker** (later examples); hence *rope-walking* vbl. sb.; **rope-way,** (*a*) (examples); (*b*) a rope used as a means of transport; **rope wrapping** = *rope brown* above.

1897 *Private Life of Queen* xxiv. 201 A very simple cornice..composed of the conventional 'egg and dart' and 'rope' borders. **1912** T. Okey *Introd. Art of Basket-Making* ix. 100 *The Rope Border*—This, a modification of the plaited border, may be carried out by numbering six stakes in succession and doubling the first two. **1953** A. G. Knock *Willow Basket-Work* 26 The simplest and smallest rope border was used on the oval buff shopping basket. **1888** *Chambers's Encycl.* II. 331/2 The rope-boring machinery of Mather and Platt of Salford..is in extensive use. **1902** *Encycl. Brit.* XXX. 763/2 In Europe rods, either of iron or wood, seem to be preferred, though rope boring is by no means unknown. **1908** R. W. Sindall *Manuf. of Paper* vi. 27 *Rope browns* are common papers made of fairly strong material of a miscellaneous character, this name having been derived from the fact that rope and similar fibre were at one time used exclusively. **1914** E. A. Dawe *Paper & its Uses* xvii. 115 Brown wrapping papers are made of various materials and in many qualities and substances. Rope browns, air-dried, cylinder-dried are three kinds. **1926** *Paper Terminol.* (Spalding & Hodge, Ltd.) 23 *Rope brown*, a quality of brown paper manufactured from old rope. **1955** S. C. Gilmour *Paper* xxii. 251 The thickness of a quality such as Rope Brown would appear to the touch to be much in excess of the same substance in an M. G. Pure Kraft. **1905** *Outing* July 415/1 Before we left that camp Rodney and Sue were sleek and fat, and my bruises and rope-burns were healed. **1944** B. A. Botkin *Treas. Amer. Folklore* i. iv. 132 The red rope-burn that he wore about his permanently stiff neck, usually hidden by a bandana, was his only diploma. **1948** Faulkner *Intruder in Dust* vii. 159 A big saddleless black mule with a rope-burn on its neck. **1965** A. Blackshaw *Mountaineering* viii. 217 (*caption*) He is wearing gloves to protect his hands from rope burns should the leader fall. **1966** M. & O. Murie *Wapiti Wilderness* v. 54 There was such friction from the mule's wild lunges that my palms were rather badly rope-burned. **1895** *Montgomery Ward Catal.* Spring & Summer 90/3 Rope Embroidery Silk..very coarse. **1897** *Sears, Roebuck Catal.* 321/2 Corticelli Rope Embroidery Silk..A course [*sic*] silk, for bold designs..when rapid work is required. **1944** R. F. Adams *Western Words* (1945) 131/2 When running an animal to be roped, the educated rope horse knows when the cowboy takes down his rope and what is expected of him. **1961** R. P. Hobson *Rancher takes Wife* i. 19 Rhino was a good rope horse. **1892** J. Nasmith *Students' Cotton Spinning* xii. 400 In arranging the blowing rooms it is now customary to separate them from the main building by the rope race. **1903** *Sci. Amer.* 23 May 392/2 In soft-coal mines the man in charge of the cable train is called a rope rider. In bringing his cars out of the mine he sits upon the ring which connects the cable with the train. **1902** *Encycl. Brit.* XXVI. 521/1 He [*sc.* the bellringer] has to bear in mind,..what bell or bells are striking immediately before or after him—this being ascertained chiefly by 'rope-sight' *i.e.*, the knack..of seeing which rope is being pulled immediately before and after his own. **1956** G. E. Evans *Ask Fellows who cut Hay* xviii. 143 The science of change-ringing is something of a mystery to the layman... 'It's all right once you get *rope-sight*,' one old ringer confided. **1975** *Islander* (Victoria, B.C.) 16 Mar. 12/3 He must start pulling his bell before the bell that he is following has sounded, so he must be able to recognize from the movement of the ropes (without hearing the sound) when he should start to pull his own rope, and this art of recognition is called 'ropesight'. **1977** *Church Times* 20 May 8/5 The ability to see one's path in this dancing maze is called ropesight, and is an essential attribute for a change ringer. **1880** L. Higgin *Handbk. Embroidery* iii. 28 Rope stitch..should..have the appearance of a twisted rope. **1932** D. C. Minter *Mod. Needlecraft* 55/2 Chain, pekinese, appliqué, Portuguese border and rope stitch..are useful for working this type of letter. **1887** *Encycl. Dict.* VI. i. 182/1 *Rope-trick*.., a juggling feat, introduced into England from America by the Brothers Davenport, in 1864. The performer was bound with ropes in a cabinet, or to a chair; the lights were then lowered, and on their being raised he was discovered at liberty, having been released, it was said, by spiritual agency. **1894** A. Lang *Cock Lane* 106 Thus, when Ibn Batuta, the old Arabian traveller, tells us that he saw the famous rope-trick performed in India—men climbing a rope thrown into the air, and cutting each other up, while the bodies revive and reunite—he very candidly adds that his companion, standing by, saw nothing out of the way, and declared that nothing occurred. **1907** Maskelyne & 'Devant' in 'D. Devant' *My Magic Life* (1931) xii. 131 We are prepared to pay a salary at the rate of £5,000 a year to any man who can perform the Rope Trick as described in the legend... He is to stand out in the open air... He is to throw one end of a rope into the air, and the other end is to be on the ground. The rope is to become stiffened; a boy is to climb up it and disappear into space. **1922** L. H. Branson *Indian Conjuring* ix. 76 (*heading*) The Indian rope trick. **1953** —— *Lifetime of Deception* xxxviii. 206 The Indian '*Jadoo-wallah*' is a much over-rated performer, particularly as the world-famous Indian rope trick has never been performed. This is a statement of fact. **1958** *Times Lit. Suppl.* 17 Jan. 26/5 These are no ugly moral questions, no probings of primitivism: Sir Maurice blandly marshals the material..and the miracle (or rope trick, according to one's viewpoint) is duly performed. **1977** *Private Eye* 4 Mar. 17/3 For what such massive buying operations did was to ensure that the Slater share price resembled the Indian rope trick, defying gravity. **1862** E. A. Hall *Diary* 2 Jan. in O. A. Sherrard *Two Victorian Girls* (1966) ii. 289 Spent an hour at the Crystal Palace and saw the rope-walker, Blondin. **1942** E. Sitwell *Street Songs* 11 We watched the sonambulists, rope-walkers, argonauts. **1881** *Gen. Statutes State of Michigan* (1882) I. 539 Any person..who shall apprentice, give away, let out or otherwise dispose of any such child to any person in or for the vocation, service or occupation of rope or wire walking..shall be deemed guilty of a misdemeanor. **1890** [see *act *sb.* 7 c]. **1957** *Encycl. Brit.* XIX. 547/1 *Rope-walking*, the art of walking, dancing and performing tricks on a rope or wire stretched between two supports. **1889** *Engineer* LXVIII. 454/1 Rope railways, as they were called, or ropeways, for transmitting minerals and goods, seem to be rapidly growing in favour, especially for mining purposes. **1928** *Daily Mail* 7 Aug. 8/5 Next week's programme includes instruction in the use of heavy derricks and aerial ropeways. **1941** 'R. West' *Black Lamb & Grey Falcon* II. 925 If you have to have a rope-way, you have to have Germans... All the decent funiculars in the world are made by a German company. **1950** tr. *Mountaineering Handbk.* (Assoc. Brit. Members Swiss Alpine Club) x. 116 To transport loads, injured people or materials over precipices, ravines, large crevasses or torrents, where possible fix a rope over the obstacle..the anchorage at the ends of a ropeway should be firm enough to meet all eventualities. **1963** *Economist* 30 Nov. 911/1 Aerial ropeways and chairlifts can be pretty profitable. **1937** Rope wrapping [see *acid-proof* adj. s.v. *acid *sb.* 4].

rope, *v.*[1] Add: **1. b.** (Further examples.)

1974 *Times* 18 Feb. 2/7 They had set out yesterday morning to climb Zero Gulley. About half way up Mr Beattey slipped and fell 100ft, landing on a ledge. Mr Thomas was roped to him. **1976** D. Clark *Dread & Water* i. 8 Redruth was climbing solo on a pretty easy pitch... Silk was roped to a partner.

absol. (Further examples.) Also with *up*.

1922 E. R. Eddison *Worm Ouroboros* xii. 177 They roped at the foot of the glacier that came down from the saddle, some five thousand feet above them. **1925** *Climbers' Club Jrnl.* XVII. 41 We roped up at the foot of the rocks at ten o'clock and serious climbing began at once. **1950** T. Longstaff *This my Voyage* ii. 16 We struck the arête at seven fifteen and after a bite, roped up. **1952** Morin & Smith tr. *Herzog's Annapurna* ix. 138 We roped up in the same order in which we had camped. **1965** A. Blackshaw *Mountaineering* vii. 198 The party should rope at the bottom of the first pitch of the climb.

d. (Further examples.)

1925 E. F. Norton *Fight for Everest: 1924* 115 It was one of our rules that any party of porters..must be met at the Col and escorted and roped over the intricate route into camp. **1976** A. White *Long Silence* ii. 18 It had been a difficult climb... He..roped me most of the way.

e. *to rope down* (intr. and trans.), to descend by means of a double rope fixed above; to make an abseil.

1931 *Climbers' Club Jrnl.* XVII. 204 The next little excitement was when we came to the top of..the Grand Diable... One has to rope down it. **1935** D. Pilley *Climbing Days* vi. 122 This roping down..is a trick one gets used to. **1943** E. Shipton *Upon that Mountain* iv. 78 We reached a gap about 30 feet deep, and roped down into it. **1945** G. W. Young *Mountain Craft* (ed. 4) iv. 152 Climbers, shy still of claiming it as a national practice, still struggle alternatively with 'rappel' and 'Abseilung', so as to put a wrapper..of dark foreign distinction about new methods of roping down. **1955** P. Bauer *Kanchen-*

junga Challenge I. i. 22 We roped down with flashes of lightning as our only illumination. **1965** A. BLACKSHAW *Mountaineering* viii. 239 (*heading*) Roping down (abseiling or rappelling).

2. (Examples with *off*.)
1889 *Cent. Dict.* s.v. rope[1] v., A space in front of the pictures was roped off to prevent injury to them. **1921** A. HUXLEY *Crome Yellow* xxviii. 298 It was the hour for the dancing..a space had been roped off. **1976** *S. Wales Echo* 23 Nov., A section of the centre had to be roped off yesterday to enable schools to use the sports facilities.

4. b. *to rope in* (further examples); also, to arrest (*rare*).
1916 'BOYD CABLE' *Action Front* 10 They..roped in my captain to identify me. **1925** D. G. MACKAIL in *Strand Mag.* Sept. 254/2 I'm sorry for you, my man, but ..another twenty-four hours, and we might have been roping you in, too. **1929** —— *How Amusing!* 108 He remembered now; they'd roped him in as a godfather. **1970** *Nature* 2 May 395/1 Despite its ability to attract private funds, the zoo has been less successful at roping in the public. **1973** E. PAGE *Fortnight by Sea* xi. 120 I've roped in the Pagets for a game, it seems she plays golf too. **1978** *Lancashire Life* Mar. 96/2 Much of it can be a do-it-yourself operation, in which the whole family can be roped in to help. **1981** N. FREELING *One Damn Thing* iv. 30 The gendarmes..sent the urban police to rope in the rest of the band.

5. b. (Earlier and later examples.)
1882 *Sydney Slang Dict.* 7/2 *Rope*, to lose a race purposely: to swindle one's backers or the public by a 'cross' or prearranged race, in which the best man or best horse is made to 'rope' or run behind. **1904** R. THOMAS *Swimming* ii. 44 A racer is said to rope when he does not exert himself to the utmost, in order to make out that he is not so good a swimmer as he really is, that he may thus get an advantage in the next handicap for which he enters.

ropeable, *a.* Add: Also *N.Z.* Also **ropable.** (Earlier and later examples.)
1874 C. DE BOOS *Congewoi Corr.* 195, I don't know a nastier smell than the smeller new togs just fresh from the tailor's goose, and the thoughter that amost made me ropable. **1919** H. LAWSON *Coll. Verse* (1969) III. 385 Don't get ropable, or moony—and, above all, don't get spoony. **1955** P. WHITE *Tree of Man* (1956) 278, I often remember how you broke that washstand at Yuruga. Mother was ropeable. **1957** D. NILAND *Call me when Cross turns Over* (1958) 216 God, she thought, as she sat down, he's ropable. **1958** *N.Z. Listener* 16 May 21/3 There was—with a walking stick, his leg in plaster. And was he ropeable! He came down and ripped into them: 'Who do you think you're going to play—a kindergarten? You're playing New Zealand. Now get cracking.' **1963** J. CANTWELL *No Stranger to Flame* viii. 125 She was going to have my kid, but she dropped it when another bloke put the acid on. I got ropeable and did her.

roped, *ppl. a.* Add: **2. a.** (Earlier and further examples.) Also *fig.* Also *roped-off*.
1829 P. EGAN *Boxiana* 2nd Ser. II. 350 Harry Jones and Bob Simmonds entered a twenty-four-foot roped ring at one o'clock. **1876** G. M. HOPKINS *Wreck of Deutschland* iv, in *Poems* (1967) 52, I steady as a water in a well, to a poise, to a pane, But roped with, always, all the way down from the tall Fells or flanks of the voel, a vein Of the gospel proffer. **1921** A. HUXLEY *Crome Yellow* xxvii. 295 In a roped-off space beyond, Mary was directing the children's sports. **1927** WODEHOUSE *Meet Mr. Mulliner* iii. 70 He seemed to be always on the point of introducing into debates on parish matters the methods which had made him so successful in the roped ring. **1932** AUDEN *Orators* III. 109 To stand with the wine-dark conquerors in the roped-off pews. **1943** J. B. PRIESTLEY *Daylight on Saturday* iv. 23 They went..to the enormous canteen. There was a roped-off space in the middle. **1955** E. HILLARY *High Adventure* 10 George Band with Sherpas ..on a roped cliff. **1965** F. SARGESON *Mem. Peon* vi. 163 His meagre, roped-off end of the..area. **1976** A. PRICE *War Game* II. 217 Posters directing motorists to roped-off fields. **1977** *Custom Car* Nov. 58/1, I can't help thinking a roped-off enclosure and a bit of creative parking for the various classes would have made for more interest.

b. (Further example.)
1935 *Encycl. Sports* 431/2 No one should ever attempt a roped climb without at least one experienced mountaineer in the party.

rope-like, *adv.* and *a.* (Earlier example.)
1840 EMERSON *Woodnotes* I, in *Dial* Oct. 244 The rope-like pine roots crosswise grown Composed the network of his throne.

rope-maker. Add: **b.** *rope-maker's eye*: a special eye made on a rope.
1883 *Man. Seamanship for Boys' Training Ships R. Navy* (Admiralty) (1886) 127 A Rope-Maker's Eye is generally made in the end of a jibstay when fitted with a slip at the jib-boom end, and has a thimble in it to receive the slip. **1911** *Encycl. Brit.* XV. 874/1 *Ropemakers' Eye*.. is formed by taking out of a rope one strand longer by 6 in. or a foot than the required eye, [etc.].

rope-over, *a. rare*[—1]. [ROPE *sb.*[1]] ? With muscles like twisted strands of rope.
1887 G. M. HOPKINS *Poems* (1967) 104 Lank Rope-over thigh; knee-nave; and barrelled shank.

roper. 4. For *U.S.* read 'chiefly *U.S.*' and add further examples.
1964 C. WILLOCK *Enormous Zoo* v. 92 At last her head was coming within range of the ropers. **1976** *Billings* (Montana) *Gaz.* 5 July 1-C/1 At Sunday's performance, cowboys in the calf roping event were the stars as each of the last five ropers managed to conquer Mike Cervi's rowdy black calfs to place in the money.

5. (Earlier examples.)
1840 *Picayune* (New Orleans) 31 Oct. 2/3 He had not well landed on the Levee, so famous for cotton bags, sugar,..'ropers in', and other 'dry goods'. **1844** J. H. GREENE *Expos. Arts Gambling* (ed. 2) 158 Those secret partners, by gamblers, are termed *ropers*, or *stool-pigeons*: their business is to delude the inexperienced into their dens of iniquity.

rope's end, *sb.* Add: **1.** Also in phr. *not to care a rope's end for*.
1858 TROLLOPE *Three Clerks* II. viii. 178 Uncle Bat.. did not care a rope's end for Undy Scott.

rope's-ending, *vbl. sb.* (Earlier example.)
1840 H. COCKTON *Life Valentine Vox* xii. 88 You shall catch, my dear, the blessedest rope's-ending you ever had any notion on yet.

rope-walk. Add: (Earlier and later examples.) Also *attrib.*
1672 *Rec. Early Hist. Boston* (1881) VII. 72 John Harrisons rope walke. **1886** *Encycl. Brit.* XX. 844/1 *Ropewalk Spinning*.—The sequence of operations in this ancient but still greatly used method of working is—(1) heckling the fibre; [etc.]. **1963** G. BLAKE *Gourock* ii. 22 It is interesting to note that the site on which was built the original Gourock, Ropework Company's rope-walk in 1777 was already marked 'Ropework' in 1721. *Ibid.* 24 The original Gourock ropewalk, 200 fathoms long and slated for half its length ran down to a rocky spit. **1971** *Daily Progress* (Charlottesville, Va.) 21 July 23/4 Born in an era of sailing vessels with their need for miles and miles of rope for riggings, the Ropewalk flourished in both world wars and declined after each.

rope-work. Add: **3.** Use of ropes in climbing.
1901 G. BELL *Let.* 8 Sept. (1927) I. vii. 127 After a great deal of complicated rope work we reached the Gemse Sattel. **1979** D. KYLE *Green River High* xvi. 211 All *I* had to do was shin a hundred feet up a rope!.. I've never been a one for rope-work, even in the gym.

4. Decoration with a rope motif.
1952 J. B. OLDHAM *Eng. Blind-Stamped Bindings* I. 11 Italian and Spanish blind bindings are so unlike English as to be easily distinguishable, with the former's characteristic leafy or rope-work frame, and the latter's rather unusual and fantastic stamps.

ropey, var. ROPY *a.* in Dict. and Suppl.

rope-yarn. Add: **3.** Used *attrib.* to designate a day given as a holiday or, more usu., a half-holiday (see quots.). Chiefly *Naval slang*.
1886 H. BAUMANN *Londinismen* 159/1 *Rope-yarn.. Sunday*, freie(r) Sonntag. **1914** *Dialect Notes* IV. 151 *Rope-yarn holiday, n. phr.*, a half holiday. **1929** F. C. BOWEN *Sea Slang* 113 *Rope Yarn Sunday*. In the British Navy, '*Make and Mend time*' q.v., on Thursday afternoon. The Americans use the term for Saturday afternoon when there are no drills or inspections, but ship's work is done. Their make and mend is on Wednesday, known as *Rope Yarn Holiday*. **1952** J. V. NOEL *Naval Terms* 184 *Rope Yarn Sunday*, any afternoon, except a week-end, that is free of work. Usually Wednesday afternoon is called *rope yarn Sunday* since liberty is often granted early on that day aboard ships in port. **1956** E. N. ROGERS *Queenie's Brood* 79 Rope-yarn Sunday is the seaman's Monday. Actually, it is a half day off and comes on a Wednesday afternoon. **1962** GRANVILLE *Dict. Sailors' Slang* 97/2 *Rope-yarn Thursday*,..the original Naval..half holiday.

roping, *vbl. sb.* Add: **1.** (Further examples.)
1883 *Man. Seamanship for Boys' Training Ships R. Navy* (Admiralty) (1886) 50 Q. What is the roping? A. The bolt rope round the edges of the sail to prevent it from rending. **1977** D. JAMES *Spy at Evening* vi. 29, I jumped. Into the black spray, clawing wildly for the rope ladder..my outstretched fingers touched the stiff, wet roping.

4. For '*U.S.* and *Austral.*' read 'chiefly *U.S.* and *Austral.*' (Further examples.) Also *roping-up*.
1907 S. E. WHITE *Arizona Nights* III. i. 241 The roping and throwing and branding..filled our days with..the unusual. **1932** BLUNDEN *Face of England* 102 The last shocks are on the wagon, the roping-up is done. **1973** *Times* 2 Oct. 15/2 Giraffes are among the most difficult animals to capture. Straight-forward roping is unsuitable because a fall is more likely to break the neck of a giraffe than of a more compact animal. **1976** *Billings* (Montana) *Gaz.* 16 June 1-C/2 Cooper, who was being pressed in the second go-round of steer wrestling, held the lead in team roping with teammate Phil Longacre at 7.34 seconds. **1979** *Tucson Mag.* Apr. 68/3 The charreada is a fast-paced program of riding, roping, music, and dancing.

7. *roping arena, horse, stick*.
1979 *Farmington* (New Mexico) *Daily Times* 27 May 10 C/5 (Advt.), 40 acres with..iron fenced corral, roping arena, etc. **1949** *Los Angeles Times* 12 July II. 2/5 The final resting place of Soap Suds, once the greatest humorist's favorite roping horse. **1976** *Billings* (Montana) *Gaz.* 27 June 8-D/1 (Advt.), Saddle horses of all kinds & roping horses for sale. **1878** E. S. ELWELL *Boy Colonists* 190 Ernest..had to get behind the animal, and by dint of prodding with the roping stick..to force it to run up towards the corner. **1888** 'R. BOLDREWOOD' *Robbery under Arms* III. xiv. 201 He stuck to his roping-stick—good, heavy-ended gum sapling, six or seven feet long.

ropy, *a.* Add: Also **ropey. 1. a.** (Further examples.)
1935 J. LAWRANCE *Painting from A to Z* xi. 103 Thick, ropey coats of paint look unsightly. **1940** H. L. HIND *Brewing* II. xxxvii. 917 The general consensus of practical brewing opinion in Great Britain seems to be that a species of coccus or 'sarcina' is nearly always to be found in samples of ropy beer. **1950** *N.Z. Jrnl. Agric.* Feb. 165/3 Stock should not be allowed to drink from stagnant pools, as these are a source of the organism responsible for ropey milk.

c. *fig.* Bad, unsatisfactory, unreliable, unwell. *slang* and *colloq*.
1942 *R.A.F. Jrnl.* 18 Apr. 10, I then commanded a scratch squadron of rather ropey machines. **1942** *Tee Emm* (Air Ministry) II. 131 It will probably show how ropy your judgement is on modern types. **1944** S. GIBBONS *Bachelor* xvi. 144, I think you must have a ropey time. Worrying about the poor, and giving all your money away and not eating much. **1945** *Gen* 30 June 51/1 He's feeling a bit ropey now, and he's going to have a bad night. **1953** E. HYAMS *Gentian Violet* iii. 42 Their aircraft are pretty ropey. **1957** *Daily Mail* 3 Dec. 14/1 It is, of course, very difficult to get waiters on New Year's Eve. If you hire them outside, you may get a few ropey types. **1959** W. D. PEREIRA *North Flight* ii. 33 You look a bit ropey, Dad, why don't you go home..and relax? **1961** *Sunday Express* 15 Jan. 4/6, I feel a bit ropey... I think I've picked up some sort of virus. **1963** *Times* 20 May 6/5 Some of the acting is a bit ropy. **1971** J. AIKEN *Nightly Deadshade* iii. 22 Mother..was crippled and Father left her... Everything was one hundred per cent ropy except that she had a little money. **1978** F. MANN *Acupuncture* (ed. 3) ix. 138 Sometimes a ropy pulse occurs in elderly people who have had many illnesses affecting several bodily systems, all of which have been only partly cured.

d. Of a cow: producing ropy milk.
1960 *Farmer & Stockbreeder* 19 Jan. 60/3 But what did farmers do? They sent all their ropy cows to F[atstock] M[arketing] C[orporation] and flogged the best in the auction mart.

2. (Further examples.)
1973 M. AMIS *Rachel Papers* 132 Otherwise it was mostly long whitened grass, frizzled bushes, and hundreds of ropey little trees, fifteen feet high. **1976** *Nature* 26 Feb. 650/1 Sample ARP 74-14-31, with a ropey surface showing flow direction, has a preserved glassy crust and a palagonite layer overlain by a thin manganese coating.

roque (rōᵘk). [An arbitrary alteration of CROQUET *sb.*; cf. ROQUET *sb.*] A form of croquet played in the U.S., differing from croquet chiefly in the use of a hard-surfaced, embanked court, ten hoops, and short-handled mallets. Also *attrib.*
1899 *Boston Even. Transcript* 15 Sept. 6/5 The players of the new croquet, having developed a new and scientific game, have adopted a new name, and call it roque. **1906** *Springfield* (Mass.) *Weekly Republ.* 30 Aug. 16 A 16-years-old lad who never before had played in a big-tournament won the national championship at roque. **1909** *Chicago Daily News* 12 Aug. 8/1 They are holding a roque tournament at Norwich, Conn. **1924** R. LARDNER in *Current Opinion* July 128/2 'Good gracious!' I said. 'Imagine being married to a woman that plays five hundred like she does and drops her teeth on the roque court!' **1954** J. STEINBECK *Sweet Thursday* viii. 55 Roque is a complicated kind of croquet. **1968** *Punch* 9 Oct. 495 Archery and golf and rackets and roque and lawn tennis have all been in and out again. **1976** *Webster's Sports Dict.* 356/2 *Roque*, a variation of croquet played with short-handled mallets on a hard-surfaced court.

Roquefort. Add: **a.** (Further examples.) (Now a proprietary name in the U.K.)
[**1766** W. C. CROKER *Compl. Dict. Arts & Sci.* I. s.v. *Cheese*, At Rochfort, in Languedoc, they make a cheese of ewe's milk.] **1885** [see *EDAM]. **1927** M. A. HULBERT *Treasures of Hundred Cooks* ix. 212 Use equal parts of Roquefort and Philadelphia cream cheese. **1933** *Gourmet's Bk. Food & Drink* ix. 136, I do not think a creamy or soft cheese is the best..nor, on the other hand, would I advise starting the meal with the brutal pungency of Roquefort. **1955** *Times* 10 May 12/4 Roquefort, a French blue veined cheese, is perhaps the best example of a cheese that is still to-day definitely 'regional'. **1963** *Trade Marks Jrnl.* 26 June 885 Roquefort... Roquefort cheese. Société Anonyme Des Caves & Des Producteurs Réunis de Roquefort (Aveyron). **1976** *National Observer* (U.S.) 23 Oct. 10/3 Other favorite menu frauds, Reeves reports, include substituting..blue cheese for Roquefort.

b. In full *Roquefort dressing*. A variety of salad dressing made with Roquefort cheese. Also used *attrib.* of a salad served with this. Chiefly *U.S.*
1943 D. POWELL *Time to be Born* ix. 210 Cheever must ..eat oysters Rockefeller and Roquefort salad dressing. **1961** J. HELLER *Catch-22* (1962) ix. 98 I've got some live Maine lobsters hidden away that I can serve you tonight with an excellent Roquefort salad and two frozen éclairs. **1962** *Listener* 11 Jan. 90/3 It is worth trying to order one of those marvellous green salads unaccompanied by the demand: 'Roquefort, thousand-isle or French?' **1968** C. DRUMMOND *Death & Leaping Ladies* i. 21 Plain salad, with a little touch of Roquefort dressing. **1973** M. & G. GORDON *Informant* xl. 152 A hamburger dinner with lettuce salad and Roquefort dressing. **1977** *Transatlantic Rev.* LX. 87 Andrea, in bad humor, portions out breakfast—leg of armadillo.., imitation roquefort dressing, a half-ration of water and sour mix.

roquesite (rǫ·kesəit). *Min.* [ad. F. *roquésite* (Picot & Pierrot 1963, in *Bull. de la Soc. franç. de Min. et de Crist.* LXXXVI. 7/2), f. the name of Maurice *Roques*, 20th-c. French geologist: see -ITE¹.] A sulphide of copper and indium, $CuInS_2$, occurring as small greyish blue crystals.

1963 *Mineral. Abstr.* XVI. 372/1 A new mineral determined by electron microprobe technique is named roquésite. It occurs as inclusions in bornite in the Charrier Cu, Sn, and Fe mine, Allier, central France. **1970** *Doklady Earth Sci.* CXCI. 138/1 During field investigation of ores from depth at a pyrite deposit in central Kazakhstan, we detected roquesite, a mineral reported in such ores for the first time. **1974** *Mineral. Abstr.* XXV. 329/1 Roquesite..occurs in grains up to 1 mm in length in bornite associated with chalcopyrite, wittichenite,.. etc. in veins cutting a Devonian volcanic-sedimentary succession.

Ro-Railer (rōᵘ,rēⁱ·ləɹ). Also **ro-railer.** [f. Ro(AD *sb.* + RAIL *sb.*² + -ER¹.] The name of an experimental vehicle, introduced by the London, Midland, and Scottish Railway, which could be adapted to run on either road or railway. (No longer current.) Cf. *road-railer* s.v. *ROAD *sb.* 12.

1931 *Times Educ. Suppl.* 31 Jan. p. iv/1 Trials of the 'ro-railer', a vehicle which..can be driven either on the railway or on the road. **1934** *Discovery* Nov. 317/1 The L.M.S. have experimented with various types [of railcar], including a 'Ro-Railer' which can run equally well on road and on rail, and more conventional Diesel-engined car. **1959** H. ELLIS *Brit. Railway Hist.* II. III. i. 334 The L.M.S. tried out, on the Stratford upon Avon and Midland Junction line, a motor bus called a Ro-Railer, with two sets of wheels which could be very quickly substituted, one for another, according to whether it were to go on road or railway.

‖ **Roriz** (rori·ʃ). The name of a wine-growing estate in the Douro valley of Portugal, used *absol.* to designate a variety of port produced there.

1873 C. M. YONGE *Pillars of House* I. ii. 30 What right had you to know that I knew the taste of Cape from Roriz? **1907** *Yesterday's Shopping* (1969) 96/1 *Ports for laying down*..Quinta Roriz. **1917** *Harrods Catal.* 1286/1 *Old bottled vintage ports*..Kopke Roriz. **1920** G. SAINTSBURY *Notes on Cellar-Bk.* iii. 38 Kopke's famous 'Roriz' did not..appeal to me.

ro-ro (rōᵘ·rōᵘ), *a.* Abbrev. of *ROLL-ON, ROLL-OFF.

1969 *Jane's Freight Containers 1968–69* p. iii/2 Ro-Ro berths were also included. **1969** *Australian* 30 Oct. 13/1 First the Scandias and now it's to be an even larger series of roll-on roll-off (Ro-Ro) ships for service in the Australia-Europe trade. **1974** *Times* 23 Jan. 16/7 Colonel Frank Bustard, one of the great shipping pioneers..was the father of the 'ro-ro' revolution. **1975** *Globe & Mail* (Toronto) 2 Oct. B14/1 It is adapted for roll-on, roll-off operation and will be served by two..ro-ro ships. **1978** *N.Y. Times* 30 Mar. D12 (Advt.), The new Farrell fleet incorporates the most sophisticated and efficient methods of cargo handling. We have breakbulk, container, LASH, RoRo and giant container vessels.

Rorschach (rǭ·ɹʃāχ). The name of Hermann *Rorschach* (1884–1922), Swiss psychiatrist, used *attrib.* and *absol.* to designate a type of projective personality test first devised by him, in which a standard set of ink blots of different shapes and colours is presented one at a time to a subject with the request that he should describe what they suggest or resemble. Also *Rorschach (ink) blot, method,* etc. Also *fig.*

1927 MOIR & GUNDLACH in *Jrnl. Exper. Psychol.* Apr. 151 Each subject was given the Rorschach test. *Ibid.*, In a classification of the individual records according to the Rorschach diagnostic tables. **1935** *Amer. Jrnl. Psychiatry* July 109 The Rorschach test has recently received considerable attention in psychiatric and psychological circles. **1942** [see *INSECURITY 1]. **1948** *Personnel Psychol.* I. 357 (*heading*) Can the Rorschach pick sales clerks? **1951** KOESTLER *Age of Longing* i. 40 The brandy..expanded slowly into a Rorschach blotch on the marble surface. **1953** A. K. C. OTTAWAY *Educ. & Society* viii. 147 The Rorschach method of giving a verbal interpretation of ink-blots. **1956** *Publ. Amer. Dial. Soc.* XXVI. 121 The social or clinical psychologist will want to go still more deeply into the individual's imaginative response to the Rorschach ink blots. **1958** *Listener* 17 July 93/2 Rorschach blots and tapestries. **1960** *Commentary* June 486/2 Rorschach (inkblot) ratings. **1966** T. PYNCHON *Crying of Lot 49* i. 18 His [*sc.* a psychotherapist's] theory being that a face is symmetrical like a Rorschach blot. **1971** *Jrnl. Gen. Psychol.* LXXXV. 295 Free associative responses and responses to ambiguous stimuli—a kind of auditory Rorschach. **1974** B. M. & D. D. BRAGINSKY *Mainstream Psychol.* vi. 118 The two most widely used psychological tests, the Rorschach inkblot test and the Draw-a-Person test (both projective tests), have also been widely researched. **1980** *Dædalus* Spring 136 The Rorschach test is effective..because it forces people to be creative.

Rörstrand (rǭ·rstrand). Also *erron.* **Rostrandt.** The name of a building in Stockholm in which a ceramics factory was opened in 1725, used *attrib.* and *absol.* to designate the varieties of pottery and porcelain manufactured there.

1881 C. SCHREIBER *Jrnl.* 7 Oct. (1911) II. 354 Stockholm, Rostrandt, and Marienberg pottery and porcelain. **1901** W. P. RIX tr. *E. Bourry's Treat. Ceramic Industries* I. i. 753 Rörstrand crockery ware. **1906** W. BURTON *Porcelain* xvi. 188 The body and the glaze of the Rörstrand porcelain are as beautiful as those of Copenhagen. **1925** B. RACKHAM tr. *E. Hannover's Pott. & Porc.* I. IV. iv. 482 Rörstrand faïence has not infrequently..an even faint violet tone. **1961** *Guardian* 3 Mar. 10/5 Foreign buyers do not want Wedgwood or Doulton or Spode or Minton to look like Arabia, Rörstrand, or Rosenthal. **1974** *Encycl. Brit. Micropædia* VIII. 669/3 *Rörstrand faience*, first faience (tin-glazed earthenware) produced in Sweden.

rort (rǭɹt), *sb. Austral. slang.* [Back-formation f. RORTY *a.*] **1.** A trick, a 'dodge'; a fraud or dishonest practice. Now freq. with qualifying word.

1936 J. DEVANNY *Sugar Heaven* 20 The cockies are supposed to pay this retention money into the bank..but normally they don't pay it in... It's the greatest rort ever. **1958** *Sunday Mail Mag.* (Brisbane) 24 Aug. 4/4 'If they don't it will be a rort.' 'But why should it be a rort?' asks the man. **1973** *Nation Rev.* (Melbourne) 31 Aug. 1441/3 Items such as the health scheme have yet to be introduced and others—such as the removal of many of the more outrageous tax rorts—could still be frustrated were there to be an early election. **1979** *Sunday Sun* (Brisbane) 7 Jan. 20/3 Many professional people.. previously were denied access to the typical expense account rort.

2. A crowd; a wild party.

1941 BAKER *Dict. Austral. Slang* 61 *Rort*,..a crowd. **1952** T. A. G. HUNGERFORD *Ridge & River* 81 Out we go on another bloody rort, so what's the use of saving a day? **1969** G. JOHNSTON *Clean Straw for Nothing* 78, I am not, strictly, a true devotee of the wild Australian 'rort' and always remorseful in my hangovers. **1972** *Sydney Morning Herald* 26 Aug. 20/3 One of her annual St Teresa's Day parties—a decorous..underworld rort in honour of St Teresa.

rort (rǭɹt), *v. slang.* [Back-formation from RORTY *a.*] **1.** *intr.* To shout, complain loudly; to shout abuse. Also, to call the odds at a race-meeting. Also with *at.*

1931 T. H. DEY *Leaves from Bookmaker's Book* ii. 35 How he could 'rort', and keep his customers on the racecourse in a perpetual roar of laughter with his witty remarks. **1935** M. HARRISON *Spring in Tartarus* III. 327 It isn't you..that I'm rorting at. **1962** GRANVILLE *Dict. Sailor's Slang* 97/2 *Rort*, to shout in argument or act truculently when charged with indiscipline... In Cockney Slang *to rort* is to 'shout the odds'.

2. (Examples both exemplify the *vbl. sb.*) (See quots.) *Austral. slang.*

1941 BAKER *Dict. Austral. Slang* 61 *Rorting*, shrewd practices, confidence trickery. **1980** *Sunday Mail* (Brisbane) 15 June 6 (*heading*) Overseas tax havens and 'rorting' claimed. $3000m a year in tax dodges.

rorter (rǭ·ɹtəɹ). *Austral. slang.* [f. *RORT *sb.* or *v.* + -ER¹.] One who engages in dishonest practices; a professional sharper or trickster.

1941 BAKER *Dict. Austral. Slang* 61 *Rorter*, a professional sharper: a hawker of worthless goods: one who practises sly dodges to obtain money. **1945, 1961** [see *poofter rorter* s.v. *POOFTER]. **1962** A. MARSHALL *This is Grass* 159 Rorters like Flogger prepared to fleece any man who stood staring around him.

rorty, *a.* Add: (Further examples.) Also in extended senses: (of persons and things) boisterous, rowdy, noisy; (of drinks) intoxicating; (of behaviour, speech, etc.) coarse, earthy, of dubious propriety; crudely comic. Also as quasi-*adv.*

1888 ''ARRY' in *Punch* 6 Oct. 156/1, I like to feel rorty and free. **1898** R. HICHENS *Londoners* xvi. 280 'Tell us a good story, Rodney—one of your rorty ones.' Mr. Rodney shrivelled. 'I fear', he murmured—'I fear I am scarcely in the—the—er—rorty vein to-night.' **1899** R. WHITEING *No. 5 John St.* ix. 95 She is Boadicea..no 'British warrior queen' of recitation, but a right-down 'raughty gal', leading her alley [*sic*] to battle against the Roman 'slops'. **1904** G. B. LANCASTER *Sons o' Men* 190 If Sandy or Towse get into a row we must back 'em up, of course. But it's been a rorty piece of work. **1914** 'BARTIMEUS' *Naval Occasions* xvii. 144 I've heard her talking like a Mother to a rorty Midshipman. **1923** — *Seaways* vii. 96 Isn't he a little man?.. Bettin' with bookies and actin' rorty. **1932** S. GIBBONS *Cold Comfort Farm* xvi. 217 Compared with the heavy, muffling darkness of the night in which the countryside was sunk, the lights looked positively rorty. **1950** 'D. DIVINE' *King of Fassarai* xxix. 255 It [*sc.* coconut milk] comes rortier if you leave it..to ferment, but it's got a kick now. **1969** W. TUTE *Matter of Diplomacy* ii. 16 The rorty brigadier must have a taste for lean stringy meat, though of course she had been a baronet's daughter and that made up for a lot. **1971** *Sunday Nation* (Nairobi) 11 Apr. 29/3 The once-called 'power roar' from the engine compartment.. never became obtrusive or 'rorty'. **1973** *Daily Tel.* 23 Aug. 6/8 He has a wide and rorty selection of illustrations. **1974** *Good Motoring* Mar. 22/1 It is..odd that such a comfortable car should have such brilliant performance ..which is characterised by a 'rorty' exhaust note. **1978** C. BEATON *Parting Years* 160 Anne Tree is likewise an oversize personality and character—rorty, Hogarthian and with exquisite understanding of character.

Rory O'More (rōᵊ·ri ōᵘmōᵊ·ɹ). *Rhyming slang.* Also **Rory O'Moore** and *ellipt.* as **Rory, rory.** [The name of a legendary Irish rebel, the eponymous hero of a popular ballad (1826) and novel (1837) by S. Lover (1797–1868), Irish writer.] **a.** The floor; also *on the Rory*, poor, penniless. **b.** A door.

1857 'DUCANGE ANGLICUS' *Vulgar Tongue* 17 Rory-O'More, *n.* floor. **1859** HOTTEN *Dict. Slang* 145 *Rory O'Moore*, the floor. **1892** 'Doss CHIDERDOSS' in *Sporting Times* 29 Oct. 1/2, I fired him out of the Rory quick. **1935** A. J. POLLOCK *Underworld Speaks* 98/2 *Rory O'More*, the door. **1936** J. CURTIS *Gilt Kid* xviii. 178 Some lousy berk must have been snooping around the place and found that rory open. **1938** F. D. SHARPE *Sharpe of Flying Squad* 332 *On the Rory*, penniless. **1953** BERREY & VAN DEN BARK *Amer. Thes. Slang* (1954) § 466/3 *Rory O'Moore*, a door. **1973** B. AYLWIN *Load of Cockney Cobblers* x. 49 *Rory O'More*, floor or door, *Rory*.

Rosalia² (rozā·liă). *Mus.* Also with small initial. Pl. **Rosalias, Rosalie.** [Prob. the personal name *Rosalia*, occurring in the title of an Italian popular song, *Rosalia, mia cara*, the melody of which employs this device.] The repetition of a phrase or passage one note higher, with the retention of the same intervals and a consequent change of key.

[**1773** C. BURNEY *Present State of Music in Germany* II. 327 The French have a term for this tediousness, which is wanting in other languages, they call it *Rosalie*.] **1801** BUSBY *Dict. Mus.* s.v., *Rosalia*, a term applied by the Italians to the repetition of a passage one note higher. **1883** GROVE *Dict. Mus.* III. 160/1 *Rosalia*,..a form of Melody, Vocal or Instrumental, in which a Figure is repeated several times in succession, transposed a note higher at each reiteration. *Ibid.* 160/2 Schumann has been recently accused of writing Rosalie, *usque ad nauseam*. **1937** G. B. SHAW *London Music in 1888–89* 30 To give the orchestra symphonic work instead of rosalias and rum-tum. **1944** W. APEL *Harvard Dict. Mus.* 652/2 *Rosalia*, a disparaging term denoting the schematic and unimaginative application of sequential treatment... The word applies in particular to sequences which, owing to the exact repetition of the intervals, involve modulation of the key to the higher second. **1954** *Grove's Dict. Mus.* (ed. 5) VII. 230/2 *Rosalia*, the name given to the identical repetition of a melody a tone higher, keeping the exact intervals of the notes.

rosaline (rōᵘ·zălīn). Also with capital initial. [App. of Fr. origin (see etym. note).] In full, *rosaline point.* A variety of fine needlepoint or pillow lace. Used esp. of Venetian or Belgian rose-point lace. Also *Comb.*

The word is not found in standard Fr. dicts., but occurs in specialist works (cf. C. Mague *Dentelles Anciennes* (1930)). Webster (1961) prefers to regard it as irreg. f. ROSE *sb.*, but its meaning and use in Eng. suggest a Fr. origin.

1900 E. JACKSON *Hist. Hand-Made Lace* vii. 66 Richness of workmanship distinguished the early eighteenth century specimens, and the firm yet delicate laces such as Rosaline Point..were especially suitable for the purpose. **1921** GALSWORTHY *To Let* I. ii. 25 'There's a bit of rosaline point in here,' he said, stopping before a shop, 'that I thought you might like.' **1953** M. POWYS *Lace & Lace-Making* vi. 47 In the Treasury of St. Marks in Venice there is a Bas d'Aube of the finest quality with smaller flowers and detail, a type of Point de Venise which is called 'Rosaline', the whirls and picots sometimes rising up to the height of half an inch and giving a moss-like effect. *Ibid.* iv. 23 Rosaline is made with the same technique as the Point d'Angleterre and Duchesse, the only difference being that it has a winky pin at the border of the braid instead of the usual edge. **1966** 'E. KYLE' *Love is for Living* iii. 27 They hadn't any rosaline perlé... Their best lacemaker is ill. *Ibid.* vi. 51 This is rosaline perlé. Here is the real rose-point. You see that the first has these small knots like pearls to diversify the pattern? **1971** *Country Life* 4 Nov. 1197/3 This *rosaline* or *point de neige* is the summit of virtuosity.

rosary. 6. a. (Further *fig.* examples.)

1951 N. MARSH *Opening Night* v. 106 Trying to cheer herself up by telling over her rosary of romantic memories. **1960** S. BECKER tr. *Schwarz-Bart's Last of Just* (1961) VI. 291 One day Fräulein Blumenthal arrived to visit, leading her rosary of tiny Levys.

rosasite (rōᵘ·zăsəit). *Min.* [a. It. *rosasite* (D. Lovisato 1908, in *Atti d. R. Accad. d. Lincei* XVII. II. 726), f. *Rosas*, name of a mine at Sulcis, Sardinia: see -ITE¹.] A carbonate-hydroxide of copper and zinc, $(Cu,Zn)_2(OH)_2CO_3$, a secondary mineral found as a bluish-green deposit on copper and zinc ores.

1909 *Jrnl. Chem. Soc.* XCVI. II. 246 (*heading*) Rosasite, a new mineral from the mines of Rosas (Sulcis, Sardinia). **1958** *Mineral. Mag.* XXXI. 501 Rosasite has not so far been reported in Britain, but we are now able to record no less than seven occurrences. *Ibid.*, The rosasite generally forms small bluish-green wart-like aggregates.

‖ **rosbif** (rǫzbif). [Fr., repr. ROAST BEEF.] **a.** In *Gastronomy*, beef (and occas. other types of meat) roasted in the English manner. Also *Comb.* and *transf.*

1846 R. FORD *Gatherings from Spain* xi. 120 Our true love for the *ros-bif* of old England. **1877** E. S. DALLAS *Kettner's Bk. of Table* 7 In the most popular cookery books of France..roast mutton and lamb are designated Rosbif de Mouton, and Rosbif d'agneau. **1897** A. BEARDSLEY *Let.* 15 Apr. (1970) 303 She..has been lecturing me about diet. Hot water and rosbif make up her programme. **1923** JOYCE *Let.* 12 July (1966) III. 78 My complexion is now cinnabar and rosbif a l'anglaise. **1972** *Country Life* 20 Jan. 159/1 The Frenchman, if given the opportunity, prefers *le rosbif anglais.* **1972** J. AIKEN *Butterfly Picnic* i. 19 How about a nice grilled steak—chicken—rosbif?

b. A French pejorative term for an Englishman. *rare.*

1858 THACKERAY *Virginians* (1859) II. iii. 23 Only my white cockade and coat had saved me from the fate which the other *canaille* of *Rosbifs* had deservedly met with.

roscherite (rǫ·ʃĕrəit). *Min.* [ad. G. *roscherit* (F. Slavík 1914, in *Bull. internat. de l'Acad. tchèque des Sciences, Prague* XIX. 109), f. the name of Walter *Roscher* (fl. 1914), German apothecary and mineral collector: see -ITE[1].] A hydrated basic phosphate of beryllium, calcium, iron, and manganese, $(Ca,Mn,Fe)_3Be_3(PO_4)_3(OH)_3.2H_2O$, sometimes also containing magnesium, found as yellowish-green to brown crystals in granite and pegmatite.

The presence of beryllium in roscherite was not discovered until 1958, the mineral previously having been believed to contain aluminium.

1916 *Chem. Abstr.* X. 31 Roscherite is a new monoclinic mineral occurring as short thick plates and also as slender prismatic and thin tabular crystals. **1958** *Amer. Mineralogist* XLIII. 824 Roscherite from the Sapucaia pegmatite mine occurs as single crystals, crystal aggregates, and granular crusts in vugs in muscovite. **1975** *Tschermaks Mineral. und Petrogr. Mitteilungen* XXII. 266 Roscherite from Lavra da Ilha, Taquaral, Minas Gerais is a magnesian roscherite.

Roscius (rǫ·siŭs, rǫ·sk-, rǫ·ʃiŭs). Also **Roshus, Rossius.** The name of Quintus *Roscius* Gallus (see ROSCIAN *a.*), used to designate an actor, usu. one of outstanding ability, success, or fame (now chiefly *Hist.*, with reference to David Garrick). Also *fig.*

1647 HERRICK *Noble Numbers* 74 Thou art that Roscius, and that markt-out man, That must this day act the Tragedian. *a* **1661** FULLER *Worthies* (1662) London 224 Edward Allin..was the Roscius of our age. *a* **1706** EVELYN *Diary* an. 1662 (1955) III. 338 His best [painting] in my opinion is Lacy the famous Rossius or comedian, whom he has painted in three dresses. **1749** W. R. CHETWOOD *Gen. Hist. of Stage* 155 Mr. George Powel, a reputable Actor, with many Excellencies, gave out that he would perform the Part of Sir John Falstaff in the Manner of that very excellent English Roscius, Mr. Betterton. **1763** BOSWELL *Jrnl.* 21 Jan. (1950) 163, I was sitting with the great Roscius of the age [*sc.* Garrick]. **1793** W. B. STEVENS *Jrnl.* 13 May (1965) 82 The little Roscius of a Baronet tortures his *Crura Podilla* into Harlequin Agility. **1804** *Times* 27 Nov. 3/1 The Young Roscius was at Covent-Garden Theatre last night. **1826** HAZLITT in *New Monthly Mag.* Jan. 38 Of our party only two persons present had seen the British Roscius [*sc.* Garrick]. **1888** KIPLING *Soldiers Three* 58 Captain dear,.. the gallery have enjoyed the performinces av a Roshus. **1958** C. OMAN *David Garrick* xiv. 372 The Garricks set out for home next day... John O'Keefe, the Dublin playwright, saw Roscius for the last time 'walking very quick (his way)' up and down the Adelphi terrace. **1973** C. PRICE *Theatre in Age of Garrick* ii. 6 To the eighteenth century, Garrick was the outstanding actor of modern times, and to call him 'Roscius' as was so often done was merely to indicate that in one respect at least England could rival ancient Rome.

roscoe (rǫ·sko). *U.S. slang.* Also **rosco** and with capital initial. The surname *Roscoe* used as a term for a gun, usu. a pistol or revolver. See also *John Roscoe* s.v. *JOHN 4.

1914 JACKSON & HELLYER *Vocab. Criminal Slang* 72 *Roscoe*,.. a revolver... 'Stash your roscoe before you come back to the kip.' **1927** *Amer. Speech.* II. 387/2 During the harvest season, individuals and gangs harvested the harvesters at the point of the *rod* or *Roscoe* (gun). **1930** *Sat. Even. Post* 28 June 161 Slide back the shutters in the steel windows, jam your roscoes through and blast hell out of everything in sight. **1930** *Amer. Mercury* Dec. 457/2 They settle him on a rosco rap. **1941** *Sun* (Baltimore) 15 Oct. 10/16 Favorite roscoes and tommy guns of gangland's paladins. **1958** *Sat. Even. Post* 20 Sept. 86/1 Mickey and a sinister young hood..waved a couple of loaded roscoes at the cashier. **1965** E. LACY *Moment of Untruth* vii. 111 'I know you're a dick, but..' ..'What makes you think that?' 'At the bull fight, when I stood up to let you pass—felt the roscoe on your hip.' **1979** E. NEWMAN *Sunday Punch* viii. 62 'You'll shoot me if I don't sell?'.. His hand went to the bulge again. 'Is that what they call a "roscoe"?'

roscoelite (rö·skoləit). *Min.* [f. the name of Sir Henry *Roscoe* (1833–1915), English chemist + -ITE[1].] A vanadium ore that is a basic silicate of potassium, vanadium, and aluminium belonging to the mica family and occurring as minute green or brown scales.

1876 J. BLAKE in *Amer. Jrnl. Sci.* CXII. 31 The mineral, to which I have given the name of Roscoelite,—in honor of Professor Roscoe, of Manchester, who has done so much for the chemical history of vanadium,—is a well marked species of mica, containing quite a large percentage of vanadium. **1943** R. D. GEORGE *Minerals & Rocks* iii. 92 As an ore of vanadium, roscoelite has been found chiefly in western Colorado. **1966** *Mineral. Abstr.* XVII. 670/1 Haradaite ($SrVOSi_2O_6$), goldmanite (calcium vanadic garnet $Ca_3V_2Si_3O_{12}$), and roscoelite ($KV_2AlSi_3O_{10}(OH)_2$) have been hydrothermally synthesized..at moderate *PT* conditions. **1974** *Encycl. Brit. Micropædia* X. 346/3 Vanadium is the 22nd most abundant element in the Earth's crust. Some commercial sources are the minerals carnotite, vanadinite, and roscoelite.

rose, *sb.* and *a.* Add: **A. I. 1. c.** *sugar of roses* (earlier and later examples).

1686 W. DENTON *Let.* in M. M. Verney *Mem.* (1899) IV. ix. 359, I could wish you would take sugar of roses with yr. asses' milke. **1922** [see *RINGOCANDY].

3. b. *rose of the sun* = ROSA SOLIS 1.

1910 KIPLING *Rewards & Fairies* 275 Excellent herbs had our fathers of old—..Cowslip, Melilot, Rose of the Sun.

II. 4. e. *to pluck a rose*: see *PLUCK *v.* 9.

f. *not to be the rose but to be near it* (and variants), phr. expressing a person's proximity to some admired person, ideal, or the like.

[**1808** F. GLADWIN tr. *Sâdy's Gûlistân* p. x, I was a worthless piece of clay, but having for a season associated with the rose, the virtue of my companion was communicated to me.] **1818** C. R. MATURIN *Women* I. x. 191 'I am not the rose,' said he, 'but I have been near the rose.' **1825** H. WILSON *Memoirs* (ed. 2) I. 234, I considered her with respect and admiration, unmixed with jealousy. This was not the rose; but she had dwelled with it. **1848** THACKERAY *Pendennis* (1849) I. ii. 11 If they were not the roses, they lived near the roses, as it were, and had a good deal of the odour of genteel life. **1866** MRS. GASKELL *Wives & Daughters* II. xviii. 181 The great reason why she did not hear of the gossip against Molly as early as anyone, was that, although she was not the rose, she lived near the rose. **1872** S. R. HOLE *Six of Spades* xii. 106 It seems to say, with the perfumed earth in the Persian fable, 'I am not the rose; but cherish me, for we have dwelt together.' **1899** H. JAMES *Awkward Age* II. viii. 84 Mrs. Grendon, though not perhaps herself quite the rose, is decidedly, in these days, too near it. **1907** E. GOSSE *Father & Son* iv. 91, I was not permitted to go forth and trade with this old person, but sometimes our servant-maid did, thereby making me feel that if I did not hold the rose of merchandise, I was very near it. **1917** 'O. DOUGLAS' *Setons* xiii. 151 It was not the rose but it was someone who at times was near the rose—and he went and sat down beside Jessie. **1979** *Country Life* 7 June 1863/4 Laura moves to Candleford Green, which, if not the rose of Candleford itself, is still nearer the rose than was Lark Rise.

g. *pl.*, expressing favourable circumstances, ease, success, etc., in various phrases, as *roses, (roses,) all the way, not all roses, everything's roses, come up roses* (U.S.).

[**1629**: see sense 4 c in Dict.] **1855** BROWNING *Patriot* in *Men & Women* I. 191 It was roses, roses, all the way. **1899** [see sense 4 c in Dict.]. **1930** A. P. HERBERT *Water Gipsies* xiii. 173 The tunnel was too much for you, eh? Well, I told you it weren't all roses on the 'Cut'. **1938** G. GREENE *Brighton Rock* VII. i. 283 'Sometimes he's bad to me. Oh, I can tell you,' she urged, 'it's not all roses.' **1948** WODEHOUSE *Uncle Dynamite* vi. 84, I should have thought you would be so glad to get back from a ghastly country like Brazil that life would have been roses, roses all the way. **1969** *Times* 12 Dec. 24 If some disaster hit us..we would have to soldier on, pretending that everything in the column was coming up roses. **1971** 'E. LATHEN' *Longer the Thread* (1972) vi. 60 'We don't have to worry about where the next thunderbolt will hit.' 'So everything's roses,' Eric Marten growled derisively. **1974** *New Yorker* 1 Apr. 95/2 (Advt.), There is a splendid hotel on a marvelous corner of Park Avenue where everything's coming up roses and crystal and gilt. **1976** C. WESTON *Rouse Demon* (1977) xviii. 89 This kid's from a good solid home. Parents are okay. Everything's roses. **1977** *Time* 7 Feb. 59/1 Aired over eight consecutive nights, *Roots* came up roses for ABC. **1977** *World of Cricket Monthly* June 42/2 Although Australia lost the Ashes, it was roses, roses, all the way for him.

h. *the last rose* (with allusion to quot. 1820), the last flowering of an era, an art form, or the like, before its end.

[**1820** T. MOORE *Irish Melodies* 119 'Tis the last rose of summer, Left blooming alone.] **1965** C. MACKENZIE *My Life & Times* IV. 147 The summer of 1912 blows in my memory like a flower of time that was; it is for me the last rose of a London that vanished during the First World War. **1978** *Times* 5 Aug. 14/6 The 'Pervigilium Veneris' is one of the most haunting incantations of love ever written. This last rose of pagan poetry is also appropriately mysterious. **1981** *Sunday Tel.* 14 June 12/8 This book is a literary curiosity. It is the last rose of a pre-Vatican II summer.

i. *to come out smelling of roses* (and variants): to emerge with an (apparently) unblemished record.

1968 'E. LATHEN' *Come to Dust* xvii. 167 No matter how you sliced it, the old grads..were not going to come out of this smelling like roses. **1976** J. PORTER *Dover & Claret Tappers* xii. 146, I intend to emerge from this business smelling of roses. If, to achieve this, I have to wash my hands in your blood, that's perfectly OK by me.

j. *roses round the door*, phr. used to denote marital (or rural) domestic happiness.

1934 L. GOLDING *Five Silver Daughters* xiii. 315 Talking about my mother and her pearls—it all sort of reminded me of the roses round the door. **1977** B. PYM *Quartet in Autumn* iv. 38 'Roses round the door and all that', as Norman used to say when Letty's retirement plans were mentioned.

5. *English rose*: see *ENGLISH *a.* 2 e.

6. a. *Wars of the Roses* (examples).

1835 M. GRAHAM *Little Arthur's Hist. Eng.* II. xxxii. 3 For more than thirty years afterwards, the civil wars in England were called the wars of the Roses. **1841** S. BAMFORD *Passages Life Radical* (ed. 2) II. xxvi. 132, I passed the Obelisk at Barnet, where the famous battle was fought in the wars of the roses. **1879** TROLLOPE *Eye for an Eye* I. ii. 30 They have held the same property since the wars of the Roses. **1939** W. S. MAUGHAM in *Hearst's Internat.* Feb. 30/2 The barony held by the first earl dated from the Wars of the Roses. **1966** A. L. ROWSE (*title*) Bosworth Field and the Wars of the Roses.

IV. 12. b. (Later examples.) Also printed on fabric, woven in a carpet, etc.

1897 *Sears, Roebuck Catal.* 290/1 Imported Paris Organdies..with colored roses, buds and leaves. **1955** R. P. JHABVALA *To whom she Will* xv. 102 She was very fine now in a pink silk kamiz with blue roses on it. **1964** C. MACKENZIE *My Life & Times* III. 13 The Surgeon's lessons [in putting] were given along the corridor.., the hole being one of the roses in the Brussels carpet. **1972** *Country Life* 6 Jan. 25/3 Many quilts [were] named after roses..Cactus Rose, Desert Rose, Rose of Sharon, Rambling Rose (whose other name was Old Maid's Ramble).

c. Also as an emblem of the rival sporting teams of Yorkshire and Lancashire.

1907 F. THOMPSON in *Athenæum* 23 Nov. 654/3 It is little I repair to the matches of the Southron folk, Though the red roses crest the caps, I know. **1954** A. W. LEDBROKE *Lancashire County Cricket* xxv. 244 The bank holiday Battle of the Roses provides..the nearest approach to the atmosphere of Sydney or Melbourne—when the crowds are orderly. But there is more than tenseness to a match between Lancashire and Yorkshire.

14. c. For (? *obs.*) read (now usu. *compass rose*) and add: More generally, a circular pattern showing the points of the compass. (Later examples.) Cf. WIND-ROSE 2.

1919 S. F. CARD *Air Navigation* ii. 11 When the chart or map contains the true and magnetic 'roses'..the conversion can be done by putting a straight edge from the centre to the true direction. **1937** M. COVARRUBIAS *Island of Bali* iv. 76 The Nawa Sangga, the magic rose of the winds, the Balinese cardinal directions. *Ibid.* ix. 280 A chicken with feathers of five colours was placed in the centre [of an offering], next to a small circular Rose of the Winds made of rice dyed in the eight different colours of the cardinal directions. **1943** [see *PELORUS]. **1951** N. MONSARRAT *Cruel Sea* I. 13 The ship was his: he was to commission and to command H.M.S. *Compass Rose*... *Compass Rose* was nothing out of the ordinary; it had to be a flower name because she was one of the new Flower Class corvettes. **1960** E. L. DELMAR-MORGAN *Cruising Yacht Equipment & Navigation* ii. 30 The dial or, as we call it these days, Pelorus or dummy compass rose, was the navigator's instrument and was in use for many centuries long before it was given magnets and mounted on a pivot.

f. *Building.* A circular, sometimes ornamental mounting through which the shaft of a door-handle may pass.

1857 *Commissioners of Patents' Jrnl.* 16 Jan. 41 Patent 37, January 5, 1857, Andrew Brundish: for mounting knobs, and in constructing and mounting roses for locks, latches and other such like fastenings. **1902** J. T. REA *How to Estimate* xi. 217, 2-in cast brass knobs with solid necks, cast rose and escutcheon. **1945** N. W. KAY in R. Greenhalgh *Building Repairs* iv. 110/1 A knob may be held by its rose and be free to swivel in it. **1957** M. T. TELLING in *Pract. Building & Decorating* II. iii. 154 To cover holes for keys and spindles, escutcheon plates and roses are fixed with small brass nails or screws.

g. A circular mounting on a ceiling through which the wiring of an electric light passes; = *ceiling rose* s.v. *CEILING *vbl. sb.* 7.

1889 *Illustr. Official Jrnl.* (Patent Office) 24 July 616/1 Improvements in roses for supporting electric lamps. **1944** A. C. GREENWOOD *Pract. Electr. Wiring & Contracting* v. 152/2 Covers of roses should screw down with an easy motion. **1967** *Times Rev. Industry* June 74/3 Electric fittings (e.g. switches, roses, lampholders, fuseboxes, junction boxes). **1977** L. R. WAKELIN *Home Electr. Repairs* 24/2 A neutral conductor must be taken to the light rose.

h. A figure in *Sword-dancing* (see quots.).

1913 C. J. SHARP *Sword Dances N. England* III. ii. 106 The leader should call 'Nut', a bar or two before the end of a strain, so that the Rose may be begun at the commencement of the next strain... The dancers leave the Nut in the hands of No. 1 and fall back into line facing the audience, returning to the original Rose position. **1933** E. K. CHAMBERS *Eng. Folk-Play* 129 There is a persistent figure..in which each dancer presses the hilt of his sword under the point of his neighbour's so as to mesh the swords together..in a form which may be anything from a pentagon to an octagon... This is called the Lock or Nut, which probably means Knot, and at Whitby the Rose. **1971** D. KENNEDY *North Skelton Sword-Dance* 9 *The Rose.* The leader raises the Lock in his right hand and all dance round clockwise.

i. An award (differentiated as the *Golden, Silver,* and *Bronze Rose*) presented at the International Television Festival at Montreux for successful light entertainment programmes.

1961 *Times* 27 May 7/5 The B.B.C.'s 'Black and White Minstrel Show' won the main prize tonight in the Montreux international television festival's Golden Rose contest. The jury awarded the first prize of a 'golden rose' and 10,000 Swiss francs..to the B.B.C. show. **1964** *Ann. Reg. 1963* 457 The C.B.S. spectacular, *Julie and Carol at Carnegie Hall*, won the top prize for light entertainment—the Golden Rose—at the Montreux International Television Festival in May. **1972** *Times* 5 May 5/3 Britain carried off both the Golden Rose and the

Silver Rose television awards here today for the best television light entertainment shows. **1975** *Times* 5 May 4 *The Goodies*, the BBC entry, has won the Silver Rose award at the television festival at Montreux... Italy won the contest and the Golden Rose... The Bronze Rose.. went to Austrian television.

16. d. The rounded end of a potato, esp. one being used for sprouting.

1851 H. Stephens *Bk. of Farm* (ed. 2) I. 630/2 The sets should be cut with a sharp knife, be pretty large in size, and taken from the rose or crown end of the tubers. **1976** *Country Life* 5 Feb. 305/4 Seed tubers of earlies [*sc.* potatoes] will be stood 'rose' or blunt end uppermost..to sprout.

e. *Geol.* = *ROCK-ROSE 5, *ROSETTE 5 e.

1911 *Proc. U.S. Nat. Museum* XXXVIII. 19 In Rockenberg occur well-developed rosettes or 'roses', often uniting in extensive groups. **1954** R. L. Parker tr. *Niggli's Rocks & Mineral Deposits* vii. 274 (*caption*) Rosette-like arrangement of tabular crystals of hematite, known as iron roses. **1955** F. H. Pough *Field Guide Rocks & Minerals* (ed. 2) II. 182 [Barite] is found in perfect imitative 'roses' of a red-brown color and sandy texture near Norman, Oklahoma. **1973** A. F. L. Deeson et al. *Collector's Encycl. Rocks & Minerals* 122/3 Gypsum 'roses' occur in many areas where gypsum has been dissolved in percolating waters which are drawn to the surface by capillary action and evaporate.

V. 19. a. *rose-bloom* (later example), *-blossom, -bough, -breath, -culture, -dust, -flake, -flower* (later example), *-fruit, -grower* (earlier and later examples), *-petal* (later example), *-prickle, -scent, -stem, -time* (later examples), *-tribe.*

1929 C. Day Lewis *Transitional Poem* II. 34 Heedless if truth maintain On the rose-bloom her station? **1878** Swinburne *Forsaken Garden* in *Poems & Ballads* (Ser. 2) 29 The foam-flowers endure when the rose-blossoms wither. **1927** E. Sitwell *Rustic Elegies* 37 Beneath the twisted rose-boughs of the heat. **1892** W. B. Yeats *Countess Kathleen* 93 Ah, leave me still A little space for the rose-breath to fill. **1846** T. Rivers *Rose Amateur's Guide* (ed. 4) II. 131 Modern gardening has made rapid strides in rose culture. **1924** E. Sitwell *Sleeping Beauty* xiii. 44, I shall be but thin rose-dust, He will be cold, unkind. **1951** L. MacNeice tr. *Goethe's Faust* 294 That noble soul which gave me right of seizure They've filched by throwing rose-dust in my eyes. **1876** G. M. Hopkins *Wreck of Deutschland* xxii, in *Poems* (1967) 58 Stigma, signal, cinquefoil token For lettering of the lamb's fleece, ruddying of the rose-flake. **1917** D. H. Lawrence *Look! We have come Through!* 60 To me it seems the seed is just left over From the red rose-flower's fiery transience. *Ibid.*, How will you have it?—the rose is all in all, Or the ripe rose-fruits of the luscious fall? *a* **1963** S. Plath *Uncoll. Poems* (1965) 9 First frost, and I walk among the rose-fruit. **1857** Rose-grower [see *rose show*, sense 23 a below]. **1920** G. Saintsbury *Notes on Cellar-Bk.* iv. 57 A friend of mine..had some official business with one of the great rose-growers in the neighbourhood of London. **1960** R. Campbell tr. J.-M. A. Gamo in *Coll. Poems* III. 85 Silken spectrum-blaze Which an eternity shot through with rays Showers with a thousand rose-petals of light. **1944** E. Sitwell *Green Song* 1 Remember the rose-prickles of bright paws Though we shall mate no more. **1859** Geo. Eliot *Adam Bede* I. xv. 279 The delicate rose-scent of his hair. **1885** A. Edwardes *Girton Girl* I. v. 111 Tintajeux Manoir with its..faded drawing-room, its light halls, its rose scents. **1960** S. Plath *Colossus* 36 Thorns on the bloody rose-stem. **1850** Mrs. Gaskell *Let.* 26 Apr. (1966) 111 The Shaens begged me to come in rose-time to them. **1912** E. Pound *Ripostes* 33 Thou keep'st thy rose-leaf Till the rose-time will be over. **1924** E. Sitwell *Sleeping Beauty* v. 26 If none of the rose-tribe can survive The snow, then how can our poppet live?

b. *rose-alley, -arbour* (later example), *-bower* (later examples), *-farm, -garden* (further examples), *-hedge, -land.*

1934 E. M. Wright *Story of Joseph Wright* viii. 232 We formed a torchlight procession down the rose-alley, and buried Mary's playfellow in her own plot of garden. **1977** *Belfast Tel.* 22 Feb. 9/6 The rose arbor in Belfast's Botanical Gardens provides little shelter from the rain. **1876** O. Wilde *Kottabos* II. x. 269 Roses are white in the rose-bower. **1975** J. O'Faolain *Women in Wall* iii. 46 'Please... Let me do it.'..'Tell,' he went to sit down in a rose bower, 'about the Call.' **1970** T. Hughes *Crow* 31 The woodpecker drummed clear of the rotovator and the rose-farm. **1910** *Granta* 5 Feb. 201 It is said..that he keeps poultry and a cow, plays simple tunes on a pan pipe, bathes every evening at sunset, and takes all his meals in a rose garden. **1936** T. S. Eliot *Burnt Norton* in *Coll. Poems 1909–35* 185 The door we never opened Into the rose-garden. **1867** A. J. Evans *St. Elmo* xxi. 292 A Cherokee rose-hedge is not more thickly set with thorns than a literary career with grievous, vexatious, tormenting disappointments. **1929** R. Bridges *Testament of Beauty* III. 88 In the New World far Pasadena's roseland.

e. *rose knot* (later example).

1947 A. Ransome *Great Northern?* i. 20 A hand..took hold of the rose knot worked in the end of the bit of rope that dangled from the clapper of a small ship's bell.

20. a. (Further examples.)

1858 W. Bagehot in *National Rev.* Apr. 455 The harsh outlines of poverty will not bear the artificial rose-tint. **1870** F. Kilvert *Diary* 13 Mar. (1938) I. 56 The mountain clad in deep snow and tinged with rose colour... As the sun set a lovely rose tint stole over the snowy mountains. **1906** W. de la Mare *Poems* 124 From the day, The rose-light ebbed away. **1916** Joyce *Portrait of Artist* (1969) v. 218 The dull white light spread itself east and west, covering the world, covering the roselight in his heart. **1922** C. Mackenzie *Altar Steps* xxvii. 315 A set [of vestments] in old rose damask for mid-Lent. **1929** Blunden *Near & Far* 47 And sounding works whose smoke lifts proud Through towers of force to yon rose-cloud. **1930** E. Pound *XXX Cantos* ii. 13 The coral face under wave-tinge, Rose-paleness under water-shift. **1932** Blunden *Face of England* 85 And that far rose-reflection burns On the dusk water far too red. **1949** Dylan Thomas *Let.* 13 Oct. (1966) 328, I have the hot and cold rose-flush comings and goings after elderberry wine last night. **1965** F. Sargeson *Mem. Peon* iv. 82, I held her hand to examine its dusky rose-bloom.

c. (Later examples.)

1916 E. & O. Sitwell *20th-Cent. Harlequinade* 23 Rose-silver haze. **1928** *T. Eaton & Co. Catal.* Spring & Summer 1/1 Felt hat... Colors Sand; Rose-Beige; Gobelin Blue. **1930** E. Pound *XXX Cantos* xvii. 78 Stone trees, white and rose-white in the darkness. **1932** H. Crane *Let.* 13 Feb. (1965) 399 Wine glasses of a smoky rose-purple transparency that set one dreaming. **1949** E. Pound *Pisan Cantos* lxxvi. 43 And within the crystal, went up swift as Thetis In colour rose-blue before sunset And carmine and amber. **1953** W. de la Mare *O Lovely England* 33 Rose-green the light where a hermit knelt, praying, His solitude verdurous, vision-like, still. **1966** C. Mackenzie *My Life & Times* V. 21 Their rose-brown flesh burnt by the sun. **1977** *Horse & Hound* 10 June 41/3 (Advt.), 14 hands 1in outstanding quality rose grey gelding, 4 yrs.

21. a. *rose-finned, -flecked, -flushed, -footed, -impearled, -lit, -shadowed, -shot, -spotted, -stained, -veiled.*

1920 Blunden *Waggoner* 20 The rose-finned roach and bluish bream. **1965** E. Bishop *Questions of Travel* 25 Hastily, all alone, a glistening armadillo left the scene, rose-flecked, head down, tail down. **1913** C. Mackenzie *Sinister St.* I. I. vi. 86 Over a red wall hung down the branch of a plum tree, loaded with creamy ovals of fruit, already rose-flushed with summer. **1942** E. Sitwell *Street Songs* 31 Then, who knows Rose-footed swan from snow, or girl from rose. **1917** G. Frankau *City of Fear* 25 Rose-impearled o'er a wonder-world Glowed the last of the sunset-gleams. **1910** A. Bennett *Clayhanger* IV. iii. 479 He left the crowded and rose-lit dining-room early. **1867** G. Meredith *Vittoria* I. i. 12 The gleam of the distant rose-shadowed snows. **1957** R. Campbell *Coll. Poems* II. 109 Freckled like rose-shot apricots. **1952** A. G. L. Hellyer *Sanders' Encycl. Gardening* (ed. 22) 73 Sepals with a white, rose-spotted, ribbon-like appendage. *a* **1973** J. R. R. Tolkien *Silmarillion* (1977) xxiv. 250 Like a white bird, shining, rose-stained in the sunset. **1952** R. Campbell tr. *Baudelaire's Poems* 46 The balcony beneath a rose-veiled sky.

b. *rose-shaped.*

1933 E. Sitwell *Five Variations* 4 And many a rose-shaped heart must lie beneath The maps on strawberry leaves. **1945** C. L. B. Hubbard *Observer's Bk. Dogs* 87 Ears rose-shaped.

22. a. *rose-ambrosial, frail, -full, heavy, -hot, -pale, -soft, -solemn, -towering.*

1936 L. B. Lyon *Bright Feather Fading* 54 Alas, no rose-ambrosial world men share Who fall from love and falling cease to be. **1927** Joyce *Pomes Penyeach* 3 Frail the white rose and frail are Her hands that gave... Rosefrail and fair..My blueveined child. **1932** E. Sitwell *Bath* iv. 68 The rose-full, rose-soft, hooped dresses are wet with dew. **1895** W. B. Yeats in *Sat. Rev.* 2 Nov. 573/1 The rose-heavy twilight. **1922** D. H. Lawrence in *English Rev.* Feb. 101 The living steel In rose-hot tips, and flakes of rose-pale snow. **1951** W. de la Mare *Winged Chariot* 50 That rose-pale cheek, loose hair, and eager tongue. *c* **1860** J. R. Lowell *Power of Sound* (1896) 9 So sang she, feeling in her bosom stir The rose-soft palms of that first murderer. **1916** Joyce *Portrait of Artist* (1969) iv. 155 It was only.. within rosesoft stuffs that he dared to conceive of the soul or body of a woman moving with tender life. **1932** [see *rose-full* above]. **1935** W. Empson *Poems* 22 Snow-puppy curves, rose-solemn dado band. **1949** S. Spender *Edge of Being* 16 To wake on peaks at dawn among the inhuman Rose-towering dreams.

b. *rose-circled, -clustered, -crowned* (later *fig.* example), *-embowered, -entangled, -festooned, -garlanded, -lamped, -wreathed* (earlier and later examples).

1975 G. Ewart *Be my Guest!* I. 32 Or I see Gertrude waving from a cottage with a very attractive rose-circled door. **1971** B. Malamud *Tenants* 50 This flower-massed, rose-clustered, floating island. **1910** R. Brooke *Hill* in *Cambr. Rev.* XXXII. 181/1 We shall go down with unreluctant tread Rose-crowned into the darkness! **1918** G. Frankau *One of Them* 257 Screen me..From my sub-conscious Freudian profanity, That rose-embowered private sitting-room. **1962** I. Murdoch *Unofficial Rose* v. xxvi. 249 He wandered towards her through a rose-entangled forest. **1929** M. Lowry *Let.* 13 Mar. (1967) 5 Of course it was..merely a rose-festooned illusion. **1917** A. Waugh *Loom of Youth* IV. viii. 322 He had done what he set out to do, he would step rose-garlanded out of the lighted room, in the flush of his success. **1925** C. Day Lewis *Beechen Vigil* 24 Like a queen of fable In rose-lamped gardens. **1847** H. W. Longfellow *Evangeline* II. iii. 108 Rose-wreathed, vine-encircled, a broad and spacious veranda. **1924** R. Graves *Mock Beggar Hall* 61 While incense burns beside the rose-wreathed couch.

23. a. rose-berry (later example); **rose bit,** a countersink bit having a conical head with a number of radial cutting teeth that meet at the tip; † **rose blanket** *U.S.*, a blanket decorated with a rose motif; **rose box,** (*b*) *Naut.* (see quot. 1976); **rose diagram,** a diagram in which values of a quantity in various directions are shown graphically according to compass bearing, in the manner of a wind-rose; **rose-fever** (earlier example); **rose gold,** delete † and (?) and add def.: an alloy of gold with a little copper, having a reddish tinge; (later examples); **rose head,** (*c*) = Rose *sb.* 17; (*d*) a spreading top on an upright rain-pipe; **rose-hip,** also = Hip *sb.*[2]; (examples); **rose hip syrup,** a syrup containing extract of rose hips, taken as a source of vitamin C; **rose-hip tea,** a beverage made from rose-hips and hot water; **rose-jar,** a jar for holding dried rose petals; **rose-petal,** used *attrib.* of various preserves, wine, etc., made from rose petals; **rose show,** an exhibition mainly or entirely of roses; **Rose Sunday** *obs.* exc. *Hist.*, the fourth Sunday in Lent; **rose-temple,** a belvedere over which climbing roses may be trained; **rose-wine** = Rosolio.

c **1921** D. H. Lawrence *Mr. Noon* iv, in *Mod. Lover* (1934) 224 Gilbert helped her to pick scarlet rose-berries, and black privet berries. **1858** *Min. Proc. Inst. Civil Engineers* XVII. 178 A 'rose-bit' is..employed, to remove the intervening metal. **1966** A. W. Lewis *Gloss. Woodworking Terms* 7 The chief type [of countersink bit] is the 'rose' bit which has radial flutes which shave away the edge of the hole. **1759** *Newport* (Rhode Island) *Mercury* 26 June 3/2 Just imported by Simon Pease, jun...best Rose Blankets. **1820** *Columbian Centinel* 8 Jan. 3/4 A great variety of Dry Goods:..Rose Blankets. **1923** *Man. Seamanship* (Admiralty) II. xviii. 305 *Gear Boxes*... Suction and delivery hoses with bends and rose boxes. **1972** L. M. Harris *Introd. Deepwater Floating Drilling Operations* App. B 238 Bilge drainage should be checked... The rose boxes and strainer plates are clear, clean and sound. **1976** *Oxf. Compan. Ships & Sea* 722/2 *Rose Box*, the name given to the strainer at the end of the suction pipe of a bilge pump... It is also widely known, particularly in yachts, as a strum box. **1938** *Bull. Geol. Soc. Amer.* XLIX. 1887 The orientation of the long axes are [*sic*] plotted as a conventional 'rose' diagram. **1956** *Q. Jrnl. Geol. Soc.* CXII. 71 A rose diagram is made showing the directions, in 10-degree classes, of the long axes of the stones. **1971** I. G. Gass et al. *Understanding Earth* xiii. 175 (*caption*) Rose diagram representing readings of dip directions of the cross laminae of either linguoid ripples or barchan dunes. **1851** E. S. Wortley *Trav.* III. 22 This complaint [*sc.* hay-asthma] is known in the United States, and is called there, rose-fever. **1901** Rose gold [see *karat]. **1948** A. Selwyn *Retail Jeweller's Handbk.* (ed. 3) x. 137 Red gold had a revival when Paris jewellers re-introduced it in jewellery in 1937–38, and other countries followed. Pale shades are called pink or rose gold. **1742** W. Ellis *Mod. Husbandman* July xxiv. 128 A Barrel..that has an Arm of Tin fix'd in with a Rose-head, that the Water may run on their Roots. **1883** *Specif. Alnwick & Cornhill Railway* 51 Four-inch rain-pipes are to be provided, with proper roseheads. **1857** Rose-hip [in Dict., sense 19 a]. **1915** *Chambers's Jrnl.* 20 Mar. 271/2 These [*sc.* plants for feeding pigs and fowls] were supplemented in the autumn by non-fattening foods, such as acorns..and rose-hips. **1976** *Norwich Mercury* 17 Dec. 3/7 They [*sc.* bird paintings] include a greenfinch with rosehips. **1942** *Q. Jrnl. Pharmacy* XV. 314 During the winter of 1941–42 the Ministry of Health experimented with two new large-scale sources of the vitamin, black-currant purée and rose hip syrup. **1972** J. Mann *Mrs. Knox's Profession* x. 82 Gripe water, rose hip syrup and everything else a baby could conceivably need. **1964** G. Hauser *Treasury of Secrets* v. 52 The pink rose hip tea ..is the great favorite at the famous Bircher-Brenner Sanatorium in Switzerland. **1973** C. Bonington *Next Horizon* xii. 175 John and Dougal settled down to their meal of dried meat and nuts, followed by rose-hip tea. **1894** *Harper's Mag.* Jan. 310/1 A rose-jar stood on one [table] in the corner. **1935** H. Edib *Clown & his Daughter* xxxvi. 201 I've brought stuffed vine-leaves and rose-petal jam, Tewfik. **1963** M. McCarthy *Group* i. 18 An Armenian restaurant in the twenties, where you got rose-petal jelly for dessert. **1968** J. Rathbone *Hand Out* vi. 36 His breakfast..consisted of sour grey bread, white cheese, rose-petal syrup and tea. **1970** *Rose Ann.* 93 Pot-pourri and rose petal jam from well-loved old recipes ..are often made at home... Home-made rose-petal wine has a delicious taste. **1975** P. Somerville-Large *Couch of Earth* vii. 115 The waiter..came over..the napkin over his arm stained with rosepetal jam. **1977** *Times* 25 Nov. (Christmas Bk. Suppl.) p. xxx/4 Experimenting with rose petal oils to soften the skin. **1857** *Florist* Apr. 122 A suggestion to Rose growers—amateurs and professionals: —why should we not have, near some central station (such as Rugby) A Grand National Rose Show? **1978** *Lancashire Life* Sept. 40 The Lakeland Rose Show this year cost £25,000 to stage. **1880** McClintock & Strong *Cycl. Bibl. Lit.* IX. 130 It is not known when the ceremony of consecrating the rose was introduced... The day is always the fourth Sunday in Lent, which is consequently known as 'Rose-Sunday'. **1891** tr. *Pastor's Hist. Popes* I. 220 Golden roses were bestowed each year on Laetare Sunday, hence called Rose Sunday. **1864** S. Hibberd *Rose Bk.* vi. 125 To form a simple rose temple is a matter of no great difficulty. **1894** *Country Gentlemen's Catal.* 295/2 Rose Temple..Price—£5. With Openings filled in to form a Summer House. Price—£7 5/-. **1852** in *Venerabile* (1930) Apr. 357 A good dinner and caffe after with rose-wine.

b. rose-briar (later example); **rose geranium,** add: or *P. graveolens*, or one of several varieties of them; also, a perfume resembling the scent of these flowers; (earlier and later examples); **rose gum,** a large gum-tree, *Eucalyptus grandis*, found in eastern Australia; **rose mahogany,** an eastern Australian timber tree, *Dysoxylum fraserianum*, of the family Meliaceæ, or its fragrant reddish wood; **rose pea,** add '17th and' before '18th century'; (earlier examples).

1932 D. H. LAWRENCE *Last Poems* 178 Rose-leaves to bewilder the clever fools And rose-briars to strangle the machine. **1832** *Chambers's Edin. Jrnl.* 7 Apr. 76/2 Thorburn bought a rose geranium, intending to ornament his shop. **1890–1** *T. Eaton & Co. Catal.* Fall & Winter 42/2 Perfumes..Italian violet, rose geranium, white heliotrope. **1939** L. MACNEICE *Autumn Jrnl.* 69 Clouding The cooling water with rose geranium soap. **1964** C. LOEWENFELD *Herb Gardening* II. 171 Rose geranium is a shrubby plant with deeply cut and divided leaves and clusters of pink and lavender flowers. **1971** *Vogue* 15 Sept. 85/1 Bubble Bath in four fragrances—Lemon Verbena, English Fern, Rose Geranium and Lavender Blue. **1947** R. H. ANDERSON *Trees New South Wales* (ed. 2) 158 Flooded Gum or Rose Gum (*Eucalyptus grandis*). A tall, frequently majestic tree. **1967** A. RULE *Forests Austral.* iii. 36 Species such as tallowwood and rose gum, occurring in the humid coastal forests of eastern Australia. **1929** W. D. FRANCIS *Austral. Rain-Forest Trees* 185 *Dysoxylum fraserianum* Benth. Rosewood, Rose Mahogany. **1958** *N.Z. Timber Jrnl.* June 59/1 Rose mahogany..resembles Honduras mahogany. **1965** *Austral. Encycl.* III. 319/2 One of the best-known and most abundant of these [trees] is the rose mahogany. *Ibid.*, Its dust, like that of rose mahogany, has an irritating effect on tender parts of the skin. **1629** J. PARKINSON *Parad.* lii. 522 The Scottish or tufted Pease, which some call the Rose Pease, is a good white Pease fit to be eaten. **1690** L. HAMMOND *Jrnl.* 2 Apr. in *Proc. Mass. Hist. Soc.* (1892) 2nd Ser. VII. 154 Wedensday, I planted my Rose pease.

c. rose-bug (earlier and later examples); **rose-hopper** = **rose leaf-hopper*; **rose leaf-hopper**, a greenish-yellow sucking insect, *Typhlocyba* (or *Edwardsiana*) *rosæ*, of the family Cicadellidæ, which attacks the foliage of roses, making the leaves pale and mottled.

1800 *Massachusetts Spy* 1 Oct. 3/4 He suggests that the Rose-bug is the pre-existing state of those worms. **1916** W. P. EATON *Idyl of Twin Fires* 207, I frequently pick rose bugs..before breakfast, very early, when they are still sleepy. **1920** WODEHOUSE *Damsel in Distress* i. 10 The small, yellowish-white insect..sometimes called a rose-hopper. [**1852** T. W. HARRIS *Treat. Insects New England Injurious to Vegetation* (ed. 2) 199 There is another little leaf-hopper that..lives upon the leaves of rose-bushes. *Ibid.* 511/2 Rose-bush leaf-hopper.] **1890** *Insect Life* II. 340 Original figures are given of..the Rose Leaf-hopper. **1939** METCALF & FLINT *Destructive & Useful Insects* (ed. 2) xvii. 585 The rose leafhopper and another common apple leafhopper, pass the winter in the egg stage in the bark. **1970** L. HOLLIS *Roses* x. 106 Rose leaf-hopper..sucks the sap and causes mottling to appear on the leaves.

24. a. rose-comb, substitute for second part of def.: also, a bird bearing a comb of this kind; also *attrib.*; (earlier and later examples); **rose fish** (earlier and later examples); **rose-madder**, the rose colour produced by madder dye or pigment; **rose-mole**, a mark or mole of a reddish colour.

1850 D. J. BROWNE *Amer. Poultry Yard* 52 The fleshy rose comb of the golden Hamburgh terminating in a sharp point behind..is seen in no other variety of fowl. **1927** HALDANE & HUXLEY *Animal Biol.* ii. 68 The original pure-bred rose-comb stock gives nothing but rose-combs. *Ibid.* 69 The offspring will clearly be blue Andalusian.., with rose-combs. **1972** *Country Life* 16 Nov. 1265/1 Of the 11 [bantams] two were cockerels of rosecomb blood... One of the two rosecombs was supposed to be a hen. **1731** R. HALE *Jrnl.* 18 June in *Essex Inst. Hist. Coll.* (1906) XLII. 223 Wee spy'd the Fin of a Whale..& Suppossing it to be a Rose fish, ran forward to see it. **1947** *Richmond* (Va.) *Times-Dispatch* 4 May B15/2 Boston showed a two-month catch of rosefish. **1975** *Globe & Mail* (Toronto) 9 Aug. 8/3 The Russians..pioneered in earlier years..such harvests as the rosefish catch off Labrador. **1886** H. C. STANDAGE *Artists' Man. Pigments* v. 52 *Madder Lakes* (Madder Carmine.., Lake or Rose Madder). **1895** *Montgomery Ward Catal.* Spring & Summer 252/3 Winsor & Newton's Oil Colors..Pink Madder, Rose Madder. **1902** *Encycl. Brit.* XXXI. 773/1 Amongst the former [*sc.* natural colouring matters] may be named..rose-madder and the madder-lakes from the alizarin and allied bodies derived from the root of the ordinary madder plant *Rubia tinctorum.* **1933** H. NICOLSON *Diary* 16 Mar. (1966) 143 They [*sc.* the Rocky Mountains] are rose-madder and blue. **1877** G. M. HOPKINS *Poems* (1967) 69 Glory be to God for dappled things—..For rose-moles all in stipple upon trout that swim.

b. rose-finch, a small European or Asian finch belonging to the genus *Carpodacus*, the males of which have red or pink plumage.

1863 T. C. JERDON *Birds India* II. 399 The Rose-finch is found as a cold weather visitant throughout the greater part of India. **1890** E. W. OATES *Fauna Brit. India: Birds* II. 212 The genus *Propasser* belongs to the Rose-finches, the males of which are characterized..by rose-coloured plumage. **1953** D. A. BANNERMAN *Birds Brit. Isles* I. 175 The eastern races of the rosefinch also winter in India.

rose, *v.*[1] Add: **2. b.** *intr.* To become rosy; to blush. *rare*—[1].

1922 HARDY *Late Lyrics* 22 You grew elate, And rosed, as maidens can, For a brief span.

rosé (rōᵘ·ze, ‖ roze), *sb.* (*a.*) [*ellipt.* for F. *vin rosé* pink wine.] **1.** A wine that is light red or pink in colour.

1897 A. BEARDSLEY *Let.* 17 May (1970) 320, I have just vomited up the meals of the last two or three days. You see your Saint Marceau (royal rosé) has been avenged. **1932** E. HEMINGWAY *Death in Afternoon* 491 *Valdepenas* is..excellent in both white and rosée [*sic*]. **1951** E. DAVID *French Country Cooking* 26 Rosés of Anjou and Tavel. **1959** *News Chron.* 9 Dec. 6/6 It says of a Portuguese Rosé: '..Pale pink but sparkling'. **1960** *House & Garden* June 118/3 A Vin Rosé from the Côte du Rhône will cost you about 8s and a Rosé from Anjou a little more. **1974** *Guardian* 24 Jan. 13/5 True rosé is made from black grapes when the skins are left in the vat for the first one to three days of fermentation. *Ibid.* 13/6 The rosé makers can adjust acidity by early or late picking.

2. *attrib.* or as *adj.* Of a wine: that is a *vin rosé*; light red or pink in colour. Also *transf.*

1959 *Good Food Guide* 34 Rosé and white Bordeaux, 10/6. *Ibid.* 199 About three dozen wines, beginning with white and rosé ordinaires at 12/6 (oddly, no red). **1960** *Harper's Bazaar* Apr. 115/2 Add 1 bottle dry *rosé* wine. **1967** A. LICHINE *Encycl. Wines* 417/2 Not to be forgotten are the rosé wines of Portugal. **1974** *Harrods Christmas Catal.* 14 Ostrich feather boa..shades of mandarin/rosé £36. **1977** *Times* 12 Feb. 7/2 Pastry, rosé meat, rough-cut pâté and lambent juices.

rose-apple. 2. (Earlier and later examples.)

1790 W. BECKFORD *Descr. Acct. Jamaica* II. 190 The orange, the rose-apple, the papa..and other productions. **1975** I. & A. MANCINELLI tr. *Bianchini & Corbetta's Fruits of Earth* 168 The rose apple is about the size and color of an apricot, with one to three seeds inside.

rose bowl. [f. ROSE *sb.* + BOWL *sb.*[1]] **1.** A bowl designed to hold cut roses; *spec.* such a bowl offered as a prize in a competition.

1895 *Montgomery Ward Catal.* 545/2 Rose Bowl, 6½ inch, imitation of heavy cut glass. **1916** *Daily Colonist* (Victoria, B.C.) 25 July 7/1 (Advt.), Brilliant Beauty Glassware Assortment..Rose Bowls—Clear crystal, beautiful design. Special, each 50c. **1958** L. DURRELL *Mountolive* xii. 232 The room was full of the scent of the pastels burning in the great rose-bowl by the telephone. **1970** P. BAIR *Tribunal* III. ii. 161 For the winner a prize of two hundred pounds was waiting, together with a handsome rose bowl. **1972** *Daily Tel.* 10 Oct. 13 Today's young people hardly know what a rose-bowl is. **1976** *South Notts Echo* 16 Dec. 3/5 The winner will receive a silver rose-bowl which is competed for annually.

2. *U.S.* (With capital initials.) The name of a football stadium at Pasadena, California, used *attrib.* and *absol.* of a football match played between rival college teams annually on New Year's Day at the conclusion of the local Tournament of Roses.

1930 *Los Angeles Times* 2 Jan. (Sports section) 1/1 Southern California's smashing victory gives that institution two wins in as many Rose Bowl games...The other triumph was scored over Penn State in 1923. **1947** *Collier's* 29 Nov. 89/2 Getting to the Rose Bowl is even simpler this year because Illinois, as the winner last year, isn't eligible to go until three years are up. **1959** *Boston Herald* 1 Jan. 75/4 When you tune in the Rose Bowl, watch the quarterbacks. **1969** *Eugene* (Oregon) *Register-Guard* 3 Dec. 1D/3 Michigan's football team began working out without equipment Tuesday in preparation for the trip to Pasadena, Calif., for the Rose Bowl game against Southern California New Year's Day. **1971** J. HENDERSON *Copperhead* xx. 244 It was Lourdes, the Rose Bowl, and a Democratic Convention all in one gargantuan jumble. **1976** *Honolulu Star-Bull.* 21 Dec. H-5/1 Michigan football Coach Bo Schembechler agrees with Southern California's John Robinson that the Rose Bowl should decide the national championship.

rosebud. Add: **2. b.** (Later non-*attrib.* example.)

1973 *Times Lit. Suppl.* 1 June 608/1 He married..a college beauty queen (a 'Rosebud' of 1922).

† c. A member of the junior section of the Girl Guides Association, now called a 'Brownie' or 'Brownie Guide' (see *BROWNIE[1] 2). *Obs.* exc. *Hist.*

1914 A. BADEN-POWELL in *Girl Guides' Gaz.* June 2/1 The age at which a Rose Bud may join the Baden-Powell Girl Guides is eight years. **1914** O. BADEN-POWELL in *Ibid.* July 3/1, I am so glad to hear that some of you are taking up the work of training Rosebuds, to follow in your footsteps. **1915** *Girl Guides' Gaz.* Jan. 15/2 Our 'Rosebuds' are growing rapidly in numbers..but we hear they are dissatisfied with their name. *Ibid.* June 3/2 (*heading*) Rosebuds or Brownies? **1973** *New Society* 27 Sept. 755/2 Brownies were started in 1910 by Baden-Powell's sister, under the name of Rosebuds.

rose-colour, *sb.* Add: **1.** (Earlier *transf.* example.)

1865 MRS. GASKELL *Wives & Daughters* (1866) I. xxv. 280 Such were the facts, but rose-colour was the medium through which they were seen.

2. (Earlier example.)

1857 TROLLOPE *Barchester T.* III. ix. 177 It was not all rose colour with Mr. Slope, although his hopes ran high.

rose-colour, *v.* (Later example in *transf.* or *fig.* sense.)

1974 M. C. GERALD *Pharmacol.* xv. 281 Stimulation of RAS results in an enhanced state of arousal to environmental stimuli,..'rose-coloring' the individual's subjective appraisal of the world around him.

rose-coloured, *a.* Add: **3.** (Earlier examples.) *rose-coloured spectacles*, used in *fig.* phrases to indicate that a person's view of something is unduly favourable, optimistic, or idealistic.

1854 C. M. YONGE *Castle Builders* iv. 56 The first rose-coloured lights in which they had viewed everything, was wearing off. **1856** DICKENS *Dorrit* (1857) I. xxxiv. 299, I don't like to dispel your generous visions, and I would give any money..to live in such a rose-colored mist. **1861** Rose-coloured spectacles [in Dict.]. **1867** A. J. EVANS *St. Elmo* xii. 157, I have a right to all my charming, rose-colored views of this world. **1921** PRINCESS P. METTERNICH *Days that are no More* iii. 104, I was young and favoured by fortune, no troubles had yet befallen me, and I saw everything through rose-coloured spectacles. **1981** *Oxford Jrnl.* 15 May 8/2 Mrs M— must be viewing Carterton crossroads through rose-coloured spectacles. Far from being vastly improved, it is becoming a ghastly eyesore.

rose du Barry (rōᵘ·z dü ba·ri). Also **rose du Barri.** [f. the name of the Comtesse *du Barry* (1746–93), a patron of the Sèvres porcelain factory.] A soft shade of pink developed *c* 1757 for use as a ground colour on Sèvres porcelain. Also *attrib.* or as *adj.* Cf. *ROSE POMPADOUR.

1856 [see *CABARET[1] 3]. **1879** C. SCHREIBER *Jrnl.* 13 Oct. (1911) II. 227 Some very fine Rose du Barry Sèvres vases. **1902** *Encycl. Brit.* XXIX. 730/1 The experts of Tôkyô and Nagoya have produced many very beautiful specimens of monochrome enamels—yellow (canary or straw), *rose du Barry*, liquid-dawn red, [etc.]. **1912** C. MACKENZIE *Carnival* xxviii. 284 The two girls followed their host to his room which was hung with rose du Barri draperies prodigally braided with gold. **1931** J. CANNAN *High Table* iii. 36 His head making a grease mark on the *rose du Barri* brocade. **1934** *Historical Colours* (Thos. Parsons & Sons) 58 Du Barry Red is sometimes wrongly called Rose du Barry. **1960** H. HAYWARD *Antique Coll.* 243/2 *Rose du Barry*, a popular misnomer for the coloured ground used on Sèvres porcelain and properly known as rose Pompadour. **1974** *Country Life* 3 Oct. 939/3 Vases of delicate pink which we know now as rose Pompadour but which used to be called rose du Barry.

rose-leaf. Add: (Further *attrib.* and *Comb.* examples.) Hence **ro·se-lea:fy** *adj.*

1854 C. M. YONGE *Heartsease* II. xviii. 50 A little pair of socks, in delicate fancy-knitting for Johnnie. 'Dear, dear mamma! her own pretty rose-leaf pattern. Think of her knitting for my Johnnie!' **1884** 'MARK TWAIN' *Huck. Finn* xxii. 222 Every lady's rose-leafy dress flapping soft and silky. **1908** [see *HALVA]. **1913** C. MACKENZIE *Sinister St.* I. II. ii. 167 As for Dora's face, Michael found it beautiful with the long-lashed blue eyes and rose-leaf complexion. **1946** L. B. LYON *Rough Walk Home* 27 On rose-leaf heights we too were born, But spirit falters, or the proud foot slips.

rosella[1]. **1.** Substitute for def.: A brightly coloured seed-eating Australian parakeet belonging to the genus *Platycercus*. (Earlier and later examples.)

1829 *Sydney Gaz.* 21 July 4/1 The doleful dying quails, And roselles [*sic*] golden. **1838** J. HAWDON *Jrnl.* 15 Mar. in *Journey New South Wales to Adelaide* (1952) 51 Parrots now appeared more numerous, Rosellas and others. **1941** *Coast to Coast 1941* 86 Thither were transferred..the assortment of rosellas and grass parrots that had in one way or another fallen into captivity. **1966** EASTMAN & HUNT *Parrots Austral.* p. ix, I rather feel that the Blue-cheeked is a very beautiful connecting link between Pale-headed and Northern Rosellas.

2. *Austral.* and *N.Z.* A sheep whose wool is beginning to fall off naturally, and which is therefore easy to shear.

1849 D. McLEOD in *Stephen's Adelaide Miscell.* III. 81 At shearing he..pick[s] all the 'Rosellas' (clean-bellied sheep). **1910** C. E. W. BEAN *On Wool Track* 193 If there is an old ewe in the pen, a 'rosella' as they call her, with most of the lower wool worn off, she goes the first. **1954** E. C. STUDHOLME *Te Waimate* (ed. 2) I. xv. 130 An old hand..would..quickly catch and shear all the 'rosellas', or easily shorn sheep. **1972** J. S. GUNN in G. W. Turner *Good Austral. Eng.* iii. 60 Few shearers recognised *flyer, cop, gunbarrel*..as terms for what is usually called a *barebelly* or *rosella*.

‖ **rosemaling** (rō·səmā:liŋ, -mǭ:liŋ). [Norw., f. *rose* rose + *maling* painting.] The art of painting (wooden implements, furniture, etc.) with decorative flower motifs. Hence **ro·se-maled, -malt** (-māld, mālt) *ppl. a.* [Norw. *-malt* pa. ppl. of *male* to paint], decorated with rosemaling; **ro·semaler,** one who practises rosemaling.

1948 *School Arts* Mar. 223/1 The Rosemaling (flower painting) of Norway has been brought to this country [*sc.* the U.S.A.] and skillfully adapted to American living by Per Lysne of Stoughton, Wisconsin. **1950** H. MAJOR *Norwegian Holiday* 88 There will be a bowl or two decorated in the colorful rose-painting (*rosemaling*) design of the district. *Ibid.* 93 (*caption*) A student must first design his rosemaling. **1953** J. STEWART *Folk Arts of Norway* iv. 87 Rosemaling..has a counterpart in the Swedish *blomstermålning* (flower painting), in the decorative painting of Russia, and in Pennsylvania Dutch art. **1956** T. BØHN in *Norwegian-Amer. Stud. & Rec.* XIX. 120 The multitude of Norwegian immigrant items grew, including such things as *rosemalt* chests, cupboards, boxes. **1972** DEAN & SMITH *Wisconsin* 145/1 Rosemaling, the colorful art of floral painting that grew up in Norway, is enjoying a booming revival in Wisconsin. **1975** LOVOLL & BJORK *Norwegian-Amer. Hist. Assoc., 1925–1975* v. 21 The museum has also conducted workshops in *rosemaling* (rose painting) and wood carving, with teachers from Norway. **1975** J. LANGLAND in *Massa-*

chusetts Rev. (Univ. of Mass.) Summer 568 They stuffed their childhood into rosemaler trunks, clamped them with iron bands locked once and for all on the eastern hemispheres. **1976** P. VIRCH *Rosemaling in Round* i. 1/2 The largest public collection of rosemaled chests, bowls, furniture and boxes can be seen in Vesterheim, the Norwegian-American museum in Decorah, Iowa. *Ibid.*, (*caption*) This collection of bowls owned by the author was painted for her by..rosemalers of Norway.

rosenbuschite (rōᵘ·zĕnbuʃəit, rōᵘzĕnbu·ʃəit). *Min.* [ad. Norw. *rosenbuschit* (W. C. Brögger 1887, in *Geol. För. i Stockholm Förh.* IX. 254), f. the name of K. H. F. *Rosenbusch* (1836–1914), German mineralogist and geologist: see -ITE[1].] A fluorine-containing aluminosilicate of calcium, sodium, zirconium, and titanium occurring as radiating groups of slender triclinic crystals of an orange or grey colour.

1890 *Jrnl. Chem. Soc.* LVIII. 1079 Rosenbuschite.. presents sufficient analogies to pectolite for it to be described as a zircon-pectolite. **1966** W. A. DEER et al. *Introd. Rock-Forming Minerals* 60 Rosenbuschite occurs as an accessory mineral in nepheline-syenite, but is a more frequent constituent of nepheline-syenite pegmatites.

rosenhahnite (rōᵘzĕnhā·nəit). *Min.* [f. the name of Leo *Rosenhahn*, U.S. amateur mineralogist, who first found it in 1962 + -ITE[1].] A hydrous calcium silicate, $(CaSiO_3)_3$.-H_2O, occurring as buff to white, tabular or lath-like, triclinic crystals.

1967 A. PABST et al. in *Amer. Mineralogist* LII. 336 (*heading*) Rosenhahnite, a new hydrous silicate from Mendocino County, California. **1973** *Nature* 5 Jan. 42/1 Thermal dehydration data showed that the molecule of water is given off very slowly at temperatures between 400 and 500°C and a single crystal of rosenhahnite transforms into an almost perfect single crystal of wollastonite, $CaSiO_3$.

Rosenkreuzian, var. ROSICRUCIAN *sb.* and *a.* in Dict. and Suppl.

Rosenthal (rōᵘ·zĕntāl). The name of Philip *Rosenthal*, founder of a porcelain factory at Selb in Bavaria *c* 1880, used *attrib.* of pottery made there.

1947 M. PENKALA *European Porcelain* 64 Rosenthal porcelain is carefully modelled and decorated. **1962** P. PURSER *Peregrination 22* xxx. 136 The tray was silver and the tea service Rosenthal china. **1970** E. PACE *Saberlegs* xvi. 152 Oranges heaped in an old Rosenthal bowl. **1977** C. MCFADDEN *Serial* (1978) i. 8/2 They spent it rapidly on ..Rosenthal china.

rose of Sharon. Add: **1. b.** (Later examples.)

1876 E. G. WHITE *Testimonies for Church* (1948) I. 19 There was a beautiful pink flower in the garden called the rose of Sharon. **1974** *Daily Colonist* (Victoria, B.C.) 23 July 20/6 The other Rose of Sharon is a real beauty whose true name is *Hibiscus syriacus*.

c. Delete *dial.* and add later examples.

1938 A. T. JOHNSON *Garden To-day* xl. 141 The old 'Rose of Sharon'.., a lowly carpeting shrub, is fairly well known. **1979** C. E. L. PHILLIPS *New Small Garden* xv. 243 There are 'carpeting' plants for covering rough places or growing under trees. The Rose-of-Sharon is one of the most useful of these.

3. Chiefly *U.S.* The name of a pattern used in quilting. Also *attrib.*

1894 *Scribner's Mag.* Sept. 363/1 Other floral designs, the sunflower, double peony, rose of Sharon hint at flower-borders lovingly tended by the over-taxed hands of a busy housewife. **1915** M. D. WEBSTER *Quilts* caption facing p. 75 Rose of Sharon. Made in Indiana about 65 years ago. It has a wool interlining instead of the usual cotton. **1929** R. E. FINLEY *Old Patchwork Quilts* xi. 126 The quilt shown..presents the original somewhat crude but very old type of 'Rose of Sharon' block. **1964** D. BRIGHTBILL *Quilting as Hobby* 88/1 The most popular pattern [of Bride's Quilts]..was the Rose of Sharon... Its name was probably derived from the Song of Solomon: 'I am the Rose of Sharon And the Lily-of-the-Valley.' **1966** D. A. HINSON *Quilting Man.* iii. 45 The Rose of Sharon quilt patterns are legion. **1974** *Times* 11 Jan. 9/5 Quilting is a special craft of [the Mennonites]..and they love the traditional patterns like Rose of Sharon.

ro·sepath. [f. ROSE *sb.* + PATH *sb.*] A pattern used in weaving.

1932 SIMPSON & WEIR *Weaver's Craft* x. 92 Other suitable 'threading drafts' will be given; but the 'Rosepath' entering offers plenty of scope for experiment and a great variety of patterns. **1960** A. GIBBS in G. Lewis *Handbk. Crafts* 103 Let us assume that we are going to use a simple pattern, Rosepath (this is a universal pattern, being found in peasant weaving throughout the world; it is capable of a very large number of variations).

rose-pink, *sb.* and *a.* Add: **A.** *sb.* **1.** (Later example.)

1877 E. S. DALLAS *Kettner's Bk. of Table* 338 The rose-pink, which is sometimes used for colouring..is obtained from the peach tree.

2. Also *fig.*, sentimentality, sentimental writing.

1872 G. MEREDITH *Let.* 3 Dec. (1970) I. 473 Read the first chapter for a specimen of modern rose-pink.

rose Pompadour (rōᵘ·z pǫ·mpădūᵊɹ). [f. ROSE *sb.* + POMPADOUR.] = *ROSE DU BARRY. Cf. POMPADOUR 2.

Considered by some authorities to be the more correct term.

1884 P. VILLARS tr. *Gasnault & Garnier's French Pottery* ix. 123 We must mention, among the most remarkable productions of the manufactory of Sèvres during the first period whose history we have briefly sketched, the beautiful ornamental vases with..the pink ground termed *rose carné* or *rose Pompadour* (sometimes erroneously called *rose Dubarry*). **1905** W. BURTON tr. *Auscher's Hist & Descr. French Porcelain* viii. 65 In 1757 the painter Xrowet invented that most famous ground-colour, rose-Pompadour. **1935** *Burlington Mag.* May 249/2 The 'claret-colour', which must have started as an attempt to ape the lovely rose Pompadour of Sèvres. **1936** *Ibid.* Dec. p. xix/2 The Sèvres porcelain especially the apple-green and *rose Pompadour* pieces. **1949** *Dict. Colours Interior Decoration* (Brit. Colour Council) III. 23/1 *Rose Pompadour*. This colour (matched to porcelain in the Wallace Collection, London) is named after Madame de Pompadour who took a great interest in the porcelain manufactury, first at Vincennes and later at Sèvres. **1960** R. G. HAGGAR *Conc. Encycl. Continental Pott. & Porc.* 386/2 *Rose Pompadour*..was invented according to Garnier by Jean Hellot, or, according to Auscher by Xhrouet... It takes its name from the Marquise de Pompadour (died 1764). **1960** H. HAYWARD *Antique Coll.* 243/2 Coalport..produced a rose Pompadour in the 19th cent. **1975** *Oxf. Compan. Decorative Arts* 135/2 An outstanding result of this [development of Sèvres, fostered by royal privileges] was the development of a series of very splendid ground-colours: dark blue in 1749,..pink ('rose Pompadour') in 1757 and so on.

ro·se-ti:nted, *a.* [f. ROSE *sb.*] = ROSE-COLOURED *a.* spec. *rose-tinted spectacles* = *rose-coloured spectacles* s.v. *ROSE-COLOURED *a.* 3.

1855 [see ROSE *sb.* 21 a]. **1885** 'MARK TWAIN' *Let.* 2 Mar. (1917) II. 452 He sold me $10,000 worth of another rose-tinted stock. **1956** C. WILSON *Outsider* viii. 245 The good-natured, eupeptic vulgarian who sees life through rose-tinted spectacles. **1966** *Listener* 20 Oct. 559/2 The official propaganda machine, whose task is to present every aspect of Soviet life through rose-tinted spectacles. **1977** *Church Times* 25 Feb. 7/2 There are no rose-tinted specs shading the very clear eyes of Elizabeth West as she describes life in her *Hovel in the Hills*.

Rosetta stone (rōᵘze·tă stōᵘ·n). [The name of a celebrated stone, bearing a trilingual inscription dating from the 2nd c. B.C., found in 1799 near Rosetta in Egypt.

The stone, now in the British Museum, bears an inscription in Greek, demotic, and hieroglyphics; the decipherment of the latter two parts of the inscription by Jean-François Champollion in 1822 led to the interpretation of all the other early records of the Egyptian civilization.]

Used *transf.* and *fig.* of something that resembles the Rosetta stone, usu. by acting as a key to some previously unattainable understanding (in quot. 1969, something indecipherable).

1902 *Encycl. Brit.* XXVI. 721/2 Although not the Rosetta stone which enabled him to decipher the minute structure of glucose and its congeners, this compound made possible for the first time the separation and identification of such compounds. **1933** H. G. WELLS *Shape of Things to Come* 24 About a third of the shorthand stuff was already represented by longhand or typescript copy in the folders. That was my Rosetta Stone. **1969** R. LOWELL *Notebk. 1967–68* 102 The typescript looked like a Rosetta Stone. **1975** *New Yorker* 29 Sept. 29/1 A knowledge of accounting is a kind of Rosetta stone. **1979** *Sci. Amer.* Mar. 72/1 The spectrum of the hydrogen atoms has proved to be the Rosetta stone of modern physics: once this pattern of lines had been deciphered much else could also be understood.

rosette, *sb.* Add: **1. a.** (Earlier and later examples.) Also, applied to such a decoration awarded to prize-winners at horse shows and similar events.

1790 *Pennsylvania Packet* 11 Dec. 3/2 Imported.. Ladies..elegant..beaded rosettees, for shoes. **1951** J. PULLEIN-THOMPSON *Radney Riding Club* ii. 31 When the ponies were fed and settled for the night Eric nailed the new rosettes beside the others in the saddle-room. **1957** R. FERGUSON *Rosettes for Jill* v. 52, I fastened my two red rosettes and the blue one on Black Boy's brow-band, and collected my prizes. **1965** T. GUNN in *New Statesman* 14 May 768/1 To enter Jerusalem on an ass.. or wear a rosette for Arsenal. **1967** *Listener* 26 Oct. 552/3, I walked up to one of the chaps and said.., pointing at the two Welsh rosettes upon his chest: 'Excuse me, what are these for?'

d. *transf.* A rose- or star-shaped symbol used in guides to hotels and restaurants to indicate the standard of service or cuisine provided.

1966 P. V. PRICE *France* 318 The famous 'stars' of Michelin, which are indicated by rosettes in the guide book, refer *solely* to the standard of the food and drink. **1974** *Country Life* 24 Jan. 167/3 (Advt.), Our AA Rosette reflects..the high standards of country house hotel-keeping of which we are justly proud. **1976** *Times* 2 Oct. 10/1 In Avignon..a truly Lucullan dinner at *Hiély-Lucullus*..the food worthy of its two rosettes in Michelin.

4. b. Also, a similar formation as a symptom of plant disease, the leaves on a stem being clustered owing to its greatly reduced internodal growth. (Further examples.)

1891 *Jrnl. Mycol.* VI. 143 The lower leaves on these tufts or rosettes roll and curl, turn yellow,..and fall early. **1937** F. D. HEALD *Introd. Plant Path.* ii. 20 Rosettes, or closely grouped clusters of leaves caused by the failure of axes to make a normal elongation. This should not be confused with the normal rosette habit of certain plants. **1952** [see next sense]. **1980** *Amateur Gardening* 18 Oct. 21 The lovely wide-faced flowers.. are held over the hairy rosettes of leaves in May and June.

c. Delete *U.S.* and substitute for def.: Any of various plant diseases in which there are rosette-like malformations of leaves. Also *rosette disease*. (Examples.)

1891 E. F. SMITH in *Jrnl. Mycol.* VI. 143 It seems best, therefore, to call it [*sc.* the disease] 'the peach rosette' until it can be determined whether it is identical with yellows. *Ibid.* 146 This rosette disease resembles yellows very closely. **1923** *Phytopathology* XIII. 41 The symptoms of the rosette disease of wheat bear certain resemblances to the symptoms of corn mosaic as described by Kunkel. **1946** *Ann. Reg. 1945* 349 K. M. Smith..has shown that the two separable complexes of tobacco rosette disease may be transmitted..by Aphis. **1950** *Times* 2 Feb. 9/2 This new discovery brings within reach a means of prevention of virus diseases which are transmitted by aphids, such as yellow virus on sugar beet, strawberry virus and rosette disease in groundnuts. **1952** tr. *Gram & Weber's Plant Dis.* 489/2 Rosette is a disease of *Lilium longiflorum* and its varieties...Infected plants have yellow leaves which remain in a basal rosette. **1972** J. T. SLYKHUIS in Kado & Agrawal *Princ. & Techniques Plant Virol.* vii. 208 Evidence that pigeon pea sterility and rose rosette are caused by viruses rests on transmission of the disease by grafting.

d. *Med.* A group of red cells bearing one factor adhering to one red cell bearing another factor, produced in tests for antigens, antibodies, and related substances on the cell surfaces.

[**1958** *Jrnl. Clin. Invest.* XXXVII. 1216/2 The antibody-sensitized red cells were seen to cluster around individual leukocytes, often producing rosette-patterns.] **1964** *Immunol.* VII. 477 Many of the peritoneal cells were seen to be coated with sheep red cells, giving, in many instances, a characteristic 'rosette' appearance. **1966** *Jrnl. Exper. Med.* CXXIII. 144 (*caption*) Rosettes of sheep red cells adsorbed onto the surface of guinea pig lung macrophages. **1971** I. M. ROITT *Essent. Immunol.* iii. 50 When lymphocytes are incubated with, say, sheep red cells, those with surface receptors for the erythrocytes will bind them to form a rosette. **1976** *Nature* 15 July 216/1 This heat treatment does not destroy the ability of the macrophages to form rosettes with sheep red blood cells.

5. a. (Earlier and later examples.)

1767 J. WEDGWOOD *Let.* 23 May (1965) 53 At Birmingham I saw a Lathe executed upon the plan of that which is full of Rosetts, and every Rosett had a projection from the edge. **1931** A. U. DILLEY *Oriental Rugs & Carpets* (caption to plate 33) India Rug of Persian star, palmette, rosette, and leaf design with border of realistic flowering plants.

d. = *ROSE *sb.* 14 g.

1896 R. ROBB *Electr. Wiring* v. 152 The holes in the socket bushing and in the rosette are little larger than enough to allow the cord to slide through them. **1904** *Electr. World & Engin.* 7 May 887/2 The finish and smoothness of the rosette are in every way admirable. **1961** C. C. CARR *Craft's Amer. Electricians' Handbk.* (ed. 8) iv. 126 The drop cord passes through the hole in the center and is attached to connections inside the body of the rosette.

e. *Geol.* = *ROCK-ROSE 5, *ROSE *sb.* 16 e.

[**1902** H. A. MIERS *Mineral.* IV. i. 249 Irregular conjunctions are distinguished as—... Rosette-shaped, when they overlap round a centre like the petals of a rose.] **1905** *Bull. U.S. Geol. Survey* No. 239. 59 The rosettes are sometimes a foot in diameter, while there is every gradation from this to submicroscopic size. **1923** *Proc. Oklahoma Acad. Sci.* III. 102 Barite and especially the form known as 'sand barite rosettes', has long attracted attention as one of the most widely disseminated of Oklahoma minerals. **1971** FEJER & WALKER tr. *H. Baegel's Collector's Guide Minerals & Gemstones* i. 31 Tabular minerals (gypsum, barite, hematite) may occasionally form rosettes ('desert roses').

f. *Engin.* An arrangement about a point of three or more coplanar lines that represent the axes of strain gauges used to determine the strain existing in a structure or material at that point.

1931 W. HOVGAARD in *Trans. Soc. Naval Architects & Marine Engineers* XXXIX. 26/1 We arrive thus at what may be called a 'rosette' of strain measurements consisting of one horizontal (longitudinal) strain, one vertical (transverse), and two at 45 degrees inclination. **1946** G. MURPHY *Advanced Mechanics of Materials* iii. 64 Valuable information concerning the stresses can be obtained by measuring the strains developed in a model or a trial design of the prototype and converting the strains into stresses. The usual procedure involves the measurement of the normal strains on a rosette of three or four intersecting gage lines at the point. **1950** M. I. HETENYI *Handbk. Exper. Stress Anal.* ix. 400 The four-gage 45° rosette combines all the advantages enumerated..for the equiangular and the rectangular rosettes. **1969** H. N. NORTON *Handbk. Transducers for Electronic Measuring Syst.* xiii. 559 Gages with multiple grids (rosettes) were developed for simultaneous measurement of strain in different directions.

6. *rosette bud, habit, symptom, virus*; *rosette-forming* adj.; **rosette gauge** *Engin.*, an assembly of strain gauges whose axes correspond to the lines of a rosette (see sense *5 f); **rosette plant** (see quot. 1934).

1977 J. L. HARPER *Population Biol. of Plants* xviii. 543 Digitalis purpurea regenerate from rosette buds if the inflorescence is damaged before the seed is required. *Ibid.* xiv. 437 The flora of Port Meadow is composed of perennial grasses..plus laterally spreading clonal dicots.. and some rosette-forming species. **1943** *Exper. Stress Anal.* I. I. 13/2 In connection with the use of wire resistance rosette gages..small corrections must sometimes be applied to the initial strain observations. **1969** H. N. NORTON *Handbk. Transducers for Electronic Measuring Syst.* xiii. 561 When using rosette gages, it is necessary to operate upon the output readings using Poisson's ratio to convert strain rates to stress. **1937** Rosette habit [see sense 4 b above]. **1903** W. R. FISHER tr. *Schimper's Plant-Geogr.* III. iv. 706 Perennial rosette-plants play a leading part, especially on alpine meadows. **1934** H. GILBERT-CARTER tr. *Raunkiaer's Life Forms of Plants* ii. 47 A transition is formed from the rosette plants in which..the foliage leaves are all gathered into a rosette at the base. **1965** *Austral. Encycl.* VII. 123/2 It [*sc.* the Western Australian pitcher-plant] is a small rosette plant. **1928** C. E. OWENS *Princ. Plant Path.* xix. 423 Potato plants which are attacked by the Rhizoctonia fungus on the underground parts sometimes show leaf-roll and rosette symptoms. **1937** K. M. SMITH *Textbk. Plant Virus Dis.* ii. 186 Numerous other [groundnut] plants in the Gambia have been observed showing typical rosette symptoms. **1960** J. E. VAN DER PLANK *Plant Path.* III. vii. 262 Rosette virus ordinarily spreads slowly from peach to peach. **1977** J. L. HARPER *Population Biol. of Plants* xvi. 488 The rosette virus of peach..kills the host rapidly.

rosette (roze·t), *v.* [f. prec. sb.] **1.** *intr. Med.* Of a cell: to form a rosette.

1969 [implied in ROSETTING *ppl. a.* below]. **1973** *Jrnl. Immunol.* CXI. 1834 Lymphocytes with binding sites for complement..do not rosette with R[abbit] R[ed] B[lood] C[ells]. **1977** *Lancet* 5 Nov. 988/1, 2%..of the lymphocytes rosetted with sheep red blood-cells (T cells).

2. *trans.* To award a rosette-like symbol to, as a mark of excellence.

1974 *Guardian* 20 Mar. 1/3 Three restaurants much rosetted by English guides—the Ritz, the Savoy, and the Mirabelle.

So **rose·tting** *ppl. a.*

1969 *Internat. Arch. Allergy* XXXV. 220 Vicarious loss of potentially rosetting cells would distort the results.

rosetted, *a.* Add: **1. a.** (Further examples.)

1901 *Bull. Geol. Soc. Amer.* XII. 166 Even the loose and less coherent matrix reveals, under the action of wind and rain, an ill-defined, though unmistakably radiate, or rosetted structure. **1955** *Mineral Abstr.* XII. 573 Rosetted crusts of silver-white semseyite on galena. **1966** D. VARADAY *Gara-Yaka's Domain* iv. 47 There they [*sc.* cheetahs]..glared up at their rosetted relative. The humourless leopard glared back at them. **1969** *Internat. Arch. Allergy* XXXV. 214 (*caption*) Typical appearance of rosetted cells obtained with the suspension-centrifugation technique. **1975** *Daily Tel.* 8 Sept. 13 Triumphantly rosetted and bristling with the familiar red-and-white battle insignia of Manchester United.

b. Of skin or pelt: marked with rosette-like blemishes.

1905 W. E. CASTLE *Heredity of Coat Characters in Guinea-Pigs & Rabbits* 75 A rosetted or rough coat is unknown in rabbits. **1960** O. MANNING *Great Fortune* I. 20 The skin was mottled purple and rosetted with yellow scabs.

c. Having been awarded a rosette.

1972 *Times* 6 May 9/3 As delicious as any rosetted *specialité*.

2. Affected with rosette disease.

1891 *Bull. U.S. Dept. Agric. Div. Veg. Physiol. & Path.* I. 48 Many of the roofs of rosetted trees were honey-combed by gum-pockets. **1937** K. M. SMITH *Textbk. Plant Virus Dis.* ii. 186 The rosetted plant may flower, but few of the pegs make any growth. **1949** BUTLER & JONES *Plant Path.* viii. 289 'Rosetted' peaches nearly always die the following autumn or winter.

rosetting (roze·tiŋ), *vbl. sb.* [f. ROSETTE *sb.* and *v. + -ING[1].] The occurrence or development of rosettes.

1948 MELHUS & KENT *Elem. Plant Path.* x. 246 These plants nearly always remain dwarfed and often show a 'rosetting' caused by the increase in the number of branches and the shortening of the internodes. **1970** *Internat. Arch. Allergy* XXXIX. 658 It is possible to obtain a rosetting reaction with antigen-coated erythrocytes around receptor-bearing dead lymphoid cells. **1978** T. T. KOZLOWSKI in Horsfall & Cowling *Plant Dis.* III. ii. 31 Symptons of mineral deficiencies include necrosis, dieback of shoots, rosetting, [etc.]. **1978** *Nature* 13 Apr. 619/2 (*caption*) Cells were tested for rosetting with IgG-OE immediately or after incubation overnight at 37 °C, and with or without trypsin treatment.

rose-water. Add: **1. c.** *rose-water bowl, dish* (later examples), *ewer* (later example); **rose-water pear** (earlier example); **rose-water pipe,** an oriental tobacco-pipe in which the smoke passes through rose water before reaching the mouth.

1629 J. PARKINSON *Parad.* III. xxi. 592 The Rosewater peare is a goodly faire peare, and of a delicate taste. **1835** N. P. WILLIS *Pencillings by Way* II. xxi. 234 A string of beads in one hand, and a splendid narghilé, or rose-water pipe, in the other. **1956** G. TAYLOR *Silver* v. 97 A rose-water dish of 1672 belonging to St John's College, Oxford. **1960** H. HAYWARD *Antique Coll.* 243/2 *Rose-water ewer and dish or basin*, used for finger-washing at table. **1968** *Canad. Antiques Collector* June 9/3 The rose water bowl or basin was like an enormous soup plate, 12 to 20 inches in diameter. It had an extra wide rim, two inches or more, around the slightly depressed center and was usually ornately decorated.

Hence **ro·se-wa:tery,** *a.*

1902 G. B. SHAW *Let.* 20 June (1972) II. 277 The comparatively rose-watery part of it [*sc.* a situation in *Mrs. Warren's Profession*].

rosewood. Add: **5*.** A shade or tint of the colour of rosewood.

1853 *Heal & Son Catal.: Bedsteads* 33/1 Parisian Bedstead, with handsome cast iron side and ends, sheet iron head and foot board, japanned rosewood. **1897** *Sears, Roebuck Catal.* 22/3 Wood stains..Perfect imitations of natural woods, Cherry, Rosewood, Mahogany, Walnut [etc.]. **1907** *Yesterday's Shopping* (1969) 145/1 Stains.. as used by the Working Ladies Guild, colours:—Rosewood, Satinwood, Oak, [etc.]. **1927** *Daily Tel.* 21 Feb. 14 (Advt.), Two-Piece Suits, Coats, &c. Available in shades of Light Grey, Rosewood, Fawn, Sand, &c. **1930** *Daily Express* 6 Oct. 13/1 (Advt.), Shades, beaver, brown, rosewood, and drab. **1971** [see *MOSS *sb.*[1] 5 d].

Rosh Chodesh, Rosh Hodesh (roʃ χō·deʃ, rōᵘʃ χōᵘ·dĕʃ). [Heb., lit. 'head of the month'.] A Jewish half-holiday observed at the appearance of the New Moon, the beginning of the Jewish month.

1879 C. E. SACHAU tr. *Albîrûnî's Chronol. Anc. Nations* xiv. 274 (*heading*) Nîsan... has only one Rosh-Ḥodesh and 30 days. **1934** WEBSTER, Rosh Ho'desh..or Cho'desh. **1963** *Times* 24 Apr. 16/1 He initiated the delightful presidential custom of inviting to his residence a representative gathering of citizens from a different ethnic group each 'Rosh Chodesh', the start of a Hebrew calendar month. **1976** G. JESSUP *No Strange God* xi. 75 The first day of every month is a semi-festival, called *Rosh Ḥodesh*, when mourning and fasting are forbidden.

Rosh Hashana (roʃ haʃanā·, rōᵘʃ hăʃōᵘ·no). Also **Rosh Hashanah, Rosh Hashonoh,** etc. [Heb., lit. 'head of the year'.] The Jewish New Year, celebrated on the first and second day of the month Tishri.

1846 *Jewish Chron.* 21 Aug. 199/1 Rosh Hashana (New Year), and Yom Kippur (Day of Atonement), were kept by most of our co-religionists. **1862** *Chambers's Encycl.* IV. 304/1 The most exalted of new-moon festivals was that of the first day of the seventh month, 'the day of remembrance of the sounding' or 'of trumpets' (Lev. xxiii. 24), to which in later times..the name of Rosh hashana (New Year) was given. **1907** I. ZANGWILL *Ghetto Comedies* 18 We lived somehow till *Rosh Hashanah* (New Year), hoping it would indeed be a New Year. **1957** L. STERN *Midas Touch* III. xx. 152 So this year you will come to *shul* maybe for *Rosh Hashona*? **1960** F. RAPHAEL *Limits of Love* II. i. 165 It's *Rosh Hashana*... I'm going to read some prayers. **1970** *Challenge* (Lubavitch Foundation) 281 *Rosh Hashonoh* is Coronation Day for G-d as our King and for Israel as His people. **1973** *Jewish Chron.* 19 Jan. 5/4 After the Munich massacre of Israeli Olympic sportsmen..it was decided that memorial prayers would be recited at the Rosh Hashana service in Copenhagen's main synagogue. **1973** *Synagogue Light* Sept. 26 Jewish residents of New York State, will join on September 26, with others of their faith throughout the world, in the observance of Rosh Hashanah. **1978** *Detroit Free Press* 16 Apr. (Record) 9/5 On September 16, 1939, the eve of Rosh Hashana..the *Luftwaffe*.. bombed the Jewish quarter of Warsaw.

Roshi (rōᵘ·ʃi). [Jap.] The spiritual leader of a community of Zen Buddhist monks.

1934 D. T. SUZUKI *Training of Zen Buddhist Monk* iv. 31 Yinji-ryō which attends on the master known as Rōshi. **1949** C. HUMPHREYS *Zen Buddhism* vii. 142 Laymen, accepted for teaching by the Roshi, may come for a period... The whole of the monastery is locked in full meditation with a queue of..monks waiting their turn for the Roshi to confirm, reject or make further suggestions for their inward labours. **1959** *Encounter* Jan. 21/1 The Zen Master, or *Roshi*, the spiritual head of the monastery. **1972** *Last Whole Earth Catalog* (Portola Inst.) 50/2 She's sort of like an elderly Zen priest, an old roshi who after years of work and study has distilled a large burden of 'knowledge' into a single gem of wisdom which he renders in a single haiku. **1974** R. C. ZAEHNER in *Times Lit. Suppl.* 6 Dec. 1389/4 Anglican priest turned Zen Rōshi, reconciled to his church shortly before his death, but belly-laughing, genial, infuriating Rōshi to the end. **1978** C. HUMPHREYS *Both Sides Circle* xv. 165 There is no likelihood of Zen roshis, in the full meaning of the term as used in the Rinzai School, arriving in Europe in sufficient numbers to give us expert training.

Rosicrucian, *sb.* and *a.* Add: Also (after G. *Rosenkreuz*) **Rosenkreuzian. A.** *sb.* Also, a member of a present-day Rosicrucian society (see sense B below).

1957 *Encycl. Brit.* XIX. 560/1 That it is not always possible to prove the existence of the order in a given country at any particular moment does not disturb the Rosicrucians, for it seems to be recognized that there occur periods when the order is deliberately 'in sleep'.

B. *adj.* (Further examples.) Now also applied to various societies that claim to continue the Rosicrucian tradition.

1837 K. H. DIGBY *Mores Catholici* VIII. vi. 193 The cabalistic learning, expressed in the unintelligible language of Theosophy, which was in the seventeenth century to be the foundation of the Rosenkreuzian society. **1959** *Chambers's Encycl.* XI. 840/2 In the mid-19th century there came into being a Rosicrucian Society in England, an offshoot of masonry, the leading figure being R. W. Little. The name has also been appropriated by American theosophy. None of these later developments can claim historical continuity with any original group. **1961** *Listener* 21 Sept. 443/2 Nothing of his marriage or his dealings with Rudolf Steiner, the Rosicrucian Order, or the Catholic Church. **1977** *Daily Times* (Lagos) 5 Jan. 2 (Advt.), Members of the Rosicrucian Order Amorc (Nigeria) have applied to be registered under the Land Perpetual (Succession) Act.

Rosicrucianism. (Later examples.)

1955 C. S. LEWIS *Surprised by Joy* iv. 62 She was.. floundering in the mazes of Theosophy, Rosicrucianism, Spiritualism; the whole Anglo-American Occultist tradition. **1961** *Listener* 21 Dec. 1089/1 For a time Satie dabbled in Rosicrucianism.

rosied, *a.* (Later example.)

1910 W. DE LA MARE *Three Mulla-Mulgars* xxii. 291 The faintly-rosied starlight.

Rosie Lee, var. *ROSY LEE.

rosier. (Later *poet.* example.)

1925 E. SITWELL *Troy Park* 88 Under a rosier Stood the Bishop Walked with a crozier.

rosin, *sb.* Add: **1. c.** *slang.* (*a*) Alcoholic drink. Cf. ROSIN *v.* 2. (*b*) A fiddler, a violinist; also, *rosin-the-bow*.

1734 *Select Trials* I. 227/1 Says I to the Gentleman, I hope, Sir, you won't forget your Coachman—a little Rozzam wou'd do very well. *Ibid.*, Rosin, strong Drink: A Metaphor first used among Fidlers. **1864** HOTTEN *Slang Dict.* 215 *Rosin*, beer or other drink given to musicians at a dancing party. *Ibid.*, *Rosin-the-bow*, a fiddler. **1901** F. E. TAYLOR *Folk-Speech S. Lancashire*, *Rozzin*, a jocular term for musician's drink. **1904** S. WATSON *Wops the Waif* (1924) iii. 9/1 A short, lame man,.. with a violin beneath his arm, suggesting the identity with the 'rosin' announced.

2. *rosin-distiller, -flux*; **rosin-back** *Circus slang*, (*a*) a horse used by a bareback rider or acrobat; (*b*) a bareback rider.

1923 C. R. COOPER *Under Big Top* 170 She is trained to the 'rosinback', as the ring horse is called. **1931** *Amer. Mercury* Nov. 353/2 *Rosinbacks*, bareback riders. **1933** P. GODFREY *Back-Stage* xvii. 213 One of the least spectacular, yet most difficult, tasks is to train the trick-rider's horse, or 'rosin-back'. These horses are massive Flemish animals, capable of supporting on their broad backs several performers at a time. **1945** C. B. COCHRAN *Showman looks On* iii. 33 A 'rosin-back' is a ring-horse used by bareback riders... Rosin is rubbed into the horse's back to help the rider to get a firm footing as he jumps from the ring on to the horse. **1974** V. CANNING *Painted Tent* iii. 51 There were a few horses in the stable, a couple of rosin backs and a small black pony. **1885** *List of Subscribers, Classified* (United Telephone Co.) (ed. 6) 207 Tar, rosin, benzole and naphtha distillers. **1960** COOKE & MARCUS *Electronics & Nucleonics Dict.* 410/2 *Rosin-core solder*, solder made up in tubular or other hollow form, with the inner space filled with rosin flux to serve as a noncorrosive flux for soldering joints. **1976** *S9* (N.Y.) May/June 101/3 For electronics work only rosin flux is used as it is non-corrosive.

Rosinante. Add: (Earlier example.)

1745 *Life & Adventures B.-M. Carew* 65 Who, enraged by their several Losses, began to curse the Doctor and his Rosinante.

Hence **Rosina·ntine** *a.*, lean, worn-out. *nonce-wd.*

1936 P. FLEMING *News from Tartary* ix. 235 Plump and naked..they [*sc.* camels] were a great contrast to our shaggy, Rosinantine beasts.

rosined, *ppl. a.* Add: Also *fig.*

1774 GOLDSMITH in *London Chron.* 28–30 Apr. 416/3 And shall I mix in this unhallow'd crew? May rosin'd lightning blast me if I do.

rosiner (rǫ·zinəɹ). *Ir.* and *Austral. slang.* Also **rosner, rossiner, rozener.** [f. ROSIN *sb.* or *v.* + -ER[1].] A drink of spirits; a stiff drink. Also *transf.*

1932 D. JOHNSTON *Moon in Yellow River* I. 35 Well, you must step across to the store some time and we'll give you a rosner. **1933** *Bulletin* (Sydney) 10 May 20/1 Fill up the cup, a rozener, a hummer! **1934** S. BECKETT *More Pricks than Kicks* 119 'And the rosiners' said Mrs Tough, 'will you have that in the lav too?' Reader, a rosiner is a drop of the hard. **1947** H. D. BROCKMAN *Fatal Days* 114 I've not had a solitary spot since four. I need a rosiner. **1954** T. RONAN *Vision Splendid* 345 Two nips that old Block had and the one I poured into Peter. They were rozeners I'll admit, but still the three I've had out of this second bottle haven't exactly been small ones. *a* **1966** 'M. NA GOPALEEN' *Best of Myles* (1977) 310 A rossiner wouldn't be bad, have a double one after this. **1973** D. STUART *Morning Star, Evening Star* 53 There's no harm in a bit of rosiner after a hard day's travel, just once in a while.

Rosminian. (Earlier examples.)

1837 L. D. SHREWSBURY *Let.* 16 Apr. in D. Gwynn *Fr. Luigi Gentili* (1951) ix. 128, I thought the Rosminians would bring their means with them. **1843** M. PATTISON *Diary* 1 Oct. in W. Meynell *John Henry Newman* (1890) iii. 32 Talk of some Rosminian Nuns coming to England.

rosner, var. *ROSINER.

rosolio. Add: Also **rossolio.** (Earlier and further examples.)

1818 'A. BURTON' *Adventures J. Newcome* IV. 238 At each Jew Agent's did he stop, Each Wine-house, and Rosolio-shop. **1850** [see *liqueur-glass* s.v. *LIQUEUR *sb.* 3]. **1973** *Times Lit. Suppl.* 14 Sept. 1064/2 He plied the abbot with sweet pink rosoglio and was then admitted to a closet in the cellar.

Ross (rǫs), *sb.*[4] The name of Sir James Clark *Ross* (1800–62), Scottish explorer, used *attrib.* and in the possessive in **Ross('s) gull,** to designate a pinkish-white Arctic gull, *Rhodostethia rosea,* formerly named *Larus rossii* in his honour by J. Richardson in 1825 (*App. W. E. Parry's Jrnl. Second Voy. N.-W. Passage 1821–23* 359).

[**1872**: see ROSY *a.* 5.] **1902** *N. Amer. Fauna* XXII. 80 Ross Gull. The first known specimen of this beautiful species was killed at Alagnak, Melville Peninsula, by James Clark Ross, in June, 1823, during Parry's second voyage. **1926** A. THORBURN *Brit. Birds* IV. 70 The Wedge-tailed Gull... A specimen of this small and very beautiful species, known also as Ross's Gull, is said to have been obtained at Tadcaster, Yorkshire, in December, 1846. **1957** L. L. SNYDER *Arctic Birds Canada* 222 The rather fragmentary information pertaining to Ross's Gull has come largely from the Old World. **1971** *Country Life* 23 Sept. 751/1 The announcement of two rare arctic gulls sighted in the north east of England last December: a Ross's gull and an ivory gull. **1976** *New Yorker* 26 Jan. 25/3 Last year around this time, a Ross's gull—the only species of gull with a conspicuously pink breast—caused a considerable stir when it arrived at Salisbury, Massachusetts, thousands of miles from its normal home, in Siberia.

Ross (rǫs), *sb.*[5] The name of Bernard R. *Ross* (1827–74), factor of the Hudson's Bay Company, used in the possessive in **Ross'(s) goose** to designate a small Arctic goose, *Chen rossii,* formerly *Anser rossii,* named in his honour in 1861 by John Cassin (*Proc. Acad. Nat. Sci. Philadelphia* 72).

1874 E. COUES *Birds of Northwest* 553 Horned Wavy; Ross' Goose. **1908** C. MAIR *Through Mackenzie Basin* 320 At Fort Chipewyan..Ross's goose is the last to arrive in the spring. **1947** C. E. GILLHAM *Raw North* 175 He kindly interpreted for me while I interviewed his natives regarding the whereabouts of the Ross's goose. **1966** W. E. GODFREY *Birds of Canada* 52/2 White or greyish-white geese with black wing tips, they are likely to be confused with Ross's Goose.

Ross (rǫs), *sb.*[6] The name of Sir Charles A. F. L. *Ross,* Scottish-born engineer and soldier, used to designate a type of rifle used by the Canadian Army, esp. in the war of 1914–18.

1906 *Canadian Mag.* Dec. 66 (Advt.), Ross Rifles... The best in the World... 303 Calibre. **1917** *Grit* (Toronto) 7 Dec. 4/5 Think of the Ross Rifle, the lame horses, the sham shoes, the Allison rake-off. **1963** *Military Arms of Canada* 43 The Ross Rifle was a straight pull bolt action rifle that was made in calibre .303 British and .280 Ross for the Canadian Government. **1972** J. MINIFIE *Homesteader* xix. 169 We had been issued Ross rifles, a heavy weapon with a straight-draw action which jammed. **1973** J. QUICK *Dict. Weapons* 377/1 *Ross .303 rifle*... Under actual trench-warfare conditions it was found unsuitable. A serious problem with this weapon is the bolt. If re-assembled wrong, it will permit firing in an unlocked position, resulting in serious injury or death to the shooter.

ross, *v.* (Earlier and later examples.)

1853 S. STRICKLAND 27 *Yrs. Canada West* II. 230 As soon as the tree is felled, a person, called a liner, rosses and lines the tree on each side. **1958** *N.Z. Timber Jrnl.* June 59/2 *Rossing,* removing the bark from logs.

Rossby wave (rǫ·sbi). *Physics* and *Meteorol.* [f. the name of Carl-Gustaf Arvid *Rossby* (1898–1957), Swedish meteorologist + WAVE *sb.*] A long wavelength fluctuation of a current in a fluid system having no divergence and subject to Coriolis force; *esp.* a lateral fluctuation of a jet stream, with wavelength comparable with the radius of the earth.

[**1951** *Jrnl. Meteorol.* VIII. 264/2 The velocity..of Rossby long waves relative to a basic current.] **1963** *Deep-Sea Res.* X. 735 Damped, stationary Rossby waves can occur in the ocean superimposed on a steady west to east flow. **1974** *Earth-Sci. Rev.* X. 203 Planetary or Rossby waves, though probably unimportant in the fluid interior of the Earth, are of interest to earth scientists in general, because of their pervasive role in the general circulation of oceans and atmospheres. **1974** *Nature* 5 Apr. 539/1 The intense Kuroshio current may generate a series of Rossby waves, which can propagate across the entire Pacific Basin. **1974** *Encycl. Brit. Macropædia* X. 163/1 If floor conditions are neither divergent nor convergent.., the absolute vorticity should not change with time... This explains the reason for the formation of long planetary waves, the so-called Rossby waves, in the upper-tropospheric flow patterns.

Rossettian (rǫ̆ze·tiăn), *a.* [f. the name of D. G. *Rossetti* (see below) + -IAN]. Pertaining to or characteristic of Dante Gabriel Rossetti (1828–82), English poet and Pre-Raphaelite artist, or his work.

1881 'V. LEE' *Let.* in P. Gunn *Vernon Lee* (1964) vii. 79 All the Rossettian poeticules. **1905** G. B. SHAW *Let.* 11 Sept. (1972) II. 555 His [*sc.* W. Morris's] old Rossettian associates called him Topsy. **1908** D. H. LAWRENCE *Let.* 9 Oct. (1962) I. 30 What's the M.R.? Mary Rose? It sounds Rossettian. **1914** G. B. SHAW *Pygmalion* (1916) III. 144 One of the beautiful Rossettian costumes which.. led to the absurdities of popular estheticism. **1927** E. SITWELL in *Daily Mail* 30 June 10/4 In provincial cities we may still find relics of Rossettian heads of fox-coloured hair. **1974** K. CLARK *Another Part of Wood* v. 179 An invitation to dine was in Rossettian language 'Come and grub with me', but the dinner was more Beardsleyan.

So **Rossettia·na** [ANA *suff.*], relics of, or information about, D. G. Rossetti.

1928 R. L. MEGROZ in *Daily Express* 28 Sept. 10/3 Sir Hall Caine has now made explicit what every careful student of Rossettiana has realised, that Lizzie Siddal committed suicide.

rossie (rǫ·si), *sb. Anglo-Ir.* [ad. Ir. *rásaidhe, rásaí.*] A wandering woman, a jilt; used as a disparaging term for a woman.

1922 JOYCE *Ulysses* 359 If they could run like rossies she could sit so she said she could see from where she was. **1927** P. S. DINNEEN *Irish-Eng. Dict.* (ed. 2) 879/1 *Rásach, aigho, acha, f.,* a rambling woman, a gipsy, a jilt; *cf.* rossie (*Dublin*); *rásaidhe, id.* **1939** JOYCE *Finnegans Wake* (1964) 327 All the prim rossies are out dress-parading. **1961** 'F. O'BRIEN' *Hard Life* v. 71 She told us all about her dear friend, Emmeline Pankhurst. Now there is a bold rossie for you if you like.

Rossi–Forel (rǫ:si fore·l). Also **Rossi Forel.** [The names of Michele Stefano Conte de *Rossi* (1834–98), Italian geologist, and François-Alphonse *Forel* (1841–1912), Swiss physician and limnologist, who in 1883 collaborated in proposing the scale (a modification of Rossi's scale of 1873).] *Rossi–Forel scale*: a ten-point scale used to measure the local intensity of an earthquake.

1885 *Science* 6 Mar. 197/1 The intensity of shocks is measured on the Rossi-Forel scale. **1900** *Jrnl. Geol.* VIII. 304 The continuous curves represent the isoseismal lines of intensities 4 and 3 of the Rossi-Forel scale. **1946** *Nature* 13 July 65/1 The shock on May 8 was apparently the most pronounced felt in Dunedin for many years. The intensity recorded there was IV–V on the Modified Mercalli Scale (equivalent to 5 on the Rossi–Forel Scale). **1976** *Daily Colonist* (Victoria, B.C.) 17 Aug. 1/1 The quake, measuring 7 on the Rossi Forel scale of 10, struck shortly after midnight.

rossiner, var. *ROSINER.

Rossinian (rǫ̆sī·niăn), *a.* [f. the name of G. A. *Rossini* (see below) + -IAN.] Pertaining to or characteristic of Gioacchino Antonio Rossini (1792–1868), Italian operatic composer, or his music.

1869 H. S. EDWARDS *Life of Rossini* v. 55 The melody, as it now exists, is eminently Rossinian in form and style. **1897** G. B. SHAW in *Sat. Rev.* 20 Mar. 290/1 Passages which are Rossinian in their reliance on symmetry of melody and impressiveness of march to redeem poverty of meaning. **1927** *Daily Tel.* 14 June 12/6 The performance..was as full of spirit and élan as the delightful Rossinian 'snippets' that help to make this ballet [*sc.* La Boutique Fantasque] perhaps the most exhilarating thing in the whole of M. Diaghileff's repertory. **1955** E. DENT in H. Van Thal *Fanfare for E. Newman* 92 We sometimes find the most tragic situation set to the most cheerful music merely because the Rossinian style demands a big *finale* and the impression of a happy end. **1977** *New Yorker* 11 July 82/1 'Un Giorno di Regno', Verdi's first comic opera, which is a bit old-fashioned for its period and full of Rossinian idioms.

rossite (rǫ·səit). *Min.* [f. the name of Clarence Samuel *Ross* (1880–1953), U.S. geologist + -ITE[1].] A hydrated calcium vanadate, $CaV_2O_6.4H_2O$, found as yellow triclinic crystals occurring in glassy masses in sandstone.

1926 FOSHAG & HESS in *Amer. Mineralogist* XI. 66 (*heading*) Rossite, a new calcium vanadate from Utah. *Ibid.*, This mineral has been called rossite, in honor of Dr. C. S. Ross of the U.S. Geological Survey. **1963** *Canad. Mineralogist* VII. 713 The crystal structure of rossite, $Ca(VO_3)_2.4H_2O$, has been determined. **1968** I. KOSTOV *Mineral.* 470 Rossite group. The group comprises exclusively vanadates of aluminium, iron, sodium, and calcium, most of which are closely related to the montroseite group of oxides.

rösslerite, var. *ROESSLERITE.

‖ **rosso antico** (rǫ·so a·ntiko). [It., lit. 'ancient red'.] **1.** The name given by Josiah Wedgwood (see WEDGWOOD) to the red stoneware produced at his Staffordshire factories.

1776 J. WEDGWOOD *Let.* 3 Mar. (1903) II. 163, I am afraid we shall never be able to make the *Rosso Antico* otherwise than to put you in mind of a red-Pot-Teapot. **1875** E. METEYARD *Wedgwood Handbk.* 28 Wedgwood made much red ware from the same Bradwell-wood clay as that used by Elers, only he glazed the insides of his vessels. Some of Wedgwood's earliest portrait medallions and bas-reliefs were in rosso antico, but the results were not satisfactory. **1976** *Times* 7 Dec. 16/3 The same American bidder paid £1,000..for a Wedgwood *rosso antico* pot-pourri vase of 1805.

2. A rich red marble found in Italy, and employed as a decoration. Also *attrib.* or as *adj.*

1816 J. DALLAWAY *Of Stat. & Sculpt.* 248 That [*sc.* the marble] of Lybia, is called, by the present antiquaries, 'rosso antico': of this marble there is no known quarry. **1848** MILL *Pol. Econ.* I. III. iv. 552 The materials of many of the ornamental articles manufactured in Italy are the substances called rosso, giallo, and verde antico. **1863** LYTTON *Caxtoniana* II. 15 The columns of its lofty portico were of the *rosso antico* marble. **1882** *Athenæum* 30 Dec. 906/1 The material altogether Tuscan, the white marble having been brought from Serravezza, the red (like a fine *rosso antico*) from the neighbourhood of Siena. **1969** *Listener* 16 Jan. 79/1 Of marbles I have found *cipollino, pavonazzetto, giallo* and *rosso antico,* but no harder materials such as porphyry or serpentine.

rossolio, var. ROSOLIO.

ros solis. 2. (Later example.)

1877 E. S. DALLAS *Kettner's Bk. of Table* 21 The Italians..brought with them into France at least two liqueurs—this acqua d'oro with a predominant flavour of rosemary; and rossolis, with a predominant flavour of sundew.

roster, *sb.* Add: Also with pronunc. (rōᵘ·stəɹ).

2. (Later examples.) Also in extended uses.

1930 *New Statesman* 3 May p. iii/1 One particular point is worth noting as to the names in this amazing roster of public enemies. **1942** E. PAUL *Narrow St.* xxxix. 337 Practically the entire roster of the Cagoulards was in the new Vichy Government. **1955** *Railway Mag.* May 365/2 This involves over 300 miles daily and is normally a 4-6-0 steam locomotive roster. **1967** W. W. NEWCOMB *Rock Art of Texas Indians* iv. 38/1 The roster of game animals which could figure prominently in human subsistence is not large. **1971** M. TAK *Truck Talk* 133 *Roster.* When the dispatch department has no immediate assignment for a driver, the driver's name is entered on the dispatch roster. **1978** *Detroit Free Press* 16 Apr. (Detroit Suppl.) 25/3 There he burned up American Association and made Tigers' roster in Spring Training, 1977.

3. *attrib.* and *Comb.*, as *roster-board, game, sheet, system.*

1963 J. LUSBY in B. James *Austral. Short Stories* 233 Thwaites..walked to the roster-board. **1977** *Weekly Times* (Melbourne) 19 Jan. 71/2 Feature of the roster games in the Kentish Cricket Association was the 6–15, including the hat-trick, by Railton's David Castles against Kimberley. **1977** R. LUDLUM *Chancellor MS.* xvii. 184 He kept mementoes... Photographs, roster sheets. **1976** B. JACKSON *Flameout* vii. 122 The roster system played unfair tricks on investigators: you could.. find yourself involved in two [air crash] investigations in three months.

roster (rǫ·stəɹ, rōᵘ·stəɹ), *v.* [f. the sb.] *trans.* To place (someone or something) on a roster.

1922 *Glasgow Herald* 26 Jan. 8 The men can be rostered up to nine hours, with overtime paid after eight hours. **1962** *Mod. Railways* May 350/1 The day Birmingham–Glasgow trains in each direction are now rostered for Type 4 diesel haulage. **1967** *Times Rev. Industry* July 65/2 Even opening on Saturday morning is a vexed question among bank staffs. The board's suggestion that staffs might be rostered..ignores the factors of personal convenience and prestige. **1970** *Railway Mag.* Oct. 561/2 The stud of 'Deltics' is regularly being rostered right up to the limit of locomotives in traffic. **1973** C. MASON *Hostage* ii. 34 Eighteen men..had been rostered on for the two shifts of the guard. **1975** *New Yorker* 13 Oct. 152/3 One of McInally's replacements, Saxon, is rostered at five feet ten and a hundred and forty pounds. **1977** *Daily Tel.* 18 Feb. 2/5, I also found examples where more staff were rostered to work on Sundays than on week-days.

Hence **ro·stered** *ppl. a.*, placed on a roster; assigned in accordance with a roster.

1973 *Daily Tel.* 13 Dec. 2/8 They [*sc.* train drivers] are continuing to do rostered overtime as agreed locally, and are only banning voluntary additional overtime and rest-day working. **1977** *N.Z. Herald* 8 Jan. 2–9/6 (Advt.), Fitter-turners will be required to work alternating shifts or a rostered day work scheme.

rösti, var. *ROESTI.

rostral, *a.* (*sb.*) Add: **4.** *Anat.* (See quot. 1975.)

1894 *Amer. Naturalist* XXVIII. 374 The two ends of the principal axis are respectively 'rostral' instead of 'cephalic' or 'oral' or 'proral'..and..'caudal' [according to Schulze]. *Ibid.* 375 Among Ascidia..there is perhaps a rostral extremity, but there is no caudal extremity in adults. **1953** *Brit. Jrnl. Psychol.* XLIV. 184 The procedures employed were..transorbital leucotomy and thermocoagulation of the cerebral cortex in the rostral portion of the frontal lobes. **1954** T. L. PEELE *Neuroanat. Basis Clin. Neurol.* iv. 39/2 Running transversely across the rostral end of the cerebral peduncles are the optic tracts. **1975** E. GARDNER et al. *Anatomy* (ed. 4) i. 5/2 Rostral means nearer the 'front end', which is taken to be the hypophysical area in the early embryo and the region of the nose and mouth in post-embryonic life.

Hence **ro·strally** *adv.*, towards the rostral part.

1936 *Jrnl. Anat.* LXX. 208 Sagittal serial sections show that rostrally it runs into continuity with the medial preoptic nucleus. **1954** T. L. Peele *Neuroanat. Basis Clin. Neurol.* iv. 38/1 Beginning at the caudal point of transection and proceeding rostrally, the following visible divisions can be made: medulla, pons,..and cerebral hemispheres. **1970** *Brain* XCIII. 42 Most of the degeneration is a little more rostrally situated than in the preceding experiment. **1978** C. Reid *Primer Human Neuroanat.* xvi. 149 A larger area of the reticular formation facilitates or augments reflexes at lower levels and this area extends rostrally through the pons and mid-brain and into the diencephalon.

rostrifacture (rǫ·strifæ:ktiŭɹ). *rare*⁻¹. [f. L. Rostrum beak: after Manufacture *sb.*] A structure made by a bird with its beak.

1884 E. Coues *Key to N. Amer. Birds* (ed. 2) 408 Distinguished as the orioles are for the dexterity and assiduity they display in their elaborate textile rostrifactures [etc.].

rostro-. Add: *rostrocaudally* adv.; **rostroca·rinate** *a. Archæol.*, of or pertaining to stone implements of a keeled and beaked shape, esp. those characteristic of the Oldowan and Sangoan cultures of the African Pleistocene, and to flint objects from the Red Crag deposits of East Anglia, formerly thought to be hand tools of late Pliocene date, but now believed to be natural formations; also *ellipt.* as *sb.*

1912 R. Lankester in *Phil. Trans. R. Soc.* B. CCII. 295 We distinguish..an anterior surface, narrowed to the form of a keel and ending in a beak (hence we call the implement 'rostro-carinate') as a consequence of the oblique direction and convergence of the lateral surfaces, which approach one another so as to leave only a narrow keel-like ridge between them. **1934** *Jrnl. R. Anthrop. Inst.* LXIV. 337 Among these large tools (which were afterwards called Sangoan), a number of well-made rostro-carinate forms is to be distinguished. **1952** *Mem. Geol. Survey Uganda* VI. ii. 64 The most finely finished product is somewhat canoe-like in shape—sharp prow, blunt stern..; the less finished or those not elaborately shaped, rather like a flat bottomed boat or rostrocarinate. **1957** J. K. Charlesworth *Quaternary Era* II. xxxviii. 1016 The Cromerian implements..are ochreous or orange-brown artefacts, often striated as at East Runton. The tools are usually made from heavy flakes but include rostrocarinates and crude Abbevillean forms. **1964** K. P. Oakley *Frameworks for dating Fossil Man* iv. 176 Some [Oldowan flakes] were beak-shaped. [*Note*, p. 263] 'Rostro-carinate', a term which is better avoided since it suggests identification with the flaked flints well known under that name from the Crags of East Anglia which are now regarded to be of natural origin. **1960** *Jrnl. Compar. Neurol.* CXV. 166/2 In the medial nucleus a topographic organization is suggested in which the nucleus has effectively made a 180° rotation rostrocaudally. **1975** *Nature* 17 Apr. 617/2 There is also a gradient, though less steep, rostrocaudally along the eminentia.

rostrum. Add: **1. a.** (Earlier example.)

1542 N. Udall tr. *Erasmus's Apophthegmes* ii. f.315ᵛ, The place called *Rostra* (where oracions wer made to the people).

2. a. (Later example.)

1974 R. Adams *Shardik* xxiv. 186 The rostra, barracoons and blocks of the slave market.

b. Also *transf.*

a **1964** G. Underwood *Pattern of Past* (1968) ix. 96 *Rostra* are sloping recumbent stones, sometimes projecting from a hillside, and sometimes half buried in a slanting position on level ground. At their upper points they mark small terminal blind springs, and their situation and appearance suggests that they may have been intended as pulpits. I have named them accordingly.

d. A platform for a policeman when superintending the traffic at a crossing.

1930 *Morning Post* 16 July 12/5 First and foremost.. there is the constable on the rostrum.

e. *Theatr.* (See quot. 1951.)

1930 W. G. Fay *Short Gloss. Theatr. Terms* 17 When it is necessary to use a rostrum to get elevation on the stage it is generally concealed behind a ground row. *Ibid.* 24 *Ramp*, a slope made of planks from a rostrum to the stage where steps are not used. **1951** *Oxf. Compan. Theatre* 678/1 *Rostrum*, any platform, from a small dais for a throne to a vast battlement, placed on the stage. It is usually made with a removable top and hinged sides, to fold flat for packing. It is reached by steps or a ramp, and quitted off-stage by 'lead-off' steps. A rostrum-front is a canvas-covered flat placed to conceal the front of the platform.

f. *Cinemat.* and *Television.* A platform used to support a camera employed in the filming of animated sequences and the like. Also *attrib.*

1951 Halas & Privett *How to Cartoon for Amateur Films* 105 Let's leave the camera on one side for the moment and consider the *rostrum*. That is the frame on which the camera and the board which holds the animation drawings are mounted. **1959** Halas & Manvell *Technique Film Animation* xix. 235 Such scenes as night bombing, wrecked aircraft, submarines under water and flying through cloud were done with one or two drawings, a little wood-carving, cotton-wool and the full use of single and multiplane shooting on the animation rostrum. *Ibid.*, *Rostrum camera*, apparatus for producing an image on cine-film. Its minimum requirements for animation work are that it must be capable of exposing one frame or film at a time when required. **1975** *Gloss. Terms Motion-Picture Industry* (*B.S.I.*) 9 *Rostrum*, adjustable but rigid support for the camera and the animation table, so constructed that they do not alter position relative to each other in an uncontrolled way. **1976** *Oxf. Compan. Film* 19/2 In the diagram, the camera (a) is shown mounted on the rostrum (US term 'animation stand'). **1977** *Broadcast* 18 Apr. 43/2 Vacancy for aerial image rostrum cameraman.

3. b. *transf.*

1782 H. Walpole *Let.* 18 May (1904) XII. 251 To-day we hear that Sir George Rodney has defeated—ay, and taken—Monsieur de Grasse in his own ship... These naval rostra arrived very opportunely to stay our impatience for a victory over the Dutch.

4. d. (Earlier example.)

1740 J. Grassineau *Mus. Dict.* 205 *Rostrum*, is the name of an instrument wherewith they rule paper for musical compositions.

rosy, *a.* (*sb.*) Add: **1. f.** *slang.* Drunk; tipsy.

1905 *Dialect Notes* III. 17 *Rosy, adj.* Slang. Drunk. **1931** *Princeton Alumni Weekly* 22 May 798/1 When 'the lid is off' one gets 'rosy',..and maybe 'passes out'. **1975** D. Bagley *Snow Tiger* xii. 104 Sure, there was drinking. Some of the boys..got pretty smashed... I was a bit rosy myself.

5. a. rosy apple, (*a*) used in skipping formulas; (*b*) (see quot. 1959²); **rosy-bill,** a South American pochard, *Netta peposaca*, which has a pink bill.

1916 N. Douglas *London Street Games* 64 Rosy apples lemon and a pear A bunch of roses shall she wear. **1959** I. & P. Opie *Lore & Lang. Schoolch.* xv. 339 The skipping formula usually begins.. Rosy apple, lemon tart, Tell me the name of your sweetheart. A, B, C, D, [etc.]. *Ibid.* xviii. 381 There are more than sixty established names for the pursuit of illegally knocking at doors... *Rosy Apple.* Derby. **1964** *Western Folklore* XXIII. 258 Rosy apples, Mama's little tart, Tell the initials Of your sweetheart! **1888** R. Hubbard *Ornamental Waterfowl* ii. v. 162 The Rosy-bill is a native of South America. **1956** G. Durrell *Drunken Forest* i. 16 Rosybills, immaculate in their gleaming black-and-grey plumage, their beaks looking as though they had been freshly dipped in blood. **1976** *Eastern Daily Press* (Norwich) 16 Dec. (Advt.), Sale, pairs black swans, Emperor, Barnacle, Egyptian, Tested, Gadwell, Shelduck, Rosybill, Carolinas, Pintails.

6. *rosy-blue, -gilt, -golden, -mauve, -red* (later example); also, *rosy-pale.*

1862 G. M. Hopkins *Vision of Mermaids* (1929), Which, lightening o'er the body rosy-pale, Like shiver'd rubies dance. **1925** V. Woolf *Common Reader* 115 The apples rosy-gilt in the afternoon sun. **1926** D. H. Lawrence *Sun* iii. 11 The child and she were now both tanned with a rosy-golden tan, all over. **1952** A. G. L. Hellyer *Sanders' Encycl. Gardening* (ed. 22) 94 [*Cattleya*] *Harrisoniana*, light rosy-mauve, variable, summer, autumn. **1956** H. Gold *Man who was not with It* (1965) xi. 89 His hungry mouth, rosy-red with fever. **1976** I. Murdoch *Henry & Cato* i. 3 Leaving New York in daylight, his plane had soon risen into a sort of radiant rosy-blue stratospheric gloom. **1978** *New York* 3 Apr. 94/3 The terrine de poisson, a rosy-pale slice of fish pâté.

7. *rosy-billed, -fleeced, -flowered, -footed* (later example), *-lipped, -muzzled, -petalled, -rayed*; also, *rosy-glistening, -rising, -torturing.*

1876 *Proc. Zool. Soc.* 399 The Rosy-billed Duck has been successfully introduced into Europe. **1936** R. Campbell *Mithraic Emblems* 57 The rosy-fleeced Arrival of the Moon. **1927** V. Woolf *To Lighthouse* i. vii. 63 A rosy-flowered fruit tree. **1928** O. Gogarty *Wild Apples* 8 Fair skin and smooth as the rosy-footed dove's wing! *a* **1918** W. Owen *Poems* (1963) 127 The crunch of boots on blue snow rosy-glistening. **1862** G. M. Hopkins *Vision of Mermaids* (1929), The waves were rosy-lipp'd. **1923** D. H. Lawrence *Birds, Beasts & Flowers* 63 Violets, Pagan, rosy-muzzled violets. **1928** Blunden *Retreat* 44 This retinue Of rosy-petalled sauntering joys. **1925** —— *Eng. Poems* 90 Others like opals rosy-rayed convene. **1916** —— *Pastorals* 19 Nothing Eastern come to us Save the rosy-rising sun. **1929** —— *Near & Far* 19 No rosy-torturing desert.

B. *ellipt.* or as *sb.* **1.** *the rosy* (*a*) (see Dict., sense 1 e); (*b*) blood; (*c*) a good time; phr. *to do the rosy*, to have a good time. *slang.*

1891 *Sporting Life* 25 Mar. 7/3 Goddard was smothered in the rosy as he went to his chair, and Choynski bled at the mouth. **1892** E. J. Milliken *'Arry Ballads* 69/2 A doin' the rorty and rosy as lively as 'Opkins's lot. *Ibid.* 77 Not *my* idea of the rosy.

2. *Naut. slang.* A ship's rubbish-bin.

1937 D. Marlowe *Coming, Sir!* ii. 46, I struggled with the heavy garbage bins, called 'rosies'. **1962** Granville *Dict. Sailors' Slang* 97/2 *The rosy*, the Merchant Navy's *gash bucket*: a 'rose by any other name'. **1966** 'L. Lane' *ABZ of Scouse* 86 *Put a crust on ther Rosy fer 'im*, he has a good appetite. *Rosy*, a ship's swill bin.

Rosy Lee, Rosie Lee (rōᵘ·zi lī·). Also with small initials. Rhyming slang for 'tea'. Also *ellipt.* as **Rosie.**

1925 Fraser & Gibbons *Soldier & Sailor Words* 246 *Rosy Lee*, tea. (Rhyming slang.) **1929** J. B. Priestley *Good Companions* i. iv. 133 'Ow about a drop o' Rosie Lee? *Ibid.* 134 We'll 'ave the Rosie now, George. **1964** A. Prior *Z Cars Again* iv. 35 This is the best cup of rosy I get all day, Janey. **1968** J. Boland *Breakdown* i. 4 Want a drop of rosie, do yer, Dad? **1970** A. Draper *Swansong for Rare Bird* ix. 90 We were having a cup of rosy lee.

rot, *sb.*¹ Add: **5.** (Further examples.) Also used of activities, objects, etc. Also as *int.* Cf. *tommy-rot* s.v. Tommy 6.

1879 M. E. Braddon *Cloven Foot* iv. 96, I thought he despised ballet-dancing. Yet this is the third time I have seen him looking on at this rot. **1880** Henley & Stevenson *Deacon Brodie* iv. 79 Portrait of George as a gay hironmonger... O rot! Hand it over, and keep yourself out of that there thundering moonlight. **1894** G. Moore *Esther Waters* xxxix. 302 All bloody rot; who says I'm drunk? **1905** H. James *Golden Bowl* vi. 74 He had not many things, none of the redundancy of 'rot' they had elsewhere seen. **1914** G. B. Shaw *Fanny's First Play* 158, I quite agree that harlequinades are rot. *a* **1953** E. O'Neill *Long Day's Journey* (1956) i. 35 It's damned rot! I'd like to see anyone influence Edmund more than he wants to be. **1977** C. McCullough *Thorn Birds* ii. 36 'What if it isn't the Eyetie girl?'..'Rot!' said Paddy scornfully.

6. (Earlier and later examples.) Usu. in phrases *the rot set in, to stop the rot.* Now chiefly in extended uses: a decline (in resources, standards, behaviour, etc.).

1868 *J. Lillywhite's Cricketers' Compan.* 61 A terrible 'rot' set in at the commencement of their second 'venture'. **1882** *Australians in Eng.* 71 After the fall of Leslie's wicket, however, a complete 'rot' set in. **1912** P. F. Warner *Eng. v. Austral.* ix. 100 Ransford..had rendered great service to his side by helping to 'stop the rot'. **1926** G. M. Trevelyan *Hist. Eng.* vi. ii. 642 By these all too drastic measures the rot of pauperism was stopped. **1930** J. B. Priestley *Angel Pavement* i. 38 He could not pretend to himself now that such pitiful economies as these could stop the rot. **1938** R. Warner *Professor* v. 113, I really don't know how the rot set in, but the process may have been something like this. **1951** C. P. Snow *Masters* xix. 157 We must take care that a rot doesn't set in. **1955** *Times* 6 June 3/1 The rot began when Appleyard came into the attack. **1958** *Spectator* 22 Aug. 251/1, I have a feeling that, recently, airlines have been allowing this precious asset to depreciate. The rot set in with the introduction of bus fares. **1969** *Listener* 17 July 68/1 The rot set in, I think, with the President's speech to the Air Force Academy at Colorado Springs in June. **1973** M. Woodhouse *Blue Bone* ii. 12, I went up to London..and that, as the saying goes, is where the rot set in.

rot, *v.* Add: **1. e.** *N. Amer.* Of sea or river ice: to melt or thaw. Cf. *Rotten *a.* 4 c.

1892 [implied in Rotting *vbl. sb.*¹]. **1977** *New Yorker* 20 June 86/2 Ice was beginning to rot.

2. b. *slang. to rot about*, to fool about, waste time. Now *rare.*

1902 E. Nesbit *Five Children & It* viii. 198 When we're all rotting about in the usual way heaps of things keep cropping up. **1909** J. R. Ware *Passing Eng.* 211/1 *Rotting about*.., wasting time from place to place. **1927** W. E. Collinson *Contemp. Eng.* 116 'To play the fool' is to rag about, rot about, fool about, play the [giddy] goat, bucket around.

3. a. Also *fig.*, to languish (*in* a place).

1927 *Scribner's Mag.* Feb. 168/1 A man must do something. It's better than rotting in the saloons in Casper. **1975** T. Allbeury *Special Collection* ii. 10 The Moscow Centre has just left them to rot. **1978** I. B. Singer *Shosha* ii. 39, I asked for Dora and he replied 'Rotting in Siberia'.

4. b. Also with *down.*

1912 Galsworthy *Inn of Tranquility* 79 'They don't do a stroke more than they're obliged,' he ended;..'Yes,' he muttered, 'the nation is being rotted down.'

c. (Earlier example.)

1811 *Weekly Reg.* 5 Oct. 86/1 (*heading*) Process for rotting hemp.

d. *slang.* To spoil, interfere with; to ruin. Also const. *up.*

1908 A. S. M. Hutchinson *Once aboard Lugger* vi. viii. 344 You rotted my show all right. **1908** D. Coke *House Prefect* viii. 104 You can see Bob's off you, and we don't want to rot the whole thing up, just when he's begun to be decent again. **1932** 'A. Bridge' *Peking Picnic* xxv. 323 I've got a complex about the whole business, and you know why. Well, that might rot it all up, at any moment. **1973** N. W. Schur *British Self-Taught* 335 To *rot* a plan is to *spoil* it. **1978** *Sunday Times* 15 Jan. 42/7 A turquoise velvet top (detested since I rotted up a quiz programme in it).

7. a. (Further examples.) Also, to abuse, denigrate. Also (in *absol.* use), to joke.

1890 W. E. Henley *Let.* 6 June in J. Connell *W. E. Henley* (1949) vii. 182 He'd have given much to hear you rotting the Alien. **1905** H. A. Vachell *Hill* vii. 155 Has anybody been rotting you? **1914** 'I. Hay' *Lighter Side School Life* vii. 181 We don't do any *work*: we just rot Duck-face. We simply rag his soul out. **1914** G. B. Shaw *Fanny's First Play* iii. 200 But I'm serious: I'm not rotting. Really and truly—. **1922** S. Leslie *Oppidan* iii. 38 A sport taking the mysterious form of 'rotting the Flea'. **1934** R. Macaulay *Going Abroad* xxx. 264 There are things one simply mustn't rot about, I feel.

rota. Add: ‖ **4.** *Mus.* A musical composition which has the form of a round; this form itself. Used esp. of medieval English songs (as 'Sumer is icumen in', where this designation appears in the original manuscript). Cf. Round *sb.*¹ 19 b.

1876 Stainer & Barrett *Dict. Mus. Terms* 381/1 *Rota*.., a Round, but the word is sometimes applied to anything with frequent repeats, as for instance a Hymn tune. **1883** Grove *Dict. Mus.* III. 180/1 It..is written for six voices, four of which sing the round proper or 'rota' (as it is termed in the Latin directions for singing it). **1944** W. Apel *Harvard Dict. Mus.* 652/2 *Rota*,.. medieval name for a round, particularly the Sumer-canon, probably with reference to the 'turnover' of the melody in the different parts. **1955** *New Oxf. Hist. Mus.* (rev. ed.) II. xi. 402 Its form, which is described in the manuscript itself as a *rota*, is that of an infinite canon. **1979** *Early Music* July 391/2 The piece in question is the famous *rota* 'Sumer is icumen in'.

5. *attrib. and Comb.*, as *rota committee, system*; **rota cut**, an interruption or reduction of power or water supplies which is imposed on different areas by rotation in time of shortage. See also sense 1 in Dict.

1935 *Planning* II. XLIV. 13 As much as possible of the actual assessment of need should be left to local rota committees, using the regional scale with fairly wide discretion. **1974** *Times* 15 Feb. 15/2 The third course..is to impose rota cuts designed..to avoid the working days of industry, and..essential services such as hospitals. **1977** *Times* 20 Apr. 5/2 Rota-cuts (when water supplies are cut off for a certain number of hours a day) might appear a less painful alternative than standpipes (involving total cut-off of domestic supplies). **1955** *Times* 25 Aug. 9/6 Only if a six-day shopping week is adopted, with a rota system to give staff a five-day week, will distribution costs be materially increased.

rota-, var. *ROTO-.

rotal, *a.* **3.** (Further example.)

1960 *Tablet* 18 June 586/2 The Rotal sentence referred to by Dr. McReavy relies on the pronouncement of Benedict XIV.

rotamer (rōᵘ·tămǝɹ). *Chem.* [f. ROTA(TIONAL *a.* + *-MER.] Any of a number of distinct conformations of a molecule which can be interconverted by rotation of part of the molecule about a particular bond; a rotational isomer.

1963 *Chem. & Industry* 29 June 1086/1 The single sharp N-methyl signal indicates magnetic averaging of signals and hence very rapid rotamer interconversion even at low temperatures. **1969** *Jrnl. Chem. Soc.* B. 1019/2 The near temperature-invariance of the n.m.r. spectrum over the range studied could be the consequence either of one minimum-energy rotomer being strongly preferred, or of insufficient difference in magnetic shielding at *N*-methyl for different rotamers. **1976** *Nature* 26 Aug. 780/1 The analysis of the side-chain rotamer population..shows that the Met, Phe, and Tyr side chains favour one of the two possible *trans-gauche* rotamers, but for each of these residues all three rotamers have significant populations.

Rotameter (rotæ·mītǝɹ, rōᵘ·tămītǝɹ). Also **rotameter.** [partial tr. G. *rotamesser* (*Chem. Rev. über die Fett- u. Harzind.* (1911) XVIII. 55), f. *rota*(*tion* ROTATION, etc.: see -METER.]

1. A proprietary name for a device with a transparent wall that is fitted into a pipe or tube and indicates the rate of flow of fluid through it.

1911 *Chem. Abstr.* V. 1695 (*heading*) The rotameter. **1914** G. LUNGE *Techn. Gas-Analysis* 50 The 'Rotameter' of the Deutsche Rotawerke, Aachen, allows of directly reading off the quality of gas (or liquid) passing through per hour. **1925** *Industr. Chem.* I. 474/2 In oxy-acetylene welding, if rotameters are inserted in the oxygen and acetylene tubes, it is possible to obtain perfect uniformity. **1949** E. CHAIN in H. W. Florey et al. *Antibiotics* II. xvii. 701 From the air-filter the air passed through a rotameter..and a check-valve..into the fermenter through the sparger. **1952** *Trade Marks Jrnl.* 18 June 555/1 *Rotameter*... Apparatus for measuring, indicating, or recording the rate of flow of gases or liquids. Rotameter Manufacturing Co. Ltd., Derwent Works, Purley Way, Croydon, Surrey; Manufacturers—29th Nov. 1948. **1979** A. L. LYDERSEN *Fluid Flow & Heat Transfer* iii. 61 Standard rotameters are delivered for connection to pipes with diameters from 3 to 150 mm.

2. Var. *ROTOMETER.

rotang. The form **rotan** is now freq. used, as being closer to the Malay. Also *attrib.* of objects made of rotan.

1821 J. LEYDEN tr. *Malay Annals* 124 The whole Siamese army retreated; and, as they took their departure, they threw down large quantities of their baggage rotans in the district of Moar, where they took root. **1927** H. M. TOMLINSON *Gallions Reach* xxxi. 242 The climbing palms, the rotans, flourished about it. **1939** *Geogr. Jrnl.* XCIV. 419 It [*sc.* the nutmeg fruit] falls to the ground with a heavy 'plop', or is gathered in a rotan cage at the end of a long stick. **1954** R. H. HOLTTUM *Plant Life in Malaya* xiii. 186 The most important group of climbing monocotyledons are the Rotans or Rattan canes. **1959** *New Biol.* XXX. 51 The rotan lashings and ladders are renewed annually. **1963** J. KIRKUP *Tropic Temper* 23 The..hall of the hotel was full of bamboo and rotan furniture. **1972** *Straits Times* (Singapore) 28 Nov. 1/2 The Government is bringing in the rotan as a new weapon to fight the drug menace in Singapore.

Rotarian (rotēǝ·riăn), *a.* and *sb.* Also occas. with small initial. [f. ROTARY *a.* and *sb.* + -AN.] **A.** *adj.* Of, pertaining to, or characteristic of the Rotary organization, a Rotary Club, or Rotarians. **B.** *sb.* A member of a Rotary Club. Cf. *ROTARY *a.* 4.

1911 (*title of periodical*) The Rotarian. **1915** *Chicago Herald* 9 Nov. 10/5 The Rotarians will observe 'Moving Picture day' at a luncheon in the crystal room of the Hotel Sherman. **1921** *Glasgow Herald* 10 Feb. 9/4 The President..said the Prince lived out consistently the motto of Rotarians, 'Service, not self'. *Ibid.* 15 June 11/1 An effective programme on education must produce a more intense study of Rotarian literature, a more liberal use of the Rotarian speakers available [etc.]. **1923** R. HERRICK *Homely Lilla* xi. 181 Lilla, on opening the newspapers, often found his name and a brief report of his remarks at a Rotarian lunch. **1928** L. NORTH *Parasites* 270 Rotarians and women's clubs wrote her letters applauding her patriotic stand for home-products. **1931** [see *MAIN STREET, MAIN STREET b]. **1935** G. GREENE *Basement Room* 141 He wouldn't have recognized himself among the rotarians. **1939** W. FORTESCUE *There's Rosemary* lv. 313, I quietly repeated the *rondeau* he had written for the Rotarian garden-party we had so lately given at Admiral's House. **1947** *Britannica Bk. of Year* (U.S.) 704/1 Rotarians throughout the world devoted their programs during the month of November to the United Nations Educational, Scientific and Cultural Organization. **1955** *Times* 9 May 3/2 The father, a pillar of rotarian society, expects the worst and is won over. **1968** M. BRAGG *Without City Wall* xxiv. 225 There, too, was the herd, just as herd-like as the Institutes, Rotarians, Churches, and Social Activators. **1976** *Time* 27 Sept. 30/1 When a Southerner calls his territory 'God's country,' he is less Rotarian than religious. **1978** G. VIDAL *Kalki* iii. 53 Dr. Ashok detached himself from a group of American secret agents (or Rotarians or salesmen).

Hence **Rota·rianism**, the Rotarian system; the way of life held to be characteristic of Rotarians.

1922 *Nation* (N.Y.) 19 Apr. p.v (Advt.), Do you know your state? How it stands in intelligence, rotarianism, bootlegging, evangelism, crime? **1928** *Daily Express* 20 June 2/5 A pantomime symbolising the story of the spread of Rotarianism throughout the world. **1942** BERREY & VAN DEN BARK *Amer. Thes. Slang* §231/1 *Rotarianism*, middle-class propriety.

rotary, *a.* and *sb.* Add: **A.** *adj.* **2. a.** (Further examples.)

1906 *Daily Colonist* (Victoria, B.C.) 6 Jan. 7/3 Big rotary snowplows and gangs of men have been unable to cope with the conditions. **1939** *Archit. Rev.* LXXXV. 76/3 The laundry is all electric, and is equipped with a Rotary Washer and Spin Dryer, and Rotary Ironer. **1960** *Which?* Mar. 48/1 The rotary mower differs from the side-wheel and roller in the way it cuts, which is a chopping action, like a scythe, rather than a shearing action, like a pair of scissors. **1963** R. R. A. HIGHAM *Handbk. Papermaking* ii. 68 Rotary screens may be divided into inward and outward flow types which may be either oscillating or stationary. **1970** *Which?* Mar. 84/2 If you have got long, rough, grass, you will still need a rotary mower. **1977** *Evening Gaz.* (Middlesbrough) 11 Jan. 10/4 (Advt.), Kenwood rotary ironer, excellent condition, £20. **1979** *SLR Camera* June 39/3 Don't put the prints in a conventional flat-bed or rotary dryer designed for drying fibre-based papers.

b. *Printing.* Designating a press in which a cylindrical printing surface is rotated continuously in contact with moving paper, usu. from a web, and the resulting method of printing.

1880 F. J. WILSON *Typogr. Printing Machines* IV. 135 Owing to the speed at which rotary machines are driven, slight difficulties frequently arise. **1899** J. SOUTHWARD *Mod. Printing* III. xvi. 148 Rotary web printing was in England first rendered practicable by engineers employed in the office of *The Times*, who produced the 'Walter Press,' which was completed in 1866. **1926** R. W. POLK *Pract. Printing* xv. 114 There are rotary presses (called sheet-fed rotaries) which print sheets of paper previously cut to size, but most of them print from large rolls of paper which feed a continuous web through the machine at a high rate of speed. **1962** *Penrose Ann.* LVI. 103 It is still too early to predict what the future will hold for the letterpress rotary machine utilizing wrapround plates, **1968** J. R. BIGGS *Basic Typogr.* 80/2 With a rotary press, in which an impression is made at every revolution of the cylinder, very high speeds are possible. **1979** P. G. NEW *Bk. Production* vi. 81 Letterpress..is taking a leaf from litho's book by adopting some of the same techniques, such as rotary printing.

c. Designating or pertaining to a system of drilling, used esp. in drilling for oil, in which the drilling column with the bit attached to it is rotated; *rotary table*, in rotary drilling, a power-driven steel turntable which is attached to the top of the drilling column and serves to rotate it.

1906 B. REDWOOD *Treat. Petroleum* (ed. 2) I. 287 The rotary system, which is in general use in the oil-fields of the coastal plain of Texas, is a modification of that invented by Fauvelle in 1845. *Ibid.* 288 There are three styles of rotary rigs in use. *Ibid.* 289 The lower end of the drilling-rod or casing with the bit attached is passed through the rotary table. **1912** E. H. C. CRAIG *Oil-Finding* viii. 150 Thus through a thick soft argillaceous group it may be found most profitable to use a rotary rig, while drop drills and under-reamers may suit a variable series containing hard calcareous bands. **1939** D. HAGER *Fund. Petroleum Industry* ix. 200 The drill is turned by means of the rotary table. **1944** B. A. BOTKIN *Treas. Amer. Folklore* IV. 493 Rivalries take such subtle forms as the feud between cable-tool drillers and rotary workers in the oil fields. **1974** *Petroleum Rev.* XXVIII. 724/3 Samples may be retrieved by conventional rotary coring. **1974** *BP Shield Internat.* Oct. 18/4 Once it's drilled all the way down to the 'rotary-table', we pull the kelly back, unscrew it, and then make it up to another 30 feet section of pipe.

4. (With capital initial.) Of or pertaining to a world-wide organization of clubs for business and professional men (of which the first, formed in Chicago in 1905, met at each member's premises in rotation) which have the aim of promoting unselfish service and international goodwill. *Rotary Club*, a local branch of this organization.

1910 *Chicago Record-Herald* 10 June 2/4 'The National Association of Rotary Clubs will be one of the most powerful factors in the civic life of the nation,' declared Paul P. Harris... 'Its membership, limited to one man in each line of business,..fighting together in the seventeen largest cities of the country, will be able to win on about any proposition they undertake.' **1921** *Glasgow Herald* 10 Feb. 9/4 Sir Harry Lauder was the guest of honour at a Rotary Club luncheon at the Hotel Cecil, London, yesterday afternoon. *Ibid.* 15 June 11/1 The subjects under consideration included Rotary education, publicity, and business methods. **1930** G. O. THOMAS *Calm Weather* 61 The Rotary Club of which I am a member is very luckily composed of such persons as are engaged in different ways of life, and deputed as it were out of the most conspicuous classes of mankind. **1945** *Business Week* (U.S.) 30 June 44/3 But final decision is to be made..at the next fully attended Rotary convention. **1951** *Britannica Bk. of Year* 558/1 Eleven young men and one young woman nominated by Rotary Clubs in Great Britain and Ireland were awarded Rotary foundation fellowships. **1963** *Sat. Even. Post* (U.S.) 9 Feb. 60/2 A new club adopts the standard Rotary constitution in its native tongue. *Ibid.* 62/3 Rotary volunteers are setting up small-business clinics in backward areas. **1972** T. P. MCMAHON *Issue of Bishop's Blood* xii. 143 He was pudgy, five-seven—the type that would fit at any Rotary luncheon in the country. **1976** *S. Wales Echo* 25 Nov. 20/4 The Rotary Club of Cardiff run a Christmas bargain shop from Tuesday next to Saturday.

5. Special collocations: *rotary camera*, a type of automatic camera, used to photograph documents, in which the subject material is moved automatically past the lens in synchronization with the film; *rotary clothes-drier* or *-line*, an approximately circular clothes line supported by spokes from a central pole and capable of rotation; *rotary converter*, an electric motor adapted for use with either alternating or direct current and capable of converting one to the other; *rotary cutting* or *cut*, a method of making veneer by rotating a log longitudinally against a knife-edge so that a layer of wood is peeled off; hence *rotary-cut* adj.; *rotary cutter*, the apparatus used in this method; (see also sense 2 in Dict.); *rotary engine*, any engine which produces rotary motion or of which the action depends upon the rotation of some part or parts; *spec.* (*a*) an aircraft engine with a fixed crankshaft around which cylinders and propeller rotate; (*b*) a Wankel engine; hence *rotary-engined* adj.; *rotary table*: see sense 2 c above; *rotary-wing*, used *attrib.* to denote any aircraft deriving its lift from aerofoils that rotate, usu. in an approximately horizontal plane.

1955 H. TEN EYCK *Gloss. Terms Microreproduction* 68 *Rotary camera*, any microfilm camera which photographs documents while they are being moved by some form of transport mechanism. **1962** A. GÜNTHER *Microphotogr. in Library* (Unesco) 18 For the production of roll microfilm..there are rotary cameras in which separate original pages and the film move synchronously. **1974** G. G. BAKER et al. *Guide to Production of Microforms* iii. 15 Some rotary cameras have been specially designed to accept continuous line-printout stationery. **1971** *Guardian* 10 Apr. 4/1 (Advt.), Rotary clothes drier with 100 foot line. **1971** *Country Gentlemen's Mag.* May 222/2 Rotary Clothes Lines..offer more line space than the conventional fixed line. **1978** P. PORTER *Cost of Seriousness* 3 A camera, an eye Of memory is recounting inches along from the pea-trellis, The cement-block fence, the rotary clothes-line. **1899** FRANKLIN & WILLIAMSON *Alternating Currents* xiii. 166 An ordinary direct current dynamo may be made into an alternator by providing it with collecting rings..in addition to its commutator. Such a machine is called a rotary converter. *Ibid.* 167 The rotary converter may be used as an ordinary direct-current dynamo or motor. **1934** *Discovery* Nov. 324/2 Their products include D.C. to A.C. rotary converters,..constant current changing dynamos and an entirely portable petrol-driven alternator. **1950** *Times Rev. Industry* Sept. 25/1 One of the first three locomotives is to have a rotary converter set and d.c. motors. **1927** KNIGHT & WULPI *Veneers & Plywood* xvii. 151 The modern methods of manufacturing veneer are practically three-fold, the oldest being sawn, the later, sliced, and the recent, rotary cut. **1974** *Encycl. Brit. Macropædia* XIX. 922/2 More than 90 percent of all veneer is rotary cut... Logs of hard woods, intended for rotary cut or sliced veneer, are softened by submersion in hot water or steam. **1936** *Archit. Rev.* LXXX. 180/3 If you produce your veneers in any required size by the rotary cutter (invented about 1892)..you superimpose something on your materials which is not natural to them according to established standards. **1973** *Materials & Technol.* VI. i. 85 The handling of veneers as they are produced by the rotary cutters varies from factory to factory. **1927** KNIGHT & WULPI *Veneers & Plywood* xvii. 148 There are four ways of converting logs into veneer... If these are to be arranged according to volume of production, rotary cutting will easily stand at the head of the list. **1957** *Encycl. Brit.* XXIII. 42/2 Veneers are also produced by means of the rotary cutting process as a raw material for plywood. **1838** Rotary engine [in Dict., sense 2]. **1887** *Encycl. Brit.* XXII. 516/2 In all rotary engines, with the exception of steam turbines,—where work is done by the kinetic impulse of steam,—there are steam chambers which alternately expand and contract in volume. **1909** *Flying: the Why & Wherefore* x. 91 The recent successes of the seven-cylinder rotary Gnome engine. **1928** C. F. S. Gamble *Story of N. Sea Air Station* xiii. 216 Although rotary engines were falling gradually into disfavour owing to their heavy lubricating-oil consumption, lack of reliability, and large head resistance, one engine was designed during this year—the Bentley Rotary..which gave excellent service in single-seater machines in 1918. **1960** C. H. Gibbs-Smith *Aeroplane* I. viii. 30 In 1887 he [*sc.* Lawrence Hargraves] invented the rotary engine (driven by compressed air) in which the cylinders and propeller revolved about a stationary crankshaft. **1968** S. E. Ellacott *Everyday Things in Eng. 1914–68* xii. 182 The Wankel rotary engine..was on show at Earl's Court in October 1967. **1969** J. D. Storer *Simple Hist. Steam Engine* i. 16 If the water or wind could be replaced by a man-made stream of steam, or hot gases, an ideal rotary engine would result. This type of heat engine is known as a turbine. **1973** H. Jones *Steam Engines* iv. 47 Between 1785 and 1800, Boulton and Watt supplied 110 rotary engines fitted with sun and planet gear to textile mills. **1909** *Westm. Gaz.* 23 Oct. 9/1 Delagrange brought out his rotary-engined Bleriot. **1973** *Times* 28 June 31/2 The Mazda RX3, now the cheapest rotary-engined car at £1,615 in Britain. **1908** Rotary-wing [see *gyropter* s.v. *Gyro-]. **1935** *Jrnl. R. Aeronaut. Soc.* XXXIX. 53 The main objects of this invention is [*sic*] to increase the stability and manœuvrability of helicopter machines, to improve the controllability of rotary wing aircraft to reduce the drag of such aircraft. **1958** *Times* 1 Mar. 7/3 A company engaged in manufacturing rotary wing aircraft is seeking permission to operate a base which would consist of a small platform built over the Thames, connected to an aircraft parking area on the river bank.

B. *sb.* **1.** *spec.* A rotary printing machine or press. (Further examples.)

1926 *Penrose's Ann.* XXVIII. 135 A battery of reel-fed litho. offset rotaries are running most efficiently. **1978** R. Clay in J. Moran *Clays of Bungay* xiii. 145 In 1938 the Company had purchased two old Cottrell sheet-fed rotaries.

2. (With capital initial.) The Rotary organization or its ideals; an individual Rotary Club. *Rotary International*, the official title (since 1922) of the world-wide organization of Rotary Clubs.

1921 *Glasgow Herald* 10 Feb. 9/4 Sir Harry Lauder.. said Rotary was like the lamplighter who came into a dark street. **1922** *Rotarian* May 234/1 No more important question can ever come before a Rotary convention than one which will be discussed at the convention in Los Angeles—a Constitution for International Rotary. **1935** D. Fahey *Mystical Body of Christ in Mod. World* vii. 112 Let us see what attitude the Catholic Church has adopted towards Rotary. **1944** B. Johnson *As Much as I Dare* 275 When the members of the Denver Rotary attend Eastern conventions they wear ten-gallon hats. **1963** *Sat. Even. Post* 9 Feb. 58 Once a mutual-aid society for Midwestern businessmen, Rotary busily promotes peace and good brotherhood on a global scale. **1977** H. Fast *Immigrants* iv. 243 I'm due to speak to Rotary in thirty-five minutes.

3. *U.S.* = *roundabout *sb.* 4 d.

1940 N. Bel Geddes *Magic Motorways* v. 91 Progress around the rotary is slow, for all cars have to weave from lane to lane and are slowed down by the cars feeding in ahead. **1955** *New Yorker* 12 Mar. 38/2 At eight the next morning we came to the first traffic rotary outside New York, in New Jersey. **1966** *PMLA* LXXXI. ii. 11/1 In my lifetime I have seen the *traffic circle* of the Middle Atlantic States become the *rotary* of New England. **1976** A. Cross *Question of Max* i. 15 She executed..several rotaries which seemed specifically designed to enable cars going in opposite directions to meet head-on.

rotatably (rotēi·tăbli), *adv.* [f. Rotatable *a.* + -ly².] In a manner that allows rotation.

1918 H. Seymour *Reproduction of Sound* 263 The stylus 9 is mounted in a lever 10 rotatably supported on a pivot 11.

rotate, *v.* Add: **3.** (Earlier and later examples.)

1861 *Trans Illinois Agric. Soc.* IV. 318 We must rotate crops. **1950** *N.Z. Jrnl. Agric.* Jan. 4/1 By rotating the calves through the paddocks ahead of the cows at intervals of 3 or 4 days. **1980** W. Safire in *N.Y. Times Mag.* 20 Jan. 10/3 She explained, 'We're going to rotate the house and we even rotate the cars. We've been separated for four months, and it's a growing experience.'

5. *U.S. Mil.* (See quot. 1973²: chiefly *pass.*) Also *intr.* for *pass.*

1944 *Yank* 4 Feb. 6 The policy on leaves and furloughs includes provision that individuals who have had two years Alaskan service and who do not desire to be rotated may volunteer for an additional Alaskan tour. **1951** *Sun* (Baltimore) 3 Nov. (B ed.) 6/2 The assurances to G.I.'s in Korea that they would be rotated home were regarded with unmodulated disbelief. **1954** *Britannica Bk. of Year 1953* 354/2 Each side might rotate up to 35,000 men a month on a man-for-man basis. **1973** *Washington Post* 13 Jan. A3/3 You look at an NLF..soldier, who can't..get R and R to Hong Kong, time off in Vungtau, and then rotate in a year back to the States. **1973** J. Quick *Dict. Weapons* 377/2 *Rotate*, to remove a person, crew, unit, or the like from service in an overseas area, from combat service, or from service in a hardship environment and to return such person, crew, or unit to service in the zone of the interior or other less exacting environment. **1976** 'B. Shelby' *Great Pebble Affair* 12 Donnelly and I rotated back to the States together.

rotating, *ppl. a.* **2.** (Further examples in sense 'rotative'.)

1975 *Saturday Night* (Toronto) July–Aug. 18/2 It has been the unions in the public service, not surprisingly, who have perfected the kind of random sniper-fire known as 'selective' strikes or 'rotating' strikes or 'twenty-four-hour' strikes. **1976** *National Observer* (U.S.) 21 Aug. 15/1 Asolo now offers nine plays in rotating repertory from mid-February to Labor Day.

rotation. Add: **1. b.** *Cryst., Math., Physics.* The conceptual operation of turning a system about an axis.

1899 W. J. Lewis *Treat. Crystallogr.* iii. 19 When the least angle which gives interchangeability is 90°, the rotation can be effected four times before the crystal returns to its original position. **1965**, etc. [see *reflection 9*].

c. *Math.* = *curl *sb.* 3 e.

1909 J. G. Coffin *Vector Analysis* v. 117 The operator $\nabla \times$ applied to **F** or curl **F** (read del cross **F** or curl of **F**), also sometimes written in German books, rot **F** (read rotation of **F**), is a new vector derived from **F**. **1911** [see *curl *sb.* 3 e]. **1923** H. Levy tr. *Runge's Vector Analysis* ii. 111 The vector field **f**, when its rotation is not zero, that is, when **f** is not the gradient of a scalar function, leads to a second vector field $\mathbf{g} = \nabla \times \mathbf{f}$. **1972** A. G. Howson *Handbk. Terms Algebra & Anal.* xxxv. 175 In physical applications, curl represents some measure of rotation (older texts often describe curl **f** as the rotation of **f** and denote it by rot **f**).

d. *Statistics.* The mathematical rearrangement of a body of data, regarded as representing a set of points in a space, so that the axes of the space come to lie in directions of particular relevance.

1935 L. L. Thurstone *Vectors of Mind* ix. 222 Each independent rotation may be regarded as a disturbance of a pair of columns in the factorial matrix. **1952** R. B. Cattell *Factor Analysis* xxi. 411 A great advance in speed in rotation processes is available now through the I.B.M. multiplier (a rotation of a 15 × 18 factor matrix can be done in a day). **1972** *Jrnl. Social Psychol.* LXXXVII. 69 Rotation to simple structure was made for five factors in each case, though not all five could be interpreted.

2. d. *Forestry.* The cycle of planting, felling, and replanting; the period of this, the (actual or planned) time between the formation or regeneration of a crop and its felling.

1888 E. E. Fernandez *Man. Indian Sylviculture* i. 6 The existence of a rotation implies the more or less simultaneous appearance of the old generation, and a similarly more or less simultaneous removal of that generation and the appearance of the new one. There can hence be no rotation in the case of selection-worked forests. **1889** W. Schlich *Man. Forestry* I. ii. ii. 170 The selection of the rotation..should be so fixed under the method of natural regeneration as to admit of a proper regeneration of the wood, whether by seed or coppice shoots. **1890** [see sense 2 a in Dict.]. **1927** *Forestry* I. 101 A more detailed investigation of the returns from quality class V forests showed that at 100 years (the financial rotation) the yield was 1.06 per cent., and at 120 years (the more usual rotation) it was 1.03 per cent. **1938** G. S. Cansdale et al. *Black Poplars* 9 The poplar is essentially a tree to be grown on short rotation. **1977** M. Clawson *Decision Making in Timber Production* 26 For many sites, the earnings from the next rotation of timber growing are highly speculative or dubious, partly because it is so far in the future.

3. *rotation axis, group*; *rotation-like* adj.

1903 Rotation axis [see *holoaxial* s.v. *holo-]. **1971** I. G. Gass et al. *Understanding Earth* i. 19/1 The stereogram of zircon..shows a four-fold rotation axis in the centre and also shows a number of reflection planes. **1974** G. Reece tr. *Hund's Hist. Quantum Theory* xiii. 177 These two-valued representations of the rotation group had been discovered by Hermann Weyl. **1952** Dylan Thomas *Let.* 11 Dec. (1966) 388 It was, I think, originally a little 'organ'..full of rotation-like gossip.

rotational, *a.* Add: **2.** *Physics.* Of, pertaining to, or designating the (quantized) energy possessed by molecules, etc., by virtue of their rotation.

1914 *Chem. Abstr.* VIII. 859 According to the quantum hypothesis the rotational energy of a mol[ecule] varies discontinuously, from which it follows that a band is made up of a series of lines whose vibration difference is a measure of the moment of inertia of a mol[ecule]. **1939** J. W. T. Spinks tr. *G. Herzberg's Molecular Spectra* I. iii. 72 The rotational quantum number *J*..gives approximately the angular momentum in units $h/2\pi$. **1950** W. J. Moore *Physical Chem.* xi. 327 A set of closely packed rotational levels is associated with each of these vibrational levels. **1973** C. Sagan *Cosmic Connection* (1974) iv. 27 Molecules undergo rotational transitions, due to the free rotation of the molecule. **1978** P. W. Atkins *Physical Chem.* xvii. 561 According to the gross selection rule, methane cannot give a rotational Raman spectrum, whereas the hydrogen molecule, and any other diatomic..can.

3. *Agric.* Applied to methods of land management in which animals are grazed on successive areas of land in turn, so that each area is empty for a time after having been grazed.

1931 H. E. Woodman et al. in *Jrnl. Agric. Sci.* XXI. 267 It may be inferred that a similar result would follow from a system of rotational grazing, where the pasture enclosures, after being closely grazed, are permitted a 3-weeks' interval of unchecked growth before being grazed again. **1950** *N.Z. Jrnl. Agric.* Apr. 307/1 Rotational cropping is now an excellent fertility builder. **1967** C. D. Blake et al. *Fundamentals Mod. Agric.* ix. 208/1 In the broad sense, rotational grazing is any system of handling animals which involves holding them for short periods on small sections of the total area of an available pasture and then regularly moving them, as a group, to other sections of the whole area. There is an infinite number of rotational grazing systems available.

rota·tionally, *adv.* [f. prec. + -ly².] In a rotational manner; by or with respect to rotation.

1894 *Phil. Trans. R. Soc.* A. CLXXXV. 817 A simple theory of free electrons in a rotationally fluid æther. **1946** *Nature* 3 Aug. 176/1 These velocities are so high that rotationally stable stars cannot be formed unless one of two conditions is fulfilled. **1950** *N.Z. Jrnl. Agric.* Jan. 4/2 Calves which are rotationally grazed. **1976** *Physics Bull.* July 292/2 Eddies of rotationally dominated turbulence. **1978** *Sci. Amer.* Jan. 122/3 The four letters p, b, d and q are rotationally similar.

rotativism (rōu·tătiviz'm, rotēi·t-). [f. Rotative *a.* + -ism.] A system whereby different political parties hold office in turn according to a pre-arranged plan.

1908 *Sun* (N.Y.) 3 Feb. 2/1 Each party held office by arrangement alternately. This arrangement was known as rotativism. **1921** *Edin. Rev.* Jan. 158 The country must in effect sink back into the slough of 'rotativism'. **1960** W. C. Atkinson *Hist. Spain & Portugal* xiii. 313 The system in Portugal was known as rotativism. **1969** I. Gilmour *Body Politic* I. i. 55 The party struggle was also a stage fight in Portugal, where the parties agreed under a system called rotativism to alternate in office.

rotativist (rōu·tătivist, rotēi·t-), *a.* (and *sb.*) [f. as prec. + -ist.] **1.** Of, pertaining to, or characterized by rotativism in politics. Also *ellipt.* as *sb.* Also *transf.*

1909 *Spectator* 12 June 918/2 The late King [of Portugal] yielded to the intrigues of the 'rotativist' parties. **1917** G. Young *Portugal* vi. 217 The collapse of the Portuguese colonial empire must come with the continuance of the struggle between rotativist Royalism and revolutionary Republicanism. **1926** *Glasgow Herald* 24 Dec. 4/7 They recalled the indifference of the electorate on the frequent occasions of general elections by order of the Rotativists. **1929** *Camb. Anc. Hist.* (ed. 2) III. 253 A regular 'rotativist' arrangement made by the son of Smendes with the Thebans by which he was to be succeeded by the Theban high-priest..and he again by a Tanite.

2. That relates to rotative movement. *rare.*

1939 A. J. Toynbee *Study of Hist.* VI. 173 Stoic and Epicurean philosophers who apparently were not put out by the incongruity between their rotativist conception of the nature of Reality and their ethical aim of Detachment.

rotator. Add: **2. a.** (Further examples.)

1930 *Jrnl. Sci. Instruments* VII. 22 It is necessary, for the purposes of wool examination, to be able..to examine the filament completely at any point by rotating it through 360°, and for this purpose a fibre rotator has been designed. **1967** *Stain Technol.* XLII. 107 The rotator consists of a 12 inch disc to which 8 glass jars.. are held firmly... It is rotated by means of a rubber belt driven by a small electric motor. **1971** *Sci Amer.* July 85/2 Perhaps a much more massive rotating object in the core of a galaxy could account for the existence of quasars. In these models the rotator must have a mass of about a billion solar masses. **1977** *Lancet* 28 May 1150/2 This allows rapid separation of antibody-bound from free T_3/T_4 by simple inversion of the assay tubes in a rotator.

b. A device for rotating an aerial.

1959 *Sears, Roebuck Catal.* Spring/Summer 884/2 TV Antenna Rotators... Turns antenna 360° per min. **1970** *Globe & Mail* (Toronto) 28 Sept. 30/4 (Advt.), Al's TV, towers, color, rotator, U.H.F., Channel 17 installed. **1974** Harvey & Bohlman *Stereo F.M. Radio Handbk.* vii. 163 For long-distance (DX) reception an aerial amplifier and/or aerial rotator are useful accessories to a high gain aerial in extracting the largest possible signal to drive the receiver into full amplitude limiting. **1977** *Gramophone* Nov. 965/1 Feeding the tuner/amplifier from a four-element J-Beam FM aerial mounted on a rotator, it was possible to receive several continental FM stations in mid-Surrey.

rotavate, rotovate (rōu·tăvēit, rōu·to-), *v.* [Back-formation from next.] *trans.* To prepare (a field, garden, etc.) with a Rotavator; to work (a substance) into the soil by means of a Rotavator. Hence **ro·ta-, ro·tovating** *vbl. sb.*; **ro·ta-, ro·tovation.**

1959 *Birmingham Post* 10 June 1/1 A new allotment.. had been 'adequately fenced, roadways constructed and the site ploughed and rotavated'. **1960** *Farmer & Stockbreeder* 26 Jan. 78/3 It is not claimed that Rotavation is suitable for all cultivations, all the time, in all soils. **1962** *Times* 11 Apr. 24/3 Garden rotovated. **1962** *Times* 3 Dec. (Agric. Suppl.) p.vii/5 The usual procedure..is to rotavate the dead herbage. **1971** *Nature* 13 Aug. 446/2 The British Ministry of Agriculture suffered some criticism for suggesting that the best way of disposing of surplus and unwanted DDT..was to rotovate it into the soil. **1977** *Jersey Even. Post* 26 July 24/6 (Advt.), Subsoiling and rotovating undertaken at competitive rates. **1978** *Rescue News* Summer 4/2 Methods of working peat include rotovation.

Rotavator, Rotovator (rōu·tăvēitəɹ, rōu·to-). Also with small initials. [f. Rot(ary *a.* + Culti)vator; see *roto-.] Proprietary names of a machine with rotating blades designed to break up or till soil.

1936 *Trade Marks Jrnl.* 1 July 808 Rotavator... Ploughs, cultivators, diggers, harrows and hoes, all being agricultural machines. Rotary Cultivators Limited. **1951** *Official Gaz.* (U.S. Patent Office) 13 Mar. 362/2 Rotary Hoes Limited, East Horndon, England. Filed Dec. 27, 1949. *Rotavator*... For ploughs, cultivators, diggers, harrows, and hoes. **1954** *Encounter* Dec. 31/2 Nobody said..that it was a handicap to have a holding so large you could *choose between* a rotavator and a proper tractor. **1959** *Times* 13 Mar. 6/6 Mr. Merricks then bid £5 and the Rotovator was knocked down to him. **1963** *Times* 17 Jan. 3/7 The machine, a 'Rotavator', breaks up the packed snow and ice into powder, so that it can be swept away. The machine has been used on Watford's football ground and there are plans to use it at racecourses. **1970** T. HUGHES *Crow* 31 The woodpecker drummed clear of the rotovator. **1971** 'S. SMITH' *Grave Affair* vii. 102 They went back to the farm for the rotavator to break up the soil. **1977** *Trade Marks Jrnl.* 21 Sept. 1895/1 *Rotovator*... Agricultural machinery and power operated agricultural implements. **1978** *Morecambe Guardian* 14 Mar. 22/3 (Advt.), Agrotiller and Landmaster Rotovators.

rotavirus (rō͞u·tăvəiᵊrɒs). *Biol.* [mod. L., f. L. *rota* wheel + VIRUS.] Any one of a genus of wheel-shaped double-stranded RNA viruses.

1974 T. H. FLEWITT et al. in *Lancet* 13 July 61/1 Since these viruses differ morphologically both from reoviruses and orbiviruses, the name 'rotavirus' is suggested for them. **1977** *Lancet* 11 June 1263/2 Rotaviruses cause acute enteritis in man and animals. **1977** *Rec. Adv. Clin. Virol.* I. 158 Rotaviruses differ both in size and shape from the reoviruses... They resemble orbiviruses in the appearance of rings..seen on some particles..; but the [rotavirus] diarrhoea viruses also differ from the orbiviruses in their smooth outline. **1979** *Brit. Med. Jrnl.* 15 Dec. 1551/1 Rotavirus infection is the commonest cause of acute non-bacterial gastroenteritis in infancy and childhood.

R.O.T.C., ROTC (rǫ·tsi; *also* āɹ,ō͞u,tī,sī). *U.S.* [Acronym f. the initials of *R*eserve *O*fficers' *T*raining *C*orps.] A military division with units established at civilian educational centres to qualify students for appointment as reserve officers.

1916 *N.Y. Times* 27 Dec. 6/1 The cap ornament for members of the Reserve Officers' Training Corps is to consist of a wreath inclosing the letters R.O.T.C. **1919** [see *DRIP *sb.* 3 b]. **1925** *Scribner's Mag.* July 15/2 He goes to the R.O.T.C. and prepares himself for a berth in the adjutant-general's office. **1936** *N.Y. Herald Tribune* 1 June 17/3 (*heading*) Flint defends the R.O.T.C. in Syracuse talks. **1959** N. MAILER *Advts. for Myself* (1961) I. 35 He had been allowed to go to this university only on the agreement..that he..was to join the R.O.T.C. and to remain in it until after graduation. **1974** *Hartsville* (S. Carolina) *Messenger* 22 Apr. 2-A/8 Early in the school year he went to Myrtle Beach Air Force Base for a military physical that was sent to all the academics and to the ROTC headquarters. **1975** *Publishers Weekly* 26 May 57/1 Out of his campus experiences he examines ROTC from the academic viewpoint. He ponders the fairness of grading prospective draftees.

rote, *sb.*² Add: **3.** *rote-like* adj.; **rote learning** (further examples); also *spec.* in *Psychol.*, the learning by rote of meaningless material designed to be free of associations, as a technique in the study of learning.

1914 *Brit. Jrnl. Psychol.* VII. 253 (*title*) The value of distributed repetitions in rote learning. **1940** G. KATONA *Organizing & Memorizing* vii. 164 We shall study the classic material used in investigating the memory, that is, rote learning of nonsense syllables. **1970** *Jrnl. Gen. Psychol.* LXXXII. 54 The similarity of the present results to those in the rote literature argues against the sharp distinction drawn between meaningful and rote learning by Ausubel. **1954** W. FAULKNER *Fable* 35 He said, repeated, rote-like, cold, unemphasised, almost telegraphic: 'Comité des Forges'.

rote, *sb.*⁶ (Further examples.)

1909 *Newfoundland Q.* Dec. 9/1 The fishermen are accustomed, in foggy weather, to find their bearings by carefully listening to the rout of the sea on the shore, which they (very correctly) call rote, or rut. **1941** T. S. ELIOT *Dry Salvages* i. 8 The menace and caress of wave that breaks on water, The distant rote in the granite teeth. **1965** S. E. MORISON in *Amer. Neptune* Oct. 236 Often have I heard a Maine man say, 'Sea's making up. Hear that rote!' *Ibid.*, T. S. Eliot doubtless listened to the rote from his parents' house, during the windless calm after a storm, or on a 'weather-breeder' day when swells from the eastward begin crashing on the 'granite teeth' of Cape Ann before a storm breaks.

rotenone (rō͞u·tĕnō͞un). *Chem.* Orig. †**-on.** [ad. Jap. *rotenon* (K. Nagai 1902, in *Jrnl. Tokyo Chem. Soc.* XXIII. 753), f. *roten* derris: see -ONE.] A toxic crystalline polycyclic ketone, $C_{23}H_{22}O_6$, obtained from the roots of several species of plant (notably derris, cubé, and timbo), which is widely employed as an insecticide in the form of a powder or an emulsified spray. Also as *v. trans.*, to treat with rotenone.

1924 *Chem. Abstr.* XVIII. 408 From air-dried roots, 0·93% crude rotenon is obtained which is mixed with waxy impurities. **1925** *Ibid.* XIX. 1708 Further analysis of rotenone, an active insecticidal principle of the root of *Derris elliptica* Benth. **1962** GORDON & LAVOIPIERRE *Entomol.* ix. 57 Fine dusts containing pyrethrum or rotenone are highly successful when employed against various insects such as fleas and lice. **1975** *New Yorker* 19 May 45/3 We poison out a small reef by squirting in emulsified rotenone, a chemical poison derived from the root of a South American plant called cubé, originally used by Indians for fishing. *Ibid.* 46/1 You rotenone a reef, and for the next hour or two you pick the samplings up. **1977** LEWIS & ELVIN-LEWIS *Med. Bot.* ii. 45 *Tephrosia cinerea*, yielding rotenone and the toxic principle tephrosin, is used in Venezuela and Africa as a fish poison.

rot-gut, rotgut. Add: **1.** (Further examples.)

1911 E. M. CLOWES *On Wallaby* vi. 164 The cattle-men, shearers, and shepherds get their internal machinery completely ruined in time by the quantity of inferior boiled sugar and fruit that they consume, and which they have inelegantly christened 'rot-gut'. **1923** C. E. MULFORD *Black Buttes* xiv. 220 Yes, even a drink of rot-gut would 'a' bought you! **1939** JOYCE *Finnegans Wake* (1964) 381 And suck up..whatever surplus rotgut, sorra much, was left by the lazy lousers of maltknights and beerchurls. **1946** *Time* 7 Oct. 10/2 For 50 years we have been hearing how the drought-smitten Jayhawkers were poisoning themselves on bootleg rotgut because we couldn't get decent liquor. **1952** E. O'NEILL *Moon for Misbegotten* IV. 173 That isn't Phil's rotgut. That's real, honest-to-God bonded Bourbon. **1969** *Private Eye* 4 July 14/3 But don't drink that rotgut. Here warm your gizzard with a tot of rum from my flask. **1976** *Times* 8 July 16/4 It was being killed mercilessly by the whisky posts with their rotgut.

2. (Further examples.) Also *transf.* and *fig.*

1877 H. RUEDE *Let.* 24 Apr. in *Sod-House Days* (1937) 57 They have a brand called 'Old Style', some of Catlin's (St. Louis) cheap rotgut tobacco, and from that price up. **1927** L. BROMFIELD *Good Woman* xiii. 140 A glass filled many times with the rot-gut whisky that Hennessy sold. **1948** F. BLAKE *Johnny Christmas* I. 5 Not a man in that line but hated Santa Ana and his Mexicans, hated their talk, the way they killed, their rot-gut laughter. **1970** J. HOWARD *Please Touch* 6 Many kinds of wine: sweet, dry, nutty, fruity, insouciant, rotgut, presumptuous and noble. **1978** *Sunday Times* (Colour Suppl.) 18 June 42/3 Traders stack their boats with liquor, rotgut whisky and cachaca, cheap spirit.

rother-beast. For *Obs.* read '*Obs.* exc. *arch.*' and add later examples.

1836 in A. R. Stedman *Marlborough & Upper Kennet Country* (1960) xxvii. 270 No burgess shall keep on the common more than two rother beasts... that is to say, kine or bullocks. **1933** *Catholic Bull.* Mar. 215 Let us read over again the overwhelmingly impressive reasonings of this great among the greatest pontiffs, then contrast the fruits of imperial connection, of Masonry, of that trade in pasturing and larding the sides of rother-beasts, to champion which the Knight of the Ranchers..has couched his lance.

Rothschild (rǫ·þstʃəild). [Name of Mayer Amschel *Rothschild* (1744–1812) of Frankfurt, and his descendants, proprietors of an international banking firm.] **1.** One who resembles a member of the Rothschild family in being exceptionally rich; a millionaire. Also in colloq. phr. *to come the Rothschild*: to pretend to be rich (see COME *v.* 28 c).

1833 CARLYLE *Sart. Res.* I. v, in *Fraser's Mag.* VIII. 670/2 All miracles have been out-miracled for there are Rothschilds and English National Debts. **1850** E. RUSKIN *Let.* 18 Apr. in M. Lutyens *Effie in Venice* (1965) I. 167 We..called on Madame Chabrillan who is married to the Rothschild of the family. **1863** GEO. ELIOT *Romola* I. I. 74 The Bardi..[were] standing in the very front of European commerce—the Christian Rothschilds of that time. **1885** H. JAMES *Little Tour in France* xii. 92 Jacques Coeur..was a Vanderbilt or Rothschild of the fifteenth century. **1893** W. S. GILBERT *Utopia* (*Limited*) I. 32 Though a Rothschild you may be..As a company you've come to utter sorrow. **1905** FARMER & HENLEY *Dict. Slang* 111/2 *To come the Rothschild*, to pretend to be rich. **1910** W. J. LOCKE *Simon* xvi. 221, I had wealth—not a Rothschild or Vanderbilt fortune but enough to assure me ease and luxury. **1938** [see *ROCKEFELLER]. **1974** J. GARDNER *Return of Moriarty* 57 A relatively young whore, Mary Jane Kelly, who sometimes came the Rothschild about her past, calling herself Marie Jeannette Kelly.

2. as *adj.* See *MOUTON ROTHSCHILD.

‖ **rôti**¹ (roti). [Fr.] In *Gastronomy*, a main course consisting of roasted meat; (a dish of) roasted meat. Also as *adj.* (with preceding sb.) and *Comb.*

1771 SMOLLETT *Humph. Cl.* III. 143 The rotis were scorched and stinking, for the honour of the fumet. **1806** J. PINKERTON *Recoll. Paris* II. vi. 102 Upon the appearance of the *roti*, the ordinary wine is changed for the richer kinds of Burgundy or Bordeaux. **1841** THACKERAY *Mem. Gourmandizing* in *Fraser's Mag.* XXIII. 714/1 Saddle of mutton rôti. **1864** MRS. GASKELL *French Life* in *Fraser's Mag.* LXIX. 440/2 The rôti and the salad follow. **1906** MRS. BEETON *Bk. Househ. Managem.* lxii. 1669 *Rôti* (Fr.), the roast..the course of a meal which is served before the entremets. **1951** *Good Housek. Home Encycl.* 639/1 *Rôti*, the meat, poultry or game course in a dinner. **1980** G. GREENE *Dr. Fischer* xvi. 114 With the Mouton Rothschild there was a *rôti de boeuf*.

‖ **roti**² (roti). [a. Hindi, Urdu *roṭī* bread, ROOTY.] A cake of unleavened bread of a type originating in India. (Now also current in the W. Indies.)

1920 *Chambers's Jrnl.* 29 May 407/1 What are two hours to an Indian peasant? They had had their *roti* (bread), and, the stomach being full, having to wait was a small matter. **1952** [see *JOHNNY-CAKE a]. **1958** J. CAREW *Black Midas* vi. 98 We bought fruit and roti from peddlers on the stelling. **1971** *Leader* (Durban) 7 May 9/1 (Advt.), Only the best is good enough... That's why I use only Bakers Homo Flour for my roti. **1971** *Advocate-News* (Barbados) 17 Sept. 6/4 Among the specialties to be presented to Barbadians by the Roti Shop are chicken, beef and shrimp roti, dholl puri and potato roti. **1974** *Socialist Worker* 9 Nov. 8/3 The starving stream in from all directions to receive a roti (a thin flat piece of bread) or perhaps two if they are lucky. **1976** *Sunday Standard* (Bombay) 11 July 4/3 Roti, the unleavened bread, is the stuff of our lives.

rotisserie (rō͞utĭ·səri). orig. *U.S.* Also **rôtisserie.** [a. F. *rôtisserie*, f. *rôtiss-*, stem of *rôtir* to roast + *-erie* -ERY.] **1.** A restaurant where meat is roasted or barbecued, freq. at a grill in the front window.

1868 *Overland Monthly* Nov. 470/1 At some of these French houses, especially designated as *rotisseriés* [*sic*], the kitchen is nominally open to inspection. **1914** S. LEWIS *Our Mr. Wrenn* i. 15 A rôtisserie, before whose upright fender of scarlet coals whole ducks were happily roasting to a shiny brown. **1925** *Restaurant News & Managem.* Dec. 10 (*caption*) An instance of successful catering to business and professional people The Rotisserie Inn, Salt Lake City. **1936** MENCKEN *Amer. Lang.* (ed. 4) 215 *Rôtisserie*, with the accent omitted, seems to be an Americanism. It signifies an eating-house wherein chickens and butcher's meat are roasted at a charcoal-grill, usually in the show-window of the establishment.

2. A cooking appliance which has a rotating spit for roasting and barbecuing meat. Also *attrib.* and *Comb.*

1953 *Home Beautiful* Apr. 133 Cooking on a rotating spit or rotisserie is high gourmet cooking. **1953** J. & M. ROBERTSON *Compl. Small Appliance Cookbk.* ii. 37 Rotisserie heat is *beside* or *above* the revolving food. *Ibid.* ii. 42 Serve with rotisserie-browned potatoes. **1960** *Guardian* 17 Mar. 9/4 All the glittering machines, the washers, the electric rotisseries. **1969** *Daily Colonist* (Victoria, B.C.) 6 Dec. 40/1 They borrowed a commercial rotisserie, got the charcoal white hot, and loaded the apparatus with 200 pounds of wild boar. **1973** *Times* 30 July 11/1 Rôtisserie spits, continuous cleaning ovens, the use of colour..these and other innovations.. are maintaining..the popularity of the gas cooker. **1978** *Lancashire Life* Apr. 125/3 There are, in fact, three variations of this cooker, the most expensive one having a built-in rotisserie and kebab attachments.

Hence (as a back-formation) **roti·ss(e)** *v. trans.* and *intr.*, to cook meat on a rotisserie; **roti·ssed** *ppl. a.*, **roti·ssing** *vbl. sb.*

1958 *Word Study* Dec. 5/1 The manufacturer has created the verb 'rotiss'. *Ibid.* 5/2 The housewife is advised to set her pointer according to what meat is being 'rotissed', and is informed that she needn't preheat when 'broiling or rotissing'. *a* **1963** P. BRACKEN *I hate to housekeep Bk.* (1969) viii. 72 She is a little scared of the rotisserie in her new double oven, so she continues to buy her chickens ready-rotissed. **1978** *Verbatim* Feb. 1/2 One San Francisco appliance dealer boasts of a stove which will not only roast and broil, it will also *rotisse*!

Rotissomat (rō͞utī·somæt). [f. *ROTISS(ERIE + -O + *-MAT.] The proprietary name of a commercial automatic cooking appliance with rotating spits for roasting meat.

1947 *Official Gaz.* (U.S. Patent Office) 8 July 187/1 Rotiss-o-mat Corporation, Astoria, Long Island, N.Y. *Rotiss-o-mat for electric rotisseries.* Claims use since January 1946. **1958** *Trade Marks Jrnl.* 9 Apr. 372/2 *Rotiss-o-mat*... Electric installations for cooking poultry and parts of such installations included in Class II. Harley Manufacturing Corporation..New York. **1960** *Observer* 13 Nov. 3/3 Chicken restaurants depend on a shiny piece of plant called a 'rotissomat', invented by the American, Sol Leder. **1961** *Times* 24 July 13/5 An Oxford supermarket has a rotissomat. **1963** M. BEADLE *These Ruins are Inhabited* xi. 160 The one near me on the London Road has installed a rotissomat.

roto (rō͞u·to). *N. Amer.* Abbrev. of *ROTOGRAVURE 2, an illustrated or pictorial (section of a) newspaper or magazine.

1932 G. A. CHAPPELL *Evil through Ages* v. 70 To-day our Sunday illustrated sections are taken up by wives and mothers..who sign testimonials, exhibit dogs, dress up as colonial dames, anything to get into the rotos. **1942** BERREY & VAN DEN BARK *Amer. Thes. Slang* §522/17 *Rotogravure section*, roto, rotogravure, roto section. **1975** *Boston Globe* 22 Feb. 7/3 (Advt.), The Bride: a special roto magazine devoted to the newlyweds and soon-to-be-weds of '75 this Sunday in The Boston Globe. **1978** *Amer. Poetry Rev.* Nov./Dec. 30/1 He was writing for the roto section of a Sunday newspaper. **1979** *Globe & Mail* (Toronto) 25 Jan. 7/3 A few publications such as Chatelaine and the rotos—Weekend and the Canadian—slept right through it, as far as ad revenues were concerned.

roto- (rō͞u·to-), in some words also *rota-*, comb. form of L. *rōta* wheel, roller and Eng. ROTARY *a.*, ROTATION, etc., as in ROTOGRAPH, *ROTOCHUTE, etc.

rotochute (rō͞u·toʃūt). [f. *ROTO- + PARA)-CHUTE *sb.*] A mechanical device with rotating blades which can be attached to objects dropped from a great height so as to slow their fall.

1949 *Jrnl. Brit. Interplanetary Soc.* VIII. 139 A new type 'high-speed' parachute, intended for use in retrieving recording equipment from high-altitude rockets, was tested recently... Ordinary parachutes were ripped to shreds after falling free into the denser atmosphere... Expelled from A-4 rockets at altitudes up to 100 miles.., the rotochute attains supersonic velocity before atmospheric density builds up and the blades begin to revolve, gradually being forced out against air pressure to assume a horizontal position. **1955** *Sci. News Let.* 5 Mar. 160/3 Supplies can now be dropped to troops from low altitudes by a 'rotochute', a bomb-shaped device with rotor blades to slow the descent. **1962** *Aeroplane* CII. 45/2 In the recovery of space vehicles, the 'rotochute' is capable—according to this company—of satisfying three basic requirements not easily met in a single recovery system.

Rotodyne (rōᵘ·todəin). Also **Rotadyne** (rōᵘ·tă-). [f. *ROTO- + *-DYNE.] A proprietary name of an aircraft equipped with rotors, capable of vertical take-off and rapid flight.

1949 *Trade Marks Jrnl.* 17 Aug. 727/1 *Rotadyne* 676,644. Rotary wing aircraft. The Fairey Aviation Company Limited,..Hayes, Middlesex. *Ibid., Rotodyne* 676,645... To be associated with No. 676,644. **1958** *Times* 9 Nov. 4/4 The..Rotodyne, the world's first vertical take-off and landing airliner. **1959** [see *ASSAULT *sb.* 8]. **1959** [see *CONVERTIPLANE].

rotogravure (rōᵘ:to,grăviūᵊ·ɹ). *Printing.* Also ‖**rotogravur**, †**rotagravure**, and with capital initial. [orig. the name of the *Rotogravur* Deutsche Tiefdrück Gesellschaft (Berlin), said to be f. the names of two other companies, *Roto*phot (Berlin) and Deutsche Photo*gravur* AG (Siegburg), adopted in Eng. with assimilation of the ending to that of PHOTOGRAVURE. The form *rotagravure* (in sense 1) is an etymologizing re-formation f. L. *rota* wheel, roller + PHOTO)GRAVURE or F. *gravure* engraving.] **1.** A method of printing by means of a rotary press with intaglio cylinders, usu. used at high speed for long print runs.

1913 *Photography* 7 Jan. 2/1 The half-tone block..has advantages for certain purposes which it does not share.. with Rotogravure. **1913** *Illustr. London News* 8 Feb. (Suppl.) p. iii/1 The rotogravur method is that more generally called the carbon. **1914** *N.Y. Times* 29 Mar. 11/1 Advance copies of the rotogravure section of *The Times* of next Sunday..awakened enthusiasm. This is the first rotogravure section to be printed upon the new rotogravure presses of *The Times*, and it contains thirty-eight additional famous paintings from the Altman collection. **1919** S. H. MORGAN in *Inland Printer* July 407/1 The proper name for the process and its product is 'rotary photogravure', and it is quite natural that in these busy times there would be an effort to abbreviate these two words. So why not use..'rota', meaning a wheel or roll, and 'gravure',..and by combining the two call it 'rotagravure' hereafter? **1940** *Chambers's Techn. Dict.* 731/1 Rotagravure. **1942** J. STEINBECK *Moon is Down* ii. 29 Lieutenant Prackle took from his pocket a folded rotogravure page and he unfolded it and held it up and looked at it. It was a picture of a girl. **1957** *Gravure* Mar. 38/3 The first use of rotogravure in a periodical occurred in 1897, when a gravure illustration was included with an article by W. Burger describing the Castle Kreuzenstein, and which appeared in the monthly bulletin of the Imperial Austrian Museum of Art and Industry. **1972** *Physics Bull.* Sept. 532/2 For high quality colour work with long runs (one million or more) rotogravure printing is universally used.

2. A sheet or other object, or a section of a newspaper or magazine, that has been printed by this process.

1914 *N.Y. Times* 29 Mar. 11/3 The rotogravures are superior to any group of reproductions I have ever seen issued in this way, except for the occasional photogravure that some publication has put forth. **1943** D. POWELL *Time to be Born* iv. 94, I suppose business experience never can quite make up for your picture in the Sunday rotogravure. **1968** L. J. BRAUN *Cat who turned on & Off* vii. 64 His pleasurable dreams were always in colour; others were in sepia, like old-time rotogravure. **1978** J. UPDIKE *Coup* (1979) v. 197 The American press loved this artful clown; in their rotogravures he looked like a negative print of Santa Claus.

rotometer (rotǫ·mĭtəɹ, rōᵘ·tomītəɹ). Also **rota-**. [f. *ROTO- + -METER.] A hand-held measuring device incorporating a small wheel whose revolutions are registered in terms of distance travelled, e.g. on a map or plan.

1901 F. W. TAYLOR *Art of Cutting Metals* (ed. 3) 91 An instrument called a 'rotameter', which we have found the best appliance for practical use in measuring the cutting speed. *Ibid.*, The small wheel..which projects beyond the rim of the rotameter is firmly pressed directly against the surface of the rotating forging. **1913** T. W. CROFT *Amer. Electricians' Handbk.* 134 The rotometer (Fig. 141), is a convenient tool for scaling distances. The little wheel is run over the course of the circuit. The pointer indicates feet direct for drawings of certain scales. **1949** R. ASHLEY *Electr. Estimating* i. 14/1 The map measure, commonly known in the profession as the 'rotometer', is considered by most electrical estimators engaged in large construction work as the most valuable of tools. **1957** G. E. HUTCHINSON *Treat. Limnol.* I. ii. 166 The shore line may be measured on the map by means of a rotometer. **1971** W. N. ALERICH *Electr. Construction Wiring* xvii. 456/2 The measuring can be done with the aid of a rotameter or an architect's scale.

roton (rōᵘ·tǫn). *Physics.* [f. ROT(ATION + *-ON¹.] A quantum or quasiparticle associated with vortical motion in a liquid, esp. in liquid helium.

1941 L. LANDAU in *Jrnl. Physics U.S.S.R.* V. 75/2 An 'elementary excitation' of the vortex spectrum might be called a 'roton'. [*Note*] This name was suggested by I. E. Tamm. **1947** *Physical Rev.* LXXII. 852/1 In Landau's theory, the excited atoms of the Bose-Einstein theory are replaced by 'rotons'. **1968** *New Scientist* 25 July 198/3 The evaporation of helium atoms due to the decay of 'rotons', the elementary rotational excitations of liquid helium. **1973** *Nature* 9 Nov. 66/1 A new type of elementary excitation, christened the ³He roton, may exist in liquid ³He-⁴He mixtures. **1977** *New Scientist* 3 Mar. 507/1 The physical nature of the roton still remains a mystery some thirty years after their existence was first postulated by Landau, although they have been detected in numerous experiments.

rotor. Add: **3.** A rotor arm.

1920 V. W. PAGÉ *Useful Hints for Motorists* iii. 89 The distributor head and rotor are made of bakelite. **1959** *Motor Man.* (ed. 36) viii. 215 Before replacing the rotor, which should also be cleaned with a petrol-damped rag and dried with a soft cloth, apply a few drops of engine oil to lubricate the cam bearing. **1975** tr. *Melchior's Sleeper Agent* III. 212 Someone's been monkeying with the jeep... The rotor! Someone's pinched the distributor rotor.

4. A cylinder mounted vertically on a ship and designed to be rotated on its axis, so that the Magnus effect will provide a forward propulsive force in a cross-wind.

1924 *Public Opinion* 14 Nov. 483/3 Very little electric power is required to work the rotors. **1924** *Glasgow Herald* 17 Nov. 4 The navigational importance of Herr Anton Flettner's 'rotor' as an auxiliary. **1925** *Ibid.* 6 Feb. 9 These towers—technically called rotors—are supported on strong internal masts, about which they are revolved by small electric motors. **1943** [see *MAGNUS EFFECT]. **1957** *Encycl. Brit.* XIX. 577/2 The inventor states that it is not intended to drive ships solely by wind rotors, but that they shall serve as an auxiliary power upon steam and motor vessels.

5. A hub with a number of radiating arms that is rotated in an approximately horizontal plane to provide the lift for a helicopter or other rotary-wing aircraft.

1930 *Jrnl. R. Aeronaut. Soc.* XXXIV. 915 The wings of the aeroplane and the rotor of the autogiro. **1945** *Tee Emm* (Air Ministry) V. 56 Note the main rotor, that is the big propeller affair on top... Get rid of any assumption that because the rotor is *above* the aircraft it is also above *you*. **1973** R. LEWIS *Blood Money* viii. 107 The helicopter..dropped lower towards the surface of the tarn until finally the downthrust of air from the rotors churned the water into a maelstrom.

6. The rotating vessel in a centrifuge.

1939 *Industr. & Engin. Chem.* Sept. 1073 The rotor or bowl must be removed for cleaning when it becomes filled with bowl cake. **1958** M. G. LARIAN *Fund. Chem. Engin. Operations* (1959) xiv. 566 The centrifuge is shown in Fig. 24. It consists of a tubular bowl rotor enclosed in a stationary casing. **1978** *Nature* 14 Sept. 147/1 Brain homogenates..are centrifuged at 100,000*g* for 18 h in a Beckman 42.1 rotor.

7. A part of an encoding or decoding machine, rotation of which changes numerous electrical circuits and thereby the code.

1946 *U.S. Patent 2,402,182* 3 The selected ratchet and pawl mechanism..then rotates the rotors one step while the contacts carried by the rotors are disengaged. **1973** H. GRUPPE *Truxton Cipher* xviii. 189 That moment in '42 when he had handed over the Truxton Cipher rotors to the Russians. **1979** *Books & Bookmen* Jan. 31/1 The object was to enable the recipient of the message to set the rotors of his own machine for deciphering that particular message.

8. A large eddy in which the air circulates about a horizontal axis. [a. G. *rotor*, introduced in this sense by J. Küttner 1938, in *Beiträge zur Physik der freien Atmosphäre* XXV. 108.]

1949 *Q. Jrnl. R. Meteorol. Soc.* LXXV. 54 The crests of waves may be capped by clouds under suitable conditions of humidity. Beautiful examples are the Helm Bars.., and the 'Rotors' associated with the Moazagotl. **1955** *Tellus* VII. 367 The stationary lee-waves produced by a big mountain often break up into turbulent whirls or 'rotors' in the lower layers of the air flow. **1960** *Aeroplane* XCVIII. 390/3 They moved downwind into the downdraught and at 2,500 ft. dropped into the rotor and its turbulence, which became especially violent from 1,500 ft. down to the ground. **1979** *Courier-Mail* (Brisbane) 15 June 6/10 It was believed that wind conditions against the cliff face caused what was known in the sport as a 'rotor'. 'The wind spins across from the hill face and grabs you,' he said.

9. *attrib.* and *Comb.*, as **rotor arm**, the part of the distributor of an internal-combustion engine which, by its rotation, successively makes and breaks electrical contacts so that each sparking plug fires in turn; **rotor blade**, each of the radiating arms of the rotor of a helicopter or other rotary-wing aircraft; **rotor cloud**, a turbulent cloud in a rotor (sense *8) in the lee of a mountain; **rotor disc**, (*a*) the space swept out by rotor blades as they rotate; (*b*) the rotor head; **rotor head, hub**, the structure at the upper end of a shaft of a rotorcraft, to which the rotor blades are attached; **rotor ship**, a ship whose motive power is derived from cylindrical rotors. See also *ROTORCRAFT.

1919 FRASER & JONES *Motor Vehicles* xviii. 195 The rotor arms are placed at right angles to each other and project from both sides of the shaft. **1964** [see *DISTRIBUTOR b (ii)]. **1968** *Listener* 25 July 109/1, I stopped the jeep in the middle of the crowd while Kim automatically removed the rotor arm and padlocked the gears. **1931** DE LA CIERVA & ROSE *Wings of Tomorrow* viii. 118 This was the only Autogiro that ever broke a rotor blade in flight. **1947** *Times* 16 Apr. 2/1 An airscrew which can be extended to the dimensions of a rotor blade such as that used in helicopters has long been sought. **1973** R. LEWIS *Blood Money* viii. 106 Crow heard the chatter of rotor-blades and saw the helicopter coming in. **1959** *Gloss. Meteorol.* (Amer. Meteorol. Soc.) 487 *Rotor cloud*, a turbulent, altocumulus-type cloud formation found in the lee of some large mountain barriers. **1967** R. W. FAIRBRIDGE *Encycl. Atmospheric Sci.* 609/1 The moazagotl condition is set up by a standing wave established when the warm chinook or foehn-type air flows down the lee slope of the mountain range, initiating a series of undulations with eddies, the rising air of which develop cumuloform rotor clouds. **1974** T. BEER *Atmospheric Waves* iv. 182 The base of the rotor cloud is near the level of the crest while the top may be several thousand feet higher. **1944** H. F. GREGORY *Anything Horse can Do* xiv. 145 The direct-control Autogiro is controlled by tilting the rotor disk in the desired direction. Actually it is accomplished by rocking the hub. **1976** B. JACKSON *Flameout* (1977) iv. 54 Klein bent to stare at the forward stages of the compressor rotor. All the wing-like blades were rooted in the rotor disk. **1931** DE LA CIERVA & ROSE *Wings of Tomorrow* vi. 93, I propose to overcome the inequality of lift by building into the rotor head a device for changing the angle of incidence of the blades as they made their circle. **1958** LAMBERMONT & PIRIE *Helicopters & Autogyros of World* 32 The rotor head..was controlled by feathering and impressed flapping. **1931** DE LA CIERVA & ROSE *Wings of Tomorrow* viii. 118 The rotor hub is almost entirely a machine shop product. **1949** *Electronic Engin.* XXI. 292/2 The testing tower..was erected to provide a means of testing rotor hubs and blades independently of helicopter aircraft. **1924** *Glasgow Herald* 17 Nov. 4 (*heading*) The rotor ship. *Ibid.* 12 Dec. 8 The Rotor ship is apparently a thing devoid of beauty. It reminds one of a match-box with two cigarettes placed vertically on top. **1926** *Ibid.* 27 Apr. 11 The big new rotorship Barbara will be launched at Bremen tomorrow. Her tonnage is 3000, and she has three rotors, each measuring nearly 100ft. in height and 13ft. in circumference. **1949** O. G. SUTTON *Sci. of Flight* iv. 84 The idea of a rotor-ship does not seem to have appealed to shipbuilders in general and it is now regarded as a scientific curiosity and no more. **1957** *Encycl. Brit.* XIX. 578/1 An ordinary sailing vessel requires to take down all her canvas in a hurricane, but the rotor ship could continue sailing, with more stability for manoeuvring.

rotorcraft (rōᵘ·tǫ̈ɹkrɑ̄ft). [f. ROTOR + CRAFT *sb.*] A rotary-wing aircraft.

1940 *Jrnl. Aeronaut. Sci.* VII. 444/1 Theoretical studies of rotorcraft vibration..were initiated about two years ago by the Kellett Autogiro Corporation. **1955** LIPTROT & WOODS *Rotorcraft* ii. 12 Rotorcraft, which is the generic name for rotary wing aircraft, may be classified under six categories... Helicopter... Gyroplane... Cyclogyro... Gyrodyne... Compound helicopter... Convertible aircraft. **1969** *New Scientist* 28 Aug. 421/1 At least 60 per cent of the loaded weight of a tactical monoplane is normally disposable... The corresponding figure for rotorcraft rarely exceeds 45. **1979** *Daily Tel.* 14 Sept. 10/5 Britain's only helicopter museum, the British Rotorcraft Museum at Weston-super-Mare, Avon, said yesterday that it had been forced to close because the local airfield lease has run out.

Rotoscythe (rōᵘ·tosəið). Also **roto-scythe, rotoscythe.** [f. *ROTO- + SCYTHE *sb.*] The proprietary name of a machine with rotating blades, designed to cut rough grass or vegetation.

1948 *Times* 20 Mar. 6/7 The roto-scythe..has come to take the place of the brushing-hook for the removal of grass and herbage too tall for the mowing machine. **1949** *Trade Marks Jrnl.* 19 Jan. 48 *Rotoscythe*... Lawn Mowers. Power Specialities Limited,..Slough, Buckinghamshire; manufacturers. **1955** *Radio Times* 22 Apr. 46/1 Rotoscythe cuts long or short, neater–quicker. **1966** 'J. BERRISFORD' *Wild Garden* i. 16 Rough grass.. must be cut (by scythe or rotoscythe).

Rototiller (rōᵘ·totiləɹ). Chiefly *N. Amer.* Also **rototiller, roto-tiller.** [f. *ROTO- + TILLER *sb.*¹] A machine with rotating blades or prongs designed to break up or till soil (registered in the U.S. as a proprietary name). Hence **ro·totilling**, the preparation of soil with a Rototiller.

1923 *Sci. Amer.* Dec. 411/1 From England comes the description of one which differs radically from the American variety in that the soil is worked by a revolving member called a miller... The rototiller is driven by a two-cycle, 8 to 10 horse-power engine. **1932** *Official Gaz.* (U.S. Patent Office) 25 Oct. 949/1 *Rototiller* for farm machine for soil cultivation. Claims use since Feb. 9, 1929. **1938** C. CULPIN *Farm Machinery* vii. 106 One of the most successful types of rotary cultivator is the small 'Rototiller' type, of which the best-known example is the

Simar Rototiller... The loose tilth produced by the Rototiller is very suitable for much horticultural work. **1959** *Times* 13 Mar. 6/6 Another man bid £5 for a rototiller. **1969** *Daily Colonist* (Victoria, B.C.) 15 July 22/5 In cultivated ground, hoeing or rototilling doesn't help much—in fact, in can spread the pest. **1974** *Globe & Mail* (Toronto) 5 Mar. 29/5 A friend of mine who deals in rototillers tells me he has more orders and enquiries this year than he's ever had. **1976** *Casper* (Wyoming) *Star-Tribune* 29 June 17/7 (Advt.) Custom plowing and rototilling, dozer work. **1978** *Sunday Star* (Toronto) 21 May A3/6 Rental agencies reported that most..of their garden tools, and especially roto-tillers, were rented for the day.

Rotovator, var. *ROTAVATOR.

‖ **rotta** (rǫ·ta). *Hist.* Also **rota.** [med. Lat.: see ROTE *sb.*¹] = ROTE *sb.*¹

1883 GROVE *Dict. Mus.* III. 179/1 *Rota*, or *Rotta*.., not, as might be supposed from its name, a species of vielle or hurdy-gurdy, but a species of psaltery or dulcimer, or primitive zither, employed in the middle ages in church music. It was played with the hand, guitar-fashion, and had seven strings mounted in a solid wooden frame. **1942** E. BLOM *Music in England* i. 12 A miniature in an eighth-century codex in the British Museum..shows King David playing on a rotta (a generic link between the lyre and the harp). **1964** S. MARCUSE *Musical Instruments* (1966) 102/2 In the 8th c., Cuthbert had mentioned the cithara that 'we' call rotta. **1977** *Early Music* July 300/1 When the musicians and minstrels adopted it [*sc.* the ancient psaltery] for their own purposes, ..they made its shape and form suitable to their convenience, applying additional strings and calling it by the vernacular name *rotta*.

rotten, *a.* Add: **I. 4. c.** orig. *N. Amer.* Of ice: weak; melting, disintegrating. (Cf. *ROT *v.* 1 e.)

c **1665** P. E. RADISSON *Voyages* (1885) 133 We cutt the ice wth hattchetts & we found places where [it] was rotten, so we hazarded ourselves often to sinke downe to our necks. **1746** T. WALKER *Diary* 20 Mar. (1889) 9 Went over ye River upon ye ice. It grew very rotten. **1795** E. P. SIMCOE *Diary* 7 Feb. (1911) 266 At Jacques Cartier the ice was so rotten I was obliged to go a league higher to cross the river with safety. **1849** J. E. ALEXANDER *L'Acadie* II. ii. 31 Thence we proceeded to Montreal, which we reached after four days and three nights of most unpleasant travel, and even dangerous, on account of exposure and the rotten ice. **1916** N. DUNCAN *Billy Topsail* xvi. 120 [The ice] had yielded somewhat—it must have gone rotten—in the weather of that day. **1935** *Monthly Weather Rev.* (Washington) LXII. 133/1 The boatman, fisherman, and lots of others ..swear that at this season [*sc.* spring] surface ice becomes rotten, or honeycombed, and sinks. **1966** T. ARMSTRONG et al. *Illustr. Gloss. Snow & Ice* Fig. 7 (*caption*) Rotten ice. The puddles on the surface have mostly joined together and in places have melted right through the ice.

II. 8. b. (Earlier and later examples.) Also in weakened sense in *rotten luck, shame*, etc. Also as intensifying word and as quasi-*adv.*

1880 'MARK TWAIN' *Tramp Abroad* xxiii. 226 I'm most rotten certain 'bout that. **1911** G. B. SHAW *Blanco Posnet* 405 You that always talk as if He never did anything without asking your rotten leave first. **1914** —— *Fanny's First Play* I. 177, I was copped in the Dock Road myself: rotten luck, wasn't it? **1922** JOYCE *Ulysses* 748 It was rotten cold too that winter. **1930** [see *electric blanket* s.v.*ELECTRIC *a.* 2 b]. **1943** [see *DUE *sb.* 4 c]. **1952** E. O'NEILL *Moon for Misbegotten* II. 107 You rotten bastard! **1959** I. & P. OPIE *Lore & Lang. Schoolch.* ix. 161 Juvenile repugnance continues to be expressed by the old standbys..rotten, rotten shame, rotten swiz. **1964** *Daily Mail* 14 Dec. 1/3 The other girls sent me up rotten when they heard about my date. **1976** M. MACHLIN *Pipeline* xli. 446, I would not say that they are your friendliest people. And sometimes they are downright rotten. **1977** *Listener* 12 May 626/2 Mr Wood is not only brave enough to send himself up rotten, but also to make a hilarious series out of the whole literary game. **1980** *Jewish Chron.* 26 Dec. (Lit. Suppl.) p. vii/2, I was the only girl among 50 reporters and of course I was spoilt rotten.

d. *to knock rotten*, to kill or stun. *Austral. slang.*

1919 W. H. DOWNING *Digger Dial.* 31 *Knocked rotten*, killed or stunned. **1941** *Coast to Coast* 179 'He pulled it down on top of him,' continued Jo... 'It knocked him rotten.' **1945** BAKER *Austral. Lang.* vi. 120 The development of an extensive vocabulary of fighting terms... *knock rotten.*

e. *Austral. slang.* Drunk. Also in phr. *to get rotten.*

1941 BAKER *Dict. Austral. Slang* 61 *Rotten, to get*, to become exceedingly drunk. **1953** T. A. G. HUNGERFORD *Riverslake* 135 Monday to-morrow—blasted work again. God, could I get rotten! **1971** J. FAMECHON *Fammo* 145 A reporter from one of the Sydney papers—he was the last to leave, rotten.

10. a. *rotten-boned, -chested, -fleshed, -livered* adjs.

1912 D. H. LAWRENCE *Let.* 3 July (1962) I. 134 My cursed, rotten-boned, pappy hearted countrymen, *why* was I sent to *them.* **1927** R. GRAVES *Poems (1914–26)* 210 As counterbalance in my mind To being rotten-boned and blind. **1969** L. MICHAELS *Going Places* 63, I..coughed again, a rasping, rotten-chested hack. **1908** HARDY *Dynasts* III. IV. vi. 417 We kings? Kings of the underground country, then, by this time, if we hadn't been too rotten-fleshed to follow the drum. **1929** R. GRAVES *Poems* 20 Lame, rotten-livered, this and that canaille.

b. *rotten-sweet*; also *rotten-woven.*

1947 M. MORRIS in B. James *Austral. Short Stories* (1963) 348 She stood over the bin inhaling the queer rotten-sweet smell of the blossoms. **1868** G. M. HOPKINS *Jrnls. & Papers* (1959) 184 In the train I was noticing that strange rotten-woven cloud.

c. (Further example.)

1936 W. GREENE *Death in Deep South* 69 You are rotten-egged out of a jerkwater town—rotten egged!—by a handful of hoodlums.

rottenly, *adv.* Delete *rare*—⁰ and add examples in sense 8 b of adj.

1905 G. B. SHAW *Let.* 29 Nov (1972) II. 584, I see.. that the papers all say that..Major Barbara [is] a rottenly undramatic play. **1927** H. WALPOLE *Jeremy at Crale* iii. 43 'They weren't half pleased at your playing so rottenly.' 'I didn't play rottenly.' **1934** D. L. SAYERS *Nine Tailors* II. 79 I'm afraid—if I go west this time—I'll be leaving you rottenly badly off, old girl.

Rotten Row. 2. (Further example.)

1975 *Listener* 30 Oct. 581/3 The majority of our line-of-battle ships had been rotting in reserve [by 1778]... Many of the battleships laid up in 'Rotten Row' were mere stacks of decayed timber.

rotting, *vbl. sb.* Add: **1.** Also *rotting-down* (in quot. *fig.*).

1916 GALSWORTHY *Sheaf* 269 Economically..such rotting-down of the boys is grievously short-sighted.

rotto (rǫ·to), *a. nonce-wd.* [f. ROTT(EN *a.* + *-O².] A jocular var. of ROTTEN *a.* 8 in Dict. and Suppl.

1922 JOYCE *Ulysses* 23 The father is rotto with money. *Ibid.* 630 There was the case of O'Callaghan..among whose other gay doings when rotto and making himself a nuisance to everybody all round he was in the habit of ostentatiously sporting in public a suit of brown paper.

Rottweiler (rǫ·twəilər, -vəilər). Also **Rott-weiler.** [a. Ger., f. *Rottweil*, the name of a town in Württemberg, West Germany + *-er* -ER¹.] A large black-and-tan dog belonging to the breed so called, having a short, coarse coat, docked tail, and a broad head with pendent ears. Also *attrib.*

1907 R. LEIGHTON *New Bk. Dog* 521/2 The Rottweil Dog, usually called the *Rottweiler Metzgerhund*, or butcher's dog of the town of Rottweil in South Germany. **1917** *Policeman's Monthly* Jan. 5/3 Nowadays four breeds of dogs are being used for police purposes: the Continental Sheepdog,..the Airedale Terrier, the Doberman Pinscher and the Rottweilers. **1939** KINNEY & HONEYCUTT *How to raise Dog* ii. 73 Very large (Breeds such as Great Danes, Newfoundlands,..mastiffs, Rottweilers, Italian bulls, and Pyrenean mountain dogs). **1948** C. L. B. HUBBARD *Dogs in Brit.* xvi. 163 Although a comparatively new arrival to Britain the Rottweiler is a very well-known dog on the Continent. **1962** *Times* 24 Aug. 1/3 (Advt.), Very special homes required by 3 Rottweiler puppies. **1963** *Guardian* 5 Jan. 5/3 Among the dogs successfully trained for police work are the Rottweiler..and the Bouvier. **1971** 'L. EGAN' *Malicious Mischief* (1972) viii. 127 Katharine thought of Labrador retrievers,..Newfoundlands, and Rottweilers. **1978** *Daily Tel.* 11 Apr. 3/6 Dulwich College staff are alleged to have been attacked by Rottweillers—German hunting dogs—belonging to a neighbour.

rotunda. Add: **2. a.** (Earlier examples.)

1780 A. YOUNG *Tour in Ireland* I. 2 In the evening to the Rotunda, a circular room, 90 feet diameter, an imitation of Ranelagh, provided with a band of music. **1808** M. WILMOT *Russ. Jrnls.* (1934) III. 316 From the Gallery one enters a Green House..in the Center of which is a rotunda for Entertaining Company.

b. *N. Amer.* The main hall of a public building; a lobby, a concourse.

1905 *Eye Opener* (Calgary) 28 Jan. 3/1 The hotels have no drinking-water tanks in their rotundas for the use of guests or local patrons—for obvious reasons. **1912** J. SANDLANDS *Western Canad. Dict.*, *Rotunda*, the hall or main entrance and waiting-room of a railway depot or an hotel. **1924** J. F. DORRANCE *Never Fire First* xiii. 134 The scene in the rotunda of Montreal's impressive Windsor Station was as lively as it was metropolitan. **1958** *Edmonton Jrnl.* 19 June 33/3 Place and Date of Sale [is] Rotunda, Fifth Floor, Natural Resources Building, Edmonton, Alberta. **1973** H. KEMELMAN *Tuesday Rabbi saw Red* vi. 41 Inside the enclosed area of the Marble, the marble-tiled rotunda, students were swarming about.

2*. *Typogr.* A type-face of gothic inspiration used in some early printed books, based on a rounded script developed in the 13th century and popularized by the Bolognese law-school; also, the manuscript hand on which this type-face was based.

1929 A. F. JOHNSON in *Library* IX. 364 This is the rounded gothic of the Italians... In typography the Germans call it Rotunda. *Ibid.*, Jenson's Rotundas had a much wider vogue than his roman. **1954** R. STOKES *Esdaile's Student's Man. Bibliogr.* (ed. 3) iv. 141 The third class of *rotunda* types..is largely an Italian style of gothic and shows a much more open quality. **1969** H. CARTER *View of Early Typogr.* iii. 50 This Italian rotunda was a somewhat cramped letter with short ascending and descending strokes... It was ideally suited to printing and printing was ideally suited to it. **1976** *Times Lit. Suppl.* 22 Oct. 1328/3 Caxton's mainstay bâtardes 2, 4, and 6 are surely best understood as belonging to the great calligraphic types of the earliest period, in fourth place after the Gutenbergian or Mainz texturas and rotundas and the Venetian romans. **1978** *Jrnl. R. Soc. Arts* CXXVI. 378/1 The widely practised 'Rotunda' hand of the Marmion, Soane, Serristori and other manuscript Hours.

‖ **Rotwelsch** (rō·tvelʃ). Also † **Rothwelsch.** [Ger., f. MHG. *rot* beggar or *rôt* red + *welsch* WELSH.] A form of slang or cant used by vagrants and criminals in Germany and Austria.

1841 BORROW *Zincali* II. III. ii. 130 The name of this [robber] jargon varies... In Germany [it is called] 'Rothwelsch' or red Italian. **1892** [see YIDDISH *a.*]. **1916** H. BRADLEY *Shakespeare's English* in *Shakespeare's England* II. xxx. 567 The Hebrew words that are so conspicuous in the contemporary *Rotwelsch* of Germany. **1934** PRIEBSCH & COLLINSON *German Lang.* 260 The lowest type of speech is the thieves' and beggars' cant known in German as *Rotwelsch* or *Gaunersprache.* **1961** *John o' London's* 30 Nov. 610 The *argot* of the French underworld, the *Rotwelsch* of Germany, is paralleled by the *Cant* of English rogues and vagabonds. **1973** *Reader's Digest* Feb. 122/2 'Please, put away that firecracker,' said the Major, lapsing into *Rotwelsch*—the slang of Vienna's underworld.

rouble. Add: **1, 2.** The rouble is now available primarily in paper form.

‖ **roucoulement** (rūkūlmaṅ). *rare.* [Fr.] The soft cooing sound made by doves. Also *transf.*

1863 J. A. SYMONDS *Let.* 12 Aug. (1967) I. 413 This *roucoulement* (cooing) in the throat is different from the yogel & seems to be peculiar to Swiss singing. **1926** E. SITWELL *Elegy on Dead Fashion* 2 Roucoulement of doves and veilèd belles.

Rouen. Add: **a.** Also used to designate earthenware of a type made at Rouen (esp. in the sixteenth and seventeenth centuries), as *Rouen faience, plate, ware.*

1863 W. CHAFFERS *Marks Pott. & Porc.* 94 From this period [*sc.* the early sixteenth century] until the middle of the XVIIth Century no notices of the Rouen Fayence have been discovered. **1869** C. SCHREIBER *Jrnl.* 11 Oct. (1911) I. 51 In all these shops there was a profusion of Rouen ware, or what pretended to be such, which proves how common it is. **1971** J. R. BERNASCONI *Collectors' Gloss.* 191 *Rouen ware*, an enamelled faience ware produced at Rouen in the 17th century. **1974** N. FREELING *Dressing of Diamond* 26 His valuable pieces of Nevers and Rouen faïence. **1977** *Western Mail* (Cardiff) 5 Mar. 14/1 Elwyn D. Thomas & Co., F.S.V.A. will Sell by Auction.. 'Dresden', 'Mason', 'Delft', 'Rouen' plates and plaques.

rouf (rōᵘf). Also **roaf, rofe, roof.** Backslang, esp. among costermongers and criminals, for 'four'; *spec.* four shillings, four pounds; a four-year prison sentence.

1851 H. MAYHEW *London Labour* I. 23/1 *Rouf-yenep*, Fourpence. **1882** *Sydney Slang Dict.* 11/2 *Roaf Yanneps*, four pence. **1950** P. TEMPEST *Lag's Lexicon* 212 All [prison] sentences are referred to in slang... 4 years, a 'lagging' or a 'rofe' (pron. 'roaf'). **1957** *Evening News* 12 Nov. 6/6 Newcomers [to Cockney slang] are a 'rouf' (4s), 'a deuce' (£2), and 'anarf' (10s). **1958** F. NORMAN *Bang to Rights* III. 138, I tried to tell them that it had been a business deal, but you know what it's like talking to a moronic coszer, so that was it I got a rouf. **1972** K. ROYCE *Miniatures Frame* v. 64 From under a pottery sugar jar..protruded two jacks... I found a roof under them.

rouge, *a.* and *sb.*¹ Add: **B.** *sb.*¹ **1. a.** (Further *fig.* example.)

1882 'F. ANSTEY' *Vice Versâ* xvii. 312, I saw through his rouge with half an eye.

c. *rouge compact.*

1931 F. L. ALLEN *Only Yesterday* v. 107 For every adult woman in the country there were being sold annually over a pound of face powder and no less than eight rouge compacts.

2. a. Also (usu. with qualifying adj.) applied to polishing powders other than ferric oxide (see quot. 1937). (Further examples.)

1937 *Industr. Minerals & Rocks* (Amer. Inst. Mining & Metall. Engineers) i. 55 Briefly, they [*sc.* metallic oxide buffing materials] consist of various iron oxides such as crocus (red-brown), rouge (red), black rouge (magnetic iron oxide) mainly for glass, green rouge (chromium oxide) mainly for platinum and stainless steels; satin rouge (lampblack) for celluloid and bone; [etc.]. **1962** R. WEBSTER *Gems* I. xx. 366 The polishing powder..may be either rouge (iron oxide), green rouge (chromium oxide), putty powder..or rotten-stone.

b. *rouge flambé* (rūʒ flaṅbe), a brilliant red glaze for porcelain, orig. Chinese, made from copper oxide.

1902 *Encycl. Brit.* XXXI. 875/2 Even the long-sought secret of the Chinese *sang de boeuf* and *rouge flambé* glazes has been worked out in Europe. **1912** A. BENNETT *Matador of Five Towns* 4 A few specimens of modern *rouge flambé* ware made at Knype. **1960** R. G. HAGGAR *Conc. Encycl. Continental Pott. & Porc.* 124/1 He succeeded in producing a fine *rouge flambé* and an admirable turquoise blue glaze. **1967** M. CHANDLER *Ceramics in Mod. World* iii. 95 Copper oxide..can—under suitable conditions in a reducing atmosphere—produce the extremely brilliant red of rouge flambé. *a* **1977** *Harrison Mayer Ltd. Catal.* 14/2 *Rouge flambe, sang de boeuf*, a red glaze originating in China, its rich colour being due to a copper glaze fired under reducing conditions.

c. *rouge de fer* (rūʒ də fẹ̄r), an orange-red enamel colour made from a base of ferric oxide and used on Chinese porcelain.

1922 *Daily Tel.* 12 June 20/5 (Advt.), A pair of famille verte baluster vases enamelled in birds and flowering prunus, in green, rouge de fer, yellow, and aubergine, 17½ in. high. **1939** *Burlington Mag.* Apr. p.xv/1 A pair of famille-verte jars and covers,..with *rouge-de-fer* borders. **1959** *Times* 3 Mar. 7/2 A pair of eighteenth century models of dogs enamelled in *rouge de fer* realized 170 guineas. **1980** *Catal. Fine Chinese Ceramics* (Sotheby, Hong Kong) 166 All in tomato-red 'rouge-de-fer' and gilding.

4. a. (Further example.) Also *fig.*

1886 Hardy *Mayor Casterbr.* I. x. 123 The rich *rouge-et-noir* of his countenance underwent a slight change. **1920** H. Crane *Let.* 18 Aug. (1965) 41, I am sure there is more of a 'rouge et noir' cast to your surrender. **1958** L. Durrell *Balthazar* iii. 61 You are not the sort of man to stake everything on a single throw at *rouge et noir*.

5. a. (Earlier and later examples.)

1805 *New Pocket Hoyle* 117 Another parcel is then dealt for rouge in a similar manner. **1867** [see *couleur 2]. **1928, 1964** [see *noir 2 b].

b. The red numbers in the game of roulette.

[**1850** *Bohn's Hand-bk. Games* 348 The other chances are also designated on the green cloth,..on one side 'l'impair, la manque, et le rouge'.] **1923**, etc. [see *manque]. **1928**, etc. [see *noir 2 a].

6. French red wine; = Red *sb.*[1] 3 b. Also in *Comb.*

1957 L. Durrell *Spirit of Place* (1969) 143 You should see..the care with which they select a good bottle of champagne..or even an ordinary rouge at a shilling **1976** N. Roberts *Face of France* xv. 153 The accompanying glass of wine..is only *rouge supérieure*.

rouge, *sb.*[2] Add: **2. b.** (Further examples.) (See also quot. 1954.)

1954 *Sun* (Baltimore) 11 Dec. 11/7 The 'rouge' is a point scored when a kick into the end zone isn't run out or when the kick goes clear through the 25-yard-wide zone. **1959** *Times* 30 Nov. (Canada Suppl.) p.xx/1 In Canada we also have the rouge, which is a kicked single point. **1966** *Weekend Mag.* (Montreal) 27 Aug. 20/2 If only our rouge were added to the American game, football..wouldn't leave a thing to be desired as a game. **1976** *Webster's Sports Dict.* 357/1 *Rouge*, Canadian football, a score of one point awarded to the kicking team when a member of the receiving team fails to run a kickoff or a punt out of his own end zone.

rouge, *v.*[1] **2. b.** (Later example.)

1954 H. Gold in *New World Writing* VI. 13 You should have seen me rouge all over.

rougeless (rū·ʒlės), *a. rare.* [f. Rouge *sb.*[1] + -less.] Lacking rouge (in quot. *fig.*).

1857 [see *intime].

‖ **rouget** (rūʒe). [Fr.] = *red mullet* s.v. Red *a.* 17 c.

1885 A. Edwardes *Girton Girl* III. v. 83 He invited me to eat red mullet with him..Rougets en papillottes, accompanied by fine old graves. **1960** E. David *French Provincial Cooking* 286 *Rouget* proper..is red mullet. **1967** G. Greene *May we borrow your Husband?* 59, I ordered a small *rouget* and a half bottle of Pouilly. **1975** *Harpers & Queen* June 110/3 We ate *rougets* next; such *rougets*, simply grilled. **1977** *Times* 28 Jan. 15/7 Loup, daurade and rouget are among the best local fish [in Nice].

Rouget cell (rūʒe). *Histology.* Also **Rouget's cell.** [tr. G. *Rougetsche zelle* (B. J. Vimtrup 1922, in *Zeitschr. f. Anat. u. Entwicklungsges.* LXV. 178), f. the name of C. M. B. *Rouget* (1824–1904), French physiologist, who described such cells in 1873 (*Arch. de Physiol.* V. 603).] = *pericyte.

1922 A. Krogh *Anat. & Physiol. Capillaries* iii. 54 As there can be no doubt that the richly ramified muscle cells on the capillary wall are the same as those originally found by Rouget in the hyaloid membrane, Vimtrup has named them after the first discoverer, and we shall speak of them henceforth as Rouget cells. **1928** [see *pericyte]. **1939** W. E. Le Gros Clark *Tissues of Body* vii. 158 In appearance, Rouget cells (or pericytes, as they have been called), are quite similar to connective-tissue cells. *Ibid.* 159 Vimtrup..reported that, in Amphibia, local contraction of capillaries always started at the site of one of the Rouget cells. **1961** G. Bevelander *Essent. Histol.* (ed. 4) x. 106 According to some authors the tubule is clasped at intervals by Rouget's cells. These are branching cells which are said to be contractile and to cause the constriction of the capillaries. **1970** T. S. & C. R. Leeson *Histol.* (ed. 2) xi. 217/1 Among the pericapillary elements, peculiar cells (Rouget cells) with long branching processes which surround the capillary wall have been described. Early studies indicated that these cells were contractile and were responsible for the contractility of capillaries. More recent work suggests that true capillaries in mammals do not possess Rouget cells and that capillary contractility is independent of them.

rough, *sb.*[1] Add: **I. 2. c.** (Further examples.)

1955 [see *bunker *sb.*[1] 4]. **1971** 'D. Halliday' *Dolly & Doctor Bird* iii. 29, I played well that morning, and the two balls I shot into the rough I recovered. **1977** *Cork Examiner* 6 June 7/2 At the 13th, Higgins was in the rough off the tee. **1980** *Guardian* 10 June 25/3 A spectator found another in the left rough and Cisco found the other in the right rough.

II. 6. c. The heavier, rougher part of housework; freq. in phr. *to do the rough.*

1946 M. Dickens *Happy Prisoner* vii. 114 Cosy discussions on clothes and curtains and women to do the rough. **1950** J. Cannan *Murder Included* iii. 39 He..suggested having a woman for the rough. **1959** *Times* 21 Nov. 1/3 No cooking or rough. **1974** 'A. Gilbert' *Nice Little Killing* v. 70 The woman who came to do the rough twice a week.

d. Sharp, acid, or harsh drink; *spec.* (*a*) *slang,* draught bitter beer; (*b*) rough cider.

1946 J. Irving *Royal Navalese* 147 'Rough', draught bitter beer. **1960** 'R. East' *Kingston Black* xiii. 129 He was selling the rough at three shillings a gallon.

III. 9. c. Applied to alum used as an adulterant in bread.

1855 *2nd Rep. Comm. on Adulteration of Food* 47 in *Parl. Papers 1854–5* VIII. 373 There are several trade names for alum; one of them, being very characteristic of its effects on the mucous surface, is 'roughs', and another is 'seasoning'. **1909** *Practitioner* Feb. 263 All the samples of bread contained alum, and an instance was mentioned of flour, with which as much as ten per cent. had been mixed... In the trade, the adulterant received the name of 'roughs'.

10. a. Delete *rare*⁻¹ and add further examples. Also, a rough sketch, layout, etc.

1710 in *Publ. Colonial Soc. Mass.* (1925) XV. 395 A rough of sundry Articles wˢ drawn up. **1796** J. Steele *Papers* (1924) I. 144 A rough of a letter which may at some future period compose part of a circular. **1936** *Punch* 12 Aug. 170/2, I don't suggest for a moment that these are *finished* ideas. They are no more than artists' roughs. **1961** Webster, ²*Rough*,..4d rough proof. **1970** R. K. Kent *Lang. Journalism* 114 *Rough*, a preliminary layout or drawing, without details. **1975** J. Butcher *Copy-Editing* ix. 48 Alterations to artwork are caused as often by authors' inadequate or incorrect roughs..as they are by draughtsmen's mistakes. **1976** *Vogue* 15 Mar. 24/1 The roughs of my column are completed.

d. Uncut precious stone; an uncut gem, esp. a diamond.

1920 in Webster. **1961** in Webster s.v., A huge piece of rough was cut to a superb gem of 128 carats. **1974** L. St. Clair *Emerald Trap* (1975) i. 6, I want lots of big roughs. Finsch, Top Wesselton, maybe some Jaeger. **1976** W. Greatorex *Crossover* 162 No thefts of rough have been reported, so I suppose they're clean?

rough, *a.* Add: **I. 1. b.** Also, having a long nap.

1848 J. Ruskin *Let.* 29 June in M. Lutyens *Ruskins & Grays* (1972) xiii. 123, I beg very *particular* thanks for the *Rough* towels. **1939** *Army & Navy Stores Catal.* 623/1 'Christy' bath towels rough brown linen pile... 'Christy' bath towels in mixed linen and cotton..a semi-rough towel for hard wear.

d. Applied to the surface of a tennis- or squash-racket on which the loops formed by the string(s) looped around others project; freq. in context of spinning a racket to decide the choice of service or ends. Opp. *smooth *a.* 1 d.

1890 [see *smooth *a.* 1 d]. **1911** C. H. B. Quennell in L. Weaver *House & its Equipment* 204 It spoils the game if, as a result of guessing 'rough' or 'smooth' [etc.]. **1973** M. Russell *Double Hit* xxv. 186 Nevil spun his racket. 'Smooth,' said Colleano. 'Rough. I'll serve.'

e. *Bacteriol.* Applied to a bacterial phenotype characterized by corrugated and irregular colonies, and by cells lacking polysaccharide capsules.

[**1920**: see *R. II. 2 a.] **1921** J. A. Arkwright in *Jrnl. Path. & Bacteriol.* XXIV. 38 The irregularity of the surface has led to this variant being called the Rough ('R') form in distinction from the Smooth ('S') form. **1949** L. R. Thompson *Introd. Microorganisms* viii. 106 Rough (R-type) colonies are characterized by a dull appearance, and a folded or uneven surface. **1974** Q. N. Myrvik et al. *Fund. Med. Bacteriol. & Mycol.* ii. 25 When freshly isolated gram-negative pathogens are cultivated in the laboratory, they often undergo a smooth to rough (S→R) colony mutation.

II. 5. c. (Earlier example.) Also, unfortunate, unreasonable, unfair.

c **1856** W. Whitman *Daybks. & Notebks.* (1978) III. 670 That's rough. **1867** 'Mark Twain' *Let.* 5 Dec. in C. Clemens *Mark Twain* (1932) 16 Another devilish thing is that the Alta [California] copyrighted the letters—that was rough. **1889** A. Lang *Letters on Lit.* 183 As we had also lots of..boomerangs..the poultry used to have rather a rough time of it. **1941** Baker *Dict. Austral. Slang* 61 *A bit rough*, unreasonable, unfair. **1942** *Yank* 23 Sept. 14 At best the going's very rough. **1944** *Yank* 4 Aug. 5 'We were 66 days on the beach at Anzio,' said Egan. 'It was rough.'

10. Also in wider use. (Further examples.) Also, miserable, dejected, in a bad way.

1883 'Mark Twain' *Life on Mississippi* lii. 513, I spent my last 10 cts for..cheese & i felt pretty rough. **1961** M. Dickens *Heart of London* II. 204 He looks rough. Someone ought to do something. Take im to ospital. **1971** C. Bonington *Annapurna South Face* xvi. 196 'I'll never make it to Camp VI,' said Nick. 'I feel dead rough.' **1972** *Times* 22 June 4/1, I felt really rough..before I was admitted to hospital.

III. 11. c. Of the sound of an internal-combustion engine: irregular, excessively noisy.

In quot. 1945 with a pun on sense 10.

1930 *Engineering* 24 Oct. 534/3 A state of affairs which would cause the engine to be 'rough' in its running. **1945** C. H. Ward-Jackson *Piece of Cake* (ed. 2) 53 When an engine sounds rough it is not well.

13. b. Of language, expression, etc.: coarse, vulgar, indelicate.

1958 *Spectator* 1 Aug. 176/2 It badly needs its rough jokes. **1961** in Webster s.v., A rough anecdote for such an audience. **1976** *Honolulu Star-Bull.* 21 Dec. E-1/4 You learn to live with the rough language so it doesn't bother you.

14. b. *rough and tough* (earlier example, used as a nickname).

c **1813** I. Pocock in M. R. Booth *Eng. Plays of 19th Cent.* (1969) I. 67, I suppose old rough-and-tough, master Grindoff, will be here presently.

d. In slang phrases *rough as bags, guts,* etc., uncouth, coarse. Chiefly *Austral.* and *N.Z.*

1919 W. H. Downing *Digger Dial.* 42 Rough as bags. **1925** Fraser & Gibbons *Soldier & Sailor Words* 246 *Rough as a sandbag*,..a term for a person who behaves unpleasantly. Uncouth. Objectionable. **1929** K. S. Prichard *Coonardoo* ii. 22 Ted was as rough as bags..a good-looking, good-natured bloke who could neither read nor write. **1938** E. Lowe *Salute to Freedom* 318 Rough as bags. Cleared his throat..and spat, just missing a pile of ribbons. **1941** Baker *Dict. Austral. Slang* 61 *Rough as a sandbag*, as for next. *Rough as bags, rough as a bag*, unpolished, crude, coarse. Esp. applied to persons. 'Rough as a pig's breakfast' is an equivalent. **1941** —— *N.Z. Slang* 53 [20th cent. N.Z. slang includes] rough as a bag (the Australians also have rough as bags), and rough as a pig's breakfast. **1946** E. G. Webber *Johnny Enzed in Middle East* 23 Smarten 'em up... Rough as bags. **1948** P. White *Aunt's Story* 34 Tom Wilcocks was as rough as bags. His neck was red and strong. The pollard had caked hard on his hard hands. **1966** G. W. Turner *Eng. Lang. Austral. & N.Z.* vi. 115 There is simile:..'rough as bags' (which I know better in the variant 'rough as sacks'). **1966** B. Beaver *You can't come Back* 118 I'm shy all right, but I'm not smooth... I'm rough as guts. **1968** F. Hardy *Unlucky Australians* 11 The old Territorian is a good bloke, rough as guts but his heart's in the right place. **1970** *Guardian* 25 July 6/1 Behan was most obviously gross and cussed and tragic and rough as ould bags. **1977** C. McCullough *Thorn Birds* x. 235 Even Dot MacPherson, the Bingelly heiress, ..was rough as bags, no posh Sydney boarding school and all that crap.

IV. 17. d. Of stationery, etc.: for use in writing rough notes or exercises; in which preliminary records are written.

1867, etc. [see *rough book*, sense 21, in Dict. and Suppl.]. **1884**, etc. [see *rough log(-book)*, sense *21]. **1928** E. Scott *War among Ladies* I. iv. 44 Blotting-paper, foolscap, 'rough' paper..were laid out. **1960** *Sc. Nat. Dict.* V. 343/2 *Jot-book*, a rough note-book. *Ibid.*, A pupil's rough exercise book. **1977** P. D. James *Death of Expert Witness* II. 101 His rough notebook?.. Anything of importance was noted in that book, and subsequently transferred to the files.

e. Applied to a vacuum of the lowest degree of evacuation.

1927 G. W. C. Kaye *High Vacua* vi. 74 For industrial purposes, such as exhausting rough vacuum mains, furnaces, or ovens, the so-called 'dry air pump' of the engineer is normally employed. **1949** S. Dushman *Vacuum Technique* iii. 141 With a 'rough' vacuum of about 10 mm mercury, such a pump could reduce the pressure to about 1 micron. **1969** *Gloss. Terms Vacuum Technol.* (*B.S.I.*) 1. 7 *Rough vacuum*, 10^5 N/m² to 10^2 N/m². 760 torr to 1 torr. [*Note*] Not intended to be precise definitions, but to provide convenient and practical subdivisions of the vacuum range. **1976** *Physics Bull.* Apr. 161/1 Medium vacuum is used extensively for freeze drying and rough vacuum is also used for specimen handling and sample transfer.

V. 21. a. rough book, (*a*) also = **rough log(-book)*; (*b*) a book in which rough notes are written, a jotter; **rough calf** (see quot. 1952); **rough cut** *Cinematogr.*, the first edited version of a film, the state of a film after preliminary editing; also *attrib.*; **rough grazing,** uncultivated land used for grazing; an area of such land; **rough log(-book)** *Naut.*, a book in which the particulars of a ship's voyage are first entered, to be written up later in the main log-book; **rough mix,** a preliminary blend of separately recorded parts of a piece of music; **rough pâté,** pâté made with coarsely-chopped or -minced meat; **rough scruff** *U.S.* = *rough-scuff;* **rough spin** *Austral. slang,* a misfortune; **rough stuff,** (*c*) unruliness, violent behaviour; **rough-tonguing,** rude speech; verbal abuse, disparaging; a scolding; **rough trade** *slang,* a tough or sadistic element among male homosexuals, esp. prostitutes; the activities of homosexual prostitutes; (see also quots. 1935, 1973).

1902 Conrad *Typhoon* v. 47 He copied neatly out of the rough-book the number of miles, the course of the ship. **1969** A. Laski *Dominant Fifth* ii. 43 She had been drawing on her rough book. **1912** Monk & Lawrence *Text Bk. Stationery Binding* 85 Rough calf or its substitutes require the surface well cleaned before tooling. **1952** A. W. Lewis *Basic Bookbinding* ii. 17 *Rough calf*, calf skin finished on the flesh side and used on books with the flesh side outermost. **1963** B. C. Middleton *Hist Eng. Craft Bookbinding Technique* 286 Rough calf was much used in the seventeenth and eighteenth centuries. **1975** *Sotheby & Co. (Hodgson's Rooms) Catal.* 31 July–1 Aug. 45 Abelard (Peter) and Heloise. Opera,..a few leaves slightly soiled, eighteenth century rough calf, slightly rubbed.

1939 *N.Y. Times* 2 Apr. x. 4/4 The only demands we have made on the producers as a Guild were to have two weeks' preparation time for 'A' pictures, one week preparation time for 'B' pictures and to have supervision of just the first rough cut of the picture. **1952** L. Ross *Picture* (1953) iii. 108 Actually, every director should make the rough cut—the film as assembled from start to finish for the first time—himself. **1957** Manvell & Huntley *Film Music* iii. 59 Functional music may be composed after the film has been shot and assembled in rough-cut. **1970** *Daily Tel.* 23 Sept. 12/3 There was no censorship apart from the cutting of a single frame at the request of an East German Government representative who saw the pictures at rough-cut stage. **1978** P. J. Kavanagh *People & Weather* vi. p. ciii, He returned to the studio with his film, triumphant... But when he put together the rough-cut he was appalled. **1932** *Jrnl. Min. Agric.* XXXIX. 37 White clover can be successfully established on certain types of rough grazings without mechanical cultivation. **1953** E. Smith *Guide Eng. Traditions* 1 'Rough grazing', wild open land over which various owners of livestock have grazing rights. **1966** I. Moore *Grass & Grasslands* iv. 30 The transition from ley to permanent pasture or meadows, thence to rough grazing and scrub, and finally to forest, is an orderly, gradual process. **1970** *Sruth* (Inverness) 16 Apr. 3/1 The reconditioning of regenerated areas of heath land and rough grazings. **1884** *Naval Encycl.* 701/2 *Rough log*, the book in which the journal of the ship is originally written. A smooth copy, signed by the watch-officers, is inspected by the commanding officer, and forwarded to the Navy Department. **1917** D. Wilson-Barker *Man. Elementary Seamanship* (ed. 7) vii. 225 Every officer keeps an account of the work..during his watch. This record he enters on a log slate, scrap, deck, or rough log, as it may be called. **1922** F. Riesenberg *Stand. Seamanship for Merchant Service* xviii. 761 The *smooth log* is a copy of the *rough log*. The latter is the original and valuable record. **1948** R. de Kerchove *Internat. Maritime Dict.* 667/2 *Ship's log book*, a nautical record compiled from entries taken from the rough log book. **1961** F. H. Burgess *Dict. Sailing* 68 *Deck log*, a ship's rough log book, in which is recorded all information about working the ship, and other events as they occur. *Ibid.* 174 *Rough log*, the deck log. **1962** G. Danton *Theory & Pract. Seamanship* xiii. 288 The Chief Officer's logbook.. is virtually a diary of the ship's activities. The information contained therein is derived from the rough logbook, which is kept by the individual Officers-of-the-watch. **1970** D. M. Henderson *Seamanship* xxvi. 464 The rough, original or chart room log-book is written up by the Officer of the Watch or Officer of the Deck. **1977** *Rolling Stone* 24 Mar., I'd sneak back in and listen to the rough mix. **1977** *Zigzag* Apr. 6/2 The way Stevie likes to work is to record something, then take a rough mix down to the country where he's got a little demo studio, and work out what he's going to put down within what's already there. **1961** G. Smith *Business of Loving* xi. 222, I settled on a rough paté, some pheasant with game chips. **1974** *Times* 4 Nov. 14/8 We chose rough country pâté and Vichyssoise to start with. **1977** P. Harcourt *At High Risk* i. 19 We had a rough *pâté de la campagne*. **1831** *Boston Even. Transcript* 1 Oct. 1/2 The roughscruf of St Louis called my deliverer a Watchenago. **1865** 'Mark Twain' in *Californian* 18 Mar. 8/2 The ruff-scruff and rag-tag-and-bob-tail of noble old Calaveras. **1924** *Truth* (Sydney) 27 Apr. 6 *Rough spin*, bad luck. **1940** F. D. Davison *Woman at Mill* 150, I had a rough spin. **1913** J. London *Valley of Moon* i. iv. 32 There's goin' to be rough stuff down there in a minute. **1915** H. L. Wilson *Ruggles of Red Gap* ii. 30 But you'll have to be firm, because he's full of tricks. And if he starts any rough stuff, just come to me. **1919** W. H. Downing *Digger Dial.* 42 *Rough stuff*, an undisciplined, reckless, indecent, disorderly or disrespectful person or thing. **1925** Chesterton *Everlasting Man* i. i. 24 His chief occupation..was.. treating women in general with what is, I believe, known in the world of the film as 'rough stuff'. **1940** Wodehouse *Eggs, Beans & Crumpets* 238 Your aunt..has a right to early information about any rough stuff that is being pulled on the premises. **1959** 'M. M. Kaye' *House of Shade* xx. 275 I'd have got that pro-Red nancy-boy before he started any rough stuff. **1978** *Lancashire Life* Apr. 73/2 The presence of a girl in a group of tipsy young men keeps them in check, however: the laughs are there but the rough stuff isn't. **1916** 'Boyd Cable' *Action Front* 98 An' I admit I felt easier after that rough-tonguin'... That slobberin' an' kissin' business..may be all right for a lot o' bloomin' Frenchies. **1919** J. Buchan *Mr. Standfast* xii. 217 He would relish the rough-tonguing of non-coms. **1956** N. Marsh *Off with his Head* (1957) ix. 191 Maids up to castle heard his great-auntie giving him a terrible rough-tonguing. **1935** A. J. Pollock *Underworld Speaks* 99/1 *Rough trade*, a person picked up on the street by a sexual pervert. **1965** *Playboy* Aug. 124/2 The gay boys call us 'rough trade'! We're the ones they date.... We're the ones they buy presents for. **1967** *Evening Standard* 11 July 10/3 The gradual destruction..of.. Boyde Ashlar..as he gets involved with what I believe is called the Rough Trade. **1973** *Amer. Speech 1970* XLV. 58 *Rough trade* n, pick-up from one of the occupations typical of tough men, such as truck drivers or dock workers. **1976** M. Machlin *Pipeline* xxxviii. 412 There were no gay bars or hangouts, and very few gays dared walk the streets in the more extravagant, deviant-type-wardrobes. Any gay activity in Fairbanks was probably confined to rough trade. **1978** C. Beaton *Parting Years* vi. 159 He made friendships too easily with the 'rough trade'. **1980** *Times Lit. Suppl.* 7 Mar. 253/3 Auden was a homosexual who..seems to have had a greater craving for a settled relationship and being loved than for rough trade or other casual excitement.

b. rough collie, a long-coated black and white, or black, tan, and white collie; **Rough Fell,** a large long-woolled sheep of the breed so called, found in parts of the Pennine area; **rough greyhound** = Deer-hound.

1806 Rough collie [see Collie]. **1872** 'Stonehenge' *Dogs Brit. Islands* (ed. 2) ii. viii. 175 The rough or shaggy-coated colley..has a fine foxlike muzzle. **1931** A. C. Smith *About our Dogs* xvii. 275 The Smooth Collie should be identical in all features with the Rough, except in coat. **1977** *Grimsby Even. Tel.* 5 May 3/5 (Advt.), Cairns, Westies, Rough Collies, Old English Sheepdogs. **1916** W. J. Malden *Brit. Sheep & Shepherding* vi. 58 The Rough Fell sheep of the moors and hills of North-west Yorkshire..and adjoining districts are clearly allied to the Scotch Black-face. **1945** J. F. H. Thomas *Sheep* ii. 30 The Rough Fell. Again a breed not numerically strong. **1960** Rough Fell [see *Exmoor]. **1888** Rough greyhound [see *fleet-hound* s.v. *Fleet *a.*[1] 4]. **1948** C. L. B. Hubbard *Dogs in Brit.* xv. 122 The Deerhound, or Rough Greyhound as it was then called, was a prized possession of the Scottish chieftain.

22. *rough-water, -weather* (earlier and later examples), *-wood*.

1833 *Chambers's Edin. Jrnl.* 1 June 141/1 Those who are tough, keep the deck in their rough-weather cloaks. **1898** H. E. A. Coate *Realities of Sea Life* xiv. 124 All hands very busy in unbending rough-weather sails and bending fine-weather ones. **1921** W. de la Mare *Crossings* 67 A garden chair beside a roughwood table. **1967** *Gloss. Terms Air-Cushion Vehicles* (*B.S.I.*) 7 *Rough water drag*, the increment in the drag during operation in rough water over the drag, under otherwise identical conditions, in calm water. **1971** *Flying* Apr. 27/1 A deep V bottom provides lower impact loads on rough-water landings. **1978** J. A. Michener *Chesapeake* iv. 184 The entire group of Quakers went..to the rough-wood house of James Lamb.

23. a. *rough-barked* (earlier example), *-edged* (further examples), *-faced* (earlier example), *-grained* (further example), *-mouthed*, *-surfaced*.

1836 J. G. Whittier *Mogg Megone* 11 The gnarlëd trunk of the rough-barked oak. **1932** D. Gascoyne *Roman Balcony* 36 Glittering, rough-edged shadows on the dull lawn. **1970** *Daily Tel.* 23 Jan. 6 Rough-edged men who cannot complete a sentence without a four-letter word. **1978** J. Carroll *Mortal Friends* ii. vii. 216 He threw himself into the fray with a fierceness that was rough-edged and merciless even for him. **1812** E. Weeton *Let.* 25 May (1969) II. 15 A rough-faced fellow, a journeyman saddler. **1962** in E. E. Evans-Pritchard *Ess. Social Anthropol.* v. 115 He represented a sultan who excels the ordinary people in body and spirit, and one gained the impression that one was dealing with a rough-grained, able and cunning man. **1899** A. Bennett *Jrnl.* 29 Oct. (1932) I. 96 The actual coarse, ignorant, crude-thinking, rough-mouthed maiden of past times. **1926** Rough-surfaced [see *offset *sb.* 10 b]. **1962** *Science Survey* XI. 166 There are smooth-surfaced vesicles, vacuoles and tubules; flattened sacs whose limiting membranes are encrusted with particles and therefore 'rough'-surfaced.

b. (Further example.)

1901 *Nature* 19 Sept. 523/2 Seven rough-keeled snakes (*Dasypeltis scabra*).

c. *rough-stalked meadow-grass* (later examples).

1901 H. M. Ward *Grasses* iii. 42 *Poa trivialis.* (Rough-stalked Meadow-grass.) Conspicuous in deep rich pastures. **1960** *Farmer & Stockbreeder* 8 Mar. 117/1 Rough-stalked meadow grass, bent, and wild white clover together with a few so-called 'weeds'.

rough, *adv.* Add: **1. a.** (Examples corresponding to sense *11 c of the adj.)

1954 L. Klemantaski tr. *Fraichard's Le Mans Story* v. 52 'The engine is running rough!' he cried. **1978** J. Gardner *Dancing Dodo* xxxviii. 308 The port engine faltered... She had started to run rough.

b. (Further examples.) Also, *to live rough*.

1960 *Guardian* 7 Dec. 1/4 He had been sleeping rough with the others on a haystack. **1974** *Whig-Standard* (Kingston, Ontario) 11 Jan. 7/1 A 'dosser... Sleeps on a bench, wrapped in a newspaper, living 'rough'. **1974** J. I. M. Stewart *Gaudy* ix. 172 We neither of us had a bean, you see, and I was just going to sleep rough. **1977** *Jrnl. R. Soc. Arts* CXXV. 148/2 There are going to be 2000 single people in London without homes sleeping rough this Christmas.

2. a. *rough-dig, -edit, -land, -school, -sketch, -sort*.

1909 *Country Life* 23 Oct. 577/1 One could see him rough-schooling younger brothers and companions. **1910** W. J. Locke *Simon* xxiv. 315 The story of his marriage is a little lunatic drama all to itself and I will tell it some day. But now I can only rough-sketch the facts. **1950** Partridge *Here, There & Everywhere* 166, I should like to rough-sketch the position occupied by him and Lewis Carroll in the chronology of the subject. **1960** *Aeroplane* XCIX. 541/2 Turning to lunar and interplanetary research, Mr. Stoller said that in 1962 three Ranger vehicles were planned to rough-land payloads on the surface of the Moon. These will be followed by the soft-landing mission. **1962** A. Nisbett *Technique Sound Studio* vii. 124 It will often be possible to rough edit without bothering to mark the tape. **1969** W. Rutherford *Gallows Set* iv. 55 This film has already been rough-edited... That means that the editor will have done all the obvious things, taken out false starts, put in the cutaway questions. **1972** H. Evans *Newsman's Eng.* i. 1 The international news..has been checked, rough-edited. **1976** *Norwich Mercury* 19 Nov. 11/3 It is advisable to rough-dig all uncropped land. **1978** *Cahiers de Lexicologie* XXXII. 31 Assembling and rough-sorting a citation collection.

b. *rough-bound, -built, -cut* (later example), *-dug, -hurled, -plucked, -scored, -split, -trimmed*.

1865 G. M. Hopkins *Poems* (1967) 20 Those crookèd rough-scored chequers may be pieced To crosses meant for Jesu's. **1870** D. G. Rossetti *Let.* 21 Apr. (1965) II. 851, I suppose the inscription at the back of the rough-bound copy sent is from the real block. **1882** W. D. Hay *Brighter Britain!* I. v. 120 Rough-split sections of the great logs. *a* **1892** J. G. Whittier in S. T. Pickard *Life & Lett. Whittier* (1894) I. i. 13 And lo! in the midst of a clearing stood The rough-built farmhouse, low and lone. **1909** *Daily Chron.* 18 Oct. 4/5 Fowls are sold both dead and rough-plucked, and alive for fattening. **1925** Blunden *Eng. Poems* 31 As wave-wise Rough-hurled they rose, With a sweet sureness. **1965** G. J. Williams *Econ. Geol. N.Z.* xiv. 221/1 During the second world war about 1½ tons of rough-trimmed mica were won from this area. **1967** E. Short *Embroidery & Fabric Collage* ii. 38 Woven silks were embellished with rich all-over embroidery which incorporated pearls and rough-cut gem stones. **1973** R. Adams *Watership Down* xx. 125 The Honeycomb was still rough-dug and half-finished. **1976** *Cumberland News* 3 Dec. 35/3 (Advt.), Oven ready and rough plucked birds.

d. *rough-editing, -landing, -schooling*.

1909 *Spectator* 30 Oct. 678/2 Sir Percy Fitzpatrick is certainly right in picking out..the 'rough-schooling of younger boys and companions'. **1959** *Fortune* July 157/1 A somewhat more difficult trip..will be the rough landing of a fifty-pound payload on the moon. **1962** A. Nisbett *Technique Sound Studio* vii. 117 *Rough editing* is assembling the main body of the programme in the right order and taking out the longer stretches of unwanted material.

rough, *v.*[1] Add: **I. 2. c.** (Earlier and later examples.) Also with inanimate object. See also sense *6 g.

1845 W. G. Simms *Wigwam & Cabin* 1st Ser. 58 She [*sc.* a bear] roughed me once or twice more with her paws. **1904** *Baltimore American* 1 Aug. 2 (*heading*) Badman roughs a train, but is shot in the hand by a plucky trainman. **1928** *Daily Mail* 25 July 12/4 Tunney knows he will be roughed and bustled around for the first few rounds. **1957** D. Niland *Call me when Cross turns Over* vi. 153 They grabbed Shelton and roughed him outside into the rising wind. **1971** *Frendz* 21 May 2/4 Cant put the rest down because the tin hats will rough my kin. **1978** *N.Y. Times* 29 Mar. B 6/5 The Mets..roughed Pete Falcone with a pair of runs apiece in the fourth, fifth and sixth innings.

II. 4. a. (Earlier example.)

c **1771** M. Suckling *Let.* in Southey *Life of Nelson* (1813) I. i. 5 What..has poor Horatio done,..that he.. should be sent to rough it out at sea?

5. c. *Austral.* and *N.Z.* To shear (a sheep) badly.

1878 'Ironbark' *Southerly Busters* 180, I allus roughs 'em when the boss Ain't on the shearin' floor. **1897** D. McK. Wright *Station Ballads* 37 But he wouldn't shear at Maimai, started in to rough them through. **1956** G. Bowen *Wool Away!* (ed. 2) 156 *Rough 'em*, the opposite to 'pink 'em', and meaning rough shearing and a bad job of the sheep.

III. 6. b. (Earlier and later examples.)

1770 C. Carroll *Let.* 25 Apr. in *Maryland Hist. Mag.* (1917) XII. 352, I think you are wrong to Have the Capitalls &c. finished there, they may be defaced in the Carriage, wh Danger would be avoided if only roughed out there. **1955** *Times* 4 Aug. 7/6 The first act has been already roughed out. *a* **1974** R. Crossman *Diaries* (1975) I. 370 By the early hours I had roughed out a reasonably intelligent script.

g. Const. *up*. To deal roughly with, assault, damage, upset, intimidate; = sense 2 c.

1942 Berrey & Van den Bark *Amer. Thes. Slang* §341/2 *Treat roughly*; '*manhandle*'... rough (up), rough-house, strong-arm, treat 'em rough. **1943** R. Chandler *Lady in Lake* (1944) xxxvi. 192 You know how to rough up a bum that hasn't any money. **1959** 'M. M. Kaye' *House of Shade* iii. 29 When am I supposed to have roughed up your room? **1963** *Times* 14 Jan. 3/1 They had roughed-up France's pack a year ago. **1970** M. Braithwaite *Never sleep Three in Bed* xi. 135 They began to rough us up and we kicked and pulled and yelled about what our dads would do if they didn't leave us alone. **1973** *Time Out* 2–8 Mar. 15/1 A lot of teachers got roughed up, but that's not to say beaten up. **1977** M. Goulder in J. Hick *Myth of God Incarnate* iii. 58 Not only must he be prepared to be roughed up by southern policemen; he must also risk assassination. **1978** *N.Y. Times* 30 Mar. D 19/4 But at that point, the Phillies dealt Bruhert a cruel blow. They roughed him up with six rapid-fire singles. **1978** J. A. Michener *Chesapeake* xiv. 864 Amos Turlock..led an expedition to Caveny's home, which had been roughed up but not destroyed.

h. *to rough down*, to give (wood) a rough, preliminary planing. Cf. Roughing *vbl. sb.* 2 b.

1960 *McGraw-Hill Encycl. Sci. & Technol.* XIV. 543/1 Flat or uniformly contoured surfaces of wood are roughed down, smoothed, or made level by the shaving and cutting action of a wide-edged blade or blades.

7. a. (Earlier and later examples.)

1770 C. Carroll *Let.* 20 Apr. in *Maryland Hist. Mag.* (1917) XII. 351 The stone cutters wish to have a draft of the Bases & Capitalls, they could rough the stones to that draft, & save a great deal of carriage. **1937** *Times* 13 Apr. (British Motor No.) p.xii/2 Machines of particular interest are the Gleason completing machine for producing differential pinions, roughed and finished at a speed of 65 seconds each, and the lapping machines.

d. To subject to a partial or preliminary evacuation. Also with *down, out*.

1948 [implied in *roughing down* s.v. *roughing *vbl. sb.* 2 b]. **1971** *Physics Bull.* July 423/2 This consists of a large ion pump and liquid N_2 cooled titanium sublimation pump combination, 'roughed' by two high capacity sorption pumps and an oil free mechanical roughing pump. **1976** A. Roth *Vacuum Technol.* v. 200 The removal of the atmospheric air from the system to some acceptable operating pressure is referred to as roughing out the system... Mechanical rotary pumps, and ejectors are the typical roughing and backing pumps.

roughage. For '*dial.* and *U.S.*' read 'orig. *dial.* and *U.S.*' and add: **1.** Also *N.Z.* (Further examples.)

1940 E. C. STUDHOLME *Te Waimate* x. 80 The first work of the settlers was to burn off the roughage on large areas of country. **1950** *N.Z. Jrnl. Agric.* Feb. 122/3 On much of the country a fairly high proportion of cattle to sheep is carried, the cattle being used largely to clean up roughage left by the sheep.

2. The indigestible fibrous matter or cellulose in vegetable foodstuffs. Also *attrib.*

1927 *Lancet* 16 July 106/1, I suspect that the advocacy of this bread was begun on the ground that the extra cellulose which it contains, forming what has been termed 'roughage', is of advantage as a mechanical irritant to the mucous membrane of the colon. **1932** *Times Lit. Suppl.* 7 Jan. 1/3 French art has had in the past its extra-artistic responsibilities, its burdens and entanglements, leading to the presence in the work of art of what corresponds to 'roughage' in food. **1948** *Good Housek. Cookery Bk.* 13 Much constipation is due to insufficient quantities of roughage in the diet. **1963** *Times* 4 Feb. 4/7 Roughage diets. **1976** *Which?* Nov. 244/3 Wholemeal bread is a simple and effective source of roughage.

b. *fig.*

1931 *Musical Times* Jan. 74/1 This was another of the oddities that we have to accept as roughage to the Hallé [orchestra] fare. **1948** C. S. LEWIS *Lit. & Life* 58 There is no roughage in a Kipling story—it is all unrelieved vitamins from the first word to the last. **1962** [see *FUNK *sb.*[2] 2]. **1963** *Punch* 23 Jan. 141/3 Twelve months in jail provided the roughage for his first book. **1974** *Times* 28 Feb. 15/3 The electorate..finally gagged on their traditional roughage of internecine strife.

rough-and-ready, *a.* Add: **2.** (Earlier examples, as a nickname.)

1843 in *Amer. Speech* (1965) XL. 132 But Rough and Ready made dem smell Gunpowder a la Poker. **1846** *Congress. Globe* 24 May 865 Col. [Zachary] Taylor..had won for himself by his gallant conduct in the field the soubriquet of 'Old Rough and Ready'.

Hence **rough-and-readiness.**

1956 *Essays in Crit.* VI. 185 Beliefs that allow Pound to be satisfied..with a surprising emotional rough-and-readiness. **1960** *Guardian* 30 Nov. 7/1 The rough-and-readiness of such Italian neo-realists as Rossellini.

rough-and-tumble, *a.*, *sb.*, and *adv.* Add: **A.** *adj.* **4.** Roughly constructed or improvised; makeshift. *rare.*

1912 KIPLING *Land & Sea Tales* (1923) 70 They heaved up their rough-and-tumble anchor, and made after a.. sailing-ship.

C. *adv.* (Further U.S. example.)

1935 Z. N. HURSTON *Mules & Men* (1970) I. viii. 178 Mr. Allen might have eaten by the rules but Cliffert and I went at it rough-and-tumble with no holds barred.

rough-and-tumbling. For *nonce-wd.* read *rare* and add further example.

1832 *Chambers's Edin. Jrnl.* I. 130/2 The scene can only be compared to a rough-and-tumbling in the back woods of America.

roughback (rʊ·fbæk). [f. ROUGH *a.* + BACK *sb.*[1]] One of several flatfishes with rough skins, esp. the long rough dab, *Hippoglossoides platessoides.* Also *attrib.*

1795 J. SINCLAIR *Stat. Acct. Scotland* XVI. 548 Flounders of all kinds, roughback, plaise. **1815** J. ARBUTHNOT *Hist. Acct. Peterhead* 15 Dab, vulgarly called Rough Back Fluke, Rochie. **1903** G. SIM *Vertebr. Fauna of Dee* 244 Long Rough Dab. 'Rochie'..'Rough-back Fluke'..is not looked upon with much favour as an article of food. **1935** *Fisheries Notice* (Min. Agric.) No.23.4 Suggested Trade Name. Rough-back... General English Equivalent. Long Rough Dab. **1973** J. GRIGSON *Fish Cookery* 281 Roughback (i American plaice) (ii rock sole; flat-fish).

rough-cast, roughcast, *ppl. a.* and *sb.* Add: **I. 1. c.** Of glass: cast in a particular manner (see next).

1939 *Archit. Rev.* LXXXV. 99 (*caption*) Bent dome of 'rough-cast' glass used, at the Saint-Gobain pavilion, Paris 1937, as a simple and elegant alternative to the ordinary opaque basin. **1973** *Technical Translation Bull.* XIX. 103 *Plate glass*..is expensive to produce owing to the need for grinding and polishing of the 'rough cast plate' produced as a first stage... Indeterminate patterns such as 'rough cast' or 'cathedral' are normally called 'cast.'

2. d. A type of glass (see quot. 1962).

1962 *Gloss. Terms Glass Industry* (*B.S.I.*) 31 *Rough cast*, rolled translucent glass, one surface of which has a definite texture, made by rolling molten glass either on a table or between rollers. **1973** [see prec. sense].

rough-casting, *vbl. sb.* **1.** (Later example.)

1977 *S. Wales Echo* 18 Jan. (Advt.), Pebble Dashing, Spar Dashing, Rough-casting, all types of Plastering carried out.

rough-draft, *v.* (Further example.)

1975 I. K. MARTIN *Regan & Manhattan File* 110 Regan wrote his own report and rough-drafted Cassidy's report as a favour.

rough-dry, *v.* Add: (Further examples.) Now more generally, to dry roughly or imperfectly. Hence **rou·gh-dried** *ppl. a.*

1900 KIPLING in *Daily Express* 12 June 4/5 Sweating men, rough-dried sweating horses with wisps of precious forage. **1942** Z. N. HURSTON in A. Dundes *Mother Wit* (1973) 222/1 He was born with this rough-dried hair. **1952** 'J. TEY' *Singing Sands* i. 8 Service..had lost its starch and its high glaze. It had become what housewives call rough-dried. **1978** P. HARCOURT *Agents of Influence* xii. 146 She..continued to rough-dry her hair on the towel.

rough-dry, *a.* (Earlier examples.)

1856 MRS. STOWE *Dred* I. 181 Clothes look rough-dry, as if they had been pulled out of a bag. **1865** M. EYRE *Lady's Walks S. of France* i. 8 The articles..are neither starched nor ironed, but simply sent home rough dry.

rough-grind, *v.* Add: So **rou·gh-ground** *ppl. a.*

1901 KIPLING *Kim* xi. 289 A clothful of *atta*—grayish, rough-ground native flour,—twists of down-country tobacco.

rou·gh-hew, *sb. rare.* [f. the vb.] Something lacking the finishing process; a preliminary version.

1889 G. M. HOPKINS *Lett. to R. Bridges* (1935) 301 It was only a sketch, a rough-hew of a song.

rough house, rough-house, *sb. slang* (orig. *U.S.*). [ROUGH *a.* 21.] An uproar, a disturbance, a row; horseplay, boisterous behaviour; a fight, a struggle.

1887 M. ROBERTS *Western Avernus* 54 He called the bridgeman a very opprobrious name, and for a moment there was great danger of a 'rough house' out of hand. **1895** [see ROUGH *a.* 21]. **1900** *Dialect Notes* II. 55 *Rough-house*, *n.* 1. A disorderly class. 2. Rough play. **1902** G. H. LORIMER *Lett. Merchant* xvi. 238 [He] said he liked things lively, but there was altogether too much rough house on Beacon Hill for him. **1906** *Dialect Notes* III. 154 *Rough-house*, *n.* Scuffle (in a room). 'The room looked like they had had a roughhouse.' Common slang. **1908** A. J. DAWSON *Finn* xix. 292 Seems to me you've been havin' a pretty rough house with somebody. **1911** R. D. SAUNDERS *Col. Todhunter* iii. 49 But an ominous cry rose from his front. 'Rush 'em, boys! Make a rough-house.' **1913** R. H. BARBOUR *Around the End* xxi. 258 The audience.. indulged in wild 'rough-house'. **1919** 'ETIENNE' *Strange Tales from Fleet* 136, I need not enlarge on the subsequent entertainments, which consisted of a sing-song followed by a 'rough house', in which a certain amount of furniture was broken. **1923** H. L. FOSTER *Beachcomber in Orient* xi. 240, I..watched Singapore fade into the distance with its memories of vice, iniquity, and general rough-house. **1933** E. O'NEILL *Ah, Wilderness!* I. 25 That's enough, now. No more roughhouse. You sit down here, Richard. **1941** *Penguin New Writing* II. 87 Someone being funny and turnin' off your juice and you keep striking at your electrode and wondering why the hell it doesn't strike and flash, and losing your temper, and then seeing the rest laughing and having a rough house for a while. **1952** [see *BOCHE]. **1973** 'B. GRAEME' *Two & Two make Five* xiii. 123 He's smaller and lighter than me; not nearly so useful in a rough house.

b. *attrib.* or as *adj.* (Also *roughhouse.*)

1898 F. P. DUNNE *Mr. Dooley in Peace & War* 25 Other gin'rals iv th' r-rough-house kind, like Napoleon Bonypart, th' impror iv th' Frinch, Gin'ral Ulis S. Grant, an' Cousin George Dooley, hired coarse, rude men. **1901** *Official Basket Ball Rules* (Spalding's Athletic Library) 49 Mr. Naismith never invented the game for 'rough house' work. **1906** *N.Y. Globe* 22 Aug. 6 On that rough-house occasion more force than was necessary was used to eject the Bryanite faction. **1919** H. L. WILSON *Ma Pettengill* ii. 74 Two or three other directors..had put him into rough-house funny plays where he got thrown downstairs or had bricks fall on him. **1932** *Amer. Speech* VII. 241 Jazz is free, Jazz is roughouse. **1938** E. BOWEN *Death of Heart* II. iv. 240 Mr. Bursely was shoved against the bookcase by Wallace Parker shoving, that rude way. .. I didn't like him to see us so rough house. **1938** R. GRAVES *Coll. Poems* 121 Time and Space Do but amuse us with their rough-house turn. **1946** *Casper* (Wyoming) *Tribune-Herald* 29 Mar. 9/3 Rocky, with his striking black hair and roughhouse tactics in the ring, has become a gallery idol.

rou·gh-house, *v. slang* (orig. *U.S.*). Also **rough house, roughhouse.** [f. the sb.] **1.** *intr.* To make a disturbance or row; to behave or act boisterously or violently; to fight or engage in horse-play *with.* Also quasi-*trans.* with *it.*

1900 *Dialect Notes* II. 55 *Rough-house*, *v.i.* To put a room in disorder. **1904** R. L. MCCARDELL *Show Girl & her Friends* 107 When they teased him about having to keep him out of the place if he did not stop rough-housing it, poor Dopey smiled..and asked if he had hurt anybody very bad. **1908** U. B. SINCLAIR *Metropolis* 57 She's always wanting to rough-house it. **1920** 'SAPPER' *Bull-Dog Drummond* ix. 239 Somebody has been rough-housing by the look of things. **1928** *Chambers's Jrnl.* Apr. 211/2 He had a veteran in combat to deal with, a man who had 'rough-housed' it all over the world. **1929** E. L. RICE *Street Scene* II. 167 Rough-housing with your kid brother. **1971** *Daily Colonist* (Victoria, B.C.) 5 May 43/2 Police spokesmen said the boys were 'rough-housing' on the grass. **1977** *Time* 10 Jan. 13/1 Twice, a broken leg set him back—once when he was caught in an avalanche while skiing, later while roughhousing with friends.

2. *trans.* To handle (a person) violently; to assail roughly; to maltreat by rough usage.

1902 H. L. WILSON *Spenders* xxxvi. 436 You rough-housed the boy considerable yesterday. **1903** *N.Y. Times* 6 Oct. 1 After the rush the classes adjourned to Massachusetts Avenue and began to 'rough house' the passing street cars. **1925** H. L. FOSTER *Trop. Tramp with Tourists* 188 The S[ocial] M[anager] must not risk the loss of their future patronage by mauling or roughhousing such as might not enjoy it, or at least tolerate it. **1928** *Daily Express* 4 Sept. 9/5 Harvey as a boxer of exceptional skill should not have allowed West to rush into close quarters and 'rough-house' him. **1938** X. HERBERT *Capricornia* (1939) xxvi. 389 He explained that when he had tried to keep order at the station he had been rough-housed. **1952** in Wentworth & Flexner *Dict. Amer. Slang* (1960) 434/1 The question of whether..gun-toting bodyguards rough-housed Swedish citizens.

Hence **rou·gh-houser** (also *attrib.* and *fig.*); **rou·gh-housing** *vbl. sb.*

1904 *N.Y. Even. Post* 2 Jan., In fiction, whether it is historic, society, or the work of literary rough-housers. **1927** *Blackw. Mag.* June 843/2 It is more than mere rough-housing. **1933** D. L. SAYERS *Murder must Advertise* v. 90 Stand by..in case there's any rough-housing. **1949** KOESTLER *Promise & Fulfilment* I. xii. 131 Apart from some rough-housing..the troops found no occasion for any martial activity. **1951** *Sun* (Baltimore) 2 Mar. 19/2 In some sections, wrestling is outdrawing boxing... Lord Carlton, who poses as a titled Englishman; the Golden Terror, a roughhouser type..have contributed to the success. **1974** H. L. FOSTER *Ribbin'* vi. 244 Many male teachers relate physically to male students through playful roughhousing where some form of physical body contact is made.

roughie (rʊ·fi). *dial.* and *slang.* Also **roughy.** [f. ROUGH *sb.*[1] + -IE, -Y[6].] **1.** A rough or rowdy; a brawler; a hooligan.

1905 *Eng. Dial. Dict.* V. 158/1 *Roughy*, *sb.* Sc. Irel. 1 A coarsely made, bullying fellow. Ant. GROSE (1790) *MS. add.* (C.) **1933** *Bulletin* (Sydney) 15 Nov. 33/1 With such a lot of roughies in the hall. **1953** *Amer. Speech* XXVIII. 118 *Rough, roughy*, *n.* A carnival roustabout, a manual labourer. **1966** W. S. RAMSON *Austral. Eng.* iv. 62 Roughie, meaning 'a coarsely made, bullying fellow' was used in both Scotland and Ireland. **1971** P. DRISCOLL *White Lie Assignment* vii. 60, I know a roughie when I see one... He's just one of those blokes who can't stay away from trouble.

2. *Austral.* In dog- and horse-racing: an outsider.

1934 'S. RUDD' *Green Grey Homestead* 155 Those who had lost a wager or two will turn to Bell and say: 'You knew something about the roughie!' **1951** CUSACK & JAMES *Come in Spinner* 40 He's a roughie so 'e'll go out at long odds. **1958** F. HARDY *Four-Legged Lottery* 14, I might just have a shilling on a roughie. **1973** *Sun-Herald* (Sydney) 26 Aug. 58/2 Punters were reluctant to support him... Consequently Pepper Moss went out as a 12–1 'roughie'.

3. *Austral.* A trick, an unfair practice; esp. in phr. *to put a roughie over.*

1939 K. TENNANT *Foveaux* II. i. 122 Kelly put a roughie over Charlie to-day. *Ibid.* III. ii. 151 'They're putting over a roughie at Central,' the secretary..mentioned casually. **1945** BAKER *Austral. Lang.* xv. 265 A *roughie*, *toughie, hottie, crookie, swiftie, smartie* will all be heard in male conversation to describe a joke or trick that is either agreeable or disagreeable. **1970** R. BEILBY *No Medals for Aphrodite* 269, I bluffed him, put a roughie over him.

roughing, *vbl. sb.* Add: **2. b.** (Further examples.) Also with *off, out* (cf. ROUGH *v.*[1] 6 b in Dict. and Suppl.; also *attrib.*).

1846 Roughing out [in Dict., sense 5]. **1883** *Proc. Inst. Mech. Engineers* 226 They are used in different machine tools principally for 'roughing out', or..rapidly reducing castings, forgings, &c., from their rough state to nearly their finished forms. **1901** *Jrnl. Inst. Electr. Engineers* XXXI. 312 Two drills should in all cases be provided, one a roughing-out drill, and the other a finishing drill. **1947** J. C. RICH *Materials & Methods of Sculpture* ix. 252 The bushhammer is a very useful and fairly rapid tool, which may be employed from the coarse, initial roughing-out stages almost to the very delicate or final stages of the carving. **1947** DYLAN THOMAS *Let.* Jan. (1966) 292 And I also worked upon the preliminary roughing-out of the script with Taylor. **1948** *Rev. Sci. Instruments* XIX. 15/1 The holding pump serves as a fore-pump for the diffusion pump during the roughing-down portion of the cycle. **1969** E. H. PINTO *Treen* 388/1 A mid-19th-century roughing off plane. **1970** R. J. SMALL *Study of Landforms* iv. 128 Many of these joints are evidently post-denudational, having appeared since the 'roughing-out' of the main elements in the landscape by Tertiary erosion.

3. (Earlier examples.)

c **1823** BYRON *Don Juan* XII. lxiii. variant line 6 in Hagelman & Barnes *Concordance to Byron's Don Juan* (1967) 682 But those who have been a little used to roughing. **1836** T. POWER *Impressions Amer.* II. 211 This little city [*sc.* Mobile] was to me one of the most attractive spots I visited south of the Potomac. I came upon it..after a severe roughing, and found a fine climate and old friends.

4. (Further example.) Also *N.Amer.*, in *Football, Ice Hockey,* and *Lacrosse*: foul tackling, punching, or pushing. Also, *roughing-the-kicker* attrib.

1938 *Sun* (Baltimore) 27 Oct. 12/6 Brooks, of Yale, broke through and rushed the kicker... Being unable to stop himself in midair, he naturally crashed into the kicker, and Michigan was given the ball for roughing the punter. **1958** F. C. AVIS *Boxing Reference Dict.* 96 *Roughing*, questionable tactics in a boxing contest, and likely to involve disqualification of the offender. **1958** *Herald-Tribune* (Grande Prairie, Alberta) 28 Feb. 5/6 Bryan McCurdy..and Bill Oakford..went off together for roughing and slashing at the 18:55 mark. **1961** J. S. SALAK *Dict. Amer. Sports* 371 *Roughing the kicker* (football), making unnecessary bodily contact with the punter, which is illegal. *Roughing the passer* (football), unnecessary roughness to a player who has thrown a forward pass. A penalty is involved for this infraction. **1968** *Globe & Mail* (Toronto) 15 Jan. 20/2 The skirmish provoked a pushing duel that netted every player on the ice, with the exception of the goalkeepers, minors for roughing. **1973** *Houston* (Texas) *Chron.* (Suppl.) 14 Oct. 5/1, I was unaware of just how specialized pro football had become until..discovering that one team's kicker had not punted the entire evening. He had, however, drawn eight roughing-the-kicker penalties... It's 15 yards and an automatic first (five yards and an automatic first for the less flagrant 'running into the kicker'). **1976** *Webster's Sports Dict.* 357/1 *Roughing the kicker* (*football*), a personal foul that results when a defensive player runs into or knocks down the kicker on a scrimmage kick without first touching or deflecting the ball... When it is called, the penalty is 15 yards from the previous spot. *Roughing the passer* (*football*), a personal foul in professional play that results when a defensive player runs into or tackles a passer after a forward pass has been thrown... When it is called, the penalty is 15 yards from the previous spot.

b. With *up*: see *ROUGH *v.*[1] 6 g.

1960 *Sunday Express* 23 Oct. 17/4 His roughing-up of George Bernard Shaw can't compare for butchery with what Mr. Mankowitz did last week to Robert Louis Stevenson. **1973** J. PATTINSON *Search Warrant* iv. 67 He could already feel the stiffness in his limbs that was the result of the roughing-up. **1977** R. BARNARD *Blood Brotherhood* xvi. 181 Their gang knifings and roughings-up.

5. *roughing filter, plane, shop*; **roughing pump**, a pump for evacuating a system from atmospheric pressure to a lower pressure at which a second pump can operate.

1904 *Rep. Brit. Assoc. Adv. Sci. 1903* 761 The other two original tanks were converted into six roughing filters containing 3 feet in depth of fine gravel, to intercept particles which have escaped the precipitation process. **1960** *McGraw-Hill Encycl. Sci. & Technol.* XIV. 543/1 The scrub or roughing plane..has heavy, rounded blades making it suitable for cleaning up rough boards. **1958** *Rev. Sci. Instruments* XXIX. 368/1 With the roughing pump pinched off..and the system then thoroughly baked out while pumping with the electronic pump, very low pressures can be achieved. **1971, 1976** Roughing pump [see *ROUGH *v.*[1] 7 d]. **1910** *Daily Chron.* 15 Jan. 7/2 The cause of the fire was the fusing of an electric motor in the 'roughing' shop [of an opticians' factory].

rough lock, rough-lock. *N.Amer.* [LOCK *sb.*[2] 4.] A device, as a chain, for slowing the passage down a slope of a vehicle or of logs. So **rou·gh-lock, rou·ghlock** *v. trans.*, to slow a vehicle by means of a rough lock, to attach chains to a vehicle so as to slow it; **rou·gh-locking** *vbl. sb.*

1859 Rough-locking [see ROUGH *adv.* 2 d]. **1884** W. SHEPHERD *Prairie Experiences* 197 The hind wheels were rough-locked, that is, a large linked chain was tied round the rim of the wheel in such a way that the wheel rides upon the chain, which drags along and cuts into the ground. **1913** E. MACLENNAN in MacLennan & Snow *Songs of Neukluk* 15 She had a skookum load of logs, but I couldn't understand With the rough-lock and the geepole how it scaped from her command. **1962** J. ONSLOW *Bowler-Hatted Cowboy* v. 46 The rough-lock bit deep into the softening ice and mud. **1973** R. D. SYMONS *Where Wagon Led* I. viii. 128 The stout sleigh groaning in protest against the logging chain rough-locked around a hind runner.

rough neck, rough-neck, roughneck. *colloq.* (orig. *U.S.*). [ROUGH *a.*] **1. a.** A rough or rowdy; a person of rough habits or quarrelsome disposition; an uncultivated or ignorant person.

1836 *Col. Crockett's Exploits & Adventures Texas* iv. 58 You may be called a drunken dog by some of the clean shirt and silk stocking gentry; but the real rough necks will style you a jovial fellow. **1903** *Sun* (N.Y.) 25 Nov. 2 The police were kept on the jump chasing away gangs of 'rough necks' (the pet name for the rowdies in Sam Park's late union) who went from building to building trying to intimidate members of the new union. **1903** *N.Y. Evening Post* 17 Aug. 7/7 His [*sc.* Sam Park's] stated income amounts to union wages from his union of 'roughnecks', as the iron-workers call themselves, as walking delegate. **1917** J. M. GRIDER *War Birds* (1927) 30 But there are a few rough-necks in every outfit that will cause trouble and get the whole bunch in wrong. **1918** [see *non-academic* s.v. *NON- 3]. **1929** J. BUCHAN *Courts of Morning* I. iii. 51 The water-front was a perfect rat-hole for every criminal in the Pacific—every brand of roughneck and dope-smuggler and crook. **1940** E. N. TEALL *Putting Words to Work* I. xxi. 147 The business man will say that if a university can afford to write such letters there is no need for a roughneck like him to bother. **1959** 'J. CHRISTOPHER' *Scent of White Poppies* vi. 91 She has me tabbed for a roughneck... She has enough on with civilizing you, without having me to cope with as well. **1972** D. HASTON *In High Places* i. 14 Jimmy was twenty-eight, and already a qualified architect; we were seventeen-year-old roughnecks. Basically I think..he was at heart a roughneck himself. **1979** *Time* 13 Aug. 28/3 Like Lewis, countless other managers and entrepreneurs are coming to Denver to live amid its comfort and culture while their hired roughnecks and miners squeeze the energy from the rural out-posts.

b. *transf.* and *fig.*

Some examples are hardly distinguishable from sense 1 a.

1916 *Rio Grande Rattler* 13 Sept. 1 Ten buck [private] packers, known in the army as 'rough necks'—a title that usually fits the situation nicely. **1916** H. L. WILSON *Somewhere in Red Gap* v. 208 And so the party moved on for an hour or two, with the roguish young roughnecks cutting up merrily at all times, pretending to be cowboys coming to town on pay day. **1918** *Dialect Notes* V. 27 *Rough-neck*, n. 1. A rowdy. 2. A woman or girl of easy morals but not a prostitute. 3. A dance, open to anyone who 'has the price', at which 'anything goes'. General. **1926** MAINES & GRANT *Wise-Crack Dict.* 13/1 *Razor back*, roughneck or stake driver in a circus. **1926** F. SCOTT FITZGERALD *Great Gatsby* iii. 59 I'm Gatsby, he said... I was looking at an elegant young roughneck. **1941** E. P. O'DONNELL *Great Big Doorstep* iv. 59 'Are you a rough-neck?' 'Yes. I'm in the bull-gang so far. I'm trying to get in the office.' **1960** [see *MAUVAIS COUCHEUR]. **1978** *Amer. Poetry Rev.* July/Aug. 36/2 He was also an intellectual roughneck.

c. A worker on an oil-rig, esp. a labourer on the floor of a rig.

1917 *Dialect Notes* IV. 421 *Roughneck, n.* A man who works about an oil derrick. **1932** *Amer. Speech* VII. 270 *Roughneck*, n., the regular term for a member of a driller's crew on a rotary rig; not applied to the driller. **1948** *Chicago Tribune* 5 Dec. 1. 14/3 Among today's roughnecks you'll find college men—petroleum engineers and geologists. **1958** *Times* 15 May 14/6 Any such rig [for oil drilling] is known throughout the industry as a wildcat, and unskilled members of drilling crews are technically classified as 'roughnecks'. **1972** *Guardian* 11 Feb. 12/1 A Dutch oilman endorsed this. 'When the exploration is over, the 'roughnecks' (local labour) will go.' **1976** M. MACHLIN *Pipeline* xi. 135 He..had worked as a Roughneck in the Louisiana area and in East Texas on the oil rigs. **1977** *Time* 14 Mar. 37/1 The centre of the rig's activities is the mud-slicked drill floor, where half a dozen roughnecks struggle day and night with heavy chains and power-driven winches to shove 90-ft.-long pieces of drill pipe into the narrow hole.

2. *attrib.* Rough; rowdy; uncultivated; characteristic of a rough-neck.

1916 H. L. WILSON *Somewhere in Red Gap* vii. 288 He really wanted..to study insect life and botany and geography and arithmetic,..instead of being killed off in a sudden manner by his rough-neck parent. **1920** C. SANDBURG *Smoke & Steel* 7 The others were roughneck singers a long ways from home. **1931** 'R. WEST' in *Time & Tide* 19 Sept. 1091, I commend to every reader the essay on 'Foreheads Villainous Low', with its entertaining satire on the new 'roughneck' movement among the intellectuals. **1973** A. HUNTER *Gently French* xiv. 128 Those risks..would be part of the fun for a roughneck Romeo. **1976** R. SANDERS in D. Villiers *Next Year in Jerusalem* 209 The roughneck genius of a Walt Whitman.

So **rou·gh-neck** *v. intr.*, to work as a roughneck on an oil-rig; **rou·gh-necking** *vbl. sb.*

1932 *Amer. Speech* VII. 270 *Roughneck*, intr. v., to work as a member of a rotary driller's crew. **1976** *Globe & Mail* (Toronto) 16 Feb. 3/1 About 200 a year are beginners ready to try roughnecking, the industry's term for the beginners' job. **1977** *New Yorker* 6 June 47/2 One.. roughnecked in the oil fields near Houston.

roughness. 1. d. For *U.S.* read *local* (chiefly *U.S.*) and substitute for def.: Fodder, hay, corn-husks, etc., as used to feed cattle or horses, as opp. grain. (Earlier and later examples.) Also *transf.*

1813 J. HARTSELL *Jrnl.* 29 Oct. in *East Tennessee Hist. Soc. Publ.* (1939) XI. 99 Did not draw aney rufness for our teeme. **1846** *Knickerbocker* XXVIII. 313 The truck's all soaked, and there can't nobody stay here to save souls without some kind of *roughness* to keep up natur'. **1859** W. DICKINSON *Gloss. Dial. Cumberland* 93 *Roughness*,..grass left for winterage. **1888** C. D. WARNER *On Horseback* iv. 142 'Roughness', we found out at the other house, meant hay in this region. **1938** J. STUART *Beyond Dark Hills* iv. 88 We don't feed the cattle anything but roughness. **1949** *Publ. Amer. Dial. Soc.* XI. 10 *Roughness*, ..fodder; roughage. **1966** *Ibid.* *1964* XLII. 22 *Roughness*, roughage: fodder, corntops, coarse hay.

e. *Bacteriol.* The quality of being rough in sense *1 e of the adj.

1929 TOPLEY & WILSON *Princ. Bacteriol. & Immunity* vii. 191 The property of colonial roughness is associated.. with a characteristic change in the method of cell division. **1934** *Jrnl. Bacteriol.* XXVII. 559 Roughness is a relative term when applied to colonial form for many rough colonies may have a smooth appearance on ordinary media. **1960** L. PICKEN *Organization of Cells* iii. 63 The roughness expresses itself in the formation of dry, membranous, or brittle colonies, with irregular margins and corrugated surface, and a granular appearance under the microscope; in contrast to the colonies of the Smooth type which are creamy or butter-like in consistency, with even margins and homogeneous in texture.

roughometer (rʌfǫ·mĭtəɹ). *U.S.* [f. ROUGH *a.* + -O + -METER.] = *PROFILOMETER 2 (*b*).

1926 *Public Roads* VII. 144/2 The roughometer consists of a rack which is attached in a vertical position to the front axle of the vehicle. **1947** *Daily Progress* (Charlottesville, Va.) 20 Mar. 8 (*caption*) State Highway Department engineers have developed the 'rough-o-meter' pictured above to detect some of the tiniest irregularities in the surface of highways.

rough-out, roughout (rʌ·faut). [ROUGH *v.*[1]] **1.** *Archæol.* A prototype of an artefact. Cf. ROUGH *v.*[1] 6 b.

1936 *Proc. Prehist. Soc.* II. 214 Some sixty odd specimens were found most of which were implements gone wrong in the manufacture or rough-outs never proceeded with. **1959** J. D. CLARK *Prehist. S. Afr.* v. 120 Unfinished roughouts are found associated with factory debris and many finely-made developed Acheulian and even later transitional forms. **1980** *Rescue News* Sept. 4/3 Many large fragments of stone roof slates in various stages of rough-out were found in the fill.

2. Used *attrib.* to designate informal outdoor clothing. *U.S.*

1963 *New Yorker* 29 June 75 Chinos, shirts, roughout jackets. **1976** *National Observer* (U.S.) 10 Apr. 21/5 One scuffed cowboy boot sits poised atop the other; the baggy, rough-out trousers are now slung low beneath the prodigious belly.

rough-rider. Add: **1.** (Earlier example.)

1733 J. BRAMSTON *Man of Taste* 17, I would with Jockies from Newmarket dine, And to Rough-riders give my choicest wine.

2. Also *fig.*

1977 T. ALLBEURY *Man with President's Mind* vi. 62 At the Pentagon end Langham's going to need a man who grinds away diplomatically. Not a rough-rider.

rough-riding, *vbl. sb.* (Earlier and later examples.)

1776 G. COLMAN *Let.* 21 July in *Private Corr. D. Garrick* (1831) I. 231 After a great deal of rough riding, I have got him to accept bills of exchange payable in two and four months. **1969** *Telegraph* (Brisbane) 17 May 3/2 Thrill-seeking boys..have discovered a dangerous new pastime—riding in tall buildings on the top of a lift cage... The boys call it 'rough-riding'.

rough shoot. [SHOOT *sb.*[1]] An act of shooting game without beaters; an area in which one has a right to shoot in this manner. So **rou·gh-shoot** *v. intr.*; **rough-shooter; rough-shooting.**

1900 [see SHOOT *sb.*[1] 1 g]. **1934** F. ELLIS *Summers of Yesterday* II. 78 It was a wild bit we had taken, sea-trout fishing, brown trout, and rough shooting, that was all. **1937** L. DURRELL *Panic Spring* vii. 113 They used to ..rough-shoot across the parklands. **1943** G. GREENE *Ministry of Fear* II. i. 122 The Home..had its own hens and pigs and a good many acres of rough shooting. **1972** 'M. INNES' *Open House* v. 42 Manage you a bit of rough shooting, too. Brought your gun? **1976** *Shooting Times & Country Mag.* 18–24 Nov. 28/2 (Advt.), A perfect fowler's or roughshooter's gun. *Ibid.* 16–22 Dec. 48/2 (Advt.), Yellow dog, 2 years, trained for rough shoot. **1976** *Evening Post* (Nottingham) 16 Dec. 21/8 (Advt.), Rough shoot wanted, 30 miles radius of Nottingham.

rou·gh-towel, *v. rare.* [ROUGH *a.*] *trans.* To rub or dry with a towel of long-napped material.

1889 E. SAMPSON *Tales of Fancy* 23 He sponged his men..and rough-towelled them.

rough-up. Add: **a.** (Further examples.)

1933 *Bulletin* (Sydney) 6 Dec. 24/4 [Bridge] The council, while signifying approval, wants to make it clear that in future all inter-State rough-ups will be its pigeon. **1951** E. RICKMAN *Come racing with Me* x. 85 This one may be fit enough in a week or two to be given a 'rough-up' (a good gallop with companions but not a formal trial).

c. A fight; a brawl.

1896 *Sessions Papers Cent. Criminal Court* 22 June, There was a little rough up, and I found myself stabbed in my arm. **1950** K. S. PRICHARD *Winged Seeds* 26 There'd 've been a rough-up in no time, and only half a dozen of us with Paddy against forty or fifty men.

d. (See quot.)

1919 V. MARSHALL *World of Living Dead* 69 The 'donkey-dipper' is another kind of pick-pocket. He works alone, and his methods are to grip, to rip, and to run. 'A dead rough-up'—thus the more scientific of the fraternity designate him in their scorn.

roughy, var. *ROUGHIE.

‖ **rouille** (rūy). [Fr., lit. 'rust'.] Mayonnaise flavoured with pimento or the like.

1951 R. CAMPBELL *Light on Dark Horse* xix. 275 No decent fisherman will eat bouillabaisse without the *rouille*. **1976** N. ROBERTS *Face of France* ix. 101 A fish soup..a *bourride*, with a spoonful of *rouille* stirred into it.

roulade. Add: **2.** *Cookery.* A dish prepared by rolling up a slice of meat or a sponge or similar base, esp. with a filling (see quots. 1969, 1975[1]). Also *attrib.*

1885 *Tasty Dishes* (James Clarke & Co.) 151 Roulades of Beef. **1958** *Catal. County Stores, Taunton* June 3 *Pâté de foie gras*..Roulade for slicing—a tin 14/9, 22/3. **1965** A. R. DANIEL *Up-to-Date Confectionery* (ed. 4) xxviii. 407/2 Roulade Slices. *Ibid.* 408/1 Spread the sheet of roulade with pink-coloured kirsch-flavoured butter icing. *Ibid.* 409/1 The Swiss..make a special type of butter-sponge sheet from which to make roulade and dresden slices. **1969** R. & D. DE SOLA *Dict. Cooking* 194/2 *Roulade*,..slice of meat, covered with forcemeat or other savoury filling, rolled up, and cooked. **1975** J. CHILD *From Julia Child's Kitchen* III. 109 A *roulade* is a flat soufflé baked in a rectangular shape, then rolled up with a filling. **1975** *Times* 18 Dec. 7/5 The roulade of avocado is..delicious. **1980** *Times* 24 May 24/3 Puddings include chocolate roulade.

rouleau. Add: **3.** (Earlier example.) Also in extended use (see quot. 1976). Also *attrib.* and *Comb.*

1820 M. EDGEWORTH *Let.* 8 June (1979) 160 Muslin gowns each trimmed with rouleaux of sattin. **1968** J. IRONSIDE *Fashion Alphabet* 105 *Rouleau*, a rounded padded belt which may be finished with a knot or bow. **1970** *Kay & Co.* (Worcester) *Catal.* *1970–71* Autumn/Winter 173/1 Deep back opening with rouleau tie fastening. **1972** *Country Life* 23 Mar. 737/3 A tweed suit..has a rouleau belt. **1974** *Janet Frazer Catal.* Spring & Summer 184/3 Nylon slip with lace trimmed rouleau straps. **1975** *Times* 14 Oct. 9/5 The hand made rouleau belts and the gold and ivory buttons. **1976** P. CLABBURN *Needleworker's Dict.* 228/3 *Rouleau*, any trimming or part of an article which is rounded or rolled. It may be in the form of piping or may mean a turned hollow tube as in the 'shoelace' shoulder straps of the 1930s and 1940s. **1977** *Daily Tel.* 4 Apr. 15/1 She wears a charming little rouleau-edged cap tilted over her brow. *Ibid.* 15/3 There were..dresses of black cotton.., and the academic robe, with high, padded rouleau neck, shone out..in most unacademic tangerines.

4. Used *attrib.* to designate a type of vase with a cylindrical body and narrow neck, made in China from the late seventeenth century, or an imitation of such a vase.

1915 R. L. HOBSON *Chinese Pott. & Porc.* II. x. 165 (*caption*) Club-shaped (*rouleau*) Vase finely painted in famille verte enamels. **1936** *Burlington Mag.* Nov. p. xix/1 *Famille-verte* vases..a large *rouleau* specimen. **1937** *Ibid.* June p. xxv/2 Other specimens of K'ang-hsi in brilliance and quality are a pair of large rouleau vases. **1964** M. MEDLEY *Handbk. Chinese Art* 81/2 *Rouleau vase* is a vase with cylindrical body, short rather flat shoulders, a short thick neck, also cylindrical, and a slightly spreading mouth, which sometimes turns up a little at the rim. The term applies to a type of vase produced from the late 17th century onward. **1977** *Times* 17 May 16/4 Two large (17½ inches) *famille verte* rouleau vases.

‖ **roulement** (rulmaṅ). [Fr., lit. 'roll, roster'.] A movement of members or equipment of the armed services; rotation of units, relief of troops. Also *attrib.*

1918 W. S. CHURCHILL in M. Gilbert *Winston S. Churchill* (1977) IV. Compan. I. 290 Although *roulement* can proceed on both sides, this is a formidable preponderance and it tells more and more as reserves are used up. **1930** *Times Lit. Suppl.* 10 July 567/1 After the Lys offensive he was in what was known as the *roulement*, the transfer of troops to the Rheims area. **1941** W. S. CHURCHILL *Second World War* (1950) III. 735 Reserves of pilots and machines should be disposed in squadrons, and thus allow *roulement* to be extended in the event of protracted fighting. **1971** H. WILSON *Labour Govt.* (1974) xix. 467 Moreover, there was a problem of rotating troops, what is known in the West as *roulement*. **1977** *Guardian Weekly* 14 Aug. 4/2 Their individual battle tours on Irish soil..Roger spent four months here once with his *roulement* unit.

roulette. Add: **2. b.** Also *roulette ball, system, -wheel* (earlier example).

1844 *Rep. Sel. Comm. Gaming* 210 in *Parl. Papers* VI. 1 Seized..2 roulette balls, 2 dice-boxes, 2 bags containing 366 counters, [etc.]. *Ibid.* 211, I seized a roulette-wheel and a quantity of gambling apparatus. **1926** A. CHRISTIE *Murder of R. Ackroyd* iii. 26 Caroline visibly wavered.. much as a roulette ball might coyly hover between two numbers. **1976** 'J. FRASER' *Who steals my Name?* xi. 134 A roulette ball has no memory... In the South of France a ball went into the same slot seven times running. **1976** P. CAVE *High Flying Birds* iv. 47, I once sold a foolproof roulette system to a professional gambler for 500 francs.

d. *Russian roulette*: see *RUSSIAN *a.* 2 d*.

5. (Earlier example.)

1835 *Brit. Cycl. Arts & Sci.* I. 508/1 A more expeditious way of multiplying the dots has been contrived in the instrument called a *roulette*, a toothed wheel, fixed to a handle which, by being rolled forcibly along the copper, produces a row of indentations.

rouletted, *pa. pple.* Add: **b.** Of archaeological objects: impressed with lines or dots by means of a cogged wheel or a comb. **c.** *gen.*

1938 *Oxoniensia* III. 28 Sherd with shell-grit; fine stabs and rouletted horizontal lines. **1939** V. G. CHILDE *Dawn European Civilization* (ed. 3) xii. 214 The 'rouletted' decoration is executed with a comb with very short teeth, separated by extremely narrow interstices, and probably with a curved edge. It yields a practically continuous line of round or, more often, rectangular dots, separated by low septa. **1969** G. BIBBY *Looking for Dilmun* xv. 323 They were Attic ware, imports from Greece itself. Some of them were even rouletted, decorated with a close pattern of semi-circles made with a toothed wheel, a characteristic which proved their Greek origin beyond a doubt. **1975** J. B. HARLEY *O.S. Maps* v. 72 It..was characterized by National Grid lines rouletted in black. [*Note*] That is, the line consists of small, closely spaced dots. **1977** *Antiquaries Jrnl.* LVII. 381 Fine wares include bowls..with a foot-stamp within rouletted circles (second century A.D.), and lead-glazed wares.

rouletting, *vbl. sb.* Add: **b.** Decorating pottery, etc., with dotted lines by means of a cogged wheel or comb; ornamentation produced in this way.

1937 *Oxoniensia* II. 19 It contained a great quantity of Roman pottery, mostly early grey ware jars but including part of a butt-beaker in fine buff ware with two zones of rouletting, and a bit of a buff amphora handle. **1973** A. H. WHITEFORD *N. Amer. Indian Arts* 148 Coins and ingots were hammered into sheets and decorated by stamping and rouletting. **1979** *Archaeology* July–Aug. 31/1 The carinated bowls were stamped with palmettes inside concentric spirals of rouletting, a technique of producing hatch lines around the central design.

Roumanian, *sb.* and *a.* Add: See also *ROMANIAN *sb.* and *a.*³, *RUMANIAN *sb.* and *a.* **A.** *sb.* **1.** (Further examples.)

1925 N. IORGA *Hist. Roumania* iii. 35 Anthropology and ethnography do not find the Slav type amongst the Roumanians. **1934** R. W. SETON-WATSON *Hist. Roumanians* i. 9 The Roumanians claim that they are the true descendants of Trajan's colonists. **1964** *Whitaker's Almanack 1965* 913/1 By the *Treaty of Berlin*..the Principality was recognized as an independent State, and part of the *Dobrudja* (which had been occupied by the Roumanians) was incorporated. **1974** M. B. BROWN *Econ. of Imperialism* xii. 296 What worries the Roumanians and other underdeveloped countries in the Soviet bloc is precisely the results of the artificial world division of labour in which they have for so long been held.

2. (Further examples.)

1925 N. IORGA *Hist. Roumania* viii. 145 Coresi.. began to publish religious works in Roumanian, or in Roumanian and Slavonic. **1933** L. BLOOMFIELD *Language* xviii. 314 A feature common to both Roumanian and the western Romance languages is presumably guaranteed as Latin. **1964** *Whitaker's Almanack 1965* 913/2 Roumanian is a Romance language with many archaic forms and with admixtures of Slavonic, Turkish, Magyar and French words.

B. *adj.* (Earlier and later examples.) *Roumanian stitch* = *Oriental stitch* s.v. ORIENTAL *a.* 3 c.

1860 *Universe* 8 Dec. 1/2 His projects extend to the formation of a great Roumanian State. **1883** R. TORCEANU *Simplified Gram. Roumanian Lang.* p. vii, The Roumanian tongue can claim..attention on more grounds than one. **1925** N. IORGA *Hist. Roumania* viii. 145 Religious manuscripts..in which the Roumanian text in red letters follows the Slavonic text in ink. **1932** D. C. MINTER *Mod. Needlecraft* 10/1 Intergradating one stitch and colour with another, as is possible with Irish stitch..and Roumanian..or satin stitch. **1934** M. THOMAS *Dict. Embroidery Stitches* 177 Roumanian Stitch consists of a long stitch across the shape tied down with a shorter slanting one in the centre. **1959** R. N. C. HUNT *Books on Communism* 37 An exhaustive study by a group of experts on aspects of Roumanian life under Communism. **1974** M. B. BROWN *Econ. of Imperialism* xii. 295 In the Roumanian dispute with Comecon, the basis of the Roumanian argument has been one that we have met before.

roumanite, var. *RUMÄNITE.

Roumelian (rume·liăn, -ī·liăn), *a.* (*sb.*) Also Rumelian. [f. as ROUMELIOTE: cf. Turk. *rum* Byzantine Greek (of Turkish nationality), *il* province.] Of or pertaining to Roumelia (see ROUMELIOTE in Dict. and Suppl.), with particular reference to Ottoman territories of the southern Balkans inhabited by Greeks and now forming parts of northern Greece and Bulgaria; of or pertaining to the form of Greek spoken there. Also as *sb.*, a Greek inhabitant of Roumelia.

1859 J. F. MAGUIRE *Rome* (ed. 2) xxviii. 323 The different languages in which poetical compositions were recited at the Polyglot Academy, for Epiphany, 1858 [were]..Danish, Roumelian, Albanian, Polish, [etc.]. **1880** E. W. HAMILTON *Diary* 29 Aug. (1972) I. 41 Colonel Wilson who is reporting on the state of the Bulgarian and Eastern Roumelian provinces finds..a better state of affairs than he expected. **1888** *Encycl. Brit.* XXIII. 655/2 This is due partly to the Christian communities, notably the Maronites and others in Syria, the Anatolian and Roumelian Greeks, and the Armenians. **1902** D. G. HOGARTH *Nearer East* 155 Most thinly peopled are the mountainous districts between the Vardar and the Rumelian plains. **1935** H. EDIB *Clown & his Daughter* xxi. 114 Why should they insult him and spit at him because he was a Rumelian?

Roumeliote. Add: Also -iot. (Earlier and later examples.)

Normally used of the area corresponding to Aetolia and Acarnania. Cf. *ROUMELIAN *a.* (*sb.*).

1835 N. P. WILLIS *Pencillings* II. xxii. 248 At the Adrianople gate, we found a large troop of horsemen.. who had accompanied a Roumeliote chief from the mountains. **1886** *Times* 5 Apr. 5/1 Instinctively the Roumeliots prefer to blame Turkey rather than Russia. **1939** A. TOYNBEE *Study of Hist.* VI. 331 The Rumeliot Greek Armatole and Klephtic ballads. **1964** A. A. PALLIS *Greek Miscellany* 144 He took the side of the Roumeliots against the party of the primates of the Morea. *Ibid.*, His hero was that greatest of Roumeliot captains, George Karaiskakis. **1969** C. M. WOODHOUSE *Philhellenes* iv. 118 The same feelings were expressed by an old Rumeliot whom James Emerson met. **1973** —— *Capodistria* xv. 347 Two Roumeliote *kapetánioi*, Grivas and Stratos, were bombarding each other..to settle a private feud. *Ibid.* xvi. 382 The Roumeliotes..were eager for action.

‖ **Roumi** (ru·mi). Also 6 Rumi, 9 Roumy. Fem. **roumia**. [ad. Arab. *rūmī* Byzantine, Pers. *rūmi* Turk, Greek.] Among Arabs, a term for a European.

1576 R. EDEN tr. *Vertomannus's Navigation & Vyages* vi. xiv. 401 They affyrmed also, that there are certayne Christian kynges (whiche they call Rumi) of great power, confynyng or borderyng on the dominions of the great Turke. **1819** J. L. BURCKHARDT *Trav. Nubia* 542 Such a misfortune had never been heard of in the time of the Islam, and before them no Roumy had ever come into these parts. **1867** 'OUIDA' *Under Two Flags* II. iii. 74 Not but what our *Roumis* are brave fellows enough; better comrades no man could want. **1924** *Public Opinion* 27 June 619/3 The Roumis had got round the flanks and were attacking the Arab Camp. **1927** *Daily Express* 17 June 9 An intelligent and up-to-date caid..in the Sahara ..answered..'most of my people are unaccustomed to the ways of the roumia (foreign woman).' **1958** *Times Lit. Suppl.* 11 July 393/4, I did happen to be the first *roumia* allowed to a remote branch of the sect who live off the beaten track.

rounce, *sb.*² Add: [Perh. ad. G. *ramsch* a variety of Skat.] (Earlier and later examples.) Also, a similar domino game. Hence **rounce** *v.*² (see quots. 1864, 1868).

1855 in *Calif. Hist. Soc. Q.* (1929) VIII. 352 Had a great rounce game, a little noise but no fun. **1857** *Hoyle's Games* 99 The Game of Rounce is played by each player taking five pieces, (after having turned for the trump, the highest piece turned deciding that point); the trump is then turned up for the trump-holder by his right hand adversary, the highest end being trump. **1864** W. B. DICK *Amer. Hoyle* 397 Rounce. This is a pleasant game [of dominoes], and from two to four may participate in it. *Ibid.*, The player who fails to take a trick with his hand is 'Rounced', i.e., sent up five points. **1868** —— *Mod. Pocket Hoyle* 196 The game of Rounce, as played in the United States, is derived from the German game of *Ramsch*, and in its principal features resembles Division Loo. *Ibid.* 197 Each trick taken in play counts one point, and if a player fail to take a trick after entering to play his hand, he is *Rounced*, that is, sent up five points, which adds a X to his score. **1975** *Way to Play* 66/1 Forty-two, or domino rounce, is an adaptation of a card game for play with dominoes. The object is to score points by winning tricks.

round, *sb.*¹ Add: **I. 2. c.** (Earlier examples.)

1660 W. DENTON *Let.* 29 Feb. in M. M. Verney *Mem.* (1894) III. xiii. 469 The Beef the best that ever was eat, I eat a whole Round last night my self. **1771** J. WOODFORDE *Diary* 5 Jan. in *Parson Woodforde Soc. Q. Jrnl.* (1970) III. I. 24, I gave them for Dinner..a Round of Beef boiled.

attrib. **1934** WEBSTER *Round steak*. **1972** 'L. EGAN' *Paper Chase* (1973) x. 161 Athelstane was..condescending to eat the best round steak cut into bite-size pieces. **1975** *Evening Herald* (Dublin) 8 May 6/7 Round steak.. dropped by 10p per pound.

e. pl. *Comm.* Articles that are naturally or artificially produced in round shapes.

1911 *Chambers's Jrnl.* 8 Apr. 297/1 Formerly 'flats' and 'rounds' used to be spoken of to distinguish the imports of this drug [*sc.* rhubarb]. **1928** *Daily Mail* 25 July 19/3 Potatoes.—Spitalfields: English Kidneys 6s to 7s, rounds 5s to 5s 6d per cwt.

5. a. Also *fig.*, a condition which displays a given subject from all aspects; three-dimensionality. Usu. in phr. *in the round*.

1931 *Times Lit. Suppl.* 31 Dec. 1052/3 One cannot tamper with a screen character who speaks like a human being..and has his being 'in the round'. **1933** *Punch* 12 July 51/2 It is not an easy part, seeing that it is the only character in the whole cast to be drawn in the round. **1948** 'M. WESTMACOTT' *Rose & Yew Tree* ix. 72 Up to now Lord St. Loo had been a name, an abstraction... Now he came into the round—a living entity. **1959** *Spectator* 7 Aug. 164/3 The camera also gives an impression in the round of the man who seems one-dimensional in print.

d. *Theatr.* In phr. *in the round*, alluding to performance on a stage or arena surrounded by the auditorium, as distinguished from a proscenium; esp. in *theatre-in-the-round*. Cf. *ARENA 5.

1944 *Bull. National Theatre Conf.* (U.S.) Apr. 19 In this country, Glen Hughes out in Seattle has operated his Studio and Penthouse theatres, playing sophisticated comedies to small audiences 'in the round'. **1948** *Sat. Rev.* 3 Apr. 24/1 'Theatre-in-the-round' is the way it is described by John Rosenfeld, who is not *a* czar but *the* czar in matters dramatic and musical in the Southwest. **1950** *Sun* (Baltimore) 8 June 16/1 The New York debut of theatre-in-the-round was off to a rousing start last week. **1958** *New Statesman* 22 Feb. 228/3 At the Mahatma Gandhi Hall, Fitzroy Square, Miss Margaret Rawlings is giving *Phèdre* in English In-the-Round. **1963** *Listener* 28 Mar. 559/2, I do object to playing to them in the round, because it gives them a chance to get at the actor physically. **1963** 'E. MCBAIN' *Ten Plus One* (1964) vii. 73 We did the play in the round... we banked rows of rented bleachers on the stage, and the performers worked in the centre. **1967** *Oxf. Compan. Theatre* (ed. 3) 941/2 Modern theatre-in-the-round first came into prominence in Russia, where in the 1930s Okhlopkov in his Realistic Theatre produced a number of Soviet plays on stages set up in the central area with the audience pressing close on all sides. **1980** *Times Lit. Suppl.* 5 Sept. 973/1 Audience involvement was not new to Tudor Drama: medieval theatre-in-the-round had already thrived on it.

e. *out-of-round* sb., the extent to which an object departs from being circular in section; also as *adj.* Hence *out-of-roundness*.

1951 C. W. KENNEDY *Inspection & Gaging* iv. 67 Standards for allowable taper, out-of-round or eccentricity should be established in every shop. **1955** W. H. CROUSE *Automotive Engines* xiv. 403 Some bearing failures may result..from a tapered or out-of-round crankpin. *Ibid.* 412 Bearings working against out-of-roundness or taper of more than 0·0015 inch will not last long. **1962** *Mod. Petroleum Technol.* (Inst. Petroleum) (ed. 3) xxvi. 848 'Out-of-roundness'..must always be expected [in a pipe] as a result either of poor manufacture or of damage in transit. **1970** K. BALL *Fiat 600, 600D Autobk.* xi. 130/2 The out-of-round must not exceed ·0004 inch. **1975** BRAM & DOWNS *Manuf. Technol.* iv. 110 Disadvantages of self-centring chucks are that they cannot clamp blank or out-of-round items to maintain accuracy. **1979** *B.S.I. News* Jan. 4/1 Yielding in stiffeners due to out-of-roundness and buckling.

III. 13. c. *spec.* A recurring succession or series *of* meetings for discussion or negotiation; one stage in such a process. Also without *const.*

1964 *Ann. Reg. 1963* 252 They disagreed on what should be the approach of the Six in preparation for the forthcoming 'Kennedy round' of negotiations. **1977** *Economist* 22 Oct. 89/1 There is still no sign (two months into the current wage round) that wages are about to go through the roof. **1978** *Internat. Relations Dict.* (U.S. Dept. State Library) 42/2 The talks, which opened in Geneva in October 1973, were called the 'Tokyo Round' because they were initiated by a declaration signed in Tokyo.

14. c. *pl. Naut.* Inspection.

1902 L. Delbos *Naut. Terms* (ed. 4) 140/1 *Rounds*, inspection. **1914** 'Bartimeus' *Naval Occasions* xviii. 158 The Sub-Lieutenant, 'standing the rounds' in the doorway. **1916** 'Taffrail' *Stand By!* 13 Except on Sundays, when the latter is specially tidied up for the 'rounds', it will not bear close investigation. **1961** F. H. Burgess *Dict. Sailing* 174 *Rounds*, inspection.

15. Also *spec.* a visit to each of the in-patients in a ward or under the care of a particular doctor or nurse.

1904 *Sci. & Art of Nursing* I. iv. 99 There is always the danger that in the haste and pressure to have all in order for the rounds of the medical staff, the minor requests of patients may be postponed. **1928** A. T. Schofield *Behind Brass Plate* xiii. 94 Samuel Fenwick, in his rounds, was very droll... After the usual examination of a new patient he performed his well-known trick. **1954** A. Huxley *Let.* 9 May (1969) 706 He [*sc.* a physician] takes foreign pupils—mostly doctors..—young men who live near by and go the rounds with him and learn by listening, answering questions and doing. **1965** Spencer & Tait *Introd. Nursing* vii. 31 It is generally considered that visitors can be in a main ward outside main meal times, sanitary rounds, rest times and doctors' rounds. **1974** G. B. Mair *Confessions of Surgeon* v. 58 When added to routine clerking, ward rounds, night rounds, dealing with emergencies,..no day had enough hours.

16. c. (Earlier examples.)

1775 C. B. Clapcott *Rules of Golf* (1935) 24 No member of this Society pay the Cadies more than one penny per round. **1834** P. Buchan *Peterhead Smugglers* 63 To gang wi' you to the links ilka morning at five o'clock to a round o' the golf. **1866** *Golfer's Year Bk.* 65 The order of play was the reverse of the wonted 'round' over Bruntsfield, in order that strangers might cope on equal footing with players who were up to the green. Each round consisted of 7 holes, and four rounds were fixed on for the decision of the Tournament.

17. b. Now usu. *pl.* Also *to make the rounds.*

1837 *Jamestown* (N.Y.) *Jrnl.* 22 Mar. 3/2 There is a story going the rounds in relation to the president-elect. **1862** O. W. Norton *Army Lett.* (1903) 55 Everything of the kind has to go the rounds, you know. **1934** H. L. Ickes *Secret Diary* (1953) I. 254 He expressed the fear that in some way I connected him with all of these stories that are going the rounds about me. **1977** *Rolling Stone* 13 Jan. 39/2 The rumor that the FBI started about her being a Soviet spy is still making the rounds at parties she no longer attends.

IV. 20. a. (Further examples.)

1928 C. Mackenzie *Extraordinary Women* x. 176 Two rounds of stingers brought the evening to a close. **1960** M. Spark *Ballad of Peckham Rye* (1964) vii. 107 Dixie, at first under the impression that Humphrey was buying the round, asked for a ginger ale. **1970** G. F. Newman *Sir, You Bastard* viii. 255 Just a slag avoiding his round. **1978** J. Porter *Dead Easy for Dover* xii. 125 The local chap had proved himself more than willing to stand his round, and Dover didn't ask more than that of anyone.

b. (Further examples.) Also, a sandwich or sandwiches made of two slices cut from a loaf of bread.

a **1902** S. Butler *Way of All Flesh* (1903) lxxii. 330 She..had made him a round of toast. **1947** A. Ransome *Great Northern?* xix. 232 Peggy was cutting rounds of bread to make potted meat sandwiches. **1974** L. Deighton *Spy Story* xvi. 162 'Have you come for your sandwiches?'..'Last night's pork, and one round of cheese.'

23. b. Also *fig.* and in attrib. phr. *round-by-round.*

1937 'M. Innes' *Hamlet, Revenge!* II. iii. 137 Gott sighed. 'You certainly know the habits of your friends. Round Two to you.' **1955** T. H. Pear *Eng. Social Differences* 246 Championship fight..with a leading article and a back-page 'round-by-round' report. **1959** *Listener* 22 Oct. 681/2 He began round two by making a fresh application for *habeas corpus*. **1961** *Times* 25 May 15/4 It is a remarkable round-by-round study in the art of politics. **1967** *Listener* 3 Aug. 147/3 By quoting, selectively, two rounds of a three-round controversy.. [you] gave an inaccurate picture of the course of the argument.

d. (Further examples.)

1921 [see *End *sb.* 20 b]. **1951** *Sport* 30 Mar.–5 Apr. 2/4 In the Amateur Cup they reached the second round, losing to Pegasus.

24. a. (Earlier examples.)

1794 C. Mathews *Let.* 28 Dec. in A. Mathews *Mem. Charles Mathews* (1838) I. vi. 129 He came forward at the end of the play.., and he had six successive rounds of applause. **1808** *Monthly Mirror* Mar. 268 The audience.. with not three, but six rounds of applause, greeted his return.

25. *ellipt.* = *round-the-houses* s.v. *Round *prep.* 1 a. *slang.*

1893 P. H. Emerson *Signor Lippo* xiv. 55 One day he walked straight into this kitchen clobbered in a black pair of rounds, tight to his legs.

round, *sb.*[2] (Further example.)

1943 T. Harsley *Find, fire, & Strike* 38 The 'round down' at the stern where the aircraft ready to take off are ranged.

round, *a.* Add: **I. 3. b.** Also *fig.* of character.

1927 E. M. Forster *Aspects of Novel* iv. 106 The test of a round character is whether it is capable of surprising in a convincing way. If it never surprises, it is flat.

c. (Further examples.) See also quot. 1960.

1788 E. Sheridan *Jrnl.* 22 Dec. (1960) vi. 138 As to gowns all kinds—Chemises—Round gowns with flounce or not. **1815** *La Belle Assemblée* June 274/1 *Morning-Dress.* Round dress of jacconet muslin. **1836** Dickens *Sk. Boz* (1837) 2nd Ser. 100 They were decent people, but not over-burdened with riches, or he would not have so outgrown the suit when he passed into those corduroys with the round jacket. **1960** C. W. Cunnington et al. *Dict. Eng. Costume* 184/2 *Round dress* or *gown*,..a term indicating a dress with joined bodice and skirt, the latter closed all round... 18th c. Occasionally made with a slight train. 19th c. No train, the term now meaning a dress without a train.

e. Designating any of several styles of circular, conical, or pill-box hat.

1795 tr. *C. P. Moritz's Trav.* 141 A fellow in a brown frock and round hat. **1804** [in Dict., sense 4]. *c* **1806** D. Wordsworth *Jrnl.* (1941) I. 303 A fine fellow..in tight clean clothes and a nice round hat. **1825** H. Wilson *Mem.* II. 175 Down came Colonel Palmer..his laced jacket covered with an old, short, brown great coat, and a shabby round hat. **1828** D. Wordsworth *Jrnl.* (1941) II. 403 Women often with round hats, like the Welsh. **1890** C. M. Yonge *More Bywords* 137 Those foolish girls thought me too fine a lady to like to be seen with her in her round hat on a Sunday. **1968** [see *Pill-box b].

5. a. *round dance*, (*a*) (further examples); also *round dancer, dancing*; (*b*) [tr. G. *rundtanz* (K. von Frisch 1923, in *Zool. Jahrb., Abt. f. Allgemeine Zool. u. Physiol. der Tiere* XL. 31], a circular movement performed by bees at their hive or nest, believed to indicate a source of food to other bees.

1919 *Ladies' Home Jrnl.* May 31/1 My dear lady, are you going to give up round dancing? **1947** A. Einstein *Mus. Romantic Era* x. 110 The sharp rhythm of round dances and torch dances. **1950** K. von Frisch *Bees* iii. 71 The round dance and the wagging dance are two different terms in the language of bees, the former meaning a source of food near the hive and the latter a source at 100 metres or more. **1952** C. R. Ribbands *Behaviour & Social Life of Bees* xix. 153 The characteristic of the 'round dance' is that the bee performs a complete circle, whereas the 'waggle dance' is a figure-of-eight. **1973** R. A. Morse *Compl. Guide Beekeeping* xiii. 203 Certain races of bees use a dance intermediate between the round dance and the wag-tail dance incorporating parts of both. **1976** *Columbus* (Montana) *News* 3 June 1/2 Mr. and Mrs. Robert Shanks, Columbus, are ardent and avid square and round dancers.

II. 7. a. (Further example.)

c **1829** D. Jerrold in M. R. Booth *Eng. Plays of 19th Cent.* (1969) I. 175, I deserve a round dozen [*sc.* thirteen lashes] for the question.

IV. 15. a. round ball, (*b*) also *spec.* an early alternative name for Base-ball (earlier examples); **round barrow** *Archæol.*, a Bronze Age burial mound of circular form; **round bilge**, a curved, as distinct from an angular or stepped, hull; also *attrib.*; hence **round-bilged** *a.*; **round cell** *Path.*, used *attrib.* = next; **round-celled** *a. Path.*, (of a neoplasm) characterized by round, undifferentiated cells; **roundeye** *slang*, a European, as distinguished from a *slant-eye* (*Slant *a.* 3); **round heels** chiefly *U.S.*, rounded heels that allow the wearer to rock backwards easily; usu. *transf.* and *fig.* (*slang*) implying the inability to remain upright, as in an incompetent boxer or sexually compliant woman; hence **round-heeled** *a.*; **round-heeler**; **round log** *U.S.*, a log that has been felled but not hewn; also *attrib.*; **round lot** *U.S.*, a unit of trade (see quot. 1962); **round timber** *U.S.*, timber that has been felled but not hewn; also *transf.*; **round towel** (earlier and later examples); **round turn,** also in colloq. (orig. *Naut.*) phr. *to bring* (*fetch*) *up with a round turn,* to check or stop suddenly; **round wood,** (*a*) = **round timber*; (*b*) short logs of small diameter from the tops of pine and spruce trees, used for box-making.

1834 R. Carver *Bk. of Sports*, This game is known under a variety of names. It is sometimes called 'round ball', but I believe that 'base', or 'goal ball' are the names generally adopted in our country. **1856** *Porter's Spirit of Times* 27 Dec. 276/3, I have thought..a statement of my experience as to the Yankee method of playing 'Base', or 'Round' ball, as we used to call it, may not prove uninteresting. **1869** J. Thurnam in *Archaeologia* XLII. 168, I propose to classify the barrows of this part of England according to the following scheme:.. I. Long Barrows. (*Stone period*)... II. Round Barrows. (*Bronze period*). *Ibid.*, In none of the..long barrows.. have objects of metal..been found... In the..round barrows, not only are there objects of stone, but..chiefly, those of bronze, and..iron... They may be regarded..as belonging to the Bronze period. **1926** M. C. Burkitt *Our Early Ancestors* vi. 151 In England we have..passage graves (generally called 'Long Barrows'..) in many places.., and stone kists (generally called Round Barrows from the circular shape of the tumuli). **1975** J. G. Evans *Environment Early Man Brit. Isles* vi. 130 Two Bronze Age round barrows known as the Burton Howes. **1980** *Encounter* May 59/1 Long barrows and causewayed camps signal the territories of the early and middle Neolithic groupings, with the henges and round barrow cemeteries appearing in the late Neolithic/early Bronze Age. **1951, 1961** Round bilge [see *hard chine* s.v. *Hard *a.* (*sb.*) 22]. **1977** *Austral. Sailing* Jan. 38/2 The round-bilged 'mouldie' hull has virtually disappeared. **1889** Round cell [see sense 17 in Dict.]. **1961** R. D. Baker *Essent. Path.* xix. 533 Malignant tumors of the thymus may arise from epithelial structures (carcinoma) or from a fibrous component (fibrosarcoma) but are perhaps most often round-cell tumors and presumably lymphomas. **1873** Round-celled [in Dict., sense 16]. **1907** J. H. Parsons *Dis. Eye* xxix. 605 Sarcoma is rare; it may be round or spindle-celled, pigmented or non-pigmented. **1961** R. D. Baker *Essent. Path.* xiii. 302 The undifferentiated sarcomas must be classified according to how they look microscopically, and may be described as spindle-celled or round-celled. **1967** *Guardian* 16 Aug. 6/5 Many Europeans have been assaulted simply because they were 'roundeyes'. **1977** 'J. Le Carré' *Hon. Schoolboy* vi. 125 In the East a roundeye could live all his life in the same block and never have the smallest notion of the secret tic-tac on his doorstep. **1957** J. Kerr *Please don't eat Daisies* 118, I know I'm just a broad, Mike. I'm a round-heeled babe. **1975** 'R. Rostand' *D'Artagnan Signature* (1976) xiv. 83 You said that as if I'm some round-heeled little chippie who dragged you to the floor. **1927** *Vanity Fair* (N.Y.) Nov. 67/2 Others contend that 'a round-heeler' was applied to street-walkers many years ago. **1926** Abbott & Weaver *Love 'em & leave 'Em* III. 109 You want people to say you got round heels. Why don't you go on the streets and be done with it? **1926** *Variety* 29 Dec. 7/4 A push-over, which means a fighter with round heels along cauliflower alley, was, by the same token, a dame on rockers. **1929** E. Wilson *I thought of Daisy* i. 16 Myra Busch is a push-over!..She's got round heels! **1944** R. Chandler *Lady in Lake* v. 35 You'd think..I'd..pick me a change in types at least. But little roundheels over there ain't even that. **1963** 'G. Bagby' *Murder's Little Helper* (1964) viii. 84 Little Miss Roundheels..specialized in gentlemen who were otherwise committed. **1975** P. de Vries *Glory of Humming Bird* xiii. 192 Her famous round heels did not seem to rule out a stern morality on other counts. **1869** S. Haycraft *Hist. Elizabethtown, Kentucky* (1921) ii. 15 In the winter time they met in the round log cabins with dirt floors. **1871** E. Eggleston *Hoosier Schoolmaster* 95 He came upon a queer little cabin built of round logs. **1884** 'Mark Twain' *Huck. Finn* xxxii. 329 Phelps's was one of these little one-horse cotton plantations..round-log kitchen. **1942** *Sun* (Baltimore) 27 Feb. 17/5 The rates charged by brokers for 'round lots' (units of 100 shares) range from 3 cents a share..to 13 cents. **1962** S. Strand *Marketing Dict.* 638 *Round lot*, a trading unit. 1) On the New York Stock Exchange, 100 shares. 2) On the Chicago Board of Trade, 5000 bushels. **1874** J. F. Rusling *Across Amer.* xxvii. 429 Snow galleries consumed in all nearly forty-five million feet, board measure, of sawed timber, and over a million and a quarter feet of round timber. **1905** *Bull. Bureau of Forestry* (U.S.) No. 61. 45 *Round timber*, pine trees which have not been turpentined. **1964** *Times Rev. Industry* Mar. 56/1 The firm has arranged with Boys and Boden to reopen the sawmill section of British Saw-mills at Welshpool from March 1 for the conversion of round timber. **1972** *Gloss. Terms Timber* (*B.S.I.*) 8 *Round timber*, felled trees, logs or poles. **1845** *Ainsworth's Mag.* VIII. 71, I at last became quite tired of him and his string of repetitions, or round towel speaking. **1908** G. Jekyll *Children & Gardens* ii. 12 If it can have a small pantry containing a water supply and a sink,..and a round towel handy, it will be better than if these necessaries were in the kitchen itself. *a* **1910** in *Amer. Speech* (1979) LIV. 99 *Round turn*,..'fetched up with a round turn'. Suddenly. **1920** Galsworthy *In Chancery* II. vi. 175 The end came swiftly on the 20th of January with a telegram... It brought him up with a round turn. **1961** F. H. Burgess *Dict. Sailing* 174 *Round turn, Bring up with a*, stop someone or something abruptly. **1910** *Timber Trades Jrnl.* 8 Jan. 37/1 The wood shipped from Archangel is the now well-known roundwood. **1930** *Aberdeen Press & Jrnl.* 3 Apr. 8 So far as the 'round wood' or 'pulp wood' is concerned, most of the Aberdeen contracts for the season are now fixed-up. **1971** *Country Life* 25 Nov. 1450/1 The cash value..from the sales of roundwood and timber..in East Anglia.

16. a. *round-barred, -bellied* (later example), *-bodied, -bottomed* (later examples), *-browed, -budded, -cheeked, -cornered* (later example), *-ended, -eyed* (further example), *-hatted, -lipped, -necked, -paned, -pollened, -soled, -spectacled, -sterned, -walled*; also *round-looking*.

1923 D. H. Lawrence *Birds, Beasts & Flowers* 143 The upstart of your round-barred, sun-round tail! **1919** J. Masefield *Reynard the Fox* 9 Round-bellied like a drinking-cup. **1963** R. P. Dales *Annelids* ii. 42 *Sternapsis* is a small, round-bodied burrower in which the septa have mostly broken down. **1909** B. Lubbock *Deep Sea Warriors* 37 Three men came.., each shouldering a 'round-bottomed chest', as the sailor's bag is called. **1964** V. J. Chapman *Coastal Veg.* iii. 73 Round-bottomed flasks are completely filled with sea water. **1921** Round-browed [see *firm-lipped* s.v. *Firm *a.* C. 1 b]. **1925** W. de la Mare *Two Tales* 95 Minute plants, their round-budded clusters showing. **1605** Marston *Dutch Courtezan* I. i. sig. B1, A softe plumpe round cheekt froe. **1871** Geo. Eliot *Let.* 17 June (1956) V. 153, I hope she will be round-cheeked and strong. **1967** Karch & Buber *Offset Processes* xii. 503 Round-cornered cards are usually purchased already round-cornered, die cut and absolutely rectangular. **1951** Whitby & Hynes *Med. Bacteriol.* (ed. 5) xx. 314 The *Clostridia* in their most typical form are straight or slightly curved round-ended bacilli 0·4μ–1·2μ × 3μ–8μ. **1960** *Farmer & Stockbreeder* 2 Feb. (Suppl.) 8/3 Square or round-ended sticks are also useful..

in building up a design. 1923 D. H. LAWRENCE *Birds, Beasts & Flowers* 160 Yellow eyes incomprehensible with thin slits To round-eyed us. 1962 *Times* 21 Dec. 10/7 A round-hatted drummer. 1906 HARDY *Dynasts* II. IV. i. 230 The Archduchess, a fair, blue-eyed, full-figured, round-lipped maiden. 1958 S. SPENDER *Fool & Princess* 161 Round-looking lips. 1962 L. DEIGHTON *Ipcress File* xxxi. 198 Jean wore a new round-necked, sleeveless.. dress in tangerine linen. 1974 *Country Life* 17 Jan. 107/1 A round-necked, sleeveless top. 1937 DE LA MARE & JONES *This Year, Next Year* 39/1 Through its round-paned window. 1909 W. BATESON *Mendel's Princ. Heredity* I. v. 93 It was..more usual to find whites exclusively produced by the cross of two extracted F_2 whites, long-pollened and round-pollened respectively. 1964 W. L. GOODMAN *Hist. Woodworking Tools* 73 It is a round-soled plane, 14in. long, with a type (b) mouth carving enclosing the date 1706. 1945 W. DE LA MARE *Burning-Glass* 53 Round-spectacled Chardin's Passion for life. 1897 J. L. ALLEN *Choir Invisible* xiii. 195 Where some round-sterned packet from New England or New Amsterdam was unloading its cargo. 1931 G. O. RUSSELL *Speech & Voice* 67 A..round-walled organ pipe.

b. *round-mouthed, -winged.*

1945 STEP & WELLS *Shell Life* 228 Such a form as *Littorina rudis*..was probably the ancestor of the Round-mouthed Snail (*Cyclostoma elegans*), which is clearly a marine snail that has been so modified that it lives far inland on the dry chalk-downs. 1907 R. SOUTH *Moths Brit. Isles* 1st Ser. 175 (*heading*) The round-winged muslin. 1908 *Ibid.* 2nd Ser. 257 In most of such aberrations the tips of the fore wings are rather more rounded than in typical specimens, and these are referable to ab. *rotundaria*, Haworth (Round-winged Wave).

c. *round-seeded* (later example).

1970 *Daily Tel.* 10 Jan. 7/3 Round-seeded peas lack the flavour of the wrinkled varieties.

17. (Further examples.)

1856 Round-bend [see *LIMERICK 2 b]. 1936 J. STEINBECK *In Dubious Battle* iv. 64 A roundwick Rochester lamp. 1940 E. MOLLOY *Electric Wiring* vi. 156 The British Standard Specification for domestic plugs and sockets is confined to the round-pin type. 1941 H. I. CHAPELLE *Boatbuilding* 44 The round-bottom model is considered by most amateur builders too difficult to construct. 1946 *Fortune* Apr. 142/1 [He] obviously doesn't want the job or he wouldn't have put in any round-figure bid that size. 1956 'J. WYNDHAM' *Seeds of Time* 231 The doctor's round-figure price made him frown. 1967 KARCH & BUBER *Offset Processes* xii. 504 Perforating machines allow round-hole perforating, like that found on postage stamps and grocery store stamps. 1968 J. ARNOLD *Shell Bk. Country Crafts* 160 Later wagons, built after 1850 or so, had round-section ironwork. 1970 *Which?* Sept. 280/2 We have criticised this plug before since it will fit into a 5-amp round-pin socket which leaves the appliance unearthed. 1976 *Woman's Day* (U.S.) Nov. 158 Following construction detail, assemble legs and stretcher with 3" roundhead stove bolts and nuts. 1979 *Nature* 7 June 537/1 (*caption*) The 5-doxylstearic acid..was dried down from chloroform/methanol (2:1 v/v) solution in a round-bottom flask. 1979 *Jrnl. R. Soc. Arts* Nov. 746/1 The round-hole capsules resemble round-hole tea ceremony rooms.

round, *adv.* and *prep.* Add: **A.** *adv.* **I. 1. a.** Also in phr. *round and round* (further examples).

1898 A. B. GOMME *Tradit. Games* II. 143 Round and round went the gallant, gallant ship. 1936 *Billboard* 11 Jan. 12/4 That latest contagion, *Music Goes Round and Round*,..is selling at the rate of 16,000 copies daily. 1977 *Washington Post* 26 Dec. c8/2 The music sells the movie. The movie sells the albums. The TV and radio and newspapers sell both. Round and round we go.

e. *all the year round* (further *attrib.* examples). Also as sb. phr. (see quot. 1883).

1883 HARDY in *Graphic* Summer 4/2 One of those curious summer shelters sometimes erected on exposed points of view, called an all-the-year-round. 1910 *Busy Man's Mag.* Feb. 58/2 Vancouver is becoming an all-the-year-round resort. 1939 G. GREENE *Confidential Agent* IV. i. 269 We want to make it an all-the-year-round resort. 1963 *Times* 5 Feb. 7/5 Equipped for all-the-year-round motoring.

g. (Earlier example.)

1857–8 in W. WHITMAN *Daybks. & Notebks.* (1978) III. 676 The Doctor has evidently been 'round some'.

III. 11. *round-turning* (later example); *round-girdled* adj.

1878 O. WILDE *Ravenna* 5 A moon of fire Round-girdled with a purple marriage-ring. 1923 D. H. LAWRENCE *Birds, Beasts, & Flowers* 25 Am I not blind, at the round-turning mill?

B. *prep.* **1. a.** Also in phr. *round and round* (further examples); *round-the-world* (further examples); **round-the-** (also †**me**) **houses,** (*a*) *Rhyming slang*, trousers (see also *ROUND *sb.*[1] 25); (*b*) *attrib. phr.* applied to a motor race or circuit following the streets of a city.

1898 A. B. GOMME *Tradit. Games* II. 122 Round and round the village, As we have done before. 1951 in *Oxf. Dict. Nursery Rhymes* 184 Round and round the garden like a teddy bear; One step, two step, Tickle you under there! 1977 *Washington Post* 26 Dec. c8/2 Travolta himself..is going round and round the country with a cordon of publicists.

Comb. 1857 'DUCANGE ANGLICUS' *Vulgar Tongue* 17 *Round me houses*,..trousers, pronounced trouses [ed. 2, 1859, trousies]. 1858 A. MAYHEW *Paved with Gold* II. x. 169 Philip intimating that, as soon as he had put on his *trousers*, he would blacken Bill's *eyes*, roared out, 'Wait till I've togged my 'round-the-houses', and then I'll cook your 'mince-pies' for you'. 1898 J. D. BRAYSHAW *Slum Silhouettes* 220 An' as fer 'is rahnd-the-'ouses, they 'ad a crease right dahn 'em. 1906 E. DYSON *Fact'ry 'Ands* xiii. 164 No man that wore 'ome-made round-th'-'ouses ever done wonders in this world. 1932 A. CHRISTIE *Peril at End House* xi. 131 It was he who financed..the expenses of the round-the-world flight. 1935 EYSTON & LYNDON *Motor Racing* iv. 38 The introduction of events run over short circuits planned within the confines of a town. These have become known as 'round-the-houses' races, the first of which was the Grand Prix of Monaco, inaugurated in 1929. 1957 S. MOSS *In Track of Speed* i. 14 The Manx Cup race in the Isle of Man, which was a sort of 'round-the-houses' contest in the environs of Douglas. 1970 *N.Z. News* 21 Jan. 16/1 Champion of the American circuit, British-born Ron Grant revelled in conditions he had not experienced before in the Wanganui annual round the houses motorcycle race. 1974 *Times* 10 Jan. 12 The West German round-the-world racing yacht, Peter von Danzig, is putting into Bluff, on New Zealand's South Island. 1974 P. WRIGHT *Lang. British Industry* x. 87 Some of it [*sc.* rhyming slang] apparently doesn't even rhyme properly; e.g. *round the houses* (trousers).

c. *round the clock, the clock round*: see *CLOCK *sb.*[1] 4. Also *Comb.*, as *round-the-year.*

1959 *News Chron.* 28 Nov. 3/1 Round-the-year sea bathing.

2. c. *colloq.* Of time: About; approximately. Cf. *AROUND *prep.* 4 b.

1928 F. N. HART *Bellamy Trial* iii. 92 It must have been round quarter to nine. 1942 PARTRIDGE *Usage & Abusage* 277/1 *Round* for *on* or *about* is a characteristic of Cockney speech: e.g. 'Meet me round seven o'clock'.

5. a. *round-the-corner* (further examples).

1881 [see *LAZY-TONGS]. 1915 A. CONAN DOYLE *Valley of Fear* I. vii. 121 You get to your point, I admit, but you have such a deuced round-the-corner way of doing it.

c. *round the wicket*: see *BOWL *v.*[1] 4 b. (Further examples.)

1867 G. H. SELKIRK *Guide to Cricket Ground* iv. 61 The discretion allowed to the bowler to deliver the ball either over or round the wicket. 1894 N. GALE *Cricket Songs* 26 If round the wicket, medium pace, Won't make the batsman budge,.. Sling him a grub. 1956 N. CARDUS *Close of Play* 14 Macaulay bowled off-spin from round the wicket. 1966 B. JOHNSTON *Armchair Cricket* 109 *Round the wicket*, a method of delivery where the bowler has his back to the stumps at the bowling end as he delivers the ball, i.e. a right-arm bowler bowls on the right-hand side of the stumps, a left-arm bowler on the left-side. 1974 *Sunday Tel.* 9 June 34/6 Titmus, fancying his chances, went round the wicket and induced the predictable catch to short leg.

d. Phr. *round the bend*: see *BEND *sb.*[4] 10 c.

round, *v.*[1] Add: **I. 4. d.** To approximate (a number) by expressing it in fewer significant figures (the rightmost digit(s) being replaced by 0 and the last unaltered digit being increased by 1 when the digit that followed is 5 (or 6) or more); to express (a number) in a less exact but more convenient form. Also with *down, off, up* (see senses 5 h, 6 e, 8 d below).

1934 in WEBSTER. 1935 SHUSTER & BEDFORD *Field Work in Math.* iv. 14 Round the following numbers to three significant figures. *Ibid.* 15 Multiply 2·87 ft. (*a*) by 3·14, (*b*) by 3·142... Round in each case to three figures. 1956 G. A. MONTGOMERIE *Digital Calculating Machines* vii. 129 The usual rule is to ignore a digit less than five and to add one in the next place for five or more. 3·54 would be rounded to 3·5, 3·55 to 3·6, 3·56 to 3·6. 1962 *B.S.I. News* Jan. 25/1 The results are either exact or have been rounded by the accepted convention to the number of significant figures given. 1966 *Rep. Comm. Inquiry Univ. Oxf.* II. p. xxxii, In the tables each figure is rounded separately. 1971 *Jrnl. Gen. Psychol.* LXXXV. 72 The loadings have been rounded to two figures.

5. *round up.* **d.** (Further example.)

1947 A. RANSOME *Great Northern?* viii. 111 The *Sea Bear* slipped on in silence towards the big white motor yacht... She rounded up perhaps forty yards away.

e. (Later *lit.* and earlier and later *transf.* examples.) Also *absol.*

1869 *Overland Monthly* III. 126 At night they 'round up' or 'corral'. 1907 C. E. MULFORD *Bar-20* 15 They shore outer be here now. They rounded up last week. 1925 E. F. NORTON *Fight for Everest 1924* 26 Kingston and I amused ourselves by trying to round up some kiang [*sc.* wild donkeys]. 1949 *Sky Line Trail* Oct. 18/1, I met some cowboys rounding up strayed horses.

transf. 1885 *Weekly New Mexican Rev.* 15 Jan. 2/5 Mr. Twitchell went down to 'round up' the gang and was so far successful as to spot the leader. 1910 *Chambers's Jrnl.* June 384/1, I have seen groups of these unfortunates 'rounded up' and marched off to the nearest police-station. 1931 *Daily Express* 15 Oct. 6/3 The star-traders of the talkies have been out rounding up fresh material from which to carve the box-office idols of the future. 1944 M. LASKI *Love on Supertax* xii. 118 They delay.. arrests in the futile hope of 'rounding up the whole gang'. 1975 P. G. WINSLOW *Death of Angel* vi. 136, I heard about your difficulty and immediately rounded up Cecil.

h. To increase (a number) when rounding it (cf. sense 4 d above) by adding 1 to its rightmost remaining digit, or by expressing it as the next higher round number.

1956 G. A. MONTGOMERIE *Digital Calculating Machines* vii. 129 In a long calculation, all these increases may accumulate, and it is better to round some of them up and some of them down. 1963 *Rep. Comm. Inquiry Decimal Currency* iv. 30, in *Parl. Papers 1962–3* (Cmnd. 2145) XI. 195 The custom with some of these goods is to round up, sometimes down, to the nearest halfpenny. 1969 *Guardian* 30 July 16/1 The Shell-Mex and BP group..will not be advising the 17,000 stations it supplies whether to 'round-up' or 'round-down' petrol prices when the halfpenny ceases to be legal tender. 1975 *Language for Life* (Dept. Educ. & Sci.) xxi. 310 Some Authorities with schools of under 100 pupils round up the number on roll to the nearest 50 and calculate their *per capita* allowance on that basis. 1976 [see *ROUNDING *vbl. sb.* 1 c].

6. *round off.* **e.** = sense 4 d above. Also *absol.*

1935 SHUSTER & BEDFORD *Field Work in Math.* iv. 14 The product given above, 20·671728 ft., should be 'rounded off' to 20.7 ft. 1945 J. P. ECKERT et al. *Description of ENIAC* (PB 86242) (Moore School of Electr. Engin., Univ. Pennsylvania) B-5 The products c_j are rounded-off to the same number of places. 1977 K. M. E. MURRAY *Caught in Web of Words* xi. 211 James had rounded off sums downwards rather than upwards—writing £900 for an actual £975 for example. 1978 GREEN & LEWIS *Sci. with Pocket Calculators* ii. 21 Many calculators..round off automatically when displaying results.

8. a. (Further examples.) Also *fig.* and *refl.*

1926 *Publishers' Weekly* 29 May 1789/2 Presently we came away. The inquiry was rounding itself out. 1937 A. L. ROWSE *Sir Richard Grenville* 10 New discoveries.. helping to round out and present at length a fairly full portrait of the man. 1947 J. C. RICH *Materials & Methods of Sculpture* Pl. 35/4 (*caption*) Rounding out the forms from the front of the sheet. 1966 *Listener* 24 Nov. 763/1 Now, with three full-length plays behind him..it is possible to round out a little that first impression. 1972 *Daily Tel.* 30 Nov. 21 Lloyds Bank's new merchant bank, set up yesterday to round out the bank's services, has no name. 1979 *Arizona Daily Star* 5 Aug. I. 1/4 The third act very satisfactorily rounds out what has long been a frustrating, partially finished production.

d. *round down*, to decrease (a number) when rounding it (cf. sense 4 d above) by making no alteration to its remaining digits, or by expressing it as the next lower round number.

1956, etc. [see sense 5 h above]. 1970 *Guardian* 19 Feb. 13/6 The new conversion table would enable prices sometimes to be rounded down, although some may be rounded up. 1971 *Daily Tel.* 9 Nov. 14 It is Post Office practice for telephone bill totals ending in ½p to be rounded down to the nearest whole penny. 1976 [see *ROUNDING *vbl. sb.* 1 c].

II. 11. c. Delete *rare*—[1] and add later example.

1911 W. JAMES *Some Probl. Philos.* vi. 99 Rationalistic philosophy has always aspired to a rounded-in view of the whole of things, a closed system of kinds.

III. 13. a. (Later example.) Now *rare.*

1941 *Penguin New Writing* II. 14 Early as it is women and old men are hunting for scraps of coal on the side of the incline. They have to be away before the police start to round.

b. Also const. *in.*

1924 GALSWORTHY *White Monkey* I. xiii. 109 He rounded-in from the Embankment towards home.

f. To turn round *on*; to assail, assault, esp. with words; to abuse, berate.

1882 *Sydney Slang Dict.* 7/2 *Round* (*on a man*),..to abuse. 1909 *Blackw. Mag.* Sept. 413/1 On one occasion.. she had rounded on him and scolded him for a full half-hour. 1932 E. BOWEN *To North* xx. 211 Cecilia did not round on Julian. 1966 *Listener* 24 Nov. 764/2 It may be possible to find a parallel in the work of other writers whose first impulse, as young men, was to round on society. 1973 *Times* 16 Nov. 4 Professor Peters also rounds on the Inner London Education Authority for exceeding its brief.

14. a. Also with *out.*

1912 *Red Mag.* Apr. 510/2, I guess she didn't know how she had rounded out in the mountain air.

d. (Earlier example.)

1879 *Missouri Republican* 22 Oct. 3/7 Are you going to 'round up' at Maj. B.'s tonight?

round about, *adv.* and *prep.* Add: **B.** *prep.* **3.** Of time, amount, etc.: about; approximately; = *AROUND *prep.* 4 b.

1913 P. REEVES (*title*) Round about a pound a week. 1926 W. R. INGE *Lay Thoughts* 182 In the Middle Ages the births and deaths in the undrained towns were both round about 50 per thousand in each year. 1961 N. CARDUS *Sir T. Beecham* 64 It was round about 1931 that he told me he was about to form a new orchestra in London.

roundabout, *sb.* and *a.* Add: **A.** *sb.* **2. b.** (Earlier and later examples.)

1823 J. F. COOPER *Pilot* I. vi. 66 The young sailor.. slipped his arms into the sleeves of a morning roundabout, covered with the trappings of his profession. 1825 in *Trans Illinois State Hist. Soc. 1910* (1912) 177, I have twelve shirts six pair Pantaloons 6 vests..two roundabouts. 1904 *N.Y. Even. Post* 7 Jan. 7 Only yesterday this young man was playing about the streets of Washington, a schoolboy in roundabouts.

c. (Earlier example.)

1844 *Lowell Offering* IV. 175 [He sat] in a large flat-bottomed 'roundabout' on the opposite side of the fireplace.

†**d.** *U.S.* A loose dressing-gown worn by women. **e.** *N.Z.* (See quot. 1861.) *Obs.*

1841 *Southern Lit. Messenger* VII. 525/1 The garment is a long, loose roundabout, connecting in front with strings, and is much worn, even at the present time. 1856 V. LUSH *Jrnl.* 17 Jan. (1971) 176 The whole lot stood quietly looking at us, clothed from top to toe in their long full roundabouts. 1861 R. B. PAUL *N.Z.* 17 [The Maori women's] usual dress is..a shapeless sack of printed calico, called a 'roundabout', tied round the neck but loose at the waist. 1874 W. M. BAINES *Narr. E. Crewe* 118, I also gave [the Maori girl] 8 yards of Navy blue print (which everyone knows is enough for a 'roundabout'). 1890 P. A. PHILIPS *Reminisc. Early Days* 7 The hostess did not dress for dinner..her usual attire being a Maori roundabout. **1895** K. D. WIGGIN *Village Watch-Tower* 103 Mother had let her slip on her new green roundabout over her nightgown.

4. b. *to gain on the swings and lose on the roundabouts*: see *SWING *sb.*[2]

d. A junction at which traffic moves one way round a central island. Cf. *ROND-POINT b, *ROTARY *sb.* 3.

1927 *Glasgow Herald* 3 Jan. 7/2 There is only one draw-back to the roundabout, and that is the inconvenience caused to pedestrians. **1937** *Times* 13 Apr. (British Motor No.) p. viii/1 Roundabouts..have the advantage of keeping vehicles on the move. **1947** *Daily Mail* 22 May 3/4 Removal of the Mansion House to make room for a big round-about. **1955** *Times* 2 Aug. 9/7 Makeshift tactics are particularly evident in the proposed treatment at Hyde Park Corner which includes an extremely complicated roundabout. **1967** *Listener* 28 Sept. 398/1 People make only occasional use of their speedometer.. on such critical occasions as the approach to roundabouts. **1977** *Belfast Tel.* 14 Feb. 5/9, 12 shots were fired at an armoured police vehicle near the roundabout at Narrow-water Castle.

B. *adj.* **1. d.** (Earlier example.)

1737 *S. Carolina Gaz.* 30 Apr.–7 May 1/1 [Drunkenness] bears no kind of Similitude with any sort of Virtue, from which it might..borrow a Name; and is therefore reduc'd to the wretched Necessity of being express'd by distant round-about Phrases.

f. Of or pertaining to a junction at which traffic moves one way around a central island. Cf. sense A. 4 d above.

1927 *Rep. Commissioner Police Metropolis, 1926* 18 During the past year round-about systems of traffic have been put into operation at Parliament Square [etc.]. **1939** *War Illustr.* 7 Oct. 127 This car was found abandoned the morning after colliding with the posts of a 'roundabout' island. **1976** *Alyn & Deeside Observer* 10 Dec. 1/6 From there it runs to Broughton in the Welsh county of Clwyd and ends at a roundabout junction.

3. b. Designating a type of chair with a rounded seat or back (see quots.). Cf. sense A. 2 c.

1741 in J. S. Moore *Goods & Chattels of our Forefathers* (1976) 286 Six India Back Chairs and a Round about Ditto with Leather seats £2 os od. **1840** *Knickerbocker* XVI. 115, I sat in my roundabout chair the other evening. **1936** F. C. MORSE *Furniture* 170 'Roundabout' chairs are met with in inventories from 1738 under various names,—'three-cornered chair', 'half round chair', 'round about chair'. **1952** J. GLOAG *Short Dict. Furnit.* 398 The round-about chair has a circular seat, either upholstered or caned, a semi-circular back, and six legs. **1960** H. HAYWARD *Antique Coll.* 84/1 Corner chairs were known in the 17th cent. and were sometimes called elbow chairs or roundabout chairs. **1966** M. M. PEGLER *Dict. Interior Design* (1967) 380 *Roundabout chair.* This chair is usually designed to fit into a corner, the square seat diagonally set and the back extending across two adjoining sides.

5. a. (Earlier and later examples.)

1802 C. FINDLATER *Gen. View Agric. Peebles* 40 The round-about fire side..was universally in use in the kitchen. **1978** T. HENDERSON *Shetland* 142 (*caption*) A round-about fire in Walls about 1910.

round-arm, *a.* and *adv.* Add: **1.** Also, of a bowler who delivers the ball thus.

[**1833** J. MITFORD in *Gentl. Mag.* Sept. 238/2 Ashby.. introduced the round bowling, by throwing the arm in a sweeping circular position.] **1836** *New Sporting Mag.* Oct. 358 Mr. Lowth is a round-arm, left handed bowler.

round-armed *a.* (earlier examples); hence **round-armer,** a round-armed delivery.

1854 Round-armed [see *BOWL *v.*[1] 4 b]. **1863** *Lillywhite's Cricket Scores* III. 43 A medium-paced round-armed bowler. **1951** R. ROBINSON *From Boundary* ii. 39 He rings in a leg-break or a round-armer now and again. **1954** J. FINGLETON *Ashes crown Year* 255 Then came Miller's..appeal..as he rapped May's pads with a round-armer.

rounded, *ppl. a.* Add: **II. 6. c.** Of a number: having been approximated by rounding; expressed in fewer significant figures. Also with advb.

1947 *Math. Tables & Other Aids Computation* II. 286 He had taken 10-figure logarithms of rounded-off quantities containing only five or six significant figures. **1953** *Proc. IRE* XLI. 1271/1 *Long Right* places the bits to be dropped into the *MQ* register; *Round* then leaves a rounded number in the accumulator. **1956** G. A. MONTGOMERIE *Digital Calculating Machines* vii. 129 A convenient rule to ensure this is to make the rounded digit even rather than odd in case of doubt. **1973** PHILLIPS & TAYLOR *Theory & Applic. Numerical Anal.* 359 If the amount neglected is exactly $\frac{1}{2}10^{-t}$ we can avoid statistical bias by forcing the last digit in the rounded number to be even.

roundel. Add: **I. 2. c..** Now only *Hist.* (Further example.)

1971 R. HOWE *Mrs. Groundes-Peace's Old Cookery Notebk.* 56 Wooden trenchers were also known as treen roundels.

5. d. (Further examples.)

1885 [see *BULLION[3] 2]. **1898** W. GANDY *Romance of Glass-Making* ix. 145 Now and then one comes across an old window—generally a cellar window—where the panes have been filled with bull's-eyes, 'roundels', or the waste centres left from the discs of crown glass after cutting. **1908** A. L. DUTHIE *Decorative Glass Processes* i. 28 Circular in form..are *roundels,* which have always been largely used in leaded lights and are characteristic of German and Italian windows. They are made in an infinite variety of colour and size. **1933** R. MOLLET *Leaded Glass Work* ii. 13 Bullions are very popular... The smaller sizes (2 or 3 in. in diameter) are sometimes called 'roundels'.

e. An identification disc painted on an aeroplane; *spec.* that of the Royal Air Force and Royal Naval Air Command, comprising a design of concentric red, white, and blue circles.

1948 *Daily Tel.* 5 July 1/1 The R.A.F. plane—I could see the roundel—was spiralling down without a tail. **1963** J. LUSBY in B. James *Austral. Short Stories* 225 Wingtip clear of the next man's, able to move forward or back and level with his roundel. **1975** T. ALLBEURY *Palomino Blonde* xxiii. 142 A helicopter came..across the bay. The RAF roundels looked fresh and clean.

rounder. Add: **I. 1. d.** For *U.S.* read *N.Amer.* and add earlier and later examples. Also *transf.*

1854 *Congress Globe* 33rd Congress 1st Sess. App. 1220/3 I have always found him a very kind and agreeable man—what the 'rounders' in New York would term a 'glover'. **1879** A. DALY *Let.* 20 Oct. in J. F. Daly *Life A. Daly* (1917) xxi. 330 [We] are old 'rounders' and familiar with the voice, gait and peculiarities of most of the actors and actresses on the American stage. **1920** C. SANDBURG *Smoke & Steel* 51 A rounder leered confidential. **1935** Z. N. HURSTON *Mules & Men* (1970) I. iv. 93 'What make de rooster crow every morning at sun-up?' 'Dat's to let de pimps and rounders know de workin' man is on his way.' **1943** W. H. CHASE *Sourdough Pot* v. 24 [She] possessed all the earmarks of a 'rounder'—the evidence of much dissipation was remarkably developed. **1962** 'K. ORVIS' *Damned & Destroyed* iv. 29 An all-night dive patronized by cheap women and rounders and drunks. **1975** *Globe & Mail* (Toronto) 7 Oct. 4/5 He agreed that rounders—a term used to describe criminals whose haunts include hotels in the Jarvis Street–Dundas Street area of Toronto—have a great fear they will be seen talking to the police.

e. *U.S. slang.* (See quot. 1903.)

1881 *Bradstreet's* 29 Jan. 51/4 The 'rounder' in alms-taking is headed off. **1903** *Charities* 3 Oct. 283 The class of persons known as 'rounders', people who go from one hospital to another seeking advice and treatment, a species of medical mendicants.

f. *U.S. slang.* A transient railway worker.

1908 *Casey Jones* (song) in *Railroad Man's Mag.* May 764/1 Come all you rounders, for I want you to hear The story told of an engineer, Casey Jones was the rounder's name, A heavy right-wheeler of a mighty fame. **1939** F. J. LEE *Casey Jones* 287 The word 'rounder' as applied to Casey must be taken as a light, affectionate appellation. **1961** *Listener* 24 Aug. 270/2 His was a six-pipe job whose moans sent every coloured 'rounder' from Chicago to New Orleans into ecstasies.

2. a. (Earlier and later examples.)

1828 W. CLARKE *Boy's Own Book* (ed. 2, London) 20 *Rounders.* In the west of England this is one of the most favourite sports with bat and ball... In Rounders, the players divide into two equal parties, and chance decides which shall have the first innings. **1854** DICKENS *Let.* 12 July (1938) II. 566 The keeping up of a 'home' at rounders. **1939** *Bull. N.Y. Public Libr.* Apr. 303 Is baseball an offshoot of rounders? **1969** I. & P. OPIE *Children's Games* 5 At Sedgley Park School in Staffordshire, about 1805, the boys were content with Kites, Marloes (marbles),..Rounders,..and even with 'playing horses'. **1977** *Cleethorpes News* 27 May 18/1 In addition to exploring the mines, they played rounders among the sheep on the hillside.

II. 5. (Earlier example.)

1774 T. PENNANT *Tour in Scotl. & Voy. Hebrides 1772* I. 99 On each side the gateway..are two rounders.

III. 11. *Newfoundland.* Small unsplit cod, freq. eaten as a delicacy.

1908 C. W. TOWNSEND *Along Labrador Coast* v. 132 The very small cod are not boned, but are salted whole. These are called 'leggies' or 'rounders'. **1966** A. R. SCAMMELL *My Newfoundland* 32 School fees could not be put on the account and the schoolmaster wouldn't accept fish, tomcods or rounders. *Ibid.* 91 When the last rounder was aboard he gave a quizzical glance at the sun. **1974** *National Geogr. Mag.* Jan. 129/2 We dined sumptuously on native dishes..'rounders' (baby cod, salted and dried whole like kippers, and boiled for breakfast).

round-faced, *a.* Add: **2.** Also, *round-faced monkey.* For *Macaques* substitute *Macaca.*

1872 *Proc. Zool. Soc.* 777 It would seem that our Round-faced Monkey, in the proportionate dimensions of fore limb to spine's length, presents closest agreement with man.

Roundhead, round-head. Add: **1. a.** (Later *transf.* and *attrib.* examples.)

1963 *Times* 11 Feb. 6/7 Now that industry is 'dis-hoarding' labour and achieving results more effectively than Roundhead policy at the Treasury. **1973** D. AARON *Unwritten War* 345 Southern magazines featured articles contrasting invidiously planter 'Cavaliers' and Yankee 'Roundheads'. **1976** *Listener* 5 Feb. 140/3 Under the Cromwellian leadership of Peter Hall, the roundheads of the new professionalism drove the cavalier dilettanti largely from the scene.

b. *N.Amer. slang.* An immigrant from northern Europe, *spec.* a Swede.

1895 *Dialect Notes* I. 393 *Roundhead,* a Swede. **1902** S. CLAPIN *New Dict. Americanisms* 341 *Roundhead,* in the North-West, frequently said of a Swede. **1931** 'D. STIFF' *Milk & Honey Route* iii. 38 Swedes are 'roundheads' or 'salve eaters'. **1976** 'TREVANIAN' *Main* (1977) iii. 57 'He's not a bad type, for a Roundhead,' Gaspard says.

c. *Ethnol.* One of a race or type of man characterized by roundness of the head. Cf. *ROUND-HEADED *a.* 1 b. *rare.*

1896 A. H. KEANE *Ethnol.* I. v. 106 Mounds differing in type from those of the round-heads.

4. (Further example.)

1908 A. W. TILBY *Eng. People Overseas* I. ii. 72 The former was strongly cavalier and episcopal; the latter was as strongly roundhead and puritan.

Hence **rou·ndheader** = sense 1 b above.

1934 J. O'HARA *Appointment in Samarra* iii. 80 The schwackies, the roundheaders..—regional names for non-Latin foreigners—probably were inside getting drunk.

round-headed, *a.* Add: **1. b.** *Ethnol.* Designating a race or type of man characterized by possessing a skull of rounded shape, usu. distinguished from a LONG-HEAD (sense 2). *rare.*

1896 A. H. KEANE *Ethnol.* I. v. 106 Mr. W. K. Moore-head..recognises two distinct mound-building races, the old long-headed, and the later round-headed intruders.

Hence **round-hea·dedness,** the state of being round-headed; the condition of having a round head.

1935 [see *HIGH FREQUENCY 1 b].

round-house, *sb.* Add: **2. b.** (Earlier example.)

1808 J. DAVIS *Post Captain* (ed. 3) i. 5, I..was obliged to get up in the night to go to the roundhouse.

3. a. (Further example.)

1971 *Country Life* 11 Nov. 1325/1 An example..is a farm building specifically termed the wheelhouse, but more popularly known as roundhouse or gin gan.

4. For *U.S.* read 'orig. *U.S.*' and add earlier and later examples. Also *fig.* and *attrib.*

1856 W. FERGUSON *Amer. by River & Rail* 249 The engine-house..is open in the centre; and this arrangement ..is much less expensive, than the 'round house', where all is covered in. **1895** *Rep. Chicago Strike 1894* (U.S. Strike Comm.) 214 A number of switch tenders, yard clerks, flagmen, tower men, and roundhouse men left their work. **1945** F. H. HUBBARD *Railroad Avenue* ii. 10 Many runners considered it smart to keep roundhouse work on an engine down to a minimum—the fewer the defects they reported, the better standing they had at the roundhouse. **1953** *Manch. Guardian Weekly* 5 Nov. 15/1 This restoration of power [over the money supply] was hailed by a writer in 'Harper's Magazine' as a..guarantee that 'the engine of inflation has been stowed firmly in the roundhouse'. **1966** M. R. D. FOOT *SOE in France* ix. 269 Six large engines in the Troyes locomotive roundhouse. **1980** *Dædalus* Spring 121 Myths provide a conceptual system through which we may understand..a roundhouse where we can move from the track of one person's reality to another's.

5. a. *U.S. Baseball.* A pitch made with a sweeping side-arm motion. Also *attrib.*

1910 *Amer. Mag.* June 224/2 The first curves discovered were of the variety now known as the 'barrel hoop' or 'round house'. **1912** C. MATHEWSON *Pitching* 19 When I first joined the Giants, I had what is known as the 'old round-house curve', which is no more than a big, slow outdrop. **1926** *Amer. Speech* I. 369/2 Pitched balls are designated by obvious terms. A 'spitter', a 'hook',..a 'round-house'.

b. *slang* (orig. *U.S.*). A blow delivered with a wide sweep of the arm. Also *fig.* Freq. *attrib.*, esp. as *roundhouse left, right.*

1920 *Collier's Mag.* 3 July 34/4 He swung a roundhouse left, square to the Kid's unprotected face. **1927** *Daily Express* 16 Dec. 3 It is necessary to take the [golf] ball cleanly, and with something akin to a 'round-house' swing from this position. **1932** J. T. FARRELL *Young Lonigan* iii. 133 They fought, slugging, socking away, rushing, swinging with haymakers and wild swishing roundhouses. **1945** *Tee Emm* (Air Ministry) V. 51 Discourage him by jabbing his snout or gills with an oar,.. and don't take round-house swings that may upset you. **1946** *Sun* (Baltimore) 14 Dec. 2/6 Mr. Collins leaped to his feet and swung a round-house right at the witness. **1948** *Ibid.* 12 May 17/6 Trainer Jimmy Jones obviously was disappointed at failure to have Coaltown [*sc.* a horse] on hand to deliver Columet's [*sic*] winning jab and round-house... Jimmy will saddle the Calumet starter. **1958** J. KEROUAC *On Road* iv. 126 Damion's girl suddenly socked Damion on the jaw with a roundhouse right. **1967** *Boston Herald* 1 Apr. 17/7 Harris built up an early lead over the baffled 29-year-old veteran with his roundhouse blows. **1976** M. MACHLIN *Pipeline* lvii. 573 Doheny's arm drew back, as though to launch a roundhouse upper-cut.

round-house *v.*, (*b*) *slang*, to hit (a person) with a round-house blow.

1974 W. GARNER *Big Enough Wreath* xi. 137 She roundhoused Smith with a white plastic handbag that must have had a brick in it.

rounding, *vbl. sb.*[1] Add: **1. a.** (Further examples.) Also with *off, out, up.*

1876 M. WHILLDIN *Descr. Western Texas* 16 It soon became evident that a place near us had been selected for 'rounding up'. **1916** *Daily News* 6 Sept. 4 There can rarely..have been a better example of the insolence of Zabernism than the 'rounding up' of crowds of unoffending people at the stations. **1932** W. C. HOLDEN *Rollie Burns* xiii. 172 Our rounding-up outfit was camped about eight miles from the Yellow House Canyon. **1936** *Trans. Philol. Soc.* 78 The rounding of *ā* to [ɔ] is in Middle English generally held to be a West Midland feature. **1947** A. EINSTEIN *Mus. Romantic Era* xi. 127 The perfect rounding-out of the form, which from the musical standpoint is entirely self-contained. **1949** *Jrnl. R. Aeronaut.*

Soc. LIII. 957/1 The cabin floor angle in the steeper types, such as Dakotas and Lancastrians, is changed as slowly as possible by slow rounding out and by landing with the tail just off the ground. **1961** E. A. POWDRILL *Vocab. Land Planning* iii. 38 The private developer refers to most forms of peripheral development as 'rounding-off', whilst the planning authority merely contends that it is not, usually without saying what rounding-off really means. **1971** P. GRESSWELL *Environment* 132 Development will be severely restricted except for a reasonable amount of infilling and/or rounding off. **1977** *Canad. Jrnl. Linguistics 1976* XXI. 176 At this level we want to state, for example, that a language has vowels which are opposed in rounding.

c. The action of *ROUND *v.*[1] 4 d. Also with *down, off, up* (cf. *ROUND *v.*[1] 5 h, 6 e, 8 d).

1935 SHUSTER & BEDFORD *Field Work in Math.* iv. 14 In computation with approximate numbers, rounding off should be done by these rules. **1953** *Proc. IRE* XLI. 1270/1 Different calculations may require different methods of rounding in order to reduce the residual rounding error to an acceptably low level. **1963** *Rep. Comm. Inquiry Decimal Currency* iii. 18 in *Parl. Papers 1962–3* (Cmnd. 2145) XI. 195 Outstanding balances would convert exactly on the changeover date, with no discrepancies which might or might not be explained by decimalisation roundings. **1973** C. W. GEAR *Introd. Computer Sci.* vi. 249 The errors introduced by rounding and truncation are initially small, but sometimes their effect is amplified by subsequent operations. **1976** C. BIRTWISTLE *Electronic Calculator* iii. 35, 23 is rounded down to 20 and 28 is rounded up to 30. Where is the critical point at which rounding down changes to rounding up? Obviously it is the half-way mark, 25.

3. a. *rounding plane*; **rounding error** = *round-off error* s.v. *ROUND-OFF *sb.* 1.

1948 *Math. Tables & Other Aids to Computation* III. 79 The operator is concerned with numerous questions of digital accuracy and the accumulation of rounding errors. **1962** A. BATTERSBY *Guide to Stock Control* 115 Allowing for rounding errors, the stockholding cost at ½ per cent would be £15. **1973** C. W. GEAR *Introd. Computer Sci.* vi. 249 The first source is called rounding error, and is due to the fact that only a finite set of all of the real numbers can be represented in the computer as floating-point numbers. **1940** *Chambers's Techn. Dict.* 732/2 Rounding plane. **1969** E. H. PINTO *Treen* 389 Different versions of the same tool, known as a stail-engine, witchet, or rounding and tapering plane.

b. rounding-off error = **round-off error*.

1945 J. VON NEUMANN in B. Randell *Origins Digital Computers* (1973) 362 A reasonable precision for many differential equation problems is given..by keeping the relative rounding-off errors below 10^{-8}. **1974** W. T. WELFORD *Aberrations Symmetrical Optical Syst.* vi. 84 The difference between them is to be calculated to a fraction of a wavelength; this may make a heavy demand on the computer when rounding-off errors are allowed for, since the computer word length may correspond to only about eight decimal digits.

roundness. Add: **1. a.** (Further *fig.* example.)

1927 E. M. FORSTER *Aspects of Novel* iv. 98 Dickens's people are nearly all flat (Pip and David Copperfield attempt roundness, but so diffidently that they seem more like bubbles than solids).

d. *out-of-roundness*: see *ROUND *sb.*[1] 5 e.

round-off, *a.* Add: **B.** *sb.* **1.** = *ROUNDING *vbl. sb.*[1] 1 c. Freq. *attrib.* as *round-off error*, the error introduced thereby.

1946 GOLDSTINE & VON NEUMANN in J. von Neumann *Coll. Wks.* (1963) V. 17 A very complicated calculation in which the accumulation and amplification of the round-off errors threatens to prevent the obtaining of results of the desired precision. **1947** *Bull. Amer. Math. Soc.* LIII. 1026 The transition from the true operations to their pseudo-operations is effected by any one of the familiar methods of round off. **1962** *Times Lit. Suppl.* 20 Apr. 268/1 Whenever approximations due to round-offs or other reasons are indicated, the degree of approximation is perfectly well determined. **1973** C. W. GEAR *Introd. Computer Sci.* vi. 258 Sometimes a bad choice of method will make the solution very sensitive to round-off or truncation errors.

2. The act of rounding off or completing an operation appropriately.

1964 *Trampolining* ('Know the Game' Ser.) 40/1 It is similar in action to the round-off in ground work tumbling.

Round Robin. Add: Now usu. with small initials. **3. a.** (Earlier and later examples.) Now used loosely of any such document signed by many persons, freq. in alphabetical order to indicate that responsibility is shared.

(*a*) **1730** *Weekly Jrnl.* 3 Jan. 3/4 A Round Robin is a Name given by Seamen, to an Instrument on which they sign their Names round a Circle, to prevent the Ringleader being discover'd by it, if found.

(*b*) **1978** B. LEVIN in K. Gregory *First Cuckoo* 13 Writers of round robins ('We, the undersigned, each in his or her personal capacity..') also choose *The Times* for preference, the second elevens being accommodated elsewhere.

transf. **1977** *N.Y. Rev. Bks.* 4 Aug. 7/1 As if to point up the homosexual theme, rather than to offer a round robin of sexuality.

b. orig. *U.S.* A tournament in which every player or team competes once with each of the others. Freq. *attrib.*

1895 *Official Lawn Tennis Bull.* 3 Jan. 1/2 The so-called round-robin tournament, where each man plays every other, furnishes the best possible test of tennis skill. *Ibid.* 3/1 No one would..argue that a man of that rating could win in a round-robin. **1904** J. P. PARET *Lawn Tennis* iii. 24 Invitation tournaments are of American origin, and the matches are generally played on what is called the 'round robin' system, each of the players meeting all of the others in turn. *Ibid.* iv. 65 The British visitors next played a round-robin at Chicago. **1943** M. KRAITCHIK *Math. Recreations* ix. 231 In a round-robin tournament among teams of four or two we must arrange a schedule by which every team meets every other just once. **1952** E. LASKER *Chess Secrets* 379 Arrange the players in groups, and have the winners, or the first two or three of each group, play a final round robin. **1974** *Times* 20 Apr. 11/1 The 'Aces' of America [*sc.* a bridge team] held their own against the Italians in the preliminary round-robin to decide who should compete in the final. **1978** *Time* 3 July 50/1 In June, the 14 survivors and the West German team..moved to Argentina to join the host country's team in an exhausting series of round-robin matches.

c. (See quot. 1976.)

1972 J. WAMBAUGH *Blue Knight* (1973) x. 171 Would you care for a round robin or a three-horse parley to-day? **1976** *Daily Tel.* (Colour Suppl.) 26 Mar. 31/4 *Round robin*, three horses linked in Up and Down bets on each pair, plus three doubles and a treble (10 bets).

Hence **round-robinee·r**, a subscriber to a round robin (sense 3 a), an importuner; **round-ro·bining**, the act of subscribing to a round robin (sense 3 a).

1933 H. P. LONG *Every Man a King* xii. 179 If ever again you fifteen round-robineers find me drowning, for Heaven's sake, let me drown! **1968** *Guardian* 13 July 8/6 On Tuesday—after much round-robining—hundreds of BBC secretaries and studio staff intend boycotting the corporation's canteen.

round-shouldered, *a.* Add: (Further *transf.* example.)

1950 H. L. LORIMER *Homer & Monuments* v. 262 Here the round-shouldered short-tanged blade [of a sword] which alone was found at Arkalochon is in the majority, but side by side with it a more serviceable type is developed.

Hence **round-shou·lderedness,** the state or quality of having round shoulders.

1940 S. SPENDER *Backward Son* 14 References to..his round-shoulderedness.

roundsman. Add: **2.** (Earlier and later examples.)

1868 *N.Y. Herald* 31 July 6/5 Patrolman Jas. Mee..is hereby appointed roundsman on the force. **1870** 'MARK TWAIN' in *Galaxy* Sept. 430/1 The rank of constable or even roundsman. **1902** *Chambers's Jrnl.* Oct. 674/1 The first grade of promotion is to roundsman... The roundsman is an important man, for on him the discipline of the patrolmen largely depends. **1937** *Sun* (Baltimore) 1 Dec. 3/1 John McAdams, a former customs roundsman, who was dismissed recently, also was accused of being a member of the smuggling ring.

3. (Further examples.)

1935 *E. Anglia Daily Times* 18 Dec. 4/2 A Lowestoft milk roundsman, who persuaded his customers to buy more than 12 per cent. more milk in three months, has won the £25 and cup awarded for salesmanship. **1977** 'M. UNDERWOOD' *Fatal Trip* xix. 106 It did not take long to discover the name of the dairy [and]..that Frey Chaytor was the roundsman.

round table, *sb.* Add: **4.** *spec.* an assembly of people for a conference or discussions at which all participants are accorded equal status (in this sense freq. *attrib.*). Also *transf.*, a collection of opinions or remarks on a particular subject.

1889 [in Dict.]. **1892** *Review of Reviews* Feb. 148/1 The subject of the 'Round Table Conference'..is what part churches should take in labour problems. **1901** H. W. PAUL *Life Gladstone* xxi. 245 The year 1887 opened with an attempt to reconcile the conflicting elements of the Liberal Party, which came to be known as the Round Table Conference. **1910** (*title of periodical*) The Round Table: a quarterly review of the politics of the British Empire. **1928** *Daily Express* 3 July 2/4 The Archbishop of Canterbury made a striking proposal yesterday for a 'round table' to discuss the future relations of Church and State. **1929** *Times* 31 Oct. 14/3 Mr. Benn himself proposed to visit India forthwith for.. a round-table conference. **1943** M. MCCARTHY in *Partisan Rev.* May–June 280 The problems..are..opened for discussion in an atmosphere reminiscent of the Chicago Round Table. **1943** *Times* 8 July 5/5 In certain instances we stayed overnight to enjoy the free and easy of a 'round table conference'. **1947** *Radio Times* 14 Mar. 1/2 Round-table controversial political discussions, which the BBC will continue to originate. **1952** D. RIESMAN in *Antioch Rev.* Dec. 418 A roundtable..of which he was chairman at the Corning Conference. **1955** *Times* 30 July 5/1 Round-table talks may be held in London about a year hence to consider a new constitution for a self-governing Singapore. **1973** *Word 1970* XXVI. 120 He took an active part in the linguistic and anthropological life of Mexico, attending conferences, round tables, and the like. **1976** *National Observer* (U.S.) 10 Apr. 1/3 The Observer convened an informal round-table talk involving six young people with differing perspectives. **1978** *Jrnl. R. Soc. Arts* CXXVI. 768/1 In 1930–31 he was Adviser to the Indian States Delegation to the Round Table Conference in London.

5. (With capital initials.) A formal association whose members meet regularly for discussion, *spec.* an organization (or a branch of it) founded in 1927, in which professional people between the ages of 18 and 40 hold discussions, debates, and similar activities, and undertake community service and the promotion of international understanding. Also allusively as *adj.*, designating the qualities or characteristics associated with the Round Table or its members.

1917 L. CURTIS *Let. to People of India* 13 The Round Table organisation..is merely a system for enabling people to unite for the study of their duties as citizens of this Commonwealth, as a guide to their own individual action. **1928** *Review of Reviews* Mar.–Apr. 253/2 At Norwich..an Association of Young Men has established a Club for young business men, meeting once a week in the evening for the reading of papers, discussions, and debates, under the title of 'The Round Table'. **1955** A. HUXLEY *Let.* 25 Mar. (1969) 739 Possibly also to go up ..and stay a few days near Puharich's Round Table Foundation outfit. **1968** *Guardian* 10 Sept. 2/7 Mr Powell was speaking to the Rowley Regis Round Table at Cradley Heath, Staffordshire. **1972** J. BURMEISTER *Running Scared* xvii. 213 The woman was..wearing carefully bleached out jeans... Round Table, thought Ginny, with a touch of country. 'I'm terribly sorry.' The voice was Round Table too. **1973** *Stand. Encycl. S. Afr.* IX. 412/2 The Round Table movement in South Africa was founded in East London in 1948. **1977** *Times of Zambia* 7 Sept. 2/4 The committee is made up of the Rotary, Round Table and Lions clubs members.

round table *v.*, **round-tabler.** Delete *nonce-uses* and add later examples.

The use in quot. 1923 is with allusion to the periodical *The Round Table* (see quot. 1910 under sense 4 above).

1923 T. E. LAWRENCE *Let.* 27 Mar. (1938) 413 You [*sc.* Lionel Curtis] have tried (Round Tabling and by mouth) to tell all whom you can reach. **1976** *National Observer* (U.S.) 1 May 19/3 They might squabble bitterly from time to time, but in the main the Round Tablers quoted each other, promoted each other, wrote books and plays and articles about each other with an incestuous zeal. **1976** *Norwich Mercury* 10 Dec., Children of Round Tablers sing for the 250 old folk from Wymondham and Attleborough who attended a Christmas party in Wymondham Central Hall on Sunday.

round-top. 2. (Further examples.)

1897 *Sears, Roebuck Catal.* 251/2 Black enameled iron, round top trunk. **1962** L. S. SASIENI *Princ. & Pract. Optical Dispensing* xii. 312 Round Top Fused [Trifocals]. **1966** J. S. COX *Illustr. Dict. Hairdressing* 129/1 *Round-top butch*, a hair style for men in which the hair is cut very short to a round contour.

round trip. orig. *U.S.* Also **round-trip.** [f. ROUND *a.* 15.] **a.** A circular tour or trip; an outward and return journey.

1860 *Railroad Guide* (Dinsmore & Co.) Sept. 142 Round trip tickets. **1868** *Putnam's Mag.* Mar. 351/1 Time for the round trip..44 hours. **1892** [in Dict. s.v. ROUND *a.* 15 a]. **1923** R. D. PAINE *Comrades of Rolling Ocean* xiii. 223 We signed for the round trip in the *Liberty Chimes*, but we don't feel like taking her all the way home. **1956** *People* 13 May 9/4 The 30-mile round trip to the lonely isle took seven hours. **1976** SCOTT & KOSKI *Walk-In* (1977) iii. 21 'Round trip?' the ticket seller asked... 'You want to go and come back?'

b. *transf.* and *fig.*

1932 *Amer. Speech* VII. 270 *Round-trip*.., one *pull-out* and the subsequent *run-in* of the drill pipe in rotary drilling. **1935** *Econ. Geol.* XXX. 739 Very deep wells may require as much as eight hours to make the 'round trip'. **1938** *Amer. Speech* XIII. 220/2 Round-trip words, i.e. from O[ld] F[rench] to Eng[lish], thence to French. **1945** L. SHELLY *Jive Talk Dict.* 33/1 *Round trip*, anything unusually good or outstanding. **1963** *Gloss. Mining Terms* (*B.S.I.*) III. 12 *Round trip*, the operation of withdrawing the drill rods and bit, etc., from the hole, of extracting core, replacing rods and bit and resuming drilling. **1973** *N.Y. Law Jrnl.* 20 July 5/1 The..Stock Exchange said yesterday it would like to attract small investors back to the stock market with a 'round trip' rate.

c. *attrib.*

1860 [see sense a above]. **1890** *Brighton* (Colorado) *Reg.* 25 Jan. 1/4 The railway company has rehashed its round-trip rate, from suburban towns to Denver. **1939** G. GREENE *Another Mexico* ii. 31 He had got a round-trip ticket to Mexico City. **1976** 'M. BARAK' *Secret List H. Roehm* v. 58 Enclosed was an Air France round-trip ticket to Montevideo. **1978** *Detroit Free Press* 5 Mar. D21/3 (Advt.), Commodore's unique Fly Free/Cruise Easy program..pays half of the lowest applicable round-trip air fare..to Miami.

Hence **round-tri·pper,** (*a*) a traveller who makes a round trip; (*b*) in *Baseball*, a home run; a batter who hits a home run; **round-tri·pping** *Econ.*, the practice of earning profit by borrowing on overdraft and relending in money markets.

1944 D. BURLEY in A. Dundes *Mother Wit* (1973) 219 That's why I'm out here..instead of being a round-tripper. **1962** P. PURSER *Peregrination 22* xii. 60 He was a tourist.. the only genuine round-tripper in the first-class. **1974** *Saturday* (Charleston, S. Carolina) 20 Apr. 5–B/4 Jeff Grantz..powered four round-trippers in one inning. **1974** *Daily Tel.* 25 May 20/3 Interest arbitrage operations, otherwise known as round tripping. **1977** *Times* 23 Nov. 29/8 It is believed there has been a good deal of 'round tripping'—borrowing in the money markets to finance purchases of CTDs at a profit. **1978** J. A. MICHENER *Chesapeake* 649 Home Run Baker..would hit in one year the unheard-of total of twelve round-trippers. **1980** *Boston Globe* 30 Mar. 76 Home runs were circuit clouts. Then they became round trippers, until George Scott renamed them taters. **1980** *Times* 5 Sept. 15/2 It becomes attractive for blue-chip corporate borrowers to take loan from their banks and re-lend the funds to the short-term money markets. This is known as 'round-tripping'.

round-up. Add: **1. b.** *transf.* (in quot. *attrib.*)

1926 J. MASEFIELD *Odtaa* 214 He took one of the big round-up stew cauldrons which lay against a wall.

2. a. For *U.S.* (and *Austr.*) read orig. *U.S.* (Earlier and later examples.) Also *fig.*

1873 in *Ann. Wyoming* (1927) V. 74 The herders of this Co. start a Round-up tomorrow... Each man picks out his stock and drives them in. **1878** J. H. BEADLE *Western Wilds* xxviii. 437 These cattle, having run wild upon the plains of western Texas, are collected by a grand 'round-up'. **1879** *Tinsley's Mag.* XXIV. 353 One's companions, when camping out on the 'round up' are often anything but desirable. **1907** S. E. WHITE *Arizona Nights* iii. 60 We had our first round-up, found the natural increase much in excess of the loss by Indians. **1909** [see *PAY *v.*[1] 10]. **1951** E. PAUL *Springtime in Paris* xv. 287 Busse, rattled as a rabbit in a roundup, bounced back to the pavement just in time to bump into the burly Chestnut Man. **1976** *Billings* (Montana) *Gaz.* 10 June 1-c/1 At the Spanagel ranch west of Forsyth all hands are in the middle of roundup and putting up hay.

b. (Earlier and later examples.)

1880 *Harper's Mag.* Feb. 380/2 We old fellows have a round up 'most every year in Denver. **1936** L. C. DOUGLAS *White Banners* iv. 70 An unexpected invitaton to read a paper at the first monthly round-up of the University Club.

c. The group of men and horses engaged in a round-up.

1878 in *Colorado Mag.* (1939) XVI. 152 Most of the round-up gone; a few still lingered at the bar. **1903** 'O. HENRY' in *Everybody's Mag.* June 519/1 The round-up had ridden on but a few moments before. *a* **1918** G. STUART *40 Yrs. on Frontier* (1925) II. 178 It was a novel sight to witness the big spring roundup pull out.

d. A survey of opinion; a résumé of facts or events; *spec.* in *Broadcasting*, a summary of newsworthy items.

1886 *Philadelphia Times* 3 May 1/1 That exception.. will probably be included in the general round-up by tomorrow. **1892** *Boston Jrnl.* 29 Nov. 3/1 Round-Up of the Boston Aldermanic Districts. **1904** F. CRISSEY *Tattlings of Retired Policeman* ii. 42 A hatchet-faced lawyer..made a quick round-up of the representatives of the corporate interests and vested rights of the state. **1932** *Sun* (Baltimore) 21 Dec. 8/2 The 'round-ups' of Congressional opinion on the war debts issue. **1949** *Lincoln County News* (Oceanlake, Oregon) 4 Aug. 3/4 Another periodic survey of censorship conditions..shows no major barriers have come down since the last roundup of the situation. **1958** *Spectator* 1 Aug. 159/1 The BBC's Middle East round-up on Saturday night was a notable project. **1962** *Listener* 22 Mar. 528/1 He presented a brilliant newsreel round-up 'Cease-fire in Algeria'. **1967** *Economist* 2 Dec. 915/1 A round-up of how America has reacted to the first rush into gold. **1974** *Radio Times* 21 Feb. 46/2 Commentary from Trinidad on the final day's play in the Second Test, together with a round-up of the day's sport.

e. The systematic rounding-up of people or of objects; *spec.* the arrest of people suspected of crime.

1899 *Chicago Rec.* 17 Jan. 12/1 A 'round-up' of all suspicious characters was begun. **1927** A. CHRISTIE *Big Four* v. 54 A short time ago a round-up was made of certain crooks and gunmen. **1943** *Sun* (Baltimore) 17 Nov. 6/1 The collection today will be of all tins accumulated since June 9, when the last such roundup took place. **1966** M. R. D. FOOT *SOE in France* ix. 264 Contacts in the Rouen police..provided reliable warnings of impending round-ups. **1978** *Detroit Free Press* 16 Apr. (Record) 9/3 The round-up began Aug. 26 at the command of the Germans, who at the same time began arresting 20,000 foreign Jews in the occupied zone.

f. = *RODEO 3 b.

1914 *World's Work* Feb. 444/2 During the three days of The Round-Up, a constant stream of humanity pours into Pendleton. **1948** *Great Falls* (Montana) *Tribune* 18 Sept. 5/4 Malta is preparing to welcome at least 5,000 people this weekend when the two-day fall roundups will be staged.

g. In *fig.* phr. *the last round-up*, death, resurrection, or the Last Judgement.

1932 G. BROWN (*song-title*) The last round up. **1940** *Hoofs & Horns* Dec. 11/1 Tom Mix..has laid down his honors..and taken the sunset trail that leads to the Last Roundup.

5. *attrib.*, as (sense 2 a) *round-up boss, camp, captain, outfit, party, wagon*; (sense 2 d) *round-up article, programme, review*; (sense 2 f) *round-up pennant, week.*

1960 V. JENKINS *Lions down Under* 14 'Potentially the greatest team ever to tour New Zealand,' was how Graeme Jenkins..described them in a round-up article. **1977** *Irish Times* 8 June 4/7 A round-up article on the celebrations written by the agency's court correspondent was delivered by hand to some London offices last night. **1920** J. M. HUNTER *Trail Drivers of Texas* 313 The round-up boss would let no one drive through the herd. **1923** R. POCOCK in *Outward Bound* Mar. 410/2 Seventeen miles across the Mesa la Sal, in Utah, brought me to a round-up camp. **1907** Round-up captain [see *CUT *sb.*[2] 23 c]. **1890** *Stock Grower & Farmer* 14 June 5/3 The herder was found by the Long S roundup outfit, about six miles west of Sulphur draw. **1885** *Weekly New Mexican Rev.* 26 Mar. 1/6 Round-up parties have already been started for that section. **1891** *Fur, Fin & Feather* Mar. 188 Wolves naturally follow in the wake of round-up parties. **1931** Y. WINTERS *Coll. Wks.* (1952) 66, I remembered.. The sprawling streets,.. The Round-up pennants. **1979** *Jrnl. R. Soc. Arts* CXXVII. 358/1 What is reported on the news, and current affairs, something very different indeed from..election round-up programmes. **1978** *Amer. Poetry Rev.* Nov./Dec. 32/3 A round-up review by George Dillon in *Poetry*. **1893** T. ROOSEVELT *Wilderness Hunter* ii. 23 Close beyond the trees on the farther bank stood the two round-up wagons. **1973** R. D. SYMONS *Where Wagon Led* I. i. 10 Two of the three men.. were out in the south country with the roundup wagon. **1924** W. M. RAINE *Troubled Waters* iv. 40 A poster.. announced Round-up Week,..roping, and other Western sports.

roundward, *a.* and *adv.* Delete *nonce-word* in Dict. and add: **A.** *adj.* (Further example.)

1927 D. H. LAWRENCE *Mornings in Mexico* 80 The reeling, roundward motion of tree-tips in a wind.

roundwise, *adv.* and *a.* Add: **2.** *adj.* **b.** = ROUNDWARD *a.* *rare*[—1].

a **1930** D. H. LAWRENCE *Apocalypse* (1932) 42 The roundwise moving of the cosmos.

roundy, *a.* **1.** (Later example.)

1882 G. M. HOPKINS *Poems* (1918) 54 As tumbled over rim in roundy wells Stones ring.

Rous (raus). *Biol.* The name of Francis Peyton *Rous* (1879–1970), U.S. physician, used *attrib.* to designate (*a*) a type of virus-induced sarcoma which afflicts birds, described by him in 1910 (*Jrnl. Exper. Med.* XII. 696); (*b*) an RNA virus which causes such sarcomata (its existence was suggested by Rous et al. in 1912 (*Jrnl. Amer. Med. Assoc.* 20 Nov. 1794/1)). So **rou·svirus.**

1911 *Jrnl. Exper. Med.* XIII. 389 We succeeded..in cultivating malignant tissues such as the Rous chicken sarcoma. **1925** W. E. GYE in *Lancet* 18 July 109/2 It has now been shown that Rous tumour No. 1 is caused by a virus which has been cultivated. **1931** *Brit. Jrnl. Exper. Path.* XII. 127 To decide whether the fragility of the Rous virus were due to its inability to resist oxidation, or whether a proteolysis were the inactivating cause. **1945** DURAN-REYNALS & SHRIGLEY in *Res. Conf. on Cancer* (Amer. Assoc. Adv. Sci.) 13/1 When the Rous tumor virus is inoculated into ducks two sets of lesions occur. **1945** H. S. N. GREENE in *Ibid.* 19/1 Dr Shrigley has succeeded in transplanting the Rous sarcoma in the anterior chambers of guinea pigs' eyes, and this is the first instance in which a virus-induced tumor has been proved to be a cancer. **1961** R. D. BAKER *Essent. Path.* xiii. 311 Carcinogenic viruses are known to produce the Rous sarcoma in chickens and the Shope papilloma of rabbits. **1961** *Lancet* 5 Aug. 301/1 The ability of cells infected with Rous-sarcoma virus to multiply has been demonstrated, but such chronically infected tumour cells cannot be considered to have recovered. **1972** *Sci. Amer.* Jan. 26/1 The rousviruses do not transfer information from RNA to RNA, as other RNA viruses do. **1977** *Nature* 15 Dec. 631 The genome of Rous sarcoma virus (RSV) is a 30–40S RNA of 10,000 nucleotides.

rousable (rau·zăb'l), *a.* [f. ROUSE *v.*[1] + -ABLE. Cf. *AROUSABLE *a.*] Capable or admitting of being roused.

1910 *Daily Chron.* 7 Mar. 8/1, I thought her endowed with a temper that might be very violent when roused, though not easily rousable. **1961** *Lancet* 5 Aug. 323/1 She was semicomatose but rousable.

rouse, *sb.*[2] Add: **3.** (Later examples.) Also *rouse-out.*

1881 C. A. STEPHENS *Knockabout Club in Woods* (1882) xi. 122 The result was a most unwelcome rouse-out shortly after ten o'clock. **1916** C. SANDBURG *Chicago Poems* 125 The silk and flare of it [*sc.* a red scarf] is a great soprano leading a chorus Carried along in a rouse of voices reaching for the heart of the world.

4. *attrib.*, as (sense 2) *rouse-parade.*

1937 D. JONES *In Parenthesis* I. 4 We've got too many buns—and all those wads—you knew they were going—why did you order them—they won't be in after rouse-parade even—they've gone.

rouse (raus), *v.*[4] *Austral.* and *N.Z. colloq.* Also **rous.** [Cf. ROUST *v.*[1]] *intr.* To scold. Freq. const. *at, on, onto*: to upbraid (someone). Hence **rou·sing** *vbl. sb.*[3]

c **1910** in G. A. WILKES *Dict. Austral. Colloquialisms* (1978) 279/2 *Rouse*, abuse or vilify. **1911** L. STONE *Jonah* v. 47 It's gittin' late; 'ow'll yer ole woman rous w'en yer git 'ome? *Ibid.* xi. 126 'E niver rouses on me. W'en 'e gits shirty, I just laugh, an' 'e can't keep it up. **1915** C. J. DENNIS *Songs of Sentimental Bloke* 88 If she 'ad only roused I might 'a' smiled. She jist seems 'urt an' crushed; not even riled. **1934** V. PALMER *Sea & Spinifex* 182 Combo's one of those sulky devils that forget nothing. .. Can't take a bit of rousing as part of the day's work. **1940** F. SARGESON *Man & his Wife* 27 Then Mrs Bowman roused on to me for putting too much sugar in her tea. **1951** D. CUSACK *Say No to Death* 30 Auntie used to rouse on me frightfully because I spent so much time on the beach. **1961** R. LAWLER *Piccadilly Bushman* 31 Don't rouse at me, Alec.

rouseabout. Add: **2. a.** (Earlier and later examples.) Also *N.Z.*

1861 [see *fleece-picker* s.v. *FLEECE *sb.* 6]. **1901** M. FRANKLIN *My Brilliant Career* xvii. 150 Joe Slocombe, the man who acted as groom and rouseabout, was waiting for me. **1909** 'S. RUDD' *From Selection to City* ix. 76 Numbers of shearers and rouseabouts had arrived on the scene before us, and the station was all astir. **1917** A. B. PATERSON *Saltbush Bill* 8 Come all you little rouseabouts and climb upon my knee. **1936** A. RUSSELL *Gone Nomad* iii. 19, I..was able to throw, skirt, and roll a fleece with the crack rouseabout of the shed. **1947** D. M. DAVIN *Gorse blooms Pale* 81 I'm not letting Joe get buggered about by any bloody fly-by-night rouseabout. **1961** *N.Z. Listener* 26 May 8/1 The rouseabout and presser had just finished clearing up. **1966** 'J. HACKSTON' *Father clears Out* 181 As a boy milker, manager, rouseabout, studmaster, and jackeroo on our place I became aware of the prevailing bad manners among some cows.

b. *transf.* An odd-job man or general worker; a casual labourer. *Austral.* and *N.Z.*

1906 E. DYSON *Fact'ry 'Ands* ii. 15 Billy the Boy, the juvenile rouseabout from the printer's flat. **1911** E. M. CLOWES *On Wallaby* iii. 64 It is to land so won and so held that every casual 'rouseabout' or street loafer feels that he has a perfect right. **1933** *Bulletin* (Sydney) 7 June 20/1 The rouseabout at Casey's pub was sacked. **1951** CUSACK & JAMES *Come in Spinner* 39 They'll probably stick you in as rouseabouts in a lunatic asylum, seeing the experience you've 'ad 'ere.

c. *attrib.*, as *rouseabout swiper, work.*

1887 J. FARRELL *How he Died* 19 It may be that the rouseabout swiper who rode for the doctor that night Is in Heaven with the Hosts of the Blest, robed and sceptred, and splendid with light. **1906** E. DYSON *Fact'ry 'Ands* xii. 148 A man was engaged to assist at the guillotines and do the rouseabout work of the factory. **1934** J. LILICO *Sheep Dog Mem.* 27 [The dogs] would head, lead, huntaway, force and back, though..they were best at rouseabout work.

rouseabout (rau·zăbaut), *v.* *Austral.* [f. ROUSEABOUT 2.] *intr.* To work as a rouseabout. Hence **rou·seabouting** *vbl. sb.*

1914 *Bulletin* (Sydney) 17 Dec. 44/2, I never done no shearin'; but I rouseabouted one year in a shed near Muttaburra. **1945** BAKER *Austral. Lang.* II. iii. 61 We., now speak of *jackerooing* (just as we speak of *rouseabouting*), for work as a station-hand. **1967** *Southerly* XXVII. 205 Writing, he said, came easier than..shearing, station rouseabouting.

rousedness (rau·zėdnės, -zd-). *rare.* [f. ROUSED *ppl. a.*[1] + -NESS.] The state of being aroused; a roused condition, alertness.

1915 D. H. LAWRENCE *Rainbow* iv. 94 And there was a kind of bristling rousedness in the room. *Ibid.* x. 261 Everywhere was a sense of mystery and rousedness.

rouser. Add: **1. b.** (Earlier example.)

1765 H. JACKSON *Ess. on Brit. Isinglass* 56 Previous to cleansing, conquassate the whole Aggregate with a Rouser.

2. a. (Earlier and later examples.)

1839 C. F. BRIGGS *Adventures H. Franco* I. xiv. 127 We never exchanged another word until we reached the fire, and then, says he to me, I tell you what, Smith, it is going to be a rouser. **1977** *Time* 24 Oct. 8/3 It cleared the way for a rouser of a speech by Thatcher.

4. (Earlier and later examples.)

1897 H. LAWSON *While Billy Boils* 85 They are all shearers, or at least they say they are. Some might be only 'rousers'. **1900** —— *Verses, Popular & Humorous* 168 The 'rouser' has no soul to save. Condemn the rouseabout! *a* **1964** E. HARRINGTON in *Penguin Bk. Austral. Ballads* (1964) 262 The rousers gave a billycan and brand new tucker bag.

rousie (rau·zi). *Austral.* and *N.Z. colloq.* Also **roussie, rousy.** [Abbrev. of ROUSEABOUT.] = ROUSEABOUT 2.

1933 *Bulletin* (Sydney) 29 Nov. 20/1 The rousie entered the office to be paid off. **1952** [see *DAGGER *sb.*[2] b]. **1956** F. B. VICKERS *First Place to Stranger* ix. 135 He tried to run all the rousies till Ivor stopped him. *a* **1964** H. P. TRITTON in *Penguin Bk. Austral. Ballads* (1964) 228 Then try to catch the rousy's eye, and softly whisper, 'Tar'. **1966** G. W. TURNER *Eng. Lang. Austral. & N.Z.* vii. 147 There are names for woolshed workers,..the *rousie* or rouseabout and the *sheepo* who fills the catching pens.

Rousseauan, *a.* Add: (Later examples). Also as *sb.* **Rousseauesque** *a.*[1] (examples), **Rousseauian, Rousseauish** *adjs.* (later examples); similarly **Rousseaui·stic, Rousseau·vian** *adjs.*; **Rousseauism** (later examples); **Rousseauist** (examples) (also as *adj.*), **Rousseauite** (later example); similarly **Rousseaua·rian.**

1775 H. WALPOLE *Let.* 3 Apr. (1904) IX. 174 The Rousseaurians [*sic*] will imagine that I interpolated the condemnation of his *Eloïse*. **1806** J. MACKINTOSH *Let.* 24 Dec. in R. J. Mackintosh *Mem. Life Sir J. Mackintosh* (1835) I. vi. 306 It is certainly a most ingenious, and the only reasonable, modification of the Lockian and Rousseauvian principle. **1889** *Cent. Dict.*, *Rousseauist*.., a follower or an admirer of J. J. Rousseau. **1905** H. G. WELLS *Mod. Utopia* v. 171 The sweetish, faintly nasty slops of Rousseauism. **1914** *Blast* 20 June 18 Blast.. Rousseauisms (wild Nature cranks). **1928** C. HOLLIS *Dr. Johnson* iii. 67 The Rousseauan argument was that man was good. *Ibid.* 68 Rousseauans had been responsible for the generalisation that man was good. **1930** H. READ *Wordsworth* iii. 131 They had taken a ward to educate.. but they did not take their duties any more seriously than a pair of Rousseauites should. **1935** D. FAHEY *Mystical Body of Christ in Mod. World* iv. 30 The Rousseauist dogma of the natural goodness of man. *a* **1937** J. L. STOCKS *Reason & Intuition* (1939) vi. 84 In modern times the Rousseauistic strain still survives. **1937** 'C. CAUDWELL' *Illusion & Reality* v. 98 Wordsworth, like

Shelley profoundly influenced by French Rousseauism. **1938** R. GRAVES *Coll. Poems* 96 And being no Rousseauist, Nor artists-of-the-world-unite. **1947** A. EINSTEIN *Mus. Romantic Era* xviii. 339 This Rousseauesque theory of the linguistic origin of music, basically wrong as it is, still reappears even in professional psychological literature of the 19th century. **1962** GREGOR & NICHOLAS *Moral & Story* v. 144 This somewhat Rousseauistic view of nature contrasts strangely with the determinist one, which Hardy runs alongside it. **1962** C. WALSH *From Utopia to Nightmare* ix. 126 Americans are Rousseauans by temperament. **1965** M. HODGART *Faber Bk. Ballads* 12 We are all Rousseauists or Wordsworthians to the degree that we are discontented with the artificiality of our culture. **1967** B. W. ALDERSON tr. *Hürlimann's Three Cent. Children's Bks. in Europe* ix. 120 The Romanticism and Rousseau-ish idealism in books about America and the Indians. **1969** J. MANDER *Static Society* 170 The 'good' Indian myth of Rousseauvian Europe. **1971** Rousseauian [see *neo-primitivism* s.v. *NEO- 1 a]. **1971** G. STEINER *Bluebeard's Castle* i. 24 What needs close attention is the extent to which critiques of urban society tend to become indictments of all formal, complex civilization as such ('civilization', of course, has in it the word for city). Rousseauist naturalism has an obvious destructive edge. **1974** *Listener* 21 Mar. 372/3 The editor of his [*sc.* Aaron Burr's] journal calls it 'Rousseauistic'... Couldn't one just call it unselfconscious? **1977** *Times Lit. Suppl.* 11 Feb. 148/2 The Machiavellian and Rousseauesque hints of subordination of church to state. **1977** in *Private Eye* 10 June 5/2 In the name of directness, of authenticity, of courage, of any number of Rousseauian virtues that belong exclusively to the noble savage. **1977** *Listener* 16 June 790/3 Throngs of Indonesians who.. appear to conform to the most elevated models of Rousseauvian *noblesse*. **1978** *Dædalus* Summer 2 The Rousseauan longing for a pastoral idyll is not yet dead.

Rousseauesque (rusōᵘ,e·sk), *a.*² [f. the name of Henri 'le Douanier' *Rousseau* (1844–1910), French primitive painter + -ESQUE.] Characteristic of the style of Rousseau.

1962 *Guardian* 9 July 5/3 She is also extremely successful in depicting Rousseau-esque foliage. **1978** A. HUXLEY *Illustr. Hist. Gardening* iii. 76 (*caption*) This Rousseauesque painting from the Jodphur [*sic*] school depicts a lush private garden.

Roussette. Add: **3.** A white wine produced primarily in the French departments of Savoy and Jura.

1926 P. M. SHAND *Bk. of Wine* v. 171 Frangy and Digny-Musièges belong to the more or less immediate neighbourhood of Seyssel, as does also a good, rusty-coloured wine called Roussette, named after the informing grape of the Savoy vineyards. **1946** G. MILLAR *Horned Pigeon* xx. 309 With the *fondue* we drank *Roussette*, an excellent local white wine which was then new to me. **1967** A. LICHINE *Encycl. Wines* 459/1 *Roussette*, the principal wine of Seyssel, in Haute-Savoie, France. It is white, flinty-dry, and made from Roussette grapes. **1968** *Vogue* 15 Apr. 121/1 To the South of the Jura lie the vineyards of the Savoy. Both red and white wines are grown, but it is the latter that are worth looking for, especially seyssel and..crépy and roussette.

roussie, var. *ROUSIE.

roust, *v.*² For '*dial.* and *U.S.*' read 'orig. *dial.* and *U.S.*' and add: **1. a.** (Further examples.) Also, to rouse or stir *up*, to raise or arouse (*from* one's bed, etc.).

1850 W. COLTON *Deck & Port* 299 We rousted our anchors this afternoon from the bed in which they have slumbered for the last six weeks. **1871** J. HAY *Little Breeches* 12 But we rousted up some torches, And sarched for 'em far and near. **1883** *Peterson Mag.* June 469/2 Awhile ago you was all rousted-up about goin' to New York village to see Mrs. Larne. **1905** J. C. LINCOLN *Partners of Tide* xi. 221 'Now, then,' he added, 'while we're waitin' for the tide to turn we might's well roust out a little more of the cargo.' **1939** J. STEINBECK *Grapes of Wrath* 123 Don't roust your faith bird-high an' you won't do no crawlin' with the worms. **1972** E. WIGGINTON *Foxfire Bk.* 169 You get up and roust up your fire. **1978** R. LUDLUM *Holcroft Covenant* xliii. 496 I've been rousted from my bed to take additional scrapings from the dead man's room.

b. *intr.* To get *up*, turn *out*; to rummage *around*.

1884 J. C. HARRIS *Mingo & Other Sk.* 162 It twon't never do in the roun' worl' for to be a-makin' faces at 'im frum the groun'. Roust up, roust up. **1900** C. C. MUNN *Uncle Terry* 172, I generally roust out by daylight. **1912** R. A. WASON *Friar Tuck* 67, I knew it was my duty to roust out an' keep Horace from gettin' more sleep'n my treatment for his nerves called for. **1941** J. STREET *In my Father's House* i. 19 Suppose you were a dominecker rooster—I mean hen... And you were in a coop and just outside the coop was a heap of grass that you wanted to roust around in. **1977** 'O. JACKS' *Autumn Heroes* v. 67 He made them go over the check lists with him... He rousted around.

2. To jostle (see quot. 1942); (esp. of police) to harass, rough up. Hence as *sb.*² *N.Amer.* (orig. *Criminals'*) *slang*.

1904 'No. 1500' *Life in Sing Sing* 252/1 *Roust*, to jostle. **1942** BERREY & VAN DEN BARK *Amer. Thes. Slang* §490/5 *Roust, rousting, rowdy-dowdy*, the act of causing a crush in a crowd or jostling the victim in order to pick his pockets. *Ibid.* §490/12 *Roust*,..to cause a crush in a crowd or jostle the victim in order to pick his pockets. **1961** RIGNEY & SMITH *Real Bohemia* p. xvi, *Roust, a*, a bust, an arrest, a raid. **1972** J. WAMBAUGH *Blue Knight* (1973) v. 68, I can't take this kind of heat. I can't take being rousted and hurt. **1976** N. THORNBURG *Cutter & Bone* viii. 193 He ran into Sergeant Verdugo, one of the detectives who had rousted him the night of the murder. **1978** R. THOMAS *Chinaman's Chance* xxiii. 234 'I'm..your friendly, conscientious chief of police.' Wu nodded slowly. 'And this is a roust, huh?' **1978** *Globe & Mail* (Toronto) 11 Jan. 8/1 Like one afternoon last spring,..when plain-clothes cops are rousting us when we're trying to do business. At the same time the bank at Church and Carleton gets robbed and the robber got away on foot.

roust (raust), *v.*³ *Austral. colloq.* [var. of *ROUSE *v.*⁴; cf. ROUST *v.*¹] *intr.* = *ROUSE *v.*⁴ Also with quasi-obj. in phr. *to roust hell out of*. Hence **rou·sting** *vbl. sb.*¹

1916 C. J. DENNIS *Songs of Sentimental Bloke* 124 *Roust* or *rouse*, to upbraid with many words. **1918** —— *Digger Smith* 82 All me roustin' leaves 'em both serene. **1938** X. HERBERT *Capricornia* xviii. 250 'All dem sister proper humbug.' 'How's that?' 'All time roustin'. All time tink we go out wid boys. We no can talk boys. But dem sister proper mad long boys demself.' **1941** S. CAMPION *Mo Burdekin* 139 And 'avin 'im roust hell outa me for it. **1970** P. WHITE *Vivisector* i. 11 He hung around Mumma, waiting for her to settle, and she didn't roust on him.

roustabout. 2. a. For *Austr.* read 'orig. *U.S.*' and add earlier and further examples. Also, a casual or unskilled labourer; a vagrant or layabout.

1877 *Harper's Weekly* 17 Mar. 3/3 The vagabonds, the roustabouts, the criminals, and all the dregs of society seem to be Democrats. **1880** A. A. HAYES *New Colorado* v. 77 He was a kind of rostabout [*sic*], or dish-washer, to a camping outfit. **1883** 'MARK TWAIN' *Life on Mississippi* li. 454 Do you mean the Roman army?—those six sandalled roustabouts in nightshirts? **1896** J. MCDOUGALL *Saddle, Sled & Snowshoe* xv. 187, I have been Mr. Woolsey's interpreter, guide, and general 'roust-about', his confidante and friend, for the past two years. **1911** H. S. HARRISON *Queed* 35 It takes a Whitney to invent the cotton gin, but the dullest negro roustabout can operate it. *a* **1918** G. STUART *40 Yrs. on Frontier* (1925) II. 179 Every man, whether owner of the largest herd or a humble roustabout, takes his orders from the captain. **1942** E. H. PAUL *Narrow St.* xix. 152 Butchers, roustabouts and helpers..toiled steadily in the lamplight. **1960** H. MILLER *Nexus* (1964) xiv. 237 I've got a good wife, only we're temperamentally unsuited to one another. I'm too common for her. Too much of a roustabout.

b. *spec.* A workman in a circus. *N. Amer.*

1931 *Amer. Mercury* Nov. 353/2 *Razorbacks*,.. Workmen who load and unload the circus train; never called *roustabouts* or *flunkeys*. **1949** *Los Angeles Times* 9 Apr. 2/3 Roustabouts from the Clyde Beatty circus appeared to offer any manual labor needed. **1957** *Harper's Bazaar* Feb. 175 He may earn his living as a petty criminal, a hobo, a carnival roustabout or a free-lance moving man in Greenwich Village. **1976** *Telegraph-Jrnl.* (St. John, New Brunswick) 4 Sept. 32/1 From a carnival *roustabout* to owner of the show in 25 years.

3. A general or manual labourer on an oil installation.

1948 H. L. MENCKEN *Amer. Lang.* Suppl. II. 763 *Roustabout*, a laborer on an oil lease, not a member of the rig crew. **1959** LARSON & PORTER *Hist. Humble Oil & Refining Co.* xii. 291 The next annual crop of new engineers was..put to work for a year as roughnecks or roustabouts. **1971** C. SIMPSON *New Australia* 518 The average young oilfield worker, called a 'roustabout', needed to have more than muscles. Technical competence was also called for. **1972** L. M. HARRIS *Introd. Deepwater Floating Drilling Operations* iv. 35 Drilling and roustabout crew requirements differ little from rig to rig. **1975** *Offshore Engineer* Dec. 54/1 (Advt.), The clothing was tested on the rig Sedco 700, operating close to the 62nd parallel, by supervisors and roustabouts on the nightshift.

roustabout (rau·stăbaut), *v.* [f. prec.] *intr.* To be, or work as, a roustabout.

1907 'O. HENRY' in *Everybody's Mag.* Nov. 593/1, I hurried the rest of the way up the river, roustabouting on a lower coast packet that made a landing for every fisherman that wanted a plug of tobacco. **1934** in *Amer. Ballads & Folk Songs* 494 When Jack is old and weather-beat, Too old to roustabout.

rouster. Add: **1.** (Further examples.)

1929 B. L. BURMAN *Mississippi* iii. 47 A rouster, with two coffee sacks tied around his body..lay on the boiler deck strumming a guitar. **1938** —— *Blow for Landing* xiv. 236 Barrels began to roll swiftly down the gang-plank, like a bass-drum accompaniment for the feet of the negro rousters. **1941** [see *COONJINE *sb.* and *v.*].

2. *U.S.* and *Austral.* = ROUSTABOUT 2 in Dict. and Suppl.

1890 in BARRÈRE & LELAND *Dict. Slang.* **1911** C. E. W. BEAN *'Dreadnought' of Darling* xxxviii. 338 There tumbled out of it all the sweepings of Sydney, all the old cripples, and beggars, and rousters in Christendom.

rousting (rau·stiŋ), *vbl. sb.*² *U.S. colloq.* [f. ROUST *v.*² + -ING¹.] (An act of) police harassment, a police raid (see also quot. 1942).

1942 BERREY & VAN DEN BARK *Amer. Thes. Slang* §490/5 *Rousting*,..the act of causing a crush in a crowd or jostling the victim in order to pick his pockets. **1960** *Washington Post* 25 Jan. 1 There's more vice on Pacific Heights and Nob Hill and there's no rousting (police raiding) up there. **1968** S. ELLIN *Valentine Estate* II. vi. 51 Rousting was the word for it. Keep pushing a man until he either left the territory or did something he could be nailed for. **1972** B. GARFIELD *Line of Succession* I. 75 The prisoners each morning complained to their lawyers of the nightly roustings. **1975** *High Times* Dec. 31/1 So far, however, the little hungo town has been spared the midnight roustings.

rousy, var. *ROUSIE.

rout, *sb.*¹⁰ (Later example.)

1912 C. MACKENZIE *Carnival* xxxiv. 358 'I'm going to have a rare old rout-out this morning,' Jenny announced.

rout, *v.*⁸ Add: **2. b.** (Further examples.) Also with *away*; *spec.* (also without const.) to cut a groove in (a wooden or metal surface), to machine or work with a router.

1818 *Trans. R. Soc. Arts* XXXV. 123 In the old way of routing the wood the grooves are torn and uneven at the bottom. **1934** *Woodworker* XXXVIII. 158/3 He first routs out his templet as suggested to the..shape he desires. **1946** C. H. HAYWARD *Light Machines for Woodwork* xii. 155 It is of special value for routing the ends of pieces..of odd shape. **1948** H. MISSINGHAM *Student's Guide Commerc. Art* II. 100 The line block is finished by first routing away all unwanted metal from the work. **1958** *New Scientist* 17 July 441/2 (*caption*) Routing an aircraft bulkhead from a solid billet of high-tensile aluminium alloy. **1960** 'N. SHUTE' *Trustee from Toolroom* vi. 131 You routed each plank all along its length to fit the next one?

3. a. (Earlier example.) Also to fetch (a person) out of a house, etc.

c **1776** H. NEWDIGATE *Let.* in A. E. Newdigate-Newdegate *Cheverels* (1898) i. 9 My Lord routed us out yᵉ moment we had breakfasted to pass sentence upon some trees that are to be fell'd.

b. (Earlier and later examples with *out*.) Also, to turn *out* (a room, etc.).

1814 JANE AUSTEN *Let.* Aug. (1952) 397 As soon as my Trunk & Basket could be routed out from all the other Trunks & Baskets in the World, we were on our way. **1929** J. MASEFIELD *Hawbucks* 101 He went home to his cellar and routed out a bottle of port. **1938** M. K. RAWLINGS *Yearling* iv. 31 He dashed in to his room and routed out his heavy cowhide brogans. **1950** R. MOORE *Candlemas Bay* III. 142 Ordinarily, he would have enjoyed routing out the fishhouse. **1973** A. CHRISTIE *Postern of Fate* I. v. 39, I shall go up and rout him out.

routing *vbl. sb.* (further examples, in sense 2 b of the vb.); also with *out*.

1935 *Times* 9 Nov. 4/4 Blind men..use, unaided, the circular saw and the routing machine (a speed of 15,000 revolutions a minute) to carve the animals. **1946** C. H. HAYWARD *Light Machines for Woodwork* xii. 147 For such work as the free-hand routing out of..the groundwork of a piece of carving it is essential that the wood is laid flat..and the machine passed over it. **1953** E. G. HAMILTON *Power Tools for Home Craftsman* vii. 231 Routing with a pattern is a fast and simple method of doing production work. **1958** *New Scientist* 17 July 441/1 The chief applications of the intricately shaped parts produced from solid metal by routing are in the aircraft industry. **1976** C. H. GRONEMAN *Gen. Woodworking* (ed. 5) xlvi. 224 (*caption*) Freehand routing of a penciled design.

route, *sb.* Add: The pronunc. (raut) is used by many speakers in the U.S. and Canada.

1. a. Also, used in various countries, esp. the U.S. and France, with a following numeral to designate a particular highway. Also *fig.*

1924 *N.Y. Times* 21 Dec. VIII. 9/7 Route 2 is the highway from Scranton Pa...to Montreal. **1933** KIPLING *Souvenirs of France* i. 18 That was the Rhone Road, Route 7. **1938** *Travel* June 37/1 From New York there are three delightful motor routes..all picking up Route 6. **1962** 'K. ORVIS' *Damned & Destroyed* v. 41 You haven't fooled me. You're on Route Zero. **1970** *Washington Post* 30 Sept. B4/1 Fredericksburg location is just off route 95.

c. *U.S.* An established stage by which post is conveyed prior to delivery.

1792 *Deb. Congress U.S.* 10 Jan. (1849) 58 The route by which the mails are at present conveyed shall in no case be altered. **1821** *Ibid.* 31 Dec. (1855) 47 Praying that the route of the mail from Savannah to Augusta..may not be altered. **1874** *Ann. Rep. Postmaster-General* (U.S. Post-Office Dept.) 209 Each railway post-office clerk..is required to attach to each package of letters he makes up a facing or label-slip bearing the address of the package, the office or route upon which it was made up.

d. *N.Amer.* A round travelled regularly by someone collecting, delivering, or selling goods, such as newspapers or milk.

1841 *Jamestown* (N.Y.) *Jrnl.* 5 May 2/4 He succeeded in obtaining possession of a route for a morning penny paper. **1849** C. MATHEWS *Moneypenny* xiii. 119 Go up-stairs, and tell Wages to give you the St. John's Park route. He'll fix your pay. **1868**, etc. [see *paper route* s.v *PAPER *sb.* 12]. **1874**, etc. [see *milk-route* s.v. *MILK *sb.* 10]. **1939** J. P. MARQUAND *Wickford Point* x. 108 Her father ran a milk route and drank hard cider. **1976** *Washington Post* 19 Apr. C14/4 (Advt.), Routes are available in the metropolitan Washington area to aggressive persons who are experienced Route Sales people.

e. Phr. *to go the route*, in *Baseball*, to pitch for an entire game; also *transf.* in *Boxing*; *fig.*, to go the full distance, to go all the way. *U.S.*

1913 *Chicago Record-Herald* 16 Mar. VIII. 1/5 This was the first complete battle Cicotte has pitched, and he was watched closely to see if he could go the route. **1926** J. BLACK *You can't Win* xvi. 230 If a Chinese doesn't like you he will keep away from you; if he does like you he will go the route. **1933** *Amer. Speech* Oct. 36/1 He went the route without being kayoed. **1948** *Chicago Tribune*

8 May II. 3/3 Bill Voiselle went the route for the Braves. 1963 I. Fleming *On H.M. Secret Service* iv. 45 She made love with the fervour and expertness of a girl who, in the American phrase, had 'gone the route'. 1974 *Index-Jrnl.* (Greenwood, S. Carolina) 18 Apr. 11/3 Steve Rogers went the route, giving up six hits.

3. a. (Earlier example.)

1751 Fielding *Amelia* I. I. ix. 68 This Letter was from his Captain, to acquaint him, that the Rout, as they call it, was arrived, and that they were to march within two Days.

c. (Earlier and later examples.)

1802 C. James *New Mil. Dict.*, s.v. *March*, His next care must be the arrangement of all its different component parts, with which he will form his column of route. 1976 *Broadcast* Dec. 17/2 There can be few occupations so completely degrading as marching in column-of-route.

4. (sense 1) *route book, card, check, marker, -mile, -mileage, number, planning, proficiency*; *route-proving* adj.; (sense 3) *route column, march* (hence as *vb. intr.*), *-marching* (earlier example); **route-goer** *Baseball*, one who goes the route (see sense 1 e above); hence **route-going** *a.*; **routeman, route man** *N.Amer.* = Roundsman 3; also, a salesman who works a particular route (see sense 1 d above); hence **routemanship; route salesman** *N.Amer.*, a salesman who works a particular route (cf. **routeman*); so **route sales, route salespeople; route sheet** *N.Amer.*, an engagement itinerary for a touring company or artist.

1910 (*title*) Route book for the British Isles. 1975 *Oxf. Compan. Sports & Games* 702/2 The correct route, which the organizers convey to the crew in route-books. 1931 *Amer. Speech* VI. 335 *Route-card*,..a table or schedule issued to show people giving the 'stands' for about ten days in advance. 1963 P. Drackett *Motor Rallying* iii. 39 British rallies require only the accurate plotting of six-figure map references plus the ability to..read from a simple route-card. *Ibid.* 37 Route checks, or passage controls, are also a feature of the majority of rallies. 1954 W. Faulkner *Fable* 6 It was a whole battalion.. emerging from the *Place de Ville* in close route column. 1967 *Boston Sunday Herald* 26 Mar. II. 3/1 The Philadelphia 76ers had five route-goers..while Hal Greer missed only one game. 1976 *Billings* (Montana) *Gaz.* 17 June 2–H/4 Doug DeCinces and Lee May each hit three-run homers to support 39-year old Mike Cuellar's first route-going performance of the season. 1918 *Nat. Laundry Jrnl.* 1 May 56/1 It really matters little whether he be known as a route man, salesman, or representative. ..Good route men are scarce. 1943 *Daily Progress* (Charlottesville, Va.) 29 May 8 (Advt.), In the face of a 40% reduction in gasoline mileage your routeman will call on you three times each week as in the past. 1976 *Billings* (Montana) *Gaz.* 2 July 9–C/1 (Advt.), Excellent opportunity for a Route Man to take over present route & expand. 1945 *U.S. Armed Forces Educ. Man.* EM 991. xiii. 136 This chapter explains the elements of routemanship. 1895 W. S. Churchill *Let.* 27 Feb. in R. S. Churchill *Winston S. Churchill* (1967) I. Compan. I. viii. 559, I went out with the regiment on Friday to a route march—which was very fine. 1909 *Blackw. Mag.* Sept. 396/1 They have all been called out to some absurd inspection, or route march, or manœuvres, or something. 1934 Webster, Route-march, v.i. 1939 *Airman's Gaz.* Dec., You route march into the local swedeville. 1977 D. Bagley *Enemy* xxix. 231 Benson had a cushy billet for a soldier in wartime. Not for him route marches in the pouring rain. 1789 *Rules & Regulations Field Exercises & Movements Army in Ireland* I. 54 In Common Route marching the same regularity of step cannot be required, as is necessary in the operation of manœuvre. 1925 *N.Y. Times* 5 Aug. 8/3 The shield of the United States was adopted today as a model for the outline of route markers for the system of national highways. 1968 M. Woodhouse *Rock Baby* xv. 148 Plenty of people cross various borders..when they can't see the route-markers. 1911 *Encycl. Brit.* XXII. 824/2 In Europe the average route-mile capital is £27,036. 1962 *Observer* 25 Mar. 1/5 Route-mileage is the length of routes, as distinct from the length of individual sets of tracks. British Railways cover about 18,500 route-miles. 1967 *Listener* 26 Jan. 123/1 A maximum of 100 m.p.h. is now possible over about 360 route-miles of British Rail. 1924 *N.Y. Times* 21 Dec. VIII. 9/7 The route number is painted in figures five inches high. 1973 D. Westheimer *Going Public* iv. 64 He memorized the route numbers of the buses. 1967 *Jane's Surface Skimmer Syst.* 1967–68 51/1 The Central Electricity Generating Board..is constantly faced with route-planning problems. 1959 Wallis & Blair *Thunder Above* iii. 15 His first trip as captain would be a route-proficiency check. 1957 *Times* 21 Dec. 5/3 The flight..completed their route-proving programme before the beginning of commercial operations. 1937 DeArmond & Graf *Route Sales Managem.* 4 Another factor in route sales distribution, the accurate anticipation of customer demand. 1937 *Job Descriptions of Laundry Industry* 253 Route-Man, Route Driver, Route-Salesman... Drives a Delivery Truck over an established route to collect washing from and deliver it to customers' houses. 1968 *Globe & Mail* (Toronto) 13 Feb. 33/7 (Advt.), Route Salesman..required by supplier of industrial garments. 1976 *Washington Post* 19 Apr. C14/4 (Advt.), *Route Sales.* Routes are available..to aggressive persons who are experienced Route Sales people. 1916 *Variety* 27 Oct. 12/2 Sam Sidman's Own Show is on the Columbia route sheet to play there. 1941 W. C. Handy *Father of Blues* xiv. 195 Each one..had been copying other pluggers' borrowed route-sheets and submitting them to me as evidence of work done by themselves.

5. (Later examples.) Also *en-route*, (N.Amer.) *enroute*.

1955 *Times* 10 May 10/3 In the course of his journey to Leeds the Prime Minister made several speeches *en route.* 1956 R. Braddon *Nancy Wake* ix. 93 He would attempt to escape somewhere en route to Gerona. 1967 *Boston Sunday Herald* 26 Mar. VI. 4/1 (Advt.), Enroute to Miami with overnight stays in Wash., D.C., [etc.]. 1976 *National Observer* (U.S.) 7 Feb. 11/3 You can take advantage of Sitmar's 'Cruise Plus' feature which allows stopovers enroute home. 1978 *Nature* 5 Oct. 363/2 US spacecraft are now en-route to Venus, Jupiter, Saturn and Uranus.

route, *v.* (in Dict. s.v. Route *sb.*). Delete '(Chiefly in railway use.)' and add further examples.

For the pronunc., see the sb. in Dict. and Suppl.

The pres. pple. is spelt *routeing* (the better form: cf. note s.v. *routing *vbl. sb.*) or *routing*.

1893 M. H. Cushing *Story of our Post Office* 235 Here are the carriers themselves, engaged in 'routing' the mail. 1926 J. Black *You can't Win* ix. 113 The papers were carefully read at night, and the next morning 'routed' through the prison. 1926 *N.Y. Times Mag.* 15 Aug. 6 Complaints were routed past the complaint department to the President's office. 1952 *Oxf. Mag.* 24 Jan. 142 An attempt is made to govern, by routing it through the Proctors, the growing spate of information. 1959 *Daily Tel.* 17 Mar. 13/2 A minute later he routed the Liverpool Street–Norwich train through. 1960 *Washington Post* 16 Nov. A16 West Germany's share of a greater European effort in NATO would have to be routed through NATO organs. 1961 L. Mumford *City in Hist.* (1966) xvi. 567 Major through-traffic streams must be routed around residential areas. 1971 P. Gresswell *Environment* 105 Others [*sc.* footpaths] might be better routed round field edges than through the middle of fields. 1971 D. Potter *Brit. Eliz. Stamps* xiii. 142 Very large postings in bulk attract substantial discounts. They are routed by second-class mail. 1977 *Daily Tel.* 20 Jan. 17/4 The organising committee intends to prevent a repetition by routeing the procession through wide streets.

b. To schedule or bill.

1916 *Variety* 22 Oct. 12/2 Rud Hynicka's show..will not play the Star and Garter next week as routed. 1932 L. C. Douglas *Forgive us our Trespasses* (1937) xiii. 253 Deducing from time-tables, Dinney hypothetically routed Joan to arrive at six-thirty on Thursday evening.

c. To direct (an electrical signal or transmission of any kind, as a telephone call) over a particular circuit or path, or *to* a particular location.

1948 J. Atkinson *Telephony* I. xii. 234/2 The group centre extends the call to the zone centre where it is routed to the distant zone centre exchange. 1956 *B.B.C. Handbk. 1957* 50 The sound components of the various contributions are routed and switched simultaneously with the vision. 1962 *Listener* 3 May 770/2 If one operator on the lunar surface wished to communicate with another operator a dozen miles away, his only method would be to route his signal by way of the Earth. 1964 F. L. Westwater *Electronic Computers* i. 6 By means of electronic switching devices a word is routed to the correct address in the store. 1973 *Daily Tel.* 22 Jan. 2/1 The dialling code for Rome is 010 39 6. The digits 010 route the call to the international automatic exchange in London, 39 routes to Italy, and the final 6 is the code number for Rome. 1973 *Physics Bull.* Feb. 109/1 The reference channel plug-in..accepts a reference signal derived from a chopper, which enables the plug-in to control and route the signal pulses to two counting channels.

‖ **route nationale** (rūt nasyonal). Pl. **routes nationales.** [Fr., = national highway.] In France, a main or trunk road constructed and maintained by the central government.

1896 A. P. Rockwell *Roads & Pavements in France* 26 The 22,000 miles of *Routes Nationales* are periodically examined with great care in order to ascertain the actual thickness of the stone layer. 1906 C. Neville *Round France in Motor* vi. 39 The next morning we ought to have continued along the Route Nationale, which goes to Macon *via* Châlon. 1924 Kipling in *N.Y. World* 23 Apr. 15/2 Route Nationale No. 20 conducts from Paris to the Spanish frontier at Bourg-Madame. 1949 M. Laski *Little Boy Lost* iii. 49 This isn't Paris—it's some shabby village away from all the *routes nationales.* 1973 G. Sims *Hunters Point* xix. 177 The frontier town of Menton.. where the French Route Nationale meets the Italian Via Aurelia.

router, *sb.*[5] **1.** Substitute for def.: A cutter that removes wood from a groove or recess, as in a router plane. (Earlier example.)

Quot. 1875 in Dict. belongs to next sense.

1818 *Trans R. Soc. Arts* XXXV. 123 With my plane, as fast as the cutters pierce the wood, the router follows after, and clears the wood out of the groove.

b. A router plane.

1846 C. Holtzapffel *Turning & Mech. Manipulation* II. 979 Mr. Wm. Lund has constructed the router..with a screw adjustment to the cutter. 1923 R. Greenhalgh *Pract. Joinery & Carpentry* xix. 245 A number of grooves are first run round the wreath [of a handrail] in suitable places, a useful tool for this purpose being the router. 1954 W. E. Kelsey *Carpentry, Joinery & Woodcutting Machinery* i. 14 Router or old woman's tooth... This is a tool for cleaning out and levelling the bottoms of trenches. 1974 G. Blackburn *Illustr. Encycl. Woodworking Handtools* 169 The Pattern Maker's Router is similar to the Router Plane, but with a machined, larger sole.

c. (See quot. *a* 1877.)

a 1877 Knight *Dict. Mech.* I. 288/2 The center-bit consists of three parts: a center point or pin..; a thin cutting point or nicker that..circumscribes the hole; and a broad chisel-edge or router, placed obliquely, and tearing up the wood within the circle marked out by the point. 1947 H. E. King *School Cert. Woodwork* vi. 63 Boring Bits... The router and nicker are sharpened on the inside only. 1955 M. M. Waters *Woodwork* 107 The nicker extends lower than the router and so engages the wood slightly ahead of it.

d. A woodworking machine similar to a spindle moulder but using a much higher speed of rotation and able to produce finished work; also, a portable hand-held version of this.

1946 W. B. McKay *Joinery* i. 24 Another form of vertical boring machine is known as a router or recessing machine or overhead spindle moulder. 1954 W. E. Kelsey *Carpentry, Joinery & Woodcutting Machinery* xvii. 517 The router has taken over a great deal of the lighter work up to 1 in. or $1\frac{1}{4}$ in. thick which was formerly done on the spindle-moulder. *Ibid.* 546 Portable electric router... This machine works on the same principle as the overhead-router. 1958 *Wall St. Jrnl.* 30 Sept. 7/4 An official..enthuses over a new power wood-working tool called a 'router'. 1976 *Arizona Republic* (Phoenix) 9 May K2/6 Harman uses a router (similar to an electric drill..) to make a hole in the center of the slice for the hand shaft to go through. 1976 *S. Wales Echo* 23 Nov. 11/5 (Advt.), One overhead router £200. Various other items for woodworking shop.

3. *attrib.*, as **router bit, cutter** = sense 1 c above; **router plane,** a plane with a cutter projecting below the sole so that the bottom of a groove or recess can be planed.

1953 E. G. Hamilton *Power Tools for Home Craftsman* vii. 230 Small router bits are usually of the single-flute type. 1976 C. H. Groneman *Gen. Woodworking* (ed. 5) xlvi. 220 Most routers use $\frac{1}{4}$- or $\frac{3}{8}$-in.-shank (6·35- or 9·52-mm-shank) router bits. *a* 1877 Knight *Dict. Mech.* III. 1995/2 *Routing-machine*, a shaping-machine which works by means of a router-cutter..revolving above a bed with universal horizontal adjustment. 1846 Router plane [in Dict., sense 1]. 1934 *Planecraft* (C. & J. Hampton Ltd.) xiv. 105 The Record Router Plane..is made both with an open and with a closed mouth. 1966 A. T. Collins *Newnes Compl. Pract. Woodworking* 30 Router planes are used for levelling and smoothing the surface on the bottom of a groove, slot or cavity which is inaccessible to an ordinary grooving plane. 1974 [see sense 1 b above].

routier[1]. (Later *Hist.* examples.)

1962 J. Needham *Sci. & Civilisation in China* IV. I. 285 Huang Shêng-Tsêng named as one of his sources a *Chen Wei Pien* (Collection of Needle Positions), which may or may not have been a specific printed book. If it was, it must have been a 'routier' or 'rutter' like the *Yüeh Yang Chen Lu Chi* (Record of Courses Set by the Needle in the Cantonese Seas), which is known to have still existed in the 18th century. 1971 S. E. Morison *European Discovery Amer.: Northern Voy.* xiv. 465 Alfonce attributes the discovery of this river to the Portuguese, and the rhymed *routier* of 1547 by Jean Mallart agrees.

‖ **routier**[2] (rutye). [Fr., f. *route* Route *sb.*]

1. *Hist.* A member of any of numerous companies of mercenary soldiers that were active in France during the later Middle Ages.

1845 *Encycl. Metrop.* XI. 620 They [*sc.* the mercenary adventurers] were named also..*Routiers*, for numerous reasons too unsatisfactory to deserve quotation. 1910 *Encycl. Brit.* II. 683/1 Arthur now resumed the war against the English, and at the same time took vigorous measures against the plundering bands of soldiers and peasants known as *routiers* or *écorcheurs.* 1924 K. Norgate *Richard the Lion Heart* ii. 53 If these Routiers could have been controlled by their employers, Henry and Richard might probably have been easily surrounded and captured. 1951 W. B. Wells tr. *Perroy's Hundred Years War* IV. i. 149 When he entered the king's service, ..Duguesclin was no more than a captain of *routiers*, fond of pillage and raids. 1961 P. Green tr. *Oldenbourg's Massacre at Montsegur* iv. 105 The *routiers*, or mercenary companies, who formed a large part of the infantry. 1965 Auden *About House* (1966) 17 Conventional Blunderbuss war and its routiers. 1970 M. Jones *Ducal Brittany* vi. 167 The payments made by John IV to the *routier* companies in 1368–9 were..rather of protection money.

2. In France, a long-distance lorry driver. Also *attrib.*

In the *attrib.* examples the reference is usually to the *Guide des Relais Routiers*, a guide-book originally designed for lorry-drivers in France.

1961 L. Durrell in *Holiday* Feb. 114 We planned to stop somewhere on the road to Béziers and have a bite of supper—Raoul knew a little place patronized by the *routiers.* 1971 *Guardian* 18 Aug. 10/5 One hotel (Routiers) stop in each direction including dinner and breakfast.. [£]9.00. 1975 *Ibid.* 27 Jan. 7/5 Setting out with your Green Card and your Routier Guide to storm the Alpine passes. 1976 *Times* 14 Feb. 13/4 A cheap and cheerful *routier* halt where..the *café au lait* came in something more like a *pot de chambre* than a cup.

routinary, *a.* Delete *rare* and add later examples. Also, in wider senses: that acts according to routine; occurring, performed, etc., routinely.

1963 V. Nabokov *Gift* ii. 105 Some sort of routinary hallucination, like a harmless domestic ghost that sits down..every evening by the fireside. 1967 D. Flakoll tr. *Asturias's Cyclone* iii. 33 'The second ball is routine... Perhaps you can tell us where..routine commences.' 'It ends the instant the ball leaves your hand. You are no longer a rutinary [*sic*] bowler. The adventure begins.' 1976 *Word* 1971 XXVII. 61 The exceptionality, for today, of prenatal assessment of foetal neurophysiology will be the routinary procedure of the future.

routine, *sb.* (*a.*) Add: **1. c.** *Theatr.* A carefully rehearsed act or sequence of actions (in dancing, singing, dialogue, etc.); a sketch, turn, or 'number'; the manner in which an act is performed. Similarly in *Gymnastics*, a performance comprising a sequence of exercises carried out either on the floor or on apparatus, usu. in competition. Also *transf.* and *fig.*

1926 *Dance Mag.* June 25/3 No one ever taught him a routine. When he hummed a tune, dance steps just came to him. **1930** *Dancing Times* July 354/2 If a student goes through the same routine of steps (I am not talking of exercises, but of combined steps constituting a dance) [etc.]. **1932** N. Coward *Words & Music* I. 9 Don't do a pratfall in your first routine. **1949** N. Marsh *Swing, Brother, Swing* xii. 280 He wasn't meant to fall. They'd altered the routine. **1956** H. Kurnitz *Invasion of Privacy* xiv. 92 Do you know the blackmail routine that Jarrold gave me tonight? **1959** Loken & Willoughby *Compl. Bk. Gymnastics* xvii. 196/1 For example, a fast, snappy mass tumbling act would be good following a slow, precise doubles balancing routine. **1963** 'E. McBain' *Ten plus One* vi. 78 What the hell is this?.. A vaudeville routine at the Palace? **1975** *Oxf. Compan. Sports & Games* 452/1 In C-difficulty routines he may perform movements such as going from a handstand between the bars and then resting again in another handstand. **1977** *Time* 22 Aug. 43/1 A teacher in Peoria had encouraged him to become a performer, and when he returned from Germany he started a routine there at a little club.

d. *Computers.* A set of instructions which performs a specific task and is stored so that it may be executed many times; now esp. one which may be part of a longer, self-contained program.

1945 J. P. Eckert et al. *Description of ENIAC* (PB 86242) (Moore School of Electr. Engin., Univ. Pennsylvania) B-3 Suppose it is desired to..carry out a computational routine of m line steps, print the final results, and then perform the same routine n times. **1948** Goldstine & von Neumann in J. von Neumann *Coll. Wks.* (1963) V. 217 We call the coded sequence of a problem a routine, and one which is formed for the purpose of possible substitution into other routines a subroutine. **1948** *Proc. IRE* XXXVI. 1453/1 The iterative methods of numerical analysis involve the repeated performance of computing routines. **1951** M. V. Wilkes et al. *Preparation of Programs for Electronic Digital Computer* iii. 22 A 'closed' subroutine is one which is called into use by a special group of orders incorporated in the master routine or main program. **1967** *Technology Week* 23 Jan. 11/2 (Advt.), Software for Sigma 5 includes..a library of mathematical, business and utility routines. **1971** Dudrap & Emery in R. A. Wisbey *Computer in Lit. & Linguistic Res.* III. 90 It is often better to provide a few assembly-code routines than to try doing character editing in 'raw' FORTRAN. **1980** K. D. Wise *Microcomputers* v. 102 Transfers of data or control between routines should occur only when the programmer specifically requests them and only as called for in the specification of the routines.

3. a. (Later examples.) Now passing into *adj.* Also, in wider senses: of a customary or standard kind; usual, typical, standard.

1940 H. Spencer *Art & Life W. Shakespeare* v. 197 No routine braggart-soldier he. **1960** 'E. McBain' *Give Boys Great Big Hand* vi. 59 'Maybe you can find some of Karl's skull on it. Isn't that what you'd like to find?' 'This is just a routine investigation, Mrs. Androvich.' **1961** W. Sargeant in Webster s.v. *routine* adj., The level of artistry..was altogether routine and uninspired. **1964** L. Deighton *Funeral in Berlin* xxvii. 146, I shouldn't worry about it. It's just a routine check. **1979** *Sci. Amer.* Dec. 112 Recently it has become routine in many laboratories and hospitals to record evoked potentials from the brain stem.

b. *Comb.*, as *routine-chained, -ridden, -sodden* adjs.

1920 *Chambers's Jrnl.* 19 June 453/2 Routine-chained staffs worked on into the night. **1929** A. Huxley *Holy Face* 64 Our routine-ridden, mechanized world of flabbily sub-human sentimentalists. **1964** M. McLuhan *Understanding Media* x. 103 The need for advanced knowledge presses on the spirits of the most routine-ridden minds. **1920** *Contemp. Rev.* June 866 The Soviet authority had to destroy everything in this department—the laws themselves, the routine-sodden institutions.

routine (ru*tī*·n), *v.* [f. prec.] *trans.* To apply a routine to; to organize according to a routine. Hence **routi·ning** *vbl. sb.*

1897 G. B. Shaw in *Sat. Rev.* 18 Dec. 712/1 No actor can possibly play leading parts of the first order six nights a week all the year round unless he underplays them, or routines them mechanically in the old stock manner. **1941** W. C. Handy *Father of Blues* iv. 39, I was consulted by Whalen and Martelle relative to routining their shows. **1948** 'La Meri' *Spanish Dancing* iv. 43 There are a variety of typical steps which can be routined at the will of the dancer. **1959** R. Condon *Manchurian Candidate* ii. 31 Yen Lo got three implantation teams started on them, staying with each team through the originating processes until he had assured himself that all had been routined with smoothness. **1976** W. Goldman *Magic* II. 65 He spent the intervening days working out his routining. Start with the flashy stuff or save those for the end?

routined (ru*tī*·nd), *ppl. a.* [f. Routine *v.* + -ed[1].] Subjected to or regulated by (a) routine.

1913 E. F. Benson *Thorley Weir* i. 22 The gleaming romance and glory that lie so close below the surface of the most routined and rutted life. **1928** *Manch. Guardian Weekly* 23 Nov. 407/2 Criticism will do well not to base on this routined output a judgment which leaves out of account the Schubert of the year of his death. **1948** 'J. Tey' *Franchise Affair* xiii. 138 One result of stepping out of a routined life was..that you couldn't..stroll home at four o'clock of an afternoon. **1964** F. Bowers *Bibliogr. & Textual Crit.* vi. iii. 180 An inexperienced.. compositor might be supposed to feel the influence of copy more strongly than a thoroughly routined workman.

routineer. (Later examples.)

1928 G. B. Shaw *Intelligent Woman's Guide Socialism* lxx. 340 The civil servant, the judge, the navy captain, the field marshal, the archbishop, however extraordinary able, gets no more than any routineer of his rank and seniority. **1956** 'H. MacDiarmid' *Stony Limits & Scots Unbound* 129 The routineer Haig, Whose lack of imagination carried him through. **1977** *National Observer* (U.S.) 22 Jan. 6/1 The innovator, in both business and the arts, is always to be contrasted..with the routineer.

routinely (ru*tī*·nli), *adv.* orig. *U.S.* [f. *routine *sb.* (*a.*) 3 a + -ly[2].] As a matter of course or of routine; according to (a) routine; by rote, mechanically.

1924 *Scribner's Mag.* Aug. 216/1 Even now I think we take policemen, professors, conductors, etc., much too routinely. **1948** A. Cooke in *Manch. Guardian Weekly* 29 Apr. 13/2 It has been routinely filed away and incorporated in the body of American dogma. **1956** *Nature* 25 Feb. 383/1 The inhibition of the enzyme by the osmium tetroxide fixative routinely used for electron microscopical preparations. **1965** *Economist* 10 July 137/3 Such infractions are routinely settled with a small bribe for the policeman. **1968** J. D. Watson *Double Helix* xviii. 129 He was only routinely enthusiastic as he went over Griffith's quantum-mechanical arguments. **1971** D. Lambert in C. Bonington *Annapurna South Face* 289 Appendicectomy is done routinely on members of expeditions to the Antarctic. **1974** J. Heller *Something Happened* 101 'What did you do today?' I ask routinely (before she can ask me).

routiner (ru*tī*·nəɹ). [f. Routin(e + -er[1].] † **1.** (see Routineer.) *Obs. rare*—[1].

2. *Teleph.* A set of equipment for testing circuits and switching apparatus in an exchange.

1929 *P.O. Electr. Engineers Jrnl.* XXII. 24 Routiners are composed of two main parts: the test and control apparatus, and the access equipment. **1948** J. Atkinson *Telephony* I. xxi. 453/1 Specially designed test boxes or routiners..are arranged to apply test conditions somewhat more onerous than the conditions normally encountered in practice. **1973** *P.O. Electr. Engineers Jrnl.* LXVI. 44/2 Trunk circuit routiners..are used to verify that a call can be established to a distant answering relay-set over each outgoing trunk circuit in turn and that the transmission loss..is within maintenance tolerance.

routing, *vbl. sb.* (in Dict. s.v. Route *sb.*). Add: Also **routeing.** Also, the action of the vb.: direction along, or allocation to, particular routes. (Further examples.)

Routeing is the better form to distinguish it from Routing *vbl. sb.* and *ppl. a.* (pronounced rau·tiŋ).

1903 *Electr. World & Engineer* 23 May 856/1 The facility which such combination lends to through routing of cars. **1930** M. Clark *Home Trade* xxiv. 198 All waste of time in the passage of any piece of work through the factory, scientific management methods endeavour to eliminate by 'routeing'. **1947** A. Harris *Bomber Offensive* 188 Against this we devised a new kind of routeing. **1964** F. L. Westwater *Electronic Computers* iii. 28 The routing and control of a sequence of pulses throughout a computer depends on an appropriate assembly of switching circuits. **1975** *Daily Tel.* 12 Feb. 14 Postal addresses are in effect routing directions. **1976** P. R. White *Planning for Public Transport* vii. 139 The weakness is that journey times between major towns are often far too long, especially in relation to potential direct routeings.

‖ **routinier** (ru*ti*nye), *a.* and *sb.* *Mus.* [Fr.: cf. Routineer.] **A.** *adj.* Of a piece of music: composed in a routine or orthodox manner. *rare.* **B.** *sb.* A conductor who performs in a mechanically correct, but uninspiring, way.

1934 C. Lambert *Music Ho!* v. 279 Walton's..mature but regrettably consonant *Belshazzar's Feast* was dismissed, particularly by the older critics, as 'routinier', conventional, and unworthy of its place in so selectly revolutionary a festival. **1970** *Guardian* 1 Jan. 8/2 Everything was first-rate with the exception of Boris himself..and the conductor Boris Khaikin, a tired routinier. **1970** *New Yorker* 26 Sept. 114/3 A new conductor..didn't seem to arouse much tension. He proved to be what is usually described as a useful *routinier*.

routinization (ru*tī*:nəizē·ʃən). [f. *routinize *v.* + -ation.] The being or becoming routine in character or operation; the action of superimposing a routine upon that which was previously less systematized or controlled.

1934 in Webster. **1946** Gerth & Mills *From Max Weber* (1947) iii. 54 By tracing out the routinization of charisma, Weber is able to assign a heavy causal weight to institutional routines. **1954** *Encounter* June 12/1 Coal mining..now—with the mechanisation of cutting and conveying—takes on much of the routinisation of factory work. **1960** *Guardian* 29 Apr. 11/1 Beatnik Tanya.. excoriates the routinisation of sex in marriage. **1965** H. Kahn *On Escalation* xiii. 258 It is a major purpose of current command-and-control efforts to facilitate the 'routinization'..of the various aspects of crisis management. **1972** A. Giddens *Politics & Sociol. in Thought of Max Weber* iii. 39 The 'routinisation' of politics—that is to say, the transformation of political decisions into decisions of administrative routine..—is specifically foreign to the demands which are most basic to political action. **1976** *National Observer* (U.S.) 26 June 17/3 We are all equally liable to the lumpish routinization of compassion both maddening and necessary.

routinize (ru*tī*·nəiz), *v.* [f. Routine + -ize.] *trans.* To subject to (a) routine; to make into a (matter of) routine.

1928 *Amer. Speech* III. 434 An investigator of nurses' training asks whether nurses are to become 'machinized and routinized'. **1937** J. Dollard *Caste & Class in Southern Town* xv. 344 All such behavior patterns have emotional value, even when they seem most routinized. **1960** W. H. Whyte *Organization Man* xxvi. 364 They know how to routinize crisis. **1965** *Listener* 24 June 925/2 Ours is a time in which man..has been mechanized and routinized. **1973** J. S. Bruner *Beyond Information Given* (1974) xvii. 300 When..the child has routinized the task of holding two objects, one in each hand, there then occurs a first storage activity. **1978** *Dædalus* Summer 70 Duty emerges..as an attempt to codify, systematize, and routinize behavior which springs from desire.

routi·nized, *ppl. a.* [f. prec.] Subject to (a) routine; made into a (matter of) routine.

1938 *Sun* (Baltimore) 21 July 18/1 There was nothing to indicate an approaching disaster in the routinized handling of the dynamite before the blast. **1945** G. Williams *Women & Work* ii. 41 Women..were mostly confined to the lower-grade, more routinised categories. **1949** M. Mead *Male & Female* xiii. 269 The baby would not eat, having very doubtfully enjoyed the routinized, cloth-enveloped experience. **1952** B. Ulanov *Hist. Jazz in Amer.* xiii. 151 The fairly tight, routinized Nichols sessions set the style. **1978** *Jrnl. R. Soc. Arts* CXXVI. 412/2 Administration is the conduct of affairs in a routinized fashion. **1981** *Times Lit. Suppl.* 27 Feb. 216/1 The twentieth century may be the century of..routinized labour.

roux. (Earlier and later examples.)

1813 L. E. Ude *French Cook* vi. 140 Cut your chops.., then fry them in a little butter, of a nice brown colour, drain this butter, and make a *roux* very *blond*. *Ibid.* xiii. 297 Put a lump of butter into a stew-pan... Then make a *roux* by mixing a little flour. When your *roux* begins to get brown, put in two large onions cut [etc.]. *Ibid.* xiv. 361 After having stewed your oysters.., you make a *roux blanc* into which you put a few small onions, [etc.]. **1845** E. Acton *Mod. Cookery* (ed. 2) iv. 97 Sauce tourneé is..rich pale gravy..thickened with delicate white roux. **1861** Mrs. Beeton *Bk. Househ. Managem.* 251 *White roux*, for thickening White Sauces... Allow the same proportions of butter and flour..and proceed in the same manner as for brown roux. **1945** *ABC of Cookery* (Ministry of Food) xiii. 51 This mixture of fat and flour is called a roux. **1965** *House & Garden* Dec. 84/4 Cook for a further few minutes to dispel the raw flour taste, then stop, if you want the *roux* white, carry on a little longer for the blonde, and longer still for a brown. **1976** *National Observer* (U.S.) 6 Nov., The roux should be brown but not burned. Do not burn or you will ruin the gravy.

rov, var. *rav.

rover[1]. Add: **3. a.** Also *spec.* (see quot. 1944).

1933 H. G. Wells *Bulpington of Blup* v. 177 They were to go as 'Rovers' to the Russian Ballet. **1944** G. B. Shaw *Everybody's Political What's What?* xxxi. 279 Complaisant critics were welcomed in the theatre even when all the stalls were sold out and they had to be content as 'rovers' without allotted seats, sitting or standing about wherever they could.

c. *Australian Rules Football* (see quot. 1969[1]). *Rugby Football*, formerly, an extra forward performing some of the functions of the scrum half and fly half. *Amer. Football*, a defensive linebacker who is assigned to move about to anticipate opponents' plays.

1894 A. Sutherland in M. Shearman *Athletics & Football* (ed. 4) II. vii. 422 The rover is an individual chosen for his quickness and readiness to go wherever he is wanted. He observes the turn of the game, and follows when he sees his own followers being overweighted by their adversaries [in Australian Rules Football]. **1909** E. G. Nicholls *Mod. Rugby Game* iv. 54 A fifth three-quarter..as the 'rover' or flying half is frequently styled. **1916** *Colliers* 30 Dec. 30/3 He is all over the field as a rover, diagnosing the play quickly and with unfailing accuracy. *a* **1917** J. E. Raphael *Mod. Rugby Football* (1918) xvii. 225, I played 'rover' for England on a memorable day at the Crystal Palace. **1927** Wakefield & Marshall *Rugger* II. vi. 268 The formation used in New Zealand... In this formation..the outsides consist of the extra forward, who may be described either as a rover or a half-back, a scrum-half, two five-eighths, a centre, [etc.]...The rover puts the ball into the scrum, while the scrum-half stands at the base of the scrum to take it out. **1954** J. B. G. Thomas *On Tour* 26 They [*sc.* the All Blacks] packed 2-3-2, with Gallaher acting as a 'rover', whose duty it was to put the ball into the scrum while the scrummage half back waited behind the scrum. **1969** Eagleson & McKie *Terminol. Austral. Nat. Football* III. 10 *Rover*, a member of the ruck, usually smaller than the other two members (*followers*), and selected for agility in capturing the ball. **1969** *Australian* 24 May 39/4 Essendon has Barry Davis back as a ruck-rover, to help captain Don McKenzie, and this should strengthen the side's following division and provide more opportunities for rovers Bob Greenwood and Don

Gross. **1970** *Univ. of Alabama Football Press Guide* 17 The rover slot was very similar to linebacking. **1975** *Oxf. Compan. Sports & Games* 385/1 A team [in Australian Rules Football] is made up of three full-forwards [etc., and]..the 'ruck'. The ruck consists of two followers and a rover, who moves with the flow of play.

d. Formerly, a member of a senior branch of the Scout Association (see Scout *sb.*⁴ 2 c). Also *rover scout.*

In 1967 this branch of the Scout Association was replaced by the venture scout branch (see quot. 1966).

1922 R. Baden-Powell *Rovering* 210 Rovers are a Brotherhood of the *Open Air* and *Service.* **1933** A. G. Macdonell *England, their England* xiii. 235 Lots of the young chaps are Rovers and don't drink so as to be an example to the Scouts and Cubs. **1959** *Chambers's Encycl.* II. 481/2 The movement in Great Britain is divided into four groups: rover scouts, i.e. young men of 18 and over; [etc.]. **1966** *Times* 10 June 11/1 The Scout Association will have three main sections—cub scouts.., aged 8 to 11; scouts, aged 11 to 16; and venture scouts (replacing senior scouts and rovers), aged 16 to 20. **1972** K. Bonfiglioli *Don't point that Thing at Me* i. 7 His bedroom is..full of fresh air; just what you would wish your Rover Scout son's room to be.

e. The name given to an R.A.F. reconnaissance patrol flown in 1940 and 1941. Also *attrib.*

1942 *R.A.F. Jrnl.* 3 Oct. 18 'Strike' and 'rover' patrols were on the board every day. **1957** R. Barker *Ship-Busters* ii. 35 The Rover was a roving commission, an armed reconnaissance against enemy shipping.. carried out by a small number of aircraft working independently.

f. Also **Rover, 'Rover.** *ellipt.* A Land-Rover (see *land *sb.*¹ 12).

1961 A. Wilson *Old Men at Zoo* iv. 207 You hop into the rover, Carter. You're frozen. **1973** G. Moffat *Lady with Cool Eye* vi. 66 Slade was taking the spare wheel off the 'Rover's bonnet. **1975** *Country Life* 13 Feb. 373/1 Some elderly sportsmen have high seats constructed on their 'rovers'..for shooting.

5. A remote-controlled surface vehicle for extraterrestrial exploration.

[**1967** *Jrnl Spacecraft & Rockets* IV. 209/1 A dynamic analysis in preliminary design of a lunar roving vehicle should have at least two basic aspects.] **1970** *Science Jrnl.* Jan. 16 The first rover is scheduled to take four trips of up to 32 km each with travel limited to 4·8 km radius from the landing site. **1971** [see *moon buggy* s.v. *moon *sb.* 16]. **1971** *Nature* 19 Nov. 125/3 The rover had a responsive steering, and..climbed slopes where the dust layer was deep enough to make walking difficult. **1972** [see *lunar *a.* and *sb.* A. 1 c]. **1978** *Sci. Amer.* Mar. 89/3 Another possibility is an unmanned surface rover capable of traversing hundreds of kilometers over a period of several years, which would be able to analyze the regolith in more detail than any satellite in orbit could.

roving, *vbl. sb.*¹ Add: **1. b.** *roving course.*

1939 P. H. Gordon *New Archery* iii. 21 Royal edict set aside places for shooting in the towns and provided long roving courses over the distances between towns.

2. b. roving commission (see quot. 1846); also *transf.* and *gen.*, (a body given) authority to pursue any inquiry or investigation in whatever quarters it may be considered necessary.

1846 [in Dict.]. **1867** *Congress. Globe* 22 Mar. 273/2, I think it would be safer to leave this matter [of certain state claims] to the direct inspection of the War Department, than to send out a roving commission. We have had enough of these roving commissions. **1894** *Congress. Rec.* 25 Apr. 4098/1 Is it a legitimate expenditure of the public money to send up consuls with roving commissions to hunt out commerce for a certain class of our people? **1930** W. S. Churchill (*title*) My early life: a roving commission. **1936** A. Christie *ABC Murders* xviii. 130, I had a kind of roving commission to purchase things for my brother. **1954** 'N. Blake' *Whisper in Gloom* I. ii. 31 Who'd you put him on to? Or was it a roving commission? **1959** *Ann. Reg. 1958* 179 The Russians opposed the Western proposal that they should be mobile and on a permanent footing on the ground that such 'roving commissions' would engage in espionage. **1981** *Listener* 1 Jan. 12/1 For several years as West Africa correspondent he had what was in effect a roving commission.

roving, *vbl. sb.*³ Add: **2. a.** (Further examples.)

1960 *New Scientist* 10 Mar. 597/1 The quantity of glass fibre applied..is governed by the rate of operation of the rollers that feed the multi-ply coil of glass fibre rovings to the cutter block. **1964** H. Hodges *Artifacts* ix. 128 Sometimes the rolag may be drawn out to a thickness approaching that of the required thread, and even given a slight twist before winding on to the distaff. Prepared fibres in this state are usually called rovings. **1972** *Physics Bull.* Nov. 663/3 The glasses are produced in continuous strands, consisting of 204, or multiples of 204, filaments which are subsequently processed into rovings or into yarns for weaving purposes. **1977** *Austral. Sailing* Jan. 51/2 The construction..sounds strong, including a hand-laid layer of woven rovings and additional strengthening in stress areas.

b. (Further examples.)

1946 A. J. Hall *Stand. Handbk. Textiles* iii. 105 The roving at this stage is about as thick as coarse string. **1972** *Physics Bull.* Nov. 663/3 S-Glass is most commonly employed in 'roving' or other unwoven forms. **1972** *Sci. Amer.* Dec. 47/2 Roving, on bobbins, is put into spinning frames, where it receives a final drawing out and the twisting necessary to make it into yarn.

roving, *ppl. a.* Add: **2. d.** Of an ambassador, journalist, etc., required to travel to various locations to deal with events as they occur.

1938 E. Waugh *Scoop* iii. i. 258 Will you accept five year contract five thousand year roving correspondent. **1946** *R.A.F. Jrnl.* May 147 This month our roving reporter..went back to Germany. **1958** *Listener* 26 June 1043/2 He was in the recent past Mr. Kishi's roving trade ambassador in south-east Asia. **1965** B. Sweet-Escott *Baker St. Irreg.* iii. 98 Staying in the Middle East as 'a kind of roving ambassador'. **1967** *Boston Sunday Globe* 23 Apr. 29/2 Boston's roving inspectors—who check on city services for the mayor. **1968** J. Drummond *Gantry Episode* ix. 72 It can't be done. Not by ordinary methods. That's why Purnell wants you as his roving reporter. **1970** A. Sinclair *Guevara* vi. 71 From 1960 onwards, Che had often served as a roving ambassador for Fidel Castro. **1972** D. Bloodworth *Any Number can Play* xii. 111 She would return..as a roving correspondent for the Worldover Syndication Service.

3. a. (Later examples.)

1951 N. Mitford *Blessing* I. ii. 17, I'm afraid she's deeply romantic, and Valhubert has a roving eye. **1968** D. Gray *Died in Red* xiv. 73 The man with the roving eye comes along, and he tells you you're wonderful. **1970** V. Gielgud *Candle-Holders* xi. 98 Angela Baynes had caught Tarzan's permanently roving eye.

row, *sb.*¹ Add: **I. 1. a.** *spec.* A line in a chorus.

1849 Thackeray *Pendennis* I. xiv. 125 Who's that gal in the second row, with blue ribbons, third from the stage. **1932** D. L. Sayers *Have his Carcase* xxiii. 303 O.K. darling. 'Aeroplane Girl', first row, song and dance. **1967** A. Wilson *No Laughing Matter* ii. 85 The thousands of silly boys who join the back row of the chorus every year.

2. d. *Mus.* = *tone-row* s.v. *tone *sb.* 11. Also Comb., as *row-note.*

1936 *Musical Q.* XXII. 14 The chief contribution towards the organization of the twelve-tone system is that peculiarly Schoenbergian concept—part abstract theory and part pure inspiration—the 'row': a semi-arbitrary arrangement of the twelve chromatic tones into a horizontal motival structure. *Ibid.* 31 Examples could be multiplied indefinitely, but,..most of them would boil down to some similar types of random distribution of the row-notes. **1958** A. Jacobs *New Dict. Mus.* 390 This method works through the 'note-row' (or 'series'), in which all the twelve notes are placed in a particular order as the basis of a work. No note is repeated within a row, which accordingly consists of twelve different notes and no others. **1965** *Listener* 20 May 757/3 An important aspect of the work is the extraction from the note-series of innumerable motivic elements and of the great variety of ways in which the row is itself presented. **1971** *Times Lit. Suppl.* 1 Oct. 1180/2 He [*sc.* Webern] was particularly partial to rows whose second half is a mirror inversion of the first.

4. a. Also *Comb.*, as **row house** *N. Amer.*, a terraced house; also (with hyphen) *attrib.*; hence **row housing.**

1936 H. Hagedorn *Brookings* i. 10 So the Brookings children moved to Baltimore..and went to live in a pleasant brick row-house with the canonical white stoop which Baltimoreans cherished. **1940** *Sun* (Baltimore) 16 Feb. 24/1 Mr. Pagon, in proposing that the entire area be rezoned from a row-house status, pointed out that [etc.]. **1949** *Ibid.* 29 Nov. 12/1 The Housing Authority's plans call for row housing. **1952** *Ibid.* 11 Jan. 12/3 The narrowest row house will be 16 feet across the front..and there will be only seven to a group. **1957** W. H. Whyte *Organization Man* xxiii. 305 A study of several new Philadelphia row-house neighborhoods. **1968** *Globe & Mail* (Toronto) 13 Feb. B2/4 There is no doubt that municipalities..would be agreeable to more realistic zoning in respect to smaller lots, row housing, etc. **1979** *Kingston* (Ontario) *Whig-Standard* 29 Mar. 21/4 The township has called for ten feet of yard between the end of a line of row houses and the next building.

b. Also *attrib.*

1871 J. M. Langford *Let.* 2 Dec. in *Geo. Eliot Lett.* (1956) V. 223 Some of the Row Houses whose subscription was partially delivered have been in for more.

e. Chiefly *U.S.* A line of cells in a prison; esp. in phr. *death row,* the part of a prison where condemned prisoners are kept.

1950 in M. McLuhan *Mech. Bride* (1967) 4/2 The doomed men..were filmed in death row yesterday afternoon. **1968** *Listener* 15 Feb. 210/2 Until he arrived, the ten prisoners in death row never left their cells, not even for exercise. **1971** *Black Scholar* Apr.–May 19/1 He is now waiting on Death Row in the Ohio Penitentiary. **1973** *Philadelphia Inquirer* 7 Oct. (Today Suppl.) 26/3 After all that time, you'd think we would all be exhilarated to be off the row. But everyone of us wanted, on some level, to go back. We didn't want to face the responsibilities of being out and having to fend for ourselves. **1973** *Publishers Weekly* 27 Aug. 231/2 Sentenced to death, he cut off his penis and has spent 23 years in a cage on a row reserved for lunatics. **1980** *Sci. Amer.* Apr. 63/3 Texas, which already has such a capital-punishment law on the books, currently ranks second in the nation, with 119 on death row.

6. a. Also *Comb.*, as **row boss** *U.S.* (see quot. 1937); **row crop** (see quot. 1930).

1930 *Amer. Speech* VI. 11 Irrigation farmers call beets, potatoes, and beans *rowcrops* in distinction from alfalfa and the grains, the *flood* crops, for in the former case the water is directed down rows instead of being allowed to flow over the whole field. **1937** *Sun Mag.* (Baltimore) 11 July 9/3 'The young ones aren't as good as their parents,' said the row boss. *Ibid.*, The term 'row boss' comes..from his being in charge of the pickers when they are working along the rows of vegetables. **1943** J. S. Huxley *TVA* 45 Indian corn and other row crops. *Ibid.* 58 Row crops are confined to the more level spots. **1950** *Engineering* 5 May 505/3 Light, medium and heavy tractors were all represented, and each group was subdivided into rowcrop and general-purpose tractors. **1960** *Farmer & Stockbreeder* 1 Mar. 125/1 We pioneered pneumatic tyred row-crop wheels. **1971** *Arable Farmer* Feb. 29/1 Wheel tractors on the farm being used solely for haulage and row-crop work. **1977** *New Yorker* 29 Aug. 48/1 So much for row-boss supervision, so much for harvest labor, so much for trucking, so much for tractor overhead, so much for fertilizer and pesticides.

b. For *U.S.* read 'orig. *U.S.*' and add later examples.

1912 J. Masefield *Widow in Bye St.* iv. 56 Bessie, the gipsy, got with child by Ern... 'I hear the gipsy has a row to hoe.' **1955** *Times* 2 Aug. 4/6 The lecturer then set himself a hard row to hoe; the scholarly correction of everything his audience may have been taught at school about King John, Runnymede, and Magna Carta. **1961** B. Ferguson *Watery Maze* v. 119 Mountbatten had therefore no easy row to hoe; but he had a definite course to steer: the invasion of France. **1969** *Listener* 26 June 894/2, I recognise full well that there are many people who always find life a pretty difficult row to hoe and our society must be a compassionate society. **1976** *New Yorker* 26 Apr. 62/3 Women have a God-damned hard row to hoe.

7*. In knitting, one line of stitches.

1800 M. Edgeworth *Parent's Assistant* (ed. 3) II. 79 Her mother's unfinished knitting lay upon a table near the bed, and Susan sat down in her wicker arm chair and went on with the row, in the middle of which her hand stopped the preceding evening. **1872** Geo. Eliot *Middlem.* II. iii. xxvi. 69 Mrs Taft who was always counting stitches and gathered her information in misleading fragments caught between the rows of her knitting. **1909** W. J. Locke *Septimus* i. 4 She counted the rows of her knitting. **1932** [see *knit *sb.* 1 a]. **1970** M. Hamilton-Hunt *Knitting Dict.* 19 Cast on in usual way, work a few rows of st st, the depth of the hem required.

II. 12. Also *transf.* of occurrences: in succession, consecutively. *colloq.*

a **1961** in Webster s.v.⁴ *row,* Won the state tourney for four years in a row. **1969** 'E. Lathen' *When in Greece* xiii. 139 Acute gastric distress..kept him awake..for a second night in a row. **1979** M. Babson *So soon done For* i. 10, I burnt the clothes he'd been wearing yesterday, and I shampooed his hair three times in a row.

14. Special Combs.: **row matrix** *Math.*, a matrix consisting of a single row of elements; **row vector** *Math.*, a vector represented by a row matrix.

1941 Birkhoff & MacLane *Survey Mod. Algebra* viii. 203 The coordinates of a vector ξ relative to a given basis in an n-space V form a one-rowed array $X = (x_1,\ldots,x_n)$, X a 'row matrix'. This may be considered as a vector in $V_n(F)$ or as a $1 \times n$ 'row matrix'. **1954** Beaumont & Ball *Introd. Mod. Algebra & Matrix Theory* i. 23 Any m by n matrix..may be thought of as an m by 1 column matrix with elements which are 1 by n row matrices. **1928** H. W. Turnbull *Theory of Determinants* iii. 36 There are two distinct types of vector, the row vector, and the column vector. **1978** *Nature* 13 Apr. 605/2 A row vector..may be derived which has elements representing the magnitude of growth response to each climatic variable.

row, *sb.*² **1. a.** (Earlier and later examples.)

1746 S. Barry *Let.* 6 June in D. Garrick *Private Corr.* (1831) I. 41 This occasioned a pleasant scene, for immediately, a terrible 'Row' ensued, between the few who paid ready money, and those who brought in his benefit-tickets. **1753** J. Poulter *Discoveries* (ed. 2) 13 He would prick again for thirty [Guineas]; we were afraid he would make too big a Row when he lost that, that is, a great Noise. **1955** *Times* 11 May 14/3 The Barons Court contest gains piquancy from a big local row which both sides expect to favour the Conservatives.

row, *sb.*³ (Earlier example.)

1832 F. Trollope *Dom. Manners Amer.* (ed. 2) I. xvi. 249 A row upon the Ohio was another of our favourite amusements.

row, *v.*¹ Add: **I. 2. c.** Also *to row in,* to conspire. *slang.*

1897 *Daily Tel.* 12 Feb. 5/7 It's very likely the sellers and the general public concerned in auction sales are anything but satisfied with the results of sales by auction where a 'knock-out' is arranged, and especially where the auctioneer 'rows in' with the crew. **1909** J. R. Ware *Passing Eng.* 211/2 *Row in,*..unfair conspiracy. From Thames life through centuries. A man 'rowed in' in a river robbery, or even a murder. **1934** P. Allingham *Cheapjack* xvi. 202, I think these boys had better row in with us...We may as well stick together. **1970** G. F. Newman *Sir, You Bastard* vii. 194 What if they try to row in? **1977** P. Moyes *To kill Coconut* vii. 99 'Rowing in' is slang for implicating somebody in a crime.

II. 8. a. (Earlier examples.) Cf. *salt river 2 b.

1828 *Reg. Deb. Congress U.S.* 2 Feb. 1341 But, sir, I will venture to say this, that, in playing this game, if the Secretary of State is not influenced by the same courtesy which governed the courtiers of the great Frederick, never to beat the monarch at chess, that he could give the President twenty-nine, and as they say in Kentucky, 'row him up salt river'. **1832** *Spirit of Times* 28 Apr. 3/1 He 'rowed' Stanberry 'up a salt creek', and is now *being* tried by the House of Representatives for his unlucky propensity. **1832** J. K. Paulding *Westward Ho!* I. ix. 77 See if I don't row you up Salt River before you are many days older.

9. e. *to row out,* to exhaust by rowing.

1928 *Daily Express* 7 Aug. 12/6 Both pairs finished in a distressed condition, Boardman being completely rowed-out.

row, *v.*[3] Add: **1. a.** (Earlier example.)
1789 *Loiterer* 14 Nov. 10 We..looked into every coach, *rowed* the waggons, examined both the boxes, the roofs, and the baskets.

b. For quot. substitute:
1789 *Loiterer* 21 Feb. 11 Racket *rowed* me up at seven o'clock—sleepy and queer but forced to get up to make breakfast for him.

2. a. Also const. *out, out of.*
1908 *Smart Set* June 143/1 Most fathers would have rowed me out of the house. **1976** *New Mus. Express* 31 July 6/4 But you get these weird, insecure feelings that they might be trying to row you out, which wasn't the case. No one was talking about sacking me.

3. Now usu. in the more limited sense 'to have a row, to quarrel noisily or heatedly'.
1890 T. A. Janvier *Aztec Treasure-House* xvi. 195 Some of these Indians are friendly, and we don't want to start a row with them if they are willing not to row with us. **1914** S. Lewis *Our Mr. Wrenn* xvii. 227 Why, Mouse! I thought you'd be glad to see me. I've never rowed with you, have I? **1970** G. F. Newman *Sir, You Bastard* viii. 209 He couldn't remember rowing. Rows were usually loud demonstrative things. **1978** R. Rendell *Sleeping Life* viii. 73 We row, of course we do, that's healthy in a marriage, but we love each other.

row-de-dow. (Earlier examples.)
1790 R. Tyler *Contrast* III. i. 42 There was a soldier fellow, who talked about his row de dow, dow, and courted a young woman. **1832** *Deb. Congress U.S.* 13 Mar. (1833) 2128 The rub-a-dub and row-de-dow excitement. **1885** *Referee* 8 Mar. 5/1 With regard to the Prince and Princess's visit to Ireland, the 'row-de-dow'—that is, we believe, the Hibernian term for it—which took place [etc.].

rowdy, *sb.*[1] **a.** (Earlier example.)
1808 W. Littell *Festoons of Fancy* (1814) 62 But it seems to this court that the loss to him would be the same, as if he had lost it among those, whom his gentlemanship is pleased to call *rowdies*.

rowdy, *v.* Add: **b.** *trans.* To treat in a rowdy manner.
1825 J. K. Paulding *John Bull in Amer.* xii. 209 Notwithstanding..their being regulated and rowdied, and obliged to cut down trees as big round as a hogshead.

rowdy-dow·, *sb.* [Cf. Row-de-dow.] Boisterous noise; uproar. Also *attrib.* passing into *adj.* and quasi-*adv.* So **rowdy-dowy** *a.*
1852 J. Labern *Popular Comic Song Bk.* 75 While Spifflicating Charlie Coker and Jane of the Hatchet-face divine, Just did the Rowdydowy Poker. **1935** W. Stevens in *Poetry* XLV. 245 The heavy bells are tolling rowdy-dow. **1946** *Time* 22 July 40 This rowdy-dow roundup is the wild-cow milking contest. **1950** *N.Y. Times* 9 July II. 1/1 To restore the old rowdy-dow of burlesque, Mr. Mike Todd and Mr. Clark have gathered a handful of authentic drolls.

rowdy-dow, *v.* [f. prec.] *intr.* To be noisy or boisterous.
1966 T. Pynchon *Crying of Lot 49* v. 110 She collided with a gang of guided tourists come rowdy-dowing out of a Volkswagen bus.

rowdy-dowdy, *a.* (Earlier and later examples.)
1854 M. S. Cummins *Lamplighter* 260 To offer herself as a champion for that rowdy-dowdy child. **1928** [see *nightman 2].

rowdying (rau·di,iŋ), *vbl. sb.* [f. Rowdy *v.* + -ing[1].] Causing a disturbance.
1839 *Picayune* (New Orleans) 26 Feb. 2/4 There *is* more quiet and less rowdying..here than in Boston, with all its anti-drinking, anti-bellringing and other anti-noise making laws. **1887** *Courier-Jrnl.* (Louisville, Kentucky) 18 Feb. 1/3 There was a good deal of noise and 'rowdying'. **1913** D. H. Lawrence *Sons & Lovers* xiii. 430 'We've heard that song before,' snapped the old man. 'Now you get off, and don't be long about it. Comin' *here* with your rowdying.'

rowdyism. (Earlier and later examples.)
1842 S. Longfellow *Let.* 8 Feb. in *Lett. Charles Dickens* (1974) III. 40/1 [Charles Dickens was] very animated and talkative,..with..the slightest tincture of rowdyism in his appearance. **1936** I. L. Idriess *Cattle King* xx. 189 Perhaps the hostility and rowdyism that the Salvation Army had to suffer..aroused his sympathy. **1955** *Times* 20 Aug. 6/1 The seriousness with which the commission regards the situation..from the relatively minor demonstration in Saarbrücken last Saturday night to the rowdyism in Neunkirchen on Wednesday night. **1976** *Southern Even. Echo* (Southampton) 15 Nov. 2/8 The problems presented by late night rowdyism.

roweite (rōᵘ·əit). *Min.* [f. the name of George *Rowe*, 20th-cent. U.S. mine official and mineralogist + -ite[1].] A basic borate of calcium and manganese, usu. also containing magnesium and zinc, first found as light brown elongated orthorhombic crystals in zinc ore at Franklin, New Jersey; (Mn,Mg, Zn)$_2$Ca$_2$B$_4$O$_7$(OH)$_6$.
1937 Berman & Gonyer in *Amer. Mineralogist* XXII. 301 The crystals of roweite are light brown in color, lath shaped and without measurable terminations. **1975** *Soviet Physics: Doklady* XX. 244/1 The isostructural nature of the (Mn, Mg) and Mn roweites and the [B$_4$O$_5$(OH)$_4$] tetraradical..met in sodium borate.

rowel, *sb.* Add: **I. 1. d.** *rowel-deep* adv. (earlier example).
1832 W. C. Bryant *Poems* 45 His spurs are buried rowel-deep, he rides with loosened rein.

II. 8. For *Obs.*—[1] read *Obs.* and add later example.
1836 *Col. Crockett's Exploits & Adventures Texas* i. 1 Though they start at the lowest rowel of the ladder.

rowel, *v.*[1] Add: **2. c.** *fig.*
1918 F. Hackett *Ireland* xii. 331 The indecency and indignity of personal subjection rowelled Parnell like a spur with teeth in it. **1931** E. Linklater *Juan in Amer.* II. xii. 137 Now the staccato ear-splitting *rafale* of cheering rowels them afresh. **1967** S. Beckett *Stories & Texts for Nothing* 42 Between the caressing voice and the fingers rowelling my neck the contrast was striking. **1975** E. Berckman *Indecent Exposure* viii. 94 Her visit..was strong enough to rowel and disturb her.

rowelled, *ppl. a.* For *rare*—[1] read *rare* and add: **b.** Pricked by rowels (example is *fig.*).
1924 R. Campbell *Flaming Terrapin* ii. 29 Rowelled by that sharp prow to hissing hate, The waves washed round her.

rowing, *vbl. sb.*[1] Add: **2. b. rowing machine,** an appliance in which exercises may be done that simulate rowing; **rowing stick** *poet.*, an oar; **rowing tank** (see quot. 1976).
1848 J. de C. Locke tr. *Montolieu's Swiss Family Robinson* 2nd Ser. I. x. 95 (*heading*) The rowing-machine. **1894** *Outing* Mar. 458/1 The exercises consist of hard work on rowing-machines or in the tank, vigorous dumb-bell exercise, and a run of two miles per day. **1935** C. Isherwood *Mr. Norris changes Trains* iv. 68 The Baron made a hobby of his figure. He tortured himself daily on an electric horse, a rowing-machine and a rotating massage belt. **1944** T. Rattigan *White Sun Shines* II. 58 If you want exercise I've got a rowing machine in the bathroom. **1977** 'E. Crispin' *Glimpses of Moon* i. 20 Exercising on a rowing-machine. **1923** E. Pound *XXX Cantos* xx. 93 Their names are not written in bronze Nor their rowing sticks set with Elpenor's. **1892** *Outing* Jan. 277/2 In 1887 the rowing tank was first put into practical use in the Yale gymnasium. **1939** Nickalls & Mallam *Rowing* iv. 87 The object of the rowing tank is to allow oarsmen to indulge in..rowing without going out on the river... Tank rowing originated in America, where ice prevents any outdoor rowing for a considerable part of the year. **1976** *Webster's Sports Dict.* 360/1 *Rowing tank*, a large tank of water containing a mock-up of a shell in which an oarsman or sculler can practice his stroke and work on technique. The effectiveness of a stroke is indicated by a meter which measures the turbulence of the water.

c. *rowing-song.*
1888 L. A. Smith *Music of Waters* p. xxvii, Rowing-songs should..also be included in this class. **1956** M. W. Stearns *Story of Jazz* ix. 96 Whereas early travelers heard rowing songs and sea shanties, later specialists found work songs.

rowing, *vbl. sb.*[3] (Earlier example.)
1832 E. Grosvenor *Let.* 15 Dec. in G. Huxley *Lady Elizabeth & Grosvenors* (1965) iv. 103 To some magistrates who behaved shabbily B. gave what was called 'a proper rowing'.

rowing, *vbl. sb.*[5] (Later example.)
1964 H. Hodges *Artifacts* x. 145 Finally, the clean felted cloth was often brushed with teazles (*teazling, rowing*) to raise a nap of fine hairs on the surface.

rowing, *ppl. a.*[2] Add: **b.** Quarrelling; disposed to quarrel.
1961 *Guardian* 20 Oct. 7/6 The grey Depression background, the rowing parents.

Rowland (rōᵘ·lănd). *Physics.* The name of H. A. *Rowland* (1848–1901), U.S. physicist, used *attrib.* and in the possessive to designate certain devices and concepts associated with his work, as **Rowland('s) circle,** a circle on which must lie the entrance slit, (curved) grating, and photographic plate of a spectrograph if all the spectral lines are to be brought to a focus on the plate; **Rowland ghost,** a spurious spectral line produced by a periodic error in the spacing of the lines of a diffraction grating; **Rowland grating,** a diffraction grating ruled on a machine built by Rowland; **Rowland('s) mounting** (see quot. 1966); **Rowland ring,** a torus made of a magnetic material whose properties it is wished to investigate and linked with a coil of current-carrying wire.
1932 *Jrnl. Optical Soc. Amer.* XXII. 245 Symmetric adjustment of the grating about the point of tangency to the Rowland circle. **1952** R. W. Ditchburn *Light* vi. 196 If then a point source of light is placed at a point Q on the circle whose diameter is equal to the radius of the grating, and which touches the grating at its centre, the spectra will be focused along the circle. This circle is known as the 'Rowland circle'. **1967** G. W. Stroke in S. Flugge *Handbuch der Physik* XXIX. 477 Eq. (25.27) is clearly satisfied on Rowland's circle. *Ibid.*, The best foci are obtained on the Rowland circle when the source is also placed on that circle. **1922** *Jrnl. Optical Soc. Amer.* VI. 419 The separations of the Rowland ghosts from the parent lines are readily deduced from the characteristics of the ruling engine. **1969** D. Richardson in R. Kingslake *Appl. Optics & Optical Engin.* V. ii. 27 In contradistinction to Rowland ghosts, which usually arise from errors extending over large areas of the grating, each satellite usually originates from a small number of misplaced grooves in a localized part of the grating. **1910** *Phil. Mag.* XX. 773, I had a polished flat plate of speculum metal, such as is used for making Rowland gratings, silver-plated and polished. **1926** R. W. Lawson tr. *Hevesy & Paneth's Man. Radioactivity* iv. i. 44 The grating space of a Rowland grating is about 10^{-4} cm. **1974** *Encycl. Brit. Macropædia* II. 235/1 Some Rowland gratings are still in use. **1901** *Physical Rev.* XII. 10 The second grating..was of 21 ft. radius, 14,438 lines to the inch. It was arranged on Rowland's mounting. **1914** *Astrophysical Jrnl.* XL. 205 It provides for a grating of 15 ft. (4·57 m) radius, and, optically considered, is the Rowland mounting with the plane of the focal circle vertical. **1966** *McGraw-Hill Encycl. Sci. & Technol.* IV. 141/1 In the Rowland mounting, camera and grating are connected by a bar forming a diameter of the Rowland circle. **1953** J. D. Kraus *Electromagnetics* v. 232 (*caption*) Rowland-ring method of obtaining magnetization curve. **1966** *McGraw-Hill Encycl. Sci. & Technol.* VIII. 51/1 When the core of the Rowland ring is initially demagnetized, **B** = 0 and **H** = 0.

rowlock. Add: Now freq. with pronunc. (rǫ·lǫ̆k).

rownsepyked (rau·nspəikĕd), *ppl. a. rare*—[1]. [f. Rounsepike.] Of a tree, having branches stripped of leaves.
1937 D. Jones *In Parenthesis* III. 39 More leper-trees pitted, rownsepykèd out of nature, cut off in their sap-rising.

row·-off. [f. Row *v.*[1] + Off *adv.*] In rowing, a race giving the losers in previous heats a second chance to qualify for the final.
1928 *Daily Tel.* 7 Aug. 12/1 Under the repechage system of rows-off between previous losers, J. Wright.. and T. D. A. Collet..had another chance in the sculling event.

row·-over. [f. Row *v.*[1] + Over *adv.*] An instance of rowing over. Cf. Row *v.*[1] 1 f.
1868 W. Brough *Field of Cloth of Gold* v. 41 Here I am you see, Coming to trial, should the plaintiff halt, Defendant claims a judgement by default. So you are mine; and I my rival crow over. It's what they call in boat-racing a row over.

Rowton (rau·tǫ̆n). The name of Montague William Lowry-Corry, 1st Lord *Rowton* (1838–1903), used *attrib.* in **Rowton (lodging-) house,** a type of cheap lodging-house intended to provide better conditions than a common lodging-house.
1892 *Times* 16 Dec. 8/1 Yesterday a large model lodging-house which has been erected by Lord Rowton at Bond-street, Vauxhall, for the accommodation of working men, was opened for the inspection of visitors. The building, which has been named 'Rowton-house', stands upon a site within a few yards of Vauxhall-cross. **1911** *Encycl. Brit.* XXIII. 789/1 In 1894 a company, Rowton Houses (Limited), was incorporated to extend the scheme, a main characteristic of which was that the houses should not be charitable institutions but should be on a paying commercial basis. **1932** Kipling *Limits & Renewals* 388 In what they call a Rowton lodging-house. **1937** H. G. Wells *Brynhild* vi. 74 One man wrote from a Rowton lodging-house on ruled paper torn from an exercise book. **1956** A. Wilson *Anglo-Saxon Att.* II. ii. 355 He had drifted from lodgings to Salvation Army hostels and Rowton Houses. **1960** C. Wilson *Ritual in Dark* I. ii. 41 It would have destroyed his appetite, like a meal in a Rowton House. **1968** *Listener* 28 Nov. 735/2 Eventually we drove him round Camden Town looking for a night's lodging. We went first to the local Rowton House. **1972** *Guardian* 19 Feb. 9/3 He ended up in a hostel, like Rowton House, for the down and out. **1977** *Vole* No. 3. 23/2 Gone is the once normal category of 'the lodger' and gone are such institutions as Rowton House, providing decent short-term accommodation for single people.

row-waggon, var. *rolwagen.

rowy (rau·i), *a.* [f. Row *sb.*[2] + -y[1].] Noisy; characterized by quarrelling.
1922 Joyce *Ulysses* 763 Hes running wild now out at night away from his books and studies and not living at home on account of the usual rowy house.

Roxbury (rǫ·ksbĕri). The name of a town in Massachusetts, used *attrib.* in **Roxbury russet** to designate a variety of green-skinned apple with russet markings, originally grown in New England.
1822 J. Thacher *Amer. Orchardist* 136 Roxbury russeting..is one of the best known, and most valuable fruits in Massachusetts. **1834** *N.Y. Sun* 23 Sept. 4/1 The sweet side of the apple is of a bright yellow colour, and the sour side of the same colour as the Roxbury Russet. **1861** [see *Baldwin]. **1880** *Harper's Mag.* Mar. 573/2 She set right to a-parin' them Roxbury russets. **1949** *Amer. Forests* Sept. 20/1 Some of the apples sound familiar: Smoke House, Roxbury Russet, Jonathan, Baldwin. **1975** *New Yorker* 11 Aug. 35/1 The first American apple of which there is any record is the now all but forgotten Roxbury Russet.

Roxy (rǫ·ksi), *sb.* The nickname of Samuel Lionel Rothafel (1882–1936), U.S. radio and film entrepreneur, used *attrib.* of persons and things connected with the chain of cinemas built by him.

1940 F. Scott Fitzgerald *Let.* 12 July (1964) 84 It's very modern to be taking dramatic criticism although it reminds me vaguely of the school for Roxy ushers. **1957** *Encycl. Brit.* XV. 868/1 The Roxy theatre,..which opened in 1927 in New York city, with a 6,250 seating capacity, cost $8,000,000 and grossed in one week $144,267. **1961** A. Berkman *Singers' Gloss. Show Business* 76 *Roxy ending*.., the fanfare ending of a song, first used at the Roxy Theatre in New York. The Roxy Ending is sometimes played at the end of a production number, or where majestic fullness is required. (Also *Paramount ending, Publix ending*).

Roy (roi), *sb.*[3] *Austral.* [f. the personal name *Roy.*] A smart, fashionable, or 'smooth' person. Also *attrib.*

1960 *Encounter* May 28 The Australian business-man or big land-owner, the button-down shirt, lightweight suit type of smoothie from the North Shore line in Sydney or the Toorak Road in Melbourne, with his spurious 'taste' and 'culture'... In current Australian terminology, this is the 'Roy' type. **1965** *Nation* (Austral.) 27 Nov. 21 Middle-class 'Roys' in sports cars and yachting jackets. **1971** F. Hardy *Outcasts of Foolgarah* xi. 143 The young executives, the in-people, call them what you like, the Roys, the jet set, the status symbol seekers from Perisher Valley to Palm Beach, and none of them worth a pinch of shit if it comes to doing an honest day's work.

royal, *a.* and *sb.* Add: **A.** *adj.* **I. 3. a.** (Further examples.)

1815 J. Mayne *Jrnl.* 3 Feb. (1909) xi. 270 The Princess of Wales was present, and towards the end of the opera she went round into the royal box. **1874** W. P. Lennox *My Recoll.* I. iii. 77, I..upon reaching the theatre dismounted, and followed the royal party into the anteroom of the royal box. **1930** E. Wallace *Lady of Ascot* x. 105 Julian had a Royal Enclosure badge, and was the only member of the party possessed of this privilege. **1958** *Spectator* 8 Aug. 201/1 The physicists, who sometimes exercise their sovereignty by barring psychology from the Royal Enclosure of the physical sciences. **1963, 1968** [see *enclosure 4 a]. **1971** H. Trevelyan *Worlds Apart* xxiv. 282 My wife did her part, showing great endurance and invariable good humour, finding herself, while I was in England, on Khruschev's right at a lively dinner in the 'Royal Box' in the Bolshoi Theatre during the celebration of Shakespeare's four hundredth anniversary. **1974** 'G. Black' *Golden Cockatrice* vii. 113 The kind of people who might one day get him into the Royal Enclosure at Ascot.

4. (Earlier and further examples of special designations.)

1592, 1769 [see Navy[1] 3]. **1786** [see Artillery *sb.* 5]. *a* **1865** Smyth *Sailor's Word-bk.* (1867) 583 Royal naval reserve. **1889** [see Engineer *sb.* 2 c]. **1911** *Shipping World* 15 Mar. 276/1 The Royal Fleet Auxiliary *Burma* ..is a vessel with considerable claims to notice. **1913** [see *flying officer* s.v. *flying *vbl. sb.* 3]. **1918** *Times* 16 Mar. 10/2 It is Our Will and Pleasure that the Air Force to be established pursuant to the said Act shall be styled the 'Royal Air Force'. *Ibid.* 28 Nov. 9/3 The three Corps will henceforth be known as the 'Royal Army Service Corps', the 'Royal Army Veterinary Corps', and the 'Royal Army Ordnance Corps'. **1922** Joyce *Ulysses* 48 Her fancyman is treating two Royal Dublins in O'Loughlin's of Blackpitts. **1935** *Ann. Reg. 1934* 23 The Minister announced that a new branch of the Territorial Army, under the name of the Royal Defence Corps, was to be formed. **1937** *Ann. Reg. 1936* 65 The King had approved the creation of a new Reserve called the Royal Air Force Reserve, which would be open only to men in civil life. **1943** [see R.E.M.E., REME]. **1946** *Times* 10 Dec. 4/4 The King has approved that the following regiments and corps shall in future enjoy the distinction of 'royal', their new titles being..Royal Army Educational Corps. Royal Army Dental Corps. Corps of Royal Military Police. Royal Pioneer Corps. **1950** *Jrnl. R. United Service Inst.* XCV. 289 In the same Army Order it was also stated that on transfer to the R.A.C. the R.T.C. would be re-designated Royal Tank Regiment. **1955** *Times* 20 July 8/7 The Queen has approved the promotion of Prince Bernhard of the Netherlands to the honorary rank of Air Vice-Marshal Royal Air Force Volunteer Reserve, with effect from July 8. **1965** *Oxford Mail* 29 June 1/4 A new Army corps will come into being next month. It is the Royal Corps of Transport made up of the Royal Army Service Corps..the Royal Engineers' transport units and the Movement Control Service.

5. b. *Royal Borough,* part of the title of three English boroughs (Kensington (and Chelsea), Kingston-upon-Thames, and Windsor) that have a royal connection.

1897 *Private Life of Queen* xxvii. 226 Our Queen..gave the plot of land..to the people of the 'Royal Borough' [of Windsor] for a recreation ground. **1901** *London Gaz.* 19 Nov. 7472/2 The King has been pleased to direct Letters Patent to be passed..granting the title 'Royal' to the Metropolitan Borough of Kensington, and ordaining and declaring that the said Borough shall henceforth be called and styled the 'Royal Borough of Kensington'. **1923** *Victoria Hist. Co. Berkshire* III. 56/2 The borough of Windsor..was from the first, as it has since remained, a royal borough, owning no overlord but the King. **1930** G. B. Shaw *Apple Cart* ii. 75 It is my intention to offer myself to the Royal Borough of Windsor as a candidate at the forthcoming General Election. **1975** G. Evans *Kensington* p. xvi, Although the granting of the title 'Royal' does not carry with it any special precedence or privilege, there are only three English Boroughs—Kensington, Kingston-upon-Thames..aud Windsor—on which the Sovereign has conferred the title. **1976** *Equals* Dec. 8/1 She is one of four Conservative councillors for the St. Mary's ward of the Royal Borough of Windsor and Maidenhead.

6. (Further examples.)

1759 in Hodges & Hughes *Sel. Naval Documents* (1927) 135 Whereas Mr. Nathaniel Peacock has been educated in the Royal Academy at Portsmouth, and is well qualified to serve His Majesty at sea. **1834** *Times* 25 Jan. 5/3 The mayor and other members were willing to show proper deference to the Royal commission. **1871** [see Commission *sb.*[1] 6]. **1873** *London Gaz.* 21 Jan. 265/1 We do therefore beg leave to recommend that your Majesty will be graciously pleased, by your Order in Council, to approve of the closing of the Royal Naval College at Portsmouth, and the founding of a College at Greenwich, to be styled 'The Royal Naval College'. **1894** *Times* 19 May 7/3 A report by Mr. R. Hunter Pringle, Assistant-Commissioner to the Royal Commission on Agriculture, has been laid before Parliament. **1907** *Times* 9 Mar. 12/2 The ninth annual dinner of the Automobile Club was held..last evening... The chairman announced that a letter had been received from the Home Office stating that his Majesty had been pleased to command that the club should be henceforth known as the Royal Automobile Club. **1926** *Daily Chron.* 13 May 1/7 The proposals in this direction tentatively made in the report of the Royal Commission should be pressed and the powers of the proposed board enlarged. **1926** *Encycl. Brit.* II. 1020/1 The constant vigilance and activity of the Royal Society for the Protection of Birds and the Selborne Society have secured legislative and administrative protection for birds. **1927** T. M. Longstreth *Silent Force* 344 We are members of the Royal Canadian Mounted Police..and I'm going to seize your ship and cargo. **1928** *Times* 24 May 11/4 The Royal Colonial Institute, which celebrates its diamond jubilee this year, has decided to change its name to 'The Royal Empire Society'. **1930** [see *National Trust* s.v. *national *a.* 5]. **1955** *Times* 15 June 8/7 The executive committee of the Royal Automobile Club, which is responsible for the conduct of motor races in the United Kingdom, is to meet to-day. **1958** *Times* 9 May 7/7 The Queen has approved, by Order in Council, that henceforth the Royal Empire Society shall be known as the Royal Commonwealth Society. **1965** *Listener* 17 June 892/6 Three royal commissions are at this moment examining the general parts of the local government body. **1971** *Whitaker's Almanack 1972* 1098/2 Royal British Legion, Headquarters, Pall Mall, S.W.1. **1976** *Fundy Tourist* (St. Stephen, New Brunswick) 1 July 1/1 The Royal Canadian Mounted Police—the words conjure up visions of red knights on slick black steeds. **1977** *R.A.F. News* 11–24 May 5/6 The collection..in aid of the Warboys Branch of the Royal British Legion Honorary Association. **1977** *Western Morning News* 1 Sept. 6/1 The following.. adhere to a code of conduct laid down by the Royal Institute of Chartered Surveyors. **1980** *Brit. Med. Jrnl.* 29 Mar. 925/1 The obvious and only course of action was a Royal Commission.

7. a. (Further examples.)

1780 T. Davies *Life David Garrick* I. xvi. 180 The king was prevailed upon to give a kind of sanction to this entertainment, by a royal command, on the first night of representation. **1863** [see Assent *sb.* 2]. **1869** *Bradshaw's Railway Manual* XXI. 298 The Fusion Bill ..was..carried through both Houses of Parliament and received the Royal assent on the 31st of July. **1976** *Times* 1 Sept. (Fashion Suppl.) p. ii /5 Norman Hartnell and Hardy Amies, both royal warrant holders.

II. 8. a. Also applied to the use of the plural pronoun 'we' by a single person to denote himself. Cf. We *pron.* 2 a.

1835 [see We *pron.* 2 a]. **1931** *N. & Q.* 6 June 414/1 The writer uses 'we' throughout—rather unfortunately, as one is sometimes in doubt whether it is a sort of 'royal' plural, indicating only himself, or denotes himself and companions. **1960** J. Rae *Custard Boys* ii. xv. 175 'In the absence of the accused we will continue with the trial.' ..He used the royal 'we', but he spoke for us all. **1964** R. H. Robins *Gen. Linguistics* vii. 287 Somewhat similar is the use of the 'royal *we*'; in strictly ceremonial circumstances reigning sovereigns in some countries (of which Great Britain is one) use what are otherwise first person plural pronouns in reference to themselves in their official or constitutional capacity. **1966** J. Cleary *High Commissioner* ii. 26 'May we ask whom you wish to see?' Monarchs and butlers, Malone thought: who else has the right to speak in the royal plural? **1975** M. Babson *There must be Some Mistake* i. 1 '*We* simply can't take it in,' Lydia drawled, her '*we*' not only royal, but universal.

d. (Later examples.) Also (chiefly *U.S. colloq.*) used as an intensifier, freq. with ironic force.

1938 G. Greene *Brighton Rock* iii. i. 99 She remembered: a face in a bar. She had a royal memory. **1951** J. D. Salinger *Catcher in Rye* iv. 27 He gave out a big yawn while he said that. Which is something that gives me a royal pain in the ass. I mean if someone *yawns* right while they're asking you to do them a goddam favor. **1960** Wentworth & Flexner *Dict. Amer. Slang* 435/1 *Royal*... Used as a term of emphasis, esp. before taboo words and expressions, most freq. in 'a royal screwing'. **1972** *Dict. Contemp. & Colloq. Usage* 24/2 *Royal screw (fuck)*,..an ultimate or complete put-down; total failure where success was expected; an unmitigated defeat or deception. **1976** *Times Lit. Suppl.* 9 July 841/2 Life principle Elspeth may be, but she is also a royal pain in the neck. **1977** C. McFadden *Serial* x. 26/2 Kate had been Harvey's idea of a royal Bengal pain in the ass for the last year.

13. b. royal antelope, a tiny antelope, *Neotragus pygmæus,* found in forested areas of West Africa; **royal Bengal (tiger),** an Indian variety of the tiger, *Panthera tigris,* distinguished by unbroken stripes.

1771 T. Pennant *Synopsis Quadrupeds* 28 Antelope.. Royal..with very short strait horns. **1871** E. G. E. Ward *Jrnl.* 3 June in D. P. Carew *Many Years, Many Girls* (1967) i. 52 One lady..had arrayed herself in a complete suit of tiger-stripes..so that she looked like a Royal Bengal. **1872** *Proc. Zool. Soc.* 639 The type of the former I believe to have been a genuine specimen of the Royal Antelope. **1964** L. S. Crandall *Managem. Wild Mammals in Captivity* 675 The royal antelope..was represented in the Zoological Gardens of London in 1914. **1964** R. Perry *World of Tiger* xv. 233 The..very rare Royal Bengal tiger is distinguished by unbroken black stripes.

14. b. *Royal Ann(e)* (U.S.) a variety of bigarreau cherry, having red skin and white flesh, or a tree bearing fruit of this kind; *Royal Sovereign,* a variety of strawberry or its large, early-ripening fruits.

1892 *Proc. R. Hort. Soc.* XV. p. lxvii, First Class Certificate. To Strawberry Royal Sovereign (votes, unanimous), from Mr. T. Laxton, Bedford. **1897** S. T. Wright *Fruit-Culture* xviii. 116 For early forcing, Royal Sovereign is a grand acquisition, as it is remarkably early and prolific, with large fruit of excellent quality. **1900** L. H. Bailey *Cycl. Amer. Hort.* I. 293/2 The Napoleon Bigarreau (locally known as Royal Ann) is the ideal for a white cherry. **1930** V. R. Gardner *Cherry* xiii. 111 The outstanding light-fleshed sweet cherry is the Napoleon,—also known as Napoleon Bigarreau and Royal Ann. Indeed it is the *one* white-fleshed sweet cherry of real commercial importance in the United States. **1941** M. L. Smith *Going to God's Country* iv. 175 It was very beautifull with all the groves of tall fir trees and the Royal Ann cherys. **1946** *Nature* 6 July 24/2 The virus..produces faint chlorotic spots on the leaves of Royal Sovereign strawberry. **1957** M. McCarthy *Memories Catholic Girlhood* viii. 202 Two kinds of cherry trees, black and Royal Anne. **1960** B. K. Wilson *Lovely Summer* i. 11 Slade is going to pick the Royal Sovereigns this afternoon.

15. royal binding (see quot. 1952); **royal flush** (earlier and later examples); formerly also = *straight flush* s.v. Straight *a.* 9 b; **royal icing,** a hard, shiny icing, the ingredients of which include egg whites; **royal jelly:** see *Jelly *sb.*[1] 2; **Royal Scot,** a familiar name for the London to Glasgow express; also, the name of the class of locomotive designed to haul this train; **Royal Stewart (tartan):** (see quot. 1975); also known as *dress Stewart* or *Royal tartan*; **royal straight (flush),** in Poker, = *royal flush* in Dict.; also *fig.*; **royal tennis** = *real tennis* s.v. *real *a.*[2] 4 e.

1929 G. D. Hobson *Bindings in Cambr. Libraries* 141 More royal bindings were turned out at this bindery [*sc.* Samuel Mearne's] than at any other. **1939** *Guide Exhib. in King's Library* (Brit. Mus.) 119 The later royal bindings do not, perhaps, maintain the same high level of excellence. **1952** J. Carter *ABC for Book-Collectors* 157 A book described as being in a 'royal binding' may be expected to have a sovereign's arms on one or both covers; but it must not necessarily be supposed that it therefore has a royal provenance. **1868** W. B. Dick *Amer. Hoyle* (ed. 5) 177 *Royal Flush,* a Straight or Sequence, all of the same suit. *Ibid.* 178 *Straight Flush,* the same as Royal Flush. **1888** B. Matthews *Pen & Ink* 197 The Straight Flush (called a Royal Flush when it begins with the ace and ends with the ten). *Ibid.* 198 The Royal Flush is not often seen; like other exalted monarchs it does not make itself common in men's eyes. **1922** [see *full house 2]. **1845** E. Acton *Mod. Cookery* xvi. 423 (*heading*) Tourte meringuée, or, tart with royal icing. **1974** *Times* 13 Nov. 12/5 Royal icing or glacé icing must be made with proper icing sugar. **1927** *Times* 27 Sept. 16/2 With the beginning of the winter train service yesterday the London, Midland and Scottish Railway introduced a non-stop run of 299½ miles... This run will be made daily by the 10 a.m. Royal Scot from London to Carlisle, which proceeds to Edinburgh and Glasgow. **1933** *Triumph of Royal Scot* 16 The locomotive which hauled the train throughout the tour was LMS Number 6100 Royal Scot, the first of 50 locomotives of the Royal Scot class to be constructed in 1927. **1942** *Model Railway News* Jan. 9/1 The exhaust steam injector on the 'Royal Scot' was omitted on the model. **1953** *Manch. Guardian* 15 Aug. 3/3 Good fortune and the fact that all the coaches were of the new all-steel type reduced casualties when the Royal Scot was derailed near Abington last Saturday. **1977** *Times* 30 Apr. 12/3 On Monday..the Royal Scot is making a celebration run from Euston to Glasgow—50 years..after the first train of that name chugged its way out of London. **1842** J. S. Stuart in *Vestiarum Scoticum* Pl. III (*caption*) The Royal Stuart. **1855, 1969** [see *hunting *vbl. sb.* 3 b]. **1975** J. Scarlett *Scotland's Clans & Tartans* 94 The origin of the Royal Stewart tartan is unknown... There is no record of the Royal Stewart sett having borne that name before the nineteenth century—little that it even existed. ..General Stewart of Garth..stage-managed George IV's visit in 1822 and costumed him in 'Royal Stewart'. **1895** W. Stevens *Let.* 4 Aug. (1967) 7 Girls charming lots of money but am always open to engagements in finance where I hold a royal straight. **1907** J. C. Harris in *Uncle Remus's Mag.* Oct. 28/3 The hand I've dealt to you is known as a royal straight flush, an' it sweeps ever' thing before it. **1962** R. Cook *Crust on its Uppers* iii. 40 They're all *diamonds*, ace, king, queen... Suppose he makes royal straight flush? *Ibid.* 41 He hasn't made royal straight. **1902** E. Miles *Racquets, Tennis, & Squash* v. xi. 270 *Note on the name 'Tennis'.*—In Tasmania the game is called Royal Tennis; in England it is occasionally called Real Tennis; and in America it is always called Court Tennis. **1912** G. Inglis *Sport & Pastime in Australia* xii. 175 Tennis—or Royal Tennis as it is often called in Australia—was first introduced into the Commonwealth by Mr. S. S. Travers about 1875... The Hobart court was originally built by Mr Travers as a private court. In 1882 it was taken over by the 'Royal Tennis' Club. **1965** *New Statesman* 6 Aug. 185/1 The royal tennis court, which is enclosed. **1977** *Times* 19 Aug. 12/8 Playing royal tennis at Hampton Court.

c. *royal blue* (earlier example), *green, purple* (later examples).

1789 J. WOODFORDE *Diary* 9 Sept. (1927) III. 139, I took 2 Inside Places in the Royal Blue Coach..to London. **1881** C. C. HARRISON *Woman's Handiwork* I. 61 The cushion-cover..has a ground of royal purple velvet. **1902** *Recipes for Colour, Paint, Varnish, Oil, Soap & Drysaltery Trades* i. 36 Royal Green. Prussiate of potash..Sulphate of iron, [etc.]. **1913** C. L. UEBELE *Paintmaking & Color Grinding* x. 171 Foremost in the line of greens is what we [*sc.* Americans] call chrome green, which, however, is known on the other side as Brunswick or royal green, an intimate mixture of chrome yellow and Prussian blue. **1951** R. MAYER *Artist's Hand-bk. Materials & Techniques* ii. 60 *Royal green*, chrome green. **1956** G. DURRELL *My Family & Other Animals* 18 The endless, meticulous curves of the sea flamed for an instant and then changed to a deep royal purple flecked with green.

16. *royal-sized.*

1974 *Publishers Weekly* 26 Aug. 302/1 A royal-sized volume containing a spectacular gallery of 306 illustrations in full colour.

B. *sb.* **2. e.** A name projected, but not adopted, in Great Britain and Australia, for a decimal unit of currency.

1920 *Rep. R. Comm. Decimal Coinage* 11 in *Parl. Papers* (Cmd. 628) XIII. 467 The second scheme (Lord Leverhulme's) proposes the creation of a new unit of 100 halfpennies to be called a Royal. *Ibid.* 12 We must regard the halfpenny and Royal scheme as impracticable. **1962** A. C. AITKEN in *Listener* 26 Jan. 159/1, I would rectify this..by simply having a pound of a dozen shillings. I will call it a 'royal'—for that has the proper sound and connotation, and, besides, a stag of twelve points is a 'royal'. **1963** *Guardian* 6 June 11/2 The Cabinet decided today that Australia's main currency units will be the Royal and the Crown... The royal, equal to 10 of the present Australian shillings, will be subdivided into 100 cents.

3. c. (Earlier example.)

1848 QUEEN VICTORIA *Jrnl.* 18 Sept. (1980) 64 A magnificent stag, 'a royal', which had dropped, soon after Albert had hit him.

5. a. Also, a royal mast.

1937 C. S. FORESTER *Happy Return* I. i. 10 He had.. noted that the wind was from the west, and just strong enough to give the ship steerage way, with all sail set to the royals. **1970** *Parade* (Austral.) June 26/2 The ship must have sunk almost instantly because when she was found two days later, only the top of one of her royals was just visible out of the water.

b. (Earlier and later examples.)

1839 *Knickerbocker* XIII. 42 Send him some ratlinstuff, so that he can set up brace-backstays abaft, and cross his royal yards, and call all hands up anchor. **1927** G. BRADFORD *Gloss. Sea Terms* 146/1 *Royal yard*, the next above the topgallant yard.

7. b. (Later example.)

1977 *Navy News* June 4/1 Next opportunity for the Hermes and 845 Squadron to work with the Royals was during Exercise Dawn patrol in the first weeks of May.

8. Short for *royal blue*.

1885 *Queen* 24 Oct. (Advt.), *Ladies' gloves*... Shades, Tan, Golden, and Royal. *c* **1900** in *American Mail Order Fashions* (1961) 30 *Sweater*, made with alternate stripes.. of..red and royal, or royal with red stripes. **1922** *Daily Mail* 11 Dec. 1 (Advt.), Beautifully made in Duvetyn or Monchon,..Black, Grey, or Royal. **1939** J. B. PRIESTLEY *Let People Sing* iv. 82 It [*sc.* a van] had been generously rather than neatly painted, in a manly scheme of crimson and royal. **1974** *Harper's & Queen* Sept. 35/1 Crêpe dress. Black, sand, mink, red, emerald or royal.

9. *ellipt.* for: **a.** The Royal Society. Also *attrib.* **b.** The Royal Show (of the Royal Agricultural Society).

1951 C. P. SNOW *Masters* v. 45 There's not been a day pass in the last three years when he hasn't reminded me that he is a Fellow of the Royal, and that I am not. *Ibid.* 49 He would not get into the Royal Society now. But as March came round each year, he waited for the announcement of the Royal elections. **1958** *Spectator* 27 June 829/2 The Royal is the shop-window of British farming. **1966** 'W. COOPER' *Mem. New Man* II. vi. 172, I was not agreeing off the cuff that Bill's getting into the Royal would necessarily enhance his prospects. **1975** *Country Life* 26 June 1676/1 Beneath the surface of a highly professional modern 'Royal', one may sense the old-time garden-party atmosphere... Verona and the Royal Show are each unique in their own way because they have evolved.

‖ **royale** (rwayāl). [Fr., lit. 'royal', in same sense.] = IMPERIAL *sb.* 8.

1842 W. C. MACREADY *Diary* 26 May (1912) II. 171 A middle-aged man..with moustache and royale oiled to points which curled up at considerable distance from his face. **1877** E. CREER *Lessons in Hairdressing* 95/2 *Royale* (or *Imperiale*), tuft of beard just below the under lip.

Royalist. Add: **1. a.** *spec.* in Canada, a United Empire Loyalist (see LOYALIST in Dict.).

1785 R. HUNTER *Quebec to Carolina* (1943) 65 The Royalists have settlements along Lake St. Francis and up to Cataraqui. **1972** J. MOSHER *Some would call it Adultery* IV. xxi. 176 'Oh, a Royalist, eh?' said the admiral, using the Yankee term for United Empire Loyalist, as they were known in Canada.

royalty. Add: **6. c.** Also, a payment made, or a portion of the production given, by a producer of minerals, oil, or natural gas to the owner of the site or of the mineral rights over it. Also *attrib.*

1896 B. REDWOOD *Petroleum* I. v. 250 Such leases are often transferred at a larger royalty, especially after the territory has been proved productive. **1949** *Our Industry* (Anglo-Iranian Oil Co.) (ed. 2) i. 8 Oil companies wishing to prospect in a foreign country have first to make an agreement with the Government of that country... This agreement determines the royalties payable. **1971** WILLIAMS & MEYERS *Oil & Gas Terms* (ed. 3) 390 The landowner's royalty is typically 1/8th of production. **1977** *Time* 5 Dec. 59/1 What had really blown was a giant natural-gas well that probably will make Lucy and her husband, Walter Parlange, royalty rich.

e. (Earlier and later examples.)

1857 MRS. GASKELL *Let.* 26 Nov. (1966) 484 He was to have the sale of them for three years..paying me a royalty of 3d on each copy sold. **1867** J. SPEDDING *Publishers & Authors* 25 In order to translate the substance of the bargain into a percentage upon the sale, (or a 'royalty', as we call it,) it is only necessary to divide the total estimated profit by the number of copies through the sale of which it is to be made. **1875** HARDY *Let.* 4 Nov. (1978) I. 40 Name of book. Copies sold in the half year. Retail price of same. 10 per cent royalty. **1974** R. RENDELL *Face of Trespass* iv. 43 He began worrying about his royalty statement. *a* **1976** A. CHRISTIE *Autobiogr.* (1977) VI. iv. 318, I had not kept any of the royalty statements sent me.

f. A periodic payment for the right or privilege of using another person's know-how under a know-how or trade secrets agreement.

1962 *Conveyancer* XXVI. 368 Some sort of lump-sum payment on the signing of the agreement will usually be appropriate, since it must be recognised that the seller runs a risk when he hands over the initial batch of information and documents. Beyond that, it is common to provide for some sort of royalty on turnover. *Ibid.* 369 The seller..will be willing to accept a reasonably widely drawn royalty clause on the basis that if the seller's methods turn out to be usable..they are certain to incorporate a good deal of indispensable information. **1973** J. P. CUNNINGHAM *Competition Law of E.E.C.* viii. 172 The know-how agreements between Happich and Gallino and between Happich and Maglum contained provisions requiring the licensees to pay royalties to Happich.

7. d. *Ir.* (See quot.)

App. a nonce-use based on Ir. *Ráth na Ríoghradh* the rath of the royalty, a name for the rath at Tara (A. J. Bliss).

1893 W. B. YEATS *Celtic Twilight* 104 They came to a royalty (a name for the little circular ditches, commonly called raths or forts, with which Ireland is covered since Pagan times).

royster, var. ROISTER.

roz (rǫz), abbrev. *ROZZER.

1971 J. WAINWRIGHT *Dig Grave* 79 Not that he gave a fart about the roz crowd. **1977** —— *Do Nothin'* v. 83 The roz has removed his helmet.

rozener, var. *ROSINER.

rozzer (rǫ·zəɹ). *slang.* [Origin unknown.] A policeman, a detective.

1893 P. H. EMERSON *Signor Lippo* xviii. 87 If the rozzers was to see him in bona clobber they'd take him for a gun. **1903** A. M. BINSTEAD *Pitcher in Paradise* iii. 75 He..nearly knocked down the rozzer in the mackintosh suit who was regulating the traffic from the middle of the road. **1936** M. ALLINGHAM *Flowers for Judge* xiii. 193 Aven't seen 'er since she went off with a rozzer. **1942** WODEHOUSE *Money in Bank* (1946) xiv. 126 You mean a rozzer? A detective? **1958** E. HYAMS *Taking it Easy* III. iii. 298 Then some nosy rozzer come up on a motorbike. **1962** R. GORDON *Doctor in Swim* v. 36 You can always try a bit of give and take with an English rozzer, and no hard feelings. **1977** 'E. CRISPIN' *Glimpses of Moon* xii. 236 The rozzers were after him, not a doubt about that.

r-process: see *R III. 7.

-rrhaphy, formative element [ad. Gr. -ῥαφία, f. ῥάπτειν to sew: see -Y[3]], used to form words denoting surgical suturing of a wound or part, as *gastrorrhaphy, hysterorrhaphy*.

-rrhoea, -rrhea, formative element [ad. Gr. -ρροια (as in διάρροια DIARRHŒA, γονόρροια GONORRHŒA), f. ῥοία flux, flow], used in various medical terms, as *LOGORRHŒA, MUCORRHŒA.

Rualla (ru͵a·lă), *sb.* and *a.* Also **Ruála, Ruwalla,** etc. **A.** *sb.* A Bedouin people; a member of this people. **B.** *adj.* Of or pertaining to this people.

1831 J. L. BURCKHARDT *Notes on Bedouins & Wahábys* I. 6 *El Raualla*..generally occupy the desert from Djebel Shammar towards the Djof, and thence towards the southern vicinity of the Hauran; but they frequently encamp between the Tigris and Euphrates. **1875** *Encycl. Brit.* II. 247/2 First, the Anezah clan, whose pasture-grounds extend from Syria southward to the limits of Jebel Shomer... Their principal subdivisions are the Sebaá on the north, the Woold-Alee on the west, and the Ruála on the south. **1888** C. M. DOUGHTY *Trav. Arabia Deserta* I. vii. 194 The poor man had been maimed thus by a Ruwàlla lance-thrust in the mouth, when riding in the North. **1917** [see *HOWEITAT]. **1918** T. E. LAWRENCE *Lett.* (1938) 248 We decided to carry out a flying attack.. with our regular troops, the Rualla horse.., and such Hauran peasants as should be brave enough to declare for us. **1926** —— *Seven Pillars* (1935) III. xxx. 174 His was the chief family of the Rualla, but Nuri had no precedence among them at birth, nor was he loved. *Ibid.*, One of the chief men of the Ruwalla. **1959** W. THESIGER *Arabian Sands* iii. 54 In Syria I..had visited the summer camp of the Rualla, a city of black tents.

ruana (ru͵ā·nă). [Amer. Sp.] A type of Colombian and Peruvian cape or poncho.

1942 F. CARPENTER *Our S. Amer. Neighbors* iii. 63 Men and women dressed in elegant clothes..meet Indians wearing native straw hats, and bright home-woven ponchos which are here called 'ruanas'. **1971** *Sat. Rev.* (U.S.) 31 July 55/2 'Knee-rugs' (about 38" × 54") which double for long skirts, ruanas, jumpers. **1974** *Times* 22 Aug. 9/3 Macindo..[is] an ethnic shop specializing in the handwork of the Northern Andes... For the winter there will be heavier wool ponchos, ruanas and serapes. **1977** *Western Living* (Vancouver) Apr. 28/3 The women folk [in Peru], dressed in broad full length skirts, rainbow coloured *ruanas* (cape-like shawls) and a variety of masculine hats.

Ruanda, var. *RWANDA.

rub, *sb.*[1] Add: **1. d.** *Naval slang.* A loan *of*. Also const. *at*.

1914 'BARTIMEUS' *Naval Occasions* xxi. 193 'Don't you take on, Taff,' said another, pushing over his pannikin of rum. ''Ave a rub at this lot.' **1919** W. LANG *Sea Lawyer's Log* xiii. 162 'Innyone as hasn't had a letter can have a rub of mines,' says Moriarty, the big Irishman, generously. **1946** J. IRVING *Royal Navalese* 147 'The rub of a dollar' means the loan of a dollar. **1948** PARTRIDGE *Dict. Forces' Slang* 158 Give us a rub of five bob till pay day!

2. c. Also *fig.*

1931 *Times Lit. Suppl.* 31 Dec. 1048/4 If he is unfortunate in having finished his task before his problem was knocked completely out of shape by England's suspension of the gold standard, that is just the 'rub of the green'. **1962** *Guardian* 5 Nov. 2/2 If applications.. reached fantastic proportions, the Government would have to consider the matter. 'At present we treat it as a rub of the green.'

8. A sound as of rubbing.

1907 R. H. BABCOCK *Dis. Lungs* xxvi. 511 If the chest be examined a friction-rub is likely to be detected on the side corresponding to the pain... The symptoms are the result of a dry, circumscribed pleurisy. *Ibid.* xxxv. 726 The so-called pleuritic friction sound or pleuritic rub..is a succession of fine crackling sounds..produced by the separation of the two pleural surfaces or by their rubbing together when rendered sticky. **1950** *Audio Engin.* Aug. 15/3 When the cause of the noise is mechanical, as in defective or ill-designed speakers, pickups and microphones, we may hear rattles,..rub, and wheeze. **1976** *Lancet* 13 Nov. 1083/1 Bronchial breath sounds and a pleural rub were present over the right middle lobe.

9. Special Combs.: **rub resistance,** the degree to which print will withstand rubbing without becoming smudged or detached; so **rub-resistant** *a.*

1958 E. A. APPS *Printing Ink Technol.* xxvii. 431 A high standard of rub-resistance is necessary in inks used for food cartons which are jostled in transport, and for display cards which are frequently handled. *Ibid.* 432 Inks which tend to give gloss and very level films are also usually fairly rub-resistant. **1967** E. CHAMBERS *Photolitho-Offset* xvi. 240 Anti-driers retard drying on the machine and modifiers such as waxes and oils control setting, flow,..and rub-resistance.

rub, *v.*[1] Add: **I. 1. c.** (Further examples.) Also *fig.*

1922 JOYCE *Ulysses* 324 The *Times* rubbed its hands and told the whitelivered Saxons there would soon be as few Irish in Ireland as redskins in America. **1966** *Listener* 30 June 936/1 The British Government has invested half a million pounds on this display of international sport and the London hotel-keepers are rubbing their hands. **1973** *Times* 30 Apr. 5/4 Cloth manufacturers of all sorts must be rubbing their hands just now, because fashion definitely calls now for a greater volume of material per garment.

5. a. Joc. phr. *not to have two pennies to rub together*, and varr., expressing lack of money or poverty.

1929 M. DE LA ROCHE *Whiteoaks* vii. 98 George, like Finch, was always hard up. Sometimes they had not between them two coins to rub together. **1977** K. O'HARA *Ghost of T. Penry* xvii. 172 I've known Mrs Bathhurst without two pennies to rub together, and always..concerned about others.

b. *to rub shoulders with* (further examples.) Also *to rub elbows (with)* (chiefly *U.S.*).

1851 CARLYLE *Life J. Sterling* I. viii. 74 One right peal of concrete laughter at some convicted flesh-and-blood absurdity, one burst of noble indignation at some injustice or depravity, rubbing elbows with us on this solid Earth. **1906** U. SINCLAIR *Jungle* xxvi. 327 Young white girls from the country rubbing elbows with big buck Negroes with daggers in their boots. **1916** L. N. PARKER *Disraeli* II. 56 You would pass him in the street without the faintest idea you had rubbed elbows with one of the world's greatest powers! **1922** JOYCE *Ulysses* 497 Have we cold feet about the cosmos? No... You have that something within, the higher self. You can rub shoulders with a Jesus, a Gautama, an Ingersoll. **1946** MEZZROW & WOLFE *Really Blues* ii. 21, I got my kicks out of rubbing elbows with all those bigtime gamblers. **1956** B. HOLIDAY *Lady sings Blues* (1973)

i. 8 A whorehouse was about the only place where black and white folks could meet in any natural way. They damn well couldn't rub elbows in the churches. **1961** in WEBSTER s.v. *rub* vb., Reports on social products rub shoulders with book reviews and notes. **1976** E. MACLAREN *Nature of Belief* iii. 20 I'm rubbing shoulders with questions of religious philosophy all the time. **1979** *Yale Alumni Mag.* Apr. (Suppl.) cn20/3 As a piano played show tunes of the 1930's, Teng rubbed elbows with George Weyerhauser of the Weyerhauser Co.

d. *to rub noses* (*with*), to touch noses in greeting, in token of friendship. Also *fig.*

This custom was practised among Eskimos, Maoris (see *HONGI *sb.*), and elsewhere in the Pacific Islands. Among Eskimos it has practically died out.

1822 G. F. LYON *Jrnl.* 28 July (1824) vi. 247 When the principal [Eskimo dancer] had pretty well exhausted himself, he walked gravely up to him, and taking his head between his hands, rubbed noses with him amidst the plaudits of all present. **1832** A. EARLE *Narr. Residence N.Z.* 159 He..rubbed noses so forcibly with me that I felt his friendship for some time. **1858** R. M. BALLANTYNE *Coral Island* xx. 242 Tararo went up to Jack and rubbed noses with him... Seeing that this was their mode of salutation..we rubbed noses heartily with the whole party. **1891** [in Dict., sense 5 b]. **1945** D. LEECHMAN *Eskimo Summer* 240 Before they had much contact with white men, the Eskimos used to rub noses on meeting old friends after a protracted absence. **1964** MRS. L. B. JOHNSON *White House Diary* 15 June (1970) 169 Lynda Bird..had enjoyed Hawaii hugely, rubbing noses with Maori children. **1973** 'D. JORDAN' *Nile Green* xx. 82 He's got three daughters and an Eskimo au pair girl... It's all this rubbing noses... It gets him down.

e. *to rub one's nose in it*: see *NOSE *sb.* 9 e.

II. 11. *rub out*: **a.** (Further *fig.* examples.)

1936 E. AMBLER *Dark Frontier* vii. 111 Rovzidski rubbed out by Red Gauntlet mob... Government fail to take action against slayers. **1946** L. B. LYON *Rough Walk Home* 24 Again the random child by robot thumb Of war rubbed out. **1950** A. LOMAX *Mr. Jelly Roll* 220 The gangsters..had promised to rub him out if he didn't stop trying to hire away their star New Orleans side-men. **1957** WODEHOUSE *Over Seventy* xii. 125 The heavy goes to his asylum, and two months later is released as cured. Upon which, he dresses up as a Siberian wolf-hound and hurries off to rub out another citizen. **1961** B. FERGUSSON *Watery Maze* xiv. 333 The first task was to destroy the enemy's radar organisation, and the R.A.F. addressed themselves to the job of rubbing out as many stations as they could. **1979** E. NEWMAN *Sunday Punch* xxiv. 214, I learned what the man muttered when the fight ended and Aubrey was declared the winner. It was: 'That Philpott-Grimes. I maybe rub him out.'

13. *rub up*: **e.** Also *ellipt.* without *the wrong way*.

1882 E. W. HAMILTON *Diary* 31 Aug. (1972) I. 328 Lord Dufferin is half inclined to advise that we should concede this to them in order not to rub up the Sultan more than we can help. **1971** *Weekend World* (Johannesburg) 9 May 6/7 Judges, magistrates, prosecutors, defence lawyers treat everybody alike, but the minor officials sure know how to rub up a non-White.

f. To caress (a person) in order to excite him or her sexually. *slang.*

1656 R. FLETCHER tr. *Martial's Epigrams* II. 102 Me thinks I scarcely am wound up by thee..to the height of Venerie... Thus Phillis rub me up, thus tickle mee. **1937** PARTRIDGE *Dict. Slang* 710/2 *Rub up*,..so to caress a person that he or she becomes actively amorous. **1939** JOYCE *Finnegans Wake* (1964) I. 203 Rubbing her up and smoothing her down, he baised his lippes in smiling mood.

g. To make clean, clear, or bright (again) by rubbing.

1847 C. BRONTË *Jane Eyre* III. viii. 183 My first aim will be..to *clean down* Moor House..; my next to rub it up with bees-wax, oil, and..cloths, till it glitters again. **1859** MRS. STOWE *Minister's Wooing* xviii. 179 He rubbed up his optical instruments to see whether they were rising in right order. **1886** F. R. STOCKTON *Casting away of Mrs. Lecks & Mrs. Aleshine* III. 111 In the mornin' I'll rub up that floor till it's as bright as new. **1974** A. ROSS *Bradford Business* 76 Even the short heavy bolts had been rubbed up with a wire brush.

III. 14. d. *to rub up*: to masturbate. *slang.*

1937 PARTRIDGE *Dict. Slang* 710/2 *Rub up*, the v. corresponding to *rub off*, 2 [*sc.* a masturbation]. **1963** C. MACKENZIE *My Life & Times* II. 115 Just as I was going down the steps into our area B— asked me if I ever rubbed up... In bed that night I tried the experiment recommended by B—.

e. *to rub off*, of qualities, etc.: to have influence *on* through close or continued contact; to be transmitted to others.

1959 N. MAILER *Advts. for Myself* v. 463 He spent years hobnobbing with gentlemanly shits and half-ass operators and some of it had to rub off on him. **1965** *Listener* 11 Nov. 761/1 There is no evidence that anything of Sickert's powerful teaching rubbed off on him. **1969** 'G. NORTH' *Procrastination of Sgt. Cluff* v. 44 How long was it since he'd begun to work with the Sergeant? How much of the Sergeant had rubbed off on him? Could he think any more except as the Sergeant thought? **1971** *Times* 9 Sept. 3/2 One hopes that something of their Christian charity and principles would rub off. **1976** E. MACLAREN *Nature of Belief* ii. 16 Jews come in contact with Zoroastrians and certain ideas rub off. **1978** *Jrnl. R. Soc. Arts* CXXVI. 185/1 Morale was lower, there was apathy and this was rubbing off on new entries.

18. rub-board, (*b*) *N.Amer.*, a wash-board; **rub rail,** a rail to protect (a vehicle, etc.) against rubbing.

1964 *Amer. Folk Music Occasional* I. 28 Clifton Chenies is no doubt the best known of the so-called 'Zydeco' musicians. This music..usually features the accordion with drum or rub-board accompaniment. **1972** *Daily Colonist* (Victoria, B.C.) 13 Feb. 22/2 Building furniture and washing clothes on a rub board in a small tub. **1961** WEBSTER, Rub rail. **1969** *Jane's Freight Containers 1968–69* 550/2 Products: G-85 fifth wheel container and general purpose trailer with cushioned rub rails. **1980** *Reader's Digest* Feb. 226/2 The car skidded..25 feet up the bridge, jumped a 5½-inch-high rub rail and hurtled..into the water.

rubabah, var. *REBAB.

rubaboo, var. *RUBBABOO.

rub-a-dub, *sb.* Add: **2.** A pub, a hotel. *Austral.* and *N.Z. rhyming slang.*

c **1926** 'MIXER' *Transport Workers' Song Bk.* 81, I gazed upon the motley crowd Within this 'rub-a-dub'. **1963** H. SLESAR *Bridge of Lions* iii. 52 He could fathom why rub-a-dub meant a pub.

So **rub-a-dub-dub** (*b*) in same sense.

1941 [see *RUBBEDY]. **1945** BAKER *Austral. Lang.* xv. 270 A hotel becomes known in rhyming slang as a *rub-a-dub-dub*—by rhyme on 'pub'. **1971** *National Times* (Austral.) 13 Dec. 20 'Let's grab some Kate and Sydney and a pint of apple fritter at the rub-a-dub-dub.'.. Translated: 'Let's grab some steak and kidney and a pint of bitter at the pub.'

‖ **ruba'i** (rubā·,ī). Also **ruba'iy.** Pl. **rubaiyat** (rū·bai(y)at, rū·bei(y)at). [Arabic *rubā'īy-ah*, f. *rubā'īy* composed of four elements.] In Persian poetry, a quatrain.

The pl. is chiefly familiar in the title of the work by Omar Khayyam (cf. *OMARIAN *a.* and *sb.*), known to English speakers in FitzGerald's version.

1859 E. FITZGERALD *Rubáiyát of Omar Khayyám* p. xii, The original Rubáiyát (as, missing an Arabic Guttural, these *Tetrastichs* are more musically called), are independent Stanzas, consisting each of four Lines of equal, though varied, Prosody; sometimes *all* rhyming, but oftener (as here attempted) the third line suspending the Cadence by which the last atones with the former Two. **1885** *Encycl. Brit.* XVIII. 656/1 Those principal forms of poetry now used in common by all Mohammedan nations—the forms of..the *rubá'í* or quatrain (our epigram, for which the Persians invented a new metre in addition to those adopted from the Arabs), [etc.]. **1934** [see *QASIDA]. **1959** *Chambers's Encycl.* X. 202/1 *Omar Khayyam*.., Persian poet and master of the *ruba'i* (quatrain)... The *Rubaiyat* have now been translated into almost all the literary languages of the world.

Rubarth's disease (rū·bāɹt). *Vet. Sci.* [Named after C. S. *Rubarth* (b. 1905), Swedish veterinary scientist, who described it in 1947 (*Acta Path. & Microbiol. Scand.* Suppl. No. 69).] An infectious disease of dogs, caused by an adenovirus, that affects chiefly the liver and is sometimes fatal; infectious canine hepatitis.

1951 *Vet. Record* 15 Dec. 833/2 We wish..to place before you certain data which we have been able to collect..regarding virus hepatitis in dogs, or Rubarth's disease, within our own kennels. **1961** C. H. D. TODD *Popular Whippet* x. 147 There are four common canine diseases, viz. two virus diseases—distemper (including hard pad variety) and Rubarths disease (a liver affection), and two bacterial diseases which affect the kidneys. **1970** A. R. JENNINGS *Animal Path.* vi. 118 Intranuclear inclusion bodies are a feature of Rubarth's disease and the inclusions have diagnostic significance.

‖ **rubashka** (ruba·ʃkă). Pl. **rubashkas, rubashki.** [Russ.] A type of blouse or tunic worn in Russia.

The pl. *rubashka* in quot. 1956 is *erron.*

1921 *Glasgow Herald* 29 Nov. 6 In North Russia during the summer the men, young and old, clean-shaven or whiskered and bearded, wear rubashkas, or blouses, of various colours, some of them even set off with touches of bright embroidery. **1924** *Blackw. Mag.* Feb. 149/1 She had opened her khaki rubashka and shown the subaltern the scar. **1956** WALLIS & BLAIR *Thunder Above* (1959) ii. 11 An orchestra, colourful in their rich silk *rubashka*, providing music that seemed to flow from the Volga. **1972** *Nat. Geographic* Sept. 401 The bearded men wore *rubashki*, the hand-embroidered blouses of old Russia.

rubato. Add: (rubā·to). (Earlier and later examples.) Also *transf.*

1883 GROVE *Dict. Mus.* III. 188/1 *Rubato*,..referring to the values of the notes, which are diminished in one place and increased in another. **1921** G. SAMPSON *English* III. 94 The natural *rubato* of civilised speech. **1925** J. A. JOHNSTONE (*title*) Rubato, or the secret of expression in pianoforte playing. **1946** J. CARY *Moonlight* ii. 9 Her old-fashioned style, indeed, with its exaggerated rubato, her swayings, murmurings, tosses of the head, might have amused or disgusted a modern audience. **1955** *Times* 9 May 3/7 His use of rubato sounded nonchalant instead of expressive in Mozart. **1977** *N.Y. Rev. Bks.* 13 Oct. 6/2 He remarks that Victorians had moved away from the hard clear notes of Wordsworth's *Lyrical Ballads*: the ballad had moved into the rubato and vibrato of the drawing room. **1979** *Early Music* July 341/1 In the Vivaldi example the *fermate* over the semiquaver rests can only be indications of *rubato*.

rubbaboo (rʌbăbū·). Also **rababoo, robiboo, rubaboo, rubeiboo,** etc. *N. Amer.* (*Obs.* exc. *Hist.*) [ult. ad. Algonquian.] A kind of soup or porridge made from pemmican.

1821 N. GARRY *Diary* 22 Aug. in *Trans. R. Soc. Canada* (1900) VI. 151 Our men are now eating Rababoo made of Pemican and Flour. **1857** P. JACOBS *Jrnl.* 72 The food that is generally prepared and eaten in these regions by voyagers is what is called 'ahrubuhboo'. I do not know what the word itself means. I spell it as I hear it pronounced. **1862** R. KENNICOTT *Jrnl.* Jan. in J. A. James *First Sci. Exploration Russ. Amer.* (1942) ii. 85 Rubbaboo is a favorite dish with the northern voyageurs, when they can get it. It consists simply of pemmican made into a kind of soup by boiling in water. Flour is added when it can be obtained, and it is generally considered more palatable with a little sugar. **1865** MILTON & CHEADLE *N.-W. Passage by Land* xv. 289 Our fare was what the half-breeds call 'rubaboo', which we made by boiling a piece of pemmican the size of one's fist in a large quantity of water thickened with a single handful of flour. **1881** E. S. FARROW *Mountain Scouting* xiii. 200 When required for use, it [*sc.* pemmican] is cut from the hard mass and either eaten cold, or is mixed with flour forming a porridge called '*robiboo*'. **1935** *Beaver* Sept. 135 One of the tastiest forms, and one more often mixed than any other for table use, was 'rubeiboo', consisting of pemmican boiled down with a mixture of potatoes, onions and other vegetables. This, when properly seasoned, was very palatable. **1969** E. W. MORSE *Fur Trade Canoe Routes* I. ii. 23 The pemmican was either sliced off and munched raw, or made with flour and water into a *potage* called 'rubbaboo'.

rubbedy, rubberdy, rubbidy (rʌ·bə(ɹ)di), altered f. *RUB-A-DUB *sb.* 2. Cf. *RUBBITY. *Austral.*

1941 BAKER *Dict. Austral. Slang* 62 *Rubberdy*.., a public house. Rhyming slang on 'rub-a-dub-dub' for 'pub'. **1957** D. NILAND *Call me when Cross turns Over* iv. 101 How about a gargle? Down to the rubberdy, come on. **1962** 'D. FORREST' *Hollow Woodheap* i. 11 'Where..is "The Eagle on the Hill"?' 'A rubbedy in South Australia.' **1969** *Melbourne Herald* 8 May 15, I was having a gargle with a cobber in a Fleet St. rubbedy. **1970** K. GILES *Murder Pluperfect* ii. 46, I met another of the Fennels down at the rubbidy. **1971** *Australian Post* 8 Apr. 40/5 There's the story of the barman in the rubbedy.

rubber, *sb.*[1] Add: **I. 4. b.** (Earlier example.)

1816 W. Y. OTTLEY *Inquiry Origin & Early Hist. Engraving* I. 81 The friction of a rubber, made of hair, or of pieces of cloth, was then applied to the paper, which was thus rubbed backwards and forwards till the impression of the engraving was transferred to the paper.

c. An article usu. consisting of a soft pad attached to a wooden handle, used for erasing chalk from a blackboard.

1880 [see *BLACKBOARD]. **1978** P. MARSH et al. *Rules of Disorder* ii. 38 They just started..chucking wooden dice at her..and blackboard rubbers.

6. Also,† a brake acting by friction on the wheels of a vehicle.

1850 R. GLISAN *Jrnl. Army Life* (1874) iv. 32 The third one [*sc.* vehicle], having no rubbers or brakes to the wheels, went so fast, down a steep hill, that the driver was thrown from his seat. **1894** T. B. SEARIGHT *Old Pike* 145 The 'rubber', called brake at this day, was not in use when the National Road was first thrown open for trade and travel. Instead,..saplings, cut at the summit of the hills, were shaped and fashioned to answer the ends of the 'rubber', and at the foot of the hills taken off and left on the roadside.

7. (Further examples.)

1898 *19th Ann. Rep. U.S. Geol. Survey* VI. B. 407 A second kind, and one much used in London for fronts, is a large, light-red brick, so soft as to be readily scratched by the knife. These are called 'rubbers'. **1977** *Listener* 20 Oct. 519/4 There is quality, too, in the kind of bricks still known as 'rubbers'—ones that have been hand-rubbed on all surfaces to achieve an immaculate join.

II. 8. a. *spec.* one who massages sportsmen or athletes (chiefly *N. Amer.*).

1895 J. L. WILLIAMS *Princeton Stories* 185 Another sub and William, the negro rubber, picked Wormsey up. **1911** *Daily Colonist* (Victoria, B.C.) 6 Apr. 9/5 A 'rubber' has been engaged by Manager Wattalet. Perhaps the use of such a term would shock the sensibilities of our ball players. The correction, therefore, is made with all haste. It is a 'masseur', who has become attached to the Victoria baseball club. **1949** *Sun* (Baltimore) 14 Oct. 27/6 The schools have hired some of the best men in the training profession. Today, they are not just rubbers; they know anatomy, physiology and chemistry. **1950** J. DEMPSEY *Championship Fighting* xxiv. 192 The 'rubber' (rub-down man) applies soothing lotions to the muscles as he kneads them with his fingers.

III. 11. a. Now also applied to any of a large range of synthetic organic polymers having properties of elasticity, etc., resembling those of natural rubber. (Further examples.)

1912 *Jrnl. Soc. Chem. Industry* 15 July 617/1 There can now be no doubt that rubber may actually be obtained synthetically by the polymerisation of isoprene and its homologues and that the synthetic product is really rubber and strictly comparable with natural rubbers. **1941** *Jrnl. R. Aeronaut. Soc.* XLV. 145 Mechanically, natural rubber is not surpassed by any synthetic rubber. However, in resistance to swelling by organic liquids.. and deterioration by sunlight or oxidising agents, synthetic rubbers have been found superior. **1961** L. MUMFORD *City in Hist.* (1966) xv. 545 The new régime was based on..new synthetic materials, like rubber, bakelite, and the plastics. **1973** *Nature* 6 Apr. 420/1 Natural rubber is still the preferred polymer for many high performance applications.

b. For *U.S.* read 'orig. *U.S.*' and add earlier and later examples; (*b*) plimsolls, esp. plimsolls worn for climbing.

(*a*) **1842** *Southern Lit. Messenger* VIII. 516/2 The *younkers* who would go 'a Maying', very prudently provided themselves with rubbers and tippets before encountering the rough southeaster. **1856** S. ROBINSON *Kansas* xii. 160 The snows..are fast melting, and mingling with the clayey soil. So, besides the burden of rubbers, one has to carry no little portion of the native earth. **1901** *Daily Colonist* (Victoria, B.C.) 22 Oct. 4/6 (Advt.), Special sale of rubbers today at 2.30 p.m. *c* **1921** D. H. LAWRENCE *Mr Noon* iv, in *Mod. Lover* (1934) 221 He went out to his motor-cycle and got it ready. He went indoors and put on his rubbers. **1951** E. PAUL *Springtime in Paris* iii. 53 An umbrella rack with a porcelain tray for rubbers. **1972** J. MINIFIE *Homesteader* xvii. 145 It [*sc.* gumbo] was notorious for its adhesive quality; it stuck to everything, pulled off rubbers—galoshes as people were beginning to call them [in 1914]. **1974** M. Z. LEWIN *Enemies Within* iv. 17 Snow made it look beautiful. I put on my rubbers and walked around. (*b*) **1925** *Jrnl. Fell & Rock Climbing Club* VII. 12 Arrowhead Ridge..Leader needs about 60 feet of rope. Rubbers. **1933** G. D. ABRAHAM *Mod. Mountaineering* v. 107 Rubbers are usually used, but I have also made the ascent in nailed boots, and in either footgear dry rocks are advisable. **1941** C. KIRKUS *Let's go Climbing* vi. 95 A climb of such difficulty is not done in boots, but in rubbers. These are ordinary plimsolls or gym shoes. **1950** T. LONGSTAFF *This my Voyage* xiv. 282 To the right of Kern Knotts Crack is a narrow vertical cracklet... It..is now a recognised climb. It is led, generally in rubbers, without any moral support of a rope from above. **1957** CLARK & PYATT *Mountaineering in Brit.* vii. 134 For the climb,..for which rubbers are recommended, all the party wore boots. **1968** P. CREW *Encycl. Dict. Mountaineering* 103/2 With the advent of P.A.'s and similar footwear, and their widespread use in Britain, the use of rubbers has diminished considerably.

c. Also *collect.*, the tyres of a vehicle; occas. used in colloq. phrases expressing speed or acceleration. Chiefly *U.S.*

a **1961** G. FELSEN in WEBSTER s.v., I'll road test her for you after we get new rubber on. **1976** N. THORNBURG *Cutter & Bone* iv. 91 The huddled figure..going round the car and out of sight for a few moments and then back into it almost immediately and laying down rubber again. **1977** *Hot Car* Oct. 61/1 There really is an incredibly large number of cars and vans cruisin' round on completely the wrong sort of rubber for the type of vehicle. **1980** J. BALL *Then came Violence* (1981) i. 7 Every patrol and supervisory car..would be burning rubber within seconds.

d. A piece of rubber for erasing pencil or ink marks. Also used of erasers made of other substances.

1788–9 [in Dict., sense 11 a]. **1891** *Catal. & Price List* (Waterlow & Sons Ltd.) 169 (*caption*) Artists' Rubber. Stationer's Rubber... Grey Vulcanised Rubber. **1907** A. E. ZAPF *Cycl. Drawing* I. 14 In making drawings, but little erasing should be necessary. However, in case this is necessary, a soft rubber should be used. **1928** [see *BUNGIE, BUNGY]. **1952** PRICE & BISHOP *Art School Self-Taught* II. iii. 275 For erasing errors, a harder rubber is needed. **1968** F. G. HOLLIDAY *Man. Stationery* v. 113 Erasers are often called 'rubbers', but today a surprisingly small proportion of them actually consists of rubber. **1973** M. AMIS *Rachel Papers* 139 Between my finger and thumb I take a rubber and bounce it up and down on the desk.

e. *U.S. Baseball* (*a*) The home plate; (*b*) the pitcher's plate (now the usual sense).

1891 *Chicago Herald* 5 May 6/1 Those same errors.. hustled two runs over the rubber. **1895** *Evening Star* (Washington, D.C.) 2 Oct. 9/3 Twirler Magee once more tried to 'make good', in a pitching sense, but..he was put out of the running, and Billy Dineen sent to the rubber. **1910** O. JOHNSON *Humming Bird* v. 54 In the breakaway Tyrell, the first to dust the rubber for the Chaperons, selected a hole in the circumambient and poked a buzzer over short. **1919** *Chicago Daily Tribune* 12 Apr. 19/2 An unfairly delivered ball is a ball delivered by the pitcher to the batsman with the bases unoccupied, while no foot is in contact with the rubber. **1950** A. DALEY *Times at Bat* 106 He hit the first pitch a mile... Still seething inwardly he crossed the rubber and returned to the dugout. **1975** *New Yorker* 14 Apr. 92/2 Seaver, too, restored memory—the cold, intelligent gaze; the unwasteful windup; the sudden forward, down-dropping stride off the rubber.

f. *slang.* A contraceptive sheath made of rubber; a condom. Cf. *rubber goods, shop* below.

1947 C. WILLINGHAM *End as Man* xiv. 173 Maybe next time you'll use a rubber. **1955** W. GADDIS *Recognitions* I. v. 184 What are you reading?.. Malthus, for Christ sake... The next thing, you'll be peddling rubbers in the street. **1968** B. TURNER *Sex Trap* viii. 53, I need more rubbers. There's only enough for about a couple of good days left. **1978** J. IRVING *World According to Garp* iv. 71 'Oh, Garp,' Cushie said. 'Don't you have any *rubbers?*'

12. a. Also used of articles made of synthetic rubber. *rubber apron, band* (hence as *v. trans.*), *bed, boat, bone, boot, bullet, clothing, coat, dinghy, garment, glove, hose* (further examples), *pants, ring* (further examples), *sheet, sheeting, shoddy, shoe, sole, suit, truncheon.*

1926 *Daily Colonist* (Victoria, B.C.) 10 Jan. 7/1 (Advt.), Women's rubber aprons. Save your frocks and save your laundry bills, too. **1977** 'M. UNDERWOOD' *Fatal Trip* xviii. 102 'Caught me just in time,' the pathologist said, peeling off his rubber apron. **1895** *Montgomery Ward Catal.* Spring & Summer 117/1 Cabinet of assorted pure rubber bands for home and office use. Assortment of sizes up to one-half inch wide and 2½ inches in length. **1919** F. HURST *Humoresque* 128 'I asked you why you was like a rubber band.' 'Aw, I give up, Miss Sadie.' ''Cause you're so stretchy, see?' **1947** J. C. RICH *Materials & Methods Sculpture* v. 121 Tape or rubber bands can be used to hold sections of a mold together for casting positives. **1962** D. LESSING *Golden Notebk.* IV. 488, I found a stack of letters rubber-banded together in one corner. **1973** 'E. MCBAIN' *Let's hear It* xv. 216 He removed the rubber band from the roll, and spread the plans on the floor. **1849** N. KINGSLEY *Diary* 26 Oct. (1914) 78 Some of the fellows went in swimming this afternoon by takeing rubber beds. **1943** J. B. PRIESTLEY *Daylight on Saturday* xxix. 219 Sometimes they got into little rubber boats and so weren't found for a day or two. **1976** J. LEE *Ninth Man* 5 The billowy outlines of the rubber boat, rapidly filling with air. **1949** N. STREATFEILD *Painted Garden* v. 48 His spare collar and lead, his water bowl, his rubber bone. **1973** E. LEMARCHAND *Let or Hindrance* viii. 91 A dog basket with a rubber bone in it. **1852** S. C. DAVIS *Jrnl.* 16 Dec. in B. A. Richards *Calif. Gold Rush Merchant* (1956) 85 Arrived at San Francisco and purchased 200 books, pamphlets, magazines, &c., also some Rubber Boots, &c. **1975** *Ecology* LVI. 538/1 In very dry years the whole bog surface..may be dry enough to walk on without rubber boots. **1971** *Guardian* 14 June 1/8 The soldiers, wearing gas masks and riot helmets, fired nine rounds of rubber bullets. **1976** P. FERRIS *Detective* viii. 150 You're half hoping I've got..a patrol group coming in with gas and rubber bullets. **1980** *Jrnl. R. Soc. Arts* July 486/1 Fire hoses as favoured on the Continent or rubber bullets favoured by the Army in Ireland. **1895** *Montgomery Ward Catal.* Spring & Summer 296/3 Medium and heavy weight rubber clothing. **1967** G. FREEMAN *Undergrowth of Lit.* x. 151 Talcum powder is also useful to apply to the body before squeezing into rubber clothing. **1850** N. KINGSLEY *Diary* 21 Nov. (1914) 157, I put on my Rubber Coat and built a chimney outside the tent. *a* **1918** G. STUART *40 Yrs. on Frontier* (1925) I. 69 Rubber coats and shoes were unknown at that time. **1939** Rubber dinghy [see *DINGHY 2 c]. **1953** *News Chron.* 2 June 2/6 Nothing had been forgotten by the crowds... Even rubber dinghies had been brought to keep off the rain. **1973** E. LEMARCHAND *Let or Hindrance* v. 54 Can't we get hold of an RAF rubber dinghy, or inflatable raft? **1921** *Dict. Occup. Terms* (1927) §608 Garment maker, rubber. **1967** G. FREEMAN *Undergrowth of Lit.* x. 152 There is a wide belief among women that sweating in rubber garments makes them slim. **1895** *Montgomery Ward Catal.* Spring & Summer 297/1 Ladies' Rubber Gloves... Men's Rubber Gloves. **1914** 'E. BRAMAH' *Max Carrados* 96 Here is a rubber glove. I have cut the wire but you had better put it on. **1932** E. HEMINGWAY *Death in Afternoon* xii. 138 The doctor..picked up the pistol in his rubber gloves. **1975** *Listener* 24 July 125/3, I have peeled off my rubber gloves and put the Fairy Liquid back on the shelf. **1939** *N.Y. Sunday News* 4 June 68/3 What do you think, they're using a rubber hose on her? Piffle! **1976** H. TRACY *Death in Reserve* xii. 100 Why don't you get your bloody rubber hoses out and your hallucinogens..and your flashing lights. **1897** *Sears, Roebuck Catal.* 783/3 Rubber pants. **1936** F. M. FORD *Let.* 6 Sept. (1965) 261 She [*sc.* Pennsylvania] led the Universe in the production of rubber pants. **1895** *Montgomery Ward Catal.* Spring & Summer 537/3 Rubber rings, for Mason fruit jars. **1970** W. H. PARKER *Health & Dis. in Farm Animals* v. 50 A more recent method of 'bloodless castration' is the use of the rubber ring. **1976** H. TRACY *Death in Reserve* xix. 146 Free bucket-and-spade, beachballs, rubber rings. **1922** *Encycl. Brit.* XXXII. 300/1 In very exacting work, such as the vulcanizing of hard-rubber sheets, curing is effected by immersion of the material in hot water. **1957** *Ibid.* XIX. 610/1 The rubber sheet is firmly pressed against the prepared fabric. **1966** MAY & MOSS *New Math for Adults Only* xii. 71/2 Such geometry..is known as topology. Youngsters call it rubber-sheet geometry because the figures can be twisted and stretched and still remain the same. **1975** I. STEWART *Concepts Mod. Math.* x. 144 Topology is sometimes described as 'rubber-sheet geometry', a whimsical and somewhat misleading description. **1976** M. MILLAR *Ask for me Tomorrow* (1977) xiii. 107 She gave him a sponge bath..on a rubber sheet on the bed. **1895** *Montgomery Ward Catal.* Spring & Summer 108/2 Nursery rubber sheeting. **1965** M. THOMAS *Grannies' Remedies* 16 Another..poultice is a piece of soft thick sheet-lint..squeezed out in hot water, and laid over the part, covered with a larger piece of thin rubber-sheeting. **1907** *Sci. Amer.* 5 Oct. 240/2 Scrap rubber, or rubber 'shoddy' as it is called, is made up principally of worn-out boots and shoes. **1844** *Knickerbocker* XXIV. 287 Old rubber-shoes! old rubber-shoes! Humble theme for heavenly muse! **1931** M. ALLINGHAM *Look to Lady* xvii. 178 They heard the soft scrape of his rubber shoes on the bole of the tree. **1897** *Sears, Roebuck Catal.* 208/1 Royal rubber soles. **1901** E. W. HORNUNG *Black Mask* vi. 112 There had been no warning step.. and my suspicious eye had searched his feet for rubber soles. **1975** G. SEYMOUR *Harry's Game* iv. 66 A night patrol, their faces blackened, rubber soles on their shoes. **1948** H. INNES *Blue Ice* viii. 205 Sweating underwater in a rubber suit. **1931** M. ALLINGHAM *Look to Lady* v. 66 A small but wicked looking rubber truncheon and..[a] Colt revolver. **1959** J. BRAINE *Vodi* iv. 69 They beat him up with rubber truncheons. The marks don't show. **1973** W. FAIRCHILD *Swiss Arrangement* viii. 94 Give this one a pair of jackboots..and he'd be just like the rest... Drench you with charm first and, if that failed, slug you with a rubber truncheon.

c. *rubber addict, latex, plantation, shop, substitute.*

1967 G. FREEMAN *Undergrowth of Lit.* x. 152 To the rubber addict 'slimwear' is a key word. **1907** *Chem. Abstr.* I. 1326 (*heading*) On the action of iodine and bromine on the resins in rubber latex. **1972** *Materials & Technol.* V. iv. 80 Rubber latex is not naturally very stable: the rubber particles coagulate spontaneously in course of time. **1911** *Encycl. Brit.* XXIII. 798/2 The experience of planters in general is in favour of the complete removal of weeds from a rubber plantation. **1948** M. LASKI *Tory Heaven* i. 6 James had..been sent to try his luck on an uncle's rubber-plantation in Malaya. **1923** in M. Box *Trial of Marie Stopes* (1967) 166 A. As a matter of fact..these things have been used by the hundreds... *Q.* Bought at rubber shops, rubber goods' shops? *Ibid.* 254 Contraceptives are for sale at what have been called, I think, rubber shops? **1936** 'G. ORWELL' *Keep Aspidistra Flying* i. 13 He'd slink into one of the rubber-shops and buy *High Jinks in a Parisian Convent.* **1940** GRAVES & HODGE *Long Week-End* vii. 105 Contraception['s]..association with the pornographic literature of rubber-shops. **1911** Rubber substitute [see *artificial rubber* s.v. *ARTIFICIAL *a.* 5]. **1935** *Chambers's Encycl.* VI. 123/2 Paints, varnishes, rubber-substitutes, oil-cloth, soft soap, &c.

13. a. *rubber-planter.*

1937 *Discovery* May 143/2 The rubber planter uses coconut shells for collecting the raw latex from his trees.

b. Also with vbl. sbs., as *rubber-collecting.*

1910 *Blackw. Mag.* May 729/1 Rubber-collecting is less laborious, but takes you into dangerous parts.

c. *rubber-boned, -booted, -caped, -coated, -cored, -cushioned, -faced, -gloved, -insulated, -jointed, -legged, -lipped, -mounted, -mouthed, -necked, -soled* (further examples), *-stoppered, -tipped, -tired* (later *fig.* examples), *-treaded.*

1958 *New Statesman* 22 Feb. 227/2 Especially fantastic is the dance of a rubber-boned neighbour (Stephen Preston). **1943** J. W. DAY *Farming Adventure* xx. 228, I dined and went down to the quay, oil-skinned and rubber-booted. **1935** W. CATHER *Lucy Gayheart* I. ix. 75 When the rubber-caped boy was gone, Lucy stood looking at the yellow envelope. **1934** WEBSTER, Rubber-coated. **1959** *Chambers's Encycl.* XII. 30/2 Some of the earliest known products of rubber, observed in Brazil, shoes and rubber-coated garments for example, possessed these faults. **1972** *Classification of Occupations* (Dept. Employment) III. 244/1 Operates machine to wind..rubber coated wire round core. **1902** *Amer. Golfer* Apr. 102/1 The advent of the rubber-cored ball has made this [*sc.* an official golf ball] a question of practical interest to all golfers. **1929** W. DEEPING *Roper's Row* xxxv. 398 Sillocks was a golf maniac, and went from Rye to Hoylake..smiting a rubber-cored ball. **1935** *Chambers's Encycl.* VI. 122/1 Innumerable other new applications, as in rubber-cored golf-balls and vulcanite fountain-pens, have caused an enormous increase in the importation of rubber. **1971** *Flying* Apr. 40/1 The free-floating rubber-cushioned engine cowling. **1911** *Encycl. Brit.* XXIII. 803/2 The required thickness of the spread sheet is very often secured by the rubber-faced surfaces of two cloths being united before curing. **1965** F. SARGESON *Mem. Peon* vii. 241 It was more as though he aimed at captivating me with his abilities as a rubber-faced comedian. **1970** *Motoring Which?* July 107/4 Bumpers lightly mounted; rubberfaced overriders front and back. **1956** P. SCOTT *Male Child* II. vii. 174 Handled by sterilized, rubber-gloved hands. **1977** B. PYM *Quartet in Autumn* x. 91 Her pink rubber-gloved hands plunged in the washing-up water. **1965** *Motor* 17 July 6/1 The wiring was rubber insulated and in poor condition. **1934** J. A. LEE *Children of Poor* (1949) 200 People go to the circus to see the rubber-jointed wonder. **1942** BERRY & VAN DEN BARK *Amer. Thes. Slang* §702/32 '*Punch-drunk*'; *dazed*,..rubber-legged. **1950** J. DEMPSEY *Championship Fighting* xxv. 200 He becomes 'rubber-legged' as he lurches about the ring. **1960** *Times* 24 Feb. 16/5 A right to the head had Luukkonen rubber legged as he stood against the ropes. **1973** M. AMIS *Rachel Papers* 180 Once, I affectionately imitated her pout; she veered away in pained bewilderment, so I changed it to an imitation of rubber-lipped Norman, claiming I had heard him on the stairs. **1947** CROWTHER & WHIDDINGTON *Science at War* iv. 166 A rubber-mounted dome was found. **1969** *Jane's Freight Containers 1968–69* 245/1 Two rubber-mounted gantry cranes are used to transfer containers. **1968** *Times* 15 Nov. 16/1 The American designers swing-a-ding-ding with such vivacity and with such rubber-mouthed, beady-eyed professionalism as to render our homemade brand soft-in-the-head amateurs by comparison. **1928** D. H. LAWRENCE *Lady Chatterley* x. 168 There was a toughness, a curious rubber-necked toughness and unlivingness about the middle and upper classes. **1932** BLUNDEN *Face of England* 114, I came to an old tree over the stream, and crossing with some disadvantage to its rubber-necked lichens, I was in an open meadow. **1957** R. CAMPBELL *Coll. Poems* II. 126 The rubbernecked, Hell-touring Thracian. **1913** E. C. BENTLEY *Trent's Last Case* v. 123 He wore rubber-soled tennis shoes. **1973** J. LEASOR *Host of Extras* iii. 49, I had not heard his rubber-soled shoes. **1927** C. B. NEBLETTE *Photography* xx. 465 The potassium pentasulphide solution thus formed is then allowed to cool, filtered and kept in a rubber-stoppered bottle tightly closed. **1913** *T. Eaton & Co. Semi-Ann. Sale Catal.* No. 36. 17/2 Rubber tipped pencils. **1926** 'C. BARRY' *Detective's Holiday* xi. 97 A sallow, unhealthy-looking man of about thirty years, who walked with the help of a stout stick and a rubber-tipped wooden stump. **1976** M. GILBERT *Night of Twelfth* i. 8 He..walked..with the aid of a rubber-tipped stick. **1901** KIPLING *Let.* May in Ld. Birkenhead *R. Kipling* (1978) xiv. 235 We were bung full of beastly spiritual pride... We went about despising things and people, unconsciously turning our ideals to mean an easy life...soft rubber-tyred. **1980** A. CROMIE *Lucky to be Alive* i. 9, I would be leaving the rubber-tired life behind. **1936** J. STEINBECK *In Dubious Battle* i. 11 He went in a dark entrance and climbed the narrow stairs rubber-treaded, the edges guarded with strips of brass.

14. Special Combs.: **rubber boa**, a short, stout, brown snake, *Charina bottæ*, belonging to the family Boidæ and found in western North America; **rubber cement**, a cement or adhesive containing rubber in a solvent; hence *rubber-cemented* adj. (also *fig.*); **rubber cheque** *slang* (orig. *U.S.*), a cheque that 'bounces'; **rubber-chicken circuit** *N. Amer. slang*, an after-dinner-speaking circuit; **rubber dam, rubberdam**: see *DAM *sb.*[1] 4 e; **rubber fetishism**, sexual fetishism which is centred on objects made of rubber; hence **rubber fetish**; **rubber goods** *pl.*, articles made of rubber; freq. *spec.* contraceptive devices; also *attrib.* and *fig.*; **rubber gum**, the sap or latex of rubber trees; **rubber ice** *N.Amer.*, thin, flexible ice; **rubber johnny** *slang*, a condom (cf. sense 11 f above); **rubber kite** *slang* = **rubber cheque*; **rubber-leather** *a.*, consisting of rubber and leather; **rubber-like** *a.*, resembling or suggestive of rubber; **rubber plant**, a tree, *Ficus elastica*, belonging to the family Moraceæ, and native to south-east Asia, the juvenile form of which is widely cultivated as a house plant for the sake of its large leathery leaves which are dark green above and pale yellowish-green beneath; **rubber-proofed** *a.*, coated or treated with rubber for water-proofing; **rubber snake** = **rubber boa*; **rubber solution**, a solution of rubber, *spec.* one used as an adhesive in the repair of tyres; **rubberware**, rubber goods; **rubberwear**, rubber clothing.

1907 R. L. DITMARS *Reptile Bk.* xxv. 211 The Rubber Boa... Size moderate. Form very stout. **1977** *Westworld* (Vancouver, B.C.) May–June 46/2 Another snake common around the lake is the rubber boa. **1895** *Montgomery Ward Catal.* Spring & Summer 525/2, 1 can rubber cement. **1939** R. STOUT *Some Buried Caesar* xii. 175 I'll close it forever and seal the crack with rubber cement. **1965** ZIGROSSER & GAEHDE *Guide Coll. Orig. Prints* vii. 107 Synthetic adhesives, such as rubber cement. **1961** W. SANSOM *Last Hours S. Lee* 246 Bossom was already home, rubber-cemented to his favourite comedian on the telly. **1962** 'E. MCBAIN' *Like Love* (1964) vi. 82 Grossman turned over the lucite-encased sketch and studied the typewritten key rubber-cemented to its back. **1927** Rubber cheque [see *BOUNCE *v.* 6 c]. **1936** WALLACE & CURTIS *Mouthpiece* i. 9 By now the woman has exhausted her credit in Vienna, issued a few rubber checks and passed on to Budapest or somewhere. **1955** J. POTTS *Death of Stray Cat* xv. 157 Jimmy was going to have a lot more to explain than just a handful of rubber cheques. **1973** R. BUSBY *Pattern of Violence* vi. 94 Have you got that blighter who's been trying to put me out of business with rubber cheques? **1959** *Maclean's Mag.* 23 May 1/1 Next year's rubber-chicken circuit is being sewed up by three Toronto women with a public-speaking agency called Canadian Celebrity Bureau. **1977** *Rolling Stone* 5 May 47/3 He spent the winter making speeches on the rubber-chicken circuit. **1954** B. KARPMAN *Sexual Offender* xix. 352 Another rubber fetish in a case reported by Payne was a mackintosh, and in this case also the patient preferred one that had been stolen. **1930** S. PARKER tr. *Stekel's Sexual Aberrations* I. v. 105 During the two years that he was engaged, he continued his rubber and glove fetishism unabated. **1951** HARTWICH & BURBURY tr. *Krafft-Ebing's Aberrations of Sexual Life* x. 173 Despite this strong rubber-fetishism he had a normal sexual relationship. **1971** E. CHESSER *Human Aspects Sexual Deviation* iii. 51 Although rubber fetishism features largely in pornographic literature, if it makes for married happiness it is impossible to see how any moral issue can arise. **1853** *Pathfinder Railway Guide* Sept. (Advt.), Goodyear's patent vulcanized rubber goods. **1897** *National Police Gaz.* (U.S.) 26 May 15/4 (Advt.), T. W. Harrison's rubber, cigar, and book stores. List of all kinds of rubber goods, French & American specialities, pessaries of every description. **1922** JOYCE *Ulysses* 533 Rubber goods. Neverrip. **1928** D. H. LAWRENCE *Lady Chatterley* x. 141 She wasn't all tough rubber-goods and platinum, like the modern girl. **1951** G. GREENE *End of Affair* III. vii. 143 They ought to have opaque glass in their doors like rubber-goods shops. **1973** A. BROINOWSKI *Take one Ambassador* xii. 187 The rubber goods factory next door. **1910** *Chambers's Jrnl.* Mar. 153/2 In these forests grow the trees which yield the finest quality of rubber-gum. **1896** *Dialect Notes* I. 423 *Rubber ice*, thin ice that bends when skated upon. **1916** *Ladies' Home Jrnl.* Apr. 101/2 'Soft as Cheese!' Doctor Rolfe concluded. 'Rubber ice and air holes.' **1962** W. O. MITCHELL *Kite* xiv. 171 Jimmy Sangster had gone through rubber ice, to be found far downstream in a back-water. **1980** *Private Eye* 29 Feb. 13/1 Even the rubber johnny merchants gave him the thumbs down. **1961** *John o' London's* 30 Nov. 610/3 A worthless cheque is a *rubber kite*. **1923** *Daily Mail* 28 May 3 A new process for the manufacture of rubber-leather compounds. **1922** *Encycl. Brit.* XXXII. 299/1 Isoprene undergoes polymerization on exposure to light with the production of a rubber-like mass. *a* **1930** D. H. LAWRENCE *Last Poems* (1932) 156 The vibration of the motor-car has bruised their insensitive bottoms Into rubber-like deadness. **1959** *Times* 27 Apr. (Rubber Industry Suppl.) p. ii/4 Some of the earliest research work on a synthetic product with rubberlike properties was carried out in this country. **1888** Rubber plant [see RUBBER *sb.*[1] 12 b]. **1908** 'O. HENRY' *Gentle Grafter* 138 The little wine-stained table..between the rakish rubber plant and the framed palazzio della something. **1959** C. MACINNES *Absolute Beginners* 81 The rubber-plants in the espressos had been dusted. **1971** *New Scientist* 9 Sept. 554/1 The prime atmospheric essential that they should be places fit for rubber plants to live in. **1934** J. A. SINCLAIR *Airships* iii. 65 The envelopes were composed of rubber-proofed fabric, two fabrics being used with rubber interposed between them, and also on the inner or gas surface. **1960** *Textile Terms & Definitions* (Textile Inst.) (ed. 4) 123 Rubber-proofed sheeting. **1897** J. VAN DENBURGH *Reptiles Pacific Coast & Gt. Basin* 156 The Rubber Snake..is not rare in the moister portions of California. **1954** R. C. STEBBINS *Amphibians & Reptiles Western N. Amer.* 352/2 Rubber Snake... Usually found in moist locations, often near, or within, coniferous woods. **1894** ALBERMARLE & HILLIER *Cycling* (rev. ed.) 471 The hole [is] discovered..and a small patch of rubber stuck over it with rubber solution. **1911** *Encycl. Brit.* XXIII. 802/1 The best solvents for rubber are carbon bisulphide, benzol and mineral naphtha, carbon tetrachloride and chloroform. These liquids, either alone or mixed, are employed in making the rubber solutions used for technical purposes. **1967** E. SHORT *Embroidery & Fabric Collage* ii. 45 It is also a useful precaution to put a spot of rubber solution onto the endings of threads on the back of the work. **1972** *Materials & Technol.* V. xiv. 516 Sometimes rubber cements are made for impregnating or proofing of fabrics, or rubber solutions are prepared for dipping or adhesive purposes. **1950** *N.Z. Jrnl. Agric.* Oct. 300/1 During the war..rubberware of any kind was very scarce. **1977** *Hot Car* Oct. 71/2 A full range of butch and beefy rubberware is also stocked both Stateside and UK. **1967** G. FREEMAN *Undergrowth of Lit.* x. 150 There is also a comprehensive catalogue of the latest range of rubberwear called 'Black Panther'. **1972** *Guardian* 2 Dec. 10/1 Allen Jones's search for potent imagery has led him into a vicarious world..[of] rubberwear and lingerie catalogues.

rubber, *sb.*[2] Add: **2.** (Earlier example.) Also at bridge.

1744 S. FIELDING *Adventures D. Simple* I. II. i. 140 The best Expedient to be found out is, to play a Rubbers at one place, and then drive their Horses to death, to get to the other time enough not to disappoint their Friends. **1886** *Biritch* 3 After each rubber there is a fresh cut for partners. **1908** *Laws of Auction Bridge* §11 At the end of the rubber the total scores..are added up. **1930** [see *AUCTION *sb.* 2 b]. **1960** J. BETJEMAN *Summoned by Bells* vi. 56 Depositing their wraps and settling down To a nice rubber. **1965** *Listener* 20 May 758/3 Even a 33 per cent. chance of game is worth taking if the reward is a 700 rubber.

3. (Examples in *Cricket.*)

1792 in H. T. Waghorn *Dawn of Cricket* (1906) 118 The first game of the rubber. **1895** J. N. PENTELOW *Eng. v. Austral.* 76 Shaw's team thus winning the rubber in fine style. **1912** J. B. HOBBS *Recovering 'Ashes'* 120 England thus decisively winning the match and the rubber by an innings and 225 runs. **1955** *Times* 10 June 4/1 It was not a sparkling partnership, but it was a sober and extremely serviceable start to the new rubber. **1975** *Cricketer* May 8/1 His side won four to one in the recent rubber in Australia.

5. *attrib.* and *Comb.*, as (sense 2) *rubber player, saver, -value*; **rubber bridge**, a type of bridge in which the hands are not replayed and in which settlement is made after each rubber; **rubber game**, a game played to determine the winner of a series; **rubber match**, a match to determine the winner of a series; also *fig.*

1936 R. LEDERER *Mod. Contract & Duplicate* 10 At Rubber Bridge you are faced by a variety of partners. **1951** E. CULBERTSON *Bidding & Play in Duplicate Contract Bridge* xv. 194 The strategy of bidding and play in total-point duplicate is almost exactly the same as the strategy of bidding and play in rubber bridge. **1977** *Times* 29 Aug. 6/4 The real experts preferred rubber bridge at which they could win hard cash. **1908** R. FOSTER *Auction Bridge* 32 It is very important not to let players make a declaration that will put them out, especially on the rubber game. **1946** J. CARY *Moonlight* ix. 68 'Of course it was always a rubber match,' Robin was saying to Amanda. 'From the first night. It didn't seem to matter at first. The really *interesting* thing was how it went bad on us.' **1976** *National Observer* (U.S.) 20 Nov. 5/1 In the rubber match this year, he seems to have sneaked by the same Sam Young with those 201 votes. **1977** *New Yorker* 25 July 58/1 In their rubber match the following year it was Miss Sutton, 6–1, 6–4. **1974** *Times* 16 Feb. 15/2 Without..a code, even the strongest rubber player..will fail to find the perfect answers. **1928** A. E. M. FOSTER *Auction Bridge for All* 201 Z's bid was a good and cheap rubber saver. **1912** F. IRWIN *Fine Pts. Auction Bridge* 166 The rubber-value is 250 points above the line.

rubber, *v.* Add: **1. a.** (Earlier and later examples.) Also const. *around, for.*

1896 ADE *Artie* xi. 100 About a dozen ringers followed us in and stood around rubberin. **1899** W. J. KOUNTZ *Billy Baxter's Lett.* 4 Up there you are likely any minute to come face to face with an Apache or some leftover Aztec rubbering around among the trees. **1910** 'O. HENRY' *Whirligigs* viii. 108 Every few minutes he would pick up his stick rifle and tiptoe to the mouth of the cave to rubber for the scouts of the hated paleface. **1916** H. L. WILSON *Somewhere in Red Gap* ii. 58 So I rubbered awhile,..and then I forgot 'em, looking at some other persons that come in. **1929** WODEHOUSE *Gentleman of Leisure* xiii. 107 Shall I rubber around and find out where is dey kept, boss? **1930** *Living Age* 1 Apr. 183 Bill Coyote..was loping around the trail and rubbering for eats. **1950** *Chicago Tribune* 24 Jan. III. 1, I just saw Moon Mullins out in the alley rubbering up here. **1974** P. DE VRIES *Glory of Hummingbird* (1975) ii. 13 The oncoming cleric who could be seen from the curtained window at which we all rubbered to be even now approaching.

b. To listen or listen *in* (on a party telephone line). *N. Amer. colloq.*

1920 S. LEWIS *Main St.* 189 Say, did you hear me putting one over on these goats that are always rubbering in on party-wires? I hope they heard me! **1948** *Southern Folklore Q.* Sept. 191 She's always rubberin' on a party line. **1963** G. H. THOMSON *Crocus Country* xxxviii. 237 No one thought it much of a crime to 'rubber', as it helped to pass the time for isolated people.

rubberdy, var. *RUBBEDY.

rubber heel, *sb.* (*phr.*) [RUBBER *sb.*[1] III + HEEL *sb.*[1]]

1. A shoe heel made of rubber.

1916 *Daily Colonist* (Victoria, B.C.) 23 July 10/6 The best rubber heel costs only 10¢ more. **1921** *Dict. Occup. Terms* (1927) §602 *Rubber heel maker*,..a moulder..engaged in moulding rubber soles and heels. **1922** *Encycl. Brit.* XXXII. 301/2 To a large degree the rubber heel has also displaced leather in medium-grade footwear.

2. One who investigates the conduct of members of his own organization; *spec.* an internal police investigator. *slang.*

1942 BERREY & VAN DEN BARK *Amer. Thes. Slang* §458/16 '*Spotter.*' (One who spys upon employees.)..rubber-heel. **1970** G. F. NEWMAN *Sir, You Bastard* 12 It was the detail that led the Rubber Heels to Shepherds Market. **1975** *Listener* 6 Feb. 163/3 'Have those five-day wonders and rubber heels never copped a drop or fitted someone up?' (Have those graduates from the Police College investigating a complaint against an officer never accepted a bribe or planted evidence?)

3. *attrib.* and *Comb.*, as (sense 2) *rubber-heel boy, inquiry, mob.*

1962 PARKER & ALLINSON *Courage of his Convictions* iv. 152 Stamper thought he'd be clever and he phoned the rubber-heel mob at Scotland Yard. **1971** *Daily Tel.* 18 Sept. 1/7 They led to investigations into the conduct of police officers by senior detectives. To all British police forces this type of investigation is known as a 'rubber heel' inquiry. **1976** P. FERRIS *Detective* vii. 110 They were the rubber-heel boys, the policemen who investigated policemen.

Hence **ru·bber-heel** *v. intr.* and *trans.*, to investigate (a colleague), to keep (an associate) under surveillance, to spy *on*; **ru·bber-heeler** = sense 2 above; **rubber-heeling** *vbl. sb.*

1959 M. PUGH *Chancer* 91 'So,' he said, 'you fancy yourself as a rubber-heeler?' The phrase usually applied to a policeman, sent to check on another policeman, and to get his facts from the underworld. The 'rubber-heeler' was disliked by criminals as much as he was disliked by the police. **1968** 'B. MATHER' *Springers* xiv. 157 But Sonia? Was she here only for her own safety—or was she rubber-heeling on me to make certain there were no slip-ups? *Ibid.* xv. 168, I was under the closest rubber-heeling and I certainly couldn't afford to interest myself in something that was no longer in my parish. **1973** —— *Snowline* iv. 49 To a brothel? Not with me rubber-heeling on him, he wouldn't... Anyhow, as a copper he'd want it for free. **1976** R. BUSBY *New Face in Hell* viii. 114 He..had..been rubber-heeled for flagrantly fabricating evidence, demoted to sergeant and sent back into uniform. **1977** F. WEBB *Go for Out* v. 71 The Metropolitan Police owned four such vehicles for use by their crime squads, rubber-heelers, or the Special Branch.

ru·bberiness. [f. *RUBBERY *a.* + -NESS.] Rubber-like quality.

1952 E. HEMINGWAY *Old Man & Sea* 125 The old man swung the club down on him..and hit only the heavy solid rubberiness. **1959** *Times* 27 Apr. (Rubber Industry Suppl.) p.vi/6 Embrittlement caused by high temperature oxidation or by loss of rubberiness in the cold must therefore be avoided. **1972** P. W. ALLEN *Natural Rubber & Synthetics* i. 1 All [rubbers] are high polymers, but of a special type possessing distinctive chemical structural characteristics which enable them to be transformed by one means or another into materials having the property of 'rubberiness'.

rubberize (rʌ·bəraiz), *v.* [f. RUBBER *sb.*[1] + -IZE.] *trans.* To treat, coat, or impregnate with rubber. Hence **ru·bberized** *ppl. a.*; **ru·bberizing** *vbl. sb.*

1912 *Chem Abstr.* VI. 1554 Hides and skins..are rubberized by treatment with hot rubber soln. consisting of Para rubber, [etc.]. **1918** *Sphere* 2 Feb. 109/2 The rubberised cotton envelope has a capacity of 77,000 cubic ft. **1925** *Sunday at Home* Mar. 346/1 The balloon..is of rubberised fabric. **1936** *Lancet* 10 Oct. 865/2 The airman wore a two-piece suit of rubberised fabric. **1951** *Oxf. Jun. Encycl.* VII. 466/1 Putting on the rubber, or 'rubberizing', takes place in several stages. **1953** J. Y. COUSTEAU *Silent World* 8 To protect myself from cold I spent days tailoring and vulcanizing rubberized garments. **1963** A. J. HALL *Textile Sci.* v. 235 Water repellency obtained by means of silicones retains its permeability to air..—this advantage is not possessed by textile materials which have been rubberised. **1967** *Jane's Surface Skimmer Syst. 1967–68* 2/2 The skirts can be manufactured simply by cutting up and bonding strips of standard rubberised cloth. **1972** *Materials & Technol.* V. xiv. 454 (*caption*) Fabric being rubberised on calender for use as conveyer belt carcase. **1977** *Field* 13 Jan. 66/4 What is the best way to clean a white rubberised riding mackintosh?

rubberneck, *sb.* and *v.* For *U.S. slang* read '*colloq.* (orig. *U.S.*)' and substitute for def.: **A.** *v.* **a.** *intr.* To crane the neck in curiosity, to gape; also, to look around, to sight-see. (Earlier and later examples.) **b.** *trans.* To stare at. Hence **ru·bbernecking** *ppl. a.* and *vbl. sb.*

1896 ADE *Artie* iii. 23, I stood around there on one foot kind o' rubber-neckin to find an openin. **1927** H. V. MORTON *In Search of England* ix. 173 Here's a great sight going on that hundreds of rubber-necking tourists would pay anything to see. **1932** D. L. SAYERS *Have his Carcase* iv. 59 She..could not waste time rubber-necking round Wilvercombe with Lord Peter. **1939** *Daily Mail* 12 Apr. 8/4 Thousands of people..have 'rubber-necked' this monstrosity [*sc.* Ming, the giant panda] until their eyes ached. **1939** *Times Lit. Suppl.* 20 May 293/3 Mr. Graves resembles some of the professional guides who showed him round when he went 'rubber-necking'. **1946** *Sun* (Baltimore) 5 Nov. 10/7 The long, vaulted centra hall..was crowded with chairs for invited guests with probably five times as many more people standing behind them. Londoners love to rubberneck on tiptoe. **1958** *Observer* 27 Apr. 6/7 Mr. Gunther has the born tourist's eye, and he can put down what he sees. He carries his rubber-necking from the pavements and the cafés to every corner into which he is allowed to penetrate. **1969** *Daily Tel.* (Colour Suppl.) 21 Nov. 73/2 Hortensio was rubber-necking like an American tourist, admiring the scenery, sniffing the breeze. **1973** J. MANN *Only Security* vi. 61 'You're not itching to get your hands on the site?'.. 'Not a bit, lovely just to rubberneck for a change.' **1977** *Time* 16 May 54/1 Wisconsin motorists may never see a purple cow, but they are rubbernecking at an enormous piebald blue one emblazoned on Farmer Hilbert Schneider's 75-year-old barn at Johnson Creek.

B. *sb.* Someone who stares; an inquisitive person; a sight-seer, a tourist. (Earlier and later examples.)

1899 *Amer. Jrnl. Sociol.* May 726 Oh, no! in the language of the shop, she was only a 'rubber-neck'. **1909** G. B. MCCUTCHEON *Truxton King* iii. 41 They are the nobility—the swells. They don't hang around the streets like tourists and rubbernecks. **1918** 'I. HAY' *Last Million* xii. 188 Attended by a respectfully interested cohort of disciples, or rubbernecks. **1937** *Daily Herald* 6 Feb. 6 One of its valuable features will be to deprive the rubber-necks, who gloat over the domestic troubles of their neighbours in the local police court, of their entertainment. **1941** J. SMILEY *Hash House Lingo* 46 *Rubber neck*, tourist. **1974** P. MCCUTCHAN *Call for Simon Shard* xiii. 119 Can you clear the place up, Inspector? Move the rubbernecks on, back to bed? **1975** C. WESTON *Susannah Screaming* (1976) xxiv. 123 Without apology, Krug shoved through the rubbernecks.

b. *attrib.* and *Comb.*, as *rubberneck party, ride, tour, tourist*; **rubberneck auto, bus, car, wagon**, a vehicle for taking people on a sight-seeing tour.

1906 'O. HENRY' *Four Million* (1916) xix. 192 The Rubberneck Auto was about ready to start. The merry top-riders had been assigned to their seats by the gentlemanly conductor. **1949** *Chicago Daily News* 13 Aug. 5/6 That's the relatively harmless impression of Skid Row seen from the rubber-neck busses. **1951** E. PAUL *Springtime in Paris* x. 175 Large rubberneck buses from travel agencies drive through, packed with sightseers from various States of the Union. **1915** *Dialect Notes* IV. 245 *Rubber-neck car, n. phr.*, sight-seeing vehicle. 'We saw several *rubber-neck cars* in Yellowstone Park.' **1916** GALSWORTHY *Sheaf* 276 There exists in America a vehicle called the 'rubber-neck' car. **1925** H. L. FOSTER *Trop. Tramp with Tourists* 326 The tourists go riding through town in rubberneck parties. **1927** *New Republic* 12 Oct. 210/2 'The Manhatters' is founded upon the idea of a rubberneck ride through this island. **1915** *Chicago Herald* 8 Nov. 4/2 The black and tans from the southern states..have been taken on a rubberneck tour. **1949** *Nat. Geogr. Mag.* Dec. 783/2 Twice daily a horse-drawn stage leaves the Plaza on a 'rubberneck' tour. **1926** *Glasgow Herald* 27 July 10 As somebody has to get it in the neck, it may as well be..the rubberneck tourist. **1942** BERREY & VAN DEN BARK *Amer. Thes. Slang* §424/2 *Rubberneck tourist*, a sight-seeing tourist. **1908** G. H. LORIMER *Jack Spurlock* xi. 321 The Major inquired loudly of Horton, the Governor's secretary, whether he was 'runnin' a blank rubber-neck waggon'. **1932** *New Yorker* 11 June 38/2 The one who stepped from the rubberneck wagon happened to be the first [Japanese lady] they had ever seen. **1943** M. FLAVIN *Journey in Dark* 174 On the rubberneck wagons the fellow with the megaphone would point it out and say: 'Residence of Stanley Adams, financier and banker.'

Hence **ru·bbernecker** = *RUBBERNECK *sb.*

1934 in WEBSTER. **1942** BERREY & VAN DEN BARK *Amer. Thes. Slang* §765/8 *Rubbernecker*, a sight-seer. **1958** *N.Y. Times* 19 Apr. 16/5 He..completed a swing that lofted the ball over the barrier. He grinned apologetically at the rubber-neckers. **1969** S. HYLAND *Top Bloody Secret* i. 61 The usual crowd of rubberneckers on the far pavement. **1974** *Spartanburg* (S. Carolina) *Herald* 22 Apr. A4/2 American rubber-neckers in Moscow or Leningrad or elsewhere, with their free and easy manners, will leave as much an impression on the Russians they meet as they will take away with them.

rubberoid (rʊ·bərɔid). Also **Rubberoid.** [f. RUBBER *sb.*[1] III + -OID.] A substitute for rubber. Also *attrib.*

Formerly a proprietary name in the U.S. Quot. 1968 seems to denote a different substance (cf. *RUBEROID, with which there may have been confusion).

1884 *Official Gaz.* (U.S. Patent Office) 8 Jan. 112/1 Composition as a substitute for hard rubber—The James D. Frary & Son Co., Bridgeport, Conn. Application filed November 26, 1883. 'The word Rubberoid.' **1910** [mentioned s.v. RUBBER *sb.*[1] II]. **1951** R. BRADBURY *Illustrated Man* (1952) 160 The city awaited the soft tread of their rubberoid boots. **1968** S. E. ROBERTS *Of Us & Oxen* x. 137 We also lost a piece of rubberoid. I don't know how such a heavy thing could have gotten away.

rubber stamp, *sb.* (*phr.*) and *v.* [RUBBER *sb.*[1] III.] **A.** *sb.* (*phr.*) **1.** (See quot. 1888.) Also, the imprint of such a stamp.

1881 *Instructions Clerks Census Eng. & Wales* (1885) 158/2 Rubber Stamp Maker. **1888** [see RUBBER *sb.*[1] 12 a]. **1954** KOESTLER *Invisible Writing* IV. xxxix. 420 Queuing up each time..to obtain the rubber-stamp which granted a further stay of a day or a week. **1957** E. H. GOMBRICH *Story of Art* xiv. 203 The result looked like any rubber stamp we use today, and the principle of printing it on paper was practically the same. **1975** J. VAN DE WETERING *Outsider in Amsterdam* (1976) ii. 24 They looked at the imprint of the rubber stamp and the signature.

2. *fig.* Used of a person or institution whose power is formal but not real; a person who or body which endorses uncritically.

1919 W. R. THAYER *Theodore Roosevelt* xxi. 334 He may have heard the exhortation 'Be your own President; don't be anybody's man or rubber stamp.' **1943** *Ann. Reg. 1942* 235 This new body..was not to have any of the traditional attributes of a Spanish Cortes. It was to be..an assemblage of Government nominees and notables, a rubber stamp. **1956** A. WILSON *Anglo-Saxon Att.* II. i. 196 The danger of the oldest of all representative bodies becoming a mere rubber stamp. **1965** *Listener* 3 June 823/2 The regional councils were attacked as being mere rubber stamps for the regional boards. **1976** *Survey* Winter 66 The governmental assemblies..are most certainly not rubber stamps for the decisions of their respective executives.

b. *attrib.* or as *adj.*

1931 *Government of Oxford* 5 Others believe that.. interest would be stimulated if Congregation could be relieved of its 'rubber stamp' duties. **1940** *Manch. Guardian Weekly* 29 Mar. 252 Lord Samuel transfixed the 1931–5 Parliament in a phrase: he called it 'The rubber-stamp Parliament'. **1946** W. S. CHURCHILL *Victory* 197 Equal opportunity for all, under free institutions and equal laws—there is the banner for which we will do battle against all rubber-stamp bureaucracies or dictatorships. **1953** *Manch. Guardian Weekly* 8 Oct. 7 The President does not want a 'rubber-stamp' Congress. **1977** *Time* 14 Mar. 23/1 This month's session of the People's Assembly, Burma's rubber-stamp parliament.

B. *v.* (With hyphen.) *trans.* **a.** To mark with the imprint of a rubber stamp; to print with a rubber stamp.

1922 *Hotel World* 13 May 2 No hotel would rubber-stamp its stationery. **1965** M. SPARK *Mandelbaum Gate* iv. 113 Abdul went to start rubber-stamping the soles of smuggled sandals. **1973** *Radio Times 50th Anniv. Souvenir* 66/1 I'd written a fan letter to Bing Crosby... I received a photo of him back—with his autograph rubber-stamped across it.

b. *fig.* To endorse or approve uncritically; to pass routinely or automatically.

1934 WEBSTER, *Rubber-stamp, v.t.* a. To sign with a rubber stamp. b. Hence figuratively, to approve, endorse, or dispose of (as a document or policy) as a matter of routine, usually without the exercise of one's judgment. **1935** *Ann. Reg. 1934* 304 Moreover the Democrats in Congress were completely at one with the Republicans.. in their dislike at appearing merely to 'rubber-stamp' measures drafted by the President. **1959** *News Chron.* 8 July 1/1 We do not believe that the purpose of a conference of our type is to rubber-stamp every declaration. **1978** S. BRILL *Teamsters* i. 15 The current trustees ..had rubber-stamped loans to mob fronts.

Hence **rubber-sta·mping** *ppl. a.* and *vbl. sb.*; **rubber-sta·mpish** *a.* [-ISH[1]], quasi-automatic, almost purely formal.

1932 L. C. DOUGLAS *Forgive us Our Trespasses* (1937) ix. 183 An hour and a half was spent..in a rubber-stampish approval of the 'tentative suggestions' sent from the faculty 'as a basis of discussion'. **1952** 'M. COST' *Hour Awaits* 24 The first letter of 1919—its address almost obliterated by rubber-stampings. **1958** *Sunday Times* 20 Apr. 16/4 He is, in a sense, a dictator, for..the Constituent Assembly is virtually a rubber-stamping body. **1969** *Daily Tel.* 26 Aug. 14 A fresh round of repressive legislation, including instant loss of employment for all who question the official line in deed or word, was all ready for rubber-stamping. **1979** *China Now* Mar./Apr. 3/3 A central working conference..took decisions of far-reaching importance. These decisions were..not just a rubber-stamping of proposals.

rubbery (rʊ·bəri), *a.* [f. RUBBER *sb.*[1] III + -Y[1].] Resembling or suggestive of rubber. Also *fig.* and *Comb.*

1907 GALSWORTHY *Country House* II. v. 147 He left his hand against the animal's warm, soft, rubbery mouth. **1928** *Collier's* 10 Nov. 20/2 He..wrapped a thick hairy arm about Dan's neck in a chancery hold and squeezed his Face into the thick rubbery flesh of his side. **1935** W. CATHER *Lucy Gayheart* I. viii. 67 Even his white skin looked harder, somewhat rubbery. **1950** J. D. MACDONALD *Brass Cupcake* (1974) x. 95 He paid off with a very rubbery check. **1959** *Washington Post* 19 Jan. A12/2 Mr. Mikoyan's responses to questions on the television program, 'Meet the Press', last evening were.. as evasive and rubbery a performance as one could imagine. **1962** *Times* 9 Apr. 4/1 His legs went rubbery as Pender smashed him with lefts and rights to the head. **1973** *Country Life* 1 Nov. 1322/1 Palms and rubbery-leaved banana plants. **1977** *People Weekly* 10 Oct. 44/2 There..are the two rubbery faces mugging through those unforgettable sketches that kept America home Saturday nights from 1950 until 1954.

rubbidy, var. *RUBBEDY.

rubbing, *vbl. sb.* Add: **5. a.** *rubbing alcohol, table.*

1955 T. STERLING *Evil of Day* iii. 37 Celia checked her vanity case to see that she had enough rubbing alcohol. **1971** *Sci. Amer.* Aug. 114/3 Spray the wax joints one at a time with rubbing alcohol. **1939** 'E. QUEEN' in *Blue Bk.* Oct. 21/2 Koyle slipped from the rubbing-table, and Barney Hawks began shooing men out of the shower-room. **1976** *N.Y. Rev.* 24 June 8/3 Lyndon Johnson liked to talk to people while..lying in bed, on his rubbing table, skinny-dipping.

b. *rubbing plate, strake* (further examples).

1969 *Jane's Freight Containers 1968–69* 550/3 The front end incorporates a rubbing plate and retractable king pin. **1928** G. CAMPBELL *My Mystery Ships* iii. 36 The hinges were outboard, and had to be covered with rubber and made to look like a rubbing strake for going alongside a jetty. **1975** *Daily Colonist* (Victoria, B.C.) 24 May 7/3 Her hull mostly white down to the rubbing strake then black to the waterline.

rubbish, *sb.* (and *a.*) Add: **2. a.** (Later examples used of people.)

1885 R. HOLLAND *Gloss. County of Chester* (1886) 293 They're nowt bu' *rubbitch.* **1976** W. TREVOR *Children of Dynmouth* v. 114 Stringer, the headmaster, was rubbish; the P.E. man went after the girls.

3. a. Delete † *Obs.* and add: Revived in mod. colloq. use.

1979 M. BOYCE *I was There!* 83/2 A side that can be easily beaten..a rubbish side, Bedworth or Nuneaton.

b. *rubbish dump, heap* (earlier and later examples), *-pile, -tip.*

1976 W. TREVOR *Children of Dynmouth* iii. 72 It's hardly irrelevant that the country for which men were prepared to give their lives has become a rubbish dump. **1878** *Jrnl. Speculative Philos.* XII. 12 In the *failures* to 'adjust'—in the rubbish-heap, according to Spenser—lies, for them, the real key to the truth. **1932** KIPLING *Limits & Renewals* 299 He very rarely went down into what had now become a rubbish-heap. **1959** C. FREMLIN *Uncle Paul* iv. 33 The five of spades would have to go on the rubbish heap after all. **1884** 'MARK TWAIN' *Huck. Finn* xxxvii. 375 The rubbage-pile in the backyard. **1889** —— *Connecticut Yankee* xix. 235 Just a rubbish-pile of battered corpses. **1922** JOYCE *Ulysses* 422 On a step a gnome totting among a rubbishtip crouches to shoulder a sack of rags and bones. **1971** *Country Life* 24 June 1597/3 Wayside flowers..are still plentiful enough..especially in waste places like rubbish tips.

c. *rubbish-collector*; also *rubbish-dumping* ppl. adj. Also instrumental, as *rubbish-filled* adj.

1965 F. SARGESON *Mem. Peon* iii. 47 It was said that one [absent-minded scholar] had arrived at the college with his household rubbish after leaving his umbrella outside his gate to be collected by the rubbish-collector. **1937** BLUNDEN *Elegy* 84 By mysterious law each place Where Nature looks most gentle and glad Attracts the rubbish-dumping race. **1954** W. FAULKNER *Fable* 385 The corporal's body..went over backward..onto the edge of the rubbish-filled trench behind it.

d. rubbish shop, store, a junk shop.

1869 C. SCHREIBER *Jrnl.* 17 June (1911) I. 17 We found a small teapot, Venetian,..in a rubbish shop in the Spaderia. **1872** *Ibid.* 14 Apr. 156 He took us to a rubbish store.., from which we got nothing but a 'Davenport' plate.

rubbish, *v.* orig. and chiefly *Austral.* and *N.Z.* [f. the sb.] **1.** *trans.* To disparage, criticize severely. Hence **ru·bbished** *ppl. a.*; **ru·bbishing** *vbl. sb.*

1953 T. A. G. HUNGERFORD *Riverslake* ii. 20 If Verity was going to tramp you for burning the tucker..he would have rubbished you long before this. **1965** *Telegraph* (Brisbane) 26 Feb. 13, I knocked him down and I hope he dies. He rubbished me to a mate of mine. **1968** *Comment* (N.Z.) June 33/2 The paper..was recently rubbished in the Catholic *Tablet.* **1972** *Guardian* 16 Oct. 8/1 This live show had a live and participating audience; so Hockney got briefly rubbished the moment his film ended. **1975** *Observer* 12 Jan. 17/1 His plight, and that of the cricketers, have both been latched on to as a chance, not to be missed, of rubbishing the Poms. **1977** *Bulletin* (Sydney) 22 Jan. 14/3 To that extent the much rubbished figures of the CES are consistent with the quite independently determined estimates of the Bureau of Statistics. **1979** *Spectator* 14 July 28/2 A conventional rubbishing of the Left and applause of the Right.

2. *Surfing.* (Chiefly in *pass.*) To tip (a surfer) off a wave.

1962 *Austral. Women's Weekly* 24 Oct. (Suppl.) 3/3 *Rubbished*, to be thrown off wave and dumped on shore. **1963** *Sun-Herald* (Sydney) 22 Sept. 84/5 The fate the board rider dreads is the 'wipe out'. This is when he is 'rubbished' or tipped violently off a wave.

rubbishry (rʊ·bɪʃri). *rare.* [f. RUBBISH *sb.* + -RY.] Rubbish; a collection of rubbish.

1894 KIPLING in *Scribner's Mag.* Dec. 670 Fillin' my bunk wi' rubbishry the Chief put overside.

rubbishy, *a.* Add: **2. a.** (Example of use of a person.)

1946 [see *LEAVABLE *a.*].

b. *Comb.*, as *rubbishy-looking* adj.

1874 'MARK TWAIN' *Lett. to Publishers* (1967) 81 You notice that the Gilded Age is a rather rubbishy looking book.

rubbity (rʊ·bɪti), shortened f. next. Cf. *RUBBEDY, etc. *Austral.*

1941 BAKER *Dict. Austral. Slang* 62 *Rubbity*.., a public house. **1957** 'N. CULOTTA' *They're a Weird Mob* (1958) vii. 104 'Where's Jimmy an' Pat?' 'Down the rubbity.' **1963** *Australasian Post* 8 Aug. 47/3 The proprietor of the local rubbity was a woman. **1968** D. O'GRADY *Bottle of Sandwiches* 54 Roebourne boasted one pub..—the rubbity—we soon became aware of what was doing around the little joint. **1973** A. BUZO *Rooted* 63 'Been down to the rubbity lately?' 'No, I haven't hit the hops for a couple of weeks.'

rubbity-dub (rɒ:bĭtidɒ·b), altered f. *RUB-A-DUB-DUB (b). *Austral.*

1957 'N. CULOTTA' *They're a Weird Mob* (1958) vii. 104 'What is a rubbity?' Joe said scornfully, 'Rubbity-dub.' **1971** *National Times* (Austral.) 13 Dec. 20/2 'Let's grab a do-or-die, have a couple of inky stinks at the rubbity dub...' Translated: 'Let's grab a pie, have a couple of drinks at the pub.'

rubble, *v.* Restrict 'Now *dial.*' to senses in Dict. and add: **1. b.** *trans.* To reduce to rubble. Also *fig.* Chiefly in *pass.* and as **ru·bbled** *ppl. a.*

1926 F. M. FORD *Man could stand Up* I. ii. 37 Things had become more rubbled—mixed up with alarums. **1945** *Daily Progress* (Charlottesville, Va.) 2 Mar. 1/8 Cologne, rubbled anew after dawn by a thousand British heavy bombers. **1953** *Encounter* Nov. 52/1 Palaces like Priam's, scarcely now to be identified among the rubbled trenches that were Ilium. **1978** *Islands* (N.Z.) Aug. 67 O Brave New World..without cities and the bombs to rubble them.

rubby (rɒ·bi). *Canad.* [f. *rubbing (alcohol)* s.v. *RUBBING *vbl. sb.* 5a: see -Y[6].] **1.** A habitual drinker of rubbing alcohol (see sense 2 below).

1950 A. PALMER *Montreal Confidential* 102 The police department has probably given up keeping score of rubbies they have fished out of the river. **1965** *Vancouver Sun* 18 Oct. 35/6 Most of the dinner guests were men off the street, rubbies, derelicts, the jobless, alcoholics, the lost ones, residents of Vancouver's Skid road. **1978** W. S. AVIS in *Occasional Papers Dept. English R. Military Coll. Canada* No.2. 45 Both skid roads remained to become run-down, unsavoury slums.., the hangouts of drifters, rubbies, and other unfortunates.

2. Rubbing alcohol, sometimes mixed with wine, etc., used as an intoxicant.

1961 *Maclean's Mag.* 29 July 36/1 A gallon of wine and two bottles of rubby and you can throw a party in the jungles that'll last all night. **1974** D. RICHARDS *Coming of Winter* i. 29 And there in the shacks the old men hard on rubby, telling stories of the war.

Also **ru:bby-du·b** [cf. also *DUB *sb.*[6]] = sense 1 above.

1950 A. PALMER *Montreal Confidential* 101 If the bum looks a bit plastered don't stop... Chances are he's a 'rubby-dub' and his mind is no doubt clouded with smoke. **1957** *Maclean's Mag.* 25 May 68/2 'We've got everything here from ex-cons to rubby-dubs,' says..one of Elliot's six provincial policemen. **1972** *Daily Colonist* (Victoria, B.C.) 7 Mar. 31/8 Mr. Minister, don't talk nonsense—don't suggest the rubby-dub has to gather up enough money for his own treatment.

rubby-dubby (rɒ·bidɒ:bi). *Angling.* [? f. RUB *v.*[1], DUB *v.*[1] 5: see -Y[6].] Minced fish such as pilchards, mackerel, etc., placed in a net-bag and used as a lure for shark and other large fish. Also *attrib.*

1957 R. ARNOLD *Compl. Sea Angler* xi. 176 As the rubby-dubby moves through the water, the oil from the broken-up bait spreads out from behind the boat, leaving an ever-widening channel down which the hungry sharks ..will cruise searching their prey. **1959** *Angling Times* 27 Feb. 6/3, I, drifting with a rubby-dubby trail, soon had a shark. **1960** *Sunday Express* 24 July 13/1 Two net bags stuffed with old pilchards and mackerel (the skipper calls it 'rubby-dubby'). **1970** *Daily Tel.* 2 May 9/3 Large fish can be attracted, like shark, with the 'rubby dubby' method. **1971** *Angling Times* 10 June 24 Ivan got over the rubby-dubby bags, and started a drift.

ru·b-down. [f. vbl. phr. *to rub down*: RUB *v.*[1] 8.] An act of rubbing down in any sense.

1885 *Boy's Own Paper* 21 Mar. 305/1 When the stick has dried in shape, trim it to taste with a sharp knife, and give it a good rub down with sand-paper. **1896** S. HALE *Let.* 4 June (1919) 299 We reached here reeking, just in time for a rubdown. **1903** [see RUB *sb.*[1] 1 c]. **1917** M. T. HAINSSELIN *Grand Fleet Days* xv. 104 To think that I should get a rub-down like this from the Admiral. **1936** J. CURTIS *Gilt Kid* xiii. 133 Just imagine getting a rub-down at the copper-house and the bogies dragging a lump of coal out of his sky. **1936** 'P. QUENTIN' *Puzzle for Fools* viii. 63 We took rubdowns and other uncomfortably beneficial treatments. **1963** X. FIELD *Under Lock & Key* xi. 143 They and their cells are searched every fortnight or so, at irregular intervals and at an unexpected moment. The 'rub downs' usually lead to their precious belongings being removed. **1965** MRS. L. B. JOHNSON *White House Diary* 5 Oct. (1970) 325 Lyndon on the table getting a rubdown and holding them in conversation. **1977** 'E. MCBAIN' *Long Time no See* viii. 123 A hawker for one of the rubdown emporiums handed her a leaflet.

Rube, var. *REUB.

rubeanic acid (rū·biænik æ·sid). *Chem.* [tr. G. *rubeanwasserstoffsäure*, f. L. *rube-us* red + G. *-an* (as in *cyanwasserstoffsäure* hydrocyanic acid) + *wasserstoff* hydrogen + *säure* acid.] Dithio-oxamide, $[CS(NH_2)]_2$, an orange-red crystalline solid formed by reaction of cyanogen and hydrogen sulphide, and employed in analysis as a reagent to detect copper.

[**1884** *Jrnl. Chem. Soc.* XLVI. 1109 (*heading*) The so-called rubeanhydric acid (cyanogen bisulphydrate).] **1891** *Ibid* LX. II. 1008 The following experiments show that the red compound ('rubeanic acid, rubeanwasserstoff') obtained by the combination of cyanogen and hydrogen sulphide behaves in many reactions as if it were dithi-oxamide, $NH_2·CS·CS·NH_2$. **1928** *Q. Jrnl. Indian Chem. Soc.* III. 118 Rubeanic acid may be regarded as a tanto-meric compound consisting of an equilibrium mixture of sym.-dithio-oxamide and sym.-di-imido-dithio-oxalic acid. **1967** *New Scientist* 2 Feb. 272/3 A test plate subjected to 500 hours accelerated weathering while protected with a polyurethane resin containing rubeanic acid shows no sign of tarnishing. **1981** *Sci. Amer.* Feb. 127/1 For a more sensitive test [for copper in silver coins] Epstein suggests using a saturated solution of rubeanic acid (dithiooxamide) in alcohol and a 20 percent solution of malonic acid.

Rube Goldberg (rūb gōᵘ·ldbəɹg). *U.S.* The name of the American humorous artist Reuben ('*Rube*') Lucius *Goldberg* (1883–1970), used *attrib.* of any unnecessarily complicated, impracticable or ingenious device of the kind illustrated by this artist. Hence **Rube Goldbe·rgian** *a.*

1956 RICE & STEINMETZ *Amish Year* 69 The whole Rube Goldberg device is hitched to a wire which runs through ringbolts attached to short poles stuck in the ground, all the way to the house. **1961** WEBSTER, Rube Goldbergian. **1962** *Time* 22 June 38 It [*sc.* Bertrand Russell's *History of the World in Epitome*] consists of a page with seven words, a drawing of the Garden of Eden,..a drawing of a Rube Goldbergian battle scene, and a few final words. **1963** *Johns Hopkins Mag.* Jan. 20 Insofar as Congress' Rube Goldberg machinery is contrived to help it wait for the propitious moment, it is much to be valued. **1977** *Time* 26 Sept. 33/1 It contains a Rube Goldbergian arrangement of pulleys, ropes and rollers. **1978** *Nature* 9 Nov. 122/3 Orchids are Rube Goldberg machines; a perfect engineer would certainly have come up with something better.

rubeiboo, var. *RUBBABOO.

rubella. Add: (Further examples.) Also *attrib.*

1962 A. SORSBY in A. Pirie *Lens Metabolism Rel. Cataract* 298 Congenital cataract..can be caused by such frankly environmental disturbances as maternal rubella. **1970** *Nature* 11 Apr. 172/1 Growth retardation occurs in rabbits congenitally infected with rubella virus. **1971** *Where* Sept. 271/1 Blindness..in an increasing proportion of cases..is linked with additional handicaps such as deafness, cerebral palsy or mental retardation (for example, 'rubella' babies often have more than one handicap).

rubelliform (rube·lifǭɹm), *a. Med.* [f. RUBELL(A + -I- + -FORM.] Resembling the characteristic rash of rubella.

1959 *Amer. Jrnl. Trop. Med & Hygiene* VIII. 104/1 The rash occurs..as blotchy, maculopapular, rubelliform or occasionally petechial lesions. **1969** *Amer. Jrnl. Epidemiol.* LXXXIX. 665/2 A rubelliform rash..mild upper respiratory symptoms and absence of Köplik's spots were the clinical diagnosis criteria. **1976** *Lancet* 6 Nov. 990/1 Three children had a rash, rubelliform in 2 cases and localised and purpuric in 1.

Rubenesque: see *RUBENSESQUE *a.*

Rubens (rū·benz). The name of the Flemish painter Sir Peter Paul *Rubens* (1577–1640), used *attrib.* in **Rubens brown**, a brown earth-colour; **Rubens hat** (see quot. 1960); **Rubens madder**, madder brown.

1860 Rubens brown [see *CASSEL]. **1885** A. EDWARDES *Girton Girl* I. xiii. 250 A distant lovely head..its waves of amber hair set off against the soft velvet of a Rubens hat. **1886** H. C. STANDAGE *Artists' Man. Pigments* vi. 67 Rubens brown is a native earth of an ochreous character. *Ibid.* 69 Rubens madder, otherwise known as Orange Russet, [etc.]. **1934** H. HILER *Notes on Technique of Painting* ii. 125 *Madder,..Rubens madder,..*etc. These names are now applied both to products from the genuine madder root, and also to those made from its synthetic colouring principles alizarin and purpurin. **1960** C. W. CUNNINGTON et al. *Dict. Eng. Costume* 185/1 *Rubens hat..*, a hat with a high crown and brim turned up on one side. **1969** R. MAYER *Dict. Art Terms & Techniques* 341/1 Rubens madder is now made from synthetic alizarin. *Ibid.* 414/1 Rubens brown is a variety of Van Dyke brown.

Rubensesque (rūbənze·sk), *a.* [f. prec. + -ESQUE.] Characteristic or suggestive of the paintings of Rubens; esp. of a woman's figure: full and rounded. Also **Rubene·sque,** *a.*

1913 *Maclean's Mag.* July 106/2 There are, no doubt, eccentric artists who prefer a Rubensesque figure, but these are the exceptions, and for most private work and school work a spare figure is far more valuable. **1925** W. DEEPING *Sorrell & Son* xx. 185 He had a view of her broad back, and her robust curves... A Rubenesque figure, sumptuous and solid. **1927** *Observer* 17 July 15/4 The models of his choice are of rather Rubenesque fullness. **1952** G. RAVERAT *Period Piece* v. 87 She had auburn hair ..a charming Rubenesque complexion, and a deep rich voice. **1957** W. CAMP *Prospects of Love* II. xiv. 89 'Was she about as big as me?'.. 'Yes, I think she was. Slightly more Rubensesque hips, if anything. But I should think her waist was the same.' **1971** R. HILL *Advancement of Learning* i. 13 The nude was Rubensesque. **1976** L. DEIGHTON *Twinkle, Twinkle Little Spy* viii. 78 The artless gesture of the *ingénue*, inappropriate for this Rubenesque wife and mother.

Rubensian (rube·nziăn), *a.* [f. *RUBENS + -IAN.] Of, pertaining to, or characteristic of Rubens or his work.

1890 *Athenæum* 18 Jan. 90 The composition is distinguished by the true Rubensian 'swing' and emphatic movement. **1940** *Burlington Mag.* June 193/2 This family, with all its Rubensian attributes, as plainly inherits something from each of Rubens's three masters. **1964** *Punch* 1 Apr. 490/2 A voluptuous Rubensian still-life. **1976** *Jrnl. R. Soc. Arts* CXXIV. 624/2 The *composition* of Constable's picture is perhaps the least Rubensian thing about it. **1979** *Amer. N. & Q.* Oct. 29/1 Rubensian themes that appear in the earlier part of Van Dyck's career.

rubeola. 2. Delete 'Now *rare* or *Obs.*' and add further examples.

1883 J. N. HYDE *Pract. Treatm. Dis. Skin* IX. i. 389 The distinction between rubeola and rötheln will be given later. **1909** C. B. KER *Infectious Dis.* ii. 21 It would be simpler if every one referred to measles as 'morbilli' and to German measles as 'rubella', and if the term rubeola were allowed to drop. *Ibid.*, Unfortunately the term 'rubeola' is..freely used to designate measles. **1947** K. WIENER *Skin Manifestations of Internal Disorders* iv. 90 The latin term rubeola is used for this disease [*sc.* German measles] in the German literature, while in the English-American terminology, rubeola designates true measles. **1969** A. B. CHRISTIE *Infectious Dis.* xii. 346 The term rubeola still lingers on as a synonym of measles, though this usage was condemned as long ago as 1909 by Ker. **1973** *Sci. Amer.* Sept. 105/1 The same principle now allows very effective immunization against poliomyelitis, tetanus, diphtheria and both kinds of measles (rubella and rubeola).

Ruberoid (rɒ·-, rū·bəroid). Also **ruberoid.** A proprietary name applied esp. to a roofing material composed of felt impregnated with bitumen. See also *RUBBEROID.

1901 *Official Gaz.* (U.S. Patent Office) 28 May 1848/1 Certain named substances of the nature of rubber. The Standard Paint Co., New York, New York. Filed Nov. 22, 1900. Ruberoid. **1902** *Trade Marks Jrnl.* 14 May 599 *Ruberoid*..Roofing pasteboard or paper and roofing felt. The Standard Paint Company Zweigfabrik Hamburg. **1910** *Ibid.* 8 June 894 *Ruberoid*... Paint and varnish included in Class 1.., and sheathing material included in Class 1 for heat insulating purposes. The Ruberoid Company Limited London. **1911** R. F. SCOTT *Jrnl.* 10 Jan. in *Last Exped.* (1913) I. iv. 111 On the outside [of the roof] is a matchboarding, then a layer of 2-ply 'ruberoid'. **1916** *Cornh. Mag.* Apr. 504 Myself and a chum had just returned..laden with 3″ by 4″ timbers and ruberoid which we found. **1921** H. G. PONTING *Gt. White South* 123 The roof..was covered with a thicker layer of ruberoid, and was lined with a single thickness of boards. **1925** *Glasgow Herald* 3 Aug. 5 The hut..was timber-built and roofed with rubberoid [*sic*]. **1934** *Trade Marks Jrnl.* 21 Nov. 1504/2 *Ruberoid*... Nails; and sectional sheets of ordinary metal for use in building. The Ruberoid Company Ltd. **1958** *House & Garden* Mar. 66/2 Roofs can be of shingles, clay tiles or, as shown here, Ruberoid felt. **1975** *Cricketer* May 47/1 (Advt.), Ruberoid Cricket Pitch is the year round match or practice wicket which can be used out of doors then lifted and re-laid for internal use.

Rubicon, *sb.* Add: **3.** Also applied to a variety of piquet. Also *absol.* (see quots.).

1882 'CAVENDISH' (*title*) The laws of Rubicon piquet, adopted by the Portland Club. **1897** R. F. FOSTER *Compl. Hoyle* 438 Rubicon piquet, for two players. The chief difference between this game and the usual form, Piquet au cent, is in the manner of declaring... Rubicons. If either or both players fail to reach 100 points in the six deals, the one having the most is the winner, and adds to his own score all the points made by the loser, with 100 in addition for game. **1950** *Hoyle's Games Modernized* (ed. 20) 76 It is only necessary to discuss the Rubicon Game, the game of 100 or 101 points being in disuse. *Ibid.*, There is another condition, namely, the establishment of 100 as a 'Rubicon'. **1973** J. SCARNE *Encycl. Games* 604 Rubicon (*piquet*), failure of the loser of a game to reach 100 points. **1975** *Way to Play* 105/1 The procedure then depends on whether these totals exceed the 'rubicon' of 100 points.

rubicundly, *adv.* (Later example.)

1980 *Daily Tel.* 6 Oct. 3/1 'We can't go on living in the 19th century,' says the rubicundly amiable secretary of St Stephen's [Club].

rubidium. Add: [Coined in Ger. by Bunsen in *Ann. d. Chem.* (1861) CXIX. 107.] **1.** Atomic number 37; symbol Rb. (Earlier and later examples.)

1861 H. E. ROSCOE in *Proc. R. Inst.* III. 326 A few days ago the speaker received a letter from Bunsen, which contains the following most interesting information:— 'The substance which I sent you as impure tartrate of Cæsium contains a *second* new alkaline metal... I propose to call the new metal "Rubidium".' **1861** *Chem. News* 27 July 44/2 Both rubidium and cæsium, the two alkali metals recently discovered by means of spectrum analysis, have a great chemical similarity to potassium. **1912** J. W. MELLOR *Mod. Inorg Chem.* xix. 359 Metallic rubidium is prepared by heating an intimate mixture of the carbonate with finely divided carbon. **1946** *Nature* 2 Mar. 269/1 Minerals richest in rubidium are the lithia micas (lepidolites) which quite frequently contain as much as 2–3 per cent Rb_2O. **1950** N. V. SIDGWICK *Chem. Elements* I. 65 Rubidium and caesium catch fire at once on exposure to air. **1974** *Encyl. Brit. Micropædia* VIII. 705/3 Rubidium, because of its electropositiveness, is second only to cesium as a proposed working fluid in plasma propulsion for deep-space probes.

2. a. *attrib.* and *Comb.*

1862 *Phil. Mag.* XXIV. 46 (*heading*) On the preparation of the rubidium compounds. **1911** *Encycl. Brit.* XXIII. 809/1 The rubidium salts are generally colourless, mostly soluble in water and isomorphous with the corresponding potassium salts. **1950** F. E. ZEUNER *Dating Past* (ed. 2) x. 334 Other minerals like hydrothermal microclines, pollucite, and rubidium-rich varieties of muscovite, may in due course become important. **1950** *Thorpe's Dict. Appl. Chem.* (ed. 4) X. 637/2 Rubidium Sulphate, Rb_2SO_4, forms rhombic crystals. **1962** F. I. ORDWAY et al. *Basic Astronautics* iv. 127 A rubidium-vapor magnetometer to measure magnetic fields in space. **1971** I. G. GASS et al. *Understanding Earth* ii. 44/2 A small amount [of strontium] is usually also incorporated into calcium-poor, rubidium-bearing potassium minerals. **1977** *Broadcast* 13 June 6/3 The MSF time signals are derived from what is loosely described as an atomic pendulum but is more correctly known as a rubidium vapour oscillation.

b. Special Comb.: **rubidium-strontium**, used *attrib.* to denote a method of isotopic dating, or results obtained from it, based upon measurement of the relative amounts in rock of rubidium 87 and its beta decay product, strontium 87.

⌊**1946** *Nature* 2 Mar. 269/1 By means of this standard, Rb/Sr ratios of five samples of lepidolite and one of pollucite were determined spectrochemically.., the resultant ages being as follows.⌋ **1950** F. E. ZEUNER *Dating Past* (ed. 2) x. 334 Minerals suitable for the rubidium/strontium method must be rich in Rb and free from non-radiogenic Sr. **1961** *Times* 25 Apr. 2/6 The Department ..is at present using both the potassium-argon and rubidium-strontium methods. **1977** A. HALLAM *Planet Earth* 184/2 Rubidium-strontium and uranium-lead measurements conclusively show that all these rocks were formed between about 3700 and 3800 million years ago.

Rubik (rū·bik). [The name of E. *Rubik*, Hungarian teacher, who patented the puzzle in Hungary in 1975.] *Rubik('s) cube*: a puzzle consisting of a cube seemingly formed by 27 smaller cubes, uniform in size but of various colours, each layer of nine or eight smaller cubes being capable of rotation in its own plane; the task is to restore each face of the cube to a single colour after the uniformity has been destroyed by rotation of the various layers.

1980 D. E. TAYLOR (*title*) Rubik's cube. **1980** D. SINGMASTER *Notes Rubik's 'Magic Cube'* (ed. 5) p. i, This edition has been retitled since the Magic Cube is now being sold as Rubik's Cube. *Ibid.* 37 Ideal [*sc.* the Ideal Toy Corp.] has renamed the cube as 'Rubik's Cube' on the grounds that 'magic' tends to be associated with magic. **1981** *Sci. Amer.* Mar. 14/1 Bűvös Kocka—the Magic Cube, also known as Rubik's Cube—has simultaneously taken the puzzle world, the mathematics world and the computing world by storm. **1981** *Bookseller* 4 July 45/1 Rubik's cube is the latest game/puzzle aimed at driving both parents and children to madness. **1981** *Daily Tel.* 9 July 14/1 Those who in recent months have been driven potty by the clicking of the intellectual's worry beads, the multi-coloured and multi-faceted Rubik Cube, will be glad to know that help has arrived.

‖ **rubinetto** (rubine·to). *rare.* [It.] A tap, a faucet (in quot. *fig.*).

a **1930** D. H. LAWRENCE *Last Poems* (1932) 157 The half-hidden private parts just a little brass tap, rubinetto, turned on for different purposes.

rubinglimmer (rū·bin,glimər). *Min.* [a. G. *rubinglimmer*, f. *rubin* ruby + *glimmer* mica, GLIMMER *sb.*[2]] = *lepidocrocite* s.v. LEPIDO- in Dict. and Suppl.

1836 T. THOMSON *Outl. Min., Geol.* I. 439 Rubinglimmer. **1837** J. D. DANA *Syst. Min.* VI. 380 Brown iron ore... The crystallized variety has been called Onegite, rubinglimmer, pyrosiderite, and Göthite. **1879** *Encycl. Brit.* X. 229/1 Hæmatite (peroxide of iron) occurs crystallized in veins through crystalline rocks,.. and sometimes in minute scales (rubin-glimmer) disseminated through the minerals of many crystalline rocks. **1919** [see *lepidocrocite* s.v. *LEPIDO-]. **1944** C. PALACHE et al. *Dana's Syst. Min.* (ed. 7) 683 Goethite... Found at numerous localities in Nassau, Westphalia, and the Rhine Provinces, Germany, especially at Siegen (does not include the rubinglimmer = lepidocrocite, found at Siegen), [etc.].

rubio (ru·bio). [Sp., lit. 'fair, blond(e), golden'.] Limonite mined in northern Spain.

1892 *Trans. Fed. Inst. Mining Engin.* III. 611 A feature of the rubio deposits is the occurrence of numerous clay 'backs' in the ore. **1901** E. H. DAVIES *Davies's Treat. Metalliferous Minerals & Mining* (ed. 6) xxviii. 280B 'Rubio' ore continues to be the principal class of ore produced [in Bilbao]. **1923** R. H. RASTALL *Geol. of Metalliferous Deposits* xv. 340 One of the most important groups of mines is that of Somorrostro in Viscaya, west of Triano. In this region four types of ore are recognized: (1) Vena... (2) Campanil... (3) Rubio, limonite, often siliceous and aluminous. (4) Carbonato. **1935** *Economist* 2 Feb. 292/2 Business in foreign ore is quiet. Whilst best rubio is nominally 17s. per ton c.i.f. Middlesborough, the tendency is upward.

ru·b-off. *slang.* [f. vbl. phr. *to rub off*: RUB *v.*[1]] An act of masturbation or manual stimulation to orgasm.

1937 PARTRIDGE *Dict. Slang* 710/2 *Rub-off*.., a masturbation. **1969** T. PARKER *Twisting Lane* 202 She charges three quid for sex, two quid for a rub-off.

ru·b-out. *U.S. slang.* Also **rubout.** [f. vbl. phr. *to rub out* s.v. RUB *v.*[1] 11 a.] A murder, an assassination, esp. of one gangster by another. Also *attrib.*

1927 D. HAMMETT in *Black Mask* May 11/2 The hombre she blamed for Paddy's rub-out. **1934** *Sun* (Baltimore) 21 Aug. 7/1 Another..witness is Mrs... Fontaine, alleged 'gang-girl' associate of 'Big George' Phillips wounded in one 'rub out' attempt. **1953** *Ibid.* 12 June 34/3 Police marked down the Messina murder as one of Baltimore's extremely rare gangland rubouts. **1959** *Washington Post* 15 Aug. A3/1 Two hoodlums were gunned to death on Chicago's West Side today and police said at least one of the executions was probably a crime syndicate 'rubout'. **1977** *Time* 10 Jan. 22/1 In what was clearly a political rub-out, the couple—who were discovered by Mrs. Tayyeb's sister, sometime Skyjacker Leila Khaled—had been killed by at least a dozen shots.

rubral (rū·brăl), *a. Anat.* [f. L. *ruber*, *rubr-* red + -AL.] Of or pertaining to the red nucleus of the brain.

1954 [see *RUBRO-]. **1972** M. L. BARR *Human Nervous System* vii. 110/2 A few rubral efferents enter the cerebellum through the superior peduncle to end in cerebellar nuclei.

rubredoxin (rubrėdǫ·ksin). *Biochem.* [f. L. *rub-er* red + *REDOX + -IN[1]: cf. *FERREDOXIN.] Any of a class of natural proteins having an iron atom co-ordinated to the sulphur atoms of four cysteine residues, and concerned in intracellular electron-transfer processes.

1965 LOVENBERG & SOBEL in *Federation Proc.* XXIV. 233/2 This protein, which we tentatively named rubredoxin has been isolated in pure form. **1970** *Nature* 4 July 16/1 An interesting set of metalloproteins, which occur in plants and bacteria, are the non-haem iron proteins, such as the ferredoxins and rubredoxins. **1977** *Jrnl. Amer. Chem. Soc.* XCIX. 3505/1 (*heading*) Theoretical studies of the oxidized and reduced states of a model for the active site of rubredoxin.

rubric, *sb.* and *a.* **I. 2. b.** Delete *rare* and add: (Further examples.) Also, an injunction, a general rule.

1891 *N.Y. Times* 28 Sept. 4/5 It is the duty of independents—the duty of all voters—..to..'weigh the merits and demerits of each candidate and each party.' ..No better rubric of conduct could be laid down. **1934** J. W. POWELL in *Webster* s.v. rubric, The groups of opinion inculcated by instruction are again found to fall into five 'rubrics'—animism, cosmogony, mythology, metaphysic, and science. **1962** W. NOWOTTNY *Lang. Poets Use* viii. 202 There are no critical rubrics or Queensberry rules about this game. **1965** G. MCINNES *Road to Gundagai* i. 13 'Don't go out too far!' A censorious well-worn rubric and I barely heard it. **1970** I. L. HOROWITZ *Masses in Lat. Amer.* i. 3 To understand the processes that go under the rubric of social development it is necessary to study masses as well as elites.

rubrician. (Earlier example.)

1843 H. MOZLEY *Let.* 23 Aug. in D. Mozley *Newman Family Lett.* (1962) 135 The notion of Puseyites or Rubricians..slipping unawares into popery is too absurd.

rubricism. (Later example.)

1978 C. HOWELL in C. Jones et al. *Study of Liturgy* II. III. x. 241 Trent ushered in four centuries of rigidity and fixation; it was an era of rubricism.

rubricize (rū·brisəiz), *v. rare.* [f. RUBRIC *sb.* + -IZE.] **a.** *trans.* To provide with a rubric or rubrics. **b.** *intr.* To make general categorizations. Hence **ru·bricizing** *ppl. a.*

1920 R. HARRIS *Testimonies* II. vii. 65 There is no reason to alter the opinion that the *Testimony* material should be rubricized. **1951** [see *CONSTELLATE *v.* 2 b].

rubro- (rū·bro), comb. form of L. *ruber* red, forming adjs. in *Anat.* with the sense 'relating to the red nucleus of the brain and (another part)', 'passing from the red nucleus to (another part)', as *rubrobulbar*, *-frontal*, *-oculomotor*, *-parietal*, *-reticular*, *-spinal*.

1902 H. MORRIS *Treat. Human Anat.* (ed. 3) v. 769 The rubro-spinal tract is formed by a number of fibres which are scattered in the anterior part of the lateral pyramid, in the posterior part of the lateral ground bundle, and in the posterior part of Lowenthal's tract. **1937** J. H. GLOBUS *Pract. Neuroanat.* 150 Others..descend to the brain stem and spinal cord as the rubroreticular and rubrospinal tracts. **1954** T. L. PEEL *Neuroanat. Basis Clin. Neurol.* xvii. 386/2 The rubro-oculomotor fibers to the third, fourth, and sixth cranial-nerve nuclei..form the most mediodorsal part of the capsule of the red nucleus. *Ibid.* 387/1 Fibers to other cranial-nerve motor nuclei, a rubrobulbar tract, are probably included in the rubral outflow. *Ibid.*, Rubrofrontal and rubroparietal fibers are described as leaving the dorsolateral surface of the nucleus and passing..to frontal and parietal lobes. **1972** M. L. BARR *Human Nervous System* vii. 110/2 Neuronal activity in the red nucleus..influences lower motor neurons through the rubrospinal tract and through rubroreticular and reticulospinal connections. **1974** D. & M. WEBSTER *Compar. Vertebr. Morphol.* xii. 290 The rubrospinal tract leaves the red nucleus, and the reticulospinal tract leaves the reticular formation.

ru·b-up. [f. vbl. phr. *to rub up*: RUB *v.*[1] 13 in Dict. and Suppl.] The act of rubbing up in any sense.

1928 G. CAMPBELL *My Mystery Ships* xiii. 245 We.. went out to the Sound for a good 'rub up' in our drill and to get everything tested. **1943** 'TAFFRAIL' *White Ensigns* 26 He would take voluntary classes of men who wanted a rub-up in gunnery or seamanship before passing for higher rating. **1953** *Chambers's Jrnl.* June 355/1 Back then to the purgatory of waiting—with no text-books for a final rub-up permitted. **1967** KARCH & BUBER *Offset Processes* vi. 227 Plates are repaired:.. 4. By 'rub up'—to bring back or strengthen spots or areas that may become weak from an unknown cause.

ruby, *sb.* and *a.* Add: **I. 5. d.** *ellipt.* Ruby port (see sense *11).

1938 G. GREENE *Brighton Rock* I. iii. 37 'Give me a glass of Ruby,' the sombre man said. **1959** W. JAMES *Word-bk. Wine* 148 Ruby is a young, deep-red wine, or a tawny which has been refreshed with a younger wine.

II. 8. a. *ruby laser.*

1961 *Ann. Reg. 1960* 396 One drawback of the ruby laser was that it produced light only in bursts. **1974** *Encycl. Brit. Micropædia* VIII. 707/1 The chromium atoms responsible for the ruby's colour are also responsible for the emission of red light when ruby is excited by radiation, as in the red light produced by a ruby laser. **1977** *Jrnl. R. Soc. Arts* CXXV. 765/1 The first ruby laser of Maiman in 1960.

b. Also *ruby-ripe*, *-sweet*.

1918 W. DE LA MARE *Sam's Three Wishes* in *Twelve Poets* 27 Ruby-ripe to see, The pixy-pears burn on yon hawthorn tree. **1920** E. SITWELL *Wooden Pegasus* 21 As isles of the cherry Or ruby-sweet berry.

10. a. *ruby-eyed*, *-tasselled*.

1919 R. C. PUNNETT *Mendelism* (ed. 5) ix. 95 In canaries, again, there are ruby-eyed cinnamon forms corresponding to the various green and yellow varieties. **1950** D. GASCOYNE *Vagrant* 38 Fatalist, Ruby-eyed. **1920** BLUNDEN *Waggoner* 55 And ruby-tasselled shepherd's rose.

11. ruby anniversary, a fortieth anniversary; **ruby-back**, used *attrib.* to designate fine Chinese porcelain enamelled on the reverse in pink or crimson; so **ruby-backed** adj.; **ruby-dazzler** *Austral.* and *N.Z. slang*, something exceptionally fine (cf. *BOBBY-DAZZLER); **ruby port**, port of a deep red colour, *spec.* that matured in wood for only a few years and fined before bottling; **Ruby Queen** *Forces' slang* (see quot. 1925); **ruby wedding**, a fortieth (occas. forty-fifth) wedding anniversary.

1962 *Guardian* 17 Nov. 5/2 The celebration of the BBC's ruby anniversary. **1915** R. L. HOBSON *Chinese Pott. & Porc.* II. xii. 213 A ruby-back saucer dish delicately painted. **1935** *Burlington Mag.* Jan. 25/2 At that period the Chinese kilns produced the ruby-back egg-shell porcelain. **1960** H. HAYWARD *Antique Coll.* 115/1 A new delicate painting style began to oust that of the *famille verte*..about 1720, and was applied especially to plates, bowls and cups and saucers of 'egg-shell' thin porcelain. The 'ruby-back' variety is coloured deep rose-pink on the reverse. **1980** *Catal. Fine Chinese Ceramics* (Sotheby, Hong Kong) 180 Compare the ruby-back cups painted with fruit in the interior sold in these rooms 29th November, 1977. **1900** F. LITCHFIELD *Pott. & Porc.* vii. 113 The most highly-prized egg-shell, which is termed 'ruby backed' china. **1970** G. C. WILLIAMSON *Bk. of Famille Rose* vii. 104 Ruby-backed pieces can be marked off as belonging to a particular group, but the division must be confined exclusively to the ruby back. **1941** BAKER *N.Z. Slang* vi. 51 Expressions..in constant use by our youngsters:..bobbydazzler, rubydazzler, dag, swinjer, [etc.]. **1941** —— *Dict. Austral. Slang* 62 *Rube*,..something esp. fine. *Rubydazzler*, as for 'rube'. **1977** W. S. RAMSON in *Quadrant* (Sydney) May 67/1 The *Australian Pocket Oxford*..is a real *beaut*, a *ryebuck* dictionary, a *ringer*, a *ripper*, a gem amongst dictionaries if not a *rubydazzler*. **1921** A. L. SIMON *Wine & Wine Trade* v. 59 It also happens sometimes that a vintage Port..will be kept in wood for a more or less extended number of years before it is bottled. The result will be a wine with less colour and strength than the early bottled vintage Port, but with more body and colour than tawny Port. This wine is often described as 'Ruby' Port. **1938** G. GREENE *Brighton Rock* I. iii. 47 Life was sunlight on brass bedposts, ruby port. **1967** A. LICHINE *Encycl. Wines* 411/2 A bottle of Vintage Port..will suffer if it is open to the air very long, though a Ruby Port or Tawny will survive better. **1925** FRASER & GIBBONS *Soldier & Sailor Words* 246 *Ruby Queen*,..an occasional nickname for any young nurse or Sister of fresh complexion. **1934** BLUNDEN *Choice or Chance* 31 With Ruby Queens We once crowned feeds of pork and beans. **1911** WEBSTER s.v. ruby *a.*, *Ruby wedding*, the forty-fifth wedding anniversary. **1963** B. SMITH *Etiquette* vii. 117 According to a former convention..the interim anniversaries are..fortieth year, Ruby Wedding. **1977** *Times* 15 Apr. 12/5 This year marks his ruby wedding as well as his retirement.

ruby-red, *a.* **b.** quasi-*sb.* (Earlier example.)

1885 [see *ISOCHROMATIC *a.* 2].

ruby-throated, *a.* Add: Also occas. used of people.

1957 O. NASH *You can't get there from Here* 68 Our ruby-throated playgirls and madcap millionaires.

rucas, ruccus, *varr.* *RUCKUS.

ruched, *ppl. a.* (In Dict. s.v. RUCHE *sb.*) Add: (Earlier and later examples.) Also *fig.*

1847 E. GRAY *Let.* 5 May in W. James *Order of Release* (1947) iii. 31 Cloaks of pale glacé silk with ruished frills round them. **1848** —— *Let.* 10 May in *Ibid.* v. 107 A stone silk dress with two broad flounces Ruched and a Brussels lace cape. **1900** *Ann. Rep. Board of Regents Smithsonian Inst. 1898* II. 703 In a broad way we may distinguish as leading types [of hemipenis] the following: The smooth; the plicate, or flounced; the calyculate, or ruched; and the disk-bearing. **1923** E. Sitwell *Bucolic Comedies* 61 Ruched as their country waterfalls, The cherried maids walk beneath the dark walls. **1932** *Woman's Weekly* 19 Mar. 467/1 The..skirt is cut in wide scallops and trimmed with ruching. Little ruched pieces..give the frock quaintness and charm. **1978** *Detroit Free Press* 5 Mar. D7/5 (Advt.), This terrific coat with its softly ruched back.

ruching. (Later examples.) Also *fig.*

1914 C. Mackenzie *Sinister St.* II. iv. iv. 914 The beginning of the street ran between two high brown walls crowned with a ruching of broken glass. **1932** [see prec.]. **1971** *Homes & Gardens* Sept. 61/2 And not only have they pounced on all the lace, all those bibs and tuckers and ruchings and veils and shawls and scarves and yard after yard of flouncing.

ruck, *sb.*[1] Add: **3. b.** *in a ruck*, in *Racing*: in one group.

1840 *Spirit of Times* 10 Oct. 380 When Randal blew his bugle, away they all flew in a ruck.

d. (*a*) *Rugby Union.* (Also *loose ruck.*) = *loose scrummage* s.v. **LOOSE *a.* 9. (*b*) *Australian Rules football.* (See quot. 1969.)

1906 Gallaher & Stead *Compl. Rugby Footballer* ix. 134 What we call a loose ruck..represents the disordered state of things occurring, for example, when..a back has slipped and stopped the play when trying to block a forward rush. One man is down, and all his other colleagues in the back division are induced to come up to his assistance. **1955** *Times* 8 Aug. 2/2 With the South African pack controlling the line outs..and driving hard from the rucks the home side looked to have a firm grip on the game. **1956** V. Jenkins *Lions Rampant* xii. 180 On the muddy ground they made rush after rush, and piled into the loose rucks as if their lives depended on it. **1967** *Australian* 17 Apr. 12 Terry Waters..was moved into the ruck in the third quarter. **1969** Eagleson & McKie *Terminol. Austral. Nat. Football* III. 10 *Ruck.* 1. The three members of a team who do not occupy fixed positions but are free to follow the play wherever it goes around the field; the ruck consists of a rover and two followers. *Ibid.* 11 *Ruck.* 2. A member of a team selected to play in the ruck, other than the rover. **1973** [see **MAUL *sb.*[1] 4]. **1979** *Times* 12 Dec. 9/1 Oxford..won most of the rucks or mauls that mattered.

4. a. (Later example.)

1922 E. Wallace *Flying Fifty-Five* xii. 70 Its jockey had given up all attempt at winning and was content to finish with the ruck.

5. (Earlier example.)

1885 'Mark Twain' *Let.* 11 Sept. (1917) II. xxv. 460 Flowers and general ruck sent to him by Tom, Dick, and Harry from everywhere.

6. *attrib.*, as (sense *3 d (a)) *ruck ball*; (sense *3 d (b)) *ruck man, -rover.*

1976 *Scotsman* 24 Dec. 16/4 The ruck ball was promptly knocked on by a centre. **1963** *Sunday Mail* (Brisbane) 24 Feb. 24/5 Dr. Eric Laithwaite,..senior lecturer in electrical engineering at Manchester University,..looks more like an uncomplicated ruckman than an ingenious scientist. **1969** Eagleson & McKie *Terminol. Austral. Nat. Football* III. 11 *Ruckman*, a member of the ruck whose function it is to take marks, and to knock the ball to the rover when the ball is thrown up or bounced by the umpire. **1977** *Age* (Melbourne) 18 Jan. 26/4 (*caption*) Fumbling is embarrassing anytime for a famous VFL ruckman and Jones covers his face in despair. **1967** *Australian* 24 Apr. 12 The brilliant Polly Farmer is now being used as a ruck-rover. **1969** Eagleson & McKie *Terminol. Austral. Nat. Football* III. 12 *Ruck-rover*, a mobile member of the ruck who is usually intermediate in size between a follower and rover.

ruck (rʌk), *sb.*[5] *colloq.* [Perh. f. **RUCK *v.*[6] or shortening of Ruction or **RUCKUS.] A quarrel, a row.

1958 F. Norman *Bang to Rights* I. 15, I didn't feel like having a ruck about this. **1960** *Times* 15 Mar. 7/7 All that gun business is—silly isn't it. I mean they were only having a ruck to start with. **1963** T. & P. Morris *Pentonville* vi. 144 The prisoner said that he had 'had a bit of a ruck with the instructor over this'. **1964** *Listener* 31 Dec. 1055/2 Squaddies and Teds, personal rucks forgotten, are fleeing from a common enemy—the law. **1976** 'P. B. Yuill' *Hazell & Menacing Jester* vi. 66 'I heard him and her having a ruck about Nicholas, that's all.' 'What kind of a row?'

ruck (rʌk), *v.*[5] *slang.* [Of unknown origin.] *intr.* **a.** To inform *on* a criminal. **b.** To give information about a crime or a criminal. **c.** *gen.* To abandon, to repudiate a person. With *on.*

1884 *Daily News* 20 Sept. 2/2, I told the prisoner that I was not going to ruck on an old pal. **1889** *Session Paper Cent. Criminal Court, 1729–1913* CX. 871 He said 'Has Cleasby *rucked*? If he has, I will b–y well kill him when I come out'—ruck means telling. **1898** J. D. Brayshaw *Slum Silhouettes* 207 Yer won't tell Mo that I told yer—will yer? If he knew as I'd rucked on him, he'd kill me. **1903** A. M. Binstead *Pitcher in Paradise* iv. 96 Your worthy parent..isn't going to ruck on you in the golden autumn of his life, just because you were denied the keen commercial instincts that led him to make a pile! **1906** E. Pugh *Spoilers* viii. 92 'I don't care,' said Deuce, defiantly... 'I ain't goin' to ruck on Dad.'

ruck, *v.*[6], var. Rux *v.*

1936 G. Ingram *Muffled Man* i. 13 'Oh, all right,' sulked Sonny. 'You ain't going to "ruck" me, are you?' **1959** C. MacInnes *Absolute Beginners* I. 109, I saw I mustn't keep on rucking him, because, after all, this was a party. **1966** P. Willmott *Adolescent Boys* vi. 112 The governor of my place is horrible... He rucks you if you take more than ten minutes for a quarter of an hour's job.

rucked, *ppl. a.*[1] Add: Also with *up*: rumpled; caught up.

1944 J. D. Carr *Till Death do us Part* vi. 64 A light-haired young man..lying on a rucked-up sofa. **1964** D. Francis *Nerve* i. 7 Mr Brewer pulled down his unconscious wife's rucked-up skirt. **1980** C. Fremlin *With no Crying* iv. 20 She'd..straightened her rucked-up skirt.

rucked, *ppl. a.*[2] [cf. **RUCK *sb.*[1] 3 d (a).] Passed from a loose scrummage.

1976 *Wymondham & Attleborough Express* 3 Dec. 26/3 The youthful, fit students started in an attractive manner while Diss resisted with strong tackling and counter attacking from rucked possession.

rucking, *vbl. sb.*[2] The action of Ruck *v.*[2]

a **1915** in W. H. Chantrey *Theatre Accounts* (1915) 67 Druggets or crumb cloths where used must be secured so as to be in no way liable to rucking.

rucking, *vbl. sb.*[3] [cf. **RUCK *sb.*[1] 3 d (a).] Loose scrummaging.

1958 [see *loose scrummaging* s.v. **LOOSE *a.* 9]. **1963** *Times* 31 May 3/4 He told New Zealanders: 'I think we can learn much from your game—particularly your forwards' rucking and driving over the ball, which we are trying to practise.' **1966** *Sunday Times* 2 Oct. 20/6 Their captain, Matthews, set an example with his rucking and gained them some valuable balls.

rucking, *vbl. sb.*[4] *slang.* [f. **RUCK *v.*[6] + -ING[1].] A reprimand; a scolding, telling-off.

1958 F. Norman *Bang to Rights* I. 41 I'll have to give her a right rucking about that. **1974** T. Barling *Shooter Man* iii. 23 Ask him. It'll only cost you a few coppers and a rucking for calling him back. **1976** E. Dunphy *Only a Game?* v. 146 Perhaps all the rucking he was taking was getting through to him, and he started doing a little bit more.

rucksack. Delete ‖ and add pronunc. (rʌ·ksæk, rʊ·ksæk). Also **rucsac, rucsack,** 9 **rücksack.** (Earlier and later examples.)

1866 *Nature & Art* I. 192/2 We therefore confidently recommend a perusal of it to all those about to grasp the 'Alpen-stock', and shoulder the 'Rücksack'. **1882** W. A. Baillie-Grohman *Camps in Rockies* 411 '*Rück-sack*', or *Stalker's Bag* is..for all sporting purposes a most useful article. **1932** *Pontings Catal.* Whitsun, Rucksacks made of a..rubber proofed twill material. **1955** *Times* 31 Aug. 6/5 She wore shorts and rode a man's bicycle, on the back of which was strapped a heavy rucksack and a spare wheel. **1969** W. H. Little in C. Cullingford *Man. Caving Techniques* iii. 33 A rucsac of a suitable kind and size will often be necessary to carry the caver's needs to the cave entrance. **1976** *Liverpool Echo* 7 Dec. 5/1 An electric drill, a sanding machine and two rucksacks worth a total of £110. **1978** *Vole* No. 7 29/1, I did manage to corner a walker in Dorset, whose rucsac nearly broke my arm when I tried to lift it.

ru·cksacked, *a.* [f. prec. + -ED[1].] Provided with or carrying a rucksack.

1909 H. G. Wells *Ann Veronica* xvi. 322 To walk beside him, dressed akin to him, rucksacked and companionable, was bliss in itself. **1973** A. Price *October Men* i. 8 Holidaying couples and rucksacked students.

ru·cksackful. [f. Rucksack + -ful.] As much as a rucksack will contain.

1971 C. Bonington *Annapurna South Face* xi. 126 Ian was therefore carrying up the entire load of fixed rope left by Nick and Martin, a rucksackful weighing around forty pounds.

ruckus (rʌ·kə̆s). orig. and chiefly *U.S.* Also **rucas, ruccus, rucus, rukus.** [cf. Ruction and Rumpus *sb.*] An uproar, a disturbance; a row, a quarrel; fuss, commotion. Also *attrib.*

The earliest examples, spelt with a single *c* or *k*, may possibly represent the variant usually spelt *rookus*.

1890 *Dialect Notes* I. 66 *Rucus* (rŭkəs): for *rumpus*. [Kentucky.] **1902** *Ibid.* II. 244 Rukus. **1909** 'O. Henry' *Roads of Destiny* xiii. 210 There shall be rucuses in Salvador..and the monkeys had better climb the tallest cocoanut trees. **1923** C. E. Mulford *Black Buttes* ii. 20 Them two bummers [*sc.* restless cattle] was raisin' more of a ruckus than usual to-night. **1934** *Sun* (Baltimore) 17 May 10/1 The ruccus in the City Hall over discharge of a municipal employé by the Mayor. **1948** F. Blake *Johnny Christmas* II. 69 With this Kiowa–'Rapaho ruckus and these picture-book soldiers that just showed up, we don't want anything more on our hands. **1963** *Economist* 12 Oct. 147/2 The ruckus kicked up by the outraged wives and mothers of America. **1972** *Time* 10 July 38/1 But then ruckus raising is Fischer's speciality. **1977** *Times Lit. Suppl.* 1 July 792/1 World Team Tennis..now actively encourages..'audience participation', a polite phrase that covers barracking, beer-cans, and the kind of ruckus that England normally only sees after a Cup Final. **1979** *Dædalus* Spring 162 Like the *graeculi* of the Roman Empire, we Europeans are still capable of raising a little cultural ruckus.

ruction. (Further examples.)

1878 A. Hume *Remarks Irish Dial.* 111 When a..ruction has been 'riz'. **1900** F. P. Dunne *Mr. Dooley's Philos.* 24 That's life in America. 'Tis a gloryous big fight, a rough an' tumble fight, a Donnybrook fair three thousan' miles wide an' a ruction in ivry block. **1905** [see **PAVVY]. **1913** [see **RIPPIT]. **1921** E. O'Neill *Diff'rent* I, in *Emperor Jones* 218 That brown gal took an awful shine to Caleb and when she saw the ship was gittin' ready to sail she raised ructions,..howlin' and screamin' and beatin' her chest with her fists. **1943** *Sun* (Baltimore) 17 Nov. 14/1 As a result of this little ruction, Baltimore is freed..from the grip of a political coalition which boded no good for the city. **1964** D. Varaday *Gara-Yaka* xii. 103 The ructions of a clash between rival tribes.

rud, *sb.*[1] **3.** (Later *Comb.* example.)

1876 G. M. Hopkins *Poems* (1967) 177 The blood-gush blade-gash Flame-rash rudred..and dingle-a-danglèd Dandy-hung dainty head.

rudaceous (rudē·ʃəs), *a. Geol.* [f. L. *rūd-us* rubble + -aceous.] Of a rock: composed of larger grains than is an arenaceous rock.

1904 A. W. Grabau in *Amer. Geologist* XXXIII. 242 In the further subdivision of the clastic rocks, texture or size of grain takes precedence over chemical composition. .. We commonly recognize these sizes of grain, 1st that larger than what is commonly considered the normal sandgrain, 2d, the sand-grain, and 3d, the rock flour or impalpable powder. The first texture is most appropriately called rudaceous. **1920** —— *Gen. Geol.* xviii. 570 Rocks of all textures may be argillaceous, those of rubbly (rudaceous) texture and those of arenaceous texture generally carrying the clay as an admixture or as part of the cement. **1949** F. J. Pettijohn *Sedimentary Rocks* vii. 196 The rudaceous subtypes..are marked by characteristic compositional and textural features. **1977** A. Hallam *Planet Earth* 168 Most sedimentary rocks, classified as either detrital or chemical-organic, are also classified according to their grain-size as rudaceous rocks, arenaceous rocks or argillaceous rocks.

rudbeckia (rʌd-, rudbe·kiă). [mod.L. (Linnæus *Systema Naturæ* (1735)), f. the name of Olaf *Rudbeck* (1660–1740), Swedish botanist + -IA[1].] A perennial herb of the genus so called, belonging to the family Compositæ, native to North America, and bearing yellow or orange flowers with a prominent conical disc of dark florets in the centre of each one.

1759 P. Miller *Gardeners Dict.* (ed. 7) s.v. Rudbeckia with oval, Spear-shaped, undivided Leaves, placed alternate. **1789** W. Aiton *Hortus Kewensis* III. 250 Broad jagged-leav'd Rudbeckia. Nat[ive] of Virginia and Canada. **1821** *Bot. Reg.* VIII. tab. 525 (*heading*) Eight-rayed Rudbeckia. **1870** W. Robinson *Wild Garden* II. 86 Newman's Rudbeckia... A very showy vigorous plant. **1908** G. Jekyll *Colour in Flower Garden* ix. 79 The fine double Rudbeckia called Golden Glow is treated in the same way. **1931** *Daily Mirror* 27 Aug. 7/3 Among the best of autumn-flowering perennials for the mixed border, or the wild garden, are the rudbeckias. **1962** *Amateur Gardening* 17 Feb. 5 A flower which makes for a bold display in the garden and as a cut flower is the rudbeckia. **1974** C. Milne *Enchanted Places* vi. 49 The penstemons, the bergamots,..the rudbeckias, the dahlias ..were still looking as lovely as ever.

rudd[1]**.** For *Leuciscus* read *Scardinius.* (Earlier and later examples.)

1526 in 'Antiquary' *Forme of Cury* (1780) 177 Fresh Sammon... Great Ruds... Baken Turbuts. **1925** J. T. Jenkins *Fishes Brit. Isles* 297 The Rudd is usually deeper in the body than the Roach. **1966** *Studia Neophilologica* XXXVIII. 130 The English name of the rudd obviously refers to the red colour of the lower fins of the fish.

Rudd[2] (rʌd). [Perh. f. the name of Margaret Caroline *Rudd* (d. 1779), a notorious courtesan, for whom the table may have been invented.] Used *attrib.* and in the possessive in *Rudd('s) table*, an elaborately appointed lady's toilet table of the late eighteenth century.

1788 in R. Fastnedge *Shearer Furnit. Designs from Cabinet-Makers' London Bk. of Prices* (1962) 14 A three foot 4 inch, rudd table, all solid, with astragal, or 2 beads, and hollow round the edge of the top, the 2 outside drawers with no quadrant boxes, a glass hung to each drawer, supported by quadrants.., plain Marlbro' feet, and an astragal round the bottom of the frame. **1793** *Cabinet-Makers' London Bk. of Prices* (ed. 2) 161 *A Rudd, or Lady's Dressing Table..* Three feet four inches long, two feet wide, three drawers in front, a glass frame hing'd to each end drawer, and supported by quadrants, a moulding on the edge of the top, plain Marlbro' legs, and an astragal round the bottom of the frame. **1892** F. Litchfield *Illustr. Hist. Furnit.* vii. 186 The names given to some of these designs [in Hepplewhite's *Guide*] appear curious; for instance: 'Rudd's table or reflecting dressing table,' so called from the first one having been invented for a popular character of that time. **1902** W. H. Hackett *Decorative Furnit. 16th, 17th & 18th Cent.* x. 124 About the year 1788, Shearer also published.. 'Household Furniture'... The nineteen plates consist of designs for secretaires, bookcases, bureaux..and what was known as a Rudd or lady's dressing table. **1970** [see *lobby chest* s.v. **LOBBY *sb.* 4].

rudder, *sb.* **2. a.** Delete note in small type, and add: **d.** An analogous flat movable structure used for controlling the motion of an aircraft; now usu. a vertical flap, hinged at its leading edge, forming part of the tailplane of an aeroplane.

The 'boat' in quot. 1804 is the gondola of a balloon.

1804 G. CAYLEY in J. L. Pritchard *Sir G. Cayley* (1961) 220 Fixed upon a universal joint a Rudder of considerable length opposing both an horizontal and vertical surface.. intersecting each other in right angles to the air. A handle to direct this Rudder must communicate with the Boat. **1843** *Mechanics' Mag.* XXXVIII. 278 The broad horizontal rudder, or tail, H, capable of being turned on its hinge to any angle, at pleasure, gives the power of ascent and descent when the propellers are used, and forms also the chief means of stability in the path of the flight. The small vertical rudder I, is for the purpose of lateral steerage. **1879** *Encycl. Brit.* IX. 321/1 M. Pénaud succeeded in overcoming the difficulty in question by the invention of what he designates his automatic rudder. This consists of a small elastic aero-plane placed aft or behind the principal aero-plane which is also elastic. **1910** R. FERRIS *How it Flies* vi. 116 The rudder for steering to left or right is mounted at the extreme rear end of the body. **1966** D. STINTON *Anat. Aeroplane* viii. 163 Aerobatic aeroplanes usually have a large portion of the fin surface lying ahead of the tailplane, or a large portion of the fin and rudder lying behind its trailing edge. **1969** K. MUNSON *Pioneer Aircraft 1903–14* 9 The operator lies prone on the lower surface, his hips resting in the cradle, and his hands grasping the roller, D_1, which actuates the front rudder, D.

e. Use or turning of the rudder, the extent to which the rudder is turned.

1918 W. G. MCMINNIES *Pract. Flying* 218 If you are turning to the right and notice wind striking your left cheek, you are side-slipping outwards, so give a little more bank or take off some rudder. **1936** W. H. MCCORMICK *Mod. Bk. Aeroplanes* x. 86 In order to turn an aeroplane to the right, right rudder is put on by moving the right-hand end of the rudder bar gently forward by means of the right foot. **1958** 'N. SHUTE' *Rainbow & Rose* ii. 49 She needed quite a bit of rudder. **1978** J. S. EVANS *Pilot's Manual* iv. 151 Let it be assumed that our aeroplane is in cruising flight, with sufficient rudder applied to prevent propwash-induced yaw.

5. b. The tail of an otter.

[**1903** H. JOHNSTON *Brit. Mammals* vii. 138 The otter.. swims and dives with great facility, and propels itself with all four limbs, using the tail as a great rudder.] **1907** *Yesterday's Shopping* (1969) 694 Horses' hoofs, deer slots, fox, hare, or otter pads cured and mounted in various styles; also fox brushes and otter rudders. **1941** H. CORY *Mammals Brit. Isles* 34 When swimming submerged the animal uses the forefeet for paddling and the hind feet, assisted by the rudder, for steering. **1965** P. WAYRE *Wind in Reeds* xi. 151 Canadian otters are larger and bulkier [than British ones] with broader and deeper heads and thicker rudders. **1976** *Scotsman* 24 Dec. (Weekend Suppl.) 2/2 He [*sc.* an otter] was coiled..with his jaws clenched, and his rudder curled round the webs of his hindfeet.

6. a. *rudder pedal, post*; **rudder-bar**, a bar operated by the pilot's feet which controls the position of an aircraft's rudder.

1912 *Q. Rev.* July 240 Machines like Dunne's, which have no separate rudder-bar allowing of foot-correction. **1918** W. G. MCMINNIES *Pract. Flying* 234 *Rudder post*, the upright member to which the rudder is hinged. **1919** PIPPARD & PRITCHARD *Aeroplane Struct.* v. 36 In some aeroplanes..the rudder bar is replaced by pedals and directional control is obtained by pressing the appropriate pedal. **1935** C. G. BURGE *Compl. Bk. Aviation* 537 *Rudder post*, the main vertical member of a rudder to which the rudder hinges are attached. **1959** Rudder-bar [see *'N, 'N']. **1966** D. STINTON *Anat. Aeroplane* viii. 139 If hinge-moments are too high to be handled efficiently, artificial forces may be transmitted through the stick and rudder-pedals by an artificial feel-system. **1976** B. JACKSON *Flameout* iv. 63 The flight data recorder..tape-recorded..the pilot's movements of the control yokes and rudder pedals, [etc.].

b. *rudder-fan, flutter, power.*

1915 S. H. CARDEN in M. Gilbert *Winston S. Churchill* (1972) III. Compan. I. 625 Large rudder power makes her sufficiently handy although starboard engines out of action. **1928** *Daily Tel.* 13 Mar. 11/3 The machine dived into the sea from a height of about 100 ft. after developing what appeared to be rudder flutter. **1930** J. S. HUXLEY *Bird-Watching* vi. 102 They became birds through the evolution of feathers out of scales... The other peculiarities of modern birds, such as..the transformation of their originally long and awkward tail, like a kite's, into an efficient rudder-fan..came later.

rudder, *v.* (In Dict. s.v. RUDDER *sb.*) Delete *rare* and add: *trans.* and *intr.* Also, to use the rudder. Also *fig.* (Further examples.)

1940 'N. SHUTE' *Landfall* 210 He glanced quickly at the cruiser to check the direction, ruddering slightly to maintain his course. **1942** *Tee Emm* (Air Ministry) II. 65 Do a quick barrel half roll..pulling the stick back.. when you are on your side, and then rudder into a steep dive. **1952** M. TRIPP *Faith is Windsock* ii. 35 Hamish pulled back on the throttles, strangling life from the engines; Bergen ruddered and braked hard. **1954** W. FAULKNER *Fable* 107 He..ruddered the tracer right onto it. **1960** S. PLATH *Colossus* 66 A pigeon rudders down. **1973** M. AMIS *Rachel Papers* 71 That afternoon,.. ruddered by perceptive questions, encouraging smiles and apt generalizations from myself, Rachel Noyes told the story of her life.

ruddering (rʌ·dəriŋ), *a.* [f. RUDDER *sb.* + -ING².] That acts as a rudder; that guides or steers. Cf. *RUDDER *sb.* 5 b.

1960 T. HUGHES *Lupercal* 46 With webbed feet and long ruddering tail. **1960** R. W. MARKS *Dymaxion World of B. Fuller* 29/2 As with the pulled (rather than pushed) wheelbarrow, the ruddering tail wheel was lifted over, rather than shoved into the traveled terrain.

rudderless, *a.* **b.** (Later examples.)

1887 W. B. YEATS *Let.* 11 Mar. (1954) 32 Please excuse this somewhat rudderless scrawl. **1977** *Oxf. Mission Q. Paper* Jan.–Mar. 15 Young folk, often rudderless in their religious thinking and experience of life.

ruddervator (rʌdəɹvēitəɹ). *Aeronaut.* [f. RUDDER *sb.* + ELE)VATOR.] A control surface designed to act as both rudder and elevator.

1962 *Flight Internat.* LXXXI. 172/1 The ruddervators are controlled from a control column horizontally mounted under the right side of the couch. **1966** D. STINTON *Anat. Aeroplane* 244 Flaps, ailerons, and 'ruddervators' were designed to incorporate the minimum number of ribs.

ruddle, *v.* Add: Also *absol.*

1960 S. PLATH *Colossus* 52 Imagine their deep hunger, deep as the dark For the blood-heat that would ruddle or reclaim.

ruddy, *a.* (*sb.*) and *adv.* Add: **A.** *adj.* **3.** *ruddy shelduck, turnstone.*

1852 Ruddy shelduck [see SHELD-DUCK]. **1954** J. DELACOUR *Waterfowl of World* I. 250 The Ruddy Shelduck is a strong and successful species which..occupies a very large range. **1909** J. & M. MACOUN *Catal. Canad. Birds* (ed. 2) 212 Ruddy Turnstone... This species is a common migrant in Newfoundland. **1938** P. A. TAVERNER *Birds of Canada* 185 The turnstone is represented in America by the Ruddy Turnstone.., rather smaller than the European form. **1972** S. BURNFORD *One Woman's Arctic* iv. 92 Only about fifty yards away, were the.. nests of two pairs of ruddy turnstones.

3*. Orig. a euphemistic substitution for BLOODY *a.* 10; now freq. used as an intensive in its own right: damnable, blasted, confounded. *colloq.*

1916 'TAFFRAIL' *Pincher Martin* ii. 28 Go on, Ginger!.. Slosh 'im one on the ruddy boko! **1924** GALSWORTHY *White Monkey* II. i. 121 Only why didn't Mr. Elderson say: 'You ruddy liar!'? **1945** [see *EUSTON ROAD]. **1968** [see *GIVE *v.* 16 c]. **1969** I. KEMP *Brit. G.I. in Vietnam* ii. 31 'Oh no!' I thought. 'The ruddy thing won't have time to open before I hit.' **1977** *Radio Times* 12–18 Nov. 69/4, I carted my ruddy topee all over India and finally abandoned it under a bed in Fort William in Calcutta.

5. a. *ruddy-bodied, -clustered, -faced* (examples), *-finned, -muzzled.*

1916 D. H. LAWRENCE *Twilight in Italy* 89 The many ruddy-clustered oranges beside the path remind me of the lights of a village. **1916** BLUNDEN *Harbingers* 34 Ruddy-finned roach and bronze carp swam. **1922** JOYCE *Ulysses* 291 The figure seated on a large boulder at the foot of a round tower was that of a broadshouldered..ruddyfaced sinewyarmed hero. **1923** D. H. LAWRENCE *Birds, Beasts & Flowers* 62 Cyclamens, ruddy-muzzled cyclamens. **1960** S. PLATH *Colossus* 79 Bronze dead dominate the floor, Resistive, ruddy-bodied.

b. *ruddy-dark, -golden, -orange.*

1927 D. H. LAWRENCE *Mornings in Mexico* 35 Calico pantaloons round his ruddy-dark waist. *Ibid.* 126 The men are naked to the waist, and ruddy-golden. *a* **1930** —— *Last Poems* (1932) 266 Green moonlight And ruddy-orange limbs stirring the limbo Of the unknown air.

B. *adv.* Used, usu. preceding an adj., as an intensifier (orig. a euphemistic substitute for BLOODY *adv.* 2: cf. sense A. 3* above): confoundedly, damnably, damned.

1914 C. BERESFORD *Mem.* I. xiii. 119 All I've got to say, is to say you've got a ruddy good billet. **1922** JOYCE *Ulysses* 420 Lay you two to one Jenatzy licks him ruddy well hollow. **1933** M. LINCOLN *Oh! Definitely* iii. 23 I'd have ruddy well..locked the door. **1959** M. GILBERT *Blood & Judgement* xiii. 139 Culver Street's been pulled down and a ruddy great block of flats put up. **1979** *Oxford Times* 28 Dec. 9/2 Most of the groups I heard there and elsewhere played too ruddy loud.

ruddy, *v.* **2.** (Later example.)

1938 W. DE LA MARE *Memory* 49 See, how the sun Ruddies through his filmy grey, Turns to light the dreaming one.

rude, *a.* and *adv.* Add: **A.** *adj.* **I. 5. e.** Fig. phr. *rude awakening*, a severe disillusionment or arousal from complacency.

1895 G. ALLEN *Woman who Did* vi. 71 Alan was often quite alarmed in his soul when he thought of the rude awakening that no doubt awaited her. **1912** T. DREISER *Financier* v. 47 Life had given him no severe shocks nor rude awakenings. **1971** *Daily Tel.* 12 June 18/1 Anyone visiting this year's Grosvenor House Antique Fair.. with the object of buying antiques on the cheap is in for a rude awakening. **1975** SHEA & WILSON *Golden Apple* IV. 248 Then comes the rude awakening: food riots, industrial stagnation, a reign of lawless looting and plunder.

II. 15. rude boy, one of a class of unemployed black youths inhabiting the poorer areas of Jamaica and typically seen as indolent and apt to commit petty crimes.

1967 *Caribbean Q.* Sept. 39 Rude bwoy is that person, native, who is totally disenchanted with the ruling system; who generally is descended from the 'African' elements in the lower class... Rude bwoys are largely centred in those urban areas that suffer from chronic depression. **1975** *Globe & Mail* (Toronto) 11 June 3/1 The rude boys, rudies or just plain rudes are the street corner toughs, hustlers, petty thieves and dealers in ganja (marijuana) **1976** D. HEBDIGE in Hall & Jefferson *Resistance through Rituals* 152 The exotica of Rastafarianism provided distractive screens behind which the rude boy culture could pursue its own devious devices unhindered and unseen. **1977** LOGAN & WOFFINDEN *New Musical Express Bk. of Rock* 414 The rude boys (outlaws) of Jamaica's shanty towns began to move into the studios, celebrating their own chosen lifestyle, which resulted in a spate of rudeboy records.

B. *adv.* **a.** (Later examples.)

1795 J. WOODFORDE *Diary* 8 Sept. (1929) IV. 226 Jane behaved quite rude this Evening. **1885** G. M. HOPKINS *Poems* (1967) 99 But ah, but O thou terrible, why wouldst thou rude on me Thy wring-world right foot rock?

b. *rude-masoned, -ripened, -rounded* adjs.

a **1889** G. M. HOPKINS *Poems* (1967) 185 Who built these walls made known The music of his mind, Yet here he had but shewn His ruder-rounded rind. **1928** BLUNDEN *Japanese Garland* 20 Over the rude-ripened vale. **1930** —— *Poems* 128 There is a sluice through whose rude-masoned stones And fissured planks our timid river falls.

rude (rūd), *sb. colloq.* [f. prec.] **a.** An impolite or unsophisticated person. **b.** = *rude boy* s.v. *RUDE *a.* 15.

1961 J. DAWSON *Ha-Ha* iv. 74 No Brains' Trust will work so long as you've always got to have a gaggle of rudes and silly old sages to balance the bright young men. **1975** [see *rude boy* s.v.* RUDE *a.* 15].

ruderal, *a.* Add: (Further examples.) Also as *sb.*, a ruderal plant.

1905 F. E. CLEMENTS *Research Methods Ecol.* iv. 263 The pioneers in impoverished or exhausted fields are uniformly ruderal plants. **1929** J. W. BEWS *World's Grasses* vi. 226 Most of the species of *Digitaria* tend to become ruderals. **1963** *New Scientist* 20 June 677/2 The more permanent colonisers [on Lake Kariba, East Africa] appear to fall into two groups, those of semi-aquatic habitats,..and ruderals of open ground. **1970** *Watsonia* VIII. 175 Weeds or ruderal plants. **1979** *Nature* 20–27 Dec. 780/2 An ecological classification of plants into competitors, stress-tolerators and ruderals.

rudery (rū·dəri). [f. RUDE *a.* and *adv.* + -ERY.] Rudeness; rude or impolite speech or behaviour; a rude remark, comment, practical joke, etc.

1932 R. ACKLAND *Strange Orchestra* II. 71 Just been having a bit of rudery, dear. **1933** DYLAN THOMAS *Let.* 25 Dec. (1966) 77, I have..been averse to including such obvious rudery in my letters to you. **1940** 'N. BLAKE' *Malice in Wonderland* II. xvi. 235 What's this? Some new rudery taken place? **1960** S. W. C. PACK *Admiral Lord Anson* i. 3 Although a superficial courtesy existed, coarseness and rudery were common. **1968** *Blackw. Mag.* CCCIII. 454/1 The lane twisted and turned, and small Sikh boys kept pace with us, their long hair tied in top-knots, chanting songs in Punjabi which I trust were not ruderies. **1979** J. SMYTH *Milestones* xviii. 230 Then suddenly he would uncoil, spring to the despatch box and reply pungently to some rudery which had appeared to float over his head.

Rudie (rū·di). *Jamaica.* Also **rudie.** [f. RUDE *a.* and *adv.* + -IE.] = *rude boy* s.v. *RUDE *a.* 15.

1967 *Caribbean Q.* Sept. 41 The number of rudie tunes on the air-waves reflects the increased status accorded Rudies by this other Afro-Jamaican society. **1974** *Howard Jrnl.* XIV. 48 This theme is a strong one in West Indian culture and is reinforced by the image of the rudie in Reggae—the super cool hooligan who always come[s] out on top. **1976** *Daily Mirror* 2 Apr. 21/2 Unemployment was, and is, constantly high, with the Rudies being the main sufferers. Their problems became a theme of ska. **1977** *Westindian World* 3–9 June 13/4 'Steppin Razor'..is a little reminiscent of the rudie tunes of the sixties.

rudiment, *sb.* Add: **1. d.** Pl. (With capital initial.) The name of the lowest class in certain Roman Catholic schools and colleges, freq. divided into the 'third', 'second', and 'first' class (of) Rudiments. Cf. *FIGURE *sb.* 22 b.

1716 [see *FIGURE *sb.* 22 b]. *a* **1799** in C. Butler *Acct. Life Alban Butler* (1799) 6 The year after Mr. Alban Butler's arrival at Douay, I was placed in the same school, under the same master, he being in the first class of rudiments, as it is there called, and I in the lowest. **1846** in *Stonyhurst Mag.* (1933) Dec. 415/2 July 25th Sun. Themes judged Rhet... 29 th. Themes judged Rudiments. **1885** J. GILLOW *Lit. & Biogr. Hist. Eng. Catholics* II. 553 At the period of his liberation Robert Gradwell was in second-class Rudiments. **1893** B. WARD *Hist. St. Edmund's Coll.* iv. 58 The two classes of 'Figures' were changed very shortly after this into three classes of 'Rudiments', and this term has survived at St. Edmund's to the present day. **1912** B. WARD *Eve Catholic Emanc.* III. xxxiv. 2 He was a boy in the 'Second of Rudiments' [*Note*] Equivalent to the Second or Third form at an English school. **1936** M. TRAPPES-LOMAX *Bishop Challoner* i. 5 The 'classes', or forms, were named Figures or Rudiments, Grammar, Syntax, Poetry, and Rhetoric, names which originally were related to the work of the class... This nomenclature is still retained in some of the English Catholic schools. **1972** *Publ. Catholic Rec. Soc.* LXIII. 142 The vast majority of students began their course..in one or other of the Rudiments classes.

rudist (rū·dist). Also **Rudista.** [a. mod.L. family name *Rudista* (J. E. Gray in *Synopsis Contents Brit. Mus.* (ed. 21, 1823) 62), f. L. *rudis* unformed + -*t*- + -A 4.] A fossil pelecypod bivalve mollusc belonging to the superfamily Rudistacea, which included cone-shaped reef-forming animals. Also *attrib.* Also **Ru-, rudi·stid** [-ID[3]], in the same sense.

1889 NICHOLSON & LYDEKKER *Man. Palæont.* (ed. 3) I. xxxvi. 734 The *Rudistæ* are..entirely extinct. **1890** *Mem. Boston Soc. Nat. Hist.* IV. 322/1 The Rudistæ are conical or cup-shaped Pelecypods with a superficially marked radial symmetry. **1935** TWENHOFEL & SHROCK *Invertebr. Paleontol.* ix. 403 The various Rudistids are especially noteworthy. **1959** *New Scientist* 1 Jan. 16/1 A good collection of fossil reef-forming corals, rudistids, and related atoll fauna. **1969** BENNISON & WRIGHT *Geol. Hist. Brit. Isles* xiv. 332 The coral-like Rudists are important, forming reef environments in Tethys. **1978** *Nature* 26 Oct. 779/2 Future editions could be improved by the inclusion of a few famous foreign examples such as the Burgess Shale fauna and a rudist reef association.

rudite (rū·dəit). *Geol.* Also **rudyte.** [f. L. *rūd-us* broken stone, rubble + -ITE[1].] Any consolidated breccia or conglomerate consisting of particles larger than sand grains; = PSEPHITE.

1904 A. W. GRABAU in *Amer. Geologist* XXXIII. 242 The consolidated rock whether conglomerate or breccia may be called a rudyte. **1920** —— *Gen. Geol.* xviii. 569 Three textural types of rock may be recognized: (1) the rubble-rock or rubble-stone, or rudyte, which when the fragments are rounded is a conglomerate and when angular a breccia; (2) the sand-rock or sandstone or arenyte; and (3) the mud-rock or mud-stone or lutyte. **1935** *Bull. Nat. Res. Council* (U.S.) XCVIII. 239 Rudite. This is a general term..for fragmental sedimentary rocks coarser than sand grains. **1959** W. W. MOORHOUSE *Study of Rocks in Thin Section* xviii. 334 The clastic sediments are classified according to size as rudytes (rudaceous), which are conglomerates, arenytes (arenaceous)..and lutytes (lutaceous). **1966** B. SIMPSON *Rocks & Minerals* xvii. 174 The quartz-rich rudites are quartz conglomerates and quartz breccias. **1971** I. G. GASS et al. *Understanding Earth* i. 31/1 The rudites are represented by such rock types as conglomerate.

rue, *sb.*[1] For 'Now *dial.* or *arch.*' read 'Chiefly *dial.* or *arch.*' and add: **1. a.** (Later examples.)

1959 *Listener* 31 Dec. 1174/2 The nature and the mixture of the ingredients in the poetry—nostalgia, bathos, irony, rue, and religious fervour. **1976** *Publishers Weekly* 8 Mar. 64/2 A mix of rue and wit that is vintage [Mort] Sahl.

ruelle. Add: **3.** In France, a small street; a lane, alley.

1908 T. E. LAWRENCE *Let.* 9 Aug. (1938) 59 Streets—mostly stairs, irregular and broken, running under archways and tunnels... Cover these ruelles with grass, heap them with refuse. **1911** O. ONIONS *Widdershins* vii. 242 He took us back along a plantain-groved street, and suddenly turned up an alley... It was a dilapidated, deserted *ruelle*.

Rueping process (rü·piŋ). Also **Rüping,** (*erron.*) **Ruping.** [Named after Max *Rüping* (fl. 1902), German timber engineer, its inventor.] An economical method of preserving wood by applying creosote to it after subjecting it to high air pressure so that the cells are permeated but not filled.

1904 S. M. ROWE *Handbk. Timber Preservation* (rev. ed.) 129 In the new Ruping process the seasoned wood is for some time (from about a half hour to an hour) exposed to a pressure of 5 atmospheres in the boiler..so that all the cells must be filled with air. **1917** A. J. WALLIS-TAYLER *Preservation of Wood* vii. 200 The Rueping Process has been patented in Great Britain... It was primarily devised with the object of reducing the cost of creosoting by preventing the heavy loss occasioned by dripping when the wood is treated by the ordinary process. **1930** H. FERGUSSON in H. Boulton *Century of Wood-Preserving* 66 The British Post Office for some little time has had all its poles done by the Rueping process. **1968** [see *empty-cell* s.v. *EMPTY *a.* and *sb.* C.].

Rufai (rufā·ˌi). Also † **Rifa'ee,** † **Rufaee, Rufa'i.** Pl. as sing. or **-s.** [Turk. *Rufai*, ad. Arab. *rifā'ī*, f. the name of Aḥmad al-*Rifā'ī* (d. 1183), the founder of this order.] A howling dervish (see quot. 1877 and DERVISH), one of an order of Muslim friars pledged to poverty and self-mortification.

1832 G. A. HERKLOTS tr. *Jaffur Shurreef's Qanoon-e-Islam* xxviii. 291 *Rufaee* or *Goorz-mar*, they originate from Syed Ahmud Kubeer, whose *fuqeers* strike the point of the *goorz* against their breasts, or into their eyes, level blows at their backs with the sword, thrust a spit through their sides, or into their eyes. **1836** E. W. LANE *Acct. Manners & Customs Mod. Egyptians* I. x. 310 The Rifa'-'ee durwee'shes are celebrated for the performance of many wonderful feats. **1868** J. P. BROWN *Dervishes* ii. 51 *Ahmed Sa'eed Rufā'ee* was the founder of the Order of the *Rufā'ees*, generally known among European travellers as the 'Howling Dervishes', from their peculiar mode of worship. **1877** *Encycl. Brit.* VII. 114/1 This leads to the Devr, or rotation, in which the Rufai, or Howling Dervishes, stand in a circle, shoulder to shoulder, each on his right foot, and swaying the body and the left leg backwards and forwards or from side to side. **1885** T. P. HUGHES *Dict. Islam* 120/1 Some..wear tall caps called *kulāhs*, made also of felt; and others, such as the Rufā'īs, use short caps called Tāqīyah, to which is added a coarse cloth. **1900** 'ODYSSEUS' *Turkey in Europe* v. 192 There are several orders..the most important being the Bektashis, the Mevlevis, and the Rufais (the two latter commonly known to Europeans as dancing and howling dervishes). **1928** W. B. SEABROOK *Adventures in Arabia* xiii. 251 The objective of our pilgrimage was a monastery of the Rufai, or Howling Dervishes—a sect fundamentally different from the Whirling Melewi—in the mountains between Hama and Aleppo. **1965** *Encycl. Islam* (rev. ed.) II. 164/2 The Sa'dis, Rifā'īs and Aḥmadīs have particular feats, peculiar to each *tarīḳa*, of eating glowing embers and live serpents or scorpions and glass, of passing needles through their bodies and spikes into their eyes.

ruff, *sb.*[3] Add: **3. b.** *Comb.* **ruff and discard** *Bridge*, an opportunity (usu. for declarer) to win a trick by ruffing in one hand while discarding a loser from the other.

1939 N. DE V. HART *Bridge Players' Bedside Bk.* xxxix. 120 If West leads a Heart, then declarer gets a ruff-and-discard which enables him to ruff the third round of either minor suit. **1972** R. MARKUS *Common-Sense Bridge* III. 102 A ruff and discard disposed of a losing club. **1977** *Bridge Mag.* July 34/2 Aunt Agatha now played the king of clubs, giving West the option of conceding a ruff and discard or leading away from his king of spades.

ruff, *sb.*[5] **1.** (Later examples.)

1927 *Melody Maker* Aug. 804/3 All the various beats used in military drumming. The stroke-and-drag paradiddle and the four-stroke ruff, for instance, are not essential. **1957** A. A. SHIVAS *Art of Tympanist & Drummer* i. 30 *Embellishments.* These are very important and much used in side drumming... The three important ones are the flam, the drag and the ruff.

Ruff (rɒf), *sb.*[10] [f. the name of W. *Ruff*, founder editor of *Guide to the Turf or Pocket racing Companion* (1842–53), a twice-yearly compendium of horse-racing information, subsequently published as *Ruff's Guide to the Turf* and since 1869 incorporating various other racing periodicals.] A colloq. abbreviation of *Ruff's Guide to the Turf*.

1854 *Sporting Rev.* Jan. 63 The racing world have in Ruff and the Book Calendar two very competent expounders of the 'forms' in which thorough-breds have 'gone' this season. **1902** in Farmer & Henley *Slang* VI. 1. 70/1. **1918** G. FRANKAU *One of Them* xxi. 159 Weep for a Shrunken Ruff, a tipless tout.

ruff, *v.*[2] Add: **2. a.** (Earlier example of present spelling.)

1813 *Hoyle's Games of Whist & Quadrille* 50 *Ruff*, and *over-ruff*, to trump a suit led, second or third hand.

b. Const. *out.* To defeat (a card, etc.) by ruffing, so as to establish master cards in the suit led; also, with suit as object.

1927 M. C. WORK *Contract Bridge* 141 *Ruffing out*, trumping the low cards of a suit before playing its high cards. **1939** N. DE V. HART *Bridge Players' Bedside Bk.* 22, I laid down dummy's Ace and King of Hearts, and then tried to ruff out the suit. **1960** T. REESE *Play Bridge with Reese* 23 If the spades are breaking as well, I can play Ace and another spade, ruff out the King of clubs and enter dummy to make two long clubs. **1967** P. ANDERTON *Play Bridge* xi. 88 South covers with his A. .. and West trumps. This procedure is known as ruffing out a suit and East now holds the master cards in the Spade suit. **1972** *Times* 20 May 13/3 She ruffed out the clubs ruffing the third round with the ♡10.

ruffer[1]. For *rare*—[0] and (See quot.) in Dict. read: **a.** = *ruffing trick* s.v. *RUFFING *vbl. sb.*[1] **b.** A card that ruffs or trumps another (see also quot. 1611 in Dict.).

1936 E. CULBERTSON *Contract Bridge Compl.* xxxix. 435 A trick made by ruffing a losing card with an otherwise worthless card of the trump suit is called a ruffer. **1974** *Country Life* 28 Feb. 453/3 This not only deprives South of a diamond ruff, but the trump trick comes back if South uses dummy's Ten as a ruffer. **1975** *Ibid.* 30 Jan. 289/3 The right way is to use his own trumps as ruffers.

ruffianing, *vbl. sb.* **2.** (Earlier example.)

1829 P. EGAN *Boxiana* 2nd Ser. II. 446 Ruffianing was all *the go* at Moulsey Hurst so slippery, Till Science took the cause in hand.

ruffianly, *a.* **1.** (Later *Comb.* example.)

1882 W. D. HAY *Brighter Britain!* I. xi. 301 A line of nine ruffianly-looking scarecrows, under review by.. head-master of the ceremonies.

ruffing, *vbl. sb.*[1] Add: Also *attrib.*, as *ruffing element, trick, value.*

1930 E. CULBERTSON *Contract Bridge Blue Bk.* iv. 60 The..characteristic of the Supporting Hand lies in the use of ruffing tricks. **1936** 'LUCIAN' *Straight Bid* xii. 126 In actual play the result is materially affected by.. ruffing values, etc. **1950** *Bridge from 'Times'* ii. 63 This is a pretty example of the use of the long trump hand to make ruffing tricks. **1952** I. MACLEOD *Bridge* xii. 143 The introduction of the ruffing element, and the problems of trump management make the play in a suit contract far more difficult and intricate. **1971** *Country Life* 22 Apr. 973/1 The ruffing element which obtains in a suit contract. **1977** *Bridge Mag.* Sept. 153/2 His ruffing values being distinctly unimpressive he quickly converted to seven no-trumps.

ruffing, *ppl. a.*[2] [f. RUFF *v.*[1]] That forms or rises in ruffs.

1865 R. D. BLACKMORE in *Macm. Mag.* XII. 33/1 The blackcocks..swell their ruffing breasts, and crow for their rivals to spar with them.

Ruffini (rufni·i). *Anat.* The name of Angelo *Ruffini* (1864–1929), Italian anatomist, used *attrib.* and with *of* to designate certain dermal sensory organs.

1900 HUBER & DEWITT in *Jrnl. Compar. Neurol.* X. 175 The author [*sc.* Ruffini] thus distinguishes this spindle, which may bear his name, from the neuro-tendinous end-organs of Golgi... The Ruffini organ is composed of connective and elastic tissue. **1928** *Amer. Jrnl. Psychol.* XL. 357 No Golgi-Màzzoni, Krause or Ruffini end-organs were discovered in the hairy parts of the human skin. **1974** D. & M. WEBSTER *Compar. Vertebr. Morphol.* x. 200 On the other hand, the end bulbs of Ruffini—flattened, bulblike endings within a fine, connective tissue network—respond to temperature increases. **1981** A. BRODAL *Neurol Anat.* (ed. 3) ii. 51 Another type of slowly adapting receptor..has a resting discharge that increases when a mechanical stimulus is applied to the skin. These receptors..are found in the dermis and appear to be Ruffini endings.

ruffle, *sb.*[1] **II. 7. b.** Substitute for def.: *pl.* Handcuffs. *slang* (? *Obs.*). For **1796** *Grose's Dict. Vulgar T.* (ed. 3) read **1785** GROSE *Dict. Vulgar T.* and add examples.

1839 W. H. AINSWORTH *Jack Sheppard* I. II. ix. 305 'I'll accommodate you with a pair of ruffles.' And he proceeded to handcuff his captive. **1840** H. COCKTON *Life Valentine Vox* xiv. 109 'Sam! here, where are the ruffles?' and the fellow addressed instantly produced a pair of handcuffs. **1912** A. H. LEWIS *Apaches of N.Y.* viii. 179 Outside they found Cohen..with the ruffles on the Ghost.

8. *attrib.* and *Comb.*, as *ruffle collar, lace; ruffle cuffed, headed* adjs.; **ruffle shirt** *N. Amer.*, (*a*) a shirt decorated with ruffles; (*b*) *transf.*, an aristocrat, a person of means; hence **ruffle-shirted** *a.*, **ruffle-shirter.**

1968 J. IRONSIDE *Fashion Alphabet* 52 *Ruffle collar*, a collar cut on the bias or circular so that it falls in a fluted ruffle round the neck. **1880** 'MARK TWAIN' *Tramp Abroad* 399, I did not get back the same drawers I sent down... I got a pair on a new plan. They were merely a pair of white ruffle-cuffed absurdities. **1927** W. DEEPING *Kitty* xxix. 370 The ruffle-headed pianist bumping up and down on his chair. **1682** J. PINNEY *Let.* 4 Sept. (1939) 15 The remnant you sent downe shall speadily be cut & sent & a ruffel lace of 2 nailes broad. **1830** *Amer. Sentinel* (Philadelphia) 27 Aug. 2/2 Where a dinner is to be got up, a few mechanics are procured to take the first rank, and the ruffle shirts fall into the rear. **1831** *American* (Harrodsburg, Kentucky) 22 July 3/1 General Jackson and his friends are lessening the burthens of the people by.. placing the Tax, on Wines, Rum,..and fine cloth such as the *Rufle* [*sic*] *shirt* gentry wear. **1838** B. DRAKE *Tales & Sk.* 64 The colonists presented, indeed, a curiously grotesque appearance, loitering about the station in ruffle shirts and coon-skin caps. **1840** J. P. KENNEDY *Quodlibet* xii. 158 If he does get on with his business, and makes a little fortune, we can call him a..Ruffle Shirt. **1848** *Knickerbocker* XVIII. 520 It was asserted..that he wore a ruffle-shirt and overshoes. **1835** A. B. LONGSTREET *Georgia Scenes* 85 The *ruffle-shirted* little darlings of the present day. *a* **1864** [see sense 7 a in Dict.]. **1876** *Harper's Weekly* 26 Aug. 691/1 They belonged to the class which the ward politicians of to-day sneer at as ruffle-shirted and silk-stockinged. **1842** *Knickerbocker* XIX. 305 Many a taunt, hitherto repressed, was thrown at the ruffle-shirters, as the town boys called them.

ruffled, *a.* Add: **a.** *ruffled shirt*, a shirt decorated with ruffles; also *transf.*, = *ruffle shirt* (*b*) s.v. *RUFFLE *sb.*[1] 8.

1754 *Calendar Virginia State Papers* (1875) I. 249, 2 fine Ruffled shirts and 2 plain shirts for themselves..sent by the Governor to them. **1768–74** [in Dict.]. **1860** O. W. HOLMES *Prof. at Breakfast-Table* i. 19 Joe Warren, the first bloody ruffled-shirt of the Revolution, was as good as born here. **1905** A. H. RICE *Sandy* 271 A few feet farther away hung a portrait of her grandfather, brave in a high stock and ruffled shirt. **1974** J. AIKEN *Midnight is Place* iv. 120 He wore black buckled shoes and a ruffled shirt.

b. (Further examples.)

1850 *Rep. Comm. Patents: Agric. 1849* (U.S.) 289 The ruffled oat is very much cultivated, and highly esteemed. **1941** J. STEINBECK *Sea of Cortez* xvii. 170 There were many of the ruffled clams with hard, thick, wavy shells.

ruffler[1]. (Later examples.)

1908 *Sears, Roebuck Catal.* 41/1 The set of attachments..consists of one ruffler, one shirring plate, one tucker. **1964** *McCall's Sewing* x. 144/2 The ruffler attachment is also capable of gathering large sections of fabric.

Rufflette (rɒ·flèt, rɒfle·t). [f. RUFFLE *sb.*[1] + -ETTE.] A proprietary name for a kind of tape that can be sewn to the top edge of a curtain, having slits at regular intervals by which curtain-hooks may be attached, and cords threaded through that enable the tape and curtain to be gathered or 'ruffled'.

1931 *Trade Marks Jrnl.* 18 Nov. 1533 The Rufflette. Use claimed from 28th September, 1922... Cotton curtain heading tapes included in Class 25. **1947** *Radio Times* 18 Apr. 22/2 (Advt.), There's more than material in curtains..there's the art of making them drape beautifully—how simple that is with 'Rufflette' curtain tape with hooks and rings. **1964** *McCall's Sewing* xvi. 280 Two types of Rufflette are available giving gathered or pleated effects. In both cases first form hem..then baste Rufflette tape to this. **1973** *Guardian* 28 Feb. 11/3 Curtains, with Rufflette tape topping, are in two sizes.

ruffly, *a.* Add: Also **ruffley.** (Later examples.)

1909 [see *HATTY *a.*]. **1980** M. G. EBERHART *Casa Madrone* ii. 30 A ruffly blouse.

ruff-scuff, alteration of *rough-scuff* s.v. ROUGH *a.* 21. (In quot. 1902, = poor fodder.)

1902 H. F. DAY *Pine Tree Ballads* 4 Drat the man who feeds out ruff-scuff, wood and wire from the swale. **1936** *N.Y. American* 13 Aug. 17/1 There is a snug harbor.. chivvied out of a city's ruff-scuff for dreamers.

rufous, *a.* Add: **1. a.** (Later examples.)

1922 JOYCE *Ulysses* 182 Glittereyed, his rufous skull close to his greencapped desk-lamp sought the face. **1977** *Time* 3 Jan. 21/1 The flat kindly face of Mr. Earl's photographs has made no print on any of them except the rufous Billy, a wily jester.

c. *rufous bee,* a solitary bee, *Andrena fulva*; *rufous rat-kangaroo,* a small marsupial, *Æpyprymnus rufescens,* found in south-eastern parts of Australia.

1926 LE SOUEF & BURRELL *Wild Animals Australasia* 234 Rufous Rat-kangaroo... General colour above coarsely grizzled rufescent grey. **1928** *Observer* 17 June 24/3 That queen of burrowers,..the rufous bee, Andrena. **1972** *Sunday Mail Mag.* (Brisbane) 3 Sept. 4 The rufous rat-kangaroo..occurs in many parts of central and south Queensland, particularly in open forest.

2. *rufous-brown* (later examples).

1953 D. A. BANNERMAN *Birds Brit. Isles* I. 300 The black crown feathers are then mostly obscured by buff or rufous-brown tips to the feathers. **1968** B. HINES *Kestrel for Knave* 26 On a shelf behind the bars stood a kestrel hawk: Rufous brown. Flecked breast, dark bars across her back and wings.

4. b. (Later examples.)

1907 R. SOUTH *Moths Brit. Isles* 1st Ser. 299 The Small Rufous..varies from pale ochreous white, through reddish shades, to a greyish brown. **1958** W. J. STOKOE *Caterpillars Brit. Moths* (new ed.) I. 281 The Small Rufous..occurring in fens and marshes.

rufus, *a.* Add: **B.** *sb.* (Also with capital initial.) **1.** *U.S. slang.* A countryman. **2.** *colloq.* A nickname for a red-haired person.

1955 D. W. MAURER in *Publ. Amer. Dial. Soc.* xxiv. 106 A farmer or yokel is called by old-timers a *rufus* (obsolescent) or a *hoosier.* **1959** I. & P. OPIE *Lore & Lang. Schoolch.* ix. 170 Red heads attract a barrage of nicknames:..reddy, red kipper, red mop, red thatch, red paint brush, Rufus, and Rusty.

rug, *sb.*[2] Add: **3. a.** (Earlier and later examples.) Now freq. of shapes other than square or oblong. *to cut a* (or *the*) *rug*: to dance (esp. to jazz music); *to pull the rug out from under someone*: see *PULL *v.* 19 k); *to sweep* (or *kick*) (something) *under the rug*: to conceal (something difficult, embarrassing, or unpleasant) in the hope that it will go unnoticed or be forgotten (cf. *CARPET *sb.* 2 e).

1808 JANE AUSTEN *Let.* 1 Oct. (1952) 212 She does not doubt your making out the Star pattern very well, as you have the Breakfast-room-rug to look at. **1930** *Heal's Catal.: Furnit.* 9 Knotted Axminster Circular Rug, designed by the late Noel Simmons, 5 ft. in diameter. **1942** *Harper's Bazaar* July 21/3 Let's dance, wanta cut a rug. **1943** *N.Y. Times* 9 May II. 5/4 Why, brother, all the cats cut a mean rug to that music. **1945** T. WILLIAMS *Glass Menagerie* vii. 107 'How about cutting the rug a little, Miss Wingfield?' 'Oh, I—' 'Or is your program filled up? Let me have a look at it. Why, every dance is taken!' **1961** D. M. DISNEY *Mrs Meeker's Money* vii. 77 The whole thing..was so far outside the normal routine.. that it practically demanded being swept under the rug. **1973** *Times* 1 Dec. 20/8 Those who used to look for reds under the beds now fear bugs under the rugs. **1976** *National Observer* (U.S.) 25 Sept. 12/4, I can see numerous problems that were rather swept under the rug in the article. **1978** M. PUZO *Fools Die* xvi. 174 Unless the government covers the whole thing up, you know, kicks it under the rug.

b. *U.S. slang.* A wig.

1940 J. O'HARA *Pal Joey* 190, I even wear a little rug up front. **1967** W. & M. MORRIS *Dict. Word & Phr. Origins* II. 75 Advertisements for men's wigs invariably refer to them as *hair pieces,* but in the trade a wig may be a *doily,* a *divot* or a *rug. Ibid.,* And a *rug?* Well, that's the works—a wig to conceal over-all baldness. **1978** *Telegraph* (Brisbane) 18 Feb. 8/2 'Now, in fact, I do wear a hairpiece in the film I'm making.'..The film for which he has donned a 'rug' as they are called, is Meteor.

6. b. *rug-chest, -fringe, -hook, -hooking, -making* (later example), *-peddler, -wool, -work* (earlier example), *-yarn*; **rug brick,** a rough-surfaced brick; **rug-cutter** *U.S. slang,* an enthusiastic or expert dancer; also *transf.*; so **rug-cutting,** dancing; **rug-ranking** *Canad.,* the system of determining the salary of a secretary in federal employment by the status of the person for whom she works; so **rug-rank** *v.*; **rug-rat** *U.S. slang,* a child.

[**1952** *Bricklaying* (Structural Clay Products Inst.) I. ii. 28 Types and Colors of Brick... The Matt faces and Rug faces can almost be placed in the same family. The degree of smoothness or roughness is almost unlimited.] **1961** WEBSTER, Rug brick. **1968** *Globe & Mail* (Toronto) 3 Feb. 43/1 (Advt.), 3 bedroom rug brick home. **1972** *Times* 19 Sept. 9/5 (Advt.), Partners desk; rug chests. **1976** *Leicester Trader* 24 Nov. 19/2 (Advt.), Rug chests... £25. **1938** *N.Y. Amsterdam News* 2 Apr. 17/1 The thousands of..rugcutters..that are being hatched daily.. are a peril. **1941** W. C. HANDY *Father of Blues* (1957) i. 6 Country gals and their..suitors got as much enjoyment.. as jitterbugs or rug-cutters get nowadays from a swing band. **1942** Z. N. HURSTON in *Amer. Mercury* July 96/1 *Rug-cutter,* originally a person frequenting house-rent parties, cutting up the rugs of the host with his feet; a person too cheap or poor to patronize regular dance halls; now means a good dancer. **1959** N. MAILER *Advts. for Myself* (1961) 107 He seemed full of strength and merriment. He would clap two geishas to him, and call across..to another soldier. 'Hey, Brown,' he would shout, 'ain't this a rug-cutter?' **1940** *Amer. Speech* XV. 205/1 *Rug-cutting,* violent, eccentric dancing. **1942** *Chatelaine* Apr. 54/2 The rug-cutting addicts discovered an older form of swing. **1947** S. LEWIS *Kingsblood Royal* 21 As I say: we don't know where Belfreda goes or what she does—rug-cutting or witchcraft or maybe she belongs to some coloured left-wing political gang. **1981** 'S. CAUDWELL' *Thus was Adonis Murdered* ix. 114 He raised again the matter of the rug-cutting expedition... The only places..where there might be dancing..looked to me formidably expensive. **1897** *Sears, Roebuck Catal.* 298/3 Wool Rug Fringe, with gimp heading 3 inches deep. **1922** JOYCE *Ulysses* 691 The upturned rugfringe. **1966** *Olney Amsden & Sons Ltd. Price List* 35 Latchet Rug Hooks... 16/- Dozen. **1967** *House & Garden* June 19/1 *Hooked rugs...* You need open-mesh canvas and a rug hooking tool which is a metal hook fitted into a wooden handle. It has a hinged metal shank at the hook end which will open and close automatically to prevent the hook getting caught in the canvas. **1974** *Aiken* (S. Carolina) *Standard* 22 Apr. 2-A/6 Rug Hooking, 9:30 a.m.–2:30 p.m., Recreation Center, North Augusta. **1976** N. ROBERTS *Face of France* iii. 39 Shops with displays of equipment for tapestry work and rug-making. **1916** J. LONDON *Let.* 12 Oct. (1966) 473 'Uncle Charley'..then proceeded to shake you down in proper money-lender,..rug-peddler fashion. **1977** *Kingston* (Ontario) *Whig-Standard* 9 Feb. 7/2 Her abilities caught the eye of some of the rising lights of her time, and the story has it that she 'rug-ranked' her way up out of the secretarial classifications. **1973** *Globe & Mail* (Toronto) 21 July 1/1 Rug-ranking..refers to the Government's method of establishing the pay level of secretaries in the same way the quality of the manager's rug is determined. It goes with the title on the door. *Ibid.,* While Mr. Drury says 'there isn't much possibility' of replacing the rug-ranking system with a point-rating system, he expresses sympathy for the problems faced by the secretaries. **1968–70** *Current Slang* (Univ. S. Dakota) III–IV. 104 *Rug rat,* a small child. **1976** *Daily Tel.* (Colour Suppl.) 16 July 10/1 He is without children; he has rug-rats instead. **1926** S. T. WARNER *Lolly Willowes* II. 114 She bought an extensive parcel..of variously coloured rug-wools. **1967** E. SHORT *Embroidery & Fabric Collage* iii. 83 A soft Persian rug wool is the easiest to sew with. **1823** E. WEETON *Let.* 21 Nov. (1969) II. 243 She is fond of rug work, and has done a great deal in a superior and beautiful manner. **1895** *Montgomery Ward Catal.* 124/3 Colored Rug Yarn... ingrain carpet yarn, assorted colors, 4 skeins to pound. **1932** D. C. MINTER *Mod. Needlecraft* 224/2 The thinner qualities of rug yarn—such as Persian, Straight, Shetland and various Thrums yarns.

rug, *sb.*[3] (Further examples.)

1622 DRAYTON *Poly-Olbion* II. xxvi. 124 Thicke Vapours, that like Rugs still hang the troubled ayre. **1969** G. M. BROWN *Orkney Tapestry* 29 The old Orkneymen had a range of words for every kind and intensity of rain—a driv, a rug, a murr..a hellyiefer.

rug, *v.*[1] Add: **1. a.** (Later example.)

1930 KIPLING *Limits & Renewals* (1932) 234 Old dry bites—when they get good hold and rugg you. That showed he must have dealt with the Beasts.

2. a. Also, to struggle.

1832 *Chambers's Edin. Jrnl.* I. 225/1 The gilly,..who comes into the town,..rugging and riving for a place in some writer's office. **1951** R. RENDALL *Orkney Variants* 24 Their lowan e'en are taakan tent O'chiels like Mansie o' the Bu Whose days upon the land are spent Ruggan wi' Taurus and the Pleugh.

rug, *v.*[3] [f. RUG *sb.*[2]] *trans.* To cover with a rug. Freq. with *up.*

1818 M. EDGEWORTH *Let.* 15 Oct. (1971) 126 He hopes to have the rooms carpetted and rugged by tuesday. **1936** F. CLUNE *Roaming round Darling* iii. 26 Many sharp turns and wattle-trees. The latter, droopy after being out all night, should be rugged up this weather. **1961** C. H. D. TODD *Popular Whippet* iii. 39 Kennels of greyhounds usually have the inmates 'rugged up' at night. **1968** E. R. BUCKLER *Ox Bells & Fireflies* vi. 93 You rugged the oxen and took the double-bitted ax from its leather fastener. **1975** D. FRANCIS *High Stakes* i. 18 He was a great horse..he would soon be rugged up nice and quiet in a stable.

ruga. Add: (Further examples.)

1913 *Cunningham's Text-bk. Anat.* (ed. 4) 1298 When this muscular layer is contracted, the scrotum becomes smaller..and the skin is thrown into folds or wrinkles called rugæ. **1962** *Gray's Anat.* (ed. 33) 1514 The loose texture of the mucous layer allows the mucous coat to be thrown into folds or rugae when the bladder is empty. **1963** J. OSBORNE *Dental Mech.* (ed. 5) ii. 40 The rugae may be accentuated with blue inlay wax. **1969** *Gloss. Terms Dentistry* (*B.S.I.*) 107 *Rugae,* the irregular ridges of the mucous membrane covering the anterior part of the hard palate.

Hence **ru·gal** *a.*

1936 KANTNER & WEST *Phonetics* (ed. 3) I. iii. 48 Attention should be drawn to the alveolar or rugal ridge which is the raised line of flesh found at the point where the teeth emerge from the gums.

Rugbeian. Add: Also **Rugboean.** (Earlier and later examples.)

1714 T. CAVE *Let.* 16 June in M. M. Verney *Verney Lett.* (1930) I. xiii. 249 We also favoured this day our two young Rugbeians and found Em well. **1971** *Times* 18 Dec. 13/7 He had, in the opinion of many people with whom I have spoken (including one eminent old Rugboean), fully captured Hughes's message.

Rugby. Add: Also with small initial. **a.** (Further examples.) Also *Comb.* **Rugby League,** an association of Rugby football clubs formed in 1922 (previously the 'Northern Union'), having rules differing from those of the Rugby Union; Rugby played according to these rules; also *attrib.*; **rugby tackle,** a tackle in which the arms are used to bring an opposing player down, as in Rugby football; **Rugby Union,** an association of Rugby football clubs formed in 1871; Rugby played according to its rules; also *attrib.*

See esp. quot. 1975.

1871 *Field* 22 July 82/2 (*heading*) *The Rugby Union.* A special general meeting of the Rugby Football Union will be held at the Arundel Hotel, Arundel Street, Strand, on Monday evening. **1874** G. H. WEST *Rugby Union Football Ann.* 2 The following clubs have now enrolled themselves under the Rugby Union. *Ibid.* 11 Since the formation of the Rugby Union, the rules of football have been somewhat modified and altered... A few hints, therefore, on the general style of play in the Rugby Union game, and also an explanation of those rules which most affect it may not be out of place. **1885** [see *ASSOCIATION II]. **1906** GALLAHER & STEAD *Compl. Rugby Footballer* xix. 265 There were fifty thousand people present—by far the biggest attendance of spectators we had ever seen at a Rugby match. **1923** *Whitaker's Almanack* 474/2 *Northern Union in 1921–22* This body is now called the Rugby League. **1926–7** *Army & Navy Stores Catal.* 721/2 Rugby jerseys (to order only). **1929** R. HARDING *Rugby* 142 It was said that a certain Rugby League Club was prepared to give me £750 to become a professional Rugby player. *Ibid.* 144 The system of professionalism which obtains in the Rugby League is the best. **1931** R. CAMPBELL *Georgiad* I. 18 Jack Squire..who ..makes a funeral of a Rugby Match. **1959** *Times* 21 Sept. 3/6 In this community of Rugby-minded souls every man..could readily appreciate the virtues of an attacking as against a defensive policy. **1959** F. GUEST *Indian Cavalryman* viii. 97 The subaltern, who was an athletic young man, immediately dived at the men in a Rugby tackle. **1960** T. MCLEAN *Kings of Rugby* viii. 57 His Rugby-playing days were over. **1961** *Times* 7 Apr. 20/7 In the matter of crowd behaviour, in fact, the Rugby-watching public can in no way afford to be smug. **1963** *Listener* 14 Feb. 300/1 David Storey's *This Sporting Life* is a *bildungsroman* of an unusual sort. Machin, its central character, is a miner turned Rugby League player. **1969** [see *LEAGUE *sb.*[2] 1 c]. **1969** *Listener* 20 Mar. 384/3 The 'sheer disorder' of the broken field of your Rugby Union game. **1975** *Oxf. Illustr. Dict., Rugby football,* one of the two main types of football (the other being Association football), played with 15 players a side (in Rugby Union) or 13 (in Rugby League), with an elliptical football punted, dropped, or passed from hand to hand, the object being to touch down behind the opponents' line and score a try, and to kick the ball over the crossbar of the H-shaped goal. **1976** J. MCCLURE *Rogue Eagle* ii. 30 Hulk's Airtex shirt and ridiculous rugby shorts. **1976** *Western Mail* (Cardiff) 27 Nov., Mid-Wales Howells Cup first round rugby tie with Mid-Glamorgan..has been postponed. **1976** *Alyn & Deeside Observer* 10 Dec. 3/7 In the second half..Chester played some excellent rugby. **1978** *Rugby World* Apr. 45 (Advt.), The *original* long playing records of Rugby Songs in the *Jock Strapp Series. Ibid.* 51 (Advt.), Top quality rugby jerseys.

b. Rugby fives, the leading form of fives: see FIVES[2].

1897 *Encycl. Sport* I. 398/2 In the Eton court..the presence of the pepper-box, the hole, and the step, make the game in practice as different from Rugby Fives as in theory it is similar. **1935** *Encycl. Sports* 270/1 A Rugby fives court, called after the school of that name, is a covered four-walled building. The walls are all plain, except that on the front wall there is a ledge or board, above which the ball must be struck to be in play. **1958** *Times* 16 Dec. 4/6 Old Oundelians..beat Rugby Fives Association..by 121 points to 70. **1975** *Oxf. Compan. Sports & Games* 870/1 Rugby fives is mainly a school, old boys', and university game.

ruge, *sb.*[1] (Later example.)

1791 A. GRAHAM in *Publ. Hudson's Bay Rec. Soc.* (1969) XXVII. IV. 117 [The tusk of the unicorn fish] is quite straight, and has a double spiral ruge on its surface.

rugged, *a.*[1] Add: **4. b.** Also *colloq.* in weakened sense: tough, difficult.

1942 *Yank* 7 Oct. 7 'Rugged' the Destroyers call the Tank Hunting Course. **1943** *Newsweek* 27 Sept. 23/1 The war here is still pretty rugged, as the boys say. **1946** *News Chron.* 30 Aug. 3/8 The first night was a bit rugged, in a way (George said). There being no bed, Mrs Cain made up the bedclothes on the concrete floor. **1953** *Manch. Guardian* 31 July 4/6 They thought it not too strenuous: it had not been easy but had been 'rugged'. **1973** J. Pattinson *Search Warrant* v. 81 If things get really rugged I just put the bite on my old man.

8. (Later examples.)

1931 *Amer. Speech* VI. 185 Frequent adjectives of encomium in book reviews are..romantic, rugged, ruthless. **1966** *Listener* 10 Mar. 363/2 Nicholas Maw's.. string quartet, a closely-knit, rugged work, product of a rich and fertile imagination. **1976** *Gramophone* Dec. 1057/2 Jochum's reading has a rugged truth combined with poetic sensibility.

9. a. *spec.* in phr. *rugged individualism.* So *rugged individualist, individuality.*

1928 H. Hoover *New Day* 154 We were challenged with a peace-time choice between the American system of rugged individualism and a European philosophy or diametrically opposed doctrines—doctrines of paternalism and state socialism. **1937** [see *deliquescent *a.* 3]. **1937** *Education* Nov. 186/1 Each of them..is a rugged individualist doing everything to satisfy his own personal desire. **1946** G. B. Shaw *Geneva* III. 76 Your pose is that of the rugged individualist, the isolationist. **1962** [see *same B. 2 d]. **1973** *Guardian* 18 June 4/4 The apolitical frame of mind which is summed up in the cliche 'rugged individualism'. **1974** *Encycl. Brit. Macropædia* V. 403/1 Cypriots are a people of rugged individuality.

b. orig. *U.S.* Of a manufactured object: strongly constructed, capable of withstanding rough usage. Also *transf.*

1921 *Wireless World* 29 Oct. 477/2 The whole design has been made robust, or, as our American friends would say, 'rugged'. **1960** *Practical Wireless* XXXVI. 302/1 The mains transformer should be a rugged component capable of secure attachment to the chassis to survive the hazards of transport. **1975** J. Wyllie *Butterfly Flood* xxvii. 128 Everybody uses Land Rovers. Good cars, too. Rugged. **1978** *Detroit Free Press* 16 Apr. (Gardening Guide) 6 (Advt.), This 19.9 hp grounds maintenance tractor is specially designed for big jobs where you need rugged, dependable power.

ruggedize (rʌ·gĕdaiz), *v.* orig. *U.S.* [f. Rugged *a.*[1] + -ize.] *trans.* To make rugged; to produce in a version designed to withstand rough usage. So **ru·ggedized** *ppl. a.*; **ruggediza·tion.**

1954 *Electronic Engin.* XXVI. 255 The recent introduction of 'ruggedized' valves. **1958** C. C. Adams *Space Flight* 198 Automatic-control mechanisms must be added to the ship so that maneuvers can be programmed into them while the men are lying all but helpless on their contour chairs. And these equipments themselves must be 'ruggedized' to withstand the very accelerations they are compensating for. **1959** *Wall St. Jrnl.* (Eastern ed.) 18 May 13/3 There are no two ways about it. Ruggedization is costly. **1962** *Daily Tel.* 21 May 10/8 A leaflet..from a New York electrical equipment firm..describes a 'ruggedised weather-proofed instrument'. **1969** *IEEE Trans. Nuclear Sci.* XVI. 314/1 An electronic subsystem packaged in a compact and ruggedized fashion suitable for operation in outer space. **1971** *Daily Tel.* (Colour Suppl.) 10 Dec. 31/4 The tubes were used extensively in the Korean War. Since then they have been miniaturised and protected—or 'ruggedised'—against the rough treatment they can expect on active service, and have spawned many instruments. **1977** *Sci. Amer.* Oct. 140/1 (Advt.), When the frequency, sinusoidal amplitude and sweep rate of the vibration levels demand the ultimate in ruggedization, consider Questar.

ruggedness. Add: **3.** Of manufactured objects: robustness, durability. Cf. *rugged *a.*[1] 9 b.

1936 *Physics* VII. 75/1 The ruggedness of the simplified extrusion plastometer has been established by over two years of practically uninterrupted service. **1971** *Physics Bull.* Nov. 644/1 (Advt.), Designed to provide the versatility required for laboratory use with the ruggedness of production line equipment.

rugger[2]. Add: (Later *attrib.* examples.) **rugger-tackle** *v. trans.* = Tackle *v.* 5 (*a*).

1914 'Bartimeus' *Naval Occasions* ix. 64 They earned their 'Rugger' colours together as scrum and stand-off halves. **1927** *Granta* 14 Oct. 9/1 He has had to be content with four years and a captaincy in the Magdalene Rugger side. **1929** *Mercury Story Bk.* 162 'Rubbish' I heard an eupeptic Rugger man protesting. **1930** R. Campbell *Poems* 10 Nor at his Rugger-Match is Squire more gay. **1937** F. Smythe *Camp Six* v. 65 The football was also very popular and Nursang did his best to form the Sherpas into a rugger scrum. **1951** M. McLuhan *Mech. Bride* (1967) 137/1 The same contrast may be seen between the rugger crowd and the soccer crowd. **1955** *Times* 3 Aug. 7/4 Gradually strength and energy returned, and in two days the Sherpas produced the expedition rugger ball. **1967** D. Pinner *Ritual* xii. 119 He rugger-tackled the policeman. **1973** D. Lees *Rape of Quiet Town* vii. 111 It was all in the spirit of a rugger club frolic.

ruggerite (rʌ·gərait). *rare.* [f. Rugger[2] + -ite[1].] One who plays Rugby football.

1951 R. Campbell *Light on Dark Horse* iv. 75 In the end his school of 'scruffy soccerites' defeated Langley's ruggerites at their own rugger.

ruggery (rʌ·gəri), *a. rare.* [f. Rugger[2] + -y[1].] Being or resembling a typical Rugby player.

1961 A. Comfort *Come out to Play* ii. 136 Gaudeamus was a large, ruggery man.

rugging, *sb.* (Later examples.)

1939 *Country Life* 11 Feb. p. xxxiii/2 (Advt.), Cheaper quality in rugging, 27/6, 25/- & 20/-. **1963** E. H. Edwards *Saddlery* xx. 149 The most simple of all is the Yorkshire boot, which consists of an oblong of stout rugging with a tape sewn along the centre.

Rugian (rū·dʒiăn), *sb.* and *a.* [f. L. *Rugii* pl., Rugians + -ian.] **A.** *sb.* A member of an ancient Germanic tribe; the East Germanic language of this tribe. **B.** *adj.* Of or pertaining to the Rugians.

1611 Coryat *Crudities* 106 Odoacer the Rugian that vsurped the Kingdome of Italy..by expelling Augustulus the last Emperour of Rome. **1845** *Encycl. Metrop.* XI. 268/1 Those united bands the Heruli, the Alani, the Scyrri, and the Rugians..constituted the military force of Italy. **1884** *Encycl. Brit.* XVII. 727/1 This Rugian war was probably an indirect cause of the fall of Odoacer. **1934** Priebsch & Collinson *German Lang.* 25 A few other Germanic languages, e.g. Skirian, Rugian, [etc.]. **1935** H. A. L. Fisher *Hist. Europe* I. x. 120 There was a bigness of scale about Theodoric which redeemed many of the grosser vices... After three years' hard fighting he eliminated from Italy the Rugian army of Odovacar, and thereafter gave thirty-six years of golden peace to that much harassed land.

rugosa (rugōᵘ·ză). [L., fem. of *rūgōsus* (see Rugose *a.*) and the specific epithet of *Rosa rugosa* (C. P. Thunberg *Flora Japonica* (1784) 213).] A hardy shrub rose belonging to the species *Rosa rugosa*, or one of its varieties or hybrids, distinguished by dark green, wrinkled leaves and large, globular, orange-red hips. Also *attrib.*

1892 W. Paul *Contrib. Hort. Lit.* 189 The Rugosa Rose. Where large showy Roses are valued these flowers will not fail to please. **1899** T. W. Sanders *Cultivated Roses* 33 Madame Georges Bruant (hybrid rugosa). **1906** *Roses* 121 Rugosas, owing to their very bushy growth, should be in separate beds. **1920** *19th Cent.* July 174 Roses innumerable—teas, chinas, rugosas, briars, and their hybrids—are asserting their decorative uses. **1943** T. C. Mansfield *Roses* ii. 18 The rugosa hybrids make exceptionally fine hedges. **1962** R. Page *Educ. of Gardener* vii. 209 The rugosa rose 'Blanc Double de Coubert' goes into every garden I make. **1977** *Vole* No. 1. 34/3 The rugosas flower for weeks and have lovely hips.

rugose, *a.* Add: **a.** *rugose mosaic*, a mosaic disease of potatoes characterized by a marked wrinkling of the leaves and increased chlorosis and dwarfing compared with other mosaics.

1923 Schultz & Folsom in *Jrnl. Agric. Res.* XXV. 52 The writers believe that most of Murphy's crinkle..is identical with the type here designated as 'rugose mosaic' with some leaf-rolling mosaic symptoms. **1967** A. E. Cox *Potato* iv. 93 The two most serious of the virus diseases, leaf roll and rugose mosaic, are transmitted from infected to healthy plants by aphids.

c. [a. mod.L. order name *Rugosa* (Milne-Edwards & Haime *Monogr. Brit. Fossil Corals* (1850) 1. p. lxiv.] Of a fossil coral: belonging to the extinct order Rugosa (or Tetracoralla), which includes horn-shaped corals with ridged surfaces.

1872 H. A. Nicholson *Man. Palæont.* I. viii. 99 It has been shown that some..abnormal Rugose corals were provided with a lid. **1935** *Geol. Mag.* LXXII. 482 The rugose corals..are a group of Palaeozoic corals. **1972** *Sci. Amer.* June 61/2 The conical or cylindrical stone tube that sheltered the second type has conspicuous external growth wrinkles on its surface; these corals are called rugose.

d. *fig.*

1942 A. L. Rowse *Cornish Childhood* vi. 133 Old Sidney was a rugose personality... I am bound to say that, rough-edged as he was with everybody, he was always very kind to me.

rugosity. Add: **2.** (Later *fig.* example.)

1969 T. E. B. Howarth *Culture, Anarchy & Public Schools* iii. 54 It may..be doubted if the new sixth-former..will take kindly to the traditionally rigorous system of the old type of sixth form. He will expect his teachers to spare him the sterner rugosities.

Ruhmkorff (rū·mkǭɪf). *Physics. Obs.* except *Hist.* The name of Heinrich Daniel *Ruhmkorff* (1803–77), German-born inventor, used *attrib.*, *absol.* and in the possessive to designate a powerful type of induction coil first made by him.

[**1852** W. R. Grove in *Phil. Mag.* IV. 500, I procured one of these apparatus from M. Ruhmkorff: the size of the coil portion of the apparatus is 6·5 inches long, 4 inches diameter.] **1855** —— in *Ibid.* IX. 1 If a small Leyden phial have its coatings connected respectively with the extremities of the secondary wire of a Ruhmkorff coil (the primary being, as usual, connected with the condenser of M. Fizean, and two wires being attached to the terminals and brought within striking distance), the noise and brilliancy of the discharges are greatly increased. **1878** *Encycl. Brit.* VIII. 103/1 The type of these is the induction coil or inductorium, sometimes called Ruhmcorff's coil, after the great Parisian instrument-maker who first brought the instrument to perfection. **1908** *Rep. Brit. Assoc. Adv. Sci. 1907* 621 The aërials connected through the secondary of a peculiarly made Ruhmkorff coil constitute one oscillating system of a low frequency. *Ibid.* 622 When the swing is worked up they burst through the spark gap, short-circuiting out the Ruhmkorff. **1971** *Sci. Amer.* May 82/2 The final phase of the coil's development was reached during the 1850's. Heinrich Daniel Ruhmkorff, a German instrument maker living in Paris, turned his attention in 1851 to the construction of better and more powerful coils... The quality of his products quickly brought him fame, and such coils soon became known as Ruhmkorff coils.

ruin, *sb.* Add: **I. 4.** (Further *fig.* examples.)

1946 B. Marshall *George Brown's Schooldays* ii. 7 Hullo, here's Abinger. He looks a fearful ruin, doesn't he? *Ibid.* xxiv. 102 A ruin's a chap who's a swot and a punk and who's rotten at games.

III. 11. a. *ruinward* adv.

1936 A. E. Housman *More Poems* 61 And on through night to morning The world runs ruinward.

b. *ruin-mound* = Tell *sb.*[2]

1911 *Encycl. Brit.* XIV 741/2 There are in Irak hundreds of ruin mounds, some of them of considerable size, covering ancient Babylonian cities. **1939** P. Carleton *Buried Empires* i. 23 Attracted by the numerous *tells*, or ruin-mounds, in his district, he set workmen to dig.

ruin, *v.* Add: **I. 3. d.** (Later examples.)

1929 E. O'Neill *Dynamo* I. ii. 28 Pa and Ma warned me linesmen were no good... they just ruined you and went their way. **1955** *Radio Times* 22 Apr. 4/3 The sentimental blatherings of Mrs. Arbuthnot who was 'ruined' by Lord Illingworth twenty years before. **1962** E. Bentley tr. *Brecht's Mother Courage* vi. 51 She's not so pretty anyone would want to ruin her.

ruinate, *ppl. a.* Add: **1. c.** *Jamaica.* Of land: exhausted, abandoned. Hence as *sb.*, land which has reverted to the wild, scrubland, 'bush'.

1835 B. M. Senior *Jamaica* 54 Lands termed 'ruinate', which means such as have been used till worn out, and then allowed to grow up in bushes and weeds. *Ibid.* 55 In three or four years after the ruinate is cleared up, the pimento begins to bear. **1847** P. H. Gosse *Birds of Jamaica* 11 We see it [*sc.* the Red-tailed Buzzard] all the year round, sailing deliberately in wide circles over the pastures and ruinates. **1894** R. T. Banbury *Jamaica Superstitions* 30 We would advise parents never to allow their little ones to wander about near woods, or ruinates by themselves.

ruinate, *v.* **1. b.** (Later *arch.* examples.)

1922 E. R. Eddison *Worm Ouroboros* xviii. 253 If I do not..remedy for you our fortunes which this bloody fool hath laboured to ruinate, spit in my face. **1935** G. Barker *Poems* 55 Time, though slowly, ruinates Love, with which it arbitrates.

ruinous, *a.* Add: **3.** (Later example.) Also *transf.*, excessively expensive.

1897 A. Beardsley *Let.* 27–28 Feb. (1970) 260 If the hotel turns out too ruinous, and our expenditure in these matters could not be controlled, then we will decide for lodgings.

‖ **rukh** (ruk). Also **ruk.** [a. Hindi *rūkh*, f. Prakrit *rukkha-* tree.] In India: a forest; a forest reserve.

1893 Kipling *Many Inventions* 191 He made no pretence at keeping a garden, for the *rukh* swept up to his door. **1928** *Blackw. Mag.* Apr. 443/1 It was a week or two before General Devi Deen came again for our ride through the *ruk.*

rukus, var. *ruckus.

rule, *sb.* Add: **I. 3. b.** *rules of the game* transf., conventions in political or social relations or the like.

1910 S. E. White *Rules of Game* xli. 644 Things change; and a man is foolish to act as though they didn't. He's just got to keep playing along according to the rules of the game. And they keep changing too. **1936** M. Mitchell *Gone with Wind* xxxi. 521 The rules of the game had been changed and..honest labor could no longer earn its just reward. **1964** Rousseas & Farganis in I. L. Horowitz *New Sociol.* 287 Operating within the rules-of-the-game of institutionalized conflict. **1974** *Daily Tel.* 15 Oct. 18/2 As leader of the Opposition Mr Heath, under the rules of the game, has the right of reply tonight to Mr Wilson's Ministerial broadcast last night.

4. b. *rules of evidence*, the legal rules that apply to the giving of evidence.

1756 *J. Gilbert's Law of Evidence* (rev. ed.) 8 The Rule of Evidence commands no farther than to produce the best that the Nature of the Thing is capable of. **1801** T. Peake *Law of Evidence* p. v, The chapter on Parol Testimony, also is in a great measure new; for the rules of evidence in this respect have been so much altered, and so much light has been thrown on them by modern decisions, that, comparatively, little is to be collected from ancient books. **1892** S. L. Phipson *Law of Evidence* p. v, I have..adhered to one uniform method of arrangement throughout—that of stating: (1) The rules of evidence..[etc.]. **1908** J. H. Wigmore in *Sel. Ess. Anglo-Amer. Legal Hist.* II. xl. 691 (*heading*) A general survey of the history of the rules of evidence. **1942** E. M. Morgan in *Model Code of Evidence* (Amer. Law Inst.) 5 The rules of evidence have been developed in myriads of cases. *Ibid.* 34 This has led to the invention of the hypothetical question, which, as Mr. Wigmore says, 'is one of the truly scientific features of the rules of Evidence'. **1956** E. C. Conrad *Mod. Trial Evidence* I. i. 15 No exceptions to the general applicability of the rules of evidence as a broad proposition has been noted. **1973** *N.Y. Law Jrnl.* 4 Sept. 3/4 This committee was not bound by the rules of evidence. It was not constrained to follow courtroom procedures.

c. *rule of law*: (*a*) a valid legal proposition; (*b*) a doctrine, deriving from theories of natural law, that in order to control the exercise of arbitrary power, the latter must be subordinated to impartial and well-defined principles of law; (*c*) spec. in English law, the concept that the day-to-day exercise of executive power must conform to general principles as administered by the ordinary courts.

(*a*) *a* **1634** E. COKE *Third Part Institutes Lawes Eng.* (1644) vii. 53 In case of life the rule of law ought to be certain. **1756** *J. Gilbert's Law of Evidence* (rev. ed.) 16 The Rule of Law that requires the greatest Evidence that the Nature of the Thing is capable of. **1768** BLACKSTONE *Comm.* III. xxiii. 383 If a whole county is interested in the question to be tried, the trial by the rule of law must be in some adjoining county. **1969** *Columbia Law Rev.* LXIX. 1168 It is clear that those rules of precedent which are binding as 'rules of practice' are also rules of law.

(*b*) **1883** J. E. C. WELLDON tr. *Aristotle's Politics* iii. §16. 154 The rule of law then..is preferable to the rule of an individual citizen. **1929** LD. HEWART *New Despotism* ii. 23 What is meant here by the 'Rule of Law' is the supremacy or the predominance of law, as distinguished from mere arbitrariness, or from some alternative mode, which is not law, or determining or disposing of the rights of individuals. **1936** F. G. WILSON *Elem. Mod. Politics* viii. 207 It is of historic importance that the rule of law in the medieval and early modern sense was the rule of superearthly law..—eternal law, divine law, natural law, and human law. **1953** T. D. WELDON *Vocab. Politics* iii. 69 Strictly speaking there is nothing difficult or impressive about 'the Rule of Law'. It is merely a convenient way of referring to the fact that associations have rules and unless those rules are pretty generally kept and enforced the association breaks down and the activity which it was designed to promote becomes impracticable. **1959** E. C. S. WADE in A. V. Dicey *Law of Constitution* (ed. 10) p. xcvii, In another sense the rule of law means the recognition of certain fundamental obligations as binding upon States in their dealings with one another... The United Nations.. claims to give effect to the rule of law. *Ibid.* p. cvii, The International Commission of Jurists considers that the basic idea uniting lawyers in many different legal systems is a conception of the rule of law. **1971** *Engineering* Apr. 54/1 Industry-wide negotiations, ending in a kind of rule-of-law. **1974** J. LAPALOMBARA *Politics within Nations* iii. 106 But the difference between the *Rechtsstaat* and constitutionalism is that the rule of law in the former is based on a concession from the ruler. **1977** *Rolling Stone* 24 Mar. 31/2 Those senators..knew of the need to continue redeeming the rule of law that Edward Levi had begun.

(*c*) **1885** A. V. DICEY *Law of Constitution* v. 172 When we say that the supremacy or the rule of law is a characteristic of the English constitution, we generally include under one expression at least three distinct though kindred conceptions. We mean, in the first place, that no man is punishable or can be made to suffer in body or goods except for a distinct breach of law established in the ordinary legal manner before the ordinary courts of the land. **1923** W. S. HOLDSWORTH *Hist. Eng. Law* (rev. ed.) iv. 405 The precocious development of our common law has..given..the opportunity for the development of those two fundamental characteristics of our English constitution—the system of self-government and the rule of law. **1933** W. I. JENNINGS *Law & Constitution* 256 The 'rule of law' in this sense means that public authorities ought not to have large powers. **1959** *Polit. Stud.* VII. 114 He [*sc.* Dicey] would not have admitted for one moment that a Rule of Law followed from the mere fact that the conduct of government had a legal basis. **1971** S. A. DE SMITH *Constitutional & Admin. Law* ii. 40 Nor would it be justifiable to examine the general concept of the rule of law at length... The concept is usually intended to imply (i) that the powers exercised by politicians and officials must have a legitimate foundation..and (ii) that the law should conform to certain minimum standards of justice. **1975** LD. HAILSHAM *Door wherein I Went* xxxvi. 253 The rule of law, an increasingly sophisticated idea..is essentially a province for an official with a foot in both camps, a sworn judge as well as a sworn Privy Councillor, with an independent duty towards the judiciary and the legal profession.

5. *to bend* or *stretch the rules*: to interpret the rules leniently, to overlook or allow an infringement of the rules; hence *rule-bender*; *rule-book* (later examples); also *fig.*

1910 W. M. RAINE *Bucky O'Connor* 13 The situation was one not covered in the company's rule book. **1945** F. H. HUBBARD *Railroad Avenue* ii. 10 Casey was never the type known as a 'rule-book engineer'. **1954** W. FAULKNER *Fable* 113 Germans fight wars by the rule-books. **1959** M. GILBERT *Blood & Judgement* xiv. 151 Some stuffy old Chief Superintendent, who's lived with one finger in the Rule Book. **1968** *Punch* 20 Mar. 417/3 Despite some fierce and not altogether rulebook tackling by their opponents, the Students were..taking the game right into the Police half. **1973** M. WOODHOUSE *Blue Bone* iv. 36 The Communists..were bound to loathe the guts of the big old families since that was what the rule book said. **1973** *Times* 2 Nov. 5/7 Trying to get other members of the European Community to 'bend the rules' so that exports can be resumed. **1977** 'O. JACKS' *Autumn Heroes* ii. 37 He bent over backwards to be straight in all his dealings... He wouldn't stretch the rules. **1978** S. BRILL *Teamsters* vii. 272 They were rule-benders (or perhaps sometimes lawbreakers) in a rule-benders and lawbreakers' world.

b. (Also with lower-case initials.) **Rules Committee**, a committee of a house of a U.S. federal or state legislature responsible for expediting the passage of bills.

1918 H. W. DODDS *Procedure in State Legislatures* (Annals Amer. Acad. Polit. & Social Sci. Suppl. No. 1) iv. 60 Enjoying as much parliamentary power as the English cabinet, the rules committee [of the New York Assembly] nevertheless escapes any measure of responsibility before the people. **1976** *National Observer* (U.S.) 12 June 5/2 Lobbying..was so intense the Rules Committee wouldn't release the legislation.

c. Followed by a number or letter: a particular regulation imposed by an institution (see quots.).

1929 *Bookman* (U.S.) July 527/2 *Rule G*, in all railroad rule books, prohibiting the use of intoxicants. **1932** *Santa Fé Mag.* Jan. 34/2 Getting drunk is *Rule b*, failing to protect your train or to flag it is 99, attending an investigation is *going on the carpet.* **1974** *Guidelines to Volunteer Services* (N.Y. State Dept. Correctional Services) 43 *Rule 5*, when a parolee must abstain from alcohol. **1976** A. MILLER *Inside Outside* 6, I would also call on those men under Rule 43 (the segregation rule), and chat with them for a while. **1977** *Times* 11 Apr. 7/7 Over 60 prisoners are in segregation 'for the maintenance of good order or discipline' under rule 43 on any one day.

II. 7. a. Also, *rule-of-brain* (nonce-wd., after RULE OF THUMB in Dict. and Suppl.)

1948 L. MACNEICE *Holes in Sky* 25 Tom and Tessy..of themselves significant, To rule-of-brain recalcitrant.

c. (Later examples.) In modern Linguistics, usu. applied to any one of a system of rules that can be formulated in such a way that together they describe all the features of a language. Freq. *Comb.*

1953 [see *morpheme-sequence* s.v. *MORPHEME c]. **1957** N. CHOMSKY *Syntactic Struct.* x. 107 A grammar has a sequence of rules from which phrase structure can be reconstructed and a sequence of morphophonemic rules that convert strings of morphemes into strings of phonemes. Connecting these sequences, there is a sequence of transformational rules. **1965** *Language* XLI. 548 Language is rule-governed behavior, and learning a language involves internalizing the rules. **1968** J. LYONS *Introd. Theoret. Linguistics* i. 48 Learning the language 'naturally' as children, they [*sc.* the speakers of a language] come to speak it according to certain systematic principles, or 'rules', 'immanent' in the utterances they hear about them. It is the task of synchronic linguistic description to formulate these systematic 'rules' as they operate in the language at a particular time. **1968** *Language* XLIV. 735 It follows from premise 1 that from proto-language *L there will be *n* rule sequences into each of *n* daughter languages. **1971** P. KIPARSKY in W. O. Dingwall *Survey Linguistic Sci.* 612 The concept of *rule opacity*..has an important role to play elsewhere in linguistic theory. **1972** *Language* XLVIII. 83 There is every reason to believe that they will allow one to get rid of the unprincipled blocking device of extrinsic rule-ordering. **1974** G. M. GREEN *Semantics & Syntactic Regularity* vi. 194 The notions of redundancy rule, structural description feature, and deep-structure constraint were necessitated by the concepts of rule government. **1976** [see *phrase-structure* s.v. *PHRASE *sb.* 7]. **1978** *Language* LIV. 41 These features trigger rules that apply only to forms bearing the corresponding rule feature... We can call this device the 'rule-feature' theory. **1979** *Trans. Philol. Soc.* 18 The rule-environment is *arbitrary*—why not a rule deleting *no* only when it is *followed* by N we might ask?

9. *work to rule*: see *WORK *v.* and *sb.*

V. 17. c. Also, (*b*) of police: to interrogate (a suspected criminal); (*c*) of a doctor of medicine: to examine (a patient).

1948 *Free-Lance Writer & Photographer* Apr. 54/2 When a P.C. stops a suspect in the street and interrogates him, he 'runs the rule over him'. **1953** *Times* 21 Oct. 1/5 Good afternoon, doctor, I don't suppose it's anything really, just a bit off-colour..thought you'd better run the—er—rule over me.

23. c. In sense 3, as *rule formulation, system*; *rule-bound* (hence *-boundedness*), *-giving*, *-governed* adjs.

1905 W. JAMES *Mem. & Stud.* (1911) v. 89 You ask for a free man, and these utopias give you an 'interchangeable part', with a fixed number, in a rule-bound organism. **1950** *Mind* LIX. 391 Why not say 'rule-giving' method? **1968** *Listener* 29 Aug. 266/2 Societies have defined and structured rule systems of reward and punishment. **1977** J. D. DOUGLAS in Douglas & Johnson *Existential Sociol.* i. 39 As Becker realized, there is almost always conflict over such presentations of rule-boundedness. **1977** A. GIDDENS *Stud. in Social & Polit. Theory* iii. 144 Universal pragmatics..attempts to reconstruct the rule systems which allow actors to communicate in any type of context. **1978** C. HOOKWAY in Hookway & Pettit *Action & Interpretation* 27 If indeterminacy obtains it is likely to infect the translation of the object language into a meta-language involved in the rule-formulation. **1978** *Listener* 30 Mar. 396/2 To try to explain how the speaker's intentions, his rule-governed intentional behaviour, relates language to the world. **1979** *Dædalus* Summer 9 Rule-bound, conventional, and traditional ethics continue to hold their own. *Ibid.* 20 It remains a normal, rule-governed collective activity.

d. rule-box, a rectangle formed by ruled or printed lines.

1928 *Publishers' Weekly* 30 June 2605 Above the stamp ..must be *printed* the words..enclosed in a rule box.

e. *pl.* used *Comb.*, chiefly in senses 3 b and 5, as *rulesmaker, rulespeople.*

1963 *Punch* 20 Mar. 416/1 Does anyone ever know the order of the draw? Yes, the rulespeople. **1974** *Sunday* (Charleston, S. Carolina) 21 Apr. 3-A/3 Rulesmakers said politicians were put in a class by themselves, 'because they get to practice all year in their daily work'. **1978** *Detroit Free Press* 2 Apr. 6E/3 Whatever the coach can do for them, Bolinger–Boden–Markovich and all the other offensive linemen around have received very big help recently from the rulesmakers in their game.

rule, *v.* Add: **I. 1. b.** (Later example.)

c **1921** D. H. LAWRENCE *Mr. Noon* viii, in *Mod. Lover* (1934) 266 It's just like him—but there you are. Those that won't be ruled can't be schooled.

5. a. *Rule, Britannia*: the usual name for a patriotic song sometimes sung on public occasions in Britain. Also as *attrib. phr.* Hence **Rule-Brita·nnia,ism** chauvinism (*nonce-wd.*).

The name is taken from the refrain of the song (see quot. 1740).

[**1740** THOMSON & MALLETT *Alfred* II. v. 42 *Ode*... Rule, Britannia, rule the waves; Britons never will be slaves.] **1806** [see BUFF *sb.*[2] 6]. *a* **1888** [used in def. of BRITON *sb.* 1 c]. **1898** *Academy* 8 Oct. 25/1 A preference for accuracy above Rule-Britanniaism. **1899** KIPLING *Absent-Minded Beggar* 1 When you've shouted 'Rule Britannia', When you've sung 'God save the Queen'. **1918** *Daily Mirror* 12 Nov. 2/1 When the strains of 'Rule, Britannia!' rang out his Majesty raised his naval cap. **1936** G. B. SHAW *Simpleton* I. 24 Let the whole earth be England; and let Englishmen rule it. (Singing) Rule Britannia: Britannia rules the wa— He blows his brains out. **1941** 'G. ORWELL' *Lion & Unicorn* 19 In England all the boasting and flag-wagging, the 'Rule Britannia' stuff, is done by small minorities. **1968** *Listener* 18 July 86/2 Judges are good at making grand Rule Britannia statements, like Judge Salmon's in 1958... 'Everyone.. is entitled to walk the streets in peace,..and free from fear.'

d. Slang phr. —— *rule(s), O.K.*, used orig. in wall graffiti to affirm the superiority of a gang, football team, etc. Freq. in *transf.* use.

1975 S. JACOBSON in *New Society* 27 Mar. 780 (*title*) Chelsea rule—okay. **1976**, etc. [see *O.K. *a.* a]. **1981** *Times* 31 June 1/1 It is a case of the tobacco industry rules, OK.

6. a. (Later example.)

1964 *Financial Times* 3 Mar. 2/3 Prices yesterday ruled fully firm for all descriptions of merino fleece and skirtings.

b. (Later examples.) Also *transf.*

1909 *Chambers's Jrnl.* June 409/1 During the past year the longest period when the wind velocity ruled below five miles per hour was only seven days. **1979** *Morning News* (Karachi) 24 May 7/1 In the jutes section Indus and Pak Jute ruled firm. Sugar shares were irregular.

II. 8. a. Also with object and complement.

1928 H. G. WELLS *Mr. Blettsworthy* iii. 154 He it was had first ruled me insane and immune from Reproof.

d. (Earlier U.S. and later examples.) Also, more generally: to eliminate as a possibility; to make impossible; to decide against.

1869 'MARK TWAIN' *Innoc. Abr.* li. 539 Though they have been ruled out of our modern Bible, it is claimed that they were accepted gospel twelve or fifteen centuries ago. **1883** —— *Life on Mississippi* xlv. 413 One of these [mules] had to be ruled out, because he was so fast that he turned the thing into a one-mule contest. **1903** J. ST. L. STRACHEY in 'Vigilans sed Æquus' *German Ambitions* p. vii, To rule out the writings of the men on whom 'Vigilans sed Æquus' has based his Letters because they are obscure..is to misunderstand the evolution of public affairs in Germany. **1925** N. E. ODELL in E. F. Norton *Fight for Everest: 1924* 335 The disadvantage of the North Col is the fact that the camp here must be pitched on snow, though under all but the worst conditions this need not rule it out. **1928** *Daily Tel.* 12 June 13/4 The possibility of a battle between the rival Southern commanders cannot be ruled out. **1966** C. MACKENZIE *Paper Lives* vi. 85 The Right Honourable Henry Upjohn thought for a moment about trying that joke at the next political meeting in his constituency but ruled it out at once. **1971** I. BUTYKAI tr. *Lukovich's Electric Foil Fencing* II. 84 Certain parts should be ruled out as being compulsory so that the combined movement should present an acceptable, applicable and expedient picture. **1976** *National Observer* (U.S.) 13 Nov. 5/2 Nothing in the group's by-laws rules out inmates, officials said, so the invitations stand. The prisoners said they were 'very pleasantly surprised' to find they could join Phi Kappa Phi.

e. With *in*, used in opposition to sense 8 d above.

1904 G. B. SHAW *Let.* 6 Dec. (1972) II. 471 It is just this personality that rules her out, whereas if we had a scrap of originality it would rule her in. **1973** *Observer* 17 June 1/1, I haven't ruled it out and I haven't ruled it in.

III. 10. b. *Comm.* With *off*: to close (the books) for the day. Also *absol.*

1977 *Times* 17 Sept. 20/4 Books were eventually ruled off within a band of 5¾–6¼ per cent. **1978** *Times* 15 Aug. 18/8 Closing balances were being found at sharply lower levels, so that books were eventually ruled off within a band of 4½ per cent to 6½ per cent. *Ibid.* 17 Aug. 21/3 Houses ruled off anywhere between 2 per cent and 4 per cent.

11. (Later *fig.* example.)

1924 R. CAMPBELL *Flaming Terrapin* i. 18 As he rose up, the moon with slanted ray Ruled for those rapid hoofs a shining way.

rule-joint. Add: Also *attrib.*

1966 A. W. LEWIS *Gloss. Woodworking Terms* 47 *Rule-joint hinge*, brass hinge with one long and one short leaf and with the countersinking for the screw heads on the opposite side to the knuckle. *Ibid.* 95 *Stay*, metal fitting which limits the movement of a door or lid, e.g. a shad stay, or a rule-joint stay.

rulelessness. (In Dict. s.v. RULELESS *a.*) (Later example.)

1969 P. ANDERSON in Cockburn & Blackburn *Student Power* 222 Durkheim's account..produced the concept of anomie—the unceasing reproduction of subjective rulelessness by a society that is defined by its ensemble of objective rules.

rule-maker. Add: Hence **ru·le-making** *sb.*

1926 *Amer. Bar Assoc. Jrnl.* XII. 599 Study..of rule-making in action in those states where the courts still retain much of their rule-making powers. **1946** *Nature* 21 Dec. 894/1 In Africa the rule-making power of native authorities can have a significant influence on future developments in this field. **1964** GOULD & KOLB *Dict. Social Sci.* 385/2 In sociology and related fields, *legislation* is sometimes applied to the function and products of rule-making by any agency, governmental or private, the rules of which are normally accepted by the persons to whom they apply. **1979** *Railway Age* 31 Dec. 14/2 The ICC Bureau of Operations agreed with the proposal to institute a rulemaking, but was less eager than the OPA to see IPD eliminated.

rule of thumb. Add: **1.** (Later examples.) Also, a particular stated rule that is based on practice or experience.

1906 [see *drill book* s.v. *DRILL *sb.*[2] 7 b]. **1965** C. D. EBY *Siege of Alcázar* (1966) vii. 135 In doubtful cases a rule of thumb applied: if the prisoner employed one servant in his household or two workers in his business, then he was a Fascist. **1967** G. F. FIENNES *I tried to run a Railway* ii. 14 George Jackson who timed by rule of thumb faster and as accurately as any Grapher. **1976** *Inorg. Chem.* XV. 1032/2 The i.r. spectra..show no apparent deviation from the rule of thumb that vibrational spectra of mixed-valence compounds are approximate superpositions of the single-valence spectra. **1976** *Southern Even. Echo* (Southampton) 11 Nov. 3/7 The rule of thumb over the tenancy of a council home should be 'follow the children'. **1977** *National Observer* (U.S.) 1 Jan. 7/2 The usual rule of thumb in the real-estate business is that a family can afford a house 2 to 2½ times its income. **1980** *Jrnl. R. Soc. Arts* Feb. 166/2 By day that same boy's master, and overlooker, and fellow-workmen, are all teaching him..that rule of thumb is the only safe guide.

2. a. (Later examples.) Also in predicative use.

1935 E. WAUGH *Edmund Campion* ii. 55 Old-fashioned priests..came to him when they found their simple, rule-of-thumb dialectics insufficient to cope with their trained opponents. **1947** E. M. FORSTER in *Harper's Mag.* July 15/2 Virginia Woolf..believed in reading a book twice. The first time she abandoned herself to the author unreservedly. The second time she treated him with severity and allowed him to get away wih nothing he could not justify. After these two readings she felt qualified to discuss the book. Here is good rule of thumb advice. **1962** W. NOWOTTNY *Lang. Poets Use* iii. 53 This attitude..however rule-of-thumb it may be, is reasonable enough. **1977** *N.Y. Rev. Bks.* 24 Nov. 16/1 Ridiculing the 'rule of thumb' methods used in the household.

b. (Later example.)

1947 [see *NOMOGRAPHER].

Hence **rule-of-thu·mbite**, a person who works by rule of thumb (*nonce-wd.*).

1916 H. G. WELLS *Mr. Britling* I. i. 16 Ruskin and Morris..were as reactionary and anti-scientific as the dukes and the bishops. Machine haters. Science haters. Rule of Thumbites to the bone.

ruler, *sb.*[1] Add: **6.** *Comb.* (sense 3 b) *ruler-straight* adj.; (sense 1) **ruler-cult** *Antiq.*, worship offered to a hereditary ruler; also *transf.*

1928 A. D. NOCK in *Jrnl. Hellenic Stud.* XLVIII. (*title*) Notes on ruler-cult. **1951** M. P. NILSSON *Cults, Myths, Oracles, & Politics in Anc. Greece* iii. 108 The ruler cult was from the age of the Epigoni the state religion of the Hellenistic monarchies in the East. **1958** *Times* 15 Nov. 9/7 Revolutionary and critical times may produce the phenomenon we call ruler-cult. **1960** *Lebende Sprachen* V. 35/3 Ruler-straight seam, schnurgerade Naht. **1963** A. LUBBOCK *Austral. Roundabout* 14 The horizon meets the sky in a ruler-straight line.

ru·lered, *ppl. a. poet.* [f. RULER *sb.*[1] (sense 3 b) + -ED[1].] = RULED *ppl. a.* 4.

1952 L. MACNEICE *Ten Burnt Offerings* 50 Steam is a dry word; the best word is water... Best in the East..on the rulered page of a Moghul garden—Cool marrow of marble spines.

ruleress. For *rare*—[0] read *rare* and add example.

1937 G. FRANKAU *More of Us* xii. 125 Was this The ruleress of waves, R.N., all-British, Who stooped to plant the Cytherean Kiss?

ru·lering, *vbl. sb. rare.* [f. RULER *v.* + -ING[1].] The action of RULER *v.*; a beating with a ruler.

1849 DICKENS *Dav. Copp.* (1850) vii. 77 Tear-blotted copy-books, canings, rulerings.

rulership. Add: **1. a.** (Later example.)

1975 F. HEER *Charlemagne* xv. 225 The Emperor dreamed that a man came to him with a present from God, a sword symbolising rulership.

c. Rulers collectively.

1964 *Listener* 11 June 945/2 The emergence of a professional Civil Service alongside an increasingly amateur political rulership.

Rules (rūlz). [pl. of RULE *sb.*] **1.** *Racing.* (*a*) Jockey Club Rules (the Rules of Racing). (*b*) National Hunt Rules.

1898 A. E. T. WATSON *Turf* vi. 128 Unauthorised meetings—that is to say, meetings not under Rules. **1976** *Horse & Hound* 3 Dec. 10/4 He is one of twin brothers who have both ridden several winners under Rules.

2. = *Australian rules* s.v. *AUSTRALIAN *a.* b.

1946 D. STIVENS *Courtship of Uncle Henry* 18 In those days..they played Rules in long pants that reached below the knee. **1965** *Austral. Encycl.* IV. 134/2 It is known as the Australian Game, National Football, or Australian Rules. In some parts it becomes merely 'Rules. **1967** *Canberra Times* 17 June 27 Victoria expects to win over W.A. in Rules. **1976** *Sydney Morning Herald* 27 May 22 Rules penalty upsets Saints.

ruling, *vbl. sb.* Add: **3. a. ruling engine,** a machine for engraving equally spaced parallel straight lines on a surface.

1901 *Physical Rev.* XII. 9 It is generally assumed in treating the grating that the lines of the ruling are of equal width and are separated by equal spaces... This cannot be the case in view of..the almost inconceivable rigidity of the ruling engine which would be necessary. **1969** D. RICHARDSON in R. Kingslake *Appl. Optics & Optical Engin.* V. ii. 28 Most ruling engines use screws as the basic indexing means. **1980** *Sci. Amer.* May 126/3 A narrow strip of phosphorescent paint was applied down the middle of this detector, which could be moved along the support with the screw of a ruling engine.

b. (Later examples.) *spec.* in *Palæography*, the lines ruled by the scribe on a page or throughout a manuscript.

1944 P. HODGSON *Cloud of Unknowing* (E.E.T.S.) p. x, Single columns of text, usually 34 lines to a page; vertical and horizontal rulings; [etc.]. **1958** *Scriptorium* XII. 51 (*title*) The ruling of the *Exeter Book*. **1963** N. R. KER *Owl & Nightingale* (E.E.T.S.) p. xii, The pencil ruling is often indistinct. **1976** *Codicologica* I. 78 Other aspects of the medieval book: the nature of parchment, ink, pricking, and ruling.

ruling, *ppl. a.* Add: **1. a.** (Further examples.)

a **1832** BENTHAM *Wks.* (1843) X. 571/2 He hates the ruling few; but he does not love the subject many. **1862** R. COBDEN *Let.* in W. L. Burn *Age of Equipoise* (1964) ii. 69 There has been a great reaction..among that which I call the ruling class, against..humanitarianism. **1943** J. B. PRIESTLEY *Daylight on Saturday* ii. 5 Cheviot..was a good engineer... He belonged to tomorrow's ruling class. **1952** D. KELLY (*title*) The ruling few. **1955** T. H. PEAR *Eng. Social Differences* i. 15 An undiscriminating ear mistakes for 'ruling-class speech' a synthetic approximation to it. **1962** L. DAVIDSON *Rose of Tibet* xv. 280 The ex-enemy was now treating quite amiably with 'ruling circles' exiled in Chumbi. **1964** T. B. BOTTOMORE *Elites & Society* i. 6 Mosca's 'political class' is nothing but the intellectual section of the ruling group. *Ibid.* iv. 71 A second group which has attracted attention as a potential ruling elite is that constituted by the managers of industry. **1972** 'R. CRAWFORD' *Whip Hand* II. i. 58 Neville, for all his blue blood, was closer to the breadline than he was... How could a ruling class produce such examples of weakness? **1979** *Dædalus* Summer 2 They are the very models of ruling-class incompetence.

b. (Later examples.)

1945 J. T. COX *Practice Church of Scotland* 104 All are elders—ministers being teaching or preaching as well as ruling elders, and the others 'ruling elders' only. In practice the terms 'elder' and 'ruling elder' are restricted to such as are members of a Kirk Session, exclusive of the minister or ministers of the charge. **1974** *Marlboro Herald-Advocate* (Bennettsville, S. Carolina) 18 Apr. 8/3 A congregational meeting has been called..for the purpose of electing one Ruling Elder to serve on the session.

rulley. (Earlier *Comb.* and later examples.)

1806 W. SHOUT in *N. & Q.* (1963) Apr. 136/1, 6 rulley load of stone—7,, 6. **1977** *Times* 14 Oct. 16/6 East Yorkshire's College of Agriculture has reverted to a strong cob, Folly, and four-wheel rulley to assist their shepherd on his rounds. **1978** J. CUMMINGS *Railway Motor Buses* I. 40 The third Stirling, fitted with a rulley body, found a home with the Mechanical Engineers Department at Hull. **1979** *Bull. Yorks. Dial. Soc.* Summer 9 When the tide rose again they sailed away to Hull where they [*sc.* the goods] were transferred on rullies to the station and entrained to Hornsea.

ruly, *a.*[2] **1.** (Later *poet.* example.)

1952 DYLAN THOMAS *Coll. Poems* 165 And truly he Flows to the strand of flowers like the dew's ruly sea.

rum, *sb.*[1] Add: **1. b.** (Earlier example.)

1779 J. WOODFORDE *Diary* 12 Aug. (1924) I. 258 At the 3 Innes for some Rum and water pd. 0.0.3.

c. For *U.S.* read *N. Amer.* and add earlier and later examples.

1800 *Upper Canada Gaz.* (York, Ontario) 5 Apr. 3/2 Many have labored to calumniate Rum, and render it unpopular, by dwelling on some of its supposed bad effects. **1851** *Voice of Fugitive* (Windsor, Ontario) 5 Nov. 2/5 Rum and Negro hate [are] the two great public evils of our time. **1918** W. A. MACKAY *By Trench & Trail* 15 No one will rejoice more than Oscar Dhu to see the demon rum utterly destroyed in Canada ere many moons. **1933** E. O'NEILL *Ah, Wilderness!* II. 74 'Never marry a woman who drinks! Lips that touch liquor shall never touch yours!'..Too bad! So fine a woman once—and now such a slave to rum! **1957** *Prairie Overcomer* (Three Hills, Alberta) Dec. 444/2 Of these two foes we cannot say whether *Rome* or *rum* is the greater adversary of the pure Gospel.

2. a. *rum-bottle* (later examples), *distillery, ration, still.*

1847 THACKERAY *Van. Fair* (1848) xxxix. 359 The three tumblers and the empty rum-bottle. **1967** A. LICHINE *Encycl. Wines & Spirits* 464/2, 7 francs..gave a customer the sugar-syrup bottle, the rum bottle, a tumbler, and left him to himself. **1774** N. CRESSWELL *Jrnl.* 4 Sept. (1925) 34 In the evening went with Mr. Perkins to see Mr. Kid's Plantation. The Sugar works and Rum distilleries are very extensive. **1816** *Mass. Hist. Soc. Coll.* 2nd Ser. IV. 124 A rum distillery was established in 1738. **1968** *Spirits* ('Know the Drink' Ser.) 32/2 Sugar factories and rum distilleries are much larger and more efficient than they were. **1923** KIPLING *Irish Guards in Gt. War* I. ii. 89 Their bivouacs..where a hot meal..and a rum-ration awaited them. **1977** *Amer. N. & Q.* XV. 135/2 Temperance campaigns, reduced rum rations, more leave, recreational programs, recruitment of higher caliber personnel, all helped to reduce alcoholism. **1914** F. C. GLASS *With Bible in Brazil* iv. 45, I recalled the big rum-still in the back-yard. **1968** *Spirits* ('Know the Drink' Ser.) 32/1 Rum stills are often fitted with 'rectifiers' which allow the least volatile elements to return to the pot.

b. *rum-maker, -seller* (earlier and later examples).

1926 J. MASEFIELD *Odtaa* i. 4 The northward provinces became sparsely inhabited by..sugar-growers, rum-makers, and copper-miners. **1781** J. GREENWOOD in *Maryland Hist. Mag.* (1910) V. 125 We..took in..seven passengers, who were sutlers or rum-sellers to Gen. Washington's army. **1900** *Congress. Rec.* 25 Jan. 1200/2 A rumseller is as bad as a polygamist. **1973** H. ROBERTSON *Grass Roots* iv. 76 There seems to be no limit to the number of offences these licenced rumsellers can commit.

d. adjs. *rum-bathed*; also *rum-brave*.

1897 G. B. SHAW *Let.* 13 May (1965) I. 762 His rum bathed hair. **1934** E. HEMINGWAY in *Cosmopolitan* Apr. 119/2, I know you haven't got any guts unless you've got rum... I want you rum-brave. I don't want you useless.

3. rum baba: see *BABA[2]; **rum baron,** a magnate in illegal liquor traffic; **rum butter,** a hard sauce made from rum and butter; **rum chaser** *U.S.*, during the Prohibition era, a coast-guard speedboat for pursuing rum-runners; **rum-cherry** *U.S.*, the wild black cherry, *Padus serotina*, or the tree bearing this fruit; **rum cocktail,** a cocktail in which rum is the principal ingredient; **rum fleet** *U.S.*, during the Prohibition era, a 'fleet' of ships engaged in rum-running; **rum-hitting** [cf. *HIT *v.* 22* b] *vbl. sb.*, excessive drinking of rum; **rum-hound** *slang*, (*a*) = *rumpot*; (*b*) a prohibition agent (*U.S.*); **rum-jar** *slang*, a type of German trench-mortar shell; **rum jelly,** a concentrated form of rum; **rum-joint** *U.S.*, formerly, a place where illicit liquor was sold; **rum-mill** *U.S.*, a tavern or liquor shop; **rumpot** *N. Amer. slang*, a habitual heavy drinker; **Rum Rebellion** *Austral. Hist.*, the rebellion against Governor William Bligh by officers of the New South Wales Corps (noted for trafficking in rum) in 1809; **Rum Row** *U.S.* (see quot. 1927); **rum-runner,** (*a*) one who smuggles or lands illicit liquor; (*b*) = *rum ship*; **rum-running** [RUN *v.* 45 c] *vbl. sb.*, smuggling or landing prohibited liquor; also as *ppl. adj.*; **rum ship,** a ship engaged in rum-running; **rum shop** *U.S.* and *Caribbean*, a shop or tavern selling rum and other liquor; a saloon.

1923 *Westm. Gaz.* 4 Apr. 8/5 Reminiscences are inevitable in any gathering of rum barons. **1975** H. WHITE *Raincoast Chron.* (1976) 12/1 A few 'rum barons' could be apprehended in the United States. **1889** A. B. MARSHALL *Cookery Bk.* ii. 38 *Rum Butter*... Prepare as in foregoing recipe, using Liquid Sunshine rum instead of brandy. **1939** [see *brandy-butter* s.v. *BRANDY *sb.* 2]. **1967** 'J. MUNRO' *Money that Money can't Buy* i. 8 Shops that sold Lakeland jet, woollens and rum butter. **1972** *Country Life* 26 Oct. 1041/1 Butter was..taken to Wigton market.. with a special delicacy called rum-butter. **1924** *Rudder* Jan. 40 Congress will be asked to appropriate many millions of dollars for a fleet of rum chasers. **1931** D. RUNYON in *Hearst's Internat.* May 64/2 She is riding in a big foreign automobile the size of a rum-chaser. **1829** A. H. LINCOLN *Familiar Lect. Bot.* 301 Wild-cherry, rum-cherry, cabinet cherry... In dense forests, it grows to a very great height. **1843** *Knickerbocker* XXI. 585 They had been feeding him upon that inebriating article of food, rum-cherries. **1908** N. L. BRITTON *N. Amer. Trees* 506 This well-known tree, also called the Black, Cabinet, or Rum cherry, is abundant in mixed forests and neglected clearings, from Nova Scotia..southward to Florida. **1949** COLLINGWOOD & BRUSH *Knowing your Trees* 256 They have a pleasant, slightly bitter taste and are sometimes used in a beverage called 'cherry bounce' hence the name 'Rum Cherry'. **1861** *Harper's Mag.* Jan. 150/2 Measures of the most vital importance are first introduced in rum-cocktails, then steeped in whisky, after which they are engrossed in gin for a third reading. **1936** A. THIRKELL *August Folly* vi. 181 Richard..had made and drunk two rum cocktails. **1976** J. VAN DE WETERING *Tumbleweed* x. 93 The iced rum cocktail went down well. **1923** *Westm. Gaz.* 4 Apr. 8/5 Off-shore is the rum fleet. **1975** J. GORES *Hammett* xvi. 113 Dom brings in most of the real Canadian from the rum fleet these days. **1910** J. MASEFIELD *Ballads & Poems* 34 There's..Stabbing, of course, and rum-hitting, Dirt, and drink, and stink, and crime. **1918** L. E. RUGGLES *Navy Explained* 120 *Rum Hound*, a boozer, or a man who likes his oil. **1920** ADE *Hand-Made Fables* 5 Just as the western Sun was ducking behind the Hills, the amateur Rum-Hounds piled out. **1951** E. PAUL *Springtime in Paris* xi. 192 What he resented was the insinuation that he was a chronic rumhound. **1916** P. MCGREGOR *Let.* 29 June in M. Moynihan *Greater Love* (1980) 21 A 'Rum Jar', the largest Hun shell known on our front, can knock in yards of trenches. **1923** KIPLING *Irish Guards in Gt. War* I. 252 Rum-jar by rum-jar, borne joyously through the dark streets. **1964** *Listener* 17 Sept. 431/1 The Germans also stepped up their mortar fire on our front-line trenches—the fearful 'rum jars'. **1976** J. VAN DE WETERING *Tumbleweed* x. 93 The rum comes from Jamaica, packed in drums, rum jelly. We mix it with water in a little factory. **1928** *Sunday Express* 24 June 8/4 One of our men started a row with one of these birds... They fought in a rum-joint and everyone joined in. **1853** *Yankee Humour & Uncle Sam's Fun* 87 Every rum-mill, groggery and tippling-shop..is a trap set by the devil to catch those who are guilty of not having over three cents. **1867** [see *DEADFALL 2 c]. **1889** BARRÈRE & LELAND *Dict. Slang* I. 238/1 *Charter the bar, charter the grocery, to* (American), to buy all the liquor in a groggery or 'rum-mill' and give it away freely to all comers. **1930** D. RUNYON in *Collier's* 1 Feb. 12/1 All he sees..is this rumpot ham. **1941** *Sun* (Baltimore) 17 Feb. 18/3 He admires good food and good whisky. 'All cooks,' he said, 'I mean, all good cooks, is rumpots.' **1966** T. H. RADDALL *Hangman's Beach* IV. xxii. 345, I had him moved in there as soon as that rumpot of a doctor was off tae the toon. **1855** W. HOWITT *Land, Labour & Gold* ii. 118 From the date of this 'rum rebellion', and the forcible deposition of poor Bligh..the system of political grants went on swimmingly. **1938** H. V. EVATT (*title*) Rum Rebellion. **1966** G. W. TURNER *Eng. Lang. in Austral. & N.Z.* i. 8 The opposition of the Corps to authority culminated in a rebellion (the 'Rum Rebellion') against Governor William Bligh. **1923** *Lit. Digest* 26 May 52/2 Small consignments are carried from there down to the 'Rum Row' of ships anchored beyond the three-mile limit of the Long Island and New Jersey shores. **1927** W. E. COLLINSON *Contemp. Eng.* 81 We all know..about..Rum Row (where the liquor ships gather outside the prohibited area). **1949** IREY & SLOCUM *Tax Dodgers* i. 26 There were three Rum Rows, one on each coast and a smaller one working in the Gulf of Mexico. **1920** *N.Y. Times* 19 Sept. 6/1 The Detroit rum runners have had a good deal of notoriety. **1925** H. L. FOSTER *Trop. Tramp with Tourists* 7 Is that a rum-runner? **1941** B. SCHULBERG *What makes Sammy Run?* xii. 291 We discovered one solitary light moving slowly along the horizon... It was a rum runner. **1980** *Smithsonian* Aug. 45 The match became known as 'the rum-runners' paradise' because so many Coast Guard patrol boats had to be diverted to control the spectator fleet. **1924** *Lit. Digest* 31 May 38/1 Rum-running in New York has received at least a temporary setback. **1926** *Scribner's Mag.* Aug. 166/2 Tully—an old friend of mine, in the rum-running game now—will get you over the line into Canada. **1930** *Aberdeen Press & Jrnl.* 1 Feb. 7/5 Grey Ghost, one of the fastest rum-running craft on Lake Erie, has been sighted locked in the ice. **1959** N. MAILER *Advts. for Myself* (1961) 65 With the things he'd done, the Marines in Nicaragua,..rumrunning in New Orleans, somehow he'd kinda forgotten that you stood a chance of dying too. **1924** Rum-ship [see *HIJACKING *vbl. sb.* and *ppl. a.*]. **1931** F. L. ALLEN *Only Yesterday* x. 245 Rum-ships rolling in the sea outside the twelve-mile limit. **1738** W. STEPHENS *Jrnl.* 10 Apr. in *Colonial Rec. Georgia* (1906) IV. 122 Those private Rum-Shops were become as common among the People, in Proportion, as Gin-Shops formerly at London. **1873** 'MARK TWAIN' *Gilded Age* xxxiii. 302 Industry and economy soon enabled him to start a low rum shop in a foul locality. **1953** S. M. SADEEK *Windswept & Other Stories* (1969) 17 Den e lead me in the rumshop. **1974** *Sunday Advocate-News* (Barbados) 24 Feb. 17/1 Well populated with rum shops and nightclubs and most recently a horse racing betting shop, the area has become the noisiest in the country.

rum, *sb.*[4] Also **rhum.** *U.S.* [Origin uncertain.] A form of rummy (*RUMMY *sb.*[2]).

1910 [see *RUMMY *sb.*[2]]. **1912** *Official Rules of Card Games* (U.S. Playing Card Co.) 15 Rum. (This is a combination of Conquian and Whiskey Poker.)..Objects of the Game.—To get rid of the cards dealt to the player by laying them out in triplets or fours, or in sequence and suit of three or more. **1913** *Chicago Record-Herald* 2 Mar. v. 6/1, I never found on one of them The kale I lose at rhum. **1921** M. C. WORK *Auction for Two or Three* 79 The modern game of Rum resembles Conquian in many respects and was at first called 'Coon Can'. **1974** *Encycl. Brit. Macropædia* XVI. 25/1 Among the mos widely played Rummy games is 500 Rum,..and its variants including Michigan Rum.

rum, *a.*[2] Add to def.: Also, bad, spurious. (Further examples.)

1783 *Session Paper Cent. Criminal Court* Oct. 952 By God, this is a rum go. *c* **1803** G. COLMAN in M. R. Booth *Eng. Plays of 19th Cent.* (1973) III. 70 Dang me, but he's a rum customer! **1847** G. W. M. REYNOLDS *Mysteries of London* III. xxv. 71/2 Work the bulls and couters rum. **1870** D. J. KIRWAN *Palace & Hovel* xxxii. 483 'Ah! that's a rum customer,' said the policeman; 'she's fly to hevery-think.' **1895** *Wales* July 323/2 What's rum is that he is one of the best 'uns in chapel. **1930** G. B. SHAW *Apple Cart* I. 3 *Pamphilius.* He must have been a rum old bird. *Sempronius.* Not rum enough to be noticed. There are millions like him. **1942** *Gen* 1 Sept. 13/1 Anything that is good in the navy is 'scran' and if it's bad it's 'rum'. **1955** J. THOMAS *No Banners* vii. 61 'This is a rum go,' Alfred said. **1971** H. A. SMITH *View from Chivo* xix. 192 A rum cove if ever I met up with one. **1977** J. I. M. STEWART *Madonna of Astrolabe* xi. 153 Some Scottish names are distinctly rum. Yours is.

Comb. (Later example.)

1955 *Times* 16 Aug. 10/5 That's a rum looking swallow.

‖ **rumaki** (rumā·ki). [Perh. altered f. Jap. *harumaki* spring roll.] An appetizer, of Oriental origin, consisting chiefly of chicken livers, water chestnuts, and bacon, marinated and broiled.

1965 R. CARRIER *Cookbk.* iii. 96 To make 24 *rumaki* (Japanese hot canapés), you will need ½ pound chicken livers, 24 half-slices of bacon, 8 water chestnuts and 24 cocktail sticks. **1972** *Village Voice* (N.Y.) 1 June 74/1 (Advt.), Chicken Liver Rumaki. **1978** *Chicago* June 221/1 Delicious Cantonese-style appetizers include superlative king crab egg rolls and the best rumaki we've ever tasted.

Ruman (rū·măn), var. ROUMAN *sb.* and *a.*

1878 *Chambers's Encycl.* VI. 512/2 Every Ruman who possesses a small yearly income is eligible for a seat in parliament. **1957** *Encycl. Brit.* XIX. 637/1 Tradition, embodied in a local chronicle of the 16th century entitled 'History of the Ruman land since the arrival of the Rumans'..gives 1290 as the date of the founding of the Walachian state.

Rumanian (rumēi·niăn), *sb.* and *a.* [Var. ROUMANIAN *sb.* and *a.* Until recently the dominant spelling in the twentieth century, but now *Romanian* is the officially preferred form.] **A.** *sb.* **1.** = *ROMANIAN *sb.* 1, ROUMANIAN *sb.* 1.

1878 *Chambers's Encycl.* X. 709/1 The choice of the Rumanians fell upon Prince Charles of Hohenzollern-Sigmaringen, who was proclaimed Prince of R. on April 20, 1866. **1902** *Encycl. Brit.* XXXII. 312/1 As regards nationality [in Rumania], there are Rumanians, 5,469,036; foreigners, 171,063; and nondescript (principally Jews), 272,241. **1935** HUXLEY & HADDON *We Europeans* vii. 213 The largest nation in the Balkan peninsula is that of the Jugoslavs.., who are largely separated from their northern brethren by the Magyars and Rumanians. **1973** HOWAT & TAYLOR *Dict. World Hist.* 1313/2 Rumanians expected this to lead to union and autonomy.

2. = *ROMANIAN *sb.* 2, ROUMANIAN *sb.* 2.

1889 in Cent. Dict. **1902** *Encycl. Brit.* XXX. 396/2 The urban and most of the rural Vlachs are bilingual, speaking Greek as well as Rumanian. **1948** A. L. KROEBER *Anthropol.* (rev. ed.) vi. 244 These Greek idioms and structure features recur in Latin-derived Rumanian. **1968** J. LYONS *Introd. Theoret. Linguistics* v. 204 The so-called 'postpositive' articles of Swedish,..Rumanian, ..Macedonian, etc. **1974** [see *ROMANIAN *sb.* 2]. **1975** *Language* LI. 411 In Rumanian, the polite pronoun..is 3rd person in form.

B. *adj.* = *ROMANIAN *a.*[3], ROUMANIAN *a.*

1878 *Chambers's Encycl.* VI. 513/1 In 1877, the entire Rumanian military force numbered 144,668 men. **1902** *Encycl. Brit.* XXXII. 313/2 The Rumanian Church is autocephalous, but holds the same dogmas as the Orthodox Greek Church. **1927** PEAKE & FLEURE *Priests & Kings* xi. 177 The painted pottery people of the Rumanian plain spread along the foot-hills on the outside of the Carpathians. **1938** *Oxf. Compan. Mus.* 819/2 The Russian development of a national music..served to some extent as an incentive to Rumanian musicians. **1950** THEIMER & CAMPBELL *Encycl. World Politics* 372/1 On 7 October 1940 German troops occupied Rumania to secure Rumanian oil..and agricultural surpluses for Germany. **1957** M. B. PICKEN *Fashion Dict.* 279/1 *Rumanian-stitch*, series of parallel stitches intersected at center by shorter stitches. **1968** J. LYONS *Introd. Theoret. Linguistics* v. 204 It is the criterion of 'interruptability' (or 'insertability') which distinguishes the English article as more 'word-like' than the Rumanian or Macedonian article. **1973** *Times* 2 Apr. 6/5 (Advt.), A fine quality Rumanian rug in superb Balkan colours.

Hence **Ruma·nianism**, Romanian identity, Romanian nationalism.

1938 *Times* 1 Jan. 11/1 The new Government believed ..in the spiritual renaissance of Rumanianism through the Christian Church.

Rumanianize (rumēi·niănəiz), *v.* [f. *RUMANIAN *a.* + -IZE.] *trans.* To make Romanian in character. Hence **Ruma:nianiza·tion.**

1922 O. JESPERSEN *Language* xi. 205 A Saxon village which had been almost completely Rumanianized. **1938** *Times* 1 Jan. 11/1 The laws for the protection of Rumanian labour, and of the Rumanianization of undertakings which..employ foreigners instead of Rumanians.

rumänite (rumēi·nəit, rū·mănəit). *Min.* Also **r(o)umanite.** [ad. G. *rumänit* (O. Helm 1891, in *Schr. d. Natürforsch. Ges. in Danzig* VII. IV. 186), f. *Rumänia* Romania: see -ITE[1].] A variety of amber containing sulphur and succinic acid and found in Romania.

1892 E. S. DANA *Dana's Syst. Min.* (ed. 6) 1004 *Rumänite*... A yellow amber-like resin obtained from different points in Rumania, as in sandstone in the Buseo district, at Telage in the Bohosa district, etc. **1904** L. J. SPENCER tr. *M. Bauer's Precious Stones* II. 554 Roumanite, or Roumanian amber, is rarely yellow, but is usually brownish-yellow to brown. **1932** G. C. WILLIAMSON *Bk. Amber* 214 The ordinary phrase of Black Amber applied by dealers to Rumanite is misleading, because its colour value is a very high one, and many examples are amongst the most lovely coloured pieces of Amber that have ever been found. **1962** R. WEBSTER *Gems* I. xxiii. 442 At several places in Romania is found an amber, named appropriately roumanite, which is said to contain less succinic acid and more hydrogen sulphide.

rumba (rʊ·mbă), *sb.* Also **rhumba.** [Amer. Sp.] An Afro-Cuban dance; a ballroom dance imitative of this, danced on the spot with a pronounced movement of the hips. Also, the dance rhythm of the rumba; a musical composition with this rhythm. Also *transf.*

1922 J. HERGESHEIMER *Bright Shawl* 112 Her life..was incredibly, wildly, debauched. Among other things, she danced, as the mulata, the rumba, an indescribable affair. **1926** *Nation* 15 Sept. 242/1 A half-dressed couple behind a slide window dancing the rumba. **1932** *New Yorker* 9 Apr. 39/2 Ceruse's tango band reminds you of every illicit Paris bender you ever had. Rumbas and tangos abound. **1934** H. MICHAEL *Peace without Honour* in J. W. Marriott *Best One-Act Plays of 1933* 135 Put on a dance record... It's a rumba. Will that do? **1939** [see *BEGUINE[2]]. **1950** A. LOMAX *Mister Jelly Roll* (1952) ii. 79 Time seemed to flow like a dreamy rhumba. **1956** M. STEARNS *Story of Jazz* iii. 26 The rhumba, which is by far the most popular outside of Cuba, is consistently diluted for Western ears and has become a fixture at fashionable American night clubs. **1958** E. BORNEMAN in P. Gammond *Decca Bk. Jazz* xxi. 264 Ellington..started it all in 1930 with his jazz rumba *Maori.* **1974** *Encycl. Brit. Micropædia* VIII. 716/1 Best known for the dancers' subtle side to side hip movements with the torso erect, the rumba is danced with a basic pattern of two quick side steps and a slow forward step. **1980** *Tablet* 26 Jan. 84/2 A group of liturgical dancers swathed in white, practising the Our Father dance. No doubt this particular excursion into religious rumba was absurd.

b. *slang.* A spree.

Perhaps an erroneous use.

1934 E. HEMINGWAY in *Cosmopolitan* Apr. 108/3 He'd been giving the nigger a dollar a day and the nigger had been on a rumba every night. I could see him getting sleepy already.

2. *attrib.* and *Comb.*, as *rumba band, competition, dancer, orchestra, record, rhythm*; **rumba-box** (see quot. 1961).

1944 H. MCCLOY *Panic* 110 The swish of a sand-filled gourd in a rhumba band. **1967** O. LANCASTER *With an Eye to Future* v. 119 The strains of 'Peanut Vendor' played by one of the newly fashionable rumba bands. **1976** *Islander* (Victoria, B.C.) 4 Jan. 2/2 As far as we know the African Bongo Tribe made the first bongo drums for the latter use in the modern rhumba band. **1961** F. G. CASSIDY *Jamaica Talk* xii. 266 As for the *rumba-box*..it is a recent invention or importation which simulates the tones of the bass viol by means of four pieces of metal of different gauges attached to a box (the resonance chamber), which vibrate when they are plucked with the fingers, and are tuned to correspond to the strings. **1976** G. SIMS *End of Web* x. 69 The Rastafarians with their home-made drums and rumba-boxes. **1944** M. SHARP *Cluny Brown* xix. 130 She entered for a Rumba competition. **1973** *Black World* Sept. 12/2 Guillén captured the vitality of Afro-Cuban life in a series of 'sones' (songs) which deal with cane cutters, rumba dancers, and folk types. **1941** B. SCHULBERG *What makes Sammy Run?* xi. 271 He was..dancing with her out on the patio to the rhumba orchestra. **1972** J. MCCLURE *Caterpillar Cop* viii. 118 Lisbet had to raise her voice.. above the rhumba record to catch his attention. **1932** *Radio Times* 8 Apr. 129 There is Southern glamour in the Rumba Rhythm of a tango tune. **1957** *Encycl. Brit.* VII. 23/2 The Rumba rhythm: one, two, three, pause; one, two, three, pause. **1970** W. APEL *Harvard Dict. Mus.* (ed. 2) 744/1 After 1930 rumba rhythms were incorporated into jazz.

ru·mba, *v.* Also **rhumba.** [f. the sb.] *intr.* To dance the rumba. Also, to move as though dancing the rumba.

1938 G. GREENE *Brighton Rock* II. i. 66 The tune the band was playing, the crowd on the floor trying to rumba. **1944** M. SHARP *Cluny Brown* xxiv. 156 Belinski at once rose, grasped the girl round the waist, and then began to rumba. **1951** E. TAYLOR *Game of Hide-&-Seek* II. i. 120 'Englishwomen should never rumba,' he told her. **1961** G. DURRELL *Whispering Land* iii. 85 He [*sc.* a fur seal] decided that the seagull should be taught a lesson, so he humped himself up indignantly and rumbaed towards it ferociously. **1970** V. CANNING *Great Affair* vii. 111 You once taught two boys to rhumba.

rumble, *sb.* Add: **1. c.** In sound reproduction, low-frequency noise originating as mechanical vibration in a turntable. Also *attrib.* and *Comb.*

1949 FRAYNE & WOLFE *Elem. of Sound Recording* xiv. 271 An additional factor that must be considered in noise measurements is the vibration or 'rumble' of the turntable. **1968** *Times* 29 Nov. (Sound of Leisure Suppl.) p. vii/1 Background noise while a record is playing can be very disturbing and it is the elimination of this noise, appropriately called rumble, which is the main concern of the manufacturers of gramophone records and record playing units. **1970** J. EARL *Tuners & Amplifiers* i. 19 Sometimes the high-pass filter is referred to as the rumble filter, since its bass attenuation characteristic significantly reduces the amplifier's response to low-frequency noises generated by the turntable unit and passed on via the disc and pickup. **1971** *Hi-Fi Sound* Feb. 67/2 With a rumble-free turntable, a player may cost as much as an entire low-budget sound system. **1977** *Time* 10 Oct. 43/1 (Advt.), There is rumble from the cutting machine in most record grooves.

d. A rumour. *U.S. colloq.*

1961 P. A. BRODEUR in *Webster* s.v., Picked up the rumble..and thought he'd pass it on just in case. **1966** 'E. MCBAIN' *Eighty Million Eyes* iv. 67 The neighbourhood rumble is that he was fooling around with one of their wives. **1974** E. McGirr *Murderous Journey* 63 The rumble is that he works for Marcello.

2. b. A street-fight between rival gangs. Also *fig. slang* (chiefly *U.S.*).

1946 *Amer. Mercury* Apr. 480 We're going to have a rumble with the Happy Gents tonight. Gang kids call these fights rumbles. **1953** Kramer & Karr *Teen-Age Gangs* p. v, A 'rumble'—a wild group fight—which gang youths consider the glamorous high point of their existence. *Ibid.* i. 4 A leader naturally headed his followers in a rumble with another gang. **1958** H. Salisbury *Shook-Up Generation* (1959) iv. 64 He would do things no other boy would dare. He would sound a cop on the beat and run away laughing. In a rumble he was like a wildcat. **1969** C. Burke *God is Beautiful, Man* (1970) 38 By the time they got the drink there was a big rumble brewin'. The Israelites set up a big crash pad and there was another gang that didn't like it and they decided they would have a real big rumble with these Moses people. **1971** P. L. Cave *Chopper* iv. 28 So I missed out on a rumble tonight. **1977** *Time* 31 Oct. 55/1 Singer Frank Sinatra seldom ducks a rumble with a reporter.

4. Also in a motor vehicle, = **rumble seat. U.S.*

1929 W. Faulkner *Sanctuary; Orig. Text* (1981) vii. 82 The car drew up... The ones in the rumble said nothing. **1939** —— *Wild Palms* 90 McCord drove them up to the lake on the Saturday night before Labor Day, the hundred dollars worth of food—the tins, the beans and rice..—in the rumble. **1941** B. Schulberg *What makes Sammy Run?* viii. 189 I'll look in the rumble... I think I have some.

6. [Perhaps a different word.] An interruption in the course of a crime; an alarm; a tip-off. *Criminals' slang.*

1911 C. G. Roe *Horrors of White Slave Trade* iv. 80, I posed as a theatrical manager..and caught many an unwary stage struck girl... I was taking small chances of being caught and in fact did not have a 'rumble' during all the time I was there. **1913** A. Stringer *Shadow* v. 93 'But he blew out for 'Frisco this morning,' contended the puzzled Sheiner. 'Shot through as though he had just had a rumble!' **1914** Jackson & Hellyer *Vocab. Criminal Slang* 73 If you walk on the main stem you'll get a rumble. **1927** D. Hammett in *Black Mask* Feb. 17/2 The neighbors give us the rumble. **1949** A. Hynd *We are Public Enemy* i. 21 The cops had gotten a rumble that..gangsters were holed up. **1949** in Wentworth & Flexner *Dict. Amer. Slang* (1960) 437/1 If there's a rumble, we do the time. **1957** *Life* 9 Dec. 57 The boys slip into town. You wouldn't think they would be noticed. But some busybody catches on and puts in a rumble.

7. *attrib.* and *Comb.*, as **rumble seat** *N. Amer.* = *dicky, dickey *sb.* 9 c; **rumble strip** (see quots. 1962 and 1975).

1912 *Collier's* 23 Mar. 20/3 She's burnin' the wind out of town in a college boy's car with big May on the rumble seat behind. **1929** M. Lief *Hangover* 301 The next morning she packed a small bag of necessaries, stowed it in the rumble seat, and drove off. **1951** T. Capote *Grass Harp* iv. 95 They'd stuffed her into the rumble-seat of Big Eddie's old coupé and driven straight to the jail. **1972** *Evening Telegram* (St. John's, Newfoundland) 5 Aug. 15/1 Three old-fashioned things you seldom see on the roads these days... Running boards, rumble seats and courtesy. **1962** *Punch* 27 June 960/2 American towns have been experimenting with 'rumble strips'—coarse-textured expanses of road surface just before cross-roads. **1974** *Oxford Times* 12 July 15/3 Rumble strips put down in the road to slow traffic had no effect. **1975** *Daily Mail* 3 Jan. 11/4 *Rumble strips*: These are tiny ridges on a road surface which cause a high-pitched whine as the car tyres pass over them... They indicate a hazard ahead.

rumble, *v.*[1] Add: **2. b.** (Earlier example.)

1803 G. Colman *John Bull* ii. ii. 19 I've rumbled on the road, all night, Frank; my bones ache.

3. d. To have a gang fight. *slang* (chiefly *U.S.*).

1959 *Listener* 29 Jan. 201/2 Do you know why a 'diddley bop' should put on a 'stenjar' to 'go down' to 'rumble' at a 'jitterbug'... That is the language of the teenage gangs of New York. **1969** S. Greenlee *Spook who sat by Door* xiv. 121 The teenage gangs..haven't been rumbling and so they have a lot of latent hostility to get rid of. **1977** 'E. McBain' *Long Time no See* viii. 116 We *was* tired, man. We been rumblin all the past month..gang-busting.

5. d. (Later examples.)

1963 *Times* 28 Jan. 9/5 Many people who even want Britain to enter the Common Market express a little joy in seeing de Gaulle rumbling your people. **1976** Ld. Annan in *Ann. Rep. Univ. Coll. (London)* 1975–76 7 It looks..as if the Department of Education and Science has rumbled the Schools Council plan for a common system of school leaving examinations, a proposal which the universities regarded with the deepest suspicion.

e. To clean in a rumble.

1904 Harbord & Hall *Metall. of Steel* xxxiv. 532 Small forged or stamped and malleable cast articles, which can be 'rumbled' bright in a shaking barrel, take the metal fairly well. **1957** *New Scientist* 7 Nov. 23/3 The thin parting bridges [of ball-bearings] are automatically severed and, after cooling, the balls are rumbled to remove the burr.

6. [Perhaps a different word.] *trans.* To get to the bottom of; to see through, understand, grasp; to recognize; to detect, discover, disturb. *slang.*

1886–96 in Farmer & Henley *Slang* (1903) VI. 75/2, I rumbled the tip as a matter of course. **1898** A. M. Binstead *Pink 'Un & Pelican* ix. 209, I soon rumbled he was in it, when I heard Ball givin' him the 'me lord' for it. **1912** C. Mackenzie *Carnival* (ed. 5) x. 126 I've properly rumbled your friends. **1925** N. Venner *Imperfect Imposter* iii. 30 He'd have rumbled me. He can't rumble me now. **1928** E. Wallace *More Educated Evans* iii. 69, I rumbled you as soon as I took a screw through the winder. **1930** P. MacDonald *Link* 74 If I hadn't had so many queer things happen to me in such a short time..I'd never have rumbled him. **1939** *Almanac for New Yorkers* 125 Some mugs rumbled us. **1956** 'A. Gilbert' *Riddle of Lady* viii. 115 The tobacconist..had been rumbled and compelled to give evidence. *Ibid.* xi. 178, I might have guessed you'd rumble me. **1959** *Encounter* Aug. 29/2 He evidently didn't rumble anything was at all unusual. **1966** J. Bingham *Double Agent* iii. 43 You've been rumbled. What's the use of a gun? **1979** E. Newman *Sunday Punch* xvi. 145 'Have you any influence with him?' 'He'd rumble that. He'd think I was your agent.'

rumbled, *ppl. a.* Add: **2.** Also *fig.*

1930 R. Campbell *Adamastor* 67 Nature..Admits no vegetable green... But with snarled gold and rumbled blue Must disinfect the sight.

rumbler. Add: **1. b.** A type of round bell on a harness, etc. Also *attrib.*

1953 A. Jobson *Household & Country Crafts* xii. 130 But at Chichester the first horse had three bells, the second four and the third five. In the case of round bells they were known as rumblers. **1961** *Countryman* LVIII. iii. 596 Some early ones had round 'rumbler' bells. **1971** *Country Life* 8 Apr. 839/2 Rumblers were another type of bell, circular with a ball inside to give them their characteristic sound. This type was quite common for cart horses or pack horses, but never used on a sheep as that animal did not give the bell the right kind of motion to make it rumble properly.

3. A machine for peeling potatoes.

1976 *Star* (Sheffield) 20 Nov. (Advt.), One 56 lb Triumph Superb Potato Rumbler, fully reconditioned, £300. **1977** *Grimsby Even. Tel.* 24 May 4/9 (Advt.), Potato room with an imperial rumbler and a Crypto chipper.

rumble-tumble. 4. Add: *Anglo-Indian.* (Further examples.)

1956 D. Walker *Harry Black* xiii. 192 'What's for breakfast?' 'Keventer's sausages and rumble-tumble,' Christian said... She went off to feed the family..on sausages and scrambled eggs. **1966** J. & R. Godden *Two under Indian Sun* iii. 54 Rumble tumble, the Indian name for scrambled eggs. **1980** D. Hart-Davis *Heights of Rimring* vii. 74 The rumble-tumble was a mighty omelette with strips of onion in it, accompanied by fried potatoes.

rumbling, *vbl. sb.* Add: **4.** Cleaning in a rumble. Also *attrib.*

1888 in *Lockwood's Dict. Mech. Engin.* 295. **1924** *Jrnl. Inst. Metals* XXXII. 294 Small articles, such as may be treated in rumbling barrels. **1965** G. J. Williams *Econ. Geol. N.Z.* xiv. 217/1 The relatively unaltered phenocrysts were experimentally removed by screening, cleaned by washing and rumbling, and analysed. **1976** *Western Mail* (Cardiff) 27 Nov., Further ancillary machines are avilable for drilling, tapping, rumbling and welding.

rumbly, *a.* (Earlier example.)

1874 L. Troubridge *Jrnl.* 3 Sept. in J. Hope-Nicholson *Life amongst Troubridges* (1966) 92 We..had the usual stuffy, rumbly drive.

rumbo[3]. Add: Also **rumbow.** (Earlier example.)

1846 *Swell's Night Guide* 130/2 *Rum bow*, rope stolen from any of the king's dock-yards.

rumbullion[1]. For *Obs.* read *'Obs.* except *Hist.'* and add: Also, a glass or drink of rum.

1972 F. van W. Mason *Roads to Liberty* 19 Katie! A brace of rumbullions. Fast as you can brew 'em!

rumbunctious, var. *rambunctious *a.*

rumbustiously (rɒmbɒ·stiəsli), *adv.* [f. Rumbustious *a.* + -ly[2].] In a rumbustious manner.

1966 *Listener* 10 Feb. 217/2 In *Horseman, Pass By!* we had a fair share of both, as well as poetry read rumbustiously by Mr O'Connor and grimly by Mr Kennelly. **1977** *Time* 5 Dec. 49/2 Lampie, the hard-drinking lighthouse keeper (played rumbustiously by Mickey Rooney), tells everyone that he has seen a dragon.

rumbustiousness (rɒmbɒ·stiəsnės). [f. as prec. + -ness.] Rumbustious character; boisterous behaviour.

1926 C. L. Graves *Hubert Parry* II. 106 In spite of his occasional exuberance and 'rumbustiousness' (a favourite word of his) he could, when the need arose, assume a wonderful dignity of demeanour. **1959** *Times Lit. Suppl.* 2 Oct. 556/4 More than one old White Russian..has felt his exiled convictions wavering a little before the rockets and rumbustiousness of the new Russia. **1977** *Gramophone* Jan. 1141/1 This come-to-the-fair rumbustiousness is well caught in the Scherzo.

rumdum, rumdumb (rɒ·mdɒm), *a.* and *sb.* Also **rumdumm** and with hyphen. *N. Amer. slang.* [f. Rum *sb.*[1] + Dumb *a.* (*sb.*).] **A.** *adj.* **a.** Stupefied through drink; unconscious; incapacitated; stupid. **b.** Humdrum.

1891 *Brooklyn Eagle* 11 Sept. 2/4 *Rum-dumb*,..stupid with continual drinking. **1922** S. Lewis *Babbitt* vii. 99 Don't faint with surprise if some of those rum-dumm liars get one good swift poke from Mike. **1936** J. Steinbeck *In Dubious Battle* i. 15. Cop slugged me from behind, right in the back of the neck... I was rumdum for a long time. **1939** —— *Grapes of Wrath* xv. 215 He jus' stan's there lookin' at that dead kid. Can't get a word of 'im. Jus' rum-dumb. **1973** *Newsweek* 12 Mar. 96 Ponicsan finds surprising depth and touching delicacy in the rumdum lives he weaves together—dime-store and dinner women, odd-job truckers and coal-mine cripples. **1975** *Islander* (Victoria, B.C.) 14 Sept. 6/1 Mr. Brown had gone on a humdinger of a toot after a lucky find and wound up in bed rumdumb with no fire in his cabin.

B. *sb.* **a.** A habitual drunkard; a stupid person. **b.** Someone of ordinary ability.

1891 *Brooklyn Eagle* 11 Sept. 2/4 *Rum-dumb*,..an habitual soak. **1916** G. A. England *Pod, Bender & Co.* 8 Why don't we lure in some rumdum of an ex-heavy-weight. **1949** N. Algren *Man with Golden Arm* i. 16 The cell was full of a drifting flesh-coloured light and the murmuring rumdums were being let out of the cells to wash. **1960** C. Hamblett in J. Pudney *Pick of Today's Short Stories* XI. 137 Other drinkers..mocked at him and called him cloth-head, or rumdum, or plain moron. **1976** *Harper's Mag.* July 72/2, I beat the rum-dums but go down before quality players.

Rumelian, var. *Roumelian *a.* (*sb.*).

Rumeliot, var. *Roumeliote.

rumenal, var. Ruminal *a.* in Dict. and Suppl.

rumenitis (rūmĕnəi·tis). *Vet. Sci.* [f. Rumen + -itis.] Inflammation of an animal's rumen.

1905 [see *reticulitis]. **1963** Jubb & Kennedy *Path. Domestic Animals* II. i. 51/1 A more common form of acute rumenitis, presumably chemical, develops after overeating on rapidly fermentable carbohydrate, usually grain. **1973** *Vet. Ann. 1972* 19 A deep haemorrhagic and necrotizing rumenitis.

rumenotomy (rūmĕnǫ·tŏmi). *Vet. Med.* [f. Rumen + -o + -tomy.] Incision into an animal's rumen.

1882 J. W. Hill *Bovine Med. & Surg.* xxiv. 587 Rumenotomy consists in removing the contents of the viscus through an artificial opening. **1973** [see *ruminal *a.* 2].

Rumford (rɒ·mfǒɹd). *Obs.* except *Hist.* The name of Count (von) Rumford (see Rumfordize *v.*) used *attrib.* to designate kitchen articles or fireplaces designed by him or improved according to systems devised by him. Also *ellipt.* as *sb.*

1810 *Agric. Museum* (U.S.) I. 42 The dinner was principally prepared hot on the ground, by means of a portable Rumford kitchen... The utility of the portable Rumford had not probably been experienced on the field on any previous occasion in New England. *a* **1817** Jane Austen *Northanger Abbey* (1818) II. v. 87 The fire-place..was contracted to a Rumford. **1831** R. Cox *Adventures Columbia River* II. xiv. 322 A bright brass footman..was suspended from the shining bars of a Rumford grate. **1854** Thoreau *Walden* 34 Spacious apartments, clean paint and paper, Rumford fire-place. **1937** M. Lansing *Mary Lyon through her Lett.* 230 All marveled at the Rumford oven, given by Deacon Safford. .. This Rumford oven was a sheet iron box with a compartment beneath in which the fire was built. **1951** *Dict. Americanisms* II. 1428/2 (*caption*) Rumford oven beside a fireplace.

rumgumptious, *a.* Add: Also **rumgumshus.** (Later example.)

1962 A. Jobson *Window in Suffolk* vi. 96 A quarrelsome person was *rumgumshus*.

Rumi, var. *Roumi.

ruminal, *a.* Add: Also **rumenal. 2.** Of or pertaining to the rumen of an animal.

1923 [see *reticular *a.* 4]. **1963** Jubb & Kennedy *Path. Domestic Animals* II. i. 52/1 The ruminal environment is, except immediately after eating, anaerobic. **1973** Hickman & Walker *Atlas Vet. Surg.* iii. 70 Rumenotomy is indicated..for the relief of rumenal impaction.

ruminant, *sb.* Add: **b.** A contemplative person. *rare.*

1940 C. S. Lewis *Let.* 22 Mar. (1966) 179 Why should quiet ruminants like you and I have been born in such a ghastly age?

ruminate, *v.* **1. a.** (Later examples.)

1928 *Oxford Poetry* 7 About your poorly-mounted majesty Stand cow-faced women ruminating sales. *a* **1961** A. Huxley in *Webster* (1961) s.v., Ruminating the contents of that last batch of letters she had received. **1975** *N.Y. Times* 26 Sept. 35/2 Mr. Rodgers has lived long, created much and filled an age with the sound of his music. Perhaps he has earned the right to ruminate..the art of autobiography.

ruminating *vbl. sb.* (later example).

1955 *Sci. News Let.* 16 July 36/2 Grazing animals frequently chew their cud for about nine hours out of every 24, and this ruminating is somewhat concentrated at night, Dr. Balch suggested.

rummage, *sb.* Add: **4. rummage sale** (*b*) (further examples); also *attrib.* and *fig.*

1910 M. Beerbohm *Let.* 15 Nov. (1964) 192 It will be a different sort of exhibition..: a *retrospective* and rummage-sale affair. **1912** *Strand Mag.* Aug. 155 Good wickets at rummage-sale prices. **1922** JOYCE *Ulysses* 737 Rummage sale a lot of trash. **1973** *Black World* Sept. 62 Your black skin Loose as a rummage sale coat. **1977** *Time* 24 Oct. 48/3 The *Road* shows were rummage sales of stuff out of vaudeville, burlesque—marvelously shoddy masterpieces of farce and fantasy, stitched together with clichés and ad libs.

rummage, *v.* Add: **I. 3. b.** (Later example with *up.*)
1889 J. K. JEROME *Three Men in Boat* iv. 57, I rummaged the things up into much the same state that they must have been before the world was created, and when chaos reigned.
5. b. (Earlier example with *out.*)
1803 *Lett. Miss Riversdale* II. 303 In rummaging out the contents of a *secrétaire*,..[she] had discovered a private drawer.
II. 8. b. Also const. *around.*
1883 'MARK TWAIN' *Life on Mississippi* iii. 36 He come rummaging around in the dark amongst the shingle bundles.

rummager. 2. (Further examples.)
1856 E. G. PARKER *Lesson of '76* 9 Layard, the great rummager of Nineveh. **1935** L. LUARD *Conquering Seas* iii. 44 Next time I'll let the rummagers put a stop to their nonsense.

rummish, *a.* (Earlier example.)
1760 DUCHESS OF NORTHUMBERLAND *Diary* 17 Aug. (1926) 26 Ld Dumfries very drunk, talk'd of being frisky & rummish.

rummy, *sb.*[1] Add: **2. a.** A habitual drunkard; an alcoholic. *slang* (chiefly *U.S.*).
1851 J. H. GREEN *Twelve Days in Tombs* 55 The learned counsel of the rummies opened his defence... the court adjourned, and the rummies repaired to *another bar* to congratulate each other upon the success of the morning. **1907** G. B. SHAW *Major Barbara* 170 Your Rummies of the tamest respectability pretending to a past of reckless and dazzling vice. **1939** [see *nut factory* s.v. *NUT *sb.*[1] 21]. **1962** E. LACY *Freeloaders* vi. 124 You'd go to pieces, become a rummy. **1975** *Publishers Weekly* 20 Jan. 67/1 A salty old rummy who specializes in pious letters pleading for help.
b. A stupid person; a blockhead; a sucker. *U.S. slang.*
1912 ADE *Knocking Neighbors* 108 She extracted a promise from Cousin and several other Desperate Characters that they would come out into the wilderness and give the Rummies a Touch of High Life. **1913** J. LONDON *Valley of Moon* 59 You'd better tell the rummy to beat it. **1937** *Reader's Digest* Oct. 36/2 Most rummies never discover they have been rooked.

rummy, *sb.*[2] orig. *U.S.* Also **rumme.** [Origin uncertain.] Any of a group of card games, similar to coon-can, the main object of which is to acquire runs or flushes of three or more cards. Also *attrib.* See also *gin rummy* s.v. *GIN *sb.*[2] 2 b, *OKLAHOMA.
1910 *Sun* (N.Y.) 10 Sept. II. 3/1 The leader this season seems to be a new round game that is called rum. Some persons have it rhum, rhummy and even rhumston. **1913** *Official Gaz.* (U.S. Patent Office) 13 May 536/2 Milton Bradley Company, Springfield, Mass. Filed Mar. 20, 1913. Rumme. **1915** *Chicago Herald* 30 Nov. 15/4 This gave him the idea the game was rummy and he spread the nines on the table. **1919** S. LEWIS *Free Air* xix. 202 He takes some kind of dope, and he cheats at rummy. **1928** L. NORTH *Parasites* 285 Sometimes they played écarté..or Rummy. **1934** W. SAROYAN *Daring Young Man* 213, I would sneak out of the bookie joint and run across the street to a rummy parlour and get into a game. **1964** A. WYKES *Gambling* vii. 164 Games of the rummy series appear to be the oldest. **1974** *Harrods Gift Catal.* 60/1 Packs of cards to play Bingo, Crosswords, Rummy and a variety of games.

rummy, *a.*[1] Add: **B.** as *sb.* An odd or unconventional person.
1975 G. V. HIGGINS *City on Hill* iv. 117 At least the rummies that swing it in Dorchester're *alive*. **1977** J. WAMBAUGH *Black Marble* (1978) vi. 72 She always had to look at the rummy to see if he was putting her on. *Ibid.*, It must be dope... This rummy's a doper!

rummy, *a.*[2] Add: (Earlier and later examples.) Also, drunken.
1834 *Jamestown* (N.Y.) *Jrnl.* 29 Jan. 1/5 The Massachusetts Masons,..like the rummy deacon, who fell from his horse—have merely 'got off to get on better'. **1843** *Amer. Pioneer* II. 372 He departed, muttering curses loud and deep, and in a voice peculiarly rummy. **1961** W. A. WHITE in *Webster* s.v., His face was blotched..his eyes were rummy, his jaw was uncertain.

rummy, *v.* [f. *RUMMY *sb.*[2]] *intr.* To obtain a hand that can be laid down at rummy; to say 'rummy' signifying this. Also const. *out.*
1929 *Encycl. Brit.* XIX. 658/2 Directly a player rummies that deal is finished, and all the hands are exposed and added up. **1966** L. DAVIDSON *Long Way to Shiloh* x. 144 'What about a game of cards?'.. She played with immense concentration and rummied out in about five minutes.

rumorous, *a.* Add: **1.** (Further examples.)
1889 W. B. YEATS *Wanderings of Oisin* 68 Wandering of yore in forests rumorous, Beneath the flaming eyeballs of the night. **1926** GALSWORTHY *Silver Spoon* I. xii. 89 The rumorous town still hummed; the sky was faintly coloured. **1970** I. MURDOCH *Fairly Honourable Defeat* II. xix. 371 It was dark outside, windy rainy rumorous darkness coming from far away.
Hence **rumoro·sity,** stir, public outcry. *rare.*
1906 JOYCE *Let.* 25 Sept. (1966) II. 166 Ibsen..seems to have disclaimed some of the rumorosity attaching to *A Doll's House.*

rumour, *sb.* Add: **2.** Also phr. *rumour has it.*
1912 J. N. MCILWRAITH *Diana of Quebec* xviii. 276 Rumour had it they were engaged. **1922** JOYCE *Ulysses* 190 Mr. Russell, rumour has it, is gathering together a sheaf of our younger poets' verses. **1957** D. ROBINS *Noble One* xi. 111 Rumour has it that when Brett went off on his trip, he was asked to give the pretty Juliet a lift..and they've *neither* of them come back. **1961** B. N. CARDOZO in *Webster* s.v., We make our blunders..as rumour has it that you make your own.
3. Comb. *rumour-factory, -mill, -monger* (further examples), *-mongering*; *rumour-ridden* adj.
1933 DYLAN THOMAS *Let.* 11 Nov. (1966) 63 Every country in this rumour-ridden world..is branded like Cain across the forehead. **1935** Rumour-monger [see *NON-ARYAN *sb.*]. **1953** in P. C. Berg *Dict. New Words* 138/2 A sincere and humble apology printed by the paper in response to charges of rumour-mongering. **1953** J. MASTERS *Lotus & Wind* vi. 76 He must come quickly for her sake—and for his own, to confront the rumourmongers and force them to eat their vile words. **1967** *Economist* 25 Mar. 1131/3 One decree, so far unused, imposing fierce penalties for rumour-mongering and another providing for custody without trial. **1973** *New Journalist* (Australia) July–Aug. 2/3 If there's any truth at all in what's been processed through the industry rumour mills, the.. journalists..might well be coming from the Sydney production lines. **1977** *Private Eye* 1 Apr. 18/3 The peculiar recent gyrations in the shares..may owe as much to the ambitious designs of certain mysterious figures..as to the myriad stories poured out by the well-primed City rumour factory. **1977** *China Now* July/Aug. 18/2 In rebellion against the People's Government, one of the..Grand Lamas went on a rumour-mongering rampage. **1979** *Time* 8 Jan. 28/1 Communications in Iran are unreliable, with the result that the country has become a vast rumor mill. **1979** *Railway Age* Nov. 34/1 Rumormongers have ranged from the *Des Moines Register*, the major newspaper of a major ICG state, to a federal official.
5. (Later examples.)
1889 W. B. YEATS *Let.* 3 Feb. (1954) I. 110 They always long for rest and to get away from the noise and rumour of the world. **1922** JOYCE *Ulysses* 388 His heart shook within the cage of his breast as he tasted the rumour of that storm. **1927** F. B. YOUNG *Portrait of Clare* 624 Her ears became aware of an unusual sound. At first she thought it was only the wind-swept rumour of one of the great munition trains. *a* **1973** J. R. R. TOLKIEN *Silmarillion* (1977) iii. 52 But many refused the summons, preferring the starlight and the wide spaces of Middle-earth to the rumour of the Trees.

rumour, *v.* Add: **2. d.** To force through rumour *into* (an action, etc.). *rare.*
1925 F. SCOTT FITZGERALD *Great Gatsby* i. 25, I had no intention of being rumored into marriage.

rumouring, *vbl. sb.* (Later example.)
1957 T. HUGHES *Hawk in Rain* 54 You hear..through all The leafy valley a rumouring of air go.

rump, *sb.*[1] Add: † **1. d.** A type of bustle. *Obs.*
1786 E. SHERIDAN *Jrnl.* 22 Jan. (1960) iii. 79 However you may tell her as a friend gradually to reduce her Stuffing as Rumps are quite out in France and are decreasing here but can not be quite given up 'till the weather grows warmer. **1807** R. SOUTHEY *Lett. from England* II. xlix. 335 There were protruberances on the hips called bustlers, another behind which was called in plain language a rump.
2. c. (Further example.) Also, corporal punishment administered on the buttocks.
1833 J. ROMILLY *Diary* 20 Mar. (1967) 31 The original bet was 1 G[ui]n[e]a, but Sedgwick proposed a rump & dozen. **1922** JOYCE *Ulysses* 323 A rump and dozen says the citizen, was what that old ruffian sir John Beresford called it but the modern God's Englishman calls it caning on the breech.
5. a. *rump-patch, roast, -steak* (earlier example).
1902 *Nature* 14 Aug. 375/2 The author states that the gaur and the gayal have a white rump-patch. **1948** A. L. RAND *Mammals Eastern Rockies* 206 Elk... Sides of body yellowish brown, rump patch lighter. **1926** *Daily Colonist* (Victoria, B.C.) 6 July 6/1 (Advt.), Small Rump Roasts, per lb. 23c. **1976** *National Observer* (U.S.) 22 May 20/4 Right in the Rump Roast. **1747** H. GLASSE *Art of Cookery* i. 6 *To Broil* Steaks..take fine Rump Steaks about Half an Inch thick.
b. *rump caucus, government, -junta, meeting, parliament* (see also sense 3 c in Dict.), *party, state.*
1933 *Sun* (Baltimore) 19 Apr. 1/7 The incipient revolt as reflected in the rump caucus of Democratic inflationists. **1861** *Richmond* (Va.) *Examiner* 4 Dec. 3/3 It may very reasonably be doubted how far General Sherman or his officers would suffer schemes so vitally important to the Rump Government to leak out through the indiscretions of loquacious volunteers. **1937** *Nation* 6 Nov. 419/1 The Franco rump government in Spain. **1977** *Time* 15 Aug. 15/2 In 1975 the Turks declared their own Turkish Federated State of Cyprus; last week the only notice this rump government took of Makarios' passing was to announce flatly that it would not recognize his successor as the leader of a united Cyprus. **1835** *Times* 19 June 2/2 The Westminster Rump-juntas of our own day. **1935** *Sun* (Baltimore) 10 Dec. 2/7 Mr. Berry..declared the meeting adjourned, and Dr. Haake and his confreres edged their way out to the sidewalk, where they theatened for a time to hold a 'rump meeting'. **1977** *New Yorker* 10 Oct. 50/3 On the eve of Eaton's ninetieth birthday.. he was summarily booted upstairs to chairman emeritus by his own board of directors at a rump meeting. **1838** *Ibid.* 17 Feb. 764/1 What prevents Congress from declaring itself perpetual—a rump Parliament? **1963** *Times* 23 May 13/4 This move is a direct reversal of the proposal, threatened by the Governor of the Gambia, that the remaining validly elected members of the House of Representatives constituted a 'rump parliament', capable of curing this difficulty. **1976** *New Yorker* 22 Mar. 98/2 Krishnan Kant recently made an eloquent and wide-ranging indictment of the emergency, a sort of *cri de cœur*, in what could properly be called the rump Parliament, inasmuch as so many of both its opposition and its Congress members have been jailed. **1959** *Ann. Reg. 1958* 121 Rump parties would continue to exist and split the anti-P.A.P. vote. **1938** *Sun* (Baltimore) 31 Oct. 8/3 Germany and Italy have consented to serve as arbiters in the dispute between Hungary and the rump Czechoslovakian state. **1940** *Tablet* 4 May 422/1 Herr Joseph Bühler..is at present a sort of head of the Governor-General's Government in the rump-State of Poland.
c. rumpsprung *a.*, sprung or become baggy in the seat; also *fig.*; hence **rumpspringing** vbl. sb.
1939 C. MORLEY *Kitty Foyle* xiii. 131 Pop creaking in his rumpsprung wicker chair. **1954** *Publ. Amer. Dial. Soc.* XXI. 35 *Rumpspringing: pres. part., n.*, of a skirt, the act of bagging in the seat, caused by sitting. An inner lining is sometimes used to prevent *rumpspringing*... *Rumpsprung: adj.* **1970** D. WATERFIELD *Continental Waterboy* ii. 11 'In my opinion,' Mrs. Neuberger told the reporters, 'Vancouver women are rump-sprung.' **1975** *Weekend Mag.* (Montreal) 31 May 9/1 In the hallway, his rumpsprung wife is making a blasé remark about the new labor code.

Rumpelstiltskin (rʊ:mpəlsti·ltskin). [ad. G. *Rumpelstilzchen.*] The name of a vindictive dwarf in German folk-tale, used allusively.
1949 G. ORWELL *Nineteen Eighty-Four* II. 181 A little Rumpelstiltskin figure, contorted with hatred. **1976** *National Observer* (U.S.) 21 Feb. 5/2 A hunch that computerized direct marketing would become the Rumpelstiltskin of American politics in the 1970s.

Rumpety, var. *RUMPTY *sb.*[2]

rumpless, *a.* Add: (Further example.) Hence **ru·mplessness,** the state of being without a rump.
1945 *Jrnl. Exper. Zool.* XCVIII. 65 The injection of solutions of certain chemicals into unincubated chicken eggs led to the appearance of increased numbers of rumpless embryos and chicks. *Ibid.* 67 Insulin produced a high degree of rumplessness. **1971** *N.Z. Med. Jrnl.* LXXIII. 340 (*heading*) Lumbo-sacral agenesis or rumplessness [in humans].

rumply, *a.* For *rare*—1 read *rare* and add later examples.
1961 *Guardian* 21 Jan. 1/1 The rumply 35 White House staff members who had been marooned. **1967** E. B. NICKERSON *Kayaks to Arctic* xviii. 176 But the water was only slightly rumply, our boat moved easily along.

Rumpty (rʊ·mpti), *sb.*[2] Also **Rumpety.** *Air Force slang.* [f. RUMP *sb.*[1], after *BUMPETY, BUMPITY *adv.*] A Farman training aeroplane, used esp. during the war of 1914–18.
1917 A. S. G. LEE *Let.* 31 Aug. in *No Parachute* (1968) vi. 103 The Maurice Farman Rumpety I learned to fly on. **1917** in *Liberty* (1926) 28 Aug. 14/1 We are going to start on Rumptys as these Henry Farman planes are called. **1934** V. M. YEATES *Winged Victory* I. x. 83 Tom told them the first time he went up was in a Rumpty, that was to say, a Maurice Farman Shorthorn, a queer sort of bus like an assemblage of birdcages. *Ibid.* 86 After Rumpties he had gone on to Avros which really were aeroplanes, and quite different to fly. **1968** J. J. HUDSON *Hostile Skies* iii. 33 The 'Rumpty', the famous Farman primary trainer.

† **rumpty,** *sb.*[3] and *a.* *Obs. Austral.* and *N.Z. slang.* [Origin uncertain.] (Something) excellent. Also **ru:mptydoo·ler.**
1941 BAKER *N.Z. Slang* vi. 51 Expressions..in constant use by our youngsters..rorter, rumpty, rumptydooler, [etc.]. **1945** *2nd N.Z. Expeditionary Force Times* 29 Jan., What a rumpty. *Ibid.* 5 Feb. 45/4 It's a rumpty. **1945** BAKER *Austral. Lang.* vi. 126 Here are some of the many synonyms for *bonzer* (it should be noted that most of them are interchangeable as nouns and adjectives).. *rumptydooler.* **1946** E. G. WEBBER *Johnny Enzed in Italy* 45 What a rumpty.

rumpus, *sb.* Add: **c.** *Comb.*, as **rumpus room** orig. *N. Amer.*, a room set aside for recreation, which does not need to be kept tidy.
1940 *Chatelaine* July 37/2 Off through a double-doored hallway can be seen the 'rumpus room', that dennish haunt of Priscilla and Rosemary. **1945** NELSON & WRIGHT *Tomorrow's House* ii. 14/2 Their daughter took over the rumpus room in the basement. **1958** J. K. GALBRAITH *Affluent Society* xiii. 151 In the more censorious social levels of American society there is already a well-developed..aversion to gadgetry... In such circles shiny rumpus rooms, imaginative barbecue pits,..and

magnificent cars no longer win acclaim. **1959** *Encounter* Sept. 50/2 Retreating to a rumpus room with ping-pong tables and do-it-yourself work-benches. **1960** *News Chron.* 30 June 6/4 How things start out on their journey to the rumpus room. **1970** J. Blackburn *Land of Promise* xvii. 222 Betty brought university friends home for many good sing-songs and games in the rumpus room which we fixed up in the basement. **1977** J. I. M. Stewart *Madonna of Astrolabe* i. 7 The festivity..became more and more of a romp. Indeed, not so much a romp as a rumpus. But this too was in order. The room was called the rumpus room.

rumpy. Add: **2.** A chicken without a tail. Also *attrib.*

[**1885** L. Wright *Bk. Poultry* 448 It is the Rumpless or Persian Cock of Latham, and the Rumpkin of others.] **1895** *Funk's Stand. Dict.* II. 1561/3 Rumpy... 2. A variety of domestic fowl in the Isle of Man and the Hebrides. **1972** *Nat. Geographic* Sept. 438/2 We used to have a number of animals that were special to the Isle of Man... There are still some hens without tails—'rumpy hens' we call them.

ru·m-strum, *v.* [Echoic.] *intr.* To strum.

1872 Hardy *Under Greenw. Tree* II. ii. viii. 23 [He'd] want to see her young figure sitting up at that quare instrume't, and her young fingers rum-strumming upon the keys.

rumti-. Add: (Earlier and later examples in imitations of sounds.) Also, used in comb. with adjs.; *rumti-too* adj., commonplace.

(*b*) **1817** Keats *Let.* 15 Apr. (1958) I. 129, I hope one of you will be competent to take part in a Trio..when you have said Rum-ti-ti you must not rum any more. **1898** G. B. Shaw *Perfect Wagnerite* 109 A little rum-ti-tum triplet. **1912** *World* 7 May 690/2 Mr. Cyril Maude makes a rather rumtifootling bishop amusing and forgivable even in his most flagrant lapses from clerical circumspection. **1974** *Listener* 31 Jan. 131/1 Try translating Goethe's *Faust* with the same metre..it's apt to sound fatally rum-ti-tum. **1976** G. Ewart *No Fool* i. 31 This is a convention, we know, of course, and a wistfulness in the rum-ti-tum might be detected.

(*c*) **1906** Galsworthy *Man of Property* i. i. 22 Did you ever see such a collection of rumty-too people? **1920** —— *In Chancery* i. i. 9 He was feeling more strongly than ever that Timothy's was hopelessly 'rum-ti-too', and the souls of his aunts dismally mid-Victorian.

rum-tum. Add: **3.** Used in imitation of a regular rhythmic sound; also *attrib.*

1898 G. B. Shaw *Perfect Wagnerite* 139 The strings play a rum-tum accompaniment. **1917** —— *London Music in 1888–89* (1937) 380 The accompaniments are a derisive rum-tum. **1922** Joyce *Ulysses* 51 Of all the glad new year, mother, the rum tum tiddledy tum. **1958** *Times* 28 Nov. 8/4 The rum-tum bars in Malcolm Arnold's *United Nations* tone-poem. **1963** *Times* 14 May 15/1 Mr. Charles Groves..brought out the rum-tum rhythms more successfully than the great arches of melody they support.

run, *sb.*^{1} Add: **I. 1. d.** (Further examples.) Also *to give* (someone) *a run for his money* (colloq.), to give (that person) satisfaction or a good return for trouble taken; to offer (him) a strong challenge.

1905 *Athenæum* 1 Apr. 397 We do not get the proper run for our money, if we may put it in sporting lingo. **1908** Chesterton *Man who was Thursday* xiii. 277 Since the beginning of the world all men have hunted me like a wolf... I have given them a good run for their money, and I will now. **1914** G. B. Shaw *Dark Lady of Sonnets* Pref. 108 If I had been born in 1556 instead of in 1856, I should have taken to blank verse and given Shakespear a harder run for his money than all the other Elizabethans put together. **1916** 'Taffrail' *Pincher Martin* ix. 160 Most of them longed for a run for their money... The graver possibilities of war did not intrude themselves upon their minds until long afterwards. **1920** A. Huxley *Limbo* 83 'We'll give you a good run for your money,' said Hyman. 'I hope they'll be feeling a little uncomfortable by the time they have done with you, Greenow.' **1948** *Sun* (Baltimore) 26 Nov. 17/1 Backers of..Egretta, a stakes-winning filly, in the Endurance 'Cap did not get a run for their money. **1952** E. O'Neill *Moon for Misbegotten* i. 14 You're a wonderful fighter. Sure, you could give Jack Dempsey himself a run for his money. **1955** *Times* 27 Aug. 6/1 Pickering said that he was going.. 'simply to satisfy the people of Bloxwich. They demand a run for their money and I will give it to them.' **1976** J. Wainwright *Bastard* i. 13 The old Beetle punches the rear wheels into the softness and with good tyres..this bus could give a snow-cat a run for its money.

e. *Cricket.* The act of running by the bowler to the bowling crease in delivering the ball; a run-up.

1836 *New Sporting Mag.* Oct. 358 The only fault is in his taking too long a run before he delivers the ball. **1891** W. G. Grace *Cricket* ix. 240 When Smith begins his run he is behind the umpire and out of sight of the batsman. .. It is rather startling when he suddenly appears at the bowling crease. **1904** P. F. Warner *How We recovered Ashes* i. 22 With a short run Relf bowls a fast medium ball. **1976** J. Snow *Cricket Rebel* 77, I finished the match with ten wickets—the five in the second innings off a short run—for 80 runs.

f. *U.S.* A movement of settlers to new land; = Rush *sb.*^{2} 4 a in Dict. and Suppl.

1894 *Daily Ardmoreite* (Ardmore, Okla.) 30 Apr. 2/1 Buckskin Joe and his followers are camped at Marlow preparatory to making a run on the Fort Sill country tomorrow. **1901** *World's Work* June 894/1 Hitherto the settlers made a 'run' for the homesteads. **1930** *Publishers' Weekly* 8 Feb. 697 On April 22, 1889, this strip was opened up with the land rush known as the famous Oklahoma Run. **1948** *Daily Oklahoman* (Okla. City) 16 May E 3/2 The nine great land openings began in 1889 with the 'run' into the area now occupied by Oklahoma City, Guthrie, Norman, Stillwater and other cities.

2. a. (Earlier and later *Comb.* examples.)

1853 F. Lillywhite *Guide to Cricketers* 32 He is a splendid field anywhere, and one of the most sure run getters to be met with. **1867** *Baily's Monthly Mag.* July 250 The wickets good, and the ground in splendid order for run-getting. *Ibid.* Dec. 137 Harrow had not a great run-getting Eleven this year. **1877** *London Society* May 416/2 The run-stealer's heart would surely be broken in his first innings. *a* **1907** F. Thompson *Sel. Poems* (1908) p. viii, And I look through my tears on a soundless-clapping host As the run-stealers flicker to and fro. **1921** G. R. C. Harris *Few Short Runs* iv. 95 We..got two of their best bats caught..by George Remnant—one of the finest fields I ever saw, and in second-class matches a wonderful run-getter. **1934** Blunden *Mind's Eye* 186 The pair amuse themselves and astonish us with slogging and run-stealing. **1950** *Sport* 7–11 Apr. 11/3 Our batsmen will find run-getting more easy. **1963** *Times* 17 Apr. 3/1 P. K. Thomas, a consistent run-scorer in the Colts, is expected to mature with the first XI experience. **1965** G. McInnes *Road to Gundagai* xii. 209 It was an era of run-getters. **1976** *0–10 Cricket Scene* (Austral.) 7/1 His career Test aggregate of 5187 leaves him fourth on the Australian run-gathering list, among the elite. **1977** *Sunday Times* 2 Jan. 28/3 Australia's reaction..was to score at a run-a-minute rate.

b. (Earlier examples.) Also *Comb.*

1856 *Spirit of Times* 6 Sept. 13/3 At the time of the adjournment the score stood fifteen runs in favor of the Union, and twelve runs for the Baltic. **1858** *By-Laws Knickerbocker Base-Ball Club of N.Y.* 20 The game shall consist of nine innings to each side, when, should the number of runs be equal, the play shall be continued until a majority of runs, upon an equal number of innings, shall be declared, which shall conclude the game. **1891** *Harper's Weekly* 23 May 391/4 As for Poole, he is the same 'run-getter' that he was last year. **1970** *Washington Post* 30 Sept. D1/2 But the Twins came back to tie it 11–11 in their half on run-scoring singles by Cardenas and Chuck Manuel.

c. *Croquet.* The passage of a ball under a bridge or hoop. Cf. Run *v.* 37 d.

1863 Mayne Reid *Croquet* 34 If a ball, after running a bridge, strike an obstacle, and recoil back through the bridge, the run remains good.

4. a. Also in *Comb.*, as **run-boat** *U.S.*, a boat which collects or transports the catch made by marine fishing vessels; also *transf.*

1911 *Rudder* Aug. 49/2 The run-boats, in the local vernacular, are schooners mostly, about 60 to 70 feet on deck, and merely run back and forth between the dredging fleet and Baltimore. **1935** *Sun* (Baltimore) 6 Feb. 13/6 Most of the catch is brought to Crisfield in large run-boats, sent to the fishing grounds by fish dealers here. **1941** *Ibid.* 17 Mar. 11/3 Large dealers here go down the bay in run-boats to buy from the catchers. **1967** *Washington Star* (Sunday Mag.) 25 June 11 The Jessie Taylor out of Smith Island, Md., is typical of the 'runboats' that bring the seafood to town. **1974** *News & Observer* (Raleigh, N. Carolina) ii. 13/2 He told me he'd run aground in his private 'run boat'.

c. (Earlier and later examples.) Now freq. an excursion or drive by car or bicycle. Also in phr. *run ashore* (Naut.), a brief period of shore leave; also (with hyphen) *attrib.*

1819 H. Cockburn *Let.* 8 Oct. (1932) 18, I also took a run t'other day to Blair Adam. **1881** *Sportsman's Year-bk.* 199 Bicycle Touring Club... The members..enjoy Club runs or tours without the heavy outlay attendant on forming a small local Club. **1902** C. L. Freeston in Harmsworth *Motors & Motor-Driving* xxi. 388 Several tours and runs also took place, the anniversary run to Southsea..being an enormous undertaking. **1912** *Motor Man.* (ed. 14) v. 163 Never start on a run without being assured that there is ample oil. **1948** Partridge *Dict. Forces' Slang* 159 *Run ashore*, a short evening's shore leave. **1959** *Motor Man.* (ed. 36) xii. 259 A party in an ordinary family car..can count its daily run, including stops, at a kilometre a minute. **1977** *Navy News* June 8/2 It was certainly a good run ashore for the ship's company, with the Principality of Monaco granting free admission to many places of interest. *Ibid.* Aug. 31/2 Also 'out of this world' are the run-ashore opportunities.

d. (Earlier example.)

1857 *Lawrence* (Kansas) *Republican* 4 June 2 The train ..made a quick and pleasant run, arriving in Jefferson City promptly in time.

e. A brisk walk or perambulation. Now usu., a dog's exercise walk.

1837 W. Tayler in J. Burnett *Useful Toil* (1974) ii. 178, I am obliged to stay within to help the sick. This is what I don't like as I like to get a run everyday when I can. **1871** 'L. Carroll' *Through Looking-Glass* iv. 79 'O Oysters,' said the Carpenter, 'You've had a pleasant run! Shall we be trotting home again?' **1967** P. Moyes *Murder Fantastical* viii. 106 'What on earth made you go off down to the river on your own?' 'I was only giving Tinker her run... There was no need to come after me.' **1977** 'J. Bell' *Such Nice Client* viii. 83, I was giving Caesar a very short run on the lead.

f. A single trip on a toboggan, sleigh, etc., down a slope or course. Cf. sense 23 d below.

1898 *Encycl. Sport* II. 473/2 A good average run down the Cresta course takes 75 seconds. **1919** [see *Luge *sb.*]. **1935** *Encycl. Sports* 178/2 The art of making good time on a run is acquired by long study of the ten banked turns. **1956** *Ski-ing* ('Know the Game' Ser.) 22/1 If the run is made too early, the snow will be as hard as iron. **1976** F. Raphael *Glittering Prizes* 57 I'll make the first run. You grab the stop watch and bugger off down to the bottom of the hill, OK?

g. *Mil.* An offensive operation, *spec.* an attack by sea or air. See also *bomb run* s.v. *Bomb *sb.* 6, *dummy run* s.v. *Dummy *sb.* 7 b. Also *transf.*

1916, etc. [see *dummy run* s.v. *Dummy *sb.* 7 b]. **1941** *Flight* 13 Mar. 204/2 The bomber had successfully bombed its target on the first run; another run was then made and incendiaries started small fires. **1944** *Hutchinson's Pict. Hist. War* 12 Apr.–26 Sept. 43 (*caption*) The aircraft is seen making its second run over the target. **1948** Auden *Age of Anxiety* i. 18 We began our run; Death and damage darted at our will. **1963** *Listener* 4 Apr. 585/2 Our patrol car got the call as 'shots fired', with the address given. My partner and I responded. In such radio 'runs' you never know what to expect. **1975** J. Grady *Shadow of Condor* vi. 109 The CIA agent.. tips us to another run, which we intercept. **1977** *Time* 30 May 46/3 For the climactic battle sequence, which includes dogfights in space and missile runs on the Death Star, Lucas gathered all the old war movies he could find and spliced together their aerial-combat footage.

h. A single or regular journey made by an aircraft; the distance thus travelled.

1912 Kipling *Diversity of Creatures* (1917) 4 DeForest, whose business it is to know the out districts, told us that it..was about half an hour's run from end to end. **1944** [see *milk-run* s.v. *Milk *sb.* 10]. **1958** 'N. Shute' *Rainbow & Rose* i. 3, I was on the Sydney–Melbourne run. **1976** *Daily Mirror* 16 July 2/1 President Amin's jet airliner was poised last night to take off for Uganda..on a whisky run.

i. A regular round (freq. one accomplished by means of a vehicle). Also in phrases *mail-run* s.v. *Mail *sb.*^{3} 4 b, *milk-run* s.v. *Milk *sb.* 10, *paper run* s.v. *Paper *sb.* 12.

1925 *N. & Q.* 21 Mar. 208/1 In the dairy trade phrases such as 'He has a milk-run' or, 'he has a milk-walk' or 'he has a milk-round' are common. **1946** [see *mail-run* s.v. *Mail *sb.*^{3} 4 b]. **1968** K. Weatherly *Roo Shooter* 38 At night when they had done the evening run on their traps they would return home. **1978** *Oxf. Diocesan Mag.* July 16/3 A Soup run was established, operating four nights a week, and we have made contact with up to forty people in derelict property in and around the town centre.

8. With advs. See main entries.

II. 9. d. A downward flow or trickle of paint when applied too thickly; the action of paint in 'running'. Cf. Run *v.* 22 b.

1935 J. Lawrence *Painting A to Z* xi. 103 Don't leave the quirks swimming in paint, or it will wrinkle, or perhaps even run down into the lower mouldings, and leave a 'run'. **1951, 1958** [see *Curtain *sb.*^{1} 1 e]. **1975** *Amer. Speech 1969* XLIV. 24 *Run*, n., the action of paint when it is applied too heavily; it can't adhere to the wall surface and begins to stream down the wall.

III. 13. e. *Oil Industry.* (A distance drilled during) a spell of drilling with a particular bit.

1880 J. F. Carll *Geol. Oil Regions* xxviii. 310 The engineer examines the steam and the water gauges and the fire, and then proceeds to sharpen the tool required for the next 'run'. **1946** M. C. Seamark in *Mod. Petroleum Technol.* (Inst. Petroleum) 94 Cores of 10–20 feet can be taken at one 'run'. **1974** R. D. Grace in P. L. Moore et al. *Drilling Practices Man.* xiv. 354 Bit records of that time [*sc.* the late 1940s] were filled with typical runs of only five to ten feet in four to five hours at depths below 10,000 feet.

f. A length of electric wiring; a distance covered by uninterrupted cable.

1905 C. C. Metcalfe *Pract. Electr. Wiring* i. 5 If the run is this length..a conductor of greater sectional area, with a negligible resistance, should be used. **1938** J. W. Sims *Elect. Installations* vii. 128 Special care should be taken to avoid metallic obstructions inside the conduit.. and bushes should be fitted at the end of a run. **1957** A. L. Osborne *Elect. in Building* ii. 20 By eliminating long unbroken cable runs, voltage drop within the building is not likely to occur. **1970** J. Earl *Tuners & Amplifiers* iv. 94 Use 15-ampere cables for runs in excess of 10 ft.

g. A tear in a knitted garment or stocking; = *Ladder *sb.* 3 b. Also *attrib.* and *Comb.* Cf. *Runner 9 d.

1922 M. B. Houston *Witch Man* xii. 146 She looked the suit over, darned a tiny run in the tights, [etc.]. **1933** *Radio Times* 14 Apr. 95, I had an awful ladder in my stocking... I scarcely ever have a run now. **1936** G. G. Denny *Fabrics* (ed. 3) i. 104 *Run resist*, knitting process which locks stitches to reduce runs in hosiery and underwear. **1938** O. Nash *I'm Stranger here Myself* 173 She stopped to moisten her finger on account of a run in her stocking. **1938** 'E. Queen' *Four of Hearts* iv. 67 You've got a run in your stocking. **1938** *Knit Goods Weekly* 15 Aug. 11 These hosiery finishes bind fibre to fibre.. strengthen the fabric..make it snag-resistant, run-resistant..add miles more wear. **1939** *Business Week* 27 May 32/1 Merchants..seem not at all worried about the inroads that this really run-resistant hosiery might make in total sales volume. **1951** in M. McLuhan *Mech. Bride* (1967) 95 Ivory Flakes care helps safeguard sheerest nylons from embarrassing, eye-catching runs. **1957** M. B. Picken *Fashion Dict.* 279/2 *Run-proof*, a knitted construction where locked loops prevent a run. *Run resist*, a type of knitting with loops so constructed as to resist the tendency to run. **1969** *Sears Catal.* Spring/ Summer 409 Run-resistant mesh-knit seamless stretch nylons. **1970** *Focus* June 15/2 The term run-resist is used on the advice of hosiery trade associations, as an 'out' under the Trade Descriptions Act, 1968. **1973** 'E. McBain' *Let's hear It* x. 146 She's noisy and vulgar; there are runs in her nylons. **1974** H. L. Foster *Ribbin'* v. 186 A female student may have a run in her stockings and will be ribbed about it.

14. d. (Earlier examples.)

1798 *Rec. Smithtown, N.Y.* (1898) 351 The grist mill house..[will] carry three run of stones with three Bolting mills. **1815** *Niles' Weekly Reg.* IX. 187/1 The whole expense in generating steam sufficient to drive two run of stones upon this principle will not exceed two hundred and twenty dollars.

f. *pl.* with *the*. An attack of diarrhoea. *colloq.*

1962 E. LACY *Freeloaders* vii. 147 I'd picked up a touch of '*la tourism*' or in basic English, the runs, from..the unwashed fruit. **1966** 'L. LANE' *ABZ of Scouse* 91 *Go like a bookie wit' ther runs*, to move very fast. **1971** B. MALAMUD *Tenants* 214 Sam Clemence, a witness from Harlem U.S.A., despite a bad case of the runs.., stands up for his friend Willie. **1976** U. HOLDEN *String Horses* ix. 112 'What can she do Lil? Please help.' 'There's nothing. Pills will only give her the runs. I don't hold with that abortion lark.'

15. a. (Further examples.) Also *spec.* a sudden movement on the part of foreign depositors to withdraw their holdings of a nation's currency by exchanging them for equivalent sums in other currencies. Freq. const. *on*.

1891 G. CLARE *Money-Market Primer* vii. 59 Country bankers,..fearing that the shock to confidence may cause a 'run' on the part of their depositors, telegraph to London for more notes. **1932** P. EINZIG *Tragedy of Pound* vii. 65 In July [1931] the failure of the Nordwolle and other commercial firms resulted in a run on several German banks. **1955** H. WILSON in *Hansard Commons* 10 June 148 More confidence has been given to the speculators, and therefore the run on sterling has temporarily stopped. **1964** S. BRITTAN *Treasury under Tories* vi. 189 Mr Thorneycroft responded to the run on the pound with his famous deflationary package. **1976** *Economist* 16 Oct. 23/3 The Bank of England reacted to the March run on sterling by using up reserves and borrowing money to try to check the exchange rate collapse.

b. (Earlier example.)

1816 JANE AUSTEN *Emma* II. vi. 97 A couple of pair of post-horses were kept, more for the convenience of the neighbourhood than from any run on the road.

19. a. *spec.* (*a*) the amount of sap drawn off when sugar maples are tapped; the amount of maple sugar produced at one time; (*b*) (*Oil Industry*) the action of transferring a quantity of oil through a pipeline, or of subjecting it to a process such as distillation; the amount of oil so treated.

(*a*) **1822** *Farmer's Diary 1823* (U.S.) sig. C 3, Sugar makers may venture to set seven or eight hundred pails to one of these pans,..in case of extra ordinary runs, which, however, do not often happen. **1890–3** E. M. TABER *Stowe Notes, Lett. & Verses* (1913) 40 The early runs are not so sweet as the later; the trees being full of frost. **1949** *Highway Traveler* Feb. 17/2 In the average season of a month..sap can be expected to run on about half of the days, while on two to five days there will be 'good runs'. **1978** N. PERRIN *First Person Rural* 84 It was no hard run—but my 104 buckets would probably yield 40 or 50 gallons [of maple sap] today.

(*b*) **1883** [in Dict.]. **1888** *Science* 12 Oct. 172/2 This past spring an oil-man..was suffocated in one of these tank-sheds while making a run of oil; viz., running the oil from the receiving-tank to the transportation or pipe-line company's tanks. **1898** *19th Ann. Rep. U.S. Geol. Survey* VI contd. 29 Usually the terms 'production' and 'pipe-line runs' are considered as synonymous, but production is always slightly in excess of runs. The expression 'pipe-line runs' means the amount of oil the pipe lines have received from the wells, and as the pipe lines do not run all the oil in the tanks at the wells, it would be remarkable if the same amount remained in the tanks at the wells at the close of each year. **1914** *Chem. Abstr.* VIII. 2247 Flushing out the vapors remaining in the still with steam so that they will not mix with the vapors from the next run. **1931** *Economist* 14 Feb. 361/1 Crude oil 'runs' to refinery stills have, therefore, been restricted to about 10 per cent. below last year's level.

c. Also, a spell of manufacturing some product; an instance or a spell of carrying out an experimental procedure, esp. one involving automatic equipment. (Further examples.)

1931 *Anatomical Rec.* XLIX. 180 In an original trial run on five albino rats..three became pseudopregnant. **1935** *Industrial & Engin. Chem.* Sept. 1074/2 In one run,..the temperature began to rise and continued to rise after the heat input to the bomb was stopped. **1951** S. JENNETT *Making of Bks.* vii. 106 When the make-ready is completed and the machine is ready to start its run the hand-feeder takes her place at the feeding board. *Ibid.* 107 The run then commences. **1971** J. E. HARRY *Plastics Fabrication & Electrotechnol.* v. 38 Preformed materials such as sheet or tube..are sometimes used instead of moulding processes for short runs of large components. **1972** *Nature* 18 Feb. 397/1 The difference observed was found consistently in different electrophoretic runs. **1972** *National Observer* (U.S.) 27 May 11/2 At first he intended to fake the run, using plain creek water in the barrels with..foam rubber pellets floating on top to simulate the head on the fermenting mash.

d. A spell of sheep-shearing. *Austral.* and *N.Z.*

a **1910** G. MEEK in A. E. WOODHOUSE *N.Z. Farm & Station Verse* (1950) 59 The record shearing run of nineteen-nothing nine. **1933** L. G. D. ACLAND in *Press* (Christchurch, N.Z.) 18 Nov. 15/7 *Run*,..stretch of work. Shearers work for an hour before breakfast, two stretches in the morning and three in the afternoon. The stretches are divided by meal-times and *smokos*. **1956** G. BOWEN *Wool Away!* (ed. 2) 157 *Run*, the shearing time worked between official stops, smokos, or meals. *a* **1964** H. P. TRITTON in *Penguin Bk. Austral. Ballads* (1964) 227 My shearing days are over, though I never was a gun: I could always count my twenty at the end of every run.

e. *Computers.* An instance of the execution of a program or other task by a computer.

1946 *Math. Tables & Other Aids to Computation* II. 151 From a series of positive values of x and y, it could form Σx, Σy, Σx^2, Σxy, Σy^2 and check them in one run. **1952** *Rev. Electronic Digital Computers* (Amer. Inst. Electr. Engineers) 17/2 The chance that the machine would get through any particular 20-minute run was independent of its chances of getting through any other 20-minute run. **1964** F. L. WESTWATER *Electronic Computers* ix. 144 It requires two runs on the computer..to solve the problem. **1971** J. B. CARROLL et al. *Word Frequency Bk.* p. xxxvi, In the particular computer run that produced this table, the number turned out to be 609,798. **1977** *Sci. Amer.* Oct. 116/2 The program and certain aspects of the discharging procedure had to be modified to overcome the problems indicated by the first computer runs.

20. a. (Later examples of *general run*.) Also *normal run*.

1957 G. RYLE in C. A. MACE *Brit. Philos. Mid-Century* 257 This question did not begin seriously to worry the general run of philosophers until..sixty years ago. **1965** G. MCINNES *Road to Gundagai* v. 87 What..set our tannings aside from the normal run..was the deliberation and the ritual. **1970** *Incorporated Linguist* IX. IV. 111 This is a book which should be of interest to the scholar and the linguistic specialist, less so to the general run of professional translators.

d. *Printing.* The total number of copies of a book, newspaper, etc., printed during a single period of press-work. Cf. *press-run* s.v. *PRESS *sb.*[1] 16 b and *print run* s.v. *PRINT *sb.* 15 a.

1909 WEBSTER *s.v. Run* n., A run of 3,000 copies on a press. **1936** *Penrose Ann.* XXXVIII. 146 Rotary printing will master any long runs. **1951** S. JENNETT *Making of Bks.* ix. 138 The film assists in the retention of moisture, and longer runs can be printed at greater speed [by collography]. **1976** *Penrose Ann.* LXIX. 132 Over half of all printing jobs involve runs under 10,000 sheets.

e. *run of the mill* (also *the mine*, etc.), the material yielded by a mill, mine, etc., as it emerges from the production process and before being sorted or inspected for quality; also *run-of-mine*, etc. Hence *fig.*, the ordinary, average, undistinguished, or mediocre type (cf. *mill run* (*d*) s.v. *MILL *sb.*[1] 10). Also in various extended and nonce-uses. Freq. as *adj.* or *attrib.* phrase.

1909 *Cent. Dict.* Suppl., *Run of the kiln*, bricks of all kinds and qualities just as they happen to come from the kiln. *Ibid.*, *Run of the mine*, coal just as it comes from the mine, large and small sizes and all qualities together. **1930** *Daily News Record* (U.S.) 17 Mar. 19/4 Suspicion has attached to the yarn producers' definition of 'inferior'. Leading users of these yarns say they interpret the word to mean 'run of the mill'. A purchase of such yarns may include various percentages of first, second and subqualities of yarn, in fact all that 'run of the mill' suggests —but the grading is done by the cloth mill. **1930** *Engineering* 20 June 811/2 This machine is intended to reduce run-of-mine coal to any size between 6in. and 1¼in. cube, in one operation. **1930** *Hearst's Internat.* Sept. 37/2 But level-headed as a wife and a darned sight better-looking than the run of the mill of wives. **1933** *Sun* (Baltimore) 14 Oct. 4/3 An ordinary, run-of-the-mill gravy. *Ibid.* 23 Dec. 8/7 The attitude of run-of-the-mine citizens on lynching. **1938** K. A. PORTER in *Southern Rev.* Winter 429 I've got a special job beside my usual run of the mill. **1939** EVANS & MCGOWAN *Guide to Textiles* 66 Run-of-the-mill is a term which in general means that the merchandise has not been inspected... Sheets and pillowcases are frequently sold as run-of-the-mill. **1940** O. NASH *Face is Familiar* 118 And in celestial circles all the run-of-the-mill angels would rather be archangels or at least cherubim and seraphim. **1941** *Sun* (Baltimore) 30 July 10/1 The balance is composed of items which, in the main, are run-of-the-mine budget pruning. **1943** B. A. DE VOTO in *Harper's Mag.* May 645/1 But what they have to say is mostly run of the mill. **1944** *Sun* (Baltimore) 17 Feb. 17/1 The growers want 25 cents a pound for wrapper leaf..and 15 cents for 'run of the crop' as against the OPA set prices of 21 for wrapper..and 10 for ungraded. **1945** 'L. LEWIS' *Birthday Murder* (1951) i. 13 Hime..has managed out of..a run-of-the-mill story, something..unusual in its effects. **1946** *Richmond* (Va.) *News Leader* 29 Nov. 15/1 That's about 80 times the cost of a hide from a 'run-of-the-mine' cow. **1950** *Engineering* 11 Aug. 131/3 The..washery will treat 750 tons of run-of-mine coal per hour. **1951** *News Chron.* 12 Dec. 4 To the ordinary run-of-the-mill bank customer these may perhaps seem lordly examples of living on overdrafts. **1952** [see *IMPERFECT *sb.* 3]. **1952** *Amer. Speech* XXVII. 264 Fabric which is shipped to a buyer just as it comes from the loom without inspection and without elimination of weaving defects is referred to as run-of-the loom. **1953** A. UPFIELD *Murder must Wait* x. 95 Her taste wasn't the usual run of the mill. **1960** E. DELAVENAY *Introd. Machine Transl.* vii. 106 It should free intellectual ability for more productive work than that of run-of-the-mill translations. **1967** *Gloss. Mining Terms* (*B.S.I.*) VIII. 23 *Run of mine* (R.O.M.), the product of a mine before sorting or cleaning. **1969** *Daily Tel.* 21 Apr. 17/7 No hard boundaries exist to separate jazz singers from run-of-the-mill night club performers. **1975** 'D. JORDAN' *Black Account* xii. 60 The difference between run-of-mine ores and washed fines. **1975** *Publishers Weekly* 9 June 52/1 Taylor's thoughtfully written, low-keyed text proves far superior to most run-of-the-battlefield 'popular' histories. **1977** *Amer. N. & Q.* XV. 117/1 Prices of run-of-the-mine books are often more difficult to ascertain than those of $500-plus items. **1978** R. LUDLUM *Holcroft Covenant* iii. 35 Althene was not your run-of-the-mill mother, as mothers were understood by this particular son. **1980** *Times Lit. Suppl.* 31 Oct. 1240/2 We are left with a pretty run-of-the-mill thriller.

IV. 22. (Earlier and further examples.) Also *Austral.* and *N.Z.*, a sheep station. Also *attrib.*, as *run cattle*, *sheep*.

The early Amer. usage in quot. 1658 is not supported by further evidence.

1658 *Rec. Brookhaven, N.Y.* (1880) 3 This land and the grass thereof for a range, or run, for to feed horses and cattle on..I have sold. **1804** *Sydney Gaz.* 12 Feb., A commodious dwelling-house [with] an extensive run for stock. **1847** A. HARRIS *Settlers & Convicts* xvi. 330 If the shepherd suffers the flock to spread, in these mountainous runs especially, they get into creeks and hollows. **1858** *Richmond-Atkinson Papers* (1960) I. vii. 421, I found that Elliot's run..was in a capital position..in a finely grassed country. **1911** C. E. W. BEAN '*Dreadnought' of Darling* i. 12 Huge 1,000,000-acre runs or little 20,000 acre homestead leases. **1930** L. G. D. ACLAND *Early Canterbury Runs* 1st Ser. i. 2 A number..sold or abandoned their runs, and came to New Zealand early in 1851. *Ibid.* 7 All run sheep had been Merinos in the old days. **1933** —— in *Press* (Christchurch, N.Z.) 18 Nov. 15/7 *Run* sheep, *run*-cattle, as opposed to paddock sheep or milking cows and hand-reared calves. **1936** F. CLUNE *Roaming round Darling* xviii. 178 Toorale.., headquarters of a run of 1,000,000 acres. **1950** *N.Z. Jrnl. Agric.* Sept. 215/1 With fertility declining pastures are becoming more difficult to control for sheep, and because of this, run cattle numbers are being increased. **1963** *Weekly News* (Auckland) 10 July 38/3 Run cattle..can be moved on a mob basis from one paddock to another. **1966** G. W. TURNER *Eng. Lang. Austral. & N.Z.* iii. 50 A *run* is a parcel of land as leased. A sheepfarmer might own several adjacent runs of land, in this sense, and the whole 'station' so formed might also be termed a run.

Comb. **1859** F. FULLER *Five Yrs. Residence N.Z.* ix. 162 The Runholder kept the remaining portion as the payment for his trouble and expense in looking after the sheep. **1864** *Sunday at Home* 17 Dec. 811/1 A small chapel has been built for the use of the inhabitants by a runholder near. **1911** W. H. KOEBEL *In Maoriland Bush* xxii. 284 His career as a run-holder is usually a fleeting one with an abrupt termination. **1930** L. G. D. ACLAND *Early Canterbury Runs* 1st Ser. 8 On the whole, runholding has not been much of a business in Canterbury. **1940** W. G. MCCLYMONT *Explor. N.Z.* xii. 130 The country they contained had been granted to run-holders in order of application.

23. c. *pl.* A place at which wagons may be loaded or unloaded. *U.S.*

1870 *Huntington* (N.Y.) *Town Rec.* (1889) III. 585 The said land..[is] sufficient..to build two runs, so called, or three runs..to load brick at. **1923** C. R. COOPER *Under Big Top* 226 Many a man [is saved] from injury at the unloading runs. **1931** *Amer. Mercury* Nov. 354/1 *Runs*, the unloading place at the railroad.

d. A slope of snow on which tobogganing, skiing, etc., are carried out. Also *transf.* Cf. sense 4 f above.

1874 [see TOBOGGAN *v.*]. **1898** *Encycl. Sport* II. 470/2 The English and American visitors to St. Moritz and Davos introduced tobogganing as a sport, and set to work to construct both toboggans and runs. **1910** [see *BOB-SLED, -SLEIGH]. **1935** *Encycl. Sports* 178/2 The most famous toboggan run in the world, the Cresta is rebuilt every year under expert supervision. **1956** *Ski-ing* ('Know the Game' Ser.) 22/1 The *piste* is artificial and either made by a large number of skiers ski-ing down a run, or [etc.]. **1961** [see *MOGUL *sb.*[2]]. **1972** 'M. YORKE' *Silent Witness* vi. 137 She took off her skis at the bottom of the run. **1974** *Rules of Game* 253/3 The brake [on a bobsleigh] is used only in emergencies, as its serrated edge damages the surface of the run. **1976** F. RAPHAEL *Glittering Prizes* 58 As he reached the top of the run, he was conscious that someone was standing there.

V. 28. a. *on the run* (further *fig.* examples, chiefly in sense 'fleeing' or 'escaping' from justice).

1909 J. B. ATLAY *Ld. Haliburton* 184 There was a widespread impression that the assailants had got the Government 'on the run', and that a vigorous campaign would show further concessions when Parliament met. **1932** *Week-End Rev.* 9 Apr. 456/2 In 'Secret Sentence' she explores another world—the world of political assassination, of criminal investigation departments, of men on the run. **1954** X. FIELDING *Hide & Seek* xi. 139 They were fugitives from justice and had been on the run in this area for over a year. **1955** *Times* 30 June 10/7 The President strongly resisted the suggestion that, as Russia was now 'on the run' it might be possible to reduce American expenditure on foreign aid. **1957** *Times* 31 Oct. 3/1 The gangster, the No. 1 Public Enemy, on the run. **1963** T. TULLETT *Inside Interpol* i. 17 If it had not been for the men in the Rue Paul Valéry he might still be 'on the run'.

e. *to get the run*: to be dismissed from one's employment. *slang.* (chiefly *Austral.*).

1889 BARRÈRE & LELAND *Dict. Slang* I. 403/2 *Get the run, to*, (English and Australian), to be discharged. **1941** [see *running shoe* s.v. *RUNNING *vbl. sb.* 17 a]. **1959** BAKER *Drum* (1960) II. 141 *Run, get the*, to be dismissed from employment.

29. b. Also, a flow *of* speech.

a **1915** JOYCE *Giacomo Joyce* (1968) 12 She stands black-robed at the telephone. Little timid laughs, little cries, timid runs of speech suddenly broken.

e. *run-of-river* adj. phr (usu. *attrib.*), denoting (an installation employing) a water supply taken directly from a river, esp. for generating hydroelectricity, with no major attempt to store water or regulate flow.

1943 STEINBERG & SMITH *Economy Loading* v. 169 In a run-of-river plant, the flow of the river must be utilized as it comes, so that this plant would normally supply the system base load. **1956** V. A. Thiemann in B. G. A. Skrotzki *Electric Generation* v. 228 Hydro stations may be classified as either peaking or run-of-river. **1964** Linsley & Franzini *Water Resources Engin.* xvi. 453 Some run-of-river plants have enough storage.. to permit storing water during off-peak hours for use during peak hours of the same day. **1965** R. G. Kazmann *Mod. Hydrol.* iv. 89 The raw water obtained from an impounded supply is generally better than that obtained from a run-of-river water source.

30. b. For *a* **1890** J. W. Palmer *New & Old* 62 (Cent.) read **1859** J. W. Palmer *New & Old* ii. 62, and add further examples. Also, *to lose (the) run of.* Now *rare.*

1872 Mrs Stowe *Oldtown Fireside Stories* 29 She hed the in and out o' the Sullivan house, and kind o' kept the run o' how things went and came in it. **1893** 'Thanet' *Stories of Western Town* 145 I've been in this block, Mrs Carleton and me, ever since it was built; and, some way, between us we've managed to keep the run of all the folks in it. **1893** 'Mark Twain' *£1,000,000 Bank-Note* 29 You couldn't afford to lose the run of business and be no end of time getting the hang of things again when you got back home. **1918** J. C. Lincoln *Shavings* xix. 320, I kind of lost run of the time.

32. b. (Earlier example.) Also *transf.*, complete freedom of action. Also *the run of one's knife.*

1807 in *N. & Q.* (1904) 11 June 478/1 And it suits to a T, To receive as your fee, The run of your teeth And five guineas a day. **1927** *Daily Mirror* 10 Dec. 9/1 Sir Granville Ryrie..began work as a cattle driver at £30 a year and the 'run of his knife', which means his food. **1974** *Broadcast* 2 Dec. 16/3 Hugh Carleton Green..allowed—nay! encouraged a group of bright and irresponsible young men and women to have the run of their teeth in the so-called 'satire' programmes.

34. Special Comb.: **run time** *Computers*, (*a*) the time at or during which a program or other task is executed; (*b*) the length of time taken by the execution of a particular task.

1965 Mitchell & Willmott *Programming Computer in Atlas Autocode* viii. 51 Each routine or block is associated with a serial number for use in tracing faults found at run time. **1968** M. V. Wilkes *Time-Sharing Computer Syst.* iv. 37 At run time, the segment number is used to enter the segment table belonging to the user whose program is running at that instant. **1972** [see *overlay *sb.* 6]. **1974** Adby & Dempster *Introd. Optimization Methods* v. 178 Colville found that the number of function evaluations proved a totally unreliable guide to run time.

run, *v.* Add: **I. 1. g.** *to run counter (to)*: see Counter *adv.* 1 and 3.

h. *Cricket.* To act as a runner (*runner 1 f) *for* (a disabled batsman).

1855 F. Lillywhite *Guide to Cricketers* 7 No substitute shall in any case be allowed to stand out or run between wickets for another person without the consent of the opposite party. **1900** W. A. Bettesworth *Walkers of Southgate* xi. 290 Mr Rutter..was..standing behind the wicket in the usual place of a man who is running for another. **1908** W. E. W. Collins *Leaves from Old Country Cricketer's Diary* xiii. 223 Once only in more than forty years, when I was hit badly on the knee-cap, I had a man to run for me.

i. *colloq.* To suffer pressingly from diarrhoea. Cf. *run *sb.*[1] 14 f.

1966 A. E. Lindop *I start Counting* vi. 92 'I said to her ..''if you lie down on that wet grass you'll come down with the running trots''—' 'And did she?' .. 'She was run, run, run, *run*! All the time.' **1967** A. Wilson *No Laughing Matter* iii. 188 Suddenly she knew by sensation the meaning of that unattractive expression 'it kept me running all night'... She was indeed kept 'running all night'.

2. b. (Further example.) Also with *in.*

1960 G. E. Evans *Horse in Furrow* xi. 151 But the danger of undersized or ill-bred stallions 'running in' with the mares on communal..pastures had become considerably less. **1972** *Country Life* 3 Feb. 288/3 The heifers.. run with the Hereford bull to produce their first calf.

c. *to run (a)round*: to associate or consort *with* (someone, esp. of the opposite sex); to court, have an affair with; similarly with *together.* Also in general sense, to go about hurriedly with no fixed goal; to go from one place or person to another. Also *transf. to run (a)round in circles*: see *circle *sb.* 1 c.

1887 in *Amer. Speech* (1950) XXV. 37/1 She used to run around with Jim Reiley. **1891** J. H. Pearce *Esther Pentreath* iii. v. 194 The speaker, a big awkward slattern, had been long trying hard..to get Casy to 'run around' with her. **1920** H. Crane *Let.* 24 Sept. (1965) 42 I've been running around talking, talking, talking and waiting for the proper persons to arrive at their offices. **1925** F. Scott Fitzgerald *Great Gatsby* vi. 125, I may be old-fashioned in my ideas, but women run around too much these days to suit me. **1929** D. Runyon in *Hearst's Internat.* July 56/1 He writes about..who is running around with who, including guys and dolls. **1940** M. Allingham *Black Plumes* iii. 19 He and Phillida ran round together quite a bit. **1940** F. & R. Lockridge *Norths meet Murder* viii. 129 You could tell me about it, and why you didn't like Brent, if it wasn't because he was running around with your wife. **1952** M. Laski *Village* xi. 161 They've been running around together for some time... She's certainly a lovely girl. **1962** [see *cruddy *a.* 2]. **1969** in Halpert & Story *Christmas Mumming in Newfoundland* 213 Since people know who the uncovered janney 'runs around with' (i.e., his friends), they will have a clue to the probable identity of the others.

4. a. Also *to run out on* (someone), to abandon, desert.

1920 H. C. Witwer in *Collier's* 15 May 57/1 Kin you imagine him runnin' out on me too? **1934** Ade *Let.* 8 Mar. (1973) 180, I received no invitation or notification and neither did John Golden and so we must not be accused of running out on our little pop-eyed friend. **1942** T. Rattigan *Flare Path* i. 25 You *were* a fool to run out on me, weren't you? **1951** M. McLuhan *Mech. Bride* (1967) 60/2 Some of the fellows were sneering that her husband was running out on her. **1962** H. Hood in R. Weaver *Canad. Short Stories* 2nd Ser. (1968) 210 I'm not running out on you. **1973** 'D. Halliday' *Dolly & Starry Bird* xv. 221, I decided I was going back to Rome. ..Johnson, on whom I was running out, listened to me with patience.

e. In weakened sense, to leave, depart (freq. with an implication of haste). Also with *along, away. Run along (with you!)* imp., used esp. to children or inferiors (cf. *get along!* s.v. Along *adv.* 2).

1816 Jane Austen *Emma* II. i. 18 'I am afraid we must be running away,' said Emma..beginning to rise... 'I, had no intention..of staying more than five minutes.' **1890** O. Wilde *Pict. Dorian Gray* i, in *Lippincott's Monthly Mag.* July 7 You are not going to run away so soon, Mr. Hallward? **1902** B. Potter *Tale of Peter Rabbit* 15 Now run along, and don't get into mischief. **1927** A. A. Milne *Now We are Six* 57 But every one says, 'Run along!' (Run along, run along!) All of them say 'Run along! I'm busy as can be.' **1933** M. Lowry *Ultramarine* ii. 62 Oh well, I'll have to put up with you. Run away and play. **1934** E. Bowen *Cat Jumps* 242 'Yes, run along with you,' she said. 'And don't be so silly again.' **1935** N. Mitchison *We have been Warned* ii. 202, I must run or the garden party will miss me. **1952** E. O'Neill *Moon for Misbegotten* i. 56 So run along now and play with your horse, and don't bother me. **1962** I. Murdoch *Unofficial Rose* vi. 62 Douglas Swann rose again, accepting his dismissal. 'No thank you, Ann, I must run.' **1965** G. McInnes *Road to Gundagai* xii. 211 Tell your Mother we're going to the flicks and I'll be back about eleven. Better run along now. **1975** A. Bergman *Hollywood & Levine* xi. 164 'Helen, we'll be running, said Wohl... There was a final chorus of good-byes.

7. a. Also, *to run to* (also *true to, up to*) *form*: of a horse, to perform in a race consistently with its previous record. Freq. *transf.* and *fig.*

1891 G. Chetwynd *Racing Reminisc.* I. 85 The result of the Prince of Wales' Stakes was interesting, as it afforded a striking proof of the way in which horses sometimes consistently run up to their form. **1934** Webster, *Run true to form, or type,* to operate as might be expected by its inherent nature. **1960** *Bedside 'Guardian'* IX. 178 This [canvassing] ran true to form until one young woman reddened and said: 'I don't think you should accost mothers on a playground.' **1970** G. F. Newman *Sir, You Bastard* viii. 253 It was simply Paul running to form, never arriving anywhere on time. **1973** D. Lessing *Summer before Dark* 227 I'd be running true to form wouldn't I? A few years in the wide world and then back to the home paddock.

b. (Earlier and later examples.) Also, to stand as a candidate for office *on* a specific issue or policy.

1826 *Virginia Herald* (Fredericksburg) 22 Nov. 3/1 Mr. Pitcher is elected Lt. Governor, by a large majority over Mr. Huntington, who ran on the same ticket with Mr. Clinton. **1851** J. A. Quitman in J. F. H. Claiborne *Life & Corr. J. A. Quitman* (1860) II. xvi. 147 A majority of the people have declared against the course of policy.. upon which alone I had consented to run as a candidate. **1859** *Knickerbocker* Oct. 372 We have never had the misfortune to run (or 'be run', as the phrase is) for Congress. **1912** M. Nicholson *Hoosier Chron.* 54 I'd go into their counties and spend every cent I've got fighting 'em if they ever ran for office again. **1929** W. Faulkner *Sartoris* ii. 67, I know what I'll do: I'll run for Congress. **1950** *Manch. Guardian Weekly* 24 Aug. 15 Mr. Dewey has sworn not to run again for the Governorship. **1964** Gould & Kolb *Dict. Social Sci.* 484/2 The Democratic candidate..ran instead on the issue, among others, that the Eighteenth Amendment should be repealed. **1967** G. F. Fiennes *I tried to run Railway* iii. 16 There's a job going as Assistant District Superintendent at Burntisland. Do you want to run for it? **1968** *Globe & Mail* (Toronto) 3 Feb. 3/8 Mr. Woodcock, who says he is running on a youth ticket, joins two other fringe candidates. **1978** *Detroit Free Press* 5 Mar. a 14/1 President Carter says he does not know whether he will run for re-election in 1980 or whether he will win if he does.

e. *to run scared*: in *U.S.* political terminology, to compete for office in a manner indicating or suggesting a fear of losing, esp. to avoid over-confidence. Also in generalized and weakened senses, to be frightened, to panic. Usu. as *pres. pple.*

1960 *Newsweek* 19 Sept. 39/1 Confident as he is of winning, Nixon intends to run hard and scared until the very last minute. **1964** G. McDonald (*title*) Running scared. **1968** W. Safire *New Lang. Politics* 389/2 The phrase is directed..to the candidate who is in the position of Thomas E. Dewey in 1948, considered a 'shoo-in'... Hindsighted politicians now say Dewey should have 'run scared'—conducted a more aggressive, fighting campaign. **1969** P. F. Simon *The Boxer* (song) 3 In the quiet rail-way sta-tion run-ning scared. **1976** *Times* 1 Mar. 7/4 President Ford..has been running scared against Reagan for many months. **1976** J. Philips *Backlash* iii. i. 116 He's big, but running very scared. **1978** *Time* 1 May 24/2 'People are running scared,' says..a Boston drug-abuse expert. 'A situation exists which borders on hysteria,' agrees the deputy director of the Illinois dangerous-drugs commission. **1978** *Washington Post* 12 June c2/1 Members of Congress who are already running scared (this is an election year).

8. b. (Earlier examples.)

1743 M. Catesby *Nat. Hist. Carolina* II. p. xxxiii, Herrings in March leave the salt waters, and run up the rivers. **1806** Lewis & Clark *Orig. Jrnls. Lewis & Clark Exped.* (1905) IV. 95 These women informed us that the small fish began to run which we suppose to be herring from their description. **1884** G. B. Goode *Fisheries U.S.: Nat. Hist. Aquatic Animals* 376 [Kingfish] occasionally run to a considerable distance up the rivers.

9. b. *to run off the rails*: see *rail *sb.*[2] 4 a, b.

10. a. Also of a torpedo: to pass through the water.

1914 F. T. Jane *Navy as Fighting Machine* xiii. 100 The 'balance chamber'. This regulates the depth at which the torpedo will run. **1942** *R.A.F. Jrnl.* 16 May 21 They dived and dropped their torpedoes, all of which ran satisfactorily.

b. Also in phr. *to run into the sand(s)*, to peter out; to come to nothing.

1931 E. Wilson *Axel's Castle* iv. 112 We may put it down to an academic assumption that English drama ended when the blank verse of the Elizabethans ran into the sands. **1956** A. L. Rowse *Early Churchills* xvii. 378 A naturally clever woman with genuine interests of the mind that ran into the sand.

c. Also *fig.*

1918 *Dialect Notes* V. 21 *Run foul of,* to meet. **1932** *Times Lit. Suppl.* 27 Oct. 792/4 He ran foul of the most powerful gang in New York and the police at the same time. **1971** *New Scientist* 27 May 533/1 Tamplin originally ran foul of the AEC when he was asked to demolish Ernest Sternglass's case.

11. a. (Further examples.)

1861 J. A. Symonds *Let.* 30 Apr. (1967) I. 287 This is just the time that I sd like to be at home... If I can, I shall run down for a day this Term. *Ibid.* 28 Oct. 314 Do you not think you cd persuade Papa to run up with me one night this week to see it? **1866** G. Meredith *Let.* 14 Jan. (1970) I. 356 A..letter disarranged the plan, which would have left me free of conscience to run down to you. **1866** Trollope *Belton Estate* xxxii, in *Fortn. Rev.* 1 Jan. 429 I'll..just run over once or twice in the year. It would not be a nice place for you to live at long. **1871** J. Blackwood *Let.* 31 Dec. in *Geo. Eliot Lett.* (1956) 230 Hamley only ran up for an afternoon and could not get to the Priory. **1885** C. M. Yonge *Two Sides of Shield* I. x. 168 He says he would run over to see me if it were not for the dragons. **1898** G. B. Shaw *Let.* 18 Oct. (1972) II. 68 Our visitors here are..Strandring and Pease, who run down occasionally, or at least intend to do so. **1902** E. Nesbit *Five Children & It* ix. 237 I'll run up to town and have some lunch at club. **1921** G. B. Shaw *Back to Methuselah* iii. 136 Why not run over and join me for the afternoon? **1972** D. Sutton in *Lett. R. Fry* I. 53 During the 1910s Fry had formed the habit of running over to Paris.

b. Also const. † *it.* Also of a company, to schedule journeys *over* a given route. Now freq. with qualifying advb., as *to run late,* (of a transport service) to be behind schedule; also *transf.* of persons.

a **1817** Jane Austen *Northanger Abbey* (1818) I. vii. 84 How long do you think we have been running it from Tetbury, Miss Morland? **1869** *Bradshaw's Railway Man.* XXI. 177 The company authorized to run over the Mid-Kent, the West End of London and Crystal Palace, ..and the West London Extension. **1954** L. MacNeice *Autumn Sequel* 161, I today, equally undefended, Not knowing if we are running fast or late, Walk through this empty train. **1956** N. Marsh *Off with his Head* (1957) vi. 113, I got called out on an urgent case and found myself running late. **1973** *Daily Tel.* 3 Feb. 14 Any attempt to discover by telephone whether an incoming flight is running late is futile. **1977** N. Marsh *Last Ditch* vi. 176 Alleyn looked at his watch. 'I'm running shamefully late,' he said.

c. To slide or travel on a sleigh or toboggan or on skis.

1887 [see Coast *v.* 13]. **1898** *Encycl. Sport* II. 472/1 Now, as each competitor is obliged to run three times,.. and as the course varies, not only day by day, but hour by hour,..a great deal of judgment is required on the part of the rider. **1935** *Encycl. Sports* 562/2 The attitudes of skiers in running vary from an almost upright one to a very low crouch. *Ibid.* 563/1 Having acquired confidence, the ability to go fairly fast, and to run straight over moderate slopes without falling, the novice can now tackle the turns. **1956** *Ski-ing* ('Know the Game' Ser.) 13/2 The fastest method of ski-ing down a slope is naturally by running straight (*schussing*).

15. d. (Earlier example.)

1731 D. Eaton *Let.* 2 May (1971) 135 We shall view the saplins at Oakly Wood on Wednesday and have the sale day on Saturday, bycause the bark runns very well.

17. b. (Examples of a motor vehicle or engine.)

1912 *Motor Man.* (ed. 14) vi. 174 When a car is running badly the owner very often comes to the conclusion, [etc.]. **1952** *Chambers's Jrnl.* Apr. 208/1 With the port outer-diesel running the exciter and the other diesels cut to no load. **1939** G. B. Shaw *Geneva* iii. 110 It's no use going on making motor cars that you know will never run. **1959** E. K. Wenlock *Kitchin's Road Transport Law* (ed. 12) 112/1 The petrol tank must not be filled..while the engine is running.

c. *transf.* Of a business, household, etc.: to function or operate.

1927 E. O'Neill *Marco Millions* ii. iii. 141 Sound common sense and a home where everything runs smooth. **1939** J. B. Priestley *Let People Sing* xiv. 416 I've got this place. It's doin' well, makin' money. But I don't want it all the time, an' now it's running easily it doesn't need me all the time. **1969** J. Barzun (*title*) The American university: how it runs, where it is going. **1974** N. Freeling *Dressing of Diamond* 84 Meals were always on time. ..The 'house' ran like silk.

d. Of a cinematographic film, recording tape, etc.: to pass between spools, to (continue to) be in motion; to be shown or played.

1931 *Discovery* Dec. 386/1 The speed at which the film was running, ninety feet per minute, made it necessary that statements should be brief. **1969** 'A. GILBERT' *Missing from her Home* vi. 84 I'd been to see a film in the afternoon, and it ran longer than I expected. **1972** *Listener* 21 Dec. 852/1 Production Assistant: 'Quiet. Going for a take. Standing by.' Director: 'Right.' Sound: 'Sound running.' Director: 'Turn over.' **1973** V. CANNING *Finger of Saturn* i. 8 The film began to run... I just watched. **1976** *Oxf. Compan. Film* 743/1 The first part, running about 3½ hours, was released as *The Wedding March*.

20. c. (Further example.) Also in *fig.* phr. *to run hot*: of persons, to become angry (cf. HOT *a.* 6 b).

1924 A. D. SEDGWICK *Little French Girl* I. iv. 31 We have our baths in the morning, and the water doesn't run very hot then. **1941** *Sun* (Baltimore) 29 July 10/7, I seen him reading across the table and called him down. He run hot and so I told him to git his money. *Ibid.*, He was so pleased with the phrase 'run hot' that he regarded himself as the gainer on balance. **1976** K. BENTON *Single Monstrous Act* v. 166 The Detective Chief Superintendent's waiting for us, and beginning to run hot, too. He's got a lot on his mind.

21. a. (Earlier U.S. examples of ice.)

c **1804** P. GASS *Jrnl.* (1807) v. 61 The ice began to run in the river. **1867** A. D. RICHARDSON *Beyond Mississippi* xi. 145 Reaching the Missouri again, I found the ice running so heavily, that it was impossible to cross.

25. a. (Further example.)

c **1865** MRS. GASKELL *Let.* 6 Oct. (1966) 777 Still the scullery tap *did not run*; & until it does that smell will go on.

d. Of a bath: to be in the process of being filled with water.

1936 J. BUCHAN *Island of Sheep* vi. 117 He's back now, for I heard his bath running. **1946** J. B. PRIESTLEY *Bright Day* x. 298 She popped her head round the door.. to tell me that a bath was running for me. **1973** 'P. REID' *Harris in Wonderland* xiv. 103 Mayer woke me at nine with a mug of tea. He was fully dressed. 'The bath's running for you,' he said. **1977** 'A. YORK' *Tallant for Trouble* xii. 184 I've a bath running.

27. c. (Further examples.) Also of a cinematographic film: (to continue) to be shown to the public.

1923 H. CRANE *Let.* 5 Oct. (1965) 149 Charlie [Chaplin] ..is here in New York at present to see that the first film he has produced in it gets over profitably... It's running now for just a week or so more at the 'Lyric' theatre. **1940** G. MARX *Let.* 5 Sept. (1967) 25 He also hates Noel Coward and even refuses to see his playlets, which are now running at El Capitan. **1976** *Oxf. Compan. Film* 646/1 Rodgers and Hammerstein's stage musical, which opened in New York in 1959 and ran for four years.

29. b. (Further examples.)

1928 R. A. KNOX *Footsteps at Lock* ix. 87 These things do run in families... In *our* family, we're always appearing when we're not wanted to. **1966** A. E. LINDOP *I start Counting* xx. 259 Runs in the family, doesn't it. Goddam bossy, both of you. You're a real little chip off the brotherly block. **1971** 'H. CALVIN' *Poison Chasers* x. 137 Curiosity..runs in the family..like wooden legs. **1973** [see *military policeman* s.v. *MILITARY *a.* 3 b].

c. Of a newspaper or magazine article: to be printed or published, to appear; to be printed without abridgement.

1928 *Amer. Speech* IV. 135 If news is 'heavy' on a 'tight day' and is permitted to 'run' in length practically as written, [etc.]. *Ibid.* The copy reader now knows whether he is to let 'copy', news articles, 'run' or must 'cut'. **1974** *Publishers Weekly* 18 Nov. 12/3 Janet Flanner's introduction to 'London Was Yesterday'.. will run in the February issue of *Travel & Leisure*.

30. b. (Later examples with *to*).

1914 G. B. SHAW *Parents & Children* p. xi, The something unpleasant may be only a look of suffering..or it may run to forcible expulsion from the room. **1939** —— *In Good King Charles's Golden Days* I. 45 Mr. Newton: your privilege with me does not run to the length of knocking my brother down. **1967** 'S. WOODS' *And shame Devil* 222 He was brilliantly attired in crimson pyjamas... Who would have thought his taste would run to the exotic?

33. b. Also const. *at*, and with a specified amount.

1924 *Sci. Amer.* Sept. 213/1 This means that the ore runs approximately four and one-half tons per gram of radium. **1940** G. MARX *Let.* 5 Sept. (1967) 24 He ran it [*sc.* a film] yesterday for the Breen office—it runs over 13,000 feet. **1960** *Bedside 'Guardian'* IX. 216 The original operetta, which runs to a bothersome two and a half hours, was compressed..into a tight, not to say breathless, hour. **1971** *Daily Tel.* 26 Oct. 1/8 Unemployment benefit is running at about £6,900,000 a week. **1973** *Country Life* 14 June 1712/2 The Historic Buildings Council grants are now running at a rate of £1½ million a year. **1978** *Nat. Geographic* Nov. 623/1 Last autumn arrests [of illegal immigrants] were running 80 a week.

II. 35. a. Also *fig.* in colloq. phr. *to run a mile*, to seek safety in flight; to evade through fear, reluctance, etc.

1949 D. SMITH *I capture Castle* v. 64 Men..run a mile from obvious fascination. **1952** 'R. GORDON' *Doctor in House* xvii. 188 The ones that run a mile if they see a nurse and talk big about staying single. **1963** A. HERON *Towards Quaker View of Sex* 67 Were a woman to whom he exposed himself to respond sexually, the average exhibitionist would run a mile. **1969** H. E. BATES *Vanished World* x. 98, I ran a mile from intellectual swank words such as 'esoteric' and 'proliferate'. **1973** J. WILSON *Truth or Dare* iv. 44 Full of talk—yet if Betty gave any of them the come-on they'd run a mile. **1977** *Gay News* 7–20 Apr. 29/1 Whenever anything reasonably likely appears on the scene Cole runs a mile and wallows in neo-platonic discussions on the..differences between lust and love.

d. *esp.* to navigate (a stream, esp. a dangerout stretch of one) in a small boat. (Earlier examples.)

1805 LEWIS & CLARK *Orig. Jrnls. Lewis & Clark Exped.* (1905) III. 23 There were five shoals neither of which could be passed with loaded canoes nor even run with empty ones. **1839** J. K. TOWNSEND in R. G. Thwaites *Early Western Trav.* (1905) XXI. xv. 358 Here Mr. M'Leod and myself debarked, and the men ran the dall. **1875** 'MARK TWAIN' *Old Times on Mississippi* ii. 37 Each of our pilots ran such portions of the river as he had run when coming up-stream.

36. c. (Earlier example.) Also to score from (a stroke) by running; cf. sense *77 i (*d*).

1744 *Laws* [of Cricket] in *New & Compl. Dict. Arts & Sci.* (1755) IV. 3459/2 If in running a notch, the wicket is struck down by a throw [etc.]. **1816** W. LAMBERT *Instr. & Rules Cricket* 35 The Striker should be careful and attentive in running both his own and partner's hits. **1878** *Sussex Archaeol. Coll.* XXVIII. 80 Cricket grounds are not larger now than then, and yet the batsmen *ran* their hits.

e. *to run rings round*: see RING *sb.*[1] 14 d in Dict. and Suppl.

f. *to run interference*: in *U.S. Football*, to move in such a way as to cause interference (cf. *INTERFERENCE 1 c). Also *fig.*

1929 JONES & WESSON *Football for Fan* ii. 23 Whether he is to charge straight ahead, cross check, pull out to run interference or to protect a pass..he must always look the same to his rivals before the ball is snapped. **1932** F. OAKES *Football Line Play* xi. 135 The most difficult block the center must make occurs when both linemen on each side of him drop back to run interference. **1947** *Partisan Rev.* May–June 236 The official liberal runs interference for the Communist with a system of intellectual evasion. **1972** J. MOSEDALE *Football* iii. 39 Nagurski was described as a 'man who runs his own interference'. **1976** *National Observer* (U.S.) 1 May 5/3 He said he wasn't going to allow *his* police to run interference for employees trying to get through a union picket line.

40. d. *slang* (orig. and chiefly *N. Amer.*). To drive past (a traffic signal showing red). Cf. *JUMP *v.* 10 b.

1935 *Harper's Mag.* June 60/2 Perhaps we even 'ran' a light, relying on the waiting cars to continue to wait until we were out of their way. **1951** *Tuscaloosa* (Alabama) *News* 28 Jan. 1/7 Mitchell..had been arrested on charges of reckless driving and running a stop sign. **1953** *Birmingham* (Alabama) *News* 8 Aug. 1/8 Wilson told officers the brakes on his..truck failed, causing him to run a red light at the intersection. **1967** *Boston Traveler* 1 June 5/6 Policeman Howard Park stopped a minister for passing a red light... 'He who runs red light gets ticket.' **1972** *Even. Telegram* (St. John's, Newfoundland 27 June 14/4 Guy forgot to turn on his lights. And ran a stop sign. A policeman pulled him over. **1978** *Guardian Weekly* 15 Jan. 13/2 Cairo drivers run red lights and drive the wrong way down one-way streets.

41. b. To darn (the heel of a stocking) before wearing in order to strengthen it.

1802 D. WORDSWORTH *Jrnl.* 24 Dec. (1941) I. 186, I have been..running the heel of a stocking. **1844** S. S. ARNOLD in *Proc. Vermont Hist. Soc.* (1940) VIII. 170 Paid Mrs. Wales for knitting silk stockings and running the heels 67 cents. **1904** *Eng. Dial. Dict.* V. 186/1 It is common to run the heels of stockings with cotton before wearing them.

c. To attach (a ribbon or similar decoration) to cloth by passing it through a series of holes in the material.

1872 *Young Englishwoman* Nov. 607/2 Run a braid or ribbon through the open row. **1908** M. MORGAN *How to dress Doll* v. 48 Ribbon is run through neck and sleeves.

42. a. Also *spec.*, to chase or hunt animals (e.g. buffalo) on horseback or (occas.) with a vehicle. Chiefly *N. Amer.*

1841 G. CATLIN *Lett. on N. Amer. Indians* I. 219 On this journey we saw immense herds of buffaloes; and although we had no horses to *run* them, we successfully *approached* them on foot. **1849** F. PARKMAN *Calif. & Oregon Trail* xxiv. 386 The chief difficulty in running buffalo..is that of loading the gun or pistol at full gallop. **1900** W. F. DRANNAN *31 Yrs. on Plains* (1901) xxi. 300, I met about thirty Kiowa Indians going out to run the buffalo near there. **1949** L. NORDYKE *Cattle Empire* 264 Horses are furnished for the care of the cattle and for other useful purposes, and they must not be used to run wild horses, or buffalo, or antelope. **1963** G. F. G. STANLEY *Louis Riel* 5 There could be no room for selfish individualism when the métis ran the buffalo. **1968** K. WEATHERLY *Roo Shooter* 130 Hunter would have to run the little doe with the Land-Rover.

c. (Earlier example.)

1767 J. WEDGWOOD *Let.* 27 May (1965) 54 The Ministry were run very hard yesterday in the House of Lords. They carried their point by a Majority of three only.

e. (Earlier example.) Also, to exhaust or defeat by constant pursuit or pressure; to destroy by excessive use.

1836 W. T. PORTER in *Spirit of Times* 9 July 162/1 It's no use to run the thing into the ground. **1947** J. STEINBECK *Wayward Bus* viii. 135 Well, start feeling good, then, and don't run it into the ground. Nobody likes sick people very long. **1955** *Times* 3 Aug. 3/7 Close marking, hard tackling, and shrewd tactical kicking, until the opposition has been 'run into the ground'. **1977** *N.Y. Rev. Bks.* 31 Mar. 21/1 Crossman during his brief tenure as editor..just about ran the paper into the ground.

43. a. Also *transf.*, esp. in political use.

1880 E. W. HAMILTON *Diary* 2 Dec. (1972) I. 83 He expressed his belief that the suspension of the Habeas Corpus a month or two ago would have arrested the evil, and as things now are the only course to take is to 'run' two measures side by side the moment Parliament meets. **1898** W. S. CHURCHILL *Let.* 5 Jan. in R. S. Churchill *Winston S. Churchill* (1967) I. Compan. II. 854 We can run Tirah and Egypt in double harness.

c. (Further examples.) Chiefly *Austral.*

1862 R. HENNING *Let.* 28 Aug. (1966) 95 He is going to run some sheep on the station, and I dare say will do very well. **1901** M. FRANKLIN *My Brilliant Career* ii. 10 Mother felt dubious of her husband's ability to make a living off a thousand acres, half of which were fit to run nothing but wallabies. **1930** L. G. D. ACLAND *Early Canterbury Runs* 1st Ser. x. 241 The dry cattle were run further out than the sheep. **1966** G. W. TURNER *Eng. Lang. Austral. & N.Z.* iii. 50 The word might be used as a transitive verb. 'He runs merinos' i.e. has merino sheep as his stock.

44. a. Also *to run* (one) *off one's feet*, to occupy or overwork to the point of exhaustion (usu. *pass.*). *to run* (one) *ragged*: see *RAGGED *a.*[1] 6.

1857 C. M. YONGE *Dynevor Terrace* II. xv. 235 Charlotte was what Martha expressively called 'fairly run off her feet'. **1937** M. ALLINGHAM *Dancers in Mourning* xxii. 279 Run off his feet, poor lad. Don't know when he sleeps. **1949** N. MITFORD *Love in Cold Climate* I. x. 107 You'd never believe that woman was nearly eighty, she could run us all off our feet. **1970** W. J. BURLEY *To kill Cat* i. 7 'I expect you've got enough to do at this time of year.' 'Run off our feet, sir.'

b. Also, to drive (one) *crazy, out of one's head. U.S. dial.*

1924 L. VOLLMER *Sun-Up* I. 13 Neither one of us is got 'nough [learning] to run us crazy. **1928** J. PETERKIN *Scarlet Sister Mary* xxv. 288 It'll run you crazy if it don' kill you. **1940** J. STUART *Trees of Heaven* I. ii. 20 Some say whiskey will run a man crazy. **1942** L. VOLLMER in *Sat. Even. Post* 22 Aug. 12/3 Fink's meanness had run his wife out of her head.

c. (Further examples.) Also with advbs.

a **1861** T. WINTHROP *John Brent* (1876) xvi. 183 But then he knows ther ain't no Utes round here to stampede his animals or run off any of his gals. **1901** W. N. HARBEN *Westerfelt* xvi. 220 He was here the night they run him off. **1911** T. DREISER *Jennie Gerhardt* I. 10 A man run us away. **1924** H. CROY *R. F. D. No. 3* xi. 189 He's got to be run out. **1946** G. FOREMAN *Last Trek of Indians* x. 195 The agent announced his intention of running out of the country any such preacher who might appear. **1949** W. GANN *Tread of Longhorns* v. 57 The city rulers felt that the marshal should have stopped the jail delivery, and for his failure to do so, he was run off the job. **1967** *Boston Sunday Globe* 23 Apr. 4/6 Something most 17-year-old girls seldom mention..rats. 'They're bad and they'd run you right out of the cellar,' she said. **1976** C. EGLETON *State Visit* xiii. 120 Some cowboy of a truck driver ran us off the road. **1977** 'E. ANTHONY' *Silver Falcon* ii. 44 Get out of Beaumont!.. There's enough of us here who loved your father to run you out.

45. a. (Later *fig.* example.)

1901 M. FRANKLIN *My Brilliant Career* xxiv. 207 The recent 'going bung' of a building society—his sole remaining prop—had run him entirely ashore.

b. Also *spec.*, to convey (someone) in a motor vehicle to a particular destination.

1909 W. J. LOCKE *Septimus* iv. 57 The chauffeur touched his cap. 'I'll run you both over to Nice,' said Clem Sypher... 'I'll run you back again.' **1924** KIPLING *Debits & Credits* (1926) 326 I'll run you out home before sun-up. I'm a haulage contractor now. **1936** L. A. G. STRONG *Last Enemy* ix. 274 'I must go over and see him.'.. 'I can't run you over to day, I'm afraid.' **1939** A. THIRKELL *Before Lunch* v. 126 'Shall I run you home?' he asked. Daphne said her bicycle was in the bottle room. **1952** 'M. INNES' *Private View* iii. 60 Better run you home first... It will save you five minutes. **1958** 'A. BRIDGE' *Portuguese Escape* viii. 128 A taxi..will take aeons. I'll run you out when it's all fixed. **1971** 'D. HALLIDAY' *Dolly & Doctor Bird* iv. 58, I ran Johnson back to my house. **1976** M. BIRMINGHAM *Heat of Sun* ix. 152 I'll run you over later... You stay and have some tea now.

49. a. (Further examples.) Also, to cause (a ball) to move rapidly in a specified direction.

1889 W. T. LINSKILL *Golf* iv. 32 In 'running' the ball with the iron..keep the hands forward in advance of the club head. **1971** *Times* 15 Feb. 9/4 He ran the ball strongly 30ft. past the hole. **1977** *Observer* 30 Jan. 24/8 Tueart made ground on the left before passing to Power, who struck a low centre and David Craig ran the ball past his own keeper.

50. a. Also *spec.* to pass (a duster, etc.) hurriedly *over* (a surface) or *under* (furniture).

1948 A. CHRISTIE *Taken at Flood* I. xvi. 95, I know service isn't up to much nowadays—but I still think they run a mop under the furniture. **1952** M. ALLINGHAM *Tiger in Smoke* xii. 190, I ought just to run a tape over the place. **1975** W. J. BURLEY *Wycliffe & Pea-Green Boat* viii. 115, I cook a meal for him occasionally and I run a vacuum over the place. **1977** J. R. L. ANDERSON *Death in City* i. 10 Emptying waste-paper baskets, running a duster over desks, and vacuum-cleaning floors.

d. *Theatr.* To move or carry (scenery) about the stage; to shift (a 'flat') along a groove. Freq. with advs., as *on, off.*

1831 J. BOADEN *Life Mrs. Jordan* I. ix. 201 English play and farce, demanding a constant succession of scenes called flats, run on suddenly for the frequent changes of place. **1889** *N.Y. Tribune* 14 July 10/5 Nearly all scenes..are mounted on wheels which enable them to be easily moved upon the stage, hence the compound verbs 'run-on' and 'run-off', which are in universal use in the theatre. The word 'move' is scarcely ever heard. **1921** G. C. D. ODELL *Shakes. from Betterton to Irving* I. iii. 99 A Shutter is the modern 'flat', run—in two pieces—on grooves from opposite wings and clamping together when they meet midway of the stage. *Ibid.* iv. 109 The second scene is 'Ambrosio's House', and may with equal certainty be attributed to a second 'flat' scene run in, on the second groove, behind the first... The next act begins again with 'the Street', which I am convinced was run on immediately at the end of the first act. **1959** W. C. LOUNSBURY *Backstage from A to Z* 102 *Running a flat*, carrying a flat.

e. *to run the rule over*: see RULE *sb.* 17 c in Dict. and Suppl.

51. a. Also, to cause (a conveyance, vehicle, etc.) to move in a particular direction, or to a specified destination.

1902 J. H. A. MACDONALD in A. C. Harmsworth *Motors & Motor-Driving* xix. 373 On this run he on one occasion got down for a moment, asking his friend to steer, which the friend did by promptly running the car off the road. **1913** *Autocar Handbk.* (ed. 5) xxi. 228 The car may be run in one way and out the other. **1970** J. PORTER *Rather Common Sort of Crime* iv. 42 She got back to Shangrila and ran the car into the garage.

b. (Earlier and further examples.) *spec.* to keep, use, and maintain (a road vehicle).

a **1817** JANE AUSTEN *Northanger Abbey* (1818) I. vii. 86 What do you think of my gig, Miss Morland?.. A friend of mine..ran it a few weeks, till..it was convenient to have done with it. *a* **1877** KNIGHT *Dict. Mech.* II. 1346/1 Attempts are being made..to run locomotives by means of liquid fuel. **1902** A. C. HARMSWORTH *Motors & Motor-Driving* iii. 38, I am running at present four cars of French construction. **1912** *Motor Manual* (ed. 14) vi. 174 A car owner had, for a long time, been running his car with a very defective lubricator. **1924** *Discovery* June 98/1 Simple..apparatus of this kind can be run off an ordinary lighting circuit. **1939** G. B. SHAW *Geneva* II. 45 No No: motor oil. The stuff you run your aeroplanes on. **1959** E. K. WENLOCK *Kitchin's Road Transport Law* (ed. 12) 78/2 The driver of every vehicle run under an A, special A, B or C license. **1973** 'D. JORDAN' *Nile Green* xxii. 87, I can't collect you. I don't run a car.

c. (Earlier and further examples.) Also in various extended uses. In *transf.* sense *esp.* to look after, manage, or control (someone, *spec.* a spy). Also *refl.* (said of a business or other organization): to function smoothly, to require little administrative interference. *to run the show*: see SHOW *sb.*[1] 16 in Dict. and Suppl.

1861 O. J. VICTOR *Hist. Southern Rebellion* I. xvii. 252/2, I suppose I will have to run the machine as I find it. **1866** *Harper's Mag.* Mar. 539/1 The real owner of a grocery.., which was 'run' nominally by another individual. **1883** *Referee* 29 Apr. 7/2 American evangelists and speculators who run salvation on much the same lines as Barnum runs his menagerie. **1888** J. BRYCE *Amer. Commonwealth* II. lxii. 446 The primaries have almost always been so carefully packed, and so skilfully 'run', that a majority of trusty delegates has been secured. **1899** R. WHITEING *No. 5 John Street* i. 4 A..coral island..'run' on principles of almost primitive Christianity. **1911** G. B. SHAW *Doctor's Dilemma* p. xxvii, He may make considerable profits at the same time by running what is the most expensive kind of hotel. **1928** E. O'NEILL *Strange Interlude* VII. 235 Why couldn't Mother let me run my own birthday? **1932** E. WAUGH *Black Mischief* viii. 295 Can't think what you see in revolutions... I suppose you ran the whole country. **1956** H. L. MENCKEN *Minority Rep.* 206 Why assume so glibly that the God who presumably created the universe is still running it? **1959** *Motor Manual* (ed. 36) xii. 265 One way of running a trial of this sort is to give each competitor a list of places. **1972** *Jrnl. Social Psychol.* Dec. 180 As a result of unexpected difficulties (early summer vacation at Patna University) only 26 groups could be run. **1974** J. MANN *Sticking Place* i. 14 He was as helpful as could be, the members always said..though of course the place pretty well ran itself. **1977** J. AIKEN *Last Movement* iv. 76 Our staff are highly efficient; the place runs itself almost without our interference.

transf. **1890** S. HALE *Let.* 2 May (1919) viii. 242 Cornelia is running me, and she is really just the right sort. **1904** CONRAD *Nostromo* I. vi. 67 He was not running a great enterprise there... He was running a man! **1931** E. F. BENSON *Mapp & Lucia* iii. 67 She wanted to run her, to sponsor her, to arrange little parties for her. **1949** *Sat. Even. Post* 23 Apr. 130/4 You're my father and all that, but I'll be damned if you run me any more. **1961** 'J. LE CARRÉ' *Call for Dead* ix. 91 The East Germans..run their agents direct from Germany. **1967** A. CHRISTIE *Endless Night* x. 89, I felt that Ellie was dependent on Greta.. that she let Greta run her. **1972** D. BLOODWORTH *Any Number can Play* xx. 206 The central Chinese department..were running you for all you were worth. **1976** SCOTT & KOSKI *Walk-In* (1977) xv. 94 Major Ch'en was running this agent.

e. *U.S.* To support or provide for (a person or family).

1871 'MARK TWAIN' in *Galaxy* Apr. 616/1 Turnips enough to run the family for two years! **1880** —— *Tramp Abroad* 225 'Pap's so po' he cain't run me no mo', so I want to git a show somers if I kin, 'tain't no diffunce what..I don't turn my back on no kind of work.' **1909** R. A. WASON *Happy Hawkins* 280 She was in the habit of estimatin' just how little nourishment it would take to run her to the next feed.

f. orig. *U.S.* To publish or print in a newspaper or magazine; *spec.* to publish repeatedly or successively (an advertisement, article, etc., or a series of such items). Also *transf.* of broadcast items.

1884 E. W. NYE *Baled Hay* 202 The business manager.. hated to lose old Balshazzar's whole trade, for he wouldn't run any of his ads unless he would take them all according to his contract. **1912** G. M. HYDE *Newspaper Reporting* iii. 30 If..the editor decides not to print the story, he *kills* it; otherwise he *runs* it. **1916** J. LONDON *Let.* 31 Oct. (1966) 479 Please send me as many prints or proofs.. of this letter of mine (if you run it). **1930** *Publishers' Weekly* 8 Feb. 667/2 The full page advertisement we ran in the New York Times..brought in more business than any advertisement we have ever run. **1950** *Time* 16 Jan. 65/3 With his vigorous news pages, Dana ran blistering editorials against Boss Tweed, the Credit Mobilier and the Whisky Ring. **1966** *Listener* 12 May 699/1 For Mr Allsop to say that the film would be shown next week was like a newspaper editor saying that he would postpone the headline of today's news to run it the following day. **1973** *N.Y. Law Jrnl.* 20 July 4/3 During the last gubernatorial election campaign in New York State, the incumbent ran some 3,000 television commercials on twenty-two different television stations. **1976** N. THORNBURG *Cutter & Bone* iii. 62 The lady who ran the ad..evidently had liked his voice.

g. To be suffering from (a fever or high temperature).

1918 A. WOOLLCOTT *Let.* 6 July (1944) 64 Baldridge.. was running a fever which worried me a little. **1926** I. MACKAY *Blencarrow* xxxii. 273, I don't like her running this temperature. **1956** A. H. COMPTON *Atomic Quest* ii. 82 The following morning, still running a low fever, I cleared these moves with Vice President Filbey. **1961** P. DOUGHERTY *Mother Mary Potter* xxviii. 245 All through Lent Mother Potter was running a high temperature and suffering greatly. **1963** 'E. MCBAIN' *Ten plus One* viii. 107, I had a little virus, I was running a small fever. **1967** C. POTOK *Chosen* xi. 189, I came home from school with a fever... I was running 103·6. **1970** D. UHNAK *Ledger* i. 17 You're warm, Christie. You must be running about a hundred and one.

h. *to run a book* [BOOK *sb.* 10 in Dict. and Suppl.], to take bets; also *transf.*

1931 *Economist* 10 Oct. 642/1 The discount marker has been inactive, and many brokers are running narrow books, and so are needing less money than usual. **1955** *Times* 12 Aug. 5/4 Powell, who explained that he had been 'running a book' in the prison.

i. To show (a film or television recording); to set (a film camera) in action. Also with *through*.

1940 [see sense 33 b above]. **1953** E. SIMON *Past Masters* III. 196 'Have you ever thought of doing anything, with that Mexican film of yours, Hamish?'.. 'If I could have it run through somewhere and have another luke at it.' **1956** H. KURNITZ *Invasion of Privacy* viii. 64 'Your film..unmistakably duplicates a heartbreaking episode experienced by my client.'.. 'We'll run the picture for your client and guarantee to substantially change any objectionable portion.' **1973** V. CANNING *Finger of Saturn* i. 8 I'll run them [*sc.* films] straight through. **1974** I. MURDOCH *Sacred & Profane Love Machine* 125 Harriet felt giddy and exposed as if very quietly, as in a silent film run in slow motion, the house had been hit by a bomb. **1974** *Daily Tel.* 2 May 3/4 Using a friend's projector and screen, he ran a short colour film taken at the wedding.

j. To perform (a test, analysis, experiment, or the like); to subject (something) to, or measure (a property) by means of, an experimental procedure.

1947 *Jrnl. Biol. Chem.* CLXVII. 553 Assays run in replicate of course give narrow limits of confidence, the limits decreasing with increasing replication. **1961** *Lancet* 5 Aug. 291/2 The mobility of the abnormal screen-globulin did not correspond with that of the Bence Jones protein when both were run in a starch gel containing 2-mercaptoethanol. **1964** ROBERTS & CASERIO *Basic Princ. Org. Chem.* ii. 29 Solids are often run as finely ground suspensions. **1970** H. MCLEAVE *Question of Negligence* (1973) xxi. 167 Could Cameron have some sort of brain lesion?.. It was imperative to run those tests. **1976** M. MACHLIN *Pipeline* lviii. 588 In a test he ran, oil soaked ice disintegrated and sank within five days, while adjacent ice did not melt at all. **1978** *Nature* 8 June 456/2 Curie temperatures were run for seven specimens, and they ranged from 222 to 272 °C, with an average of 248 °C.

k. *Computers.* To perform (a computation), execute (a program or other task), investigate (a problem), etc., on a computer.

1952 *Rev. Electronic Digital Computers* (Amer. Inst. Electr. Engineers) 12/3 The last problem in this field has not yet been run, but the study has shown that the entire gamut of stock control for a large supply office can be covered by the computer in approximately 3 weeks time. **1968** E. O. JOSLIN *Computer Selection* iv. 70 One should examine each class of programs to determine the equipment required to run that class of program through the computer. **1973** *Computers & Humanities* VII. 225 Instructors considering adopting this text can be assured that the programs accompanying the flowcharts do work since all solutions have been run. **1977** [see *program library* s.v. *PROGRAM, PROGRAMME *sb.* 4].

52. a. See also FACE *sb.* 7 b in Dict. and Suppl.

b. (Earlier examples.)

1789 *Maryland Jrnl.* 2 Jan. 3/2 It was agreed to run the following ticket in their respective Districts. **1792** A. HAMILTON *Let.* 10 Oct. in *Wks.* (1886) VIII. 286 Either Governor Clinton, or Mr. Burr,..is to be run in this quarter as Vice-President, in opposition to Mr. Adams. **1825** J. K. PAULDING *John Bull in Amer.* v. 85 [They] talk of running him for the next governor.

c. (Earlier U.S. examples.)

1835 P. HONE *Diary* 16 Mar. (1889) I. 134 This is a club..where they sup, drink champagne and whiskey punch, talk as well as they know how, and run each other good-humouredly. **1860** J. G. HOLLAND *Miss Gilbert's Career* 349 Now what's the use of running a feller?

e. *slang.* To report or hand over (someone) to the police, etc. *spec.* in *Mil.* use, to bring a charge against (someone).

1909 E. WYRALL *Spike* iii. 17 In tramp language, to be 'run' is to be handed over to the police. **1919** *Athenæum* 18 July 632/2 'Running a man' means bringing a charge against him for orderly room. **1925** FRASER & GIBBONS *Soldier & Sailor Words* 247 *Run, to*, to report or charge anyone with an offence. **1930** BROPHY & PARTRIDGE *Songs & Slang 1914–1918* 157 Let them spades alone or I'll run yer. **1933** 'G. INGRAM' *Stir* xii. 188 Was any of you monkeying with the cocoa last night?.. If I find out who it was, I'll run 'im and make it 'ot for him. *a* **1935** T. E. LAWRENCE *Mint* (1955) II. iii. 107 We are supposed to have a flight-lieutenant over us. I saw one, when the Sergeant Major ran me.

f. To manipulate or falsify, esp. in phr. *to run the odds*.

1922 JOYCE *Ulysses* 312, I heard So and So made a cool hundred quid over it, says Alf... He let out that Myler was on the beer to run the odds and he swatting all the time.

g. *to run one's mouth*, to talk profusely or excessively, to chatter; to complain. Cf. *to shoot (off) one's mouth* s.v. SHOOT *v.* 23 g in Dict. and Suppl. *U.S.* and *Black slang*.

1940 W. FAULKNER *Tomorrow* in *Sat. Even. Post* 23 Nov. 39/1 Drunk still & running his mouth. **1954** in CASSIDY & LE PAGE *Dict. Jamaican Eng.* (1967) 388/1 Yu run yu mout fe not a ting, all de talk yu talk fe nutten. **1970** C. MAJOR *Dict. Afro-Amer. Slang* 98 *Run (one's) mouth*, to talk excessively; to complain. **1973** *Black Panther* 24 Mar. 14/3 Maybe you call working running your mouth on these TV programs. **1977** *Time* 13 June 50/1 All there is to real estate is running your mouth a bit, knocking on doors and asking people if they want to sell their house.

h. *to run a game*: to obtain money by deceit or trickery; freq. const. *on*. *U.S. Blacks.*

1967 J. HORTON in *Trans-Action* Apr. 6/2 Their reasons for disapproving of hustling were not moral. Hustling meant trouble... Others said there was not enough money on the street or that it was too difficult to 'run a game' on people. **1973** T. KOCHMAN *Rappin' & Stylin' Out* 162 Other operators on the street who are looking for a chance to 'whup' (Chicago) or 'run' (Los Angeles, New York) 'a game' (trick someone out of some money) are known as 'slicks' or 'slicksters'. **1974** H. L. FOSTER *Ribbin'* ii. 30 This is..the behavior that urban blacks use to 'run a game on the man'. *Ibid.* iv. 160 He knows how to 'run a game' to get what he desires from people. **1975** *Language* LI. 246 If we look at a number of Los Angeles examples of black 'put down' terms (e.g... *to run a game on someone*..) and K's example *to mount someone*, we can see that such expressions..are positive and kinetic.

53. f. (Earlier and later examples.)

1823 *Practical Builder* ix. 376 When the mould is ready, the process of running the cornice begins. **1893** J. P. ALLEN *Pract. Building Construction* xxi. 337 Cornices, and other ornamental mouldings,..are 'run' in plaster by means of 'horsed mouldings', running on a wood ground fixed on the wall, truly horizontal, the required depth of the cornice. **1966** C. LLOYD *Building Construction* 115 (*caption*) Cornice mould run in situ in coarse plaster, using a sheet zinc profile.

g. *Bridge.* To take an uninterrupted succession of tricks in (a particular suit), to take (a number of tricks) in that way, to play (one's cards in a suit) in that way.

1929 M. C. WORK *Compl. Contract Bridge* iv. 21 The bidder..is insured against having his adversaries open and 'run' that particular suit. **1976** *Country Life* 29 Jan. 250/1 South drew trumps..then ran three Club tricks.

56. c. Also *spec.* without *const.*, to cause water to flow into (a bathtub); to pour out water for (a bath).

1933 R. HICHENS *Paradine Case* xxvi. 277 His valet was running the bath. **1955** W. GADDIS *Recognitions* II. i. 341 When Basil Valentine got home, he ran his bath immediately. **1958** OSBORNE & CREIGHTON *Epitaph for George Dillon* I. 20 I'll go and run myself a bath. **1971** *Ink* 12 June 15/1 Anna..asks if she should run her bath. **1974** 'M. ALLEN' *Super Tour* vi. 225 Be a good boy. You can begin by running me a hot bath.

g. To cause water to flow over (something) held *under* a tap.

1921 in *Sc. Nat. Dict.* (1968) VII. 448/2 To run one's hands under the tap. **1972** *Guardian* 18 Aug. 11/3 Boil the pasta..then drain and run under the cold tap. **1979** *Daily Tel.* 24 Aug. 14 One wine expert commented: 'This is just the same as running a bottle under the tap. It would ruin any decent wine.'

III. With prepositions, in specialized uses.

59. run across—. (Earlier and later examples.)

1880 'MARK TWAIN' *Tramp Abroad* xxi. 202 If I don't run across you in Italy, you hunt me up in London before you sail. **1903** 'C. E. MERRIMAN' *Letters from Son* 151, I keep running across Job Withers. **1930** D. RUNYON in *Collier's* 20 Dec. 32/3 Now in the summer of 1928 I am in Halifax.., when I run across Louie the Lug.

61. run against—. b. (Earlier and further examples in sense 'to encounter suddenly or casually'.) Also *to run up against* (fig.), to meet with difficulty, obstruction, or opposition from (a person or thing).

1821 P. Egan *Life in London* II. v. 285 Such is the *hypocrisy* displayed on the one side, and the saucy low independence exhibited on the other, which are to be *run against* every day in 'Life in London'! **1886** [see *up against* s.v. Up *adv.*[1] 24]. **1914** 'High Jinks, Jr.' *Choice Slang* 23 Running up against a stone wall. **1924** *Truth* (Sydney) 27 Apr. 6 *Run against*, to meet. **1960** A. Munro in R. Weaver *Canad. Short Stories* (1968) 2nd Ser. 278, I had run up against the simple unprepossessing materialism which was the rock of their lives.

64. run into—. c. Also, *to run into money* (see quot. 1934). *U.S. colloq.*

1934 Webster s.v., *Run into money*, to amount to a considerable sum; to cost a considerable amount. **1973** N. Meyer *Target Practice* (1975) ii. 20 You realize this could run into money?.. I generally get a hundred dollars a day plus expenses.

h. orig. *U.S.* To encounter, meet by chance.

1902 G. H. Lorimer in *Sat. Even. Post* 22 Feb. 11/1 You're just about due now to run into a smart Aleck buyer. **1926** E. O'Neill *Great God Brown* I. ii. 35 The one time I ran into him, I thought he told me he'd destroyed all his pictures. **1934** 'A. Bridge' *Peking Picnic* vi. 60 Mrs. Leroy and the Kuniangs, walking with Derek Fitzmaurice on the City Wall, ran into Miss Ingersoll and Henri Delache. **1954** Koestler *Invisible Writing* xv. 164, I ran into Hahn as I was getting off the Number Eleven tram. **1977** A. Morice *Scared to Death* iii. 21, I expect she's run into one or two acquaintances.

66. run out of—. b. (Further examples.) Also with inanimate subject.

1929 D. Mackail *How Amusing!* 244 He had run out of tobacco the night before. **1938** Mrs. Belloc Lowndes *Diary* 29 Sept. (1971) 165, I ran out of methylated in the last war. **1966** *New Statesman* 14 Oct. 546/2 There was a popular line about the Tories running into Europe because they had run out of ideas. **1970** *Amer. Speech 1968* XLIII. 59 Those who participated were asked to fill their cars with a small amount of gasoline and then have the cars run out of gas on one of the highways leading to the New York World's Fair. **1971** [see *let *v.*[1] 29 b]. **1973** J. Porter *It's Murder with Dover* viii. 71 Do you mind just hanging on for a second, sir? I've-errun out of cigarettes.

c. In various colloq. phrases, as *to run out of road*: to approach the end of the roadway (usu. on failing to turn into a bend); also *transf.* and *fig.*; hence *to run out of track*, etc.; *to run out of steam*: of persons, to exhaust one's energy, ideas, etc.; also of things.

1961 Run out of steam [see *post-Christmas* s.v. *post- B. 1 a]. **1961** *Sunday Tel.* 9 July 6/3 When he [*sc.* the motorist] 'runs out of road', he gets severely 'bent'. **1965** Priestley & Wisdom *Good Driving* xii. 83 'Coming unstuck' or 'running out of road' are the light-hearted expressions used by the motor racing fraternity for an experience which can be the far-from-amusing result of attempting to take a bend with the 'wrong' camber at too great a speed. **1968** *Times* 29 Nov. 13/4 It is losing energy more rapidly than other slower pulsars, and is likely to 'run out of steam' soonest. **1969** R. V. Beste *Next Time I'll Pay* xv. 235 If Sequierez's appearance had meant anything, it was that the Cultural Attaché to Her Britannic Majesty's Embassy in Madrid had run out of rope. **1970** *Listener* 19 Nov. 710/3 The real-life situation of the superstar simply running out of road gives the work a clearly recognisable integrity of plot. **1973** D. Francis *Slay-Ride* vii. 78 When I'd run out of steam, they would begin to nod while they listened. **1974** *Country Life* 26 Dec. 2009/2 At Zahedan in southern Iran I ran out of railway. **1975** I. S. Black *Man on Bridge* xii. 170 Munro..drove till he ran out of track. **1977** *Times* 11 June 11/3, I chose not to hire one [*sc.* a motor-bike], having run out of road on a 350 some years back. **1977** *Gramophone* Dec. 1191/1 The disc input.. tends to run out of steam at the low frequency end.

67. run over—. f. Also, to go over with a machine. Cf. sense 50 a above.

1969 *Guardian* 17 July 11/5 When you've..hoovered the landing..you could just run over Mr Neville's carpet.

g. (Earlier example.) (Cf. sense 78 i below.)

1794 J. Woodforde *Diary* 15 Feb. (1929) IV. 96 A very young Man coming back from Norwich to day with an empty Waggon, falling under it was run over by it.

h. *U.S. colloq.* To impose upon, treat with contempt; to push (someone) around.

1836 *Spirit of Times* 9 July 162/2, I would not advise any man to run over me, for I ask no man any odds further than civility. **1914** B. Tarkington *Penrod* xxv. 264 I've stood enough around here for one day, and you can't run over *me*, Georgie Bassett. **1929** W. Faulkner *Sound & Fury* 227 You may think you can run over me like you do your grandmother and everybody else.

68. run through—. f. To rehearse, repeat, go over (a procedure, role, or the like).

1975 Cowie & Mackin *Oxf. Dict. Current Idiomatic English* 269/2, I think I've grasped your main proposals, but would you mind running through them once again? **1980** K. Hagenbach *Fox Potential* xvi. 157, I ran through it for her without the grim details... When I had finished the story, Frankie put her hand on my thigh.

69. run to—. b. (*b*) (Further examples.) Now freq. const. *can, could*, etc.

1924 H. De Sélincourt *Cricket Match* iii. 76 [He] only gave it me..because he knows I couldn't run to one of my own. **1931** T. R. G. Lyell *Slang, Phrase & Idiom* 653 *B.* 'How much do they want for it?' *A.* 'Five hundred pounds.' *B.* 'I'm afraid I can't possibly run to that.' **1953** E. Simon *Past Masters* III. 156 Bits and pieces in the press, posters if we can run to them. **1970** *Alberta Hist. Rev.* Summer 1/1 Frame houses..needed to be heated and insulated with something of the modern thoroughness to be at all tolerable; and few men could run to it.

(*c*) (Earlier and later examples.)

1883 *Daily Tel.* 4 Oct. 3/2 What I *should* like is a nice pair of spectacles, and, as far as my money would run to it, everything else accordin', sir. **1900** P. White *West End* v. 40, I always had an idea that the guv'nor had some money, but I didn't imagine it would 'run' to this. **1931** T. R. G. Lyell *Slang, Phrase & Idiom* 653 I've only got ten shillings, and..it certainly won't run to twenty-four!

(*d*) To manage to provide, go so far as to have.

1880 *Punch* 25 Dec. 298/2 A red 'un [*sc.* button-hole] with maiden'air trimmings is what I consider O.K. Suits my style and complexion, yer know, so I runs to it once in a way. **1934** G. B. Shaw *On Rocks* I. 208 Weve got nothing out of this. We dont run to Spanish in the Isle. **1960** *Bedside 'Guardian'* IX. 215 Some of the others [*sc.* theatres] run to 1930-ish chrome and glass fittings. **1973** 'M. Innes' *Appleby's Answer* xv. 128 Am I right.. in remembering that Gibber [*sc.* a village] runs to a tea-shop?

e. Now usu. *to run to seed.* (Further example; also earlier and further *transf.* examples.)

1740 Fielding *Champion* 15 Mar., For Virtue itself by growing too exuberant, and (if I may be allowed the Metaphor) by running to Seed changes its very Nature, and becomes a most pernicious Weed of a most beautiful Flower. **1861** *N.Y. Herald* 23 Nov. 4/5 Can such a country be..permitted to run to seed? **1873** *Amer. Jrnl. Insanity* Apr. 559 We believe somewhat in moral depravity and in accepting the results of our father's sins, but carried to the extent advocated by the Doctor, it is Calvinism run to seed. **1893** *Burpee's Farm Ann.* 65/1 It comes early and stands a long while before running to seed. **1924** A. Huxley *Little Mexican* 249 He pictured a large, blonde, barmaidish personage, thirty-one and not yet married, running a bit to seed. **1953** J. Wain *Hurry on Down* iv. 66 He was plump, but not yet running to seed; aged about forty-five to fifty. **1956** G. Durrell *Drunken Forest* iii. 62 At one time she must have been a handsome woman, but now she had run slightly to seed. **1976** *National Observer* (U.S.) 27 Nov. II. 2/3 Today there is a striking resemblance among many of the 1,000 or so residents, and most of the youngsters run to tow-head.

g. *U.S.* Of persons: to have a preference for or a leaning towards (something); to favour.

1873 'Mark Twain' *Gilded Age* xxxiii. 307 We had Dr. Spooner a good while, but he runs so much to emetics.. that we changed off and took Dr. Leathers. **1896** —— in *Harper's Mag.* Aug. 346/2 In my nature I have always run to pie, whilst in his nature he has always run to mystery.

71. run with—. c. orig. and chiefly *U.S.* Of persons: to associate with (a person or group), to befriend.

1909 *Dialect Notes* III. 365 *Run with..*, to associate with, go in the company of. **1914** B. Tarkington *Penrod* xiv. 126 You fellers have treated me nice—and some day you come over to my yard; I'd like to run with you fellers. You're the kind of fellers I like. **1922** E. O'Neill *Hairy Ape* vi. 64 If I can't find her I'll take it out on de gang she runs wit. **1946** Mezzrow & Wolfe *Really Blues* (1957) 378 *Run with*, associate with. **1969** G. Donaldson *Fifteen Men* xiv. 240 He ran with a crowd of kids known as 'Les Snobs'. **1975** *New Review* May 70/1 Hunter Thompson, who ran with the Hell's Angels for eighteen months to write *The Hell's Angels.*

IV. With adverbs, in specialized uses.

72. run away. b. Also *transf.* Freq. used jocularly in the negative (as, *it won't run away*) to give assurance of the permanence or fixity of something or someone.

1882 C. M. Gaskell in *Nineteenth Cent.* Sept. 460 The landowner has been credited with the..most valuable form of security;..it could not 'run away'. **1888** C. M. Yonge *Beechcroft at Rockstone* II. xxi. 191 The charms of 'the halls of Ivor'..which, after all, would not run away. **1908** A. Bennett *Old Wives' Tale* IV. iii. 515 There's no earthly reason why you should go back... The house won't run away. **1928** A. M. M. Douton *Bk. with Seven Seals* 21 Sunday will be round again in a week, and Park Chapel won't run away. **1942** A. E. W. Mason *Musk & Amber* i. 15 'What of Grest [*sc.* an estate] meanwhile?' 'Grest won't run away, Sir.' **1973** J. Porter *It's Murder with Dover* vii. 65 What's your sweat? This Tiffin bird's not going to run away.

transf. **1920** E. O'Neill *Beyond Horizon* III. i. 152 You've spent eight years running away from yourself. **1934** —— *Days without End* I. 36 It's a rocky road.. this running away from truth in order to find it? **1944** B. Hutchison *Hollow Men* vi. 79 It's his mask. It fools nearly everybody. He's always running away from himself. **1966** *Listener* 17 Nov. 718/2 The whole of the world ran away from the pound, and if this doesn't reveal an inflationary situation, what does?

d. (Further *transf.* examples.)

1935 *Industrial & Engin. Chem.* Sept. 1074/2 'Ethylene at a temperature above 350°C. and under a pressure of 175 kg. per sq. cm...decomposes with explosive violence.' Fortunately, this was not found to be the case, but in many experiments the temperature 'ran away'. **1945** *Rev. Mod. Physics* XVII. 482 If the reaction was not to 'run away', it was essential to make use of neutrons of very low energy in the individual steps of the chain process. **1946** [see *oil operated* s.v. *oil *sb.*[1] 6]. **1953** *Times* 31 Oct. 2/7 We have no practical experience of what happens if a reactor runs away. **1959** C. Hodder-Williams *Chain Reaction* xviii. 198 When the pile 'ran away', one of the heat-exchangers burst with the increased steam pressure.

73. run down. b. (Later examples of (*b*).)

1897 A. Beardsley *Let.* 22 Nov. (1970) 396, I am abominably ill; I ran down at Paris quite alarmingly. *Ibid.* 22 Dec. 410, I had run down terribly before I came here and was quite shattered by the journey.

m. (Earlier example.)

1737 *London Mag.* Oct. 542/1 Our directing the next Payment to be made to the Bank would, I believe, possess the Generality of Mankind with an Opinion that we were resolved to abolish the Company.., which would of course run the Price of their Stock down to very near Par.

n. To reduce or bring (an activity, operation, organization, etc.) to a halt gradually or progressively.

1861 C. M. Yonge *Young Step-Mother* vii. 74 Miss Meadows began one of her tangled skeins of words.. and Mr. Kendal, knowing..that the only chance of a conclusion was to let her run herself down, held his tongue. **1976** A. Price *War Game* I. vi. 118 We're running down the Incident Room, it's true. But we're not giving up. **1977** *Times* 18 Aug. 15/8 Over the past few years, Volkswagen has been progressively running down its 'beetle' production in Germany... Only 100 cars a day are at present produced.

o. *U.S. slang.* To rehearse or perform (a piece of music); to recite (verse).

1948 *Down Beat* 1 Dec. 10 We ran down three new instrumentals and a vocal for Baubles Buxon! **1959** G. Kanin *Blow up Storm* 19, I distributed the parts and we ran it down. **1960** *Jazz Rev.* Nov. 12 When we rehearsed an arrangement that no one had seen before, we'd run it down once or twice. **1961** R. Russell *Sound* i. 10 Bernie struck off a rich chord and began running the tune down in his immaculate post-Teddy Wilson style. **1969** H. R. Brown in T. Kochman *Rappin' & Stylin' Out* (1972) 205 The teacher expected me to sit up in class and study poetry after I could run down shit like that. **1975** R. S. Gold *Jazz Talk* 228 *Run down*, ..to perform, usually in rehearsal, a piece of written music.

p. *to run it down*: to describe or explain a situation in full; to tell the whole truth about a subject. *U.S. slang.* (Freq. in Black English.)

1964 T. Cade in *Massachusetts Rev.* Summer 622, I tried to figure out the best way to run it down to this girl right quick that they didn't have to live in this town. **1967** J. Horton in T. Kochman *Rappin' & Stylin' Out* (1972) 22 Street repartee at its best is a lively way of 'running it down', or of 'jiving'. **1970** G. Jackson *Let.* 17 Mar. in *Soledad Brother* (1971) 236 Write me a letter..and run it down; school, politics, futurities. I want to know it all. **1972** B. G. Cooke in T. Kochman *Rappin' & Stylin' Out* 48 This gesture of lowering the lip is a result of the emphatic manner in which they are 'running it down'.

74. run in. d. Also without *to.* (Earlier example.) *to run in and out* (*of* one another's homes, etc.): to make frequent informal visits (to one another).

1857 [see *get *v.* Etym. note]. **1876** C. M. Yonge *Womankind* xi. 81 A little croquet, a great deal of chatter; and worse than all, much running in and out among near neighbours. **1952** M. Laski *Village* iv. 77 It's lucky it's so far away; at least they can't be running in and out of each other's homes every minute. **1958** A. White tr. *Colette's Claudine in Paris* iv. 30 Just a few yards from here, there's a delightful flat, and we'd be practically on each other's doorsteps.... We could be always running in and out... it would be nice for Claudine and for you too.

g. (Earlier and later examples.) Also in *Naval* use (see quot. 1962).

1859 G. W. Matsell *Vocabulum* 76 *Run in*, arrested. **1889** *N. & Q.* 20 July 49/1 The respectable gentleman who ..takes my part if I get 'run in' by the police. **1909** J. R. Ware *Passing Eng.* 212/1 Thus hooked he is 'run in', where..he is treated for 'D.T.'s'—the origin of most amok—when he either recovers or is passed into an asylum. **1933** J. Cary *Amer. Visitor* 35 Cottee was over the boundary, so I'm going to run him in. **1938** [see *fowl *sb.* 1 d]. **1948** Partridge *Dict. Forces' Slang* 159 I've warned you, the next time you are adrift I'll run you in to the First Lootenant. **1951** *New Yorker* 15 Dec. 94 'Am I going to have to run you in?' the policeman asked. **1962** Granville *Dict. Sailors' Slang* 98/2 *Run in*, place a man in the Commander's report or bring him before the Officer-of-the-watch.

i. (Earlier and later examples.)

1817 *Ackermann's Repository* Jan. 53/1 A row of straw-colour ribbon is run in next to the border. **1900** F. M. Ford *Let.* Oct. (1965) 13, I took hold of that young woman and ran in every bit of her charm I could think of and then smashed in all the repulsion I could think of.

k. To operate (new machinery, esp. a motor vehicle or its engine) at reduced speed or load until it has reached a normal working condition. Also *refl.*, said of the machinery. Also *fig.*

1919 W. H. Berry *New Traffic* (*Aircraft*) xv. 86 Some engineers suggested that the flight should be used to 'run in' the engines. **1925** *Morris Owner's Manual* xvi. 103 It must, of course, clearly be understood that when an engine is new and stiff much more heat is developed than is the case when it has run itself in. **1934** *Punch* 6 June 629/1 Never start a new engine on the self-starter. The battery and dynamo need running-in before you use them. **1939** N. Monsarrat *This is Schoolroom* III. xvii. 390 Anthea bought a car, we ran it in. **1953** A. White tr. *Colette's Cat* iv. 109 We're going out to Rambouillet for lunch in the forest. I've got to run the car in. **1959** *Listener* 2 Apr. 603/1 If you are running-in a new car, and conscientiously keeping down to a maximum of thirty miles an hour, [etc.]. **1961** H. Nicholson *Let.* 1 June

(1968) 395 Kennedy 'must run himself in' before he can inspire confidence. **1972** *Guardian* 18 Sept. 11/4 My car offers its apologies for curious behaviour: 'Running In' is plastered across its back. **1973** A. BEHREND *Samarai Affair* iii. 31 Having thus ticked over gently during the previous ten minutes, the committee had now run itself in for the major business of the afternoon.

75. run off. c. (Further examples.)
1925 *Daily Tel.* 13 May 4/3 On purchasing that company it was decided to allow its marine business to run off. **1955** *Times* 3 May 15/1 In the first quarter of this year the surplus has tended to run off.

d. Also *to run off at the mouth*: to talk excessively; to talk nonsense. Cf. sense 52 g above. *U.S. slang.*
1909 *Dialect Notes* III. 403 *Runnin' off at the mouth*,.. loquacity; talking too much. Used of one excessively loquacious. 'He's got a bad case of runnin' off at the mouth.' **1942** BERREY & VAN DEN BARK *Amer. Thes. Slang* §151/6 *Talk nonsense*... go *or* run off at the mouth. *Ibid.* §189/3 *Be talkative*... run (off) at the mouth. **1951** *Rochester* (N.Y.) *Democrat & Chron.* 12 Sept. 14/6 Culio... A run-of-the-mob gunsel—till he runs off at the mouth! **1962** A. LURIE *Love & Friendship* xi. 223 I'm a pig coming over here and running off at the mouth, probably boring you to hell. **1976** *National Observer* (U.S.) 28 Aug 1/1 The man they simply ran off at the mouth about here, Jimmy Carter.

k. To produce or turn out (duplicated copies, etc.).
1889 *Cent. Dict.* 5271/2 *To run off*,.. In printing, to take impressions of; print: as, this press will run off ten thousand every hour; to run off an edition. **1901** MERWIN & WEBSTER *Calumet 'K'* vi. 106 Now, we'll write to Mr. Brown—no,.. I'll do that one myself. You might run off the other and I'll sign it. **1932** A. J. WORRALL *Eng. Idioms* 78 This machine will run off eighty copies per minute. **1970** H. MCLEAVE *Question of Negligence* xxvii. 229 They had trundled in a portable X-ray machine... They ran off six plates.

l. *Austral.* and *N.Z.* (See quots.)
1933 L. G. D. ACLAND in *Press* (Christchurch, N.Z.) 25 Nov. 15/7 *Run off*,..(3) To separate: e.g., 'I will *run off* the strangers when we draft the mob'. **1965** J. S. GUNN *Terminol. Shearing Industry* II. 15 *Run-off*, to take a group of sheep from the flock without necessarily 'cutting out' all of this group or 'drafting' them into special lots, for example 'I'll run off some fats'.

76. run on. a. (Further examples in *Racing*.)
1971 *Rand Daily Mail* 4 Sept. 23/4 Fighting Heart was running on when he beat Desert Oil over 1 000 metres. **1977** *Field* 13 Jan. 56/1 Trainers had no way of knowing whether their fastest puppies had that ability to 'run on', an endowment with stamina so essential for Altcar honours.

h. (Further examples.) Also, to set (an advertisement) as continuous text rather than displayed matter.
1951 S. JENNETT *Making of Bks.* xv. 256 Some manuscripts and some of the early printed books avoided paragraph divisions and ran all paragraphs on, indicating the commencement of each by means of a paragraph mark. **1973** F. JEFKINS *Advertising made Simple* I. i. 17 By classified we mean not only that the advertisements are small and run-on but that they are grouped together under identifying headings. *Ibid.* III. xvii. 200 *Displayed classified*, or *semi-display*—advertisements in the classified section which are not merely run on, but set out and possibly illustrated.

77. run out. c. (*a*) (Later examples.)
1965 A. NICOL *Truly Married Woman* 103 'Oxygen,' Doc said. 'We ran out last week, sir, I forgot to tell you,' the nurse said. **1972** J. WILSON *Hide & Seek* vi. 106 'Haven't you got any?' asked Alice. 'No—no, I've run out,' he said.

(*c*) Of a crop variety: to lose its distinguishing characteristics in successive generations.
1890 *Bull. Cornell Agric. Exper. Station* XXI. 88 We are still confirmed in our belief that varieties of tomatoes are unstable and that they soon 'run out'. **1901** I. P. ROBERTS in L. H. Bailey *Cycl. Amer. Hort.* III. 1418/1 Old varieties [of potatoes] which have 'run out' often find their way into a locality where conditions are superior. **1957** DUNCAN & ROSS *Growing Field Crops* 10 Sometimes disease and insect invasions reverse the process of plant improvement by adjustment. When this happens, varieties are said to run out.

d. (*c*) (Earlier example.)
1875 *Baily's Mag.* July 162 Mr Greenfield in particular running out almost to every ball and driving it along the ground.

†(*d*) *Cricket.* To be run out. Cf. sense 77 m below. *Obs.*
1828 *Boy's Own Bk.* 22 When a striker has run out, the notch they were running for shall not be reckoned. **1860** F. LILLYWHITE *Eng. Cricketers' Trip to Canada & U.S.* 20 Hayward contrived to run out. **1876** *Haygarth's Cricket Scores 1855–75* V. 368 Five ran out on the Bradford side.

h. (Further examples.) Also without complement, to win.
1928 *Daily Tel.* 26 June 11/7 He went on to lead 4–2 in the third set, and then at 5–4, had three set balls before running out. **1941** G. HEYER *Envious Casca* xii. 219 [She] miscued... 'You'll run out now.' **1959** *Times* 19 Mar. 17/5 Then Borch began to smash brilliantly and ran out for the game. **1960** E. S. & W. J. HIGHAM *High Speed Rugby* xxi. 289 In ninety-nine cases out of a hundred, a fitter team will run out winners. **1976** *Bridgwater Mercury* 21 Dec., British Cellophane's second team ran out 4-1 winners against Bridgwater Police in the fourth division of the Somerset Squash League.

i. (*c*) (Later example.)
1977 *New Yorker* 10 Oct. 152/2 He then dropped service again, after which Connors ran out the set, 6–2.

(*d*) *Cricket.* To score from (a hit) by running. Freq. *imp.*
1856 *Househ. Words* 2 Feb. 60/2 When you holloa out... 'Run it out!' **1886** J. PYCROFT *Oxf. Memories* II. xxi. 89 There were no bounds, all hits were run out. **1898** J. A. GIBBS *Cotswold Village* xi. 234 'Come six, Podder!' I shouted, amid cries of 'Keep on running!' 'Run it out!' etc., from spectators and scouts alike. **1908** W. E. W. COLLINS *Leaves from Old Country Cricketer's Diary* xi. 180 Run it out, sir, run it out. I hope you'll get six.

l. (*c*) (Further example.)
1911 *Chambers's Jrnl.* Sept. 596/2 When you have read it over, I will run out another copy.

m. (Earlier and further examples.) Also, of a batsman: to cause one's partner to be run out.
1750 in H. T. Waghorn *Cricket Scores 1730–73* (1899) 47 Tom Bell (run out) 0. **1823** M. R. MITFORD in *Lady's Mag.* July 391/1 Joel Brent..ran out his mate, Samuel Long. **1860** *Baily's Monthly Mag.* Aug. 364 His only perceptible fault was his tendency to run himself and others out. **1900** P. F. WARNER *Cricket in Many Climes* I. iv. 59 Dick Berens ran me out when I was well on my way to a hundred. **1912** —— *England v. Australia* xii. 134 Hitch and Strudwick between them ran out Tumilty. **1933** M. LOWRY *Ultramarine* ii. 80 You go in first and run out the chief steward. **1974** *Times* 4 Feb. 1/1 A decision whereby Kallicharan..was given run out for 142 off the last ball of the day..was later reversed.

78. run over. i. Of a vehicle, etc.: to knock down and pass over (someone); to injure or kill by knocking down. Also *transf.* Freq. in *pass.*
The passive use is indistinguishable from that of sense 67 g.
1932 L. GOLDING *Magnolia St.* I. vii. 114 He is so small the driver hardly notices him till he has very nearly run him over. **1954** T. S. ELIOT *Confid. Clerk* III. 109 *Eggerson*: ..Unfortunately, the father died suddenly... *Lady Elizabeth*: He was run over. By a rhinoceros In Tanganyika. **1970** [see *ROAR *v.* 3 e]. **1978** *Daily Tel.* 1 Nov. 19/6 Mann appeared to be more concerned about the damage to his motor-cycle than the youth he had run over.

81. run up. d. (*a*) (Later example.)
1870 [see *BREAK *v.* 8 c].

f. (Further example.)
1970 *Field* 16 Apr. 703/1 Stanley and Michael Lunt, father and son who between them won three amateur championships and ran up in a fourth.

g. (*a*) (Further examples in *Cricket*.)
1955 *Times* 25 Aug. 3/3 The South Africans ran up 467 runs for the loss of eight wickets. **1977** *Sunday Times* 2 Jan. 28/3 They ran up 322 for four wickets despite a rain-soaked outfield.

(*d*) (Earlier example.)
1870 W. W. FOWLER *Ten Yrs. in Wall St.* xxiv. 394 They stepped into the gap, and ran up the price again.

i. (*e*) To raise (a flag) to the top of a mast, etc. Also *fig.* (see quot. 1962).
1901 G. B. SHAW *Devil's Disciple* I. 28 Run up the American flag on the devil's house. **1930** E. M. BRENT-DYER *Chalet Girls in Camp* v. 76 Nearer the lake were the two flag-poles, and the flags would be run up at six o'clock the next morning. **1938** A. J. LIEBLING *Back where I came From* 27 He run up the American flag. **1962** S. STRAND *Marketing Dict.* 639 *Run it up the flag pole*, a Madison Avenue jargon for trying out any idea. Full expression: 'Let's run it up the flag pole and see who salutes it.' **1964** MRS L. B. JOHNSON *White House Diary* 21 May (1970) 143 They had already provided a flag pole and we ran up the flag while they all gave the Pledge of Allegiance. **1966** *New Statesman* 25 Mar. 409/2 The decision was made—in the admen's jargon that comes naturally to Tory strategists—to run it up the flagpole and see if anyone saluted.

(*f*) To run (an aircraft engine) quickly while it is out of gear in order to warm it up. Also *intr.*
1938 W. O. MANNING *Flight Handbk.* iii. 77 These [wheel brakes] are used..for holding the aeroplane while the engine is being 'run up'. **1942** *R.A.F. Jrnl.* 3 Oct. 26 Intermittently, the sound of engines running up overcomes the wind. **1958** 'N. SHUTE' *Rainbow & Rose* i. 33 Billy Monkhouse had got the Auster out and was running it up outside the hangar. **1976** *Farnborough 76* (Soc. Brit. Aerospace Companies) 11/1 Inboard engines '2' and '3' are run up first, then the outboards '1' and '4' follow.

j. (*a*) (Later *transf.* examples.)
1965 *New Statesman* 19 Mar. 458/3 Were one to ask a computer to run up a composite 18th-century man, the result would be remarkably like Dr Burney. **1974** 'J. LE CARRÉ' *Tinker, Tailor* ix. 68 In KL I had them run me up a British passport.

(*c*) Now usu. to make (a garment, etc.) by sewing quickly or simply.
1977 *Lancashire Life* Nov. 74/1 The women keep it clean, scrubbing floors, washing curtains, running up new ones on the machine [etc.]. **1979** P. DRISCOLL *Pangolin* iii. 38 The tailors who ran up suits in twenty-four hours.

V. 82. Collocations used attributively or as sbs. **run and fell** *Needlework* (see quot. 1968); also *attrib.*; **run-flat** *a.*, applied to a kind of tyre on which a vehicle may run after a puncture has occurred; **run-sheep(y)-run** *N. Amer.* and *Sc.*, a children's hiding game (see quot. 1909).
1882 CAUFEILD & SAWARD *Dict. Needlework* 428/1 *Run and fell*..is a method sometimes adopted in lieu of Over-sewing, and employed in making seams, either in underlinen, or in the skirts and sleeves of dresses. **1961** M. SPARK *Prime of Miss Jean Brodie* iii. 69 In the worst cases they unstitched what had been done and did it again, saying 'This'll not do', or 'That's never a run and fell seam'. **1968** J. IRONSIDE *Fashion Alphabet* 99 *Run-and-fell*, a seam similar to a flat-fell but only one row of machining shows. The two edges are seamed together, one is trimmed close to stitching and the other turned under and then laid flat against the main part of garment and machined. **1976** P. CLABBURN *Needleworker's Dict.* 230 *Run and fell seam*,.. type of seam worked on fairly light fabrics, commonly used for children's garments and undergarments, but now often superseded by other varieties. **1946** R. STORRS *Dunlop in War & Peace* xi. 61 As the name *Run Flat* (*Bullet-proof*) *Tyre* suggests, a bullet may penetrate this tyre, but there is no immediate deflation. **1958** A. G. DONNITHORNE *Brit. Rubber Manuf.* iv. 39 New kinds of tyres were produced to meet service demands in the two World Wars, such, for example, as Dunlop's 'run-flat' tyre. **1973** *Guardian* 30 May 9/3 The Dunlop Denovo 'run-flat' tyre, designed to end the dangers of punctures at high speed, and to enable the motorist to continue his journey without changing the wheel, will be available in October. **1905** *Dialect Notes* III. 93 *Run, sheep, run*,.. a kind of hide and seek in which the participants hide together. **1909** J. H. BANCROFT *Games* 6 The author found a good example of folklore-in-the-making in the game usually known as 'Run, Sheep, Run!' in which a band of hidden players seek the goal under the guidance of signals shouted by a leader. **1949** M. MEAD *Male & Female* 456, I set myself to study changing patterns of run, sheepy, run or prisoner's base. **1962** W. STEGNER *Wolf Willow* I. i. 15 The open field beside Down's where we used to play run-sheep-run in the evenings. **1968** *Sc. Nat. Dict.* VII. 447/1 Rin-sheep-rin. **1969** I. & P. OPIE *Children's Games* iv. 173 'Run, Sheepie, Run' (Cumnock [in Scotland]). **1975** *Islander* (Victoria, B.C.) 4 May 2/1 It seems to me I played run-sheep-run there.

run, *ppl. a.* Add: **II. 9. a.** (Earlier example.)
1774 T. PENNANT *Tour in Scotl.* (ed. 3) 287 Some of the walls, all of run lime, do as yet remain.

10. (Earlier example.)
1822 T. CREEVEY in *Creevey Papers* (1903) I. x. 236, I met..the Duke [of Wellington]... It has been a damned serious business,' he said... 'It has been a damned nice thing—the nearest run thing you ever saw in your life.'

11. (Earlier and later examples.) Also, exhausted by running; worn out.
1876 *Coursing Calendar* 147 Troapham proved herself a rare stayer, for she was fearfully run in her first course. **1917** G. BELL *Let.* 13 Jan. (1927) I. xv. 393, I wonder you have time to write me such splendid long letters! You really must not do it when you feel dreadfully run.

13. a. (Earlier example.)
1865 F. B. PALLISER *Hist. Lace* xxxvi. 424 To France must be assigned the application of the Jacquard system to the net-frame, and consequently the invention of machinery lace. Shawls and large pieces in 'run lace', as it is termed, had previously been made after this manner.

14. *run-after*, sought after; popular; *run-on* (further examples); *run-out* (earlier examples); *run-over*, (*a*) of (the heels of) shoes: worn down on one side; (*b*) = *run-on*.
1878 *Trans. Illinois Dept. Agric.* XIV. 144 The long, lank hog of the old, run-out breed has given place to the improved Poland China. **1880** *Rep. Vermont Board Agric.* VI. 28 The first condition of fertility we have, even in these run-out pastures. **1882** G. M. HOPKINS *Lett. to R. Bridges* (1955) 158 The question of what they call run-on lines and the rhymes or other final words belonging is difficult. **1906** 'O. HENRY' in *N.Y. World Mag.* 8 July 8/1 'Smoky' was dressed in..run-over shoes, and trousers of the 'serviceable' brand. **1908** R. W. CHAMBERS *Firing Line* vi. 75 I've heard that you are the most assiduously run-after girl at Palm Beach. **1919** *Ladies' Home Jrnl.* Mar. 89/4 '*Why* do my heels run-over?' Run-over shoe heels are more than unsightly. They are warning of incipient foot trouble. They are usually due to a weakness of the foot structure which permits the foot to 'give' outwardly or inwardly in walking. **1931** *Times Lit. Suppl.* 15 Jan. 43/2 His rules about mid-verse pause and run-over lines. **1946** B. MACDONALD *Egg & I* xvi. 175 Reddish cotton stockings, run-over shoes. **1955** *Ess. & Stud.* VIII. 61 The madcap movement of the run-on lines perfectly parallels the hither-thithering of the trapped mind. **1965** R. E. LONGACRE in *Language* XLI. 74 Such imbedding of sentence within a phrase has special phonological characteristics (level, run-on intonation, and lack of pause before termination of the imbedding phrase). **1978** J. A. MICHENER *Chesapeake* 667 He wore run-over shoes, baggy trousers, torn shirt and smashed hat, items which he rarely changed. **1979** *Dictionaries* I. 15 The question arises of whether run-on entries will be defined or not.

run-about. Add: **1. a.** Also, an assistant, a dogsbody.
1957 [see *GARDE CHAMPÊTRE]. **1959** M. SUMMERTON *Small Wilderness* i. 15 He hadn't relished my taking a job as a tea-maker and general runabout on a ritzy household magazine. **1976** J. FRASER *Who steals my Name?* xv. 186 A constable was kept on duty as a part-time secretary to the chief superintendent, a run-about, a screen protecting his privacy.

b. (Earlier example.)
1775 J. WOODFORDE *Diary* 13 June (1924) I. 163 His whole Face..was uncommonly ugly, not unlike one of the runabout gipsies.

4. (Further examples.)
1900 ADE *Fables in Slang* 155 He took her riding in his new Runabout every Evening. **1900** *Motor-Car World* I. 130/2 A new small car... It is known as the University Runabout. **1912** *Chambers's Jrnl.* Feb. 144/1 The 'auto-carrier'..gives everything that the small runabout motor-car can offer. **1930** *Punch* 2 Apr. 374/1 Just ahead of us was a small runabout car. **1949** *Chicago Tribune* 18 Sept. 34/2 Among some 70 old-time cars will be a one

cylinder 1904 Cadillac runabout, [etc.]. **1956** *News Chron.* 1 Nov. 8/5 It is the latest in a line of economy runabouts—the Mark E Bond Minicar. **1968** 'J. Le Carré' *Small Town in Germany* ii. 24 The pavements are obstructed by the runabout cars of British Counsellors' wives. **1980** *Times* 7 Mar. 25 Whereas the Mini is really a Town runabout, the Metro is conceived as a family car that will be more comfortable for longer runs.

5. A light aircraft.

1904 A. Santos-Dumont *My Airships* xxii. 282, I determined to build a small air-ship runabout for my pleasure and convenience only. **1922** *Westm. Gaz.* 14 Nov. 3/6 Arrangements are being made..to launch the first power-driven runabout of the air. **1932** *Flight* 13 Oct. 952 The machines would have been the forerunners of cheap aerial runabouts. **1959** *Economist* 3 Jan. 58/2 A small aircraft need not be barred from using a big airport provided that it carries radio. But many of the smallest runabouts have no radio. **1966** P. O'Donnell *Sabre-Tooth* vi. 87 The twin-engined de Haviland Dove, the six-passenger aircraft which plied as a runabout from the valley..to Kabul. **1977** 'J. Le Carré' *Hon. Schoolboy* xii. 273 'Is that a single-engined plane?'.. 'Kind of executive runabout kind of thing.'

6. orig. and chiefly *U.S.* A small motor-boat.

1932 *Daily Progress* (Charlottesville, Va.) 7 Sept. 10/3 This event will be followed by..two free-for-all outboard races and a race for runabouts not over 50 horsepower. **1946** *Sun* (Baltimore) 16 Sept. 12 (*caption*) The D, E, F and G Class service and racing runabouts leave the starting line in the second heat. **1966** T. Pynchon *Crying of Lot 49* iii. 64 'Help,' said Di Presso, looking back.. across the lake. Another runabout had appeared and was headed toward them. **1970** J. Cleary *Helga's Web* xv. 274 He had started up the motor of the runabout and cruised quietly back to the yacht. **1975** B. Garfield *Hopscotch* ii. 27 A little motor runabout zipped past the barge.

‖ **runanga** (rū·naŋa). *N.Z.* Also with capital initial. [Maori.] In Maori society, an assembly or council. (See also *whare runanga* s.v. *whare.)

1858 J. Morgan *Let.* 21 June in *Richmond–Atkinson Papers* (1960) I. 411 This arrangement was proposed by Potatau's *runanga*. **1861** A. S. Atkinson *Jrnl.* 18 Nov. in *Ibid.* 727 The King party will not..accept the new runanga system. **1862** —— *Jrnl.* 5 Feb. in *Ibid.* 744 One man, the head of the Runanga, shall have £100 a year, 7 Runanga men £70 each, [etc.]. **1905** W. Baucke *Where White Man Treads* 33 He..carves effigies of his tribe-founders and heroes on the memorial posts of his runanga house, that when the elders meet to discuss matters of state, the presence of his dear dead may preside, and guide the thoughts of the council. **1946** *Jrnl. Polynesian Soc.* June 157 *Runanga*, assembly; council; so, *whare-runanga*, meeting-house. **1967** J. Metge *Maoris of N.Z.* ii. 33 As a group, the kaumātua formed a community council (*runanga*) which advised and could influence the chief. **1975** D. Scott *Ask that Mountain* (1976) ii. 41 Discussion and debate was reserved for the *runanga*, the council of leaders and elders.

run-around. Restrict *U.S. colloq.* to sense in Dict. and add: Also as one word. **1.** (Earlier and later examples.)

1857 *Knickerbocker* XLIX. 97 There comes us a 'run-round' on the end of our pen-finger. **1913** J. London *Valley of Moon* III. iv. 352 His finger was hurting too much, he said... 'It might be a run-around,' Saxon hazarded. **1968** Leider & Rosenblum *Dict. Dermatol. Words* 364 *Run(-)around*.., is colloquial for inflammatory conditions of the soft parts about nails and conveys the idea of tendency to extend circularly.

2. *colloq.* (orig. *U.S.*). Deceit, evasion; behaviour likely to mislead or cause inconvenience, esp. in phr. *to give* (someone) *the run-around*.

1915 *Chicago Herald* 2 Dec. 13/4 Pitts is satisfied that he is the victim of the grandest run-around ever put over on a boxing promoter. **1924** H. C. Witwer in *Cosmopolitan* Jan. 84/2 If you wanted to give William a run around why not say we were Cleopatra and Salome and be done with it? **1929** J. P. McEvoy *Hollywood Girl* i. 3 All I get is the run around—that nothing today, my dear, but keep in touch with us, you never know what is liable to turn up. **1933** *Sun* (Baltimore) 24 Nov. 20/4 The fans were given the runaround in the third race here yesterday. **1934** E. S. Gardner *Case of Lucky Legs* xiii. 191 A small-town dentist.., and you think that fits you to give me a run-around in a murder case. **1938** O. Nash *I'm Stranger here Myself* 115 Humanity must continue to follow the sun around And accept the eternal run-around. **1944** 'N. Shute' *Pastoral* ii. 27 Perhaps her boy friend was giving her the run around. **1950** 'S. Ransome' *Deadly Miss Ashley* ix. 109 He had already taken more than enough of a run-around from her. **1960** W. Haggard *Closed Circuit* iv. 43 My instructions are to..give him the runaround and soften him up. **1973** J. Wainwright *Devil You Don't* 176, I don't trust you... It could be a runaround. **1979** E. Newman *Sunday Punch* xix. 164 We were seeing a deliberate run-around by Smith.

3. *Printing.* Type set in shorter measure so as to fit at the side of an illustration.

[**1934** V. Steer *Printing Design & Layout* 327/2 *Run Round Block*, type set to surround a block.] **1949** Melcher & Larrick *Printing & Promotion Handbk.* 260/2 The use of run-arounds increases the cost of type composition and is often avoided on that account. **1978** *Verbatim* May 7/1 It is extremely difficult (and expensive) to program a computer to set run-arounds.

4. *colloq.* (orig. *U.S.*). A short journey or excursion. Also *attrib.* and *fig.*

1954 *Ties* (U.S.) Dec. 14/2 Steve operates the Little Southern's passenger train and local freight on regular-style train orders, with 'meets' and 'runarounds' carefully scheduled. **1976** *Broadcast* 29 Nov. 7/3 Over 1600 [people] have said they would become 'runaround drivers', ferrying around the elderly and infirm. **1977** *Time Out* 28 Jan.–3 Feb. 15/3 LBC's runaround with Alexander Walker on the week's new films.

runaway, *sb.* (and *a.*) Add: **I. 1. c.** Also *transf.* of (part of) a railway train.

1945 G. B. Grundy *55 Yrs. at Oxf.* i. 17 The eight trucks of a luggage train which I had seen were runaways.

2. a. (Further examples.) Also (*U.S.*) of horses: an act of bolting. Also *transf.* of a railway train or wagons.

1850 L. H. Garrard *Wah-to-Yah* xxi. 291 Three of the muleteams, made handsome runaways. **1898** *Kansas City* (Missouri) *Star* 18 Dec. 1/5 Miss Agnes Peterson was hurt in a runaway caused by the driver of an express wagon. **1967** G. F. Fiennes *I tried to run Railway* iv. 32 We never had a runaway. **1971** *Leader* (Durban) 7 May 16/4 Occasional runaways by Derrick Norris and Elijah Adams looked dangerous at times, but failed to bring home any goals. **1975** *Budget* (Sugarcreek, Ohio) 20 Mar. 7/8 Jacob D. Shetler had a runaway recently. He wanted to haul wood to saw, when the horses took off.

b. = Runway 1 a. *colloq.* (chiefly *U.S.*).

1868 *Fur, Fin, & Feather* 205 After a hard pull after a deer, or a long and tiresome vigil on a 'run-away', nothing is so vexatious as a miss-fire. **1944** *Living off Land* ii. 32 Carry a few snares..set them on the runaways through the grass or bushes... Set the noose in a spot where the runaway is narrow.

c. *transf.* (*ellipt.* uses of senses 4 and 6 in Dict. and Suppl.)

1947 *Sun* (Baltimore) 8 Jan. 18/1 The [stock-market] ticker tape frequently was idle until the final hour when sufficient offerings arrived to quicken the pace. There was nothing like a run-away, however. **1967** *Boston Sunday Herald* 14 May 2-5/2 Nineteen hits, 14 walks and three big innings added up to a 26-4 runaway for Bates over Brandeis Saturday. **1976** 'G. Black' *Moon for Killers* ii. 23 That book didn't need promoting. It was a runaway.

d. *Science.* Uncontrolled departure of a system from its usual or intended equilibrium.

1955 *Sci. Amer.* Oct. 60/3 Although reactors are designed so that there is a built-in tendency to overcome runaways automatically, accidents are always possible. **1957** *Practical Wireless* XXXIII. 684/1 Damage might result due to the heating effect of the lamp raising the temperature of the junction causing a 'run away', irreparably damaging the photo-transistor. **1973** *Physics Bull.* July 411/2 The danger of runaway of a fusion reactor is minimal, for the total deuterium and tritium in the reactive zone would be only about 0·25 g per 1000 MW of output power. **1974** *Nature* 29 Mar. 399/1 When the mass accreted exceeds $\sim 10^{-5} M_\odot$ nuclear energy generation becomes violent enough to drive a thermal runaway typical of novae.

II. 3. a. (Further examples.) Also (*U.S.*) of slaves.

1699 *N. Carolina Colonial Rec.* (1886) I. 514 A particular law..injoyns all persons on a penalty to apprehend runaway Negroes. **1784** J. F. D. Smyth *Tour U.S.A.* II. 102 Run-away Negroes have resided in these places for twelve, twenty, or thirty years and upwards. **1804** R. Sutcliff *Trav. N. Amer.* (1811) iii. 58 Whenever he saw a Negro whom he judged to be a runaway slave, he would.. jump from his work-board. **1852** *Morning Courier* (N.Y.) 8 Oct. 2/2 She causes a reward to be offered for the recovery of a runaway slave 'dead or alive', when no reward with such an alternative was ever heard or dreamed of south of Mason and Dixon's line. **1885** 'Mark Twain' *Huck. Finn* xxxviii. 325 On the scutcheon we'll have a.. crest, a runaway nigger, *sable*, with his bundle over his shoulder. **1977** *Time* 30 May 14/2 Rhodesian officials shrugged off Kaunda's declaration as the diplomatic equivalent of a mosquito bite, but the brutal civil war in the runaway British colony continues.

b. (Earlier example of *runaway match* and later example of *runaway marriage*.)

1838 Mrs. Gaskell *Let.* 17 Aug. (1966) 27 Wm has promised..to marry you if it comes to a runaway match. **1921** Runaway marriage [see *film actress* s.v. *film *sb.* 7 c].

4. a. (Further examples.)

1957 [see *hair-raising* adj. s.v. *hair *sb.* 10]. **1958** Hayward & Harari tr. *Pasternak's Dr. Zhivago* II. ix. 268 Revolutionaries who take the law into their own hands are horrifying, not as criminals, but as machines that have got out of control, like a run-away train.

fig. **1960** *New Left Rev.* Sept.–Oct. 40/1 More important than sympathy actions for and with Negroes, the sit-ins stimulated a similar burst, a run-away brush fire of activity for all sorts of other aims. **1971** *Fremdsprachen* XV. 45 The site of an oil tanker wreck and a runaway underwater oil well. **1973** *N.Y. Law Jrnl.* 1 Aug. 4/7 The third occurrence of pacemaker failure involved the supplying of an accelerated beat by the second pacemaker. This is a situation commonly known as a 'runaway' pacemaker.

b. In general use, of economic, natural, etc., conditions: thoroughly out of control, developing at an ever-increasing rate; unrestrained, rampant.

1925 *Scribner's Mag.* July 59 All of them expressed relief that predictions of a 'runaway market' for staple products had not been fulfilled. **1936** *Sun* (Baltimore) 23 Nov. 2/4 Because such an oversupply of excess funds might provide the basis for 'runaway' credit expansion, the board is considering increasing reserve requirements. **1949** *Ibid.* 3 Mar. 2/7 Representative Eberharter.. warned against making the home relief program 'too attractive', pointedly asserting that some states already were showing a 'runaway' tendency. **1967** *Listener* 21 Dec. 807/2 Lots of aspects of the world..are..'in a runaway condition'; population growth, technological growth, the destruction of Nature, to name only three. **1974** *Ibid.* 21 Feb. 235/2 If the miners' dispute is settled on very inflationary terms..it's going to be runaway inflation in Britain. **1980** *Times* 9 Jan. 12 The private pocket, not the public purse, is the best defence against runaway inflation.

c. Of commercial sales, etc.: immeasurable, overwhelming. *spec.* in phrases *runaway best seller, success.* Also *fig.*

1953 L. Z. Hobson *Celebrity* iii. 31 If *The Good World* should develop a runaway sale in bookstores, this windfall might reach a *hundred* and fifty-two thousand. *Ibid.* xii. 180 So this was what a 'run-away best seller' meant. **1960** *Harper's Bazaar* July 18/2 The season's runaway best-seller. **1968** M. Jones *Survivor* ii. 27 *Down in Flames* had been such a runaway best-seller in 1946 that there were bound to be people who remembered it. **1971** *Sunday Times* (Johannesburg) 28 Mar. 6/5 This film was a runaway box-office success. **1976** Botham & Donnelly *Valentino* ix. 71 His plan was a runaway success.

6. (Earlier example.)

1877 *Illust. London News* 2 June 515/3 The only other noteworthy feature..was the runaway victory of Lady Lumley in the Stanley Stakes.

7. In U.S. industrial terminology, designating a plant which is transferred from one location to another in order to prevent trade-union activity or evade labour regulations. Also applied *transf.* to a ship sailing under a *flag of convenience* (see *flag *sb.*[4] 1 f).

1949 *Dict. Labor Law Terms* 71 *Runaway shop*, a plant transferred to destroy union effectiveness and to evade bargaining duties. **1952** J. A. Morris *Woolen & Worsted Manuf. Southern Piedmont* iv. 118 Even though few 'runaway plants' are involved in the southern woolen and worsted movement, the effect of unions is nevertheless felt. **1954** *West Coast Sailors* 1 Oct. 4/1 Why has Mr. Rothschild started this program to assist operations of runaway foreign flags? **1957** Clark & Gottfried *Dict. Business & Finance* 308/1 In the textile and apparel industries, especially, many such runaway shops have left the New England and Middle Atlantic states over a period of years, and relocated in the South. **1960** *Wall St. Jrnl.* 15 Mar. 14 On the high seas, according to the maritime unions, are 1,695 'runaway' flag ships which have owners of one nationality and registry of another... Registered in Panama, Liberia and Honduras..these ships are described as flying 'flags of necessity' by operators and 'flags of convenience' by seamen. *Ibid.*, The union claimed that the use of foreign technicians was the equivalent of a 'runaway shop'. **1967** *Ibid.* 12 Dec. 1 Runaway plants set up by U.S. companies just inside Mexico to utilize cheap labour will come under increasing attack from the AFL-CIO.

run-back. [f. Run *v.*] **1.** The action or fact of running backwards.

1926 *Gloss. Terms Electr. Engin.* (Brit. Engin. Stand. Assoc.) 140 *Runback preventer*, a system of connection in a tramcar controller such that, in the event of the car running backwards, the motors act as short-circuited generators and thus exert a braking action. **1929** A. T. Dover *Electric Traction* (ed. 2) viii. 183 Where the motors are cross-connected for braking..the braking positions of the controller are effective for both directions of motion of the car, and may, therefore, be used for preventing a run-back. **1973** P. Dickinson *Green Gene* ii. 41 He wanted to see whether any usable figures were available for..the mid-nineteenth century, enough at least for him to construct a crude model and attempt a run-back.

2. The additional space located at either end of a lawn tennis court.

1908 A. W. Myers *Compl. Lawn Tennis Player* 213 At Auteuil..the run-back is inadequate and the timbered roof too low. **1927** *Daily Express* 30 May 3/5 The proper run-back for a court should be 21 ft. from the base-line to the stop-netting. **1977** *Club Tennis* Mar. 15 Where economy of space and/or money are important considerations a size of 33.53m × 16.46m (110ft × 54ft) which gives a 4.88m (16ft) run back is entirely adequate for the average home player.

3. *Amer. Football.* (See quot. 1976.)

1944 *Sun* (Baltimore) 6 Oct. 14/1 The 'one-man gang's' total net gain was 275 yards, 243 yards gained in 22 times carrying the ball from scrimmage, and 37 yards gained in two kickoff runbacks. **1949** *Lafayette Alumnus* (Lafayette Coll., Easton, Pa.) 24 Oct. 1/2 Winston Williams was outkicking Delaware's Smith and the Maroon had a slight edge on runbacks. **1971** L. Koppett *Guide to Spectator Sports* ii. 59 The receiving team can attempt a 'runback' at any time, even after a fumble. **1976** *Webster's Sports Dict.* 364/1 *Runback*,..a run made to advance the ball after catching a kick or punt or after intercepting a forward pass.

runcible (rʊ·nsib'l), *a.* [Prob. a fanciful alteration of Rouncival.] A nonsense word used by Edward Lear in *runcible cat, hat*, etc., and esp. in **runcible spoon**, in later use applied to a kind of fork used for pickles, etc., curved like a spoon and having three broad prongs of which one has a sharp edge.

The illustrations provided by Lear himself for his books of verse give no warrant for this later interpretation.

1871 E. Lear *Owl & Pussy-Cat* in *Nonsense Songs*, They dinèd on mince, and slices of quince, Which they ate with a runcible spoon. **1872** —— *More Nonsense* 235 The Dolomphious Duck, who caught Spotted Frogs for her dinner with a Runcible Spoon. **1877** —— *Laugh-*

able Lyrics 24 He has gone to fish, for his Aunt Jobiska's Runcible Cat with crimson whiskers! **1888** —— *Nonsense Songs & Stories* (ed. 6) 8 His body is perfectly spherical, He weareth a runcible hat. **1895** —— *Ibid.* (new ed.) 76 What a runcible goose you are! *Ibid.* 77 We shall presently all be dead, On this ancient runcible wall. **1926** *N. & Q.* 11 Dec. 430/2 A runcible spoon is a kind of fork with three broad prongs or tines, one having a sharp edge, curved like a spoon, used with pickles, etc. Its origin is in jocose allusion to the slaughter at the Battle of Roncevaux, because it has a cutting edge. *Ibid.*, Does a 'runcible' hat mean one of the sort called a trilby? In that case a 'runcible' spoon may be one with prongs or teeth. **1949** Partridge *Name into Word* 373 'He weareth a runcible hat.' Thus Edward Lear in 'Self-Portrait', where the hat is a 'topper' with a sharp rim. Now, a *runcible spoon* (Lear, 1871) is not a spoon at all but a pickle fork, broadly and triply tined, one tine being sharp-edged and curved like a spoon... The word *runcible* has been built in the architectural style of fencible; indeed, it may constitute a blend of Roncevaux and fencible (capable of defending). **1969** R. & D. De Sola *Dict. Cooking* 195/2 *Runcible spoon*, not a spoon but a fork with three broad curved prongs, used for serving appetizers. **1979** *Washington Post* 25 Mar. N6/2 A runcible spoon..is a large, slotted spoon with three thick, modified fork prongs at the bowl's end, and a cutting edge on the side.

run-down, *ppl. a.* Add: **3.** (Further example.) Also *transf.* of appliances not run by clock-work. Cf. also quot. 1866 at sense 5 below.

1974 A. Goddard *Vienna Pursuit* iv. 141 As though a run-down gramophone had been rewound, he went on. **1977** E. Ambler *Send no more Roses* x. 231 On the bench was a trickle charger with spring-clip connectors on long leads for attaching the thing to a run-down battery.

4. (Further examples.) *spec.* of districts, etc.: decayed, shabby, seedy.

1929 T. Wolfe *Look Homeward, Angel* xxxix. 612 He was offered employment..on the teaching staff of the run-down military academy. **1938** M. Brinig *May Flavin* iv. 369 The particular district was one of cheap run-down rooming houses. **1948** H. Lawrence *Death of Doll* iv. 75 Run-down neighbourhood but respectable; rooming houses and railroad flats. **1953** K. Tennant *Joyful Condemned* xxxii. 309 A run-down little suburban house with..a broken wooden verandah. **1962** A. Lurie *Love & Friendship* iv. 71 The streets of run-down two- or four-family frame houses. **1977** *New Yorker* 27 June 24/3 The church, a structure in American-Gothic style.. dominates a run-down neighborhood.

5. (Earlier and later examples.)

1866 Geo. Eliot *Let.* 12 Feb. (1956) IV. 232 George.. was a little benefited, but only a little. He is too far 'run down' to be wound up in a very short time. **1889** *Jrnl. Mental Sci.* XXXV. 200 Her general appearance gave the idea of being 'run down' in bodily health. **1916** [see *nervy *a.* 5]. **1927** C. Connolly *Let. c* 24 Jan. in *Romantic Friendship* (1975) 219, I am sorry you are run down. **1938** E. Waugh *Scoop* I. ii. 32 Once or twice when Mrs. Salter complained of being run down, they had visited prosperous resorts on the East Coast.

ru·ndown, *sb.* Also run-down and as two words. [f. Run *v.*] **1.** *U.S. Baseball.* An action whereby defensive players attempt to tag out a runner caught off base between them. Also *attrib.*, as *rundown play*.

1908 *Spalding's Base Ball Guide* 69 Chance forced Tinker and then working the steal stunt for a run down was put out. **1946** *Sun* (Baltimore) 27 May 15 (*caption*) Charlie Keller, the Yankee's slugger, is shown being caught in a rundown in the ninth inning of the first game. **1971** L. Koppett *N.Y. Times Guide Spectator Sports* i. 30 Less reprehensible mixups occur on rundown plays. **1978** *Detroit Free Press* 5 Mar. c 3/1 Chilly, wet weather prevented the pirates from a scheduled workout on pickoffs, rundowns and cutoff throws.

2. *U.S. horse-racing slang.* A list of entries and betting odds. Chiefly *attrib.* (see quot. 1942).

1935 *Sun* (Baltimore) 12 Jan. 7/8 Sergt. Ignatius Benesch, who led the raiders, said the bookmaking activities were being carried out on the second floor... Sergeant Benesch and his squad took several telephones and a quantity of run-down sheets to the station as evidence. **1942** Berrey & Van den Bark *Amer. Thes. Slang* §733/2 *Rundown board*, the bookmaker's board on which is posted the sheet of entries and odds; *rundown sheet, slate*, a list of entries and betting odds posted by a bookmaker. **1948** *Sun* (Baltimore) 17 Dec. 12/5 He observed Yateman making off with a board containing run-down sheets, while Hoffman was attempting to flee with a money bag and race-bet slips. **1951** *Publ. Amer. Dial. Soc.* xvi. 55 *Run down*,..the current change of odds in a booking establishment, caused by fluctuations of opinion or by a flurry of betting. *Ibid.* 56 *Run down sheet*,..a printed list provided for the patrons of the book. It contains the day's entries and the morning line odds and is used by the gambler to keep track of the fluctuations in odds.

3. *slang* (orig. *U.S.*) A (usu. verbal) listing of items of information; a summary or brief account of pertinent facts; a short description.

1945 *Sun* (Baltimore) 21 Feb. 7/4 In between taking care of the general's two uniforms..Orderly Powder gave inquiring correspondents a short rundown. **1949** *Tuscaloosa* (Alabama) *News* 8 Oct. 1/8 Here's a quick run-down of major disputes which already have made idle more than a million workers. **1953** *N.Y. Times* 29 June 29/1 A run-down on market conditions for various steel products follows. **1960** *Guardian* 21 Sept. 6/2 The movie guide provides a brief run-down on each film and assesses its suitability for children. **1966** T. Pynchon *Crying of Lot 49* v. 105 John Nefastis..brought out his Machine... 'You know how this works?' 'Stanley gave me a kind of rundown.' **1971** *Farmer & Stockbreeder* 23 Feb. 8/2 He gave a strangely fragmented rundown of British Rail policy as it affected horticulture in the West. **1977** I. Shaw *Beggarman, Thief* III. i. 184 I'm going to tell them they got to give me a complete rundown on the family.

4. A gradual and sustained reduction in the size or scope of an organization, enterprise, or activity.

1948 *Hansard Commons* 8 Mar. 931, I feel that the timing of the run-down [of the Navy] has not been very satisfactory. **1955** *Times* 5 Aug. 7/1 A few minor financial worries have also intruded. So far all have been surmounted, and the 'run down' of British forces is proceeding swiftly and smoothly. **1957** *Economist* 21 Dec. 1068/2 If informal agreements can be reached with newly independent Commonwealth countries about the pace of the run-down of their balances, so be it. **1960** *Guardian* 10 Nov. 3/3 The telegraph service again showed a deficit, but the rate of run-down in the traffic has been checked. **1973** *Listener* 14 June 785/3 By attracting people away from the city centre, they [*sc.* ringways] generate the run-down of the city centre. **1978** *Daily Mirror* 12 Jan. 2/2 They produced a report which could lead to an even swifter and more drastic rundown in the industry than has been planned.

rune². Add: **1.** (Further *transf.* examples.) Also, applied to a letter or character of a non-Germanic alphabet (esp. in fictional writings) having a resemblance to the Germanic runes.

1883 I. Taylor *Alphabet* 201 An adaptation or survival of the 'Slavonic Runes', the existence of which is however entirely hypothetical. **1937** J. R. R. Tolkien *Hobbit* i. 30 Look at the map..and you will see there the runes in red. **1948** D. Diringer *Alphabet* II. v. 314 The monumental inscriptions are written in a runic character, termed Kök Turki runes. **1954** J. R. R. Tolkien *Fellowship of Ring* v. 339 They were written by many different hands, in runes, both of Moria and of Dale, and here and there in Elvish script. **1958** *Everyman's Encycl.* (ed. 4) IX. 461/1 Orkhon Inscriptions (also known as Siberian, Early Turki, Pre-Islamic Turki or Kök Turki Runes) are the earliest epigraphical monuments written in Turki. **1961** M. Savill tr. *E. Doblhoffer's Voices in Stone* ix. 289 Babinger sent a photograph..to the decipherer of the Old Turkish runes, Vilhelm Thomsen. **1968** U. K. Le Guin *Wizard of Earthsea* iv. 67 He studied the Further Runes and the Runes of Éa, which are used in the Great Spells. *a* **1973** J. R. R. Tolkien *Silmarillion* (1977) 322 *Cirth*, the Runes, first devised by Daeron of Doriath.

2. c. (Further examples.) *spec.* a cryptic or magic verse, an incantation; a lament.

1870 D. G. Rossetti *I saw Sibyl at Cumæ* in *Coll. Wks.* (1886) I. vi. 378 'I saw the Sibyl at Cumæ' (One said)... 'She hung in a cage, and read her rune.' **1900** A. Carmichael *Carmina Gadelica* I. p. xx, The wife knew many secular runes, sacred hymns, and fairy songs. **1908** Somerville & 'Ross' *Further Experiences Irish R.M.* viii. 211 She chanted..words in measured cadence... By the time this rune had been repeated three times she was in the hall. **1922** Joyce *Ulysses* 203 There he keened a wailing rune.—*Pogue mahone! Acushla machree!* **1936** W. Holtby *South Riding* I. i. 20 Curses could be lifted by spells. Midge was always trying them, inventing her own runes and incantations. **1949** *New Yorker* 22 Oct. 38/2 (*title*) Runes for an old believer. **1973** G. M. Brown *Magnus* i. 23 Tana repeats a small bridal rhyme, a rune of fertility, the meaning of which is not at all clear but she has learned it from her grandmother. **1977** P. Fitzgerald *Knox Brothers* i. 32 Eddie had begun on Kennedy's Latin Grammar; there were more inexplicable runes for Wilfred to repeat in the nursery: 'Caesar adsum jam forte—Cæsar had some jam for tea.'

3. a. *rune-carver* (further examples), *-collector, -cutter, -rister* (further *arch.* example), *-singer, -writer* (further example).

c **1865** E. Charlton in *Archæologia Æliana* VI. 131 The ignorance of the Rune cutter has transposed one or two of the letters. **1883** Vigfusson & Powell *Corpus Poeticum Boreale* I. 571 Bali, a Swedish Rune carver from Upland, appears to have lived about the end or middle of the eleventh century. **1898** I. M. Anderton tr. *Comparetti's Trad. Poetry of Finns* I. i. 5 The first rune collectors..only considered and published detached songs, and did not think of classifying them. **1904** *Saga-Bk. of Viking Club* III. iii. 320 The..uniformity can only be explained by supposing that there were professional rune-writers, travelling over the country and inscribing stones. **1908** *Ibid.* V. ii. 258 To the right of the stem is an inequality in the stone, which the rune-cutter (*rune-rister*) apparently wished to avoid. **1927** E. V Gordon tr. runic inscription in *Introd. Old Norse* 170 Biari has the temple, a wise rune-carver. **1962** C. L. Wrenn in Davis & Wrenn *Eng. & Medieval Stud. presented to J. R. R. Tolkien* 316 If the 'first fronting' had in fact not yet been completed in the dialect of the rune-cutter. **1963** S. B. F Jansson in Browne & Foote *Early Eng. & Norse Stud.* ix. 112 In all probability the rune-carver wished his rune-ribbon to start and end at the same level on the stone. **1972** *Funk's Stand. Dict. Folklore* 382/1 Lönnrot himself said, 'Because I am sure that not one of the rune-singers could surpass me in the knowledge of the runes, I used my right to put together the songs as it seemed best.'

b. *rune font, -stone* (further examples).

1883 Vigfusson & Powell *Corpus Poeticum Boreale* II. 589 A Swedish Rune-stone has the roasting-scene of l. 4 carved upon it. **1931** *Times Lit. Suppl.* 9 July 548/1 The discovery of the Eggjum rune-stone in 1917. **1962** P. G. Foote tr. *S. V. B. Jansson's Runes of Sweden* 163 The finest of the rune fonts is the one..carved by the Gotlander Sigraf. **1980** K. Randsborg *Viking Age in Denmark* 32 The persons mentioned on the early rune-stones were connected with royal power.

c. *rune-inscription, -letter, -lore, -maiden, -master, -name, -poem, -song, -worship; rune-blazoned, -inscribed* (further example), *-like* (further example) adjs.; **rune-ribbon**, the carved scroll on a runic stone in which the runes are engraved; **rune-row**, a runic alphabet; **rune-tree**, (*a*) = *tree-rune* s.v. Tree *sb.* 10 c; (*b*) (see quot. 1899).

1938 W. de la Mare *Memory* 76 A subtle Serpent.. Raised its rune-blazoned head. **1898** *Saga-Bk. of Viking Club* II. ii. 337 Asfrid..raised a..gravehaugh over the body of her husband, whereon she set up a rune-inscribed stone in his honour. **1931** C. L. Ewen *Hist. Surnames* iii. 65 The rune-inscribed crosses. **1925** *Saga-Book of Viking Soc.* IX. ii. 272 The rune-inscriptions..must be assigned to the first part of the 11th century. **1937** J. R. R. Tolkien *Hobbit* iii. 64 'What are moon-letters?'.. 'Moon-letters are rune-letters.' **1965** C. L. Wrenn in Bessinger & Creed *Medieval & Linguistic Stud.* 50 The seven rune-like symbols just mentioned. **1868** G. Stephens *Runic Mon.* I. 94 (*heading*) Rune-lore. **1959** R. W. V. Elliott *Runes* iii. 30 Other pagan rites and customs that went hand in hand with rune-lore. **1906** C. M. Doughty *Dawn in Britain* I. ii. 80 Her covert image..and holy cart Shall her rune-maiden ministers, in the lake, Wash. **1965** R. Derolez in Bessinger & Creed *Medieval & Linguistic Stud.* 33 A simple formula such as..'unknown Danish runemaster > Hrabanus Maurus', is tempting but dangerous. *Ibid.* 34 One might..suppose that a 'rune master'..would resort to runes if asked to write the names in full. **1970** Foote & Wilson *Viking Achievement* ix. 312 Once the act of carving stone had developed in southern Scandinavia, Swedish sculptors and rune-masters experimented to bring it to fruition. **1879** I. Taylor *Greeks & Goths* xviii. 117 Let us compare these.. Ogham names with the corresponding rune names. **1927** E. V. Gordon *Introd. Old Norse* 161 The first letter of each rune-name gives the value of the rune. **1974** *Eng. Stud.* LV. 512 The inscriber of the Franks Casket normally represented the voiceless dorsal fricative by 'g', so that for him the rune-name would have been *eg*. **1861** D. H. Haigh *Anglo-Saxon Sagas* 16 In the Anglo-Saxon rune-poem, the following stanza occurs:- Ing wæs ærest, mid East-Denum, (etc.). **1879** Vigfusson & Powell *Icelandic Prose Reader* 457 The idea is..possibly taken from some such English poem as the Exeter Codex Rune Poem. **1962** C. L. Wrenn in Davis & Wrenn *Eng. & Medieval Stud. presented to J. R. R. Tolkien* 316 The Old English, Old Norse, and Icelandic rune-poems. **1963** S. B. F. Jansson in Browne & Foote *Early Eng. & Norse Stud.* ix. 111 All that was visible..was a short section of the rune ribbon, with some carved lines above it. **1868** G. Stephens *Runic Mon.* I. 105 All the *oldest* written Runerows are Futhorcs. **1955** J. R. R. Tolkien *Return of King* 397 It was often called *Angerthas Moria* or the Long Rune-rows of Moria. **1973** R. I. Page *Introd. Eng. Runes* xii. 190 The common English rune-row had twenty-eight [characters] or more to the Germanic twenty-four. **1868** G. Stephens *Runic Mon.* I. 105 As for there being any 'German' people whatsoever..who.. practist heathen rites and used Rune-songs and Rune-books and Rune-carvings in incantations and divinations —why the thing is ridiculous. **1892** S. A. Brooke *Hist. Early Eng. Lit.* I. 192 These phrases are from the *Rune Song*. **1927** E. V. Gordon *Introd. Old Norse* 161 The usual forms of this fuþark..are given in the Rune-Song. **1863** J. M. Mitchell tr. runic inscription in *Mesehowe* 51 Cut to our late Father these Rune Trees, (He was a) leader on the West Sea. **1879** I. Taylor *Greeks & Goths* xviii. 129 The characteristic of the five classes of the rune trees would be (1) branches; (2) forks; (3) loops; (4) crooks; (5) roots. **1899** A. H. Keane *Man, Past & Present* ix. 341 A great feature of the system were the 'rune-trees', made of pine or birch bark, inscribed with figures of gods, men, or animals, which were consulted on all important occasions. **1940** F. Scott Fitzgerald *Let.* Dec. (1964) 100 But be sweet to your mother at Xmas despite her early Chaldean rune-worship which she will undoubtedly inflict on you.

rune (rūn), *v. rare.* [f. Rune².] *intr.* To compose or perform poetry or songs; to lament.

1936 M. Franklin *All that Swagger* i. 7 He was wont to rune to himself as he sat alone, thrust aside by his sons as childish. **1964** Auden in *Listener* 1 Oct. 575/2 Our handful Of clients at least can rune.

Runge–Kutta (ru·ŋgə ku·ta). *Math.* The names of Carl David Tolme *Runge* (1856–1927) and Martin Wilhelm *Kutta* (1867–1944), German mathematicians, used *attrib.* to designate a method of approximating to solutions of differential equations.

1930 J. B. Scarborough *Numerical Math. Analysis* xiii. 274 In the special case where dy/dx is a function of x alone the Runge-Kutta method reduces to Simpson's rule. **1950** *High-Speed Computing Devices* (Engin. Res. Associates) vii. 128 By the Runge-Kutta method, the formulas which are applied are given below. **1975** *Nature* 9 Oct 516/2 Membrane action potentials were computed with Hodgkin-Huxley equations, modified for *Myxicola*, using a modified fourth-order Runge–Kutta algorithm, and the six-parameter model. **1980** *Daily Tel.* 16 Sept. 2 (Advt.), It has 128 program steps that fulfil practically every function a mathematician needs. From setting a program for the definite integral by the Simpson's rule.. to the Runge-Kutta method.

runic, *a.* and *sb.* Add: **A.** *adj.* **1. a.** (Further examples.)

1948 [see *rune² 1]. **1962** G. Clauson *Turkish & Mongolian Stud.* v. 72 The Runic alphabet is in a class by itself. **1968** W. S. Allen *Vox Graeca* i. 37 Special symbols are found only in the Old Germanic Runic and Old Celtic Ogham systems of writing. **1973** *Cassell's Encycl.*

World Lit. i. 412/1 *Orhon Inscriptions*, the most important of the oldest surviving specimens of the Turkish language. .. They are inscribed in the Turkish runic alphabet.

d. Of or pertaining to runes; concerned with runes.

1861 J. Farrer *Let.* 28 Sept. in J. M. Mitchell *Mesehowe* (1863) p. viii, I shall send one to an English Runic scholar. **1862** P. A. Munch in J. Farrer *Notice Runic Inscr. Orkneys* 29 In the later times of the Runic period. **1868** G. Stephens *Runic Mon.* I. 94 The 'Scandinavian Futhork' is..a peculiar modification and compendium of the common Runic traditions. *Ibid.* 410 This runic drama was not yet ended. **1881** *Yorkshire Archæol. & Topogr. Jrnl. 1879–80* 54 His learning was of a very varied character. 'Anglo-Saxon' and Runic lore was that by which he was best known. **1953** *Saga-bk. Viking Soc.* XIII. 281 Random runic studies in the eighteenth century. **1973** R. I. Page *Introd. Eng. Runes* i. 3 It was the scholars of the late seventeenth and early eighteenth centuries who put English runic studies on a sound basis. *Ibid.* 4 His [*sc.* George Hickes's] *Thesaurus* contained a large amount of runic material. *Ibid.*, Runic knowledge. *Ibid.* viii. 113 A living runic tradition there.

B. *sb.* **2. b.** One of the runic alphabets. Also in *pl.*, runic characters collectively (*rare*).

1863 J. M. Mitchell *Mesehowe* 32 It is probable that only one or two of the best educated in each ship could write or read the Runic. **1868** G. Stephens *Runic Mon.* I. 94, 4 of these [letters] (the h— for which the Runic prefers the Phœnician mark for ch—, the z, the gh and the sh) are more or less wanting in the Runic. *Ibid.* 157 In Scandinavian-runics, when the w had quite died out. *Ibid.* 159 In Scandinavian-runics the old rune for y lingers on for a time. **1886** T. Le Marchant Douse *Introd. Gothic of Ulfilas* I. 16 Of the foregoing letters, *urus* and *faihu* are runes..*bairka, eis, ôthal*, and perhaps, *quairthr*, common to runic and Greek. **1961** M. Savill tr. *E. Doblhoffer's Voices in Stone* ix. 280 The traveller discovered an impressive granite monument engraved with three inscriptions:.. the third in 'Siberian' runic. **1963** *Times* 4 June 14/6 And after thousands and thousands and thousands of years, and after Hieroglyphics, and Demotics, and Nilotics, and Cryptics, and Cufics, and Runics, and Dorics, and Ionics, and all sorts of other ricks and tricks..the fine old easy, understandable Alphabet—A, B, C, D, E, and the rest of 'em—got back into its proper shape again for all the Best Beloveds to learn when they are old enough.

runically, *adv.* [f. Runic *a.* + -al + -ly[2].] In a runic manner; with runes.

1920 *Times Lit. Suppl.* 28 Nov. 779/3 Runically inscribed objects contained in..better known public collections.

run-in. Also **run in. 1.** (See Run *sb.*[1] 8.)

2. *colloq.* (chiefly *U.S.*). A quarrel, argument, or row; a clash or fight. Usu. in phr. *to have a run-in* (*with* someone).

1905 'H. McHugh' *You can search Me* 82 Sorry we had the run in but it was all my fault. **1912** C. Mathewson *Pitching in a Pinch* viii. 180 Fred Tenny has said for a long time that Mr. Klem gives him a shade the worst of it on all close ones because he had a run in with that umpire one day when they came to blows. **1920** I. Ostrander *How Many Cards?* xii. 145 The cook at the de Forests' two doors away had a run-in with that Sarah, the butler's wife, and she won't speak to any of them. **1930** D. Runyon in *Collier's* 20 Dec. 32/3, I am all tired out..from getting a slug in my chest in the run-in with Jerk Donovan's mob in Jersey. **1945** G. Marx *Let.* 16 Feb. (1967) 50 Your father and I have many run-ins these days... He can't get it into his thick skull that I have come of age. **1952** A. Barin *With Hope, Farewell* 44, I 'ad a run-in with the caterers, too. **1962** A. Lurie *Love & Friendship* ii. 31, I had a run-in with the Administration about it last spring. **1979** 'A. Hailey' *Overload* I. iii. 19, I hear you had a run-in with Nancy Molineaux.

3. The approach of an aircraft to a dropping point or landing place; = *run-up 1 d.

1943 *Combined Operations* (Min. of Information) ii. 19 Two lights—a red switched on when the pilot is beginning his run-in to the dropping zone and a green indicating that the moment to jump has arrived. **1944** *Hutchinson's Pict. Hist. of War* 27 Oct. 1943–11 Apr. 1944. 366/2 An aircraft would be mortally wounded during its attacking run in but would not crash until after that attack had been well and truly pressed home. **1958** 'Castle' & 'Hailey' *Flight into Danger* x. 137 We must have plenty [of fuel] in hand for a long run-in over the ocean, if I decide..to ditch. **1958** P. Kemp *No Colours or Crest* (1960) v. 88 On the first run-in the aircraft would loose the containers and the 'free drops'. **1971** R. Dentry *Encounter at Kharmel* ix. 158 Alden reached his bedroom window in time to see the Cherokee..lose height for its run-in on to the strip.

4. An introductory statement or event; an approach (to a subject).

1961 *Clergy Rev.* Oct. 627 Mr Derrick provides a run-in to Fr Brown's story in the form of a Prologue. **1962** A. Nisbett *Technique Sound Studio* viii. 140 Remember not to start fading up until the run-in is complete. **1966** 'A. Hall' *9th Directive* i. 13 He sensed I would try to refuse the mission... He poured some more lime to give himself a last chance of planning his run-in. 'This is a special job,' he began.

5. *Criminals' slang.* A place to which stolen goods are driven and in which they are concealed.

1959 J. Gosling *Ghost Squad* iii. 43 He tipped us off to the whole plot, gave the address of the 'run-in'—the place where the stolen goods were cached—and the names of the thieves. *Ibid.* x. 130 The normal method was to hire a van from a small lorry-owner, run the van to the warehouse, break in, load the van, take the contents to a 'run-in'—usually a shed or garage in the central London area—and return the van. **1962** D. Warner *Death of Bogey* iv. v. 163 Just waiting to hear that the lorry reached the run-in. It's late. *Ibid.* 170 Sapper Neal and a bunch of the Sparrow boys been seen cruising around this manor in a car like they was looking for something. Is the run-in round here? **1970** P. Laurie *Scotland Yard* vi. 129 It's a run-in for stolen lorries.

6. *Comb.*, as **run-in groove**, on a gramophone record, the blank groove traversing the annular area outside the grooves carrying the recording; **run-in shed** *U.S.*, an open-fronted shelter in which horses are housed.

1962 A. Nisbett *Technique Sound Studio* viii. 146 If the disc is being played from the start, or if there is no sound definite enough to be used as a cue, it will be necessary to count the revolutions from the run-in groove. **1976** *Gramophone* Sept. 510/1 It..moves the stylus to the run-in groove of the record. **1964** *Blood-Horse* 26 Dec. 1874/1 Kelly has built a pair of L-shaped run-in sheds... The run-in sheds—unlike three sided Madden sheds used on many Blue Grass horse farms—are closed on only two sides, the north and west. **1977** J. W. Evans et al. *Horse* xxiii. 723 Flies, hot weather, cold rains, and strong, cold winds seem to bother horses, and run-in sheds provide adequate protection from these conditions.

runkle, *v.* Add: Also (*rare*) in colloq. use. Also with *up*.

1929 E. Bowen *Joining Charles* 188 She..pulled down the sofa loose-cover where it had 'runkled' up. **1958** M. Allingham *Hide my Eyes* viii. 85 He looked so neglected with his green tights runkled round his ankles.

runless (rʊ·nlės), *a.* [f. Run *sb.*[1] + -less.] In *Baseball* and *Cricket*: devoid of runs; unable to score.

1921 *Daily Colonist* (Victoria, B.C.) 7 Oct. 11/4 The New York Americans made world's series history today.. leaving the New York Nationals runless. **1963** *Times* 30 May 4/7 Devereux, a left-hander of medium pace, rendered the patient Tebay runless and strokeless for lengthy periods by the simple expedient of bowling a shade short of a good length.

runnel (rʊ·n'l), *v.* [f. Runnel[1].] *trans.* To form streams or channels in (a surface); to channel or furrow. Hence **ru·nnelled** *ppl. a.* Cf. Runnelling *a.*

1933 G. Barker *Thirty Preliminary Poems* 13 And sparkling veins Escape in dark wooded places Runnelling like willow trees The lachrymose moist soil. **1947** *New Writing* XXXI. 164 Their faces were black with coal dust, runnelled with sweat. **1970** R. J. Small *Study of Landforms* ix. 309 These pediments were..usually 'runnelled', and dissections of up to 15–20 ft in depth were not uncommon. **1977** P. Scupham *Hinterland* 19 A disenfranchised demon wears His runnelled face in sour grotesque, A conduit for the tumbling skies.

runner. Add: **I. 1. d.** *N.Amer.* One who chases or hunts buffalo. Now *Hist.* Cf. Run *v.* 42 a in Dict. and Suppl.

1837 W. Irving *Captain Bonneville* I. xvii. 286 'It was a beautiful sight,' says the captain, 'to see the runners, as they are called, advancing in column, at a slow trot, until within two hundred and fifty yards of the outskirts of the herd, then dashing on at full speed, until lost in the immense multitude of buffaloes.' *Ibid.* II. xi. 173 The 'runners', then, as they are called, mounted on fleet horses, and armed with bows and arrows, moved slowly and cautiously toward the buffalo. **1974** *Publishers Weekly* 11 Mar. 46/2 The early buffalo runners (hunters).

e. *Baseball.* = *base runner* s.v. *Base *sb.*[1] 20 b.

1845 [see *balk *sb.*[1] 5 b]. **1857** *Spirit of Times* 7 Feb. 372/3 Mr. Thos. Leavy..mans the first base, and rare it is, that a runner reaches the first base, if the ball is passed up quickly. **1948** *Lawton* (Oklahoma) *Constitution* 4 July 12/2 If the pitcher doesn't keep the runners close to base, the best catcher in baseball can't throw them out.

f. *Cricket.* One who runs on behalf of a disabled batsman. (Cf. *Run *v.* 1 h.)

1862 J. Pycroft *Cricket Tutor* 4 Having the luck to be lamed by a sprain, I was allowed a runner. **1908** W. E. W. Collins *Leaves from Old Country Cricketer's Diary* xiii. 219 Once, then, only in my life have I acted as runner for another batsman. **1971** *Times* 16 Feb. 7/6 His knee is stiff..and unless it improves he may need the help of a runner.

g. *N. Amer.* One who runs ahead of a dog-sledge in order to find or clear a path in snow.

1867 *Ann. Rept. Smithsonian Inst. 1866* 309 The man was a famous runner, and despite the disadvantage of small tripping snow-shoes..he would have reached the houses before them had not the line that confined the snow-shoe on his foot broken. **1921** *Beaver* (Winnipeg) June 27/2 The 'runner's' duty is to travel in front of the dogs picking out and breaking the trail. It is also his duty to clear away with an axe any trees which may have been blown across the road. **1930** L. Munday *Mounty's Wife* iv. 60 [We] were making a trip..without a runner (that is, an Indian guide who goes ahead of the dogs to break trail). **1971** T. Boulanger *Indian Remembers* 62 From Norway House..the runner was Old John Clark... In Berens River..the runner was Donald Bittern.

3. a. (Further examples.) Also used to designate one whose employment also involves the fetching and carrying of articles; an assistant; *spec.* in *U.S.* prison terminology, a prisoner entrusted with special duties; *Mil.* an orderly; a soldier who carries messages, esp. along the front line.

1830 *5th Ann. Rep. Boston Prison Discipline Soc.* 7 [At the Charlestown prison] there is, however, a class of men, consisting of ten or twelve, called *runners* and *lumpers*, whose duty consists in moving about the yard. **1912** T. Dreiser *Financier* lxvi. 679 Some of the prisoners, after long service were used as 'trusties' or 'runners', as they were locally called; but not many. **1917** G. S. Gordon *Let.* 13 Feb. (1943) 69, I was searching for the Hqs. of a Battn. and there wasn't a living soul above ground to ask except myself and my runner. **1929** R. C. Sherriff *Journey's End* III. iii. 116 Stanhope sits at the table and begins to write a short report... Stanhope calls 'Runner!' as he writes. A soldier comes from the servants' dug-out. **1933** *Sun* (Baltimore) 17 Apr. 14/4 Clifton had been assigned to the odd-jobs duties of a 'runner' on the first floor of the south wing, where both his and Kellam's cells were located. **1960** J. Grant *Come again, Nurse* xxvii. 180 The theatre runner opened the doors and said quietly: 'Mr. Spindells has arrived, sir.' **1974** *Guidelines to Volunteer Services* (N.Y. State Dept. Correctional Services) 43 *Runner*, inmate whose job is to deliver things around the prison. **1976** F. Warner *Killing Time* I. i. 6 I'd sooner be in the assembly trench waiting to go over the top than a runner. **1976** 'W. Trevor' *Children of Dynmouth* v. 100 Mrs Abigail took round Meals on Wheels with Miss Poraway as her assistant, or runner, as the title officially was.

e. (Earlier and later examples.) Also *spec.* one who provides custom for a lawyer.

1824 *Microscope* (Albany, N.Y.) 21 Feb 183/3 Our wholesale property-speculators and their gentry in livery, called *runners*. **1836** C. R. Gilman *Life on Lakes* I. 31 [At Oswego] a struggle began between the runners of the two boats. **1948** *Chelsea* (Massachusetts) *Record* 30 Nov. 8/7 Unethical lawyers, plus their hired 'runners', probation officers, jail attaches and police officers were 'selling' justice in the courthouse corridors to ignorant criminal defendants. **1951** *Life* 25 June 119/1 [They] employed 15 runners to give school children free samples of heroin and ridicule those who wouldn't try it as 'squares'. **1974** *Times* 21 Jan. 6/6 If there is a car crash, one of the first people on the scene is likely to be a 'runner', who has heard about it by tuning in to police radio frequencies. He will point out that the victim needs a lawyer immediately, and will sign him up with one on the spot.

f. A freelance antique dealer.

1969 R. Quest *Cerberus Murders* xxviii. 153 He was a free-lance—the trade term is 'runner'—picking up antiquities here and there and selling them at a profit. **1976** G. Sims *End of Web.* xii. 86 Klein is a sort of runner.. buys things in the country and sells them to West End dealers. **1978** *Observer* 16 Apr. 38/3 There are 'runners' going from shop to shop, detecting the margin of a bargain and taking the merchandise one step nearer to Bond Street.

4. b. *N.Amer.* A horse trained for hunting buffalo. Now *Hist.* (Cf. sense 1 d above.)

1858 J. Palliser *Jrnl.* 31 July (1863) 90 Breakfast finished, our 'runners' saddled and mounted, the whole party moved slowly on... Having ascended the slightly elevated ridge we then beheld our game, four or five thousand buffalo. **1971** J. McDougall *Parsons on Plains* viii. 63 From all parts of the camp riders came forth, many of them leading their runners, so as to have them as fresh as possible for the coming race.

c. *transf.* A roadworthy motor vehicle; phr. *good runner*, a motor vehicle which runs well.

1948 Partridge *Dict. Forces' Slang 1939–1945* 159 *Runner*, a vehicle that was in running order, as opposed to one that was off the road. **1972** *Fairbanks* (Alaska) *Daily News-Miner* 3 Nov. 23/7 (Advt.), '67 Chrysler Newport, stick shift, winterized, a good runner. $750. **1975** *Drive* Spring 40/2 We were asked to collect a car from a chap who had stripped it to service an identical second car... We found a car standing in the drive. So naturally we took it. But it was the runner we towed away. The wreck was in the garage. **1978** *Cornish Guardian* 27 Apr. 22 (Advt.), Peugeot 204 Saloon. Sun roof. Good runner.

5. e. Substitute for def.: Any of several carangid fishes found in tropical or temperate seas, esp. *Elagatis pinnulatus, Caranx crysos* (= *hardtail a), or *C. ruber*.

1884 [see Shoemaker 2 a]. **1902** [see *hardtail a]. **1905** D. S. Jordan *Guide Study of Fishes* II. xvii. 272 Most like the true mackerel are the 'leather-jackets', or 'runners', forming the genera *Scomberoides* and *Oligoplites*. **1913** C. F. Holder *Game Fishes of World* xxii. 211 There are a number of smaller allied fishes which are game in every sense, if taken with appropriate tackle, as the Runner (*Caranx crysos*). **1952** L. L. Mowbray in J. O. La Gorce *Bk. Fishes* (rev. ed.) 210 The runner (bottom—*Caranx ruber*) ranges throughout the West Indies and Florida, and strays northward along the southern United States. *Ibid.*, The runner and other jacks are the terror of small fishes. **1966** Leim & Scott *Fishes Atlantic Coast of Canada* 247 Blue runner. *Caranx crysos* (Mitchill). *Ibid.* 248 Although there are few actual records it is believed that the blue runner occurs sparingly along the Nova Scotian coast in the late summer months. **1975** J. G. Walls *Fishes Northern Gulf of Mexico* 201 Rainbow runner. *Elagatis bipinnulata* (Quoy & Gaimard)... A popular sportfish which is not uncommon offshore.

f. *U.S.* A black snake, the racer, *Coluber constrictor*.

1795 T. Todd *Let.* Feb. in S. Williams *Nat. & Civil Hist. Vermont* (1809) I. 485 In a field in Connecticut..I approached with caution within twenty feet of a black snake, about seven feet long, having a white throat, and of the kind which the people there call runners. **1855** W. G. Simms *Forayers* xxxix. 456 Push forward, quick as a runner (black snake).

g. In full, *runner duck*. A small white or fawn duck belonging to the breed so called and distinguished by an erect posture.

1895 W. Cook *Ducks* (rev. ed.) 96 Many cross-bred Indian Runner ducks have been sold as pure. **1900** *Reliable Poultry Jrnl.* Apr. 207/2 The Runners are particularly adapted to the market poultry man's needs. **1918** E. A. Taylor *Runner Ducks* ii. 15 The Runner Duck differs from all other breeds in that it has an upright carriage, which ensures the running gait. **1921** *Daily Colonist* (Victoria, B.C.) 29 Oct. 4/3 Anyone who has used runner ducks' eggs can hardly discern in cooking the difference between these and hens' eggs. **1937** [see *Kerry[2]]. **1960** L. Bonnet *Pract. Duck-Keeping* xiii. 116 The Indian Runner was the prolific layer of the duck world.

6. Also *spec.* = *run-boat* s.v. *Run *sb.*[1] 4 a. *U.S.*

1881 E. Ingersoll *Oyster Industry* 164 Another branch of the trade conducted by vessels, generally known as runners... The runner will anchor near some tonging-ground, and an empty basket or a small flag will be hoisted to the masthead as a signal that she is ready to receive oysters. **1890** [in Dict.].

7. a. Also freq. with qualifying sb.: see *gun-runner* s.v. Gun *sb.* 15, *rum-runner* s.v. *Rum *sb.*[1] 3, etc. Also *slang* (chiefly *U.S.*), one engaged in conveying prohibited goods (as drugs, liquor) secretly.

1930 *Amer. Mercury* Dec. 457/2 *Runner*, one who transports liquor from the border to inland towns. 'He's a torpedo for a big runner.' **1963** T. Tullett *Interpol* v. 65 Members of the gang, known as 'runners', were sent to Paris, or Marseilles, to pick up the drug. **1963** *Amer. Speech* XXXVIII. 276 A student is not permitted to buy liquor; hence, should he want some, he must find someone to obtain it for him. Such an intermediary is termed a *runner*. **1971** E. E. Landy *Underground Dict.* 163 *Runner*,.. person carrying a drug between buyer and seller.

8. c. (Earlier and further examples.) Also, the leader of a (freq. Black) street gang.

1874 M. N. Forney *Catechism of Locomotive* 547 Every locomotive runner should..have an exact knowledge of the engine intrusted to him. **1893** M. Holley *Samantha at World's Fair* i. 4 His parents..[were] good respectable..people..and runners of a cheese factory. **1945** F. H. Hubbard *Railroad Avenue* ii. 9 Dispatchers regarded him as a 'fast roller', a runner who could be depended upon to get his train over the road 'on the card'. **1962** *Amer. Speech* XXXVII. 135 *Runner*,..a locomotive engineer. **1972** C. H. Fuller in W. King *Black Short Story Anthol.* 142 'He coulda' done you in,' Rosalee enjoined... 'He's the *runner* of Tenth and Montgomery—Reuben is 'Little Blood', girl!' *Ibid.* 145 'Durango,' the *runner*, stood to the rear of his troops and when they were ready nodded to 'Cornbread' the warlord, who moved to the center of the street screaming challenges. **1973** *Philadelphia Inquirer* (Today Suppl.) 14 Oct. 29/1 Often nobody even knows who the runner (gang leader) is.

II. 9. d. = *Run *sb.*[1] 13 g.

1928 L. North *Parasites* 42 His quick eye detected a neatly darned spot near the heel of one, and a laboriously-checked runner in the other. **1931** M. de la Roche *Finch's Fortune* xvii. 257 Alayne noticed a long 'runner' on the shoulder of her knitted jumper. **1942** in H. Wentworth *Amer. Dial. Dict.* (1944) 525/1 She wears my finest evening gowns, gets runners in my hose.

10. e. A tool used in decorating pottery (see quots.).

1893 E. A. Barber *Pottery & Porcelain of U.S.* i. 9 Incised ornamentation is sometimes added by the use of a small wheel, bearing an engraved device on the edge, called the 'runner', which is held in a frame. **1974** Savage & Newman *Illustr. Dict. Ceramics* 250 *Runner*, a pointed tool used to decorate the body of a piece of pottery while it is cheese-hard and revolving on the potter's wheel.

f. The rotor or wheel of a turbine.

1908 S. F. Walker *Steam Boilers, Engines & Turbines* v. 317 The moving wheels or runners consist of wrought-steel discs. **1916** R. L. Daugherty *Hydraulics* xi. 179 The part of the turbine upon which the water does its work is called the runner. **1947** G. F. Wislicenus *Fluid Mech. Turbomachinery* i. 1 The most essential part of all types of turbomachinery is a vane-carrying rotating element, the 'runner', operating inside a stream of fluid or under its influence. **1972** J. M. K. Dake *Essent. Engin. Hydraulics* vi. 172 These concepts are applied to the runner of reaction pumps.

13. b. Also *spec.* in *Mountaineering* = *running belay* s.v. *Running *ppl. a.* 23 c.

1956 C. Evans *Kanchenjunga* xii. 126 Runner—a 'running belay' made by threading the climber's rope through a ring fixed to the mountain. **1956** [see *chock *sb.*[1] 8]. **1971** D. Haston in C. Bonington *Annapurna South Face* xvii. 206 The rope ran out so I tied all my aid slings and runners together. **1973** C. Bonington *Next Horizon* xii. 179 I'm thirty feet above my last runner, time for another but the skin of ice is too thin to take ice screws.

14. a. (Earlier example.)

1747 [see *sleigh runner* s.v. Sleigh *sb.* 4].

c. orig. *U.S.* A long narrow strip of (freq. embroidered) cloth, usu. placed along or across a table as an ornament.

1889 *Harper's Bazar* 20 Apr. 284/2 (*caption*) Embroidered table runner. *Ibid.* (Suppl.) 2/4 The cream-colored canvas grenadine centre of this table runner is a yard and three quarters long and twelve inches wide. **1904** *Buffalo Commercial* 2 June 6 Two long linen runners, one each way of the table, are now used in preference to the whole cloth or doilies. **1922** *Daily Mail* 11 Dec. 14 The illustrated table runner..was decorated at each end with a simple design. **1932** *Modern Weekly* 5 Mar. 997 Such a lovely runner to add a freshening touch to your dining-table. **1974** M. Ingate *Sound of Weir* ii. 11 On the lace runner on the dressing table was a photograph.

d. A long narrow rug or strip of carpet, used esp. in a hall or on a staircase.

1901 J. K. Mumford *Oriental Rugs* vii. 95 *Makatlik*, or 'runners'.—These are what we know as 'hall' or 'stair' rugs. **1910** S. Humphries *Oriental Carpets, Runners & Rugs* 251, I have used the term 'runners', instead of 'strips' (as some call them), because the latter description might lead one to suppose that only a fragment of a carpet was intended, whereas the runner is distinct and complete in itself... Runners are, in fact, very long rugs. **1918** V. O. Freeburg *Art of Photoplay Making* 236 He tries the stairs vaguely again, and, losing his balance at the top, grasps the 'runner' which pulls loose and wraps itself around him as he rolls down. **1937** M. Allingham *Dancers in Mourning* xvi. 200 Petals lay on the imitation parquet..and on the imitation Persian runner in the hall. **1947** [see *body carpet* s.v. *body *sb.* 30]. **1955** C. Smith *Speaking Eye* xiii. 140 The corridor was yellow with a pale green runner. **1960** *News Chron.* 12 Sept. 6/4 A good buy in Oriental carpeting is the..runner. **1972** 'H. Carmichael' *Naked to Grave* i. 8 The entrance hall had a runner of royal-blue carpet down the centre with parquet flooring on either side. **1977** *Times* 9 Sept. 16/3 In the carpet section a rare pair of Shiraz runners were bought..for £1,500.

15. a. (Earlier and later examples.)

1815 *Niles' Reg.* IX. 201/2 [We] moved the one-half of the arch off sideways, forty-six feet, on to the runners one hundred and eighty-five feet long. **1939–40** *Army & Navy Stores Catal.* 1077/2 Curtain fittings... 'Huntband' Glide... 4 Runners to the foot. **1952** Granville *Dict. Theatrical Terms* 155 *Runner*,..a curtain track. **1960** *Practical Wireless* XXXVI. 328/2, 1 nylon ball-bearing curtain runner.

b. A long horizontal beam, girder, or other member (see quots.).

1891 *Notes on Building Constr.* (new ed.) II. x. 216 The capsills or 'runners' [of a gantry]..are supported by struts. **1932** Dowsett & Bartle *Pract. Formwork & Shuttering* i. 1 Propped shuttering [for floors] consists, generally, of 'sheeting' or 'decking' laid on joists..supported by heavier timbers, called 'binders' or 'runners', resting on upright 'props'. **1960** O. Skilbeck *ABC of Film & TV* 112 *Runners*, overhead girders with their depending tackle, from which, on modern stages, lamps and even complete prefabricated sets are hung. **1968** *Gloss. Formwork Terms* (*B.S.I.*) 21 *Runner*. 1. A longitudinal member spanning across a number of support members to lace them together. 2. One of a pair of supports running parallel to the axis of the centering for a deep arch or tunnel. One runner is above the other and they are separated by folding wedges. 3. See 'ledger' [= a horizontal timber supported on posts or hangers and carrying joists].

c. (See quot. 1940.)

1891 *Notes on Building Constr.* (new ed.) II. x. 209 Sometimes in very bad soil long planks called 'runners', having sharp ends shod with iron, are substituted for the poling boards. **1928** W. Simpson *Foundations* vii. 176 When test pits are of considerable depth, say, 40 ft., it is necessary to 'double set' the timbers, in which case two, or more sets of runners are used to reach the bottom. **1940** *Chambers's Techn. Dict.* 734/2 *Runners*, a form of sheet pile much used for timbering wide excavations. It consists of short planks shaped to a chisel point at one end and usually shod with thin steel strip, so that as each runner is driven in, it wedges up against its neighbour. **1963** M. J. Tomlinson *Foundation Design & Construction* ix. 538 In water-bearing sands and silts continuous support will have to be given to the face by means of timber runners or poling boards or by steel trench sheets or sheet piling.

18*. *Typogr.* (See quot. 1956.)

1888 C. T. Jacobi *Printers' Vocab.* 117 *Runners*, figures or letters placed down the length of a page to indicate the particular number or position of any given line. **1926** W. H. Slater *What Compositor should Know* III. 16 Runners are generally used in translations, and then only when the author has written a running commentary on the peculiarities of the original. **1956** *Bookman's Conc. Dict.* 259/2 *Runners*, letters or figures placed in the margin of a page opposite lines at regular intervals for assistance in reference (especially in poetry).

runnerless (rʌ·nəɹlĕs), *a.* [f. Runner 12 + -less.] Of a strawberry plant, esp. an alpine one: not producing runners.

1956 *Dict. Gardening* (R. Hort. Soc.) *Suppl.* 118/2 Baron Solemacher. (Alpine.) This is runnerless and makes large plants. **1957** E. Hyams *Speaking Garden* ix. 114 The most useful of these [mutants]..was a runnerless strawberry. **1981** *Country Life* 25 June 1846/2 The new French Bordurella perpetual [strawberry], virtually runnerless, and therefore a suitable plant for flower borders.

runner-up. Add: Also runnerup; pl. runners-up, runner-ups. **1. b.** (Further examples.)

1949 *Cavalier Daily* (Univ. of Virginia) 22 Oct. 1/3 The last issue of the magazine will announce the award winner and the runner-ups. **1955** *Times* 16 May 13/4 Miss Garvey, twice runner-up was unable to play. **1976** *Burnham-on-Sea Gaz.* 20 Apr., Highbridge soccer team Bristol Bridge look like losing their chance of finishing runners-up in the second division of the Bridgwater and District Sunday Football League. **1976** *Billings* (Montana) *Gaz.* 27 June 8-F/6 Other accomplished cowboys attending the rodeo include Royce Smith..who was runnerup for the world title twice.

c. *transf.* and *fig.*

1932 *New Yorker* 11 June 24/3 Blyth Daly is the horsy young lady who serves as runner-up to the Brat in offensiveness. **1949** *Sat. Rev. Lit.* (U.S.) 11 June 38/2 It was a 'runner-up' for the *Herald Tribune* award. **1974** *Times* 9 Nov. 10/5 Shirley Gee's *Stones* was runner up in the *Radio Times* play competition.

3. *attrib.*, as *runner-up list, prize.*

1925 *Scribner's Mag.* Oct. 384/1 At the tournament dance..he was called out for the runner-up prize in the fourth division. **1976** *National Observer* (U.S.) 18 Dec. 6/4 Britain's Queen Elizabeth II and Prince Philip made the runner-up list, as did Alistair Cooke, Shirley MacLaine, [etc.].

running, *vbl. sb.* Add: **I. 1. a.** Also *spec.* in *Cricket*, the action of making runs; also in phr. *running between* (*the*) *wickets*.

1744 *Laws* [of Cricket] in *New & Compl. Dict. Arts & Sci.* (1755) IV. 3460/1 They [*sc.* the Umpires] are sole judges of all hindrances, crossing the players in running, and standing unfair to strike. **1833** *New Sporting Mag.* V. *Cricketers' Reg.* 12 The steady manner in which Pilch bowled rendered the running very difficult throughout. **1877** *Encycl. Brit.* VI. 580/1, 21 Or if in running the wicket be struck down by a throw..before his bat (in hand) or some part of his person be grounded over the popping crease. **1897** *Encycl. Sport* I. 225/2 The art of running between wickets, without coming to a misunderstanding with one's partner, is indispensable. *Ibid.* 226/1 Every information should be given to one's partner that may help him in running. **1906** A. E. Knight *Compl. Cricketer* ii. 87 Some of the best running between wickets ever witnessed has been shown by Australian teams, who rarely miss a possible run. **1963** A. Ross *Australia 63* vii. 151 Catching and running between the wickets apart, England had at least given as good as they had got. **1976** *Milton Keynes Express* 23 July 39/3 David Berrill and Finch with some firm strokes and quick running between the wickets took the score to 61 all out after 17.3 overs.

2. a. Also *fig.* of a person, the action of standing as a candidate or competing (*for* an office). Cf. Run *v.* 7 b. orig. *U.S.*

1830 *Wiscasett* (Maine) *Citizen* 20 Aug. 3/2 Such politicians..bet on a candidate's running for the Chief Magistracy of the Union or of a single State, precisely as they would bet on the running of a race horse. **1870** *Nation* (N.Y.) 7 July 1/1 He has never failed in getting such offices as he wanted, the record of his 'running' being about as good as that of any man in the country. **1910** *Sat. Even. Post* 24 Dec. 16/2 There was less excuse for his running on the liquor ticket. **1961** T. H. White *Making of President 1960* iv. 86 Kennedy..felt that running for the Presidency was his most important full-time business and Senate attendance took second place.

c. (*d*) (further examples).

1923 Galsworthy *Captures* 161 Dinner was certainly a disharmonic feast: little Mrs Weymouth..and the Countess subdued, Radolin artificial, our scoundrel and myself had to make the running. **1954** I. Murdoch *Under Net* v. 80 'Where did you meet Madge?' I asked. I wasn't going to let him make all the running. **1958** *Times* 13 Sept. 7/2 First Russia turns on the heat in the Middle East and then it is China's turn to make the running. **1971** *Sunday Nation* (Nairobi) 11 Apr. 18/1 When he begins courting, he is unsure of himself, half-frightened of the girl, so she has to make the running. **1977** B. Freemantle *Charlie Muffin* vi. 65 You'll have to be bloody careful. Let Kalenin make the running.

e. (Further *fig.* examples.) Similarly, *in the running*. Also const. *for* (some prize or objective).

(*a*) **1906** *Dialect Notes* III. 149 'Isn't Jack sweet on the girl I saw with that fellow?' 'No, he's out of the running.' **1918** Galsworthy *Five Tales* 304 When a man is very old and quite out of the running, he loves to feel secure from the rivalries of youth, for he would still be first in the heart of beauty. **1930** G. B. Shaw *Apple Cart* I. 34, I think I am in the running. That is why I do not feel bound to accept this ultimatum. By signing it I put myself out of the running. **1949** M. Mead *Male & Female* xvi. 341 His married daughter, who with each step that she takes towards maturity puts him more definitely out of the running.

(*b*) **1886** H. Baumann *Londinismen* 162/2. *c* **1926** 'Mixer' *Transport Workers' Song Bk.* 65 And I never strike a top-job That the other fellows get, For I'm out upon my 'lonesome', And not in the running yet. **1930** W. S. Maugham *Cakes & Ale* xi. 120 It may be that posterity will scrap all the best-sellers of our day, but it is among them that it must choose. At all events Edward Driffield is in the running. **1950** W. Cooper *Scenes from Provincial Life* IV. ii. 235 It was one of the events in which Frank was hoping to shine, since he was in the running for victor ludorum. **1975** N. Blakiston in C. Connolly *Romantic Friendship* 5, I was in the running for playing in the school eleven.

7. d. With *out*. The disappearance of the characteristics of a particular variety of a crop.

1891 *Proc. Western N.Y. Hort. Soc.* 86 By 'running out' is meant the disappearance of the characteristics of any variety... Running out, therefore, is not necessarily deterioration. **1918** Babcock & Clausen *Genetics in Relation to Agric.* xviii. 340 The so-called 'running-out' of varieties can be prevented by reasonable care to avoid mixing seed and by occasional mass selection from the field. **1949** C. C. Lindegren *Yeast Cell* xxvii. 2 The degeneration or 'running out' of hybrids showing heterosis has been one of the principal problems of hybrid vigor. **1952** tr. *Gram & Weber's Plant Dis.* 361/2 (*heading*) 'Running out' or 'decline' of strawberry crops.

e. With *off*. = *run-off 4.

1921 *Jrnl. Pomol.* II. 160 Investigations relating to the 'Running off' or dropping of Black Currant Fruits before they are ripe. **1939** H. Wormald *Dis. Fruits & Hops* ix. 181 Running off is not caused by a parasite, but is a result of defective pollination.

II. 11. c. (Later examples.)

1832 D. J. Browne *Sylva Amer.* 232 The scraping is a coating of sap which becomes solid before it reaches the boxes, and which is taken off in the fall and added to the last runnings. **1872** *Trans. Dept. Agric. Illinois* IX. 73, I have a plantation five or six years old, parts of which still grow fine fruit, with two runnings annually.

V. 15. c. *U.S. colloq.* Teasing; scolding. Cf. RUN *v.* 52 c in Dict. and Suppl.

1832 S. SMITH *Life & Writings Major Jack Downing* (1833) 158, I feel a little put out with Dr Burnham for an unhansome running he gave me 'tother day. **1902** J. CORBIN *Amer. at Oxford* ii. 16 The freshman breakfast is nothing in the world but a variation of the 'running' that is given newcomers in those American colleges where fraternity life is strong. **1936** *Nat. Geogr. Mag.* LXIX. 799/1 Much of this 'running', or badgering, is in the spirit of fun.

d. *running in*, the process of operating a new machine (*spec.* the engine of a motor vehicle) at reduced power in order to establish proper working.

1935 *Jrnl. R. Aeronaut. Soc.* XXXIX. 159 Tapered piston rings reduce the running-in period considerably. **1963** R. F. WEBB *Motorists' Dict.* 189 The object of running-in is to enable microscopic irregularities in the working surfaces to become burnished. **1968** 'M. FINCH' *Eye with Mascara* viii. 80 A little rev-up from time to time is good for running-in.

16. b. *log running*: see *LOG *sb.*[1] 9.

VI. 17. a. *running clothes, costume, costs, drawers, expenses, ground* (earlier and later examples), *pants, shorts, suit, track, vest*; **running brand** *U.S.*, a cattle brand made with a running iron (see next); also = next; **running iron** *U.S.*, a straight branding iron used (freq. illegally) for altering cattle brands; also *fig.*; **running light,** (*a*) *Naut.* = *navigation light* s.v. *NAVIGATION 8; (*b*) one of a set of small lights located on the front, rear, or sides of a motor vehicle that remain illuminated during the running of the vehicle (see quots.); **running order,** (*a*) a condition in which a machine, etc., will function; (also qualified by *well, badly,* etc.); the condition in which a road, etc. is fit to be used (cf. *working order* s.v. WORKING *vbl. sb.* 16 b; (*b*) *Theatre* and *Broadcasting* the sequence in which scenes or parts of a programme are presented; **running shoe,** a (freq. spiked) shoe for running (usu. *pl.*); also *fig.*, esp. in (orig. *N.Z.*) phr. *to give* (one) *his running shoes* (see quots.); **running time,** (*a*) (earlier example); (*b*) the time occupied by the running of a machine, performance, etc.; so, a schedule. Also *RUNNING BOARD.

1884 SWEET & KNOX *On Mexican Mustang through Texas* xii. 160 The other, called a running brand, is a long piece of iron curved at the end. **1934** *Denver* (Colo.) *Post* 4 Aug. 10/3 A running brand..[is] a brand made with a straight poker called a 'running iron', and used like a pencil. *a* **1727** in *Gentl. Mag.* (1791) LXI. I. 199 No money allowed when I run any way under twenty miles. To find my own stockings and pumps, and to have my running clothes washed in the house. **1916** W. OWEN *Let.* 14 Mar. (1967) 385, I shall consider my running clothes as my Birthday Present. **1907** *Sports Trades Jrnl.* X. 25 (Advt.), Running costumes. **1913** *Autocar Handbk.* (ed. 5) i. 14 Depreciation is a large item generally included amongst running costs. **1979** *Homes & Gardens* June 153/2 Keep running costs to a minimum by placing the freezer in a cool, well ventilated room and ensuring that it is full. **1903** *Sports Trades Jrnl.* III. 101 (Advt.), Running drawers, running vests. **1904** *N.Y. World Mag.* 1 May 6/6 This does not include running expenses. **1744** *Laws* [of Cricket] in *New Dict. Arts & Sci.* (1755) IV. 3459/2 When the ball is hit up, either of the strikers may hinder the catch in his running ground. **1927** E. V. GORDON *Introd. Old Norse* 196 Let the adventurous steed of the sand's heaven explore the broad running-ground of ships. **1894** *McClure's Mag.* July 101/2 The running-irons, or *guachos*,..are now considered bad form by progressive cattlemen. **1913** L. V. KELLY *Range Men* 16 But the running or round iron was most favored, as it was easily and secretly made by cutting a wagon-iron in two and using the rounded end. **1945** *Everybody's Digest* Aug. 89 Of a dying man, the puncher might say: 'Death's got the runnin' iron on him brandin' him for the Eternal Range.' **1968** R. F. ADAMS *Western Words* 261/1 *Running iron*, a branding iron made in the form of a straight poker or a rod curved at the end... In the 1870's a law was passed in Texas forbidding the use of this iron in branding. This was a blow aimed at the brand blotter, whose innocent single iron would tell no tales. **1881** *Naval Encycl.* 439/2 *Light*,..the term for all lamps or lanterns used on ship-board; as, *running lights, signal-lights, mast-head lights*, etc. **1948** R. DE KERCHOVE *Internat. Maritime Dict.* 613/1 *Running lights*, a general term applied to the various lights carried from sunset to sunrise by different classes of vessels when under way. **1971** M. TAK *Truck Talk* 135 *Running lights*, a tractor-trailer's clearance lights. **1975** *Times* 21 Aug. 3/2 Volvo cars..are to be fitted with 'running lights', special side lights switched on automatically with the ignition. **1977** *Observer* 3 Apr. 37/8 The working group appointed by the Nordic Road Safety Council has proposed that the use of running lights be made mandatory in daytime all year round in Denmark, Finland, Sweden and Norway. **1978** H. WOUK *War & Remembrance* xx. 192 Unescorted, floodlights on a white hull, brilliant running lights, huge red cross painted on her side. **1850** N. KINGSLEY *Diary* 4 Mar. (1914) 112 Got up steam again today and tried the larboard engine and have got both in running order. **1860** A. SHERWOOD *Gazetteer of State of Georgia* (ed. 4) 152 Soon, say in summer of 1861, much will be in running order. **1875** *General Statutes of State of Michigan* I. (1882) 829 Every corporation owning a road in use shall..draw over the same the merchandise and cars of any other corporation..: Provided, such cars are of the proper gauge, are in good running order, and properly loaded. **1902** 'O. HENRY' in *Ainslee's Mag.* Apr. 209/2 The running order of the bank was smooth and clean, and that had facilitated his work. **1939** N. COWARD *Play Parade* II. p. x, *Running order*, a list of the Scenes in their correct order. **1948** [see *RUNNER 4 c]. **1961** G. MILLERSON *Technique Television Production* x. 186 A running order, prepared from this script after the technical planning meeting, will contain a breakdown of the entire studio operations throughout the show. **1977** B. LANGLEY *Death Stalk* ii. 21 If you're editing a programme and you're not prepared for it [*sc.* an item], it can knock hell out of your running order. **1930** L. W. OLDS *Track Athletics* i. 4 The running pants should have plenty of room in the hips. **1884** *Spectator* 26 July 975/2 The running-shoes must be doffed for good and all. **1913** C. MACKENZIE *Sinister St.* I. I. vii. 107 Every evening there was steady practice..in spiked running-shoes on the grass-track. **1941** BAKER *N.Z. Slang* vi. 53 *To give a person his running shoes*, to dismiss a person from office .., which is an extension of the phrase *to get the run*, to be dismissed or fired. **1943** J. A. W. BENNETT in *Amer. Speech* XVIII. 92 Only a few current phrases can be traced to their creators. One of these is 'to give a man his running shoes', coined by a New Zealand Minister of the Crown as a vivid substitute for the English 'sack' or the American 'fire'. **1960** WENTWORTH & FLEXNER *Dict. Amer. Slang* 438/1 *Running shoes, give someone his*, to dismiss someone, as a suitor or an employee; to terminate a personal or business relationship, usu. in anger. **1963** B. PEARSON *Coal Flat* vi. 111 Like Bob Semple used to say about hit-and-run drivers—give them their running shoes. **1979** *Tucson* (Arizona) *Citizen* 20 Sept. 6A/1 President Carter is losing ground by waiting to put on his official re-election running shoes. **1912** E. W. HJERTBERG *Athletics in Theory & Practice* xii. 54 The running shorts should be wide and should not sit tightly anywhere, whatever movement one happens to make. **1974** *Times* 10 Apr. 13/2 A lifelessly wordless eccentric in running shorts. **1905** GRAHAM & CLARK *Pract. Track & Field Athletics* 9 Sufficient capital to purchase a running suit and a pair of spiked shoes,..and a spare hour somewhere in the course of the day are all that are required to give any one a chance to develop his latent possibilities. **1806** W. CLARK in *Lewis & Clark Exped.* (1905) V. 294 Emence herds of Buffalow about..is at this now running time with those animals. **1897** KIPLING *Capt. Cour.* ix. 195 Our runnin' time from San Diego to Chicago was 57.54. **1911** H. S. HARRISON *Queed* xii. 143 Queed..pulled into supper only three minutes behind running-time. **1952** GRANVILLE *Dict. Theatrical Terms* 156 *Running time*, the actual time the play takes in performance, act by act, excluding intervals and final curtain calls, which are logged separately. **1962** D. R. COX *Renewal Theory* vii. 80 Suppose that a machine is subject to stoppages and call the time necessary to restart a stopped machine a repair-time. There is thus an alternating sequence of running-times and repair-times. **1977** A. MORICE *Murder in Mimicry* II. x. 176 Even in normal running time my first entrance did not come for ten minutes. Nevertheless..I got to the theatre with two hours to spare. **1883** *Harper's Mag.* Oct. 416/2 The running track, commonly used for trotting as well, has..seen some notable achievements. **1907** *St. Nicholas* June 694/1 'And a new running track', added Dick. **1903** Running vest [see *running drawers* above].

b. (Earlier and later examples with *down*.) Also with *about, in*.

1966 J. DERRICK *Teaching Eng. to Immigrants* iv. 155 Traditional children's games..are mainly running-about games which are probably more suited to the playground..than to the classroom. **1825** *Spirit of Public Jrnls. 1823* 315 Mr. Joseph Arnold being thus foiled in his running-down scheme, placed his jarvey right across the road. **1856** DICKENS in *Househ. Words* XIII. 554/2 The landsman was relating his experience..of a fearful running-down case in the Channel. **1931** *Times* 16 Jan. 14/2 He acquired a large practice, esp. in running-down cases. **1968** *Times* 29 Nov. 13/3 The running-down rate of the pulsar implies that it has a lifetime of the same order as the Crab nebula. **1930** *Engineering* 4 Apr. 439/1 In the running-in process, it has usually been necessary for the engine to be carefully watched..to prevent damage from over heating or seizing. **1957** *Railway Mag.* June 438/1 This is part of a regular two-day running-in roster from Crewe Works. **1973** 'J. ASHFORD' *Double Run* iii. 18 The driver ignored both the fifteen m.p.h. factory speed limit and the forty-five running-in limit.

running, *ppl. a.* Add: **I. 1. b.** Also, a constant supply of water from a tap, main, or the like.

1912 M. L. FULLER *Domestic Water Supplies for Farm* xx. 151 In very few ways, if any, may the drudgery be so readily lessened or the pleasures and comforts of rural life so increased as by the installation of running water in the houses & barns. **1936** G. MITCHELL *Dead Men's Morris* i. 16 We got no runnen water endoors round this part. **1946** A. HUXLEY *Let.* 21 Apr. (1969) 543 There is running water, electric light and bottled gas, so that the fundamentals are all right. **1961** L. MUMFORD *City in History* xv. 466 A collective water system with running water available for every house. **1974** O. MANNING *Rain Forest* I. iii. 52 There's no running water, the sani-cans stink.

c. *running ice*, ice which moves downstream in blocks and sheets. *N. Amer.*

1913 W. OGILVIE *Early Days on Yukon* iii. 44 In this it satisfactorily succeeded, when running ice put a stop to further mining operations. **1922** H. A. CODY *King's Arrow* xxi. 101 The bark canoe seemed like a thing of life as it cut through the water... It had battled with running ice; it had been borne over innumerable portages. **1959** M. SHAND *Summit & Beyond* iv. 65 The Mounted Police sent out warnings that no more small boats could be used on lakes and rivers on account of the running ice. **1968** [see *CEILING *vbl. sb.* 6 c].

3. c. (Further example.)

1975 *Times* 4 Sept. 19/3 If the water is very hot it stops people washing things under a running tap.

4. Also of the eyes or nose. *running sore*: also *fig.*, a constant nuisance or irritation; a long-lasting trouble or problem.

1807 E. WEETON *Let.* 18 Nov. (1969) I. 50 As to the running eyes and noses of which you request me to give you the exact number. **1961** C. COCKBURN *View from West* ix. 117 At that time the National Union of Journalists was as a running sore to the anti-Communists of the T.U.C. **1964** J. P. CLARK *Three Plays* 82 Do forgive my running nose. **1973** *Times* 21 Nov. 6 Running sore of London staff shortages may defy short-term cure.

II. 7. e. *running mate,* a horse entered in a race in order to set the pace for another horse from the same stable which is intended to win. Also in *transf.* use, a fellow candidate (*of* someone), usu. one standing for a subordinate office, and *spec.* the vice-presidential candidate in U.S. presidential elections; *gen.*, a partner, colleague, spouse, etc. orig. and chiefly *U.S.*

1868 H. W. WOODRUFF *Trotting Horse of Amer.* xxxvi. 284 He has been..especially great for his knack at going with a running-mate. **1883** *Illustr. Sporting & Dramatic News* 30 June 399/2 'How fast do you think she can trot with a running-mate?' the reporter asked; a 'running-mate' it is, perhaps, unnecessary to explain, being a horse harnessed to a pole, which gallops or 'runs' while the other trots. **1900** *Rev. of Reviews* Jan. 7/2 A better man could hardly be selected as Mr. McKinley's 'running mate'. **1902** B. WHITLOCK *13th District* 61 There were.. pictures of the candidate himself,..and pictures, too, of his 'running mate', the candidate for vice-president. **1911** *Munsey's Mag.* Mar. 865/2 His running-mate, Elizabeth Brice, in spite of the eyes she makes, also inspires liking. **1935** *N. Amer. Rev.* Mar. 275 Nast's representation of a running-mate by a tag on the coat-tail of the head of the ticket is a fair indication of popular interest and respect. **1944** *Newsweek* 31 July 25/1 The substitution of Sen. Harry S. Truman of Missouri for Vice President Henry A. Wallace as Mr. Roosevelt's running mate. **1953** *Economist* 25 July 258/1 Eisenhower and his running-mate, Senator Nixon, spoke in stern criticism. **1958** *Listener* 21 Aug. 255/1 From President Nasser's point of view, the Sudan would be a far more desirable running-mate in the United Arab Republic than Syria. **1968** R. F. ADAMS *Western Words* 261/1 *Running mate*, a cowboy's term for his pal or his wife. **1968** W. SAFIRE *New Lang. Politics* 389/1 In horseracing, a single stable will often enter two horses in a race, the lesser horse used as a pacesetter and called a running mate. This second horse usually vanishes into obscurity. **1972** D. H. LAURENCE *Bernard Shaw: Coll. Lett. 1898–1910* 188 A similar letter had been posted..to women voters, appealing to them to vote for Shaw and his five Progressive running-mates to protect women's rights in the Borough. **1973** 'D. HALLIDAY' *Dolly & Starry Bird* i. 2, I..shared digs with my running mate, a photographer. **1977** *Irish Times* 8 June 8/6 His running-mate, Alice Glenn, received 1,240 first preferences in Dublin North-Central in 1973.

8. f. *running dog* [tr. Chinese *zǒugǒu*, f. *zǒu* to run + *gǒu* dog]: in communist terminology, one who is subservient to counter-revolutionary interests; a lackey (see *LACKEY *sb.* 1 c). Also in generalized use.

1937 E. SNOW *Red Star over China* IX. iv. 325 Vanguards of young Moslems were..urging the overthrow of the 'Kuomintang running-dog'. **1961** tr. *Mao Tsetung's Sel. Works* IV. 284 Without a revolutionary party,..it is impossible to lead the working class and the broad masses of the people in defeating imperialism and its running dogs. **1968** *Guardian* 13 July 9/5 The Kremlin's fears that the Czechoslovak revolution has become a treacherous running dog of the West. **1969** R. QUEST *Cerberus Murders* xxi. 119 This is how we worked—we were not a team and I was certainly not his running-dog. **1970** [see *housenigger* s.v. *HOUSE *sb.*[1] 23]. **1977** 'E. CRISPIN' *Glimpses of Moon* xi. 226 'Imperialist running-dogs,' said the hunt saboteuse. **1978** J. UPDIKE *Coup* (1979) iii. 98 He admired the French, he admires the polluting Americans and their new running dogs the Chinese.

g. *running back*: in American football, a back whose function is to run carrying the ball.

1924 *Collier's* 20 Dec. 38/4 There has been no running back in football history who had these baffling, bewildering qualities to such an extent. **1962** R. WALKER *Compl. Bk. Backfield Play* ii. 28 What distinguishes a back from a linesman? Many ends would make outstanding running backs. **1967** R. GRAVES *Guide to Mod. Football Offense* vi. 47 In discussing techniques and drills involved in backfield play, we will place the position of fullback and tailback under the classification *running backs*... Since the play of the quarterback is uniquely different from that of running backs, the fundamental requirements of his position will be discussed separately. **1971** L. KOPPETT *Guide to Spectator Sports* ii. 50 And the halfback and fullback are simply 'running backs'. **1979** *Arizona Daily Star* 5 Aug. (Parade Suppl.) 6/1 Susie Forton played running back and middle linebacker for the Vikings.

9. Also *running moss* = CLUB-MOSS (earlier and later examples); *running postman* = *coral-pea* s.v. *CORAL *sb.*[1] 9.

1845 Running moss [see *MOUNTAIN LAUREL]. **1898** E. E. MORRIS *Austral Eng.* 247/1 *K[ennedya] prostrata* is called the Coral Pea..or Running Postman. **1917** H. H. RICHARDSON *Fortunes R. Mahony* I. ix. 87 The short-lived grass was picked out into patterns by the scarlet of the Running Postman. **1945** E. STEP *Wayside & Woodland Ferns* (ed. 2) 129 These local names [for common club-moss] are..numerous... Others are..Lamb's-tail, Running Moss, Robin Hood's Hatband, [etc.]. **1962** Running postman[see *coral-pea* s.v. *CORAL *sb.*[1] 9].

11. a. Also in phr. *running rhythm*, used by G. M. Hopkins to denote common English metre.

c **1883** G. M. Hopkins in *Poems* (1967) 45 The poems in this book are written some in Running Rhythm, the common rhythm in English use, some in Sprung Rhythm, and some in a mixture of the two. Common English rhythm, called Running Rhythm above, is measured by feet of either two or three syllables. **1957** N. Frye *Anatomy of Criticism* 263 The sixteenth century was a period of experiment, mainly in verse *epos* or running rhythm, to use Hopkins's term. **1970** J. T. Shipley *Dict. World Lit. Terms* (ed. 3) 284/2 *Running rhythm*, the common Eng[lish] rhythm, measured by feet of 2 or 3 syllables... Opp[osed] by G. M. Hopkins to sprung rhythm.

III. 14. a. Also in various (chiefly *U.S. Sporting*) phrases, as *running attack, game, start* (see quots.).

1910 W. Camp *Bk. Foot-Ball* viii. 306 Probably there is greater fascination in the running game than in any other department of foot-ball... There is no play that brings the spectators to their feet to such wild enthusiasm as a good run. **1929** D. Runyon in *Hearst's Internat.* July 125/1 Dave the Dude is more corned than anybody else, because he has two or three days running start on everybody. **1961** J. S. Salak *Dict. Amer. Sports* 375 *Running play*,..a play during which there is a runner and which is not followed by a kick or forward pass from behind scrimmage line. **1971** L. Koppett *Guide to Spectator Sports* ii. 56 To stop a running attack, a defensive line must hold its ground. **1976** *Webster's Sports Dict.* 160/2 *Flying start*, auto racing, a start of a race in which the competitors are already moving as they cross the starting line or receive the starting signal (also called *running start*). **1977** *New Yorker* 10 Oct. 177/1 Princeton, which has another useful quota of real heavyweights..has as well a sturdy running attack, now that Isom is paced by Larson.

d. Also *running battle*. Also, any military engagement which constantly changes its location. Also *transf.* (in later use, perh. influenced by sense *17 a).

1916 'Taffrail' *Pincher Martin* xvii. 317 The *Mariner* and various other destroyers were present with the battle-cruisers throughout the first shock of the engagement and the running fight which ensued. **1928** G. B. Grinnell *Two Great Scouts* iv. 65 The Pawnee warriors sprang on their horses and set out in pursuit of the enemy. During a running fight, the Pawnees killed a number of Sioux. **1945** *Ann. Reg. 1944* I. 2 The raiders.. carried on a running fight with German fighter planes. **1967** in G. Marx *Groucho Lett.* 13 (*heading*) Running battle with Warner Brothers. **1974** [see *motor-cycle *sb.*].

e. *running repairs*, hurried, minor, or temporary repairs made to machinery, equipment, etc., while in service. Also *transf.*

1913 *Autocar Handbk.* (ed. 5) i. 16 He [*sc.* the chauffeur] should do most of the running repairs, such as tyre repairs. **1924** Kipling *Debits & Credits* (1926) 166 We'd been sent back for rest an' runnin'-repairs, back pretty near our base. **1951** N. Marsh *Opening Night* vi. 134 He..effected a number of what he called running repairs to her make-up and hair. **1957** *Encycl. Brit.* XVIII. 935/2 Most yards of any considerable size also include, or have adjacent, facilities for servicing of, and running repairs to, cars and locomotives. **1971** D. J. Smith *Discovering Railwayana* x. 59 *Running repairs*, small scale repairs carried out in a 'running' or engine shed. **1973** K. Benton *Craig & Jaguar* vii. 89 Your nose is shiny..Make some running repairs while we leave you for a moment.

f. *running jump*, a jump preceded and augmented by a run. Usu. *fig.*, esp. in phr. *to take a running jump (at oneself)*, freq. used colloq. as an expression of hostility, contempt, or indifference to someone.

1914 E. A. Powell *Fighting in Flanders* i. 18 Thompson took a running jump. **1920** S. Lewis *Main Street* xxxv. 415 There aint a town..got a better chance to take a running jump..right up into the two-hundred-thousand class. **1933** M. Lowry *Ultramarine* ii. 76 You go and take a running jump at yourself. **1953** A. Upfield *Murder must Wait* xi. 104 Tell your Chief Commissioner to take a running jump at himself. **1954** J. B. Priestley *Magicians* vi. 120 The public can take a running jump at itself. I stopped liking people a long time since. **1959** 'R. Macdonald' *Galton Case* xii. 97 Tell him to take a running jump in the Truckee River and do us all a favor. **1968** *Landfall* XXII. 22 If you think I'm subsidizing you..you can take a running jump at yourself. **1972** M. Gilbert *Body of Girl* xx. 180, I told her to take a running jump at herself. The only person who could make trouble for *me* would be old Henry Prior.

g. *running fix*, a fix obtained by determining bearings at different times and making allowance for the distance covered by the observer in the interval.

1916 S. F. Card *Navigation Notes & Examples* vii. 32 A running fix is the position obtained from two position lines by observations at different times, allowing for the run in the interval. **1942** *Tee Emm* (Air Ministry) II. 82 Here's a good tip to save yourself a running fix. **1974** K. Wilkes *Pract. Yacht Navigator* (ed. 2), ix. 119 The accuracy of the running fix depends on the correctness of the direction and distance travelled over the ground between the two bearings.

IV. 17. a. (Further examples.) Also, continually produced or maintained; constantly repeated or recurring.

1966 *This is Bill-Broking* (Allen, Harvey & Ross Ltd.) 34 *Running yield*, the interest rate on an investment, expressed in terms of a percentage on the capital invested. **1966** *Listener* 17 Nov. 732/1 A series of comic set-pieces linked into a wildly slapstick context by carefully contrived running gags. **1973** *Daily Tel.* 7 Mar 21 At the issue price of £99½ the 1980 stock will give a running yield of 9·05 p.c. and a gross redemption yield of 9·10 p.c. to 1980. **1973** *Times* 30 Oct. 4/6 As he walked the Dalai Lama gave a running audience.

e. *running commentary*, a sustained series of comments on events, actions, utterances, etc., as they occur; a continuous description of an event in progress, *spec.* a broadcast report of a game, contest, or race.

1811 C. Lamb in *Reflector* iv. 342 The writings of Fuller are usually designated by the title of quaint... But.. his way of telling a story, for its eager liveliness, and perpetual running commentary of the narrator happily blended into the narration, is perhaps unequalled. **1824** *Mirror of Literature* 17 Jan. 44/2 The Count's running commentary upon these evolutions, too, is a *chef d'oevre* in the art of reasoning. **1853** R. S. Surtees *Mr. Sponge's Sporting Tour* lxi. 348 His pleasure was, perhaps, damped by a running commentary he overheard through the lattice-window of the stable. **1858** *Chambers's Jrnl.* 4 Dec. 359/1 (*heading*) Bill Fustian's running commentary on the doings of the respectable classes. **1883** J. M. Barrie *Auld Licht Idylls* xii. 239 He loved to recite long screeds from Spenser, with a running commentary on the versification and the luxuriance of the diction. **1905** *Pall Mall Mag.* July 40/2 She gasped and..trembled out her tale of horrors, while..her daughter,..in the exasperating fashion of the chorus in a Greek play, kept up a running commentary, emphasising the points. **1927** *B.B.C. Handbk. 1928* 140/1 Running commentaries fall easily under two different headings—Sporting and purely Descriptive. **1929** *B.B.C. Year-Bk. 1930* 146 Tennis..provides excellent material for a running commentary, although the commentators find the strain of following the strokes.. with an instantaneous spoken description very great. **1931** *Discovery* Dec. 386/1 This was the first scientific film of its kind to be synchronized with the running commentary. **1946** G. N. M. Tyrrell *Personality of Man* vi. xviii. 158 Then there is Mrs. Willett's running commentary. She is always there, interjecting her own comments. **1966** B. Johnston *Armchair Cricket* 26 He has to comment rather than give a *running* commentary which is basically what happens with football or racing on television. **1969** M. Pugh *Last Place Left* xvii. 124, I drank tea with my back to the floor but Katriona gave me a running commentary until Nell rejoined me. **1977** D. Bennett *Jigsaw Man* iv. 71 I'll give you a sort of running commentary... Reorient you... The village is on the right.

f. *running set* (see Set *sb.*[2] 14), a country dance, originating in the Appalachian Mountains, in which the dancers perform a number of figures in quick succession.

1918 C. Sharp *Country Dance Book* v. 9 The Running Set..differs materially from any other known form of the Country-dance. **1927** *Observer* 27 Nov. 14/5 He got.. from elsewhere in that district, the 'running set'—a fine dance which has been received here with outspoken enthusiasm. **1938** *Times* 10 Jan. 10/4 Two American dances, the Running Set and the Big Set, were shown. **1964** W. G. Raffé *Dict. Dance* 431/2 *Running set*, an English square dance in quick time, preserved in villages of the Appalachian Mountains, in North America. *Ibid.*, Danced by four couples (sometimes more), the *Running Set* consists of an Introduction and some fourteen figures, which follow each other without pause. **1974** *Encycl. Brit. Micropædia* IX. 501/2 Historians trace the square dance to two derivatives of English country dance: the Kentucky running set, a rhythmic, complicated figure dance derived from pre-17th-century English round dances; and the cotillon.

VI. 22. b. *running mould* (Plastering), a pattern moving on fixed guides and used to shape cornices and other mouldings.

1825 [see Run *v.* 53 f]. **1911** *Encycl. Brit.* XXI. 786/1 Plain, or unenriched, mouldings are formed with a running mould of zinc cut to the required profile. **1955** N. W. Kay et al. *Mod Building Encycl.* 483/2 Solid cornices are..formed in the position they are to occupy, by a running mould, called a horse, which runs along guides fixed to the walls.

23. c. *running belay* (Mountaineering), a belay (see *belay *sb.*) through which the climbing rope runs freely, and which acts as a pulley if the climber falls.

1941 T. A. H. Peacocke *Mountaineering* ii. 26 Without the use of slings, running belays are unsatisfactory. **1946** Leonard & Wexler in *Sierra Club Bull.* Dec. 91 He [*sc.* G. W. Young] is fully aware of the dynamic belay, referring to it as the 'running belay', one of the 'expert belays' that only great skill and strength can hope to regulate. **1956** C. Evans *On Climbing* iii. 52 When negotiating a difficult pitch, the leader will, if possible, arrange running belays at intervals... He..drives a piton into a crack, and runs his rope through a snap-link clipped to the..piton. **1968** P. Crew *Encycl. Dict. Mountaineering* 87/1 Apart from the ease of carrying, the fact that the sling goes *through* a nut, instead of *round* a chockstone, often makes the running belay more mechanically sound. **1973** C. Bonington *Next Horizon* xx. 274 Don went up..quicky and smoothly without bothering to protect himself with running belays.

24. b. *running bowline* († *knot*), a bowline adapted to form a noose.

1726 Defoe *Four Years Voyages of Capt. George Roberts* 110, I got ready another Rope, at the end of which I made a running bowling knot, and the Noose so as to keep it open with one Hand. **1823** [see Bowline[1] 2]. **1883** *Man. Seamanship* (Admiralty) 89 *Q.* What is a running bowline used for..? *A.* It is used for throwing over anything out of reach, or anything under water. **1911** *Encycl. Brit.* XV. 872/1 Running bowlines are formed by making a bowline round its own standing part... It is the most common and convenient temporary running noose. **1932** E. M. Brent-Dyer *Chalet Girls in Camp* vii. 111 The rope was swung down, and as it stopped swinging, Miss Wilson knew that Jo had it safely. 'Running bowline!' she called down. **1968** E. Franklin *Dict. Knots* 24 *Running bowline*, the knot which was universally used at sea whenever a noose was needed. Useful for commencing to tie a parcel.

25. a. (Earlier and later examples.)

1848 E. C. P. in C. H. Hartshorne *Eng. Medieval Embroidery* 128 An inner line of yellow floss silk in a running stitch. **1967** E. Short *Embroidery & Fabric Collage* iii. 86 Although traditionally carried out by hand in running or back stitch, the quilting can be done on the sewing machine.

26. b. With advbs., as *running-down* (in sense 73 a of the vb.).

1968 *Times* 29 Nov. 13/7 A running-down pulsar might be found. **1973** L. Cooper *Tea on Sunday* xxiv. 177 For what was supposed to be a running-down business it all looked remarkably active.

27. *running fit*: (see quots.).

1908 S. H. Moore *Mech. Engin. & Machine Shop Practice* vii. 184 A running fit is designed to allow the surfaces in contact to move or revolve freely over each other. *Ibid.*, Two formulas are given for running fits; one for close running fits, to be used in ordinary work.., and the other for free running fits, to be used for high-speeds, heavy pressures, rocker shafts, etc. **1953** W. H. Armstrong *Mech. Inspection* iv. 51 A running fit is one in which an allowance is made so that a shaft will be free to rotate in a bearing. **1964** S. Crawford *Basic Engin. Processes* xiv. 290 Running fits.., tolerances which allow the shaft to rotate freely in the hole.

ru·nning-board. Also **running board.** [f. Running *vbl. sb.*] **† 1.** A narrow gangway on either side of a keel-boat. *U.S. Obs.*

1817 *Essex Inst. Hist. Coll.* (1866) VIII. 240 Our boat being very deep..[we] were obliged to give up after being at the expense of putting on running boards. **1834** H. Brackenridge *Recoll.* iv. 37 One night..I..lay..on the running board (a plank at the edge of the boat, on which the men walk in pushing with the pole). **1843** *Amer. Pioneer* II. 271 Keel-boats..were provided with running boards, extending from bow to stern, on each side of the boat... The crew, divided equally on each side, set their poles near the head of the boat, and bringing the end of the pole to their shoulders, with their bodies bent, walked slowly down the running board to the stern.

2. a. A foot-board extending along the side of a locomotive, railway wagon, or tram, or one extending along the roof of a railway wagon. orig. and chiefly *U.S.*

1860 Clark & Colburn *Recent Practice Locomotive Engine* 51/2 The cab, domes, 'running-board', and other matters of external finish, are very much the same on most American engines. **1874** M. N. Forney *Catechism of Locomotive* 337 The running-boards are planks..placed on each side of the boiler to enable the locomotive runner or fireman to go from the cab to the front end of the engine when it is running. **1889** *Cent. Dict.*, *Running board*,..(*a*) A narrow platform extending along the side of a locomotive. (*b*) A horizontal board along the ridge of a box freight-car or the side of an oil-car, to form a passage for the trainmen. **1903** *Electrical World & Engin.* 14 Nov. 795/2 The 'mule' has two large hooks for the towropes and has also a running board and guard hand rail. **1917** C. Mathewson *Second Base Sloan* 284 The cars that buzzed and clanged their way past Wayne were filled to the running-boards. **1930** *Amer. Speech* V. 277 *Running-board* is a bit puzzling, but the speculation that it was derived from the old summer trolleys, now almost extinct in the north, is at least permissible. **1940** *Life* 4 Mar. 50/2 The rear-end brakeman..makes an inspection tour along the 'running board', looking for loose brake beams or hot boxes. *a* **1966** 'M. na Gopaleen' *Best of Myles* (1968) 187 Particularly if the running board of the tram was already crowded with fat women.

b. A foot-board located on either side of a motor vehicle between the front and rear mudguards.

1907 S. Krausz *Practical Automobile Dict.* 26 *Running-board*, s., marchepied, s.m. **1910** *Sears, Roebuck Motor Buggy Booklet* 28 With the addition of running boards connecting front and rear fenders, convenient for shopping or business where frequent getting in and out is necessary. **1914** E. A. Powell *Fighting in Flanders* vii. 169 A big grey car shot down the road... Clinging to the running-board was her English chauffeur. **1927** M. de la Roche *Jalna* xii. 136 Wakefield mounted the running board and held the Michaelmas daisies out to her. **1929** *Daily Express* 14 Jan. 6/3 Heath, leaning over the running-board, shouted some unintelligible words. **1932** Kipling *Limits & Renewals* 139 Phil sat down on the running-board of Mr. Haman's car. **1959** *Motor* 7 Oct. 246/2 The body sides have now been carried out towards the rear to narrow down the running boards and reduce the protruding width of the rear wings. **1965** M. Bradbury *Stepping Westward* viii. 380 They sat on the running-board of the car. **1974** *Country Life* 17 Oct. 1104/1 There is the Volkswagen Beetle... Here in the 1970s we still have a car with very rounded lines, small windows, a very cramped interior and outside running boards.

3. A device used in positioning overhead power lines which enables several conductors to be pulled simultaneously using a single pulling line.

1898 E. J. Houston *Dict. Electr. Words* (ed. 4) 911/1 *Running-board*, a device employed in the construction of a heavy overhead line, consisting in placing a number of reels of wire, usually ten or more, on a spindle, and arranging a piece of wood as a cross-arm to which ten or more wires are attached, harnessing horses to the cross-piece, and then dragging the running board away as the wires are paid out from the reels, and passing them over their appropriate cross-arms, where they are at once secured to the insulators by line-men. **1964** E. B. KURTZ *Lineman's & Cableman's Handbk.* (ed. 4) xiv. 7 Tension stringing of bundled conductors. Usually two or three conductors are pulled simultaneously by one pulling line with the use of a unidirectional articulated running board.

running gear. orig. and chiefly *U.S.* Also **running-gear.** [f. RUNNING *ppl. a.*; in senses 1 and 3 a the plural form is used interchangeably with the singular.] **1.** The moving parts of a mill or other large machine.

1662 *Rec. East-Hampton, N.Y.* (1887) I. 201 Mr Backer shall have seven pounds for this yeare for tendinge the mill and maintayninge the runninge geares that is coggs and rounds. **1725** *New England Courant* 18–25 Jan. 2/2 The Wind... carry'd off the Top of the Mill, with the Shaft, Vanes, and running Geer, and brake them to Pieces. **1834** in J. S. Bassett *Southern Plantation Overseer* (1925) vi. 73 The runinge geares that is hear I cant under take to pick a crop with them. **1901** MERWIN & WEBSTER *Calumet 'K'* xiv. 262 Down in the cellar putting in the running gear for the 'cross-the-house conveyors'.

2. The rope and tackle used in handling (part of) a boat; = *running rigging.*

1838 J. F. COOPER *Homeward Bound* II. iii. 55 The standing rigging are the bones and gristle; the running gear the veins in which her life circulates. **1856** E. K. KANE *Arctic Explorations* II. iii. 48 We can burn hemp cable and cast-off running-gear. **1911** J. BARTEN *Compl. Naut. Pocket Dict.* 165/1 Running gear. **1962** A. G. COURSE *Dict. Naut. Terms* 163 *Running gear*, ropes, tackles, etc., that move in the course of ship handling or cargo working.

3. a. The wheels and axles of a cart or carriage. Also *transf.* and *fig.*

1857 D. H. STROTHER *Virginia Illustrated* 230 A shadowy group was dimly visible, a carriage mounted on the running-gear of a wagon, and drawn by four horses. **1876** [in Dict. s.v. RUNNING *ppl. a.* 22]. **1904** *N.Y. World* (Mag. Sect.) 1 May 6/1 The running gear is dark red and the upholstering is drab. **1916** *Dialect Notes* IV. 348 *Running gear*, the remnants or 'carcass' of a fowl served up cold. **1923** *Ibid.* V. 208 *Runnin' gears*, Those portions of a wagon other than the box or bed. **1924** F. R. BECHDOLT *Tales of Old-Timers* 363 The boy was driving a span of horses hitched to the running-gear of a lumber-wagon. **1941** *Amer. Speech* XVI. 24/1 Of a skinny person. 'He's got the running-gears of a katydid.' **1948** E. N. DICK *Dixie Frontier* xix. 208 The driver..fastened a big deep box on the axle or the front wheels of a wagon running-gear. **1953** RANDOLPH & WILSON *Down in Holler* viii. 184 When an airplane crashed and burned, my neighbor viewed the wreckage. 'It looks *like the runnin'-gears of a grasshopper*,' said he. **1972** J. S. HALL *Sayings from Old Smoky* 53 (Someone or something) 'looks like the runnin' gears of a crow's nest'.

b. The wheels, axles, and suspension of a railway locomotive, carriage, or wagon; the steering, suspension, and wheel systems of a motor vehicle.

1877 *11th Ann. Rep. Proc. Master Car-Builders Assoc.* 57 Probably every one of us who has experience in handling foreign cars can fully realize the importance of our draw bars and oil-boxes, and, in fact, of all the running gear of the car. **1889** *Nat. Car & Locomotive Builder* Mar. 35/1, I have always believed that the running gear of railway rolling stock should be constructed of such strength and with such intelligence as to give it a high factor of safety. **1900** *Motor World* 8 Nov. 100/1 The motor is located centrally of the vehicle, and is hung on the upper section of the running frame, which is spring supported from the main tubular running gear. **1905** *Motor Man.* (ed. 7) v. 85 Periodical cleaning and inspection of all the running gear is..the best possible insurance against breakdowns. **1919** FRASER & JONES *Motor Vehicles* xxvi. 270 The parts of a motor vehicle not included in developing and transmitting power are classified under the general heading of running gear. This includes such parts as frames, springs, axles, wheels, brakes, steering gear, etc. **1932** *New Yorker* 14 May 32/2 It was a club-sedan,..with red running gear. **1957** *Encycl. Brit.* XIV. 284/1 The mechanical parts include those portions of the locomotive which make it suitable as a vehicle, *i.e.*, the running gear, and the cab or superstructure. **1959** *Motor Man.* (ed. 36) v. 99 What is often referred to as the running gear comprises the steering system, the springing or suspension, the brakes and the wheels and tyres. **1969** *Northern Territory News* (Darwin) *Focus '69* 13/2 (Advt.), Semi-trailer tippers. Tough structural design, coupled with the best hoist and running gear available, assures down time reduced to periodic servicing.

runny (rʌ·ni), *a.* [f. RUN *v.* + -Y[1].] **a.** Tending to run or flow; having the consistency of liquid, fluid, not set; soft, melting, watery; (of eggs, etc.) soft-centred.

1817 *Niles' Reg.* XII. 165/2 This flour would prove similar to a previous baking of new flour (which was *runny*). **1904** *Eng. Dial. Dict.* V. 185/2 *Runny*,..inclined to liquefy. **1913** G. STRATTON-PORTER *Laddie* vii. 210 He slid in a whole plateful of bread, another of cake... Then we took some of every thing that wasn't too runny. **1935** M. MORPHY *Recipes of All Nations* 73 A well-made purée should be almost 'runny'—only just sufficiently thick to be eaten with a fork. **1937** *Evening News* 23 Mar. 15/5 (Advt.), No runny butter or sour milk: no more waste. **1951** *Good Housek. Home Encycl.* 524/1 A 'runny' jelly is very difficult to manipulate. **1957** J. FRAME *Owls do Cry* (1958) II. 103 Haven't I told you..to leave the egg till it's..hard, that I don't like them runny? **1972** K. LO *Chinese Food* I. 43 Eggs are sometimes scrambled with minced meat, mushrooms, onions, lard and some good broth. The dish is called Runny Yellow Egg (*Liu Huang Ts'ai*), and is another good runny dish to eat with rice.

b. Of the nose: running, discharging mucus.

1951 J. STEINBECK *Log from 'Sea of Cortez'* p. xxxii, She was a red-eyed..woman with a runny nose. **1969** A. LURIE *Real People* (1970) 85 All he had produced so far was a slow pathetic drip and trickle, as if the fat marble cherub poised above the marble bowl had a bad runny nose.

Hence **ru·nny-no:sed** *a.*

1972 J. WILSON *Hide & Seek* ii. 32 A couple of runny-nosed children..tried to get on [the roundabout] too. **1976** M. HARTMANN *Leap for Sun* i. 28 Big-arsed nannies squatting on the pavements surrounded by runny-nosed kids.

‖ **runo** (rū·no). Also **Runo**; pl. **runot, runos.** [Finnish: cf. RUNE[2].] In Finland, a short poem or song on an epic or legendary subject; *spec.* one of the songs which together constitute the Kalevala, = RUNE[2] 2 b.

[**1802** J. ACERBI *Travels* I. xxiii. 301 The species of verse is called *runic*, from the ancient Gothic word *runoot.* *Ibid.* 317 These songs, called *jauho runot* or *mill-songs*, are..sung to a slow plaintive air.] **1895** *Oracle Encycl.* II. 653/1 It was long known that there lived amongst the Finns a great number of lyrics known as *Runot* ('Runic songs'). *Ibid.*, The discovery that many of these *Runot* could be dovetailed into a true and noble epic, based on the old myths. **1898** I. M. ANDERTON tr. *Comparetti's Tradit. Poetry of Finns* I. i. 3 There is one word, *runo*, which characterises and distinguishes the traditional poetry of the Finns. **1944** W. APEL *Harvard Dict. Music.* 266/2 Next follow the *runos* (sung to the traditional poems of epic characters, called 'runes'), which are melodic and rhythmically vigorous **1954** *Grove's Dict. Mus.* (ed. 5) III. 238/1 The ancient melodies of the period following are the beautiful *runo* tunes mentioned above. *Ibid.*, Sibelius..has a distinctive *runo* style of his own. **1963** B. J. TIMMER tr. *De Vries's Heroic Song & Heroic Legend* vii. 143 Lönnrot was a folklorist, who set himself the task of collecting the older poetry of the Finns, in particular the epic songs or *runot.* **1974** *Encycl. Brit. Macropædia* VI. 910/2 Elias Lönnrot.., who composed this master-piece [*sc.* the *Kalevala*] by combining short popular songs (*runot*) collected by himself among the Finns, had absorbed his material so well, and identified himself so completely with the *runo* singers.

runo-. Add: **runolo·gical** *a.*, pertaining to runes or runology; **runologist** (earlier and later examples); **runology** (earlier example).

1962 *N. & Q.* Dec. 451/2 Values he could have taken from contemporary runological works. **1965** R. DEROLEZ in Bessinger & Creed *Medieval & Linguistic Stud.* 31 No satisfactory explanation has been offered for this runological revolution. **1977** *Ann. Bibliogr. Eng. Lang. & Lit. 1974* 214 The runological placing of the Caistor-by-Norwich inscription. **1847** I. A. BLACKWELL in M. Mallet *Northern Antiquities* (ed. 2) i. 247 These celebrated Runologists..arrived at the same interpretation of the characters. **1971** S. E. MORISON *European Discovery Amer.: Northern Voy.* iii. 76 Every leading runologist of Scandinavia and Germany who has deigned to examine the inscription has called it a clumsy forgery. **1862** J. FARRER *Notice Runic Inscr. Orkneys* p. ix, My very imperfect acquaintance with Runology.

run-off. Add: Also **runoff.** Pl. **run-offs.**

1. a. Delete *U.S.* and add: The amount of water that is carried off an area by streams and rivers after having fallen as precipitation; the water itself; also, water that runs straight off the ground without first soaking into it.

1910 *Westm. Gaz.* 19 Feb. 2/2 Iron ore, which stains all the other streams..and the run-off of the night's rain to the colour of tanyard. **1929** WEAVER & CLEMENTS *Plant Ecol.* ix. 190 It [*sc.* rainfall] may be of such a torrential nature that only part of it can be absorbed and the rest is lost as run-off. **1957** G. E. HUTCHINSON *Treat. Limnol.* I. iv. 229 A number of independent estimates of total runoff have been made by attempting to sum the rate of discharge of the rivers of the world. **1959** *Listener* 10 Sept. 378/2 The run-off from the winter snowfields of the Australian Alps. **1969** *Physics Bull.* Oct. 410/1 Calculated by subtracting runoff from rainfall, annual evaporation ranges from about 16 in per year in the north of England to 19 in per year in the Thames valley. **1970** T. HILLERMAN *Blessing Way* xiii. 109 He stopped at a pool where runoff had been trapped in a pocket of rocks. **1978** J. IRVING *World according to Garp* iv. 81 The runoff from the rain—washing over the Steering School, rinsing everything clean.

b. The process or fact of water, or what the water contains, running off from an area; an instance of this; (*N. Amer.*) the period when such a process occurs, esp. the spring thaw.

1935 *Discovery* Aug. 219/2 The rapid run-off causes disastrous floods at lower levels. **1944** F. CLUNE *Red Heart* 6 West of the Darling..the thirsty red soil soaks every particle of rain that falls, with no surplus for a run-off. **1949** W. VOGT *Road to Survival* v. 104 The rate of runoff can be reduced on even the steepest land. **1962** W. O. MITCHELL *Kite* iii. 25 As soon as the sky is blue and the run-off starts—down town every Saturday morning. **1972** *Times* 26 June 12/2 Sewage and run-off of fertilizer from agricultural land is eliminating desirable fish. **1980** *Beautiful British Columbia* Summer 4 This bucolic alternative becomes impossible when the snow flies and during spring runoff, as Duffey Lake Road then becomes impassable.

c. *attrib.*, as *run-off map, rate, water.*

1892–3 Run-off map [in Dict., sense 1]. **1937** *Sun* (Baltimore) 1 July 24/3 Slowing up the run-off rate of heavy rainfall. **1939** C. W. TOWNE *Her Majesty Montana* 95 Our farmers are fortified by thousands of dams for the storage of run-off waters for livestock needs and to supply irrigation for feed and hay crops. **1979** A. HAILEY *Overload* III. viii. 229 Hydroelectric power next year might be reduced by twenty-five percent because of the lack of runoff water.

2. a. (Earlier and later examples.) Also in other kinds of contest.

1873 *Carthusian* June 56 Hanson and Jeaffreson ran a dead heat for second place... The run-off for the second prize was won by Hanson. **1963** H. GARNER in R. Weaver *Canad. Short Stories* (1968) 2nd Ser. 49 'You tryin' out for the bowling team, Eric?' he asked. 'Sure thing. You?' 'May as well. Run-offs are on Thursday night.' **1973** *Shooting Times & Country Mag.* 7 July 19/3 If the judges have difficulty in arriving at a result, they can arrange a more difficult 'run-off' for the top dogs.

b. Chiefly *U.S.* An election held to decide the issue between the two candidates who gained the largest number of votes in a previous indecisive election. Freq. *attrib.* or as *adj.*, esp. in *run-off primary* (see PRIMARY *sb.* 6 in Dict. and Suppl.).

1924 *Lit. Digest* 6 Sept. 8/2 Texas..has a double primary. If no one has a majority in the first primary election, a later 'run-off' primary is held, in which the voters choose between the two candidates receiving the highest number of votes at the first balloting. **1933** *Sun* (Baltimore) 15 Sept. 3/4 A. H. Carmichael, of Tuscumbia, and B. L. Malone, of Decatur, will face each other in a run-off primary October 3 for the Democratic nomination to Congress from the Eighth Alabama district. **1944** *Ibid.* 31 May 7/1 (*heading*) Alabama run-offs watched for clue to group's strength. **1954** *Economist* 31 July 365/2 In Oklahoma Senator Kerr failed to gain the necessary clear majority of the votes cast, and was threatened with having to fight a 'run-off' election against a rival millionaire, Mr Roy Turner. **1959** B. & R. NORTH tr. *M. Duverger's Polit. Parties* (ed. 2) II. i. 220 In primaries in the South where the nomination is conducted at a single ballot the Democratic party generally divides into two factions;..in the system with two successive primaries.. the second or run-off primary operating in the event of no candidate securing an absolute majority at the first primary—the factions tend to increase in number. **1965** *N.Y. Times* 7 Dec. 4/2 (*heading*) De Gaulle silent on whether he will enter runoff. **1966** MRS. L. B. JOHNSON *White House Diary* 4 June (1970) 386 Today is the Democratic primary runoff and we had come home to vote. **1968** *Listener* 27 June 826/1 If General de Gaulle's victory at the polls is confirmed by the run-off vote next Sunday, he may well see this as a mandate for his projected social reforms. **1973** *Times* 31 Mar. 5/4 His nearest rival, Señor Ricardo Balbin, announced he would not contest a runoff. **1977** *Time* 21 Nov. 29/1 The gloves are expected to come off when Briscoe faces former City Councilman Jim McConn, a Houston developer, in a run-off next week.

3. a. The action or process of running off a person or thing in other senses of the vb.; a quantity run off or removed; *spec.* the material run off or produced by a mechanical process; a print run.

1843 J. H. GREEN *Exposure of Gambling* 96 The adversary, fearing that his hand is really the better hand, will, in preference to risking more, throw up his own hand, and forfeit what has already been bet. This is a run-off, as well as in cases where he has no money enough to meet the proposed bet. *a* **1948** L. G. D. ACLAND *Early Canterbury Runs* (1951) 393 *Run off*,..sheep counted out from a mob without being drafted; e.g., 'I cannot buy the whole line. I will take a run off of 300.' Usually *fair r.o.* **1952** *Bull. Poetry Soc. Amer.* Oct. 4 An impromptu and rather novel program was offered: a run-off of a phonograph recording of a broadcast made in 1948 of poems from the PSA *Anthology.* **1967** A. L. LLOYD *Folk Song in England* i. 27 Several of these [broadsides] were produced in massive run-offs. **1972** *Times* 30 Oct. 19/4 Insurance companies are seldom capable of an accurate assessment of the outstanding liabilities on their current portfolio of business (a 'run-off'). **1979** *Church Times* 26 Oct. 7/3 The low price for such a well-produced volume must indicate a large run-off.

b. An instance of running off a railway or road.

1855 *Chicago Western Times* 9 Aug. 1/8 The frequency of these run-offs demands the special attention of all railroad directors. **1872** W. S. HUNTINGTON *Road-Master's Assistant* 87 It is best always to keep spare [switch] rods on hand, to be used in case of a run-off. **1970** *Courier-Mail* (Brisbane) 19 Mar. 6/2 An invitation.. to the Transport Minister..to discuss whether runoff roads could be a means of preventing semi-trailer accidents in the Adelaide hills.

4. The dropping of fruit before it is ready for picking; = *running off* s.v. *RUNNING *vbl. sb.* 7 e.

1921 *Jrnl. Pomol.* II. 170 If frost caused the 'Run off' on half the bush, why did it not do so on the other? **1974** *Daily Tel.* 6 June 6/4 A grower at Cropthorne, Worcestershire, said the level of fruit 'run-off'—unformed fruit shrivelling and falling from trees—was much higher than usual through lack of moisture.

5. *N.Z.* Also *run-off paddock.* (See quot. 1933.)

1933 *Press* (Christchurch, N.Z.) 25 Nov., *Run off*, paddock used with turnips or green feed on which the sheep may camp and get what extra feed they can. **1950** *N.Z. Jrnl. Agric.* Apr. 366/3 Utilisation of the heavier pockets [of coastal land] and sand dunes is complementary, the latter being used mainly as a winter run-off. *Ibid.* 389/1 During early winter they [*sc.* ewes] are rationed turnips, fed good hay, and driven off their turnip break on to a large run-off paddock daily.

6. *slang.* An act of urination.

1961 PARTRIDGE *Dict. Slang* Suppl. 1255/2 *Run off, have a*, to urinate. **1967** H. W. SUTHERLAND *Magnie* ix. 117 What with the cold and the beer she was bursting for a run off again... The nearest ladies she knew was at Pier Head.

ru·n-out. Also run out, runout. [f. RUN *v.*]

1. *Founding.* † **a.** (See RUN *v.* 82.) *Obs.*

b. Leakage of molten metal from a cupola or a mould.

1888 *Lockwood's Dict. Mech. Engin.* 296 *Run out*, the escape of metal from a mould during the act of pouring, due to open joints somewhere. **1901** *Shop & Foundry Practice* (Colliery Engineer Co.) IV. xxxv. 20 If there is any breaking of joints by drawing the pattern or from a straining of the cope, allowing large fins or a run out, the metal will run into the vent channels..and fill them with iron. **1928** *Proc. Inst. Brit. Foundrymen* XX. 366 In Fig. 1—an ordinary scullery copper—it is quite obvious that if there be a runout there is little chance of saving the casting. **1960** R. LISTER *Decorative Cast Ironwork in Gt. Brit.* ii. 56 Possible defects in castings are manifold, and may be in the form of blow holes, unfused chaplets, wrong grain-structure, fractures, distortions, runouts, [etc.].

2. *Cricket.* (See RUN *sb.*[1] 8.)

1851 *Bell's Life* 21 Sept. 6/5 (*heading*) The 'runs out' and 'runs lost' at cricket. **1867** G. H. SELKIRK *Guide to Cricket Ground* vii. 122 Never run past the wicket, unless to save a run out, when you can stop yourself. **1891, 1892** [see RUN *sb.*[1] 8]. **1930** *Morning Post* 16 July 11/6 Only once..during their many long partnerships has a run-out been recorded. **1950** W. HAMMOND *Cricketers' School* xv. 140 He broke the wicket from 30 yards away in one of the most startling run-outs I have ever seen. **1976** *Milton Keynes Express* 2 July 41/6 If it had not been for three run-outs they might have got nearer their mammoth target.

3. *Mountaineering.* The length of rope required to climb a single pitch; also *transf.*, a pitch climbed by means of a single length of rope.

1920 [see *BELAYING *vbl. sb.* 2]. **1965** A. BLACKSHAW *Mountaineering* vii. 195 There are exceptions such as the routes on the Idwal Slabs in North Wales where many pitches involve run-outs of eighty feet or more. **1971** D. HASTON in C. Bonington *Annapurna South Face* xvii. 206 It was a long and tortuous pitch done in one run-out on one of our big ropes. *Ibid.* 214 My immediate prospect was a three hundred foot run-out to the top of the gully. **1972** —— *In High Places* ii. 28 It's slightly awkward to do full run-outs with three people on the rope.

4. An act or instance of running out, fleeing, or escaping; also *attrib.*, esp. in U.S. slang phr. *to take a run-out powder*, to withdraw; to leave, abscond; cf. *POWDER *sb.*[1] 2 h.

1920 *Our Navy* Aug. 33/1 The 'Wilmington' challenged us to a boat race, but when we slapped up a sack of good Chinese taels to back our team the 'Wily Willie' took a run-out powder and called off the race. **1928** *Amer. Mercury* May 80/1 The fair charmer has taken 'a run-out with the bank roll.' **1933** D. RUNYON in *Collier's* 28 Jan. 7/4 Well, The Sky says he sees no way of meeting these obligations and he is figuring the only thing he can do is to take a run-out powder. **1943** *Richmond* (Va.) *Times-Dispatch* 23 Aug. 2/1 (*heading*) Kiska forces disappointed by run-out. **1952** POHL & KORNBLATH in *Galaxy Sci. Fiction* July 147/2 You crossed us up with that cowardly run-out. *a* **1953** E. O'NEILL *Hughie* (1959) 14, I stuck it till I was eighteen before I took a run-out powder. **1968** 'E. PETERS' *Grass Widow's Tale* viii. 114 They came back for their money, just when she had everything planned for her run-out.

5. A mock auction. Cf. MOCK *a.* 2. Usu. with def. article or *attrib.*

1934 P. ALLINGHAM *Cheapjack* vii. 72 The London Mob were working the R.O. This is short for the 'Run Out'. **1938** F. D. SHARPE *Sharpe of Flying Squad* xv. 171 'Run out' shops disposing of valueless jewellery worked in conjunction with the pickpockets. *Ibid.* xxvii. 280 Run Out Shops have given me a good deal of work. Many of the methods of the Run Out Mob and their premises on which they hold their mock auctions of worthless junk range from small and cheap set-ups on the race-courses..to elaborate dens of swindle in the West End. **1939** J. B. PRIESTLEY *Let People Sing* x. 258 He told me his old partner, Charlie, had left him to join the run-out boys from Brum—that is, the gang from Birmingham running a fake auction—and, by the way, if anybody wants to see me lose my temper just let 'em talk as if I was on the run-out game. **1943** *Police Jrnl.* Mar. 69 *Run-out mob*, a gang that conducts mock auctions. **1959** *News Chron.* 16 Nov. 5 The run-out men..are mock auctioneers who draw large crowds with their showman's patter... As well as in Petticoat Lane, they operate in many of the seaside towns during the summer.

6. *Engin.* Deviation of a wheel, drill, etc., from its proper course; the extent of this.

1946 W. H. CROUSE *Automotive Mech.* xxiv. 512 Wobble or 'run-out' of the wheels can be checked by spinning the front wheels and holding a piece of chalk against the rim or side wall of the tire. **1951** C. W. KENNEDY *Inspection & Gaging* ii. 28 Common terms..are squareness, parallelism, waviness,..eccentric, run-out and out-of-line. **1975** BRAM & DOWNS *Manuf. Technol.* vii. 194 An important point of design is to reduce end thrust, to prevent bowing and flexing, producing as a consequence hole run-out and short drill-life. **1977** *Hot Car* Oct. 58/1 Subsequent to machining the wheels undergo a rigorous testing programme checking for run-out and wobble.

7. *Skiing.* = *OUTRUN *sb.* 4.

1956 *Ski-ing* ('Know the Game' Series) 13/2 These [nursery slopes] should be of average steepness at the top, have a gentle gradient in the middle and a long flat run out so that the ski will come to a stop naturally if the skier is unable to control them. **1974** *Rules of Game* 239/1 There must be a wide, gently sloping, and unobstructed run-out at the finish [of a ski-slope].

8. On a gramophone record, (the blank groove traversing) the annular area between the label and the grooves carrying the recording. Freq. *attrib.* as *run-out groove.*

1962 A. NISBETT *Technique Sound Studio* viii. 150 If the surface noise on the run in and run out of the two records is not sufficient..a 'blank'..record can be used to lend continuity of background. **1975** *Gramophone* May 2048/3 A new TD 145 turntable..has an automatic lift and shut-off device relying on electronic sensing of the run-out groove. **1976** *Ibid.* Nov. 768/2 What puzzles me is that both these discs do in fact bear the re-make matrix numbers on both label and needle run-out.

9. Special Comb. : **run-out table** (see quot. 1948).

1948 T. LYMAN *Metals Handbk.* 12/2 *Runout table*, in a rolling mill a plane area at the receiving end, for holding rolled metal. **1973** J. G. TWEEDDALE *Materials Technol.* II. 99 Most commonly, a hot semicontinuous extrusion press..is placed horizontally so that the extruded product can be discharged straight on to a 'run-out' table and never has to carry its own weight in tension whilst in its weakened hot state.

ru·n-over. Also runover. [f. RUN *v.*] **1.** (See RUN *sb.*[1] 8.) (Further examples.) Also, an instance of overrunning a time limit.

1937 *Printers' Ink Monthly* May 42/1 *Runovers*, occasions when the [radio] program itself overruns its allotted time. **1947** J. BERTRAM *Shadow of War* VI. 203 The shifts of the P.O.W. in stowing his loot, and..the *amount* that can be carried by one man on his own person, even through a 'run-over' and a 'strip-search'. **1963** *Times* 27 Sept. 12/4 Lord Home, the Foreign Secretary, today met Mr. Dean Rusk, the American Secretary of State, for nearly three hours and had what was called 'a very full runover' of matters of mutual concern.

2. In *Printing*, etc., the action or an instance of continuing matter into a margin, or on to a subsequent line or page.

1934 WEBSTER, *Run-over*, an extension, as of printed matter, beyond the space allotted; overmatter; also, U.S., the part of an article continued from a preceding page. **1956** N. R. KER *Pastoral Care* 21 The runover to avoid breaking a word at the end of the last line on fos. 49v, 50v, 68r, marked by a dot at the end of the line and another before the runover itself. **1969** in Halpert & Story *Christmas Mumming in Newfoundland* 192 The placing of the speech designations has been regularized, the run-over of lines in narrow newspaper columns abandoned, [etc.]. **1976** H. MACINNES *Agent in Place* ix. 96 The typescript finished each line neatly—no runovers onto the right-hand margin.

runt, *sb.* Add: **1. b.** (Further example.)

1928 R. CAMPBELL *Wayzgoose* ii. 58 The Sacred Carrot with the golden rind, Whose magic runt..The more one nibbled it, the larger grew.

2. d. (Further examples.) In *gen.* use, a small pig that is weakly or undernourished.

1939 V. C. FISHWICK *Pigs* I. i. 19 Such piglings grow well and are a sound proposition. They are not regarded as 'runts', a term which is here used to describe a pig that is in poor condition. **1939** *Nature* 23 Sept. 552/2 Radiographic examination of a 'runt', the small starveling pig, shows evidence of arrested growth in the skeleton. **1977** P. R. ENGLISH et al. *Sow* viii. 163 One can have a litter in which most piglets are thriving well but in which one or two are obviously suffering from malnutrition and are in danger of becoming nutritional 'runts'.

3. c. (Further examples.) Also used in weakened sense as a term of abuse.

1896 *Dialect Notes* I. 423 *Runt*, worthless fellow. (Cowboys.) *c* **1926** 'MIXER' *Transport Workers' Song Bk.* 52 As a slimy runt, I'm it! **1930** *Amer. Speech* V. 119 The expression 'little runt' was merely contemptuous. **1936** *Nat. Geogr. Mag.* June 787/2 A cadet's height determines his assignment, the tall men going to the 'flanker' companies, A and M, the 'runts' to companies F and G in the center. **1956** J. CANNON *Who struck John?* 228 You're Conn McCreary, a fat runt. You're tiny. **1958** *Chicago Tribune* 9 Feb. (Comics Feature Mag.) 9 'Anyhow, who'd ever think of connecting that runt with *this* deal?' 'Maybe you're right! But just the same I'm going to keep my beady eye on young Mister Dondi.' **1969** I. & P. OPIE *Children's Games* viii. 234 'Come on you miserable runts,' we say, and one of the runts runs up the steps, only to be thrown over the side of the railing.

d. (Earlier and later examples.)

1819 M. WILMOT *Let.* 8 Dec. (1935) 32 What think you of my *deeply* regretting not having brought a white Tabinet gown. 'Tis admired here beyond satin, and my old *runt* has in consequence been jinkumbobbed out of Mamselle and white satin till the poor dear old dress..is become the most admired thing I have. **1973** *Amer. Speech 1969* XLIV. 249 In official terminology, ground signals are referred to as *dwarf* signals, but railroad men call them *pots*, because they are round and silver, or *runts*, because they are small in comparison with the signals on bridges that span the tracks.

runted, *a.* Delete '*Obs.* exc. *dial.*' and add later examples.

1951 E. PAUL *Springtime in Paris* iii. 50 The myriads of chimney pots and vents are like runted gargoyles which look up toward scudding clouds and mackerel skies instead of downward. **1961** R. P. HOBSON *Rancher takes Wife* ii. 38 Two runted pearl-gray kittens purred and rubbed themselves against Rich's legs. **1976** T. HEALD *Let Sleeping Dogs Die* v. 87 Runted little dogs here are. No wind and dreadful temperaments.

ru·n-through. Also runthrough. Pl. run-throughs, runs-through. [f. RUN *v.*] **1.** A (freq. hasty or cursory) rehearsal of a play, a radio or television programme, etc. Also *gen.* a performance or showing (of a play, film, etc.), esp. a preview.

1923 WODEHOUSE *Inimitable Jeeves* x. 104 It must have been about a week after this rummy little episode that George Caffyn called me up and asked me if I would care to go and see a run-through of his show. **1930** J. DOS PASSOS *42nd Parallel* IV. 287 She felt it in her bones that the play would be a hit..and Mr Freelby said Ike Gold.. had sat through the runthrough with the tears running down his cheeks. **1946** *Life* 2 Dec. 51 The director, handsomely played by Sam Wanamaker, talks of his theatrical troubles until the star, Mary Grey, appears. There begins a run-through of a play about Joan of Arc, with Mary in the lead. **1952** S. KAUFFMANN *Philanderer* (1953) xiii. 217 She had to go back for the final run-through. **1957** DUNCAN & BONE *Oxf. Pkt. Bk. Athletic Training* (ed. 2) v. 71 Minor adjustments being made before competition after practice runs-through. **1959** *Times* 10 July 9/1 The two gentlemen were felicitously played at this public *première* (as at the private run-through half a year ago) by Mr. Stephen Manton and Mr. Bruce Boyce. **1963** *Ann. Reg. 1962* 421 *Christopher Sly*, a chamber opera by Thomas Eastwood, heard in Britain only in a public run-through in 1960, was given its first staging at Pforzheim. **1973** *Times* 17 Oct. 11/2, I.. immediately asked about rehearsals. I was told there would be run-throughs with a full orchestra but without the chorus and other principals. **1973** E. LEMARCHAND *Let or Hindrance* xiv. 177 The film..has been very recently edited... Like a run-through of this last part? **1977** S. BRETT *Star Trap* v. 53 The..cast assembled for a pre-tour run-through.

2. A brief survey (of facts); a summary, a concise account.

1947 *Sun* (Baltimore) 20 Mar. 1/6 The Big Four conference which, at the conclusion of the ninth session tonight, had accomplished little more than a run-through of German issues on which the Council is split. **1957** [see *FADO]. **1963** *Listener* 7 Mar. 432/2, I gave a group of young Russians a quick run-through of Eng. Lit. from Hopkins and Hardy to Amis and Osborne. **1973** A. HUNTER *Gently French* iv. 36 Tell me about Quarles... Give me a quick run through.

3. The fact or an instance of running trains through intermediate points without stopping for crew changing, loading, etc.

1964 *Canad. Labour* Dec. 31/3 Representatives of the non-operating railway unions met in Montreal with officials of the running trades to work out a common policy on rail abandonments, runthroughs and other technological changes. **1967** *Canad. Ann. Rev. 1966* 29 The implementation of the Freedman report on railway run-throughs. **1969** *Jane's Freight Containers 1968–69* 125/3 To improve interline service, the Frisco is cooperating with connecting rail carriers to pre-block traffic in run-through trains—avoiding intermediate terminal switching operations.

runting (rʊ·ntiŋ), *vbl. sb.* [f. RUNT *sb.* + -ING[1].] **1.** The birth or development of (laboratory) animals that are small for their kind.

1959 *Jrnl. Exper. Med.* CX. 522 Runting is the result of an immunological reaction of foreign cells against a tolerant host. **1974** *Nature* 11 Oct. 548/2 In some litters all rats grew normally and there was no runting. **1978** *Ibid.* 27 July 365/2 In the colony described here there has been no evidence of the runting syndrome frequently seen in conventional nude mice.

2. (See quot.) *slang.*

1976 *Drive* July–Aug. 37/2 In the [ice-cream] trade, giving kids small portions when no parents are about is called 'runting'.

runtish, *a.* Add: **1.** Also, of human beings.

1969 N. COHN *AWopBopaLooBop* (1970) x. 89 He grew up small, runtish, with bad hair and unhealthy skin. **1974** 'R. TATE' *Birds of Bloodied Feather* ii. 30 The child.. was about thirteen, runtish and not very clean.

runty, *a.* Add: **1.** (Further examples.) Also *Comb.*

1848 in Farmer & Henley *Slang* (1903) VI. 84/2 'No indeed,' ses another little runty-lookin' feller—we've got enuff to do to take care of our own babys in these diggins. **1903** J. LONDON *People of Abyss* xii. 143 We cannot understand the starved and runty toiler of the East End.. till we look at the strapping Life Guardsmen of the West End. **1938** M. K. RAWLINGS *Yearling* xiv. 156 Us Baxters is all runty and tough. **1972** *New Yorker* 22 Jan. 100/2 A young English mother..gets herself sexually awakened by a runty Italian actor... If Miranda were more intelligent and Oreste less swinish, their obsessive affair might touch us deeply. **1974** *Sci. Amer.* Nov. 61/1 The treated birds were runty and deficient in lymphocytes; all cell-mediated immune functions were suppressed.

run-up. Add: Also run up, runup. **1. b.** (Further examples.) Also *attrib.* Chiefly in *Golf.*

1907 'I. HAY' *Pip* III. xi. 339 Anything in the shape of a run-up ball would be trapped. **1931** *Daily Express* 31 Jan. 9/5 Compston, playing a run-up shot to the first green, shouted after the ball, 'Hit the stick.' **1955** *Times* 2 May 4/1 On most of Friday he putted well, and his run-ups were often in the highest class. **1963** *Times* 14 Jan. 3/7 Agate won back the 13th, where he played a run-up to the hole.

c. A run made in preparation for jumping, throwing, etc., in *Athletics*; in *Cricket*, the bowler's approach to the bowling crease before delivery.

1897 *Encycl. Sport* I. 52/2 Pace in the run-up supplies the impetus; spring enables the jumper to lift himself into the air. **1919** F. A. M. Webster et al. *Success in Athletics* x. 83 The last stride must be a short one, so that the jumping leg may be gathered well under the body for the spring. This accounts for the run-up, which must be most assiduously practised. **1929** G. M. Butler *Mod. Athletics* ix. 120 *The run-up.* The first essential of successful long jumping is speed in the approach. *Ibid.* 122 Should the run-up be inaccurate, there will be a loss of at least a foot. **1948** K. S. Duncan *Oxf. Pkt. Bk. Athletic Training* iv. 62 Practise and standardize the run-up, cross step and throwing stance. **1959** *Times* 17 June 6/6 Horner, with his upright stance and utter immobility during the bowler's run-up. *Ibid.* 24 Aug. 4/2 She was handicapped..in the long jump by a crumbling run-up. **1966** B. Johnston *Armchair Cricket 1966* 97 If the batsmen attempt to steal a run during the bowler's run-up [etc.]. **1974** *Rules of Game* 18/3 The parallel lines may be crossed during run-up, but the competitor must be between them when the javelin is released. **1977** J. Laker *One-Day Cricket* 48 The length of a bowler's run-up is limited to 15 yards.

d. = *run-in 3.

1942 *R.A.F. Jrnl.* 27 June 8 Another Stirling and a Wellington adopted almost identically the same run-up as ourselves. **1958** 'N. Shute' *Rainbow & Rose* ii. 43, I went up again and circled round... 'I'm going to do a dummy run.'.. I took a longer run-up this time. **1976** 'G. Black' *Moon for Killers* vii. 99 A small, single-prop job was coming in for a landing..its turn completed, the run-up going to be towards us.

e. A period of time or series of occurrences leading up *to* some important (freq. political) event; an action which prepares the way for one on a larger scale.

1966 *Sunday Times* 20 Nov. 48/2 The Petit Palais show offers, also, invaluable evidence in its drawing section of the ways in which Picasso manoeuvred during the crucial run-up to the 'Demoiselles d'Avignon'. **1968** *Listener* 5 Dec. 761/1 The run-up to the election of Oxford's new Poetry Professor has aroused a good deal of mirthful interest. **1970** *Daily Tel.* 2 Jan. 14 The 1970s open, with the approach and run-up to the most critical General Election in a generation. **1975** M. Kenyon *Mr. Big.* v. 47 Heathrow was the run-up to the train job because there had to be capital. **1976** *Nature* 29 July 344/2 Remaining hitches in reactor technology can, it is argued, be straightened out during the 20-year run-up to a commercial FBR network. **1977** *Film & Television Technician* Jan. 1/2 During the run-up to the overtime ban..the Trade Press was uniformly critical of the employers.

3. On the *U.S. Stock Market*, a rapid increase in the price or value of a commodity. Now also in *gen.* use.

1935 *Sun* (Baltimore) 13 Apr. 17/8 Corn advanced to 1 to 1¼ cents a bushel, but cotton was reactionary after Thursday's run-up. **1942** *Ibid.* 1 Oct. 21 Laclede gas preferred had a runup of 6½ points. **1953** *Ibid.* 30 Oct. B-28/1 A fast runup in the final dealings gave the stock market one of its sharpest boosts of the year yesterday. **1958** *Wall St. Jrnl.* 3 Dec. 27/4 Referring to the recent sharp run-up and activity in Walworth Co. stock, amid talk of merger possibilities, Fred W. Belz, president, said [etc.]. **1976** *National Observer* (U.S.) 6 Mar. 4/3 The price scare and runup in the futures prices in recent weeks 'says to me that farmers deep down inside know that this crop is not lost'. **1978** *Daily Tel.* 15 Sept. 21/4 Money market analysts have been watching a rapid run-up in short-term, negotiable bank certificates of deposit and commercial paper traded by corporations. **1979** *Time* 13 Aug. 26/3 The industry most severely dented by the oil run-up is auto manufacturing.

4. The running of a motor or mechanical device until it attains normal working or speed; warming up.

1943 *Yank* 26 Feb. 6 Last summer the intensive heat raised hell with us AMs in making engine run-ups for regulation check on props, [etc.]. **1946** *Happy Landings* July 3/1 Correct use of air filters and observing precautions against dust during run up are matters for the pilot to remember. **1958** 'Castle' & 'Hailey' *Flight into Danger* i. 16 In the run-up each engine in turn is opened to full throttle and the mags tested separately. **1959** W. S. Sharps *Dict. Cinematogr.* 126/2 *Run up*, the term given to the passage of film or a magnetic recording medium through a camera or recorder before the correct recording speed is obtained; or through a projector or other machine before the first subject image or sound is reached. **1962** A. Nisbett *Technique Sound Studio* viii. 139 The reproducer may take as much as a second or so to run up... Check this run-up time by using a recording of pure tone.

runway. For 'Chiefly *U.S.*' read 'orig. *U.S.*' and add: Also **run-way. 1. a.** (Earlier and later examples.)

1833 C. F. Hoffman *Winter in West* (1835) I. 202 The numerous deer-runways,..and innumerable tracks of rackoons, wolves, and bears, showed us that we were upon a favourite hunting ground of the Pottawattamies. **1855** *Knickerbocker* XLV. 193 The sound of the rifle has by this time brought the other hunters from their runways. **1908** A. J. Dawson *Finn* x. 168 Reynard picked up the dead rabbit and..trotted leisurely down the runway towards his own earth. **1948** A. L. Rand *Mammals Eastern Rockies* 45 Four of them [*sc.* species of shrews] are terrestrial animals, often making little runways through the moss. **1953** P. Provencher *I live in Woods* xii. 117 In winter the rabbit runway is easily distinguished in the snow. **1977** *Sci. Amer.* May 106/2 Rats in the laboratory have logged endless miles in runways, mazes and activity wheels.

b. (Earlier and later examples.)

1871 W. M. Lewis *People's Pract. Poultry Bk.* 8 The hennery should be placed in a warm, dry location..with runways ample to allow of plenty of exercise. **1913** J. London *Valley of Moon* xiv. 459 A goodly portion was devoted to white-washed henhouses and wired runways wherein hundreds of chickens were to be seen. **1949** *Sat. Even. Post* 9 Apr. 59/2 He even had a plan for one in his desk; the runways were to be painted green outside and whitewashed inside.

2. a. (Earlier and later examples.) *spec.* in *Theatr.* use (see quot. 1926); also in *Fashion*, a raised gangway on which models parade when exhibiting clothes.

1883 E. W. Howe *Country Town* iv. 20 Pushing this into my wagon with the assistance of his wife, after we had first made a run-way of boards, I hauled him to Fairview. **1901** Merwin & Webster *Calumet 'K'* xiii. 246 A runway from the hoist to the end of the building. **1912** 'W. Lawton' *Boy Aviators' Flight for Fortune* ix. 102 The rolling glide down the runway was made..and at last the bow of the *Sea Eagle*'s hull struck the water. **1926** *Amer Speech* I. 437/2 *Runway*, a platform built at stage level and extending part way down the center aisle of the theater. Used in burlesque and musical comedy for the presentation of chorus numbers. **1929** *Variety* 11 Sept. 54 Muggs still going for burlesque want that close-up of flesh which the runway provides or they won't give the teasers a tumble. **1941** B. Schulberg *What makes Sammy Run?* xii. 287 The solid glass desk looked like a burlesque runway. **1961** *Sunday Times* 3 Dec. 29/2 Advertising is the next fattener of bank accounts, then fashion photography and finally live modelling on the runways at fashion shows. **1971** C. Fick *Danziger Transcript* 95 Fourteen skinny models rehearsing on a runway. **1979** *Tucson Mag.* Mar. 12/3 Producer Spots Baxter's lifeless body stretched out on the runway of his great stage.

b. A specially prepared surface on an airfield for the taking off and landing of aircraft.

1923 *Aviation* 8 Oct. 445/1 (*caption*) A wonderful landmark—Boston Airport with its T type runways. **1926** *Nat. Geogr. Mag.* Sept. 363/2 We got off the end of the runway at a terrific speed. **1930** *Flight* 7 Feb. 194/1 To make it usable for aircraft, cinders have been laid to form three runways and these are raised above the rest of the unprepared ground. **1943** *Times* 16 Dec. 3/4 In northern Burma the U.S. Air Forces destroyed runways and dumps and burned barrack areas. **1957** *Economist* 21 Sept. 922/2 The sprawling Tachikawa airfield on the northern fringes of Tokyo is regularly the scene of 'anti-base' demonstrations by Japanese who uproot boundary fences, plant flagpoles on the runways and skirmish with the police. **1977** *Whitaker's Almanack 1978* 572 There was an official death toll of 576 when two Boeing 747 jumbo jets ..collided on the runway at Santa Cruz airport.

4. (Example.)

1874 B. F. Taylor *World on Wheels* II. vii. 250 Like the dusty 'run-ways' of thy brooks, soft pulses have grown dry and dumb.

5. *attrib.* and *Comb.*, as (sense *2 b) *runway aerodrome, marker, strip*; **runway light,** each of a series of lights marking the course of a runway.

1933 *Jrnl. R. Aeronaut. Soc.* XXXVII. 3 Detroit, where a purely runway aerodrome has been developed. **1951** *Gloss. Aeronaut. Terms* (*B.S.I.*) III. 24 *Runway lights*, lights defining a runway to indicate the area of taking-off and landing. **1958** 'Castle' & 'Hailey' *Flight into Danger* xi. 154 Put out your runway lights, except zero-eight. **1976** 'A. Hall' *Kobra Manifesto* xv. 200 The flick-flick-flick of the runway lights, falling away. **1939** *Air Ann. Brit. Empire* 65 A new metal runway marker has been introduced in order to improve the safety of aeroplane landings. **1937** *Sun* (Baltimore) 21 Apr. 9/6 The field should be equipped with boundary and beacon lights and the area of the runway strips outside of the paved portion should be sod.

Hence **ru·nwayed** *a.*, provided with a runway; consisting of runways.

1948 *Hansard Commons* 15 Mar. 1806 Two-fifths of a runwayed airfield is covered with concrete runways. **1949** *Jrnl. R. Aeronaut. Soc.* LIII. 903/1 Large grass areas on runwayed aerodromes are a liability in upkeep, except insofar as grass drying is a revenue-earning aspect.

Runyonesque (rʌ:nyənɛ·sk), *a.* [f. the name *Runyon* (see below) + -esque.] Characteristic of or resembling Alfred Damon *Runyon* (1884–1946), U.S. journalist and author, or his writings. Also **Runyonese** (-ī·z), slang or underworld jargon characteristic or suggestive of that used in the short stories of Runyon.

1938 *Times Lit. Suppl.* 22 Jan. 59/2 A good many people appear to think that 'runyonese'..is not only vulgar but also pernicious. **1938** *N.Y. Times* 28 Feb. 19/1 For a Runyonesque panel the casting director had the marvelous good fortune to find Edward G. Robinson and Ruth Donnelly to play Mr. and Mrs. **1950** *Observer* 22 Oct. 7/4 It is hard to comment on the quality of translation without seeing the original, and Mr. Maclaren-Ross had had to cope with that appallingly difficult problem of specialised slang. Mr. Maclaren-Ross's solution is Runyonesque, probably the most suitable, but still inevitably tending to denationalise the book. **1953** P. Bonner *SPQR* xvii. 150 Runyonese..is the patois which best illustrates the swath which this character is cutting. **1955** *Time* 6 June 109/1 Ruth was singing in obscure Chicago nightclubs when she first encountered a Runyonesque character who called himself Colonel Martin Snyder. **1964** *Amer. Speech* XXXIX. 304 He gives details of murders, gang wars, robberies, and the activities and special talents of such Runyonesque members of Costa Nostra as Vincent 'Jimmy Blue Eyes' Alo, [etc.]. **1964** E. P. Hoyt *Gentleman of Broadway* xvi. 249 Librarians were surprised that Runyon continued to be popular long after his style of slang and much of the language which was called 'Runyonese' had been thoroughly absorbed in American English. **1980** *Jewish Chron.* 4 Jan. 15/5 Its characters are a little self-consciously drawn, notably a pair of Runyonesque policemen.

rupestral, *a.* Add: Also as *sb.*, a rupestral plant. (Further examples.)

1926 J. J. Walker *Nat. Hist. Oxford Distr.* 104 Many of these [alpine species] are rupestrals. **1932** G. C. Druce *Comital Flora Brit. Isles* p. xiii, A 'rupestral' may also be a wet or a dry lover. **1970** *Watsonia* VIII. 115 Unlike most species of *Hieracium* it is usually a soil plant rather than rupestral.

rupestrine *a.* (example); **rupestrean,** also **rupe·strian** *a.*, done on rock or cave walls.

1896 A. H. Keane *Ethnology* 137 The carvings on the dolmen *des marchands*, Brittany, are almost identical with those of the so-called 'rupestrian inscriptions' of Tunisia and South Algeria. **1934** 'H. MacDiarmid' *Stony Limits & Other Poems* 52 Look over this beach. What ruderal and rupestrine growth is here? **1952** O. R. Gurney *Hittites* 215 The powerful rupestrian art of the later [Hittite] empire was probably stimulated by the rulers. **1967** M. Bullock tr. *Lommel's World of Early Hunters* iv. 127 The influence of rupestrian art on Negro art, particularly Negro sculpture, has not been elucidated. When we speak of African art we have grown accustomed to thinking only of Negro art, ignoring the rock-paintings or referring to them only marginally.

rupiah (rūpī·ă). [Indonesian, f. Hind. *rūpiyah*: see Rupee.] The basic monetary unit of Indonesia, equal to 100 sen.

1947 *Encycl. Brit. Bk. of Year* 307/2 The new Indonesian republic on Oct. 30 [1946] began the issue of its own currency, the rupiah, and on Dec. 1 declared its value to be 1·9 per U.S. dollar. **1952** *Ann. Reg. 1951* III. 335 The estimated deficit in the Budget was reduced to Rupiahs 987 million. **1959** 'M. Derby' *Tigress* iv. 154 Traders..preferred to sell..in free markets for honest currency instead of government controlled prices in semi-worthless Indonesian *rupiahs*. **1964** *Asia Mag.* 27 Sept. 17/2 A fantastic rise in the rupiah costs of Indonesian projects. **1973** D. May *Laughter in Djakarta* ii. 33 He gave her a hundred rupiah note. **1977** *Time* 16 May 14/1 You start dropping in 10,000-rupiah ($24) notes until he says that's enough and closes the drawer.

rupt (rʌpt), *a. rare.* [f. as Rupt *v.*] Broken, craggy.

1916 Blunden *Harbingers* 66 Run, echo, up the tarn's rupt wall.

ruptured, *ppl. a.* Add: **3. ruptured duck** *U.S. Forces' slang*, (*a*) a damaged aircraft; (*b*) the discharge button given to ex-service men, with reference to its eagle motif.

1930 'W. W. Windstaff' in S. Longstreet *Canvas Falcons* (1970) xvii. 291, I began to look for a place to bring down my ruptured duck, oil spitting in my face. **1945** *Time* 29 Oct. 11/1 The design of the present discharge button is not popular (G.I.s know it as the 'ruptured duck'). **1953** R. Chandler *Long Goodbye* xxxiii. 202 He was wearing a British Army Service badge. Their version of the ruptured duck. **1955** A. Morgan *Great Man* 34 Just another guy in a sailor suit with a ruptured duck and a set of discharge papers. **1959** W. Faulkner *Mansion* xii. 333 The ex-soldier or -sailor or -marine with his ruptured duck pushing the perambulator with one hand.

rupturing, *vbl. sb.* Restrict *Bot.* to sense in Dict. and add: **2.** *attrib.* **rupturing capacity** *Electr. Engin.*, a measure of the ability of a circuit-breaker to withstand the surge produced by its operation.

1916 C. C. Garrard *Electr. Switch & Controlling Gear* ii. 54 The remaining considerations which determine the rupturing capacity of an oil circuit breaker apart from size, robustness, quickness of break and, of course, the quality of the oil used, are length and number of breaks under oil, or speaking generally the capability of the switch to bring a large quantity of oil into intimate contact with the arc so as to smother the same as effectively as possible. **1930** *Engineering* 24 Jan. 97/3 These circuit breakers were designed for a rupturing capacity of 1,000,000 kva. **1970** J. Shepherd et al. *Higher Electr. Engin.* (ed. 2) xvii. 560 It is normal practice to specify the rupturing capacity of circuit breakers in kilovolt-amperes or megavolt-amperes. This practice is well established but may be criticized as not being logical, since the breaking capacity in megavolt-amperes is obtained from the product of short-circuit current and recovery voltage.

rural, *a.* and *sb.* Add: **A.** *adj.* **7.** Special collocations, as *rural district council*, the local council of a rural district (see District *sb.* 3 b); abbrev. **R.D.C.*; *rural free delivery* (U.S.), the free delivery of mail to a rural area with limited local postal services; *rural industry*, an industry or manufacture carried out in the country; (*Women's*) *Rural Institute* (Sc.), a Women's Institute (see quot. 1958); *rural municipality* (Canad.), an administrative division of a province; *rural route* (N. Amer.), a rural mail-delivery route; *rural science*, the study of rural concerns, esp. agriculture; *rural slum*, a country dwelling in disrepair; *rural–urban* adj., designating comparison or interchange between country and town; *rural urbanization*, the investment of the country with an urban character.

1894, 1895 Rural district council [see *district-council* s.v. DISTRICT *sb.* 6]. **1929** [see *COUNCIL-HOUSE 2]. **1974** *Times* 1 Apr. 14/1 In all, 422 authorities take over the functions of the 1,385 existing authorities—counties, boroughs, urban and rural district councils. **1893** M. H. CUSHING *Story of our Post Office* 1006 A very important effect of the rural free delivery has been to increase the pay of postmasters where it has been tried. **1900** *Congress. Rec.* 16 Jan. 873/1 The rural free delivery service has come to stay. **1930** J. M. STAHL *Growing with West* viii. 109, I talked upon rural free delivery to many thousands. **1944** *N.Y. Times* 19 Oct. 23/2 Mr. Stahl first proposed the establishment of the rural free delivery service in 1879. **1892** *Pall Mall Gaz.* 23 June 2/1 There is little hope of the general establishment of rural industries as long as the Post Office treats country districts with such scant consideration. **1949** 'J. TEY' *Brat Farrar* xxiv. 219 Mrs Stack,..being interested solely in rural industries, represented a Fixed Point in the flux of an agricultural show. **1958** *Listener* 6 Nov. 746/3 Are the efforts of the Rural Industries Organization being bent in the right direction? **1973** *Country Life* 28 June 1904/2 Twenty-seven small rural industries serving agriculture will be represented. **1922** *Scottish Women's Rural Institutes Handbk.* 1921 24 The Badge of the Scottish Women's Rural Institutes may be obtained from..London. **1932** 'O. DOUGLAS' *Priorsford* xxvii. 242 'Have you heard how many teams are going in for the Festival?'.. 'Seven. Three of them Rural Institutes.' 'The Rurals are very good as a rule.' **1958** *Everyman's Encycl.* XII. 637/1 In Scotland there is a similar [to the Women's Institutes] but quite independent organisation, and the title 'Rural Institutes' is used. **1861** *Nor' Wester* (Red River Settlement, Canada) 15 Aug. 1/4 Such was the state of things in Canada until 1847, when the Canadian Legislature passed an act (4 & 3 Vic. cap 10) to extend the municipal system to districts (now counties) and other rural municipalities. **1904** *Univ. Toronto Stud. Hist. & Econ.* II. 140 The council of a rural municipality is made up of a reeve and not less than four nor more than six councillors, the number being fixed by by-law. **1945** G. W. BROWN *Canad. Democracy in Action* (1947) vii. 84 One of the reasons for the apparent confusion is that rural municipalities go by different names in different provinces. **1964** *Naicam* (Sask.) *Sentinel* 26 Mar. 2/3 A meeting of the council of the Rural Municipality of Pleasantdale No. 398 was held in the R.M. office Wednesday. **1898** *Ann. Rep.* (U.S. Post Office Dept.) 163 Nine rural routes were carefully laid out by special agents of the free delivery service. **1956** *Chatham* (Ont.) *Daily News* 14 June 2/6 Entrants will be accepted from Thamesville and surrounding rural routes. **1965** *Globe & Mail* (Toronto) 15 Oct. 7/1 George Harris Hees of Bay Street, Toronto, St. James Street, Montreal, and, within the last month, of Rural Route 5, Cobourg. **1914** Rural science [see *HOUSECRAFT]. **1939** *Nature* 18 Feb. 305 (*heading*) Training teachers of rural science. **1976** *Daily Times* (Lagos) 24 May 13/3 In order to promote sufficient interest in the tillage of the land subjects like nature study and rural science should be made compulsory in all primary schools. **1958** P. POLLACK *Picture Hist. Photogr.* III. 350/2 The somber, seamy existence endured by Americans living in rural slums. **1972** L. LAMB *Picture Frame* i. 13 Why..should an extremely sophisticated exponent of abstract expressionism decide to set up his easel in..this rural slum? **1975** *Times* 10 Sept. 18/3 The site enveloped a rural slum community. **1957** R. K. MERTON *Soc. Theory & Soc. Structure* (1962) xviii. 592 Differences in rural–urban distribution of the two religions ..may be seen. **1970** B. ROBERTS in I. L. Horowitz *Masses in Lat. Amer.* x. 346 The career experiences of low-income families, such as rural–urban and intra-urban migration. **1974** tr. *Wertheim's Evolution & Revolution* 198 Intensified rural–urban relationships might equally increase the revolutionary potential while..facilitating communication lines for revolutionaries. **1970** J. COTLER in I. L. Horowitz *Masses in Lat. Amer.* xii. 436 As a result of the confluence of urban ruralization and of rural urbanization, there has been a change in the patterns of social stratification of Mancha India.

B. *sb.* **3.** ellipt. for: (*a*) *(*Women's*) *Rural Institute*; (*b*) **Rural District Council* (rare).

1932 [see (*Women's*) *Rural Institute*, sense A. 7 above]. **1940** 'O. DOUGLAS' *House that is our Own* viii. 82 'She takes to do wi' the Nursing and the Rural.' 'The Rural?' 'Aye, ye ken, Women's Rural Institute.' **1952** M. LASKI *Village* iv. 71 The new Housing Estate..the Walbridge Rural is going to put down at the bottom of Archery Lane. **1967** I. TAIN *Cherrycake Death* ii. 15 The Rurals were generally held to fulfil a need in the district. **1973** A. MACVICAR *Painted Doll Affair* x. 113 Jessie's out at a Women's Rural and Moira's at night school.

rurban (rɒ̄·ɹbăn), *a.* [f. R(URAL *a.* + URBAN *a.*] Combining the characteristics of country and town; designating an area sharing rural and urban ways of life.

1918 C. J. GALPIN *Rural Life* iii. 64 The word *rurban* is formed by blending *rural* into *urban*. **1932** *Times Lit. Suppl.* 11 Feb. 86/2 The science of towns..shows itself a science with technical terms, such as 'conurbation' and 'rurban'. **1939** O. E. BAKER in *Agric. in Mod. Life* I. ix. 165 Should..rural and urban merge in what has been called a 'rurban' civilization the cultural consequences would also be profound. **1945** H. H. BALK in *Econ. Geogr.* XXI. 108/2 A rurban area has very definite advantages over a strictly agricultural or rural area from the farmer's point of view. **1961** *New Yorker* 28 Oct. 43/3 In an article about the spread of highways and housing developments from cities to former farmland, we came upon a reference to 'the rurban explosion'. **1981** *Country Life* 2 July 7 To draw attention to his unsatisfactory rural-urban development, the Second Land Utilisation Survey has given it a distinctive name: rurban fringe.

Hence **ru·rbanism**, the properties of town and country life regarded as interacting and inseparable; **ru·rbanist**, an advocate of rurbanism; **rurbaniza·tion** the susceptibility of town life to rural influences.

1918 C. J. GALPIN *Rural Life* iii. 64 The idea of rurbanism is that..the open country is an element in the clustered town, and the town is a factor of the land, and the civilization, culture, and development of rural people are to be found in conjunction with town and small city, and not apart. *Ibid.*, The rurbanist boldly attempts to adjust anew the malrelations of the farm to the cluster. **1931** N. CARPENTER *Sociol. City Life* xiv. 453 Urbanized societies are those in which the cultural effects of 'rurbanization' are to be found. **1943** C. L. WHITE *Regional Geogr. Anglo-America* xiii. 403 Rather than have three fourths to four fifths of our population reside in great cities, O. E. Baker recommends rurbanism. **1959** *Economist* 30 May 850/1 Millions of city dwellers have swarmed into the countryside to set a new and increasingly widespread pattern of life which is sometimes called 'rurbanisation', sometimes 'urbiculture'. **1976** *National Observer* (U.S.) 10 July 6/4 He calls the young back-to-the-landers the 'vanguard of a new ruralism'. Another way to look at it is the 'rurbanization' of America, he says.

Ruritania (rūᵊritēⁱ·niă). [Name of the scene of Anthony Hope's novels *The Prisoner of Zenda* (1894) and *Rupert of Hentzau* (1898); f. L. *rūri-s, rūs* country + *-tania* as in *Lusitania*.] An imaginary kingdom of Central Europe: used allusively for a scene of court romance and intrigue in a modern setting, or for a petty state; more generally, any imaginary country.

[**1894** 'A. HOPE' *Prisoner of Zenda* i. 9 There came on a visit to the English Court a certain prince, who was afterwards known to history as Rudolf the Third of Ruritania.] **1897** G. B. SHAW in *Sat. Rev.* 30 Jan. 115/2 If Mr Alexander..had produced it and Sodom's Ende and so forth at a series of *matinées* of the 'Saturday Pop' class, financing them from the exchequer of the Kingdom of Ruritania [etc.]. **1929** —— *League of Nations* 8 Let us suppose that Ruritania is given a mandate to govern Lilliput provisionally for Lilliput's good. **1939** *Flight* 21 Sept. 249/1 One cannot expect every Ruritania to maintain an air arm equal to that of the Germans. **1956** A. WILSON *Anglo-Saxon Attitudes* 154 Inge..looked like the queen of some Northern Ruritania at the novel's happy ending. **1965** *New Statesman* 23 Apr. 638/1 Britain is being slowly pushed out of the main manufacturing export markets, and is taking refuge in the luxury trades... I suppose if we can't make our living in any other way, it will have to do. But let's not kid ourselves about a renaissance. This is national senescence, the Road to Ruritania. **1976** *Times* 9 Mar. 17/2 The right tactics..are to let the central bank of Ruritania drive the price of sterling down against itself.

Ruritanian (rūᵊritēⁱ·niăn), *a.* (*sb.*) [f. prec. + -AN.] Of, pertaining to, or characteristic of Ruritania, esp. with reference to the romantic or fanciful associations of the name; hence used with reference to any imaginary country. Also as *sb.*, an inhabitant or supporter of a Ruritania, or a person endowed with Ruritanian attributes or characteristics; more generally, an imaginary inhabitant of a country.

1894 'A. HOPE' *Prisoner of Zenda* i. 9 Prince Rudolf.. was adroitly smuggled off by the Ruritanian ambassador. *Ibid.* ii. 24 Every Ruritanian knows Duke Michael. **1896** G. B. SHAW in *Sat. Rev.* 11 Jan. 39/1 Our common sense which, if aroused, must immediately put a summary stop to the somewhat silly Ruritanian gambols of our imagination. **1902** *Daily Chron.* 21 Nov. 5/4 'The Traitors' is a spirited example of what may be called Ruritanian romance. **1920** H. G. WELLS *Outl. Hist.* xxxvii. 601 He [*sc.* Mirabeau] had..indulged in a sort of Ruritanian flirtation with the queen. **1935** *Punch* 20 Mar. 335/1 The third volume of *The Story of My Life* by Marie, Queen of Roumania..consists almost entirely of entries in the author's diaries. A book for Ruritanians and royalists. **1944** H. G. WELLS *'42 to '44* II. 52 The planners count noses and claim this or that district because there are 59 per cent. alleged Ruritanians here, or because 42 per cent. of the people there belong to the Lutheran Church. **1950** 'P. WOODRUFF' *Island of Chamba* v. 71, I do enjoy it, ..the alternations between rich farce, charming comedy and Ruritanian politics. **1958** *Times* 20 May 10/5 In the Ruritanian world of mountain Lebanon almost anything can happen. **1969** G. GREENE *Travels with my Aunt* I. xii. 113 The Montreux Palace in baroque Edwardian like the home of a Ruritanian King. **1977** *Times* 5 Nov. 15/3 The modern world..invaded the 'ruritanian charm' of the travel writers.

rurp (rɒ̄ɹp). *Mountaineering.* [f. initial letters of *r*ealized *u*ltimate *r*eality *p*iton.] A type of very small piton.

1968 P. CREW *Encycl. Dict. Mountaineering* 104/2 *Rurp*,..a very small American chrome-molybdenum piton, designed for use in hair-line cracks. **1972** D. HASTON *In High Places* ix. 104 A rurp—the smallest piton, about the size of a postage stamp. **1976** *Times* 13 Nov. 12/6 A curious armoury of pegs, rurps, sky hooks, bolts, and bongs now form the armoury of the modern [rock] climber.

ruru (rū·rū). *N.Z.* [Maori.] The morepork, *Ninox novæseelandiæ*; = MOPOKE, MOREPORK 1 in Dict. and Suppl.

1859 A. S. THOMSON *Story of N.Z.* I. I. i. 25 The natives call the owl Kou-Kou or Ru-ru. **1862** A. S. ATKINSON *Jrnl.* 22 Aug. in *Richmond-Atkinson Papers* (1960) I. xiii. 782 Old Potatau had likened himself to a ruru mobbed by a flock of popokateas. **1905** W. BAUCKE *Where White Man Treads* 48, I..heard snatches of an ancient witch karakia being muttered round the corner, wherein a ruru..is the medium of destruction.

Rus (rʊs, rūs). Also 9 **Russ.** [Russ. *Rus'* (see RUSS *sb.* and *a.*), Arab. *Rūs*; cf. medieval Gr. *οἱ Ῥῶς*.] The name of a group of Swedish merchant warriors who established themselves around Kiev and the Dnieper in the ninth century, whose settlements gave rise to the later Russian principalities.

1845 *Encycl. Metrop.* XXIV. 225/1 The Vareghi (*conquering*) Russ, one of the enterprising Tribes of Scandinavia, whose fleets had appeared in the Bosphorus during the first half of the IXth Century. **1876** V. THOMSEN *Relations betw. Anc. Russia & Scandinavia* II. 37, I am going to..corroborate..the Scandinavian origin of the Russ. **1918** R. BEAZLEY et al. *From Varangians to Bolsheviks* I. i. 3 Both the name of *Rus* and the fact of a Russian people and Russian States are due to them [*sc.* the Scandinavians]. **1927** E. V. GORDON *Introd. Old Norse* p. xxi, From the Swedish founders of this kingdom ..Russia takes its name, for the Swedes were known in the east as Rus. The population of the kingdom of the Rus was..mainly Slavonic, and the Rus themselves gradually lost their traditions and language. **1948** G. VERNADSKY *Kievan Russia* vi. 138 in Kiev the prince's retinue..consisted of the Swedish Rus. **1965** H. M. SMYSER in Bessinger & Creed *Medieval & Linguistic Studies* 92 In 921, Ibn Faḍlān..described..a tribe of Swedish Rūs Vikings, or, more accurately, Rūs armed merchants, and..a funeral which these Rūs accorded one of their chief men. **1976** H. R. ELLIS DAVIDSON *Viking Road to Byzantium* I. iv. 56 It is in the ninth century that we first hear of the Rus, who were well known to Arab geographers, and whom the Byzantine Greeks called *Rhos*... For most western scholars, the name *Rus* is taken primarily to denote the Scandinavian settlers in Russia, particularly those established at Kiev in the ninth century. *Ibid.* 62 There is..general agreement that in the ninth century the important Rus state on the Dnieper around Kiev was formed.

rusa. Substitute for def.: Either of two deer, *Cervus equinus* or *C. unicolor*, native to southern Asia. Cf. SAMBUR. (Earlier and further examples.)

1783 W. MARSDEN *Hist. Sumatra* 94 Deer: *rooso*: *keejang*. There are variety of the deer species; of which some are very large. **1839** T. J. NEWBOLD *Straits of Malacca* I. vii. 436 Of the genus Cervus, are the Kijang.., the Rúsa or Cervus Hippelaphus. **1958** J. SLIMMING *Temiar Jungle* ii. 23 A few yards away were the tracks of a *Rusa*, a Malayan deer.

rusbank (rö·sbaŋk). *S. Afr.* Also **rus-bank, rustbank,** etc. *Pl.* **rusbanks, rusbanke, rust banken.** [Afrikaans, f. *rus(t)* rest + *bank* bench.] A wooden settle or couch, usu. with a seat of woven leather thongs or riempies. Also *attrib.*

1880 J. NIXON *Among Boers* 216 Hans was seated on the 'rustbank', smoking a short wooden pipe. **1902** W. DOWER *Early Annals of Kokstad* 25 The few very rough seats and the rust banken..were occupied by the men, the women sat on the floor. **1910** D. FAIRBRIDGE *That which hath Been* xxiii. 277 The baas and huisvrouw..came out on their stoeps and sank into the capacious chairs and rust-banks. **1935** P. SMITH *Platkops Children* 76 After that was a long white house with a big stoep an' rus'-banks at each end. **1939** S. CLOETE *Watch for Dawn* 29 How alike all these Boer houses were. Each had the same rough, home-made riempie-seated rus-banks. **1947** *Cape Times* 5 Feb. 14 The farm-house has a huge dining-room with a massive centre table and, along one wall, the district's longest rustbank. **1965** M. G. ATMORE *Cape Furniture* 77 At all times the rustbank has been a 'multiple chair' in which the form was copied from the single chair of the time. **1971** *Evening Post* (Port Elizabeth) 8 May 20 The Furniture: Round Hand-made Stinkwood and Yellowwood Table on Pedestal Leg: three Yellowwood and Stinkwood Rusbanke. **1971** *Daily Dispatch* (East London) 8 Sept. 18 Old Rusbank-type Lounge Suite. **1972** *Grocott's Mail* (Grahamstown) 22 Feb. 1 Rusbank with riempie seat.

‖ **rusé** (rüze), *a.* Also fem. **rusée,** Pl. **rusés.** [Fr.] Given to ruses, sly, cunning; deceitful, deceptive. Also as *sb.*

1761 G. COLMAN *Jealous Wife* III. 45 Your Ladyship, I hope, has no Objections to my being a little *rusé*, for I must have Her, 'pon Honour. **1847** DISRAELI *Tancred* II. IV. iii. 189 Aberdeen and Sir Peel will never give her this advice; their habits are formed. They are too old, too *rusés*. **1889** G. MEREDITH *Let.* 20 Sept. (1970) II. 980 *Rusée* that you are! **1903** A. BENNETT *Truth about Author* i. 8, I..ordered the old rusé self to exploit the self just born. **1923** G. ATHERTON *Black Oxen* viii. 33 She was certainly *rusée*. **1938** H. G. WELLS *Apropos of Dolores* ii. 31 We hunted for five of the most rusé tennis balls I have ever known... They changed colour according to their surroundings. **1940** G. ARTHUR *Concerning Winston Spencer Churchill* 143 It was a most successful, if rather rusé, coup, but when anyone spoke of it as a military measure Kitchener would always say that Winston Churchill must have a large share of the credit. **1955** A. L. ROWSE *Expansion of Elizabethan England* x. 399 As a commander, he [*sc.* Sir Francis Vere] was exceedingly *rusé*. **1968** *Listener* 13 June 779/1 The values are unsurprising—the baby, the reliable if *rusé* Italian director, the true choice at the end. **1973** C. M. Woodhouse *Capodistria* v. 110 They constantly used of him [*sc.* Capodistria] the conventional epithets which seemed to fit his nationality—wily, *rusé*, supple, crafty.

‖ **ruse de guerre** (rüz də gɛ̄r). Pl. **ruses de guerre.** [Fr., lit. 'ruse of war': see Ruse *sb.*] A course of action intended to deceive an enemy in war; a stratagem. So, in extended uses, a justifiable trick.

1807 *Naval Anecdotes* vii. 185 We consider the whole of this singular passage as a kind of *ruse de guerre* to divert the public censure from Lord St. Vincent's Admiralty in regard to the supply of stores. **1814** M. Edgeworth *Patronage* III. xxxii. 302, I..thought even your praises of Rosamond's disposition..might only be *ruse de guerre*, or *ruse d'amour*. **1888** *Academy* 10 Nov. 300/2 Stubborn party duels, *ruses de guerre*, and all the heiving and hacking of the parliamentary fray. **1915** F. Piggott *Neutral Merchant* i. 11 By a *ruse de guerre*, or stratagem of war, I understand the adoption of some means of deceiving the enemy in war, some device out of the ordinary course of fighting. **1919** G. B. Shaw *Peace Conference Hints* vii. 99 These deceptions are necessary as *ruses de guerre*. **1922** J. Buchan *Huntingtower* v. 84 'It was an abominable lie.'..'Not at all. It was a necessary and proper *ruse de guerre*.' **1938** C. S. Forester *Flying Colours* i. 8 That had been a legitimate *ruse de guerre* for which historical precedents..could be quoted. **1962** *Times* 24 Apr. 12/6 It [*sc.* martial music] was no longer used as a *ruse de guerre*.

rush, *sb.*[1] Add: **5. a.** *rush-bottom.*

1831 J. M. Peck *Guide for Emigrants* II. 105 In all the rush bottoms they [*sc.* cattle] fatten during the severe weather on rushes.

b. *rush-bottom* (also as *adj.*), *-house*, *-matting*, *-rope* (later example), *-seat* (also as *adj.*), *-work* (later examples).

1792 A. Young *Trav. France* I. 24 Oak chairs with rush bottoms. **1809** 'D. Knickerbocker' *Hist. N.Y.* I. III. iii. 258 The young ladies seated themselves demurely in their rush-bottom chairs. **1866** D. G. Rossetti *Let.* 20 May (1965) II. 598 If there is anything besides rush-bottoms and ascetic glasses on which I should be glad to offer a fundamental remark..it is this. **1923** W. Deeping *Secret Sanctuary* xiii. 138 He made a move to sit down, and she saw him take one of the straight-backed rush-bottoms. **1960** J. Stroud *Shorn Lamb* iii. 27 Facing the magistrates ..was a single rush-bottom chair. **1835** Rush-house [see Raupo]. **1926–7** *Army & Navy Stores Catal.* 1103/4 Rush matting, 36 in. wide — per yard. 4/9. **1942** E. Waugh *Put out More Flags* ii. 108 The floor was covered in coarse rush matting and in places by bright Balkan rugs. **1964** *New Statesman* 14 Feb. 271/4 (Advt.), Rush-matting made-to-measure 2s. sq. ft. Rush-seated Italian chairs 9 gns a pair. **1922** Joyce *Ulysses* 508 Woman undoing with sweet pudor her belt of rushrope, offers her allmoist yoni to man's lingam. **1896** *Heal & Son Catal.* 156 Ebonised Rush-Seat Chair—£0 4 9 Ebonised Chair, Rush Seat £0 6 3. **1918** *Ibid.* 25 Dark Oak Rush-seat Arm chair, 35/-. **1949** R. Harvey *Curtain Time* i. 6 And soon the audience would begin to gather, first for the rush seats in the gallery, then for the balcony and the main floor. **1971** *Country Life* 18 Feb. 366/3 The square drop-in rush seat was originally upholstered. **1934** E. Bowen *Cat Jumps & Other Stories* 190 She had discovered that Miss Weekes morris-danced, that she did rush-work. **1959** *Observer* 15 Mar. 14/5, I have just had a rustic chair reseated... Very neat rushwork. **1977** *Vogue* Feb. 115/2 A Connemara Craft Centre with ceramics, rushwork, tweeds.

6. b. *rush-bordered* (further example), *-bottomed* (earlier and later examples), *-matted*, *-plaited*, *-seated* (further examples), *-seating*.

1912 W. de la Mare *Child's Day* 26 A green, rush-bordered pool. **1753** S. Fielding *Adv. David Simple* (ed. 2) V. VII. ii. 178 His Candle falling off the Table, set fire to a Rush-bottomed Chair. **1840** C. F. Hoffman *Greyslaer* II. III. i. 96 The apartment..was large and rudely furnished, containing only..a small cherry-wood table and a few rush-bottomed chairs. **1867** A. D. Richardson *Beyond Mississippi* xi. 131 The adjacent settlers came..in heavy ox-wagons sitting upon rush-bottomed chairs. **1902** *Chambers's Jrnl.* July 471/2 Here were..ancient rush-bottomed chairs, an old corner-cupboard with glass doors [etc.]. **1918** *Heal & Son Catal.* 2 Rush-bottomed Chair. **1976** 'D. Halliday' *Dolly & Nanny Bird* v. 60 A creak from the stairs..or the sounds of the rushbottomed chair I had used when feeding Benedict. **1960** C. Day Lewis *Buried Day* x. 226 Our stone-floored, rush-matted living-room..felt at first like an Aeolus' cave of draughts. **1939** F. Thompson *Lark Rise* xv. 273 His wide, rush-plaited hat. **1952** M. Laski *Village* viii. 135 A long rush-seated oak stool. **1977** *Times* 3 Sept. 11/3 Rush-seated chairs and homely local service. **1926** *Daily Colonist* (Victoria, B.C.) 14 July 5/1 We do old-fashined rush seating also chair recaning... The Red Cross Workshop. **1979** *Jrnl. R. Soc. Arts* CXXVII. 453/2 The pieces to be shown will demonstrate the variety of the skills learned by the students..—rush-seating, marquetry, turning, [etc.].

rush, *sb.*[2] Add: **1. a.** Also, the movement of large numbers of people at a specified time or season to or from work, recreation, shops, etc.; *gen.*, haste, urgency; excessive activity.

1924 G. B. Shaw *Saint Joan* p. vii, His accuser.. might have been picked out of any first class carriage on a suburban railway during the evening or morning rush from or to the City. **1925** H. Crane *Let.* 1 Dec. (1965) 220 Selling books in stores during the Christmas rush. **1931** H. Nicolson *Diary* 22 Aug. (1966) 88, I have learnt that rapidity, hustle and rush are the allies of superficiality. **1932** E. Bowen *To the North* vi. 51 She had not come down all this way..in the middle of what she and Peter considered the Whitsun rush. **1939** [see *after- I. 1]. **1943** E. B. White *Let.* 13 Aug. (1976) 243, I would like to discuss my publishing life with you some time... There is no rush about it, however, as I have no book ready to go. **1951** E. Paul *Springtime in Paris* ix. 157 The easter rush of tourists..had crowded the St. Sulpice district to overflowing. **1973** [see *office worker* s.v. *office *sb.* 12].

b. (Further examples.) Also, a rushing sensation in the body; a thrill (of fear, pleasure, etc.); a drug-induced euphoria, = *flash *sb.*[2] 1 h. *colloq.*

1916 'Boyd Cable' *Action Front* 113 At nine, sharp to the tick of the clock, the rush, rush, rush of a field battery's shells passed overhead. **1922** Joyce *Ulysses* 509 He couldn't get a connection. Only, you know, sensation. A dry rush. **1971** *Frendz* 21 May 11/1 When you start smoking one type of Hash, the best rushes come during the first day of smoking. (Assuming the Hash is good). **1976** *National Observer* (U.S.) 23 Oct. 6 Methadone is addictive, too, but it doesn't give the pleasurable 'rush' that heroin addicts speak of. **1979** *Washington Post* 25 Mar. N5 Never again was there anything quite like the rush we got from the simple fact of spring.

d. *pl. Cinemat.* The first prints of film resulting from a period of shooting; the preliminary showing of such film; = *daily *sb.* 4.

1924 G. R. Chester *On Set & Off* xvii. 206 Isidor Iskovitch sat very cockily exhibiting to his friend and boss ..some thousands of feet of 'rushes' on his pet picture, 'the Woman's Half'. **1927** L. Fawcett *Films Facts & Forecasts* xiv. 130 A good many pictures are entirely remade, and sometimes sequences are ordered to be reconstructed when the 'rushes' (short lengths of film) are seen during actual production. **1934** [see *daily *sb.* 4]. **1940** *Manch. Guardian Weekly* 15 Nov. 355 We were shown 'stills' of Mr. Gielgud's Disraeli and..in a private theatre we saw 'rushes' of the previous day's work. **1952** [see *daily *sb.* 4]. **1956** B. Holiday *Lady sings Blues* (1973) xv. 126 Every night after we'd finished work at six o'clock, Blondie would rush to the projection room to see the rushes. **1962** *Movie* Sept. 31/2 For Rouch, the ideal film of this title would be the four hours of 'rushes', without cuts or montage. **1969** *New Yorker* 29 Nov. 160/2 Nothing makes us more aware of staginess than actors reciting poetry outdoors—as directors of Shakespearean movies discover when they look at their first day's rushes. **1976** C. Bermant *Coming Home* II. iv. 160 My function was to write the outline script as a rough guide for the film crew. Then, when the rushes were available, I re-wrote to fit the pictures.

e. Used *fig.* in phrs. *bum's rush*, see *bum *sb.*[4] 1 b; *to get a rush*, of a girl or woman: to be the recipient of frequent attentions from men; *to give* (someone, *spec.* a girl or woman) *a rush*: to lavish attention on (that person) in the form of social engagements and entertainment. *colloq.*

1928 *Amer. Speech* III. 221 To say that a girl 'certainly gets a big rush' means that she has many desirable dates, and is 'cut' a lot at dances. **1934** J. O'Hara *Appointment in Samarra* (1935) i. 20 Wilhelmina Hall..was still the best dancer in the club, and was getting the best rush. **1938** E. Bowen *Death of Heart* II. iv. 249, I don't think most girls appreciate friendship; all they want is to be given a rush. **1940** Wodehouse *Eggs, Beans & Crumpets* 93 He's been giving me the rush of a lifetime. **1953** H. Waugh *Last seen Wearing* 71 She goes round with another guy..and I think he was giving her pretty much of a rush. **1956** W. H. Whyte *Organization Man* (1957) 252 An actor..comes to town from the city for a short stay. He gives her a mild rush, and she dreams of a glamorous life with him. **1969** A. Lurie *Real People* 18 She certainly wasn't prepared for the rush she got, probably for the first time in her life... You've got to admit she's not madly attractive.

f. In *attrib.* use passing into *adj.*, denoting rapidity of movement, haste, or urgency. Also *ellipt.* as quasi-*adv.*

1879 W. Whitman *Daybooks & Notebooks* (1978) I. 145, I am told that Saturday is a real rush day. **1896** Rush order [in Dict., sense 9]. **1900** J. London *Let.* 15 Mar. (1966) 102 This isn't sharpshooting, but repelling a rush attack of a body of men. **1901** C. Moffett *Careers of Danger* 381 Already the mail clerks are swarming at the pouches, like printers on a rush edition. **1901** Merwin & Webster *Calumet 'K'* vii. 126 But if you ever try to put me on a rush job, I'll quit and buy a small farm. **1904** *N.Y. Herald* 17 Sept. 1 He stated that six weeks' rush work would be required to repair the boilers to make them serviceable and the ship seaworthy. **1929** T. H. Burnham *Engin. Econ.* xv. 199 Rush orders are difficult to put through, even in well-organized works. **1933** D. L. Sayers *Murder must Advertise* viii. 126 Mr. Copley..was left working overtime upon a rush series of cut-price advertisements for Jamboree Jellies. **1933** Balmer & Wylie *When Worlds Collide* i. 24 You see, Tony, some—some things were being sent rush, by airplane. **1939** C. Day Lewis *Child of Misfortune* II. vi. 241 Christmas was a rush-time of services, visits to the sick, parties for the children and old people of the parish. **1946** *Ann. Reg. 1945* 40 There should be a three weeks' interval..so as to avoid a rush election. **1955** 'A. Gilbert' *Is she Dead Too?* viii. 151 She was gone before he arrived on the scene. It was a rush job. **1958** [see *one *numeral a.* 29* b]. **1965** Mrs L. B. Johnson *White House Diary* 2 July (1970) 292 So I got a rush appointment with Mr. Per and went over for a permanent. **1968** *Listener* 8 Aug. 176/3 It was an odd life at Oxford at the time because most people had just come out of the army and were going in for quick degrees, sort of rush degrees. *a* **1974** R. Crossman *Diaries* (1975) I. 238 They are horrifyingly superficial—merely a collection of the facts available to central government with one or two rush-job social surveys and some very hasty conclusions. **1977** R. V. Hudson in Bond & McLeod *Newslett. to Newspapers* II. 123 His expertise earned him an assignment to rush work and the highest wage among some fifty printers.

3. a. (Later examples in *N. Amer.* use.)

1970 *Globe & Mail* (Toronto) 28 Sept. 18/6 Fleming was Hamilton's leading ground gainer with four catches for 66 yards and nine rushes for 42 more. **1979** *Honolulu Advertiser* 8 Jan. C-1/1 Larry's strong rush helped keep pressure on Ram quarterback Pat Haden.

c. (Earlier and later examples.)

1860 *Yale Lit. Mag.* XXVI. 22 As a basis, a Rush tacitly assumes that it is promoting a rivalry that is proper and praiseworthy. **1916** C. A. Eastman *From Deep Woods to Civilization* 68 The two classes met in a first 'rush'. **1937** *Amer. Speech* XII. 156 *Cane rushes*, or encounters between freshmen carrying canes and sophomores seeking to break them were an institution at the University of Nebraska in the late '80's of the last century. They were vigorous affairs and fraternity rushing may well have had name from them.

d. *U.S.* A round of entertainment in which candidates for admission to a fraternity or a sorority participate. Also *attrib.*, as *rush party*, *week*, etc.

1899 A. H. Quinn *Pennsylvania Stories* 60 It was not long before Theta Chi gave him a bid to a rush smoker. **1918** *Dialect Notes* V. 27 The object of the many attentions of a frat-rush. **1931** *Kansas City Times* 24 Sept. 20/6 Aunt Phoebe Tilden read where so many colleges are having rush parties. **1940** *Sun* (Baltimore) 16 Sept. 2/8 (*heading*) Rush week for C. of C. **1944** *Greeley* (Colo.) *Daily Tribune* 24 Sept. 3/5 Formal rush week for all sororities on the campus will be Oct. 1 to Oct. 6. **1964** Rush week [see *pledge week* s.v. *pledge *sb.* 7]. **1970** *Guardian* 23 Apr. 11/4 What is called the Rush Programme. Girls who want to be 'rushed', i.e. who want to join a sorority, put their names down for sororities (the screening process) and 'rush' to about 30 or 40 parties. **1979** *Arizona Daily Star* 19 Apr. 6/2 Jennifer Johnston.. was elected assistant rush chairman.

4. a. (Earlier and later examples.)

1848 *Morning Courier & New-York Enquirer* 11 Dec. 2/1 There is a general rush for the new found *Dorado*. **1849** *Merchant's Mag.* XX. 60 In May, the gold itself began to come into the town. And then began the rising and the rush. **1893** [see *gold-rush* s.v. Gold[1] 10 a]. **1897** *Boston Globe* 29 Aug. 6/6 There are only about 1600 new Americans in the mines... There are plenty of supplies there for those already in but not for any big rush late in the fall. **1908** E. J. Banfield *Confessions of Beachcomber* II. ii. 288 A party of bushmen, fresh from the excitement and weariness of the Gilbert rush. **1911** C. E. W. Bean *'Dreadnought' of Darling* xxxv. 306 A friend of the writer's, who was in Coolgardie from the time when the rush there first started, tells of how first the waistcoat came onto the mining field. **1935** *Chambers's Encycl.* VI. 459/2 Only in 1896 was gold found in such abundance as to create a rush [to the Klondike]. **1947** R. Peattie *Sierra Nevada* 60 The discovery in 1859 of a glittering silver bonanza in Washoe County, Nevada, started a frantic rush over the mountains to Virginia City. **1955** *Bull. Atomic Sci.* Mar. 88/2 Thus the uranium boom began. The rush has grown rather than quieted, but there are healthy signs of stabilization. **1966** 'J. Hackston' *Father clears Out* 104 Following on this 'rich' find, the big Red Range rush set in. **1972** *Standard Encycl. Southern Africa* V. 227/1 By then [*sc.* 8 Sept. 1886] the rush of diggers had already set in, so that fully 3 000 people were estimated to be scattered along the Rand by this time.

b. (Further examples.)

1900 H. Lawson *Story of Oracle* in *Stories* (1964) I. 435 My Uncle Bob was mates with him on one of those rushes along there—the Pipeclay, I think it was, or the Log Paddock. **1966** 'J. Hackston' *Father clears Out* 52 Why is he so poor now, after finding all the rich reefs and rushes?

5. b. (Earlier and later examples.)

1841 *Daily Picayune* (New Orleans) 10 Dec. 2/2 They all travel round to the old brushing ground where they 'go it with a rush'. **1846** S. F. Smith *Theatrical Apprenticeship & Anecdotal Recollections* 152 When you find yourself in possession of *four aces*, go it with a perfect rush. **1898** *McClure's Mag.* X. 352 The gray-backs came through with a rush. **1903** G. B. Shaw *Man & Superman* III. 138 The complete reality comes back with a rush. **1914** T. Dreiser *Titan* i. 3 Chicago, when it finally dawned on him, came with a rush on the second morning. He had spent two nights in the gaudy Pullman..when the first lone outposts of the prairie metropolis began to appear. **1934** A. Christie *Parker Pyne Investigates* 53 She stared at Mr Parker Pyne with a desperate intentness. Suddenly she spoke with a rush.

c. (*all*) *in a rush* (and variants): phrs. denoting rapidity, liveliness, briskness, suddenness, or haste.

1859 Hotten *Dict. Slang* 84 *Doing it on the rush*, running away, or making off. **1876** 'Mark Twain' *Tom Sawyer* xviii. 149 He is always in such a rush that he never thinks of anything. **1877** G. M. Hopkins *Spring* in *Poems* (1967) 67 That blue is all in a rush With richness. **1890** Kipling *Barrack-Room Ballads* (1892) 11 An 'appy day with Fuzzy on the rush Will last an 'ealthy Tommy for a year. **1901** H. James *Sacred Fount* iv. 75 Last night she was on the rush. **1916** 'Taffrail' *Pincher Martin* i. 11 Take a pride in yourself, an' obey all orders at the rush. **1938** *Sun* (Baltimore) 8 June 8/8 Later in the season they [*sc.* soft crabs] drop off almost altogether until late July or in August, when they seem to come back all of a rush. **1962** E. B. Atwood *Regional Vocab. Texas* iii. 71 *To leave in a rush.* The most common single expression for hurried departure is *light a shuck.* **1971** *Cassell's Mod. Guide to Synonyms* 502 The slow, jolting pace of one who is in no rush.

9. rush dodge, the act of overcoming or disarming a person by means of a rush;

rush line (earlier and later examples); also *fig.*; **rush-release,** the action or an instance of producing and marketing a gramophone record in the shortest possible time; so *rush-release* vb. trans. Also *RUSH HOUR.

1888 'R. BOLDREWOOD' *Robbery under Arms* II. ii. 19 It's no use trying the rush dodge with them. **1887** *Century Mag.* XXXIV. 891/2 Across the field stretch the football infantry, the 'rush-line' or 'rushers'. **1906** *Life* 4 Oct. 366 We hear of a surprising prevalence among the young men..of the disposition to get into the political rush-line. **1923** R. D. PAINE *Comr. Rolling Ocean* i. 3 The unlucky young men who were left in his wake when he tore through a rush-line. **1976** *Webster's Sports Dict.* 365/1 *Rush line*, the defensive line of a football team. **1966** *Melody Maker* 16 July 4 The group's 'Pet Sounds' LP—rush-released by EMI—entered the MM's best-selling LPs chart this week at number nine. **1968** *Ibid.* 22 June 2 The Regal Zonophone label is rush-releasing the new Move E.P. **1978** *New Musical Express* 11 Feb. 4/2 Radiators From Space have just finished recording their new single..and Chiswick hope to have it ready for rush release on February 17.

rush, *v.*² Add: **3. b.** Also, without connotations of violence, to convey (someone or something) rapidly or urgently.

1914 S. LEWIS *Our Mr. Wrenn* 214 I'll make Tom rush us a growler of beer. **1927** U. SINCLAIR *Oil!* 264 It was our job to rush them supplies. **1935** in A. P. Herbert *What a Word!* v. 143 She was rushed to Alton Hospital, where her condition is critical. **1947** *Milwaukee Jrnl.* 29 Oct. 2 Uncle Tom doesn't scurry around to rush us a loan. **1958** [see *JERRICAN, JERRYCAN]. **1966** L. COHEN *Beautiful Losers* I. 107 Rush to me the *free* book on the Home Method of Slenderizing Heavy Legs. **1971** *Sunday Express* (Johannesburg) 28 Mar. 7/5 (Advt.), Rush me my..illustrated Guide. **1976** *Star* (Sheffield) 3 Dec. 10/7 My husband to be was rushed into hospital for a serious operation.

4. a. (Further examples.) Also, in weakened senses, to accomplish or produce rapidly; to expedite; to hurry or hustle. Also with *off, through*, etc.

1883 'MARK TWAIN' *Life on Mississippi* li. 452 Since there was so much time to spare that nineteen years of it could be devoted to the construction of a mere towhead, where was the use, originally, in rushing this whole globe through in six days? **1901** *Chambers's Jrnl.* Apr. 210/1 Candida rushed her news. **1918** W. OWEN *Let.* 19 Aug. (1967) 569 I rushed off a note in time for this evening's post. **1938** *Amer. Speech* XIII. 156/1 *Bootleg 'em*, to rush a special order through outside of regular channels. **1946** *R.A.F. Jrnl.* May 161 Do not through nervousness rush your replies. **1947** *Sun* (Baltimore) 8 Nov. 6/2 Representative Knutson..announced his intention of rushing the special session with a 'quickie' bill for income-tax reduction. **1949** SHURR & YOCOM *Mod. Dance* 5 Head of Developing and Printing at Willoughby's Camera Stores, Inc., who rushed prints and supplies through in record time. **1974** *Times* 1 Feb. 2/8 Nevertheless, Mr Campbell Adamson, director general, emphasized that the CBI was 'rushing' a council meeting, a somewhat unprecedented action, to consider Mr Heath's letter. **1976** M. MACHLIN *Pipeline* lxi. 517 If you ask me..he's rushing the whole thing and I think that these ULCC'S—these ultra-big tankers—are a mistake.

c. (Earlier and later examples.) Also *ellipt.*

1887 J. PAYN *Glow-Worm Tales* II. 44 That a fraud had been committed on us was certain, and a fraud of a very clumsy kind... He had 'rushed us' as, the phrase goes. **1930** BROPHY & PARTRIDGE *Songs & Slang 1914–1918* 158 *How much did they rush you?* meant 'How much did you have to pay?' **1931** T. R. G. LYELL *Slang, Phrase & Idiom* 655 *Rush a person*,..to overcharge a person; to make him pay an exorbitant price. *A*. 'How much d'you say you paid for this car?' *B*. 'Two hundred and fifty pounds.' *A*. 'My word! they rushed you, all right! It's not worth a penny more than £120.' **1973** N. W. SCHUR *British Self-Taught* 340 *Rush*,..soak. For instance: 'How much did they rush you for that sherry?' To rush is to charge, with the distinct implication that the price was too high.

d. To hurry or pressure (a person); now freq. *pass.* (passing into *ppl. a.*), of a person: to have much to do in a limited time, to be hard-pressed by shortage of time (also with the activity or the period of time as subject). Hence in colloq. phrases *to be rushed around, to be rushed off one's feet* (or *legs*) (cf. *run off one's feet* s.v. *RUN *v.* 44 a).

a **1890** [in Dict., sense 4 b]. **1902** W. N. HARBEN *Abner Daniel* 268 Wish I had more time at my disposal..but I really am rushed, to-day particularly. **1911** M. BEERBOHM *Let.* 2 Oct. (1964) 204, I wish you would tell Sister Loveridge..that I was so 'rushed' that I had not time to go and see anybody. **1916** E. FENWICK *Diary* 14 Feb. (1981) 111 Just rushed off my legs the whole day long. **1923** H. CRANE *Let.* 6 Feb. (1965) 118, I have been so rushed around with too much society that I have not yet got at the review for your study. **1924** *Ibid.* 5 Mar. (1965) 177 What with one's work, one's friends, books, writing, eating and sleeping, things are certainly rushed! **1937** W. H. SAUMAREZ SMITH *Let.* 20 Sept. in *Young Man's Country* (1977) ii. 91 I've been so rushed off my feet that I've not had a moment to do anything except work. **1943** D. POWELL *Time to be Born* x. 225 Amanda's too rushed right now to attend to these details. **1944** C. HIMES *Black on Black* (1973) 196 'State yo' plan, Charlie Chan—then scram!' 'Don't rush me, don't rush me.' **1947** M. MORRIS in B. James *Austral. Short Stories* (1963) 345 She..waited on the tables in Gleeson's dining-room when they were rushed. **1963** *Listener* 31 Jan. 223/2 Lentil soup requires little preparation, and, on a rushed day, takes kindly to the pressure cooker. **1965** *Listener* 4 Nov. 724/2 The elegant Harley Street consultants, the fatherly GPs, the harassed hospital house surgeons,.. those 'you can talk to' and those who are 'rushed off their feet'. **1966** 'J. HACKSTON' *Father clears Out* 203 In fact, I rushed her so, that I flabbergasted her, got her rattled. **1977** *Oxford Star* 22 Dec. 1/1 Shopkeepers have been rushed off their feet rolling out the barrel at Sainsburys, the Co-op, [etc.].

e. *U.S.* Of fraternity or sorority members: to entertain (a new student) in order to assess his or her suitability for membership, or to offer him or her membership.

1896 W. C. GORE in *Inlander* Jan. 149 *Rush*,..to entertain a student in various ways, with the view of inducing him to join a fraternity. **1922** S. LEWIS *Babbitt* xxvi. 309 He was on the committee for the Freshman Hop, and..he was being 'rushed' by two fraternities. **1924** P. MARKS *Plastic Age* vii. 62 He ought to be a good man for the fraternity... We've got to rush him sure. **1946** E. B. THOMPSON *Amer. Daughter* x. 173 There were a lot of students who weren't rushed or pledged who found solace in the Y, in literary or musical clubs, but not Dora. **1970** [see *RUSH *sb.*² 3 d].

f. To court the affection of (a girl or woman) by means of frequent entertainment, 'dating', etc. orig. and chiefly *U.S.*

1899 F. NORRIS *McTeague* xi. 226 Marcus had 'taken up with' Salna a little after Trina had married, and had been 'rushing' her ever since. **1922** F. SCOTT FITZGERALD *Beautiful & Damned* II. i. 144 With one she had gone to New Haven..she had been flattered because 'Touch down' Michaud had 'rushed' her all evening. **1932** 'B. ROSS' *Tragedy of X* 71 He had 'rushed' her, she said, for several months, and they had decided to announce their engagement. **1938** E. BOWEN *Death of Heart* II. iv. 249 That may be because you are so young that no fellow has started to rush you yet. **1955** F. A. COLLYMORE *Barbadian Dialect* 73 Who's the girl your brother's rushing now?

5. b. (Earlier and later examples.) Also, in extended uses, to attack (someone) by means of a sudden rush; to 'go for' (a person).

1863 A. S. ATKINSON *Jrnl.* 29 May in *Richmond-Atkinson Papers* (1960) II. 47 There were two sets of pits (called *rifle* pits by courtesy) the first were rushed but the Maoris ran & got all away. **1930** L. G. D. ACLAND *Early Canterbury Runs* viii. 196 The cook took up his gun and ordered him off, but the man rushed him and the cook shot him dead. **1934** WODEHOUSE *Right Ho, Jeeves* xvi. 197 Damn it, they'd rush the platform. **1937** C. HINES *Nigger* in *Black on Black* (1973) 131 He tried to shift the wire to his right hand so he could flay her with it, but she rushed him, clawing and biting. **1939** *Sun* (Baltimore) 23 Aug. 1/2 The shots were fired by Gerald Blowers.. after about fifty pickets rushed a milk truck on which he was riding. **1962** WODEHOUSE *Service with Smile* iii. 42 'Your sermon was a success, I trust?' 'Well, they didn't rush the pulpit.'

c. *to rush one's fences*: see *FENCE *sb.* 5 c.

d. (Earlier and later examples.)

1862 *Otago: Goldfields & Resources* 26 The Highlay [goldfield]..has been rushed, condemned, almost deserted, and yet survives. **1872** *Daily Tel.* 9 Feb. 3/3 The place was 'rushed'—an expressive word,..which signifies that the diggers swarmed to the spot in such crowds as to render merely foolish any resistance which an owner might be inclined to make. **1878** I. L. BIRD in *Leisure Hour* 5 Oct. 635/2 Even their [*sc.* Indians'] 'reservations' do not escape seizure practically; for if gold should 'break out' on them, they are 'rushed'. **1973** *Nation Rev.* (Melbourne) 31 Aug. (Suppl.) 1/1 It was first explored by Hume and Hovell, then opened up by cattlemen, rushed by gold seekers, and finally developed as a prosperous agricultural area.

6. e. (Further examples.) Also, to hurry, to hasten. Freq. with *(a)round* (hence *rush-round* attrib. phr.); *to rush round in circles*: see *CIRCLE *sb.* 1 c.

1914 'HIGH JINKS, JR.' *Choice Slang* 22 We rush off shopping. **1916** W. OWEN *Let.* 18 Mar. (1967) 386, I am obliged to rush into Romford for Running Clothes for a Run announced for the 17th. **1923** H. CRANE *Let.* 9 May (1965) 134 Of course I have been rushing around to a lot of other agencies. **1958** *Spectator* 20 June 807/2 Young Asia and young Africa delight to pull the legs of rush-round correspondents. **1965** G. MCINNES *Road to Gundagai* xii. 216, I..tore out of the room and rushed off to school. **1973** [see *NOSE-BAG 3]. **1976** F. RAPHAEL *Glittering Prizes* 23 'It's C7, Third Court, St John's. Only I've got to rush.' 'I shall be there.'

f. (Earlier and later examples of *to rush it.*)

1856 in B. H. Hall *College Words & Customs* (rev. ed.) 365 Leg it, put it, rush it, streak it, *Run* and worship God. **1976** L. SANDERS *Hamlet Warning* (1977) ix. 79 She laughed and looked up at him. 'Well, let's not rush it, Loomis.'

g. In American football, to run carrying the ball; to gain ground by running with the ball.

1949 *Lafayette Alumnus* (Lafayette College, Easton, Pa.) 24 Oct. 1/1 The Maroon had made 9 first downs rushing, three by passing and one by penalty. **1974** *Cleveland* (Ohio) *Plain Dealer* 13 Oct. C. 1/3 The Buckeyes rushed for 359 yards as quarterback Cornelius Greene and wingback Brian Baschnagel each scored twice. **1979** *Tucson* (Arizona) *Citizen* 20 Sept. 10 D/7 The Warrior running game hasn't been as effective as McKee would like, having rushed for only 133 yards in the first two games.

rushed, *ppl. a.* Add: (Further examples.) Also, made of rushes.

1918 *Heal & Son Catal.: Cottage Furnit.* 31 Jacobean Chair, in Dark Oak with rushed seat. **1957** A. CLARKE *Later Poems* (1961) 67, I think of rushed bones, Bogland, in furnaces, grown greener.

rushee (rʊʃiː). *U.S. College slang.* [f. RUSH *v.*² + -EE¹.] One who is 'rushed' (see *RUSH *v.*² 4 e); a candidate for membership of a fraternity or sorority.

1916 *Dialect Notes* IV. 279 *Rushee*,..a girl being 'rushed' for a college fraternity. 'The chapter has some good-looking rushees this year.' Widespread at Nebraska University. **1928** *Amer. Speech* III. 220 *Rushee*,..an individual who is being rushed by fraternities or sororities. **1940** *Sun* (Baltimore) 16 Sept. 2/8 It [*sc.* a telegram] requested a report on the character, family and scholarship of a rushee. **1942** *College Topics* (Univ. Virginia) 12 Oct. 1/2 (*heading*) Rushees navigate to houses by maps. **1960** *Amer. Speech* XXXV. 104 The girl rushee who does not have 'tights-omania' will be blackballed in short order.

rusher². Add: **3.** (Further examples.) Also, any player who rushes (see *RUSH *v.*² 6 g).

1969 *Internat. Herald Tribune* 6 Nov. 13/6 Floyd Little, leading rusher in the American Football League, suffered a sprained right knee. **1974** *Cleveland* (Ohio) *Plain Dealer* 13 Oct. C. 6/2 Wellington carried 12 times for 129 yards to lead all rushers. **1979** *Tucson* (Arizona) *Citizen* 3 Oct. 1D/4 The seventh-leading rusher in the city.

rush hour. Also **rush-hour.** [f. RUSH *sb.*² + HOUR.] A period of the day during which the movement of people is at its height, esp. one during which large numbers of people are travelling to or from work. Also *attrib.*

1898 [in Dict. s.v. RUSH *sb.*² 9]. **1907** 'O. HENRY' *Trimmed Lamp* 233 As solid as granite in the 'rush-hour' tide of humanity, stood the Man from Nome. **1926** *Daily Graphic* 13 May 1 (*caption*) The 'rush hour' at Earl's Court yesterday. Travelling discomforts are mitigated by much good humour and politeness. **1931** *Morn. Post* 18 Aug. 6/4 Rush-hour trains held up. **1932** D. L. SAYERS *Have his Carcase* iv. 50 The place is like the Corner House in the rush hour. **1955** *Times* 17 June 9/4 Even now, great congestion is caused by traffic entering and leaving the park, particularly in the rush hours. **1961** I. MURDOCH *Severed Head* xxvii. 221 Through the rush-hour traffic the god that protects drunken men protected me. **1973** 'M. INNES' *Appleby's Answer* iii. 32 It was the first of London's evening rush-hours, and their taxi made only a tedious stop-go progress. **1977** B. PYM *Quartet in Autumn* ii. 17 A woman, slumped on a seat on the Underground platform while the rush hour crowds hurried past her.

rushing, *vbl. sb.* Add: **b.** (Later examples in Football.) Cf. *RUSH. *v.*² 6 g.

1966 ROTE & WINTER *Lang. Pro Football* 111. 134/2 *Rushing*,..offensive yardage gained by running with ball. **1970** *Globe & Mail* (Toronto) 26 Sept. 36/5 Raimey..is leading the Eastern Football Conference in rushing. **1972** J. MOSEDALE *Football* x. 143 He led the league in rushing in 1942 and 1946.

d. *rushing bases*, a children's game, = *King Cæsar* s.v. *KING *sb.* 5.

1849, 1969 [see *KING *sb.* 5].

e. *U.S.* The process of entertaining candidates for fraternities and sororities and of selecting those who are suitable (see *RUSH *v.*² 4 e). Also *attrib.*

1901 *Independent* (N.Y.) 15 Feb. 392/1 The inter-fraternity contract..limited the 'spiking' or 'rushing' (terms covering all methods of competing for desirable members) to ten days. **1910** *Collier's* 23 July 16/3 My four friends..admitted that during this so-called 'rushing' for new members there was considerable rivalry among sororities. **1929** *Daily Maroon* (Chicago) 8 Oct. 2/1 No pledges are made until the fourth day of rushing week. **1931** *Kansas City Star* 10 Oct., Fraternity rushing is entirely over and the freshmen have been told their place in life. **1942** *College Topics* (Univ. Virginia) 12 Oct. 1/2 Rushing got underway and first year-men sought in the darkness for the various fraternity houses. **1946** *Life* 18 Nov. 114/2 Howard has a normally lively interest in extracurricular activities like football, swimming, college dances..fraternity and sorority rushing. **1957** *Encycl. Brit.* IX. 701/2 All of the fraternities aim to be select and to choose their members carefully from the mass of incoming students, the rushing, as the process of selection is called, being well organized and supervised by the older members. **1972** C. S. OGILVY *Tomorrow's Math.* (ed. 2) ii. 37 On college campuses where the fraternity system flourished, it was customary to allow each fraternity to choose..whom it should invite to become members. There were rules and 'codes of rushing', but even so..many undergraduates never had a chance to get into any fraternity.

rushing, *ppl. a.* Add: (Further examples.) Also *fig.*

1881 W. G. MARSHALL *Through America* (1882) 93 Each and all of these have done a 'rushing' business during the past year. **1915** *N.Y. World* 7 Aug. 1/3 All this time the soda-water stands were doing a rushing business.

rushlight. Add: **1. b.** (Earlier example.)

1827 G. GRIFFIN *Holland-Tide* 326 It was neither like sun-light, nor moonlight, nor the light of the stars, nor fire, nor rush light.

c. Also of persons.

1866 *Yale Lit. Mag.* Apr. 229 Peters told him that good scholars were looked upon here as mere rush-lights.

2. *rushlight box, holder, love.*

1934 L. B. LYON *White Hare* 34 And dowsed in dark Their little rush-light love. **1937** *Discovery* Jan. 12/1 Rushlight holders (examples of which date from the 15th century onwards but are commonly of the 18th or early

19th) are generally in iron but might be..merely split sticks. **1955** G. Stevens *In Canadian Attic* 23 Light for domestic purposes was first supplied by the campfires; next came the rushlight holder. **1969** E. H. Pinto *Treen* 123 Rush-light boxes. These containers..usually of oak or mahogany and mostly dating from the 18th century, are rare and seldom identified correctly. **1969** *Canadian Antiques Collector* Jan. 19/2 An interesting item you may be able to pick up is a 'Rushlight-holder'.

rushy (rʊ·ʃi) *a.*[2] [f. Rush *sb.*[2] + -y[1].] Quick, hurried. Also as *adv.*, in a rush, hurriedly.

1908 H. G. Wells *War in Air* iv. 153 Too soon, Bert my boy—too soon and too rushy. **1976** W. Trevor *Children of Dynmouth* i. 34 It was all half joking, all quick and rushy, his mother laughing her shrill staccato laugh, Rose-Ann laughing also, neither of them listening to him.

‖ **rus in urbe** (rū·s in ɜ̄ːɪbe), *phr.* [a. L. *rūs in urbe* country in city.] The creating of an illusion of the countryside in a city; an urban building, garden, prospect, etc., which suggests the countryside. Also *attrib.* So **rus-in-u·rbe-ish** *a.*

1759 Gray *Let.* 24 July (1827) II. 40, I am now settled in my new territories commanding Bedford gardens, and all the fields as far as Highgate and Hampstead..; so *rus-in-urbe-ish*, that I believe I shall stay here. **1795** tr. *C. P. Moritz's Travels* 68 In Grosvenor-square..there is a little circular wood, intended, no doubt, to give one the idea of *rus in urbe*. **1804** A. Seward *Life of Dr. Darwin* i. 16 To this *rus in urbe*..resorted..a knot of philosophic friends. **1841** W. M. Thackeray in *Fraser's Mag.* XXIV. 393/2 A very handsome country place..a first-rate *rus in urbe*, as the great auctioneer called it when he hammered it down. **1873** A. J. Munby *Diary* 21 May in D. Hudson *Munby* (1972) 330 P. A. Taylor is going to sell this charming rus in urbe; ample widespreading old country house, with timbered lawns, and acres of garden. **1939** 'N. Blake' *Smiler with Knife* ii. 33 This..is a remarkably non-committal room. Not so much *rus in urbe* as *suburbia in rure*. **1963** *Times* 6 Apr. 11/3 The Rumanian passion for *rus in urbe* exceeds even the English. **1968** *Times* 15 Oct. 7/1 It is a natural progression of the rus in urbe feeling of fashion this autumn. **1976** *Times* 9 Aug. 10/8 Two foxes..live in a corner of the allotments—which seems to be taking *rus in urbe* too far.

Ruski, var. Rusky *a.* and *sb.*[2] in Dict. and Suppl.

Ruskin[4]. Add: *Ruskin work* = *Ruskin linen*. **Ruskinese** *sb.* (earlier and later examples), *a.* (earlier example); **Ruskinia·na**, memorabilia of Ruskin; **Ruski·nianly** *adv.*, in a Ruskinian manner; **Ruskinism** (earlier and later examples); **Ru·skinist** = Ruskinian *sb.*; **Ru·skinite** *sb.* and *a.* = Ruskinian *sb.* and *a.*; **Ru·skiny** *a.*, designating the style admired by Ruskin.

1863 *Macmillan's Mag.* Nov. 67/2 'Laying by', therefore, in Ruskinese, can only mean simple hoarding. **1863** G. M. Hopkins *Let.* 10 July (1938) 55, I..hope you will approve some of the sketches in a Ruskinese point of view. **1933** *Scrutiny* II. 1/2 Almost every page is littered with clichés, floating in Ruskinese, and quotations from Horace are liberally applied. **1931** *Times Lit. Suppl.* 18 June 492/2 Every scrap of Ruskiniana is now scattered to all quarters. **1978** *Lancashire Life* July 50/4 It was the Severns' ill-luck to preside over the gradual running-down of Brantwood after 1918, a process completed after Arthur's death in 1931, in his ninetieth year, by the sale of household effects and Ruskiniana. **1974** Sherwood & Pevsner *Buildings of England: Oxfordshire* 325 Capitals of the French Early Gothic foliage type but also Ruskinianly naturalistic. **1851** 'An Architect' *Something on Ruskinism* p. iv, These few pages do not pretend to exhibit a portraiture of Ruskinism, or anything like one. **1940** E. Gill *Autobiogr.* vii. 277 Anything that looks like Ruskinism in my subsequent development is chiefly due to the fact that we both accepted the same first principles. **1969** *Daily Tel.* 8 Feb. 15/4 For long there have been a few devoted Ruskinists in this country and America. **1889** *St. James's Gaz.* 31 July 9/1 (*heading*) The travels of a Ruskinite's letter. **1899** G. B. Shaw *Let.* 17 Oct. (1972) II. 113 On the whole, the wooden figures [in the Alhambra], which classical & Ruskinite tourists alike disdain, are the things best worth looking at. **1975** *Maclean's Mag.* May (B.C. Suppl.) 6 As far back as 1890, a utopian community of Ruskinites had set up shop in the Fraser Valley. **1963** *Bookseller* 20 July 248/1 It was Ruskin who introduced linen cut-work to England and it is sometimes called Ruskin work, but..the proper name [is]..*Linen Cut-Work*. **1977** M. Green *Children of Sun* (rev. ed.) iii. 135 Harold [Acton] liked the Brighton Pavilion, but not the grey Gothicism, nor the Ruskiny ruins.

Rusky, *a.* and *sb.*[2] Delete *rare* and add: *slang* or *colloq.* Also **Roosky, Ruski, Russki** (now the most usual form), **Russky.** (Earlier and later examples.) Hence **Ru·sski-land,** Russia.

1858 F. Duberly *Let.* July in E. E. P. Tisdall *Mrs Duberly's Compaigns* (1963) vi. 197 Was I the Englishwoman who had gone with the armies to make war against the Ruski? **1919** *Amer. Legion Weekly* 22 Aug. 22/1 Large numbers of lowly 'Rooskies' plodded through the weary days. **1919** *Our Navy* (U.S.) Nov. 15/1 The Russkis were friendly to us because we had a lot of rubles. **1920** *Amer. Legion Weekly* 12 Mar. 5 A. E. F. Siberia..en route to Russki-land. **1923** D. York *Company A* 50 A little Russki at one side drew our attention. **1937** G. Frankau *More of Us* xiii. 135 To Mussolini's braves and Hitler's huskies Left we the task of tackling Stalin's Russkies. **1948** M. Laski *Tory Heaven* i. 14 People like the Russkis and the Yanks like dealing with gentlemen. **1957** V. Nabokov *Pnin* 71 He and Serafima, his large, cheerful, Moscow-born wife..would throw Russki parties every now and then, with Russki hors d'oeuvres. **1959** C. MacInnes *Absolute Beginners* 55 We've got to produce our own variety, and not imitate the Americans—or the Ruskis, or anybody. **1961** *Even. Bull.* (Philadelphia) 29 Mar. 22/3 (*caption*) Keeping up with the (Russki) Joneses. **1978** I. B. Singer *Shosha* ii. 38 A Russky with all these qualities is awaiting you there.

Rusnak, Rusniac, Rusniak, vars. *Russniak *sb.* and *a.*

Russ, var. *Rus.

Russell[1]. (Earlier and further examples of *Russell cord.*)

1873 [see *Persian cord* s.v. *Persian *a.* 2]. **1896** *Woman's Life* 11 July 179/2, I cannot say that the coarse blue alpaca in various shades of navy blue and prune finds favour in my eyes... It reminds me too much of the fearsome fabric known as Russell cord, that in the far-off days of my childhood constituted my school dresses. **1940** *Chambers's Techn. Dict.* 735/1 *Russel cord* (textiles), a dress fabric of plain weave, with a cord effect; made from cotton warp and worsted or mohair weft, the warp being in tapes. **1966** *Guardian* 25 Apr. 7/2 Russell cord is the right stuff for stuff wearers.

Russell[2] (rʊ·sĕl). The name of Patrick *Russell* (1727–1805), Scottish physician and naturalist, used *attrib.* and in the possessive in **Russell('s) viper** to designate a venomous snake, *Vipera russellii*, found in India, Burma, and Thailand, distinguished by a yellowish-brown skin marked with black rings or spots, and first named *Coluber russellii* in his honour by G. Shaw in 1797.

[**1797** G. Shaw *Naturalist's Miscellany* VIII. pl. ccxci (*caption*) The Russelian Snake. *Ibid.*, Dr. Patrick Russel ..presented the elegant specimen here figured to the British Museum.] **1908** E. P. Stebbing *Man. Elem. Forest Zool. India* xii. 182 The Russell's Viper is one of the most deadly of all snakes. **1937** L. Bromfield *Rains Came* I. i. 7 With the first splattering drop of rain they would come swarming out of old roots and crannies in the wall—the cobras, the Russell's vipers, the fierce little kraits. **1940** *Lancet* 17 Aug. 195/1 It was decided to determine how far commercial preparations of Russell-viper venom would meet these requirements. **1961** *Listener* 2 Nov. 735/2 Russell's Vipers, when I have caught them, were always very sluggish. **1972** M. Richardson *Fascination of Reptiles* xv. 158 Another snake which Indian snake charmers sometimes carry around in their baskets is Russell's viper.

Russell[3] (rʊ·sĕl). The name of Bertrand Arthur William *Russell*, 3rd Earl Russell (1872–1970), mathematician and philosopher, used *attrib.* and in the possessive in connection with a paradox concerning the set of all sets that do not contain themselves as members: the condition for it to contain itself is that it should not contain itself.

1922 tr. *Wittgenstein's Tractatus* 57 Herewith Russell's paradox vanishes. **1937** *Jrnl. Symb. Logic* II. 31 This contradiction corresponds to Russell's paradox. **1950** W. V. Quine *Methods of Logic* (1952) §42. 249 This difficulty is called *Russell's paradox*, for its discoverer (1901). **1963** G. T. Kneebone *Math. Logic* iv. 127 Russell's antinomy..this is the paradox of the class $\{x/x\notin x\}$. **1967** *Encycl. Philos.* V. 46/1 *Russell's Paradox*,..Russell.. came upon a new paradox, that of the set of all sets that do not contain themselves as elements. A set r, the 'Russell set', is defined by the following condition: for every x, $x\epsilon r$ if and only if $x\epsilon x$. By substitution we obtain: $r\epsilon r$ if and only if $r\epsilon r$. **1977** Bell & Machover *Course in Math. Logic* x. 462 Unfortunately..(1.2) is untenable even when $k=0$, because it leads to the well-known Russell paradox.

Russell[4] (rʊ·sĕl). The name of George *Russell* (1857–1951), English gardener, used *attrib.*, esp. in **Russell lupin,** to desginate a large perennial lupin belonging to a variety of *Lupinus polyphyllus* developed by him, introduced in 1937, and distinguished by long racemes of papilionaceous flowers in one or two of a wide range of colours.

1937 *My Garden* XI. 332 The 'Russell Lupins'..would be more correctly described as a new 'race' rather than an improvement of an old. **1957** A. Bloom *Hardy Perennials* 229 The famous Russell strain..has superseded all others in recent years. *Ibid.* 230 Russell Lupins ..have few dislikes other than over-rich or limy soils. **1974** *Country Life* 17 Jan. 72/3 George Russell, a Yorkshire gardener, was attempting to improve the perennial lupin and found..one that had sported to a new shape of flower... Virtually all subsequent lupins have been of the 'Russell' type. **1979** *Guardian* 25 Aug. 9/6 We grow Russell lupins as a hobby.

Russell body (rʊ·sĕl). *Path.* [Named after William *Russell* (1852–1940), Scottish pathologist, who described it in 1890 (*Brit. Med. Jrnl.* 13 Dec. 1356–60).] A hyaline mass of immunoglobulin produced in numbers in, and sometimes extruded by, plasma cells in excessive response to challenge by antibodies.

1913 O. C. Gruner *Biol. of Blood-Cells* vi. 276 The intracellular Russell bodies are considered the result of myelin degeneration of the cell-substance. **1970** Passmore & Robson *Compan. Med. Stud.* II. xxv. 39/2 Sometimes the fabrication of antibody within plasma cells is so excessive that hyaline masses of protein (Russell bodies) are deposited in their cytoplasm. **1977** R. B. Thompson *Disorders of Blood* xxxii. 508/2 Occasionally Russell bodies are present... They are intracellular acidophil hyaline bodies which can be produced in animal cells by injections of bacteria and can be found in many organs and tissues.

Russell fence (rʊ·sĕl). *Canada.* Also **Russel fence, rustle fence.** [Said to derive from the name of Mr. *Russell*, its inventor.] A fence in which the top rail lies in the crux of crossed posts and the lower rails hang suspended from it by looped wires.

1932 N. M. Jamieson *Cattle in Stall* 75 There was the rustle fence, with boom on top and centre. **1953** *Canad. Geogr. Jrnl.* Dec. 226/2 The Russell fence has..been patented and Russell, the inventor, succeeded..in collecting royalties from people who built fences on his model. It consists of pairs of crossed posts,..but the rails are hung from the crotches and from each other in wire loops. **1962** A. Fry *Ranch on Cariboo* i. 4 It was Russel fence, an ingenious stake and rail structure held together by heavy wire and named, I'm told, after the man who invented it. **1968** *Islander* (Victoria, B.C.) 29 Dec. 16/4 The contract price for a log fence would be around $400 a mile while a Russel fence of the same length could be had for $150. **1971** W. Hillen *Blackwater River* xiii. 122 This..falcon would have been seen sitting on nearly any Russell fence..a few years back. **1972** R. Wright *Cariboo Mileposts* 14 (*caption*) A typical Cariboo scene of a Russell fence, cattle and pine trees.

Russellian (rʊse·liăn), *a.* and *sb.* [f. the name *Russell* (see *Russell[3]) + -ian.] **A.** *adj.* Designating the mathematical or philosophical ideas of Bertrand Russell; characteristic of or pertaining to Russell (in quot. 1956, *spec.* of *Russell's paradox*: see *Russell[3]). **B.** *sb.* An adherent of Russell's ideas. Hence **Ru·ssellism,** the system of Russell's thought and practice.

1923 C. D. Broad *Sci. Thought* xiii. 534 Physical objects in the Russellian sense. **1934** R. Campbell *Broken Record* 145 Russellism and Waughism seem to me to be as tyrannical and brutal..as Arnold-of-Rugby-ism. **1937** *Discovery* Feb. 61/1 The Russellian 'calculus of propositions'. **1950** *Mind* LIX. 344 Neither Aristotelian nor Russellian rules give the exact logic of any expression of ordinary language. **1954** R. Wells in *Word* X. 235 Thus Wittgenstein has played a major part in all three branches of the Russellian movement. *Ibid.* 245 Examples ..have been separately discussed by various Russellians and Wittgensteinians. **1956** G. E. M. Anscombe tr. *Wittgenstein's Remarks on Found. of Math.* v. 166 The Russellian contradiction is disquieting, not because it is a contradiction, but because the whole growth culminating in it is a cancerous growth. **1972** *Listener* 27 Jan. 119/1 His interest is the more Russellian one of getting the system to work. **1977** *Language* LIII. 74 Perhaps he is taking a Russellian view of definite descriptions.

russellite (rʊ·sĕləit). *Min.* [f. the name of Arthur E. I. M. *Russell* (1878–1964), English mineralogist + -ite[1].] A tetragonal mixed oxide of bismuth and tungsten, $Bi_2O_3.WO_3$, found as pale yellow or green fine-grained masses.

1938 Hey & Bannister in *Mineral. Mag.* XXV. 42 We propose for the mineral the name russellite, in honour of Mr. Arthur Russell. *Ibid.* 49 Russellite..occurs at the Castle-an-Dinas wolfram mine, St. Columb Major, Cornwall, as pale yellow fragments. **1944** *Ibid.* XXVII. 2 Two pellets of comparatively pure russellite about the size of split peas were found to show on their rounded surfaces blebs of bright gold easily visible to the naked eye. **1970** *Ibid.* XXXVII. 705 Russellite $Bi_2O_3.WO_3$ occurs in a small pegmatite near Poona, Western Australia.

Russell–Saunders (rʊ·sĕl sǭ·ndəɪz). *Physics.* [The names of Henry Norris *Russell* (1877–1957), U.S. astrophysicist, and Frederick Albert *Saunders* (1875–1963), U.S. physicist; they first described the scheme in *Astrophys. Jrnl.* (1925) LXI. 38.] *Russell–Saunders coupling*, an approximation employed in a procedure for describing the possible energy states which can be adopted by a set of electrons in an atom; = *LS-coupling* (s.v. *L II. 6* b); also *Russell–Saunders scheme, state*, etc.

[**1927** *Zeitschr. f. Physik* XL. 532 Im Russell–Saunderschen Schema.] **1928** *Physical Rev.* XXXI. 957 In most spectra there is a different coupling of the quantum vectors, the Russell–Saunders coupling, which is responsible for normal multiplets. **1935** Condon & Shortley *Theory of Atomic Spectra* vii. 208 The Russell–Saunders terms corresponding to the configurations s^x and p^x. **1961** Walker & Straw *Spectroscopy* I. i. 87 It will be assumed..that Russell–Saunders coupling applies to the individual momentum vectors associated with the electrons. **1962** Cotton & Wilkinson *Adv. Inorg. Chem.* xxvi. 574 Just as the set of five d orbitals is split apart by the electrostatic field of surrounding ligands to give two or more sets of lower degeneracy, so also are the various Russell–Saunders states of a d^n configuration. **1966** D. H. Whiffen *Spectroscopy* xi. 141 Weak transitions disobeying these selection rules..are not at all uncommon and their existence implies that the Russell–Saunders scheme is not accurately applicable. **1967** W. R. HINDMARSH *Atomic Spectra* iii. 27 The assumption of negligible spin-orbit interaction on which the Russell–Saunders coupling scheme is based.

Russenorsk (rʊ·sənɒ̄ɹsk). [Norw.] A pidgin of Russian and Norwegian used by fishermen.

1964 E. PALMER tr. *Martinet's Elem. General Linguistics* v. 155 *Russenorsk*, the product of contacts between Russian and Norwegian fishermen on the shores of the Arctic Ocean, which had an ephemeral existence but has been adequately described. **1974** L. TODD *Pidgins & Creoles* i. 6 Russenorsk, a pidgin now almost extinct, arose from the contact of two Indo-European languages, Russian and Norwegian, as a means of facilitating communication between Russian and Norwegian fishermen. **1974** *Encycl. Brit. Macropædia* VI. 1063/2 Pidgins..are not true languages since they are derivations from two or more parent tongues. An example is Russenorsk (from Russian and Norwegian), used by Norwegian fishermen with Russian traders.

russet, *sb.* and *a.* Add: **B.** *adj.* **1. b.** (Earlier and later examples.)

1629 J. PARKINSON *Parad.* III. xix. 587 The Russet pippin is as good an apple as most of the other sorts of pippins. *Ibid.* xxi. 592 The russet Catherine is a very good middle sized peare. **1929** M. DE LA ROCHE *Whiteoaks* vii. 99 'H'm,' grunted Finch, tearing a bite from a russet apple. **1970** *Globe & Mail* (Toronto) 28 Sept. 5/1 (*caption*) Seventy-eight acres of..Russet and Tolman Sweet apple trees, all of them laden with ripe fruit.

d. *russet-brown* (later example), *-gold.*

1861 J. G. WHITTIER *Cobbler Keezar* in *Poet. Wks.* (1898) 84/2 Yellow and red were the apples, And the ripe pears russet-brown. **1959** E. POUND *Thrones* cii. 82 The colour..As lacquer in sunlight haliporphuros, russet-gold In the air.

e. *Comb.*, as *russet-clad, -faced, -haired, -skinned.*

1849 THOREAU *Week Concord Riv.* 19 It may be many russet-clad children lurking in those broad meadows. **1897** W. B. YEATS *Secret Rose* 80 A russet-faced boy..sat ..watching the swallows. **1936** M. H. BRADLEY *Five-Minute Girl* ix. 159 A small girl of eight, hazel-eyed, russet-haired. **1878** G. M. HOPKINS *Lett. to R. Bridges* (1955) 48 He [*sc.* a seaman]..is..russet-of-morning-skinned With the sun, salt, and whirling wind.

Hence **ru·ssetly** *adv.*, with a russet colour; in a russet state. *poet.*

c **1864** E. DICKINSON *Poems* (1955) II. 687 Though Pyramids decay And Kingdoms, like the Orchard Flit Russetly away.

russeted, *ppl. a.* (in Dict. s.v. RUSSET *v.*) Add: *spec.* (of fruit and vegetables) rough-skinned; (of their skin) rough. (Further examples.)

1917 [see next]. **1930** *Jrnl. Pomology & Hort. Sci.* VIII. 299 Examination of the russeted fruit revealed the presence of the fungus already mentioned. **1950** SMOCK & NEUBERT *Apples & Apple Products* iii. 29 This periderm is a cork cambium and is capable of forming cork-like cells which result in the russetted appearance of some fruits. **1978** *Sci. Amer.* June 64/3 The 'Idaho' potato..is the most prized of the North American varieties because of its large size, pulpy interior,..and russeted (textured) skin.

russeting, *vbl. sb.* (In Dict. s.v. RUSSET *v.*) Add: *spec.* The roughening of the skin of normally smooth-skinned fruit, esp. apples. (Further examples.)

1917 *32nd Ann. Rep. Maine Agric. Experiment Station* 86 These plots have been introduced solely..as a basis of comparison with other sprays..with respect to scab control and the production of fruit russetting and foliage injury... This treatment has increased the number of russetted apples from 5 to 10 per cent. **1928** C. E. OWENS *Princ. Plant Path.* xxv. 609 Bordeaux is apt to cause leaf injury and russeting of fruit..in moist weather. **1974** *Nature* 8 Feb. 337/3 The most insidious type of damage is russeting, and fruit skins are sensitive to certain fungicides in May and June.

Russia. Add: **2. a.** *Russia braid* (earlier examples), *duck* (earlier examples), *iron, matting* (earlier example), *sheet-iron* (earlier example).

1847 *Lady's Newspaper* 11 Dec. 566 Gentleman's waistcoat. Material—blue..cloth, and green or amber Russia braid. **1873** *Young Englishwoman* Nov. 572/1 Travelling toilet of brown cashmere, braided with brown of a darker-shade in Russia and Breton braid. **1761** *Essex Inst. Hist. Coll.* (1912) XLVIII. 95 Best prime Russia Duck **1822** M. EDGEWORTH *Let.* 6 Feb. (1971) 344 His Russia duck jacket and trowzers. **1897** *Sears, Roebuck Catal.* 127 We make it [*sc.* a stove] lined and unlined, and in smooth steel and planished iron (usually called Russia iron). **1901** *Daily Colonist* (Victoria, B.C.) 12 Oct. 8/7 (Advt.), 'Famous' Air-Tights [*sc.* stoves]. Built for light service. Will burn rough blocks of wood. Made of Russia iron. **1839** J. J. AUDUBON *Ornithol. Biogr.* V. 504 The nest..has uniformly been built of Russia matting. **1859** *Rep. Comm. Patents 1858* (U.S.) I. 530 The process of manufacturing sheet-iron, to possess most of the qualifications of 'polished Russia sheet-iron'.

Russian, *sb.* and *a.* Add: **A.** *sb.* **1. a.** *Great, Little, White Russian* (earlier examples). See also WHITE *a.* 11 e in Dict. and Suppl.

1845 *Encycl. Metrop.* XXIV. 225/1 Two principal branches are distinguished, rivals of each other, and still cherishing the bitterest animosity—the Russians *great* and *little*, and the Poles. **1854** J. S. MAXWELL *Czar & his People* xxiii. 125 The Great Russian is predominant among the various peoples of the empire. **1866** *Chambers's Encycl.* VIII. 380/2 The 50,500,000 Russians..are divisible into—1. Great Russians..2. Little Russians.. 3. White Russians.

b. Delete *rare*—¹ and add later examples.

1866 *Chambers's Encycl.* VIII. 388/2 The Russians adopt the same expedient with the Greeks, viz., of selecting the bishops from among the monks. **1963** T. WARE *Orthodox Church* viii. 165 It is not without reason that the expressions 'Soviet Church' and 'Soviet Patriarch' have now become common in the mouth of Russians.

c. (Earlier and later examples.)

1845 D. MACKENZIE *Emigrant's Guide* 118 These wild *Russians*, as they are here called, will..clear at the first leap a stockyard six feet in height. **1848** H. W. HAYGARTH *Recoll. Bush Life Austral.* xii. 135 Though he had been among horses since he was a child, his present lot were a set of the veriest 'Russians' (Anglicè, wild things) *he* ever had anything to do with. **1945** BAKER *Austral. Lang.* iii. 68 An old term worth noting, since it has been obsolete for half a century or more, is *Russians* for wild stock.

2. Also *Comb.*, as *Russian-speaking.*

1960 *Amer. Speech* XXXV. 163 The material..was gathered among the Russian-speaking population. **1976** 'M. BARAK' *Secret List of Heinrich Roehm* vii. 77 You need Russian-speaking agents to infiltrate Russian circles.

3. Also *ellipt.* for *Russian cigarette.*

1892 [see *EGYPTIAN *sb.* 5 b]. **1937** R. CHANDLER in *Dime Detective Mag.* Nov. 43/2 There were three long cigarettes..Russians, with hollow mouthpieces. **1963** N. FREELING *Because of Cats* x. 163 He had juju cigarettes too; like Russians, with a big mouth piece, and pretty loose.

B. *adj.* **1. a.** Also with distinguishing adjs., as *Great, Little, White Russian* (see sense A. 1 a in Dict. and WHITE *a.* 11 e in Dict. and Suppl.).

1911 C. J. HOGARTH tr. *V. O. Kluchevsky's Hist. Russia* I. xiii. 203 The Great Russian stock stands to the Little Russian in the proportion of three to one, and the Little Russian to the White Russian in a similar ratio. **1918** R. BEAZLEY et al. *Russia, from Varangians to Bolsheviks* I. iii. 79 The principality of Moscow had become a Great Russian nation, the Prince of Moscow a Great Russian sovereign. **1942** L. B. NAMIER *Conflicts* 8 The conflict with Russia turned on Poland's dominion over vast stretches of land inhabited by White Russian and Little Russian peasantries. **1963** *Times Lit. Suppl.* 31 May 388/4 The growth of Great-Russian jingoism.

Comb. **1963** R. I. MCDAVID *Mencken's Amer. Lang.* v. v. 265 *Nudnik*..is widely used by Russian-Jewish immigrants. **1976** *Times* 15 May 14/8 Sholem Aleichem came from a middle class Russian–Jewish background.

2. a. *Russian bear* (later *fig.* examples); *Russian Blue*, a lightly built short-haired cat belonging to the breed so called, distinguished by greyish-blue fur, green eyes, and large pointed ears; *Russian long-hair(ed) (cat)*, a stocky, long-coated cat with a relatively short tail, belonging to a breed once so called but no longer a distinct group; *Russian pony*, a small, hardy, roan pony belonging to a breed originally developed in Russia; cf. *COSSACK 2 b; *Russian sable*, the heavy dark fur of the sable, *Martes zibellina*; cf. SABLE *sb.*¹ 1 a; *Russian wolfhound* = *BORZOI.

1737 POPE *1st Epistle 2nd Bk. Horace Imitated* 22 No Lord's Anointed, but a Russian Bear. **1806** M. EDGEWORTH *Leonora* II. lxix. 121 It would really be pleasant to have a Czar at one's feet... The ancients represent Cupid riding the Numidian lion, and why should he not tame the Russian bear? **1972** C. SHORT *Naked Skier* xxvi. 147 All the gay, waltzing and slightly frenetic set-up [of Vienna] can be shattered at an instant by the roar of a Russian bear. **1977** W. FEAVER *When We were Young* 19 The political cartoon figures—British lion, Russian bear, German eagle. **1889** H. WEIR *Our Cats* 66 The Blue Cat was at first shown as the Archangel cat, then Russian blue, Spanish blue, Chartreuse blue, and..the American blue. **1933** E. BUCKWORTH-HERNE-SOAME *Cats* xxxvii. 164 Russian Blues, so called because they were originally brought from Russia, are now known as 'Foreign Blues'. **1953** A. WHITE tr. *Colette's Cat* viii. 191 I'll withdraw.. into my cold room..under the protection of..a Russian Blue cat. **1971** W. J. BURLEY *Guilt Edged* viii. 132 Trotsky is our cat—a Russian blue. **1976** *Loughborough Monitor* 26 Nov. 2/3 (Advt.), Ready for Christmas.. Russian Blue Kittens. **1889** H. WEIR *Our Cats* 30 The Russian long-haired cat..differed from the Angora and the Persian in many respects. **1939** [see *Burmese cat* s.v. BURMESE *a.* b]. **1972** ING & POND *Champion Cats of World* 72 The Russian Longhair..apparently had an even more woolly coat, and a shorter tail. **1898** J. D. BRAYSHAW *Slum Silhouettes* 151 I'm off to the Cattle Market to buy one o' those little Rooshian ponies. **1903** A. BENNETT *Truth about Author* xvi. 214 Arrival of the second post on a Russian pony that cost fifty shillings. **1936** A. W. SEABY *Brit. Ponies* 144, I stopped before a strange looking old light roan pony between the shafts of a sweep's cart. It was a Russian pony the owner averred. **1871** Russian sable [see *doll-land* s.v. *DOLL *sb.*¹ 5]. **1930** M. BACHRACH *Fur* xxi. 322 There probably has never been a peltry that has enjoyed such popularity..for so long a period of time as the Russian Sable. **1952** 'M. COST' *Hour Awaits* 152 The fur was sable, and Russian sable. **1973** D. ORGILL *Jasius Pursuit* x. 99 He took one of the fur coats... It was a magnificent garment—Russian sables. **1872** G. H. LEWES *Jrnl.* 28 Dec. in *Geo. Eliot Lett.* (1956) V. 352 He took us up to Lady Paget to see a superb Russian Wolf-hound. **1922** R. LEIGHTON *Compl. Bk. Dog* ix. 141 There is not a more elegant and graceful dog than the Borzoi or Russian Wolfhound... The wearer of a lovely silky coat, he is essentially a spectacular animal. **1941** B. SCHULBERG *What makes Sammy Run?* viii. 157 She walked.. with a haughty pride, the way one does with Russian wolfhounds. **1976** BOTHAM & DONNELLY *Valentino* viii. 59 He bought a pair of Russian wolfhounds (white).

b. *Russian olive* (U.S.), the oleaster, *Elæagnus angustifolia*, a spiny shrub with silvery leaves belonging to the family Elæagnaceæ, native to Europe and western Asia, and naturalized in parts of western North America; *Russian poplar* (Canada), a poplar native to north-east Asia, *Populus maximowiczii*, which has leathery leaves with whitish undersides; *Russian thistle* (U.S.), a tumbleweed, *Salsola kali*, a creeping prickly herb belonging to the family Chenopodiaceæ; = SALTWORT 1; *Russian vine*, a fast-growing deciduous climbing plant, *Polygonum baldschuanicum*, of the family Polygonaceæ, native to southern Turkestan and bearing clusters of white or pink flowers.

1938 W. R. VAN DERSAL *Native Woody Plants U.S.* 119 Russian olive... A large shrub to small tree; introduced from Europe and Western Asia. **1951** T. H. KEARNEY et al. *Arizona Flora* 586 Russian-olive, native of the Old World, often cultivated as an ornamental in the United States. **1972** W. A. WEBER *Rocky Mt. Flora* 173 The Russian Olive..is cultivated throughout the region at lower elevations. **1950** E. A. MCCOURT *Home is the Stranger* ii. 19 Around the farmyard ran a stunted, ill-kempt wind-break of Russian poplar. **1965** I. REEKIE *Melita Trail* ii. 6 He planted the first grove of trees in the community—ash, cottonwood, Russian poplar, and Manitoba maples. **1894** *Amer. Folk-Lore* VII. 97 *Salsola Kali*, var. *Tragus*, Moguin, Russian thistle, Russian cactus. **1898** *Monthly S. Dakotan* I. 103 Only tiny triangular spots remained dry in the lee of broken corn-stalks and scattered Russian thistles. **1939** *Nat. Geogr. Mag.* Aug. 262/2 The Russian thistle..is a relative of beets and spinach in the family of the 'goosefoots'. **1971** *Country Life* 2 Sept 583/1 In autumn the Russian Thistles..ran freely before the wind at thirty miles an hour. **1948** N. CATCHPOLE *Flowering Shrubs & Small Trees* vii. 156 A vigorous climber, and the quickest growing one known in our gardens..is commonly called the Russian vine. **1963** *Oxf. Bk. Garden Flowers* 164/2 Russian Vine..is, in fact, a native of Bokhara, and is a rampant twining plant which will quickly smother any unsightly object in one season. **1977** K. O'HARA *Ghost of T. Penry* iv. 25 The stone arch ..was half-blocked by the ruins of a ramshackle gate overgrown with Russian vine.

d. *Russian bagatelle, braid, crash, diaper, poker.*

1850, etc. Russian bagatelle [see *COCKAMAROO]. **1953** R. SENHOUSE tr. *Colette's Gigi* 25 The Russian braid of her nightdress. **1973** *Country Life* 15 Feb. 425/1 Black wool suit, the jacket..trimmed with Russian braid. **1932** Russian crash [see *nurse cloth* s.v. *NURSE *sb.*¹ 8]. **1827** *Hallowell* (Maine) *Gaz.* 20 June 4/4 (Advt.), Received.. Russian Diaper. **1957** SIMPSON & WEIR *Weaver's Craft* (ed. 8) xiii. 165 *Russian diaper.*—This has a total of 26 threads to each pattern,..and it can also be used quite successfully as a border to some of the other patterns, for curtains, covers, etc. **1970** T. LILLEY *Projects Section* x. 121 He plays Russian poker in the mess. *Ibid.* xvii. 232 In Russian Poker there are four players: each has thirteen cards which he arranges in three hands—two of five cards and one of three. These hands are each arranged in poker fashion... Three players play against the fourth—the banker—and the bank changes after every fourth deal.

d*. Special collocations: *Russian ballet*, a style of ballet developed at the Russian Imperial Ballet Academy and popularized in the West by Sergei Diaghilev's Ballet Russe from 1909; also a group of dancers trained in this style; *Russian Bank* (*Banker, banque*), a card game similar to solitaire but played by two persons; *Russian bath* = *Turkish bath* s.v. TURKISH *a.* 2 a; also *fig.*; *Russian boot*, a leather boot that extends to the calf, usu. with a wide cuff; *Russian cigarette*, a cigarette with a hollow pasteboard filter; *Russian dancer*, one who performs a Russian folk-dance; *Russian dinner*, a style of dinner in which fruit and wine are placed at the centre of a table and courses are served from a side-board; *Russian doll*, any of a set of hollow wooden dolls, the smallest of which fits inside the next smallest, and so up to the largest; *Russian dressing*, a savoury dressing with a mayonnaise base; *Russian Easter egg*, an artificial egg shell designed as a container for presents given at Easter; *Russian egg*, a poached egg served on a lettuce leaf with mayonnaise; *Russian* (*spring–summer*, etc.) *encephalitis*, a viral encephalitis transmitted by wood ticks; *Russian Revolution*, the overthrow of the Tsar and the eventual establishment of the Bolshevik form of government in Russia between February and October (Old Style) 1917; cf. *October Revolution* s.v. *OCT-

OBER 3 and *REVOLUTION *sb.* II; *Russian roulette*, an act of bravado in which a person loads (usu.) one chamber of a revolver, spins the cylinder, holds the barrel to his head, and pulls the trigger; also *fig.*; *Russian salad*, a salad of vegetables with mayonnaise; *Russian scandal*, (*a*) a game in which a whispered message, after being passed from player to player, is contrasted in its original and final versions; (*b*) gossip inaccurately transmitted; *Russian tea*, (*a*) tea grown in the Caucasus or a drink made from this; (*b*) any tea laced with lemon or rum.

1911 *Westm. Gaz.* 3 June 2/3 She disapproved of early morning tea and auction bridge, of ski-ing and the two-step, of the Russian ballet and the Chelsea Arts Club ball. **1928** A. CHRISTIE *Mystery of Blue Train* xxxi. 261, I never saw anything in this Russian ballet... Too highbrow for me. **1937** J. LAVER *Taste & Fashion* viii. 110 The overwhelming wave of Orientalism which swept over Parisian society..was due to..Paul Poiret and the Russian ballet. **1947** *Ballet Ann.* I. 68 Diaghileff, in search of inspiration, made straight for Paris, *chic* and *chi-chi*, and so Russian ballet became *Ballet Russe.* **1973** W. TUTE *Resident* ii. 36 As you know the Russian ballet is the best in the world. **1915** W. DEL MAR *Rules of Russian Bank* 1 The game of Russian Bank is played by two persons each with a pack of fifty-two cards. The object of the game is to dispose of the cards. **1930** A. WOOLLCOTT *Let.* 26 Apr. (1944) iv. 85 We played backgammon or Russian Bank all the way over [the Atlantic]. **1930** 'E. QUEEN' *French Powder Mystery* xv. 118 Not many people know how to play Russian banque. **1970** R. LOWELL *Notebk.* 121 Ford, playing Russian Banker. **1804** M. WILMOT *Let.* 24 Apr. in *Russ. Jrnls.* (1934) I. 94 The true Russian Bath admits a Vapour which I cou'd not support. **1863** C. LEVER *Day's Ride* in *All Year Round* 16 Feb. 455/1 It is a sort of intellectual Russian bath, in which the luxury consists in the exaggerated alternative between being scalded first and rolled in the snow afterwards. **1961** L. MUMFORD *City in Hist.* xiii. 386 In the seventeenth century..the bath was re-introduced as a foreign importation, a luxury..: the so-called Turkish or Russian bath. **1975** A. HAILEY *Moneychangers* II. vi. 193 Mr Quartermain likes either a sauna or a Russian bath wherever he is. **1915** in C. Willett Cunnington *Eng. Women's Clothing* (1952) iv. 132 The fashionable side-lacing Russian boots with fawn cloth tops and patent leather fronts, 21/- a pair. **1926** WODEHOUSE *Heart of Goof* iii. 108 You bet your Russian boots I was! **1977** V. S. PRITCHETT *Gentle Barbarian* xiii. 212 Turgenev..wandered about in heavy Russian boots. **1905** C. MACKENZIE *Diary* 30 Mar. in *My Life & Times* (1964) III. 222 A lazy young man..who used to smoke Bobbie's Russian cigarettes. **1926** C. BEATON *Diary* 24 Apr. in *Wandering Yrs.* (1961) 87 Smoking Russian cigarette after Russian cigarette. **1940** E. HEMINGWAY *For whom Bell Tolls* ii. 20 Robert Jordan..brought out one of the flat boxes of Russian cigarettes... They were long narrow cigarettes with pasteboard cylinders for mouth pieces. **1972** J. WAINWRIGHT *Requiem for Loser* iii. 52 They sipped tea, smoked Russian cigarettes and discussed this and that. **1913** MRS. P. CAMPBELL *Let.* 25 Mar. in *B. Shaw & Mrs. Campbell* (1952) 102 Russian dancers were imitated—shoes kicked off—hair came down. **1931** C. REMFRY-KIDD tr. *Colette's Renée Néré* I. i. 9 The Russian dancers are trying to get warm... They shout 'Yonk!' all together. **1851** *London at Table* I. 26 We have already alluded to a Russian dinner, which is the best and most economical. It is always served hot from the kitchen, and as the entrées are not exposed to the public gaze, there may be fewer of them; the joints served at the side-board by an experienced artist, are more palatable and tempting than when carved on the table. **1868** M. JEWRY *Warne's Model Cookery* 56 The present fashion of Russian dinners is fast banishing the necessity for promiscuous carving. **1937** K. BLIXEN *Out of Afr.* ii. 135 Those Russian wooden dolls which will unscrew, and have then got another doll inside them, and another inside that, and which are sold under the name of Katinka. **1967** C. FREMLIN *Prisoner's Base* xvi. 114 Each item in the dream was fitting into her interpretation like a set of Russian dolls. **1922** *Hotel World* 15 Apr. 15/1 Russian Dressing. **1938** L. BEMELMANS *Life Class* II. ii. 127 The salad, covered with Russian dressing, is a mixture of endives..pineapple..cream cheese with chopped chives. **1976** *Billings* (Montana) *Gaz.* 1 July, In medium bowl, thoroughly combine ½ cup Russian dressing, ground beef, and breadcrumbs. **1949** H. C. BAINBRIDGE *P. C. Fabergé* iv. 67 (*heading*) The Imperial Russian Easter Eggs. **1955** W. GADDIS *Recognitions* III. v. 903 Like a Russian Easter Egg, this Thing had a tiny window in one end. **1932** M. F. DANIELS tr. *F. Nietlispach's Cold Dishes & Hors-D'œuvre* I. 16 *Russian Eggs.* Poach the eggs, strain and cool. Arrange on a lettuce leaf..cover with mayonnaise and sprinkle with..minced ham and a little chopped parsley. **1969** G. LYALL *Venus with Pistol* vii. 39, I yelled an order for.. Russian eggs... It comes up a salad the size of the Garden of Eden. **1943** *Science* 12 Mar. 246/1 (*heading*) Close relation between Russian spring–summer encephalitis and louping-ill viruses. **1948** OLITSKY & CASALS in T. M. Rivers *Viral & Rickettsial Infections of Man* viii. 192/1 Russian Far East encephalitis (Synonyms: Russian spring–summer encephalitis; Russian spring or summer encephalitis; Russian forest-spring encephalitis; Russian tick-borne encephalitis; Russian endemic encephalitis). *Ibid.*, Russian Far East encephalitis is a disease occurring in spring and early summer, mainly in the Far East provinces of the Soviet Union and less frequently in European and Siberian Russia. **1976** W. L. DREW *Viral Infections* i. 7 Group B [*sc.* arboviruses] includes the viruses of St. Louis encephalitis, yellow fever, and dengue, as well as the viruses of Russian encephalitis and hemorrhagic fever found in Europe and Russia. [**1805** C. WILMOT *Let.* 7 Dec. in *Russ. Jrnls.* (1934) II. 208 The famous 28th of June 1762, the day of the Russian Revolution. **1907** I. ZANGWILL *Ghetto Comedies* 399 We are a Labour party... We have the whole Russian Revolution on our shoulders.] **1917** C. P. SCOTT *Let.* 25 Mar. in D. Ayerst *Guardian* (1971) xxvii. 403 Don't you feel the Russian revolution rather stirring in your bones? **1919** *Mr. Punch's Hist. Great War* 176 A 'History of the Russian Revolution' has already been published. **1922** *Encycl. Brit.* XXXII. 319/2 The history of the Russian Revolution starts with the gradual dissolution of all fundamental institutions and notions. **1945** 'G. ORWELL' in *Common Wealth Rev.* Nov. 12/1 The failure of the Russian Revolution—failure, that is, in the sense that the Revolution has not fulfilled the hopes that it aroused twenty-five years ago. **1977** *Times* 26 Mar. 12/4 A history-teaching colleague suggested that it might have been better if the Russian Revolution had never taken place. **1937** G. SURDEZ in *Collier's* 30 Jan. 16 'Did you ever hear of Russian Roulette?'.. With the Russian army in Rumania, around 1917,..some officer would suddenly pull out his revolver,..remove a cartridge from the cylinder, spin the cylinder, snap it back in place, put it to his head and pull the trigger. **1946** *N.Y. Post* 23 Oct. 5/2 The game was 'Russian Roulette', and the odds were 5–1. **1956** 'M. INNES' *Appleby plays Chicken* I. ii. 18 'Is it done with a revolver..with one of the six chambers loaded?' 'No. That's Russian roulette.' **1960** *Guardian* 27 July 16/4 This party..had 'played Russian roulette with American strength and American progress'. **1976** *Lancet* 9 Oct. 776/2 Abusive parents are often the scarred survivors of generations of reproductive russian roulette. **1879** M. JEWRY *Warne's Model Cookery* (new ed.) 456/2 *Russian Salad*... Cold boiled beetroot; cold carrots [etc.] ..smoked salmon, or white meat of chicken and tongue. Cut the vegetables into pieces all of one size, add the salmon..mix with Mayonnaise sauce. Garnish with anchovies. **1940** M. DICKENS *Mariana* iii. 64 'I'll tell you something, Tich,' said Uncle Geoffrey beginning on his Russian salad. **1973** 'S. HARVESTER' *Corner of Playground* I. viii. 70 He had carved the cold roast chicken and served it with Russian salad. **1873** L. TROUBRIDGE *Jrnl.* 28 Aug. in J. Hope-Nicholson *Life amongst Troubridges* (1966) vi. 50 We played Russian Scandal in the train, which was very jolly. **1873** C. M. YONGE *Pillars of House* IV. xxxviii. 126 Susie has been well lectured on Russian scandal! **1893** —— *Girl's Little Bk.* 17 Do not repeat it [*sc.* gossip]. You will probably make Russian scandal of it, and the next person will add to it. **1929** H. G. WELLS *King who was King* ii. 59 '*We used to play a game called Russian scandal*'... The screen shows a row of young people... The first whispers to the second, who whispers to the third, and so on. **1953** 'P. WENTWORTH' *Ivory Dagger* lxii. 209 There used to be a game called Russian scandal. Something was whispered from one to another, and you have no idea what it would come out like by the time even a few people had had the handling of it. **1960** G. E. EVANS *Horse in Furrow* xiii. 177 Stories passed from one to another are proverbially incorrect as 'Russian scandal'. **1862** M. B. CHESNUT *Diary* 25 June in C. V. Woodward *M. Chesnut's Civil War* (1981) 395 They had Russian tea, champagne, a samovar. **1884** G. MEREDITH *Let.* 24 Mar. (1970) II. 732 Bid him arrive by half-past five, that the thirsty troop may be refreshed by Russian tea. **1930** L. G. D. ACLAND *Early Canterbury Runs* v. 111 The publican offered to make him some 'Russian tea'... 'Russian tea' turned out to be ordinary tea well laced with rum. **1952** 'R. CROMPTON' *William & Tramp* vii. 217 She said he had lemon in his tea 'stead of milk an' I know that's called Russian tea. **1975** *Times* 1 May 15/3 There is Russian tea, a long leaf variety grown in the foothills of the Caucasian mountains. **1976** *Eastern Even. News* (Norwich) 9 Dec. 8/1 Tins of Russian, Formosa or Jasmine tea are about 68p for half a pound.

Russianism. Add: **2. b.** Soviet communism as practised by the Russians.

1933 *Catholic Times* 21 Apr. 5/1 One of the reasons for the great success of Russianism was the austerity of many of its leaders and the complete self-sacrifice of many of its rank and file.

c. A Russian custom.

1957 V. NABOKOV *Pnin* iii. 71 Shy graduate students would be taught vodka-drinking rites and other stale Russianisms.

3. b. A Russian idiom.

1957 V. NABOKOV *Pnin* iii. 87 Her fluent and flashy New York English, with..soft lapses into furry Russianisms. **1962** *Amer. Speech* XXXVII. 279 (*title*) Russianisms in the American press. *Ibid.*, Russianisms are divided here into three main groups: loanwords, foreignisms, and calques. **1967** *Listener* 19 Jan. 99/3 Professor Markov allows the occasional Russianism to show through in his introduction, which isn't perfectly idiomatic.

Russianist (rʊ·ʃǎnist). [f. RUSSIAN *sb.* + -IST.] A student of Russian language and literature.

1976 *Times Lit. Suppl.* 23 Jan. 79/4 The occupational obsessions of Russianists writing on Chekhov. **1980** *Ibid.* 19 Sept. 1018/4 Joe Andrew will be known to most British Russianists as a co-chairman of the Neo-Formalist circle.

Russianness (rʊ·ʃǎn,nės). [f. RUSSIAN *a.* + -NESS.] The quality or state of being Russian.

1937 *Sunday Times* 21 Nov. 9/2 His [*sc.* Lenin's] essential Russianness had not been weakened by culture; it had not been Westernised by foreign contacts. **1954** U. WEINREICH in Saporta & Bastian *Psycholinguistics* (1961) 382/2 We may characterize the utterance by the feature of 'Russianness' or 'Englishness'. **1968** *Economist* 9 Nov. p. x/2 This book is an account of the author's life-long love affair with Russianness: not with Russia, past or present, but with a Russianness conceived in the nursery as a daydream of the trans-Siberian railway. **1973** *Observer* 4 Feb. 37/3 Wilson is worrying away about the peculiarities of the Russian language and the astonishing Russianness of Russians. **1977** V. S. PRITCHETT *Gentle Barbarian* ii. 27 The Russian disease..the ever shadowy figure of Russianness.

Russic, *a.* For *Obs.*[−1] read *Obs.* and add later *poet.* example.

1757 J. DYER *Fleece* IV. 399 Culder's woofs, and those of Exe and Frome,..Thither by Russic caravans are brought.

Russification. (Later examples.)

1936 *Discovery* Feb. 50/1 The education provided by the Russian authorities was..entirely subordinated to the policy of 'Russification' uncompromisingly adopted since the suppression of the Polish rebellion in 1863. **1972** *Times* 15 May 14/4 In the non-Russian republics one can get a 'feel' for the way people reach to russification. **1976** A. POWELL *Infants of Spring* x. 173 An increasing policy of Russification resulted in much unrest there [*sc.* in Finland]. **1976** *Survey* Spring 188 Ukrainians, Byelorussians, Lithuanians and Latvians..are exposed to intensive Russification. **1979** *Daily Tel.* 29 Nov. 18 The policy of the Soviet Union in the Baltic countries is to annihilate their peoples by enforced Russification and deportation.

Russify, *v.* Add: (Earlier and later examples.) Hence **Ru·ssifying** *ppl. a.*

1865 QUEEN VICTORIA *Let.* 23 May in R. Fulford *Your Dear Letter* (1971) 27 Good Alice seems quite Russified. **1924** [see *PRUSSIFICATION]. **1954** KOESTLER *Invisible Writing* x. 110 The natives were drawn into the towns, educated, Russified and Stalinised. **1960** E. R. GOODMAN in J. A. Fishman *Readings Sociol. of Lang.* (1968) 731 The..denigration of Stalin left the Russifying impact of Stalin's linguistic policy intact. **1973** *Listener* 5 Apr. 444/2 The Party instructions were to Russify the *Moscow News.* **1974** *Encycl. Brit. Macropædia* XVI. 47/1 His [*sc.* Ivan III's] churches, the original aspect of which has been altered by successive russifying restorations, were clearly in the Italian style.

Russki (now the most usual form), **Russky,** varr. RUSKY *a.* and *sb.*[2] in Dict. and Suppl.

Rusniak, *sb.* and *a.* Add: Also **Rusnak, Rusniac, Rusniak. a.** *sb.* (Examples of the language.)

1862 [see RUTHENIAN *sb.* 2]. **1894** A. LEFÈVRE *Race & Lang.* 239 Little Russian, Rusniac, or Ruthene. **1955** R. JAKOBSON *Slavic Lang.* (ed. 2) 4 Ukrainian dialects are classified into Northern, Southeastern, Southwestern, and Carpathian groups; the marginal dialects (called Rusnak) of the latter group are Slovak-influenced.

Russo-. Add: **a.** *Russo-American, -Byzantine, -Chinese, -Czech, -French, -German, -Greek* (later example), *-Japanese, -Persian, -Polish* (later example), *-Slavonic, -Swedish.*

1814 tr. *G. H. von Langsdorff's Voyages & Travels* II. 99 At our arrival, we found this new settlement of the Russio-American [*sic*] Company in want of almost all the necessaries of life. **1977** *Gramophone* June 56/3 A Russian conductor..and a Russo-American concerto which I haven't heard him play before. **1889** *Cent. Dict.*, Russo-Byzantine. **1973** *Country Life* 6 Dec. 1913/1 Russo-Byzantine work in purple and gold. **1903** G. BELL *Let.* 20 May (1927) I. viii. 162 We had to go to the renowned Russo-Chinese bank to change our notes. **1949** I. DEUTSCHER *Stalin* 418 The Russo-French and the Russo-Czech alliances were concluded. **1897** E. A. BARTLETT *Battlefields of Turkey* ii. 39 Two such evenly poised camps as the Russo-French League and the German monarchies. **1928** L. ROBINSON *Let.* in *Lett. S. O'Casey* (1975) I. 266 The second act in the modern Russo-German manner is very fine. **1972** D. DAKIN *Unification of Greece* ix. 126 Phillipon..was sent to..Athens in the hope of improving Russo-Greek relations. **1906** A. BENNETT *Let.* 6 Mar. (1966) I. 70 The last trick of bringing the Russo-Japanese war into the story. **1953** A. SMITH *Blind White Fish in Persia* iii. 50 Further along the coast there was a Russo-Persian Caviare industry but their fleet was not visible. **1926** Russo-Polish [see *EXPRESSIONISM]. **1959** G. NANDRIŞ *Handbk. Old Ch. Slavonic* I. 20 In the later period Russo-Slavonic, Old Serbian, and Old Croatian texts show a regular epenthetic *L*. **1974** *Encycl. Brit. Macropædia* XVI. 60/2 Russo-Swedish relations were settled during the Napoleonic era.

b. Russophil(e (further examples), **Russophobe** (further examples); **Russophobia** (earlier and later examples); **Russophobism** (earlier example), **Russophobist** (earlier adj. example).

1897 E. A. BARTLETT *Battlefields of Thessaly* ii. 38 There was a curious outburst of Russophile writing in a portion of the English Press. *Ibid.* iii. 46 One great factor in the game..is also ignored by our English Russophiles. **1946** R. CAPELL *Simiomata* III. 153 The new Foreign Minister..is a socialist and Russophil. **1967** C. SETON-WATSON *Italy from Liberalism to Fascism* ix. 342 Aehrenthal..had the reputation of an extreme conservative and Russophil. **1971** *Daily Tel.* 11 May 9/4 It is true that as a result of our history we have been and still are Russophile. **1946** G. STIMPSON *Thousand Things* 250 The war party, the Russophobes, who urged Prime Minister Disraeli to side with the Turks, against the Russians, became known as jingoes. **1966** R. BLAKE *Disraeli* xxvi. 607 The more Turcophobe Gladstone became, the more Russophobe was Disraeli. **1836** J. S. MILL in *Westm. Rev.* XXV. 276 Ministers are smitten with the epidemic disease of Russo-phobia. **1980** *Daily Tel.* 8 July 14, I fear that it might only serve to conceal the ever lurking presence of good old 19th-century British Russophobia. **1880** E. W. HAMILTON *Diary* 25 Aug. (1972) I. 37 It is extraordinary what amount of Russophobism pervades the royal mind. **1882** *Ibid.* 4 June (1972) I. 284 She may have the Russophobist and anti-Russian party in power again in this country.

Russonorsk (rʊ·sonǭɹsk). [f. Russo- + Norw. *norsk* Norwegian.] = *Russenorsk.

1966 R. A. Hall *Pidgin & Creole Lang.* I. i. 12 On a basis of Russian and Norwegian, there grew up a pidgin known as Russonorsk, which was used..between Russian and Norwegian fishermen along the Arctic coast of Norway. **1977** C. F. & F. M. Voegelin *Classification & Index World's Lang.* 311 Russonorsk can be said to be a Russian-based pidgin-creole, but might just as well be said to be Norwegian-based.

rust, *sb.*[1] Add: **9. a.** *rust-free*; *rust-bearded*.

1922 Joyce *Ulysses* 238 A sailorman, rustbearded, sips from a beaker. **1951** Whitby & Hynes *Med. Bacteriol.* (ed. 5) iii. 30 Iron in the form of rust-free filings..reduces the oxidation-reduction potential of liquid media.

b. *rustblack*, *-brown* (later example), *-red* (later examples).

a **1915** Joyce *Giacomo Joyce* (1968) 15, I kissed her stocking and the hem of her rustblack dusty skirt. **1977** *Lancashire Life* Nov. 56/2 By May 19 these were six [eggs]—tiny, white and rust-brown speckled. **1937** V. Woolf *Years* 297 The down was soft rust-red on its wings. *a* **1963** S. Plath *Ariel* (1965) 21 A sunken rust-red engine.

c. Special Combs.: **rust-resistant, -resisting** *adjs.*, (of a metal) made so as not to rust; (of a plant) not liable to rust disease; so **rust-resistance.**

1911 *Jrnl. Agric. Sci.* IV. 99 Have any results of a definite progressive nature in the physiology of rust-resistance been yet obtained? **1940** J. C. Hudson *Corrosion Iron & Steel* ii. 10 The use of rust-resisting steels has hitherto..been confined to definite fields of service, in which rust resistance is of primary importance. **1947** *Ann. Rev. Microbiol.* I. 78 The population shifts of physiologic races show the practical need for extensive replication in time and space in testing varieties for stem rust resistance. **1907** *Jrnl. Agric. Sci.* II. 127 In some countries a careful search has already been made for rust-resistant varieties, but on the whole, with comparatively little success from the economic point of view. **1930** H. Goldschmidt tr. *Müller-Hauff & Stein's Automobile Steels* iv. 142 Krupp was the first to use rust-resistant steel. **1947** *Ann. Rev. Microbiol* I. 78 The case of Ceres wheat..illustrates this point. This rust-resistant variety was distributed in 1926, and by 1934 was grown on more than four million acres. **1964** *Abraham & Straus Catal.* Jan. 29 Rust-resistant, lightweight, aluminium ladder. **1891** R. Wallace *Rural Econ. Austral. & N.Z.* iv. 72 A sample of rust-resisting wheat from Queensland. **1909** *Chambers's Jrnl.* Nov. 766/1 The steel used is a special light, thin, rust-resisting, seamless metal. **1962** *Sci. Survey* XXI. 332 'Stainless steel' (more correctly 'rust-resisting steel') is now familiar in both domestic and industrial applications.

10. rust bucket *N. Amer. colloq.*, an old and rusty ship; also *Austral. colloq.*, a rusty old car; **rust disease** = sense 6 a; **rust hypha,** a hypha of a rust fungus.

1945 *Seafarers' Log* 8 June 2/2 C. M. Chaney, J. D. Riffle and R. R. Ullan were dispatched to one of the more notorious rust buckets as Quartermaster and AB's respectively. **1959** *Wall St. Jrnl.* 13 Oct. (Eastern ed.) 1/6 To try to get the jump on the weather, ore carriers..'will put every rust bucket that floats into the ore trade'. **1969** *Sunday Mail* (Brisbane) 9 Nov. 15/4 (*heading*) Car trade-ins fit for scrap. Dealers stuck with 'rust-buckets'. **1979** F. Forsyth *Devil's Alternative* 7 The *Garibaldi* an amiable old rust-bucket out of Brindisi. **1902** W. Watson *Thompson's Gardener's Assistant* (rev. ed.) II. 600/1 (Index), Rust disease on vines—cause and treatment. **1975** *Times* 30 May 16/5 A team of scientists at Wye College has discovered in the tobacco plant a naturally produced fungicide effective against the 'rust' diseases which are commonly destructive to important food crops, vegetables and garden flowers. **1909** W. Bateson *Mendel's Princ. Heredity* 25 Miss Marryat found that the rust-hyphae are checked before entering the stomata of the resistant plants.

rustbank, var. *rusbank.

rusted, *ppl. a.* Add: (Later *fig.* example). Also, stuck or lodged as a result of rusting, and with *in* and *up*.

1924 J. Masefield *Sard Harker* II. 82 The catch of this beastly revolver seems to have jammed... I'm afraid it's rusted-in, or something. **1929** J. M. Ross in *Oxford Poetry* 36 The Purple Beech..brandishing aloft his burnt, dark, rusted leaves. **1967** E. Short *Embroidery & Fabric Collage* i. 18 A piece of rusted up metal..could be noted in a sketch-book. **1972** *Guardian* 15 Mar. 10/2, I don't ever feel that I get rusted-up. I don't think I could have done this play if I'd been rusted-up.

rusticated, *ppl. a.* Add: **3. b.** Of pottery: (see quot. 1936).

1936 *Proc. Prehistoric Soc.* II. 19 Rusticated pottery, *i.e.* pottery of which the surface has been roughened all over as a method of decoration. **1939** V. G. Childe *Dawn Europ. Civilization* (ed. 3) 338 Definitions of certain terms, descriptive of *ceramic decoration*, here used in a special or restricted sense... Rusticated—by roughening the surface, generally covered with a thick slip, by pinching with the fingers, brushing, etc. ('barbotine'). **1967** *Antiquaries Jrnl.* XLVII. 202 Somersham..is further known for its imposing 'pot-beaker', with rusticated finger-decoration. **1977** G. Clark *World Prehistory* (ed. 3) x. 448 Impressed and rusticated pottery was supplemented by polychrome painted Tupiguarini ware.

rustiness. 2. (Later example.)

1900 G. B. Shaw *Let.* 14 Mar. (1972) II. 156 In the old days I was always standing between Bland and the rustinesses that used to come from his Tory imperviousness to the Radical notions with which Socialism was adulterated.

rustle, *v.* **4.** For '*U.S. colloq.*' read 'orig. *U.S. colloq.*' and add: **b.** (Earlier and further examples.) Now usu. with *up*.

1844 *Spirit of Times* 14 Sept. 343/3 He nailed my thumb in his jaws, and rostled up a handful of dirt & throwed it in my eyes. **1891** *Advance* 29 Jan. 101/2 Some of the members have arranged..to go out on the hills and 'rustle up' wood. **1903** A. Adams *Log of Cowboy* xxi. 332 Honeyman being excused on agreeing to rustle the wood and water. **1919** *Punch* 29 Jan. 87/1 All George's performances in the art of rustling bivvies rank as star. **1931** 'Dean Stiff' *Milk & Honey Route* viii. 81 Kid, you go out and rustle some breakfast and meet us at the water tank. **1944** M. Laski *Love on Supertax* iii. 45 Do you think you can rustle me up something to eat? **1959** *Spectator* 11 Sept. 331/1 They put on their programme with such costumes as they could rustle up from Edinburgh's shops. **1978** G. Greene *Human Factor* v. ii. 243 We may not be able to rustle up more than an omelette, Muller. Pot luck.

c. Of animals: to forage (for). Also *absol.* and *transf.*

1881 *N.Y. Times* 18 Dec. 4/3 Cattle, in winter, 'rustle' for food by nosing through the snow to the dried grass beneath. **1913** L. V. Kelly *Range Men* 109 The [Red River] settlement took up the ranching of cattle, the turning out of herds to rustle their own living. **1916** 'B. M. Bower' *Phantom Herd* xiv. 243 He turns you out thinking he'll let you rustle for yourself awhile. **1924** R. Campbell *Flaming Terrapin* iv. 61 As shepherd winds drove forth their foamy sheep To rustle through the verdure of the deep. **1925** *Chambers's Jrnl.* Mar. 168/1 It is accustomed to rustle its living through the long severe winters of its habitat. **1955** J. C. Ewers in *Bull. U.S. Bureau Amer. Ethnol.* No. 159. 42 Unless the snow was too deep..(i.e. over ca. 2 feet) they [*sc.* horses] generally could rustle enough food..to gain a meagre subsistence. **1961** R. P. Hobson *Rancher takes Wife* vii. 111 The range horses never had to be fed hay, but rustled all year round. **1966** H. Marriott *Cariboo Cowboy* ii. 32 One year with another most of the cattle, except the calves, bulls, and thin cows, all rustled out in most of these ranges for most of, if not all, the winter.

d. To gather, round *up*; also with *in* and *out*.

1896 G. W. Dice *Life* vi. 30, I was more fortunate than ever this time, and..'rustled up' a good big herd of cattle, which we shipped to Kansas City. **1903** A. Adams *Log of Cowboy* iv. 53 Our foreman..sent Honeyman to rustle in the horses. **1924** A. J. Small *Frozen Gold* iii. 81 Why ain't you rustlin' a crowd of the boys up to corral the swabs? **1947** 'N. Blake' *Minute for Murder* v. 101 He's to rustle out all his men..and post them round the building. **1965** G. McInnes *Road to Gundagai* x. 183 Well, go and rustle up the rest of them.

e. To steal (cattle, horses, etc.) by rounding them up. Also *transf.* and *absol.*

1902 A. H. Lewis *Wolfville Nights* xv. 234, I claims that this Bowlaig b'ar is guilty of rustlin' the mails an' must.. be hanged. **1910** W. M. Raine *B. O'Connor* xix. 299 We're after them for rustling a bunch of Circle 33 cows. **1916** 'B. M. Bower' *Phantom Herd* xiv. 243 You hold a grudge against your dad, and you rustle from him mostly. **1948** *Range Riders Western* May 30/1, I ain't ever rustled a cow in my life. **1951** L. MacNeice tr. *Goethe's Faust* 163 One rustles cattle, one a wife.

rustler. Add: **2. b.** (Later examples.) Now also outside the U.S. and in extended and *transf.* uses.

1908 J. M. Sullivan *Criminal Slang* 20 *Rustler*, a horse thief. **1964** *Wall St. Jrnl* 9 Jan. 1/4 He covered the orange rustlers with a double-barreled shotgun. **1971** *Daily Tel.* 19 Apr. 2/1 East Anglian farmers were warned to beware of pig rustlers after 15 sows and five pigs.. were stolen. **1977** *Oxford Times* 16 Sept. 5/5 Police trying to round up horse rustlers in Oxfordshire have admitted the efforts often prove futile.

rustling, *vbl. sb.* Add: **3.** Stealing (esp. cattle) from farms, ranches, etc. Also *transf.* and *attrib.*

1893 *Aberdeen* (S. Dak.) *Sun* 5 Jan. 7/4 Rustling cattle is an exciting trade and very profitable, but extremely hazardous. **1907** [see *cattle-rustling* s.v. *cattle 8 a]. **1924** C. E. Mulford *Rustlers' Valley* x. 118 There had been no signs of rustling for months. **1937** *Sun* (Baltimore) 23 Oct. 3/2 Battle front of the cotton-rustling racket..is the Fabens Island area..comprising 3,000 acres of rich cotton land. **1942** E. Paul *Narrow St.* ix. 69 These crows had learned that living in Paris, near the central markets.., was easier than rustling in the country, exposed to the farmers' shotguns. **1963** *Wall St. Jrnl.* 11 Oct. 9 Add 'orange rustling' to the list of crimes against society. **1976** *Evening Post* (Nottingham) 14 Dec. 6/2 It's the peak of the shoplifting season..a time for turkey rustling and Christmas tree thefts.

rustly, *a.* (Later examples.)

1936 M. Mitchell *Gone with Wind* xlviii. 851 She wanted a tafetta petticoat..so rustly that the Lord God would think it was made of angels' wings. **1959** *N.Z. Listener* 13 Mar. 5/4, I always wrapped my sandwiches in cloth rather than rustly paper.

ru·stproof, *a.* [See Proof *a.* 1 b.] **a.** Of metal: not susceptible to corrosion by rust; rust-resistant.

1691 [s.v. Rust *sb.* 9 a]. **1907** *T. Eaton & Co. Catal.* Spring & Summer 215/3 Three large cupboards..each one has metal rust proof bottom. **1931** *Chambers's Jrnl.* June 414/1 (*caption*) A new rust-proof coating. **1960** *Farmer & Stockbreeder* 19 Jan. 45/2 Rust-proof heavy gauge pressed steel bowl. **1972** *Sat. Rev.* (U.S.) 27 May 4/2 The early safety-razor blades rusted, so I had to dry them... But soon came rustproof steel.

b. Of a plant: resistant to infection by rust.

1931 J. S. Huxley *What dare I Think?* i. 36 We can now produce relatively rust-proof wheat.

rustproof (rʊ·stprūf), *v.* [f. the adj.] *trans.* To make rustproof.

1910 *Cycling* 2 Feb. 95 (*heading*) Rust-proofing the bicycle. **1953** *Archit. Rev.* CXIV. 393 Before despatch each link was tested for size and strength and 'rust-proofed' by immersing it, when hot, in an oil bath and heating it again on removal until the oil dried on the surface. **1977** 'E. Crispin' *Glimpses of Moon* xii. 252 Was it practicable to rustproof metallic structures, as one did cars?

Hence **ru·stproofed** *ppl. a.* Also **ru·stproofer,** one who makes something rustproof.

1925 *Morris Owner's Man.* 83 The K.L.G. is a detachable plug consisting of three parts—a rustproofed steel body and gland nut and an insulated central electrode. **1960** *Farmer & Stockbreeder* 22 Mar. 138/2 (Advt.), Storage Bin. Substantially made from rust-proofed steel. **1976** *Globe & Mail* (Toronto) 4 Dec. 1/2 Car dealers were often able to avoid liability in those situations by saying that the customer's contract was with the rustproofer alone.

ru·stproofing, *vbl. sb.* [f. prec. + -ing[1].]

1. The action or process of making something rustproof. Also *attrib.*

1918 *Aviation* 1 Aug. 40/2 The increased cost of.. processes of rust-proofing..has turned attention to the safety transparent, rust-proof and acid-proof finish. **1931** *Machinery* Oct. 111/2 News comes from England of the development of a new process known as the 'thermo-zinc' rust-proofing method. **1941** Steinbeck & Ricketts *Sea of Cortez* xiv. 135 The eventual disintegration of a stick of wood or a piece of iron..is assured, even though it may be delayed by such protection..as is afforded by painting and rustproofing. **1980** *Times* 29 Feb. 19 Rust-proofing methods are available which can delay by about five years the onset of corrosion.

2. A substance with which something is made rustproof.

1976 *Time* 20 Dec. 57/2 (Advt.), Each car receives 2 separate coats of rustproofing.

rusty, *a.*[1] Add: **I. 4. c.** Delete 'Now *rare*' and add later examples. Also *transf.*

1924 R. Campbell *Flaming Terrapin* iii. 47 Huge carrion crows came rasping rusty jaws. **1936** J. B. Priestley *They walk in City* vii. 192 All the time his rusty voice went on and on, half jeering at himself, half mocking the audience. **1938** M. K. Rawlings *Yearling* x. 95 They [*sc.* cranes] made a great circle against the sunset, whooping their strange rusty cry that sounded only in their flight. **1967** G. F. Fiennes *I tried to run Railway* ii. 14 At 87 [he] talked in his slow, rusty voice as if he were still on the job.

II. 9. d. *rusty spot* = *red spot 2.

1900 *Bull N.Y. Agric. Exper. Station* No. 183. 188 'Rusty Spot' is the name given to small yellowish-red points or patches scattered quite evenly throughout the mass of the cheese and having the general appearance of iron rust. *Ibid.* 189 Connell..isolated from a rusty spot cheese an organism which he called *Bacillus rudensis.* **1958** E. M. Foster et al. *Dairy Microbiol.* ii. 20 *Lactobacillus plantarum* var. *rudensis* and *Lactobacillus brevis* var. *rudensis* have been implicated as causes of rusty spot defect in Cheddar cheese.

10. b. *rusty-dusty* (later examples). Also as *sb.*, the buttocks. *Black English.*

1953 W. Burroughs *Junkie* iv. 42 A negro voice was singing, 'Get up, get up, woman, off your big fat rusty-dusty.' **1970** C. Major *Dict. Afro-Amer. Slang* 99 *Rusty dusty*, the buttocks.

c. rusty-back (fern), the scale fern, *Ceterach officinarum*; (further examples).

1908 E. Step *Wayside & Woodland Ferns* 50 The development of the sori gives a distinctly red hue to the underside and justifies the name Rustyback. **1945** A. B. Jackson *Step's Wayside & Woodland Ferns* (ed. 2) 57 The Rusty-back Fern is pretty generally distributed in England. **1960** P. Taylor *Brit. Ferns & Mosses* 120 The Rusty-back Fern is mainly confined in Europe to the Mediterranean region, extending northwards up the Atlantic coast to Great Britain. **1976** *Westmorland Gaz.* 10 Sept. 10/2 Interest was aroused..by seeing the Rusty-back and Wall-rue ferns on a wall.

11. a. *rusty-voiced*; *rusty-old*.

1912 W. Owen *Let.* 2 July (1967) 148 A taciturn, rusty-voiced man. **1917** —— *Poems* (1963) 57 Finished fields, and wire-scrags rusty-old.

rutabaga. Delete *rare* and add *U.S.* For Latin name substitute *Brassica napus* var. *napobrassica*. Add: = Swede 3. Also *attrib.* (Earlier and later examples.)

1799 J. B. Bordley *Essays & Notes on Husbandry* 30 The new turnip, called roota baga, is likely to stand our winters. **1833** W. Sewall *Jrnl.* 20 June (1930) 149/2 Finished planting potatoes. Sowed rutabaga turnips. **1916** *Yukon Territory* (Canada Dept. Interior) 213 The type shape is similar to a rutabaga, but the roots are smooth without laterals. **1951** O. Nash *Family Reunion* 107 We gobbled like pigs On rutabagas and salted figs. **1975** *New Yorker* 10 Nov. 176/2 Pertly written by pertly pretty housewives who have discovered organic gardening and how to rub two rutabagas together to feed four happy, whimsical tots—such books glut the shelves. **1976** [see *oyster plant* s.v. *oyster 5 d].

ruthenium. Add: **b. ruthenium red,** an intensely coloured red mixed-valence complexsa lt of ruthenium, $[(NH_3)_5Ru^{III}ORu^{IV}(NH_3)_4ORu^{III}(NH_3)_5]Cl_6$, obtained by air oxidation of a solution containing ammonia and ruthenium (III) chloride, and employed as a microscopic strain.

1912 *Chem. Abstr.* VI. 297 (*heading*) Differentiation of natural textiles and artificial silks by means of ruthenium red. **1950** N. V. SIDGWICK *Chem. Elements* II. 1472 The colour of ruthenium red itself can be detected in solutions more dilute than one in a million. **1978** *Sci. Amer.* Jan. 86 (*caption*) In both preparations the cells were stained with ruthenium red, which is taken up by any polysaccharide glycocalyx fibers that are present.

ruther (rʊ·ðəɹ), *adv.* [Repr. a U.S. colloq. or dial. pronunc. of RATHER.] = RATHER *adv.*

1872 [see *HOLD *v.* 42 c]. **1929** *Amer. Mercury* Sept. 47 Ruther be in cornfield workin' hard, Than be buck private in National Guard. **1938** M. K. RAWLINGS *Yearling* viii. 71 I'd ruther they hunted their way and leave me hunt mine. **1942** W. FAULKNER *Go down, Moses* 59, I ruther never to know than to find out later I have been fooled. **1970** M. CHISHOLM *McAllister says No* vi. 48 I'd ruther have him in front of me than behind.

ruther, var. *RATHER *sb.*

1935 Z. N. HURSTON *Mules & Men* I. ii. 49 Her tongue is all de weapon a woman got... She could have had mo' sense, but she told God no, she'd ruther take it out in hips. So God give her her ruthers. She got plenty hips, plenty mouf and no brains. *Ibid.* vii. 162 You didn't figger Ah was draggin' behind you when you was bringin' dat Sears and Roebuck catalogue over to my house and beggin' me to choose my ruthers. **1949** *Richmond* (Va.) *Times-Dispatch* 26 Dec. 6/5 In the Smokies,..to take one's preference is to 'have your ruthers'.

Rutherford (rʊ·ðə̆ɹfə̆ɹd). *Physics.* [The name of Ernest *Rutherford* (1871–1937), New Zealand-born English physicist.] **1.** Used *attrib.* and in the possessive to designate concepts developed by him, as **Rutherford('s) (scattering) formula** or **law,** a mathematical expression of Rutherford scattering; **Rutherford model,** a model of the atomic nucleus devised to account for Rutherford scattering; **Rutherford scattering,** elastic scattering of charged particles by the electric fields of atomic nuclei; = **Coulomb scattering*; hence **Rutherford-scatter** *v. trans.*

1931 G. GAMOW *Constitution of Atomic Nuclei* iv. 85 The ratio of the observed scattering to that given by Rutherford's formula for a given angle falls to a minimum and then rises again. **1961** POWELL & CRASEMANN *Quantum Mechanics* xii. 465 Coulomb scattering of low-energy protons, for which the classical cross section is given by the Rutherford formula. **1931** G. GAMOW *Constitution of Atomic Nuclei* iv. 84 If..the potential barrier is high enough compared with the energy of the α-particle..deviations from Rutherford's law will be small. **1970** I. E. MCCARTHY *Nuclear Reactions* I. i. 8 The first example of nuclear information being obtained from measurements of the differential cross-section as a function of momentum transfer is the Rutherford law for elastic scattering. **1930** J. BUCKINGHAM *Matter & Radiation* iii. 59 The Rutherford model. **1968** M. S. LIVINGSTON *Particle Physics* ii. 17 The nucleus of the Rutherford model must have a diameter of less than 10^{-12} cm. **1974** G. REECE tr. *Hund's Hist. Quantum Theory* iv. 62 The formula remains true in Bohr's theory, while (4) is also valid for the Rutherford model of the atom. **1977** *Nature* 6 Jan. 35/2 A beam of ^{32}S ions is Rutherford scattered backwards from the sample and the energies of the scattered ions are measured. **1928** *Proc. R. Soc.* A CXVIII. 548 This gives the Rutherford scattering formula exactly for all velocities of the incident particles. **1935** J. DOUGALL tr. *Born's Atomic Physics* v. 126 It can actually be proved that Rutherford's scattering formula is strictly valid in wave mechanics also. **1977** *Nature* 6 Jan. 36/1 The Z^2 dependence of the Rutherford scattering cross section has been taken into account.

2. (Usu. written **rutherford.**) A unit of radioactivity orig. equal to one million disintegrations per second; later defined as the quantity of any particular nuclide exhibiting this degree of activity.

The curie is the more usual unit; one rutherford is approximately $2{\cdot}7 \times 10^{-5}$ curie.

1946 CONDON & CURTISS in *Physical Rev.* LXIX. 673/1 Since the curie was named in honor of M. and Mme. Curie, the co-discoverers of radium, it is natural to select the name 'rutherford' for the new unit. The appropriate abbreviation is 'rd' which conflicts with the abbreviation of no other well-accepted physical unit. The micro-rutherford would become one disintegration per second. **1947** *Nucleonics* Oct. 34/2 A carefully defined new unit, the rutherford (rd), has been proposed for general use. Ambiguities as a result of choice of numerical values, failure to distinguish between beta rays per sec and distintegrations per sec, and extensions to arbitrary and undefined gamma-ray intensities, can then be avoided. **1958** S. GLASSTONE *Sourcebk. Atomic Energy* (ed. 2) xvii. 521 In 1948, the Committee on Standards and Units of Radioactivity of the National Research Council (United States)..favored the adoption of the proposal..that the term 'rutherford' be used to designate a quantity of radioactive material giving 10^6 disintegrations per second. **1962** H. D. BUSH *Atomic & Nuclear Physics* iv. 84 The standard unit adopted is the curie... Another unit, which has not achieved universal acceptance, is the rutherford.

rutherfordine (rʊ·ðə̆ɹfə̆ɹdīn). *Min.* [ad. G. *rutherfordin* (W. Marckwald 1906, in *Centralbl. f. Mineral.* 763); see *RUTHERFORD + -INE[5].] An orthorhombic uranyl carbonate, $UO_2.CO_3$, found as yellow fibrous masses, esp. in association with uraninite in East Africa.

1907 *Mineral Mag.* XIV. 409 *Rutherfordine*, a yellow uranyl carbonate, $UO_2.CO_3$, resembling uranochre in appearance and resulting by the alteration of uraninite. **1955** *Science* 1 Apr. 473/1 In actual crystals of rutherfordine, faults occur in the stacking of layers; regions in which the sequence of layers corresponds to structure A are occasionally terminated by regions in which the layers follow the sequence of structure B. **1959** HOGAN & GILBERT in G. J. Williams *Econ. Geol. N.Z.* (1965) xiii. 206/2 The yellow uranium mineral is rutherfordine which is consistent with the carbonate cement in the rock.

rutherfordite[1] (rʊ·ðə̆ɹfə̆ɹdəit). *Min.* [f. the name *Rutherford* (see below) + -ITE[1].] A name given to a poorly characterized yellow-brown form of fergusonite found in gold mines in Rutherford County, North Carolina.

1851 C. U. SHEPARD in *Proc. Amer. Assoc. Adv. Sci.* IV. 312 (*heading*) Rutherfordite. **1852** *Amer. Jrnl. Sci.* LXIV. 344 By its translucency, rutherfordite is readily distinguished from samarskite, which it otherwise closely resembles. **1880** *Ibid.* CXX. 57, I have detected along with the samarskite of this locality a few very small crystals..nearly identical with those found in the sands from the gold washings of Rutherford, N.C., named by me as rutherfordite, and which I now consider as belonging to the species fergusonite. **1966** Z. LERMAN tr. *Vlasov's Geochem. & Mineral. Rare Elem.* II. xi. 430 Synonyms of fergusonite: rutherfordite.., bragite.., tyrite.., arrhenite..and sipylite.

ru·therfordite[2]. *Min.* [f. as *RUTHERFORDINE: see -ITE[1].] Used as a synonym of *RUTHERFORDINE.

1922 N. H. & A. N. WINCHELL *Elem. Optical Mineral.* II. v. 88 Rutherfordite (UO_2CO_3) is orthorhombic (?), finely fibrous. Soft... Color yellow, earthy. An alteration product of uraninite. Rare. **1971** *Mineral. Mag.* XXXVIII. 104 Recommendations of the Commission on minerals for which more than one name is in common use. .. Rutherfordine, not rutherfordite.

rutherfordium (rʊðəɹfō͡ə·ɹdiə̆m). *Chem.* [f. *RUTHERFORD + -IUM.] (A name proposed for) an artificially produced transuranic element, atomic number 104. Symbol Rf. Cf. *KURCHATOVIUM.

1969 *Science* 5 Dec. 1254/1 Scientists from the Lawrence Radiation Laboratory of the University of California announced results of chemical experiments on element 104 and used the occasion [*sc.* 17–19 Nov. 1969] to propose a new name. Albert Ghiorso..suggested that the element be called rutherfordium for Lord Rutherford 'the great pioneer of nuclear science'. **1970** A. GHIORSO et al. in *Physics Lett.* XXXII. B. 95/1 We have proposed that the element 104 be named rutherfordium. **1971** *Inorg. & Nuclear Chem. Lett.* VII. 1115 As not until 1969 did the American researchers at Berkeley also succeed in obtaining element 104..there is no ground to use the name rutherfordium proposed by them. **1971** *Nature* 26 Feb. 603/1 Certain questions have been raised regarding the validity of our work on the discovery of two alpha-emitting isotopes of element 104 (rutherfordium). **1975** [see *NIELSBOHRIUM].

ruthfully, *adv.* Restrict *Obs.* to sense 2 and add: **1.** (Later example.)

1936 'M. INNES' *Death at President's Lodging* xv. 246 No change, he reflected ruthfully a moment later, was to be got from Empson that way.

rutic, *a.* Add: Now † *Obs.* Substitute for def.: *rutic acid*: **a.** = RUTIN in Dict. and Suppl. **b.** Capric acid.

rutilant, *a.* Delete 'Now *rare*' and add later examples. Also *fig.*

1917 A. HUXLEY *Let.* 30 Sept. (1969) 135 Behemoth His eyes are little rutilant stones Sunk in black basalt. **1944** S. PUTNAM tr. *E. da Cunha's Rebellion in Backlands* i. §4. 35 Diminutive-leafed opuntias,..bordered with rutilant flowers. **1954** *Times Lit. Suppl.* 2 July 425/4 There are certain magical elements constantly working against the proof-corrector—a being less rutilant, but not less vulnerable, than Tchaikovsky's Prince. **1956** K. WATSON *Source* 46 Rutilant the trail in space Of some recurrent meteor.

Hence **ru·tilance** [-ANCE], rutilant quality (*rare*).

1922 JOYCE *Ulysses* 691 He..ignited it in the candle-flame, applied it when ignited to the apex of the cone till the latter reached the stage of rutilance.

rutilated (rū·tilē̆itĕd), *a. Min.* [f. RUTIL(E + -ATE[2] + -ED[2].] Of quartz: containing needles of rutile. Cf. SAGENITE.

1889 [in Dict. s.v. RUTILATE *v.*]. **1977** A. HALLAM *Planet Earth* 136 Rutilated quartz contains orientated needles of rutile.

rutile. (Further examples.)

1951 *Chambers's Jrnl.* Sept. 568/2 Both the principal titanium minerals, ilmenite and rutile, are present in the black sands of streams and beaches in many parts of the world. **1965** *Sunday Mail Mag.* (Brisbane) 17 Jan. 11 Rutile was also needed as a flux for electric welding rods, armaments, ship building, tanks, etc. **1971** *Materials & Technol.* II. viii. 502 Still more spectacular fire is seen in synthetic rutile (titanium oxide) which can also be made by flame-fusion. **1971** *Jrnl. Oil & Colour Chemists' Assoc.* LIV. 849 Film volume measurements..showed a shrinkage of 6 per cent during six weeks of ageing at 25°C in the laboratory, for unpigmented and rutile titanium dioxide pigmented alkyd films.

rutin. Delete entry and substitute:

rutin (rū·tin). *Chem.* Also † **-ine.** [a. G. *rutin* (A. Weiss 1842, in *Pharm. Centralbl.* XIII. 903), f. L. *rūta* RUE *sb.*[2]: see -IN[1].] A yellow crystalline phenolic glycoside, $C_{27}H_{30}O_{16}$, found in several plant species (notably common rue, buckwheat, and capers) which possesses vasopressor properties and is taken to reduce blood pressure.

1857, etc. [in Dict.]. **1967** *Times Rev. Industry* Feb. 118/1 (Advt.), High blood pressure? Rutin, the natural product, has helped thousands of sufferers. **1977** *Martindale's Extra Pharmacopoeia* (ed. 27) 1697/2 Rutin was formerly used in the treatment of disease states characterised by capillary bleeding associated with increased capillary fragility but evidence of its value is inconclusive.

rutted, *ppl. a.* Add: Also *fig.*

1913 [see *ROUTINED *ppl. a.*]. **1957** G. RYLE in C. A. Mace *Brit. Philos. in Mid-Cent.* 259 Equations are not mere records of deeply rutted associations of ideas.

ru·tter[2]. Also ritter. [f. RUT *v.*[2], RIT *v.*[1] + -ER[1].] A spade for cutting or slitting peat turf.

1877 [see RIT *v.*[1] 1 b]. **1923** *Chambers's Jrnl.* 12 May 370/1 The rutter is a two-handed spade, the blade heart-shaped and sharp. **1975** *Times* 27 Aug. 8/5 A curved rutter is used for cutting the [peat] turf, a long-handled spade or flaughter for removing it.

ru·tter[3]. *N. Amer.* [f. RUT *sb.*[2] or RUT *v.*[4] + -ER[1].] A kind of plough used by lumberjacks for making tracks for sleighs.

1969 L. G. SORDEN *Lumberjack Lingo* 100 *Rutter*, a form of plow for cutting ruts in an iced logging road for the runners of a sleigh. It was often combined with a snowplow. The roads were sprinkled with water from the water tank and frozen to make ice roads. **1972** *Islander* (Victoria, B.C.) 19 Nov. 4/3 The lumbermen had a unique system of hauling logs. In early fall, while the ground was still soft, they would build a rutter. Using the front bob of a wide logging sleigh, a small V-shaped plow was welded to the point of each sleigh runner. Then the sleigh bob was taken to the top of the proposed logging road, turned around, and twin tracks were then plowed eight inches deep and six inches wide down to the main camp.

ruttier. (Later *Hist.* examples of form *rutter.*)

1937 *Geogr. Jrnl.* XC. 386 It appears that there were existing rutters up to this point. **1962** [see *ROUTIER[1]]. **1971** S. E. MORISON *European Discovery Amer.: Northern Voy.* v. 138 The rutters (*routiers*), unofficial coast pilots of the period [*sc.* the sixteenth century], were written primarily for finding one's way along European shores. **1973** D. DIVINE *Opening of World* v. 85 An English Rutter, the northern and slightly less refined version of the *portolano*, describing a harbour entrance in 1295.

rutting, *vbl. sb.* Add: **b.** *rutting call, -wrath.*

1937 *Discovery* Oct. 314/1 The rutting call of the stag. **1893** KIPLING *Seven Seas* (1896) 59 And when the first September gales have slaked their rutting-wrath, The great man-seal haul back to the sea.

ruttish, *a.* Delete *Obs.* and add later examples. Also, of or pertaining to sexual excitement.

1938 R. GRAVES *Coll. Poems* 158 A score of bats bewitched By the ruttish odour Swoop singing at his head. **1977** *Daily Tel.* 2 Dec. 15/5 He returns to ogling the field with his ruttish chum.

Ruwala, var. *RUALLA.

rux (rɒks), *sb.*[2] *Naut. slang.* [Origin unknown: cf. RUX *v.* in Dict. and Suppl. and *RUCKUS.] Disturbance, uproar.

1918 *Blackw. Mag.* CCIV. 68/1 Harker, who for fifteen months had haunted the shadows on the look-out for just such a 'rux', whose ear caught every illicit sound. **1931** KIPLING *Limits & Renewals* (1932) 196 The nastiest rux I ever saw, when a boy, began with 'All hands to skylark.' *I* don't hold with it. *Ibid.* 200 I've seen worse ruxes in my time, but a quicker breeze-up—never!

rux, *v.* Add: **2.** To vex, worry. *rare.*

1887 KIPLING *Plain Tales* (1888) 60 'E [was] too busy to rux 'isself about p'raids.

Ruy Lopez (rū·i lō͡u·pez). *Chess.* [The name of *Ruy López* de Segura (fl. 1560), Spanish bishop and writer on chess, who developed this opening.] A chess opening characterized by the moves 1 P–K4, P–K4; 2 Kt–KB3, Kt–QB3; 3 B–Kt5.

1876 *Encycl. Brit.* V. 594/2 The following are given as indicative illustrations of certain of the leading openings. .. Ruy Lopez. **1894** *Yale Wit & Humor* 49/1 Our [chess] team appears to have executed a masterly flank movement in 'retaking the exchanged Pawn in the Ruy Lopez'. **1958** [see *NIMZO-INDIAN *a.*]. **1976** *Milton Keynes Express* 2 July 40/5 He opened with the Ruy Lopez and won in 20 moves.

Rwanda (rwæ·ndă, ru,æ·ndă). Also **Ruanda.** **a.** A Bantu language of East Africa. **b.** An East African people; the inhabitants of the country of Rwanda. **c.** An East African republic (founded 1961), formerly kingdom. Also *attrib.* Hence **Rwa·ndan** *sb.* and *a.*, **Rwande·se** *a.*

1902 H. H. JOHNSTON *Uganda Protectorate* II. 969 Urunyaruanda is spoken in Ruanda, or Bunya-ruanda, south of Ankole... English, *ant*... Ruanda, *entwzi*. **1924** SMITH & SHARP *Ruanda's Redemption* 18 (*heading*) Receipts for Kigezi and Ruanda work 1920–23. *Ibid.* 22 The only literature in the Ruanda language is a translation of the four Gospels. **1939** L. H. GRAY *Foundations of Lang.* 405 Homburger's classification [of Bantu languages] is as follows:..(2) *Ruanda*, north-east of Tanganyika. **1959** *Listener* 29 Oct. 740/1 The Ruanda and Urundi of that trusteeship territory, the Belgian Congo, Uganda and Tanganyika. **1969** J. C. KING *Evangelicals* vii. 60 A similar tight-knit group within Church of England Evangelicalism is the Ruanda movement. This consists of people influenced by the East African revival movement, through the Ruanda Mission. **1973** *Times* 11 Dec. (Zaire Suppl.) p. vii/9 On our return to Goma we passed a memorial to 23 wardens killed while defending the park against Zairian, Ugandan and Rwandese poachers. **1974** *Encycl. Brit. Micropædia* VIII. 737/3 In 1969, an estimated 3,600,000 Rwanda occupied an area of roughly 10,000 square miles. **1974** *Encycl. Brit. Macropædia* XVI. 109/1 The first impression given by the Rwandan landscape is that it resembles an immense green park dominated by banana plantations. *Ibid.* 109/2 Traditionally, Rwandans believe in a supreme being called Imana. **1979** *Brit. Med. Jrnl.* 15 Dec. 1560/1 We slowly came to appreciate the fabric of a Rwandan home, from the mud walls without to the complex and supportive family within.

rya (rī·ă). Also **ryiji, ryijy.** [Sw. *rya* in same sense; cf. Finnish *ryijy*.] A Scandinavian type of knotted pile rug. Also *attrib.*

1957 B. PEPIS *Guide Interior Decorating* iv. 124 The only remotely luxurious note is the small, brightly colored heavily piled 'rya' rug, an adaptation of a Finnish design. **1960** *Guardian* 20 July 4/6 Rya rugs are a very old form of Finnish folk art. *Ibid.* 4/7 Ryas..were used in everyday life up to the sixteenth century. **1960** H. HAYWARD *Antique Coll.* 245/2 *Ryijy rugs*, Finnish rugs made in the old Norse tradition of knotted pile technique, which may go back to the Danish Bronze Age. **1964** G. LYALL *Most Dangerous Game* xviii. 139 The only shot I fired hit the ryiji on the floor. **1972** *Homes & Gardens* Aug. 28/2 The choice of rugs ranges from Axminster..to the wildest, woolliest rya imaginable. **1975** 'E. LATHEN' *By Hook or by Crook* vi. 55 When rya rugs first came into fashion..she had..become a trend setter.

rybuck, var. *RYEBUCK *a.* (*adv.*) and *int.*

Rydberg (ri·dbɔːg). *Physics.* The name of Johannes Robert *Rydberg* (1854–1919), Swedish physicist. **1.** Used *attrib.* and in the possessive to designate various concepts developed by him, as **Rydberg('s) constant,** an atomic constant, evaluated from several of the fundamental constants of physics, which appears in the formulae for the wave numbers of lines in all atomic spectra (in the case of a hypothetical atom whose nucleus has infinite mass, equal to $2\pi^2me^4/ch^3$, where m and e are the rest mass and charge of the electron, c is the speed of light, and h is Planck's constant); see also *R III. 4; **Rydberg correction,** a correction term appearing in the formula for the energy of the single electron in the outermost shell of hydrogen-like atoms, arising because the inner shells do not screen the electron completely from the nucleus; **Rydberg('s) formula,** an empirical formula giving the wave numbers of frequencies of the lines in the spectral series of atoms and simple molecules.

1913 *Phil. Mag.* XXVI. 489 An attempt to explain the appearance of Rydberg's constant in the formula for the line-spectrum of any element. **1920,** etc. [see *R III. 4]. **1937** *Ann. Reg. 1936* II. 61 Birge..pointed out that the substitution of well-established values for e/m and h/e in the Bohr formula for the Rydberg constant gives a value for e nearly half of 1 per cent less than the others. **1955** C. G. DARWIN in W. Pauli *Niels Bohr* 7 There can be few other cases in science where a theory has been made which succeeds in yielding a particular number—here Rydberg's constant—from quantities all of which are known, without the admissibility of any adjustable constant to help in doing so. **1979** *Sci. Amer.* Mar. 74/3 Later refinements have complicated Rydberg's empirical formula for the wavelengths of spectral lines, and so the Rydberg constant is now defined as this combination of m, e and h. **1927** J. W. FISHER tr. *Born's Mechanics of Atom* iii. 160 Rydberg was the first to suggest this form and verified it by measurements of numerous spectra. We shall therefore denote the quantity δ as the Rydberg correction. **1936** *Discovery* Jan. 28/1 The quantisation of the Rydberg correction into multiples of a fundamental unit. **1974** G. REECE tr. *Hund's Hist. Quantum Theory* vii. 95 Schroedinger in 1921 realized that the essential point for the interpretation of the large 'Rydberg corrections' was that the s orbits dipped deep into the atom. **1913** *Phil. Mag.* XXVI. 12 The constant K entering in Rydberg's formula is the same for all substances. **1974** G. REECE tr. *Hund's Hist. Quantum Theory* vii. 97 In 1914 A. Fowler, inspired by Bohr's theory of the He^+ lines, showed that for the doublet series of these elements Rydberg formulae held with $4R$ and that they therefore belonged to Mg^+ and Ca^+.

2. (Also written **rydberg.**) **a.** A unit of energy given by $e^2/2a_0$ (approximately $2{\cdot}425 \times 10^{-18}$ joule), where e is the electronic charge and a_0 is the radius of the first Bohr orbit for a nucleus of infinite mass. Freq. *attrib.* as *Rydberg unit*.

1935 *Jrnl. Chem. Physics* III. 563/2 The first choice would lower all [energy] values by 2·3 Rydberg units. **1944** *Physical Rev.* LVI. 336/1 The energy difference of curves III and IV is 0·44 Rydberg units more in Fig. 5 than it is in Fig. 4. **1954** *Ibid.* XCIV. 1519/2 (*caption*) Energy integrals (in Rydbergs) for diamond. **1975** *Nature* 27 Mar. 297/2 If gas accretion by this object produces all the ionising radiation required to maintain the H II region at the galactic centre, the luminosity of this radiation is $L_i = 1{\cdot}9 \times 10^8 L_\odot$..if the energy per photon is 2 rydberg.

b. A name proposed for the unit of wave number, cm^{-1}; = *KAYSER.

1951 C. CANDLER in *Nature* 21 Apr. 649 Call 'cm.$^{-1}$' by some new name, such as 'Rydberg', however, and the difficulty disappears. Absorptions can be conveniently recorded in 'kilo-rydbergs'... The name 'Rydberg' was suggested to me many years ago by Prof. H. Dingle.

rye, *sb.*[1] Add: **3. a.** (Earlier and later examples.) Also *Canad.*

1835 J. H. INGRAHAM *South-West* II. 56 The painful effects of 'old rye' in the abstract upon the body. **1860** *Grumbler* (Toronto) 19 May 3/3 And, tho' the crowd may smile at me, I'll take some neat 'old rye'. **1873** G. W. PERRIE *Buckskin Mose* xvii. 248 But for the quantity of rye we had all of us been swallowing, the others must have seen through this impudent operation as I had done. **1913** J. LONDON *Valley of Moon* 392 Some drink rain and some champagne..; But I will try a little rye. **1930** D. RUNYON in *Collier's* 1 Feb. 12/3 Wilbur is a great hand for drinking Scotch, or rye. **1945** P. CHEYNEY *I'll say she Does!* iii. 66, I..finish off my rye an' pour myself another four fingers. **1974** E. MCGIRR *Murderous Journey* 31 He slopped along..towards the living-room bar. I took a straight rye.

b. *Comb.* in the names of drinks, as *rye-and-dry* (see *DRY *sb.* 2 c), *rye-and-ginger, rye-and-orange, rye-and-soda, rye-on-the-rocks.*

1909 G. ADE *Let.* 24 Mar. (1973) 45, I have just had a rye & soda. **1942** *Tee Emm* (Air Ministry) II. 127 Say? What's mine? A Rye and dry. **1956** 'N. SHUTE' *Beyond Black Stump* 5 'What's it to be?' 'Orange juice,' said the young man. Mr Johnson ordered it, with rye on the rocks for himself. **1963** R. I. MCDAVID *Mencken's Amer. Lang.* 168 Canadian topers have an array of combinations..as *rye and orange* (Canadian whiskey and orange pop). **1964** *Time* (Canada ed.) 31 Jan. 7/1 Accepting a rye and ginger, Mike Pearson then went back to writing out a personal report.

3*. *ellipt.* Rye-bread.

1941 [see *PASTRAMI]. **1969** [see *MAYO]. **1971** 'O. BLEECK' *Procane Chron.* xiv. 123 A Danish sardine sandwich..between two thick slices of German rye. **1976** H. MACINNES *Agent in Place* v. 48 A ham on rye with a gallon of coffee.

4. b. *ryebloom; ryehigh* adj.

1922 JOYCE *Ulysses* 261 The bag of Goulding, Collis, Ward led Bloom by ryebloom flowered tables. *Ibid.* 282 O'er ryehigh blue. Bloom stood up.

5. rye and Indian (also **Injun**) (**bread**) *U.S.*, bread made from a mixture of rye and (Indian) cornmeal; **rye brome** (**grass**), add: *Bromus secalinus*; (earlier and later examples); **rye coffee** *U.S.*, a drink resembling coffee, made from roasted rye; **rye waltz** *N. Amer.* (see quot.).

1840 *Knickerbocker* XVI. 18 There were eggs and fried ham,..rye-and-Indian bread. **1887** A. W. TOURGÉE *Button's Inn* 224 She passed around a hot plateful of toasted slices of 'rye and Indian'. **1932** L. I. WILDER *Little House in Big Woods* iv. 45 She baked salt-rising bread and rye 'n' Injun bread and Swedish crackers. **1812** W. WITHERING JR. *Withering's Brit. Plants* (ed. 5) II. 210 Smooth Rye Brome-grass...In corn-fields. **1954** C. E. HUBBARD *Grasses* 67 'Rye Brome' was no doubt introduced into the British Isles long ago with the seeds of cereals. **1769** *Boston Gaz.* 16 Oct. 1/3 And as true Daughters of Liberty, they made their Breakfast upon Rye Coffee, and their Dinner was partly made of that sort of Venison called Bear. **1877** H. RUEDE *Jrnl.* 13 June in *Sod-House Days* (1937) 99 Most people out here don't drink real coffee, because it is too expensive... So rye coffee is used a great deal—parched brown or black according to whether the users like a strong or mild drink. **1951** L. CRAIG *Singing Hills* iv. 31 Every one had coffee... When I tasted mine I thought, for a moment, that poison had been put in it; it certainly was not like anything I have ever tasted before, for never before had I drunk rye coffee. **1941** W. C. HANDY *Father of Blues* ii. 16 The waltz was popular, as was also the rye waltz, a combination of three-four and two-four tempos.

rye (rəi), *sb.*[3] *slang.* [ad. Romany *rai* gentleman; cf. Skr. *rāj* to rule.] A man, gentleman. Also *Comb.*, as **rye mort,** a lady (in quot., *attrib.*); **rye mush,** a gentleman. See also *Romany rye* s.v. *ROMANY[3] 3 b.

1851 BORROW *Lavengro* II. xxvi. 242, I had always..been a great favourite with Mrs. Petulengro, who had frequently been loud in her commendation of the young rye, as she called me. **1857** —— *Romany Rye* I. vi. 74 Gentility will carry the day, madam, even with the young rye. He will ask words of the black lass, but beg the words of the fair. **1936** J. CURTIS *Gilt Kid* 55 He did not feel choosey; why, he could be a rye mush himself for one night. *Ibid.* 232 Anyone taking a quick look at her might think she was on the up-and-up. She would give that impression too, to anyone who heard her talk and saw her act. Though.. she would have to give up that rye mort touch. **1939** —— *What Immortal Hand* xiv. 151 If she's gone and got herself tangled up with a lot of rye mushes she don't want to have nothing to do with a gaol-bird like me.

ryebuck (rəi·bʌk), *a.* (*adv.*) and *int. slang* (chiefly *Austral.*). Now *obsolescent.* Also **ribuck, rybuck, rye buck,** etc. [Origin uncertain: perh. ad. G. *reibach*, var. of *rebbach* profit, ad. Yiddish (Heb.) *revaḥ*: cf. RYBECK.]

A. *adj.* Good, excellent; genuine; *ryebuck shearer*, an expert or 'gun' shearer (see *GUN sb. 13*). Also as *adv.*

1859 G. W. MATSELL *Vocabulum* 55 My pals have got up a bene moey to send to the head bloke, and if it comes off rye buck, I shall soon vamose from the stir. **1895** *Bulletin* (Sydney) 9 Feb. 15 I'm ryebuck and the girl's okay. **1906** E. DYSON *Fact'ry 'Ands* x. 132 'It's rybuck, girls,' said Feathers. 'Yer on velvet. Ther firm's willin' t' accept responsibility fer ther actions iv it's dooly accredited cat, 'n' pays compensation.' **1916** C. J. DENNIS *Moods of Ginger Mick* 92 But the reel, ribuck Australia's 'ere among the fightin' men. **1918** R. H. KNYVETT *Over There* viii. 82 They even knew our slang, for here was 'The 'Fair Dinkum' Store', and across the way 'Ribuck Goods'. *a* **1957** in Stewart & Keesing *Old Bush Songs* (1957) 267 There's a bloke on the board and I heard him say I couldn't shear a hundred sheep a day, But some fine day I'll show him the way And prove I'm a ryebuck shearer. **1965** J. S. GUNN *Terminol. Shearing Industry* I. 16 *Ryebuck shearer*, see *gun*. *Ibid.* I. 30 *Gun*, a really fast shearer, also known as a 'ryeback [*sic*] shearer', but not the same as the fastest in the shed (see *ringer*).

B. *int.* An expression of agreement or assent.

1859 G. W. MATSELL *Vocabulum* 76 *Rybuck*, all right; straight, it will do; I am satisfied. **1898** *Bulletin* (Sydney) 17 Dec. (Red Page), *Rye-buck* (all right) is no doubt an abbreviation of 'all right, my buck'. **1911** L. STONE *Jonah* I. 11 'Oh! I don't suppose you'll be missed,' replied Chook, graciously. 'Rye buck!' cried Jonah. **1916** C. J. DENNIS *Songs of Sentimental Bloke* 21 We kin get an intro, if we've luck. 'E sez, 'Ribuck'. *Ibid.* 72 'E'en in the days when she's no longer fair She's still yer wife,' 'e sez. 'Ribuck,' sez I. **1933** *Bulletin* (Sydney) 27 Sept. 42/2 'We'll meet you at the yards.' 'Ryebuck, Boss,' said The Gov'ner civilly.

rye-grass. 1. (Earlier and later examples.)

1712 J. MORTON *Nat. Hist. Northants.* ix. 482 Rye-grass is with us accounted the best thing in the World for Wood-land in Enclosures. **1931** R. BEALE *Bk. Lawn* iv. 48 Rye grass mixtures..are recommended for heavy soils. **1961** R. M. PATTERSON *Buffalo Head* vi. 216 The rocks were all hidden and a magnificent growth of rye-grass was swaying in the wind. **1979** *Buffalo* (N.Y.) *Evening News* 18 May II. 22/2 The new turf-type perennial rye-grasses available today are real beauties.

Ryeland (rəi·lănd). The name of a district in Hereford & Worcester, where the breed was first developed, used *attrib.* and *absol.* to designate a sheep belonging to the small, hornless breed so called, which is a good producer of both wool and meat.

[**1801** J. POWELL *Let.* in *Ann. Agric.* (1808) XLV. 6 The hardiness of the Ryelanders..is proverbial, as milkers.] **1802** J. SOMERVILLE *Let.* 12 Nov. in *Facts & Observations relative to Sheep* (1803) 10 The same land, which carried forty-five breeding ewes, was immediately stocked with 150 Ryelands in their stead. *Ibid.* 12 We.. sent this Ryeland mutton to market. **1837** W. YOUATT *Sheep* vii. 258 The distinguishing breed of sheep in Herefordshire is the Ryeland, so called from a district in the southern part of the county. *Ibid.* 260 The Ryeland sheep..quickly fattens. **1861** MRS. BEETON *Bk. Househ. Managem.* xiv. 323 Eleven varieties have been reared in this country of the domesticated sheep..embracing.. the Ryeland; South-Down; the Merino. **1912** R. LYDEKKER *Sheep & its Cousins* v. 101 The modern Ryeland.. retained the diminutive proportions of the ancestral breed. *Ibid.*, Ryeland wool was formerly regarded as the finest produced in the British Islands. **1929** W. C. COFFEY *Productive Sheep Husbandry* (ed. 2) xxi. 173 The Ryeland originated in Herefordshire, early in the nineteenth century. **1971** *Farmers Weekly* 19 Mar. 83/1 Both Suffolk and Ryland [*sic*] rams have been used this season.

ryiji, ryijy, vars. *RYA.

Rylean (rəi·liăn) *a. Philos.* [f. the name of Gilbert *Ryle* (1900–76), English philosopher + -AN.] Of, pertaining to, or characteristic of Ryle's theories or his approach to linguistic philosophy or philosophical behaviourism.

1958 *Times Lit. Suppl.* 10 Oct. 581/1 The first part of this book gives an account, in roughly Rylean terms, of different senses of 'know', and of the relations between 'knowing that' and 'knowing how'. **1963** W. SELLARS *Sci., Perception & Reality* v. 178 What I shall call a Rylean language, a language of which the fundamental descriptive vocabulary speaks of public properties of public objects located in Space and enduring through Time.

1966 *Philos. Rev.* LXXV. 99 Farrer shrinks..from the Hobbist mortalism that would naturally go with this Rylean view of body and mind. **1971** G. J. WARNOCK in Wood & Pitcher *Ryle* 273 It was the answer which his very Rylean proforma of a solution temptingly left room for.

‖ **ryo** (ryō). Also 9 rio, riyo. [Jap.] A former Japanese monetary unit (see quots.).

1871 A. B. MITFORD *Tales of Old Japan* I. 70 A Japanese noble will sometimes be found girding on a sword, the blade of which unmounted is worth from six hundred to a thousand riyos, say from £200 to £300. **1876** W. E. GRIFFIS *Mikado's Empire* (1877) II. 610 In popular language, the terms *hiyaku* (hundred), *fun, mommé*, and even *riō* (4 mommé, 5 fun), do not represent any coin, but are used to denote values. They are expressions belonging to the period when money was computed by weight only. **1899** L. HEARN *In Ghostly Japan* vi. 103 The sum of a hundred ryō in gold. **1915** F. BRINKLEY *Hist. Jap. People* xxxi. 438 The gold *ryō* represented 2 *koku*, or 30 *yen* of modern currency, the silver *ryō* representing 3 yen. *Ibid.* xxxii. 444 Gold..was much more valuable in China than in Japan. Ten *ryō* of the yellow metal could be obtained in Japan for from twenty to thirty *kwan-mon* and sold in China for 130. **1938** D. T. SUZUKI *Zen Buddhism & its Influence on Japanese Culture* I. vii. 160 Two loads of gold were equivalent in the currency of the time to 12,000 *ryo*. **1964** *Japan* (Unesco) (rev. ed.) i. 45/2 It is said that between 1601 and 1647 about 4,800,000 *ryō* (one *ryō* contained four *me* of pure gold) of gold and 750,000 *kan* of silver were paid to foreign countries. **1972** *Mainichi Daily News* (Japan) 6 Nov. 7/4, I will kill anyone or accept a mission of the sword for five hundred ryo in gold.

‖ **ryokan** (ryōᵘ·kăn). [Jap.] A traditional Japanese inn or hostelry.

1963 *Maclean's Mag.* 9 Mar. 37 The most charming hotel I ever stayed at was a Japanese ryokan in the mountain spa of Kinugawa north of Tokyo. **1968** *Sat. Rev.* (U.S.) 23 Dec. 57/2 Stay in a 17th-century *ryokan*—inn. **1970** *Guardian* 12 Dec. 6/6 The *ryokans*, country inns, are worth the slight additional expense over Westernized hotels. **1972** *Times* 8 May (Japan Suppl.) p. viii/2 The site..contains a magnificent temple and several *ryokan*—traditional Japanese inns. **1979** *Amer. Poetry Rev.* Mar./Apr. 45/2 Several ferries, sighted from the small balcony of our private Ryokan overlooking the beach, circle Dogashima Bay from dawn to dusk.

Ryvita (rəivī·tă). [f. RYE *sb.*¹ + L. *vīta* life.] The proprietary name of a type of crispbread.

1925 *Trade Marks Jrnl.* 18 Feb. 385 Ryvita..Bread. John Edwin Garrat, 96 Southwark Street, London SE1 Manufacturer. **1926–7** [see *CRISPBREAD]. **1930** A. BENNETT *Imperial Palace* xxii. 142 Oldham softly entered with the tea-tray... 'I've brought you some hot ryvita in case you should fancy it, sir.' **1937** 'G. ORWELL' *Road to Wigan Pier* vi. 95 A millionaire may enjoy breakfasting off orange juice and Ryvita biscuits. **1953** R. FULLER *Second Curtain* v. 79 A girl..carrying a plate of Ryvita spread with paste. **1967** *Trade Marks Jrnl.* 22 Mar. 368/1 Ryvita..Bread, crispbread and biscuits (other than biscuits for animals). The Ryvita Company Limited.. London. **1974** *Times* 19 Oct. 6/6 He had inadvertently eaten the toast (possibly Ryvita).

S

S. Add: **I. 1. b.** *s-aorist* (Philol.), in certain Indo-European languages, an aorist formed from the verbal stem by adding *s* and the ending; a sigmatic aorist.

1895 CONWAY & ROUSE tr. *Brugmann's Compar. Gram. Indo-Gmc. Lang.* IV. 371 Special vowel-grades for the root-syllable, as in the *s*-aorist.., cannot be made out for the parent language. **1933** C. D. BUCK *Compar. Gram. Greek & Latin* 281 The distinctive IE aorist is the *s*-aorist formed from the root by the addition of *s* and the secondary endings. **1962** C. W. WATKINS *Indo-Europ. Orig. Celtic Verb* I. 55 The more common situation in Vedic is one where a root athematic present has an s-aorist associated with it.

2. c. *S-curved, -decorated, -scrolled, -shaped* (later examples) adjs.; *S-bend, -curve* (later example), *-ornament, -rope, -scroll, -sofa, -trap, -turn.*

1930 *Motor* 10 June 892/2 We were negotiating an S bend on the proper side of the line on a main road. **1931** D. L. SAYERS *Five Red Herrings* xi. 115 The road makes a very sharp and dangerous S-bend. **1975** R. BROWNING *Emperor Julian* x. 187 The northern section of the frontier formed a great S-bend. **1977** R. E. HARRINGTON *Quintain* xii. 109 Fronck negotiated an s-curve, and.. pulled the Ford out onto a straight stretch. **1940** *Burlington Mag.* Mar. 81/2 The wings with their S-curved shape. **1961** M. W. BARLEY *Eng. Farmhouse & Cottage* IV. i. 189 An English boat came into Boston in 1628 with 3,500 tiles aboard, and the earliest references to pantiles, the S-curved roofing tile, occur in the 1630s. **1963** G. DANIEL in Foster & Alcock *Culture & Environment* ii. 21 The S-decorated pottery which may be a degeneration of the duck motifs found on Early Iron Age pottery in Brittany and north Spain. **1934** *Burlington Mag.* Sept. 120/2 A finely-carved double-headed eagle, resting on a symmetrical S-ornament at the bottom. **1883** W. S. GRESLEY *Gloss. Coal-Mining* 234 *S-rope*, the winding rope which passes round the under side of the drum from or to the pulley; so called because it takes the form of the letter S. **1934** *Burlington Mag.* Sept. 120/2 The symmetrically inverted S-scroll. **1956** G. TAYLOR *Silver* vii. 143 The graceful and irregular S- and C-scrolls that are the chief ingredient of the style in its linear form. **1934** *Burlington Mag.* Sept. 125/2 The lambrequin 'apron' and the S-scrolled legs both, I would suggest, came to Europe from India. **1955** R. FASTNEDGE *Eng. Furnit. Styles* iii. 77 Early examples with S-scrolled legs and bun feet were frequently decorated with floral, or later, seaweed, marquetry. **1937** T. RATTIGAN *French without Tears* II. ii. 57 From sideways on it's a bit S-shaped, if you know what I mean. **1966** *Publ. Amer. Dial. Soc.* XLII. 3 *Chicane*,..an S-shaped curve of a race track. **1906** W. DE MORGAN *Joseph Vance* xxvi. 211, I found myself sitting beside Miss Spencer on a thing like an S in the back drawing-room... As I sat by Miss Spencer on the S-sofa. [**1882** S. HELLYER *Lect. Sci. & Art Sanitary Plumbing* iii. 108 About the first form of trap used for fixing under water-closets was the syphon or round-pipe trap, *i.e.*, a pipe bent and recurved in the shape of the letter ∽.] **1885**, **1976** S trap [see *P trap* s.v. *P III. 1]. **1920** A. J. L. SCOTT *Sixty Squad* 56 Putting in a couple of 'S' turns, he made a good slow landing. **1973** *Times* 3 Mar. 15/2 The Labour Party has done an S-turn when the Government has merely done a U-turn.

4. a. S (*Bacteriol.*) = *SMOOTH *a.*; S., strain (of virus etc.), *spec.* in S.19, S19 = *strain 19* s.v. *STRAIN *sb.*[1]; S.A., s.a., sex appeal; S.A., S-A (*Med.*), sino-auricular or -atrial: S.A., small arms; S.A., S/A [F. *société anonyme*; also It. *società anonima*, Sp. *sociedad anónima*], in France, Italy, etc., a limited or joint-stock company; S.A. = *STURMABTEILUNG; S.A.A., small arm(s) ammunition; S.A.C., senior aircraftman; SAC (*U.S.*), Strategic Air Command; S.A.C. EUR., SACEUR, Saceur (also with pronunc. sæ·kiŭɹ), Supreme Allied Commander Europe; S.A.C.W., senior aircraftwoman; S.A.E., Society of Automotive Engineers (used *spec.* to designate a scale of viscosity used for lubrication oils); S.A.E., s.a.e., stamped addressed envelope; S.A.L., South Arabian League; SAM, surface-to-air missile; S & L (*U.S.*), savings and loan (association); S and M, S–M, sadism and masochism, sadomasochism; SAR, search and rescue; S.A.S., Special Air Service; SAT (*U.S.*), scholastic aptitude test; S.B., simultaneous broadcast; S.B., Special Branch; S.B., stretcher bearer; S.B.A., sick-berth attendant; SBA (*U.S.*), Small Business Administration; S.B.A.C., Society of British Aerospace Companies (formerly Society of British Aircraft Constructors); SBM, sbm, single buoy moor(ing); SBR, styrene-butadiene rubber; S.C., s.c., self-contained; SC, structural change (in Transformational Grammar); SCAP (also with pronunc. skæp), Supreme Commander Allied Powers (in Japan); also used *transf.* of the Command Headquarters; Sc.D. [L. *Scientiæ Doctor*], Doctor of Science; S.C.F., Save the Children Fund; scf, standard cubic feet (i.e. cubic feet of gas at standard temperature and pressure); SCLC (*U.S.*), Southern Christian Leadership Conference; S.C.M., State Certified Midwife; S.C.M., Student Christian Movement; SCP, single-cell protein; S.C.R., senior common room (orig. and chiefly in the University of Oxford); SCR (*Electronics*), silicon-controlled rectifier; S.C.U.A., Suez Canal Users' Association; S.D., s.d., semi-detached (house); S.D., sequence date; S.D. = *SICHERHEITSDIENST; s.d., S.D. (*Statistics*), standard deviation; SD, structural description (in Transformational Grammar); S.D.A., Scottish Development Agency; S.D.E.C.E. [F. *Service de documentation étrangère et de contre-espionnage*], the official counter-intelligence agency in France; S.D.F., Social Democratic Federation; hence *S.D.F.er*; S.D.L.P., Social Democratic and Labour Party; S.D.O., Subdivisional Officer; S.D.P., Social Democratic Party; S.D.R., special drawing right (usu. *pl.*); S.D.S. [G. *Sozialistischer Deutscher Studentenbund*], the Federation of Socialist Students (in West Germany); SDS (*U.S.*), Students for a Democratic Society; s.e.(m.), S.E.(M.) (*Statistics*), standard error (of the mean); S.E., S/E, Stock Exchange; S.E.A.C. (also with pronunc. sī·æk), South East Asia Command; SEC (*U.S.*), Securities and Exchange Commission; SECAM [F. *séquentiel couleur à mémoire* colour sequence by memory], a colour television system developed in France and widely used; SEM, scanning electron microscope, microscopy; S.E.N., State Enrolled Nurse; S.E.T. (also with pronunc. set), selective employment tax; S.F., San Francisco; S.F., s.f., science fiction; S.F. = *SINN FEIN; S.F.A., Scottish Football Association (cf. F.A. s.v. *F III. 3); S.F.A., Sweet Fanny Adams (cf. F.A. s.v. *F III. 3, *FANNY ADAMS 2); S.F.I.O. [F. *Section française de l'Internationale ouvrière*, French section of the workers' International], the French socialist party, known since 1969 as the *Parti Socialiste*; s.h., shit-house; S.H.F., s.h.f. (*Radio*), superhigh frequency; S.H.O., Senior House Officer; s.h.p., S.H.P., shaft horsepower; SI [F. *système international (d'unités)*], International System of Units (see *SYSTÈME INTERNATIONAL and *INTERNATIONAL *a.* 1 c); S.I.D. s.i.d. (*Radio*), sudden ionospheric disturbance; SIDS, sudden infant death syndrome; S.I.N.S., ship's inertial navigation system; S.I.S., Secret Intelligence Service; S.I.W., self-inflicted wound (see also quot. 1929); S.J., Society of Jesus (cf. JESUIT *sb.*); S.L.A., Symbionese Liberation Army; SLBM, submarine-launched ballistic missile; SLCM, submarine-launched cruise missile; SLE (*Med.*), systemic lupus erythematosus; S level, Scholarship (also, Special) level (of the General Certificate of Education examination); S.L.P., Scottish Labour Party; SLR (*Photogr.*), single-lens reflex (camera); S–M: see S and M above; S.M., sergeant-major; S.M., short metre (cf. SHORT *a.*, *sb.* and *adv.* 26); S.M., s.m., stage manager; S.M.L.E., short magazine Lee-Enfield (rifle); S.M.M.T., Society of Motor Manufacturers and Traders; S.M.O.N. (see *SMON as main entry); SMPTE (*U.S.*), Society of Motion Picture and Television Engineers; SNCC (*U.S.*), Student Nonviolent Co-ordinating Committee; S.N.C.F. [F. *Société Nationale des Chemins de Fer*], the French State railway authority, also used for the railway system itself; S.N.F., s.n.f., solids, non-fat; SNG, simulated, substitute, or synthetic natural gas; S.N.O., Senior Naval Officer (cf. N.O. s.v. *N II. 1); S.N.P., Scottish National Party; SNU (sniū) *Astr.*, solar neutrino unit (see quot. 1970); S.O., standing order; S.O.B., s.o.b. (chiefly *U.S.*), son of a bitch, also silly old bastard, etc.; S.O.E., Special Operations Executive; S. of S., Secretary of State; S.O.L., s.o.l., soldier (also strictly, shit, surely: see quot. 1917) out of luck (*U.S.*); SOP, standard operating procedure (*U.S.*, orig. *Mil.*); S.P., s.p., starting price; S.P.A.B., Society for the Protection of Ancient Buildings; S.P.C.K., Society for the Promotion of Christian Knowledge; S.P.D. [G. *Sozialdemokratische Partei Deutschlands*], the Social Democratic Party in West Germany; S.P.E., Society for Pure English; S.P.G. (earlier examples); S.P.Q.R. [L. *Senatus Populusque Romanus*], the Senate and People of Rome; also in joc. adaptations, esp. = small profits, quick returns; S.P.R., Society for Psychical Research; SQ [f. *s*tereophonic-*q*uadraphonic], a designation (proprietary in the U.S.) of audio equipment used with reference to a system of quadraphonic recording and reproduction; S.R., Socialist Revolutionary (Party); S.R., Southern Railway; S.R., Special Reserve; sr, steradian; S–R, stimulus–response *adj.* (in Psychol.); SRBC (*Med.*), sheep red blood cell(s); S.R.M.N., State Registered Mental Nurse; S.R.N. State Registered Nurse; sRNA († S-RNA) (*Biol.*), soluble RNA; SRO (*U.S.*), single-room occupancy; S.R.O. (orig. *U.S.*), standing room only; SRS(-A) (*Med.*), slow-reacting substance (of anaphylaxis); S.S. = *SCHUTZSTAFFEL; S.S., secret service, security service; SS, social security (benefit); S.S., steamship: also s.s., ss. (examples); SSB, ssb (*Radio*), single side-band (transmission); SSBN [Submarine (symbol SS), Ballistic, Nuclear], a nuclear-powered ballistic missile submarine; S.S.N., severely subnormal; SSPE (*Path.*) subacute sclerosing panencephalitis; SSR, secondary surveillance radar; S.S.R. [Russ. *Sovétskaya Sotsialistícheskaya Respúblika*], Soviet Socialist Republic (cf. *U.S.S.R.); SSRC, Social Science Research Council; SST, supersonic transport; S.T.C., short-title catalogue, esp. *A Short-Title Catalogue of Books Printed in England, Scotland, and Ireland 1475–1640*, by A. W. Pollard and G. R. Redgrave, first published in 1926; STD (*Teleph.*), subscriber trunk dialling; STOL, stol., short take-off and landing; S.T.V., single transferable vote; SU (*Physics*), special unitary (*sc.* group): used with following numeral denoting the number of rows and of columns in the matrices that can be used to represent it, as *SU*(3): cf. *SPECIAL *a.*; SV (*Med.*), Simian virus: used, freq. with following numeral to identify the strain, as the designation of various viruses isolated from monkeys or cultures of monkey cells; s.v. = *sub verbo, sub voce* s.v. SUB *Latin prep.* in Dict. and Suppl.; also s.vv., *sub verbis* (followed by more than one citation); SVD, swine vesicular disease; S.W., small women('s size); S.W.A.(L.)K., SWA(L)K, sealed with a (loving) kiss; SWAT (*U.S.*), Special Weapons and Tactics; s.w.g., S.W.G., standard wire gauge; SWP, Socialist Workers' Party; S.W.R., s.w.r., standing-wave ratio. See also (as main entries) *SAGE, *SALT, *SAVAK, *SEATO, *SHAEF, *SHAPE, *SNAFU, *SOGAT, *S.O.S., *STP, *SWANU, *SWAPO.

1920 J. A. ARKWRIGHT in *Jrnl. Path. & Bacteriol.* XXIII. 359 The appearance of colonies on agar of the two forms is different. The S form makes smooth, round, domed, shiny, translucent colonies; the R form grows in colonies which have a more or less jagged outline. **1974** [see *ROUGH *a.* 1 e]. **1949** *Vet. Rec.* LXI. 318/1 Each animal was inoculated intravenously with approximately 20 times the recommended vaccine dose of S.19 in a volume of 50 ml. **1960** *Farmer & Stockbreeder* 26 Jan. 89/1 As the animals are ready to go out on the early spring grazing they are collected together on the farms for vaccination with S19. **1978** *Amer. Jrnl. Vet. Res.* XXXIX. 884/1 Lymphocyte stimulation..was detected in 3 steers which had been vaccinated with S19 but not with lymphocytes from 5 nonvaccinated heifers. **1926** *Amer. Mercury* Dec. 465 The girl is a looker with an armful of S.A. (sex appeal). **1932** P. MACDONALD *Maze* 216 A Gallic young woman with apparently some looks and, let us say, 98 per cent. vigorous S.A. **1961** *John o' London's* 6 July 57/2 Surely one of Hollywood's finest character actresses—all this and blonde S.A. too. **1974** E. MCGIRR *Murderous Journey* 96, I saw you and the dame go into her apartment... I expected you to take longer. Losing the old s.a., Piron? [**1907** *Jrnl. Anat. & Physiol.* XLI. 175 (*caption*) *s.a.j.*, sino-auricular junction.] **1908** J. MACKENZIE *Dis. Heart* p. xix, Sino-auricular node (s.-a. node.) **1910** *Jrnl. Physiol.* XLI. 69 This observer finds no altered rhythm as the result of destruction of the S-A node by burning. **1944** C. P. ANTHONY *Textbk. Anat. & Physiol.* v. 177 It is named the sinoatrial node but is usually referred to simply as the S.A. node... It is also called the 'pacemaker' of the heart. **1974** M. C. GERALD *Pharmacol.* xxi. 386 Digitalis directly depresses the conducting tissues responsible for carrying the excitatory impulse from the S.A. node pacemaker. **1876** VOYLE & STEVENSON *Mil. Dict.* (ed. 3) p. x, *S.A.*, small-arms. **1888** *Man. Field Service—Army Signallers* (War Office) 12 Pins, linch, 3rd class (or 2nd class, steel, if for cart, ammunition, S.A.). **1924** *Regulations Equipment of Army (Provisional)* (War Office) II. i. 4 Eyepieces, rubber, sights, telescopic, S.A., No. 2. **1921** *London Directory* 1707/1 Geneva, Switzerland. Mondiale Express Transports S/A. **1938** E. AMBLER *Cause for Alarm* v. 83 There it was in black and white—Società Anonima Braganzetta, Torino. I had found S.A. Braga of Turin! **1977** 'J. LE CARRÉ' *Hon. Schoolboy* iv. 80 Indocharter, Vientiane SA..was an overseas Chinese company. **1931** W. LEWIS *Hitler* II. 60 The abovementioned defence-service.. received the name of *Storm-detachments—S.A.*, in memory of the 'heroic onset of the at that time mere handful'. **1934** *Ann. Reg. 1933* 168 On February 22 Goering incorporated picked S.A. men as auxiliary Police Corps. **1955** *Times* 15 Aug. 4/4 A picture of him..wearing S.A. uniform and with his right arm raised. **1968** *Listener* 19 Sept. 358/3, I do not even know the difference between the SA and the SS, so how can I make such a film. **1977** *Daily Tel.* 17 Nov. 36/7 The SS (Schutzstaffel) emerged as a powerful force after the 1934 purge which eliminated the SA (Sturmabteilung), the brown-shirted thugs who helped bring Hitler to political prominence. **1876** VOYLE & STEVENSON *Mil. Dict.* (ed. 3) p. xi, *S.A.A.*, small-arm ammunition. **1907** *Field Service Pocket Bk.* ii. 50 A total of 500 rounds S.A.A. will be maintained in the field..for every man, whether combatant or not, included in an expeditionary force. **1954** J. MASTERS *Bhowani Junction* I. xi. 95, I rummaged in the table drawers and found a list:..1,000 feet of slow-burning fuse; 12,000 rounds of SAA .303 Mark VIII Z. **1952** *R.A.F. Rev.* Jan. 11/1 Under the New Trade Structure I am now expected to pass a SAC board to qualify as a Corporal and gain the increase in pay. **1970** *Athanian* 1 Apr. 31/1 The club is an 'All Ranks' affair ranging from an S.A.C. to a Sqn Ldr. **1947** *Army & Navy Bull.* 1 Feb. 8/3 General St. Clair Streett, SAC Deputy Commander since its activation last March, received a new assignment in the War Department. **1958** *Times* 8 May 11/6 Right now, therefore, the S.A.C. crew in a S.A.C. plane is the west's number one deterrent to the Kremlin. **1974** *Publishers Weekly* 16 Dec. 22 (Advt.), H. Bruce Franklin, Melville Scholar, former SAC officer, and tugboat mate. **1951** *Army Information Digest* July 27 Supreme Allied Commander Europe (*SACEUR*). **1953** *Britannica Bk. of Year* 752/2 Saceur, Supreme Allied Commander, Europe. **1958** *Economist* 1 Feb. 393/1 Its [*sc.* Britain's] dwindling proportion of the forces at Saceur's disposal. **1959** *Times Lit. Suppl.* 13 Feb. 79/2 Proposals for placing the missile bases under the command of S.A.C.EUR...do not, as Mr. Moore says, really change the situation. **1964** *Ann. Reg. 1963* 162 Approval was given to the assignment of the British V-bomber force..to the Supreme Allied Commander Europe (SACEUR). **1979** *Observer* 25 Nov. 34/3 SACEUR, Supreme Allied Commander Europe, the military head of NATO; currently the American General Bernard W. Rogers. **1951** *R.A.F. Rev.* Sept. 34/3 The R.A.F.'s qualifying trade test leads to promotion to Senior Aircraftsman or SACW. **1977** *R.A.F. News* 30 Mar.–12 Apr. 18/1 The only WRAF rider, SACW Jennie Hye of West Drayton, put up a plucky 44·42. **1924** *Jrnl. Soc. Automotive Engineers* XV. 31/1 The fact that the present S.A.E. numbers for crankcase lubricating oil specifications were used..is of interest. **1966** *McGraw-Hill Encycl. Sci. & Technol.* XIII. 313/1 The carburizing steels..which have the greatest ability to harden..are SAE 3310 and 4320. **1967** KARCH & BUBER *Offset Processes* x. 475 The pump oiler should be filled every 25 to 50 hours of running time with ≠105SAE or equivalent pure mineral oil. **1974** *Encycl. Brit. Macropædia* XIV. 188/2 In the U.S., the Society of Automotive Engineers established a system of SAE numbers to indicate the viscosity at a particular temperature, 0°F (−18°C). Oils in common use have SAE numbers varying from 5 to 50. *Ibid.*, An oil designated 10W/40 has the viscosity of an SAE 10W oil at 0°F.., and of an SAE 40 oil at 210°F... Such an oil will help start an engine in winter (hence the suffix W) and will lubricate well under running conditions in summer. **1939** 'F. O'BRIEN' *At Swim-two-Birds* i. 15 To all my friends forwarding 6d. and two S.A.E.'s I will present this three-star cast-iron plunger. **1962** *Woman's Own* 15 Sept. 69/3, I will send you a leaflet on this subject on request (s.a.e., please). **1966** *Punch* 26 Jan. 116/3 That stream of SAEs for the free, illustrated brochure. **1977** *Vogue* Dec. 90/2 Send a SAE for the catalogue. **1966** *Economist* 29 Oct. 457/3 The much publicised series of talks between federal ministers, SAL leaders and a couple of dissident sheikhs..has come to nothing. **1970** H. TREVELYAN *Middle East in Revolution* 218 The original Nationalist party, the South Arabian League, known as SAL, were in decline. **1958** *Chambers's Techn. Dict.* 983/2 SAM. **1975** R. JACKSON *South Asian Crisis* v. 107 The Indian SAM missile systems were improved. **1979** P. NIESEWAND *Member of Club* xv. 122 Tanks, armoured cars, SAM missiles..are being landed at Beira. **1951** *Business Week* 22 Sept. 152/2 (*heading*) 'Thin Ice' for S & L's. **1967** *Economist* 25 Mar. 1145/2 Some Californian S & Ls suffered near runs on their accounts as savers began to doubt their solvency. **1976** *National Observer* (U.S.) 25 Dec. 7/1 The result is that institutions that finance a large volume of home purchases, as S&Ls do, may not be able to afford to be as generous on longer-term deposit rates. **1965** *Acronyms & Initialisms Dict.* (Gale Research Co.) 645 *S & M*,..sadism and masochism (generic term). **1966** *Realist* May 19/3 Remember the S–M ads: 'seeks discipline', 'seeks uniforms', 'seeks leather and rubber'. **1975** *New Yorker* 26 May 32/2 Death is by far the most controversial and hottest subject in America, ranking twenty-five shock points above transsexuality, school busing, S & M, and interracial cloning. **1977** *Time* 15 Aug. 31/1 The streets teemed with whores, transvestites and the S–M crowd dangling slave bracelets and chains. **1955** R. J. SCHWARTZ *Compl. Dict. Abbrev.* 159/1 *SAR*,..search and rescue. **1958** *Oxf. Mail* 1 Aug. 6/6 SAR..has two squadrons situated at ten stations mainly around the south and east coasts. **1977** *R.A.F. News* 5–18 Jan. 3/1 An SAR Wessex was scrambled from Manston the following morning. **1945** M. JAMES *Born of Desert* xxi. 319 As the continental offensive developed and gained weight, so the S.A.S. probed deeper and deeper into the enemy lines. **1960** B. A. YOUNG *Artists & S.A.S.* xix. 46 The S.A.S. first went into action on November 16, 1941, when their target was the enemy airfields at Gazala and Tmimi, and their object to cripple the enemy's air before General Auchinleck launched his attack a few days later. **1976** G. SEYMOUR *Glory Boys* xvi. 221 The SAS anti-hi-jack force had been lifted by Wessex helicopter from their base camp. **1961** A. ANASTASI *Psychol. Testing* (ed. 2) ix. 226 A number of tests have been specially developed for use in the admission, placement, and counseling of college students. An outstanding example is the Scholastic Aptitude Test (SAT) of the College Entrance Examination Board. **1971** E. ASHBY *Any Person, Any Study* ii. 59 Taken together with SAT scores the information is as good as any measure yet devised to predict academic performance in college examinations. **1974** A. LURIE *War between Tates* ii. 39 Until very recently, girls like her, whatever their SAT scores, didn't usually go to graduate school. **1923** J. REITH *Diary* 29 Aug. (1975) ii. 132, I read the News Bulletin at 7.00 p.m.—the first real SB. **1929** *B.B.C. Year-Bk. 1930* 310 One or two transmissions are, perhaps, being sent to the provinces via the S.B. lines... Tests are being taken of outside broadcasts or incoming S.B. **1964** L. DEIGHTON *Funeral in Berlin* xxxvii. 228 'Makes me curious about the locked room,' said the young S.B. man. **1975** O. SELA *Bengali Inheritance* iv. 34 Special Branch won't like it... But you will need some assistance from SB—the files at least. **1917** A. G. EMPEY *Over Top* 307 S.B., stretcher bearer. The motive power of a stretcher. He is generally looking the other way when a fourteen-stone Tommy gets hit. **1919** W. DEEPING *Second Youth* xix. 168 'Ere, you blitherin' S.B.'s, get a move on. **1942** PARTRIDGE *Dict. Abbrev.* 87/2 *S.B.A.*, Sick-Bay Attendant. **1964** J. HALE *Grudge Fight* iii. 44 'Got a nice new one for you,' said the sick bay attendant to Adams, meaning the needle which glittered in space for a moment before the S.B.A. rammed it into his arm and pressed the plunger. **1953** *Newsweek* 24 Aug. 62/3 The new Small Business Administration whirled into rapid action... SBA..will keep some functions formerly performed by the..Small Defense Plants Administration. **1976** *Billings* (Montana) *Gaz.* 27 June 2-D/8 They file for Small Business Administration (SBA) loans and get on the long HUD list for trailers. **1932** *Flight* 1 July 601 The Flying Display arranged by the S.B.A.C., with the co-operation of the Air Ministry, at Hendon last Monday must be counted a success. **1951** *R.A.F. Rev.* Oct. 13/2 It flew faster than any aircraft has ever flown before in an S.B.A.C. show. **1968** C. SIMS *Royal Air Force* xi. 174 An item in the S.B.A.C. show. **1973** HOBSON & POHL *Mod. Petroleum Technol.* xxix. 945 A development during recent years has been the so-called Single Buoy Mooring (SBM) which may be either a fixed tower or a large buoy to which the ship is moored bow on. **1975** *Offshore Engineer* Sept. 33 (*heading*) Pioneering new sbm system off coast of Anglesey. **1975** *Petroleum Rev.* XXIX. 324/1 Floating hose conveys the crude from the SBM into a tanker. **1956** *Rubber World* May 239/2 The use of the term 'butadiene-styrene rubber' and the coding 'SBR'. **1971** G. J. VAN DER BIE et al. in C. M. Blow *Rubber Technol. & Manuf.* iv. B. 84 Emulsion SBR, for long the only synthetic general purpose rubber, has blossomed from the few 'hot' types produced during World War II into the multiplicity of grades now available in 'cold' types. **1920** *Dalton's Weekly Advertiser* 10 Jan. 3/2 (Advt.), House or S.C. Flat wanted by married couple. **1975** *Irish Independent* 27 May 18/1 (Advt.), Newly furnished hall flat, completely s.c., own door, double bedroom. **1977** *Weekly Times* (Melbourne) 19 Jan. 58/7 (Advt.), Clean, SC, ground level flats, acc. 2 to 6. **1964** E. BACH *Introd. Transformational Gram.* iv. 61 The second part of the rule specifies the *structural change* (SC) by means of variable signs. **1966** A. KOUTSOUDAS *Writing Transformational Gram.* i. 24 There are different notational conventions for writing a T-rule; rule (8) above can also be written..SC: x_1—x_2—x_3 → x_3—x_1—x_2. **1946** *Newsweek* 12 Aug. 43/3 Again SCAP (Supreme Commander for the Allied Powers, the official designation of the occupation) left the implementation up to the Japanese. **1978** C. HUMPHREYS *Both Sides of Circle* xii. 131 The formal opening took place of our own Empire Building near that of S.C.A.P. (headquarters of the American army). **1885** *Ordinances Univ. Cambr.* p. viii, *Students in Science and Letters.* Proceeding to the Degrees of Sc.D. and Litt.D. **1917** J. R. TANNER *Hist. Register Univ. Cambr.* 195 Sc.D. Robes and hood of scarlet cloth, both lined with silk shot with pink and light blue. **1979** *Oxford Univ. Gaz.* 1 Mar. 554/2 University Preachers... Sunday, 11 March, at 10.15 a.m. D. E. Broadbent, C.B.E., M.A., D.Sc. (M.A., Sc.D. Cambridge, Hon. D.Sc. Southampton). **1921** *Ann. Rep. Save the Children Fund* 4/1 During the year under review, the S.C.F. has succeeded in making the needs of the children widely known throughout the United Kingdom and the British Empire. **1967** *Punch* 1 Mar. 292/2 'A simple pleasure,' said the SCF supervisor, 'but one that flat-dwelling kids just don't have.' **1974** *Petroleum Rev.* XXVIII. 794/2 The combined recoverable reserves of the field are estimated to be in the order of 1·5 to 2·0 × 10⁹ barrels of oil, with some 3·0 × 10¹² scf of associated gas. **1959** L. D. REDDICK *Crusader without Violence* xii. 205 There was so much.. rumor about friction between the SCLC and NAACP that King scampered up to New York. **1968** L. LOKOS *House Divided* x. 375 SCLC called upon the President to de-escalate the war unilaterally. **1973** *Freedomways* XIII. 8 Recent action taken by the leaders of..SCLC..is a most welcome development. **1935** *Nursing Mirror & Midwives' Jrnl.* 2 Feb. p. xx/3 (Advt.), S.C.M. required... General training not essential. **1955** *Times* 8 July 2/5 Candidates must be S.R.N., S.C.M., and should preferably have had similar experience in a Teaching Hospital. **1924** *Fellowship of Students* (Student Christian Movement) 49 The work of the S.C.M. must be closely related to the developing work of the Churches. **1948** H. G. G. HERKLOTS in M. Warren *Triumph of God* vii. 180 Now it was men and women who had been schooled in the S.C.M., who accepted its 'interdenominational position', who were planning the Edinburgh Conference. **1976** A. LOCKLEY *Christian Communes* vi. 55 The SCM headquarters were moved out of London in 1974 to Wick Court, a Jacobean mansion near Bristol, where the central staff attempted to live communally. **1971** *Nature* 16 Apr. 430/1 The big attraction of SCP is the possibility of utilizing cheap raw materials as fermentation substrates. **1976** *Jrnl. R. Soc. Arts* CXXIV. 580/2 It might be more economical to convert part of our oil supplies into food by using it as a substrate for microorganisms, to produce 'Single Cell Protein' (SCP) that could be used as the raw material for the textured meat substitutes that were referred to earlier. **1923** D. K. HORNE in G. Bailey *Lady Margaret Hall* v. 94 Each student..is placed under a tutor, who is almost invariably one of the resident members of the S.C.R. **1964** M. HUTT in D. Daiches *Idea of New Univ.* iii. 49 Falmer House belongs neither to the Union nor the SCR. **1965** *New Statesman* 7 May 734/1 Mr Soyinka..knows the SCRs of Ibadan and Ife. **1976** A. CROSS *Question of Max* vi. 73 If..I had one wish right now, it would be to be connected for a time with an Oxford college and dine at the high table, chat in the SCR. **1963** *New Scientist* 13 June 600/1 The SCR, at the outset, is basically an 'insulator'. It does not allow current to pass. **1975** D. G. FINK *Electronics Engineers' Handbk.* VII. 52 During forward-bias operation.., the *pnpn* structure of the SCR is electrically bistable and may exhibit either a very high impedance (OFF state) or a very low impedance (ON state). **1956** *Times* 22 Sept. 10/4 The members of the Suez Canal Users' Association (S.C.U.A.) shall be those nations which have participated in the second London Suez conference and which subscribe to the present declaration, and any other adhering nations. **1970** H. TREVELYAN *Middle East in Revolution* 100 The Menzies Mission..was followed by the second conference of the 'users', the formation of the 'users' ' association and the realisation that the S.C.U.A., the skewer as we called it, had a blunt point. **1939** *London Weekly Advertiser* 7 June 6/4 £70 Exclusive.—S.D. Modern House, three beds, etc., near Dyke Road Park. **1975** *Evening Herald* (Dublin) 8 May 10/2 (Advt.), Very unusual 4 bedroomed s.d. in cul de sac. **1901** W. M. F. PETRIE *Diospolis Parva* i. 6 We now make a first division into fifty equal stages, numbered 30 to 80, termed *sequence dates* or S.D. **1939** —— *Making of Egypt* vii. 55 This period (S.D. 60–75) has no generally distinctive culture. **1944** *Jrnl. Near Eastern Stud.* III. 110 Petrie distinguished it from Gerzean by naming it the Third Predynastic of Semainean, ranging from Sequence Dates 60/63 to S.D. 76. **1950** G. E. DANIEL *Hundred Yrs. of Archaeol.* v. 176 He started his sequence with S.D. 30,.. and carried on to dynastic times at S.D. 80. [**1940** H. KOEHLER *Inside Gestapo* ii. 30 Heydrich's power is much more founded on the Security Service of the Reich Fuehrer S.S. (shortened SD. RFSS.) than on the Gestapo.] **1947** H. TREVOR-ROPER *Last Days of Hitler* i. 28 Otto Ohlendorf was head of *R.S.H.A. Amt III* (also called S.D. or *Sicherheitsdienst*). **1968** *Listener* 8 Aug. 174/3, I was wearing my old SD cap which I'd brought through the whole war. **1974** A. WILLIAMS *Gentleman Traitor* xiii. 212 The father had returned to Germany in 1938..and had served in the SD, the civil arm of the S.S. **1902** *Biometrika* I. 206, σ_1 is the S.D. of the organ. **1973** *Nature* 31 Aug. 587/2 The mean (±s.d.) IQ then was 98·7 (±7·1) with no precocity. **1978** *Jrnl. R. Soc. Med.* LXXI. 659 Twin, malformed or grossly autolysed fetuses, and any which were ⩾ 2 s.d. below the mean for the gestational age group, were excluded. **1964** E. BACH *Introd. Transformational Gram.* iv. 61 The first part of the rule is a *structural description* (SD..) specifying the class of strings (in the terms of their analysis by P markers) to which the rule applies. **1975** *Studies in Eng. Lit.: Eng. Number* (Tokyo) 170 The term 'obligatory'..has generally been understood to mean that an obligatory rule must apply to a phrase-maker which meets the SD of that rule. **1975** *Glasgow Herald* 17 Dec. 1 (*heading*) S.D.A. pledge quick action. **1976** *Scotsman* 15 Dec. 5/1 Capital restructuring..will give the SDA one-third of the shares at a cost of £60,000. **1966** *Economist* 22 Jan. 301/2 His superior in SDECE admitted last week that this was true. **1966** M. WOODHOUSE *Tree Frog* viii. 58 There is Defensive Intelligence and Active Intelligence... In France, the Ministry of the Interior and S.D.E.C.E. **1972** K. BENTON *Spy in Chancery* xvii. 193 They have a.. gentleman's agreement..with both MI6 and CIA—and with the French SDECE, too, I think. **1893** G. B. SHAW *Let.* 24 Apr. (1965) I. 390 My remarks..were not levelled at the I.L.P., but at the S.D.F. **1910** CHESTERTON *George Bernard Shaw* 68 Bernard Shaw was thrown early into what may be called the cosmopolitan club of revolution. The Socialists of the S.D.F. call it 'l'Internationale'. **1957** R. HOGGART *Uses of Literacy* xi. 261 They worked for Hyndman's S.D.F. in the 'eighties, and for the I.L.P. in the 'nineties. **1980** 'FIRST' & SCOTT *Olive Schreiner* iv. 109 The Democratic Federation [of 1881] became the Social Democratic Federation (SDF) in 1883. **1936** S.D.F.er [see *MORRISITE]. **1970** *Times* 22 Aug. 3/1 'The S.D.L.P. is the only institution that can bring about reform in Northern Ireland,' he said. **1974** *Freedom* 25 May 8/1 Willing followers of the power seekers of the IRA, SDLP and all the 'loyalist' organisations. **1978** D. MURPHY *Place Apart* vi. 117 An elderly woman then observed, 'What we need is a sort of cross between the Provos and Stickies and SDLP.' **1936** W. H. S. Smith *Let.* 21 June in *Young Man's Country* (1977) i. 9 I've been in correspondence with the present S.D.O. **1947** *Civil & Milit. Gaz.* 9 Apr. 2/4 'Youngsters are attached to S.D.O.s to learn their jobs. **1977** W. H. S. Smith *Young Man's Country* iii. 103, I was welcomed by several clerks in the S.D.O.'s office. **1908** *Times* 18 Apr. 10/1 The delegate..declared that as a militant force the S.D.P. could desire no more suitable antagonist than the scion of the aristocracy who represented Rossendale. **1912** R. Macaulay *Views & Vagabonds* ii. 24 We stand for all the principles of the Fabian Society, the S.D.P., and..so forth. **1961** C. Tsuzuki *H. M. Hyndman & Brit. Socialism* viii. 164 In October 1907 this progress and the desire to emulate the Labour Party encouraged the executive to change the name of the Federation to the Social Democratic Party (S.D.P.). **1981** *Times* 27 Mar. 1/1 (*heading*) SDP launched with aim of 'reconciling the nation'. *Ibid.* 3 (Advt.), If you share our aims you can join the *SDP* by filling in the application and returning it with a subscription. **1967** *Guardian* 28 Aug. 1/7 It will be up to the managing director of the IMF.. to initiate and suggest the size of any proposed allotment of special drawing rights (SDRs). **1972** *Penguin Dict. Econ.* 382 The S.D.R...is an entry in a member country's bank balance with the I.M.F. **1976** 'J. Davey' *Treasury Alarm* iii. 43, I happened to hear some Treasury folk gossiping..and I find that SDRs, which baffled me, are Special Drawing Rights. **1968** *Times* 19 Apr. 10/4 The extreme left-wing Federation of German Socialist Students (S.D.S.). **1977** in R. Crossman *Diaries* III. 77 In West Berlin on April 11th there was an attempt to assassinate Rudi Dütschke, left-wing leader of the militant Socialist Students' League (S.D.S.). **1961** *Mademoiselle* Aug. 335/2 'Students have a mystique about action,' says Al Haber, president of the nationwide Students for a Democratic Society... Haber..has traveled to many campuses this year to establish new S.D.S. groups. **1965** *Moderator* Winter 14/2 SDS was re-formed in 1962, at which time the Port Huron statement defined its purposes. **1974** H. L. Foster *Ribbin'* iii. 92 The SDS and some third world groups sold drugs to college students to earn money and keep their cause going a few years ago. **1946** C. E. Weatherburn *Math. Statistics* vi. 110 This S.D. is usually called the standard error (S.E.) of the number of successes in a sample of size *n*. *Ibid.* 111 A deviation from the mean less than twice the S.E. is regarded as not significant. **1964** F. N. Kerlinger *Foundations Behavioral Res.* ix. 167 $SE_M = 2·73$. **1971** *Nature* 1 Jan 62/1 On these assumptions, the mean number (±s.e.) of skeletomotor nerve fibres in normal nerves was 191±26. **1974** *Ibid.* 23 Aug. 654/1 The mean concentration of prolactin in the peripheral blood of women during the cycle is 15±1 (±s.e.m.). **1927** *Financial Times* 7 May 6/5 (*heading*) S.E. Clerks' Provident Fund. **1942** Partridge *Dict. Abbrev.* 88/2 *S/E*, Stock Exchange. **1978** *Times* 23 Jan. 15/1 A Stock Exchange investigation..is now awaiting examination by the SE Council. **1944** *SEAC: Daily Newspaper of South East Asia Command* (Calcutta) 10 Jan. 1/1 First light is breaking over this awakening city as the birthday issue of SEAC (pronounce it See-ack) comes flying off the presses. **1945** *Daily Mirror* 15 Aug. 1/1 There is an Army warning against expecting the quick homecoming of SEAC troops. **1971** R. Russell tr. *Ahmad's Shore & Wave* xv. 159 In those days he [*sc.* Lord Mountbatten] was the head of S.E.A.C., and was there on leave. **1934** *Time* 16 July 46/1 The S.E.C. will take over enforcement of the Securities Act of 1933. **1955** *Times* 29 Aug. 11/3 Banks..have indicated an interest if the S.E.C. provides a means of registering them. **1966** *Economist* 1 Oct. 46/3 The SEC has steadfastly opposed the exchange's efforts to limit trading in listed stocks to members only. **1978** *Financial Times* 3 Mar. 18/2 The setting-up of a body like the SEC is a last resort. **1962** *Rep. Comm. Broadcasting 1960* 218 in *Parl Papers 1961–2* (Cmnd. 1753) IX. 259 Our attention has..been drawn to another system of colour-transmission, the 'SECAM' system. This might..prove a serious rival to the NTSC system. **1968** [see PAL s.v. *P II]. **1978** *Gramophone* Aug. 391/1 All the major video protagonists have mounted elaborate press launches of their systems, suitably adapted to the PAL TV format commonly used in Europe instead of the SECAM standard employed elsewhere. **1968** *Proc. Symp. Scanning Electron Microscope* 3/1 The scanning electron microscope, or SEM, as I shall henceforth call it. **1974** SEM [see *macerate *sb.*]. **1961** *Nursing Mirror & Midwives' Jrnl.* 26 May 760/1 Male S.E.N. or Nursing Auxiliaries required for duties in acute wards & departments. **1964** G. L. Cohen *What's Wrong with Hospitals?* ix. 192 Negro domestics abounded, but the S.E.N. school was conspicuously white. **1977** *R.A.F. News* 22 June–5 July 13 (*caption*) SACW Margie Lee, an SEN, nursing a premature baby in the maternity unit at RAF Hospital Wegberg. **1966** *Financial Times* 4 May 1/1 Most Fleet Street papers seized on the payroll tax (SET) as the Budget's main news point. **1966** *Observer* 8 May 9/1 The main virtue of S.E.T. is that it is indirect. *a* **1974** R. Crossman *Diaries* (1975) I. 508 My first reaction to S.E.T. was that in terms of farming at Prescote Manor as well as in terms of building it was absolutely unbearable. *c* **1875** *Pocket Exchange Guide San Francisco* 178 S.F. Ten-Cent Parcel Delivery Co.—16 Post. **1975** B. Meggs *Matter of Paradise* ix. iii. 267 One year at the University of Wisconsin, then moved to S.F. with her boyfriend, drummer in a rock-band. **1929** *Sci. Wonder Stories* June 92/3 The S.F. Magazine. (Science-Fiction). **1948** G. Conklin *Treas. Sci. Fiction* p. ix, Many SF writers are feeling the urgent need for social controls over our physical powers. **1954** I. Asimov in *Mag. Fantasy & Sci. Fiction* Oct. 69 (*title*) The foundation of S.F. success. **1959** *Times Lit. Suppl.* 20 Mar. 166/2 Both are by O.K.-names in the s.f. world. **1968** *Punch* 10 Jan. 69/3 Let's take a step *beyond* in the company of Ray Bradbury..and other (mainly *sf*) bloodcurdlists. **1969** *Daily Tel.* 16 Oct. 22/7 Two regular themes in S.F. are the world dominated by a, usually evil, visionary and the world run by a Great Computer. **1973** 'D. Halliday' *Dolly & Starry Bird* viii. 108 Johnson ..was looking as everybody looks when they first step into an electronic workshop. That is blasé. This is the fault of the S.F. kiddie shows on the telly. **1975** Felton & Fowler *Best, Worst & most Unusual* 44 Arguably, it is the peak of sf film in its long history. **1980** *Times Lit. Suppl.* 7 Nov. 1263/1 The reason for preferring the old established and unpretentious 'sf' need not baffle us. The use of 'sci-fi' was clearly intended to imply a jaunty insider's knowledge coupled with a modern..demonstration of slick neologism. **1922** Lady Leslie *Let.* 17 Mar. in M. Gilbert *Winston S. Churchill* (1977) IV. Compan. iii. 1809 The Union Jacks are being silently stored away—the SF flag floats on the orange Hall. **1973** *Irish Times* 2 Mar. 8/3 Sherlock J. (S.F.)... 2,488. **1882** *Football* 4 Oct. 4/1 The match would be played under the supervision of the S.F.A. **1974** *Evening News* (Edinburgh) 9 Apr. 18/8 The SFA stipulated that no game could be cancelled at such an early hour on the strength of a weather forecast. **1933** *Bulletin* (Sydney) 14 June 12/3 Ask any modern sailor who has been refused an issue of pay or rations 'What luck?' and he will be apt to reply 'Sweet Fanny Adams', or just 'S.F.A.', meaning that he received nothing. **1935** *Ann. Reg. 1934* i. 172 Thus at Toulouse the S.F.I.O. (the French section of the Workers' International) sought..to form an entente with the Communists against Fascism. **1977** *Compar. Politics* IX. 364 The Popular Front, with its broad policies of alliance extending past the SFIO to the radical party..responded to Soviet and Comintern demands. **1949** E. Pound *Pisan Cantos* lxxvii. 52, I heard it in the s.h. a suitable place To hear that the war was over. **1948** *Prof. Papers Inst. Post Office Electr. Engineers* No. 197. 3/1 S.H.F. systems are those operating in the range 3,000 to 30,000 Mc/s, 10 to 1 cm. wavelength. **1958** *Electronic Engin.* XXX. 276/1 The radio repeater design is based on the principle of amplification at intermediate-frequency with reconversion to s.h.f. and the use of a travelling-wave amplifier to deliver the final output power. **1965** *Acronyms & Initialisms Dict.* (Gale Research Co.) 638 *SHO*,..Senior House Officer. **1976** *Proc. R. Soc. Med.* LXIX. 818/1 A hypothetical increase in the number of graduates to over 5000 by 1980 would require about 18 000 SHO and registrar posts in 1982. **1931** *Times Trade & Engin. Suppl.* 24 Jan. p. iv/3 Six vessels, of 10,500 s.h.p. **1972** C. Mudie *Motor Boats & Boating* 28 The most important is SHP which is Shaft Horse Power or power delivered to the propeller shaft. **1961** SI [see *international *a.* 1 c]. **1970** *Nature* 2 May 473/2 Editors of scientific journals have been recently accused of forcing some unwilling scientists to adopt SI units. **1971** *Inside Kenya Today* Mar. 30/1 The Engineering and Construction Industries can go ahead with the change-over to the Metric System, but in particular in its modernized version called the 'Système International d'Unités' or the SI as it is popularly known in all languages. **1973** tr. *Internat. System of Units* 1 The 11th CGPM [*sc.* General Conference of Weights and Measures] (1960), by its Resolution 12, adopted the name *International System of Units*, with the international abbreviation SI, for this practical system of units of measurement. **1977** *Westworld* (Vancouver, B.C.) May–June 34/1 Canada..is one of the last major countries still using the imperial system of measurements instead of the International System of Units—universally known as SI. **1955** *Sci. News Let.* 29 Jan. 72/2 Polarized radio waves may also be a solution to the problem caused by 'SID's', or sudden ionospheric disturbances, when the sun may hurl out a great tongue of flame from which hydrogen atoms bombard the earth about 20 hours later. **1968** *Radio Communication Handbk.* (ed. 4) xii. 8/2 Ionospheric storms are often preceded (by approximately two days) by what are called sudden ionospheric disturbances (s.i.d.). **1970** J. B. Beckwith in A. B. Bergman et al. *Sudden Infant Death Syndrome* 15, I personally feel the term 'Sudden Death Syndrome' should at least be amplified to include the word 'infant'... I should like, therefore, to cast my vote for the term 'Sudden Infant Death Syndrome' (SIDS). **1980** *Sci. Amer.* Apr. 52/1 The phenomenon, which is also known by its initials SIDS (pronounced as letters rather than as a word), is defined clinically as the sudden, unexpected death of an apparently healthy infant for whom a routine autopsy fails to identify the cause of death. **1958** *Listener* 13 Nov. 779/2 The 'Nautilus' used a fully integrated apparatus of this kind called the Ship's Inertial Navigation System—inevitably contracted into its initials, 'S.I.N.S.' **1979** A. Fox *Threat Warning Red* i. 2 He could check those latitude and longitude figures against the readings on the SINS dials on the bulkhead. **1939** J. Reith *Diary* 21 Apr. (1975) iv. 227 Meeting in the foreign secretary's room, where I have never been before. Present: Halifax, Chatfield, Hoare, Cadogan, Leeper, CID secretary and Admiral Sinclair, the hush-hush SIS chief. **1964** G. Lyall *Most Dangerous Game* xiii. 91 You're SIS—one of the Foreign Office boys. What the mob would call The Secret Service. **1978** R. V. Jones *Most Secret War* vii. 63 While my evenings were spent discussing cryptography, my days went in perusing the S.I.S. files. *a* **1918** W. Owen *Coll. Poems* (1963) 74 (*title*) S.I.W. **1929** *London Mag.* Dec. 629/2 'What really coopered him, was being in charge of an S.I.W. just before Armistice.' 'What is an S.I.W.?' I said. 'A hospital for self-inflicted wounds.' **1975** P. Fussell *Gt. War & Mod. Memory* viii. 294 The final two lines of 'S.I.W.' tell us how the victim of the self-inflicted wound was buried. **1822** *Catholic Miscellany* May 208 H. More Hist. Prov. Ang. S.J. p. 467. **1916** Joyce *Portrait of Artist* iv. 187 The Reverend Stephen Dedalus, S.J. His name in that new life leaped into characters before his eyes. **1967** *Cath. Dict. Theol.* ii. 1/2 J. A. Jungmann SJ, *Handing on the Faith*..contains much recent information. **1974** *Time* 18 Feb. 16/1 The S.L.A. emblem is a seven-headed cobra. **1978** *Maledicta 1977* I. 123 Terrorists have come to rely on the press to deliver their graphic messages to the world—the Hanafi Muslims in Washington, the PLO at the Munich Olympics, the SLA in Oakland. **1967** *New Scientist* 9 Feb. 340/2 To achieve overwhelmingness, especially in the face of Russia's ABM effort, Mr. McNamara proposes to produce and deploy the Poseidon SLBM. **1973** *Sci. Amer.* Feb. 14/2 The primary SALT I restrictions..impose numerical ceilings on both land-based intercontinental ballistic missiles (ICBM's) and submarine-launched ballistic missiles (SLBM's). **1979** *Financial Rev.* 28 Sept. 10/3 The strategic deterrent is conceived as a triad consisting of bombers armed with nuclear weapons, submarine-launched ballistic missiles (SLBMs) and land-based intercontinental ballistic missiles (ICBMs). **1972** *Time* 19 June 17/3 The Pentagon is also asking for $20 million to get started on another submarine-based missile, the SLCM (Submarine-Launched Cruise Missile). **1975** *Bull. Atomic Sci.* XXXI. 13 *SLCM*, submarine-launched cruise missile. **1979** *Observer* 25 Nov. 34/1 *Cruise Missile*... Can be ground-launched (GLCMs, known as Glickums)..or launched from submarines (SLCMs). **1958** *Jrnl. Clin. Invest.* XXXVII. 876/1 The serum of patients with systemic lupus erythematosus (SLE) has been shown to contain factor(s) with a special affinity for nucleohistone (NH). **1978** *Jrnl. R. Soc. Med.* LXXI. 149 This is..the first case in which SLE has been reported in a patient with Hashimoto's thyroiditis and pernicious anaemia. **1951** *Times Educ. Suppl.* 8 June 466/1 (Advt.), Wanted for January, 1952, Senior English Mistress. The work includes G.C.E. at O., A., and S. levels. **1973** *Guardian* 28 June 13/3 Jonathan Mestel is 16 and has just finished his A and S level maths and physics exams. **1975** *Glasgow Herald* 23 Dec. 4/2 Mr Sillars said the SLP did not believe oil was a Scottish resource, but something to be used for the benefit of the entire United Kingdom. **1976** *Times* 23 Jan. 14/3 The new threat which the SLP presents..is untimely. **1964** *Colour Photogr.* Mar.–Apr. 68/3 With one manufacturer recently introducing a half-frame SLR, I wondered if this type of instrument would replace its larger brother. **1971** *Amateur Photographer* 13 Jan. 80/3 (Advt.), Nikkorex F, f2 Nikkor, w/meter, S.L.R... £69. **1977** J. Hedgecoe *Photographer's Handbk.* 14 Because of the SLR's worldwide popularity the newest and most advanced electronic and optical technology tends to be designed to suit this camera before the others. **1890** Webster 1923/2 *S.M.*,.. sergeant major. **1953** J. Masters *Lotus & Wind* v. 70 It wouldn't affect his chances of promotion to S.M. **1973** J. Wood *North Beat* xiii. 163 He had been the first company S.M. to earn a Bar to the decoration in the division. **1764** A. Williams *Universal Psalmodist* (ed. 2) 57 [Tune] Southwell. Psalm 90th Dr W. S.M. **1832** J. Jowett *Man. Parochial Psalmody* 12 St. Bride's. S.M. **1909** W. H. Frere in *Hymns Anc. & Mod.* p. lvi/2 The whole musical balance was now altered [by the influence of T. Ravenscroft's *Psalmes* of 1621]: the D.C.M. and P.M. tunes had hitherto formed the bulk of the collection, with a few C.M. and S.M. tunes to supplement them. **1909** J. R. Ware *Passing Eng.* 212/2 S.M. (*Theatrical*), stage manager. **1952** Granville *Dict. Theatr. Terms* 172 When artistes have settled into their parts, the S.M. (as he is known) may hand over the book to his assistant. **1972** V. C. Clinton-Baddeley *To study Long Silence* ii. viii. 82, I was still in the theatre when the S.M. found him. **1909** *Army & Navy Gaz.* 27 Mar. 297/3 (*heading*) S.M.L.E. Rifle. **1958** J. A. Barlow *Elem. Rifle Shooting* (ed. 5) p. xii, The S.M.L.E...will shortly be replaced by a self-loading rifle. **1914** *Autocar* 2 May 817/1 The R.A.C., the A.A. and M.U., and the S.M.M.T. **1958** *Economist* 1 Nov. 435/2 If it were desired to try to stop the rush at some point there is no salient that looks capable of being held and no one body that could do it—not the Finance Houses' Association, not the Industrial Bankers, not the SMMT nor the Hire Purchase Trade Association. **1978** *Dumfries & Galloway Standard* 21 Oct. 7/6 Although organising international motor shows is but one function of the SMMT, it is best known for this role. **1950** *Jrnl. Soc. Motion Pict. & Television Engin.* Mar. 389 SMPTE Officers and Committees..are published annually in the April issue of the Journal. **1959** W. S. Sharps *Dict. Cinematogr.* 11. 129/2 In Britain, the *British Kinematograph Society* was created originally as the British branch of the S.M.P.T.E. **1975** G. J. King *Audio Handbk.* viii. 191 The l.f. bands adhere to the SMPTE (Society of Motion Picture and Television Engineers) requirements for IMD analysis. **1960** *Atlanta Daily World* 18 Oct. 1/3 There was no announcement of formal action on SNCC's proposed march on the polls on election day. **1961** *Commonweal* 15 Dec. 311/1 This fall the S.N.C.C. has been concentrating on recruitment on white campuses. **1971** J. Bishop *Days of M. Luther King* iv. 369 The Student Nonviolent Coordinating Committee had been in that part of Selma for eighteen months... SNCC was in Marion too. **1949** *Progress French Nat. Railways Oct. 1948* 28 (*colophon*) S.N.C.F. 1949. **1963** *Times* 23 May 13/6 French Railways (SNCF) most closely resemble B.R. in size. **1976** A. White *Long Silence* vi. 46 The S.N.C.F. did not permit the express trains to stop at Colauvin. **1944** *Jrnl. Dairy Res.* XIII. 53 Milk has been deteriorating in quality (s.n.f. content) during the last two or three years. *Ibid.*, This extra labour would detect adulterated samples which yet had over 8·5% s.n.f. **1960** *Farmer & Stockbreeder* 16 Feb. 66/3 A Milk Marketing Board survey ..had shown an average of 3·7 per cent butter-fat and 8·75 s.n.f. for the breed. **1976** *Burnham-on-Sea Gaz.* 20 Apr. (Advt.), Butterfats 4%. S.N.F. 8·83%. Total 12·83%. The cows have not been prepared for sale in any way. **1972** E. N. Tiratsoo *Natural Gas* (ed. 2) i. 15 The incipient shortage of natural gas..led to the adoption of the CRG process..as the basis of what is planned to be the world's largest reforming plant producing SNG ('substitute natural gas'). *Ibid.* viii. 149 Simulated natural gas (SNG)..has been extensively used as an intermediate fuel to facilitate the changeover of industrial plants from manufactured town gas to full-scale natural gas supply. **1974** *Natural Gas* (Shell Internat. Petroleum Co.) 11 Apart from LNG, which is natural gas cooled to the liquid state, there are three main possible supplementary sources of supply, namely low-calorific-value gas from coal, synthetic natural gas (SNG) from oil or coal, and methanol derived from natural gas. **1977** K. A. D. Inglis in P. A. Stockil *Our Industry Petroleum* (Brit. Petroleum Co.) (ed. 5) 26 As supplies of natural gas run short..systems for the manufacture of substitute (or synthetic) natural gas (SNG) are being developed. **1914** A. B. Milne in *Publ. Navy Rec. Soc.* (1970) CXV. 146 Have requested S.N.O., Gibraltar, to keep special lookout for *Strassburg*. **1955** C. S. Forester *Good Shepherd* ii. 264 SNO meant senior naval officer in accordance with British usage, not one of those odd collections of letters like DSO or MBE which merely meant a decoration. **1970** A. J. Marder *From Dreadnought to Scapa Flow* V. i. ii. 17 The S.N.O. on the spot..would not allow him to have a go at the *Goeben* as soon as it was known that she was aground. **1935** *Glasgow Herald Index 1934* 231/1 Compton

Mackenzie addresses first S.N.P. mtg. in Edin., 21 Ap. **1977** M. WALKER *National Front* viii. 215 It may have been, as the SNP posters said 'Scotland's Oil' but a goodly portion of it had already been used by British Governments to guarantee foreign loans. **1970** BAHCALL & ULRICH in *Astrophysical Jrnl.* CLX. L58 We have expressed the counting rate in solar-neutrino units: 1 SNU ≡ 10^{-36} capture per target atom per second. **1972** *Ann. Rev. Astron. & Astrophysics* X. 28 The best present estimates suggest..that the ultimate sensitivity of the current 10^5-gallon experiment will be set by the cosmic-ray background at $\sim$0·4 SNU. **1976** J. KLECZEK *Universe* ii. 78 It is usual to specify the rate of the neutrino capture reactions..in terms of so-called solar neutrino units (SNU or 'snew') which are such that 1 SNU corresponds to 10^{-36} captures per target Cl atom per second. **1844** T. E. MAY *Treat. Parliament* xii. 215 A division is effected in the lords by the not-contents remaining within the bar, and the contents going below the bar. [note] Lords' S.O. No. 22. **1929** G. F. M. CAMPION *Introd. Procedure House of Commons* iv. 136 S.O. No. 11 of 1888 (the so-called 'Ten Minutes Rule'). **1976** in R. Crossman *Diaries* II. 75 It was only when the S.O. was redrafted in 1967 that M.P.s could make full use of its possibilities. **1918** H. V. O'BRIEN *Wine, Women & War* (1926) 286 What an S.O.B. that fellow is! **1930** E. POUND *XXX Cantos* x. 45 That monstrous swollen, swelling s.o.b. Papa Pio Secundo. **1934** C. STEAD *Seven Poor Men of Sydney* iv. 120 That s.o.b. Montagu got me the job 'ere, you know. **1955** AUDEN *Shield of Achilles* iii. 79 And all poor s-o-b's who never Do anything properly. **1962** L. DEIGHTON *Ipcress File* xxxii. 211 Just a simple case of a couple of well-informed S.O.B.s. **1975** 'E. LATHEN' *By Hook or by Crook* xvi. 154 A stubborn SOB who doesn't give a damn. **1948** *Jrnl. R. United Service Inst.* XCIII. 212 An S.O.E. base was established alongside General Eisenhower's Headquarters in Algiers from the outset, primarily for work into France. **1968** D. LAMPE *Last Ditch* xi. 113 SOE, the most special of the Special Forces, had just been set up under the cover of the Ministry of Economic Warfare. **1978** G. GREENE *Human Factor* III. i. 104 Over his head were a retired businessman who had once been connected with the rival wartime service SOE, and a retired general who had fought in the Western Desert. **1905** W. S. CHURCHILL *Let.* 28 Oct. in R. S. Churchill *Winston S. Churchill* (1969) II. Compan. I. 402 Of course the S of S must always control the Viceroy. **1922** G. BELL *Let.* 4 Dec. (1927) II. xxii. 658, I sent you by post the yearly report to the S. of S., a very silly sort of Xmas present. **1958** L. DURRELL *Mountolive* iv. 92 My dear chap..if you propose to make an issue of it with the S. of S. I can't help it. **1917** R. LORD *Captain Boyd's Battery A.E.F.* (1920) ii. 24 S.O.L.—Payroll abbreviation for Soldier, adapted to mean Soldier Out 'a Luck or Certainly Out 'a Luck, according to the way you spell it. Applicable to everything from death to being late for mess. **1921** J. DOS PASSOS *Three Soldiers* II. iii. 99 'We shall have to put him down A.W.O.L. You know what that means?'.. 'I guess he's S.O.L.'; this from someone behind Fuselli. **1946** B. C. BOWKER *Out of Uniform* iii. 48 As the phrase went, they were 'SOL' ('surely' out of luck). **1942** *Yank* 2 Sept. 14/2 Our regimental SOP in reference to any MP reports on enlisted men. **1961** B. FERGUSSON *Watery Maze* x. 248 The Americans had evolved what they call a Standard Operating Procedure, or S.O.P., which was thoroughly unsatisfactory. **1980** S. KING *Firestarter* 335 There will be two Shop men along, partly to act as stewards and partly to keep an eye on you. SOP, you know. **1911** s.p. [see *JOB *sb.*[2] 4 e]. **1928** E. WALLACE *More Educ. Evans* ix. 201 You backed that horse s.p. with every unfortunate bookmaker in England. **1974** G. F. NEWMAN *Price* ii. 60 What's the full SP, Trevor? **1937** *Q. Rep. Soc. Protection Anc. Buildings* I. I. 4 From that moment almost it can be said that the S.P.A.B. was born. **1943** J. LEES-MILNE *Ancestral Voices* (1975) 234 At an S.P.A.B. meeting I found a small attendance considering a matter of the first importance, whether or not to protest in the press against the night bombing of historic German cities. **1978** *Jrnl. R. Soc. Arts* CXXVI. 477/1 The Canterbury Cloisters have been discussed by the SPAB recently as being a *bad* example of restoration. **1861** *Sat. Rev.* 23 Nov. 535/2 Strong in S.P.G. and S.P.C.K. **1892** C. M. YONGE *Old Woman's Outlook* x. 240 A charming book of my childhood, which I rather believe belonged to the S.P.C.K. **1939** J. CARY *Mr. Johnson* 10 Johnson's idea of a civilized marriage, founded on..a few novels approved by the S.P.C.K., is a compound of romantic sentiment and embroidered underclothes. **1969** *Listener* 24 Apr. 586/2 Judas looking for all the world like an SPCK Jesus, all gently waving locks and sad benevolence. **1921** *Labour Monthly* Oct. 344 We may say, without presumption, that the S.P.D. (German Social-Democratic Party) is the party which deserves above all others the title of Republican Party. **1947** *Partisan Rev.* Mar.–Apr. 143 The arduous theorists of the SPD were steeped in German pedantry. **1976** T. ALLBEURY *Only Good German* ix. 58 Both the SPD and the CDU had offered him party seats in the Bundestat. **1913** R. BRIDGES *(title)* S.P.E. [manifesto of the Society for Pure English]. **1919** —— *Let.* 22 June (1940) 147 Is there any reason for delay about the S.P.E. **1923** J. M. MURRY *Pencillings* 268 Such is the appearance—neat, decorous, small, discreet—of an S.P.E. tract. **1948** *S.P.E. Tract* LXVI. 177 When I addressed myself to the honourable, melancholy task of writing the obsequy of S.P.E., I revived fond memories by turning over my file. **1839** C. FOX *Jrnl.* 22 Aug. (1883) v. 53 Mary Coleridge..read a letter from Macaulay describing the state of feeling into which one of Samuel Wilberforce's sermons had thrown him, who is now on a tour westward for the S.P.G. **1854** V. LUSH *Jrnl.* 16 Feb. (1971) 153 We settled to write to the Bishop and request him in conjunction with the Revd Mr Venn and Revd Mr Hawkins, secretaries of C.M.S. and S.P.G.—to select a master for us. **1565** J. JEWEL *Replie M. Hardinges Answeare* 294 Beda..expounded these foure solemne letters *S.P.Q.R.* in this wise. *Stultus populus quærit Romam. Foolishe Folke Flee to Rome.* **1621** I. SYLVESTER *Lacrymæ Lacrymarum* in *Du Bartas, His Diuine Weekes*, This loss (alas!) which unto All belongs!.. To all the world; except S.P.Q.R. **1881** *N. & Q.* 8 Jan. 34/2 S.P.Q.R. .. The following interpretation of these letters may amuse your readers. They form part of the decoration of the Adam ceiling of the Court Room of the Bank of England, and on a remark by a visitor that they seemed very incongruous in such a place, 'Not at all,' said one of my colleagues; 'they stand for small profits and quick returns.' **1927** E. J. P. BENN *Trade* iii. 52 Our grandfathers used to talk of small profits and quick returns. 'S.P.Q.R.', which most schoolboys of my time imagined had something to do with the early Romans, was a very favourite shop sign. **1977** L. MEYNELL *Hooky gets Wooden Spoon* xiv. 180 'So far he seems to have steered clear of anything big.' 'Wise man. S.P.Q.R. Small profits quick returns.' **1978** P. FINNEY *Crow Goddess* 112 'What does that say?' he asked, pointing at the label. 'S.P.Q.R.—the Senate and People of Rome.' **1883** *Proc Soc. Psychical Res.* p. i, The Council of the S.P.R. have from time to time received letters from Members and Associates. **1926** A. CONAN DOYLE *Hist. Spiritualism* I. viii. 185 No serious attempt of any sort, up to the formation of the S.P.R., was made to understand or explain a matter which was engaging the attention of millions of minds. **1937** A. HUXLEY *Let.* 17 Feb. (1969) 415 Broad's presidential address to the SPR is interesting in this context. **1968** M. COLLIS *Somerville & Ross* xiv. 157 Arthur Balfour, who for a time was President of the S.P.R. **1971** B. BAUER et al. in *Jrnl. Audio Engin. Soc.* XIX. 639/1 We..'encode' (combine) the four channels into two by using a special 'matrix', or linear additive circuit.., which we called the SQ (for stereophonic-quadraphonic) matrix encoder. **1973** *Official Gaz.* (U.S. Patent Office) 20 Nov. TM 138/2 Columbia Broadcasting System, Inc., New York, N.Y. Filed Dec. 6, 1971... The mark represents the stylized lettering 'SQ'. For pre-recorded phonograph records, and pre-recorded tapes... First use June 10, 1971. **1976** *Listener* 23 Dec. 846/1 Discs in compatible quadraphonic/stereo pressings utilising the SQ system. **1919** *Round Table* IX. 286 The British Labour Party is described as 'worse than the right S.R.'s'. **1967** *Soviet Stud.* XVIII. 449 The SR's were able to obtain absolute majorities even in Petrograd and Moscow. **1974** T. P. WHITNEY tr. *Solzhenitsyn's Gulag Archipel.* I. I. ii. 30 The Left SR's had been cleverer and had gone on pretending longer that they were allies of the one and only consistent party of the proletariat. **1923** *Southern Railway Mag.* Sept. p. xvi (Advt.), For All Southern Railway Staff ..Halden Estates Co., Ltd. (S.R. Proposition). **1959** *Chambers's Encycl.* XI. 490/1 Subsequently S.R. lines west of Exeter were transferred to the Western region. **1967** J. JOYCE *Story Passenger Transport in Britain* vii. 186 Nationalisation came in 1948 when the 'Big Four'—the LMS, LNER, GWR and SR..became the all-embracing 'British Railways'. **1908** *Army & Navy Gaz.* 26 Dec. 1241/3 The latter officer joins the 3rd (S.R.) Batn. **1919** W. S. CHURCHILL in M. Gilbert *Winston S. Churchill* (1977) IV. Compan. I. 466 The Regular Army and such SR & TF officers and men as must be retained. **1923** KIPLING *Irish Guards in Gt. War* I. 44 Major Webber, 'S.R.' (this is the first time that the Diary makes mention of the Special Reserve), arrived the day before. **1963** *Recommendations for Letter Symbols, Signs & Abbreviations* (*B.S.I.*) VI. 26 Steradian... sr. **1977** J. NARLIKAR *Struct. Universe* vii. 223 The survey is over 3 sr..in the sky. **1935** C. L. HULL in *Psychol. Rev.* XLII. 502 A trace conditioned reaction in an S → R relationship. **1948** E. R. HILGARD *Theories of Learning* xii. 349 Woodworth gradually shifted from his *S-R* motto. **1967** [see *neo-behaviourism* s.v. *NEO- 1 a]. **1977** *Dædalus* Fall 120 When Chomsky demonstrated that the simple application of S-R learning theory to chained responses is inadequate in principle as an account of grammar, he could not be ignored. **1971** *Nature* 23 Apr. 531/1 While investigating the interaction between antigen-antibody-complement complexes and lymphoid cells, we have noticed that sheep red blood cells (SRBC) adhered to a surprisingly large proportion of human peripheral blood lymphocytes forming clusters ('rosettes'). **1977** *Lancet* 19 Feb. 394/2 These eight dilutions and two control tubes..were tested for the formation of rosettes between human lymphocytes and S.R.B.C. **1946** *Nursing Times* 11 May p. ix/1 Mental Ward Sisters..required, S.R.M.N., or holding R.M.P.A. Certificate. **1965** *Nursing Mirror & Midwives' Jrnl.* 2 Apr. (Suppl.) 18/1 (Advt.), Applicants must be S.R.N., S.R.M.N. **1922** *Ibid.* 1 July 261/1 The Scottish General Nursing Council..'unanimously adopted' the resolution as to the undermentioned initials.. General Trained..[England] S.R.N...[Scotland] R.G.N. **1926** *Ibid.* 25 Dec. p. x/3 (Advt.), General, S.R.N., fever, and mental nurses Wanted for private work. **1974** R. INGHAM *Yoris* ii. 5 She was wearing her stiff white nurse's uniform with..the small brooch on her left breast bearing the initials SRN. **1957** M. B. HOAGLAND et al. in *Biochim. & Biophys. Acta* XXIV. 216 This is apparently a low molecular weight RNA (S-RNA) with different metabolic properties from the high molecular weight RNA of the ribonucleoprotein of the microsomes. **1963** F. H. C. CRICK in *Progr. in Nucleic Acid Res.* I. 196 Holley and his collaborators fractionated yeast sRNA by countercurrent distribution. **1971** D. J. COVE *Genetics* x. 146 If the sRNAs act as adaptor molecules, recognising the codon of the amino acid they carry, then it is to be expected that they will have somewhere in their sequence, three adjacent bases which are complementary to that codon, and able therefore to specifically hydrogen bond to it. In all the sRNAs whose sequence has been analysed, this has been found to be true. **1941** SRO [see *PALSY *sb.*[2]]. **1966** *Social Work* Oct. 32/1 The clustering of unattached individuals, many of whom are economically dependent and chronically ill, in licensed SRO buildings is a recognizable pattern. **1977** *New Yorker* 27 June 85/3 Queens has only nine of New York's several hundred S.R.O. buildings (the letters stand for 'single-room occupancy', and the tenants..are often present or former drug addicts). **1890** *Texas Siftings* 15 Nov. 13/1 At the Grand Opera House Bobby Gaylor, in the Irish Arab, called out the S.R.O. sign. **1903** 'O. HENRY' in *McClure's Mag.* July 333/1 After one reading of the Declaration of Independence in New York I've known the S.R.O. sign to be hung out at all the hospitals and police stations. **1970** *Islander* (Victoria, B.C.) 5 Apr. 16/2 The 1970 edition [of an annual concert], held on March 3,..was an SRO success. **1939** SRS [see *slow-reacting substance* s.v. *SLOW *adv.* 2 a]. **1955** W. E. BROCKLEHURST in *Jrnl. Physiol.* CXXVIII. 1 P The occurrence of a slow-reacting substance together with histamine, in the perfusate coming from the isolated lung of a guinea-pig during anaphylactic shock, has been reported previously. .. The substance has been provisionally named 'SRS-A' (slow-reacting substance in anaphylaxis) to differentiate it from the considerable number of ill-defined gut-contracting substances to which the term 'SRS' has been applied. **1958** *Pharmacol. Rev.* X. 422 When egg yolk is incubated with cobra venom a slow reacting substance (SRS-C) is formed. **1964** W. G. SMITH *Allergy & Tissue Metabolism* i. 14 Evidence for the existence of chemical mediators of anaphylaxis other than histamine has existed since 1940. Recent work on one of these, the slow reacting substance of anaphylaxis (SRS-A), led to the discovery that the hypersensitive state exerts a profound influence on tissue metabolism. **1979** *Nature* 6 Sept. 14/2 SRS has now been identified as a novel cysteinyl derivative of arachidonic acid. **1932** H. NICOLSON *Diary* 5 Jan. (1966) 105 The former would correspond to the S.S. or *Schutzstaffel* organisation of the Nazis. **1938** *Encycl. Brit. Bk. of Year* 125/1 They are known as the 'SS'..or Elite Hitler Protective Guard, now under the command of Heinrich Himmler. **1945** *Daily Mirror* 8 May 3/2 S.S. men went through the streets driving people out of their homes. **1958** *New Statesman* 19 Apr. 505/2 The nature of his work compelled him to form intimate relationships with members of two rival German organisations, the *Abwehr*, or Counter-Intelligence, and the SS. **1968** *Listener* 19 Sept. 359/1, I myself had only one sound-camera, and just before the opening of the Games a squad of SS men tried to take it away from me by force. **1975** W. CRAIG *Strasbourg Legacy* i. 4 A short, red-faced officer, resplendent in his black SS uniform, read from a memorandum. **1933** C. MACKENZIE *Water on Brain* xviii. 276 Katzenschlosser, the American S.S. man. **1969** *Sun* 12 Feb. 5/5 An advance party of 60 State Department men arrived from Washington on Monday. Probably 20 of them were SS men. (They do actually call them that in the U.S.). **1979** *Maclean's Mag.* 9 Apr. 29/1 The Trudeau government was pressuring the SS for better intelligence..about suspected FLQ cells in Quebec. **1963** F. D. FAWCETT *Cycl. Init. & Abbrev.* 140/1 *SS*,.. Social Security. **1973** *Freedom* 21 July 5/2 Hardly any squatter draws SS and parasites on society. **1975** *New Society* 20 Nov. 412/3 Tez thinks he'll be a rock star.. tomorrow. Meanwhile he's having trouble getting it together and lives off the SS. **1980** L. CODY *Dupe* xxiii. 168 The father was knocked off in a pub bombing..and.. the family's been on the SS ever since. **1868** *Times* 1 July 2/2 (Advt.), To sail 9th of July, the Liverpool and Australian Navigation Company's s.s. *Great Britain*. **1870** *Weekly Standard* (Buenos Aires) 12 Jan. 7/5 Departures. Per ss. Flamsteed on the 9th Jan. **1876** W. S. LINDSAY *Hist. Merchant Shipping* IV. xv. 558 *(caption)* S.S. 'Victoria'. **1907** *Shipping World* 16 Jan. 111 (Advt.), S.S. 'Lusitania' is being fitted with Passenger Lifts. **1955** *Times* 5 July 11/3 Things have gone very wrong indeed when British vessels suffer the treatment received by the ss. Anshun. **1956** SSB [see PEP s.v. *P II]. **1976** *S9* (N.Y.) May/June 5/2 If, however, you don't want to go for ssb, then by all means buy the best radio you can find with the largest number of features. **1969** *New Acronyms & Initialisms* (Gale Research Co.) 389 SSBN, Fleet Ballistic Missile Submarine (Nuclear powered). **1973** *Washington Post* 13 Jan. A23/3 Gormley's proposals..stem from his realization that SSBN's are the only survivable, non-provocative, anti-proliferative nuclear deterrent forces, existing or planned. **1961** *Forward Trends* V. IV. 47 The Guild Art Exhibition was in two main parts. All of it, naturally, dealing with the use of art with S.S.N., E.S.N., and backward children. **1967** *Punch* 19 Apr. 557/1 Down below the plimsoll line of an IQ of fifty are the erstwhile imbeciles and idiots, now classed as SSN—severely subnormal. **1972** *Observer* 20 Aug. 7/8 A sixth of the children in the SSN (severely sub-normal) department of this school are boys like these. **1968** *Neurology* XVIII. II. 48/2 Our data suggest that SSPE is caused by the measles virus, or a virus immunologically indistinguishable from the measles virus. **1974** SSPE [see *panencephalitis* s.v. *PAN- 2]. **1962** *Aeroplane* 21 June 6/3 Secondary surveillance radar (SSR), the so-called answer to the air traffic controller's prayer, does not appear to be so near, or as technically perfect, as one is led to believe. **1977** *R.A.F. News* 22 June–5 July 9 (Advt.), Experience is required of approach and long range surveillance equipment plus SSR, HF, VHF and UHF radio equipments. **1926** *Encycl. Brit.* III. 429 The population of the Union of Socialist Soviet Republics and its principal parts was, in 1924... Ukraine S.S.R... 27,700,000. **1947** *Whitaker's Almanack* 972/1 Uzbekistan comprises the former feudal states of Bokhara and Khiva and the Kara Kalpak S.S.R. **1977** R. PERRY *Dead End* vi. 77 He elected to resume his studies in the Turkmen SSR. **1967** *Economist* 11 Feb. 501/1 Under the direction of Dr Michael Young, the SSRC has begun to deliver the goods. **1975** M. BRADBURY *History Man* ii. 20 He was now..a research student, with an SSRC grant. **1977** *Dædalus* Summer 62 The major funding agencies, the NSF, NIMH, SSRC, Ford Foundation, etc., should be approached to provide the basis for a series of 'summit' meetings among the leaders of the various modes of 'anthropologizing'. **1961** *Fortune* June 161/1 Now in the preliminary design stage is the supersonic transport, or SST. **1969** *Listener* 6 Mar. 313/2 Russia is talking about getting her SST into passenger use before the end of 1970. **1977** *New Yorker* 27 June 86/3 The Concorde's sponsors believe that if the plane doesn't get New York landing rights the SST enterprise will end in financial disaster. **1932** *N. & Q.* 16 July 45/2 He published seven books of airs, of which the above is the sixth, at various dates between 1604 and 1638 (S.T.C. 7460–67). **1952** J. CARTER *ABC for Bk.-Collectors* 164 STC, a landmark in enumerative bibliography and one of the most frequently quoted of reference books, has recently been reprinted. **1962** DAVIS & WRENN *Eng. & Medieval Stud.* 270 The edition is attributed to 1550 in *S.T.C.* under no. 4817. **1958** *New Scientist* 4 Dec. 1421/1 In planning a scheme for STD it is very desirable that the dialling procedure should be simple and easy to understand. **1963** *Engineering* 25 Jan. 176 STD is not limited to the United Kingdom—it exists on both the Continent and America. **1973** J. WAINWRIGHT *Pride of Pigs*

169 She..picked up the receiver, waited for the S.T.D. pips to stop, said 'Hello?' **1977** P. STREVENS *New Orientations Teaching Eng.* viii. 105 STD code, oh-three-one. **1956** *Aeronaut. Engin. Rev.* Mar. 48 This type, or types, of airplane can..be called Short Take-Off and Landing, or STOL, airplanes. **1959** *Times Rev. Industry* July 80/1 Any s.t.o.l. aircraft can use quite short airstrips. **1974** *Sci. Amer.* Mar. 83/3 If STOL and VTOL aircraft, including helicopters, become accepted as a major means of intercity transport, traffic density will increase substantially. **1975** E. HILLARY *Nothing venture, Nothing Win* xvi. 260 The answer was to build an airfield and use STOL. **1953** BATHAM & THORPE *To All who are interested in Democracy* 14 The National Union of Teachers elects its officers and executive by the S.T.V. **1974** *Times* 12 Mar. 15/4 This is the single transferable vote (STV). Its effect is to ensure that every vote is of equal value, and that nearly every voter has an MP of his choice. **1955** B. HIGMAN *Appl. Group-Theoretic & Matrix Methods* xii. 175 (*table*) Special unitary [matrix group] *SU*(*n*). **1967** G. G. HALL *Appl. Group Theory* vi. 84 *SU*(*n*). The special unitary group is the subgroup of *U*(*n*) whose matrices have a determinant of unity. **1977** *Nature* 4 Aug. 469/1 It provides a classification of a totally different nature to the canonical isospin, strangeness (SU(2) and SU(3)), beloved of group theorists which classifies objects of the same spin. **1956** R. N. HULL et al. in *Amer. Jrnl. Hygiene* LXIII. 205/1 The agents isolated will be referred to as 'Simian viruses' (S.V.) until such time as a definite association with some other host or identification can be established. *Ibid.* 214/1 A large number of production samples has not been studied for S.V. contamination but of those that have been assayed a few have been found to contain S.V.$_2$ only. **1957** *Ann. N.Y. Acad. Sci.* LXVII. 414 (*caption*) Agents received from other laboratories and temporarily classified as SV's. **1967**, etc. [see *POLYOMA]. **1970** *New Scientist* 29 Jan. 194/1, SV40 occurred as a contaminant in many of the earlier batches of polio vaccine.., but has had no discernible effect on Man. **1977** *Time* 18 Apr. 48/2 He hoped to insert a monkey virus, SV40, into *E. coli.* **1864** *N. & Q.* 12 Mar. 211/2 See Richardson *On the Study of Words*, and *Dict.*, s.vv. 'Lord', 'Lady'. **1962** *Ibid.* Aug. 304/2 *Lotus-eating* (O.E.D. s.v. *Lotus-eater*). **1976** *Classical Q.* XXVI. 310 For this incorrect form of the name of the elder Suetonius, cf. *OCD* s.v. Suetonius. **1981** *Times Lit. Suppl.* 2 Jan. 6/2 One receives no help if one tries to check it sv, 'music'. **1973** *Vet. Rec.* 3 Mar. 234/1 On occasion some pigs have shown no abnormal behaviour although they had widespread lesions of SVD. **1975** G. P. WEST *Black's Vet. Dict.* (ed. 11) 747/1 SVD has been transmitted to laboratory workers. **1980** *Times* 15 Sept. 14/4 SVD cannot be distinguished from foot-and-mouth disease (FMD) on the farm. [**1917** *Harrod's Gen. Catal.* 1385/2 S. Wm's... Wm's... O.S. Wm's.] **1926–7** *Army & Navy Stores Catal.* 674/3 White drill coat... Sizes S.W., W. and O.S. **1974** *Harrods Xmas Catal.* 7 Sophisticated wrap... SW, W, or WX. **1925** FRASER & GIBBONS *Soldier & Sailor Words* 274 *SWAK*, from the initials S.W.A.K.—i.e., Sealed with a Kiss. A common superscription on the envelopes of letters to sweethearts from sailors and soldiers. **1948** PARTRIDGE *Dict. Forces' Slang* 185 *S.W.A.K.* was the commonest (Sealed With a Kiss), with the variant *S.W.A.L.K.*, the *L* in this case standing for 'Loving'. **1952** E. WAUGH *Men at Arms* III. viii. 312 The old soldiers wrote SWALK on the envelope, meaning 'sealed with a loving kiss'. **1971** R. QUEST *Death of Sinner* xvi. 154 They [*sc.* the letters] might represent a sentence like S.W.A.K... Girls at school sometimes wrote it on the backs of envelopes. It means 'sealed with a kiss'. **1973** 'D. HALLIDAY' *Dolly & Starry Bird* xi. 164, I posted him a long letter with SWALK on it to make him laugh. **1968** *Time* 19 July 18/3 Two hundred marksmen have been assigned to a squad named S.W.A.T. (Special Weapons and Tactics), designed to pick off snipers and to eliminate..the need for indiscriminate police gunfire. **1979** *Tucson* (Arizona) *Citizen* 28 Apr. 1A/1 Police said a SWAT team bombarded the vehicle with tear gas and gun blasts. **1911** *Motor Manual* (ed. 13) ii. 50 The 'secondary' winding, composed of many turns of fine wire (42 or 44 s.w.g.). **1953** *Electronic Engin.* XXV. 66, 1200 turns 36 S.W.G. enamelled copper. *a* **1977** *Harrison Mayer Ltd. Catal.* 50/1 The working ends are fabricated from 15swg stainless steel which will not rust. **1938** *Socialist Appeal* 22 Jan. 2/4 The S.W.P. will advocate the continuance of the class struggle. **1943** *Fourth International* Aug. 234/1 The new movement of the masses was developing outside the SWP. **1977** *Times* 8 Sept. 12/3 In true Marxist fashion, the SWP looks forward to the withering away of the state. **1961** *Amateur Radio Handbk.* (ed. 3) xiii. 358 The ratio of maximum to minimum voltage at the crest and trough of the standing wave, is called the voltage standing wave ratio (v.s.w.r., often abbreviated to s.w.r.). **1976** *S9* (N.Y.) Feb. 62/2 The column will also contain useful information about adjusting antennas, dope about SWR (standing-wave-radio) measurements, and all that good stuff.

b. S.A., South Africa(n), South America(n), South Australia(n); S.A.P., Sap, South African Party; S.E., S.W., also used to designate a London postal district.

1864 *N. & Q.* 6 Feb. 117/1 Cape Town, S.A. **1891** W. S. CHURCHILL *Let.* 27 Sept. in R. S. Churchill *Winston S. Churchill* (1967) I. Compan. I. v. 270 Mama has got a big map of S.A. on which she follows your route. **1933** J. CARY *Amer. Visitor* iv. 39 We were in S.A. together—the yeomanry. **1967** L. MEYNELL *Mauve Front Door* xv. 214 A bottle of S.A. sherry. **1890** WEBSTER, *S.A.*, South America. **1930** E. POUND *XXX Cantos* xii. 55 And the bust-up of Brazilian securities (S.A. securities). **1864** *South Austral. Advertiser* 17 Oct. 2/4 Share List... S.A. Insurance... S.A. Gas. **1944** *Living off Land* iv. 82 The S.A. family..could have been saved had they carried sufficient drinking water. **1971** *Sunday Australian* 8 Aug. 11/2 Senator Hannaford of SA suffered a heart attack. **1920** S. BLACK *Dorp* 9 The scornful word 'Sappers', which he knew to be a term of contempt applied by members of Hertzog's Party (the Nationalists) to all those of the Botha-Smuts element or 'SAP'. **1933** J. C. SMUTS *Let.* 7 Oct. in *Sel. Smuts Papers* (1973) V. 567 It may be a case of Sap predominance, with a Nat prime minister with a small following of his own. **1935** *Ann. Reg. 1934* I. 132 Around him rallied those S.A.P. men who vowed with him that a surrender of principles was too heavy a price to pay. **1972** *Sunday Times* (Johannesburg) 3 Sept. 2 Nats, Progs, Saps all climb in to make mischief. **1977** *Jrnl. Commonwealth & Compar. Politics* XV. 7 The networks of rural and provincial notables originally fused together by the South African Party (SAP) gave it majorities in the Cape, Transvaal, and Orange Free State. **1857** *Punch* 7 Feb. 51/2 Rowland Hill has just divided London's waste of brick by ten... Pimlico is in S.W., Brompton fast, and Chelsea mild. *Ibid.*, Yonder dismal hole S.E., Southwark. **1885** *List of Subscribers, Classified* (United Telephone Co.) (ed. 6) 62 Atkinson & Co, Westminster Bridge Road, S.E. **1934** DYLAN THOMAS *Let.* Dec. (1966) 147, 5 Redcliffe Street, London, S.W.10... Dear Bert. **1968** *Listener* 19 Dec. 810/2 In between the bombing raids, the doodle-bugs and the V2s they'd improvised a splendid life in SE20.

d. In *Biol.* S or *S* (also s) = Svedberg unit: used after a number to denote the (often characteristic) sedimentation coefficient of a subcellular body.

1942 [see *SVEDBERG]. **1942** W. B. BRIDGMAN in *Jrnl. Amer. Chem. Soc.* LXIV. 2350/2 The average values of s_{20} ..varied from 60 to 70 *S* (one Svedberg unit, $S_1 = 1 \times 10^{-13}$ c.g.s. units). **1944** *Jrnl. Exper. Med.* LXXIX. 310 Its sedimentation constant of approximately 800 S is higher than either of those associated with A virus. **1977** M. W. BERNS *Cells* iv. 71 In the eukaryotic organism, it appears that 18s and 28s cytoplasmic ribosomal RNAs are produced from a larger 45s ribsomal RNA molecule that is cleaved in a stepwise sequence that produces several intermediate size RNA molecules. **1978** *Nature* 5 Oct. 461/1 Both reconstituted 30S and reconstituted 50S particles containing mutant 16S and (23+5S) RNA, respectively, could form 70S couples with their complementary native subunits only in the presence of higher Mg^{2+} concentration.

II. Symbolic uses. **5.** *s* or *S* (*Physics* and *Chem.*) = sharp: orig. used to designate one of the four main series of lines in atomic spectra, but now more frequently applied to electronic orbitals, states, etc., possessing zero angular momentum and total symmetry.

1890 J. R. RYDBERG in *Phil. Mag.* XXIX. 335 Mg (S_2) [denotes] the (whole) second sharp series of Mg. **1922** A. D. UDDEN tr. *Bohr's Theory of Spectra* III. iii. 97 He [*sc.* Schrödinger] assumes that the 'outer' electron in the states corresponding to the *S* terms—in contrast to those corresponding to the *P* and *D* terms—penetrates partly into the region of the orbits of the inner electrons during the course of its revolution. **1926**, etc. [see *L 6* b]. **1930** [see *K 3 f]. **1935** PAULING & WILSON *Introd. Quantum Mech.* v. 142 Only for *S* states (with $l = 0$) is the wave function different from zero at $r = 0$. **1963** F. A. COTTON *Chem. Applic. Group Theory* viii. 193 An *s* orbital is totally symmetric in the O_h environment. **1978** P. W. ATKINS *Physical Chem.* xiv. 433 Whereas the s-orbitals all have non-zero values at the nucleus, the p-orbitals vanish there.

6. [Initial letter of *secondary*.] Used, chiefly in *S wave*, to denote an earthquake wave which oscillates transversely to the direction of propagation, a shear wave; so named because secondary waves arrive at a given place later than primary waves. (See also *P III. 3.)

1908, etc. [see *P III. 3]. **1913** G. W. WALKER *Mod. Seismol.* vi. 39 A pronounced movement corresponding to the arrival of the longitudinal disturbance, and..a pronounced movement when the transversal disturbance arrives, both of which have travelled by the brachistochronic path... These are..identified with the beginning of the first phase P and the second phase S of a seismogram. **1937** WOOLDRIDGE & MORGAN *Physical Basis Geogr.* ii. 16 The velocities of both P and S waves increase with depth, to a depth of approximately three-tenths of the radius. **1955** *Sci. Amer.* Sept. 57/1 S waves travel at about two thirds of the speed of P waves. **1971** I. G. GASS et al. *Understanding Earth* iii. 54/1 The core is liquid..as can be shown from its inability to transmit shear waves, the *S* waves of earthquakes.

7. In *Physics, s* and *S* denote the quantum numbers of spin angular momentum of one electron and a group of electrons, respectively. [Introduced by F. Hund 1926, in *Zeitschr. f. Physik* XXXVI. 658.]

1926 *Bull. Nat. Res. Council* (U.S.) No. 57. 5 Electronic angular momentum in units of $h/2\pi$... *s*. **1932** BACHER & GOUDSMIT *Atomic Energy States* 6 The spin moments *s* of the individual electrons form, together, a definite resultant spin moment *S*. **1966** D. H. WHIFFEN *Spectroscopy* xi. 134 One must be careful not to confuse *S* meaning a state with $L = 0$, with *S* the value of the total electron spin. **1970** G. K. WOODGATE *Elem. Atomic Struct.* iv. 57 There is no integration in the normalization condition.., and there is no approach to the classical limit in the sense that $s \to \infty$ because *s* is confined to the value ½ only.

8. S is used to denote one of the two directions of twist (see quot. 1935); so *S-spun*, etc.

1935 *Proc. Amer. Soc. for Testing Materials* XXXV. I. 448 A yard or cord has 'S' twist if, when held in a vertical position, the spirals conform in slope to the central portion of the letter 'S', and 'Z' twist if the spirals conform in slope to the central portion of the letter 'Z'. **1950** A. V. PRINGLE *Theory of Flax Spinning* xiii. 45 Because the outer fibrils in flax ultimates are arranged in 'S' twist spirals it is considered that a stronger yarn or thread can be spun when the final twist is inserted 'Z'-wise. Hence yarns for weaving are always spun Z-wise, but yarns for twisting are commonly spun S-wise. **1964** H. HODGES *Artifacts* ix. 129 Thus, if the threads are S-spun the ply will normally be Z-spun.

9. [Initial letter of *slow*.] *s-process* (Astr.): a process thought to occur in giant stars by which heavy atomic nuclei are produced from other nuclei over a long time scale by a combination of neutron captures and more rapid beta decays.

1956 [see *R III. 7]. **1971** *New Scientist* 27 Apr. 248/2 The solar-system proportions of many heavy elements reflect the results expected from the s-process, but the lighter elements defy quantitative explanation. **1977** [see *R III. 7].

10. *S meter*: a meter on a radio that indicates the strength of a received signal.

1939 *A.W.A. Technical Rev.* IV. 187 It is preferable that the S-meter be available for signal strength comparisons when the receiver gain is manually controlled. **1962** *B.B.C. Handbk.* 130 The more expensive short-wave receivers include such additional features as..'comprehensive band-spread' and 'S' meter or magic eye, which facilitate accurate tuning. **1976** PERKOWSKI & STRAL *Joy of CB* ix. 96 The output is about four times the talk power (6 dB) of AM, equivalent to a difference of one 'S' meter unit, or slightly better.

11. *S-matrix* (Physics): a scattering matrix, i.e. a matrix of probability amplitudes that occurs in the expression of the initial wave functions in a scattering process in terms of all the possible final wave functions. [After G. *matrix S* (W. Heisenberg 1943, in *Zeitschr. f. Physik* CXX. 521).]

1945 C. MØLLER in *Matematisk-Fysiske Meddelelser* XXIII. I. 18 The discrete energy values are completely independent of the form of the *S*-matrix. **1964** W. K. HEISENBERG in *Cambr. Rev.* 24 Oct. 47/1 The S-matrix elements for complicated processes will be functions of many variables. **1974** *Nature* 15 Mar. 265/1 He begins by developing the mathematical description starting from the Minkowski formalism of space-time, passing briefly through field theory, finally arriving at the S-matrix formalism which is to form the basis for the rest of the investigation.

12. *S-band*: the range of microwave frequencies between 1550 and 5200 megahertz, used for radio communication and radar.

1946 *Radar: Summary Rep. & Harp Project* (U.S. Nat. Defense Res. Comm.) 143/2 *S-band.* Refers to wavelengths of the order of 10 cm. **1952** REINTJES & COATE *Princ. Radar* (ed. 3) i. 33 Radar equipment operating..in the S, X, and K bands is called microwave radar. **1965** FILIPOWSKY & MUEHLDORF *Space Communications Techniques* ii. 111 S-band high power transmitters in the 2000 to 2400 Mc range are being provided for future Earth to spacecraft deep-space communications, with power ratings from 10 KW to 100 KW. **1970** N. ARMSTRONG et al. *First on Moon* xi. 257, I haven't heard a word from those guys, and I thought I'd be hearing them on your S-band relay. **1974** *Encycl. Brit. Macropædia* XV. 370/1 Early in the war, the British had developed an airborne S-band..radar for bombing, called the H2S.

13. *Chem.* [Abbrev. of L. *sinister* left.] *S* is used to designate (compounds having) a configuration about an asymmetric carbon atom in which the substituents, placed in order according to certain rules, form an anticlockwise sequence when viewed from a particular direction. Opp. *R* III. 6.

1956, 1971 [see *R III. 6]. **1973** *Nature* 6 Apr. 367/3 In these experiments, the R(−) isomers..were considerably more active than the alternate S(+) configuration.

14. *S* denotes the strangeness quantum number of sub-atomic particles.

1956 M. GELL-MANN in *Nuovo Cimento* IV. Suppl. 852 Since we have $S = 0$ for ordinary particles and $S \neq 0$ for 'strange' ones we shall refer to *S* as 'strangeness'. **1965** C. M. H. SMITH *Nuclear Physics* xi. 734 In the final state the total strangeness is zero as Λ^0 and K^+ have *S*-values of -1 and $+1$ respectively. **1973** L. J. TASSIE *Physics of Elem. Particles* vi. 54 The K^- is the antiparticle of the K^+, and has $S = -1$.

15. *Particle Physics.* [Repr. *strange*; also understood as = *singlet* or *sideways*.

'The letters u and d stood for "up" and "down" (that is to say, isotopic spin projection up and down) and s stood for "strange", with "singlet" (isotopic spin singlet) as a supplementary meaning. "Sideways" was a joke that I used from time to time.'—M. Gell-Mann, let. to Ed.]

s is used to designate one of the three quarks originally postulated by Gell-Mann, viz. the 'strange' quark, which has zero isospin and charge $-\frac{1}{3}$.

1964 [see *QUARK *sb.*]. **1964** *Physics* I. 74 There is a triplet *t* of fermion fields corresponding to three spin ½ quarks: the isotopic doublet *u* and *d*, with charges ⅔ and $-\frac{1}{3}$ respectively, and the isotopic singlet *s*, with charge $-\frac{1}{3}$. **1973** *Physics Lett.* XLVII. B. 365/2 Even if there is a fourth 'charmed' quark u' in addition to the usual u, d, and s, there are still three colors. **1975** *Physics Bull.* Apr. 177/1 There are two nonstrange quarks, u and d, a doublet under SU(2), and a strange quark s which is a singlet under SU(2). **1975** L. H. RYDER *Elem. Particles & Symmetries* xi. 192 Let us..take up the suggestion of Gell-Mann in 1964 that the three basic particles, which he called quarks, do not have the same hypercharge *Y* as *p*, *n* and Λ, but are as shown in Figure 2. (*u* and *d* stand for isospin up and down, *s* for singlet.) **1975** *Sci. Amer.* Oct. 43/1 The third quark, *s*, is needed only to construct strange particles, and indeed it provides an explicit definition of strangeness: A strange particle is one that contains at least one *s* quark or *s̄* antiquark. **1977** *Nature* 21 July 204/1 Quark model enthusiasts have been having a field day predicting..the properties of new 'charmed' hadrons composed of c-quarks together with the old u, d and s-quarks. *Ibid.* 204/2 Each flavour of quark (u, d, s or c) comes in each of the three colours, but hadrons are always combinations of quarks with no net colour.

s'. Add: **2.** = So *adv.* Now *colloq.* (Written continuously with the succeeding word.) Cf. S'ELP.

1607 SHAKES. *Cor.* IV. vi. 120 You have brought A trembling vpon Rome, such as was neuer S'incapeable of helpe. **1930** M. ALLINGHAM *Mystery Mile* xxi. 200 'It anythink yer see, and 'it like 'ell—s'long as it ain't me. **1947** K. TENNANT *Lost Haven* i. 20 Man brings his own booze, and gets shot out without s'much as one drink of it.

's. Add: Also written as a separate word.

1. b. = *it is.* Chiefly *poet.* or (in imitation of informal or careless speech) *colloq.*

1599 SHAKES. *Much Ado* III. iv. 9 By my troth's not so good, and I warrant your cosin will say so. **1933** H. C. BAILEY *Mr. Fortune Wonders* 98 You wouldn't blame your dear boy! Your only one! 's too bad. **1951** J. WYNDHAM *Day of Triffids* i. 25 'S that bloody comet, b—it! Thash what done it.

c. = *that's*, esp. in phr. *'sright* (and varr.) = *that's right* (see *RIGHT *a.* 7 e). *colloq.*

In some uses represented erron. by *s'*.

1939 M. HARRISON *What are we waiting For?* 99 'It was two years last August: wasn't it, Fred?' 'Sri,' said Fred. **1958** C. WATSON *Coffin, scarcely Used* xix. 174 'I thought he had only one funeral today.' 'S'right.' **1968** S. WOODS *Past Praying For* III. 245 'Wednesday, the twenty-second of September?' ''sright.' **1969** N. FREELING *Tsing-Boum* x. 64 'Man to see you, chief. Says you're expecting him.' ''s right.' **1977** 'M. UNDERWOOD' *Fatal Trip* xxv. 153 'Did they all leave together?' ''Sright.' 'By car?' ''Sright.'

5. Now also *colloq.*, esp. in phr. *so's* = *so as* (see So *adv.* and *conj.* 29; As *adv.* 21 a). (Further examples.)

1867 J. T. TROWBRIDGE in *Our Young Folks* Mar. 133 Soon's I've got the hang o' the thing,..I'll astonish the nation. **1942** *R.A.F. Jrnl.* 16 May 2 We heave sandbags and pull ropes and tie knots..till we get so's we don't notice the weather. **1948** D. BALLANTYNE *Cunninghams* I. 5 He had a system for using up the day so's time didn't drag too much. **1955** W. MOORE *Bring Jubilee* iii. 28 You're a gloomy gus, Hodge. Tain't's bad's that. **1970** 'R. LLEWELLYN' *But we didn't get Fox* ii. 22 I'm sore's hell, but that's the situation!

6. = *does*: see Do *v.* A. 2 c. *colloq.*

1934 N. BELL *Winding Road* xxii. 611 When's Parliament reassemble, Stephen? **1938** N. MARSH *Artists in Crime* xvii. 253 What's he know about it? **1966** J. HACKSTON *Father clears Out* 22 That fellow was most disheartening. What's he know about gold! **1980** 'M. UNDERWOOD' *Crime upon Crime* i. 7 What's he do?.. I wondered if he belonged to one of those hush-hush outfits?

-s, *suffix*[2]. A shortened form of the hypocoristic dim. suffix -SY, added to the same classes of words, as *Babs, Toots; ducks* (see *DUCK *sb.*[1] 3 c), *moms.*

saab, sa'ab, varr. SAHIB in Dict. and Suppl.

Saadian (sā·diăn), *a.* Also **Sadian, Sa'dian.** [f. Arab. *Sâadi, Sa'dī*, the name of a 16th- and 17th-cent. dynasty of sharīfs in Morocco + -AN.] Of or belonging to the Sa'dī dynasty.

[**1899** B. MEAKIN *Moorish Empire* vii. 116 In consequence of..the assertion that this family only belonged to the Beni Sâad, it was contemptuously known as the Sâadi dynasty.] **1951** W. BLUNT *Black Sunrise* iv. 40 In the sixteenth century..Marrakesh had risen again under the Sadian kings. **1963** *Guardian* 27 Feb. 15/3 There are two marvellous things to see [in Marrakesh]—the Saadian tombs, and the Souks, or covered bazaars. **1971** J. M. ABUN-NASR *Hist. Maghrib* viii. 205 The Sa'dian *Sharifs* were able to organize a religio-political movement which eventually unified Morocco.

‖**saaidam** (sai·dam). *S. Afr.* Also **zaai-** and with capital initial; pl. **-damme, -dams.** [Afrikaans, f. *saai* to sow + *dam* DAM *sb.*[1]] A basin of land enclosed by artificial earthen walls, designed to receive flood-water for its irrigation. Also *attrib.*

1925 R. DEAKIN *Southward Ho!* vii. 79 The raising of crops with the help of *saaidams*..would transform the scene. **1937** MARAIS & SIM in D. J. Seymore *Handbk. for Farmers in S. Afr.* (S. Afr. Dept. Agric. & Forestry) 704 The so-called 'saaidam' system is practised. **1947** *S. & E. Afr. Year Bk. & Guide* 551 From Kotjeskolk to Sak River the branch line runs through the fertile Fish River valley along which large 'Zaaidams' have been made. Cultivation by zaaidams is carried out by diverting the flood water..into extensive areas enclosed by dams. **1953** *Cape Argus Mag.* 2 June 1/6 'Koos Nel' constructed the first large 'Saaidam' in the North-West. **1955** J. H. WELLINGTON *S. Afr.* I. 385 Saaidam irrigation is practised along the Sak river... The sowing 'dam' is a basin bordered by low earthen walls into which the flood waters are diverted. **1972** *Stand. Encycl. S. Afr.* V. 445/1 There is considerable irrigation, including the unique system whereby flood-water is diverted into shallow basins, known as 'saaidamme'. **1975** *Ibid.* XI. 422/2 In the North-Western Cape wheat is grown on saaidams.

‖**saal** (zāl). *rare.* Also **Saal.** [Ger.; cf. SALLE.] A large room or hall. (Used with reference to European countries, esp. Germany.)

1855 GEO. ELIOT in *Fraser's Mag.* LI. 702/1 A more interesting place to visitors is the library, which occupies a large building not far from the Schloss. The principal *Saal*..is ornamented with some very excellent busts. **1876** —— *Dan. Der.* I. II. xv. 291 Sir Hugo saying as they entered the large *saal*—'Did you play much at Baden, Grandcourt?' **1978** *Chicago* June 52/1 The Chicago Public Library offers tours of this splendid building—it ranks with the best of the European saals.

Saale (zā·lə). *Geol.* The name of a river in E. Germany used *attrib.* with reference to the third (penultimate) glaciation of the Pleistocene epoch in northern Europe, equivalent to the Riss glaciation in the Alps.

1937 W. B. WRIGHT *Quaternary Ice Age* (ed. 2) x. 136 In several places two deposits of loess are separated from one another by glacial formations, indicating that loess formation preceded the advance of the Saale Ice-sheet. **1945** F. E. ZEUNER *Pleistocene Period* iii. 76 The most remarkable feature of the Ukrainian succession is the moraine of the Dnjepr lobe of the Saale glaciation. **1959** WELLS & KIRKALDY *Outl. Hist. Geol.* (ed. 4) xix. 368 The Gipping and Lowestoft Boulder Clays must be correlated with the Saale and Elster glaciations respectively. **1971** R. F. FLINT *Glacial & Quaternary Geol.* xxiv. 628 The distribution of the extensive Saale drift is generally well defined, though in places it is not differentiated clearly from the Elster. **1979** *Nature* 18 Jan. 172/1 It lies between Saale glacial deposits and the sands of the Last (Weichselian) Glaciation (isotope stages 2, 3, 4 and 5a–5d).

Saalian (zā·liăn), *a.* (*sb.*) *Geol.* [ad. G. *saalisch* (H. Stille 1920, in *Nachr. v.d. K. Ges. d. Wissensch. z. Göttingen* (Math.-phys. Kl.) 219), f. *Saale* (see prec.): see -IAN).] Designating, or pertaining to, a minor orogenic episode in Europe which is believed to have occurred in the Permian period. Also *ellipt.* as *sb.* Also **Saa·lic** *a.*

1931 GREGORY & BARRETT *Gen. Stratigr.* 19 The Saalian is represented in England by the Armorican which is earlier than Middle Permian. **1933** *Proc. Leeds Philos. & Lit. Soc.* (*Sci. Sect.*) II. 456 (*table*) Saalian folding. **1937** A. L. DU TOIT *Our Wandering Continents* vii. 156 The relatively weak Saalian and Pfalzian Phases marked out the end of the Lower and Upper Permian respectively in the central Variscan zone. *Ibid.* xvi. 309 The Saalian was weak in Europe and the Urals, but strong in both west and east—in the Caribbean and Appalachians and along the southern margin of Asia. **1969** BENNISON & WRIGHT *Geol. Hist. Brit. Isles* x. 244 The pre-Permian unconformity of north-east England may be due to the Asturic Phase or to the (later) Saalic Phase. **1973** P. J. BUREK in Tarling & Runcorn *Implications Continental Drift to Earth Sci.* II. 822 The closing of the Ural trough along with the formation of the Uralides (Saalian orogenic phase). **1974** *Encycl. Brit. Macropædia* XIV. 99/1 In Europe, orogenic and igneous activities were on a much smaller scale than they had been in the Carboniferous. Here, two minor orogenies..are generally named Pfälzian (post-Early Permian) and Saalian (Late Permian).

Saam(e, var. *SAMI.

Saan, var. *SAN[2].

Saanen (sā·nĕn). The name of a small town in the canton of Berne, Switzerland, used *attrib.* and *absol.* to designate (a member of) a breed of white goats which was first developed in the region.

1908 'HOME COUNTIES' *Case for Goat* iii. 26 Something is now heard of the white Saanen. **1909** G. J. G. JENSEN *Goat-Keeping for All* ii. 7 Saanen Goats.—Some two or three specimens of this breed were recently imported by Mr. H. E. Hughes, of Broxbourne. **1920** C. J. DAVIES *Goat-Keeping for Milk Production* i. 14 The white breed of Switzerland takes its name from Gessenay in Berne... In England the variety is usually known as the Saanen. **1948** A. HUXLEY *Ape & Essence* (1949) 125 Three-horned and robed impressively in a white Saanen soutane the great man is sitting with a couple of two-horned Familiars at a large table. **1976** *Denbighshire Free Press* 8 Dec. 17/6 (Advt.), Territone goats, Anglo Nubian British Saanen.

Saar (zāɹ). The name of a river in West Germany, a tributary of the Moselle, used *attrib.* and *absol.* to designate a white wine produced in this region.

1905 G. MEREDITH *Let.* 1 Mar. (1970) III. 1515 Can it be a Moselle? Or a Saar wine. **1967** A. LICHINE *Encycl. Wines* 474/1 The Saars can outclass the Moselles in the best years... Saar wines..are always classed with the Moselles. *Ibid., Kauzem.* Very delicious wines, heavier, fuller, rounder than most Saars.

Saarlander (zā·ɹlandəɹ). [Ger., f. *Saarland*, the name of a West German *Land*; cf. prec.] An inhabitant of Saarland. Also *attrib.* or as *adj.*

1955 *Times* 4 May 10/1 A Gaullist senator complained that the Government, in accepting the Franco-German consortium, had excluded the Saarlanders. **1975** *Times* 18 June 25/3 The iron and steel works..were returned to German control at the request of the Saarlanders. **1980** E. LEATHER *Duveen Let.* xv. 175 He was a Saarlander, and a dedicated Nazi. *Ibid.* 178 His ancestors had been.. Saarlander plumbers.

saater, var. *SAETER, SETTER.

sabadilla. Add: Also, a preparation of this for medicinal or agricultural use. (Further examples.)

1890 HUGHES & DAKE *Cycl. Drug Pathogenesy* III. 759 We have thought it better to omit the symptoms belonging to them, lest they should prove as worthless as those.. which were observed in a boy suffering from tape-worm before he took Sabadilla 30, and which (naturally) disappeared after 46 ells of the worm had been passed. **1907** *Brit. Pharmaceutical Codex* 241 Sabadilla consists of the dried ripe seeds of *Schoenocaulon officinale*,..a tall herbaceous plant growing on the low mountain slopes in Mexico, Guatemala, and Venezuela. **1946** *Richmond* (Va.) *Times-Dispatch* 4 Feb. 4/1 A powerful new insecticide has been developed from a long-known plant... The new bug killer is known as sabadilla. **1977** *Martindale's Extra Pharmacopoeia* (ed. 27) 796/2 Sabadilla was formerly used as a parasiticide, especially for pediculosis capitis, in the form of ointment..or vinegar.

sabadine (sæ·bădīn). *Biochem.* Also † **sabatine.** [ad. G. *sabadin* (E. Merck 1891, in *Arch. der Pharm.* CCXXIX. 164): see SABADILLA and -INE[5].] A veratrum alkaloid ester, $C_{29}H_{47}NO_8$, present in sabadilla seeds.

1891 *Jrnl. Chem. Soc.* LX. II. 844 The author has isolated two alkaloïds from sabadilla seeds, *Asagræa officinalis.* Sabadine is best separated as the nitrate. **1951** A. J. HENNIG et al. in *Jrnl. Amer. Pharmaceut. Assoc.: Sci. Ed.* XL. 168 Evidence has been obtained of at least five additional alkaloids in the water-soluble portion, crude fraction D..of sabadilla alkaloids. One of the new alkaloids has been obtained in crystalline state and given the name 'sabatine'. **1962** *Jrnl. Med. & Pharmaceut. Chem.* V. 693 Sabatine was found to be identical with sabadine. ..On historical grounds, the names sabadine and sabine (for the ester and alkamine respectively) deserve preference. **1976** *Jrnl. Neurochem.* XXVII. 1271/2 Veratrine sulfate consisted of the alkaloids veratridine, cevadilline, sabadine and cevadine.

Sabæan, Sabean, *a.* and *sb.* Add: Also Sabaean. **A.** *adj.* Also, of or pertaining to the language of the Sabæans (see below).

1883 [in Dict.]. **1886, 1902** [see *MINÆAN *sb.* and *a.*]. **1968** [see *LIHYANIC *sb.*]. **1974** *Encycl. Brit. Macropædia* I. 620/1 The Sabaean offshoot, a graceful and elegant script consisting of 29 letters, spread into Africa, where it became the progenitor of the Ethiopic alphabet.

B. *sb.* **b.** The language of the Sabæans, a dialect of Old South Arabic.

1905 G. BELL *Let.* 23 Feb. (1927) I. 196 A mass of rocks all covered with inscriptions..one..very like the oldest script of Yemen Sabaean. **1910** J. BUCHAN *Prester John* xi. 183 It must have been some old sacred language—Phoenician, Sabæan, I know not what—which had survived in the rite. **1951** [see *MINÆAN *sb.* and *a.*].

sabal (sēi·băl). [Generic name (M. Adanson *Familles des Plantes* (1763) II. 495), perh. a. S. Amer. native name.] A fan palm of the genus so called, or a related fossil plant, belonging to the family Palmaceæ and native to tropical America. Cf. PALMETTO.

1812 *Curtis's Bot. Mag.* XXXV. 1434 (*heading*) Dwarf Sabal, or Swamp Palmetto. **1902** L. H. BAILEY *Cycl. Amer. Hort.* IV. 1593/1 The Sabals have proved a great success. **1975** *Islander* (Victoria, B.C.) 20 Apr. 14/2 Leaves from sabal have been found around Nanaimo.

sabalo. (Examples.)

1889 in *Cent. Dict.* [**1904** W. M. GALLICHAN *Fishing & Trav. Spain* xvi. 161 These traps were set for the sábalos, or shad.] **1938** V. HEILNER *Salt Water Fishing* xii. 195 Look at all the big marlin Hemingway has taken. And of course sabalo. **1965** A. J. MCCLANE *Stand. Fishing Encycl.* 924/2 Tarpon... Also known as the *sabalo* (Spanish), this species is considered by many anglers as the king of gamefishes.

sabatia, var. *SABBATIA.

Sabatier (sabatye). *Photogr.* Also (*erron.* but more commonly) *Sabattier.* The name of Armand *Sabatier* (1834–1910), French physician and scientist, used *attrib.* and in the possessive to designate a process and an effect developed by him, as † **Sabatier's amphi-positive process,** the process of image-reversal giving rise to the Sabatier effect; **Sabatier effect,** partial or complete reversal of an image on film or paper, resulting from exposure to unsafe light after partial development. Cf. SOLARIZATION 1 in Dict. and Suppl., *PSEUDO-SOLARIZATION.

1894 E. L. WILSON *Cyclopædic Photogr.* 329/1 Sabatier's Amphi-Positive Process. The peculiarity of this process consists in the pictures being the result of a superposition, or entangling of two images, one negative, the other positive. **1930** tr. *L. P. Clerc's Photogr.* xvi. 138/1 A similar phenomenon is observed when white light is momentarily admitted to the room while the normal image is still weak. (Sabatier effect.) **1939** M. NATKIN *Fascinating Fakes in Photogr.* 58 Solarisation, sometimes called Sabatier effect, has been known for a very long time. **1956** [see *SOLARIZATION 1 a]. **1970** C. B. NEBLETTE *Fund. Photogr.* v. 52 If a photographic material is exposed, developed, washed but not fixed and then exposed to diffused light and again developed, a positive image or a combination of a positive and a negative image is obtained... This is known as the Sabattier effect (Sabatier, 1850). **1970** M. J. SETHNA *Photography* xii. 180 Actually producing the Sabatier effect is not an easy matter. **1976** K. I. & R. E. JACOBSON *Imaging Syst.* v. 105 Although the Sabattier effect has been ascribed to the screening effect of the negative image produced by the first exposure and development on the printing by the second exposure onto the underlying emulsion, desensitization by the products of development is a more likely explanation.

sabatine, obs. var. *SABADINE.

‖ **sabayon** (sabayoṅ). [Fr., ad. It. *zabaione* zabaglione.] A dessert or sauce made with egg yolks, sugar, and white wine, whipped together, thickened over a slow heat, and served hot or cold. Also *attrib.* and *Comb.*

1906 *Mrs. Beeton's Bk. Househ. Managem.* lxii. 1669 (*heading*) Sabayon..Pudding sauce, composed of cream or milk, sugar, white wine, and eggs. **1939** A. SIMON *Conc. Encycl. Gastron.* I. 46/2 (*heading*) Sabayon sauce. 4 egg yolks. 1½ oz. sifted sugar. 2 gills Marsala wine. **1960** V. NABOKOV *Invitation to Beheading* i. 13 Excellent sabayon! Should still like to know if it will be long now. **1973** *Sat. Rev. World* (U.S.) 18 Dec. 48/3 *Sabayon* reeling from an overdose of Grand Marnier. **1975** *Times* 31 May 7/4 There were..triumphs:..the white wine sauce for sole paillard, and the sabayon au kummel.

Sabba-day. Now *rare.* Also **Sabber-day**, etc. U.S. colloq. var. of SABBATH-DAY. Also *Comb.*, as **Sabba-day house**, a house used for rest in the interval between church services; = *noon-house* s.v. *NOON *sb.* 6 b.

c **1772** T. BURBANK in *Essex Inst. Hist. Coll.* (1920) LVI. 292 Thare was in the yeare 1738 a great athcak one sabbady. **1858** *Harper's Mag.* Nov. 856/2 A thousand terrible thoughts rushed into her mind;..above all, the loss of her 'Sabber-day' dinner. **1868** H. W. BEECHER *Norwood* 47 Duties never conflict, you said, only Sabby-day morning last. **1876** J. E. TODD *John Todd* 40 Near by were a number of rough, stone-built 'Sabba'-day houses, where they flocked at noon, for warmth in winter (they had chimneys), and coolness in summer. **1891** [see *noon-house* s.v. *NOON *sb.* 6 b]. **1935** J. C. LINCOLN *Cape Cod Yesterdays* 5, I knew that, when I next dressed, it would be in the prim and stiff and spotless garments befitting what Grandmother often said her mother used to call 'Sabba' Day'.

sabbatarial (sæbătēə·riăl), *a. rare*—¹. [f. L. *sabbatāri-us* (see SABBATARIAN *a.* and *sb.*) + -AL.] Favouring or tending to the observance of the Sabbath.

1867 TROLLOPE *Last Chron. Barset* II. lxxiii. 294 The archdeacon had been very stoutly anti-sabbatarial when the question of stopping the Sunday post to Plumstead had been mooted in the village.

Sabbath. Add: **4.** *Sabbath dress* (later example), *-tide*; *Sabbath-dark* adj.; (objective and objective genitive) *Sabbath-breaking* sb. and adj. (further examples), *-keeping* sb. (earlier examples); **Sabbath candle**, a candle lit shortly before dusk on the eve of the Jewish Sabbath; **Sabbath goy** [*GOY], a Gentile who performs for Orthodox Jews tasks forbidden to the latter on the Sabbath; = *shabbos-goy* s.v. *SHABBOS b; **Sabbath lamp**, a lamp lit on the eve of the Jewish Sabbath; **Sabbath loaf**, a plaited loaf eaten on the eve of the Jewish Sabbath; **Sabbath school** (*a*) (earlier and later U.S. examples).

1815 MILLS & SMITH *Rep. Missionary Tour* 29 Sabbath-breaking, profanity and intemperance prevail [in New Orleans] to a fearful extent. **1918** H. G. WELLS *Joan & Peter* v. 96 Secularists and socialists..planned..to..plunge the whole world into vice and rapine and Sabbath-breaking. **1958** B. HAMILTON *Too Much of Water* iii. 59 Charity can do without help from the proceeds of vice and Sabbath-breaking. **1978** P. BAILEY *Leisure & Class in Victorian Eng.* ii. 39 Certain magistrates..prosecuted sabbath-breaking cricket players. **1892** I. ZANGWILL *Children of Ghetto* I. viii. 191 She, at least, would never fail to light the Sabbath candles. **1967** *Listener* 20 July 83/3 My mother..stopped lighting the Sabbath candles..but still spoke as constantly to God. **1945** DYLAN THOMAS *Let.* 30 July (1966) 280, I went to the Edwinsford Arms, a sabbath-dark bar. **1977** H. KAPLAN *Damascus Cover* (1978) iv. 35 Girls in white Sabbath dresses laced with colored embroidery. **1977** *Listener* 24 Mar. 382/3, I was a Sabbath *goy*; that is, for a penny or two, I lighted fires and performed other chores forbidden to orthodox Jews on Saturday, or Friday evening. **1977** *Times* 8 June 4/3 My host had been a sabbath *goy*, that is he had lighted fires for the orthodox on the sabbath. **1643** W. WALWYN *Power of Love* 32 Men are not pleased except salvation be proved to be very difficult to bee obtained, it must still depend either on our beleeving.., or repenting,..or Sabbath-keeping,..or else man is not pleased. **1832** F. TROLLOPE *Domestic Manners of Americans* I. xviii. 284 The waiving the sabbath-keeping by the proprietor, was for his own convenience. **1850** G. AGUILAR *Vale of Cedars* xxxiv. 281 It was..the Sabbath eve... The Sabbath lamps were lighted. **1892** I. ZANGWILL *Children of Ghetto* I. v. 139 For three things a woman dies in childbirth, for not separating the dough, for not lighting the Sabbath lamps, for not —. *Ibid.* II. xviii. 79 The Sabbath loaves shaped like boys' tip-cats—with a curious plait of crust from point to point, and thickly sprinkled with a drift of poppy-seed, and covered with a velvet cloth embroidered with Hebrew words. **1951** L. W. LEONARD *Jewish Cookery* v. 26 *Challah*, in twist form or Biblical beehive coil, is the Sabbath loaf of white bread. It is customary to place two *challas* under a special napkin... The two loaves are symbolic of the 'two portions of manna' which fell for the Sabbath. **1972** H. KEMELMAN *Monday Rabbi took Off* xlvii. 271 The candles were already lit and the table set with the two braided Sabbath loaves. **1820** *Rec. Early Hist. Boston* (1909) XXXIX. 131 The application for liberty to use the Boylston school house on Fort hill for a Sabbath school..was granted. **1832** W. D. WILLIAMSON *Hist. State of Maine* III. 688 *Sabbath-schools*..[were established] in Philadelphia, about 1811, and have since spread over the United States. **1866** J. C. GREGG *Life in Army* 209 It was sung by the colored Sabbath School children. **1900** *Congress. Rec.* 23 Jan. 1104/2 A wonderful petition is rolled in..from Sabbath schools, sectarian churches, and societies. **1945** J. BETJEMAN *New Bats in Old Belfries* 48 And so my thoughts this happy Sabbathtide.

sabbatia (sæbēⁱ·ʃiă). Also **sabatia.** [mod.L. (M. Adanson *Familles des Plantes* (1763) II. 503 as *Sabatia*), f. the name of Constantino and Liberato Sabbati, 18th-cent. Italian botanists + -IA¹.] An annual or perennial herb of the genus so called, belonging to the family Gentianaceæ, native to eastern North America, and bearing clusters of pink or white flowers.

1814 *Curtis's Bot. Mag.* XXXIX. 1600 (*heading*) Dichotomous sabbatia. **1847** W. DARLINGTON *Agric. Bot.* 260 Angular sabbatia. Centaury. **1902** L. H. BAILEY *Cycl. Amer. Hort.* IV. 1594/2 Sabbatias require a light, sweet soil. **1949** *Natural Hist.* June 278/3 On grassy, pine-sprinkled savannas, in the company of gaudy sabbatias, insignificant burmannias, and orange habenarias. **1972** F. PERRY *Flowers of World* 123/1 *Sabatia* (*Sabbatia*) are annual or biennial [*sic*] plants from North America with erect branching stems... The plants contain a bitter principle and when dried are used as a tonic.

Sabbatian, *a.* and *sb.*² Add: **A.** *adj.* (Further examples.)

1941 G. G. SCHOLEM *Major Trends in Jewish Mysticism* viii. 284 The swift rise and the sudden collapse of the Sabbatian movement in 1665 and 1666, from Sabbatai Zevi's proclamation of his messianic mission to his renunciation of Judaism. **1974** *Times Lit. Suppl.* 20 Sept. 1024/5 The seventeenth-century mystical Messiah, Sabbatai Sevi (1626–1676), and the Sabbatian heresy named after him.

B. *sb.* (Further examples.)

1974 *Encycl. Brit. Micropædia* IX. 99/1 A sect of Muslim Sabbatians—the Dönme of Salonika—survived him [*sc.* Shabbetai Tzevi]. **1977** *N.Y. Rev. Bks.* 14 Apr. 27/1 The antinomian energies of the Sabbatians..did in fact feed the subsequent currents of enlightenment and reform in Western Europe.

Sabbatianism (further examples).

1941 G. G. SCHOLEM *Major Trends in Jewish Mysticism* viii. 297 Sabbatianism as a movement was long identified with its more extreme, antinomian and nihilistic aspects. **1977** *N.Y. Rev. Bks.* 14 Apr. 28/1 The way was thus prepared for the mighty swell of Sabbatianism.

sabbatic, *a.* Add: **b.** = *SABBATICAL *a.* 2 c. *rare.*

1905 *N.Y. Even. Post* 23 Sept. 8 Professors Hull and Durham are spending their sabbatic year in Europe. **1970** *Newslet. Amer. Dial. Soc.* Nov. 7 Budget requests may include..up to two-thirds of sabbatic, academic, or other leave pay offered by an applicant's institution.

sabbatical, *a.* Add: **2. c.** orig. *U.S.* Designating a period of leave from duty granted to university teachers at certain intervals (orig. every seven years) for the purposes of study and travel; *spec.* in *sabbatical year* (cf. sense 2 a in Dict.). Now freq. used *transf.* of rest or absence from other occupations, professions, or activities. Also *sabbatical officer*, one granted sabbatical leave (from work or study) for the performance of a certain office.

[**1880** *Ann. Rep. Pres. & Treas. of Harvard Coll. 1879–1880* 19 The Corporation adopted, on the 31st of May, 1880, new rules with regard to leave of absence for professors and assistant professors... The Corporation have decided that they will grant occasional leave of absence for one year on half-pay, provided that no professor have such leave oftener than once in seven years.] **1886** E. N. HORSFORD *Scheme adopted by Trustees, Wellesley Coll.* 8 To each of the heads of the above departments the Sabbatical Grant contemplates that every seventh year of her academic service from a given date, she shall be eligible to have..a year's leave of absence, to be passed in Europe, and with it her half-yearly salary. If for any reason an eligible officer declines the Sabbatical Year, the grant in her case may be offered to another equally eligible. **1892** W. JAMES *Let.* 13 July (1920) I. 321 Only why talk of 'sabbatical' years? **1905** *N.Y. Even. Post* 23 Sept. 8 Professors Allinson, Sears and Hill are spending their sabbatical year of absence in foreign travel and study. **1926** B. RUSSELL *On Education* III. xviii. 242 Every university teacher ought to have a Sabbatical year (one in every seven) to be spent in foreign universities or in otherwise acquiring knowledge of what is being done abroad. **1949** *Time* 18 Dec. 12/2 Kennan announced that he was leaving the State Department 'on sabbatical leave'. **1962** *Times* 12 Apr. 18/2 The break-up of his subsequent marriage impels him to escape from England and to spend a 'sabbatical year' in travel. **1972** *Nature* 4 Feb. 277/2 On sabbatical leave from the Department of Therapeutic Research, University of Pennsylvania School of Medicine. **1976** *Postmaster* (Merton Coll., Oxf.) 30 A union of university students, with clearly defined objectives, and with no sabbatical officers. **1976** *Gramophone* Apr. 1575/3 I'm doing it on May 9th with Rostropovich in the last concert before I take off a sabbatical year, promised to my wife when I reached sixty.

B. *sb.* A period of sabbatical leave; a sabbatical year (cf. sense 2 c above). Freq. in phr. *on* (*a*) *sabbatical.*

1934 in WEBSTER. **1946** H. HOWE *We Happy Few* 18 Then when Papa had his sabbatical, we went to Paris. **1958** *Manch. Guardian* 7 June 1/6 Parliament will be reconstituted after a six-month sabbatical. **1961** *Harper's Bazaar* Dec. 47/2 The ultimate in holidays is the 'sabbatical', a term which business is taking over from the academic world. **1978** L. HEREN *Growing up on The Times* iii. 102 Pat found a furnished flat, which belonged to an academic on a sabbatical in the United States.

Sabber-day, var. *SABBA-DAY.

sabe (sā·be, sā·ve), *v.* [Re-formation after, or re-borrowing of, Sp. *sabe*: see SAVEY, SAVVY *v.* in Dict. and Suppl.] = SAVEY, SAVVY *v.* Cf. *QUIEN SABE.

1850 *California Courier* (San Francisco) 6 Sept. 2/3 Ha! *Sabe* that? **1874** [see SAVEY, SAVVY *v.*]. **1903** A. ADAMS *Log of Cowboy* vi. 37 Girls, you know, sabe each other that way. **1907** S. E. WHITE *Arizona Nights* i. 9, I sabed that they'd seen the original exhibit your Uncle Jim was making of himself.

sabe (sā·be, sā·ve), *sb.* [See prec.] = SAVEY, SAVVY *sb.*

1872 B. HARTE in *Atlantic Monthly* Mar. 352/2 Did n't hev no more *sabe* than to come round yar with sickness in the house and no provision. **1892** [see SAVEY, SAVVY *sb.*]. **1913** J. LONDON *Valley of Moon* 311 We ain't got the *sabe*, or the knack, or something or other. **1931** *Lariat* Apr. 53 You ain't got much sabe.

Sabei, var. *SEBEI.

Sabellian, *a.*² and *sb.*² Add: **a.** *adj.* Also, of or pertaining to the language of the Sabellians. **b.** *sb.* Also, any of the numerous dialects of Italic spoken by the Sabellians.

1904 C. D. BUCK *Gram. Oscan & Umbrian* 3 The Oscan-Umbrian group..includes also the dialects of most of the minor tribes of central Italy, which may be conveniently designated as Sabellian. *Ibid.*, Strictly speaking the Samnite tribes were Sabellian, and their language, the Oscan, a Sabellian dialect. **1939** [see *Latino-Faliscan* s.v. *LATINO-]. **1939** [see *MARSIAN *sb.* and *a.*]. **1972** W. B. LOCKWOOD *Panorama Indo-Europ. Lang.* 58 A few early inscriptions characterised as Sabellian show that this dialect was closely akin to Oscan.

‖ **sabha** (săbā·). [Hind. *sabhā* assembly.] In India, an assembly; a council or society (see quots.). Cf. *LOK SABHA, *RAJYA SABHA.

1922 A. B. KEITH in *Cambr. Hist. India* I. iv. 96 The power of the king [in Vedic India] cannot have been in normal circumstances arbitrary or probably very great. There stood beside him as the mode of expression of the will of the people the assembly, which is denoted by the terms *samiti* and *sabha* in the Saṃhitā. **1936** J. NEHRU *Autobiogr.* xli. 323 All manner of allied or sympathetic or advanced organisations had been declared unlawful—kisan sabhas and peasant unions. **1950** M. MASANI *Our Growing Human Family* vii. 66 Some of these ancient Indian republics were extremely democratic... They had popular assemblies of all the people called the samiti and a parliament elected by the people called the sabha. **1968** *Jrnl. Mus. Acad. Madras* XXXIX. 119 Hardly 250 to 300 kritis are sung in the concerts of today—in spite of the availability of Music Sabhas. **1974** *Encycl. Brit. Micropædia* VIII. 747/3 *Sabhā*.., an important unit of self-government in Hindu society. It is basically an association of persons who have common interests, such as members of the same endogamous groups, but may also be an intercaste group (*e.g.*, a *mazdūr sabhā*, or association of labourers). The *sabhā* differs from the *pañcāyat* (caste or subcaste council) in that its scope is much larger.

‖ **sabi** (sā·bi). [Jap.] In Zen Buddhist philosophy, a quality of simple, restrained, and mellowed beauty.

1932 B. L. SUZUKI *Nōgaku* 15 The feeling of *sabi* or *shibumi* is the essence of the art of Nō. **1938** D. T. SUZUKI *Zen Buddhism* I. ii. 17 *Sabi* consists in rustic unpretentiousness or archaic imperfection, apparent simplicity or effortlessness in execution, and richness in historical associations. **1948** *Introd. Classic Jap. Lit.* (Kokusai Bunka Shinkōkai) p. vi, This new spirit was restrained by the persistence of traditional ideas as..in the appreciation and cultivation of 'mellowness' (*sabi*, patina) in literature. **1965** W. SWAAN *Jap. Lantern* xvi. 184 A quality most valued in architecture and art connected with the tea-ceremony is that of *sabi* or *wabi*. **1979** S. COE in I. Webb *Compl. Guide Flower Arrangement* xvii. 227/3 The first [mood] is *sabi*, a sense of loneliness which comes from being completely detached, and seeing things as if they are happening by themselves.

Sabian, *a.* (Earlier example.)

1787 W. JONES in *Asiatick Researches* (1790) II. 8 It is generally asserted, that the old religion of the Arabs was entirely Sabian; but I can offer so little accurate information concerning the Sabian faith, or even the meaning of the word, that I dare not yet speak on the subject with confidence.

sabin (sēⁱ·bin). *Acoustics.* Also **sabine** and with capital initial. [f. the name of Wallace Clement *Sabine* (1868–1919), U.S. physicist.] A unit of sound absorption equal to the absorbing power of one square foot of perfectly absorbing surface; = *open window unit* s.v. *OPEN *a.* (*adv.*) 22 c.

1934 *Jrnl. Acoustical Soc. Amer.* VI. 101 Total absorption—600 units (Sabine—0·50 sec.). **1936** *Gloss. Acoustical Terms* (*B.S.I.*) 22 The unit of equivalent absorption is termed an absorption unit. When the unit of area is a square foot, this unit is called a sabin. **1956** *IRE Trans. Audio* IV. 21 *A* is the absorption of the room in sabins. **1968** [see *open window unit* s.v. *OPEN *a.* (*adv.*) 22 c]. **1969** *Daily Tel.* 5 Nov. 5/1 The Professor assembled 10 miniskirted secretaries in a physics department's reverberation chamber... The 10 girls averaged a sabine count of 2·5 each, whereas a similar test in 1964, when skirts were longer, produced an average sabine count of 4·6. Twice as much sound was therefore absorbed in 1964. **1975** G. J. King *Audio Handbk.* i. 23 A room of total surface area 111·45 m² (1200 ft²),..and 0·2 coefficient of absorbency, signifying that 20% of the sound is absorbed .., would have a total absorbency of almost 240 sabins.

Sabine, *a.* and *sb.*[1] Add: **A.** *adj.* **a.** (Earlier and further examples.)

1600 Holland tr. *Livy's Romane Hist.* I. 8 And the youth of Rome upon a token and watch-word given, fell on every side to carrie away the Sabine maidens. **1606** Jonson *Hymenaei* sig. Cᵛ, The Speare, which (in the Sabine tongue) was called Curis. **1784** Cowper *Let.* 3 July (1904) II. 219, I may..refresh my spirits by a little intercourse with the Mantuan and the Sabine bard. **1822** M. Wilmot *Jrnl.* 19 Apr. in *More Lett.* (1935) 165 We set out..to seek for Horace's Sabine Farm at the back of Mt Lucretiles. **1823** Byron *Don Juan* IX. vii. 8 You, my Lord Duke!..half a million for your Sabine farm Is rather dear!

b. Of or pertaining to the Sabine language.

1888 [see *MARRUCINIAN *sb.* and *a.*]. **1977** *Word 1972* XXVIII. 7 They are obviously Italic (Sabine), not really Latin words.

B. *sb.*[1] **c.** The Italic language of the Sabines.

1834 W. Gell *Topogr. Rome* II. 381 Cata, in Sabine, says Varro, means pointed. **1933, 1939** [see *MARSIAN *sb.* and *a.*]. **1974** [see *MARRUCINIAN *sb.* and *a.*].

d. Sabine wine. *rare.*

1863 Whyte-Melville *Gladiators* x. 153, I talked myself well-nigh hoarse, and stayed out the drinking of two flagons of sour Sabine to boot.

Sabine[2] (sæ·bəin). The name of Sir Edward *Sabine* (1788–1883), British explorer, soldier, and President of the Royal Society, used *absol.*, *attrib.*, or in the possessive in **Sabine('s) gull** to designate *Xema sabinii*, an Arctic gull with a forked tail, grey head, and black collar, first named *Larus sabini* in his honour by his brother Joseph Sabine in 1818 (*Trans. Linn. Soc.* XII. 522).

1852 P. C. Sutherland *Jrnl. Voy. Baffin's Bay* II. 88 Sabine and ivory gulls, and other birds,..were on their flight up the Channel. **1886** *Code Nomencl. & Check-list N. Amer. Birds* (Amer. Ornithologists' Union) 91 (*heading*) Sabine's Gull. **1958** *Evening Telegram* (St. John's, Newfoundland) 6 May 30/5 Few people have the opportunity to see Sabine's gulls as they rarely come south. **1972** S. Burnford *One Woman's Arctic* ii. 43 Once only I saw a solitary sabine.

sabine, var. *SABIN.

sabinene (sēⁱ·binīn). *Chem.* [ad. G. *sabinen* (F. W. Semmler 1900, in *Ber. d. Deut. chem. Ges.* XXXIII. 1464), f. L. (*Juniperus*) *sabin-a* (see Savin, savine) + *-en* -ene.] A colourless liquid bicyclic terpene, $C_{10}H_{16}$, found in a number of essential oils, notably oil of savin.

1900 *Jrnl. Chem. Soc.* LXXVIII. i. 454 When oil of savin is distilled, a fraction, forming 30 per cent. of the whole, boils between 162° and 170°, and consists principally of a terpene, $C_{10}H_{16}$, which the author terms sabinene. **1942** *Jrnl. Org. Chem.* VII. 399 The presence of α-terpinene in this case, is due probably to isomerization of sabinene under the conditions of the experiment. **1976** *Nature* 22 Apr. 726/2 Terpenes with an exomethylene bond (for example, sabinene, nopinene and camphene) show three strong peaks in the Raman spectrum around 920, 877 and 856 cm^{-1}.

Sabinian (săbi·niăn), *sb.* and *a.*[1] *Roman Law.* [ad. L. *Sabinianus*, f. *Sabinus* (see below).] **A.** *sb.* A follower of Massurius Sabinus, a celebrated jurist in the time of the emperor Tiberius. **B.** *adj.* Of or pertaining to Massurius Sabinus or his views.

1862 T. Mackenzie *Stud. in Roman Law* 13 Capito.. was the chief of the rival sect, called after two of his followers Sabinians or Cassians. **1886** E. E. Whitfield tr. *Salkowski's Inst. & Hist. Roman Law* 47 The opposition..arises between the two schools of Law..the Proculians and Sabinians. **1903** F. P. Walton *Hist. Introd. Roman Law* xvii. 137 We frequently read that the Proculian view upon some question was so and so, and that the Sabinian view differed from it. **1907** S. L. Phipson *Law of Evidence* (ed. 4) xlvi. 558 The old controversy between the Proculians and the Sabinians, between the logical, inferential or liberal school of interpreters, and the grammatical or literal. **1953** A. Berger *Encycl. Dict. Roman Law* 687/1 Among the prominent Sabinians after Sabinus and Cassius were Lavolenus, Gaius, and Julian. **1977** A. Watson *Nature of Law* vii. 102 Even in the second century A.D. one of the two famous schools of jurists, the Sabinian, argued that barter should be included within the contract of sale.

Sabi·nian, *a.*[2] *rare.* [f. Sabine *a.* and *sb.* + -ian.] = Sabine *a.*

1902 Belloc *Path to Rome* 432 Rome was hidden by the low Sabinian hills.

Sabin vaccine (sēⁱ·bin). *Med.* [Named after Albert Bruce *Sabin* (b. 1906), Russian-born U.S. microbiologist who developed the vaccine in 1955.] A vaccine against poliomyelitis made from attenuated viruses of the three serological types and administered orally.

1955 *Brit. Med. Jrnl.* I. 24/1 (Index), Vaccination; human trial of Sabin (live) vaccine. **1961** *Lancet* 30 Sept. 756/2 Administration of candied live Sabin vaccine led to a sharp reduction in poliomyelitis incidence and complete prevention of a seasonal rise in incidence during summer and autumn months. **1978** *Daily Tel.* 13 June 16 The production of anti-polio vaccine in America is being imperilled because India has stopped the export of rhesus monkeys, needed for processing Salk and Sabin vaccines, in the past few months.

Sabiny, var. *Sapiny.

Sabir (săbīᵊ·ɪ, ‖ sabir). Also (in *transf.* sense) **sabir.** [Fr., a. *sabir* 'to know' in the language invented by Molière for a song in *Le bourgeois gentilhomme* (1670), prob. ad. Sp. *saber* to know.] A French-based pidgin language used in parts of North Africa; also, = *lingua franca*; also *transf.* and *attrib.*

1867 'Ouida' *Under Two Flags* III. i. 18 'You are great warriors,' he cried, in the Sabir tongue. **1939** L. H. Gray *Foundations of Lang.* 37 *Sabir*, a mixture of French, Spanish, Italian, Greek, and Arabic, which serves as a *lingua franca* for the Mediterranean ports. **1964** E. Palmer tr. *Martinet's Elem. Gen. Linguistics* v. 155 These somewhat sketchy tools of communication are often called *sabirs* after the language which long flourished in the Mediterranean ports and is also known as the *lingua franca.* **1972** R. Mayne *Europeans* iv. 58 The multinational institutions of the Common Market are gradually developing a modern administrative *sabir* compounded from French, German, Italian, and even English. **1974** *Florida FL Reporter* XIII. 17/1, I cannot agree that the 'Sabir Pidgins'..at least are special formations. Rather, they were transmitted by maritime routes—and in some frontier situations. **1978** *Language* LIV. 338 It seems clear that temporal priority must be granted to the contact system used with North Africans of the western Mediterranean ('Sabir') over that used with Black Africans (the reconnaissance language). *Ibid.*, Eastern Sabir, the pidgin used by pilgrims and merchants in the eastern Mediterranean, was, however, much more destructured than the Western Sabir recorded in the Portuguese documents.

sabji, var. Subjee in Dict. and Suppl.

sabkha (sa·bχa, sa·bka). *Geogr.* Also **sabquha, sebk(h)a.** Pl. **sabkha(s), sebakh.** [ad. Arab. *sabḵah* a saline infiltration, salt flat.] A flat, salt-encrusted depression, usu. just above the water-table, that is subject to periodic flooding and evaporation, resulting in accumulation of alternating layers of æolian clays and salts, and is found esp. in N. Africa and Arabia. Cf. *chott, *kavir, *playa 1, Shott in Dict. and Suppl.

1878 [see Shott]. **1891** [see *chott]. **1909** Groom & Balfour tr. *E. Warming's Œcol. of Plants* lviii. 233 Here also may be placed the *shotts* and *sebakh* of North Africa, depressions which contain salt water during the rainy season, but many of which are dry and covered with incrustations of salt in summer. **1911** G. Bell *Let.* 23 Feb. (1927) I. xii. 280 The ground here is what the Arabs called 'sabkha', soft, crumbly salt marsh, sandy when it is dry and ready at a moment's notice to turn into a world of glutinous paste. **1937** *Trans. Connecticut Acad. Arts & Sci.* XXXIII. 110 In the smaller sebkas, comparable in dimensions to Carson Lake, the water is less salt, and supports a more varied fauna. **1957** R. J. H. Church *W. Afr.* xiv. 231 There is, in the north, a succession of salt encrusted mud-flats (sebkhas), marshy only after rare rains, which are remnants of former lagoons. **1963** [see *kavir]. **1964** *Nature* 23 May 759/1 The coast of the Sheikdom of Abu Dhabi, Trucial States, ..is bordered for most of its length by low coastal flats which stand just above normal high-tide level. These flats are known locally as sabkha. **1972** *Sci. Amer.* Dec. 29/3 Sabkhas became an object of considerable interest to geologists soon after it was realized that certain types of ancient rock formation are practically identical with the sabkha sediments; both are characterized by the presence of nodular anhydrite and stromatolitic dolomite. **1973** *Nature* 20 July 145/1 The Triassic sabkhas were not all coastal sabkhas, or tidal flats, some may have been continental sabkhas, or playa flats. *Ibid.* 7 Sept. 29/2 The cores..show microalternations of organic matter and carbonate (sometimes replaced by chert) which closely resemble Recent supratidal deposits in the Persian Gulf (sabquha),..which are a product of a hot dry climate and hypersaline marine conditions with frequent drying out of the sediment. **1977** A. Hallam *Planet Earth* 157 Many modern desert coasts are bordered by salt marshes, usually known as sabkhas. **1980** D. Creed *Scarab* v. 39 The long flat distances of the sabkha..the time-worn cliffs, the unbroken blue of the sky.

sable, *sb.*[1] Add: **1. b.** For 'pencil' read 'brush'. (Further examples.) Cf. *kolinsky.

1899 [see *red sable* s.v. *red *a.* 19 a]. **1958** M. L. Wolf *Dict. Painting* 41 Modern painters' brushes are in two general types: bristle, or coarse hair, usually that of the pig; and fine hair, made of sable, or so-called 'camel hair'. **1973** F. Taubes *Painter's Dict.* 207 Sables are standard painting tools for all water-based mediums—watercolor, acrylic, casein, gouache, etc.—which require large, thin passages of fluid color.

2. b. Short for *sable coat.*

1975 R. Stout *Family Affair* xiv. 123, I..went to the hall with Mrs Bassett's mink or sable or sea otter and held it for her. **1977** J. Crosby *Company of Friends* xvi. 105 She eyed the sable some more... In a few more years they would be hanging that coat on the wall..like a painting.

3. (Earlier example.)

1785 *Daily Universal Reg.* 1 Jan. 4/3 About 140 tons of old Sable and Gurioff's iron saved out of the Westmoreland.

4. a. *sable coat* (later example; hence *-coated* adj.); *sable-trimmed* adj.

1928 Sable coat [see *ask *v.* 5 d]. **1978** F. Maclean *Take Nine Spies* 336 The seductive, sable-coated countess ..on the Orient Express. **1922** Joyce *Ulysses* 457 A sabletrimmed brick quilted dolman.

sable, *sb.*[2] and *a.* Add: **A.** *sb.* **6.** *sable-gowned, -tinted* adjs.

1848 J. G. Whittier in *National Era* 14 Dec. 198/5 The sable-gowned divine..shall prove Their trade accordant with the Law of Love. **1918** G. Frankau *One of Them* II. xvi. 121 Hat thrown aside from tresses sable-tinted.

B. *adj.* **2. a.** *his sable majesty* (also, *excellency*): applied to a dark-complexioned potentate; *spec.* the Devil.

1867 G. H. Lewes *Let.* 8 Aug. in *Geo. Eliot Lett.* (1956) IV. 384 Here he translated the Bible, and here he wrestled with Satan, flinging (like a true literary antagonist) his ink-stand at his sable majesty's head, and staining the whitewashed wall. **1875** J. D. Lang *Hist. Acct. New South Wales* (ed. 4) I. xi. 393 If Her Majesty could have commissioned the Prince of Darkness to represent her in the Colony.., I doubt not but his sable Excellency would have received a Farewell Address of respect. **1881** [see Majesty 2]. **1895** *Photos* 8 June 10 His sable majesty.. is a man of great force of character.

sablefish (sēⁱ·b'lˌfiʃ). *N. Amer.* [f. Sable *a.* + Fish *sb.*[1]] A grey- or black-skinned fish of the family Anoplopomatidæ, esp. *Anoplopoma fimbria*, found in the Pacific off the western coast of North America.

1936 P. S. Barnhart *Marine Fishes S. Calif.* 61 Family Anoplopomatidae. Sablefishes... *Anoplopoma fimbria* (Pallas). Sablefish... In northern waters this fish becomes very fat and is much valued for food. **1964** G. C. Carl *Some Common Marine Fishes Brit. Columbia* 48 The sablefish..is smoked and sold under the name of 'black cod'. **1972** *Islander* (Victoria, B.C.) 16 Apr. 13/3 Should black cod, or sablefish, prove to be unrewarding, she is designed to convert easily for tuna fishing. **1975** *Sci. Amer.* Oct. 88/3 The flatnose codling, the sablefish and the arctic sleeper shark are common inhabitants of the bottom off the coast of southern California and Lower California.

sabliere[1]. (Canad. examples.)

1800 Henry & Thompson *Jrnl.* 23 Oct. in E. Coues *New Light Early Hist. Greater Northwest* (1897) I. iii. 123 Oak logs..contg. 100 ft. for the sableries. **1809** D. Thompson *Jrnl.* 18 Nov. (1950) 64 Men put up the partition Wall of my Room & finished the Walls the Sablier Beams Roof Beams &c which ended the Day.

Sabme, var. *Sami.

sabot. Add: **2. c.** Any device fitted inside the muzzle of a gun to hold or support the projectile to be fired (as when they are of different calibres).

1950 Scott & Richardson *Fin Stabilized Projectile Devel. for 3 inch/70 Gun* (NAVORD Rep. 1537: AD 857–242) 3 Removal of the sabot by spin can be disregarded as the projectile acquires little, if any, spin in the smooth bore tube... The type of sabot developed by the Germans during World War II, and operating primarily by muzzle blast with the assistance of the air stream, is the simplest in design. **1954** K. W. Gatland *Devel. Guided Missile* (ed. 2) ii. 47 Models launched from guns in the new supersonic free-flight wind-tunnel are protected in the gun barrel by plastic 'sabots' which keep the models correctly aligned and act as pistons. **1957** E. Burgess *Guided Weapons* iv. 100 The models..which are being tested are launched through a smooth-bore gun by means of a discarding sabot. **1963** *Dict. U.S. Mil. Terms* (U.S. Dept. Defense) 188 *Sabot*, lightweight carrier in which a subcaliber projectile is centered to permit firing the projectile in the larger caliber weapon. The carrier fills the bore of the weapon from which the projectile is fired; it is normally discarded a short distance from the muzzle. **1975** I. V. Hogg *German Artillery of World War Two* 267 An enormous range of sabot shells was developed in Germany with the intention of either increasing the range of field guns or reducing the time of flight of anti-aircraft shells.

5. (See quot. 1966.)

1962 *Internat. Art Treasures Exhib., Victoria & Albert Mus.* 20/2 A Louis XV parquetry table à écrire..raised on cabriole legs with gilt bronze sabots. **1966** M. M. PEGLER *Dict. Interior Design* (1967) 383 *Sabots*... Decorative metal coverings for the feet of wood furniture ..appeared in the 18th century, and were made of bronze doré, bronze, brass, etc. **1980** *Country Life* 3 July 11/2 A ravishing writing desk... The cabriole legs are framed by moulded ormolu borders reaching down to pierced sabots.

6. In baccarat and chemin de fer, a shoe: see *SHOE *sb.* 5.

[**1963** C. GRAVES *None but the Rich* 3 Baccarat, in fact, is chemin-de-fer played with a fixed bank, chemin-de-fer taking its name from the fact that the 'shoe' (in French, *sabot*), as the deal box is known, moves like a toy railway train round the table each time the dealer loses.] **1964** A. WYKES *Gambling* vii. 177 (*caption*) The *sabot* from which the 'chemmy' cards are dealt. **1966** P. O'DONNELL *Sabre-Tooth* vi. 93 The sabot containing the six packs of cards, recently shuffled and stacked by the croupier. **1977** X. FIELDING *Money Spinner* 162 Finally they are placed in the 'shoe' or *sabot*, from which the banker deals them one by one.

sabotage (sæ·bŏtɑ̄ʒ, ‖ sabɔtɑ̄ʒ), *sb.* [Fr., f. *saboter* to make a noise with sabots, to perform or execute badly, e.g. to 'murder' (a piece of music), to destroy wilfully (tools, machinery, etc.), f. *sabot*: see SABOT and -AGE.] The malicious damaging or destruction of an employer's property by workmen during a strike or the like; hence *gen.* any disabling damage deliberately inflicted, esp. that carried out clandestinely in order to disrupt the economic or military resources of an enemy. Also *transf.*, *fig.*, and *attrib.*

1910 *Church Times* 11 Nov. 631/2 We have lately been busy in deploring the *sabotage* of the French railway strikers. **1916** *Sydney Morning Herald* 18 Oct., A shearing rouseabout,..charged..with having written a letter to Senator Lynch, threatening him and certain other Labour politicians and employers of Australia with acts of sabotage. **1918** E. S. FARROW *Dict. Mil. Terms* 528 *Sabotage*, wanton destruction of property to embarrass or injure an enemy; such as the smashing of machinery, flooding of mines, burning of wheat and grain, destroying fruit and provisions, dynamiting reservoirs and aqueducts, tying up railroads, etc. **1920** *Glasgow Herald* 26 June 7 Forces are at work in Germany for the sabotage of the Treaty. **1931** W. MARTYN *Scarlett Murder* iv. 53 He was in that mood of smouldering rage which only sabotage would slake. **1948** *N.Y. Jrnl. American* (Sunday Mail ed.) 9 May 1/5 Berger and Dasch gave..'full and complete' identification of all connected with the sabotage plot. **1955** *Times* 27 Aug. 6/7 These were the most considerable sabotages of telephone lines which have yet occurred in this area. **1958** *Spectator* 20 June 791/3 The most recent attack on him has been for cultural sabotage. **1977** *South China Morning Post* (Hong Kong) 22 July 1/4 The border flare-up began on July 12, the radio said, when a four-man Libyan sabotage squad was arrested after crossing the border armed with machineguns and explosives. **1978** T. ALLBEURY *Lantern Network* vii. 86 Langlois had led six-man teams on fifteen sabotage missions. **1979** *Tucson* (Arizona) *Citizen* 20 Sept. 11A/5 The PLO has provided guns and sabotage devices to its IRA friends.

Hence **sa·botage** *v. trans.*, to ruin, destroy, or disable deliberately and maliciously (freq. by indirect means); **sa·botaging** *vbl. sb.*

1918 *New Appeal* 7 Dec. 1/2 Testimony..that the companies are sabotaging the government. **1920** *Glasgow Herald* 20 Aug. 7 When the miners threaten to sabotage the commerce of the country struggling to get back to pre-war prosperity. **1923** *Ibid.* 4 Jan. 4 The sabotaging of the Dual Monarchy, the revolt of the Yugoslav troops, [etc.]. **1934** C. LAMBERT *Music Ho!* v. 303 Technically speaking it [*sc.* the atonal school] sabotaged the moribund romantic tradition. **1941** *Sun* (Baltimore) 22 Mar. 24/1 The fireworks bill..was passed by the Senate tonight..despite eleventh-hour attempts to sabotage it or delay enactment. **1975** *Times* 14 Jan. 14/3 [Michael Foot] defended the social contract and weighed into the press for sabotaging it.

sabota lark (săbōᵘ·tă lāɹk). [f. *sabota*, native name of the bird adopted as its specific name (A. Smith *Rep. Exped. for Exploring Central Africa* (1836) 47) + LARK *sb.*[1]] A buff-coloured lark, *Mirafra sabota* or *M. nævius*, of the family Alaudidæ, found in southern Africa.

1884 R. B. SHARPE *Layard's Birds S. Afr.* (rev. ed.) 526 Sabota Lark... Sir Andrew Smith procured this lark on the arid plains north of Latakoo. **1896** H. A. BRYDEN *Tales S. Afr.* v. 109 There, too, are the thick-billed lark, the Sabota lark, with its clear ringing call, and a few other—but not many—small birds. **1948** C. D. PRIEST *Eggs of Birds breeding in S. Afr.* 67 Sabota Lark... In grass on the ground, at times the cup-shaped nest not being well concealed. **1964** P. A. CLANCEY *Birds Natal & Zululand* 293 The sabota lark commences to breed in October.

saboteur (sæ·bŏtəɹ, ‖ sabɔtör). Also fem. **saboteuse.** [Fr.] One who commits sabotage.

1921 tr. *W. Rathenau's New Society* 125 The *saboteurs* of labour. **1931** *Observer* 11 Jan. 20/2 Two managers of a dairy were dubbed saboteurs and sentenced to..imprisonment for letting two hundred tons of butter spoil. **1947** J. MULGAN *Report on Experience* xii. 148 The men who were killed had been *saboteurs*, or gleaners of information for the Allies, patriots in their own quiet and dangerous way. **1973** E. PACE *Any War will Do* III. 199 They're too chicken to send in their paratroopers, and they're not smart enough to send in saboteurs. **1977** Saboteuse [see *PIG *sb.*[1] 6 b]. **1977** *South China Morning Post* (Hong Kong) 22 July 1/3, 12 members of the 9th Libyan Armoured Division were taken prisoner along with 30 saboteurs. **1980** *Daily Tel.* 20 Mar. 1/5 Two fox-hunt saboteurs who had appeared as prosecution witnesses against hunt followers.

sabquha, var. *SABKHA.

Sabra (sæ·bră). [ad. mod.Heb. *ṣābrāh* prickly pear.] **1.** (Also with small initial.) A Jew born in Palestine (see *PALESTINIAN *a.* and *sb.*) or, after 1948, in Israel (see *ISRAEL 3). Also *attrib.*

1945 *Zionist Rev.* 16 Nov. 8/2 Of course I was born here. No, I am not a new immigrant, not even an old one; I am a *sabra*. **1946** KOESTLER *Thieves in Night* I. ii. 9 They were Sabras—nicknamed after the thorny, rather tasteless fruit of the cactus, grown on arid earth, tough, hard-living, scant. *Ibid.* II. ii. 95 These Sabra-boys regard a glass of wine as something like opium or hashish. **1949** —— *Promise & Fulfilment* 222 He is a *sabra*, with a pleasant open face and good physique. **1958** M. E. SPIRO *Children of Kibbutz* p. x, My research problem, therefore, was restricted to the relationships between kibbutz child training and *sabra* (one born and raised in a kibbutz) personality. **1971** *Times* 28 Sept. (Israel Suppl.) p. iv/4 Only two of the 18 Ministers in Israel's Government are *sabras*, native Israel Jews... There is no *sabra* university president. **1977** *Time* 4 July 16/1 Begin's predecessor, Yitzhak Rabin, was a nonobservant Sabra who often seemed uncomfortable wearing a yarmulke and unfamiliar with the words of daily prayers.

2. (See quots.)

1970 *House & Garden* Nov. 139/1 Sabra is a new liqueur from Israel..a blend of Jaffa orange and chocolate. **1975** *Times* 11 Jan. 11/5 Sabra, the Israel liqueur made with bitter oranges and a very bitter Swiss chocolate.

sabre, *sb.* Add: **1. a.** (Further *fig.* examples.)

1922, etc. [see *sabre-rattling* vbl. sb. and ppl. adj., sense 4 a below]. **1928**, etc. [see *sabre-rattler*, sense 4 a below]. **1949** *Western Folklore* VIII. 112 To rattle the saber. To threaten military action. **1968** *Listener* 29 Aug. 259/2 The antique apparatus of Soviet diplomacy complete with rattling sabres and dutiful crowd noises from the Warsaw satellites, was mobilised in the hope of strengthening the Old Guard in the Czechoslovak party. **1976** *Times* 27 Jan. 1/3 At least a few Conservatives.. doubt whether Mrs Thatcher was prudent to appear to rattle sabres and remind electors that women national leaders..have sometimes looked more warlike than men. **1978** J. A. MICHENER *Chesapeake* 704 Orators from many southern states came north to excite voters against the dangers of black franchise, and sabers rattled as ancient battles were recalled.

c. In Fencing, a weapon with a flattened blade and blunted cutting edge, either curved or straight, lighter than the *ÉPÉE; the exercise of fencing with sabres.

[**1880** J. M. WAITE *Lessons in Sabre* p. xi, I have had the honour of instructing the following Clubs in both Fencing and Sabre:—The London Fencing Club [etc.].] **1910** *Encycl. Brit.* X. 252/1 Just as the practice of the 'small' or thrusting sword gave rise to two rival schools, the French and the Italian, that of the sabre or cutting sword..became split up into two main systems, Italian and German. **1927** L. BERTRAND *Cut & Thrust* vi. 75 He was..a resplendent figure..waving..a light and fragile silver-plated sabre. **1935** *Encycl. Sports* 531/1 In fencing with the sabre, the upper part of the body is the sole target, and the hits are made by cuts. **1952** *Fencing* ('Know the Game' Ser.) 5 To hit at foil, épée and sabre, is to strike the opponent with the point of the sword so that it fixes clearly and distinctly and has a character of penetration. **1954** R. CROSNIER *Fencing with Sabre* I. 22 At sabre, the distance between two fencers is such that body or head cannot be hit when the opponent lunges fully. **1971** I. BUTYKAI tr. *Lukovich's Electric Foil Fencing* II. 166 This is also in support of what is described above about the application in sabre of feints with the body. **1978** G. WRIGHT *Illustr. Handbk. Sporting Terms* 32 If, in foil and sabre, hits are equal, the bout continues until a deciding hit is landed. *Ibid.* 33 The ancestors of the sabre include the eastern sabre, the English broadsword, and the cavalry sabre.

4. a. *sabre-fencer, -fencing, -play, -player, -stroke*; *sabre-like* adj.; **sabre leg** (see quot. 1952); also *attrib.*; **sabre-rattler**, a reckless militarist; one who threatens violent action; **sabre-rattling** *vbl. sb.*, military aggression; threatening violent action; aggressive blustering; also as *ppl. adj.*; **sabre saw**, a portable electric saw with a narrow reciprocating blade, used for cutting curves.

1952 *Fencing* ('Know the Game Ser.) 26 Modern sabre fencers..have developed a technique when attacking, of directing the blade, changing its direction, and striking, by means of wrist actions and finger manipulation. **1954** R. CROSNIER *Fencing with Sabre* I. 28 Sabre fencers who have progressed in technique and sword control, acquire the ability to change their grip, slightly, when attacking or defending. **1927** L. BERTRAND *Cut & Thrust* vi. 77 The rules of sabre-fencing are eminently practical. **1954** R. CROSNIER *Fencing with Sabre* 14 When reading this text-book, some may accuse me of having approached the subject of sabre fencing with the mind of a confirmed foilist. **1975** *Oxf. Compan. Sports & Games* 304/2 It is.. necessary to have..a president to control the bout and award hits according to the rules and conventions applicable to sabre fencing. **1952** J. GLOAG *Short Dict. Furnit.* 404 *Sabre leg*, a hollow curved leg of rectangular section, so called because of its resemblance to the curve of a cavalry sabre. It was copied from the seats and thrones depicted on Greek and Roman vases, and was introduced towards the end of the 18th century. After 1815, it was sometimes called a Waterloo leg. In chairs of cheap quality the front edge is usually rounded. **1963** *Times* 2 Mar. 5/4 A small walnut kneehole desk made £220 (Quinney's), six sabre-leg Regency dining chairs £160. **1974** *Country Life* 5 Dec. (Suppl.) 78/2 A George III Sofa Table..with swept sabre legs. **1934** WEBSTER, Saber-like. **1962** D. NICHOLS *Echinoderms* i. 20 *Machaeridia*, bilaterally symmetrical worm-like remains with a skeleton of imbricating plates. Greek: 'sabre-like'. **1880** J. M. WAITE *Lessons in Sabre* p. vi, The English method of sabre play..could be considerably improved. **1927** L. BERTRAND *Cut & Thrust* vi. 81 In..observance of this maxim [sc. *sciabola in mano*] lies the *alpha and omega* of all sabre-play. **1954** R. CROSNIER *Fencing with Sabre* I. v. 26 The Hungarian principle..maintained that sabre play was a combination of finger-play and wrist work, conducive to light, rapid, and precise blade actions. **1880** J. M. WAITE *Lessons in Sabre* p. vi, Sabre players, as a rule, have not been fencers, or at least have been fencers with trifling skill. **1928** *Daily Express* 6 Dec. 5/2 There is no reason for supposing that the child Napoleon will grow up a sabre-rattler. **1975** *Times Lit. Suppl.* 6 June 625/4 When he [*sc.* Churchill] came to the rescue of Montagu in the stormy Amritsar debate, he incurred the disgust of the sabre-rattlers. **1922** *Weekly Dispatch* 19 Nov. 8 A policy of adventure, sabre-rattling, and reckless expenditure. **1928** *Observer* 26 Feb. 16/4 A sabre-rattling gesture against a nation with whom we have been at peace for more than a hundred years. **1958** HAYWARD & HARARI tr. *Pasternak's Dr. Zhivago* I. iv. 105 You have to swagger about in an officer's uniform too, you have to do your own bit of sabre-rattling. **1973** 'I. DRUMMOND' *Jaws of Watchdog* x. 136 A sabre-rattling pink-hating American. **1977** C. MCCULLOUGH *Thorn Birds* ii. 40 Look at the way that saber-rattling Churchill sent our men into something as useless as Gallipoli! **1977** *Time* 24 Oct. 8/1 Despite saber-rattling rhetoric, a steel war is far from inevitable. **1953** R. J. DE CRISTOFORO *Power Tool Woodworking for Everyone* v. 179 Saber saws are usually confined to heavy cutting when curves are not too severe. **1976** M. MACHLIN *Pipeline* xxviii. 334 The group carried two battery operated saber-saws with hacksaw blades in their chucks. **1980** *Sci. Amer.* Mar. 29/2 A big saber saw, its diamond blade able to cut a four-foot slab at one pass (beyond the two-foot reach of the biggest rotary blades), requires some 25 horsepower, delivered by hydraulic flow from its engine trailer nearby. **1854** TENNYSON *Charge of Light Brigade* in *Wks.* (1896) 222/2 Cossack and Russian Reel'd from the sabre-stroke Shatter'd and sunder'd.

b. sabre-toothed, *a.* (*fig.*), ferocious; **sabre-tooth(ed) cat** = *sabre-toothed lion, tiger*; **sabre-toothed lion,** for 'the genus MACHAIRODUS' substitute 'the subfamily Machærodontinæ'; **sabre-tooth** *sb.* (later example).

1906 E. INGERSOLL *Life Animals: Mammals* 86 A divergent branch..developed amazingly throughout most of the Tertiary period,..to which Cuvier gave the name of 'saber-tooth cats'. **1933** A. S. ROMER *Vertebr. Paleont.* xv. 294 In sharp contrast are the saber-toothed 'cats', Machaerodontinae... In the saber-tooths the upper canines were exceedingly long stabbing and slicing structures. **1968** *Times* 21 Dec. 2/3 There was a sabre-toothed scrummage of photographers. **1973** Sabretooth cat [see *MACHÆRODONT *a.*]. **1975** J. G. EVANS *Environment Early Man Brit. Isles* i. 21 Three species of mammal considered to have become extinct prior to the Hoxnian .. a sabre-toothed cat (*Homotherium latidens*) and two voles. **1977** *Times* 14 Mar. 5/3 Henry Howard, Earl of Surrey..fell in the sabre-toothed power struggle for the succession when Henry VIII was dying.

sabreur. Add: **a.** (Further example.) See also *BEAU SABREUR.

1969 N. FREELING *Tsing Boum* ix. 59 Castries the cavalryman, swaggering sabreur.

b. A sabre-fencer.

1927 L. BERTRAND *Cut & Thrust* vi. 81 How to acquire this touch is a question the would-be sabreur has to answer. **1952** *Fencing* ('Know the Game' Ser.) 26 Sabreurs attack more often by means of a 'Flèche', than by means of a lunge. **1958** *Oxf. Mag.* 13 Mar. 377/1 The Cambridge sabreurs challenged our supposed superiority in the sabre. **1978** G. WRIGHT *Illustr. Handbk. Sporting Terms* 35 (*caption*) The flèche attack demonstrated by a sabreur.

sabrina neckline (săbrī·nă). *U.S.* Also with capital initial. [f. *Sabrina*, the title of a film (1954), in which the actress Audrey Hepburn appeared wearing a dress with such a neckline.] A neckline with ties at the shoulders.

1959 E. HEAD *Dress Doctor* ix. 119, I had to console myself with the dress, whose boat neckline was tied on each shoulder—widely known and copied as 'the *Sabrina* neckline'. **1967** *Boston Sunday Herald* 30 Apr. v. 4/2 The bride wore an 18th century gown of white satin sabrina neckline with a long bodice trimmed with pearls and crystals and a train fastened at the shoulders with bows. **1976** *Columbus* (Montana) *News* 3 June 2/4 The bride's gown fashioned with chantilly lace basque bodice with long fitted sleeves and sabrina neckline, had a full skirt with petal overskirt of organza.

sabugalite (săbiū·gălait). *Min.* [f. *Sabugal*, name of a town in Beira Province, Portugal + -ITE[1].] A mineral of the autunite group, $HAl(UO_2)_4(PO_4)_4.16–24H_2O$, first found as yellow crystals in a number of mines in Portugal, and also prepared artificially.

1951 C. FRONDEL in *Amer. Mineralogist* XXXVI. 671 Sabugalite is a new member of the autunite group with the composition $HAl(UO_2)_4(PO_4)_4.16H_2O$. **1959** *Ibid.* XLIV. 420 The average index of refraction of the synthetic product indicated a value of about 1·57, which is within the range of indices given by Frondel for natural sabugalite. **1959** [see *SALÉEITE].

sabulite (sæ·biuləit). *Mil.* [f. L. *sabul-um* sand + -ITE[1].] A high explosive consisting of ammonium nitrate with some TNT and calcium silicide.

1914 *Daily Consular & Trade Rep.* 17 June 1641 Tests were recently made..of a new explosive called sabulite, which will be manufactured at Coguitlam, British Columbia. **1914** *Mining & Engin. World* XLI. 676/1 Sabulite, a recent invention by a Belgian explosive expert, had a thorough and satisfactory test..a few days ago. **1919** E. DE B. BARNETT *Explosives* IV. 114 Very similar explosives in which calcium silicide is used in place of aluminium are also manufactured, Sabulite being an explosive of this class. **1940** *Thorpe's Dict. Appl. Chem.* (ed. 4) IV. 464/1 Military sabulite contained ammonium nitrate 78%, trinitrotoluene 8% and calcium silicide 14%, the latter constituent increasing the heat of explosion.

sabzi, var. SUBJEE in Dict. and Suppl.

sac[2]. Add: **3.** (Earlier example.)

1814 M. BIRKBECK *Journey through France* 18 In three days the same postillion left our sac at the hotel unopened, not an article missing.

4. sac-winged bat, a South American bat belonging to the genus *Saccopteryx* or closely related genera of the family Emballonuridæ, distinguished by the pouch-like scent gland found in the wing membrane of the males.

1891 W. S. DALLAS in P. M. Duncan *Cassell's Nat. Hist.* I. v. 313 The Striped Sack-winged [*sic*] Bat is rather a small species. **1939** G. M. ALLEN *Bats* ix. 139 Still more remarkable..are the South American sac-winged bats,.. in which a large pouchlike gland is present in the membrane that extends from the fore shoulder to the wrist. **1964** E. P. WALKER et al. *Mammals of World* I. 235/1 Sac-winged bats generally roost in groups of 3 to 30 individuals.

sac[3], sacch (sæk). *slang.* [Abbrev. SACCHARINE *a.* and *sb.*] A saccharine tablet.

1961 PARTRIDGE *Dict. Slang* Suppl. 1257/1 *Sac*, a *sac*charine tablet: coll. (domestic, and small traders'): heard in 1917, but not gen. until 1942. **1968** 'E. TREVOR' *Place for Wicked* vi. 79 Sacchs. You couldn't get them down there.

Sac, var. *SAUK. **Saca**, var. *SAKA. **sac à commis**, var. *SAGAKOMI.

sac-à-lait. (Earlier and later examples.)

[**1877** C. HALLOCK *Sportsman's Gazetteer* 378 Goggle-eyed Perch;..sac-a-lac (New Orleans Creoles).] **1903** T. H. BEAN *Fishes N.Y.* 463 Still other names of local application [for the calico bass] are barfish, bitter head, tinmouth, *sac-a-lait*, lamplighter, [etc.]. **1931** W. A. READ *Louisiana-French* 67 In Louisiana the final *t* of *sacalait* is silent. **1937** *Zeitschr. für Französische Sprache & Literatur* LXI. 82 *Sacalait*, the Louisiana name for the crappie.., commonly thought to have been suggested by the beautiful white flesh or the silvery appearance of this fish. The actual source of the name is Choctaw *sakli*, 'trout', French *sac à lait* being merely a typical example of folk etymology. **1949** *New Orleans Times-Picayune Mag.* 16 Oct. 20/3 If you run out of bait while the bream, sacalait, and other fish are practically jumping into the boat, then the lily is your friend. **1973** *Trailer Travel* Jan. 73/2 You can catch large-mouth bass, channel cats, breams, and sac-a-lait or crappie.

sacaline, var. *SACHALINE.

sacate, zacate (sǎkā·te, zā-). Also **Zacate**. [ad. Mexican Sp. *zacate* grass, hay, ad. Nahuatl *çacatl, zacatl* grass, reed.] Any of several grasses grown in Mexico, the southern U.S.A., and the Philippines, and used for hay or fresh forage; fodder made from such a grass. Cf. next.

1848 J. W. ABERT *Rep. Exam. New Mexico 1846–'47* 29 As there were no pasture grounds near the village, I was forced to buy 'zacate' for my mules. **1891** G. VASEY *Illustr. N. Amer. Grasses* (U.S. Dept. Agric. Div. Bot.) I. II. (*facing plate* XX), [*Sporobolus wrightii* is] a tall coarse grass, growing in dense tufts, commonly called Saccaton or Zacate. **1921** *Blackw. Mag.* Nov. 659/1 The jungle almost obliterated the track. He cut it down with his *machete*.., and, pushing his tired beast through *sacate* and bamboo, emerged..on a gravelly bank. **1977** A. V. BOGDAN *Trop. Pasture & Fodder Plants* 44 *Axonopus affinis* Chase... Carpet grass;..Zacate amargo. *Ibid.* 45 *Axonopus compressus* (Swartz) Beauv. Carpet grass;.. Zacate amargo. *Ibid.* 92 *Cynodon dactylon* (L.) Pers... Bermuda grass;..Zacate Bermuda.

sacaton, zacaton (sæ·kǎtōᵘn, zæ·-, ‖ sakatō·n). Also **sacatone**, † **saccato**, † **saccaton(e)**, and with capital initial. [ad. Mexican Sp. *zacatón*, augmentative of *zacate* (see prec.)] Any of several coarse, tough grasses grown in Mexico and the southern U.S.A. and used for hay, esp. species of *Sporobolus* and *Epicampes*; *alkali sacaton*, a tussock grass, *Sporobolus airoides*, able to survive drought and alkaline soils. Cf. prec.

1865 *Harper's Mag.* Jan. 147/1 The grass consists of three principal varieties; the sacatone, a coarse, thick, and strong variety, growing in bunches; the mesquit..and the grama. **1886** *Outing* Dec. 223/2 We came upon a caved-in well, a wide hollow with a black bottom, covered with high rank grass, the Mexican *zacaton*. **1891** G. VASEY *Illustr. N. Amer. Grasses* (U.S. Dept. Agric. Div. Bot.) I. I. (*facing plate* XXV), It [sc. *Muhlenbergia distichophylla*] is one of the grasses called saccato. *Ibid.* (*facing plate* XXVII), This [sc. *Epicampes macroura*] is another of the grasses called saccato, or saccatone. **1929** J. W. BEWS *World's Grasses* v. 201 Two species of the S.W. States are important forage grasses in the arid or semi-arid regions of Nebraska, Arizona, and Texas—*S*[*porobolus*] *wrightii* Munro, 'Saccaton', and *S. airoides* Torr., 'Alkali Saccaton' or 'Alkali Drop-seed'. **1936** J. A. MCKENNA *Black Range Tales* 177 The Indians.. crept from rock to rock; they crawled like snakes from one bunch of sacatone to another. **1942** CASTETTER & BELL *Pima & Papago Indian Agric.* 22 Along the edges and in the openings of the forests of these two drainages, sacaton grass (*Sporobolus Wrightii*) thrives. **1968** F. W. GOULD *Grass Systematics* v. 265 *Sporobolus airoides* (Torr.) Torr., alkali sacaton, is a characteristic bunchgrass of alkaline areas in the western states. **1972** G. DURRELL *Catch me a Colobus* ix. 194 The zacaton grass..is tall—as much as three feet high—a very pale golden-yellow in colour, and it grows in huge tussocks all over the soft, black, volcanic soil. **1977** A. V. BOGDAN *Trop. Pasture & Fodder Plants* 181 *Panicum maximum* Jacq. Guinea grass;..Zacaton (Mexico).

sacbrood (sæ·kbrūd). [f. SAC *sb.*[2] + BROOD *sb.*] A fatal viral disease of bee larvæ.

1913 G. F. WHITE in *Circular Bureau Entomol., U.S. Dept. Agric.* No. 169. 1 Sacbrood..is no new disease. *Ibid.* 3 There is, therefore, a disorder attacking the brood of bees in which [the] brood dies, but in which there has not been demonstrated any microorganism to which the cause of the trouble could be attributed. For this disease the name of 'sacbrood' is here suggested. *Ibid.*, Many larvæ dead of this disease can be removed from the cell without rupturing their body wall. When thus removed they have the appearance of a small closed sac. This character suggested the name 'sacbrood'. **1928** R. W. GLASER in T. M. Rivers *Filterable Viruses* viii. 281 The number of colonies that die as a direct result of sacbrood is comparatively small; the loss of individual bees, however, in the aggregate is enormous. **1967** K. M. SMITH *Insect Virol.* v. 95 Not much is known of the biology of sacbrood but at the moment the virus has only been recorded from the larvae of the honeybee.

saccacom(m)i(s), varr. *SAGAKOMI.

saccade. Delete ‖ and add: Also with pronunc. (sǎkā·d). **b.** A brief, rapid movement of the eye from one position of rest to another, whether voluntary (as in reading) or involuntary (as when a point is fixated).

1953 *Jrnl. Optical Soc. Amer.* XLIII. 495/2 These [types of eye movement] include relatively large slow waves, saccades, and slow drifts of fixation. **1962** *Ibid.* LII. 571/2 The eye does not move continuously along a line of print in reading, but executes a regular alternation of rapid jumps, called saccades, and fixational pauses. **1967** *New Scientist* 20 Apr. 156/1 Apart from a rapid trembling which plays a part in the mechanism of perception itself, there are two main types of eye-movement: slow 'drifts' away from the target image, and rapid jerks or 'saccades' tending to recentre it. **1971** *Sci. Amer.* June 35/2 Each saccade leads to a new fixation on a different point in the visual field. Typically there are two or three saccades per second. **1974** *Nature* 22 Mar. 308/3 Some observers can learn to suppress small saccades completely, without decreasing the accuracy of fixation or the visibility of the target.

saccadic (sǎkæ·dik), *a.* [f. prec. + -IC.] **1.** Of the nature of or pertaining to a saccade or saccades (sense *b).

1916 R. DODGE in *Psychol. Bull.* XIII. 422 German and Scandinavian writers are commonly using the descriptive class term 'saccadic' to denote the rapid eye-movements for which we have only the arbitrary name of 'type 1'. I am not sure with whom the term originated, but it seems worth adopting. *Ibid.* 423 He independently rediscovers and thus confirms a number of eye-movement phenomena; such as the inability to see during saccadic movements. **1940** R. S. WOODWORTH *Psychology* (ed. 12) xiv. 478 The saccadic movement carries the eyes from one object to another, while the pursuit movement follows a moving object. **1948** *Brit. Jrnl. Psychol.* XXXVIII. 144 In a task such as reading, where we wish to observe different parts of the field successively, it can be shown by photography that the eye makes jerks, or 'saccadic movements', having a mean duration of 0·03 to 0·05 sec. **1954** *A.M.A. Arch. Ophthalm.* LII. 710 Most experimenters have found that all voluntary movements executed in the absence of a moving visual stimulus are saccadic. **1977** DELL'OSSO & TROOST in Brooks & Bajandas *Eye Movements* 52 Saccadic palsy with normal pursuit occurs in both congenital and acquired ocular motor apraxia.

2. *gen.* Jerky, discontinuous.

1937 SCOTT & VLASTOS *Towards Christian Revolution* 247 Marxists are disposed to charge Christians with.. failure to appreciate the saccadic movement of history. **1951** J. S. BRUNER *Beyond Information Given* (1974) vi. 92 The reader may object that our model of the information-confirming cycle seems too saccadic, too jumpy. **1980** *Times Lit. Suppl.* 18 Jan. 54/2 From these things—parties, cafes, trips, gigs—a saccadic inconsequential life is made.

Hence **sacca·dically** *adv.*

1962 *Jrnl. Optical Soc. Amer.* LII. 572/2 One can produce conditions of stimulation under which the saccadically moving eye will not be able to see as well as the fixating eye. **1964** *Jrnl. Physiol.* CLXXIV. 259 In Fig. 11B is also shown what can never be measured in practice, the net active-state tension needed to drive the eye saccadically. **1975** *Nature* 1 May 68/2 When the cage was rotated, the bird showed the classical optomotor response of the head: alternately stabilising in visual space and saccadically moving to a new position.

saccarist, var. *SACRIST 2.

saccato, saccaton(e, varr. *SACATON, ZACATON.

sacch: see *SAC[3].

saccharase (sæ·kărēiz). *Biochem.* [f. med.L. *sacchar-um* sugar + *-ASE.] Invertase, sucrase.

1920 *Chem. Abstr.* XIV. 2344 Influence of the temperature and the acidity upon the formation of saccharase. **1930** J. B. S. HALDANE *Enzymes* ix. 168 In the case of saccharase the amount of substrate transformed is proportional over wide ranges both to the enzyme concentration and the time. **1973** *Enzyme Nomenclature* (Commission on Biochem. Nomenclature) 217/2 β-Fructofuranosidase... Other Names: Sucrase, Invertase, Invertin, Saccharase, β-*h*-Fructosidase.

saccharescent (sækăre·sənt), *a. rare.* [f. as SACCHARINE *a.* and *sb.* + -ESCENT.] Exuding sugar; sugary. Also *absol.* as *sb.* (In quots. *fig.*)

1930 E. POUND *XXX Cantos* xv. 65 The saccharescent, lying in glucose, the pompous in cotton wool. **1979** *Sunday Tel.* 15 July 12/7 A. C. Benson..dispensed saccharescent sweetness and cosy light through a number of best-sellers.

saccharhinoceros (sækărəinǫ·sĕrəs). *nonce-wd.* [Blend of SACCHARINE *a.* and *sb.* and RHINOCEROS.] A lumbering person with an excessively effusive or affectedly sentimental manner. *So* **saccharhino·ceroid** *a.*

1951 R. CAMPBELL *Light on Dark Horse* xvii. 240 The saccharine of false purity exuded from every pore of this saccarhinoceros advocate of virtue. *Ibid.* 241 The saccharhinoceros went off rumbling out some inarticulate phrases about 'Impertinence'. *Ibid.* 251 Sennacheribs.. lost his head completely, and seemed to be about to make a sort of saccharhinoceroid charge.

saccharic, *a.* Add: Also *loosely*: sweet.

1945 R. HARGREAVES *Enemy at Gate* 138 Anything from porter and sour Crimean wine to..exalted, if saccharic champagne.

saccharide. Substitute for entry:

saccharide (sæ·kărəid). *Chem.* [f. med.L. *sacchar-um* sugar + -IDE.] † **a.** A substance formed in the fermentation of melted sugar (see quot. 1862). *Obs.* [Introduced in Fr. by A. Gélis 1859, in *Compt. Rend.* XLVIII. 1062.]

Quot. 1857 in Dict. is wrongly dated. The word occurs first in the second edition (1862).

1860 *Q. Jrnl. Chem. Soc.* XII. 376 Researches on melted sugar, and on a new principle—saccharide: by A. Gélis. **1862** W. A. MILLER *Elem. Chem., Org.* (ed. 2) 78 According to Gélis, when sugar which has thus been melted is dissolved in water it furnishes a solution which when fermented with yeast yields only half the quantity of alcohol that ordinary sugar would have produced, a peculiar body to which he gives the name of saccharide ($C_{12}H_{10}O_{10}$) remaining in solution. It exerts a slight rotatory power to the right upon a beam of polarized light.

† **b.** A compound formed by the action of an acid on a sugar. *Obs.* [Introduced in Fr. by M. Berthelot 1860, in *Ann. de Chim. et de Phys.* LX. 94.]

1862 H. WATTS tr. *Gmelin's Handbk. Chem.* XV. 316 By heating dextro-glucose with (organic) acids, compounds are formed..which belong to the class of saccharides.

c. A sugar, esp. a monosaccharide; freq. used unsystematically to denote any mono- or oligosaccharide or a simple derivative of such a compound. [Introduced as G. *saccharid* by B. Tollens in *Kurzes Handb. d. Kohlenhydrate* (1888) 16.]

1895 THOMSON & BLOXAM *Bloxam's Chem.* (ed. 8) 705 The above considerations have given rise to a classification of the carbohydrates into (1) saccharides or monoses, ..(2) disaccharides or bioses,..(3) polysaccharides or polyoses. **1914** *Chem. Abstr.* VIII. 2716 (*heading*) Resolution of racemic saccharides by means of optically active amyl mercaptan, and some mercaptals. **1932** *Analyst* LVII. 374 By reducing the concentration of nitric acid, it is possible to obtain a mixture which reacts rapidly with saccharides and not with polysaccharides. **1955** *Stain Technol.* XXX. 286 Methods for the demonstration of saccharide, fatty acid, amino acid, vitamin and ketosteroid were chosen for testing. **1973** *Jrnl. Biochem.* (Tokyo) LXXIV. 144/2 Changes in the CD [sc. Circular Dichroism] bands at 295 and 305 nm on adding saccharides, acetamides or alcohols were monitored to study the interaction with lysozyme. **1974** *Amer. Jrnl. Physiol.* CCXXVI. 720/1 Hyperosmolarity with these saccharides [*viz.* glucose, mannitol, raffinose] caused sustained reduction of spontaneous frequency.

saccharilla (sækări·lă). *Disused.* [app. fancifully f. L. *sacchar-um* sugar.] A kind of muslin.

1851 *Illustr. Catal. Gt. Exhib.* III. 480/1 Saccharilla book muslin. *Ibid.*, Saccharilla mull muslin. *a* **1877** KNIGHT *Dict. Mech.* II. 1503/2 s.v. *Muslin*, Varieties are known as..lawn, saccharilla, harness. **1884** *Encycl. Brit.* XVII. 109/2 Plain, striped, and figured grenadines, and saccarillas.

saccharin. **2.** Add to def.: *o*-sulphobenzoic imide, $C_7H_5NO_3S$. (Further examples.)

1893, etc. [see *DULCIN b]. **1918** G. FRANKAU *One of Them* xvii. 128 Swiftly and cloying-sweet as saccharine In Governmental tea, a week had melted. **1973** J. G. TWEEDDALE *Materials Technol.* II. vii. 164 Many pharmaceutical products (including the sweetening substance saccharine) originated from coal-gas waste. **1977** *N.Y. Times Mag.* 15 May 88 It seems to strike most people as absurd, even outrageous, that saccharin has been indicted, convicted and condemned as a carcinogen. **1977** *New Yorker* 27 June 24/2 Only recently, the press has devoted acres of space to the subject of saccharin.

attrib. **1926–7** *Army & Navy Stores Catal.* 480/1 Saccharine tablets. bot. 100 -/10. **1968** *Canad. Antiques Collector* Nov. 21/2 During World War II still another use was found for these decorative little boxes..as containers for saccharin pills. **1978** G. FOX *Amok* iii. 25 Lenore took a tiny saccharin pill.., grimaced as she dropped it into her coffee. **1978** E. MALPASS *Wind brings up Rain* iv. 43 He pushed the bag of sugar into a drawer. If she wanted a cup of tea she could use her saccharine tablets.

saccharine, *a.* and *sb.* Add: **A.** *adj.* **5.** (Further examples.)

1933 *Punch* 16 Aug. 178/1 Here is actually a Viennese film based not on copious draughts of The Blue Danube (with sugar), but on the crisper life which must presumably exist in that city, even in defiance of the saccharine mirage which appears to be the fondest of Hollywood's illusions. **1934** C. LAMBERT *Music Ho!* II. 106 Such a saccharine melody as 'None but the Weary Heart'. **1951** *Essays in Crit.* I. III. 289 The saccharine honeymoon by the seaside. **1955** W. GADDIS *Recognitions* II. ii. 370 A saccharine line drawing of a woman. **1970** K. MILLETT *Sexual Politics* II. iii. 92 It was enough for him to rely on sentiment, a vague nostalgia about the heroic middle ages, and saccharine assertions about The Home. **1976** *Amer. N. & Q.* XIV. 147/2 The parable is saccharine and simplistic. Its sentimental treatment..asks for the cheap pity of melodrama and offers too easy a solution.

saccharined (sæ·kărind), *a.* [f. SACCHARINE *a.* and *sb.* + -ED².] Excessively sweet and sugary in tone.

1962 *Punch* 13 June 916/1 The recipe here [in a BBC series] has a queasy mélange of saccharined goodies with disc jockies selecting tunes by pop composers [etc.]. **1973** O. SELA *Portuguese Fragment* (1974) xxi. 118 A saccharined voice announces that your flight will be delayed.

saccharinity. (In Dict. s.v. SACCHARINE *a.* and *sb.*) (Further *fig.* examples.)

1932 B. DE VOTO *Mark Twain's Amer.* viii. 191 Similar items in saccharinity..had created a brummagem reputation. **1971** A. BURGESS *MF* i. 15 Loewe suddenly smiled with horrible saccharinity. **1977** *Times Lit. Suppl.* 18 Feb. 176/2 Juxtapositions of venom and saccharinity, iciness and boredom.

saccharinize (sæ·kărinəiz), *v.* [f. SACCHARIN + -IZE.] *trans.* To sweeten by adding saccharin. Freq. *fig.*, to make agreeable; to render inoffensive. Hence **sa·ccharinized** *ppl. a.*

1971 S. MARCUS in *Atlantic Monthly* Apr. 95 His praiseworthy intention to bring great genius before large numbers of readers comes to seem suspect in the light of the corrupt and corrupting means he employs in censoring, simplifying, and saccharinizing it. **1977** *New Scientist* 27 Oct. 208 The House..would require such a notice to be displayed only at the shop or other retail outlet where 'saccharinised' products are actually bought.

saccharolytic (sæ:kăroli·tik), *a.* *Biochem.* [f. SACCHARO- + *-LYTIC.] Of or pertaining to the chemical breakdown of carbohydrates; able to effect this.

1908 *Jrnl. Med. Res.* XVIII. 86 Bacillus coli showed but a weak sugar-splitting power, the saccharolytic action ceasing after twenty-four and sometimes after eighteen hours. **1928** L. E. H. WHITBY *Med. Bacteriol.* xv. 154 Saccharolytic organisms are so-called on account of their marked power of producing acid and gas in a carbohydrate medium. **1975** R. R. GILLIES *Lect. Notes Med. Microbiol.* xiv. 81 The six antigenically distinct types show variation in their saccharolytic and proteolytic activities.

Saccharomycetes (sæ:kăroməisī·tīz, -ts), *sb. pl.* [mod.L., f. generic name SACCHAROMYCES (J. Meyen 1838, in *Archiv für Naturgeschichte* IV. II. 100) + MYCETES.] A group name for yeasts, esp. those now included in the family Saccharomycetaceæ.

1884 W. B. GROVE *Synopsis Bacteria & Yeast Fungi* ii. 57 The saccharomycetes, or Yeast Fungi, are unicellular plants, which multiply themselves by budding. **1902** *Encycl. Brit.* XXVIII. 560/2 No satisfactory proof has as yet been given that Saccharomycetes are derivable by culture from any higher form. **1906** G. MASSEE *Text-bk. Fungi* I. 54 In the Saccharomycetes, or Yeasts, three modes of spore-formation are known. **1958** J. LODDER et al. in A. H. Cook *Chem. & Biol. Yeasts* i. 13 The fission yeasts were placed in a subfamily of their own,..separated from the Saccharomycetes.

saccharose. Add: **a.** = *DISACCHARIDE. Now *Obs.* (Further example.)

1911 [see *GLUCOSE 1 b].

b. = *SUCROSE b.

1876 [in Dict.]. **1928** A. B. CALLOW *Food & Health* i. 15 Each molecule of saccharose is composed of one atom of glucose (also called dextrose or grape sugar), and one atom of fructose (also called laevulose or fruit sugar). **1962** *Nature* 22 Sept. 1201/1, I have isolated two melibiose-fermenting yeasts,..which..are capable of fermenting maltose, but which neither ferment nor assimilate saccharose. **1979** *Digestion* XIX. 213 The jejunal absorption of either an elemental solution (amino acids, glucose and glucose oligosaccharides), or of nonelemental diet (chicken meat,..glucose, saccharose, maltose and dextrin maltose, corn and wheat oils) were compared in 25 healthy subjects.

Saccopastore (sa:kopastōᵊ·re). The name of a village near Rome used *attrib.* in **Saccopastore cranium, skull,** to designate the remains of a Neanderthal type of *Homo sapiens* found there in 1929.

1934 S. SERGI in *Proc. 1st Internat. Congr. Prehist. & Protohist. Stud. 1932* 50 The dimensions of the Gibraltar skull are slightly larger than those of the Saccopastore skull. *Ibid.* 51 The Saccopastore cranium does not at present permit of a complete examination. **1973** B. J. WILLIAMS *Evolution & Human Origins* xi. 181/2 In terms of dimensions and overall form the Saccopastore skull is much like the earlier Steinheim skull.

sacculus. Add: **2. b.** *Microbiol.* A bag-shaped macromolecule present as a structural element in the cell walls of some bacteria.

1964 WEIDEL & PELZER in *Adv. Enzymol.* XXVI. 194 Sacculi, as we shall call bagshaped macromolecules of the kind discussed here, are objects located on that border where Organic Chemistry merges into Morphogenesis and Morphology... A sacculus is not merely a complex chemical compound; it is, in a truly biological sense, a morphological entity. **1972** *Nature* 25 Feb. 426/2 Penicillin has been shown to interfere with the biosynthesis of the structural element of the bacterial cell wall, the sacculus. **1973** R. G. KRUEGER et al. *Introd. Microbiol.* v. 189/2 The mucopeptide sacculus obtains much of its structural rigidity from the repeating β-1,4-glycosidic bonds between the polysaccharide monomers.

‖**sac de nuit** (sak də nwi). ?*Obs.* [Fr.] A night-bag, a travelling bag.

1814 M. BIRKBECK *Journey through France* 18 An article of our baggage was missing... It was a *sac de nuit* containing sundries of some value. **1819** M. WILMOT *Let.* 3 Sept. (1935) 10 My invaluable Parisian pelisse..was only crammed, on second thoughts, to fill up a chink in my sac de nuit. **1845** R. FORD *Hand-bk. for Travellers Spain* I. I. 17 The company makes itself responsible for baggage..at relative allowances for *sacs de nuit*, portmanteaus, and trunks. **1860** *Once a Week* 8 Dec. 646/2 A little black *sac-de-nuit*.

sacerdoce. For *rare*⁻¹ read *rare* and add later example.

1926 R. FRY *Transformations* 58 Sir Claude Phillips was a great High Priest [of art history]..and..had to the full the sense of his sacerdoce.

sacerdos. For *Obs.* read *rare* and add later examples.

1930 E. POUND *XXX Cantos* xxix. 135 As who with four hands at the cross roads By King's hand or sacerdos' are given their freedom. **1949** —— *Pisan Cantos* lxxx. 92 Torn from the *sacerdos* hurled into unstillness.

‖**sacerdotium** (sæsəɹdōᵘ·ʃiŏm, sækəɹdōᵘ·tiŏm). [a. L. *sacerdōtium*: see SACERDOCY.] **a.** = SACERDOCY. **b.** The dominion of the Church in mediæval Europe.

1931 *Times Lit. Suppl.* 20 Aug. 628/2 The unhappy Episcopus..nearly lost his 'sacerdotium' in consequence. **1955** *Times* 2 July 7/3 When later the regular universities grew up the journey from Paris to Oxford, though arduous, was a routine event in the life of a scholar. This easy movement within the European *Studium*—as it called itself in grand contrast to the *Imperium* and *Sacerdotium*—was killed like many other good things by the rise of nationalism. **1956** *Scottish Jrnl. Theol.* IX. 174 Does the consecration of a bishop confer a new *character*? Or does it simply give him authority and grace to perform functions inherent in the *sacerdotium* or *ordo* of the presbyter, but not at present exercised by presbyters? Historically the *sacerdotium*, or ministry of the Word and Sacraments, was at one time regarded as particularly the characteristic of the bishop rather than of the presbyter.

sachaline (sæ·kalin, -īn). Also **sacaline.** [ad. the specific epithet of *Polygonum sachalinense* (F. Schmidt in C. J. Maximowicz *Primitiæ Floræ Amurensis* (1859) 233), f. *Sakhalin*, name of an island north of Japan.] A large perennial knotweed, *Polygonum sachalinense*, of the family Polygonaceæ, native to Japan and bearing clusters of small greenish flowers and very large oval leaves which are sometimes used as fodder.

[**1882** *Garden* 22 Apr. 280/2 (*heading*) The Sachalian knotweed.] **1901** L. H. BAILEY *Cycl. Amer. Hort.* III. 1393/2 Sacaline... Exceedingly vigorous plants, spreading rapidly from the tips of strong underground shoots. **1905** W. J. SPILLMAN *Farm Grasses U.S.* xv. 234 The two most prominent fads of this kind in recent years were sachaline, a well-nigh worthless representative of the smartweed family, and penicillaria. **1943** FERNALD & KINSEY *Edible Wild Plants* iii. 176 The leafy summits of young stems of Sachaline..cooked as a potherb..are as good as or superior to French Sorrel. **1952** L. & J. BUSH-BROWN *America's Garden Bk.* (ed. 2) xii. 535 Perennials blooming in September and October... Sacaline. **1975** *Daily Colonist* (Victoria, B.C.) 9 Oct. 6/1 A fast-growing weed threatening new growth in forests [is] sachaline, a bamboo-like weed from eastern Europe.

sachem. **2.** (Earlier and later examples.)

1684 in *Documents Colonial Hist. New-York* (1853) I. 402 Wee have put ourselves under the Great Sachim Charles that lives over the Great Lake. **1836** O. W. HOLMES *Song for Centennial Celebr. Harvard Coll.* in *Poems* (1849) 194 And, when at length the College rose, The sachem cocked his eye At every tutor's meagre ribs Whose coat tails whistled by. **1861** *Charleston* (S. Carolina) *Mercury* 29 Mar. 1/2 The Sachems of the Black Republican party did not appreciate the peculiarity of the times when they enacted the Morrill Tariff. **1942** E. PAUL *Narrow St.* xx. 164 [André] Breton, the pontifical sachem, turned to Trotsky and became an enemy. **1972** *Science* 16 June 1222/2 Chairman of the study group was Detlev W. Bronk, former president of Rockefeller University, president of the academy from 1950 to 1962, and himself a grand sachem of the advisory system. **1973** *Caribbean Contact* Feb. 2/2 It's the customs and immigration sachems, though, who must get top billing as the real purveyors of theatre in this world within a world. **1977** *Time* 18 July 26/3 Most party sachems are lining up behind either Incumbent Abraham Beame or Governor Hugh Carey's choice.

‖**Sachertorte** (za·χərto:rtə). Also **Sacher Torte, sachertorte.** [Ger., named after *Sacher*, proprietor of a hotel in Vienna, or the hotel itself + *torte* cake.] A rich chocolate cake of a kind orig. made in Vienna.

1906 *Mrs. Beeton's Bk. Househ. Managem.* lii. 1543 *Sacher torte.* (German chocolate tart.) **1954** 'M. COST' *Invitation from Minerva* 133 That crowning achievement of the Viennese table: *Sachertorte*. **1961** W. BUCHAN *Helen All Alone* 58 Large..cups of coffee..with brioches and sachertorte. **1974** *Times* 5 Apr. 16/3 Ice-cream, butterscotch,.. Sachertorte, pears, Baked Alaska. **1978** M. DICKENS *Open Bk.* i. 4 A rather formal tea, with damp cucumber sandwiches and *Sachertorte*.

sachet. Add: **4.** A small sealed bag-like container, now usu. of plastic, for holding a liquid, a powder, or air.

1917 *Harrod's Gen. Catal.* 358/3 Shampoo Sachets... box 1/0. **1941** N. MARSH *Death & Dancing Footman* (1942) ii. 42 The sachets used in permanent waving. **1970** *Which?* June 169/1 Jackets using air-filled sachets should be very safe too. **1975** C. F. ROSS *Packaging of Pharmaceuticals* I. 4 *Powders*.. are sometimes presented in single-dose containers. These may include sachets, filled automatically on suitable strip-packaging machines using paper, aluminium foil, plastics films or laminations of these.

‖**Sachlichkeit** (za·χliχʸkəit). [Ger., = 'objectivity'.] Objectivism, realism; *spec.* in the fine arts = *NEUE SACHLICHKEIT.

1930 *Times Lit. Suppl.* 24 Apr. 341/4 The prevailing note is one of indifference, of complete detachment, of *Sachlichkeit*. **1938** C. FULLMAN tr. *P. Thoene's Mod. German Art* 9 The general characteristics to be found in contemporary German painting..belong to the spiritual categories of a post-war world: Despair and its concomitants—satire and irony; realism, matter-of-fact-ness, *Sachlichkeit*. *Ibid.* 95 Max Beckmann has called his form 'transcendental *Sachlichkeit*'. **1968** *Listener* 3 Oct. 436/1 A generation of excellent artist-designers, such as Bruno Paul, Hans Poelzig and the brothers Taut, all worked in the spirit which was already associated with the word *Sachlichkeit*, which—taken literally—means 'thingness'; it is usually translated as 'matter-of-fact', 'realistic', 'sober', 'objective', and gained currency in matters of art and design early in this century.

‖**Sachverhalt** (za·χferhalt). *Philos.* Pl. **Sachverhalte.** [Ger., = status rerum (Grimm).] Esp. with reference to the philosophy of Wittgenstein and phenomenology, a state of affairs, an objective fact.

1922 B. RUSSELL in *Wittgenstein's Tractatus* 9 Facts which are not compounded of other facts are what Mr Wittgenstein calls *Sachverhalte*. **1931** W. R. B. GIBSON tr. *Husserl's Ideas* 461 The 'substantive' quality attaches to the 'Substrat' underlying the 'Sachverhalt', as well as to the 'Sachverhalt' itself. **1932** A. H. GARDINER *Theory of Speech & Lang.* i. 26 The unit of speech is the sentence and hence the 'thing' signified by every such unit is always of a complex kind—a state of things, as we might say, or a *Sachverhalt*, if we prefer to use the convenient German equivalent. **1950** *Mind* LIX. 266 That new type of object called the *Sachverhalt* or State of Affairs (the Meinongian 'Objective'). **1972** J. N. FINDLAY *Meinong's Emotional Presentation* p. xv, We become aware of what Husserl called variously states of affairs (*Sachverhalte*) or propositions.

sack, *sb.*[1] Add: **I. 1. f.** *Criminals' slang.* A pocket.

1699 B. E. *New Dict. Canting Crew, Sack*,..a Pocket. **1858** A. S. MAYHEW *Paved with Gold* III. iii. 265 I've brought a couple of bene coves, with lots of the Queen's pictures in their sacks. **1955** *Publ. Amer. Dial. Soc.* XXIV. 125 Rarely one hears the side coat pocket called a *sack*.

g. (*a*) A hammock; a bunk; (*b*) a bed; freq. as *the sack*; *to hit the sack*: see HIT *v.* 11 c. *slang* (chiefly *U.S.*; orig. *Naval*).

1829 *Sailors & Saints* II. iv. 92 There was no more to do, nor hand him below, and bundle him into his sack. **1883** MELTON & OLIPHANT *Cruise of U.S.S. Galena* 48 We were congratulating ourselves that the drills were over and retired to our 'dreaming sacks'. **1942** *Chevron* 17 Jan. 4/3 *Sack*, bunk. **1943**, etc. [see HIT *v.* 11 c]. **1947** *Reef Points 1947–48* (U.S. Naval Acad., Annapolis) 219 *Flake out*, to utilize one's sack between Reveille and Taps. **1950** 'D. DIVINE' *King of Fassarai* vi. 41 The first time I came on board you were lying in your goddam sack. **1952** in Wentworth & Flexner *Dict. Amer. Slang* (1960) 439/2 Let me stay in the sack all day. **1963** 'E. MCBAIN' *Ten Plus One* xv. 194 Helen seems to think a little more than necking took place... She seems to think you all crawled into the sack. **1968** J. UPDIKE *Couples* ii. 168 Women with that superheated skin are usually fantastic in the sack. **1977** I. SHAW *Beggarman, Thief* III. x. 342 Probably in the sack, he thought, with that fellow with the beard.

h. A bag, large or small, made of paper or the like; *paper sack*: see *PAPER *sb.* 12. *U.S.*

1904, etc. [see *PAPER *sb.* 12]. **1928** *Dialect Notes* VI. 60 A paper bag is always a *sack* or a *poke*, since *bag* means scrotum in the hill country. **1933** *Collier's* 28 Jan. 8/1 While he is at the ball game, he buys himself a sack of Harry Stevens' peanuts. **1956** B. HOLIDAY *Lady Sings Blues* (1973) viii. 77, I got so tired of scenes in crummy roadside restaurants over getting served, I used to..sit in the bus and rest—and let them bring me out something in a sack. **1974** M. G. EBERHART *Danger Money* v. 56 Greg paid for the food and took the sacks to the station wagon.

i. A base in baseball. Cf. *BAG *sb.* 1 c. *U.S.*

1914 LARDNER & HEEMAN *Mar. 6, 1914* 30 We've larruped out th' four-sack poke And scored among a salvo. **1922** E. J. LANIGAN *Baseball Cycl.* III. 47 Until 1920, a notable athlete..could skip around the circuit in the ninth..and, although unmolested, receive credit for a group of stolen sacks. **1938** H. E. WEST *Baseball ScrapBk.* 20 Before he reached the keystone sack the umpires flagged him down and sent him back to bat over again.

j. In American football, an act or occasion of tackling a quarter-back behind the scrimmage line before he can make a pass.

1972 S. DELUCA *Football Playbk.* 370 *Sack*, when the quarterback is thrown for a loss while attempting to pass. **1974** [see *quarterback sack* s.v. *QUARTERBACK *sb.* 3]. **1978** *Detroit Free Press* 2 Apr. 6E/3 Other changes have been made, this year and in recent years, to put juice into the offence, the feeling being that people come to see touchdowns and not quarterback sacks. **1980** *Washington Star* 3 Nov. D3, I would have to say the sacks were the difference in the game.

k. *sad sack*: see as main entry.

3. *to hold the sack*: to be saddled with an unwelcome responsibility. *U.S.*

1904 W. H. SMITH *Promoters* xxiv. 343 They are the ones that are always left to hold the sack. **1921** C. E. MULFORD *Bar-20 Three* xii. 140 Long an' Thompson are holding the sack. They're scapegoats for th' whole cussed gang. **1929** *Univ. Kansas Graduate Mag.* Apr., We will be holding the sack for an additional..deficit of nearly $1000. **1936** E. S. GARDNER *Case of Stuttering Bishop* xii. 191 Perhaps you didn't plan to drag me into the case and leave me holding the sack, but it sure looks as though you did. **1954** W. FAULKNER *Fable* (1955) 176 You might leave your own kinfolks holding the sack, but these are the sheriff's friends.

4. (Further examples.)

1913 J. STEPHENS *Here are Ladies* 102 Getting the 'sack' is an experience which wearies after the first time. **1935** D. GARNETT *Beany-Eye* I. 34 If I just give him the sack he won't get another job and will get into a brawl and be sent to prison again. **1937** 'G. ORWELL' *Road to Wigan Pier* I. i. 11 If they failed to secure a minimum of twenty orders a day, they got the sack. **1958** *Times Lit. Suppl.* 16 May 274/1 Always late, crumpled and scruffy, perpetually in debt, hourly expecting the sack, Greave takes refuge from the horrid realities of life in Mittyesque fantasies, pretending he is a high-powered American salesman.

III. 7. a. *sack-barrow* (later example), *-cart*, *-end* (example fig.), *-pile*, *-pocket*; (sense *1 j) *sack pack*. **b.** *sack-carrier*, *-hauling*. **c.** *sack-wise* adv.

1979 *Daily Tel.* 10 Nov. 10/6, I stuff the bags till I can hardly drag them, and then have to move them on a sack barrow. **1745** W. ELLIS *Agriculture Improv'd* in *Mod. Husbandman* VII. I. 124 So..that Sack-carriers or Cornporters convey the bought Wheat..to such Loft or Granary. **1966** 'L. LANE' *ABZ of Scouse* p. iv, Merseyside's prosperity depended mainly..upon the crate-handlers, the sack-carriers and the horse-whackers, or in the most up-to-date cliché, the 'service industries'. **1963** *Times* 14 Jan. 10/7 My duties, on the other hand, were many and varied. They included propelling a two-wheeled vehicle, known to the initiated as a sack-cart, for long distances, delivering parcels at the houses of well-to-do customers. **1969** *Listener* 8 May 640/3, I used to have to get them [*sc.* sacks of flour] onto what we call a sack-cart, a trolley, shoot them into a bin. **1937** E. MUIR *Journeys & Places* 26 Proud history has such sackends. **1965** A. BLACKSHAW *Mountaineering* III. xvii. 420 If sack hauling is unavoidable use a separate rope. **1976** *Time* 13 Sept. 68/2 On defense, the Colts' front four is largely unknown to fans but not to opposing quarterbacks. Pittsburgh's fearsome front four has the rep, but it was the Colts' 'Sack Pack' that led the league in dumping passers last season. **1897** 'MARK TWAIN' *Following Equator* xxviii. 273 He saw a white linen figure stretched in slumber upon a pile of grain-sacks... The form whirled itself from the sack-pile. **1938** F. D. SHARPE *Sharpe of Flying Squad* xiv. 154 Others [*sc.* shoplifters] have spacious sack pockets underneath their skirts large enough to contain a roll of cloth, a dress, or a small suitcase. **1923** D. H. LAWRENCE *Birds, Beasts & Flowers* 178 And all her weight, all her blood, dripping sack-wise down towards the earth's centre.

8. sack-bag (earlier example); **sack-bearer**, the larva of an American moth of the family Lacosomidæ, which makes cases from leaves; **sack chair** (see quot. 1970); **sack drill, duty** *U.S. Naval slang*, sleep; time spent in bed; **sack kraft**, a type of strong brown paper used esp. for making large paper sacks; **sack lunch** *N. Amer.*, a packed lunch; a lunch in a paper bag; **sack paper** = **sack kraft*; **sack race** (examples); **sack-racing** (example); **sack ship** *Canad. Hist.*, a large vessel used for transportation in the Newfoundland fisheries; **sack-shouldered** *a.* (*nonce*), carrying a sack on the shoulders; **sack time** *slang* (orig. *U.S. Forces'*), time spent in bed; sleep; bedtime; **sack-worthy** *a.*, deserving of the sack (sense 4).

1842 S. S. ARNOLD *Diary* 28 Oct. in *Proc. Vermont Hist. Soc.* (1940) VIII. 160 Mr. Gleason borrowed a sack bag to carry up his cocoons in. **1842** T. W. HARRIS *Treat. Insects New Eng. Injurious to Vegetation* 298 The Germans give these insects a more characteristic name, that of *sackträger*, that is sack-bearers. **1895** J. H. & A. B. COMSTOCK *Man. Study of Insects* xviii. 358 Melsheimer's Sack-bearer... The larva of this species feeds on oak. **1954** BORROR & DELONG *Introd. Study Insects* xxvi. 524 The Lacosomidae are called sack-bearers because the larvae make cases from leaves and carry the cases about. **1970** [see *POLYSTYRENE]. **1976** 'Z. STONE' *Modigliani Scandal* IV. v. 188 Dee was lying in a sack chair, naked. **1946** *Calif. Folklore Q.* Oct. 387 The Navy Man enjoys resting or sleeping. A sailor who retires *hits the sack, sacks in, sacks out, gets in some sack drill*,..*or gets some shut-eye*. **1954** WEBSTER Add., Sack duty. **1960** WENTWORTH & FLEXNER *Dict. Amer. Slang* 440/1 *Sack duty*, sleep; time spent sleeping. **1963** *Economist* 11 May 555/1 Reed's will take..the paper—sack kraft—into its own mills for conversion. **1972** *Daily Colonist* (Victoria, B.C.) 18 June 24/1 Others brought blankets and sack lunches early Saturday and sat sprawled on the grass. **1975** J. GRADY *Shadow of Condor* (1976) v. 91 There was still enough room for the sack lunch he would buy at the restaurant and his two thermos jugs, one for coffee, one for milk. **1957** V. S. SMITH *Introd. Paper & Papermaking* 125/1 (Index), Sack paper. **1968** Sack paper [see *KRAFT]. **1859** GEO. ELIOT *Adam Bede* II. xxv. 195 Here is the prize for the first sack race. **1945** G. MILLAR *Maquis* x. 207, I got up in the sleeping-bag and crossed the floor in it like a child doing the sack-race. **1967** Mrs. L. B. JOHNSON *White House Diary* 12 Sept. (1970) 568, I was wild about the sack races! **1887** *World Almanac* 103 (*heading*) Sack-racing records. **1732** E. FALKINGHAM *Let.* 4 Oct. in *Calendar State Papers Amer. & W. Indies 1732* (1939) 225 Which fish they sell to the British sack ships, for bills of exchange. **1907** J. G. MILLAIS *Newfoundland* viii. 160 In 1527, the little Devonshire fishing ships were unable to carry home their large catch, so 'sack ships' (large merchant vessels) were employed to carry the salt cod to Spain and Portugal. **1965** W. S. MACNUTT *Atlantic Provinces* 14 Its larger vessels, now known as 'sack ships', appeared on the scene at St. John's, taking no part in the catching of the cod, and serving primarily as freighters and transporters. **1922** JOYCE *Ulysses* 429 A sack-shouldered ragman bars his path. **1944** *Yank* 18 Feb. 4 The biggest difference between the Scouts and other doughboys is their sacktime conversation. **1945** *House Beautiful* Jan. 39 Sack Time means just lying on your cot doing nothing. **1949** in Wentworth & Flexner *Dict. Amer. Slang* (1960) 440/1, I didn't have any sack time. **1959** *Alfred Hitchcock's Mystery Mag.* Feb. 74/1 Last night, when I was just getting eyes for some sack time, this bear falls up to my pad, a type looking to score for free. **1974** L. DEIGHTON *Spy Story* xix. 204 I'll make sure they kick your ass from sun-up to sack-time. **1942** D. F. BRUCE *Dimsie carries On* xxi. 197, I can't just sack her for talking to a man in the road, even if he happens to be one for whom we have no great liking; there's nothing sack-worthy in that.

sack, *sb.*[3] Add: **2. b.** *sack-holding* ppl. adj.

1858 W. BAGEHOT in *National Rev.* Oct. 474 Falstaff is a sort of sack-holding paunch.

sack, *sb.*[4] Add: **2. a.** (Earlier examples of *sack coat*.)

1847 S. S. MAGOFFIN *Diary* 26 Aug. in *Down Santa Fé Trail* (1926) 253 The general was dressed in his famed old gray sack coat. **1869** S. BOWLES *Our New West* v. 100 My last winter's thick pantaloons and heavy sack coat.. completed my clothing.

b. sack suit, a suit with a straight, loose-fitting jacket; a lounge suit. Hence **sack-suited** *a.*

1895 *N.Y. Dramatic News* 6 July 14/4 Four button sack suit, $25. **1907** H. LAWSON in Murdoch & Drake-Brockman *Austral. Short Stories* (1951) 68 He wore a saddle-tweed sac suit two sizes too small for him. **1960** B. KEATON *Wonderful World of Slapstick* 116, I cleaned up, got into a natty sack suit, and brushed my hair. **1978** J. RAVEN *Triad Consignment* iii. 26 Those sack-suited characters in B-pictures.

3. (May belong under SACK *sb.*[1]) A cut of dress, being short, unwaisted, and usu. narrowing at the hem; a dress in this style; also *sack dress*.

Fashionable during the second half of the 1950s.

1957 *Punch* 18 Sept. 333 After all, the *belted* sack-dress, in some form or another, is a perennial we have known all down the years, flowering chiefly in the suburbs and the provinces. **1957** *Daily Mail* 26 Sept. 4/2 The sack has swept London like a prairie fire. *Ibid.* 10 Oct. 10/3 A sack, however well cut, needs a tallish figure, and it *must* be very short and tight at the hemline. **1958** *Observer* 21 Sept. 9/3 If there's still a sack to be seen, next week it will acquire a drawstring below the bust. **1959** *Listener* 8 Jan. 56/2 The sack is out. Now, it's the Empire line. **1959** *Times* 25 July 7/4 Hence the rapid disappearance of the A line, the Z line, the *sac*, and the rest of the hideous devices for disguising the fact that women really look their best when they wear bright colours and bulge (moderately) in the proper places. **1969** *Listener* 14 Aug. 206/3 The next big fashion thing was the Sack, and after that the waist, if it was indicated at all, was round the knees or the hips or the diaphragm. **1973** *Guardian* 10 Apr. 13/3 Lagerfeld shows signs of the sack coming back. **1975** 'M. FONTEYN' *Autobiogr.* II. iv. 173 Elizabeth [Taylor] was wearing a 'sack' dress, the latest fashion.

sack, *v.*[1] Add: **1. d.** In American football, to tackle (a quarter-back) behind the scrimmage line before he can make a pass.

1969 *Internat. Herald Tribune* 6 Nov. 13/4 If you're sacked it's second and 17. **1974** *Plain Dealer* (Cleveland, Ohio) 27 Oct. 7-C/3 Despite all the problems the Buckeye defense managed to sack Anderson three times and picked off three of his passes. **1976** *Washington Post* 4 Sept. D1/5 Kilmer..was sacked hard early in the second quarter by Bears tackle Ron Rydalch.

4. b. *pass.* with *in*, *out*, or *up*: to be in bed or asleep. Cf. sense 8 below.

1954 BERREY & VAN DEN BARK *Amer. Thes. Slang* (ed. 2) §251/11 Asleep,..sacked out. *Ibid.* §892/3 In bed,..sacked out. **1959** W. FAULKNER *Mansion* xii. 280, I was all right. I had had it. I had it made. I was sacked up. **1965** 'R. L. PIKE' *Police Blotter* iii. 56 His punk grandson took it when the old man was sacked in one night.

5. a. (Active examples.) Also *transf.* and *fig.*, esp. (*a*) to reject (a suitor), to jilt; (*b*) to expel from school.

1861 H. MAYHEW *London Labour* II. 469/1 Ah! she's a good kind creetur'; there's no pride in her whatsumever —and she never sacks her servants. **1882** R. D. BLACKMORE *Christowell* III. xi. 160 He had never known more than one girl, worth the end of a cigar—and that one had sacked him. **1907** G. B. SHAW *Major Barbara* II. 214 When trade is bad..and the employers az to sack arf their men, they generally start on me. **1914** 'I. HAY' *Lighter Side School Life* vii. 191 Tommy..arrives home one afternoon in a taxi in the middle of term, and announces..that he has been 'sacked'. **1929** *Amer. Speech* V. 20 When a hillman anounced that 'Lucy done *sacked* me' he meant that his sweetheart had refused him a date, or rejected his proposal of marriage. **1930** *Punch* 2 Apr. 376/3 If it doesn't turn out well I shall sack the lot of you. **1933** *Sun* (Baltimore) 8 May 8/2 The general contention that competition must be sacked in favor of some scheme of controlled coöperation. **1955** *Times* 21 July 13/4 The difficulties were due to the failure of nationalization and ..the remedy was to sack the Coal Board, [etc.]. **1970** G. F. NEWMAN *Sir, You Bastard* iii. 110 Scotty sacked the policemen who had arrived in the patrol car; they could add nothing. **1977** *Times Lit. Suppl.* 14 Jan. 24/1 He hated the two and a half terms he spent as a boy there before, aged twelve.., he was sacked.

8. *intr.* With advbs. **a.** *to sack in*: to turn in, to go to bed; also, to lie in. *slang* (orig. *U.S.*).

1946 [see *sack drill* s.v. *SACK *sb.*[1] 8]. **1951** in Wentworth & Flexner *Dict. Amer. Slang* (1960) 440/1 Shut up and sack in. **1962** 'S. RANSOME' *Without Trace* x. 107 After she left I had some more drinks and sacked in. **1966** D. F. GALOUYE *Lost Perception* xvi. 168 'I let you sack in this morning,' he told Gregson, 'so you could stockpile your energy.' **1967** 'T. WELLS' *What should you know of Dying?* iii. 41 Benedict's call, at about nine o'clock, woke me up... I'd planned to sack in till about eleven. **1976** N. THORNBURG *Cutter & Bone* iii. 79 Listen, pal, before I sack in..why don't you tell us.

b. *to sack out*: to go to bed, to have a sleep, to doss down. *slang* (orig. and chiefly *U.S.*).

1946 [see *sack drill* s.v. *SACK *sb.*[1] 8]. **1951** *Arkansas Democrat* 3 July 14/5 Well, it's time to sack out. **1961** 'E. LATHEN' *Banking on Death* viii. 66 The radio said the roads were closed, so I said the hell with it and sacked out on the couch. **1970** J. HANSEN *Fadeout* vii. 55, I was getting ready to sack out. I'd just had a shower. **1971** *Daily Tel.* 19 July 3/2 Many young travellers..are faced with the choice of curling up in a doorway or 'sacking out' in one of London's parks. **1977** *New Yorker* 9 May 46/1 One night we missed the last train. We sacked out in the waiting room in Grand Central.

c. *to sack down*: to go to bed. *slang*.

1956 F. HERBERT *Dragon in Sea* 84 Want me to bring up some sandwiches before I sack down? **1978** E. V. CUNNINGHAM *Case of Russian Diplomat* i. 11, I lost a night's sleep... How about I sack down for a few hours?

sackable (sæ·kǎb'l), *a.* [f. SACK *v.* 5 a + -ABLE.] For which one may be sacked; justifying the sack. So **sackabi·lity**, liability to be sacked.

1975 *Financial Times* 13 Jan. 25/6 Mr. Carew thinks that to-day's average British executive has had sackability built into him from childhood. **1975** *Daily Tel.* 3 Oct. 6/5, I admit I may have been impetuous in writing what I did about the school, but every word is truth. I don't consider publication of the truth to be a sackable offence.

sackbut. Add: **1.** Now used again in the performances of some early music. (Later examples.)

1972 *Register of Early Music* Autumn 19 (*heading*) People who have expressed an interest in:— Cornetts, Serpents, Sackbuts and Early Brass. **1973** *Early Music* I. 48 (Advt.), Brass Instruments... Sackbuts, Renaissance and Baroque trumpets by Meinel & Lauber. **1978** *Early Music Gaz.* Jan. p. 11/3 *Cornett and Sackbut* is a new magazine for all players of early lip-reed instruments.

sackbutter, var. SACKBUTER.

1916 STANFORD & FORSYTH *Hist. Mus.* ix. 180 *Four* sackbutters were enough for her grandfather. *Ibid.* 188 The other three are playing on brass instruments with slides. One may call them simply trombones. These are the *Royal Sackbutters.*

sackcloth. Add: **1. d.** *sackcloth-bound* adj.

1843 J. G. WHITTIER *Lays of My Home* 14 And mate with maniac women, loose-haired and sackcloth-bound.

sackclothed, *a.* Add: Also *fig.* (Later examples.)

1922 BLUNDEN *Shepherd* 23 And rising floods gleam silver on the verge Of sackclothed skies and melancholy grounds. **1924** R. CLEMENTS *Gipsy of Horn* ix. 169 Half-bred negroes and Indians, sackclothed and uncivilised.

sacked, *ppl. a.*² [f. SACK *v.*¹ + -ED¹.] **1.** That has been put into a sack; stored in a sack.

1895 *Funk's Stand. Dict.* s.v. sack¹ *vt.*, Sacked grain. **1937** E. HEMINGWAY *To have & have Not* II. i. 78 The man went on slowly lifting the sacked packages of liquor and dropping them over the side. **1970** D. WATERFIELD *Continental Waterboy* i. 3 The trouble with lock gates built of sacked mud is that they do not ordinarily open easily.

2. That has been 'given the sack'; dismissed, discharged (from employment or office). Also *absol.*

1934 G. B. SHAW *On Rocks* 148 The exterminated, or, as we call them, the evicted and sacked, try to avoid starvation. **1981** *Daily Tel.* 10 Sept. 8/8 (*heading*) Pay out for sacked heart man.

sa·cker². *U.S.* [f. SACK *v.*¹ 6 + -ER¹.] One engaged in sacking logs.

1902 S. E. WHITE *Blazed Trail* lii. 360 It was noon. The sackers looked up in surprise.

sa·cker³. *N. Amer.* [*SACK *sb.*¹ I i.] A baseman in baseball. (Usu. preceded by ordinal number indicating the base position.)

1914 LARDNER & HEEMAN *Mar. 6, 1914* 46 He once was the world's most famous first sacker. **1926** *Amer. Speech* I. 369/2 Basemen are 'sackers'. **1938** H. E. WEST *Baseball Scrap Bk.* 158 Wally Pipp became the Yankee first sacker in 1915, and Lou Gehrig succeeded him ten years later and is still going strong. **1944** *College Topics* (Univ. Virginia) 30 Mar. 3 Bob Bryon, first sacker from North Carolina State, seems assured of the first base position. **1958** [see *HOME-BREW 2]. **1974** *Anderson* (S. Carolina) *Independent* 22 Apr. 7A/1 As proof of his defensive prowess, Hargrove led the WCL first sackers in fielding with a .988 percentage.

sackie (sæ·ki). [Local name in Guyana.] Any of several small parrots found in northern South America, esp. *Pionites melanocephala*, which has black, blue, and green plumage.

[**1916** C. CHUBB *Birds Brit. Guiana* I. 340 The 'Macusis' call it [*sc.* the black-headed caique] *Sackuih.*] **1951** E. MITTELHÖLZER *Shadows move among Them* III. ii. 260 Sackies kept up a gay twittering. **1969** S. M. SADEEK *Windswept* 3, I would..imitate the kiss-ka-dees and sackies as they sang.

sacking, *vbl. sb.*¹ **1.** (Later examples.)

1958 *Daily Sketch* 2 June 1/2 This will not mean sackings as the buses are 3,000 men short now. **1970** G. F. NEWMAN *Sir, You Bastard* vi. 183 The normal fracas following a sacking would bring too much attention to Sneed when he stepped into the vacancy.

sacking, *sb.*³ Add: **1.** Also *transf.* of other material used for the same purpose.

1843 'R. CARLTON' *New Purchase* I. xxi. 199 Next was a sacking of clapboards pinned down; and then a very thick straw bed.

3. *sacking bottom* (earlier examples), *needle*; *sacking-wrapped* adj.

1744 J. HEMPSTEAD *Diary* (1901) 425 [I was] fitting a new Bedstid that I Sent with Sacking Bottom. **1841** G. CATLIN *Lett. on N. Amer. Indians* I. 191 A sacking-bottom, made of the buffalo's hide. **1868** G. G. CHANNING *Early Recoll. Newport, R.I.* 254 Sometimes it [*sc.* the bedstead] was furnished with a 'sacking bottom'. **1970** A. H. WHITEFORD *N. Amer. Indian Arts* 67/1 Sacking needles are used to insert the final weft threads. **1952** M. ALLINGHAM *Tiger in Smoke* viii. 129 One small sacking-wrapped bundle.

Sacky, var. *SAUK.

‖ **sacra** (sæ·kră), *sb. pl.* [ad. L. *sacr-a* sacred things, rites, etc., neut. pl. of *sacer* sacred.] Things endowed with sacred significance.

1819 S. FLEMING *Sherburne's Misc. Poems* p. xiii, The poems are of a miscellaneous description: some being amatory, which the Author styles Erotica;..and others of a graver cast, to which he applies the titles of Ethica and Sacra. **1903** J. E. HARRISON *Prolegomena to Study of Greek Relig.* iv. 126 Probably on this day the magical *sacra* lay upon the altars where the women placed them. *Ibid.* 132 Special cakes..were provided for them, but whether to eat or to carry as *sacra* does not appear. **1945** *Mind* LIV. 77 The contemplation of *sacra* gives rise to motor attitudes—shouting, prancing, rolling on the earth —which are no doubt in the first instance self-expressive. **1959** *Listener* 14 May 853/2 Plato..included the *sacra* in his concept of play. **1964** V. W. TURNER *Forest of Symbols* (1967) iv. 102 In the Lesser Eleusinian Mysteries of Athens, *sacra* consisted of a bone, top, ball, tambourine, apples, mirror, fan, and woolly fleece.

sacral, *a.*² Add: Also with pronunc. (sæ·crăl). (Later examples.) Also *gen.*, set apart for a religious purpose, sacred; pertaining to that which is sacred.

1912 J. E. HARRISON *Themis* p. xi, The *dromenon* in its sacral sense is, not merely a thing done, but a thing *re*-done, or *pre*-done with magical intent. **1958** R. F. C. HULL tr. *Jung's Psychol. & Relig.* in *Coll. Wks.* XI. 350 Any sacral action, in whatever form, works like a vessel for receiving the contents of the unconscious. **1974** R. HELMS *Tolkien's World* i. 24 Tolkien's profoundly suggestive insights into the sacral nature of the human imagination parallel Blake's rather than Arnold's. **1977** *Church Times* 10 June 10/2 A kind of apostolic succession of kingship, temporal and sacral intermingled to form a regal high priesthood. **1977** J. N. M. WIJNGAARDS *Did Christ rule out Women Priests?* vii. 66 The Old Testament priests had to offer frequently at specified sacral times. **1979** *N.Y. Rev. Bks.* 25 Oct. 15/1 Moon recently announced in that sacral third person he uses in public appearances, 'he will go to Germany.'

sacrality (săkræ·liti). Chiefly *Anthrop.* [f. SACRAL *a.*² + -ITY.] Sacral character.

1958 W. R. TRASK tr. *Eliade's Birth & Rebirth* iii. 59 Sacrality, spirituality, and immortality are expressed in images that, in one way or another, signify the beginning of life. **1964** R. MANHEIM tr. *Eliade's Mystery & Spiritual Regeneration* in *Papers from Eranos Yearbks.* V. 26 It is not the natural phenomenon of birth that constitutes the mystery; it is the revelation of feminine sacrality, that is, of the mystical bond between life, woman, nature, the godhead. **1977** J. N. M. WIJNGAARDS *Did Christ rule out Women Priests?* vii. 64 Christ replaced a priesthood based on sacrality by a priesthood based on grace.

sacralization (sæ:krălaizē¹·ʃən). *Anthrop.* [f. next + -ATION.] The action or fact of endowing with sacred qualities. Also *transf.* Cf. *DESACRALIZATION.

1918 *Encycl. Relig. & Ethics* X. 897/1 This 'sacralization' is not proved for sacrifice generally, either savage or civilized. **1937** C. CAUDWELL *Illusion & Reality* vi. 112 To the capitalist commodity-fetishism takes the form of sacralisation of the common market-denomination of all commodities—money. **1954** B. & R. NORTH tr. *Duverger's Pol. Parties* I. ii. 122 Totalitarian parties are in the 'sacred' category... The Party is personified (with a capital letter: a typical characteristic of 'sacralization'), the all-powerful infallible, protective, transcendent Party. **1958** G. W. BROMILEY tr. *Barth's Church Dogmatics* IV. II. 667 It [*sc.* the Church] may fall victim either to alienation (secularisation) or self-glorification (sacralisation). **1976** *Times Higher Educ. Suppl.* 6 Aug. 7/4 [Stanley] Spencer's sacralization is often concerned with transforming profane, urban or suburban icons. **1980** *Times Lit. Suppl.* 8 Aug. 902/5 Unexpected, if partial, justifications of.. boredom in church, learning by rote, the sacralization of war.

sacralize (sæ·krălaiz), *v.* *Anthrop.* [f. SACRAL *a.*² + -IZE, after F. *sacraliser* (see quot. 1899).] To endow with sacred significance (freq. through ritual); to set apart from ordinary life or use as sacred.

[**1899** HUBERT & MAUSS in *l'Année Sociologique* III. 215 Pour employer la terminologie que nous voudrions faire admettre: ils se sacralisent et, en même temps, désacralisent pour les autres l'espèce totémique.] **1933** E. E. EVANS-PRITCHARD in *Ess. Social Anthropol.* (1962) vii. 134 Exchange of blood in such situations [*sc.* blood-brotherhood] sacralizes and endows with sanctions a politico-economic transaction. **1957** V. W. TURNER *Schism & Continuity in an Afr. Society* x. 294 In the past doctors drove the uninitiated away..from areas in the bush which they had sacralized for ritual purposes. **1967** *Listener* 11 May 616/3 In spite of his call to sacralize secularity, there is little expectation of transcendence here. **1972** S. TUGWELL *Did you receive Spirit?* ix. 75 It is only where action and contemplation have become secularised (or sacralised, for that matter..), that any contradiction appears.

sacrament, *sb.* Add: **2. e.** *the last sacraments*, Holy Communion and Extreme Unction administered to the dying; (see also quot. 1920); *the sacrament of the sick*, in the Roman Catholic Church, Extreme Unction (now officially termed the Anointing of the Sick).

1760 in J. O. Payne *Old English Catholic Missions* (1889) 29 Jan. 7, William Hornby died at Middleham. He had the last sacraments. **1893** E. BELLASIS *Mem. Serjeant Bellasis* viii. 184 He left him..to go and tell the Curé.. that the Serjeant ought to have the last Sacraments without delay. **1920** *Encycl. Relig. & Ethics* XI. 574/1 At Cwm Yoy, in the Black Mountain, on the way to Llanthony, the people have at a funeral what they call 'the Last Sacrament'. The coffin is brought out and placed on trestles, and beer and cake are then partaken of by the guests and persons assembled.., before the funeral procession starts. **1966** 'HAN SUYIN' *Mortal Flower* i. 41 The priest..with a Chinese choir boy holding the implements of Extreme Unction,..myself and my sisters assembled in Father's hospital room, to witness..the last sacraments of the Church. **1972** S. TUGWELL *Did you receive Spirit?* xi. 98 It is painful,..and at times comic, to read the Fathers of Trent arguing about the sacrament of the sick. **1975** *N.Y. Times* 26 Oct. 1/5 A mass was held in the Prado Palace at which he [*sc.* Franco] took communion and received the sacrament of the sick, a religious ritual that used to be known as the last rites. **1981** *Church Times* 4 Sept. 9/4 He was the priest in the famous photograph giving the Last Sacraments (a term seldom used now) to the wounded and dying on what the Irish call 'Bloody Sunday'.

3. d. *sacrament of the present moment*, any and every moment regarded as an opportunity for the reception of divine grace.

1921 E. J. STRICKLAND tr. *de Caussade's Abandonment to Divine Providence* I. i. 3 What treasures of grace lie concealed in these moments filled, apparently, by the most ordinary events... O Bread of Angels! heavenly manna!.. Sacrament of the present moment! **1930** J. CHAPMAN *Spiritual Lett.* (1935) 83 The whole point of the 'Sacrament of the present moment' is that it is a..sacrament; it is God's action, God's will. **1943** O. WYON *School of Prayer* iii. 38 God makes His will known to us through the things that happen every day... Once we see it, our whole life is lifted on to a higher plane. This way of living has been described as *The Sacrament of the Present Moment.* **1967** J. N. WARD *Use of Praying* iii. 36 There is the use of the 'Jesus Prayer'... There is the cultivation of the 'sacrament of the present moment'. **1979** *Tablet* 22/29 Dec. 1251/2 We miss the many-splendoured thing in the goings-on of daily life, but it is there, totally transforming it and bestowing the sacrament of the present moment on those who are willing to accept it.

6. sacrament day, a day on which Holy Communion is celebrated; **sacrament house**, delete † and add later examples; **sacrament Sabbath** = *Sacrament Sunday*; **Sacrament Sunday** (earlier example).

1687 W. SEWALL in *Mass. Hist. Soc. Coll.* (1878) 5th Ser. V. 176 May 15th was our Sacrament-day. **1765** T. LINDSEY *Let.* 1 Nov. in *N. & Q.* (1942) 1 Aug. 62/2 Being a sacrament-day, I could but barely ask the former how he did as he went out of the church. **1826** A. CONSTABLE *Let.* 10 Oct. in J. Constable *Corr.* (1962) 228 Golding din'd with me on Sunday (Sacrament day). **1876** C. SCHREIBER *Jrnl.* 16 July (1911) I. 464 Many objects of the rarest interest—a dance of death (1742).., a sacrament house. *Ibid.* 24 July 470, I saw a fine Sacrament house, the third I have met with. **1975** A. MAYCOCK *Malling Abbey* (rev. ed.) 15 The nuns enter their choir from the cloister.., passing..on the right a circular sacrament house on which the light falls from a conical shaft immediately above it. **1816** in *Sc. Nat. Dict.* (1971) VIII. 3/2 'Twas sacrament Sabbath and much had been laid in. **1957** E. E. EVANS *Irish Folk Ways* xviii. 253 The 'sacrament Sabbaths' of Presbyterian Ulster were great gatherings having something of the nature of fairs. **1768** J. WOODFORDE *Diary* 9 Oct. (1924) I. 80 David Maby.. dined with us, being Sacrament Sunday.

sacramentalism. Add: **2.** The theory that the natural world is a reflection or imitation of an ideal, supernatural, or immaterial world.

1936 C. S. LEWIS *Allegory of Love* ii. 45 The attempt.. to see the archtype in the copy, is what I mean by symbolism or sacramentalism. **1963** H. BLAMIRES *Christian Mind* II. vi. 175 A living Christian mind would elucidate for the young a finely articulated Christian sacramentalism which would make sense of, and give value to, the adolescent's cravings towards the grandeur of natural scenery, towards the potent emotionalism of music and art, and towards the opposite sex.

Sacramentarian. Add: **B.** *sb.* **2.** (Earlier example.)

1732 J. WESLEY *Let.* 18 Oct. (1931) I. 130 Some of the men of wit in Christ Church..made a pretty many reflections upon the Sacramentarians, as they were pleased to call us.

sacramented, *ppl. a.* *rare*⁻¹. Consecrated, made sacred, sealed by a sacrament.

1914 R. BROOKE in *New Numbers* I. 116 They'll..sell Love's trust And sacramented covenant to the dust.

sacre, *v.* Add: **2. a.** (Later *arch.* example.)

1976 N. ROBERTS *Face of France* xxv. 229 French kings, with rare exceptions have been sacred in Reims Cathedral.

‖**sacré** (sakre), *sb.* [Fr., cf. SACRÉ *v.*] (The utterance of) the word 'sacré' as a profane imprecation.

1828 LYTTON *Pelham* I. xix. 148 He uttered a short, low, laugh..; and, pushing through the atmosphere of *sacrés* and *mille tonnerres*..strode quickly to the door.

‖**sacré** (sakre), *a.* [Fr.: cf. prec.] Holy, sacred, used in various French oaths, as *sacré bleu* (sakre blö), also *sacre bleu, sacrebleu*, a euphemism for *sacré Dieu*; *sacré Dieu* (sakre dyö); *sacré nom* (sakre noṅ), *sacré tonnerre* (sakre tonęr).

1768 STERNE *Sentimental Journey* II. 134 If there is but a cap-full of wind in or about Paris, 'tis more blasphemously *sacre Dieu*'d there than in any other aperture of the whole city. **1869** 'MARK TWAIN' *Innoc. Abr.* xxvii. 294 'Is, ah—is he dead?' 'Oh, *sacre bleu*, been dead three thousan' year!'. **1901** S. J. WEYMAN *Count Hannibal* i. 1 Sacré nom, am I King, or a dog of a —. **1905** BARONESS ORCZY *Scarlet Pimpernel* i. 10 '*Sacré tonnerre*,' said the captain. **1923** W. L. Locke *Moordius & Co.* ii. 23 *Sacre-bleu!* the world had changed since 1870. **1974** K. Benton *Craig & Tunisian Tangle* vi. 63 But *sacre bleu!* you can't depend on that.

sacred, *a.* and *sb.* Add: **A.** *adj.* **3. b.** *Sacred Blood,* the blood of Christ; *sacred concert* (examples); *sacred music* (examples); *sacred orders* [eccl. L. *ordines sacri*], the holy or major orders.

[**1709** J. Bingham *Origines Ecclesiasticæ* II. iii. i. 9 The Clergy of the Superior Orders are commonly called the ἱερώμενοι Holy and Sacred, as in Socrates and others.] **1726** J. Ayliffe *Parergon* 184 The first [*sc.* sub-deacons, deacons, and priests] the Canon Law..stiles Sacred Orders. **1832** *Rep. Sel. Comm. Dramatic Lit. with Minutes of Evidence* 50 in *Parl. Papers 1831–2* VII. 1, I thought it would be a better thing to represent plays than to give a pretended sacred concert. **1836** *Penny Cycl.* VI. 374/1 The clerical orders of the Catholic church are divided into two classes, *sacred* and *minor* orders. **1862** in N. Longmate *Hungry Mills* (1978) viii. 113 Never was so much sacred music heard upon the streets of Manchester as during the last few months. **1884** Addis & Arnold *Cath. Dict.* 622/1 The orders of bishop, priest, deacon, and (but only since the thirteenth century) subdeacon are called sacred' or 'greater'. **1900** *Cornish Echo* 30 Mar. 4/4 Wesley Chapel Falmouth. *Sacred Concert* by Truro Wesleyan Church Choir. **1901** Procter & Frere *Prayer Bk.* xvi. 650 The Sacramentary of Serapion gives forms of ordination only for the three sacred orders. **1920** Wodehouse *Jill the Reckless* (1922) xvi. 230 It is the custom of the dwellers in Atlantic City..to attend a species of vaudeville performances—incorrectly termed a sacred concert—on Sunday nights. **1922** Chesterton *Ballad of St. Barbara* p. vii, In the grey rocks the burning blossom Glowed terrible as the sacred blood. **1934** *Daily Gleaner* 5 Jan. 21/2 *Sacred Concert*..A fine programme of sacred songs, instrumental music and recitations will be presented at St. Thomas' Church, Bath, on Sunday. **1950** *Cornishman* 12 Jan. 4/2 Sacred Concert by Ludgvan Male Choir with Elise Harvey, guest soloist. **1965** *New Statesman* 19 Nov. 794/3 We are made aware of the ideas of the period—notably the Pope's own contributions to the Franciscan v. Dominican battle about the Sacred Blood. **1978** *Listener* 24 Aug. 244/4 By 1733 Bach had written the vast majority of his sacred music.

7. sacred circle, an exclusive company, an élite; **sacred egoism** = *Sacro egoismo; **sacred way,** a route used by religious processions, pilgrims, etc.

1939 *Country Life* 11 Feb. 156/1 The courses, however, which have been admitted into this sacred circle—Westward Ho! for the Amateur Championship, Carnoustie for the Open, and Troon and St. Anne's for both meetings, have all been of a certain ancient standing. **1928** H. W. Schneider *Making Fascist State* i. 11 Salandra's policy of 'sacred egoism', of bargaining with both sides to see who would promise Italy the most for her neutrality, is both disgraceful and useless. **1970** R. A. H. Robinson *Origins of Franco's Spain* iv. 186 Aguirre still pursued a policy of sacred egoism and held aloof from non-Basque causes. **1884** A. Lang in M. Hunt tr. *Grimm's Household Tales* I. p. xiv, Amber and jade and slaves were carried half across the world by the old trade-routes and sacred ways. **1910** *Encycl. Brit.* II. 883/2 The chain..of Aegaleos, through a depression in which was the line of the sacred way, where the torchlight processions from Athens used to descend to the coast. **1937** G. Mitchell *Come away, Death* i. 31 Now we go to Eleusis along the Sacred Way, to penetrate the meaning of the Mysteries. **1971** Garside & Wilkins tr. *Ceram's Gods, Graves & Scholars* (ed. 2) xxiii. 292 The Sacred Way of Babylon ran..from the outer city walls to the Gate of Ishtar.

sacred cow. [f. Sacred *a.* + Cow *sb.*[1]] **1.** The cow as an object of veneration amongst Hindus.

1891 J. L. Kipling *Beast & Man in India* vi. 116 The Muhammedan..creed is in opposition to theirs [*sc.* the Hindus] and there are rankling memories of a thousand insults to it wrought on the sacred cow. **1972** E. J. Sharpe in Hinnells & Sharpe *Hinduism* xxxvii. 121 As every visitor to India knows, the 'sacred cow' is not as a rule particularly well looked after. **1979** E. H. Gombrich *Sense of Order* vi. 167 The couch in Tutankhamun's tomb ..was shaped like a sacred cow, ready to carry the pharaoh into the other life.

2. *fig.* (orig. *U.S.*). **a.** *Journalism.* (*a*) someone who must not be criticized; (*b*) copy that must not be altered or cut.

1910 *Atlantic Monthly* Mar. 308/1 In the office these corporations were jocularly referred to as 'sacred cows'. **1922** U. Sinclair *They call me Carpenter* xxvi. 92 It doesn't matter, because I couldn't use the story. Mr. Stebbins is one of our 'sacred cows'. **1923** O. G. Villard *Some Newspapers* 143 The editors gave me their word that there is..no list of men to be attacked and no 'sacred cows' (i.e., favourites to be spared) in their shop. **1936** W. E. Hall *Reporting News* 430 Sacred cow—copy which is not to be changed or cut. **1940** R. E. Garst *Headlines & Deadlines* 206 *Sacred cow,* slang for a subject or story in which the publisher or higher editors are interested and which must be printed. **1973** B. Broadfoot *Ten Lost Years* xxxi. 351 Newspapers had a lot more sacred cows than they do now.

b. An idea, institution, etc., unreasonably held to be immune from questioning or criticism.

1936 M. Mitchell *Gone with Wind* xiii. 240, I think of my brother, living among the sacred cows of Charleston, and most reverent towards them. **1955** *Bull. Atomic Sci.* Feb. 62/2 The need for widespread secrecy has become a sacred cow, a belief hedged by the deepest emotions and accepted without question by many Americans. **1961** L. Mumford *City in Hist.* vi. 182 Economic exploitation, slavery, war, specialized life-time labor... Plato's polis relied for daily meat and drink on these sacred but diseased cows. **1962** *Listener* 5 July 10/2 Business is the 'sacred cow' here. **1963** *Richmond* (Va.) *Times-Dispatch* 16 Dec. 19/1 Military bases..are sacred cows in Congress. **1967** Coulthard & Smith in Wills & Yearsley *Handbk. Managem. Technol.* 207 A new movement, variously described as 'management by objectives', 'improving management performance' or 'performance planning', now promises to sweep away some of the 'sacred cows' of management development. **1971** *Country Life* 4 Nov. 1223/3 By clearing away any sacred-cow reputation clinging to the master he stirs the reader to look for himself. **1978** *Maledicta 1977* I. 111 He has for many years attacked most of their sacred cows and revealed them to be dry and motheaten skins. **1978** L. Heren *Growing up on The Times* iv. 152, I was not an Establishment man. I had often caused trouble for the paper because of my refusal to give proper obeisance to sacred cows.

Sacred Heart. 1. The heart of Jesus, regarded as an object of devotion; similarly, *Sacred Heart of Mary. Feast of the Sacred Heart* (R. C. Ch.), a festival observed on the Friday in the week following Corpus Christi; also *ellipt.*

1765 (*title*) The devotion to the Sacred Heart of Jesus. **1793** J. Berington in *Panzani's Memoirs* p. xxxii, He might be busied in preparing a gay posey of devotion to the *sacred heart of Mary.* **1823** C. Butler *Contin. A. Butler's Lives Saints* 228 The devotion to the sacred Heart was sanctioned by all the prelates of the neighbouring country. **1833** M. Arundell *Let.* 30 June (1894) vii. 47/2 You will pity me however confined to a sick bed during all my favourite feasts, Whit-Sunday, Corpus Christi, Sacred Heart! **1853** J. B. Dalgairns *Devotion to Heart of Jesus* i. 59 Symbols, which are also realities, as the Sacred Hearts of Jesus and Mary, the Five Wounds, or the Precious Blood of our Lord. **1881** G. M. Hopkins *Sermons* (1959) 100 (*heading*) For Sunday June 26 1881 being the Sunday..nearest the Feast of the Sacred Heart (which this year is to be kept on Monday the 27th). **1924** E. Leahy tr. *Bainvel's Devotion to Sacred Heart* ii. ii. 103 To St Margaret Mary and her revelations is really due the inception of the devotion to the Sacred Heart in the form that has received the Church's sanction. **1945** J. Betjeman *New Bats in Old Belfries* 25 As Thy Sacred Heart displays Lush Kildare of scented meadows, Roscommon, thin in ash tree shadows,..Kneeling all in silver haze? **1967** K.-H. & B. Kruger tr. *Rahner's Theol. Investigations* III. xxii. 331 The Sacred Heart devotion in the doctrine and practice of the Church both past and present manifests itself under many aspects and forms. **1977** B. Lucas tr. *De Foucauld's Lett. from Desert* iv. 69, I was determined to write..to tell you how close I shall be to you on the feast of the sacred Heart.

2. *transf.* **a.** A form of prayer used in private devotions to the Sacred Heart.

1815 J. Milner in F. C. Husenbeth *Life J. Milner* (1862) xvi. 288 Spiritual Reading afternoon.—Grace, Rosary, Sacred Heart. **1881** G. M. Hopkins *Sermons* (1959) 102 When we say the Sacred Heart it is of Christ himself we are thinking and not of his heart only.

b. A devotional picture of the Sacred Heart.

1931 *Jrnl. Amer. Folk-Lore* XLIV. 413 Pictures of Saints, etc., are used also [in voodoo magic in America]... Sacred Heart of Jesus. For organic diseases. **1941** A. White *Let.* 22 Mar. in *Hound & Falcon* (1965) 108, I prefer the Catholic Church with all the awful Sacred Hearts and Little Flowers and the rest to the still more awful bleak 'tastefulness' of the others. **1977** M. Kenyon *Rapist* iv. 40 Above the door..hung the Sacred Heart in lurid primaries.

3. Used as (part of) the name of several religious orders and of schools run by them; freq. *attrib.* and *ellipt.*

1885 H. James *Little Tour in France* iii. 22 The modern buildings (of the Sacred Heart)..are in the vulgar taste which seems doomed to stamp itself on all new Catholic work. **1907** E. Wharton *Fruit of Tree* ii. 20 A girl who was at the Sacred Heart in Paris with me. **1919** T. S. Eliot *Sweeney among Nightingales* in *Poems,* The nightingales are singing near The Convent of the Sacred Heart. **1965** A. White *Hound & Falcon* 20 Even in my day Tunbridge Wells was always said to be much less strict... [*Note*] Another Sacred Heart convent. **1973** *Guardian* 25 Apr. 15/3 Mr Joe Faye..of the Sacred Heart School, Redcar... The 12-man governing board of Sacred Heart (a Catholic maintained school.) **1974** V. Canning *Mask of Memory* i. 19 Gave the sweets to the Sacred Heart children on the beach.

sacrificable, *a.* For *rare*—1 in Dict. read *rare* and add: also, rightly or properly to be sacrificed.

1973 *N.Y. Law Jrnl.* 27 Feb., No citizen's individuality is sacrificable to expediency.

sacrifice, *sb.* Add: **3. c.** *sacrifice of praise* (*and thanksgiving*): a phr. drawn from biblical sources (e.g. Lev. vii. 12, Ps. l. 14, 23 (R.V., etc.), Heb. xiii. 15) used *gen.* for an offering of praise to God, and liturgically in the anaphora of many post-Reformation Eucharistic rites, tr. *sacrificium laudis* of the Latin Canon of the Mass.

1535 Coverdale *Heb.* xiii. 15 Let vs therfore by him offre allwayes vnto God the sacrifice of prayse. **1549** *Bk. Common Prayer* f. cxxviii[v], Entierely desiryng thy fatherly goodnes, mercifully to accepte this our Sacrifice of praise and thankes geuing. **1611** Bible *Jer.* xvii. 26 Bringing sacrifices of praise vnto the house of the Lord. **1864** F. Pierpoint *For the Beauty of the Earth* (hymn) in O. Shipley *Lyra Eucharistica* (ed.2) 340 Christ, our God, to Thee we raise This our Sacrifice of Praise. **1877** E. Daniel *Prayer-Bk.* 296 That sacrament in which we offer our sacrifice of praise and thanksgiving for the redemption of the world. **1884** Addis & Arnold *Cath. Dict.* 564/1 The Mass is a sacrifice of adoration, of praise and thanksgiving. **1980** *Alternative Service Bk. 1980* 132 Accept through him, our great high priest, this our sacrifice of thanks and praise.

5. a. Delete (*nonce-use*) and add later examples.

1915 *Truth* 30 June 1068/1 Being convinced that his 'trade sacrifice' will result in increased business. **1976** *Billings* (Montana) *Gaz.* 5 July 9-c/8 (Advt.), Yaesu FT101 base, desk mike, antenna & tripod. *Sacrifice.* **1976** *Evening Advertiser* (Swindon) 31 Dec. 17/2 (Advt.), Bargain: 1971 Ford Escort 1100..genuine sacrifice, £380 only.

b. *Baseball.* = *sacrifice hit* (see 6 in Dict.).

1880 *Inter-Ocean* (Chicago) 29 June 8/3 Force's winning run came off a wild throw by Ward, a sacrifice and single. **1904** R. H. Barbour *Bk. School & Coll. Sports* 173 When the batsman is looking for a sacrifice keep the ball high. **1912** C. Mathewson *Pitching in a Pinch* xii. 261 Snodgrass got a base on balls and journeyed to second on a sacrifice. **1968** *Washington Post* 4 July c2/8 Willie McCovey threw wildly trying to force the Atlanta pitcher at second on a sacrifice. **1976** *Billings* (Montana) *Gaz.* 6 July 3-c/1 Rookie Butch Hobson drove in three runs with a sacrifice and a single.

c. *Chess.* The action of *Sacrifice *v.* 3 e.

1915 J. du Mont tr. *Lasker's Chess Strategy* i. iv. 25 White..prefers to end up with a magnificent sacrifice. **1933** H. Phillips *Week-End Problems Bk.* 310 The key-move..offers double sacrifice with a cross-check. **1952** E. Lasker *Chess Secrets* 122 With this Bishop sacrifice Janowski tears down his opponent's defenses. **1977** *Guardian Weekly* 25 Dec. 23/5 Black took 80 minutes to decide to accept this strong pawn sacrifice.

d. *Bridge.* = **sacrifice bid(ding).*

1952 *Bridge Mag.* Apr. 39/2 Five clubs is only two down, a good sacrifice against five spades. **1964** Frey & Truscott *Offic. Encycl. Bridge* 480/1 One will earn a fat score with one's sacrifice only when most of the field is bidding game with his opponents' cards. **1974** [see *Make *sb.*[2] 10].

6. *sacrifice bringer, sale;* **sacrifice bid(ding)** *Bridge,* (making) a bid higher than the contract that one expects to be able to fulfil, in order to prevent opponents from making a score greater than the penalty one is likely to suffer; **sacrifice bunt** *Baseball,* a bunt that puts the batter out whilst allowing a base runner to advance; **sacrifice fly** *Baseball,* an outfield fly that is caught so that the batter is put out but which allows a base runner to advance after the ball is caught; **sacrifice hit** (earlier example); **sacrifice meat,** meat eaten at a feast following the offering of a sacrifice to a deity.

1932 H. Phillips *One Hundred Contract Bridge Hands* 115 This is a good example of a 'sacrifice bid'... South now bids Four Hearts as probably a cheaper 'sacrifice' (even if doubled) than that of the game. **1959** *Listener* 13 Aug. 262/1 The hidden value of a part score has a bearing also on sacrifice bidding at the game level. **1964** Frey & Truscott *Offic. Encycl. Bridge* 481/1 A hidden advantage of sacrifice bidding is the chance that the opponents will be pushed one higher and will go down. **1923** D. H. Lawrence *Birds, Beasts & Flowers* 149 And you, great bird... Can be put out of office as sacrifice bringer. **1974** *Anderson* (S. Carolina) *Independent* 24 Apr. 5B/2 Jack Brohamer..moved to second on Buddy Bell's sacrifice bunt. **1970** *Globe & Mail* (Toronto) 25 Sept. 31/1 Roger Freed's sacrifice fly..helped Baltimore stretch its lead to 4-1 in the fifth. **1979** *Arizona Daily Star* 22 July c5/5 Butch Wynegar also drove in a run in the sixth with a sacrifice fly to help Goltz raise his record to 9-6. **1881** *N.Y. Herald* 21 July 8/3 The Metropolitans scored another run on two pretty singles, a passed ball and a sacrifice hit. **1926** D. H. Lawrence *David* iv. 24 They be all there, waiting for the sacrifice meat. **1902** G. H. Lorimer *Lett. Self-Made Merchant* x. 129 It was the record-breaking, marked-down sacrifice sale of the year on dogs.

sacrifice, *v.* Add: **3. c.** To sell or get rid of at a sacrifice, esp. in commercial use. Also *absol.*

1850 *Punch* XVIII. 130/2 A newspaper advertisement announces that 'A Professional gentleman is instructed to sacrifice *three* young sound *Horses* at half their cost.' We wonder what deity horses could be sacrificed to? **1903** Farmer & Henley *Slang* VI. 91/1 *Sacrifice*..to sell regardless of cost. **1930** *San Antonio* (Texas) *Light* 31 Jan. 14/7 (Advt.), Owner Must Sacrifice Must sell at bargain. **1947** E. Hodgins *Mr. Blandings builds his Dream House* ii. 23 'Farm dwelling..original beams..will sacrifice', The *New York Times* advertisement had said.

d. *Baseball.* (*a*) *intr.* To make a hit which advances another player, the batter being put out. (*b*) *trans.* To advance (another player) in this way.

1905 *Sporting Life* 2 Sept. 4/1 Lumley's effort to sacrifice resulted in a short pop fly. **1912** C. Mathewson *Pitching in a Pinch* ix. 202 Brown sacrificed, sending Kling to second. **1971** L. Koppett *N.Y. Times Guide Spectator Sports* i. 31 When a batter walks, is hit by a pitch, sacrifices (by bunting so that other runners advance even though he is out),..he is not charged with an official time at bat. **1974** *News & Courier* (Charleston, S. Carolina) 22 Apr. 9-A/3 Denny Doyle..was sacrificed to second. **1975** *Verbatim* Sept. 5/1 But Joe Ferguson did something much more drastic than that: *He sacrificed Garvey home!*

e. *Chess.* To put or leave (a man) in a

position where it can be captured without equivalent loss by one's opponent, in order to gain a future advantage.

1915 J. DU MONT tr. *Lasker's Chess Strategy* II. 224 White decides to sacrifice a Knight in order to open the files in the centre for his Rooks. **1952** E. LASKER *Chess Secrets* 54 White could sacrifice a piece for three Pawns. **1969** A. GLYN *Dragon Variation* vii. 193 They'd both sacrifice every piece on the board. By the middle-game they'd just have the two Kings left. *Ibid.* ix. 271 He tried to break the stranglehold by sacrificing first a Knight and then a Rook. **1974** HARTSTON & KEENE *Karpov–Korchnoi 1974* 66 Korchnoi plucks up his courage and sacrifices his K-side in order to create a passed pawn of his own.

f. *Bridge. intr.* To make a sacrifice bid.

1952 PHILLIPS & REESE *Bridge with Mr. Playbetter* xiv. 59 He must take all possible measures to prevent Hurry sacrificing in Five Clubs. **1959** *Listener* 22 Jan. 189/2 Is it possible, under the Laws, to sacrifice at the level of Eight? **1962** *Ibid.* 13 Sept. 410/3 Over Four Hearts North could raise to six. No doubt, in that event, East-West would sacrifice in Six Spades. **1964** FREY & TRUSCOTT *Offic. Encycl. Bridge* 480/2 Be alert to sacrifice against confident auctions when it appears that everyone else will be in game too.

4. To kill (an experimental animal) for scientific purposes.

1903 *Jrnl. Physiol.* XXIX. 83 The animal was sacrificed on the 315th day after the 1st lesion had been established. **1926** J. S. HUXLEY *Ess. Pop. Sci.* 282 When, after a couple of months, the dog was sacrificed, it was found..that the histological character of the cells had changed, cross-striations arising in them. **1944** *Jrnl. Immunology* XLIX. 316 The animals were sacrificed by a blow on the head and the small intestine was immediately removed. **1971** *Sci. Amer.* July 55/1 In rats we destroyed the mitral cells in the olfactory bulb by surgical intervention and, after a survival time of from three to five days, sacrificed the animal to conduct a microscopic examination of the fibers leading from these cells.

sacrificial, *a.* Add: **4.** Involving or being an anode of a metal that is used up when protecting another metal against electrolytic corrosion.

1861 *Mechanics' Mag.* 5 Apr. 229/1 A curious statement made in the House of Commons, a few days ago, induces us to offer a few remarks on what may be called, appropriately enough, 'the sacrificial function in metals'. .. Failing..to achieve what was intended of it, the copper-protecting process of Davy ceased to be employed; but the failure of it is that which alone concerns us here, as illustrating what we would wish to convey by the words *sacrificial metal.* **1937** U. R. EVANS *Metallic Corrosion Passivity & Protection* xii. 531 The protection method is sacrificial, the valuable iron boiler being protected by sacrificing the easily replaceable zinc. **1949** *Jrnl. R. Soc. Arts* XCVII. 598 A sufficient cathodic current density may be impressed upon structures of iron or steel by the use of external anodes of magnesium, aluminium or zinc, the anode undergoing 'sacrificial corrosion'. **1968** *Rep. Progr. Appl. Chem.* LIII. 69 It was better to use an all-nickel coating..rather than a copper undercoat where sacrificial corrosion resulted in complete loss of plate. **1976** *Daily Tel.* 25 Nov. 7/1 It is common practice to fit the pipes with collars of a zinc alloy, which act as 'sacrificial anodes', corroding in preference to the steel pipe. **1978** *Metals* (Shell Internat. Petroleum Co.) 7 Zinc is ideal as a sacrificial metal for the corrosion-protection of steel.

sacrificially, *adv.* [f. SACRIFICIAL *a.* + -LY[2].] In a sacrificial manner.

1937 L. C. DOUGLAS *Forgive us our Trespasses* i. 2 'Wish you was a-goin' along'... 'No,' Martha would reply, sacrificially, 'somebody's got to stay on th' place.' **1972** *Daily Tel.* 7 Sept. 18 Our officers and staff who serve so sacrificially year in and year out..are not men who have come to terms with squalor.

sacrilege, *sb.*[2] (Later *poet.* example.)

1802 W. S. LANDOR *Poetry* 7 Thrown prostrate on the earth, the Sacrilege Rais'd up his head astounded.

sacrilegious, *a.* Add: Now usu. with pronunc. (sækrili·dʒəs).

sacrist. Add: **2.** Also 8 **saccarist.** An officer in the University of Aberdeen (formerly King's and Marischal Colleges); orig. a cleric whose responsibilities included the furnishings of the church, later a senior janitor or head porter with some ceremonial duties.

1638 *King's Coll.* (Aberdeen) *Minutes* 27 Dec., In the visitatioun of the Kinges Colledge of the Universitie of Aberdeine..convenit..Mr. Alexander Ross doctor of divinitie, principall of the said Colledge,..Mr. Gilbert Ross, cantor, and Patrick Innes, sacrist. *a* **1670** [in Dict.]. **1732** in A. M. Munro *Rec. Old Aberdeen* (1899) I. 256 Robert Gordon, Saccarist in the King's College. **1792** J. SPALDING *Hist. Troubles* I. 127 Mr. David Lindsay Parson of Belhelvie, was said to be moderator of this committee, to the which committee upon the 24th of March were summoned in name of the assembly and moderator, the principal of the King's College of Old Aberdeen, the four regents, the canonist, Doctor of Medicine, civilist, sacrist, and janitor, founded members thereof. **1825** *Aberdeen Censor* Dec. 210 Enrolled as a student in divinity, by paying six shillings to the sacrist of Marischall College and a moiety to the library. **1865** G. MACDONALD *Alec Forbes* II. ii. 8 A long broom which the sacrist had been using to clear foot-paths. **1902** *Minutes Aberdeen Univ. Court* V. 250 The Joint Committee were of the opinion that appropriate costumes, including robes and hats, for the two sacrists, could be procured for £15. **1965** *Aberdeen Univ. Rev.* Autumn 70 No ceremony is complete without the presence of the sacrist (or sacrists) robed in purple, with a tricorne hat trimmed with gold upon his head, and bearing his silver, bell-headed, mace.

sacristaness. Add: Also *fig.*

1924 C. C. MARTINDALE *St. Paul* xi. 141 The city of Ephesus was the sacristaness of the great Artemis and of the image that fell from heaven.

sacro-[2]. Add: *sacrospinous, -tuberous, -uterine;* **sa:cro-ilii·tis,** inflammation of the sacro-iliac joint.

1934 *Acta Rheumetologica* VI. xxIII. 7/1 All the cases of Spondylitis adolescens..so far examined, have radiographically shown indications of bilateral infection of both sacro-iliac joints, (Sacro-ileitis) usually in the form of ankylosis. **1936** *Brit. Jrnl. Radiol.* IX. 127 (*caption*) Complete ankylosis of the sacro-iliac joints—the end-result of a chronic sacro-iliitis. **1977** *Lancet* 17 Sept. 591/1 Around the classic centre, rigid spine with radiographic sacro-iliitis, there is a very large fringe of milder forms of spondylitis. **1910** H. W. CATTELL *Lippincott's New Med. Dict.* 845/1 *Sacrospinous ligament* = sacrosciatic ligament, lesser. **1913** *Gray's Anat.* (ed. 18) 354 The sacrospinous ligament (small sacrosciatic ligament) is thin, and triangular in form. **1967** G. M. WYBURN et al. *Conc. Anat.* vi. 163/2 The short sacrospinous ligament lies anterior to the sacrotuberous ligament and extends from the spine of the ischium to the lower part of the sacrum and coccyx. **1910** H. W. CATTELL *Lippincott's New Med. Dict.* 845/1 *Sacrotuberous ligament,* = Sacrosciatic ligament, great. **1925** *Jrnl. Amer. Med. Assoc.* 31 July 307/2 Von Meyer..described the rotary movement of the sacrum, and showed..the restraint put on this rotation by the sacrotuberous and sacrospinous ligaments. **1962** *Gray's Anat.* (ed. 33) 531 The sacrotuberous ligament..is placed at the lower and posterior part of the pelvis. **1967** Sacrotuberous [see *sacrospinous* above]. **1888** W. H. & H. T. BYFORD *Pract. Med. & Surg.* (ed. 4) ii. 83 Two fingers carried high up in the posterior fornix vaginae can usually feel the semi-circular folds of the sacro-uterine ligament extending outward, backward and upward. **1946** R. W. TE LINDE *Operative Gynecol.* vii. 125/1 Pushing back the mucosa in the attempt to see the peritoneum exposes each sacro-uterine ligament.

‖**sacro egoismo** (sa·kro egoi·zmo). [It., 'sacred egoism': see *SACRED *a.* 7.] Nationalism without scruples in relationships with other states. Also *transf.*

[**1914** A. SALANDRA in G. Fumagalli *Chi l'ha Detto?* (1958) 560 Anima sevro..da ogni sentimento che non sia quello della illimitata ed esclusiva devozione alla Patria nostra, del *sacro egoismo* per l'Italia.] **1944** *Zionist Rev.* 21 Apr. 6/3 Characteristic of our present attitude is the suggestion that my insistence on 'using every means for the pursuit of our own aims', sounds rather like the doctrine of *sacro egoismo.* **1947** 'G. ORWELL' *Eng. People* 15 Power politics, 'realism', *sacro egoismo* and the doctrine that the end justifies the means. **1981** J. SUTHERLAND *Bestsellers* xi. 126 The adolescent's values..*sacro egoismo,* refusal to form lasting relationships, machismo.

sacsac (sæ·ksæk). [Pidgin.] A local name in Papua New Guinea for the sago palm, *Metroxylon sagu.* Also *attrib.*

1947 I. L. IDRIESS *Isles of Despair* xxiv. 163 Sago from the sac-sac palm. **1962** *Coast to Coast 1961–62* 55 We told them where they would find the sago-palms, the sacsac, to plait for walls and roof.

Sacta, Sacti, varr. *SAKTA, *SAKTI.

sad, *a.* Add: **III. 11.** *sad-faced* (later examples), *-garbed, -hearted* (later example), *-lidded, -looking, -making, -serene, -smiling, -sweet, -visaged;* **sad-ass** *N. Amer. slang,* used *attrib.* as a term of abuse; also **sad-assed** *a.*

1971 *Black World* Apr. 63 How is Philadelphia?.. Thats one sad-ass city..bout to sink into the ground. **1974** D. SEARS *Lark in Clear Air* xiii. 158 A few general comments on sad-assed, puritanical sons-of-bitches individually and collectively. *c* **1893** A. W. PINERO in M. R. Booth *Eng. Plays of 19th Cent.* (1969) II. 285, I knew her when she was a sad-faced, pale baby. **1947** J. MULGAN *Report on Experience* xi. 126 In the streets were sad-faced men and women, still hungry and no longer happy. **1971** *Where?* Oct. 309/1 Indeed, one might argue that there is an urgent and essential need to produce this quality of communal participation and commitment if our society is to survive. Not that this means a sadfaced approach. **1848** J. R. LOWELL *Poems* 2nd Ser. 167 He looks a sachem, in red blanket wrapt,..'mid some council of the sad-garbed whites. **1952** C. DAY LEWIS tr. *Virgil's Aeneid* I. 16 And spoke these words of comfort to his sad-hearted friends. **1921** D. H. LAWRENCE *Tortoises* 35 His black, sad-lidded eye sees but beholds not. **1961** C. MCCULLERS *Clock without Hands* iv. 78 The red lamp with ragged fringes, two obviously broken chairs and other pieces of sad-looking furniture. **1930** E. WAUGH *Vile Bodies* xii. 208 'My dear, isn't that rather sad-making for you?' 'I'm desperate about it.' **1955** J. D. SALINGER *Franny* in *New Yorker* 29 Jan. 30/3 But just so tiny and meaningless and—sad-making. **1960** J. STROUD *Shorn Lamb* xxiii. 251 You were watching the end of an epoch; that's always rather sad-making. **1933** W. DE LA MARE *Fleeting* 17 How sad-serene the abandoned house. **1928** BLUNDEN *Undertones of War* 4 And there, sad-smiling,.. were two or three of the convalescent squad. **1909** E. POUND *Exultations* 12 Ye know somewhat the strain, the sad-sweet wonder-pain of such singing. **1925** J. GREGORY *Bab of Backwoods* iii. 33 He managed to get his one free arm about her, hugging her tight while he said good-bye; Bab would never forget that terribly sad-sweet moment. **1953** S. KAUFFMANN *Philanderer* xiv. 233 A lamp-lighted restaurant table, the distant sad-sweet music, all these flowed together in a comfortable alcoholic haze. **1869** 'MARK TWAIN' *Innoc. Abr.* xxxiv. 370, I never saw such.. starving, sad-visaged, broken-hearted looking curs in my life.

saddhu, var. *SADHU.

saddle, *sb.* Add: **I. 1. d.** Ellipt. for *saddle brown* in sense 10 below.

1976 *Billings* (Montana) *Gaz.* 26 June 14-A/3 (Advt.), The perfect handbag for carrying everything in Saddle, Tan or Rust. **1977** *West Briton* 25 Aug. 31/5 (Advt.), 1974 (Oct.) Lancia Fulvia 3 Coupe, finished in maroon with saddle interior.

II. 4. a. *spec.* in *Geol.,* a depression along the axis of an anticline, concave in longitudinal section and convex in transverse section.

1886 T. M. READE *Origin of Mountain Ranges* xvi. 187 (*caption*) Saddle in lower Silurian rocks between Clarach Bay and Aberystwyth, formed by the junction of anticlinal and synclinal curves. **1928** E. R. LILLEY *Geol. Petroleum & Natural Gas* xii. 293 Where the amount of oil and gas is sufficient only to fill the distinctly domed portions of the fold, the saddle is normally water-bearing. **1952** *Q. Jrnl. Geol. Soc.* CVIII. 16 Individual anticlines have lengths of up to 250 miles, following long straight courses and rising and falling into culminations and saddles. **1977** *Offshore Engineer* May 52/1 The structure is a tilted fault block with hydrocarbons trapped on the upthrown side of a normal fault in two culminations separated by a saddle.

c. *Mining.* = *saddle reef* in sense 10 below; *spec.* one that is anticlinal rather than synclinal.

1872 *Rep. Vermont Board Agric.* 630 The miners were quarreling about false and true veins, horses of rock and saddles of ore. **1908** J. M. MACLAREN *Gold* II. 368 In working the saddles, prospecting for lower saddles is effected by sinking shafts designed to strike a 'leg' of an underlying saddle, from whence stopes are carried up to the crest of the anticline. **1937** W. H. EMMONS *Gold Deposits of World* vii. 528 As many as 24 quartz saddles in an anticline have been passed through from the surface to a depth of 2,200 feet. **1950** DAVID & BROWNE *Geol. Commonwealth of Austral.* II. xxvii. 196 Inverted saddles are smaller and less common than saddles, but they have given profitable yields in several mines.

5. j. An insulating device designed to be fitted around an electrical wire or conduit to help to hold it in place.

1888 D. SALOMONS *Managem. Accumulators & Private Electr. Light Installations* (ed. 3) II. ii. 107 Leather saddles answer well to keep the wires in place. **1930** F. C. RAPHAEL *Electr. Wiring of Buildings* vi. 91 Multiple saddles are used if two or more lengths of conduit run together. **1969** H. A. MILLER *Pract. Wiring* I. v. 34 It is good practice to secure single runs by clips and multiple runs by saddles.

k. *Dentistry.* The basal part of a denture, which replaces alveolar tissue and bears the artificial teeth.

1907 H. J. GOSLEE *Princ. & Pract. Crown & Bridge-work* xxiv. 443 The saddle should now be swaged of 30 to 32 gauge platinum, trimmed to the proper outline, fitted in the mouth with the caps in place, and then soldered thereto with platinum solder. **1930** I. G. NICHOLS *Prosthetic Dentistry* xli. 638 The various materials employed in rebasing saddles are: modeling compound, plaster, and wax. **1962** BLAKE & TROTT *Periodontol.* iv. 39 The free end saddle, which cannot be supported by occlusal rests, always presents a problem.

l. A fire-clay bar for supporting ceramic ware during glazing.

1911 A. B. SEARLE tr. *Bourry's Treat. Ceramic Industries* (ed. 2) xii. 399 The pieces, especially plates, may be placed upright in rectangular saggers, kept up at the bottom by rectangular saddles and at the top by a series of thimbles. **1930** —— *Encycl. Ceramic Industries* III. 74/2 *Saddle,* a type of support usef for plates, etc. in a saggar. It consists of bars of triangular cross-section. Two of these are laid parallel to each other on the bottom of the saggar, and the plates are stood on end across these. **1964** H. HODGES *Artifacts* i. 39 These setters vary considerably in shape, and their names are usually adequately descriptive—saddle, stilt, spur, thimble, pin. **1967** M. CHANDLER *Ceramics in Mod. World* iii. 102 Thimbles, saddles, and stilts are made of fireclay and so designed that the weight rests only on sharp points.

7. c. (Earlier and later examples.)

1854, etc. [see *saddle feather, saddle hackle (feather),* sense 10 below]. **1976** J. BATTY *Understanding Old Eng. Game* (ed. 2) 58 *Saddle,* that part of the back of a male bird nearest to the tail which includes long feathers known as saddle hackles.

8*. a. A piece of leather stitched across the instep of a shoe, often in a contrasting colour.

1930 *Footwear Organiser* Jan. 37/1 The tie shoe is a development of the one-bar, with a bar or saddle fastened in the centre by means of a fancy lace or ribbon tie through eyelets. **1948** R. T. WILCOX *Mode in Footwear* 170 (*caption*) Saddle oxford—white elk—brown calf saddle—red rubber sole—worn since the 1920's. **1972** *N.Y. Times* 3 Nov. 8/1 (Advt.), In bone leather with a blue saddle..in big girl sizes 5 to 9 medium width.

b. Ellipt. for *saddle shoe* in sense 10 below.

1972 *N.Y. Times* 3 Nov. 8/1 (Advt.), Everyone loves our bumpy, bouncy saddle—the shoe that sparks up the classics.

8.** *Math.* A saddle point.

1952 W. HUME-ROTHERY et al. *Metall. Equilibrium Diagrams* xxx. 262 (*heading*) Diagrams involving intermediate compounds: saddles. *Ibid.*, The highest point in the saddle, *R*, will be a maximum in the direction of the eutectic valleys, and at this point the solidus line.. touches the liquidus. **1978** *Nature* 7 Sept. 76/1 They explain..Thom's listing of the ways in which critical points of functions (that is, maxima, minima and saddles) of *n* variables can coalesce as k parameters vary.

III. 9. Simple attrib., as *saddle-cover, -horn* (earlier and later examples), *-lining, -load, -pad, -paste, -pouch*; with the sense 'used for riding', as *saddle mare* (later example), *stock*; *saddle-peaked* adj.; in the names of affections incident to the use of the saddle, as *saddle boil, sore, -weariness*; objective, as *saddle-stitching*.

1816 U. BROWN *Jrnl.* 20 Aug. in *Maryland Hist. Mag.* (1916) XI. 151 Cumberland's Back is Compleatly full of Saddle Biles & in a full fever. **1884** 'MARK TWAIN' *Huck. Finn* ii. 8 He said they rode him all over the world..and his back was all over saddle-boils. **1977** *Times Lit. Suppl.* 8 Apr. 422/1 His [*sc.* Mark Twain's] more excruciating experiences (seasickness, saddle boils, the running war against vermin). **1676** S. SEWALL *Diary* 27 Oct. (1878) I. 27 Saddle Cover [was] lost. **1895** M. A. JACKSON *Mem. Stonewall Jackson* (ed. 2) xx. 403 A superb English saddle, bridle, holsters, saddle-cover. **1926** T. E. LAWRENCE *Seven Pillars* (1935) VIII. xcii. 508 Afterwards we slept on our saddle-covers, the tanned fleece hooked last of all over the saddle-load to make a slippy and sweat-proof seat for the rider. **1856** A. CARY *Married* 184 The bridle rein was twisted around the saddle horn. **1926** T. E. LAWRENCE *Seven Pillars* (1935) VII. lxxxviii. 490 She [*sc.* a camel]..was docile and smooth to ride, turning left or right if the saddle-horn were tapped on the required side. **1971** D. C. BROWN *Yukon Trophy Trails* i. 20, I hung the box by a string from the saddlehorn and climbed on. **1919** J. MASEFIELD *Reynard* I. 5 Some.. Brushed at saddle-flaps or hove Saddle-linings to the stove. **1926** Saddle-load [see *saddle-cover* above]. **1975** *Islander* (Victoria, B.C.) 7 Sept. 16/2 His reports usually dealt with his saddlemare, Snippet, and her unexpected foal. **1750** J. HEMPSTEAD *Diary* 30 Mar. (1901) 546, I mended my old Sadle pad. **1971** J. MCDOUGALL *Parsons on Plains* xv. 135 Then I dressed, and putting a saddle-pad on, rode her [*sc.* a mare] all the afternoon. **1917** *Harrods Gen. Catal.* 537/4 Harrods' Saddle Paste. Per tin... 0/6. **1919** J. MASEFIELD *Reynard* I. 5 The savour Of saddle-paste and polish spirit. **1939–40** *Army & Navy Stores Catal.* 767/2 Propert's Saddle Paste..1/–. **1869** 'MARK TWAIN' *Innoc. Abr.* xlix. 521 Saddle-peaked Hattin, traditional 'Mount of Beatitudes'. **1926** T. E. LAWRENCE *Seven Pillars* (1935) VIII. xcvi. 532 We followed dragging my few things in their light saddle-pouch. **1946** M. C. SELF *Horseman's Encycl.* 354 Riders with bad seats will often give a horse saddle sores. **1962** C. STORR *Lucy runs Away* v. 26 I've ridden two miles... I've got saddle sores. **1954** E. JENKINS *Tortoise & Hare* xii. 149 A small suitcase..was being repaired by the local ironmonger, who did saddle-stitching for the farmers. **1903** A. ADAMS *Log of Cowboy* 17 Then the entire saddle stock was driven in, so as to be at hand in case a hasty change of mounts was required. **1948** F. BLAKE *Johnny Christmas* II. 75 He went directly on to the door and pushed it open, passing in among the oxen and saddle-stock of the fort. **1909** *Chambers's Jrnl.* June 347/1 In a general way, the word Bush recalls to the writer..the sun and dust and saddle-weariness of the great gray inland plains.

10. saddle-bill = *saddle-billed stork*; also *attrib.*; **saddle-blanket** (earlier and later examples); **saddle block** *Obstetrics*, the technique of anæsthetizing the perineal region by a low spinal injection; freq. *attrib.*; **saddlebred** *a.*, bred to have the gaits of an American Saddle Horse; also *ellipt.* as *sb.*; **saddle bronc** *U.S.*: in a rodeo, a bronco ridden with a saddle; freq. *attrib.* as *saddle bronc riding* (also *ellipt.* as *saddle bronc*); **saddle brown,** the tan colour of saddle-leather; **saddle-burned** *a.*, chafed by a saddle; **saddle club,** a riding club; **saddle-coloured** *a.*, (of complexion) saddle brown, tanned; **saddle embolus** *Med.*, an embolus straddling the fork of an artery, esp. the aorta, so as to block both branches; **saddle feather** = *saddle hackle* (*feather*) below; **saddle-gall** (later example); **saddle graft,** a graft made by saddle grafting; **saddle gun** *U.S.*, a gun carried on the saddle of a horse; **saddle hackle (feather),** any of the long feathers growing backwards from the saddle of a cock; so **saddle-hackled** *a.*; **saddle horse,** (*a*) (see sense 9 in Dict.); (*b*) (see quot.); **saddle-leaf,** substitute for def.: = TULIP-TREE 1 a; (earlier and later examples); **saddle mark,** (*a*) a mark or patch on a horse's back produced by the friction of a saddle; (*b*) (see quot. 1963); **saddle-notch** (see quot. 1930); hence as *vb. trans.* and **saddle-notched** *a*; **saddle oxford,** a saddle shoe in the Oxford style; **saddle point** *Math.*, (*a*) a point at which a curved surface is locally level but at which its curvature in two directions differs in sign, i.e. for a surface defined by a function f of x and y, a point at which $\partial f/\partial x = \partial f/\partial y = 0$ and $(\partial^2 f/\partial x^2)(\partial^2 f/\partial y^2) < 0$; (*b*) in a zero-sum game, the joint outcome of the two parties following their unmixed optimal strategies, where these exist; **saddle quern** (earlier and further examples); **saddle reef** *Mining*, a reef or vein of ore between the strata in the curve of an anticline or syncline; **Saddle Rock** *local U.S.*, a large oyster; in full *Saddle Rock oyster*; **saddle-rug** (examples); **saddle scabbard** *N. Amer.* (see quot. 1944); **saddle-shaped** *a.* (further example of sense 'anticlinal'); **saddle shoe,** a shoe with a saddle (sense 8* a); **saddle shoulder** *Fashion*, a square-cut shoulder on a jersey, etc., that is an extension of the sleeve; also *attrib.*; **saddle-sore** *a.* (further examples); **saddle-stone,** (*b*) (example); **saddle thrombus** *Med.* = *saddle embolus* above; **saddle tramp** *N. Amer. slang*, a vagrant on horseback; **saddle vein** *Mining* = *saddle reef* above; **saddle wire,** (*b*) *Bookbinding*, a wire staple passed through the back fold of a single gathering; usu. *attrib.*; hence **saddle-wired** *a.*

1906 W. L. SCLATER *Birds S. Afr.* IV. 43 (*heading*) Saddle-bill, or African Jabiru. *Ibid.* 44 The Saddle-bill is found all over tropical Africa. **1947** J. STEVENSON-HAMILTON *Wild Life S. Afr.* xxxiv. 289 The saddle bill or jabiru (*Ephippiorhynchus sinegalensis*)... They are striking-looking birds; the forepart of the long bill crimson, the centre black, and the saddle or shield which comes just above the nostrils, bright yellow. **1973** *Times* 11 Dec. (Zaire Suppl.) p. vii/5, I was able to identify a saddle-bill stork. **1817** E. P. FORDHAM *Let.* 26 July in *Personal Narr. Travels* (1906) 98 My cloak and saddle-blanket, spread on the floor, form my couch. **1925** C. JACOBSON *Life Story Jeff Davis* xxviii. 234 When I licked that gang at Little Rock during the last campaign, they went around on the streets with their faces looking as long as a saddle blanket. **1973** A. H. WHITEFORD *N. Amer. Indian Arts* 75 Twill weaving is done by the Navajo in making saddle blankets. **1946** PARMLEY & ADRIANI in *Southern Med. Jrnl.* XXXIX. 194/2 The term 'saddle block analgesia' is well chosen inasmuch as it is not only descriptive but is also free from the word spinal which sounds very, very dangerous to most obstetric patients. **1974** PASSMORE & ROBSON *Compan. Med. Stud.* III. xl. 17/2 Low spinal anaesthesia (saddle block) involves the injection of local anaesthetic into the C[erebro] S[pinal] F[luid] of the subarachnoid space. *Ibid.*, The incidence of serious complications is low and saddle block is popular in North America. **1974** Saddlebred [see *pleasure-horse* s.v. *PLEASURE *sb.* 6]. **1976** *Horse & Hound* 10 Dec. 73/1 (Advt.), 2 beautiful colts to mature 15 hands 2 in by American saddlebred Goldmount Bourbon Genius. **1977** *Islander* (Victoria, B.C.) 18 Sept. 6/1 Lancer, an American saddlebred, who is nearly eight. **1949** G. ROUNDS *Rodeo* 49 (*heading*) Saddle Bronc Rodeo. **1956** *N.Y. Times Mag.* 23 Sept. 47/2 Rodeo people call them broncs, but never broncos if they are saddled. Otherwise, they're 'bareback horses'. Saddle broncs usually are larger. Neither are apt to be vicious. Most can be halter-led. *Ibid.*, A saddle bronc ride, which requires more skill, lasts ten [seconds]. **1973** *Houston Chron.* 14 Oct. (Suppl.) 2/3 Texas Prison Rodeo features bareback riding, saddle bronc riding, calf tussles, clowns and other events. **1976** *Columbus* (Montana) *News* 3 June 1/4 The rodeo picks up again at 1:00 p.m. Sunday. Events are saddle bronc, bull riding, steer wrestling, [etc.]. **1977** *New Yorker* 6 June 48/2 He rode dogies and then steers and saddle broncs. **1961** WEBSTER, Saddle brown. **1975** *Cleveland* (Ohio) *Plain Dealer* 31 Mar. 24-D (Advt.), Perfectly matched Rocker-Recliner or Swivel Rocker in handsome, saddle-brown Masland Duran vinyl. **1941** J. STEINBECK *Sea of Cortez* xvi. 160, I removed the saddle to see whether he might not be saddle-burned. **1946** *Carleton Coll.* (Northfield, Mass.) *Bull.* Mar. 85 The Saddle Club, open to students proficient in horsemanship. **1962** A. SAMPSON *Anat. of Britain* xvi. 258 Guards officers..have their own club in Mayfair, their own polo club, cricket club, saddle club, flying club, shooting club. **1977** *Navy News* June 18/3 Services saddle clubs have been helped. **1854** 'LOGAN' *Master's House* 260 That 'saddle-colored' nigger grinning at me..would be all the better for about 'forty-five', well laid on. **1900** KIPLING *Land & Sea Tales* (1923) 39 The saddle-coloured sons of the soil looked down their noses. **1936** M. MITCHELL *Gone with Wind* xxxiii. 553 A saddle-colored negro of middle age. **1937** *Ann. Surg.* CVI. 909 Incisions have been made very close to the aorta, in either one or the other iliac arteries, and successful removals of saddle emboli accomplished. **1974** J. D. MAYNARD in R. M. Kirk et al. *Surgery* xi. 236 Retrograde catheterisation to the bifurcation of the aorta will allow dislodgement of a saddle embolus. **1854** L. A. MEALL *Moubray's Treat. Poultry* 128 The hackle and saddle feathers are straw colour. **1901** *Nature* 4 July 233/1 Manipulation of the tail-feathers..would not account for the likewise abnormal elongation of the saddle-feathers. **1946** WINTER & FUNK *Poultry Sci. & Pract.* (ed. 2) iii. 55 Castrated males grow longer neck, saddle, and tail feathers than do cockerels. **1946** K. TENNANT *Lost Haven* (1947) xiv. 224 The smooth patch of grey rock that looked like a saddle gall. **1951** *Dict. Gardening* (R. Hort. Soc.) II. 917/1 (*caption*) Saddle graft. **1959** *New Biol.* XXX. 38 He.. made a saddle graft between the two plants then, when the graft had taken, he cut transversely across the graft-union so that the wound callus formed would be a mixture of tissues from the two plants. **1886** *Outing* (U.S.) VIII. 7/1, I..had with me the little forty-sixty Winchester saddle gun. **1949** *10 Story Western* May 21/1 They jerked the saddle guns from their scabbards. **1854** L. A. MEALL *Moubray's Treat. Poultry* 85 The saddle hackle and back feathers. **1855** *Poultry Chron.* III. 44/1 Should the saddle-hackle feathers of the Silver Spangled cock be spangled, or perfectly white? **1951** W. H. SILK *Bantams & Miniature Fowl* iv. 26 Neck and saddle hackle are silvery-white as free from black striping as possible... Saddles and wing-bows are rich yellow or orange, shading to silvery-white in saddle-hackle. **1976** Saddle hackle [see sense 7 c above]. **1855** *Poultry Chron.* III. 209/2, I consider the really perfect hen-feathered cocks vastly superior in plumage to the long-feathered saddle-hackled. **1958** J. HISLOP *From Start to Finish* viii. 67 The best way to [learn]..is to practise on a saddle-horse (a wooden stand, upon which saddles are cleaned). **1820** C. MATHEWS *Let.* 31 Aug. in A. Mathews *Mem. C. Mathews* (1839) III. vii. 149 If you have not got any in the grounds, a saddle-leaf tulip is beautiful. **1931** W. N. CLUTE *Common Names of Plants* 39 The tulip-tree (*Liriodendron tulipifera*) was called saddle-leaf because the young leafblades in the bud were bent back across the petiole in such a way as to retard the growth of the tip and make it appear as if cut square across. **1908** *Animal Managem.* (War Office) 32 Saddle marks are extremely common, in fact it is the exception to find an old troop horse without them. **1963** BLOODGOOD & SANTINI *Horseman's Dict.* 172 *Saddle mark*, hair left unclipped on a horse's back in the shape of a saddle; usual in clipping hunters. **1976** *Horse & Hound* 10 Dec. 67/2 (Advt.), Bay mare... Some saddle marks. **1930** J. BEAMES *Army without Banners* 12 He disdained the clumsy 'squaw notch', where one log sits simply in a shallow groove cut in the one below, and fitted them neatly into place with the 'saddle notch', a triangular ridge cut to fit closely into a deep V in the log above. **1974** *Islander* (Victoria, B.C.) 8 Sept. 4/2 After the logs were peeled David..saddle-notched each log and fitted them into place. **1976** *Amer. Speech 1973* XLVIII. 166 In the South the saddle-notch was favored, while in the Mid-Atlantic and Midwestern areas V-notching was preferred. **1967** *Dict. Canadianisms* 651/2 *Saddle notch*, a saddle-notched joint. **1977** *New Yorker* 27 June 58/3 He and Lilly built a..cabin of unpeeled, saddle-notched logs. **1948** R. T. WILCOX *Mode in Footwear* 165 (*caption*) Saddle oxford of the period—black or brown and white. **1967** A. WEST in *Coast to Coast 1965–66* 212 Onto her feet she secured a pair of saddle oxfords that were too big by wrapping the laces around her ankles. **1922** G. N. WATSON *Treat. Theory Bessel Functions* viii. 235 The points [u_0, v_0, $Rf(w_0)$] are saddle points, or passes, on the surface. **1946** H. & B. S. JEFFREYS *Methods of Math. Physics* xvii. 472 Through any saddle-point it will be possible to draw at least two curves such that ϕ is constant along them. **1960** A. RAPOPORT *Fights, Games, & Debates* vii. 136 A saddle point is an entry in the game matrix which is the smallest in its row and the largest in its column. **1966** S. BEER *Decision & Control* xviii. 467 In the inadequate game-theoretic model, neither side can exploit information about the other, because the game has a fixed saddle point. **1973** *Listener* 21 June 826/2 We can conceive of a kind of space that has saddle-points in it, over which massive bodies slide in some directions more easily than in others. **1867** *Archaeol. Jrnl.* XXIV. 246 A 'saddle-quern', resembling that found at Ty Mawr, was sent to the museum of the Institute at the Hull meeting, 1867. **1938** *Proc. Prehist. Soc.* IV. 35 The true saddle-quern..was a two-handed implement allowing only a to-and-fro movement of the upper stone. **1978** A. & G. RITCHIE *Anc. Monuments Orkney* 41 The original rubbing stones were found beside this massive saddle quern, together with a pile of crushed razor-shells. **1860** *Mining Surveyors' Rep.* (Mining Dept., Victoria) Aug. 216 The Wellington Reef..is what is termed by miners a saddle reef, or, in other words, a vein of quartz branching from the cap in two distinct underlies, viz. one to the east and the other to the west. **1906** J. PARK *Text-bk. Mining Geol.* ii. 49 The gold-bearing veins at Cape Terawhiti, near Wellington, in New Zealand, are interesting examples of saddle-reefs which exhibit both an anticlinal and synclinal arrangement. **1975** E. HILLARY *Nothing venture, Nothing Win* (1977) xviii. 351 Saddle reefs of quartz in the goldfields of Victoria, Australia, and on the west coast of New Zealand. **1852** *Lantern* (N.Y.) II. 158/1 Oyster House sages..acknowledge that for a consideration they will puff anything from Saddle Rock Oysters to Fancy soap. **1865** J. H. BROWNE *Four Years in Secessia* 279 The stewing of 'Saddle-Rocks' in a chafing dish, or the preparation of a lobster salad, was as far as I had ever advanced in the mysteries of the cuisine. **1881** E. INGERSOLL *Oyster-Industry* 244 *Fancy Oysters.*—In New York, these are 'Saddle Rocks', 'Blue Points', etc. *Ibid.* 247 *Saddle Rock Oysters*, a trade name in New York for the largest and finest oysters. **1679** *Rec. Court of New Castle on Delaware* (1904) 361, 2 saddle Ruggs & 3 old Blancketts. **1931** A. U. DILLEY *Oriental Rugs & Carpets* Pl. 20 (*caption*) Kerman Saddle Rug. **1898** H. S. CANFIELD *Maid of Frontier* 185 His horse came up to his ranch..with the gun still in the saddle scabbard. **1944** R. F. ADAMS *Western Words* 137/1 *Saddle scabbard*, a heavy saddle-leather case in which to carry a rifle or Winchester when riding. The gun fits in as far as the hammer, leaving the stock exposed. **1973** R. D. SYMONS *Where Wagon Led* VI. xviii. 280 He couldn't get at his rifle which was in the saddle scabbard. **1950** DAVID & BROWNE *Geol. Commonwealth of Austral.* II. xxvii. 176 A few of the ore-bodies appear to be saddle-shaped. **1941** J. C. FURNASS *How Amer. Lives* 272 You could paint an accurate oil portrait from those data alone, right down to the socks and saddle shoes. **1958** *Listener* 31 July 157/2 A young American boy and girl, dressed in teenage style of blue jeans, suede saddle shoes, and peach-coloured polo shirts. **1974** D. RAMSAY *No Cause to Kill* I. 6 Saddle shoes. Brown and white... Of all things! Who wore saddle shoes nowadays? **1957** M. B. PICKEN *Fashion Dict.* 280/2 *Saddle shoulder sleeve*, sleeve with shoulder extended into neckline somewhat like raglan, but square-cut in 'saddle' effect. **1969** *Sears Catal.* Spring/Summer 20 Classic Cardigan... Saddle shoulders add a well tailored look. **1978** *Detroit Free Press* 2 Apr. (Detroit Suppl.) 21 (Advt.), Crew neck pullover with saddle shoulder. **1956** R. BRADDON *Nancy Wake* xv. 178 It's just that damned bicycle. I'm so saddle-sore I could die. **1975** *Times* 8 Feb. 10/5 What if riding pales and saddlesore guests seek other diversions? **1932** G. M. BOUMPHREY *Story of Wheel* 42 The 'saddle-stone', which had a hollow face in which a smaller stone was rubbed backwards and forwards. **1933** *Ann. Surg.* XCVIII. 262 At about the point of bifurcation of the deep and superficial femoral is a constricted portion with a saddle thrombus which shows beginning organization. **1937** *Ibid.* CVI. 908 The..patient was operated upon rather late, after the saddle thrombus developed, by the transabdominal route. **1942** BERREY & VAN DEN BARK *Amer. Thes. Slang* § 913/10 *Saddle..tramp*, a cowboy who rides from ranch to ranch living on Western hospitality. **1962** E. LUCIA *Klondike Kate* 7 Most of them [*sc.* prostitutes] led wretched lives,..attached to gamblers, card sharps..saddle tramps, gun-slingers and rogues. **1979** *Radio Times* 5–11 May 23/2 Kirk Douglas back on the range for King Vidor, in the one about the saddle tramp up against the barbed wire. **1935** STOČES & WHITE *Structural Geol.* 293 Saddle veins are filled openings..which were similarly formed in the arches and troughs of folded beds. **1977** A. HALLAM *Planet Earth* 314/3 Saddle veins are lens-shaped, concave below and convex above. **1911** WEBSTER, Saddle wire stitch. **1948** R. R. KARCH *Graphic Arts Procedures* xii. 301 Saddle-Wire bound booklets are the simplest and cheapest in form... The cover and pages are held by two or more stitches on saddle-wire booklets, which allows them to lie flat and open. **1967** V. STRAUSS *Printing Industry* x. 659/1 Saddle wire stitching produces a completely flat-opening book. **1967** KARCH & BUBER *Offset Processes* xii. 492 Saddle-wired books lie flat when open, and may be folded upon themselves.

saddle, *v.* Add: **1. d.** *S. Afr.* *to saddle off* = OFF-SADDLE, OFF-SADDLE *v.*

1835 J. W. D. MOODIE *Ten Yrs. S. Afr.* I. 65 He..asked us if we would 'saddle off' our horses.

e. *trans.* To enter (a horse that one has trained) in a race.

1928 *Daily Mail* 25 July 14/2 Scott will not saddle Lamintone for the Church House Handicap Plate (2.30) at Liverpool. **1947** *Sun* (Baltimore) 11 June 17/4 Palmer Sowers, of Washington, saddled two winners on the program and might have made it three had not Jockey J. Keenan lost a stirrup in the final drive of the second race. **1970** *Globe & Mail* (Toronto) 25 Sept. 32/3 Trainer Glen Magnusson..saddled three successive winners. **1976** *Southern Even. Echo* (Southampton) 13 Nov. 15/3 The Bishop Auckland trainer should start successfully by saddling Clever Prince to win the Threlkeld Handicap Chase.

6. c. To attach after the manner of a saddle.

1831 J. J. AUDUBON *Ornith. Biogr.* I. 303 The nests were fixed to a horizontal bough, but were not *saddled* upon it so deeply as those of the Wood Thrush are. **1881** *Amer. Naturalist* XV. 217 Our nest..was saddled to a horizontal limb after the fashion of our wood pewee. **1940** *Bull. U.S. Nat. Museum* No. 176. 321 It was about 30 feet from the ground, saddled on a horizontal branch of a maple over the trail.

saddleback, *sb.* and *a.* Add: **A.** *sb.* **4. b.** (Earlier and later examples.)

1770 G. CARTWRIGHT *Jrnl.* 2 Oct. (1792) I. 40 They returned with three shellbirds and a saddleback. **1932** J. BARBOUR *Forty-Eight Days Adrift* vi. 61 A 'saddle-back' coming towards us..was a good sign we were getting near land.

d. Substitute for def.: A New Zealand wattle-bird, *Creadion* (or *Philesturnus*) *carunculatus*; (later example).

1966 *Weekly News* (Auckland, N.Z.) 1 June 17/1 A pair of saddlebacks point like hunting dogs... They snap from one rigid position to another, head down, tail erect, wattles a blood crimson, the fragmented sunlight burnishing the chestnut saddle on their backs.

g. The brown and green larva of the moth *Sibine stimulea*, which has stinging spiny hairs and is found in southeastern North America.

1895 J. H. & A. B. COMSTOCK *Man. Study of Insects* xviii. 225 The Saddle-back Caterpillar... Its most characteristic feature is a large green patch on the back. **1943** *Sun* (Baltimore) 9 Sept. 16/7 The Saddleback is of the family *Eucleidae*. **1954** [see *10[2]].

h. A parti-coloured black and white pig belonging to the breed so called. Also *saddleback pig*.

1919 (*title*) The Wessex Saddleback Pig Society's herd book. **1927** *Daily Tel.* 6 Dec. 9/2 Mr. Douglas Vickers' herd of Wessex saddlebacks at Temple Dinsley, Hitchin. **1978** E. DOWNING *Keeping Pigs* iii. 25 The Large Black and the Saddleback are still hardy. **1981** *Times* 25 May 10/6 The Johnstone Cup..was won by the cider firm, Whiteways..with British saddleback pigs.

i. The African black-backed jackal, *Canis mesomelas*.

1947 J. STEVENSON-HAMILTON *Wild Life S. Afr.* ii. 23 The side-striped jackal..began to decrease... Its place had been taken by the black-backed jackal... It may be that it contracted and died from the same disease as affected the wild dog, and from which the saddle-back..remained..immune. **1964** D. VARADAY *Gara-Yaka* vii. 61 A pair of saddle-back jackals coming into view from the sands of an ant-bear hole.

j. The North American Arctic shrew, *Sorex arcticus*.

1948 A. L. RAND *Mammals Eastern Rockies* 51 The saddle-back shrew with its red-brown sides and tricolour pattern is the most beautiful of our shrews. **1966** R. L. PETERSON *Mammals E. Canada* 38 *Sorex arcticus* Kerr—Arctic or Saddle-back Shrew. *Ibid.* 38/1 The young do not show the distinct dorsal band or 'saddle back'.

B. *adj.* **1.** (Examples of *saddleback chair*.)

1904 M. BEERBOHM *Let.* 3 Jan. (1964) 155 There is nothing to do except to sit in the hall on a saddle-back chair. **1981** P. VANSITTART *Death of Robin Hood* III. iii. 142 The dulled crimson sofa and saddleback chairs.

2. Also *saddleback caterpillar, jackal, pig, shrew*: see sense A. 4 above.

saddle-backed, *a.* Add: **1.** Also of furniture.

1910 A. BENNETT *Clayhanger* II. xxi. 313 He would begin to establish himself in a saddle-backed, ear-flapped easy-chair.

b. Placed astride like a saddle.

1878 J. H. BEADLE *Western Wilds* xxx. 487 Colorado is divided nearly down the center by the main chain of the Rocky Mountains—or, in miner's phrase, 'saddle-backed across the range'.

4. Also used of other animals with similar markings, as *saddle-backed shrew* = *SADDLEBACK *sb.* 4 j.

1927 H. H. T. JACKSON *Taxon. Rev. Amer. Long-Tailed Shrews* 69 A specimen of the American saddle-backed shrew..was mentioned as early as 1772.

saddle-bag. Add: **1.** (Earlier and later examples.) Also a bag attached behind the saddle of a bicycle.

1773 H. FINLAY *Jrnl.* (1867) 43 The rider had saddle bags quite full besides. **1780** W. FLEMING in N. D. Mereness *Trav. Amer. Colonies* (1916) 651 Capt. Pawling ..had gone back for my saddlebags. **1901** DUNCAN & SCOTT *Allen & Woodson Counties, Kansas* 619 The doctor of 1858,..with saddle-bags like paniers to a pack mule, would make a strange comparison with the well-dressed and well-barbered M.D. of the present era. **1920** *Cycling* 12 Aug. p. xvii/3 (Advt.), Few pigskin saddle bags, 9 by 6 by 4, 17s 6d, post 9d. **1940** J. BETJEMAN *Old Lights for New Chancels* 49 Kant on the handle-bars, Marx in the saddlebag. **1965** D. MURPHY *Full Tilt* p. xi, Apart from the normal accessories—saddle-bag, bell, lamp and pump—she carried only pannier-bag holders on either side of the back wheel. **1973** R. T. WAY *Bicycle* 63/2 For normal day-to-day riding, a small saddlebag is all that is needed—it only has to take a cape, cap, tools, snack and camera.

2. Also *ellipt.*, a saddle-bag chair.

1919 C. DANE *Legend* 82 'There's your chair. Isn't that always your chair?'..But he did not take the saddle-bag near Anita's own seat.

sa·ddle-bag, *v.* *U.S.* Also (*rare*) **saddle-bags.** [f. the sb.] *intr.* To double round an obstruction.

1884 'MARK TWAIN' *Huck. Finn* xiii. 114 They lost their steering-oar..and saddle-baggsed on the wreck. **1898** *Derrick's Handbk. Petroleum* 32 A boat..laden with 1,500 bbls. of oil, 'saddle-bagged' on pier of Oil Creek bridge. Boat and contents a total loss. **1901** W. F. FOX in *6th Ann. Rep. N.Y. State Forest, Fish & Game Comm.* 254 Sometimes the long, floating mass [*sc.* a lumber raft] would swing in the wind and current so that it would 'saddle-bag' on the head of the bar below the dam. **1905** *Terms Forestry & Logging* (U.S. Dept. Agric. Bureau Forestry) 45 *Saddlebag*, as applied to a boom, to catch on an obstruction and double round it.

saddle seat. **1.** The seat of a saddle.

1822 J. FOWLER *Jrnl.* 28 Apr. (1898) 135 We then passed threw Some low Hills a little East of South Seven miles to the River and Crossing over found the Watter up to the Saddle Sceats. **1850** *Rep. Comm. Patents* 1849 (U.S.) I. 263 The bent tension springs CC, for supporting the saddle seat. **1963** BLOODGOOD & SANTINI *Horseman's Dict.* 170 *Waist*, saddle-seat at its narrowest point.

2. See SADDLE *sb.* 10.

3. a. A seat made by the crossed hands of two persons.

1913 *Amer. Jrnl. Insanity* Jan. 575 She..suggested that a couple of gentlemen..should clasp their hands so as to form a 'saddle seat' for her, and thus she rode from the platform to the car.

b. A chair seat resembling a saddle (see quot. 1960); also, a chair with such a seat.

1934 in WEBSTER. **1952** J. GLOAG *Short Dict. Furnit.* 406 *Saddle Seat*, a solid wooden seat with two shallow depressions separated by a slight central ridge, suggesting the shape of a saddle. It is used on many types of Windsor chair. **1960** H. HAYWARD *Antique Coll.* 246/1 Some late 18th cent. chairs have a gently curving seat sloping down in the centre which is described colloquially as a saddle seat. A slightly different form is found on Windsor chairs where the centre of the wooden seat is shaped to resemble a saddle. **1976** *County Life* 27 May (Suppl.) 486/1 Late 18th century wheel-back armchairs with saddle seats and X-frame legs.

saddle stitch, *sb.* **a.** *Bookbinding.* A stitch of thread or a wire staple passed through the back fold of a booklet while it lies open on a saddle-shaped support.

1934 WEBSTER, Saddle stitch. **1956** A. WILLIAMSON *Methods Bk. Design* xix. 331 The whole is fastened together by a saddle-stitch which passes through the spine fold. **1960** G. A. GLAISTER *Gloss. Bk.* 365/1 *Saddle stitch*, a method of stitching brochures or pamphlets by placing them open astride a saddle-shaped support and stitching through the back.

b. *Needlework.* (See quot. 1964.)

1962 W. BUTLER *Dolls' Dressmaking* 92 This trim shirt has saddle-stitch outlining the cuffs, collar and front opening. **1964** *McCall's Sewing* ii. 31/2 *Saddle stitch*, a decorative top-stitch made by taking longer stitches on top and shorter ones underneath. **1974** H. MCCLOY *Sleepwalker* viii. 157 Glove seams were mended, too, with a special stitch like the saddle stitch.

Hence **sa·ddle-stitch** *v. trans.*; so **sa·ddle-stitched** *a.*; **sa·ddle-stitching** *vbl. sb.* (see also *SADDLE *sb.* 9). Also **sa·ddle-stitcher,** a device that performs saddle-stitching.

1923 H. A. MADDOX *Dict. Stationery* 69 *Saddle Stitching*, the method of wire stitching pamphlets and single section books through the centre of the fold. **1933** J. MASON in W. Atkins *Art & Pract. Printing* V. viii. 193 Thread-stitching machines are widely used for pamphlets, exercise books, and note-books. They will saddle-stitch a single section. **1947** C. TALBOT *Compl. Bk. Sewing* xxi. 144/2 Saddle-stitching is a very smart..finish for tailored clothes. It can be done in self-colour or definite contrasts. **1948** *Words into Type* 546 *Saddle stitched*, stitched through the back, the thread, silk, or wire showing on the back and in the middle fold. **1958** *Times* 6 Oct. 13/1 The next figure wears a coat designed in France and made in a supple taupe-coloured suède with saddle-stitching along the seams in a lighter shade. **1961** *Harper's Bazaar* Feb. 75 A short-sleeved white shirt, saddle-stitched..round the collar. **1964** *McCall's Sewing* xiii. 239/2 *Saddle stitching*. Take short stitches through the garment and facing an even distance from the edge. The stitches on the top side are longer than the stitches on the underside. **1967** V. STRAUSS *Printing Industry* x. 659/1 The cover of saddle-stitched books is usually, but not necessarily, of paper. **1973** *Country Life* 11 Oct. 1089 The suit..in 100% wool, with deep centre vent and impeccable saddle stitched lining. **1974** *McGraw-Hill Yearbk. Sci. & Technol.* 121/2 The most popular methods of binding soft-cover books are saddle stitching, side stitching, and perfect or patent binding. **1975** M. BANISTER *Bookbinding as Handcraft* xiii. 114/1 Like the Swingline Saddle Stitcher, this one also clinches its own staples. **1979** *Jrnl. R. Soc. Arts* July 485/2 The work involved..collating and folding the sheets and the covers, and saddle-stitching the copies with stainless steel staples.

saddling, *vbl. sb.* Add: **2.** *saddling enclosure*; *saddling paddock*, also (*Austral. slang*) a nickname for a bar in the Theatre Royal, Melbourne, frequented by prostitutes in the nineteenth century; also, a similar bar elsewhere; hence, a known place of rendezvous; (earlier and later examples).

1876 *Argus* (Melbourne) 1 July 4/4 The stranger sees that the women, possibly picking up a male companion, all enter the apartment which was previously closed, and which is now guarded by swing doors. Curiosity will doubtless prompt him to enter, and he will find himself in the far-famed 'saddling paddock' of the Royal. *Ibid.* 4/5 The existence of the 'saddling paddocks' is a scandal established with a forethought for the courtesan's benefit which is an eternal disgrace to their promoters. **1909** J. R. WARE *Passing Eng.* 213/1 *Saddling-paddock* (*Australian*), place of amusement or rather place of assignation. **1958** G. CASEY *Snowball* iii. 29 The ribald, popular name of the enclosure round the Government Dam was 'the saddling paddock'. **1969** *Sun* (Melbourne) 12 July (Turf Guide) 4/2 The AJC new grandstand in the saddling paddock at Randwick will be open on August 4. **1969** *Sun-Herald* (Sydney) 13 July 33/1 Mr Swales told us he could not get through to the stewards on the phone and gave us permission to return to the saddling enclosure to put our case to the stewards.

Sadean (sā·diăn, sē̆i-), *a.* Also **Sadeian, Sadian.** [f. the name of the Count de *Sade* (see SADISM) + -AN.] Of, pertaining to, or characteristic of de Sade.

1960 *20th Cent.* Mar. 206 The Sadian dream of the unleashed subconscious. **1963** N. GEAR *Divine Demon* 5 There were also many fantastic accounts of his life which obscured the facts in a mist of Sadeian mythology. **1978** R. HAYMAN *De Sade* xiv. 228 Baudelaire was the first poet to express modern alienation, but his negativity is Sadean.

sadful, *a.* For † *Obs. rare*[−1] read *rare* and add later example.

1884 'MARK TWAIN' *Huck. Finn* xvii. 158 She could write about anything..just so it was sadful.

sadhana (sā·danā). *Indian Philos.* Also **sadhan** and with capital initial. [Skr. *sādhanā* dedication to an aim; *sādhana* means to the goal, etc., f. *sādh* to succeed, attain.] (See quots.)

1898 K. L. SARKAR *Hindu System of Relig. Sci. & Art* vii. 137 Worship and prayer (Sadhana and Upashana) are in the main of two kinds. *Ibid.* 138 Some leaders of those sects in which *sakama sadhana* (selfish prayer) prevails, are more or less driven to give preference to that blank conclusion of Rationalism called *Nirvan Mukti* (merger in the Infinite One.) **1909** S. TATTAVABHÚSHAN *Philos. of Bráhmaism* i. 2 Bráhmaism..presents itself to us in three aspects,—(1) as a creed, (2) as a system of *Sâdhan* or spiritual culture, and (3) as a scheme of social reform. **1921** C. ELIOT *Hinduism & Buddhism* II. xxxii. 282 *Siddhi* is produced by Sâdhana, or that method of training the physical and psychic faculties which realizes their potentialities... It is part of Sâdhana to arouse..energy and make it mount from the lower to the higher centres. **1932** N. K. BRAHMA *Philos. of Hindu Sādhanā* ii. 13 The term '*Sādhanā*' is a current Bengali expression... Its literal meaning is 'that by which something is performed' or more precisely 'means to an end'. In the sphere of religion, it is always used to indicate the essential preliminary discipline that leads to the attainment of the spiritual experience which is regarded as the *summum bonum*... *Sādhanā* includes all the religious practices and ceremonies that are helpful to the realisation of spiritual experience. **1941** K. G. MASHRUWALA *Practical Non-Violence* 48 Violence is born of a narrow conception of 'I' and 'Mine'. The search and discipline of non-violence (the *Sadhana of Ahimsa*) consists in a constant and progressive widening of that conception. **1958** V. RAGHAVAN in W. T. de Bary et al. *Sources of Indian Tradition* xiii. 303 As Indian philosophy aims at experiencing the Truth, all the schools include disciplines (*Sādhanas*), practical means for the attainment of the spiritual goal. **1968** *Indian Music Jrnl.* V. 33 After seven years of Sādhanā..[he] was appointed the principal teacher of Lahore branch. **1972** P. HOLROYDE *Indian Music* vii. 252 The artistic search through feeling out the sādhana of the musical art is, as a result, inward and contemplative.

sadhu (sā·du). Also **saddhu** and with capital initial. [Skr. *sādhú* good, pious, holy man, saint, f. as prec.] In India, a holy man or sage.

1845 *Encycl. Metrop.* XXI. 672/2 When their [*sc.* spiritual guides'] sanctity is such, that they are believed to have the power of securing or withholding divine blessings, they are styled Sád'hú (saint). **1901** KIPLING *Kim* xi. 291 He switched out his..turban-cloth and.. rolled it over and under about his loins into the intricate devices of a Saddhu's cincture. **1920** *Glasgow Herald* 25 May 9 He put on the saffron robe of the Sadhu. **1924** *Blackw. Mag.* Oct. 481/2 The temple's guest-chamber, kept for visiting *sadhus* and *sanyasis*. **1955** *Times* 10 Aug. 8/3 A procession of sadhus or 'holy men' is said to have left Pathankot on the Kashmir frontier. **1958** L. DURRELL *Balthazar* x. 208 The old man was a judge in India... He dresses like a *saddhu*... You English are eccentrics. **1968** *Indian Music Jrnl.* V. 32 The philosophical discussions which his father had with the Scholars and sādhu-s who came to see him. **1978** *Times Lit. Suppl.* 3 Feb. 145/2 The Hindu Sadhus were pythons of the psychic world, whose slumbrous coils contained, and at the same time hid, the force of a battering ram.

Hence **sa·dhu,ism**, the principles or practices of a sadhu; **sa·dhuship** [-SHIP 3 b], in *his sadhuship*, a humorous title for a sadhu.

1903 J. C. OMAN *Mystics, Ascetics & Saints of India* xii. 278 (*heading*) The future of Sadhuism. **1914** W. G. LAWRENCE *Let.* 2 Apr. in *Home Lett. T. E. Lawrence* (1954) 519 It's wonderful to see and hear the way the students listen to him owing to their respect for his old sadhuship. **1979** F. OLBRICH *Sweet & Deadly* vii. 74 Holiness is a game to them [*sc.* hippies], a cheap thrill—instant Sadhuism.

Sadian, var. *SADEAN *a.*

Sadian, Sa'dian, varr. *SAADIAN *a.*

sadic (sā·dik, sēi-), *a.* [f. the name of the Count de *Sade* (see SADISM) + -IC.] = *SADEAN, SADISTIC *adjs.*

1919 R. FRY *Let.* 5 Jan. (1972) II. 443 A pretty bad melodrama..a Sadic German Jew who starts the worship of Astarte. **1926** T. E. LAWRENCE *Seven Pillars* I. i. 5 What now looks wanton or sadic seemed in the field inevitable. **1928** *Daily Tel.* 6 Nov. 10/6 The oily warder.. finds a Sadic pleasure in flogging the life out of his helpless charges. **1976** *Times Lit. Suppl.* 17 Sept. 1147/4 There's a new genre coming into focus..which may illuminate thanatos, celebrate the death wish or merely exploit a sadic lechery.

Sadie Hawkins (sēi·di hǭ·kinz). *U.S.* The name of a character in the cartoon strip *Li'l Abner* by 'Al Capp' (Alfred Gerald Caplin, 1909–79), used *attrib.* to designate a day early in November on which, according to a 'tradition' in the cartoon series, women can propose marriage to men, demand dates with them, etc., or to designate events taking place on that day.

1939 *Daily Mirror* (N.Y.) 4 Nov. 21 Sadie Hawkins Day!! **1940** *Ibid.* 2 Nov. 12 Oh, happy Sadie Hawkins Day! Befo' the sun goes down Ah'll catch me a man, daid or alive!! *Ibid.* 8 Nov. 39 The first 'gun'! The Sadie Hawkins Day Race is on. **1941** *Sun* (Baltimore) 3 Nov. 15/2 Rulman also promised a free marriage to women who catch a man in the Sadie Hawkins footrace. **1942** *Ibid.* 27 Oct. 16 Your chances are four times as good of marrying up wid him on Sadie Hawkins Day as on Leap Year Day—Sadie Hawkins Day comes once *every year*. **1952** *Ibid.* 28 Feb. 32/2 The dean..was the only man to get away in the Sadie Hawkins Day race this afternoon. **1977** *Guardian Weekly* 20 Nov. 19/1 Much of Li'l Abner has been absorbed into American folklore—Sadie Hawkins Day, when sexual roles are reversed and girls chase and catch their men.

sad-iron. (Earlier and later examples.)

1761 *Newport* (Rhode Island) *Mercury* 3 Nov. 4/3 To be sold by Naphtael Hart, jun... sad Irons, Tellescopes, [etc.]. **1815** *Niles' Weekly Reg.* IX. 94/2 Sad irons [were manufactured]. **1936** M. MITCHELL *Gone with Wind* I. v. 84 Hands like sadirons when it comes to reins. **1964** F. O'ROURKE *Mule for Marquesa* 99 Washday smell,.. don't forget to damp and starch, spit on the sadiron.

sadism. Add: Now usu. with pronunc. (sēi·diz'm). (Later examples.) Now understood as cruelty that evidences a subconscious craving and is apparently satisfied, sexually or otherwise, by the infliction of pain on another by means of aggressive or destructive behaviour or the assertion of power over that person; also *loosely*, deliberate or excessive cruelty morbidly enjoyed.

1924 J. RIVIERE et al. tr. *Freud's Coll. Papers* II. xxii. 261 We should not be astonished to hear that under certain conditions the sadism or destruction instinct which has been directed outwards can be introjected. **1937** H. G. WELLS *Brynhild* vii. 116 He..with an expression of impish sadism..prodded his sceptre into young Bates. **1943** H. READ *Politics of Unpolitical* ii. 18 Sadism is the unconscious impulse to acquire unrestricted power over another person, and to test the fullness of this power by destroying that other person. **1952** *Times Lit. Suppl.* 11 Jan. 28 Feeling [in France] had been bruised by the war [of 1914–18], but it had not been forced (as happened after the Second World War) to find..an outlet in sadism or violence. **1965** H. DEUTSCH *Neuroses & Character Types* ix. 132 Such observations led Freud to assume that it is the same aggression whether it is attached to the libidinal impulses in the form of sadism or whether..it is incorporated in the superego and made the expression of its severity. **1974** I. BIEBER in S. Arieti *Amer. Handbk. Psychiatry* III. xv. 318/2 In my view sadism is a maladaptive response to threat; it is a paranoid constellation in which the victim is a personified representative of a variety of irrationally perceived threats. **1979** M. GLASSER in I. Rosen *Sexual Deviation* x. 281 The distinction I am making between aggression and sadism may be illustrated by some simple examples.

sadist. Add: Now usu. with pronunc. (sēi·dist). (Examples.) Also, more generally, someone who derives satisfaction from inflicting pain or asserting his or her power over others. Also as *adj.*

1919 H. WALPOLE *Secret City* I. x. 68 There was something almost sadist..in the old gentleman's observation of Markovitch's labours. **1919** M. K. BRADBY *Psycho-Anal.* x. 133 The need for a greater outlet of emotion and energy in daily life where the sadist has capacity for ruling others by the strength..of his personality. **1920** *Glasgow Herald* 9 Sept. 6 The fatal policy which has given a handful of political cranks, aided by hired mercenaries and sadist abnormals, the right to stand for Russia. **1934** H. G. WELLS *Exper. Autobiogr.* II. ix. 760 Those mucky little sadists, Stalky and Co. **1954** B. KARPMAN *Sexual Offender* xix. 355 Every sadist possesses certain elements of masochism. **1962** C. ALLEN *Textbk. Psychosexual Disorders* vii. 105 Those who retain a sentimental view of the blue-eyed innocence of the child naturally find it difficult to imagine..that the ruthless ferocity of the sadist originates at that time. **1974** J. BANCROFT *Deviant Sexual Behaviour* v. 120 Some interesting studies of suppression of fantasy have been carried out. An example is a sadist treated by Marks.

sadistic, *a.* Add: Now usu. with pronunc. (sădi·stik). (Earlier and later examples.) Also, more generally, of or characteristic of a sadist; also *Comb.*, as *sadistic-anal* adj., relating to sadism that is typical of the anal stage of development; *sadistic-masochistic* adj. = *SADO-MASOCHISTIC *a.*

1892 C. G. CHADDOCK tr. *Krafft-Ebing's Psychopathia Sexualis* iii. 170 The pain of tight lacing, experienced by himself or induced in women, is a delight to him,—sadistic-masochistic element. **1915** C. R. PAYNE tr. *Pfister's Psychoanal. Method.* 78 The sadistic-masochistic instinctive tendency. **1922** J. RIVIERE tr. *Freud's Introd. Lect. Psycho-Anal.* 289 Regression of..the Libido to the antecedent stage of the sadistic-anal organization. **1929** B. RUSSELL *Marriage & Morals* 98 He drowns his dissatisfaction..by the sadistic pleasure to be derived from watching prize-fights or persecuting radicals. **1936** H. G. WELLS *Anatomy of Frustration* xx. 255 He hated people who nursed 'wrongs'. The 'wrongs' of Ireland—of India—of women, roused an almost sadistic impatience in him. **1946** H. PEARSON *Life O. Wilde* xvi. 319 Like all people who believe in punishment, he [*sc.* the governor of Reading Gaol] was vindictive and sadistic by nature, modelling himself on the God of his fathers as depicted in the Old Testament. **1952** *Times Lit. Suppl.* 15 Feb. 124/3 The vicarious sadistic lust for power of a disappointed man. **1954** B. KARPMAN *Sexual Offender* ix. 101 He admits drawing pictures of a sadistic nature; the torture of females, perversion of corpses. **1973** 'E. MCBAIN' *Let's hear It* xiv. 209 Teddy normally enjoyed films, except when she was submitted to the excesses of a sadistic *nouvelle vague* camera. **1977** A. SHERIDAN tr. *Lacan's Écrits* vii. 270 Regression is no more dependent on the need in demand than sadistic desire is explained by anal demand.

sadistically (sădi·stikăli), *adv.* [f. prec.: see -ICALLY.] In a sadistic manner; cruelly.

1922 G. B. SHAW in S. & B. Webb *Eng. Prisons under Local Govt.* p. ix, When such people are..sadistically excited by reports of the White Slave traffic, they clamor to have sentences of two years' hard labor supplemented by a flogging. **1936** F. M. FORD *Let.* 6 Sept. (1965) 261, I believe that publishers should be as sadistically punished as possible. **1951** M. MCLUHAN *Mech. Bride* (1967) 16/2 The rest of the program fits this pattern by allowing Charlie to ride sadistically over a number of carefully selected victims. **1963** *Times* 12 Jan. 4/1 The east wind continued to blow sadistically at Littlestone yesterday.

saditty (sæ·dĭti), *a.* *U.S. Blacks.* Also **seditty.** [Orig. unknown.] Affecting an air of superiority.

1967 *Jet* 20 July 43 Eartha..is considered 'seditty' by many Negroes. **1971** C. MITCHELL-KERNAN in T. Kochman *Rappin' & Stylin' Out* (1972) 318 That's all I hear lately—soul food, soul food. If you say you don't eat it you get accused of being saditty. **1973** *Black World* Aug. 61/2 Them big man-eatin' dogs them saddity niggers had roun' the house.

Sadler (sæ·dlәɹ). The name of John *Sadler* (fl. 1871–80), British botanist, used *attrib.* or in the possessive in **Sadler('s) oak** to designate *Quercus sadleriana*, an evergreen shrub with serrate leaves, found in parts of western North America and named in his honour by Robert Brown in 1871 (*Ann. Mag. Nat. Hist.* 4th Ser. VII. 249).

1908 N. L. BRITTON *N. Amer. Trees* 338 Sadler's oak.. is an interesting shrub of the high mountains of northwestern California and adjacent Oregon, with sharply serrate leaves. **1939** L. ROWNTREE *Flowering Shrubs Calif.* ix. 149 When the endemic..Sadler's Oak or Deer Oak, has room to do as it pleases,..it takes on the shape of an inverted pyramid. **1951** H. E. MCMINN *Illustr. Man. Calif. Shrubs* 83 Deer Oak. Sadler Oak. An evergreen shrub, 2 to 8 feet high, with many slender flexible stems from the base.

sadly, *adv.* Add: **9. b.** As a sentence adverb: regrettably, unfortunately.

1973 *Times* 16 Feb. 19/4 The Headmaster of Winchester College asks: 'Is there any other ancient cathedral city in Western Europe with so much fast, heavy, long-distance traffic planned to run so near?' Sadly, the answer is 'Yes, York'. **1974** *Times Lit. Suppl.* 7 June 607/3 No one would dispute the pointed courage of Camus's early journalistic campaigning. Sadly, though, this does not make him a great artist. **1978** *Lancashire Life* July 44/3 Sadly, his collection was sold and dispersed throughout the world after his death.

sado- (sēi·do), *Psychol.*, comb. form of SADISM or SADISTIC *a.* (in Dict. and Suppl.). Cf. also *SADO-MASOCHISM.

1935 [see *SADO-MASOCHISM]. **1954** B. KARPMAN *Sexual Offender* ix. 131 Alcohol is the illegitimate satiation of appetite which she fights in obsessionalism based on sado-necrophilia. **1964** *Observer* 30 Aug. 28 Client prints paperbacks for all tastes from (I think) the nasty sado-snobbism of poor Fleming to Tolstoy. **1970** *Guardian Weekly* 11 Apr. 19 A kind of all-senses collage assembled from bits of girlie photos, tropical stills, and mock-ups of sado-erotic temple carvings. **1976** *New Yorker* 26 Apr. 121/1 Given the sado-erotic content of the film... one tends to make Grace a woman. **1980** R. LUDLUM *Bourne Identity* xiii. 195 The sado-romantic myth turns into a brilliant, blood-soaked monster who brokers assassination.

sado-maso (sēi·domæ·so), *a.* (*sb.*) Slang (chiefly *U.S.*) abbrev. of *SADO-MASOCHIST; *SADO-MASOCHISTIC *a.*

1970 *Time* 23 Feb. 54/1 A gang of seminude galley slavettes..bend to the oar under a whip cracked by everyone's favorite sado-maso slave queen, Raquel Welch. **1973** *Listener* 22 Feb. 237/1 He passed..the spill-out of the sado-maso bar... At present, the sado-masos are in the ascendant. **1978** M. PUZO *Fools Die* xxiv. 277 No fantasies could be spun around them unless you were into sado-maso stuff.

sado-masochism (sēi·domæ·sŏkiz'm). *Psychol.* Also **sadomasochism.** [f. *SADO- + MASOCHISM.] The co-existence of Sadism and Masochism in one individual; the need both to inflict and to suffer pain or to assert power over another and to be submissive combined as one psychic condition evidenced in sexual relationships (freq. in a fantasied manner) or socially, as an outlet for aggressive or destructive impulses. Also *transf.* and *fig.*

1935 L. BRINK tr. *Stekel's Sadism & Masochism* I. p. v, I do not claim that I have solved the perplexing problem of sadomasochism. **1937** M. HIRSCHFELD *Sexual Anomalies* xvi. 302 Thus it is quite correct to speak of sado-masochism and, quite logically, many sadists are, simultaneously, also masochists. **1959** *Listener* 16 Apr. 683/3 The sado-masochism of the Christian ascetic tradition. **1963** A. HERON *Towards Quaker View of Sex* 67 Clinical instances of sado-masochism are not sufficiently numerous to constitute a threat to society. **1975** T. ALLBEURY *Special Collection* xvii. 114 I've been covering a vice-ring..in Mayfair... It specializes in sado-masochism..every thing from thumb-screws to a crucifix. **1977** *Early Music* July 415/3 The *Art of Fugue* is invariably presented in 'complete' performances which strike one rather as exercises in musical sado-masochism.

Hence **sa:do-ma·sochist**, one afflicted with the condition of sado-masochism; also *attrib.* or as adj.; **sa:do-masochi·stic** *a.*

1935 L. BRINK tr. *Stekel's Sadism & Masochism* I. p. v, The literature concerning sadomasochistic disorders is extraordinarily abundant. *Ibid.* iv. 60 All sadomasochists are affect-hungry individuals. **1942** *Observer* 15 Nov. 3/6 Sado-masochistic fusions of instinct are an all-important factor in the unconscious development of character. **1951** M. MCLUHAN *Mech. Bride* (1967) 10/1 This sado-masochist mechanism of punch and get punched will be found everywhere. **1963** *Jrnl. Amer. Psychoanal. Assoc.* XII. 306 Abraham stressed the importance of the sadomasochistic elements in his patient. **1977** *Gay News* 24 Mar. 3/2 Study and encounter groups for sadomasochists, transvestites and Jewish homosexuals are the latest projects of Pastor Douce. **1980** *Times Lit. Suppl.* 25 Apr. 459/4 His [*sc.* Somerset Maugham's] relationship with Haxton, the only person with whom he established intimacy, was sado-masochistic.

sad sack (sæ·d sæk). *slang* (chiefly *U.S.*). [The name of a cartoon character invented by G. Baker, U.S. cartoonist.] A stupid and blundering member of the armed services; an inept, ineffectual, and unfortunate person; a social or occupational misfit. Also *transf.* and *attrib.*

[**1942** *Yank* 17 June 7 (*caption*) The Sad Sack.] **1943** *Sun* (Baltimore) 28 Dec. 14/6 A forlorn look, a G.I. haircut, an oversized fatigue uniform and all the paraphernalia that goes with them branded me as a typical 'sad sack'. **1951** M. McLuhan *Mech. Bride* (1967) 68/2 Model mother saddled with a sad sack and a dope. **1953** *Word Study* May 5/1 Everyone knows of the sensitive misfit, the 'sad sack' who suffers a good deal of spiritual depression, the result of an unfortunate maladjustment to service routine. **1967** *New Yorker* 15 Apr. 148/3 Mr. Goldman's movie sweeps up a dustpanful of young Village sad sacks and patronizes them. **1971** J. Gray *Red Lights on Prairies* iii. 58 A sad-sack of a shack town on Pile of Bones Creek. **1973** *Observer* (Colour Suppl.) 15 July 21/4 On the whole the pre-1914 spinster had been something of a sad sack. **1974** T. P. Whitney tr. *Solzhenitsyn's Gulag Archipel.* I. I. v. 222 These sad-sack spies, with the milk hardly dry on their lips. **1978** *Listener* 31 Aug. 286/4 The sad sack of a hero, who speaks in the first person, is called Lewis Redfern.

‖ **sadza** (sæ·dză). [Native name.] In southern and eastern Africa, a porridge made of ground maize.

1950 *Cape Times Week-end Mag.* 3 June 2/3 Manaas had gorged himself with *sadza* and his little stomach was distended. **1965** *Observer* 7 Nov. 2/3 Each family owns its few acres of land from which it produces its main diet of maize (made into a porridge called sadza) and pumpkin. **1975** M. Hartmann *Game for Vultures* vi. 79 Marunga pecked at the greasy stew and dry sadza. **1979** P. Niesewand *Member of Club* xiii. 88 The sadza—thick, starchy maize meal porridge—bubbled in tins.

‖ **saeta** (sa,e·tă). Also **saetta**. [Sp., lit. = arrow.] An unaccompanied Andalusian folk-song, sung during religious processions.

1923 *Chambers's Jrnl.* Mar. 213/1 Somewhere in the crowd a woman is singing a *saeta*, sad and undulating, like no other music on earth. **1939** Spender & Gili tr. *Lorca's Poems* 19 Among troubled *saetas* And stars of crystal. **1966** *New Statesman* 26 Aug. 297/1 Clusters of microtones which resemble nothing so much as the ululations of the *saeta* singers in the Easter Day procession in Seville. **1977** P. Somerville-Large *Eagles near Carcase* vi. 123 He hummed a high nasal tune which I recognized as a *saetta* I had last heard sung to a Seville Madonna during Holy Week.

saeter, setter (sē̆i·təɹ, se·təɹ). Also **saater, sæter, saether, sater, seater, seter.** [ad. ON. *sætr* mountain pasture; cf. Norw. *sæter, seter*; Sw. *säter*. In sense 2 a directly from Norw.

In sense 1, the word in some examples may represent ON. *setr* a homestead, a residence (see esp. quot. 1931). The two are common formative elements in placenames of the Northern Isles, and cannot always be distinguished (see J. Jakobsen *Etymol. Dict. Norn Lang. in Shetland* (1932), s.v. *seter*).]

1. *Shetland* and *Orkney*. A meadow associated with a dwelling; a summer pasture in the out-field.

1576 in D. Balfour *Oppressions 16th Cent. in Orkney & Zetland* (1859) 72 The said Magnus complenis upon the said Laird, that quhair he had ane steding, callit Sater, lying in Brassay, of four merk and ane half land..: nevertheless, quhen he had gottin bot ane ȝeiris crope thairoff, he put him furth of the same. *c* **1772** in A. C. O'Dell *Historical Geogr. Shetland Islands* (1939) II. xi. 239 Feued property and udal comprehend the lands of Shetland of all denominations Setter-lands excepted. **1795** *Statistical Acct. Scotl.* XIV. 321 As to our meadows, they are always called *Seaters*. Though I am little acquainted with the Norwegian language, I understand a *Seater* to be a place for maintaining milch cows; and these *Seaters* are to this moment properly adapted for it. **1822** S. Hibbert *Descr. Shetland Isles* 427 In the ancient Shetland language, the green pasturage attached to a dwelling was named a Setter or Seater. **1931** *Proc. Orkney Antiquarian Soc.* IX. 27/2 Just beyond the Wideford Burn..lies the three-farthing land, skatland, of Grymesetter. Next adjacent lies the 'quoyland' of Grymesquoy... Both names point to an original farmer *Grimr*. He apparently settled there on a 'setter' just before skat was imposed on the Orkney lands. **1939** A. C. O'Dell *Historical Geogr. Shetland Islands* II. xi. 246 The 'Setter Lands', or areas settled since Norwegian times, as revealed by a MSS Scatt Rental of 1824 have been mapped, and the distribution reveals mainly an intensification in the Norwegian settlement [over that of the Merk Lands]. **1952** H. Marwick *Orkney Farm-Names* III. 229 In Orkney..there is no evidence of sæters, and accordingly in the present work no derivation [of farm-names] from *sætr* is suggested.

2. a. In Scandinavia, a mountain pasture where cattle remain during the summer months. Also *attrib.*

1799 Malthus *Diary* 9 July (1966) 132 His cows are now gone to pasture on the mountains—to Saaters, as they seem to call it. **1841** H. Martineau *Feats on Fiord* vi. 161 The mountain pasture belonging to a farm is called its Seater. **1882** Lees & Clutterbuck *Three in Norway* 56 This sæter is in a most beautiful situation, perched on a little flat bit of ground on the mountain side. **1924** *Contemp. Rev.* Feb. 236 Part of a herd of sixty or seventy ..had wandered down from the *fjeld* into the *saether*. **1940** J. Buchan *Memory Hold-the-Door* viii. 191, I do not mean the Swiss alp or the Norwegian saeter pasture, for these are on too large a scale. **1968** G. Jones *Hist. Vikings* II. ii. 82 Increasingly the husbandman came to have his own upland grazing, his seter (*seter*, Swedish *säter*). Sometimes the seter was of a permanent nature.

b. A mountain dairy or farm on such a pasture.

1923 G. F. Barbour *Life Alex. Whyte* xxii. 451 He and Dr. Sutherland Black..drove seventy miles up the Saetersdal..picnicked for several days in a fishing 'saeter'. **1926** *Public Opinion* 25 June 585/2 Mountain farms were being turned into saeters. **1931** *Hardy's Anglers' Guide* 42 The angler taking up his quarters at a small farm or 'saeter'. **1955** M. E. B. Banks *Commando Climber* vi. 106 The local farmer and his wife in a neighbouring *saeter*.. always moved about their wooded farm on skis.

saetta, *var.* *saeta.

‖ **saeva indignatio** (sɔi·va indignā·tio). [L.] 'Savage indignation', an intense feeling of contemptuous anger at human folly. (Orig. and in later allusive use with reference to the epitaph of Swift: see quot. *a* 1745.)

[*a* **1745** Swift *Wks.* (1841) I. p. lxxi/1 (*epitaph*) Hic depositum est corpus Jonathan. Swift... Ubi saeva indignatio Ulterius cor lacerare nequit.] **1853** Thackeray *Eng. Humourists of Eighteenth Cent.* i. 32 The 'sæva indignatio' of which he [*sc.* Swift] spoke as lacerating his heart..breaks out from him in a thousand pages of his writing, and tears and rends him. **1900** F. M. Ford *Let.* Oct. (1965) 12 You haven't enough contempt, enough of the *saeva indignatio*. **1928** W. B. Yeats in *Exile* Spring 5 Swift beating on his breast in sibylline frenzy blind Because the heart in his blood-sodden breast had dragged him down into mankind... *Saeva Indignatio* and the labourer's hire. **1957** R. Speaight *Life H. Belloc* xxi. 529 The furniture of home itself, the laughter and the love of friends—must he leave them, too? Yes, he exclaimed, with a *saeva indignatio* worthy of his master Swift, he must. **1969** *Punch* 1 Jan. 34/1 There was Solzhenitsyn's *The First Circle*..which..fell short of greatness because it was too docile. It lacked *saeva indignatio*. **1972** *Eng. Stud.* LIII. 280 It lacks the poised humour which saved Aluko's earlier characters from becoming mere sitting ducks for his *saeva indignatio*.

Safaitic (safāi·tik), *a.* Also **Safahitic.** [f. the Arab. place-name *Safa* in Syria, SE of Damascus + -itic (see -ite[1]).] Of or pertaining to an ancient Semitic language known only from inscriptions probably of the first centuries AD discovered near Safa.

1905 G. Bell *Let.* 24 Oct. (1927) I. xi. 225 I'm going to his house tomorrow to look over some Nabathean and Safaitic inscriptions and discuss what is to be found in Nejd. **1911** *Encycl. Brit.* XXIV. 626/1 To the first centuries of the Christian era belong the thousands of Arabic inscriptions, found in the wild, rocky districts south-east of Damascus, which are commonly termed Safaitic, after Safa, a locality in their neighbourhood. **1939**, etc. [see *Lihyanic *sb.*]. **1951** A. M. Honeyman in H. H. Rowley *Old Testament & Mod. Study* ix. 270 A new Pars Quinta has been projected to cover the Safaitic, Lihyanite, and Thamudic material. **1976** *Times* 3 Sept. (Qatar Suppl.) p. iv/9 From..the end of the first millennium BC,..a Safaitic inscription by a warrior to Du-Shara, high god of the Nabataeans.

safari (săfā·ri), *sb.* Also † **sefari.** [Swahili, journey, expedition, f. Arab. *safar* journey.]

1. a. A journey; a cross-country expedition, often lasting days or weeks, orig. in E. Africa and on foot, especially for hunting; now often with motorized vehicles, for tourism, adventure, or scientific investigation. Often in phr. *on safari*.

[**1860** *Harper's Mag.* Oct. 630/1 Safari! safari los! a journey, a journey to-day!] **1907** J. H. Patterson *Man-Eaters of Tsavo* vi. 61 [He] had left me and gone on *safari* (a caravan journey) to Uganda. *Ibid.* xi. 119 They join another caravan and begin a new *safari* to the Great Lakes. **1922** H. B. Hermon-Hodge *Up against it in Nigeria* iv. 54, I am an indifferent marksman both at range and on safari. **1928** *Daily Express* 16 Nov. 9 The royal safari—as a shooting expedition of this nature is described in Africa—is complete to the minutest detail. **1935** E. Hemingway *Green Hills of Africa* II. iii. 46 We had gone on a foot safari to hunt rhino in the forest. **1958** L. van der Post *Lost World of Kalahari* iv. 74 It was time we did another safari together. **1964** C. Willock *Enormous Zoo* ii. 23 Justin Tokwar's account of his historic porter safari to the Nile. **1970** *Drum* (E. Afr. ed.) Feb. 27/5 The time when safari in Tanzania meant roughing it will soon be over and visitors can enjoy the awe-inspiring scenery..and the relaxation of miles of unspoiled tropical beaches in comfort and luxury. **1976** *San Francisco Examiner* 30 May (Sunday Scene) The safari is organized to be an inside view of the naturalist's Africa.

b. *transf.* and *fig.*

1958 *Spectator* 22 Aug. 249/3 The London Studio are performing for a group of ten, for each other. And as long as they pursue this safari down a cul-de-sac, this is all the audience they will either attract or deserve. **1975** T. Dinesen *My Sister, Isak Dinesen* vi. 79, I cannot help seeing it like our safari sometime in the future, in which we shall remember all the shauries as shadows and smile at them. **1977** P. Hill *Liars* viii. 105 His educated hands went on safari down her stomach.

2. A hunter's or traveller's party or caravan.

1890 F. Lugard *Diary* 2 Feb. (1959) I. 92 A Safari is by no means an easy thing to manage, especially at first. **1892** *Daily News* 15 July 5/6 It would be a great thing if the next sefari (caravan) brought up a small Nordenfelt or Hotchkiss gun. **1901** *Ann. Rep. Board of Regents Smithsonian Inst. 1900* 433 We collected our safari of one hundred and thirty Manyema carriers. **1909** W. S. Rainsford *Land of Lion* vi. 141 Be always careful to look for signs of crocodiles,..and warn your safari to be careful. **1928** *Blackw. Mag.* Oct. 549/1 It is seldom indeed that a safari passes through the bush without some news of it being 'telegraphed' ahead by the natives.

3. *attrib.* and *Comb.* **a.** *gen.*, as *safari accounts, coach, horn, lodge, path, plan, ranch, work*. **b.** Designating articles of clothing suitable for wearing on safari, or made in a similar fashionable style, as *safari boot, hat, jacket, kit, shirt, suit*. **c.** Of furniture, etc. (proprietary name): designed for use whilst on safari or otherwise travelling, as *Safari (camp) bed, chair, mattress*. **d.** Special Combs.: **safari ant,** a nomadic, carnivorous, African ant of the subfamily Dorylinæ, esp. one belonging to the genus *Anomma*; **safari camp** *Austral.*, a camp in the outback; **safari look** (see quot. 1968); **safari park,** an area of parkland where wild animals are kept in the open and through which visitors may drive in motor vehicles.

1890 F. D. Lugard *Diary* 30 Jan. (1959) I. ii. 89 Discussed a plan for working safari accounts &c. with Dick. **1926** D. Strickland *Through Belgian Congo* vi. 94 The driver or safari ant is perhaps, from an entomological standpoint, the most interesting. **1966** B. Kimenye *Kalasanda Revisited* 51 Safari ants..those large, shiny black insects whose jaws clamp into flesh. **1976** K. Thackeray *Crownbird* ix. 189 A crawling mass of siafu, large safari ants with big pincers. **1945** *Trade Marks Jrnl.* 7 Mar. 123/2 *Safari*... Beds (furniture). Hounsfield Limited, 81, Morland Road, Croydon, Surrey, manufacturers. **1976** M. Birmingham *Heat of Sun* vii. 110 [We] dragged a safari bed from the bottom of the linen cupboard and set it up in..my room. **1970** *Times* 20 May 7/1 Mr. Lea was said to have been wearing..khaki trousers, and brown safari boots. **1977** H. Innes *Big Footprints* III. iii. 292 [We] took our safari boots off and dabbled our bare feet in a pool. **1969** *Northern Territory News* (Darwin) *Focus '69* 97/1 More are being encouraged here by small plane links between Darwin and Arnhem Land safari camps, as well as other outback attractions. **1972** V. Canning *Rainbird Pattern* ii. 39 The inner room, smaller, contained a safari camp bed with the appropriate bedclothes. **1977** *Bulletin* (Sydney) 22 Jan. 65/1 One lives 48 kilometres away on the Nourlangie safari camp. **1967** H. Harrison *Technicolor Time Machine* (1968) viii. 75 Slithey was leaning back in her safari chair while her wig was being combed. **1973** 'S. Harvester' *Corner of Playground* III. vii. 224 A safari coach of rich Americans drew up. **1968** J. Ironside *Fashion Alphabet* 144 *Topee* or *Safari hat*, shaped like a pith-helmet with rounded crown and brim sloping down, slightly wider at the back and front. **1977** H. Innes *Big Footprints* II. iii. 179 Her eyes, shaded by the safari hat, were gazing towards the distant mountains. **1928** *Blackw. Mag.* Oct. 549/1 The sound of a safari horn came drifting across the bush. **1972** *Vogue* Feb. 86 Safari jacket, unlined seersucker. **1977** M. Allen *Spence in Petal Park* xii. 50 She was wearing a gold roll-neck sweater and a brown suede safari jacket. **1928** *Daily Express* 29 Nov. 1/1 The Prince, dressed in safari kit. **1964** C. Willock *Enormous Zoo* iii. 34 The safari lodge at Mweya was unexpectedly losing money. **1975** 'D. Jordan' *Black Account* xxxii. 163 There was a safari lodge with hot water and white sheets. [**1968** J. Ironside *Fashion Alphabet* 27 *Safari*. This is a White-hunter look that has been in and out of fashion since the beginning of the twentieth century. Details such as belted and vented jackets..imitation pith helmets and epaulettes..in both skirt and trouser suits.] **1969** *Sears Catal.* Spring/Summer 40 Cape, Top and Pants Set for the total safari look. **1974** *Times-Picayune* (New Orleans) 4 Oct. IV. 1 (Advt.), The safari look with shell and slacks in beige, belted jacket in brown. **1971** Safari mattress [see *garden umbrella* s.v. *garden *sb.* 4 a]. **1969** *Times* 1 Oct. 14/2 Opened early this summer Windsor Safari Park covering an area of 140 acres on the north edge of Windsor Great Park has proved very successful. **1977** B. Pym *Quartet in Autumn* v. 45 There would be visits to a safari park and to the stately homes that offered the best attractions. **1920** *Blackw. Mag.* Feb. 205/1 A good safari path winds through a deep valley in the Livingstone Mountains. **1890** F. D. Lugard *Diary* 3 Apr. (1959) I. iv. 170 Had a long talk over Safari plans and worked out the details of my idea of food supply &c. **1975** 'D. Jordan' *Black Account* xix. 104 Angel Engelbrecht has a safari ranch in Northern Transvaal. **1968** *Vogue* 15 Apr. 77 Safari shirt in brave bright red Linoseta over navy blue supraline trousers. **1967** *Observer* 26 Feb. 29/3 (*heading*) Safari suit. The most convincing and adaptable fashion from Paris. **1979** P. Niesewand *Member of Club* xv. 115 A mild-mannered American.. wearing a light blue safari suit. **1890** F. D. Lugard *Diary* 17 Jan. (1959) I. i. 75 A fine body of men..ready to take service with the Company in fort and station building, shamba making, and safari work.

Hence as *v. intr.*, to go on safari; also *transf.*

1908 *Times Lit. Suppl.* 19 Nov. 413/1 Mr. Chapman then has safaried twice for pleasure to British East Africa. **1936** *Punch* 5 Aug. 164/1 I've safaried in Sahara, And I've wandered in Peru. **1971** L. Gutteridge *Cold War in Country Garden* I. iii. 55 The two men went up-country and safaried around for a while. **1977** W. McIlvanney *Laidlaw* xxxiv. 160 The receptionist was waiting... In the time it took Harkness to safari to her desk, she didn't look up once.

Safavid (sæ·făvid), *a.* and *sb.* Also **Safawid.** [ad. Pers. *ṣafawī* (see Sophy[1]) + patronymic suff. *-id*.] **A.** *adj.* Of or pertaining to a ruling dynasty in Persia (1501–1736). **B.** *sb.* A member of this dynasty.

1911 *Encycl. Brit.* XXI. 233/2 By the fall of the Safawid dynasty Persia lost her race of national monarchs. **1957** *Ibid.* XVII. 574/1 The Safawid dynasty did not actually come to an end until Nadir Shah usurped the throne in 1736. **1972** *Country Life* 20 Jan. 155/3 The numerous flasks of wine for which the Safavid Kings had such a weakness. **1975** *New Yorker* 13 Oct. 31/3 'This is not a catalogue,' Mr. Ross said, 'because many of the objects now on view will help you sort out the Timurids from the Safavids.'

safe, *sb.* Add: **1. b.** (Earlier example.)

1820 *Rec. Early Hist. Boston* (1909) XXXIX. 174 A fire proof safe in the Selectmens room for the security of the records.

3. A tray laid under plumbing fixtures to receive spilled water.

1862 *Illustr. Catal. Internat. Exhib., Industr. Dept., Brit. Div.* II. No. 6392 Patent Bath, sienna marbled inside, verdantique outside. Taps and safe fitted. **1896** T. E. COLEMAN *Sanitary House Drainage* xvi. 129 The floor of the bath-room should be laid with mosaic..the bath standing within a properly constructed safe, which may be made of slate, marble, glazed earthenware, or tiles. **1956** GUMBRILL & SMITH *Blake & Jenkins's Drainage & Sanitation* (ed. 11) vii. 215 The lead safe sometimes placed under the cistern must have a waste pipe which should be carried through an external wall.

4. A contraceptive sheath. *colloq.*

1897 *Science of Generation* xx. 235 The use of various mechanical contrivances, such as French Safes, Condom Sheaths, etc., is also objectionable. **1959** V. PACKARD *Status Seekers* (1960) xi. 155 Young Italian-American men..of high-school age regularly carry 'safes' or condoms. **1979** E. KOCH *Good Night Little Spy* x. 94 Just in time he remembered his safe. He took it out of his pants pocket.

5. The operative position of a firearm's safety device; the state in which a gun cannot be fired. Cf. SAFETY 8.

1920 G. BURRARD *Notes on Sporting Rifles* 71 One may ..fail to stop a dangerous charge through the rifle being at 'safe'. **1967** V. CANNING *Python Project* ii. 31, I hope you've got that damned thing on 'safe'? **1978** F. ROSS *Sleeping Dogs* 127 The safety catch was off. He clicked it to 'safe' and tossed it on the carpet.

6. *attrib.* and *Comb.* (chiefly sense 1 b): simple attrib., as *safe-door, -key, -robbery*; objective, as *safe burster, buster, -maker, -making, -opener, -robber*; **safe-blower** orig. *U.S.*, a safe-robber who uses explosive material to burst open safes; hence **safe-blowing** *vbl. sb.*; **safe-breaker** orig. *U.S.*, a robber who breaks open safes; hence **safe-breaking** *vbl. sb.*; **safe-cracker** orig. *U.S.* = **safe-breaker*; hence **safe-cracking** *vbl. sb.*

1873 G. LENING *Dark Side N.Y. Life* 148 Namely, first those who burst open the safe with gunpowder,—'safe blowers'. **1951** WODEHOUSE *Old Reliable* iv. 51 Are you a safeblower magically gifted with the art of buttling, or a butler who has somehow picked up the knack of blowing safes? **1972** *Times* 12 May 2/8 A former safe-blower..claimed to have got away with a total of £10,000 at a cost of 20 years in different jails. **1928** H. ASBURY *Gangs of N.Y.* x. §2. 217 [Marm Mandelbaum] also offered advanced courses in burglary and safe-blowing. **1970** 'D. HALLIDAY' *Dolly & Cookie Bird* viii. 113 We amuse ourselves with safeblowing. **1870** M. H. SMITH *20 Yrs. Wall St.* xxv. 320 A safe-breaker from Boston, a bank-robber from Philadelphia, a New York thief, have each their own way of doing things. **1977** J. WAINWRIGHT *Nest of Rats* I. vii. 46 The genuine peterman—the safe-breaker who takes a personal pride in pitting his wits against those of the safe-makers. **1934** WEBSTER, Safebreaking. **1937** 'M. INNES' *Hamlet, Revenge!* II. ii. 115 The burglary and safe-breaking had been unsuccessful. **1981** 'M. HEBDEN' *Pel is Puzzled* vii. 61 Two years for attempted safe-breaking in Lyons. **1873** G. LENING *Dark Side N.Y. Life* 148 Then those who, not using powder, have recourse to mechanical means, these are 'safe bursters' *par excellence*. **1934** WEBSTER, Safecracker. **1960** *Times* 27 May 18/6 His hero, Bob, is an (almost) reformed safe-cracker. **1977** D. BAGLEY *Enemy* xiv. 111 The chief safe-cracker was a man I'd met before. **1934** WEBSTER, Safecracking. **1937** 'M. INNES' *Hamlet, Revenge!* II. iii. 130, I know something about this safe-cracking business. **1967** *Times* 28 Feb. (Canada Suppl.) 31 Montreal claimed that it had more..safecrackings than any other city in the world. **1977** D. BAGLEY *Enemy* xiv. 111, I..found the safe-cracking team at work. **1894** 'MARK TWAIN' in *Century Mag.* XLVIII. 22 The safe-door was not open. **1911** *Encycl. Brit.* XXIII. 997/1 Where larger quantities of valuables had to be preserved than a safe would conveniently hold, a safe-door of larger dimensions would be made and attached to a masonry or brick room. **1894** 'MARK TWAIN' in *Century Mag.* XLVIII. 22 His plan was, to..steal the safe-key..and then go back and rob the safe. **1911** *Encycl. Brit.* XXIII. 996/2 Well-authenticated experiments performed by safe-makers on their own and other makers' productions. **1977** Safe-maker [see **safe-breaker*]. **1886** *Encycl. Brit.* XXI. 144/1 The ingenuity of inventors has..effected much in safe-making. **1970** H. TREVELYAN *Middle East in Revolution* 251 The combination lock was stuck and only the girls, who had been evacuated, could open the safe. Miraculously, an amateur safe-opener appeared and did the trick. **1873** G. LENING *Dark Side N.Y. Life* 148 The safe robber..usually obtains access to houses by means of false keys. **1959** J. CARY *Captive & Free* xxvii. 124 He might have been a test pilot, a racing motorist, an explorer, a climber of Himalayan peaks; or perhaps a cat burglar, safe-robber, or hold-up man. **1886** *Frank Leslie's Pop. Monthly* XXI. 47/2 The Egerton safe-robbery..had baffled all the detectives in town.

safe, *a.* Add: **I. 4.** (Later example of *with* (*a*) *safe conscience*.)

a **1817** JANE AUSTEN *Northanger Abbey* (1818) I. xiii. 231 Now we may all go to-morrow with a safe conscience.

II. 7. Also const. *for*.

1697 [in Dict.]. **1917** W. WILSON in *Sel. Addresses* (1918) 195 The world must be made safe for democracy. Its peace must be planted upon the tested foundations of political liberty. **1929** H. W. NEVINSON *English* viii. 63 It was believed by some that the Great War was waged to make the world safe for democracy, and the result has been that democracy was destroyed in many European countries. **1932** J. FORTESCUE in *Eighteen-Sixties* 244 The pain of seeing the world made safe for that most unsafe and lowering of influences, vulgarity. **1932** A. P. HERBERT in *Punch* 15 June 653/2 The last few years of the War were directed by the great brains up above to thinking out new ways of making the War safe for the infantry. **1963** J. F. KENNEDY in *Evening Star* (Washington, D.C.) 10 June A-7/4 And if we cannot end now our differences, at least we can help make the world safe for diversity.

9. c. (Earlier example.) Cf. *the sure*(*r*) *side* s.v. SURE *a.* 1 e.

1811 JANE AUSTEN *Sense & Sens.* III. iv. 78 Determining to be on the safe side, he made his apology in form as soon as he could say any thing.

11. a. Also *spec.* in *Cricket*.

1823 *Lady's Mag.* July 387/1 Samuel Long..is..so steady a [cricket] player! so safe! **1851** J. PYCROFT *Cricket Field* x. 185 The safest pair of hands in England. **1897** K. S. RANJITSINHJI *Jubilee Bk. Cricket* ii. 18 'A safe field'..signifies that the fielder may be relied upon to stop hits that come within reasonable distance of him, and to hold practically all catches. **1975** *Oxf. Compan. Sports & Games* 648/2 A bulky left-handed batsman of safe and unspectacular method.

b. Also in proverbial phr. *better* (*to be*) *safe than sorry*.

[**1837** S. LOVER *Rory O'More* II. xxi. 148 'Jist countin' them,—is there any harm in that?' said the tinker: 'it's betther be sure than sorry'.] **1933** *Radio Times* 14 Apr. 125/1 Cheap distempers very soon crack or fade. Better be safe than sorry. Ask for Hall's. **1958** [see *LIGHTSHIP]. **1962** A. NISBETT *Technique Sound Studio* vii. 120 For tapes that are to be broadcast it is better to be safe than sorry. **1972** J. WILSON *Hide & Seek* vii. 128 It's not that I want to shut you in... But—well, it's better to be safe than sorry.

c. *to play safe*: see *PLAY *v.* 18 f.

14. safe area, during the war of 1939–45, an area not liable to be attacked or invaded; **safe deposit** (further *attrib.* examples); **Safe-hand, safe(-)hand**, applied *attrib.* and *absol.* to a variety of courier services available for confidential documents; also as *adv.*; **safe hit** *Baseball* (see quot. 1895); **safe house**, a place of refuge or rendezvous for those wanted by the authorities, engaged in spying, etc.; **safe lamp, light**, restrict † to sense in Dict. and add: (*b*) *Photogr.*, a translucent filter for use on a dark-room light, coloured according to the sensitivity of the materials used; also, a lamp that produces such a dim, coloured light; so **safe-lighting** *vbl. sb.*, **-lighted, -lit** *ppl. adjs.*; **safe period**, the part of the menstrual cycle during which conception is least likely; **safe seat** *Pol.*, a parliamentary seat which is likely to be retained at an election with a large majority; **safe-tray** = *SAFE *sb.* 3.

1944 *Ourselves in Wartime* 175 The threat of invasion, and the air-blitz of 1940–1941 over London and the provinces stimulated evacuation afresh... Many thousands of children were removed to safe areas, and.. over 620,000 children were settled in reception areas. **1944** *Daily Tel.* 11 July 2 Married couple wanted. Safe area (Alva, Scotland). **1882** *Century Mag.* Mar. 769/1 They did not ask for the key of the safe-deposit box, or for other evidence. **1970** K. ROOS *What did Hattie See?* x. 92 You don't give a dame a key to your safe deposit box. **1947** LD. MOUNTBATTEN *Let.* 12 June in *India Office Rec.* 1450 GG 43 Coll. I. p. 31 Please follow it up with the letter, which should be sent by safehand of pilot. **1965** 'W. HAGGARD' *Hard Sell* xi. 113 The rumblings from London..had ceased with a Safehand letter from the Minister. **1975** N. LUARD *Robespierre Serial* iv. 16 Delivered safe-hand by courier eight months before, the letter stated briefly that Darley had been approached by an individual who'd indicated he might be interested in political asylum. *Ibid.* 17 A second safe-hand letter had arrived. **1867** *Ball Player's Chron.* 6 June 2/3 Flagg afterward made his base by a safe hit. **1895** G. J. MANSON *Sporting Dict.* 98 *Safe Hits*, this term is applied to high balls sent from the bat with just force enough to carry them over the heads of the infields, but not far enough out for the outfielders to catch. **1897** *Encycl. Sport* I. 77/2 Immediately the batsman hits a fair ball, he endeavours to get to first base... He may get there on a safe hit made by the succeeding batsman. **1963** J. JOESTEN *They call it Intelligence* I. iv. 44 A so-called 'safe house'..is usually a piece of extra-territorial property owned by a particular embassy. **1969** H. MACINNES *Salzburg Connection* xv. 212 So that is what it was: a safe house. They could shelter several people here..while new passports and identities were being faked. **1979** H. KISSINGER *White House Years* xxi. 889 A seedy little apartment in an old brownstone that the CIA had used as a safehouse. **1968** *Gloss. Terms Offset Lithogr. Printing* (*B.S.I.*) 11 *Safelamp*, a lamp providing light of a spectral composition to which a photographic material is relatively or completely insensitive. **1978** *Amateur Photographer* 2 Aug. 131/1 With a 150-watt enlarger lamp, two 25-watt lamps in the safelamps and a 60-watt lamp in the illuminator there is no risk of overload. **1903** A. PAYNE *Pract. Orthochrom. Photogr.* 90 Red sensitive plates..may be used with a safe light. **1932** *Discovery* Sept. 292/1 These infra-red plates are..easy to manipulate in the dark room with a lamp screened by a greenish yellow safe-light filter. **1976** J. MCCLURE *Rogue Eagle* vi. 98 If..he'd had the orange safe-light turned on..the film would have fogged instantly. **1977** J. HEDGCOE *Photographer's Handbk.* 51 These features make the paper convenient to handle in an orange safe-lighted darkroom. *Ibid.* 39 Printing papers and films intended for copying black and white originals have this sensitivity, allowing the use of bright orange safe-lighting. **1979** *Amateur Photographer* 10 Jan. 75/1 Electronic timers are far more accurate than relying on peering at your watch in a safelit dark-room. **1918** M. STOPES *Wise Parenthood* iv. 31 Some people..may find the comparative security of a 'safe period' sufficient. **1923** —— *Contraception* ii. 14 The proper form of contraceptive must be one available at *any* time by the pair: and so the 'safe period' often advocated by those who pose as moralists is not satisfactory. **1934** *Jrnl. Amer. Med. Assoc.* 10 Feb. 452/2 The woman determines her 'safe period' on the basis of her shortest cycle, and also of her longest cycle. The overlapping 'safe days' constitute her 'safe period'. **1936** C. G. HARTMAN *Time of Ovulation in Women* xviii. 183 There is an absolute Safe Period for the monkey female. *Ibid.* xix. 192 Announcement of failures of the Safe Period is a daily occurrence. **1956** A. HUXLEY *Adonis & Alphabet* 284 In the kind of society which has the most urgent need of birth control, the Safe Period Method is almost useless. **1971** *Petticoat* 17 July 6/3 The safe period should more correctly be known as the safer period. You are less likely to conceive then, but that is all. **1976** *Winter's Crimes 8* 180 The so-called safe period won only limited approval... She couldn't let herself be pregnant. **1891** W. FRASER *Disraeli & his Day* 491 A material element in the future of Constitutional Government is the non-existence of safe seats. **1939** W. I. JENNINGS *Parliament* ii. 27 The influence of a great landowner... May Secure nomination by the local Conservative association and so enable the person nominated to acquire a safe seat. **1974** *Times* 13 Feb. 4/6 Redistribution can make a safe seat marginal. **1886** *Encycl. Brit.* XXI. 715/2 Under most plumbing fixtures it is usual to place a safe-tray to receive any water accidentally spilt. **1912** G. THOMSON *Mod. Sanitary Engin.* xvi. 142 When built-up baths were in use, safe trays were an indispensable part of the installation.

15. *safe-buttressed, -enshrined, -going, -sequestered* (later example), *-swung* ppl. adjs.

1918 G. FRANKAU *One of Them* xxxii. 249 O Empire thrice and four times blessed by Fate, Safe-buttressed on ten thousand O.B.E.s! **1926** W. DE LA MARE *Memory* in Kipling & de la Mare *St. Andrews*, Keeps she for me, then, safe-enshrined—Cold of the north—those bleached grey streets. **1874** TROLLOPE *Way we live Now* (1875) I. xlvii. 296 In this safe-going country young men perhaps are not their own masters till they are past thirty. **1930** R. CAMPBELL *Poems* 17 Safe-sequestered in some rural glen. **1900** KIPLING in *Century Mag.* Jan. 407 Safe-swung above the glassy death.

safe, *v.* Delete † *Obs. rare* and add: (Later examples.) **b.** *intr.* and *trans.* In *Mountaineering*, to belay. Also const. *up*. Hence **sa·fing** *vbl. sb.*

1940 *Tararua Tramper* July 6 The real uses for alpine work may be divided into three: Step-cutting, 'safing' (by which I mean anchoring or belaying), and control during descent. *a* **1945** E. R. EDDISON *Mezentian Gate* (1958) xxxviii. 202, I am sick..of for ever climbing mountains safed with a dozen ropes held by a dozen safe men. **1960** M. REDGROVE in *Pick of Today's Short Stories* XI. 194 His mountain-sense stabbed a quick reproach and he dragged his attention back to safing Creade up. **1969** *Word Study* Apr. 6/1 To avoid having any unused explosive going off in the faces of members of the post-recovery team, the capsule must be disarmed or *safed*. **1972** *New Scientist* 14 Dec. 645 'Safing' procedures were now being carried out by the astronauts while Launch Control itself tried to identify the cause of the cut-off. **1974** 'J. LE CARRÉ' *Tinker, Tailor* xxv. 215 We tossed them agents we could do without, we gave them good communications, safed their courier links.

safeguard, *v.* Add: **c.** To 'protect' (a native manufacture or industry) against foreign imports. Cf. *SAFEGUARDING *vbl. sb.* b.

1926 *Encycl. Brit.* III. 445/2 (*heading*) Four classes of goods safeguarded. **1928** *Manch. Guardian Weekly* 10 Aug. 105/1 By appointing a Royal Commission to inquire into the expediency of safeguarding the iron and steel industries. **1929** *Morning Post* 5 Feb. 14/4 Safeguarding Wool.

safeguardance (sēⁱ·fgāːɹdəns). *rare.* [f. SAFEGUARD *v.* + -ANCE.] Safeguarding, protection.

1908 HARDY *Dynasts* III. v. v. 213 To all eyes it is imperative That some mode of safeguardance be devised.

safeguarding, *vbl. sb.* Add: **b.** The protection of native manufactures and industries against foreign imports. Also *attrib.*

[**1903** *Daily Mail Year Bk.* 149/1 *Protection* is the name given to the system of safe-guarding from foreign competition, native industries by the imposition..of duties.] **1921** *Act* 11 & 12 *Geo. V* c. 47 Part I, Safeguarding of Key Industries. **1925** *Times* 10 Feb. 12/4 The idea of introducing a general Safeguarding of Industry Bill has been abandoned. **1926** H. BELL in F. W. Hirst *Safeguarding* p. vi, Protection is no longer called 'Tariff Reform'. It is called 'Safeguarding of Industries' or 'Buy British Goods' or 'Merchandise Marks'. **1932** G. D. H. COLE *Brit. Trade & Industry* 366 The McKenna and Safeguarding duties.

safekeep, *v. rare.* [Back-formation f. SAFEKEEPING *vbl. sb.*] *trans.* To keep safe, protect.

1966 *Anchor Bible* XVI. *Psalms* i. 6 But Yahweh shall safekeep the assembly of the just, While the assembly of the wicked shall perish. **1972** *Harper's Mag.* Oct. 80 Banking on Dictys to safekeep her, I'd set out for Samos.. to learn about life from 'art'.

safener (sēⁱ·fnəɹ, -fənəɹ). [f. SAFE *a.* + -EN[5] + -ER[1].] A substance that reduces the harmfulness to plants of other substances, esp. one in an insecticide or fungicide.

1942 *Industr. & Engin. Chem.* Apr. 498/1 The principal use of zinc as a spray is for the control of peach bacterial spot and as a 'safener' for arsenate of lead sprays on peach. **1950** J. C. Walker *Plant Path.* xvi. 647 Glyceride oils are..good safeners for copper sprays. **1975** *Big Farm Managem.* June 61/2 George Moore considers Eradicane to be the important herbicide for the British market at present. This is the chemical which has a built-in 'safener' which protects maize from the herbicide which would otherwise kill it.

safety. Add: **1. a.** (Examples of 'safety in numbers'.)

1816 Jane Austen *Emma* II. i. 2 She determined to call upon them and seek safety in numbers. **1886** C. M. Yonge *Chantry House* II. xii. 112 They all came creeping down after her, feeling safety in numbers. **1914** T. Dreiser *Titan* xvii. 140 Perhaps he was beginning to run around with other women. There was safety in numbers—that she knew. **1941** E. Howie *Murder for Christmas* xi. 135 The old adage—there's safety in numbers—may very well apply here. **1973** 'S. Woods' *Yet she must Die* 115 'Lydia was flirtatious. But nobody took that seriously, least of all the men concerned.' 'Safety in numbers, in fact.'

g. (Earlier example.) *to play for safety*: see *play *v.* 18 f.

1857 M. Phelan *Game of Billiards* (ed. 2) iv. 65 Playing for safety.—When you forego a possible advantage, in order to leave the balls in such a position that your opponent can make nothing out of them.

h. *safety first*: see as main entry in Suppl.

6. (Further examples.) Now usu. as *safety factor.*

1909 Webster, Safety factor. **1916** W. H. Molesworth *Spons' Electr. Pocket-Bk.* 482/1 Safety factor, aerial conductors. **1971** L. Pilborough *Inspection of Chem. Plant* ii. 16 Factors of safety for many metallic materials at temperatures up to 650°F may vary from 4 to 5 in the U.K. **1973** C. Sagan *Cosmic Connection* (1975) iii. 17 Its orbit [*sc.* that of Pioneer 10] was not disturbed by an errant asteroid—the safety factor was estimated as 20 to 1.

8. (Further examples.)

1936 Hemingway in *Hearst's Internat.* Sept. 168/1 He had the safety on and..he lowered the rifle to move the safety over. **1968** K. Weatherly *Roo Shooter* 11 The shooter picked up the smaller rifle and brought it to his shoulder, flipping the safety off with his thumb. **1972** *Shooting Times & Country Mag.* 27 May 13/3 Never push the safety off until the moment of shooting.

9*. a. (*a*) *N. Amer. Football*, an act of carrying the ball into one's own end zone; a score of two points awarded against a team for this; (*b*) *Polo* (see quots. 1905).

(*a*) **1881** *Proc. Intercollegiate Conventions Conf.* in P. H. Davis *Football* (1911) 469 If the game still remains a tie the side which makes four or more safeties less than their opponents shall win the game. **1910** W. Camp *Bk. of Foot-Ball* ii. 54 A 'safety' is made when a side are so sorely pressed that they carry the ball behind their *own goal line*. **1941** *Charlottesville* (Va.) *Daily Progress* 14 Jan. 11 If a legal forward pass is incomplete in the offensive team's end zone, it is to be ruled an incompleted pass instead of a safety. **1950** *Chicago Tribune* 26 Feb. 20/2 A blocked kick and safety can be credited against him. **1972** J. Mosedale *Football* iv. 48 The ball hit a goal post and was ruled a safety—the winning margin.

(*b*) **1905** T. F. Dale *Polo* xvi. 309 Whenever a player either accidentally or intentionally gives the ball an impetus with his mallet which carries the ball over the goal line he is defending, and it touches nothing except the goal-post or the ground after leaving his mallet, it shall be deemed a safety. *Ibid.* 310 A safety (an excellent word, by the way, to define what we describe as a hit behind to save their goal by the defending side) counts as −½. **1931** 'Marco' *Introd. Polo* ii. iv. 72 In America, hitting the ball over one's own line is called hitting a 'safety'; since it is occasionally safer to do this when one can't clear the ball, than to leave it in position for a certain goal to be scored. **1959** *Times* 3 Aug. 2/1 Lucas managed to force in a safety and this was followed by Harper's run. **1973** H. Disston *Beginning Polo* x. 119 'Technical' fouls, such as hitting the ball behind your own goal line (a safety).

b. *ellipt.* for *safety match.*

1900 J. Vaizey *About Peggy Saville* v. 31, I..go in for safeties, which 'strike only on the box'. **1927** R. A. Knox *Three Taps* iv. 39 That match worries me... Those are ordinary safeties. This is a smaller kind. **1938** S. Beckett *Murphy* xii. 263 Whether..it was a Brymay safety that exploded the mixture, or a wax vesta.

c. *Baseball.* A safe hit.

1905 *Sporting Life* 9 Sept. 2/3 Harry whaled away at the ball and hit it on a line over short stop for a safety. **1917** C. Mathewson *Second Base Sloan* 105 Billy White led off with a safety to left. **1931** *Randolph Enterprise* (Elkins, W. Virginia) 9 July 5/3 The locals hammered out 15 hits on the first contest while the visitors collected eight safeties. **1968** *Washington Post* 4 July c2/8 Pappas ..gave up six safeties in the seven innings he pitched. **1976** *Billings* (Montana) *Gaz.* 5 July 3-c/1 Carlos Pimental and Scott Meade led Billings' 12-hit attack with three safeties apiece.

d. *ellipt.* for **safety razor*.

1924 Kipling *Debits & Credits* (1926) 165 'You could with a Safety, though,' said Anthony. And, indeed..one might have shaved in it with comfort. **1925** *Punch* (Almanack No.) 2 Nov. p. iv, When you decided to use a 'safety', instead of the old solid hollow-ground razor, why did you do so? **1932** D. L. Sayers *Have his Carcase* iv. 62 A young man who had so much difficulty with his razor would be more likely to change over to a safety and use a new blade every few days.

e. *N. Amer. Football. ellipt.* for **safety man* (*b*).

1931 K. K. Rockne *Coaching* iii. 19 The safety who always catches the punts, but never brings them back very far is more valuable than the 'flash' who brings them back quite a distance, but is inclined to fumble. **1969** *Eugene* (Oregon) *Register-Guard* 3 Dec. 1D/2 Washington State's Eric Dahl was supposed to be the top sophomore defensive back, but in retrospect, the writers should have given that nod to UCLA's 5-9 safety, Ron Carver. **1976** *Honolulu Star-Bull.* 21 Dec. H-3/1 'You can't cry over spilled milk,' said Chuck Foreman. 'We're just glad we're going to be there.' Minnesota strong safety Jeff Wright concurred.

f. *N. Amer.* A metal-ringed outlet for a stove-pipe in the roof of a tent, etc.

1962 M. E. Murie *Two in Far North* I. iv. 40 The pipes from the many stoves went out through the roofs through galvanized-iron drums called 'safeties'. **1968** C. Helmericks *Down Wild River North* I. v. 83 You could hear a breeze sigh across the tent, rattling the tin safety against the little stove pipe.

10. *safety bar, barrier, carabiner, device, equipment, harness, inkstand, line, lock* (examples), *-mechanism, rail* (later examples), *rope, seat, sling, snap, spring, strap*; also designating items of protective clothing, as *safety boot, helmet, jacket, shoe, suit*; gen., as *safety code, margin, measure, regulation, standard*; *safety-conscious, -related* adjs.; **safety belt,** a protective or restraining belt; *spec.* (*a*) a belt in an aeroplane to hold a passenger in his seat, esp. on take-off or landing; (*b*) a belt in a motor vehicle to hold the wearer in his seat in the event of a collision or emergency stop (cf. *seat belt* s.v. *seat *sb.* 29); **safety boat,** delete † and add earlier and later examples; **safety box,** (*a*) a box with a surface on which safety matches can be ignited; (*b*) a safe-deposit box; **safety cab,** (*b*) a tractor cab designed with a view to safety in use; **safety catch,** a catch or stop attached to a mechanical contrivance as a safe-guard, esp. in hoisting apparatus or on the trigger of a gun; **safety chain,** a chain providing additional security; *spec.* (*a*) a subsidiary chain connecting railway-cars, etc., together; (*b*) a chain securing a watch or jewellery to the clothing; (*c*) (see quot. *a* 1877); (*d*) a chain on a door preventing opening beyond a certain point; **safety committee,** a committee appointed to deal with safety in a place of work, etc.; **safety curtain:** in theatres, a fire-proof curtain which can be lowered to protect the main body of the theatre from fire on or behind the stage; **safety deposit** (chiefly *attrib.*) = *safe deposit* s.v. Safe *a.* 14 in Dict and Suppl.; so as *v. trans.*, to place or store in a safe deposit; **safety engineer,** a person trained in accident prevention and the organization and implementation of (esp. industrial) safety measures; hence **safety engineering; safety-film,** a slow-burning film specially prepared for cinematographic work; **safety fuse,** (*b*) *Electr.*: see *fuse *sb.*[5]; **safety glass,** toughened or laminated glass; **safety island, isle,** a traffic island constituting a safety zone; = Refuge *sb.* 3 c; **safety man,** a person responsible for safety; *spec.* (*a*) a person whose work is to guard a temporarily disused mine-shaft in readiness for the resumption of work; (*b*) *N. Amer. Football*, the defensive back who plays in the deepest position; **safety net:** chiefly in circuses, a net to prevent injury in the event of a fall from a height; also *fig.*; **safety officer,** a person responsible for safety in a factory, etc.; **safety paper,** paper specially prepared to guard against the tampering with or counterfeiting of banknotes, etc.; **safety play,** (*a*) *Billiards* (see sense 1 g in Dict. and Suppl.); (*b*) *Bridge* (see quots.); † **safety plug,** (*a*) a plug or stopper that allows the quick release of contents when their presence becomes unsafe, *spec.* one of fusible metal that melts when the contents become too hot; (*b*) an electrical fuse; **safety razor,** a razor in which the blade is prevented by a guard from cutting the skin during shaving; also *attrib.*; **safety representative,** a representative of the workforce on an industrial safety committee; **safety rod** *Nuclear Engin.*, a rod of a neutron-absorbing material which can be inserted into a reactor in an emergency to slow or stop the reaction; **safety switch** (see quot. 1940); **safety touch(down)** *N. Amer. Football* = *safety 9 a; **safety vault,** a vault or strong room for the safe custody of valuables; **safety vent,** an outlet affording safety; *spec.* = sense *9* f; also *fig.*; **safety zone,** (*a*) an island or part of a road or square where pedestrians may wait in safety for buses, etc.; (*b*) an area round the Americas in which warlike activities were to be proscribed during the war of 1939–45; also *transf.*

1963 E. H. Edwards *Saddlery* xiv. 99 Numerous so-called 'safety bars'... These ingenious devices, which were hinged in various ways to open up and release the stirrup leather when occasion demanded, have largely disappeared. **1951** *Gloss. Aeronaut. Terms* (*B.S.I.*) III. 25 *Safety barrier*, a net or other contrivance by means of which an aircraft that misses the arresting gear is brought to rest. **1858** Safety belt [in Dict.]. **1911** *Aero* 8 Apr. 6 Safety belt made for monoplanists. **1948** 'N. Shute' *No Highway* iii. 56 Then she pulled out the safety belt from behind the seat and showed him how to clasp it round his body. **1955** *Sci. News Let.* 17 Sept. 181/1 He would not drive without a safety belt. **1962** *Which?* Jan. 5/1 Safety belts should really be an integral part of car safety. **1976** S. Barstow *Right True End* III. xiii. 195 Now he wants to sit with his mother in front. I lengthen the safety-belt and strap them in together. **1976** P. Cave *High Flying Birds* iii. 40 Blood pounding in my head and lungs bursting, I was only dimly aware of the safety-belt catch finally coming free to let me float gently towards the surface. **1840** *Niles' Reg.* 4 Apr. 71/2 Lake, sound and sea going steamers [are] to have an equipment of..safety boats sufficient to carry all the passengers and crew. **1976** *Yachts & Yachting* 20 Aug. 369/1 On the first day a race was abandoned..because one safety boat was unserviceable (despite the presence of mark boats and spectator boats which could have doubled as safety boats in an emergency). **1967** *Times Rev. Industry* Mar. 16/3 Their shoe arose out of their earlier interest in the safety boot market. **1977** *West Briton* 25 Aug. 5/2 Mr. Cock..wore safety boots, leather gloves and carried a torch as he climbed down into the tank. **1902** 'Mark Twain' *Double-Barrelled Detective Story* II. 131, I hold in my fingers a burnt Swedish match—the kind one rubs on a safety-box. **1926** J. Black *You can't Win* x. 133 If I get snared by the bulls they won't know I've got a safety box. **1965** *Farmer & Stockbreeder* 21 Sept. 58/2 (Advt.), Safety cab by Clydebuilt... For your positive safety Clydebuilt has enormous structural strength, N.I.A.E. tested under rigorous conditions. **1973** *Times* 17 Nov. 6/1 All new tractors sold to farmers after September 1, 1975, would have to be fitted with a safety cab in which the noise level did not exceed 90 decibels. **1972** D. Haston *In High Places* xii. 148 Sliding back down the ropes was something of a joke: you just fixed a safety carabiner and ran down the line. **1877** *Encycl. Brit.* VI. 75 Various forms of safety catch and disengaging hooks. *a* **1884** Knight *Dict. Mech.* Suppl. s.v. *Safety Catch*, Safety catches attached to the cage are held away from the guides while the weight of the cage hangs on the rope. **1908** *Chambers's Jrnl.* 26 Dec. 61/2 The door can be opened a few inches and yet be held by the safety-catch. **1928** *Daily Mail* 31 July 5/3 Thinking the safety-catch was fixed she handled the revolver carelessly and the trigger fell. **1962** *Daily Tel.* 6 July 1/8 An electronic 'safety catch' which could be released only by a coded radio signal from headquarters. **1970** H. Trevelyan *Middle East in Revolution* 35 He had therefore imposed a limit on trade with the Communists: what he called his safety catch. **1973** 'R. MacLeod' *Nest of Vultures* 8 The gun was a Mauser and the safety catch was off. **1841** C. H. Gregory *Managem. Locom. Engine* 10 The draw-bar connecting the Engine and Tender must be secure, and the safety-chains attached. **1845** *Business Advertiser & Gen. Directory Chicago* 122 Clocks, Jewelry, Gold Safety Chains, Gold Fob Chains. **1851** *Illustr. Catal. Gt. Exhib.* III. 674/1 Safety chain brooches, for effectually fastening a lady's dress. *a* **1877** Knight *Dict. Mech.* III. 2016/1 *Safety-chain*, a slack chain which attaches a truck to a car-body and limits the excursions of the former as it slues round. **1965** D. Francis *Odds Against* x. 138 A nervous grey haired elderly man opened the front door on a safety chain. **1972** M. J. Bosse *Incident at Naha* i. 23, I called through the door, 'Who's there?' and opened it only to the length of the safety chain. **1973** J. Stubbs *Dear Laura* i. 21, I wonder whether you could not look at the safety chain of my new brooch? **1976** *Billings* (Montana) *Gaz.* 30 June 9-D/1 (Advt.), New tow bar and safety chain for pinto Datsun, Toyota, Vega, etc. **1954** (*title*) Institute of Petroleum Marketing Safety Code. **1961** *Lancet* 12 Aug. 365/2 A safety code for workers exposed to ionising radiations in industry is laid down. **1971** *Guardian* 22 June 6/6 Moving pavements..could become a major form of city transport with the adoption of a new safety code to supersede the existing 2 mph speed limit. **1945** *Proc. Inst. Mech. Engin.* CLII. 149 Safety engineering is advancing in experience and practice, and is receiving an impetus by the appointment of safety officers and safety committees by many important firms. **1961** *Sunderland Echo* 14 Jan. 2/1, 120,000 miners each received a letter from the divisional chairman urging them to be more safety conscious. **1973** C. Bonington *Next Horizon* xxi. 291 It seemed bitterly ironic that the person in the team who was, perhaps, the most safety-conscious should have been caught out by this cruel act of fate. **1909** *Weekly Budget* 21 Aug. 4/6 The safety curtain at the Lyceum went on strike one evening last week. **1912** *Theatreland* 11 Oct. 4/2 It was left to his successor, Richard Brinsley Sheridan, to stand sponsor for the iron 'safety' curtain. **1974** J. Gardner *Return of Moriarty* 303 Dr. Night had the stage cleared, the safety curtain lowered. **1891** 'Mark Twain' *Lett. to Publishers* (1967) 280 Yes, the statement was what I wanted... I sent it to Whitmore to be safety-deposited. **1892** *Ibid.* 304 As fast as Halsey delivers the securities to you I want you to put them in a box in a Safety Deposit Vault, and keep the key yourself. **1936** L. C. Douglas *White Banners* v. 86 She maintained a safety deposit-box there which she occasionally visited. **1978** S. Sheldon *Bloodline* xxxix. 350 A safety-deposit box in Zurich, contents unknown. **1884** *Harper's Mag.* Dec. 118/1 If the elevator has a safety device. **1929** *Daily Express* 7 Nov. 8/4 All the latest safety devices, such as four-wheel or six-wheel brakes, and safety glass. **1971** *Reader's Digest Family*

Guide to Law 580 An employee working in a place from which he could fall more than 6 ft 6 in. must be provided with a safety device, such as fencing, where this is 'reasonably practicable'. **1934** Webster s.v. *Safety adj.* 2, Safety engineers. **1945** *Proc. Inst. Mech. Engin.* CLII. 166/1 The management of a mechanical engineering works should be just as much safety engineers as those claiming to be specialists in that direction. **1974** *Encycl. Brit. Macropædia* XVI. 138/1 The safety engineer is concerned with reducing both the frequency with which accidents occur and the frequency with which they threaten. **1945** Safety engineering [see **safety committee*]. **1977** *Jrnl. R. Soc. Arts* CXXV. 668/2 The effective application of safety engineering must go hand in hand with an understanding of management techniques. **1969** Safety equipment [see *chastity belt* s.v. *chastity 6]. **1971** *Reader's Digest Family Guide to Law* 612/1 If..the employer can prove that he..provided the necessary safety equipment, he may not have to pay damages. **1928** *Daily Mail* 25 July 5/5 All the film used is safety film. **1959** W. S. Sharps *Dict. Cinematogr.* 84/2 *Cellulose acetate base*.., a slow burning safety film base. **1981** *Daily Tel.* 10 Feb. 12/4 We have been able to keep up to schedule because we stockpiled safety film when the price was low. **1922** *Tatler* 4 Oct. p. xii (Advt.), Another striking testimony for the Triplex Safety Glass. **1935** [see *armoured *ppl. a.* 3]. **1950** *Engineering* 10 Feb. 167/3 The cab is..fitted with safety-glass windows. **1964** L. Deighton *Funeral in Berlin* xix. 111 The safety glass shattered into milky opacity. **1920** *Flight* 9 Sept. 978/2 Attention is drawn to the necessity of ensuring that the fitting and maintenance of safety belts and harness in aircraft is secure and functions properly. **1937** C. Boff *Boys' Bk. of Flying* xvii. 185 The pupil, in the rear cockpit, held the aeroplane on its back, with the startled instructor, in the front cockpit, holding on for dear life... His safety harness should have been properly secured, but it wasn't. **1972** D. Francis *Smokescreen* i. 7, I sat in the driving seat of a..sports car... [It] would not start until the safety harness was fastened. **1961** J. H. Goodier *Dict. Painting & Decorating* 247 Modern safety helmets are often made from resin bonded fibreglass, with a head harness of polythene. **1973** *Daily Tel.* 6 June 14/1 Britain's turbanned Sikh motor-cyclists are not alone in having problems with the new law making it compulsory for riders to wear crash helmets (sorry, *safety* helmets). **1869** J. C. Patteson *Let.* 24 Nov. in C. M. Yonge *Life J. C. Patteson* (1874) II. xi. 391 Patent safety inkstands—these things are useful on board ship. **1873** C. M. Yonge *Pillars of House* II. xx. 180 Felix..his safety ink-stand planted in the sand. **1933** *Sun* (Baltimore) 4 Apr. 3/4 A few years ago safety islands were placed in the middle of some of Cambridge's principal thoroughfares to safeguard the lives of pedestrians. **1965** J. Von Sternberg *Fun in Chinese Laundry* vii. 189, I met the man..on one of the safety islands for pedestrians in the middle of Piccadilly Circus. **1934** *Transit Jrnl.* Nov. 437/1 Serious accidents in which fast moving automobiles crashed into the ends of safety isles in Baltimore. **1971** *Rand Daily Mail* (Home Owner) 27 Mar. 16/4 (Advt.), Wetlook diving suits... Safety jackets. **1976** A. Price *War Game* i. 46 There was a cowman in the road ahead, bright in his orange-banded safety jacket. **1957** R. G. Collomb *Dict. Mountaineering* 134 *Safety Line*, an independent rope attached to a climber's waistline when he is making an abseil. **1973** C. Bonington *Next Horizon* xix. 262 Alastair Newman had swum across first and McLeod followed, after tying on a safety-line. *a* **1877** Knight *Dict. Mech.* III. 2017/1 *Safety-lock*. 1. (*Lock*). A lock so contrived as not to be opened by a picklock or without the proper key... 2. (*Fire-arms*.) One provided with a stop or catch to prevent accidental discharge. **1970** *Which?* July 217/1 Most had a safety lock to prevent you exposing the film by accident. **1928** *Sunday Dispatch* 23 Dec. 3/4 These officials, known as 'safety men', will eat their dinner in semi-darkness hundreds of feet below the surface of the earth. **1929** *Daily Express* 7 Nov. 2/4 'Although,' she said, 'I am not a safety man myself, I have lived twenty-five years with a safety man, so I think I may claim to know a little how things work.' **1931** K. K. Rockne *Coaching* iii. 19 In catching punts the safety man stands with both feet flat on the ground. **1962** C. Forsyte *Diving Death* xx. 161 As Left began to get into his diving things again he wished..that somebody could be left in the boat as safety man. **1972** J. Mosedale *Football* ix. 135 He scored from four yards out, running straight over the safety man. **1967** W. Soyinka *Kongi's Harvest* 40 Five minutes. That's enough of a safety margin isn't it? It had better be! **1934** Webster s.v. *Safety* adj. 2, Safety measures. **1959** *Petroleum Handbk.* (ed. 4) 379 The safety measures at installations and depots are..based on the elimination of all possible sources of ignition from all areas where dangerous concentrations of petroleum vapours are at all likely. **1972** *Classification of Occupations* (Dept. Employment) II. 78/1 *Safety officer*. Advises on industrial safety and organises and co-ordinates accident prevention and safety measures within an organisation. **1977** P. Johnson *Enemies of Society* xv. 197 The technique of all-purpose explanation is completed by another safety-mechanism. **1950** P. Tempest *Lag's Lexicon* 183 *Safety net*, the steel nets spread across the hall, from landing to landing on the first floor, to prevent accidents, attempts at homicide, suicide, etc. **1953** *Economist* 11 July 87/1 A genuine flexibility, 'worked out' in the market, is compatible with the security of floor prices, or more accurately of 'safety net' prices that would protect the farmer against serious losses. **1958** *Spectator* 22 Aug. 249/3 Acrobatic tricks no commercial management would risk without a safety net. **1965** 'W. Haggard' *Hard Sell* iv. 45 The fire chief was speaking into the walkie-talkie..and men were running with a safety net. They spread it and held it. **1971** *Guardian* 29 July 11/6 An open invitation..to let costs rise in expectation of a taxpayers' safety net. **1974** G. Mitchell *Javelin for Jonah* xi. 137 He had been with a travelling circus..but they dismissed him... He had begun to insist on having a safety-net for his act. **1978** D. A. Stanwood *Memory of Eva Ryker* xxiii. 215 It'll be the first time..without Dr. Stanford's help... A triple somersault, with no safety net. **1939** *Engineering* 18 Aug. 215/2 The Chief Inspector of Factories..was prepared to call together a committee representing makers of presses, ..safety officers,..and factory inspectors. **1976** *Guardian* 15 Apr. 1/4 The firm's safety officers wearing breathing apparatus went down the tunnel..to see that all the men had escaped. **1851** *Illustr. Catal. Gt. Exhib.* iii. 540/1 White and coloured safety paper for bankers' cheques. **1967** Karch & Buber *Offset Processes* 553 Safety Paper, paper treated usually by printing a design in a light tint which protects the sheet against forgery. **1896** Safety play [see *balk *sb.*[1] 9]. **1959** *Listener* 3 Sept. 370/1 The safety play, properly so called, is a play that risks the loss of a trick which can be spared to guard against the possible loss of a trick which cannot be spared. **1964** *Official Encycl. Bridge* 481/2 A safety play is the play of a suit in such a manner as to protect against an abnormal or bad break in that suit, thereby either eliminating or minimizing the danger of losing the contract. **1977** *Cleethorpes News* 6 May 29/4 Sid's superb safety play in this last frame..stood him in good stead. **1837** P. Nicholson *Pract. Masonry* ii. viii. 145 In the case..of any choking up of the connection-pipes, the stoker has merely to lift the safety-plugs, and clear out the pipes, by introducing a rod of iron into them. **1869** *Appleby's Illustr. Handbk. Machinery & Iron Work* p. xiii/1 (Index), Safety plugs, fusible. **1882** *Engineering* 7 July 11/3 Every lamp in the electrolier has its safety plug. **1887** *Ibid.* 11 Nov. 503/2 The fusible safety plug illustrated.. has been adopted by the South Wales and Monmouthshire Boiler Insurance Company. **1890** J. W. Urquhart *Electr. Light Fitting* v. 163 The usual safety plugs are marked with the number of ampères of current they can carry without fusion. **1923** *Power Engineer* XVIII. 475/2 (*heading*) Safety plug for heavy oil engines. **1940** *Chambers's Techn. Dict.* 154/2 *Check rail*.., a third rail laid on a curve alongside the inner rail and spaced a little from it, to safeguard rolling-stock against derailment due to excessive thrust on the outer rail. Also called.. *safety rail*. **1964** *Eng. Stud.* XLV. 23 A pulpit is a raised safety-rail in the bows of a yacht or motor cruiser. *a* **1877** Knight *Dict. Mech.* III. 2018/1 Safety-razor. **1903** *Hardwareman* 11 July 53 (Advt.), Something new in safety razors. **1921** A. Huxley *Crome Yellow* xxiv. 262 The packet of safety-razor blades. **1973** 'R. MacLeod' *Nest of Vultures* 8 The fair-haired man had shaved that morning. A safety razor shave by the smooth shine of his cheeks. **1956** A. Toynbee *Historian's Approach to Relig.* xviii. 238 The need for safety-regulations would not be eliminated if atomic power were to be applied exclusively to pacific and beneficent uses. **1971** *Reader's Digest Family Guide to Law* 580/1 Employees must observe safety regulations so that they do not endanger themselves or other workers. **1976** *National Observer* (U.S.) 28 Aug. 9/1 General Motors Corp. has been ordered to..pay a $400,000 penalty to the United States for refusing to notify owners of a safety-related defect. **1977** *Jrnl. R. Soc. Arts* CXXV. 676/2 Safety representatives will have the legal right to paid time off from work for undertaking these functions and for undergoing training for them. **1950** *Chem. & Engin. News* 4 Dec. 4257 The Argonne heavy water reactor is equipped with two control rods, two safety rods, and three shim rods. The safety and control rods are each formed of a 3·5-inch tubular sandwich of 1/32-inch cadmium placed between two aluminium tubes. **1971** *New Scientist* 13 May 389/1 The safety rods of a nuclear reactor are for use in emergencies when the neutron flux within the reactor core has to be immediately reduced. **1845** *Times* 31 July 1/5 Carriage for the Continent.—A Travelling Britzska, with every possible travelling appendage, namely eight trunks and imperials, two drag shoes and staff, safety ropes, pair and four horse bars, solid flap and German shutter. **1935** *Discovery* Mar. 73/1 For the descent..it is essential..to make constant use of the safety-rope. **1975** G. Moffat *Miss Pink* xii. 168 He wouldn't have fallen backwards... The safety rope would have held him. **1966** *Observer* 17 Apr. 21/3 The most hopeful sign is the emergence of the 'safety seat',..bolted firmly to the floor, with belts built-in. **1976** *Star* (Sheffield) 26 Nov. (Advt.), K. L. Jeenay Safety Seat. £8. **1943** *Sun* (Baltimore) 31 Mar. 13/2 A worker will be required to fill in a form showing..that the employer does not furnish safety shoes to him, that he needs the shoes to protect his health and safety [etc.]. **1974** *Encycl. Brit. Macropædia* XVI. 144/1 Safety shoes have been developed for protection in a wide variety of situations. **1974** H. MacInnes *Climb to Lost World* xi. 192, I had a karabiner and safety sling running on the other rope. **1932** Safety snap [see *karabiner]. **1862** Safety spring [see *bradoon]. **1960** *B.S.I. News* June 8/2 Finally, Mr. NcNeill considered the question of 'safety' standards. **1976** 'R. B. Dominic' *Murder out of Commission* i. 7 You're in the Atomic Energy Commission... You can bring Ben up to date on safety standards. *a* **1877** Knight *Dict. Mech.* III. 2018/2 *Safety-strap*.., an extra back band passing over the seat of a gig-saddle..; used as a safeguard on light trotting harness. **1938** R. G. Collingwood *Princ. Art* xi. 240 The child's finding itself..wheeled about in a perambulator with a safety-strap round its waist. **1963** *Amer. Speech* XXXVIII. 207 The safety straps that are snapped or tied..from the ski to the boot to prevent run-away skis. **1917** *Chambers's Jrnl.* Oct. 702/2 A recently-invented life-saving apparatus, known as the 'ever-warm safety-suit', goes far towards removing this danger. **1974** *Times* 21 Feb. 3/4 (Advt.), Safety suits. **1940** *Chambers's Techn. Dict.* 293/2 *Emergency stop*, a switch installed in a lift-car, or other similar piece of equipment, by means of which the power to the operating motor can be cut off. Also called a *safety switch*. **1944** *Engineering* 8 Sept. 192/3 Investigation..revealed that some time previously the safety switch had failed. **1904** 'R. Connor' *Prospector* 38 With a brilliant series of passes the 'Varsity quarters and halves work the ball through the McGill twenty-five line, and by following hard a high punt, force the captain to a safety touch. **1958** *Edmonton* (Alberta) *Jrnl.* 7 Aug. 7/2 Flying wing Jack Hill..booted three converts while guard Don Walsh picked up two points on a safety touch. **1970** *Globe & Mail* (Toronto) 25 Sept. 33/3 The Panthers conceded a safety touch for Humberside's other points. **1887** *Century Mag.* XXXIV. 889/2 A 'safety' touch-down counts two points against the side which makes it. **1957** *Encycl. Brit.* IX. 472/2 No penalty was attached to the safety touchdown until 1881. **1846** T. L. McKenney *Mem.* I. 26 One set [of vouchers was] for the Treasury Department, one for my office proper, and the third for a safety vault. **1902** A. D. McFaul *Ike Glidden* xvii. 129 The safe suddenly became the people's depository and safety vault. **1963** *Times Lit. Suppl.* 26 Apr. 297/2 Using his diary as a safety-vent. **1968** C. Helmericks *Down Wild River North* i. vi. 86 The little stovepipe rattled and scratched against the tin safety vent of the tent. **1915** *Policeman's Monthly* Oct. 3/2 (*caption*) Safety zone at near-side car stop, Detroit. **1921** *Daily Colonist* (Victoria, B.C.) 8 Apr. 9/4 Mr. E. S. Harris asked the board to make some provision for 'safety zones' on the busiest streets of Victoria. **1939** *Daily Tel.* 18 Dec. 7/2 The safety zone would help the Allies, by keeping German submarines out of, roughly, a third of the Atlantic. **1940** J. Betjeman *Old Lights for New Chancels* 56, I will labour for Thy Kingdom, Help our lads to win the war, Send white feathers to the cowards Join the Women's Army Corps, Then wash the Steps around Thy Throne In the Eternal Safety Zone.

safety first. A maxim or slogan inculcating the necessity of taking precautions for the avoidance of accident. Also *attrib.*; occas. applied to the safest kinds of investment.

Various safety-first campaigns (in factories, schools, etc.) were organized in Britain in the early-twentieth cent. The slogan is said to derive from the American railway industry (see *Encycl. Brit.* (1926) III. 446). It was widely used as a slogan in Conservative election posters in 1922 and (with reference to Stanley Baldwin) in 1929.

1873 *Cassell's Mag.* Nov. 71/2 A system that would go on the motto of safety first. **1914** G. M. Price *Mod. Factory* 138 Corporations which have within the last five years taken up the slogan of 'safety first' and have done great work in accident prevention. **1924** J. S. C. Bridge *Hist. France* II. 118 The so-called battles were conducted under the rules of a carefully framed code, of which 'safety first' was the unacknowledged watchword and inspiration. **1927** [see *narrow-beamed* s.v. *narrow *a.* 7]. **1927** *Daily Mail* 5 Aug. 3/1 (*heading*) Rising 'Safety First' Stocks. **1931** *Daily Mirror* 27 Aug. 4 These and other safety first signs are being introduced all over the Dominion. **1932** *Daily Mail* 2 July 3/1 The volume of business transacted in 'safety-first' stocks was probably not so large as earlier in the week. **1936** A. Christie *Cards on Table* xiii. 130 The moment you begin..adopting as your motto 'Safety First'—you might as well be dead. **1944** *Living off Land* iii. 61 Where the ground appears to be in the least unsafe, it should *always* be timbered as an essential 'safety-first' principle. **1953** Earl Winterton *Orders of Day* xi. 153 Mr Davidson was accused by many Conservatives, at least in private, of being responsible for the defeat of the Government and the invention of the Party's election slogan, 'Safety First'. **1964** S. Duke-Elder *Parsons' Dis. Eye* (ed. 14) xxvi. 377 Every attempt should be made by the provision of comfortable goggles and by educative means, such as 'Safety First' notices. **1965** A. J. P. Taylor *Eng. Hist. 1914–1945* viii. 282 The cause had a strong appeal for many Conservatives who wanted something more exciting than Baldwin's Safety First. **1977** J. Wainwright *Nest of Rats* i. ix. 64 The Koh-i-noor's twin sister... The glitter deserving of all that sophisticated safety-first garbage.

Hence **safety-fi·rster**, a person unwilling to take risks.

1928 *Daily Express* 19 Nov. 5 Many women would dislike the uncertainty, so the safety-firster, the shy, the unadaptable, and the disliker of change should keep their permanent posts and be thankful they have them. **1929** E. Linklater *Poet's Pub* xi. 140 You're trying to persuade me to be cowardly and middle-aged, a safety-firster.

sa·fety-pin, *v.* [f. the sb.] *trans.* **a.** To pin *on* or attach with a safety-pin; also *fig.* **b.** To attach a safety-pin or safety-pins to; to put a safety-pin into.

1919 'K. Mansfield' *Let.* 30 Oct. (1928) I. 270 Her ears which are neatly buttonholed on to the sides of her head and not just safety-pinned on as most babies' are. **1960** P. A. Bennett in J. Pudney *Pick of Today's Short Stories* xi. 12 The buttons on my coat will have to be sewn on.. so she safety-pinned them on. **1971** *Country Life* 6 May 1087/1 Fortunately, I had sent the engineer over the side to safety-pin the bombs beforehand. **1975** *Listener* 6 Feb. 176/1 Delysia dressed me in her clothes, safety-pinned me all down the back.

safety-valve. Add: **2.** Also *attrib.*

1925 I. A. Richards *Princ. Lit. Crit.* xxxi. 232 If we do not..try to bring under this Safety-valve heading work with which it has no concern, it may be granted that in some cases the explanation is in place. **1956** 'J. Wyndham' *Seeds of Time* 100 There had been nothing worse than safety-valve grumbling. **1964** R. Miliband in I. L. Horowitz *New Sociol.* 868 What Mills condemned in Safety-valve welfarism was not the welfare.

Hence **sa·fety-valving** *vbl. sb.* (*nonce-use*), letting *off* or discharging as though through a safety-valve.

1965 K. Amis *James Bond Dossier* ix. 93 Violent films, TV shows and the like are useful in safety-valving off our private aggressions.

safflower. Add: **2.** The oil from the seeds is also used in cooking, making margarine, etc. (Further examples.)

1974 *Nature* 13 Dec. 519/2 No work is at present supported at international level on oil seeds such as sunflower, safflower and rapeseed, although their oils are important in the diets of many developing countries. **1980** *Holistic Health News* (Berkeley, Calif. Holistic Health Center) Sept./Oct. 8/3 Mix together: 1 cup of oil, safflower works well. 1½ teaspoons of sea salt.

3. (Further examples.)

1968 *Globe & Mail* (Toronto) 17 Feb. B7 Safflower seed

oil has especially good stability for cooking and frying oils. **1971** H. McCloy *Question of Time* I. iii. 28 Margarine made with safflower oil (butter is as bad for arteries as eggs).

saffra(a)n (săfrā·n). [Afrikaans, f. Du. *zaffraan* yellow.] A large evergreen forest tree, *Cassine crocea*, of the family Celastraceæ, found in coastal areas of south-eastern Africa, and bearing yellowish bark and clusters of greenish flowers followed by white plum-shaped fruit; also, the hard light brown wood of this tree. Also *attrib.*

1819 C. G. Curtis *Acct. Colony Cape of Good Hope* 72 Saffran hout... Close and hard. **1831** G. Greig *S. Afr. Almanac* 187 The other woods most in request, and found in Albany are..Red and White Pear, Saffran. **1854** L. Pappe *Silva Capensis* 11 Saffronwood; Saffraan-hout. Branches much spreading. **1950** *Cape Argus* 22 Apr. (Mag. Section) 2/3 He points to a..saffraan, as the oldest inhabitant of the Cape Town gardens. **1953** *Ibid.* 28 Feb. (Mag. Section) 3/7 Near the fountain were some high Saffraan pear trees. **1957** *Cape Times* 26 July 11/1 Holes are being dug..for about 80 shade trees. The species agreed upon..are saffraan and milk-wood. **1973** *Eastern Province Herald* (Port Elizabeth) 28 May 13 A typical wagon of the Great Trek period would have had..wheel falloes of hard pear or saffraan.

saffron, *sb.* and *a.* Add: **A.** *sb.* **6. a.** *saffron flower.*

1910 W. de la Mare *Three Mulla-Mulgars* viii. 108 A little bunch of faded saffron-flower. **1970** Simon & Howe *Dict. Gastron.* 332/1 The English town of Saffron Walden was an important producer [of saffron] and its town arms still have three saffron flowers pictured within the turreted walls.

b. (parasynthetic and with pa. pples.) *saffron-clad, -coloured* (later example), *-flavoured, -robed, -spotted* adjs.

1881 O. Wilde *Poems* 106 Beheld an awful image saffron-clad. **1931** W. Faulkner *Sanctuary* (1981) xviii. 175 A final saffron-colored light lay upon the ceiling. **1959** I. & P. Opie *Lore & Lang. Schoolch.* xii. 243 Simnel Cake, a rich saffron-flavoured fruit cake with almond icing. **1971** *Guardian* 5 July 18/5 The saffron-robed members of the [Hare Krishna] order. **1945** J. Betjeman *New Bats in Old Belfries* 26 Little fields with boulders dotted, Grey-stone shoulders saffron-spotted.

c. saffron bun, a bun flavoured with saffron; **saffron milk cap,** an edible orange-coloured funnel-shaped agaric, *Lactarius deliciosus*; **saffron rice,** rice flavoured with saffron; **saffron-wood** (earlier example); = *Saffra(a)n.

1852 C. M. Yonge *Two Guardians* i. 12 A feast..of saffron buns, Devonshire cream, and cyder. **1922** Joyce *Ulysses* 158 Saffron bun and milk and soda lunch in the educational dairy. **1977** *West Briton* 25 Aug. 3/4 Each child received a saffron bun and a bottle of pop. **1954** E. M. Wakefield *Observer's Bk. Common Fungi* 55 Saffron Milk Cap..is recognisable by the orange milk which quickly turns green on exposure to the air. **1972** *Times* 23 Sept. 14/5 The..'Saffron Milk Cap' is harmless and eagerly sought. **1926** T. E. Lawrence *Seven Pillars* (1935) iii. xxxvii. 217 They took very long about the food and it was not till near noon that at last it came: a great bowl of saffron-rice, with a broken lamb littered over it. **1973** R. Parkes *Guardians* ii. 42 Dan helped himself to another portion of saffron rice, annointed it with curry and tabasco. **1854** Saffron-wood [see *saffra(a)n].

Hence **sa·ffronic** *a.* (*rare*) = Saffrony *a.*

1949 E. Sitwell *Canticle of Rose* 245 Then the King who is part of the saffronic dust.

safranin. Add: **a.** Now *Obs.* **b.** Now more commonly **safranine** (-īn). Also, any of a large class of azine dyestuffs (chiefly red) related to this, which are obtained typically by coupling of diazotized aromatic mono-amines with aromatic diamines. Sometimes with following letter designating particular compounds. (Earlier and later examples.)

1872 *Jrnl. Chem. Soc.* XXIV. 271 (*heading*) Preparation of saffranine [*sic*]. *Ibid.* 828 Safranine when treated with aniline yields a purple dye. **1905** Cain & Thorpe *Synthetic Dyestuffs* xviii. 134 The first technical production of Safranine under this name was carried out under the French patents of Felix Duprey in 1865, but without success. **1911** I. W. Fay *Chem. Coal-Tar Dyes* xii. 298 Mauve, the very first dye prepared by Perkin in 1856, has been shown..to be a true safranine. **1952** K. Venkataraman *Chem. Synthetic Dyes* II. xxv. 766 The simplest Safranine (Safranine B; Phenosafranine; CI 840) is obtained by oxidizing a mixture of *p*-phenylenediamine and aniline to the indamine by means of dichromate and hydrochloric acid, and boiling the solution to convert the blue indamine into the red Safranine. **1971** R. L. M. Allen *Colour Chem.* viii. 124 Safranine T is used for dyeing tannin-mordanted cotton, bast fibres, wool, silk, polyacrylonitrile fibres, leather and paper.

safrol. Substitute for entry:

safrole (sæ·frǭᵘl). *Chem.* Formerly **safrol** (-ǫl). [ad. F. *safrol* (Grimaux & Ruotte 1869, in *Compt. Rend.* LXVIII. 928) f. *sas)safr(as* Sassafras: see -ol, *-ole.] A colourless, liquid, bicyclic, aromatic ether, $C_{10}H_{10}O_2$, which occurs in a number of essential oils, esp. oil of sassafras of which it is the major constituent.

1869 *Chem. News* 16 July 35/1 The oil further contains safrol, $C_{10}H_{10}O_2$, boiling at between 231° and 233°. **1884** *Jrnl. Chem. Soc.* XLVI. 1338 Safrole is the main constituent of the essential oil of sassafras. **1922** [see *pinene]. **1950** *Thorpe's Dict. Appl. Chem.* (ed. 4) X. 656/1 Oil of sassafras is obtained from *Sassafras officinale* Nees..and contains 78% safrole... Safrole is also found as a constituent of many essential oils especially those derived from the order *Lauraceæ*. **1970** *New Scientist* 30 July 232/2 There are very many substances used as food ingredients..which might, like the safrole in root beer, be found to be toxic. **1976** *Nature* 22 July 252/1 After many generations of people had enjoyed the natural flavour of sassafras, it turned out that safrole, the substance responsible for this, caused cancer in rats.

sag, *sb.*[2] Add: **3. a.** (Earlier examples.)

1727 in *Amer. Speech* (1940) XV. 387/1 Thence along the North Side of the Mountains to a Corner Several Saplins by a Sagg. **1850** *Rep. Comm. Patents 1849: Agric.* (U.S.) 443 Strawberries are met with..on the edges of 'sloughs' or 'saggs'.

b. *fig.*

1868 W. James *Let.* 15 May in R. B. Perry *Tht. & Char. W. James* (1935) I. 512 Such an event rather dislocates my mind from its habitual 'sag' in contemplating the world. **1938** E. Bowen *Death of Heart* iii. i. 323 Behind the opaqueness of her features control permitted no sag of tiredness.

4. Also, in a business or programme of development.

1897 E. Hough *Story of Cowboy* 334 Then in time came ..the 'sag' in the cattle business. **1946** *Sun* (Baltimore) 20 Aug. 8/2 (*heading*) The sag in the housing program. *a* **1974** R. Crossman *Diaries* (1975) I. 555 The Chancellor had cut back local-authority spending on mortgages... In that case, I said, he must permit us to use public-sector building to make up for the sag.

5. *attrib.* and *Comb.*, as **Sagbag,** the proprietary name of an informal chair consisting of a large bag filled with polystyrene granules which accommodates itself to the form of the sitter; also **sagbag; sagbend,** the curved stretch of pipe below the point of inflexion in the S-shaped length of pipeline as it is lowered on to the sea bed from a barge (cf. *over-bend *sb.*); **sag pond,** a pond whose basin is the result of earth movement associated with a fault; **sag wagon** *Cycling* (see quot. 1961); also *transf.*

1974 *Observer* 13 Jan. 23/6 (*caption*) Polystyrene sagbag in various colours of canvas..from..Habitat. **1974** *Trade Marks Jrnl.* 18 Dec. 2520/2 *Sagbag*... Furniture; chairs and settees: seats and seating... cushions (not for medical or surgical purposes);..Habitat Designs Limited, Hithercroft Road, Wallingford, Berkshire; Merchants. **1978** *Evening Standard* 28 Apr. 18/4 June Mendoza's picture of La Rippon, shoeless in a denim jump-suit and reclining fetchingly in a purplish sag-bag. **1969** *Preprints 1st Ann. Offshore Technol. Conf.* II. 37/2 To prevent excessive bending in the sag bend a straight stinger must discharge the pipe very near to the bottom. **1975** *Petroleum Rev.* XXIX. 309/1 A pipe tensioning system has been provided which will avoid buckles in the sagbend. **1933** *Calif. Jrnl. Mines & Geol.* XXIX. 197 Numerous little water-holding depressions known as sag ponds mark the site of local subsidences. **1974** Gribbin & Plagemann *Jupiter Effect* x. 114 And yet in the San Francisco Peninsula, where memories of 1906 should prompt some caution, lines of so-called sag ponds, which geologists use as a clear indicator of the fault line, have been filled in to make building land! **1961** Partridge *Dict. Slang* Suppl. 1257/1 *Sag-wagon*, a van that, following a [cycle] race, picks up exhausted riders. **1963** *Times* 6 June 5/7 When, later, Selaru had gear trouble they both gave up the struggle for the solace of a sag waggon. **1977** C. McFadden *Serial* (1978) xlvii. 102/2 You wanna come along in the bus in case I need a sag wagon?

sag, *v.* Add: **2. c.** (Earlier example.)

1870 W. W. Fowler *Ten Yrs. in Wall St.* xxv. 393 The price grew firmer when two or three men were observed selling quietly large amounts, and then the price sagged to 250.

6. *intr.* and *trans.* To play truant (from). *Liverpool local.*

1959 I. & P. Opie *Lore & Lang. Schoolch.* xvii. 372 *Sagging.* This is definitely the prevailing term [for playing truant] amongst delinquents in all parts of Liverpool. **1965** *Woman* 28 Aug. 8, I re-visit childhood haunts in Liverpool, meet the next generation in the Cathedral grounds where we used to 'sag'—that is, play truant. **1966** F. Shaw et al. *Lern Yerself Scouse* 45 *I'm saggin skewl*, I am playing truant.

saga[1]. Add: **1. b.** Also, a novel or series of novels recounting the history of a family through several generations, as *The Forsyte Saga*. Now freq. in weakened use, a long and complicated (account of a) series of more or less loosely connected events.

[**1891** R. L. Stevenson *Let.* 19 May (1899) II. 231 Henry Shovel has now turned into a work called 'The Shovels of Newton French'.., which work is to begin in 1664..and end about 1832... I mean to make it good; it will be more like a saga.] **1895** Hall Caine *Bondman* (ed. 4) p. viii, I have called my story a Saga, merely because it follows the epic method. **1919** J. Galsworthy *Let.* 25 Nov. in H. V. Marrot *Life & Lett. J. Galsworthy* (1935) iv. i. 485, I have just finished a sequel to *The Man of Property*, and, in accordance with the scheme I broached to you..have still one story and a third novel in further sequel to write, to make the whole of *The Forsyte Saga*. **1935** D. L. Sayers *Gaudy Night* iii. 51 She felt she would rather be tried for life over again than walk the daily treadmill of Catherine's life. It was a saga, in its way, but it was preposterous. **1942** 'M. Innes' *Daffodil Affair* ii. 89 Appleby and Hudspith were scarcely in a position to give it the dispassionate appraisal of literary critics; the saga had a sort of aura of alligator which made it uncomfortable hearing. **1952** *Times Lit. Suppl.* 1 Jan. 15/3 The latest, no doubt the logical, development of the 'life with mother' saga is the chronicle of pregnancy and childbirth. **1959** *Listener* 18 June 1074/1 The Burrell Collection..is still, after a long saga of misadventures, looking for a site. **1970** *Nature* 18 Apr. 197/1 By now, the daily newspapers will tell how the saga of Apollo 13 has been finished. **1977** 'E. Crispin' *Glimpses of Moon* x. 190 Rousing themselves hastily from the morbid fascination induced by this saga, Thouless, Padmore and the Major all went into action. **1978** H. Wouk *War & Remembrance* xlix. 497 '*Found* her! Where?' 'In Marseilles. Told me about it for two hours over dinner. It's a saga.'

¶ **2.** (Earlier and further examples.)

1845 B. Thorpe in *J. M. Lappenberg's Hist. Eng.* I. 90 The poem of Beowulf.., in which the old Anglian saga is ennobled by an Anglo-Saxon of the eighth century. **1855** Geo. Eliot in *Fraser's Mag.* July 55/1 The libretto is founded on the old German *saga* of the Venusberg and the knightly minstrel Tannhäuser. **1881** H. Morley *Longer Works in Eng. Verse & Prose* I. i. 1/1 Most ancient of English poems is the old saga which tells how Beowulf rescued Hrothgar from the attacks of Grendel. **1898** T. Arnold *Notes on Beowulf* v. 71 Whether the Sigemund–Siegfried saga is of Scandinavian or German origin. **1903** L. F. Anderson *Anglo-Saxon Scop* 16 The great number of sagas learned by the scop of *Beowulf* is expressly mentioned... It was praiseworthy in a scop to have learned not only the more familiar sagas, but some not generally known. **1912** R. W. Chambers *Widsith* 15 How much of this is history, and how much saga, it is not easy to say. **1960** M. B. McNamee in *Jrnl. Eng. & Gmc. Philol.* LIX. 199 At least by the eleventh century, the mysterious serpent-infested mere of Anglo-Saxon saga had provided a means of making the story of Christ and Satan and Hell graphic to the Anglo-Saxon imagination.

3. *saga-age, -cycle, -hero*; **saga boy** *W. Indies*, [perh. f. a different word], a well-dressed lounger, a playboy.

1897 W. P. Ker *Epic & Romance* iii. 230 In the material conditions of Icelandic life in the 'Saga Age' there was all the stuff that was required for heroic narrative. **1956** Peterson & Fisher *Wild Amer.* xxxiii. 354 The.. Eskimos used to drive the geese across the tundra..and net them..a method of wildfowling known..in Iceland, where it became a great art in the Saga Age. **1949** *Human Relations* II. 358/2 This change in behaviour is clearly demonstrated by men who have been to Aruba, Curacao, Trinidad, or U.S.A., and who have acquired some money. .. In this group the 'Saga-Boys' are to be found—flamboyantly dressed men with exaggerated manners and mannerisms and somewhat aggressive tendencies. **1959** V. S. Naipaul *Miguel St.* xi. 118 Eddoes was a real 'saga-boy'. This didn't mean that he wrote epic poetry. It meant that he was a 'sweet-man', a man of leisure, well-dressed, and keen on women. **1966** P. Sherlock *West Indies* xi. 143 Saga boys dressed in sheath-like saga pants, 'peg-top trousers' and saga coats called Bim-Bams. **1892** S. A. Brooke *Hist. Early Eng. Lit.* I. 104 The first saga-cycle includes the songs sung concerning the earlier deeds of Beowulf before he became king. **1899** W. H. Schofield tr. *S. Bugge's Home of Eddic Poems* 172 In the oldest reference to this saga-hero, in *Widsith*, 21, we read: *Hagena* [*wéold*] *Holmrygum*.

sagaciate (sǎgē[1]·ʃi,ē[1]t,-æ·ʃu-), *v. U.S. dial.* Also **segashuate,** etc. [App. jocularly f. Saga-ci(ous *a.* + -ate[3].] **a.** *intr.* To thrive or prosper. (Freq. used when inquiring after one's health.)

1832 *Boston Transcript* 2 Aug. 2/3 Well, Clem, how do you sagatiate dis lubly wedder? **1842** *Literary Gaz.* 1 Jan. 6/3 How does your copperosity sagaciate this morning? **1880** J. C. Harris *Uncle Remus* ii. 24 'How duz yo' sym'tums seem ter segashuate?' sez Brer Rabbit, sezee. **1890,** etc. [see *corporosity]. **1906** *Dialect Notes* III. 154 How are you sagashawatin'? **1976** K. Bonfiglioli *Something Nasty in Woodshed* xi. 131 My symptoms started to sagashuate again but Jock blocked my every move to slink back into bed.

b. *nonce-uses.*

1904 A. Morrison *Green Eye of Goona* v. 181 The police sagaciate that Pooley must ha' gone straight to London. **1909** 'O. Henry' *Roads of Destiny* xxii. 366, I sagatiated in your associations once, if I am not mistaken.

sagakomi (sægăkǭᵘ·mi). *N. Amer.* Also 8 **segockimac,** 8— **sac à commis,** 9— **sac-cacom(m)i(s).** [a. Ojibwa *sakākkomin* bearberry.] = Bearberry a, b; also, the leaves of this plant used with, or as a substitute for, tobacco.

In quot. 1934 wrongly applied to madroño, *Arbutus menziesii*, another member of the Ericaceæ.

1703 L. A. Lahontan *New Voy. N. Amer.* II. 53 They are forc'd to buy up Brasil Tobaco, which they mix with a certain Leaf..call'd Sagakomi. **1778** J. Carver *Trav. Interior Parts N. Amer.* 31 A weed that grows near the great lakes..is called by the Indians Segockimac, and creeps like a vine on the ground,..bearing a leaf about the size of a silver penny, nearly round... These leaves, dried and powdered, they likewise mix with their tobacco. **1823** J. Franklin *Narr. Journey to Polar Sea* 741 Jackashey-puck..has received the name of *Sac à commis*, from the trading clerks carrying it in their smoking bags. **1836** G. Back *Narr. Arctic Land Exped.* ix. 257 We passed many sandhills, variegated by the..plant, called..by the traders 'sac à commis'. **1837** *Trans. Lit. & Hist. Soc. Quebec* III. 91 Saccacommi [is] frequently used to smoke in lieu of tobacco, by the traders engaged in the fur countries. **1890** L. F. R. MASSON *Bourgeois de la Compagnie du Nord-Ouest* II. 102 *Graine d'ours*, bear berry, also called *sac à commis*, a creeping plant which is smoked, and which the clerks put in their sacs. **1910** F. W. HODGE *Handbk. Amer Indians.* II. 407/2 Sagakomi. The name of a certain smoking mixture, or substitute for tobacco, applied also to the bearberry bush..or other shrubs the leaves and bark of which are used for the same purpose. **1934** L. L. HASKIN *Wild Flowers Pacific Coast* 263 The coast Indian name for it [*sc.* madroño] seems to have been *saccacomis*, upon which the French constructed a pun, calling it *sac-a-commis*.

sagamité. a. (Earlier and later examples.)
c **1665** P. E. RADISSON *Voyages* (1885) 40 Then my father made a speech shewing many demonstrations of vallor, broak a kettle full of Cagamite with a hattchett. **1744** J. DE CHAMPIGNY *Present State Louisiana* 22 They were employed in..making Sagamité and baking it. **1880** G. W. CABLE *Grandissimes* 26 They sat down to bear's meat, sagamite and beans. **1916** F. W. WAUGH *Iroquois Foods* 91 Probably no corn or other food is referred to so frequently as hominy, or sagamité, as it was more familiarly known to the early French. **1931** W. CATHER *Shadows on Rock* IV. iii. 193 Cécile did not want much breakfast... She had sagamite and milk. **1940** E. J. PRATT *Coll. Poems* (1958) II. 256 It was the middle room that drew the natives, Day after day, to share the sagamite And raisins, and to see the marvels brought From France. **1963** *Beaver* Autumn 17/2 Their [*sc.* the Hurons'] sagamité, a kind of corn porridge that drew excruciatingly long faces from the early Frenchmen, was, nevertheless, remarkably nourishing.

sagashuate, etc., varr. *SAGACIATE.

sage, *sb.*[1] Add: **2. b.** *sage-and-onion stuffing* (earlier example).
1861 MRS. BEETON *Bk. Househ. Managem.* 241 (*heading*) Sage-and-onion stuffing, for geese, ducks, and pork.
4. Delete '?' (Earlier example.)
1805 M. LEWIS *Jrnl.* 12 May in *Orig. Jrnls. Lewis & Clark Exped.* (1904) II. 29 The wild hysop sage..and some other herbs also grow in the plains and hills.
4*. The colour of sage.
1881 C. C. HARRISON *Woman's Handiwork* I. 20 A ground of sage or of Pompeian red velvet. **1971** *Vogue* 15 Sept. 129/1 Suit..sizes 10–16: colours: brown/white, burnt orange/white, olive/sage.
5. a. *sage-ash*, *-scrub*.
1923 D. H. LAWRENCE *Birds, Beasts & Flowers* 147 An eagle at the top of a low cedar-bush On the sage-ash desert. **1927** —— *Mornings in Mexico* 136 Across the grey desert..low, grey, sage-scrub was coming to pallid yellow.
b. sage-brush (earlier and later examples); also in *Comb.*, as **Sagebrush State**, popular name of Nevada (formerly also applied to Wyoming); **sage-bush** (later examples); **sage-green**, also as adj.; (earlier and later examples); **sage-grey** *a.* = *sage-green* in Suppl.; **sage-willow** (earlier example); **sage-wood**, (*b*) a small tree or shrub, *Buddleia salviifolia*, of the family Loganiaceæ, found in southern Africa and bearing leaves like those of common sage and racemes of white or purple flowers; also, the hard, heavy wood of this tree.
1850 K. WEBSTER *Gold Seekers of '49* (1917) iii. 84 We were compelled to tie our mules to sage brush to keep them from straying away. **1861** 'MARK TWAIN' *Lett.* (1917) I. 54 On the plains, sage-brush and grease-wood grow about twice as large as the common geranium. **1893** L. WAGNER *Significance of Names* 35 Nevada is also called..*The Sage-Brush State*, from the wild artemesia covering the plains. **1907** S. E. WHITE *Arizona Nights* 191 We began to toil in the ankle-deep sand of a little sage-brush flat. **1917** *Boston Even. Globe* 11 Apr. 16/4 Nevada has been known for many years as the Sagebrush State. **1934** G. E. SHANKLE *State Names* ii. 155 The sobriquet, the *Sagebrush State*, applied to Wyoming, refers to the fact that wild sage (*Artemisia tridentata*) grows on the desert sections of this State. **1946** D. C. PEATTIE *Road of Naturalist* v. 53 A few forms like sagebrush or creosote bush..repeat themselves for fifty miles on end. **1976** *Billings* (Montana) *Gaz.* 20 June 10-c/2 Sagebrush, Silver and Battle Born State are nicknames for Nevada, first explored by the Spaniards in 1776. **1976** *Sci. Amer.* Oct. 20/3 Strong lives with his wife and 11-year-old daughter in pine and sagebrush country overlooking the Rio Grande. **1977** J. F. FIXX *Compl. Bk. Running* ii. 25 We are in a canyon surrounded by mountains, trees and sagebrush. **1902** 'MARK TWAIN' in *Harper's Mag.* Jan. 269/2 He started on a run, racing in and out among the sage-bushes. **1977** J. L. HARPER *Population Biol. Plants* xx. 604 Woodland dominated by pinyon pine..is intimately associated with *Artemisia* sage-bush communities. **1810** *Repository of Arts* (Ackermann) Apr. 262/2 Light sage green, or cream-coloured kerseymere breeches. **1929** [see *DEMI-SEMI]. **1976** *Star* (Sheffield) 20 Nov. 10/2 (Advt.), Bed-settee with arms. Teak frame. Sage green expanded vinyl. **1923** D. H. LAWRENCE *Birds, Beasts & Flowers* 190 Day has gone to dust on the sage-grey desert. **1846** G. B. EMERSON *Rep. Trees & Shrubs Mass.* 256 The sage willow is a slender, hoary plant, or a spreading tufted bush. **1854** L. PAPPE *Silva Capensis* 31 Sage-wood... Wood hard, tough, heavy. **1932** WATT & BREYER-BRANDWIJK *Medicinal & Poisonnous Plants S. Afr.* 140 Sagewood, Saliehout,..is possibly used medicinally by the Hottentots. **1973** *Stand. Encycl. S. Afr.* IX. 458/2 The sagewood..belongs to the rather heterogeneous family Loganiaceæ.

c. sage cock (earlier and later examples); **sage hare** (example); **sage hen**, substitute for def.: = *sage cock*; (earlier and later examples); **sage rabbit**, substitute for def.: one of several small hares of western North America, esp. *Sylvilagus nuttallii*; (earlier example).
1840 A. WISLIZENUS *Ausflug nach Felsen-Gebirgen 1839* ix. 49 Sage cock, cock of the plains. **1917** T. G. PEARSON *Birds Amer.* II. 30/1 The Sage Cock has a sharp cackle. **1868** *Amer. Naturalist* II. 536 The Sage Hare..is more rare near Fort Benton. **1843** J. WILLIAMS *Jrnl.* 27 July in *Narr. Tour to Oregon* (1921) 14 The sage hen is found here also. **1917** [see *COCK sb.[1] 10]. **1962** E. LUCIA *Klondike Kate* viii. 170 A great flight of sagehens darkening the sky. **1846** R. B. SAGE *Scenes Rocky Mts.* p. iv, [The] sage rabbit..is nearly three times the size of the common rabbit.
d. *attrib.* or as *adj.* Resembling the colour of sage (sense 1). Cf. sense 4* above.
1785 E. SHERIDAN *Jrnl.* 5 July (1960) 59, I have one [plume of feathers] for mine [*sc.* a hat] of dark sage, pink and white feathers. **1820** M. EDGEWORTH *Let.* 8 June (1979) 160 My two tabbinets, sage and fawn ditto have done excellent service, new furbished. **1904** *T. Eaton & Co. Catal.* Spring & Summer 187/1 All-wool carpet..in red and sage colorings.

SAGE, Sage (sē̆ⁱdʒ), *sb. Mil.* [Acronym f. the initial letters of '*s*emi-*a*utomatic *g*round *e*nvironment'.] A name given to an early warning and air defence control system covering the United States and Canada. Freq. *attrib.*
1955 *N.Y. Times* 25 Sept. IV. 2/2 Some time in 1954—the exact date has not been disclosed—the National Security Council gave the Air Force the go-ahead on a project..called Sage. **1958** *Times* 23 July 9/6 Sage is basically a computer..which will evaluate all the information received from the early warning networks, guide missiles and aircraft to their targets, and even work out which is the best weapon to use in a particular situation. **1958** *Electr. Engin.* LXXVII. 793/1 At the present time, excluding other connecting weapons systems, there are three main types of data systems used in the SAGE system. Grouped according to use, these are ground-to-ground, ground-to-air and radar data systems. **1961** *Aeroplane* C. 115/1 Construction has started on the new SAGE (semi-automatic ground environment) defence system which is to be introduced into Canada during this year. **1971** E. LUTTWAK *Dict. Mod. War* 44/2 Guidance is by command direct from the SAGE Air Defence System supplemented by radar homing for final interception.

saggar, seggar, *sb.* The forms saggar, sagger are now usual. **1.** Also, more widely, a case made of refractory material or cast or wrought iron used to protect objects while in a furnace, esp. as in Dict. and also during annealing of iron castings. (Further examples.)
1888 *Lockwood's Dict. Mech. Engin.* 298 Saggers, cast-iron boxes used for packing the castings and sifted red hæmatite, in readiness for the annealing oven, in the process of manufacture of malleable cast iron. **1928** H. M. BOYLSTON *Iron & Steel* v. 151 If the parts are small..they are packed with a mixture of rolling-mill scale or scale from saggers and brick-bats or sand. The packed pots, or saggers, are then heated in an annealing furnace. **1960** *Times Rev. Industry* July 22/1 A rich iron ore is packed, together with coke breeze (the reducing agent) and limestone, into clay containers called saggars (the term is taken from the pottery industry, and in fact the process is very similar to that used in making pottery). **1964** H. HODGES *Artifacts* i. 39 Some glazed wares need to be protected from the direct flame, and..this may be done by placing them in lidded boxes called saggars (saggers or seggers). **1967** M. CHANDLER *Ceramics in Mod. World* ii. 79 The ceramist uses saggers only when he must. **1977** R. FOURNIER *Illustr. Dict. Pract. Pottery* (rev. ed.) 196/2 With the coming of cleaner fuels, smaller kilns, and 'continuous' firing the use of the saggar has declined sharply and it is becoming difficult to purchase them.
2. *saggar-clay* (earlier example).
1786 J. WEDGWOOD *Let.* 13 Feb. (1965) 292 With regard to Sagar clays, they cannot be judged of from their external appearance.

saggar, *v.* Add: Hence **sa·ggaring** *vbl. sb.*
1901 W. P. RIX tr. *Bourry's Treat. Ceramic Industries* xiii. 718 The great trouble of burning porcelain, looked at from all points, is saggering.

saggy, *a.*[2] Add: Also *colloq.*
1977 'L. EGAN' *Blind Search* ii. 30 An old saggy couch to sleep on.

sagina (sădʒəi·nă). [a. L. *sagīna* fatness, adopted as a generic name by Linnæus (*Systema Naturæ* (1735)).] A small annual or perennial mat-forming herb of the genus so called, belonging to the family Caryophyllaceæ, esp. *S. pilifera* or *S. procumbens*, which are sometimes used instead of grass as lawn plants; = PEARLWORT.
1962 R. PAGE *Educ. of Gardener* iv. 132 A smaller, sunken oval..set out in a chessboard design with squares of stone alternating with squares of sagina. **1972** *Country Life* 23 Mar. 676/2 During recent years continental exhibitors at flower shows have employed turves cut from prostrate, moss-like sagina, and lawns of this have met with limited success in Germany.

sagittal, *a.* Add: **3.** *Optics.* Pertaining to or designating the plane that contains the chief ray from an off-axis point source and those rays that are brought to a point in the further (radial) line image formed by an astigmatic system (in a plane at right angles to the sagittal plane).
1902 MANN & MILLIKAN tr. *Drude's Theory of Optics* iii. 50 All the rays emitted by *P*..cross the axis at the same point P_2. The beam made up of such rays is called a sagittal beam. It has a focal point at P_2. **1910** J. P. C. SOUTHALL *Geom. Optics* vii. 333 Following the usage of most modern writers, we shall call the incident and refracted rays lying in the planes $\bar{\pi}$, $\bar{\pi}'$, respectively, the Sagittal Rays. [*Note*] 'Sagittal' is a term borrowed from Anatomy... Some writers..prefer..the word 'equatorial' instead of sagittal. **1936** H. T. FLINT *Geom. Optics* vii. 150 This line and $P_2P_2{}^1$ are the focal lines of the astigmatic reflected pencil,..the sagittal and tangential lines respectively. **1972** O. N. STAVROUDIS *Optics of Rays* xii. 226 These skew rays, called sagittal rays, also pass through opposite sides of both the circle on the exit pupil and the ellipse on the image plane... Any fan of sagittal rays from the fixed object point will converge to..the sagittal focus... The tangential focus and the sagittal focus are the astigmatic foci.
sagitally *adv.* (examples).
1950 *Jrnl. Compar. Neurol.* XCII. 142 The right postcentral sulcus..its lower limb running almost sagitally. **1977** *Lancet* 29 Oct. 930/2 The pineals were removed, bisected sagitally, homogenised, and stored at −20°C.

Sagittarian (sædʒitēᵊ·riăn), *sb.* and *a.* *Astrol.* [f. SAGITTARI(US + -AN.] **A.** *sb.* A person born under Sagittarius (22 November–21 December), the ninth sign of the Zodiac. **B.** *adj.* Of, pertaining to, or characterized by Sagittarius; born under Sagittarius.
1911 I. M. PAGAN *Pioneer to Poet* ix. 126 The chief characteristic of the fully developed Sagittarian is his extraordinary power of mental activity. **1924** C. E. O. CARTER *Conc. Encycl. Pychol. Astrol.* 11 Psychologically the progressiveness of the Sign shows as Hope, reaching forward into the future... The belief in immortality is typically Sagittarian. **1940** R. GLEADOW *Astrol. in Everyday Life* ix. 210 Sagittarian luck depends very much upon Jupiter's condition. **1950** C. FRY *Venus Observed* I. 12 Your birthday? No, you're a Sagittarian. This is only October. **1964** L. MACNEICE *Astrol.* iii. 96 In music the Sagittarian type is Beethoven. **1979** J. LEASOR *Love & Land Beyond* i. 12 He enjoyed the ultimate privilege of freedom which, as a Sagittarian, he put..beyond price.

Sagittarius. Add: **3.** *Astrol.* = *SAGITTARIAN *sb.* Also without article.
1940 R. GLEADOW *Astrol. in Everyday Life* ix. 209 No one, of course, can think more quickly than Gemini; but Sagittarius can guess; he is very intuitive. **1969** 'V. PACKER' *Don't rely on Gemini* (1970) i. 3 'Was Pope John a Gemini?' 'Oh no... He was a Sagittarius.' **1970** *Guardian* 27 Apr. 1/1 The Labour member for Bebington is a Sagittarius. **1979** S. RIFKIN *McQuaid in August* (1980) vi. 35 It is clear to me you're Sagittarius. You're prompt, calm, and very reliable.

sago. Add: **3.** *sago pudding* (later example).
1973 'D. JORDAN' *Nile Green* xxiii. 92 A notorious property developer..was spooning sago pudding into his face.

saguaro. Add: Also **sahuaro, sugarro.** Substitute for def.: A large branching cactus, *Carnegiea gigantea*, found in desert regions of southwestern North America. (Earlier and later examples.)
1856 *Wild West* (San Francisco) Oct. 4/6 There are in this region a few Indian rancharies, to which the *Papagos* resort to gather the fruit of the *sugarro.* **1864** S. MOWRY *Arizona & Sonora* 161 Gradually appear..scattered saguaras. **1881** *Amer. Naturalist* XV. 982 By far the most conspicuous form is..the 'saguara' cactus. **1907** S. E. WHITE *Arizona Nights* 220 [The] snake..looked just like a sahuaro stalk. **1916** E. C. PEIXOTTO *Our Hispanic Southwest* 64 Tall saguaros reared their fluted columns like giant candelabra. **1933** *Sun* (Baltimore) 27 Sept. 15/6 The Southwest's giant tree cactus, or sahuaro, is susceptible to crown gall. **1955** [see *CHOLLA]. **1968** W. GARNER *Deep, Deep Freeze* xxxii. 261 Drieter slipped behind a great saguaro with a girth matching his own. **1978** *Times* 21 Aug. 10/6 We could tell this was the real desert because we glimpsed our first saguaro cactuses—those monstrous plants, some more than 100 years old and standing up to 15 feet high. **1979** *Arizona Daily Star* 1 Apr. (Advt. Section) 16/7 This parcel [of land] is dotted with native sahuaro.

sah (sā), colloq. and (U.S.) dial. var. SIR *sb.* Cf. *SUH.
1893 H. A. SHANDS *Some Peculiarities of Speech in Mississippi* 54 *Sah* (sa), Negro for *sir.* **1901** W. CHURCHILL *Crisis* I. i. 5 'But, Ephum! Say, Ephum!' 'Yes sah.'

Sahaptin (sâhæ·ptin), *sb.* and *a.* Also † **Sahapotin, Shahaptan.** [Southern Interior Salish *Sʔaptnx* Sahaptin, Nez Percé; of uncertain ulterior etymology.] **A.** *sb.* **a.** Formerly, a (member of an) American Indian tribe of the Snake River basin, also called the *NEZ PERCÉ; also, any of several groupings of the Nez Percé and others believed to be linguistically related. Now applied to a number of closely related North American Indian peoples of the Columbia River basin. **b.** The language or language grouping of any of these peoples. **B.** *adj.* Of or pertaining to any of these peoples or their language.

1836 A. Gallatin in *Trans. Amer. Antiquarian Soc.* II. 264 (*map*) Sahapotins. **1841** *Jrnl. R. Geogr. Soc.* XI. 225 The first and more northern Indians of the interior may be denominated the Shahaptan Family, and comprehends ..the Shahaptan, or *Nez Percés*..; the Kliketat..; and the Okanagan. **1846** H. Hale *U.S. Exploring Exped.: Ethnogr. & Philol.* 198 The South-Oregon division. To this belong the *Sahaptin* family (Nez-percés and Walla-wallas), [etc.]. **1918** J. E. Rees *Idaho Chronol.* 109 Their earliest home was upon the Columbia River and when they were pushed southward the Salish called them 'Shahaptans', meaning 'strangers from up the river'. **1918** *Internat. Jrnl. Amer. Linguistics* I. 176, I have.. gathered voluminous data supporting previously expressed contentions concerning the genetic relationship between Lutuamian, Wailatpuan, and Sahaptin. **1921** E. Sapir *Language* 222 The presence of postpositions in Upper Chinook..is clearly due to the influence of neighboring Sahaptin languages. **1940** M. W. Smith *Puyallup-Nisqually* 22 If he spoke Sahaptin, it is also certain that he spoke Salish. **1947** B. A. De Voto *Across Wide Missouri* 11 Ethnologists use the name which the Flatheads bestowed on them, the Shahaptan, of uncertain meaning but perhaps a designation of the country they lived in. **1965** *Canad. Jrnl. Linguistics* X. 125 Jacobs also has published a considerable quantity of Sahaptin texts. **1971** *Language* XLVII. 840 The northernmost example, the Sahaptin and Nez Perce shift of $n > l$, is reversed in comparison to the more southern shifts.

Sahara. Add: **1. b.** (Earlier example.)

1855 Dickens *Holly-Tree Inn* in *Househ. Words* Extra Christmas No. 2/2 The bleak wild solitude..was a snowy Saharah.

2. A shade of brown or yellow. Also *attrib.*

1923 *Daily Mail* 9 Oct. 1/1 Colours: Lemon,..Fawn, Sahara, Mole. **1930** *Daily Express* 8 Sept. 11/5 The suit is stocked in shades of sand, Sahara Brown and Grey. **1970** 'D. Halliday' *Dolly & Cookie Bird* ii. 12 He was.. broad-shouldered, with that super kind of Swedish suède jacket in Sahara sand colour. **1974** *Times* 4 May 5/2 Bathroom suites in..honeysuckle, orchid, midnight blue, sahara, black. **1976** *Yorkshire Evening Press* 9 Dec. 20/2 (Advt.), 1971 Opel Rekord coupe in Sahara Gold.

Saharan, *a.* (In Dict. s.v. Sahara.) Add: **B.** *sb.* **a.** One of a group of languages spoken in the eastern Saharan region. **b.** A member of a people living in the Sahara, *spec.* native to or inhabiting the former Spanish Sahara on the Atlantic coast.

1963 J. H. Greenberg *Lang. Afr.* vi. 130 To the.. grouping which consists of Songhai, Saharan, Maban, Fur and Coman in addition to Chari-Nile, the name Nilo-Saharan is given. **1970** *Daily Tel.* 30 June 16 The men from the Spanish Sahara, known as 'Saharans', now in Egypt have two main objectives. **1975** *N.Y. Times* 8 Nov. 26/2 The referendum under international supervision, recommended by a United Nations commission, will be difficult to conduct fairly among mostly illiterate and nomadic Saharans.

Saharaui, var. *Sahrawi.

Sahelian (săhī·liăn), *a.* [f. *Sahel*, proper name of the region + -ian.] Of, pertaining to, or designating the belt of land in West Africa south of the Sahara desert which comprises parts of Senegal, Mauritania, Mali, Niger, and Chad and is mostly savannah.

1973 *Nature* 28 Sept. 194/2 The present drought situation and the probable long term trends now seriously threaten the economic and political viability of the Sahelian states of West Africa. **1973** *Times* 30 Oct. 16/6 The exhibition shows the effects of the drought in the Sahelian region of West Africa. **1976** *New Society* 29 Apr. 220/2 Africa's poorest region, the Sahelian 'famine belt' from the Atlantic to Lake Chad, was once a place of fabulous wealth. **1980** *Spectator* 21 June 18 Next come the even more gruesome aid donors, whose antics Markham witnessed during the terrible Sahelian drought a few years ago.

sahib. Add: Also **saab, sa'ab** and with pronunc. (sāb). **1. a.** (Further examples.) Also affixed to Indian and Bangladeshi titles and names.

1886 Kipling *Departmental Ditties* (ed. 2) 7 Rajah Rustum..Heaped upon the Bukshi Sahib wealth and honours manifold. **1921** E. M. Forster *Let.* 1 Apr. in *Hill of Devi* (1953) 60 The Palace is inhabited by four chief people—me, H.H., Malarao Sahib, and Deolekr Sahib. **1971** *Shankar's Weekly* (Delhi) 4 Apr. 8/1 Here we are grappling with basic issues and our director saab is bothered about mixed metaphors and split infinitives. *Ibid.* 21/4 He then went to Lalaji's house outside which Vijay was furiously pacing up and down. 'Yes, sa'ab,' he meekly announced his arrival. **1977** 'D. MacNeil' *Wolf in Fold* ii. 18 The native nodded. 'I understand, Ogilvie sahib. I believe also that the *risaldar* sahib will help.' **1978** F. Olbrich *Desouza pays Price* iii. 12 A gentleman would like to see you, Inspector saab.

b. *transf.* A gentleman; someone considered socially acceptable.

1919 W. Deeping *Second Youth* xxv. 212, I happen to know Colonel Horseley out there; he's a sahib, and quite big, one of the biggest things I've met. **1928** D. L. Sayers *Unpleasantness at Bellona Club* ix. 102 'Is the fellow a sahib?' 'Good God, no! Looks like an attorney's clerk or something.' **1952** A. Grimble *Pattern of Islands* 24 A sahib, naturally..right kind of breeding, right kind of school. **1977** *Listener* 28 July 123/1 Being a muff can be as arduous a vocation as being a sahib.

2. *Comb.*, as **sahib-log** [Urdu *log* people, caste], the European gentlefolk in India.

1848 J. H. Stocqueler *Oriental Interpreter* 199/2 *Sahib logue*, the common appellation given to European gentlemen in India. **1927** W. H. Todd *Tiger, Tiger!* vii. 117 The 'sahib-log' were after him. **1953** P. Scott *Alien Sky* I. iv. 42 The *Sahib-log* lived in whitewashed bungalows. **1978** 'M. M. Kaye' *Far Pavilions* ii. 30 The troopers.. asserted that all the Sahib-log in Meerut were dead.

Sahib-dom (sā·ibdəm). ? *Obs.* [f. Sahib + -dom.] The quality or condition of being a sahib.

1901 Kipling *Kim* ix. 215 'Oah!' said Kim, firmly resolved to cling to his Sahib-dom. **1909** M. Diver *Candles in Wind* iv. 45 A creature without either the birthright of caste, or the prestige of Sahib-dom.

sahibhood (sā·ibhud). [f. as prec. + -hood.] = prec.

1946 [see *Negroness]. **1953** J. Trench *Docken Dead* vii. 104 He looked round for admiration..at..the evidence of sahibhood. **1977** A. Wilson *Strange Ride R. Kipling* i. 23 The need to assert his lost sahibhood.

‖**sahitya** (sā·hitya). [Skr., association, agreement; composition, literature; lyrical verse.] The lyrical verse which forms part of an Indian dance-song (see quots.).

1953 F. Bowers *Dance in India* 46 Three types of singing, determined by the nature of the dance, are performed in Bharata Natya: (1) Ordinary poetic songs with words for abhinaya portions, called *sahitya*. **1965** E. Bhavnani *Dance in India* v. 34 Then comes the rendering in gesture language and emotional acting, the explanation of a song or *Sahitya* which are devotional sentiments in lyrical verse form and are the text to be interpreted. **1968** *Jrnl. Mus. Acad. Madras* XXXIX. 8 The Raga chosen for the song aptly conveys the sentiment expressed by the Sahitya. **1971** *Shankar's Weekly* (Delhi) 18 Apr. 24/1 One of the sisters was out to prove that they could tackle the swaraprasthara to coincide terminally with the point of commencement of the sahitya.

Sahiwal (sā·hivāl, -wāl). Also **Sanhiwal.** [The name of a town in the central Punjab, Pakistan.] A cow or bull belonging to the breed so called, originally native to Pakistan but now used in tropical regions elsewhere, distinguished by small horns and a hump on the back of the neck; also, the breed itself. Also *attrib.*

1916 *Rep. Agric. Research Inst. & Coll., Pusa 1914–15* 10 Two herds are now being maintained at Pusa, one of selected Sanhiwal (Montgomery) cows and their descendants, the other of cross-bred Ayrshire-Sanhiwal cattle. **1919** *Rep. Progress Agric. in India 1917–18* v. 182 Experiments with crossing the ordinary *desi* cow of good stamp with the Hissar, Sahiwal and Kosi strains are in progress. **1941** *Empire Jrnl. Exper. Agric.* IX. 11 The Sahiwal has reached in 25 years a level of milking performance which foreign breeds would have taken more than a century to attain. **1959** R. B. Kelley *Native & Adapted Cattle* v. 71 Sahiwal cattle are also known as Montgomery cattle. *Ibid.* 75 Most Sahiwals are red. **1968** *Sunday Mail Mag.* (Brisbane) 7 July 5/1 We have 1200 head of cattle—Ayrshires; four horses and a few sahiwals. **1970** *Kenya Farmer* Feb. 13/1 The range of breeds in Kenya is now very considerable. For dairy, there are Ayrshire, Friesland, Guernsey and Jersey; for dual purpose, Brown Swiss, Red Poll and Sahiwal.

Sahli (sā·li). *Med.* The name of Hermann *Sahli* (1856–1933), Swiss physician, used *attrib.* and in the possessive with reference to a method he devised for determining the hæmoglobin content of the blood by converting a sample into acid hæmatin and adding water until the colour matches a standard.

1906 R. C. Cabot *Physical Diagnosis* (ed. 3) xxiii. 465 Sahli's instrument..must be obtained from one of the firms recommended by him. *Ibid.* 569/2 (Index), Sahli's test for hæmoglobin. **1931** Osgood & Haskins *Textbk. Lab. Diagnosis* II. ix. 354 The ordinary type of Sahli apparatus is worthless because the acid hematin used as the standard fades too rapidly. *Ibid.* 347 Diluted to the 100 mark in a Sahli tube. **1956** *Nature* 17 Mar. 524/1 No significant change was noted in the red-cell count; but there was a drop in the hæmoglobin-level from 81 to 70 per cent when tested by the Sahli method. **1974** Passmore & Robson *Compan. Med. Stud.* III. xxi. 2/1 The Hb of blood is measured colorimetrically after it has been converted to a stable form. The methods available use acid haematin, oxyhaemoglobin or cyanmethaemoglobin. The simplest is the Sahli method.

sahlinite (sā·linəit). *Min.* [f. the name of Carl A. *Sahlin* (1861–1943), manager of a Swedish ironworks + -ite[1].] A basic monoclinic arsenate and chloride of lead found as pale yellow scales in dolomite at Långban, Sweden.

1934 G. Aminoff in *Geol. Foreningen Förhandlingar* LVI. 493 (*heading*) Note on a new mineral from Långban (Sahlinite). **1951** C. Palache et al. *Dana's Syst. Min.* (ed. 7) II. 775 Sahlinite... Monoclinic. In aggregates of small thin scales. **1968** I. Kostov *Mineral.* 467 Sahlinite has perfect cleavage on {010}.

Saho (sā·ho), *sb.* and *a.* Also † **Shiho, Shoho.** [Cushitic.] **A.** *sb.* **a.** A (member of a) Cushitic-speaking people of Eritrea. **b.** The language or dialect of this people. **B.** *adj.* Of or pertaining to this people or their language.

1790 J. Bruce *Trav.* III. v. iii. 68 The Shiho were once very numerous; but, like all these nations having communication with Masuah, have suffered much by the ravages of the small-pox. **1831** S. Gobat *Jrnl.* 22 May (1834) iv. 291, I have just passed three very disagreeable months, in the midst of the savage Shohos. **1842** Isenberg & Krapf *Jrnl.* 30 Apr. (1843) 521 The Governor promised this morning that he would send to the next Shoho village for a guide to take us to Arkeeko. *a* **1860** W. C. Plowden *Trav. Abyssinia* (1868) i. 23 The Shihos, a nomad race to the southward of Massowah. *Ibid.* xviii. 360 There are two roads, through the countries of two tribes of Shihos, leading to Adowah, the one through the tribe called Asowarta, the other, Tora... These two tribes form the Shiho nation, and occupy the mountainous tracts between Massowah and Christian Abyssinia. **1883** R. N. Cust *Sk. Mod. Lang. Afr.* I. ix. 128 (*heading*) Saho *or* Shiho *or* Shoho. *Ibid.* 129 The Saho bring down their herds in the rains to graze. **1885** [see *Danakil *sb.* and *a.*]. **1932** W. L. Graff *Lang.* xi. 404 The most important dialects [of Cushitic] are Bedja, Saho and Afar. **1960** E. Ullendorff *Ethiopians* iii. 40 The Saho tribes live in the coastal depression between Massawa in the north, the gulf of Zula in the east, and the escarpment of the Akkele Guzay in the west. **1962** G. A. Lipsky et al. *Ethiopia* iv. 47 Almost all the Saho-speaking tribes are located in Eritrea. *Ibid.* vii. 113 The Saho and Dānākil people also are Moslem. **1968** M. Abir *Ethiopia* vi. 132 Most of the Sahos and their Belau rulers left Arkiko and the surrounding area, and escaped into the mountains. **1972** *Language* XLVIII. 847 His list can be supplemented with examples from..Chinantec, Saho, Slave.

Sahrawi (sarā·wi). Also **Saharaui.** [a. Arab. *ṣaḥrāwī* (whence Sp. *saharaui*) of the desert, f. *ṣaḥrā'* desert, Sahara.] An inhabitant of Western (formerly Spanish) Sahara, a Saharan; also *collect.*, the people itself. Also *attrib.*

1976 *Times* 27 Feb. 14/1 Self-determination for the Sahrawi people is a prerequisite for any settlement. *Ibid.*, Polisario should be recognised as the legitimate representative of the Sahrawis. **1976** *Times Lit. Suppl.* 16 Apr. 466/2 In either case the Saharauis will hardly be the beneficiaries. *Ibid.*, The inner working and tensions of Saharaui society. **1977** *Guardian Weekly* 6 Nov. 12/4 Two French technicians..taken away along with 24 Mauritanian workers by a Sahrawi guerrilla unit... The Sahrawi are not agents of subversion, but people who want back the homeland [*sc.* Western Sahara] they were forced to quit. **1980** J. Mercer *Canary Islanders* 264 In 1975 Spain handed over the Spanish Sahara and the Saharaui people to Morocco and Mauretania, in exchange for economic and other benefits. This led to the current war between the occupying neo-colonial powers and the Saharauis (Polisario).

saht-bai, var. *sat-bhai. **sahuaro,** var. Saguaro in Dict. and Suppl.

sahukar, var. Soucar.

1913 J. M. Keynes *Indian Currency & Finance* iv. 95 Notes, even of the value of Rs. 5, are looked upon with distrust by the village yokels and even by the village sahukars. **1930** *Economist* 12 Apr. 820/1 The majority.. consists of rural sahukars, who, though shrewd, are primitive in their methods, and prefer the use of cash and notes to cheques and bills. **1936** J. Nehru *Autobiogr.* xxxix. 302 The tenant's position was even worse. He was also a *sahukar's* serf.

saice, var. Syce.

Saigonese (səigonī·z), *collect. sb.* [f. *Saigon* (now Ho Chi Minh City), formerly the capital of South Vietnam + -ese.] The people of Saigon. (No longer in official use.)

1967 [see *high *adv.* 9 b]. **1975** *Daily Tel.* 1 May 1 Laughing guerillas..drove through the streets exchanging waves and banter with the Saigonese.

sail, *sb.*[1] Add: † **1. d.** *Aeronaut.* Applied to a flat aerodynamically structured part of an aircraft. *Obs.*

1808 G. Cayley *Aeronaut. & Misc. Note-bk.* (1933) 64, I tried a small square sail in one plane, with the weight nearly in the same, & I could not perceive that the centre & resistance differed from the centre of bulk. **1817** *Phil. Mag.* L. 35 The sketch..represents a side view of the arrangement of the moving and steering sails of a balloon on the wing plan. **1837** *Mechanics' Mag.* XXVI. 421/2 From the hinder mast C a sail may be conveniently braced to either side, so as to act as a rudder, and thus preserve a steady course. **1902** F. Walker *Aërial Navigation* viii. 118 A head sail *i* and stern sails *h*, h^1 had braces and halliards for steering... The sails *h*, h^1 acted as aëroplanes as well as for steering purposes. **1903** —— *Pract. Kites & Aëroplanes* ii. 25 The 'leeches', or free edges of the sails ..are double-stitched around a leech-rope.

3. c. Also *fig.*

1893 'Mark Twain' *Lett. to Publishers* (1967) 348 A well-organized business..an enterprise not experimental but under full sail.

8*. The conning-tower of a submarine.

1959 *Jane's Fighting Ships* 414/1 'The sail', as the conning tower is now called on nuclear submarines. **1963** *Guardian* 1 Mar. 1 The Ethan Allen looked like any other submarine though the conning tower—which they call the sail these days—was much larger than usual. **1968** *New Scientist* 26 Dec. 704/2 Photographs of the wreckage show that the *Scorpion* split in two at the point on the hull where the 'sail' (the new name for the conning tower) is mounted near the forward end. **1974** L. Deighton *Spy Story* xviii. 190 The great submarine threaded its way out through the Sound... The skipper came down from the sail.

9. a. *sail area*; **b.** *sail-stiffening* adj.

1898 W. F. Jackson in W. A. Morgan *'House' on Sport* I. i. 19 Traditions are still heard of boats lurking behind barges..to dart out at the last moment with something surprising in the way of sail area. **1976** *Oxf. Compan. Ships & Sea* 947/2 There was no form of handicap on size or sail area. **1945** P. Larkin *North Ship* 35 Increasingly to fear Sail-stiffening air.

10. sailboard orig. *U.S.*, a surf-board or light sail-boat which is propelled by wind caught in its sail; also as *v. intr.*; hence **sailboarder, sailboarding** *vbl. sb.*; **sail-boat**: for '? *rare*' read 'chiefly *N. Amer.*' and add earlier and later examples; **sail curtain** = Curtain *sb.*[1] 2 a; **sail-duck** (earlier example); **sail-flying** = *sailplaning *vbl. sb.*; **sail-maker** (later example in aeroplane construction); **sail plan** (see quot. 1961); **sail wing**, the sail of a hang glider with its framework; (the structures described in quots. 1972, 1974 differ from one another).

1962 D. Klein *Beginning with Boats* iv. 95 Another boat that may tempt you because it can give you a great deal of fun at rather low cost is what is called a *sailboard*—that is, a sort of surfboard equipped with centerboard, rudder, and sailing rig. **1978** B. Webb tr. *Brockhaus & Stanciu's Sailboarding* 8 You can ski in any mountainous region where there is snow, just as you can sailboard on any water, whether it be an ocean or a reservoir. **1980** *Daily Tel.* 15 Sept. 2 (*caption*) A 22ft-long sailboard made for two..being demonstrated at Southampton. **1974** A. H. Drummond *Sailboarding* 10 The surfboarder catches a wave and uses its energy to surf along. The sailboarder does just about the same thing, except that he uses a sail to capture the energy of the wind... Thus, sailboarding is surfing using wind power. **1978** *Times* 5 Apr. 8/5 Beau Vallon is the island's most visited beach... Enthusiasts use it for sail-boarding, water-skiing, para-gliding, diving and goggling. **1979** *Yachts & Yachting* 9 Nov. 1433/3 Wandering sailboarders could be pleased with a complete cover for their board. **1798** C. Williamson *Descr. Genesee Country* iii. 19 The number of sail-boats have greatly increased on the Lake. **1831** M. Holley *Texas* (1833) 47 From Brazoria to Bolivar, I came in a sail-boat. **1911** J. C. Lincoln *Cap'n Warren's Wards* xxi. 333 He had gone to see the sail-boat man. **1956** M. Duggan *Immanuel's Land* 64 A flatbottomed sailboat on the slope shifted almost afloat, and settled again into the mud. **1977** E. Leonard *Unknown Man No. 89* xxi. 211 A painting..of..a sailboat with the mast broken off. **1941** J. Masefield *Gautama* 52 The red sail-curtain droops. **1776** T. Pennant *Tour in Scotl. & Voy. Hebrides 1772* II. 143 At present the manufactures have risen to a great pitch: for example, that sail-cloth, or sail-duck, as it is here called, is very considerable. **1931** A. Gymnich in V. W. Pagé *Henley's ABC of Gliding* 148 By sailflying we understand a flight without any kind of motor or other driving power in which the energy required for the flight without loss in altitude, is taken solely from the air currents. **1944** T. Horsley *Soaring Flight* 71 The chapter on soaring sites will have given an indication of the winds used in the simplest sail-flying. **1916** H. Barber *Aeroplane Speaks* 103 All is now ready for the sail-maker to cover the surface with fabric. **1953** J. Masefield *Conway* 298 As it happens, we have the sail-plan of her sister-ship. **1961** F. H. Burgess *Dict. Sailing* 178 *Sail plan*, a diagram to show a boat's rig and measurements. **1962** C. H. Gibbs-Smith *Sir George Cayley's Aeronautics 1796–1855* xiii. 129 It is interesting to find at the present time (1962) a powered aeroplane using flexible sail-wings: this is the American Ryan 'Flex Wing' which has plastic-coated nylon wings supported in a delta plan by only three rigid spars, which meet at the front; one is central and the other two spread out to form the sides of the triangle. **1972** *Daily Tel.* (Colour Suppl.) 13 Oct. 9 A sail wing is a device shaped rather like an extremely ambitious paper dart and is made from dural aluminium and nylon. From a point at its centre hangs an 'A' frame... The pilot hangs in space upon an arrangement structurally similar to a child's swing, complete with a narrow wooden seat. **1974** *Sci. Amer.* Dec. 141/1 The sail wing consists of a tubular spar that supports the leading edge of a fabric envelope and a set of short, rigid booms at the tip and foot of the spar between which a slender cable is stretched to form the trailing edge of the wing. **1978** P. O'Donnell *Dragon's Claw* xiv. 293 The sail-wing rested on the grass... They stood surveying the wing.

sail, *sb.*[3] Delete † *Obs.* and *Arch.*, and add later example.

1924 H. J. Butler *Motor Bodywork* xviii. 276 Some of the lighter types of delivery van are made with a recessed rocker side... The body is then built up to the seat line by means of, say, an $1\frac{1}{4}$" hardwood rocker side lapped on vertically, or with a slight sail, into the bottom side.

sail, *v.*[1] Add: **I. 4. a.** (Examples referring to aircraft.)

1897 [see *glider 2 a]. **1910** *Daily Mail Year Bk.* 149/2 The Gross was compelled to descend, after sailing above the enemy's line.

b. (Earlier example.)

1866 'Mark Twain' *Speeches* (1923) 13 The Kanaka, without spur or whip,..sailed by us on the old plug.

5. b. (Earlier examples.) Also in weakened sense, to glide over a surface; to pass rapidly or smoothly.

1819 M. R. Mitford *Let.* 18 Mar. (1925) 161 Just as we were at our merriest, in sailed Madam J—, like a tragedy queen. **1836** W. Dunlap *Thirty Years Ago* I. ii. 22 Mrs. Epsom sailed majestically about the house. **1876** 'Mark Twain' *Tom Sawyer* v. 58 Then there was a wild yelp of agony and the poodle went sailing up the aisle. **1909** R. A. Wason *Happy Hawkins* 10, I flopped onto a pony an' sailed out to a little glen. **1949** W. Awdry *Tank Engine Thomas Again* 50 He remembered the Level Crossing. There was Bertie fuming at the gates while they sailed gaily through. **1979** C. Egleton *Backfire* xii. 135 He sailed through Immigration and collected his suitcase.

c. (Earlier example.) Also, to launch *into* or attack; also *fig.*

1856 'Q. K. P. Doesticks' *Plu-ri-bus-tah* iv. 69 'Sailing in', without regard to Any of the laws of 'Fancy'. **1883** 'Mark Twain' *Life on Mississippi* xxvi. 246 Old General Pillow..sailed in, too, leading his troops as lively as a boy. **1903** A. H. Lewis *Boss* iv. 52 Half an hour before six, blow your whistle an' sail in. **1934** R. Campbell *Broken Record* ii. 33, I sailed into him with a beauty on the ear. **1936** F. Clune *Roaming round Darling* xvii. 173, I sailed into Mrs O'Malley's cooked meat and damper.

‖**sailab** (sai·lāb). Also **sailaba.** [Hindi, Punjabi *sailāb(ā)* flood, torrent f. Pers. *sail* flowing + *āb* water.] A method of cultivation used in the Indus basin in Pakistan and northern India in which the land is irrigated by flood-water from the rivers.

1916 J. Douie *Panjab, N.W. Frontier Province & Kashmir* xiv. 142 'Unirrigated' embraces cultivation dependent on rain (*bárání*) or on flooding or percolation from rivers (*sailáb*). **1960** *Indus Basin Devel. Fund Agreement* 30 in *Parl. Papers 1961* (Cmnd. 1527) XXXVII. 501 Pakistan may also withdraw such waters from each of the following Tributaries..for irrigation of that part of the following areas cultivated on *sailab*. **1962** *Times* 2 June 11/6 The annual migration follows a restricted round which includes short halts for cultivation by the *sailaba* method. Rough earthen bunds are built in the wadis to form a trap for the soil wash from the occasional flash floods and the sorghum and millet seeds are sown in these small patches of saturated soil. **1973** N. D. Gulhati *Indus Waters Treaty* iii. 43 The total area in the Indus basin, along different rivers, cultivated annually after inundation or *sailab*, was about 2·17 million acres... This cultivation was referred to as *sailab*.

sailable, *a.* Delete 'or *Obs.*' and add: **2.** (Later example.)

1976 *New Scientist* 16 Dec. 646/2 A sailable expanse of water.

sailcloth. Add: **3.** Also used for other garments, upholstery, etc. (Earlier and later examples.)

1873 *Young Englishwoman* Jan. 39/1 This hunting pouch consists of a back, front, and flap of grey sailcloth, lined with dark green American cloth. **1881** C. G. Harrison *Woman's Handiwork* I. 48 Among other washing fabrics used in art needlework are *crash*.., *twilled cotton, duck, sail-cloth*, [etc.]. **1962** R. P. Giles *Fabrics for Needlework* iv. 79 Sail-cloth. A very strong, firm, canvas-type fabric made in different weights... Not originally intended for a clothing fabric but nowadays the lighter weights are used for jeans, sportswear, and even summer dresses and skirts. **1979** *Arizona Daily Star* 5 Aug. (Parade Suppl.) 14/1 (Advt.), Comfortable, carefree sailcloth casuals that go their fun-loving way on soft and springy crepe soles.

sailer. Add: **3.** *Baseball.* (See quot. 1961.)

1937 *Sun* (Baltimore) 28 May 14/7 There were two strikes and three balls on Cochrane when Hadley threw his ill-fated 'sailer'. **1961** J. S. Salak *Dict. Amer. Sports* 379 *Sailer* (baseball), a pitched fast ball that takes off, that is, sails. **1975** *New Yorker* 17 Nov. 158/2 The throw, however, was a horrible sailer that glanced off Burleson's glove and went on into center field.

sailing, *vbl. sb.*[1] Add: **2. b.** fig. *plain sailing* (see main entry). Also with similar qualifying adjs.

1827, etc. [see Plain Sailing *sb.*]. **1841** Lytton *Night & Morning* II. viii. 118 'Oh! then it's all smooth sailing,' replied the other. **1927** H. Crane *Let.* 19 Dec. (1965) 313 After a good deal of fair 'sailing' since arriving here—I am now convinced that 'flying' is even better. Right now however..I am 'all fives' on the ground. **1959** *Daily Tel.* 15 Oct. 12/2 Brilliant sailing in the comparatively calm waters of the Post Office.

4. a. *sailing club, date, day* (earlier example), *match* (earlier example); **sailing-line,** (*b*) a line (Line *sb.*[2] 22) of sailing vessels; **sailing master** (earlier U.S. example); **sailing orders** (earlier *fig.* example); **sailing rule,** a rule of the sea, to prevent the collision of ships, etc.

1810 E. Weeton *Let.* 5 Sept. in *Jrnl. of Governess* (1969) I. 293 A sailing club consisting of four or five young men of fortune, have conducted the annual Regattas. **1973** G. Moffat *Lady with Cool Eye* vii. 73 The inspector, meeting the traffic superintendent in the local sailing club, chanced to mention Mrs. Wolkoff's latest protest. **1906** J. London *Let.* 1 Dec. (1966) 227 All..that you wanted answered..was my sailing-date. **1839** in M. Johnson *Amer. Advertising, 1800–1900* (1960), The sailing days of the above ship have been altered. **1905** *Chambers's Jrnl.* May 366/1 Sailing-lines to the West Indies..give Bermuda a wide berth. **1779** in *New Hampsh. Hist. Soc. Coll.* (1863) VII. 194 Appointed—Curtis Sailing Master of the armed ship Hampden. **1810** E. Weeton *Let.* 15 Aug. in *Jrnl. of Governess* (1969) I. 284 You must not suppose that Mr. and Mrs. P. or myself were in the boat during the sailing match. **1796** W. Scott *Let.* 26 Sept. (1932) I. 56 Your sailing orders are—If the subject is casually introduced to treat it lightly. **1877** *Regulations for Government of Navy of U.S.* 185 *Steering and sailing rules*,.. Art.15. If two ships, one of which is a sailing-ship, and the other a steamship, are proceeding in such directions as to involve risk of collision, the steamship shall keep out of the way of the sailing-ship. **1976** *Oxf. Compan. Ships & Sea* 954/1 The actual sailing rules embody in general the Rule of the Road as it affects sailing vessels.

b. *sailing-boat* (earlier and later examples), *dinghy*, *-packet* (earlier example), *-ship* (earlier example), *vessel* (examples); *sailing-chariot* (earlier example).

1721 *New-England Courant* 14 Aug. 2/2 On the 4th Inst. at Night were drowned going to Thomsons Island in a small sailing-Boat, Mr. Heskew, [etc.]. **1976** *Oxf. Compan. Ships & Sea* 960/2 A sailing boat with masts stepped as above but sloop-rigged on the foremast would be termed a yawl. **1759** Johnson *Rasselas* I. vi. 35 He ..found the master busy in building a sailing chariot. **1930** A. P. Herbert *Water Gipsies* vi. 55 Sailing-dinghies, eights and single-scullers. **1975** *Oxf. Compan. Sports & Games* 1123/1 To take part, all a man needs is a yacht,.. or a sailing dinghy as small as 12 ft. (3.65 m.) long. **1842** Dickens *Let.* 17 Feb. (1974) III. 66 There is a sailing-packet from here to England tomorrow. **1871** D. G. Rossetti *Let.* July (1967) III. 959 They are coming back..by sailing-ship. **1748** B. Franklin *Exper. & Observations Electricity* (1751) I. 38 In the wake of every sailing vessel. **1976** Sailing vessel [see *sailing rule* above].

sailing, *ppl. a.*[2] (Earlier and later examples of *sailing course*.)

1807 T. D. W. Dearn *Bricklayer's Guide* 50 Then proceed to take the sailing course, and the wall on either side the chimney. **1946** Holgate & McDougall *Bricklaying* v. 63 An attractive method of making an all-brick coping more effective is by first laying on top of the wall a course of three-quarter bats as headers and after completing the coping, filleting this 'sailing' course with cement mortar.

sail-off. *N. Amer.* [f. Sail *v.*[1] + Off *adv.*, after *play-off*, *row-off*.] **a.** An additional sailing contest to decide between tied contestants. **b.** A series of sailing contests or races held to decide a championship.

1949 *Sun* (Baltimore) 19 July 14/6 The Miller Series at Gibson Island last week end also was sail-off of the home star fleet's championship tie between Ron Blizzard, with Snowflake and Dave Dunigan who sails Lodestar. **1955** *Ibid.* 27 June 13/1 There will be two unlucky sailors next week end when the tie is broken by a sudden death sail-off. **1970** *Times* 19 Aug. 6/6 The winner of the France-Australia sail-off will meet America for the Cup. **1972** *Even. Telegram* (St. John's, Newfoundland) 5 Aug. 15/5 Small-boat sailing..is gaining in popularity and the skippers might like to show what they can do in an annual sail-off.

sailor. Add: **4.** (Earlier and later examples.)

1890 *Demorest's Family Mag.* June 504/2 Boat-shaped, wide-brimmed sailors in white..are worn by either boys or girls for play-hats. **1891** *Delineator* Sept. 230/1 *Ladies' felt sailor hat* —A stylish and dressy sailor is pictured here in a dark brown felt. **1922** H. Titus *Timber* xxix. 252 She pulled the straw sailor tighter over her golden hair. **1943** D. Powell *Time to be Born* x. 227 Her smart little toasted straw sailor with floating pink veil. **1979** D. Eden *Storrington Papers* vi. 68 Miss Featherstone had whipped off her modest sailor and arranged the light-as-air confection on her head.

5. a. *sailor-blue* adj.; (appositive) *sailor-boy* (earlier example), *-king*.

1930 J. Dos Passos *42nd Parallel* I. 91 She was waiting for him..looking like a Gibson girl with her neat sailor-blue dress. **1978** J. Krantz *Scruples* iii. 65 Perhaps his height came from his father, but the bright blond hair and sailor-blue eyes were pure Swedish Viking. **1835** J. E. Alexander *Sk. Portugal* x. 245, I..engaged a Portuguese sailor-boy..to accompany me to Africa. **1911** Fletcher & Kipling *School Hist. Eng.* 91 He [*sc.* Edward III] was merchant-king, sailor-king, soldier-king. **1965** Finer & Savage *Sel. Lett. J. Wedgwood* i. 38 [The Royal patronage] was again extended in 1830 by William IV, the 'Sailor King'. **1975** B. Meyrick *Behind Light* xii. 149 King George, the Sailor King, because he had served at sea.

b. sailor collar (see quot. 1968); **sailor hat** (examples); hence **sailor-hatted** *a.*; **sailor knot** = *sailor's knot*; hence **sailor-knotted** *a.*; **sailor-man,** (*a*) (earlier example); (*b*) a sailing-barge(man); **sailor pants** *U.S.*, flared trousers such as those worn by sailors; **sailor suit,** a suit similar to that of an ordinary seaman, worn mainly by small boys; hence **sailor-suited** *a.*; **sailor top,** a jerkin similar to that worn by sailors; also applied to a ladies' blouse of this design; **sailor trousers** *U.S.* = **sailor pants*.

1895 *Montgomery Ward Catal.* 79/2 Guipure Open work sailor collars. **1932** 'E. M. Delafield' *Thank Heaven Fasting* II. v. 223 A grey satin blouse, with a black bow in the front of the square sailor collar. **1968** J. Ironside

Fashion Alphabet 52 *Sailor*, A collar cut deep and square at the back, narrowing to a '*V*' in the front. It is often trimmed with braid—as worn by sailors. **1974** *She* Jan. 52/2 Braided jacket with square-back sailor collar, £8·50. **1980** *Times* 22 Oct. 10/7 Sailor collar, shift shape and hip belt. **1873** *Young Englishwoman* Mar. 131/2 Brown velvet sailor hat of two shades. **1912** A. BENNETT *Matador of Five Towns* 46 A quite little girl..with a short frock and long legs, and a sailor hat (H.M.S. *Formidable*). **1976** *Vogue* Jan. 48 White tunic..with white duck American sailor hat. **1909** E. NESBIT *Daphne in Fitzroy St.* x. 152 'It's only me, miss,' said the sailor-hatted charwoman. **1872** 'MARK TWAIN' *Roughing It* lxii. 447 Black silk neck-cloth tied with a sailor knot. **1939** T. S. ELIOT *Old Possum's Bk. Pract. Cats* 14 The curtain-cord she likes to wind, and tie it into sailor-knots. **1923** W. J. LOCKE *Moordius & Co.* viii. 109 With deft fingers she gave his sailor-knotted tie a twist and a pull. **1761** G. COLMAN *Jealous Wife* III. 45 The Irish Sailor-Man, for whom I prevailed on your Lordship to get the Post of a Regulating Captain. **1948** *Sea Breezes* VI. 337/2 From Colchester sails Francis & Gilder's large fleet of 'sailor-men'. **1951** H. BENHAM *Down Tops'l* 187 *Sailorman*, the London River term for either a sailing-barge or a sailing-bargeman. **1961** G. FOULSER *Seaman's Voice* i. 20 The winter of 1936–7 was a rough one, with a lot of windbound intervals for the 'sailormen'. **1931** H. CRANE *Let.* 13 June (1965) 373 My usual household white sailor pants and shirt. **1976** *National Observer* (U.S.) 2 Oct. 18/1 Today Stramler is in white sailor pants and a T-shirt. **1880** *Harper's Mag.* Aug. 337/2 Excursionists in sailor suits were playing croquet. **1885** C. M. YONGE *Nuttie's Father* II. xii. 145 We can't persuade ourselves to cut his hair, and it looks so lovely on his sailor suit. **1946** G. MILLAR *Horned Pigeon* iv. 53 He wore a sailor suit that was much too small for him—clothing that had been provided when a Messerschmitt had shot his Blenheim down into the sea. **1976** *Times* 27 Feb. 10/5 Susanna Agnelli was born in 1922... She and her brothers and sisters were dressed in sailor suits, blue in winter, white in summer. **1960** *Times* 3 Aug. 5/2 A juvenile delinquent cousin who appears sailor-suited in the first act. **1977** *Times* 7 May 9/1 The sailor-suited members of the Vienna Boys' Choir. **1913** C. MACKENZIE *Sinister St.* I. I. v. 80 He..wished that he were not compelled to wear a sailor-top that was slightly shabby. **1916** JOYCE *Portrait of Artist* (1969) i. 12 He had a blue sailor top on. **1962** G. AVERY *Greatest Gresham* i. 20 She had..a navy blue sailor top to her blue serge suit. **1971** *Vogue* Dec. 70 Gabardine trousers. Sailor top with big bow. **1851** M. REID *Scalp Hunters* xx. 69 *Calzoneros* of green velveteen. These are cut after the fashion of sailor-trousers,—short-waist—tight round the hips, and wide at the bottoms.

c. sailor's blessing *Naut. slang*, a curse; also **sailors' blessing**, such rigging or tackle as eases the sailors' work; **sailor's farewell** *Naut. slang*, a parting curse; † **sailor's hat** *Obs.* = *sailor hat*; **sailors' home** (earlier example); **sailor's knot** (earlier example); **sailor's pleasure** *Naut. slang* (see quots.); † **sailor's suit** *Obs.* = *sailor suit* above.

1876 F. W. H. SYMONDSON *Two Years abaft Mast* ii. 56 Poor 'doctor' not unfrequently comes in for a 'sailor's blessing' (a growl). **1944** J. MASEFIELD *New Chum* 166 Being almost new had all the latest sailors' blessings; nothing above her royals, double topgallant yards, a spike jib boom and no spanker gaff. **1937** PARTRIDGE *Dict. Slang* 722/1 *Sailor's farewell*, a parting curse. **1974** *Listener* 10 Jan. 50/3 The sole baker there..found himself ruined, and in some anger he gave the village a sailor's farewell and announced that he was off. **1862** *Englishwoman's Domestic Mag.* V. 142/1 Two styles of *hat*.. seem to be equally in favour this season—one, the sailor's hat with straight brim; the other, the turned-down or bell-shaped hat. **1885** *Outing* 7 Nov. 138/2 Their round straw hats, with flat-topped crowns, and shape usually termed by Americans 'sailor's hat'..were trimmed with a plain white ribbon around the crown. **1839** *New Orleans Commerc. Appeal* 18 Apr. 2/2 (*heading*) Public meeting to promote the establishment of a Sailors' Home. **1843** POE *Mystery of Marie Rogêt* in *Ladies' Compan.* (N.Y.) Feb. 165/2 The 'sailor's knot' with which the bonnet-ribbon is tied. **1856** C. NORDHOFF *Merchant Vessel* 132 Others take what is called, *par excellence*, 'sailor's pleasure', in overhauling their chests, bringing their best clothing on deck to air, and counting over their stock of tobacco and pipes. **1932** J. W. HARRIS *Days of Endeavour* 57 They must have a sailor's pleasure on Sunday to see what can be raked up. *Ibid.* 232 *Sailor's pleasure*, overhauling contents of sea-chest and bag, and airing go-ashore clothes. **1933** P. A. EADDY *Hull Down* v. 122 Sunday at sea in a deep-water sailing-ship, especially if the weather is fine, and nearing port the sole topic of conversation, means 'sailor's pleasure'. **1869** G. MEREDITH *Let.* Dec. 19 (1970) I. 406 You should see Willie Godson in his sailor's suit.

sailorship (sē¹·ləɪʃip). *rare.* [f. SAILOR + -SHIP.] Seamanship; the skill of a good seaman.

1820 J. SEVERN *Let.* 20 Sept. in H. E. Rollins *Lett. John Keats* (1958) II. 343 Keats this Morning brags of my sailorship. **1856** C. NORDHOFF *Merchant Vessel* 111 Fancy seizings and lashings bore witness to the sailorship of the mates and crew.

sailplane (sē¹·lplē¹n). Also **sail-plane.** [f. SAIL *sb.*[1] + PLANE *sb.*[3]] A heavier-than-air aircraft without an engine (or having only a small engine which is not normally used except to take off); = *GLIDER 2 a (but see quot. 1971).

1922 *Flight* XIV. 545/2 The gliding angle of a good 'sail-plane' might be in the neighbourhood of 1 in 16 or 1 in 18. **1933** *Sun* (Baltimore) 5 Aug. 15/5 During the day sport planes circled about his sailplane. *Ibid.* 23 Sept. 4/5 Federal officials..will gather..to witness a demonstration in sailplane flying. **1935** *Ibid.* 17 May 1/4 The cheapest flight from London to Paris was made this evening when Robert Kronfeld..landed..in his sailplane driven by a motor-cycle engine of five horsepower, having consumed $1.50 in fuel for the 210-mile flight. **1940** *Illustr. London News* CXCVII. 85/1 The type of sailplane (or, to use the popular, but less correct, term, 'glider') required for use in transporting troops must, of course, be very large. **1950** *Chambers's Jrnl.* 137/2 In tropical countries some birds utilise these thermals, as they are called by sailplane pilots, and indeed make no attempt to fly until the air has warmed up. **1961** *New Scientist* 18 May 362/2 The Olympia 460 is what is called a 'standard' class sailplane. That is to say, it has a span of only 15 metres instead of the 19 metres allowed in the open class for world championship flights. **1971** N. ELLISON *Brit. Gliders & Sailplanes* 9 The terms 'gliders' and 'sailplanes' nowadays are somewhat synonymous. When these terms were first introduced a sailplane was defined as 'a glider having a sinking speed of less than 0·8 metres (2·625 feet) per second'. Today, nearly all motorless aircraft are sailplanes and capable of soaring flight, i.e. flying without loss of height or gaining height.

Hence **sa·ilplaner**, in the same sense; **sai·l-planing** *vbl. sb.*, the flying of sailplanes, gliding; also *transf.*

1923 *Flight* XV. 34/2 In order to encourage gliding and sailplaning in America, the National Aeronautic Association of U.S.A. have appointed a sub-committee to deal with this form of flying. **1930** *Daily Express* 8 Sept. 16 The first lesson in the art of sail-planing. **1962** *Punch* 15 Aug. 237/2 It [*sc.* the fulmar] makes distance at sea.. by sailplaning and tacking. **1973** *Sci. Amer.* Dec. 134/2 The cockpit panel of a serious sailplaner shows 10 dials, plus radio, oxygen gear and cameras. **1977** *Maclean's Mag.* 2 May 58/2 For recreation they have turned to such exotic and often dangerous sports as..sailplaning.

sainfeldite (sē¹·nfeldəit). *Min.* [a. F. *sainfeldite* (R. Pierrot 1964, in *Bull. de la Soc. franç. de Min. et de Crist.* LXXXVII. 180/1), f. the name of P. *Sainfeld* who collected the material: see -ITE[1].] A hydrous arsenate of calcium, $Ca_5H_2(AsO_4)_4.4H_2O$, occurring as small rosettes of transparent monoclinic crystals.

1964 *Chem. Abstr.* LXI 14371 Three new naturally occurring minerals, which were already known as synthetic compounds, were weilite.., rauenthalite.., and sainfeldite. **1972** *Bull. de la Soc. franç. de Min. et de Crist.* XCV. 33/2 Sainfeldite is the least hydrated member of the group including vladimirite, $Ca_5H_2(AsO_4)_4.5H_2O$, and guérinite, $Ca_5H_2(AsO_4)_4.9H_2O$.

saint, *a.* and *sb.* Add: **A.** *adj.* **4. c. St. Augustine grass,** a coarse grass, *Stenotaphrum secundatum*, native to the southeastern United States and central America and named after a town in Florida; **St. Bees Sandstone,** a pebbly sandstone occurring in thick beds in northwest England, formerly regarded as Upper Permian but now as Lower Triassic; **St. Bernard('s) lily,** a perennial herb, *Anthericum liliago*, belonging to the family Liliaceæ and bearing racemes of white flowers; **St. Brigid('s) anemone,** a plant belonging to a garden race of *Anemone coronaria*, bearing single or double red or blue flowers; **St. Bruno's lily,** a rhizomatous perennial herb, *Paradisea liliastrum*, which resembles St. Bernard's lily but has larger flowers (cf. LILY 1 b); **St. Dabeoc's heath,** an Irish heath, *Dabœcia cantabrica* or one of its varieties, belonging to the family Ericaceæ and bearing white, pink, or purple flowers; **St. George's mushroom,** a creamy-white, flattened mushroom, *Tricholoma gambosum*; **St. Kilda (field, house) mouse,** a variety of the long-tailed field mouse, *Apodemus sylvaticus hirtensis*, or the house mouse, *Mus musculus muralis*; **St. Kilda wren,** a local variety of the wren, *Troglodytes troglodytes hirtensis*, with paler plumage; **St. Leger** (further examples); **St. Louis encephalitis** [*St. Louis*, city of Missouri, U.S.], a severe viral encephalitis transmitted by mosquitos; **St. Patrick's cabbage** (see CABBAGE *sb.*[1] 2).

1905 W. J. SPILLMAN *Farm Grasses U.S.* xiii. 196 St. Augustine grass occurs along the Atlantic coast from Charleston, S.C., southward. **1968** F. W. GOULD *Grass Systematics* v. 203 St. Augustine grass is relatively coarse. [**1836** *Trans. Geol. Soc.* IV. 398 The red sandstone of St. Bees Head is unquestionably the exact equivalent of the upper red sandstone of that series.] **1865** E. W. BINNEY in *Mem. Lit. & Philos. Soc. Manchester* II. 373 Fine-grained red sandstone, laminated and ripple-marked, same as that seen at Moat,.. Maryport, and other places, which may be conveniently called St. Bees sandstone. **1946** L. D. STAMP *Britain's Struct. & Scenery* xxii. 224 The St. Bees Sandstone,..of New Red Sandstone age, forms the red cliffs of St. Bees Head. **1969** BENNISON & WRIGHT *Geol. Hist. Brit. Isles* xi. 265 In this case the base of the St. Bees Sandstone, of Bunter age, may also be diachronous. **1883** W. ROBINSON *Eng. Flower Garden* 26/2 The St. Bernard's Lily..grows from 1 foot to 2 feet high, producing single, sometimes branched flower-spikes. **1900** W. D. DRURY *Bk. Gardening* x. 315 The St. Bruno and St. Bernard Lilies..are fast becoming popular. **1964** H. RAMSBOTHAM tr. *Schauenberg's Bulb Bk.* III. 106 St. Bernard's Lily..is a common plant in Alpine meadows. [**1894** *Jrnl. R. Hort. Soc.* XVII. p. liv, Award of Merit. To Anenome St. Brigid's strain..from Earl Cowper, Panshanger, Hertford (g[ardener] Mr. Fitt).] **1902** *Ibid.* XXVII. p. lxxxvi. Award of Merit. To the Alderborough strain of St. Brigid Anemones. **1939** W. FORTESCUE *There's Rosemary* lxxix. 408 We had the joy..of seeing his beautiful frail hands caress the petals of flaming St Brigid Anemones and slender tulips which bordered the drive of the Domaine. **1971** *Country Life* 2 Sept. 543/3 St. Brigid's anemones. Sown in April, they flower from August. **1795** *Curtis's Bot. Mag.* IX. 318 (*heading*) Savoy Anthericum, or St. Bruno's Lily. **1883** W. ROBINSON *Eng. Flower Garden* II. 26/2 The major variety of the St. Bruno's Lily has much larger flowers than the type. **1964** H. RAMSBOTHAM tr. *Schauenberg's Bulb Bk.* III. 204 The English name of this lovely Alpine plant [*sc.* St. Bernard's Lily] is 'St. Bruno's Lily'. **1863** R. C. A. PRIOR *On Pop. Names Brit. Plants* 195 St. Dabeoc's Heath, from an Irish saint of that name, a species found in Ireland. **1978** P. ROWE-DUTTON tr. *van de Laar's Heather Garden* 130 St. Dabeoc's Heath. A low, evergreen Irish native with broad fresh green leaves, silvery beneath. **1891** M. C. COOKE *Brit. Edible Fungi* iv. 34 'St. George's mushroom'..makes its appearance about the time of St. George's Day. **1966** *Oxf. Bk. Flowerless Plants* 134/2 'St. George's Mushroom'..grows in undergrowth on the edges of woods..and in open grassland. **1899** G. E. H. BARRETT-HAMILTON in *Proc. Zool. Soc.* 78, I have now before me..a fine adult pair..of the St. Kilda Mouse. **1913** —— *Hist. Brit. Mammals* II. 540 (*heading*) The St Kilda Field Mouse. *Ibid.* 661 (*heading*) The St Kilda House Mouse. **1960** M. BURTON *Wild Animals Brit. Isles* 78 St. Kilda field mouse..with brown under parts. *Ibid.* 88 Since the human inhabitants left the island in 1930, the St. Kilda mouse has become extinct. **1976** *Islander* (Victoria, B.C.) 7 Mar. 3/3 The St. Kilda house mouse has become extinct. *Ibid.*, The St. Kilda field mouse is also larger. **1884** H. SEEBOHM in *Zoologist* VIII. 333 Those ornithologists who regard the climatic races of this bird as distinct species, will probably come to the conclusion that the St. Kilda Wren is one of the most distinct. **1914** [see WREN 1 b]. **1944** J. S. HUXLEY *On Living in Revolution* ix. 96 The St. Kilda wren..was for some time classified as a separate species. **1976** *Islander* (Victoria, B.C.) 7 Mar. 3/3 The St. Kilda wren is unique. **1847** THACKERAY *Van. Fair* (1848) xxxiv. 302 He and his father fell to talking about odds on the St. Leger. **1930** *Daily Express* 11 Sept. 9/5 The St. Leger was run in almost ideal conditions. **1977** *Times* 10 Sept. 22/1 Thirteen runners have finally stood their ground for this year's St Leger..at Doncaster this afternoon. [**1933** *Jrnl. Amer. Med. Assoc.* 9 Sept. 860/2 (*heading*) The St. Louis encephalitis epidemic.] **1934** *Ibid.* 18 Aug. 462/2 The virus of St. Louis encephalitis had an almost exclusively neurotropic activity. **1962** GORDON & LAVOIPIERRE *Entomol.* xix. 130 As regards western equine encephalomyelitis and St. Louis encephalitis..the important vector appears to be *Culex tarsalis*. **1977** *Jrnl. Virol.* XXII. 608 The antigenic determinants of St. Louis encephalitis, Japanese encephalitis, and dengue virus envelope and nucleocapsid proteins were examined by solid-phase competition radioimmunoassay. **1851** C. A. JOHNS *Flowers of Field* I. 240 S[*axifraga*] *umbrosa* (London Pride or St. Patrick's Cabbage). **1976** *Church Times* 14 May 14/5 Other flowers with religious or curious folk-names are 'Yellow Archangel'..; 'St. Patrick's Cabbage' (one of the saxifrages); [etc.].

‖ **d.** Similarly found in various place- or personal names of French origin, as **St. Cloud** (sæṅklū), used *attrib.* to designate porcelain or faïence made at St. Cloud, Seine-et-Oise, in the late-seventeenth and eighteenth centuries; **St. Emilion** (sæntemilyoṅ), the name applied to various wines produced in the region of St. Emilion, Gironde, in south-west France; **St. Galmier** (galmye), an effervescent natural mineral water from St. Galmier, Loire, in central France; **St. Honoré** (onore) (see quot. 1964); usu. *attrib.*, as *gâteau St. Honoré*; **St. Paulin** (polæṅ), a kind of cheese (see quots.); **St. Porchaire** (pōrʃēr), used *attrib.* to designate a kind of earthenware made at Saint-Porchaire, Deux-Sèvres, France, in the sixteenth century; **St. Raphael (wine)** (rafaʸel), an aperitif wine from St. Raphael, Var, in France.

[**1699** M. LISTER *Journey to Paris* 138, I saw the *Potterie of St. Clou* with which I was marvellously well pleased.] **1721** M. W. MONTAGU *Let.* June (1966) II. 6 If you have not allready laid out that small Summ in St. Cloud ware, I had rather have it in plain Lutestring. **1870** C. SCHREIBER *Jrnl.* 17 Feb. (1911) I. 71 We found an exquisite pâte tendre St. Cloud group. **1978** *Times* 4 Mar. 10/7 The Garrick Club have..Thomas King's cane with a fine St Cloud porcelain handle. **1833** C. REDDING *Hist. Mod. Wines* v. 142 St. Emilion has plenty of body, and superior flavour. **1981** P. FOX *Satan's Messenger* II. xviii. 133 You don't serve a Château Lafite to two hundred people... The St. Emilion would be perfectly adequate. **1883** *Encycl. Brit.* XVI. 436/1 Classes I. and II. of alkaline waters..are very abundant on the Continent, and.. some of the best-known ones enumerated below are ..French..St. Galmier, Pougues, Chateldon. **1912** BEERBOHM *Seven Men* (1919) 114 'Apollinaris? St. Galmier? Or what?' I asked. He preferred plain water. **1907** *Yesterday's Shopping* (1969) 55/2 *Iced & Fancy Cakes*... Gâteaux St. Honore..each 1/5. **1964** A. LAUNAY *Caviare & After* 143 *Saint Honoré*, a rich, round pastry filled with cream and topped with crystallized fruits. **1968** V. CANNING *Melting Man* v. 120 He.. came back with a concoction that made me feel I would never want to eat again... 'It is a *Saint-Honoré*. He was, you know, once Bishop of Amiens and is the patron saint of pastry-cooks. **1968** D. HOPKINSON *Incense-Tree* i. 6 Her dinner parties were graced with.. Gâteau St Honoré. **1956** A. SIMON *Cheeses of World* 73 *Saint-Paulin* is a semi-hard cheese made from cow's milk. .. The Trappists of..Tamié..used to sell their cheese as *St. Paulin*, but it is now sold as *Fromage de Tamié*. **1958** *Catal. County Stores, Taunton* June 9 *Cheese*..St. Paulin—each 5/6. **1971** *Sunday Times* (Colour Suppl.) 28 Mar. 34/3 *Saint-Paulin*, resembles Port Salut in texture, taste and origins. First made in a Norman monastery, it is a rich yellow whole cow's milk cheese, at once soft and firm to the touch and very mildly ripe to taste. **1899** P. GLAZIER *Man. Hist. Ornament* 81 Henri-deux, or St Porchards ware, now more properly described as Oiron ware, originated at St Porchard in 1524. **1925** E. HANNOVER *Pott. & Porc.* III. i. 15 Specimens of the 'Henri II' (St. Porchaire) ware, which is also extremely rare, have repeatedly been offered for sale..in our own days. **1960** [see *HENRI DEUX]. **1975** *Times* 20 May 16/4 One of the greatest rareties in..European ceramics, a St. Porchaire ewer, is to be offered for sale... St. Porchaire wares were made between about 1525 and 1565 and only 60 pieces have survived... St. Porchaire ware, also known as *faience de Henri II*.. was rediscovered by the public, like Palissy ware, as a result of the 1862 'Special Exhibition of Works of Art' at the South Kensington Museum. **1899** HARDY *Let.* 23 Aug. in *One Rare Fair Woman* (1972) 83, I have taken one bottle of St Raphael wine—and it has picked me up. **1951** [see *LILLET]. **1971** *Guardian* 3 June 9/4 St. Raphael and Dubonnet are the sweetest [aperitifs]. **1980** E. LEATHER *Duveen Let.* xii. 138 Glasses of St Raphael and Vichy water were ordered.

B. *sb.* **2. a.** Also, a monk or anchorite, esp. in phr. (*is*)*land of saints*, Ireland.

1888 CHESTERTON *Ballad of White Horse* v. 102 His men were all as thin as saints. *Ibid.* 103 Though Ireland be but a land of saints, and Wales a land of thieves. **1904** C. WALSH in J. McCarthy *Irish Lit.* I. p. xvii, Her nationality and her national spirit have been recognized during the last twenty years as they never were since the days when Ireland was the 'island of saints and scholars', the land of intellectual light and leading in Europe. **1938** W. B. YEATS *New Poems* 13 My father upon the Abbey stage, before him a raging crowd. 'This Land of Saints' and then..'Of plaster Saints'. **1964** *Welsh Hist. Rev.* II. 122 The migrations of the 'saints' from Britain can be dated almost exclusively to the sixth century. *Ibid.* 123 We can picture these early British 'saints' (monks) seeking solitary places at home and abroad in which to serve God. **1979** *Guardian* 1 Oct. 2/8 It was the Pope's arrival at Dublin Airport..which truly set the distinctive character of this personal pilgrimage to his 'island of saints'.

3. a. Also used by the Plymouth Brethren of their own members.

1838 G. V. WIGRAM *Let.* in T. S. Veitch *Story of Brethren Movement* (1933) iv. 59 The question I refer to is 'How are the meetings for communion of Saints in these parts to be regulated?' **1866** H. GROVES *Darbyism* ii. 25 God so ordered it, that the anathemas which had divided the assemblies in Plymouth, should fall upon the saints assembling at Bethesda in Bristol. **1907** E. GOSSE *Father & Son* iii. 72 She now had the care of a practised woman, one of the 'saints' from the Chapel. **1978** *Times Lit. Suppl.* 26 May 573/1 Critical intelligence and the world of the Plymouth Brethren proved..incompatible: growing up meant leaving the Saints.

4. a. Also in colloq. use, an extremely good or long-suffering person.

1852 THACKERAY *Esmond* III. iii. 92 'O how good she is, Harry,' Beatrix went on to say, 'O what a saint she is!' **1978** R. BARNARD *Unruly Son* xvii. 186 My mother.. always thought about me. She was a saint.

6. saint's day, (*b*) = NAME-DAY 1.

1943 E. M. ALMEDINGEN *Frossia* iii. 149 It is my saint's day, we have guests coming. **1980** 'J. LE CARRÉ' *Smiley's People* xxiii. 272 Felicity had called her in..to have Russian company on her saint's day.

saint, *v.* Add: **2. b.** (Later example.)

a **1910** 'MARK TWAIN' in C. B. Taylor *Margins on Thackeray's 'Swift'* (1935) 47 It would have been enough merely to have forgiven Swift in this paragraph—not sainted him.

sainted, *ppl. a.* Add: **2. b.** Used trivially as an expletive in phr. *my sainted aunt* (also *mother*)!

1869 'MARK TWAIN' *Innoc. Abr.* v. 52 'Twenty-five cigars, at 100 reis, 2500 reis!' Oh, my sainted mother! **1916** M. DIVER *Desmond's Daughter* II. ii. 50 My sainted aunt! You did ought to have been in the anteroom just now. **1919** F. HURST *Humoresque* 114 Your sainted mither!.. It's only because she was sainted I'm lettin' ye up in on her. **1921** [see *AUNT 5]. **1926** 'SAPPER' *Final Count* v. 141 Oh! my sainted aunt! don't tell me that old gorse bush was Carl Peterson. **1939** WODEHOUSE *Uncle Fred in Springtime* xvii. 256 'Oh, my aunt! Don't tell me she's changed her mind and wants the stuff after all?' .. 'Exactly.' 'Oh, my sainted bally aunt!' **1971** R. ROBERTS *Classic Slum* viii. 127 Self-consciously we incorporated weird slang into our own oath-sprinkled banter—'Yarooh!' 'My sainted aunt!' 'Leggo!' and a dozen others.

St. Elmo (sĕnt e·lmo). Also † **St. Elm, St. Helmo, San Telmo, sant-elmo.** [A corruption, via *Sant'Ermo*, of the name of *St. Erasmus* (martyred 303), Italian bishop and patron saint of Mediterranean sailors; cf. It. *fuoco di Sant'Elmo*.] Used in the possessive, *absol.*, and with *of* to denote the luminous appearance of a naturally occurring corona discharge about a ship's mast or the like, usually in bad weather. Now usu. as *St. Elmo's fire*; = CORPOSANT, HELENA.

1561 Sant-elmo [see CORPOSANT a]. **1621** J. CHAMBERLAIN *Let.* 21 July (1939) II. 390 His comming was taken for a goode presage, like the appearing of St. Elmo after a tempest. **1774** Fires of St. Helmo [see FIRE *sb.* A. 10 b]. **1814** tr. *G. H. Von Langsdorff's Voy. & Trav.* II. iv. 102 In the winter months the air is often so charged with electricity, that for many hours together in the darkest nights a bluish green electrical light, called St. Helen's, or St. Elm's fire, may be seen. **1845** *Encycl. Metrop.* IV. 135/1 The fire of St. Elmo, so frequently seen upon the masts of vessels in the mediterranean, and from very early times connected with the names of Castor and Pollux, meets with a very simple explanation on the principle of a pointed conductor imbibing electricity. **1882** *Encycl. Brit.* XIV. 633/2 This glow is known to sailors as St Elmo's (San Telmo's) fire, in old days Castor and Pollux. **1942** *Tee Emm* (Air Ministry) II. 56 St. Elmo's Fire..is caused by the aircraft passing through a charged area of cloud and thus charging up itself... A glow, and in more extreme cases long streaks of fire appear at the propellers, wing-tips or nose. **1956** G. DURRELL *My Family & other Animals* xvii. 235, I tell you, we'll find the chimney covered with Saint Elmo's fire one night, and before we know where we are we'll be drowned in our beds by a tidal wave. **1969** M. A. UMAN *Lightning* 244 Ball lightning and St. Elmo's fire are sometimes confused. St. Elmo's fire is a corona discharge from a pointed conducting object in a strong electric field. Like ball lightning, St. Elmo's fire may assume a spherical shape. Unlike ball lightning, St. Elmo's fire must remain attached to a conductor, although it may exhibit some motion along the conductor. Further, St. Elmo's fire can have a lifetime much greater than the lifetime of the usual ball lightning. **1976** *Scotsman* 20 Nov. (Weekend Suppl.) 1/1 The top of the mast was surrounded with an eerie pale green phosphorescence. This was St. Elmo's Fire—known and feared by seamen of old—caused by static electricity.

St. Kildan (sĕnt ki·ldăn). Also † **St. Kildean, St. Kildian.** A nátive or inhabitant of the island of St. Kilda in the Outer Hebrides.

The island is now the property of the National Trust for Scotland. The last native inhabitants were formally evacuated on 29 Aug. 1930.

1764 K. MACAULAY *Hist. St. Kilda* v. 77 The St. Kildians are too wise or too good protestants, to neglect their secular affairs on the festival days of Columba and Brendan. **1819** D. WEBSTER *Topogr. Dict. Scotl.* 375/2 One of the St. Kildans coming to Harris, was attacked with the small-pox, and died. **1842** J. WILSON *Voyage round Coasts of Scotl.* II. i. 9 In another moment we stood on Terra-Kilda... The small group of St. Kildeans.. seemed cheered by our arrival. **1861** R. CHAMBERS *Domestic Ann. Scotl.* III. 181 Mr. Macaulay..mentions.. that not only is a St. Kildian's person disagreeably odoriferous to a stranger, but 'a stranger's company is..as offensive to them.' **1939** *Geogr. Mag.* X. 73/2 Stac Lee.. was much more easily and more often climbed by the St. Kildans than Stac an Armin. **1965** T. STEEL *Life & Death of St. Kilda* 10 The St. Kildan can only be described as a St. Kildan, and his island home little else than a republic. **1980** *Times* 22 July 4/2 It is 50 years since the last St Kildans elected to leave the island.

St. Lucian (sĕnt lū·ʃən), *sb.* and *a.* **A.** *sb.* A native or inhabitant of St. Lucia in the West Indies. **B.** *adj.* Of or pertaining to St. Lucia.

1844 H. H. BREEN *St. Lucia* v. 169 The early refugees, being unwilling to gratify the curiosity of the St. Lucians ..had rallied their numerous inquiries. **1952** S. SELVON *Brighter Sun* viii. 149 Ah sorry for all dem Grenadians and St. Lucians who come over here to make money. **1955** *Caribbean Q.* IV. II. 99 St. Lucian life has had a consistency and continuity rare in the New World. **1971** *Advocate-News* (Barbados) 17 Sept. (Guyana Suppl.) p. i/1 Barbadians, St. Lucians, St. Vincentians, Grenadians, Dominicans..all of them Guyanese by definition though not by birth..these are the people one meets in almost every hinterland settlement in Guyana. **1973** *Caribbean Contact* Feb. 4/2 In a brief conversation with the St. Lucian born elevator attendant..Salkey records valuable information. **1978** *Daily Tel.* 11 Mar. 13/1 Because of the to-ing and fro-ing of the two languages, it takes a St. Lucian to understand another St. Lucian when he breaks out into the local Creole patois.

saintpaulia (sĕntpǭ·liă). [mod.L. (H. Wendland 1893, in *Gartenflora* XLII. 321), f. the name of Baron Walter von *Saint-Paul* (1860–1910), German explorer + -IA[1].] A stemless perennial herb of the genus so called, belonging to the family Gesneriaceæ, native to East Africa, and bearing ovate hairy leaves and clusters of violet, pink, or white flowers; esp. a pot plant of the species *Saintpaulia Ionantha*, the African violet.

1895 HOFMARSCHAL BARON ST. PAUL in *Curtis's Bot. Mag.* CXXI. 7408 The *Saintpaulia* was discovered by my son, who lives in East Africa. **1946** M. FREE *All about House Plants* xv. 127 If you carefully examine a Saintpaulia which has been growing in the house all winter you will see..that it has split up into several crowns. **1961** *Amateur Gardening* 14 Oct. 27/2 It would be best to divide the saintpaulia when it finishes flowering. **1974** *Times* 5 Oct. 12/2 Millions of African violets, saintpaulias, are sold every year, but vast numbers do not live for long in houses or flats.

Saint-Simonian, *a.* and *sb.* Add: (Earlier and later examples.) **Saint-Simonist** (earlier example); also *attrib.* or as *adj.*; **Saint-Simonianism** (earlier and later examples), **-Simonism** (earlier example).

1829 J. S. MILL *Let.* 7 Nov. in *Wks.* (1963) XII. 40, I object altogether to the means which the St Simonists propose for organizing the *pouvoir spirituel*. **1830** —— *Ibid.* 9 Feb. 45 His objections to the Saint-Simonian philosophy. *Ibid.* 48 France must pass through several states before it arrives at St Simonism. **1831** *Ibid.* 20–22 Oct. 76 A Christian would be positively less fit than a St Simonian (for example), to form part of a national church. **1833** *Ibid.* 25 Nov. 193 The great majority have retained of St Simonianism about as much as is good and true, dropping the rest. **1952** F. A. VON HAYEK *Counter-Revolution of Sci.* iv. 144 The greatest of the Saint-Simonians..and the medium through whom many of them had received the doctrine of the master, was Auguste Comte. **1953** S. SPENDER *Creative Element* ii. 54 At the end of *Une Saison en Enfer* Rimbaud seems, indeed, to wish to reconcile Christianity with Saint-Simonist socialism. **1974** *Times Lit. Suppl.* 25 Jan. 66/2 He suggests that Heine saw himself as a Saint Simonian prophet and that Saint Simonianism, not the 1830 revolution, drew him to Paris. **1976** A. W. GOULDNER *Dialectic of Ideol.* xii. 274 The surprising continuities between the Saint-Simonian formulations and the Weberian.

St. Trinian's (sĕnt tri·niănz). The name of a girls' school invented by the cartoonist Ronald Searle (b. 1920) in 1941. Used *absol.* and *attrib.* to designate allusively the characteristic style of hoydenish behaviour, school uniform, etc., of the girls in the cartoons and the subsequent associated books and films.

Searle's daughters attended St. Trinnean's school in Edinburgh.

[**1941** R. SEARLE in *Lilliput* IX. IV. 313 (*caption*) Owing to the international situation the match with St. Trinian's has been postponed. **1948** D. B. WYNDHAM LEWIS in R. Searle *Hurrah for St. Trinian's* 8 Those typical English Roses, the girls of St. Trinian's, a nightmare synthesis of Roedean, Heathfield and Wycombe Abbey.] **1958** *Times* 20 May 11/4 How the girls of to-day, finishing at St. Trinian's or taking their degrees at St. Jude's, will smile with affectionate tolerance at these meagre achievements in the scholastic line. **1961** *Guardian* 3 Mar. 10/4 A St Trinian's type of schoolgirl. **1964** C. DALE *Other People* iv. 88 She was big and fat and pasty... In her school uniform..she looked a complete St. Trinian's type. **1972** *Guardian* 25 Jan. 9/2 Louis Feraud..includes a group of dresses called schoolgirl frocks..Lolita lives again, and one longs for the innocence of St Trinian's. **1977** 'D. CORY' *Bennett* iii. 93 His high-pitched St Trinian's giggle. **1981** R. BARNARD *Sheer Torture* xi. 121 Aunt Kate..an overgrown product of St Trinian's.

sais, saïs, varr. SYCE. (Further examples.) Also [a. Arab. *sā'is*] in African and Asian use.

1887 KIPLING *Plain Tales from Hills* (1888) 28 He.. deserved a V.C., if it were only for putting on a *sais*'s blanket. **1924** L. ECKENSTEIN *Tutankh-aten* ii. 24 The *saïses* running on either side of the chariots as only outrunners in Egypt can run. **1927** R. J. H. SIDNEY *In Brit. Malaya Today* 143 The Malay *saises* will all be playing cards. **1936** W. H. S. SMITH *Let.* 26 June in *Young Man's Country* (1977) ii. 11, I said good-bye to Peter and his sais yesterday morning. **1953** J. MASTERS *Lotus & Wind* viii. 113 I'll walk back to your bungalow with you. My sais can bring Beauty along. **1975** T. DINESEN *My Sister, Isak Dinesen* v. 56 The sais (horse-keeper) was to bring the horses up after us.

Saiva (ʃəi·vă), *sb.* and *a.* [a. Skr. *śaiva* relating, belonging, or sacred to Siva; a worshipper or follower of Siva.] **A.** *sb.* A member of one of the three great divisions of modern Hinduism, exclusively devoted to the worship of the god Siva as the Supreme Being. **B.** *adj.* Of or pertaining to this division of Hinduism.

1810 E. MOOR *Hindu Pantheon* 15 *Saivas* or worshippers of Siva. **1842** *Penny Cycl.* XXII. 65/2 The great Saiva reformer, Sankara Acharya. **1876** *Encycl. Brit.* IV. 210/1 The *Śaiva*, *Vaishnava*, and *Sākta* sects. **1974** *Encycl. Brit. Macropædia* VIII. 893/2 Most Śaiva worship is not systematic but a complex amalgam of pan-Indian Śaiva philosophy and local or folk worship.

Hence **S(h)ai·vism** = SIVAISM; **S(h)ai·vite** *sb.* and *a.* = SIVAITE.

1867 R. MILMAN *Jrnl.* 21 Nov. in F. M. Milman *Mem. R. Milman* (1879) iii. 48 This temple is reckoned..the holiest shrine in India..among Shaivites. **1877** MONIER WILLIAMS *Hinduism* viii. 97 Śaivism and Vaishṇavism are not opposite or incompatible creeds. **1882** *Encycl. Brit.* XIV. 228/1 Saivite gods or devils. **1924** E. M. FORSTER *Passage to India* xxxvii. 323 They cantered..past a Saivite temple, which invited to lust, but under the semblance of eternity. **1956** R. REDFIELD *Peasant Society & Culture* 88 The important Vaishnavaism and Shaivism are theistic and ethical. **1969** *Indo-Asian Culture* Oct. 70 Both Saivism and Vaishnavism were popular in Srihatta and the neighbouring region during the late Gupta and mediæval times. **1972** 'E. PETERS' *Death to Landlords!* x. 153 A Saivite sadhu seated in contemplation.

saj (sadʒ). [Hindi.] The Indian laurel, *Terminalia tomentosa*, a tropical tree of the family Combretaceæ, native to India and Burma and bearing terminal spikes of yellow flowers; also, the dark hardwood produced by this tree and others of the genus. Also *attrib.*

1839 E. W. LANE tr. *Arabian Nights* II. xiii. 384 Its door was of sáj, adorned with brilliant gold. **1931** J. W.

BEST *Tiger Days* xii. 173 Nobler trees take their place; the stately saj and the dark-limbed ebony. **1952** J. MASTERS *Deceivers* viii. 88 The man..started back..and began to run toward a thin line of saj trees bordering the road.

Saka (ʃæ·kă), *sb.* and *a.* Also **Çaka, Saca.** [Skr. *Śaka*; cf. Gr. pl. Σάκαι, L. pl. *Sacæ*.] **A.** *sb.* **a.** (A member of) an ancient Indo-Scythian people originating in central Asia. **b.** The language of this people, = *KHOTANESE *sb.*

[**1601** P. HOLLAND tr. *Pliny's Nat. Hist.* VI. xvii. 123 Beyond the realme Sogdiana, inhabit the nations of the Scythians. The Persians were wont to call them in generall Sacas, of a people adjoining unto them, so named. **1795** J. NOTT tr. *Catullus' Poems* I. xi. 35 Whether he treads Hircanian ground; Or seeks the gentle Arab's home; The Parthians, for the dart renown'd; Or mid the Sacæ's doom'd to roam.] **1880** H. W. BELLEW *Races of Afghanistan* ii. 18 The province itself derived its name of Sákistán..from the Sáka, who were probably the same people as the Sáká Hámuvarga mentioned in the tables of Darius. **1934** AHMAD & AZIS *Afghanistan* vii. 45 Driven from their home in Central Asia the Sakas migrated into Kashmir. **1961** [see *Indo-Scyth* s.v. *INDO-[1]]. **1966** G. S LANE in Birnbaum & Puhvel *Anc. Indo-European Dial.* 223 Of the fifty-one words submitted as possible borrowings from Iranian, twenty-one are attested in Saca (Khotanese), or on various grounds appear to be for the most part of Saca origin. **1972** W. B. LOCKWOOD *Panorama Indo-European Lang.* 237 The Persians are said by Herodotus to have called the various Scythian tribes Saka... Rich manuscript remains of Saka came to light in Turkestan... The language of Khotan is called Khotanese Saka or simply Khotanese... Saka appears to survive in the mountains to the west. **1974** *Encycl. Brit. Macropædia* I. 173/1 Iranian tribes of nomadic Śaka.. seem, before 130 BC, to have made a pact with the Parthians and to have settled in Sīstān whence they spread eastward..into India.

B. *adj.* **a.** Of or pertaining to this people or their language. **b.** In Indian chronology, designating or pertaining to an era reckoned from A.D. 78

1883 [see *MAHAYANA]. **1886** *Encycl. Brit.* XXI. 854/1 The ancient Aryan inscriptions usually employ the Saka (Salivahana) era, dating from 79 A.D. **1923** *Cambr. Hist. India* I. xxiii. 585 It was in consequence of its long use by the Çaka princes of western India that the era has become generally known in India as the Çaka era—a name which effectually disguises its origin, and one which has in no small degree perplexed modern scholars in their endeavours to unravel the secret of Kamishka! **1932** W. L. GRAFF *Lang.* 371 Other Middle Iranian documents, especially known through recent discoveries, represent the Sogdian and Saka dialects. **1956** R. PIERIS *Sinhalese Social Organization* II. 92 The Śaka era was made use of in all legal instruments... It is said to date from a king Saka. **1958** O. CAROE *Pathans* iv. 63 Greek or Macedonian soldiers were needed to guard the frontier marches against the Saka nomads. **1974** *Encycl. Brit. Macropædia* IV. 574/2 The Śaka, or Salivāhana, era (AD 78), now used throughout India, is the most important of all. It has been used not only in many Indian inscriptions but also in ancient Sanskrit inscriptions in Indochina and Indonesia. The reformed calendar promulgated by the Indian government from 1957 is reckoned by this era. It is variously alleged to have been founded by King Kaniṣka or by the Hindu king Salivāhana or by the satrap Nahapāna.

Hence **Sa·kian** = *SAKA *sb.* b.

1933 L. BLOOMFIELD *Language* iv. 63 Other medieval Iranian languages, which have been identified as *Parthian*, *Sogdian*, and *Sakian*. **1939** [see *KHOTANESE *sb.* and *a.*].

sakabula (sakabu·lă). *S. Afr.* Also **sac(c)aboola**, etc. [a. Zulu *iSakabuli* widow-bird.] The long-tailed widow-bird, *Euplectes progne*, of the family Ploceidæ, the male of which is black, with red patches on the wings and very long tail-feathers. Also *fig.*

1877 LADY BARKER *Year's Housekeeping S. Afr.* ix. 179 Lynx tails hung down like lappets on each side of her face which was over-shadowed and almost hidden by the profusion of sakabula feathers. **1885** RIDER HAGGARD *King Solomon's Mines* viii. 127 They wore upon their heads heavy black plumes of Sacaboola feathers, like those which adorned our guides. **1896** H. L. TANGYE *In New S. Afr.* iv. 105 One of the most strange inhabitants of the Transvaal is a small black bird, the Sakabula. **1912** *E. London Dispatch* 20 July 3 They bartered the highly prized tail feathers of the sakaboola bird. **1937** S. CLOETE *Turning Wheels* 362 A saccabula, gorgeous in his black spring feathers, his wings blotched with red, flew past them followed by his wives that were grey and dull. **1951** R. CAMPBELL *Light on Dark Horse* x. 144 The finest variety [of widow-bird], the 'Sakabula', is quite a common sight. **1973** *Weekend Post* (Port Elizabeth) 28 Apr. 3 The long-tailed black widow birds commonly known as sakabullas.

Sakai (sā·kai), *sb.* (and *a.*) Also 9 **Sakkye.** [Malay, lit. subject, dependent.] **a.** An aboriginal people of the Malay peninsula (loosely used of Malayan aborigines collectively); a member of this people. **b.** The language of the Sakai. Also *attrib.* or as *adj.*

1839 T. J. NEWBOLD *Pol. & Statistical Acct. Straits of Malacca* I. vii. 421 The Semangs, Sakkye, or Orang Bukit, men of the hills. **1886** *Jrnl. Anthrop. Inst.* Feb. 285 In this state of Perak there is at present besides the Sakais one other race, the Sĕmang. *Ibid.*, The Sakai race inhabits the left bank of the Perak River. **1906** [see *JAKUN]. **1920** R. J. WILKINSON *Hist. Peninsular Malays* (ed. 2) i. 3 The fair wavy-haired aborigines known as the Sakai inhabit both sides of the Malayan main range. *Ibid.* 8 The grammar..of Sakai is extraordinarily complex and inflected. **1932** L. GOLDING *Magnolia St.* III. vi. 538 The people seemed stranger to him than the pygmies of the African jungle or the Sakais of Malaya, who live up in the hills and make their clothes out of the bark of trees. **1952** P. D. R. WILLIAMS-HUNT *Introd. Malayan Aborigines* i. 1 *Sakai*, used generally for Aborigines is a derogatory term which is disliked by most jungle dwellers. **1966** *Telegraph* (Brisbane) 18 Nov. 2/3 Malaya's aborigines, the little brown jungle men called Sakai, tried out a little modern technology. **1977** P. THEROUX *Consul's File* 43 The local *sakais*—they might have been Laruts—had deported some wild monkeys there.

sakawinki. Add: Also **sak(k)iwinki(e).** (Further examples.) Also, a South American squirrel monkey of the genus *Saimiri*.

1954 G. DURRELL *Three Singles to Adventure* i. 38 'What are they?'.. 'Squirrel monkeys, but I don't know what they call them here.' 'Sakiwinkis, Chief.' **1958** J. CAREW *Black Midas* vi. 102 Behind us, sakki-winki monkeys chattered, and toucans screamed. *Ibid.* vii. 155 Red howlers roared..and tinamous and saki-winkies joined in.

sake, *sb.* Add: **4*.** (See quot. 1879[2]). *nonce-use.*

1876 G. M. HOPKINS *Wreck of Deutschland* xxii, in *Poems* (1967) 58 Five! the finding and sake And cipher of suffering Christ. **1879** —— *Henry Purcell* in *Ibid.* 80 Let him oh! with his air of angels then lift me, lay me! only I'll Have an eye to the sakes of him, quaint moonmarks, to his pelted plumage under Wings. **1879** —— *Lett. to R. Bridges* (1955) 83 *Sake* is a word I find it convenient to use:..it is common in German, in the form *sach.* It is the *sake* of 'for the sake of'... I mean by it the being a thing has outside itself, as a voice by its echo, a face by its reflection,..a man by his name, fame, or memory, *and also* that in the thing by virtue of which especially it has this being abroad,.. as for a voice and echo clearness; for a reflected image light, brightness;..for a man genius, great achievements... In this case it is, as the sonnet says, distinctive quality in genius.

saké. Add: Now usu. with pronunc. (sā·ki). (Further examples.)

1916 [see **brown rice*]. **1917** E. POUND *Lustra* 189 We drink our parting in saki. **1931** G. B. SANSOM *Japan* I. iii. 52 The new season's rice and *sake* of the new brew. **1947** R. BENEDICT *Chrysanthemum & Sword* v. 101 Every sip of *sake* doled out to them before going into battle. **1947** J. BERTRAM *Shadow of War* 273 The guards looted the *saké* from their own stores. **1958** G. MIKES *East is East* 56 Drinking *sake*, watching dancing and listening to singing. **1978** M. PUZO *Fools Die* xxxv. 409 She kept filling my cup with some sort of wine, the famous sake, I guessed.

attrib. **1957** A. THWAITE *Home Truths* 53 And fill my *saké* cup again. **1960** B. LEACH *Potter in Japan* v. 118 An immense sake bowl was filled with about 4 gallons of hot wine. **1979** 'J. MELVILLE' *Wages of Zen* ii. 17 Otani held out his *sake* cup and she refilled it.

Sakel: see next.

Sakellaridis (sækĕlæ·ridis), **Sakellarides** (-idīz). Also shortened to **Sakel** (sæ·kĕl). [The name of Σακελλαρίδης, a Greek cotton-grower who originated the variety.] The name of a superior variety of Egyptian cotton, widely grown in the early 20th century.

1912 W. L. BALLS *Cotton Plant in Egypt* vi. 105 The main varieties at present cultivated on a commercially important scale are Yannovitch and Sakellaridis in the 'fine-spinning' group; [etc.]. *Ibid.* 106 One of the cherished fables of the practician teaches that heavy crops and fine staple cannot co-exist. The inaccuracy of this belief, though long suspected, has only recently been proved by the Sakel variety. **1915** J. A. TODD *World's Cotton Crops* xiv. 276 Sakellarides, or Sakel, as it is commonly called, is a comparatively new variety, dating from about 1907. **1931** *Times* 17 Nov. 13/1 With Sakellaridis at 7d. per lb. **1953** *New Biol.* XIV. 49 The famous Sakellarides variety, selected by a Greek of that name in the early years of this century, has become a parent of most or all of the better quality Egyptian varieties now being bred. **1955** CHRISTIDIS & HARRISON *Cotton Growing Probl.* iii. 119 After 1887, a number of varieties acquired prominence; among them..Sakellaridis or Sakel (1909).. could be mentioned. All are now extinct, even Sakel. **1958** BROWN & WARE *Cotton* (ed. 3) iii. 71 In 1918 several crosses were made between Pima and Sakel (Sakellarides), the latter having become the most prominent variety in Egypt following Mit Afifi.

sakhaite (sæ·kheˌəit). *Min.* Also **sahaite.** [ad. Russ. *sakhaĭt* (I. V. Ostrovskaya et al. 1966, in *Zapiski vsesoyuznogo min Obshchestva* XCV. 193), f. *Sakha*, name of the locality in Siberia where it was discovered: see -ITE[1].] A hydrous borate and carbonate of calcium and magnesium, the crystals of which belong to the cubic system and occur as greyish white masses.

1966 *Chem. Abstr.* LXV. 3567 A new mineral, called sakhaite.., was found during study of magnesian skarns in Siberia. **1970** *Canad. Mineralogist* X. 694 The formula of sakhaite was recalculated in an attempt to determine whether a relationship existed between sakhaite and harkerite. **1975** *Soviet Physics Doklady* XIX. 559/1 We have studied the synthetic analog of sahaite..under hydrothermal conditions in the CaO–MgO–B_2O_3–CO_2–H_2O system.

Sakmarian (sakmæ·riăn), *a. Geol.* [ad. Russ. *Sakmarskiĭ* (first used as a stratigraphical term by A. Karpinsky 1874, in *Zap. Imperatorskago Min. Obshchestva* IX. 269), f. *Sakmara*, name of a river in the Southern Urals: see -IAN.] Name of a stage in the Lower Permian in the Soviet Union; of or pertaining to this stage and the rocks that characterize it, and the geological age during which they were deposited. Freq. *absol.*

1936 V. E. RUZHENTSEV in *Problemý Sovetskoĭ Geologii* VI. 506 The upper Carboniferous is overlain in complete conformity by the Permian system which begins with Schwagerina beds. The writer defines by the name Sakmarian the whole of the deposits with Schwagerina princeps Ehr. and with the Ammonoid fauna described for the first time from the Sakmara river... The Sakmarian consists of sandy-argillaceous beds among which there are many conglomerates. **1960** *Bull. Geol. Soc. Amer.* LXXI. 1766/2 It is now the official usage of the Geological Survey of the U.S.S.R. to draw the base of the Permian below the Sakmarian and equivalent beds in the Ufa Plateau. **1963** D. W. & E. E. HUMPHRIES tr. *Termier's Erosion & Sedimentation* i. 20 Lakes and marshes are known in the northern hemisphere which were contemporaneous with the Stephanian and Sakmarian glaciers of the Southern hemisphere. **1974** *Nature* 8 Feb. 396/1 McLachlan and Anderson have recorded orthocerid nautiloids, the brachiopod *Attenuatella*, [etc.]..from the base of the succession near Kimberley. They favoured a Sakmarian age for this marine incursion.

Sakta (ʃā·ktă). Also 9 **Sacta.** [a. Skr. *śākta* relating to power or to the Sakti; a worshipper of the Sakti.] A member of one of the principal sects of modern Hinduism which worships the Sakti or divine energy, especially as identified with Durgā, the wife of Siva. Also *attrib.* Cf. *SAIVA *sb.* and *a.* Hence **Sa·ktism**, the worship of the Sakti.

1810 E. MOOR *Hindu Pantheon* 116 Those, of whatever sect, who worship exclusively the female power..are called Sactas. **1845** *Encycl. Metrop.* XXIV. 443/1 The Hindús are almost always either 1. Vaïshnavas..; 2. Saïvas..; or 3. Sáktas. **1877** MONIER WILLIAMS *Hinduism* ix. 123 Tāntrism, or Śāktism, is Hindūism arrived at its last and worst stage of medieval development. **1920** [see *NADA[1]]. **1931** G. MACMUNN *Relig. India* 69 The Sakta groups have borrowed much from aboriginal practices and influence. *Ibid.* 160 The really secret cult of Saktism. **1974** *Encycl. Brit. Macropædia* VIII. 896/2 The Tantric movement is not rarely inextricably interwoven with Śāktism. *Ibid.* 897/2 Śākta adepts are trained to direct all their energies toward the conquest of the Eternal.

Sakti (ʃa·kti). Also 9 **Sacti; Shakti** and with small initial. [a. Skr. *śakti* power, divine energy, f. *śak* to be able.] In Hindu religion, the female principle, esp. when personified as the wife of a god, as Durgā is the Sakti of Siva, etc.; supernatural energy embodied in the principle.

1810 E. MOOR *Hindu Pantheon* 10 All the principal, and several of the secondary deities..have wives assigned to them, who are called Sacti. **1842** *Penny Cycl.* XXII. 67/1 That thou, united with thy Sakti, dost in sport create the universe from thy own substance. **1862** MRS. J. B. SPEID *Our Last Yrs. in India* vii. 174 Seresvati, the goddess of letters, &c., Lackshmi, of prosperity, and Kali or Parvati, of destruction... These three goddesses, under the name of the Sactis, sometimes receive an exclusive worship. **1871** J. GARRETT *Classical Dict. India* 540 The Sakti is said to have originated in God, the Supreme Being... There are many special forms of Sakti-worship. **1918** J. WOODROFFE *Shakti & Shâkta* 49 According to Shâkta doctrine each man and woman contains within himself and herself a vast latent magazine of Power or Shakti. **1922** JOYCE *Ulysses* 499 It has been said by one: beware the left, the cult of Shakti. **1937** M. COVARRUBIAS *Island of Bali* x. 339 Every Balinese believes that his body, like an electric battery, accumulates a magic energy called *sakti* that enables him to withstand the attacks of evil powers... This *sakti* is not evenly divided; some people are born with a capacity to store a higher charge of magic than others; they become the priests, witch-doctors, and so forth, endowed with supernatural powers. **1962** A. HUXLEY *Island* xiii. 213 Paintings of tropical animals, Bodhisattvas and their bosomy Shaktis. **1968** A. WARHOL *A* 421 He doesn't have any bhakti it's all shakti. **1972** D. BLOODWORTH *Any Number can Play* xviii. 184 In thirty times thirty years will come one with the ears of the Buddha and with the *sakti*... Supernatural power. **1977** *N.Y. Times Mag.* 4 Dec. 144 Joya's famous *shakti*, or spiritual energy.

sakura (sakū·rā). [Jap.] A flowering cherry tree belonging to one of the many varieties bred from various species of *Prunus*; also, the blossom or wood of a tree of this kind.

1884 tr. *J. J. Rein's Japan* II. iii. 471 *Yoshino*..once the residence of the anti-emperors, a famous old place with many Sakura (Prunus pseudocerasus). **1892** F. T. PIGGOTT *Garden of Japan* 19 *P[runus] pseudocerasus*—*sakura*, with enormous pink double flowers. **1911** *Encycl. Brit.* XV. 175/2 The wood used is generally that of the cherry-tree, *sakura*, which has a grain of peculiar evenness and hardness. **1948** C. INGRAM *Ornamental Cherries* 13 Will you please tell me why you are so very fond of our

Sakura—our Cherries? **1963** *Times* 22 Apr. 11/7 Famous songs such as '*Sakura, Sakura*' (Cherry blossom, Cherry blossom) elicited no gleam of sentiment. **1970** J. Kirkup *Japan behind Fan* 41 The season when the *sakura* or cherry blossom blooms.

† **sal**[3] (sæl). *Theatr. slang. Obs.* Abbrev. of Salary *sb.* 1.

1844 E. R. Lancaster *Manager's Daughter* (ed. 2) in *Oxberry's Budget of Plays* I. 110/1 Who does he suppose was to cut comic mugs before noblemen, without being paid double sals.? **1870** O. Logan *Before Footlights* xxxii. 433 'You're earning your sal easy,' says Clown to him with some reproach. **1885** *Househ. Words* 29 Aug. 350/1, I say that part of this money shall be shared among us as 'sals', and some of the remainder shall be used for mounting the guv'nor's panto.

sal[4] (sæl). [f. S(ilicon + Al(uminium).] **1.** *Petrogr.* One of the two primary categories erected by Cross, Iddings, Pirsson, and Washington to classify igneous rocks and their characteristic minerals, and broadly including those rich in non-ferromagnesian aluminous and siliceous minerals such as quartz, feldspars, and feldspathoids. Hence **salic** (sæ·lik) *a.*[2], of or pertaining to this category of rocks. Cf. *femic *a.*

1902 W. Cross et al. in *Jrnl. Geol.* X. 573 To express concisely the two groups of standard minerals and their chemical characters in part, the words *sal* and *fem* have been adopted. The former is employed to designate group I, mnemonically recalling the *s*iliceous and *al*uminous character of its minerals. **1902**, etc. [see *femic *a.*]. **1931** A. Johannsen *Descr. Petrogr. Igneous Rocks* I. viii. 86 The classes are determined by the salic-femic ratio. The five classes are: I. Persalic. Ratio sal:fem greater than 7·00 [etc.]. **1974** I. S. E. Carmichael et al. *Igneous Petrol.* ii. 48 The most generally used index of magmatic evolution is the differentiation index (DI) proposed by Thornton and Tuttle (1960); this is simply the weight percentage of the..salic components quartz.., albite.., orthoclase.., nepheline.., leucite.., and kalsilite.

† **2.** *Geol.* Also **Sal.** [a. G. *Sal* (E. Suess *Das Antlitz der Erde* (1909) III. ii. xxiv. 626), f. *S*(*i*+*Al*, chem. symbols for silicon and aluminium.] = *sial (now superseded by that term). *Obs.*

1909 [see *Nife]. **1922** *Geol. Mag.* LIX. 338 Wegener accepts the terminology of Suess, except that he follows Pfeffer in writing Sial instead of Sal. *Ibid.* 340 The boundary of the Sal should therefore be drawn at the foot of the continental slope, where the continental masses begin to rise from the ocean-floor. **1954** R. L. Parker tr. *P. Niggli's Rocks & Mineral Deposits* xi. 476 A granite-gneiss association takes the upper hand and is the reason for calling the entire outer crust the sial crust (sial or sal, containing Si and Al, besides alkalies, as the most important elements).

salable, var. Saleable *a.*

salad. Add: **3.** *salad bowl* (earlier and later examples), *cream* (further example), *-eater, fork, leaf, plate* (examples); **salad bar** chiefly *U.S.*, a servery from which a salad may be obtained; **salad basket,** (*a*) a wire basket in which superfluous moisture is shaken from the constituents of a salad after washing; (*b*) *slang* [tr. Fr. *panier à salade*], a police van, 'Black Maria'; **salad days:** also *attrib.* in *sing.*; **salad servers,** a large spoon and fork for serving salads.

1976 *Amer. Speech 1974* XLIX. 116 *Salad bar*, counter in many restaurants, with ingredients from which the diner can make his own salad. **1978** *Times* 23 Apr. 12/6 The..assistant manageress..led me to the salad bar with its two kinds of salad, four kinds of bread and four kinds of salad dressing. **1906** *Mrs. Beeton's Bk. Househ. Managem.* xxxv. 1092 Where a salad basket is not available, the materials should be well drained and shaken in a colander. **1962** P. Brickhill *Deadline* vi. 83 A row of large 'Black Marias', or, as I learned, '*paniers à salade*' (salad baskets) as the French call them. **1966** J. Dos Passos *Best Times* (1968) ii. 54 The French cooks were already out..whirling the salad around in wire salad-baskets to dry it. **1975** H. McCutcheon *Instrument of Vengeance* iii. 52 There will be a salad basket here soon... What you call, I think, a Black Maria. **1773** J. Wedgwood *Let.* 21 Nov. (1965) 156 Sa[lad] Bowles, and boats. **1867** Trollope *Last Chron. Barset* I. xxxii. 267 A bitter leaf will now and then make its way into your salad-bowl. **1921** *Daily Colonist* (Victoria, B.C.) 22 Oct. 7/7 (Advt.), China salad bowls—hand painted. **1980** *Berkeley Graduate* Oct. 5/2 Even in California, the salad bowl of the nation, thousands of people were hungry. **1976** D. Clark *Dread & Water* ii. 26 A woman..was shaking salad cream from a bottle. **1953** Dylan Thomas *Under Milk Wood* (1954) 60 She whispers to her salad-day deep self. **1963** *Times* 8 Mar. 15/4 This was a young concerto for a young pianist —it was, we have tried to suggest, not such a salad-day reading. **1947** Auden *Age of Anxiety* (1948) iii. 70 The parlour cars and Pullmans are packed also With scented assassins, salad-eaters Who murder on milk. **1917** *Harrods Gen. Catal.* 892/2 Glass salad forks... Prices on application. **1978** *Detroit Free Press* 5 Mar. A17/5 (Advt.), Stainless tableware..setting includes salad fork, dinner fork, [etc.]. **1927** Joyce *Pomes Penyeach*, The still garden where a child Gathers the simple salad leaves. **1881** C. C. Harrison *Woman's Handiwork* iii. 219 The little salad-plates were silver-gilt. **1976** G. McDonald *Confess, Fletch* (1977) xxxii. 150 Sylvia entered with salad plates. The salad consisted of..cold, canned peas. **1907** *Yesterday's Shopping* (1969) 148/2 Salad Servers, boxwood..set 1/1. **1978** 'M. Delving' *No Sign of Life* v. 94 Betsy is a carver... She carves the handles of salad servers and jugs for me.

‖ **salade niçoise** (salad nīswɑz). [Fr., = salad of, or from, Nice in the south of France.] A variety of salad (see quots.).

1955 E. David *Bk. of Mediterranean Food* 160 There may be anchovies, gherkins, artichoke hearts, lettuce... *Salade niçoise*..is made with the same variety of ingredients. **1960** —— *French Provincial Cooking* 145 (*heading*) *Salade niçoise*..The ingredients depend upon the season and what is available. But hard-boiled eggs, anchovy fillets, black olives, and tomatoes, with garlic in the dressing, are pretty well constant elements in what should be a rough country salad, rather than a fussy chef's concoction. **1969** C. Irving *Fake!* vii. 86 A gallery, as Elmyr put it, 'like a *salade niçoise*, a little bit of everything, mostly for the American tourists'. **1975** *Times* 22 July 14/3 Eight dinner guests fed on *salade niçoise* made with fresh French beans.

‖ **saladero** (saladēə·ro). [Sp.] In Spain and Latin America, a slaughter-house where meat is also prepared by drying or salting.

1870 *Weekly Standard* (Buenos Aires) 19 Jan. 8/5 The sales of saladero ox and cowhides during the last fifteen days. **1885** *Encycl. Brit.* XIX. 762/2 The principal prison in the capital of the kingdom [*sc.* Spain] was nothing more than a converted slaughter house where pigs were killed and salted, as its name, the Saladero, implied. **1902** *Encycl. Brit.* XXXI. 461/2 The increase in the herds of recent years has caused the owners of *saladero* establishments in Argentina and Uruguay to try the working of factories in Paraguay for the preparation of *tasajo* (jerked beef). **1930** C. F. Jones *S. Amer.* xviii. 403 As a lean animal served the purposes of the saladero, or salting establishment, the native cattle proved quite satisfactory. **1960** H. S. Ferns *Brit. & Argentina in 19th Cent.* xiii. 416 The old-fashioned *saladeros* supplying the domestic market with fresh meat and foreign markets with dried and salted meat were faced with severe difficulties. **1973** M. Kochan tr. *F. Braudel's Capitalism & Material Life* iii. 135 *Charque*, boned and dried meat produced in the saladeros of Argentina (once again intended for slaves and the European poor), was to all practical purposes invented at the beginning of the nineteenth century.

‖ **Salagrama** (ʃālagrā·ma). Also **Salagram** and with small initial. [a. Skr. *śālagrāma* (see Shalgram).] = Shalgram. Freq. *attrib.*

1801 H. T. Colebrooke in *Asiatick Researches* VII. 240 A Sālagrāma stone ought to be placed near the dying man. **1833** R. Everest in *Ibid.* XVIII. ii. 111, I have several times looked for such among the Salagrams in the Hindoo temples. **1913** J. N. Farquhar *Crown of Hinduism* 267 If he recognizes Vishnu, he may possess a discus, a *salagrama* stone, a conch shell or a *tulsi* plant. **1920** —— *Outl. Relig. Lit. India* vii. 293 The more usual symbols are: Vishnu, the Śālagrāma pebble.

salak (sala·k). Also **salac.** [Malay.] A thorny palm tree belonging to the genus *Salacca*, native to tropical south-east Asia, esp. *S. edulis*, or its pear-shaped edible fruit.

1820 J. Crawfurd *Hist. Indian Archipelago* I. iv. 445 The *Salak*, affords a fruit about the size of a pullet's egg, which consists of a hard stone, enveloped by a firm white pulp, which is covered by thin husks. **1856** B. Seemann *Pop. Hist. Palms* 345 Nothing is recorded of the other species of this genus,—for instance,..the Salak of Penang. **1937** M. Covarrubias *Island of Bali* v. 105 *Salak*, a pear-shaped fruit that grows on a palm, tastes like pineapple, and is covered by the most perfect imitation snake-skin. **1952** W. March *October Island* x. 125 He made up a poem from the names of the palm trees..and..would recite it... Salak, pigafettia, orania palindan,.. And the great royal palm. **1981** *Oxf. Encycl. Trees of World* 259/2 Many palms have edible fruits though rather few are widely cultivated for this product, amongst them Salac (*Salacca edulis*) of southeast Asia.

salal. Substitute for def.: An evergreen shrub, *Gaultheria shallon*, belonging to the family Ericaceæ, native to western North America, and bearing racemes of pink or white flowers followed by edible purple berries. Also *attrib.* (Earlier and further examples.)

1825 D. Douglas *Jrnl. Trav. N. Amer.* (1914) 104 *Gaultheria shallon*; called by the natives 'Salal' not 'Shallon'. **1833** W. F. Tolmie *Jrnl.* 29 Aug. (1963) 230 Have supped on Sallal & at dusk, shall turn in. **1884** C. Phillipps-Wolley *Trottings of Tenderfoot* 140 In front lay in the river-bed a grove of cottonwood, and the bush I think British Columbians call 'sal lal'. **1926** *Daily Colonist* (Victoria, B.C.) 11 July 16/3, I caught my foot in a trailing vine and ploughed head first into the salal bushes. **1946** [see *black-cap 5]. **1952** *Beaver* Sept. 7/1 Fireweed blazes in the rear and salal sprouts out of the unpainted totem poles. **1977** J. Gillis *Killers of Starfish* (1979) xii. 105 She started to lead the way through Mike's pile of salal cuttings.

salamander, *sb.* Add: **3. d.** (Earlier and later examples.)

1755 H. Glasse *Art of Cookery* (ed. 5) 331 Put it in the Oven to brown, or do it with a Salamander. **1943** F. Thompson *Candleford Green* iii. 54 The smith then heated red-hot one end of a large, flat iron utensil known as the 'salamander' and held it above the plate until the rashers were crisp and curled. **1958** *Observer* 18 May 10/5 Caramelise the sugar by passing a red hot salamander very close to the surface till the sugar melts.

e. (Earlier example.) Also (*N. Amer.*), a workman's brazier.

1873 *Chicago Tribune* 3 Feb. 1/7 It caught fire from the 'salamander' used in drying the plaster. **1944** S. Bellow *Dangling Man* 107, I warmed myself at a salamander flaming in an oil drum. **1971** R. Lewis *Fenokee Project* viii. 151 They caught a glimpse of twinkling lights... 'Salamanders... The workers over there have set up fire pots made out of punctured oil drums.'

4. (Earlier and later examples.)

1805 M. Lewis *Jrnl.* 9 Apr. in *Orig. Jrnls. Lewis & Clark Exped.* (1904) I. 289 Their work resembles that of the salamander common to the sand hills of the States of South Carolina and Georgia. **1834** J. J. Audubon *Ornith. Biogr.* II. 264 Thousands of 'mole-hills', or the habitations of an animal called 'the salamander'..presented themselves. **1885** *S. Florida Sentinel* 8 Apr. 1/6 The gophers (Florida salamanders) proved its [*sc.* the garden's] destruction. **1943** A. G. Powell *I can go Home Again* 225 The small burrowing rodent..which others call the gopher, we called the salamander. **1964** W. H. Burt *Field Guide to Mammals* (ed. 2) 136 Southeastern pocket gopher..(Salamander).

6. salamander safe (earlier examples); now *obs.*

1840 *Merchant's Mag.* (U.S.) II. 280 The Salamander Safe. **1845** in C. Cist *Cincinnati Misc.* I. 194/2 These Salamander safes are made of stout, wrought bar and plate iron,.. lined with a chemical preparation, which is a non-conductor of heat, and is indestructible by fire. **1852** *Hunt's Merchants' Mag.* XXVI. 256 In April, 1833 I [*sc.* C. J. Gayler] patented my 'Double Fire Proof Safe'. The same year the name 'Salamander' was applied to it, for the reason that one had been subjected to a very intense heat for a long time, and fully protected its valuable contents.

Hence **salama·nderish** *a.* (*rare*—[1]).

1921 W. de la Mare *Mem. Midget* xxxii. 225 Even my salamanderish body sometimes gasped like a fish out of water.

salamander, *v.* Add: **c.** *Cookery.* To brown by means of a salamander. Hence **sala·mandering** *vbl. sb.*

1878 *Amer. Home Cook Bk.* 65 When it is cooked, glaze the top and salamander it. **1943** F. Thompson *Candleford Green* iii. 54 Another cooking process..which perhaps may have been peculiar to smithy families was known as 'salamandering'.

salame. Delete ‖. **1.** Now usu. in form **salami** (sălā·mi), constr. *sing.* (Further examples.)

1937 *Time & Tide* 11 Sept. 1209/1 Everyone carried a basket with their food for the day—red wine, long rolls of bread, salami, cherries. **1956** A. Wilson *Anglo-Saxon Att.* ii. iii. 363 Tea at Slough was a curious meal. There was *salami* and *mortadella* and caraway bread. **1973** C. Bonington *Next Horizon* x. 146 We had a mass of high protein food; nuts, cheese, salami [etc.].

2. *attrib.* and *Comb.*, as *salami sandwich, sausage*; **salami tactics**, the piecemeal attack on or elimination of (esp. political) opposition (see quot. 1952).

1925 N. Coward *Fallen Angels* in *Three Plays* 258 At the last moment he said he wanted a Salami sandwich. **1977** C. McFadden *Serial* (1978) xlviii. 102/2 I'm not going back to the same old lifestyle with..me making salami sandwiches all the time. **1946** G. Millar *Horned Pigeon* iii. 50 The driver handed out a bit of Salami sausage and a small flask of wine. [**1947** *Time* (Latin Amer. ed.) 9 June 25/1 In Budapest, the citizens considered that the Smallholders' Party had been wrecked. 'Rakosi has eaten the last of the salami', was the word.] **1952** *Times* 19 May 7/3 Mr. Rákosi describes one stage in it as 'salami tactics', by which slices of the Small-holders' Party were cut away and its strength worn down, even while the Small-holders' leader was Prime Minister and Mr. Rákosi his deputy. **1964** *Spectator* 29 May 731/2 Castro's skilful use of 'salami tactics' was helped by their prevailing reluctance to be considered 'witch-hunters'. **1978** *Times* 28 Apr. 17/7 If these salami tactics are continued it will not be long before they [*sc.* Kew Gardens] are closed on every public holiday.

salarian, *a.*[2] Restrict † *Obs.* to sense in Dict. and add: **b.** *Salarian Way*, the name of an ancient road, the *Via Salaria*, running from Rome north-east to Reate (now Rieti) and later extended to the Adriatic.

[*a* **900**: see Way *sb.*[1] 1 c.] **1866** tr. *P. Guéranger's Life St. Cecilia* viii. 87 Two figures in the cemetery of Priscilla in the Salarian Way, have been reproduced by Agincourt. **1945** R. Hargreaves *Enemy at Gate* 38 The Salarian Gate stood upon the Salarian Way, the road by which the Romans had been accustomed to carry sea-salt up to the country of the Sabines.

salariat (sălēə·riăt). [a. F. *salariat*, f. L. *salārium* (see Salary *sb.*) after *proletariat* Proletariate, -at.] The salaried class; salary-earners collectively.

1918 Reckitt & Bechhofer *Meaning of Nat. Guilds* iv. 85 Hypnotized by the round 'O' in the figure of their pay, the salariat feel that they really are important members of the industry. **1922** *Q. Rev.* Apr. 288 The 'salariat' is almost as much enslaved as the proletariat. **1926** *Glasgow Herald* 2 Feb. 8/2 Departmental economies, involving..savings on the salariat. **1937** *Daily Herald* 8 Feb. 13/2 Sir Walter Citrine..stressed the fact that technological progress had enormously increased the importance of the 'salariat'. **1965** *Sunday Times* 17 Jan. 4/1 Mr. Iain Macleod..said..'The age of the Salariat is here, and the age of the wage earner is passing.' **1971**

Oxford Times 26 Nov. 7/2 Most of its members came from the British salariat—he [*sc.* Clive Jenkins] preferred this to the usual term white collar workers. **1978** *Listener* 26 Jan. 106/1 The professions and the salariat.

salary, *sb.* Add: **3.** *salary bracket, -earner, man, officer, scale*; *salary-fixing* vbl. sb.

1969 L. Hellman *Unfinished Woman* vi. 62 We were in what was called 'the same salary bracket'. **1926** *Socialist Rev.* Oct. 47 A minority of salary-earners receive also unearned incomes of varying sizes. **1961** *Guardian* 25 Oct. 1/7 The machinery for salary-fixing in the universities is complicated. **1719** in A. McF. Davis *Tracts Currency Mass. Bay* (1902) 193 Salary Men, Ministers, School-Masters, [etc.]..are pincht and hurt more than any. **1962** *Spectator* 29 June 846/2 Expensive cameras are being crowded out as the ultimate dream of what the Japanese call 'salarymen'. They are being replaced by a little bubble of an automobile. **1816** *Deb. Congress U.S.* 4 Dec. (1854) 240 The only difference between a salary officer and a per diem, is simply in the mode of payment, and not in the amount. **1940** R. S. Lambert *Ariel & all his Quality* xi. 302 Grade and salary scales were defined, and every employee informed where he stood.

‖ **salaud** (salo). [Fr., f. *sale* dirty.] A French term of abuse: filthy beast, 'swine', 'bastard'.

1962 D. Lessing *Golden Notebk.* III. 374 Jules said he would only pay me three hundred dollars for it. Salaud! **1967** C. L. Markmann tr. *F. Fanon's Black Skin White Masks* 11 When in the words of a gang of *salauds* it is no longer possible to find the sense of non-sense. **1971** E. Paul *Reluctant Cloak & Dagger Man* xv. 177 'Salaud,' Jean whispered... 'For that you are going to die.' **1977** Fontana & Van de Water in Douglas & Johnson *Existential Sociol.* iii. 109 In *Nausea* Sartre referred to the others as *salauds* ('swine'). They live a smug existence, feel no anguish, and easily find meaning and justification in their lives.

salbutamol (sælbiū·tămǫl). *Pharm.* [f. Sal(icyl + But(yl + Am(ine + -ol.] A white crystalline sympathomimetic agent which is used esp. as a bronchodilator in the treatment of asthma and is given as tablets of the sulphate or as an aerosol; 1-(4-hydroxy-3-hydroxymethylphenyl)-2-t-butylamino-ethanol, $C_{13}H_{21}NO_3$.

1969 *Brit. Jrnl. Dis. Chest* LXIII. 173 Salbutamol is a new, metabolically stable adrenergic stimulant apparently more specific than either isoprenaline or orciprenaline for adrenergic β_2-receptors. **1977** *Lancet* 23 Apr. 908/2 Aerosolised salbutamol 1500 μg had no significant effect on lung function. *Ibid.* 13 Aug. 354/2 In 208 women in premature labour oral salbutamol 8 mg 6-hourly prolonged pregnancy for more than 2 days in 90% of patients. **1980** *Brit. Med. Jrnl.* 29 Mar. Advt. between pp. x and xi, A metered-dose aerosol delivering 100 mcg salbutamol BP per actuation.

salchow (sæ·lkǫv, sæ·lko). *Skating.* Also **Salchow.** [f. the name of Ulrich *Salchow* (1877–1949), Swedish figure skater, who invented it.] In full, *salchow jump.* A jump in which the skater takes off from the inside back edge of one skate and lands, after a complete rotation, on the outside back edge of the other.

1921 B. Meyer *Skating* 113 *Salchow jump*, outside forward three with jump from the back inside edge to the outside back edge of the other foot. **1930, 1959** [see *axel]. **1968** *Daily Tel.* 6 Dec. 15/6 An inspired Haig Oundjian took the men's title. He never put a foot wrong and his brilliant triple salchow was the jumping highlight of this meeting. **1976** *Times* 19 Jan. 9/7 Beginning with a perfect triple salchow and a soaring double axel, Miss Pötzsch went through her programme with rare charm.. marred only by a two-footed landing of a double salchow. **1980** *Times* 25 Jan. 9/3 The British champion did play for safety by eliminating the two triple jumps he is not totally sure of, the lutz and toe salchow.

Saldanha (sældā·nă). The name of a bay in western Cape Province, South Africa, used *attrib.* in **Saldanha man, skull,** to designate a fossil hominid belonging to an archaic form of *Homo sapiens* or the fragments of it found at Hopefield by Singer and Jolly in 1953.

1953 M. R. Drennan in *S. Afr. Jrnl. Sci.* L. 8 (*caption*) Side view of the skull-cap of Saldanha Man. *Ibid.* 8/2 The Saldanha skull is thus somewhat shorter..than..the Rhodesian skull. **1954** *Amer. Jrnl. Physical Anthropol.* XII. 349 Fluorine tests also revealed that *Mesochoerus* and *Paleoloxodon* lived contemporaneously with Saldanha Man. *Ibid.* 352 The Saldanha skull..at present consists of a fairly complete 'cap' or vault. **1959** J. D. Clark *Prehist. S. Afr.* iv. 83 Saldanha Man may..be considered to be representative of the kind of 'proto-Australoid' individual who was responsible for the final expression of the Earlier Stone Age cultures in southern Africa at the end of the Middle and beginning of the Upper Pleistocene. **1973** B. J. Williams *Evolution & Human Origins* xi. 184/2 The later find of the Saldanha skull provided another specimen almost identical to that of Rhodesian Man.

Saldanier (sældānīᵊ·ɹ). *S. Afr. Hist.* Also **Saldanhar** (-ā·ɹ). [Afrikaans, f. the name of *Saldanha* Bay in Cape Province (cf. prec.).] A member of a Hottentot group that, in the seventeenth century, inhabited the region of Saldanha Bay; an African cattle-dealer.

[**1607** W. Keeling in R. Raven-Hart *Before Van Riebeck* (1967) 36 Saldanians alias Cafares.] **1838** D. Moodie tr. *J. van Riebeck's Jrnl.* in *Record* I. 16 In the evening some of the Saldania Ottentoos came to the Fort... These two Saldaniers were much bolder and livelier men than the Strandlopers who daily live with us, but still having the same language and clothing. *Ibid.* 22 The Saldaniers..lay in thousands about Salt River with their cattle in countless numbers. **1900** A. H. Keane *Boer States* p. xviii, *Saldaniers*, originally the Hottentots of the grassy Saldanha Bay district, who had always plenty of cattle to sell to the Dutch East India Company's people; later, any native livestock dealers. **1972** *Stand. Encycl. S. Afr.* V. 606/2 As soon as they arrived in South Africa the Portuguese..followed by the Dutch colonists in 1652, came into contact with a yellowish brown pastoral people at the Cape. The colonists at first called them Kaapmans and Saldanhars, but later on the name 'Hottentot'..became firmly established.

sale, *sb.*[2] Add: **1. c.** (Earlier examples.)

1866 *Chambers's Jrnl.* 30 June 402/2 (Advt.), Enormous and incredible sale.., for ten days only!!! **1875** L. Troubridge *Life amongst Troubridges* (1966) 124 We.. found a vague little shop where a sale was going on and everything was too ridiculously cheap. We bought some-little silk scarves for a penny three farthings each. **1880** [see *clearance sale* s.v. *clearance 10].

d. *Bookselling.* The ordinary trade rate.

1900 *What will it Cost?* 48 [Trade phrases] *Sale*, 30% discount off published price.

2. f. Now usu. *sale or return*, and freq. *attrib.* (Later examples.)

1952 E. Coxhead *Play Toward* iv. 100 The tickets.. were distributed on a sale-or-return basis to every child in the school. **1954** L. Durrell *Let.* in *Spirit of Place* (1969) 122 The local bookseller..has been pestering me to help him re-arrange his shop... Is there any sale or return system? **1973** *Times* 17 Apr. 23/2 A clause forcing direct-sales firms to offer their goods on a 'sale or return' basis. **1978** S. Hodges *Gollancz* vii. 154 Reg Dignum, the London traveller, persuaded Victor to let him sell it [*sc. Guilty Men*] 'on sale or return', a practice which the firm normally never agreed to.

g. *sale of work*, a sale of articles that have been made by members of an association, congregation, or the like, held on behalf of some charitable, religious, or political object. Also, a commercial sale of handiwork.

1859 in F. K. Prochaska *Women & Philanthr. 19th-c. Eng.* (1980) 258 (*title*) Second annual report of the association for the sale of work by ladies of limited means. **1873** *Young Englishwoman* May 258/1 Can the Editor inform M.A.B. of any repository where needle or network by distressed gentlewomen is removed and sold for their benefit? (New Society for Sale of Work, North Audley Street W). **1890** *New Road Chapel Monthly Visitor* Feb. 18b/1 Sale of work and mothers' meetings. **1905** *Grand Mag.* June 810 Ladies..are informed that..a shop or gallery for the sale of work is shortly to be opened. **1917** F. Klickmann *Between Larch-Woods & Weir* ii. 21 The vermilion satin cushion embroidered with yellow eschscholtzias, that had lain in a trunk in the attic since the last Sale of Work but two. **1969** Joyce *Finnegans Wake* (1964) 446 'Tis post purification we will, sales of work and social service, completing our Abelite union by the adoptation of fosterlings. **1973** A. Behrend *Samarai Affair* iv. 54 A ride round the farm, a coffee morning or a Conservative sale of work. **1976** M. Hinxman *End of Good Woman* vii. 99 The success of the last sale of work.

h. *sale and lease-back*: see *lease-back.

3. a. *sale catalogue, -goer, shop* (earlier and later examples); **sale day,** (*a*) the day on which a sale is held; (*b*) *Austral.* and *N.Z.*, a market-day; **sale-leaseback** = *sale and lease-back* (*lease-back); **sale-yard** *Austral.* and *N.Z.*, an enclosure in which livestock is sold.

1792 J. Lackington *Mem. First 45 Yrs.* xxxi. 329, I soon after this proposed printing a sale catalogue. **1852** *Fraser's Mag.* June 723/2 When he [*sc.* a wholesale bookseller] subscribes a book, or issues a sale catalogue. **1910** *Quaritch's Catal.* No. 286 (*title*) Sale-Catalogue of the library of David Garrick. **1840** *Spirit of Times* 25 Apr. 90/2 Sale days. **1898** *Bulletin* (Sydney) 26 Mar. 31/1 Tuesday was sale-day. Monday afternoon was devoted to the yarding of cattle and the yarding and drafting of innumerable sheep. **1937** *Burlington Mag.* Nov. p. xix/1 Let us hope..that this game..will end on the sale-day. **1948** N. Scanlan *Rusty Road* i. 12 Thursday was Sale Day..market day, they would call it in England, but there was no market in these small New Zealand towns. **1927** *Daily Express* 4 July 3/3 Sale-goers are advised to remember the date. **1973** *N.Y. Law Jrnl.* 1 Aug. 5/3 Private placement of mortgages, joint ventures, sale-leasebacks on income properties and land, [etc.]. **1978** *Detroit Free Press* 5 Mar. B1/2 The sale-leaseback arrangement, which enables the farmer to raise money for new equipment despite low farm prices. **1757** *Connoisseur* (ed. 2) III. 151, I am sure we have cast-off cloaths sufficient to furnish a sale-shop. **1922** Joyce *Ulysses* 285 In Lionel Marks's antique saleshop window..candlestick melodeon oozing maggoty blowbags. **1957** *Beaver* Autumn 38/1 The 'Saleshop' classification marked a modest type of urban transition, from fur trade to general store operation. **1976** *Derbyshire Times* (Peak ed.) 3 Sept. 18/5 (Advt.), Self service grocery stores with modern detached house... Spacious living accommodation..plus saleshop 31ft. × 19ft. 6 ins. fully fitted for the trade. **1901** M. Franklin *My Brilliant Career* iv. 18 He was a familiar figure at the Goulburn sale yards every Wednesday. **1934** [see *backing *ppl. a.*]. **1975** *N.Z. Jrnl. Agric.* Sept. 61/1 Normally stud stock are sold either from yards on the farm itself, or by auction at recognized centrally situated saleyards.

b. *sales appeal, area, campaign, chart, correspondent, curve, figures, force, girl, -goer, graph, -lady* (earlier and later examples), *-manager, -master* (later example), *message, outlet, -people, -person, presentation, promoter, promoting, promotion, volume*; **sales clerk** *N. Amer.*, a shop asistant; **sales drive,** an energetic effort to sell goods extensively; hence **sales-drive** *v. trans.*; **sales engineer,** a salesman with technical knowledge of his goods and their market; hence **sales engineering; sales pitch** [*pitch *sb.*[2] 5 b] = **sales talk*; hence **sales pitchery; sales rep**: colloq. abbrev. of next; **sales representative,** one who represents a commercial firm to prospective customers and solicits orders; a traveller (cf. Representative *sb.* 4 a in Dict. and Suppl.); **sales resistance,** the ability or disposition to resist buying something offered for sale; also *fig.*; hence **sales-resistant** *a.*; **sales room** (examples); **sales slip,** a slip of paper recording the price of an article and other details of its sale; **sales talk,** persuasive rhetoric designed to promote the sale of goods or (*transf.*) the acceptance of an idea; **sales tax,** a tax levied on the retail sales of commodities.

1931 C. Bedell *Seven Keys to Retail Profits* iii. 36 Instead of using a $20 bill to give him *two* profit opportunities, a double sales appeal, many a retailer spends the entire twenty for a quantity of one item. **1936** *Jrnl. R. Aeronaut. Soc.* XL. 289 In the case of commercial aircraft, at any rate, by the gain in 'sales appeal' resulting from the general air of cleanness. **1966** *B.B.C. Handbk.* 39 Another sales area which has great potential—the distribution of programmes for non-theatric use in schools, universities, training colleges. **1969** D. C. Hague *Managerial Econ.* III. xiii. 288 We talk of price wars, sales campaigns, marketing strategies. **1959** 'F. Newton' *Jazz Scene* iv. 72 Rhythm and blues have not only swamped ordinary pop music in America and Britain, at least in terms of the sales-chart, [etc.]. **1934** Webster, Sales clerk. **1968** *Globe & Mail* (Toronto) 17 Feb. 39 A 19-year-old Toronto sales clerk. **1979** *Honolulu Advertiser* 8 Jan. D-3/9 Sales Clerk..full time and part time. Apply at B.S. Co. Ward Warehouse. **1951** in M. McLuhan *Mech. Bride* (1967) 41/3 A book that ought to be read by all advertising writers, sales correspondents, editors and business-paper writers. **1961** *Evening Standard* 14 July 20/3 Sales Correspondent in an expanding Mail Order Organization. **1946** Sales curve [see *roof *sb.* 2 a]. **1969** 'J. Morris' *Fever Grass* ix. 81 You know I'm worth it. Just watch your sales curves. **1951** M. McLuhan *Mech. Bride* (1967) 144/2 Every success drive and sales drive is committed to erasing this [*sc.* resistance] in all its varieties. **1962** *Punch* 21 Nov. 754/1 To..sales-drive their dish-washing machines. **1942** *Sun* (Baltimore) 16 July 2/6 Three self-styled 'sales engineers' stood to garner commission on millions of dollars of Government war work. **1969** *Sales Engineer* Mar. 29/1 (Advt.), A Sales Engineer is any person who is directly or indirectly selling technical products to industry. Sales Engineering is not a trade, it is a profession, and the readers of *Sales Engineer* are professionals. **1966** G. N. Leech *Eng. in Advertising* x. 99 The only criterion of success known to the advertising profession—sales figures. **1934** Webster, *Sales force*, the sales clerks or sales agents of an establishment. **1974** *Times* 9 Mar. 24/6 (Advt.), Opportunity for a girl..to join Sales Force in the exciting new ski development of Anzère. **1980** M. Babson *Queue here for Murder* ii. 21 Soon the Bonnard's sales force would start clocking in, and..after that the customers. **1887** *Courier-Jrnl.* (Louisville, Kentucky) 2 Feb. 4/7 In order to cripple his old partner, he offered superior inducements to the sales girls to go with him. **1978** M. Kenyon *Deep Pocket* xi. 136 The squeak of a salesgirl flattened against a wall. **1925** *Glasgow Herald* 6 Jan. 7/2 The large number of men among the sales-goers. **1967** R. Jeffries *Deadly Marriage* i. 8 I've returned with firm orders for three parlour-sheds... That'll put the old graph up... The sales graph. **1856** *Daily Alta California* (San Francisco) 29 Oct. 4/3 (Advt.), *Wanted*—By a young lady, a situation as *saleslady* in a dry goods, trimming, or millinery store. **1928** *Sunday Dispatch* 5 Aug. 5/6 An amatory porter and a sales-lady sitting on some dirty steps on the Underground. **1976** *Billings* (Montana) *Gaz.* 20 June 8-D/5 (Advt.), Mobile Lot-Imperial Park. All city utili. Call Real Estate saleslady Geri Erickson, 252-0264. **1913** *Writer's Mag.* Nov. 184/2 *The Accountant*, Detroit, Mich., is in the market for interesting business stories—material of interest to business managers, advertising and sales managers, [etc.]. **1933** H. Nicolson *Diary* 5 Jan. (1966) 131 We are then met by..the sales-manager of Doubleday Doran. **1979** R. Perry *Bishop's Pawn* i. 13 My cover as sales manager for a multinational electronics firm. **1922** Joyce *Ulysses* 392 A worthy salesmaster that drove his trade for live stock and meadow auctions hard by Mr Gavin Low's yard in Prussia street. **1966** G. N. Leech *Eng. in Advertising* iii. 30 The kernel of the sales message..has to be in some way special and different for each product. **1957** C. Smith *Case of Torches* iv. 46 We must..keep the Belgian company as healthy as possible otherwise we stand to lose their valuable sales outlets. **1977** *Times* 5 Nov. 12/7 For.. the purchasers of holidays, there will be..a wider choice of sales outlets. **1876** *Scribner's Monthly* Feb. 599/2, I walked through the crowds of purchasers and salespeople. **1976** *Evening Standard* 14 June 24/8 (Advt.), 2 salespeople required to manage small gift shop. **1978** *Tucson Mag.* Dec. 33/1 If you find pleasure in being the only customer in the midst of a convention of used car salespeople, you'll love buying stereo equipment in Tucson. **1920** *Harper's Mag.* June 86 We have long been familiar with *salesman* and *saleswoman*—even, alas! with *saleslady*; and the latest member of the family to whom we have been introduced to, *salesperson*, a name intended to apply to employee of either sex. **1928** *Publishers' Weekly* 10 Nov. 1962/2 We shall be glad to send a complimentary copy of the novel on request to any retail salesperson to read. **1955** *Sun*

(Baltimore) (B ed.) 12 Sept. 10/7 The 'pencil box' she bought for her grandson and which the salesperson called a 'companion', wasn't a box at all. **1976** *Evening Standard* 14 June 24/5 (Advt.), Salespersons required for expanding Northern based home improvement company. **1980** *Times* 18 Feb. 12/6 One of those cheap department stores where you may browse for several weeks without even locating a salesperson at all. **1962** *Listener* 18 Jan. 133/2 Ditchburn went through a masterly sales pitch. **1976** *National Observer* (U.S.) 19 June 1/5 In fact, as things turned out, it was an extraordinary sales pitch for Reagan himself. It drew $600,000 and made Reagan the new conservative star. **1980** *Jrnl. R. Soc. Arts* Feb. 145/2 Managers are impatient and practical people who, having accepted our sales pitch, will want to learn how to use what they have bought. **1968** *Punch* 7 Aug. 206/1 Close scrutiny reveals the fan of a camp follower beneath the canopy; or, perhaps, then as now, she was sketched in merely as a piece of crypto-sexual sales-pitchery. **1947** *Fortune* Nov. 175/1 (Advt.), They bring real 'theater' to a sales presentation. **1981** W. H. HALLAHAN *Trade* iv. 111 My firm is doing the sales presentation for the Essen Arms Company. **1935** *Punch* 4 Sept. 264/1 The great advantage of being a Sales Promoter is that the working hours are short. *Ibid.*, Sales Promoting is one of those lovely jobs in which it is impossible to judge by results. **1916** *(title)* Sales promotion by mail: how to sell and how to advertise. **1964** A. WYKES *Gambling* iii. 70 A young Indian businessman..went to Tokyo on a sales-promotion visit for his firm. **1979** *Jrnl. R. Soc. Arts* CXXVII. 346/2 Ingenuity, in..sales promotion..creates better value for the customer. **1969** *Observer* (Colour Suppl.) 23 Mar. 23/3 Sales reps in their company cars are my number-one headache. **1979** *Business Traveller* Nov.–Dec. 46/1 The sales rep has been sweating it out..in the hope of clinching a much bigger deal. **1949** *Daily Tel.* 21 Nov 2/5 Experienced Sales Representatives. **1981** 'E. FERRARS' *Experiment with Death* iv. 83 He's a sales representative for a firm of confectioners. **1925** *New Yorker* 4 July (verso front cover), 'Beggar on Horseback' presents no sales resistance problem... The buying public flocks. **1933** P. FLEMING *Brazilian Adventure* I. x. 88 Girls..sold flags for the Red Cross... Posters exhorted them to 'give our young men courage': an injunction which I suppose they thought it would be easier to obey if they first broke down the young men's sales resistance. **1972** M. BABSON *Murder on Show* xvi. 185 Heaven help you the day some woman gets her hooks into you—you've no sales resistance at all. **1979** E. H. GOMBRICH *Sense of Order* i. 19 In the history of Greek rhetorical theory such 'sales resistance' developed into an aesthetic prejudice on the part of purists against all forms of verbal fireworks. **1957** *Times Lit. Suppl.* 22 Mar. 174/3 His sympathies are so one-sidedly Jewish that he sometimes makes a reader sales-resistant. **1840** *Knickerbocker* XVI. 226 Ejecting a crowded audience from his sales-room, because an unlucky wight had the temerity to bid six-pence for a tattered copy of Paradise Lost. **1929** W. FAULKNER *Sanctuary* (1981) xvi. 186 The block..was filled by a row of automobile sales-rooms. **1981** *Times* 20 July 18/5 Used vehicle outlets..in.. 'upmarket' salesrooms. **1962** *Lebende Sprachen* VII. 35/3 *Sales slip*, Barverkaufsschein, Kassenzettel. **1965** G. JACKSON *Let.* 25 Feb. in *Soledad Brother* (1971) 64, I asked Robert to send me some shoes... They have to be sent from Sears by the salesman, cost no more than $25, have the price or sales slip in the box. **1976** *New Yorker* 23 Feb. 35/1 Do you have a sales slip? **1926** *Amer. Speech* II. 97/2 Slang is regularly employed, especially in the 'sales-talk' letters [sent by business firms], but it must have a definite snap and appropriateness. **1933** *Punch* 1 Feb. 122/2 'No sales-talk?' 'No... These bolts sell themselves.' **1968** MRS. L. B. JOHNSON *White House Diary* 1 Aug. (1970) 697 Mayor Richard Daley..was giving Lyndon a sales talk about coming to Chicago. **1974** N. MARSH *Black as he's Painted* ii. 52 Motivated by sales-talk and embarrassment, he bought..a cat bed-basket. **1921** *Daily Colonist* (Victoria, B.C.) 27 Oct. 2/6 An important decision affecting the Dominion sales tax was rendered by Judge Gunn here. **1940** *Economist* 31 Aug. 282/1 To secure additional tax revenue, the sales tax has been raised from 5 to 10 per cent [in New Zealand]. **1978** *N.Y. Times* 30 Mar. B1/2 His anti-government attitude and promise to veto any sales tax or income tax the Legislature may pass has won him many followers. **1959** *Listener* 26 Mar. 552/2 In order to increase the sales-volume of a new shade of lipstick.

sale, *v.* For *rare*$^{-1}$ read *rare* and add later *trans.* example.

1922 JOYCE *Ulysses* 555 Lovely ladies saling gloves.

2. *intr.* To hold a sale; to shop at the sales. Hence **sa·ler**, a person who frequents sales; **sa·leing** *vbl. sb.* All now *rare* or *Obs.*

1901 *Sketch* 3 July 443/1 To go 'saleing' in Bond Street. **1902** *To-Day* XXXV. 447/1 All London is 'saleing' at the present moment. **1928** *Daily Express* 19 June 3/2 Men went 'sale-ing' at lunch time. **1928** *Morning Post* 25 June 8 Many experienced 'salers' will tell you that it is an excellent plan to go to the sales with an open mind. **1928** *Daily Express* 5/3 Dec. 5/3 'Saleing' has become a specialised art. **1929** *Ibid.* 8 Jan. 3/4 The great furniture houses are 'saling'.

saleability. Add: Also irregularly **salesability.** (Further examples of the various spellings.)

1940 E. GILL *Autobiogr.* vii. 195 The man who buys in order to sell can only judge of good by the saleability of what he has bought. **1940** M. LOWRY *Let.* 27 July (1967) 33 Whit..has not..wanted to say anything..until some verdict has been reached..as to its salesability. **1972** *Nature* 28 Jan. 232/2 One is forced to the conclusion that the title was chosen with an eye to salability. **1975** *Language* LI. 447 It was a common practice..for grammatical works by well-known scholars to be more or less extensively emended and refashioned by later publishers, in order to enhance their usefulness and saleability. **1976** *Publishers' Weekly* 1 Nov. 70/1 Undoubtedly it enhances gift book salability. **1979** *SLR Camera* Jan. 14/2 Subjects of universal and eternal—as far as saleability was concerned—content.

saleable, *a.* Add: **1. a.** Also *absol.* or as *quasi-sb.*

1945 *Sun* (Baltimore) 4 Aug. 8/7 Five hundred salables were offered and 2,500 went directly to packers. **1946** *Ibid.* 15 Jan. 10-O/2 Salables amounted to 2,500 head, compared with 5,000 head marketed a week ago.

‖ **sale Boche, sale boche** (sal bɒʃ). [Fr., f. *sale* dirty + *BOCHE.] A French term of abuse for a German.

1919 C. MACKENZIE *Sylvia & Michael* iii. 85, I get called *sale boche* if I open my mouth. **1934** D. L. SAYERS *Nine Tailors* 189 A man..called him *sale Boche*—but Jean knocked him down. **1938** L. BEMELMANS *Life Class* I. iv. 67 'Go away!' he repeated. '*Sale Boche!*' I called him a French pig. **1979** D. ROBINSON *Eldorado Network* vi. 53 Marty..blasted off the complete clip in the general direction of Mola's camp. '*Sales boches!*' he spat.

saléeite (sæ·le͡ɪ,ait). *Min.* orig. **saléite;** also without accent. [ad. F. *saléite* (Thoreau & Vaes 1932, in *Bull. de la Soc. géol. de Belgique* XLII. 96), f. the name of Achille *Salée* (d. 1932), Belgian palæontologist: see -ITE[1].] A hydrated phosphate of magnesium and uranium, $Mg(UO_2)_2(PO_4)_2 \cdot 10H_2O$, which occurs as yellow crystals in association with torbernite as an oxidation product of uranium minerals.

1934 *Chem. Abstr.* XXVIII. 5372 Saleite is the Mg analog of autunite. **1940** *Mineral. Mag.* XXV. 643 Saleeite. A. Schoep... The correct form of saleite. **1951** *Amer. Mineralogist* XXXVI. 681 Under the microscope, the saléeite from Portugal appears as rectangular plates with the corners sometimes truncated at 45°. **1959** in G. J. Williams *Econ. Geol. N.Z.* (1965) xiii. 206/2 The yellow coating of secondary uranium mineral..forms small plates and is an unidentified member of the sabugalite-saleeite-novacekite group.

Salem (sēⁱ·lĕm). [Name of a place in Gen. xiv. 18 (Heb. *Shālēm*), understood to be another name for Jerusalem and to mean 'peace' (Heb. *shālōm*).] Occasionally (chiefly in the nineteenth century) adopted by Methodists, Baptists, Independents, etc., as the name of a particular chapel or meeting-house. Hence used as a synonym for 'nonconformist chapel'. Cf. BETHEL 2, EBENEZER 2, ZION.

1857 GEO. ELIOT in *Blackw. Mag.* July 62/1 The Independent chapel, known as Salem, stood red and conspicuous in a broad street. **1880** TROLLOPE *Duke's Children* III. iii. 27 Every Salem and Zion and Ebenezer in his large parish would be closed. **1935** A. CRUSE *Victorians & their Bks.* iv. 66 Most Churchmen really did look down upon the Dissenters... The congregations that gathered in the Bethels and Ebenezers and Salems.. were, for the most part, made up of the less educated and less polished classes. **1963** W. H. BOORE *Valley & Shadow* ix. 43 Salem, Bryncoed, was square and dumpy... The place was private, too—just the Lord and His elect. **1970** *Guardian* 1 Aug. 9/8 The grey chapels called Salem and Zion.

Salempore. Add: (Later examples of spelling *salampore.*)

1883 B. MITFORD *Through Zulu Country* xv. 189 On shelves against the walls are arranged blankets, Salampore cloth, [etc.]. **1928** E. SITWELL *Five Poems* 15 Gaze d' Ispahan and bulchauls, salampores.

sale price. [SALE *sb.*[2]] **a.** Retail price. **b.** A price fetched at auction. **c.** A price reduced for a sale (sense 1 c).

1793 [see SALE *sb.*[2] 3]. **1866** *London Society* Mar. 258/2 The sale price of the 'Marriage à la Mode' cannot therefore be again tested. **1897** *(title)* The sale prices of 1896. **1902** *To-Day* XXXV. 123/1 Some people, so long as they see 'Sale Price'..written on a card pinned to some goods, are content to pay any price. **1940** C. MILBURN *Diary* 31 Aug. (1979) 55, I bought an evening frock in 1919 at sale price for £18 18s. od. **1970** R. JEFFRIES *Dead Man's Bluff* xix. 185 She'd been in and tried on some fur coats, including a mink at sale price. **1974** N. FREELING *Dressing of Diamond* 138 My wife gets her hairdressing free and her clothes at sale prices. **1980** M. BABSON *Queue here for Murder* i. 6 A diagonal red line through the original price and the sale price below it.

Hence **sa·le-price** *v. trans.*, to set at a price for sale.

1959 *Time* 2 Nov. 6/2 In Seattle, the suburban Grinnell & McLean furniture store ballyhooed 'Mother-in-law-Mattresses', sale-priced at $9·95. **1978** *New York* 3 Apr. 74 (Advt.), And for just $50 more, we'll transform the Sofa into a queen-sized sleeper convertible! Of course, we've also sale-priced the pieces separately.

saleratus. (Earlier examples.)

1837 S. GRAHAM *Treat. Bread-Making* 46 Pearlash or saleratus is also used by them in considerable quantities. *attrib.* **1846** *Knickerbocker* XXVII. 510 The white sal-æratus cake and the 'water bewitched' are quickly devoured. **1853** MRS. A. L. WEBSTER *Improved Housewife* 130 Salaeratus Biscuit.

Salesian (sălī·ʃăn, sălī·ʒăn), *a.* and *sb.* [ad. *Salésien*, f. the name of St. François de *Sales* + *-ien* -IAN.] **A.** *adj.* Of or pertaining to St. Francis of Sales (1567–1622), Roman Catholic mystic, or to communities founded by him or living according to his rule, as the nuns of the order of the Visitation founded in 1610 under his direction, and societies founded by St. John Bosco for the rescue of poor and neglected children. **B.** *sb.* A follower of St. Francis of Sales or a member of a Salesian order; a Brother or Sister of one of the orders founded by St. John Bosco.

1836 *Account Conversion of L.T.H. to Holy Catholic Church* 18 Till I had examined the Rules and visited a Convent of Salesian Nuns. **1884** *Month* Jan. 46 His [*sc.* Bosco's] institution henceforth went by the name of 'The Oratory of St. Francis of Sales', and his co-labourers were called 'Salesians'. **1884** H. B. MACKEY *St. Francis de Sales's Treat. Love of God* p. xxxiii, S. Francis also had his special characteristics, which, therefore, are not French but Salesian. **1890** LADY MARTIN tr. *Villefranche's Life Dom Bosco* xx. 232 His first missionary expedition.. included ten priests and coadjutor Salesian Brothers. **1912** *Catholic Encycl.* XIII. 399/1 The Salesians established themselves at Battersea in London. **1928** J. BRODRICK *Life & Work Cardinal Bellarmine* I. ix. 182 There is an added quality in his work, a characteristic Salesian grace which is the best part of it. **1930** *Tablet* 4 Oct. 425/1 This learned and zealous Salesian is already known as one of the ablest men in the Church to-day. **1964** F. D. PARKER *Central Amer. Republics* vi. 179 Five Franciscans and one Salesian. **1974** *Oxf. Dict. Chr. Ch.* (ed. 2) 190/2 *St. John Bosco* (1815–88)... In 1859 he founded the 'Pious Society of St. Francis de Sales', commonly known as the 'Salesians'.

salesite (sēⁱ·lzait). *Min.* [f. the name of Reno H. *Sales* (1876–1969), U.S. geologist + -ITE[1].] A very rare basic iodate of copper, $CuIO_3(OH)$, found as bluish-green orthorhombic prisms at Chuquicamata, Chile, and also prepared synthetically.

1939 PALACHE & JARRELL in *Amer. Mineralogist* XXIV. 388 Salesite is an iodate of copper first found by the junior author in 1936 on the west side of Bench E-4 at the south end of the open pit at Chuquicamata, Chile. **1962** *Acta Crystallographica* XV. 1106/1 Rotation and Weissenberg photographs of the artificial $CuIO_3(OH)$..indicate that it is identical with salesite in cell dimensions and the distribution of intensities.

salesman. Add: **c.** In various *transf.* senses.

1912 J. SANDILANDS *Western Canad. Dict.*, *Salesman*, a commercial traveller, a drummer, a store counter-man, or a man who canvasses real estate. **1930** *Amer. Speech* VI. 134 *Salesman*, confidence man. **1937** *Daily Herald* 15 Jan. 12/8 Increased employment means that people are replacing old-fashioned furniture for [*sic*] new, and the attractive designs made possible by veneering are good salesmen. **1942** BERREY & VAN DEN BARK *Amer. Thes. Slang* § 507/3 *Pimp*; *procurer*..crack salesman,.. salesman. **1944** *Amer. N. & Q.* IV. 10/2 A transportation company in New Jersey now refers to its drivers and motormen as 'salesmen'. **1945** MENCKEN *Amer. Lang.* Suppl. I. 588 American milk-wagon drivers are called *milk-salesmen* and bakers' deliverymen *bread-salesmen*. **1968–70** *Current Slang* (Univ. S. Dakota) III–IV. 105 *Salesman*, n. Pimp; one who sells anything.

salesmanship. Add: (Later examples.) Also *fig.*

1930 *Economist* 20 Dec. 1164/2 The Prince of Wales, who is shortly leaving for Buenos Aires, where he will open the British Empire Trade Exhibition, delivered an outspoken address on salesmanship. **1936** *Discovery* Apr. 129/2 Consult any of the books on psychology and salesmanship so numerous on the market. **1937** WODEHOUSE *Ld. Emsworth & Others* v. 172 When a woman is to all intents and purposes waiting for a demon lover, it requires super-salesmanship to induce her to accept on the this-is-just-as-good principle an Ernest Plinlimmon. **1960** *Farmer & Stockbreeder* 12 Jan. 102/2 Salesmanship in food is liable to be overrated because nothing is more distasteful than..food, when you have had enough.

saleswoman. Add: (Later examples.)

1916 D. H. LAWRENCE *Amores* 97 She puts me away like a saleswoman whose mart is Endangered by the pilferer on his quest. **1932** L. GOLDING *Magnolia St.* III. vi. 548 She's one of the leading saleswomen in our firm.

Hence **sa·leswomanship**, the position of a saleswoman; the character of being a (good) saleswoman.

1973 M. AMIS *Rachel Papers* 28 Gloria held the assistant pet-food saleswomanship in, handily, a Shepherds Bush emporium. **1977** *Church Times* 29 Apr. 11/2, I felt that a little saleswomanship might be a good thing.

salgram, var. SHALGRAM. **salic,** *a.*[2]: see *SAL[4] 1.

salic (sēⁱ·lik), *a.*[3] *Soil Sci.* [f. L. *sal* salt + -IC.] Applied to a soil horizon which is at least 15 cm. thick and is enriched with salts more soluble in water than gypsum (see quot. 1971).

1960 *Soil Classification* (U.S. Dept. Agric.) v. 60/1 A salic horizon is a horizon 6 inches or more thick with secondary enrichment of salts more soluble in cold water than gypsum. **1970** E. M. BRIDGES *World Soils* iii. 24/2 These soils develop a surface encrustation of salt... Such soils possess salic horizons. **1971** *Gloss. Soil Sci. Terms* (Soil Sci. Soc. Amer.) 26/2 A salic horizon is 15 cm or more in thickness, contains at least 2% salt, and the product of the thickness in centimeters and per cent salt by weight is 60% cm or more.

salicaceous, *a.* Add: Also *transf.* (*joc.*), made of willow.

1963 *Times* 13 June 13/3 This makes one wonder whether any of the aforetime Latinists ever called a bat a salicaceous implement.

salicetum (sælisī·tǝm). Also **salictum.** Pl. **saleceta, -cetums.** [f. L. *salix, salic-* willow + *-ETUM.] A plantation of willows, esp. a collection of different species and varieties of willow.

1776 A. HUNTER *Evelyn's Silva* xx. 252 In order to raise a Salictum, or a plantation of Willows for timber, the ground must be dug or plowed; and the cuttings for this purpose should be of the last year's shoot. **1838** J. C. LOUDON *Arboretum* I. I. 129 Woburn Abbey, where a salicetum, or salictum..was planted in 1825. *Ibid.* III. 1477 A Salictum is the only scene in which a complete collection of willows can be displayed to advantage. **1853** C. G. B. DAUBENY *Oxford Bot. Garden* (ed. 2) 16 Salicetum. On the opposite side of the garden outside of the walls, and bordering upon the river, there existed a few years ago a tolerably good collection of Willows. **1875** *Encycl. Brit.* III. 422/1 Mr. William Scaling..cultivates a salictum of about 100 acres. **1926** *Nat. Hist. Oxford District* 73 Many interesting Willows which were formerly grown in the Salicetum in the Botanic Gardens. **1952** G. TAYLOR *Victorian Flower Garden* x. 153 The Willow garden, or salicetum, as it was called, slightly antedates the pinetum. **1972** S. C. WARREN-WREN *Willows* ii. 32 A salictum should be a sizeable area of ground set aside for the express purpose of growing a fully representative group of willows. *Ibid.* 33 It may be considered wise to have two salicta. **1978** A. HUXLEY *Illustr. Hist. Gardening* ix. 307 The numerous species of *Salix* were gathered into salicetums or sally gardens.

salicyl. Add: **sa:licyla·ldehyde,** *o*-hydroxybenzaldehyde, $C_7H_6O_2$, a colourless volatile liquid having an odour of bitter almonds, which is found in oil from meadowsweet and related species, and is used esp. in perfumery.

1869 [in Dict., s.v. SALICYL *attrib.*]. **1896** W. T. BRANNT *Animal & Vegetable Fats* (ed. 2) II. xix. 274 Salicylaldehyde..exists in the oils of meadow sweet and of other species of *spiraea.* **1973** *Nature* 4 May 37/2 Several compounds with specific odours, such as 2,4-pentanedione, morin, salicylaldehyde and acetic acid, are well known chelating agents for heavy metals.

salicylate. Substitute for def.: A salt or ester, or the anion (o-$C_6H_4(OH)COO^-$), of salicylic acid. (Further examples.)

1964 W. G. SMITH *Allergy & Tissue Metabolism* iii. 40 Salicylate inhibits both the 'in vitro' activation of permeability globulin and its action on capillaries. **1972** *Sci. Amer.* Jan. 92/3 Physicians have found that most patients coming to the emergency room of a hospital with massive bleeding of the upper gastrointestinal tract have taken salicylates within the preceding 24 hours. **1977** *Addictive Dis.* III. 284 Researchers have called attention to the hazard to pregnant women of the easy accessibility of over-the-counter drugs such as salicylates.

salie (sa·li). Also **saliehout, zalie.** [Afrikaans, a. Du. *salie* sage.] = *sage-wood* (*b*) s.v. *SAGE *sb.*[1] 5 b.

1819 C. G. CURTIS *Acct. Colony Cape of Good Hope* 72 Saly hout..Hard and heavy. **1908** F. C. SLATER *Sunburnt South* 11 Wild-willows and feathery-flowered *zalie* trees grew in..profusion. **1932** [see *sage-wood* s.v. *SAGE *sb.*[1] 5 b]. **1952** *Cape Times* 2 Aug. 9/3 Among indigenous trees, three are milkwood, salie and Kafir plum. **1973** *Stand. Encycl. S. Afr.* IX. 459/1 Saliehout... Tall, much-branched shrub..with large, simple, opposite, grey-green leaves.

salience. Add: **2. b.** *Social Psychol.* The quality or fact of being more prominent in a person's awareness or in his memory of past experience.

1938 H. D. SPOERL tr. *Stern's Gen. Psychol. from Personalistic Standpoint* iv. 74 The different proportions of salience and embedding give the process and content of every experience its special character. **1938** G. W. ALLPORT *Personality* xx. 553 At other times..consciousness is embedded..more deeply; there is less clearness, less salience. Salience represents an act of pointing, a directedness of the person toward something that at the moment has special significance for him. **1953** C. I. HOVLAND et al. *Communication & Persuasion* v. 155 We shall refer to the degree to which..a specific group is present and prominent in a person's 'awareness' as the *salience* of that group. **1958** W. C. SCHUTZ *FIRO* vii. 147 If the reaction to the anxiety is withdrawal from interchange in that area, the area acquires a negative salience in that the actor tries to avoid it. **1965** T. M. NEWCOMB et al. *Social Psychol.* iii. 58 The difference between the centrality of an object to an individual and the closely related matter of its *salience.* **1972** *Jrnl. Social Psychol.* Aug. 256 Relatively low Salience problems..produced shifts predominantly towards greater risk.

saliency. Add: **2. b.** *Social Psychol.* = *SALIENCE 2 b.

1965 T. M. NEWCOMB et al. *Social Psychol.* ii. 37 The notion of saliency has an interesting counterpart in the information storage of modern 'thinking machines' or large computers.

salient, *a.* Add: **A.** *adj.* **5. b.** Also *Psychol.*, standing out or prominent in consciousness.

1938 H. D. SPOERL tr. *Stern's Gen. Psychol. from Personalistic Standpoint* iv. 74 Dissonance is constant by being augmented or diminished. All experience consequently tends to become either *salient* against or *embedded* with the totality. **1938** G. W. ALLPORT *Personality* xx. 553 The most important of all facts about consciousness is that it is graded; sometimes it stands out, as it were, against the diffuse background of personal life. It is *salient*... The more salient an experience, the greater its objective meaning. **1953** C. I. HOVLAND et al. *Communication & Persuasion* v. 161 A communication will produce more immediate change when the opposing group norms are at a low level of salience than when they are highly salient. **1965** T. M. NEWCOMB et al. *Social Psychol.* ii. 37 We shall use the term 'salient' to describe stored information that has been prompted to the forefront of the individual's conscious thought.

6. Electr. *salient pole*, a type of field pole used in electrical machinery in which the energizing coil is wound on a pole-piece projecting inside the yoke of a stator assembly or outside the cone of a rotor assembly.

1886 S. P. THOMPSON *Dynamo-Electric Machinery* (ed. 2) vii. 121 This pattern differs from that of the better known 'A' Gramme in using salient poles instead of having the 'consequent poles' at the middle points of the electromagnets. **1920** *Whittaker's Electr. Engineer's Pocket-Bk.* (ed. 4) 169 The turbo-alternator is now the standard a.c. generator, and is almost invariably built with a cylindrical (or non-salient pole) rotor, the salient pole construction being confined to slow-speed alternators and water turbine-driven alternators. **1962** [see *ALTERNATOR]. **1970** J. SHEPHERD et al. *Higher Electr. Engin.* (ed. 2) x. 331 An alternative arrangement to having uniform slotting on both sides of the air-gap is to have salient poles around which are wound concentrated coils to provide the field winding. The salient poles may be on either the stator or the rotor.

B. *sb.* **2. a.** A narrow projection or spur of land extending from a larger feature; a spur-like area of land, esp. one held by a line of offence or defence, as in trench-warfare; *spec.* (freq. with *the* and capital initial) that at Ypres in western Belgium, the scene of severe fighting in the war of 1914–18.

1864 W. G. MITCHELL in *War of Rebellion* (U.S. War Dept.) (1891) 1st Ser. XXXVI. I. 359 Conducted General Wright to a point near the Salient we had captured. **1903** A. F. MOCKLER-FERRYMAN *Milit. Sketching & Reconnaissance* ix. 88 Select..a line of level to be assumed as a crest-line, so situated that when drawn-in it will show the shape of all the principal salients and re-entrants. **1914** *War Illustr.* 5 Dec. 366/1 The British salient at Ypres fascinated the Kaiser. **1915** *N.Y. Tribune* 8 May 9/2 The salient at Ypres always has been dangerous. Formerly it made a semi-circular loop, with Ypres a little above the centre. After this successful movement of the Germans it took the shape of the eye in a hook and eye. **1927** R. H. MOTTRAM *Spanish Farm Trilogy* 238 Poperinghe was the railhead for that essentially English battle-field, the Ypres Salient. **1944** *Daily Progress* (Charlottesville, Va.) 2 Oct. 9/4 The British drove five miles north of the village of Oss at the north-western corner of their salient to the Maas. **1972** K. BONFIGLIOLI *Don't point that Thing at Me* xix. 172, I had almost succeeded in becoming..'Mad Jack' Mortdecai, V.D. and Scar, the ice-cool toast of the Ypres Salient. **1974** *News & Courier* (Charleston, S. Carolina) 28 Apr. A-1/6 An officer identified in a national radio interview as Yoav, commander of the southern salient.

b. *fig.*

1936 [see *industrial psychologist* s.v. *INDUSTRIAL *a.* e]. **1969** *Daily Tel.* 31 Oct. 18 With this week's pamphlet on 'The Police and the Citizen'..he will be taking the council into a very hot salient indeed.

salientian (sēɪliˌe·ntʃiăn, -e·ntiăn), *a.* (and *sb.*) *Zool.* [f. mod.L. name of order *Salientia* (J. N. Laurenti *Synopsis Reptilium* (1768) 24), f. L. *salient-em* (see SALIENT *a.* and *sb.*) + -IA[1]: see -AN.] = *ANURAN *a.* Also as *sb.*

1948 *Evolution* II. 29/2 The general trend of modified salientian ontogeny is towards withdrawal of development from water. **1951** [see *CALCAR[2] 2]. **1956** *Nature* 18 Feb. 342/2 How, then, can the salientian trends so clearly shown in the hind limbs and girdle..be correlated with the absence of a functional sacrum? **1973** ESTES & REIG in J. L. Vial *Evolutionary Biol. Anurans* i. 43 This hypothesis does not afford an answer..to the question of placement of salientian origins.

saligram, var. SHALGRAM.

salina. Delete ‖ and add: Also, a low, marshy area of land near the coast (orig. *Jamaican*). (Further examples.)

1756 P. BROWNE *Civil & Nat. Hist. Jamaica* 356 The Samphire of Jamaica... This plant is common in all the Salinas on the south side of Jamaica: it abounds with alkalious salts, but the manufacture of this commodity has not been yet attempted in that island. **1774** E. LONG *Hist. Jamaica* I. II. iv. 474 In making roads to traverse the salinas, or level grounds adjacent to the sea, and in swampy places, a *stratum* should first be laid. **1811** W. J. TITFORD *Sk. Hortus Bot. Amer.* 33 Herbaceous marsh samphire..grows in great plenty in Jamaica, on the Salinas and Marshes near the sea coast. **1889** *Nat. Geogr. Mag.* I. IV. 334 Beyond the narrow gateway in the hills, less than three miles of level swampy *salinas* reach to the surf of the Pacific.

Salina[2] (sălǝi·nă). *Geol.* The name of a town (now a part of Syracuse) in New York State, used *attrib.* and *absol.* to designate a group of sub-stages of the upper Silurian in New York State and adjacent areas, characterized by thick shale formations that contain beds of rock-salt; of or pertaining to this group or the time when it was deposited.

1863 J. D. DANA *Man. Geol.* III. ii. 246 With the opening of the Salina period there was a change by which shales or marls and marly sandstones, with some impure limestones, were formed over a portion of New York. **1905** H. RIES *Econ. Geol. U.S.* vi. 129 The vast beds of rock salt which occur in the Salina (Monroe) are exploited along the Detroit and St. Clair rivers. **1906** CHAMBERLIN & SALISBURY *Geol.* II. 388 Gypsum..is present in the Salina series. **1949** C. O. DUNBAR *Hist. Geol.* ix. 193 In central New York the salt-bearing shales of the Salina group..succeed the Niagaran limestone. **1960** R. L. BATES *Geol. Industr. Rocks & Minerals* vi. 216 An aggregate salt thickness of at least 1800 feet has been penetrated in oil test wells in the central part of the Michigan Basin, where the top of the Salina is some 8000 feet below the surface. **1974** *Encycl. Brit. Micropædia* VIII. 810/3 The Salina Group consists of two shale formations that attain a thickness of more than 300 metres (1,000 feet).

Hence **Sali·nan** *a.*

1909 *Jrnl. Geol.* XVII. 245 (*heading*) The Middle Siluric or Salinan. **1924** C. SCHUCHERT *Textbk. Geol.* (ed. 2) II. xxi. 264 Cayugan or Upper Silurian..Salinan.

saline, *a.* and *sb.* Add: **A.** *adj.* **1. b.** (Earlier and further examples.)

1789 in J. M. Brown *Polit. Beginnings Kentucky* (1889) 255 Kentucky in general appears to be a limestone soil.. abounding in..saline springs, which by simple evaporation plentifully supply the country with salt. **1840** in *Trans. Michigan State Agric. Soc.* (1855) VI. 289 Several saline springs and deer-licks were examined in the valley and vicinity of Maskego river.

5. b. *saline solution* = *physiological saline* s.v. *PHYSIOLOGICAL *a.* 2 b.

1833 J. FORBES et al. *Cycl. Pract. Med.* II. 213/2 In extreme cases, or when the practitioner is not called in till the very last stage of fever, Dr. Stevens thinks life may be occasionally saved by injecting a saline solution into the veins. We have lately adopted this saline treatment in some cases of typhous fever. **1890** F. TAYLOR *Man. Pract. Med.* 105 The intravenous injection of saline solutions has appeared to do good in some cases of profound collapse. **1932** L. N. KATZ in *Practitioners Libr. Med. & Surg.* I. XXV. 1170 Isotonic saline solution injected subcutaneously or intravenously is valuable. **1971** A. C. GUYTON *Basic Human Physiol.* xx. 223/2 The arterial pressure remained normal until the animals were required to drink 0·9 per cent saline solution.

B. *sb.* **3. b.** = physiological saline (see *PHYSIOLOGICAL *a.* 2b). Also *attrib.*

1926 S. WRIGHT *Appl. Physiol.* vi. 245 If saline is injected intravenously into a normal animal, a condition of hydræmic plethora results. **1951** [see *HYPERTONIC *a.* 2]. **1952** E. F. DAVIES *Illyrian Venture* ix. 160 Saline injections followed, bottles hung above me, needles feeding into my arm. **1956** A. C. GUYTON *Textbk. Med. Physiol.* xxvi. 304/2 If the sodium chloride solution is isotonic with the body fluids (that is, the injected saline has exactly the same crystalloidal osmotic activity as do both the extracellular and intracellular fluids), it does not increase or decrease the crystalloidal osmotic pressure of the extracellular fluid. **1971** *Nature* 11 June 344/2 Cholera can be treated by killing the bacteria with antibiotics such as tetracycline and replacing the body fluid lost through diarrhoea with saline.

salinely (sēɪ·lǝinli), *adv. rare.* [f. SALINE *a.* + -LY[2].] In a saline or salty manner.

1929 W. FAULKNER *Sartoris* III. ix. 268 He still felt nausea, and he drank long of the tepid water from the tap. Immediately it welled salinely within him.

salinification (săli:nifikēɪ·ʃǝn). [f. SALINE *a.* + -IFICATION.] The action or process of becoming, or causing to become, saline.

1911 WEBSTER, *Salinification*, process of making salt. *Rare.* **a 1961** in *Webster*, s.v., The..salinification of many agricultural soils. **1979** B. L. C. JOHNSON *Pakistan* v. 78/2 It may be necessary for Sind to restrict its irrigated area in order to ensure that whatever water is applied is given in sufficiently copious quantities to avoid salinification.

salinity. Add: **2.** Special Comb.: **salinity crisis** *Geol.* and *Geogr.*, a period of increased evaporation and salinity in the Mediterranean at the end of the Miocene epoch which resulted in the local disappearance of marine life.

1967 C. RUGGIERI in Adams & Ager *Aspects Tethyan Biogeogr.* 286 The Gibraltar straits (probably the true asylum for the Indo-Pacific relicts during the salinity crisis of the Upper Miocene). **1977** A. HALLAM *Planet Earth* 231/1 This evaporative phase..is known as the 'salinity crisis' because of the extreme effect which it had upon the marine fauna and flora present in the late Miocene Mediterranean.

salinization (sæ:linǝizēɪ·ʃǝn). [f. SALINE *a.* and *sb.* + -IZATION.] The accumulation of salts in the soil.

1928 A. A. J. DE 'SIGMOND in *Proc. & Papers 1st Internat. Congr. Soil Sci.* I. 334 Circumstances under which only the salinization took place, giving no chance for alkalization. **1951** W. P. KELLEY *Alkali Soils* iv. 77 Salinization is the initial step in the formation of an alkali soil. **1973** *Nature* 12 Jan. 105/2 With the available evidence strongly indicating salinity to be the primary cause of woodland mortality, it is necessary to offer some reason for the rapid and widespread salinization of Amboseli basin.

salinometer. Delete the clause beginning '*esp.*' and add further examples.

1963 G. L. Pickard *Descriptive Physical Oceanogr.* vi. 86 One of the great advantages of the electrical salinometer is that it uses a null-balance method. **1977** M. G. Gross *Oceanogr.* (ed. 2) v. 127 Salinometers are commonly used for salinity determinations on oceanographic ships and at shore-based laboratories.

Hence **salino·metry,** the use of a salinometer; measurement of the salinity of water.

1907 in Webster. **1964** *Oceanogr. & Marine Biol.* II. 104 Magazine loading of samples and automatic print-out of results have been achieved for radioactive samples, and similar developments in salinometry would not be impossible.

Salisbury steak (sǭ·lzbəri stēɪk). *U.S.* Also with small initial. [f. the name of J. H. *Salisbury* (1823–1905), American physician specializing in the chemistry of foods + Steak.] A variety of hamburger steak initially promoted by Salisbury.

1897 A. K. Eccles *Man. what to Eat* 9 To cook the Salisbury steak..place the Cakes on the broiler, turning frequently until done. **1914** D. C. C. L. Roper *Scientific Feeding* ii. 61 *Salisbury steak.* Secure some fresh, thick, sliced round steak. Scrape or grind in a meat-cutting machine, and mould into flat, round cakes. Have an iron spider very hot and oiled... Lay the meatcake in, and turn from side to side till cooked sufficiently. **1945** Mencken *Amer. Lang.* Suppl. I. 429 During World War I an effort was made by super-patriots to drive all German loans from the American vocabulary. *Sauerkraut* became *liberty cabbage, hamburger steak* became *Salisbury steak.* **1953** R. Chandler *Long Goodbye* xix. 117 After a while I ..ate one of Rudy's 'world-famous' salisbury steaks, which is hamburger on a slab of burnt wood, ringed with browned-over mashed potato, supported by fried onion rings and one of those mixed-up salads which men will eat with complete docility in restaurants. **1966** L. J. Braun *Cat who could read Backwards* vii. 80 'I'll eat with you' said Quilleran... Odd ordered Salisbury steak. **1970** T. Coe *Wax Apple* xxiii. 162 Two plates of that kind of outsize hamburger usually called Salisbury steak and frequently served in places where large numbers of people are being fed without a choice of menu.

Salish (sēɪ·lɪʃ). Also † **Salisk, Selish.** [Southern Interior Salish *séˀliš* Flat-heads, Northern Okanagan *siylx* Salish: of uncertain ulterior etym.] **1. a.** Formerly, an American Indian tribe of N.W. Montana, also called the Flat-heads (see Flat-head 1); now used to designate a group of American peoples, including the Flat-heads, inhabiting the N.W. United States and S.W. Canada.

The group is freq. subdivided geographically into *Coast(al)* and *Interior Salish.*

1831 W. A. Ferris *Life in Rocky Mts.* (1940) v. 88 They [*sc.* Flat-head Indians] call themselves in their beautiful tongue, 'Salish', and speak a language remarkable for its sweetness and simplicity. **1881** *Encycl. Brit.* XII. 826/2 Selish or Flat Heads. **1910** F. W. Hodge *Handbk. Amer. Indians* II. 415/2 Salish... Formerly a large and powerful division of the Salishan family, to which they gave their name, inhabiting much of w. Montana and centering around Flathead lake and valley. **1933** W. Schmidt *High Gods in N. Amer.* vii. 111 Of the three Amerindian groups whose religions include a High God, the Selish are the most recent. **1978** *Amer. Poetry Rev.* Sept./Oct. 15/3 The organization of the animal kingdom by a lunar divinity occupies a predominant place..in the myths of the Salish of North America.

b. The name of a group of languages spoken by the Salish. (In quot. 1848, the language of the Flat-heads.)

1848 R. G. Latham in *Jrnl. Ethnol. Soc. London* I. 158 *The Salish.*—This is an anonymous vocabulary from Duponceau's collection... It is evidently closely akin to the Okanagan. **1923** A. L. Kroeber *Anthropol.* v. 120 Chinook and Coast Salish, indeed, are in contiguity, and one may therefore have taken up the trait in imitation of the other. **1929** [see *Mosan *sb.*]. **1940** M. W. Smith *Puyallup-Nisqually* 20 Although the language of the Puyallup-Nisqually is classified as Salish, the people themselves used no special language names. **1977** C. F. & F. M. Voegelin *Classification & Index of Worlds' Lang.* 302 The argument for leaving Salish unaffiliated with respect to phylum classification is given by Voegelin and Voegelin (1967).

2. *attrib.* or as *adj.*

1849 in *Ex. Doc. 31st U.S. Congress 1 Sess. Senate* (1850) No. 52. 170 The *Salisk* or *Flat Head* Indians occupy from Bitter Root river, a fork of the Columbia, all the country that is drained by that stream down to what is called the Hell Gate. **1902** *Encycl. Brit.* XXV. 373/1 The Shoshone, Shahaptin, and Salish tribes are of middle stature. **1933** L. Bloomfield *Language* 470 Quilleute, Kwakiutl, and Tsimshian..distinguish between visibility and invisibility in demonstrative pronouns; the latter peculiarity appears also in the neighboring Chinook and Salish dialects. **1965** *Canad. Jrnl. Linguistics* Spring 159 Several other Coast Salish languages distinguish by sex of referent in the older generation. **1977** *Islander* (Victoria, B.C.) 2 Oct. 14/1 She has in her studio..a Salish loom.

Salishan (sēɪ·lɪʃăn), *sb.* and *a.* [f. prec. + -an.] **A.** *sb.* = *Salish 1 b. **B.** *adj.* Of or pertaining to the Salish people or language group.

a **1886** J. W. Powell in *7th Ann. Rep. U.S. Bureau Amer. Ethnol.* (1891) 104 Eastern Vancouver Island to about midway of its length was also held by Salishan tribes. **1897** [see *Kwakiutl]. **1902** G. W. James *Indian Basketry* (ed. 2) v. 51 They are of the Salishan stock. **1937** H. H. Turney-High *Flathead Indians of Montana* i. 11 That much of the North Pacific Coast is inhabited by Salishan people is a well-known ethnological fact. That a portion of western Montana is also inhabited by a Salishan group of tribes is also well-known. **1940** H. Vogt *Salishan Stud.* 1 During my stay with the Kalispel Indians..I had the opportunity of taking down some material on Spokan and Colville, Salishan languages related to Kalispel. **1959** E. Tunis *Indians* viii. 112/2 Not far from the Kutenai, in southern Canada, lived the Salishan tribes, speaking a language that has no traceable connection with any other Indian speech. **1965** *Canad. Jrnl. Linguistics* Spring 88 In Salishan, Kutenai, Quileute and Nootka a *k-* or *q-* seems to be added in the numeral 'three'. **1973** *Amer. Speech 1969* XLIV. 232 Chinook jargon is a pidginized Chinukan-derived contact vernacular with Nootkan, Salishan, English, French, and Algonkian lexical elements. **1977** *Language* LIII. 502/2 In the Salishan languages, as elsewhere on the Northwest Coast, much of the burden which in other languages falls on the syntax is shouldered by the principles of word structure.

‖**salita** (sali·ta). Pl. **salite, salitas.** [It.: see Sally *sb.*[1]] In Italy, an upward slope or incline, a stretch of rising ground.

1910 H. G. Wells *Hist. Mr. Polly* i. 35 Other countrysides have their pleasant aspects... Italy gives salitas and wayside chapels, and chestnuts and olive orchards. **1937** E. Pound *Fifth Decad Cantos* xliii. 16 The kalypygous Sienese females Get that way from the *salite* That is from continual plugging up hill. **1949** —— *Pisan Cantos* lxxx. 89 And Italy one eucalyptus pip From the salita that goes up from Rapallo. **1967** P. E. H. Durston *Mortissimo* xii. 100 A short, bulky Italian..strolled casually toward the steep *salita* leading up to the Pincio.

saliva. Add: **1.** Also *fig.*

a **1957** R. Campbell tr. *F. García Lorca's Romance de la Guardia Civil* in *Coll. Poems* (1960) III. 63 The Virgin cures the children With the saliva of the stars.

2. (See quot.)

1969 P. Hollister *Encycl. Glass Paperweights* 303 *Saliva,* unwanted string or conglomerate of small bubbles that may be the result of insufficient expulsion of internal air or cooling of the gather during assembly.

3. *attrib.*, as *saliva gland*; **saliva ejector,** † **extractor** *Dentistry*, a device incorporating a suction pump, for removing saliva from the mouth during a dental operation; **saliva test,** any scientific test performed on a sample of saliva.

a **1884** Knight *Dict. Mech.* Suppl. 778/1 *Saliva ejector,* an instrument for carrying off the accumulating saliva in dental operations. **1897** E. C. Kirk *Textbk. Operative Dentistry* vii. 157 An excessive flow of saliva is uncomfortable to the patient, by its accumulation it impedes the operation... During the preparation of accessible cavities ..the accumulation may be carried off by the use of a saliva ejector. **1931** N. Bennett *Dental Surg.* (ed. 2) xix. 774 The saliva ejector when first introduced met with considerable opposition, but its use is now almost universal, and if simple aseptic precautions are taken no objection can possibly be found to its adoption. **1963** C. R. Cowell et al. *Inlays, Crowns, & Bridges* v. 53 This permits a saliva ejector to be used, which retracts the tongue and keeps the teeth dry. **1877** J. Taft *Operative Dentistry* (ed. 3) vi. 176 Various pumps were devised for removing the saliva... All..have been superseded by the introduction and use of the rubber dam and saliva extractor... The profession is indebted..for the latter to Dr. J. E. Fisk. **1915** W. Owen *Let.* 13 Mar. (1967) 327, I noticed that my saliva-glands were a trifle addled. **1939** *New Yorker* 8 July 77/1 You might like to know something about just what the New York Racing Commission does to prevent tampering with horses. Every winner gets a saliva test. **1973** J. Thomson *Death Cap* i. 9 The saliva test will prove that the person who licked the stamp belongs to the 'O' blood group. **1975** *Times* 21 May 3/4 Detectives have taken their first saliva test in the hunt for the Cambridge rapist.

Hence **sali·va** *v. intr.*, to salivate; **sali·vaed** *a.*, flecked or covered with saliva.

1939 G. Greene *Confidential Agent* i. ii. 84 He felt her hand rest on his knee: she wasn't romantic, she had said: this was an automatic reaction, he supposed, to the deep seats and the dim lights and the torch songs; as when Pavlov's dogs saliva'd. **1975** J. Goulet *Oh's Profit* xxx. 187 Oh's salivaed middle finger had stumbled across a pocket of ants directly in front of the television.

salivarian (sælivēə·riăn), *a. Biol.* [f. mod.L. *Salivaria*, name of a section of the genus *Trypanosoma* (C. A. Hoare 1964, in *Jrnl. Protozool.* XI. 203/1), fem. of L. *sālīvā-rius* (see Salivary *a.*): see -an.] Used to designate those species of *Trypanosoma* which occur in the bloodstream of the secondary host, and are transmitted from its mouth when it bites a vertebrate. Cf. *Stercorarian *a.*

1969 *Jrnl. Protozool.* XVI. 466 (*heading*) A new organelle of bloodstream salivarian trypanosomes. **1971** P. C. C. Garnham *Progr. Parasitol.* iii. 27 The earlier evolution of these mammalian trypanosomes... At first.. eliminated in the faeces on to the inhospitable ground..; next, in the 'stercorarian' trypanosomes..passed in the faeces and..transferred to the mucous membrane of the new host; finally and best, in the 'salivarian' trypanosomes..the organisms..reach..salivary glands and when the insect next bites, the infection inevitably enters the new host. **1977** Soltys & Woo in J. P. Kreier *Parasitic Protozoa* I. vi. 241 *Trypanosoma* (*N.*) *congolense* is a small salivarian trypanosome and varies in length between 8 and 24 μm. **1977** J. M. Mansfield in *Ibid.* viii. 310 Unlike other stercorarian trypanosomes, *T. rangeli* infects the hemolymph and salivary glands as well as the alimentary canal of its intermediate host. **1980** *Nature* 24 Jan. 383/2 Infection rates of salivarian trypanosomes (subgenera *Nannomonas, Duttonella* and *Trypanozoon*) in the tsetse fly *Glossina.*

salivarium (sælivēə·riŏm). Pl. **salivaria.** [f. Saliva + -arium; cf. med.L. *salivarium* a linen cloth used to catch discharged spittle (DuCange).] A spittoon, esp. one genteelly disguised with a lid, ornamental casing, etc.

1883 *Graphic* 25 Aug. 194 (Advt.), Inlaid Walnut Salivarium, 6s. 9d. **1939** Joyce *Finnegans Wake* (1964) ii. 286 With his primal handstoe in his sole salivarium. **1960** [see *non-U *a.* and *sb.*].

salivate, *v.* Add: **2. c.** *fig.* To display one's relish *at* some prospect or anticipated event, to 'lick one's lips'.

1970 *Guardian* 11 May 10/3 On May 1, the American military were delighted to be unleashed into the Cambodian sanctuaries. One officer said of his colleagues: 'They've been salivating at the prospect of this for months.' **1977** *Times* 1 Nov. 14/6 The double LP set has sold two million copies in America. Pye, who are marketing the records in Britain, are salivating at the sales prospects.

salix (sēɪ·lɪks, sæ·lɪks). [a. L. *salix* willow.] = Willow *sb.* 1.

1775 T. Blaikie *Diary Scotch Gardener* (1931) 61, I found..several sorts of *salixes.* **1965** P. Wayre *Wind in Reeds* viii. 96 A hazel hen feeding quietly among the salix and lichens.

Salk vaccine (sǭlk). *Med.* [Named after Jonas Edward *Salk* (b. 1914), U.S. virologist, who developed the vaccine in 1954.] The first vaccine developed against poliomyelitis, made from viruses of the three immunological types inactivated with formalin.

[**1954** *Brit. Med. Jrnl.* 6 Mar. 593/2 This is..the first large-scale trial of Dr. Salk's vaccine.] **1954** *Jrnl. Amer. Med. Assoc.* 10 July 1021/1 There is no chance that injections of Salk vaccine will cause human Rh-negative subjects to produce Rh antibodies. **1958** *Oxford Mail* 22 Aug. 1/9 Chicago has been completely free from polio this year for the first time, states the Health Department, which credited this to the extensive use of Salk vaccine. **1964** [see *killed *ppl. a.* 1 c]. **1976** M. Grossman in W. L. Drew *Viral Infections* ix. 246 The Salk vaccine is no longer manufactured nor used in the United States.

salle. Add: **1. a.** (Earlier and later examples.)

1765 H. Walpole *Let.* 5 Dec. (1904) VI. 375 You may go into the *petit cabinet*, and then into the great *salle*, and the gallery. **1913** H. James *Small Boy & Others* xxv. 359, I..enjoyed the commemorative show of Delaroche given ..in one of the rather bleak *salles* of the École des Beaux-Arts.

b. = *salle de jeu* (see sense 2 below).

1886 C. M. Yonge *Chantry House* II. xv. 144 Martyn was doing his best for him..while Lady Peacock was at the *salle.* **1966** G. Greene *Comedians* i. iii. 89, I watched him leave the *salle.* He had over three hundred dollars to change now. **1970** 'J. Morris' *Candywine Devel.* xxiii. 247 He stood at the big roulette table in the main *salle.*

c. = *salle d'armes* (see sense 2 below).

1961 F. C. Avis *Sportman's Gloss.* 197/1 *Salle*, the fencing hall or studio, often open to the public. **1973** *Where* Mar. 73/3 Among the luxuries enjoyed by school C..a fencing salle. **1975** *Oxf. Compan. Sports & Games* 306/2 A few schools, such as that of the famous *Angelos* and the *London Fencing Club*, founded in 1848, kept the sport alive in a few London *salles*, some public schools, and the universities.

2. salle d'armes (sal darm), a fencing-room, school or club; **salle d'attente** (earlier and later examples); **salle d'audience** (sal dodyãns), a court-room; **salle d'eau** (sal do), a wash-room, shower-room; **salle de jeu** (sal də ʒö), a gambling house or room; **salle des pas perdus** (sal de pā pɛrdü), a waiting-hall (at a law-court, station, etc.), lobby; **salle privée** (sal prīve), a private gambling room in a casino.

1885 E. Castle *Schools & Masters of Fence* x. 159 How different a 'salle d'armes' in Paris or London in those days from the old Italian schools of Queen Bess and Henri III. **1902** G. B. Shaw *Let.* 4 Mar. (1972) II. 269 There should be a salle d'armes where stage combats & wrestlings could be practised. **1952** *Fencing* ('Know the Game' Ser.) 19/1 In a friendly encounter in the Salle d'Armes (Fencing Room) or Club, the sporting tradition of acknowledging a hit has been jealously preserved. **1863** *Miss Jemima's Swiss Jrnl.* 26 June (1963) i. 9 Passengers..are locked in the *salle d'attente* until the arrival of the train. **1909** E. Nesbit *Daphne in Fitzroy St.* iv. 44 The rout of dark-skinned, browbent, hurrying, preoccupied French folk.. in the *salle d'attente* at the station. *a* **1666** Evelyn *Diary* an. 1644 (1955) II. 98 Within are severall Chambers, Courts, Treasures &c above that most rich and glorious Sale de l'Audiens. **1957** L. Durrell *Spirit of Place* (1969) 138 Of course no lavatories and *salle d'eau* a rarity. Even in this lovely villa we wash from a bucket. **1964** *Punch* 14 Oct. 573/3 Town-dwellers in France who have a *salle d'eaux* [*sic*]..of their own. **1968** D. Torr *Treason Line* 130 They were in the *salle des jeux* [*sic*], the hushed sanctuary of the temple of chance. **1901** V. BETHELL *Monte Carlo Anecdotes* 4 In the year 1858 a grand banquet was held to inaugurate the opening of his *Salle-de-Jeux*. **1839** *Indispensable Eng. Vade Mecum Paris* 135 The most remarkable hall is that named *la salle des Pas-Perdus*, being 222 feet long, by 84 wide. **1885** H. JAMES *Little Tour in France* xvii. 120 The curious *salle des pas perdus*, or central hall, out of which the different tribunals open.. is a feature of every French court-house. **1977** *Listener* 10 Feb. 183/1 The image is growing on me of Limbo as a large railway terminus..where the dead hang about in a *salle des pas perdus*. **1930** E. WAUGH *Labels* ii. 35 The cinema producer's version of the *salles privées*, with jewelled courtesans and ribboned grand-dukes, is a thing of the past. **1976** H. MACINNES *Agent in Place* xiv. 153 There were two wings..the left one consisted of the *Salle Privée*.

3. With varying pronunc. (sāl, sǭl). Also † **saul.** The finishing department of a paper-mill, in which sheets of paper are examined, sorted and packed.

1819 *Rees's Cycl.* XXVI. s.v. Paper, The paper, being sufficiently dried for the last time, is carried to the building where it is examined, finished, and pressed: this is called the *Saul*. **1854** C. TOMLINSON *Cycl. Useful Arts* II. 364/1 The paper..is taken down, carried to a building called the Saul..where it is examined, finished, and pressed. **1888** CROSS & BEVAN *Paper-Making* 175 The sheets of paper are now ready to be examined before being finally sent away from the mill. This is done in the 'Finishing-house', or 'Salle' as it is sometimes called. **1946** H. WHETTON *Pract. Printing & Binding* xxviii. 345/1 If the paper is being sold in sheets it goes to the 'salle' or finishing department, where each sheet is examined top and bottom..and sorted. **1976** *Oxford Times* (City ed.) 12 Mar. 1/7 Sogat members at Wolvercote Mill could not recommend acceptance of the management's latest proposals for the 70 men in the salle.

sallee, var. *SALLY *sb.*[4]

sallow, *sb.* Add: **4. b. sallow (wattle),** one of several Australian acacias that resemble willows in habit or foliage.

1884 A. NILSON *Timber Trees New South Wales* 21 *A[cacia] dealbata*.—Silver Wattle; Sallow. **1965** *Austral. Encycl.* VII. 539/2 *A[cacia] longifolia, A. mucronata* and several related species with long flower-spikes are known as sallow wattles in Victoria.

sallow, *a.* Add: **c.** Also *sallow-hued, -thinking*.

1910 W. DE LA MARE *Three Mulla-Mulgars* 81 There came spindling along an old sallow-hued Earth-mulgar. **1606** MARSTON *Parasitaster* III. sig. E1, A blacke hayred, pall-fac'de, sallowe thinking Mistresse.

† **Sally** (sæ·li), *sb.*[3] *Obs.* Corruption of SAL ENIXUM. Also **Sally Nixon.**

1879 G. LUNGE *Sulphuric Acid* II. ii. 19 Sulphate known as 'nitre-cake', 'salonix' (=sal enixum), or 'sally'. **1882** W. CROOKES *Dyeing & Tissue-Printing* 81 The crystallized sulphate of soda, known..in many dye-houses as Sally Nixon.

sally (sæ·li), *sb.*[4] *Austral.* Also **sallee.** [Variant of SALLOW *sb.*] One of several eucalypts or acacias that resemble willows in habit or appearance; (see quot. 1965).

1884 A. NILSON *Timber Trees New South Wales* 22 *A[cacia] falcata*.—Hickory; Sally;.. Willow. **1889** J. H. MAIDEN *Useful Native Plants Austral.* 149 *Acacia falcata*, ..'Hickory'. 'Lignum-Vitae'. 'Sally'. *Ibid.* 250 *Eucalyptus stellulata*,..'Sally' or 'Black Gum'. *Ibid.* 335 *Acacia falcata*... Called variously 'Hickory',..and 'Sally' or 'Sallee'. **1932** R. H. ANDERSON *Trees New South Wales* 58 Snow Gum or White Sally. *Ibid.*, Black Sally..Also known as Sally or Muzzlewood. **1941** BAKER *Dict. Austral. Slang.* 62 Sally: an acacia. **1949** J. WRIGHT *Woman to Man* 17 In the olive darkness of the sally-trees Silently moved the air. **1957** *Forest Trees Austral.* (Austral. Forestry & Timber Bureau) 96/2 Swamp gum or broad leaved sally..occurs in cold and damp situations. *Ibid.* 144/1 White sallee is usually only 30–60 feet in height. **1965** *Austral. Encycl.* VII. 539/2 Sallee, or sally, a corruption of the English 'sallow' which is applicable to certain willow species..and commonly used for Australian eucalypts and wattles that are supposed to resemble them in habit or foliage. Black sallee and white sallee are the names standardized in the timber trade for the cold-loving *Eucalyptus stellulata* and *E. pauciflora* respectively. *Acacia floribunda* and *A. prominens* are among the eastern wattles which have been called sally.

Sally (sæ·li), *sb.*[5] *colloq.* [Alteration of SALVATION (ARMY).] **1. a.** The Salvation Army. Also with *the*, and *attrib.*

1915 *N.Y. World Mag.* 9 May 14/3 *Sally*, nickname for Salvation Army. **1931** 'D. STIFF' *Milk & Honey Route* v. 52 The Salvation Army, more intimately known in Hobohemia as 'The Sally'. **1977** *Gay News* 7–20 Apr. 7/3 (*heading*) Sally soldier... A Salvation Army social worker who indecently assaulted young boys was sent to jail for three years at the Old Bailey recently.

b. A member of the Salvation Army; usu. *pl.*, the Salvation Army.

1936 I. L. IDRIESS *Cattle King* xx. 189 The surest place to find Sid Kidman, when in town on a Saturday night, was among the crowd around the 'Sallies'. **1942** BERREY & VAN DEN BARK *Amer. Thes. Slang* §327/4 *Sally*, a Salvation Army girl. **1957** D. NILAND *Call me when Cross turns Over* ii. 31 The woman that runs it, she used to be some sort of a high-up with the Sallies down in Sydney. **1966** A. LA BERN *Goodbye Piccadilly* iv. 43 The constable recommended the Salvation Army hostel... Why not? Better men than Dick Blamey have slept with the 'Sallies'. **1977** C. MCCULLOUGH *Thorn Birds* iii. 65 It's a hotel for the workingman run by the Sallies.

2. A Salvation Army hostel.

1931 'D. STIFF' *Milk & Honey Route* 213 *Sallies*, Salvation Army hotels and industrial workshops. **1966** *New Statesman* 1 Apr. 479/2 Julie Felix sang against the Salvation Army—and we were..miles away from the sad Sally where the meth-drinkers are deloused. **1977** *Church Times* 18 Nov. 9/1 He knew that the only other places to find a bed—the 'Sally', the Cyrenian shelter, even the fairly distant 'Spike'—would not have him that night.

3. *Comb.*, as **Sally Ann(e)** [colloq. alteration of *Army*], the Salvation Army; a Salvation Army hostel; **Sally Army,** the Salvation Army.

1927 *Amer. Speech* II. 387/1 *Sally Ann* is the sobriquet for Salvation Army. **1961** W. A. HAGELUND *Flying Chase Flag* iii. 48 Now you go see the Major at the Johnson Street Sally Anne about some meal tickets and beds. **1976** *New Society* 5 Aug. 290/3 The Salvation Army?.. You'd never get me sleeping there... Everyone knows you pick all sorts of things up from the Sally Ann. **1961** E. WILLIAMS *George* xxiii. 386 Your dear Brother Tom has celebrated his thirteenth birthday with buying a uniform for the Sally Army. *Ibid.* xxvi. 441 Tom sat uneasily polishing his Sally-Army trumpet. **1978** *Guardian* 9 Aug. 7/5 At Christmas, the Sally Army gave her a slap-up lunch.

sally, *v.*[2] Add: **4. a.** Also **saully.** To move, sway, or run from side to side (see quot. 1887 and cf. SALLY *sb.*[1] 7); to progress by making a rocking movement from side to side. *dial.* and *Naut.*

1825 J. T. BROCKETT *Gloss. North Country Words* 181 *Sally*, to move or run from side to side; as is customary with the persons on board of a ship after she is launched. **1887** D. DONALDSON Jamieson, Suppl. 210 To *Sally*, *Saully*,.. to move or run from side to side, as children do in certain games, and as workmen do on board a ship after it is launched; to rock or swing from side to side, like a small boat at anchor; also, to rise and fall, like a ship on a rough sea. **1972** *Daily Tel.* 15 July 3/8 He told the court that he was 'sallying' down Lowther Street when a policeman stopped him. Asked by the Judge what 'sallying' meant, he said: 'I was just sitting on the saddle pushing the bike along with my foot on the kerb.'

b. *trans.* To rock (a stationary or slow-moving ship) by running from side to side in order to assist its progress. *Naut.*

1919 E. SHACKLETON *South* i. 33 The engines running full speed astern produced no effect until all hands joined in 'sallying' ship.

Sally Lunn. Add: **1.** (Earlier example.)

1780 P. THICKNESSE *Valetudinarian's Bath Guide* (ed. 2) iii. 12, I had the misfortune to lose a beloved brother in the prime of life, who dropt down dead as he was playing on the fiddle at Sir Robert Throgmorton's, after drinking a large quantity of Bath Waters, and eating a hearty breakfast of spungy hot rolls, or *Sally Luns*.

2. Applied loosely to several varieties of yeast and soda bread, esp. in the southern United States. Also *attrib.*

1901 *Picayune's Creole Cook Bk.* (ed. 2) 407/2 Sally Lunn is nothing more than the old breakfast dish known to the Creoles for generations as 'Pain à la Vieille Tante Zoë'. **1933** F. M. FARMER *Boston Cooking-School Cook Bk.* (rev. ed.) 53 Sally Lunn Tea Cakes... Make like Raised muffins. **1976** M. G. EBERHART *Family Fortune* vii. 70 Alice was tucking food away..Alice asked for more Sally Lunn.

Sally Nixon: see *SALLY *sb.*[3]

sallyport. 3. (Earlier example.)

1814 JANE AUSTEN *Mansf. Park* III. vii. 161 The three boys..determined to see their brother..to the salley-port.

Salmanazar (sælmănē[i]·zăɹ). Also **Salmanasar.** [ad. *Salmanasar*, the form in the Vulgate of the name of *Shalmaneser*, King of Assyria (II Kings xvii, xviii).] A large size of wine-bottle. Cf. *BALTHAZAR, JEROBOAM, *REHOBOAM 2.

1935 A. L. SIMON *Dict. Wine* 225 *Salmanazar*, the fancy name given to a fancy bottle large enough to hold a dozen reputed quarts, or 9·60 litres, equal to 338·025 fluid ounces. **1959** *Gloss. Terms Packaging* (B.S.I.) 28 *Salmanazar*, a wine bottle—capacity 12 reputed quarts. **1962** [see *BALTHAZAR]. **1978** *Daily Tel.* 13 June 16/2 Edward Heath is to be given a salmanazar of champagne... A salmanazar contains the equivalent of 14 ordinary bottles.

salmine (sæ·lmīn). *Biochem.* Also **-in** (-in). [ad. G. *salmin* (A. Kossel 1896, in *Zeitschr. f. physiol. Chem.* XXII. 180), f. L. *salm-o* salmon: see -INE[5].] A protein, one of the protamines, isolated from the sperm of the salmon and related species.

1896 *Jrnl. Chem. Soc.* LXX. I. 582 The sulphate [of the protamine] from salmon sperm has the formula $C_{16}H_{31}N_9O_3,H_2SO_4$. That from sturgeon sperm has rather different solubilities in sodium chloride solutions, and the names *salmine* and *sturine* are suggested by [*sic*] the two protamines. **1949** *Proc. Soc. Exper. Biol. & Med.* LXX. 494/1 Salmin, an acid hydrolysis, was shown to yield arginine, proline, serine, valine, alanine, and isoleucine. **1963** F. HAUROWITZ *Chem. & Function of Proteins* (ed. 2) ii. 18 Heterogeneities have also been discovered..in the protamines clupein and salmine of fish sperm.

salmon, *sb.*[1] and *a.* Add: **A.** *sb.* **3.** (Earlier example.)

1873 [see *PAPER *sb.* 8 b].

4. a. *salmon boat, fishery* (earlier example), *mousse, paste* (PASTE *sb.* 1 d), *river* (later examples); *salmon fly* (later examples), *gaff*.

1894 *Rudder* Mar. 77 White Class—Salmon boat, Canthelpit, Captain Jacobsen. **1905** J. LONDON *Tales of Fish Patrol* 23 The salmon boat got out its oars. **1732** *Calendar State Papers: Colonial Ser.* (Publ. Rec. Office) (1939) XXXIX. 226 The salmon fishery is still carried on in the several rivers and to advantage. **1856** 'STONEHENGE' *Man. Brit. Rural Sports* v. ii. 246/1 Salmon-flies are made on the same principle as the trout-flies. **1927** M. ASQUITH *Lay Sermons* v. 106 The Durham Ranger and Black Dog are salmon-flies. [**1907** *Yesterday's Shopping* (1969) 669/3 Gaffs..Salmon and Pike.] **1922** JOYCE *Ulysses* 558 Follow the footpeople with knotty sticks, salmongaffs. **1936** LUCAS & HUME *Au Petit Cordon Bleu* 43 Put a little of the aspic into a pan... Run a thin coating of this jelly on the top of the salmon *mousse*. **1972** K. STEWART *Times Cookery Bk.* vi. 84 Salmon mousse... Allow several hours for mousse to chill. [**1917** *Harrods Gen. Catal.* p. lxvii/6 Salmon..and Shrimp Paste.] **1939** T. S. ELIOT *Old Possum's Bk. Pract. Cats* 45 You might now and then supply.. Some potted grouse, or salmon paste. **1771** G. CARTWRIGHT *Jrnl.* 29 May (1792) I. 127 At the head of this place we found a very fine salmon river. **1886** *Critic* 16 Oct. 183 A map and an annotated list of salmon-rivers locate them chiefly north of the St. Lawrence. **1968** R. M. PATTERSON *Finlay's River* 88 The Yukon, a salmon river with a name nobody had ever heard of and which was not to be found on any map.

b. *salmon-fisher* (earlier and later examples).

a **1670** [see COBLE[1] 1]. **1771** T. PENNANT *Tour in Scotl. 1769* 148 Near is a cave, where the Salmon-fishers lie during the season. **1925** F. SCOTT FITZGERALD *Great Gatsby* vi. 118 He had been beating his way along the south shore of Lake Superior as a clam-digger and a salmon-fisher.

4. c. salmon bass *S. Afr.* = *KABELJOU; **salmon berry,** substitute for def.: *N. Amer.*, one of several species of *Rubus*, esp. the white-flowered *R. chamæmorus* and *R. parviflorus* or the pink-flowered western raspberry, *R. spectabilis*; also *attrib.*; (earlier and later examples); **salmon coble** (further examples); **salmon-colour** (earlier example); **salmon disease,** (*a*) a fatal epidemic skin disease of salmon; (*b*) = *salmon poisoning* below; **salmon gum** (see quot. 1883); **salmon-pink,** an orange-pink shade (cf. sense B in Dict.); **salmon poisoning,** a fatal disease of dogs on the Pacific Coast of North America which affects lymphoid tissue and the central nervous system and is caused by rickettsias present in flukes infesting ingested salmon; **salmon pool** (further examples).

1929 *Hardy's Anglers' Guide* (ed. 51) 48 The Kabeljaauw, known in Natal as Salmon Bass..runs to as much as 150 lbs. **1957** S. SCHOEMAN *Strike!* iii. 70 The very big ones are variously referred to as..salmon, salmon bass and often even Cape salmon if caught from East London to Durban. **1844** A. SYLVESTER *Jrnl.* in *Oregon Hist. Q.* (1933) XXXIV. 359 A salmon berry..being put into the mouth of a fish [*sc.* a salmon], destroys the charm. *a* **1861** Salmon-berry [see *HIAQUA]. **1901** J. GRINNELL *Gold Hunting in Alaska* 16 The other day we picked three quarts of salmon berries. **1971** *Islander* (Victoria, B.C.) 14 Mar. 16/2 Directing their steps toward the beach..they hurried..through the salmonberry thicket. **1977** J. GILLIS *Killers of Starfish* (1979) xxii. 217 A precipitous tangle of salmonberry and alder. **1881** W. GREGOR *Notes Folk-lore N.-E. Scotl.* 146 In going past a salmon cobble in the harbour, a fisherman would not have allowed his boat to touch it. **1973** W. ELMER *Terminol. Fishing* iii. 78 The salmon coble..differs in structure from the rest of the cobles. **1813** J. CONSTABLE *Let.* 30 June (1964) II. 109 The paper will be a sort of salmon color and the sofa & chairs crimson. **1880** *Proc. R. Soc. Edin.* X. 242, I am led to believe that the so-called salmon disease does not depend upon a pre-diseased condition of the fish. **1950** *Amer. Jrnl. Path.* XXVI. 617 (*heading*) The pathology and etiology of salmon disease in the dog and fox. **1964** G. W. STAMM *Dog Owner's Vet. Guide* 79 Salmon disease has been successfully treated with certain sulfa drugs and with penicillin. **1971** D. MILLS *Salmon & Trout* iii. 91 The salmon is subject to a number of diseases... The diseases include furunculosis, Dee disease, kidney disease, salmon disease,..and columnaris. [**1883** F. VON MUELLER *Eucalyptographia* IX, *Eucalyptus salmonophloia*... A tree, when aged, attaining to fully 100 feet in height, known vernacularly as the 'Salmon-colored Gumtree', in allusion to the smooth grey and somewhat purplish bark of an oily lustre.] **1934** *Bulletin* (Sydney) 24 Oct. 20/3 A Digger mate and myself saw three salmon gums, trees of the Westralian wheatbelt and eastern goldfields. **1969** CHIPPENDALE & JOHNSTON *Eucalypts* 72/1 The salmon gum has been regarded as an indicator of good, loamy soil on which much of the West Australian wheatbelt is developed. **1884** Salmon-pink [see *CREVETTE]. **1979** *Country Life* 24 May 1618/3 The salmon-pink of dawn. **1925** *Jrnl. Amer. Vet. Med. Assoc.* LXVI. 638 A microscopic cyst has been found in the muscle of 'sore-back' salmon. When these fish were fed to dogs typical symptoms of so-called salmon poisoning were produced. **1974** T. MCGINNIS *Well Dog Bk.* 74 This fluke is host to an organism (a rickettsia) which causes a severe disease called salmon poisoning. **1874** W. LENNOX *My Recoll.* II. 72 My guide then informing me that within three miles there were several salmon pools, I lost no time in proceeding there. **1892** Salmon pool [*EASY B. 4 b].

Salmonella (sælmǫ̆ne·lă). *Bacteriol.* Also **salmonella.** Pl. **-ellæ, -ellas,** (*erron.*) **-ella.** [mod.L. (coined in Fr. by J. Lignières 1900, in *Bull. de la Soc. centrale de Méd. Vét.* XVIII. 389), f. the name of Daniel Elmer *Salmon* (1850–1914), U.S. pathologist + L. *-ella* (see -EL².).] **1.** A member of the genus of pathogenic, Gram-negative, rod-shaped bacteria so called, which includes some causing food poisoning, typhoid, and paratyphoid in man and various diseases in domestic animals.

1913 H. J. HUTCHENS tr. *Besson's Pract. Bacteriol.* 442 Lignières proposed to designate all those organisms which had the morphological and cultural attributes of the bacillus of hog-cholera..by the name Salmonella after Salmon. **1920** *Lancet* 10 Jan. 96/2 So long as there appeared to be but two types in this group of the Salmonellas,..there was little need to find a name in common for them. **1932** J. H. DIBLE *Rec. Adv. Bacteriol.* (ed. 2) iv. 79 White..adduces evidence of the presence of common antigenic complexes, relating these to the enteric and food-poisoning salmonellas. **1944** L. R. THOMPSON *Introd. Microorganisms* xix. 269 Salmonella have been ingested with meats, fish,..dairy products,..and drinking water. **1951** *Chambers's Jrnl.* Oct. 588/1 Dr. Williams Smith and Professor J. C. Cruickshank have been inquiring into the danger cats and dogs may convey by acting as reservoirs of the salmonellæ, noxious bacteria which cause food-poisoning in man. **1979** *Daily Tel.* 19 Sept. 12/8 Twenty-seven of 64 samples of poultry manure yielded salmonella. **1980** *Brit. Med. Jrnl.* 29 Mar. 928/2 Zoonotic pathogens, such as salmonellas.., may be present in any type of slurry.

2. = *SALMONELLOSIS.

1962 *Telegraph* (Brisbane) 27 Aug. 32/2 He believed there was a risk in the sale of kangaroo meat. It..carried Q fever and salmonella. **1977** *Shooting Times & Country Mag.* 13–19 Jan. 27/3 There is still the possibility of such diseases as forms of Salmonella (now a notifiable disease) being spread over a wide area.

3. *attrib.*

1916 A. I. KENDALL *Bacteriol.* xv. 344 These organisms are variously known as the hog cholera, Salmonella, Gärtner, enteritidis, intermediate, paracolon or paratyphoid group. **1920** *Lancet* 10 Jan. 95/1 The whole Salmonella group is considered a particularly variable one. **1925** J. W. BIGGER *Handbk. Bacteriol.* xxviii. 259 There are two chief types of bacilli which are responsible for isolated cases or epidemics of food poisoning... Both these are exceedingly closely related to B[acillus] paratyphosus B, and together with it form what is called the 'Salmonella' group. **1963** *Lancet* 19 Jan. 161/1 Most outbreaks of salmonella infection result from the contamination of a single article of food which is then eaten by a number of individuals. **1979** *Daily Tel.* 9 Aug. 7/3 A woman..died in hospital after an outbreak of salmonella food poisoning.

salmonellosis (sæ:lmǫ̆nelōᵘ·sis). *Path.* Also **Salmonellosis.** [ad. F. *salmonellose* (J. Lignières 1901, in *Recueil de Méd. Vét.* VIII. 416), f. prec.: see -OSIS.] Infection with or a disease caused by salmonellæ.

1913 in DORLAND *Med. Dict.* (ed. 7). **1931** *Nomencl. Diseases* (Min. of Health) (ed. 6) 104 *Bacterium (Salmonella) enteritidis..suipestifer.* Causes of epidemic food-poisoning in man (Salmonellosis) and occasionally of paratyphoid fever. **1947** *Ann. Rev. Microbiol.* I. 324 The classical case of the salmonellosis..is that of a generalized infection, namely that of typhoid fever. This human clinical picture has its close parallel in animal salmonellosis. **1965** *N.Z. News* 13 Apr. 3/1 Several thousand sheep have died since Christmas in salmonellosis outbreaks among stock in the Rotorua and Waikato districts. **1970** W. H. PARKER *Health & Dis. in Farm Animals* xiii. 178 Outbreaks of Salmonellosis in stock are a matter of concern for public health.

salmonid. Delete *rare* and add later examples. Also *attrib.* and as *adj.*

1895 B. DEAN *Fishes, Living & Fossil* viii. 186 Eggs of Salmonids are deposited loosely in 'nests' on a clean, gravelly bottom. **1931** J. R. NORMAN *Hist. Fishes* xiii. 268 When the climate was considerably colder the range of migratory Salmonids extended much farther south. **1964** *Oceanogr. & Marine Biol.* II. 178 Further changes have been reported to occur after fertilization of the ova in another salmonid, the rainbow trout. **1970** *New Scientist* 19 Feb. 353/1 Ulcerative dermal necrosis..attacks salmon and other salmonid fish. **1975** *Nature* 14 Aug. 528/2 Fish farming in the UK has grown slowly in the freshwater and marine salmonid field under commercial patronage. **1978** *Ibid.* 2 Mar. 77/1 Evidence of large-scale gene loss following tetraploidy has been reported in both salmonid and catostomid fish.

salmonize, *v.* Add: Also, to (attempt to) introduce salmon into (a river, etc.) So **sa:lmoniza·tion;** also **sa·lmonizing** *vbl. sb.*

1870 *Sat. Rev.* 30 Apr. 576/1 Why should I be 'chaffed' about the salmonization of the Thames? The Thames once produced plenty of salmon; why should not the Thames produce salmon again? **1901** *Chambers's Jrnl.* Sept. 585/2 It does not seem quite fair that a few gentlemen should be able to prevent the salmonising of such a large extent of water as is here indicated.

salmon-trout. 2. (Earlier and later Amer. examples.)

1705 *Boston News-Let.* 15–22 Oct. 2/1 Our men were refresh'd with variety of Fish, especially Salmon Trouts, some whereof 2 foot long. **1806** W. CLARK *Jrnl.* 13 Mar. in *Orig. Jrnls. Lewis & Clark Exped.* (1905) IV. 166 The Salmon Trout are seldom more than two feet in length. **1848** E. BRYANT *What I saw in California* xi. 158 He had taken with his hook about a dozen salmon-trout. **1939** *Nat. Geogr. Mag.* Feb. 212/2 Both of these species [*sc.* Dolly Varden and blackspotted trout] are known in some localities as 'salmon trout'.

salmony (sæ·məni), *a.* [f. SALMON *sb.*¹ and *a.* + -Y¹.] Somewhat salmon-coloured.

1935 E. FARJEON *Nursery in Nineties* 237 She has one evening dress..a salmony-pink brocaded with bunches of lemon-coloured flowers. **1948** V. S. PRITCHETT in E. Bowen et al. *Why do I Write?* 12 Lichfield..a nice, dull little place in glazed salmony Midland brick. *a* **1974** R. CROSSMAN *Diaries* (1977) III. 805 Anne looked fresh and exquisite, too, in her lovely salmony red suit.

salon. Add: Now also with pronunc. (sæ·loṅ, sæ·lǫn). **1. a.** (Earlier example.)

1699 M. LISTER *Journey to Paris* 196 The Castle is..most commodious. The Great Salon and the Gallery are extreamly well Painted.

3. b. ‖ **salon des refusés** (de refüze). [Fr., exhibition of rejected work], an exhibition ordered by Napoleon III in 1863 to display pictures rejected by the official Salon; also *fig.*

1896 J. C. BECKWITH in J. C. Van Dyke *Mod. French Masters* III. 220 His [*sc.* Manet's] works became known..at the exhibitions of the pictures refused at the Salon, which were for several years gathered together and shown in a building generously provided by the government, and called the Salon des Refusés. **1932** KONODY & LATHOM *Introd. Fr. Painting* xiii. 194 *Déjeuner sur l'herbe* [by Manet]..rejected by the Salon,..was exhibited in the *Salon des Refusés*, and frowned on by Louis Napoleon. **1981** *Listener* 1 Jan. 4/3 Roy Jenkins plus Shirley Williams..plus the non-reselected MPs in the *salon des refusés*.

4. An establishment in which the trade of a beauty specialist or hairdresser is conducted.

1913 *Vogue* 1 June 106/1 (Advt.), Firming the skin is the new process used exclusively by Elizabeth Arden... It is administered at the Salon by experts. **1917** *Harrods Gen. Catal.* 397 Enshrined in an atmosphere of refinement and artistic comfort, *Harrods Hairdressing Salons* are a favourite resort with ladies. **1932** *New Yorker* 9 Apr. 68/3 See the telephone book for nearest Salon. **1956** ASHLEY & STEVENSON *Hair Design & Colour* i. 12 The salon itself, as a background to modern hair-styling, must inevitably play a highly important part in creating the right atmosphere. **1973** A. MACVICAR *Painted Doll Affair* vii. 82 My wife swears it's much better than the expensive 'salon' she used to go to in Glasgow.

5. a. *attrib.*, as (sense 2) *salon philosopher, science, volume, -writer*; (sense 3) *salon furniture, norm, -piece, vocabulary*; (sense 4) *salon facial, service, treatment.*

1974 *Times* 27 Aug. 9/2 All the products Marisa uses in the salon facials can be bought. **1973** R. HAYES *Hungarian Game* ii. 18 An incredibly tasteless collection of Regency and Salon furniture in the drawing room. **1942** WYNDHAM LEWIS *Lett.* (1963) 324 The artist is labelled 'decadent' who departs from the Salon norm..by the Hitlerite pundit of 'sanity'. **1947** A. EINSTEIN *Music in Romantic Era* iii. 26 The perfect type of the 'cultured musician' in the 19th century is represented by Franz Liszt, who was an essayist and salon philosopher. **1974** *Impressionism* (R. A. Catal.) 8 Daubigny..moved to narrow the distinction between outdoor study and Salon-piece. **1977** P. JOHNSON *Enemies of Society* xv. 203 Not a true discipline at all, but..a salon science. **1974** *Harrods Christmas Catal.* p. ii, Make a Gift of Beauty with a Gift Token..to the value of whichever Salon Service or Treatment you require. **1963** *Times* 6 Mar. 13/2 The liveliest part is that of a tramp-artist with ragged costume and salon vocabulary. **1957** *Times Lit. Suppl.* 20 Dec. 778/2 The work has higher claims than that of being merely a salon volume designed for presentation. **1944** L. MACNEICE *Christopher Columbus* 13 Radio's contemporary triangle..insists on a function of words which salon-writers are perhaps too apt to forget; this function is communication.

b. *attrib.* (passing into *adj.*) and *Comb.* with (occas. derogatory) reference to light music played as in a fashionable salon.

1914 *Étude* Oct. 708/1 Nearly all compositions for the piano by modern composers are Salon Music. **1935** *Vanity Fair* (N.Y.) Nov. 38/1 He's not making a salon man of me. **1946** R. BLESH *Shining Trumpets* xii. 266 So this music sings, not in the African tones of jazz, but in bathetic and sentimental accents. It is salon music. *Ibid.* 268 The reverse record side..is precisely like the mood-music prevalent today in the special salon-swing. **1947** A. EINSTEIN *Music in Romantic Era* xvii. 331 He was a somewhat eccentric salon-composer. **1948** MENCKEN *Amer. Lang.* Suppl. II. 706 A performer who..undertakes conventional music is a *commercial, salon-man, long-underwear* or *long-hair.* **1949** KOESTLER *Promise & Fulfilment* III. i. 301 Middle-class families in the Tel Aviv cafés applauded..the Russian marches played by salon orchestras in the Viennese style. **1950** BLESH & JANIS *They all played Ragtime* iv. 77 It is unsyncopated and in a light salon vein. **1955** *Times* 12 July 5/5 A Prelude and Fugue for string orchestra by Moszkowski..combined learned and *salon* styles with surprising success. **1979** *Guardian* 5 May 14/5 Jones..wrote the music for such skittish romances as Girl from Utah..and San Toy. Excerpts from these propped up many a salon orchestra's repertoire.

‖ **salone** (salō·ne). [It.: see SALOON.] **1. a.** = SALON 1 a. **b.** = SALON 1 b. (Only with reference to Italy.)

1902 H. JAMES *Wings of Dove* X. xxxiii. 515 She received me..in that glorious great *salone.* **1912** BEERBOHM *Christmas Garland* 134 A wintry Venetian sunshine poured in through the vast windows of his *salone.* **1960** E. BOWEN *Time in Rome* v. 140 The cavalier..charged through the *salone* and out again on to the balcony. **1969** 'I. DRUMMOND' *Man with Tiny Head* v. 74 He had despised her at their first meeting, in the huge Uccello *salone.*

‖ **salonfähig** (zalo·ṅfē:,iχʸ), *a. rare.* [Ger.] Fit for (polite) society; socially respectable.

1905 W. JAMES in *McClure's Mag.* May 3/2 Neither in dress nor in manner did he ever grow quite 'gentlemanly' or *Salonfähig* in the conventional and obliterated sense of the terms. **1980** *Encounter* May 41/1 The Austrian initiative, whatever its underlying motivations, serves to lend an air of cultured respectability to a blood-stained struggle and to render Arafat *salonfähig* in Western Europe.

salonnière (sălǫniēᵊ·ɹ). [Fr., f. SALON.] A woman who holds a salon; a society hostess.

a **1922** T. S. ELIOT *Waste Land Drafts* (1971) 27 Fresca's arrived (the Muses Nine declare) To be a sort of can-can salonnière. **1925** A. HUXLEY *Those Barren Leaves* II. i. 86 Mrs. Aldwinkle the salonnière, the hostess, the giver of literary parties and agapes of lions—is she not classical? a household word? a familiar quotation? **1964** *New Statesman* 10 Apr. 572/2 For a time she [*sc.* Beatrice Elvery] worked in the Co-operative Stained Glass Studio run by Sarah Purser, a patriotic *salonnière.* **1976** S. J. DARROCH *Ottoline* iv. 60 Being a hostess gave many women a chance to use talents and abilities that would otherwise have had no outlet. They turned their houses into cultural or intellectual oases, or merely centres of gossip. And a few did so in such a style that they qualified for the exalted title of salonnière.

saloon. Add: **4. a.** (Earlier and further examples.) Also, the passenger cabin of an aeroplane. Also quasi-advb. in *to go* (etc.) *saloon.*

c **1835** in M. Johnson *Amer. Advertising, 1800–1900* (1960), Fare to Bristol—In main Saloon, and cuddy state rooms, Thirty-Five Guineas; in fore and lower saloons, Thirty Guineas. **1882** W. D. HAY *Brighter Britain!* I. ii. 57 If you can compass the means, go saloon—the extra comfort on a long voyage is well worth the extra price. **1884** *Whitaker's Almanack* (Advt. section) 20 These large, highest classed and full-powered Steamships..are fitted up in the latest and most approved fashion to ensure the comfort of Passengers, having the Saloon on Upper Deck. **1892** [see STEERAGE 5]. **1921** *Daily Mail Year Bk.* 27/1 Eight passengers..in armchair seats in a draught-proof saloon. **1930** *Daily Express* 6 Oct. 2/3 R101 swept around in a wide circle, visible only by her red and green navigating lights and the glow of the illuminated saloons.

b. (Earlier simple examples.)

1842 *Illustr. London News* 18 June 89/1 Previous to the departure from Paddington, the Royal Saloon, the fittings of which are upon a most elegant..scale, were tastefully improved by bouquets. **1850** C. SCHREIBER *Jrnl.* 17 June (1950) 243 We had a saloon carriage. **1859** *First Impressions New World* 214 There were four of these [state rooms], besides a general saloon in the middle; but the whole was greatly inferior to the elegance of Mr. Tyson's car on the Baltimore and Ohio Railway. **1886** *Encycl. Brit.* XX. 247/1 Saloon carriages are occasionally used, so called because two or more of the ordinary compartments are merged in one.

c. A type of motor car with a closed body for four or more passengers. Cf. *SEDAN 1 c.

1908 *Motor Manual* (ed. 11) iii. 92 Other forms of bodies fitted to more expensive cars include the brougham, landaulet, saloon, double phaeton, [etc.]. **1927** B. K. SEYMOUR *Three Wives* I. x. 157 He..secured the services of a Buick saloon. **1935** AUDEN & ISHERWOOD *Dog beneath Skin* 12 Brought in charabanc and saloon along arterial roads. **1955** *Times* 6 June 7/7 A chauffeur-driven saloon draws up with a single passenger in the back—a prim little boy reading a school book. **1971** *Daily Tel.* 13 Apr. 2/4 A new saloon with front-wheel drive and transversely-mounted engine..is announced today by Fiat. **1976** BOTHAM & DONNELLY *Valentino* vii. 48 The street, where a gleaming new four-door Ford saloon was parked.

5. a. (Earlier example.)

1851 [see *ICE-CREAM *attrib.*].

b. = *saloon theatre* below.

1864 G. A. SALA *Robson* 14 The place was a 'saloon'—that is to say, drinking and smoking went on during the performance, but the pieces put upon the stage were all of a high class. **1902** *Encycl. Brit.* XXXI. 46/2 The principal 'saloons' were the 'Effingham' in the Whitechapel Road, the 'Bower' in the Lower Marsh, Lambeth, [etc.]. **1974** *Encycl. Brit. Micropædia* VII. 130/1 'Saloon' became the name for any place of popular entertainment; 'variety' was an evening of mixed plays; and 'music hall' meant a concert hall that featured a mixture of musical and comic entertainment.

6. (Earlier and later examples.) Also, in British use, a refreshment bar in a theatre; a separate bar in a public house (as opposed to *public bar*), = *saloon bar* below.

1841 *Southern Lit. Messenger* VII. 764/1 After going into the saloon (grog-shop) to 'freshen the nip'—..they led me into the upper tier of boxes. **1841** DICKENS *Let.* 28 Dec. (1969) II. 454 This note is about the saloon... The refreshments are preposterously dear... There ought to be a boxkeeper to ring a bell or give some other notice of the commencement of the overture to the afterpiece. **1854** *Harper's Mag.* Apr. 586/2 As I re-entered the bar-room labeled 'saloon', of mine inn. **1902** 'N. GUBBINS' *Dead Certainties* 106 Exactly thirty days from the day upon which I first entered the accursed swing-doors of the Bull and Beehive, late one night, a stranger entered the 'saloon'. **1946** *Amer. Speech* XXI. 277 The English saloon-keeper was the keeper of the 'saloon', or as it would now be termed 'refreshment bar', in a London theatre. **1949** *Columbus* (Ohio) *Sunday Dispatch* 16 Oct. C1/3 He returned to Westerville in 1887 and opened a saloon at a new location on State St. **1969** HOUSE & STOREY *Lett. Charles Dickens* II. 454 Macready had gone to great lengths to civilize the saloon. **1976** *National Observer* (U.S.) 28 Aug. 13/1 People have been tossed out of saloons in downtown Utica, N.Y., with more style.

7. b. saloon bar, a separate bar in a public house offering more comfort, services, etc. than the public bar; **saloon car,** (*b*) = 4 c above; **saloon-keeper** (earlier and later examples); also in British use, the keeper of a refreshment bar in a theatre; **saloon man** *U.S.*, one who frequents drinking saloons; **saloon theatre:** see THEATRE *sb.* 2 in Dict. and Suppl.

1902 G. HILL in G. Sims *Living London* II. 292/3 The distinction between the 'private' bar and the 'saloon' bar is subtle... The saloon bar is the ante-chamber of the billiard room. **1932** L. GOLDING *Magnolia St.* I. iii. 45 The Public Bar, nothing like so grand as the Saloon Bar, nothing like so cosy as the Private Bar. **1977** 'J. GASH' *Judas Pair* ii. 17 The saloon bar was crowded. **1915** *Motor Manual* (ed. 18) xi. 135 Landaulets, cabriolets, and saloon cars. **1931** D. L. SAYERS *Five Red Herrings* xv. 167, I observed Mr. Gowan's saloon car standing before the door. **1974** *Country Life* 17 Oct. 1112/1 In post-war years we have had some very exciting saloon-car racing. **1849** *Theatrical Mirror* 10 Sept. 21 The 'Mirror' is supplied at most moderate prices to the Saloon Keepers, in order to enable them to sell it to advantage. **1873** 'MARK TWAIN' *Gilded Age* lix. 530 Leave the true source of our political power..in the hands of saloon-keepers. **1944** B. A. BOTKIN *Treas. Amer. Folklore* I. 131 He followed the construction of a new line on the Southern Pacific Railroad as camp saloon-keeper. **1977** *Times* 9 July 9/1 His grandfather was a poor tenant farmer..who became a saloon keeper. **1870** J. W. MCCLUNG *Minnesota* 213 Spring Valley, with 400 population..and no saloon. 'Saloon men cannot live in Spring Valley.' **1915** J. LONDON *Star Rover* ii. 9 You can weave the political pull of San Francisco saloon-men and ward heelers into a position of graft.

saloonist. a. (Earlier and later examples.)

1870 *Territorial Enterprise* (Virginia, Nevada) 3 Mar. 3/2 (*heading*) New saloonists. **1946** *Chicago Daily News* 8 Nov. 18/2 Saloonists voted out of business in the Woodlawn local option election talk of going to court to upset the vote.

‖ **salopette** (salopɛt). [Fr.] A pair of overalls or dungarees of a kind worn orig. in France by workmen and later introduced for general wear, esp. as a skiing garment. Also in *pl.*

1972 *Guardian* 31 Oct. 11/2 Basically, the salopette is a Frenchman's overalls with a high waist, a bib front and adjustable shoulder straps, modified for skiing only by a snow cuff fitting snugly round your ankles. **1973** *Country Life* 21 June 1847/2 A summer salopette suit in glazed cotton. **1974** N. FREELING *Dressing of Diamond* 130 The old man..in his sleeveless vest and bib-and-brace *salopette*. **1977** *Guardian* 16 Mar. 9/1 Peter Blacklay is a doctor and he made a pair of bright red and blue nylon salopettes in a weekend. **1978** *Daily Tel.* 2 Feb. 15/4 Salopettes are far warmer and more comfortable..than stretch ski pants. **1980** *Woman's Jrnl.* Jan. 35/1 He wears a navy blue salopette.

Salopian, *a.* and *sb.* Add: **A.** *adj.* **b.** Designating a variety of porcelain made at the former Caughley manufactory (closed 1814) near Broseley, Shropshire in the late eighteenth and early nineteenth centuries. Also *transf.* Cf. *CAUGHLEY.

1850 J. MARRYAT *Coll. Hist. Pott. & Porc.* ix. 182 The Salopian ware is very similar to the Derby in pattern and colouring. **1857** —— *Hist. Pott. & Porc.* xii. 297 The early Salopian porcelain was originally made..at Caughley. **1910** J. F. BLACKER *ABC of Collecting Old Eng. China* (ed. 3) iii. 49 Salopian blue is somewhat similar in tone to that of Worcester. **1933** W. B. HONEY *Eng. Pott. & Porc.* II. xii. 190 The Caughley porcelain was known as 'Salopian'. *Ibid.* 191 The Salopian blue-painting..was mostly cribbed from Worcester and Chantilly. **1957** *Encycl. Brit.* XVIII. 354/1 Some Liverpool factories and that at Caughley (the 'Salopian' factory)..may be regarded as offshoots of Worcester.

c. *Geol.* Of, pertaining to, or designating an alternative division of the Silurian comprising the Wenlockian and (lower) Ludlovian. Freq. *absol.*

1879 C. LAPWORTH in *Ann. & Mag. Nat. Hist.* III. Table facing p. 455 Silurian System: Middle Division (Salopian). **1880** —— in *Ibid.* V. 48 The second natural division of the Silurian system is undoubtedly Murchison's Great Mudstone series, which includes the so-called Wenlock and Lower Ludlow groups... In Shropshire this great mudstone or *Salopian* formation is by far the most important physical group in the Silurian. **1883** J. E. MARR *Classification of Cambrian & Silurian Rocks* 42 No higher Salopian beds, and no Downtonian beds occur in North Wales, partly perhaps owing to subsequent denudation. **1929** O. T. JONES in Evans & Stubblefield *Handbk. Geol. Gt. Brit.* III. iv. 92 In certain areas Lapworth's term Salopian is sometimes useful, since the line of separation between Wenlock and Ludlow, represented by that between Lower and Upper Salopian, is not easy to determine. **1940** *Q. Jrnl. Geol. Soc.* XCV. 335 (*heading*) The geology of the Colwyn Bay district: a study of submarine slumping during the Salopian period. *Ibid.* 374 The strike of these structures..indicates that the floor of the Salopian area in the Colwyn Bay region sloped from north to south. **1971** *Jrnl. Geol. Soc.* CXXVII. 104 Lapworth's..term *Salopian* was eventually extended upwards by O. T. Jones..to include the whole of the Ludlow as well as the Wenlock. It is thus still employed from time to time... It finds no place in our classification.

B. *sb.* **b.** A pupil of Shrewsbury School.

1866 *Blackw. Mag.* Apr. 432/2 He has left us specimens of Latin verses of which even modern Salopians might be proud. **1898** *Public School Mag.* Dec. 487/2 'Swilling', a substitute for baths, is still an institution, of which every Salopian is proud. **1932** PENDLEBURY & WEST *Shrewsbury School* xi. 82 Nearly 2,000 Salopians saw active service... A sum of money was set aside to assist in the education of the sons of Old Salopians who had been killed. **1964** P. COWBURN *Salopian Anthol.* p. vi, This book..is to enable Salopians..to know what has been written about this particular school.

‖ **salotto** (salǫ·tto). Also (erron.) **salotta;** pl. **salotti.** [It. dim. f. SALA¹.] In Italy, a drawing-room, reception room; a lounge.

1918 G. FRANKAU *One of Them* xii. 87 Can we repay those..midnight cocktails of your flowered *salotti*. **1924** D. H. LAWRENCE in M. Magnus *Mem. Foreign Legion* 51 So we went into the salotta. 'Oh, what a beautiful room,' he cried. **1930** E. POUND *XXX Cantos* xxvii. 126 In the salotto of that drummer's hotel. **1932** *Times Lit. Suppl.* 21 Jan. 38/3 Her prototype..can always be found in the cheerless *salotto* of a certain kind of Florentine pension.

Salpausselkä (sa·lpauselkä). *Physical Geogr.* Also **-selka.** [Finnish.] Each of two long, wide end moraines in southern Finland that are regarded as marking the last readvance of the ice sheet at the end of the Pleistocene.

1923 *Bull. de la Commission Géologique de Finlande* No. 60. 8 The southern slope toward the Gulf of Finland and Lake Laatokka (Ladoga)..consists of two faces of different grade: (1) The larger inner part, the Lake District of Finland, extending to the belt of the recessional moraines of Salpausselkä ('the damming ridge') and (2) the narrower bow-shaped Coast zone between the Salpausselkä and the coasts of Lake Laatokka and the sea. **1937** WOOLDRIDGE & MORGAN *Physical Basis Geogr.* xxii. 390 The great sand and gravel ridge which extends from east to west through Finland and is known as the Salpausselka. **1957** J. K. CHARLESWORTH *Quaternary Era* II. xxxi. 675 The Salpausselkä readvance,..of 12,000 years ago, has been linked with a temporary increase of snowfall. *Ibid.* xlii. 1172 The First or Outer Salpausselkä has a maximum altitude of 70–80 m, an average width of 2·5 km. **1968** R. W. FAIRBRIDGE *Encycl. Geomorphol.* 919/1 The upper boundary of the Pleistocene..must lie somewhere between 10,000 and 10,500 years B.P., and may be defined as..the time equivalents of sediments overlying the terminal moraines of the Valders (in North America) or the Salpausselkä (in Europe).

salpicon. Delete ? *Obs.* and add earlier and later examples. Also used as a garnish for vol-au-vents and the like.

1723 J. NOTT *Cook's & Confectioner's Dict.* sig. Gg7, Make a Hole in your Piece of roast Meat..and pour the Salpicon into the Hole. **1877** E. S. DALLAS *Kettner's Bk. of Table* 81 *Bouchées*—Morsels—These are small Vol-au-vents..filled with a salpicon of chicken, game or fish. **1906** *Mrs. Beeton's Bk. Househ. Managem.* lxi. 1651 Salpicon.—This name is applied to the various mixtures used in filling timbales, bombs, patty-cases. **1936** LUCAS & HUME *Au Petit Cordon Bleu* 44 Mix the sauce into the salmon, mushrooms, and onions and pour this *salpicon* on to the bottom of the dish. **1965** E. DAVID *French Provincial Cooking* (ed. 2) 99 *Salpicon.* May be one of a score of mixtures comprising flavouring vegetables, herbs, ham, veal, fish or meat but always cut into very small dice and bound into a thick white or brown sauce. Used as a stuffing, or as a garnish for little tartlets or *vols-au-vent*. **1977** *Time* 25 Apr. 17/2 He makes..a saddle of boned lamb stuffed with a mousse of chicken, accompanied by a salpicon of kidneys, brains and sweetbreads.

salpiglossis. For 'mod.L.' read 'mod.L. (H. Ruiz & J. Pavon *Floræ Peruvianæ et Chilensis Prodromus* (1794) 94)' and substitute for def.: An annual or perennial herb of the genus so called, native to Chile and bearing funnel-shaped flowers of various colours. (Earlier and later examples.)

1827 W. J. HOOKER *Exotic Flora* III. 229 (*heading*) Straw-coloured Salpiglossis. **1915** H. H. THOMAS *Bk. Hardy Flowers* 392 The great improvement in the size and colour of the flowers..renders the Salpiglossis very desirable for beds and groups in the border. **1931** A. N. SCOTT tr. *Carossa's Boyhood & Youth* v. 72 A whole host of the most beautiful salpiglosses. **1962** R. PAGE *Educ. of Gardener* xii. 328, I remember a fantastic planting of yard-high salpiglossis in warm reds. **1979** *Daily Tel.* 26 May 30/2 The handsome salpiglossis..will do very well from a May sowing out of doors.

salpingo-. Add: **salpinge·ctomy** [*-ECTOMY], excision of a Fallopian tube; **salpi·ngogram,** an image of the Fallopian tubes obtained with X-rays or ultrasound; **sa:lpingogra·phic** *a.*, of or pertaining to salpingography; **salpingo·graphy** [ad. G. *salpingographie* (F. Schoker 1925, in *Zentralbl. f. Gynaekol.* XLIX. 290)], the process or technique of obtaining salpingograms; **salpingo·lysis** [mod.L. (coined in Fr. by P. E. Goullioud 1914, in *Lyon Médicale* CXXII. 689): see *-LYSIS], the removal of adhesions that constrain the Fallopian tubes in abnormal positions with respect to the ovaries and hence prevent conception; **salpingo-oöphorectomy** (examples).

1888 W. H. & H. T. BYFORD *Pract. Med. & Surg.* (ed. 4) 816/2 (Index), Salpingectomy. **1897** *Amer. Jrnl. Med. Sci.* CXIV. 497 (*heading*) The stump after salpingectomy. **1978** G. VIDAL *Kalki* i. 5 In perfect health and with maximum publicity at the Marie Stopes Clinic in Daly City, I underwent a bilateral partial salpingectomy, better known as 'Band-Aid Surgery'. **1927** *Surg., Gynecol. & Obstetr.* XLV. 140/2 By means of roentgenological study after the injection of iodized oil, an accurate uterogram and salpingogram, visualizing the entire internal female generative tract, may be obtained in cases in which the Fallopian tubes are not occluded. **1964** BROWNE & MCCLURE BROWNE *Postgrad. Obstetr. & Gynaecol.* (ed. 3) xii. 158 If the salpingogram seems normal and tubercle is suspected, an endometrial biopsy should be done. **1927** *Surg., Gynecol. & Obstetr.* XLV. 132/2 Rosenblatt..reported his salpingographic observations on three women who had submitted to the Alexander-Adams operation for sterility. **1935** *Ibid.* LX. 228/1 Salpingography is..of value in determining the presence or absence of tubes in patients who have had a previous operation on the adnexa but are uncertain of its nature. **1976** G. BERCI *Endoscopy* xvii. 236/1 The use of combined laparoscopy and intra-operative salpingography employing television fluoroscopy with aimed spot films allows the most complete evaluation of uterine and tubal anatomy conducted during a single procedure. **1937** *Amer. Jrnl. Obstetr. & Gynecol.* XXXIII. 39 When the occlusion is at the fimbriated end [of the fallopian tubes], simple release of adhesions may suffice to restore the patency of the tube (salpingolysis). **1980** *Fertility & Sterility* XXXIV. 223/1 In Table 1 are listed the pregnancy rates after bilateral salpingolysis, bilateral salpingostomy, [etc.]. **1890** *Johns Hopkins Hosp. Bull.* I. 57/1 Eight cases of salpingo-oöphorectomy for fibroids are symptomatically relieved of their pressure symptoms. **1977** *Proc. R. Soc. Med.* LXX. 189/2 Fig 1 shows the ureter deliberately exposed in relation to a clamp placed across the infundibulopelvic ligament during the course of a hysterectomy and left salpingo-oophorectomy.

salsa (sa·lsă). [Sp.; cf. SAUCE *sb.*] ‖ **1.** *Cookery.* A variety of sauce served with meat. Also *Comb.*

1846 R. FORD *Gatherings from Spain* xi. 132 What sort of a stew is it? Let me smell and taste the *salsa*. **1935** J. STEINBECK *Tortilla Flat* xvi. 289 Her two sons..carried a wash-tub of salsa pura between them. **1973** *Listener* 18 Jan. 98/2 Serve the meat... Horse-radish, *salsa verde*, spicy tomato sauce..all go very well. **1978** *Tucson Mag.* Dec. 84/3 Steak and salsa rate high.

2. [Amer. Sp.] A kind of dance music of Latin American origin which incorporates elements of jazz and rock music; a dance performed to this music.

1975 *New Yorker* 29 Sept. 41/3 The group I play with consists of some Latin kids who are not afraid to break out of pure salsa. **1975** *N.Y. Times* 11 Nov. 61/5 Take the sound and percussion rhythm of an eight-piece Latin band; add a mixture of mambo, cha cha and merengue dance steps;..simmer gently for about 10 to 15 minutes on a crowded dance floor; add a pinch and a squeeze and you have it—salsa. **1976** *Monitor* (McAllen, Texas) 21 Oct. 5B/3 The Caribbean has given us gentle calypso and Trinidad's brash steel bands,..the spicy latin 'salsa' of Puerto Rico and the whimsical chants and big beat of Jamaican reggae. **1978** *Detroit Free Press* 5 Mar. D16/5 San Juan's major hotels have lounge bands that specialize in salsa (Latin rhythm with a jazz beat). **1981** *Weekly Guardian* 12 July 17/1 Salsa music drifts out of the bar as a group of grease-spattered youths tinker with the engine of a new Toyota.

salt, *sb.*¹ Add: **2. d.** (Further examples.) Now freq. *with a pinch of salt.*

1948 F. R. COWELL *Cicero & Roman Republic* xvi. 243 A more critical spirit slowly developed, so that Cicero and his friends took more than the proverbial pinch of salt before swallowing everything written by these earlier authors. **1949** V. GROVE *Language Bar* ii. 29 Even if we accept such a statement with a pinch of salt, it is an undisputable fact that its writer did look upon Latin as a guiding mistress. **1965** M. SHADBOLT *Among Cinders* xxvi. 258, I take what he says with a half-pound of salt, after his review of that play. **1981** J. S. BRATTON *Impact of Victorian Children's Fiction* ii. 41 We must take William Jones's enthusiasm about the eag erness of [tract] readers with a pinch of salt.

i. *to rub salt in one's wounds*: to behave or speak to someone so as to aggravate a hurt already inflicted.

1944 [see *CURL *v.*¹ 1 c]. **1967** WODEHOUSE *Company for Henry* x. 182 He could see that Henry was deeply stirred, and he had no wish to rub salt in his wounds. **1973** *Guardian* 16 Feb. 13/8 Mr Nixon's treatment for war wounds is rubbing salt in them.

3. a. (Further examples.) Now also applied to a person or persons of great worthiness, reliability, honesty, etc.

1916 G. B. SHAW *Androcles & Lion* p. xv, They may not be the salt of the earth, these Philistines; but they are the substance of civilization. **1931** T. R. G. LYELL *Slang, Phrase & Idiom* 659 If he's a friend of yours, you're a lucky man, for if ever a fellow was one of the salt of the earth, he is. He's the best man I've ever met, in every way. **1948** E. S. GARDNER *D.A. takes Chance* x. 103 Eve was a mighty fine girl, and her mother is the salt of the earth. **1951** E. M. FORSTER *Two Cheers for Democracy* I. 56 If you don't like people, kill them, banish them, segregate them, and then strut up and down proclaiming that you are the salt of the earth. **1953** WODEHOUSE

Performing Flea 78 You dine with the President on Monday, and he slaps you on the back and tells you you are the salt of the earth, and on Tuesday morning you get a letter from him saying you are fired. **1976** N. THORNBURG *Cutter & Bone* vi. 148 And such *good* friends they were too. Real salt of the earth.

5. b. *salt of lemon*, potassium hydrogen oxalate, used to remove ink-stains and iron-mould from linen (earlier and later examples); *Carlsbad* (or *Karlsbad*), *Vichy salts*, salts prepared from the mineral springs in these places, or imitations of them; *Everitt's salt* (see quot. 1939); † *Preston salts*, a variety of smelling-salts.

1810 *New Family Receipt-bk.* 349 Essential Salt of Lemons. **1858** P. L. SIMMONDS *Dict. Trade Products*, *Preston-salts*,..smelling-salts..containing carbonate of ammonia in small pieces, with a drachm of the following mixture added, viz. oils of bergamot, cloves, and lavender, and the strongest solution of ammonia. **1866** *Chambers's Encycl.* VIII. 453/2 The celebrated Preston smelling-salts are scented with oils of cloves and pimento. **1868** *Ibid.* X. 75/2 Ink-stains..require to be taken out with ..the essential salts of lemon. **1890** BILLINGS *Med. Dict.* I. 482/1 *Everitt's salt*, a compound of cyanide of iron and potassium, formed when potassium ferrocyanide is decomposed by sulphuric acid. **1895** *Army & Navy Co-op Soc. Price List* 15 Sept. 696/1 Carlsbad Salts. *Ibid.* 710/2 Vichy Salts, Effervescing. **1901** *To-Day* 1 Aug. 38/1 'Eisiklene Hat Wash', which I find far superior to oxalic acid, salts of lemon, or any of the usual articles used for the purpose. **1908** *Chem. Abstr.* II. 3126 Artificial crystallized 'Karlsbad salts' as sold on the market is really impure Na_2SO_4. **1939** *Thorpe's Dict. Appl. Chem.* (ed. 4) III. 471/2 Ferrous potassium ferrocyanide, $K_2Fe[Fe(CN)_6]$, (Everitt's salt) is produced by heating saturated potassium ferrocyanide solution for 40 hours at 90°C with an equal volume of 20% sulphuric acid. **1960** *Chem. Abstr.* LIV. 8120/2 Hexametaphosphate ..combined with 34% Vichy salts..gives a detergent which restores the original whiteness of superpolyamide textiles. **1977** *Martindale's Extra Pharmacopoeia* (ed. 27) 1459/1 Artificial Carlsbad Salt... A crystallised preparation of sodium sulphate 55, potassium sulphate 1, sodium chloride 10, and sodium carbonate 35. *Ibid.*, Artificial Vichy Salt. Anhydrous sodium sulphate 40, anhydrous sodium phosphate 20, potassium bicarbonate 35, sodium chloride 75, sodium bicarbonate 830.

c. (*a*) (Earlier example.)

1741 RICHARDSON *Pamela* II. 247 Mrs. Jewkes held her Salts to my Nose, and I did not faint.

(*b*) Also, *like a dose of salts*: see *DOSE *sb.* 2 c.

6. Also, † *ethereal salt*, an ester.

1876 *Encycl. Brit.* V. 553/2 The thio-acids also form ethereal salts. **1905** GOODCHILD & TWENEY *Technol. & Sci. Dict.* 633/2 Salts like ethyl acetate, derived from an organic acid and an alcohol, or from an alcohol and an inorganic acid, are called ethereal salts or esters.

12. a. *salt-spoon* (earlier example), *-spoonful* (earlier example), *-warehouse*. **b.** (objective, etc.) *salt-burner*; *salt-blue*, *-bright*, *-caked*, *-eaten*, *-free*, *-licked*, *-strewn*, *-tanged*, *-wavy*, *-white* (further examples), *-worn* adjs.

1922 Salt-blue [see *sea-death* s.v. *SEA *sb.* 18 d]. **1930** E. POUND *XXX Cantos* xvii. 79 And in her hands sea-wrack Salt-bright with the foam. **1910** G. T. ZOËGA *Conc. Dict. Old Icelandic* 346/2 [*Salt*]-*karl*,..salt-burner. **1975** C. FELL tr. *Egil's Saga* iv. 5 Those who worked in the forests and the salt-burners and all those who hunt..had to pay his taxes. **1903** J. MASEFIELD *Ballads* 19 Dirty British coaster with a salt-caked smoke stack. **1916** JOYCE *Portrait of Artist* (1969) iv. 170 Picking a pointed salteaten stick out of the jetsam among the rocks, he clambered down the slope of the breakwater. **1909** *Practitioner* Dec. 867 When nephritis occurs, the child is given milk for some days, and then a salt-free diet, or at least one poor in salt. **1977** J. CHEEVER *Falconer* 49 A salt-free diet..no salt added. **1962** A. SAMPSON *Anat. of Britain* xvi. 264 In the past the air force has been led by aviators, as the navy has been led by saltlicked admirals. **1820** M. EDGEWORTH *Let.* 4 June (1979) 144 Salt spoons never to be seen. **1837** DICKENS *Pickw.* xlviii. 518 Tom Smart beat him in the drinking by about half a salt-spoon-full. **1892** W. B. YEATS *Countess Kathleen* i. 24 My curse upon the salt-strewn road of monks. **1933** W. DE LA MARE *Fleeting* 119 This wide salt-tanged vast of air. **1883** 'MARK TWAIN' *Life on Mississippi* xli. 423 The old brick salt-warehouses clustered at the upper end of the city. **1912** E. POUND *Ripostes* 27 That I on high streams The salt-wavy tumult traverse alone. **1922** JOYCE *Ulysses* 50 A corpse rising saltwhite from the undertow, bobbing landward, a pace a pace a porpoise. **1961** A. SILLITOE *Key to Door* xxvii. 426 Water foamed into salt-white patches below the stern. **1921** W. DE LA MARE *Veil* 78 And the ocean water stirs In salt-worn casemate and porch.

c. salt bath, a bath of a molten salt or salts, as used in annealing; **salt bridge** *Chem.*, (*a*) a tube containing an electrolyte (freq. in the form of a gel) which provides electrical contact between two solutions; (*b*) a structure linking parts of a large molecule by means of a polar bond; *spec.* one formed between an acidic and a basic group; **salt-burn** = *salt-sore*; **salt bush** (further examples); also found in arid regions elsewhere; **salt-cake,** (*a*) (earlier example); **salt cedar,** a tamarisk, *Tamarix gallica*, growing as a shrub or small tree in warm parts of the United States; **salt dome,** a dome-shaped geological structure formed around and over a salt plug, often the source of oil or other minerals; also, a salt plug; **salt glaze:** also *transf.*, ceramic objects to which salt glaze has been applied; hence as *v. trans.*; **salt lake** (see main entry below); **salt-like** *a.*, *spec.* in *Chem.*, ionic; applied esp. to those hydrides which contain the anion H^-; **salt mine,** also *joc.* (esp. in *pl.*) with allusion to the practice of sentencing offenders to labour in a salt mine; *spec.* one's work or place of employment; **salt plug,** an approximately cylindrical mass of salt, typically a mile in diameter and several miles deep, which has been forced upwards by subterranean pressure, distorting the overlying strata and forming a salt dome; **salt-raker** (earlier example); **salt-shaker** *U.S.* = *salt-sprinkler*; **salt sore,** a sore caused by exposure to salt water; **salt-spreader,** a vehicle that spreads salt on roads in order to melt snow and ice; hence **salt-spreading** *vbl. sb.* and *ppl. a.*; **salt tablet,** a tablet of salt that is swallowed, usu. to replace salt lost in perspiration.

1913 *Lockwood's Dict. Mech. Engin.* (ed. 4), *Salt bath furnace*, a type of hardening furnace in which the temperature is regulated by the employment of fused salts. **1925** *Jrnl. Iron & Steel Inst.* CXI. 536 The purification of fused salt baths composed of equal parts of sodium and potassium chlorides by the addition of boric acid and charcoal is also dealt with. **1980** *Railway Gaz. Internat.* Jan. 59/2 Molten salt bath nitriding and induction hardening caused bore distortion. **1915** *Jrnl. Amer. Chem. Soc.* XXXVII. 2781 Bjerrum's method of extrapolation..is to add, to the voltage obtained by using 3·5 *M* KCl as a salt bridge, the difference between this voltage and that obtained by using 1·75 *M* KCl as the salt bridge. **1929** H. T. S. BRITTON *Hydrogen Ions* viii. 109 These two solutions are connected through the 'salt bridge', a narrow inverted U-tube, containing saturated KCl solution. **1965** *Jrnl. Molecular Biol.* XIII. 656 This arrangement would allow the α-amino group of one β-chain to form a salt-bridge with the α-carboxyl group of its symmetrically related partner, resulting in the formation of two salt bridges on either side of the dyod axis. **1978** P. W. ATKINS *Physical Chem.* xii. 347 Another way of eliminating the junction potential is to connect the two half-cells with a salt bridge formed by dissolving potassium chloride in a water-soluble jelly. **1978** *Nature* 23 Nov. 362/1 Protein subunits in the two layers of the disk of tobacco mosaic virus have very similar conformations. Much of the bonding between subunits is polar, including salt-bridge systems. **1917** D. H. LAWRENCE *Look! We have come Through!* 37 Nevertheless, once, the frogs, the globe-flowers of Bavaria, the glow-worms Gave me sweet lymph against the salt-burns. **1901** M. FRANKLIN *My Brilliant Career* xxii. 185, I listened with interest to stories of weeks and weeks spent..crossing widths of saltbush country. **1909** COULTER & NELSON *New Man. Bot. Rocky Mts.* (ed. 2) 165 Atriplex L. Saltbush. Orache. **1911** C. E. W. BEAN '*Dreadnought' of Darling* xv. 144 The grass might die off and the salt bush wither up. **1936** I. L. IDRIESS *Cattle King* ii. 10 He had never seen saltbush before. He felt strangely attracted by this little grey bush; its sombre colouring typical of the area. **1940** E. C. JAEGER *Desert Wild Flowers* 53 It [*sc.* the hoary saltbush] is one of the most widely distributed of American salt-bushes. **1944** *Living off Land* ii. 42 Lucerne leaves, nettles, saltbush and milk thistles can all be used as substitutes for spinach. **1973** *Stand. Encycl. S. Afr.* IX. 480/1 Several species of *Atriplex*..are known as saltbush. *c* **1702** C. FIENNES *Journeys* (1947) I. 49 The thinner part [of the salt] runns through on Moulds they set to catch it which they call Salt Cakes. **1881** *Harper's Mag.* Apr. 731/1 Salt cedars and stunted live-oaks..were the only trees growing from the thin soil. **1973** *Tucson* (Arizona) *Daily Citizen* 22 Aug. 58/3 We wound up tramping..through the mud and salt cedars. **1908** *Science* 28 Feb. 348/1 The expansive force of the salt from the crystallizing source will be very circumscribed and the salt domes local in character. **1928** E. R. LILLEY *Geol. Petroleum & Nat. Gas* xvi. 376 The salt dome..is known in areas where it does not appear to be associated with oil. **1945** M. F. GLAESSNER *Princ. Micropalaeont.* ix. 232 Lower Tertiary, Cretaceous, and Upper Jurassic microfossils (foraminifera and ostracodes) have been described from the salt-dome area..between the northern shore of the Caspian sea and the southern foothills of the Ural Mountains. **1964** W. C. PUTNAM *Geol.* vi. 134/1 Many of the Gulf Coast salt domes are crowned with an irregular covering of limestone, anhydrite, gypsum, and occasionally suphur, termed the cap rock. **1976** *Billings* (Montana) *Gaz.* 5 July 4-A/2 It not only will transmit needed crude oil to the Midwest, it also will make usable the vast salt domes of the Williston basin for strategic storage of crude. **1967** M. CHANDLER *Ceramics in Mod. World* ii. 52 Porous drainpipes are still often salt-glazed, a process that is unique among glazing processes. **1968** J. ARNOLD *Shell Bk. Country Crafts* 236 The studio potters produce various kinds of terracotta.. and saltglaze. **1977** *Ashmolean Mus. Rep. Visitors 1975–76* 23 A selection of white salt-glaze from the Church bequest. **1928** *Chem. Abstr.* XXII. 3343 (*heading*) Salt-like hydrides. **1952** D. T. HURD *Introd. Chem. Hydrides* iii. 23 The salt-like hydrides are very susceptible to hydrolysis in aqueous solution. **1965** PHILLIPS & WILLIAMS *Inorg. Chem.* I. xvii. 619 The non-interstitial carbides are, in some senses, intermediate in character between the metallic interstitial carbides and the reactive salt-like carbides. **1963** *Times* 13 May 3/1 Rhodes is back in favour after a year or two in the saltmines for throwing. **1966** L. DEIGHTON *Billion-Dollar Brain* xvii. 186 We finished our milk. 'Back to the salt mines,' said Harvey. **1975** B. GARFIELD *Hopscotch* xxvii. 281 I'd better get back to the salt mines. I've got a lot of unfinished jobs. **1977** *Listener* 10 Nov. 616/2 Harding was summoned by Sir John Reith and..sent off to the salt-mines of Manchester. **1918, 1944** Salt plug [see *PLUG *sb.* 2 l (ii)]. **1967** M. T. HALBOUTY *Salt Domes* vi. 87/2 Oil and formation waters migrated from sediments surrounding the salt plug and were trapped in porous sections of the cap rock. **1837** A. MALLORY *Let.* 20 Apr. in J. J. Audubon *Ornith. Biogr.* (1839) V. 257 Several of the fishermen, and salt-rakers,.. frequent the keys to the windward of this place. **1895** Salt shaker [see *pepper shaker* s.v. *PEPPER *sb.* 5]. **1931** W. CATHER *Shadows on Rock* II. i. 50 His ragged jacket was as much too tight as the trousers were too loose, and this gave him the figure of a salt-shaker. **1977** B. ROUECHÉ *Fago* (1978) I. iv. 72, I..picked up the kitchen salt shaker and rubbed it clean. **1908** N. DUNCAN *Every Man for Himself* v. 140 [*Armenian loq.*] An' thee salt-sores from thee feeshin' is on thee han's. **1979** F. FORSYTH *Devil's Alternative* 7 Those parts submerged in sea water soft and white between the salt-sores. **1951** *Sun* (Baltimore) 21 Dec. B32/6 The Board of Estimates is expected to approve today the purchase of 25 latest-type salt spreaders. **1962** *B.S.I. News* Feb. 8/1 One London council whose salt-spreading was hindered because supplies had become 'rock-hard'. **1962** *Times* 27 Nov. 13/2 For the motorways, a fleet of snow ploughs and heavy salt-spreading vehicles is at constant readiness, day and night. The salt-spreaders can cover the whole of the M.1 at 40 to 50 m.p.h., within an hour. **1944** *Living off Land* v. 102 The cure is a pinch of salt, or one of the salt tablets now provided for the purpose, on the back of the tongue before each drink. **1976** A. PRICE *War Game* II. iv. 230 A heavy leather buff-coat..trapped the sweat and delayed the dehydration... So even though the salt tablets..were necessary, the discomfort was endurable.

SALT (sǫlt). Also **S.A.L.T., Salt.** [Acronym f. the initials of *S*trategic *A*rms *L*imitation *T*alks.] Negotiations, involving esp. the U.S.A. and the Soviet Union, aimed at the limitation or reduction of nuclear armaments. Freq. *attrib.*

The last element, which is freq. redundant in *attrib.* uses, is also understood as *Treaty*.

1968 MRS. L. B. JOHNSON *White House Diary* 1 July (1970) 693 When and where the talks would start, we do not know. They are being referred to as Strategic Arms Limitation Talks (SALT). **1969** *New Scientist* 14 Aug. 314/2 The progress of SALT is likely also to be slow. **1972** *Guardian* 6 June 4/4 The Secretary for Defence..told Congress today that the United States could not afford to relax its defence effort in spite of the SALT agreement. **1973** E. OSERS tr. *Waldheim's Austrian Example* xv. 196 The first ceilings set by the Salt Talks may prove to be an important landmark in limiting the arms race. **1975** *Daily Tel.* 23 Sept. 14/3 Whether the SALT discussions were a success or not is a matter of embittered controversy. **1976** *Survey* Summer-Autumn 24 The need for a further agreement in SALT remains paramount, given the threat to human survival posed by the nuclear arms race. **1979** *Sci. Amer.* Feb. 30/1 As the Senate prepares to debate the ratification of the new treaty emerging from the second round of strategic-arms-limitation talks (S.A.L.T. II) between the two superpowers.

salt, *a.*[1] Add: **1. a.** *salt finger*, one of a number of alternating columns of rising and descending water produced when a layer of water is overlain by a denser, more salty layer; so *salt fingering*, the occurrence of salt fingers; *salt spray*, used *attrib.* to denote a test in which an article is subjected to a spray of salt water, and the associated apparatus.

1918 *Proc. Amer. Soc. Testing Materials* XVIII. 237 (*heading*) Method of making the salt-spray corrosion test. **1945** *Electroplated Coatings of Nickel & Chromium on Steel & Brass* (*B.S.I.*) 18 Salt spray cabinet. **1962** *B.S.I. News* Feb. 18/2 A frequently-used test for determining resistance to corrosion is the salt spray test. **1967** *Deep-Sea Res.* XIV. 599 The opposite situation of a stable temperature gradient made unstable with a little salt leads to the formation of 'salt fingers'. *Ibid.* 606 Because of salt fingering, salt will escape across the bottom of this layer faster than heat. **1970** *Materials & Technol.* III. ix. 704 Exposure to a continuous mist of salt water, the so-called salt-spray test,..does not truly simulate atmospheric exposure. **1977** *Sci. Amer.* Oct. 147/1 The warm salty water of the Mediterranean sets up the conditions for salt fingering as it flows through the Straits of Gibraltar and over the fresher, cooler waters of the Atlantic. **1978** J. A. KNAUSS *Introd. Physical Oceanogr.* ix. 187 It would appear that..at least some of the microstructure in the ocean is caused by salt fingers.

c. Also *salt flat*, a flat expanse of land covered with a layer of salt; *salt meadow* (chiefly *N. Amer.*), a meadow liable to be flooded by salt water (further examples).

1656 *New Haven* (Connecticut) *Town Rec.* (1917) I. 288 It was don..by the cattell hurrying dówne in to ye salt meddows. **1789** J. MORSE *Amer. Geogr.* 287 There are large bodies of salt meadow along the Delaware. **1873** J. L. CRAWFORD in D. Eagan *6th Ann. Rep. Commissioner of Lands, Florida* (1874) 97 Hundreds of salt-works were erected upon the 'salt-flats' along the sea-shore within the limits of Wakulla. **1881** *Harper's Mag.* Jan. 254/2 The sluggish river winds through tracts of salt-meadow. **1931** *Amer. Speech* VII. 5 Sometimes the hunter found that he could make his best 'killings' at the 'salt licks' or 'salt flats' frequented by the buffalos. **1952** E. F. DAVIES *Illyrian Venture* i. 20 Why was the plain white? Was it snow? No, it looked more like salt flats. **1966** T. H. RADDALL *Hangman's Beach* III. xix. 286 A fringe of farms and salt meadows along the shore. **1972** *Guinness Bk. Records* (ed. 19) 128/2 The highest speed attained by any wheeled land vehicle is 631·368 m.p.h...on the Bonneville Salt Flats, Utah, on 23 Oct. 1970... The highest speed attained by a wheel-driven car is 429·311 m.p.h... on the salt flats at Lake Eyre, South Australia, on 17 July 1964.

2. a. (Further examples.) *salt rising*: see RISING *vbl. sb.* 15 in Dict. and Suppl.; *salt side* (U.S.), salt pork (cf. SIDE *sb.*[1] 3).

1892 O. WISTER *Jrnl.* 25 Nov. in *Out West* (1958) 143 We fried some bread..and I cooked some salt side. **1961** *Amer. Speech* XXXVI. 266 The term *salt side* is probably a similar blend of Northern *salt pork* and Midland *side meat*, terms for bacon.

in phr. used attrib. or Comb. **1747** H. GLASSTONE *Art of Cookery* ix. 114 A Salt-Fish Pye. Get a Side of Salt-Fish, lay it in Water all Night [etc.]. **1966** M. WOODHOUSE *Tree Frog* x. 76 We fought our way through thick salt-beef sandwiches.

b. *salt horse* (earlier example); also *transf.*, a naval officer with general duties.

1836 MARRYAT *Mr. Midshipman Easy* III. i. 11 Why you stay in Midshipman berth—eat hard biscuit, salt pig, salt horse? **1914** F. T. JANE *Navy as Fighting Machine* viii. 69 A non-specialist officer (known colloquially as 'salt horse') serves as a watch-keeper. **1917** 'TAFFRAIL' *Sub.* v. 115 Next came Lieutenant Hinckson, the senior 'salt horse', two and a half striped Lieutenant. **1946** J. IRVING *Royal Navalese* 149 *Salt horse, A*, an officer who has not specialised in gunnery, torpedo, etc. and does not intend to. **1957** D. MACINTYRE *Jutland* ii. 33 Here was a simple 'salt-horse', indeed, and such were not often selected, in time of peace, for the higher ranks of the Service. **1960** J. BISSET *Commodore* 17 Officers in big ships called destroyer-officers 'salt horses'—meaning non-specialists, a term of disdain.

3. b. Also *salt grass* (U.S.), one of a number of grasses growing in salt meadows or dry plains, esp. *Distichlis spicata* and several species of *Spartina* (earlier and later examples); *salt hay* (U.S.) hay made from salt grass (earlier and later examples).

1648 in *Mass. Hist. Soc. Coll.* (1852) 4th Ser. I. 204 Salt hay and fresh there thousands are of acres I do deeme. **1704** *Early Rec. Providence, Rhode Island* (1894) V. 224 The which sd Cove is a place of Salt Grass called Thatch. **1732** J. HEMPSTEAD *Diary* 23 Sept. (1901) 252, I went to Mamacock & fetcht a L[oa]d of Salt hay alias Rushes. *a* **1816** B. HAWKINS *Sk. Creek Country* (1848) 43 Such is the attachment of horses to this moss, or as the traders call it, salt grass. **1843** *Knickerbocker* XXII. 34 Range your eye along the summits of the salt hay-stacks. **1910** J. HART *Vigilante Girl* xxv. 350 The little stream..ran from the spring through bunches of salt grass. **1952** L. & J. BUSH-BROWN *America's Garden Bk.* (ed. 2) xii. 446 Salt hay is one of the most satisfactory materials mentioned [for winter mulching]. **1972** R. G. KAZMANN *Mod. Hydrol.* (ed. 2) v. 175 Salt grass will survive when the water table is as much as 12 ft below the land surface.

salt, *v.*[1] Add: **1. b.** (Earlier and later examples.)

1849 N. P. WILLIS *Rural Lett.* viii. 355 'Calm as the shadow of a rock across the foam of a cataract', would be a neat thing to 'salt down' for Calhoun or Van Buren. **1931** *Kansas City* (Missouri) *Star* 19 Sept. 12/5 It is a well known fact that all gamblers salt away their ill-gotten gains and die inordinately rich. **1952** *New Statesman* 17 May 578/2 Many palms itched for the millions that the Nationalists had salted away. **1959** *Times* 22 Apr. 8/4 Undisclosed profits were 'salted away' in banks in Eire and Rhodesia. **1966** *Economist* 9 Apr. 172/3 Members of previous governments, some of them now restricted to their homes, have salted away enormous sums of hard currency in foreign banks during their period of office. **1974** *Socialist Worker* 26 Oct. 3/1 The press, the experts and the pontificators see nothing wrong or hypocritical in the fact that the Banks can salt away these millions and make still more in this time of crisis.

d. Also in active use: *trans.*, to render (an animal) immune by inoculation; *intr.* of an animal: to become immune by suffering a disease.

1898 *Cape of Good Hope Agric. Jrnl.* 9 Jan. 6 The expression *to salt a beast* means to render the animal immune to the disease, to immunize him. **1906** *Rep. Brit. Assoc. Adv. Sci. 1905* 545 Dr. Edington..reports that..by inoculating mules with Heart-water blood he has been able to salt them against Horse-sickness. **1912** *S. Afr. Agric. Jrnl.* July 54 All farmers agree that cattle which recover [from Lamziekte] do not *salt* from the disease, in other words, there is no immunity.

2. c. Also, to sprinkle (a roadway) with salt in order to melt snow or ice (later example).

1977 *Oxford Jrnl.* 2 Dec. 12/4 Roads will only be salted when it is absolutely certain a cold snap is on the way.

3. Delete *Obs.* and add later examples.

1747 H. GLASSTONE *Art of Cookery* i. 3 Never salt your roast Meat before you lay it to the Fire, for that draws out all the Gravy. **1882** MME. BOUCHARD *How to live on Nothing* 17 All roasts should be peppered as well as salted, very little flour dredged over, and they should be served with a thick gravy. **1931** E. WEIR *When Madame Cooks* v. 55 After cleaning the fish..Salt and pepper the inside of each half and then grill them like a steak. **1965** *New Statesman* 5 Nov. 692/3 He..took up his knife and fork. He carefully salted his egg.

5. b. *U.S. colloq.* To reprimand or dress down.

1904 *Springfield* (Mass.) *Weekly Republ.* 9 Sept. 6 Senator Depew salts down William Allen White, who has stated that the senator tried to bully the president. **1913** J. LONDON *Valley of Moon* viii. 61 You're too fresh to keep... You need saltin' down.

6. c. Also more generally in *Chem.*, to reduce the solubility of, or precipitate (an organic substance) by adding an electrolyte to the solution; similarly *to salt in*, to increase the solubility of (an organic compound) by adding an electrolyte to the solvent.

1928 [see *CORTIN]. **1933** *Chem. Rev.* XIII. 91 There are numbers of cases in which the addition of certain salts increases the solubility of particular non-electrolytes causing them to be 'salted in'. **1939** *Thorpe's Dict. Appl. Chem.* (ed. 4) III. 286/2 The power of these electrolytes in 'salting out' organic compounds from their solutions. **1966** MAHLER & CORDES *Biol. Chem.* ii. 58 From the data in this figure, it is clear that at low ionic strengths the protein is salted in and at high ionic strengths the protein is salted out.

d. For 'cattle' read 'livestock' and add earlier and later examples. *N. Amer.*

1783 'J. H. ST. JOHN DE CRÈVECŒUR' *Sk. 18th-Cent. Amer.* (1925) 111 We..salt our cattle regularly once a week... From the horses to the sheep everyone must have a handful given them. **1819** E. DANA *Geogr. Sk. Western Country* 234 It is rare in this country that cattle are either fed, salted, or sheltered. **1852** [see *lick-log* s.v. *LICK *v.* 8]. **1931** *Amer. Speech* VI. 359 The absence of a salt sage diet on the summer range necessitates 'salting mutton'... Every second or third day one or two fifty-pound sacks of salt for every fifteen hundred sheep will be emptied into 'salt troughs' on the 'bed grounds'. **1968** R. M. PATTERSON *Finlay's River* 240 The packer..decided to leave those two [horses] here on the meadows to fill up and recuperate. He would salt them here.

8. (Further example.)

1977 *New Yorker* 29 Aug. 54/3 That made it easy for me to salt their accounts, and that's what I did. I began putting checks from company accounts into their personal accounts, and from there into oblivion via dummy companies.

9. (Earlier and later examples.) Also *transf.* and *fig.*

1852 in *Pioneer* (San Francisco) (1855) Mar. 146 The quicksilver which was procured at the Ranch, for the testing of the quartz, the victims declared was 'salted'; and they accused the *Rancheros* of conniving at the fraud. **1863** W. H. GOODE *Outposts of Zion* III. 415 The grounds have been 'salted'—gold dust scattered to deceive. **1880** *Harper's Mag.* Dec. 88/1 The deacon had stuck in a bit of Scriptur so's to salt it like. **1924** G. B. STERN *Tents of Israel* vii. 114 The Nong-Khan mine had been cleverly 'salted'... Only spinel sapphires, of practically no value, were to be found in it. **1951** *Times* 13 Dec. 4/6 (*heading*) Gold samples 'salted'. **1966** W. S. RAMSON *Austral. Eng.* vii. 148 One interesting and now probably obsolete expression is *to salt a claim*, meaning 'to sprinkle salt over the dirt', the salt having the appearance of gold-dust and giving the impression that the miner concerned has 'struck it rich'. **1968** A. S. ROMER *Procession of Life* xviii. 296 The gravel pit it would seem, was 'salted' by someone (? Dawson) with specimens to be later excavated as seeming authentic fossils. **1977** J. B. HILTON *Dead-Nettle* ii. 20, I shall want to see some evidence that there really is a seam. No salting it, no faking..your first job is to collect your showing.

salta (sæ·ltă). [f. L. *saltāre* to leap, perh. imitating HALMA.] A game played on a checkerboard of 100 squares by two persons with fifteen pieces each, with the object of occupying the opponent's side of the board.

1901 *Daily Express* 23 Mar. 8/7 Salta is played on a board of 100 squares, each player having fifteen pieces. *Ibid.*, Like in the first international salta tournament.., a chess master has again held his own against the draughts and salta experts who competed. **1904** E. B. TWEEDIE *Behind Footlights* viii. 153 She [*sc.* Sarah Bernhardt]..plays Salta with her son. This game is a kind of draughts. **1969** R. C. BELL *Board & Table Games* II. iii. 59 Salta was invented about 1900, and is played on the black squares of a continental draughtsboard of 10 × 10 squares.

sa·lt-and-pe·pper, *a.* Applied to things and materials (esp. hair) which are of two or more colours, one being light. Cf. PEPPER-AND-SALT in Dict. and Suppl. Also applied *transf.* to places, schemes, etc., in which black and white persons are mixed. orig. and chiefly *U.S.*

1915 *Sat. Even. Post* 2 Jan. 8/3 Hattie Krakow ran her hand over her smooth salt-and-pepper hair. **1959** *Wall St. Jrnl.* 12 Aug. 19/2 Houston is considering the 'salt and pepper' plan which has been widely suggested but not yet used. It calls for initial integration in schools where there is least objection from parents and expansion into other areas later. **1966** J. S. COX *Illustr. Dict. Hairdressing* 130/2 *Salt and pepper hair*, a head of hair in which the hairs are of at least two different colours, one of which is white. **1971** *New Yorker* 21 Aug. 3 (Advt.), Braid-bound suit of salt and pepper tweed. **1972** *Ibid.* 23 Dec. 38/3 Detroit is a salt-and-pepper situation. A great mix of black and white. **1973** M. AMIS *Rachel Papers* 52 In common with every American over eight and under twenty-five, he looked like a middle-aged American sports-writer: freckled pinhead, cropped salt-and-pepper hair. **1978** R. LUDLUM *Holcroft Covenant* vi. 79 Thick eyebrows, the coiled, matted hair an odd mixture of black and white. Salt-and-pepper eyebrows.

saltarello. Add: Pl. **saltarelli, -ellos. 1.** (Further examples.)

1876 STAINER & BARRETT *Dict. Mus. Terms* 383/2 Saltarelli are frequently found as movements or separate pieces in harpsichord and pianoforte music. **1928** E. CANZIANI *Through Apennines & Lands of Abruzzi* iv. 55 At Mascione, when the *saltarella* is danced, if lovers quarrel, the man or the woman kneels and asks, '*Cosa hai fatto?*' **1968** *Listener* 22 Aug. 249/3 The orchestra takes over from the voices and provides what might be regarded as a cue for dancing—as in the *saltarello* episode (in 'Sloth'). **1976** *Early Music* Oct. 457/1 Two of them are included on the Telefunken record already mentioned: the third of the manuscript's four saltarellos and 'Chominciamento di gioia'. **1980** *Ibid.* July 406/3 Apart from some isolated examples which have appeared in various anthologies, including some of the saltarelli and the popular *Lamento di tristano*, transcriptions have been restricted to scholarly editions.

Saltash (sǫltæ·ʃ). The name of a fishing-port in Cornwall used *attrib.* in **Saltash luck** (occas. **catch**), a thankless or fruitless task that involves getting wet through. *Naut. slang.*

1914 'BARTIMEUS' *Naval Occasions* xxiii. 225 One of the securing chains wants tautening... 'Saltash Luck' for some one! **1946** J. IRVING *Royal Navalese* 149 *Saltash luck*, a wet and thankless task such as securing up a bower anchor's slips in a seaway with the forecastle streaming with spray. **1962** GRANVILLE *Dict. Sailors' Slang* 99/2 *Saltash catch or Saltash luck*, 'a wet arse and no fish'. This West Country phrase has long been in use at sea, both in the Royal and Merchant Navies... It is believed to have originated in the lucklessness of fishermen at Saltash near Plymouth who sit on the bridge and catch nothing but the tide.

saltate, *v.* Restrict *rare* to sense in Dict. and add: **2.** *Physical Geogr.* To move by saltation (sense *1 d); also *trans.* (causatively). Chiefly as **saltating** *ppl. a.* (further examples).

1941 R. A. BAGNOLD *Physics Blown Sand & Desert Dunes* viii. 104 The energy supplied to the saltating grains by the wind. **1961** N. D. OPDYKE in A. E. M. Nairn *Descript. Palaeoclimatol.* iii. 47 Millet seed sand grains..show very high sphericity and roundness values due to their mode of transport which tends to round off the individual grains while they are being saltated. **1969** *Nature* 23 Aug. 792/2 Larger particles may be moved, not by the wind itself, but by momentum exchange with saltating grains. **1976** R. C. SELLEY *Introd. Sedimentol.* vi. 172 In a situation such as a river channel,..gravel will be rolling along the bottom, sand will sedately saltate, and silt and clay will be carried in suspension.

saltation. Add: **1. d.** *Physical Geogr.* A mode of transport of hard particles over an uneven surface in a fluid stream (as a wind or river), in which they progress in leaps, and on falling to the surface either bounce up for another leap or impart their momentum to other particles which on rising are accelerated forward by the stream. Cf. *SALTATE *v.* 2.

1908 W. J. MCGEE in *Bull. Geol. Soc. Amer.* XIX. 199 Transportation may be regarded as the general movement of earth matter seaward by streams; it comprises carriage of material (*a*) in solution, (*b*) in suspension, and (*c*) in what may be denoted saltation. **1941** R. A. BAGNOLD *Physics of Blown Sand & Desert Dunes* ii. 20, I shall use the name 'saltation' for the motion of sand in air, but without prejudice to the question of whether or not the mechanism which causes the grain to jump from the surface is the same in the two fluids. In air it is certainly the impact of a grain with the surface; but this is rarely so in water. **1962** READ & WATSON *Introd. Geol.* I. iv. 206 The mechanisms of transport in the sea are similar to those already described in connection with rivers, namely, suspension, rolling and saltation. **1977** A. HALLAM *Planet Earth* 50 The sand grains suspended in the air are the smaller ones, movement of larger particles being along the ground by saltation—by a series of jumps.

3. *Biol.* **a.** A mutation, esp. one with marked effects on several characters.

The 'saltations' studied by de Vries (see quot. 1906) are now known to have been translocations, which in *Œnothera* with its unusual system of chromosomes lead to large phenotypic changes.

1870 [see sense 1 c in Dict.]. **1906** *Pop. Sci. Monthly* June 485 The name 'saltation', or in recent years 'mutation', has been applied to extreme fluctuation, the immediate cause of which is unknown. *Ibid.*, Experiments of Dr. Hugo de Vries on the saltations of the descendants of an American form of evening primrose. **1919** *Jrnl. Exper. Zool.* XXVIII. 381 In our opinion, the attempted distinctions between 'saltations', 'mutations', and 'variations of slight degree' have led rather to confusion of thought than to clearer thinking. To us these are all a single class, 'mutations'. **1930** R. A. FISHER *Genetical Theory Nat. Selection* vii. 163 Unless such a resemblance formerly existed a gradual mimetic evolution is precluded, and we should be forced to admit that the mimetic females arose as sports or saltations totally unlike their mothers. *Ibid.* 164 A single saltation from a male of the same species. **1963** E. MAYR *Animal Species & Evolution* xv. 435 The sudden origin of new species, new higher categories, or quite generally of new types by some sort of saltation has been termed macrogenesis.

b. Change of phenotype occurring within a fungal colony.

1922 F. L. STEVENS in *Bull. Illinois Nat. Hist. Surv.* XIV. v. 157 The existing differences in definition and usage of the term mutation, as also our very limited knowledge of cytological conditions in the genus Helminthosporium and our ignorance as to whether it has sexual stages, have led me to select the term saltation for the variations here discussed. **1926** *Ann. Bot.* XL. 223 Changes of a more lasting nature may be conceived as arising gradually as a response or adaptation to certain growth conditions, or by sudden jumps. The latter type of phenomenon, which is known to occur in a considerable number of fungal genera,..is usually described as a 'mutation', or more conservatively as a saltation. **1940** J. RAMSBOTTOM in J. S. Huxley *New Systematics* 414 The morphological range is often so great that a single saltation will give what would be considered as a new species. **1978** *Nature* 29 June 755/1 The common and poorly understood phenomenon of frequent somatic variation in certain supposedly haploid fungi (saltation) may perhaps be due to the loss of extra chromosomes that had been acquired previously.

Hence **salta·tional** *a.*, of, pertaining to, or occurring by means of saltation.

1963 E. MAYR *Animal Species & Evolution* xv. 435 The reorganization of the gene pool, required for successful speciation, is (except in the case of polyploidy) never saltational. *Ibid.* 437 Some saltational postulates are based on the assumption of essentially invariant evolutionary rates. **1978** *Sci. Amer.* Sept. 41/1 Even T. H. Huxley..could not accept the gradual origin of higher types and new species; he proposed a saltational origin instead.

saltationist (sæltēɪ·ʃənist), *a.* and *sb. Biol.* [f. SALTATION + -IST.] **A.** *adj.* Of or pertaining to saltationism. **B.** *sb.* One who supports or advocates saltationism.

1954 R. A. FISHER in J. S. Huxley et al. *Evolution as Process* 93 Darwin's criticism of the saltationist theory of M. Mivart. **1978** *Sci. Amer.* Sept. 44/1 They were essentialists and saltationists, and they looked on mutation as the probable driving force in evolution. **1980** *Nature* 4 Dec. 430/1 T. H. Huxley himself was unable fully to accept Darwin's gradualism, and preferred the saltationist camp.

So **salta·tionism**, the theory that new species arise suddenly as a result of major mutations.

1975 KELLY & MCGRATH *Biology* vii. 213/2 DeVries.. insisted that a new species could arise by the introduction of a single mutation in an organism. His theory, called saltationism.., has been disproved, with one exception. **1978** *Sci. Amer.* Sept. 41/1 Saltationism was also popular with such biologists as Hugo De Vries, one of the rediscoverers of Gregor Mendel's laws of inheritance. **1979** M. RUSE *Darwinian Revolution* ix. 249 There were scientific reasons why many favored saltationism.

saltative (sæ·ltătiv), *a. rare.* [f. SALTATE *v.* + -IVE.] = SALTATORY *a.* 2 a.

1829 [implied in SALTATIVENESS]. **1911** *Law Rep., King's Bench* I. 654 These Scotch sheep are of a peculiarly wandering and saltative disposition.

saltatory, *a.* and *sb.*[1] Add: **A.** *adj.* **2. a.** (Example in *Physical Geogr.*)

1908 *Bull. Geol. Soc. Amer.* XIX. 199 The coarser particles due to corrosion..and to washing move forward at ever varying rates in saltatory fashion, the variable or leaping movements arising largely in combinations of friction with inertia.

d. *Physiol.* Used to designate the mode of transmission in a myelinated nerve in which the nerve impulse 'jumps' from node to node.

1934 *Amer. Jrnl. Physiol.* CX. 308 The pictures could be accounted for if progression were saltatory and by a process such as Lillie (1925) has described as occurring in the iron wire model... Here, due to reactivation by eddy currents flowing around the segments, activity progresses in jumps from node to node and consequently is more rapid than in the simple model. **1949** *Jrnl. Physiol.* CVIII. 339 The finding..that a large decrease in node spacing can occur without a drop in conduction velocity is shown not to conflict with the theory of saltatory conduction. **1977** *Proc. Nat. Acad. Sci.* LXXIV. 211/1 Myelinated nerve conducts by transmission of electrical excitation from node to node through local electrical circuits. This 'saltatory' mode of conduction results from a discontinuity in the excitability properties of the axon: excitable regions (nodes) alternate with nonexcitable passive core conductors (myelinated internodes).

e. *Biol.* Of the movement of small particles within cells: proceeding in directed jerks.

1964 L. I. REBHUN in Allen & Kamiya *Primitive Motile Syst. in Cell Biol.* 503 Particles may at one time undergo Brownian movement and suddenly undergo a process converting this to sudden, discontinuous motion, i.e., saltatory motion. **1970** *Nature* 7 Feb. 559/1 It may well be.. that microtubules in brain function in the saltatory transport of material and vesicles from their site of formation in the cell body to their site of utilization at the synaptic endings. *Ibid.* 5 Sept. 1006/2 Translocation has been pictured as a saltatory interaction between enzyme-containing vesicles and fibrous proteins, chiefly microtubules.

3. Biol. *saltatory replication*, a hypothetical evolutionary event in which very many identical copies of a short section of DNA are added to a genome.

1968 R. J. BRITTEN in *Carnegie Inst. Year Bk. 1966–7* 72/2 *Saltatory replications*, the hypothetical events by which families of hundreds of thousands of similar nucleotide sequences are produced in the DNA of an organism. .. Families are produced in a time short compared to the time required for their loss by divergence (a few hundred million years). **1968** —— & KOHNE in *Ibid.* 84/1 Events in which very many copies [of a DNA segment] are made in a short time interval (saltatory replication). Evidence is now available which clearly indicates saltatory replication. *Ibid.* 88/1 A saltatory replication producing 100,000 copies of the right sort of gene is a candidate for a genetic event with immense potentiality. **1970** *Nature* 12 Dec. 1043/2 Such gene expansion has been designated saltatory replication and is illustrated in Fig. 1 C.

salt-box. Add: **1. c.** *U.S.* Used *attrib.* or *absol.* to designate a kind of frame-house which resembles a salt-box in shape, having two storeys at the front and one at the back.

1876 J. S. INGRAM *Centennial Exposition* 717 One of the chief oddities of the Exhibition—the Hunter's Cabin. It was built of logs in the 'salt-box' style and entirely open in front. **1900** J. DE F. SHELTON *Salt Box House* i. 17 Colloquially, it was called a 'salt-box house', its lines repeating those of the wooden salt-box that hung in the kitchen chimney. The ridge-pole was set far to the front, from which a short roof sloped..down to the outer line of the ceiling of the ground floor. **1934** *Sun* (Baltimore) 14 Aug. 10/6 The first of the salt boxes were almost always made by adding the lean-to to the two-room house. **1944** *Sat. Rev.* (U.S.) 2 Sept. 30/1 (Advt.), New England saltbox in scenic New York setting. **1952** F. ALLEN *Big Change* II. viii. 126 New England salt-box-type houses with attached garages. **1967** V. SILTER *Biltmore Call* 57 Some were remodelled farm houses..and some were old saltboxes..and some were just plain old country houses. **1976** *New Yorker* 22 Mar. 125/1 Cunningly combining painted backcloths, a two-story saltbox frame, and picturesque detail in the way of furniture and properties, Ming Cho Lee's decor for the six different settings was at once varied, realistic, and romantic.

salt-cellar. Add: **c.** *colloq.* Each of the pronounced hollows at the base of a thin neck. (Usu. with reference to young women.)

1870 O. LOGAN *Before Footlights* 26, I was a child of the most uninteresting age..a tall scraggy girl, with red elbows, and salt cellars at my collar-bones, which were always exposed, for fashion at that time made girls of this age uncover neck and arms. **1880** F. BELTON *Random Recoll. Old Actor* vi. 87 The bones of her elbows were painfully prominent, with enormous salt-cellar hollows in her neck. **1913** 'O. ONIONS' *Story of Louie* I. i. 25 The copper-haired girl with the long thin neck and the 'salt-cellars' showing through her white flannel blouse. **1913** *Queen* 17 May 35 (Advt.), 'Saltcellars' and thinness of the neck and shoulders. **1964** P. WHITE *Burnt Ones* 162 She was so thin, but he loved her even for her salt-cellars.

salt chuck. *N. Amer. colloq.* [Chinook jargon, f. SALT *a.*[1] + *CHUCK *sb.*[6]] In western Canada and north-western U.S.: the sea, the ocean.

1868 F. WHYMPER *Trav. Alaska* iv. 45 An Indian, paddling in his 'frail kanim' on the great 'salt chuck' or sea, was swallowed—canoe and all—by a great fish. **1874** C. HORETZKY *Canada on Pacific* 132 A thick heavy mist hung over the valley, completely hiding the Cascade range which we had now to enter and pass through before reaching the 'salt-chuck'. **1909** E. I. DENNY *Blazing the Way* I. vii. 120 The fish, of many excellent kinds, from the 'salt chuck', brought fresh and flapping to our doors, in native baskets by Indian fishermen. **1938** G. CASH *I like Brit. Columbia* 61 Unless you are camped near a log dump—which means where a logging company is dumping logs into the salt chuck—you have quite a time gathering enough. **1958** R. G. LARGE *Skeena* (ed. 3) x. 65 Sailing the salt-chuck easily, o'er an oft familiar route. **1964** L. LINTON *Of Days & Driftwood* iv. 24 Even the gulls, screeching over the gray saltchuck..were giving their last accolade to summer. **1975** *Islander* (Victoria, B.C.) 27 July 14/2 In 1905, most people lived close to the saltchuck and along Rainey Creek.

Hence **sa·lt-chucker**, a sea-water angler.

1958 in R. E. Watters *Brit. Columbia* 216 It is the spirit that counts, and that spirit extends to trying to make life happier for thousands of scattered salt-chuckers. **1963** *Sun* (Vancouver) 20 July 15/1 Now, however, with an average of almost two fish per short outing of a few hours each trip, I'm wearing the saltchucker's smug smirk.

salted, *ppl. a.* Add: **2. a.** Now used esp. of prepared foods, as *salted almond, peanut*, etc. (Further examples.)

1892 *Encycl. Pract. Cookery* I. 15/1 Salted and 'Devilled' Almonds. **1921** A. HUXLEY *Crome Yellow* xix. 202 Georgiana ate only an olive, two or three salted almonds, and half a peach. **1935** M. MORPHY *Recipes of All Nations* 775 Salted Green Peas, first cooked in cinders and then salted like almonds, are among Persian delicacies. **1954** 'R. CROMPTON' *William & Moon Rocket* iv. 85 Salted nuts..potato crisps.. celery. **1970** E. DAVID *Spices, Salt & Aromatics in Eng. Kitchen* 231 Salted almonds, whatever the promises held out by the words vacuum-sealed or oven-fresh on tins and jars are not to be bought. **1972** A. MACVICAR *Golden Venus Affair* v. 49, I ordered a Pym's No. 1... We munched salted peanuts.

4. (Earlier and later examples.)

1864 T. BAINES *Explorations in S.W. Afr.* xv. 418 He asked carefully 'whether the horse was salted' (i.e. acclimatised by having recovered from the horse sickness). **1977** BUXTON & FRASER *Animal Microbiol.* II. xlviii. 634/1 Horses and mules that have recovered from a natural attack of horse sickness are generally more resistant to disease than other equines and are known as 'salted', as are animals that have survived for a number of years in badly infected areas without ever showing obvious signs of the disease.

5. (Earlier and later examples.)

1862 *California Mag.* Jan. 355/1, I lost my $2,000 by buying a 'salted' claim. **1949** *This Week Mag.* 15 Oct. 27/4 They are occasionally called upon by unscrupulous characters whose main object is to sell them a 'salted' mine.

saltery. Add: **3.** *N. Amer.* A factory where fish is prepared for storage by salting. Now chiefly *Hist.*

1903 *Sci. Amer. Suppl.* 21 Mar. 22751/3 During 1900 there was but one saltery operated solely as such in this district. It is situated on the Nushagak and had an output of 7,186 barrels of red-fish and 536 barrels of king salmon for the season. **1960** M. SHARCOTT *Place of Many Winds* viii. 132 A few bricks and a couple of rotted and barnacled pilings tell of a long-forgotten cannery or saltery. **1972** L. HANCOCK *There's a Seal in my Sleeping Bag* ix. 218 Alert Bay was once a small saltery to preserve salmon prior to shipment to Victoria.

‖ **saltimbocca** (sæltimbǫ·kă). [It., f. *saltare* to leap + *in* IN *prep.* + *bocca* mouth.] A dish consisting of rolled pieces of veal and ham cooked with herbs. Also in *Comb.*, as *saltimbocca (alla) Romana.*

1937 M. MORPHY *Good Food from Italy* 89 (*heading*) Veal and Ham à la Romana [Saltimbocca alla Romana]. **1959** *Good Food Guide* 224 Escalope Cordon Bleu, 'rather like a Roman Saltimbocca only deep fried in batter'. **1960** *Harper's Bazaar* Oct. 154/2 *Saltimbocca* combines paper-thin slices of veal with *prosciutto* and a sage leaf. **1969** G. GREENE *Travels with my Aunt* I. xiii. 126 He put a lot of *saltimbocca Romana* into his mouth. **1977** C. MCCULLOUGH *Thorn Birds* xvii. 447 I'll have pâté, some scampi and a huge plate of saltimbocca. **1978** *Chicago* June 237/1 [There are] half a dozen veal dishes (Saltimbocca alla Romana—with prosciutto, butter, herbs, and marsala—is a specialty), [etc.].

saltine (sǫ·ltīn). orig. and chiefly *U.S.* [f. SALT *sb.*[1] + -INE[4].] A salted cracker or thin crisp biscuit.

1907 *Grocery World* 4 Nov. 40/2 Crackers and cakes... Orange Cookies... Quaker City Mixed... Salted Strips... Saltines [etc.]. **1914** H. C. SHERMAN *Food Products* viii. 287 Crackers,..Pretzels... Saltines... Soda crackers (etc.). **1933** E. O'NEILL *Ah, Wilderness!* II. 63 Mrs. Miller. (as Norah comes back with a dish of saltines—begins ladling soup into the stack of plates before her). *c* **1938** *Fortnum & Mason Price List* 19/1 Southern American Biscuits..Saltines..2/3. **1958** E. S. WARNER *Silk-Cotton Tree* xvii. 177 The Head was passing around a box of soggy-looking saltines. **1969** 'E. LATHEN' *Murder to Go* xiv. 134 'Would anybody..like some crackers?'.. He delayed his own departure until the appearance of a dish of saltines. **1975** *New Yorker* 14 Apr. 104/3, I sought him out in his office at Hi Corbett Field (where he was lunching on two Cokes and some saltines crumbled into a cup of soup). **1980** R. L. DUNCAN *Brimstone* v. 89 Have my lunch brought in. Milk and saltines.

saltiness. (Later example in *fig.* sense.)

1934 A. WOOLLCOTT *While Rome Burns* 26 Hansoms have the advantage of semi-privacy, and what their drivers lack in chic they make up in saltiness.

salting, *vbl. sb.* Add: **2. a.** (Earlier and later examples in sense 9 of the vb.)

1856 *Santa Barbara* (Calif.) *Gaz.* 21 Feb. 2/5 The best yield I have seen is eighteen cents to the pan, and this was without any 'salting'. **1869** 'MARK TWAIN' *Lett.* (1917) I. 164 When it was discovered that those lumps were melted half dollars and hardly melted at that, a painful case of 'salting' was apparent. **1949** *Sun* (Baltimore) 31 Oct. 3/4 Farrell and others pointed out that 'salting'.. along nine miles of river shore would be pointless and profitless. **1951** *Times* 13 Dec. 4/6, ——, works manager, of Malvern, Johannesburg, was found Guilty at the Rand criminal sessions to-day on two counts of *falsitas* in the 'salting' (fraudulent enrichment) of the basal and leader reef third deflection core samples of the Erdeel 5 mine. **1972** *Courier-Mail* (Brisbane) 20 June 5/3 (*heading*) Cutler denies nickel salting.

b. Chem. *salting in, out* (cf. *SALT *v.*[1] 6 c).

1857 [in Dict., sense 2 a]. **1905** *Jrnl. Physiol.* XXXII. 329 The only method which, according to our present knowledge, leaves proteids absolutely unaltered is that of 'salting out'. **1926** R. WRIGHT in *Jrnl. Chem. Soc.* 1203 The mutual lowering of solubility which takes place when an electrolyte and an organic substance are dissolved together in water..is the basis of the process of 'salting out' when an organic compound is driven out of aqueous solution by the addition of a salt. What may be termed 'salting in' is the reverse phenomenon, that is, a mutual increase in solubility of electrolyte and organic compound when added to the same solvent, which in this case is not pure water but aqueous alcohol. **1939** *Thorpe's Dict. Appl. Chem.* (ed. 4) III. 286/2 The 'salting out' effect of electrolytes on hydrophilic colloids is due to their dehydrating action as well as to their power of neutralising the charge. **1957** G. E. HUTCHINSON *Treat. Limnol.* I. ii. 183 Salting out of charged silt particles by water of compensation currents. **1970** A. L. LEHNINGER *Biochem.* vii. 133 Salts containing divalent ions..are far more effective at salting-in than salts such as NaCl, NH_4Cl, and KCl.

4. (sense 1) *salting-pan* (earlier example), *-shed.*

1816 JANE AUSTEN *Emma* II. iii. 43 My mother was so afraid that we had not any salting-pan large enough. **1889** W. B. YEATS *Wanderings of Oisin* 82 Times from the saltin' shed..I scarce could drag my feet. **1961** N. FROUD et al. tr. *Montagné's Larousse Gastronomique* 493/2 The fish is transported from the boat to the salting sheds.

saltire. Add: Also, a cross having this shape.

1970 H. BRAUN *Parish Churches* viii. 104 The 'saltire' or diagonal cross formed of two struts crossing, was nearly always formed of two serpentine timbers. **1974** *Northern Times* (Golspie, Sutherland) 2 Aug. 3/4 The gift was a saltire—a St. Andrew's Cross in blue and white with the arms of the cross outlined in gold thread.

salt lake. [SALT *a.*[1]] A saline lake, usu. one with no outlet to the sea so that salts brought in by rivers accumulate in it; *esp.* one which is not particularly alkaline (cf. *bitter lake* s.v. *BITTER *a.* 1 c).

1763 J. BELL *Trav. from St. Petersburg* I. 289 We set up our tents near a lake of brackish water, called Solonoy-Osera, or the salt lake. *Ibid.* 326 The 22d, we quitted the salt lake. **1836** *Penny Cycl.* VI. 343/2 A great number of smaller and larger salt lakes. **1882** [see *BITTER *a.* 1 c]. **1923** J. S. HUXLEY *Ess. Biologist* i. 34 A salt-lake shrimp could tolerate an even higher concentrate of brine. **1970** [see *EXOGENETIC *a.* 2 b].

saltlessness. (Later example in *fig.* sense.)
1867 QUEEN VICTORIA *Let.* 13 Feb. in R. Fulford *Your Dear Letter* (1971) 121 There is great bitterness in the constant depression..and total saltlessness of my life.

salt-lick. Add: (Further examples.) Also *fig.* Now chiefly *N. Amer.*
1859 J. PALLISER *Jrnl.* 16 Feb. (1863) 129 A splendid ram..had been caught by setting a snare in a path leading to a 'salt-lick'. **1922** *Beaver* May 7/2 They [*sc.* bighorn sheep] being in the habit of seeking the salt-licks early in the morning and again late in the evening. **1948** C. DAY LEWIS *Poems 1943–47* 75 The sea rolled up like a blind, oh pitiless light Revealing, shrivelling all! Lacklustre weeds My hours, my truth a salt-lick. **1965** R. MCKIE *Company of Animals* vii. 113 Jim went at first light to check which animals were visiting a small salt-lick in the jungle. **1976** N. THORNBURG *Cutter & Bone* viii. 202 Immediately she was weeping in his arms, her face a lovely saltlick to his mouth.

salt-marsh. Add: **b.** (Further examples.)
1862 *Harper's Mag.* Nov. 737/2 'Salt-marsh fly'—is a nuisance found everywhere..near salt marshes. **1932** *Sun* (Baltimore) 23 Aug. 4/7 The salt marsh mosquito causes intense discomfort. **1972** SWAN & PAPP *Common Insects N. Amer.* xxii. 592 Salt-marsh Mosquito: *Aedes sollicitans. Ibid.*, The California Salt-marsh Mosquito..breeds in salt marshes and tide pools along the Pacific coast.
c. *attrib.* in general use.
1937 *Discovery* Apr. 98/2 The occupation was brought to an end with the onset of salt-marsh conditions. **1960** J. J. ROWLANDS *Spindrift* 91 The salt-marsh hayfields are favorite stopping-places for geese and ducks on their northward flight. **1975** J. G. EVANS *Environment Early Man Brit. Isles* vii. 180 Later stages in the saltmarsh succession form good sheep pasture.

‖**salto** (sa·lto). [It., leap; cf. SALTUS.] **1.** salto mortale (mǫrtā·le) [It., = fatal jump, somersault], a daring or flying leap (as of a trapeze artist, etc.); also *fig.*, a step that involves risk; an unjustified inference, a 'leap of faith'.
1896 W. CALDWELL *Schopenhauer's Syst.* vii. 361 He really solved it [*sc.* the question of altruism] only by a *salto mortale.* a **1910** W. JAMES *Ess. Radical Empiricism* (1912) ii. 67 The transcendentalist..holds knowing to consist in a *salto mortale* across an 'epistemological chasm'. **1937** J. M. MURRY *Necessity of Pacifism* vii. 115 England will take this glorious *salto mortale* into a more human future. **1952** R. MANNING-SANDERS *Eng. Circus* IV. xvii. 237 Let us look..at the act of the two Codonas,..after Alfredo, in 1922, had mastered that wonderful feat, the *salto mortale*, or triple somersault. **1968** M. GUYBON tr. *Solzhenitsyn's First Circle* (1971) xxviii. 164 He was escorted up another flight of steps—where, as in a circus during the *salto mortale*, there were nets to catch him if he jumped off. **1977** *Language* LIII. 44 While the enclitic nature of the copula is beyond question in itself, inferring 'aphaeresis' as a phenomenon consequential upon it has involved an epistemological 'salto mortale' which has not been very successful.
2. *Gymnastics.* A somersault.
1972 B. TAYLOR et al. *Olympic Gymnastics* iii. 35 With more advanced movements (such as a double back salto or double twisting back layout), a spotting belt is sometimes used. **1974** *Rules of Game* 36 *Compulsory exercises*... Arms backward, two or three running steps into forward piked salto, land on one leg. **1980** *Sunday Times* 20 July 28/2, I will show you a new dismount off the beam... It is a double Salto off one leg with half a turn.

Saltoun (sǭ·ltən). [Proper name: see quot. 1886.] A variety of artificial trout fly (see quots.).
1886 F. M. HALFORD *Floating Flies* v. 90 Saltoun. *Wings.* Palest starling. *Body.* Black silk, ribbed with silver wire. *Hackle and Whisk.* Pale ginger cock. *Hook.* oo or ooo. A very useful summer fly, invented by and named after the late Lord Saltoun [prob. Alexander Fraser, 17th Lord Saltoun, d. Feb. 1886], a prominent member of the old Stockbridge Club. **1892** M. O. MARBURY *Favorite Flies* (ed. 2) 379 (*heading*) Frederic M. Halford's floating flies for dry-fly fishing... No. 223 Saltoun. **1926** *Chambers's Jrnl.* 13 Feb. 164/1 There's a two-pounder at the stream-mouth that has risen twice to the saltoun. **1931** *Hardy's Anglers' Guide* (ed. 53) 66 Lake and Sea Trout Flies... No. 44. Saltoun. **1961** A. C. WILLIAMS *Dict. Trout Flies* (ed. 3) 302 *Saltoun*, an old pattern and a one-time favourite on the chalk streams. After falling into disuse, it has been revived in recent years as a lake fly.

salt rheum. **2.** For *U.S.* read *N. Amer.* and add: **a.** (Earlier and later examples.)
1809 E. KENDALL *Trav. Northern Parts U.S.* I. 325 In the neighbourhood, the greater number of patients that it attracts appear to be such as labour under scrofulous diseases. That, of which I heard the name in everyone's mouth, is the *salt rheum.* **1877** R. J. BURDETTE *Rise & Fall of Mustache* 291 'Centennial Cordial and American Indian Aboriginal Invigorator'..has absolutely no equal for the cure of..salt rheum. **1901** *Daily Colonist* (Victoria, B.C.) 26 Oct. 8/1 This preparation seems to have magnetic powers in stopping the dreadful itching, burning sensations of salt rheum and eczema.

salt river. *U.S.* [SALT *a.*[1]] † **1.** A river which is tidal a considerable distance from its mouth. *Obs.*
1659 *Early Rec. Providence, Rhode Island* (1892) I. 97 A percell of land..lieth upon the salt River at the furthermost side of the towne boundes. **1704** *Ibid.* (1894) V. 224 Sd Cove..lieth adjoyneing to the North side of the salt River called Pautuckett. **1791** W. BARTRAM *Trav. N. & S. Carolina* I. iv. 29 Numerous small rivers and their branches: these they call salt rivers, because the tides flow near to their sources.
2. a. The name of a river (perh. one in Kentucky) used as *attrib. phr.* to designate the inhabitants of the American backwoods region, esp. with reference to their uncultivated manner of speech. Also applied to the speech, etc., of these people. Now only *Hist.*
1828 *Western Intelligencer* (Hamilton, Ohio) 26 Dec. 1/4 A 'Salt River Roarer'. One of these two fisted backwoodsmen, 'half horse, half alligator, and a little touched with the snapping turtle'. **1835** *Knickerbocker* V. 403 They [*sc.* speeches in Congress] are chiefly made up of extracts from the common school collection of lessons for reading and speaking, sprinkled with scraps of dog-Latin, and a sort of patois, called Salt-river roaring. **1835** T. FLINT in *Athenæum* July 511/2 There is, in fact, a well-known rivalry between the collectors of the Downing dialect of New England, and the Crocket or Salt River dialect of the South and West. **1947** J. CONROY *Midland Humor* p. x, The ring-tailed roarers and Salt River screamers of the half-horse and half-alligator breed, both male and female, were ordinarily combinations of physical might and mother wit which enabled them to outsmart invaders from other regions.
b. *fig.* In slang phr. *to row* (someone) *up Salt River* and varr., to defeat (a political opponent); to overcome, send to oblivion. Also with intransitive vb., to be defeated or overcome, to go to oblivion; to get drunk. Freq. in allusive and proverbial uses. Now *rare.*
The simplest of the numerous explanations offered for this usage is that which connects it with sense 2 a; see H. Sperber and J. N. Tidwell in *Amer. Speech* (1951) XXVI. 241–7.
1828, etc. [see ROW *v.*[1] 8 a in Dict. and Suppl.]. **1830** *Cincinnati Chron.* 2 Jan. 1/2 He replied he didn't 'smoak me', and unless I cut cable in short order, he'd roar me up salt river. **1832** *Washington* (Ohio) *Herald* 17 Nov. 3/4 The Jackson boys of Ohio have been enabled to give them another ride 'up Salt River'. **1838** *Bentley's Misc.* IV. 588, I can drink till the world gets too old to move. While another man rows up Salt River, I'm only putting the fire out in the forest. *Ibid.*, Rowing up Salt River is a slang term for getting intoxicated. **1852** *Chicago Democrat* 11 Nov., One Thomas Holt, lately a clerk in The Chicago Post Office, when last seen,..was on his way up 'Salt River' with Gen. Scott. **1880** in J. C. Andrews *Pittsburgh Post Gaz.* (1936) xvi. 218 For Salt River—The River Boat Democracy left its Wharf Tuesday, Nov. 2, 1880 bound up Salt River in search of the late lamented Samuel J. Tilden. **1941** L. D. BALDWIN *Keelboat Age on Western Waters* 97 It'd shore be harder'n rowin' up Salt River to find a cleverer parcel o' fellers 'n them keelers.

salt spring. [SALT *a.*[1]] A flow of salt water or brine out of the earth; a brine-spring, brine-well. Also as *attrib. phr.*
1601 HOLLAND tr. *Pliny's Nat. Hist.* II. xxxi. vii. 416 In some parts of Spaine there be salt springs. *a* **1647** [see SALT *a.*[1] 1]. **1683** J. PETTUS *Fleta Minor* I. 321 Of Salt-Petre, Vitriol, Allum and Salt Springs. **1748** J. HILL *Hist. Fossils* 382 The Sea-water and Salt-springs sustain it [*sc.* alimentary salt]..in a liquid form. **1782** T. PENNANT *Journey Chester to London* 27 The Britons, who had, in several places, plenty of salt-springs. **1834** *Phil. Mag.* IV. 31 The comparative strength of the salt springs of that country at different depths. **1839** G. ROBERTS *Dict. Geol.*, *Salt Springs*, which contain a large quantity of common salt, obtained from them by mere evaporation. **1852** J. REYNOLDS *Hist. Illinois* 86 They discovered in the present county of Galatin, salt springs. **1853** *Trans. Mich. Agric. Soc.* IV. 9 The twenty-two sections of salt spring lands now unappropriated.

saltus. Add: Now used in unnaturalized Latin form (further examples). Also in *Comb.* Cf. *salto mortale* s.v. *SALTO 1.
1894 A. C. FRASER *Locke's Essay Annotated* II. IV. xii. 348 The inductive *saltus*, which transcends this datum. **1913** E. W. HOBSON *Squaring the Circle* ii. 18 There is no jumping to the limit as the supposed end of an essentially endless process, to be reached by some inscrutable *saltus.* **1923** G. B. SHAW in *Nation & Athenæum* 10 Feb. 714/2 He [*sc.* Wright] was hampered not only by the mistakes of Pasteur, but by a remarkable *saltus empiricus* made by a famous bacteriological acrobat..named Metchnikoff. **1934** A. C. EWING *Idealism* viii. 407 One can..pass from one to the other without a *saltus in aliud genus.* **1951** J. HOLLOWAY *Lang. & Intelligence* iii. 55 There must be a *saltus naturae*, an innate idea of symbolization must come to fruition.

salt water, *sb.* and *a.* Add: **B.** *attrib.* as *adj.* **a.** Also *salt-water taffy* (TAFFY[1], var. form of TOFFEE), a type of confectionery made chiefly from corn syrup and sugar, freq. sold at North-eastern (chiefly New Jersey) seaside resorts. *U.S.*
1894 *Official Gaz.* (U.S. Patent Office) 17 July 410/1 (*caption*) The representation of a four masted schooner with the words '*The Original Atlantic City Salt Water Taffy*'. **1910** H. T. PECK *New Baedeker* II. vi. 309 And there are also itinerant venders of every sort of edible..from 'salt-water taffy'..down to peanuts and 'hot dogs'. **1933** *Nat. Geogr. Mag.* May 520/2 Next to the visitor, Atlantic City's biggest 'Industry' is the making and shipping of 'salt-water taffy'. Legend says that in the early eighties a man had a candy stand on the beach. One day an unusually high tide splashed over a batch of old-fashioned, pulled taffy on a slab. Being an enterprising person, he told his customers that he had something new—'salt-water taffy'. **1954** W. RICHMOND *Choice Confections* xxi. 385 This formula produces a salt water taffy or kiss of very fine quality... The formula can be used for regular kiss-shaped pieces or long sticks of salt water taffy. **1960** J. J. ROWLANDS *Spindrift* 65 Through the grimy windows of the salt-water taffy counter you see the cold steel arms of the taffy puller motionless and empty-handed. **1979** *United States 1980/81* (Penguin Travel Guides) 48 Vermont cheese and maple syrup, salt-water taffy along the New Jersey shore..are all specialties of their respective regions.
c. *U.S.* and *W. Indies.* Used to designate a recent, usu. black, immigrant (see quots.).
1774 E. LONG *Hist. Jamaica* II. III. iii. 410 The Creole Blacks differ much from the Africans, not only in manners, but in beauty of shape, feature, and complexion. They hold the Africans in the utmost contempt, stiling them, 'salt-water Negroes', and 'Guiney birds'; but value themselves on their own pedigree. **1818** H. B. FEARON *Sk. Amer.* 93 If I had my will there should never be a salt-water man employed in the States. *a* **1820** B. H. LATROBE *Jrnl.* (1905) iii. 63 The ferryman..is one of several who are children of a man and woman, negroes, brought from Africa—called here salt-water negroes. **1855** F. DOUGLASS *My Bondage* 323 The salt water slave who hung in the guards of a steamer..has, by the publicity given to the circumstance, set a spy on the guards of every steamer departing from southern ports. **1961** F. G. CASSIDY *Jamaica Talk* viii. 156 A sort of half-way condition between the creole Negro and the salt-water Negro was the *salt-water Creole*—one born during the voyage to Jamaica. **1966** *Publ. Amer. Dial. Soc.* 1964 XLII. 39 Irish informants use *turkey* and *saltwater turkey* to designate a recent immigrant.

salty, *a.*[1] Add: **A.** *adj.* **3.** (Later example.)
1978 J. A. MICHENER *Chesapeake* 359 When Captain Turlock learned that his mate had studied with the rector, there was salty discussion of that churchman's habits.
4. *U.S. Naut. slang.* Of a sailor: tough; hard-bitten; aggressive. Cf. SALT *sb.*[1] 11.
1920 H. R. CHAMBERS *U.S. Submarine Chasers in Mediterranean* ii. 12 We were all very 'salty' and 'rolled' fore and aft along the deck instead of walking. **1926** ANDERSON & STALLINGS *Three Amer. Plays* III. 73, I lived with a Spanish girl at Cavite back in '99... In those days I was salty as hell, a sea-going buckaroo. **1926** J. W. CROSLEY *Bk. Navy Songs* II. 24 A salty bunch of Ensigns we, from the great Atlantic Fleet, And we're here to learn the reason why a valve must have a seat. **1939** *Sat. Even. Post* 23 Dec. 6/1 He was a salty old regular, with one of those wedge-shaped figures and an ugly underslung face of the texture and color of seamed leather. **1941** M. GOODRICH *Delilah* iii. 210 The consensus was that Delilah's men now, for some reason, thought they were 'salty' and were looking for trouble.
5. *U.S. slang.* Angry, irritated; hostile. *to jump salty*: to undergo a sudden change of mood or outlook; to become annoyed or angry (with someone).
1938 *Amer. Speech* XIII. 314/1 *Jump salty*, implies an unexpected change in a person's attitude or knowledge. The person may become suddenly angry, or an unhipped person may become hipped. **1938** *N.Y. Amsterdam News* 26 Feb. 17/2 Let's sound a high C on the postoffice man whose Girl Friday is 'jumpin' salty' 'cause he won't Reno the wife who thinks but isn't sure. **1944** C. CALLOWAY *Hepsters Dict.*, *Salty*, angry, ill-tempered. **1952** C. BROSSARD *Who walk in Darkness* xi. 67 Why do you have to get so salty when people want to have fun? **1958** *Partisan Rev.* XXV. 292 That man jumped salty on me. **1967** J. A. WILLIAMS *Man who cried I Am* xvi. 187 Oops! The dozens, is it? I made you salty eh? **1975** P. G. WINSLOW *Death of Angel* vi. 137 He was furious when I said I didn't have any [money] and got very salty.
B. *sb.* Also **saltie.** A sea-going ship (as opposed to LAKER[1] 4). *N. Amer.*
1959 *Ottawa Citizen* 29 Apr. 53/1 Sixty or more ocean ships—called 'salties' by lake seamen—and inland ships were expected to be in transit today. **1961** *Times* 24 Apr. 16/6 Hundreds of miles eastward again the 'salties' are converging from all over the world, soon to thread the canals and locks linking our vast ocean-like lakes, and bringing a nostalgic Atlantic tang into the very heart of the Dominion. **1966** *Kingston* (Ontario) *Whig-Standard* 5 Jan. 19/7 The only saltie to visit Kingston that year, the 17,170 ton Malmanger of Norway, sailed with her holds only half full of grain. **1971** *Cleveland* (Ohio) *Plain Dealer* 14 Dec. c7 (*heading*) British salty will be last in Cleveland this season.
Hence **sa·ltily** *adv.*
1926 R. MACAULAY *Crewe Train* II. ix 172 Arnold's old flannel trousers were rolled above his knees; his white, slim, long legs glistened saltily beside Denham's firm, brown ones. **1945** C. MANN in B. James *Austral. Short Stories* (1963) 77 After a time he did not so much hear and saltily smell those myriad fish. **1955** *Times* 7 July 5/1 Parents should teach a straightforward, 'saltily realistic' approach to sexual questions. **1958** *Times* 24 Dec. 3/6 The drawings pay marked attention to the arts. Constable.. is accompanied by..the young Brangwyn, saltily caught by Phil May.

‖**salud** (salu·ð), *int.* [Sp., = (good) health: see SALUTE *sb.*[1]] A toast before drinking: 'cheers!', 'good health!'
1938 E. HEMINGWAY *Fifth Column* I. ii. 7 Salud, Comrade Stamp Collector. **1940** G. GREENE *Power & Glory* II. ii. 139 'I will have a little brandy.' 'Salud!' **1961** J. WELCOME *Beware of Midnight* xi. 140 '*Salud*,' she said, lifting her glass. **1973** G. GREENE *Honorary Consul* III. iii. 148 'That is a very large whisky.'.. 'Large? Why, it is only half as big as mine. *Salud!*'

saluki (sălū·ki). Also **selugi, sleughi; slogie, slokee, sloug(h)i, slughi.** [ad. Arab. *selūḳī*, f. *Saluḳ* the name of a town in the Yemen.]

A large, lightly built hound belonging to the breed so called, with feathered tail and feet and large pendant ears; formerly called the Persian greyhound. Also *attrib.*

1809 J. G. JACKSON *Acct. Empire of Marocco* v. 31 They often hunt the gazel with the (slogie) African greyhound. **1844** J. H. D. HAY *Western Barbary* xiii. 89/2 The beaters kept good and steady line, and woe to the wild ones that showed themselves to..the swift-footed slokees on the plain. **1891** 'OUIDA' in *N. Amer. Rev.* Sept. 316 The Siberian and the Persian greyhounds are one and the same breed; called *sleughi* in Persia and Arabia. **1913** *Dress & Vanity Fair* (N.Y.) Oct. 110/2 Among them is a Saluki or gazelle hound. **1924** *Blackw. Mag.* Jan. 24/2 Among them..a few Selugis, Persian greyhounds of as ancient and pure a strain as our own. **1924** G. BELL *Let.* 13 Feb. (1927) II. xxiii. 684 When I came in at 4 from the office I found Marie sitting in the garden looking like a female St. Jerome, with a needle for a book, a slughi dog for a lion and a tame red-legged partridge standing solemnly beside her instead of a quail. **1926** *Public Opinion* 30 July 102/2 A tall great sloughi came out of the house, beating his tail against the posts of the verandah. **1928** *Evening News* 5 May 9 He was requested by the Bey to bring him back a really fine English slougi. **1931** C. S. JARVIS *Yesterday & To-day in Sinai* xi. 212 A Saluki hunt on camel-back. **1938** J. W. DAY *Dog in Sport* i. 18 The fleet gazelle-hound of the desert, ancestor of the graceful, tassel-eared Saluki of to-day. **1945** C. L. B. HUBBARD *Observer's Bk. Dogs* 134 Being a member of the Greyhound family, the Saluki is extremely old and of the purest descent. It traces back to about 5,000 years B.C., when it was little different to the modern dog of the Arabs of to-day. **1953** A. SMITH *Blind White Fish in Persia* ii. 41, 100 miles along it there was a tea house, just a hut with a man outside smoking a hookah and a boy with two Salukis. **1973** *Country Life* 8 Feb. (Suppl.) 33/3 (Advt.), Afghans and Salukis, also Ibizans and Pharoahs (with whom we will be at Crufts). **1978** *Times* 7 Jan. 12/2 Bahrain's pure-bred saluki hound, which recently came close to extinction as a pedigree strain, is making a comeback.

‖ **salumeria** (salu*meri*·a). [It., grocer's or pork-butcher's shop, f. *salume* salted meat f. *sale* salt (L. *sal* salt).] A delicatessen.

1926 R. HALL *Adam's Breed* I. v. 42 There was Fabio's salumeria..his wares—the sausages, the paste, the rich yellow oil, the..Chianti. **1967** P. JONES *Fifth Defector* ii. 10, I was just coming out of the Salumeria in Via Canzotti... Where we get that delicious smoked cheese?

saluresis (sæliuri·sis). *Med.* [f. as next + DI)URESIS.] The renal excretion of a greater quantity of salts than is usual. Cf. next.

1959 *Lancet* 25 Apr. 866/1 The urinary output of salt is raised... The saluresis soon abates. **1975** *Aviation, Space & Environmental Med.* XLVI. 1358/1 Exogenous mineral-corticoid prevents the diuresis, saluresis, and kaluresis.

saluretic (sæliure·tik), *a.* and *sb.* *Med.* [f. L. *sal* salt + DI)URETIC *a.* and *sb.*] **A.** *adj.* Promoting the renal excretion of salts. **B.** *sb.* A saluretic drug. Cf. prec.

1959 *Lancet* 25 Apr. 866/1 Recently a more potent saluretic agent, hydrochlorothiazide, has become available. .. The saluretic and antidiuretic actions were interdependent. **1964** L. MARTIN *Clin. Endocrinol.* (ed. 4) i. 53 Restriction of protein and salt in the diet has been advised, and hydrochlorthiazide may be used for its saluretic effect. **1975** *Jrnl. Pediatrics* LXXXVI. 831/2 In newborn infants the saluretics are the diuretics of choice. *Ibid.* 832/1 Mannitol has..been used successfully, either alone or with one of the saluretic agents.

‖ **salus populi suprema lex (esto).** Latin phr. (occurring in Cicero *De Leg.* III. iii. 8): the safety of the people must be the supreme law. Also *ellipt.* as *salus populi*. Similarly *salus rei publicae*.

1612 BACON *Essaies* xxvii, Judges ought above all, to remember the Conclusion of the Romaine twelve Tables; *Salus populi suprema lex*, and to know that Lawes, except they bee in order to that end, are but things captious, and Oracles not well inspired. **1617** J. CHAMBERLAIN *Let.* 10 May (1939) II. 74 Necessitie hath no law, and yf *salus populi* be *suprema lex*, in this case *salus regis* was included too. **1788** GIBBON *Let.* 29 Nov. in *Wks.* (1796) I. 193 In so new a case the *salus populi* must be the first law. **1794** [see *political science* s.v. *POLITICAL *a.* 6]. **1836** J. F. DAVIS *Chinese* I. vi. 251 These are contained in their sacred books, whose principle is literally, *salus populi suprema lex*. **1845** H. BROOM *Legal Maxims* i. 1 Salus Populi Suprema Lex... Hence there are many cases in which individuals sustain an injury for which the law gives no action. **1910** CHESTERTON *G. B. Shaw* 89 The real and ancient emotion of the *salus populi*, almost extinct in our oligarchical chaos. **1963** *Times* 8 Mar. 13/5 In matters concerning the safety of the state, the definition of which can be safely left to our Courts of Law, *salus rei publicae* must surely still be *suprema lex*? **1978** *Times* 10 May 17/5, I do not wish to pursue the arguments for and against birching..except to express doubts as to whether the vague and potentially dangerous maxim 'salus populi suprema lex'..is really the best possible guideline to be recommended to a court of law for the determination of a legal issue.

‖ **salut** (salü), *int.* [Fr., lit. 'health'; cf. *SALUD *int.*, SALUTE *sb.*[1]] A toast: 'cheers!', 'good health!'

1933 E. HEMINGWAY *Homage to Switzerland* in *Scribner's Mag.* Apr. 206/2 'Prosit,' said Johnson... The other two porters said 'Salut'. **1938** L. DURRELL *Spirit of Place* (1969) 53 All the Best. I hope to look you two up soon..Salut—Larry. **1966** L. COHEN *Beautiful Losers* I. 4 Salut F., old and loud friend! **1976** 'TREVANIAN' *Main* (1977) xiii. 253 She lifts her glass. 'Salut?' 'Salut.'

‖ **salut** (salü), *sb.* Also with capital initial. [Fr., ellipt. for *salut du Saint Sacrement*, salutation (or benediction) of the Blessed Sacrament.] In French Roman Catholic churches: an evening service of Benediction (at which the Host is exposed and the hymn 'O Salutaris Hostia' is sung).

1694 J. DRUMMOND *Let.* 30 Mar. (1845) 17 One may be either offering the Holy Sacrifice in conjunction with the priests of God, or singing the praise of the Almighty God at the Saluts, or hearing exhortations. **1815** E. WYNNE *Diary* 15 Sept. (1952) xxxi. 536 We went into church while the *Salut* was going on. **1843** C. BRONTË *Let.* 2 Sept. in W. Gérin *C. Brontë* (1967) xiv. 241, I found myself opposite to Ste Gadule, and the bell..began to toll for evening 'salut'. **1853** —— *Villette* xii. 43/2 At sunset or the hour of *salut*, when the externes were gone home. **1901** *Month* Sept. 268 The word *salut*, which is still in French-speaking countries the name most commonly employed to designate the service of Benediction, preserves the memory of an institution which most probably must be regarded as the primitive stock, upon which the Exposition of the Sacred Host and the blessing imparted with It are only an excrescence. **1967** W. GÉRIN *C. Brontë* xiii. 188 The great bell..ringing to Matins, Vespers, and to 'Salut' throughout the catholic year.

salutation. Add: **1. c.** *esp.* in the Church of England: 'The Lord be with you'. (Later examples.)

1929 E. C. THOMAS *Lay Folk's Hist. Liturgy* II. v. 182 In 1552 the Salutation and Kyrie [in Morning Prayer] were postponed to the Creed. **1978** D. M. HOPE in C. Jones et al. *Study of Liturgy* II. III. ix. 231 The people said 'Amen' at its [*sc.* the Epistle's] conclusion and the Gospel continued..after the salutation by the celebrant.

salutatorian. (Later examples.)

1943 *Lafayette Alumnus* (Lafayette Coll., Easton, Pa.) Nov. 1/1 Lloyd Felmly..was salutatorian of his class. **1977** *Transatlantic Rev.* LX. 130 Elwood was valedictorian; I was salutatorian.

salutatory, *a.* and *sb.* Add: **A.** *adj.* **b.** Also in high schools.

1940 W. L. FINK *Evaluation Commencement Pract. Amer. Public Secondary Schools* ii. 25 Time would not permit all of the members of the class to speak. Accordingly, certain pupils chosen on the basis of scholarship alone were given the honor of delivering the salutatory and valedictory addresses. **1947** E. A. KAUMP *High School Commencement Bk.* (rev. ed.) 93 (*heading*) The Salutatory. *Ibid.*, The Salutatory address is another honor speech..given by the student who makes the second highest average during the high school years.

B. *sb.* **2. a.** (Earlier example.)

1869 'MARK TWAIN' in *Buffalo* (N.Y.) *Morning Express* 21 Aug. 2/3 Your new editor feels called upon to write a 'salutatory' at once.

b. (Earlier and later examples.) Also in high schools.

1779 *Pennsylvania Packet* 7 Oct. 1/1 John Woodword [gave] the salutatory in Latin. **1864** *Harper's Mag.* Sept. 501/1 Still another is the burlesque philosophical oration and the half Latin, half Saxon Salutatory. **1905** *N.Y. Even. Post* 12 June 12 The annual class day exercises of the University of Pennsylvania were held to-day. H. B. Taylor delivered the salutatory. **1932** *School Life* May 165/1 On 85 occasions fond..parents had listened to the same old story: Salutatory, oratory, valedictory. **1947** [see A. b above].

salute, *sb.*[1] Add: **3. d.** With defining term prefixed, denoting the attitude adopted by the saluter, or his affiliation, as **raised-arm salute,** a salute made with the arm outstretched at an angle of about 45° from the vertical; **clenched fist salute,** a raised-arm salute with fist clenched (chiefly in communist use); **Hitler** or **Nazi salute,** a raised-arm salute with hand outstretched.

1935 [see *HITLER]. **1937** V. BARTLETT *This is my Life* x. 165 Hundreds of arms went out in the Hitler salute, hundreds of voices yelled the *Horst Wessel Lied.* **1943** D. GASCOYNE *Poems 1937–1942* 5 The centurions..Greet one another with raised-arm salutes. **1959** *Chambers's Encycl.* XII. 173/2 Special forms of salute, the clenched fist salute of the Communists, the 'Roman salute' of the Fascists and the Hitler salute, have been a feature of modern political life. **1969, 1974** [see *NAZI *adj.*]. **1976** *Times* 13 Nov. 4 (*caption*) Clenched fist communist salutes from a group of Madrid car workers who had earlier voted to join the strike. **1977** *Times* 27 Jan. 6/8 Riot police looked on impassively here [*sc.* Madrid] today as a massive crowd of mourners..gave the clenched fist Marxist salute at the funeral of five lawyers gunned down on Monday night by right-wing terrorists.

saluting, *vbl. sb.* Add: **b.** *saluting-base.*

1961 *John o' London's* 19 Oct. 447/2 All the Queen's horses..gallop right past the saluting-base. **1976** C. EGLETON *State Visit* ix. 88 The Queen had climbed on to the saluting base... The Queen left the dais to inspect the Guard of Honour.

Salvadorean (sælvădō^ə·riăn), *a.* and *sb.* Also **Salvadoran, -ian.** [f. El *Salvador* (see below) + -AN.] **A.** *adj.* Of or pertaining to El Salvador, a republic in Central America. **B.** *sb.* A native or inhabitant of El Salvador.

1886 *Encycl. Brit.* XXI. 268/2 The tree from which it [*sc.* Balsam of Peru] is obtained grows naturally nowhere else in the world except in a limited part of the Salvadorian seaboard known as the Balsam coast. **1887** *U.S. Consular Rep.* XXIII. No. 82. 292 However great the advantage given to the Salvadorean debtor by English commercial codes,..American is worth 3 per cent. more than English gold. **1895** *Handbk. Salvador* (*Bull. Bureau Amer. Republics No. 58*) 79 Salvadorians are such either by birth or naturalization. **1909** 'O. HENRY' in *McClure's Mag.* July 330/1 For a Salvadorian he was not such a calamitous little man. **1941** C. M. WILSON *Central Amer.* (1942) iii. 52 The distinctly Salvadoran Feast of the Holy Savior. **1947** M. LOWRY *Let.* Nov. (1967) 159 Mlle. Zaza, wife of Salvadorean new passenger. **1969** *Guardian* 19 July 8/2 The quarter of a million Salvadoreans in Honduras. **1979** *Daily Tel.* 20 Apr. 4/4 Another hostage, a Salvadorean who was the Israeli honorary consul. **1980** *Ibid.* 11 July 19/7 A Mexican and a Salvadoran have been charged.. with illegally smuggling a group of aliens..into the United States. **1981** *Times* 24 Feb. 13/4 The victory of the Salvadorians is certain.

salvage, *sb.* Add: **2. c.** In wartime, esp. the war of 1939–45: the saving and collection of waste material, esp. paper, for recycling; also *transf.*, those who organized and carried out this collection.

1918 *Times* 2 Mar. 3/5 A National Salvage Council has been set up with the approval of the War Cabinet to deal with the problems of civil salvage and the recovery of waste products generally. **1942** *Oxford Mag.* 29 Jan. 147/1 Next week sees the end of the great drive for salvage of waste paper. **1943** *Punch* 20 Jan. 51/3 Careless of salvage we tore wildly at the wrapper and turned eagerly to the last page. **1944** M. LASKI *Love on Supertax* i. 13 A large pile of empty bottles bore witness to the family's constant failure to remember which day the salvage called. **1946** R. LEHMANN *Gipsy's Baby* 118 Found last week in turning out old papers for salvage. **1961** E. S. TURNER *Phoney War* xx. 291 Some notable gestures were made that summer [in 1943] by persons whose idea of sacrifice was not fulfilled by lending money to the State at interest or putting out old love-letters for salvage.

3. c. Waste material, esp. paper, suitable for recycling. (Cf. sense 2 c above.)

1939 *Times* 11 Nov. 8/4 The salvage department will collect and organize the use of salvage. **1942** *Times Lit. Suppl.* 9 May 229/2 Recently,..a perfect copy of Von Gerning's 'Tour Along the Rhine', with colour plates by Ackermann, was sent to his firm as salvage, together with other fine volumes. **1943** G. WINN in S. Briggs *Keep smiling Through* (1975) 187 Queen Mary.., whenever she sees salvage lying around unclaimed—bones, bottles, scrap iron—Her Majesty stops the car, has it picked up, and taken home in triumph to the village dump. **1945** 'R. CROMPTON' *William & Brains Trust* xi. 204 We'll say we're collectin' salvage if anyone comes. **1951** *Good Housek. Home Encycl.* 237/2 The local Councils in many districts still undertake the collection of salvage. **1959** *Chambers's Encycl.* XII. 176/1 Industrial salvage arises in some form at nearly all factories. Apart from waste paper and canteen scraps, there are textile and chemical wastes, used oils, metal scrap, sawdust [etc.]. **1978** CADOGAN & CRAIG *Women & Children First* x. 213 Older children could help the war effort; they..collected salvage, joined fire-watching rotas.

4. *salvage brigade, campaign, collector, -drive, -dump, man, operation, sack*; *salvage-minded* adj.; **salvage archæology, excavation** = *rescue archæology, excavation* s.v. *RESCUE *sb.* 3 c.

1967 G. H. GROSSO *Cave Life on Palouse* in *Encycl. Sci. Suppl.* (Grolier) 30 'Salvage archaeology' became a way of life for anthropologists in Washington after Grand Coulee Dam created Roosevelt Lake more than 20 years ago. **1977** *Jrnl. R. Soc. Arts* CXXV. 199/1 If the Canada Council spent 90 per cent of its funds on salvage archaeology in California, for example, defenders would be very hard to find. **1890** W. BOOTH *In Darkest England* II. ii. 115, I propose to establish in every large town..'A Household Salvage Brigade',..entrusted with the task of collecting the waste of the houses in their circuit. **1942** P. JEPHCOTT *Girls growing Up* iii. 47 Ordinary time-table lessons are supplemented by..salvage campaigns. **1941** 'R. CROMPTON' *William does his Bit* vii. 165 (*heading*) William—the Salvage Collector. **1975** S. BRIGGS *Keep smiling Through* 187 The salvage collector assured her that the letters would not be read, but suggested that she could tear them into small pieces. **1942** *Ann. Reg. 1941* 335 Such special occasions as a War Weapons Week or a Salvage Drive. **1952** R. A. KNOX *Hidden Stream* p. vii, My store of back-numbers is full to bursting again, and calls for a fresh salvage-drive. **1943** *Punch* 14 Apr. 321/1 Since picking out of the salvage-dump a book entitled Half-Hours with the Stars, my father, a municipal dustman, has become keen on astronomy. **1972** *Even. Telegram* (St. John's, Newfoundland) 29 June 14/3 Provision for the preservation or salvage-excavation of archaeological and historical sites. *a* **1945** in S. Briggs *Keep smiling Through* (1975) 187 The war is driving Hitler back But here's one way to win it: Just give your salvage men the sack And see there's plenty in it. **1942** *R.A.F. Jrnl.* 13 June 23 (*caption*), I want all you hut orderlies to *get* salvage-minded and *stay* salvage-minded. **1919** 'SAKI' *Fate* in *Toys of Peace* 200 The billiard table..was not the best place to have chosen for the scene of salvage operations. **1975** *Globe & Mail* (Toronto) 4 June 2/2 Even filet mignon and Spencer steaks from Mr. Dumais' meat salvage operation went into hamburger. **1942** *Times Lit. Suppl.* 9 May 229/2 Before dropping books into the salvage sack, owners have been urged..to consult the nearest public or university librarian or literary friend.

salvage, *v.* Add: **2.** *U.S.* and *Austral.* To take (esp. *euphem.* by misappropriation) and make use of (unemployed or unattended property).

1918 *Stars & Stripes* 8 Feb. 2 *Salvage*, to rescue unused property and make use of it. **1919** S. PRENTICE *Padre* xv. 266 When he came out five minutes later it was gone; someone had 'salvaged' it again. **1919** K. D. MORSE *Let.* 1 Jan. (1920) vi. 206 The boys were setting off pyrotechnics of all sorts 'salvaged' from the dump. **1920** RIGGS & PLATT *Hist. Battery F* 15 We manœuvered around and got a loaf of bread and anything else we could 'salvage' before the M.P.'s were put guarding it. **1928** J. B. WHARTON *Squad* i. 40 If you two'll collect up all the canteens, we'll go off an' see what we can salvage. **1941** BAKER *Dict. Austral. Slang* 63 *Salvage, to*: to steal, purloin.

3. To save and collect (waste material, esp. paper) for recycling.

1943 *Ann. Reg. 1942* 313 The great national campaign to salvage paper for re-pulping resulted in..the destruction of many..irreplaceable volumes.

Hence **sa·lvaged** *ppl. a.*, **sa·lvaging** *vbl. sb.*

c **1920** J. F. McGRATH *War Diary* 171 Salvaged rabbits, chicken, beer, and wine to add to the rations. **1951** *Manch. Guardian* 20 Apr. 6/7 His salvaging rather from the morgue of the Rules Committee of the Marshall Plan. **1969** R. EMERSON *Judging Delinquents* x. 275 Hard-core, discredited delinquents most in need of salvaging.

salvageable (sæ·lvĕdʒăb'l), *a.* [f. SALVAGE *v.* + -ABLE.] Capable of being salvaged. Also *fig.*

1976 *New Yorker* 24 May 115/1 Some urban experts suggest that the blacks who were salvageable were swept up and out into the suburbs—into decent jobs, and all that. **1977** *Custom Car* Nov. 20/1 Result: one completely junked digger with only the engine salvageable. **1981** *Times* 2 Mar. 10/4 The party is still salvageable..but it will not be saved if its best members leave it.

salvar, var. *SHALWAR.

Salvarsan (sæ·lvāɪsæn). *Pharm.* Also **salvarsan.** [a. G. *salvarsan*, f. L. *salv-āre* to save + G. *ars-enik* ARSENIC *sb.*^{1} + *-an* -AN.] A former proprietary name for *ARSPHENAMINE. Now chiefly *Hist.*

1910 *Official Gaz.* (U.S. Patent Office) 23 Aug. 987/2 Farbwerke vorm. Meister Lucius & Brüning, Höchst-on-the-Main, Germany. Filed Feb. 23, 1909. *Salvarsan.* **1910** *N.Y. Med. Jrnl.* 3 Dec. 1137/1 Ehrlich followed up the arsenic compounds, and after many, many trials, changes, and improvements, placed, carefully and well prepared, dioxydiamidoarsenobenzol or 'salvarsan', to give it its trade name, before the profession. **1911** *Brit. Med. Jrnl.* 14 Jan. 100/1 The remedy has rapidly undergone improvements and successively become '606 ideal', '606 hyperideal', and now 'Salvarsan'. **1913** A. B. REEVE *Poisoned Pen* iii. 91 In these tubes I have the now famous salvarsan. **1913** *Times* 9 Aug. 3/1 The spirillum of relapsing fever, cultures of which after treatment with salvarsan were no longer capable of infecting mice. **1927** *Glasgow Herald* 29 Dec. 4/1 Setting right a joint by manipulation is different from killing a spirochaete with salvarsan. **1937** M. COVARRUBIAS *Island of Bali* (1972) x. 352 But the reluctance of the Balinese to undertake foreign treatment, the forbidding cost of Salvarsan, and the natural promiscuity do not help the situation. **1956** B. HOLIDAY *Lady sings Blues* (1973) ii. 24 At the hospital they were giving everybody shots of salvarsan for syphilis—only it was called 'bad blood' then. **1973** *Sci. Amer.* Sept. 106/3 In 1907 Paul Ehrlich of Germany, after long travail, succeeded in synthesizing Salvarsan, an arsenic compound that would kill *Treponema pallidum*, the microorganism that causes syphilis.

salvation. Add: **1. e.** Phr. *to work out* (*one's own*) *salvation*; freq. *fig.*, to be independent or self-reliant in striving towards one's goal.

1535 [see sense 1 a in Dict.]. **1678** S. BUTLER *Hudibras* III. i. 86 With Crosses, Relicks, Crucifixes, Beads, Pictures, Rosaries and Pixes: The Tools of working out Salvation, By meer Mechanick Operation. **1818** KEATS *Let.* 9 Oct. (1931) I. 243 The Genius of Poetry must work out its own salvation in a man: It cannot be matured by law and precept, but by sensation and watchfulness in itself. **1881** T. R. DAVIDS tr. *Buddhist Suttas* I. vi. 114 Decay is inherent in all component things! Work out your salvation with diligence! **1891** [see sense 1 d in Dict.]. **1911** L. T. HOBHOUSE *Liberalism* iv. 80 Let every people be free to work out its own salvation. **1948** A. J. TOYNBEE *Civilization on Trial* x. 210 It is for other Muslims to work out their salvation for themselves as may seem good to them. **1957** A. THWAITE *Ess. Contemp. Eng. Poetry* ix. 142 His [*sc.* Robert Graves'] self-imposed isolation from English literary life has left him free to work out his own poetic salvation and to take an idiosyncratic view of what everyone else is writing. **1981** *Daily Tel.* 12 Jan. 14/3 There are those..who resist the radicals' attempts to force their 'rights' upon them, and prefer to work out their own salvation.

f. (With initial capital.) *ellipt.* for (a member of) the Salvation Army.

1889 *Longman's Mag.* Feb. 407 My father says he is shamed to be called an Inglishman when he sees how the Salvation is knocked about and prossecuted. He says people will hold a drunken man up, but will knock a Salvation down.

4. *salvation banner*; *salvation-contemning* adj.; **salvation history** = *HEILSGESCHICHTE; **Salvation Jane** = *Paterson's curse* s.v. *PATERSON; **Salvation lassie** = *LASS 1 d.

1931 R. CAMPBELL *Georgiad* II. 33 One or two whose love is not unfurled Like a salvation banner to the world. **1919** KIPLING *Years Between* 63 Drunk with enormous, salvation-contemning Love for a tinker. **1959** *Times Lit. Suppl.* 20 Mar. (Relig. Bks. Section) p. vi/4 Such people are also rejecting the Incarnation, Crucifixion and Resurrection as events in 'salvation-history'. **1962** [see *KERYGMA]. **1977** E. QUINN tr. *Küng & Lapide's Brother or Lord* 20 We ought to ask..how far the Jew..can help us to reach a more authentic understanding of Jesus: an understanding which brings home to us afresh the continuity of salvation history. **1911** *Jrnl. Dept. Agric. S. Austral.* XV. 305 (*heading*) Salvation Jane. **1912** *Ibid.* XV. 679, I went to considerable trouble..in cutting down every plant of 'Salvation Jane' on a portion of my farm. **1937** LADY ROCKLEY *Some Canadian Wild Flowers* 5 There are tracts in New South Wales and South Australia covered with a Viper's Bugloss..but there it is a noxious weed reprobated by the names of 'Paterson's Curse' and 'Salvation Jane'. **1970** P. W. MICHAEL in R. M. Moore *Austral. Grasslands* xxiii. 356/2 *Phalaris tuberosa* has been shown to give excellent control of Salvation Jane or Paterson's curse in south-eastern South Australia. **1891** A. JAMES *Diary* 7 Apr. (1965) 188 Lifting up her voice in prayer as she knelt among the Salvation lassies. **1972** P. M. HUBBARD *Whisper in Glen* iv. 34 These slight, intense men had to have their pound of flesh, whether it was a blowsy trollop..or a Salvation lassie.

Salvation Army. Add: **2.** *attrib.*

1881 W. CORBRIDGE *Salvation Mine* (recto front cover), Salvation Army Stores, 101 Queen Victoria Street. **1910** 'SAKI' *Lost Sarijak* in *Reginald in Russia* 16 The corpse was that of a Salvation Army captain. **1920** H. BEGBIE *Life W. Booth* II. ii. 17 Blasphemous handbills, supposed to be circulated by Salvation Army Officers. **1921** M. L. CARPENTER *Angel Adjutant* v. 49 The wives of Salvation Army Bandsmen make their sacrifices. **1921** J. LAW *Curate's Promise* xv. 133 He saw..two officers..go into a large Salvation Army Hostel for women. **1928** H. CRANE *Let.* 27 Mar. (1965) 320, I finally had to finish the night in a ward of the Salvation Army Hotel. **1956** [see *ROWTON]. **1966** [see *SALLY *sb.*^{5} 1 b]. **1972** P. M. HUBBARD *Whisper in Glen* iv. 34 A Salvation Army lass with the body of a Rubens Venus. **1978** *Lancashire Life* Sept. 90/2 In her latest picture..she shows a Salvation Army band playing hymns in a northern town some time between 1920 and 1930.

salvationist. Add: **2.** One who rescues from peril; a saviour.

1971 *Daily Tel.* 4 May 14 Our great wartime leader, and I think salvationist, Sir Winston Churchill.

3. *attrib.* or as *adj.*

1934 WEBSTER, *Salvationist*, n. & adj. **1943** J. S. HUXLEY *Evolutionary Ethics* vii. 56 What I may call salvationist ethics, aimed at achieving salvation in a supernatural other life. **1959** A. F. WRIGHT *Buddhism in Chinese Hist.* iv. 81 Salvationist Buddhism..is neither an anomaly nor a temporary aberration of an otherwise 'rational' people.

salva·tionize, *v.* [-IZE.] *trans.* To convert, save, preach salvation to.

1927 *Scribner's Mag.* Feb. 118/2 Molly never could get over bein' salvationized. Some persons, when they get salvationized, get more joyous and happy. *a* **1930** D. H. LAWRENCE *Phoenix II* (1968) 439 Power..isn't bossing, or bullying, hiring a manservant or Salvationizing your social inferior.

Salvatorian (sælvătōᵊ·riăn), *sb.* [f. L. *salvātor* (It. *salvatore*), saviour + -IAN.] A member of a Roman Catholic congregation, the Society of the Divine Saviour, founded in Rome in the late nineteenth century. Also *attrib.* or as *adj.*

1903 F. M. STEELE *Monasteries & Relig. Houses Gt. Brit. & Ireland* 188 (*heading*) The Fathers of the Society of the Divine Saviour, or the Salvatorians. **1909** *Catholic Encycl.* V. 53/2 The Salvatorians have establishments in Italy, Sicily, Austria, Poland. **1931** *Tablet* 22 Aug. 252/2 Father Melchior Geses, a German Salvatorian of the mission of Shaowu in the Vicariate of Foochow. **1962** L. SMITH *Salvatorians* 7 The chief ways in which the Salvatorians play their part in the work of the Church for the salvation of souls, is by contributing their particular spirit to the ministry of external work, in preaching and teaching, in assisting the parochial clergy, in the Mass and administration of the sacraments, as well as in the specialized tasks of educational and youth work. **1979** *Tucson* (Arizona) *Citizen* 20 Sept. 5A/1 In 1970, the Salvatorian Fathers filed for bankruptcy, the first instance of legal insolvency in the history of the Church in this country... The Salvatorians, LaSalettes and Paulines—essentially unregulated by virtue of their religious status—were able to float bonds in violation of normal Securities and Exchange Commission requirements that money raised be spent on the advertised purpose.

salvatory, *a.* (Later examples.)

1921 *Challenge* 18 Feb. 241/2 Salvatory and reconstructive work. **1922** J. Y. SIMPSON *Man & Attainment of Immortality* xiv. 334 The fact of Christ remains, solitary and salvatory. **1958** J. LODWICK *Bid Soldiers Shoot* III. vii. 222 The murderer has but a single advantage: the patient police, who, in extended order, beat the bush in search of him, or of the macabre *trouvaille* of his hastily buried victim, do not..believe that they will encounter either, personally. Therefore, when they do..a salvatory hiatus follows.

‖ **salva veritate** (sæ·lvā ve:rĭtā·te), *advb. phr.* [L.] Saving the truth, without infringement of truth.

1930 P. P. WIENER tr. *Nicod's Found. Geom.* III. v. 141 It will be found in all cases necessary and sufficient that these two relations be *equivalent*, that is to say,..that one can be replaced by the other and the field of one by the field of the other, *salva veritate*, in every proposition containing nothing besides logical or mathematical expressions. **1957** [see *inter-substitutability* s.v. *INTER- 2 a]. **1963** J. LYONS *Structural Semantics* iv. 56 Attempts to handle synonymy in terms of substitutability throughout the language *salva veritate* are generally regarded as unsatisfactory.

salve, *sb.*^{1} Add: Now freq. with pronunc. (sælv). **c.** (Later examples.)

1896 *Leeds Mercury Weekly Suppl.* 21 Nov., Put plenty o' sauve on him an' tha'll get owght aht on him 'at iver tha wants to. **1908** J. M. SULLIVAN *Criminal Slang* 21 *Salve*, getting on the right side of the arresting officer. **1926** MAINES & GRANT *Wise-Crack Dict.* 14/1 *Spread the salve*, soft, conciliatory talk.

salve, *v.*^{1} Add: Now freq. with pronunc. (sælv).

salvia. For (Tournefort 1700) substitute (J. P. de Tournefort *Institutiones Rei Herbariæ* (1700) I. 180), and add: Also *attrib.* and *fig.* (Later examples.)

1923 D. H. LAWRENCE *Birds, Beasts & Flowers* 66 If there were salvia-savage Bolshevists To burn the world back to manure-good ash, Wouldn't I stick the salvia in my coat! **1941** E. P. O'DONNELL *Great Big Doorstep* ii. 28 There were humming-birds working around a wild salvia bush in the grove. **1963** W. BLUNT *Of Flowers & a Village* 222 Mrs. Stringer insisted upon my going round to see her salvias.

salvific, *a.* Delete † *Obs. rare* and add later examples.

1946 R. A. KNOX *Epistles & Gospels* 223 A salvific law, promising life to Israel only, might have seemed to contravene them [*sc.* the promises of God]; not a purely damnific Law like that of Sinai. **1958** *Times Lit. Suppl.* 17 Oct. 599/3 Stephen would have seen in the Crucifixion nothing 'salvific', but only the latest in a series of crimes committed against the prophets of the pure religion of Moses. **1967** E. R. FAIRWEATHER in Clark & Davey *Anglican/R.C. Dialogue* (1974) iv. 49 Anglican theology has revealed no sympathy with..any other doctrine which would minimize the reality and the salvific role of Christ's human will. **1979** J. HICK in M. Goulder *Incarnation & Myth* vi. 199 It is no longer acceptable..to assume the salvific uniqueness of one's own religion.

salvo, *sb.*^{2} Add: **2. b.** (Later examples in wider applications.)

1924 'W. FRANK' (*title*) Salvos, an informal book about books and plays. **1955** *Times* 26 May 4/3 It [*sc.* a broadsheet] was intended to be the 'hush-hush' weapon, which by triumphant revelation at the last moment and, by its powerful propaganda salvo, would bring to submission any wavering voters still about. **1971** *Daily Tel.* (Colour Suppl.) 21 May 18/3 They can stay on deck,..watch salvoes of gannets plummet in white streaks to the sea. **1977** W. M. SPACKMAN *Armful of Warm Girl* 43 He bought her the Hindu nose-jewel..and gently slipped it on (which with little salvoes of apologetic kisses she had at once slipped off, and never worn again).

d. Of bombs dropped from aircraft.

1942 *R.A.F. Jrnl.* 27 June 36 A..change of course saved the ship from a direct hit from the salvo dropped by the leading aircraft. **1949** *Sun* (Baltimore) 17 Oct. 1/5 These loads are dropped either in 'chain' (a trail of bombs, blasting out a path between two and three miles long) or in 'salvo', where the scores of 500-pounders tumble out of the bays together in an 'area' bombing operation.

Salvo (sæ·lvo), *sb.*^{3} *Austral. colloq.* [f. SALV(ATIONIST + -O^{2}.] A member of the Salvation Army; *pl.*, the Salvation Army.

1896 *Bulletin* (Sydney) 31 Oct. 27 (*title*) The Salvo's Error. **1908** C. H. S. MATTHEWS *Parson in Austral. Bush* xxvii. 256 Well, I was rared a Carthlick, but I haven't followed it up much. To tell ye the truth, I class 'em all alike—priests, parsons, 'salvos', and all the lot of 'em. **1942** J. SWEENEY in Murdoch & Drake-Brockman *Austral. Short Stories* (1951) 382 We come to the Salvo hut where there is a big joker sitting on a form drinking coffee and eating biscuits. **1952** J. CLEARY *Sundowners* iii. 144 I've only met one other Rupert... That was when I was in the Salvos. **1962** A. UPFIELD *Will of Tribe* ix. 87 Can't help bringing out old clichés. The Salvo padre at Derby was down on them but we learned them quick. **1968** *Telegraph* (Brisbane) 29 June 16/6 Hundreds of former Diggers have similar stories of the morale-boosting work done by the 'Salvos'. **1978** R. MCKIE *Bitter Bread* 77 When workers everywhere got their notices and the slump showed every sign of lasting, the Salvos decided to open a doss house.

salvo, *v.* Add: Also *transf.* and with sense 'to drop a salvo of (bombs)'.

1895 H. G. HUTCHINSON *Peter Steele, Cricketer* vii. 155 He had just made his century, and been salvoed with applause. **1943** *Yank* 17 Dec. 5 The pilot feathered the props and kept on; the Fort limped in over the target and salvoed its bombs.

‖ **salvoconducto** (salvokondu·kto). [Sp.: see SAFE-CONDUCT *sb.*] A pass, safe-conduct.

1955 W. GADDIS *Recognitions* II. vi. 545 What happened! What happened to Huss? John Huss, enticed by a salvoconducto up to Constance, where three bishops sat on his case, and he was burned. **1957** P. KEMP *Mine were of Trouble* i. 13 Just beyond the Spanish barrier we halted; Vicuña went into the control hut to report and to collect my *salvoconducto*.

salvy, *a.* (Earlier U.S. example.)

1861 *Trans. Ill. Agric. Soc.* IV. 103 Care should be taken not to work it too much, as it will hurt the grain of the butter and make it salvy.

salwar, var. *SHALWAR.

Salyrgan (sæ·lɜɪgăn). *Pharm.* Also **salyrgan.** A proprietary name (orig. used in Germany) for *MERSALYL.

1924 *Official Gaz.* (U.S. Patent Office) 10 June 270/1 H. A. Metz Laboratories, Inc., New York,..*Salyrgan*...

Preparations for the treatment of spirochetal and other infectious diseases and as a diuretic. Claims use since about Apr. 11, 1924. **1924** *Trade Marks Jrnl.* 15 Oct. 2285 *Salyrgan*... Farbwerke vorm. Meister Lucius & Brüning... Hoechst am Main, Germany; Manufacturers.—16th August 1924. **1928** *Canad. Med. Assoc. Jrnl.* XVIII. 45/1 Salyrgan was first introduced as an antiluetic mercurial agent. **1956** *Internat. Rev. Cytol.* V. 223 Experiments..indicate that salyrgan strongly inhibits the hydrolytic splitting of the high-energy phosphate bonds of ATP. **1976** *Amer. Jrnl. Clin. Path.* LXV. 685/1 High concentrations of salyrgan.. shortened the lag period.

sam, *sb.*[1] Add: **2.** (Later examples.) Also without const.: an oath, a promise.

1939 J. Masefield *Live & Kicking Ned* 115 On that I swop my solemn sam. **1940** M. Allingham *Black Plumes* xii. 138 Upon my Sam I think you're both mad. **1966** 'J. Hackston' *Father clears Out* 71 He'd see that things were righted, upon his Sam he would.

Sam, *sb.*[2] Abbrev. of Sambo (sense 2) in Dict. and Suppl.

1867 W. H. Dixon *New Amer.* II. ii. 13 Sam—all negroes there are Sams—may be a Methodist. **1877** L. Hearn *Genius Loci* in *Cincinnati Commercial* 12 Aug. 6/4 I'm Rag-a-back Sam, And I don't care a d—m, Fur I sooner-be a nigger dan a poor white man. **1938** *Amer. Speech* XIII. 152/1 *Sam*, a negro who demeans himself to secure favor with white people. **1964** L. Nkosi *Rhythm of Violence* 4 Black Sams! Why don't they do somethin' so we can handle this once and for all! **1973** K. Johnson in T. Kochman *Rappin' & Stylin' Out* 148 *Sam*, a common name of black males, it is used to refer to any black male. In addition, the story character, Sambo, was black; perhaps the label derives from 'Little Black Sambo'.

sam, *v.*[1] **2.** (Further examples.)

1824 W. Carr *Horæ Momenta Cravenæ* 11 If shoe nobbud cud git a bit a naturable rist, shoe wod sam up strength fast. **1934** J. B. Priestley *Eden End* i. 10 I've been up in the back garret, samming up these old clothes for the doctor.

sam, *v.*[2] Add: Also **samm.** Hence **sammed** *ppl. a.*; **sa·mming** *vbl. sb.*

1885 A. Watt *Art of Leather Manuf.* xii. 151 The butts are next piled in a heap to *sam*, or *samm*, as it is termed, for several days, by which the leather becomes tempered, or in an uniformly moist and softened condition. **1909** H. G. Bennett *Manuf. of Leather* xx. 256 *Samming* is an exceedingly important operation by which leather is brought into a uniformly half-dry condition, this state being quite necessary for many of the finishing operations... The 'sammed' condition may be obtained in three ways—by drying out completely and then wetting back by dipping through water (often tepid) and leaving 'in pile' for some hours; by drying the wet goods in suspension to the required consistency and no further, wetting back any parts that have become drier than the bulk and leaving in pile for a time to become uniform; and by machine samming, in which case the superfluous moisture is removed by the pressure of machine rollers.

‖ **samadh** (sămā·d). [See next.] The tomb of a holy man or yogi who is assumed to have achieved samadhi rather than to have died. Cf. *Samadhi 1 b.

1828 *Asiatick Researches* XVI. 39 A temple, sacred to the deity whom they worship, or the *Samádh*, or shrine of the founder of the sect, or some eminent teacher. **1888** Kipling *Departmental Ditties* (1890) (ed. 4) 80 They made a *samádh* in his honour, A mark for his resting-place. *Ibid.* 82 Thus the *samádh* was perfect, thus was the lesson plain. **1891** Monier Williams *Brahmanism & Hinduism* 179 A native of Oudh, whose samadh or tomb is at Katwa. **1964** A. Swinson *Six Minutes to Sunset* i. 16 A dilapidated domed *samadh* (or tomb).

‖ **samadhi** (sămā·di). *Indian Philos.* [Skr. *samādhi* a placing together, f. *sam* together + *ā* prefix + *dhā* to place (see Do *v.*).] **1. a.** The state of union with creation into which a perfected yogi or holy man is said to pass at his apparent death. **b.** The voluntary burial of such a person before death in anticipation of this state; the site of the burial of a holy man (cf. prec.).

1795 *Asiatick Researches* IV. 218 Dhritara'shtra, in the state of *Samadhi*, quitted his terrestrial form to proceed to the..beatitude, which awaited him. **1891** Monier Williams *Brahmanism & Hinduism* 261 When such a man dies in India, his body is not burnt but buried, because in fact he is not supposed to die at all. He is believed to lie in a kind of trance, called Samadhi. **1925** *Glasgow Herald* 24 Sept. 7 The Sadhu did not commit suicide, but performed the religious rite of Samadhi. **1968** *Jrnl. Mus. Acad. Madras* XXXIX. 13 Something more beautiful and commodious must be built at his Samadhi to commemorate his work. **1979** *Times of India* 17 Aug. 34 The Janata party had betrayed the oath taken at Gandhi's samadhi that they would fulfil his dreams of a nationalist, socialist India by forming connections with the RSS, he said.

2. The highest state of meditation, in which the distinctions between subject and object disappear and unity with creation is attained; the last stage of yoga.

1827 *Trans. R. Asiatic Soc.* I. 25 The collection of *Yóga-sútras*..is distributed into four chapters or quarters..: the first on contemplation (*samád'hi*)..[etc.]. **1850** [see *Dhyana]. **1913** [see *Raja yoga]. **1939** A. Huxley *After Many a Summer* ii. i. 189 Baby..is now walking about in a state of perpetual *samadhi*. **1958** J. Sykes *Quakers* i. i. 31 A moment almost of group samadhi, of the displacement of all by God's Being, and Becoming. **1960** J. Hewitt *Yoga* i. 7 By a programme of bodily and mental self-discipline we who move on lower levels of consciousness can achieve Samadhi (union with divine consciousness). **1965** *New Statesman* 16 Apr. 616/2 Ramakrishna's ability to pass into a trance-like state of 'higher spiritual awareness' known as samadhi. **1971** *Shankar's Weekly* (Delhi) 11 Apr. 22/2 From time to time, the Swamiji would come out of his samadhi to frown at the opening and closing of the compartment door. **1977** L. A. Govinda *Creative Meditation* iii. vi. 135 Though samadhi may be the culmination in the meditative experience, we cannot remain in that state.. but have to return to the world.

Samain, var. *Samhain.

Samaj (sămā·dʒ). Also **Somaj.** [a. Hindi and Bengali *samāj* society, f. Skr. *samāja* a meeting with, f. *sam* together + *aj* to drive.] An assembly or congregation in India; a church or religious body, as in *Brahmo Samaj* (see *Brahmoism).

1875 C. M. Davies *Unorthodox London* 2nd Ser. (ed. 2) 193 The present representative of the Bramo Somaj in London, was to preach at Mr. Conway's chapel. **1876** *Encycl. Brit.* IV. 201/1 He gave a printing-press to the Samáj. *Ibid.* 201/2 They encourage the establishment of branch Samájes in different parts of the country. **1884** [see Progressive *a.* 4]. **1913** J. N. Farquhar *Crown of Hinduism* 76 The truths of religion which they find there are the doctrines taught by the Samāj. **1948** [see *Sarvodaya]. **1958** W. de Bary et al. *Sources of Indian Tradition* xxii. 629 The Ārya Samāj (the Society of the Āryas, or 'noble men') which he [*sc.* Dayānanda] established at Bombay in 1875 has since reflected the militant character of its founder, and from its stronghold in the Punjab has contributed to the rise of Hindu nationalism.

Saman[1] (sā·măn). [a. Skr. *sāman* chant.] A sacred text or verse forming the third of the four kinds of Vedas; the name of the Veda thus formed. Also *attrib.* So **Samaveda** (sā·mă₁vē:dă), the name of the third Veda.

1798 *Asiatick Researches* V. 364 Prayer..on beginning a lecture of the Samaveda. **1843** *Penny Cycl.* XXVI. 171/1 These are the ǀRĭch, Yajush, Sâman, and Atharvan'a. *Ibid.*, The Sâmaveda contains songs of lyrical character to be recited with melancholy. **1886** *Encycl. Brit.* XXI. 277/1 The sâman-hymnal consists of two parts, viz., the *Sâmaveda-samhitâ*, or collection of texts (rich) used for making up sâman-hymns, and the *Gâna*, or tune-books. *Ibid.* 278/1 The *Vamśa-brâhmaṇa*, a mere list of the Sâmaveda teachers. **1900** J. G. Frazer *Golden Bough* (ed. 2) I. i. 92 A particular hymn of the ancient Indian collection known as the Samaveda. **1913** J. N. Farquhar *Crown of Hinduism* 77 The *Sāman*, *Yajus*, and *Atharvan* exhibit the same polytheism. **1954** *Grove's Dict. Mus.* (ed. 5) IV. 456/1 The Sāmans (sacrificial chants) may, though rarely, be heard nowadays. **1968** *Jrnl. Mus. Acad. Madras* XXXIX. 105 *Samkirtana* is in itself *Brahman* and is greater than *Sama-veda.*

saman[2] (samā·n). Also **samaan, samang.** [a. Amer. Sp. *samán*, f. Carib *zamang.*] = *guango, Zamang. Also *attrib.*

1888, etc. [see *monkey-pod* (*tree*) s.v. *monkey *sb.* 17 b]. **1951** J. C. Fennessy *Sonnet in Bottle* ii. iii. 46 The huge tents of the saman trees were islands of blackness in the cooling streams of night air. **1958** G. Lamming *Of Age & Innocence* ii. vii. 117 The tall black samaan tree at the curve of the hill-top. **1960** *Times* 10 Mar. 18/3 The saman trees..were full of holders of tree tickets. **1963** [see *guango]. **1968** E. Lovelace *Schoolmaster* viii. 120 Christiana was sitting on the trunk of a fallen samaan tree in the shade near the cocoa house. **1974** *Times* 5 Feb. 12/4 Queen's Park Oval is unlike its namesake at Kennington. Where the gasholders should be there are some fine samaan trees, with a range of low, wooded hills right behind them.

Samang, var. *Semang.

samango (samæ·ŋgo). [Native name.] In full, *samango guenon* or *monkey*. An African monkey, *Cercopithecus mitis*, which has blue-grey fur with black markings.

1888 *Proc. Zool. Soc.* 564 The most notable additions during the month were:—..the Small-clawed Otter..the Samango Monkey. **1894** H. O. Forbes *Hand-bk. Primates* II. 71 (*heading*) The Samango Guenon. **1912** J. Stevenson-Hamilton *Animal Life in Afr.* xvi. 260 The Samango monkey..extends from the eastern part of Cape Colony, through Portuguese East Africa, and the whole of Rhodesia. **1932** S. Zuckerman *Social Life Monkeys & Apes* xi. 185 The Samango monkey is encountered in the forests of eastern South Africa. *Ibid.*, Very near where the Samangos were seen, I came across a party of seven Vervet monkeys. **1967** J. R. & P. H. Napier *Handbk. Living Primates* 104 (*caption*) Samango monkey..grooming.

samara. Add: Also with pronunc. (sămā·ră). (Further examples.)

1960 [see *achene]. **1976** *New Yorker* 12 Jan. 66/2 The best-known samara is the maple key, which is much larger than the fruit of the birch.

Samaritan, *sb.* and *a.* Add: **A.** *sb.* **a.** (Later examples.)

1957 *Oxf. Dict. Chr. Ch.* 1211/1 *The Samaritan Pentateuch*, a slightly divergent form of the Pentateuch in Hebrew, current since pre-Christian times among the Samaritans. It is the only part of the OT accepted by the Samaritans. **1965** M. Spark *Mandelbaum Gate* iv. 91 Those Israelites, Samaritans, those boys. **1977** *Sci. Amer.* Jan. 100/1 Although the kingdom of Samaria vanished long ago, the Samaritans still survive today as perhaps the smallest ethnic minority in the world.

b. Freq. in full, *good Samaritan*; also *transf.*, a kind and helpful person; hence (nonce-wds.) *good Samaritanism, good Samaritanship.*

1640 N. Rogers (*title*) The good Samaritan, or an exposition on that parable, Luke x. ver. xxx–xxxviii. **1840** J. Ruskin *Let.* 4 July in *Lett. to College Friend* (1894) 11 You have sacrificed half a Good Samaritanship to insult your friends with letters of brown paper. **1846** [in Dict.]. **1898** 'A. Hope' *Rupert of Hentzau* iii. 42 Good Samaritans but not men of war, they returned to where I lay senseless on the ground. **1919** M. Beer *Hist. Brit. Socialism* i. v. 74 The new order would act as a good Samaritan and pour oil and wine into the wounds of the nation. **1923** *Virginia Law Rev.* Apr. 423 It is unreasonable that the priest and the Levite should go free while the good Samaritan should be forced to undergo the ordeal and expense of a trial. **1925** A. Huxley *Those Barren Leaves* ii. vi. 156 On the faces of all my good Samaritans I noticed an expression of child-like earnestness. **1930** H. Redwood *God in Slums* 14 A co-opted partner in every kind of Good Samaritanism. **1950** T. S. Eliot *Cocktail Party* i. ii. 49 Don't you realise how lucky you are To have *two* Good Samaritans? *a* **1953** E. O'Neill *Touch of Poet* (1957) i. 9 Sure, the good Samaritan was a crool haythen beside you. **1963** *Reader's Digest* May 89/1 The best known and most effective curb of the malpractice-suit racket is California's so-called Good Samaritan law. **1977** *Times of Zambia* 7 Sept. 1/6 Shawa started as a Good Samaritan, trying to separate a fight in which Mr Sichinga was involved.

c. *the Samaritans*, an organization founded in London in 1953 that offers counselling by telephone to those in distress or contemplating suicide; hence as *sing.*, a member of this organization. Also (in sing.) *attrib.*

[**1953** *Church Times* 27 Nov. 854/5 The Rev. Chad Varah..intends to open a 'Good Samaritan' centre—on the telephone.] **1960** *Times* 29 Nov. 6/6 The vast majority of those who came to the Samaritans were not mentally ill... The Samaritans had helped people of all types, from a duke to a dustman. **1967** *Guardian* 8 June 3/5 The most common reasons for people calling the Telephone Samaritans for help in the Greater Manchester area..were depression, anxiety, and mental illness. **1969** *Listener* 10 Apr. 508/1 The girl..works for Oxfam and wants to be a Samaritan. **1973** J. Seabrook *Loneliness* 115 I'd break down, I'd be all trembling. I used to ring the Samaritans. I don't know what I'd have done without the man who was my counsellor. **1977** *Hongkong Standard* 14 Apr. 13/3 (Advt.), Discouraged/Depressed? Dial the Samaritans, day or night. **1978** M. Dickens *Open Bk.* xxi. 186 The Samaritans is a world-wide fellowship of men and women of all ages, creeds and races, dedicated to befriending people who are desperate enough to want to kill themselves. *Ibid.*, I went to the Samaritan centre in London to talk about the isolated and lonely people who I knew must be among their callers.

B. *adj.* **a.** Also *Comb.*, as (sense b of the sb.) *samaritan-like* adj.

1973 E.-J. Bahr *Nice Neighbourhood* vi. 64 We callously discussed how Samaritan-like we'd been, having John over for dinner.

Samaritanism. 1. (Later example.)

1973 *Sci. Amer.* Jan. 80/1 Of all the multifarious forms of Jewish religious expression that arose, only two have survived and flourish today... A marginal survivor is Samaritanism, maintained by a tiny group of Samaritans..who continue to worship on their holy Mount Gerizim.

samarium. Substitute for entry:
samarium (samēᵊ·riŏm). *Chem.* [mod.L., coined in Fr. (P.-É. Lecoq de Boisbaudran 1879, in *Compt. Rend.* LXXXIX. 214): see *Samarskite and -ium.] A hard grey metallic element of the lanthanide series, found in small quantities in monazite sand, samarskite, and other rare earth minerals. Symbol Sm; atomic number 62.

1879 *Jrnl. Chem. Soc.* XXXVI. 890 A new metal to which the author gives the name Samarium. **1907** *Athenæum* 31 Aug. 244/3 A sulphide of calcium containing a trace of the rare element samarium. **1923** U. R. Evans *Metals & Metallic Compounds* II. 233 If an attempt is to be made to obtain pure compounds of samarium, europium, or gadolinium, the double magnesium salts are more satisfactory. **1955** *Sci. News Let.* 12 Mar. 164/1 Rare earth metals, such as samarium and europium, have long remained a mystery, simply because there was not enough of them available to find out what they could be used for. **1969** *New Scientist* 28 Aug. 430/2 Storage densities of 100 000 bits of information per square inch may be achieved with an orthoferrite containing samarium and terbium. **1974** *Encycl. Brit. Micropædia* VIII. 829/2 In addition to its more stable trivalent state, samarium..has a +2 oxidation state... Trivalent samarium..forms a series of yellow salts and solutions. **1977** *Gramophone* Oct. 590/1 (Advt.), It has an unusually tiny, samarium cobalt (rare earth) magnet of remarkably high power. **1980** *Sunday Times* 24 Aug. 14/8 The magnet within which the coil fits is now made of samarium cobalt.

sama·ria, substitute for def. in Dict.: the oxide Sm_2O_3, a cream-coloured solid; (earlier and later examples).

1885 *Jrnl. Chem. Soc.* XLVIII. ii. 1025 The spectrum of a phosphorescent mixture of samaria 90 parts, and yttria 10 parts, in high vacua, shows none of the lines of yttrium, but is almost a facsimile of the spectrum of pure samarium. **1974** *Encycl. Brit. Macropædia* XV. 516/1 Mosander's didymia was resolved into several oxides—samaria (samarium; 1879), praseodymia.., neodymia.., and europia.

Samarra[2] (sămā·ră). The name of a city in northern Iraq, used in phr. *an appointment in Samarra* to indicate the inevitability of death. Also *transf.*

In Maugham's play (see quot. 1933), the servant to a merchant meets Death in the market-place at Baghdad, and flees to Samarra to escape his clutches. When questioned by the merchant, Death explains his surprise at seeing the servant, replying as in quot. 1933.

1933 W. S. MAUGHAM *Sheppey* III. 112, I was astonished to see him in Bagdad, for I had an appointment with him to-night in Samarra. **1934** J. O'HARA (*title*) Appointment in Samarra. **1971** A. PRICE *Alamut Ambush* xi. 133 He had ridden out innocently..and had set up his own appointment in Samarra. **1973** *Times* 28 June 16/8 All Mr Heath's justified complacency as he watches the Labour Party destroying itself will avail him little if, come the next General Election, his own rendezvous with destiny turns out to be an appointment in Samarra.

samarskite. Substitute for entry: **samarskite** (sæ·māɹskəit). *Min.* [ad. G. *samarskit* (H. Rose 1847, in *Ann. d. Physik* LXXI. 166), f. the name of Col. M. von *Samarski*, 19th-cent. Russian mining official: see -ITE[1].] A complex niobate and tantalate of yttrium, uranium, and iron, with small quantities of other metals including lanthanides, which is found as velvet-black or dark brown monoclinic prisms in granite pegmatites.

1849 J. NICOL *Man. Mineral.* 285 Samarskite... Rhombic; isomorphous with columbite..mostly imbedded in flat, somewhat polygonal grains. **1947** *Proc. Indian Acad. Sci.* A. XXV. 405 The samples of samarskite were secured from the Kodanda Rama mine in Nellore District. **1973** T. MOELLER in J. C. Bailar et al. *Comprehensive Inorg. Chem.* IV. xliv. 49 Minerals of lesser importance include..samarskite, an yttrium earth–iron–calcium–uranyl niobate–tantalate, found in North Carolina, the Ural Mountains, and Madagascar.

Samaveda: see *SAMAN[1].

samba (sæ·mbă), *sb.*[1] [Pg., of Afr. origin.] A Brazilian dance of African origin; a ballroom dance imitative of this; also, a piece of music such as accompanies this dance. Also *attrib.*

1885 W. MOBERLY *Rocks & Rivers Brit. Columbia* 17 It was here I first saw the graceful South American dance—the Zemba Queca (I am not certain how it is spelt). **1911** B. MIALL tr. *P. Denis's Brazil* xiii. 324 It is during these festivals that the negro dances are performed; the *Coco* and the *Samba*. **1929** H. MILES tr. *P. Morand's Black Magic* p. i, 1919—Darius Milhaud arrives from Brazil. He..plays me those Negro *Sambas* which are shortly to serve for the music of his *Bœuf sur le Toit*. **1939** *Britannica Bk. of Year* (U.S.) 201/1 The samba is the national dance of Brazil, much as the fox trot is in the United States... In 1938, the samba was just beginning to make its way in the New York night clubs. **1942** D. PIERSON *Negroes in Brazil* ix. 248 It was of these *Bahianas* that Carmen Miranda sang when she recently captivated Broadway with the staccato notes of the rollicking *samba* by Dorival Caymmi, 'Que é a Bahiana tem?' *Ibid.* 249 The *samba*, or *samba batida*, a regional form of the old *batuque*, although it has now been taken over by the upper classes and in a modified form become not only one of the most characteristic musical forms but also one of the favorite dances of Brazil, is still enjoyed in its primitive simplicity by the Bahian lower classes. **1949** M. DICKENS *Flowers on Grass* ix. 240 Mervyn and Wanda were doing a Samba. **1950** J. VEDEY *Band Leaders* 132 He [*sc.* Edmundo Ros] states that many of the numbers published as Sambas are not really Sambas at all. .. In 1940..the Rumba was the only known dance of its kind, played in either slow or fast tempo. The Samba, which Ros himself actually introduced, followed. *Ibid.* 144 Who are these thousands of people packing the Palais de Danse and jiving wildly to the sambas and Bop arrangements of the popular bands? **1954** J. STEINBECK *Sweet Thursday* xxviii. 199 The crazy trumpet put a samba beat to the 'Wedding March'. **1965** W. SOYINKA *Road* 21, I have not seen any other tout who would stand on the lorry's roof and play the samba at sixty miles an hour. **1974** *Down Beat* 18 July 26/3 Zoot, Jaki and Al all get their say in a medley of sambas. **1977** *Gramophone* Aug. 353/3 Barlow specializes in the more traditional sequined ballroom fare of quicksteps, waltzes, foxtrots, a tango, cha cha chas, a samba, slow rumbas, a pasodoble and jive. **1979** P. FOX *Mantis* iv. 62 Great driving-music: hard rock Samba, plenty of guitar.

samba (sæ·mbă), *sb.*[2], var. SAMBO (sense 1).

1958 J. CAREW *Wild Coast* ix. 126 It please me eyes to see you growing up into a proper samba man. **1959** J. MORRIS *Adversary* i. 9 A couple of upcountry *corregidors*.. had three girls between them... One of them looked like a *samba*. **1974** *Black World* Aug. 55 The Dirty Tricks store window featured a grotesque, black-purple mask of a 'samba' sister with a bone through its nose.

samba (sæ·mbă), *v.* [f. *SAMBA *sb.*[1]] *intr.* To dance the samba. Also *fig.*

1950 in WEBSTER Add. **1959** 'J. DRUMMOND' *Black Unicorn* xviii. 128 He put his arm round my waist, and started trying to make me samba. **1972** *Time* 22 May 9/3 Brazil had sambaed away with the talks. **1975** *Times* 14 Apr. 12/4, 37 couples..were required to cha-cha, samba, rumba and paso doble. **1979** C. WOOD *James Bond & Moonraker* xi. 111 How do you kill five hours in Rio if you don't samba?

samba, var. SAMBUR in Dict. and Suppl.

‖ **sambal** (sæ·mbăl, ‖ sambal). Also **sambaal, sambel.** [Malay.] A highly seasoned condiment, of Malayan and Indonesian origin, consisting of raw vegetables or fruit prepared with spices and vinegar and used as a relish; found also in other (esp. *S. Afr.*) cookery. Cf. *POL SAMBOL.

1815 A. PLUMPTRE tr. *Lichtenstein's Trav. S. Afr.* II. iv. xxxiii. 84 *Sambal* is a mixture of gherkins cut small, onions, anchovies, Cayenne pepper, and vinegar. **1817** S. RAFFLES *Hist. Java* I. 98 The most common seasoning.. is the lombok; triturated with salt, it is called *sámbel*. **1839** T. J. NEWBOLD *Brit. Settlements in Straits of Malacca* II. xii. 178 The ordinary food of Malays..is rice, and in times of scarcity, sago seasoned with a little salt fish, Blachang, the caviar of the East, made with acid fruits, &c., into a variety of condiments termed Sambals. **1871** *Cape Monthly Mag.* June 334 They make a sort of chutnee out of quinces, which they call 'sambal'. **1933** L. AINSWORTH *Confessions Planter in Malaya* 145 The usual small side-dishes containing what are known as 'sambals', which consist of such things as fried ground nuts, shredded cucumber, burnt grated coconut, Bombay duck and red and green chillies. **1942** S. CLOETE *Hill of Doves* xxiii. 328 He thought of food once more—bobotee; breede, made of mutton ribs; cucumber sambal. **1950** *Cape Times* 7 June 16/1 Her letter has reference to *melktert*, brandied peaches, *kreef frikkadels*, quince *sambaal*—all things which are becoming a lost art to us. **1953** DU PLESSIS & LÜCKHOFF *Malay Quarter* i. 15 The spicy stew is enhanced by means of various *sambals* or condiments. **1971** L. CHARTERIS *Saint & People Importers* iii. 24 Order me some samosas, lamb curry, pilau rice, dhal, and all the sambals you can crowd on the table. **1978** *Courier-Mail* (Brisbane) 26 Oct. 25/3 We ordered..a made-on-the-premises sambal mixing pineapple, capsicum and mild chillies in soy sauce, sugar and vinegar.

‖ **sambaquí** (sambakī·). [Tupi.] A form of shell heap, found on the S. Brazilian coast, resulting mainly from the action of the wind and the sea, in which remains of prehistoric and historic cultures have been found; also *attrib.* (See quot. 1946.)

1944 S. PUTNAM tr. *E. da Cunha's Rebellion in Backlands* ii. 50 The pre-Columbian of the 'Sambaquis'. **1946** A. SERRANO in J. H. Steward *Handbk. S. Amer. Indians* I. iii. 401 The word 'sambaquí' is of *Tupi-Guaraní* origin and means 'hill of shells'. *Ibid.* 403 The sambaquís are littoral cordons or concentrations of shells, broken and reshaped by natural forces. *Ibid.* 404 Artifacts in the most ancient sambaquís, which are farthest from the sea, correspond to the primitive culture of Lagoa Santa. *Ibid.*, The prevailing idea..has been that of a cultural unity—a single sambaquí culture—that is distinctive and characteristic of these deposits. It is no longer possible to maintain this. **1953** *Jrnl. R. Anthrop. Inst.* LXXXIII. 60 On the coast, the classic *sambaquí* culture, called the 'Southern Phase', may succeed the chipped-axe phase. **1977** G. CLARK *World Prehist.* (ed. 3) x. 447 There is evidence from the shell mounds or sambaqui sites that intensive exploitation of coastal resources had begun.

‖ **sambar** (sa·mbar). Also **sambhar.** [Tamil.] In South Indian cookery, a highly seasoned lentil gravy. Also *attrib.*

1957 S. RANGARAO *Good Food from India* vii. 68 Sambar powders go well into meat curries. **1967** M. WALDO *Internat. Encycl. Cooking* II. 541/2 *Sambar*, (Indian), a highly seasoned vegetable and lentil dish. **1972** *Indian Express* 28 Dec. 10/1 South Indian dishes—idli, dosa and sambhar—have become popular. **1973** *Times* 19 June (Bombay Suppl.) p. xv/3 The food of South India, especially the idli (spongy rice cakes) with sambar (liquid lentil juice) should not be missed. **1976** *Sunday Standard* (India) 11 Jan. 10/4, I distribute bread to these children everyday. I've also brought sambar to go with it. **1977** *Sunday Times* (Colour Suppl.) 27 Nov. 35/4 The food is as authentic as it is in Madras—..*sambar* (the thick lentil gravy cooked with vegetables and tamarind juice).

Sambo. Add: **2.** (Earlier and later examples.) Now used only as a term of abuse. Also *attrib.*, esp. with reference to the appearance or subservient mentality held to be typical of the black American slave.

1704 *Boston News-Let.* 2 Oct. 2/2 There is a Negro man taken up supposed to be Runaway from his Master,.. calls himself Sambo. **1735** J. ATKINS *Voy. to Guinea, Brazil & W. Indies* 170 If you look strange and are niggardly of your Drams, you frighten him; *Sambo* is gone, he never cares to treat with dry lips. **1781** I. JACKSON *Divorce* II. 34 So then, Sambo, you want to be in the fashionable world, I see?.. Timothy, show the black Gentleman downstairs. **1818** 'A. BURTON' *Adventures J. Newcome* IV. 222 His Steward was a scoundrel Sambo, And in his own conceit a d—d beau; A true Barbadian being born, He others held in utter scorn. **1922** JOYCE *Ulysses* 322 *Black Beast Burned in Omaha, Ga.* A lot of Deadwood Dicks in slouch hats and they firing at a sambo strung up on a tree with his tongue out and a bonfire under him. *Ibid.* 436 Tom and Sam Bohee, coloured coons in white duck suits, scarlet socks, upstarched Sambo chokers and large scarlet asters in their buttonholes leap out. **1927** G. B. SHAW *Doctors' Delusions* (1932) 137 When a vivisector says, in effect, 'I have a dread secret to wrest from Nature: so you must license me to sacrifice a guinea pig', the Sambo in us assents. **1957** [see *BOOT *sb.*[3] 1 e]. **1959** S. ELKINS *Slavery* 227 What, then, of the 'reality' of Sambo? Did the Sambo role really become part of the slave's 'true' personality? **1962** L. DEIGHTON *Ipcress File* xix. 123 'I'd just better be right about you pale-face,' he said. 'You'd just better had, Sambo.' **1969** *N.Y. Rev. Bks.* 13 Mar. 3/1 The reasons for the development of the 'Sambo' response of the Negro slave to his environment which help to explain the paucity of slave revolts in America. **1969** *Guardian* 1 Apr. 7/4 The brothers wore Afro costume... Their loose jigging and gestures, open-mouthed, Sambo style, reverberated with their long solid jammed numbers. **1973** *Times Lit. Suppl.* 2 Mar. 230/2 The 'Sambo' stereotype of the loyal, lazy, affectionate and child-like slave. **1977** *Times* 10 June 8/5 A white Zambian..had called him a black sambo during the struggle for independence.

sambok, var. SJAMBOK.

sambook. Add: Also **sambuq.** (The usual spelling is now *sambuk.*) Also *attrib.* (Later examples.)

1906 H. W. SMYTH *Mast & Sail* 307 The Red Sea *sambuk* is generally from 18 to 20 tons only. **1938** F. STARK *Jrnl.* 1 Mar. in *Winter in Arabia* (1940) 201 A king..sent for one thousand virgins from Somaliland across the sea; they were all shipped in a sambuq. **1942** [see *MASHWA]. **1963** *Times* 1 Feb. 14/6 They want a sambuq to meet them at Bir Sukaiya at noon next Wednesday—it's three hours' sail by sambuq from there to Perim. **1974** *Nat. Geographic* Sept. 333 (caption) *Sambuk*, once the most common of Arab dhows, has ferried generations of Moslem pilgrims from Africa towards Mecca. **1975** *Financial Times* 31 Oct. 5/4 The monsoon was pushing the seas too high, even for the sturdy *sambuq* fishing boats.

Sam Browne (sæm braun). [The name of Sir *Sam*uel James *Browne* (1824–1901), British general, who invented it.] In full, *Sam Browne belt*: a belt with a supporting strap that passes over the right shoulder, worn by commissioned officers of the British Army and also by members of various police forces, etc. Also *transf.*, a commissioned officer.

1915 *Punch* 6 Oct. 288/3 Military Wedding Equipment. Sam Browne belt, single brace and frog, best bridal leather. **1916** E. C. MIDDLETON *Aircraft* xvi. 114 Should he be posted to the Army wing he will probably present himself to an astonished and apoplectic adjutant wearing two cross straps to his 'Sam Browne'. **1919** *Amer. Legion Weekly* 5 Sept. 27 It wasn't the privates or the acting corporals or the full-fledged Sam Brownes who had a monopoly on this particular quality. **1933** J. CARY *Amer. Visitor* xvii. 278 Stoker in a Sam Browne and Gore with a huge Webley strapped to his waist were interrogating Sam and Henry. **1942** E. WAUGH *Put out More Flags* i. 55 Taking in every detail of his uniform, the riding boots, Sam Browne belt, the enamelled stars of rank. *Ibid.*, I heard they had stopped wearing cross straps on the Sam Browne. **1972** J. WAMBAUGH *Blue Knight* (1973) i. 16, I loosened my Sam Browne for the joy of eating. **1977** 'A. YORK' *Tallant for Trouble* i. 13 He wore the khaki shorts and bush jacket, and the Sam Browne belt, of a police officer.

‖ **sambuca**[2] (sambu·kă). Also **sambucca,** and with capital initial. [It., ad. L. *sambūc-us* elder tree: see SAMBUCENE.] An Italian liqueur resembling anisette.

1971 P. PURSER *Holy Father's Navy* xv. 121 They stared at me, coffee cups and brandies and *sambuccas* half-raised to lips. **1975** *Times* 11 Jan. 11/5 Sambuca, from Italy.. contains liquorice. **1977** *New Yorker* 20 June 26/1 It got so cold that..when they tried to pour anisette or Sambuca into their coffee in the early mornings to warm up, they sometimes found it frozen in the bottle.

sambunigrin (sæmbiunəi·grin). *Chem.* [ad. F. *sambunigrine* (Bourquelot & Danjou 1905, in *Compt. Rend.* CXLI. 598), f. mod.L. *Sambucus nigra*, taxonomic name of the common elder (f. L. *sambūcus* elder + *niger* black): see -IN[1].] A colourless crystalline glycoside of the nitrile of *d*-mandelic acid, found in the leaves of the elder and having the formula $C_6H_5{\cdot}CH(CN){\cdot}O{\cdot}C_6H_{11}O_5$.

1905 *Jrnl. Chem. Soc.* LXXXVIII. I. 912 The leaves of *Sambucus nigra* contain only traces of emulsin; it is therefore possible to extract from the air-dried or the fresh leaves the glucoside sambunigrin $C_{14}H_{17}O_6N$, which crystallises from ethyl acetate in long, colourless needles. **1965** ANSELL & GIGG in S. Coffey *Rodd's Chem. Carbon Compounds* (ed. 2) Ic. ix. 104 It [*sc.* hydrogen cyanide] is widely distributed in plants in the form of..glycosides of the cyanohydrins of various aldehydes and ketones (amygdalin, prunasin, sambunigrin,..etc.).

sambuq, var. SAMBOOK in Dict. and Suppl.

sambur. Add: Also **samba.** Substitute for def.: Either of two large deer, *Cervus unicolor* or *C. equinus*, native to southern Asia. (Further examples.)

1874 H. H. COLE *Catal. Objects Indian Art S. Kensington Mus.* ii. 107 Strips of sappan wood.., ebony and sambur horn dyed green. **1913** L. WOOLF *Village in Jungle* ii. 25 He showed them the sambur lying during the day in the other great caves. **1950** J. H. WILLIAMS *Elephant Bill* xi. 166, I once jumped into a creek, ten yards from a tiger, that was..eating a freshly killed samba deer. **1964** LD. MEDWAY in Wang Gungwu *Malaysia* I. iii. 57 This large group includes several animals widespread in South-east Asia such as the..Sambar and Barking Deer. **1969** J. LEASOR *Week of Love* v. 92 A dapper man..with sambur skin shoes.

Samburu (sæmbu·ru), *sb.* and *a.* [Native name.] **A.** *sb.* **a.** A pastoral people of mixed Hamitic stock inhabiting northern Kenya; a member of this people. **b.** The Nilotic language of this people. **B.** *adj.* Of or pertaining to this people or their language.

1896 W. A. CHANLER *Through Jungle & Desert* vii. 281 They said they had originally belonged to the Berkenedji or Samburu tribe. *Ibid.* 306 On our way to the new zeriba we were approached by a band of 100 Samburu. **1927** W. M. ROSS *Kenya from Within* xxiv. 436 Heavy pressure was brought to bear on the local Government to grant land in actual use by the Samburu tribe to one or more of the European sheep-ranchers. **1947** [see *MASAI]. **1959** A. MOOREHEAD *No Room in Ark* iv. 100 The Samburu.. are a tall fine slender people with something of the ancient Egyptians about them. **1964** J. HILLABY *Journey to Jade Sea* 81 Lelean said something uncomplimentary in Samburu. **1965** P. SPENCER *Samburu* p. xxii, Pardopa clan was typical of less than a half of the Samburu clans. **1976** D. TOPOLSKI *Muzungu* xiv. 222 He answered, just as chattily in Samburu. *Ibid.* 223 An uncircumcised man is still considered to be a boy amongst the Samburu.

same, *a.* (*pron.*, *adv.*). Add: **I. 6.** *same difference*, the same thing, no difference. *colloq.*

1945 E. WILSON *I am gazing into my 8-ball* xx. 106 'That fluff from my office.' 'Fluff?' laughed Miss Lawrence. 'Fluff, doll, same difference.' **1951** J. CORNISH *Provincials* II. i. 130 'I found you.' '*I* found *you*.' 'Same difference.' **1976** A. HILL *Summer's End* viii. 115 'In the first place,' he said, 'these'm *boats*, not barges.' 'Same difference,' Noggie insisted.

II. 7. a. Colloq. phr. (*the*) *same but* (or *only*) *different*: almost the same; subtly different.

1942 BERREY & VAN DEN BARK *Amer. Thes. Slang* §16/9 *Same but different*, nearly the same. **1977** *Lancashire Life* Nov. 60/1 More seasoned observers may remark that the scene's the same, only different.

8. (Later examples.)

1914 G. B. SHAW *Pygmalion* (1916) III. 157 *Pickering.* We have taken her to classical concerts and to music.. halls; and its all the same to her: she plays everything.. she hears right off when she comes home. **1962** L. DEIGHTON *Ipcress File* 8 If it's all the same to you, Minister, I'd prefer you to make a note of the questions, and ask me afterwards.

III. 10. *same-aged*, *-named*, *-natured*, *-sexed*, *-sidedness*, *-sized* (later example); also *same-day*, *-sex*, *-size* attrib.; **same-level** *Social Science*, analogous; that uses an established principle in one field of research for the explanation or analysis of phenomena in another field.

1949 M. MEAD *Male & Female* xiv. 285 He will frown upon the same-aged youth who has a reputation for active premarital sex relations. **1967** *Punch* 22 Feb. 258/3 And such cleaning and pressing, a same-day service like you never seen. **1934** J. T. WISDOM in *Aristotelian Soc. Suppl. Vol.* XIII. 66 When the psychologist says 'I am in awe of you' means 'I fear and admire you' he is giving a more ostensive but still same-level translation of the first sentence. **1936** *Mind* XLV. 442 All material analysis is 'same-level analysis'. **1958** M. ARGYLE *Relig. Behaviour* xii. 141 A third kind of theory explains an empirical result by showing that it is an example of a law in another field of research—this will be called a 'same-level' theory. *Ibid.* 143 This is clearly a 'same-level' explanation, postulating that religion is learnt by the same processes of socialization as are other attitudes and beliefs. **1954** S. DUKE-ELDER *Parsons' Dis. Eye* (ed. 12) xxviii. 473 In vertical palsies the paresis is due to failure of the 'same-named' rectus muscle (in the left superior area, the left superior rectus) or the most 'crossed-named' oblique muscle (right inferior oblique). **1696** J. SERGEANT *Method to Sci.* I. ii. 20 The same Causes upon the same-natur'd Subjects, must work the same Effects. **1949** M. MEAD *Male & Female* xiv. 284 Their sex, lightly anchored to the model of the same-sex parent. **1917** Same-sexed [see *FRATERNAL *a.* c]. **1977** *Lancet* 24 Sept. 657/2 There is sometimes same-sidedness in familial breast cancer. **1967** KARCH & BUBER *Offset Processes* v. 151 Set the camera for same-size reproduction. **1951** W. DE LA MARE *Winged Chariot* 32 On every nut there swelled the same-sized husk.

B. *absol.* and as *pron.* **2. d.** (*the*) *same again*: another drink of the same kind as the last; *same here*: the same (thing) applies to me; my case is similar; I agree; (*the*) *same to you*; I say the same thing to you (as you have just said); freq. used as a retort.

1896 W. C. GORE in *Inlander* Jan. 150 *Same here!* I agree. **1907** A. P. MCKISHNIE *Gaff Linkum* xi. 59 'I've enj'yed th' ride in th'moonlight jest as much as I enj'yed th' singin' school.' 'Same here,' said Mr. Goosecall. **1911** G. B. SHAW *Blanco Posnet* 404 *Blanco.* Dearly beloved brethren —*A Boy.* Same to you, Blanco. **1913** KIPLING *Diversity of Creatures* (1917) 288 'Do you know I've broken this man's neck?' 'Same here,' I says. **1925** *New Yorker* 17 Oct. 12/2 The same to you. **1929** D. H. LAWRENCE in *Star Rev.* Nov. 624 It is as if the young girl said to the young man today: I rather like you, you know. You are so thrillingly repulsive to me.— And as if the young man replied: Same here! **1938** L. MACNEICE *Earth Compels* 22 What will you have now? The same again? **1949** G. B. SHAW *Buoyant Billions* II. 21 A chain shopkeeper, not a country squire. *She.* Same here: my father is a famous lucky financier. **1959**, etc. [see *KNOB *sb.* 1 e]. **1962** *Sunday Times* 19 Aug. 18 'I'm a rugged individualist: I think for myself.' 'Me too.' 'Same here.' **1972** H. KEMELMAN *Monday Rabbi took Off* xxi. 136 'To tell the truth, I think it was the *rebbitzin* that wrote it and he signed it.' 'Same here.' **1975** D. O'SULLIVAN in D. Marcus *Best Irish Short Stories* (1977) II. 90 A thump on the counter brought the barmaid... 'Same again, ladies?'

4. a. (Later examples.)

1901 M. FRANKLIN *My Brilliant Career* viii. 56 A big red-bearded man..had received a letter from Mrs. Bossier instructing him to take care of me. He informed me also that he was glad to do what he termed 'that same'. **1926** in H. W. Fowler *Mod. Eng. Usage* 512/1 Sir,—Having in mind the approaching General Election, it appears to me that the result of same is likely to be as much a farce as the last. **1966** G. W. TURNER *Eng. Lang. in Austral. & N.Z.* vi. 135 A different influence of written language is seen in the use of *same* as a pronoun equivalent to *it*, as in 'put the tailboard up and secure same with a length of wire' from New Zealand (Wally Crump, 1964), a facetious borrowing of lawyer's English which is quite common. **1973** *N.Y. Law Jrnl.* 24 July 4/4 The following sentence in a brief is typical of its misuse as a noun: 'Waldbaum purchased the soda..then stacked it on the shelves in order to sell the same.'

5. b. pl. *Linguistics.* Features or utterances that are identical.

[**1926** BLOOMFIELD in *Language* II. 155 Within certain communities successive utterances are alike or partly alike... That which is alike will be called *same.* That which is not same is *different.* This enables us to use these words without reference to non-linguistic shades of sound and meaning. **1948** B. BLOCH in *Ibid.* XXIV. 10 Successive phonotations composed wholly of the same articulations are *the same.* Other aspects are different.] **1961** R. B. LONG *Sentence & its Parts* xvii. 378 The evidence of history warrants our regarding the italicized words in the following pairs as 'sames' in spite of the differences in meanings. We rode in the day *coach.* We went with the football *coach* [etc.]. **1962** [see *FORM *sb.* 5 c]. **1964** CRYSTAL & QUIRK *Syst. Prosodic & Paralinguistic Features in Eng.* iv. 49 We should..only subsequently look for the correlations between postulated 'sames' of tension and formal items in the linguistic and situational context which will enable us to make statements of meaning. **1977** *Trans. Philol. Soc. 1975* 9 Certain configurations in languages typically result from the principled ('lawful') divergence over time of original sames.

C. *adv.* and in adverbial phrases. **1. a.** (Examples with omission of *the.*) Also, in weakened sense: just as, as.

1857 'S. SONDNOKKUR' *Ryde fro Ratchda to Manchistur* (ed. 2) IV. 9 Aw kuddunt elp wundurin..wether it wur to put iz grund coffi in, saym uz wi dun o whoam. *Ibid.* VI. 14 Thir wur o rattlin saym uz uv o lot a peawur looms. **1884** 'MARK TWAIN' *Huck. Finn* ii. 10 Strange niggers would ..look him all over, same as if he was a wonder. **1930** W. FAULKNER *As I lay Dying* 4 She ought to taken those cakes when she same as gave you her word. **1933** M. LOWRY *Ultramarine* i. 16 He knows bloody well same as myself it doesn't pay to shout and be unkind to youngsters. **1957** L. P. HARTLEY *Hireling* viii. 65 But I shouldn't be able to serve them personally, same as I do now. **1975** *Listener* 6 Feb. 174/1 There was no work... They were all bad years, because, same as I say, there was nothing.

c. *same like*: just like, the same as, in the same manner as. *dial.*, *illiterate*, or *joc.*

1898 W. P. RIDGE *Mord Em'ly* x. 142 Beef Pudding same like Mother makes! **1922** E. O'NEILL *Anna Christie* II. 134 Two my bro'der dey gat lost on fishing boat same like your bro'ders vas drowned. **1928** J. PETERKIN *Scarlet Sister Mary* iv. 47 E weddin-dress fits em same like a green shuck fits a young ear o corn. *Ibid.* xix. 207 I'll lay down on de ground an' holler same like a dog. *Ibid.* xxi. 227 'How you do today?' 'Fine. Same like a lamb a-jumpin.' **1959** A. CHRISTIE *Cat among Pigeons* ix. 107 'See no evil, hear no evil, think no evil. Same like the monkeys,' observed Sergeant Percy Bond. **1968** 'L. EGAN' *Serious Investigation* vi. 78 But same like the gent in Holy Writ, Beware the anger of a patient man. **1973** G. MITCHELL *Murder of Busy Lizzie* xv. 185 Ain't going to be no share-out. Same like the boy with the apple-core, if you happen to know that story. **1980** I. MURDOCH *Nuns & Soldiers* vii. 382, I have rich friends, same like you.

samey (sē^i·mi), *adv.* and *a.* *dial.* and *slang.* [f. SAME *a.* (*pron.*, *adv.*) + -Y^6.] **A.** *adv.* *all the samey* = SAME *adv.* 2.

1897 KIPLING *Captains Courageous* x. 221 All the samey, something's got to be done about it.

B. *adj.* Identical, characterized by sameness; lacking in variety, monotonous. Hence **sa·meyness.**

1929 E. RAYMOND *Family that Was* iii. 49 The days that followed, becoming 'samey'.., sank out of memory's sight. **1959** *Sunday Times* 19 July 10/6 Many of his pictures of expensive men and women on expensive horses seem samey. **1962** *Listener* 11 Jan. 90/3 All that 'samey' food and the lack of service. **1969** M. TRIPP *Malice & Maternal Instinct* iv. 25 Arthur never varied his approach or technique. Arthur was samey. **1977** *Oxf. Times* 9 Dec. 17/3 Their thick sound tends towards sameyness, but the songs have enough character to retain one's interest. **1978** *Illustr. London News* Nov. 142/2 She moves beautifully and does all that a dancer could do to differentiate steps that are samey.

Samfrau (sæ·mfrau). *Geol.* [See quot. 1937.] The name of a geosyncline postulated to have extended across *GONDWANALAND.

1937 A. L. DU TOIT *Our Wandering Continents* iv. 62 A major geosyncline..traversing Bolivia, north and central Argentina, Cape, Weddell Sea, passing east of King Edward VII Land and through Edsel Ford land, crossing Tasmania and the eastern part of Australia to New Guinea... This feature, which seems to have played so vital a rôle during the evolution of Gondwana,..can conveniently be called the 'Samfrau' Geosyncline—a contraction of the words 'South America—South Africa—Australia'. **1959** *New Biol.* XXIX. 14 A further example of this type is the Samfrau geosyncline, of which Du Toit has suggested the remnants now occur in South America, South Africa, and Australia. **1971** M. H. P. BOTT *Interior of Earth* vii. 202 Examples [of good fits of tectonic features on the assumption of continental drift] include..the fitting together of the Samfrau orogenic belt of Gondwanaland.

samfu (sa·mfū). Also **samfoo.** [Cantonese *sāam-fu.*] A suit consisting of jacket and trousers worn by Chinese women, particularly in Malaysia and Hong Kong; also worn by men. Freq. *attrib.*, as *samfu jacket*, *trousers.*

1955 D. MOORE *We live in Singapore* 41 Her thin, pendulous breasts hung down inside her *samfoo* jacket like malignant deformities. **1963** J. KIRKUP *Tropic Temper* ii. 23 Chinese girls in samfu, a kind of flowered pyjama suit with short flaring jacket. **1966** D. FORBES *Heart of Malaya* iv. 47 A Chinese woman dressed in a white peasant smock and blue *samfu* trousers. **1967** A. CORDELL *Bright Cantonese* iv. 51 The people..came..to the bath, pulling their samfoo jackets over their heads. *Ibid.* vi. 69 He brought white samfoo trousers and a jacket heavily stained with crimson flowers. **1969** J. BENNETT *Dragon* ii. 19 She was wearing a *samfu*, the blue or black suit which looks like the Viet Cong pyjama uniform. **1975** O. SELA *Bengali Inheritance* ii. 20 The witness was a frail, elderly Chinese... He wore a tattered black *samfoo.*

Samgha, var. *SANGHA.

‖ **Samhain** (saun; sau·in, sa·win). Also **Samain, Samhainn.** [a. Ir. *samhain* (Sc. Gaelic *samhuinn*), OIr. *samain.*] The first day of November, celebrated by the ancient Celts as a festival marking the beginning of winter and of the new year according to their calendar; All Saints' Day or Hallowmass. Also *attrib.* Cf. BELTANE.

The OIr. form *samain* is used only with reference to the ancient Celts. 'Samhain Eve' (quot. 1904) and 'the night of Samhain' (quot. 1910) are different renderings of Ir. *oidhche Shamhna* 'Hallowe'en'.

1888 J. RHYS *Lect. Orig. & Growth Relig. as illustr. by Celtic Heathendom* v. 518 The Samhain feast..was, like the Greek Apaturia, partly devoted to business..otherwise the feast, which occupied, not only Samain or the first of November, but also the three days before and the three days after it, was given up to the usual games. **1904** W. B. YEATS *Stories of Red Hanrahan* 1 The barn where some of the men were sitting on Samhain Eve. **1910** J. M. SYNGE *Deirdre of Sorrows* I. 5 And it raining since the night of Samhain. **1917** J. M. CLARK *Vocab. Anglo-Irish* vii. 27 Irish folk-lore has kept alive words of such classic associations as..Samhain and shanahus..which mean.. 'All-Hallowtide' (Nov. 1) and 'a friendly chat' respectively. **1949** J. A. MACCULLOCH *Celtic & Scandinavian Religions* I. viii. 58 Samhain, which means 'summer end', naturally pointed to the fact that the powers of blight, typified by winter, were beginning their reign. But it may have been partly a harvest festival. **1957** W. R. KERMACK *Scottish Highlands* 153 At Samhain (Hallowe'en, 31st October, the beginning of Winter) the Lewismen made libation to the sea-god Shony, who could send them plenty of seaweed to manure their fields. **1958** T. G. E. POWELL *Celts* iii. 117 At *Samain*, sacrifices were certainly offered although no material descriptions have survived. **1968** *New Larousse Encycl. Mythol.* 236/1 The [Celtic] year began on what is now the first of November with the feast of *Samain*... The ordinary people felt less sanguine about the possibility that on the eve of *Samain* the people of the *side* left their domain and wandered in the world of man. **1970** *Q. Rev. Guernsey Soc.* XXVI. 60 These four were the feast of Beltainn the great Sungod in May; mid-summer, mid-August..and Samhainn or Hallowmass (November 1).

Sam Hill (sæm hil). *N. Amer. slang.* Also **sam hill, samhill.** [Orig. unknown.] A euphemism for hell; used especially in expressions of impatience or irritation preceded by *in* or *the* with an interrogative word.

1839 *Havana (N.Y.) Republican* 21 Aug. 1/4 What in sam hill is that feller ballin' about? **1868** J. T. TROWBRIDGE *Three Scouts* vi. 26 When you might a'married!—why in Sam Hill didn't ye, then? **1894** 'MARK TWAIN' in *St. Nicholas* Jan. 257/2 Hateful people..giving me Sam Hill because I shirked. **1909** *N.Y. Even. Post.* 10 Apr. (Sat. Suppl.) 3/5 How in Sam Hill can she do it? She's just as hot when she gets to bilin' p'int as she'll ever be. **1918** M. E. FREEMAN *Edgewater People* 314 What in Sam Hill made you treat him so durned mean fur? **1927** W. JAMES *Cow Country* 77 What the Sam Hill do you think we are out here, servants? **1948** *Salt Lake Tribune* 18 Dec. 10/7 He wondered who the Sam Hill the 'senator' was. **1962** H. GREEN *Time to pass Over* xii. 147 Why in the samhill didn't you step in and stop them, Mike. **1973** B. BROADFOOT *Ten Lost Years* xxiii. 262 He probably never could have figured what the Sam Hill was going on.

Samhita (sa·mhitā). Also **sanhita.** [Skr. *saṃhitā* union, connection, f. *sam* together + *dhā* to place.] A text treated according to sandhi; a version of the vedas which is the continuous text formed from the pada or separate words by the appropriate phonetic sound changes. Also *attrib.*

1805 H. T. COLEBROOKE in *Asiatick Researches* VIII. 476 Tradition..reckons sixteen Sanhitas of the Rigveda. **1843** *Penny Cycl.* XXVI. 171/1 The Rigveda is the first in order and its Sanhitā contains mantras..to the elemental deities. **1887, 1917** [see *PADA b]. **1920** J. N. FARQUHAR *Outl. Relig. Lit. India* i. 26 The Veda as handed down in the various schools..soon showed considerable differences.

It has come down to us in four distinct forms called Saṁhitās. **1953** in K. W. Morgan *Relig. of Hindus* vii. 265 The Upaniṣhads are the philosophic and mystical elaboration of the truths first revealed to the Seers and recorded in the Saṁhitās. **1974** *Encycl. Brit. Micropædia* X. 375/3 The foremost collection, or Samhitā, of such hymns..is the Ṛgveda.

Sami (sā·mi, sām). Also † **Salme-Same; Saam(e, Sabme,** etc. [Lappish *Sami* (in earlier orthography, *Sabme, Samek*) of uncertain ultimate etym.; cf. also Sw. and Norw. *Same*.] The native name of the Lapps; occas. *sing.*, a Lapp.

This word is preferred to *Lapp* by scholars.

1797 *Encycl. Brit.* IX. 572/1 The Laplanders call themselves *Salme-Same*, and *Salmen-Almatjeh*. **1842** *Penny Cycl.* XXIII. 390/1 They [*sc.* the Laplanders] call themselves Sami. **1864** *Chambers's Encycl.* VI. 38/1 The Lapps, who call themselves the *Sami* or *Sahmelads*, are a physically ill-developed, diminutive race. **1935** S. J. Beckett *Wayfarer in Norway* xx. 145 The Lapps call themselves Sami or Sahmelads, whilst they call the Finns Suomi (which, like the name Finn, means 'Fen', or marsh-dwellers). **1957** R. Paine *Coast Lapp Society* I. i. i. 3 The people whom we know as Lapps have their own name for themselves—*sabme*, plural *sāmek*. In academic circles inside Scandinavia, the Lappish term is now replacing any other... Outside Scandinavia, however,..*sabme* is not widely understood. **1964** S. Dunn et al. tr. E. D. Prokof'yeva in Levin & Potapov *Peoples of Siberia* 547 Some scholars have compared the name 'Samoyed' with the Lappish (Saam) words 'same-yedne' ('land of the Saams'). This is based on the fact that the territory settled by the Nentsy.. was in earlier times inhabited by the Lapps (Saams). **1968** [see *pot *sb.*[1] 13 f]. **1977** *Daily Colonist* (Victoria, B.C.) 19 June 22/3 The..reindeer herder is one of the Saame, better known as Lapps. **1980** *Times* 8 Feb. 14/7 The 2,000 or so Lapps, or more accurately Sami, who live in this area.

Samian, *a.* and *sb.* Add: **A.** *adj.* (Earlier and later examples of pottery.) Also *ellipt.* and with small initial. **Samian ware** (earlier example).

1779 T. Pownall in *Archæologia* V. 287 The one [*sc.* vessel] is a red sort, the Ionian, or particularly the Samian, which is most commonly found. *c* **1841** W. T. P. Shortt *Sylva Antiqua Iscana* 110 The great quantity of fragments of Roman Red Ware, especially of that beautiful description, known to the ancients by the generic term of Samian, is not by any means the least interesting of the curiosities dug up in the city of Exeter, of late years. **1844** *Gentl. Mag.* July 35/2 Whether that singularly beautiful red glazed earthenware.. of which such vast quantities have been since exhumed in every part of England and France where their respective records have assigned a Roman station, be really the identical Samian pottery of Pliny, is, I think, a question yet to be decided. **1848** *Jrnl. Brit. Archaeol. Assoc.* Apr. 2 The Samian ware is found throughout this country almost wherever Roman remains are met with. **1958** Stanfield & Simpson *Central Gaulish Potters* I. 52 Black slip samian has a pinkish-red or buff-coloured core. **1967** *Antiquaries Jrnl.* XLVII. 192 It seems most likely that the later samian has come from pits dug into the rampart. **1981** P. Salway *Roman Britain* 202 Mr B R Hartley's study of the dies for the makers' stamps on samian pottery reveals that the amount of samian bearing the same stamps which comes from the two Walls is negligible.

samiel. Add: Now with pronunc.: (sa·miĕl). (Later examples.)

1832 J. Bell *Syst. Geogr.* IV. 231 The most dreadful of all winds is the famous semoum or samiel,..which prevails in the desert bounded by Bassora, Bagdad, Aleppo, and Mekka, and the effects of which are suffocation and immediate putrefaction of the body. **1962** [see *leveche].

samisen. Add: Also 7 **shamshin,** 9 **samsi, samishen,** 9– **shamisen; shamisan.** (Earlier and further examples.)

1616 R. Cocks *Diary* 9 Oct. (1883) I. 188 The *tuerto* that plaid on the *shamshin*. **1822** F. Shoberl tr. *Titsingh's Illustr. Japan* 94 Several young females came to bear them company, playing on the *samsi*, and dancing. **1840** *Chinese Repository* Dec. 630 The *samishen* is a three-stringed guitar, and is usually played with a plectrum. **1871** A. B. Mitford *Tales of Old Japan* I. 243 The *shamisen*, a sort of banjo. **1880** I. Bird *Unbeaten Tracks in Japan* I. 134 Yuki plays the *samisen*, which may be regarded as the national female instrument. **1936** K. Sunaga *Japanese Music* i. 19 The instrument employed as the accompaniment for the songs of geisha girls..was the *samisen*... It might be described as a three-stringed, rectangular banjo. **1955** E. Pound *Classic Anthol.* ii. 115 And words soft as the shamisan Distinguish the thick-faced man. **1964** I. Fleming *You only live Twice* i. 18 [Bond was] far from being..bewitched by the inscrutable discords issuing from the catskin-covered box of the three-stringed *samisen*. **1970** J. W. Hall *Japan* x. 227 The music of the *shamisen*. **1972** *Times* 18 Sept. 5/4 Guests knelt on tatami and used chopsticks to eat while geisha girls played the samisen.

samite. Add: Also *fig.*, *attrib.*, and *Comb.*

1938 R. Graves *Coll. Poems* 63 Into their many-shielded, samite-curtained, Jewel-bright hall where twelve Kings sit at chess. **1971** 'A. Burgess' *MF* xvii. 191 There were fireworks out tonight, thudding and searing the samite air.

samiti (sæ·mĭti). Also **samity.** [Hind. *samiti* meeting, committee.] In India and Bangladesh, an assembly or committee.

1930 M. L. Darling *Rusticus Loquitur* v. 124 The 250 Mahila Samitis or Women's Institutes founded in Bengal by Mrs G S Dutt. **1950** M. Masani *Our Growing Human Family* 41 The village assembly, known in Europe as the Folk-moot and in India as the Samiti. **1962** *Times* 26 Jan. (Survey of India) p. vi/6 Presidents of the various block *samitis* in a district form the *zila parishad*. **1975** *Bangladesh Times* 19 July 8/8 All the members of the Board of Directors of Bangladesh National Bidi Sramik Samabaya Samity.. have also applied for membership of the national party. **1976** D. Hiro *Inside India Today* 50 What then emerged was a three-tiered system whereby the old district boards.. were replaced by Zilla parishads (i.e. district councils) with responsibility for co-ordinating development plans to be channelled through panchayat samitis (i.e. council committees) consisting of a number of popularly elected panchayats encompassing one or more villages—all interlinked through indirect elections. This system, popularly known as the panchayat raj, was first introduced..in 1959.

‖ **samizdat** (sæ·mizdæ̆t, səmizda·t). Also with capital initial. [Russ., abbrev. of *samoizdátel'stvo* self-publishing house, f. *samo-* self + *izdátel'stvo* publishing house.] The clandestine or illegal copying and distribution of literature (orig. and chiefly in the U.S.S.R.); an 'underground press'; a text or texts produced by this. Also *transf.* and *attrib.* or as *adj.* Phr. *in samizdat*, in this form of publication.

1967 *Times* 6 Nov. (Russia Suppl.) p. xxii/4 A vast and newly educated [Soviet] population..do not pass around the precious *samizdat* (unpublished) manuscripts. **1968** tr. I. A. Yakhimovich *Let.* in *Probl. of Communism* July–Aug. 48/1 One must not speculate with the honor of the state, even if a certain leader wants to end *samizdat*. **1968** *Time* 27 Sept. 22/2 Those lines [of Solzhenitsyn] have not been published in the Soviet Union. But they are nonetheless read and passed from hand to hand in *samizdat*, the readers' answer to Soviet censorship. **1970** *New Statesman* 20 Feb. 241/1 The underground distribution of manuscripts and their publication abroad means that the *samizdat* writers have—at least in the eyes of the authorities —opted out of the Soviet scheme of things. **1971** *Guardian* 15 July 13/8 Nicolae Ceausescu's latest puritanical damper on 'Bourgeois Influences' in Rumania coincides with the first case of underground 'Samizdat' literature to come from there. **1973** R. Rosenblum *Mushroom Cave* 55 I've told you how effective the samizdat network has been in circumventing the repression of criticism. **1977** M. Walker *National Front* vii. 182 The NF *samizdats* which did so much to pollute the atmosphere of NF life during the year [*sc.* 1975]. **1977** *Time* 28 Nov. 30/2 An exhibit of clandestine *samizdat* in the Correr Museum. **1978** *Manch. Guardian Weekly* 27 Aug. 7 Jiri Hrusa's novel 'The Questionnaire', which was printed by the Prague Samizdat. **1980** *Times Lit. Suppl.* 3 Oct. 1094/4 The strongest works to have come out since 1962—Solzhenitsyn's *The First Circle* [etc.].. —have appeared, and could only appear, in *samizdat*.

Hence **samizda·tchik** [Russ. *-chik*, agent suffix], one who takes part in the writing, copying, and distribution of *samizdat* material (pl. *samizdatchiki*).

1972 *N.Y. Times Mag.* 10 Sept. 92 To fill their reserves.. the *samizdatchiki* seek ties with other cities... They arrive with copies of the originals, which have been given abroad. **1979** *N.Y. Times Bk. Rev.* 20 May 3/2 He assiduously collects information for the samizdat journals..writes pseudonymous articles for samizdat and spends weeks on end retyping the Chronicle and other materials from Moscow in multiple copies. He is the quintessential *samizdatchik*.

Samkhya, var. *Sankhya.

‖ **samlor** (sæ·mlǭɪ). Also **samlo.** [Thai.] Chiefly in Thailand, a three-wheeled vehicle, freq. motorized, used as a taxi.

1955 *Times* 6 May 11/6 Let him be insidiously towed in a motor *samlor* round this town of Bangkok. **1960** R. Kirkbride *Innocent Abroad* xi. 82 We crossed a humped bridge.. in the city, dodging about amongst cycle-rickshaws and samlors. **1963** 'Han Suyin' *Four Faces* 54 Peter would photograph her in front of the temples of Angkor, stepping down from a *samlo*, the three-wheeled vehicle, man-propelled, in use in Cambodia. **1974** *Time* 7 Jan. 50/2 The Assembly even includes a *samlor* driver, who intends to park his three-wheel smoke-belching minitaxi at the National Assembly building.

Sammy (sæ·mi), *sb.* Also **Sammie.** [Familiar dim. of the name *Samuel*: see -y[6].] † **1.** *slang.* A ninny, simpleton. Also in *Comb. Obs.*

1837 E. Howard *Old Commodore* II. iii. 54 You have been sammy-foozled by a rascally swindler. **1838** R. B. Peake *Quarter to Nine* i. ii. 10 What a Sammy, give me a shilling more than I axed him! **1897** F. T. Jane *Lordship Passen and We* xv. 165 Simple Sammy, as we called Mr. Pote, the new pastor.

2. *slang.* In British use: an American soldier in the war of 1914–18, so called from the name *Uncle Sam* (see Uncle *sb.* 2 c). Now *rare* or *Obs.*

1917 *Punch* 13 June 384/2 As a term of distinction and endearment [for the American 'Tommies'] Mr. Punch suggests 'Sammies'—after their uncle. **1917** *Nation* (N.Y.) 16 Aug. 164/1 The 'Sammies' whom the headlines are featuring. **1918** *Stars & Stripes* 29 Mar. 4/1 A Sammie may be defined as an American soldier as he appears in an English newspaper or a French cinema. It is a name he did not invent, does not like, never uses and will not recognize. **1921** *Glasgow Herald* 8 July 7/2 While a French soldier costs on average 13 francs 37 per day,..a 'Tommy' costs 31 francs 69, and a 'Sammy' 59 francs 30.

sammy, *v.* Add: (Earlier and later examples.) Also, to dampen (leather that has been allowed to dry out) slightly.

1885 C. T. Davis *Manuf. Leather* xxix. 502 The eleventh step, which consists in 'sammying' the hides, is then carried into effect. **1922** A. Rogers *Pract. Tanning* xv. 449 After the leather has been dried out, in order to set the fiber it must again be dampened back or sammied before carrying out the finishing process. **1974** P. W. Blandford *Country Craft Tools* xv. 199 The currier used a 'sleaker' to force out dirt, then the hide was 'sammied' by rolling either between a pair of rollers or under a heavy brass roller.

Samnite, *sb.* Add: **b.** A type of gladiator. **c.** The language of the Samnites.

1600 Holland tr. *Livy's Romane Hist.* ix. 344 The Campaines upon a pride, and inveterate hatred that they bare against the Samnites, used to arme their swordplayers and fensers at the sharpe (which was a solemne sight and pastime they had at their great feasts) with this same attire, and termed them in mockerie, by the name of Samnites. **1859** B. W. Dwight *Mod. Philol.* i. 187 The Umbro-Samnite Dialects: Umbrian; Samnite or Oscan; Volscian; Marsian. **1882** [see *Marsian *sb.* and *a.*]. **1957** *Encycl. Brit.* X. 383/2 The Samnites fought [in gladiatorial contests] with the national weapons—a large oblong shield, a vizor, a plumed helmet and a short sword. **1971** M. Grant *Cities of Vesuvius* iii. 74/1 Down to the first century BC, 'gladiator' and 'Samnite' were synonymous terms; and then the latter became the name of a particular type of gladiator.

Samoan, *sb.* **a.** (Earlier examples.)

1856 J. C. Patteson *Let.* in C. M. Yonge *Life J. C. Patteson* (1874) I. vii. 262 Another crew arrived with a Samoan teacher... I rode out pick-a-back on the Samoan, Leonard following on a half-naked Anaitean. **1871** C. M. Yonge *Pioneers & Founders* ix. 250 These Samoans, though they deified many animals, had no temples, idols, priests, nor sacrifices.

samoleon, var. *simoleon.

samosa (sămō̆ᵘ·să). Also **samoosa, samusa.** [Hind.] A triangular pastry fried in ghee or oil, containing spiced vegetables or meat.

1955 R. P. Jhabvala *To whom she Will* ix. 67 Another plate was filled with..samusas. **1960** — *Householder* i. 54 'They have made vegetable samusas with our tea,' Romesh told his father. **1971** *Weekend* (Colombo) 12 Sept. 6/3 (Advt.), Rizwana for cool cool Faluda and fresh hot Samosa. **1974** N. Gordimer *Conservationist* 131 What'd you find to buy?—..Samoosas.—..He puts the neat, crisp, greasy triangle whole into his mouth. **1978** [see *pakora].

Samoyed, *sb.* and *a.* Add: Also **Samoyede.** **A.** *sb.* **1.** (Earlier and further examples.)

1589 A. Jenkinson in Morgan & Coote *Early Voy. Russia & Persia* (1886) I. 36 The Tartars and Gentiles, called Samoyedes. **1841** [see *Ostyak]. **1911** *Encycl. Brit.* XXIV. 118/1 The language now spoken by the Samoyedes belongs to the Finno-Ugrian group, and is allied to Finnish but has a more copious system of suffixes. **1944** [see *Nenets]. **1972** *Language* XLVIII. 206 The Samoyeds make up only one small group of scattered tribes among the many non-Russian peoples who have inhabited Siberia.

2. Also with small initial. A white or buff dog belonging to the breed so called, once used as working dogs in the Arctic, and distinguished by a thick, shaggy coat, stocky build, pricked ears, and a tail curled over the back. Also *attrib.*

1889 *Pall Mall Gaz.* 30 Apr. 6/2 A beautiful brown silky-haired sharp-eared Samoyed dog. **1905** [see *laika]. **1914** N. Newnham-Davis *Gourmet's Guide to London* liii. 340 [He] brought me in..to look at a delightful little Samoyede puppy. **1922** R. Leighton *Compl. Bk. Dog* vii. 98 The white Samoyed is one of the most beautiful of all dogs. **1934** [see *malamute]. **1954** M. K. Wilson tr. *Lorenz's Man meets Dog* ix. 90 Pointed muzzles, obliquely set Mongolian eyes and pricked ears pointing sharply upwards..that fascinating expression which distinguishes Greenland sledge-dogs, Samoyeds and Huskies. **1977** G. Marton *Alarum* 61 The well-fed passengers..probably expected to be carried across immense ice fields by rough Samoyed dogs.

B. *adj.* (Earlier and later examples of use as a quasi-*sb.*)

1822 tr. *Malte-Brun's Universal Geogr.* I. xxiii. 571 The Tunguse is a dialect of the Mantchou; the Samoyede differs from it. **1956** J. Whatmough *Language* 28 In the north, Samoyede, a member of the same family as the Finnish dialects.

sampan[1]. Add: **3.** *Comb.*, as **sampan-wallah** [Wallah], a boatman in charge of a sampan.

1932 *Times Lit. Suppl.* 29 Sept. 693/3 In time he became a sampan-wallah. **1934** 'G. Orwell' *Burmese Days* vii. 123 The successful sampan-wallah turned and discharged at his rival a mouthful of spittle.

sampan[2] (sæ·mpăn). [Khoi-khoin *samban*.] = Tampan in Dict. and Suppl.

1898 W. C. Scully *Between Sun & Sand* i. 8 The ground beneath is full of the dreaded 'sampans', which bury themselves in the flesh and cause serious injury. **1920** *Glasgow Herald* 2 Sept. 4 The minor plagues of scorpions and 'sampans'.

samphire. Add: **3.** *samphire-bush* (later example), *-gatherer*, *-greens.*

1928 V. Woolf *Orlando* iv. 148 Closer and closer they drew, till the samphire gatherers, hanging half-way down the cliff, were plain to the naked eye. **1941** I. L. IDRIESS *Great Boomerang* ii. 10 Out among the samphire bushes lay huddled the little cloud of sheep. **1970** S. TRUEMAN *Intimate Hist. New Brunswick* iii. 57 Come home with thoughts of periwinkles, dulse, maple cream, samphire greens. **1971** *Country Life* 28 Oct. 1132/3 The reference to samphire, which for most of us means *King Lear*, the blinded Gloster and the wretched samphire-gatherer on Dover cliff.

sampi (sæ·mpəi). Also **sanpi.** [Late Gr. σαμπῖ, prob. f. ὡς ἂν πῖ like pi.] The modern name for an ancient Greek numeral (ϡ) = 900, which has been hypothetically identified with one of several sibilants in early Greek alphabets.

1833 *Penny Cycl.* I. 385/2 The letter *tsadi* has no representative in the Greek alphabet, unless, indeed, it bear any relation to the Greek figure called *sanpi*, which, however, was never used, as far as it is known, for an alphabetic character. **1875** *Encycl. Brit.* I. 609/2 Herodotus..speaks of the 'same letter which the Dorians call σάν, the Ionians σίγμα'; and though *san* was no letter of the Ionic alphabet, the compound *sampi* (= σαν+πι) denoted 900. **1912** E. M. THOMPSON *Introd. Greek & Lat. Palaeogr.* vii. 91 A symbol derived from the old letter *san*,..which, from its partial resemblance to *pi*, was called *sampi* (= *san*+*pi*), for 900. **1968** W. S. ALLEN *Vox Graeca* i. 58 This stage [*sc.* affricate stage of [ts]] is probably represented by some early Asiatic Ionic inscriptions which show in such cases a special letter **T**.., which may be derived from the Semitic '*tsade*' (and perhaps survives in the numeral symbol ϡ = 900, now known by the late Byzantine name of σαμπῖ < ὡς ἂν πῖ).

sample, *sb.* Add: **2. c.** A specimen taken for scientific testing or analysis.

1878, 1882 [in Dict., sense 2 a]. **1895** J. C. GUERNSEY *Urinalysis including Blanks* 11 If a sample of urine cannot be analyzed immediately upon its receipt, add ten to fifteen grains of salicylic acid. **1938** LUNDELL & HOFFMAN *Outl. Methods Chem. Analysis* iii. 21 In a chemical analysis, the first consideration is the use of a sample that truly represents the material under test. **1950** RACE & SANGER *Blood Groups in Man* i. 3 The reactions when different cell samples are tested against parallel titrations of the same antisera. **1973** J. G. DICK *Analytic Chem.* ii. 32 Samples of impure acidic substances were analyzed by a neutralization method.

d. *Statistics.* A portion drawn from a population, the study of which is intended to lead to statistical estimates of the attributes of the whole population.

1903, 1922 [see *POPULATION² 2 d]. **1944** H. G. WELLS *'42 to '44* 42 He would get answers to his questions from Samples of his Consumers. **1951** [see *MID-RANGE 1]. **1961** *Listener* 9 Nov. 780/2 There is the social survey of, say, the Young and Wilmott kind, with its planned interviews of samples. **1979** *Church Times* 9 Mar. 2/2 A nationally representative sample of 956 people was interviewed for the survey.

6. a. (Further examples.)

1895 W. SCHLICH *Man. Forestry* III. I. iv. 66 Having ascertained the volume of the sample plot, that of the whole wood can be calculated. **1970** G. A. & A. G. THEODORSON *Mod. Dict. Sociol.* 361 The extent to which generalizations based on sample data may be considered applicable to the total population from which the sample was drawn depends on the method used to select the cases included in the sample and the size of the sample. **1978** C. H. STODDARD *Essent. Forestry Pract.* (ed. 3) vi. 119 Timber estimators also measure and tally the trees in the strips or sample plots. **1978** R. V. JONES *Most Secret War* xix. 156 Maita had stayed in Salisbury because she was nervous about London, but she wanted to come for a sample weekend, and when would I recommend?

a*. General *attrib.*, as *sample investigation, method, study, survey* (hence *sample-survey* vb. trans.).

1930 *Economist* 1 Nov. 801/2 Even so, his impressions are inevitably based on 'sample' investigations and must be read with these limitations in mind. **1944** H. G. WELLS *'42 to '44* 43 The sample method of dealing with human affairs is exemplified by various uses to which we can put a jury. **1965** J. MEUVRET in Glass & Eversley *Population in Hist.* xxi. 516 Other sample-studies in parish registers..have revealed analogous results. **1966** *Economist* 12 Nov. 682/3 The development of economic knowledge sample-surveyed in these articles has been matched by a growing use of economists in business and government. **1975** *Listener* 6 Feb. 187/3 The study of human behaviour by..sample surveys.

a.** Used *attrib.* to denote various statistical attributes of a sample, as *sample average, mean, range,* etc.

1939 A. E. TRELOAR *Elements Statistical Reasoning* x. 137 The standard error of the sample mean. **1941** *Ann. Math. Statistics* XII. 91 (*heading*) Determination of sample sizes for setting tolerance limits. **1947** O. L. DAVIES *Statistical Methods Res. & Production* ix. 217 One [chart] on which the sample averages $\bar{x}$ are recorded and the other on which sample ranges *w* are recorded. **1971** HICKMAN & HILTON *Probability & Statistical Analysis* ix. 153 The sample variance..is said to be a point estimator of the population variance in the same sense that the sample mean..is a point estimator of the population mean.

b. sample book, a book containing samples of fabrics for prospective buyers; **sample bottle,** a bottle in which samples of fluid from the body may be collected; **sample case,** a case containing samples carried by a travelling salesman; **sample room,** (*a*) and (*b*) (earlier examples).

1938 *Burlington Mag.* Apr. 200/2 The distinguished firm of weavers, whose sample-books of 100 years and more ago are still in existence. **1976** P. CLABBURN *Needleworker's Dict.* 232/1 Old sample books still in existence are of the greatest value in telling later generations what was in fashion at a particular date. **1977** *Belfast Tel.* 22 Feb. 8/6 Doctors' hands.., little sample bottles, having your arm draped in black as your blood pressure is taken. **1875** *North Alabamian* (Tuscumbia, Alabama) 30 Sept. 3/3 We were not glad to see him, as he had left his sample case at home. **1935** [see *KEISTER 1 a]. **1971** D. E. WESTLAKE *I gave at the Office* 123 A salesman rapping his knuckles on his sample case in a waiting room. **1865** G. A. SALA *My Diary in Amer.* II. 46 Sometimes the bar is at the side, screened off, and genteelly disguised under the name of 'sample room'. You enter ostensibly to purchase cherries, and immediately 'put yourself outside' a 'tot' of Bourbon. **1869** W. H. BREWER *Rocky Mountain Lett.* (1930) 10 'Saloons', 'barrooms', 'sample-rooms', 'liquor stores', 'lager beer', etc., furnish most of the signs on the places of business. **1887** *Grip* (Toronto) 21 May 10/2 One of the drug travellers insisted..that the clerk..had, in the north sample room, first nicknamed Albendis 'Chippy'. **1892** *Hist. Rev. York County* (Pa.) 62/1 To the side is the reading and sample-rooms for the commercial traveler.

sample, *v.* Add: **5. a.** (Examples of use with inanimate subj.)

1974 HARVEY & BOHLMAN *Stereo F.M. Radio Handbk.* v. 119 The composite audio signal voltage is sampled at the midpoints by a train of short pulses and the sampled voltage level is held between pulses. **1978** *Nature* 13 July 135/2 A synchronous gating circuit..samples the V_2 signal at a selectable phase ('phase lock'), converting it to a proportional d.c. voltage.

6. To provide with samples.

1935 A. P. HERBERT *What a Word!* iii. 83 From a firm of 'Publishers and Educational Contractors for Handicraft Materials':..'We shall welcome the opportunity of *sampling* you with anything you would like to see.' 'We are *sampling* Norway with the new articles.' **1946** K. T. KELLER in *Chrysler Corp. Ann. Rep.* XXI, The limited production to date of our new models has been inadequate to properly sample our dealers.

7. *Comb.*: **sample-and-hold** *adj. phr. Electronics,* applied to a circuit or technique in which a varying voltage is sampled periodically and the sampled voltage is retained in the interval until the next sampling.

1966 M. SCHWARTZ et al. *Communication Syst. & Techniques* vi. 244 One difficulty in PAM systems used for time-division switching is that the short samples do not deliver very much average signal power to the individual receiving channels. The difficulty can be remedied by the use of a sample-and-hold circuit. **1974** HARVEY & BOHLMAN *Stereo F.M. Radio Handbk.* v. 119 Using this sample-and-hold technique, good channel separation, low distortion and low subcarrier breakthrough may be realized. **1979** C.-T. CHEN *One-Dimensional Digital Signal Processing* 435 The conversions between analog and digital signals are performed by sample-and-hold (S/H) circuits, analog-to-digital (A/D) converters, and digital-to-analog (D/A) converters.

sampled, *ppl. a.* Add: **2. sampled data,** data supplied at regular intervals, rather than continuously; freq. *attrib.*, designating a system whose behaviour is modified by such data.

1951 *Trans. Amer. Inst. Electr. Engin.* LXX. 1779/1 The design of a sampled-data servo system is as direct as the design of a conventional system. *Ibid.* 1779/3 A control system makes use of sampled data when it is impossible to supply continuous data to all its parts. **1955** J. G. TRUXAL *Automatic Feedback Control System Synthesis* ix. 500 Servomechanisms which operate on sampled data: *i.e.*, systems for which the input (or the activating signal) is represented by samples at regular intervals of time, with the information ordinarily carried in the amplitudes of the samples. **1968** *Brit. Med. Bull.* XXIV. 252/1 The breathing mechanisms must include a form of 'memory' and a so-called 'sampled data' system.

sampler, *sb.*¹ **5.** Delete † *Obs. rare* and add later examples.

1972 T. KOCHMAN *Rappin' & Stylin' Out* p. xv, Minimally necessary would be a comparative sampler of the diverse preaching styles that exist in the black community. **1975** *Booksellers Weekly* 15 Sept. 55/3 The authors also include a sampler of foreign menus: continental, Italian, Greek, Mexican, oriental, Indonesian. **1976** *National Observer* (U.S.) 17 Jan. 14/1 (Advt.), Try this Vermont Sampler... We'll send you, on approval, our Vermont cob-smoked ham..and 1 lb. of our delicious cob-smoked bacon.

6. That which contains a sample or representative selection; *spec.* a gramophone record of examples of a performer, type of music, etc.

1969 *Nature* 10 May 599/1 This paperback is a sampler of letters, periodicals, and reports in the United States relating to the publication late in 1859 of Charles Darwin's 'Origin'. **1970** *Melody Maker* 20 June 27/4 We are promised jazz releases from A. & M. Records commencing shortly with a jazz sampler. **1977** *Linlithgowshire Jrnl. & Gaz.* 15 Apr. 6/6 And one of the best ways to start is with Atlantic Record's sampler containing numbers from the albums 'War Babies', 'Abandoned Luncheonette' and 'Whole Oates'.

7. *attrib.* and *Comb.*, as (sense 3 b) *sampler rhyme*; (sense *6) *sampler album* (*ALBUM¹ 6), *collection, record.*

1977 *Zigzag* Mar. 28/3 He's also doing a sampler album, with sleeve notes too, I think. **1973** A. DUNDES *Mother Wit* p. xii, There are already sampler collections of raw folklore data available. **1975** *Gramophone* May 2024/1 Gustav Leonhardt Portrait. Sampler Record. **1951** W. DE LA MARE *Winged Chariot* 51 My cross-stitch sampler-rhyme.

sampler, *sb.*² Add: **1.** Also, one employed in any other form of sampling. (Further examples.)

c **1950** G. VAN DELDEN *I have Plan* i. 15 He..came to the mine.., so they put him on the staff as a sampler. **1971** J. B. CARROLL et al. *Word Frequency Bk.* p. xviii, The responsibility for judging whether or not a textual segment was an essentially English sentence was left to the sampler.

2. A device for obtaining samples for scientific study.

1902 *Bull. U.S. Fish Comm.* 1901 XXI. 58 (*caption*) Soil sampler, after Delbecque. **1927** *Bull. Nat. Res. Council* (U.S.) No. 61. 237 A modification of the Davis peat-sampler. *Ibid.* 238 In deeper water the other sampler had to be used. **1946** *Geogr. Jrnl.* CVII. 164 The core-sampler gave relatively short cores or none at all... The piston-sampler constructed by Dr. Kullenberg—a modification of the original vacuum core-sampler—secured practically undisturbed cores down to a maximum depth of over 3600 metres. **1959** *Jrnl. Sci. Instruments* XXXIV. 3 (*heading*) Impaction sampler for size grading air-borne bacteria-carrying particles. **1974** *Nature* 25 Oct. 678/2 The air samplers do not register this excess presumably because the size of the spray particles is beyond the upper limit of collection of the sampling duct.

sampling, *vbl. sb.* Add: **2.** (Further examples in *Statistics.*)

1924 J. STAMP *Stud. Current Probl. Finance & Govt.* 12 A second development of statistics, along the lines of the theory of probability, is in the important principle of 'sampling'... Under certain conditions 20 per cent., or even 5 per cent., samples may yield satisfactory and reliable results. **1935** *Brit. Birds* XXVIII. 332 Sampling is an attractive labour-saving device, but it presents a number of obstacles and pitfalls, and needs to be used with considerable caution. **1973** *Jrnl. Genetic Psychol.* CXXII. 249 This wide sampling yields a measure of a generalized expectancy of reinforcement.

3. *attrib.*, as *sampling method, rate, survey*; **sampling distribution,** the theoretical frequency distribution of a statistic, as calculated from a sample, over all samples of the same size and kind; **sampling error,** error due to the use of a sample which does not perfectly characterize the population from which it is drawn.

1928 *Proc. R. Soc.* A. CXXI. 654 (*heading*) The general sampling distribution of the multiple correlation coefficient. **1967** R. C. CAMPBELL *Statistics for Biologists* ii. 32 A sample statistic..has a sampling distribution. This last term is slightly misleading, because all the distributions we have considered arise from sampling; the name is however usually reserved for the distribution from sample to sample of a statistic calculated from each sample. **1914** *Psychol. Rev.* XXI. 109 The correlation (compensated for sampling errors) between any two columns. **1955** *Times* 8 July 7/3 It is anticipated that..the estimated total population of the Sudan will have a sampling error of substantially less than 1 per cent. **1974** *Times* 11 Feb. 15/3 Polls are subject to considerable sampling error. **1943** *Ann. Math. Statistics* XIV. 289 The accuracy of a sampling method may be measured by the variance of the estimate of the quantity which is of interest. **1975** *Listener* 6 Feb. 187/3 We accept sampling methods in our everyday life. **1947** *Bell Syst. Techn. Jrnl.* XXVI. 396 Any input wave can be represented by a series of regularly occurring instantaneous samples, provided that the sampling rate is at least twice the highest frequency in the input wave. **1978** *Gramophone* Apr. 1789/2 The Sound Stream recorder, which sells for $70,000, is a full 6-bit binary conversion and recording system, with a sampling rate of 48K, frequency response to 17kHz,..and a tape speed of 30ips. **1960** *Amer. Speech* XXXV. 176 The picture is probably as true as a sampling survey can give. **1972** H. KURATH *Stud. Area Linguistics* 76 A sampling survey carried out on a modest scale can reveal important aspects of the dialectal structure.

‖**sampot** (sanpo). [Fr., ad. Cambodian *sampuet.*] A kind of Cambodian sarong.

1931 *N. & Q.* 22 Aug. 127/1 The women of Cambodia make *sampots.* These are the long and wide sashes of silk of many colours which they bind around their waists. **1957** *Encycl. Brit.* IV. 641/2 Both sexes wear the *sampot* (a copious sort of loincloth) which the men supplement with a short jacket, the women with a long scarf draped around the figure or a long clinging robe. **1963** 'HAN SUYIN' *Four Faces* 100 The woman in a Cambodian *sampot* and blouse.

samprasarana (sæmprăsā·rănā). *Philol.* [Skr. *samprasāraṇa*, lit. 'a stretching out, extending', f. *sam-* together + *pra-* forth + *-sāraṇa* extension.] In Sanskrit, the interchange between the vowels i, u, ṛi, lṛi and their corresponding semi-vowels y, v, r, l; hence, a similar process in other Indo-European languages.

1861 T. GOLDSTÜCKER *Pāṇini: his Place in Sanskrit Lit.* 169 It is probable, therefore, that Pāṇini did not invent these terms, but referred to them as of current use. On the other hand, he distinctly defines..*upadhá, lopa, samprasárana*, and *abhyása.* **1888** J. WRIGHT tr. *K. Brugmann's Elements Compar. Gram. Indo-Gmc. Lang.* I. 473 Vowel absorption often happens in languages with predominantly expiratory accentuation... If the absorption happens in such a manner that the syllable retains its value as a syllable, which is only possible, if another sound is able to undertake the part as bearer of the syllabic accent, we call the process samprasāraṇa (after the Indian grammarians). **1916** A. A. MACDONELL *Vedic Gram. for Students* 5 The Samprasāraṇa series. Here the accented high grade syllables *ya, va, ra*..interchange with the unaccented low grade vowels *i, u, ṛ*. **1933** L. BLOOMFIELD *Language* xxi. 384 When a relatively sonorous phoneme is non-syllabic, it often acquires syllabic function; this change is known by the Sanskrit name of *samprasarana*. **1968** *Language* XLIV. 278 The forms *x^{u}arta- and *u̯arta- are correct: they are doubtless full grade replacements for the zero grade in samprasarana roots.

‖ **Samsam** (sæ·msæm). Now chiefly *Hist.* [Malay.] A person of mixed Malayo-Thai origin from the west coast of the Malay peninsula (see quot. 1961).

1836 J. Low *Diss. Soil & Agric. Penang* viii. 293, I believe there are some converts also amongst the Samsams, or mixed descendants of Siamese and Malays. **1839** T. J. Newbold *Pol. & Statistical Acct. Straits of Malacca* I. 420 The Samsams are a race of Malays who have adopted the religion and language of the Siamese. **1883** *Encycl. Brit.* XV. 322/2 A mixed Malayo-Siamese people, commonly known as Samsams, form the bulk of the population in the lower parts of Ligor and Sengora, and in the north of Kedah. **1961** L. D. Stamp *Gloss. Geogr. Terms* 403/1 *Samsam*.., a person of mixed Siamese–Malay origin, especially characteristic of the State of Kedah under Siamese suzerainty from 1821 to 1909.

‖ **samsara** (samsā·ra). *Indian Philos.* Also **sangsara.** [Skr. *saṃsāra*, a wandering through, f. *sam* prefix expressing completeness + *sṛ* to run, glide, move.] The endless cycle of death and rebirth to which life in the material world is bound; also *attrib.* Hence **samsa·ric** *a.*

1886 *Encycl. Brit.* XXI. 289/1 The notion of saṃsâra has become an axiom, a universally conceded principle of Indian philosophy. **1913** J. N. Farquhar *Crown of Hinduism* v. 213 All souls, whether living as gods, demons, men, animals, or plants, are afloat on the stream of transmigration (*saṁsāra*). **1928** W. Y. Evans-Wentz *Tibet's Great Yogi* p. xvi, The golden fish..symbolizes sentient beings immersed in the Ocean of Sangsaric (or Worldly) Existence. **1930** S. N. Dasgupta *Yoga Philos.* 67 The metaphysics of the saṃsāra cycle in connection with sorrow, origination, disease, rebirth. **1935** W. Y. Evans-Wentz *Tibetan Yoga* 16 The Sangsāra, or external universe, is a psycho-physical compound of mind; matter, as we see it, being crystallized mental energy. **1963** 'Mayananda' *Tarot for Today* xi. 140 It [*sc.* Stellar Power] can be distributed and assimilated by the Earth and Solar System, generally, thus producing all the minutiæ of Samsaric detail. **1966** R. F. C. Hull tr. *Jung's Ulysses* in *Coll. Wks.* XV. 127 Ulysses..is for Joyce.. the higher self who returns to his divine home after blind entanglement in *samsara*. **1977** L. A. Govinda *Creative Meditation* I. x. 43 The basic qualities of human individuality binding us to our worldly existence (*samsāra*) are at the same time the means of liberation and enlightenment.

samsi, var. Samisen in Dict. and Suppl.

‖ **samskara** (sanskā·ra). *Indian Philos.* Also 9 **sanscara, sanskara.** [Skr. *saṃskāra* a making perfect, preparation, f. *sam* together + *kṛ* to make, perform.] **1.** A purificatory ceremony or rite marking a stage or an event in life; one of twelve rites enjoined on the first three classes of the Brahman caste.

1807 *Asiatick Researches* IX. 288 The *Jainas*..admit the same division into four tribes, and perform like religious ceremonies, termed *sanscaras*, from the birth of a male to his marriage. **1832** *Ibid.* XVII. 309 Some of the original rites are still preserved..in such of the Sanskaras, or purificatory ceremonies as are observed at the periods of birth, tonsure, investiture, marriage, [etc.]. **1891** Monier Williams *Brāhmanism & Hindūism* (ed. 4) 353 Twelve purificatory rites, called Sanskāras were prescribed in the ancient collections of domestic rules..for the purification of the three higher castes. **1913** J. N. Farquhar *Crown of Hinduism* ii. 104 Debendranath Tagore..rebelled against the polytheistic and idolatrous character of the sacraments (*saṁskāras*) of the Hindu family. **1962** R. Zaehner *Hinduism* vii. 201 Saṁskaras or sacraments play an important part throughout the life of a Hindu. **1977** B. Saraswati *Brahmanic Ritual Trad.* p. xii, Of all the social institutions, the institution of the *samskaras* serves as the corner-stone of the total cultural complex of the brahmanic society.

2. A mental impression, instinct, or memory.

1827 *Trans. R. Asiatic Soc.* I. 562 Thence comes passion (sanscára), comprising desire, aversion, delusion, &c. **1875** Monier Williams *Indian Wisdom* iii. 79 *Saṇskāra*, implying —*a.* impetus as the cause of activity; *b.* elasticity; *c.* the faculty of memory. **1896** 'Swāmi Vivekānanda' *Yoga Philos.* 233 *Samskāra*, impressions in the mind-stuff that produce habits. **1930** N. Dutt *Aspects Mahayana Buddhism* iii. 94 They have been blinded by avidyā (ignorance of the Truth), from which have followed the saṃskaras (impressions). **1952** H. Zimmer *Philos. of India* III. ii. 324 The noun saṁskāra, signifying 'impression, influence, operation, form, and mold', is one of the basic terms of Indian philosophy. **1977** J. Hewitt *Yoga & Meditation* v. 42 The other is that which consists only of *Samskaras*, being brought on by the practice of the cause of complete suspension.

Sam Slick (sæm slik). *U.S.* The name of a peddling clock-seller, hero of a series of stories by T. C. Haliburton (1796–1865), Nova Scotian judge and political propagandist, used *transf.* of a type of smooth-spoken and sharp-practising New Englander, and hence *gen.* of any resourceful trickster or 'spiv'. Also *attrib.*

1897 R. G. Haliburton in *Haliburton: a Centenary Chaplet* 26 Sixty years ago the Southern States were familiar with the sight of Sam Slicks. **1916** M. Aiken *Canada in Flanders* I. 118 A 'hyphenated' voice..cried out peevishly next evening: 'Say, Sam Slick, no dirty tricks tonight.' **1944** B. A. Botkin *Treas. Amer. Folklore* III. 358 For Yankee trickiness or slickness the name Sam Slick has become proverbial. **1962** *Amer. Speech* XXXVII. 84 Other items of the standard vocabulary of this 'Sam Slick' American were suggested rather than directly quoted.

Samsoe (sæ·mso). Also **Samso, Samsø.** In full, *Samsoe cheese*: a firm, buttery cheese from the Danish island of Samsoe.

1953 G. P. Sanders *Cheese Varieties & Descriptions* 124 Swiss Cheese is made in many other countries besides Switzerland... Danish Swiss is called Samso. **1955** *Times* 10 May 12/4 Samsoe cheese..takes its name from the island of Samsoe. **1968** *Vogue* 15 Apr. 42/2 You need 8 oz. Danish Blue cheese, 4 oz. Samsoe cheese. **1968** L. Deighton *Continental Dossier* 8 Local dishes are rare—specialities are found country-wide, like..'Samsø'—the Cheddar of Denmark. **1976** M. Patten *Barbecue & Outdoor Eating* 27/2 Grate 12 oz (350 g) Danish Samsoe cheese and slice 2–3 tomatoes.

Samson. Add: Also, except in senses 1 and 6, with small initial. **1.** *Samson-like* adj. and adv. (later examples); *Samson-passion.*

1796 Southey *Joan of Arc* IX. 359 By experience rous'd shall man at length Dash down his Moloch-gods, Samson-like And burst his fetters. *a* **1821** Byron *Don Juan* (1956) III. lvii. variant line 8 And make him Samsonlike—more fierce with blindness. **1929** Blunden *Near & Far* 49 Joy's masque and fashion of Time's Samson-passion Deceived no lark that springs from weed and clod.

3. For ? *Obs.* in Dict. read 'Now *Hist.*' and add later examples.

1965 E. Tunis *Colonial Craftsmen* iv. 95 The wheelwright ..pulled the joint hard together with a large threaded clamp called a samson. **1968** J. Arnold *Shell Bk. Country Crafts* 163 There was a samson, for drawing felloes together when the strakes were being nailed on.

5. *Logging* (see quots.). Hence **sa·mson** *v.*

1905 *Terms Forestry & Logging* (U.S. Dept. Agric. Bureau Forestry) 45 *Sampson*, an appliance for loosening or starting logs by horsepower. It usually consists of a strong, heavy timber and a chain terminating in a heavy swamp hook. *Ibid.*, *Sampson a tree, to*, to direct the fall of a tree by means of a lever and pole. **1913** [see *kilhig]. **1971** F. C. Ford-Robertson *Terminol. of Forest Sci., Technol. Pract. & Products* 148/2 *Killig*.., *Pushpole*.. = *Sampson* (USA). A stout pole, sometimes notched into the tree stem at one end and braced against the base of a peavey handle at the other, used to push a small tree manually in the desired direction.

6. Samson fox [in allusion to Judges xv. 4], a fox belonging to a variety of the North American red fox, *Vulpes fulva*, in which the fur lacks guard hairs and so has a scorched appearance. Also *absol.*

1910 E. T. Seton *Life-Hist. Northern Animals* II. xxxii. 709 Another freak is the 'scorched' or 'Samson Fox'. **1921** N. M. W. J. McKenzie *Men of Hudson's Bay Company* xvii. 160 Foxes that were burned like these were [what] we called 'Samsons', and were useless. **1933** E. Merrick *True North* 305 He said he weren't goin' to..go clear into Canada to trap a few weasels and samson foxes. **1948** A. L. Rand *Mammals Eastern Rockies* 105 The Samson fox is a freak, in which the guard hairs are lacking.

Samsonite[1] (sæ·msənəit). Also **samsonite.** [f. Samson + -ite[1].] **1.** A variety of dynamite having an inert base of borax and salt.

1909 *Jrnl. Soc. Chem. Industry* 31 Aug. 915/2 The Secretary of State has made an Order adding the following explosives to the schedule..Nobel Ammonia Powder.. Samsonite..Titanite No. 1. **1915** A. Marshall *Explosives* 213 A charge of undoubtedly hard frozen Samsonite exploded whilst being rammed home with a wooden rammer. **1921** *Glasgow Herald* 28 Feb. 11 Illegal possession..of 2980 gelignite cartridges, 10 samsonite cartridges. **1936** E. Hart *Shotfirer's Man.* viii. 95 He then charged the shothole with 8 ozs. of Samsonite No. 3 and fired it.

2. A proprietary term in the U.S. for a make of suitcases, briefcases, and other items of luggage, etc. Chiefly *attrib.*

1939 *Official Gaz.* (U.S. Patent Office) 21 Feb. 538/2 Shwayder Bros., Inc., Denver, Colo. Filed Oct. 17, 1938. *Samsonite Streamlite.* For trunks, suitcases, and traveling bags. Claims use since Apr. 18, 1938. **1963** *Times* 24 Apr. 16/4 After this generous present, it is a bit of a come-down for the eight regional winners to receive 'Samsonite bridge tables and chairs'. **1969** J. Gardner *Compl. State of Death* iv. 40 The file was dropped into a slim brown Samsonite brief-case. **1971** D. MacKenzie *Sleep is for Rich* vi. 196 The samsonite case would carry a hundredweight without collapsing. **1977** *Time* 28 Feb. 47/1 Just now, Linda is cooling out in Los Angeles after months of bashing about in planes and buses like a piece of lost Samsonite. **1977** C. McFadden *Serial* (1978) xliv. 94/2 She dragged the Samsonite over the threshold.

samsonite[2] (sæ·msənəit). *Min.* [ad. G. *samsonit* (Werner & Fraatz 1910, in *Centbl. f. Mineral.* 331), f. the name *Samson* (see quot. 1910) + *-it* -ite[1].] A sulphide of silver, antimony, and manganese which occurs as black prisms with a metallic lustre.

1910 *Mineral. Mag.* XV. 430 Samsonite... Found with pyrargyrite and pyrolusite in the Samson mine, St. Andreasberg, Harz. **1968** I. Kostov *Mineral.* 173 Samsonite ($Ag_4MnSb_2S_6$) is a mineral of peculiar composition, containing up to 5·96% Mn and crystallizing in the monoclinic system. **1969** *Acta Crystallographica* B. XXV. 1004/2 The presence of two atomic polyhedra—the squat pyramids, SbS_3, and slightly deformed octahedra, MnS_6,—is the most characteristic feature of the crystal structure of samsonite.

Samson's post. 2. b. (Earlier and later examples.)

1865 *Harper's Mag.* Apr. 573/2 The walking-beam is a heavy horizontal piece of timber, supported in the centre by a Samson-post. **1960** C. Gatlin *Petrol. Engin.* iv. 45/1 The walking beam is supported by the sampson post, and imparts the reciprocating motion to the drilling line.

Samuelite (sæ·miuĕləit). [f. the name of Sir Herbert Louis *Samuel*, first Viscount Samuel (1871–1963), Liberal politician + -ite[1].] A supporter of Sir Herbert Samuel; used *spec.* to designate a member of the official Liberal Party, which was led by Samuel, subsequent to the secession in 1931 of the Liberal National Party under Sir John Simon (see *Simonite). Freq. *attrib.*

1931 *Times* 13 Oct. 14/4 The Liberal Party was split into at least three well-marked divisions. There were the Simonites, who had thrown in their lot boldly with the national cause; the Samuelites, about whom he [*sc.* Churchill] was unable to give any correct information; and the Lloyd Georgeites. **1931** A. Sinclair *Let.* 3 Nov. in J. Bowle *Visct. Samuel* (1957) xvii. 286 If you will forgive me saying so..we don't want to be called..Samuelite Liberals as opposed to Simonite Liberals. **1936** *Ann. Reg.* *1935* 87 Against it [*sc.* the Government] were..the Liberals without prefix, led by Sir Herbert Samuel, and commonly known as 'Samuelites'. **1952** Visct. Simon *Retrospect* x. 180 The Samuelite Liberals supported the vote of censure. **1976** C. Cook *Short Hist. Liberal Party 1900–1976* x. 118 In March 1932, the National Government's decision to introduce the Import Duties Bill provoked a rebellion by the Samuelite Liberals.

Samuel-Smilesian: see *Smilesian.

samurai. Delete ‖ and '(Unchanged in the plural)' and add: Pl. **samurai,** occas. **samurais.**

1. a. (Earlier and later examples.)

1727 J. Scheuchzer tr. *Kaempfer's Hist. Japan* II. i. 396 'Tis from thence they are call'd *Samurai*, which signifies persons who wear two swords. **1795** tr. *C. P. Thunberg's Trav. Europe, Afr., & Asia* (ed. 2) III. 123 The people in office at this place, who wore two sabres, were called *Samrai*. **1841** *Chinese Repository* X. 17 Class 4 is that of the *samorai*, or military, and consists of the vassals of the nobility. **1896** L. Hearn *Kokoro* x. 172 The fear of the dead was held not less contemptible in a samurai than the fear of man. **1898**, etc. [see *bushido]. **1904**, etc. [see *heimin]. **1972** *Mainichi Daily News* (Japan) 6 Nov. 7/7 The Samurai were distinguished in dress most easily by the swords they wore.

b. *transf.* and *fig.*

1905 H. G. Wells *Mod. Utopia* ix. 259 These people constitute an order, the *samurai*, the 'voluntary nobility', which is essential in the scheme of the Utopian State. **1918** G. Frankau *One of Them* xx. 151 Stern mitred prelates; Law-lords; back-woods Samurais Who flung to consequence a scornful 'Damn your eyes'. **1934** H. G. Wells *Exper. Autobiogr.* II. ix. 735, I have told already..how I tried to make the Fabian Society into an order of the Samurai. **1977** *Time* 24 Jan. 17/2 Yukio Mishima, the right-wing literary samurai who committed spectacular hara-kiri in 1970.

2. *attrib.* and *Comb.*, as *samurai code, ethic, order, spirit, sword, warrior*; *samurai-minded* adj.

1971 *Times Lit. Suppl.* 20 Aug. 984/1 The samurai code embraced more than the practice of Zen and the ethics of Japanese forms of Confucianism. **1970** *Newsweek* 7 Dec. 32/2 The Japanese militarists of the 1930s twisted the ancient samurai ethic into the ideology of Fascism. **1938** *Times* 17 Feb. 16/1 In private conversation business men will unequivocally express disapproval of the course of events, a minority of *samurai*-minded ultra-patriots being the only exceptions. **1906** G. B. Shaw *Let.* 24 Mar. (1972) II. 614 A proposal for a set of observances of the Samurai order. **1923** Samurai spirit [see *bushido]. **1961** I. Murdoch *Severed Head* xix. 155 Was it..when I saw her cut the napkins in two with the Samurai sword? **1977** *National Observer* (U.S.) 15 Jan. 5 Hayakawa..went on to even more fame as the 'samurai warrior' president of San Francisco State University.

samusa, var. *samosa.

samyama (samya·ma). *Indian Philos.* Also **sanyama.** [Skr. *saṃyama* restraint, control of the senses, f. *sam* together + *yam* sustain, hold up (*yāma* rein, bridle, self-control).] The name given to the three final stages of meditation in yoga, which lead on to *samadhi*, or the state of union.

1828 *Trans. R. Asiatic Soc.* III. 164 That which removes sin is Brahmanhood. It consists of..*Neyama*, and *Ripavas*, and *Dan*,..and *Sànyama*. **1884** R. C. Bose *Hindu Philos.* 160 Three internal subservients, attention, contemplation, and meditation, collectively called by the name of 'subjugation' (sanyama). **1899** Max Müller *Six Syst. Indian Philos.* vii. 459 It is difficult to find a word for Saṁyama, firm grasp being no more than an approximate rendering. It is this Saṁyama, however, which leads on to the Siddhis, or perfections. **1959** E. Wood *Yoga* xiii. 237 *Sanyama* is then a definite tool of mind, which can be used to gain knowledge of various kinds. **1978** D. N. Bradshaw tr. *Oki's Meditation Yoga* iii. 84 People usually assume that there are many preparations to be made before entering samyama, but the method of Yoga is simple and clear.

san[1] (sæn). [Gr. σάν.] The name (first recorded by writers of the sixth century B.C.) for a sibilant (M) found in early Doric scripts (later displaced by sigma), which has been compared with various Semitic sibilants and *SAMPI.

1584 B. RICH tr. *Herodotus' Famous Hystory* I. f.44v, All the wordes in theyr language which consist of 4 or more sillables do commonly end in one letter: which letter the Dores cal San the Iones Sigma. **1709** I. LITTLEBURY tr. *Herodotus' Hist.* I. I. 89 All Names representing the Person or Dignity of a Man, terminate in that letter which the Dorians call San, and the Ionians Sigma. **1860** *Chambers's Encycl.* I. 169/2 In accommodating itself [*sc.* the Phoenician alphabet] to the necessities of the Greek tongue..the name *Sigma* was transferred to *San*. **1912** [see *SAMPI]. **1915** J. SANDYS tr. *Pindar's Odes* 559 In olden days, the lay of the dithyramb was wont to wind its straggling length along, and the sibilant *san* was discarded. **1933** [see *KOPPA]. **1961** L. H. JEFFERY *Local Scripts Arch. Greece* I. ii. 33 By the second half of the fifth century, the sign of *san* was no longer in use, except in conservative Crete, and as an emblem on the coins of Sikyon.

San[2] (sān). Also **Saan**. [Bushman, app. of Khoikhoi (Hottentot) origin: cf. Nama *sā* to inhabit.] **a.** The name used for themselves by the Bushmen of southern Africa (see BUSHMAN 1); also *attrib.* **b.** The principal language of the Bushmen.

1876 *Encycl. Brit.* IV. 575/1 Bushmen..so named by the British and Dutch colonists of the Cape, but calling themselves *Saab* or *Saan*, are an aboriginal race of South Africa. **1878** K. JOHNSTON *Africa* xxiv. 440 The Bushmen or San are the nomads of the Kalahari. **1881** [see *NAMA *a.*]. **1907** *Rep. Brit. Assoc. Adv. Sci. 1906* 689 They are called Baroa by the Basuto, Abatwa by the Kafirs, San by themselves. **1930** [see *KHOIKHOI]. **1944** M. OLDEVIG *Sunny Land* v. 50, I had the rare good fortune to come upon a Saan Bushman, one of the few who still inhabit parts of the Namib desert. **1967** D. S. PARLETT *Short Dict. Lang.* 73 The Khoin or 'Click' languages..comprising to the south Bushman (San), to the north Hottentot (Nama) [etc.]. **1974** J. FLINT *Cecil Rhodes* i. 9 South Africa was the home of the San (the so-called Bushmen). **1977** C. F. & F. M. VOEGELIN *Classification & Index World's Lang.* 201 South African Khoisan. Central... 36. San = Saan.

san[3] (san). [Jap.: a contraction of the more formal *sama*.] A Japanese honorific title, equivalent to Mr., Mrs., etc., suffixed to personal or family names as a mark of politeness; also *colloq.* or in imitation of the Japanese form, suffixed to other names or titles (cf. *MAMA-SAN).

When suffixed to a female personal name, and in more polite endearment, *san* is often coupled with the prefix *O-* (see quot. 1922).

1878 C. DRESSER in *Jrnl. Soc. Arts* XXVI. 175/1 Mr. Sakata, or, as they would say Sakata San, who was appointed ..as one of my escort through Japan. **1891** A. M. BACON *Japanese Girls & Women* xi. 304 He is a person to be treated with respect,—to be bowed to profoundly, addressed by the title San, and spoken to in the politest of languages. **1922** JOYCE *Ulysses* 321 The fashionable international world attended *en masse* this afternoon at the wedding... Miss Grace Poplar, Miss O Mimosa San. **1952** T. J. MULVEY *These are your Sons* vii. 146 'You go away, O'Reilly-san?' the little girl asked. **1964** I. FLEMING *You only live Twice* i. 16 'Bondo-san,' said Tiger Tanaka, Head of the Japanese Secret Service, 'I will now challenge you to this ridiculous game.' **1968** *Guardian* 23 Feb. 11/4 Corpsman Kenneth Corner..told her [*sc.* a Vietnamese girl]: 'It's going to be all right baby-san, it's going to be all right.' **1972** J. BALL *Five Pieces of Jade* xiv. 188 It would make me the greatest pleasure, Nakamura san.

San[4] (sæn). Also **san.** Colloq. abbreviation of SANATORIUM (esp. in sense *3).

1906 R. BROOKE *Let.* 1 Apr. (1968) 47, I started this disease..rather badly, and as the San. was full, we were put into a room in the house. **1914** 'I. HAY' *Lighter Side School Life* iii. 71 Broken neck, inflammation of the lungs, ringworm, and leprosy, old son... You are going to the San. **1936** M. KENNEDY *Together & Apart* III. 174, I was in quarantine for mumps, so I stayed in our school San. all the holidays. **1945** [see *KNOW *v.* 1 b]. **1976** 'D. FLETCHER' *Don't whistle 'Macbeth'* 45, I sounded like some old-fashioned matron, soothing the felled captain of the First Eleven in the san.

sanakatowzer (sæ:năkătaʊ·zəɪ). *Naut. slang. rare.* Also with capital initial. [Of uncertain origin: cf. TOWSER *sb.* and *bandowzer* in *D.A.E.*] An extremely forceful blow; something particularly large or powerful, such as a heavy wave.

1903 KIPLING in *Collier's Weekly* 15 Aug. 9/3 Mr. Ducane catches 'im a sanakatowzer of a smite over the 'ead with the flat of 'is sword. **1920** *Blackw. Mag.* Apr. 501/2 She shipped one Sanakatowzer that nearly swamped her.

sanaphant (sæ·năfænt). *Electronics.* [f. *SANA(TRON + *PHANT(ASTRON.] (See quots.)

1949 B. CHANCE et al. *Waveforms* v. 200 Although somewhat more complex than the screen-coupled phantastron, the sanatron and sanaphant can generate waveforms..as short as 1 μsec. **1955** *Electronic Engin.* XXVII. 397/2 This undesirable loading may be avoided by the use of the sanaphant circuit, in which the gating waveform is obtained by amplification of the voltage developed across a small resistor inserted in the cathode circuit of the charging valve. **1960** COOKE & MARCUS *Electronics & Nucleonics Dict.* 413/2 *Sanaphant*, a linear time-delay circuit similar to the sanatron, differing chiefly in the connections between the two pentodes.

Sanatogen (sănæ·tŏdʒĕn). A proprietary name for a tonic wine.

[**1898** *Official Gaz.* (U.S. Patent Off.) 14 June 1657/2 Dietetic albuminous preparations. Bauer, Cie Berlin... Sanatogen... Used since October 25, 1897.] **1924** G. B. STERN *Tents of Israel* xii. 173 She dispensed a share in her jellies and Sanatogen and grapes. **1936** H. NICOLSON *Let.* 28 Apr. (1966) 259 Tell Gwen I do not need Sanatogen at present. **1939** *Trade Marks Jrnl.* 1 Mar. 290/1 *Sanatogen Tonic Wine*... Genatosan Limited, 43, Regent Street, Loughborough, Leicestershire; manufacturers.

sanatorium. Add: Also with pl. sanatoriums. **1.** (Earlier and later examples.) Also *fig.*

1839 *London Med. Gaz.* XXV. 406/2 Dr. Southwood Smith, Dr. Arnott, and some other gentlemen, have it in contemplation to establish, under the name of 'Sanatorium', an institution..where patients are provided with board and medical treatment on the payment of a certain sum per week. *Ibid.* 407/2 We anticipate..that the parties who have set about the Sanatorium will abandon the scheme before it has been brought into actual operation. **1934** DYLAN THOMAS *Let.* 15 Apr. (1966) 104, I don't want to see my books; a library is a sanatorium of sick minds. **1973** *Sci. Amer.* Sept. 130/2 The care of the mentally ill in distant upland sanatoriums.

3. A room or building in a boarding school for the accommodation of the sick. Cf. *SAN[4].

1860 *Eton Gloss.* 30 Sanatorium. The Hospital—a modern improvement—where a boy seized with any infectious and dangerous illness is at once sent. **1901** *Eton Boy's Lett.* 98 They dont take measels to the Sanatorium as they arent dangerous. **1914** 'I. HAY' *Lighter Side School Life* iii. 71 When dragged from the scrummage he was in a half-fainting condition. He revived as he was being carried to the Sanatorium. **1981** E. NORTH *Dames* iv. 75 Should Sister move the general's daughter to the sanatorium?.. Polio was about at Eton..where many girls had brothers.

sanatron (sæ·nătrǫn). *Electronics.* [Perh. irreg. f. SANITARY *a.* (cf. quot. 1951): see *-TRON.] A circuit which generates a saw-tooth output waveform on receipt of a short trigger pulse, used in time-bases and similar applications.

1946 *Jrnl. Inst. Electr. Engineers* XCIII. IIIA. 1191/1 The circuit, known as the Sanatron, is illustrated in Fig. 5. **1951** O. S. PUCKLE *Time Bases* (ed. 2) ix. 181 The Royal Air Force used many slang terms. The name 'Sanatron' has been derived from the term 'sanitary', meaning satisfactory. **1955** *Electronic Engin.* XXVII. 397 /2 Examination of the sanatron circuit also shows that the gating waveform is obtained by partial differentiation..and amplification of the sweep waveform. **1966** *McGraw-Hill Encycl. Sci. & Technol.* XIII. 645/1 The basic sanatron delay circuit, of which there are a number of variations, combines in two pentode tubes the function of a gate waveform generator, clamp and linear saw-tooth generator.

sanbornite (sæ·nbǫɹnəit). *Min.* [f. the name of Frank *Sanborn* (d. 1945), U.S. mineralogist + -ITE[1].] A triclinic silicate of barium, $BaSi_2O_5$, which occurs as white or colourless plates at a locality in California, and has been artificially prepared.

1932 A. F. ROGERS in *Amer. Mineralogist* XVII. 161, I am indebted to Mr. Frank Sanborn of the Division of Mines, Department of Natural Resources, State of California..for the specimen which contains the new mineral, sanbornite, herein described. **1950** *Jrnl. Amer. Ceramic Soc.* XXXIII. 43/1 Point *M*, the quintuple point for the fields of sanbornite, tridymite, and mullite..is therefore a eutectic. **1968** I. KOSTOV *Mineral.* 381 The structures of apophyllite, sanbornite, and gillespite are similar and correspond to a layered type with basic silicon sheets of condensed wollastonite chains.

Sancerre (saṅsę̄r). The name of a city in the Cher department of central France, used *attrib.* and *absol.* to designate a light white (occas. red) wine produced in its neighbourhood.

1787 A. YOUNG *Jrnl.* 1 June in *Trav. France* (1792) I. 13 We are now in Berri... We drank there excellent Sancere wine, of a deep colour, rich flavour, and good body. **1946** A. L. SIMON *Conc. Encycl. Gastron.* VIII. 148/2 *Sancerre*, a noted white wine..sold..under the name of *Château de Sancerre*. **1962** P. BRICKHILL *Deadline* iv. 61, I ordered a bottle of Sancerre and it came well chilled. **1977** C. MCCARRY *Secret Lovers* vii. 86 Cathy would take a half-bottle of Sancerre.

Sancho[2] (sæ·nʃo). The forename of *Sancho* Panza, the squire of Don Quixote (see DON *sb.*[1] 1 c, QUIXOTE *sb.*) used allusively of one who is a companion or foil to a quixotic person.

1870 D. G. ROSSETTI *Let.* 15 Mar. (1965) II. 817 He [*sc.* Stillman] is a complete Don Quixote in every way, and with such a Sancho as myself to back him, we ought not to lack for adventures. **1934** R. CAMPBELL *Broken Record* 10 Humanity can be divided roughly into two classes, the Quixotes and the Sanchos.

‖ **sancocho** (sanko·tʃo). [Amer. Sp., a. Sp. *sancocho* half-cooked meal, f. *sancochar* to parboil.] In South America and the Caribbean: a rich soup containing meat, plantain, yucca, etc. (see quot. 1969).

1939 C. BROWN *S. Amer. CookBk.* 78 Sancocho, a truly native dish with its tropical ingredients, takes the place in the Dominican Republic of the pucheros encochidos in cooler Latin-American countries. **1954** M. WALDO *Compl. Round-the-World Cookbk.* 361 The wonderful soup-stew of Latin countries, *sancocho*, is undoubtedly the [Dominican Republic] people's choice for a national dish. **1969** R. & D. DE SOLA *Dict. Cooking* 199/2 *Sancocho*,..Latin-American souplike stew containing fish, fowl, meat, seafood, vegetables, and spices. **1977** *Time* 22 Aug. 23/1 Following a meal of *sancocho* (Panama's national soup) and hot chili sauce, Torrijos offered the following comments.

‖ **sancta simplicitas** (sæ·ŋktă simpli·sitæs, sa·ŋkta simpli·kitās), *Latin phrase.* [L. 'holy simplicity'.] An expression of astonishment at another's naïvety. Also used *substantivally.*

These are said to have been the dying words of John Huss (1373–1415), Bohemian religious reformer and martyr, provoked by the sight of a simple peasant adding wood to the fire about his stake.

1847 F. A. KEMBLE *Let.* Dec. in *Rec. Later Life* (1882) III. 278 Miss L— ingenuously replied, 'Oh dear! that she'd never thought of that...' *Sancta Simplicitas!* **1889** G. B. SHAW in *Star* 13 July 4/4 She..thinks it would be too much to ask the public to listen to two sonatas. *Sancta simplicitas!* too much! **1894** M. BEERBOHM in *Yellow Bk.* Apr. 65 The day of sancta simplicitas is quite ended. **1936** *Times Lit. Suppl.* 31 Oct. 870/1 Setting and character perfectly fused..the *sancta simplicitas* of the Reverend Micah Balwhidder. **1963** L. MEYNELL *Virgin Luck* iv. 84 'Me? I've never had a bet in my life. I don't even know how to.' '*O Sancta simplicitas.* I wish I didn't.' **1980** —— *Hooky & Prancing Horse* xi. 187 'How on earth did you get in?' '*Sancta simplicitas*..which means you are still wet behind the ears.'

sanctification. Add: **4.** *slang.* Blackmail, esp. the extortion of political favours from a diplomat. Cf. *SANCTIFY *v.* 9.

1975 *Observer* (Colour Suppl.) 23 Nov. 25/3 *Sanctification*, blackmail for the purposes of extracting political favours from a victim, not money. **1977** J. GARDNER *Werewolf Trace* x. 87 He told himself to be careful. They were not above trying a bit of sanctification.

sanctify, *v.* Add: **9.** *slang.* To blackmail (a person), esp. for the purposes of extracting political favours. Cf. *SANCTIFICATION 4.

1977 J. GARDNER *Werewolf Trace* vii. 71 Can't you sanctify him, or give him a dose of measles? Isn't that how you people talk about blackmail and murder? *Ibid.* xiv. 127 They've sanctified Maubert... It's what they call it. They've made him holy, separated him. Blackmailed him.

sanction, *sb.* Add: **2. d.** *Pol.* Esp. in *pl.*, economic or military action taken by a state or alliance of states against another as a coercive measure, usu. to enforce a violated law or treaty.

1919 G. B. SHAW *Peace Conference Hints* vi. 84 Such widely advocated and little thought-out 'sanctions' as the outlawry and economic boycott of a recalcitrant nation. **1935** *Punch* 25 Dec. 728 'And you,' we replied in great excitement, 'are the very man to give it to him. Come, now, put on your beard, fly over to Italy, and—sanctions or no sanctions—put into his stocking your One Hundred and Eighty-Ninth Volume.' **1937** A. HUXLEY *Ends & Means* ix. 109 Military sanctions *are* war. Economic sanctions, if applied with vigour, must inevitably lead to war-like reactions on the part of the nation to which they are applied, and these war-like reactions can only be countered by military sanctions. **1943** H. A. WALLACE in *N.Y. Times* 26 July 10/6 He witnessed the collapse of sanctions under the League of Nations. **1948** P. D. WHITTING in M. Beloff *Hist.* 356/1 Abyssinia was annexed by Italy in May, 1936. Sanctions were dropped two months later. **1965** *New Statesman* 9 Apr. 562/2 Given sufficient pressures to ensure the cooperation of British firms and banks operating in Rhodesia..sanctions could work if they were maintained for an extended period. **1981** *Guardian* 20 July 12/2 If Israel is to be stopped from riding roughshod over Western interests in the Middle East.., American sanctions may have to be a lot more convincing.

9. a. *attrib.* and *Comb.*, as (sense *2 d) *sanction-breaker, -buster, -busting*; *sanction-induced* adj.

1968 *Guardian* 25 Apr. 1/8 British citizens would be able to come to Britain from Rhodesia 'unless they are known sanction breakers or supporters of the illegal regime'. **1973** *Times* 8 June 27/1 (*heading*) Dutch move to stop the sanction busters. **1973** *Guardian* 16 Apr. 1/6 The Smith regime in Rhodesia has carried out its most spectacular coup in sanction-busting..with the triumphant announcement that three Boeing-707 jet airliners have been delivered. **1974** A. WILLIAMS *Gentleman Traitor* xii. 186 He studied the.. South African and Rhodesian economies, and how these interlocked with the complex methods of Sanction-Busting. **1970** D. GOLDRICH et al. in I. L. Horowitz *Masses in Lat. Amer.* v. 192 We can project the possibility..of sanction-induced parochialism on the part of formerly more highly politicalized actors.

b. *attrib.* and *Comb.* in *pl.* (sense *2 d), as *sanctions-breaker, -breaking, -buster, -busting*; *sanctions-busting* adj.

1973 R. LEWIS *Blood Money* viii. 110 *Scathe* would not be publishing an exposé on the German businessman, sanctions-breaker or not. **1935** *Times* 7 Nov. 14/6 It may be taken for granted..that the German conception of neutrality does not permit of what might be described as 'sanctions-breaking'. **1976** P. DRISCOLL *Barboza Credentials* I. ii. 29 Countries whose laissez-faire attitudes had encouraged sanctions-breaking. *Ibid.* III. i. 92, I had one immediate concern: the British consulate. Sanctions-buster or not, I was in desperate need of their help. **1970** *Observer* 1 Mar. 4/4 It is disappointed that so little is being done to..promote the campaign against the sanctions-busting ships. **1975** M. Hartmann *Game for Vultures* ii. 22 He had started seriously in the sanctions busting game.

sanction, *v.* Add: **4.** To impose sanctions upon (a person), to penalize.

A use of doubtful acceptability at present.—Ed.

1956 *Universe* 27 July 1/1 (*heading*) Let Church sanction road killers. **1978** *Daily Mail* 29 Nov. 9/1 Sir Geoffrey Howe..referred to Ford's being 'sanctioned'... Nobody.. made a protest about this violence being done to the English language (or about normal meanings being stood on their head).

sanctionable, *a.* Delete *rare* and add examples.

1927 A. Kocourek *Jural Relations* 441 *Sanctionable acts*, unlawful acts which are visited by a sanction. **1944** *Scrutiny* XII. 155 The only sanctionable activities unconnected with religion are parlour games. **1976** *Interdisciplinary Sci. Rev.* I. 182/1 It was our visit to the Flower Children..that suggested to me the need for an alternative to the polar position—the need for a totally new and socially sanctionable drug.

sanctioneer (sæːŋkʃənɪə·ɹ). [f. Sanction *sb.* + -eer.] = *sanctionist 1.

1937 G. Frankau *More of Us* v. 53 Ask not of him—my noble sanctioneers Whose peaceful intents of such warlike mood are. **1965** *Observer* 21 Nov. 3/2 The 'sanctioneers', as they are coming to be called, are highly satisfied with Mr. Heath. **1967** *Economist* 7 Jan. 19/1 South West Africa would offer the sanctioneers a far more permanent bridgehead, the chance of applying sanctions, in effect, against apartheid itself.

sanctioning, *ppl. a.* Add: **1. b.** That imposes or maintains sanctions. Cf. *sanction *sb.* 2 d. *rare.*

1976 *Individualist* Dec. 66/2 South Africa will surely fall, and another great satellite state will have been created in a powerful strategic position. Have the 'sanctioning' countries considered this?

sanctionism (sæ·ŋkʃəniz'm). *rare.* [f. Sanction *sb.* + -ism.] The theory of economic or military sanctions; advocacy of such sanctions.

1938 *Nation* (N.Y.) 29 Jan. 115/2 The struggle against the 'highly civilised hordes of sanctionism'.

sanctionist (sæ·ŋkʃənist), *sb.* (and *a.*). [f. Sanction *sb.* + -ist.] **1.** One who advocates or supports the employment of sanctions. Cf. *sanction *sb.* 2 d.

1935 *Observer* 6 Oct. 18/3 The 'News Chronicle', a sanguinary sanctionist, had a displayed article last week called 'Christmas is coming'. **1937** A. Huxley *Ends & Means* ix. 111 Sanctionists reply by asserting that the mere display of great military force by League members will be enough to deter would-be aggressors.

2. *attrib.* passing into *adj.*

1935 *Observer* 6 Oct. 18/3 British policy and the sanctionist mania were originally based on the delusion that Signor Mussolini was bluffing. **1936** *Empire Rev.* LXIII. 145 Sanctionist policy. **1937** A. Huxley *Ends & Means* ix. 112 According to sanctionist theory, the League is to take military action in order to bring about a just settlement of disputes.

Sanctoral. Delete † *Obs.* and add: Also with small initial. (Later examples.)

1955 A. A. King *Liturgies of Relig. Orders* iii. 195 The mediaeval sanctoral was similar to that in many of the calendars of the time. **1975** *Church Times* 7 Mar. 8/4 Priests of the Society of Retreat-Conductors gave him a desk and something described as a coffee-table calendar of the Church's year and sanctoral.

sanctuary, *sb.*[1] Add: **II. 5. d.** An area of land within which (wild) animals or plants are protected and encouraged to breed or grow.

1879 A. P. Vivian *Wanderings in Western Land* xiii. 299 The suggestion..of setting apart certain districts as 'sanctuaries', within which the buffalo should never be molested, is one well worthy of consideration. **1887** [see *bird sanctuary* s.v. *bird *sb.* 9]. **1897** *Cornh. Mag.* Jan. 37 The national forests will become, as the New Forest is now in some measure, sanctuaries for all the animals *feræ naturæ* of England. **1909** *Bull. N.Y. Zool. Soc.* June 511/2 Around the coast there is gradually being extended a chain of insular bird sanctuaries that means much to the avifauna of North America. **1943** J. S. Huxley *TVA* 54 Game management areas and game refuges or sanctuaries have been set up. **1975** M. Russell *Murder by Mile* iii. 26 The glen's by way of being something of a bird and animal sanctuary. **1978** *Country Life* 16 Nov. 1632/1 Rare and vulnerable plants and animals will be protected by setting aside 'sanctuaries'.

sand, *sb.*[2] Add: **1. h.** *Soil Sci.* Applied *spec.* to particles whose sizes fall within a specified range, and to soils having a specified proportion of such particles (see quots.). Hence *sand-size* sb. (adj.).

1873 E. W. Hilgard in *Amer. Jrnl. Sci. & Arts* CVI. 337 (*table*) Coarse Sand, 80–90 (1/180) mm... Finest Sand 20–22 (1/180) mm. **1900** R. Warington *Lect. Physical Properties Soil* i. 8 Coarse sand 0·5–1·00 mm... Fine sand 0·1–0·25 mm. **1925** P. Emerson *Soil Characteristics* i. 6 The different soil particles are designated according to size as follows... Very coarse sand 2·0 to 1·0 millimeters... Very fine sand 0·1 to 0·05 millimeter. *Ibid.* 7 The United States Bureau of Soils recognizes the following classes [of soil]:..*Sand*: more than 25 per cent very coarse, coarse and medium sand, less than 50 per cent fine sand, more than 20 per cent silt and clay. **1952** L. M. Thompson *Soils & Soil Fertility* ii. 8 Based on size of soil particles there are three fractions, sand, silt, and clay. **1957** Sand-size [see *sedimentological *a.*]. **1964** K. W. Butzer *Environment & Archeol.* x. 158 The modified Wentworth grade scale..is most widely used in North America. It has the following logarithmic subdivisions:..sand 0·064–2 mm., silt 0.004–0·064 mm... The non-logarithmic, modified Atterberg scale widely used in Europe has slightly different nomenclature... coarse sand 0·2–2·0 mm... fine sand 0·02–0·06 mm., silt 0·002–0·02 mm. **1971** *Gloss. Soil Sci. Terms* (Soil Sci. Soc. Amer.) 14/2 *Sand*, a soil particle between 0·05 and 2·0 mm in diameter. *Ibid.* 18/1 *Sand*, soil material that contains 85% or more of sand; percentage of silt, plus 1·5 times the percentage of clay, shall not exceed 15. **1972** J. G. Cruickshank *Soil Geogr.* ii. 55 The products of physical weathering are usually large on the particle size scale; that is, they are stone, gravel, or sand size and less commonly as small as silt size.

i. A fashionable shade resembling the colour of sand.

1923 *Daily Mail* 13 Feb. 13/2 (Advt.), Artificial silk hose ..in black, white, beaver, nude, cinnamon, sand, suede. **1930** *Daily Express* 6 Oct. 5/6 (Advt.), Imitation nutria fur sets... In dark grey, fawn, beaver, sand, and nutria. **1971** *Guardian* 28 Sept. 11/2 (*caption*) Quilted raincoat... In sand, orchid, or damson. **1979** *Country Life* 24 May (Suppl.) 55 (Advt.), The new Renault 5..comes in black, silver, blue or sand.

2. b. (Later examples.)

1873 Trollope *Phineas Redux* I. vi. 53, I complain of no injustice. Our castle was built upon the sand. **1905** G. L. Dickinson *Mod. Symposium* 77, I have been watching..one building after another laboriously raised by each speaker in turn, only to collapse ignominiously at the first touch administered by his successor. And why? For the ancient reason, that the structures were built upon the sand. **1920** Galsworthy *In Chancery* ii. iii. 151 She put out her hand to him. 'I feel you're a rock.' 'Built on sand,' answered Jolyon. **1963** *Times* 9 Jan. 4/2 On slower courts the story with Hughes would be different, but here, where even the best stroke is not an outright winner until it has died, his game is indeed built on sand.

d. *to bury* (or *hide*) *one's head in the sand* (and allusive varr.): to ignore unpleasant realities.

In some quots. with direct reference to the legendary belief that an ostrich buries its head in sand when threatened.

1844 [see *ostrich[1] 2 a]. **1899** W. H. D. Rouse in North tr. *Plutarch's Lives* VI. 345 Like the ostrich that hides his head in the sand. **1916** W. Wilson in *N.Y. Times* 2 Feb. 1/1 America cannot be an ostrich with its head in the sand. **1929** L. MacNeice in *Oxford Poetry* 24 Asking..Whether it would not be better To hide one's head in the warm sand of sleep. **1937** F. P. Crozier *Men I Killed* vii. 137 Our new system of rearmament is at least..encouraging our Colonel Blimps to hide their heads, stupidly like the ostrich, in the sand! **1946** E. O'Neill *Iceman Cometh* iii. 201 He thrusts his head down on his arms like an ostrich hiding its head in the sand. **1976** *Star* (Sheffield) 29 Oct. 10/4 The people of England should not bury their heads in the sand and say it can't happen here.

7. a. Delete † *Obs.* and add later examples.

1918 L. E. Ruggles *Navy Explained* 20 Bread is called 'punk'; sugar, 'sand'. **1935** A. J. Pollock *Underworld Speaks* 86/1 *Pass the sand*, pass the sugar. **1945** *California Folklore Q.* 19 Oct. 46 Joe with cow and sand. **1971** M. Tak *Truck Talk* 100 *Load of sand*, a cargo of sugar.

b. (Earlier and later examples.)

1867 G. W. Harris *Sut Lovingood* 102, I tell yu he hes lots ove san' in his gizzard; he is the best pluck I ever seed. **1872** *Newton Kansan* 5 Dec. 3/3 We hope to see Mr. Pettibone with sufficient 'sand in his craw' for this new position [*sc.* police judge]. **1875** B. Harte *Tales of Argonauts* 71 Blank me if I didn't think he was losing his sand, till he walked to position. **1924** Galsworthy *Forest* iv. ii. 120 By Jove, Mr. Farrell, there's sand in you. Tell me, isn't he ever ashamed of himself? **1933** J. Buchan *Prince of Captivity* iii. i. 264 A plain face with nothing showy about it, but all the horse-sense and sand in the world. **1954** 'W. Henry' *Death of Legend* 4 You losing your sand, Buck?

e. *to raise sand* (U.S.): to create a disturbance; to make a fuss.

1892 *Dialect Notes* I. 231 'To raise sand' is slang [in Kentucky] for to get furiously angry, the same as 'to raise Cain'. **1893** H. A. Shands *Some Peculiarities of Speech in Mississippi* 74 *Raise sand*,..to create a disturbance, to raise a row. **1948** *Sun* (Baltimore) 1 Dec. 17/4 Boudreau raised sand but the decision stuck. **1970** C. Major *Dict. Afro-Amer. Slang* 96 *Raise sand*,..to make an outcry; to brawl; to fight.

9. a. *sand-barge, -beach* (earlier examples), *-canyon, -cart, -flat* (earlier and later examples), *-heap* (later examples), *-island, -knoll, -land* (later examples), *-line, -mound, -pile, -reef, -sack, -sea, -spit, -stretch, -vein.*

1840 R. H. Dana *Two Yrs. before Mast* 225 We were as deep as a sand-barge. **1887** S. Samuels *From Forecastle to Cabin* 197 My ship was loaded as deep as a sand barge. **1709** J. Lawson *New Voy. Carolina* 151 The Sand-Birds.. frequent our Sand-Beaches. **1728** J. Comer *Diary* 7 Apr. (1893) 50 A schooner..was cast on shore on a sand beach at Westport. **1806** *Deb. Congress U.S.* (1852) 9th Congress 2 Sess. App. 1117 They passed a number of sand-beaches, and some rapids. **1939** Auden & Isherwood *Journey to War* 120 Sand-canyons, guarded by fantastic sandy spires and pinnacles. **1788** Cowper *Let.* 1 Feb. in R. Southey *Life & Wks. W. Cowper* (1836) VI. 117 Thinking myself an ass, and my translation a sand-cart. **1825** J. Constable *Let.* 1 Aug. (1966) IV. 97 A scene on Hampstead Heath, with broken foreground and sand carts. **1834** *Chambers's Edin. Jrnl.* III. 233/3 It was like subjecting a pampered palfrey all of a sudden, to the sorrows of the sand-cart. **1923** *Glasgow Herald* 30 Jan. 9 There is generally a so-called sandcart, a sort of squat fly with an awning for two. **1773** in E. W. McMullen *Eng. Topogr. Terms in Florida* (1953) 190 From this point runs a sand flat 1¼ mile from the shore of Anastasia Island. **1794** *Trans. Soc. Promotion Agric., Arts, & Manuf.* (U.S.) I. 143 He..kept him in a very poor pasture adjoining a creek where creek-thatch grew on sand-flats. **1826** J. J. Audubon *Ornithol. Biogr.* II. 41 The dead fish that frequently are found about the sand-flats of rivers. **1922** Joyce *Ulysses* 41 Unwholesome sandflats waited to suck his treading soles. **1854** C. M. Yonge *Heartsease* II. iii. xv. 327, I hope she will take her down to the sand-heap, where the children have been luxuriating all morning. **1974** *Times* 5 Oct. 12/2 That sand-heap played a large part in his method of teaching. **1840** Poe *Jrnl. of Julius Rodman* in *Compl. Wks.* (1902) IV. 43 Sand-island. **1975** *Offshore Engineer* Dec. 16/3 A sand island could engulf a conventional steel or concrete platform. **1916** Joyce *Portrait of Artist* (1969) iv. 172 A ring of tufted sandknolls. **1963** *Times* 10 June 7/1 This is 73 percent above the average of 16 other sandland farms carrying cattle and sheep as well as growing corn. **1972** *Plant Dis. Reporter* LVI. 695 This pathogen spread rapidly into all the tomato sand-land areas of Florida. **1891** W. B. Yeats *John Sherman & Dhoya* ii. 185 By the.. edge of the lake..there suddenly stood before him a slight figure, at the edge of the narrow sand-line, dark against the glowing water. **1872** 'Mark Twain' *Roughing It* v. 51 He.. climbs the nearest sand-mound, and gazes into the distance. **1921** *Daily Colonist* (Victoria, B.C.) 8 Apr. 4/2 Organized playgrounds were a valuable asset to any city—a playground in which there were sandpiles and wading pools for the little ones. **1976** *National Observer* (U.S.) 30 Oct. 16/5 She recalls playing 'kick the can' and burying each other in sand piles. **1883** 'Mark Twain' *Life on Mississippi* xxiv. 267 You can tell a sand-reef—that's all easy. **1973** *Publ. Amer. Dial. Soc.* lx. 8 The mainland is..cut off from the Atlantic by the long lines of sand reefs called the Outer Banks. **1889** W. B. Yeats *Wanderings of Oisin* iii. 49 But prone on the pathway, prone struggling, They lay 'neath the sand-sack at length. **1936** M. H. Mason *Paradise of Fools* xix. 218 When we finally get stuck in the middle of the Sand Sea..you'll have to carry everything. **1976** L. Deighton *Twinkle, twinkle, Little Spy* ii. 13 This road skirted the edges of the Sahara's largest sand-seas. **1854** V. Lush *Jrnl.* 5 Feb. (1971) 151 The boat beat about all the afternoon and towards evening ran fast upon the sandspit off the mouth of the Mungamungaroa Creek. **1910** S. P. Hyatt *Diary of Soldier of Fortune* xv. 161 The town..stands on a little sandspit which juts out from a mangrove-circled bay. **1934** *Discovery* May 130/1 One result of the storm was that a sand spit was built out across a bay. **1974** *Nat. Geographic* Dec. 785/1 Its reef supported two islets, one a mere sandspit and the other some 350 yards long. **1930** E. Pound *XXX Cantos* ii. 9 Glare azure of water, cold-welter, close cover. Quiet sun-tawny sand-stretch. **1922** Blunden *Shepherd* 28 Where the sand-vein still bubbles its clear spring.

b. *sand-castor, -shaker, -strewer; sand-loving, -teasing* adjs.

1897 'H. S. Merriman' *In Kedar's Tents* xxv. 281 Vincente was writing at the table... He smiled as he shook the small sand-castor over the paper. **1924** [see *Battersea]. **1940** R. Graves *Sergeant Lamb of Ninth* 206 The chest was filled with pens, ink, paper, sand-castors. **1915** R. Lankester *Diversions of Naturalist* 17 The rare sand-loving plants of the dunes. **1967** *Oceanogr. & Marine Biol.* V. 505 Sand-loving species such as the tectibranch gastropod *Philine aperta.* **1958** *Washington Post* 26 June A1/8 They [*sc.* microphones] would be located where the old and now empty 'sand shakers', once used as blotters, are placed on each desk. **1972** *Country Life* 3 Feb. 272/3 It [*sc.* a 1652 inkstand] opens to reveal..on the right a sand-shaker. **1975** *New Yorker* 26 May 105/3 (Advt.), Sterling Silver Salt and Pepper Reproductions of the original sand shakers used by George Washington at Mt. Vernon. **1922** Joyce *Ulysses* 428 Through rising fog a dragon sandstrewer, travelling at caution, slews heavily down upon him, its huge red headlight winking. **1865** G. M. Hopkins *Poems* (1948) 33 Eye greeting doves bright-counter to the rook, Fresh brooks to salt sand-teasing waters shoaly.

c. *sand-blanched, -built* (earlier and later examples), *-buried* (later example), *-cleaned, -faced, -laden, -obliterated, -rubbed, -silted, -smothered, -stained.*

1932 W. Faulkner *Light in August* v. 105 A smooth, sandblanched floor. **1788** T. Dwight *Triumph of Infidelity* 6 As sand-built domes dissolve before the stream,..The structure fled. **1916** Joyce *Portrait of Artist* (1969) iv. 160 The music passed..over the fantastic fabrics of his mind, dissolving them painlessly and noiselessly as a sudden wave dissolves the sandbuilt turrets of children. **1960** Auden *Homage to Clio* 58 A sand-buried site. **1891** W. B. Yeats *John Sherman & Dhoya* 17 Our sand-cleaned doorsteps. **1931** *Times Lit. Suppl.* 3 Sept. 668/2 Hand-made and sand-faced [tiles]. **1976** *Liverpool Echo* 7 Dec. 11/2 They were hand-made, sand-faced Flemish bricks, mellowed by time and totally irreplaceable. **1902** D. G. Hogarth *Nearer East* 72 The chief ranges run north and south, weathered to fantastic outlines by the sand-laden winds and keen frosts of winter nights. **1955** P. Larkin *Less Deceived* 41 Those few forbidding signs Of the continuous coarse Sand-laden wind, time. **1938** D. Gascoyne *Hölderlin's Madness* 47 The sand-obliterated face. **1922** V. Woolf *Jacob's Room* i. 13 Wind-swept, sand-rubbed, a more unpolluted piece of bone existed nowhere. **1945** C. Mann in Murdoch & Drake-Brockman *Austral. Short Stories* (1951) 259 It broke through the sand-silted block. **1924** Lawrence & Skinner *Boy in Bush* 11 Clogged,..sand-smothered, that's what we are. **1916** A. Huxley *Burning Wheel* 50 Who marked the land-weeds and the sand-stained foam.

d. *sand-rimmed, -roofed, -wharfed.*

1857 J. G. Whittier *Poetical Wks.* II. 231 Mine the sand-rimmed pickerel pond. **1845** Longfellow *Belfry of Bruges* 50 Whole villages of sand-roofed tents. **1930** Blunden *Poems* 318 So unexpected and so beautiful That they live on in the sand-wharfed pool.

e. adverbial, as *sand-blond, -sized, -toned* adjs.; locative, as *sand-groping* vbl. sb.;

sand-bogged, -burrowing, dwelling, -marooned, -mounded adjs.

1953 C. Day Lewis *Italian Visit* ii. 32 The hills are sand-blond. **1959** A. Upfield *Bony & Black Virgin* xi. 88 Lots of drift sand now. We'd find it rougher in the ute. Be sand-bogged a lot. **1963** R. P. Dales *Annelids* i. 29 Such protonephridia..are found in phyllodocids and in the sand-burrowing nephthyids. **1911** F. O. Bowen *Plant-Life on Land* 128 Certain sand-dwelling plants. **1963** R. P. Dales *Annelids* ii. 43 In lugworms, in the fusiform sand-dwelling opheliids. **1924** Lawrence & Skinner *Boy in Bush* 21 They walked off the timber platform into the sand, and Jack had his first experience of 'sand-groping'. **1946** W. de la Mare *Traveller* 19 Meagre his saddlebag as camel's hump When, sand-marooned, she staggers to her doom. **1921** —— *Veil* 24 Rent hull, and broken mast, She sprawls sand-mounded. **1965** G. J. Williams *Econ. Geol. N.Z.* xx. 365/2 In them [*sc.* sandstones] the clay mineral occurs as large sand-sized aggregates. **1977** A. Hallam *Planet Earth* 24/2 Somewhat larger particles, sand-sized grains, offer sufficient air resistance to be briefly heated to incandescence by friction before being entirely destroyed in the upper atmosphere. **1916** *Chambers's Jrnl.* Sept. 635/2 In the midst of the mass of sand-toned uniforms.

10. a. sand-ball (earlier example); **sand-bar** (earlier and later examples); also, a sandbank in the course of a river or close to a beach; **sand-bar willow,** a North American shrub or small tree, *Salix longifolia*; **sand blow,** the removal or deposition of large quantities of sand by the wind; a place where this has occurred; **sand-body** *Geol.*, a permeable underground mass of sand or sandstone (which may contain oil); **sand boil** *U.S.*, an eruption of water through the surface of the ground; **sand-castle,** a structure of sand resembling the form of a castle, of the kind made by a child on the beach; also *fig.*; **sand cay** [Cay], a small sandy island, usu. elongated parallel to the shore, freq. found on a coral reef and there composed of fine coral debris; = **sand key*; **sand-clock** = Sand-glass 1; **sand-club,** (*a*) (example); (*b*) orig. *U.S.*, = *sand-iron* (b); **sand core,** a compact mass of sand that is dipped into molten glass and withdrawn, so as to serve as a core in the making of a hollow vessel; freq. *attrib.*; **sand-crack,** (*a*) substitute for def.: a fissure in a horse's hoof; (without *a* and *pl.*) a condition so characterized; (later examples); **sand crater** (earlier example); **sand culture** *Bot.*, a hydroponic method of plant cultivation in which the plants are rooted in beds of purified sand supplied with nutrient solutions, used esp. to determine their mineral requirements; a culture of this kind; usu. *attrib.*; **sand-devil,** in Africa, a small whirlwind; **sand drown,** chlorosis of plants caused by magnesium deficiency in the soil; **sand filter,** a filter used in water purification consisting of layers of sand arranged with coarseness of texture increasing downwards; **sand garden,** in Japanese landscape gardening, an open space covered with sand, the surface of which is raked into a pattern; so **sand gardening,** the practice of this style of landscape design; **sand glacier** *Geomorphol.* (see quot. 1972); **sand grain** *Printing* (see quot. 1906); also *attrib.*; **sand-groper** (earlier and later examples); **sand-grown** *a.*, designating a native of Blackpool; **sand-happy** *a.* (see *-happy); **sand-hog** *U.S.*, a man who works underground, as in a caisson or in foundation-work; also *fig.*; **sand-hole,** (*c*) a hole in sand; **sand-iron,** (*b*) (earlier example); **sand key** *U.S.* [Key *sb.*[3]] = **sand cay*; **sand-lime,** used *attrib.* to denote a type of brick made by baking sand with a proportion of slaked lime under pressure; **sand-painting,** the technique used esp. by the Navajo Indians of painting with coloured sands; an instance of this; **sand-picture** (examples); also more *gen.*, a design made in sand; **sand pie,** wet sand formed by a child into the shape of a pie; **sand-plain** (earlier example); **sand-pump** (earlier example); **sand ripple,** one of a series of small parallel ridges or undulations in the surface of sand; **sand shadow,** an accumulation of sand to the lee of an obstruction; **sand-shoe** (later examples); **sand-slinger** *Founding* (see quot. 1948); **sand-smoke,** a whirlwind or sandstorm; **sand-stock (brick)** (later examples); **sand-storm,** now usu. written as one word (later examples); also *fig.*; **sand-table,** (*a*) a sand-covered surface on which letters or designs can be drawn and erased or models placed and removed; (*b*) = *sand-trap 1; **sand-tray,** (*a*) = **sand-table* (a); (*b*) = *sand-box 2 e; **sand-wash** *U.S.*, a sloping surface of sand spread out by an intermittent stream; **sand wave,** a wave-like formation in sand; *spec.* in *Physical Geogr.*, an undulation similar to a megaripple but on a larger scale; **sand-wedge** = *sand-iron* (b).

1846 *Jewish Manual, or Pract. Information Jewish & Mod. Cookery* iv. 212 Sand-balls are excellent for removing hardness of the hands. **1766** J. Bartram *Jrnl.* 29 Jan. in W. Stork *Descr. E. Florida* 55 Towards the opposite shore there is a sand-bar. **1782** T. Jefferson *Notes State of Virginia* ii. 9 The Missisipi, below the mouth of the Missouri, is always muddy, and abounding with sand bars, which frequently change their places. **1796** A. Ellicott *Jrnl.* (1803) 14 The fog was so thick that we could neither discover sand-bars nor logs. **1897** *Outing* (U.S.) XXX. 50/2 This one sheet of water formed a small harbor to the lee of a sand-bar. **1935** M. M. Atwater *Crime in Corn-Weather* i. 2 The little river—at this season no more than a network of shallow runnels between thirsty sand bars. **1968** W. Warwick *Surfriding in N.Z.* 10/3 At a beach break..the takeoff area is always changing due to drifting sand-bars. **1884** C. S. Sargent *Rep. Forests N. Amer.* 168 Sand-Bar Willow... Very common throughout the Mississippi River basin. **1975** M. C. Davis *Near Woods* v. 64 A natural hedge of sandbar willows accompanied us for twenty yards or so into the lake. **1922** *Chambers's Jrnl.* XII. 428/2 The drifting sand held sway... Towns and villages were devastated by it... Sand-blow alone did not complete the desolation. For months great areas were covered with water. **1934** *Antiquity* VIII. 182 Vast sand-blows begun by cattle breaking down the dunes. **1980** *National Trust* Spring 15/1 They were isolated from the sea by the extraordinary thirteenth- and fourteenth-century sand-blows. **1910** R. H. Johnson in *Oil Investors' Jrnl.* 20 Feb. 70/3 The necessity of conceiving the shape of the sand body as something different from the shape of the actual oil-containing reservoir is of great importance. *Ibid.*, I have found this of considerable value in predicting the shape of a 'sand-body'. **1911** —— in *Econ. Geol.* VI. 809 In order to emphasize the importance of shape I have suggested that the term sand-body be adopted, from the analogy of the word ore-body, to describe the reservoir, i.e., continuous mass of sand or sandstones sufficiently porous to be capable of containing oil and gas in commercial quantities. **1927** *Petroleum Devel. & Technol. 1926* (Amer. Inst. Mining Engin. Petroleum Div.) 202 He is also enabled to determine such vital subsurface conditions as (1) porosity, (2) density, (3) saturation, and (4) thickness of sandbodies. **1937** *Daily Progress* (Charlottesville, Va.) 2 Feb. 1/8 Dread 'sand boils' bursting up in the heart of..Cairo [Illinois] forewarned of deeply undermined barriers guarding the..city today... The eruptions sprang from the terrific pressure of the flooded Ohio River waters slowly eating their way beneath the..levels. **1939** W. Faulkner *Wild Palms* 24 Even those who..had probably never before seen more water than a horse pond..could (and did) talk glibly of sandboils. **1954** *Encounter* Oct. 9/1 The owners of the..plantations along the Big River confederated..to hold the sandboils and the cracks. **1976** C. S. Brown *Gloss. Faulkner's South* 167 A sandboil must be neutralized promptly. This is done by building a wall of sandbags around it so that a column of water will be built up above it to equalize the pressure. **1854** C. M. Yonge *Castle Builders* v. 63 The children are.. dabbling after sea-weed and shells, and building sand castles. **1925** H. G. Wells *Christina Alberta's Father* I. iv. 95 They had..camped on the beach while Mr. Preemby and Christina Alberta had made sand-castles. **1975** C. A. Haddad *Moroccan* i. 5 We tried to build a sandcastle romance out of our few short months in the [desert] sand. **1980** D. Newsome *On Edge of Paradise* vii. 228 Playing like children on the beach..making sand-castles. **1934** T. Wood *Cobbers* xvii. 219 You do not see it [*sc.* the Barrier Reef]... You see instead islands... Islands which are sand-cays covered with birds. **1937** *Geogr. Jrnl.* LXXXIX. 138 Sand-cays may occur on almost any reef, but they are most typical of the inner reefs of the outer barrier. **1968** R. W. Fairbridge *Encycl. Geomorphol.* 972/2 During hurricanes, sand cays are liable to be swept clear of vegetation and may disappear completely in a single storm. **1865** *Student & Schoolmate* June 177 One evening, fifty years ago, the noiseless 'sand-clock' in Squire Allen's bar-room was fast running down. **1964** *Listener* 24 Dec. 1011/3 The watch makers of Nuremberg were still turning out sand clocks on the egg-timer principle. **1873** *Winfield* (Kansas) *Courier* 11 Sept. 1/7 A weapon of a peculiarly dangerous and for a time mysterious nature..is a sand club, formed by filling an eel skin with sand. **1912** *Punch* 15 May 380/2 Incidentally I am pleased to know that Americans call a niblick a sand-club. **1977** P. Alliss *Play Golf with P. Alliss* 57 If you play on a heavy course with hard muddy bunkers then you will need a sand club with a sharpish leading edge. **1894** W. M. F. Petrie *Tell El Amarna* iv. 27 A tapering rod of metal was taken..; on the end of this was formed a core of fine sand... The rod and core were dipped in the melted glass... When the whole was finished, the metal rod in cooling would contract loose from the glass; it could then be withdrawn, the sand core rubbed out, and the vase would be finished. **1933** *Antiquity* VII. 421 In the technique of glass-manufacture..the process of pressing into a mould as distinct from modelling on a sand-core came into vogue. **1934** *Greece & Rome* May 140 Vessels of glass made by the sand-core technique, a process well known in Egypt during the eighteenth dynasty. **1962** D. Harden *Phoenicians* xi. 154 From the seventh to the third century sand-core fabrics made up the bulk of existing glass vessels. **1903** Somerville & 'Ross' *All on Irish Shore* 82 The glow from the fire illumined the smith's sardonic grin of remembrance. 'She had a sandcrack in the near fore that time, and there's the sign of it yet.' **1934** A. Russell *Tramp-Royal in Wild Austral.* xix. 120 This in a country where the hooves of horses develop sandcrack. **1976** *Horse & Hound* 3 Dec. 53 (Advt.), Daily use after sand-crack, seedy-toe, brittle or contracted feet, encourages the natural growth of healthy horn. **1856** Thoreau *Jrnl.* 9 Apr. (1949) VIII. 268, I..sit on the edge of that sand-crater near the spring by the railroad. **1916** *Soil Sci.* II. 208 The sand culture solutions giving low yields of tops are characterized by a wide range in the Mg/Ca ratio. **1936** *Phytopathology* XXVI. 279 Soil cultures were similarly prepared and kept with the sand cultures under the same conditions. **1940** [see *gravel culture* s.v. *Gravel *sb.* 9]. **1978** *Fluoride* XI. 76 In *Helianthus annus* seedlings grown in sand culture for five weeks the concentration of fluoride in the root and shoot was generally proportional to the concentration in the substrate. **1901** *Lancet* 16 Mar. 771/1 A number of small whirlwinds, called 'sand-devils', which would pass slowly along sucking up quantities of sand and any light articles such as pieces of paper. **1977** H. Innes *Big Footprints* iii. ii. 282 There was nothing visible..except here and there the dancing whirl of a sand devil. **1922** *Science* 22 Sept. 341/2 The popular name of this chlorosis is 'Sand Drown', a term referring to the fact that the disease is likely to occur in aggravated form in the more sandy portions of the field after heavy rainfall. **1968** B. C. Akehurst *Tobacco* v. 96 Magnesium deficiency (called sand drown) is shown by a characteristic chlorosis that starts with the tips of the bottom leaves, spreads across them and moves up the plant in a similar manner. **1894** Rafter & Baker *Sewage Disposal in U.S.* xiv. 267 Sand filters have considerable capacity for storing the nitrogenous matter at one period and later on converting it into nitrates. **1977** F. M. Middleton in H. I. Shuval *Water Renovation & Reuse* i. 13 Sand filters have been used for many years. **1936** T. Tamura *Art of Landscape Garden in Japan* 225 (*caption*) A sand garden carefully raked to print lines and waves. **1965** 'S. Harvester' *Assassins Road* iii. 32 The lighted windows showed patches as desolate as a Japanese sand-garden. **1975** R. L. Duncan *Dragons at Gate* (1976) iii. 89 Calder only half heard what she was saying,..fixing his attention on the sand garden. **1960** *Spectator* 16 Feb. 261/1 It's an uneasy, foreign respect—the sort one feels for minor, inscrutable Japanese arts such as Noh or sand-gardening. **1875** *Encycl. Brit.* III. 599/1 Among the less ordinary geological phenomena [of the Bermudas] may be mentioned the 'sand glacier' at Elbow Bay. **1897** *Geogr. Jrnl.* IX. 286 Wind blowing outwards from a deep sand tract forms a horizontal plateau terminated by a talus as steep as the sand can rest. Under these conditions the encroachment of sand recalls the manner of advance of a glacier, and to this formation I restrict the term 'sand glacier'. **1919** *Proc. R. Soc. Victoria* XXXI. 416 The typical forms of sand accumulation known as 'sand glaciers', which have been described in various parts of the world are due to sand being blown up the sides of hills or mountains, thence finding a passage through any passes or saddles, and spreading out on the opposite sides to form wide fan-shaped plains. **1972** *Gloss. Geol.* (Amer. Geol. Inst.) 627/2 *Sand glacier.* (*a*) An accumulation of sand that is blown up the side of a hill or mountain and through a pass or saddle, and then spread out on the opposite side to form a wide fan-shaped plain. (*b*) A horizontal plateau of sand terminated by a steep talus slope. **1906** Goodchild & Tweney *Technol. & Sci. Dict.* 203/1 Sand Grain... A ground is laid as for etching; a sheet of sandpaper is then laid face downwards on the plate, which is passed through the printer's press with sufficient pressure for the grains of sand to pierce the ground. **1960** H. Hayward *Antique Coll.* 248/1 A sand-grain aquatint is obtained from a plate which has been pulled through the press with a piece of sand paper to roughen its surface. **1896** H. Lawson *Let.* 3 Sept. (1970) 62 W[estern] A[ustralia] is a fraud... The old Sand-gropers are the best to work for or have dealings with. **1934** [see *Bananaland]. **1946** K. S. Prichard *Roaring Nineties* 214 'I'm a sand-groper,' she snapped... 'Don't know anything about London or Paris.' **1974** *Sunday Tel.* (Austral.) 30 June, Mining millionaire Lang Hancock has a sizeable number of sandgropers prepared to support his view that Western Australia should be detached from the rest of the nation. **1969** *Listener* 6 Mar. 300/1 Natives of Blackpool are called sand-grown men. **1972** *New Society* 16 Nov. 394/2 The 'sand-grown-'uns' (the Blackpool-born). **1943** *Fortune* Dec. 268 A British Tommy on the North African desert.. may have gone..'sand happy'. **1944** J. Gunther *D Day* 129 Many are what the officers call 'sand-happy'; this is a phrase almost equivalent to punch-drunk, except that it does not mean lack of fighting instinct. **1961** *Times* 14 Sept. 15/2 Captain Scott, weathered, expatriate, sand-happy. **1903** *Century Mag.* Nov. 43/1 The tunnel workers, or 'Sand Hogs', enter the lower chambers of the shield. **1904** *N.Y. Even. Post* 11 Jan. 3 The men who are employed as 'sandhogs' or excavators in the caisson for the new Manhattan Bridge. **1940** R. Chandler *Farewell, My Lovely* xiii. 98 He just got through working as a sandhog on the San Jack tunnel. **1965** *National Observer* (U.S.) 13 Dec. 12/1 Those who view Mr. Sweeney and his Appalachian Commission associates as 'sandhogs' are the other poverty operations. **1977** N. Hynd *Sandler Inquiry* xvii. 130 George McAdam was a 'sandhog'. *Ibid.* 131 The sandhogs were the British agents in oil intelligence. **1897** *Encycl. Sport* I. 457/1 Golf may be played..where the..whins, sand-holes and banks, supply the conditions which are essential to the proper pursuit of the game. **1910** W. de la Mare *Three Mulla-Mulgars* xx. 267 Home he goes to his leaf-thatched huddle or sand-hole. **1935** W. Empson *Poems* 22 By jackal sandhole to your air flung wide. **1862** Sand-iron [see Niblick]. **1775** B. Romans *Conc. Nat. Hist. E. & W. Florida* App. p. xli, We found ourselves surrounded by three very small low sand keys (full of prickly pears). **1829** in *Amer. State Papers: Naval Affairs* (U.S. Congress) (1861) IV. 968 An effort is now making to form a naval establishment on the insulated cluster of sand keys called the Dry Tortugas. **1837** J. W. Williams *Territory of Florida* 23 Anclote Sound is sheltered on the west, by Anclote, Jacs and Sand Keys. **1880** G. W. Cable *Grandissimes* v. 34 A beautiful land of low, evergreen hills..[looked] out across the pine-covered sand-keys of Mississippi Sound. **1930** J. F. Dobie *Coronado's Children* xviii. 308 They landed the Laffites on a barren sand key with just enough provisions to keep them alive a few days. **1937** *Geogr. Jrnl.* LXXXIX. 143 The reefs which bear a sand-key, and on which there is no sub-aerial accumulation of coral-shingle, have a least depth of water of 3 feet. **1910** *Encycl. Brit.* IV. 521/1 The so-called sand-lime bricks are now made on a very extensive scale in many countries. **1933** *Archit. Rev.* LXXIV. 225/2 (*caption*) The whole of the internal walls are faced with cream sand-lime bricks. **1966** W. G. Nash *Brickwork* I. i. 30 There are four classes of sand-lime bricks. **1902** W. Hough in *Rep. U.S. Nat. Museum 1900* 467 The ceremonial sand painting of the Hopi and Navajo, where the most beautiful effects are secured by allowing sand in slender streams of different colors to fall from the hand guiding it over the surface to form designs. **1908** *Encycl. Relig. & Ethics* I. 826/2 The sand-paintings..may be regarded as actual pictorial prayers. **1963** G. S. Maxwell *Navajo Rugs* (1973) iii. 47 Sandpainting rugs are woven copies of actual sandpaintings. **1978** T. Hillerman *Listening Woman* i. 3 Tell me more about how these sand paintings got messed up. **1957** J. Kirkup *Only Child* xiv. 188 There was a man who made wonderful sculptures in the damp sand... Once,..he made a low-relief sand-picture of the Shields Town Hall. **1970** G. Savage *Dict. Antiques* 369/2 Apart from the work of Zobel, sand-pictures are rarely signed, and must be identified from their characteristics. **1975** *Times* 6 Dec. 11/5 A collection of sand pictures, mostly made in the Isle of Wight. **1835** C. F. Hoffman *Winter in West* I. 148 A bevy of rosy little girls..were making 'sand pies' on the bank of the river. **1980** M. Drabble *Middle Ground* 181 Girls in a concrete playground, making sand pies. **1818** A. Eaton *Man. Bot.* (ed. 2) 291 On the sand plains, at the foot of Pine-rock, in New-Haven, a [juniper] root..often sends off shoots. **1865** *Harper's Mag.* Apr. 573/2 A sand-pump is a metal case from five to ten feet in length, constructed with a valve at the bottom. **1879** T. D. Forsyth in E. D. Morgan tr. *Prejevalsky's From Kulja to Lob-Nor* 27 The upheaval of the Gobi..causes an entirely independent direction of profile.. to that of the sand-ripples which cover it. **1897** *Geogr. Jrnl.* IX. 279 The uniformity of the wind-ripple pattern is at all times remarkable. In water-formed sand-ripples no such uniformity has been recorded. **1941** R. A. Bagnold *Physics of Blown Sand & Desert Dunes* xi. 144 A sand ripple is merely a crumpling or heaping up of the surface, brought about by wind action, and cannot be regarded as a true wave in a strict dynamical sense. **1960** B. W. Sparks *Geomorphol.* xi. 248 The formation of sand ripples is closely connected with the process of saltation. **1941** R. A. Bagnold *Physics of Blown Sand & Desert Dunes* xiii. 188 Deposits caused directly by fixed obstructions in the path of the sand-driving wind... These sand shadows and sand drifts are dependent for their continued existence on the presence of the obstacle. **1971** I. G. Gass et al. *Understanding Earth* xiii. 184/2 Left behind protecting shells or pebbles are elongate mounds of sand ('sand-shadows') which give the beach a distinctive appearance. **1916** J. B. Cooper *Coo-oo-ee* xvi. 235 In the circumscribed space of the vessel, the men, clad in their blue dungarees, wearing white sand-shoes, prepared themselves for their future battles. **1931** V. Woolf *Waves* 16 Those are Louis' neat sand-shoes firmly printing the gravel. **1948** J. Betjeman *Sel. Poems* 79 Don't empty children's sand-shoes in the hall. **1965** S. T. Ollivier *Petticoat Farm* vii. 96 Rather than walk the dusty road in their freshly cleaned sparkling white sandshoes the girls took a short cut across the paddocks. **1979** *Guardian* 23 May 31/4 The sand shoe and school sandal look which was justifiably popular last summer. **1928** *Jrnl. Iron & Steel Inst.* CXVII. 805 Stripping machines are mounted on turntables, which bring the flasks within range of a sand-slinger, and then delivers them to the mould conveyor. **1948** J. E. Garside in H. W. Baker *Mod. Workshop Technol.* I. iii. 65 For the ramming of sand moulds, a machine known as the 'sand slinger' is often used. It ejects a stream of sand vertically downwards at a high speed, so that the sand is rammed by impact with the pattern. **1930** T. S. Eliot tr. *St.-J. Perse's Anabasis* 49 These sandsmokes that rise over dead river courses. **1956** *Archit. Rev.* CXIX. 257/2 Leicestershire sandstock bricks are used in the panel on the west elevation. **1973** *Parade* (Austral.) Oct. 28/3 'Sandstock' (handmade) bricks were made from clay in the valley. **1928** H. Crane *Let.* 27 Apr. (1965) 325 Efforts for a foothold in this sandstorm [*sc.* Hollywood] are still avid. **1966** 'J. Hackston' *Father clears Out* 139 We missed the old..weather... Missed our blinding sandstorms even. **1978** A. & G. Ritchie *Anc. Monuments Orkney* 43 The people who were forced to abandon their homes in the final sandstorm had been using essentially the same sort of pottery vessels as their ancestors who founded the settlement. **1812** N. J. Hollingsworth *Address Madras Syst. Educ.* p. ix, To the finger and sand-table may succeed the pencil and slate. **1911** *Encycl. Brit.* XX. 728/2 To get rid of them [*sc.* impurities] the esparto pulp when washed and bleached is run from the potcher into storage chests, from which it is pumped over a long, narrow serpentine settling table or 'sand-table'. **1928** *Daily Tel.* 7 Aug. 4/4 A thorough groundwork of tactical knowledge has been formed by sand-table and week-end schemes during the winter. **1955** F. G. Patton *Good Morning, Miss Dove* 13 One group..modelled clay caribou for the sand table. **1963** R. R. A. Higham *Handbk. Papermaking* ii. 67 With rifflers and sand tables the stock is passed at approximately 0·5% consistency along narrow channels. **1969** E. H. Pinto *Treen* 423 The sand table is a very ancient device and may be referred to by Isaiah 'Now go write it before them in a table'. **1971** J. Wainwright *Last Buccaneer* II. 243 'What..is a sand-table?'..'It's usually a tray, filled with sand. The army uses them. It's possible to mould the sand into the contours of geographic locations for demonstrating military tactics.' [**1817** A. Bell *Instructions for Conducting Schools through Agency of Scholars Themselves* II. i. 68 For writing on sand, smooth and level (trays or) boards, ten inches wide, with ledges on every side of an inch deep..are prepared.] **1893** *N. & Q.* 25 Mar. 233/1 Economy being a great feature in the plan, the sand trays..were adopted. A full account of the system was published by the S.P.C.K. in 1840. **1968** *Guardian* 23 Aug. 7/6 A livid deputation approached me, waving the kitten's sand-tray. **1972** *Country Life* 6 Jan. 31/2, I was also interested in the 19th-century sand tray or abacus in the north aisle. This was used for teaching children to write with a wooden stick on the sand. **1901** *Science* 4 Jan. 38/1 From this point the party worked down the sandwash of Rio San Ignacio (or Rio Altar) to the coast of the Gulf of California, where the Tepoka Indians lived until recently. **1937** *Discovery* Jan. 24/1 The sandwashes surrounding the wells in the Gobi. **1948** *Sierra Club, S. Calif. Chapter, Schedule* No. 129. 69 The campsite will be in the sand wash at the mouth of the Fan Hill Canyon. **1819** Sand-wave [in Dict., sense 9 a]. **1899** *Geogr. Jrnl.* XIII. 624 The sand-waves which corrugate the beds of streams and rivers. **1902** 'Mark Twain' in *Harper's Mag.* Jan. 269/2 He started on a run, racing in and out among the sage-bushes a matter of three hundred yards, and disappeared over a sand-wave. **1917** *Bull. Geol. Soc. Amer.* XXVIII. 915 Cross-bedding..probably represents in many instances one phase of a phenomenon called sand waves, which are nothing more than current-made ripple-mark[s] of mammoth proportions... The crests are often 15 to 35 feet apart and rise from 2 to 3 feet above the troughs. **1939** W. H. Twenhofel *Princ. Sedimentation* vi. 190 The sand waves or antidunes move up-current as the individual sands move down-current. **1978** *Nature* 14 Sept. 101/2 Sandwaves are the largest scale of bedform.., with average heights and wavelengths markedly larger than those of megaripples. **1937** H. Longhurst *Golf* I. xxii. 196 No chapter on bunker play would be complete without a description of..the..sand wedge. **1952** *Chambers's Jrnl.* May 298/1, I couldn't use a sand-wedge in a bunker because I hadn't the strength to swing it. **1971** 'D. Halliday' *Dolly & Doctor Bird* xv. 215 Wallace Brady..landed in the long, pale trap in front of the green and stayed there doing explosive shots with a sand-wedge.

b. sand bird (earlier and later examples); **sand boa,** a snake of the genus *Eryx*, found in north and east Africa and south and east Asia; **sand crab,** also *fig.*; (earlier and further examples); **sand dab,** (*a*) substitute for def.: either of two eastern North American flatfishes, the American plaice, *Hippoglossoides platessoides*, or the windowpane, *Scophthalmus aquosus*; (earlier and later examples); **sand dollar,** substitute for def.: a flattened, irregular sea urchin belonging to the order Clypeastroida; (further examples); **sand fiddler** *U.S.*, a small burrowing fiddler crab of the genus *Uca*; **sand-fish,** (*c*) *S. Afr.* = *moggel; (*d*) *S. Afr.*, the beaked salmon, *Gonorhynchus gonorhynchus*; **sand goanna,** an Australian monitor lizard, *Varanus gouldii*; **sand goby,** the common goby, *Pomatoschistus minutus*; **sand-lance** = *sand-launce*; **sand lizard,** (*a*) (later examples); (*b*) *U.S.*, a fringe-toed lizard of the genus *Uma* or the striped race-runner, *Cnemidophorus sexlineatus*; **sand-mason,** substitute for def.: a burrowing polychæte tube-worm belonging to the genus *Lanice*; also *attrib.*; (later examples); **sand monitor,** (*b*) = **sand goanna*; **sand perch,** substitute for def.: a small bass, *Roccus americanus*, found in marine and fresh water in eastern North America; (earlier and later examples); **sand-runner** (examples); **sand-shark,** (*a*) one belonging to the family Carchariidæ, esp. *Carcharias taurus*; (later examples); (*b*) = *guitar-fish* s.v. *guitar *sb.* b; (later examples).

1709 J. Lawson *New Voy. Carolina* 151 The Sand-Birds are about the Bigness of a Lark, and frequent our Sand-Beaches. **1917** T. G. Pearson *Birds Amer.* I. 234 White-rumped Sandpiper..Sand-bird. **1910** R. L. Ditmars *Reptiles of World* IV. 233 The Sand Boas, *Eryx*, are degenerate burrowing species,..with a flat body, very stumpy tail, a small head,..and tiny eyes. **1970** *E. Afr. Standard* 23 Jan. 6/4 These [snakes] include..a sand boa and two boa constrictors. **1844** J. E. DeKay *Zool. N.Y.* VI. 6 This [sc. *Platycarcinus irroratus*] and the succeeding species [sc. *P. sayi*] are both designated by our fishermen as the Spotted Crab and Sand Crab. **1883** Sweet & Knox *On Mexican Mustang through Texas* 24 The calling of each other names, such as 'sand-crabs' and 'mud-turtles', is one of the harmless ways in which they ventilate their spleen. **1946** K. Tennant *Lost Haven* (1947) xii. 199 The little cream sand-crabs swift as impatient foam. **1952** W. J. Dakin *Austral. Seashores* xv. 190 The sand bubbler-crab... This little crab may be found..resting at the bottom of a vertical chimney-like burrow. **1955** V. Palmer *Let Birds Fly* 108 No, you ol' sandcrab, you don't know Charlie. **1839** D. H. Storer *Rep. Ichthyol. Mass.* 143 *Platessa dentata*..known by the fishermen as the 'Sand-dab' in the Boston market. **1903** T. H. Bean *Fishes N.Y.* 726 Sand Dab..is also known as the rusty dab. **1924** J. A. La Gorce et al. *Bk. Fishes* 15/1 The Sand Dab, lying on the sand, has harmonizing blotches imprinted all over the upper part of its body. **1954** J. Steinbeck *Sweet Thursday* xxiv. 155 Joe Elegant ordered sand dabs for supper. **1884** *Bull. U.S. Nat. Museum* No. 27. 123 The so-called 'sand dollar'..inhabits the east coast. **1923** *N. & Q.* 18 Aug. 133/1 The stone pies appear to be the fossilized remains of certain echinoderms kindred to the North American sand-dollar. **1962** [see *keyhole *sb.* 4]. **1969** R. Lowell *Notebk. 1967–68* 70 His face an azure sand-dollar on the pail of a child. **1976** *National Observer* (U.S.) 6 Nov. 17-A/4, I stare down at the water-stained sand, hoping to find a sand dollar. **1852** C. H. Wiley *Life in South* 30/1 Sand-fiddler,..the local name for a small animal of the shell-fish kind. **1973** *Publ. Amer. Dial. Soc.* LX. 1 The long beaches are left to the sun and the surf, the sand fiddlers, the gulls and the pelicans. **1925** *Ann. S. Afr. Mus.* XXI. 125 Beaked Salmon or Sand Fish... Greyish brown above, silvery below. **1946** L. G. Green *So Few are Free* x. 135 The sandfish..migrates at spawning time. **1947** [see *moggel]. **1949** Vesey-Fitzgerald & Lamonte *Game Fish of World* v. 375 The sandfish, a species of *Labeo* characterised by the inferior position of the mouth, is another common inhabitant of this river system [*sc.* the Olifants river]. **1953** J. L. B. Smith *Sea-fishes S. Afr.* 87 Sandfish or Beaked Salmon (Austral.). **1968** K. Weatherly *Roo Shooter* 119 A sand goanna..has no respect for snakes at all; he would give most of them a very rough time of it. **1911** F. Ward *Marvels of Fish Life* ii. 13 The sand goby..merely scoops out a hollow. **1935** D. B. Wilson *Life of Shore & Shallow Sea* viii. 88 Sand gobies..could not possibly see the bait. **1971** *Nature* 21 May 150/2 Other workers have found that the scarcity of the sand goby in inshore waters is matched by an increase offshore. **1905** D. S. Jordan *Guide to Study of Fishes* II. xxix. 521 The small family of sand-lances..comprises small, slender, silvery fishes, of both Arctic and tropical seas. **1975** *New Yorker* 12 May 80/3 The sand lances had both the length and the diameter of standard pencils. **1910** R. L. Ditmars *Reptiles of World* III. 173 The Sand Lizard or Striped Race-Runner..is the only species of its genus ranging into the southeastern portion of the United States. **1915** E. G. Boulenger *Reptiles & Batrachians* I. iv. 81 The Sand Lizard..is a very local creature with us, confined to sandy heaths. **1928** *Bunker's Mag.* Jan. 73 The little sand lizards so common in West Texas possess the same ability to snap off their tails when they get into a tight corner. **1954** R. C. Stebbins *Amphibians & Reptiles Western N. Amer.* 224/1 Buried sand lizards can sometimes be frightened from the sand. **1979** *Jrnl. R. Soc. Arts* CXXVII. 405/2 The heathland..is the habitat of reptiles such as the smooth snake and sand lizard. **1935** E. G. Boulanger *Nat. Hist. Seas* v. 77 Another common worm is the Sand Mason.., the tubes of which few can have overlooked. **1977** *Radio Times* 12–18 Nov. 19/1 Now he has photographed the denizens of mudflats: sea urchins, sand-mason worms, and the dog-whelk. **1975** H. G. Coggar *Reptiles & Amphibians Austral.* 236/1 Gould's Goanna or Sand Monitor... A widespread species subject to considerable geographic variation in colour, pattern and size. **1878** C. Hallock *Sportsman's Gazetteer* 378 Sand Perch, or Bachelor Perch;..Apparently a cross between the yellow belly and silver perch. **1946** *Richmond* (Va.) *Times-Dispatch* 4 Aug. IV. 4-D/2 There is always the likelihood of catching.. sand perch and blue-nosed perch. **1965** A. J. McClane *Stand. Fishing Encycl.* 737/1 The sand perch..is one of the small sea basses distributed from North Carolina to Texas. **1894** A. Newton *Dict. Birds* III. 813 Sand-runner, like the foregoing [*sc.* sand-plover], but perhaps sometimes used more for Sandpiper. **1913** H. K. Swann *Dict. Eng. & Folk-Names Brit. Birds* 205 Sand Runner: The Dunlin. Also the Ringed Plover and the Sanderling on the Humber. **1979** *Bull. Yorks. Dial. Soc.* Summer 7 We would find eggs on the sand at the sea side of the Point laid by a bird we called a sand runner. **1938** A. H. Verrill *Strange Fish* ix. 92 Certain species of sharks..may be considered harmless to man. Such are the sand-sharks and dogfish. **1949** W. W. Small in Vesey-Fitzgerald & Lamonte *Game Fish of World* v. 381 A sandshark (really a shovelnose skate)..can give an angler hell. **1961** E. S. Herald *Living Fishes of World* 17/2 Sand sharks—Family Carchariidæ. **1968** D. O'Grady *Bottle of Sandwiches* 51 He said it was only a sand-shark, or shovel-nose.

c. sand cherry, substitute for def.: a shrub or small tree, *Prunus pumila*, of central North America, or a related species, *P. besseyi*, of the western states; also, the fruit of these plants; (earlier and later examples); **sand flower** = Sandwort; **sand grass,** (*b*) *N.Z.* = *pingao; **sand lily,** (*a*) *U.S.*, a stemless rhizomatous herb, *Leucocrinum montanum*, belonging to the family Liliaceæ and bearing clusters of fragrant white flowers; (*b*) a bulbous plant, *Pancratium maritimum*, belonging to the family Amaryllidaceæ, native to the Mediterranean region, and bearing fragrant white flowers; = *sea-daffodil* s.v. Sea *sb.* 23 f; **sand myrtle,** substitute for def.: a small evergreen shrub, *Leiophyllum buxifolium*, of the family Ericaceæ, native to eastern North America and bearing pink or white flowers; (earlier and later examples); **sand-oat** = *sand-reed* in Dict. and below; **sand pear,** substitute for def.: an oriental species of pear, *Pyrus pyrifolia*; (earlier and later examples); **sand-reed,** substitute for def.: the marram grass, *Ammophila arenaria*; cf. Marram 1; (later examples); **sand spurry** (earlier and later examples); **sand verbena** *N. Amer.*, a trailing herb of the genus *Abronia*, belonging to the family Nyctaginaceæ, found in western North America, and bearing clusters of fragrant red, yellow, or white flowers; **sand-weed** = Sandwort.

1778 J. Carver *Trav. N. Amer.* 30 Near the borders of the Lake [Michigan] grow a great number of sand cherries. **1800** A. Henry *Jrnl.* 17 Aug. in E. Coues *New Light Early Hist. Greater Northwest* (1897) I. ii. 40 We found an abundance of sand-cherries, which were of an excellent flavor. **1970** J. H. Gray *Boy from Winnipeg* 55 When we tired of that [*sc.* swimming] we would go picking sand-cherries. **1916** W. de la Mare *Songs of Childhood* (rev. ed.) 80 Alliolyle where the sand-flower blows Taught three old apes to sing. **1937** Dylan Thomas in *Life & Letters* Spring 70 He stumbled on over sand and sandflowers like a blind boy in the sun. **1905** Sand grass [see *pingao]. **1959** A. H. McLintock *Descr. Atlas N.Z.* 31 Planting of sand grass, lupins, and, in places, pines..is needed to protect farm land. **1909** Webster, *Sand lily*, a white-flowered scapose liliaceous plant..of the western United States. **1929** *Encycl. Brit.* XIX. 939/1 Sand Lily..native to plains and mountain valleys from South Dacota and Nebraska west to California. **1951** T. H. Kearney et al. *Arizona Flora* 177 The star-lily or sand-lily..is to be looked for in northern Arizona. **1956** G. Durrell *My Family & Other Animals* xvi. 215 The smooth curve of the dune..was the only place on the island [*sc.* Corfu] where these sand lilies grew, strange, misshapen bulbs buried in the sand, that once a year sent up thick green leaves and white flowers above the surface. **1973** Hitchcock & Cronquist *Flora Pacific Northwest* 691 Fl[ower]s white, rather showy, borne in clusters... Sand lily, star lily. **1814** F. Pursh *Flora Americana* I. 301 *Ammyrsine buxifolia*..known by the name of Sand-myrtle among the inhabitants of New Jersey. **1882** *Harper's Mag.* June 71 Of the smaller shrubs now in bloom we find the sand-myrtle, with its terminal umbel-like clusters of small pinkish flowers. **1943** R. Peattie *Great Smokies & Blue Ridge* 266 Tangled growths of rhododendrons..with some amounts of mountain laurel, blueberry, smilax, and occasionally sand myrtle. **1881** *Encycl. Brit.* XII. 60/1 The dunes show a tendency, except where the Dutch prevent it by planting wood or sand-oats, to wear away on the side towards the sea. [**1629** J. PARKINSON *Parad.* III. xxi. 593 The Sand peare is a reasonable good peare, but Small.] **1880** [see *KIEFFER]. **1951** *Dict. Gardening* (R. Hort. Soc.) IV. 1722/2 Sand Pear... Edible var[ietie]s are grown in China and Japan. **1849** W. H. HARVEY *Sea-Side Bk.* i. 12 The sand-reed..naturally grows on the sandy shores of Europe. **1879** *Scribner's Monthly* Sept. 651/1 After laboriously cleaning their fish, they laid them among the sand-reeds. **1910** *Encycl. Brit.* XIII. 590/2 The most common plant here is the stiff sand-reed. **1975** M. C. DAVIS *Near Woods* i. 3 On a wave-lashed slope, this sand reed measures land's end. **1866** Sand spurry [see SPURREY 2]. **1960** *Oxf. Bk. Wild Flowers* 112/2 The Cliff Sand Spurrey (*S. rupicola*), found on rocky coasts in the south and west, has glandular hairy stems... Sand Spurrey (*S. rubra*), common in sandy and gravelly places, is a rather hairy plant. **1898** A. M. DAVIDSON *Calif. Plants* 174 The wild four o'clock and the sand verbena are classed in this group [of beautiful weeds]. **1929** *Encycl. Brit.* XIX. 940/1 The white sand-verbena,..with very numerous fragrant flowers, occurs from Iowa to Idaho. **1946** D. C. PEATTIE *Road of Naturalist* i. 16 Pervading the sunny waste with fragrance, rose sprawling sand-verbenas. **1849** D. G. ROSSETTI *Let.* 18 Oct. (1965) I. 78 Curse the big mounds of sand-weed!

sand, *v.* Add: **3. a.** (Later examples with *up*.)

1918 GALSWORTHY *Five Tales* ix. 61 They would..sand up his only well in the desert. **1956** PETERSON & FISHER *Wild Amer.* xxxiv. 369 Novashtoshnah, which means 'the new growth' (newly sanded up from island to peninsula), is the northeast point of St. Paul.

5. a. Also in phr. *to sand and canvas*, to clean thoroughly. Also *fig.* orig. *Naut. slang*.

1912 J. MASEFIELD in *Eng. Rev.* Oct. 345 Unless you're clean we'll sand-and-canvas you. **1914** *Dialect Notes* IV. 151 *Sand and canvas*,..to clean. **1933** P. A. EADDY *Hull Down* 187 The Mate was anxious to get on with the 'sand and canvasing' of the bright work.

b. = SANDPAPER *v.*

1928 E. W. HOBBS *Mod. Furnit. Veneering* vii. 84 The wood finish..is sprayed on, allowed about three hours to dry, and sanded lightly with No. 400 waterproof paper and water. **1939** PATTOU & VAUGHN *Furnit.* II. vi. 197 Sand all first coaters with the grain and do not lap the sanding more than necessary. **1958** *Listener* 11 Sept. 399/1 After sanding the piece of furniture, you will be using oil paint to give a hard, durable surface. **1976** F. E. SHERLOCK *Enjoying Home Carpentry & Woodwork* xi. 116 When the project has been glued and cleaned-up.., it must be sanded.

6. *intr.* To become clogged or bunged *up* with sand.

1926 *Summary of Operations, California Oil Fields* (Calif. State Mining Bureau) Oct. 9 The well..stopped of its own accord, probably sanding up.

sandal, *sb.*[1] Add: **4.** *sandal-footed* adj.; *sandal-mark, -shoe*; **sandal-foot,** used *attrib.* and *absol.* to designate a kind of stocking with a non-reinforced heel, suitable for wearing with sandals.

1959 *Vogue* June 71 Coming in..are the sandal-foot stockings... Aristoc have fully-fashioned sandal-foots. **1970** *Focus* June 10/2 Sandalfoot is used to indicate a vision or non-reinforced heel. **1978** *Detroit Free Press* 2 Apr. 2B (Advt.), Sheer, sandalfoot pantyhose with bone or self-colour panty knit right in. **1927** D. H. LAWRENCE *Mornings in Mexico* 83 A white, sandal-footed man following with the silent Indian haste. **1949** R. CAMPBELL tr. St. John of the Cross in *Coll. Poems* I. 167 Tracking your sandal-mark The maidens search the roadway for your sign. **1603** Sandal-shoe [see *sandal shoon* in Dict.]. **1882** W. D. HAY *Brighter Britain!* II. 127 Sandal-shoes upon their feet.

sandalwood. Add: Also **sandal-wood.** **3.** A perfume derived from sandalwood oil.

1865 E. RIMMEL *Bk. Perfumes* viii. 143 Indra..appears very partial to scent, for he is always represented with his breast tinged with sandal-wood. **1973** G. BUTLER *Coffin for Pandora* viii. 161 Her heavy scent of heliotrope and sandal-wood.

4. A fashion shade resembling the colour of sandalwood, a light yellowish brown. Also as *adj.*

1926 *Daily Express* 1 Sept. 10 (Advt.), Shades of mulberry, sandalwood, purple, [etc.]. **1927** *Ibid.* 26 Feb. 5 This attractive model is designed in sandalwood face-cloth. **1937** [see *MIST *sb.*[1] 1 e]. **1976** *Country Life* 26 Feb. 502/3 Stockings..in..a browny colour called Sandalwood.

5. *Comb.*, as **Sandalwood English** = *BEACH-LA-MAR; **sandalwood oil**; a strongly aromatic oil obtained by distillation of sandalwood (*Santalum*), used in perfumes and cosmetics and formerly as a genito-urinary antiseptic.

1922 JESPERSEN *Language* 216 The so-called *Beach-la-mar* (or Beche-le-mar, or Beche de mer English); it is also sometimes called Sandalwood English. **1936** S. ROBERTSON *Devel. Mod. Eng.* iv. 89 Beach-la-Mar or Sandalwood-English, spoken..all over the Western Pacific. **1950** J. C. FURNAS *Anat. Paradise* v. 355 *Beach-la-mar* (sometimes Sandalwood English) is the specific name of this pidgin. **1971** I. F. HANCOCK in D. Hymes *Pidginization & Creolization of Lang.* VII. 523 Melanesian Pidgin English, also known as Neo-Melanesian, Sandalwood English, Bêche-de-mer, Beach-la-mar, etc. **1851** *Illustr. Catal. Gt. Exhib.* IV. 878/2 Sandal-wood oil..from Mangalore and Canara. **1901** W. H. WHITE *Text-bk. Pharmacol. & Therapeutics* 586 Sandal-wood oil is very similar in its action to the oils of copaiba and cubebs. **1952** KIRK & OTHMER *Encycl. Chem. Technol.* IX. 589 The Australian sandalwood oils and the West Indian sandalwood oils are distilled from different species. **1965** F. SARGESON *Memoirs of Peon* v. 109 He was so knowledgeable about the virtues of copaiba and sandalwood oil,..not to mention a chemist who would be of great assistance to me.

sandar, pl. of *SANDR, SANDUR.

Sandawe (sandā·we). Also **Sandawi.** [Native name.] The name of a tribe in central Tanzania having racial, cultural, and linguistic affinities with the Hottentots; a member of this tribe; their language; also *attrib.* or as *adj.*

1924 *Jrnl. Afr. Soc.* XXIV. 26 Farther to the south-east, another 'click' language is met with, the Sandawi. **1925** *Ibid.* XXIV. 219 A section of Wanyaturu some 5,000 strong, who for generations have lived with them, accepting the rule of the Sandawi headmen. *Ibid.* 226 The Sandawi is a bowman. *Ibid.* 334 For a description of the Sandawi language I must refer to some notes by Father Lemble... Its most interesting feature is its clicks. **1947** *Jrnl. R. Anthrop. Inst.* LXXVII. 61/1 The Sandawe are a tribe, some 21,000 strong, inhabiting part of the Kondoa Irangi District..in the Central Province of Tanganyika. **1958** J. P. MOFFETT *Handbk. Tanganyika* v. 158 The members of the Sandawi tribe occupy the south-western part of the Kondoa District. **1963** in Oliver & Mathew *Hist. E. Afr.* iii. 60 It should be added that the pastoralism of the Hottentots *seems* to be older and more deep-seated than that of the Sandawe. **1974** *Encycl. Brit. Macropædia* XVII. 1029/2 During the Stone Age, bands of hunter-gatherers of the Bushmen type inhabited parts of the country [*sc.* Tanzania]. The Sandawe are vestiges of this early group.

sand-bag, sandbag, *sb.* Add: Now usu. as one word. **2. e.** (Earlier example.)

1808 E. WEETON *Let.* 8 Nov. in *Jrnl. of Governess* (1969) I. 123 Scarce a window or a door was permitted to be opened. My room window was fastened down, and stuffed with sand-bags.

sandbag, *v.* Add: **1. b.** *intr.* To attend to sandbags.

1928 *Sat. Even. Post* 4 Feb. 100/2 One of the chauffeurs had just finished fueling the plane. 'You fly her,' said Andy. 'I'll sandbag.'

2. (Earlier and later examples.) Also *fig.*, to bully or coerce; to criticize or lambaste.

1887 *Courier-Jrnl.* (Louisville, Kentucky) 2 Feb. 6/2 The next day Claytor turned up at Central Station with a fairy story that he had been sand-bagged on his way home. **1901** *Congress. Rec.* 23 Jan. 1345/1 [This district] is lying in wait, as it were, from one year's end to the other, awaiting an opportunity to sandbag the public. **1903** 'O. HENRY' in *Ainslee's Mag.* Feb. 59/2 About what figure had you and the kalsominer agreed to sandbag the state for? **1919** *Daily News* 12 Mar. 8/1 While the [German] revolution was being side-tracked in Parliament it was being sand-bagged in the proletariat. **1973** *Globe & Mail* (Toronto) 4 May 6/1 Each will attempt to sandbag the Liberals into adopting its policies. **1974** *Listener* 27 June 818/1 Mr Heath and Mr Wilson sandbagging each other at televised press conferences.

3. *Poker.* To refrain from raising at the first opportunity in the hope of raising by a greater amount later.

1940 O. JACOBY *On Poker* v. 36 The time to sandbag is when you have three of a kind or better. **1950** G. S. COFFIN *Poker Game Compl.* vi. 71 Jacks back sometimes offers a fine chance to sandbag. **1977** D. ANTHONY *Stud Game* i. 7 He fondled his stack of blue chips. He was sandbagging me. I gave him the same dose of silence. **1978** *Sci. Amer.* July 112/3 By under-representing a strong hand (sand-bagging) and thus keeping his opponents from folding a player may increase the pot he expects to win.

sa·ndbagged, *ppl. a.* [f. SANDBAG *v.* + -ED[1].] Having or equipped with sandbags. Also *fig.*

1916 *Blackw. Mag.* May 615/2 He had betaken himself..to a blockhouse which guarded a section of the..railway... The outlook from this sand-bagged sanctuary was extensive and curious. **1930** WODEHOUSE *Very Good, Jeeves!* viii. 223 The Snettisham..was standing there with a sand-bagged look watching her nominee pass right out of the betting. **1940** *Economist* 20 July 91/2 Claims under personal accident ..were higher, for the black-out and sand-bagged pavements produced many minor injuries. **1952** DYLAN THOMAS *Coll. Poems* 43 Man-in-seed, in seed-at-zero, From the star-flanked fields of space, Thunders on the foreign town With a sand-bagged garrison. **1959** I. JEFFERIES *Thirteen Days* ii. 26 The Yehudi convoys used to form up..with iron-clad buses and sand-bagged lorries. **1977** *Time* 21 Feb. 14/1 The demilitarized zone in Nicosia..separates sandbagged Turkish- and Greek-Cypriot gun emplacements.

sandbagger. Add: **1.** (Earlier and later examples.) Also *fig.*

1882 G. W. PECK *Peck's Sunshine* 203 Suppose all the men that have been robbed in the past year by cowardly sand-baggers, could have 'put up their hands'. **1893** *Chicago Tribune* 26 Apr. 6/4 One of the Chicago papers recently complained that Illinois had no first-class highwaymen. It must have overlooked the legislative 'sand-baggers'. **1929** C. E. MERRIAM *Chicago* 343 A matter to be carefully watched here [in subcommittees of the city council] is room for blackmail, even in the case of worthy measures unless the sandbaggers are offset by those of an opposite persuasion. **1981** P. MCCUTCHAN *Shard calls Tune* xiii. 148 Senglea..had had its quota of sandbaggers once, evil men who lurked upon roofs and swung heavy sandbags to strike sailors on the head so that their pockets could be rifled.

2. *Poker.* One who sandbags. Cf. *SANDBAG *v.* 3.

1940 O. JACOBY *On Poker* v. 36 In this event the sandbagger intends to raise. **1950** G. S. COFFIN *Poker Game Compl.* v. 56 We have bet aces up so many times in last position when all checked after the draw, and butted into triplets and sandbaggers.

sand-blast. Add: **2.** Also, a blast of sand-laden liquid. (Further example.)

1913 V. B. LEWES *Oil Fuel* iii. 69 A big gusher would, by sand-blast action, cut through the chilled steel shields in a few days.

sand-blasted *a.*, delete *nonce-wd.* and add further examples; **sand-blaster** (further examples); also, = SAND-BLAST 1.

1920 *Public Health Rep.* (U.S. Public Health Service) XXXV. 518 (*heading*) The efficiency of certain devices used for the protection of sand blasters against the dust hazard. **1937** U. R. EVANS *Metallic Corrosion Passivity & Protection* xiii. 545 A roughened (sand-blasted) surface appears necessary for good adhesion. **1974** *Nature* 5 Apr. 502/1 Abraiding freshly made implements in a tumbling mill, or sandblaster. **1975** M. BRADBURY *Hist. Man* iii. 44 Another [student] brought a sand-blaster and cleaned off the walls of the basement. **1975** *New Yorker* 19 May 11/3 (Advt.), Polished and sandblasted stainless-steel sculptures. **1976** 'TREVANIAN' *Main* (1977) iv. 76 The sandblasters have cleaned..a façade that used to bear the comfortable patina of soot... For months now, they have been sand-blasting the building.

sand-blast, *v.* [f. SAND *sb.*[2] + BLAST *v.*; cf. SAND-BLAST.] To subject to a blast of sand or the like, esp. so as to clean or polish. Also *fig.*

1888 *Texas Siftings* 6 Oct. 6/3 'Sleigh-bells! Well, I'll be sand blasted!' said the business man. 'What do you mean by trying to sell sleigh-bells in this section of the country? Don't you know it never snows here?' **1924** *Jrnl. Inst. Metals* XXXII. 294 The present-day practice is to sand-blast almost every article which is to be metal sprayed. **1939** A. K. LOBECK *Geomorphol.* xi. 376 (*caption*) The sand grains have been sand-blasted away but the more durable binding silica..has resisted the attack. **1972** *Timber Trades Jrnl.* 3 June 47/1 The metal surfaces to be coated are first sand-blasted to remove grease and impurities. **1979** H. MCCLOY *Smoking Mirror* 176 The old buildings..had been sand-blasted to preserve their fabric.

Hence **sa·nd-blasting** *vbl. sb.*

1904 GOODCHILD & TWENEY *Technol. & Sci. Dict.* 257/1 Sand blasting is another method of producing an etched effect upon glass. **1935** H. R. SIMONDS *Finishing Metal Products* xii. 105 The term 'sand blasting' is commonly used to describe the application of an abrasive material under pressure to surfaces to be cleaned or otherwise treated. Even when steel grit is used as the abrasive, the term 'sand blasting' is frequently retained. **1977** *New Yorker* 24 Oct. 42/1 Dissolution, leaching, sandblasting, cracking and melting of fireproof doors.

sand-blind, *a.* (Examples in *poet.* use.)

1864 G. M. HOPKINS *Poems* (1967) 15 Are you sand-blind? Slabs of water many a mile Blaze for him all this while. **1938** W. DE LA MARE *Memory* 46 Hope..Led sand-blind Despair To a clear babbling wellspring And laved his eyes there.

sand-box. Add: **2. d.** A small low-sided sand-pit (cf. *SAND-PIT 3). Chiefly *U.S.*

1937 [see *HUH *int.*]. **1968** *Globe & Mail* (Toronto) 17 Feb. 39 Divided they stand not unlike urchins defying each other in the sandbox. **1969** [see *MICKEY MOUSE 1]. **1976** *National Observer* (U.S.) 8 May 20/4 All the men in her life, from sandbox playmate to lip-smacking savage.

e. A box kept indoors and filled with sand or other material for a cat to defecate in.

1967 L. J. BRAUN *Cat who ate Danish Modern* viii. 73 Qwilleran showed Koko the new location of his sandbox and gave him his old toy mouse. **1971** J. MCCLURE *Steam Pig* viii. 98 The *Daily Post*..an evening rag not worth putting in the cat's sand-box. **1974** M. G. EBERHART *Danger Money* (1975) iv. 40 I've fixed up a sandbox for the cat.

sand-boy. Add: **1.** (Earlier and further examples of the proverbial phr.) Now commonly *as happy as a sandboy*.

1821 P. EGAN *Life in London* II. v. 289 Logic..appeared to be as happy as a sand-boy, who had unexpectedly met with good luck in disposing of his hampers full of the above-household commodity. **1928** *Daily Express* 17 Mar. 3/1 The King was in his element here... He was happy as a sandboy. **1958** *Daily Sketch* 2 June 11/3 Brimming with health, polished like a Derby cup, happy as a sandboy. **1973** *Perthshire Advertiser* 17 Feb. 18/3 It isn't hot, but they're as happy as sandboys.

sand-bur (sæ·ndˌbɜɪ). *U.S.* Also **sand-burr.** [f. SAND *sb.*[2] + BUR *sb.*] The small prickly fruit of any of several plants, esp. a bur-grass of the genus *Cenchrus* or an annual herb, *Franseria acanthicarpa*; also, any of several plants bearing such a fruit. Also *attrib.*

1830 W. A. FERRIS *Life in Rocky Mts.* (1940) vi. 28 These grass-knots, are called 'Sand-burrs'. **1834** A. PIKE *Prose Sk. & Poems* 48 To add to our comforts, the ground here was covered with sand-burs. **1867** E. EGGLESTON in *Little Corporal* Sept. 37/1 A bad name..sticks to you like a sand-burr. **1896** [see SAND *sb.*[2] 10c]. **1904** *Topeka* (Kansas) *Daily Capital* 11 June 4 A sandbur will grapple on to a man's coat tail and stay there all day just to get a chance to fall into his bed at night. **1948** F. BLAKE *Johnny Christmas* I. 39 Weatherby stalked back to his bed, knocked the sandburs from his socks, and..pulled his blankets over his ears. **1957** L. EISELEY *Immense Journey* 69 There passed before my eyes the million airy troopers of the milkweed pod and the clutching hooks of the sandburs. **1971** *Country Life* 4 Nov. 1193/1 These [impurities] include the long spiky seeds of shepherd's needle..and the viciously armed burs of the sand-bur grasses..from South America.

sa·nd-cast, *v. Founding.* [f. SAND *sb.*² + CAST *v.*] *trans.* To make (a casting) by pouring molten metal into a sand mould.

1949 C. J. SMITHELLS *Metals Ref. Bk.* 596 Nearly all alloys can be sand cast, including relatively hot short materials. **1952** WOOD & VON LUDWIG *Investment Castings for Engineers* xvii. 371 The preference for location of bosses in parts which are to be sand cast is on internal surfaces rather than external ones.

So **sa·nd-cast** *ppl. a.*; **sa·nd casting** *vbl. sb.*, (*a*) an object cast in a sand mould; (*b*) the process of casting in a sand mould.

1934 *Jrnl. Inst. Metals* LIV. 103 A sand-cast ingot. **1939** *Light Metals* II. 361 (*heading*) The production of aluminium-alloy sand castings. **1949** C. J. SMITHELLS *Metals Ref. Bk.* 596 Sand casting offers the widest scope of all the casting processes. *Ibid.*, In weight, sand castings range from less than an ounce up to more than 100 tons. **1960, 1964** [see *gravity die-casting* s.v. *GRAVITY 8 b]. **1967** A. H. COTTRELL *Introd. Metall.* xiii. 184 In sand casting a wooden pattern of the required shape, slightly enlarged to allow for shrinkage of the casting, is firmly packed in sand in a moulding box... A green sand casting is made in sand bonded with clay. **1981** *Pop. Hot Rodding* Feb. 22/1 The only engine components that should be changed are the pistons, and only if they are of sand-cast manufacture.

sande (sa·nde). Also **sandee,** and with capital initial. [W. Afr.] The name of a cult for women based on secret rites of initiation, etc., widespread amongst tribes in Sierra Leone and Liberia. See also *PORO.

1803 T. WINTERBOTTOM *Acct. Native Africans Sierra Leone* II. 235 In the river Sherbró,..which is inhabited by Bulloms, there is a society of girls called Sandee girls, who, besides being initiated into various mysteries, are instructed to dance in public. **1930** *Harvard Afr. Exped. 1926–27* I. v. 83 Most of the tribes in Liberia still practice certain ceremonies connected with the initiation of both boys and girls in the bush schools... The..girls' school is known as *sande.* **1954** R. LEWIS *Sierra Leone* i. 9 Quite a number of the mauve- and green-uniformed but nubile-looking schoolgirls who walk in crocodile through the streets will be rushed through Sande in the holidays. **1968** HARRIS & SAWYER *Springs of Mende Belief* i. 2 *Sande*..plays a more restricted role in the community. Its main concern is to cultivate in adult women the qualities of wifehood and motherhood. *Ibid.* vi. 104 This accusation..includes..any attempts to watch the masked *sande* dancers remove their head-piece.

Sandemanian, *sb.* and *a.* Add: Also erron. **Sandimanian, Sandymanian.** (Earlier and further examples.)

1766 B. STEVENS *Let.* 21 Jan. in E. Stiles *Extracts from Itineraries & Other Misc.* (1916) 566 In the late times of oclocracy some small damages have been done to the Sandimanian meeting house. **1773** *Massachusetts Gaz.* 8 Apr. 3/1 The Fire likewise communicated to the Sandemanian Meeting House. **1926** A. HUXLEY *Let.* 10 Aug. (1969) 272 Faraday..was at once a Sandemanian and a Fellow of the Royal Society. **1935** B. RUSSELL *Relig. & Sci.* vii. 171 Faraday was a Sandymanian, but the errors of that sect did not seem, even to him, to be demonstrable by scientific arguments.

sander, *sb.* Add: **3.** A sand-papering machine.

1895 in *Funk's Stand. Dict.* **1930** *Engineering* 23 May 688/1 The combination consists of a saw-table,..a disc sander. **1975** M. BRADBURY *Hist. Man* iii. 43 Students.. with a rented sander exposed, and then waxed yellow with a rented waxer, the good old wood of the floors.

sandesh (sa·ndeʃ). [a. Bengali *sandesh* a sweetmeat.] An Indian sweetmeat resembling cheese fudge.

1944 in D. K. Gupta *Best Stories Mod. Bengal* I. 72 She.. pushed a plate full of Sandesh towards me. **1953** R. GODDEN *Kingfishers catch Fire* xi. 122 *Sandesh,* which is like toffee, and *jilibis* that are rings of clear sugar. **1966** J. & R. GODDEN *Two under Indian Sun* iv. 103 Indian sweets, jillipis or sāndesh. **1973** *Times* 19 June (Bombay Suppl.) p. xv/3 West Bengal's rosogollas and sandesh.

sand-fly. 1. a. Substitute for def.: A small blood-sucking fly belonging to the family Simuliidæ or Psychodidæ or a biting midge of the family Ceratopogonidæ. (Later examples.)

1907 FOUNTAIN & WARD *Rambles Austral. Naturalist* xi. 121 The sand flies..irritated us greatly. **1932** [see *owl fly* s.v. *OWL *sb.* 7 b]. **1947** I. L. IDRIESS *Isles of Despair* xxxii. 214 Barbara was fortunate that it was beautiful weather;..no hellish mosquitoes or burning sandflies to torture her naked hide. **1962** GORDON & LAVOIPIERRE *Entomol. for Students of Med.* xxi. 141 Members of the family Simuliidæ are widely known as 'buffalo-flies' and 'black flies', but in some parts of the world, as in Australia, they are ..designated by other names such as 'sandflies' or 'midges'. **1972** SWAN & PAPP *Common Insects N. Amer.* xxii. 595 The biting midges..include some very annoying pests, variously called no-see-ums, punkies, sand flies, moose flies, and gnats.

3. sand-fly fever, an acute viral fever transmitted by flies of the genus *Phlebotomus.*

1911 DORLAND *Med. Dict.* (ed. 6) 629/2 *Phlebotomus papatasii* [printed *papatassii*]..is thought to convey by its bite an infection known as sandfly fever. **1936** *Indian Jrnl. Med. Res.* XXIII. 870 The lesion in dengue fever.. differs to some extent from that in sandfly fever. **1962** GORDON & LAVOIPIERRE *Entomol. for Students of Med.* v. 26 There remain certain virus infections, such as sandfly fever and dengue, which cause disease in man, but for which no animal reservoir has, as yet, been demonstrated.

sandfracing, sand fracing (sæ·ndfrækiŋ), *vbl. sb. Oil Industry.* Also **-fraccing, -fracking.** [f. SAND *sb.*² + FRAC(TUR)ING *vbl. sb.*] A method of stimulating production from an oil field by forcing fluid containing sand grains into the reservoir rock. So **sa·ndfrac** *sb.*, a name for this process; **sand frac(k** *v. trans.* and *absol.*, to apply this treatment to (an oil field).

1953 *Petrol. Engineer* XXV. B108/2 This well had two sandfrac treatments, using..round grained sand. **1957** *Times* 11 Dec. 16/4 It is believed that sandfracing and drilling in proven areas will maintain the present rate of production. **1960** *Oil & Gas Reporter* XII. 1034 After the well was completed, Phillips contracted with *D* to sand frack. *Ibid.* 1035 Phillips arranged..to sand frack the producing formation to increase productivity. **1961** *Ibid.* XIV. 111 On December 9, 1959, Gregg et al. requested the Commission to enter field rules including one which would authorize any operator to 'sand frac' by using a maximum of 20,000 gallons of fluid and 40,000 pounds of sand per well. **1961** *Texas Law Rev.* XXXIX. 359 It is suggested that compulsory pooling is a workable and effective method of solving the small tract problem and, more specifically, the issues arising from an alleged trespass caused by sand-fracing.

sandhi (sa·ndi). *Philol.* Also †**sundhi,** and with capital initial. [a. Skr. *saṃdhi* junction, combination, f. *sam* together + *dhā* to place (see DO *v.*).] The term applied orig. by Sanskrit grammarians to assimilative changes occurring in Sanskrit in the final and initial sounds of words in a sentence (*external sandhi*), and in the final sounds of stems in word-formation (*internal sandhi*); extended by modern philologists to analogous phenomena in other languages.

1806 W. CAREY *Gram. Sungskrit Lang.* I. iii. 15 (*heading*) Of Sundhi, or the permutation of letters occasioned by the junction of syllables. **1841** H. H. WILSON *Introd. Gram. Sanskrit Lang.* ii. 8 The changes to which letters are subject for the sake of euphony are numerous, and carefully defined, forming that part of Sanskrit grammar which is termed..Sandhi, 'a holding together', 'a function'. **1888** H. SWEET *Hist. Eng. Sounds* 15 An equally primitive stage is preserved in the Sanskrit sandhi, only here it is generally the end of a word that is modified. **1888** J. WRIGHT tr. *Brugmann's Elem. Compar. Gram. Indo-Europ. Lang.* I. 501 Owing to the scantiness of the Umbrian–Samnitic materials, handed down to us, it remains doubtful at what period certain processes of sandhi took place in Latin. **1901** A. A. MACDONELL *Sanskrit Gram.* p. ii, The rules of Sandhi are based chiefly on the avoidance of hiatus and on assimilation. **1933** *Eng. Stud.* XV. 41 O[ld] E[nglish] *æt þam ende,* which became *atten ende,* and then, through sandhi, *at an ende.* **1939** [see *MORPHOPHONEMICS *sb. pl.*]. **1952** [see *NUCLEAR *a.* (and *sb.*) 1 c]. **1976** *Language* LII. 212 There is ample evidence that much of Sanskrit external sandhi is the result of sweeping generalizations.

2. *attrib.* and *Comb.*

1888 J. WRIGHT tr. *Brugmann's Elem. Compar. Gram. Indo-Europ. Lang.* I. 488 The fettered language of the Vedas already furnishes the proof that the sandhi-system of the classical Sanskrit is not a thing of natural growth. **1933** L. BLOOMFIELD *Language* xxiii. 418 There resulted sandhi-alternants of words like *water*:..['wɔtə]..['wɔtər iz]... This..resulted in the sandhi-form *the idea-r is*... English sandhi-alternation is limited largely to cases like the above. **1935** *Amer. Speech* X. 86/1 The sandhi customs are different in English from what they are in Dutch. *Ibid.*, A preliminary statement of the sandhi rules of the dialect or language studied. **1945** *Mod. Lang. Notes* Dec. 539 The sandhi-affricate formed in the sequence *right here.* **1961** R. E. KELLER *German Dialects* 264 This sandhi-lenition is not indicated in the orthography of the *Lux[emburger] W[ör]t[er]b[uch].* **1969** *Eng. Stud.* Suppl. p. lxxxi, At a conservative estimate twenty-two of the above twenty-eight instances support a spoken *sandhi*-distribution of voiced and voiceless final consonants. **1975** *Language* LI. 551 Words may have more than one form, due to sandhi processes such as French liaison and elision.

sand-hill. Add: **b. sand-hill crane,** substitute for def.: a North American crane, *Grus canadensis*; also *absol.*; (earlier and later examples).

1805 W. CLARK *Jrnl.* 31 Oct. in *Orig. Jrnls. Lewis & Clark Exped.* (1905) III. 176 Jo killed a Sand hill Crane. **1834** J. K. TOWNSEND *Narr. Journey Rocky Mts.* (1839) i. 12 We observed great numbers of the brown, or sandhill crane,.. flying over us. **1907** W. O. LILLIBRIDGE *Where Trail Divides* 115 He can..stalk a sandhill crane where there isn't cover to hide your hat. **1938** C. H. MATSCHAT *Suwanee River* 186 He seen the sandhills a-dancin' their matin' dance. **1949** *Natural Hist.* Oct. 378/1 Once heard. the far-reaching call of the sand-hill crane is a sound that can never be forgotten. **1960** R. T. PETERSON *Field Guide Birds of Texas* 79 Sandhill Crane..A long-legged, long-necked gray bird with a bald red forehead. **1977** *New Yorker* 9 May 113/1 He had later seen a pair of sandhill cranes.

d. *Canad. pl.* A region of southeastern Alberta; in the mythology of Plains Indians, the abode of departed spirits.

1949 J. G. MACGREGOR *Blankets & Beads* 113 Nothing marks the spot where some mighty chief or minor brave sleeps, while his spirit travels the trails of the Great Sand Hills. **1957** *Camsell Arrow* (Edmonton, Alberta) Christmas 77/1 The sun dance site is in the heart of the 50-mile-square Blood reserve about 40 miles south of Lethbridge. There are situated the sacred sand hills and the happy hunting grounds for departed spirits. **1959** N. SLUMAN *Blackfoot Crossing* 13 Little Tree would have to go unadorned to the Sand Hills, for her daughter could not part with the red glass beads. **1963** R. D. SYMONS *Many Trails* xiii. 138 He [*sc.* a missionary] had been saying that it would not be long now before he [*sc.* an Indian] would be called to the Sand-hills. **1975** *Alberta Hist.* Spring 16/2 Indians tell that a blizzard came up and blue and yellow lightning coloured the sky when Wolf Collar's ghost departed for the Sand Hills, the home of the dead.

sand-hiller (earlier and later examples).

1848 *Congress. Globe* 30th Congress 1st Sess. App. 137/1 The thing is whispered even among the sandhillers of South Carolina. **1850** E. P. BURKE *Reminisc. Georgia* 205 These people are known at the South by such names as crackers, clay-eaters, and sand-hillers. **1872** [see *piney-woods cracker* s.v. *PINEY WOOD b]. **1944** [see *piney-woods tacky* s.v. *PINEY WOOD b]. **1958** H. BABCOCK *I don't want to shoot an Elephant* 155 Barefooted and shirtless, the sandhiller was sprawled listlessly on the porch when I arrived.

sandhya (sa·ndyā). [a. Skr. *saṃdhyā* a holding together, junction: cf. *SANDHI.] **a.** Twilight. **b.** The period which precedes a yuga or age of the world. **c.** Morning or evening prayers.

1868 *Chambers's Encycl.* X. 327/1 A long mundane period of years, which is preceded by a period called *Sandhya,* 'twilight'. **1876** MONIER WILLIAMS *Indian Wisdom* (ed. 3) 248 The two Sandhyas of sunrise and sunset. **1891** —— *Brahmanism & Hinduism* 401 The first act of the Morning Sandhyā Service..is sipping water. **1913** J. N. FARQUHAR *Crown of Hinduism* 164 The daily devotions (sandhya) are restricted to the three castes. **1971** *Leader* (Durban) 7 May 9/4 They were all saying the 'sandhya', the evening prayers. In perfect Hindi! **1974** *Encycl. Brit. Micropædia* VIII. 850/1 *Sandhyā*.., Hindu religious acts performed by the twice-born (the three higher castes) at the three divisions of the day (morning, noon, and night).

Sandinista (sa:ndinī·stă), *sb.* (*a.*) [Sp., f. the name of Augusto César *Sandino* (1893–1934), Nicaraguan nationalist leader + *-ista* -IST.] A supporter of Sandino; a member of the revolutionary Nicaraguan guerrilla organization founded by him or of a similar organization founded in his name in 1963. Also *attrib.* or as *adj.*

1928 *Nation* (N.Y.) 29 Feb. 232/2 Everybody from here on was a Sandinista; the trail was full of Sandinistas. **1931** *Foreign Affairs* (N.Y.) IX. 499 A purely objective view of the facts hardly warrants calling the Sandinistas 'bandits'. **1954** *Southwestern Social Sci. Q.* (U.S.) Sept. 140 The Guardia's inability to destroy the *Sandinista* movement did not permit the early withdrawal of the marines. **1967** N. MACAULAY *Sandino Affair* iii. 55 On November 2 [1926] he led this force in an attack on the two-hundred-man government garrison at Jícaro, near San Albino. The Sandinistas killed some of the defenders. **1974** *N.Y. Times* 29 Dec. 1/4 The guerrillas, members of the so-called Sandinista Front, were said to have demanded the release of some 40 political prisoners. **1977** *Time* 31 Oct. 16/1 Others, like the Sandinista guerrillas of Nicaragua or the Islamic Marxists of Iran, have specific targets. **1980** *Ann. Reg. 1979* 66 A new Government, formed by the Sandinistas, was quickly recognized by the US.

sand lot. Add: Also with hyphen and as one word. **1.** (Earlier and later examples.) Also used *absol.* in the political sense; in literal use, a plot of empty or undeveloped land, esp. in a town or suburb.

1878 *N.Y. Tribune* 14 Aug. 4/3 Mr. Kearney, the 'sandlot orator' of California..came East with the prestige of a victorious leader. **1880** *San Francisco News Let.* 3 July 10/1 The Sand-lot barely escaped a Kilkenny fight on Sunday last. **1885** *Mag. Amer. Hist.* Feb. 201/2 One Dennis Kearny [*sic*]..made his headquarters in what were known as the 'Sand lots', near San Francisco. **1898** G. F. ATHERTON *Californians* 37 She drew Helena into a sand lot opposite. **1913** J. LONDON *Valley of Moon* 78 I've known [about his bad thumb] since he first got it as a kid fightin' in the sandlot at Watts Tract. **1930** J. DOS PASSOS *42nd Parallel* 192 The scorched sandlots and pinebarrens laid out into streets. **1949** *Sun* (Baltimore) 8 Jan. 9/5 The survey revealed that of the 18 direct fatalities [in football games] occurring in 1948, 6 were in 'sandlots'. **1978** *Verbatim* May 13/1 The sandlot in Washington Square has a sign 'Sandlot reserved for children and their guardians'.

2. Used *attrib.* (now usu. as one word) with reference to sports and games of the kind played by amateurs in a sand lot.

1890 *Breeder & Sportsman* (San Francisco) (Base Ball Suppl.) 7 June 3/3 Why. 'skates' and 'wafters' are kept in the team simply because at one time they were alleged good players by some sand lot critic. **1921** *Daily Colonist* (Victoria, B.C.) 10 Apr. 10/1 The National Baseball Federation, the governing body of the sandlot baseball, today went on record as opposing the 'Black Sox'. **1932** *Sun* (Baltimore) 6 Sept. 14/4 The Bugle nine will be composed of the pick of sand lot teams. **1942** *Short Guide Gt. Brit.* (U.S. War Dept.) 12 'Village cricket' which corresponds to sandlot baseball. **1954** *Encounter* Oct. 8/2 Interpret what this goddamn cotton market is going to do tomorrow, and we can both quit chasing this blank blank sandlot ball team. **1964** R. MURPHY *Pond* iv. 64 He played sandlot football in the afternoons. **1979** *Amer. Poetry Rev.* Mar./Apr. 24/1 Just once the kid with bad eyes hit a home run in an obscure sandlot game.

sand lotter, also with hyphen and as one word; (*b*) one who plays in a sandlot team.

1889 *Breeder & Sportsman* (San Francisco) 14 Dec. 485/1 The local sports kicked like old sand-lotters; they visited the judges stand..and told the poolseller that their money would never be paid. **1979** *N.Y. Times* 6 Aug. c2/1 These White Sox..are stocked with college players, sandlotters and, as Lonborg says, 'guys who love the game but, well, have some deficiencies'.

‖ **sandolo** (sæ·ndǒlo). Also **sandalo** (pl. **-i**), *erron.* **sandola.** [It.] A flat-bottomed rowing-boat of the kind used in the waterways of Venice.

1928 D. H. LAWRENCE *Lady Chatterley* xvii. 314 He was a sandola man, a sandola being a big boat that brings in fruit and produce from the islands. **1940** V. WOOLF *Roger Fry* iv. 100 Row out across the lagoons in a sandolo. **1962** N. MITFORD *Water Beetle* 123 Young men..ferry tourists from the steamer to the village in sandolos. **1966** J. G. LINKS *Venice for Pleasure* 223/2 Take a gondola or the smaller *sandolo* from Burano. **1969** B. MALAMUD *Pictures of Fidelman* vi. 154 Sandali sailed under bridges, heaped high with eggplants. **1974** *Encycl. Brit. Macropædia* XIX. 72/2 There are almost as many different kinds of watercraft in Venice as there are surface vehicles in a mainland city, from the dainty little *sandolo*, rowed standing with crossed oars, to giant ocean liners.

Sandow (sæ·ndo). The name of Eugen *Sandow* (1867–1925), Russo-German exponent of physical culture, used as the type of a strong man; also applied *attrib.* and in the possessive to exercises, an exercise machine, and societies endorsed by him. Also *fig.*

1898 *Physical Culture* I. 112/2 If 'Cantab' had proposed the theory that Sandow's system would have produced as good a ten-stone oar as Oxford training made of Mr. Kent, he would have stated a definitely arguable proposition; for if Sandow's system is to be applied to rowing at all, this is one of the results we shall immediately ask it to produce. **1905** W. B. YEATS *Let.* July (1954) III. 454, I have got into my routine here... To this I have added Sandow exercises twice daily. **1911** L. STONE *Jonah* I. ix. 100 He threw down the hammer with the air of a Sandow. **1914** C. MACKENZIE *Sinister St.* II. III. ii. 531 They talked instead of Sandow exercises and mountain-climbing. **1932** A. HUXLEY in *Lett. D. H. Lawrence* p. xiii, How bitterly he [*sc.* Lawrence] loathed the Wilhelm-Meisterish view of love as an education, as a means to culture, a Sandow-exerciser for the soul. **1947** N. COWARD *Peace in our Time* I. iv. 51 Nora: You're thinner than you were when—when you went away. Stevie: I'm Sandow to what I was when I left the prison camp. **1947** C. GRAY *Contingencies* i. 21 A complete fallacy.. that it is possible for aesthetic sensibility to be imparted ..by any such methods of spiritual jerks or intellectual Sandow exercisers. **1952** D. DAVIE *Purity of Diction in Eng. Verse* 175 He [*sc.* G. M. Hopkins] has no respect for the language, but gives it Sandow-exercises. **1962** *Listener* 2 Aug. 166/2 The founding of hundreds of Sandow physical-culture clubs throughout England and Wales. **1965** F. SARGESON *Mem. Peon.* v. 116 Anyone who engaged in Sandow exercises.

Hence **Sa·ndowism,** the principles of physical culture advocated by Sandow.

a **1930** D. H. LAWRENCE *Phoenix* (1936) 656 Physical training and Sandowism altogether is a ridiculous and puerile business.

sand-paper, sandpaper, *sb.* Add: Now usu. as one word. **1. b.** *fig.* Chiefly *attrib.* or as *adj.*, rough, abrasive, aggressive.

1953 'N. BLAKE' *Dreadful Hollow* II. xi. 145 The voice which had that sandpaper timbre of the overdriven. **1976** *Time* 20 Dec. 22/1 With his sandpaper style and naked drive for power, Burton had quite a few enemies.

Hence **sa·ndpapery** *a.*, resembling sandpaper, rough.

1957 V. NABOKOV *Pnin* 22 The sandpapery side of his head. **1970** E. MCGIRR *Death pays Wages* iii. 53 He.. massaged a sand-papery jaw. **1975** T. ALLBEURY *Special Collection* xi. 77 His hand was dry and sandpapery.

sand-pit. Add: Also as one word. **3.** A space in a garden or park enclosed by low walls and filled with sand in which children may play.

1898 G. B. SHAW *Candida* I. 80 A park..containing..a sandpit..imported from the seaside for the delight of children. **1908** G. JEKYLL *Children & Gardens* xi. 90 You will find out endless ways of playing with the sand-pit. **1937** T. ADAMS *Playparks* 49 Sandpits are not desirable in crowded playgrounds of large towns. **1959** *Oxf. Mail* 11 Mar. 6/4 Nurseries featuring merry-go-rounds, sand-pits, and attendants dressed as clowns are supplied free of charge. **1960** F. G. LENNHOFF *Exceptional Children* vii. 138 He found some release through child-like games..including sandpits and mud. **1976** 'D. HALLIDAY' *Dolly & Nanny Bird* ix. 118 Grover..was given half an Italian Easter egg and was sick in the sandpit.

‖ **sandr, sandur** (sæ·ndŭr, sæ·ndŭɹ). *Physical Geogr.* Pl. **sandar**; also **sandr, sandrs, sandurs.** [a. older Icel. *sandr* (pl. *sandar*) SAND *sb.*[2] In mod. Icel. the sing. is spelt *sandur.*] A broad, flat or gently sloping, sheet of glacial outwash.

1893 *Proc. Boston Soc. Nat. Hist.* XXVI. 172 This would lend much support to the theory that the sand and gravel plains of the Cape, of Long Island, and of the outlying islands, are to be regarded as confluent fan-deltas built up by streams issuing from the ice sheet, at times when its edge lay along the northern margin of the plains. They are therefore homologous with the sandr of Greenland,..and the gravel fans of Alaska. **1899** *Geogr. Jrnl.* XIII. 299 Here they [*sc.* glacial streams] cover vast areas with gravelly or sandy deposits, the equivalent of the 'sandr' of Iceland. **1937** W. B. WRIGHT *Quaternary Ice Age* x. 138 The outer moraine is distinguished from the inner by its great development of *sandr* or outwash sand plains. The inner moraine here lacks the *sandr* altogether. **1946** F. E. ZEUNER *Dating Past* v. 113 Analysis of the zones of moraines and sandrs of the Scandinavian Glaciation confirmed that there were at least three major glaciations. **1969** J. L. DAVIES *Landforms Cold Climates* xi. 180 The Icelandic sandurs have an overall gradient of about 1 : 200 to 1 : 250. **1976** H. M. FRENCH *Periglacial Environment* viii. 177 Periglacial sandar are particularly well developed in the broad valleys which drain towards the Beaufort Sea in the western Arctic.

sa·nd-trap. [f. SAND *sb.*[2] + TRAP *sb.*[1]] **1.** A device for separating sand and other impurities from a stream of water or pulp passing through it, esp. in the manufacture of paper.

a **1877** KNIGHT *Dict. Mech.* III. 2027/2 *Sand-trap*, a device for separating sand, etc., from water flowing through a pipe. **1885** *Encycl. Brit.* XVIII. 221/2 From them the pulp is pumped into the supply-box, which communicates with the sand-traps by means of a regulating cock. **1927** T. WOODHOUSE *Artificial Silk* 22 These sand traps are long, shallow, wooden troughs, the bottoms of which are covered by suitable rough-haired felt and baffle plates. **1963** R. R. A. HIGHAM *Handbk. Papermaking* ii. 68 Sand traps..are the small recesses in the trough of a beater or breaker which are covered with a perforated metal plate.

2. *Golf.* A bunker. Also *fig.*

1922 WODEHOUSE *Clicking of Cuthbert* iv. 99 As for the deep sand-trap in front of the seventh green, he spent so much of his time in it that there was some informal talk..of charging him a small weekly rent. **1927** *Daily Express* 29 Oct. 3/3 We cannot eliminate from the game that part of it which is played within the confines of the sandtraps. **1971** 'D. HALLIDAY' *Dolly & Doctor Bird* xv. 212 He doesn't like soft sculpted sand-traps, which he likes to call bunkers. **1980** *Amer. Speech* LV. 127 Sixteen pages of notes and documentation attest to the authors' concern for accuracy and good scholarship, even though the inevitable sandtraps occur where nonspecialists attempt specialized courses.

sandveld (sæ·ndvelt, ‖ sæ·ntfelt). Also **sand veld, sand-veld, zandveld.** [a. Afrikaans, f. *sand* SAND *sb.*[2] + *veld* VELDT, VELD.] In southern Africa, (the name of) a region of light sandy soil.

1824 W. J. BURCHELL *Trav. S. Afr.* II. ix. 242 The plains on the other side [of the Langberg], are called by the name of *Zandveld*. **1873** *Cape of Good Hope Blue Bk.* App. p. JJ3, Several hundred trees have been planted along the main road to Cape Town..on 'Zandveld'. **1919** *S. Afr. Geogr. Jrnl.* III. 73 The Free State farmer in the early spring-time treks to the 'sand veld' with his stock. **1937** MARAIS & SIM in D. J. SEYMORE *Handbk. Farmers in S. Afr.* (Dept. of Agric. & Forestry, S. Afr.) 704 In the sandveld the production of a grain crop is not easy—the soil is a light sand, not particularly fertile. **1939** 'D. RAME' *Wine of Good Hope* I. xiii. 158 They left the last of the wheat and came to a queer sand-veld. **1944** M. OLDEVIG *Sunny Land* vi. 51 The Kalahari, the waterless sandveld of Bechuanaland and South West Africa. **1953** D. LESSING *Five* iii. 121 This..was farming country,..a pocket of good, dark, rich soil in the wastes of the light sandveld. **1959** [see *AFRICANDER, AFRIKANDER 3]. **1964** *Listener* 6 Aug. 192/1 He plants the first rose on the burnt sandveld.

Sandwich, *sb.*[1] Add: **2. Sandwich tern,** a black, grey, and white tern, *Sterna sandvicensis*, found in Europe and Africa.

1785, 1888 [see TERN *sb.*[1]]. **1914** *Chambers's Jrnl.* May 308/1 These birds are the ring-ouzel..and the sandwich tern. **1934** *Discovery* Oct. 293/1 Many species like the.. Sandwich tern, and puffin are growing scarcer. **1968** [see *MACHINE *sb.* 3]. **1971** *Country Life* 18 Feb. 356/2 Two birds, at least, which breed nowhere else in Spain, have important colonies here: the black-headed gull and the Sandwich tern.

sandwich, *sb.*[2] Add: **1. a.** Now made of almost any filling or spread, occas. with only one slice of bread, as in *open* or *open-faced sandwich* (see *OPEN *a.* (*adv.*) 22 c), or with biscuits, sliced buns, or cake. The specifying word now freq. denotes form as well as contents: *club* (see *CLUB *sb.* 20), *Dagwood, Denver, hero* (see *HERO *sb.* 5), *peanut butter* (see *PEANUT b), *poor boy* (see *POOR *a.* (*sb.*) 8), *submarine sandwich* (see *SUBMARINE *sb.*). (Earlier *fig.* example.)

1925 S. LEWIS *Arrowsmith* xxiv. 280 You might bring me a Denver sandwich from the Sunset Trail Lunch. **1932** G. GREENE *Stamboul Train* I. i. 11 Get me a sandwich... I'm so empty I can hear my stomach. **1954** *Good Housek. Cookery Bk.* (rev. ed.) 443/1 Buns and cakes, provided they are not too sweet may be cut in thin slices and used for sweet sandwiches. **1977** *Rolling Stone* 16 June 12/1 Our past albums were like Dagwood sandwiches because you had to listen to them 30 or 40 times on very sophisticated equipment to hear everything we'd dub in. **1978** G. MITCHELL *Mingled with Venom* iv. 37 Take Diana the smaller of my two sponge sandwiches.

fig. **1790** T. WILKINSON *Mem.* III. 154, I will, by way of a sandwich, halt for a few minutes refreshment, and present the reader [etc.].

b. A form of training involving alternate periods of practical and theoretical instruction. Freq. *attrib.* or as *adj.* (cf. sense 3 below).

1913 FLEMING & BAILEY *Engineering as Profession* ii. 113 A sandwich arrangement comprising short alternating periods of technical and practical training until the full course in each is completed. **1955** *Times* 14 July 2/6 This professional training scheme is organized over four or five years on a 'sandwich' basis. **1961** *Technology* Aug. 197 For its support of the sandwich principle *Technology* has often been taken to task by teachers in the colleges of advanced technology. **1965** *Listener* 2 Dec. 887/2 An undergraduate comes up in October, spends two terms in the college. In April he begins his first six-month spell in industry... This is the Brunel sandwich evolved over the past eight years. **1972** *Guardian* 20 June 18/6 The polytechnics..have a special interest in sandwich degree courses .., either the thick sandwich, with one year out of a total of four spent in an industrial job, or the thin sandwich, during which the student spends alternating periods..in college and in industry. **1980** *Jrnl. R. Soc. Arts* Feb. 157/1 We have a lot to learn and the sandwich graduates may possibly help to bridge that gap.

c. A laminated board or panel consisting of a layer of light-weight material situated between and bonded to two thin sheets of a strong material, used in light constructions, esp. in aircraft.

1944 *Use of Wood for Aircraft in U.K.* (U.S. Forest Products Lab. Publ. No. 1540) 21 The fuselage..is composed of a plywood and balsa wood sandwich about 1/2 inch thick. **1946** *Rep. & Mem. Aeronaut. Res. Comm.* No. 1987. 2 The various kinds of sandwich considered are those in which the faces are of steel or duralumin, and the fillings of onazote, balsa wood or plywood. **1954** D. M. DESOUTTER *All about Aircraft* viii. 134/2 Corrugated metal..makes a good filling for sandwiches. In this kind of sandwich two thin sheets are held apart by the corrugated metal between, and they are attached to it by welding or any other means. **1976–7** *Sea Spray* (N.Z.) Dec./Jan. 86/3 The Adelaide boat, built of foam/glass sandwich in a highly sophisticated layup technique was designed as a good all-rounder.

d. Used *attrib.* in *Chem.* to denote (complexes having) a structure in which a metal atom is bonded between two parallel cyclic ligands in different planes, as in ferrocene.

1952 *Jrnl. Amer. Chem. Soc.* LXXIV. 4971/2 A projection on the (*x, y*) plane concomitant with the 'sandwich' structures proposed by Wilkinson [et al.]..immediately appeared. **1966** PHILLIPS & WILLIAMS *Inorg. Chem.* II. xxvii. 336 It does not appear that the benzene ring can act as a bridging sandwich-ligand, but two metal atoms can be 'sandwiched' between two benzenes. **1973** *Nature* 2 Nov. 3/1 Wilkinson used the name 'sandwich compounds' for the metallocenes. **1974** *Ibid.* 11 Jan. 85/1 In the so-called 'sandwich' molecules $(C_6H_6)_2Cr$ and $(C_5H_5)_2Fe$, the metal atoms are symmetrically placed between the rings.

3. (in sense 1 a) *sandwich bar, bell, bread, counter, grill, loaf* (also ellipt.), *lunch, paper, shop, spread, supper* (later example); (in sense *1 b) *sandwich course, student, system, training*; **sandwich-board man** = sense 2; also *fig.*; **sandwich boy,** (*a*) = sense 2; (*b*) a student on a sandwich course; **sandwich cake** = *layer cake* s.v. *LAYER *sb.* 5; **sandwich case** (later examples); **sandwich construction,** the structure or method of fabrication of sandwich panels; **sandwich flag,** a miniature flag that identifies the filling of a sandwich; **sandwich panel,** a panel constructed as a sandwich.

1955 H. SMITH *Making Money in Catering Business* vi. 51 (*heading*) Analysis of operating costs of a small provincial snack and sandwich bar. **1971** E. PAUL *Reluctant Cloak & Dagger Man* x. 122, I found a sandwich bar, settled on a stool and ordered sandwiches and beer. **1977** *Lancashire Life* Mar. 101/1, I once met a chap who worked behind the counter of a sandwich bar at a railway station. **1922** JOYCE *Ulysses* 284 Under the sandwichbell lay on a bier of bread one last, one lonely, last sardine. **1890** W. BOOTH *In Darkest England* p. xv, The expense of providing boards for 'sandwich' boardmen. **1936** W. B. YEATS *Lett. on Poetry* (1940) 124 When I excluded Wilfred Owen..I did not know I was excluding a revered sandwich-board Man of the revolution. **1961** K. REISZ *Technique Film Editing* (ed. 9) ii. 199 Sandwich-board man carrying airline advertisement placard. **1835** *Bell's Life in London* 11 Oct. 1/1 The Sandwich boy took the hats and bonnets at the street-door. **1958** *Daily Mail* 19 Sept. 11/3 The first of the 'sandwich boys'..have won diplomas in technology. **1971** B. MALAMUD *Tenants* 103 A loaf of sandwich bread on the table. **1911** C. E. W. BEAN *'Dreadnought' of Darling* xxv. 221 The thin layer of jam or chocolate in a sandwich cake. **1929** J. B. PRIESTLEY *Good Companions* I. ii. 54 Mrs. Chillingford said this with immense gusto, then went slap into a piece of sandwich cake. **1968** 'P. HOBSON' *Titty's Dead* vi. 70 At her elbow stood a pot of strong Indian tea and half a sandwich cake. **1908** Sandwich-case [see *patch pocket* s.v. *PATCH *sb.*[1] 8]. **1948** F. THOMPSON *Still glides Stream* ii. 40 'That fool of a groom'..had carried off with him his mistress's sandwich case. **1944** *Use of Wood for Aircraft in U.K.* (U.S. Forest Products Lab. Publ. No. 1540) 3 The sandwich construction so effectively used in the Mosquito fuselage consists of birch plywood faces and a balsa core, affording a relatively thick section of high strength and rigidity, and good sound and thermal insulating qualities. **1946** *Rep. & Mem. Aeronaut. Res. Committee* No. 1987. 2 Considerable interest has recently been shown in the possibilities of the so-called 'sandwich' construction in the design of stressed-skin wings and fuselages. **1963** H. R. CLAUSER et al. *Encycl. Engin. Materials & Processes* 587/1 The largest single reason for the use of sandwich construction and its rapid growth to one of the standard structural approaches during the past 10 years is its high strength or stiffness-to-weight ratio. **1913** S. STORY *Spirit of Paris* 1 Cafés..have been elbowed away by vulgar bars and automatic sandwich counters. **1960** R. E. WOLF tr. *T. Henrot's Belgium* 189 Department stores with low-price sandwich counters. **1978** 'A. STUART' *Vicious Circles* 3 The sandwich counter of the Bar Roma..Russian salad, prosciutto, baby pizzas. **1955** *Times* 15 July 9/7 This can be arranged in the 'sandwich' course, which alternates periods of study in college with periods of training in industry. **1957** *Technology* Apr. 44/4 Up to fifteen of these students will be Vickers undergraduate apprentices using the 'thick' sandwich course. **1966** *New Scientist* 13 Oct. 8/2 Most of the 2000 first-degree students are on sandwich courses which generally last 4½ years. **1972** *Accountant* 5 Oct. 436/1 The first paper was on sandwich courses. **1980** *Jrnl. R. Soc. Arts* Feb. 155/1 The apathy of senior management to design was felt in our BA (Hons) 4-year Sandwich course. **1907** *Yesterday's Shopping* (1969) 352 B/3 (*heading*) Sandwich flags. *Ibid.*, Stamped in Gold and Colours, with different names such as—Anchovy..Tongue..Foie Gras. **1950** *Vogue* Aug. 100/3 Intellectuals..spend very little on..sandwich flags. **1962** F. T. DAY *Introd. to Paper* viii. 87 Sandwich flags are designed to distinguish party dishes. **1955** Sandwich grill [see *MASTER *sb.*[1] 30]. **1937** D. L. SAYERS *Busman's Honeymoon* iv. 83 How many loaves would you be wanting? .. A cottage and a sandwich. And a small brown? **1943** C. MILBURN *Diary* 30 Jan. (1979) 166, I got two sandwich loaves. **1978** F. WELDON *Praxis* xxii. 194 On the estate bread was a sandwich loaf and the cheese cheddar or processed. **1932** D. L. SAYERS *Have his Carcase* i. 9 She carried ..little..beyond a pocket edition of *Tristram Shandy*, a vest-pocket camera, a small first-aid outfit and a sandwich lunch. **1959** *Economist* 3 Jan. 26/2 About 15 per cent of men eat a sandwich lunch. **1973** K. BENTON *Craig & Jaguar* vi. 67 There will be a sandwich lunch for us on the way. **1946** *Rep. & Mem. Aeronaut. Res. Comm.* No. 1987. 2 A sandwich panel is one in which a thick sheet of a relatively weak 'filling' is interposed between two thin sheets of a more orthodox structural material, such as steel, duralumin or plywood. **1953** *Archit. Rev.* CXIV. 132/3 Walls are sandwich panels made up of two asbestos cement sheets with a cellular core. **1963** H. R. CLAUSER et al. *Encycl. Engin. Materials & Processes* 586/2 When a sandwich panel is loaded as a beam, the honeycomb and the bond resist the shear loads while the facings resist the moments due to bending forces, and hence carry the beam bending as tensile and compressive loads. **1923** T. S. ELIOT *Waste Land* iii. 14 The river bears no empty bottles, sandwich papers. **1924** [see *CARTON[2] b]. **1970** 'D. HALLIDAY' *Dolly & Cookie Bird* vii. 108 The empty packets of cigarettes, the greasy sandwich paper. **1948** MENCKEN *Amer. Lang.* Suppl. II. 580 Eat shop, sandwich shop. **1967** A. BAILEY in L. Deighton *London Dossier* 55 Sandwich shops abound to feed the mid-day lunch-hungries. **1978** *Detroit Free Press* 2 Apr. 11A/2 Business at the sandwich shops and stores on the edge of the campus was brisk. *c* **1938** *Fortnum & Mason Price List* 37/2 Sandwich Spread—per glass 10½d. **1950** A. WILSON *Such Darling Dodos* 134 Dainty bridge rolls filled with sandwich spread. **1972** R. P. JHABVALA *New Dominion* I. 69 Your ketchup—and this is something new—sandwich spread—I thought you'd like to try it for your tea. **1963** *Times* 24 May (London Underground Suppl.) p. xv/4 The quaintly described dip. tech. sandwich student has his place. **1975** *Times* 1 Sept. 10/8 The difficulty of finding places for sandwich students. **1954** J. BETJEMAN *Few Late Chrysanthemums* 26 Settles down to sandwich supper and the television screen. **1919** *Proc. Inst. Automobile Engineers* XII. 450 This training should be taken along with their apprenticeship... The sandwich system has been in existence in Glasgow for over 70 years. **1940** *Nature* 21 Dec. 812/2 Some large firms testify highly to the value of the product of such a 'sandwich' system. **1956** *Ibid.* 3 Mar. 412/1 All its departments have increased their facilities to students,..and in particular the 'sandwich system' has been established. **1971** *New Scientist* 1 Apr. 36/2 Industry is not yet prepared to cooperate sufficiently with educational establishments to make the sandwich system work as it should. **1957** *Technology* Mar. 10/3 Student apprentices, on completing their first two years sandwich training, are also transferred to the main works. **1978** *Jrnl. R. Soc. Arts* CXXVI. 347/1 The Tech's part-time study, which was a form of sandwich training.

Sandwich (sæ·ndwitʃ), *sb.*[3] The name of a town on Cape Cod, Massachusetts, U.S.A., applied to a factory and to glass produced there from 1825 to 1888.

1881 C. C. HARRISON *Woman's Handiwork* III. 227 American finger-bowls..are made at the sandwich factory in Massachusetts. **1922** *Antiques* Feb. 57/2 Until recently no one had taken the trouble to look into the sources of sandwich glass. **1935** J. C. LINCOLN *Cape Cod Yesterdays* 164 The buttery shelves of every house in our town were filled with Sandwich glass at that period. **1947** R. P. COFFIN *Yankee Coast* 276 Long shelves across the north windows, every inch of them covered with sandwich glass drinking the pure north light. **1964** J. CLEARY *Flight of Chariots* vi. 251 She bought four-poster beds, Windsor chairs, Sandwich glass, hooked rugs.

sandwich, *v.* Add: **2.** (Later *fig.* examples.) Also, to place (different elements) alternately.

1900 *Times* 7 July 10/1 To offend the ear still further these calls of screeching boys are sandwiched by 'Any seat, Sir, but the first four rows'. **1924** H. DE SÉLINCOURT *Cricket Match* iv. 104 He liked to sandwich the weak and the strong, the swift and the slow. **1937** 'G. ORWELL' *Road to Wigan Pier* ii. 29 The miner does that journey to and fro, and sandwiched in between..are seven and a half hours of savage work. **1942** *R.A.F. Jrnl.* 27 June 30 Since the D.H. was sandwiched between them..he was almost pulverised. **1957** *Technology* Mar. 16/2 Mechanical engineering students at Hendon Technical College sandwich eight weeks of study with eight weeks of factory work. **1977** *Time* 30 May 40/3 He sits in a rocker sandwiched between speakers blaring the hard rock music of the Grateful Dead.

intr. for *refl.* **1931** *Times Lit. Suppl.* 18 June 484/2 Tobogganing and their other misdemeanours agreeably sandwich with the humours of the always optimistic Waterall.

sandwiching *vbl. sb.* (earlier example).

1877 E. S. DALLAS *Kettner's Bk. of Table* 334 In puff paste the butter and the paste are separate and there is no mixing or kneading—only what may be called fine sandwiching.

sandy, *a.* Add: **5. a.** *sandy-haired* (earlier example).

a **1817** JANE AUSTEN *Persuasion* (1818) IV. iii. 49 Colonel Wallis's companion..certainly was not sandy-haired.

b. sandy hill crane = *sand-hill crane* s.v. SAND-HILL b in Dict. and Suppl.; **sandy pear** = *sand pear* s.v. SAND *sb.*[2] 10 c in Dict. and Suppl.

1819 D. THOMAS *Trav. Western Country* 210 A bird inhabits this country called the sandy hill Crane. **1825** Sandy hill crane [see *LEY var. LYE *v.*[2]]. **1884** tr. *A. de Candolle's Orig. Cultivated Plants* 233 Sandy Pear, Chinese Pear.

sa·nd-yacht. Also **sand yacht, sandyacht.** [f. SAND *sb.*[2] + YACHT *sb.*] A sail-driven craft mounted on a three- or four-wheeled chassis, used for sailing on sand.

1912 *Car* 6 Nov. 458/2 Some of the sand-yachts have three wheels; others have four wheels. **1924** F. M. FORD *Joseph Conrad* IV. 227 Knocke was just within the Belgian border. You could run in a sand-yacht in front of the dunes, right to Sluys. **1960** L. LAMPLUGH *Sixpenny Runner* ii. 21 By sailing he meant sand-yacht sailing..along the four-mile stretch of sands. **1967** *Daily Tel.* 21 Feb. 15/1 Sand yachts in the first race across the Sahara..are 70 miles from Tindouf. **1970** R. MARR in *Sports Stories for Boys* 309 The *Sandsprite* was a sand yacht, a sleek, streamlined vessel of gleaming aluminium and scarlet enamel, mounted on three motor-cycle wheels. **1980** *West Lancs. Even. Gaz.* 23 June 5 Action from the sandyacht racing at Fylde International Sand Yacht Club.

Hence **sand-yachter,** one who uses a sand-yacht; **sand-yachting** *vbl. sb.* and *ppl. a.*; **sand-yachtsman** = *sand-yachter* above.

1922 *Car* 6 Nov. 458/2 (*heading*) Sand-yachting on the Belgian coast. **1937** *Illustr. London News* 21 Aug. 315 Sailing the desert at 45 m.p.h.: the thrilling sport of sand-yachting at an R.A.F. station in Egypt. **1960** L. LAMPLUGH *Sixpenny Runner* vii. 76 Keith had spent most of the week with the sand-yachters..on Brenstowe beach. *Ibid.* xv. 157 His sand-yachting pals. **1967** *Sunday Times* 28 May 19 Forty sand yachtsmen from six countries had a disappointing day at St. Annes, Lancashire, yesterday when races for the international..sand yacht championships were unable to be started. **1970** *Daily Tel.* 23 May 9 Sensible sand-yachters wear a crash helmet. **1973** *Country Life* 25 Jan. 218/1 Ideal wind speeds for sand yachting are between 12 and 20 m.p.h. **1980** *West Lancs. Even. Gaz.* 23 June, The following Fylde sandyachters were chosen for the British team.

sanely, *adv.* (Earlier example.)

1803 M. EDGEWORTH *Let.* 19 Mar. (1979) 101, I am not famous for judging sanely of strangers.

san fairy ann (sæn fēə·ri æn). *slang.* Also **san ferry ann,** etc. [Jocular form repr. F. *ça ne fait rien* 'it does not matter', said to have originated in army use in the war of 1914–18.] An expression of indifference to, or resigned acceptance of, a state of affairs. Also *ellipt.* as **Fairy Ann.**

1919 W. H. DOWNING *Digger Dial.* 43 *San ferry ann*,..it doesn't matter. **1921** *Amer. Legion Weekly* 8 Apr. 14 Son fairy Ann. **1922** B. A. COLONNA *Hist. Company B, 311th Infantry* 78 If he did not sign he did not get paid and often when he does sign he don't get paid. So 'sanferriens'. **1924** *Radio Times* 19 Dec. 589/1 My mottoe's still san fairy Han. **1927** H. KIMBER *San Fairy Ann* ix. 312 'There is a magic charter,' he whispered. 'It runs, "San Fairy Ann".' **1930** KIPLING *Thy Servant Dog* III. 88 We said we were wonderful brave dog... He said 'Fairy Ann! Fairy Ann!' **1941** W. P. CROZIER *Diary* Mar. in D. Ayerst *Guardian* (1971) xxxiv. 544 Gradualness, san faery ann. **1956** F. B. VICKERS in *Coast to Coast 1955–6* 72 'Ya. Good night.' 'San ferry ann, Joe.' 'Which means black you, Jack, I'm all right,' Tom shouted. **1965** L. BRAIN *It's Free Country* xx. 181 'I wish you'd thought of my ulcer before you—' he began, and then broke off. 'Oh, san fairy anne!' **1973** *Times* 22 June 20/1 (Advt.), San fairy Ann... It doesn't matter to us whether it is fixed wing or helicopter because we sell the best of both.

‖ **Sanfan** (sa·nfan). Also **San-fan, San Fan** and with small initial. [Chinese *sānfǎn*, f. *sān* three + *fǎn* anti-, against.] Used *attrib.* to designate an official campaign conducted in China in 1951–2 against corruption, waste, and bureaucratism in State affairs. Cf. *WUFAN.

1956 *Contemp. China 1955* I. 63 The *san-fan* movement directed against the 'three evils' of corruption, waste and bureaucracy in state institutions and enterprises. **1966** F. SCHURMANN *Ideol. & Organization in Communist China* v. 318 The regime resorted to terror to enforce controls. This took the form of the Three-Anti (*Sanfan*) and Five-Anti (*Wufan*) movements. The *Sanfan* campaign which started in the winter of 1951 was directed against corruption, waste, and bureaucratism. **1971** H. TREVELYAN *Worlds Apart* viii. 98 The early campaigns were followed by the 'San-fan' and 'Wu-fan' movements, the so-called Three Antis and Five Antis, directed against corrupt Government officials and businessmen, but doubtless also against the politically unreliable. **1974** tr. *Wertheim's Evolution & Revolution* 333 In the early fifties, the *San Fan* (three-anti) campaign was directed at all kinds of malpractices in the newly built state apparatus.

Sanfedist (sæ·nfĕdist), *sb.* (and *a.*) [ad. It. *sanfediste* (also used), f. *santa fede* holy faith, used in the title of the society known as the Bande della Santa Fede + -IST.] A member of an Italian political and military organization of the late 18th and early 19th centuries loyal to the Papacy and hostile to republicanism. Also *attrib.* or as *adj.*

1842 F. W. FABER *Foreign Churches* II. 268 It has been asserted..that among the higher orders of society in the Papal States another party has been formed, which includes within itself a few of the princes of the Church and affords some disquiet to the Austrian embassy at Rome. The members of this society call themselves Sanfedists. It is indeed but a revival of old Guelphic principles... The Sanfedists are said to have arisen in 1780 as an anti-Austrian party at Turin, Gregory VII, and Sixtus V, being the great objects of their admiration. **1881** *Encycl. Brit.* XIII. 486/1 In a short while, the Carbonari societies, with Sanfedisti and many other revolutionary associations, had extended their organization through the length and breadth of the peninsula. **1920** J. P. TREVELYAN *Short Hist. Ital. People* xxvii. 475 During the reign of..Leo XII..Romagna was ravaged by the blood feuds of Carbonari and Sanfedisti. **1960** E. E. Y. HALES *Revolution & Papacy* vii. 123 The most interesting..Sanfedist leader was Cardinal Ruffo. *Ibid.* xvi. 264 During Leo's..reign—he died on February 10, 1829—the discontent in the Papal States..grew more serious. The policy of using the Sanfedists..was now encouraged from Rome, with a view to suppressing..the secret societies. **1965** C. HIBBERT *Garibaldi & his Enemies* I. iv. 48 At Ancona twenty-eight *Sanfedisti*, murderous anti-liberals who acted in the name of the faith, were assassinated.

Sanforized (sæ·nfŏrəizd), *a.* Also **sanforized.** [f. the name of *Sanford* L. Cluett (1874–1968), U.S. inventor of the process + -IZE + -ED[1].] **a.** A proprietary name for cotton and other fabrics which have been preshrunk by a special process. Also *transf.*

1930 *Official Gaz.* (U.S. Patent Office) 30 Sept. 737/1 Cluett, Peabody & Co., Inc., Troy, N.Y... *Sanforized* for piece goods of cotton, linen, woolen, silk, rayon, and combinations thereof. **1938** *Times* 21 Feb. 11/1 A water-repellant finish is demonstrated at the stand of the Bleachers' Association, where Sanforized cotton and linen cloths are shown. **1939** *Trade Marks Jrnl.* 24 May 706/2 *Sanforized*... Piece goods of textile material but not including cotton piece goods. Cluett, Peabody & Co., Inc.,..Troy, New York..; manufacturers. **1944** T. D. CLARK *Pills, Petticoats & Plows* 221 A frugal backwoods customer adequately sized up the complications of the 'sanforized' era in men's clothing when he sauntered into the Harbour Pitts store. **1952** M. STEEN *Phoenix Rising* i. 21 If this were the States.. you'd be in a tuxedo and a sanforized shirt. **1963** *New Yorker* 15 June 78 Made in the Orient of fine Sanforized cotton. **1970** *Which?* Nov. 340/1 Some jeans carried a Sanforised label. **1975** G. HOWELL *In Vogue* 104/2 In shops people were asking for uncrushable fabrics like zingale, and for cottons, linens and spun rayons which were Sanforized—preshrunk. **1978** *Church Times* 25 Aug. 8 Soap-operas featuring sanforised nurses or grubby Lancastrians—everyday stories of boring folk.

b. *fig.*

1968 *Observer* (Colour Suppl.) 11 Feb. 24 (Advt.), The Sanforized Big Car. £567. The Imp is the big car shrunk small before it reaches you. **1970** S. J. PERELMAN *Baby, it's Cold Inside* 130 The next time I go shopping for naïve art, I'll make bloody well sure it's Sanforized.

Hence **Sa·nforizing,** this process.

1948 *Time* 11 Oct. 91/3 The company was also lucky in its Vice President Sanford Cluett, the original families' only remaining executive. Cluett was an experiment-minded man. His tinkering had turned up Sanforizing. **1963** A. J. HALL *Textile Sci.* v. 241 Recently the inventors of the Sanforizing machine have been able to use a 2-inch thick rubber belt in a modified machine and so enable fabrics to be shrunk up to 20% in length.

San Franciscan (sæn fræ̆nsi·skăn), *sb.* and *a.* [f. *San Francisc(o* (see below) + -AN.] **A.** *sb.* A native or inhabitant of San Francisco in California, U.S.A. **B.** *adj.* Of or pertaining to San Francisco.

1875 *Scribner's Monthly* July 277/2 San Franciscans are remorseless critics. **1886** F. C. BAYLOR *On Both Sides* iv. 227 The glasses rattled as if in a San Franciscan earthquake. **1899** KIPLING *From Sea to Sea* II. xxv. 8 It may be this sense of possible disaster..that makes San Franciscan society go with..a whirl. **1949** *Los Angeles Times* 6 June 2/5 San Franciscans wear overcoats and furs even in the summer. **1960** PARTRIDGE *Charm of Words* 55 Beatniks, as the San Franciscan press christened members of the Beat community. **1973** S. COHEN *Diane Game* (1974) iv. 43 I'm afraid I've become a San Franciscan. **1977** W. MARSHALL *Thin Air* ii. 16 His soft San Franciscan accent.

sang (sæŋ), *sb.*[2] *U.S.* colloq. abbrev. of GINSENG.

1843 'R. CARLTON' *New Purchase* I. xxvii. 256 The storekeeper was obliged to book the nine and a quarter cents, to be paid in 'sang'. **1886** *Harper's Mag.* June 58/2 Formerly, digging 'sang', as they call ginseng, was a general occupation. **1897** W. E. BARTON *Sim Galloway's Daughter-in-Law* 20 The sang was short this year. **1948** E. N. DICK *Dixie Frontier* 32 He spent some time digging ginseng, or 'sang' as they called it. **1978** *Nat. Parks & Conservation Mag.* Feb. 18/1 Hunters of 'sang', as ginseng is known in Virginia and West Virginia, can tell..exciting stories about finding the 'big root' or 'patch'.

attrib. **1859** BARTLETT *Dict. Amer.* (ed. 2) 379 *Sang-hoe*, the implement used in gathering ginseng. **1878** C. B. COALE *Life & Adventures Wilburn Waters* xxi. 124 These hill-sides are a godsend to 'sang-diggers'. **1899** M. G. KAINS *Ginseng* 31 The average 'sang' digger has very little conscience. **1927** K. EUBANK *Horse & Buggy Days* 53 The trail of death which lasted for twenty years started over the ownership of a 'sang-digger' hog. **1949** J. NELSON *Backwoods Teacher* xxii. 233 Thar I was in them deep woods huntin' sang roots. **1975** C. BOGUE in E. Wigginton *Foxfire 3* 247 A man could go 'sang' hunting and return with a fortune.

Hence as *v. intr.*, to gather ginseng; **sa·nging** *vbl. sb.*

1848 BARTLETT *Dict. Amer.* 282 *Sang*,..is or was also used in Virginia as a verb; *to go a sanging*, is to be engaged in gathering ginseng. **1859** *Ibid.* (ed. 2) 379 In Alleghany Co., Maryland, is Sang Run near which is a well-known 'sanging ground'. **1877** *Field & Forest* III. 40 Why, I have sanged all over it [*sc.* the mountain]. **1892** J. L. ALLEN *Blue-Grass Region of Kentucky* 249 In the wildest parts of the country.. entire families may still be seen 'out sangin'. **1975** C. BOGUE in E. Wigginton *Foxfire 3* 247 With some domestic sale, as well as a continuing foreign market, 'sanging' became a business.

‖ **sang** (sɒŋ), *sb.*³ Also **srang**; pl. **-**, (anglicized) **-s.** [Tibetan *s(r)ang* ounce.] A former Tibetan unit of currency, consisting of 100 *sho*; a coin or note of this value.

1902 S. C. DAS *Journey to Lhasa & Central Tibet* vii. 182 The Government revenue for each *kang* is, on an average, fifty *srang* (125 rupees), or about one hundred and fifty *khal* of grain. **1947** *Whitaker's Almanack* 886/2 The present currency [of Tibet] is reckoned in *sangs*... The 1939 value was about 8 sangs = 1 rupee. **1962** R. A. G. CARSON *Coins* 545 Since 1935 on various srang values in silver..has been the lion with a background of mountains. **1962** L. DAVIDSON *Rose of Tibet* ix. 174 The current yuan went 330 to the Tibetan sang: the sang six and a half to the rupee. **1970** R. D. TARING *Daughter of Tibet* xviii. 242 Thubtenla lent me six hundred *sangs* (about £6). **1974** D. NORBU *Red Star over Tibet* ii. 36 His profits and premium from Chang Thang amounted to 600 *sang*.

sang, var. *SHENG[1].

Sanga (sæ·ngă). [Amharic.] A bull or cow belonging to the East African breed so called, distinguished by large, lyre-shaped horns. Also *attrib.*

1814 H. SALT *Voy. Abyssinia* 258, I was gratified by the sight of the Galla oxen, or Sanga. **1862** *Chambers's Encycl.* IV. 583/1 Galla Ox, or Sanga, a remarkable species or variety of ox inhabiting Abyssinia. **1912** R. LYDEKKER *Ox & Its Kindred* vii. 160 These Galla or Sanga cattle are generally white and have small or no humps, their muzzles being black... In stature these oxen are very large. **1959** J. D. CLARK *Prehist. S. Afr.* xi. 283 The indigenous long-horned African breed—the Sanga cattle. **1970** W. J. A. PAYNE *Cattle Production in Tropics* I. ii. 46 East Africa is the most likely centre of origin of the earliest Sanga cattle.

sangar: now the usu. form of SUNGAR in Dict. and Suppl.

sangaree, *v.* (Earlier example.)

1835 J. H. INGRAHAM *South-West* I. 115 [Devotees of domino are] clustered around the tables, with a tonic, often renewed and properly sangareed, at their elbows.

sang-de-bœuf. Add: (Earlier and later examples.) Also *transf.*, a ceramic glaze of this colour; porcelain bearing such a glaze.

1881 C. C. HARRISON *Woman's Handiwork* II. 104 A number of antique Chinese vases in high glaze, sang de bœuf, céladon, gray, rose, mandarin, yellow. **1900** F. LITCHFIELD *Pott. & Porc.* iv. 45 The pottery made in self-colour, such as *sang de boeuf*. **1957** MANKOWITZ & HAGGAR *Conc. Encycl. Eng. Pott. & Porc.* 88/2 The monochrome copper-red glazes of the Chinese were successfully imitated in the closing decades of the nineteenth century by Bernard Moore and the Burtons. These glazes were designated *Sang de Boeuf* and 'Flambé'. **1960** O. MANNING *Great Fortune* II. 121 She had seen an Italian tea-set of fine *sang-de-bœuf* china. **1965** D. TORR *Diplomatic Cover* vi. 102 A scholarly, balding man..was examining a plain deep red vase. Janine was saying,..'It's a genuine Lang Yao sang de boeuf, seventeenth century.' **1972** *Trans. Oriental Ceramics Soc.* XXXVIII. 47 All these transmutations can be seen..in the *sang de boeuf* bowl No 231 where the almost colourless rim shows faintly green. **1974** SAVAGE & NEWMAN *Illustr. Dict. Ceramics* 254 *Sang-de-bœuf*,..a brilliant red glaze which exhibits patches resembling the coagulation of ox-blood... The colouring agent was copper oxide fired in a reducing atmosphere, and it was developed in China during the Ch'ing dynasty.

sanger, var. SUNGAR in Dict. and Suppl.

Sängerfest (se·ŋəɹfest). *U.S.* Also **Saengerfest**, *erron.* **Sangfest.** [a. Ger. *sängerfest*, f. *sänger* singer + *fest* *FEST.] A choral festival.

1865 *Harper's Weekly* 5 Aug. 490/2 Arrangements were made for the Saengerfest, which will be celebrated at Philadelphia in 1867. **1903** *Forest & Stream* 24 Jan. 78 It is thought that the event will attract several hundred shooters from all over the United States, as the Saengerfest will be in progress here the week of the shoot. **1950** 'D. DIVINE' *King of Fassarai* xxvii. 241 They've got a *Sangfest* on down at the *falu*... Teresa's leading the choir. **1966** *Amer. Speech* XLI. 13 In 1853 the first *Sängerfest* took place in New Braunfels [Texas], at which singing societies from neighboring towns participated. Several *Sängerfests* still take place annually.

‖ **sangha** (sa·ŋa). *Buddhism.* Also 9 **Thanga**; **samgha** and with capital initial. [Hind. *saṅgha*, Skr. *saṃgha*, f. *sam* together + *han* to come in contact.] The community or order of monks. Also *transf.*

1858 P. BIGANDET *Life or Legend of Gaudama* 234 The Budhist Religious constitute the Thanga, or assembly of the Perfect. They are the strict followers of Budha. **1876** *Encycl. Brit.* IV. 429/2 The Sangha, or Society, as Buddha's order of mendicants was called. **1921** C. ELIOT *Hinduism & Buddhism* III. xxxvi. 71 The Sangha has always shown a laudable reserve in interfering directly with politics... In 1886, when the British annexed Burma, the Head of the Sangha forbade monks to take part in the political strife. **1951** E. CONZE *Buddhism* ii. 53 The core of the Buddhist movement consisted of monks... The entire 'brotherhood' of monks and hermits is called the *Samgha*. The Samgha naturally always formed only a small minority of the Buddhist community. **1968** T. WOLFE *Electric Kool-Aid Acid Test* xxi. 292 Boise in that moment is in the tiny knot of Perfect Pranksters, the inner circle, ascending into the the *sangha* for good! **1978** C. HUMPHREYS *Both Sides of Circle* xii. 135 The adoption of Twelve Principles became my major Buddhist activity in Japan, and their later presentation to the Sanghas and leading Buddhists of Thailand, Burma and Ceylon was..my major interest in those countries.

sanglier. (Further examples.)

1805 J. SIBLEY *Let.* 10 Apr. in *Deb. Congress U.S.* (1852) 9th Congress 2 Sess. App. 1104 There were innumerable quantities of..deer, foxes, sangliers, or wild hogs [etc.]. **1842** W. TOLMIE *Jrnl.* 7 May in *Physician & Fur Trader* (1963) 356 The Sanglier or wild boar is still found there. **1896** C. M. YONGE *Release* II. xiii. 198 It is like having to do with a set of tame pigs..turned loose among the wild sangliers.

Sango (sæ·ŋgo). [Native name.] An African language of the Adamawa-Eastern group of the Niger—Congo family, *spec.* that pidginized version of Sango spoken as a lingua franca in the Central African Republic and elsewhere in central Africa.

1948 M. GUTHRIE *Classification Bantu Lang.* 74 Full classified list of the Bantu languages... Zone B... Group 10... B.14 Cira, i-(Saŋgo). **1955**, etc. [see *NGBANDI]. **1967** W. J. SAMARIN *Gram. of Sango* 17 Sango is a creolized language because it stands in somewhat the same relationship to vernacular Sango as Haitian Creole to French. **1971** B. MAFENI in J. Spencer *Eng. Lang. W. Afr.* 112 Pidgin languages have been known to develop in circumstances where no master–servant relationship existed between the groups in contact. Pidgin Sango, spoken in the Central African Republic, is a good example. **1977** C. F. & F. M. VOEGELIN *Classification & Index World's Lang.* 128 *Sango*,..a lingua franca..with many French and Bantu words.

Sangoan (sæŋgōᵘ·ăn), *a. Archæol.* [f. the place-name *Sango* Bay in Uganda + -AN.] Of, pertaining to, or designating a palæolithic culture in central Africa, roughly contemporary with the Mousterian culture in Europe, and the people and tools associated with it. Also *absol.*, this culture.

[**1924** *Man* XXIV. 169 The large tools of the Sango types..are now known to occur practically wherever extensive beds of quartzite crop out.] **1931** L. S. B. LEAKEY *Stone Age Cultures of Kenya Colony* x. 232 Kamasian pluvial. Sub-divisions unknown but may include Mr Wayland's Kafuan and Sangoan. **1952** *Geol. Survey Uganda Memoir* VI. II. 64 The typical Sangoan pick is an elongated steep-sided, double-ended implement with small flat dorsal and large ventral faces... The most finely finished product is somewhat canoe-like in shape. **1959** J. D. CLARK *Prehist. S. Afr.* ii. 40 The cultures of the First Intermediate period.. can be subdivided into two contemporary cultures—the Fauresmith and the Sangoan. **1969** *Geol. Survey Uganda Memoir* X. 87 The occurrence of tranchets and pressure flaked lances, together with mint-fresh, steeply flaked duck-head and other small hand axes..invites correlation with the latest Sangoan or upper Lupemban. **1977** G. CLARK *World Prehist.* (ed. 3) i. 34 The leading artefacts of the Sangoan continued to be bifacial, including core-axes, picks and narrow lanceolate forms.

Sangrado. (Earlier *fig.* example.)

1812 BYRON *Works* (1898) II. 429 After feeling the pulse and shaking the head over the patient, prescribing the usual course of warm water and bleeding—the warm water of your mawkish police, and the lancets of your military—these convulsions must terminate in death, the sure consummation..of all political Sangrados.

‖ **sangre azul** (sa·ŋgre aþū·l). [Sp.] The 'blue blood' of the old and aristocratic Spanish families (see note s.v. BLOOD *sb.* 8).

1834 [see BLOOD *sb.* 8]. **1846** F. FORD *Gatherings from Spain* xix. 259 *Sangre azul* is the ichor of demigods which flows in the arteries of the grandees. **1876** *Gentl. Mag.* Nov. 601 The sephardim..once contained the *sangre azul* of the nation. **1975** H. MCCLOY *Minotaur Country* vii. 74 Carlos.. was the embodiment of *sangré azul*.

Sangria (sæŋgrī·ă). Also **sangría.** [a. Sp. *sangría* (see SANGAREE).] A cold drink of Spanish origin composed of red wine variously diluted and sweetened.

1961 'J. WELCOME' *Beware of Midnight* x. 119 Hugo ordered a dry Martini for himself and a jug of *Sangria* for the others..'It's a sort of Spanish Pimms.' **1966** *House & Garden* Dec. 79/3 Visitors to Spain soon become familiar with sangría—the national iced wine cup. The simplest form consists of slices of fruit..soaked in a rough Spanish red wine and with a little water..and ice added. **1972** D. LEES *Zodiac* 107, I ordered a pitcher of sangria to go with the couscous. **1978** *Times* 23 Apr. 12/8 There was time for a glass of the house Sangria (a sweet wine tasting of Cherry-ade).

sangsara, var. *SAMSARA.

sanguinaria. For 'mod. L.' in etym. read 'mod. L. (J. J. Dillenius in Linnæus *Systema Naturæ* (1735))' and add earlier example.

1808 [see *Jersey tea* s.v. *JERSEY[2]].

sanguinary, *a.* (and *sb.*) ¶ **4.** (Examples.)

1890 KIPLING in *Macm. Mag.* LXI. 155/1 This is sanguinary. This is unusual sanguinary. Sort o' mad country. **1891** —— *Lett. of Marque* xv. 110 'Eres this sanguinary down mail a stickin' in the eye of the Khundwa down! **1910** G. B. SHAW *Lett. to Granville Barker* (1956) 168 The inhabitants raise up their voices and call one another sanguinary liars. **1942** *Tee Emm* (Air Ministry) II. 131 Lovely crate, but lousy on the approach with that sanguinary great nose sticking up in front of you.

sanguine, *a.* and *sb.* Add: **A.** *adj.* **5.** *sanguine-flowered* adj.

1922 JOYCE *Ulysses* 44 His fustian shirt, sanguine-flowered, trembles its Spanish tassels at his secrets.

sanguinity. 2. (Later example.)

1979 *Time* 8 Jan. 72/2 Nevertheless, Lasch, a history professor.., legitimately finds cracks of doom in our sanguinity.

sanhita, var. *SAMHITA. **Sanhiwal**, var. *SAHIWAL.

‖ **san hsien** (san ʃyen). *Mus.* Also 9 **san heen, hien; san-hsien.** [Chinese *sānxián*, f. *sān* three + *xián* string of musical instrument.] A Chinese three-stringed plucked instrument with a long neck and oval-shaped body. Cf. SAMISEN.

1839 *Chinese Repository* May 43 The *san heēn*. Three-stringed guitar... The *san heēn* is played as an accompaniment to the *pepa*, as its sounds are low and dull. **1848** S. W. WILLIAMS *Middle Kingdom* II. xvi. 169 The *san hien*, or three stringed guitar, resembles a rebeck in its contour. **1874** *Jrnl. North-China Branch R. Asiatic Soc.* VIII. 115 The *San-hsien* is usually played as an accompaniment to the *P'i-p'a*, its sound being low, and dull, and deficient in character. **1917** *Encycl. Sinica* 388/2 Hsien tzû or San hsien is a three-stringed instrument with a small oval body covered above and below with snake-skin, and a neck about thirty inches long. There are no frets. It is played with a plectrum of jade. **1933** N. WALN *House of Exile* 204 An orchestra..played serpent-bellied *san hsien*. **1954** *Folk Arts of New China* 34 Before he came to Peking, the blind minstrel Han Chi-hsiang, as he frankly admitted, was somewhat complacent about his technique on the *san hsien* (a Chinese three-stringed musical instrument). **1975** C. P. MACKERRAS *Chinese Theatre in Mod. Times* 22 The other principal plucked instruments are the *yüeh-ch'in* and the *san-hsien*, both of which function as secondary accompanying instruments in many dramatic styles... The name *san-hsien* means 'three strings'... It produces a characteristic twanging sound.

Sanibin (sæ·nibin). Also **Sani-bin** and with small initial. [f. SANI(TARY *a.* + BIN *sb.*] The proprietary name of a receptacle for refuse.

1921 *Trade Marks Jrnl.* 16 Mar. 550 Sanibin. 411,006. Bins and the like Receptacles... Robert Bailey and Son Limited,..Stockport, Cheshire; Manufacturers of Surgical Dressings. **1963** *Spectator* 1 Mar. 273/2 Cosi-jade sanibins. **1966** A. E. LINDOP *I start Counting* xviii. 219 Under the sink where he kept the Sani-bin. **1975** *Listener* 25 Dec. 879/1 A blaze in one of the downstairs sani-bins.

sanidinite. (Examples.)

1887 *Mineral. Mag.* VII. 227 The blocks of sanidinite and laacher-trachyte occur of all sizes up to masses measuring two feet in diameter... The sanidinite consists principally of sanidine, or of sanidine and nosean. **1916** J. A. THOMSON in David & Priestley *Brit. Antarctic Exped. 1907–9: Geol.* II. 139 Trachytes appear to have the power of converting inclusions of such rocks as older trachytes, gneisses and granulites into sanidinites. **1962** *N.Z. Jrnl. Geol. & Geophysics* V. 395 The finest examples of sanidinites..were obtained from a zone of yellowish-green glass, in some places as much as half an inch in thickness, formed at the contact between porcellanite and overlying basalt.

sanification (sænifikē̆ⁱ·ʃən). *rare.* [f. SANIFY *v.*: see -FICATION.] The action or process of making healthy.

1895 W. JAMES *Let.* 16 June (1920) II. 21 Just about to get a little health into me, a little simplification and solidification and purification and sanification.

Sanio (sæ·nio). *Bot.* The name of Gustav *Sanio* (1832–91), German botanist. † **a.** [First designated, as *Sanio'sche balken*, by C. Müller 1890, in *Ber. d. Deutsch. Bot. Ges.* VIII. 23.] Used in the possessive and with *of* to designate a thickening of the primary wall or medial lamella separating or inclosing pits in wood, esp. of the radial walls of tracheides in gymnosperms. *Obs.*

1891 *Jrnl. R. Microsc. Soc.* 488 'Sanio's Bands' in the Coniferæ.—By this term (*Sanioische Balken*) Herr C. Müller proposes to designate the beams or thickenings commonly found in the xylem-elements, chiefly in the tracheids of Coniferæ. **1915** *Jrnl. Linn. Soc.: Bot.* XLI. 462 All the Indian species of *Pinus* show Sanio's rims. **1916** *Ann. Bot.* XXX. 425 Sanio's bars are small rods crossing the tracheides, cambium, and phloem elements in many conifers. **1920** *Bot. Gaz.* LXX. 431 Considerable importance was attached for some years to the presence or absence of 'bars' or 'rims' of Sanio. **1935** C. J. CHAMBERLAIN *Gymnosperms* xi. 245 A cytological study of the origin and development of the bordered pit and the bars and rims of Sanio would be interesting.

b. *Sanio's law*: any of a set of empirical results that describe the growth of tracheides in conifers.

1903 MUDGE & MASLEN *Class-bk. Bot.* ii. 51 It follows rom Sanio's law that the elements of the phloem and xylem, unless subjected to subsequent disturbances, should be arranged in radial rows. **1915** BAILEY & SHEPARD in *Bot. Gaz.* LX. 66 (*heading*) Sanio's laws for the variation in size of coniferous tracheids. *Ibid.* 70 It is evident from Table V that Sanio's second law is applicable to *Picea rubens* as well as to *Pinus sylvestris*. **1961** *Forestry* XXXIV. 125 The foundation of the study of tracheid and fibre-length variation was laid by Sanio (1872) who presented his results of studies on Scots pine (*Pinus sylvestris*) in a set of five conclusions which, for some time now, have been regarded as 'Sanio's Laws'. **1975** S. CARLQUIST *Ecol. Strategies of Xylem Evol.* 5 The variations noted in Sanio's laws have been confirmed for a number of conifers and dicotyledons.

‖ **sanitar** (sænitā·ɹ). [Russ.] In Russia, a hospital attendant; *spec.* a medical orderly in the army.

1916 H. WALPOLE *Dark Forest* I. i. 33 Then I came to Petrograd and through the English Embassy found a place in one of the hospitals, where I worked as a sanitar for three months. **1927** —— in *Daily Express* 21 Dec. 8/6 He was my servant during part of 1915, when I was a sanitar in the Russian army. **1933** —— *Vanessa* IV. 674 The sanitars began to dig a grave. **1974** F. FARMBOROUGH *Nurse at Russian Front* II. 30 The 1st *Letuchka*, (Flying Column).. was staffed with four surgical sisters,..two doctors,..about 30 *sanitars* (ambulance orderlies) and an officer.

sanitarian, *sb.* and *a.* Add: **A.** *sb.* **b.** *U.S.* A public health officer.

1946 *Richmond* (Va.) *News* 20 Mar. 4/2 A field trip to observe high-temperature, short-time pasteurization was one of the high-lights today of the closing session of the Virginia Association of Milk Sanitarians. **1974** *Index-Jrnl.* (Greenwood, S. Carolina) 23 Apr. 12/1 J. D. Kirby, chief sanitarian with the health department, said the vaccine is 'the safest, most reliable yet perfected and is specified by the Public Health Services'. **1976** *National Observer* (U.S.) 23 Oct. 10/2 The boss is Dale Reeves, senior public-health sanitarian and head of the consumer-protection program.

sanitary, *a.* Add: **1. a.** Also *sanitary reform, reformer.*

1850 C. KINGSLEY *Alton Locke* I. i. 4 A sanitary reformer would not be long in guessing the cause of my unhealthiness. **1857** —— *Two Years Ago* II. iv. 68 Sanitary reform is thrust out of sight, simply because its necessity is too humiliating to the pride of all. **1884** *Times* 4 Oct. 4/5 Dr Jaeger's sanitary woollen system has been adopted by some of our most eminent sanitary reformers. **1966** N. LONGMATE *King Cholera* xi. 112 The sanitary reformer triumphed over the cleric: the churches were shut for one whole Sunday. **1974** H. R. F. KEATING *Underside* iv. 41 There's an immense amount to be done in sanitary reform.

b. (Further examples.)

1877 T. L. NICHOLS *Herald of Health Almanack* 21 (Advt.), O for the muse of Dryden, or of Pope To hymn thy praises, *Sanitary Soap*! **1934** A. HUXLEY *Beyond Mexique Bay* 2 The last word in cocktail bars and peach-pink sanitary fittings. **1940** *Chambers's Techn. Dict.* 740/1 *Sanitary ware*, ..glazed earthenware used for some sanitary fittings. **1977** *Times* 30 July 10/4 Plain colours..in bath and sanitary ware.

2. Delete small-type note and add further example.

1861 TROLLOPE *Orley F.* (1862) I. xxxi. 229 The judge, though he rode everyday on sanitary considerations, had not a sportsman's celerity in leaving and recovering his saddle.

3. Special collocations: **sanitary belt**, a belt to which a sanitary towel is attached; **Sanitary Commission** *U.S. Hist.*, one of various commissions established to supervise matters of health and sanitation, *spec.* that set up by the U.S. government in 1861 to care for soldiers and their dependants during the Civil War; **sanitary engineer**, one whose profession is the design, construction, or maintenance of sanitary appliances or sewerage; a plumber; hence **sanitary engineering**; **sanitary inspector**, an officer appointed to inspect sanitary conditions, a public health inspector; **sanitary napkin** (*U.S.*), **pad, towel,** a pad worn by women to absorb menstrual flow.

1908 *Sears, Roebuck Catal.* 998/2 The EZ Sanitary Belt.. fits the body so smoothly that it is not felt when either worn over or under garments. **1969** B. MALAMUD *Pictures of Fidelman* ii. 55 He trotted to get her anything she had run out of—drawing pencil, sanitary belt, safety pins. **1861** *N.Y. Times* 25 June 4/4 A week ago we noticed the formation in Washington of the Sanitary Commission for the volunteers, and its approval by the Army Medical Bureau and by the Government. **1898** *Kansas City* (Missouri) *Star* 19 Dec. 2/5 The sanitary commission's work can all be done by a state veterinarian. **1949** J. B. HERRICK *Mem. 80 Yrs.* 1 A clearer war memory is that of the fair of the Sanitary Commission, held in Chicago in the summer of 1865. **1873** B. LATHAM *Sanitary Engin.* Pref., The whole range of works in which the Sanitary Engineer is engaged. **1901** *Daily Colonist* (Victoria, B.C.) 5 Oct. 6/2 The septic tank system of sewerage..is highly recommended by some of the most eminent sanitary engineers in Europe and America. **1974** 'M. YORKE' *Mortal Remains* v. iv. 156 Her grandfather had been a sanitary engineer, making lavatory basins. **1868** B. LATHAM (*title*) Inaugural address..before the Society [of Engineers]..upon..the results of sanitary engineering. **1957** *Encycl. Brit.* XVIII. 740/2 A barrister by profession, he [*sc.* Edwin Chadwick] mastered the elements of sanitary engineering, then a little-understood science. **1863** *Times* 24 June 7/5 We shall leave it to the report of the sanitary inspector... He was astonished..to find the rooms so nice and clean. **1897** *Act* 60 & 61 *Vict.* c. 38 The expression 'sanitary inspector' means a sanitary inspector appointed by the local authority. **1907** *Nature* 21 Feb. 400/1 Among the recommendations are..the provision of an expert staff of inspectors under the medical officer, whose title shall be altered from that of 'Inspector of Nuisances' to 'Sanitary Inspector'. **1943** *Our Towns* (Women's Group on Public Welfare) iii. 88 A Sanitary Inspector gave evidence that the majority of houses have outside W.C.'s only. **1956** *Act* 4 & 5 *Eliz. II* c. 66 § 1 Sanitary inspectors appointed under the local Government Act, 1933, or the London Government Act, 1939, shall henceforth be designated public health inspectors. **1977** *Lancashire Life* Dec. 92/3 Not only did Christopher become Burnley's first fire brigade chief and first sanitary inspector. **1917** W. J. ROBINSON *Sex Knowledge for Women & Girls* vi. 45 Menstrual blood.. is discharged from the uterus..to the outside, where it is caught on cotton, sanitary napkins or some other pad. **1975** D. RAMSAY *Descent into Dark* 74 She had experienced no traumas over the change from sanitary napkins to tampons. **1926** *Daily Colonist* (Victoria, B.C.) 2 Jan. 7/7 (Advt.), The hazards of the old-time sanitary pad have been supplanted with a protection both absolute and exquisite. **1974** *Times* 27 Apr. 1/6 One [line]..will always have to be sold cheaply.. denture powder, sanitary pads and tampons, nappies. **1881** *Trans. Obstetr. Soc.* XXII. 188 Dr. Galabin showed the new ladies' sanitary towels manufactured by Messrs. Southall, Barclay, & Co., of Birmingham. They were extremely light and soft, and contained a pad of absorbent cotton wool. **1896** *Eng. Illustr. Mag.* Aug. 8/2 (Advt.), Ladies will find the use of Southalls' Sanitary Towels in assorted sizes to be a great convenience and a great saving. **1917** *Lancet* 28 July 145/2 (*heading*) The destruction of sanitary towels and surgical dressings. *a* **1935** T. E. LAWRENCE *Lett.* (1938) 503 You'd think they'd have had some other place for their sanitary towels. **1977** B. FREEMANTLE *Charlie Muffin* iii. 33 On the wall..there was still a white outline where the sanitary-towel dispenser had been.

sanitation. Add: **1.** Also *spec.* (the provision of) toilet facilities.

1901 V. BETHELL *Monte Carlo Anecdotes* p. xii (Advt.), *Hotel Metropole...* Sumptuous private suites, excellent cuisine, perfect sanitation. **1934** M. V. HUGHES *London Child* x. 117 Sanitation was not known at Reskadinnick, neither earth nor water nor any such thing.

2. In *Comb.*, designating a person or vehicle employed in the removal and disposal of domestic refuse, as *sanitation man, truck, van* (*U.S.*).

1939 *N.Y. Times* 16 Sept. 19/2 Sweepers and drivers..will be known as 'sanitation men'. **1975** *New Yorker* 8 Sept. 111/1 The city paid the sanitationmen $713,500 at time-and-a-half rates to clean up the debris that had accumulated because the strikers had refused to collect it. **1958** *N.Y. Times* 18 Nov. 26/6 'Some kind of job action' by the crews of sanitation trucks can be expected. **1974** *Anderson* (S. Carolina) *Independent* 23 Apr. 3B/4 Among the critically hurt was a crewman on a sanitation truck that happened to be picking up refuse at the..building. **1973** *Times* 27 Aug. 5/7 My wife explained that this caper was weightier than that by defining dust cart as Garbage truck, or, in Current American, sanitation van.

sanitize, *v.* Delete *rare* and add: **1.** (Further examples.)

1950 C. A. LAWRENCE *Surface-Active Quaternary Ammonium Germicides* vi. 90 It can be said that dishes are sanitized by adequate cleaning. **1968** *National Observer* (U.S.) 22 Apr., His demand: an injunction directing the companies to sanitize their smoke or close down. **1971** *Listener* 11 Nov. 659 Air-conditioning sanitises the air. **1978** *Detroit Free Press* 5 Mar. 20/2 (Advt.), This formula permanently and completely removes urine and sanitizes your carpet.

2. *transf.* and *fig.*, esp. (*U.S. slang*) to render more acceptable, clean up, as by the removal of undesirable, improper, or confidential material.

1934 *N.Y. Times* 7 July 2/4 New words are being manufactured at NRA's code factory... Leon Henderson, economic adviser, has just turned out two which may some day find their way to dictionaries. 'Sanitize' is one. Mr. Henderson says it means putting 'sanity and sanitation in business'. **1966** *Amer. Speech* XLI. 300 After it [*sc.* a document] has been *sanitized*, or redrafted to remove the secret information. **1974** *News & Courier* (Charleston, S. Carolina) 28 Apr. A–10/4 Aides claim the transcripts are accurate, but they have been 'sanitized' to delete Nixon's profanity and character slurs spoken in confidence. **1977** *Rolling Stone* 13 Jan. 38/1 The Congressional Joint Committee on Atomic Energy reacted to the criticism by trying to sanitize the report. **1978** *Listener* 30 Mar. 394/3 The language of the Pentagon is designed (if I may use an Americanism) to sanitise disagreeable realities and disreputable motives. **1978** *Guardian Weekly* 27 Aug. 15/4 NBC also has said that the rape scene was essential to the film's artistic integrity, although the network sanitized the scene after the furor created by the initial showing. **1980** *Times Lit. Suppl.* 7 Nov. 1258/4 A writer has no duty to sanitize his imagination; if defilement is what Potter most wants to write about, write about it he should. But..we do not have to like the taste of greasy hamburger.

Hence **sa·nitized** *ppl. a.*

1950 C. A. LAWRENCE *Surface-Active Quaternary Ammonium Germicides* vi. 93 In those tests in which the number of bacteria did not exceed 100 per swab, the glasses were considered adequately sanitized regardless of the chemical agent used. **1970** *Nature* 17 Oct. 203/2 The commission found no consensus..that explicit sexual materials (the commission's sanitized word for 'pornography') should be banned. **1973** *Ibid.* 5 Oct. 231/1 The 'sanitised' transcripts of the proceedings have contained virtually no discussion of the possible implications of the programme. **1973** *Philadelphia Inquirer* (Today Suppl.) 7 Oct. 44/2 The towels are in place, the bed's made, even the 'sanitized' slip is still over the toilet. **1977** N. FREELING *Gadget* IV. 173 A hotel with..sanitized lavatory seats. **1979** G. ROBERTSON *Obscenity* 274 The press published the original text, juxtaposed with the sanitised version prepared by the Corporation, after the director and dramatist had publicly protested against 'this new and Orwellian form of political censorship'.

sanitizer (sæ·nitəizəɹ). [f. SANITIZE *v.* + -ER[1].] A substance which sanitizes: a disinfectant, or a preservative of food.

1950 *Jrnl. Milk & Food Technol.* XIII. 63/2 The most recent trend has been toward the use of the quaternary ammonium detergent sanitizer. **1968** SHAFFER & STUART in Lawrence & Block *Disinfection, Sterilization & Preservation* x. 160/1 Acceptances of chemicals as sanitizers have been based in the past on tests conducted under conditions of actual use. **1979** *Nature* 19 Apr. p. xvii/1 The Brentchem range of 14 specifically developed detergents, sanitisers and ancillary products for use in laboratories has been recently improved.

San Joaquin (sæn wǫkī·n). [The name of a river in southern California.] *San Joaquin Valley fever*: = *COCCIDIOIDOMYCOSIS.

1958 *New Biol.* XXVII. 65 [Coccidioidomycosis] was originally known as the San Joaquin Valley fever from the part of California with which fatalities from the disease were associated. **1974** M. C. GERALD *Pharmacol.* xxvi. 450 (*table*) *Coccidioides*—San Joaquin Valley fever.

Sanka (sæ·ŋkă). Chiefly *U.S.* [Repr. abbrev. form of F. *sans caffeine* without caffeine.] The proprietary name of a make of decaffeinated coffee.

1923 *Official Gaz.* (U.S. Patent Office) 14 Aug. 251/1 Société Anonyme Fabriques de Produits de Chimie Organique de Laire, Issy, France... *Sanka*... Teas and coffees; tea and coffee extracts, both dry and liquid, and tea and coffee substitutes. Claims use since Mar. 19, 1910. **1933** *Ibid.* 18 Oct. 642/1 Sanka Coffee Corporation, New York... *Sanka.* For coffees. **1952** *Trade Marks Jrnl.* 17 Dec. 1176/1 *Sanka*... Coffee. General Foods Corporation.., New York. **1964** H. CAMPBELL *Why did They name It...?* 10 Dr. Roselius named the new product *Sanka*—a contraction of the French phrase *sans caffeine*. **1975** *New Yorker* 26 May 28/1 For breakfast, he ordered orange juice, a boiled egg (five minutes), toast and Sanka. **1978** G. VIDAL *Kalki* viii. 192 Giles served Jason Scotch. Prager asked for Sanka. 'I have an ulcer,' he said.

‖ **Sankaracharya** (ʃaŋkarātʃā·riă). Also **sankaracharya.** [Skr.] The name and title of Sankara Acharya, a famous teacher of Vedānta philosophy (prob. of the eighth century A.D.), used as the title of one of various Indian religious teachers and leaders.

1947 K. M. PANNIKAR *Survey of Indian Hist.* xii. 133 Soon, however, especially after the disappearance of Buddhism, the Mutts became centres of luxury like the great abbeys and the Sankaracharyas who presided over them assumed pontifical dignities. **1960** KOESTLER *Lotus & Robot* i. 54 The nearest to an authoritative position..was attributed to the five Sankaracharyas, leaders of an important Traditionalist sect. **1969** *Cultural News from India* Nov. 43 The annual *Agama Silpa Vidwat Sadas* inaugurated a few years ago by the Sankaracharya of Kanchi Kamakoti Peetam bids fair to be an event of increasing importance and to establish a wholesome tradition. **1977** *Times* 20 Jan. 6/8 India's mass spectacle of faith during the Kumbh Mela Fair started before dawn... Many sages—sankaracharayas, nahatmas [*sic*] and guru—rode on elephants or in chariots.

Sankhya (sā·ŋkiă). Forms: 8–9 **Sanchya**; 9– **Sankhya, Samkhya.** [Skr. *sāṃkhya*, lit. = relating to number, prob. referring to the 'enumeration' of the twenty-five principles of the philosophy.] One of the six orthodox systems of Hindu philosophy, based on a dualism of matter and soul.

1788 G. CAUL in *Asiatick Researches* I. 344 Both these works contain a studied and accurate enumeration of natural bodies and their principles; whence this philosophy is named Sánc'hya. **1808** H. T. COLEBROOKE *Amarasimha's Cósha; or, Dict. Sanskrit Lang.* III. iv. § xxvi, The third quality, according to the Sán'chya system of philosophy: darkness or illusion, contrasted to truth and passion. **1838** *Penny Cycl.* XII. 234/1 The *Sánkhya* system of philosophy.. maintains that true knowledge can alone secure perfect deliverance from evil. **1877** MONIER WILLIAMS *Hinduism* 193 The Sānkhya philosophy, founded by a sage named Kapila, though probably prior in date, is generally studied next to the Nyāya, and is more categorically dualistic. **1934** J. BAILLIE *And Life Everlasting* v. 117 In opposition to such monism, arose the dualistic Sankhya system. According to this teaching human souls are not all united in one impersonal *atman*, but exist separately, each in its own right. **1957** *Encycl. Brit.* XII. 251/1 The *Sāmkhya* is a reaction against the idealistic monism of the Upanishads. It believes in a real matter and an infinite plurality of individual souls which are not emanations of a single world-soul. **1959** *Listener* 17 Sept. 431/2 This [religion] again has resemblances to Brāhmanism and to Sānkhya. **1977** J. HEWITT *Yoga & Meditation* iii. 19 Yoga borrows extensively from the Samkhya (or Sankhya) system.

San Luiseño: see *LUISEÑO.

sanmartinite (sænmā·ɹtinəit). *Min.* [f. *San Martin*, name of a town in San Luis Province, Argentina + -ITE[1].] Monoclinic zinc tungstate, $ZnWO_4$, usu. also containing some iron, calcium, and manganese, found as dark brown microcrystalline aggregates in quartz, in association with scheelite.

1948 ANGELELLI & GORDON in *Notulae Naturae* (Acad. Nat. Sci. Philadelphia) 9 Apr. 1 (*heading*) Sanmartinite, a new zinc tungstate from Argentina. *Ibid.* 2 While usually compact, the sanmartinite may be quite porous, and in color varying from dark brown to dark gray depending upon the amount of admixed scheelite. **1968** I. KOSTOV *Mineral.* 483 Sanmartinite is a zincian member $(Zn,Fe)WO_4$, containing about 18% ZnO.

sannyasi. Now the most usual form of SUNNYASEE, SUNNYASI in Dict. and Suppl.

Sanocrysin (sē[i]nokrəi·sin). *Pharm.* Also sano-, -chrysin. [a. Da. *sanocrysin*, irreg. f. L. *sān-us* healthy, SANE + -O + Gr. *χρυσ-ός* gold + *-in* -IN[1].] A colourless crystalline complex salt of gold, sodium (dithiosulphato)-aurate(I), $Na_3[Au(S_2O_3)_2].2H_2O$, formerly used in the treatment of tuberculosis.

A proprietary term in the U.S.

1924 H. MØLLGAARD *Chemotherapy of Tuberculosis* ii. 24 The compound built by this synthesis is registered under the name: Sanocrysin. **1924** *Brit. Med. Jrnl.* 8 Nov. 870/2 Arrangements have been made for producing it in bulk in Denmark under the name 'sanocrysin'. **1925** *Official Gaz.* (U.S. Patent Office) 10 Mar. 255/1 *Sanocrysin*... Medicine for phthisis. Claims use since Mar. 16, 1924. **1926** D. MASTERS *How to conquer Consumption* 103 Möllgaard's treatment is generally referred to..as the 'gold treatment', because it consists of a metallic compound of gold, which the discoverer has named 'sanocrysin'. **1929** *Daily Express* 7 Jan. 4 In the treatment of consumption..by sanochrysin. **1943** *Thorpe's Dict. Appl. Chem.* (ed. 4) VI. 117/2 Sodium aurothiosulphate..has been of considerable interest since 1924 when it was introduced..under the name 'Sanocrysin' for the treatment of tuberculosis. **1965** *Biochem. Pharmacol.* XIV. 1174 Gold sodium thiosulphate ('Sanochrysin'), Platinum Chemicals Ltd., Asbury Park, N.J., U.S.A.

‖**sanpaku** (sanpa·ku). [Jap., lit. 'three white', f. *san* three + *haku* white.] Visibility of the white of the eye below the iris, as well as on either side. Also *attrib.* or as *adj.*

1963 *N.Y. Herald Tribune* 18 Aug. 23/1 George Ohsawa, the Japanese philosopher and prophet of the Unique Principle walked through the streets of New York yesterday... There were many beautiful girls... But so many *sanpaku*. **1964** T. WOLFE in *N.Y. Herald Sunday Mag.* 12 Jan. 15/2 Abdul Karim Kassem, President Ngo Dinh Diem and President Kennedy; all *sanpaku* and, now, all shot to death, all destroyed by the fate of the *sanpaku*. **1965** W. DUFTY tr. *Sakurazawa Nyoiti's Macrobiotics* (1972) 60 Any sign of sanpaku meant that a man's entire system—physical, physiological and spiritual—was out of balance. **1970** W. BURROUGHS JR. *Speed* 162 Had I had a rose, I'd have held it in my teeth all morning with sanpaku eyeballs.

San Pellegrino (sæn pelegri·no). The name of a village in Lombardy, used *attrib.* and *absol.* to designate a mineral water obtained from springs there; a bottle or glassful of this water.

1924 W. STORMONT *Summer in Italy* (ed. 2) 174 The following is an abridged classification of the principal waters:.. Affections of the Stomach and Intestines: Agnano,..San Pellegrino, Telese. **1953** G. COOPER *Your Holiday in Italy* (ed. 2) II. 49 Mineral waters *aranciata* (made from oranges—ask for 'San Pellegrino'). **1964** H. ROSE *Your Guide to N. Italy* II. 94 San Pellegrino mineral water is mentioned in historical literature as early as the twelfth century. **1965** 'W. HAGGARD' *Hard Sell* xi. 116 To drink?... A bottle of Recoardo. No Recoardo? Then San Pellegrino. **1971** M. MCCARTHY *Birds of Amer.* 283 He had had noodles, a salad, and a small San Pellegrino. **1981** R. THOMAS *Mordida Man* xxviii. 242 In front of Abedsaid was a small bottle of San Pellegrino mineral water.

sanpi, var. *SAMPI.

sans, *sb.* Add: Also **Sans** (esp. as the proper name of particular type-faces). (Examples.)

1927 A. J. WATKINS *Advertisement Lay-Out & Copy-Writing* 116/2 *Serifs*,..not present on block letters or sans type. **1932** H. A. MADDOX *Printing* (ed. 2) iii. 40 (*caption*) Sans-serif (Gill Sans in light, medium, and bold). **1959** O. MILLS *Stairway to Murder* ii. 16 Brash cardboard notices in harsh Sans letters. **1966** BERRY & POOLE *Annals Printing* 208/1 Modern sans include Futura (1927), Cable (1927), [etc.]. **1969** J. WAINWRIGHT *Big Tickle* 124 The double-column headline was in Sans Heavy Italic. **1978** *Antiques & Art Monitor* 28 Oct. 19/2 The result was a series of type-faces, 'Perpetua' and 'Sans', which remain some of the noblest and least fussy in the world.

sans, *prep.* Add: **1.** Freq. *joc.* (Further examples.)

1901 G. B. SHAW *Admirable Bashville* III. 324 And my blows unpaid, Sans stakes, sans victory, sans everything I had hoped to win. **1922** L. STRACHEY *Let.* 6 Feb. in *Let.: V. Woolf & L. Strachey* (1956) 97, I am sans eyes, sans teeth, sans prick, sans..but after that there can be no more sanses. **1929** *Oxford Poetry* 45 Here, foundling and cheat, my Lord Parvenu suns His armorial lie, sans remorse and sans pother. **1942** *Tee Emm* (Air Ministry) II. 78 *Sans* rank, *sans* aircraft, *sans* everything to show off about, he'll be just a foolish little figure. **1970** *Nature* 28 Feb. 781/2 The specimen, though sans its right hind paddle, is a fine example of *Ichthyosaurus platyodon* (Conybeare). **1975** *Publishers Weekly* 18 Aug. 58/2, 75 relevant illustrations sans razzle-dazzle. **1977** *Rolling Stone* 30 June 68/1 It offers anxiety enough for the Rhodesians themselves, ..to face the prospect of starting life afresh in some harsher, colder country, sans servants, sans swimming pool, sans sunshine, sans supremacy. **1979** A. HAILEY *Overlord* III. i. 196 The result was a high-quality recording, sans commercials, which the adults and other families watched later at their leisure.

2. a. sans blague, you don't say! I don't believe it!; **sans dire**, without saying anything, without mentioning (something specified); **sans doute**, doubtless, no doubt; **sans-pareil**, restrict † to subst. use in Dict. and add: (*b*) (as two words) unique, unequalled; **sans phrase**, (further examples); also, without exceptions or qualifications; **sans recours** (Law) [cf. RECOURSE *sb.*[1] 4 b], 'without recourse (to me)', an endorsement on a bill of exchange absolving the endorser or any other party from liability as such party; **sans-souciant** *a. rare*, carefree, unworried.

1922 JOYCE *Ulysses* 398 A drenching of that violence, he tells me, *sans blague*, has sent more than one luckless fellow in good earnest posthaste to another world. **1967** *New Yorker* 25 Feb. 39/1 *Aristide*..I happen to be only forty-four. *Auto-coiffeur. Sans blague?* I would have put you at twice that age. **1881** TROLLOPE *Ayala's Angel* II. xxviii. 68 I ain't. You might as well let that accident pass, sans dire. **1890** E. DOWSON *Let.* 17 June (1967) 154 *Sans doute* you know your way by this time. **1918** 'K. MANSFIELD' *Let.* 11 Jan. (1977) 90 A pimp getting in [a train] to hold a seat for some super-pimp gave me such a blow in the chest that it is blue today. I thought: 'This is Marseilles, *sans doute*.' **1962** *John o' London's* 20 Sept. 287/1 This conducted tour..must be quite *sans pareil* for..candour. **1885** *Encycl. Brit.* XVIII. 793/2 This study gives us the science of empirical psychology, or, as it is now termed, psychology *sans phrase*. **1919** D. RUSSELL *Let.* Nov. in *Tamarisk Tree* (1975) v. 78, I got him to accept sans phrase for the moment. **1956** *Ann. Reg. 1955* 8 If they chose to expel him, he would become Independent *sans phrase*. **1961** J. WILSON *Reason & Morals* iii. 161 Thus we might say (almost *sans phrase*, as some early Christian authorities did) 'sex is bad'. **1976** *Times Lit. Suppl.* 26 Mar. 337/1 A. J. P. Taylor is the representative historian of our century... He is a historian *sans phrase*, not a man using history as the vehicle for other gifts. **1874** J. B. BYLES *Treat. Law Bills of Exchange* (ed. 11) v. 38 A safe and proper mode in which an agent may indorse, so as to avoid personal responsibility, is by adding the words, *sans recours* or *without recourse to me*. **1974** D. W. FIDDES *Business Terms, Phr. & Abbrev.* (ed. 14) 184 Sans recours is a phrase used in the endorsement of bills and notes. When an endorser wishes to free himself of responsibility, he adds the words *Sans Recours*, or *Without recourse to me*. **1826** W. SCOTT *Jrnl.* 10 Mar. (1972) 109, I have in my odd sans souciant character a good handful of meal from the grist of the Jolly Miller who—once Dwelld on the river dee.

‖**sansa** (sæ·nsa). Also **sanse, zanza, zanze.** [Marungu (Bantu), ad. Arab. *ṣanj*, Pers. *sinj* cymbals.] An African musical instrument consisting of a wooden box having at the top tongues of bamboo or iron which the performer vibrates with his thumb and fore-fingers. Cf. **Kaffir piano*, *MARIMBA.

1864 C. ENGEL *Music Most Anc. Nations* 14 Nos. 4, 5, and 6 show the notes of three *zanzes*. **1874** —— *Descr. Catal. Musical Instruments S. Kensington Museum* (ed. 2) 297 The *zanze*, or sansa, is to be found principally among the Negro tribes of upper and lower Guinea. **1876** STAINER & BARRETT *Dict. Mus. Terms, Zanze*... Known also by the names of mambira, ambira, marimba, ibeka, vissandschi, in different parts of Africa. **1909** *Cent. Dict. Suppl.*, Sanse. **1929** *N. & Q. Anthropol.* (ed. 5) II. 299 The 'musical-box' is an elaborated mechanical analogue of the *sansa*. **1970** *Guardian* 24 Apr. 9/1 They improvise together on the xylophone, sansas (thumb pianos), guitar, or piano. **1975** S. MARCUSE *Mus. Instruments* (rev. ed.) 455/1 *Sansa*, linguaphone consisting of tuned metal or split-cane tongues fitted to a wooden board or resonator, so that one end of the lamellae can vibrate freely. *Sansa* is the name of the linguaphone among the Marungu people of the Congo; by extension it has come to be used in a generic sense for all similar instr[ument]s.

sanscara, var. *SAMSKARA.

sansculotte. 1. (Earlier and later *gen.* examples.)

1794 LD. TORRINGTON *Diary* 5 May (1938) IV. 10 Nor do I hope to live to see the Sans Culottes of this land laying all distinction waste. **1927** G. B. SHAW *Gt. Composers* (1978) I. 18 Mozart was still to him the master of masters.. but he was a court flunkey in breeches while Beethoven was a Sansculotte. **1940** [see *DEFLATE *v.* 2 b]. **1955** *Times* 18 July 6/1 So it is the crowd of *sans autos*—the modern *sansculottes*?—who are left to swarm over the streets, empty of all but the buses (each with its little crest of Tricolor flags for the occasion) and taxis, to celebrate with a certain fervour their annual rites. **1969** *N.Y. Rev. Bks.* 30 Jan. 8/1 The term plebs is convenient for the *sans-culottes* and similar movements made up mainly of small shopkeepers, artisans, journeymen; proletariat for factory workers.

sansculottism. (Earlier example.)

1794 J. B. S. MORRITT *Let.* 22 May (1914) ii. 32 His enemies charge him with sansculottism.

sansei (sæ·nsē[i]). [Jap., f. *san* three, third + *sei* generation.] An American born of nisei parents (see *NISEI); a third-generation Japanese American.

1945 in WEBSTER Add. **1950** *Amer. Speech* XXV. 242 Further distinctions lie in other colloquialisms such as *sansei* ('third generation'), the few descendants of *nisei*. **1971** *Newsweek* 19 Apr. 108/1 Aoki says bluntly that nisei and sansei (second and third generation) are too educated and don't work hard enough. **1975** *Time* (Canad. ed.) 20 Oct. 39/1 Carl Takamura, a young sansei (third generation) state legislator.

sanserif. Add: Also **sans serif.** Cf. CERIPH. (Further examples.)

1961 *Guardian* 17 June 14/6, I saw a..truck bearing in white sans serif capitals the name Fay Improvement Company. **1970** *Brit. Printer* July 77/2 Bold sans serifs have remained popular on posters up to the present day. **1976** *Visible Language* X. 88 Sans serif, to him, was the best, if not the only kind of type suitable for the modern world.

sansevieria (sænsīvi[ə]·riă). Also **sanseveria, sanseviera.** [mod.L. (C. P. Thunberg *Prodromus Plantarum Capensium* (1794) I. 65), f. the title of Raimond de Sansgrio, Prince of Sanseviero (1710–71) + -IA[1].] A herbaceous perennial of the genus so called, belonging to the family Liliaceæ, native to tropical Africa or south-eastern Asia, and bearing racemes of white or greenish flowers and rosettes of stiff, erect, variegated leaves yielding a strong white fibre; also called bowstring hemp. Also *attrib.*

1804 *Curtis's Bot. Mag.* XIX. 739 (*heading*) Chinese Sanseveira. **1851** *Illustr. Catal. Gt. Exhib.* IV. 882/2 Liliaceous plants, such as..the Sanseviera, the pine-apple, and even the plantain. **1899** F. V. KIRBY *Sport E. Central Afr.* xxiv. 268 Quantities of the sansevieria plants..yield a valuable fibre. **1955** *Sci. News Let.* 2 Apr. 213/2 Kenaf is seen as a substitute for jute, sanseveria for manila hemp. **1959** J. D. CLARK *Prehist. S. Afr.* ix. 248 The knife or scraper used by the Hukwe Bushmen in Northern Rhodesia for shredding *sansevieria* leaves to obtain fibre for rope and string is also made of wood. **1961** [see *MOTHER-IN-LAW 4]. **1976** *Hortus Third* (L. H. Bailey Hortorium) 1002/2 Sansevierias are commonly grown as durable porch and house plants.

Sansi (sā·nsi). Also **Sansiya, sansya.** [Origin uncertain (see quot. 1896).] A low-status caste group of the Punjab, India; a member of this group. Also *attrib.*

1882 E. J. GUNTHORPE *Notes on Criminal Tribes* xiii. 78 Kunjurs are..a branch of the great family of Sansya robbers, who claim their descent from Sainsmull. **1883** D. C. J. IBBETSON *Outl. Panjâb Ethnogr.* vi. 311 The thieving Sánsis are said to admit any caste to their fraternity except the Dhedhs and Mhangs; and the man so admitted becomes..a Sánsi. **1896** W. CROOKE *Tribes & Castes North-Western Provinces & Oudh* IV. 277 Sânsiya. A vagrant thieving tribe... Of their name no satisfactory account has been given. Some derive it from the Sanskrit *svâsa*, 'breathing', or *srasta*, 'separated', others with *svagânika*, 'one who has to do with dogs', or *svapâka*, 'dog-cooking', a person of a degraded and outcaste tribe, who, by the older law, was required to live outside towns, to eat his food in broken vessels, to wear the clothes of the dead, and to be excluded from all intercourse with other people... The Sânsiya is no doubt the near kinsman of the other degraded wandering races who occupy the same part of the country, such as the Kanjar. **1901** KIPLING *Kim* iv. 86 They meet a troop of long-haired, strong-scented Sansis, with baskets of lizards and other unclean food... The Sansi is deep pollution. **1931** E. A. H. BLUNT *Caste System N. India* ix. 149 The Beriya, Bhantu, Habura, Karwal, and Sansiya..may be regarded as offshoots of a single nomadic race. **1972** S. R. SHARMA in F. Singh *Hist. Punjab* III. xvi. 366 Prostitution had come to be associated with certain castes—Kanjai, Bangali, Sansi and Pema.

Sanskara, var. *SAMSKARA.

Sanskritic, *a.* (Earlier example.)

1848 MAX MÜLLER in *Rep. Brit. Assoc. Adv. Sci. 1847* XVII. 336 There is still another more Sanscritic termination in *e*, for the locative of words ending in a consonant or the vowel *a*.

Sanskritist. (Earlier example.)

1853 W. D. WHITNEY in *Jrnl. Amer. Oriental Soc.* III. 292 This little work..gave perhaps the most powerful impulse to that movement which has since carried all Sanskritists irresistibly to the study of the Vedas.

Sanskritize, *v.* Add: **b.** *trans.* To adapt to the beliefs or practices of a high Hindu caste. **Sanskritization** (examples corresponding to sense *b of the vb.).

1952 M. N. SRINIVAS *Relig. & Society among Coorgs of S. India* ii. 30 A low caste was able..to rise to a higher position in the hierarchy by adopting vegetarianism and teetotalism, and by Sanskritizing its ritual and pantheon. In short, it took over, as far as possible, the customs, rites, and beliefs of the Brahmins... This process has been called 'Sanskritization' in this book, in preference to 'Brahminization', as certain Vēdic rites are confined to Brahmins and the two other 'twice-born' castes. *Ibid.* 38 Some Coorg families are more Sanskritized than their neighbours. **1964** *Diogenes* XLV. 99 (*heading*) Sanskritization and cultural mobility. **1974** tr. *Wertheim's Evolution & Revolution* iii. 240 Even if a sub-group within a caste..achieved a certain measure of prosperity and aiming at a higher status through 'sanskritization', has constituted itself as a separate sub-caste, [etc.].

Sansya, var. *SANSI.

Santa Ana (sæ·ntă æ·nă). *U.S.* Also **Santa Anna, Santana** (sæntæ·nă). [Sp., = Saint Anne.] A hot, dry, föhn-type wind of desert origin, freq. strong and dust-laden, which blows on the coastal plain of southern California after being channelled and heated adiabatically during its descent of the Santa Ana Mountains. Also *Santa Ana wind.*

The suggestion made in some dicts. that this is named after Antonio Lopez de *Santa Anna* (?1795–1876), Mexican revolutionary leader and president, seems without foundation.

1887 *Ann. Meteorol. Rev. Calif. 1886* (Calif. State Agric. Soc.) 128 Another health-giving, but extremely disagreeable wind, is the 'Santa Ana', or 'norther'. *Ibid.*, The 'Santa And' wind receives its name, because it frequently issues from the Santa Ana Pass. **1889** G. DAVIDSON *Pacific Coast: Coast Pilot of Calif.* (U.S. Coast & Geodetic Survey) (ed. 4) 40 In November, 1888, when the Santa Ana wind had passed its greatest strength, a reverse current of wind was drawing along the shore from Anaheim Landing towards Newport Bay. **1915** *Nature & Sci. Pacific Coast* (Amer. Assoc. Adv. Sci.: Pacific Coast Comm.) 22 Known locally as Santa Anas, these wind storms constitute the most disagreeable feature of the weather in the great valley of the south. **1931** A. A. MILLER *Climatol.* viii. 150 The Santa Annas of southern California and the Northers of the Sacramento Valley are hot, dry winds. **1941** B. SCHULBERG *What makes Sammy Run?* iv. 56 The music came at us like a Santa Ana wind. **1970** KOENIG & DIXON *Children are Watching* xxi. 181 Out in the sunset the Santana scoured the beach and hurled fine sand with enough force that hands cupped protectively over eyes. **1972** C. WESTON *Poor, Poor Ophelia* xi. 58 Santa Ana wind, he thought. No fog tomorrow, desert heat instead. **1973** R. HAYES *Hungarian Game* xliii. 248 A Santa Ana, that dry desert wind, blew away the smog.

Santa Claus. Add: Also *dial.* and *colloq.* **Santy. a.** (Earlier examples.) Also, a person wearing a red cloak or suit and a white beard, to simulate the supposed Santa Claus to children, esp. in shops or on shopping streets. Also *transf.*, *fig.*, *attrib.*, and *ellipt.* as *Santa.*

1773 *N.Y. Gaz.* 26 Dec. 3/1 Last Monday the Anniversary of St. Nicholas, otherwise called St. A Claus, was celebrated at Protestant-Hall. **1808** *Salmagundi* 25 Jan. 407 The noted St. Nicholas, vulgarly called Santaclaus—of all the saints in the kalendar the most venerated by true hollanders, and their unsophisticated descendants. **1886** P. STAPLETON *Major's Christmas* 201 Papas and mammas..planned the Santa Claus performance which was to come when the inquisitive eyes were closed in slumber. **1821** *Weekly Visitor* IV. 262/1 For time immemorial the Dutch had a tradition, that there existed a being of no *earthly birth*, who was called *Santa Claus.* **1909** *Chicago Daily News* 10 Aug. 8/3 Uncle Sam is by no means an impartial Santa Claus. **1913** *Sat. Even. Post.* 6 Dec. 50/1 If you want to act the part of Santa this Christmas. **1925** T. DREISER *Amer. Trag.* (1926) I. II. xxix. 356, I know something Santy has brought my Dad that he'll like. **1932** J. BEAMES *Gateway* vi. 108 You're just as kiddish as what you was when you'd be up at three in the mornin' to see what Santy had brung you. **1934** *Amer. Mercury* May 5/2 The Santa Claus theory of relief may be appropriate to a genuine emergency like an earthquake or a big fire. **1943** K. TENNANT *Ride on Stranger* iii. 24 Come on down, Ma. Come and see what Santa's brought you. **1956** H. GOLD *Man who was not with It* (1965) xxxii. 310 It was practically Christmas, too, with all the Santy Clauses peddling in the streets. **1957** [see *GOOD-TIME *a.*]. **1973** 'D. HALLIDAY' *Dolly & Starry Bird* i. 2 The Zodiac Trust is the Santa Claus of worldwide astronomy. A private foundation richly funded.., it makes grants to struggling centres. **1975** *Times* 10 Dec. 4/4 Being a man was a genuine occupational qualification for a Santa Claus. **1976** M. MACHLIN *Pipeline* ix. 103 A huge, heavy-set man,..with a bushy unkempt Santa Claus beard, walked unsteadily toward their table. **1976** *Scotsman* 24 Dec. (Weekend Suppl.) 1/1 Stop rakin', Rikki. Santy says ye've had enough. **1976** *Scottish Daily Express* 27 Dec. 2/8 She was one of nine women charged with prostitution in Dallas, Texas, for propositioning Vice Squad officers disguised as Santas. **1977** *Times* 24 Dec. 16/5 Santa must have been updated over the years. Presumably girls hang out their tights now, instead of a solitary stocking.

b. (*collect. sing.*) Christmas presents; Christmas delicacies. *U.S. dial.*

1929 W. FAULKNER *Sound & Fury* 107 Buy yourself some Santy Claus. **1939** *These are our Lives* (Federal Writers' Project, U.S.) 22 One Christmas we ask him for fifty dollars for some clothes and a little Santy Claus for the chil'en.

Santa Gertrudis (sæ·ntă gəɹtru·dis). The name of the Santa Gertrudis division of the King Ranch, Kingsville, Texas, used to designate a breed of large red-coated beef cattle suitable for hot climates, developed there between 1910 and 1940 by crossing Brahmans and Shorthorns; an animal of this breed. Also *attrib.*

c **1946** R. J. KLEBERG *Santa Gertrudis Breed of Beef Cattle* 8 The bull on the ranch known as 'Monkey'..marks the real beginning of the improved breed of Santa Gertrudis cattle. *Ibid.* 11 Santa Gertrudis calves at eight months of age will average over 500 pounds. **1949** *Jrnl. Heredity* XL. 115/1 One of the most noteworthy contributions to livestock breeding has been the creation and development of the Santa Gertrudis breed of beef cattle. **1955** *Times* 16 July 11/5 The Zebu and Santa Gertrudis breeds are suitable in country where grasses lack nutriment for a great part of the year. **1960** *Times* 1 Oct. 7/7 A remarkable artificial insemination programme [in Queensland]..aims to transform a herd of 30,000 Shorthorn cattle into one of 70,000 high grade Santa Gertrudis. **1962** *Listener* 6 Dec. 956/1 Mr Joyce had introduced Santa Gertrudis cattle from Texas. **1978** J. B. FRIEND *Cattle of World* 148/2 The Santa Gertrudis today carry approximately ⅝ Shorthorn blood and ⅜ Brahman blood.

Santal² (sæ·ntal). Also **Santhal, Sonthal.** [Native name.] A Kolarian people of north-eastern India; a member of this people. Also, the language of this people (see next). Also *attrib.*

1852 J. PHILLIPS *Introd. Sántál Lang.* i. 1 *The Sántál*, having been hitherto an unwritten language, has..no characters of its own. *Ibid.* 3 Pronouns in Sántál, are.. completely interwoven with the declension of nouns. **1866** [see *MUNDA *sb.* and *a.*]. **1873** L. O. SKREFSUD *Gram. Santhal Lang.* p. iii, Santhali is the language spoken by a people called by foreigners the Santhals or Santals, inhabiting the western frontier of Lower Bengal. *Ibid.* i. 8 *Semi-consonants.* k', ch', t', p'. The sounds, which these letters represent, are peculiar to the Santal language... The 'Schnalz-laute' (click-sounds) mentioned by Dr. Lepsius, as existing in some of the African languages, appear to have some similarity to these Santal jerks. **1891** MONIER WILLIAMS *Brahmanism & Hinduism* (ed. 4) xxii. 578 We came to what appeared to be a good typical example of a Santal village-community. **1891** KIPLING *City of Dreadful Night* 85 We have any amount of Sonthals besides Mahomedans and Hindus of every possible caste. **1936** *Times Lit. Suppl.* 3 Oct. 788/4 The pictures of Sonthal life are evidently based on personal and intimate knowledge. **1941** J. H. HUTTON in L. O'Malley *Mod. India & West* xii. 422 The ignorance and honesty of the Santal enabled the first adventurous traders from the plains to make rapid fortunes out of the hill-men. **1969** *Illustr. Weekly of India* 27 July 29/1 Santal women do not wear much jewellery. **1971** *Ibid.* 25 Apr. 42/2 (*caption*) Resettled Santhals in the Malkanagiri zone of Dandakaranya Project. The Santhals are also found in the border districts of West Bengal. **1974** W. G. ARCHER *Hill of Flutes* i. 19 Flanked by rows of tall palmyra palms, Santal villages have an air of genial comfort. *Ibid.* 24 Within this neat and ordered setting most Santals lead calm and happy lives.

Santali (sæntā·li), *sb.* and *a.* Also 9 **Santalee; Santhali, Sonthali.** [f. prec. + adj. suff. *-i.*] **A.** *sb.* The Munda language of the Santals. **B.** *adj.* Of or pertaining to the Santals or their language.

1873 [see *SANTAL²]. *c* **1875–9** E. L. BRANDRETH *On Non-Aryan Lang. India* 7 The Santali verb..has twenty-three tenses. **1891** KIPLING *City of Dreadful Night* 96 Sonthali..is more elaborate than Greek. **1927** *Other Lands* July 138/2 At one house I was presented with a burnt arm to examine, and having no Santali with which to explain that I was not a doctor, the only thing to do was to look at it carefully and express, by nods and smiles, great satisfaction at the state of its progress. **1961** WEBSTER, Santhali. **1969** [see *MADAL]. **1974** *Times* 18 Apr. 16/6 Elmhirst took his first group of students into the Moslem, Hindu and Santali villages of the district early in 1922. **1974** W. G. ARCHER *Hill of Flutes* 343 The Santali Language. According to Grierson's Linguistic Survey, Santali is an Austro-Asiatic Language.

santalol (sæ·ntălǫl). *Chem.* [f. SANTAL + -OL.] Either of two isomeric terpenoid alcohols, $C_{15}H_{24}O$ (known respectively as α- and β-*santalol*), which are fragrant liquids found in sandalwood oil.

1895 *Pharm. Jrnl.* I. 118/1 Chapoteaut, after a very careful study of the oil, announced some time ago that it consisted almost entirely of two bodies, $C_{15}H_{26}O$ [*sic*], an alcohol termed santalol, and $C_{15}H_{24}O$, probably the corresponding aldehyde. **1935** *Jrnl. Chem. Soc.* 312 Tautomerism is observed also in the two santalols themselves, since they yield on ozonolysis both formaldehyde and acetylcarbinol. **1966** *McGraw-Hill Encycl. Sci. & Technol.* XIII. 497/2 Santalol occurs in sandalwood oil and is used in perfumery. **1976** *Nature* 5 Aug. 487/2 The essential oils D-bornyl acetate, α- and β-santalol and several plant sesquiterpene hydrocarbons have been shown to induce sexual excitement in male American cockroaches.

Santa Lucia (sæ·ntă lutʃī·ă). The name of a range of mountains in southwestern California, used *attrib.* in **Santa Lucia fir** to designate the bristlecone fir, *Abies bracteata*, which is native to the region.

1905 *Occasional Papers Calif. Acad. Sci.* IX. 7 Santa Lucia Fir is found in only a few cañons of the Santa Lucia Mountains in Monterey County. **1948** *Sierra Club Bull.* (San Francisco) Mar. 137 Among these were the Santa Lucia fir..and hosts of others. **1965** *Listener* 20 May 742/3 You mentioned a Santa Lucia fir just now, and you were saying that in its original habitat it is sadly depleted. **1977** *Daily Colonist* (Victoria, B.C.) 7 Aug. 1/1 The Marble Cone fire has destroyed two-thirds of the Ventana Wilderness Area, home of the Santa Lucia fir which grows nowhere else.

‖ **santé** (sante), *int.* Also in anglicized form **santy** (sæ·nti). [Fr., lit. 'health'.] An exclamation used as a salutation before drinking. Cf. HEALTH *sb.* 6.

1903 KIPLING *Traffics & Discoveries* (1904) 43 Here's santy to us all! **1952** P. FRANKAU *Wreath for Enemy* I. 18 She cried, '*Santé, santé*' raising her glass to each of us. **1966** J. FOWLES *Magus* iv. 21 She had poured herself a whisky. '*Santé.*' **1975** D. GRAY *Ride on Tiger* iv. 30 He raised his own glass of champagne and said, '*Santé!*' **1980** P. HARCOURT *Tomorrow's Treason* II. ii. 141, I watched him..pour us each a generous tot. '*Santé!*' He grinned.

‖ **santeria** (santerī·ă). Also **Santeria.** [Sp., lit. 'holiness, sanctity'.] An Afro-Cuban religious cult with many Yoruba elements.

1950 *Southwestern Jrnl. Anthropol.* VI. 64 The worship of African deities, as it is practised in Cuba today, is known as *santeria.* The deities and the men and women who work with them are known by the Spanish words *santos, santeros*, and *santeras*, or by the Yoruba words *orisha, babalorisha*, and *iyalorisha.* **1953** [see *SANTERO 2]. **1956** *Publ. Amer. Dial. Soc.* XXVI. 34 In Cuba the practitioners of a religion known as Santeria use a variety of African language called Lucumí in their religious services. **1972** W. R. BASCOM *Shango in New World* 20 A second major center of santeria in the United States, perhaps even more important than Miami, is New York City, where a Shango temple has been established. Apparently this has attracted not only Cuban refugees but also Puerto Ricans and New York Negroes.

‖ **santero** (santē·ro). Fem. **santera.** [Sp.] **1.** In Mexico and Spanish-speaking areas of south-western U.S.: a maker of religious images.

1931 R. L. BARKER *Caballeros* xiii. 333 As the colonists became more securely rooted on the prados and mesas of Nuevo México certain men developed greater proficiency as carvers and painters. They were called santeros, the saint-makers, who signed and dated their work on the backs of the santos de retablos. **1944** *Horizon* Jan. 23 At about the same period [*sc.* 18th and 19th centuries] the *santero* of New Mexico produced for religious needs starkly primitive paintings and sculpture (*retablos* and *bultos*). **1951** *Western Folklore* Apr. 153 The following material about *santeros* was collected in the San Luis Valley, where there still remains a definite *santero* tradition... Southern Colorado is..the one remaining place where something may still be learned of the *santero* and his art.

2. A priest (or priestess) of a religious cult, esp. *santeria.*

1950 [see *SANTERIA]. **1953** *Language* XXIX. 157 Lucumí is a term here used to refer to a language spoken in Cuba by practitioners of the religion known as *Santería.* In Cuba both the *santeros* and the language are often called Lucumí. **1972** W. R. BASCOM *Shango in New World* 20 Refugee santeros and santeras have..spread to many other parts of the New World. **1977** *N.Y. Rev. Bks.* 4 Aug. 27/3 He did many odd jobs for his neighbors,..served as a *santero*, or priest, in two religious cults.

santo. Add: **2.** A wooden representation of a saint or other religious symbol from Mexico or south-western U.S.

1834 A. PIKE *Prose Sk. & Poems* 146 The santos and other images had been brought from Mexico. **1948** F. BLAKE *Johnny Christmas* I. 19 The lines of prayer benches, the altar with its tapestry and candlesticks, the religious santos set in niches. **1976** *National Observer* (U.S.) 1 May 18/1 *Folk sculpture USA*... Santos from the Southwest, trade signs, voodoo cult objects.

Santobrite (sæ·ntŏbrəit). [f. the name of the Mon*santo* Chemical Company.] A proprietary name for preparations of sodium pentachlorophenate (s.v. *PENTA-), used as a fungicide, wood preservative, insecticide, etc.

1936 *Official Gaz.* (U.S. Patent Office) 2 June 14/2 Monsanto Chemical Company, St. Louis, Mo... *Santobrite.* For preservatives for wood, lumber, and other cellulosic materials. Claims use since Apr. 2, 1936. **1938** [see *pentachlorophenate* s.v. *PENTA-]. **1944** *Trade Marks Jrnl.* 29 Nov. 567/1 *Santobrite*... Insecticides, germicides, algicides, [etc.]. **1959** [see *pentachlorophenate* s.v. *PENTA-]. **1971** N. E. HICKIN *Wood Preservation* 89 The technical materials are also known as 'Santobrite' (the Monsanto Chemical Co.) and 'Dowicide G' (the Dow Chemical Co.).

Santo Domingan (sæ·nto domi·ŋgăn), *a.* [f. *Santo Domingo* (see below) + -AN.] Of or pertaining to Santo Domingo, former name of the Dominican Republic, and also the name of a district, and of the capital city of the Dominican Republic.

1934 in WEBSTER. **1947** J. C. RICH *Materials & Methods Sculpture* x. 291 The West Indian *Swietenia mahogani* is marketed as Cuban, Santo Domingan, or Spanish mahogany. .. Santo Domingan mahogany is one of the hardest and heaviest varieties. **1976** B. LECOMBER *Dead Weight* x. 118 A little Santo Domingan whore.

santon. Add: **3.** Chiefly in Provence: a figurine adorning a representation of the manger in which Christ was laid.

1926 E. I. ROBSON *Wayfarer in Provence* xviii. 226 The little home-made crèches, the simple figures known as the Santons,..the pastoral ceremonies..at the famous midnight mass of Les Baux, are all witnesses to the way in which the Nativity story went home to the hearts of the Provençals. **1952** *Spectator* 10 Oct. 478/1 The pretty *santons*, the traditional clay figures of the Holy Family and the ancient trades of Provence. **1963** G. K. WILKINSON *Guinea-Pigs* xii. 189 Christmas will soon be on us and I hope that you will arrange the Holy Crêche and the Santons in the church. **1976** N. ROBERTS *Face of France* iii. 40 These days *santons*, the little pottery crib figures introducing characters from daily life..into the Nativity scene, are known far beyond their native Provence.

Santonian (sæntōᵘ·niăn), *a. Geol.* [ad. F. *Santonien* (H. Coquand 1857, in *Bull. de la Soc. géol. de France* XIV. 749) f. *Santon*, native or characteristic of Saintes, a town in Charente-Maritime Dept. (f. L. *Santoni* or *Santones*, ancient name of a people of Aquitania), + *-ien* -IAN.] Name of a stage in the Upper Cretaceous in France and adjacent areas, corresponding to the middle Senonian and to part of the Upper Chalk in Britain; of or pertaining to this stage and to the strata which characterize it, or the geological age during which it was deposited. Freq. *absol.*

1869 H. COQUAND in *Q. Jrnl. Geol. Soc.* XXV. 239, I have divided the Cretaceous formation of the south-west [of France] in the following manner..Santonian stage (of Saintes). **1885** A. GEIKIE *Text-bk. Geol.* (ed. 2) 833 This stage [*sc.* the Senonian]..consists mainly of white chalk separable into the two divisions of: 1st, Micraster (Santonian) sub-stage composed of chalk beds [etc.]. **1924** C. SCHUCHERT *Text-bk. Geol.* (ed. 2) II. xxxviii. 537 Upper Cretaceous [of Europe]... Senonian... Santonian. **1971** *Nature* 18 June 439/2 Misfit motion in the African plate closed this rift in Santonian time. **1974** *Encycl. Brit. Micropædia* VIII. 886/2 In northern Europe the Santonian is represented by the Granulaten Chalk, the equivalent of portions of the Upper Chalk in Great Britain.

Santorin (sæntŏrī·n, sæ·ntŏrin). Also **santorin, Santori·ni.** [ad. Gr. *Σαντορίνη* Santorini, former name for Thira, ad. It. *Sant' Irene* St. Irene, Italian name for the island.] In full *Santorin earth*. A natural volcanic ash, similar to pozzolana, found on the island of Thira in the Cyclades.

1868 WATTS *Dict. Chem.* V. 191 *Santorin*, an argillaceous mineral, occurring on the island of Santorin, which yields an excellent cement. **1876** *Min. Proc. Inst. Civil Engineers* XLV. 291 For hydraulic works on the Mediterranean coast Santorin earth recommends itself through facility of excavation and lading and economical transport at sea. **1951** LADOO & MYERS *Non-Metallic Minerals* (ed. 2) 407 Santorini or Santorin earth is a variety of pumice mined on Santorin Island (Greece), used in making pozzuolana cement. **1971** *Materials & Technol.* II. ii. 106 Cements ground together with siliceous materials other than pozzolan—such as santorin earth (Greece), trass..and diatomaceous earth (USA)—are also named pozzolan cement.

Santos (sæ·ntǫs). The name of a port in Brazil, used *ellipt.* and *attrib.* of coffee exported from there.

[**1885** C. F. VAN D. LAËRNE *Brazil & Java: Rep. Coffee-Culture* x. 267 The second or Santos zone lies..between 21 and 24 degrees S.L. but a little further landwards, as it does not begin till about 150 kilometers from Santos. *Ibid.* 289 The coffee-shrub in the Santos zone is much larger than the coffee-shrub in the Rio zone, besides being almost twice as productive.] **1888** C. G. W. LOCK *Coffee* vi. 112 As to impurities:—San Domingo is usually very dirty; Ceylon, East India, Rio, Santos, Martinique, and Java, generally well prepared and clean. **1899** [see *JAMAICA b]. **1956** A. E. HAARER *Mod. Coffee Production* xvii. 398 Though an ever-increasing number are beginning to pick ripe coffee and prepare it by the wet method,.. most planters still follow the old dry method. Of the latter there are two kinds, those who process only ripe cherry and take more care in its preparation,..and those who strip the crop from the trees at the stage when most of it is ripe... The first of these two methods produces a softer and milder product such as Santos coffee. **1975** *Times* 6 Mar. 7/7 Blue Sumatra, 82 p per pound..very strong aroma. Santos, 72 p, the best Brazilian, rich flavour.

‖ **san ts'ai** (san‚tsəi). Also **san-ts'ai.** [Chinese *sāncǎi*, f. *sān* three + *cǎi* colour.] Chinese pottery, esp. of the Tang dynasty, decorated in three colours; decoration in three enamel colours applied to pottery and porcelain. Also *attrib.*

1901 C. MONKHOUSE *Hist. & Descr. Chinese Porc.* I. caption facing p. 35 Squirrel and grapes: *San-ts'ai* water pourer. **1906** S. W. BUSHELL *Chinese Art* II. ii. viii. 37 For a typical example of the *san ts'ai*, or 'three-coloured', decoration *sur biscuit*, see the pictures..of a fish-shaped water pourer, which is painted with the brownish-purple, green, and yellow enamels of this *genre*. **1915** R. L. HOBSON *Chinese Pott. & Porc.* II. x. 151 The Dresden collection is peculiarly rich in this kind of *san ts'ai*. **1959** H. CHEVALIER tr. *Grousset's Chinese Art & Culture* vi. 292 The main categories of Ming ceramics are..: 1. *San-ts'ai* or 'three-colours', namely green.., yellow.., and aubergine-violet. **1972** *Trans. Oriental Ceramics Soc.* XXXVIII. 29 The combination of green, blue and yellow-brown glaze which constitutes the famous T'ang polychromes ('three-colour ware', *san-ts'ai*) appear to belong..to the first half of the 8th century. **1978** P. VAN GREENAWAY *Man called Scavener* xi. 159 A priceless san ts'ai bowl.

santy: see *SANTÉ. **Santy (Claus:)** see *SANTA CLAUS. **Sanusi, Sanusiya(h:** see *SENUSSI; **sanyama:** see *SAMYAMA.

sanyas(s)i, sanyas(s)in, varr. SUNNYASEE, SUNNYASI in Dict. and Suppl.

s-aorist: see *S I. 1 b.

Saorstát Éireann (sī·rstāt ē·rʸən, sē·r-). [Ir., = The Free State of Ireland.] = *Irish Free State* s.v. *IRISH *adj.* 2 c. Also *ellipt.* as **Saorstát.**

1922 *Bille um Bun-reacht Shaorstáit Eireann (Constitution of Saorstát Eireann Bill)* 2 Article 1. The Irish Free State/ Saorstát Eireann is a co-equal member of the community of nations. **1923** *Glasgow Herald* 18 June 9/8 One was Article 12 where the Northern Government was entitled to pass a resolution against entrance into the Saorstat. **1924** W. B. YEATS *Senate Speeches* (1961) 69 Your Committee is gravely impressed by the responsibility now laid upon the Saorstat towards the Irish people. **1938** S. BECKETT *Murphy* 197 Turf is compulsory in the Saorstat, but one need not bring a private supply to Newcastle.

sap, *sb.*[1] Add: **1. b.** (Later examples.)

1865 G. M. HOPKINS *Poems* (1967) 169 My sap is sealed, My root is dry. **1942** T. S. ELIOT *Little Gidding* i. 7 Between melting and freezing The soul's sap quivers. **1961** B. J. CHUTE *Moon & Thorn* iv. 37 An old man..gave her a more than reflective look as she passed, the sap still plainly rising in his branches.

d. Cytology. *cell sap* [tr. G. *zellsaft*] (see quot. 1875); *nuclear sap*, the fluid within the nuclear membrane.

1875 BENNETT & DYER tr. *J. Sachs's Text-bk. Bot.* I. i. 62 The term Cell-sap may be understood in a wider or in a narrower sense. In the former it would express the collective mass of all fluids by which the cell-wall, the protoplasm-body, and all other organised structures of the cell are saturated, and would also embrace the fluids contained in the vacuoli of the protoplasm; in a narrower sense the latter only is ordinarily designated as cell-sap. **1884** *Jrnl. Bot.* XXII. 124 The rich, violet-coloured cell-sap in the flower of *Justicia speciosa*..crystallizes very easily into minute slender prisms. **1887** *Jrnl. R. Microsc. Soc.* 979 Linin and paralinin, the substance respectively of the nuclear threads..and of the intermediate matrix or 'nuclear sap'. **1955** *Internat. Rev. Cytol.* IV. 293 Another suggestion for the origin of nucleolar material is that it is formed from nuclear sap. **1971** VILLEE & DETHIER *Biol. Princ. & Processes* vi. 152 The activation of amino acids for protein synthesis, the process of glycolysis and many other reactions occur in the soluble cell sap. *Ibid.* xvi. 499 The plant cell, inside its cellulose wall, has one or more large vacuoles filled with cell sap. **1975** *Nature* 4 Sept. 21/1 Similar preparations were..made from rat liver chromatin but after previous removal of 'nuclear sap' which contains soluble nuclear proteins. **1978** B. S. BECKETT *Illustr. Biol.* xxxi. 62/1 As root hairs take up water their cell sap is diluted and soon becomes a weaker solution than the sap of cells deeper inside the root.

4. b. *U.S. slang.* A club; a short staff. So *saps* (see quot. 1899).

1899 'J. FLYNT' *Tramping with Tramps* 396 *Saps*, a clubbing with weapons made from saplings. **1915** *N.Y. World Mag.* 9 May 14/3 *Sap* or *sapstick*, a crutch, cane or club. **1926** J. BLACK *You can't Win* vii. 83 The town marshal would then appear with a posse armed with 'saps', which is short for saplings, young trees. **1932** J. DOS PASSOS *1919* 436 He could hear the crack of saps on men's skulls. **1940** R. CHANDLER *Farewell, my Lovely* xxvi. 116 He had the sap out this time, a nice little tool about five inches long, covered with woven brown leather. **1955** W. FOSTER-HARRIS *Look of Old West* vii. 218 Its [*sc.* a quirt's] handle, or butt, would probably be loaded with an iron spike or with buckshot, thus giving you a handy sap when you needed one. **1974** D. SEARS *Lark in Clear Air* iv. 49 His main staff of office was a lead sap that must have weighed two pounds.

7. a. *sap-flow, -pressure; sap-clear, -filled, -rife* adjs.; **sap-rot** (further examples); **sap-stain,** discoloration of sap-wood, esp. a bluish discoloration by fungi; so **sap-stained** *a.*, **sap-staining** *sb.* and *a.*; **sap-sucker** (earlier and further examples); **sap-whistle**: delete † and add later example.

1953 E. SITWELL *Gardeners & Astronomers* 31 The gardener plays upon his sap-clear flute. **1915** D. H. LAWRENCE *Rainbow* xiii. 383 Her own world of warm sun and growing, sap-filled life was turned into nothing. **1935** C. DAY LEWIS *Time to Dance* 64 We remember them as the glowing fruit remembers Sap-flow and sunshine. **1976** *Sci. Amer.* May 104/3 Hales measured the springtime sap pressure by placing open mercury manometers on a cut vine. **1942** W. FAULKNER *Go down, Moses* 326 Wet and saprife spring in their ordered immortal sequence. **1918** J. W. HARSHBERGER *Mycol. & Plant Path.* xxxv. 545 Sap-rot (*Polystictus versicolor* (L.), Fr.).—*Polystictus versicolor* is one of the most cosmopolitan species of fungi known... It grows on the sapwood of every species of deciduous tree known. It is the most serious of all the wood-rotting fungi, destroying probably 75 per cent. of the timber used for railroad ties. *Ibid.* 558 Sap-rot (*Daedalea quercina* (L.) Pers).—One of the most important enemies of structural oak, produces a soft, mushy decay of the wood. **1971** *Country Life* 4 Nov. 1224/2 The chestnut for the frames is cleft..soon after cutting to prevent sap rot. **1910** *Bot. Gaz.* L. 142 The examination of microscopic sections of this sap-stained lumber reveals the fact that the colored substance, produced by the chemical reaction, is most conspicuously developed in the wood rays and wood parenchyma cells. *Ibid.*, Favorable conditions for sap-staining are found during warm weather. *Ibid.* 147 Sap stain is in general produced in two ways, by the attacks of fungi and by chemical discoloration. **1921** *Phytopathology* XI. 214 As a sap-staining organism *Lasiosphaeria pezizula* has been previously reported by Humphrey. **1953** F. T. BROOKS *Plant Dis.* (ed. 2) xii. 199 Several species of Ceratostomella and allied genera, together with many Fungi Imperfecti, cause sap-stain or blueing of the sap-wood of soft and hard timber felled for lumber, and of pulp-wood... Affected wood is reduced in marketability as the stain is unsightly in timber used for certain purposes. **1976** B. M. BAKSHI *Forest Path.* III. 280 Sap staining fungi..do not cause any wood decay. *Ibid.* 281 The fungi causing soft rot, like those causing sap stain, belong to the Ascomycetes and Fungi Imperfecti. **1805** LEWIS & CLARK *Jrnl.* 8 Apr. in *Orig. Jrnls. Lewis & Clark Exped.* (1905) VI. 187 [I saw] the small woodpecker or sapsucker as they are sometimes called. **1834** J. J. AUDUBON *Ornith. Biogr.* II. 81 The Downy Woodpecker..is best known in all parts of the United States by the name of Sap-sucker. **1941** *Sun* (Baltimore) 25 Jan. 6/1 The cardinals have been flashing to and fro, and the flickers and sapsuckers and the tiny snowbirds. **1962** T. A. IMHOF *Alabama Birds* 329 These far-ranging woodland birds are called Peckerwoods and Sapsuckers in the South. **1971** *Islander* (Victoria, B.C.) 13 June 13/2 A sapsucker tapped out an accompaniment on his favorite tree. **1979** *Bull. Yorks. Dial. Soc.* Summer 7 Here's a sap whistle, lads er aw alike, Here's en aad knife, en a nut off a bike [in a boy's pocket].

b. *N. Amer.* With *spec.* reference to the sap of the sugar maple, as *sap beer, -boiling, bucket, -cider, -gatherer, -house, -kettle, pail, pan, season, sled, syrup, trough, tub, weather, works, yield*; **sap-boiler** (in Dict., sense 7 a); **sap-bush,** a grove of sugar-maples; **sap neckyoke** = **sap yoke*; **sap orchard** = **sap bush*; **sap porridge** (see quots.); **sap run,** an increased flow of sap in a sugar-maple tree; **sap spout,** a spout through which sap is drawn from a sugar-maple tree; **sap sugar** = *maple sugar* s.v. MAPLE 3; **sap tree,** the sugar maple, *Acer saccharum*; **sap weather,** the kind of weather that encourages the flow of sap in a sugar-maple tree; **sap yoke,** a yoke used for carrying sap pails.

1950 H. & S. NEARING *Maple Sugar Bk.* ix. 202 The other maple product is sap beer. **1876** Sap-boiling [see sense 7 a in Dict.]. **1845** S. JUDD *Margaret* I. iii. 12 [Here were] frows, sap-buckets, a leach-tub. **1969** E. H. PINTO *Treen* 94 A maple sap bucket of coopered pine,..is shown... The wire loop, for suspending it on a nail below the sap incision in the tree, can be seen in the photograph. **1980** *Blair & Ketchum's Country Jrnl.* (Brattleboro, Vermont) Oct. 102/1 I've used mine [*sc.* a wooden packboard] to carry 200 sap buckets up the washed-out road to the sugar-house and to carry finished gallons of syrup back down. *a* **1882** T. WEED *Autobiogr.* (1883) I. ii. 12, I now look with great pleasure upon the days and nights passed in the sap-bush. **1845** J. F. COOPER *Chainbearer* II. v. 60, I don't think anything of bringing you..a little water,.. nor should I had we any beer or sap-cider. **1874** *Rep. Vermont Board Agric.* II. 719 The 'sap-gatherer' or 'draw-tub', as it is called, is a hogshead containing from one hundred to one hundred and fifty gallons. **1917** D. CANFIELD *Understood Betsy* vii. 110 The sap-house, where Cousin Ann and Uncle Henry were making syrup. **1939** I. B. WOLCOTT *Yankee Cook Bk.* 338 Any one who.. returns to the sap house. **1904** M. E. WALLER *Wood-Carver of 'Lympus* ii. 51 [I] drew trees and sheep and loggers' camps on the flat stones beneath the crotch set for the sap-kettles. **1968** E. R. BUCKLER *Ox Bells & Fireflies* iv. 77 You thought..about the sap kettle in the cool green shadow, waiting to be emptied at noon. **1905** W. M. WEBB in A. E. Cowles *Past & Present City of Lansing & Ingham County, Michigan* 441 One neighbor whittled out brooms... Another gauged the sap neckyokes and another made ox yokes. **1861** *Boston Herald* 12 Apr. 2/6 Owners of sap orchards can afford to work day and night. **1947** K. M. WELLS *Owl Pen Reader* (1969) I. 44 Jim..followed him, hanging sap pails to the already dripping spouts. **1874** *Rep. Vermont Board Agric.* II. 729 Russia iron is the best material for home made sap pans as the niter can be removed from it more easily. **1842** *Amer. Pioneer* I. 346 'Sap porridge',..when made of sweet corn meal, and the fresh sacarine juice of the maple, afforded both a nourishing and a savory dish. **1948** E. N. DICK *Dixie Frontier* 290 Corn-meal mush was a regular supper dish. In the spring it was made with maple sap and was known as sap porridge. **1876** J. BURROUGHS *Winter Sunshine* 119 A 'sap-run' seldom lasts more than two or three days. **1950** H. & S. NEARING *Maple Sugar Bk.* ix. 202 Maple vinegar..is made of sap run at the end of the season. *Ibid.* iii. 48 Much of the boiling was done far from home, and the sugar makers camped out in the deep woods until the sap season was over. *Ibid.* v. 98 The loaded sap sled..moves down rather easily. **1878** *Rep. Vermont Board Agric.* V. 105 We now have the Eureka sap spout, the tin bucket, [etc.]. **1949** *Highway Traveler* Feb. 16/2 A sap spout, or 'spile' as your boss may call it, is driven into the opening with a few taps of a hammer. **1800** C. D. R. D'ERES *Mem.* 63 The squaws in particular, would make me many and valuable [presents]..consisting of sap sugar. **1895** S. O. JEWETT *Life of Nancy* 105 [She] handed us sap sugar on one of her best plates. **1951** T. CAPOTE *Grass Harp* i. 11, I could hear the tantalizing tremor of their voices flowing like sapsyrup through the old wood. **1843** *Knickerbocker* XXII. 161 One felled the proper trees, taking care to leave the sap-trees, the sugar-maple, untouched. **1804** T. G. FESSENDEN *Orig. Poems* (1806) 41 Your love I well repaid By..a sap-trough neatly made. **1840** [see sense 7 a in Dict.]. **1897** R. E. ROBINSON *Uncle Lisha's Outing* x. 84 These 'ere boots... They're stiffer'n sap troughs. **1872** *Rep. Vermont Board Agric.* I. 215 When I was a boy I purchased one hundred sap tubs, and commenced sugaring on my own hook. **1950** H. & S. NEARING *Maple Sugar Bk.* vi. 137 The 20-degree-night and the 45-degree-day, sunny-days and cold-night formula for sap weather is very far from telling the whole story. **1832** J. J. STRANG *Diary* 19 Feb. in M. M. Quaife *Kingdom of St. James* (1930) 202, I expect to dismiss my school soon and leave the place..for the people want their boys to work in the sap works. **1849** *Knickerbocker* XXXIII. 279 '*The Sugar Bush*' has vividly recalled to memory..the pale blue smoke curling up from the 'sap-works'. **1950** H. & S. NEARING *Maple Sugar Bk.* iv. 82 There is some evidence that length of trunk plays a part in sap yield. **1878** *Rep. Vermont Board Agric.* V. 105 The sap was lugged with sap yoke and pails on their shoulders.

sap, *sb.*[4] Add: **2.** Study, book-work. *Eton College slang.*

a **1862** Q. HOGG *Let.* in E. M. Hogg *Quintin Hogg* (1904) ii. 32 The night before last I..worked the whole night... I hope I shall take well after all my sap. **1901** *Quiet Evening* in *Eton Echoes* 13 Soon a drowsiness steals o'er you, and all thought of 'sap' is banished.

sap, *sb.*[5] (Later examples.)

1930 *Sat. Even. Post* 26 July 145/1 In some ways Angelo's a sap, but I never thought he'd get himself in a spot like that. **1940** WODEHOUSE *Quick Service* xix. 240 You were a sap to come away. **1945** 'N. SHUTE' *Most Secret* vii. 154 But when you come to think of it, I'd have been a sap. **1959** I. & P. OPIE *Lore & Lang. Schoolch.* x. 181 The word 'sap'..the children define as meaning a sissy or a softy ('soft in that he does not do anything wrong'), and suggest other moist alternatives, as 'milksop', 'soppy date', a 'wet', or a 'drip'. **1968** *Globe & Mail* (Toronto) 3 Feb. 35/1 Bobby Mull.., is a sap if he accepts less than $ 100,000 from the tight-fisted..management. **1973** 'H. HOWARD' *Highway to Murder* vi. 72 My brother was a prize sap... Guess he knows better now.

sap, *v.*[1] Add: **2. d.** To erode by glacial sapping (*SAPPING *vbl. sb.*[1] 2 b).

1910 *Geogr. Jrnl.* XXXV. 269 Lack of glacial scratches or polish in uplands sapped by this process should not be allowed to weigh too heavily in reconstructing the glacial history of the district. **1940** *Geogr. Rev.* XXX. 81 Whether these glaciers, when at their maximum thickness, were able to sap vigorously the very bottom of the head walls.. is a little doubtful.

sap (sæp), *v.*[4] *U.S. slang.* [f. SAP *sb.*[1]] *trans.* To hit or club (someone) with a sap (see *SAP *sb.*[1] 4 b). Also with *up* and *intr.* in *to sap up on* (someone).

1926 J. BLACK *You can't Win* vii. 83 The posse fell upon the convention and 'sapped up' on those therein assembled and ran them..out of town. **1926** *Clues* Nov. 162/1 *Sapped*, beaten up. **1931** 'D. STIFF' *Milk & Honey Route* 213 *To get sapped* means to be clubbed by the bulls. **1935** A. J. POLLOCK *Underworld Speaks* 101/1 *Sapped*, struck with a club or billy by a police officer. **1940** R. CHANDLER *Farewell, my Lovely* xxxviii. 178 He slumped sideways and clawed at a corner of the desk, then rolled on his back. It was nice to see someone else get sapped for a change. **1971** *Black World* Apr. 65 My eye was swole... I remember how you sapped me up somethin awful.

Sapei, var. *SEBEI.

sapele (săpī·li). The name of a port on the Benin River, southern Nigeria, used to designate the reddish-brown hardwood timber of *Entandophragma cylindricum*, a large West African forest tree belonging to the family Meliaceæ. Also *attrib.*

1904 *Timber Trades Jrnl.* 2 Apr. 740/2 A fair amount of the African wood [*sc.* mahogany]..was sold. There were submitted 346 lots of Lagos..69 logs of Sapeli, Benin, padouk, birch and Gaboon logs. **1914** E. W. FOSTER *Notes Nigerian Trees & Plants* 20 The wood..has been exported to Europe under the name of 'Unscented Mahogany' presumably to distinguish it from the 'Sapele Scented Wood'. **1928** *Sunday Express* 29 July 15/4 We take the most handsome pieces of burr walnut, of rosewood and sapele mahogany... We place these on the surface of our furniture in such a way that they provide all the beauty and decoration that is needed. **1936** *Nature* 9 May 790/1 The following woods amongst others have been used: laurel wood,..Sapele. **1954** *Archit. Rev.* CXV. 189/3 Display shelves are of sapele wood supported by light steel rods, cellulosed black and orange. **1958** [see *MANSONIA]. **1960** *News Chron.* 21 Apr. 6/2, 11 steps, with treads of sapele (an African hardwood), lead to a landing above the hall. **1964** R. W. J. KEAY et al. *Nigerian Trees* 265 This [*sc. Entandophragma cylindricum*] is one of Nigeria's largest and finest trees, producing the well known Sapele Wood. **1972** 'K. ROYCE' *Miniatures Frame* ix. 117 A board room..with steel tubular chairs running the length of a sapele mahogany table. **1981** *Times* 24 Apr. 12/2 Great sapele logs are stacked along the banks of the Oubangy river.

sap-head. (Earlier U.S. example.)

1798 T. G. FESSENDEN in *Farmer's Weekly Museum* 2 Jan. 4/1 The poet nimbly trips it back—Over the Union courses rapid, And squibs each Jacobinick saphead.

‖ **saphir d'eau** (safīr do). Also **sapphir(e) d'eau.** [Fr., lit. 'sapphire of water'.] A translucent blue variety of cordierite occurring in Sri Lanka; = *water-sapphire* s.v. WATER *sb.* 29.

In Fr. the term was orig. used by mineralogists to refer to blue quartz.

1820 R. JAMESON *Syst. Mineral.* (ed. 3) I. 174 The sapphire d'eau of collectors. **1897** L. FLETCHER *Introd. Study Mineral.* 106 Cordierite is a silicate of magnesium, iron and aluminium; its transparent variety is the *Saphir d'eau* of jewellery. **1925** KRAUS & HOLDEN *Gems & Gem Materials* II. 165 Ceylon is the most important locality, and the gems from that country have sometimes been called *saphir d'eau*, or 'water sapphire'. **1936** H. P. WHITLOCK *Story of Gems* 175 Iolite. This silicate of magnesium, aluminium and iron is better known as *water-sapphire* (saphir d'eau).

sapient, *a.* and *sb.* Add: **A.** *adj.* **3.** *Anthrop.* Of, pertaining to, or characteristic of modern man, *Homo sapiens.*

1971 *Nature* 28 May 213/1 At sites in East Africa can be seen evidence of the various stages of human evolution—the older levels have the remains of the australopithecines and the younger levels have, in succession, early hominines and, finally, fully sapient types. **1976** *Ibid.* 5 Aug. 487/1 It [*sc.* the Ndutu cranium] differs from Swanscombe and Steinheim in its occipital curvature and in that the mastoid of Steinheim is sapient in form.

sapiential, *a.* Add: **2.** Also applied to similar writings in Old English.

1970 *N. & Q.* Dec. 445/1 Old English sapiential poetry has received a good deal of scholarly attention.

sapin. Delete † *Obs.* and add later examples.

1793 E. WYNNE *Diary* 14 Sept. (1935) I. xii. 216 Not such Sapin and Pine woods as in the Country of St. Gall but Oak's. **1813** A. HENRY *Jrnl.* 14 Dec. in E. Coues *New Light Early Hist. Greater Northwest* (1897) II. xxiv. 772 The place is deeply shaded with spruce, pine, sapin, etc. **1927** *Brit. Weekly* 1 Sept. 470/3 Across the valley..are the mountain slopes, with the valiant *sapins* sending their spear points, in massed formation, to the highest level at which a tree can grow.

Sapiny (sæ·pini). Also **Sabiny, Sapin, Saviny.** [Native name.] = *SEBEI.

1909 A. C. HOLLIS *Nandi* I. 2 It seems probable that the tribes allied to the Nandi who live on or near Mount Elgon (the Lako, Kony, Mbai, Sabaut, Sapin, Pôk, and Kâpkara) are only a section of the migrants. **1964** Sabiny [see *KIPSIGIS]. **1977** C. F. & F. M. VOEGELIN *Classification & Index World's Lang.* 323 *Nandi*... Sapiny = Sabei = Savei = Sebei = Saviny = Kamecak (572,000; Uganda).

Sapir–Whorf hypothesis (săpīᵊ·ɹ hwōᵊɹf). [f. the names of Edward *Sapir* (1884–1939) and Benjamin Lee *Whorf* (1897–1941), American linguists.] A hypothesis, first advanced by Sapir in 1929 and subsequently developed by Whorf, that the structure of a language partly determines a native speaker's categorization of experience. Cf. *WHORFIAN *a.*

1954 H. HOIJER *Language in Culture* I. 93 The central idea of the Sapir–Whorf hypothesis is that language functions, not simply as a device for reporting experience, but also..as a way of defining experience for its speakers. **1954** —— in *Mem. Amer. Anthropol. Assoc.* LXXIX. 95 Differences..which reflect a people's habitual and favorite modes of reporting, analyzing, and categorizing experience, form the essential data of the Sapir–Whorf hypothesis. **1956** J. B. CARROLL in B. L. Whorf *Lang., Thought, & Reality* 27 Whorf's principle of linguistic relativity, or, more strictly, the Sapir–Whorf hypothesis (since Sapir most certainly shared in the development of the idea) has..attracted a great deal of attention. **1976** *Word* 1971 XXVII. 242 This is 180 degrees different from what has been known about the Sapir–Whorf hypothesis, which advocates that it is language that has the power to dictate man's world view in a tyrannical way.

sapogenin. Add: In mod. use, a generic term for any of the steroid aglycones of the saponins. (Further examples.) [Coined in G. by P. A. Bolley 1854, in *Ann. d. Chem. u. Pharm.* XC. 216.]

1916 *Jrnl. Biol. Chem.* XXVIII. 443 Hydrolysis [of a new saponin] yielded a sapogenin. **1955** *Sci. Amer.* Jan. 57/1 The steroid part of a saponin is called a sapogenin. **1977** LEWIS & ELVIN-LEWIS *Med. Bot.* ii. 19/2 Some of the plants having useful steroidal sapogenins include *Dioscorea* spp. (yams, Dioscoraceae), *Agave* spp., and *Smilax* spp. (Liliaceae).

saponaria (sæpŏnēᵊ·riă). [med.L. *sāpōnāria* (see SAPONARY *a.* and *sb.*), adopted as a generic name by Linnæus (*Systema Naturæ*, 1735).] = SOAPWORT 1. Cf. SAPONARY *sb.* 1, SAPONER.

1865 M. EYRE *Lady's Walks S. of France* vii. 87, I gathered..eye-bright, saponaria, and ling. **1900** J. M. ABBOTT in W. D. Drury *Bk. Gardening* vii. 237 Saponarias.. are dwarf hardy annuals..of the Pink family. **1951** *Dict. Gardening* (R. Hort. Soc.) IV. 1865/2 Saponarias mostly grow readily in well-drained soils.

saponarin (sæpǫ̆nēᵊ·rin). *Chem.* Formerly also **-ine.** [a. G. *saponarin* (G. Barger 1902, in *Ber. d. Deut. Chem. Ges.* XXXV. 1296), f. med.L. *sāpōnār-ia* (see below and SAPONARY *a.* and *sb.*) + *-in* -IN[1].] A white or pale yellow crystalline flavonoid diglycoside, $_2C_7H_{30}O_{15}$, first found in soapwort, *Saponaria officinalis.* Hence **saponare·tin** [*-ETIN], a monoglycoside derived from this by hydrolysis.

1902 *Jrn. Chem. Soc.* LXXXII. I. 387 Saponarin dissolves in about 1000 parts of hot water and crystallises on cooling in minute, birefringent needles. **1905** G. BARGER in *Rep. Brit. Assoc. Adv. Sci. 1904* 531 Unless the solution be dilute, a second product of hydrolysis separates as a thick yellow oil, which has not yet been obtained crystalline. The name saponaretin is suggested for it. **1923** *Nature* 25 Aug. 304/2 The formation of a glucoside (saponarine) in the mitochondria. **1950** *Thorpe's Dict. Appl. Chem.* (ed. 4) X. 687/1 Saponarin..dried in air is a white powder, but after drying *in vacuo* becomes pale yellow. **1967** *Chem. Abstr.* LXVI. 10485/2 Saponaretin..was obtained by chromatog[raphy] of flavonoids on a polyamide column. **1969** *Acta Chemica Scandinavica* XXIII. 2910/2 At the time of Molisch's investigation the constitution of saponarin was not known. It is now identified as isovitexin-7-glucoside (apigenin-6-*C*-7-*O*-diglucoside).

saponification. Add: **b.** *saponification equivalent* (further examples); now usu. defined in terms of the amount of alkali required to saponify a particular quantity of oil, *spec.* the number of milligrammes of potassium hydroxide required by one gramme of oil; also *saponification number, value.*

1895 PEARMAIN & MOOR *Aids to Analysis of Food & Drugs* 89 The saponification value of an oil may be stated in terms of alkali absorbed per cent., or the number of grammes of the oil which would be saponified by one litre of normal solution of alkali, which is usually known as the 'saponification equivalent'. **1896** *Analyst* XXI. 192 The ether value thus obtained, added to the acid value, gave the saponification number. **1944** *Industrial & Engin. Chem.* (*Analytical Ed.*) XVI. 53 The indicator..is therefore recommended for use in the determination of acid numbers and saponification equivalents. **1946** F. SCHNEIDER *Qualitative Organic Microanalysis* vi. 163 For the identification of the acid portion of the ester use the titrated solution from the determination of the saponification equivalent. **1964** C. J. BONER *Gear & Transmission Lubricants* iii. 68 The saponification number divided by two will give a close approximation of the percentage of fat in a compounded oil. **1975** *Materials & Technol.* VIII. I. 17 The saponification value..expressed as the number of milligrams of potassium hydroxide required to saponify one gram of fat.

saponin, -ine. Add to def.: In mod. use, any of a large class of steroid glycosides obtained from plants, which are usu. toxic (esp. to fish), causing hæmolysis, and are characterized by the property of foaming in aqueous solution. (Further examples.)

The spelling *saponin* is now usual.

1891 *Jrnl. Chem. Soc.* LX. II. 1531 The author [*sc.* R. Kobert] considers that there are a series of saponins of the general formula $C_nH_{2n-8}O_{10}$, several of which are known. **1916** *Jrnl. Biol. Chem.* XXVIII. 443 A new saponin, $C_{24}H_{40}O_{14}$, was isolated from the rootstock of *Yucca filamentosa.* **1953** C. W. & E. SHOPPEE in E. H. Rodd *Chem. Carbon Compounds* II. B. xix. 1035 Saponins..are haemolytic when injected into the bloodstream of animals and therefore highly toxic intravenously but comparatively harmless when ingested. **1977** LEWIS & ELVIN-LEWIS *Med. Bot.* ii. 19/2 The recent importance of plant steroidal compounds, especially the steroid saponins, is their suitability as cortisone and hormone precursors.

sapotoxin (sæ·potǫksin). *Chem.* Also **-ine.** [a. G. *sapotoxin* (R. Kobert 1887, in *Arch. f. exper. Path. u. Pharm.* XXIII. 241), f. med.L. *sāpōnāria* (see below and SAPONARY *a.* and *sb.*): see TOXIN.] A saponin found in the bark of the Chilean soap-bark tree, *Quillaja saponaria*; also, any markedly toxic saponin.

1891 *Jrnl. Chem. Soc.* LX. 1532 The sapotoxin of *Agrostemma githago* (corn cockle)..is absorbed both by the subcutaneous tissues and by the intestinal canal, and thus acts as a dangerous poison. **1892** *Ibid.* LXII. 350 The sapotoxin of *Agrostemma* has the same composition as those of *radix saponariæ albæ* and of quillaja bark, but differs from them in its physiological properties. **1924** C. T. KINGZETT *Chem. Encycl.* 486 Saponins from quillaya bark..are stated to consist of one-third quillajic acid and two-thirds of a body named sapotoxin. **1927** *Glasgow Herald* 11 June 4 The saponine and sapotoxine in effluents from beet-sugar factories. **1941** *Martindale's Extra Pharmacopœia* (ed. 22) I. 910 Quillaia... Contains quillaic acid..and sapotoxin, $C_{17}H_{26}O_{10}$..closely allied to saponin.

sapped, *ppl. a.* Add: Also, eroded or broken off by glacial sapping.

1972 J. G. MCCALL in C. Embleton *Glaciers & Glacial Erosion* xi. 220 The general lack of any further frost action on the 'sapped' blocks of rocks which formed the moraine and screes in the area.

sapphir(e) d'eau, var. *SAPHIR D'EAU.

sapphire. Add: **1. f.** A sapphire used as a stylus for gramophone records.

1943 *Electronic Engin.* XVI. 121/2 The portion of the wire between the ribbon and the sapphire provides sufficient vertical compliance to minimise mechanical noise. **1957** [see *playing-life* s.v. *PLAYING *vbl. sb.* 2]. **1964** P. J. GUY *Disc Recording & Reproduction* vii. 99 In the author's experience some sapphires have a very much shorter life.

2. b. A sapphire mink (see sense *3 c).
1951 *Genetics* XXXVI. 575 Several color phases result from the combination of two or more of these mutant genes, the sapphire..and the 'red-eyed' pastel..being of most commercial importance at the present time.

3. a. *sapphire needle, point, stylus* (all = sense *1 f); *sapphire-shot* adj.; **sapphire quartz**, a rare indigo-blue variety of quartz; = SIDERITE[1] 5.
1940 *Chambers's Techn. Dict.* 740/1 Sapphire needle. **1943** *Gramophone* Dec. 107/2 In the last two years of manufacture of radiograms in this country practically all of them came thru with sapphire needles as standard equipment. **1899** *T. Eaton & Co. Catal.* Spring & Summer 191 Graphophone Supplies... Recorder, with sapphire point, $5.00. Reproducer, with sapphire point, $5.00. **1972** *Country Life* 28 Dec. 1777 We..listened avidly to Mr Alfred Heather's rendering of *I'll sing thee songs of Araby* on our sapphire-point Pathé gramophone. **1868** J. D. DANA *Syst. Min.* (ed. 5) 193 Siderite, or Sapphire-quartz. Of indigo or Berlin-blue color. **1904** L. J. SPENCER tr. *M. Bauer's Precious Stones* 488 Sapphire-quartz (azure-quartz or siderite) is a blue, crystalline quartz... It is used to a very small extent and is correspondingly low in price. **1971** *Country Life* 3 June 1382/3 Quartz, however, may be variously tinted:..sapphire quartz—blue; [etc.]. **1883** G. M. HOPKINS *Poems* (1967) 95 Yet such a sapphire-shot, Charged, steepèd sky will not Stain light. **1947** *Gramophone* Oct. 74/1 This..has the..replaceable sapphire stylus, for which the makers claim 1,000 playings before replacement is necessary. **1974** *Encycl. Brit. Macropædia* XVII. 54/1 When, between 1933 and 1935, attempts were made to use sapphire styli with electrical pickups weighing 50 to 150 grams.., record wear was found to be excessive.

c. sapphire mink, a variety of mink with blue fur (see also sense *2 b); also, the fur of this animal.
1960 *Guardian* 26 Aug. 6/4 A generously wide sapphire mink stole. **1974** *Genetika* XII. II. 109 The interactions between genes are demonstrated to result in a significant rearrangement of cells and the development of a new pigmentation type in sapphire minks. **1976** *S. Wales Echo* 25 Nov. 22/7 (Advt.), Full-length Sapphire Mink, £850.

Sapphist. Add: (Examples.) So **sapphi·stically** *adv.*, in the manner of a Sapphist.
1913 R. BROOKE *Let.* 13 Dec. (1968) 547 A woman.. who loved Lulu sapphistically. **1923** V. WOOLF *Diary* 19 Feb. (1978) II. 235 She is a pronounced Sapphist, & may..have an eye on me. **1925** [see *PÆDERAST]. **1975** 'M. ORR' *Rich Girl, Poor Girl* (1977) xviii. 247 Winifred knew herself to be..a Sapphist on the prowl for a desirable *jeune fille*.

sappiness. 2. (Example.)
1943 *New Yorker* 20 Feb. 22/1 She was..convinced.. that a floppy feminine hat was a symbol of celluloid sappiness.

sapping, *vbl. sb.*[1] Add: **2.** *Physical Geogr.* **a.** Undercutting by water, esp. backward erosion by a waterfall of softer layers of rock at its base; headward erosion of hillsides by springs.
1863 [in Dict.]. **1902** W. M. DAVIS in *Bull. Mus. Compar. Zoöl.* XXXVIII. 328 Whatever flood plains may have been produced during the excavation of the present basin floor, the streams have now so well taken advantage of their opportunity for lateral corrosion or 'sapping' that terraces at high and intermediate levels are everywhere obliterated. **1932** W. H. EMMONS et al. *Geol.* vi. 133 As the swirling water back of the falls loosens the soft, shaley formation it removes it piecemeal and undermines the capping limestone, until finally it remains as an inadequately supported overhanging ledge from which large masses of rock plunge into the pool at the bottom of the falls. This process of undercutting is termed sapping. **1936** *Proc. Geologists' Assoc.* XLVII. 40 A coombe formed in jointed chalk by the sapping back of springs. **1957** *Ibid.* LXVIII. 31 There remains the curious series of right-angled bends in the Ravensburgh Valley system, which has been attributed to sapping along major joints. **1970** R. J. SMALL *Study of Landforms* ii. 53 On rocks such as chalk and limestone the actual sources of streams are extended into escarpments and steep slopes by the process known as 'spring sapping'. This involves underground chemical erosion, surface stream erosion, and slumping of moistened debris around the springhead.

b. Undermining by glacial erosion; (*loosely*) plucking; *spec.* erosion of rock slopes by frost action under the margins of a glacier.
1899 W. D. JOHNSON in *Science* 20 Jan. 106/1 An unrecognized process was set forth, that of sapping, whose action is horizontal and backward... The tendency of the sapping process is to produce benches and cliffs. **1938** *Geol. Mag.* LXXV. 261 As the wall at the head of the cirque retreats under the action of sapping and plucking, immediately downstream the ice abrades and smoothes. **1954** *Jrnl. Glaciol.* II. 421 In accounting for these features [*sc.* roches moutonnées] the assumption ordinarily made is that rock has been removed by plucking or sapping from the downstream side, leaving that face steep and irregular. **1968** R. W. FAIRBRIDGE *Encycl. Geomorphol.* 741/1 The walls have been kept steep and caused to retreat by the collapse of unsupported rock faces as they have been undercut by the process of glacial 'sapping'... The explanation of sapping appears to be found in rending and disintegration of rock by the freeze-and-thaw process. **1972** J. G. MCCALL in C. Embleton *Glaciers & Glacial Erosion* xi. 217 The term sapping, as used here, implies frost-riving on the rock slopes under the margins of a glacier. It is produced by the freezing of any water which flows in under the 'cold' glacier and, in the case of cirques, it results in a horizontal retreat of the headwall.

sapping, *vbl. sb.*[2] (Earlier and later examples.)
1821 *Salt-Bearer* No. 26. 303 When at Eton, boxing, rowing, cricket, and even *sapping*, had by turns the honour of possessing a stall in his hobby stable. **1922** S. LESLIE *Oppidan* iv. 48 That..was why *sapping* was unnecessary.

sappy, *a.* Add: **2. b.** (Later example.)
1948 F. R. LEAVIS *Great Tradition* ii. 111 *The Portrait of a Lady* belongs to the sappiest phase of James's art, when the hypertrophy of technique hadn't yet set in.

7. Also as *sb.* Hence **sa·ppyhead**, a foolish person. Cf. SAP-HEAD.
1922 JOYCE *Ulysses* 114 Martin could wind a sappyhead like that round his little finger without his seeing it. **1930** D. H. LAWRENCE *Nettles* 23 You know that they've got to think that they're happy... Oh so happy, you sappy.

sapric (sæ·prik), *a. Soil Sci.* [f. Gr. σαπρ-ός rotten, putrid + -IC.] Of a soil or soil horizon: characterized by the presence of highly decomposed organic material.
1965 FARNHAM & FINNEY in *Adv. Agronomy* XVII. 138 In the classification of organic soils presented here, only three types of horizons are considered diagnostic... These are the fibric, mesic, and sapric horizons, listed in order of increasing decomposition. **1972** J. G. CRUICKSHANK *Soil Geogr.* vi. 187 At the other extreme, sapric.. soils or horizons are well decomposed and contain a high proportion by weight of mineral material.

† **saprine.** *Chem. Obs.* Also -in. [ad. G. *saprin* (L. Brieger *Untersuchungen über Ptomaine* (1885) II. 46), f. as prec.: see -INE[5].] A ptomaine of doubtful identity isolated from putrefying flesh.
1887 [see CADAVERINE]. **1894** *Watts's Dict. Chem.* IV. 346/2 Saprine is isolated by means of its platinochloride. **1910** *Practitioner* June 830 Ptomaines obtained from putrid meat and other albuminous bodies:..Saprin $C_5H_{16}N_2$.

‖ **sapristi** (sapristi), *int.* [Fr., corruption of *sacristi* in same sense.] An exclamation of astonishment, exasperation, etc.; a mild oath.
1839 THACKERAY *Cox's Diary* in *Comic Almanack 1840* 33 Shouting out, 'Aha!' and '*Sapprrrristie!*' **1867** 'OUIDA' *Under Two Flags* II. i. 3 Sapristi! And what did he say? **1932** A. CHRISTIE *Peril at End House* xxii. 244 And the card—*my* card! *Ah! Sapristi*—she has a nerve! **1957** O. NASH *You can't get there from Here* 97 So when I sight my island home I'll salvage but a single tome, Which is—what should it be, *sapristi*, But any book by Agatha Christie? **1966** A. CHRISTIE *Third Girl* ii. 10 Ah *Sapristi!* That must be a woman—undoubtedly a woman. **1972** A. MACVICAR *Golden Venus Affair* i. 9 Sapristi, what a condition he's in!

saprobe (sæ·proᵘb). *Biol.* [f. Gr. σαπρό-ς putrid + β-ίος life; cf. G. *saprobie* (Kolkwitz & Marsson 1902, in *Mittheilungen aus der K. Prüfungsanstalt f. Wasserversorgung und Abwässerbeseitigung* I. 46).] Any organism that derives its nourishment from decaying organic matter.
1932 G. W. MARTIN in *Bot. Gaz.* XCIII. 427 The word *saprophyte* and its derivatives, implying that a fungus is a plant, can be replaced by saprobe (σαπρός + βίος), which is without such implication. **1952** C. J. ALEXOPOULOS *Introd. Mycol.* i. 30 Fungi obtain their food either as parasites or saprobes. Some are obligately parasitic or saprobic. **1971** G. C. AINSWORTH *Ainsworth & Bisby's Dict. Fungi* (ed. 6) 518 Saprobe is the preferred usage for fungi.

saprobial (sæprōᵘ·biăl), *a. Ecol.* [f. *SAPROB(IC *a.* + -IAL.] Serving as a measure of saprobity.
1965 *Hydrobiologia* XXV. 523 The secondarily introduced methods of statistical calculation and expression of saprobial indices may only pretend an exact mathematical basis. **1970** J. SCHWOERBEL *Methods Hydrobiol.* vii. 155 The saprobial valency is better characterized than the allotment to a single zone of the saprobic system.

saprobic (sæprōᵘ·bik), *a. Ecol.* [f. G. *saprob-ie* *SAPROBE + -IC.] **a.** Characterized by the prevalence of decaying organic material; *spec.* = *polysaprobic* adj. s.v. *POLY- 1; *saprobic system*, a system by which a body of polluted water is divided into zones characterized by the presence of certain organisms that are treated as indicators of the degree of pollution.
1913 *Bull. Illinois State Lab. Nat. Hist.* IX. x. 498 We will distinguish..three stages of impurity, by use of the following terms applicable both to the waters themselves and to the characteristic organisms, given here in the order of a diminishing impurity, namely: (1) septic or saprobic [etc.]. **1925** [see **polysaprobic* adj.]. **1967** A. F. BARTSCH in Olson & Burgess *Pollution & Marine Ecol.* VI. 294 Various North American biologists have expressed doubt as to the applicability of the saprobic system to coastal and estuarine environments. **1971** R. J. BENOIT in L. L. Ciaccio *Water & Water Pollution Handbk.* I. iv. 255 The general relationship between the saprobic zones and the zones shown by oxygen sag curves has been illustrated. **1975** D. F. WESTLAKE in B. A. Whitton *River Ecol.* iv. 126 In general macrophytes are not good indicators for use in the saprobic system of classifying rivers.

b. Pertaining to or characteristic of a saprobe; deriving nourishment from decaying organic matter.
1932 *Bot. Gaz.* XCIII. 429 The nutrition of the Phycomycetes is saprobic or parasitic. **1960** H. B. N. HYNES *Biol. Polluted Waters* xiii. 161 Complex organic..molecules encourage the growth of saprophytic plants and saprobic animals. **1976** *Nature* 27 May 336/2 The free-living saprobic form found in soil is mycelial.

Hence **sapro·bical** *a.* = *SAPROBIAL *a.*; **saprobi·city** = *SAPROBITY.
1961 *Arch. Hydrobiol.* LVII. 405 Tables of the saprobical valency of species studied by the authors as well as examples of the saprobiological evaluation are appended. **1971** *Ann. Rev. Microbiol.* XXV. 565 The rate of multiplication of the test organism, i.e., optimum biomass produced, is considered to be an integrated biological measure of the content of biologically active organic nitrogen in the water and thus a measure of the saprobicity. **1975** G. A. COLE *Textbk. Limnol.* iv. 61/2 Saprobicity, the total of all the processes that are antithetical to primary production, is another classification of heterotrophy.

saprobiology (sæprobəi,ǫ·lodʒi). [f. as next + BIOLOGY.] The study of saprobic environments.
1958 *Ecology* XXXIX. 547/2 It can be stated in terms used in saprobiology that the polysaproby was changed into alpha-mesosaproby. **1965** *Hydrobiologia* XXV. 524 The applicability in practice is..the main criterion of an applied scientific branch, as saprobiology is.

Hence **sa:probiolo·gical** *a.*; **saprobio·logist**.
1960 *Biol. Abstr.* XXXV. 3801/2 The saprobiological analysis is based on the determination of approximately 8,500 organisms. **1965** *Hydrobiologia* XXV. 526 Such problems as the influence of different amino acids..on the stimulation of the growth of *Sphaerotilus* and *Leptomitus* cannot be solved by the saprobiologists alone. **1971** *Ann. Rev. Microbiol.* XXV. 574 Caspers & Karbe..have proposed a saprobiological classification of waters.

saprobiotic (sæprobəi,ǫ·tik), *a. Biol.* [f. Gr. σαπρός putrid + βιωτικ-ός pertaining to life.] = *SAPROBIC *a.*
1940 *Chambers's Techn. Dict.* 740/2 *Saprobiotic*, feeding on dead or decaying animals or plants. **1950** P. D. F. MURRAY *Biology* xlvii. 52 A saprobiotic organism (the term covers 'saprozoic' and 'saprophytic') is one which lives on the dead bodies of other organisms or their inanimate products. **1960** E. N. WILLMER *Cytol. & Evolution* ix. 151 Many flagellates..depend for their energy supplies on the extraction of materials dissolved in the fluid in which they are swimming, i.e. they lead a saprobiotic existence.

Hence **saprobio·tically** *adv.*
1957 G. E. HUTCHINSON *Treat. Limnol.* I. ix. 623 Living plankton metabolizing its reserves or living saprobiotically.

saprobity (sæprōᵘ·bĭti). *Ecol.* [f. *SAPROB(IC *a.* + -ITY.] The degree to which the decomposition of organic material is occurring in an aquatic environment.
1956 *Archiv für Hydrobiol.* LI. 389 Utilization of the running water Macroorganism as Indicators of the water saprobity degrees (sensu Kolkwitz-Marsson). **1965** *Hydrobiologia* XXV. 523 The saprobity system is applicable only to organic pollution undergoing bacterial decomposition and it is useless for the assessment of the effects of poisons or other pollutional matters. **1973** BAYLY & WILLIAMS *Inland Waters & their Ecol.* xii. 254 The 'saprobity indices' of several European workers..are indirect measures of pollution based upon a combination of chemical, bacteriological, and biological features.

saprolite (sæ·prolәit). *Geol.* [f. Gr. σαπρός putrid + -LITE.] Soft, clay-rich, thoroughly decomposed rock formed *in situ* by chemical weathering of igneous and metamorphic rocks.
1895 G. F. BECKER in *16th Ann. Rep. U.S. Geol. Survey* III. 289, I propose the term *saprolite*. *Ibid.* 290 The deposits referred to..are gold-bearing saprolites. **1935** *Jrnl. Geol.* XLIII. 745 In the Appalachian Piedmont of the southern states, weathering has reduced the granitic rocks to an extensive mantle of incoherent clay, or saprolite, that in places extends to a depth of over 100 feet. **1948** *Prof. Papers U.S. Geol. Survey* No. 213. 125/2 The upper parts of the lodes were in the saprolite zone and were worked as residual placer deposits, but at the base of the saprolite these deposits graded into solid lodes. **1977** A. HALLAM *Planet Earth* 48/1 Chemical weathering can produce a rotted rock-form known as a saprolite, which is the product of chemical changes which have taken place *in situ*.

Hence **saproli·tic** *a.*; **sa:prolitiza·tion**, the process of formation of saprolite.
1904 L. J. SPENCER tr. *Bauer's Precious Stones* 361 Several crystals of rhodolite were found..embedded in a decomposed saprolitic rock. **1970** D. CARROLL *Rock Weathering* iii. 20 Extensive areas in arid Western Australia are underlain by saprolitic rocks on which lateritic profiles have developed (probably in the Pliocene). *Ibid.*, Saprolitization also occurs in rocks that are covered by later deposits that protect them from erosion. An example is saprolitization under a cover of river gravel or sand through which water percolates.

sapropel (sæ·propel). *Geol.* [a. G. *sapropel* (H. Potonié 1904, in *Sitzungsber. Ges. naturforsch. Freunde Berlin* 13 Dec. 243), f. as next.] An unconsolidated nitrogen-rich slime or sludge, formed of incompletely decomposed aquatic micro-organisms, esp. algæ, found in anaerobic environments on the bottoms of lakes and seas.

1907 *Rep. Brit. Assoc. Adv. Sci. 1906* 748 The sapropel is formed from the excrements and bodies of completely aquatic animals and plants which have lived in stagnant water, and therefore, because the water is stagnant, do not decay completely. *Ibid.*, Cannel coal..is a fossil sapropel. **1929** H. B. MILNER *Sedimentary Petrogr.* (ed. 2) 335 The coal-substance has been regarded by Potonié as 'sapropel', a solidified jelly-like carbonaceous slime. **1970** *Nature* 17 Oct. 200/1 Cores from the Mediterranean's three deep basins also yielded dolomites,..diatomites and organic sapropels. **1978** *Ibid.* 16 Nov. 259/2 The preservation of non-siliceous algae is uncommon, although found in the sapropel deposits of the USSR.

sapropelic (sæpropeˑlik), *a. Geol.* and *Zool.* [ad. G. *sapropelisch* (R. Lauterborn 1901, in *Zool. Anzeiger* XXIV. 50), f. Gr. σαπρός putrid + πηλός mud, earth, clay: see -IC.] Found in, characterized by, or derived from sapropel.

1901 *Jrnl. R. Microsc. Soc.* 144 'Sapropelic' Fauna... Dr. R. Lauterborn uses the term '*sapropelische*' to denote the organisms found in the muddy debris covering the bottom of stagnant fresh-water pools. **1918** [see *HUMIC *a.*]. **1963** D. W. & E. E. HUMPHRIES tr. *Termier's Erosion & Sedimentation* xi. 239 The presence of a sapropelic bottom inhibits aerobic life over the whole of the lower part of the basin. **1966** [see *HUMIC *a.*]. **1971** *Nature* 31 Dec. 508/1 They [*sc.* labyrinthodonts] are never found in humic coals, but usually in sapropelic coals, laid down in the deep anaerobic mud which formed in stagnant conditions.

saprophile, *sb.* (Example of *fig.* use.)

1934 S. BECKETT *More Pricks than Kicks* 67 A little saprophile of an anonymous politico-ploughboy setting him off.

sapskull. (Later example.)

1974 J. AIKEN *Midnight is Place* i. 11 Idiot! Sapskull! How dared you write?

Saraband[2] (sæˑrăbænd). Also **Sarabend, Serabend,** etc. [ad. *Saravand*, name of a district in western Iran.] A kind of Persian rug characterized by a pattern of leaf or pear forms. Also *attrib.*

1901 J. K. MUMFORD *Oriental Rugs* vi. 68 The 'pear' [*sc.* a motif] seems to have..original association with Persia... In the Sarabands..it covers the whole field. *Ibid.* xi. 197 The Saraband rugs are made in the district of Sarawan. **1913** W. A. HAWLEY *Oriental Rugs* ix. 130 In Mir-Sarabends one of two threads encircled by a knot is doubled under the other at back. In Royal Sarabends each is equally prominent. **1931** [see *palm-leaf pattern* s.v. *PALM-LEAF c]. **1943** *Burlington Mag.* May 130/2 A Saraband carpet, the property of Mrs. Gilbert Russell. **1962** C. W. JACOBSEN *Oriental Rugs* 278 Choicest antique Sarabends will have as many as 350 knots to the square inch. **1975** 'E. LATHEN' *By Hook or by Crook* viii. 78 An old and valued customer was..closing a deal for an old and valued Saraband. **1975** *Oxf. Compan. Decorative Arts* 612/1 Serabend rugs with all-over cone designs.

Saracen. Add: **4. Saracen's corn,** also = *Saracen corn* or buckwheat, *Fagopyrum esculentum.*

1600 R. SURFLET tr. *Stevens & Liebault's Maison Rustique* I. xi. 53 Let her cause to be ground amongst her corne beanes, pease, fetches or sarrasins corne in some small quantitie. **1804** M. WILMOT *Russ. Jrnls.* (1934) I. 123 So many different sorts of Corn..the Sarazens' Corn so white, the flax with its blue flowers, the peas so green.

Sarah (sēᵊˑră). [f. *s*earch *a*nd *r*escue *a*nd *h*oming.] Name given to a portable radio transmitter used by wrecked airmen to signal their position to rescue ships or aircraft. Also *attrib.*

1955 *Times* 31 Aug. 8/3 'Sarah', the device demonstrated yesterday, weighs only about 3lb. and can be carried in a Mae West. It contains a beacon battery of 24 hours operating capacity which can send signals to a Shackleton aircraft 75 miles away. A wrecked airman can start 'Sarah' working quite easily and can speak on it to those who are searching for him. **1956** *Times* 18 July 10/7 Tryout for 'Sarah'..'Sarah', the R.A.F.'s new air-sea rescue system, had its first real test yesterday. **1962** S. CARPENTER in *Into Orbit* 59 One of these beacons, a British invention called 'Sarah'—for 'Search and Rescue and Homing'—put out the signal that helped tell the search planes exactly where I was. *Ibid.* 60 There was one Sarah beacon aboard the capsule.

saralasin (săræˑlăsin). *Pharm.* [Contraction of 1-*sar*-8-*ala*- angioten*sin*, f. SAR(COSINE + ALA(NINE + *angioten*)*sin* (f. ANGIO- + *HYPER)TENSIN).] A synthetic octapeptide which blocks the pressor action of hypertensin II, thereby reducing high blood pressures.

1974 *Lancet* 28 Dec. 1535/1 Angiotensin-II blockade by the competitive antagonist sar[1]-ala[8]-angiotensin II ('Saralasin')... Blockade of angiotensin II with saralasin has been advocated. **1977** *Ibid.* 24/31 Dec. 1317/1 Two types of renin-angiotensin inhibitor have been tested in renal hypertension—competitive antagonists of angiotensin II, such as saralasin, and inhibitors of the converting enzyme.

Saramaccan (særămæˑkăn), *sb.* and *a.* Also **Saramak(k)an.** [f. the name of the river *Saramacca* in Surinam.] **A.** *sb.* **a.** A native or inhabitant of the upper reaches of the river Saramacca. *rare.* **b.** A creole language of this region; = *Jew Tongo* s.v. *JEW *sb.* 3 c. **B.** *adj.* Of or pertaining to the people or language of this region.

1959 J. VOORHOEVE in *Word* XV. 436 (*title*) An orthography for Saramaccan. *Ibid.* 437 The phoneme analysis was based on a Saramaccan story and a series of testwords. *Ibid.*, The Rev. Schmidt is a Saramaccan by birth. **1961** *Compar. Stud. Society & Hist.* III. 278 Saramakkan is spoken only by the Bush Negroes on the upper reaches of the Surinam or 'Saramakka' river. **1968** [see *Jew Tongo* s.v. *JEW *sb.* 3 c]. **1970** *Language* XLVI. 408 (*title*) A Saramaccan narrative pattern. **1976** *Amer. Speech 1974* XLIX. 141 Saramakkan and other creoles of the Americas with a higher proportion of African linguistic content are recognized tone languages.

Saran (sărænˑn). orig. *U.S.* Also **saran.** A proprietary name for PVC, esp. as a film. Also *Saran Wrap* (hence *Saran-wrapped* adj.).

1940 *Official Gaz.* (U.S. Patent Office) 26 Nov. 809/2 The Dow Chemical Company, Midland, Mich. Filed Sept. 27, 1940. *Saran* for thermoplastic synthetic resins comprising polymers and co-polymers derived from vinylidene chloride. Claims use since Aug. 21, 1940. **1942** [see *POLYVINYLIDENE]. **1948** *Textile Colorist* Feb. 46/3 Plastic Sales Division—of the Dow Chemical Company has formally released its trademark rights to the name 'saran' permitting it to become the descriptive name of the product. **1958** *Trade Marks Jrnl.* 26 Nov. 1214/2 *Saran*.. Wrapping (packaging) materials included in Class 16 in the form of films. The Dow Chemical Company..Manufacturers. **1966** N. SIMON *Odd Couple* II. i. 64 After the.. leftovers have been Saran-Wrapped—what do we do? **1968** T. WOLFE *Electric Kool-Aid Acid Test* xxvii. 391 Dresses made out of..supermarket Saran Wrap. **1969** W. R. R. PARK *Plastics Film Technol.* vi. 161 The three plies, 'Saran' 18 (outer), PVC 88 (center), and 'Saran' 22 (inner) each serve a specific function. **1974** D. E. WESTLAKE *Help* ii. 15, I was stretching Saran Wrap over the toilets. **1979** *Maclean's Mag.* 21 May 9/1 Clark began by granting interviews in a separate compartment aboard his plane but by the fifth week of the campaign, Tory campaign manager Lowell Murray sensed that the party was taking the heat for a Saran-Wrapped strategy. **1980** *Yachts & Yachting* 29 Feb. 656/2 Blown saran to produce an easily worked filler.

‖ **sarangi** (sāˑraŋgi). Also 9 **sarungee.** [Skr.] An Indian musical instrument resembling a violin. Cf. *SARINDA.

1851 *Illustr. Catal. Gt. Exhib.* IV. 913/2 Sarungee and bow, or Hindoostanee fiddle. **1886** GONDAL *Jrnl. of Visit to Eng. in 1883* 155 Those niceties of sweet sounds which a *sitar* or a *sárangi* can alone give. **1891** C. R. DAY *Mus. & Mus. Instruments S. India* vi. 93 The use of Sârangi in Southern India..is rapidly being discontinued. **1921** [see *ESRAJ]. **1929** *Radio Times* 4 Jan. 38/3 The *sarangi* has a sweeter, slightly deeper tone than the violin. **1969** [see *DILRUBA]. **1980** *Early Music* July 351/2 This, as can be heard when listening to recordings of the sarangi, does not chop a note from the string but leaves a small *bruyard* to escape.

Saratoga. Delete 'prob.' in etym. and add: **1.** (Earlier examples.)

1858 *N.Y. Tribune* 26 July 3/1 The Saratoga Trunk is an article that has been a theme of story for some time. **1874** B. F. TAYLOR *World on Wheels* I. ix. 72 It is not a carpet-bag, nor a valise nor a Saratoga.

2. In Combinations: **Saratoga chips, (fried) potatoes** *U.S.*, thinly-sliced fried potato served cold, potato crisps; **Saratoga water** *U.S.*, a mineral water obtained from the springs at Saratoga.

1880 F. M. A. ROE *Army Lett.* (1909) 262 The Saratoga chips were delicate and crisp. **1947** *Reader's Digest* Feb. 95/2 She compromised on..a broiled lobster drenched with butter, Saratoga chips, and a fancy ice cream. **1973** *Daily Colonist* (Victoria, B.C.) 4 Feb. 24/2 An Indian—an American Indian—was a chef in Saratoga, N.Y., in 1853 when he had an order for French fries—sliced thin. He sliced them too thin and they came out crunchy, and for the next 40 or 50 years, they were known as Saratoga chips. **1876** M. N. HENDERSON *Cooking* 194 Nothing deteriorates more by getting cold or keeping than fried potatoes (with the exception of Saratoga fried potatoes, which are served cold). **1877** *Golden Hours* Apr. 187/2 (*heading*) Saratoga Potatoes. **1911** *Oysterman & Fisherman* Mar. 25/2 Serve with oysters... French-fried or Saratoga potatoes. **1829** *Amer. Advertiser* (Philadelphia) 29 July 3/6 (Advt.), Fresh Saratoga or Congress Spring Water. **1893** *Harper's Mag.* Jan. 323/1 In front of me was the sign: 'Saratoga water. All you wish for five cents.' **1969** R. & D. DE SOLA *Dict. Cooking* 200/1 *Saratoga water*, any of several mineral waters bottled at their source in Saratoga Springs, New York.

sarbut (sāˑɹbɒ̆t). *local slang.* Also **sarbot, sarbutt.** [App. a proper name.] In Birmingham: a police informer. Also as *v. intr.* = INFORM *v.* 7 b.

[**1896** *Birmingham Daily Mail* 17 Apr. 2/5 'Old Sarbot' says that..the Corporation have no legal powers to superannuate them from the rates.] **1897** *Ibid.* 5 Aug. 3/1, I knew him as one of those men who were engaged by the police for the purpose of putting up robberies and then giving information about them... They are called touts, 'sarbuts' or something else. **1928** F. C. TAYLOR *Language of Lags* in *Word-Lore* Oct. 122 Should one of the fraternity turn informer, he is for ever afterwards known as a *nark*, a *sarbot*, a *copper*. *Ibid.* 124 May be she'll sarbot to the D. who clobbered the kids. **1969** R. BUSBY *Robbery Blue* iii. 24 Your sarbut's story wasn't good enough... We were fooled. **1976** —— *New Face in Hell* viii. 110 The hand-picked city crime squad..recruited their 'sarbuts', the city slang for informants. **1978** *Daily Mail* 25 Jan. 12/2 In Birmingham an informer..is a 'sarbutt'.

sarc (sāɹk). *rare.* Abbrev. of SARCASM. Cf. *SARKY *a.*

1926 E. WALLACE *Square Emerald* xv. 236 She always knew when her young lady was indulging in what Lucretia described as 'sarc'.

Sarcee (sāˑɹsi), *a.* and *sb.* Also † **Sursee, Sussee, Sarsee, Sarsi.** [ad. Blackfoot *saaxsíiwa*; 18th-c. forms ad. Cree *sasiw*, pl. *sasiwak.*] **A.** *adj.* Of or pertaining to the Sarcee or their language (see below). **B.** *sb.* **a.** An Athapaskan people of Alberta in Canada; a member of this people. **b.** Their language.

[**1772** M. COCKING *Jrnl.* 1 Dec. in *Trans. R. Soc. Canada* (1909) II. II. 111 There are 4 Tribes, or Nations, more, which are all Equestrians Indians, Viz... Pegonow or Muddy-water Indians & Sassewuck or Woody Country Indians.] **1790** E. UMFREVILLE *Present State of Hudson's Bay* i. 78 Those Indians from whom the Peltries are obtained are known to us by the following names, *viz.* The Ne-heth-aw-a Indians. The Assinne-poetuc Indians. The Fall Indians. The Sussee Indians [etc.]. **1801** A. MACKENZIE *Voy. from Montreal* p. lxxi, The Sarsees, who are but few in number, appear from their language, to come.. from the North-Westward, and are of the same people as the Rocky-Mountain Indians. **1820** D. W. HARMON *Jrnl. Voy. & Trav. Interior N. Amer.* 313, I have been acquainted with fifteen different tribes of Indians, which are the.. Black feet Indians, Blood Indians, Sursees [etc.]. **1904** *Jrnl. Amer. Folklore* July–Sept. 180 (*heading*) Traditions of the Sarcee Indians. *Ibid.*, The Sarcee Indians of Alberta, N.W.T., Canada, claim to have belonged at one time to the Beaver Indians. **1915** *Univ. Calif. Publ. Amer. Archaeol. & Ethnol.* XI. III. 190 The Sarsi are an Athapascan-speaking group of Indians who have been closely associated with the Northern Blackfoot of Alberta. **1919** *Anthropol. Papers Amer. Mus. Nat. Hist.* XVI. IV. 273 The text itself was dictated by Eagle-ribs..a younger son of the head chief of the Natsilt'inna, one of the four Sarsi bands. *Ibid.*, A.. running account of the sun dance was recorded as a text in Sarsi. **1921** E. SAPIR *Language* 213 The buffalo culture of the Plains (Sarcee). **1933** L. BLOOMFIELD *Language* iv. 72 The Athabascan family covers all but the coastal fringe of northwestern Canada (Chipewyan, Beaver, Dogrib, Sarsi, etc.). **1936** D. MCCOWAN *Animals Canad. Rockies* ix. 81 Amongst the Stony and Sarcee Indians there was formerly a vague superstition imposing a sort of taboo on the cougar. **1965** *Language* XLI. 171 Harry Hoijer and Janet Joël, 'Sarsi nouns'. **1965** [see *ATHAPASCAN, -PASKAN *sb.* 2]. **1973** A. H. WHITEFORD *N. Amer. Indian Arts* 92 Checks, diamonds, and terraced triangles were old patterns among the..Sarcee. **1977** T. A. SEBEOK *Native Lang. Americas* II. 316 The term Mountain..has been applied also to groups speaking Beaver, Chipewyan, Kaska, Sarsi, Slave, Tsetsaut and Yellowknife.

sarcenchyme. Add: Hence **sarcenchyˑmatous** *a.*

1888, 1900 [see *CHONDRENCHYMA].

sarco-. sarcomere, ˌsarcosome: delete defs. and see as main entries.

sarcococca (sāɹkokǫˑksă). [mod.L. (J. Lindley 1826, in *Bot. Reg.* XII. 1012), f. SARCO- + Gr. κόκκος seed.] A small evergreen shrub of the genus so called, belonging to the family Buxaceæ, native to India, China, and Malaysia, and bearing clusters of white, often fragrant, flowers followed by black or red berries.

1914 W. J. BEAN *Trees & Shrubs Hardy in Brit. Isles* II. 500 The hardy Sarcococcas, all Chinese, are neat and pleasing shrubs,..the flowers white, fragrant. **1972** *Country Life* 16 Mar. 624/2 Equally valuable for winter flowering are the evergreen sarcococcas.

sarcocyst (sāˑɹkosist). *Microbiology* and *Vet. Sci.* [f. SARCO- + CYST.] **a.** A cyst in muscle tissue containing spores or sporoblasts of sarcosporidia. **b.** An individual of the genus *Sarcocystis* of sarcosporidia.

1892 G. FLEMING tr. *Neumann's Treat. Parasites & Parasitic Dis.* VI. i. 662 The Sarcocysts of Miescher are very frequent—at least, in certain countries and at certain periods. **1932** GAIGER & DAVIES *Vet. Path. & Bacteriol.* xxii. 333 The sarcocyst in the muscles is the only stage of the parasite which is known. *Ibid.* 334 Sarcocysts may die *in situ.* **1938** SOUTHWELL & KIRSHNER *Guide Vet. Parasitol. & Entomol.* (ed. 2) ii. 19 Sarcocysts are included in the Sporozoa, though it is doubtful if they really belong to this class. **1970** [see *SARCOSPORIDIUM].

Hence **sarcocyˑstic** *a.*

1927 [see *SARCOSPORIDIAL *a.*]. **1979** *Acta Leidensia: Scholae Medicinae Tropicae* XLVII. 46 Schizogonic and sarcocystic stages.

sarcoid, *a.* and *sb.* Add: **A.** *adj.* **2.** *Path.* Pertaining to or resembling sarcoidosis.

1935 *Proc. Soc. Exper. Biol. & Med.* XXXIII. 403 A sarcoid lesion of the skin..was removed. **1962** *Lancet* 26 May 1107/2 Sarcoid tissue obtained from a skin lesion was suspended in saline solution. **1976** EDINGTON & GILLES *Path. in Tropics* (ed. 2) xi. 522 The presence [in Crohn's disease] of a sarcoid reaction in the tissues of the bowel wall, and regional lymph nodes.

B. *sb.* **2. a.** *Path.* Sarcoidosis; also, a tumour resembling a sarcoma.

1899 C. BOECK in *Jrnl. Cutaneous & Genito-Urin. Dis.* XVII. 543 (*heading*) Multiple benign sarkoid of skin. **1941** *Arch Ophthalm.* XXVI. 358 The term sarcoid was adopted by Boeck in 1899 for lesions simulating sarcomas and leukemic conditions of the skin. He believed the condition to be one only of the skin. Later he recognized his mistake in the term and changed it to multiple miliary lupoid. **1963** JUBB & KENNEDY *Path. Domestic Animals* II. x. 565/1 Sarcoids are usually multiple and occur most frequently about the base of the ear, on the neck, and on the lower limbs. **1977** *Proc. R. Soc. Med.* LXX. 484/2 Greenberg *et al.* (1964) found parotitis in 23 (6%) of 388 patients suffering from sarcoid. **1978** *Price's Textbk. Pract. Med.* (ed. 12) III. 275/2 Subcutaneous telangiectases or haemangiomata become visible in some patients. The latter may develop into small tumours or 'sarcoids' up to a centimetre across.

b. *Comb.*, as *sarcoid-like* adj.

1943 *Arch. Dermatol. & Syphilol.* XLVII. 62 Sarcoid-like lesions have..been produced by the injection of bovine tubercle bacilli of low virulence into rabbits. **1968** A. ROOK et al. *Textbk. Dermatol.* xxvi. 937/1 Beryllium causes either a local or a systemic sarcoid-like reaction.

sarcoidal (sāɹkoi·dăl), *a. Path.* [f. prec. + -AL.] = *SARCOID *a.* 2.

1961 *Jrnl. Amer. Med. Assoc.* 4 Nov. 476/1 Employing a suspension of human sarcoidal tissue as test material. **1962** *Lancet* 26 May 1108/1 If sarcoidosis were produced by many agents..then a series of sarcoidal test-tissues would presumably be necessary.

sarcoidosis (sāɹkoidōᵘ·sis). *Path.* [f. as prec. + -OSIS.] A chronic disease characterized by the widespread appearance of sarcoid granulomata derived from the reticuloendothelial system.

1936 *New England Jrnl. Med.* CCXIV. 346 (*heading*) Hutchinson–Boeck's disease (generalized 'sarcoidosis'). **1955** *Lancet* 26 Mar. 640/2 There is no general agreement on whether any form of treatment is effective for pulmonary sarcoidosis. **1975** *Guardian* 25 Feb. 6/1 He recorded a verdict of death from natural causes after hearing that Mrs Rogers died of acute adrenal insufficiency due to sarcoidosis, a chronic illness which can affect all the organs of the body.

sarcolemma. Add: Hence **sarcole·mmal** *a.*, of or pertaining to the sarcolemma.

1912 *Brain* XXXIV. 370 In some places the sarcolemmal nuclei were much increased in numbers. **1974** *Nature* 1 Mar. 69/2 Our data favour the hypothesis that sarcolemmal sensitivity to ACh is regulated by a mechanism located in or near the muscle membrane.

sarcoma. Add: Also with pl. **sarcomas.**

1. b. Now applied to almost any malignant tumour not derived from epithelial tissue. (Further examples.)

1971 *Nature* 21 May 147/2 In human populations only about 10 per cent of cancers are sarcomas; the other 90 per cent are carcinomas—cancers of tissues of epithelial, not mesodermal, origin. **1975** *Sci. Amer.* Nov. 64/2 The cancers are divided into three broad groups. The carcinomas arise in the epithelia... The much rarer sarcomas arise in supporting structures such as fibrous tissues and blood vessels. The leukemias and lymphomas arise in the blood-forming cells.

sarcomere (sā·ɹkomīᵊɹ). *Anat.* [f. SARCO- + *-MERE.] A unit of a myofibril in striated muscle, consisting of a dark band and the nearer half of each adjacent pale band.

1891 E. A. SCHAFER in *Proc. R. Soc.* XLIX. 281 The segment of a sarcostyle comprised between two transverse membranes may be termed 'muscle-segment' or 'sarcomere'. **1897** *Jrnl. Anat. & Physiol.* XXXI. 336 [Schäfer] regards the sarcostyle as divided at regular intervals by Krause's transverse membranes into 'muscle segments' or 'sarcomeres', which are only new names for Krause's 'muscle caskets'. **1930** W. BLOOM *Maximow's Text-bk. Histol.* viii. 205 In the invertebrates (arthropods)..sarcomeres as long as 17μ have been found. The length of the sarcomere and the physiologic peculiarities of the muscle have not..been correlated. **1970** T. S. & C. R. LEESON *Histol.* (ed. 2) ix. 162/2 It is customary to consider the muscle fibril as composed of structural units. Each unit extends between adjacent z lines and is termed a sarcomere. **1980** CRAWFORD & JAMES in R. Owen et al. *Sci. Foundations Orthopaedics & Traumatol.* x. 68/1 Changes in sarcomere length occur by movement of the thick myosin filaments along the thin actin filaments, their own length remaining unchanged.

sarcomic (saɹkōᵘ·mik), *a. nonce-wd.* [f. SARCOMA + -IC.] = CANCEROUS *a. fig.*

1958 J. STEINBECK *Once there was War* p. xx, We are poisoned in our souls by fear, faceless, stupid sarcomic terror.

sarcophagize, *v.* Add: Also *intr.* for *pass.* (*nonce-use*).

1953 E. SITWELL *Gardeners & Astronomers* 9 The hue of honey sarcophagising or of sard.

sarcoplasmic (sāɹkoplæ·zmik), *a. Anat.* [f. *sarcoplasm* s.v. SARCO- + -IC.] Of, pertaining to, or containing sarcoplasm; *sarcoplasmic reticulum*, the characteristic endoplasmic reticulum of striated muscle.

1891 *Internat. Monatsschrift für Anat. u. Physiol.* VIII. 229 The optical effect produced by the enlarging sarcoplasmic accumulations will involve more and more of the segment. **1902** *Encycl. Brit.* XXXI. 733/1 The muscle-cells of the ventricles are thicker, less sarcoplasmic, and more clearly striated than the auricular muscle. **1948** *Jrnl. Neurol., Neurosurg. & Psychol.* XI. 78/1 The dense areas showed an accumulation of pale oval sarcoplasmic nuclei. **1953** BENNETT & PORTER in *Amer. Jrnl. Anat.* XCIII. 69 The disposition of the larger masses of this sarcoplasmic reticulum is interpreted as evidencing an arrangement entirely analogous to the cross-fiber reticulum of Thin (1876), Melland (1885)..and others. **1970** T. S. & C. R. LEESON *Histol.* (ed. 2) ix. 164/2 Sarcoplasmic reticulum corresponds to the endoplasmic reticulum of other cell types, but its membranes are not associated with ribosomes. The sarcoplasmic reticulum comprises an extensive, continuous system of membrane-limited sarcotubules enclosing each myofibril as in a net. **1970** *Nature* 31 Oct. 417/2 The group of muscle fibres in the centre of the section show sarcoplasmic basophilia.

sarcopterygian (sāːɹkǫptəri·dʒiăn). [f. mod. L. name of subclass *Sarcopterygii* (A. S. Romer 1955, in *Nature* 16 July 126/2) + -AN: see SARCO- and PTERYGO-.] A fossil or living fish belonging to the subclass Sarcopterygii, distinguished by fleshy fins.

1966 A. S. ROMER *Vertebr. Paleontol.* (ed. 3) v. 71/2 Many later sarcopterygians have simple bony scales. **1974** D. & M. WEBSTER *Compar. Vertebr. Morphol.* v. 96 Among the sarcopterygians there are striking differences between the pectoral girdles of the living lungfish, Dipnoi, and the living coelacanth, *Latimeria*.

sarcoptid (sāɹkǫ·ptid). [f. mod.L. family name *Sarcoptidæ*, f. generic name *Sarcoptes* (P. A. Latreille *Hist. Nat. Crustacées & Insectes* (1802) III. 67): see SARCOPTES and -ID³.] An itch or mange mite of the family Sarcoptidæ. Also *attrib.* or as *adj.* Also **sa·rcopt** in the same sense.

1870 A. S. PACKARD *Guide Study of Insects* 666 Various Sarcoptids occur on birds. **1892** G. FLEMING tr. *Neumann's Treat. Parasites Domestic Animals* I. v. 121 The sarcopt of scabies..has the body slightly oval. **1932** L. VAN ES *Princ. Animal Hygiene* xliii. 736 Sarcopts are the most common cause of mange in dogs. **1962** GORDON & LAVOIPIERRE *Entomol. for Students of Med.* xliv. 264 (*caption*) The life-cycle of a sarcoptid mite.

sarcosome (sā·ɹkosōᵘm). *Biol.* [ad. G. *sarcosom* (G. Retzius 1890, in *Biol. Untersuchungen* Neue Folge I. 76): see SARCO- and *-SOME⁴.] A large mitochondrion found in striated muscle.

1899 [in Dict. s.v. SARCO-]. **1912** *Amer. Jrnl. Anat.* XIV. 5 The 'exoplasmic granules' (J granules and Q granules) and the 'endoplasmic granules' of Holmgren correspond to the 'Sarcosomes' of Retzius which in turn correspond to Kölliker's true interstitial granules. It is possible that Retzius and Holmgren may have occasionally confused fat droplets with sarcosomes. **1919** *Anat. Rec.* XVI. 217 The wing muscle of the mantis furnishes an exceptionally favorable material for the investigation of the interfibrillar sarcoplasmic granules, or 'sarcosomes', characteristic of insect wing muscle. **1956** *Physiol. Rev.* XXXVI. 3 It is proposed in this article..to use the term sarcosome in its original sense as a general term to describe the lipoprotein granules which lie between the myofibrils and which can be seen with the light microscope. **1970** *Sci. Amer.* Feb. 101 The specialized mitochondria of the myocardial cell are unusually large; they are called sarcosomes.

sarcosporidiosis (sāːɹkosporidiōᵘ·sis). *Vet. Sci.* [f. next + -OSIS.] Infection with, or a disease caused by, sarcosporidia.

1893 *Bull. Bureau Animal Industry, U.S. Dept. Agric.* No. 3. 80 Barrows' description renders it almost certain that this was a case of sarcosporidiosis. **1953** R. P. HALL *Protozool.* vi. 326 Sarcosporidiosis of man is apparently rare, although cases are reported occasionally. **1978** AYERS & JONES in K. Benirschke et al. *Path. Laboratory Animals* I. i. 14/1 Sarcosporidiosis is probably the most common parasitic disease of the heart seen in laboratory animals.

sarcosporidium (sāːɹkospori·diŏm). *Microbiology* and *Vet. Sci.* Also **Sarco-**. Pl. **-sporidia.** [mod.L., ad. F. *sarcosporidie* (G. Balbiani, in *Jrnl. de Micrographie* (1882) VI. 262, (1883) VII. 87): see SARCO- and SPORIDIUM.] A spore-forming protozoan of the genus *Sarcocystis* that is a common parasite in the muscle tissue of many vertebrates, esp. domestic and laboratory mammals. Usu. *pl.*

1891 *Jrnl. Compar. Med. & Vet. Arch.* XII. 693 The small cysts found in the muscular fibres of various animals and known as Sarcosporidia. *Ibid.*, The negative results obtained..from feeding meat infected with sarcosporidia to various animals. **1927** *Indian Jrnl. Med. Res.* XV. 142 It is suggested that this parasite is an undescribed species of sarco-sporidium infecting the human host. **1930** *Jrnl. Parasitol.* XVI. 111 From the economic standpoint Sarcosporidia are of chief interest to the veterinarian rather than the physician. **1970** JUBB & KENNEDY *Path. Domestic Animals* (ed. 2) I. ii. 121/2 Of those parasites with an affinity for muscle, the ubiquitous Sarcosporidia are the most common. The sarcocysts may be found in the Purkinje cells as well as in the myocardial fibres and normally appear to be of little detriment.

Hence **sa:rcospori·dial** *a.*, **-spori·dian** *a.* and *sb.*

1903 E. A MINCHIN in E. R. Lankester *Treat. Zool.* I. II. 301 The dangerous effects of the Sarcosporidian parasites. **1913** *Proc. Cambr. Philos. Soc.* XVII. 221 (*heading*) *Sarcocystis colii*, n. sp., a Sarcosporidian occurring in the red-faced African mouse bird. **1924** HEGNER & TALIAFERRO *Human Protozool.* xi. 372 (*caption*) Sarcosporidian spores. **1927** *Indian Jrnl. Med. Res.* XV. 142 Sarcocystic (Sarcosporidial) infection is common in cattle. **1949** C. A. HOARE *Handbk. Med. Protozool.* xiv. 271 Sarcosporidial infection has been reported in the muscles of the heart, larynx, tongue and the extremities. **1957** SMITH & JONES *Vet. Path.* xx. 704 Myocarditis... Sarcosporidial.. cysts are common in the heart muscle.

Sard, *a.* and *sb.*² Add: Also ‖ **Sarde. B.** *sb.* **1.** (Further examples.)

1845 *Encycl. Metrop.* XXIV. 318/2 The Sards are greatly attached to the pleasures of the table. **1889** C. EDWARDES *Sardinia & Sardes* vi. 147 The foreman was a Sarde of an advanced type. **1932** [see *SARDINIAN *sb.* 2]. **1968** *Listener* 29 Feb. 267/1 No Sard will betray another... There's the unwritten law of *omerta*, of silence.

2. = *SARDINIAN *sb.* 2.

1885 [see *LOGUDORO]. **1889** C. EDWARDES *Sardinia & Sardes* iii. 59 Modern Sarde is what Sardinia's conquerors made it—a language much more nearly kin to Latin than Italian. **1957** *Whitaker's Almanack 1958* 899/1 Sard, the dialect of Sardinia, is accorded by some authorities the status of a distinct Romance language. **1975** *Times Lit. Suppl.* 25 Apr. 452/4 Gramsci was a humane and intelligent man, but in no sense an 'authority' on anything except Mussolini's prisons and Sard.

‖ **sardana** (saɹdā·nă). [Sp.] A popular Catalan dance performed to pipes and drum.

1922 *Glasgow Herald* 28 Apr. 8 The music played by amateur orchestras, even in small villages, to the Sardanas or national Catalonian dances is delightful. **1934** C. LAMBERT *Music Ho!* III. 172 The Catalan sardanas..have added to their primitive basis sophisticated and foreign elements. **1953** *Observer* 13 Sept. 9/2 To describe the new local dance, the Sardana from Spanish Catalonia, Mr. O'Brian has essayed a poetic prose. **1965** *Listener* 10 June 877/3 Spain retains small keyless shawms..and also has modern keyed forms in the sardana bands of Catalonia. **1976** D. MUNROW *Instruments Middle Ages & Renaissance* 40/3 The Catalonian *coblas* of north-eastern Spain which play for the *sardana*, the 'national' dance of the region.

sardine². Add: **1. b.** (Earlier example.)

1870 L. M. ALCOTT *Old-Fashioned Girl* xiii. 266 We've got sardines, crackers, and cheese.

d. In colloq. phr. *to be packed* (*in*) *like sardines*: to be crowded or confined tightly together, as sardines in a tin.

1911 W. OWEN *Let.* 12 Sept. (1967) 80 The entrance hall.. where for half an hour the boys stand waiting packed like sardines. **1922** *Dialect Notes* V. 172 We were packed in there like sardines in a box. **1974** *Daily Mirror* 11 Nov. 4/3 Lodgers at a lorry drivers' digs hit by a horror blaze were 'packed in like sardines', it was claimed yesterday.

e. *pl.* (const. as *sing.*) A party game of hide-and-seek, in which each seeker joins the hider upon discovery until one seeker remains. Also *sardines-in-the* (also *a*)-*box* (U.S.).

1924 in Mendel & Meynell *Weekend Bk.* 241 *Sardines* is gaudier still. Only one player hides, all the others seek; the first to find him hides with him, the next..squashes in alongside,..till everybody's hiding in the same spot but one Seeker. **1925** F. SCOTT FITZGERALD *Great Gatsby* v. 82 'Hide-and-go-seek' or 'sardines-in-the-box' with all the house thrown open to the game. **1935** N. MARSH *Enter Murderer* xx. 242 Give us all the light in the house. I refuse to play sardines with Mr. Hickson. **1959** J. BYROM *Take only as Directed* xiii. 147, I remembered the big linen-chest... I had once hidden there playing Sardines. **1960** N. HALE *New England Grilhood* 113 We used to play hide-and-go-seek, and a game called sardines-in-a-box. **1962** B. COBB *Murder: Men Only* iv. 37 That game—'Sardines,' isn't it?—in which men hide with girls in cupboards. **1974** N. FREELING *Dressing in Diamond* 116 Tomorrow is a holiday... So we weekend... And play sardines. **1980** G. M. FRASER *Mr. American* xiii. 259 The festivities were strictly of the nursery variety..musical chairs, 'sardines', and hide-and-seek.

2. *sardine boat, fishing, fleet*; *sardine can, sandwich, tin*; *sardine-packed* adj.; **sardine box** (earlier example).

1927 L. RICHARDSON *Brittany & Loire* 128 The early type of sardine boat had no overhang—a long, straight keel, straight stem. **1976** F. GREENLAND *Misericordia Drop* II. xiii. 161 A converted sardine-boat. **1855** *Harvard Mag.* I. 266 O ghosts of innumerous sardine-boxes, and emptied cracker-kegs. **1977** *Modern Railways* Dec. 484/1 The first run was with an eight-car formation of this stock forming the 18.00 down Clacton packed to sardine-can condition. **1979** P. DRISCOLL *Pangolin* ii. 22 The tram..was more crowded than usual..a clanking sardine can. **1775** J. SCHAW *Jrnl. Lady of Quality* (1921) iv. 220 Above a hundred boats engaged in the sardine fishing. **1939** H. M. MINER *St. Denis* ii. 23 There is still some commercial eel-and sardine-fishing, but this has declined. **1942** 'A. BRIDGE' *Frontier Passage* iv. 65 The many-coloured dancing shapes of the sardine-fleet. **1917** WYNDHAM LEWIS *Let.* Sept. (1963) 92, I am now absolutely sardine-packed with the quintessence of the prosperous slums of a Protestant country. **1954** B. MALAMUD in *Partisan Rev.* Nov.–Dec. 587 Leo fixed tea and a sardine sandwich. **1978** F. WELDON *Praxis* vii. 42 She had lit the fire and made sardine sandwiches. **1890** W. BOOTH *In Darkest Eng.* II. ii. 121 Most of the toys which are sold in France on New Year's Day are almost entirely made of sardine tins. **1933** M. ALLINGHAM *Sweet Danger* xv. 187 'Leave that smelly little sardine tin [*sc.* a motor car] alone.'... 'The exhaust smells a little, but that's nothing.' **1973** 'A. HALL' *Tango Briefing* x. 124 A rip-string and I pulled it, opening the polyester like a sardine-tin.

sardine (sāɹdī·n), *v. colloq.* (orig. *U.S.*). [f. SARDINE².] *trans.* To pack closely, as sardines in a tin; to crowd, cram, press tightly.

1895 W. C. GORE in *Inlander* Dec. 114 *Sardine*,..to pack closely, side by side. 'We sardined ourselves in front of the Law Building and howled.' **1896** *Advance* 24 Dec. 916/2 There are 350 people outside.., and in some way we are going to sardine them in. **1940** H. WALPOLE *Roman Fountain* vii. 124 We were pressed back and sardined together. **1953** DYLAN THOMAS *Under Milk Wood* (1954) 69 Mrs Probert..is the one love of his sea-life that was sardined with women. **1968** *N.Y. Times* 22 Apr. 36 Hundreds of thousands of people..will be sardined into the famous amusement park. **1977** *New Yorker* 11 July 79/1 Once sardined in place, they are subject to terrifying hazards in case of fire.

Sardinian, *a.* and *sb.* Add: **A.** *adj.* **c.** Designating a Romance language (or group of dialects) spoken by the Sardinians.

1835 G. C. LEWIS *Origin & Formation Romance Lang.* i. 48 Niebuhr..says that 'specimens of the Sardinian language from the civilized districts exhibit peculiarities which are more than varieties of dialect'. **1960** W. D. ELCOCK *Romance Lang.* v. 474 In..perceiving that the 'outlandish' character of Sardinian speech lay in its approximation to Latin the poet-philologist [Dante] had almost divined the truth concerning the origin of the Romance languages. **1974** *Encycl. Brit. Macropædia* XV. 1029/1 It is sometimes said that these last two [*sc.* Sassarian and Gallurian] are not Sardinian dialects but rather Corsican.

d. *Sardinian warbler*, a black, brown, and white warbler, *Sylvia melanocephala*, found in the Mediterranean region.

1909 C. WHYMPER *Egyptian Birds* 209 Sardinian Warbler ..Rare. **1954** D. A. BANNERMAN *Birds Brit. Isles* III. 150 In Sicily..the Sardinian warbler is the commonest warbler. **1971** *Country Life* 1 July 27/3 Our most familiar sounds by day were..the chatter of Sardinian warblers among the mastic bushes.

B. *sb.* **2.** A Romance language (or group of dialects) spoken in Sardinia.

1813 *Q. Rev.* Oct. 259 Bolognese.., Sicilian.., Sardinian. **1841** *Penny Cycl.* XX. 427/1 A book was published at Cagliari, in both Sardinian and Italian, called 'Moriografia Sarda'. **1894** W. M. LINDSAY *Latin Lang.* ii. 34 Short *ŭ* and *ŏ* of Latin are distinguished not only in Sardinian.., but also in Roumanian and in the Latin element of the Albanian language. **1932** G. F.-H. BERKELEY *Italy in Making* I. iv. 52 French was permitted for the Savoyards and Valdostani, Genoese for the Ligurians, and Sardinian for the Sards. **1965** W. S. ALLEN *Vox Latina* i. 25 At what period such a [phonetic] change took place it is impossible to say, but Sardinian suggests that it was very late. **1974** *Encycl. Brit. Macropædia* XV. 1026/1 On linguistic grounds Sardinian (not the language of an independent nation since the 14th century) and Occitan (the medieval Provençal) are usually regarded as languages rather than dialects. *Ibid.* 1029/1 The first documents in Sardinian are legal contracts dating from about 1080.

sardonic, *a.* Add: **c.** *Comb.*, as *sardonic-looking* adj.

1921 D. H. LAWRENCE *Tortoises* 29 She is..A little sardonic-looking, as if domesticity had driven her to it.

Hence **sardo·nicism**, the quality or state of being sardonic; an instance of this; a sardonic remark.

1928 *Daily Express* 6 Jan. 8/3 The old Spartan régime has gone, but there is a relentlessness about the public school system that engenders secret terrors at every turn. It may be the fear of ridicule, or the sardonicisms of a satiric master, or one of a dozen things. **1930** W. DE LA MARE *On Edge* 197 A corrosive sardonicism had come into her voice. **1940** W. FAULKNER *Hamlet* II. i. 100 He would speculate now and then with cold sardonicism. **1964** *Listener* 29 Oct. 667/2 Because familiarity with the role has made Sean Connery feel able to play Bond more relaxedly, an agreeable sardonicism has been added to the earlier deliberately overdone Superman masculinity.

Sardoodledom (saɹdū·d'ldəm). [f. blend of the name of Victorien *Sardou* (1831–1908), French dramatist + DOODLE *sb.* + -DOM.] A fanciful word used to describe well-wrought, but trivial or morally objectionable, plays considered collectively; the characteristic milieu in which such work is admired.

1895 G. B. SHAW in *Sat. Rev.* 1 June 725/2 (*heading*) Sardoodledom. **1897** —— in *Ibid.* 17 Apr. 410/2 It is rather a nice point whether Miss Ellen Terry should be forgiven for sailing the Lyceum ship into the shallows of Sardoodledom for the sake of Madame Sans-Gêne. **1931** *Times Lit. Suppl.* 1 Jan. 2/1 The 'cup-and-saucer' comedy of Robertson and what Mr. Shaw christened 'Sardoodledom' ..opened a new phase of theatrical history. **1959** *Listener* 30 July 186/3 Sardoodledom is not forgotten. **1960** *Times* 15 Jan. 16/1 We do not want to try to rebut Shaw's criticism of 'Sardoodledom'.

saree. Restrict ‖ to sense b and add: The form *sari* is now common, esp. in writings outside India. (Further examples.)

1908 [see *CHOLI]. **1930** *Aberdeen Press & Jrnl.* 6 May 6, I was struck today by the international character of London. Indians in gay saris, a group of Japanese,..all passed me. **1960** [see *CHOLI]. **1969** *Hindu* 3 Aug. 12/4 A petition on behalf of over 4,000 handloom weavers of Salem and other parts of Tamil Nadu was presented to the Rajya Sabha on Tuesday urging the immediate implementation of the order reserving manufacture of coloured sarees for the handloom sector. **1969** *Femina* (Bombay) 26 Dec. 8/4 The piece-de-resistance of the show, a smart zip-up sari, found great favour with the foreigners in the audience. **1971** [see *MANIPURI *a.* and *sb.*]. **1971** R. RUSSELL tr. *A. Ahmad's Shore & Wave* i. 14 Love for the dark-skinned maidservants in their grubby sarees. **1976** *Leicester Trader* 24 Nov. 22/1 (Advt.), Also we clean..dresses, bedspreads, sarees, etc.

2. *attrib.* and *Comb.*

1936 J. FLANNER in *New Yorker* 22 Aug. 65/1 The Hindu hockey team, and its handsome, sari-clad womenfolk. **1955** R. P. JHABVALA *To whom She Will* xiv. 96 Radha.. would walk into a sari-shop, because she was so fond of looking at nice silks. **1968** *Guardian* 19 Sept. 7/3 Embroidered sari silks for evening dresses. **1978** 'M. M. KAYE' *Far Pavilions* xxvi. 392 There was little chance of seeing her..save as a sari-shrouded figure on the occasion of her marriage.

Hence **sa·reed** *a.*, wearing a saree.

1958 E. A. ROBERTSON *Justice of Heart* xv. 212 The sari'd head wagged slower. **1975** O. SELA *Bengali Inheritance* vii. 53 Oval-eyed, smiling sareed girl with skin like brown silk.

Sargasso. Add: **a.** Also *fig.*, esp. in sense 'a confused or stagnant mass'.

1934 DYLAN THOMAS *18 Poems* 12 The dry Sargasso of the tomb Gives up its dead to such a working sea. **1968** A. C. CLARKE *2001: Space Odyssey* xlii. 206 It had swept him across the Galaxy, and dumped him..in this celestial Sargasso. **1976** *Listener* 12 Feb. 182/3, I started the week with a careful schedule and ended in bed with 'flu, lost in a Sargasso of phone-ins, pop, news, avant-garde operas and the reminiscences of David Niven. **1977** *Mystery Writers' Choice* 62, I waited..adrift in a sargasso of conflicting feelings.

b. Sargasso Sea: also *fig.*

1961 P. SOLOMON in B. E. Flaherty *Psychophysiol. Aspects Space Flight* III. 275 Deprived of sensory input, the mind is cut adrift and regresses inexorably into that Sargasso Sea of the primary process, where time disappears, ..where vivid, multicolored hallucinations swirl and befuddle the senses. **1966** C. H. HAPGOOD *Maps of Anc. Sea Kings* ii. 25 We found ourselves in a veritable Sargasso Sea of uncertainties. **1966** J. RHYS (*title*) The wide Sargasso Sea. **1979** P. O'CONNOR *Into Strong City* I. xix. 68, I was experiencing a severe London pea-soup fog... I swam through an impenetrable ochre sargasso sea.

sargassum (saɹgæ·səm). [mod.L. (G. E. Rumpf *Herbarium Amboinense* (1755) VI. tab. 76): see SARGASSO.] **a.** A large floating seaweed of the genus so called, found in masses in warm or temperate seas. Cf. GULF-WEED, SARGASSO.

1905, etc. [see sense b below]. **1951** G. M. PAPENFUSS in G. M. Smith *Man. Phycol.* vii. 119 *Sargassum*..forms immense floating masses in the Sargasso Sea, between the West Indies and the coast of North Africa. **1969** J. M. KINGSBURY *Seaweeds of Cape Cod* 116 The berry-like bladders..serve to identify *Sargassum* or 'gulfweed' as it is sometimes called.

b. sargassum angler, fish, a small toadfish, *Pterophryne histrio*, which lives in clusters of sargassum; **sargassum weed** = sense a above.

1961 Sargassum angler [see *sargassum weed* below]. **1905** D. S. JORDAN *Guide to Study of Fishes* II. xxxi. 549 (*caption*) Sargassum-fish. **1928** W. BEEBE *Beneath Tropic Seas* iii. 26 An unexpected performance was suddenly staged in the jar of sargassum fish. **1962** K. F. LAGLER et al. *Ichthyol.* iv. 119 The sargassum fish (*Pterophryne*) and the alga-resembling seadragon..are the most frequently cited examples of the extension of the skin into flaps. **1928** W. BEEBE *Beneath Tropic Seas* iii. 24 On several days great masses of sargassum weed drifted into the bay. **1961** E. S. HERALD *Living Fishes of World* 283/1 The sargassum angler can make slight changes in its colour pattern to match its background, but seems to be limited to those shades found in the sargassum weed.

sarge² (sāɹdʒ). orig. *U.S.* Also **Sarg(e), serg.** Colloq. abbrev. of SERGEANT *sb.* (Freq. used as a term of address.) **a.** *Mil.* = SERGEANT *sb.* 9 a. Also *Comb.*

1867 W. L. GOSS *Soldier's Story* 98 You look hungry too, Sarg. *Ibid.* 258 Sarge, the Colonel has got his mad up, and you'll be sent into the stockade. **1913** *Sat. Even. Post* 5 Feb. 6 'Sergeant Tanner?' asked the bartender incredulously. 'The sarge,' replied Kennedy with some satisfaction. **1919** W. H. DOWNING *Digger Dial.* 43 *Sarge* (n.), sergeant. **1929** F. A. POTTLE *Stretchers* (1930) 238 But sarge, I've been out since five without a bite. **1940** PARTRIDGE *S. P. E. Tract* LV. 191 The Regular Army's pre-1914 slang.. consisted mainly of words from Hindustani and Arabic..and abbreviations (..*sarge* 'sergeant'). **1958** M. K. JOSEPH *I'll soldier no More* ix. 166 Hey, sarge, there's another bugger out in the middle of the field. **1973** *Jewish Chron.* 19 Jan. 14/2 We are never allowed to forget the grim and earnest purpose behind the farcical square-bashing and sarge-baiting.

b. = SERGEANT *sb.* 10.

1926 *Scribner's Mag.* Aug. 193/2 'Quiet, serg.,' volunteered the desk man. 'Too quiet,' corrected the sergeant. **1934** J. M. CAIN *Postman always rings Twice* x. 115 Just a few minutes, sarge. **1938** G. GREENE *Brighton Rock* III. i. 106 'You aren't pulling my leg, are you?' the sergeant said. 'Not this time, sarge.' **1959** M. GILBERT *Blood & Judgement* i. 15 Garn, Sarge, *this* isn't Guy Fawkes, it's Father Christmas. **1977** 'J. BELL' *Such a Nice Client* xi. 106 'I want you over here,' said Sergeant Thomas... 'Right, sarge,' answered the constable.

Sargonid (sā·ɹgǭnid), *sb.* and *a.* Also **-ide.** [f. the Akkadian royal name *Sargon* + *-id*, after SELEUCID, etc.: cf. -ID³.] **A.** *sb.* A member of the Assyrian dynasty founded by Sargon II (ruled 722–705 B.C.), which remained in power until the fall of Assyria in 607 B.C.

1887 Z. A. RAGOZIN *Assyria* ix. 295 (*heading*) The Sargonides. **1913** H. R. HALL *Anc. Hist. Near East* x. 516 Sennacherib was the first Sargonid who no longer went forth to war himself.

B. *adj.* **1.** Of, pertaining to, or designating this dynasty.

1913 H. R. HALL *Anc. Hist. Near East* x. 517 (*heading*) Sargonide dynasty. **1925** *Cambr. Anc. Hist.* III. ii. 43 The days of the 'Sargonid' dynasty. *Ibid.* 45 A fanciful genealogy of the Sargonid house.

Sarik, var. *SARYK.

Sarin (sā·rin). Also **sarin.** [Ger., of unknown origin.] The name of an odourless organophosphorus nerve gas.

1951 *Acta Physiol. Scandinavica* Suppl. No. 90. 106 (*table*) Isopropoxy-methyl-phosphoryl-fluoride (sarin). **1967** *New Scientist* 26 Jan. 196/3 At Newport, Indiana, there is a plant making Sarin,..and loading it into rockets, land mines and artillery shells. **1968** *Observer* 16 June 9/1 By the end of the war, three of these gases—compounds of phosphorus—were known in Germany: tabun, sarin and soman. **1978** A. MELVILLE-ROSS *Blindfold* ii. 18 Bad stuff 'Sarin'. Nerve gas containing fluorine and phosphorus... Absorption through the skin..means paralysis and death.

‖ **sarinda** (sā·rindā). Also 9 **sarindah.** [Hind., dial. var. of *sārangi* *SARANGI.] An Indian stringed musical instrument played with a bow (see quots.).

1851 *Illustr. Catal. Gt. Exhib.* IV. 913/2 Musical Instruments... Sarindah or fiddle..from Moorshedabad. **1872** *Catal. Special Exhib. Anc. Musical Instruments* (S. Kensington Mus.) 35 *Sarinda.* A kind of Violin. **1921** H. A. POPLEY *Music of India* vii. 109 The Sārindā is another variety of the sārangī, peculiar to Bengal. **1944** W. APEL *Harvard Dict. Music* 801/1 In India fiddles called *sarinda* have truly fantastic shapes such as only the Indian fancy could have produced. **1964** S. MARCUSE *Musical Instruments* 456/2 *Sārindā*, folk sārangī of India, with thin wooden body of irregular shape, and skin belly covering only the lower part of the body, short neck, 3 gut or hair strings that are bowed. **1969** [see *DILRUBA]. **1977** G. WELLS in *Early Music* Apr. 250/2 A sarinda from Northern India.

sark, *v.* **2.** (Later example.) Also, to cover with sarking felt or boards.

1961 *Guardian* 21 Feb. 2/7 (Advt.), Other kinds of Sisalkraft will insulate buildings, cure concrete, sark roofs. **1977** *Belfast Tel.* 19 Jan. 24/2 (Advt.), Roofspace partly floored, sarked and felted.

Sarkese (sāɹkī·z), *sb.* and *a.* [f. the place-name *Sark* (see below) + -ESE.] **A.** *sb.* **a.** *collect.* Also **Sarkees.** The inhabitants of the Channel Island of Sark. **b.** The language of Sark, a variety of Norman French. **B.** *adj.* Of or pertaining to Sark.

1845 G. W. JAMES *Sark Guide* vii. 78 Most of the Sarkese now manufacture their own lobster pots... The Sarkese certainly love money even to a fault. **1882** D. F. S. *Channel Islands* 77 The kind-hearted Sarkese thought the sentence too severe... The good Sarkese women kept her company. **1928** L. E. HALE tr. *J. L. V. Cachemaille's Island of Sark* 105 This..harbour..has a history of its own, interesting to the Sarkese, and also to the tourist. **1935** E. PLATT *Sark as I found It* iv. 29 The Sarkees adore litigation. **1957** *Sunday Times* 10 Feb. 3/8 The debates in the *Parlement* are conducted in Sarkese which is apparently a slightly modernised version of Ancient Norman. **1958** J. W. DAY *Lady Houston* ix. 127 No other race of people but the Sarkese speak it [*sc.* 'Norman-French'] today. **1965** 'J. CHRISTOPHER' *Wrinkle in Skin* vi. 71 He had been one of the Sarkees engaged in the carriage business. **1978** *Times Lit. Suppl.* 26 May 572/5 Some of the Sarkese still reproach her with fraternization with the Germans.

sarking, *vbl. sb.* Restrict *Sc.* and *north.* to sense 2 and add: **1.** (Further examples.) Also, the action of SARK *v.* 2 (in Dict. and Suppl.).

1926–7 *Army & Navy Stores Catal.* 308/2 Ruberoid Sarking Felt. Rolls contain 24 sq. yds. **1957** *Archit. Rev.* CXXI. 354/4 In addition to these they will show their extensive range of general purpose papers for sarking and damp-proofing. **1958** *N.Z. Timber Jrnl.* July 73/1 *Sarking boards*, close boarding to carry roof tiles, shingles, or slates. Thin boards used as a lining. *Ibid.*, *Sarking felt*, a bituminous underlining placed beneath slates or tiles.

sarky (sā·ɹki), *a. colloq.* [f. abbrev. of SARCASTIC *a.* + -Y[1]: cf. *SARC.] Sarcastic. (Widely used amongst schoolchildren.) Also in *Comb.* Hence **sa·rkily** *adv.*; **sa·rkiness.**

1912 D. H. LAWRENCE *Let.* 1 Feb. (1962) I. 97 Why are you so sarky? **1924** H. DE SÉLINCOURT *Cricket Match* iii. 46 He says it sarky-like and sneering. **1930** *Diary of Public School Girl* 76 Made some currant buns. Bob very sarky about them. **1949** E. TAYLOR *Wreath of Roses* vii. 107 She's funny with Ernie, very sarky sometimes the way she answers him back. **1958** C. WATSON *Coffin, scarcely Used* iii. 25 The bland and (he had heard) 'sarky' inspector. **1965** *New Statesman* 30 July 163/1 John's saturnine profile, George's sarkiness, Paul's ageing chorister naughtiness and Ringo's deadpan outsider appeal are well brought out by David Watkin's restless camera. **1967** M. WADDELL *Otley Pursued* xv. 139 'Eating it would have been bad for your digestion, I suppose,' she said sarkily. **1977** 'J. BELL' *Such Nice Client* xvi. 161 You needn't be sarky, I've never refused you.

Sar-Major (sāɹmē[i]·dʒəɹ). Also **Sarmajor,** etc. and with small initial. Mil. colloq. abbrev. of SERGEANT-MAJOR 2. (Freq. used as a term of address.) Cf. *SARGE[2]; *SARN'T.

1919 W. H. DOWNING *Digger Dial.* 43 *Sarmajor*, Sergeant-major. **1958** P. SCOTT *Mark of Warrior* I. 26 Thank you, Sar-Major. I congratulate you on your staff. **1969** D. CLARK *Nobody's Perfect* iii. 109 There's some..think because a man's been a sar' major he'll want to turn the place into a training depot. **1974** P. MCCUTCHAN *Call for Simon Shard* i. 6 What's up, Sar-Major?

‖ **sarmale** (saɹmā·le), *sb. pl.* Also **sarmalas** and in sing. **sarmala.** [Romanian.] A Romanian dish of forcemeat and other ingredients wrapped in leaves, esp. cabbage or vine leaves.

1945 A. L. SIMON *Conc. Encycl. Gastron.* VII. 107/2 *Sarmalas.* Rub a little garlic on some raw beef and mince the beef with a little ham, a scrap of onion, parsley and other seasonings. Dip some spinach or young vine leaves in hot water and roll up the mince in them... Braise very slowly. **1958** W. BICKEL tr. *Hering's Dict. Classical & Mod. Cookery* 509 *Sarmale,* Saurkraut Rolls: ground beef and pork mixed with boiled rice, seasoned with garlic, salt, pepper and finely chopped onions, wrapped in leaves of cabbage pickled in whole heads and rolled together. **1969** *Listener* 2 Jan. 31/1 Local dishes include sarmale (meat and rice in pickled cabbage leaves). **1970** 'M. UNDERWOOD' *Silent Liars* II. xii. 131 First we have mamaliguta... Then Sarmale which are meat balls in cabbage leaves.

Sarmatian, *sb.* Add: **b.** The language of the Sarmatians, known only from Greek inscriptions in the southern U.S.S.R., and now regarded as a member of the Iranian group.

1922 O. JESPERSEN tr. R. Rask in *Language* ii. 39, I divide our family of languages in this way: the Indian.. Iranic..Thracian..Sarmatian (Lettic..and Slavonic),.. Gothic..and Keltic. **1939** L. H. GRAY *Foundations of Lang.* 320 Old Sakian..and Old Sarmatian are preserved only in a few proper names and glosses. **1972** W. B. LOCKWOOD *Panorama of Indo-Europ. Lang.* 235 The exiguous records of the Median language are of the same character as those of Scythian and Sarmatian.

sarmientite (sāɹmie·ntəit). *Min.* [f. the name of Domingo Faustino *Sarmiento* (1811–1888), Argentinian educator and statesman + -ITE[1].] A monoclinic hydrated basic arsenate and sulphate of ferric iron, $Fe_2(AsO_4)(SO_4)(OH).5H_2O$, found as pale yellow-orange microcrystalline nodules.

1941 ANGELELLI & GORDON in *Notulae Naturae* (Acad. Nat. Sci. Philadelphia) 16 Sept. 1 (*heading*) Sarmientite, a new mineral from Argentina. **1941** *Science* 26 Sept. (Suppl.) 9/1 Called sarmientite.., the new mineral is found in fair-sized nodules of great purity, of a pale yellow-orange color, in iron sulfate deposits of the Santa Elena mine. **1968** *Amer. Mineralogist* LIII. 2081 When heated at 300° C for one hour sarmientite yields a buff colored product, amorphous to X-rays.

sarnie (sā·ɹni). *slang.* Also **sarney.** [Prob. f. *sarn-*, repr. colloq. or (north.) dial. pronunc. of initial element of SANDWICH *sb.*[2] + -Y[6], -IE.] = SANDWICH *sb.*[2] 1. Freq. in *pl.*

1961 PARTRIDGE *Dict. Slang* Suppl. 1259/1 *Sarnies,* sandwiches. **1966** F. SHAW et al. *Lern Yerself Scouse* 39 *Sarneys, abnabs,* sandwiches. **1973** *Observer* 22 Apr. 27/5 Most people clamour for tea and sarnies within an hour, but I'm funny where dope's concerned. **1980** *Times* 11 Sept. 8/1 Questions like the protein content of bacon butties..and the vitamin rating of corned beef sarnies.

Sarn't (sāɹnt). Also **Sarnt, sar'nt,** etc. and with small initial. Mil. colloq. abbrev. of SERGEANT *sb.* 9 a. (Freq. used as a term of address.) Also **Sarn't-major** = SERGEANT-MAJOR 2. Cf. *SAR-MAJOR.

1930 BROPHY & PARTRIDGE *Songs & Slang* 159 *Sarnt,* a smart and soldierly pronunciation of sergeant. Only used before the N.C.O.'s surname, e.g. 'Sarnt Smith', but 'Here's the Sergeant'. Also in *Sarnt-Major,* but here it could be used without the surname. **1945** *Gen* 30 June 50/1 An erb would turn up from no-where, come up to the sarnt and 'Flight Sarnt So-and-So's compliments, Sarnt, and can A. C. Actor be released from polo practice'. **1946** [see *PEE *v.*[2] 2 b]. **1959** I. JEFFERIES *Thirteen Days* i. 21 'Ah, Sar'nt,' he said, nodding to my salute. **1972** G. BELL *Villains Galore* vii. 85 'Get out of there. Sarn't major...' They got out and were searched. The sergeant-major was thorough. **1972** F. DURBRIDGE *Bat out of Hell* v. 157 Let me put you in the picture, Sar'nt. **1978** R. MARK *Office of Constable* iii. 39 A bugler whose lip split whilst blowing the single-note half-hour call provoked the falsetto scream, 'Sarn't major... Take his name for idle blowing of the 'orn.'

‖ **sarod** (sarō[u]·d). Also **saroda, sarode,** etc. [Hindi.] An Indian stringed musical instrument of Persian origin, variously bowed or plucked. Also *attrib.* and *Comb.*

1865 *Proc. R. Irish Acad.* IX. 1. 115 *Sarrooda,* may be called the tenor or second fiddle... The *sarrooda* is..powerful but..difficult of execution; and it combines the effect of a guitar..and the violin. **1898** B. A. PINGLE *Indian Music* (ed. 2) ii. 58 On the..Saroda..the limit of a Ghasita is not fixed. **1921** H. A. POPLEY *Music of India* vii. 109 The *Sāroda* or *Sarrawat* is a sārangi played with the plectrum instead of the bow. **1957** *New Oxf. Hist. Music* I. iv. 224 The *sarod,* played with a plectrum held between the fingers, has no frets. **1961** *Observer* 26 Nov. 28/1 Two sarod recitals. Srimati Sharan Rani. Foremost woman sarod player, acc. by Chatur Lal (tabla). **1961** *Guardian* 8 Dec. 10/6 Sharan Rani, the famous Indian sarode player, was.. in London today. **1975** R. P. JHABVALA *Heat & Dust* 96 They had a tape playing of sarod music.

‖ **saron** (sā·rǫn). [Javanese.] An Indonesian musical instrument, normally having seven bronze bars which are struck with a stick.

1817 T. S. RAFFLES *Hist. Java* I. viii. 470 The *sáron*.., the *démong*.., and *selántam*.., are *staccátos* of metallic bars, and a sort of bells placed on a frame. They contain a regular diatonic scale, and nearly two octaves. **1940** C. SACHS *Hist. Mus. Instruments* (1942) xii. 239 The Javanese *saron* cannot have been constructed much earlier than 900 A.D. The modern saron has a wooden resonance box which frequently is carved in the shape of a crouching dragon...Sarons are constructed in four main sizes an octave apart. **1961** [see *metallophone* s.v. *METALLO-]. **1964** S. MARCUSE *Mus. Instruments* 457/1 *Saron,* metallophone of Bali and Java, first depicted at Borobudur (*ca.* 800). In modern sarons the bars are set above a wooden trough resonator.

sarong. Restrict ‖ to sense 2. **1. a.** Substitute for def.: The Malay national garment, resembling a skirt, which consists of a long strip of (often striped or brightly-coloured) cloth worn round the waist and sometimes the chest by both sexes. (Its use is not restricted to Malaysia.) (Further examples.)

1911 *Encycl. Brit.* XVII. 483/1 The silk is imported raw and is re-exported in the form of Malay clothing (*sarongs*) of patterns and quality which are widely celebrated. **1923** D. H. LAWRENCE *Kangaroo* i. 6 Somers had..opened the bags, so she fished out an Indian sarong of purplish shot colour, to try how it would look across the table. **1953** G. M. DURRELL *Overloaded Ark* ix. 166 Here he removed his sarong and proceeded to bathe. **1965** R. MCKIE *Company of Animals* iv. 77 They..pulled up their checked sarongs to spit between their crossed legs. **1971** *Sun* (Colombo) 20 Sept. 5/2 When it comes to crossing a stream groin deep the man in sarong has an advantage over the one in long trousers.

b. *attrib.* and *Comb.*

1913 L. WOOLF *Village in Jungle* vii. 193 In the roof between the thatch he found the two sarong cloths. **1944** *Film Star Parade,* Dorothy Lamour... Paramount tested her for the leading part in 'Jungle Princess' and it was thus that she first became the 'sarong girl'. **1972** M. SHEPPARD *Taman Indera* 40 Thin cut out panels with another sarong design were fitted into the end wall at the same level. **1979** W. H. CANAWAY *Solid Gold Buddha* xiii. 95 Both men wore sarong-like lower garments.

Hence **saro·nged** *a.*, wearing or attired in a sarong.

1934 R. V. C. BODLEY *Jap. Omelette* iii. 19 The good-natured smile of the saronged Malays and their cousins the Sudanese and Madoerese concealed no sinister thoughts. **1962** *Punch* 18 July 106/1 We barely have time to settle down from the last lot of celluloid raptures enacted beneath our palms when some other super-colossal unit arrives to shoot further bouts of saronged amour.

Saronic (sarǫ·nik), *a.* [ad.L. *Saronicus,* Gr. Σαρωνικός.] Of, pertaining to or designating the *Saronic Gulf,* a part of the Aegean Sea between Attica and the Peloponnese. Also † **Saro·nian** *a.*

1601 HOLLAND tr. *Pliny's Nat. Hist.* I. IV. iv. 73 The one side thereof is called the Corinthian gulfe, the other, the Saronian. **1845** *Encycl. Metrop.* XIX. 725/1 To the Myrtoan Sea belonged the deep Saronic Gulf, (Σαρωνικός). **1890** J. G. FRAZER *Golden Bough* I. i. 6 Hippolytus..had been killed by his horses on the sea-shore of the Saronic Gulf. **1956** A. TOYNBEE *Historian's Approach to Relig.* I. 44 The pinnacle of Acrocorinthus a stone's throw away, just across the Saronic gulf. **1977** *Times* 11 June 11/3 Spetses..one of the Saronic islands.

Sarouk (sarū·k). Also **Saruk.** The name of a village near Arak in Iran, used *attrib.* or *absol.* to designate various types of rug made there.

1900 J. K. MUMFORD *Oriental Rugs* xi. 204 Persian magnates..never demur at the loose colours which are the only drawback to the Saruks. **1913** W. A. HAWLEY *Oriental Rugs* ix. 126 Probably not one in a score..of the Sarouks now offered for sale in this country was woven there. **1920** [see *KASHAN]. **1931** A. U. DILLEY *Oriental Rugs & Carpets* iv. 121 The best Saruks are now all woven in Sultanabad. **1962** C. W. JACOBSEN *Oriental Rugs* iii. 32 In the City of Arak..and in the surrounding villages, a good many thousand Sarouks have been woven each year, especially for the American market. *Ibid.* II. 281 The early Sarouks were very fine and short pile rugs... No large Sarouks were made until about the turn of the century. **1975** 'E. LATHEN' *By Hook or by Crook* x. 97 A Sarouk, gleaming on the wall like a Rembrandt. **1977** *Times* 10 Sept. 14/6 A Saruk carpet of about 1930 fetched £2,100 in Sotheby's sale..yesterday.

‖ **sarpanch** (sa·ɹpantʃ). [Hindi–Urdu, = head arbitrator, foreman of a jury or council.] In India: the head of a panchayat or village council.

1963 F. G. BAILEY *Politics & Social Change* I. i. 55 In order to run the panchayat one of the..members is selected as head and another as his assistant. The head is called the 'Sarpanch' and his assistant is the 'Naib Sarpanch'. **1971** *Hindustan Times* (New Delhi) 7 Apr. 12/4 They went around with Girdhari Lal, the village sarpanch. **1976** D. HIRO *Inside India Today* 50 Forty to fifty panchayats are banded together to form a panchayat samiti (covering a population of 30,000 to 100,000). Its membership consists of the sarpanches of the constituent panchayats and ten co-opted members.

sarrusophone. (Further examples.)

1894 G. B. SHAW in *World* 7 Mar. 23/1, I want a craftsman to take the matter up, with the object, not of inventing some new instrument like the saxophone or sarrusophone which nobody wants, but of giving us back the old instruments. **1926** WHITEMAN & MCBRIDE *Jazz* ix. 196 The sarrusophone, which is made in seven or more sizes, is named with the wood winds although it is metal. For this reason, it is sometimes mistakenly called a metal oboe. **1975** *Gramophone* Oct. 611/3 Since the nine encyclopaedic columns..nowhere spell out the forces required by Schmitt's score, I feel justified in giving them here:.. two bassoons, sarrusophone, two E flat clarinets [etc.].

sarsartie, Sarsi, varr. *SOSATIE, *SARCEE.

Sart (sāɹt), *sb.*[2] and *a.* [Turki.] **A.** *sb.* **a.** A member of a settled people of mixed Turkoman and Iranian descent, living as town-dwellers and traders in Turkestan and parts of Afghanistan. Cf. *TAJIK. **b.** The Eastern Turkic dialect of Uzbek spoken by the Sarts. **B.** *adj.* Of or pertaining to this people or their language.

The name is widely used, with varying degrees of exactness, to designate the sedentary people of this region. They are thus contrasted with the Kurds and others, by whom the term is considered derogatory. Other commentators view the Sarts as an ethnologically distinct people.

1871 R. B. SHAW *Visits to High Tartary* ii. 26 All the Khokandees whom I met with in Eastern Toorkistân agreed in affirming that Sart is merely a word used by the Kirghiz to denote all who do not lead a nomad existence like themselves, whether they be Tajiks or Oosbeks. **1879** *Encycl. Brit.* IX 85/2 Tajiks..in the chief towns and central districts, who are known as Sarts, show a large infusion of Uzbeg and other Turki blood. **1898** BEALBY & HEARN tr. *Hedin's Through Asia* v. 61 Guided by some Sart boys, I threaded my way through a labyrinth of narrow lanes. **1900** 'ODYSSEUS' *Turkey in Europe* iii. 101 Sart, though now commonly used as a name for the Jagatai Turkish spoken in those provinces [sc. Fergana, Turkestan, etc.] is, strictly speaking, not a linguistic designation, but denotes a dweller in cities and a merchant, as distinguished from a countryman and agriculturist, called Tajik. **1920** *Glasgow Herald* 31 Aug. 8 It is among the highly intelligent Sarts and Tadjiks, speaking Persian and Arabic fluently and many of them conversant with Hindustani, that the Bolshevists find their cleverest agents. **1946** F. M. BAILEY *Mission to Tashkent* iii. 36 Sart writers sometimes refer to themselves as Turks but this word is..misleading. **1953** O. CAROE *Soviet Empire* iii. 34 It was to sedentary dwellers of this kind, whether bilingual or speaking only Tajik, that the true Turks formerly applied the pejorative appellation of 'Sart'. **1954** PEI & GAYNOR *Dict. Linguistics* 190 *Sart,* an Asiatic language; member of the Central Turkic group of the Altaic sub-family of the Ural-Altaic family of languages. **1964** R. A. PIERCE in N. J. Couriss tr. *Pahlen's Mission to Turkestan* 10 Pahlen..regarded the Sarts as a distinct ethnic group with their own language. Originally..the word was applied to the sedentary, and.. urban, population of Turkestan without any reference to race or language. A Sart might..be of Tadzhik.., Uzbek.., or of mixed Iranian and Turkic stock; and..speak.. Tadzhik or Uzbek... There is no such thing as a Sart language. During the Soviet régime the word acquired a derogatory significance and is now no longer used.

sartorially (sāɹtō[ə]·riăli), *adv.* [f. SARTORIAL *a.* + -LY[2].] With regard to clothes.

1905 W. J. LOCKE *Morals of Marcus Ordeyne* xii. 146 When she puts her foot upon my sartorially immaculate knee. **1916** —— *Wonderful Year* xvii. 245 Like a woman clothes-starved for years..Martin ran sartorially mad. **1928** *Daily Express* 16 Apr. 3/4 Sartorially magnificent in all-over woolly tights. **1970** *Daily Tel.* 30 Dec. 9/2 Sartorially speaking, men are at last catching up with the women. **1972** *Ibid.* 14 Mar. 13/7 Sartorially, the beginning of the Chinese 'thaw' is to be seen in the gaily-coloured clothes worn by girls and women. **1974** 'M. UNDERWOOD' *Pinch of Snuff* ii. 12 The club's most sartorially elegant member.

Sartrean, Sartrian (sā·ɹtriăn), *a.* Also **Sartreian.** [f. the name of *Sartre* (see below) + -AN, -IAN.] Of, pertaining to, or characteristic of the French writer and philosopher

Jean-Paul Sartre (1905–80), his writings, or his existentialist philosophy. Hence as *sb.*, an admirer of the ideas of Sartre.

1948 [see *COMMITMENT 6 c]. **1949** E. L. MASCALL *Existence & Analogy* vi. 126 Given their atheist dogma, the Sartrians are quite right in asserting that existence is absurd, that the world does not make sense. **1951** N. ANNAN *Leslie Stephen* viii. 247 In the 'forties Sartrian Existentialism..was a bizarre attempt to justify the duties to society which are inescapably binding upon individuals, who, whether they like it or not, are forced to commit themselves. **1958** *Spectator* 25 July 141/2 That unique Sartrean blend of intellectual and moral disintegration. **1961** *Encounter* June 42/2, I cannot claim to be either a Sartrian or a Thomist. **1962** *Listener* 24 May 920/2 From the Sartrian standpoint, Rousseau went about this enterprise in the wrong way. **1970** J. D. CAUTE *Fanon* iii. 35 Fanon's prose reverberates with Sartreian concepts, phrases, dialectical juxtapositions, paradoxes and essentialist abstractions. **1975** J. SYMONS *Three Pipe Problem* xix. 218 Were they both dead, joined in a permanent squabble in some Sartrean hinterland? **1977** *New Yorker* 16 May 147/1 Soyinka discusses material..with ample cross-references to Greek drama, Nietzschean aesthetics, Jungian philosophy and Sartrean opinionizing.

Saruk, var. *SAROUK.

Sarum. (Further examples.)

1929 S. LESLIE *Anglo-Catholic* x. 117 His ritual was simple: two lights, Sarum Use and Sarum colours with simple vestments of linen. **1954** O. CHADWICK *Founding of Cuddesdon* v. 133 This was just the time when the old-fashioned cassock was giving way to the Sarum cassock, which was intruding from about 1887 onwards and conquering by 1897. **1957** *Oxf. Dict. Chr. Ch.* 1209/1 In the years preceding the Reformation the output of Sarum books was enormous. The much increased knowledge which has followed their discovery..has led to the revival of Sarum customs and ornaments in many English cathedral and parish churches. **1966** J. BETJEMAN *High & Low* 55 And there we'll sing the Sarum rite Tae English Hymnal airs. **1972** C. STEPHENSON *Merrily on High* iv. 64 SS. Philip & James, very Sarum, and St. Margaret's close by very western, were the centre of great turmoil at one stage when the vicar of Phil & Jim was making it western and the vicar of St. Margaret's was busy taking off the six candles from the altar and substituting two while introducing Sarum practices. **1974** *Encycl. Brit. Micropædia* VIII. 908/3 The Sarum chants resemble Gregorian ones in the use of free rhythm, modes.., psalm tones.., musical form, and the addition of tropes.

‖ **sarvodaya** (saɹvo·daya). [Skr., f. *sárva* 'all' + *udayá* 'uplift, prosperity'.] The welfare of all; the name given to the new social order advocated by the Indian leader M. K. Gandhi (1869–1948) and his followers. Also *attrib.*

[**1908** M. K. GANDHI (*title*) Sarvodaya.] **1919** *Bombay Chron.* 8 Apr. 713 The committee has selected the following prohibited books for dissemination:..*Sarvodaya* or *Universal Dawn* by M. K. Gandhi. **1941** K. G. MASHRUWALA *Practical Non-Violence* (1946) 45 This is the civilization of Sarvodaya (the wellbeing of all). **1948** *Harijan* 4 Apr. 54/2 *Samaj*, which corresponds more to brotherhood than to association. .. The Sarvodaya Samaj has been established to strive.. towards a society based on Truth and Non-violence, in which there will be no distinction of caste or creed. **1954** B. KUMARAPPA *Sarvodaya* (1958) p. iii, Sarvodaya, as the welfare of all, represents the ideal social order according to Gandhiji. Its basis is all-embracing love. **1962** B. SMITH *Portrait of India* vi. 45 Vinoba..became at Gandhi's death, the leader of the *Sarvodaya* movement of selfless service. *Ibid.* 46 Gandhi's *sarvodaya* embodied the idea of regeneration in the individual and in society. **1965** E. LINTON *World in Grain of Sand* ix. 163, I thought of the Gandhians in their present dilemma as expressed later at the Sarvodaya Conference at Vedchi. **1971** *Peace News* 10 Sept. 8/2 The concept of the freedom march was born in the minds of Indian Sarvodaya workers. **1974** *Times* 7 Dec. 5/4 The village is conceived of in Gandhian or *sarvodaya* terms as a miniature, self-governing republic. **1978** *Times Lit. Suppl.* 3 Feb. 121/2 India's own homespun village socialist movement known as *Sarvodaya* acquired its name, significantly, from the word used by Gandhi to translate the title of Ruskin's book, *Unto This Last.*

sarwan, var. SURWAN.

Saryk (sarĭ·k). Also **Sarik.** [Native name.] **a.** One of several Turkic tribes inhabiting the Turkmen Soviet Socialist Republic; a member of this tribe. **b.** *attrib.* Used to designate a carpet or rug made by this tribe, similar in design to a Bokhara carpet. Also *absol.*

1885 E. W. HAMILTON *Diary* 9 Apr. (1972) II. 831 The news reached me that the Russian Colonel—Alikhanoff—attacked the Afghans at Penjdeh on the 30th,..and that Alikhanoff had actually instigated the Sariks (a Turcoman tribe in that neighbourhood) to attack the English party... The Sariks fortunately declined the offer. **1889** G. CURZON *Russia in Central Asia* v. 96 Transcaspia..includes.. the minor oases inhabited by the Sarik and Salor Turkomans. **1899** SKRINE & ROSS *Heart of Asia* II. iv. 268 The Merv oasis was inhabited by the Sâriks,..who were engaged in a struggle with the Khivans. **1922** H. CLARK *Bokhara, Turkoman & Afghan Rugs* p. xiv, In the course of years I acquired..specimens of Salor, Saryk..and Afghan Turkoman rugs... A Saryk Turkoman rug of the early 18th century, nearly square in shape and of wonderful colouring. **1957** C. W. HOSTLER *Turkism & Soviets* ii. 69 The Turkmens are divided into seven main tribes (the Chauders,..Sariks, Salors and Ersaris). **1960** H. HAYWARD *Antique Coll.* 248/2 *Saryk rugs*, Turkestan rugs, generally not so fine in texture as Bokhara rugs.., but bearing a similar design. **1962** C. W. JACOBSEN *Oriental Rugs* II. 286 Even today nine out of ten dealers have never heard of the name 'Saryk'. **1964** *Sunday Times* (Colour Suppl.) 19 Jan. 25 Sarik. Carpet from a Turcoman tribe almost destroyed by the Tekkes in the last century. **1974** *Encycl. Brit. Macropædia* XVIII. 800/1 The number of people in other tribes (the Salyr, Saryk, Groklen, and Choudor) fluctuated between 20,000 and 40,000.

sas, var. *SASS *sb.* **sasaitie,** var. *SOSATIE.

Sasak (sā·sak), *sb.* and *a.* Also 9 **Sassak.** [Native name.] **A.** *sb.* One of the Malay inhabitants of the island of Lombok. Also, the language of the Sasaks. **B.** *adj.* Of or pertaining to the Sasaks.

1817 T. S. RAFFLES *Hist. Java* II. p. cxcviii, Comparative vocabulary of the Bugis, Makasar, Mandhar, Bûton, Sásak, Bíma, Sembáwa, Tembóra and Endé Languages. **1869** A. R. WALLACE *Malay Archipel.* I. xi. 256 Beyond Mataram..is Karangassam, the ancient residence of the native or Sassak Rajahs before the conquest..by the Balinese. *Ibid.* 270 The aborigines of Lombock are termed Sassaks. They are a Malay race... They are Mahometans. **1897** E. J. TAYLOR tr. *W. Cool's With Dutch in East* III. 121 The language of the Sassaks is totally different from that spoken by the Balinese; although the Sassaks have borrowed many words from their neighbours, still they are unable to understand each other's language. **1937** M. COVARRUBIAS *Island of Bali* ii. 30 In 1885 there was a rebellion of Sasaks, the vassals of the Balinese in Lombok... The Sasak chiefs complained to the Dutch, asking to be freed from the tyranny of the Balinese princes. **1954** E. D. LABORDE tr. *C. Robequain's Malaya, Indonesia, Borneo & Philippines* II. xii. 24 Balinese Hinduism is isolated between Java and Lombok, for Islam has..almost wholly won over Lombok... Sasak converts to Islam form the great majority..of the population. **1961** P. KEMP *Alms for Oblivion* xi. 163 Almost nine-tenths of this population are Sasaks, a simple agricultural people of Malay stock. *Ibid.* 166 We enlisted the Eurasian as an extra interpreter, for..he spoke Dutch, Malay, Balinese and Sasak. **1965** *Language* XLI. 294 Madurese, like some of its neighboring languages (Sundanese, Javanese, Balinese, and Sasak), has socially determined choices of words. **1974** *Encycl. Brit. Micropædia* VI. 308/3 The population of Lombok is composed largely of Sasaks of Malay origin.

Sasanian, var. SASSANIAN *a.* and *sb.* in Dict. and Suppl.

Sasanid, var. SASSANID *sb.* and *a.* in Dict. and Suppl.

sasanqua (săsæ·nkwă, -kă). Also **sasank(w)a.** [Jap. *sasankwa* mountain tea-flower.] An evergreen shrub, *Camellia sasanqua*, belonging to the family Theaceæ, native to Japan, and bearing fragrant white or pink flowers and seeds yielding an edible oil also used in the production of silk and soap.

1866 LINDLEY & MOORE *Treas. Bot.* I. 207/2 *C. Sasanqua* (Sasanqua is the Japanese name of the plant) is found in many parts of China and Japan. **1878** *Trans. Asiatic Soc. Japan* VI. 216 A kind of evergreen with poplar-like leaves..is called *Sasanka* by the Japanese. **1884** tr. *J. J. Rein's Japan* 441 In November and December Sasankwa and Cha..blossom. **1962** J. L. THRELKELD *Camellia Bk.* i. 3 In the gardens of Japan the sasanqua predominates.

sasatie, var. *SOSATIE.

sash, *sb.*[2] Add: **3. sash cramp** (see quot. 1964); **sash-door** (earlier examples); **sash-pane,** each of the panes of glass in a sash-window.

1964 J. S. SCOTT *Dict. Building* 275 *Sash cramps*, cramps between 2 and 5 ft long used for clamping sashes during gluing. **1969** E. H. PINTO *Treen* 381/2 Wooden cramps. The general run of both G cramps and sash cramps are too familiar to need any special description. **1726** D. EATON *Let.* 25 Sept. (1971) 60, I think the sash door at Little Deen ought to be oak, and these planks we have will do very well. **1739–40** RICHARDSON *Pamela* (1740) I. 95 In this green Room was a Closet, with a Sash-door and a Curtain before it. *c* **1806** D. WORDSWORTH *Jrnl.* (1941) I. 311 The dwelling-house was distinguished from the outer buildings..by a chimney and one small window with sash-panes.

sashay (sæʃē^i·), *sb.* *N. Amer.* [f. next.] **1.** A venture, a sally; an excursion, trip, or expedition.

1900 G. ADE *More Fables* 184 Lutie never got out of her Dream until she made a bold Sashay with a Concert Company. **1935** H. L. DAVIS *Honey in Horn* 15 If you yank him out for any all-night sashay on these roads, you ought to be ashamed of yourself. **1941** *Sat. Even. Post* 16 Aug. 68/3 On my first sashay into the flying field. **1952** E. B. WHITE *Let.* 6 Apr. (1976) 355 Spring is making little sashays about coming to town, but it has been a fairly unconvincing demonstration so far. **1961** R. M. PATTERSON *Buffalo Head* v. 183 He could make a long sashay north along the foot of the range. **1968** —— *Finlay's River* 147 Swannell, Copley and Alexander and the two dogs..set out for a three-day sashay up the strong creek that flowed into the Ingenika.

2. A step in square dancing (see quot. *c* 1940). Also *transf.* and *attrib.*

c **1940** *Square Dance* (Writers' Program, Illinois) 40 The Sashay is a series of short quick steps directly to the side, either to the right or to the left... The gent holds the lady's left hand in his right, and her right hand in his left. **1941** R. J. MCNAIR *Western Square Dances* XIX. 78 The Sashay step is a quick side step. **1956** R. HOLDEN *Contra Dance Bk.* iv. 45 Sashay, the American chassez. **1971** *Flying* (N.Y.) Apr. 49/1 It's got a marvelous sort of sashay movement because it's such a big airplane that when you roll you can feel those booms kind of rolling around behind you. **1974** 'J. MARKS' *Mick Jagger* 32 The juvenile Jagger... Trying a few quick sashays and eating a banana.

sashay (sæʃē^i·), *v.* *colloq.* (chiefly *U.S.*). Also **sasshay.** [Now the dominant form of SASHY *v.*] **1.** *intr.* **a.** To perform a chassé, esp. in square dancing; freq. *transf.*, to perform a movement similar to the chassé. **b.** To glide, walk, or travel, usu. in a casual manner. **c.** To move diagonally or sideways; to travel an irregular path; to wander or saunter. **d.** To move or walk ostentatiously, conspicuously, or provocatively; to strut or parade. Freq. with *adv.*

1836 *Franklin Repository* (Chambersburg, Pa.) 4 Oct. 1/3 If you don't sashay across, button your lip, and go home quietly, you and I will have to promenade all around, and swing corners into the watch house. **1865** 'MARK TWAIN' in *Californian* 18 Mar. 8/1 For all they're so handy about keeping her sashaying around from shanty to shanty ..none of 'em's ever got a good word for her. **1878** F. H. HART *Sazerac Lying Club* 83 S'pose, gentlemen, that we sashay up to the bar. **1888, 1891** [see SASHY, SAS(S)HAY, *v.*]. **1905** *Dialect Notes* III. 64 They sashayed back and forth to beat the band. **1913** C. E. MULFORD *Coming of Cassidy* v. 80 Logan..is about thirty miles east. You must 'a sashayed some to get only this far in four days. **1917** H. GARLAND *Son of Middle Border* xv. 163 At dancing parties they balanced or 'sashayed' in *Honest John* or *Money Musk.* **1935** Z. N. HURSTON *Mules & Men* I. v. 113 John was callin' for de new set: 'Choose yo' partners.'..'Sashay all.' **1942** E. PAUL *Narrow St.* ix. 74 He staggered eastward toward the Panthéon and I sashayed westward to the rue Lafayette. **1944** C. HIMES *Black on Black* (1973) 201, I picked up my sack and sorta sashayed off. **1949** K. M. WELLS *Owl Pen Reader* (1969) III. 246 Fireflies danced by Moonstone Creek. They dipped and cavorted, they sashayed like a million wee stars gone mad. **1951** E. PAUL *Springtime in Paris* v. 114 Instead of continuing toward the rue de la Huchette, Christophe hopped and sashayed to the left. **1960** F. RAPHAEL *Limits of Love* I. iii. 41 A large Negro..was sashaying through the crowd towards them. **1968** J. UPDIKE *Couples* iv. 311 Sashaying from the shower nude, her pussy of a ferny freshness. **1973** S. ALSOP *Stay of Execution* (1974) II. 201 Stewart brought a pretty..girl friend home. As she sashayed through the living room, Andrew remarked, 'I like the way she wiggles her things.' **1978** J. A. MICHENER *Chesapeake* 270 He hoped that Nelly Turlock would not sashay in, demanding dividends for her family. *Ibid.* 545, I see her sashayin' past in a dress I know she stole from Miss Susan.

2. *trans.* To cause (someone or something) to sashay; to walk or parade (a person); to carry or convey (an object); to manœuvre (a vehicle).

1928 L. H. NASON *Sergeant Eadie* 130 What the hell good a rifle does to me sashayin' these jugheads up an' down the road, I don't know. **1944** J. S. PENNELL *Hist. Rome Hanks* 189 Take them guns thar—tuck 'em from the Yanks at the fust battle of Manassas, an' been a-farin' 'em eveh since an' sashayin' 'em all oveh hell an Vuhginny. **1963** T. PYNCHON *V.* i. 22 Rachel would gee and haw this MG around Route 17's bloodthirsty curves and cutbacks, sashaying its arrogant butt past hay wagons. **1977** J. GARDNER *Werewolf Trace* i. 17 'James Bond rules. Okay?' chuckled Bud, sashaying the car neatly between a pair of taxis.

Hence **sasha·ying** *vbl. sb.* and *ppl. a.*

1935 R. STOUT *League of Frightened Men* xx. 272 It did mean his sashaying out of the house twice in two days, which was an all-time record. **1976** *New Yorker* 8 Mar. 109/1 He'd start with a fusillade of rim shots, sink into a sashaying figure that strode back and forth between his tomtoms.

sashed, *ppl. a.*[1] Add: *sashed window* (earlier examples).

1816 JANE AUSTEN *Emma* II. vi. 98 He stopt for several minutes at the two superior sashed windows which were open. *Ibid.* III. xiv. 260 A brick house, sashed windows below, and casements above.

sashed (sæʃt), *ppl. a.*[2] [f. SASH *v.*[1] or *sb.*[1] + -ED[1,2].] Dressed or adorned with a sash.

1869 'MARK TWAIN' *Innoc. Abr.* vii. 69 Turbaned, sashed and trowsered Moorish merchants. **1894** [see SASH *v.*[1]]. **1970** *Daily Tel.* 27 Apr. 14 A good sashed white midi coat for £25.

‖ **sashimi** (sæ·ʃimi). [Jap., f. *sashi* pierce + *mi* flesh.] A Japanese dish consisting of thin slices of raw fish served with grated radish or ginger and soy sauce. Also *attrib.* or as *adj.*

1880 I. L. BIRD *Unbeaten Tracks in Japan* I. 239 The preparation of raw fish cut into oblong strips called *sashimi.* **1920** *Japan Advertiser* 22 Aug. 5 Sashimi or arai..is raw tai, tunny or kare, served with horseradish. **1933** P. PETO *Recipes Rare from Everywhere* 29 *Sashimi.* The fish is skinned, cleaned and cut into fillets about $\frac{1}{16}$ inch thick;

it is arranged on a dish and garnished with fresh thinly sliced vegetables, and is eaten with Shoyu blended with Japanese shredded horseradish. **1936** K. TEZUKA *Jap. Food* 14 *Sashimi* (raw sea-bream, flounder, tunny, etc. cut into thin slices). **1959** R. KIRKBRIDE *Tamiko* vii. 54 They had hors d'oeuvres of raw wild vegetables, sashimi, thin slices of raw tuna [etc.]. **1967** *Guardian* 8 Dec. 8/2 Finding fish fresh enough to serve sashimi (raw) is very difficult. **1969** R. HOWE *Far Eastern Cookery* 189 *Sashimi*..is a truly Japanese speciality... I took myself to a small *sashimi* bar..and ordered *sake*. **1973** J. GORES *Final Notice* x. 60 Waiting for the Japanese waitress to arrive with the sukiyaki and sashimi. **1978** *Maclean's Mag.* 13 Nov. 47/1 Each spring the tiny fishing village 20 miles south of Halifax prepares to satisfy the yearnings of 100 million Japanese for sashimi.

sashy, sas(s)hay, *v.*: see *SASHAY *v.*

sasquatch (sæ·skwɒtʃ). *Canad.* Also **Sasquatch.** [Salish.] A name for a huge, hairy, man-like monster supposedly inhabiting the north-west of the U.S. and Canada. Also *collect.* and *attrib.*

1929 *Maclean's Mag.* 1 Apr. 61/1 The strange people, of whom there are but few now—rarely seen and seldom met—..are known by the name of Sasquatch, or, 'the hairy mountain men'. **1950** C. P. LYONS *Milestones on Mighty Fraser* 28 Indian lore has it that a mysterious race of giants, known as the Sasquatch, live in the high mountains around Harrison Lake. **1958** *Encycl. Canadiana* IX. 233/1 Known originally to the Indians..as Saskehavas (wild men), they are called by the..whites Sasquatch (hairy men). **1966** *Globe Mag.* (Toronto) 11 June 3/3 Most villagers relate every Sasquatch sighting to the amount of alcohol they insist must have been consumed immediately prior to the monster's appearance. **1971** W. HILLEN *Blackwater River* xi. 108 Stories of strange lights and huge, wild, hairy men, or 'sasquatch', circulate periodically, usually toward spring. **1972** L. HANCOCK *There's a Seal in my Sleeping Bag* vi. 123 We scanned the steep forested slopes of the pass for Sasquatch. **1974** *New Yorker* 25 Feb. 92/2 The Northwest's legendary Sasquatch, a huge, humanoid seven-or-so-foot creature akin to the Abominable Snowman of Tibet. **1976** *Toronto Star* 31 Jan. 7/1 A nine-man team, using computerized information and electronic detection gear, will go sasquatch hunting in British Columbia in April or May. **1977** *New Yorker* 20 June 72/2 It was lumpy, pitted, pocked, rough, ugly—an apparent filling from the tooth of a Sasquatch. **1979** T. GIFFORD *Hollywood Gothic* (1980) v. 53, I feel like a sasquatch has been using me for a soccer ball.

Sasquehanno, etc., obs. varr. *SUSQUEHANNOCK.

sass (sæs), *sb. U.S. colloq.* Also **sas.** [var. SAUCE *sb.*] **1. a.** = SAUCE *sb.* 4 a.

1775 J. STEVENS *Jrnl.* 5 May in *Essex Inst. Hist. Coll.* (1912) XLVIII. 43 Steven Barker come down & brought us som sas. **1836** B. TUCKER *Partisan Leader* II. xxxv. 124 The fellow talked to me about living at home on codfish, and potatoes, and cider, and pies, and *all sorts of sass*. **1860** *Knickerbocker* July 102 White turnip, yellow turnip, or any sort of sass, long sass, or short sass. **1945** M. LYON *Fresh from Hills* iv. 46 A family could get along without garden sass.

b. = SAUCE *sb.* 4 b.

1913 H. KEPHART *Our Southern Highlanders* xiii. 293 Your hostess, proffering apple sauce, will ask, 'Do you love sass?'

2. = SAUCE *sb.* 6 b.

1835 [see *CHUNK *v.*[1] 1]. **1853** G. C. HILL *Dovecote* 88 I've a precious good mind to duck you for your sass! **1876** 'MARK TWAIN' *Tom Sawyer* i. 23 If you give me much more of your sass I'll take and bounce a rock off'n your head. **1880** J. C. HARRIS *Uncle Remus* iv. 31 Brer Rabbit wuz bleedzed fer ter fling back some er his sass. **1897** 'O. THANET' *Missionary Sheriff* 21, I shall take more advantage of it if you give me any sass. **1935** J. T. FARRELL *Judgement Day* ii. 25 It must have been something of the old Studs Lonigan left in him that led to his not taking sass, risking a fight. **1967** P. WELLES *Babyhip* iii. 46 Is this what we get? Sass? No gratitude. **1977** *Time* 3 Jan. 21/1 If she's mostly given over now to laughter, pride and sass, she has earned her fun.

sass (sæs), *v. U.S. colloq.* [var. SAUCE *v.*]

1. *trans.* = SAUCE *v.* 4 d.

1856 'J. PHOENIX' *Phoenixiana* xvi. 125 While the squire..sasses all respectable persons With his talk of pills he's invented. **1867** 'MARK TWAIN' *Celebr. Jumping Frog* 166 You ought never to 'sass' old people—unless they 'sass' you first. **1887** [see SAUCE *v.* 4 d]. **1896** *N.Y. Dramatic News* 18 July 2/3 When he was requested to desist he 'sassed' the officer. **1920** S. LEWIS *Main Street* ix. 118 There had to be one man in town independent enough to sass the banker! **1929** W. FAULKNER *Sound & Fury* 67 Dont you sass me, nigger boy. **1956** W. H. WHYTE *Organization Man* (1957) VII. xxvi. 358 If little Johnny sasses Mrs. Erdlick just once more. **1966** K. L. MORGAN in A. Dundes *Mother Wit* (1973) 602/1 She wanted to know if it was all right to 'sass' the woman the way she did since she was 'trash'. **1978** J. A. MICHENER *Chesapeake* 536 'But, Missy, I done clean it.' 'Don't you sass me!' she screamed.

2. *intr.* To speak impertinently; *to sass back*, to reply impertinently, to 'answer back'.

1880 J. C. HARRIS *Uncle Remus* iv. 29 You been runnin' roun' here sassin' after me a mighty long time. **1884** 'MARK TWAIN' *Huck. Finn* (1885) xxvii. 237 The king sassed back, as much as was safe for him. **1891** O. W. HOLMES *Over Teacups* 154, I suppose Me-Number-Two will 'sass back'. **1976** *National Observer* (U.S.) 24 July 10/3 No teacher chooses to teach students who are sleeping or throwing chalk or sassing.

Hence **sa·ssing** *vbl. sb.*

1962 W. H. GASS in Foley & Burnett *Best Amer. Short Stories* 112 Listen to me, Jorge, I've had enough to your sassing. **1967** P. WELLES *Babyhip* iii. 48 'Don't you get hysterics,' Mrs Green warned, 'or I'll throw cold water on you. I'll have none of this sassing.' **1977** *New Yorker* 6 June 48/3 Far worse than any welts he ever got when his father or Abel beat him in the shed for misbehaving or sassing.

sassafras. Add: **1. b.** The wood or timber of this tree.

1728 *Rec. Early Hist. Boston* (1883) VIII. 222 No Popler, ..Sassifax, Black ash, Basswood, or Ceder Shall be Corded up. **1900** *19th Ann. Rep. U.S. Bureau Amer. Ethnol. 1897–98* I. 422 Sassafras is tabued as fuel among the Cherokee..perhaps for the practical reason that it is apt to pop out of the fire when heated. **1921** C. C. DEAM *Trees of Indiana* 165 Floors were made of sassafras to keep out the rats and mice.

2. a. (Later examples.)

1863 *Rio Abajo Weekly Press* (Albuquerque, New Mexico) 14 Apr. 2/3 Sassafras.—Those who use this drink will find [etc.]. **1871** E. EGGLESTON *Hoosier Schoolmaster* 88 He drank his glass of water, having declined even her sassafras. **1912** M. NICHOLSON *Hoosier Chron.* 44 Sassafras in the spring, and a few doses of quinine in the fall,..were all the medicine that any good Hoosier needed.

3. *sassafras-bush*; **sassafras soap** (earlier example); **sassafras tea** (later U.S. examples).

1848 G. C. FURBER *Twelve Months Volunteer* 54 The field, or the larger part of it, growing up with tall weeds and sassafras bushes. **1944** T. D. CLARK *Pills, Petticoats & Plows* 261 The graveyard is scraped bare of crab grass,..Johnson grass and sassafras bushes to give them a 'cared-for' appearance. **1860** J. G. HOLLAND *Miss Gilbert's Career* 108 Arthur took his accustomed seat at the head of the table, with Leonora at his right hand,.. [in an] atmosphere of sassafras-soap. **1817** T. DEAN in *Indiana Hist. Soc. Publ.* (1918) VI. 324 We took some bread and sassafras tea. **1960** I. WALLACH *Absence of Cello* 41 Perry sipped a cup of sassafras tea.

Sassanian, *a.* and *sb.* Add: **a.** *adj.* (Further examples.) Also, of, pertaining to, or characteristic of the period of this dynasty.

1928 C. DAWSON *Age of Gods* iv. 84 In historical times we find the influence of the Sassanian culture of Persia following very much the same paths. **1929** E. C. THOMAS *Lay Folks' Hist. Liturgy* I. v. 22 Persia..was conquered by the Mohammedans in 651, thus ending the native Sassanian dynasty, which was founded in 223 B.C. **1940** *Burlington Mag.* July 31/1 An important feature in Sasanian and Muslim architecture. **1958** A. TOYNBEE *East to West* 167 On bas-reliefs of the Sasanian age one is shocked to find the goddess Anahita holding her ground beside Ormuzd. **1971** R. RUSSELL tr. *Ahmad's Shore & Wave* viii. 93 Strange houses. One like a dreadnought..one in Japanese style, one displaying Sassanian arches. **1977** *Ashmolean Mus. Rep. Visitors 1975–76* 17 (*title*) Parthian and Sasanian metalwork in the Bomford collection. **1980** J. LEES-MILNE *Harold Nicolson* xiv. 303 The Sassanian city of Istakh, destroyed during the Arab conquest in the seventh century A.D.

b. *sb.* (Further examples.)

1931 A. W. SEABY *Art in Life of Mankind* 80 The Sasanians were as bitter enemies of the Christian eastern or Byzantine empire as they had been of pagan Rome. **1976** *Nature* 10 June 472/1 The Venus–Jupiter conjunction of 650 was one recorded by the Chinese; this conjunction was later regarded by Masha'allah as signifying the fall of the Sasanians and the rise of the Arabs.

Sassanid, *sb.* and *a.* Add: Also **Sasanid.**

a. *sb.* (Later examples.) **b.** *attrib.* and *adj.* (Earlier and later examples.) Also = *SASSANIAN *a.*

1867 C. M. YONGE *Pupils of St. John* xvii. 270 The Sassanid princes had taken up all the traditions of their supposed ancestry. **1904** F. C. BURKITT *Early Eastern Christianity* 25 The rise and decay of Christianity in the Sasanid Empire. **1910** [see *AQUAMANILE]. **1929** E. C. THOMAS *Lay Folks' Hist. Liturgy* I. v. 22 In A.D. 202 Abjar IX., Prince of Edessa, adopted Christianity, but this Church [in Persia] was barely tolerated by the Parthians and often persecuted by the Sassanids. **1958** A. TOYNBEE *East to West* 165 The capital of the Sasanid Persian Empire's Arab wardens of the Arabian marches. **1977** *Field* 31 Mar. 525/1 For the early Persian dynasties such as the Archamedians and Sassanids, the rug may have been used as a gift from one ruler to another.

sassatje, var. *SOSATIE.

Sassella (sæse·lă). Also **sassella.** [It.] The name of a red wine from the Valtellina district, Lombardy, in Italy.

1935 A. L. SIMON *Dict. Wine* 227 *Sassella*, one of the best red wines of the Valtellina (Lombardy). **1967** A. LICHINE *Encycl. Wines & Spirits* 330/1 In this district [*sc.* Valtellina], centred around the town of Sondrio, the three almost identical red wines are Sassella, Grumello, and Inferno, all from Nebbiolo grapes grown on the more manageable Alpine slopes. **1970** *House & Garden* May 140/2 Of all the Lombardy wines..I have most enjoyed..sassella—a red wine. **1975** 'S. MARLOWE' *Cawthorn Jrnls.* xix. 166 A bottle of the dark, velvety Sassella stood on the table.

sasshay: see also *SASHAY *v.*

sassy (sæ·si), *a. colloq.* (orig. and chiefly *U.S.*). [Var. SAUCY *a.*[1]] Impudent, saucy, 'cheeky'; outspoken, provocative; conceited, pretentious; self-assured, spirited, bold; vigorous, lively; stylish, 'chic'. Also quasi-*adv.*

[**1815** D. HUMPHREYS *Yankey in Eng.* I. 22 'Ah, you sly boots. Don't be saucy.' 'Saisy!']. **1833** S. SMITH *Life & Writings J. Downing* 128 If I should give out now.., them are sassy chaps in Portland would laugh at me. **1862** C. F. BROWNE *A. Ward his Book* 200 A hansum yung gal, with..a sassy little black hat tipt over her forrerd, sot in the seat with me. **1870** 'MARK TWAIN' *Lett. to Publishers* (1967) 38 And then I talked sassy to him for a page or two. **1880** J. C. HARRIS *Uncle Remus* ii. 24 Brer Rabbit pacin' down de road..dez ez sassy ez a jay-bird. **1908** J. H. SHINN *Pioneers & Makers Arkansas* xxxii. 258, I have seen sassy people, but of all sassy people in the world Arkansassy people are the worst. **1917** T. H. COMSTOCK *Man thou Gavest* 12, I kept the sassy little hen. **1936** WODEHOUSE *Laughing Gas* vii. 77 Have you ever had to look after a sassy, swollen-headed, wisecracking child star? **1945** L. SAXON et al. *Gumbo Ya-Ya* xii. 233 My ma was hard-headed and sassy, and she'd talk right back to anybody, Massa or nobody. **1958** J. KEROUAC *On Road* I. x. 75 You can fill your filthy belly and get fat and sassy right before my eyes. **1961** *New Statesman* 11 Aug. 193/2 The film..is big and sassy, full of generous visual effects. **1969** N. COHN *A Wop Bopa Loo Bop* (1970) xviii. 169 They looked at the things the Who did and analysed them and thought up sassy names for them. If the Who smashed up their instruments..was that violence? Certainly not: it was auto-destruction. **1974** K. MILLETT *Flying* (1975) III. 368 Celia's voice sweet brave sassy, 'Of course I'll be okay.' **1977** *Time* 7 Feb. 57/1 He has..a stand-up lush of an ex-wife..whose sassy words rain mockery on all. **1977** *Spare Rib* July 50/1, I learned a lot of things from the Beatles about sassiness. I always thought they were sassy, that was my label for them. **1979** *Arizona Daily Star* 5 Aug. I. 10/4 She plays a leading character, Persona Non Grata, a hip, wise, slightly sassy new friend of Alic. **1980** W. SAFIRE in *N.Y. Times Mag.* 21 Sept., The Oxford American Dictionary, a sassy and helpful addition to any library. *Ibid.* 9 Nov., He initials 'MFC', a sadly sassy signal that means 'measure for coffin'.

Hence **sa·ssily** *adv.*; **sa·ssiness.**

1976 C. WESTON *Rouse Demon* (1977) xii. 56 'Go ahead, ask me something,' he urged sassily. **1976** 'TREVANIAN' *Main* vi. 128 Now that his first panic is over, something of his haughty sassiness returns.

sastruga (sæstrū·gă). Chiefly as pl. **sastrugi** (-i). [a. G. *sastruga*, f. dial. Russ. *zastrúga* small ridge, furrow, f. *zastrugát'* to plane, smooth, f. *strug* plane.] One of a series of irregular ridges formed on a snow surface by wind erosion and deposition, aligned parallel to the direction of the prevailing wind.

1840 E. SABINE tr. *von Wrangell's Narr. Exped. Polar Sea* vii. 146 We were guided by the wave-like stripes of snow (sastrugi) which are formed, either on the plains on land or on the level ice of the sea, by any wind of long continuance. *Ibid.* 147 It often happens that the *true* permanent sastruga has been obliterated by another produced by temporary winds. **1878** E. L. MOSS *Shores of Polar Sea* vi. 42 The sloping shore hills are barred with 'sastrugi'—wind-made ridges of snow—but the abrupt scooped-out rifts between them are smothered over with fleecy powder in gentle undulations. **1911** R. F. SCOTT *Jrnl.* in *Last Exped.* (1913) I. 517 The hard surface gave place to regular sastrugi. **1937** *Geogr. Jrnl.* LXXXIX. 195 He remarks on sastrugi 6 inches high, then for three days very few. **1960** *Times* 17 Feb. 10/3 Much of the traverse was conducted over a difficult surface rippled with *sastrugi*. **1975** E. HILLARY *Nothing venture, Nothing Win* xiii. 243 The surface, which had appeared so smooth from above, was..liberally peppered with large sastrugi—some of them up to three feet in height. **1979** R. FIENNES *Hell on Ice* v. 70 The sastruga ripples we encountered along the summit ridges.

satai, var. *SATAY.

Satan. Add: **3.** Also *Comb.*, as *Satan-mad*; **Satan monkey**, substitute for def.: the black saki, *Chiropotes satanas*, which is found in dense forest in parts of South America and has thick reddish-black fur; (examples).

1918 W. DE LA MARE *Motley* 51 Not simple happy mad like me,..But that foul Satan-mad. **1906** E. INGERSOLL *Life of Animals: Mammals* 44 (*caption*) Black Saki, Cuxio, or Satan Monkey. **1941** J. S. HUXLEY *Uniqueness of Man* ix. 205 Others, like..the Satan monkey with his fine beard, are curiously reminiscent of ourselves.

Satanist. 1. Delete 'Now *rare*' and add later examples.

1926 C. CONNOLLY *Let.* 16 May in *Romantic Friendship* (1975) 126, I think he's a satanist. **1974** *Encycl. Brit. Macropædia* XIX. 899/2 Such modern satanists as Aleister Crowley and Gerald Gardner. **1976** *Eastern Even. News* (Norwich) 29 Nov., The sisters..are on the trail of a group of Satanists, believed to have caused a young man's death.

4. A writer of the 'Satanic school'.

1921 *Glasgow Herald* 9 Apr. 6/3 Thus he [*sc.* Baudelaire] is a Satanist in the Miltonic sense of a rebel against stifling power.

satay (sæ·tēɪ). Also **satai, saté.** [Mal. *satai, sate*, Indonesian *sate.*] An Indonesian and Malaysian dish, consisting of small pieces of meat grilled on a skewer and usually served with a spiced sauce.

1934 *Willis's Singapore Guide* 149 'Satai' I am given to understand was introduced into this Country by the Chinese, the word being spelt 'Satae', meaning three pieces of meat. **1937** M. COVARRUBIAS *Island of Bali* v. 108 The *saté* can be made of pork or chicken, but turtle remains the favourite of the Balinese of Den Pasar. **1955** P. ANDERSON *Snake Wine* II. vi. 163 The Malays crouch over their portable stoves, fanning the embers below sticks of spicy broiled goat known as *satay*. **1967** L. DEIGHTON *London Dossier* 56 You can eat Malay Satay in the Singapore restaurant in Allen Street, W8. **1971** *Carry Singapore in your Pocket* (Singapore Tourist Promotion Board) (ed. 3) 30 One of the most famous Malay dishes is satay which is tenderised and spiced mutton, chicken or beef barbecued over charcoal and dipped in a chilli-hot peanut sauce. They are served skewered. **1971** *National Geographic* Jan. 16/2 Saté consists of bits of meat skewered on bamboo slivers, grilled over charcoal, and served with a spicy peanut sauce. **1976** *Outdoor Living* (N.Z.) I. II. 64/1 The sate is Asia's answer to the shishkebab. The sate is usually all meat, beautifully spiced and traditionally served on small wooden skewers. **1980** *Times* 5 July 11/2 A menu that ranges from Indonesian satay..to Persian khoresh faisinjan.

‖ **sat-bhai** (sātbāi). Also **saht-bai, sathbhai.** [Hind. *sātbhāī*.] An Indian jungle babbler, *Turdoides striatus*, a large brown bird with a long tail and slightly curved bill; = SEVEN SISTERS 4.

1863 T. C. JERDON *Birds of India* II. 65 It [*sc.* the large grey babbler] leaves the jungles and wilds, and becomes the familiar and unscared..*Sat bhai*. **1886** KIPLING *Departmental Ditties* (ed. 2) 62 The blue jay screams and flutters where the cheery *sát-bhai* dwell. **1928** H. WHISTLER *Pop. Handbk. Indian Birds* 32 The vernacular name [of the jungle babbler] is 'Sathbhai', the Seven Brethren. **1953** S. ALI *Birds of Travancore & Cochin* 28 A frowzled, untidy-looking earthy brown bird..invariably in flocks of half a dozen or so, whence its popular Hindustani name Sātbhai (= seven brothers). **1978** 'M. M. KAYE' *Far Pavilions* ii. 27 The normal noises of an Indian morning:.. the harsh cry of a peacock..and the chatter and chirrup of tree-rats, *saht-bai* and weaver-birds.

satchel, *sb.* Add: **2. satchel charge** (see quot. 1973).

1961 in WEBSTER. **1969** *New Yorker* 20 Sept. 145/1 Setting off satchel charges and other explosives at police stations. **1973** J. QUICK *Dict. Weapons* 385/1 *Satchel charge*, a number of blocks of explosive taped to a board fitted with a rope or wire loop for carrying and attaching. **1977** *Time* 20 June 6/3 The troops used satchel charges to widen the gap made by the armored car, causing thunderous explosions that awoke sleeping villagers.

sate, *v.* Add: **1. e.** *intr.* (for *refl.*). To become sated. *rare.*

1869 BROWNING *Ring & Bk.* IV. XI. 179 Let me turn wolf, be whole, and sate, for once.

sate (sē^{i}t), *sb. Blacksmithing.* [Var. SET *sb.*^{1}] A heavy chisel or punch used for cutting metal. Cf. SET *sb.*^{1} 33 in Dict. and Suppl.

1906 T. MOORE *Handbk. Pract. Smithing & Forging* ii. 15 The cold sate..is a very simple tool in itself, and easy to make. *Ibid.* 17 The hot sate..is made in much the same way as the cold sate. **1942** W. H. ATHERTON *Workshop Pract.* (ed. 2) V. 198 Making two small holes..by slitting with the hot sate and opening out slightly..will widen the hole sufficiently to take a drift of the size required. **1962** [see *SET *sb.*^{1} 33].

saté, var. *SATAY.

sateen. Add: **2.** *Comb.*, as *sateen-backed* adj.

1939–40 *Army & Navy Stores Catal.* 629/2 Down quilts.. Figured Rayon Marocain, Sateen backed. **1960** *Farmer & Stockbreeder* 15 Mar. (Suppl.) 4/1 This wool-lined, sateen-backed quilted pad, with elastic waist belt, fits snugly.

sateless, *a.* Add: Also const. *in*.

1935 L. LUARD *Conquering Seas* 6 The heedless voice of the land sateless in greed.

satellite, *sb.* Add: **2. c.** A man-made object placed (or designed to be placed) in orbit around an astronomical body (usu. the earth).

[**1880** W. H. G. KINGSTON tr. *Verne's Begum's Fortune* xiii. 180 A projectile, animated with an initial speed twenty times superior to the actual speed, being ten thousand yards to the second, can never fail! This movement, combined with terrestrial attraction, destines it to revolve perpetually round our globe... Two hundred thousand dollars is not too much to have paid for the pleasure of having endowed the planetary world with a new star, and the earth with a second satellite.] **1936** *Discovery* Sept. 299/2 The scheme for building a metal outpost satellite and propelling it in a fixed orbit 600 miles above the earth's surface. **1945** A. C. CLARKE in *Wireless World* Oct. 305/2 This 'orbital' velocity is 8 km per sec. (5 miles per sec), and a rocket which attained it would become an artificial satellite, circling the world for ever with no expenditure of power. **1955** *Times* 30 July 6/1 The satellite is expected to be about the size of a basketball, and will be shot into the upper atmosphere by a rocket, where it will circle the earth at an altitude of between 200 and 300 miles at a speed of about 18,000 miles an hour. **1956** *Spaceflight* I. 6/2 After the Earth satellite stage, the next target will almost certainly be the Moon. **1957** *Ibid.* 49/1 Each satellite will be launched into its orbit by being ejected from the third stage of a multiple stage rocket. **1957** *Times* 7 Oct. 8/1 The Russian satellite soaring over the United States seven times a day has made an enormous impression on American minds. **1961**, etc. [see *communication(s) satellite* s.v. *COMMUNICATION 12]. **1964** *Ann. Reg. 1963* 185 Among other notable American achievements in space during the year was the launching of a communications satellite. **1972** *Computers & Humanities* VII. 49 An experiment..was conducted during the fall of 1971 at Stanford, where users were able to communicate with a computer by using NASA's ATS-1 experimental satellite. **1977** *Times* 16 Dec. 16/1 Killer satellites are small spacecraft. They carry an explosive charge which destroys itself and any nearby satellite on detonation.

6. a. A country or state politically or economically dependent upon and subservient to another.

[**1776** T. PAINE *Wks.* (1796), II. 24 In no instance hath nature made the satellite larger than its primary planet; and as England and America..reverse the common order of nature, it is evident that they belong to different systems: England to Europe, America to itself.] **1800, 1827** [in Dict., sense 2b]. **1930** *Economist* 8 Nov. 844/2 Do they portend a military alliance against France between a Fascist Italy and a Fascist Germany, with a bevy of East European satellites—Bulgaria, Albania, Hungary, Austria —to balance Poland and the Little Entente? **1936** *Pacific Affairs* Sept. 404 Outer Mongolia may well be called a satellite of the Soviet Union. **1941** *Ann. Reg. 1940* 204 This [*sc.* the Tripartite Pact of the Axis Powers] made Hungary a mere satellite of Germany. **1948** *Sun* (Baltimore) 9 Jan. 1/2 Several of the Soviet Union's satellites. **1974** M. B. BROWN *Econ. of Imperialism* xii. 286 Cuba is not a satellite of the USSR in the same sense that other Latin American States are satellites of the USA. **1977** *Time* 21 Feb. 8/1 In Czechoslovakia, East Germany, Poland and even some of the less volatile satellites, the Russians and their local rulers are being forced to put out brushfires of discontent.

b. A community or town that is economically or otherwise dependent on a nearby larger town or city.

1912 G. R. TAYLOR in *Survey* (N.Y.) 5 Oct. 14/2 In some sections of the South scarcely a city of any size lacks one or more satellites thrumming with spindle and shuttle. **1935** *Archit. Rev.* LXXVII. 188 (*caption*) 19th Century. Came the railways and with them the first general exodus, suburbs and satellites springing up round the railway stations. **1947** [see *OVERSPILL *sb.* a]. **1958** *Manch. Guardian* 30 June 6/2 And if Manchester itself is some way from Tatton, Manchester's proposed satellite at Lymm is much nearer. **1977** *R.A.F. News* 27 Apr.–10 May 8/2 No. 50(B) Squadron was then based at Skellingthorpe, west of Lincoln (a satellite of Swinderby).

7. *Spectroscopy.* A spurious or subordinate spectral line; *spec.* one caused by an irregularity in the positions of lines in a diffraction grating. Also *satellite line*.

1904 *Astrophysical Jrnl.* XIX. 118 The appearance and disappearance, according to circumstances, of the satellite lines still remains a most curious fact. **1924** *Phil. Mag.* XLVIII. 501 On moving the eyepiece back, the line broadened and a faint black 'satellite' split off from it, moving slowly across the grating. **1945** R. A. SAWYER *Exper. Spectrosc.* vii. 175 It often happens that satellites or diffuse edges will be observed for strong lines at the best obtainable focus. **1969** [see **Rowland ghost*]. **1971** *Physics Bull.* July 388/3 The centre line is due to Rayleigh scattering and the satellites arise from transverse (T) and longitudinal (L) phonons.

8. *Anat.* Chiefly as *satellite cell*. Each of the cells that go to make up the membrane surrounding the nerve cell bodies in many ganglia, analogous to the Schwann cells that surround their axons; also, formerly, a Schwann cell.

[**1908** G. MARINESCO in *Compt. Rend. Hebdom. des Séances et Mém. de la Soc. de Biol.* LXV. 99 De toutes ces recherches, il résulte qu'il existe à l'état normal un équilibre entre la nutrition des cellules satellites et celle des cellules des ganglions sensitifs.] **1928** W. PENFIELD in E. V. Cowdry *Special Cytol.* II. xxx. 1055 Specific stains showed the perivascular and perineuronal oligoglia satellites to be definitely increased. **1954** M. SINGER in R. O. Greep *Histology* xi. 216 Each cell body of spinal, cranial, and autonomic ganglia is completely encapsulated by a thin membrane composed of so-called satellite cells which contains small, scattered, and flattened nuclei. **1958** *Exper. Cell Res. Suppl.* V. 33 The structural characteristic which is present in all fibers so far studied..is the Schwann or satellite cell which..appears everywhere to enclose the axon. **1960** G. CAUSEY *Cell of Schwann* v. 69 The regeneration of nerve fibres and their satellite cells in the tail of the tadpole. **1971** W. M. COPENHAVER et al. *Bailey's Textbk. Histol.* (ed. 16) x. 259/1 When these companion cells are in association with a nerve cell body.., they are called satellite cells; when they provide ensheathment for axons, they are called neurilemma cells, or cells of Schwann.

9. *Cytology.* A short section of a chromosome demarcated from the rest by a constriction (if terminal) or by two constrictions (if intercalary). [The sense is due to S. G. Navashin, who used Russ. *spútnik* satellite (*Izvestiya Imper. Akad. Nauk* (1912) VI. 378).]

1926 C. D. DARLINGTON in *Jrnl. Genetics* XVI. 246 Chromosome 'G' is seen to be approaching the pole with the satellite foremost; this means that the satellite is endowed with special responsiveness to the attraction of the pole. **1960** *Lancet* 14 May 1063/2 In some chromosomes the additional criterion of the presence of a satellite is available (table 1), but in view of the apparent morphological variation of satellites, they and their connecting strands are excluded in computing the indices. **1975** A. & D. LÖVE *Plant Chromosomes* I. i. 26 A secondary constriction may demarcate a short part of the chromosome, either intercalary or, most frequently, terminally. Such a terminal piece is called a satellite.

10. *Bacteriol.* A bacterial colony growing in culture near a second colony which is the source of a diffusible substance which promotes the growth of the first but is not produced by it; or consequently shows accelerated growth, or resists a substance which would otherwise poison it. Usu. *attrib.*

1938 in Dorland & Miller *Med. Dict.* (ed. 18) 1243/1. **1940** M. FROBISHER *Fund. Bacteriol.* (ed. 2) xxv. 355 (*caption*) 'Satellite' formation by *Hemophilus influenzae* on 'chocolate-agar' plate. **1943** *Jrnl. Bacteriol.* XLV. 522/1 The development of satellites depended upon the concentration of sulfonamide, the susceptibility of the satellite strain, the temperature of incubation, and the size of the inoculum of both satellite and inhibitor. **1975** *Jrnl. Clin. Microbiol.* I. 90/2 The satellite growth of *Haemophilus* species around a colony of *Staphylococcus* can be attributed not only to NAD but also to catalase, which is produced by staphylococci.

11. *Molecular Biol.* A portion of the DNA of a genome distinguished from the rest of the genome by its distinctive base composition and density. Freq. *attrib.*

1961 S. KIT in *Jrnl. Molecular Biol.* III. 711 The mean buoyant densities of the principal and the satellite mouse DNA bands were 1·701 and 1·690 g cm^{-3}, respectively. **1962** *Ibid.* IV. 439 Calf thymus satellite was found at the same position in each of three different DNA preparations isolated from thymus tissue obtained from different animals. **1970** *New Scientist* 27 Aug. 406/1 Discovered originally in the mouse, where it constitutes some 10 per cent of the total DNA in each cell of the animal, satellite DNA can be distinguished from the rest by its different density, and by the fact that it apparently consists of repeating base sequences—i.e., multiple copies of a given sequence repeated again and again. **1977** REES & JONES *Chromosome Genetics* ii. 22 Exceptional DNA segments may have an unusually high or low G + C content. When plotted, these fractions appear as heavy or light satellites respectively at the tails of the 'main-band' DNA. Heavy satellites are found in the guinea pig and in human DNA. Light satellites ..are less common.

12. Used *attrib.* to designate a computer or computer terminal distant from, but connected to and serving, a main computer.

1966 C. J. SIPPL *Computer Dict. & Handbk.* 278 As a satellite system the real-time system relieves the larger system of time consuming input and output functions as well as performing preprocessing and postprocessing functions. **1970** O. DOPPING *Computers & Data Processing* vi. 95 Input data in cards or paper tape are converted to magnetic tape by the satellite computer. **1971** E. F. SCHOETERS in B. de Ferranti *Living with Computer* viii. 68 The way in which their huge networks of small satellite computers, or calculating terminals, connected to big machines in London behave..will show just how much more work has to be done.

13. *attrib.* and *Comb.*, as (sense *2 c) *satellite camera, communication(s), killer, launcher, navigation, observatory, programme, -tracking*; *satellite-borne* adj.; *satellite-to-home* adj. phr.; (sense *6) *satellite city, community, country, government, nation, state, town, township*; **satellite airfield,** an airfield auxiliary to and serving, if necessary, as a substitute for a larger airfield; **satellite photo(graph),** a photograph taken from an artificial satellite; so **satellite photography; satellite picture,** a satellite photograph; **satellite station,** (*a*) an artificial satellite; *spec.* (see quot. 1950); (*b*) a secondary radio station which receives and retransmits programmes, so as to improve local reception; **satellite telescope,** a telescope in orbit beyond the range of atmospheric distortion; **satellite television,** television in which the signal is transmitted via an artificial satellite.

1941 F. H. JOSEPH *Lett. Home from Brit. at War* (1942) 38 Clear skies over West Raynham's satellite airfield, Massingham. **1951** O. BERTHOND tr. *P. Clostermann's Big Show* I. 20 We spent the last three weeks of our training at Montford Bridge, a small satellite airfield lost in the hills. **1968** *Wall St. Jrnl.* 25 Sept. 36/1 Flight delays at World Chamberlain and the satellite airfields are almost non-existent. **1962** W. B. THOMPSON *Introd. Plasma Physics* i. 4 Recently, rocket- and satellite-borne counters have detected belts of energetic radiation, electrons and ions, high above the earth's atmosphere. **1974** *Sci. Amer.* June 132/2 Within less than a decade the bulk of transoceanic telephony (and all transoceanic television) has become satellite-borne. **1963** Satellite camera [see *satellite picture* below]. **1966** P. O'DONNELL *Sabre-Tooth* xiv. 185 The end of the journey..was on neutral ground, in an area where spy-plane or satellite cameras would never seek. **1912** G. R. TAYLOR in *Survey* (N.Y.) XXIX. 5 Oct. 23/1 Like camp sutlers, the traffickers in demoralization are quick to follow the trail of satellite cities. **1960** *Washington Post* 20 Dec. A14 They urge that the growth of this region from some 4 million to 9 million persons in the remainder of this century be organized in a pattern of some 50 new satellite cities, each of 75,000 to 150,000 population. A dozen of them would fill the corridor between Baltimore and Washington. **1977** *New Yorker* 13 June 94/2 The new Taichung port..is to include a separate satellite city. **1959** J. H. STRAUBEL et al. *Space Weapons* 243 (Index), Satellite communication. **1960** *Signal* XIV. 32/1 A means of communication is needed that will immediately provide several hundred channels linking key cities throughout the world. This requirement will be filled by a satellite communication system. **1961** *Times Rev. Industry* Feb. 26/3 Last autumn a team of British experts visited the United States to discuss with their opposite numbers the feasibility of establishing a satellite communications system. **1964** *Economist* 1 Aug. 481/2 Complex legal controversies arising from satellite communications systems. **1946** *Nature* 13 July 39/2 The Manchester request for compulsory powers to buy land for the creation of satellite communities. **1970** R. Stavenhagen in I. L. Horowitz *Masses in Lat. Amer.* vii. 254 Not only in the city but also in the 'satellite communities' is commerce usually in Ladino hands. **1956** *Times* 7 Feb. 8/5 Dropping leaflets over the satellite countries..was begun by Radio Free Europe in April, 1954. **1969** A. G. Frank *Latin Amer.* (1970) i. 4 Relations between the satellite underdeveloped and the now developed metropolitan countries. **1976** B. Freemantle *November Man* iv. 43 The Americans actually believe we [*sc.* the Russians] are going to withdraw all our troops from the satellite countries. **1949** Koestler *Promise & Fulfilment* I. xii. 133 Experts of the Foreign Office..tried to set up a puppet Jewish Agency as a kind of satellite Government. **1977** *Guardian Weekly* 2 Oct. 15/2 A new weapon that could destroy Soviet satellites in space... Vought is expected to have a battle version of the satellite killer ready to test in space in about two years. **1977** *Time* 17 Oct. 32/1 The U.S. will now emphasize efforts to design an American satellite killer to defend against the Soviet version. **1959** *Daily Tel.* 2 July 5/5 This satellite launcher is about 110 ft long and 15 in in diameter at the base. **1961** *New Scientist* 19 Jan. 133/1 Several of these countries will discuss the specific proposal for the development of a satellite-launcher based on *Blue Streak.* **1916** C. M. Meredith tr. *F. Naumann's Central Europe* vi. 180 What is meant by a satellite nation..? We might also say a planet State. Such States have their own life. **1956** E. E. Cummings *Let.* 26 Nov. (1969) 253 Urging (via night & day broadcasts) the socalled satellite nations to revolt from colossal Russia. **1967** *Oceanogr. & Marine Biol.* V. 145 In February 1965 *Atlantis* II returned to the area to carry out a hydrographic and coring survey of this area using a satellite navigation system and ship-board computer for the location of this small area. **1975** *Offshore Progress—Technol. & Costs* (Shell Briefing Service) 7 With satellite navigation, however, the rig can fix its own position by computer, processing signals received from orbiting satellites. **1953** J. N. Leonard *Flight into Space* 159 They suspect that the human intellect is approaching a boundary of mystery which its present tools cannot penetrate. Some of them feel that the satellite observatory may be the necessary tool. **1976** H. Kemelman *Wednesday the Rabbi got Wet* xii. 61 The noon broadcast had been almost entirely devoted to..Hurricane Betsy. There were..satellite photos of the eastern coast. **1963** Van Dijk & Rutherford in Wexler & Caskey *Rocket & Satellite Meteorol.* 305 Satellite photographs were obtained of a cut-off low over southeast Australia. **1977** A. Hallam *Planet Earth* 43 (*caption*) A satellite photograph of the Andes. **1971** P. O'Donnell *Impossible Virgin* v. 107 I'll have it checked by our own Map Section... There's *something* there which is detectable by satellite photography. **1963** Van Dijk & Rutherford in Wexler & Caskey *Rocket & Satellite Meteorol.* 305 Facility in interpretation of meteorological satellite pictures can best be achieved by exercises in which clouds of known type and distribution are charted and compared with pictures of the same cloud taken by satellite camera. **1977** L. P. White *Aerial Photogr. & Remote Sensing for Soil Survey* vii. 73 Early examination of coverage of this kind did, however, serve to indicate the possibility of using automatic satellite pictures for purposes other than meteorology and oceanology. **1959** *Daily Tel.* 13 May 1 Britain has decided to take the essential steps to enable scientists here to participate in a satellite programme. **1916** C. M. Meredith tr. *F. Naumann's Central Europe* vi. 181 Round about the satellite States there still exists a certain mass of unorganised national material. **1943** *Ann. Reg. 1942* 176 Their [*sc.* Pan-Germans'] plan was that Germany..should carve out in the Danube basin several satellite states. **1950** *Sun* (Baltimore) 17 July 11/2 Fortifications toughening the ragged western borders of central Europe's satellite states. **1976** *Survey* Summer–Autumn 41 Here was the authentic voice of the unconscious Western desire to believe that the satellite states of the Soviet Union were free. **1945** *Wireless World* Oct. 306 (*caption*) Three satellite stations would ensure complete [radio] coverage of the globe. **1950** W. Proell *Handbk. Space Flight* 174 *Satellite station*, synonym for space station... *Space station*, a habitable vehicle placed in a satellite orbit around a planetary body, for use in refueling of space ships, communications relaying, or military use. **1954** E. Pangborn *Mirror for Observers* (1955) I. i. 21, I understand men will have their first satellite station in a very short time, four or five years. **1959** *Times Lit. Suppl.* 30 Oct. 631/4 The cost of building a moon rocket at a satellite station, including the fuel of the rockets carrying the materials, he estimates as £40m. **1959** *Proc. Inst. Electr. Engineers* V. 416/1 A number of low-power satellite stations are therefore planned... They will be designed to..pick up signals from an existing B.B.C. station and retransmit them on a different channel for local reception. *Ibid.*, The B.B.C.'s plan for extending and improving the coverage of the television service and of..sound services on v.h.f. by building low-power satellite stations in various parts of the country. **1962** *Rep. Comm. Broadcasting 1960* 197 in *Parl. Papers 1961–2* (Cmnd. 1753) IX. 259 It is possible to provide low-powered relay stations..to extend coverage still further...These satellite stations..have been planned as a stage by stage project. **1951** J. P. Marbarger *Space Med.* 26 If we turn such a satellite telescope to the outer reaches of the universe, the planets and the stars, we shall find observation conditions which no terrestrial observatory could equal. **1960** *Aeroplane* XCIX. 358/1 It turns out that this is a design study into a stabilised platform for a small satellite telescope. **1966** *B.B.C. Handbk.* 53 The BBC's first satellite television transmissions were shown in 1962. **1971** L. Koppett *N.Y. Times Guide Spectator Sports* xii. 194 Satellite television. **1967** *Economist* 1 July 32/2 What about lasers? What about direct satellite-to-home broadcasting?..Perhaps the only way in which the federal government could expect to keep abreast of the developments in communications technologies would be to set up a Department of Communication. **1973** *Computers & Humanities* VII. 226 The uses of such wonders as switched data networks, computer terminals, mobile radio transceivers, and satellite-to-home-receiver television transmission. **1925** C. B. Purdom (*title*) The building of satellite towns. **1929** *Times* 17 July 17/6 Since neither complete decentralization nor the proposal to 'departmentalize' the government of Greater Paris is found to give general satisfaction, the system of 'satellite towns' has been suggested as a way out. **1933** *Archit. Rev.* LXXIV. 166/2 The proposed formation of a ring of satellite towns around the immediate radius of London. **1946** F. J. Osborn *Green Belt Cities* I. 182 *Satellite Town.* This term was first used in Great Britain in 1919 as an alternative description of Welwyn Garden City... Some planning writers have thoughtlessly renewed the old confusion by using the term Satellite Town to describe an Industrial Garden Suburb. It is better reserved for a Garden City or country town, at a moderate distance from a large city, but physically separated from that city by a Country Belt. **1955** *Sci. Amer.* Jan. 40/3 As population continues to move from cities out to ever more distant suburbs and satellite towns [etc.]. **1971** *Rand Daily Mail* 27 Mar. 3/7 A giant new satellite township near Pretoria..will provide housing..for about 200 000 White people. **1958** A. Budrys in Aldiss & Harrison *Decade 1950s* (1976) 68 I'm assigned to the satellite-tracking station. **1969** *Listener* 20 Feb. 233/2 Satellite tracking is not as easy as it appears.

14. *attrib.* passing into *adj.* That is a satellite to something else; subsidiary, subordinate; associated; ancillary.

1892 B. Potter *Jrnl.* 8 Aug. (1966) 245 We..found the thirteen or fourteen vans drawn up in the town square, and covered with a tarpaulin, with several satellite peep shows. **1923** N. Shaw *Forecasting Weather* v. 115 Two detached secondary or satellite depressions. **1931** *Economist* 17 Oct. 699/1 The Indian currency and..the various 'satellite' currencies of the Crown Colonies and Possessions. **1939** *Oxoniensia* IV. 13 Post-holes 1.., 3 and 6 were also provided with from two to four satellite sockets and slots for supports. **1949** *Caribbean Q.* I. III. 43 A central model farm..would carry on intensive dairy farming... The satellite farms would be run by skilled farmers. **1957** *Observer* 8 Sept. 7/3 When fashion makes a decisive move innumerable satellite trades are affected. **1965** B. Sweet-Escott *Baker St. Irregular* iii. 77 This was to be their home for the next four years and became in due course surrounded by a series of satellite premises. **1967** *Boston Sunday Globe* 23 Apr. (Mag.) 33/1 Satellite clinics for children and pregnant mothers..run jointly by several Harvard affiliated hospitals and the City of Boston. **1969** *Wall St. Jrnl.* 1 Dec. 9/1 Pan Am..is trying to sell passengers on use of the 'satellite' terminal facilities around the New York metropolitan area. **1972** *Accountant* 26 Oct. 518/2 Satellite reports, or supplementary reports, would be prepared for the particular interests of particular users. **1976** *NBR Marketplace* (Wellington, N.Z.) III. 37/2 The satellite seminar was joined by dozens of doctors and nurses. **1976** *Offshore Engineer* July 20/3 A cluster of 10 wells with four satellite wells for water and gas injection.

satellite (sæ·tĕləit), *v.* [f. prec.] **1.** *intr.* To orbit like a satellite.

1959 *IRE Trans. Military Electronics* III. 62/2 Mission periods of the order of one year (including a brief period..of satelliting about the target planet).

2. *trans.* To transmit by way of a communications satellite.

1974 *Listener* 14 Dec. 826 The telephone woke me. It was Peter Lynch, our contact in Tel Aviv (from where our film was being satellited). **1976** A. Davis *Television* iv. 50 During the war in Cyprus in 1974, film shot by British cameramen was flown to Tel Aviv where it was processed, then satellited to Rome, where it was fed into the Eurovision network. **1978** *Broadcast* 23 Oct. 5/1 BBC TV News reporter Bob Friend..satellited the pictures to London from Tai Pei.

satellited (sæ·tĕləitĕd), *a.* [f. Satellite + -ed[2].] **1.** (In Dict. s.v. Satellite.)

2. *Cytology.* Having a satellite or satellites (*satellite *sb.* 9).

1934 L. W. Sharp *Introd. Cytol.* (ed. 3) xviii. 319 (*caption*) Synaptic configurations..after deletion of portion of shorter arm of satellited chromosome. **1938** *Jrnl. R. Microsc. Soc.* LVIII. 103 Every primary diploid plant or animal generally has one pair of satellited chromosomes which..produce by fusion a single nucleolus. **1971** *Nature* 21 May 195/1 In the Australasian superfamily Dasyuroidea, all species have seven pairs of chromosomes, the autosomes including..two small pairs of chromosomes of which one has a satellited short arm.

satellitism (sæ·tĕləitiz'm). [f. Satellit(e + -ism.] **1.** *Bacteriol.* The occurrence of satellites (*satellite *sb.* 10); the promotion of bacterial growth by the proximity of a colony of different bacteria.

1951 Whitby & Hynes *Med. Bacteriol.* (ed. 5) xvi. 282 Staphylococci secrete enough of the factor to stimulate growth of *H*[*æmophilus*] *influenzæ*; colonies of the latter on a blood plate are always larger when they lie near a staphylococcal colony (satellitism). **1975** *Jrnl. Clin. Microbiol.* I. 89 (*heading*) New satellitism test for isolation and identification of *Haemophilus influenzae* and *Haemophilus parainfluenzae* in sputum.

2. *Pol.* The fact or condition of being a satellite (state); the role of a satellite.

1955 O. Lattimore *Nationalism & Revolution in Mongolia* 41 (*heading*) Anatomy of satellitism. **1962** —— *Nomads & Commissars* viii. 155 Stalin..and Mongolia's loyalty to the Soviet alliance bring up the question of satellitism. **1964** *Economist* 10 Oct. 101/1 Only by helping to create a state much closer in strength to the superpowers can we escape satellitism or neutralism. **1969** D. Widgery in Cockburn & Blackburn *Student Power* 137 Wilson's satellitism to Washington forces an attack on Government spending.

satellitosis (sætlĕəitōᵘ·sis). *Path.* [f. Satellit(e + -osis.] A proliferation of neuroglial cells around nerve cells in the brain.

1928 W. Penfield in E. V. Cowdry *Special Cytol.* II. xxx. 1055 From this satellitosis a perivascular and even a perineuronal leucocytic infiltration must be carefully distinguished. **1969** Brown & Bertke *Textbk. Cytol.* xxiii. 549 Oligodendrocytes..may increase in number during aging to produce a satellitosis, which is often seen in aging organs. **1979** *Jrnl. Compar. Path.* LXXXIX. 490 Some of the ganglion cells showed satellitosis.

satellize (sæ·tĕləiz), *v.* [f. Satell(ite + -ize.] **1.** *intr.* To cluster *about. rare.*

1916 E. V. Lucas *Variety Lane* 60 A little band of important men hurried up, satellizing about a quiet, gentle-looking but distinguished man.

2. *trans.* To make into a political or economic satellite.

1951 *Melbourne Herald* 16 Apr., Dr. W. E. Stanner..introduced..the verb *to satellise.* Dr. Stanner used it when referring to other countries which, in given conditions, Russia might *satellise.* **1965** *Observer* 19 Sept. 2/3 Pakistan..will not become a satellite of India; but..she will not be satellised by China either.

Hence **satelliza·tion**, the action of making into a satellite; the condition or process of being satellized; **sa·tellized** *ppl. a.*

1958 *Times* 13 May 8/5 Mr Rountree, Assistant Secretary of State..told the committee:..'Satellization of the Middle East now seems less a danger than it did a few months ago.' **1962** *Economist* 12 May 551/2 A small communist country which..wants to escape satellisation by China. **1968** 'Han Suyin' *Birdless Summer* I. iii. 56 Japan's terms were the permanent satellization of China. **1969** A. G. Frank *Latin Amer.* (1970) i. 7 The satellized national, regional, and local metropoles in Latin America find that their economic development is at best a limited or underdeveloped development. **1976** *Globe & Mail* (Toronto) 18 June 7/3 In spite of the somewhat unsure character of its national identity and its excessive satellization by the American economic and cultural empire, Canada-without-Quebec has enough 'difference' left, [etc.].

satelloid (sæ·tĕloid). [f. Satell(ite + -oid.] A craft designed to follow approximately a free-fall orbit, but to expend power to overcome air resistance or to change its course.

1955 *Times* 3 Aug. 8/5 He has constructed a special earth satellite, the 'Satelloid' which goes to an altitude of 100 miles and from there is moved forward by an engine. **1956** *Jrnl. Brit. Interplanetary Soc.* XV. 166 Dr. Krafft A. Ehricke, of the guided missile group of Convair, has suggested that a weakly-powered satellite might be placed in a lower orbit than that required for an unpowered satellite, and used the word 'satelloid' to describe such a vehicle when discussing it at the I.A.F. meeting in Copenhagen. He said that the satelloid might be placed in an orbit at 80 miles altitude. **1960** *Aeroplane* XCVIII. 496/1 The authors examine various statements which have been made by U.S. military leaders on the merits of arching ballistic missiles, jump-down bombs, variable orbit satelloids, and boost-glide devices.

satem (sā·təm). *Philol.* Also **satəm.** [f. Avestan *satəm* hundred, from its pronunciation with (s), as opposed to *centum: first used by P. von Bradke 1890 in *Über Methode und Ergebnisse der avischen Alterthumswissenschaft* I. iv. 63.] A name given by philologists to one, chiefly eastern, group of Indo-European languages, distinguished by their use of sibilants where the corresponding sounds in cognate words in the western group (cf. *centum) are velar stops.

1901, etc. [see *centum]. **1933** L. Bloomfield *Language* xviii. 316 Many scholars suppose that the earliest traceable division of the Primitive Indo-European unity was into a western group of so-called '*centum*-languages' and an eastern group of '*satem*-languages'. **1952** O. R. Gurney *Hittites* vi. 119 The main characteristics of the Indo-Iranian (or so-called 'Satem') languages (change of original *k* to *s*, *qu* to *k*, and *e* and *o* to *a*). **1973** *Word 1970* XXVI. 3 The time when the back velar stops moved forward in satem languages.

sater, var. *saeter, setter.

sathbhai, var. *sat-bhai.

'satiable, colloq. reduced form of Insatiable *a.* Used in phr. *'satiable curiosity* in allusion to Kipling's *Just So Stories* (see quot. 1900).

1900 Kipling *Just So Stories* (1902) 63 There was one Elephant..—an Elephant's Child—who was full of 'satiable curtiosity, and that means he asked ever so many questions. **1963** L. Egan *Run to Evil* i. 6 Talk about the Elephant's Child... Nobody could really dislike the Brandon boy, even with his 'satiable curiosity. **1974** K. Benton *Craig & Tunisian Tangle* v. 52 She's like the Elephant's Child, full of 'satiable curiosity.

satiated, *ppl. a.* Add: (Later examples, esp. in sense of *satiation b and *satiety 1 e.)

1935 Adams & Zener tr. *Lewin's Dynamic Theory of Personality* viii. 255 Both agreeable and disagreeable tasks are comparatively more rapidly satiated than neutral ones. **1969** J. D. Davis et al. in *Jrnl. Compar. & Physiol. Psychol.* LXVII. 407 Intake of milk by fasted rats was reduced 50% below normal after their blood had been transfused with that of satiated rats. **1975** Schneider & Tarshis *Physiol. Psychol.* xvi. 283 These studies have shown that the size of the cells in the ventromedial hypothalamus are larger and thus presumably more active in satiated animals than in deprived animals.

satiation. Add: **b.** *Psychol.* The point at which satisfaction of a need or familiarity with a stimulus reduces or ends an organism's responsiveness or motivation. Also *attrib.*

1935 Adams & Zener tr. *Lewin's Dynamic Theory of Personality* viii. 254 The progressive process of satiation is evidenced by such typical criteria as variation, dissolution of the whole.., inattention, forgetting. **1944** Köhler & Wallach in *Proc. Amer. Philos. Soc.* LXXXVIII. 276/1 We propose to call only the alterations of *T*-objects 'figural after-effects' and to refer to the affection of the medium as 'satiation'. **1954** Woodworth & Schlosberg *Exper. Psychol.* (rev. ed.) xiv. 426/1 Satiation..is not offered as an explanation of the illusion itself, but as a cause of its reduction and final destruction. **1967** J. R. Millenson *Princ. Behavioral Analysis* (1969) xv. 367 There are drive operations that reduce or eliminate reinforcing value... The most universal of these is *satiation*—repeatedly presenting the reinforcer until it loses its power to reinforce. **1975** Schneider & Tarshis *Physiol. Psychol.* xvi. 276 Studies have confirmed the notion that the ventromedial hypothalamus comes into play during satiation to inhibit eating. *Ibid.* 283 The transfused rats no longer seemed to be hungry... Davis took this to mean that the blood does carry an off, or satiation, signal. **1978** F. Leukel *Essent. Physiol. Psychol.* xii. 197/2 Satiation stimuli are more readily aroused.

satiety. Add: **1. e.** *Psychol.* Satisfaction of a need (esp. hunger) as it is registered physiologically; also *attrib.* and *Comb.*, as *satiety hormone, mechanism, process*; **satiety centre**, an area of the brain concerned with the regulation of food intake.

1951 *Amer. Jrnl. Physiol.* CLXIV. 186 The physiological release of enterogastrone is apparently not involved in the production of satiety. **1962** *Science* CXXXV. 374/2 The so-called 'feeding center' of the lateral hypothalamus and the 'satiety center' of the medial hypothalamus are well known. **1969** J. D. Davis et al. in *Jrnl. Compar. & Physiol. Psychol.* LXVII. 407/1 Is food intake..regulated by a 'satiety hormone' which terminates feeding when it reaches a threshold level? **1971** K. H. Pribram *Lang. of Brain* x. 192 Somehow the lesion had impaired the patient's *feelings* of hunger and satiety and this impairment was accompanied by excessive eating! *Ibid.* 195 The term 'motivation' can be restricted to the operations of appetitive 'go' processes..and the term 'emotion' to the operations of affective 'stop' or satiety processes of equilibrium. **1974** J. Olds in W. R. Adey et al. *Brain Mechanisms* vii. 379 In one of these areas, known as the 'satiety center', destruction of tissues caused animals to overeat and become obese. **1975** F. P. Valle *Motivation* xii. 227 There are several hypotheses regarding the variables that govern the activity of the 'satiety center' in the ventromedial nuclei. **1977** N. R. Carlson *Physiol. of Behav.* xii. 324 The fact that we stop eating before a significant amount of food is digested makes it necessary to postulate a satiety mechanism. *Ibid.* 325 Satiety has many sources, from several kinds of detectors. **1978** F. Leukel *Essent. Physiol. Psychol.* xii. 203/1 The first center is the ventromedial nucleus of the hypothalamus. This nucleus appeared to function as a satiation, or satiety, centre.

satin, *sb.* (and *a.*) Add: **I. 1. c.** A woman's satin dress.

1787 'T. Wignell' *Contrast* I. 2 She is to be married in a delicate white sattin. **1866** Mrs. Gaskell *Wives & Daughters* I. xxvi. 287, I remember the time when Mrs Kirkpatrick wore old black silks..and now she is in a satin. **1932** [see *low-cut* s.v. *low *adv.*]. **1958** J. Cannan *And be a Villain* iv. 100 A high-waisted pomegranate satin with gold lace sleeves.

4. (Earlier and later examples.)

1845 J. R. Planché *Golden Fleece* I. 13 An ardent spirit, known By several names..Some 'Cupid's eye water' the liquor call, 'White Satin' some. **1934** T. S. Eliot *Rock* ii. 66, I brought you along a drop o' satin. Four glasses and all.

5*. A domestic rabbit belonging to the breed so called, developed in America during the early 1930s by Walter A. Huey and distinguished by smooth fur with a satin-like sheen. Also *attrib.*

1934 W. L. Cotta in *Fur Animals* Aug. 3/1, I take great pleasure in describing, for the first time publicly, the most amazing rabbit of all time, the Satin Havana. **1935** *Small Stock Mag.* Aug. 7/2 Anything in the nature of a boom will do the satin more harm than good. **1946** *Amer. Rabbit Jrnl.* XVI. 44/2 In 1936 the American Satin Rabbit Breeders Association was organized. *Ibid.* 45/1 With the exception of the Satin Havanas, none of the Satin breeds have an Approved Working Standard. **1947** *Fur & Feather* 9 May 191/3 The Satin..a beautiful animal..comes in various colours, white, an orange, blue, black... Its fur feels like satin. It is a breed about nine years old and was started from a freak litter of Havanas. **1957** J. C. Sandford *Domestic Rabbit* i. 2 A second mutation of a coat character is the Satin. *Ibid.* 3 The Satin coat has also been combined with a number of colours. **1979** G. R. Scott *Rabbit Keeping* i. 26 The Satin rabbit is another mutation. *Ibid.*, The early Satins were ivory in colour.

II. 6. b. (Later examples.)

1913 C. Mackenzie *Sinister St.* I. I. vii. 103 Boys emerged from the tuckshop, sucking gelatines and satin pralines and chocolate creams. **1930** E. Pound *XXX Cantos* vii. 27 Square even shoulders and the satin skin, Gone cheeks of the dancing woman. **1975** P. Moyes *Black Widower* v. 56 A single big tear ran down her black satin cheek. **1977** *Hot Car* Oct. 59/2 The finish will be a nice satin which is a sod to keep clean.

c. Delete † *Obs.* and add later example.

1912 W. de la Mare *Listeners & Other Poems* 8 Her satin bosom heaving slow With sighs that softly ebb and flow.

7. a. *satin-like* adj. (earlier and later examples); **b.** *satin-clad, -frilled, -purfled, -sandalled, -shimmering* adjs.

1881 'Mark Twain' *Prince & Pauper* xxxii. 349 Satin-clad officials are flitting and glinting everywhere. **1949** Blunden *After Bombing* 25 Enchanting poppies satin-frilled. **1699** M. Lister *Journey to Paris* 59 A very smooth Sattin-like Skin. **1919** E. Pound *Quia Pauper Amavi* 16 There is a satin-like bow on the harp. **1862** G. M. Hopkins *Poems* (1967) 10 And trample and tread The satin-purfled smooth to foam. **1917** Blunden *Poems* (1930) 44 Satin-sandalled Chloes glimmering. **1952** R. Campbell tr. *Baudelaire's Poems* 89 On satin-shimmering, downy avalanches.

8. a. **satin-finish**, also any effect resembling satin in texture or surface produced on materials in various ways; **satin leather, satin oil**, leather finished so as to resemble satin; **satin-paper** (earlier examples); **satin weave** (see quot. 1897); **satin wire** (see quot. 1925).

1865 Mrs. Stowe *House & Home Papers* 157 For satin finish,..American papers equal any in the world. **1929** *Encycl. Brit.* XXIX. 7/2 Frequently the surface [of glass] had been dulled by acid so as to produce a 'satin' finish. **1959** *Gloss. Packaging Terms* (*B.S.I.*) 32 *Satin finish*, a decorative matt finish mechanically or chemically applied to aluminium and tinplate sheets. **1969** *New Yorker* 27 Sept. 92/3 (Advt.), It's Norway Pewter with the gleaming, never-tarnish satin finish. **1972** *Homes & Gardens* Mar. 106/2 They [*sc.* paints] are obtainable in gloss, semi-gloss, eggshell and satin finishes. **1974** *Harrods Christmas Catal.* 8 Housecoat in washable satin-finish flocked nylon. **1802** *Monthly Mag.* XIV. 203/2 White and chamois leather.. are evidently in danger of being beat out of the market by the English satin-leather. **1903** L. A. Flemming *Pract. Tanning* xiv. 264 Wax calf and satin leather are finished upon the flesh or inner side. **1971** T. C. Collocott *Dict. Sci. & Technol.* 1033/1 *Satin leather*.., leather with a perfectly smooth finish and without grain marks. **1895** *Montgomery Ward Catal.* Spring & Summer 517/3 Men's Satin Oil Congress Gaiters. **1897** C. T. Davis *Manuf. Leather* (ed. 2) xxviii. 424 This blacking is for satin oil, glove grain, plow grain, oil grain and dongola. **1834** M. Edgeworth *Tour in Connemara* (1950) 55 Mr. Jones wrote me as elegant a note as ever you saw on satin paper. **1840** Thackeray in *Fraser's Mag.* XXI. 684/1 I'll keep everything: the red wax, because it's like your lips; the black wax, because it's like your hair; and the satin paper, because it's like your skin! **1897** Stephenson & Suddards *Text Bk. Ornamental Design Woven Fabrics* 104 What is known in textile manufacturing as a satin weave, which is a construction of cloth where the weft comes to the surface in greater proportion than the warp, or *vice versa*, in a certain definite order. **1964** *McCall's Sewing* iv. 52/2 Satin weaves produce smooth, lustrous fabrics. **1969** *Sears Catal.* Spring/Summer 20 Blazer stripes in a satin weave on sand beige. **1899** in A. Adburgham *Shops & Shopping* (1964) xxii. 261 Satin wire. **1925** G. E. Martin *Make your Own Hats* (rev. ed.) i. 4 *Satin wire*, the thickest wire used in millinery, covered with a padding of cotton and then wrapped with silk; sometimes used for head line and edge wires. **1966** Satin wire [see *millinery 3].

b. **satin bell** = *mariposa lily; **satin-flower**, (*e*) a small herb of the genus *Sisyrinchium*, esp. *S. douglasii*, which is native to western North America and has grass-like leaves and small blue or purple flowers; **satin walnut** (earlier and later examples); **satin wave**, a white moth, *Sterrha subsericeata*; **satin-wood**, add: esp. *Fagara flava*; also, the similar yellowish wood of any of several African or Australian trees, esp. *Daphnandra micrantha* or *Zanthoxylum brachyacanthum*; also, any of the trees producing this timber; the colour of this timber; (earlier and later examples).

1898 A. M. Davidson *Calif. Plants* 123 Mariposas are.. sometimes called globe tulips,..the satin-bell or fairy's lantern. **1925** W. L. Jepson *Man. Flowering Plants Calif.* 237 White Globe Lily..Also called Snow-drops, Indian Bells, and Satin Bells. **1882** G. P. Lathrop *Echo of Passion* iv. 76 Marigolds and satin-flowers..were growing in the midst of rank weeds. **1971** *Daily Colonist* (Victoria, B.C.) 18 Apr. 22/2 Numerous clumps of satin flower blend their purple hued petals with the rosy shooting star. **1897** G. B. Sudworth *Nomencl. Arborescent Flora U.S.* 205 Sweet Gum..Satin Walnut. **1949** Collingwood & Brush *Knowing your Trees* 247/1 Sweetgum..is frequently marketed as satin walnut. **1908** R. South *Moths Brit. Isles* 2nd Ser. 117 The Satin Wave... The wings of this species are glossy whitish. **1958** W. J. Stokoe *Caterpillars Brit. Moths* II. 29 The Satin Wave..is widely distributed throughout England and Wales. **1792** G. Imlay *Topogr. Descr. W. Territory N. Amer.* 214 Satin-wood tree. Not classed. **1799** *Times* 1 June 4/1 (Advt.), Cabinet articles.. in mahogany, satin, and other woods. *Ibid.*, Valuable, and seasoned stock of Mahogany and satin wood in lots, planks, boards, and veneers. **1884** A. Nilson *Timber Trees New South Wales* 50 *D*[*aphnandra*] *micrantha*.—Satin-wood; Light yellow-wood... Timber fragrant, quite yellow when fresh. *Ibid.* 125 *Z*[*anthoxylum*] *brachyacanthum.* Satinwood; Thorny Yellowwood. **1902** G. S. Boulger *Wood* v. 97 About 1750, Satinwood..became fashionable for coach-panels. **1907** *Yesterday's Shopping* (1969) 145/1 Stains.. as used by the Working Ladies Guild, colours:—Rosewood, Satinwood, Oak, [etc.]. **1908** [see *obeche]. **1920** [see *afrormosia]. **1926–7** [see *maple 2 b]. **1936** R. H. Anderson *Trees New South Wales* 127 Socket Wood.. is also known as Light Yellow-wood, Satin Wood, and occasionally as Sassafras. **1958** *N.Z. Timber Jrnl.* July 73/2 There is a great variety of satinwoods. **1962** S. Wynter *Hills of Hebron* v. 73 The indent where the pulse beat was smooth, like satinwood.

c. **satin beauté**, a soft finely woven material with a dull crêpe back and brilliant satin finish; **satin de chine**, a silk fabric with a silk finish; **satin de laine** (earlier example); **satin de Lyon(s)** (see quots.).

1922 *Daily Mail* 18 Dec. 8 Her gown, in the Early Italian style, will be of cream satin beauté. **1928** *Times* 9 May 10/6 A draped gown of lavender satin beauté, embroidered with silver. **1880** L. Higgin *Handbk. Embroidery* ii. 14 '*Satin de Chine*', and other silk-faced materials of the same class. **1895** *Army & Navy Co-op. Soc. Price List* 15 Sept. 1095/1 Satin de Lyon..Satin de Chine, for dress linings. **1969** R. T. Wilcox *Dict. Costume* 303/2 *Satin de chine*,..was known in medieval Europe... Because of its exquisite texture, it became a court favorite. **1851** Satin de laine [see *Mousseline 1 b]. **1881** C. C. Harrison *Woman's Handiwork* II. 115 Satin de Lyons, of a fine close quality, may be used with water-colors. **1915** L. Harmuth *Dict. Textiles* 137/2 *Satin de Lyon*, silk satin made with a twilled back, and finely striped face, used for lining. **1969** R. T. Wilcox *Dict. Costume* 303/2 *Satin de lyon*, satin with a ribbed back. Used for masculine evening wear trim such as top hat, waistcoat, lapel or trouser stripes.

satined, *ppl. a.* Add: **a.** (Later example.) Also, having a satin-finish. **b.** Clothed in satin.

1817 Jane Austen *Venta* in *Minor Wks.* (1954) VI. 457 The Lords & the Ladies were sattin'd & ermin'd. **1897** *Sears, Roebuck Catal.* 415 Solid Sterling Silver [bracelet], chased satined links.

satinize, *v.* Add: Hence **sa·tinized** *ppl. a.*

1972 *Guardian* 18 July 11/2 Satinised cotton trousers. **1975** *Harper's & Queen* June 96 Shocking pink shawl in satinised cotton.

satire (sæ·təiəɹ), *v.* [f. the sb.] *trans.* = Satirize *v.* 2 a.

1905 S. Joyce in *Lett. J. Joyce* (1966) II. 104 He doesn't think the critics will approve, or the people satired. **1961** in *Amer. Speech* XXXVI. 138 Hawthorne in his story 'Earth Holocaust' satires Emerson's idea of books.

satirism. Delete † *Obs.* and add later example.

1950 *Scrutiny* XVII. II. 145 What strikes one in reading, however, is not so much the variety of these satirisms..but simply their ubiquity.

satisfaction. Add: **5. e.** *Psychol.* The satisfying of a need or desire as it affects or motivates behaviour.

1911 E. L. Thorndike *Animal Intelligence* vi. 244 The Law of Effect is that: Of several responses made to the same situation, those which are accompanied or closely followed by satisfaction to the animal will..be more firmly connected with the situation, so that when it recurs, they will be more likely to recur. **1922** R. S. Woodworth *Psychol.* xix. 488 Dancing also gives a chance for muscular activity which is obviously one source of satisfaction in the more active games. **1951** J. M. Fraser *Psychol.* xiv. 161 Another group of satisfactions can be drawn, not perhaps from the work itself, but from the surroundings in which it is carried out. **1966** Katz & Kahn *Social Psychol. of Organizations* xii. 363 If there is one confirmed finding in all the studies of worker morale and satisfaction, it is the correlation between the variety and challenge of the job and the gratifications which accrue to workers. **1976** R. H. Moos *Human Context* viii. 265 Once workers feel competent with the transition, they often report long term gains in satisfaction or morale.

III. 7. **satisfaction note** *Insurance*, an acknowledgement of satisfaction with repairs made to a car signed by one claiming repair costs from an insurance company; **satisfaction theory** *Theol.* = *doctrine of satisfaction* (see sense 3 in Dict.).

1971 *Reader's Digest Family Guide to Law* 533/1 When repairs [to a car] are finished, the policy-holder is usually asked to sign a satisfaction note... Before signing, inspect the vehicle carefully and, if possible, take it for a test drive. **1973** *Times* 15 Dec. 19/7 Normally you will have to sign a 'satisfaction note' for the repairers before you can regain possession of your car after it has been repaired. **1932** Satisfaction theory [see *Anselmic *a.*]. **1969** *Dict. Christian Theol.* 23/1 Anselm..in his work *Cur Deus Homo?*,..interpreted the doctrine [of atonement] in terms of the 'satisfaction' or 'juridical' theory.

satisfiable, *a.* Restrict *rare* to sense a and add further examples of sense b.

1942 W. S. Churchill *End of Beginning* (1943) 228 All these conditions were satisfiable around 23rd October. **1944** *Annals Math. Stud.* XIII. 91 Formulas which are valid (or satisfiable) in every domain of individuals. **1952** R. L. Wilder *Introd. Foundations Math.* ii. 26 An axiom system Σ is satisfiable if there exists an interpretation of Σ. **1978** *Sci. Amer.* Jan. 106/3 When the machine is given a yes instance of a problem in *NP*, its operation is described by a satisfiable sentence, whereas the operation of a machine given a no instance is described by a sentence that cannot be satisfied.

Hence **sa:tisfiabi·lity.**

1944 *Annals Math. Stud.* XIII. 90 We may study the decision problem from the point of view either of validity or of satisfiability, instead of that of provability. **1952** R. L. Wilder *Introd. Foundations Math.* ii. 26 Where a system [of axioms] is consistent, we are usually unable to tell the fact from I. I. But..we have a very simple test showing 'satisfiability' in the sense of I.3. **1977** *Word 1972* XXVIII. 285 Something which, with Hockett, we may term the 'productivity' of the description, one of the fundamental conditions of its acceptability or 'satisfiability'.

satisfice, *v.* Restrict *Obs.* exc. *north.* to sense in Dict. and add: **2.** *intr.* To decide on and pursue a course of action that will satisfy the minimum requirements necessary to achieve a particular goal. Hence **sa·tisficer**; **sa·tisficing** *ppl. a.* and *vbl. sb.*

1956 H. Simon in *Psychol. Rev.* LXIII. 129/2 Evidently, organisms adapt well enough to 'satisfice'; they do not, in general, 'optimize'. *Ibid.* 136/1 A 'satisficing' path, a path that will permit satisfaction at some specified level of all its needs. **1957** —— *Models of Man* IV. 205 The key..appeared to lie in substituting the goal of satisficing, of finding a good enough move, for the goal of minimaxing, of finding the best move. **1958** March & Simon *Organizations* vi. 141 To optimize requires processes several orders of magnitude more complex than those required to satisfice. **1963** G. P. E. Clarkson in A. R. Oxenfeldt *Models of Markets* II. 340 Two important innovations..have occurred... The first of these is the modified concept of rational behavior known as 'satisficing'... Important changes in the theory of the firm have been brought about by the introduction of the satisficing concept of behavior. **1967** H. Simon in N. Rescher *Logic of Decision & Action* i. 19 It is easy to see how GPS can be made into a satisficer. **1973** *N.Y. Times* 11 Feb. III. 1/2 Big business executives don't really try to maximize profits but '*satisfice*'—that is, they try to make enough profit to keep stockholders and boards of directors happy without bringing the wrath of government regulators, consumer groups or business competitors down on them. **1977** P. N. Khandwalla *Design of Organizations* xi. 404 To the seat-of-the-pants 'satisficer', scientific analysis may be acceptable in dealing with relatively trivial problems. **1977** Janis & Mann *Decision Making* ii. 32 A much more serious flaw of this complex form of satisficing lies in its failure to ensure that the alternatives retained are..superior to those eliminated.

‖ **satori** (sătō^ə·ri). *Zen Buddhism.* [Jap., = spiritual awakening.] A sudden indescribable and uncommunicable inner experience of enlightenment. Also *transf.* Hence **sato·ric** *a.*, pertaining to or inducing satori.

1727 J. G. Scheuchzer tr. *Kæmpfer's Hist. Japan* I. III. vi. 242 This profound Enthusiasm is by them call'd *Safen*, and the divine truths revealed to such persons *Satori*. **1921** A. Waley *Nō Plays of Japan* 58 The only escape from this 'Wheel of Life and Death' lies in *satori*, 'Enlightenment', the realization that material phenomena are thoughts, not facts. **1921** D. T. Suzuki in *Eastern Buddhist* May 33 The power to see into the nature of one's own being lies also hidden here [in the subconscious]. Zen awakens it. The awakening is known as *Satori*, or the opening of a third eye. **1933** —— *Ess. Zen Buddhism* 2nd Ser. I. 21 When you have satori you are able to reveal a palatial mansion made of precious stones on a single blade of grass; but when you have no satori, a palatial mansion itself is concealed behind a simple blade of grass. **1949** C. Humphreys *Zen Buddhism* ii. 33 *Satori*, the immediate experience of truth as distinct from understanding about it. **1957** *New Yorker* 31 Aug. 35/1 It takes at least ten years of meditation and *koans* to attain even one flash of *satori*. **1968** T. Wolfe *Electric Kool-Aid Acid Test* viii. 102 It was as if Cassady..was in a state of satori, as totally into this very moment, Now, as a being can get. **1970** W. Burroughs Jr. *Speed* vii. 154 His music was improvised to fit short declarations and imaginary rhyming words, prayers and questions to the audience that he fit together in a satoric sound that brought me back to and into the running water. **1974** *Sci. Amer.* Oct. 140/2 Thought, like the kingdom of life, grows and evolves slowly; the book focuses on 'the inner work of synthesis' and not on the claimed *satori* of one chance page.

satrangi, satranji, satringee, satrunjee, varr. Sitringee in Dict. and Suppl.

satsang (satsa·ŋ). *Indian Philos.* Also **Satsang.** [ad. Skr. *satsaṅga* association with good men, f. *sat* good man + *saṅga* association.] A spiritual discourse, a sacred gathering.

1929 J. N. Farquhar *Mod. Relig. Movements in India* iii. 171 As in Theosophy, you may be a Rādhā Soāmi and yet remain a Hindu, a Muhammadan or a Christian... Yet it is definitely stated that the religion is for all, and that outside the Satsaṅg there is no salvation. **1971** *Shankar's Weekly* (Delhi) 4 Apr. 5/4 Local communists had been watching with uneasiness at this priest's continual attendance at kirtans and satsangs and were even of the mind that he should be denounced as a CIA spy. **1972** *Times* 23 Oct. 12/1 There [in Delhi] they will sit at the boy's feet, listen to his spiritual discourses (*satsangs*) or just enjoy his physical presence. **1977** *New Society* 30 June 672/3 The 'satsangs' (spiritual discourses) given at the recent Wembley festival.

Satsuma. Delete ‖ and add: Now (esp. in sense 2) freq. with pronunc. (sætsū·mă). Also **Satzuma.** **1.** Also *absol.*

1880 T. W. Cutler *Grammar Jap. Ornament* 16 Modern Satsuma is largely decorated at Tokio and elsewhere. **1909** M. Diver *Candles in Wind* ix. 86 Roses..filling every available bowl, even the sacred Satzuma. **1974** Savage & Newman *Illustr. Dict. Ceramics* 255 True Satsuma is comparatively rare outside Japan.

2. (Freq. with small initial.) A small tangerine belonging to a variety of *Citrus reticulata* so called; also, the variety itself. Also *attrib.* as *Satsuma orange.*

1882 E. S. Hart in *Proc. 18th Session Amer. Pomological Soc. 1881* 67/1 One [variety of tangerine] from Japan called Satsuma, bore a temperature of 16°. **1905** *Flora & Sylva* III. 66/1 Satsuma, an early fruiting Mandarine. **1909** *Circular Bureau Plant Industry U.S. Dept. Agric.* XLVI (*title*) The limitation of the Satsuma orange to trifoliate-orange stock. **1922** [see *mikan]. **1926** H. H. Hume *Cultivation of Citrus Fruits* xxix. 477 Satsuma oranges are susceptible to the disease. **1943** Webber & Batchelor *Citrus Industry* I. v. 551 The Satsuma was first introduced into the United States in 1876 by Dr. George R. Hall... It is characteristic of Satsuma fruits that although they mature and fill with juice..the rind frequently remains green or shows only slightly colored. **1967** [see *clementine]. **1980** 'M. Yorke' *Scent of Fear* vii. 64 She bought..some tangerines—or satsumas, as they were called nowadays.

sattrangee, var. Sitringee in Dict. and Suppl.

sat-upon (sæ·t,ŏpǫn), *ppl. a.* *colloq.* [See Sit *v.* 26 d.] Downtrodden, humiliated, 'squashed'.

1892 *Times* 30 July 8/2 In his concession, where he is an apologetic and much sat-upon importation, the foreign resident does no harm. **1893** *Chambers's Jrnl.* 25 Feb. 128 With that sat-upon sort of man..you never know where he may break out.

saturability. (In Dict. s.v. Saturable *a.*) (Example.)

1979 *Nature* 19 Apr. 747/2 If the direct linkage EGF–receptor complex is a complex of EGF and its physiological receptor, the saturability for reversible EGF binding and direct complex formation should be similar.

saturable, *a.* Add: (Later examples.)

1966 *Electronics* 31 Oct. 44 The transmittance of the saturable absorber increases with the light flux. **1979** *Nature* 19 Apr. 748/2 A stereospecific, saturable, high affinity binding site for ³H-diazepam has recently been characterised in membrane fractions isolated from the brains of mammals.

b. Of magnetic systems: capable of retaining a saturating magnetic field (see Saturate *v.* 4 b). *Saturable reactor*: an iron-cored coil whose impedance to alternating current can be varied by varying the direct current in an auxiliary winding so as to change the degree of magnetization of the core.

1944 W. D. Cockrell *Industr. Electronic Control* x. 84 Another device by means of which we make deliberate use of the saturating effect for loads both large and small is the saturable reactor. **1956** [see *ferro-resonance* s.v. *ferro-1 c]. **1962** F. I. Ordway et al. *Basic Astronautics* v. 187 The flux gate magnetometer..consists essentially of a flux gate of two, identical, high-permeability, saturable coils, oppositely wound with identical coils. **1966** *McGraw-Hill Encycl. Sci. & Technol.* XII. 37/1 Saturable-core reactors are used to control large alternating currents where rheostats are impractical. Theater light dimmers often employ saturable reactors. **1975** D. G. Fink *Electronics Engineers' Handbk.* XIII. 82 The response time of saturable reactors is the combination of the time constants of the control circuit and of the gate-winding circuit.

saturate (sæ·tiurĕt), *sb.* *Chem.* [f. the vb.] A saturated fat or fatty acid.

1959 R. H. Potts in E. S. Pattison *Industr. Fatty Acids* ii. 13 In selecting a raw material, one always considers that more saturates can be made if required, but the unsaturated requirements must be purchased with the raw material. **1977** *Nature* 3 Nov. 2/2 Pursuit of the lipid hypothesis does not mean just swapping polyunsaturates for saturates.

saturate, *v.* Add: **2. c.** *Mil.* To overwhelm (enemy defences) by aerial attack, esp. by intensive bombing.

1942 *Times* 1 June 4/3 The plan for saturating the defences of Cologne was an undoubted success. **1943** *Times* 12 Mar. 8/4 Air Marshal Sir Arthur Harris and his commanders and staffs have displayed extraordinary fertility in tactical ideas. The monster raids saturating the enemy's active and passive systems of defence is one example. **1944** *Ann. Reg. 1943* I. 74 The ultimate possibility of saturating the enemy's defences both on the ground and in the air. **1956** A. H. Compton *Atomic Quest* 228 The areas attacked were saturated with bombs.

d. To supply (a market) to the point of over-satisfaction of demand for a product.

1958 *Engineering* 4 Apr. 435/1 The Swiss vehicle market, if not saturated, seems to be reaching a certain stabilisation of demand. **1976** 'G. Black' *Moon for Killers* i. 18 The market was saturated, and Robert bought two thousand of them at a throw-away price. **1978** *Times Lit. Suppl.* 27 Jan. 84/5 *Man watching* will saturate the market and maintain its well-deserved primacy.

3. a. Also, to cause to become saturated (see *saturated *ppl. a.* 3 b).

1866 *Notices Proc. R. Inst. Gt. Brit.* IV. 419 This new molecule—we call it hypochlorous acid—we open again: again two attraction units are liberated and saturated by a second atom of bivalent oxygen. **1926** H. G. Rule tr. *J. Schmidt's Text-bk. Org. Chem.* 26 Thiele assumes that all such unsaturated compounds possess a double bond, but that the two affinities do not completely saturate one another, leaving a certain residual affinity or partial valency in excess on each carbon atom. **1972** *Materials & Technol.* V. x. 282 Such isomers may arise from the addition of hydrogen at a double bond which is normally not saturated by natural processes. **1977** *Lancet* 20 Aug. 401/1 Many dietitians tell patients not to re-use the oil more than once because reheating is thought to saturate the double bonds.

b. *Physiol.* To cause (tissues of the body) to retain the greatest amount of inert gas possible at the given pressure during a saturation dive.

1965 *Jrnl. Appl. Physiol.* XX 1269/2 The decompression schedule after and while breathing helium takes longer than with nitrogen because the helium saturates a greater proportion of the body tissues. **1971** J. Salzano et al. in C. J. Lambertsen *Underwater Physiol.* 347 (*heading*) Arterial blood gases, heart rate, and gas exchange during rest and exercise in men saturated at a simulated seawater depth of 1000 feet. **1974** *Encycl. Brit. Macropædia* X. 926/1 For any given depth,..there is a saturation point, at which body tissues are saturated with inert gas; after that, no matter how long a worker stays under pressure his decompression time does not increase.

4. b. (Further examples in *Magnetism.*)

1891 S. P. Thompson *Electromagnet* iv. 151 The iron is..more saturated round the edge than at the middle... If the edge is already far saturated you cannot by applying higher magnetizing power increase its magnetization much. **1928** [see sense 6 below]. **1962** R. D. Pettit in G. A. T. Burdett *Automatic Control Handbk.* v. 18 The core flux is initially saturated negatively.

5. *Electronics. trans.* To cause or maintain a state of saturation in (a device or a current); *pass.*, to be in a state of saturation. Cf. *saturation 3 d, f.

1919 J. A. Crowther *Ions, Electrons, & Ionizing Radiations* ii. 17 The effects when the current is not saturated are in general very complex. **1956** J. C. Logue in L. P. Hunter *Handbk. Semiconductor Electronics* xv. 30 It is possible to have a high degree of saturation or just barely to saturate the transistor. **1962** Simpson & Richards *Physical Princ. Junction Transistors* xvi. 388 The base current chosen must be sufficient to saturate the transistor. **1969** J. J. Sparkes *Transistor Switching* i. 18 This equation applies only when the transistor is saturated. **1976** Millman & Halkias *Electronic Fund. & Appl.* iv. 81 A knowledge of h_{FE} tells us the minimum base current..which will be needed to saturate the transistor.

II. 6. *intr.* To reach or exhibit a condition of saturation, in any sense; to reach a state in which no further change or increase is possible.

1928 *Observer* 17 June 26/3 The essential thing is the current that can be carried without any danger of saturating the core... If the core saturates there will at once be a falling-off in the quality of reception. **1947** F. G. Spreadbury *Electronics* iv. 184 The thermionic current does not truly saturate, but continues to increase slowly. **1953** *Physical Rev.* XCI. 632/2 As the rf level is increased, the peak amplitudes labeled M_1 and M_2 in Fig. 2 saturate quite readily. **1957** R. D. Middlebrook *Introd. Junction Transistor Theory* ii. 28 The hole flow very soon reaches a limit as the potential is increased. This occurs when all the available holes are being drawn out of the *p*-region. The electron current saturates in a similar way. **1962** R. D. Pettit in G. A. T. Burdett *Automatic Control Handbk.* v. 21 When the flux in element A saturates, that in element B is unsaturated. **1969** J. J. Sparkes *Transistor Switching* iii. 74 The circuit can be designed so that the output transistor saturates. **1975** *Nature* 6 Nov. 85/1 Figure 1 shows that the steady-state amplitude saturates at a relatively low stimulus level. **1976** [see *saturation 3 a]. **1977** *Nature* 21 Apr. 709/1 This ratio tends to saturate for crystallite sizes less than 40 Å.

saturated, *ppl. a.* Add: **2. b.** *transf.* Filled to capacity; *spec.* in *Econ.*, of a market in which demand is completely satisfied.

1962 S. Strand *Marketing Dict.* 653 *Saturated market*, the ultimate point of absorption of a product or service within a territory. Now limited to parts replacement. **1965** *Monthly Economic Let.* (First National City Bank, N.Y.) Apr., Household durables with 'highly saturated markets'—those which the vast majority of families already have, such as refrigerators or black-and-white television sets—achieved sales gains through growing replacement demand.

3. a. (Further examples.) In mod. use, applied to solutions containing as much solute as is possible in equilibrium conditions (in contrast to those that are supersaturated).

1939 *Thorpe's Dict. Appl. Chem.* (ed. 4) III. 452/2 Removal of solvent from a saturated solution at this point results in the solution becoming supersaturated. **1978** P. W. Atkins *Physical Chem.* viii. 220 If a lump of solid is left in contact with a solvent it will dissolve until the solvent has become saturated. The saturated solution corresponds to the case in which the chemical potential of the pure solid is equal to the chemical potential of the solute in the saturated solution.

b. Orig., applied to compounds which contained the greatest possible proportion of some element, and to (the chemical 'affinities' of) atoms, radicals, etc., which had entered into chemical combination to the maximum extent. Now applied to organic compounds, molecules, groups, etc., which have structures containing the greatest possible numbers of hydrogen atoms, and hence have no multiple bonds between carbon atoms; occas. applied also to carbon atoms in such structures.

1866 *Notices Proc. R. Inst. Gt. Brit.* IV. 429 We have thus been led..to a distinction of a novel kind, that of finished and unfinished molecules; or, to use the more frequently employed expression, that of saturated and non-saturated compounds. **1876** *Phil. Mag.* II. 167 The group OH is related in one case to a carbon atom a large number of whose affinities are already 'saturated' (to use a common term). **1888** [in Dict., sense 3]. **1935** A. K. Anderson *Essent. Physiol. Chem.* iv. 67 Chemically, fats differ from oils in that fats contain saturated fatty acids whereas oils contain rather large quantities of unsaturated fatty acids. **1949** *Thorpe's Dict. Appl. Chem.* (ed. 4) IX. 6/2 In the higher land-animals the most abundant component acids are always the monoethenoid oleic and the saturated palmitic acid. **1961** [see *POLYUNSATURATED *a.*]. **1968** MURTHY & NATHAN *Org. Chem. made Simple* vii. 122 A saturated carbon atom may be represented by a model showing only the tetrahedrally directed linkages. **1971** *Jrnl. Gen. Psychol.* LXXXV. 155 Increasing the amount of saturated fat..resulted in a similar increase in the excitatory process. **1976** *Sci. Amer.* Mar. 35/2 Such multiple-ring, or polycyclic, compounds are said to be saturated if all the bonds of the carbon atoms, beyond the minimum needed for carbon–carbon bonding, are linked to hydrogen atoms.

c. *Min.* and *Petrol.* Of a mineral (see quot. 1913). Of a rock: containing neither free quartz (or some other specified oxide) nor any undersaturated minerals.

1913 S. J. SHAND in *Geol. Mag.* Decade V. X. 508 Of the various minerals which enter into the composition of igneous rocks, about one-half are capable of forming in presence of free silica... These may..be termed saturated minerals. *Ibid.* 510 A rock which contains only saturated minerals may be termed a saturated rock. **1947** [see *OVERSATURATED *ppl. a.*]. **1951** TURNER & VERHOOGEN *Igneous & Metamorphic Petrol.* iii. 54 Saturated minerals are those which are compatible with excess silica under magmatic conditions, and are therefore commonly associated with quartz. **1968** B. BAYLY *Introd. Petrol.* vi. 53 All saturated rocks fall within the shaded area in Fig. 6·1. The commonest such rocks are made of feldspar with pyroxene or amphibole.

4. b. *Electronics.* Characterized by or exhibiting saturation (senses *3 d, f); of or pertaining to a device in such a state.

1896 *Phil. Mag.* XLII. 394 For a given intensity of radiation the current through the gas does not exceed a certain maximum value whatever the electromotive force may be, the current gets, as it were, 'saturated'. **1899** *Ibid.* XLVII. 160 The gas tends to become more readily saturated with diminution of pressure. **1933** *Proc. IRE* XXI. 1667 The practical limitation of this 'saw-tooth' generator lies in the fact that there is no such thing as a completely saturated thermionic tube. **1956** J. C. LOGUE in L. P. Hunter *Handbk. of Semiconductor Electronics* xv. 11 It is necessary to impose an upper limit on r_c in the saturated region. This is to ensure that the voltage drop between the emitter and collector terminals is small when the transistor is in a saturated state. **1967** *Electronics* 6 Mar. 122/2 They permit a whole spectrum of products with the highest speed possible with saturated logic. **1977** TAUB & SCHILLING *Digital Integrated Electronics* i. 18 When a base current I_B is supplied, the transistor is able to furnish a current $I_C = h_{FE}I_B$. If the current I_C is actually less than $h_{FE}I_B$, the transistor is said to be in saturation. However, such is the case because of the constraint imposed by the circuit and not by the transistor. Hence, strictly, we should speak of a saturated circuit and not a saturated transistor.

c. *saturated diving* = *saturation diving* s.v. *SATURATION 5.

1968 *New Scientist* 17 Oct. 125/2 The important element in saturated diving is that after six days or six months of exposure to a given depth or pressure, the diver requires a single, fixed decompression period. **1971** *Petroleum Rev.* July 248/1 Saturated diving requires a considerable increase in equipment sophistication and diver training.

saturation. Add: **3. a.** (Further examples in *Chem.* Cf. *UNSATURATION.) More widely in *Physics*, a condition or phenomenon in which a quantity (usu. the value of some property) no longer increases in response to an increase in the magnitude of some external influence, or ceases to alter in the usual way; *spec.* in *Spectroscopy* (see quot. 1976). See also senses 3 c, d, f following.

1866 *Notices Proc. R. Inst. Gt. Brit.* IV. 422 The saturation of these two units [of attraction] by the trivalent nitrogen atom. **1902** J. B. COHEN *Theoret. Org. Chem.* xvii. 240 The saturation of one unsaturated carbon atom necessitates that of the other. **1964** N. G. CLARK *Mod. Org. Chem.* vi. 89 By partial saturation of this triple bond with hydrogen, an olefin is produced. **1968** A. A. BAKER *Unsaturation in Org. Chem.* vi. 71 His formulas..illustrate the progressive saturation of a diatomic carbon molecule to acetylene, to ethylene, and to completely saturated ethane. **1948** *Physical Rev.* LXXIII. 683/1 As H_1 is increased, the thermal contact between spin system and lattice eventually proves unable to cope with the energy absorbed by the spin system, the spin temperature rises, and the relative absorption..diminishes. It is the onset of this saturation effect which has been used to measure the spin-lattice relaxation time. **1953** *Ibid.* XCI. 206/2 From the saturation of the absorption and a measurement of the rf field, a spin-lattice relaxation time of approximately one millisecond is calculated. **1959** G. TROUP *Masers* iii. 37 If the energy density of radiation falling on an assembly of molecules having an excess upper state population is increased, there comes a time when the energy of induced emission is no longer linearly dependent on the incident radiation energy density. This phenomenon is known as saturation. **1961** G. R. CHOPPIN *Exper. Nuclear Chem.* v. 62 The higher the atomic number of the scattering material, the larger is f_b [back-scattering factor]. Also, f_b increases with thickness up to a saturation thickness beyond which it is a constant. **1972** MCFARLANE & WHITE *Techniques of High Resolution N.M.R. Spectroscopy* v. 55 The gross observable effects of saturation are a general broadening of the spectrum with associated loss of peak height and resolution. **1976** D. SHAW *Fourier Transform N.M.R. Spectroscopy* ii. 20 Saturation is the equalisation of the population in the ground and the excited state which occurs because relaxation from the excited state is slow and with a strong exciting field a dynamic equilibrium can be set up. In this equilibrium the number of nuclei in the upper and lower states become [*sic*] equal, and the signal saturates, or disappears.

c. *Magnetism.* The condition of being as strongly magnetized as possible, or so strongly magnetized that an increase in magnetizing force produces no appreciable increase in magnetization.

1837, 1864 [in Dict., sense 3]. **1920** *Whittaker's Electr. Engineer's Pocket-bk.* (ed. 4) 144 In addition to the limitations imposed by saturation, the parts of the magnetic circuit where the flux is continually changing in value are further restricted by losses due to eddy-currents and hysteresis. **1962** *Newnes Conc. Encycl. Electr. Engin.* 463/2 The coercivity is the magnetizing force necessary to remove the magnetism completely from a specimen which has been magnetized to saturation. **1974** *Encycl. Brit. Macropædia* XI. 333/2 It was suggested in 1907 that a ferromagnetic material is composed of a large number of small volumes called domains, each of which is magnetized to saturation.

d. *Electronics.* The condition in which increase in the potential difference between two electrodes in a gas-filled or evacuated vessel leads to no increase in the current flowing between them, owing to the limitations of the gas as a current-carrier or the electrode as an electron-emitter.

1896 *Phil. Mag.* XLII. 394 It is evident that this saturation must occur if the current destroys the conducting power of the gas. **1899** *Ibid.* XLVII. 158 The great difficulty in producing complete saturation, i.e. to reach a stage when all the ions produced reach the electrodes, may be due to one or more of three causes. **1947** R. LEE *Electronic Transformers & Circuits* v. 116 In plate-modulated class C amplifiers, sufficient excitation must be applied so that grid saturation still obtains at 100 per cent modulation; otherwise output would not be proportional to plate voltage. **1962** D. F. SHAW *Introd. Electronics* x. 192 Other cathode materials, such as metallic oxides, do not exhibit full saturation.

e. *Psychol.* A term used in mental testing based on the theory of two-factor analysis put forward by C. S. Spearman (1863–1945) for the degree to which the general factor (*g*) saturates the specific factor or ability in question; also *attrib.*

1904 C. S. SPEARMAN in *Amer. Jrnl. Psychol.* XV. 276 Intellective saturation, or extent to which the considered faculty is functionally identical with General Intelligence. *Ibid.* 277 Mathematics, for example, has a saturation of 74 and Common Sense has one of about 96. **1927** *Psychol. Bull.* XXIV. 392 Slocombe..applies the intellective saturation formula of Spearman to nine group tests. **1940** C. L. BURT *Factors of Mind* xii. 299 Let us suppose that both the variances for the different factors and the saturation coefficients for the different tests are everywhere equal. **1951** R. H. THOULESS *Gen. & Social Psychol.* (ed. 3) xxiii. 367 This degree of dependence on the general factor was called by Spearman the saturation with *g* of the ability in question; the term more commonly used at the present time is the general factor loading.

f. *Electronics.* The state of operation of a transistor in which the collector current becomes independent of the base voltage, arising when the base-collector junction becomes forward-biased.

1956 J. C. LOGUE in L. P. Hunter *Handbk. of Semiconductor Electronics* xv. 48 In pulse-type computer systems, the length of time that the transistor is driven into saturation is controllable. **1962** SIMPSON & RICHARDS *Physical Princ. Junction Transistors* xvi. 389 'External' control causes the 'on' position to be largely independent of transistor parameters..and makes heavy base overdrive possible without danger of saturation. **1975** D. G. FINK *Electronics Engineers' Handbk.* XVI. 13 When the collector current I_C reaches its maximum possible value.., saturation occurs and the collector junction becomes forward-biased.

g. The retention by the blood of the greatest amount of inert gas possible under the given pressure, as during a saturation dive (see sense 5 below); also *transf.*, a saturation dive.

1971 J. K. SUMMITT et al. in C. J. Lambertsen *Underwater Physiol.* 519 A study of five trained men during compression to a simulated depth of 1000 FSW, during subsequent saturation at this pressure for 77 hr and 30 min, and during decompression. **1974** *Encycl. Brit. Macropædia* X. 926/1 Reasonably safe and efficient decompression from saturation at depths up to 600 feet..can be accomplished by a decompression at the rate of 15 minutes per foot.., or about 100 feet..per day. **1975** *BP Shield Internat.* May 5/1 In excess of 14,000 diver man hours were spent in saturation without a single decompression problem or lost time accident. **1975** *Offshore Engineer* Dec. 7/2 A 17-day saturation involving six divers at depths of up to 260m carried out by Strongwork Diving (International) has given a British company a new record.

4. (Further examples.) Cf. *HUE *sb.*[1] 3 c.

1966 [see *HUE *sb.*[1] 3 c]. **1967** E. SHORT *Embroidery & Fabric Collage* i. 12 The hues are all used at their full strength or saturation, i.e. they are not diluted in any way by black or white. **1970** *Nature* 19 Sept. 1183/1 Discrimination tests revealed that sorters identified stamps most easily if seven colours were used each at two distinct levels of saturation, for example, dark blue and light blue, dark green and light green. **1978** *Sci. Amer.* Mar. 87/3 The color pictures were generated by first determining the spectral irradiance of Mars in each of the regions and then computing the hue, brightness and saturation of color for the range of wavelengths to which the human eye is sensitive.

b. *transf.* The name of a control on a colour television set used to adjust the quality of colours in the picture.

1964 M. S. KIVER *Color Television Fundamentals* (ed. 2) v. 144 There is also a color saturation control to adjust the vividness or depth of color. **1967** *Punch* 12 Apr. 532/3 It is good to be able to report that the colour sets shown at the Ideal Home Exhibition in London..had one colour control only. For reasons impossible to conjecture it is labelled 'Saturation'. Twisting this knob does not release a jet of water, however; it simply changes the picture from black-and-white to any strength of colour desired. **1968** *Guardian* 5 July 8/5 There is a secondary colour knob marked either 'saturation' or 'colour' which enables you to control the shade you receive. **1974** A. G. PRIESTLY *Receiving PAL Colour Television* v. 103 A good saturation control is not easy to design. The control itself is usually situated on the front of the receiver for use by the viewer.

5. *saturation charge, recording, time, weapon*; **saturation current**, the greatest current that can be carried by a gas or electronic device (cf. senses 3 d, f above); **saturation dive**, a dive made with the diver's blood-stream saturated with an inert gas, usu. helium or nitrogen, at the pressure of the surrounding water, so that the time required for decompression afterwards is independent of how long the dive lasts; so **saturation diver, diving** *vbl. sb.*; **saturation point**, the state or condition at which saturation begins; the limit of acceptance; freq. *fig.*; **saturation (vapour) pressure** *Physics* (see quot. 1969).

1969 Saturation charge [see *saturation time* below]. **1896** *Phil. Mag.* XLII. 403 The saturation current depends only on the number of conducting particles produced by the rays. **1929** *B.B.C. Year-bk. 1930* 450/2 As the anode voltage applied to a three-electrode valve is increased, the anode current also increases up to a point, when a further increase in anode voltage does not increase the anode current. This maximum value of the current is called the 'saturation current'. **1954** L. M. KRUGMAN *Fund. Transistors* iii. 43 The saturation current is composed of two components. The first is formed by thermally generated carriers which diffuse into the junction region. The second component is an ohmic characteristic which is caused by surface leakage across the space charge region. **1976** MILLMAN & HALKIAS *Electronic Fund. & Appl.* iv. 79 In addition to the variability of reverse saturation current with temperature, there is also a wide variability of reverse current among samples of a given transistor type. **1966** *Sci. Amer.* Mar. 27/1 It is clear..that the 'partial pressure' of oxygen should be kept between about 150 and 400 millimeters of mercury during the at-depth phase of a long saturation dive. **1974** *Daily Tel.* 22 Feb. 7/6 The record saturation dive in the North Sea was 621ft. The diver took a day to get down, and after surfacing spent 3½ days in a decompression chamber. **1970** *Sci. Jrnl.* Feb. 15 The *Argyronète*, a self-propelled submersible combining a house in which saturation divers can live (under sea bottom pressure) and a conventional submarine with a crew at normal atmospheric pressure. **1974** *Encycl. Brit. Macropædia* X. 926/1 In practice, saturation divers are compressed slowly to working pressure, generally in the deck chamber, and are then transferred as needed to and from the work site sealed in the diving bell. **1975** *BP Shield Internat.* May 5/4 It is..not uncommon for saturation divers to spend from two to three weeks under saturation conditions. **1966** *Sci. Amer.* Mar. 27/1 Although this 'saturation diving' is efficient, it imposes an extra technical burden, because the schedules for the ultimate decompression must be calculated and controlled with particular care. **1970** *New Scientist* 26 Mar. 617/2 The experiment successfully demonstrated the feasibility in scientific research of saturation diving—a technique which relies on the fact that once the body tissues become saturated with gases breathed under pressure, the time to remove them during decompression remains the same no matter how much longer the person stays at that pressure. **1974** *Daily Tel.* 22 Feb. 7/6 Bone necrosis is a growing fear connected with saturation diving. **1976** *Offshore Platforms & Pipelining* 122/3 Any diving inspection beyond the 140-ft. depth, which requires any appreciable time on the bottom, is carried out by using saturation diving. **1858** Saturation point [in Dict.]. **1902** *Encycl. Brit.* XXXIII. 631/2 It is a fair inference that similar behaviour would be observed up to the saturation-point if surface condensation could be avoided. **1927** *Sunday Times* 13 Feb. 2 Those controlling the industry realize that the world production of motor-cars has by no means reached saturation point. **1932** WODEHOUSE *Louder & Funnier* 71, I rather fancy that sinister jewel-trackers have about reached saturation-point. **1977** *Times* 30 Apr. 3/3 The popularity of the forest may have reached saturation point. **1884** Saturation pressure [in Dict.]. **1902** *Encycl. Brit.* XXXIII. 631/1 The values of the saturation-pressure have been very accurately determined for the majority of stable substances. **1975** D. G. FINK *Electronics Engineers' Handbk.* XXIII. 56 There are two methods of recording called saturation and nonsaturation. With saturation recording, material under the head is fully saturated throughout the material thickness. **1969** J. J. SPARKES *Transistor Switching* i. 23 The turn-off time is divided into two parts. First the saturation time,..during which the saturation charge..is used up and the collector current does not significantly change. Second, the fall time. **1955** *Sci. Amer.* Mar. 74/2 For every temperature there is a 'saturation vapor pressure' at which the rates of escape and of deposit at a step balance. Under these conditions the crystal does not grow. It can grow only when the vapor is supersaturated. **1969** *Gloss. Terms Vacuum Technol.* (*B.S.I.*) I. 9 *Saturation vapour pressure*, the pressure exerted by a vapour when in equilibrium with its solid or liquid phase. **1955** *Bull. Atomic Sci.* Jan. 14/3 The construction of 'saturation weapons' became possible when it was discovered that under certain circumstances a tiny amount of matter transforms into a tremendous amount of energy.

b. Designating an activity intended to achieve the complete saturation of its object; orig. *Mil.*, referring to intensive bombing operations, esp. in *saturation bombing*; hence *saturation bomb* vb.; more widely, applied to an intensive operation in the fields of marketing, advertising, security, and the like.

1942 *Sun* (Baltimore) 15 Oct. 13/5 The fact that only nine bombers were lost..was taken to mean that the 'saturation technique' was used to crowd so many planes over the area in a short raid that the strong defenses..were swamped. **1943** *Time* 7 June 29/3 According to U.S. testimony, the precision bombing of the American forces is more effective, ton for ton, than the saturation bombing of the R.A.F. *Ibid.* 30 Aug. 33/2 The greatest air force the world has known: a combination of the daylight precision bombing planes of the U.S. Eighth Air Force and the heavy nighttime saturation raiders of the R.A.F. *Ibid.* 6 Sept. 36/3 Of the 73 raids Berlin had experienced, this was the worst, the first of the kind of saturation raids that had wrecked Hamburg. **1944** *Times* 28 Mar. 4/5 A great weight of high-explosives and incendiaries pounded Essen in a 'saturation' attack which lasted just under half an hour. **1957** CLARK & GOTTFRIED *Dict. Business & Finance* 314/2 *Saturation* selling involves making a product available in every outlet in an area, and using every possible means of sales promotion. **1958** *Listener* 5 June 950/3 Mrs. Ancsa's father had been killed in a saturation air-raid. **1962** *Economist* 2 June 920/3 The large number of copies of each film necessary for this so-called 'saturation release'. **1966** *Times* 12 July 11/3 It is simply not true to say that America has engaged in saturation bombing. **1971** *Wall St. Jrnl.* 13 Aug. 14/1 He came to realize such journalism is possible through 'saturation reporting'. **1975** R. H. RIMMER *Premar Experiments* (1976) i. 19 The days when we believed we could change things—like the draft, or the saturation bombing of Vietnam, or the Pentagon running the universities. **1977** *Time* 28 Nov. 29/2 As the deadline arrived.., West Germany's national airline responded with a policy of saturation security for its 411 daily scheduled flights worldwide. **1979** P. NIESEWAND *Member of Club* xxi. 165 The Cubans were saturation bombing the camp. **1981** I. A. GORDON in *N.Z. Listener* 18–24 Apr., The big idea behind the saturation-bombing of consumers with a trade-name is to persuade you that X (and not Y or Z) is the brand to remember.

Saturday. Add: **3.** *Saturday-afternooner*; **Saturday penny**, a penny or small sum of money given to a child on Saturday as pocket-money.

1906 Saturday-afternooner [see *early-closer* s.v. *EARLY *a.* 7]. **1972** *Homes & Gardens* Apr. 60, I am old enough to remember the small child's pocket money called the 'Saturday penny'. **1979** *Church Times* 27 Apr. (Mayflower Suppl.) p. iii/2 When I was in trouble with my Mum and Dad and they wouldn't give me my 'Saturday penny'..I had at least twelve other homes where there were relations where I could go and 'con' them for a penny.

Saturdaying (sæ·təɹdēɪˌiŋ, -diˌiŋ), *vbl. sb.* [f. SATURDAY + -ING[1], after Russ. *subbótnik*.] An English rendering of *SUBBOTNIK. So **Sa·turdayite.**

1920 *Manch. Guardian* 5 Feb. 9/7 In Moscow it has been found worth while to set up a special bureau for 'Saturdayings'. **1920** *Contemp. Rev.* Oct. 504 For members of the Bolshevik party, 'Saturdaying' had become compulsory. **1932** C. HOGARTH tr. *Kollontai's Free Love* 233 She will persuade you..that it is necessary..to deny oneself everything that gives joy, to live only for the 'Saturdayites'.

Saturday night. [SATURDAY 3.] **1.** Used *attrib.* of activities taking place on or as on a Saturday night, esp. some form of revelry.

[**1847** H. MELVILLE *Omoo* xii. 49 The evening of the last day of the week was always celebrated by what is styled on board of English vessels, 'The Saturday-night bottles'. Two of these were sent down into the forecastle, just after dark.] **1896** 'M. RUTHERFORD' *Clara Hopgood* xii. 121 Saturday-night drunkenness and looseness in the relations between the young men and young women. [**1938** G. GREENE *Brighton Rock* III. 124 'Saturday,' he thought, 'today's Saturday,' remembering the room at home, the frightening weekly exercise of his parents which he watched from his single bed. *Ibid.* VII. 320 The Boy was shaken again with his nocturnal Saturday disgust. He couldn't blame his father now... You couldn't even blame the girl.] **1942** BERREY & VAN DEN BARK *Amer. Thes. Slang* § 509/17 *Saturday-night habit, week-end habit*, indulgence in small amounts of narcotics at irregular intervals. **1951** *Evening Sun* (Baltimore) 27 Mar. 4/1 The graduate 'hype' was a 'student' or 'hoosier fiend' who 'dabbled' with drugs occasionally. He had what is known as 'chippy habit', a 'Saturday night habit', or an 'ice cream habit'. **1963** R. I. McDAVID *Mencken's Amer. Lang.* xi. 742 Most cats consider it necessary to probe the mystic depths with the assistance of wine, a joint of pot.., peyote buttons and large infusions of invigorating jazz music—..in any event indulged in with friends as part of the Saturday night kicks. **1964** *New Statesman* 17 Apr. 606/2 Is the Saturday-night blind..any less characteristic of the modern urbanised proletariat than of the traditional rural peasantry? **1976** *N.Y. Times Mag.* 10 Oct. 111/2 [In the southern States of the U.S.] there were all those cross burnings, lynching bees and Sairday Nite Socials.

2. *spec. attrib.* uses: *Saturday night palsy* or *paralysis*, temporary local paralysis of the arm, esp. wrist drop, after it has rested on a hard edge for a long time, as during sleep following a bout of drinking (*colloq.*); *Saturday night pistol* (*U.S. colloq.*) = **Saturday night special*; *Saturday night soldier*, a member of a volunteer army, as opp. a regular soldier; *Saturday night special* (*U.S. colloq.*), a cheap, low-calibre pistol or revolver such as might be used by a petty criminal.

1927 I. S. WECHSLER *Textbk. Clin. Neurol.* III. 249 The frequent occurrence of wrist drop in alcoholics who fall asleep and lean heavily on the arm has given rise to the common designation of 'Saturday night palsy'. **1942** *Sun* (Baltimore) 23 Apr. 22/2 A similar ailment is called 'shelter paralysis'—formerly known as 'Saturday night paralysis' because its victims were generally payday tipplers. **1951** E. PAUL *Springtime in Paris* xii. 216 Berthe was suffering from what is known in the United States as Saturday-night paralysis,..when drunken men go to sleep in gutters, with one arm across a sharp kerbstone. **1974** PASSMORE & ROBSON *Compan. Med. Stud.* III. xxxiv. 35/1 Wrist drop thus produced is known as a 'Saturday night palsy'. **1929** M. A. GILL *Underworld Slang*, *Saturday night pistol*, 25 automatic. **1917** A. G. EMPEY *Over Top* 311 *'Terrier'*, Tommy's nickname for a Territorial or 'Saturday-night soldier'. **1974** *Maclean's Mag.* Oct. 30/1 My husband was a Saturday Night soldier, the militia, and he couldn't wait for the war and when it started, zoom, he was called up and then he was happy. **1968** *N.Y. Times* 17 Aug. 1/1 Title IV of that law bans the importation of the cheap, small-caliber 'Saturday night specials' that are a favorite of holdup men. **1976** *Pioneer* (Big Timber, Montana) 30 June 4/2 A ban on 'Saturday Night Special' handguns. **1977** C. McFADDEN *Serial* xlvi. 98/1 I'm not packing a Saturday-night special, *really*.

Hence **Saturday nighter**, a person who attends an entertainment on a Saturday night; **Saturday-night** *v. intr.*, to spend a Saturday night in enjoyment or revelling.

1962 D. LESSING *Golden Notebk.* IV. 462 The fellows were out Saturday-nighting true-hearted, the wild-hearted Saturday-night gang of true friends. **1966** *Listener* 24 Mar. 422/2 The Korean script announced that *Dr No* was showing inside. So he was..and half the population of Korea was inside, too..all of us lapping up James Bond like Surbiton Saturday nighters.

Saturn. 2. (Further examples.)

1964 R. H. BAKER *Astronomy* (ed. 8) viii. 225 Saturn is encircled by three concentric rings... There is no gap between the bright ring and the crape ring. **1974** *Encycl. Brit. Macropædia* XVI. 274/2 Saturn has ten satellites... Janus, the most elusive and closest to the planet, was found by A. Dollfus in 1966.

Saturnalia, *sb. pl.* Add: **2.** (Earlier example.)

1775 *Answer to Pamphlet, entitled Taxation no Tyranny* 61 Thus you would establish a Saturnalia of cruelty, and expose these devoted men to the brutality of their own slaves.

Saturnian, *a.* Add: **1. a.** (Earlier example.)

1612 J. SELDEN in Drayton *Poly-olb.* sig. A4, This later age..hath, in our greatest Latine Critiques..so receiued that Saturnian Language, that, to Students in Philology, it is now growne familiar.

3. a. Delete † and add later example in the sense 'due to the baleful influence of Saturn'.

1922 W. B. YEATS *Seven Poems & Fragment* 6 Stretch out your limbs and sleep a long Saturnian sleep.

c. *Physics.* Of or pertaining to a model of the nuclear atom in which electrons are assumed to orbit in rings around a central nucleus, thus resembling the appearance of Saturn. Now *hist.*

1904 H. NAGAOKA in *Phil. Mag.* VII. 445 The system differs from the Saturnian system considered by Maxwell in having repelling particles instead of attracting satellites. *Ibid.* 455 There are various problems which will possibly be capable of being attacked on the hypothesis of a Saturnian system, such as chemical affinity and valency. **1911** *Phil. Mag.* XXI. 688 Nagaoka has mathematically considered the properties of a 'Saturnian' atom which he supposed to consist of a central attracting mass surrounded by rings of rotating electrons. **1967** D. TER HAAR *Old Quantum Theory* iii. 31 Nagaoka (1904) had considered earlier the properties of a 'Saturnian' atom. **1974** G. REECE tr. *Hund's Hist. Quantum Theory* iv. 56 Nuclear types of atom included..the 'Saturnian system' of H. Nagaoka (1904).

saturnian (sătʊ̈·ɹniăn), *sb.*[3] [f. mod.L. generic name *Saturnia* + -AN.] = *SATURNIID *sb.*

1842 T. W. HARRIS *Treat. Insects Injurious to Vegetation* 276 These insects..belong to a family called Saturnians.

saturniid (sătʊ̈·ɹniˌid), *a.* and *sb. Ent.* Also **Saturniid.** [f. mod.L. family name *Saturniidæ*, f. generic name *Saturnia* (F. von P. Schrank *Fauna Boica* (1802) II. 149): see SATURNIAN *a.* and *sb.*[2]] **A.** *adj.* Of, pertaining to, or belonging to the family Saturniidæ, which includes large, mainly tropical moths with a few species of temperate regions. **B.** *sb.* A moth of the family Saturniidæ.

1892 W. L. DISTANT *Naturalist in Transvaal* 122 The fine Saturniid moth *Urota sinope*. **1928** G. H. CARPENTER *Biol. Insects* xii. 378 The large Chinese Saturniid silk-moth.. is represented in Japan and Java by readily distinguishable forms. **1952** *Bull. Amer. Mus. Nat. Hist.* XCVIII. 355/1 The saturniid moths appear to be most closely related to the small South American families Oxyteridae and Cercophanidae. *Ibid.* 365/2 The eyes of saturniids are large in relation to the head. **1964** [see *LASIOCAMPID *sb.* and *a.*]. **1979** *Smithsonian* X. 68 (*caption*) Saturniid moth..is one of the many colorful insects harbored in Costa Rica's forests.

‖ **satya** (sa·tya). [Skr.] In Indian philosophy: truth, truthfulness.

1943 C. S. LEWIS *Abolition of Man* i. 10 Righteousness, correctness, order, the *Rta*, is constantly identified with *satya* or truth, correspondence to reality. **1956** E. WOOD *Yoga Dict.* 139/2 *Satya.* (Truthfulness). The second of the abstinences. **1974** *Encycl. Brit. Macropædia* VIII. 900/1 The ancient ideals of *ahimsā*, chastity, observances, and *satya* (Truth, which he [*sc.* Gandhi] identified with God) were the main principles of his undogmatic doctrine and social and political practice. **1975** DASTUR & AIYAR in H. M. Patel et al. *Say not the Struggle Nought Availeth* 192 In Gandhi's view, truth (*satya*) and non-violence (*ahimsa*) were inter-related.

‖ **satyagraha** (satyā·graha). [a. Skr. *satyāgraha* insistence on truth, f. *satya* truth + *āgraha* pertinacity.] The Indian form of passive resistance, as formulated by M. K. Gandhi. Also *transf.* and *attrib.*

1920 M. K. GANDHI *Non-Co-operation* (1921) 46 But all the painful experience that I then gained did not in any way shake my belief in Satyagraha or in the possibility of that matchless force being utilised in India. **1928** V. G. DESAI tr. *Gandhi's Satyagraha in S. Afr.* xii. 173 A small prize was therefore announced in *Indian Opinion* to be awarded to the reader who invented the best designation for our struggle... Sr. Maganlal Gandhi..suggested the word 'Sadagraha', meaning 'firmness in a good cause'. I.. corrected it to 'Satyagraha'. Truth (Satya) implies love and firmness (Agraha) engenders and therefore serves as a synonym for force. I thus began to call the Indian movement 'Satyagraha', that is to say, the Force which is born of truth and love or non-violence, and gave up the use of the phrase 'passive resistance'. **1929** *Daily Express* 10 Jan. 1/5 The ex-soldiers expressed their intention of performing satyagraha until their leader was released. **1930** *Aberdeen Press & Jrnl.* 7 Apr. 7/1 The 'Untouchables', dissatisfied with his campaign, have threatened counter satyagraha. **1955** *Times* 5 July 10/5 But there were signs of official uneasiness; Sikh dignitaries were arrested before offering satyagraha, Press censorship was imposed in Amritsar, [etc.]. **1958** *Economist* 26 July 280 Delay in producing this Bill was one of the grievances advanced by the Tamil minority when they launched their satyagraha campaign in the spring. **1963** *Times* 3 May 12/2 Negro and white youngsters, organized by bodies such as the student non-violent coordinating committee and the south Christian leaders' conference, will be offering their own kind of satyagraha throughout the deep south. **1969** *Pioneer* (Lucknow) 13 Aug. 7/7 A batch of 12 girls were taken into custody.. when they staged satyagraha in support of a separate Telengana. **1976** *Times* 23 Jan. 9/2 The opposition..is pursuing its campaign of *satyagraha* (non-violent demonstration) in traditional Indian style. **1980** *Times Lit. Suppl.* 21 Nov. 1339/1 For him [*sc.* Michael Scott], the world desperately needs a moral force which will work for justice. He finds this in *satyagraha*, the soul-force, more positive than non-violence or passive resistance, an active weapon of good in its perennial fight against evil.

So **satya·grahi** (with pl. **satyagrahi** or **satyagrahis**), **satya·grahist**, an exponent or practitioner of *satyagraha.*

1928 V. G. DESAI tr. *Gandhi's Satyagraha in S. Afr.* xx. 233 Rama Sundara was the first Satyagrahi prisoner. *Ibid.* xlv. 468 Only thus could the Satyagrahis..bring their struggle to a triumphant end. **1930** *Aberdeen Press & Jrnl.* 6 Mar. 8/6 He [*sc.* Gandhi] will be accompanied by a band of satyagrahists or home rule volunteers, who will march on foot. **1934** H. MILLER *Tropic of Cancer* 102 The little band of Satyagrahists imitated the devotion of their master. **1968** H. J. N. HORSBURGH *Non-Violence & Aggression* i. 22 Belligerents do, and satyagrahi do not, claim finality for their interpretation of a just settlement. **1976** *New Yorker* 24 May 43/1 According to Gandhi, a satyagrahi, or votary of satyagraha, is governed by the belief that the soul can be saved from evil in the world, and so helped along in its search for Brahma, by truth and truth alone.

satyr. Add: **6.** *satyr-brood, forest, -spring, -talk*; *satyr-charming, -hairy, -haunted, -like* (earlier example), *-shrewd* adjs.

1924 E. SITWELL *Sleeping Beauty* i. 11 Smiling dim as satyr-broods. **1883** J. G. WHITTIER *Bay of Seven Islands* 31 Calm as the hour, methinks I feel A sense of worship o'er me steal; Not that of satyr-charming Pan. **1933** E. SITWELL *Five Variations* 2 Mowhair for satyr forests. **1953** —— *Gardeners & Astronomers* 29 Like the first budding of the small red satyr-hairy leaves upon the fruit-boughs. **1924** —— *Sleeping Beauty* xv. 53 From satyr-haunted caverns drip These lovely airs on brow and lip. **1835** POE in *Southern Lit. Messenger* I. 637/2 Satyr-like figure of Mentoni himself. **1928** BLUNDEN *Retreat* 38 And almost catch the horned and rude Woodgod at gaze ere satyr-shrewd He dodges by. **1922** E. SITWELL *Façade* 7 Like red Furred buds of satyr-springs long dead. **1944** L. MACNEICE *Springboard* 49 Not smut but satyr-talk, not clever but wise.

satyress. (Later examples.)

1952 [see *NIXIE[1]]. **1978** *Daily Tel.* 12 Apr. 14/4 A Tiepolo drawing, 'A Centaur with a Satyress', was bought for £4,000.

saty·rically, *adv. rare.* [f. SATYR.] In the manner of a satyr.

1887 SWINBURNE *Let.* 14 Aug. (1962) V. 209, I have written a poem..called 'Pan and Thalassius'... Pan is figured in all his different shapes or phases..lord of the mystery of earth and immanent godhead of—or in—the terrene All: only not of the human soul, the stars, Urania, and the sea—on whose general behalf the intruder in his domain has the last word—while recognizing the folly and falsehood of the cry that 'Pan is dead'..over which premature cry the old wood-god chuckles satyrically.

Satyrid (săti·rid), *sb.* and *a.* [a. mod.L. family name *Satyridæ*, f. generic name *Satyrus* (P. A. Latreille & J. B. Godart *Encyclopédie Méthodique* (*Insectes*) (1819) IX. 11): see SATYR and -ID[3].] **A.** *sb.* A small, usually brown, butterfly belonging to the subfamily Satyrinæ of the family Nymphalidæ. **B.** *adj.* Of or pertaining to a butterfly of this kind.

1901 D. Sharp in *Cambr. Nat. Hist.* VI. vi. 348 The species of the genus *Pierella* connect these transparent Satyrids with the more ordinary forms. **1912** H. Rowland-Brown *Butterflies & Moths* viii. 79 The Continental Satyrids..and our 'Grayling',..well-nigh invisible on the tree trunks where they love to perch. **1936** *Discovery* Dec. 370/2 A shining silvery insect..quite different from the general run of Satyrid butterflies. **1963** V. Nabokov *Gift* ii. 126 His father accompanied him up a trail through the pinewoods in order to show him, with a smile of condescension for this European trifle, the Satyrid recently described by Kuznetzov, which was flitting from stone to stone. **1975** *Zool. Jrnl.* CLXXVII. 333 *Zethera hestioides* Felder, a Philippine Satyrid..shows unimodal mimicry.

satyrish (sæ·tĭriʃ), *a.* [f. Satyr + -ish[1].] Characteristic of a satyr (sense 1); erotic, sensual.

1932 W. Faulkner *Sartoris* iii. vi. 233 Simon chuckled again, unctuously, a satyrish chuckle rich with complacent innuendo. **1937** J. C. Powys *Maiden Castle* v. 198 His satyrish pleasure in the exposed curves of her limbs.

satyromaniac (sæ:tĭromēⁱ·niæk), *a.* and *sb.* [f. Satyr + -o + -maniac.] **A.** *adj.* Of a man: exhibiting excessive sexual desire. **B.** *sb.* A man who exhibits excessive sexual desires; a sex maniac.

1889 *Cent. Dict., Satyromaniac, a.* and *n.* I. *a.* Affected with satyromania. II. *n.* A person affected with satyromania. **1892** G. B. Shaw *Let.* 12 Aug. (1965) I. 360, I hear from Oxford that de Mattos is ravishing every maiden in the country...York Powell writes to me privately urging the importance of dissociating ourselves from the satyromaniac W. S. de M. **1909** —— *Let.* 22 June (1972) II. 847, I have read the play...It is made impossible by your nymphomania. There are two men in it.., one a satyromaniac, the other a mere imaginary male figment to focus the nymphomania of all the women. **1944** D. L. Sayers *Let.* 18 Oct. in J. Brabazon *D. L. Sayers* (1981) x. 112 All Satyromaniacs, sadists, connoisseurs in rape.

Satzuma: see *Satsuma.

sauce, *sb.* Add: **1. a.** Also with qualifying *adj.*, as *black, brown, hard, white sauce.*

Occas., in the names of sauces taken unchanged from French into English, found with the qualifying word following; in such cases the Fr. pronunc. (sos) may be heard. *sauce Robert* (sos robɛ̄r), now the usual form of *Robert sauce* (in Dict.) See also *allemande *sb.* 3, *Béarnaise, *Mornay, Soubise 2.

1573 'C. Hollybande' *French Schoole-maister* 114 Cut some of these loynes of the hare, drest with a blacke sauce. **1723** J. Nott *Cook's & Confectioner's Dict.* sig. Bb6, *To dress Pikes* à la Sainte Robert [*sic*]..make your Sauce Robert in the following manner. *Ibid.* sig. Dᵛ, *Artichokes with white Sauce*... Make a Sauce for them with the Yolks of Eggs, a Drop or two of Vinegar, and a little Gravy. **1806** J. Simpson *Compl. Syst. Cookery* 293 Pigs feet au gratin, ears shredded, and sauce robert. **1845** E. Acton *Mod. Cookery* iv. 116 *Bechamel.* This is a fine French white sauce, now very much served at good English tables. *Ibid.* 130 *Sauce Robert*... Large onions,..butter,..flour... Gravy... Mustard. **1884** White sauce [in Dict.]. **1909** *Cent. Dict.* Suppl., *Hard sauce*, a creamy sauce of butter and sugar, usually flavoured with vanilla or the like. **1911** Webster, Brown sauce = Espagnole sauce. **1928** S. Lewis *Man who knew Coolidge* i. 103 A..Plum Pudding..with both hard and soft sauce. **1935** 'R. Hull' *Keep it Quiet* xxix. 279 A brown substance.. called generally 'Sauce Robert', which disfigures cutlets and suchlike. **1939** A. L. Simon *Conc. Encycl. Gastron.* I. 29/2 In U.S.A., a Hard Sauce is made with one measure of fresh butter to two of castor sugar... A squeeze of lemon is then added... It is usual, in some States,..to add some Brandy or Rum... In England, a similar sauce is called Brandy Butter or Rum Butter. **1960** *Good Housek. Cookery Bk.* (rev. ed.) 196/1 The foundation of all brown and white sauces in which flour is the thickening agent is the roux, formed by cooking the butter and flour together. For white sauces the butter should be melted, the flour added and the two stirred and cooked together until well incorporated. The liquid should then be added by degrees. **1974** E. McGirr *Murderous Journey* 90 His man had a certain way with Sauce Robert which gave it an added piquancy. **1981** M. C. Smith *Gorky Park* iii. 304 She'd brought cartons of spaghetti with meat, clam and white sauces.

d. *U.S. slang.* (See quot.)

1919 E. V. Rickenbacker *Fighting Flying Circus* p. xi, *Sauce*, petrol or gasoline.

e. *slang* (orig. *U.S.*). Alcoholic liquor; occas., a narcotic drug.

1940 J. O'Hara *Pal Joey* 114 It made him sad and he almost began hitting the sauce. **1953** W. Burroughs *Junkie* (1972) xiii. 134 The first thing you have to do is cut down on the sauce and build up your health. You look terrible. **1960** Wodehouse *Jeeves in Offing* xvii. 176 Her first husband,..was..a constant pain in the neck to her till one night he most fortunately walked into the River Thames while under the influence of the sauce and didn't come up for days. **1970** M. Braithwaite *Never sleep Three in Bed* vi. 66 Which means any occasion when any group of the brothers and sisters..have got into the sauce. **1975** N. Freeling *What are Bugles blowing For?* xii. 74 Castang found a narcotics squad cop...Patricia was known, but not well. 'She got off the sauce for nearly a year.' **1976** W. Trevor *Children of Dynmouth* v. 114 'You often get loonies in joints like that,' he remarked on the street. 'They drink the sauce and it softens their brains for them.' **1978** H. C. Rae *Sullivan* i. ii. 25 You're not in debt, on the sauce, going gay... I can't blackmail you.

2. *fig.* Also in Fr. phr. *sauce piquante.*

1821 Hazlitt *Table-T.* Ser. I, *Character of Cobbett* 121 How fine were the graphical descriptions he sent us from America:..what a fine *sauce piquante* of contempt they were seasoned with! **1934** C. Lambert *Music Ho!* iii. 206 They are only thorns protecting a fleshy cactus—a sauce piquante poured over a nice juicy steak.

7. *sauce-bottle, -bowl, -tureen* (earlier and later examples); *sauce-stained* adj.

1925 Hodkin & Cousen *Textbk. Glass Technol.* v. 49 Glasses..of the type usually used for ordinary white flint glass, for medical, paste, and sauce bottles, and for those used in machines with automatic feeding devices. **1973** *Country Life* 1 Nov. 1313/1 The autumn gathering [of mushrooms] went to make ketchup, put up in old sauce bottles. **1765** J. Wedgwood *Let.* 2 Mar. (1965) 29, I have sent the Green & Gold Sauce bowles and stands..in a box. **1922** Joyce *Ulysses* 44 His breath hangs over our saucestained plates, the green fairy's fang thrusting between his lips. **1772** J. Wedgwood *Let.* 17 Feb. (1965) 119, I thank you.. for the hint respecting the sauce Terrine. **1776** [see Tureen β]. **1971** *Country Life* 1 Apr. 765/2 At the dining table, the classical urn was, of course, readily applied..to the now popular sauce tureen.

sauce, *v.* **1. a.** Delete *arch.* and add later examples.

1973 *Jewish Chron.* 2 Feb. 19/1 If..I choose to sauce them, then I find the ordinary four-to-a-fish fillets quite suitable. **1975** *Times* 4 Oct. 12/4 A sole dish..said to be sauced with cream, wine and egg... The pale yellow sauce tasted sour.

4. d. (Earlier and later examples.) Also *transf.*

1862 H. Adams *Let.* 10 Jan. in N. Longmate *Hungry Mills* (1978) iv. 61, I found myself this morning sarsed through a whole column of *The Times* and am laughed at by all England. **1892** B. Potter *Jrnl.* 6 Oct. (1966) 274 He puts on wrong postage..and will sauce anybody who is unprovided with small change; he wants reporting. **1962** D. Lessing *Golden Notebk.* ii. 274 He sauced her with his eyes; sitting up broad, solid, pink-cheeked; very sure of himself.

sauce-boat. Add: **2.** *Archæol.* A vessel of the Early Helladic and Early Cycladic cultures resembling a sauce-boat and prob. used for drinking or pouring liquids.

1967 R. Higgins *Minoan & Mycenean Art* ii. 55 Sauce-boats like the popular Mainland variety..were decorated with an all-over wash. *Ibid.* iii. 67 Favourite shapes are now the so-called 'sauceboats', a very common type whose function is unknown. *Ibid.* iii. 70 Only one form of gold or silver plate has been recorded from mainland Greece for this period. That form, known in two surviving examples, is a translation into gold of the common pottery 'sauceboat' shape. **1977** G. Clark *World Prehist.* (ed. 3) iv. 157 Another unusual ceramic vessel common to the three areas is the sauce-boat which also occurs in Early Helladic Greece in gold.

saucebox. Add: Also *attrib.*

1825 in C. E. Pearce *Life & Times Madame Vestris* (1923) 116 We thought that the stamping sort of sauce-box air with which she marched away to the tune of the 'Dashing White Sergeant' was too much in keeping with her notorious male-attire exhibitions. **1969** V. C. Clinton-Baddeley *Only a Matter of Time* 89 He hadn't used 'camp' for several weeks—not since his sauce-box notice of *Idomeneo.*

saucepan. Add: **2.** *saucepan brush*; **saucepan lid,** rhyming slang for (*a*) a 'quid', a one-pound note; (*b*) a 'kid', a child.

1926-7 *Army & Navy Stores Catal.* 181/1 Steel saucepan brush. Each— -/6. **1944** C. Milburn *Diary* 30 Dec. (1979) 260 A few oddments at the ironmonger's..a dish mop, a baking tin, a colander, a saucepan brush. **1952** *Observer* 12 Oct. 5/3 Won't dish-mops, saucepan-brushes and swabs, rubbers, and all kitchen cloths one day be of nylon? **1951** P. Hoskins *No Hiding Place!* xvii. 191/2 *Saucepan lid*, £1 note. **1960** J. Franklyn *Dict. Rhyming Slang* 119/1 *Saucepan lid*,..kid.

saucepanful (sǭ·spănful). [f. Saucepan + -ful.] The contents of a saucepan; the amount a saucepan will hold.

1868 Dickens *Holiday Romance* ii, in *All Year Round* 8 Feb. 206/2 The other Princes and Princesses were squeezed into a..corner to look at the Princess Alicia turning out the saucepan-full of broth, for fear..they should get.. scalded. **1976** *Horse & Hound* 3 Dec. 34/4 Two or three saucepansful may be needed simultaneously and it is a good idea to put a spoon in the glass when dispensing. **1980** J. O'Faolain *No Country for Young Men* iv. 71 Judith boiled a saucepanful [of water].

saucer. Add: **2. c.** = *flying saucer* s.v. *flying *vbl. sb.* 3. Also *attrib.*

[**1878** *Denison* (Texas) *Daily News* 25 Jan., in C. & J. Lorenzen *UFOs* (1969) i. 10 When directly over him it [*sc.* a flying object] was about the size of a large saucer and was evidently at a great height.] **1947** *Daily Progress* (Charlottesville, Va.) 5 July 1/4 Describing what they saw as flat, translucent plates 12 to 15 inches in diameter, several Port Huron, Mich., residents reported seeing the 'saucers'. **1958** *Times Lit. Suppl.* 16 May 274/3 The author declares he was arrested while camping out in a fertile saucer district and narrowly escaped a mental examination court. It all affords a good occasion to re-tell certain saucer stories the author inquired into. **1966** *McGraw-Hill Encycl. Sci. & Technol.* V. 363/2 Light reflections from material objects account for most reports of saucers. **1978** D. A. J. Seargent *UFO's* vi. 122 People frequently shy away from traditional religions and look for salvation from the 'saucers'.

3. (Earlier example.)

c **1702** C. Fiennes *Journeys* (1947) iii. v. 177, I went to this Newcastle in Staffordshire to see the makeing the fine tea-potts cups and saucers of the fine red earth.

4. So (*slang*), an eye. Also *attrib.*

1864 M. Lemon *Jest Bk.* 185, I always know when he has been in his cups by the state of his saucers. **1958** *Spectator* 22 Aug. 246/2 Nor were they wasting any saucer stares on National Savings or 'Taking up a Career in the Midland Bank'.

7. b. *saucer-barrow, -brooch, -cloud, -hat*; **saucer bath,** a wide shallow bath usu. kept in a bedroom and used for sponging oneself down; **saucer-buried** *a.*, formerly in the southern U.S., applied to a Black person whose burial was paid for by donations placed in a saucer laid on or near the corpse; hence **saucer-burial**; **saucerman,** a being imagined or believed to be the pilot or passenger of a flying saucer. **c.** *saucer-blue* adj.

1941 *Proc. Prehist. Soc.* VII. 88 The saucer-barrow may be defined as a low mound, generally one or two feet high.. enclosed in a ditch and outer bank. **1899** Somerville & 'Ross' *Some Experiences Irish R.M.* ii. 38 A conspicuous object outside the door was a saucer bath full of something that looked like flour. **1927** G. Murray *Classical Trad. in Poetry* 4 He used a sponge and a tooth-brush and a saucer bath. **1951** C. V. Wedgwood *Last of Radicals* i. 19 The patriarchal old gentleman, who rose every morning to a cold saucer-bath. **1925** W. de la Mare *Miss Jemima* 12 She was staring about her..with her saucer blue eyes. **1912** *Archaeologia* LXIII. 167 The find included no less than four saucer brooches, one decorated with the star with incurved sides..and three with spirals. **1965** A. H. Smith in Bessinger & Creed *Medieval & Linguistic Stud.* 61 The presence of artifacts in the Avon valley cemeteries, like applied, disc, and saucerbrooches..has been interpreted as a mixed culture. **1963** P. Pollack *Photography* xxvii. 351/1 A picture of a saucer burial taken in Alabama. **1925** Du B. Heyward *Porgy* i. 25 It had even become a grievous reproach to have a member of the family a 'saucer-buried nigger'. **1911** H. S. Walpole *Mr. Perrin & Mr. Traill* iv. 72 Faint blue skies, dim and shining like clear glass with a hard yellow sun stuck like a tethered balloon between saucer-clouds. **1940** M. Sadleir *Fanny by Gaslight* i. 30 My own tartan frock..and tiny saucer hat. **1965** J. Potts *Only Good Secretary* iv. 68 Her head, topped with its black saucer hat. **1967** *Time* 4 Aug. 40/2 Barney and Betty Hill..whose 'abduction' by saucermen during an auto trip was described in the fast-selling book [etc.] **1971** *New Scientist* 30 Sept. 722/1 Visiting saucermen from Mars might well report back to base that all our Gods must be hard of hearing.

sau·cer, *v.* [f. the sb.] **1.** *intr.* To be saucerlike; to take the shape of a saucer, be as shallow as a saucer.

1925 W. de la Mare *Broomsticks* 112 The immense starry sky that saucered in the wide darkness of the Moor. **1977** *Times* 19 Nov. 1/6 They prophesy that the rate is now 'saucering' and that after a brief dip into single figures it will rise again.

2. *trans.* To make saucerlike; to shape (something) like a saucer.

1934 Webster, *Saucer, v.t. & i.* To make or be saucerlike. **1977** *Whitaker's Almanack 1978* 1058/1 The site has been successfully 'saucered' to disguise the bulk and reduce the overall height.

3. *trans.* To pour (a liquid) into a saucer, esp. from a cup.

1938 *Atlantic Monthly* Oct. 552/2 'Want a sasser o' sorghum?... The visitor would 'sasser' some sorghum. **1944** A. Clarke *Coll. Plays* (1963) 246 Mind you don't utter A word..Until you have eaten six slices of bread With plenty of butter—and saucered your tay! **1951** H. Giles *Harbin's Ridge* x. 100 Granny saucered her coffee and blew on it. **1978** *New Yorker* 9 Jan. 41/3 Have you ever heard the old Texas expression 'saucered and blowed'?.. If a cowboy's coffee is too hot, he puts some in a saucer and blows on it. A cowboy will say to a friend, 'Take mine, it's already saucered and blowed.' Jim needs to get the energy bill saucered and blowed.

saucer eye. Add: (Later examples without supernatural associations.)

1970 'D. Halliday' *Dolly & Cookie Bird* vi. 78 She still had the huge saucer eyes I remembered, with false eyelashes and then spikes drawn in under the lashes. **1976** G. Moffat *Short Time to Live* v. 48 'This is the astonishing thing—' she turned to Miss Pink with saucer eyes.

saucer-eyed, *a.* Add: (Further examples.) Also *transf.*, of an expression, emotion, etc.

In quot. 1968 the sense is 'susceptible to seeing flying saucers'.

1843 *Ainsworth's Mag.* IV. 5 The frightful, open-mouthed, saucer-eyed expression of wonder. **1934** A. Woollcott *While Rome Burns* 57 He rushed at me in saucer-eyed excitement. **1968** *Listener* 27 June 823/1 As if people haven't tended in such matters to see the expected thing in the expected form, as if they were unlikely to go saucer-eyed to their vigils. **1978** J. Irving *World According to Garp* xvii. 361 Garp looked for the strange saucer-eyed girl. **1979** N. Freeling *Widow* xvii. 108 I've been shot at... Don't look so saucer-eyed..don't let's dramatize.

saucerful. Add: Also, the contents of a saucer, and *fig.* (Earlier and further examples.)

1852 Mrs. Gaskell *Cranford* (1853) viii. 156 She..mixed a saucer-full for him, and put it down for him to lap. **1917** D. Canfield *Understood Betsy* vi. 123 She herself ate three saucerfuls. **1927** [see *grape-nuts* s.v. *grape *sb.*[1] 9]. **1944** M. Laski *Love on Supertax* viii. 77 A saucerful of margarine. **1973** K. Giles *File on Death* ii. 48 Here, sit at the table, and I'll give you a saucerful.

saucerian (sǭsīᵊə·riăn), *a* and *sb.* [f. SAUCER + -IAN.] **A.** *adj.* Of or pertaining to a flying saucer (see *FLYING *vbl. sb.* 3). **B.** *sb.* **a.** A believer in the existence of flying saucers. **b.** An entity which travels by flying saucer.

1950 *Jrnl. Brit. Interplanetary Soc.* IX. 300 This passage.. surely deserves immortality. We..happen to believe it is true—but perhaps not in the saucerian sense that the author intended. **1965** *New Society* 9 Sept. 14/4 The definition of the situation in occult terms began in 1950 with the publication of..the first saucerian book complete with little green men..looked upon by saucerians as the beginning of the tradition. **1973** C. SAGAN *Cosmic Connection* (1975) vi. 43 Likewise, the category of contact story, now quite fashionable in some UFO enthusiast circles, of sexual contact between human and saucerian..must be relegated to the realm of improbable fantasy. Such crossings are about as reasonable as the mating of a man and a petunia.

saucerization (sǭ:sərəizēⁱ·ʃən). *Surg.* [f. SAUCER + -IZATION.] The surgical excision of bone or flesh so as to leave a shallow saucer-shaped cavity. So **sau·cerize** *v. trans.*

1928 P. LEWIN *Orthopedic Surg. for Nurses* xv. 252 In chronic osteomyelitis the entire infected area must be removed, the so-called 'saucerization'. **1940** *Lancet* 13 July 32/1 No method of treating such a case can compare with closed plaster after saucerisation, which may include laying open all heavily infected areas. **1946** *Jrnl. Bone & Joint Surg.* XXVIII. 19 The wounds are saucerized and then packed. **1964** W. A. LARMON in L. Davis *Christopher's Textbk. Surg.* (ed. 8) xxv. 1105/1 This operation is termed saucerization because the bone cavity is made as shallow and broad as possible by the surgeon.

‖ **saucier** (sosye). [Fr.] A sauce cook.

1961 *Evening Standard* 14 Sept. 29/3 (Advt.), Saucier required for first class London Club. Interesting position with good wages. **1976** *National Observer* (U.S.) 10 Apr. 5/1 She..gained 10 pounds that could be attributed almost entirely to the magic of the finest sauciers in town. **1980** J. CARTWRIGHT *Horse of Darius* xvii. 269 Chef Leon..took three under-chefs, a *saucier*, a vegetable cook, and his desert chef.

saucisson. Add: **1.** (Later examples.) Freq. with Fr. qualifying words designating spec. types of sausage. Also *attrib.*

Following Fr. usage the term usu. describes a sausage which does not need to be cooked, as opp. to a *saucisse*.

1958 W. BICKEL tr. *Hering's Dict. Cookery* 31 *Marinated sausage*: saucissons à l'huile: sliced cervelat, marinated in French dressing with chopped onions. *Viennese sausage*: saucissons de Vienne: heat up in boiling water, serve with grated horseradish, mustard, saurkraut or goulash sauce. **1962** *Harper's Bazaar* Aug. 69/1 A few slices of *saucisson d'ail* and *saucisson sec.* **1965** *House & Garden* Jan. 60 *Saucisson à l'ail* (*garlic sausage*), a type that includes many of the large sausages such as saucisson de Lyon and cotechino. *Saucisson d'Arles* (*Arles sausage*)..is dried and delicately seasoned. *Saucisson de Lyon*, a sausage from Lyon made of pork, with fat and lean mixed. **1972** *Guardian* 11 Mar. 15/3 [The] Brasserie du Nord..is noted..for its *saucisson* and *rognon* dishes. **1975** *Women's Jrnl.* Sept. 73/3 We started off with a plate of beetroot and tomato and *saucisson*. **1980** J. DITTON *Copley's Hunch* I. ii. 60 A little *saucisson sec*, bread and apples.

sauconite (sǭ·kǭnəit). *Min.* [f. *Saucon*, name of a valley near Bethlehem, Pennsylvania + -ITE¹.] A clay mineral of the montmorillonite group containing a high proportion of zinc.

1875 F. A. GENTH *Prelim. Rep. Mineral. Pennsylvania* v. 120 The first [peculiar clay] occurs at the Ueberoth Zinc Mine near Friedensville, Lehigh county, where it has been discovered by Prof. W. Th. Roepper, who named it 'Sauconite'. **1946** *Amer. Mineralogist* XXXI. 414 Sauconite proves to be a member of the montmorillonite group of minerals in which three bivalent zinc ions proxy two trivalent alumina ions in octahedral positions in the lattice structure. **1968** I. KOSTOV *Mineral.* 373 Additional representatives of the sub-groups are the following corresponding varieties:.. Zn-saponite (sauconite) with about 35% ZnO.

saucy, *a.*¹ Add: **2. b.** Now freq. in coy use: 'daring', smutty, suggestive.

1962 *Times* 13 Apr. 18/4 The comedy is all reduced to relentlessly 'saucy' sniggering farce. **1975** *Radio Times* 3 Apr. 17 George Formby..died 15 years ago. His songs, especially the saucy ones, have passed into legend. **1977** *News of World* 17 Apr. 9/7 He [*sc.* Mozart] won a reputation as a bed-hopping gambler and earned a fortune... Experts unearthed the saucy truth when they studied the great man's personal accounts.

3. (Later example.)

1904 A. BENNETT *Great Man* vi. 50 He ate a little of the lean, leaving a wasteful margin of lean round the fat..; then he unobtrusively laid down his knife and fork. 'Come, Henry,' said Aunt Annie, 'don't leave a saucy plate.'

‖ **saudade** (saˌuda·di). [Pg.] Longing, melancholy, nostalgia, as a supposed characteristic of the Portuguese or Brazilian temperament.

1912 A. F. G. BELL *In Portugal* i. 7 The famous *saudade* of the Portuguese is a vague and constant desire for something that does not and probably cannot exist, for something other than the present, a turning towards the past or towards the future; not an active discontent or poignant sadness but an indolent dreaming wistfulness. **1936** R. GALLOP *Portugal* xi. 262 In a word *saudade* is yearning: yearning for something so indefinite as to be indefinable: an unrestrained indulgence in yearning. **1957** R. CAMPBELL *Portugal* p. ix, It [*sc.* Portugal] is an intensely poetic country, and it is the country of *saudade*, that mysterious melancholy which sighs at the back of every joy. **1976** *Gramophone* Aug. 320/1 The vigour and the *saudade*, the two Brazilian qualities with which the Preludes are imbued, are here replaced by a *gaucho* nostalgia.

Saudi (sau·di, sǭ·di, saˌū·di) *sb.* and *a.* [ad. Arab. *sa'ūdi*, f. the name *Sa'ūd* (see below) + *-I.] **A.** *sb.* **a.** A member of the Arabian Sa'ūd dynasty, the rulers of Nejd since the eighteenth century and of the kingdom of Saudi Arabia since 1932. **b.** = *SAUDI ARABIAN *sb.* **B.** *adj.* **a.** Of or pertaining to the Sa'ūd dynasty. **b.** = *SAUDI ARABIAN *a.*

1933 K. WILLIAMS *Ibn Sa'ud* i. 18 Muhammad took Riyadh... The Sa'udis could neither forget nor forgive their humiliation. *Ibid.* 23 Was the star of the Sa'udi scion.. not to appear? *Ibid.* ii. 28 Arabia knew that a Sa'udi was.. again master of Riyadh. **1949** *Britannica Bk. of Year* 51/1 A fraternal declaration which it was hoped would be the beginning of friendlier relations between the Saudi and Hashimi dynasties. **1957** *Encycl. Brit.* II. 169/1 The name Arabia is quite often used, incorrectly, when reference is intended to the Saudi kingdom only. **1959** W. THESIGER *Arabian Sands* xii. 227 At that time I was dressed as a Saudi. *Ibid.* xiii. 245 They were dressed in Saudi fashion, in long white shirts, gold-embroidered cloaks, and white head-cloths. **1962** *Listener* 5 Apr. 587/1 The Saudis could not bear the thought of an expansion of Hashimite power into Syria. **1974** *Encycl. Brit. Macropædia* XVI. 275/2 The 10,000 Saudi Arabs employed by Aramco..are exposed to modern industrial skills, technology, [etc.]. **1976** *Daily Record* (Glasgow) 22 Nov. 15/2 While I was there, Lebanese and Saudis in exquisite white silk suits, sipped pink champagne and peeled off £20 tips to English waitresses. **1976** *Star* (Sheffield) 3 Dec. 14/7 Sheffield workers got a pat on the back..for helping to save a Saudi customer waiting.

Hence **Sau·dian, Sau·dite** *adjs.*

1949 [see *HASHIMITE *a.* and *sb.*]. **1950** W. THEIMER *Encycl. World Politics* 378/1 Some experts believe that the Saudian oilfields contain one-half of the world's oil reserves.

Saudi Arabian (sau·di ărēⁱ·biăn, sǭ·di ărēⁱ·biăn), *a.* and *sb.* Also **Sa'udi Arabian,** and with hyphen. [f. *Saudi Arabia* (see below): cf. *SAUDI *sb.* and *a.*, ARABIAN *a.* and *sb.*] **A.** *adj.* Of or pertaining to Saudi Arabia, a kingdom founded in 1932 by Abdul Aziz ibn Sa'ūd (1882–1953), comprising the greater part of the Arabian peninsula. **B.** *sb.* A native or inhabitant of Saudi Arabia.

1934 *Times* 23 Nov. 13/7 Sheikh Hafiz Wahba, the Saudi Arabian Minister to the Court of St. James's, is about to return to Mecca. **1947** K. PHILBY *Let.* in F. Maclean *Take Nine Spies* (1978) vii. 251 Ignorance and arrogance make a bad combination, and the Saudi Arabians have both. **1951** *Britannica Bk. of Year* 48/1 Syria undertook to supply Syrian goods for Saudi-Arabian consumption. *Ibid.*, The Saudi Arabian province of Hasa on the Persian Gulf. **1959** *Chambers's Encycl.* I. 504/2 The financial strength of the Sa'udi Arabian government has been greatly increased by the granting of foreign concessions for oil and minerals. **1959** G. A. LIPSKY *Saudi Arabia* i. 2 Loyalty to the family.. and loyalty to the tribe are the strongest bonds felt by most Saudi Arabians. **1976** *Alyn & Deeside Observer* 10 Dec. 9/6 A group of Saudi Arabians in Chester, celebrated one of their own religious feasts last week.

sauerbraten (sauᵊ·ɹbrā:t'n, ‖ zau·ərbrā:tən). *U.S.* [Ger., f. *sauer* sour + *braten* roast meat.] A dish of German origin consisting of oven- or pot-roasted beef that has been marinaded in vinegar with peppercorns, onions, garlic, and bay-leaves before being cooked.

1889 B. K. KRAMER *'Aunt Babette's' Cook Bk.* 62 (*heading*) Sauerbraten. **1923** *Ladies' Home Jrnl.* Mar. 133/1 A demure little Mennonite maid..will invite you cordially to 'sit up' to a table arrayed with the wealth of cup cheese and pot cheese and sugar cakes and *sauerbraten* and noodles and all the rest of the savory dainties..on the menu of a Pennsylvania Dutch family. **1931** *Better Homes & Gardens* Mar. 44/3 The Sauerbraten mit Kartoffelklossen—that pot roast with the wonderful sauce. **1938** L. BEMELMANS *Life Class* I. i. 29 They lived on a diet of sauerbraten and cabbage. **1964** S. BELLOW *Herzog* 80 We eat in twenty minutes. Good chow. Sauerbraten. **1966** N. FREELING *King of Rainy Country* 84 There was a very good delicate sauerbraten, with almonds and raisins in it, not too vinegary. **1978** *Detroit Free Press* 16 Apr. (Detroit Suppl.) 28/2 Or the sauerbraten, the German version of roast beef, is always good, marinated with a vinegar mixture which later is used to make the rich brown gravy.

sauerkraut, sourcrout. Add: For the full history of the anglicized form, see SOUR CROUT, SOUR-CROUT. The usual form is now *sauerkraut*. (Further examples.)

1863 P. S. DAVIS *Young Parson* 48 [You] eat the best of roast beef, while I have to put up with sauerkraut and spec. **1892** S. BARING-GOULD *Strange Survivals* vi. 130 Such an umbrella..was sufferable as spread over an old woman vending *sauerkraut*. **1945** C. A. PRICE *German Settlers in S. Austral.* ii. 14 Various Silesian recipes such as..Sauerkraut (pickled cabbage), etc., made their appearance and even penetrated to the English colonists. **1973** *Times* 29 Dec. 10/2 The stereotypes of the German as a man born with a monkey wrench in his hand and eating vast quantities of sausage and sauerkraut..should really be discarded. After all, the French eat more sauerkraut.

2. *U.S. slang.* (Often with capital initial.) A German. Cf. *KRAUT 2.

1841 H. J. MERCIER *Life in Man of War* 232 Yes, old sour-crout, and you'd be *dirty too* if you were..in that infernal shot-locker as long as these fellows have been. **1858** J. A. STONE *Put's Golden Songster* 41 Sauer-Kraut was looking for a Justice of the Peace. **1909** *Sat. Even. Post* 3 July 7 I'll expurgate you, you old Dutch Sauerkraut!

3. *attrib.* and *Comb.*, as *sauerkraut barrel, cutter*; **sauerkraut-eater** *slang* = sense 2 above.

1888 *Century Mag.* Mar. 807/1 The representative Americans of the present day..[are] the Micks and the Pats, the Hanses and the Wilhelms, redolent still of the dudeen and sauerkraut barrel. **1969** *Canadian Antiques Collector* Aug. 21/1 Another..bargain is a primitive sauerkraut cutter, which she..purchased for twenty-five cents. **1918** R. BRAMBLETT *Let.* 9 June in K. Cowing *Dear Folks at Home* (1919) 217 We will scatter those 'sauerkrauter eaters' [*sic*] before the summer is over.

‖ **sauf** (sōf), *prep.* [Fr.: cf. SAVE *quasi-prep.* and *conj.*] Used for: except for, apart from.

c **1844** H. TAYLOR *Let.* in F. A. Hayek *John Stuart Mill & Harriet Taylor* (1951) 115 Your liability to take an over large *measure* of people—sauf having to draw in afterwards. **1847** J. S. MILL *Let.* 9 Mar. in *Wks.* (1963) XIII. 708, I have had a book to write..which I have now..completed, sauf the revising. **1864** G. MEREDITH *Let.* 1 June (1970) I. 259 Her Papa can't bear to lose her, though he always lets his daughters have their way in this matter, *sauf* the guarantee of moral character.

‖ **saugrenu** (sogrənü), *a.* Also fem. pl. **saugrenues.** [Fr.] Absurd, preposterous, ridiculous.

1876 W. JAMES *Let.* 5 July in R. B. Perry *Tht. & Char. W. James* (1935) I. 371 The *saugrenu*, comic Shakespeare scenes. **1889** E. DOWSON *Let.* 18 Oct. (1967) 110, I have many adventures to tell you of—some assez saugrenues. **1908** 'ODYSSEUS' *Turkey in Europe* (ed. 2) xiii. 440 The Great Powers of Europe are very like ordinary prejudiced individuals, not to say the lower animals. What they shy at one day, what they denounce with diminishing invective as impossible, revolutionary *saugrenu*, or crude, they accept a few years later as a matter of course. **1933** *N. & Q.* CLXV. 378/2 If we take 'chevalier' as addressed by Christ to the poet, do we not get merely a retort—frigid, and, by reason of the historical association a little *saugrenu*?

Sauk (sǭk). Also **Sac**; 8 **Sacky, Sax.** [ad. Canad. F. *Saki*, f. Ojibwa *osāki*; cf. Sauk *asākiwa* person of the outlet.] An Algonquian Indian people inhabiting parts of the central United States, formerly in Wisconsin, Illinois, and Iowa, now in Oklahoma and Kansas; a member of this people. Also, the language of this people, a dialect of Fox. Also *attrib.* or as *adj.*

1722 D. COXE *Descr. Carolana* 48 The Nations who dwell on this River, are Outogamis,..Sacky, and the Poutouatamis. **1762** [see *MENOMINEE]. **1789** *Deb. Congress U.S.* 25 May (1834) 41 The treaties..with the sachems and warriors of the Wyandot, Delaware,..and Sac nations,.. appear to have been negotiated [etc.]. **1810** Z. M. PIKE *Acct. Expeditions Sources Mississippi* App. I. 20 The Sauks and Reynards are planting corn. **1810** in *Deb. Congress U.S.* (1853) 12th Congress 1 Sess., App. 1858 A considerable number of Sacs went..to see the British superintendent. **1835** [see *MENOMINEE]. **1836** J. HALL *Statistics of West* 53 On this prairie is a small village of the Sauk and Fox Indians. **1877** L. H. MORGAN *Anc. Society* II. vi. 169 The Shawnees had a practice, common also to the Miamis and Sauks and Foxes, of naming children into the gens of the father or of the mother or any other gens. **1881** *Encycl. Brit.* XII. 832/1 The *Sacs* and *Foxes*, now one tribe, located in Indian Territory, were originally separate, living near Green Bay, Wisconsin... A few still remain in Iowa, Nebraska, and Kansas. **1933** L. BLOOMFIELD *Language* iv. 72 The Algonquian family..includes the languages of..the Great Lakes region (..Menomini, Sauk, Fox, Kickapoo, [etc.]). **1946** G. FOREMAN *Last Trek of Indians* 187 Treaties were thus made with the following tribes: Delawares, Kansas, Sauk and Foxes of the Mississippi, Sauk and Foxes of the Missouri, [etc.]. **1972** J. MOSEDALE *Football* i. 3 The famous Sac and Fox warrior, Chief Blackhawk. **1974** *Encycl. Brit. Micropædia* VIII. 921/1 In the 1970s there were about 1,000 Sauk. **1978** *Handbk. N. Amer. Indians* XV. 654 Organized as the Sac and Fox tribe of Indians of Oklahoma under the Oklahoma Indian Welfare Act of 1936, the Sauk had an elected chief and business committee.

sauna (sǭ·nă, ‖ sau·na), *sb.* [Finn.] A bath-house or bathroom in which the Finnish steam bath is taken; the steam bath itself, taken in very hot steam produced by throwing water on to heated stones. Also *attrib.* and *Comb.*, as *sauna bath, heat, stove, suite*; **sauna-like** *a.*, oppressively hot and steamy.

1881 P. D. DU CHAILLU *Land of Midnight Sun* II. xvii. 206 One of the most characteristic institutions of the country is the *Sauna* (bath-house), called *Badstuga* in Swedish. **1897** E. B. TWEEDIE *Through Finland in Carts* iii. 42 Every house in the country, however humble that house may be, boasts its *bastu*, or bath-house, called in Finnish *Sauna*. **1936** *Discovery* Apr. 110/1 A speciality of Finland which everyone who visits the country ought to try is the *Sauna*—the special steam-baths which Finnish people from time immemorial have been in the habit of taking. **1939** *Daily Tel.* 18 Dec. 1/5 The Finnish soldiers..continue to take their celebrated 'sauna' steam baths wherever they are stationed. **1957** A. BUCHWALD *I chose Caviar* 31 But in Finland a sauna is not just a bath—it is a way of life. A sauna is to a Finn what a pub is to a Britisher, what a café is to a Frenchman, what a television set is to an American.

1959 *Times* 2 Dec. 5/4 A move to make British business men sauna bath conscious begins next week with the opening of a Finnish-style sauna in the City of London... City Wall sauna, as it is called, has the requisite little wooden rooms with a stove containing a pile of heated stones on to which water is sprinkled to produce the sauna heat, and showers and rest cubicles. Bunches of leafy birch twigs will also be available, price 2s. 6d., for bathers to whisk up their circulation; the sauna itself costs 15s. **1971** *Country Life* 26 Aug. 512/3 It stands in six acres, with frontage to the river, and has a..sauna bath, stables, [etc.]. **1975** *N.Y. Times* 13 Apr. x. 1/2 The sauna, otherwise known as the Finnish bath, is a wood-lined room with benches built up toward the ceiling. A special sauna stove (today, usually electric) heats small rocks piled atop it and the rocks in turn radiate a dry heat. **1976** *Times* 22 July 4/4 The sauna-like conditions of the Oxford court during the [last] five weeks. **1978** *Morecambe Guardian* 14 Mar. 15/3 Preparing for the play involved the cast in a trip to the sauna suite at Lancaster Baths.

sau·na, *v.* [f. the sb.] *intr.* To take a bath in a sauna, to visit a sauna.

1967 J. Eastwood *Little Dragon from Peking* iv. 28 Do you sauna? **1972** *Vogue* June 118/1 You could retire here to..shower, sauna, ring your friends.

saunter, *v.* Add: **2. b.** Also, to travel by vehicle in a slow and leisurely manner.

1932 R. Fry *Let.* 6 June (1972) II. 671 We sauntered through North Italy and saw a lot of lovely things.

3. Delete † and add: Also *trans.* (Further examples.)

1926 D. H. Lawrence *Plumed Serpent* ix. 153 Sauntering the day away. **1970** *Daily Tel.* 14 Nov. 9/3 If you're not fond of boats you soon will be..sauntering the sunny quay, watching the gulls.

saurian, *a.* and *sb.* Add: **A.** *adj.* **3.** Also *fig.*

1864 W. Bagehot in *National Rev.* XVIII. 525 Much of *Tristram Shandy* is a sort of antediluvian fun, in which uncouth Saurian jokes play idly in an unintelligible world. **1929** G. Mitchell *Mystery of Butcher's Shop* i. 8 Mrs. Beatrice Lestrange Bradley..smiled the saurian smile of the sand lizard and basked in the sun. **1940**—— *Brazen Tongue* vi. 67 Lady Selina had never approved..the deep affection of her daughter Sally for this oddly saurian aunt. **1970** [see *morning-glory 1].

B. *sb.* **2.** Also *fig.*

1923 H. G. Wells *Men like Gods* i. i. 13 A car with the voice of a prehistoric saurian warned him. **1953** A. Huxley *Let.* 25 Sept. (1969) 684 The mesozoic reptiles of the Ford Foundation are being as mesozoic as ever... Hutchins has recently flown to New York and has promised to do what he can with the saurians. **1974** V. Nabokov *Look at Harlequins* (1975) ii. i. 130 He was one of the very few larger saurians in the *émigré* marshes.

saurischian, *a.* and *sb.* Insert in etym. after *Saurischia*: (H. G. Seeley 1887, in *Proc. R. Soc.* XLIII. 170). (Later examples.)

1933 A. S. Romer *Vertebr. Paleontol.* ix. 181 We shall here use a conservative classification which divides the saurischians into two suborders. *Ibid.* 184 (*caption*) The manus in saurischian dinosaurs. **1970** *Nature* 11 Apr. 109/1 It was carnivorous and is thus classified in the Theropoda within the saurischian dinosaurs. **1973** J. Updike *Museums & Women* 197 The two saurischians entered his party with the languid confidence of the specially cherished. **1977** *Radio Times* 17 Dec. 45 One of the liveliest of these disputes concerns the two great groups of dinosaurs, the saurischians (with hip-bones like those of lizards) and the ornithischians.

sauropod, *a.* and *sb.* Insert in etym. after *Sauropoda* (O. C. Marsh 1884, in *Nature* 20 Nov. 68/2). **b.** *sb.* For 'order' substitute 'suborder'. (Later examples.)

1933 A. S. Romer *Vertebr. Paleontol.* ix. 189 A first step in sauropod development is perhaps illustrated by *Anchisaurus*. *Ibid.* 190 The sauropods were massively built. **1971** *Nature* 15 Jan. 153/1 The great herbivorous dinosaurs known as sauropods are inevitably the most impressive exhibit in any natural history museum. **1976** *Ibid.* 8 Apr. 559/2 The laminar bone of sauropod dinosaurs is indistinguishable from that of some of the larger artiodactyls and it is presumed that this indicated a similar metabolism.

sausage, *sb.* Add: **2. c.** = **sausage-balloon*.

1858 *Househ. Words* 30 Jan. 168/1 Down came the grand royal blue sausage. **1874** *Belgravia* Aug. 170 This sausage was incased in the ordinary net-work and dependent shrouds, encircled by the ordinary hoop, and sustaining the ordinary car—a big circular basket capable of containing four persons comfortably. **1916** J. Buchan *Battle of Somme* 20 Captive balloons, the so-called 'sausages', glittered in the sunlight. **1916** J. R. McConnell in *World's Work* Nov. 53/2 Norman Prince became obsessed with the idea of bringing down a German 'sausage', as the observation balloons are called. **1928** C. F. S. Gamble *Story N. Sea Air Station* xx. 356 While the first pilot brings the boat down to 1,000 feet and flies over the air station to have a careful look at the 'sausage' to confirm the wind direction. **1929** Hall & Niles *One Man's War* 164 A balloon job is either a success or a failure the very first time you try, as the crew on the ground haul in their 'sausage' at the first note of warning from the observers. **1940** [see *obbo].

d. *slang.* A German. Also *attrib.* ? *Obs.*

1890 Barrère & Leland *Dict. Slang* II. 203/2 *Sausage game* (billiards), a German game. **1909** *Sat. Even. Post* 3 July 30 The durned old beer-swillin' sausage! **1919** *Athenæum* 8 Aug. 727/2 The German was known by several names, as 'Jerry',..'Sausage', [etc.]. **1923** J. Manchon *Le Slang* 255 *Sausage*..sobriquet de l'Allemand. **1929** E. A. Dolph *Sound Off!* 186 In the World War..our soldiers not only sang about the 'Huns', 'Krauts', and 'sausages', but they even took a fling at the..French.

e. *slang.* A German trench-mortar bomb, so called because of its shape. ? *Obs.*

1915 [see *Bath Oliver* s.v. *Bath *sb.*[2] 2 a]. **1918** H. W. McBride *Emma Gees* 164 At first we called them 'sausages', then 'rum-jars'..then they became 'flying pigs'. **1926** F. M. Ford *Man could stand Up* ii. v. 184 What the Germans called *Minenwerfer* might project what our people called sausages.

f. *colloq.* A person, esp. in phr. *silly old sausage* and varr.

[**1900** *Dialect Notes* II. 57 *Sausage*, 1. A person easily imposed upon. 2. An easy-going, inoffensive person.] **1934** W. Gibson *Fuel* 72 His mother's stopped Waving, to wipe her eyes, the silly old sausage! **1955** 'A. Gilbert' *Is she Dead Too?* ii. 38 Dr Grieve..was a silly old sausage. **1972** K. Bonfiglioli *Don't point that Thing at Me* v. 54 Very good customer of mine..Very nice old sausage. **1977** *Harper's & Queen* Nov. 308/4 He's only had five letters, the dear old sausage.

g. colloq. phr. *not a sausage* (and varr.), nothing at all.

1938 M. Allingham *Fashion in Shrouds* xix. 349 I've been..to Ben's and I dropped in at Conchy Lewis's. Not a sossidge [*sic*] anywhere. **1943** P. Brennan et al. *Spitfires over Malta* 29 Nothing happened, & we came back very brassed off, not having seen a sausage. **1955** J. Bingham *Paton Street Case* viii. 139 Don't go and quarrel with the old geezer, or he'll cut you off without a sausage. Hang on, and you'll get the lot. **1963** V. Nabokov *Gift* iii. 179 Time flies, he gets older, she blossoms out—and not a sausage. Just walks by and scorches you with a look of contempt. **1970** P. Laurie *Scotland Yard* iii. 69 We do this for three nights and don't get a sausage—we stop lots of people but they're all relatively straight. **1978** J. Wainwright *Ripple of Murders* 134 'Anything?' 'Not a sausage, Dick.' **1981** *Times* 29 June 12/6 Mr Healey said the press did not print Labour's actual policies. 'Not a sausage.'

h. A length of padded fabric that can be placed at the foot of a door to stop draughts.

1961 Partridge *Dict. Slang Suppl.* 1259/1 *Sausage*,.. a draught-excluder placed at foot of a door. **1962** *Times* 10 Feb. 11/3 Red twill coated, sand filled sausages along window ledges. **1977** *Times* 30 Apr. 20/1 Keeping the maximum heat indoors by..using sandfilled sausages against gaps under doors.

4. a. *sausage-shop* (earlier examples); **b.** *sausage-eating* adj.; **c.** *sausage-finger*; *sausage-pink*, *-shaped* (later examples) adjs.

1913 'Saki' *When William Came* xii. 206 A highly civilized race like ours..is not going to be held under for long by a lot of damned sausage-eating Germans. **1922** Joyce *Ulysses* 324 And as for the Prooshians and the Hanoverians,..haven't we had enough of those sausageeating bastards? **1910** *Practitioner* Jan. 33 The fingers..as large at their tips as at their base—the so-called sausage fingers. **1922** Joyce *Ulysses* 59 The ferreteyed porkbutcher folded the sausages he had snipped off with blotchy fingers, sausagepink. **1926** J. S. Huxley *Ess. Pop. Sci.* 251 It will become simpler.. and finally be converted into a sausage-shaped semi-opaque mass of tissue. **1956** *Nature* 18 Feb. 320/2 Dr. Dessens mentioned a small sausage-shaped (presumably organic) type of particle. **1767** Sterne *Tr. Shandy* IX. v. 12 A Jew who kept a sausage shop in the same street. **1873** Sausage-shop [see *corner *sb.*[1] 2 b].

d. sausage balloon, (*a*) an elongated aeronautical balloon; † (*b*) *slang*, a kite balloon used for observation (*obs.*); **sausage board,** a surf-board rounded at both ends; **sausage-burger** [*burger], a hamburger made with sausage meat; **sausage curl** (later examples); also, *esp.* a horizontal curl (see quots.); **sausage dog** *colloq.*, a dachshund; † **sausage-eater** *slang*, a German (*obs.*); **sausage machine,** a machine for manufacturing sausages; also *fig.*, esp. with reference to an institution that is held to 'process' its members so that their views, outlook, etc., are routinely identical; also *attrib.*; **sausage-meat** (earlier examples); also *attrib.*; **sausage roll** (earlier examples); **sausage toad** *colloq.* (see quot. 1937); **sausage-tree,** an evergreen tree, *Kigelia pinnata*, belonging to the family Bignoniaceæ, native to tropical Africa, and bearing red, bell-shaped flowers followed by pendulous, hard-shelled fruits shaped like large sausages.

1874 *Belgravia* Aug. 170, I am not, at this length of time, quite certain as to whether the body of the 'sausage' balloon was provided with two valves—one at each end of the cylinder—or whether there was but a solitary trap for the emission of gas at the convexity of the summit. **1916** F. M. Ford *Let.* 28 July (1965) 67 The air is full of sausage balloons, swallows, larks & occasional aeroplanes. **1917** 'Sapper' *No Man's Land* 97 A row of sausage balloons like a barber's rash adorned the sky. **1930** Blunden *De Bello Germanico* 79 Daylight relieving still prevailed, despite the hovering sausage-balloons. **1965** J. Pollard *Surfrider* ii. 18 Or it might be a 'sausage board'—straight for most of its length and rounded at both ends. **1970** *Studies in English* (Univ. of Cape Town) I. 28 Older designs [of surfboard] include the *sausage board*; rounded at both ends. **1942** *Better Homes & Gardens* Aug. 41/3 (Advt.), Sausageburgers. Add 1 tsp. Heinz Horseradish (soaked 10 minutes in 1 tbs. water) to 1 lb. bulk pork sausage. Shape into four cakes. Pan-broil, turning often. **1979** *Good Housekeeping* Nov. 367/2 *Sausage burgers*. 450g..pork sausagemeat. 125g..fresh white breadcrumbs [etc.]. **1966** J. S. Cox *Illustr. Dict. Hairdressing* 131 *Sausage curl*, a wide, croquignole-wound curl. Not to be confused with a spirally-wound drop or hanging curl. **1968** J. Ironside *Fashion Alphabet* 198 *Sausage curls*, similar to ringlets but laid horizontally. **1974** *Country Life* 28 Mar. 712/3 Pearls, ringlets and sausage curls. **1938** J. W. Day *Dog in Sport* v. 77 From Royal circles the snaky 'sausage dog' permeated downward through the aristocracy to the ranks of the common or show-bench exhibitors. **1958** L. Durrell *Mountolive* xv. 298 The door..opened and a dispirited-looking sausage-dog waddled into the room. **1972** *Country Life* 21 Dec. 1727/3 They poke fun at my toy German sausage dog. **1918** *Sat. Even. Post* 22 June 70 The sausage eaters decided to drop a few samples on our escadrille. *c* **1840** C. Webb *Vagrant* i. i. 14 *Coco*. [*Furiously*.] Why you infernal old Tomahawk!—you Patent Mangler!—you Sausage Machine to young men! **1850** *New England Farmer* II. 379 Sausage or Mincing Machine. This is a small, compact machine, remarkably strong and durable. **1860** [in Dict., sense 4 b]. **1889** Kipling in *Pioneer Mail* 20 Nov. 647/3 They will be sorry that they began tampering with the great sausage-machine of civilization. **1934** R. Mackenzie *Maitlands* ii. 64 When I became a schoolmaster I was full of hope... But I soon saw I was just part of a sausage-machine. **1960** *Encounter* Jan. 40/2 Producing a stock of plays and playwrights to feed the relentless sausage-machines of the drama departments. **1976** *Howard Jrnl.* XV. i. 55 Rise in the incidence and severity of juvenile delinquency may increase pressures towards an even more 'sausage-machine' and delinquency-orientated approach.., with no better results. **1723** J. Nott *Cook's & Confectioner's Dict.* sig. Hh4[v], Lay in..some Sausage-meat fry'd. **1741** E. Smith *Compl. Housewife* (ed. 10) 66 Slice a penny white loaf..and work it in well with your Sausage-meat. **1845** E. Acton *Mod. Cookery* xi. 301 (*heading*) Sausage-meat cake; or, pain de porc frais. **1861** Mrs. Beeton *Bk. Househ. Managem.* x. 249 (*heading*) Sausage-meat stuffing, for Turkey. **1852** *1st Rep. Commissioners Exhib. 1851* App. xxix. 150 Sausage Rolls [consumed] 28,046. **1875** V. Lush *Jrnl.* 30 Jan. (1975) 157 Mrs O'Keefe and Mrs Spencer sent a large quantity of peaches and Mamma sent sausage rolls for the teachers. **1937** Partridge *Dict. Slang* 728/1 *Sausage toad*, sausage toad-in-the-hole: eating-houses' coll[oquialism]: late C. 19–20. **1958** B. Pym *Glass of Blessings* xiv. 159 Would you even have sausage toad if I ordered it? **1915** L. H. Bailey *Stand. Cycl. Hort.* III. 1738/1 The 'fetish-tree' and 'sausage-tree', is offered in S[outhern] Calif[ornia], and specimens may be expected in botanical collections in the W. Indies. **1944** *Sun* (Baltimore) 6 Dec. 8–D/3 An 'Admirer Visiting in Florida' sends me a colored picture postal-card view of a sausage tree... There they hang, the sausage-like seed pods, amid a background of wonderful green foliage. **1956** E. E. Evans-Pritchard *Nuer Relig.* xii. 298 The man who has committed incest.. cuts in two the fruit of a sausage-tree. **1962** *Times* 9 Oct. (Uganda Suppl.) p. viii/4 The incredible sausage-tree with its dangling woody fruits. **1977** D. Beaty *Excellency* xii. 133 The sausage trees with heavy fruits shaped like giant loofahs.

sausage, *v. rare.* [f. prec.] *trans.* To subject (a person or thing) to treatment reminiscent of the manufacture or shape of a sausage.

1922 Joyce *Ulysses* 500 He is sausaged into several overcoats. **1949** Dylan Thomas *Let.* 13 Oct. (1966) 329 So that I won't..have at once to set into motion again the.. little machines that sausage out crumbs and coppers for me. **1951** N. Mitford *Blessing* ii. ii. 168 'Sometimes they only sausage them.' 'They what?' 'Tie them up like sausages, brr round and round.' **1965** *Sunday Times* (Colour Suppl.) 11 July 9/2 Once or twice we had a bit of an indiscretion, might sausage a motor into an island, or over a muddy pasture.

Saussurean (sos[i]ū·riăn), *a.* Also **Saussurian.** [f. the name *Saussure* (see below) + -an.] Of, pertaining to, or characteristic of the Swiss scholar Ferdinand de *Saussure* (1857–1913) or his linguistic theories. Hence as *sb.*, an adherent of these theories; also **Saussu·reanism.**

1937 J. Orr tr. *I. Iordan's Introd. Romance Linguistics* iii. 194 His [*sc.* Gilliéron's] linguistic is descriptive, or, in the Saussurian terminology, 'synchronic'. **1939** P. Christophersen *Articles* 16 A word has thus two aspects: verbal image and meaning (in the well-known Saussurean terms: *signifiant* and *signifié*). **1943** *Language* XIX. 55 In its essence it is Saussurean, but differs in certain respects also from the practices of the major European groups that follow the teachings of Saussure. **1952** *Word* VIII. 264 Eleven papers are devoted to general problems and methodology, among them..the Saussurean opposition between synchrony and diachrony. **1954** *Word* X. 391 Orthodox Saussureanism of the Geneva school. **1968** J. Lyons *Introd. Theoret. Linguistics* ix. 429 This fact is expressed in Saussurean terms by saying that each language imposes a specific *form* on the *a priori* undifferentiated *substance* of the content-plane. **1971** [see *parole *sb.* 2*]. **1975** Lass & Anderson *Old Eng. Phonol.* iv. i. 117 Without adhering to the Saussurean dichotomy one can still realize that diachronic evidence does not crucially determine choices for synchronic ordering. **1977** *Language* LIII. 391 The history of Saussureanism—perhaps one of the most challenging topics that a historian of linguistics could undertake. *Ibid.* 398 As a Saussurean, K views with suspicion any suggestion 'that linguistics might not yet have reached the status of an autonomous science'.

saussurite. Add: Also **sau·ssuritized** *ppl. a.*, converted into saussurite, or having component minerals converted into saussurite.

1907 J. S. Flett in W. A. E. Ussher *Geol. Plymouth & Liskeard* 101 There are..saussuritized residues of felspar. **1954** *Mineral. Mag.* XXX. 525 The high density..of the rock..distinguishes it from saussuritized gabbros. **1974** *Nature* 25 Jan. 195/2 The plagioclase of the gabbros is often saussuritised.

|| **saut** (s*o*). [Fr., = 'leap'.] **1. Saut Basque** (also in pl. and with small initials), a dance of the French Basque provinces (see quots.).

1895 L. Grove *Dancing* x. 313 The *Mutchico*, or *Saut Basque*, of the French Basque provinces, is held during winter nights in large kitchens or on threshing-floors. **1930** R. Gallop *Bk. of Basques* iv. 56 A hundred years ago it was not unusual to see the village priest lead the *Saut Basque* on a Sunday evening. *Ibid.* vi. 104 The *jantziak* or *sauts basques*..are neither wholly ritualistic nor yet purely recreational. **1948** 'La Meri' *Spanish Dancing* iv. 39 The *Sauts Basques* is also danced by men and women and is now recreational, although its origin is ritualistic... The Sauts is better known in the French provinces of the Basque country than in the Spanish. **1964** W. G. Raffe *Dict. Dance* 445/1 *Saut Basque*, a dance of French Basque provinces, especially Basse Navarre, where it has two forms—a recreational dance in a large kitchen or on a threshing-floor; and a more ceremonial form, out of doors.

2. *Ballet.* A leap in dancing; chiefly used in the names of special steps, as *saut de Basque, saut de l'ange* (see quots. 1957).

1948 A. Chujoy tr. *Vaganova's Basic Princ. Classical Ballet* vii. 91 Saut de basque... Both legs in this pas should be fully turned out. **1952** Kersley & Sinclair *Dict. Ballet Terms* 84 *Saut*, a jump in which the dancer springs off both feet and lands in the same position. **1957** G. B. L. Wilson *Penguin Dict. Ballet* 240 *Saut de Basque*, lit. a Basque jump. Turning step performed in the air with one leg straight and the other in a retiré position. *Ibid.* 241 *Saut de l'ange*, lit. angel's jump. Similar to a temps de poisson..but the body is held obliquely to the ground in the direction of travel. **1972** H. J. Summers *Guide to Ballet* 155 *Saut de l'ange*, an angel's jump, or a forward leap with the body obliquely to the ground and arms *en couronne* and legs slightly bent. **1976** *New Yorker* 24 May 146/1 From this one performance, I seem to recall Baryshnikov landing from a double saut de basque in a split on the floor.

sauté, *sb.* (Later examples of *sauté pan.*)

1846 A. Soyer *Gastron. Regenerator* 341 Melt two ounces of butter in a sauté-pan. **1960** E. David *French Provincial Cooking* 68 Few English kitchens seem to possess sauté pans.

sauté, *v.* (Later examples.)

1907 [see *Jardinière 2]. **1953** Rombauer & Becker *Joy of Cooking* 73/1 Dice bread and sauté it in butter. **1968** *Globe Mag.* (Toronto) 13 Jan. 16/3 Halve frankfurters lengthwise. Melt butter in heavy skillet, add onion and saute over low heat until just tender but not brown.

Sauterne. Add: The correct Fr. form, now usual in the U.K., is *Sauternes.* (Later examples.)

1895 *Army & Navy Co-op. Soc. Price List* 165 Sauternes... 18/0. **1908** [see *Sauvignon a]. **1959** W. James *Word-bk. Wine* 168 The sauternes-types made in Australia, South Africa, and California are most frequently a well-sulphured mixture of white wine and fortified grape juice. **1967** A. Lichine *Encycl. Wines* 486/2 The wines to be met with in many other places in the world which call themselves sauternes—or even sauterne, as if to justify bad practice by bad spelling—are not what they claim to be.

‖ **sautoir** (sotwār). [Fr.: cf. Saltire.] A long necklace consisting of a fine gold chain usu. set with jewels.

1936 *N.Y. Times Mag.* 6 Dec. 10/1 It was the era of sunbursts, sautoirs, immense brooches and flaming diamonds. **1957** M. B. Picken *Fashion Dict.* 284/1 *Sautoir*.., long jeweled chain of gold. **1960** *Times* 29 Mar. 22/7 A pearl and diamond sautoir. **1969** R. T. Wilcox *Dict. Costume* (1970) 304/1 *Sautoir*, a long, fine gold or silver chain upon which women carried a watch, or a small gold or silver chain purse, or, perhaps, a medallion. **1980** *Times* 18 Oct. 7/4 Sautoirs, or long neckchains..were very popular at the beginning of the century.

sauve-qui-peut. Add: (Further examples.) Also as a phrase in the original Fr. sense. Hence as *vb.*, to stampede or scatter in flight.

1875 *Encycl. Brit.* III. 321/2 *Sauve qui peut* was the universal cry; and..in less than six weeks above seventy banking establishments were swept off. **1939** tr. *E. N. Marais's My Friends the Baboons* iii. 35 All the baboons do in such a case is *sauve qui peut* with an alarm-call that makes the mountains echo. **1964** *Reading Teacher* Dec. 211/1 Working-class whites, themselves anthropologically unsophisticated, join the *sauve qui peut* in search of a suburban haven. **1973** *Times* 26 Nov. 15/4 It is difficult to understand the Government's present policy, or indeed that of any of the oil users. *Sauve qui peut* will serve no one well in the long run. **1980** *Guardian* 11 Nov. 10/8 It is in those hallowed halls of the UN..that I feel most keenly the theatre of anarchy; of sauve-qui-peut.

Sauveterrian (sōᵘvte·riăn), *a. Archæol.* [ad. F. *Sauveterrien* (E. Octobon 1930, in *Actes XV Congr. Internat. d'Anthrop. & Archéol.* (1931) 332), f. *Sauveterre* (see below) + -ian.] Of, pertaining to, or designating the mesolithic culture of which remains were first discovered at Sauveterre-la-Lémance, in Lot-et-Garonne, France. Also *absol.*

1940 C. F. C. Hawkes *Prehist. Foundations Europe* iii. 50 We are..in the region of Azilian tradition, but the industry might almost equally well be a 'Middle Tardenoisian', with its crescentic and angular microliths and its moderate but not excessive development of micro-burin technique, and the French now propose to call such industries in general Sauveterrian, reserving the name Tardenoisian in a strict sense for the later stage. *Ibid.* 66 In Britain,..microlithic technique was never carried beyond the Middle Tardenoisian or Sauveterrian stage. **1952** *Proc. Prehist. Soc.* XVIII. 109 Since then, the discovery of mesolithic tools which preceded the Tardenoisian on the Causses west of the Massif Central has added 'Sauveterrian' to the terminology. **1963** E. S. Wood *Collins Field Guide Archaeol.* iv. 50 The character of the mesolithic of all but the south-east and east of England shows affinities with the French mesolithic culture called *Sauveterrian*. *Ibid.* 103 The mesolithic people of the Sauveterrian were particularly fond of rock-shelters. **1975** *Nature* 3 July 33/2 This radiocarbon evidence from the Pennines indicates conclusively that simple 'broad blade' microlithic industries identical to those of Thatcham and Star Carr precede 'narrow blade' (sometimes termed 'Sauveterrian') industries with small scalene triangles and rod-like microliths. **1975** J. G. Evans *Environment Early Man Brit. Isles* v. 92 On the high moors of north-east Yorkshire another group of industries, also Mesolithic.., occurs. These..contain..a profusion of microliths. The name Sauveterrian—after the type site in France of Sauveterre-la-Lémance—has been applied to them.

‖ **Sauvignon** (sovinʸoṅ). [Fr.] **a.** A white grape of France; the white wine made from this grape. Also *attrib.* or as *adj.*

1846 C. Cocks *Bordeaux* ii. 142 The following are the names of the most esteemed white wines. 1. The *Sauvignon*, of a yellowish or greyish brown-spotted wood. **1875** H. Vizetelly *Wines of World* 18 The fine white wines of the Gironde are produced from the Sauvignon and Semillon grapes, the former of which yields a limpid, perfumed, delicate-flavoured, amber-coloured, heady wine. **1888** *Encycl. Brit.* XXIV. 604/2 The principal vines used in the Médoc are..for white wines, the Semillon, the Sauvignon, and the Muscatelle. **1908** E. & A. Vizetelly *Wines of France* 82 Sauternes and the better Graves..are chiefly the produce of the Sauvignon and Semillon grapes. **1935** Schoonmaker & Marvel *Compl. Wine Bk.* v. 142 Corvo, a..dry white wine, made..out of two native Sicilian grapes blended with the famous Sauvignon grape of Sauternes. **1959** W. James *Word-bk. Wine* 168 *Sauvignon*, one of the three white grape varieties used in Sauternes and grown to a limited extent in South Africa, Australia, and California for high-quality white wines. **1969** V. Rose *Loire* 30 Pouilly-Fumé..is made from the Sauvignon grape. **1973** *Times* 30 June 11/4 Wines made solely from the Sauvignon Blanc grape..are now to be found in many of the French wine regions. *Ibid.* 11/5 Many merchants list Sauvignons. **1976** *Times* 6 Mar. 13/5 A classic Sauvignon..comes from Haut Poitou..with the steely flavour of this great great..wine of astonishing quality.

b. Short for Cabernet-Sauvignon, a black grape of France; also the red wine made from this grape.

1846 C. Cocks *Bordeaux* ii. 140 The *Carmenère*, or grosse *Vidure*, called also *grand Carmenet, Carbonet*, or *Sauvignon*, has..grapes..of a bright colour. **1895** *Army & Navy Co-op. Soc. Price List* 166 'Imperial', from finest Sauvignon grapes. **1907** *Yesterday's Shopping* (1969) 97/3 Sauvignon..(Burgoyne) 16/0. **1917** *Harrods Gen. Catal.* 1289/2 Sauvignon, full bodied..1/11. **1952** A. Lichine *Wines of France* 46 The wine..comes from a vineyard planted two-thirds in Cabernet Franc and Sauvignon... No white wine is made.

sav, abbrev. of Saveloy.

1936 J. Curtis *Gilt Kid* 75 Cup o' tea, sav and a slice. **1969** C. Drummond *Odds on Death* vi. 130 Some home-made savs—not the shop kind.

Savage (sæ·vėdʒ), *sb.*² The name of Arthur *Savage*, inventor, of Brooklyn, N.Y., used *attrib.* and *absol.* as a brand name (proprietary in the U.S.) of a repeating rifle produced by him in 1894, and of other firearms produced by the Savage Arms Company.

1892 *Ann. Rep. Chief of Ordnance to Secy. of War* (U.S.) App. IX. 224 *Savage*... This arm was brought before the board by Mr. Arthur Savage, of Brooklyn, N.Y. **1902** *Encycl. Brit.* XXXII. 657/2 The Savage magazine rifle, model 1899, is a 'hammerless', lever-action repeating arm. **1903** *Kynoch Jrnl.* Feb.–Mar. 62/1, I had my ·301 Savage. [**1914** *Official Gaz.* (U.S. Patent Office) 18 Aug. 989/2 Savage Arms Company, Frankfort, N.Y. Filed Apr. 25, 1913... Particular description of goods.—Rifles, Pistols, and Cartridges. Claims use since Jan. 1. 1906.] **1964** H. L. Peterson *Encycl. Firearms* 30/2 This system was later used by the Mexican Obregon pistol and in a slightly modified form by Savage pistols. **1968** *Globe & Mail* (Toronto) 17 Feb. 1/1 Police seized a battered, old ·303-calibre Savage hunting rifle.

savage, *v.* Add: **4.** Also *transf.* and *fig.*

1923 *Public Opinion* 2 Sept. 103/2 Human lust and hatred has first savaged them to death. **1926** *Bulletin* 9 June 13 He is much too severe on the form of novels—the Cogglesby comedy in 'Evan' is savaged, for example. **1929** Chesterton *Poet & Lunatics* 107, I can no more see him savaging somebody like poor young Saunders than I can see him kicking a crippled child. **1962** I. Murdoch *Unofficial Rose* xxxiv. 319 Once he stroked it [*sc.* a picture] absently, as he had done when it was his, and was savaged by an attendant. **1963** [see *cut *ppl. a.* 6]. **1977** *Time* 26 Dec. 36/1 Minnelli is only the latest in a long line of actresses savaged by Simon.

† **savagerous** (sæ·vėdʒərəs, sævæ·dʒərəs), *a. U.S. dial. Obs.* Also **sawagerous, servagerous, sevagerous.** [f. Savage *a.* + Dang)erous *a.*] Fierce, wild, violent, dangerous. Also as quasi-*adv.*

1832 F. Trollope *Dom. Manners Amer.* I. xiii. 186 The visitor took it [*sc.* a dagger] up, and examining it with much emotion, exclaimed, 'What! do you really jab this into yourself sevagerous?' **1837** R. M. Bird *Nick of Woods* I. iv. 71 The strongest men in Kentucky, and the most sevagerous at a tussle. **1845** W. T. Porter *Big Bear of Arkansas* 121 They war mighty savagerous arter likher. **1850** *Wilmington* (N. Carolina) *Commercial* 7 Mar. 1/6 Of all the untiring, unaccountable, and unspeakable 'Savagerous' rumpuses ever kicked up Cape Horn takes the banner. **1859** 'Dow, Jr.' *New Patent Sermons* 263 A very sawagerous creature called the Youknowcan. **1866** C. H. Smith *Bill Arp* 54 It [*sc.* Habeas Corpus] is, perhaps, *when suspended*, the most savagerous beast that ever got after tories and traitors. **1927** *Amer. Speech* II. 363/2 *Servagerous* (adj.), very active. 'That is a servagerous coon dog.'

SAVAK (sæ·væk, sa·vak). [Acronym f. the initial letters of Persian *Sāzmān-i-Attalāt Va Amniyat-i-Keshvar* National Security and Intelligence Organization.] The secret intelligence organization of Iran, established in 1957 and disbanded in 1979.

1967 *Time* 6 Oct. 47/2 All candidates must be approved by SAVAK, his powerful security police. **1975** *New Yorker* 8 Dec. 128/2 They speak matter-of-factly of a conspiracy that includes the C.I.A. and SAVAK (the Iranian secret police) and the Sheriff of Cole County. **1976** *Maclean's Mag.* 17 May 41/3 This is a police state ruled over by one of the most ruthless secret police forces in the world, the dread SAVAK. **1977** *Time* 28 Nov. 36/2 Documented charges by both Amnesty International and the International Red Cross that Iran's secret police organization, SAVAK, had systematically persecuted dissidents. **1979** M. McCarthy *Cannibals & Missionaries* i. 18 SAVAK, the Shah's secret police, would scarcely have the same sociable attitude as the New York State wardens and guards. **1981** *Times* 13 Aug. 2/2 A former member of Savak, the Shah of Iran's secret police, killed himself..after being told he was to be deported back home.

savannah. Add: The hitherto obs. form **savana** now has some currency. **1.** (Further examples.) In mod. use, an open plain of long grass, freq. with scattered drought-resistant trees, such as is characteristic of certain tropical and subtropical regions having distinct wet and dry seasons; grassland or vegetation of this kind.

1836 N. Isaacs *Trav. & Adventures E. Afr.* I. vi. 88 This we did for the purpose of calling at some hamlets and savannas, in our course, to obtain cattle and curiosities. **1903** W. R. Fisher tr. *Schimper's Plant-Geogr.* 261 Tropical grassland, wherever it has not been modified by human agency, occurs chiefly as savannah, more rarely as steppe. **1920** M. E. Hardy *Geogr. of Plants* iii. 142 The treeless savana is called 'campo vero';..if the savanas are strewn with clumps of low trees, they are 'serrados'. **1926** D. H. Campbell *Outl. Plant Geogr.* viii. 292 The outstanding feature of this savanna was a noble fan-palm..which formed groves of considerable extent. **1955** *Times* 28 May 7/6 The Rupununi river flows almost due north through Southern British Guiana. On either side are the wide open savannahs, broken only here and there by small clumps of stunted sandpaper bushes and groups of anthills. **1957** P. Dansereau *Biogeogr.* ii. 73 The somewhat drier types [of climate]..show a very uneven distribution of rainfall and generally support woodland or savana. **1958** L. van der Post *Lost World of Kalahari* vii. 123, I met a man..walking out of the bush into a long savannah of buffalo grass. **1968** R. W. Fairbridge *Encycl. Geomorphol.* 979/2 Savanna passes in drier regions to steppe or desert, and in wetter areas into savanna woodland. **1969** S. M. Sadeek *Windswept & Other Stories* 29 The cart rolled on..into the savannah of sagebush and beezie-beezie reeds and razor-grass. **1974** H. F. Garner *Origin of Landscapes* v. 267/2 The small forest areas on savannahs differ botanically in no great measure from more continuous rain forest elsewhere. **1976** West & Augelli *Middle Amer.* (ed. 2) ii. 47/1 One of the most puzzling features of the natural vegetation in the tropical rainy areas of Middle America is the presence of large expanses of grassland, called 'savannas', in areas that receive as much as 80 to 100 inches of rain annually, with no dry period or a quite short one... The largest of the humid savannas is found along the Caribbean margin of Nicaragua and northeastern Honduras.

b. *spec.* In the West Indies and Guyana, a particular tract of such land within definable limits; a meadow, a paddock.

1934 J. Rhys *Voyage in Dark* i. i. 4 When the black women sell fishcakes on the savannah they carry them in trays on their heads. **1952** S. Selvon *Brighter Sun* i. 13 Opposite the school was a large savannah on which cattle and donkeys grazed. **1960** *Tamarack Rev.* XIV. 48 Mittelholzer..took a walk every evening about five or six around the Port-of-Spain savannah. **1964** S. M. Sadeek *Windswept & Other Stories* (1969) 19 You don't have to go galavanting the settlements and savannahs like some coot.

2*. *U.S.* A tract of low-lying damp or marshy ground.

1671 in *S. Carolina Hist. Soc. Coll.* (1897) V. 333 You will finde..great Creeks, mar[s]hes, or Savanoes on the other side. **1737** J. Wesley *Jrnl.* 2 Dec. (1910) I. 401 There is a little [soil] of a better kind, especially in the savannahs,..so they call the low, watery meadows, which are usually intermixed with pine-lands. **1895** *Dialect Notes* I. 380 *Savannah*, stretch of bog or moorland. **1905** *Bull. Bureau of Forestry* (U.S. Dept. Agric.) No. 64. 7 Loblolly is the first pine to take possession of the savannas, or marshy pairies. **1938** J. R. Carpenter *Ecol. Gloss.* 236 *Savannah*, a tract of damp level land with a growth of grass or reeds (S[outhern] U.S.).

3. c. Special Combs.: **savannah forest, woodland,** grassland similar to savannah but with a denser growth of trees, though not enough to provide continuous cover; **savannah grass,** a stoloniferous carpet grass, *Axonopus compressus,* native to tropical and subtropical America.

1903 W. R. Fisher tr. *Schimper's Plant-Geogr.* 260 The Savannah-forest..is more or less leafless during the dry season, rarely evergreen, is xerophilous in character, usually, often much, less than twenty meters high, park-like, very poor in underwood, lianes, and epiphytes, rich in terrestrial herbs, especially in grasses. **1958** G. Lienhardt in Middleton & Tait *Tribes without Rulers* 99 Boundaries between different political communities are often not apparent to the eye in such savannah-forest areas. **1756** P. Browne

Civil & Nat. Hist. Jamaica 137 The small Savannah Grass with echinated valves..grows in the Savanna about Kingston. **1859** G. W. PERRY *Turpentine Farming* 9 Every kind of turf should be turned over, such as..wire grass, savanna grass, and broom-sage grass. **1954** *Farmer's Guide* (Jamaica Agric. Soc.) 232 Savannah Grass—Carpet Grass (*Axonopus compressus*)...In the West Indies it is an important pasture grass. **1970** A. T. SEMPLE *Grassland Improvement* viii. 177 In Malaya, fertilizer trials with savanna grass ..showed a marked response. **1976** P. D. DRISCOLL *Barboza Credentials* v. iv. 233 A parade-ground, now overgrown with savanna grass. **1903** W. R. FISHER tr. *Schimper's Plant-Geogr.* 836/2 (Index), Savannah woodland. **1960** N. POLUNIN *Introd. Plant Geogr.* xiv. 442 Savanna-woodland ..is found very widely in tropical and subtropical regions including much of Cuba and elsewhere in the Caribbean, Brazil and northern Argentina, East and central Africa.., and occupying much of India and China as well as of northern and eastern Australia. **1968** Savannah woodland [see sense *1].

‖ **savarin** (savaræn). [f. the name of Anthelme Brillat-*Savarin* (1755–1826), French gastronome.] A light, ring-shaped cake made with yeast, soaked in syrup flavoured with liqueur, and served with fruit and cream. Also *attrib.*

1877 E. S. DALLAS *Kettner's Bk. of Table* 402 Little has been said about the Bath bun, the Banbury cake, the Scotch shortbread, the Brioche, the Baba, the Savarin, the Gauffre. **1894** G. DU MAURIER *Trilby* I. II. 127 The cakes were of three kinds—Babas, Madeleines, and Savarins... The Savarin..is shaped like a ring, very light, and flavoured with rum. **1928** J. RHYS *Postures* xviii. 180 A savarin, an éclair, two meringues—the ones you like, and I've ordered tea. **1943** A. L. SIMON *Conc. Encycl. Gastron.* IV. 115/1 Savarin paste. **1958** [see *BABA[2]]. **1963** R. CARRIER *Great Dishes of World* xv. 252 The *savarin* cake mixture..is the basis of rum baba as well as many other famous sweets. *Ibid.* 253 Butter a deep cake tin or savarin mould and half-fill it with dough. **1969** *Daily Tel.* 12 Nov. 15/6 A hinged cake-tin with two interchangeable bases, one for deep sponges, the other—fluted, with a funnel—for savarins.

savate. Add: Also *Comb.*, as *savate kick*.

1969 J. FREDMAN *Fourth Agency* xi. 104 He came at me in a crouching horizontal leap and dealt me a great big savate kick. **1975** P. AUDEMARS *Nightmare in Rust* xi. 157 He..launched a tremendous *savate* kick at the base of the old man's spine.

save, *sb.*[2] Add: **2.** (Later examples.) Now. usu. such an action performed by the goal-keeper.

1942 *Sun* (Baltimore) 26 Jan. 4/1 Gil Schuerholz..made astounding saves all afternoon. **1954** *Encounter* Feb. 58/2 The highlights of a [football] game, a spectacular save, a balanced evasive run..become evocative images. **1960** B. LIDDELL *My Soccer Story* x. 68 One save of Bert's..was of the truly miraculous type... The ball..sped like a bullet towards the left-hand corner..but with a marvellous leap..Bert turned it over the bar. **1977** *News of World* 17 Apr. 23/4 Arsenal lost the match the precise second that Liverpool's England goalkeeper Ray Clemence made a world-class save from Frank Stapleton.

3. *Bridge.* = *SACRIFICE *sb.* 5 d. Freq. in phr. *cheap save*.

1927 *Observer* 31 July 14/5 Now consider the position if Z had doubled 'Six Hearts' instead of going on with Spades.. which would have saved the game and rubber. A cheap save and well worth while! **1928** A. E. M. FOSTER *Auction Bridge* IV. 200 (*heading*) A good save on majority bidding. **1974** *Country Life* 3 Oct. 975/3 A hand from a recent session. .. Trying for a cheap save.

save, *v.* Add: **I. 1. b.** Also used colloq. in *fig.* phr. *to save* (someone's) *life*, to give timely assistance, esp. a stimulating drink.

1914 [see *GESUNDHEIT]. **1938** E. WAUGH *Scoop* I. ii. 14 God bless you, Julia. You've saved my life. **1950** 'J. TEY' *To love & be Wise* xii. 153 Saved my life, you have! I missed the bus. **1955** M. ALLINGHAM *Beckoning Lady* iv. 62 Tea, darling? Bless you, you're saving my life. **1977** D. BAGLEY *Enemy* xxviii. 218 'A sherry,' she said. 'A sherry, to save my life.'

f. Hyperbolically in trivial use, as *to save* (one's) *life* (or occas. *soul*): usu. following statement in negative, denoting lack of ability or intention to do something.

1848 TROLLOPE *Kellys & O'Kellys* III. v. 106, I shan't remain long. If it was to save my life and theirs, I can't get up small talk for the rector and his curate. **1873** C. M. YONGE *Pillars of House* III. xxvii. 88 'Does she go to their church?' 'Oh no, she wouldn't to save her life—she thinks it quite shocking.' **1893** YONGE & COLERIDGE *Strolling Players* iii. 21, I couldn't act to save my life. **1916** A. BENNETT *These Twain* III. xix. 436 'What will you have to eat?' said Maggie. 'Nothing. I couldn't eat to save my life.' **1920** E. O'NEILL *Beyond Horizon* III. i. 128, I couldn't get to sleep to save my soul. **1941** J. CARY *Herself Surprised* xxxiv. 82 It took even Bill six months to get her into a motor, when motors came in, and she wouldn't telephone now to save her life. **1973** E. BERCKMAN *Victorian Album* 192 She must have..dressed in record time, but to save my life I couldn't tell you how she looked or what she had on.

8. f. Hence *save-face* adj. = *face-saving* ppl. adj. s.v. *FACE *sb.* 27. Also *absol.* as *sb.*

1917 *Chambers's Jrnl.* Jan. 13/2 The civilian native staff had bolted at the first sign of trouble, 'going to report to the authorities' being their 'save face' for it! **1935** *Times* 7 Oct. 9/4 The closing phase of the War—namely, a save-face, patched up peace. **1966** R. STANDISH *Widow Hack* i. 8 A save-face formula to enable Janet to plead *force majeure*.

9. e. *to save the situation*, to avert disaster.

1907 W. RALEIGH *Shakespeare* v. 135 If Cordelia had been perfectly tender and tactful, there would have been no play. The situation would have been saved. **1908** A. BENNETT *Old Wives' Tale* IV. ii. 467 Those dogs saved the situation, because they needed constant attention. **1922** J. WILLIAMSON *Short Hist. Brit. Expansionism* v. iii. 514 Starvation more than once threatened annihilation, but on each occasion the timely arrival of food-ships saved the situation.

12. a. For † *Obs.* read *Obs.* exc. *Hist.* and add later examples.

1946 A. HUXLEY *Let.* 3 Sept. (1969) 547 My primary preoccupation is the achievement of some kind of over-all understanding of the world, directly and, at one remove, through the building up of some hypothesis that accounts for the facts and 'saves the appearances'. **1957** O. BARFIELD (*title*) Saving the appearances. **1981** *Country Life* 26 Feb. 528/3 His single professional aim is to perceive order in the physical world, not merely to save the appearances but to discover an ordered reality.

II. 17. b. (Further examples.) Now used esp. with reference to or in exhortations concerning the purchase of savings certificates, etc., instead of consumer goods.

1916 *War Savings* Oct. 12/2 A large number of circulars headed 'Save for England' have been distributed by the school children. *Ibid.* 13/1 Men and women are saving in Gloucestershire who never saved before because they have been taught that their 6d. per week..will help to end the War. *Ibid.* 16/1 Men are encouraged to save and help their country by joining the Association. **1942** J. A. SCHUMPETER *Capitalism, Socialism & Democracy* xviii. 210 Nor am I going to ask the reader to rely on the individual comrades' propensity to save. **1948** G. CROWTHER *Outl. Money* (ed. 2) v. 169 By every imaginable device of publicity people are exhorted to save. **1961** E. S. TURNER *Phoney War* xx. 292 This was merely an ingenious way of getting people to save. **1969** *Whitaker's Almanac 1970* 353/1 The Chancellor..went on to introduce a contractual savings scheme—for which he said he was glad to appropriate (from the Conservatives) the title 'Save As You Earn'. **1978** *Times* 15 Mar. 21/8 The publication of Keynes' *General Theory* by its emphasis on the propensity to save (rather than the propensity to import) as the major cause of the insufficiency of demand,, diverted attention from Harrod's approach.

18. d. *to save one's breath* or *wind*, to refrain from wasting one's argument or energy on a lost cause. (Perh. an ellipt. use of the proverbial phr. *to keep* (*save*, etc.) *one's breath to cool one's porridge*: see PORRIDGE *sb.* 4 in Dict. and Suppl.)

1926 F. W. CROFTS *Inspector French & Cheyne Mystery* xi. 146 If your story's going to be more lies about St John Price and the Hull succession you may save your breath. **1941** MENCKEN in *New Yorker* 24 May 22/1 He might very well have saved his wind, for Bill soon had him. **1952** E. CALDWELL *Lamp for Nightfall* iv. 36 Now stop making me mad, talking about a new dress that you haven't any need of. Save your breath for something dearer. *Ibid.* x. 101 You'd better be saving your wind for road work, and for doing chores.

saved, *ppl. a.* Add: **1. b.** *saved by the bell* (Boxing) (see quot. 1971); hence *fig.* in general use, saved (as from an unpleasant occurrence) by timely interruption.

[**1932** *Ring* Nov. 3 Floored in the first session by a terrific right to the jaw, the bell saving the Jersey boy at the count of seven. **1954** F. C. AVIS *Boxing Dict.* 98 *Saved by bell*, a boxer saved from being counted out because the end of the round is signalled.] **1959** A. SILLITOE *Loneliness of Long-Distance Runner* 31 'Ain't it next door to a pub, then?' I wanted to know. He answered me sharp: 'No, it bloody well aint.'..'Then I don't know it,' I told him, saved by the bell. **1963** *Times* 18 May 8/5 If, in future, the bell interrupts a count, the count will continue until the boxer is counted out—unless he gets up in the meantime... The expression 'saved by the bell' will, therefore, become an anachronism. **1971** L. KOPPETT *N.Y. Times Guide Spectator Sports* v. 116 If a man is knocked down in the closing seconds of a round, so that the bell rings ending the round before the count of 10 has been reached, he can be 'saved by the bell'. **1976** G. SIMS *End of Web* i. 13 Had he been saved by the bell... Was there still a chance of some lovers' games?

Savei, var. *SEBEI.

saver. Add: **5.** (Further examples.) Also *transf.*

1917 A. B. PATERSON *Three Elephant Power* 17 'I had a quid on,' he says. 'And..I had a saver on the second, too.' **1950** N. CARDUS *Second Innings* 163, I..suggest a saver each way on Gunga Din. **1958** G. CASEY *Snowball* xvii. 168 A lot of people who had bet on Benny—and made sure of a saver on the Negro—put on a few shillings more at the ringside. **1974** RATHER & GATES *Palace Guard* II. v. 51 Nixon..decided to slap a deuce or two on a couple of long shots, as a 'saver'—just in case.

savey, savvy, *sb.* (and *a.*). Add: The form **savvy** is now usual. **A.** *sb.* (Further examples.)

1923 R. CUMMINS *Sky-High Corral* 31, I don't just get the savvy of this. **1936** W. R. TITTERTON *Chesterton* II. iii. 138 Which idea..Armstrong actively disliked because, having more savvy than I had, he saw it meant death to his doctrine. **1951** K. CRICHTON *Marx Brothers* x. 134 He had bounce, stage savvy, and the optimism of a Rotarian. **1964** E. B. WHITE *Let.* 1 Feb. (1976) 515, I felt deeply envious of their skills, their savvy, their self reliance, and their general deportment. **1974** *Publishers Weekly* 11 Feb. 58/1 Full of baseball savvy, the book is also at times very funny. **1978** J. CARROLL *Mortal Friends* v. i. 496 Kennedy's reputation was for more savvy than that. He knew his history, didn't he, and its humbling lesson?

B. *adj.* Of persons, etc.: having practical sense, quick-witted; knowledgeable, wily, experienced. Also wise to (something).

1905 K. INGLEWOOD *Patmos* I. ix. 124 'How very savvy of you to think of that,' he said. **1946** *Calif. Folklore Q.* Oct. 377 From the safe landing of an airplane which has followed the homing radio beam (beacon), a person who is thinking clearly, performing an act correctly, that is, who is *savvy*, is *in the groove* or *on the beam*. **1964** H. WAUGH *Missing Man* xiii. 65 The kid might give himself away and Lambert's savvy enough to pick it up. **1974** *Publishers Weekly* 27 May 65/1 Norman Two Bull is a modern and savvy 15-year-old Sioux. **1975** BYFIELD & TEDESCHI *Solemn High Murder* iv. 77 She's older and been around and savvy to a lot of things the rest of them aren't. **1978** *Guardian Weekly* 5 Feb. 15/5 They are savvy hands, and if they do not speak persuasively they do speak precisely. **1980** *Economist* 16 Aug. 51/3 A savvy tenant putting a deposit on his house gains a 12-month option to buy at the price ruling when he made the deposit.

savey, savvy, *v.* Add: Also **savee**; the form **savvy** is now usual. Also, to understand, comprehend. Freq. used in the interrogative (= 'do you understand?') following an explanation to a foreigner or to one considered slow-witted. Also *absol.*

1850 L. H. GARRARD *Wah-to-Yah* 105 You've got so much 'fofarraw' stuck 'bout you, this child didn't savvy at fust! **1897** A. H. LEWIS *Wolfville* 45 You've got to quit; savey? **1908** E. J. BANFIELD *Confessions of Beachcomber* II. iii. 315 'You savee?' The 'savee' touched Harry's dignity. 'What for you say savee? You take me for a blurry Chinaman?' **1914** S. LEWIS *Our Mr. Wrenn* iv. 59 Gotta do what I say, savvy? **1917** [see *CHAIR *sb.*[1] 1 d]. **1920** D. H. LAWRENCE *Touch & Go* II. 49 *Gerald.* Yes, I want to be told. *Anabel.* That's rather mean of you. You should savvy, and let it go without saying. *Gerald.* Yes, but I don't savvy. **1933** M. LOWRY *Ultramarine* iii. 128 Let's have two starboard lights. Savee starboard lights? **1949** *True* Jan. 61/3 When there are ladies present, we say it in Mexican. The hounds savvy either. **1955** *Times* 27 July 10/6 The secretary was a literate man who 'savvied book'. **1964** E. PALMER tr. *Martinet's Elem. Gen. Linguistics* v. 155 Everywhere we find the word *savvy* 'know', which..is automatically used by a monoglot English speaker who tries to make himself understood by a foreigner.

Savile Row (sæ·vil rōᵘ). The name of a street in London celebrated for fashionable and expensive tailoring establishments, used *attrib.* to designate such tailors, their styles, or wares, esp. men's suits.

1896 G. B. SHAW in *Sat. Rev.* 13 June 597/2 A suit turned out by a Savile Row tailor. **1934** *Cornh. Mag.* Sept. 366 Sinai, like a Savile Row tailor,..does not display its goods in the shop window for all to see. **1946** A. CHRISTIE *Hollow* xxiv. 206 She took in the Savile Row cut of Edward's clothes. **1948** 'J. TEY' *Franchise Affair* xii. 126 'I'll come along and help.' 'Not in that Savile Row suit, you won't.' **1955** T. H. PEAR *Eng. Social Differences* vii. 172 The tendency to conform with fashion, but not its extremes, marks the Savile Row tailor. **1972** M. FARHI *Pleasure of your Death* ii. 43 Van Loon..looked like a foetus—stillborn in a Savile Row suit.

saving, *vbl. sb.* Add: **4.** Now usu. with *pl.* **savings**: **savings account**, a deposit account; **savings and loan** *U.S.*, used *attrib.* to designate a co-operative association which operates in the manner of a building society, though now offering additional services, as loans for purchases other than houses, and the issue of cheques to account-holders; also *absol.*; **savings book**, a book in which an official record is kept of sums deposited and withdrawn by the holder and of interest accrued; **savings-box** = *saving-box*; (**war**) **savings certificate**, introduced February 1916, renamed 1920, (**national**) **savings certificate**, a certificate declaring that the holder has invested a small sum in government funds, encashable at any time with accrued interest, and usually maturing after five or ten years. Cf. SAVINGS BANK.

1911 *Daily Colonist* (Victoria, B.C.) 29 Apr. 8/6 Encourage your boy to save by opening a savings account for him. **1978** S. SHELDON *Bloodline* xxxix. 350 A London savings account with a balance of twenty-five thousand pounds. **1978** *Washington Post* 16 Feb. F5/4 (Advt.), You earn a high 6% on regular savings accounts. **1980** *Travel & the TSB* (Trustee Savings Bank Central Board), You'll need to show your Savings Account passbook and some identification. [**1877** *Acts & Resolves Gen. Court Mass.* ccxxiv. 613 The words 'coöperative saving fund and loan association' shall form a part of the name. **1882** *Chicago Business Directory* 86/1 Union Savings, Loan & Building Assn.] **1884** *Lakeside* (Chicago) *Ann. Directory of Business 1884–5* 1489/1 Sharpshooters' Building, Savings and Loan Association. **1887** *Laws of State of N.Y.* dlvi. 720 All associations formed under the provisions hereof shall be known as co-operative savings and loan associations; and the name of every association, so formed, shall contain as a part thereof the words Co-operative Savings and Loan Association. **1921** *Proc. 34th Ann. Convention N.Y. State League of Savings & Loan Assoc.* 7 They believe in the State organization of savings and loan associations. **1962** J. H. EWALT *Business Reborn* i. 3 The typical predepression association [was] known more often as a building and loan than as a savings and loan. **1975** *New Yorker* 5 May 98/3 The Gibraltar Savings Association, of Houston, which is a subsidiary of the Imperial Corporation of America, a holding company that owns a number of savings-and-loan companies in four of the Western states. **1936** N. STREATFEILD *Ballet Shoes* xv. 232, I was quite ashamed of your savings book... I care..that you have a nice lot saved for when you are grown up. **1977** 'J. FRASER' *Hearts Ease in*

Death ix. 103 The proprietor..was standing beside the Post Office counter when Aveyard came in, pushing a savings book..through the grille. *c* **1863** T. TAYLOR *Ticket-of-Leave Man* II. 32 I've put away a shilling every week out of my savings... It's all here. (Goes to table, and..puts a savings-box into his hand.) **1922** JOYCE *Ulysses* 30 Three, Mr Deasy said, turning his little savingsbox about in his hand. **1978** *Church Times* 27 Jan. 14/1 (*heading*) Savings box for Lent. **1916** *Times* 19 Feb. 5/1 The new War Savings Certificates, which can be bought from today for 15s. 6d. each at any money-order office. **1919** *Saving* 3 Dec. 140/2 Leyton school children have bought Savings Certificates to the value of over £48,000. **1920** *Act* 10 & 11 *Geo. V* c. 12 (*title*) An Act..to extend to National Savings Certificates the enactments relating to War Savings Certificates. **1927** W. DEEPING *Doomsday* xix. 209 Seventy-five pounds in Savings Certificates. **1932, 1941** [see *National Savings Certificate* s.v. *NATIONAL *a.* 5]. **1961** E. S. TURNER *Phoney War* x. 131 If I buy three Savings Certificates at 15s. each the State will have to pay me interest and eventually repay my capital. **1978** F. MACLEAN *Take Nine Spies* vii. 235 Into his Foreign Office black leather briefcase..he crammed nearly £300 in notes and a bundle of Savings Certificates.

saving, *ppl. a.* Add: **3.** Now freq. in phr. *saving grace*.

1910 W. G. COLLINGWOOD *Dutch Agnes* 168 She plied me with questions until I was very nearly tormented into confession. But I had the saving grace, I trust, to remember John Bell's adage of *Vir sapit qui pauca loquitur*. **1932** J. B. PRIESTLEY *Self-Selected Ess.* 282 Here, in its plain lack of ideas, is the saving grace of this dull company. **1960** C. DAY LEWIS *Buried Day* viii. 170 Tchehov..has indeed said, but with all the saving grace of his felicitous compassion, that we are not put on the earth to be happy. **1978** *Lancashire Life* Oct. 36/1 In all the shouting, the bitter recriminations, there was the saving grace of native good humour.

Saviny, var. *SAPINY.

saviour. Add: **4. b.** Special combinations: **saviour's blanket, flannel,** in Sussex and Kent, a local name for several plants with greyish downy leaves, esp. lamb's ears, *Stachys lanata*, or mullein, *Verbascum thapsus*.

1882 H. FRIEND *Gloss. Devonshire Plant Names* 10 In Sussex the small plant (*Stachys lanata*) with a similar leaf is called 'Saviour's Blanket'. **1927** V. WOOLF *Jrnl.* 4 July (1980) III. 144 They [*sc.* slightly furred cheeks] are like saviours flannel, of which she picked me a great bunch, in texture.

‖ **savoir** (savwaɹ). [Fr., = to know.] Knowledge. Used *ellipt.* for SAVOIR FAIRE or SAVOIR VIVRE.

1823 LADY BLESSINGTON *Jrnl.* 12 Aug. in E. Clay *Lady Blessington in Naples* 64 Glad as I was to profit by the *savoir* of Sir William Gell.., yet I could have wished to ramble alone. **1911** A. BENNETT *Card* x. 236 He had latterly acquired a considerable amount of social *savoir*. **1952** W. STEVENS in *Nation* 6 Dec. 519 It is as if We had come to an end of the imagination, Inanimate in an inert savoir.

savoir faire. (Later examples.)

1897 E. A. BARTLETT *Battlefields of Thessaly* iv. 74 He was a fine powerful man, with plenty of courage and *savoir faire*. **1924** *Granta* 25 Apr. 361/2 He had, it seems, spent previously some months at Deauville and Paris..and there acquired that polished French and developed that *savoir-faire*, both so typical of him. **1965** A. RENOIR in Bessinger & Creed *Medieval & Linguistic Stud.* 159 If he is indeed the speaker's husband and Wulf her lover, we could hardly expect him to stretch the limits of *savoir faire* to the point of offering the latter a cup of mead at the family table. **1974** J. BETJEMAN *Nip in Air* 28 A luncheon and a drink or two, a little *savoir faire*——.

Savonarola (sævǫnǟrōᵘ·lă). [The name of the Dominican monk, Girolamo *Savonarola* (1452–98), famed for his fierce opposition to ecclesiastical, moral, and political licence and corruption.] **1.** Used allusively to designate someone considered puritanical in attitude, esp. in regard to the arts.

1916 G. B. SHAW *Androcles & Lion* p. xv, They save society from ruin by criminals and conquerors as well as by Savonarolas and Knipperdollings. **1963** W. K. ROSE in *Lett. Wyndham Lewis* (1963) III. 122 This might change abruptly to an angry, mind-scourging Savonarola. **1980** R. LUDLUM *Bourne Identity* xvi. 252 He was a Savonarola, but without religious principles, only his own odd morality.

2. In full, *Savonarola chair*. A kind of folding chair typical of the Italian Renaissance (see quots.).

1918 G. L. HUNTER *Italian Furnit. & Interiors* (1920) I. p. iv, Of Italian chairs there are more types than were until recently known to exist:..folding 'X' chairs of the type sometimes called 'Savonarola', wonderful 'Dante' chairs. **1927** EBERLEIN & RAMSDELL *Pract. Bk. Ital., Span. & Port. Furnit.* 71 The really correct name for both the so-called 'sedia Dantesca' and the so-called 'sedia Savonarola' is *sedia del campo* or *field chair*... Being readily portable when folded up, they were carried on campaigns... These chairs were likewise commonly used by the Florentines for resting, dining, writing and reading... The finest of the 'Savonarola' chairs were made of walnut. **1969** *Observer* 11 May (Colour Suppl.) 17 Savonarola's folding chair..gave its name to this characteristic piece of Renaissance furniture—a savonarola. **1972** *Country Life* 23 Mar. 723/1 Knowledgeable inspection of the oak will reveal these shams which have been sold under such names as Dante and Savonarola chairs.

Hence **Savonaro·lan** *a.*

1960 K. CLARK *Looking at Pictures* 184 Savonarolan puritanism has made Botticelli renounce the physical beauty which he still thought appropriate to the blessed spirits in his Dante drawings. **1976** *Jrnl. R. Soc. Arts* Mar. 167/2 Michelangelo himself, of course, had a strong strain of Savonarolan puritanism in his background.

Savonius (săvōᵘ·niŏs). The name of Sigurd J. *Savonius* (*fl.* 1930), Finnish engineer, used *attrib.* to designate a device developed by him consisting of two opposed semicylindrical blades (see quot. 1948), used in various forms to measure the speed of air and water currents and as a windmill rotor in the generation of electricity from wind power.

1925 *Mech. Engin.* Nov. 912 In slow winds the Savenius [*sic*] wing rotor might have to be provided with an auxiliary motor... In strong winds, however, its own turning moment would be sufficient. **1948** P. C. PUTNAM *Power from Wind* vi. 101 The Savonius rotor was a vertical cylinder sliced in half from top to bottom, the two halves being pulled apart by about 20 per cent of the diameter... In principle it resembled a cup anemometer... The Savonius design possessed fairly high efficiency. **1955** E. W. GOLDING *Generation of Electricity by Wind Power* xii. 197 The Savonius rotor has the two halves of the bent sheet displaced so that the wind can pass between them... A number of Savonius type machines were built some years ago but only in small sizes. **1963** G. L. PICKARD *Descriptive Physical Oceanogr.* vi. 79 An alternative..is the Savonius rotor which is not sensitive to vertical motion. **1974** *Undercurrents* Mar.–Apr. 3/3 A double Savonius rotor windmill directly driving a screw pump.

Savonnerie (savǫnəri). [Fr., lit. 'soap factory', f. *savon* soap.] The name of a factory established in a former soap works in Paris in the 17th century, used *attrib.* and *absol.* to designate hand-knotted pile carpets made there. Also used of similar products from elsewhere in France.

1876 *Encycl. Brit.* V. 129/2 The most celebrated and artistic textures of this class are the Aubusson, Savonnerie, and Beauvais carpets of France. **1899** R. GLAZIER *Man. Hist. Ornament* 118 About 1590, some carpets called Savonnerie were made in the Louvre, the technique being somewhat similar to the Persian carpets. **1912** *Loan Exhib. Tapestries, Carpets & Silk Fabrics from Mobilier Nat. Paris* (Victoria & Albert Mus.) 4 The chief characteristic of the Savonnerie carpets was the application of the technical methods used in..Oriental specimens to designs prepared in the contemporary style of French decorative art. **1922** KENDRICK & TATTERSALL *Hand-Woven Carpets* I. I. vii. 73 The factory of the Savonnerie, which has provided a generic name for all French hand-knotted carpets, was founded in 1626. **1933** *Burlington Mag.* Dec. p. xxiv/2 Savonnerie panels in silk, brocades etc. **1949** N. MITFORD *Love in Cold Climate* II. iv. 225 My Savonnerie, my Sèvres, my sanguines, all my treasures gone and I confess I am very low about it. **1966** M. JARRY *Carpets of Manuf. de la Savonnerie* 18 Le Château de Fontainebleau..is fitted up with Savonnerie carpets. **1972** K. BONFIGLIOLI *Don't point that Thing at Me* i. 2 That..is a valuable Savonnerie rug. **1977** *Times* 11 Oct. 17/6 The sale will contain..16 antique Oriental carpets and one Savonnerie.

savoursome (sē¹·vəɹsŏm), *a.* Also 6 **savorsome.** [f. SAVOUR *sb.* + -SOME¹.] Full of savour (in various senses).

1595 CHAPMAN *Ovid's Banquet of Sence* xxxii, Come soueraigne Odors, come..Wax hotter ayre, make them more sauorsome. **1922** *19th Cent.* Sept. 513 Hot savoursome shellfish the inn people gave us. **1958** *Times* 9 Oct. 7/1 Mr. Derek Francis is a savoursome Casca.

Savoy. Add: **2.** (Earlier example.)

1723 J. NOTT *Cook's & Confectioner's Dict.* sig. Fᵛ, *Savoy Biskets*... Eggs..Rose-water..Sugar..beaten as thick..as Cream... The finest flour... Bake.

3. The name of the *Savoy* Theatre in London, used *attrib.* to designate the Gilbert and Sullivan operas originally presented there by the D'Oyly Carte company.

1889 G. B. SHAW in *Star* 13 Dec. 2/4 A new Savoy opera is an event of no greater artistic significance than..a new oratorio by Gounod. **1893**—— in *World* 11 Oct. 23/2 The announcement of a new Savoy opera always throws the middle-aged playgoer into the attitude of expecting a surprise. **1902** *Encycl. Brit.* XXXIII. 56/2 The Savoy operas did not aim at intellectual or emotional grandeur, but at providing innocent and wholesome pleasure. **1907** W. S. GILBERT in *Daily Mail Year Bk.* 90/1 Savoy opera.. was snuffed out by the deplorable death of my distinguished collaborator, Sir Arthur Sullivan. **1930** *Times* 22 Mar. 13/4 Savoy Opera is a tree deeply rooted in our national fantasy. **1961** *Sunday Times* 30 Apr. 12/3 Today only the Savoy operettas and the Bab Ballads remain alive to judge him [*sc.* W. S. Gilbert] by.

Savoyard, *sb.* and *a.* Add: **A.** *sb.* **3.** A member of the D'Oyly Carte company which originally played at the Savoy theatre in productions of the Gilbert and Sullivan operas. **b.** A devotee of the Savoy operas. Cf. *SAVOY 3.

1890 W. S. GILBERT (*title*) Songs of a Savoyard. **1893** G. B. SHAW in *World* 11 Oct. 24/2, I enjoyed it [*sc.* Utopia Limited] and..the majority of Savoyards will share my appreciation of it. **1908** R. BARRINGTON *Rec. 35 Years' Exper. Eng. Stage* xxi. 265 To have been an 'old Savoyard', that is to say, one of the original company, seems to confer not only a great measure of dignity but..a greater spiritual activity in old age. **1922** *Glasgow Herald* 26 July 9/1 The death is announced of Mr George Thorne, the famous Savoyard..well known to the older generation of Glasgow admirers of Gilbert and Sullivan. He..appeared regularly with the [D'Oyly Carte] company at the Royalty Theatre, Glasgow. **1930** *Times* 24 Mar. 15/5 As an old Savoyard and senior vice-president of the Gilbert and Sullivan Society, I.. heard with dismay Mr. Henry Lytton's tentative announcement of his possible retirement. **1961** *Times* 12 Dec. 5/3 In *Trial by Jury*..we remarked with horror..an anachronism as horrible to the designers of Printing House Square as is the fear of a rock 'n roll *Mikado* to good Savoyards. **1977** *Times* 14 July 12/7 While..the words and music of Gilbert and Sullivan are the main attraction, Savoyards have a powerful respect for the spirit of the original productions. **1978** *Lancashire Life* Feb. 62/1 My music teacher was the mother of Martyn Green the world-famous Savoyard, who was a Boltonian.

B. *adj.* (Earlier and later examples.)

1741 M. W. MONTAGU *Let.* 15 Nov. (1966) II. 259 This Town [*sc.* Chambéry]..is wholly inhabited by the poor Savoyard Nobillity. **1905** LD. COLERIDGE *Story of Devonshire House* xvi. 239 You will find the girl in the garden with a coarse Savoyard straw hat. **1975** P. TOPPING in Setton & Hazard *Hist. Crusades* III. v. 154 The Savoyard prince secretly intrigued with Theodore despite his agreements with Venice.

savvy: see also *SAVEY, SAVVY *sb.* (and *a.*), *v.*

saw, *sb.*¹ Add: **1. c.** A flexible saw used as a musical instrument, played with a bow.

1931 *Daily Mail* 6 Oct. 16/3 Saw solos. **1938** *Oxf. Compan. Mus.* 872/1 *Singing saw.* This is an ordinary hand saw which is held between the player's knees and played on by a violin bow; its blade is meanwhile bent, under a lesser or greater tension, by the player's left hand, so producing the different pitches. **1961** *Times* 18 Jan. 15/5 An instrument believed to be wholly new in the orchestra pit, the musical saw. **1977** *Times* 14 Dec. 14/8 The Anal Zephyr Trio *does* exist..(apart from the pianist) it includes a saw and bottles.

5. c. *saw-backed* adj.

1903 KIPLING *Five Nations* 176 The same old saw-backed fever-chart. **1924** R. CAMPBELL *Flaming Terrapin* v. 77 The angel cowboys..Vaulting on the saw-backed ridges Where they tear the sky to strips. **1961** C. H. D. TODD *Popular Whippet* 33 One is often asked about a 'saw-backed' dog and what can be done about it.

5. d. saw-doctor, (*b*) a craftsman who maintains saws in an efficient condition; **saw-grass,** (*b*) (earlier example); **saw-log** (earlier and later examples); **saw palmetto,** also, a small cluster palm, *Acoelorrhaphe wrightii*, of southern Florida and central America; (earlier and later examples); **saw-scale** = *saw-scaled viper*; **saw-scaled viper,** a small venomous rough-scaled snake, *Echis carinatus*, of the family Viperidæ, found in Africa and southern Asia; **saw-shark,** substitute for def.: a small shark of the family Pristiophoridæ, found in southern seas from Africa to Australia and distinguished by a saw-like flattened snout; (later examples); **saw-timber,** timber suitable for sawing into boards or planks; **saw-whet,** for *U.S.* read *N. Amer.* and substitute for def.: a small dark brown owl, *Ægolius acadica*, found in eastern North America; (earlier and later examples).

1936 A. M. RUST *Whangarei Early Reminisc.* 163 Timber was being got..along its..foreshore. Hundreds of bushmen ..were employed besides stackers, saw doctors, benchmen and mill-hands in the different sawmills. **1949** J. L. CARVEL *One Hundred Years in Timber* ix. 140 No sawmill can function long without efficient tool-rooms, and at the City Saw Mills the saw-shop and grinding-shop supply these essentials. These are supervised by the saw-doctor. **1977** *Belfast Tel.* 22 Feb. 22 (Advt.), C. D. Monninger Ltd. require Saw Doctor to take charge of the day-to-day running of their new Belfast Service Centre. **1822** W. H. SIMMONS *Notices E. Florida* ii. 24 They were obliged to defend their horses' feet with wrappings of cow-hide, in order to prevent their being injured by the sharp saw grass. **1799** D. W. SMYTH *Short Topogr. Descr. Upper Canada* 32 The saw logs are conveyed to this mill in a very remarkable manner. **1916** *Daily Colonist* (Victoria, B.C.) 1 July 6/6 The timber returns for the month of May..show that the total scale of sawlogs for the Province amounted to 94,771,871 ft. [etc.]. **1971** *Timber Trades Jrnl.* 14 Aug. 38/1 It is estimated that quantities from British forests should increase significantly in the next decade and with the improving quality of sawlogs home producers can look forward to obtaining an increasing share of consumption of sawnwood. **1797** B. HAWKINS *Let.* 18 Feb. in *Georgia Hist. Soc. Coll.* (1916) IX. 85 The whole country was a pine barron, with wiregrass and saw palmetto. **1894** B. TORREY *Florida Sketch-Bk.* 3 The ground [was] covered thickly with saw palmetto. **1938** M. K. RAWLINGS *Yearling* xxv. 317 The bears were..eating the berries of the saw palmetto. **1942** S. KENNEDY *Palmetto Country* 4 Shrub-like saw palmetto underlies the pine flatwoods. **1964** J. HILLABY *Journey to Jade Sea* 121 Saw-scales sound like kettles of boiling water. **1935** N. L. CORKILL in *Sudan Notes & Records* XVIII. 245 The Carpet or Saw-scaled Viper is usually considered to be a form restricted to a sandy habitat. **1966** C. SWEENEY *Scurrying Bush* xii. 168 A very violent saw-scaled viper crawled out into the open, hissing and rustling its scales against each other. **1906** D. G. STEAD *Fishes Austral.* xii. 236 The Little Saw-Shark..is a small species, having a somewhat flattened body, and attaining a length of about 4 feet. **1931** J. R. NORMAN *Hist. Fishes* iii. 35 In..one of the Saw Sharks..there may be as many as six or seven [gill-clefts]. **1961** E. S. HERALD *Living Fishes of World* 49/1 The four known species of saw sharks have small pectoral fins with the gill openings just ahead of these fins. **1932** *Sun* (Baltimore) 17 Sept. 4/6

The cutting is always done selectively, large trees being taken for saw timber for new buildings and repairs, and weed trees and defective trees for fuel. **1979** *Sci. Amer.* Feb. 65/3 In the Western national forests, which constitute.. 50 percent of the nation's entire supply of standing saw-timber. **1834** J. J. AUDUBON *Ornith. Biogr.* II. 567 The Little Owl is known in Massachusetts by the name of the 'Saw-whet', the sound of its love-notes bearing a great resemblance to the noise produced by filing the teeth of a large saw. **1894** *Outing* XXIII. 406/1 The little 'saw whet' under his tiny glass globe. **1949** *Amer. Forests* Oct. 23/1 The saw-whet owl has a peculiar voice. **1959** W. R. BIRD *These are Maritimes* vi. 183 Now I rather like the little fellows [*sc.* owls], especially the saw-whets. **1977** *New Yorker* 5 Sept. 24/1 Saw-whet owls and long-eared owls roost in evergreens in winter.

saw, *v.*[1] Add: **2. c.** (Later example of a cellist.)

1977 J. CROSBY *Company of Friends* v. 36 Czernowski sawed away at Mozart.

d. *trans.* Phr. *to saw wood,* to attend to one's own affairs; to continue working steadily. *U.S. colloq.*

1894 *Congress. Rec.* 24 Jan. 1347/2 Is it possible that the framers of the bill hold a grudge against the voters who 'sawed wood' last November? **1909** 'O. HENRY' *Options* 75 During all these wintry apostrophes, Barbara, cold at heart, sawed wood—the only appropriate thing she could think of to do. **1913** F. H. BURNETT *T. Tembarom* xxix. 359 Say nothing and saw wood... It means 'shut your mouth and keep on working'. **1933** J. BUCHAN *Prince of Captivity* III. i. 264 He sees the next job and sits down to it—stays still and saws wood, as Lincoln said.

e. Phr. *to saw a chunk* (*length, piece*) *off,* to copulate. *slang.*

1961 PARTRIDGE *Dict. Slang* Suppl. 1259/2 *Saw off a chunk* or *a piece*, to coït: Canadian: since ca. 1920. **1977** J. WAINWRIGHT *Do Nothin'* v. 86 The act is..known, in polite circles, as 'copulation'. Known, in less polite circles, as..'sawing a length off'.

2*. *transf.* With reference to the sound made by sawing; *to saw gourds,* etc., to snore loudly. *slang* (orig. *U.S.*).

1870 F. H. LUDLOW *Heart of Continent* ii. 91 In five minutes..we were all 'sawing gourds' together in the land of Nod. *a* **1897** 'R. SANDERS' *Sk. Country Life* (1898) xxx. 188 When the day's work is done..he can draw his bobtail night shirt about him..knowin that while he sleeps and dreams and saws gourds his worldly possessions are growin. **1939** J. WORBY *Spiv's Progress* ii. 12 I've been in the town and got the grub while you've been sawing them off. **1946** *Penguin New Writing* XXVIII. 184 The deaf-mute was asleep and sawing them off horribly. **1961** PARTRIDGE *Dict. Slang* Suppl. 1259/2 *Saw them off*, to snore; to sleep soundly. .. Ex the noise made with a saw clumsily handled. **1980** A. FOX *Kingfisher Scream* iii. 49 Rosemary would be asleep too now, with Don sawing wood beside her.

sawagerous, var. *SAVAGEROUS *a.*

‖ **sawah** (sā·wă). Also 8 **sawoor; sawa.** [Malay.] In Malaysia and Indonesia: an irrigated rice-field.

1783, 1839 [see *LADANG]. **1937** M. COVARRUBIAS *Island of Bali* iv. 71 The most striking element of the Balinese landscape is the ever present ricefield, the *sawa*, a patch of land filled with water held by dikes cut out of the red earth. **1961** P. KEMP *Alms for Oblivion* vii. 105 The slopes are terraced with superb skill in tier after tier of *sawas*, or small paddy-fields, that produce each year two crops of the finest rice in South-East Asia. **1978** *Times* 25 Mar. 13/1 All around us were the..rice-fields. We had watched the ploughing of the water-logged *sawahs*.

sawbill. a. (Earlier and later examples.)

1763 tr. *A. S. Le Page du Pratz's Hist. Louisiana* II. II. ii. 235 We are disturbed in the night, by the hideous noise of the numberless water-fowls,..such as cranes, flamingo's, wild geese, herons, saw-bills, ducks, &c. **1833** W. F. TOLMIE *Jrnl.* 1 Sept. (1963) 232 Saw the Sawbill Duck once or twice riding down on a log. **1835** *Ibid.* 12 June 311 Shot a sawbill with rifle at the upper end of lake. **1894** A. NEWTON *Dict. Birds* III. 814 Sawbill, a name commonly given to the Goosander and Merganser. **1973** *Nature West Coast* (Vancouver Nat. Hist. Soc.) 167 The 'toothed' bill, a necessity for holding slippery fish, has earned this bird [*sc.* the red-breasted merganser] the name 'sawbill'.

sawbuck (sǭ·bɒk). *U.S.* [ad. Du. *zaagbok* trestle, saw-horse: cf. SAW *sb.*[1] and BUCK *sb.*[7]]

1. a. = BUCK *sb.*[7]

1862 *Rep. Comm. Patents: Agric. 1861* (U.S.) 141 The sheep is then laid upon his back in a kind of sawbuck. **1869** [see SAW *sb.*[1] 5 d]. **1877** R. J. BURDETTE *Rise & Fall of Mustache* 308 You might as well tell a joke to a sawbuck as to his wife. **1906** W. CHURCHILL *Coniston* 390 He was standing with his foot upon the sawbuck and the saw across his knee. **1920** S. LEWIS *Main Street* 83 In back yards their sawbucks stood in depressions scattered with.. flakes of sawdust. **1948** *Sat. Even. Post* 10 July 83/2 I'd roped everything around the ranch—calves, hounds, horses, fence posts, sawbucks.

b. In full, *sawbuck* (*pack*)*saddle.* A pack-saddle shaped like a sawbuck.

1881 E. W. NYE *Bill Nye & Boomerang* 67 This summer, however, I will get me a little blue jackass and put a sawbuck on his back. **1907** S. E. WHITE *Arizona Nights* ii. 12 We skirmished around and found..a sawbuck saddle with kyacks. **1913** *Outing* Jan. 425/1 The most practical equipment for pack animals is the ordinary crosstree or sawbuck pack saddle for all-round use. **1933** F. H. CHELEY *Camping Out* 461 While the Government has adopted the aparejo as its pack saddle, the cross-tree or sawbuck is the best one for ordinary use. **1938** M. THOMPSON *High Trails of Glacier National Park* 138 If you are going on a camping trip you utter an instinctive protest as your packer cinches up the 'sawbuck' packsaddle and loads his animal.

2. *slang.* **a.** Ten dollars; a ten-dollar note. Also *double sawbuck* (*a*) s.v. *DOUBLE *a.* A. 6.

In allusion to the x-shaped (Roman x = 10) ends of the sawyer's buck: cf. also *BUCK *sb.*[8] dollar.

1850, etc. [see *double sawbuck* (*a*) s.v. *DOUBLE *a.* A. 6]. **1852** *Oregon Statesman* 13 Nov. 1/1 Dod rabbit it, there goes another 'saw-buck', on the plag'uey jack. **1870** J. H. B. NOWLAND *Early Reminisc. Indianapolis* 315 In former years he was ever ready to..risk what he called a 'sawbuck' (a ten dollar note), on his success. **1933** [see *BITE *sb.* 1 i]. **1973** J. WAMBAUGH *Blue Knight* ii. 41, I gave him a ten, which was just like folding up a sawbuck and sticking it in his arm. He'd be in the same shape twelve hours from now.

b. A ten-year prison sentence. Also *double sawbuck* (*b*) s.v. *DOUBLE *a.* A. 6.

1925 *Flynn's* 25 Mar. 511/1 *Sawbuck*,..a ten-year sentence. **1929** *Sat. Even. Post* 13 Apr. 50/4 A prisoner with ten years brings in a saw-buck. **1938** D. CASTLE *Do Your Own Time* iii. 28 'I'm doing two saw-bucks.' 'Oh, yeah? Whatever that is.' 'Two ten spots. Twenty years.' **1945, 1950** [see *double sawbuck* (*b*) s.v. *DOUBLE *a.* A. 6].

‖ **Sawbwa** (sǭ·bwa). Also **Chobwa, Tsaubwa,** etc. [Burmese.] The hereditary ruler of a Shan state in Eastern Burma.

1800 M. SYMES *Acct. Embassy to Kingdom of Ava* xvi. 375 We were told that there were fifty-six Chobwas dependent on the Birman state; if it be true, their territories must be very inconsiderable. **1829** J. CRAWFURD *Jrnl. Embassy to Court of Ava* xv. 395 The only class of public officers which can be called hereditary under the Burmese Government, are the Thaubwas, or Saubwas, the tributary princes of the subjugated countries. **1858** H. YULE *Narr. Mission sent to Court of Ava* xiii. 303 The Tsaubwas..retain all the forms and appurtenances of royalty. **1875** H. A. BROWNE *Jrnl.* 18 Jan. in *Reminisc. Court of Mandalay* (1907) 67 Kut-Loon.. is in the jurisdiction of the Maing-maw Tsawbwa, or Chinese Shan chieftain. **1911** *Encycl. Brit.* XXIII. 892/1 Politically, where not under the direct control of Chinese magistrates, the tribes are organized under their own chiefs, who are recognized by the Chinese government and endowed with official rank and title. In Burmese such native chiefs are termed *Sawbwa*. **1929** F. T. JESSE *Lacquer Lady* III. 276 The Shan Sawbwas were in open revolt. **1962** *Listener* 25 Oct. 646/2 Some of the Shans, led by some of the Sawbwas, agitated for separation from Burma. **1973** *Dict. World Hist.* 1378/2 The Shans have retained their racial identity and a high degree of separatism, with numbers of small states each until recently having its own ruling chief. The chiefs were known as Sawbwas, Myosas, or Ngwegunhmus, according to rank.

sawder, *sb.* Add: Also without *soft.*

1854 D. G. ROSSETTI *Let.* 11 May (1965) I. 193 MacCrac.. offers £50 for the water-colour, with all manner of soap and sawder into the bargain. **1880** 'C. E. CRADDOCK' in *Atlantic Monthly* Jan. 103/2 That ain't the right sort o' sawder fur a candidate.

sawdust, *sb.* Add: **3. a. sawdust game** *U.S. slang,* a type of confidence trick.

1872 G. P. BURNHAM *Mem. U.S. Secret Service* 404 A new device for skilful robbery of the uninitiated has been introduced..known as the 'Sawdust' or 'Circular' Game. **1939** *Times Lit. Suppl.* 9 Sept. 530/2 We hear all about..the 'sawdust game', (selling bad notes).

b. With reference to the use of sawdust for strewing the floor of a place of public entertainment (as a circus, etc.) or (U.S.) the arena used by a travelling evangelist.

1864 P. PATERSON *Glimpses of Real Life* xii. 120 As good as the general run of sawdust plays. **1883** Sawdust artist [in Dict., sense 3]. **1883** Sawdust ring [see RING *sb.*[1] 12 a]. **1913** *Collier's* 26 July 7/3 And down the aisle, 'hitting the sawdust trail', they come in ones and twos and dozens, until 476 have stood before that multitude to shake the evangelist's hand and signify their intention of starting another life. **1915** T. S. ELIOT in *Catholic Anthol.* 2 One-night cheap hotels And sawdust restaurants with oyster-shells. **1946** S. H. HOLBROOK *Lost Men of Amer. Hist.* 312 Many of these suddenly patriotic pleaders..like repentant sinners at a revival, hurried down the sawdust path. **1964** A. WYKES *Gambling* vii. 170 The terms 'carpet joint' and 'sawdust joint' meant broadly the degree of luxury or squalor to be expected in American gambling saloons. **1977** *Time* 11 July 41/2 Sawdust Evangelist Rex Humbard, likes to exhort: 'You'd better straighten out and fly right with God.' **1978** M. PUZO *Fools Die* xiv. 152, I spent the day going through all the casinos in town on the Strip and the sawdust joints in the center of town.

sawed, *ppl. a.* Add: **1. b.** *sawed-off,* short, undersized. Freq. of persons, etc.: below average height. Also *ellipt.* Cf. *SAWN *ppl. a.* 2. *U.S. colloq.*

1887 C. B. GEORGE *40 Yrs. on Rail* 22, I remember..the little sawed-off cars jolting along the uneven track. **1901** S. E. WHITE *Westerners* 220 Most marvellous was a clean-limbed, deep-chested, slender running horse, accompanied by a sawed-off English groom. **1902** G. H. LORIMER *Lett. from Self-Made Merchant* 160, I didn't understand football, but understood that little sawed-off. **1919** *Dialect Notes* V. 65 A tall girl never looks well dancing with a sawed-off. **1930** J. DOS PASSOS *42nd Parallel* 100 Two soldiers on guard, toughlooking sawedoff men. **1947** *Richmond* (Va.) *Times-Dispatch* 9 Nov. B7/7 Grover Jones, the sawed-off fullback who played one war year for Penn. **1973** *Black World* Jan. 63/1, I..heard her say to that little sawed-off runt she calls a man..., 'I think she tried to communicate with me.'

c. *sawed-off* (U.S.): used to designate a (shot)gun of which the barrel has been specially shortened to make it easier to handle and give a wider field of fire. Also *ellipt.* Cf. *SAWN *ppl. a.* 2 a.

1898 *Scribner's Mag.* Jan. 86/2 There was another roar from the messenger's sawed-off shotgun. **1912** W. M. RAINE *Brand Blotters* 80 The 'shotgun messenger' was indolently rolling a cigarette, his sawed-off gun between his knees. **1930** *Sat. Even. Post* 26 July 145/1 The other laughed harshly. 'Did they knock him off?' he grunted. 'Nothin' but a sawed-off full in the chest an' half a dozen shots from an automatic as a chaser!' **1935** 'L. FORD' *Burn Forever* 255 He'd have used a revolver, a sawed-off shotgun or a sub-machine gun. **1962** A. LURIE *Love & Friendship* xiv. 280, I suppose a sawed-off shot-gun would be more his speed. **1977** *Time* 16 May 18/1 He pulled out a sawed-off sub-machine gun.

sawfish. Add: Now applied esp. to the saw-sharks of the family Pristiophoridæ (cf. *saw-shark* s.v. SAW *sb.*[1] 5 d in Dict. and Suppl.). (Later examples.)

1880 A. C. L. G. GUNTHER *Introd. Study of Fishes* 335 These Sharks [*sc.* Pristiophoridæ] resemble so much the common Saw-fishes as to be easily confounded with them. **1934** *Sun* (Baltimore) 6 July 1/7 A saw fish measuring ten feet nine inches..was landed. **1978** O. WHITE *Silent Reach* xii. 124 Sometimes you catch sawfish and barramundi there.

sawmill. Add: (Earlier Amer. *attrib.* examples.)

1654 *Suffolk County* (Mass.) *Deeds* (1883) II. 26, I Edward Colcott..doe hereby giue..vnto Thomas Rucke..one third pte of a saw mill worke. **1716** *Duxbury* (Mass.) *Rec.* (1893) 113 We began at the waste gate belonging to the saw mill.. and run from said gate Easterly as the old saw mill dam stood. **1818** T. G. FESSENDEN *Ladies' Monitor* 35 His elbows, hoofs and paws That rip and rend and rive like saw mill-saws.

sawmiller (earlier example).

1845 THOREAU *Jrnl.* 5 July (1949) I. 361, I lodged at the house of a saw-miller last summer.

sawn, *ppl. a.* Add: **2.** *sawn-off* (now more usu. than *sawed-off* exc. in *N.Amer.*). **a.** Of a (shot)gun: = *SAWED *ppl. a.* 1 c.

1915 A. CONAN DOYLE *Valley of Fear* vi. 113 In the latter was a sawn-off shot-gun, so he came with the deliberate purpose of crime. **1937** N. MARSH *Vintage Murder* ii. 14 A salute of two sawn-off shotguns. **1959** *Encounter* July 59/1 A fifteen-year-old highschool boy who had taken a sawn-off shotgun into the classroom and blown off the head of a classmate. **1978** R. WESTALL *Devil on Road* xx. 186 A sawn-off shotgun ..sprays lead like a hose.

b. = *SAWED *ppl. a.* 1 b. *colloq.*

1936 R. CAMPBELL *Mithraic Emblems* 162 Yet could I trudge in sawn-off trousers, And redden up like logs at Yule. **1944** *Coast to Coast 1943* 56 He was a sawn-off little bloke, and they reckoned there couldn't have been much grass about when he was born. **1954** 'J. CHRISTOPHER' *22nd Cent.* 104 It's a little sawn-off town up in Scotland. **1960** J. MORTIMER *Call me Liar* 431 Found him, have you?..That sawn-off, bald, damp-eyed old hundred per cent British duodenal with..no convictions known.

sawn (sǭn), *sb.* Austral. slang abbrev. of SAWNEY *sb.* 2.

1953 K. TENNANT *Joyful Condemned* xvii. 145 I'm always getting into trouble through sawns. **1961** PARTRIDGE *Dict. Slang* Suppl. 1259/2 *Sawn*, a softy, a 'dope': low Australian.

sawoor, var. *SAWAH.

saw-pit. Add: **b.** *N.Amer.* A wooden framework serving the function of a saw-pit.

1876 H. W. RAVENELL in *Yale Rev.* (1936) XXV. 763 The saw-pit was a rude structure about seven feet high, made of strong posts set in the ground wide enough apart to hold one or two pieces of heavy pine timber, and the sawyers, one above and one beneath, sawed out one hundred feet per day. **1961** J. W. ANDERSON *Fur Trader's Story* x. 87 Next they would erect, from smaller trees in the vicinity, what we used to call a saw-pit, which was not really a pit at all but a frame set entirely above the ground.

saw tooth. Add: **1. c.** *Electronics.* A waveform showing a slow linear rise and rapid linear fall, or the reverse; a voltage or current varying in this way. Usu. *attrib.*, as *saw-tooth generator, waveform.*

1933 *Proc. IRE* XXI. 1666 The variation of intensity of both horizontal and vertical deflecting fields plotted against time is of a 'saw-tooth' shape. **1935** M. G. SCROGGIE *Television* iv. 37 The sudden charge of the condenser, followed by a slower discharge, yields a saw-tooth wave-form. **1940** [see *KEYSTONE *v.*]. **1942** *Electronic Engin.* XIV. 666/2 The time-base circuit is..adapted for single sweep operation and the saw-tooth generated can be expanded symmetrically with respect to the centre of the tube. **1947** R. LEE *Electronic Transformers & Circuits* ix. 251 Probably the most common application of sawtooth amplifier transformers is to provide a linear sweep to horizontal plates of a cathode ray oscilloscope. **1969** J. J. SPARKES *Transistor Switching* iii. 63 All sawtooth-wave generators integrate a constant voltage or current with respect to time.

2. saw-tooth roof, a roof with a serrated profile incorporating windows in the steeper sides, which face in the direction of the equator.

1900 *Engineering* 9 Feb. 173/2 The factory consists of four bays, each covered with a saw-tooth roof running east and west, and glazed on the north side only. **1942** ASHER & HEAL *Send no Money* 58 It had plenty of windows, a sawtooth roof to provide light, and it was airy and spacious. **1966** L. COHEN *Beautiful Losers* I. 10 The sun was just coming up over the sawtooth roof of the factory next door.

sawyer. 3. (Earlier example.)
1786 E. BEATTY *Diary* 6 Sept. in *Mag. Amer. Hist.* (1877) I. 312/2 Arrived at Guyandot this evening and lay all night off its mouth in rapid water—obliged to make fast to a sawyer.

sax, *sb.*[1] **1.** (Later examples.)
1968 *Medium Ævum* XXXVII. 130 The Hailfingen, Württemberg, sax. **1972** G. JONES *Kings, Beasts, & Heroes* I. i. 20 Wiglaf pierces the dragon's unarmoured underbelly, and..draws his sax and severs him at the middle.

sax (sæks), *sb.*[2] Colloq. abbrev. of SAXOPHONE. **1.** = SAXOPHONE 1 in Dict. and Suppl. For *alto sax, tenor sax*, etc., see under first element in Suppl.
1923 *N.Y. Times* 7 Oct. IX. 2 *Sax*, a saxophone. **1926** *Picture-Play Mag.* July 3/2 (Advt.), How I used to envy Laura playing beautifully mellow notes on her sax. **1931** *Amer. Mercury* Dec. 426/1 'Mom,' he said, 'is my old sax still around here?' **1943** J. B. PRIESTLEY *Daylight on Saturday* xi. 68 The works dance band, that *Elmdown Six* in which Jack Brimber played the tenor sax. **1955** L. FEATHER *Encycl. Jazz* 64 A bass sax might be used as a rhythm instrument. **1976** N. ROBERTS *Face of France* ix. 102 The moan and scream and shudder of sax and trumpet and drums in the band.
2. = SAXOPHONIST.
1926 *Melody Maker* Mar. 4 Then, for a certainty, you have heard some bad saxes! **1943** J. B. PRIESTLEY *Daylight on Saturday* iv. 21 In the canteen tomorrow..the Elmdown Six will perform. And I'm one of them. Jack Brimber—tenor sax. **1975** J. MCCLURE *Snake* vi. 86 I'm the tickler. Pianist... Drums and sax were here, but they've gone..to get pissed.
3. *attrib.* and *Comb.*, as *sax-man, -player*; **sax section**, the wind section of a dance or jazz band.
1955 L. FEATHER *Encycl. Jazz* 118 Christy, June, *singer*... Married Kenton's tenor saxman, Bob Cooper. **1972** *Jazz & Blues* Sept. 10/1 Clarence Ford, sax-man with Fats Domino, is typical in this respect. **1926** WHITEMAN & MCBRIDE *Jazz* iii. 67 'Well,' said the biggest sax player, 'we didn't know what you would want us to do.' **1980** M. BOOTH *Bad Track* ix. 158 The sax-player could see a tired desperation..in her eyes. **1932** *Melody Maker* Jan. 11/2 Eddie Pratt, Sid Cole, and Stanley Quiddington, saxophones, the latter being previously together as Jay Whidden's sax section. **1977** J. WAINWRIGHT *Do Nothin'* viii. 124 The sax section—Ric..fills it out, with the tenor..he doubles clarinet (like most sax men).
Hence **sa·xist**, a saxophonist.
1939 *Melody Maker* 13 May 3 (*heading*) Dutch saxist collects band. **1952** B. ULANOV *Hist. Jazz in Amer.* (1958) xv. 178 Harry Carney joined the band..first as an alto saxist. **1969** *Guardian* 23 Aug. 6/4 No tenor saxist of the fifties would take the stand without a one-note stutter in his vocabulary. **1975** *Gramophone* Aug. 375/3 'The Foremost!' is devoted to three tenors and a baritone saxist from the bop era.

Sax, var. *SAUK.

saxe. Add: Also **Saxe.** (Further examples.) Also *ellipt.* for *saxe blue.* **saxe blue** (further example).
1917 in G. Howell *In Vogue* (1975) 24/1 Afternoon Gown... In grey, saxe, navy, nigger, rose, and black. **1922** JOYCE *Ulysses* 441 In smart Saxe tailormade, white velours hat and spiderveil. **1939–40** *Army & Navy Stores Catal.* 607/3 Slippers...Red, Green, Saxe, Navy. **1959** G. D. PAINTER *Proust* I. vii. 87 Comparing the what-not on which she kept her Saxe figurines to an altar. **1974** *Harrods Christmas Catal.* 20 Cashmere cardigan... Natural, vicuna-colour, saxe, Harvard blue. **1980** *Radio Times* 29 Nov.–5 Dec. 34/1 Pyjamas... *Grey* trimmed *Wine, Saxe Blue* trimmed Navy.

sax-horn, saxhorn. (Earlier and later examples.)
1844 *Illustr. London News* 14 Dec. 384/2 The Sax Horn.. unites the powers of the French horn and those of the cornet-à-piston. **1939** [see *ALTHORN]. **1977** *Gramophone* May 1680/2 The piece works very well because the saxhorn family is able to offer a suitably mellifluous sound.

Saxin (sæ·ksin). Also **saxin.** A proprietary name for artificial sweeteners and other products (see quots. 1897, 1964).
1897 *Trade Marks Jrnl.* 28 July 696 *Saxin*... Chemical substances prepared for use in medicine and pharmacy, but not including those prepared for use in the cure of corns and warts and not including any goods of a like kind to any of these excluded goods. Henry Solomon Wellcome,.. London, E.C.; manufacturing chemist. **1918** 'K. MANSFIELD' *Let.* 17 Feb. (1928) I. 130 I've just made myself a glass of boiling tea, very weak, with saxin. **1964** *Trade Marks Jrnl.* 19 Aug. 1366/2 *Saxin*... Flavourings and essences, none being essential oils; and sweetening materials included in Class 30.

saxist: see *SAX *sb.*[2]

saxitoxin (sæksitǫ·ksin). *Biochem.* [f. mod.L. *Saxi-domus*, name of a genus of clams (f. L. *sax-um* rock + -I- + *domus* home) + TOXIN.] A toxic alkaloid ($C_{10}H_{17}O_4N_7{\cdot}2HCl$) synthesized by dinoflagellates of the genus *Gonyaulax* (which cause 'red tides') and accumulated by molluscs which feed on these, which thereby become toxic to man.
1962 *Jrnl. Amer. Chem. Soc.* LXXXIV. 2266/1 Saxitoxin, the paralytic poison isolated from toxic Alaska butter clams (*Saxidomus giganteus*),..is among the most toxic known substances. **1968** *New Scientist* 27 June 706/2 PSP [paralytic shellfish poison] is now known as saxitoxin and there is an extensive literature which dates back at least to the year 1778. *Ibid.*, It would appear that saxitoxin is a perhydropurine derivative into which are incorporated two guanidino moieties. **1977** *Sci. Amer.* Dec. 30/3 A tiny dose of saxitoxin—the 'red tide' toxin—can kill a man who weighs 500 million times as much as it does.

Saxo- (sæ·kso), combining form of SAXON *sb.* and *a.* [L. *Saxo-*], prefixed to ethnic adjs. in the sense 'Saxon and —', as in *Saxo-Danish, -Norman* adjs.
1798 tr. J. C. Adelung in A. F. M. Willich *Elem. Crit. Philos.* II. p. cxxiii, In the Saxon and Saxo-Danish periods, the national taste..was still much too rude to exhibit this corruption. **1932** C. J. W. MESSENT *City Churches of Norwich* 25 The base is supposed to be Saxon, or Saxo-Norman, that is built by Saxon labour under Norman direction. **1980** *Rescue News* No. 23. 2/3 A rim of Saxo-Norman pottery.

Saxon, *sb.* and *a.* Add: **A.** *sb.* **1. b.** (Further example.) Also, an Englishman as distinct from a 'Latin'.
1908 M. BEERBOHM *Let.* 23 Dec. (1964) 180 The Latins are born actors, while the Saxons have to train themselves up to the scratch. **1977** *Times Lit. Suppl.* 1 Apr. 394/3 In 1962 Ewart Milne returned to Ireland after more than twenty years in the land of the Saxon.
B. *adj.* **3. b.** *Saxon blue, green* (later examples).
1968 E. BRILL *Old Cotswold* v. 85 It is sometimes mixed with indigo, or in the old days with woad, to give what dyers call Saxon Green. **1976** *Southern Even. Echo* (Southampton) 12 Nov. (Advt. Suppl.) 14/3, 1973 Vauxhall Viva. Saxon blue... £1095.

Saxonism. Add: **1. b.** The doctrine or practice of employing English words of purely Anglo-Saxon derivation in preference to words of foreign origin.
1926 FOWLER *Mod. Eng. Usage* 514/2 Saxonism is a name for the attempt to raise the proportion borne by the originally & etymologically English words in our speech to those that come from alien sources. **1952** W. D. JACOBS *William Barnes Linguist* ii. 45 If Latinism had its failings, Saxonism manifested great excellences.

Saxonist. Add: **b.** An advocate of the use of English words of purely Anglo-Saxon origin. Cf. *SAXONISM 1 b.
1926 FOWLER *Mod. Eng. Usage* 228/1 While the plain Englishman is content that *events* should *happen*, the Saxonist..requires that there should be *happenings*, & the anti-Saxonist..that things should *eventuate*. **1934** J. J. HOGAN *Outl. Eng. Philol.* II. vii. 68 The Saxonists failed with *wheelman* 'cyclist'.

Saxony, *sb.* Add: **1. a.** (Earlier example.)
1842 *Punch* III. 74/2 House-painters, and others, will obstinately refuse to do their daily work in superfine Saxony.
b. *spec.* This wool used in making carpets. Also, a synthetic material resembling Saxony used similarly.
1910 S. HUMPHRIES *Oriental Carpets* iv. 300 *Saxony Pile Carpets.*—Made in precisely the same way as the Brussels variety... The Saxony Brussels and Saxony Velvet yarns. **1924** R. BEAUMONT *Carpets & Rugs* viii. 298 Examples in Saxony or the longer variety of 'velvet' carpet... In.. Saxony velvets the design and colour element may be as clearly delineated as in Wiltons. **1933** *Heal & Son Catal.* Carpet..; seamless 'Saxony', various colours. **1976** *Daily Colonist* (Victoria, B.C.) 3 Oct. 3/3 (Advt.), A well-constructed, full-bodied saxony nylon that is versatile and long-wearing.

saxophone, *sb.* Add: **1.** Also preceded by qualifying adj. (or quasi-adj.), as *soprano, alto* (see *ALTO *a.* b), *tenor* (see *TENOR *a.* 1), *baritone*, and *bass saxophone*, in descending order of pitch. (The instrument is widely used in modern dance and jazz bands.) Cf. *SAX *sb.*[2]
1927 *Melody Maker* Aug. 767/1 Then Mr. Billy Childs proved his excessive lung power by the force he put into blowing the soprano saxophone. **1934** S. R. NELSON *All about Jazz* ii. 57 The other saxophones in common use in the band are the tenor, baritone, soprano and bass. **1954** *Grove's Dict. Mus.* (ed. 5) VII. 434/2 Occasionally in the years just before 1917 the tenor saxophone did supplement the trombone and the soprano the clarinet, particularly in the rather larger and more highly organized bands on the Mississippi river boats. **1969** *Punch* 12 Feb. 245/3 A vaguely modal thrash headed by Lynn Dobson on flute and soprano saxophone. **1977** *Listener* 17 Feb. 215/3 Modern tenor-saxophone playing.
2. One who plays the saxophone; a saxophonist.
1929 H. MILES tr. *P. Morand's Black Magic* I. 48 The saxophone was a handsome tall fellow. **1938** D. BAKER *Young Man with Horn* III. i. 141 Rick met them... In the order of their presentation they were drums, saxophone, and trombone. **1949** N. MARSH *Swing, Brother, Swing* vi. 119 The first saxophone muttered something about hitting the high spots.
3. *attrib.* and *Comb.*
1927 *Melody Maker* May 489/2 Can you imagine anything worse than a saxophone section playing a nice legato movement and the banjo plonking away for all he is worth,.. and killing the good work of the saxes. **1954** *Grove's Dict. Mus.* (ed. 5) VII. 434/1 From time to time saxophone quartets..have appeared on the concert platform. **1973** *Advocate-News* (Barbados) 24 Feb. 3/6 (Advt.), Attention all musicians..Just arrived:..Trombone Stands..Saxophone Stands. **1976** A. WHITE *Long Silence* i. 10 We'd.. have a jolly time dancing to saxophone music until the small hours.
Hence **saxopho·nic** *a.*, of or pertaining to a saxophone; **saxophonist** (further examples).
1926 WHITEMAN & MCBRIDE *Jazz* ii. 34 Sleep for nights became a saxophonic mockery. *Ibid.* iii. 81 He noticed that a saxophonist was absent one night. **1958** *Times* 3 Dec. 14/6 The bassoon of Mr. Karl Kolbinger, which achieves an old fashioned diapason tone or a modern saxophonic reediness as he requires. **1970** *Daily Tel.* 19 May 16/4 Johnny Hodges, Duke Ellington's masterful alto saxophonist. **1976** *New Yorker* 15 Nov. 6/1 Alto saxophonist James Vass..will front his own quartet.

saxophone (sæ·ksǒfōᵘn), *v.* [f. the sb.] *intr.* To play on the saxophone. Also *fig.*, to produce a loud and raucous noise. Hence **sa·xophoning** *vbl. sb.*
1927 *Sunday Express* 28 Aug. 5/2 America's noise was gramophoned everywhere, and bawled and saxophoned. **1928** *Daily Express* 17 Mar. 9/7 Ten pairs of Communist lungs gave vent to a chorus of as syncopated invectives as one could wish. The parties of the Centre and Right saxophoned back. **1952** B. ULANOV *Hist. Jazz in Amer.* (1958) xxi. 288 Other boppers' trumpeting or saxophoning just doesn't fit.

say, *sb.*[1] Add: **3. say-cast** = *COW-TAIL 2.
1940 *Chambers's Techn. Dict.* 742/2 *Say-cast*, the coarse part of a fleece, at the tail end. **1945** [see *COW-TAIL 2].

say, *sb.*[4] **2.** For † *Obs.* read 'now chiefly *Sc.*' and add later examples.
1704 S. KNIGHT *Jrnl.* 4 Oct. (1972) 14 So I remembred the old say, and suposed I knew Sarah's case. **1880** W. T. DENNISON *Orcadian Sketch-Bk.* 7 A' to' hid's an' auld say an' a true say. **1923** R. L. CASSIE *Heid or Hert* xii. 52 A' the says o' her deid midder wud come back tull her.
3. b. For 'U.S.' read 'orig. U.S.' and add earlier and later examples.
1838 *Jamestown* (N.Y.) *Jrnl.* 11 July 1/5 One thing I am determined on, and that is, that the folks who succeed best in hauling the Two Pollies in the stream shall have *the say* in rigging on her up for the voyage. **1944** M. PANETH *Branch Street* 99, I had the 'say' now.

say, *v.*[1] Add: **B. 1. a.** Also *fig.*, of things: to suggest, to indicate. Phrs. *I won't* (or *wouldn't*) *say no to* (something, usu. a food or drink): I would like; *to say the word*: see WORD *sb.* 7; *who says —?*, with an item of food as object: who would like —?
1898 J. D. BRAYSHAW *Slum Silhouettes* 158 'Who says pudden? Mister What's It—a little piece?' **1910** H. G. WELLS *Hist. Mr. Polly* vi. 193 Sit down, everyone... Who says steak-and-kidney pie? **1939** A. THIRKELL *Before Lunch* iv. 85, I wouldn't say no to toast and honey. **1958** V. H. COLLINS *Second Bk. Eng. Idioms* 194, *I won't say no*, I won't refuse..often only a genteel way of saying 'Thank you'. **1970** P. LAURIE *Scotland Yard* iii. 68 To me drugs say beatniks, layabouts..kids going to ruin. **1972** A. ROSS *London Assignment* 33 His shirt said custom-made silk even at that distance.
c. With an inanimate item as subject: to communicate or represent; *esp.* of a clock, calendar, etc., to show (a certain time or date); of a notice, to state (a certain message).
1930 W. FAULKNER *As I lay Dying* 237 The clock said twenty past twelve. **1944** M. LASKI *Love on Supertax* xi. 103 On the door..Clarissa found a notice saying, 'Welfare Officer. Knock and enter.' **1951** W. FAULKNER *Requiem for Nun* II. i. 112 A clock on the wall says two minutes past two. **1973** W. J. BURLEY *Death in Salubrious Place* v. 105 The perpetual calendar said Wednesday August 25th. **1975** S. JOHNSON *Urbane Guerilla* I. 23 A sign said, 'Statue of Liberty—ticket office other side of building.' **1975** *Language for Life* (Dept. Educ. & Sci.) vi. 88 To teach a child that 'kuh-a-tuh' says 'cat' is to teach him something that is simply incorrect.
2. a. (Later *fig.* examples.) *spec.*, with a sum of money as subject, used as a formula to bet or wager *that* (something is the case).
1954 W. TUCKER *Wild Talent* xii. 184 A dollar says you won't come back. **1962** D. LESSING *Golden Notebk.* II. 230 The set of his shoulders said that he was listening, so she went on. **1974** L. DEIGHTON *Spy Story* xviii. 194 'A quid,' I said. 'You're on,' said Ferdy... 'And I've got a pound that says you're wrong,' said Schlegel. That's how I lost two quid. **1975** J. GORES *Hammett* iii. 28 I've got twenty at four-to-seven that says the semifinal is a draw. **1976** *Listener* 8 Apr. 427/3 This same man has since been in contact, and wants to go on another job with us..—which, to me, says that he is happy that what could be done was done under the circumstances at the time.
b. Also *transf.* and *fig.*, to convey, communicate; to mean; to indicate.
1881 H. JAMES *Portrait of Lady* I. xviii. 222 I'm afraid there are moments in life when even Beethoven has nothing to say to us. **1893** E. SALTUS *Madam Sapphira* 57 What would a Scotch and soda say to you? **1932** J. BUCHAN *Sir W. Scott* xii. 333 Venice, Tirol, Munich, Heidelberg said nothing to him. **1932** R. CAMPBELL *Pomegranates*, They change and tremble As the lips they most resemble When one red kiss is all they say. **1951** M. MCLUHAN *Mech. Bride* (1967) 80/2 By juxtaposition and contrast he is able to 'say' a great deal. **1955** M. LASKI *Apologies* 14 No, not actually like it, but—..it just doesn't say anything to me. **1966** *Listener* 10 Nov. 694/1 A Californian who knew the difference between summer and fall, no matter

what the skies and the thermometer say. **1977** H. Fast *Immigrants* v. 302, I raised a hundred and sixty thousand dollars of San Francisco money that says so. **1977** *Jrnl. R. Soc. Arts* CXXV. 602/1 Titian, in the nature of what he can and does 'say' is at least as close to Cézanne or Francis Bacon..as he is to Sannazaro or Aretino.

Proverbial phrase. (Further examples.)

1736 Gray *Let.* Dec. (1900) I. 4 Though I say it, that should not say it, there positively is not one that has a greater esteem for you. **1817** Keats *Let.* 4 Sept. (1958) I. 150 This here Beast though I say it as shouldn't..can sing. **1818** *Blackw. Mag.* II. 214/2 My adversary might find it, however, (though I say it that shouldn't say it) in the vulgar phrase, rather a *tough job.* **1842** Dickens *Let.* 1 May (1974) III. 229, I do believe, though I say it as shouldn't, that they [*sc.* Dickens's children] *are* good 'uns. **1863** H. E. P. Spofford *Amber Gods* 148 Though I say it thet shouldn't say it. **1889** E. Dowson *Let.* 5 Mar. (1967) 45, I recognize in it, thou' I say it as shouldn't what Pater calls 'a delicate tact of omission'. **1892** C. M. Yonge *Cross Roads* i. 13 Ours is reckoned one of the best choirs.. though I say it as should not say it.

c. (Later examples.)

1840, etc. [see *it *pron.* 3 f]. **1894** 'R. Andom' *We Three & Troddles* xv. 130 Giants are always wicked people. It says so in the children's books. **1900** B. Pain *Eliza* 54 'You told me it was port!' 'So it is.' 'It says tonic port on the label.' **1977** S. Brett *Star Trap* xii. 134 'Christopher Milton is thirty-eight, at least.' 'But it says in the programme—' 'Charles, Charles, you've been in the business too long to be so naïve.'

l. *when all is said and done* (and slight varr.): after all, in the long run, nevertheless, on balance.

c **1560** T. Ingelend *Disobedient Child* sig. A iii, Whan all is saide and all is done, Concernynge all thynges both more and lesse. **1583** B. Melbancke *Philotimus* sig. S iij, It must be as ye woman will, when all is said & done. *a* **1785** J. H. Stevenson *Wks.* (1795) I. 137 And yet, when all is said and done, This something's nothing but a Pun. **1886** [see Rumourer]. **1928** M. Wilkinson *Edict of Nantes* (C.T.S.) 29 When all is said Bâville was responsible for a good deal of cruelty. **1930** 'Sapper' *Finger of Fate* 162 But when all is said and done, a prospective son-in-law is as important as any letter. **1937** 'G. Orwell' *Road to Wigan Pier* iv. 73 When all is said and done, the most important thing is that people shall live in decent houses and not in pigsties. **1952** M. Laski *Village* v. 98 After all, Friday's pay-day when all's said and done. **1981** R. Barnard *Mother's Boys* iv. 49, I know. Still, when all's said and done—.

m. *what do you say to —?*: what is your response to —?; *fig.*, how would you like —?, how would — suit you?

1592 [in Dict., sense 2 b]. **1833** J. Constable *Let.* 11 Jan. (1966) IV. 391 What do you say to all or any of Mr. White's 'says'—his dogmatical manner has force. **1851** Mrs. Stowe *Uncle Tom's Cabin* (1852) II. xxiii. 77 What do you say to a game of backgammon? **1929** *Melody Maker* Jan. 20/2 What do you say to a beaker of 'the boy'? **1948** M. Laski *Tory Heaven* vi. 84 I'm getting a bit peckish. .. What do you say to us going out and looking for a bite? **1980** M. Gilbert *Death of Favourite Girl* ii. 23 What do you say we go outside and get a breath of fresh air?

n. *that is saying* (*little, much,* etc.) (and varr.): that is to concede (little, much, etc.); used to qualify or intensify a previous statement; *it says much for* (and varr.): it is much to the credit of; *to say that* (or *one thing*) *for*: to concede (the previous or following statement) as one point in favour of.

1806 C. Wilmot *Let.* 23 Mar. in *Russ. Jrnls.* (1934) ii. 223 Her Lenity makes their Lot better perhaps than that of others, but that's saying very little for the System. **1849** C. Brontë *Let.* 5 Apr. in C. Shorter *C. Brontë & her Circle* (1896) xvi. 440, I cannot perceive that she is feebler now than she was a month ago, though that is not saying much. **1853** Lytton *My Novel* III. ix. ix. 48 No, I will say one thing for English statesmen, no man amongst them ever yet was the richer for place. *Ibid.* x. xx. 202 They beat the New Yorkers in manners. I'll say that for them. **1876** J. Blackwood *Let.* 18 May in *Geo. Eliot Lett.* (1956) VI. 253 She remarked that..if people were no wiser in their speculations about more serious subjects..it did not say much for human wisdom. **1917** E. Fenwick *Diary* 13 Nov. in *Elsie Fenwick in Flanders* (1981) 183 The worst and hardest day I've had for weeks and that's saying a good deal. **1942** E. Paul *Narrow St.* vii. 59 He had with him a battery of the stuffiest lawyers in the Paris bar, and that is saying a lot. **1946** E. O'Neill *Iceman Cometh* ii. 138 Sure. Harry's the greatest kidder in this dump and that's saying something! **1956** B. Holiday *Lady sings Blues* (1973) xix. 154 Fishman had been around before the concert was a sellout, you could say that for him. **1965** *New Statesman* 30 Apr. 670/1 It says a good deal for Mr Eyre that he..is the one Mr Powell himself seems to have favoured most. **1969** K. Giles *Death cracks Bottle* vi. 64 The most impecunious peer in Ireland, which is saying something. **1975** *New Yorker* 1 Dec. 47/3 Houtek was a Railroad Baron and acted the part, but he liked to make others feel important too, I will say that for him.

o. *you('ve) said it*: you are absolutely right; you have got the point completely; I agree with you entirely.

1919 C. H. Darling *Jargon Bk.* 50 You said it, you said the right thing and I agree with you. **1925** E. Hemingway *Undefeated* in *This Quarter* I. ii. 208 'If you stand in with Retana..you're a made man.'.. 'You said it,' the other waiter..said. 'You said it then.' **1929** E. Linklater *Poet's Pub* ii. 34 'Peace is too exciting..' said Joan. 'You've said it, Miss Benbow.' **1947** 'N. Blake' *Minute for Murder* i. 9 'What do they find?' 'Chay-oh [i.e. chaos],' replied Nigel.. 'You said it.' **1970** N. Streatfeild *Thursday's Child* vii. 52 'It is a big place, there must be a lot of servants needed.'.. 'You've said it.'

p. *to say it with* (something): to express one's feelings, make one's point, etc., by the use of (that thing); *esp.* and orig. in phr. *say it with flowers,* advertising slogan of the Society of American Florists, freq. in general and *fig.* use.

1918 *Florists' Review* 3 Jan. 12/2 The slogan will be 'Say It With Flowers', and every florist who deals with the public should make that phrase a conspicuous feature of his advertising from the day the first S.A.F. page appears. **1921** I. Berlin (*song-title*) Say it with music. **1925** *New Yorker* 21 Feb. 8 (*heading*) Say it with scandal. **1928** C. Sandburg *Good Morning, America* 17 Behold the proverbs of a people, a nation... Say it with flowers. Let one hand wash the other. The customer is always right. **1932** Wodehouse *Hot Water* vi. 114 Here's this Gedge bird shoutin' about the plumbing of this Chatty-o and not saying it with flowers, neither. **1960** G. Mikes *How to be Inimitable* 33, I used to say it with flowers... More gallant, no doubt... But with *cognac* it is so much quicker. **1974** G. Mitchell *Javelin for Jonah* xiv. 175 'Why did you knife your science master?' 'We disagreed... So I say it with knives.'

q. *you can say that again,* phr. expressing whole-hearted agreement with a previous speaker's statement. *colloq.* (orig. *U.S.*).

1942 *Richmond* (Va.) *Times-Dispatch* 29 Dec. 11/5 Arthur Murray keeps in step with his hobby, Broadway idiom... If you agree [to something said] you nod and add, 'You can say that again, brother.' **1950** *Sun* (Baltimore) 1 May 12/2 The Senator wrote..that he did not 'believe that savings caused by decreases in essential services constitute constructive economy.' Senator Lehman can say that again. **1960** *Observer* 20 Mar. 10/4 *Mary*:..Andy, it's serious! *Andy*: You can say that again! **1973** *Nature* 12 Oct. 339/2 'I feel that here is an area that has not been thought out completely', he writes; he can say that again. **1974** 'E. Lathen' *Sweet & Low* xi. 102 'Everybody here is waiting for Dreyer..to put some support into this market.'.. 'You can say that again!' The fervent statement came from a total stranger. **1981** R. Barnard *Mother's Boys* vii. 70 'These teenagers are all alike, aren't they?' 'You can say that again,' snarled Lill.

3. a. *you don't say so!* (earlier and later examples); similarly *you don't say!* (orig. *U.S.*), occas. also used sarcastically; *as they say*: phr. used to mark a preceding or following expression as being proverbial or hackneyed; *if you say so*: phr. denoting acceptance of a statement or an order, usu. with grudging or placatory overtones.

1779 F. Burney *Diary* Feb. (1842) I. 183 No, you don't say so? **1842** S. Kettell *Quozziana* 14 'We shall have an explosion before long, that will shake the State of Massachusetts to its uttermost foundations.' 'You don't say so!' exclaimed I, in unfeigned alarm. **1899** R. Whiteing *No. 5 John St.* xiv. 128 You don't say so; why, I'm going to a meeting at his mother's house. **1912** Mulford & Clay *Buck Peters, Ranchman* iv. 84 'An' I could never see how he done it.' 'You—don't—say,' was Buck's thoughtful comment. **1930** A. P. Herbert *Water Gipsies* xxii. 321 Ernest, as they say, 'saw red'. **1932** L. Golding *Magnolia Street* i. x. 171 'Father, indeed!.. As much 'is father as I'm Queen Alexandra!' 'You don't say!' murmured Mr. Briggs. **1955** L. P. Hartley *Perfect Woman* xiii. 121 She lets me go, and then catches me again. It's a game, as they say. **1956** H. Kurnitz *Invasion of Privacy* iii. 30 'Okay. We've got a deal.'.. 'If you say so, George. Anything you say.' **1959** E. H. Clements *High Tension* iii. 40 'Didn't you have a lodger, though, some time last year?' The factor..was obviously..troubled at having told a lie. 'If you say so, Kilmorrin.' **1962** N. Marsh *Hand in Glove* ii. 67 'The Scorpion's not here, George.' 'You don't say,' Mr. Copper bitterly rejoined. **1976** J. Bingham *God's Defector* vii. 101 'You can..watch who goes in, can't you?' 'If you say so.' 'I do say so.' **1977** J. Thomson *Case Closed* iii. 43 Water under the bridge, as they say. **1979** R. Jeffries *Murder begets Murder* xiii. 83 'Heard the latest, Bert?.. That young filly was murdered.' 'You don't say, sir!'

b. *says who?*: 'who says so?', used to challenge a previous speaker's remark. Occas. with retort ¶ *says me*; cf. ¶ *says you* below. *slang* (chiefly *U.S.*). Also parenthetic phr. *shall we say* (in quot. 1973, *attrib.* with ironic force).

1914 Kipling *Let.* 15 Sept. in Ld. Birkenhead *Rudyard Kipling* (1978) xviii. 279 Much water, or shall we say much blood, has flowed under the bridges since they were written. **1931** M. Gilman *Sob Sister* x. 143 We can park a car there and spoon—says who! **1932** 'Spindrift' *Yankee Slang* 32 *Says who?,* challenge to a remark—what right have you to 'say so'? **1938** C. B. Kelland *Dreamland* vii. 86 'Miss Higg, you are guilty of reprehensible waste.' 'Says Who?' 'Says me.' **1968** *Listener* 30 May 699/1, I think the play may, shall we say, amplify light which does already exist but doesn't seem to have been noticed. **1971** *Black World* June 81/2 'I just asked.' 'Had no business asking.' 'Says who?' 'Me, stupid!' **1973** E.-J. Bahr *Nice Neighbourhood* x. 104 Joe Walsh, Jack's shall-we-say housemate. **1977** J. Crosby *Company of Friends* viii. 116 It's not one [*sc.* a news story] of ours..I read it with—shall we say, total astonishment. **1977** J. Porter *Who the Heck is Sylvia?* xvi. 151 'One should never break promises to children.' 'Sez who?'

¶ *says you*: also used in the present tense to convey doubt about, or contempt for, the remark of a previous speaker (freq. in form *sez you*). *slang* (orig. *U.S.*).

1927 Dunning & Abbott *Broadway* ii. 108 Steve's a fine fellow and he's just out for some innocent fun—Says you— Says I—. **1931** *Amer. Speech* VI. 205 *Says you,* you say no, but I don't believe you. 'Says me' is the answer. **1931**, etc. [see *sez]. **1932** J. Brophy *English Prose* v. 61 Oh yeah! Says you!—an expression of scornful disbelief. **1951** Wodehouse *Old Reliable* iv. 53 Says you, if I may use a homely phrase indicating doubt and uncertainty. **1981** M. C. Smith *Gorky Park* iii. iii. 328 'He's a murderer.' 'Says you.'

5. a. Delete † *Obs.* and add: In modern use: (*a*) const. *for*; (*b*) without const., the personal object being understood from the context.

1906 *Dialect Notes* III. 154 The doctor said for me not to eat a pickle. **1929** E. Hemingway *Farewell to Arms* xii. 87, I woke Georgetti, the other boy who was drunk, and offered him some water. He said to pour it on his shoulder and went back to sleep. **1934** D. L. Sayers *Nine Tailors* 72 'Why is that kept locked, Mr. Godfrey?'.. 'So Rector said to fix a lock the way they couldn't get the trap-door open.' **1946** *Publ. Amer. Dial. Soc.* vi. 26 She said for us to be there by eight o'clock. **1955** W. Denlinger *Complete Boston* i. 158 Without asking the price, the woman said to buy the dog. **1959** *Times* 20 June 7/7 Father said for Chris to take one of the lanterns. **1965** *New Statesman* 30 Apr. 687/1 On no other terms than as a parody could the book [*sc.* N. Mailer's *American Dream*] carry conviction. Its first sentence pals up with Jack Kennedy; its last paragraph includes a message from the grave from Marilyn Monroe ('Marilyn says to say hello').

10. (Further examples.) **d.** Immediately following a word or phrase to show that it represents a supposition, an instance, an approximation, or the like.

1927 *New Republic* 12 Oct. 208/1, I daresay the drummer sees no difference between Gary and, say, Newark. **1937** 'G. Orwell' *Road to Wigan Pier* vi. 100 If he were, say, an Indian or Japanese coolie, who can live on rice and onions, he wouldn't get fifteen shillings a week—he would be lucky if he got fifteen shillings a month. **1938** W. Stevens *Connoisseur of Chaos* in *Parts of World* (1942) 49 An upper, particular bough in, say, Marchand. **1940** W. Faulkner *Hamlet* i. ii. 40 In Ratliff it was that hearty celibacy as of a lay brother in a twelfth-century monastery—a gardener, a pruner of vines, say. **1944** S. Bellow *Dangling Man* 85 Little since then has worked upon me with such force as, say, the sight of a driver trying to raise his fallen horse. **1951** W. Faulkner *Requiem for Nun* iii. 231 To boil for an instant to the surface like a chip or a twig—a match-stick or a bubble, say, too weightless to give resistance for destruction to function against. **1966** *Listener* 15 Sept. 388/3 A production volume of say, 20,000 units a year. **1977** L. Meynell *Hooky gets Wooden Spoon* iii. 40 Come in about six, say. **1977** *Proc. Classical Assoc.* LXXIV. 14 In very special circumstances, you might be pressured into parenthood; say, you came from a particularly respected royal line which your subjects felt should continue.

11. a. (Earlier and later examples of *so to say.*)

1823 M. R. Mitford in *Lady's Mag.* Sept. 501/2 My flowers..withered and faded and pined away; they almost, so to say, panted for drought. **1966** *Listener* 10 Feb. 210/1 The part of the picture so to say nearest you, the foreground, the front plane, is painted to represent a doorway..which frames the main subject of the picture beyond.

c. *to say nothing of . . .*: used to refer in passing to subjects that might be used to strengthen the speaker's case; cf. *not to mention (so-and-so)* (Mention *v.* 1 a).

1934 Webster, *Say nothing of,* not to take into consideration (something too important to be neglected). **1962** *Home Managem.* (Homecraft Ser.) 27 Much damage is caused to dressing-table and bed-side table tops by spilled cosmetics and perfumes, to say nothing of marks..caused by that early-morning cup of tea. **1966** *Listener* 28 July 126/1 In an industry that has experienced Northcliffe, Hearst, and Beaverbrook, to say nothing of Bartholomew and Cudlipp, this seems unlikely. **1976** J. Crosby *Nightfall* xxxii. 191 Elf was her revolutionary sister-in-arms... To say nothing of her lover.

12. b. *I say* (later examples); also (theatr.) *I say, I say, I say,* formula used to introduce a joke; also as *attrib. phr. say*: for 'U.S.' read 'N. Amer.'; (earlier and later examples.)

1830 F. Trollope *Notebk.* in *Domestic Manners Americans* (1949) 427 Say! **1852** *Lantern* (N.Y.) I. 122/1 Say—d'you run with our machine? **1913** J. London *Let.* 20 Nov. (1966) 410 The galley stove kept going..and hot coffee—say! **1931** *Punch* 24 June 692 (*caption*) Patient (being shown into very modern consulting-room): 'I say, I didn't come to be operated on.' **1932** W. Faulkner *Light in August* viii. 172 Well, say. Can you tie that. **1967** *Listener* 3 Aug. 154/3 The sort of performers who, every summer up and down the coasts of England, bounce cheerfully on to a number of creaking stages, shouting 'Hello, hello, hello!' or 'I say, I say, I say!' **1968** M. Richler in R. Weaver *Canad. Short Stories* 2nd Ser. 191 The middle-aged couple alighted from the car. 'Say,' Mr Cooper said, 'you've got quite a baby here.' **1968** in Partridge *Dict. Catch Phrases* (1977) 104/2 A character, mid-stage, is interrupted by a 'comic' rushing up to him yelling 'I say, I say, I say'. First character shushes him off with 'Kindly leave the stage'; intruder persists with some fatuous question. **1969** *Listener* 6 Mar. 314/1 Making idiotic jokes—'I say, I say' jokes. **1976** *Times* 3 Feb. 14/3, I say, I've been to the ballet. **1976** P. Dickinson *King & Joker* viii. 114 They..grinned inanely with heads bent..and legs in the pose of a comedy routine duo. 'I say I say I say,' said Louise, 'your public face isn't as good as mine, darling.'

d. *I'll say*: used to denote enthusiastic assent (either *absol.* or with object or dependent clause). Also *I'll say so.*

1924 *Dialect Notes* V. 276 *Say:* I'd —, I'll — (both approv.). *Ibid.* 277 *So*:..I'll say — (agreement). **1926** *S.P.E. Tract* xxiv. 123 *I'll say it is,* it's my opinion, certainly. **1926** MAINES & GRANT *Wise-Crack Dict.* 10/1 *I'll say so*, emphatic agreement. **1943** N. MARSH *Colour Scheme* vi. 99 'Does he want to keep him quiet?'.. 'I'll say! Too right he wants to keep him quiet.' **1945** P. CHEYNEY (*title*) I'll say she does. **1954** E. MCLEOD tr. *Colette's Vagabond* I. iv. 35 'Hullo, Stephen! Good house?' 'I'll say!' **1960** N. HILLIARD *Maori Girl* 93 'Do you miss home much?' 'I'll say. Not so much now, though.' **1972** G. DURRELL *Catch me a Colobus* v. 95 Would we, by any chance, be interested in a pair of leopards? 'I'll say we would! Why? Do you know where there are some?' **1974** S. WOODS *Done to Death* 218 'You've taken what might have been a knock down blow with a good deal of courage.' 'I'll say she has,' said Hugh. **1979** 'J. LE CARRÉ' *Smiley's People* (1980) iv. 53 'He was a declining asset, as all ex-agents are.'.. 'I'll say,' said Strickland *sotto voce*.

‖ **saya** (sa·ya). [Sp.] In Spain and Spanish-speaking countries, a dress or outer garment worn by women (see quots.).

1841 G. BORROW *Zincali* I. II. v. 305 This female Gypsy fashion..is more properly the fashion of Andalusia, the principal characteristic of which is the saya, which is exceedingly short, with many rows of flounces. **1845** R. FORD *Hand-bk. Spain* I. ii. 196 This male *sagum* is the type of the modern *saya*, Arabic *sayah*, a long outer garment, which is always black, and is put over the indoor dress on going out. **1846** —— *Gatherings from Spain* xxiii. 323 The transparent, form designing *saya* of the lady, heightens the charms of a faultless symmetry which it fain would conceal. **1857** C. M. YONGE *Dynevor Terrace* II. ix. 132 A full dark purple satin skirt..was plaited low on the hips, and girded loosely with a brightly striped scarf. The head and upper part of the person were shrouded in a close hood of elastic black silk webbing, fastened behind at the waist, and held over the face by the hand... 'Ah, you found me out,' cried Rosita... 'I have the like *saya y manto* ready for you. Come, we will be on the Alameda [in Lima].'

sayable, *a.* Add: **B.** *sb.* That which can be said; a statement which it is possible to make.

1937 *Essays & Studies* XXII. 136 The meanable crystallized and fixed in the sayable. **1957** G. RYLE in M. Black *Importance of Lang.* (1962) 169 It is the foreign relations, not the domestic constitutions of sayables that engender logical troubles and demand logical arbitration. **1969** J. S. CUNNINGHAM *Powers that Be* 3 Infant sayables Along the seamy permeable Undersides of words.

Saybolt (sēⁱ·bǫlt). The name of George M. *Saybolt* (d. 1924), U.S. chemist, used *attrib.* to designate an apparatus he invented for measuring the kinematic viscosity of liquids, esp. oils, by measuring the time taken by a fixed quantity of liquid to pass through a standard capillary tube under specified conditions; so *Saybolt viscosity*, the viscosity so measured, usu. expressed as *Saybolt seconds*.

1886 B. REDWOOD in *Jrnl. Soc. Chem. Industry* 29 Mar. 124/2 The viscometer designed by Mr. G. M. Saybolt, inspector to the Standard Oil Company of New York, is before you... The Saybolt viscosimeter is not,..as at present constructed, suitable for use at very high temperatures. **1925** A. B. THOMPSON *Oil-Field Exploration & Development* I. xi. 520 The viscosity of oils is generally measured in one or other of three types of instruments, the Engler, Redwood and Saybolt viscosimeters, or viscometers. **1955** KIRK & OTHMER *Encycl. Chem. Technol.* XIV. 763 Viscosity is normally reported simply as Saybolt Universal or Saybolt Furol seconds, but it may be converted to centistokes by means of appropriate tables. **1968** SNELL & HILTON *Encycl. Industr. Chem. Analysis* VI. 295 The Saybolt Furol viscosity of a bituminous material is the time, in sec, that it takes 60 ml of sample to flow through the calibrated Furol orifice of the Saybolt viscometer tube, measured under carefully controlled conditions.

sayee (sēⁱ|ī). *rare.* [f. SAY *v.*¹ + -EE¹.] A person to whom something is said.

a **1902** S. BUTLER *Ess. Life* (1904) 183 It takes two people to say a thing—a sayee as well as a sayer... The belief on A.'s part that he had a *bonâ fide* sayee in B., saves his speech *quâ* him, but it has been barren and left no fertile issue.

‖ **sayonara** (sayōnara, səiǭ·nă·ră). [Jap.] Good-bye. As *sb.*, a farewell, a leave-taking; also *attrib.* As *v. trans.*, to say 'sayonara' to.

1875 *Colburn's United Service Mag.* Oct. 185 'Sionara!' (good bye), is your answer. **1880** *Golden Days for Boys & Girls* 3 Apr. 71/4 After this speech they all cried: 'Sayonara (farewell), Momotaro!' **1892** KIPLING *Lett. of Travel* (1920) 51 A traveller who has been 'ohayoed' into half-a-dozen shops and 'sayonaraed' out of half-a-dozen more. **1908** LADY R. CHURCHILL *Reminiscences* (1973) xiii. 252 Many *sayonaras* were exchanged. **1910** *Pacific Monthly* XXIII. 259/2 He is a bad man. You go away! *Sayonara!* **1952** T. J. MULVEY *These are your Sons* vii. 146 The Sisters had arranged the children in the stiff and formal formation for the '*sayonara*'. **1965** *This is Japan 1966* 106 The Honourable Sex Shop then rescued me from an embarrassing and even disastrous *sayonara* at Kobe. **1972** *Mainichi Daily News* (Japan) 6 Nov. 7/4 The International Camera Club of Japan will hold a special Sayonara party for outgoing Chairman John Thorpe, Tues., Nov. 8. **1977** J. WAMBAUGH *Black Marble* (1978) iii. 25 If I ever knew for sure what I suspect about you, Philo, it'd be sayonara, baby.

Say's law (sēⁱz lǭ). *Econ.* [f. the name of Jean Baptiste *Say* (see below).] The theory propounded by the French economist Jean Baptiste Say (1767–1832) that supply creates its own demand.

[**1817** D. RICARDO *Princ. Polit. Econ.* xix. 401 Is the following quite consistent with M. Say's principle?] **1934** *Encycl. Social Sciences* XII. 351/1 At any given time in one market area there could be only a single price relationship of each good to any other good there offered in exchange, so long as competition held sway. This tendency involved the fixation not only of an identity of offering price among different sellers of the given good to the same (prospective) buyer but also of an identity of the offering price to different (prospective) buyers of the given good from the same seller. This is the substance of what has been denominated Say's law. **1936** J. M. KEYNES *Gen. Theory Employment* iii. 26 Say's law, that the aggregate demand price of output as a whole is equal to its aggregate supply price for all volumes of output. **1969** *Daily Tel.* 21 Apr. 14/2 If Say's Law had been true there could have been no unemployment. **1972** T. SOWELL *Say's Law* i. 3 The idea that supply creates its own demand—Say's Law—appears on the surface to be one of the simplest propositions in economics.

say-so, *sb.* Delete 'Now *dial.* and *U.S.*' and add further examples. Also in extended senses: (*a*) an affirmation or assertion; (*b*) authority, authorization; (*c*) the right of consultation, a 'voice' (in some decision). Freq. in phr. *on the say-so of* (a person): according to, on the authority of (that person).

1824 *Niles' Reg.* 10 Apr. 84/2 The whole number of republican members in 1824 (on the *say-so* of Messrs. Gales and Seaton) is 216. **1902** W. N. HARBEN *Abner Daniel* 5, I think I've got a right..to have a say-so in this kind of a trade. **1902** S. E. WHITE *Blazed Trail* 195 In questions of policy mine is the say-so every trip. **1924** 'W. FABIAN' *Sailors' Wives* xvi. 186 'Give 'em to me.' 'Not without Bob's sayso.' **1937** *N. & Q.* CLXXII. 305/1 The labour of scholars is nothing to them; they prefer the say-so of some casual maker of legend long since disproved. **1947** J. MULGAN *Report on Experience* v. 53, I expect major-generals and upwards have a good deal of say-so. **1956** D. MEADOWS *Eliz. Quintet* iii. 204 Perhaps he truly believed the rest of the story—on the say-so of his assistant. **1967** *Boston Sunday Herald* 30 Apr. (Bedding Suppl.) 9/1 Another place to give your husband more say-so is in the selection of a bed. **1978** S. BRILL *Teamsters* ii. 69 Giacalone and Provenzano had set up the meeting and the subsequent murder on the say-so of higher-ups in organized crime.

‖ **saz** (saz). [Turk., ad. Pers. *sāz* musical instrument.] A stringed instrument similar to the tamboura, found in Turkey, North Africa, and the Near East.

1870 C. ENGEL *Descr. Catal. Musical Instr. in S. Kensington Museum* 26 *Saz*, a small kind of *tamboura*... The *saz* is chiefly used by the *Sho'ara*, i.e. 'Poets', who are itinerant musicians and bands of the Mussulmans. *Double saz*, inlaid with various woods and mother-of-pearl. **1918** A. A. STANLEY *Catal. of Stearns Collection of Musical Instr.* IV. 150 *Saz*, tanbur type... Algeria... Slender neck with two flat heads. Wire strings. *Ibid.* 155 *Saz*... Egypt. Pear-shaped body of some soft wood. **1957** T. SLESSOR *First Overland* iv. 48 Umtaz played his *saz* and sang. It was an instrument like an Elizabethan mandolin, and gave a strumming, jangling accompaniment to the folk-songs. **1969** J. RATHBONE *With my Knives I know I'm Good* xiii. 103 We.. sang Turkish and Russian songs to a saz which he played well. **1977** *Early Music* July 437/1 The Early Music Consort of Melbourne (medieval harp, saz, lute, rauschpfeife, [etc.]). **1980** M. BAR-ZOHAR *Deadly Document* ix. 158 The music of the strolling accordion and *saz* players.

‖ **saza** (sa·za). [ad. Luganda *'ssaza*.] In Uganda, an administrative area; a county.

1950 *Times* 13 Feb. 3/2 Exempted from payment are those persons who, in the opinion of the Resident, are entirely free from blame—that is to say, non-natives and the inhabitants of eight sazas which throughout the disturbances were trouble-free. **1955** *Times* 25 Aug. 6/5 Mr. Kintu is a saza chief. **1958** E. WINTER in Middleton & Tait *Tribes without Rulers* 158 Toro as a whole, is divided into seven large administrative areas called sazas which may be translated as counties. **1964** C. WILLOCK *Enormous Zoo* iv. 58 The *saza* chief—an important man in the local [Ugandan] hierarchy—turned out a posse.

Sazarac (sæ·zəræk). orig. and chiefly *U.S.* Also **Sazerac.** [Origin unknown.] A cocktail consisting of whisky, pernod or absinthe, bitters, and syrup, served usu. with a slice of lemon. Also *attrib.*, as *Sazarac cocktail*.

1941 *Louisiana: Guide to State* (Writers' Program) 230 The most celebrated of New Orleans cocktails—the Sazerac—is a mixture of whisky, bitters, and sugar, served in a glass mixed with absinthe. **1946** C. H. BAKER *Gentleman's Compan.* II. 122 The best drinks produced in New Orleans stick to the ancient simple formula—and please, please, never try to vary it; for if you do you'll not be drinking a true Sazarac. **1958** E. DUNDY *Dud Avocado* I. i. 18 So many marvellous new drinks..sazaracs and slings and heaven knows what else. **1961** F. CRANE *Reluctant Sleuth* viii. 66 Regan had liked Sazarac cocktails. **1963** M. MALIM *Pagoda Tree* xxii. 145 Then came the sazaracs. I remember having a word with Canthrop B beside the bar quite early on. He took charge of the bar, to superintend the mixing of this Fine Old Southern cocktail. 'I'm doubling up on the absinthe' he said gleefully. **1978** G. VIDAL *Kalki* iv. 93 We had each polished off a pair of Sazerac cocktails, a local killer [in New Orleans].

‖ **S-bahn** (e·s bān). [Ger., abbrev. of (*stadt*) *schnellbahn* (urban) fast railway.] In some German cities. a fast (sub)urban railway line or system.

1962 I. FLEMING *Living Daylights* in *Octopussy* (1966) 79 Feeling more encouraged, he took the S-Bahn back into the city. **1974** *Encycl. Brit. Macropædia* II. 851/2 East Berlin runs the S-Bahn..elevated railway system started in 1871 as a connecting system to a rail net in and out of the city. [**1976** P. R. WHITE *Planning for Public Transport* iv. 74 The creation of links across city centres..to enable S-bahn trains to offer better accessibility within the central area. **1980** G. SEYMOUR *Contract* v. 63 We should take the U-Bahn to Alexander Platz, then the S-Bahn.

S-band: see *S 12. **S-bend:** see *S 2 c.

scab, *sb.* Add: **4. b.** (Earlier and further examples.) Also, in extended uses: a person who refuses to join a strike or who takes over the work of a striker; a blackleg; a strike-breaker.

1777 *Bonner & Middleton's Bristol Jrnl.* 5 July, To the Public. Whereas the Master Cordwainers have gloried, that there has been a Demur amongst the Men's and Women's Men;—we have the Pleasure to inform them, that Matters are amicably settled... The Conflict would not been [*sic*] so sharp had not there been so many dirty Scabs; no Doubt but timely Notice will be taken of them. **1792** in A. Aspinall *Early Eng. Trade Unions* (1949) 84 What is a scab? He is to his *trade* what a traitor is to his *country*... He first sells the journeymen, and is himself afterwards sold in his turn by the masters, till at last he is despised by both and deserted by all. **1806** *Trial of Boot & Shoemakers* (Federal Soc. Journeymen Cordwainers, U.S.) 74, I concluded at that time I would turn a *scab*, unknown to them, and I would continue my work and not let them know of it. **1889** C. H. SALMONS *Burlington Strike* 259 The man who takes the place of another when that other engages in a struggle with a corporation, is a 'scab'. **1903** W. T. MILLS *Struggle for Existence* xxxv. 493 The 'scab' is no longer the unorganized and hungry worker, waiting at the factory gate. **1926** [see *bitter-ender* s.v. *BITTER- *a.* and *adv.*]. **1938** *Sun* (Baltimore) 8 Sept. 3/1 He had instructed pickets not to call non-strikers 'finks' or 'scabs' or other epithets. **1974** *Socialist Worker* 26 Oct. 13/2, 180 women walked out. But 70 stayed in... The scabs soon found out what it was like to be hated.

attrib. and *Comb.* **1850** *Morning Chron.* 11 Feb. 5/6 Having thus given the characteristics and conditions of the 'legal', or honourable trade, I next turn my inquiry to the state of the labouring men, women, and children employed by the slop-masters, who are distinguished from the 'wages' (or legal) shops by the terms '*illegal*', '*scab*', or '*slaughtershop*' *keepers*. **1926** *Socialist Rev.* June 10 The Labour Press.. cannot descend to 'scab' printing. **1940** M. LOWRY *Let.* 7 May (1967) 31 Two years as a scab lavatory attendant in Saskatchewan. **1958** *Spectator* 15 Aug. 225/2 British writers, forced to become scab-labour, are undermining it, completely against their wishes. **1977** C. MCCULLOUGH *Thorn Birds* iii. 60, I suppose some scab contractor undercut me.

5. scab weed *N.Z.*, a low-growing plant of the genus *Raoulia*, adapted to poor conditions.

1927 L. COCKAYNE in R. Speight et al. *Nat. Hist. Canterbury* 143 *Raoulia lutescens*... Scabweed. **1933** *Discovery* Sept. 292/1 The bare land patchily covered by flat 'scab weed' looks horribly diseased. **1955** J. K. BAXTER *Fire & Anvil* iii. 78 It survives many droughts..like the scabweed in Central Otago.

scab, *v.* Add: **3. a.** (Earlier and later examples.) Also with *it* as quasi-obj. and *trans.* in phr. *to scab a job*: to perform, or employ another to perform, the job of a striking worker.

1806 *Trial of Boot & Shoemakers* (Federal Soc. Journeymen Cordwainers, U.S.) 75 Their business was to watch the *Jers* [*sc.* journeymen] that they did not *scab* it. **1889** C. H. SALMONS *Burlington Strike* 357 The men..declared that they had never scabbed a day in their lives. **1895** *Rep. on Chicago Strike June–July, 1894* (U.S. Strike Commission) 308 If there is a strike ordered I will be damned if I am going to scab. **1898** *Scribner's Mag.* Oct. 445/2, I won't scab any man's job. **1932** E. WILSON *Devil take Hindmost* xxi. 223 Several speakers protest..that the companies only want to get them out so that they can scab the job. **1969** *Times* 30 Oct. 10/7 Frantic calls to friends.. summoned..a driver who was prepared to scab as a special favour. **1969** *Daily Tel.* 16 May 27/7 Peaceful pickets outside all entrances will discourage all students from scabbing on the strike.

b. *trans.* To treat or label (a person or a firm employing scab labour) as a scab; to ostracize (a person who is a scab). *rare.*

1806 *Trial of Boot & Shoemakers* (Federal Soc. Journeymen Cordwainers, U.S.) 73 They told me if I did not come to the body, I was liable to be *scabb'd*. *Ibid.* 77 In a little time after this his shop was scabbed. **1888** *Montreal Daily Herald* 21 Feb. 1/5 Engineers and others who refused to hoist or handle coal during the late effort to 'scab' the collieries. **1922** F. B. YOUNG *Pilgrim's Rest* vi. 409 [The rioting strikers] went away, saying they'd come back again and scab us to-night.

scabbard, *sb.*¹ Add: **1. a.** Also, a sheath in which a rifle, submachine gun, or similar firearm is kept.

1923 *Dialect Notes* V. 220 *Scabbard*, holster, any leather sheath for a weapon. **1941** E. HEMINGWAY *For Whom Bell Tolls* xxi. 264 From the scabbard on the right of his saddle projected the stock and the long oblong clip of a short automatic rifle. **1979** *Navajo Times* (Window Rock, Arizona) 24 May 19/2 (Advt.), Truck seat cover. Rifle scabbard & map pouch!

scabbing, *vbl. sb.* Add: **3. a.** The action of SCAB *v.* 3 in Dict. and Suppl.; refusal to strike on the part of a worker or employment of scab labour by a firm. Also *fig.*

1944 *Sun* (Baltimore) 28 Nov. 9/2 The worker who strikes while the war is on is guilty of scabbing. **1956** *Ibid.* 2 Feb. 18/1 Under a PSC order..the company would not be in a position of 'scabbing'. **1973** *Telegraph* (Brisbane) 28 July 5/2 In trades union circles the deadliest of sins is 'scabbing' while your union is on strike.

scabby, *a.* Add: **1. a.** *scabby mouth* (Austral. and N.Z.), a viral disease of sheep characterized by ulceration around the mouth.

1938 J. R. GREIG et al. *Hutyra's Special Path. & Therapeutics* (ed. 4) 579 (*heading*) Lip and leg ulceration, scabby mouth. **1950** *N.Z. Jrnl. Agric.* Aug. 100/2 On farms where scabby mouth occurs each new crop of lambs should be vaccinated, and this is most conveniently done at marking. **1966** V. G. COLE *Dis. Sheep* 217 Scabby mouth can be transmitted to the hands of persons handling affected sheep.

scabies. Now always with pronunc. (skē¹·bīz).

scabland (skæ·blænd). *U.S. Physical Geogr.* [f. SCAB *sb.* + LAND *sb.*] Flat, elevated land consisting of igneous rock with a patchy covering of poor, thin soil and little vegetation, and deeply scarred by channels of glacial or fluvioglacial origin; *spec.* that forming part of the Columbia Plateau, Washington State, U.S.A. Freq. *pl.*

1923 J. H. BRETZ in *Bull. Geol. Soc. Amer.* XXXIV. 577 The 'Scablands' are lowlands among the groups of 'Palouse Hills', plane in a general way, but diversified by a multiplicity of irregular and commonly anastomosing channels and rock-basins eroded in basalt, and containing meadows, swamps, and lakes... The local name refers to the absence of soil over much of these tracts, the basalt outcropping in ledges and over considerable level areas. **1923** —— in *Jrnl. Geol.* XXXI. 617 The terms 'scabland' and 'scabrock' are used in the Pacific Northwest to describe areas where denudation has removed or prevented the accumulation of a mantle of soil, and the underlying rock is exposed or covered largely with its own coarse, angular débris. *Ibid.* 620 The channeled scablands are the erosive record of large, high-gradient, glacier-born streams. **1943** *Science* 10 Sept. 229/1 The rock basins of the scablands are found in the wider channels particularly, and rock basins are an almost universal feature of glaciated regions. It is the channels with their included low mesas which are the unique feature of the scablands. **1956** C. RELANDER *Drummers & Dreamers* 235 The River People were virtually forgotten in their deep desolation of sagebrush, basaltic cliffs, raw umber hills and scabland. **1966** *N.Z. Jrnl. Geol. & Geophysics* IX. 130 (*heading*) Antarctic scablands. **1976** C. L. MATSCH *N. Amer. & Great Ice Age* vi. 74 At peak stage Lake Missoula had a surface area of about 7,500 km² and contained an estimated 2,000 km³ of water. All this water is thought to have discharged westward in a matter of a few days... This great flood moved boulders with diameters greater than 10 m and scoured a system of coulees across the Columbia Plateau. This great tract of flood-eroded topography is called the channeled scablands.

scabrous, *a.* Add: Now freq. with pronunc. (skæ·brəs). **1. c.** Encrusted, begrimed. Chiefly *U.S.*

1939 *Listener* 19 Jan. 157/1 A once bewitching villa, now scabrous, awaits the knacker. *a* **1961** J. REYNOLDS in Webster s.v., [The] shell of the house is scabrous with lichen and mildew. **1962** P. H. JOHNSON *Error of Judgement* xxxiii. 240 In this early glow, the tattered and scabrous paintwork on the porticos looked like a covering of dead leaves, ivy, or virginia creeper, brittle at the end of autumn. **1967** T. KENEALLY *Bring Larks & Heroes* ii. 16 In its [*sc.* a hut's] bay of scabrous timber, it was altogether a poor comment on Halloran's vehemence. **1969** *N.Y. Rev. Books* 2 Jan. 14/1 Trudging over countless guts of cement that ran like slag in Gehenna, I stuffed my scabrous shoes with newspapers.

4. (Later examples.) Now freq. used in various extended senses: nastily abusive, disgusting, repulsive.

Cf. quot. 1862 under sense 1 b.

1951 M. KENNEDY *Lucy Carmichael* II. i. 79 One shouldn't believe a word Emil says. I ventured to ask them.. about Terrific Charles, because Emil is always particularly scabrous about him. **1969** *N.Y. Rev. Books* 16 Jan. 32/4 Without going into scabrous detail, might he not have given us just a teeny hint as to *why* 'the experience convinced me the union was indeed for decentralization'? **1973** *Times* 24 May 19/1 [Scandals] create hysteria because they appeal to a scabrous and irrational element in the human mind. **1979** *London Rev. Bks.* 25 Oct. 10/1 His propaganda pieces grow more outrageously scabrous.

scabrously, *adv.* (Later example.)

1977 *N.Y. Rev. Books* 14 Apr. 8/2 The first of the book's three sections, in which a non-existent and uninhabited Ibansk is carefully and at times scabrously described.

scacchic (skæ·kik), *a. rare.* [f. It. *scacchi* chess + -IC.] Of or pertaining to chess.

1860 in W. Fiske *Chess Tales* (1912) 159 Stern old fellows were these scacchic sages! They considered the laws of chess as inviolable as those of the Medes and Persians. *Ibid.* 163 Since first the scacchic art was brought from the land of India. **1959** *Information Bull. Libr. Congress* 27 Apr. 238 The Chess Club has elected the following officers to guide its scacchic destinies during 1959.

scad⁷ (skæd). *colloq.* (orig. *U.S.*). Also **skad.** [Origin unknown.] **a.** A dollar. Usu. *pl.* in sense 'money'.

1858 *Hutching's Mag.* Aug. 85/2 Why he seed Bill and lifted him two scads. **1884** E. W. NYE *Baled Hay* 59 We have mercenary motives... We desire the scads. **1902** W. HARBEN *Abner Daniel* ix. 70 Ef he kin possibly raise the scads to pay the tax. **1909** *Amer. Mag.* Nov. 1 This land of our dads..is a dinger at nailing the scads. **1933** J. V. ALLEN *Cowboy Lore* IV. 154 He would deal for you both day and night Or as long as he had a scad. **1959** E. POUND *Thrones* xcvii. 22 Canute opposing Byzantium, 20 scads to the dinar, 100 scads to the mark (of accountancy).

b. Chiefly *pl.* A large amount; 'heaps'.

1869 *Overland Monthly* III. 131 A Texan never has a great quantity of anything, but he has 'scads' of it..or 'Scadoodles'. **1904** W. H. SMITH *Promoters* ii. 52 What did England do when she found she could raise scads of opium in India, but had no market for it? **1923** M. S. WATTS *Luther Nichols* II. iv. 214 The old girl surely did have it—scads of it. **1931** E. LINKLATER *Juan in Amer.* II. xvi. 176 And the pay? Skads of dough. Oodles and oodles of money. **1950** O. NASH *Family Reunion* 89 There's a scad o' things that to make a house a home it takes. **1956** 'N. SHUTE' *Beyond Black Stump* x. 297 It's water... Skads and skads of it, under Lucinda Station. Clear, cool water. **1977** D. BAGLEY *Enemy* xv. 121 He's installed a scad of microprocessors in that control board. **1980** *Telegraph* (Brisbane) 9 Apr. 53/6 They supply pay envelopes in scads to clients.

scaf. Restrict † *Obs.* to sense 2 and add: Also **scaffie, scaffy, scaph, skaffie. 1.** (Later examples.) Also *attrib.* in *scaffy boat.* Now *Hist.*

1781 *Aberdeen Jrnl.* 29 Oct., A large boat or scaff was put ashore two miles to the eastward of this place. **1877** E. W. H. HOLDSWORTH *Sea Fisheries* 168 The Buckie boats, known as 'Scaffs' or 'Scaffy boats', are of an entirely different build from the other Scotch craft. **1906** H. W. SMYTH *Mast & Sail* v. 100 From Portsoy westwards along the Banff and Moray coasts, and round the eastern seaboard of Ross-shire, until within the last forty years, the 'Skaffie' or 'Buckie Skaffie', as it was often known, was universally used in the herring fishing. *Ibid.* 436 *Skaffie, or scaith*, a type of Scotch lugger with raked stem and stern posts, used principally on the coastline between Frasersburgh and Dornoch, and apparently of Norse origin. **1914, 1927** [see *FIFIE, FIFIE]. **1959** *Banffshire Jrnl.* 6 Jan. 4 Open sailing boats, lug-sail rigged, called herring luggers or more familiarly 'Scaffies'.

scaffold, *sb.* Add: **B. 1. a.** (Later *fig.* example.)

1889 G. M. HOPKINS *Poems* (1967) 107 But man—we, scaffold of score brittle bones.

7. Also, a framework upon which tobacco is dried.

1784 J. SMYTH *Tour U.S.A.* II. 134 When the tobacco plants are cut and brought to the scaffolds. **1886** C. G. W. LOCK *Tobacco* 75 Some prefer hanging the tobacco on scaffolds in the field until it is ready to be put in the barn and cured by the fire. **1888** *Encycl. Brit.* XXIII. 424/2 Red shipping qualities [of tobacco] are prepared by leaving the cut stems either in the field or hung on scaffolds in the barns for a few days to wilt and wither in the air.

scaffy (ska·fi). *Sc. colloq.* Also **scavvy.** [dim. of SCAVENGER *sb.*] A street sweeper; a dustman. Also *attrib.*

1853 W. BLAIR *Chron. Aberbrothock* 19 Hecklers, an' wabsters, an' baxters, an' scaffies, an' wives, an' bairns, dowgs an' cats. **1876** J. SMITH *Archie & Bess* 25 Scaffies and leeries crackin' like pea-guns. **1892** W. M. ADAMSON *Betty Blether's Corr.* 74 Tin cans intendit for the scaffy cairt. **1918** *Kelso Chronicle* 1 Nov. 2 She often is too late for the Scaffy Bucket. **1931** J. HALL *Holy Man* iii. 37 Geordie, the road scavvy, was wearily trundling his little hand-cart up the steep slope of the village street. **1933** J. GRAY *Lowrie* 41 Dere's da scaffy fur takkin awa ony coarn o' bruck an' ess. **1967** *Buchan Observer* 7 Feb. 2 Not up in the morning early enough to catch the 'scaffy cairt'. **1978** *Scotsman* 30 June 10/7 The scaffies are now under the Environmental Health Department.

scaffy: see *SCAF.

scag (skæg). *U.S. slang.* Also **skag.** [Origin unknown.] **1.** A cigarette; a cigarette stub.

1915 *Dialect Notes* IV. 235 *Scag*, cigarette stub. **1928** *Amer. Speech* III. 454 *Skag*, a cigarette; to smoke. **1936** *Nat. Geogr. Mag.* LXIX. 778/2 A cigarette is a 'skag' (and cadets may not smoke in public).

2. Heroin.

1967 'G. BAGBY' *Corpse Candle* (1968) ix. 121 Acid, grass, skag? **1973** E. BULLINS *Theme is Blackness* 152 Most of the guys that we usta swing with are gone, man. In jail, on wine or scag. *Ibid.* 157 This scag they been sellin' me lately makes me hear funny. **1976** R. CONDON *Whisper of Axe* I. iv. 18 Addicts, prostitutes, skag merchants..the amoral and the lost. **1977** N. ADAM *Triplehip Cracksman* xiii. 138 I'm no junkie myself, never touched the scag, never even used the White Dragon Pearl.

scala (skē¹·lă). *Anat.* [L., = 'ladder'.] Each of two passages (the *scala tympani* below and the *scala vestibuli* above) into which the spiral tube of the cochlea is divided by a bony spiral lamina and which communicate at the apex of the spiral; also, the *scala media* or central duct of the cochlea, situated between these two passages and shut off from them by two membranes.

1712 *Bibliotheca Anat., Med., Chir.* II. 214/2 We have discover'd two Channels into which the Cochlea is divided by the Septum, called Scalæ, or Ladders; one of wnich..is called the Scala Tympani: But the other..is called the Scala Vestibuli. **1803** C. BELL *Anat. Human Body* III. 430 Or it [*sc.* the vibrating motion] must pass from the scala vestibuli into the scala tympani. **1872** *Gray's Anat.* (ed. 6) 596 The space between the membrane of Reissner and membrana basilaris is generally described as the Scala media, Canalis membranacea, or Canalis cochleæ, and this is the nomenclature which will be used here. **1902** D. J. CUNNINGHAM *Text-bk. Anat.* 717 The two scalæ communicate with each other through the opening of the helicotrema at the apex of the cochlea. **1945** [see *REISSNER]. **1974** *Encycl. Brit. Macropædia* V. 1123/2 The interior of the cochlea is divided longitudinally into three spiral ramps or scalae: the scala vestibuli,..the scala tympani,..and the scala media.

scalable, *a.* Restrict *rare* to sense in Dict. and add: **II. 2.** Capable of being measured or graded according to a scale.

1936 *Psychol. Monogr.* XLVII. I. 15 A few [traits] seem common enough to be regarded as comparable from one individual to another. These might be called common or scalable traits. **1944** *Amer. Sociol. Rev.* IX. 147/1 The example..of desire to go to school is a fictitious version of data that have actually proved scalable for the Army. **1968** W. A. SCOTT in Lindzey & Aronson *Handbk. Social Psychol.* (ed. 2) II. xi. 222 A measure of the degree to which the set of items is scalable, that is, represents a unidimensional attribute. **1977** R. H. BROWN in Douglas & Johnson *Existential Sociol.* ii. 81 The questionnaire was particularly attractive as a measuring device because it standardizes responses, making them easily scalable and retrievable, in principle by anyone.

3. Capable of being changed in scale. *rare.*

1977 *Jrnl. R. Soc. Arts* CXXV. 770/1 Such lasers are scaleable since large volumes could be pumped uniformly.

Hence **sca·lability**, the property of being scalable.

1944 *Amer. Sociol. Rev.* IX. 141/2 It may well be that the formal analysis for scalability may help clarify uncertain areas of content. **1959** *Psychol. Rev.* LXVI. 51/2 Ordinarily, when scalability is found, it is assumed that a unidimensional continuum exists. **1960** BROWN & GILMAN in J. A. Fishman *Readings Sociol. of Lang.* (1968) 270 We tested all 28 items for scalability and found that a subset of them made a fairly good scale. **1978** *Sci. Amer.* Nov. 44/2 It took demonstrations of the scalability of the technology and tests of improved beam focusing..to catalyze an effort that led to support by the AEC.

scalar, *a.* and *sb.* Add: Now usu. with pronunc. (skē¹·lăɹ). **A.** *adj.* **2.** (Earlier and further examples).

1846 W. R. HAMILTON in *Phil. Mag.* XXIX. 26 The algebraically real part may receive, according to the question in which it occurs, all values contained on the one scale of progression of numbers from negative to positive infinity; we shall call it therefore the scalar part, or simply the scalar of the quaternion, and shall form its symbol by prefixing, to the symbol of the quaternion, the characteristic Scal., or simply S. **1911** *Encycl. Brit.* XXVII. 962/2 The mass of a body, the pressure of a gas, the charge of an electrified conductor, are instances of scalar magnitudes. **1932** R. GANS *Vector Analysis* ii. 58 Let W..be a scalar..property of a field, and let it be regarded as a function of the position and of the time. **1964** N. N. HANCOCK *Matrix Analysis Electr. Machinery* ii. 18 A 'scalar' matrix is a diagonal matrix in which all the elements on the principal diagonal are equal.

3. Of or pertaining to a musical scale (SCALE *sb.*³ 4).

1928 G. COOKE *Theory of Music* ii. 18 One cannot.. over-emphasise the importance of these groups of notes in the theoretic study of scalar development. *Ibid.* vi. 77 The variety inherent in modulation and scalar variety. **1946** R. BLESH *Shining Trumpets* ii. 25 The basic material is recast in its scalar compass and its tonal intervals. **1959** M. T. WILLIAMS *Art of Jazz* (1960) xi. 106 Sliding tones peculiar to the scalar and harmonic structure. **1966** *New Statesman* 11 Feb. 204/1 The integration of triadic and scalar elements within a serial or non-tonal field.

4. Of or pertaining to a graduated scale (SCALE *sb.*³ 9).

1959 G. D. MITCHELL *Sociology* 130 Very often there is an identity of functional and scalar status. **1974** G. LEECH *Semantics* ii. 21 A selection from indefinitely many possible scales, which in any case would only provide for associative meaning in so far as it is explicable in scalar terms.

B. *sb.* **1.** (Earlier and later examples.) More widely, a quantity having magnitude but no direction, and representable by a single real number.

1846 [see sense 2* of the adj.]. **1903** [see *NON-DIRECTIONAL *a.* (*sb.*)]. **1932** R. GANS *Vector Analysis* i. 2 We shall denote scalars by ordinary type and vectors by heavy type. **1965** PATTERSON & RUTHERFORD *Elem. Abstr. Algebra* v. 145 By a scalar we shall mean an entity determined by a single real number and by a vector we shall mean an entity determined by both a positive real number, measuring magnitude, and a direction in space.

2. *attrib.* (some of the following may be regarded as collocations of the adj.): **scalar field**, a map from a space to the real line (see quot. 1932); **scalar function**, a function whose value is a scalar; **scalar multiplication,** multiplication of a vector by a scalar to give another vector; **scalar product** = *inner product* s.v. *INNER *a.* (*sb.*²) 1 k; **scalar triple product**, a scalar function of three three-vectors $((a_1, a_2, a_3), (b_1, b_2, b_3), (c_1, c_2, c_3))$ which can be calculated as $(a_1 b_2 c_3 + b_1 c_2 a_3 + c_1 a_2 b_3 - a_1 c_2 b_3 - b_1 a_2 c_3 - c_1 b_2 a_3)$, being the volume of the parallelepiped which has the three vectors as three coincident edges.

1932 R. GANS *Vector Analysis* i. 1 The field is called a scalar field or a vector field according as the quantity associated with the field is a scalar or a vector. **1959** M. R. Spiegel *Vector Analysis* i. 3 The temperature at any point within or on the earth's surface at a certain time defines a scalar field. **1974** G. Reece tr. *Hund's Hist. Quantum Theory* xv. 207 It was therefore a major advance when Pauli and Victor Weisskopf developed the quantum theory of a scalar field. **1956** A. A. Townsend *Struct. Turbulent Shear Flow* iii. 35 The double-correlation function depends only on a single scalar function. **1972** A. G. Howson *Handbk. Terms Algebra & Anal.* xxvi. 126 Functions such as *f* are often referred to as vector-valued functions and are denoted by symbols printed in bold type so as to distinguish them from real-valued or scalar functions. **1901** Gibbs & Wilson *Vector Analysis* i. 13 The laws which govern addition, subtraction, and scalar multiplication of vectors are identical with those governing these operations in ordinary scalar algebra. **1968** A. P. Armit *Advanced Level Vectors* ii. 25 (*heading*) Scalar multiplication of a vector..in terms of cartesian components. **1878** Scalar product [see Vector 2]. **1932** R. Gans *Vector Analysis* i. 17 By the scalar product of two vectors **A** and **B** we mean a scalar of magnitude equal to the product of the absolute values and the cosine of the angle between the vectors. **1941, 1968** Scalar product [see *inner *a.* (*sb.*²) 1 k]. **1901** Gibbs & Wilson *Vector Analysis* ii. 68 The second triple product is the scalar product of two vectors, of which one is itself a vector product, as $\mathbf{A}\cdot(\mathbf{B}\times\mathbf{C})$ or $(\mathbf{A}\times\mathbf{B})\cdot\mathbf{C}$. This sort of product has a scalar value and consequently is often called the scalar triple product. **1959** M. R. Spiegel *Vector Analysis* ii. 17 The product $\mathbf{A}\cdot(\mathbf{B}\times\mathbf{C})$ is sometimes called the scalar triple product or box product and may be denoted by [**ABC**]. **1964** E. Œ. Wolstenholme *Elem. Vectors* ii. 38 If **a, b, c** are three vectors, any pair of them may be multiplied vectorially to form a new vector **d**, the third of the original vectors may then be multiplied by **d**, either scalarly to form what is known as a scalar triple product, or vectorially to form..the vector triple product.

scalarly (skē^i^·lăɹli), *adv. Math.* [f. Scalar *sb.* + -ly².] In such a way as to yield a scalar.

1964 [see *scalar triple product* s.v. *scalar *sb.* 2].

scald, *sb.*⁵ (Later examples.)

1909 G. B. Shaw *Press Cuttings* 37 G'lang, you young scald: if I had you here I'd teach you manners. **1919** —— *O'Flaherty V.C.* 179 What do you mean, you lying young scald, by telling me you were going to fight agen the English?

scalded, *ppl. a.*¹ Add: **a.** Also in proverbial phr. *like a scalded cat.* Hence *scalded-cat raid* (see quot. 1945).

1934 [see *mark *sb.*¹ 12 e]. **1943** *Times* 6 Nov. 2/1 The *Luftwaffe*..were now using a new type of twin-engine fighter-bomber... From the French coast to Westminster Bridge was a distance of 85 miles. In and out they flashed across it at their fastest speeds—like scalded cats. **1945** L. E. O. Charlton *Britain at War* IV. 80 When a small force of enemy raiders crossed the coast and penetrated towards London on November 8th, 1943,..three of them were destroyed. One of the aircraft brought down was..one of the new twin-engine fighter-bombers described by Sir Archibald Sinclair, Secretary of State for Air, a few days previously when he spoke of 'scalded cat' raids on London and the South Coast. **1977** *Hot Car* Oct. 75/3 We have driven a converted V6 and it certainly went like a scalded cat. **1977** C. McCullough *Thorn Birds* ii. 45 Meggie hopped out like a scalded cat and dressed herself without even asking for help. **1980** *Herald* (Melbourne) 9 Apr. 7/4 How does it go, old boy? Like a scalded cat.

c. Of land: so poor as to support little if any vegetation. *Austral.*

1936 K. C. McKeown *Insect Wonders of Australia* xx. 163 The eggs are deposited, as a general rule, upon the 'scalded plains' of the interior, but the insects will avail themselves of almost any area of hard bare ground. **1948** N. C. W. Beadle *Vegetation & Pastures of Western New South Wales* vi. 58 Scalded surfaces are in general devoid of vegetation, even in the best seasons. **1977** *Weekly Times* (Melbourne) 19 Jan. 17/2 Deep gullies and scalded country are evidence of the worst abuses of valuable farming country.

scald-headed, *a.* (Earlier (*fig.*) example.)

1802 C. Wilmot *Let.* 19 Oct. in *Irish Peer on Continent* (1920) 102 Grim scaldheaded Mountains.

scalding, *vbl. sb.* **1. d.** (Earlier U.S. example.)

1865 *Trans. Illinois Agric. Soc.* V. 208 Here is no swaying of trees to the east, no scalding of the west side of the trunks in the sun.

scale, *sb.*¹ Add: **1.** For † *Obs.* read *Obs.* except *S. Afr.* and add later examples.

1946 P. Abrahams *Mine Boy* iii. 26 Joseph nodded, slapped Xuma heartily on the back and offered him a scale of beer... He smiled and took the scale. Xuma put the scale to his lips, then passed it to Daddy. **1953** P. Lanham *Blanket Boy's Moon* v. iii. 274 Drink a scale of fine home-brewed kaffir beer with us. **1969** *Post* (Golden City, S. Afr.) 6 Apr. 14 Gave her R1 and told her to buy a scale of KB from Mathebula. **1970** *Drum* Oct. 8, I found myself firmly grasping a plastic scale.

4. *to turn the scale* (earlier example).

1777 P. Thicknesse *Year's Journey* I. iii. 18 As he is a good seaman, and has a clean, convenient, nay an elegant vessel, I would rather turn the scale in his favour.

5. (Later example.)

1935 [see *Algol¹].

6. *attrib.* and *Comb.*, as *scale maker* (earlier example), *man*; **scale house** *U.S.*, a place in which large scales, as for weighing animals, are kept.

1754 *South Carolina Gaz.* 5 Feb. 3/1 A Scale-House Beam, Scales and Weights, compleat. **1870** *Trans. Illinois Agric. Soc.* VII. 442 In this division of the stock yards there are three scale houses. **1885** *Rep. Indian Affairs* (U.S.) 80 To the southeast..is our large cattle corral..with scales and scale-house. **1655** in *Suffolk County* (Mass.) *Deeds* (1885) III. 209, I John Saers of Casco bay scale maker..Haue bargained & Sold..one Island. **1783** in L. Chalkley *Chron. Scotch-Irish Settlement Virginia* (1912) I. 232 It is certified that the scale man is Peter Hane. **1930** *Amer. Speech* VI. 13 [Sugar beets] first go to the washer man, then to the hopper which rests upon the weighing apparatus, operated by the scale man.

scale, *sb.*² Add: **7. c.** *U.S. slang.* A coin; money.

1872 Schele de Vere *Americanisms* 296 Among the less generally known terms [for money] are..*wherewith, shadscales*, or *scales* 'for short'. **1874** B. F. Taylor *World on Wheels* 28 Promise him a 'scale'—scale, skilling, shilling. **1889** J. S. Farmer *Americanisms* 472/2 *Scales*, a common term for money; an abbreviation of Shadscales. **1929** *Amer. Speech* V. 152 The waitress received much scale at the hotel.

12. scale-fish, (*a*) (later examples); (*b*) (earlier example); **scale-reading,** the interpretation of the pattern of scales on a fish as an indicator of its age, history, etc.; an examination of scales for this purpose; so **scale-reader.**

1856 J. Reynolds *Peter Gott* xix. 254 Four hundred quintals of fish, heavily salted, such as are in demand for the use of the negroes on the plantations. These fish are called scale fish; they consist of hake and haddock. **1936** *Discovery* Jan. 16/1 The food of the natives consisted of various animals..but never scale fish, which seem to have been the object of a curious taboo. **1967** *Nat. Fisherman* Nov. 11-c The term 'scalefish' is used in the Bahamas for fish proper as opposed to shellfish and crustaceans. **1930** G. H. Nall *Life Sea Trout* iii. 28 It is the business of the scale reader to decipher how it [*sc.* the scale] reflects the growth, and to explain how this provides a clue to the life history of the individual fish. **1968** B. Vesey-Fitzgerald *World of Fishes* ii. 30 An expert scale-reader can tell the age of a fish accurately. **1912** *Salmon & Trout Mag.* No. 4. p. i (Advt.), The latest and most authoritative publication on the new science of scale reading. **1938** B. Curtis *Life Story Fish* iii. 29 Using scale-readings, he can construct the life-history of a species with far fewer specimens than he could in any other way. **1971** D. Mills *Salmon & Trout* xii. 281 The data from such scale readings can then be incorporated into the construction of growth curves.

scale, *sb.*³ Add: **5. c.** *Psychol.* A graded series in terms of which the measurements of such phenomena as sensations, attitudes, or mental attributes are expressed; sometimes preceded by the name of the person to whom a particular scale is attributed (as *Binet scale*; cf. *Guttman scale), or some other qualifying word.

1898 G. F. Stout *Man. Psychol.* I. ii. § 5. 31 Thus, if we have a scale of increasing gradations of intensity, we may take as our point of departure any given intensity in the scale. We can then arrange other intensities in relation to this, proceeding by intervals which we judge to be equal. **1917** Pintner & Paterson (*title*) Scale of performance tests. *Ibid.* i. 11 The Stanford Revision adheres more closely to the original Binet Scale. **1929** Thurstone & Chave *Measurement of Attitude* ii. 22 A list of 130 statements was prepared, expressive of attitudes covering as far as possible all gradations from one end of the scale to the other. *Ibid.* iv. 59 The scale-values represented by the 45 statements. **1960** *Jrnl. Pol.* XXII. 647 Scale analysis is now common enough in political science to justify omission of the details. **1966** T. M. Newcomb et al. *Social Psychol.* xiv. 429 The scale was a revision of the original Bogardus scale. *Ibid.* 498 The Likert scale may seem..a natural way of drawing attitude measurements and combining them. *Ibid.* 523 'Neutral' items in Thurstone scales are a source of considerable nonvalidity. **1972** *Jrnl. Social Psychol.* LXXXVI. 105 The scale dimension of like–dislike was used as the source of names. **1977** K. G. Shaver *Princ. Social Psychol.* v. 193 We have grouped the respondents in terms of a nominal scale: a scale of measurement by which the observations can be classified, but not ordered. *Ibid.* 194 Regardless of the distance between scores, when the data can be rank ordered (usually from the most favorable to the least favorable) they constitute what is known as an ordinal scale of measurement. *Ibid.* 196 When the numbers we assign to identify observations *do* tell us something about the distances between observations (while also providing us with a logical order), those numbers are said to constitute an interval scale of measurement. *Ibid.* 198 If an interval scale is constructed with an absolute zero point, rather than with an arbitrary one, that scale becomes..a ratio scale.

6. c. *scale of* (*two*, etc.): a scale of arithmetical notation having as radix the number given, used *attrib.* and *absol.* to designate a form of scaler (see *scaler³ 4) in which an output pulse is produced when a number of input pulses equal to the specified radix has been received.

1871 [in Dict., sense 6 b]. **1932** C. E. Wynn-Williams in *Proc. R. Soc.* A. CXXXVI. 318 As the recording..values of the 'dial' units are, respectively, 2^0 or 1, 2^1 or 2, and 2^2 or 4, and since the meter indicates the total number of groups of 2^3 or 8, the counting is carried out according to a 'scale of two', the three thyratron dials recording 'units', 'twos' and 'fours' and the meter 'eights', instead of units, tens, hundreds, and thousands. **1933** *Ibid.* CXXXIX. 621 The impulses are then applied to a 'scale of two' thyratron counting circuit. **1948** *Nucleonics* Nov. 49/1 Scale-of-*N* circuits are important tools for counting radiations in nuclear physics, as well as for various other applications. **1950** *Progr. Nuclear Physics* I. 109 A scale of five can be made by the use of a form of ring circuit with five valves with their cathodes connected together. **1963** B. Fozard *Instrumentation Nuclear Reactors* viii. 75 A cascade arrangement of six scales-of-two gives an over-all scale factor of 2^6 or 64.

7. a. (Earlier example.)

1780 *Acts & Resolves Massachusetts* (1886) V. 1413 The following scale shall be the rule..for settling the rate of depreciation on all contracts.

b. *spec.* A graduated table of wage or salary rates; *transf.*, a wage or salary in accordance with such a table.

1921, etc. [see *Burnham]. **1930** [see *beggar *v.* 3]. **1957** [see *label *sb.*¹ 7 c]. **1968** *New Yorker* 18 May 45/2 Pookie's Pub..is not the highest-paying club in town. I make about scale, or about a hundred and fifty a week. **1977** *Times Educ. Suppl.* 21 Oct. 2/5 There seems to be a case for possible demotion from scales.

12. b. *Photogr.* The range of exposures (defined as the product of the light intensity and the time) over which a photographic material will give an acceptable variation in density. Also *transf.*

[**1891** *Jrnl. Soc. Chem. Industry* 28 Feb. 104/1 By variations in the time of development it is possible to produce secondary negatives in which the scale of tones is either contracted or extended. **1920** L. A. Jones in *Jrnl. Franklin Inst.* CLXXXIX. 480 If this scale of negative densities is too great for printing on the papers which are available, we can reduce the scale by lowering the contrast of the negative.] *Ibid.* 482 The total scale of the paper may be defined as the range of light intensities, expressed either in log exposure or exposure units, which can be reproduced by the paper as perceptibly different densities. **1942** C. E. K. Mees *Theory Photographic Process* xix. 736 If all different gradations on the negative are to be rendered as different gradations in the print, the scale of the paper must be at least as great as the difference between the maximum and minimum densities of the negative. **1967** *Electronics* 6 Mar. 127/1 The persistence of the scope that was necessary for a raster scan took five seconds from top to bottom, and did not have enough grey scale for good pictures. **1970** G. L. Wakefield *Practical Sensitometry* viii. 83 A medium speed film is likely to have an exposure scale of at least 1,000 to 1 and it can be even bigger. On a log basis this is a range of 3·0 and higher. As a rule, the faster the material the larger the exposure scale.

c. *economy* (*economies, economics*) *of scale*, the relative gain in output or saving of costs derived from an increase in the size of plant or of a firm.

1944 A. Cairncross *Introd. Econ.* vi. 61 The economies of large-scale production—called for short 'economies of scale'—may be either 'internal' or 'external'. *Ibid.* xv. 195 Economies of scale, and economies of scale alone, make costs fall as output increases. **1953** Stonier & Hague *Textbk. Econ. Theory* x. 221 Over relatively low levels of output it is likely that increasing returns to outlay will occur, because with larger output there are economies of scale to be reaped. **1966** A. Battersby *Math. in Management* ix. 220 A picture of the familiar 'economy of scale' which results from spreading the fixed costs over a large number of items. **1972** *Observer* 20 Aug. 9/7 The economics of scale, that much-abused phrase, used to justify any increase in size.

13. b. Also with ellipsis of *adj.* Also with *sb.*, as *on a world scale.*

1904 H. James *Golden Bowl* I. i. ii. 26 Maggie's too wonderful—her preparations are on a scale! **1968** *Times* 15 Oct. 16/7 Possible arrangements on a world scale are affected by the telescopes available.

16. *attrib.* and *Comb.*, as (sense 9) *scale-bar, -reading* (earlier and further examples); (sense 11) *scale model*; (sense 7) *scale fee*; **scale effect,** an effect occurring when the scale of something is changed, as a result of contributory factors not all varying in proportion; *spec.* (see quot. 1940); **scale factor,** a numerical factor by which each of a set of quantities is multiplied; **scale height,** the vertical distance over which an atmospheric parameter or other quantity decreases by a factor *e* (= 2·718 . . .).

1974 *Nature* 18 Oct. 647 (*caption*) Fully developed vegetative colonies (1 month old) on liquid surface (scale bar, 0·5 cm). **1917** *Rep. & Mem. Advisory Comm. Aeronaut.* (1921) No. 374 (*heading*) Report of the scale effect subcommittee. **1930** *Engineering* 20 June 802/2 The skin friction of the plate gives a slightly erroneous velocity distribution under the model car... Still, the errors due to these imperfections are hardly likely to be so much greater than other unavoidable uncertainties, arising from scale effect and the varying conditions of full-scale operations. **1940** *Chambers's Techn. Dict.* 743/1 *Scale effect*, the effect of a change in Reynolds number upon the measured results in the performance of aerodynamic bodies. **1978** H. C. H. Armstead *Geothermal Energy* xv. 244 With conventional thermal power plants the capital cost per kilowatt installed is sensitive to what is generally known as the 'scale effect'; that is to say, a very large plant will tend to cost less per kilowatt than a small plant of similar type. **1979** *Daily Tel.* 15 Aug. 12/5 If you were trying to apply this concept to a Jaguar, you would need about a 20-litre engine—it only works because of the scale effect.. on a very small car. **1948** *Electronics* Apr. 127/1 The corresponding initial voltages must be computed and the integrators set accordingly, using the correct scale factor. **1963** [see sense *6 c]. **1968** P. A. P. Moran *Introd. Probability Theory* v. 244 Thus S_n has the same distribution as the X_i but increased by the scale factor $n^{\frac{1}{2}}$. **1975**

Sci. Amer. Nov. 120/2 The price paid for conformality is a distortion of the scale factor that increases with distance from the centre of the map. **1970** *Which?* Mar. 72/2 They saved the solicitor's scale fee on the price of the house they were buying or selling. The higher the price of the house, the higher the fee. **1937** S. CHAPMAN in *Rep. Progr. Physics* III. 44 *H* may then be interpreted as a unit of height-measurement relative to which, at the given level, the rate of upward decrease of log *p* is unity... The term 'height of the homogeneous atmosphere' is clearly not appropriate when *H* varies with height, and the name (local) 'scale-height' may be suggested. **1976** *Sci. Amer.* Mar. 53/1 In the sun or in the earth's atmosphere the size of the dominant energy-carrying cells is on the order of one scale height. **1978** *Nature* 26 Oct. 726/1 Suppose that 10^{38} ergs $^{-1}$ of X rays are emitted by the pulsar... Assume the scale height of the photons is 3×10^8 cm. **1934** *Planning* I. XXII. 6 This is not, therefore, a scheme but a scale model for one, intended to show precisely what is involved. **1952** 'T. HINDE' *Mr. Nicholas* v. 87 He had..small features ..as neat as a scale model. **1868** Scale-reading [see *ELECTROMETRY]. **1962** L. S. SASIENI *Optical Dispensing* v. 110 A slight turn..will have the effect of moving both scale-readings in the same direction.

scale, *v.*² Add: **2. c.** *Austral.* and *N.Z. slang.* To defraud or cheat (someone), to steal (something). In phr. *to scale a train* or *tram*, to ride without paying on public transport; also *intr.*

1916 A. WRIGHT *Under Cloud* 32 'How'd that happen,' asks Bill Odzon. 'Didn't think anyone could scale you.' **1941** BAKER *N.Z. Slang* vii. 62 When we are taken down financially we are *scaled.* **1945** —— *Austral. Lang.* v. 103 A *steel jockey* is a tramp who scales a train or rides without paying. *Ibid.* 106 One can *get scaled*, in the sense of being done down, when overcharged for goods. **1953** 'CADDIE' *Sydney Barmaid* xiv. 132 Better..than for them to be getting about the streets with snotty noses, and scaling trams. **1953** D. CUSACK *Southern Steel* 3 Bumping in on the back of the old steam trams, too often scaling on the footboards because he hadn't the money to pay the penny fare.

scale, *v.*³ Add: **II. 4. b.** (Later examples.) Also *loosely*, to reduce.

1933 *Sun* (Baltimore) 5 Apr. 8/2 The indebted farmer gets his mortgage debt scaled down, but with that scaling down the payment of interest again becomes the vogue. **1934** [see next sense]. **1937** *Physical Rev.* LI. 1027/1 (*heading*) Vacuum tube circuits for scaling down counting rates. **1952** M. LASKI *Village* v. 95 Hospitality had been empirically scaled down to a universally possible level. **1979** *Daily Tel.* 19 May 2/1 The original pay claim for a 30 per cent. rise has been scaled down to 16 per cent.

c. With *up*: to increase in amount or size according to a fixed scale or standard; to increase from a small scale to a larger scale. Also *absol.*

1891 *Daily News* 17 Jan. 2/5 The scaling up instead of scaling down the London, Chatham, and Dover stock. **1934** W. NELSON *Seaplane Design* vi. 64 Scaling the size of existing floats and hulls up and down can be done to arrive at the dimensions of a new design. **1972** *Aquaculture* I. 182 During the summer of 1971, the project was scaled up in size and moved out-of-doors. **1973** *Times* 28 Nov. 19/5 If the pilot plant can be scaled up at this figure it offers great hopes for the development of these abundant fuel reserves. **1975** *Nature* 17 Jan. 149/3 There will probably be no need to scale up since the existing plant can cope with 50 tons every 24 hours. **1977** *Undercurrents* June–July 7/1 It remains doubtful whether the process..can work safely and effectively when 'scaled-up' to commercial size. **1979** *Sci. Amer.* Jan. 45/1 Several organizations are currently scaling up from laboratory-size cells to units of demonstration size.

d. To measure or represent (a quantity) in exact proportion to its absolute size or according to an arbitrary defined scale.

1885 W. PENMAN *Land Surveying* ix. 127 An area to the scale of 1 chain = 1 inch was scaled and found to give 12 ac. 1 ro. 01 pls. **1898** F. E. DIXON *T. Baker's Rudimentary Treat. Land & Engin. Surveying* (ed. 17) xii. 182 It sometimes happens that a distance is scaled on a plan using..a wrong scale. **1923** *Rep. Internat. Air Congr., London, 1923* 63 Not only is it difficult to scale the printed forms with accuracy, but there is no assurance that the silhouette corresponds closely with the model tested in the wind channel. **1940** *Amer. Jrnl. Psychol.* LIII. 336 (*caption*) The curve shows how pitch, scaled in subjective units.. varies with frequency. **1951** S. S. STEVENS *Handbk. Experim. Psychol.* i. 23/1 These operations are limited ordinarily by the peculiarities of the thing being scaled. **1951** H. P. BECHTOLDT in *Ibid.* xxxiii. 1240/2 Multiple-category qualitative variables representing intensive dimensions are 'scaled' in various ways, and numerical scores are determined. **1966** T. NEWCOMB et al. *Social Psychol.* (ed. 2) 506 In a most interesting approach to problems of scaling attitudes..Guttman..began to examine items apparently ordered on the basis of 'difficulty'. **1971** J. B. CARROLL et al. *Word Freq. Bk.* p. xxvii, The base line of Graph 1 is scaled, not in terms of ϕ, but in terms of a further transformation of ϕ to the Standard Frequency Index. **1976** B. S. PHILLIPS *Social Res.* (rev. ed.) ix. 211 Select or construct those items that you wish to scale.

e. To alter (a quantity or property) by changing the units in which it is measured; to change the size of (a system or device) while keeping its parts in constant proportion.

1954 *Computers & Automation* Dec. 20/2 *Scale*, computation. To change the scale (that is, the units) in which a variable is expressed so as to bring it within the capacity of the machine or program at hand. **1966** R. C. CARTER *Introd. Electr. Circuit Analysis* vii. 239 Once the desired design performance has been achieved in the low-frequency prototype laboratory model, all factors involving frequency and impedance may be scaled to the desired operating range. **1974** *Physics Bull.* Mar. 98/3 The symmetry transformation consists of scaling the physical dimensions *d* of the system according to $d \rightarrow \lambda d$. If the equilateral triangle of figure 1 is scaled then although the size is changed, the geometric shape and all the dimensionless properties of the triangle such as the angles remain unchanged. **1978** *Sci. Amer.* Dec. 128/2 The radio waves, completely unattenuated by the intervening dust, can be scaled several orders of magnitude in frequency to predict the true intensity of the optical radiation.

f. *intr.* Of a quantity or property: to vary according to a defined rule or principle.

1974 *Physics Bull.* Mar. 98/3 The invariance of all dimensionless properties can be used to determine whether the figure scales or not. **1978** *Nature* 20 Apr. 737/3 Surprisingly the limiting torque, even at optimised pressures, scales only at [*recte* as] $T^{\frac{1}{4}}$.

7. *trans.* Of a scaler (see *SCALER³ 4): to count (electrical pulses). Also *absol.*

1938 *Rev. Sci. Instruments* IX. 221/1 The circuit either scaled correctly or no counts were registered. **1947** *Ibid.* XXIV. 322/1 Although not developed as a high-frequency instrument, the model will scale a regular pulse input up to frequencies of the order of 100 kc/s.

scaled, *ppl. a.*⁴ Add: **2. a.** That has been measured by a scale or varied in a determined proportion.

1885 W. PENMAN *Land Surveying* ix. 127 The scaled area is less than the actual one, indicating shrinkage of the paper. **1938** *Rev. Sci. Instruments* IX. 221/1 The fluctuational analysis of the scaled counts occurring at an average rate of ten per minute indicated a scaling factor of 22 to 1. **1960** ROGERS & CONNOLLY *Analog Computation in Engin. Design* x. 261 The following scaled voltage equivalents are suitable for representing the variables of the problem; $2\dot{x}$, $20\dot{x}$, $200x$, $10h$, $10t$. **1976** ATTEWELL & FARMER *Princ. Engin. Geol.* vii. 525 (*caption*) Scaled distance attenuation relationships for blasting in a rock.

b. *scaled-up*: that has been increased proportionately in amount or size in all its parts. Similarly *scaled-down.*

1944 P. WILKINSON *Aircraft Engines of World 1944* 38 The 12-cylinder 1,300 h.p. Jumo 211-J is a scaled-up version of the Jumo 210. **1947** A. E. SLATER in A. C. Douglas *Gliding & Advanced Soaring* i. 12 The earliest recorded attempts to fly, as well as the legendary ones, usually began with an attempt to reproduce a scaled-up bird's wing, often to the extent of putting feathers on it, in the belief that such a structure was inherently able to keep itself up, once it got well aloft. **1953** *Trans. Soc. Instrument Technol.* V. 126/2 The pilot unit is not usually constructed unless the manufacturer is satisfied that he will eventually proceed to the erection of a full-scale plant. It is a scaled-down version of such a plant. **1963** BIRD & HUTTON-STOTT *Veteran Motor Car* 49 B.S.A. cars..were virtually scaled-down Daimlers. **1973** *Lebende Sprachen* XVIII. 7/2 Go-ahead for a scaled-up version of the engine giving a 30 percent increase in original thrust. **1977** *Time* 19 Sept. 43/1 Anyone with a driver's license and a few dollars can safely savor some of the adrenaline-pumping, gut-clutching fever of Grand Prix racing on a minitrack, in a scaled-down Formula I speedster.

scalene, *a.* and *sb.* Now usu. with pronunc. (skē¹·lĭn). **A.** *adj.* **2.** (Later examples.)

1934 [see *SCALENOTOMY]. **1962** *Gray's Anat.* (ed. 33) 600 The scalene muscles, in particular the Scalenus medius, are important accessory muscles of inspiration.

B. *sb.* **2.** (Example.)

1978 [see *SCALENOTOMY].

scalenotomy (skē¹lĭnǫ·tŏmi). *Surg.* [f. SCALEN(US + -O + -TOMY.] Division or section of a scalene muscle.

1934 ROMANIS & MITCHINER *Sci. & Practice Surg.* (ed. 5) II. xi. 449 To produce further collapse of the apex, the operation of phrenic avulsion may be supplemented by a section of the scalene muscles. This is easily done through the same incision (scalenotomy). **1978** J. E. BATEMAN *Shoulder & Neck* (ed. 2) xv. 633/1 In some instances..the involvement of the paraspinal muscles, and the scalenes in particular, is prominent. Considerable relief..may be obtained by simple scalenotomy.

scaler². Add: **3.** *Austral.* and *N.Z. slang.* (See quots.)

1924 *Truth* (Sydney) 27 Apr. 6 *Scaler*, a fraud. *c* **1926** 'MIXER' *Transport Workers' Song Bk.* 5 (*title*) The Scaler... He waits until his dues are due, The bloke who does a scale. **1932** C. WILLS *Rhymes of Sydney* (1933) 13 See the shoppers, toppers, tabs, Scalers by the score, Hopping off, Dropping off, Darting into shore. **1945** BAKER *Austral. Lang.* v. 106 A *scaler* is a person who rides in a vehicle without paying, or one who decamps with money with which he has been entrusted.

scaler³. Add: **4.** An electronic pulse-counter, suitable for high count-rates, in which a display or recording device is actuated after a fixed number of pulses has been received and added electronically.

1945 H. D. SMYTH *Atomic Energy for Military Purposes 1939–45* 140 The scaler was set at zero. **1953** *Sci. Amer.* Mar. 105/3 As a series of pulses flows into the scaler a voltage builds up step by step... When the cut off point is reached, the tube begins to conduct and the condenser discharges, sending a single pulse from the tube's output. **1964** *Analytical Chem.* XXXVI. 2221/1 Development of the pipping scaler was stimulated by..experimental work in which it was necessary to determine time *vs.* concentration curves having a duration of a second or less. **1977** N. FREELING *Gadget* II. 87 That's a PM—sorry, photomultiplier tube... Sends signals here, to the amplifier, through here, that's the discriminator, to here, the scaler. **1980** J. W. HILL *Intermediate Physics* xxiii. 220 These are connected to about 400V obtained usually from a scaler, a piece of electronic apparatus which can count very rapidly using either 'dekatrons' or a digital display.

scale-up (skē¹·lʌp), *sb.* (*a.*) [f. vbl. phr. *to scale up* (*SCALE *v.*³ 4 c).] The action or result of increasing the scale of something. Also as *adj.*

1945 H. D. SMYTH *Gen. Acct. Devel. Atomic Energy Mil. Purposes* viii. 82 Should the several steps in the separations process have to be developed partly by the empirical approach, there would be less risk in the scale-up of a precipitation process. **1953** *Industr. & Engin. Chem.* May 990/1 All the dimensions of the larger are *x* times those of the smaller. We call *x* the 'scale-up factor'. **1965** *Amer. Scientist* LIII. 280 These tanks are modeled.. with a scaleup factor of about two. **1967** *Jane's Surface Skimmer Systems 1967–68* 49/1 In general layout, the craft represents a 'scale-up' of the configuration tested with the Raduga. **1979** *Sci. Amer.* July 79/3 The design of the 1899 kite was the basis for a scale-up version that was small enough to be flown as a kite but large enough to support a man.

scalewise (skē¹·lwəiz), *a.* and *adv.* [f. SCALE *sb.*³ 4 + -WISE.] **A.** *adj.* = *SCALAR *a.* 3. **B.** *adv.* In the manner of a scale; in respect of a scale.

1931 G. JACOB *Orchestral Technique* ix. 81 Eighteenth-century trumpet parts were written very high because of the impossibility of obtaining scale-wise passages on the natural instrument except amongst the very high harmonics. **1959** *Listener* 8 Jan. 80/2 The opening cantabile theme, descending scalewise, continuously flows into more ornate melismata. **1977** *Early Music* Oct. 535/2 The interaction of *tirades* (scale-wise flourishes)..always requires some arbitrary adjustment by the player.

scaley, var. *SCALY *sb.*

scalic (skē¹·lik), *a. Mus.* [f. SCAL(E *sb.*³ 4 + -IC.] = *SCALAR *a.* 3.

1933 *Times Lit. Suppl.* 2 Mar. 139/1 'The Rebel Stranger' ..shows in its seven versions how a tune may develop by blending scalic with figural features of melody. **1960** *Times* 5 Mar. 9/6 A scalic tune, that can sound quite unpromising. **1971** *Daily Tel.* 5 Apr. 10/3 Kempff will sometimes pedal scalic passages and is apt to be crowded out by violin accompaniments. **1979** *Early Music* Oct. 545/1 Babell's elaborations are always scalic, and on the first page of 51 the same passage, repeated sequentially, is embellished three times in an identical manner.

scaling, *vbl. sb.*³ Add: **2.** (Further examples.) Also, measurement or grading of attributes; variation of size or scale; the action of a scaler.

1807 G. GREGORY *Dict. Arts & Sci.* II. 757/3 The plan being laid down, the content of the field may be found by scaling. **1929** F. N. FREEMAN in C. Murchison *Found. Experim. Psychol.* xviii. 721 The purpose of such scaling may be merely to secure items which are equally spaced in difficulty or it may also be to weigh the pupil's performance in terms of the difficulty of the items which he passes. **1938** *Rev. Sci. Instruments* IX. 221/1 No variations in the scaling factor were found for pulses varying in amplitude by a factor of six. **1949** *Nucleonics* Feb. 67/2 Several scale-of-2 circuits in tandem provide net scaling factors of 4–8–16–32–64, etc. Other designs, utilizing 'ring scalers' or modified scale-of-16 scalers yield decimal scaling ratios (10–100–1000). **1968** FOX & MAYERS *Computing Methods for Scientists & Engineers* v. 89 It is desirable that all rows and columns of [matrix] **A**, and also of **b**, should be of reasonable size... This can always be arranged..by appropriate scaling of the rows and columns. **1975** *IEEE Trans. Nuclear Sci.* XXII. 1580/1 Simple start-stop scaling, count = 8, frequency 53 MHz. **1979** *Sci. Amer.* July 120/3 One such manifestation of movement into a marginal niche is the scaling down of body size.

scaling (skē¹·liŋ), *ppl. a.*² [f. SCALE *v.*³ + -ING².] That scales, in the senses of SCALE *v.*³ II in Dict. and Suppl.

1937 *Rev. Sci. Instruments* VIII. 414/1 The ultimate efficiency..is determined by the resolving power of the first stage of the scaling circuit. **1937** *Physical Rev.* LI. 1027/1 The ultimate efficiency that can be reached is fixed by the resolving power of the scaling down circuit. **1950** *Atomics* Sept. 255/1 The simplest scaling circuit is the 'scale of two'. **1961** G. R. CHOPPIN *Exper. Nuclear Chem.* iii. 43 The scaling system selects every *n*th pulse to pass on to the mechanical registers.

scallion. a. For Now *dial.* read *U.S.* **c.** Add: = *spring onion* s.v. SPRING *sb.*¹ 7 b. **d.** *U.S.* = LEEK 1. (Later U.S. examples.)

1902 L. H. BAILEY *Cycl. Amer. Hort.* IV. 1622/2 Scallion, a name for the Shallot; also used for onions that do not make good bulbs but remain with thick necks. **1943** H. M. FOX *Gardening for Good Eating* ix. 135 When the [onion] seedlings are thinned, they can be eaten as scallions. **1963** [see *dandelion greens* s.v. *DANDELION 3]. **1965** P. DE VRIES *Let me count Ways* xii. 159 Several stalks of crisp celery and a scallion or two left over from my lunch. **1969** *Yearbk. Agric.* (U.S. Dept. Agric.) 189/2 Green onions, shallots, and leeks are sometimes called 'scallions'. **1978** *Chicago* June 217/1 Other delicacies might be fresh crab legs..and transparent noodles studded with shrimp, scallions, and black mushrooms.

scallom (skæ·ləm), *sb. Basket-making.* [Of obscure origin: see SCALLUM *v.* in Dict. and Suppl.] A stake or rod, of which a thin or spliced end is wrapped round another stake to form a base or frame of a basket; the method of weaving baskets thus.

1912 T. OKEY *Art of Basket-Making* vii. 75 Bottoms and covers may also be made on hoops and scalloms. *Ibid.* Gloss. 154 *Scallom,* a method of forming the rigid inner frame of a bottom or cover, or of staking up a basket. **1929** A. G. KNOCK *Fine Willow Basketry* 18 *Scallom,* a stake, or the equivalent of a bottom-stick or lid-stick which has been affixed by looping its thinned end round a hoop or the outside stick of a bottom. **1959** *Gloss. Terms Packaging* (*B.S.I.*) 16 *Scallom,* the spliced end of a stake which is wrapped round the bottom outside stick and woven into the next two scalloms. **1959** D. WRIGHT *Baskets & Basketry* iv. 115, 5 scalloms of No. 12 cane run from end to end. *Ibid.* vi. 136 *Scallom,* method of fixing stakes to a ring of willow or cane.

scallom, *v.*: see SCALLUM *v.* in Dict. and Suppl.

scallop, *sb.* Add: **3.** (sense 1) *scallop bed, boat, dredge* (earlier example), *-fishery, net; scallop-edged* adj.

1977 *N.Z. Herald* 8 Jan. 1–2/3 Scallop beds around the Coromandel Harbour could be wiped out within five years if the onslaught of spiked dredges used mainly by holiday-makers continued. **1977** *New Yorker* 15 Aug. 46/1 The Sniktaw III, a forty-foot *scallop boat,* is moving rapidly south-ward down the channel. **1884** *U.S. National Mus. Bull.* No. 27. 268 Implements [used in shellfish fishery include]..Scallop-dredge. **1856** W. WHITMAN *Leaves of Grass* (ed. 2) xi. 214, I saw..the scallop-edged waves in the twilight. **1967** R. S. CHURCHILL *Winston S. Churchill* II. viii. 274 A splendid scallop-edged silver tray presented by all his colleagues in the Government. **1886** *Amer. Naturalist* XX. 1001 It is only between Cape Cod and New Jersey that any commercial scallop-fishery exists. **1881** E. INGERSOLL *Oyster-Industry* 247 *Scallop Net,* the small dredge used in catching scallops.

scalloped, *ppl. a.* Add: **2.** (Further examples.)

1877 *Home Keeper's Guide* 45 Scalloped tomatoes. **1884** *New Kentucky Home Cook Bk.* 157 Scalloped potatoes. **1925** W. G. R. FRANCILLON *Good Cookery* (ed. 3) 435 *Scalloped Oysters*... Butter a scallop shell. Arrange layers of crumbs, oysters, and butter alternately... Bake. **1936** *Farmhouse Fare* 10 *Scalloped Meat with Macaroni*... Arrange..cooked macaroni, meat, and gravy in alternate layers...cover the top with browned breadcrumbs...bake. **1960** *Woman* 23 Apr. 51/1 Scalloped Ham... Layer potatoes, onions and ham in the casserole... Pour in milk... Bake in moderate oven. **1975** B. WOOD *Killing Gift* (1976) v. iv. 243 Scalloped potatoes..next to the roast.

scallopini (skælopī·ni). Also in It. form ‖ **scaloppine.** [ad. It. *scaloppine,* pl. of *scaloppina,* dim. of *scaloppa* *ESCALOPE.] A dish consisting of very thin slices of meat (esp. veal) sautéed or fried.

1950 E. HEMINGWAY *Across River & into Trees* 103 The scaloppine with Marsala. **1957** F. & R. LOCKRIDGE *Tangled Cord* (1959) vi. 73 The waiter..heated and served scallopini. **1975** *Times* 6 Sept. 9/1 In Cardiff..it is easier to find well-cooked scaloppine and cannelloni than anything in the native tradition. **1977** J. WAMBAUGH *Black Marble* (1978) iv. 46 Sal Moroni got arrested for throwing a Sicilian cook out the window of an Italian restaurant for overcooking his scallopini.

scallum, *v.* Add: The more usual form is now **scallom.** (Later examples.) Hence **sca·llomed** *ppl. a.*, **sca·lloming** *vbl. sb.*

1912 T. OKEY *Art of Basket-Making* vii. 80 When the side stakes are scallomed on. **1929** A. G. KNOCK *Fine Willow Basketry* 61 To the curved part of the hoop, eight stakes are now scallomed. *Ibid.* 62 In scalloming a long tongue is formed at the butt-end of the stake. **1959** D. WRIGHT *Baskets & Basketry* ii. 45 The sticks are scallomed, that is: thinned down to a long, flat point and taken round the frame... Scalloming is easier to work with willow than with cane because the rods kink and stay rigid when dry. *Ibid.* iv. 114 This basket and its lid are made on a scallomed base.

scallywag, scallawag. Add: **1.** Also *attrib.*

1885 G. B. SHAW *Let.* 4 Sept. (1965) I. 138 Any socialist of the plentiful 'scallawag' type. **1926** *Glasgow Herald* 10 Sept. 11 Go back to your scallywag union. **1957** *Listener* 17 Oct. 608/2 Voyez, that rather scallywag wanderer who was dismissed by Wedgwood.

2. (Earlier and further examples.) Also *attrib.*

1862 *Charleston* (S. Carolina) *Mercury* 9 Aug. 1/3 This invaluable class is composed..of ten parts of unadulterated Andy Johnson Union men, ten of good lord and good devil-ites, five of spuss and seventy-five of scallowags. **1867** *Nation* (N.Y.) 12 Dec. 470/1 The Macon *News* has to print in full the names of thirteen persons..described (as having 'voted the Scalawag ticket'). **1888** J. BRYCE *Amer. Commonwealth* II. II. xliv. 164 A group of such 'scallawag' members.. increase their legislative income.

Hence **scallywa·ggery,** (*a*) roguery, (*b*) political opportunism; **sca·llywagism** = *scallywaggery* (*a*); **sca·llywagging** *vbl. sb., ppl. a.*

1897 *Daily News* 9 Dec. 7/1 The stages of accumulating merit for the fighting man, as Lord Charles gives them, appear to be first robbing orchards, next hatred of a life at the desk, and finally scallywagism. *Ibid.*, Robbing orchards and general scallywaggery is not within them [*sc.* disqualifications for military service]. **1911** H. S. HARRISON *Queed* iv. 45 The morning *Post* was an old paper... It had crucified carpet-baggism and scalawaggery upon a cross of burning adjective. **1915** W. J. LOCKE *Jaffery* xii. 158 He was fed up with scalliwagging all over the place. He wanted a season in town! **1962** *Punch* 9 May 735/1 Wilkes is worth writing about..for all his scallywaggery. **1977** *Times* 18 Aug. 6/1 Mr Frank Johnson.. has unimpeachable credentials as a civil rights defender. Governor George Wallace of Alabama once denounced him as 'a scallywaggin', integratin', carpet-baggin' liar'.

scalogram (skēⁱ·logræm). *Psychol.* [f. SCAL(E *sb.*³ 6 + -O + -GRAM (perh. by analogy with *cardiogram* s.v. *CARDIO-).] A diagram showing the numerical values assigned to responses and persons in an attitude test, designed esp. to analyse whether the questions relate to the same factor and the results are scalable. Also *attrib.* and *Comb.*: **scalogram analysis,** the analysis of results revealed by a scalogram; **scalogram board,** a board with movable slats on which the results are recorded.

1944 L. GUTTMAN in *Amer. Sociol. Rev.* IX. 139/2 The results of the analysis are presented and easily assimilated in the form of a 'scalogram', which at a glance gives the configuration of the qualitative data. *Ibid.* 144/1 The scalogram boards used in practical procedures are simply devices for shifting rows and columns to find a scale pattern if it exists. **1950** S. A. STOUFFER *Measurement & Prediction* i. 9 The approach which was developed in the Research Branch under..Louis Guttman has been named scalogram analysis. *Ibid.*, The scalogram hypothesis is that the items have an order such that, ideally, persons who answer a given question favorably all have a higher rank on the scale than persons who answer the same question unfavorably. **1970** E. J. WILKINS *Introd. Sociol.* v. 81 The items in this type of scalogram are accorded points, both positive and negative, and they are also of a cumulative nature. **1973** *Times Lit. Suppl.* 2 Nov. 1332/2 The second [kind of historical explanation] sublimates personality, thrives upon roll-call votes and produces a scalogram to measure regularity or deviance as its finest achievement. **1978** T. H. POISTER *Public Program Anal.* x. 362 The development of the coefficient of reproducibility (also referred to as scalogram analysis) is useful for assessing the..internal consistency of a Guttman scale.

scaloppine, var. *SCALLOPINI.

scalp, *sb.*¹ Add: **2. c.** *U.S.* The skin from the head of an animal preserved as proof of its death (usu. in order to obtain a bounty).

1703 *Narragansett Hist. Reg.* (1884–5) III. 162 All persons who shall kill any Sheep or Lambs..shall be obliged to carry in the Skalp with Ears of the same. **1847** J. S. ROBB *Streaks of Squatter Life* 80 He can git a bonus for wolf-scalps. **1890** *Stock Grower & Farmer* 22 Feb. 3/1 The bounty law must be fixed up so that scalps will be paid for. **1901** DUNCAN & SCOTT *Hist. Allen & Woodson Counties, Kansas* 15 [The county board] offered a bounty of twenty-five cents for wolf scalps.

b. (Earlier and later examples.)

1759 W. MASON *Let.* 25 Jan. in *Corr. of Thomas Gray* (1935) II. 612 Criticks like Indians are proud of the number of scalps they make in a Manuscript. **1928** T. E. LAWRENCE *Lett.* (1938) 571 It riles me unbearably to lose my scalp to a lot of fellows round whom I can make rings. **1977** *R.A.F. News* 11–24 May 19/1 Convincing wins..for the RAF under-21 hockey team... The Navy provided the first scalp.

6. b. *scalp-massage.*

1930 A. BENNETT *Imperial Palace* xxiii. 143 An electric scalp-massage. **1977** J. AIKEN *Last Movement* vii. 125, I always gave her scalp massage in the evenings..her shaved hair was taking its time about growing back.

c. *scalp-dance* (earlier example), *-hunter* (earlier and later examples); **scalp-money** (earlier example); **scalp ticket** orig. *U.S.*, a ticket sold by a scalper (see SCALPER² 2 a); **scalp yell,** a shout celebrating the taking of a scalp.

1791 J. LONG *Voyages* 35 The dances among the Indians are many and various,..[including] the scalp dance. **1835** R. M. BIRD *Hawks of Hawk-Hollow* I. 79 He acquired a singular reputation as a bold and successful scalp-hunter. **1937** T. RATTIGAN *French without Tears* II. i. 37, I can't quite see what my novel has got to do with the machinations of a scalp-hunter. **1975** *Observer* (Colour Suppl.) 23 Nov. 25/3 Once the scalp-hunters get the word that such-and-such a diplomat wants to defect or to become an out-and-out agent they enjoy priority over the sanctifiers and all the other categories of black operations people. **1704** in G. Sheldon *Hist. Deerfield, Mass.* (1895) I. 299 That the sum of Sixty Pounds be allowed and Paid to the Petitioners..as Scalp money. **1880** G. A. SALA *Amer. Revisited* 201/1 There are 'round trip' tickets which are something more than return, tickets; and finally, there are 'scalp' tickets, which you can deal in and discount. **1941** BAKER *Dict. Austral. Slang* 68 *Scalp ticket,* the return half of a train ticket. **1792** H. H. BRACKENRIDGE *Mod. Chivalry* I. v. ii. 113 A warrior..separates it [*sc.* a scalp] from the head, giving, in the mean time, what is called the scalp yell. **1913** J. LONDON *Valley of Moon* 465 He drew his finny prize to the bank..with the scalp-yell of a Comanche. **1947** *National Geogr. Mag.* July 108/1 The hundreds of scientists being marshaled there are pioneers more potent than any who fought when war drums rolled along the Mohawk, scalp yells quivered on the valley air, and the frontier was aflame.

scalp, *v.*² Add: **1. a.** (Earlier and later *absol.* and *fig.* examples.)

1759 W. MASON *Let.* 25 Jan. in *Corr. of Thomas Gray* (1935) II. 612 If you don't let them [*sc.* critics] scalp they'll do you no service. **1939** 'A. BRIDGE' *Four-Part Setting* ii. 16 Henry is plain sailing, of course—he's quite simply scalped... He's always being scalped. It's his own fault—he will chase women so. **1973** D. KYLE *Raft of Swords* (1974) x. 99 Calder took a taxi to Heathrow airport. Inevitably he would be scalped on the cab fare.

2. a. (Earlier example.)

1825 J. LORAIN *Pract. Husb.* 335 The Yankee farmer first chops the fallen timber, then scalps off the grubs level with the ground.

scalp, *v.*² Add: **2. c.** *Metallurgy.* To remove the surface layer of (metal); to remove (the surface) *from* metal.

1922 *Brass World & Plater's Guide* XVIII. 96 After the slabs are cooled they are sent to the overhauling machines where a thin layer of metal is scalped from the surface. **1922, 1949** [implied in *SCALPING *vbl. sb.*² 2]. **1958** A. D. MERRIMAN *Dict. Metallurgy* 305/1 Other methods used to scalp the ingot are by chipping, milling, planing or by means of the oxyacetylene torch.

4. (Earlier and later examples.) Also *absol.*

1886 *Harper's Mag.* July 213/2 [The scalper buys] any quantity of grain that may be offered, sells it at an advance of 1/8 cent per bushel, thus scalps the market. **1897** *Boston Globe* 29 Aug. 39/5 The broker himself would be selling the stock at 104 in New York, thereby 'scalping' one-fourth and making a handsome profit at no risk. **1902** G. H. LORIMER *Lett. Merchant* 201, I saw what looked like a safe chance to scalp the market for a couple of cents a bushel. **1948** *Sun* (Baltimore) 26 Nov. 18/2 The Stadium attendants told me they are the same men.. who scalp at other games,..selling 60-cent tickets for $1. **1977** *Time* 19 Dec. 66/1 The generous benefactor to down-and-out friends wore the same loud waistcoats as the pinchpenny negotiator who scalped outmatched publishers.

scalped, *ppl. a.*¹ Add: **c.** *Metallurgy.* Having had the surface layer removed.

1958 *Times Rev. Industry* June 53/1 Scalped wire bars.. seen in the place of the familiar round extrusion billet. **1965** *Gloss. Terms Copper, Zinc & Alloys* (*B.S.I.*) 15 *Scalped stock* (*for other than tube*), stock intended for further fabrication from which the surface has been removed by machining to improve the quality of the final product.

scalper². Add: **1.** (Earlier example.)

1760 S. NILES in *Mass. Hist. Soc. Coll.* (1837) 3rd Ser. VI. 174 This reminds me of an account we had of a notable old scalper among [the Indians].

2. a. (Earlier example.)

1875 *Chicago Tribune* 8 Dec. 12/3 The new town grew up to be..the great commercial centre of rail-road 'scalpers'.

b. (Earlier example.)

1886 *Harper's Mag.* July 213/2 The 'Pit' is the scalper's delight.

c. *slang* (orig. *U.S.*). A speculator who obtains tickets for a popular entertainment and sells them for more than their face price.

1869 *Harper's Mag.* Sept. 623/2 Where theatres are all the run, And bloody scalpers come to trade. **1935** *Time* 26 Aug. 27/1 Comedian Joe Brown..is locked out of his dressing room by mistake on his opening night and is compelled to pay $20 to a ticket scalper to get into the theatre in time for his entrance cue. **1948** *Sun* (Baltimore) 26 Nov. 18/2 Since these 60-cent tickets are sold, or supposed to be sold, only to students, the question is how the scalpers obtained them. **1969** *Truth* (Melbourne) 12 July 24/7 I'm sure scalpers wouldn't buy lottery tickets. **1977** *Rolling Stone* 16 June 12/2 The Palladium shows sold out in a few hours and scalpers have been getting up to $75 per ticket. **1978** G. VIDAL *Kalki* vi. 137 One-third of the tickets for the rally..are now in the hands of scalpers who are selling the most desirable seats..for as high as one thousand dollars a-piece!

d. *U.S.* (See quots.)

1874 J. G. McCOY *Hist. Sketches Cattle Trade* 292 So soon as an incoming train is announced nearing the stock yards, the hurrying tramps of solicitors, called 'Scalpers', may be heard hustling toward the unloading platform. If there is a shipper on the train whose stock is not consigned, they..[present] the business cards of the commission firms which have the Scalpers employed. **1930** *Amer. Speech* X. 271/2 *Scalper,* one who buys feeder cattle and resells to farmers and feeders at a profit. A speculator.

3. (Earlier and later examples.)

1837 R. M. BIRD *Nick of Woods* II. xviii. 245 Captain Ralph Stacpole did..meet another Injun-savage in the woods..with gun, axe, and scalper. **1947** B. DE VOTO *Across Wide Missouri* 32 The Company is sending..100 dozen 'common scalpers' and 55 dozen more expensive knives for murder with style.

4. (Later example.)

1950 *Engineering* 13 Jan. 30/1 [In flour milling] the endosperm released..and sifted out in the scalpers consists of particles of various sizes.

scalpette (skælpe·t). [f. SCALP *sb.*¹ + -ETTE.] (See quots. 1887, 1960.)

1881 in J. Lichtenfeld *Princ. Mod. Hairdressing* 35 (Advt.), J. Lichtenfeld's Illustrated Catalogue contains Illustrations and Description of..Invisible Scalpette Fringes, Bébé Scalpette, [etc.]. **1887** E. CREER *Board-Work* vii. 97 What is a scalpette?.. I..consider it to signify an artificial covering for concealing a deficiency of hair, or to cover a bald place upon the female head—but not a wig. **1924** *Chambers's Jrnl.* Oct. 669/1 Skilled hair-workers who will make up wigs, scalpettes. **1960** C. W. CUNNINGTON et al. *Dict. English Costume* 190/1 *Scalpette,*..a false front of invisible net to which luxuriant tresses are attached. **1961** E. S. TURNER *Phoney War* vii. 54 My private drill consists of taking off my scalpette, putting it into the sponge bag and then slipping the latter with its closed outlet downwards into the hip pocket.

scalping, *vbl. sb.*² **2.** (Further examples.)

1922 *Jrnl. Inst. Metals* XXVIII. 881 Rolling data for brass and bronze, scalping, annealing, and pickling.

1949 J. E. GARSIDE *Process & Physical Metall.* viii. 123 It is becoming general practice in the case of non-ferrous alloys to subject slabs and billets to a surface machining operation known as 'scalping' prior to cold-rolling. **1960** *New Scientist* 19 May 1269/2 The machine..is used for scalping. By scalping, the quarryman means separating the dirt from the mine output before the stones are passed into the crusher. **1967** *Gloss. Highway Engin. Terms* (*B.S.I.*) 25 *Scalpings*, hard material extracted as being unsuitable for crushing and screening. **1975** *Bristol Evening Post* 19 Feb. 1/4 The firm plan to protect Portway and services underneath from impact, possibly with a blanket of steel plating topped by scalping and sand.

scaly, *a.* Add: **8. scaly-bark (hickory)**, substitute for def.: the shagbark hickory, *Carya ovata*, or its edible nuts; cf. HICKORY 1; (earlier and later examples); **scaly-tail** = *scale-tail* s.v. SCALE *sb.*[1] 12; so **scaly-tailed** *a.*

1775 J. ADAIR *Hist. Amer. Indians* 360 Filberts.. are as sweet and thin-shelled, as the scaly bark hiccory-nuts. **1785** T. JEFFERSON *Notes on Virginia* vi. 63 Scaly bark hiccory. **1814** F. PURSH *Flora Amer.* II. 637 This useful tree is known by the name of..Scaly-bark Hickory, on account of its bark, which is torn in loose fragments. **1852** MAYNE REID *Desert Home* 198 The tree is known among backwoodsmen as the 'scaly bark'. **1906** 'O. HENRY' *Rolling Stones* (1912) 8, I saw..a little flaxen-haired man with a face like a scaly-bark hickory-nut. **1921** *Brit. Mus. Return* 97 in *Parl. Papers* XXVII. 651 A West African Scaly-tail (*Anomalurus erythronotus*), and an Ituri Scaly-tail (*Anomalurus pusillus*). **1964** L. S. CRANDALL *Management of Wild Mammals in Captivity* 229 The life-histories of the scaly-tails are not well known. **1962** M. BURTON *Syst. Dict. Mammals of World* 121 Scaly-tailed Flying Squirrels..not related to true squirrels. **1964** E. P. WALKER et al. *Mammals of World* II. 750/2 Scaly-tailed squirrels den in hollow trees. **1975** P. W. HANNEY *Rodents* ii. 30 There are no flying squirrels in Africa, but in the west of the continent their niche is filled by..the Anomaluridae or scaly-tailed squirrels.

scaly (skēⁱ·li), *sb. S. Afr.* Also **scaley.** [f. the adj.] A large yellow-fish, *Barbus natalensis*, of the family Cyprinidæ, found in certain rivers in Natal.

1947 K. H. BARNARD *Pict. Guide S. Afr. Fishes* 56 The well-known Scaley..of Natal is a near relative of the Yellow-fish. **1971** *Rand Daily Mail* (Johannesburg) 27 Mar. 23/3 An interesting observation last week was the presence of shoals of scalies in the Bushmans river. **1975** *Stand. Encycl. S. Afr.* XI. 563/1 The Natal scaly..reaches 5 kg and is restricted to the Pongola system and the rivers of Natal.

scam (skæm), *sb. slang* (orig. and chiefly *U.S.*). [Origin obscure.] **1. a.** A trick, a ruse; a swindle, a racket (*sb.*[3] 3). Also *attrib.*

1963 *Time* 28 June 48/2 He..worked..as a carny huckster... 'It was a full scam.' **1971** *Harper's Mag.* Feb. 89 A gambling house is a sitting duck to every con man or outlaw who comes through; he is invariably convinced that he has a scam that you have never seen before. **1972** *Sunday Mail* (Brisbane) 2 July 19/6 It was necessary to the success of the latest 'scam' that it be worked in places where $25 chips were constantly in play. **1975** J. F. BURKE *Death Trick* (1976) iv. 64 Hustling of any kind he could live with in his hotel, dope-dealing, selling ass, almost any scam, even burglary. **1976** M. MACHLIN *Pipeline* v. 58 Gamblers, pimps, whores, conmen, and scam artists of every persuasion were drawn to the scene like sharks. **1978** M. PUZO *Fools Die* xii. 131 The bribe-taking scam had been going on for nearly two years without any kind of hitch.

b. *spec.* A fraudulent bankruptcy (see quot. 1966). Also *attrib.*

1966 *Wall Street Jrnl.* 9 Sept. 1/1 (*heading*) 'Fat Man' Scolnick & 'scams'... They're known as 'scam' operators, promoters who set up ostensibly legitimate businesses, order large amounts of merchandise on credit, sell it fast and strictly for cash—and then go 'bankrupt', leaving their creditors unpaid. **1968** J. M. ULLMAN *Lady on Fire* (1969) xiv. 181 'The main plan's to go bankrupt... The suppliers will be stuck with unpaid bills for millions. There's a name for that—' 'Scam game,' Forbes said. **1974** *N.Y. Times* 8 July 26/1 Organized crime is stealing millions of dollars from the public through planned fraudulent bankruptcies, called 'scams' by the underworld.

2. A story; a rumour; information.

1964 *Guardian* 8 July 7/6 'People want the 1930s all over again: a thousand naked chorus girls dancing in a pink smog under crystal chandeliers on a revolving staircase on an Alp.'.. 'Didn't someone tell us once that Hollywood went bust with that scam?' **1966** *Amer. Speech* XLI. 281 *Lowdown, scam, the word*, information. **1972** W. MCGIVERN *Caprifoil* (1973) viii. 137 There's been a security break... He's scheduled a press conference... The scam is he's going to break what we know on Spencer. **1972** J. WAMBAUGH *Blue Knight* (1973) i. 28, I paid them [*sc.* informers] from my pocket, and when I made the bust on the scam they gave me, I made it look like I lucked on to the arrest. **1976** *New Musical Express* 17 Apr. 10/2 No, still no scam on Donny and Marie.

scam (skæm), *v. slang* (orig. and chiefly *U.S.*). [Origin obscure: cf. prec.] *intr.* and *trans.* To perpetrate a fraud; to cheat, trick, or swindle. Hence **sca·mming** *vbl. sb.* (in sense 1 b of *SCAM *sb.*).

1963 *Time* 28 June 48/2 My boss was scammin' from the public, and I was scammin' from him. **1966** *Wall Street Jrnl.* 9 Sept. 1/1 'Scam' originally was a carnival term meaning 'to fleece the public'. **1974** *Whig-Standard* (Kingston, Ont.) 9 Apr. 4/1 Scamming..is a form of criminal bankruptcy in which a front man buys out a legitimate firm and then uses the credit rating of the firm to buy large quantities of merchandise. *Ibid.* 4/3 Scamming, he said, ranks second only to bookmaking in financial importance to criminals. **1977** *New Yorker* 30 May 96/2 Local citizens.. try to avoid being scammed by the familiar tergiversations of city politicians.

scamphood. For *nonce-wd.* in Dict. read *rare* and add earlier example.

1845 J. S. LE FANU *Cock & Anchor* I. xvii. 257 He was ripe for the domestic virtues, and ought to renounce scamphood.

scampi (skæ·mpi), *sb. pl.* [a. It. *scampi.*] **1.** Also in *sing.* **scampo.** = *Dublin Bay prawn* s.v. *DUBLIN.

1928 RUSSELL & YONGE *Seas* xiv. 316 It is extremely plentiful in the Adriatic and is sold in the Italian ports under the name of 'Scampo'. **1953** P. BONNER *SPQR* viii. 70 Those little *scampi* are not enough for hungry fishermen. **1966** *Punch* 28 Sept. 483/3 The mysterious scampo which we see in this country, an animal which appears to have no head, is in fact the tail of the Dublin Bay Prawn. **1972** *Daily Tel.* 5 May 2/6 Scampi..make deep burrows in the mud..and thus easily escape the trawling nets of fishermen.

2. a. (A dish of) these prawns eaten as a delicacy, usu. coated with breadcrumbs and fried in oil, or boiled and served with (garlic) sauce.

1930 E. WAUGH *Labels* vi. 158, I ate *scampi* at Cavaletto and felt no ill effects. **1951** N. BALCHIN *Way through Wood* xii. 176 You look like a man who's been gazing on the scampi when they're blown. **1958** A. WILSON *Middle Age of Mrs Eliot* II. 268 It's sure to be scampi or snails or something I couldn't eat. **1962** D. LESSING *Golden Notebook* II. 244 This theme takes us through scampi and the main course. **1978** *Times* 11 Apr. 16/4 Bartolomeo Calderoni... introduced scampi to Britain. *Ibid.* 16/5 As for the scampi, he imported them from Venice's Grand Hotel..when he was head chef at Quaglino's in the 1930s.

b. *attrib.* and *Comb.*

1959 *Good Food Guide* 46 Scampi Provençales and duck Grand Marnier can be arranged to order. **1960** *House & Garden* July 60/3 Such memorable dishes as scampi risotto. **1966** D. SKIRROW *It won't get You Anywhere* vi. 32 What about a little schmaltzy restaurant down the King's Road? Or..maybe further up the river in the scampi belt? **1977** *Chicago Tribune* 2 Oct. VI. 19/1 The scampi marsala and the baked clams also were worthy antipasti choices as was the cannelloni bechamel. **1980** *West Lancs. Evening Gaz.* 7 Jan. 11 (Advt.), Vacancies for full-time/part-time scampi processors.

scan, *sb.* Add: **1. a.** (Further examples.)

1970 O. DOPPING *Computers & Data Processing* xvii. 277 If the computer were to continue the forward scanning, four scans would be needed. **1973** W. MCCARTHY *Detail* ii. 90 The air marshals scanned their bodies with their eyes. Ben passed through. I guess this scan works, he thought.

b. The action or practice of scanning with a beam, aerial, or detector. Cf. *SCAN *v.* 6 f.

1937 *Discovery* Nov. 330/1 This..scheme is modified by leaving out alternate lines during alternate scans, a technique which improves the definition and reduces flicker. **1955** *Sci. Amer.* June 41/1 When Hey published his discovery after the war, radio astronomers began an intensive radio scan of the Sun. **1958** *Times* 2 May 7/2 One of these provided the long-range warning, while the others made a coordinated scan of various sections of the target area as the structure rotated. **1966** M. WOODHOUSE *Tree Frog* xxi. 155 Say that echo's your drone up there... Then you get your vertical scan radar for altitude. **1972** *Sci. Amer.* Jan. 57/1 The rate of scan that produces a micrograph is often much lower than the scanning rate in television.

2. A single line or sweep produced by or in a scanning action (cf. *SCANNING *vbl. sb.* 2 b); also, an entire raster.

1934 J. H. REYNER *Television* ix. 103 The separation between the centres of the lenses was equal to the width of the picture scan. **1945** *Electronic Engin.* XVII. 689 The scan to fly-back ratio is constant for all time base velocities. **1952** *Jrnl. Lab. Clin. Med.* XXXIX. 153 The counter is moved alternately back and forth, with an ½ inch vertical displacement for each sweep or scan over the area occupied by the thyroid gland. **1966** *Electronics* 17 Oct. 114 The large spike at the beginning of each scan is a turnaround transient. **1967** [see *FIELD *sb.* 16 d]. **1975** D. G. FINK *Electronics Engineers' Handbk.* xx. 7 The half line, left over at the end of the field scan, displaces the next field downwards by a full line, and interlacing is achieved.

3. An image, diagram, etc., obtained by scanning; *spec.* in *Med.* = *SCINTISCAN.

1953 *Nucleonics* Nov. 45/1 Fig. 13 presents the coincidence scan and unbalance scan of a patient who showed a regrowth of tumor beneath an area of previous resection. **1956** *Jrnl. Neurosurg.* XIII. 347 (*heading*) This scan is in the posterior-anterior orientation of the head. **1969** M. CRICHTON *Andromeda Strain* I. 22 We'll want a flyby over that town... And a complete scan. **1971** *Guardian* 6 Feb. 1/7 There were, as the first scan of the [lunar] landscape showed, a few very large boulders. **1976** *Woman's Day* (U.S.) Nov. 164/2, I might ask for bone, liver and brain scans to make sure there had not been any metastasis to other parts of my body. **1978** *Nature* 14 Dec. 733/2 (*caption*) Absorbance scans of..SDS-polyacrylamide gels.

4. Special Comb.: **scan-column index,** a tabular representation of coded information concerning or contained in a set of documents, for use in information retrieval.

1962 J. O'CONNOR in *Amer. Documentation* XIII. 205/1 Place the document number in the left-hand column. Then, for each indexing term assigned to that document, look up the column and character abbreviation for the term, and in that column enter that character. I call an index of this form a Scan Column index. **1965** M. E. STEVENS *Automatic Indexing* vi. 118 Tabledex, the Scan-column Index, and similar tools provide to some extent a display of prior associations between index terms. **1971** A. GILCHRIST *Thesaurus in Retrieval* 140 The scan-column index. This is another book-form coordinate information retrieval system..in which all the item numbers are listed numerically in the first column, the other columns containing descriptors, allotted to those items. A separate table indicates which column would be searched for a particular descriptor. To facilitate searching, descriptors have been reduced to symbols.

scan, *v.* Add: **6. b.** To search (literature, a text, a list, etc.) quickly or systematically for particular information or features.

1926 *Rec. Geol. Surv. India* LIX. 202 On scanning this table it will be observed that the pyrope molecule is present in quantity..only in one garnet. **1950** *Amer. Documentation* I. 81 The rapid selector employs an optical-electronic system for scanning a reel of motion picture film on which are entered both abstracts and corresponding index entries. **1966** *Computers & Humanities* I. 12 Some [articles] are so superficial that the reader for whom the volume is designed would do better to scan the most recent ACLS list of computerized research projects in the humanities. **1967** C. BERNERS-LEE in Wills & Yearsley *Handbk. Management Technol.* 7 Some computer manufacturers supply.. suites of statistical programs for scanning files to accumulate the required statistics and then to analyse them in one of a number of ways. **1967** *Times Rev. Industry* July 89/2 Without guide lines as to where the company wants to go, scanning environmental information becomes directionless. **1970** O. DOPPING *Computers & Data Processing* xvii. 277 The computer first scans the table from the beginning to the end comparing the first record with the second, the second with the third, etc. **1972** *Computers & Humanities* VII. 19 Dilligan examines the extent to which linguistic orientation toward prosody serves as the basis for computer programs to scan large bodies of English verse. **1973** *Nature* 31 Aug. p. xiii/1 (Advt.), He or she will be required to scan incoming literature, undertake literature searches.

c. To cause (an area, object, or image) to be systematically traversed by a beam or detector; to convert (an image) into a linear sequence of signals in this way for purposes of transmission or processing.

1928 *Television* Nov. 9/1 One feature which is wrongly quoted by critics relates to how a scene is scanned. **1933** *Proc. Wireless Section Inst. Electr. Engineers* VIII. 219/2 Nipkow in 1884 proposed..to transmit the picture point by point, or to scan the picture. **1953** AMOS & BIRKINSHAW *Television Engin.* I. iv. 52 The electron beam is made to scan the target in a series of nearly horizontal lines. **1954** *Nucleonics* Jan. 60/1 By placing tracing paper and carbon paper between the stylus and the drawing table, the distribution of radioactivity in an area being scanned is recorded. **1962** A. NISBETT *Technique Sound Studio* iv. 81 A replay head scans a slightly greater length of tape than would be suggested by the size of the gap. **1967** *Nursing Times* 18 Aug. 1093/1 Not so well known is the use of radio-isotopes in radiography, to enable various organs of the body to be 'scanned' to investigate function, or the presence of tumours. **1968** *Brit. Med. Bull.* XXIV. 191/2 Radiographs..and so on..can also be digitally structured for insertion in a computer... They are scanned line by line (television-wise) by a 'flying-spot scanner', and passed through an analogue-to-digital converter which..encodes the contrast level of each point, as a row of holes. **1969** *Times* 15 Mar. 7/8 The photographs are scanned point by point by a photoelectric device. **1975** D. G. FINK *Electronics Engineers' Handbk.* xx. 79 Hard-copy facsimile systems generate a signal by systematically scanning the subject copy and producing a current corresponding to its light-intensity variations.

d. *intr.* To carry out scanning. Const. various preps.

1934 J. H. REYNER *Television* viii. 95 By causing the spot on the cathode ray screen to scan over a suitable area the image of the spot traverses the whole of the film. **1948** 'N. SHUTE' *No Highway* v. 147 What interested me most, however, as in every technical paper that one scans through quickly, was the paragraph headed 'Conclusions'. **1953** A. T. STARR *Radio & Radar Technique* i. 46 For the purpose of homing on a ship or aircraft, it is sufficient to scan through a relatively small angle in azimuth, say ±30°. **1961** G. MILLERSON *Technique Television Production* ii. 20 A gun in the picture-tube..produces such a stream of electrons, and this is made to scan over the powdered screen in a regular series of sweeps. **1965** 'J. LE CARRÉ' *Looking-Glass War* xviii. 204 He may start with the wrong crystal... It's safest for base to scan with so many crystals. **1975** *Physics Bull.* July 327/1 As the beam repeatedly scans across the faceplate, charge is accumulated. **1979** *Sci. Amer.* Mar. 82/1 Given a source of light that is monochromatic but tunable, an absorption spectrum can be measured by passing the light through a sample of the gas and scanning continuously through the frequencies surrounding a line in the spectrum.

e. *trans.* To traverse or light upon (a constituent element) as part of the scanning of the larger whole.

1937 A. M. TURING in *Proc. London Math. Soc.* XLII. 233 The machine moves so that it scans the square immediately to the right of the one it was scanning previously. **1937** *Discovery* Nov. 329/1 When the dots are being scanned, the transmitted signal depends on the relative brightness of the dots in turn. **1961** G. MILLERSON *Technique Television Production* ii. 19 As each element is scanned and gives up its information, it becomes 'wiped clean'.

f. To cause (a beam, etc.) systematically to traverse an area; to cause (an aerial) to rotate or oscillate to this end.

1960 E. V. Truefitt in R. F. Hansford *Radio Aids to Civil Aviation* v. 328 The nodding heightfinder is so called because the aerial performs a nodding motion which scans the radar beam in elevation. **1972** *Sci. Amer.* Nov. 40/3 The beam is positioned and focused by scanning the beam over the sample surface and detecting the change in the emission of secondary and reflected electrons as the beam passes over surface detail. **1973** Meyer & Mayer *Radar Target Detection* i. 15/1 If the antenna is scanned sufficiently slowly, more than one pulse may be transmitted and received while the antenna beam sweeps across a given reflecting point. **1976** *Physics Bull.* Oct. 437/1 The proton beam was scanned right across the annulus and hole. **1977** *Sci. Amer.* Sept. 123/3 A much smaller area..is exposed, and the exposure is repeated by either stepping or scanning the image over the wafer.

scanned *ppl. a.* (later examples).

1937 *Proc. London Math. Soc.* XLII. 231 We may call this square the 'scanned square'. **1953** Amos & Birkinshaw *Television Engin.* I. iv. 52 To avoid keystone effect and obtain a true rectangular scanned area, the line saw-tooth current is modulated by the field saw-tooth current so that the angular sweep in the horizontal plane is decreased as the beam moves up the mosaic. **1975** D. G. Fink *Electronics Engineers' Handbk.* xx. 8 Color television standards use the back porch to position the color burst, an eight-cycle burst of color subcarrier..that synchronizes the color-subcarrier oscillator at the end of each scanned line.

Scand (skænd). Colloq. abbrev. of Scandinavian *sb.*

1930 J. Masefield *Wanderer of Liverpool* 14 The others, all Scands, from North Europe, not knowing a word Of English. **1965** *Sun* 28 Sept. 4/5 She is still reckoned a world beauty. How does she do it, this middle-aged Scand? **1973** H. Miller *Open City* ix. 87 She had spent four days among the stodgy, unsubtle Scands on his behalf.

scandal, *sb.* Add: **1. c.** *scandal of particularity* [tr. Ger. (see quots. 1930, 1936)], the difficulty of seeing the particular man, Jesus, as the universal Saviour. Cf.* particularity 1.

1930 tr. G. Kittel in Bell & Deissmann *Mysterium Christi* ii. 31 The scandal of particularity..is the problem of history. Can a particular historical happening be peculiar? Can it be significant *sub specie aeternitatis*? And above all, can this particular occurrence be either peculiar or significant? **1936** C. H. Dodd *Apostolic Preaching & its Development* iv. 219 'Like a strange people left on earth After a judgment day.' This view of the historical status of the events comprised in the coming of Christ introduces us at once to what Professor Gerhard Kittel, in *Mysterium Christi*, calls '*das Ärgernis der Einmaligkeit*', 'the scandal of particularity'. **1961** *Listener* 9 Mar. 435/2 We do no service to religion by reducing either term of the problem, the total mystery of the Godhead or the scandal of particularity. **1979** C. F. D. Moule in M. D. Goulder *Incarnation & Myth* iv. 86 The 'scandal of particularity' is by no means a denial but rather a confirmation of the ubiquity and continuity of God's activity.

7. scandal sheet, a newspaper that is notorious for publishing scandalous or sensational stories.

1904 Ade *True Bills* 110 The Scandal Sheets never show up my Family History. **1939** R. Chandler *Big Sleep* xi. 82 The deal has to be closed to-night or they give the stuff to some scandal sheet. **1974** M. House et al. *Lett. Charles Dickens* III. 363/2 The *Age* and *Satirist*, though infamous indeed, were mere weekly scandal-sheets of no influence or political import. **1981** C. R. Lajeunesse *Dead Man Running* xi. 33 Nobody pays attention to that scandal sheet, let alone reads it.

Scandihoovian (skæːndihū·viăn), *sb.* (and *a.*) Also **-huvian.** *slang* (chiefly *N. Amer.*). Arbitrary jocular alteration of Scandinavian *sb.* Also as *adj.*

1929 F. Bowen *Sea Slang* 117 *Scandihoovian*, any Scandinavian; used as an alternative to *Scandiwegan* or *Scowegian*, but generally in mild contempt. **1966** *Publ. Amer. Dial. Soc.* *1964* xlii. 39 Applied to all Scandinavians ..were *scoop*, *Scandihuvian*, and *Scandie*. **1968** *Amer. Speech* XLIII. 303 There's plenty of color in his [*sc.* the logger's] language too... His 'snuff' is *Scandihoovian dynamite*. **1973** B. Broadfoot *Ten Lost Years* xi. 120 Salt cod! Ugh! Even a Scandihoovian couldn't take that.

Scandiknavery (skæːndinēɪ·vəri). *nonce-wd.* [Fanciful blend of Scandinavian *a.* or *sb.* and Knavery.] Deceit or trickery by Scandinavians.

1939 Joyce *Finnegans Wake* 47 We'll have a free trade Gaels' band and mass meeting For to sod the brave son of Scandiknavery. **1971** S. E. Morison *European Discovery Amer.: Northern Voy.* iii. 72 Michael A. Musmanno's *Columbus was First* (1966) is an amusing, emotional assault on what he calls 'Scandiknavery'.

Scandinavian, *a.* Add: **2.** Applied to a style of furnishing, etc., in a Scandinavian manner, esp. as characterized by simplicity of design and the use of pine-wood.

1959 R. Condon *Manchurian Candidate* ii. 19 All of the furniture was made of blond wood in mutated, modern Scandinavian design. **1964** L. Deighton *Funeral in Berlin* vi. 42 There was Scandinavian-style East German furniture in the room. **1968** S. B. Hough *Sweet Sister Seduced* xxviii. 163 He looked around the room, at the Scandinavian chairs, at the window curtains, and the Hi-fi in the corner. **1972** C. Fremlin *Appointment with Yesterday* xi. 83 Visions of colourful teenage rooms in the Sunday colour-supplements, with Scandinavian wood window-seats, and bright cushions. **1979** M. Eden *Document of Last Nazi* xxix. 171 A neat, cold-looking room, with.. Scandinavian furniture.

B. *sb.* **2.** The various languages of the Scandinavian peoples considered as a unit; *spec.* North Germanic, a subdivision of the Germanic group of Indo-European languages spoken principally in Scandinavia.

1766 J. Cleland *Way to Things by Words* 63 A sense which it also specifically has in the old Scandinavian. **1822** tr. *Malte-Brun's Universal Geogr.* I. 568 The Mœso-Gothic,..the Icelandic and modern Scandinavian, in its two principal dialects the Swedish and the Danish, constitute the Gothic branch. **1888** J. Wright tr. *Brugmann's Elem. Compar. Gram. Indo-Gmc. Lang.* I. 10 Norse (or Scandinavian)..down to the Viking period (800–1000 a.d.) was practically a single language. **1933** L. Bloomfield *Language* iv. 59 While the language of the Lombards seems to have been of the West Germanic type, the others, including Gothic, were closer to Scandinavian. **1954** Pei & Gaynor *Dict. Linguistics* 148 *North Germanic*, a branch of the Germanic group of the Indo-European family of languages; it comprises Icelandic, Swedish, Danish, Norwegian, Faroese and Gotlandic (or Gutnian). Also called *Scandinavian*. **1966** W. P. Lehmann in Birnbaum & Puhvel *Anc. Indo-Europ. Dial.* 18 The occurrence of a third singular form without *-t* in the three coastal dialects of West Germanic and in Scandinavian gives evidence of interrelations between these dialects subsequent to the earliest dialect division of Proto-Germanic. **1978** W. White in W. Whitman *Daybooks & Notebooks* I. 69 Rasmus B. Anderson..Professor of Scandinavian at the University of Wisconsin.

Scandinavianize (skæːndinēɪ·viănəiz), *v.* [f. Scandinavian *a.* + -ize.] *trans.* To render (place-names, etc.) Scandinavian in form or character. So **Scaːndina·vianized** *ppl. a.*; hence **Scaːndinaːvianiza·tion.**

1924 Mawer & Stenton *Introd. to Survey of Eng. Place-Names* iv. 60 English names often appear in a Scandinavianised form. **1933** *Times Lit. Suppl.* 20 Apr. 271/3 The distribution of place-names..is conclusive proof that all but the south-western Corner of Northamptonshire was Scandinavianized to a far greater extent than has been realized. **1937** *Harvard Stud. & Notes in Philol. & Lit.* XX. 155 *Cyninges-clif*, High Coniscliffe... The modern form shows adaptation of the first el[ement] to ON *konungr* for OE *cyning*; for further examples [of] a similar Scandinavianization see..'Connington'. **1956** I. S. Maxwell in D. L. Linton *Sheffield* 131 Those settlements sited somewhat farther from the rivers whose names also contain Scandinavian elements or have been Scandinavianized. **1959** C. L. Wrenn *Word & Symbol* (1967) 24 It would seem..that the Irish word [*cros*] came into Old English rather through Scandinavianised Irish settlers than direct. **1962** H. R. Loyn *Anglo-Saxon England* (1963) i. 60 Only occasionally, as in the Wreak valley..is there overwhelming Scandinavianization of the place-name structure. **1970** *Jrnl. Eng. Place-Name Soc.* II. 12 Rudston YE 98 (originally OE **rōd-stān*) appears in the Bruce fief with the second element scandinavianised to *-stein*, *Rodestein* 332v beside DB *Rodestan*. *Ibid.*, The second element has probably been scandinavianised to *-heim*. **1981** *N. & Q.* Apr. 177/1 In the Danelaw the Grimston(e) names have been taken to be partial scandinavianizations of earlier English names.

scandium. Substitute for def.: A silvery white metallic element, the 'eka-boron' of Mendeleev, which is found in small quantities in association with rare-earth metals (among which it is often classified) and in some tin and tungsten ores, and forms colourless salts in which it is trivalent. Symbol Sc; atomic number 21. (Add further examples.) Hence **sca·ndia,** the white oxide, Sc_2O_3. [*scandium* first formed in Sw. (L. F. Nilson 1879, in *Öfversigt af K. Vetenskaps-Akad. Förh.* XXXVI. iii. 47).]

1880 *Jrnl. Chem. Soc.* XXXVIII. 7 Scandium forms but one oxide, scandia, Sc_2O_3. **1922** *Nature* 17 June 799/1 The extraction and purification of scandium from thorveitite of Madagascar. This mineral, which contains 42 per cent of scandium oxide, is fused with soda and the silica removed by washing. **1955** *Sci. News Let.* 11 June 374/3 Studies made by Britain's Hydraulics Research Station and the Atomic Energy Research Establishment have shown that very finely ground glass containing radioactive scandium oxide moves with the mud when mixed with it in the River Thames. **1974** *Encycl. Brit. Micropædia* VIII. 944/3 Nilson discovered..its oxide, scandia, in the rare-earth minerals gadolinite and euxenite. *Ibid.*, Scandium is now produced on a small scale mostly as a by-product of uranium extraction from the mineral davidite (about 0·02 percent scandium oxide). Very few uses.. have been developed.

Scanian (skēɪ·niăn), *a.* (*sb.*) [f. med.L. *Scania*, ad. ON *Skáni* or *Skáney*, the province of Skane in south Sweden + -an.] **1.** Of or pertaining to the province of Skåne.

1895, etc. [see below]. **1932** *Times Lit. Suppl.* 28 Apr. 306/3 The unrounded *o*, which sometimes becomes the 'sorry caterwaul' of Scanian Swedish. **1963** J. Sahlgren in Brown & Foote *Early Eng. & Norse Studies* 176 The formation of Scanian place-names.

2. a. Designating the first glaciation of the Pleistocene in northern Europe, roughly corresponding to the Günz glacial in the Alps. Also as *sb.* Now *rare.*

1895 J. Geikie in *Jrnl. Geol.* III. 246 *Scanian.* The earliest glacial deposits of northern Europe occur in Skåne—the old division of southern Sweden—hence the provisional name I suggest. *Ibid.* 263 Not a trace of the Scanian bowlder-clay has been recognized in Britain **1903** A. Geikie *Text-bk. Geol.* (ed. 4) II. 1313 Scanian or 1st Glacial Epoch, represented only in the south of Sweden (Scania), which was overridden by a large Baltic glacier. To this period may belong..the oldest terminal moraines and fluvio-glacial gravels of the Arctic lands. **1910** *Encycl. Brit.* XII. 59/1 Although it is admitted that no strict correlation of the European and North American stages is possible, it has been suggested that..the Kansan may represent the Saxonian;..the Jerseyan, the Scanian; [etc.]. **1957** J. K. Charlesworth *Quaternary Era* II. xxxvi. 921 J. Geikie, a constant advocate of multiplicity, postulated six glaciations, named Scanian, Saxonian, Polandian, [etc.]. **1972** R. G. West *Pleistocene Geol. & Biol.* (ed. 2) xi. 219 (*table*) Scanian.

b. Designating a stade in the retreat of the ice-sheet at the end of the last Pleistocene glaciation in northern Europe, (corresponding to the end of the Würm glacial in the Alps) and the resulting stadial moraines. Also as *sb.*

1937 Wooldridge & Morgan *Physical Basis Geogr.* xxiii. 413 The retreat [of the Scandinavian ice-sheet] was punctuated by pauses, marked by well-developed stadial moraines. We have thus the Pomeranian Moraine, the Scanian Moraine (13,700 b.c.) and the Salpausselka of Finland. **1963** R. A. Daly *Changing World of Ice Age* ii. 54 During the third substage, which will be referred to as the Scanian, the front retreated to the position of one of the strong moraines in central Finland, where it bears the name 'First Salpausselkä Moraine'.

scannable, *a.* (Later examples.)

1936 W. de la Mare *Wind blows Over* 37 How narrow a circle of its waters was actually scannable from where she stood. **1975** *Nature* 28 Aug. 703/1 The charges can be liberated optically, in which case the device acts as a scannable photo-detector array, already on the market in the form of hand-held TV cameras.

scanner. Add: **1.** (Further example.)

1967 *Times Rev. Industry* July 89/2 A really sensitive scanner can pick up a bit of information which to most people would be..irrelevant but which to him assumes significance.

3. a. Any device for scanning or systematically examining all parts of something.

1927 *Public Opinion* 18 Feb. 152/3 Place the 'telegraph card' on an endless band passing at a fixed rate under the 'scanner', while at the other end a reproduction soon tumbles into a basket. **1952** *Progress* Spring 34 The Time-Springdale electronic scanner was used to make, from an Ektachrome transparency, the negatives needed for the colour reproduction. **1958** *Times Rev. Industry* July 25/3 A beam-scanner with an output window of pure aluminium foil is fitted to the accelerator. **1970** *New Scientist* 27 Aug. 420/3 Trials with an airborne infrared scanner over the leaking oil well..demonstrated that oil shows up clearly on the scanner. **1977** *Listener* (N.Z.) 15 Jan. 10/1 Scanners are an important innovation because of their superior diagnostic capabilities over alternative techniques, and the enhanced degree of patient safety and comfort they offer. **1977** *Time* 27 June 25/3 Using elaborate 'scanners' to monitor police radio channels, reporters were often at the spot of a reported sighting before the guards and dogs.

b. *Television.* Any of several devices that permit the sequential transmission of an image or its subsequent reconstruction in a receiver.

1929 Sheldon & Grisewood *Television* xiv. 162 Another decided advantage of the drum-scanner is its compactness. **1958** *Observer* 12 Oct. 1/3 There is..a television-type scanner which can transmit pictures of the perpetually unseen far side of the moon. **1975** D. G. Fink *Electronics Engineers' Handbk.* xx. 31 Flying-spot scanners are used in broadcast stations in Europe for both color and monochrome film reproduction.

c. A transmitting and receiving radar aerial, usu. one that rotates or oscillates in order to scan a large area.

1946 *Electronic Engin.* XVIII. 360/2 The speed of rotation of the scanner when manually controlled can be varied from 0 to 4 r.p.m. in either direction. **1965** *New Scientist* 15 July 130/1 The radar scanner continuously sweeps the sky, sending out its impulses and receiving back the reflected impulses. **1970** H. A. Taylor *Airspeed Aircraft since 1931* 172 The raised fuselage also permitted the aircraft to be loaded with the retractable air-to-surface-vessel (asv) scanner, below and aft of the control cabin.

d. *fig.*

1959 *Listener* 8 Jan. 83/2 The selectivity of your mind—your mental scanner—will quickly reveal what there is to be thought about. **1964** *Ann. Reg.* *1963* 403 Work by an Oxford psychologist..suggested that the mechanism.. involved the use of a 'scanner' in the brain which sifted through a large number of possible names.

4. Special Comb.: **scanner fo(u)nt,** a type-writing font that can be read by an optical character-recognition device.

1968 *Amer. Documentation* Jan. 74/2 A secretary types each record for scanner input, using a standard typewriter fitted with an ASA scanner font golfball. *Ibid.*, The optical character reader..reads standard ASA scanner font: 26 alphabetic characters (all upper case), 10 digits, and 25 punctuation and special characters. **1969** *Computers & Humanities* III. 132 Each item to be entered into the file is coded; typed in asa scanner font; read by an optical scanner ..onto magnetic tape; and, finally, entered into an infol file.

scanning, *vbl. sb.* Add: **2. b.** The action of systematically traversing with a beam or detector, esp. in *Television.*

1927 *Bell System Technical Jrnl.* VI. 552 We have thus available in television the same artifice..that is, of scanning, or running over the elements of the image in sequence. **1933** *Discovery* May 156/2 As much as 120-line scanning was used, thus permitting very fine detail indeed. **1936** *Electr. Commun.* XV. 187/1 The most recent demonstration of television in Italy was at Milan in April, 1936. The equipment employed electronic scanning for transmission. **1971** *Amat. Photographer* 13 Jan. 65/2 The system [for reading videotape] was later superseded by transfer scanning, using four magnetic heads on a 2 in diameter drum rotating at 14,400 rpm almost at right angles across 2 in tape, pulled past at 15 ips. **1975** D. G. Fink *Electronics Engineers' Handbk.* xx. 7 Interlaced scanning is achieved by making the horizontal (line-scanning) rate an odd multiple of one-half the vertical (field-scanning) rate.

c. The rapid or systematic searching of textual material for particular information or features.

1937 *Discovery* Sept. 256/2 A random scanning of the list reveals many names familiar to the British Association. **1954** *Amer. Documentation* V. 18/2 Speeds of operation are such as to permit scanning and correlating of generic and specific aspects of indexes in a reasonable time. **1967** *English Studies* XLVIII. 60 (*heading*) An archive of older Scottish texts for scanning by computer. **1970** O. Dopping *Computers & Data Processing* xvii. 277 The misplaced record has only been moved one step, and if the computer were to continue the forward scanning, four scans would be needed. **1975** *Language for Life* (Dept. Educ. & Sci.) viii. 115 The intermediate skills, so essential in word attack in the early stages, are at work in skimming, scanning, and the extraction of meaning in the more complex reading tasks of the later stages.

4. *auditory scanning*: the emission of short pulses of sound and detection of echoes from nearby objects, thought to be used by dolphins for the location and ranging of submerged objects.

1960 W. N. Kellogg in *Psychol. Record* X. 26 Since the noises which make up the echoes are emitted by the dolphin itself, the activity as a whole amounts to a kind of scanning by sound. We suggest the term *auditory scanning*, therefore, as a good name for both the acoustic and the general behavior comprising this elaborate pattern of activity. **1963** *Language* XXXIX. 464 The dolphin's auditory scanning is shown to consist of the emission of a continuous series of sound signals for echolocation plus binaural localization.

5. *attrib.* and *Comb.*, as *scanning movement, speed*; **scanning coil,** any of four coils arranged in pairs around the neck of a cathode-ray tube, the magnetic field of which is varied so as to cause the electron beam to trace out a raster pattern on the screen of the tube; **scanning disc,** a rotating disc having a spiral of holes near the edge, used in mechanical systems of television to provide a sequential scan of a scene by optical means for transmission and to permit reconstruction of the scene at the receiver; **scanning electron microscope,** a form of electron microscope in which an electron beam is scanned in a raster pattern across the specimen; an electrical signal is obtained by collecting and amplifying secondary electrons emitted by the specimen and is applied to a cathode-ray tube scanned in synchronism with the electron beam; hence *scanning electron micrograph, microscopy*; **scanning field** = *RASTER *sb.*[2] a; **scanning line** = *LINE *sb.*[2] 7 i; **scanning raster** = *RASTER *sb.*[2] a; **scanning spot,** the spot where an incident beam (usu. of electrons or light) strikes the surface it is scanning.

1938 J. H. Reyner *Testing Television Sets* iv. 41 The function of the transformer is to step-down the voltage applied to the scanning coil which operates with a correspondingly larger current. **1978** *Broadcast* 27 Nov. 15/2 Camera heads are still stuck with bulky camera tubes, scanning coils, splitter blocks and such paraphernalia. **1927** *Wireless World* 20 Apr. 685/1 This film was then repeated for an observer by means of a receiving equipment involving the use of a suitable neon tube and a scanning disc. **1975** D. G. Fink *Electronics Engineers' Handbk.* xx. 82 An exciter lamp illuminates the subject copy via a curved mirror, and an objective lens images the reflected light to an aperture plate in front of a scanning disk. The scanning disk is opaque except for a transparent spiral, which curves outward from the center of the disk. **1962** *Nature* 6 Oct. 82/1 Figs. 1 and 2 are scanning electron micrographs. **1979** *Sci. Amer.* Sept. 30/3 Wonderful drawings..complemented by scanning electron micrographs. **1953** *Proc. Inst. Electr. Engineers* C. II. 246/2 The main advantage of the scanning electron microscope for transparent specimens is that the resolution is not affected by energy losses of the electrons in the specimen, which in the conventional electron microscope give rise to chromatic aberration. **1972** *Sci. Amer.* Jan. 55/2 The scanning electron microscope is capable of a range of magnifications that overlaps the range of the light microscope or hand magnifying glass at the low end and the range of the transmission electron microscope at the high end. **1966** D. G. Brandon *Mod. Techniques Metallogr.* 51 Image formation by.. scanning electron microscopy. **1975** J. I. Goldstein et al. in Goldstein & Yakowitz *Practical Scanning Electron Microsc.* i. 3 The purpose of this brief historical introduction is to point out the pioneers of scanning electron microscopy and in the process trace the evolution of the instrument. **1935** *Television Today* I. 247/1 Such a scanning field is known as a 'raster'. **1975** D. G. Fink *Electronics Engineers' Handbk.* xx. 5 The lines of the second scanning field fall between the lines of the first field. **1929** Scanning line [see *LINE *sb.*[2] 7 i]. **1933** *Discovery* Oct. 318/1 The new German standard picture, consisting of 180 scanning lines, is officially considered sufficient for the opening of regular transmissions. **1960** in *Rep. Comm. Broadcasting* 334 in *Parl. Papers 1961–2* (Cmnd. 1753) IX. 259 There was.. a significant difference in the visibility of the scanning lines—the 625-line pictures being..noticeably better than the 405-line pictures. **1958** *Observer* 12 Oct. 15/4 Every few minutes, the radio telescope makes small scanning movements, up and down and from side to side. This helps to fix the direction of the radio signals from the rocket to within half a degree. **1935** *Television Today* I. 247/2 The production of a scanning raster on the cathode-ray tube of a television receiver by electrical means involves the application of two voltages of saw-tooth wave form to the two pairs of deflecting plates of a cathode-ray tube. **1975** D. G. Fink *Electronics Engineers' Handbk.* xx. 33 The starting point for generating color pictures is the optical and electronic superposition of the red-, green-, and blue-tube scanning rasters. **1929** Sheldon & Grisewood *Television* xii. 126 The scanning speed may be greatly increased by use of a series of oppositely rotating lens-discs. **1934** *Sun* (Baltimore) 20 Aug. 2/3 A tiny metal mirror, mounted on a slender rod and vibrated at scanning speeds, was presented..as..the solution of one of television's major problems. **1929** Sheldon & Grisewood *Television* xiii. 139 Since the scanning spot has finite dimensions, its response to an abrupt change in the surface being viewed will be less sharply defined than the original. **1975** D. G. Fink *Electronics Engineers' Handbk.* xx. 5 The electron beams that create the scanning spots are approximately circular, but their intensity is not uniform.

scant, *v.* **II. 7.** For 'Now *rare*' read 'Now chiefly *U.S.*' and add later examples.

1969 *New Yorker* 6 Sept. 111/1 Several thousand..men were on duty in the streets that day, while, presumably, Securitate was not scanting its duties elsewhere. **1977** *N.Y. Rev. Books* 14 Apr. 5 (Advt.), No thinker or movement is dismissed as too radical, no issue is scanted as too controversial.

scanting, *ppl. a.* Add: **b.** Decreasing, diminishing. *rare.*

1916 Kipling *Tales of 'The Trade'* 107 It was necessary to go down at once and waste whole minutes of the precious scanting light.

scantling, *sb.* Add: **2. b.** Also with reference to aircraft.

1933 [see *FRAME *sb.* 11 i]. **1978** *Jrnl. R. Soc. Arts* CXXVI. 681/2 Figure 3 indicates the comparative scantlings for compression structures having the same load carrying capacity.

7. a. (Further examples.)

1958 *Chambers's Techn. Dict.* 743/2 *Scantling*.., a piece of timber of thickness from 2 to 4 in. and of width from 2 to 4½ in. **1965** 'Lauchmonen' *Old Thom's Harvest* ii. 15 The young girl walked round the pickets that had fallen off the rotten scantling runners of the wooden part of the fence. **1972** *Gloss. Terms Timber* (*B.S.I.*) 21 *Scantling.* 1. *Softwood.* A piece of square-sawn timber 50 mm to under 100 mm thick and 50 mm to under 125 mm wide. 2. *Hardwood.* Timber converted to an agreed specification such as waggon oak scantlings. Otherwise any squared-edged piece of dimensions not conforming to other standard terms.

b. (Earlier examples.)

1703 tr. *H. van Oosten's Dutch Gardener* IV. xii. 225 You must keep your Scantling or Boares whereon your Pots stand very neat. **1743** *Colonial Rec. Georgia* (1906) VI. 68 The Reverend Mr. Bolzius [petitioned] this Board to allow him a Quantity of Boards, Planks, and Scantling. **1785** T. Jefferson *Notes on Virginia* xv. 279 The private buildings are very rarely constructed of stone or brick; much the greatest portion being of scantling and boards.

scanty, *a.* Add: **B.** *sb.* Now only *pl.* Underwear, esp. short knickers or panties for women. *colloq.* (orig. *U.S.*).

1928 J. P. McEvoy *Show Girl* (*title-page*), The hottest little wench that ever shook a scanty at a tired business man. **1929** M. Lief *Hangover* 269 There's no law in New Jersey forcing a husband to look at his wife's scanties, is there? **1934** T. Smith *Bishop's Jaegers* 5 Whereas men.. still struggle along with the old-fashioned..name of drawers..woman have far outstripped them. Theirs must be known now by such frivolous..appellations as panties, scanties..step-ins..and other similar..terms. **1944** E. Carr *House of All Sorts* 101 A puff of wind from the open door caught and ballooned the scanties. **1951** M. Dickens *My Turn to make Tea* iv. 73 No don't go, dear. You've seen me in my scanties, anyway. **1959** 'O. Mills' *Stairway to Murder* vii. 75 'Now you've got some midnight-blue scanties.' He held up Charles's underpants apologetically. **1964** J. Hale *Grudge Fight* I. i. 22 Bennet, who always looks after number one, is wearing Scapa scanties next to the skin. Long underpants and a long-sleeved vest made of thick, oily wool. **1977** *Time* 24 Jan. 46/1 Maddie's blue scanties emerge from the M.P.s' briefcases at inauspicious moments and whip through the air like naval pennants.

scapa, var. *SCARPER *v.*

scape, *sb.*[1] Add: **7.** **scape-pipe** *U.S.* = *escape pipe* s.v. Escape *sb.*[1] 8.

1838 E. Flagg *Far West* I. 51 The stern roar of the scape-pipe, gave evidence of the fearful power summoned up to overcome the flood. **1949** E. Hungerford *Wells Fargo* 22 This craft, in her neat coat of immaculate white, and her yellow stacks, 'scape pipes and upper works, and her gayly striped paddle-houses, was a pretty sight.

scape, *sb.*[3] Add: (Further examples as second element of combs.) See also *CITYSCAPE, *LUNARSCAPE, *MOONSCAPE, *ROOFSCAPE, etc.

1908 'O. Henry' *Gentle Grafter* 6 The third day of the rain it slacked up awhile in the afternoon, so me and Andy walked out to the edge of the town to view the mud-scape. **1930** *Sat. Rev. Lit.* 27 Dec. 486/3 One may..strive to..obtain a meager impression—starved, wry glimpses—of the private mindscape beyond. **1972** G. S. Fraser in Cox & Dyson *20th-Cent. Mind* II. xi. 382 Stephen's associations [in Joyce's *Ulysses*] are not really loose, he composes elaborate moodscapes in sub-Paterian prose. **1973** *Ar Internat.* Mar. 49/2 Raffael's minutely dabbed garnish color..has more in common with the jungle-scapes and frottages of Max Ernst. **1975** *Times Lit. Suppl.* 28 Nov. 1409/3 The 'largest oil painting in the world' (a sea-cum-strandscape by the rightly overlooked Jacob Mesdag). **1977** 'J. McVean' *Bloodspoor* xvii. 208 The two figures..were as much part of the desert winterscape now as the thorn barbs or the wheeling constellations in the sky above.

scape (skēⁱp), *sb.*[4] [Origin unknown: perh. f. Scape *sb.*[3] (see *INSCAPE *sb.*).] In the terminology of G. M. Hopkins: a reflection or impression of the individual quality of a thing or action. Hence **scaped, sca·pish** adjs.; **sca·ping.**

1868 G. M. Hopkins *Jrnls. & Papers* (1959) 170 The types of the two thieves..were in the wholeness and general scape of the anatomy original and interesting. (The prominence of the peculiar square-scaped drapery etc. in Holbein and his contemporaries is remarkable.) **1869** *Ibid.* 194 It is just the things which produce dead impressions, which the mind..has made nothing of and brought into no scaping, that force themselves up in this way afterwards. **1874** *Ibid.* 245, I saw also a good engraving of his *Vintage Festival*, which impressed the thought one would also gather from Rembrandt..of a master of scaping rather than of inscape. For the vigorous rhetorical but realistic and unaffected scaping holds everything but no arch-inscape is thought of. *Ibid.* 247 W. L. Wylie—*Goodwin Sands*—Fiery truthful rainbow-end; green slimy races of piers; all clean, atmospheric, truthful, and scapish. **1883** —— *Sermons & Devotional Writings* (1959) II. ii. 136 Our action leaves in our minds scapes or species, the extreme 'intention' or instressing of which would be painful. *Ibid.*, The soul then can be instressed *in* the species or scape of any bodily action..and so *towards* the species or scape of any object, as of sight, sound, taste, smell. **1948** W. A. M. Peters *Gerard Manley Hopkins* i. 2 The suffix 'scape' in 'landscape'..posits the presence of a unifying principle which enables us to consider part of the countryside..as a unit..but so that this part is perceived to carry the typical properties of the actually individed whole..'Scape' comes to stand for that being which is an exact copy or reflection of the individual whole on which it is dependent for its existence.

scape, *int.* Add: Also used for the brambling's call.

1962 *Times* 6 Nov. 14/4 The bramblings' harsh and nasal call-note, usually written 'scape'.

scapegoat (skēⁱ·pgōᵘt), *v.* [f. the sb. or back-formation from *SCAPEGOATING.] *trans.* To make a scapegoat of (someone); to subject to scapegoating. Hence **sca·pegoated** *ppl. a.*; **sca·pegoater.**

1943 *Jrnl. Abnormal & Social Psychol. Clin. Suppl.* XXXVIII. 143 Persons who had been inclined to scapegoat him originally. *Ibid.* 151 The immediate and desired objective of the scapegoaters was to relieve their feelings of frustration, of fear [etc.]. **1972** *Guardian* 27 Dec. 12/3 We either scapegoat the individual..or we scapegoat society. **1974** S. G. Shoham *Society & Absurd* IV. iv. 162 The child becomes a receptacle for the ressentiment of the scapegoater. **1976** *Child's Guardian* Winter 13/3 Oliver's problems illustrate one of the great difficulties in trying to help a scapegoated child. Often the parent/child relationships are so complicated that they seem to need each other in order to continue hurting each other. **1977** R. L. Duncan *Temple Dogs* (1978) I. ii. 55 A company is really too large to scapegoat.

scapegoating (skēⁱ·pgōᵘtiŋ). [f. Scapegoat + -ing[1].] The action or practice of making a scapegoat of someone; *spec.* in *Psychol.*, aggressively punitive behaviour directed for whatever reason against other (weaker) persons or groups.

1943 Veltfort & Lee in *Jrnl. Abnormal & Social Psychol. Clin. Suppl.* XXXVIII. 138 Scapegoating is a phenomenon wherein some of the aggressive energies of a person or group are focused upon another individual, group, or object. **1950** T. Adorno et al. *Authoritarian Personality* xi. 409 Lack of insight into one's own shortcomings and the projection of one's own weaknesses and faults onto others..probably represents the essential aspect of..scapegoating. **1962** *Listener* 7 June 1002/2 Speaking of scapegoating in new housing blocks, she tells of patients who have actually been robbed finding it difficult to obtain a hearing because they were suspected of paranoid delusions. **1977** C. Husband in H. Giles *Lang., Ethnicity & Intergroup Relations* ix. 234 The intervention of Powell at a singularly propitious moment..propelled the already vigorous scapegoating process into an unmanageable level.

scapegrace, *sb.* Add: **2.** *N. Amer.* The red-throated loon or diver, *Gavia stellata.*

1835 J. J. Audubon *Ornith. Biogr.* III. 24 In the neighbourhood of Boston, and along the Bay of Fundy, they are best known by the names of 'Scape-grace' and 'Cape-racer'. **1917** T. G. Pearson *Birds Amer.* I. 15 Red-throated Loon.. Cape Racer; Scape-grace. **1957** W. L. McAtee *Folk-Names Canad. Birds* 2 Red-throated Loon..scape-grace (Rationalization of Cape Race [where it is often seen]).

scapeless (skē¹·plės), *a.*³ [f. *SCAPE *sb.*⁴ + -LESS.] In the terminology of G. M. Hopkins: lacking scape, without distinctive and individual quality.

1874 G. M. HOPKINS *Jrnls. & Papers* (1959) 245 Scapeless aimless background of tapestry, a cannon, and so on. *Ibid.* 248 The feet not inscaped but with a scapeless look they sometimes no doubt have..and veined too, which further breaks their scaping.

scaph, var. *SCAF.

scaphopod (skæ·fopǫd). *Zool.* [ad. mod.L. class name *Scaphopoda* (H. G. Bronn *Klassen & Ordnungen des Thier-reichs* (1862) III. II. 524), f. SCAPHO- + Gr. πούς, ποδ- foot.] (See quot. 1935); = *tusk-shell* s.v. TUSK *sb.*¹ 3. Also *attrib.*

1913 B. B. WOODWARD *Life of Mollusca* iii. 47 A true Scaphopod (*Dentalium*) and representatives of the more primitive Ammonoidea..likewise came into existence in the Devonian epoch. **1935** TWENHOFEL & SHROCK *Invertebr. Paleontol.* ix. 360 Scaphopods are small, marine, bilaterally symmetrical mollusks with an external, curved and tapering tubular shell open at each end. *Ibid.* 362 The scaphopod shell is composed of aragonite. **1975** *Nature* 11 Dec. 555/3 Molluscs, primarily bivalves but also scaphopods and various gastropods,..progress through soft substrates.

scapigerous, *a.* (Earlier example.)

1859 D. BUNCE *Travels with Dr. Leichhardt* 29 *Xanthoria*, or grass-tree, three species of which enlivened the landscape with their scapigerous white blossoms.

scapolitization (skæ:pǫlitəizē¹·ʃən). *Geol.* [f. SCAPOLITE + -IZE + -ATION.] The alteration of alumino-silicate minerals of igneous rocks into, or their replacement by, minerals of the scapolite group. Also **scapo·litize** *v. trans.*; **scapo·litized** *ppl. a.*

1909 A. HARKER *Nat. Hist. Igneous Rocks* xii. 302 (*caption*) Apatite vein with scapolitized borders. *Ibid.* 383/1 (Index), Scapolitization. **1924** *Mineral Abstr.* II. 227 Chemical analyses by Pisani on fresh and scapolitized material from Pouzac show that the alteration is accompanied only by addition of sodium chloride. **1932** A. HARKER *Metamorphism* xvi. 255 This widespread scapolitization..is doubtless related to the mechanical conditions proper to regional metamorphism, which facilitate the permeation of the rocks by volatile bodies. **1936** *Nature* 29 Feb. 366/2 Gabbroid rocks were intruded..and were followed by late-stage solutions which scapolitised the sediments, turned the gabbro into epidiorite and chloritised the Basement schists. **1954** *Jrnl. Geol. Soc. Australia* I. 6 The current-bedded sediments are scapolitized calcareous rocks. *a* **1965** A. W. G. WHITTLE in G. J. Williams *Econ. Geol. N.Z.* (1965) xiv. 227/1 A large amount of titanite was introduced as anhedra during scapolitization, commonly aggregated to form elongated veins within the rock.

scapulimancy. Also: Also **scapulomancy.** (Further examples.)

1911 J. HASTINGS *Encycl. Relig. & Ethics* IV. 817/1 Scapulomancy is mentioned by Jāḥiẓ together with palmistry and another mode of augury.., viz. divination by the gnawing of mice. **1937** R. H. LOWIE *Hist. Ethnol. Theory* xi. 184 Speck and Cooper have traced scapulimancy from northern Europe through Asia to Eastern North America. **1961** G. CLARK *World Prehistory* viii. 199 It will be recalled that the practice of scapulomancy..can be traced back to the 'Neolithic' Lung-shan culture. **1973** T. R. TREGEAR *Chinese* i. 19 The bones used in their scapulimancy were incised by markings which are the earliest form of Chinese writing.

scar, *sb.*² Add: **1. a.** (Later examples of *transf.* use.)

1884 'MARK TWAIN' *Huck. Finn* (1885) ii. 24 We..pulled down the river..to the big scar on the hillside, and went ashore. **1929** W. FAULKNER *Sartoris* IV. 305 He sat his horse in the faint scar of the road. **1946** *R.A.F. Jrnl.* May 172 Their repair work had been so rapid that we could find few scars in the main part of the city.

3. scar tissue, the fibrous connective tissue of which scars are formed; also *fig.*

1875 T. HOLMES *Treat. Surg.* xxi. 386 When the scar-tissue remains permanent, although the scar is ugly and of lower organisation than the natural parts, yet it causes no important inconvenience. **1932** F. BEEKMAN *Office Surg.* xii. 291 Keloids appear most frequently in individuals of races who have a predisposition for the formation of excessive scar tissue. **1957** A. HUXLEY *Let.* 12 Jan. (1969) 815, I have just embarked on a new treatment aimed at getting rid of some of the scar tissue on my corneas. **1975** *New Yorker* 1 Dec. 55/2 'It leaves scar tissue,' one former campaign manager said. 'There's no way it can't have a deep impact on the candidate's psyche and physical condition.' **1978** J. IRVING *World according to Garp* iii. 53 The brave face was naked, the eyes clear and challenging, the scar tissue everywhere.

scarab. Add: **1.** Now also *scarab beetle.*

1921 C. A. EALAND *Insect Life* vi. 179 We do not possess in this country [*sc.* Great Britain] any of the Scarab Beetles, sacred to the ancient Egyptians. **1958** 'W. HENRY' *Seven Men at Mimbres Springs* vii. 73 Young Sanchez [packed] a cottonwood slingshot and six or eight smooth stones suitable for anything up to bullfrogs or scarab beetles.

scarbroite. Now regarded as a carbonate, not a silicate. (Further example.)

1960 *Mineral. Mag.* XXXII. 353 Scarbroite, a fine-grained but compact deposit obtained from fissures in the sandstone on the north Yorkshire coast, is shown by chemical analysis to have an idealized formula $Al_2(CO_3)_3 \cdot 12Al(OH)_3$.

scarce, *adv.* **2. d.** (Further examples.)

1915 G. FRANKAU *Tid'apa* ii. 14 A scarce-breathed, flickering soul-wave, discoded but conscience-deep. **1921** W. DE LA MARE *Veil* 35 There came, scarce-heard, Claws, fluttering feathers, Of deluded bird. **1922** BLUNDEN *Shepherd* (ed. 2) 53 In the scarce-glimmering boles. **1935** C. DAY LEWIS *Time to Dance* 33 Like a bird scarce-fledged they flew, whose flying-hours are few. **1951** W. DE LA MARE *Winged Chariot* 57, I match that child with this scarce-changed old man.

scarcity. Add: **2. b. scarcity value** (later examples); *scarcity price* (example).

1883 Scarcity value [see *monopoly value* s.v. *MONOPOLY 7]. **1920** *Times* 5 June 15/3 Profits made on selling commodities at scarcity prices since then would escape the levy. **1936** J. M. KEYNES *Gen. Theory Employment* xxiv. 377 Our aim of depriving capital of its scarcity-value. **1972** 'G. BLACK' *Bitter Tea* (1973) x. 162 She was a blonde. They have a great time in the Orient, scarcity value.

7. *scarcity root* (example).

1787 J. WOODFORDE *Diary* 29 June (1926) II. 330 Sr. Willm Jernegan sent me by Mr. Custance a Treatise on the Plant called Scarcity Root.

scare, *sb.*² Add: **4.** *scare-headline, -story*; **scare-buying** *U.S.* = *panic buying* s.v. *PANIC *sb.*² 3 b; **scare-head** (earlier and later examples); hence as *v. trans.*, to furnish with a scare-head; to display as a scare-headline; **sca·re-headed** *ppl. a.*; **scare tactic,** a stratagem or ruse which seeks to manipulate public reaction by the exploitation of fear; usu. *pl.*

1944 *Sun* (Baltimore) 23 Nov. 15/3 The sharply restricted supply of cotton goods..comes at a time when so-called 'scare' buying of such commodities is in boom proportions. **1959** *Wall St. Jrnl.* 4 May 1/1 Steel customers have been buying heavily for weeks, in anticipation of a strike... This 'scare buying'..boosted steel-making to a scheduled 94·4% of the industry's rated capacity last week. **1887** *Courier-Jrnl.* (Louisville, Kentucky) 15 Feb. 6/4 The 'scare' head which follows..is an evidence that the country paper tries hard to keep pace with the times and its metropolitan contemporary. **1902** F. NORRIS *Responsibilities of Novelist* (1903) 300 The name of the leading lady or leading man is 'scare-headed' [on theatre bills]. **1911** H. S. HARRISON *Queed* xviii. 219 The..penny evening paper..scare-headed a jaundiced account of the affair. **1926** *Scribner's Mag.* Sept. 251/1 If he is at all impressionable, a glance at the scare-heads will utterly ruin what otherwise might have been a successful day. **1951** E. PAUL *Springtime in Paris* v. 95 Metal workers were uneasy, having been stamped with scareheads against the Marshall Plan. **1971** *Sci. Amer.* May 10/2 Professor Reuterdahl's recent article in the *Dearborn Independent* is given its real place by the scare-head of the cover, which asks, in 3/4-inch letters, 'Is Einstein a Plagiarist?'. **1889** W. D. HOWELLS *Hazard of New Fortunes* II. 281 He read..the deeply scare-headed story of Conrad's death. **1892** J. KIRKLAND *Story of Chicago* I. xxxii. 381 The newspapers blazed with what are technically called 'scare headlines'. **1912** KIPLING *Uses of Reading* in *Book of Words* (1928) 87 The other made bad worse by shouting what was no better than a newspaper scare head-line. **1960** *Guardian* 11 Apr. 1/1 Rumours circulated..that the Government might introduce martial law, but this appeared to have been purely a scare story. **1977** P. JOHNSON *Enemies of Society* vii. 94 The technique of the lobby is to put out a scare-story, and then move on quickly to a fresh one when scientific investigation proves the first one unfounded. **1979** *Time* 8 Jan. 40/1 The scare stories are based on phony evidence or plain prejudice. **1967** *Punch* 8 Nov. 719/1 This alleged address from Zinoviev, the President of the Comintern..left an *Angst* about Tory scare-tactics from which Transport House has never recovered. **1973** *Black Panther* 17 Mar. 8/1 (*caption*) Boxes of poisoned lettuce have had to be destroyed. This is no 'scare tactic', it is for real. **1976** *Survey* Summer–Autumn 191 The slickers in the Pentagon are using their annual scare tactics in support of bigger budgets.

scare, *v.* **1. d.** For *U.S.* read 'orig. and chiefly *U.S.*' and add earlier and later examples. Also (*fig.*), to procure, obtain, 'rustle up'. *colloq.*

1846 *Spirit of Times* 25 Apr. 97/1 He is also to send us the rattles of the biggest snake ever scared up in 'Old Norf Caline'. **1852** H. C. WATSON *Nights in Block-House* 169 Ad was equal to two or three common men in scarin' up and shootin' red-skins. **1890** *Stock Grower & Farmer* 1 Feb. 4/2 A country the like of which can not be 'scared up' in many thousands of miles travel. **1913** J. LONDON *Night-Born* 262 Los Angeles must be on the dink when this is the best you can scare up. **1922** GALSWORTHY *Loyalties* II. ii. 71 Let's cut it and get out to Nairobi. I can scare up the money for that. **1940** *New Yorker* 13 Jan. 31/2 A young woman who had somehow contrived to scare up a permit to leave the country. **1952** J. JONES *From Here to Eternity* xii. 145 Maybe I can scare you up some [work]. **1961** *Listener* 2 Nov. 738/1 Professor Ford has always managed to scare up a few distinguished contributors. **1976** H. NIELSEN *Brink of Murder* ii. 21 Why don't you relax..and then we'll scare up some dinner.

2. (Later U.S. example.)

1869 'MARK TWAIN' *Innoc. Abr.* 440 This creature has scared at everything he has seen to-day.

3. (Further examples.) Freq. in negative, esp. with *easily* or *easy.*

1941 *Sun* (Baltimore) 4 Jan. 6/2 Whatever else they do or fail to do, the Irish don't scare easily. **1951** 'M. SPILLANE' *One Lonely Night* iv. 61 They're the kind of people who scare easily. **1967** O. RUHEN in *Coast to Coast 1965–6* 192 The horse won't scare, but take it easy. **1972** *Village Voice* (N.Y.) 1 June 5/2 'We don't scare easy,' his cousin said as I went out the door.

scarecrow, *sb.* Add: **2. c.** *Mil. slang.* Used in the war of 1939–45, to designate weapons or manœuvres which had a purely deterrent effect (see quots.).

1943 T. DUDLEY-GORDON *Coastal Command at War* iv. 41 This was the squadron..which flew the Scarecrow Control. ..No one knows how many times a U-Boat captain was forced to keep submerged because a Tiger Moth, which *might* be dangerous, was doing a scarecrow on him. **1952** M. TRIPP *Faith is Windsock* ii. 41 Two daylight attacks on Solingen... Gigantic blobs of oily smoke hung in the sky... It was their first experience of the German terror weapon, the scarecrow. **1966** L. MIALL *Richard Dimbleby, Broadcaster* 39 A great gush of flame and smoke showed the bursting of a 'scarecrow', the oddity designed by the Germans to simulate a heavy bomber being shot down, and so to put any of our less experienced pilots off their stroke.

3. Delete † (*obs.*) from sense 'a lean, gaunt figure' and add later examples.

1932 E. MUSPRATT *Wild Oats* v. 96 He was a great gaunt scarecrow, bent and crippled by disease. **1959** I. & P. OPIE *Lore & Lang. Schoolch.* ix. 169 Thin people inspire almost as many names and jokes as fat people, but..the names..are merely descriptive, as:..scarecrow, scraggy, skin and bones.

scaredly (skēə·ıdli), *adv.* [f. SCARED *ppl. a.* + -LY².] In a scared manner.

1901 G. B. SHAW *Devil's Disciple* I, in *Three Plays for Puritans* 18 *To Essie.* Essie: did you say amen? *Essie* (scaredly). No. **1978** G. VAUGHAN *Belgrade Drop* xi. 74 Savka said suddenly, scaredly: 'I hope to God you're sure!'

scaredy-cat (skēə·ıdi,kæt). *slang.* [f. SCARED *ppl. a.* + -Y⁶ + CAT *sb.*¹] A timorous person, a coward; = *fraidy cat* s.v. *'FRAID *a.* Also as *adj.*, scared. Also *ellipt.*, as *scaredy.*

1933 D. PARKER *After Such Pleasures* (1934) 86 It's so nice to meet a man who isn't scaredy-cat about catching my beri-beri. **1948** D. BALLANTYNE *Cunninghams* 173 Sydney called them scaredy-cats because they wouldn't run like he had. **1959** I. & P. OPIE *Lore & Lang. Schoolch.* x. 185 The boy..who will not take part in a prank..is a 'scaredy', a 'scare-baby'. **1965** 'LAUCHMONEN' *Old Thom's Harvest* xii. 149 You can play hard-to-get but don't look so scaredy-cat. **1980** H. R. F. KEATING *Murder of Maharajah* iii. 57 You know your mother, always was a scaredy-cat.

scaremonger. Add: Hence as *v. intr.*, to spread alarming reports; **sca·remongering** *ppl. a.*

1966 *New Statesman* 14 Jan. 38/3 The new Home Secretary, Roy Jenkins, commented on TV that the *Express* story was 'premature and slightly scaremongering'. **1976** 'D. HALLIDAY' *Dolly & Nanny Bird* ii. 28 You scaremongered all the way through. You created panic.

scarer. Add: *spec.* (usu. as *bird-scarer*) a person or thing (other than a traditional scarecrow) for frightening birds away from crops.

1930 H. H. THOMAS *Pop. Gardening Ann.* 24 A good cheap scarer on the market is obtainable in the shape of a black cat's head. **1953** R. GODDEN *Kingfishers catch Fire* xiii. 157 The bird-scarers had come to watch over the cherry crop. **1961** *Times* 7 Jan. 8/6, I could not make out whether the contents were a bird-scarer or a child's rattle. **1971** *Country Life* 16 Sept. 682/1 We were much troubled by an explosive bird-scarer in a field of barley adjoining our house.

scarf, *sb.*¹ Add: **3. e.** (Earlier example.)

1823 C. MATHEWS *Let.* 17 Feb. in A. Mathews *Mem. C. Mathews* (1839) III. 368 And also two scarfs, I think they are called.

7. *scarf-end, -tie.*

1868 G. M. HOPKINS *Note-bks. & Papers* (1937) 115 Fine afternoon with snow-white flying scarf-ends in the clouds. **1922** JOYCE *Ulysses* 440 In an oatmeal sporting suit.., tony buff shirt, shepherd's plaid Saint Andrew's cross scarftie. **1976** *Billings* (Montana) *Gaz.* 16 June 9-c/5 (Advt.), This dress is a breeze—buttons up one side to the flutter of a scarf tie.

scarf, *sb.*² Add: **3. scarf-joint** (further examples).

1919 S. F. WALKER *Electr. Mining Machinery* xx. 154 A scarf joint is..good if it is well made and very carefully bound. **1948** F. WIGHTMAN *Wind is Free* ii. 33 It had to be hoisted with a block & tackle on sheerpoles to bring it up to where its scarph joint fitted into the one cut on the forward end of the keel timber.

scarf, *sb.*⁵ Add: **2.** *Forestry.* A V-shaped incision cut in a trunk during felling, to govern the direction in which the tree is to fall; also, the sloping surface left by such an incision.

1863 *8th Ann. Rep. Maine Board Agric.* 36 The bark of the stock opposite the scarf with a thin sliver of wood is cut down. **1887** J. D. BILLINGS *Hardtack & Coffee* (1888) 180 When an army first went into camp trees were cut with the scarf two or three feet above the ground. **1903** R. J. CLOW *Pillar of Salt* iii. 55 It meant a bit of work to cut down a tree seven feet in diameter... Stello cut in the inside scarf and I put in the back chip. **1926** K. S. PRICHARD *Working Bullocks* xxxii. 296 Half-dozen men..stood on their rough-barked logs... The scarf showed ruddy as a wound in the logs. **1962** J. N. WINBURNE *Dict. Agric. &*

Allied Terminology 673/1 *Scarf*,..the beveled cut on a log or stump which results from undercutting a tree in felling.

scarf (skɑ̄ɹf), *sb.*[6] U.S. slang var. SCOFF *sb.*[2] **1932** *Evening Sun* (Baltimore) 9 Dec. 31/5 *Scarf*, food. **1944** D. BURLEY *Orig. Handbk. Harlem Jive* 81 'Pick up on the scoff, cherub.'.. The 'scoff' or 'scarf' in the above simple statement is dinner food, meals. **1961** RIGNEY & SMITH *Real Bohemia* p. xvi, *Scarf*, food; eat, believed to have come from a French chef, Scarfannelli. **1973** L. SNELLING *Heresy* II. iv. 89 How's for a bit of scarf, my tummy's anguished.

scarf, *v.*[2] **1. a.** (Later example of var. form.) **1976** *Yankee* Apr. 109/1 He forced me to scarph the keel timbers in watertight sections.

scarf, *v.*[3] Restrict *Whaling* to sense in Dict. and add: **2.** *N.Z. Forestry.* To cut a scarf in (timber). Also *back-*, *belly-scarf* (see quot. 1928). Cf. *SCARF *sb.*[5]
1899 J. BELL *Shadow of Bush* xiv. 83 The smaller trees ..had been 'scarfed', or cut partly through in readiness, and skilfully, so that each, when struck, might again in its turn strike and bring down another. **1904** 'G. B. LANCASTER' *Sons o' Men* 164 He..scarfed the timber for the saw. **1928** P. T. KENWAY *Pioneering in Poverty Bay* v. 38 He will 'belly-scarf' and 'back-scarf' the lot, that is to say he will cut about a third through on both the lower and higher sides.

scarf (skɑ̄ɹf), *v.*[4] U.S. slang var. SCOFF *v.*[2] **1.** Also *absol.* and const. *up* and *down.*
1960 R. G. REISNER *Jazz Titans* 164 *Scarf*, eat. **1968** C. ARMSTRONG *Balloon Man* viii. 98 They don't want to faint from hunger, so..they scarf up what they call a bite before they go. **1974** *Black World* June 77/1 King Dust would sit there, 'scarfing', as he called it, in silence. **1975** *High Times* Dec. 80/3, I can pick jimsonweed and chop it up and scarf it down as well as the next guy. **1976** R. CONDON *Whisper of Axe* II. xviii. 265 Let's..scarf up some of that osso bucco.

scarfed, *ppl. a.*[1] Add: (Further examples.) Cf. SCARVED *ppl. a.* in Dict. and Suppl.
1920 BLUNDEN *Waggoner* 53 The lispering aspens and the scarfed brook grasses With wakened melancholy writhe the air. **1967** *Boston Sunday Herald* 30 Apr. v. 5/1 (Advt.), Shaped and scarfed for cool summer perfection in rayon and silk.

scarfed, *ppl. a.*[2] Add: Also **scarphed.** (Later example.)
1975 *Anglo-Saxon England* IV. 187 D. M. Wilson has noted that long ships with scarphed keels were built in Scandinavia in the thirteenth century.

scarify, *v.*[1] Add: **scarifying** *vbl. sb.* (earlier example in sense 3 a of vb.); **sca·rifyingly** *adv.*[1]
1865 W. WHITE *Eastern England* xvi. 222 The engine.. is ready for ploughing, scarifying or drain-cutting. In working the scarifier, the large iron pully is anchored on the edge of the ditch. **1921** D. CANFIELD *Brimming Cup* II. xi. 182 How scarifyingly he would laugh at me.

scarify (skēᵊ·rifəi), *v.*[2] *slang* (orig. *dial.*). Also **scarrify.** [Irreg. f. SCARE *v.* + -IFY, perh. after TERRIFY *v.*] *trans.* To scare, frighten; to terrify.
1794 A. THOMAS *Newfoundland Jrnl.* (1968) 107 If a Clergyman was to make his appearance in his Canonical Robes at one of the Outharbours I have little doubt but the Weomen and Children would be scarified out of part of their senses. **1897** G. FORD *Larramys* xxxii. 231 Vine rider! Scarify mos' volks to death, 'er wüd, I reckon. **1901** 'A. FORBES' *Odd Fish* 149 It will be more likely to scarrify 'er if I tells 'er nigh twelve o'clock. **1961** 'F. O'BRIEN' *Hard Life* vii. 53 You want to scarify the divils in the town of Kinnegad? **1966** *New Statesman* 14 Jan. 51/3 There are almost forgotten casualties like *disinterested* and *jejune* and *scarify* (which was once used to mean *to wound*, not as a smart synonym for *to scare*).
Hence **sca·rified** *ppl. a.*[2], **sca·rifying** *ppl. a.*; **sca·rifyingly** *adv.*[2]
1895 MEREDITH *Amazing Marriage* II. xxix. 330 Here I'm like a cannon for defending the house, needs be, and all inside flies off scarified. **1916** M. WEBB *Golden Arrow* iv. 26 Fixing a scarifying gaze on the truant. **1924** N. COWARD *Rat Trap* I. 12, I suppose it's silly nerves, but to be on the brink of a great happiness is a scarifying feeling. **1963** *Times* 13 June 16/7 A comic role (scarifyingly overdone). **1973** *Times* 17 Jan. 17/5, I would support the comparison with a historical rationale which may be deeply disturbing, even scarifying, but it is certainly not motivated by sensationalism or propaganda.

scarily, *adv.* Add: **1.** (Earlier example.)
1845 W. G. SIMMS *Wigwam & Cabin* 1st Ser. 107 My heart as cold as ice, and jumping up and down as scarily as a rabbit's.
2. Frighteningly, unnervingly.
1967 *Economist* 19 Aug. 664/2 Shell is running a scarily fine operation with a smaller proportion than most companies of its tanker needs provided by its own fleet and with relatively short charters. **1978** L. BLOCK *Burglar in Closet* xi. 94 He'd come scarily close to the truth.

scarlet, *sb.* and *a.* Add: **B.** *adj.* **3. a. scarlet-chested (grass) parrakeet, parrot,** a small blue and green parrot with a red breast, *Neophema splendida*, found in parts of southern Australia.
1901 A. J. CAMPBELL *Nests & Eggs Austral. Birds* II. 654 (*heading*) Scarlet-chested Grass Parrakeet. **1931** N. W. CAYLEY *What Bird is That?* 152 Scarlet-chested Parrot... Rarely recorded, then only as isolated pairs. **1938** —— *Austral. Parrots* 283, I had the pleasure of seeing the Scarlet-chested Parrakeet living happily and breeding freely. **1977** *Weekly Times* (Melbourne) 19 Jan. 23/3 Mrs Jones (West Hobart) would be interested to hear from any reader who would exchange orange-breasted wax-bills for scarlet-chested parrots.
4. a. scarlet letter chiefly *U.S.*, a representation of the letter *A* in scarlet cloth which persons convicted of adultery were condemned to wear, as described in the novel by Hawthorne (see quot. 1850); also in *fig.* and allusive use (cf. BRAND *sb.* 4 b); **Scarlet Pimpernel** (see also sense 4 c in Dict.), the name assumed by the hero of a series of novels by Baroness Orczy (1865–1947), a dashing but elusive Englishman who rescued potential victims of the French Reign of Terror, used allusively; also *attrib.*; cf. *PIMPERNEL 3*; † **scarlet runner** *Obs. Mil. slang*, a soldier, with reference to his scarlet jacket; also *pl.*, a scarlet military uniform; **scarlet woman,** now used to mean: a notoriously immoral woman; a prostitute.
1850 N. HAWTHORNE (*title*) The scarlet letter. **1872** *Cincinnati* (Ohio) *Times & Chron.* 28 May 2/1 A grand mass meeting in Gotham the other night consecrated Apollo Hall by unfurling therein the scarlet letter—we mean banner—of Woodhull and Free Love. **1882** *Internat. Rev.* Mar. 301 Polygamy is the scarlet letter upon the brow of this young commonwealth which proclaims her deep shame and forbids her entrance into the sisterhood of States. **1944** W. J. CARRINGTON *Safe Convoy* 112 However, a few minutes later when the unwanted visitor arrived, she directed her venomous tongue against the daughter whom she branded from head to foot with verbal scarlet letters. **1965** M. DRABBLE *Millstone* 20, I walked around with a scarlet letter embroidered upon my bosom..but the A stood for Abstinence, not for Adultery. **1977** D. ANTHONY *Stud Game* xxi. 132 You hard-shelled Baptist prig. You can't see past the scarlet letter, can you? **1958** E. H. CLEMENTS *Uncommon Cold* vii. 178 As for cloak-and-dagger work on the moor, what price your family of Scarlet Pimpernels? **1958** *Observer* 25 May 15/5 George Baker..appears as a Scarlet Pimpernel type. **1961** *Guardian* 24 May 11/3 A wartime Scarlet Pimpernel organisation which rescued thousands of East European Jews from the Nazis. **1977** M. DRABBLE *Ice Age* III. 287 The image of Anthony as Scarlet Pimpernel, flying out to rescue stepdaughter in distress. *c* **1864** BROUGH & HALLIDAY *Area Belle* 7 Who are you calling bluebottle?—you scarlet runner! **1920** G. FRANKAU *Peter Jackson* VII. 78 'A few of our old militia uniforms.' 'Not the old scarlet-runners?'.. 'The identical, sir, with the old white facings.' **1853** T. PARKER *Theism, Atheism, & Popular Theology* 131 Atheism turns the soul out of doors, and the flesh has no better time of it; no, has a worse time, with its scarlet woman 'tinging the pavement with proud wine too good for the tables of pontiffs'. **1924** in H. Havelock Ellis *Stud. Psychol. Sex* (ed. 3) II. 124, I sought out a scarlet woman in the streets of —— and went home with her. **1977** M. KENYON *Rapist* x. 115 'Is this me?' She was holding..a turtle-neck jersey dress... 'Or would you hazard it's..old-fashioned for the scarlet woman of the bogs?'
b. scarlet ibis (later examples); **scarlet rose-finch,** *Carpodacus erythrinus* (cf. *rose-finch* s.v. *ROSE *sb.* 24 b).
1835 J. J. AUDUBON *Ornith. Biogr.* V. 62, I have found the Scarlet Ibis less numerous than even the Glossy Ibis. **1971** *Country Life* 22 July 220/1 The vivid colouring of the scarlet ibis is as expressive of the South American tropics as the bright colours of macaws and toucans. **1884** H. SEEBOHM *Hist. Brit. Birds* II. 47 The Scarlet Rose-finch is not particularly interesting at its breeding-grounds. **1976** J. T. R. & E. M. SHARROCK *Rare Birds in Britain & Ireland* 284 Scarlet Rosefinch..breeds from Germany and southern Sweden eastwards to Kamchatka.
c. scarlet maple (earlier and later examples); **scarlet runner,** substitute for def.: a red- or white-flowered climbing bean, *Phaseolus coccineus*, or its edible pods; (earlier and later examples).
1768 P. MILLER *Gardeners Dict.* (ed. 8) s.v. *Acer.* I have observed, upon cutting off branches from the scarlet Maple in February, a great quantity of a very sweet juice hath flowed out. **1813** H. MUHLENBERG *Catal. Plant. Amer. Sept.* 95 Scarlet, white, red, or soft maple. **1916** E. T. SETON *Woodcraft Man. for Girls* 292 Red, Scarlet, Water, or Swamp Maple... Noted for its flaming crimson foliage in fall, as well as its red leaf-stalks, flowers, and fruit earlier. **1786** J. ABERCROMBIE *Gardener's Daily Assistant* p. vii, A list of kitchen-garden plants... Kidney Bean (Dwarf)..Scarlet Runner. **1806** B. MCMAHON *Amer. Gard. Cal.* 580 Bean, The Dwarf Kidney... Running kinds..Scarlet Runners. **1908** *Garden* 25 Apr. 205/2 Possibly there is not a vegetable grown that is a more general favourite among amateurs than the climbing bean known as the Scarlet Runner. **1969** *Oxf. Bk. Food Plants* 36/1 The Scarlet Runner is by far the most popular green bean in Britain.

scarlet fever. Add: † **c.** *joc.* A passion for soldiers, with reference to their scarlet uniforms. *Obs.*
1861 B. HEMYNG in H. Mayhew *London Labour* (1862) Extra vol. 235 Nurse-maids..are always ready to succumb to the 'scarlet fever'. A red coat is all powerful with this class. **1890** BARRÈRE & LELAND *Dict. Slang.* II. 206/1 Ladies who run after military society are said to have *scarlet fever.*

scarper (skā·ɹpəɹ), *v. slang.* Also **scapa, scarpa.** [Prob. ad. It. *scappare* to ESCAPE, get away; reinforced during or after the war of 1914–18 by *scapa* from Cockney rhyming slang *Scapa Flow*, to go.] **a.** *intr.* To depart hastily, run away; to escape, make one's get-away.
1846 *Swell's Night Guide* 43 He must *hook it* before 'daylight does appear', and then scarper by the back door. **1861** H. MAYHEW *London Labour* III. 48/1 When I was scarpering with my culling in the monkey. **1931** M. ALLINGHAM *Look to Lady* xxiv. 253 Round up this lot now and scarpa yourselves. **1933** G. INGRAM '*Stir*' iii. 45 'I'll be punching you up the belly if you don't scarper,' threatened Smith. **1954** M. PROCTER *Hell is City* II. i. 44 Wi' my record I thought I'd better scarper before I got dragged into trouble. **1970** *Private Eye* 27 Feb. 16 Take this lolly and scarpa for lawd's sake. **1972** A. DRAPER *Death Penalty* v. 37 Ben..shouted, 'Scapa. Everyone scapa.' **1974** *Sunday Post* (Glasgow) 21 July 16/4 His panic became unbearable. He jumped out of bed and scarpered! **1977** 'E. CRISPIN' *Glimpses of Moon* vii. 111 He's downstairs now with the others—and they're keeping a sharp eye on him; he won't have a chance to scarper again.
b. *trans.* To depart or escape from (a place); usu. in phr. *to scarper the letty*, to leave one's lodgings without paying the rent (cf. *LETTY).
1937 PARTRIDGE *Dict. Slang* 731/2 *Scarper*,..to decamp from... *Scarper the letty*, to leave one's lodgings without paying. **1957** [see *LETTY].
Hence as *sb.* in phr. *to do a scarper*, to run away, 'do a bunk'.
1958 F. NORMAN *Bang to Rights* 63 We had all planned to do a scarper.

‖ **scarpetti** (skaɹpe·ti), *sb. pl.* [It., pl. of *scarpetto*, a small shoe.] Rope-soled shoes worn for rock-climbing, esp. in the North Italian Alps. Cf. *KLETTERSCHUH.
1897 O. G. JONES *Rock-Climbing in Engl. Lake District* p. xxiv, The Cumberland crags are too smooth to make *scarpetti* (*Kletterschuhe*) worth trying. **1907** G. D. ABRAHAM *Compl. Mountaineer* xxviii. 463 If the conditions become wet or icy, rubber soles are a snare and a delusion; scarpetti should be carried as a reserve. **1923** —— *First Steps to Climbing* vi. 71 They [*sc.* rubber-soled shoes] were preferable to the scarpetti, or rope-soled boots, which are the standard Dolomite wear. **1931** *Times Lit. Suppl.* 19 Feb. 129/3 On it [*sc.* Mount Blanc], climbing guideless, they practise every modern refinement, the use of crampons, scarpetti and the rappel. **1941** C. KIRKUS *Let's go Climbing!* vi. 96 Scarpetti—rope soled shoes used in the Dolomites—are coming into favour in this country. **1956** C. EVANS *On Climbing* ii. 32 In the Alps there have been other kinds of friction footwear... The rag-soled scarpetti of the Dolomites.

scarved, *ppl. a.* Add: (Further examples.) Cf. SCARFED *ppl. a.*[1] in Dict. and Suppl.
1958 M. STEWART *Nine Coaches Waiting* v. 54 Philippe and I went out..coated and scarved against the breeze. **1972** F. WARNER *Lying Figures* III. 21 Scarved, laughing children, scuffing the leaves! **1976** *New Yorker* 8 Mar. 41/2 The lottery sellers were gloved and scarved.

scary, *a.*[1] Add: **1.** (Further examples.)
1938 J. STEINBECK *Long Valley* 14 It would be a lonely life for a woman, ma'am, and a scarey life too, with animals creeping under the wagon all night. **1955** E. COXHEAD *Figure in Mist* iv. 123 We're over the scary part now. **1960** *Guardian* 27 Oct. 9/5 This is real scarey. **1961** G. GREENE *Burnt-Out Case* VI. iii. 237 Goodness, I'm glad to be here. It was really scary driving all the way alone. **1975** *New Yorker* 21 Apr. 105/1 It's something scary you don't have to believe in. **1975** *University* (Princeton Univ.) Winter 9/1 The latter showed that energy consumption, per person, could easily double by 2000. That's pretty scary, with energy resources almost sure to decline. **1977** *Times Lit. Suppl.* 11 Feb. 145/4 (Advt.), Set against a background of sinister ritual, vengeance and murder, a novel to be read at one scarey sitting. **1978** *Nature* 20 July 199/1 The procession was headed by figures dressed in radioactive protection gear, clearly intended to be scary. **1981** *Listener* 1 Jan. 23/3 The threat..is pretty scary.
2. (Earlier and later examples.) orig. and chiefly *N. Amer.*
1800 M. L. WEEMS *Let.* 29 Dec. in *Works & Ways* (1929) II. 160, I have always been very scary about our monies. **1903** J. VAIZEY *Pixie O'Shaughnessy* ix. 107 She was too frightened to own up last night—you know what a scarey little thing she is. **1907** J. M. SYNGE *Let.* 25 Apr. (1971) 128, I have been getting a little bit scary about your extravagance. **1951** L. CRAIG *Singing Hills* vi. 45 He'd a been right smart proudified of your not being scary. **1970** N. STREATFEILD *Thursday's Child* xxxii. 218 He was as scary of being seen as a wild deer.

scat (skæt), *sb.*[5] *U.S. slang.* [Origin obscure.] Whisky.
1914 JACKSON & HELLYER *Vocab. Criminal Slang* 73 *Scat, noun*, general circulation. Whiskey. Derived by suggestion from 'skey' (skee), the termination of 'whiskey'. **1949** PARTRIDGE *Dict. Underworld* 597/2 *Scat*, whiskey... Perhaps proleptic: it causes intelligence to *scat*, to scatter, to vanish. **1955** *Publ. Amer. Dial. Soc.* XXIV. 161 Peter men don't punch much guff as a rule, but sometimes the scat will loosen them up for some good yarns.

scat (skæt), *sb.*[6] (and *a.*) *Jazz.* [Prob. imitative: see quot. 1929.] **a.** A style of improvised singing in which meaningless but expressive syllables, usu. representing the sound of a musical instrument, are used instead of words. Freq. *attrib.* passing into *adj.* (see also b below).

1929 *Melody Maker* Apr. 369/1 This particular type of vocalism is known as 'Scat' singing. This name undoubtedly owes its origin to the almost inevitable way of starting any line with 'Scat-da-doo'. A very fine example of this 'Scat Singing' is in 'Candy Lips' by Louis Armstrong's Washboard beaters.., the label rightly describing it as 'Scat' chorus by Clarence Williams. **1933** D. RUNYON in *Collier's* 28 Jan. 41/1 She has to play against a scat band. **1937** *Amer. Speech* XII. 182/2 *Scat*, a style of singing in which the vocalist scorns the lyrics, substituting meaningless but expressive syllables of his own improvisation. **1946** R. BLESH *Shining Trumpets* x. 229 The pattern..was derived.. from attempts of white singers of popular tunes to imitate the rhythmic Negro scat song. **1963** *Times* 27 Dec. 4/7 The exhilarating and often quasi-instrumental vocal duetting, sometimes in scat or in falsetto, behind the melodic line. **1977** *Rolling Stone* 24 Mar., Jarreau is a sophisticated cabaret artist whose vocal mimicry and jazz-man scat account for much of his onstage success.

b. *Comb.*, as **scat-singing** *sb.*, singing in this style; also as adj.; hence **scat-singer** and (as a back-formation) **scat-sing** *v. trans.* and *intr.*

1929 [see above]. **1934** A. BOWLLY *Modern Style Singing* xxiv. 118 Current records should be the best guide of how..to 'scat' sing. **1936** *Amer. Mercury* May p. x/2 *Scat singer*, a hi-de-ho shouter. **1949** L. FEATHER *Inside Be-Bop* v. 39 The swing era produced such notable 'scat' singers as Leo Watson. **1952** B. ULANOV *Hist. Jazz in Amer.* (1958) xx. 252 She pressed the full impact of her scat-singing personality into record grooves. **1957** *Amer. Speech* XXXII. 275 Many bop phrases seem to derive from the nonsense syllables of scat-singing, which, in turn, is simply the voice imitating the sound of an instrument, the first known instance of which, so the story goes, occurred when Louis Armstrong dropped his lyric sheet in the middle of a 1926 recording date and was forced to improvise the words. **1962** 'K. ORVIS' *Damned & Destroyed* iv. 29 A hot-jazz man.. with..a misplaced confidence in his ability as a scat-singer. **1968** P. OLIVER *Screening Blues* vi. 205 With a fierce line in 'scat' singing which had the 'dirty tone' of a muted trumpet, Mary Dixon sang with no apparent restraint. **1974** *New Yorker* 29 Apr. 73 Scat-singing Ella Fitzgerald doesn't just see an audience. **1976** *National Observer* (U.S.) 20 Nov. 24/3 He didn't invent scat singing any more than Louis Armstrong did, but it's a technique he perfected. **1978** *Fanfare* (Toronto) 10 May 11/2 She sings Twisted, scat sings it, tosses her head back, shakes her lion's mane, pushes her voice into a falsetto that does no little damage to the eardrums. **1978** *Maledicta 1977* I. 222 *Fang Dang* would *scat-sing* the melody (i.e. using nonsensical words or 'vocalese' to 'sing' the parts of the instrumentation).

scat (skæt), *sb.*⁷ [ad. Gr. σκατ-, σκῶρ dung.] **1.** Dung; (*pl.*) droppings.

1950 in WEBSTER Add. **1959** E. COLLIER *Three against Wilderness* xx. 207 Whenever I travelled the game trails, my eyes were alert for any coyote scat (manure) deposited on them. **1966** C. SWEENEY *Scurrying Bush* iv. 48 The speculation when finding a spoor or scat. **1977** *Devon Wetlands* (Devon County Council) xix. 74 The two signs of Otters most likely to be found are their footprints and their droppings (usually known as scats or spraints)... Recognising spraints requires some practice particularly to avoid confusing them with Mink scats. **1977** *New Yorker* 27 June 70/3 We avoid a mound of bear scat.

2. *slang.* Heroin. Cf. *SHIT *sb.*¹ 1.

1970 *Lebende Sprachen* XV. 103/2 *Scat*, heroin. **1972** D. E. WESTLAKE *Cops & Robbers* (1973) ii. 39 You're dealing in machismo, man, just like I'm dealing in scat.

scat (skæt), *v.*⁴ *Jazz* (chiefly *U.S.*). [f. *SCAT *sb.*⁶] **a.** *intr.* To perform scat-singing; to sing or improvise with meaningless syllables.

1935 *Metronome* Apr. 54/3 Cab scats through this pair in his best Harlem manner. **1941** *Daily News* (Chicago) 11 June 24/1 Johnny..didn't know the words to the second verse. Instead he sang 'sho-ho-ho', and discovered he liked it that way. Since his audience liked it too, he..has been 'scatting' ever since. **1975** *New Yorker* 26 May 6/1 He and Buddy Rich..launch a series of fusillading four-bar breaks, in which..Torme scats in the Ella Fitzgerald mode.

b. *trans.* To sing or improvise (a song) by replacing the words by meaningless syllables.

1946 MEZZROW & WOLFE *Really Blues* (1957) 104 Louis Armstrong riffed and scatted them. **1958** *Gramophone* Dec. 331/2 Only a couple of songs are scatted. **1973** *Black World* Aug. 58/1 Could scat all Prez's solos note for note in the right key.

Hence **sca·tting** *vbl. sb.*

1946 MEZZROW & WOLFE *Really Blues* (1957) viii. 119 The first time Old Gatemouth ever put his scatting on wax. **1952** B. ULANOV *Hist. Jazz in Amer.* (1958) xx. 252 In 1946 she coined the whole new scatting vocabulary. **1973** S. HENDERSON *Understanding New Black Poetry* 57 The most interesting technical feature of the poem, however, is the singing and scatting of two songs connected with Coltrane.

scat, *int.* and *v.* Delete 'jocularly' and add earlier and later examples. Also in phr. *quicker than scat.*

1838 'T. TITTERWELL' *Yankee Notions* 52 Drive her away! 'scat her away! *Ibid.* 56 Stop, there! whisht! scat! **1860** J. S. JONES *Green Mountain Boy* I. iii. 13 I'll have the square discharge him quicker than s'cat. **1896** J. F. B. LILLARD *Poker Stories* ix. 210 We chucked him two watches and 380 dollars in cash quicker'n scat. **1917** D. CANFIELD *Understood Betsy* x. 229 Ann and I hitched up quicker'n scat. **1931** M. ALLINGHAM *Look to Lady* xiv. 145 Shoo! Shoo! Scat! We've got a policeman coming. **1950** 'D. DIVINE' *King of Fassarai* xviii. 147 Get the hell out of it! .. I told you kids to scat. **1977** H. GREENE *FSO-1* xvii. 152 Set the breakfast table out here in the drawing room. And then, scat!

scatback (skæ·tbæk). *U.S. Football.* [BACK *sb.*¹ 21: see SCAT *int.* in Dict. and Suppl.] A fast-running backfield player.

1946 *Sun* (Baltimore) 16 Dec. 15/1 They made it 14-0.. with an intercepted pass by Dante Magnani, the scatback from St. Mary's of California. **1948** *Sport Life* Nov. 70/1 The Bears have signed scatback J. R. Boone. **1976** *National Observer* 13 Nov. 1/1 He is slim and muscular-looking—a scatback set to run for daylight.

Scatchard (skæ·tʃɑːd). *Biochem.* [The name of George *Scatchard* (1892–1973), U.S. physical chemist, who published a form of such analysis in 1949 (*Ann. N.Y. Acad. Sci.* LI. 660–72).] *Scatchard plot*, a graph of the concentration of a solute absorbed by a protein, membrane, cell, or the like against its concentration in the surrounding medium; *Scatchard analysis*, the use of such graphs to deduce the number and nature of the binding sites on the protein, etc.

1958 EDSALL & WYMAN *Biophys. Chem.* I. xi. 617 (*heading*) The Scatchard plot of $\bar{v}$/(A) against $\bar{v}$. **1970** *Arch. Biochem. & Biophysics* CXLI. 623/2 (*caption*) Scatchard plot for binding of cytochrome *c* to normal rat liver mitochondria. **1975** *Nature* 13 Nov. 154/2 (*caption*) Scatchard plot of insulin-membrane interaction in two representative preparations from 10 control..and 10 diabetic.. animals. *Ibid.* 27 Nov. 339/2 Scatchard analysis of the binding data revealed a class of receptors for 5-α-dihydrotestosterone of uniform affinity. **1978** *Ibid.* 12 Oct. 553/2 (*caption*) Scatchard analysis of interaction between diazepane and 'endogenous inhibitor' of Na^+-independent ^{3}H-GABA binding.

scatological (skæːtǫlǫ·dʒikăl), *a.* [f. SCATOLOGY: see -ICAL.] Of or pertaining to scatology (senses 1 and 3); characterized by a preoccupation with obscenity.

1924 F. M. FORD *Some do Not* II. ii. 237 The late Mr. Duchemin was a scatological—afterwards a homicidal—lunatic. **1959** J. KIRKUP tr. *S. de Beauvoir's Mem. Dutiful Daughter* I. 82 There was one phrase grown-ups were always using: 'It's not proper!'.. At first I had taken it to have a scatological connotation. **1960** G. MAXWELL *Ring of Bright Water* ix. 123 As a useful by-product of his [*sc.* the otter's] impish sense of humour, the cattle tended to keep farther from the house, thus..reducing the number of scatological hazards to be skirted at the door. **1969** *Daily Tel.* 13 Mar. 23/2 The scatological streak in the man, his disgusted-disgusting jokes about excreting nymphs. **1979** *London Rev. Bks.* 25 Oct. 8/2 One might almost assume from a few of these scatological diatribes that he thought there was something intrinsically disgusting about physical love.

scatology. **3.** Delete *rare* and add later examples.

1936 R. QUINTANA *Mind & Art of Jonathan Swift* VI. ii. 360 From scatology one turns with relief to the capital verses entitled *Helter Skelter*. **1959** N. O. BROWN *Life against Death* xiii. 179 The most scandalous pieces of Swiftian scatology are..*The Lady's Dressing Room, Strephon and Chloe, Cassinus and Peter.* **1975** *Publishers Weekly* 22 Sept. 134/1 Funny, albeit unintentional scatology in the [zodiacal] Sign abbreviations.

scatter, *sb.* Add: **1. b.** *transf.* in Linguistics.

1934 J. R. FIRTH *Papers in Linguistics 1934–51* (1957) ii. 4 All the common phonetic contexts of each phoneme should be stated, and the contextual spread or 'scatter' of the phonemes compared. This knowledge of the contextual scatter of a phoneme will be found of the greatest importance for the statement of our future sound laws. **1935** —— in *Trans. Philol. Soc.* 45 The frequency of reference to sex had necessarily extended what I term the formal scatter of the word, and we now have *sexed, sexless, sexy, sexiness,* even *sexology.* **1963** J. LYONS *Structural Semantics* vii. 178 One point that seemed to be of relevance in the inquiry was the defective formal 'scatter' of the lexeme εἰδέναι.

2. Delete 'small' and *rare* and add later examples. Also *spec.* in *Archæol.*

1943 V. SACKVILLE-WEST *Eagle & Dove* iii. 17 A sick woman with a scatter of high-spirited children to control would welcome any method of keeping them quiet. **1954** J. B. MITCHELL *Historical Geogr.* iii. 73 A scatter of Scandinavian settlers in a district primarily English. **1959** *Listener* 12 Mar. 449/2 The ascendancy of the U.S.A., along with that of the U.S.S.R., has relegated the scatter of European nations to subsidiary status. **1974** C. TAYLOR *Fieldwork in Medieval Archaeol.* ii. 27 Much of it [*sc.* the information] will probably be vague, such as notes of pottery scatters, low banks, water-filled ditches and possible old quarries. **1977** *Christian* IV. 109 The human race is not a scatter of individuals.

3. *Statistics.* The degree to which repeated measurements or observations of a quantity differ; that which is measured by the variance.

1921 R. S. WOODWORTH *Psychol.* (1922) xii. 273 Usually there is some 'scatter' in the child's successes. **1923** *Proc. R. Soc.* A. CII. 357 The question arises as to how much of the 'scatter' of the Gaussian curve is due to error of observation, inexperience in making the readings, accidental variations, etc., and how much is due to a real difference in the physiological equipment of the observer. **1934** *Brit. Jrnl. Psychol.* XXIV. 344 The I.Q.'s of the boys showed a wider scatter than those of the girls. **1963** B. FOZARD *Instrumentation Nucl. Reactors* vii. 70 A commonly used measure of the dispersion or scatter of a number of observed values about the central values is the standard deviation. **1968** *Brit. Med. Bull.* XXIV. 246/2 Most observations are subject to considerable scatter, especially where mammalian systems are used, and statistical procedures of varying complexity are called for.

4. a. The scattering of light or other radiation.

1942 *Tee Emm* (Air Ministry) II. 145 Preventing the 'light scatter' which comes from scratched Perspex or slightly dirty windscreens. **1962** H. C. WESTON *Sight, Light & Work* (ed. 2) vi. 206 It is better that the increased illumination required by older eyes should be provided by 'warmer' illuminants so that 'hazing' due to scatter within the eyes is minimised.

b. *spec.* with reference to radio waves, freq. denoting the use of scattering within the atmosphere to extend the range of radio communication. Freq. *attrib.*

1950 *Proc. IRE* XXXVIII. 412/2 For two-directional antennas of beam width Θ facing one another, the greatest angle of scatter that need be considered is Θ. **1956** *Ann. Reg. 1955* 155 It was announced that a revolutionary new system of communications, known as 'scatter', which was not susceptible to jamming,..would be introduced. **1958** *Times* 30 Apr. 6/6 A range of tropospheric scatter transmitting and receiving equipment. **1966** *McGraw-Hill Encycl. Sci. & Technol.* XIII. 439/1 Radio relay systems are usually more suitable than the scatter systems for overland use where intermediate radio relay stations can be constructed. **1977** *Lancs. Life* Nov. 83/2 On the radar screen shown here, Manchester is permanently blacked-out because of 'scatter' from buildings and nearby high ground, to avoid masking approaching precipitation.

5. *Comb.* **scatter diagram, plot** *Statistics*, a diagram having two variates plotted along its two axes and in which points are placed to show the values of these variates for each of a number of subjects, so that the form of the association between the variates can be seen.

1925 F. C. MILLS *Statistical Methods* x. 366 The equation to a straight line, fitted by the method of least squares to the points on the scatter diagram, will express mathematically the average relationship between these two variables. **1937** YULE & KENDALL *Theory of Statistics* (ed. 11) xiv. 275 The scatter diagram in two dimensions may be generalised to three dimensions, and may also be used as a mental construct for higher dimensions, though no actual model can of course be made. **1960** [see *KARYOGRAM b]. **1971** *Nature* 9 Apr. 390/2 Scatter diagrams were drawn to show mean concentrations of albumin, γ-globulin, fibrinogen and cholesterol against age. **1971** *Jrnl. General Psychol.* LXXXV. 266 Inspection of the scatter plot..indicates that any index of relationship would be misleading. **1973** *Jrnl. Genetic Psychol.* CXXII. 45 Guilford's triangular scatterplot conceptualization of intelligence–creativity relationship seemed most congruent with the present..data.

scatter, *v.* Add: **4. c.** *Baseball.* Of a pitcher: to yield hits only at intervals and so restrict scoring.

1892 *Chicago Herald* 25 May 6/1 Young kept the hits well scattered. **1954** *Post-Herald* (Birmingham, Alabama) 7 June 7/2 Winning pitcher was Dave Benedict, who relieved in the first inning and scattered four hits the rest of the way. **1976** *Billings* (Montana) *Gaz.* 27 June 2-F/4 Joaquin Andujar scattered 10 hits Saturday to pace the Houston Astros to a 3-0 victory over the Cincinnati Reds.

5. e. More widely, to deflect, diffuse, or reflect (radiation, particles, or the like) in a more or less random fashion. Also *absol.* (Further examples.)

1878 LD. RAYLEIGH *Theory of Sound* II. xv. 139 If the primary sound be a compound musical note, the various component tones are scattered in unlike proportions. **1891** HURTER & DRIFFIELD in W. B. Ferguson *Photogr. Res. F. Hurter & V. C. Driffield* (1920) 146 Captain Abney has discovered that negatives 'scatter' so much light that our instrument cannot possibly measure all the light which a negative transmits. **1911** *Phil. Mag.* XXI. 675 In these calculations, it is assumed that the α particles scattered through a large angle suffer only one large deflexion. **1938** R. W. LAWSON tr. *Hevesy & Paneth's Man. Radioactivity* (ed. 2) vii. 75 Hydrogen nuclei alone behave differently, for they scatter [neutrons] very much more strongly than would be expected from the magnitude of the cross-section of hydrogen nuclei. **1955** HUETER & BOLT *Sonics* vi. 232 This limits the sound pressure that can be transmitted beyond the point where cavitation first occurs since the bubbles present will scatter and dissipate a part of the sound energy. **1955** C. G. DARWIN in W. Pauli *Niels Bohr* 6 There were a few α-particles scattered through such broad angles, even right backwards, that no conceivable compound effect could possibly explain them. **1959** *Listener* 18 June 1057/1 The distortions introduced by scattering a signal from such a surface might not be too serious. **1971** *Sci. Amer.* June 61/2 Since the neutron and the proton respond to the electromagnetic force, they scatter electrons aimed at them.

f. *intr.* *Physics.* Of radiation, particles, etc.: to undergo scattering.

1971 *Nature* 16 July 167/2 The double reflexion mechanism gives way to multiple reflexions, that is, a ray is trapped in surface cavities before scattering out, randomizing the polarization. **1975** *Ibid.* 25 Sept. 275/1 The majority of the energy is carried by phonons which inelastically scatter at the interface. **1980** *Sci. Amer.* July 57/1 Inside it an entering gamma-ray photon typically scatters off several electrons in succession.

7. a. **scatter bomb**, a bomb that scatters its material over a wide area; also *fig.*; **scatter bombing** *vbl. sb.*, bombing carried out haphazardly over an area; **scattershot** orig. and chiefly *N. Amer.*, the shot contained in a scatter-charge; also used *fig.* (chiefly *attrib.*)

to designate something of a random, haphazard, or indiscriminate character (cf. *SCATTER-GUN 2); **scatter-site** *a. U.S.* = *scattered-site* s.v. *SCATTERED *ppl. a.* 2 b.

1961 WEBSTER, Scatter bomb. **1973** J. QUICK *Dict. Weapons & Mil. Terms* 386/1 Fragmentation bombs or fragmentation clusters, as well as certain incendiary bombs equipped with bursters, are scatter bombs. **1977** *Rolling Stone* 16 June 43/2 Okay, Scorsese is a violent scatter-bomb. **1977** *Daily Tel.* 3 Aug. 5/5 West Germany's new scatter bomb..comprises more than 1,000 mini-bombs which can be fired in different patterns by rockets triggered from the cockpit. **1940** *Aeroplane* 13 Sept. 314/1 The scatter-bombing..must at times have sorely tried pilots who had seen the effects of it. **1961** WEBSTER, Scattershot. **1965** *Economist* 19 June 1393/2 The President's..scatter-shot efforts to reduce the government's spending. **1967** *Boston Globe* 5 Apr. 51/2 Jack Nicklaus is more concerned over his scattershot driver than the threat of mumps. **1972** *Publishers' Weekly* 10 July 42/2 Shirley Green brings more scattershot curiosity than serious learning to her 'history'. **1974** *State* (Columbia, S. Carolina) 27 Feb. 18-A/6 When demagogic politicians ride the land firing scatter shot, nobody..is safe unless he shares their prejudices. **1978** R. STEVENS *Law & Politics* 505 The future of the judicial role in England..may lie far more with subtle use of judicial restraint than with scattershot judicial activism. **1972** *N.Y. Times* 3 Nov. 16/2 The scatter-site housing dispute in Forest Hills. **1977** *New Yorker* 27 June 85/2 Jimmy Carter's mention of his belief in ethnic purity..in response to a *News* reporter's question about scatter-site housing.

b. *attrib.*, passing into *adj.* Designating one of a number (intended to be) scattered decoratively here and there, as *scatter cushion, pin, rug*, etc. orig. *U.S.*

1933 'E. QUEEN' *Siamese Twin Mystery* I. ii. 30 A living-room..dotted with armchairs and small scatter-rugs. **1946** *Negro Digest* Aug. 51/1 Its large living room has a vaulted ceiling and arched beams, and the floor is covered with deer skins and scatter rugs. **1957** J. D. SALINGER in *New Yorker* 4 May 123/1 Three domestic Oriental scatter rugs, extremely worn, were on the floor. **1960** *Woman* 5 Mar. 19/1 Scatter cushions have become a favourite furnishing accessory. **1960** I. WALLACH *Absence of Cello* 13 She stopped first at the jewelry counter where she sneered at some scatter pins. **1966** T. PYNCHON *Crying of Lot 49* ii. 36 Bracelets then, scatterpins, earrings, a pendant. **1974** J. IRVING *158-Pound Marriage* 104 The bed..had pitched the mattress and us across the scatter rug. **1976** L. DEIGHTON *Twinkle, twinkle, Little Spy* xviii. 185 There [were]..scatter-cushions on the floor. **1980** P. HARCOURT *Tomorrow's Treason* I. i. 31 The floor was..wood with a couple of bright scatter mats.

scatteration. Delete *rare* and add later examples. Also, the fact or condition of being scattered.

1880 'MARK TWAIN' *Tramp Abroad* xix. 183 A raft..hit the pier in the center and went all to smash and scatteration like a box of matches struck by lightning. **1892** KIPLING *Lett. of Travel* (1920) 40 A household spreads itself over plots, maybe, a quarter of a mile apart. A revenue map of a village shows that this scatteration is apparently designed. **1910** *Blackw. Mag.* July 24/1 Here there is a scatteration, but the tufters..are stopped and laid on to the line of a single stag. **1930** R. FRASER *Rose Anstey* xlix. 328 At night she stared from her bed at a great scatteration of stars. **1936** *Burlington Mag.* June 261/1 The gilt frame of the mirror is not a strong enough colour to correct the consequent scatteration. **1965** *Economist* 6 Feb. 509 A growing desire to end what Mr Walter Lippmann calls 'globalism and scatteration' in foreign policy in favour of a concentration on America's 'primary vital interests'. **1965** D. OWEN *Eng. Philanthropy* IV. xx. 559 'Scatteration' philanthropy—spending too small amounts on too many agencies or individuals.

scatter bomb, bombing: see *SCATTER *v.* 7 a.

scattered, *ppl. a.* Add: **2. b.** *scattered-site* (U.S.), used *attrib.* to designate public housing (esp. for low-income families) distributed throughout a city rather than concentrated in a few areas. Also *absol.* in *pl.* (unhyphenated) as *sb.*

1956 *Jrnl. Housing* May 163/1 (*heading*) Scattered site projects. *Ibid.* 'We have inaugurated a new policy that not only permits but encourages the use of small scattered sites,' PHA Commissioner Charles E. Slusser told delegates. **1958** *Ibid.* Jan. 11 (*caption*) Diagrammatical sketch of the City of Cedartown, showing the seven sites on which the Cedartown Housing Authority constructed..the first scattered-site project in the nation. **1959** *Ibid.* Nov. 359/2 In many areas the row house has been adapted for scattered-site use. **1966** *Daily Progress* (Charlottesville, Va.) 12 Aug. 10/1 'Scattered-site' housing is an alternative to high-rise, low-income apartments.

4. c. More widely, of electromagnetic radiation generally and sub-atomic particles: subjected to scattering. (Further examples.)

1878 LD. RAYLEIGH *Theory of Sound* II. xv. 139 If a number of small bodies lie in the path of waves of sound,..the exaltation of the higher harmonics in the scattered waves involves a proportional deficiency of them in the direct wave after passing the obstacles. **1906** *Phil. Mag.* XII. 144 From measurements of the width of the band due to the scattered α rays, it is easy to show that some of the α rays in passing through the mica have been deflected from their course through an angle of about 2°. **1926** R. W. LAWSON tr. *Hevesy & Paneth's Man. Radioactivity* iii. 39 The whole of the scattered radiation also enters the electroscope. **1966** *McGraw-Hill Encycl. Sci. & Technol.* XIII. 438/2 Although radio waves at these frequencies are not reflected by the ionosphere, it has been found that if large amounts of power are radiated, scattered energy will be received over relatively long distances beyond the horizon. **1970** I. E. MCCARTHY *Nuclear Reactions* i. 5 In addition to elastically scattered α particles, two groups of protons..were observed. **1978** P. W. ATKINS *Physical Chem.* xvii. 546 If the molecules are excited by the light during the collision they withdraw some energy from the photons, and so the scattered light emerges with a lower frequency than the incident light.

scatterer. Add: **1.** Also, something which scatters; a device for broadcasting seed.

1868 *Rep. Iowa State Agric. Soc. 1867* 227 The seed is scattered by a vibrating scatterer.

2. *Physics.* Anything which scatters radiation, particles, or the like.

1930 A. B. WOOD *Textbk. Sound* III. 282 The amplitude of the secondary waves varies directly as the volume of the 'scatterer'. **1931** [see *IMPURITY 3 b]. **1936** *Nature* 1 Feb. 185/2 The product of the 140 sec. half-period is enhanced in the case of all scatterers [of neutrons] investigated except carbon and aluminium. **1959** *Listener* 18 June 1057/1 If it [*sc.* the moon] were behaving as a uniform scatterer of radio waves. **1973** *Nature* 7 Sept. 38/2 The beam [of protons]..is made to strike a scatterer of lead or copper. **1977** R. KATZ *Ziggurat* (1978) vi. 59 Beryllium..was an excellent reflector, or 'neutron scatterer', because it had an atomic structure more dense than any other element. **1977** *Sci. Amer.* Oct. 90/2 In synthetic-aperture radar the interference pattern from each scatterer on the terrain is recorded..as a narrow broken line parallel to the edge of the data film.

scattergram (skæ·təɹgræm). *Statistics.* A contraction of *scatter diagram* s.v. *SCATTER *sb.* 5.

1938 A. E. WAUGH *Elem. Statistical Method* ix. 235 This is the method of plotting the data on a scatter diagram, or scattergram, in order that one may see the relationship. **1966** *Jrnl. Neurophysiol.* XXIX. 812 To see how latencies and phases change with frequency, scattergrams can be made comparing each interval with the latency or phase of the spikes that occur during the interval. **1973** B. J. WILLIAMS *Evolution & Human Origins* xii. 215/2 In Figure 5.1 we saw a scattergram of a spurious correlation between R_o and heart disease. **1980** *Amer. Speech* LV. 226 The reader is told to calculate..*z*'s for inter-group differences, scattergrams, and correlation coefficients.

scatter-gun. For *U.S. colloq.* read 'orig. and chiefly *N. Amer.*' and add: **1.** (Earlier and later examples.)

1836 H. R. HOWARD *Hist. V. A. Stewart* 140, I have a choice scatter-gun. **1910** *Blackw. Mag.* Feb. 285/1 All round Muttra shooting with a scatter-gun is varied and good. **1923** J. H. COOK *Fifty Years on Old Frontier* I. 4 Pigeon shooting was good..for anyone who owned or could borrow a 'scatter-gun'. **1932** 'D. YATES' *Safe Custody* ix. 198 We've thirteen men, and between us we've got six pistols and three scatter-guns. **1968** *Punch* 1 May 624/1 He hands his trunk to this Puerto Rican who's carrying..a sawn-off scatter-gun. **1973** R. D. SYMONS *Where Wagon Led* I. iv. 51 Once in a while one of us would pack a scatter gun and get a brace or two of prairie chicken.

2. *fig.* (*attrib.* in quots.). Cf. *scattershot* s.v. *SCATTER *v.* 7.

1952 J. STEINBECK *East of Eden* II. xiv. 150 A scattergun method for dealing with unpleasant facts. **1963** *Daily Progress* (Charlottesville, Va.) 6 Feb., Republicans agreed..to a 'scattergun plan'. Each representative wrote the name of his choice..on a secret ballot. There were no nominations and no debate. **1974** *Publishers Weekly* 4 Feb. 70/1 Farson sets it all down with a scattergun assertiveness that inevitably turns up contradictions. **1980** *Times Lit. Suppl.* 15 Aug. 913/1 Stuart Holland's scatter-gun polemic embodies many of the misconceptions which now threaten to dominate the Labour Party's attitude to Europe.

Hence as *v. intr.* (*fig.* in quot.) and **sca·tter-gunner.**

1968 R. M. NIXON in W. Safire *Before the Fall* (1975) I. vi. 72 If we scatter-gun too much we are not going to have an impact. **1969** *Daily Colonist* (Victoria, B.C.) 8 Nov. 20/1 Two traps will be in operation and all scattergunners are invited to compete. **1980** *Outdoor Life* (U.S.) (Northeast ed.) Oct. 104/2 Scatter-gunners bag approximately 50 million of them each hunting season.

scattering, *vbl. sb.* Add: **1.** (Further examples in *Physics.* Cf. *SCATTER *v.* 5 e.)

1911 *Proc. Manchester Lit. & Philos. Soc.* LV. p. xviii (*heading*) The scattering of the α and β rays and the structure of the atom. **1942** J. D. STRANATHAN *'Particles' Mod. Physics* xi. 405 On the theory of multiple scattering an entirely negligible number of particles should be scattered at large angles. **1950** *Nature* 30 Dec. 1103/2 It is..probable that turbulent scattering..plays an important part in determining the signals received from high-power metre-wave transmitters at distances greater than about 100 miles. **1955** HUETER & BOLT *Sonics* iii. 85 Scattering at the grain boundaries is one important cause for the absorption of ultrasonic waves in metals. **1974** G. REECE tr. *Hund's Hist. Quantum Theory* iv. 56 In 1903 J. J. Thomson worked out from the intensity of scattering of X-rays that the number of electrons must be roughly equal to the atomic weight. **1975** D. G. FINK *Electronics Engineers' Handbk.* XVIII. 91 At frequencies in the 30- to 100-MHz region, regular but weak propagation by ionospheric scattering is obtained.

3. Special Comb.: **scattering angle** *Physics*, the angle through which a scattered particle or beam is deflected.

1913 *Phil. Mag.* XXVI. 711 It is a different matter..when the scattering angle is only about 1/10 of a degree, as in the present experiment. **1950** *Nature* 30 Dec. 1102/2 A great simplification of the results is effected by restricting the discussion to small angles (beam-widths and scattering angles). **1970** I. E. MCCARTHY *Nuclear Reactions* I. i. 9 We see that for a given scattering angle particles of higher energy come closer to the nucleus.

scattering, *ppl. a.* **2. a.** Substitute for def.: *Physics.* That causes scattering (of light, radiation, particles or the like). (Further examples.)

1911 *Phil. Mag.* XXI. 675 It is essential that the thickness of the scattering material should be so small that the chance of a second encounter involving another large deflexion is very small. **1938** R. W. LAWSON tr. *Hevesy & Paneth's Man. Radioactivity* (ed. 2) ix. 95 A strong pencil of α-particles of definite velocity is allowed to strike a thin sheet of the scattering substance. **1958** *Times* 30 Apr. 6/6 The forward scatter technique..in this case uses the troposphere as the scattering medium. **1970** D. W. TENQUIST et al. *University Optics* II. ii. 84 If the incident light photon of energy $h\nu$ impinges upon a molecule of the scattering medium and the energy state of this molecule changes from E_1 to E_2, the energy of the Raman scattered photon is given by $h\nu-(E_2-E_1)$.

b. *scattering layer* (Oceanogr.), any of a number of layers in the sea which give rise to strong acoustic echoes owing to the presence of a high concentration of living organisms.

1942 *Reverberation Stud. at 24 Kc* (Univ. Calif. Div. War Res. Rep. U7) 48 (*heading*) Deep scattering layers. *Ibid.* 49 Observations indicate that deep scattering layers, in a given area, may appear and disappear and yet persist for periods as long as a month or perhaps even longer. **1948** *Nat. Geogr. Mag.* Sept. 277/2 So incredibly numerous are such sea creatures that this layer of ocean life actually returns an echo of the sound sent down by the Fathometer. The echo from this so-called 'scattering layer' is sometimes so strong that it causes navigators to think they are sailing over a shoal. **1972** J. WILLIAMS *Oceanogr.* 53 At night this deep scattering layer..is centered near the sea surface...In the morning it moves down into the depths again. **1977** CLAY & MEDWIN *Acoust. Oceanogr.* vii. 237 A great deal of data, particularly the frequency dependence of scattering layers, are obtained by using explosive sources.

scatterometer (skætərǫ·mĭtəɹ). [f. SCATTER *sb.* + -OMETER.] A radar designed to provide information about the roughness or the profile of a surface from the way it scatters the incident microwaves.

1966 *Electronics* 14 Nov. 44 A spacecraft, using a Scatterometer, has to fly over a pock-marked area of the lunar surface only once to get a detailed profile of the terrain. **1978** *Nature* 22 June 586/2 Seasat-A is primarily a 'proof of concept' mission designed primarily to discover how effectively the microwave equipment which it carries—a scanning radiometer, a radar scatterometer, a synthetic aperture radar, and a radar altimeter—can provide useful scientific information for oceanographers, meteorologists and commercial sea-users.

scattershot, -site: see *SCATTER *v.* 7.

scattery, *a.* Add: **b.** Scatter-brained. *rare.*

1924 J. GALSWORTHY *White Monkey* I. v. 33 The scattery enthusiasm of the sucking publisher. **1928** —— *Swan Song* III. i. 226 He himself knew how to wait, but did this modern young man, so feather-pated and scattery?

scattiness (skæ·tinės). [f. *SCATTY *a.*[2] + -NESS.] The quality or condition of being scatty or scatter-brained.

1959 S. GIBBONS *Pink Front Door* iv. 52 For all her scattiness, Daisy was a good child. **1959** A. BUCHAN *Spare Chancellor* v. 118 Catherine Gladstone with the characteristic scattiness of the Glynnes and the Lytteltons always referred to Lowe's followers as 'The Dolomites'. **1976** E. BERCKMAN *Be All & End All* v. 62 A peculiar combination of scattiness accompanied by a desperate concentration. **1977** 'M. INNES' *Honeybath's Haven* viii. 82 The spectacle of [Hamlet's] random and intermittent scattiness is confusing.

scatty (skæ·ti), *a.*[1] *U.S. Underworld slang.* [Of unknown origin; cf. SCOTTY *a.*] Bad-tempered.

1909 W. H. DAVIES *Beggars* xxvi. 205 Nearly all men that live in common lodging-houses..are..more or less short-tempered, or as they say—'scatty'. **1927** *Dial. Notes* V. 461 *Scatty*, ill-natured.

scatty (skæ·ti), *a.*[2] *colloq.* [Prob. f. SCATT(ERBRAINED *a.* + -Y[1].] Of a person: scatter-brained; driven distracted, mad; of a story, etc.: illogical and absurd.

1911 J. W. HORSLEY *I Remember* xi. 254 Cockney slang was far more familiar to me than most..'scatty' for mad. **1934** *Punch* 17 Jan. 74/1 Simpson, who lives opposite, says it [*sc.* the house] was preying on his mind... 'Another week and I should have been scatty,' he explained. **1951** M. KENNEDY *Lucy Carmichael* II. i. 83 She is amusing in a breathless, scatty sort of way. **1956** J. DICKSON CARR *Patrick Butler for Defence* iii. 26 If we tell this scatty story about an impossible murder, they won't believe one word we say. **1972** 'J. BELL' *Death of Poison-Tongue* i. 11 Do you mean you know who the person is who spreads wicked lies about the neighbours? Don't the ones attacked do anything if they know the person? It sounds utterly scatty. **1977** *News of World* 17 Apr. 16/7 My scatty friend..had later gone into the butchers and loudly asked for a shepherd to make a pie with. **1980** J. MCCLURE *Blood of Englishman* i. 11 The scatty receptionist had looked at him with twinkling eyes.

scaurie. Add: Also **scory, scurrie.** (Earlier and further examples.)

a **1795** G. LOW *Fauna Orcadensis* (1813) 122 The Brown and White Gull..Orc. Scory..is the scarcest of the Gull-kind in Orkney. **1822** [see *ICELAND]. **1918** T. MANSON *Humours of Peat Commission* I. 125, I mind haein a tame scorie..whin I wis a boy. **1960** *People's Jrnl.* (Dundee) 12 Mar. 9/2 Ah'm fair deav't wi' the awfa scraichin' o' the scurries.

scavenge, *v.* Add: **2. b.** To extract and collect (anything that can be used or eaten) from discarded material.

1922 JOYCE *Ulysses* 158 Saw her in the viceregal party when Stubbs the park ranger got me in with Whelan of the *Express*. Scavenging what the quality left. High tea. Mayonnaise I poured on the plums thinking it was custard. **1971** J. S. WEINER *Man's Natural History* v. 199 Big-game hunters, living by means of scavenging dead mammoths. **1977** *Times Lit. Suppl.* 7 Jan. 9/5 In Kingston [Jamaica].. 'scuffling' (dealing in whatever can be scavenged).

3. (Later examples.) Also, to borrow; to thieve; to search through rubbish *for* (leftovers or unwanted objects).

In quot. 1960 simply 'to search thoroughly'.

1938 *Sun* (Baltimore) 17 June 3/4 A woman relief investigator said aged men whom she recognized as relief clients were 'scavenging' at a market for discarded sprigs of celery. **1941** BAKER *Dict. Austral. Slang* 63 *Scavenge, to*, to borrow: to act the petty thief. **1960** P. S. BEAGLE *Fine & Private Place* xiv. 252 She..scavenged frantically in her purse, trying to hold back a sneeze until she found a handkerchief. **1978** S. TENNENBAUM *Rachel, the Rabbi's Wife* (1979) x. 340 Rachel worked hard to refurbish her studio... She scavenged for pieces of furniture, and found an old armchair, a small table, and a low couch without a cushion.

4. a. *trans.* To remove (the combustion products) from the cylinders of an internal-combustion engine. Also *absol.*, and with the engine or cylinder as object. Cf. *SCAVENGING *vbl. sb.* 2.

1894 [implied in *SCAVENGING *vbl. sb.* 2 a]. **1903** *Amer. Inventor* 15 Aug. 78/3 The engine under description scavenges thoroughly and completely upon the return stroke of the pistons. **1954** E. J. KATES *Diesel & High-Compression Gas Engines* ii. 23 Just as before, this helps to get the exhaust gases out, or scavenges them. **1961** K. ČASLAVSKÝ tr. *Mackerle's Air-Cooled Motor Engines* xviii. 376 With a mixing ratio $\lambda > 1$ the cylinder charge is increased by the amount of air contained in the exhaust gas not scavenged from the cylinder. **1966** *McGraw-Hill Encycl. Sci. & Technol.* VII. 208/2 Most medium and large two-cycle diesel engines are usually equipped with blowers to scavenge the cylinders after the working strokes and to supply the air required for the subsequent cycles. **1975** M. J. NUNNEY *Automotive Engine* x. 246 The development of the two-stroke cycle of operation is generally attributed to Dugald Clerk who, in 1878, adopted this principle for a successful design of engine that was scavenged by a separate pumping cylinder.

b. *Chem.* To combine with or remove (free radicals, electrons, or other species).

1955 *Jrnl. Amer. Chem. Soc.* LXXVII. 3245/2 This would mean that all of the radicals which are being scavenged are swept from the solution by the mercaptan. **1966** W. A. PRYOR *Free Radicals* xxi. 324 An added free radical species will inhibit the process..if it scavenges S· but does not react with S to convert it to S·. **1974** *Sci. Amer.* Dec. 71/1 Z is eventually restored to neutrality by scavenging four electrons from two water molecules. **1978** *Nature* 1 June 374/1 Newly formed amorphous iron hydroxides seem to scavenge phosphate and silicate from solution.

Hence as *sb.*, = *SCAVENGING *vbl. sb.* 2 a. Freq. *attrib.*

1912 A. P. CHALKLEY *Diesel Engines* vi. 156 On the up stroke the scavenge ports..are closed before the exhaust ports. **1925** *Glasgow Herald* 1 Apr. 11/2 This new type of engine, with its straight through scavenge and absence of air and exhaust valves. **1930** *Engineering* 21 Nov. 645/3 The scavenge pumps for the Junkers engine are mounted on the locomotive frame. **1949** T. D. WALSHAW *Diesel Engine Design* xviii. 338 Typical figures for an engine supercharged to give 50 per cent. increase in available B.H.P. are: 30 per cent. through scavenge (i.e. a volume of air equal to 30 per cent. of the cylinder volume is swept through the exhaust valve), and the amount of overlap would be about 135°. **1955** *Know your Tractor* (Shell) i. 11 The air for combustion assists removal of the exhaust gases; it is therefore known as 'scavenge' air, and its admission to the engine as 'scavenging'. **1957** [see *LUBE *sb.* and *v.*]. **1975** A. J. WHARTON *Diesel Engines: Questions & Answers* 19 Even in slow running engines, this allows only a very short period of time for scavenge to be completed.

scavenger. Add: **3*.** *Chem.* A substance or species which scavenges (sense *4 b) free radicals or other species.

1955 *Jrnl. Amer. Chem. Soc.* LXXVII. 3244 The demonstration that various radical scavengers such as butyl mercaptan, α, α- diphenyl-β-picrylhydrazyl.., iodine and oxygen do not capture the decomposition products quantitatively. **1961** G. R. CHOPPIN *Exper. Nuclear Chem.* xii. 196 The presence of even small amounts of impurity, especially if it has a high affinity for radicals (a scavenger), causes decomposition. **1970** *Financial Times* 13 Apr. 20/4 Manganese is probably the most important 'minor' metal used in the steel industry, being used as a de-oxidiser and scavenger to combine with sulphur. **1974** C. C. PATTON in P. L. Moore et al. *Drilling Practices Manual* xv. 397 Scavengers can also be added to a drilling fluid to remove small amounts of hydrogen sulfide. **1978** *Nature* 23 Nov. 347/2 Hydroxyl is the most reactive trace species in the troposphere and is therefore the dominant scavenger of many anthropogenic substances.

4. scavenger hunt orig. *U.S.*, a game in which people try to collect certain miscellaneous objects from the neighbourhood.

1940 *Sun* (Baltimore) 1 Nov. 7/3 Eight young persons on a scavenger hunt sponsored by a Westport High School sorority went to the Sixty-third street police station willingly to obtain signatures of policemen. **1963** 'E. McBAIN' *Ten Plus One* xi. 136 We're two college kids on a scavenger hunt... We're supposed to bring back a hibernating bear. **1977** *Times* 24 Dec. 10/2 The outdoors scavenger hunt is a good exercise after overeating. **1980** *Jewish Chron.* 18 July 25/5 Sunday, July 27. Car Rally/Scavenger Hunt.

scavenging, *vbl. sb.* Add: **2. a.** Removal of combustion products from the cylinders of internal-combustion engines. Also as *ppl. a.*

1894 *Work* 17 Feb. 73/3 Questions such as late ignitions, scavenging, varying explosive charges [etc.]. **1896** B. DONKIN *Text-bk. Gas, Oil, & Air Engines* (ed. 2) I. xix. 269 The increase in economy obtained with the new (1894) 'scavenging' Crossley–Atkinson engine. **1915** *Illustr. London News* 13 Mar. 340 Scavenging-pump for expelling used gases at the end of each stroke. **1924** *Times Trade & Engin. Suppl.* 29 Nov. 250/3 As is usual with large Sulzer engines the scavenging air is supplied from electrically driven turbo blowers installed in the engine-room. **1954** E. J. KATES *Diesel & High-Compression Gas Engines* ii. 24 Instead of rotary blowers, many two-cycle diesels employ what is called crankcase-scavenging. *Ibid.* 25 The outside atmospheric pressure then pushed open the scavenging valve and permitted a fresh supply of air to enter the crankcase. **1962** J. M. DOHERTY *Diesel Locomotive Practice* ii. 25 To obtain efficient scavenging in two-stroke engines, the air is always admitted to the cylinder under pressure. **1975** M. J. NUNNEY *Automotive Engine* x. 248 The mean effective pressures developed by a two-stroke engine..depend upon its scavenging efficiency.

b. *Chem.* The action of *SCAVENGE *v.* 4 b.

1955 *Jrnl. Amer. Chem. Soc.* LXXVII. 3245/2 There must be two reactions which produce the dinitrile, one which is subject to scavenging by the mercaptan and one which is not. **1978** *Nature* 1 June 374/1 Lal *et al.* have shown that from 12 to 15% of dissolved silicate can be removed from seawater by scavenging during precipitation of finely dispersed ferric hydroxide.

scavvy, var. *SCAFFY.

scawtite (skǭ·təit). *Min.* [f. the name *Scawt* (see quot. 1930) + -ITE¹.] A hydrated carbonate and silicate of calcium which occurs as minute, colourless, monoclinic crystals.

1929 *Nature* 7 Dec. 896/1 C. E. Tilley: On scawtite... This new monoclinic mineral, with composition $6CaO.4SiO_2.3CO_2$, occurs in the contact zone between the chalk and the dolerite. **1930** C. E. TILLEY in *Mineral. Mag.* XXII. 224 It is proposed to designate this new mineral scawtite, from the original locality, Scawt Hill, Co. Antrim. **1957** *Amer. Mineralogist* XLII. 387 A zone about ten inches thick between the larnite zone and the limestone consists essentially of scawtite. The scawtite rock is greyish-white, dense and flinty. **1973** *Acta Crystallographica* B. XXIX. 73 Scawtite contains 2 units of $Ca_7(Si_6O_{18})(CO_3).2H_2O$ in a monoclinic cell.

sceau, erron. form of *SEAU.

‖ **Sceaux** (sōᵘ). The name of a town near Paris used *attrib.* and *absol.* to denote tin-enamelled faience made there in the latter part of the eighteenth century, often painted with floral and figure subjects and modelled in the form of figures.

1884 GASNAULT & GARNIER *French Pottery* 182 (Index), Sceaux mark on faïence. **1903** M. L. SOLON *Old French Faïence* 125 An anchor, in allusion to the dignity of the Duke de Penthièvre, High Admiral of France, or the stencilled name: 'Sceaux', are the marks of the productions. **1948** A. LANE *French Faïence* x. 40 In the 1770's the factory apparently looked for inspiration to Sceaux faïence and Sèvres porcelain. *Ibid.* 42 The Sceaux faïence-painting was of a very high quality. **1960** R. G. HAGGAR *Conc. Encyl. Continental Pott. & Porc.* 421/1 Enamelling..gives a distinctive quality to Sceaux faience. **1971** L. A. BOGER *Dict. World Pott. & Porc.* Pl. 283 (*caption*) Cruet frame and two cruets, enameled faïence. French, Sceaux, c. 1760. **1974** *Country Life* 24 Jan. 129/3 (*caption*) Sceaux faience duck tureen.

scena. Add: **1.** In quot. 1825 for SCENE 13 read SCENE 5 d.

scenario, *sb.* Delete ‖ and add: Now usu. with pronunc. (sĭnā·rio, sĭnɛ̄ᵊ·rio). **1. a.** (Earlier and later examples.) Also, in extended use, a sketch or outline of the plot of a ballet, novel, opera, story, etc. Also *transf.* and *fig.*

1878 G. H. LEWES *Jrnl.* 28–29 Apr. in *Geo. Eliot Lett.* (1956) VII. 13 Schemed a scenario from *Daniel Deronda.* **1903** A. M. BINSTEAD *Pitcher in Paradise* ii. 51 The small card of *data* which forms the 'scenario' from which these stories are being constructed. **1911** O. ONIONS *Widdershins* 279, I myself have drafted a rough scenario of the form it appeared to me the 'Life' might with advantage be cast in. **1923** WODEHOUSE *Inimitable Jeeves* xviii. 250 'Jeeves!' 'Sir?' 'I'm in the soup.' 'Indeed, sir?' I sketched out the scenario for him. 'What would you advise?' **1924** —— *Bill the Conqueror* ix. 159 A young man in a vivid check suit came out, a small young man with close-set eyes and the scenario of a moustache. **1929** C. K. S. MONCRIEFF tr. *Proust's Captive* iii. 493 No doubt the scenario [of a series of events in the narrator's life] was not merely different but almost opposite. **1947** A. EINSTEIN *Music in Romantic Era* xvi. 284 He outlined a scenario, and..obtained a completed libretto from Somma. **1953** WODEHOUSE *Performing Flea* 69 Today I reached page 254 and have a very detailed scenario of the rest. **1955** W. DEAN in H. Van Thal *Fanfare for Ernest Newman* 59 Trianon..an inveterate compiler of librettos and ballet scenarios for all three Paris opera houses. **1977** *Dædalus* Summer 73 Thus the dramatic scenario—frequently the enactment of a sacred narrative—now becomes a performative mode sui generis.

b. *Cinemat.* A film script with all the details of scenes, appearances of characters, stage-directions, etc., necessary for shooting the film.

1911 [see *picture-play* s.v. *PICTURE *sb.* 6 a]. **1919** F. HURST *Humoresque* 184 So many times it comes up in the scenarios and the picture-plots..how money don't always bring happiness. **1922** WODEHOUSE *Girl on Boat* ix. 144 Fate, thought Sam, had constructed a cheap, mushy..five-reel film scenario. **1926, 1930** [see *CONTINUITY 6]. **1934** *Punch* 18 Apr. 426/2 The film is still full of real characters, not the pasteboard subsidiaries we meet so often in modern American scenarios of love and murder. **1937** A. HUXLEY *Let.* 15 Dec. (1969) 429 Unless in the interval I get any news about a scenario I wrote while out in Hollywood. **1941** *Spectator* 10 Oct. 355/1 Miss Bette Davis..has proved her genius for breathing life into scenarios which have been synthesized from the more extravagant..of ancient theatrical situations. **1950** T. S. ELIOT *Cocktail Party* I. i. 14 They did a film But they used a different scenario. **1969** M. STEINBECK *On Stage* 165 Strictly speaking a scenario is a film script. It is not used very much. Usually one hears film script.

2. A sketch, outline, or description of an imagined situation or sequence of events; esp. (*a*) a synopsis of the development of a hypothetical future world war, and hence an outline of any possible sequence of future events; (*b*) an outline of an intended course of action; (*c*) a scientific model or description intended to account for observable facts. Hence, in weakened senses (not easily distinguishable from sense 1 a *transf.* and *fig.*): a circumstance, situation, scene, sequence of events, etc.

The over-use of this word in various loose senses has attracted frequent hostile comment.—Ed.

1962 H. KAHN *Thinking about Unthinkable* v. 143 A scenario results from an attempt to describe..some hypothetical sequence of events... Scenarios may explore and emphasize an element of a larger problem such as..the process of 'escalation' of a small war. *Ibid.*, The scenario is an aid to the imagination. *Ibid.* 146 The scenario begins by assuming a crisis; everybody is on edge. A Soviet missile is accidentally fired. **1965** 'R. L. PIKE' *Police Blotter* xi. 185 If you hadn't tried to build up a big scenario with that self-defense crap, if you had just kept your big mouth shut, it might have held us up. **1966** 'W. COOPER' *Memoirs of New Man* I. viii. 103, I admired the beauty and simplicity of his plan—or 'scenario', as the case might be. **1968** *Guardian* 21 Feb. 7/1 Germany then plans to produce a so-called 'scenario' for arriving at an arrangement with Britain. **1968** *Listener* 20 June 791/1 The Hudson Institute..is an organisation largely devoted to preparing what it likes to call 'scenarios of the future'. **1969** M. CRICHTON *Andromeda Strain* viii. 87 The President would face four circumstances (scenarios) in which he might have to issue the Cautery order. **1971** *Observer* 27 June 1/3 Several of the computer 'scenarios' include a catastrophic and sudden collapse of population. **1974** *Nature* 15 Feb. 445/2 As a possible scenario we assume the previously reported pulses to be the chance superposition of more frequent, randomly occurring subpulses. **1975** *Sci. Amer.* Jan. 29/2 Some meteoriticists boldly construct multistage scenarios of condensation, agglomeration, accretion, heating, metamorphism and differentiation to explain the accumulated facts. **1975** *N.Y. Times* 29 Mar. 11/1 There is a certain narrative element in this whacky art, but it would be a brave man who tried to extract a single coherent scenario from any single picture or construction. **1976** *Daily Tel.* 13 Feb. 1/8 Speculation..about the likely scenario when the Cuban-armoured units reach the point..when they will encounter South African forces. **1976** *Sci. Amer.* Oct. 79A/2 Many of the models we have mentioned here are better characterized by the term scenario... There is so little detailed information that the proposals should not be dignified by the term model. Nevertheless, a good scenario can sometimes lead to a good model. **1977** C. MCCARRY *Secret Lovers* ix. 112 I'll give you the scenario... You're free to modify it..in the light of conditions in the field. **1977** *Time* 18 Apr. 46/2 By escaping from the lab and multiplying, their scenario goes, it could find its way into human intestines. **1978** J. IRVING *World According to Garp* viii. 157 The good-byes that Garp imagined conducting with Alice were violent scenarios. **1980** *Jrnl. R. Soc. Arts* July 474/2 The best scenario..that we can envisage is one in which all those who want to do formal work will have an opportunity of doing two or three days a week.

3. *attrib.* and *Comb.* in sense 1, as *scenario department, editor, picture, production, sketch, writer, writing.*

1921 B. TARKINGTON *Let.* 2 July in *On Plays* (1959) 65 About your scenario dep't [*sic*] friend's suggestion. **1959** W. S. SHARPS *Dict. Cinematogr.* 127/1 *Scenario Editor*... The title usually applied to the person in charge of the story department of a film producing company. **1929** W. S. CHURCHILL *World Crisis* V. vii. 122 Mr. Baker detracts from the vindication of his hero by the absurd *scenario* picture which he has chosen to paint. **1945** *Amer. Cinematographer* Mar. 122 (*heading*) Trials of making a scenario production. **1921** B. TARKINGTON *Let.* 30 Mar. in *On Plays* (1959) 50, I am sending you the scenario sketch for a picture of 'Beaucaire'. **1914** R. GRAU *Theatre of Science* 224 We have seen the last of the amateur scenario writer. **1939** C. ISHERWOOD *Goodbye to Berlin* 101, I thought you took an interest in the cinema?' He's miles the best young scenario writer. **1976** BOTHAM & DONNELLY *Valentino* xi. 82 The woman considered to be the best scenario writer of the day, June Mathis. **1928** H. CRANE *Let.* 27 Mar. (1965) 321 Maybe scenario writing eventually.

Hence **scena·rio** *v. trans.*, to make a scenario of (a story, book, or idea); to sketch *out*; also **scena·rioi:ze, sce·narize.**

1918 *Dial. Notes* V. 13 'The *scenarioizing* of a drama.' Moving Picture advertisement. **1922** A. BENNETT *Let.* 17 Jan. (1966) I. 300, I had attempted to scenario-ize the story and had failed to do it properly. **1922** *Moving Picture Stories* 14 July 26/3 'Clarence'..is already scenarioized and requires only the producer's final approval. **1927** *Sunday Express* 21 Aug. 4 The films were scenarioised, directed, cut, edited, distributed, and exploited by him. **1946** *Amer. Speech* XXI. 304/2, 1946 Press-sheet of RKO Radio Pictures, Inc. Geoffrey Homes is now at the RKO studios scenarizing his best seller, 'Build My Gallows High'. **1953** WODEHOUSE *Performing Flea* 23 So far I have scenarioed it out to about the 40,000 word mark. **1974** *Daily Tel.* (Colour Suppl.) 6 Dec. 42/1 Tonight's entertainment is a fashion show. 'I hear they've got it all scenarioed out,' says Bernie.

scenarist (sĭnā·rist). *Cinemat.* [f. SCENAR(IO + -IST.] A scenario writer.

1920 *N.Y. Times* 24 May 20/4 'Old Lady 31', taken by June Mathis as scenarist and John E. Ince as director from Rachel Crother's play. **1925** *New Yorker* 28 Nov. 26/2 You never can tell just what happened to the tale when it fell into the hands of the gifted scenarists. **1932** A. BUCHANAN *Films* v. 92 Every shot..is recorded by the scenarist in his script. **1941** B. SCHULBERG *What makes Sammy Run?* vii. 153 Sammy Glick, prominent scenarist and playwright. **1958** *Times Lit. Suppl.* 15 Aug. p. xxviii/1 The opening passages of *Bleak House* are a supreme evocation of atmosphere which no contemporary scenarist could equal. **1966** *New Statesman* 30 Sept. 488/2 Miss McCarthy could yet prove to be a born scenarist. Film largely robs her work of its overbearing, destructive omniscience. **1977** *Times* 10 June 15/4 Wenders explains that he and his scenarist, the playwright Peter Handke, both happened to read the book at the same time. **1977** *Time* 12 Sept. 60/1 Can an English playwright turned Hollywood scenarist find, in his late 40s, happiness and the right woman?

scene. Add: **1.** (Earlier *transf.* and later examples.)

1612 W. STRACHEY *Trav. Virginia* (1953) I. vi. 78 By their howses, they have sometymes A Scæne or high Stage raised like a Scaffold..covered with Matts, which..is a Shelter and serves for such a covered place, where men vsed in old tyme to sitt and talke. **1924** A. HUXLEY *Let.* 29 Apr. (1969) 229 A Palladian theatre with fixed scene and various other delights.

7. b. Also (with hyphens) as *attrib. phr.*

1955 H. ROTH *Sleeper* ix. 69 His behind-the-scenes directors must have trusted him. **1959** *Manch. Guardian* 23 July 6/6 One version of the behind-the-scenes nterview. **1959** 'S. RANSOME' *I'll die for You* xii. 134 He was quietly directing his official resources into a wide, behind-the-scenes investigation.

8. a. (Further examples.)

1926 *Melody Maker* Sept. 61 Since 'Nelly Kelly's Cabaret' came on the scene, it's put fresh kick into dancing. **1936** W. H. SAUMAREZ SMITH *Let.* 26 June in *Young Man's Country* (1977) ii. 11, I rode out after breakfast to the scene of action. **1946** ROSENTHAL & ZACHERY *Jazzways* 16 By 1907, Bolden had disappeared from the scene, confined to an insane asylum. **1963** D. OGILVY *Confessions Advt. Man* (1964) ii. 26 By the time I came on the scene, the big advertisers had grown more cautious. **1968** *Jazz Monthly* Apr. 8/1 People like Buddy Collette, Red Callender,..were the big time musicians on the scene then. **1979** 'E. FERRARS' *Witness before Fact* xv. 150, I don't know what things were like for you before he arrived on the scene, perhaps not so good.

c. *the scene of the crime*, the place where a crime has been committed. Also *attrib.*, as *scene(s)-of-crime*, used *esp.* to designate (a member of) a civilian branch of the police force concerned with the collection of forensic evidence.

1923 A. CHRISTIE *Murder on Links* iv. 51 Now, Monsieur Poirot, you would without doubt like to visit the scene of the crime. **1931** D. L. SAYERS *Five Red Herrings* xvi. 175 He didn't take the body with him... Now he's got to get back to the scene of the crime. **1943** G. GREENE *Ministry of Fear* I. v. 67 A few elderly men in the C.I.D...might..visit the scene of the 'crime'. **1954** F. CHERRILL *Cherrill of the Yard* iii. 38 Scenes of Crime prints. *Ibid.* 39 By this arrangement it became much easier to carry out a search with a single Scenes of Crime mark which had been classified in accordance with the single fingerprint system. **1961** *Observer* 21 May 5/3 The War Office have placed an order.. for thirty-eight 'Scene of Crime Kits', to issue to their security-men. **1971** R. LEWIS *Error of Judgment* i. 38 The scene-of-crime unit upstairs have discovered nothing, but one of the constables..came up with a glove. **1972** *Police Rev.* 8 Dec. 1601/2 Certain duties such as those of scenes-of-crime officers..were not performed by the R.U.C. **1977** P. HILL *Liars* iii. 33 The Scene of Crime man went over.. the cottage for fingerprints.

d. Some portion of human activity (as delimited by a preceding *adj.* of place, time, etc.); the realm or sphere (of an activity or interest indicated by a preceding *attrib. sb.*).

1931 *Times Lit. Suppl.* 15 Oct. 786/3 Mr. Masters..is no optimistic observer of the contemporary American scene. **1938** D. BAKER *Young Man with Horn* I. v. 52 If Rick had grown up in the present scene he'd probably have had his head perpetually inside a walnut radio cabinet listening to this one or that one playing a tea dance. **1943** H. READ *Politics of Unpolitical* vii. 98 There have been times when he was bored with the social scene, and 'doodled' while he stared hopelessly into the future. **1949** *Ebony* Nov. 24 (*heading*) The jazz scene. **1959** L. LIPTON *Holy Barbarians* I. i. 40 Something was happening on the poetry scene in Venice West. **1970** *Daily Tel.* 9 Jan. 3/6 Wilson was not mixed up with the drug scene. **1974** *Howard Jrnl.* XIV. 108 (Advt.), One of the most forceful and controversial writers on the magisterial scene. **1977** *Listener* 17 Feb. 214/2 Without that little building at Swiss Cottage..London's theatre scene would be much duller.

e. *slang* (orig. *U.S. jazz* and *beatniks'*). A place where people of common interests meet or where a particular activity is carried on. Hence, more loosely, an activity or pursuit (esp. a fashionable or superior one); a situation, event, or experience; a way of life. Freq. in phrases, as *a bad scene*, an unpleasant experience; *to make the scene*, to participate in an event or activity; to arrive (somewhere); (*to go*) *on the scene*, (to become) involved in some activity, esp. drug-taking; (*not*) *one's scene* (and varr.), (not) what one enjoys or finds interesting.

There is some overlap with sense d above.

1951 E. PAUL *Springtime in Paris* vi. 125 'Nobody comes on this scene wearin' any green,' said another taller Negro. **1957** *N.Y. Times Mag.* 18 Aug. 26/3 *Scene*, any place where musicians play or gather; by extension, any place where people meet or any event they attend. Thus, 'Let's make the country scene this week-end.' **1958** G. LEA *Somewhere there's Music* xxi. 179 Something on the scene you don't dig. *Ibid.*, It was a bad scene. It scared me, man. **1958** *Look* 19 Aug. 65/2 The regulars who 'make the scene'. 'The scene', geographically, is a narrow area running about four blocks along Grant Avenue in San Francisco's North Beach district. *Ibid.* 67/1 Like many on 'the scene', she is attracted to Zen Buddhism. **1964** *New Society* 20 Feb. 8/2 What happens to the young drug taker? It can be described ..by actually going through the experience, going 'on the scene'. **1966** *New Statesman* 1 July 26/2 Her final surrender to Clive Francis seems unlikely: his jeans are too baggy for her scene. **1966** *Melody Maker* 15 Oct. 6/6, I decided I wanted to play jazz more than any other scene. **1967** *Punch* 18 Oct. 574/3 They come here to work because it's exciting and new and because it's the scene. **1968** M. RICHLER *Cocksure* xiii. 74 Like we're having a scene on Saturday night. At Timothy's pad. **1969** *Oz* Apr. 32/1 We've all got different scenes. The whole thing is to get to know each other's trips... Are you on an acid scene? **1970** [see *MAKE *v.*[1] 65 b]. **1975** D. LODGE *Changing Places* ii. 84 Washing up was more his scene than body language. **1977** I. SHAW *Beggarman, Thief* I. viii. 101 He could take a look at the scene and blow if he didn't like it.

11. *to make a scene* (later examples). Also, *to create a scene, to have a scene*.

1957 *Sunday Mail* (Glasgow) 10 Feb. 11 *Kick up a storm*—to cause trouble, or create a scene. **1958** [see *BRACE *v.*[1] 5 c]. **1959** T. S. ELIOT *Elder Statesman* II. 61 I've made him understand That the doctors want you to be free from worry. He won't make a scene. **1970** G. F. NEWMAN *Sir, You Bastard* viii. 255 Two of them rose and followed him out. 'Don't let's have a scene,' one of the Rubber Heels said... The other ran his hands over Sneed's jacket.

13. (senses 5 and 6) *scene-change*; **scene-dock** (earlier and later examples); **scene-painted** *a.*, painted with scenes; **scene-painter** (further examples); also *transf.*; **scene-painting** (earlier example in *fig.* sense); **scene-plot** (examples); **scene-room** (earlier examples); **scene-setting**, *vbl. sb.* and *ppl. a.*, setting a scene; usu. *transf.* and *fig.*; so **scene-setter**; **scene-steal** *v.*, to appropriate more than one's fair share of attention by one's performance in a scene; so *scene-stealer* (also *transf.*), *scene-stealing* ppl. adj.

1952 W. GRANVILLE *Dict. Theatrical Terms* 158 *Scene-change*, the striking of one scene and the erection of another. **1962** A. NISBETT *Technique Sound Studio* ix. 153 When a situation calls for a scene change the simplest form that this can take is a slow fade to silence over about ten seconds, a pause of three or four seconds, and an equally slow fade in. **1871** E. L. BLANCHARD *Diary* 9 Mar. in Scott & Howard *Life E. L. Blanchard* (1891) II. 395 Then to Standard [Theatre]..go behind the scenes and see the wonderful scene dock. **1916** [see *BACK STAGE, BACKSTAGE *sb.* and *adv.*]. **1977** *Times* 1 Nov. 14/6 The [Wexford] Opera House..[has] no scene-dock, no workshops, no adequate dressing-rooms. **1918** W. OWEN *Lett.* (1967) 558 Scene-painted boulders, and all the arts and deceitful devices of Victoria. **1824** Scene-painter [see *MASTER *sb.*[1] 24 d]. **1853** [see *CHURRIGUERESQUE *a.*]. **1821** H. C. ROBINSON *Diary* 2 Dec. (1967) 71, I have finished *Waverley*... Its merit lies in portrait and scene painting. **1847** W. C. MACREADY *Diary* 20 Oct. (1912) II. 375 Made one scene plot of 'Van Artevelde', and sent it with note to Stanfield. **1933** P. GODFREY *Back-Stage* i. 19 The stage-manager, with every detail of the scene-plot in his head, stands directing the whole. **1737** *Daily Advertiser* 4 Feb., And the Scene-Rooms, Green and Dressing Rooms, to be on the outside of the last mention'd Measure. **1826** J. O'KEEFFE *Recoll.* II. 39 The author is often brought into the scene-room to give his opinion on the progress of their work. **1859** E. FITZBALL *35 Yrs. Dram. Author's Life* II. 124 The celebrated Mr Grieve, and his two sons, Thomas and William, the most perfect scene painters in the world..in their scene-room, genius always found a welcome footing. **1974** *Times* 16 Apr. 16/3 Miss Tanburn will kick-off one of the panel discussions with a half-hour scene-setter. **1978** *Language* LIV. 353 Only three functions—*subject*, *topic*, and *relator*—are assigned by the rules of H's sample and DDG of English, although a fourth (*scene-setter*) is mentioned in the text. **1963** *Times Lit. Suppl.* 17 May 358/3 A biographer with a sense of character, an eye to scene-setting. **1968** P. FOOT *Politics of Harold Wilson* 11 The two most important scene-setting subjects are food and the weather. **1972** M. GILBERT *Body of Girl* xx. 183 With a little care and scene-setting it could be made to look very convincing. **1977** D. WILLIAMS *Treasure by Degrees* iii. 34 The Prince's finery and the size of his entourage—natural scene-setting for an important Arab. **1976** *Woman's Weekly* 6 Nov. 6/2 Trish Van Devere, who not only plays Beauty in the movie (and guess who scene-steals as the Beast!) but in real life also happens to be Mrs George C. Scott. **1978** *Radio Times* 18–24 Mar. 16/3 Director Jules Dassin's wife Melina Mercouri turns every trick to scene-steal from Morley and Ustinov. **1955** T. STERLING *Evil of Day* xviii. 193 These lousy actors are all scene-stealers. **1960** *Vogue Pattern Book* No. 4. 51 The addition of demure puffed sleeves makes it the scene-stealer of more sedate occasions. **1977** M. HINXMAN *One-Way Cemetery* xiii. 94 It's not the leading role, but it's a scene-stealer. **1963** *Times* 29 Jan. 11/1 Mr. Craig's is a good, workmanly Cavaradossi, a little stiff and never scene-stealing. **1980** *Times Lit. Suppl.* 21 Mar. 323/2 A small but scene-stealing knockabout part.

‖ **scène à faire** (sẹn a fẹ̄r'). *Theatr.* Pl. **scènes à faire.** [Fr., lit. 'scene for action'.] The most important scene in a play or opera, made inevitable by the action which leads up to it. Also *transf.*

1893 *Manch. Guardian* 24 Oct. 8/3 The subject of the 'Dame aux Camellias' trying to begin life over again, and to live as if the past had never been, has often been essayed, and the *scène à faire* of her confrontation..with the inexorable reality of things has been often and sometimes admirably composed. **1921** P. LUBBOCK *Craft of Fiction* vii. 102 Thackeray's skill betrays him... His climax, his *scène à faire*, has been insufficiently prepared for. **1922** W. S. MAUGHAM *On a Chinese Screen* xlviii. 188 He was asking for the *pièce bien faite*, the *scène à faire*, the curtain, the unexpected, the dramatic. **1948** F. R. LEAVIS *Great Tradition* ii. 112 The brilliant art with which James, choosing his *scènes à faire*, works in terms of dramatic presentation. **1965** *New Statesman* 10 Dec. 943/2 A big added *scène à faire* in the council chamber gave Verdi a chance for the creation of an ensemble that looks forward very clearly to the third act of *Otello*. **1969** *Listener* 13 Feb. 220/2 Robert Hoffman acts badly, and the *scène à faire* in a wobbling rowing boat..is a triumph of embarrassment. **1980** *Times* 14 Mar. 13/8 They do, eventually, get a *scène à faire* (which, so often, proves to be a *scène à ne faire*) in which she tries to treat him as Louis XV.

scenery. Add: **2. a.** Also, that used in film and television.

1959 W. S. SHARPS *Dict. Cinematogr.* 127/1 *Scenery*, the various parts and accessories used on the set to represent the actual scene of an action. **1960** O. SKILBECK *ABC of Film & TV* 11 Scenery which may be viewed in close-up must be more convincing than that of the theatre. **1961** G. MILLERSON *Technique Television Production* 142 By special electronic equipment, we can place one camera's performers and/or scenery in the background picture provided by another picture source.

b. So phr. *part of the scenery*.

1970 N. MARSH *When in Rome* viii. 221 He..must often hang about the premises... Part of the scenery as it were. **1971** 'H. CALVIN' *Poison Chasers* v. 65 Dai had mentioned her to me as an interesting part of the local scenery. **1977** *Times* 4 July 12/4 Inexperienced Mabel..was allowed to sing the old things in harmony. I was, at first, only part of the scenery.

scene-shifter. (Later examples.)

1908 [see *LEGIT., LEGIT]. **1957** L. DURRELL *Justine* II. 102 Quick as a scene-shifter the station packs away advertisement after advertisement. **1978** *Lancashire Life* Apr. 35/3 A saviour came in the shape of little Alfie Gee—part-time electrician and scene-shifter... 'Shuffle off the stage sideways,' he whispered, 'and don't drop it, man.'

scenic, *a.* Add: **1. d.** (Earlier examples.)

1824 R. HUMPHREYS *Mem. J. Decastro* 16 It is that [part] of the scenic department from whence the borders of chambers or clouds drop, to complete each different scene. **1827** J. BOADEN *Mem. Mrs. Siddons* II. xix. 292 A benefit proportioned to the pains that have been taken in the scenic department of our stages. **1854** C. A. MOWATT *Autobiography of Actress* 48 Costumes and rehearsals and scenic effects.

e. *scenic artist*, a painter or designer of scenery for the stage. orig. *U.S.*

1840 *Spirit of Times* 21 Nov. 456/3 C. L. Smith..is the scenic artist of the Theatre. **1877** W. R. ALGER *Life Edwin Forrest* II. 581 John Wiser, a scenic artist, arranged and painted it. **1919** G. B. SHAW *Great Catherine* 114 It was quite easy for Patiomkin to humbug Catherine as to the condition of Russia by conducting her through sham cities run up for the occasion by scenic artists. **1930** SELDEN & SELLMAN *Stage Scenery & Lighting* ii. 31 Before the scenic artist can start to make scenery it is necessary that he learn thoroughly the form of scenery. **1971** BURRIS-MEYER & COLE *Scenery for Theatre* (rev. ed.) ii. 22 The designer is a member of the scenic artists' union.

3. a. (Later examples.) Also, of a window or the like: designed to afford a landscape view. Now chiefly *N. Amer.*

1937 *Discovery* Oct. 306/2 Small-holders in scenic areas. **1967** *Boston Sunday Herald* 26 Mar. VI. 3/1 (Advt.), See the scenic glories of our great continent. **1970** *Globe & Mail* (Toronto) 26 Sept. 30/1 (Advt.), The Canadian, one of the world's great trains... Soft music. Air conditioning... Scenic Domes..all the way. **1971** *New Yorker* 9 Oct. 170/3 (Advt.), Golf on scenic course. **1978** *N.Y. Times* 30 Mar. B17/2 (Advt.), Floor to ceiling scenic windows.

b. Applied to a road that has been planned and landscaped so as to provide fine views. orig. and chiefly *N. Amer.*

1914 H. MACNAIR (*title*) Scenic motorway; a motor tour de luxe. **1916** *Road Maps & Tour Bk. Western N. Carolina* (N. Carolina Good Roads Assoc.) 149 The Asheville–Murphy Scenic Highway through Swain County will afford scenery unsurpassed by any section of the country. **1934** *Popular Mechanics* Aug. 238/1 The modern de luxe highway cruiser..may take you and your baggage safely and inexpensively anywhere along historic and scenic highways. **1935** *Nature Mag.* Mar. 101 Let us hope that there will be a policy of scenic road construction. **1943**

J. S. HUXLEY *TVA* ix. 60 The Norris Freeway..is a scenic highway on which access is limited to a very few points, and where no building is allowed within several hundred yards on either side. **1959** W. B. SNOW *Highway & Landscape* 111 For specialized types of highway, scenic parkways particularly, the national standards may not always be entirely appropriate. **1967** *Boston Sunday Herald* 26 Mar. II. 9/1 A 7·4-mile Appleton Ridge Scenic Drive became a women's project in 1966. The women got the town to bulldoze the rough spots on a dirt road, cut bushes to open up magnificent views, and provide a stretch for 'slow drivers who really want to enjoy the scenery'. **1979** D. CLARK *Heberden's Seat* i. 7 Masters had suggested that they should find a scenic route and take their time.

4. a. (Earlier example.)

1845 *Punch* VIII. 247/1 To criticise a Picture by Stanfield.—Begin by unqualified praise; then commence detracting,..on the score of..'scenic effect of the figures'; and conclude by a wish he had never been a scene-painter.

b. With reference to wallpaper: creating a continuous scene or landscape on the walls of a room.

1924 N. MCCLELLAND *Historic Wall-Papers* xii. 279 (*heading*) Some famous scenic papers and their owners. **1929** C. C. OMAN *Victoria & Albert Museum: Calul. Wall-Papers* 63 The earliest scenic wall-papers..were produced by hand-painting. **1951** L. & W. KATZENBACH *Pract. Bk. Amer. Wallpaper* vi. 61 This scenic wallpaper pictures a tropic Haiti. **1976** *National Observer* (U.S.) 25 Sept. 9/1 Now about all that remains is the neon-red carpet and 'scenic' wallpaper that once surrounded a bathtub.

scenic (sī·nik), *sb.* [f. the adj.] **1.** = SCENE 6 *fig. rare*—[1].

1891 G. MEREDITH *One of Our Conquerors* III. vi. 125 She passed into music, as she always did under motion of carriages and trains, whether in happiness or sadness: and the day being one that had a sky, the scenic of music swung her up to soar.

2. A scenic film or photograph; a film or photograph the subject of which is natural scenery.

1918 *N.Y. Times* 25 Nov. 11/3 Robert C. Bruce has a scenic at the Rivoli entitled 'A Wee Bit Odd', which is entertaining pictorially in spite of labored wit in the subtitles. **1922** *Ibid.* 2 July VI. 3/3 The short comedies, scenics, travel films and other so-called non-dramatic productions are so much better than the photoplays when they are at all good. **1971** *Amateur Photographer* 3 Mar. 23/1 A cine columnist's thoughts thankfully turn from the interiors he had intended to shoot..to the spring scenic he has for years been intending to make... I like scenics and am not put off by objections that they are old-fashioned... So are trees and meadows. **1979** *SLR Camera* June 56/2 Scenics, particularly townscapes, at night are best shot while there is still some tone in the sky.

3. Short for 'scenic wallpaper' (see *SCENIC *a.* 4 b).

1951 L. & W. KATZENBACH *Pract. Bk. Amer. Wallpaper* vi. 65 While the composition of this scenic is traditional, it is executed in a technique that is distinctly modern. **1966** M. M. PEGLER *Dict. Interior Design* (1967) 393 *Scenic*, a wallpaper mural usually made up of three or four panels that create a continuous scene, vista, or design. **1972** E. A. ENTWHISTLE *French Scenic Wallpapers 1800–1860* v. 35 *Les Monuments de Paris*..was different from most of the other scenics. **1976** B. GREYSMITH *Wallpaper* 92 The most striking examples of the new French manner were the 'scenics', the term used to describe *trompe l'oeil* landscapes on a grand scale, not repeating but creating a complete scene around the walls of a room.

4. Short for *SCENIC RAILWAY.

1968 D. BRAITHWAITE *Fairground Architecture* viii. 125 In structural form there was little difference between the 'Scenic' and the earlier switchback.

5. A scenic pattern or design.

1977 *Chicago Tribune* 2 Oct. v. 9 (Advt.), Make slipcovers, draperies of 100 % cotton prints in florals, scenics, geometrics.

scenic railway (sī·nik rē[i]·lwe[i]). [f. SCENIC *a.* + RAILWAY *sb.*] A switchback or miniature railway running through artificial representations of beautiful or spectacular scenery, as an attraction at fairs, etc.

1894 *Official Guide Calif. Midwinter Exposition* 130 (*heading*) Scenic railway. *Ibid.*, It must not be supposed that gravity alone is the motive power in the Scenic Railway. **1908** [see SCENIC *a.* 3]. **1917** *Jrnl. Exper. Psychol.* II. 158 The popularity of such amusements as 'scenic railways', the sole attraction of which lies in the fright on the steep inclines, suggests that fear may be pleasant—at least retrospectively. **1923** H. C. WITWER in *Cosmopolitan* Aug. 46/1 You're a woman, a good looker with more curves than a scenic railway. **1926** T. E. LAWRENCE *Seven Pillars* (1935) III. xxxii. 184 About their crests ran narrow veins of granite-coloured stone, generally in pairs, following the contour of the skyline like the rusted metals of an abandoned scenic railway. **1930** E. WAUGH *Labels* 200 There were switch-backs and scenic railways on which empty cars swooped and swerved through breath-taking descents. **1968** [see *GALLOPER 1 b]. **1973** 'M. INNES' *Appleby's Answer* iii. 33 Shaftesbury Avenue..was like going through a 'scenic' railway in a Brobdingnagian fun-fair. **1980** *Times* 4 Oct. 12/8 One of the sights worth seeing was the drunks on the new 60 mph 'Super-looping' scenic railway.

Scenicruiser (sī·nikrū̆:zəɹ). *U.S.* Also with small initial. [f. SCENI(C *a.* + CRUISER.] The proprietary name of a line of luxury coaches equipped for long-distance travel, esp. for touring areas of scenic beauty.

1954 *Business Week* 17 July 33/2 Greyhound is wagering heavily that the Scenicruiser will rejuvenate its business. **1955** *American Mag.* Jan. 92/2 We were riding in a new Greyhound 'Scenicruiser'. **1959** *Official Gaz.* (U.S. Patent Office) 13 Jan. TM77/2 The Greyhound Corporation, Chicago...Scenicruiser. **1965** M. BRADBURY *Stepping Westward* viii. 403 They ate fast..and returned to the scenicruiser. **1974** *Encycl. Brit. Macropædia* XVIII. 721/2 The Sceni cruiser introduced in the United States in 1954 for trans-continental use..utilizes air suspension and has six wheels. **1976** *Yellowstone Explorer* July 8/1 (*heading*) Scenicruiser mini voyages. *Ibid.*, Your captain will keep you posted as the scenicruiser glides along.

scent, *sb.* Add: **5. scent-bottle,** (*a*) (further example); (*b*) a bottle designed to contain scent.

1856 C. M. YONGE *Daisy Chain* I. xxv. 262 She flew for the scent-bottle, while her father bent over Margaret. **1895** *Army & Navy Co-op. Soc. Price List* 714/2 Scent Bottles—Fancy,—A large assortment in Stock. **1917** *Harrods Gen. Catal.* 219 Sterling silver and cut glass scent bottle. **1930** T. S. ELIOT tr. *St.-J. Perse's Anabasis* 37 And a man strode forth at the threshold of the desert—profession of his father: dealer in scent-bottles. **1975** J. O'FAOLAIN *Woman in Wall* iii. 55 Translucent scent-bottles of glass and alabaster.

scenter. (Later example.)

1977 *Islander* (Victoria, B.C.) 13 Nov. 3/1 And now, in November, the rain is..a scenter of soil, a painter of stones.

scentless, *a.* Add: **3.** Also of a day on which there is no scent for the hounds to follow.

1885 *Field* 4 Apr. 428/1 That dry, scentless cycle of days. **1921** *Ampleforth Jrnl.* Jan. 137 On October 16th we hunted the high country, after a scentless day at Tom Smith's Cross on the previous Wednesday. **1976** *Horse & Hound* 3 Dec. 30/3 They had an exciting, if rather scentless, morning, catching a brace of foxes, the last one within 20 yards of the kennel gates!

4. scentless mayweed, a perennial herb, *Tripleurospermum maritimum* (formerly *Matricaria inodora*), belonging to the family Compositæ and bearing white, yellow-centred flowers and finely divided leaves.

1800 J. E. SMITH *Eng. Bot.* X. 676 (*heading*) Corn feverfew. Scentless may-weed. **1857** A. PRATT *Flowering Plants & Ferns Gt. Brit.* III. 315 Scentless Mayweed.. puzzles the young botanist by belying its name, and having an odour which, though not aromatic, is powerful and unpleasant. **1914** A. R. HORWOOD *Story of Plant Life Brit. Isles* I. 140 The Scentless Mayweed..has a larger flower and a generally darker green colour [than the stinking mayweed]. **1931** M. GRIEVE *Mod. Herbal* II. 524/1 The Scentless Mayweed owes its generic name to its reputed medicinal properties. **1975** E. J. GIBBONS *Flora of Lincolnshire* 232 Scentless Mayweed... Native. Weed of cultivation.

scenty (se·nti), *a. rare.* [f. SCENT *sb.* + -Y[1].] Smelling of scent; scented.

1937 G. FRANKAU *More of Us* x. 111 Yet, ere he handed scenty lace-edged flax back, Long to his seat in knightly honour rooted The hero cleaved. **1963** D. BALLANTYNE *And the Glory* 148 There was the warm and scenty smell of her body.

sceptic, skeptic, *a.* and *sb.* Now usually spelt *sceptic* in the U.K. and British Commonwealth and *skeptic* in the U.S. Similarly all the derivatives, *scepticism/skepticism*, etc.

scepticism, skepticism. 1. (Earlier example.)

1652 N. CULVERWEL *Light of Nature* 150 He [*sc.* Pyrrho] perswades men to encline to his Scepticisme.

† Sceptism. Add. Also 6 **sceptisme**. (Earlier and later examples.)

1652 N. CULVERWEL *Light of Nature* 153 *Des-Cartes* the French philosopher..will be fain to stop and stay in Sceptisme... He that will not cast Anchor upon these, condemnes himself to perpetual Sceptisme. **1737** A. BAXTER *Enq. Hum. Soul* (ed. 2) II. 21 That kind of Scepticism called Egomism.

sch. In words derived from Yiddish in which initial (ʃ) precedes a consonant, there is much variation in written English between *sch-* and *sh-*; however (following the German usage) *sch-* seems to be the prevailing spelling, except before *t*, where German would use simple *s-*: here *sh-* is the usual form, as it is before vowels. For the two main types see *SCHLEMIEL, *SCHMO, *SCHNOOK, etc., and *SHTICK. Such words are extremely common in the U.S. but are rarely encountered in Great Britain.

schaalstein, schalstein (ʃā·lʃtəin). *Geol.* Also **schaallstein**, and partly translated as **schaalstone** (ʃā·lstō͡ᵘn). [Ger., f. *schale* (formerly *schaale*) skin, shell + *stein* stone. See also SHALE *sb.*[2] and SCALE *sb.*[1]] **† a.** = WOLLASTONITE. *Obs.*

1804 R. JAMESON *Syst. Min.* I. 519 (*heading*) Schaalstein.—Werner. *Ibid.* 520 It is named schaalstone, which in German intimates that it is composed of lamellar distinct concretions. I have not been able to find any English word synonymous to the German, so that I am under the necessity of adopting it. **1819** W. PHILLIPS *Elem. Introd. Mineral.* (ed. 2) 300/1 (Index), Schaallstein. **1836** T. THOMSON *Outl. Min., Geol.* I. 129 Bisilicate of Lime. Table spar, schaalstein, grammite, wollastonite of Hauy.

b. Any of several basic or calcareous tuffaceous rocks, usu. laminated in structure, affected by low-grade metamorphism; a slaty or sheared greenstone.

1866 P. H. LAWRENCE tr. *von Cotta's Rocks classified & Described* II. iv. 311 Some part at least of what has been called schalstein belongs to the tufa formation. **1882** A. GEIKIE *Text-bk. Geol.* 165 Schalstein.—Under this name German petrographers have placed a variety of rocks which consist of a green, grey, red, or mottled diabase-tuff impregnated with carbonate of lime and mixed with calcareous and argillaceous mud. **1897** —— *Ancient Volcanoes of Gt. Brit.* II. xxix. 36 Some layers of this tuff assume a finely foliated appearance by the development of pale leek-green folia, which show slickensided surfaces parallel with the bedding. The rock then presents one of the usual appearances of schalstein. **1909** W. A. E. USSHER et al. *Geol. Country around Bodmin & St. Austell* vi. 44 North of Bury Down..the Middle Devonian Slates are associated with schalsteins. **1974** E. LEHMANN in G. C. Amstutz *Spilites & Spilitic Rocks* 23 In the Lahn syncline..of Western Germany, the central rock complex, of upper Middle Devonian and lower Upper Devonian age, consists of so-called 'schalstein'. Any consistency, however, suggested by that old miner's term, is not reflected in the petrographic character of the rock.

schaapsteker, var. *SKAAPSTEKER.

Schabzieger (ʃa·pˌtsīgəɹ). Also **Chapsager, -ziger, Schabzeiger, Schabziger,** etc. [Ger.: see SAPSAGO.] A kind of hard green cooking cheese made in Switzerland from curds, and flavoured with melilot. In full, **Schabzieger Käse.**

1837 *Penny Cycl.* VII. 15/2 The green Swiss cheese, commonly called *Schabzieger*, which is made in the canton of Glarus. **1846** Chapsager [see SAPSAGO]. **1866** LINDLEY & MOORE *Treas. Bot.* s.v. *Melilotus*, Schabzieger or Chapziger. **1879** *Encycl. Brit.* X. 636/1 *Glarus*... The *Schabzeiger, Schotter Käse, Kräuterkäse*, or 'green cheese', made of skim milk, whether of goats or cows, mixed with butter-milk and coloured with powdered *steinklee* (*Melilotus cœrulea*), is still largely manufactured. **1887** R. BENTLEY *Man. Bot.* (ed. 5) 534 They [*sc.* flowers and seeds of *Melilotus officinalis*] are used to give flavour to the 'Schabzieger'. **1892** *Mrs. Beeton's Bk. Househ. Managem.* xli. 894 Shabzieger is a cheese exceedingly strong both in smell and taste. **1950** *Chambers's Encycl.* VI. 371/1 *Glarus*... The green cheese called Schabziger is wholly made here. **1955** *Times* 10 May 12/4 Schabzieger, a Swiss green cheese, may well be considered regional by virtue of its limited appeal. **1958** *Catal. County Stores, Taunton* June 9 *Cheese*..Schabzieger, for grating—each 1/6. **1969** R. & D. DE SOLA *Dict. Cooking* 202/1 *Schabzeiger Käse* (German—scraped whey cheese), hard greenish cheese used in cooking and somewhat like sapsago, its American counterpart.

schadchen, var. *SHADCHAN.

‖ **Schadenfreude** (ʃā·dənfroidə). Also with small initial. [Ger., f. *schaden* harm + *freude* joy.] Malicious enjoyment of the misfortunes of others.

[**1852** R. C. TRENCH *Study of Words* (ed. 3) II. 29 What a fearful thing is it that any language should have a word expressive of the pleasure which men feel at the calamities of others; for the existence of the word bears testimony to the existence of the thing. And yet in more than one such a word is found... In the Greek ἐπιχαιρεκακία, in the German, 'Schadenfreude'. **1867** CARLYLE *Shooting Niagara: & After?* III. 12 Have not I a kind of secret satisfaction, of the malicious or even of the judiciary kind (*schadenfreude*, 'mischief-joy', the Germans call it, but really it is *justice*-joy withal), that he they call 'Dizzy' is to do it.] **1895** C. LOWE *German Emperor William II* ix. 256 But the *Schadenfreude*, or malicious joy, of the French was premature. **1901** *Q. Rev.* CXCIII. 316 Sometimes it [*sc.* Queen Victoria's smile] would be coyly negative, leading the speaker on, the lips slightly opened, with a suggestion of kindly fun, even of a little innocent *Schadenfreude*. **1902** *Contemp. Rev.* May 662, I am persuaded that what (no doubt by a slip of undesigned candour) is described in the recent *Life of Claude Bernard* by an eminent English physiologist as the '*Joys* of the Laboratory', are very real 'joys' to the vivisector; that is, *Schadenfreude*,—Pleasure in the Pain he witnesses and creates. **1902** C. HAGUE tr. *Brentano's Origin of Knowledge of Right & Wrong* 85 Pleasure at the misfortunes of others (Schadenfreude) is bad on the first ground. **1920** F. HAMILTON *Days before Yesterday* iv. 118 The particular sentiment described in German as 'schadenfreude' 'pleasure over another's troubles' (how characteristic it is that there should be no equivalent in any other language for this peculiarly Teutonic emotion!) makes but little appeal to the average Briton except where questions of age and of failing powers come into play. **1939** *Palestine Post* 31 Aug. 6/3 There appears to be a certain amount of 'Schadenfreude' in London..at Germany's failure to get the German–Soviet Pact ratified. **1947** AUDEN *Age of Anxiety* (1948) I. 14 The *Schadenfreude* of cooks at keyholes. **1974** K. CLARK *Another Part of Wood* i. 8 Arthur Rackham..certainly had a vein of *schadenfreude* (what is now misleadingly described as sadism) and took an intense delight in scraggy fingers. **1977** 'E. CRISPIN' *Glimpses of Moon* iv. 62 Solidarity or no solidarity, Widger was not wholly without *Schadenfreude* at seeing his informative colleague discomfited for once. **1978** 'A. STUART' *Vicious Circles* 15 For a Russian..there is a curious fascination, mixed with *Schadenfreude*, about..titles and honours lists.

schafarzikite (ʃăfā·ızikəit). *Min.* [ad. G. *schafarzikit* (J. A. Krenner 1921, in *Zeitschr. f. Kristallogr.* LVI. 198), f. the name of Ferenc *Schafarzik* (1854–1927), Hungarian mineralogist: see -ITE¹.] A tetragonal antimonite of iron, first found as red to red-brown prismatic crystals with a metallic lustre in a stibnite mine in Slovakia.

1922 *Mineral. Mag.* XIX. 348 Schafarzikite... Red, tetragonal crystals found with kermesite (and resembling this in appearance) at Pernek, Hungary, contain iron and phosphorus. **1955** M. H. HEY *Index Min. Species* (ed. 2) 271 Schafarzikite... Isostructural with artificial tetragonal $FeSb_2O_4$, but the one analysis approaches $Fe_5Sb_4O_{11}$. **1975** *Tschermaks Mineral. und Petrogr. Mitteilungen* XXII. 236 The crystal structure of schafarzikite, $FeSb_2O_4$,..has been refined... The Fe atoms are surrounded octahedrally by six oxygen atoms, the Sb atoms form with three oxygen atoms a flat trigonal pyramid.

schairerite (ʃēᵊ·rərəit). *Min.* [f. the name of John F. *Schairer* (1904–70), U.S. geochemist + -ITE¹.] A sulphate and fluoride of sodium, Na_3FSO_4, usu. also containing chlorine, first found as colourless rhombohedral crystals in the salt crust of Searles Lake, San Bernardino Co., California.

1931 W. F. FOSHAG in *Amer. Mineralogist* XVI. 134 For this new species, a sulfate and fluoride of soda, the name schairerite is proposed in honor of Dr. J. F. Schairer of the Geophysical Laboratory of the Carnegie Institution, who studied the quaternary system Na_2SO_4–NaF–NaCl–H_2O, in which this compound plays a prominent part. **1963** *Doklady Earth Sci.* CXXXIX. 839/1 We succeeded in discovering schairerite in totally different conditions—nepheline syenite pegmatites of Alluayv Mountain in the Lovozero massif (Kola Peninsula). **1971** *Amer. Mineralogist* LVI. 177 All but the smallest and most perfect schairerite crystals are affected by voids or imperfections.

‖ **schalet(e** (ʃa·lėt, ʃale·t). *Jewish Cookery.* Also **schaleth.** [app. a Ger. variant of Yiddish *tsholnt.*] **a.** A kind of baked fruit pudding. **b.** A Sabbath dish of meat, potatoes, and vegetables, prepared on a Friday and baked slowly overnight.

1943 A. SIMON *Conc. Encycl. Gastronomy* IV. 27/1 *Schaleth* is an old favourite among Jewish cookery recipes.. a pudding made of..apples..raisins and sultanas..spices.. and baked under a cover of a hard wheat paste. **1949** *Housewife* May 2/2 The traditional Saturday lunch-dish is the Schalet, a stew of meat and beans, prepared on the Friday and left to cook at the back of the stove. **1956** L. BLANCH *Around World in Eighty Dishes* 99 Schalète (from Israel)... An apple and raisin cake. **1966** J. GARDNER *Amber Nine* iii. 40 'Best Schalete I've ever tasted.'..'Kosher, of course.' **1970** L. M. FEINSILVER *Taste of Yiddish* ii. 172 Heine, in discussing the merits of *schalet*, or *tsholnt*, expressed regret that 'the Christian Church, which borrowed so much that was good from ancient Judaism, should have failed to adopt *schalet* as its own'.

‖ **Schallanalyse** (ʃa·lanalǖ:zə). *Philology.* [Ger., lit. 'sound analysis'.] (See quot. 1931.)

1930 [see *MOTORIC *a.* a]. **1931** *Year's Work Mod. Lang. Studies* I. III. 126 Sievers's 'Schallanalyse'..is a method of restoring the accentuation of a given textual record by registering and analyzing the reaction of a trained observer, who responds instinctively and directly to the psychological compulsion exerted by the text on any one who reads it aloud. **1939** L. H. GRAY *Found. Lang.* ii. 44 One must exclude from linguistics proper all consideration of rhythm (including the so-called *Schallanalyse*). **1947** C. L. WRENN *Poetry of Cædmon* 3 But it is made very clear at the outset of this [*sc.* Sievers's] exposition of *Schallanalyse* that only those who possess certain qualities in their motor nerves can participate in such experiments or judge of their effects. **1953** K. SISAM *Studies in Hist. of Old Eng. Lit.* vi. 103 Sievers, using arguments from 'Schallanalyse' which I cannot follow, concludes that the translator of *Genesis B* produced the whole work *Genesis A* and *B* by a process of compilation and revision.

schallerite (ʃæ·lərəit). *Min.* [f. the name of Waldemar T. *Schaller* (1882–1967), U.S. mineralogist + -ITE¹.] A reddish-brown basic silicate, arsenate, and chloride of iron and manganese crystallizing in the rhombohedral system.

1925 R. B. GAGE et al. in *Amer. Mineralogist* X. 9 The name schallerite is proposed for the mineral after Dr. Waldemar T. Schaller, of the United States Geological Survey, Washington, D.C. *Ibid.*, Schallerite occurs in seams or on cleavage faces in the massive zinc ore. **1970** *Soviet Physics: Crystallogr.* XV. 40/1 This has made it possible to carry out a systematic derivation of the possible polytype modifications of pyrosmalite and to determine the structures of schallerite and friedelite.

schalstein, var. *SCHAALSTEIN.

schanse. Add: Also **schans, schanz, skans.** (Further examples.)

1885 J. NIXON *Complete Story Transvaal* xi. 200 They found the Boers intrenched in a series of *schanses* (stone-works, breast high), along the northern ridge of the valley. **1894** B. MITFORD *Renshaw Fanning's Quest* xxii. 177 Lucky, I took the precaution of building a *schanz*,—eh? **1929** D. REITZ *Commando* ix. 75 We were sustaining heavy casualties from the English *schans* immediately in front of us. **1969** J. SELBY *Boer War* 15 Boers digging defense works and building stone schanzes. **1974** in J. Branford *Dict. S. Afr. English* (1978) 218/1 The British thought the Boers would be hiding behind these skanses or heaps of stone.

schappe (ʃæp, ‖ ʃa·pə). [a. G. *schappe* silk waste.] A fabric or yarn made from waste silk (orig. by removal of the gum by fermentation). Hence **schappe** *v. trans.*, to ferment (waste silk) in order to remove gum; **scha·pping** *vbl. sb.*

1885 *Harper's Mag.* July 246 Now they [*sc.* waste cocoons] are spun into yarn,..and made into *schappe* or 'spun silk' fabrics, not as lustrous as reeled silk goods, but stronger and cheaper. **1909** WEBSTER, Schapping, n. **1921** BEAUMONT & HILL *Dress, Blouse, & Costume Cloths* 94 The 'Schappe' or 'steeping practice' consists in placing the supply of waste silk in jacketed pans. **1957** *Textile Terms & Defs.* (*Textile Inst.*) (ed. 3) 124 *Schapping*, a continental method of degumming, applied to silk waste, that removes part of the gum by a fermentation process. Up to 10 per cent of gum may remain on the fibre. **1969** A. J. HALL *Stand. Handbk. Textiles* (ed. 7) iii. 129 Spun or schappe yarns which are short fibred and free or partly free from silk-gum are made from silk waste.

schapska (ʃæ·pskă). Also **chapska.** [Fr. *chapska, schapska*, ad. Pol. *czapka* cap.] A flat-topped cavalry helmet.

1894 *Daily News* 27 Mar. 5/4 Helmets, shakos, chapskas, and other head coverings were to be had in great profusion. **1909** WEBSTER, Schapska. **1918** E. S. FARROW *Dict. Mil. Terms* 536 *Schapska*, a military helmet or shako, first worn by the Polish lancers. **1930** *Times Educ. Suppl.* 19 July (Home & Classroom Section) p. iv/2 Spahis, in their baggy trousers, their burnouses,..their chapskas, their boléros, and all the other items of equipment,..followed. **1936** C. S. FORESTER *General* ii. 16 Put on again the glories of blue and gold, schapska and plume, lance pennons and embroidered saddlecloths. **1951** J. MASTERS *Nightrunners of Bengal* xxiv. 331 A horseman galloped up... He wore..a black schapska with a gold bag tied to its side.

schatchen, var. *SHADCHAN.

‖ **Schatz** (ʃats). Also **schatz.** [Ger., lit. 'treasure'.] In Germany: a term of endearment for a woman; a (German) girl-friend or female companion. Also dim. **Schätzi, Schatzi(e.**

1907 M. A. VON ARNIM *Fräulein Schmidt & Mr. Anstruther* xlii. 174 The trumpeter and his *Schatz* sat quietly in the kitchen. **1956** *Amer. Speech* XXXI. 142 A sizable body of German words and idioms has entered the lingo of Army troops in Germany and Austria... *Schatzi*, or sometimes *shots* (= German *Schatz*), is a sweetheart. **1966** E. WEST *Night is Time for Listening* vi. 190 He sat at a table in Pommler's..the place bulging with GI's, *Schatzis*, and miscellany. **1970** L. SANDERS *Anderson Tapes* xi. 30 Oh, *Schatzie*, I stopped wanting many years ago. Now I just accept. **1971** D. MACKENZIE *Sleep is for Rich* vi. 198 We've been through all this before, *schatz.* **1972** L. P. BACHMANN *Ultimate Act* xxiii. 209 'Are you all right, *Schätzi?*' she asked... 'What's *Schätzi?*' 'You. It's an old-fashioned translation of 'chéri' into German.' **1976** P. HENISSART *Winter Quarry* viii. 83 *Schatz*, I know my business.

Schaumann (ʃau·măn). *Med.* [Name of J. *Schaumann* of Stockholm, who described them (*Acta Med. Scand.* (1941) CVI. 239, etc.).] *Schaumann('s) body*: a rounded, laminated body containing iron and often calcium, numbers of which are common inside giant cells in sarcoidosis tissue.

1955 P. A. HERBUT *Pathology* xii. 342 Schaumann bodies are deeply bluish staining, concentric, lamellated, multiple contoured, iron- and calcium-positive concretions of variable sizes. **1976** ROBBINS & ANGELL *Basic Path.* (ed. 2) xii. 421/1 The distinctive..morphologic feature of sarcoidosis.. is the noncaseating granuloma... In 80 to 90 per cent of these granulomas, laminated concretions of calcium and proteins, known as Schaumann's bodies, can occasionally be found within giant cells.

schchi, var. STCHI in Dict. and Suppl.

sched (ʃed, sked), colloq. abbrev. of *SCHEDULE *sb.* 4 b.

1958 R. STOW *To Islands* iv. 88, I took your telegram.. to send to the doctor, but it was too late for the sched... I felt the wireless and it was cold. **1963** L. DIACK *Labrador Nurse* III. xviii. 91 There was the radio-telephone..and there was always a daily 'sched' at twelve noon.

schedule, *sb.* Add: **2.** (Earlier and later examples with reference to the British income tax.)

1803 *Income Tax Act* 43 *Geo. III* c. 122 s. 1 in *Statutes United Kingdom* (1804) I. 1012 During the Term herein mentioned, there shall be raised, levied, collected, and paid, throughout Great Britain, the several Duties and Contributions in the Schedules contained in this Act, marked (A) (B) (C) (D) and (E). **1902** KIPLING *Traffics & Discoveries* (1904) 29 'You'll only be an additional expense to me as a taxpayer. Think of Schedule D,' he says, 'and take parole.' **1966** B. E. V. SABINE *Hist. Income Tax* ii. 35 The tax was for the first time divided up into the well-known five schedules. Schedule A charged tax on the amount of land and buildings; Schedule B covered farming profits; Schedule C taxed fundholders in respect of annuities payable out of any public revenue... Schedule D was divided into the six cases which are still familiar today and brought into charge various forms of profit and interest.. and Schedule E embraced the charge on income from offices and employments of profit and annuities and pensions. **1970** *Money Which?* Mar. 4/2 Schedule A. Income from rents and other receipts from property which is unfurnished (formerly Case VIII of Schedule D, but reclassified as Schedule A as from 6 April 1970).

4. a. For 'chiefly *U.S.*' read 'orig. *U.S.*' and add earlier and further examples. Also in extended sense, a programme or plan of events, operations, etc. Freq. in phrs. *according to, before, behind, on,* etc., *schedule* (*time*).

In the sense 'a printed time-table of arrivals and departures of trains, buses, aeroplanes, etc.', the use remains chiefly *N. Amer.*

1863 O. W. NORTON *Army Lett.* (1903) 282 That is all that ever caused the name to be printed on anything but time-tables and schedules of a one-horse railroad. **1866** C. H. SMITH *Bill Arp* 21 We tried our durndest to comply with your schedule. **1881** A. A. HAYES *New Colorado* vii. 94 As he [*sc.* the engineer] rounded the curves in about half of schedule time. **1884** Schedule time [in Dict.]. **1901** O. WISTER in *Lippincott's Monthly Mag.* Aug. 193 As a delayed train makes the last few miles high above schedule speed. **1904** *Newark Evening News* 13 June 6 It is on the schedule for the new Equal Taxation Commission to organize to-morrow. **1906** 'O. HENRY' *Rolling Stones* (1912) 22 Tuesday, the day set for the revolution, came around according to schedule. **1909** *Springfield* (Mass.) *Weekly Republican* 19 Aug. 10 The train was running exactly on schedule when the party left it. **1911** C. E. PERSONS *Labor Laws & their Enforcement* 109 Most important of these enforced concessions was the temporary reduction to a ten-hour [factory] schedule at Fall River. **1927** *Daily Tel.* 1 Mar. 6/4 The material must be finished on time, routed on schedule, and delivered at exactly the psychological moment. **1961** *Lancet* 29 July 230/1 In investigations into new treatment schedules, close co-operation between the clinician and the laboratory is essential. **1968** *Globe & Mail* (Toronto) 3 Feb. 35/9 The standing in the Metro Junior B Hockey League is beginning to appear like a jig-saw puzzle as the schedule enters its final week. **1975** M. RUSSELL *Murder by Mile* ix. 93 How far behind schedule are you now? **1977** I. SHAW *Beggarman, Thief* II. i. 119 He looked up the schedule of the planes flying out of Brussels to New York. **1980** *Nature* 24 Apr. 654/1 Preparations for the launch, begun on 2 April, are going ahead on schedule following the arrival of the Lo2 launcher at Kourou.

b. An agreed period of time during which a radio transmission may be made; time allocated to listening for transmissions.

1958 'N. SHUTE' *Rainbow & Rose* i. 9, I should say they've closed down for the night. They'll be speaking on the morning schedule, at seven o' clock. **1974** D. KYLE *Raft of Swords* xiii. 143 We'd better watch this six o'clock schedule like hawks.

schedule, *v.* Add: **1.** (Later examples.) Hence, in extended uses: to place (something) on a programme of future events; to arrange for (a person or thing) to do something or *for* an event.

1898 T. N. PAGE *Red Rock* 478 The trial would come off as already scheduled. **1904** *N.Y. Even. Post* 30 Sept. 1 The archbishop is scheduled to speak this afternoon at the Academy of Music. **1922** JOYCE *Ulysses* 313 It was a historic and a hefty battle when Myler and Percy were scheduled to don the gloves for the purse of fifty sovereigns. **1931** H. F. PRINGLE *Theodore Roosevelt* I. xiv. 190 The advance took place as scheduled. **1958** 'N. SHUTE' *Rainbow & Rose* i. 7 There was a Dakota freighter scheduled to leave for Hobart..at one o'clock. **1968** *Globe & Mail* (Toronto) 17 Feb. B 7 (Advt.), *Wanted* Masonry Superintendent, to take complete charge of a young masonry construction firm. Must be able to..schedule jobs, assist in bidding etc. **1976** *Columbus* (Montana) *News* 3 June 2/3 Kristy McFarland.. is scheduled for back surgery June 4. **1976** *Sunday Times* (Lagos) 1 Aug. 22/2 Two top Nigerian lawn tennis players.. are scheduled for the Zambian Open Championships. **1979** *Tucson* (Arizona) *Citizen* 20 Sept. 3A/1 A spokesman for St. Paul [Hospital] said an autopsy was scheduled.

3. To include (a building, etc.) on a list of buildings that are to be preserved and protected for architectural or historic reasons.

1921 *Report of Ancient Monuments Advisory Committee* 5 The Commissioners of Works are bound to prepare and publish a list of all monuments the preservation of which is reported by any of the three Ancient Monuments Boards to be of national importance, and to inform the owners of their intention to include them and of the penalties hereinafter mentioned. This is called scheduling a monument. **1960** *Twentieth Century* Nov. 480 A decaying polygon.. scheduled as being of architectural or historical interest. **1971** P. GRESSWELL *Environment* 23 Ancient Monuments are 'scheduled' by the Department of the Environment.

scheduled, *ppl. a.* Add: **a.** (Later examples.)

1911 G. B. SHAW *Doctor's Dilemma* p. xx, Treatment varies widely from doctor to doctor, one practitioner prescribing six or seven scheduled poisons for so familiar a disease as enteric fever. **1921** *Report of Ancient Monuments Advisory Committee* 6 A scheduled monument.. whether public or private may not be in any way damaged. **1931** H. F. PRINGLE *Theodore Roosevelt* III. v. 568 He insisted..upon making a scheduled speech. **1952** 'J. TEY' *Singing Sands* ix. 130 Most of us fly scheduled routes, but some fly tramps. **1970** *Guardian* 31 Dec. 18/3 BEA will be able to offer seats on scheduled flights to package tour holidaymakers..at knock-down prices. **1976** *Southern Even. Echo* (Southampton) 16 Nov. 3/7 A scheduled meeting with Mr. Ford will not take place until the following week.

b. In specific collocations: **Scheduled Caste** (**or class**), in India, a category of persons in the lowest castes, or Untouchables; **scheduled territory,** between 1947 and 1972, any of a group of countries, mostly within the British Commonwealth, with currencies linked to sterling; the sterling area; after 1972 (see quot. 1977; the Republic of Ireland has now ceased to be part of the sterling area); **Scheduled Tribe**, in India, a group of aborigines who do not observe the taboos of caste.

1935 *Government of India Act* 25 & 26 *Geo. V* c. 42 1st. sched. § 26 The 'scheduled castes' means such castes, races or tribes or parts of or groups within castes, races or tribes, being castes, races, tribes, parts or groups which appear to His Majesty in Council to correspond to the classes of persons formerly known as 'the depressed classes'. **1943** B. R. AMBEDKAR *Mr. Gandhi & Emancipation of Untouchables* iii. 15 Under the Government of India Act of 1935 the Untouchables are designated as 'Scheduled Castes'. **1975** Y. B. DAMLE in H. M. Patel et al. *Say not the Struggle Nought Availeth* 143 Students belonging to the scheduled and backward classes tend to be less than ten per cent of the total students in most of the states. **1947** *Act* 10 & 11 *Geo. VI* c. 4 § 1 (3) In this Act..the expression 'the scheduled territories' means the territories specified in the First Schedule to this Act, so, however, that the Treasury may at any time by order amend the said Schedule, either by the addition or exclusion of territories. **1964** *Financial Times* 12 Mar. 19/5 The Scheduled Territories are the British Commonwealth (except Canada), the Irish Republic, British Trust Territories, British Protectorates and Protected States, Burma, Iceland, the Hashemite Kingdom of Jordan, Kuwait, Lybia, South Africa and South West Africa, Western Samoa. **1972** *Statutory Instruments* II. I. 2926 The Scheduled Territories now consist only of the United Kingdom, the Channel Islands, the Isle of Man, and the Republic of Ireland. **1977** *Guide to United Kingdom Exchange Control* (Bank of England) 6 The Scheduled Territories at present comprise the United Kingdom, including the Channel Islands and the Isle of Man, the Republic of Ireland and Gibraltar. **1957** G. S. GHURYE *Mahadev Kolis* i. 4 Many sections of Kolis describe themselves as Mahadev Kolis in order to be able to claim the special benefits of the Scheduled Tribes. **1972** *Times of India* 28 Nov. 13/2 (Advt.), This post is unreserved, however, preference will be given to Scheduled Caste|Scheduled Tribe candidates.

scheduler (ʃe·diuləɹ, *U.S.* ske·diuləɹ). [f. SCHEDULE *v.* + -ER[1].] **1.** One who draws up a schedule or arranges activities in accordance with one.

1952 *Antioch Rev.* Dec. 426 After school there are music lessons, skating lessons, riding lessons, with mother as chauffeur and scheduler. **1957** *Electronic Engin.* XXIX. 179/1 The two schedulers interpret the required data-processing operations in terms of machine functions. **1978** *Sci. Amer.* Mar. 124/2 The priority list *L* is an ordering of the tasks according to the preferences of the scheduler. **1979** H. KISSINGER *White House Years* xxii. 923 The schedulers had arranged for a visit to the Vatican in the afternoon. **1980** *Daily Tel.* 18 June 8/7 So far the Radio 3 schedulers have mostly been able to replace these concerts with records of the works that would have been played.

2. a. A machine, esp. a computer, that can arrange a number of planned activities into the order in which they should take place.

1962 *Times* 26 Oct. (Spencer Steelworks Suppl.) p. xiv/3 The finishing end scheduler is the coordinating and planning authority for the whole finishing process. *Ibid.*, The finishing end scheduler prepares and revises production schedules.

b. *Computers.* Any of several control programs that arrange jobs or the computer's operations into an appropriate sequence; also, a part of the hardware designed to perform a similar function.

1966 C. J. SIPPL *Computer Dict. & Handbk.* 279/2 The scheduler is called at regular intervals to decide which program in memory is to be run... A program may be terminated temporarily by user intervention to the scheduler, or it may suspend its own operation. **1968** *Communications Assoc. Computing Machinery* XI. 349/1 The part of the system responsible for handling block and wakeup instructions will be called the scheduler. *Ibid.* 357/2 All the external interrupt lines are directed into the scheduler, which.. loops constantly, examining them. **1973** C. W. GEAR *Introd. Computer Sci.* iv. 168 When a job is terminated, the scheduler uses the space for another job and puts the output on a work list for the output processor.

scheduling, *vbl. sb.* Add: The action of entering in or drawing up a schedule; *esp.* the preparation of a timetable for the completion of the various stages of a complex project; the co-ordination of many related actions or tasks into a single time-sequence. (Further examples.)

1957 *Proc. Conf. Operations Res., Computers, & Management Decisions* (Case Inst. Technol.) 63/1 A minimum of constraints were used to define the models of the cut-and-fill operation and of construction scheduling. **1959** *Naval Research Logistics Q.* (U.S.) VI. 131 There is an indication of the possibility of constructing special algorithms to exploit the structure of certain of the 'classical' scheduling problems. **1964** A. BATTERSBY *Network Analysis* ix. 138 A fairly simple arrow diagram..usually contains about 150 to 200 activities and forms the basis for the overall scheduling. **1967** *Times Rev. Industry* Mar. 15/1 Scheduling times on much plant and equipment are long and one can do little about rephasing such spending in the short term. **1976** P. R. WHITE *Planning for Public Transport* viii. 170 A graphic timetable of this type can be used for scheduling purposes. **1977** *Rep. Comm. Future of Broadcasting* iv. 35 To our mind an executive Broadcasting Commission..would be bound to be drawn into the details of scheduling..in making decisions about individual programmes. **1978** *Sci. Amer.* Mar. 129/3 In critical-path scheduling the tasks are assigned to processors according to the length of the various precedence chains they head in the diagram of precedence constraints. **1980** *Times* 29 Nov. 5/8 The scheduling of an interim stop in Athens after the airliner took off.

Scheele's green (ʃēⁱ·ləz grīn). *Chem.* [f. the name of Karl Wilhelm *Scheele* (1742–1786), German-born Swedish chemist, who first prepared it.] A hydrated form of copper arsenite, $Cu_3(AsO_3)_2.xH_2O$, formerly used as a pigment in calico printing and wallpaper manufacture.

1819 W. T. BRANDE *Man. Chem.* v. 274 Mixed with a solution of sulphate of copper, a precipitate of a fine apple-green colour falls, called from its discoverer, Scheele's green, and useful as a pigment. **1935** *Discovery* Sept. 261/2 The dark green background of a so-called Holbein portrait was recently found, on..analysis.., to consist of Scheele's green, a copper arsenate discovered in 1778. **1967** *Jrnl. Colour Group* 92/2 Scheele's green and emerald green, both copper arsenates, lost their popularity [with artists] because of their poisonous effects. **1973** J. D. SMITH in J. C. Bailar et al. *Comprehensive Inorg. Chem.* II. xxi. 609 Yellow silver arsenite..and copper arsenite (Scheele's green) may be precipitated from neutral solutions.

schefflera (ʃe·flərǎ). [mod.L. (J. R. & G. Forster *Characteres Generum Plantarum* (1776) 45), f. the name of J. C. *Scheffler* of Danzig + -A 2.] An evergreen shrub or small tree of the genus so called, belonging to the family Araliaceæ, native to many tropical or subtropical regions, and bearing large compound leaves and clusters of small white, greenish, or red flowers, followed by small berries.

1954 F. KINGDON-WARD *Berried Treasure* xviii. 164 The slim rigid spikes of Schefflera, like tall black candles, give a Gothic dignity to this little palm-like tree. **1976** *National Observer* (U.S.) 25 Sept. 9/2 We couldn't buy a schefflera that big for $50. **1978** *Homes & Gardens* Apr. 32/1 Some philodendrons and scheffleras..do well in most places, given reasonable light.

Scheherazade (ʃěhe:rǎzā·d, ʃěhiᵊ:r-, -zā·də). The name of the female narrator of the *Arabian Nights*, used allusively as the type of a (usu. young and attractive female) teller of long or numerous stories.

1851 DICKENS *Let.* 25 Oct. in W. Gérin *E. Gaskell* (1976) xii. 123 My dear Scheherazade,—For I am sure your powers of narrative..must be good for at least a thousand nights and one. **1872** O. W. HOLMES *Poet at Breakfast-Table* iii. 87, I had noticed that the Young Girl—the story-writer, our Scheherazade, as I called her—looked as if she had been crying or lying awake half the night. **1896** G. B. SHAW *Let.* 5 July (1965) I. 634 Or are you only a flattering storytelling Scheherezade? **1946** L. P. HARTLEY *Sixth Heaven* i. 4 'I'm afraid it will be a long story,' he said..'Waste no time in self-depreciation, Scheherazade, but..take up your tale.' **1973** G. BUTLER *Coffin for Pandora* viii. 192 You're a teller of tales, young lady... Quite a Scheherazade. **1978** M. PUZO *Fools Die* xxix. 343 During that happy time, a blond Scheherazade, she told me the story of her life. **1981** A. FRASER *Splash of Red* i. 11 That's *another* story I shall tell you... I shall be Scheherazade.

Scheiner (ʃəi·nəɹ). *Photogr.* The name of Julius *Scheiner* (1858–1913), German astrophysicist, used, usu. *attrib.*, with reference to a way of measuring and expressing the speed of photographic emulsions that he devised, as *Scheiner degree, scale, sensitometer, speed, system*; **Scheiner number**, a number depending on the logarithm of the least exposure that will give a visible image on development.

1900 *Astrophysical Jrnl.* XI. 91 In a simple experiment with the aid of Scheiner's sensitometer equal degrees of blackening were produced by continuous exposures of 96, 72, 48, 24, 12 secs. *Ibid.* 98 Remarks on the Scheiner sensitometer. **1911** A. WATKINS *Photography* iii. 47 In the case of Wynne, Scheiner, and Warnerke numbers..there is not the same direct proportion between the numbers. *Ibid.* 332 (Index), Scheiner speeds. **1918** J. R. ROEBUCK *Science & Practice of Photogr.* 225 'n' is the Scheiner degree and 'A' has the value in this case of about 4·4. **1936** *Discovery* June 192/2 The rating [of the exposure meter] agreeing more or less with the Scheiner system. **1938** S. G. B. STUBBS et al. *Modern Encycl. Photogr.* II. 1105/1 The so-called 'Scheiner speeds' quoted by Continental manufacturers are in reality not Scheiner speeds at all, as all 'Scheiner' measurements are now carried out by the Eder–Hecht method. **1942** C. B. NEBLETTE *Photography* (ed. 4) xiii. 419 The ratio of the exposures between consecutive steps on the Scheiner sensitometer is as 1:1·27. **1962** *Ibid.* (ed. 6) xx. 267/1 The Scheiner speed number was obtained originally by exposing the negative material in a sensitometer with a sector wheel having exposure steps numbered from 1 to 20, with a log exposure difference of 0·15. *Ibid.* 267/2 In 1931, the German photographic industry replaced the then meaningless Scheiner numbers by a new German standard (DIN) speed. **1963** JERRARD & MCNEILL *Dict. Sci. Units* 106 The Scheiner scale was devised in 1898..and was first used commercially by the Secco Film Company of Boston, Mass. in 1899. **1973** *Focal Dict. Photogr. Technol.* 544 Scheiner speed was expressed in degrees, every increase of 3° corresponding to a doubling of the working speed.

‖ **Scheitholt** (ʃəi·tˌhǫlt). [Ger., f. *scheit* log + dialectal *-holt* wood.] A former stringed instrument of central Europe, a precursor of the zither.

1961 A. BAINES *Musical Instr. through Ages* 210 The simplest forms [of zither], as Alpine *Scheitholt*, *épinette des Vosges*, and the Dutch *hummel*..have a long narrow hollowed-out sound-box, placed on the knees or on a table. **1976** D. MUNROW *Instr. Middle Ages & Renaissance* 33/4 Various names have been used for the string drum including *Scheitholt* and *tambourin*.

Schellingian (ʃeli·ŋiǎn), *a.* [f. *Schelling* (see below) + -IAN.] Of or pertaining to the German philosopher, F. W. J. von Schelling (1775–1854), or to his doctrines. Hence as *sb.*, a follower of Schelling. Also **Schellingism** (ʃe·liŋiz'm) [ad. G. *Schellingismus*], the system of philosophy taught by Schelling; **Sche·llingist**, a disciple of Schelling.

1865 tr. *Strauss's New Life of Jesus* I. 190 Similar instances may be brought forward from the history of the Schellingian philosophy. **1865** J. H. STIRLING *Secret of Hegel* I. I. v. 275 Once in Jena, we have to see him a declared Schellingian. **1865** W. PATER *Appreciations* (1889) 75 Schellingism, the 'Philosophy of Nature', is indeed a constant tradition in the history of thought. **1874** MORRIS & PORTER tr. *Ueberweg's Hist. Philos.* II. 114 Kantism, the renewed Spinozism (Schellingism), and Herbartism lay conjoined and undeveloped in the doctrine of Leibnitz. **1894** C. S. PEIRCE *Let.* 28 Jan. in R. B. Perry *Tht. & Char. of W. James* (1935) II. 416 If you were to call my philosophy Schellingism transformed in the light of modern physics, I should not take it hard. **1895** C. GARNETT tr. *Turgenev's On the Eve* iv. 30 My father was a learned man, a Schellingist. **1967** *Encycl. Philos.* VII. 260/2 The most important of the Russian Schellingians were Professor D. M. Vellanski..and Prince V. F. Odoyevski. *Ibid.* 261/2 In his early Schellingian period he [*sc.* Belinski] stressed aesthetic activity.

schelm, var. SKELLUM in Dict. and Suppl.

schema. Add: Also pl. **schemas. 1. a.** (Earlier and later examples.)

1796 F. A. NITSCH *View of Kant's Princ.* 103 The Schema of a Category is no picture of anything. **1961** B. M. MILMED *Kant & Current Philos. Issues* iv. 81 For both Kant and Lewis..the image is empirical, a reproduction of past experience, while the schema, through which the image becomes part of a criterion of empirical meaning, is a priori in its role as a definition of the experience to be interpreted by it. **1963** A. PAP *Introd. Philos. of Sci.* vi. 102 The schemas correspond to the following principles of logic: the principle of the hypothetical syllogism..; a statement implied by a true statement is true [etc.]. **1966** E. S. CASEY tr. *Dufrenne's Notion of A Priori* viii. 156 Now, if the schema is the *a priori* in its original state, is it not the *a priori* in its corporeal state as well?

b. *Neurol.* and *Psychol.* An automatic, unconscious coding or organization of incoming physiological or psychological stimuli, giving rise to a particular response or effect.

1920 H. HEAD *Stud. in Neurol.* II. IV. v. 605 For this combined standard, against which all subsequent changes of posture are measured before they enter consciousness, we propose the word 'schema'. **1926** M. GABAIN tr. *Piaget's Lang. & Thought of Child* v. 236 This schema may be thought to apply only to 'whys', but it is obvious that other types of question..are more or less incorporated in it. **1932** —— tr. *Piaget's Moral Judgment of Child* ii. 20 The child is undoubtedly trying..to understand the nature of the marbles and to adapt its motor schemas to this novel reality. **1950** W. R. BRAIN in D. Richter *Perspectives in Neuropsychiatry* 138 The schema would then develop by becoming a resonator to a pattern received from any part of the corresponding sensory cortex and 'learned' by repetition, and would thus be the basis both of simple recognition and of abstraction. *Ibid.* 139 The schema is a neurophysiological disposition..which plays an essential part in perception and action, speech and thought... It may prove to be the bridge between body and mind. **1964** *Listener* 25 June 1029/1 Again, Koestler uses the idea of the 'schema' to discuss memory, but he does not mention that Bartlett..wrote a whole book..precisely to develop that very idea. **1971** J. Z. YOUNG *Introd. Study Man* xxi. 277 Many, however, are very useful, especially the concept of a 'schema'. In Piagetian language this is described as a 'cognitive structure which has reference to a class of similar action sequences'. **1978** HOCHBERG & BROOKS in J. W. Senders et al. *Eye Movements & Higher Psychol. Functions* v. iv. 295 If visual momentum is the impetus to obtain sensory information, and to formulate and test a schema, it should be reflected by the frequency with which glances are made.

2. a. (Later examples.) Also in extended use.

1895 J. SULLY *Stud. of Childhood* x. 353 Number is here as little attended to as in the radial arrangements. It is worth noting that this *schema* seems to be widely diffused among children of different nationalities. **1943** H. READ *Educ. through Art* v. 121 All previous writers on the subject have attempted to trace the evolution of the schema, from the first chance recognition of a resemblance in the child's.. scribblings..to an outline or two-dimensional schema. **1960** E. H. GOMBRICH *Art & Illusion* v. 168 We shall never know what Rubens' children 'really looked like', but this need not mean we are forever barred from examining the influence which acquired patterns or schemata have on the organization of our perception. **1971** E. KRAMER *Art as Therapy* vi. 127 A five- or six-year-old child who is in the process of discovering various schemata that unmistakably denote for him men, women,..or animals is..enormously increasing his power of expression. **1981** *Times Lit. Suppl.* 10 July 783/2 He painted what the schemata of Rembrandt and J. R. Cozens enabled him to see.

b. In *gen.* use, a hypothetical outline or plan; a theoretical construction; a draft, design.

1939 E. MUIR *Present Age* i. 30 When he [*sc.* H. G. Wells] tried to reinstate society again his society was a schema, not an actual society such as Fielding described. **1947** *Partisan Rev.* XIV. 231 In the countries where capitalism really triumphed, it has yielded with far better grace..than the Marxist schema predicted. **1978** N. MARSH *Grave Mistake* iv. 123 The gardens today bear little resemblance in concept to this exquisite *schema*.

3. *Eccl.* A draft canon or decree submitted to either of the Vatican Councils for discussion.

1870 T. MOZLEY *Let.* 24 Mar. (1891) II. 273 The Council has been sitting on three successive days... Today makes the fourth given to the amended *Schema* on matters of faith. **1930** E. C. BUTLER *Vatican Council* I. x. 199 Two months elapsed during which the deputation worked at the remodelling of the schema. **1963** *Ann. Reg. 1962* 370 The first schema presented for discussion, Liturgy, seemed relatively innocuous.

schematic, *a.* Add: **B.** *sb.* A schematic representation; a diagram.

1929 R. T. A. DENNISON *Private Automatic Branch Exchanges* vii. 187 In Fig. 5, a general P.A.B.X. schematic is given. **1949** *Electronic Engin.* XXI. 366/1 The amplifier, the schematic of which is shown here, consists of a two-stage unit in which the pulses are indicated by flashes on a neon light. **1961** *New Scientist* 16 Mar. 684/2 (*caption*) A schematic of a rotary copying machine working on the distillation principle. **1971** H. A. WHITAKER in W. O. Dingwall *Survey Linguistic Sci.* 154 Further differentiation..may be seen in the schematic of the pyramid and extra-pyramid motor systems in Figure 3. **1978** R. LUDLUM *Holcroft Covenant* v. 68 It was not out of the ordinary for long-range projects in faraway places to employ consulting architects, men whose names would not appear on schematics or blueprints but whose skills would be used.

schematism. Add: **4.** (Earlier example.) Also in *Psychol.* (cf. *SCHEMA 1 b).

1796 F. A. NITSCH *View of Kant's Princ.* 103 Our conceptions of figures and pictures originate in the schematism of the pure intellect. **1951** GATTEGNO & HODGSON tr. *Piaget's Play, Dreams & Imitation* viii. 220 Two peculiarities..remind us once again of the sensori-motor schematism of stage VI, but this time on the new plane of concepts in the process of formation. **1974** *Nature* 8 Mar. 177/1 This kind of knowledge (or understanding) is conceptualised as being based on a hierarchy of operative schemes (Piaget calls it 'schematism').

schematization (skiːmătəizēɪ·ʃən). [f. SCHEMATIZE *v.* + -ATION.] **1.** The act or process of reducing to a scheme or formula; formulation in a regular order, organization according to a conventional pattern or preconceived system.

1904 W. JAMES *Let.* 31 July in R. B. Perry *Tht. & Char. of W. James* (1935) II. 151 To me the whole Munsterbergian Circus seems a case of the pure love of schematization running mad. **1937** *Proc. Prehistoric Soc.* III. 36 A natural tendency towards schematisation accounts for the rendering of the lowest zone. **1953** *Trans. Philol. Soc. 1952* 16 Overschematization..has also left its mark on the study of Old English. **1962** W. NOWOTTNY *Lang. Poets Use* vi. 123 'Formal relationships' have already appeared..in connection with verse structure, not with schematization at the level of diction. **1979** *London Rev. Books* 25 Oct. 21/4 It is a curiously French combination: on the one hand, a Cartesian ..sense of schematisation, [etc.].

2. A hypothetical organization of schemata; an analytical or tabular representation of data.

1940 *Mind* XLIX. 320 The schematization of our primitive space to the more precise form is evidently correlated in some way with the conformation, structure, and distribution of our sense-organs. **1956** *Scottish Jrnl. Theol.* IX. 399 The sharply hostile and antithetic presentation of the debates [of Jesus with the Jewish authorities], where a dualistic schematisation points to a presupposition other than the relativism of merely human squabbles. **1973** A. J. POMERANS tr. *Piaget & Inhelder's Memory & Intelligence* xix. 341 It seems clear that the 'raw' memory plays no more than a limited role in these responses while schematizations are of considerable importance. **1979** *Amer. Pol. Sci. Rev.* Mar. 168/1 It rests on images, predicative assimilations, schematizations and imaginative illustrations of various sorts.

schematize, *v.* **2.** (Earlier and later examples.)

a **1866** J. GROTE in *Jrnl. Philology* (1872) IV. 56 The *phonism* of one language differs from that of another in, 1st. The different radical phones used in it. 2nd. The different distribution of these among the noems, and 3rd. The different laws and ways in which the phones are schematized. **1913** A. S. PRINGLE-PATTISON *Idea of God* (1917) 293 When we do try to schematize the fact [*sc.* that there can be no barrier between the finite consciousness and the Being in which its existence is rooted] for ourselves, we either eliminate the characteristics of selfhood..or..lose hold of the creative unity. **1954** *Circulation* X. 14/2 These reactions which seem to be enzymatic transformations may be schematized as follows.

schematized, *ppl. a.* (Later example.)

1946 R. G. COLLINGWOOD *Idea of Hist.* 109 The whole world of events in time is thus a schematized representation of the world of logical or conceptual relations.

scheme, *sb.*[1] Add: **5. d.** Also, an outing or excursion (*obs.*).

1789 JANE AUSTEN in *Loiterer* 12 Sept. 6 That glorious achievement, A Scheme to Town. **1813** —— *Pride & Prejudice* III. ix. 166, I did not once put my foot out of doors... Not one party, or scheme, or any thing.

7. b. *scheme of colour*: now chiefly = *colour scheme* (in both senses) s.v. *COLOUR *sb.*[1] 18. Freq. *ellipt.*

1897 *Private Life of Queen* ii. 15 The general scheme of colour is crimson and cream and gold. This scheme of paint prevails throughout the suite. **1925** R. W. G. HINGSTON in E. F. Norton *Fight for Everest: 1924* 265 Certain of the little birds are decidedly conspicuous, and in some cases we see the obvious reason why they do not require a protective scheme. *Ibid.* 267 Its [*sc.* a locust's] scheme of colour was grey and black with delicate transverse bands across its thighs. **1969** J. CHEEVER *Bullet Park* ii. 31 Nubbly stretchy reps look completely out of place in my decorating scheme.

schemozzle, schepsel, varr. *SHEMOZZLE, *SKEPSEL.

Scherbius (ʃɛ̄ə·ɹbiŭs). *Electr.* The name of Arthur *Scherbius* (*fl.* 1906), German engineer, used *attrib.* with reference to a method which he devised for regulating and changing the speed of large a.c. induction motors, in which the voltage applied to the rotor is altered according to the load by means of a separate commutator motor and flywheel assembly wired in series with it.

1910 *Electrician* 8 July 513/2 In the Scherbius motor the compensating winding is connected to the brushes in opposition to the armature. **1928** *Engineering* 24 Aug. 247/2 The speed regulation of the motors is controlled by a Scherbius set. **1962** *Newnes Conc. Encycl. Electr. Engin.* 515/1 A considerable number of variable-speed induction motors with Scherbius control has been built in the past for outputs up to several thousand horse-power, particularly for steel-mill drives. **1973** J. M. D. MURPHY *Thyristor Control of A.C. Motors* x. 160 In the Scherbius system..a rotary converter rectifies the slip power, and the rectified output drives a d.c. motor which is mechanically coupled to a squirrel-cage induction generator.

Schering (ʃɛ̄ə·riŋ). *Electr.* The name of Harald Ernst Malmsten *Schering* (1880–1959), German engineer, used *attrib.* and in the possessive with reference to an alternating-current bridge circuit which he devised for measuring the capacitance and power factor of insulating materials.

1926 *World Power* V. 238/2 Of the many bridges so far developed, the Schering bridge is the most suitable for high voltage work. **1928** *Engineering* 13 Jan. 50/1 The Schering bridge is operated by a fixed-frequency valve oscillator, with a frequency of 800 periods per second. **1958** J. SHEPHERD et al. *Higher Electrical Engin.* iii. 64 The Schering bridge was developed to measure the loss resistance of dielectrics, line insulators, cables and high voltage capacitors under high voltage conditions (up to 100kV). **1975** D. G. FINK *Electronics Engineers' Handbk.* XVII. 29 Schering's bridge is widely used for measuring capacitance and dissipation factors.

scherm. Add: [Also Afrikaans *skerm.*] (Earlier and further examples.) Also, **a** temporary dwelling used by nomads.

1835 A. SMITH *Diary* 4 Nov. (1940) II. 272 Have neither cattle nor chiefs, cut all the hair off, use red clay, have no fixed residence, make skerms under a bush. **1864** T. BAINES *Explor. in S.-W. Afr.* 131 Two or three scherms for night-shooting had been thrown up. **1894** E. GLANVILLE *Fair Colonist* xxiv. 186 The gentlemen, you know, will take a tent, and our dining-room will be a skerm. 'Good gracious! what is that?' 'A large canvas drawn over the waggon-top and stretched out to some trees, with canvas sides and an open front.' **1936** C. BIRKBY *Thirstland Treks* x. 118, I saw white men living in *skerms*—huts made of matting laid over frames of thorn-bush boughs. **1943** D. REITZ *No Outspan* 70 Lion roared about our skerm. **1960** *Africa* 4 Oct. 343 It always amuses me to speak of residence when I visualize the nomadic !Kung..building their nest-like grass shelters (scherms) for a stay of a few weeks. **1963** R. LEWCOCK *Early 19th Cent Architecture in S. Afr.* viii. 137 In the small frontier farmhouses cooking was done in the open air, behind a simple screen shelter, or 'skerm'.

Schermuly (ʃɜ̄·ɹmuli). The name of William *Schermuly* (1857–1929), English inventor, used *attrib.* and *absol.* as proprietary names of apparatus comprising a line-carrying rocket fired from a pistol, used in life-saving at sea.

1922 *Life-Boat* Feb. 243/1 The Line-Throwing Gun... The two appliances to which chief attention was given were the Coston gun, an American invention..and the Schermuly Portable Rocket Apparatus. **1933** R. B. CHENEVIX-TRENCH *Jrnl.* 28 Sept. in *Mariner's Mirror* (1979) LXV. 274 One line was fired by a Schermuly pistol. **1947** *Trade Marks Jrnl.* 30 July 443/2 *Schermuly*... Pyrotechnic articles, cartridges, and apparatus for firing rockets. The Schermuly Pistol Rocket Apparatus Limited,..Newdigate, Surrey; Manufacturers. **1960** E. L. DELMAR-MORGAN *Cruising Yacht Equipment & Navigation* ix. 111 The Schermuly..are of sealed metal case construction and embody a sealed-in mechanical ignition device. **1973** B. CALLISON *Web of Salvage* x. 134 With the Schermuly pistol angled upward and to windward. **1979** P. FERRIS *Talk to Me about England* II. 103 Jarre picked his way aft... Hansen [was] tearing the wrapper from a Schermuly rocket.

schertelite (ʃɜ̄·ɹtĕləit). *Min.* [f. the name of Arnulf *Schertel* (1841–1902), Bavarian chemist: see -ITE[1].] A hydrated acid phosphate of ammonium and magnesium, $(NH_4)_2Mg_3H_4(PO_4)_4.8H_2O$, found as small water-soluble orthorhombic crystals in deposits of bat guano in caves near Ballarat, Victoria.

1902 R. W. E. MACIVOR in *Chem. News* 9 May 217/1 To prevent all future confusion, I have now decided to call this interesting mineral Schertelite [*sic*]. **1963** *Amer. Mineralogist* XLVIII. 639 Schertelite dissolves rapidly and incongruently in water with the formation of struvite. Exposure of schertelite to the atmosphere for several months results in alteration of the surface of the crystals, apparently to an intimate mixture of struvite and monoammonium phosphate.

scherzetto, scherzino: see next entry.

scherzo. Add: Now usu. with pronunc. (skɛ̄ə·rtso). (Earlier and later examples.) Also *Comb.*, as *scherzo-like* adj.

1852 GEO. ELIOT *Let.* 13 Nov. (1954) II. 67, I went to one of Jullien's concerts..and endured the Polkas for the sake of Zampa and Mendelssohn's Scherzo. **1931** *Times* 19 Feb. 10/1 The contrasts of solemnity and recklessness in the slow movement and scherzo were made particularly vivid. **1962** *Times* 20 June 15/2 The scherzo-like middle movement. **1976** *Scotsman* 20 Nov. 9/5 It was an exquisitely controlled and subtle performance,..delightfully airy in the scherzo-like variation.

fig. **1911** O. ONIONS *Widdershins* 265 'Scherzos in Silver and Grey!' he chuckled. **1955** *Sci. News Let.* 25 June 411/3 The mockingbird [will]..ring in bits from the repertories of other birds, with catcalls and rusty-hinge squeaks by way of scherzo interludes. **1964** *Listener* 12 Mar. 447/1 The play is a ruthless little fantasia (well named a *scherzo*).

Hence in dim. forms **scherzetto** (-e·to), **scherzino** (-ī·no), a short passage or piece of music with the character of a scherzo.

1884 F. NIECKS *Conc. Dict. Mus. Terms* 273 *Scherzino*, a short or light scherzo. **1907** T. S. WOTTON *Dict. Foreign Mus. Terms* 169 *Scherzettino, scherzetto*.., a little scherzo. **1954** *Grove's Dict. Mus.* (ed. 5) VII. 480/2 *Scherzino* or *Scherzetto*... The words are occasionally used for a short or very slight piece in the character of a scherzo. **1961** *Times* 3 Jan. 3/4 Fricker's octet..was well chosen..for the sociability of its scherzetto. **1963** *Times* 28 Jan. 5/2 Nothing could have been..more playful than the little scherzino movement in the *faschingsschwank aus Wien*. **1978** *Gramophone* June 95/2 There is quite a well articulated performance of the Mab *scherzetto* by Rémy Corazza.

scheulie, var. *SCHOOLIE.

schiacciato, var. *STIACCIATO.

Schick (ʃik). *Med.* The name of Bela *Schick* (1877–1967), Hungarian-born U.S. pædiatrician, used *attrib.* and *absol.* to designate a test he devised consisting in the intradermal injection of diphtheria toxin: the absence of an erythematous reaction indicates previously acquired immunity to diphtheria. [Described by Schick in *Münchener med. Wochenschr.* (1908) LV. 504–6.]

1916 *Jrnl. Immunol.* I. 203 This principle is applied today in the so-called Shick [*sic*] test of immunity to diphtheria. **1927** R. MUIR et al. *Man. Bacteriol.* (ed. 8) xvii. 478 If a positive Schick is present in addition, the reaction due to the unheated toxin will be more marked. **1955** *Sci. News Let.* 9 Apr. 229/3 The Schick test, familiar to many school children, tells whether or not 'shots' to protect against diphtheria have been effective. **1971** D. LAMBERT in C. Bonington *Annapurna South Face* 290 A test known as the Schick Test may have to be done beforehand.

Hence **Schick-positive** (**-negative**) *adjs.*, showing (failing to show) an erythematous reaction in the Schick test.

1927 R. MUIR et al. *Man. Bacteriol.* (ed. 8) xvii. 476 If the suspected carrier is Schick-positive, i.e. non-immune, the organism is likely to be non-virulent. **1932** *Ibid.* (ed. 9) xvii. 507 The proportion of Schick negative reactions increases with age much as in Europe; also the blood of Schick negative reactors contains diphtheria antitoxin. **1944** L. E. H. WHITBY *Med. Bacteriol.* (ed. 4) xiii. 237 Hospital nurses should always be actively immunized if they are Schick-positive. **1951** WHITBY & HYNES *Ibid.* (ed. 5) xiii. 239 Infants born of Schick-negative mothers are themselves immune to diphtheria for the few months during which maternal antibodies persist in the circulation.

Schiff (ʃif). *Chem.* The name of Hugo *Schiff* (1834–1915), German chemist, used *attrib.* and in the possessive to designate things he devised or investigated, as **Schiff('s) base,** any organic compound having the structure $R^1R^2C{=}NR^3$; **Schiff('s) reaction,** the action of aldehydes of restoring the magenta colour to Schiff's reagent; **Schiff('s) reagent,** an acid solution of fuchsin (magenta, rosaniline) decolorized by sulphur dioxide or potassium metabisulphite; **Schiff('s) test,** the Schiff reaction employed as a test for aldehydes.

1892 *Jrnl. Chem. Soc.* LXII. II. 1189 Schiff's bases, derived from aromatic aldehydes, have a similar constitution to benzylidenaniline, PhN:CHPh, which serves as the type of these compounds. **1915** P. E. SPIELMANN tr. *V.*

von Richter's Org. Chem. 383 Hydrocyanic acid attaches itself similarly to the oximes..and to the Schiff bases. **1951** I. L. FINAR *Org. Chem.* I. xiii. 257 Primary amines combine with aromatic aldehydes to form Schiff bases. **1971** *Nomencl. Org. Chem.* (I.U.P.A.C.) (ed. 2) 258 Compounds $R^1R^2C=NR^3$ have the class name 'azomethines'. When the nitrogen atom is substituted, this class of compound has the generic name 'Schiff's bases'. **1975** *Nature* 30 Oct. 823/2 In visual pigments, retinal is bound by way of a Schiff base linkage to the protein. **1894** PERKIN & KIPPING *Org. Chem.* I. viii. 122 Aldehyde may be detected..by the 'magenta' or 'rosaniline test' (Schiff's reaction). **1897** *Chem. News* 9 July 23/2 (*heading*) Schiff reaction applied to acid fuchsine. **1951** I. L. FINAR *Org. Chem.* I. viii. 123 Ketones do not give Schiff's reaction. **1897** *Jrnl. Chem. Soc.* LXXII. II. 468 The author [*sc.* B. von Bittó] has also studied the behaviour of Schiff's reagent (a 0·025 per cent. solution of magenta decolorised by passing sulphurous anhydride through it)..with a number of aldehydes and ketones. **1929** EVERS & ELSDON *Analysis of Drugs & Chemicals* 279 The proportion of formaldehyde may be determined by the use of Schiff's reagent. **1964** M. HYNES *Med. Bacteriol.* (ed. 8) xxvii. 412 Schiff reagent. **1902** J. B. COHEN *Theoret. Org. Chem.* ix. 128 A further reaction for aldehydes is known as Schiff's test. **1949** ENGLISH & CASSIDY *Princ. Org. Chem.* xi. 202 Advantage is taken of the greater reactivity of aldehydes toward bisulfite in the Schiff test for aldehydes. **1972** NORMAN & WADDINGTON *Mod. Org. Chem.* xii. 174 The addition of an aldehyde to this colourless solution restores the pink colour of the dye (Schiff's test).

Schilder's disease (ʃi·ldəɪz). *Path.* [The name of Paul Ferdinand *Schilder* (1886–1940), U.S. neurologist and psychiatrist, who described the disease in 1912 (*Zeitschr. f. die gesammte Neurol. u. Psychiatrie* X. 1–60).] A disease characterized by degeneration of the neurones of the brain, esp. in the occipito-temporal lobes, leading to blindness, deafness, and death.

1940 HINZIE & SHATZKY *Psychiatric Dict.* 475/1 Schilder's disease or encephalitis periaxialis diffusa, is a slowly progressive degenerative disease of the brain occurring mainly in children and young people. **1961** R. D. BAKER *Essent. Path.* xxii. 599 Diffuse cerebral sclerosis, one form of which has been called Schilder's disease, is a widespread demyelination of the cerebral hemispheres alone. **1966** WRIGHT & SYMMERS *Systemic Path.* II. xxxiv. 1284/2 A feature of Schilder's disease is that the subarcuate fibres are spared, as in some cases of multiple sclerosis.

schilling[1]. Add: Now, an Austrian unit of currency, equivalent to 100 groschen; a coin or note of (multiples of) this value.

1924 *Times* 23 June 11/1 The Austrian new Schilling..which is being issued to the public over the counters of the Austrian National Bank since Monday last [*sc.* 16 June]. **1932** *Daily Tel.* 8 Oct. 2/3 New bonds will not be issued for a smaller amount than 50 schillings. **1948** G. CROWTHER *Outl. Money* (ed. 2) ix. 312 In the countries that suffered the worst inflation, entirely new currencies were introduced (the reichsmark in Germany, the schilling in Austria, the pengö in Hungary, in place of marks and crowns). **1978** J. IRVING *World according to Garp* v. 94 'It costs five hundred schillings,' the whore said.

Schilling[2] (ʃi·liŋ). *Med.* The name of Victor *Schilling* (1883–1960), German hæmatologist, used *attrib.* and in the possessive to designate a method of classifying and counting white blood cells, and the results so obtained; (proposed by Schilling in *Deutsch. med. Wochenschr.* (1911) XXXVII. 1159).

1922 *Jrnl. Amer. Med. Assoc.* 11 Mar. 769/2 (*heading*) The Schilling differential blood count. **1924** *Ibid.* 20 Dec. 2055/1 (*heading*) Schilling's hemogram. **1927** A. PINEY *Rec. Adv. in Hæmatol.* 276/1 (*Index*), Schilling index. **1935** WHITBY & BRITTON *Disorders of Blood* iv. 77 In Schilling's method all the data of an ordinary total and differential leucocyte count, as well as a simplified nuclear count, are correlated and considered in the form of a 'hæmogram'. **1972** F. NOUR-ELDIN *Haematol.* iv. 20/2 In practice, this method is more useful than the Schilling haemogram which is based on dividing the granulocytes into four groups.

Schilling[3] (ʃi·liŋ). *Med.* [The name of Robert Frederick *Schilling* (b. 1919), U.S. physician, who described the test in 1953 (*Jrnl. Lab. & Clin. Med.* XLII. 946–7).] *Schilling test*, a test, used esp. for pernicious anæmia, in which a small oral dose of radioactively labelled vitamin B_{12} is followed by a much larger unlabelled dose administered intramuscularly: subsequent excretion of the label in the urine is reduced if there is malabsorption by the gut.

1955 *Gastroenterol.* XXIX. 654 The radioactive material ..which appears in the urine under the conditions of the Schilling test has the same distribution coefficient between ammonium sulfate saturated urine and *n*-butanol as pure vitamin B_{12}–Co^{60}. **1976** *Lancet* 13 Nov. 1087/2 The Schilling test was repeatedly normal.

‖ **Schimpfwort** (ʃi·mpfvōᵊrt). Pl. **Schimpfwörter** (-vörtəɪ). [Ger., f. *schimpf* insult + *wort* WORD.] An insulting epithet, a term of abuse.

1949 R. K. MERTON *Social Theory & Social Structure* v. 153 The community at large, however, evidently emphasizes the imperfections of bureaucracy, as is suggested by the fact that the 'horrid hybrid', bureaucrat, has become an epithet, a *Schimpfwort*. **1974** *Amer. Speech* 1971 XLVI. 84 Reinhold A. Aman..lists under *Schimpfwörter*: emotive language and verbal aggression, including cuss words, swear words, terms of abuse, insults, [etc.]. **1978** *Verbatim* Winter 3/2 For the Nazis, the word provided a wonderfully Protean term of abuse, a *Schimpfwort* of unparalleled virtuosity.

‖ **schinken** (ʃi·ŋkən). [Ger.; cf. SCHINKEL.] German ham. Also in *Comb.*, as **schi·nkenwurst** (-vūrst), ham sausage.

1848 THACKERAY *Van. Fair* lxii. 563 The little boy..consumed schinken, and braten, and kartoffeln, and cranberry jam. **1957** S. STRONG *Good Food from Vienna* 89 (*heading*) Baked ham (Gebackener Schinken). **1962** [see *PICON]. **1967** M. WALDO *Internat. Encycl. Cooking* II. 549/1 *Schinkenwurst*.., ham sausage. **1978** *Sunday Times* (Colour Suppl.) 21 May 78/2 Schinkenwurst, fleischwurst and herb leberwurst will provide a wealth of tastes. **1979** P. FRIEDMAN *Termination Order* (1980) viii. 129 He got a plate of *schinken* and salad.

Schiötz (ʃyöts). *Ophthalm.* Also **Schiøtz.** The name of Hjalmar *Schiøtz* (1850–1927), Norwegian physician, used *attrib.* and in the possessive to designate a type of tonometer he devised for measuring the tension of the sclera, and to denote readings made with such a tonometer.

1913 TÖRÖK & GROUT *Surg. of Eye* vi. 173 More accurate information can be had by the use of a Schiötz tonometer. **1917** A. DUANE *Fuchs's Text-bk. Ophthalm.* (ed. 5) II. i. 83 In Schiötz's tonometer a collar..bears at its lower end a concave plate..which is fitted to the curvature of the cornea. **1918** [see *HYPOTONIC *a.* 1 b]. **1964** [see *LACHRYMATE *v.*]. **1964** S. DUKE-ELDER *Parsons' Dis. of Eye* (ed. 14) x. 113 The type of tonometer should always be cited and the reading expressed in this form—20 mm. Hg (Schiötz).

schipperke. Substitute for def.: A small black dog belonging to the breed so called, distinguished by pointed, erect ears, a large ruff of longer fur on neck and chest, and usually a docked tail. (Later examples.)

1912 'SAKI' *Unbearable Bassington* xiv. 263 A small black dog, something like a schipperke,..ran from behind my chair. **1950** A. C. SMITH *About our Dogs* xxii. 327 The Schipperke Club standard states that the head is of the foxy type. **1976** A. POWELL *Infants of Spring* iii. 56 The 'odd' lady..used to breed schipperkes, small black dogs from the Netherlands, with sharp ears and curly tails.

Schirmer (ʃə·ɪməɪ). *Ophthalm.* [The name of Otto *Schirmer* (1864–1917), German ophthalmologist, who proposed the test in 1903 (*Archiv f. Ophthalm.* LVI. 197).] *Schirmer('s) test*: a test in which the end of a strip of filter paper is placed on the surface of the eye over the lachrymal duct: the rate at which it is moistened indicates the rate of lachrymal secretion.

1935 *Trans. Amer. Ophthalm. Soc.* XXXIII. 428 Schirmer's test read 3 mm. O.S., 5 mm. O.D., in five minutes. **1941** *Amer. Jrnl. Ophthalm.* XXIV. 21/1 The Schirmer test shows zero to 6–8 mm. in 5 minutes, whereas the lower limit of the normal is 15 mm. according to Schirmer. **1977** *Lancet* 12 Nov. 1027/2 Schirmer's test, which is often reported in the assessment of eye complaints in patients who are taking beta-adrenergic-receptor blocking drugs, is misleading and inaccurate.

schism. The pronunc. (skiz'm), though widely regarded as incorrect, is now freq. used for this word and its derivatives both in the U.K. and in North America.

schismogenesis (sizmodʒe·nėsis). *Anthrop.* [f. SCHISM *sb.* + -O + -GENESIS, after *biogenesis*, *parthenogenesis*, etc.] A term proposed for the origin of differentiation between groups or cultures caused by the reciprocal exaggeration of behaviour patterns and responses that may result in the destruction of social balance. Hence **schismoge·nic** *a.*

1935 G. BATESON in *Man* XXXV. 181 A position is set up in which the behaviour X, Y, Z, is the standard reply to X, Y, Z. This position contains elements which may lead to progressive differentiation or *schismogenesis*. **1936** R. FIRTH *We, the Tikopia* p. vii, Attempts are made to analyse cultures in terms of Schismogenesis. **1940** *Brit. Jrnl. Psychol.* Oct. 133 The growth or divergence between the two kinds of game [*sc.* rugby football]..is an excellent example of what Bateson has called 'schismogenesis'—the development of cultural traits in opposition and divergence. **1949** G. BATESON in M. Fortes *Soc. Structure* 47 In schismogenic theory it was tacitly assumed that the individuals would maximize intangible..variables such as prestige, self-esteem, or even submissiveness. **1969** B. MCLAUGHLIN *Stud. in Soc. Movements* 477 Norman Miller, 'Formal Organization and Schismogenesis', unpublished paper.

schistic, *a.*[2] For † *Obs.* read *rare* and add later example.

1931 *Discovery* Nov. 355/2 Around the melting snow in schistic soil *Androsace hedreantha* was flowering in hundreds.

schistosity. (Earlier and later examples.)

1885 *Nature* 8 Oct. 558/2 The Arnaboll (Hebridean gneiss) can be traced..from spots where it retains its original strike and petrological characters, to others where it acquires the normal strike and mineralogical features of the ordinary Sutherland schists. The old planes of schistosity become obliterated, and new ones are developed. **1908** *Mineral. Mag.* XV. 145 To the imperfect substitution of dissolved kaolin by mica and secondary quartz and resultant gravitation under the pressure of superincumbent masses may, in like manner, be attributed schistosity in Zinnwald greisen. **1919** *Amer. Jrnl. Sci.* XLVII. 203 Geinitz called attention to the delicate ruffling of the surface of schistosity of many slates, which may represent an analogous phenomenon of friction. **1951** *Jrnl. Geol.* LIX. 68 The ice..forms along joints, planes of schistosity, or any other available fractures. **1977** A. HALLAM *Planet Earth* 175/3 Deformation and the development of schistosity may result in the complete obliteration of primary planar features such as sedimentary bedding.

schistosome (ski·stosōᵘm). *Zool.* [ad. mod.L. *Schistosoma* (D. F. Weinland *Tapeworms in Man* (1858) 87), f. Gr. σχιστό-ς divided + σῶμα body; cf. *-SOME[4].] Any member of the trematode genus *Schistosoma* (formerly *Bilharzia*), of which the cercariæ are parasitic on fresh-water snails and the adults of certain species are parasitic in man, inhabiting the blood vessels; a blood fluke.

1905 *Brit. Med. Jrnl.* 7 Jan. 11 (*caption*) Two male schistosomes. *Ibid.* 12/1 A distinctive feature of this schistosome is the absence of ciliated warts on the integument. *Ibid.* 12/2 The habitat of the new schistosome is mainly arterial. **1931** BLACKLOCK & SOUTHWELL *Guide to Human Parasitol.* xvii. 144 Unlike all other digenetic trematodes, no rediae are produced at any time of the life history of the schistosomes, the asexual multiplication taking place in the sporocyst stage. **1955** *Nature* 19 Nov. 981/2 An important snail host in one country may be refractory or only slightly susceptible to the same species of schistosome from another region. **1968** *Sci. Jrnl.* Oct. 7/1 An infected human excretes anything from a few to a million schistosome eggs a day. **1970** G. R. TAYLOR *Doomsday Bk.* 92 The high schistosome infection rate in Lower Egypt.

Hence **schistoso·mal** *a.*; also **schistoso·micide** *Pharm.* [-CIDE], a substance which kills schistosomes; **schi:stosomici·dal** *a.*

1931 BLACKLOCK & SOUTHWELL *Guide to Human Parasitol.* iii. 13 Protozoal, e.g. amoebic, and helminthic, e.g. schistosomal, dysenteries, are not the only forms which may occur in the tropics. **1954** *Trans. R. Soc. Tropical Med. & Hygiene* XLVIII. 446 (*heading*) A new series of schistosomicides. *Ibid.*, No other known schistosomicide shows a corresponding degree of activity. *Ibid.*, During the last seven years a search for drugs with schistosomicidal activity has been carried out in these laboratories. **1965** *Ann. Trop. Med. & Parasitol.* LIX. 304 (*heading*) Bacteriological and immunological findings in the presence of schistosomal infection. **1978** *Nature* 22 June 628/1 Despite the efforts ever since in the search for more effective schistosomicides, few drugs can be considered as antischistosomal agents of proven value. *Ibid.* 628/2 Although further studies are needed, oxamniquine seems to be an effective schistosomicidal oral drug suitable for use in endemic areas.

schistosomiasis (ski:stosoməi·ăsis). *Path.* [f. mod.L. *Schistosoma* (see prec.) + *-IASIS.] Disease caused by infection with parasites of the genus *Schistosoma*, characterized by chronic symptoms esp. of the digestive and urinary systems, and sometimes by fever.

1906 *Philippine Jrnl. Sci.* I. 89 A second Chinese case of schistosomiasis has been recorded. **1963** O. BRELAND *Animal Life & Lore* ii. 110 The parasite causing snail fever (or schistosomiasis) must pass through stages in freshwater snails before it can attack man. **1977** J. DIDION *Bk. Common Prayer* I. iv. 25 Isabel's children suffered gastrointestinal bleeding from..schistosomiasis. **1979** *Jrnl. R. Soc. Arts* Dec. 51/2 Zinc losses from the body are abnormally high due to a high incidence of hookworm infestation and schistosomiasis causing bleeding and excessive losses of sweat.

Hence **schistoso·mial** *a.*, pertaining to or characteristic of schistosomiasis.

1934 R. GIRGES *Schistosomiasis* v. ii. 194 It [*sc.* bladder irritability] may be mistaken for enlargement of that gland and remain undiagnosed as schistosomial for a considerable period.

schistosomulum (skistosǫ·miŭlŏ̆m). *Zool.* Pl. **-somula.** Also anglicized as **-somule.** [mod.L., f. as prec. + L. *-ulum*, neut. of *-ulus*, diminutive ending.] A parasite of the genus *Schistosoma* which has entered its adult host but is not yet mature. Cf. prec.

Also erroneously used as *schistosomula* sing., *schistosomulæ* pl.

1924 FAUST & MELENEY *Studies on Schistosomiasis* I. 4 To test his hypothesis he attempted to recover schistosomula from the peripheral vein. **1934** R. GIRGES *Schistosomiasis* II. ii. 56 Entering the lymphatics or blood-vessels, schistosomula proceed..to the liver of the host. **1961** *Exper. Parasitol.* XI. 209/2 The gland cells appeared to collapse after exhaustion of their contents and no replacement of secretion was encountered even in schistosomules which had been in skin for as long as 11 days. **1961** *Jrnl. Parasitol.* XLVII. 891/2 This interval..allowed the schistosomulae to reach the hepatic portal system. **1975** *Nature* 6 Mar. 17/3 The stage in the life cycle most susceptible to the immune response is the schistosomula, the young form that penetrates the skin and migrates to the blood vessels in which the adult develops. **1975** *Jrnl. R. Soc. Arts* May 363/2 The cercaria..then penetrate the skin, lose their tails and change to yet another stage called a schistosomule, which is much like an adult worm but smaller. **1978** *Parasitology* LXXVII. 282 The number and location of schistosomulum deaths will have a considerable influence on the pattern of migration out of the skin.

Hence **schistoso·mular** *a.*

1975 *Nature* 28 Aug. 727/1 Sera from five patients infected with *S[chistosoma] mansoni* were used as sources of anti-schistosomular antibody in different experiments.

schiz (skits), *sb.* and *a. slang* (chiefly *N. Amer.*). Also **schitz.** [Abbrev. of *SCHIZOID *a.* and *sb.* or *SCHIZOPHRENIC *a.* and *sb.*]

A. *sb.* A schizophrenic person; *spec.* one who experiences a drug-induced hallucination.

1955 [see *NEEDLE *sb.* 3 b]. **1967** A. LURIE *Imaginary Friends* xii. 174 How can you tell what a schiz like her is going to do? **1973** T. PYNCHON *Gravity's Rainbow* 131 There's a long-time schiz..who believes that *he* is World War II.

B. *adj.* Schizophrenic.

1960 A. HUXLEY *Let.* 28 July (1969) 894, I imagine you cd find out a great deal—given your special knowledge of schiz symptoms. **1964** C. HODDER-WILLIAMS *Main Experiment* II. xvi. 207 Typically schitz, you know. They never can resist symbolic compulsions. **1969** —— *98·4* xii. 155, I took their damn drugs and..I nearly went schitz.

Hence **schi·tzy, schi·z(z)y** *a.*, schizophrenic; *spec.* exhibiting or suffering from the effects of hallucinogenic drugs.

1968 'R. MACDONALD' *Instant Enemy* xxv. 157 What's the matter with her? Schitzy? **1972** D. ANTHONY *Blood on Harvest Moon* xxvii. 237, I feel schitzy. The grieving widow's mask—well, sometimes it's no mask. **1975** *New Yorker* 20 Jan. 31 This friend of mine—a bit of a schizzy dude, to be sure—has been telling me that if we go on muddying up the ecosphere, [etc.]. **1975** SHEA & WILSON *Golden Apple* 142 The awkwardness of their first efforts would be published in all the psychiatric journals as proof of the regressive and schizzy nature of their unsocial and unnatural impulse toward walking. **1977** *Time* 3 Jan. 56/2 So does Director Pierson, as he captures the schizzy, druggy, enclosed, exploding tension of rock superstardom. **1979** D. ANTHONY *Long Hard Cure* xvi. 130 If you stay here long enough, you can get too dependent on the Retreat... You become a little schitzy yourself.

schizanthus (skitsæ·nþǿs). [mod.L. (H. Ruiz & J. Pavon *Floræ Peruvianæ et Chilensis Prodromus* (1794) 6), f. SCHIZO- + Gr. ἄνθος flower.] = *poor man's orchid* s.v. *POOR MAN 4 a.

1823 *Curtis's Bot. Mag.* I. 2404 (*heading*) Wing-leaved Schizanthus. **1908** *Garden* 30 May 263/3 Much has been done in the way of improving the Schizanthus. **1931** *Daily Tel.* 21 May 17/1 The pansy-flowered schizanthus. **1959** [see *poor man's orchid* s.v. *POOR MAN 4 a]. **1963** *Times* 1 May 14/4 The County Borough of East Ham occupies the middle of the hall with a group of schizanthus varieties and sweetly scented stocks. **1979** *Daily Tel.* 19 May 15/5 It is schizanthus, a thick bushy plant with leaves like parsley and a riotous show of flowers, pink, crimson, white and purple.

schizo (ski·tso), *sb.* and *a.* Slang abbrev. of *SCHIZOPHRENIC *a.* and *sb.* **A.** *sb.*

1945 N. BALCHIN *Mine Own Executioner* vi. 92 He just sank back into that queer not-really-there mood that schizos have. **1955** 'E. C. R. LORAC' *Ask Policeman* vii. 87 Let's assume a split personality..a schizo, as they say nowadays. **1961** J. I. M. STEWART *Man who won Pools* III. 203 He might have been a schizo..for all the tie-up there seemed to be between the Phil of this rational conversation and the Phil who wanted Jean Canaway. **1972** 'L. EGAN' *Paper Chase* xii. 194 He had a long history of violence and was diagnosed as a schizo.

B. *adj.*

1957 M. GAIR *Sapphires on Wednesday* x. 120, I think he must have a split mind—be schizo or something. **1958** A. HUXLEY *Let.* 16 Dec. (1969) 858 I'm glad to hear that your schizo research goes forward satisfactorily. **1960** *Harper's Bazaar* Aug. 50/2 He had gone stereo in April... Cheaper than going schizo. **1977** J. AIKEN *Last Movement* v. 89 Gertrude was a kind of belle Otèro-cum-Phaedra..and Hamlet perfectly epicene and schizo.

schizo-. Add: **schizochro·al** *a. Palæont.* [Gr. χρώς skin], applied to certain trilobite eyes in which the cornea is divided to form several discrete lenses; **schi·zocœly** (-sīli) *Zool.*, schizocœlic mode of formation (of a cœlom).

1889 J. M. CLARKE in *Jrnl. Morphol.* II. 254 The character of the visual area in the trilobites is twofold; (*a*) it may be covered by a smooth, continuous epithelial film or cornea, through which the lenses of the ommatidia are visible by translucence, and (*b*) the cornea may be transected by the protrusion of the sclera and limited to the surfaces of the ommatidia... The first group may be designated by the term Holochroal; the second group by the term Schizochroal. *Ibid.* 266 The schizochroal eyes of the Trilobites are aggregated and not properly compound eyes. **1976** *Nature* 13 May 130/1 Trilobites of the suborder Phacopina had schizochroal eyes, in which comparatively few large separate lenses are distributed over the eye surface. **1962** D. NICHOLS *Echinoderms* i. 14 A coelom..can arise as a split in the mesoderm (schizocoely) or as an outgrowth of the gut cavity or enteron (enterocoely). **1978** *Nature* 4 May 23/2 In this context, the mode of formation of the coelom (enterocoely, schizocoely, gonocoely) is of secondary importance.

2. *Psychol.* With pronunc. (skitso-, skidzo-). Used to repr. *SCHIZOPHRENIA, as in **schizota·xia** [Gr. τάξις order, arrangement], a genetically determined defect in the functioning of the nervous system which has been suggested as predisposing to schizophrenia; hence **schizota·xic** *a.* and *sb.*; **schi·zothyme** *sb.* and *a.* [Gr. θυμός mind, temper], (characteristic of) a person who is introverted and imaginative, and so regarded as tending to schizophrenia rather than to manic-depressive illness; hence **schizothy·mic** *a.*; also **schizothy·mia**, schizothymic constitution or temperament; **schi·zotype,** a personality type in which schizophrenia is potentially or actually present; hence **schizoty·pal, -ty·pic** *adjs.*; **schi·zotypy.**

1962 P. MEEHL in *Amer. Psychologist* XVII. 830/1 This neural integrative defect, which I shall christen schizotaxia, is all that can properly be spoken of as inherited. *Ibid.*, The imposition of a social learning history upon schizotaxic individuals. *Ibid.* 831/1 All schizotaxics become, on all.. existing social learning regimes, schizotypic in personality organization. **1966** I. B. WEINER *Psychodiagnosis in Schizophrenia* i. 7 Persons with schizotaxia acquire a personality organization called schizotypy that is characterized by four core behavior traits... These schizotypic traits are universally learned by all schizotaxic persons... Whereas most schizotypes remain compensated, those who are confronted with certain causal environmental influences ..are likely to decompensate into clinical schizophrenia. **1974** S. ARIETI *Interpretation of Schizophrenia* (ed. 2) xlv. 697 A minority of schizotaxics..are 'potentiated into clinical schizophrenia'. *Ibid.*, Schizotaxia is a necessary but not sufficient condition in the etiology of schizophrenia. **1925, 1932** Schizothyme [see *cyclothyme* adj. and sb. s.v. *CYCLO-]. **1936** A. HUXLEY *Eyeless in Gaza* viii. 87 'What a lot of ribs you've got!' she said at last. 'Schizothyme physique,' he answered. **1952** H. READ *Philos. Mod. Art* iv. 84 If in the end we describe..Michelangelo as a typical 'schizothyme', the common reader is not much the wiser. **1964** I. M. SMITH *Spatial Ability* vii. 229 He found the creative significantly more schizothyme, self-sufficient, withdrawn, sophisticated, desurgent and radical. **1972** *Encycl. Psychol.* III. 180/1 The schizothyme is characterized by..'a conscious contrast between the ego and the outside world', 'a touchy or indifferent withdrawal from the mass of his fellow men', the predominance of 'dreams, ideas or principles'. **1940** H. G. WELLS *Babes in Darkling Wood* IV. ii. 335 Schizothymia, the psychoanalysts would have called this sort of dreaming. **1964** I. M. SMITH *Spatial Ability* ix. 287 The hyperactivity.., nervousness and anxiety seem..more closely related to introversion or schizothymia than to extraversion. **1925** W. J. H. SPROTT tr. *Kretschmer's Physique & Char.* xiii. 223 The group of wits..ironists and satirists whose nature is indicated by the names, Heine, Voltaire,..Nietzsche. This group belongs quite decidedly to the schizothymic side. **1951** *Mind* LX. 287 The ethical question is not whether one should be cyclothymic like Goering or schizothymic like Himmler in one's destructiveness; rather it is whether one should be destructive at all, and, if so, towards what. **1961** *Lancet* 23 Sept. 712/1 Hereditary factors were more important for excitability, the cyclothymic–schizothymic scale, and super-ego strength. **1953** S. RADO in *Amer. Jrnl. Psychiatry* CX. 409/2 In this sense the patient suffering from an open schizophrenic psychosis is a schizophrenic phenotype, engendered by a schizophrenic genotype in its interaction with the environment... For psychodynamic purposes I shall abbreviate the term schizophrenic phenotype to schizotype. *Ibid.* 410/1 The ensemble of psychodynamic traits peculiar to the schizotypes may be called schizotypal organization. **1962, 1966** Schizotypic, -typy [see *schizotaxia* above]. **1962** *Amer. Psychologist* XVII. 830/2 The most important research need here is development of high-validity indicators for compensated schizotypy. **1965** G. E. DANIELS et al. *New Perspectives in Psychoanal.* 109 Variants of the schizophrenic disorders like—schizoid personality, schizotypal,..and pseudo-neurotic schizophrenia. **1974** S. ARIETI *Interpretation of Schizophrenia* (ed. 2) xlv. 697 All schizotaxics become schizotypic in personality organization, but most of them do not decompensate and never develop a psychosis. **1978** P. O'BRIEN *Disordered Mind* iv. 75 Such syndromes are now officially classified as Schizotypal Personality Disorders.

schizo-affe·ctive, *a.* (*sb.*) *Psychol.* Also without hyphen. [f. SCHIZO- + AFFECTIVE *a.*] Exhibiting symptoms of both schizophrenia and manic-depressive psychosis. Also as *sb.*, a schizo-affective person.

1933 I. L. POLOZKER in *Amer. Jrnl. Psychiatry* XC. 123 We have been in the habit of labeling these cases as psychopathic personalities with schizoid make-up... I think the name of schizoaffective is more appropriate. **1933** J. KASANIN in *Ibid.* 126 My cases are not necessarily schizo-affective psychoses but schizoaffective personalities. **1965** J. POLLITT *Depression & its Treatment* iii. 38 Another criterion of schizo-affective disorder is the appearance of typical features of schizophrenia in circumscribed episodes. **1974** *Nature* 18 Jan. 160/2 All of the schizo-affectives had a history of at least five episodes of mania, hypomania or depression. **1976** SMYTHIES & CORBETT *Psychiatry* x. 185 Cases of schizoaffective psychosis where there is much admixture of depressive symptoms may require a tricyclic anti-depressant in addition. **1979** *Daily Tel.* 19 May 3/6 Dowdeswell had had a schizo-affective psychosis which had been cured but could recur.

schizoid (ski·tsoid, skidz-), *a.* and *sb. Psychol.* [a. G. *schizoid* (E. Kretschmer *Körperbau und Charakter* (1921) ix. 96): see *SCHIZO- 2 and -OID.] **A.** *adj.* Resembling or tending towards schizophrenia, but with milder or less developed symptoms, e.g. an absence of delusions.

1925 W. J. H. SPROTT tr. *Kretschmer's Physique & Char.* xii. 208 One may for convenience call the transitional stages between illness and health, and the pathological abortive forms, 'schizoid' and 'cycloid'. **1931** *Times Lit. Suppl.* 17 Sept. 692/4 Professor Kretschmer manages to convey the impression that all philosophers and tragedians are schizophrenic, or at least 'schizoid'. **1938** *Oxford Times* 8 Apr. 23/5 He said Phillips was of what would be called 'schizoid type' but he could not agree that in the case of a split mind the subject could not distinguish between right and wrong. **1949** KOESTLER *Insight & Outlook* xxiv. 343 The frequent occurrence of infantile and schizoid features in the psychic make-up of poets. **1957** A. HUXLEY *Let.* 18 Nov. (1969) 830 Dr. Abram Hoffer..has treated several hundred patients under his care with 3 to 4 grammes of niacin—with striking success in many cases of schizoid neurosis. **1960** R. D. LAING *Divided Self* ix. 149 It is..not always possible to make sharp distinctions between sanity and insanity, between the sane schizoid individual and the psychotic. **1964** M. ARGYLE *Psychol. & Social Probl.* iii. 35 Withdrawn, schizoid people..produce a tense, uneasy atmosphere. **1976** SMYTHIES & CORBETT *Psychiatry* vi. 95 The 'schizoid' individual has usually been a lone wolf since childhood. **1977** A. SHERIDAN tr. *Lacan's Écrits* i. 5 The schizoid and spasmodic symptoms of hysteria.

b. *transf.* and *fig.*, freq. = *SCHIZOPHRENIC *a.* b.

1955 G. S. FRASER in J. Wain *Interpretations* 233 It is a kind of poem which could only have been written in the age that invented the phrase 'dissociation of sensibility' and that thought of the schizoid state as the typical occupational risk of intellectuals. **1959** *Times* 20 Feb. 14/5 It was a schizoid programme... On the one hand Daniel Jones's new fifth symphony..; on the other, a bizarre coupling of two..sets of variations on Paganini's celebrated A minor caprice. **1959** N. MAILER *Advts. for Myself* (1961) 173 'It's all schizoid,' Sam said. 'Modern life is schizoid.' **1960** *Spectator* 6 May 652 (*heading*) The schizoid state [*sc.* South Africa]. **1964** J. JACKSON et al. *Rayden's Practice & Law of Divorce* (ed. 9) iii. 155 Such schizoid situations reflect little credit on the law. **1974** 'R. TATE' *Birds of Bloodied Feather* ix. 176 He was schizoid..partly clever, partly stupid... I think he wanted to be found out. **1977** *Ripped & Torn* VI. 10/1 The best track..is 'Energy', a piece of schizoid trash. **1977** *Proc. R. Soc. Med.* LXX. 398/1 The principle..serves to emphasize that, if the tumour is to be cured, the surgeon must approach the problem in an almost schizoid frame of mind.

B. *sb.* A schizoid person; also *loosely*.

1925 W. J. H. SPROTT tr. *Kretschmer's Physique & Char.* x. 149 We sometimes find schizoids, who look just as if they had already been through a schizophrenic psychosis before they were born. **1938** S. BECKETT *Murphy* ix. 168 An emaciated schizoid..his left hand rhetorically extended.., his right, quivering and rigid, pointing upward. *a* **1941** F. SCOTT FITZGERALD *Tender is Night* (rev. ed., 1953) I. ix. 48 She's a schizoid—a permanent eccentric. *a* **1957** J. CARY *Captive & Free* (1959) xii. 57 Preedy has been taken to pieces by experts. They say, 'The typical schizoid—a little Hitler. You find him everywhere—the village boy who goes from Mass to do murder is the basic type.' **1970** *Science* 16 Jan. 251/1 Though unsatisfactory, the only means of identifying many—perhaps most—schizoids remains genealogical, and a clinical understanding of the schizoid can best be gained by reading descriptions of abnormal relatives of schizophrenics. **1975** D. LODGE *Changing Places* i. 6 Flown by pilots long gone over the hill, alcoholics and schizoids.

Hence **schizoi·dal** *a.*

1938 S. BECKETT *Murphy* iv. 49 'That long hank of Apollonian asthenia,' groaned Neary, 'that schizoidal spasmophile.' **1973** F. JOHNSON *Alienation* ii. 63 The discovery of latent schizoidal themes can be found routinely in individuals whose social functioning would in no way suggest..the existence of such 'splitting'.

schizoidia (skitsoi·diă, skidz-). *Psychol.* [ad. G. *schizoidie* (E. Bleuler 1922, in *Zeitschr. f. die gesammte Neurol. u. Psychiatrie* LXXVIII. 373), f. *schizoid* *SCHIZOID *a.* and *sb.*: see -IA[1].] The schizoid state, esp. when regarded as caused by the same genetic disorder as schizophrenia.

1940 in HINSIE & SHATZKY *Psychiatric Dict.* 475/1. **1970** *Science* 16 Jan. 253/1 By including schizoid disease (schizoidia), this hypothesis extends that of Slater... The view that schizoidia and schizophrenia are a single disease genetically is supported by their clinical similarity. **1973** MCCLEARN & DEFRIES *Introd. Behavioral Genetics* xi. 275 Twin data are utilized to support the hypothesis that schizoidia and schizophrenia are manifestations of the same underlying genetic disease. **1976** EHRMAN & PARSONS *Genetics of Behav.* xi. 276 Schizoidia may be defined as a pre- or potentially schizophrenic mental state.

schizont (skəi·zǫnt). *Zool.* [a. G. *schizont* (F. Schaudinn 1900, in *Zool. Jahrb., Abt. f. Anat. u. Ontogenie* XIII. 213), f. Gr. σχίζ-ειν to split (cf. SCHIZO-) + ὀντ-, ὤν, pres. pple. of εἶναι to be, exist.] In Protozoa, a cell that divides asexually to form daughter cells; *esp.* in Sporozoa, a multinucleate cell that divides asexually to form merozoites.

1900 *Jrnl. R. Microsc. Soc.* June 336 In the author's [*sc.* Schaudinn's] nomenclature this process of asexual multiplication is known as schizogony, the mother cells are schizonts, and the daughter cells merozoites... They may grow rapidly.., and become converted into schizonts. **1912, 1957** [see *GAMONT]. **1974** *Nature* 22 Nov. 268/1 Three different sorts of vaccine are at present being investigated: irradiated sporozoites from the mosquito, extracts from schizonts (developing stages in the blood) and emulsified merozoites (the stages which pass between blood cells).

schizonticide (skəiz-, skizǫ·ntisəid). *Pharm.* Also **schizonto-**. [f. prec. + *-icide*, as in *parricide, tyrannicide*, etc., or + -O + -CIDE.] A substance that kills schizonts.

1943 *Jrnl. Infectious Dis.* LXXIII. 11/2 In textbooks.. quinine and atabrine are considered to be 'schizonticides', whereas plasmochin is called a 'gametocide'. **1944** W. N. BISPHAM *Malaria* x. 133 Quinine is not as satisfactory as atabrine as a schizonticide in the treatment of *P[lasmodium] falciparum*. **1963** E. PAMPANA *Textbk. Malaria Eradication* viii. 211 Drugs that act on the asexual forms, as schizontocides. **1970** W. PETERS *Chemotherapy & Drug Resistance in Malaria* v. 139 The main outcome of this investigation was to pinpoint mepacrine as a safe and potent schizontocide, superior to quinine against all human malaria species. **1977** *Martindale's Extra Pharmacopoeia* (ed. 27) 343/2 The 8-aminoquinolines..have a marked effect on gametocytes..but are not effective blood schizonticides.

Hence **schizontici·dal, -oci·dal** *adjs.*

1963 P. F. RUSSELL et al. *Pract. Malariol.* (ed. 2) xix. 503 Recent trials with relatively non-toxic schizonticidal drugs..have had some more promising results. **1963** *Terminol. Malaria* (World Health Organization) iv. 66 Schizontocides or blood schizontocides ('schizontocidal drugs'..) act on asexual erythrocytic stages of the parasite. **1979** *Amer. Jrnl. Trop. Med. & Hygiene* XXVIII. 937/1 By the early 1970's over 200,000 compounds had been screened for blood schizonticidal activity.

schizophrene (ski·tsofrīn, ski·dz-). *Psychol.* [ad. G. *schizophren*, f. *schizophrenie* *SCHIZOPHRENIA.] A schizophrenic, or a person with a predisposition towards schizophrenia. Also *attrib.* and *loosely*.

1925 W. J. H. SPROTT tr. *Kretschmer's Physique & Char.* x. 147 In the schizophrene group, still less than in the circular, can we separate the healthy from the diseased. **1936** *Scrutiny* V. 248 Comparing the psychology of the schizophrene with that of the modern artist. **1945** *Times* 26 Apr. 6/5 No one would claim Beethoven as an example of the highly integrated personality but he is no schizophrene, as Dr. Carner calls Mahler outright. **1968** *Listener* 29 Aug. 260/2, I have heard a saloon-bar customer, a postman by profession, address the barmaid as: 'You dreamy schizophrene.' **1977** 'D. CORY' *Bennett* ii. 76 Schizophrenes are often held to be people of exceptional charm.

schizophrenese (skitsofrĕnī·z, skidz-). *Psychol.* [f. next + -ESE.] Disordered speech as manifested by a schizophrenic.

1964 *Internat. Psychiatry Clinics* I. 829 The speech deficiencies are not consistent from one schizophrenic child to another. One is thus not justified in referring to 'schizophrenese'—that is, a specific and positive schizophrenic speech pattern. **1976** SMYTHIES & CORBETT *Psychiatry* v. 67 It is helpful to do an amytal or pentothal interview. The schizophrenic patient often loosens up and talks 'schizophrenese' (the typical speech disorder of schizophrenia).

schizophrenia (skitsofrī·niă, skidz-). *Psychol.* [ad. G. *schizophrenie* (E. Bleuler 1910, in *Psychiatrisch-Neurol. Wochenschr.* XII. 171), f. Gr. φρήν mind: see SCHIZO- and -IA[1].] A mental disorder occurring in various forms, all characterized by a breakdown in the relation between thoughts, feelings, and actions, usu. with a withdrawal from social activity and the occurrence of delusions and hallucinations.

Used in the U.S. with a broader meaning than in Britain (cf. quots. 1979, 1980).

The pronunc. (skits-), i.e. with short (i) and with (ts), is prob. influenced by the Ger. pronunc. (sxʸits-).

1912 *Lancet* 21 Dec. 1730/1 This little volume is a translation of a series of articles by Professor Bleuler which appeared..during 1910 and 1911, in which he advances a theory of the negativism so frequently met with in dementia praecox or schizophrenia. **1925** J. RIVIERE tr. *Freud's Unconscious* in *Collected Papers* IV. 129 In schizophrenia a great deal is consciously expressed which in the transference neuroses can be demonstrated to exist in the Ucs only by means of psycho-analysis. **1944** E. A. STRECKER *Fund. Psychiatry* vii. 123 In spite of the fact that schizophrenia and manic-depressive are divergent and alien to each other in psychopathology, there are clinical situations in which the differential diagnosis is difficult. **1945** W. SADLER *Mod. Psychiatry* xxxix. 464 Among the trends of schizophrenia is the persistent tendency to shun reality. **1958** M. ARGYLE *Relig. Behaviour* ix. 107 By the psychoses we mean the clinical conditions of schizophrenia, mania and depression, paranoia, epilepsy, together with certain organic states. **1964** *Internat. Psychiatry Clinics* I. 743 While many of these cases can be grouped into the classic forms of schizophrenia, such as simple, catatonic, hebephrenic, or paranoid, others cannot be so classified and will, therefore, be diagnosed as mixed or undifferentiated types of schizophrenia. **1979** *Internat. Rehabilit. Med.* I. 79/1 It was found that hospital psychiatrists in New York included under 'schizophrenia' part of what British hospital psychiatrists diagnosed as mania, psychotic depression, and personality disorder. **1980** J. ASHTON *Everyday Psychiatry* v. 33 His [*sc.* Bleuler's] use of the word in a wide sense has influenced the practice of Swiss and American psychiatry to the present day, so that 'American schizophrenia' ranges from apparently minor personality disorders with a range of emotional reactions, through to the major deterioration of personality that is recognized as schizophrenia by British psychiatrists.

b. *transf.* and *fig.*

1933 T. S. ELIOT *Use of Poetry & Use of Criticism* v. 99 For a poet to be also a philosopher he would have to be virtually two men; I cannot think of any example of this thorough schizophrenia, nor can I see anything to be gained by it. **1945** 'G. ORWELL' in *Polemic* I. 40 Some nationalists are not far from schizophrenia, living quite happily amid dreams of power and conquest which have no connection with the physical world. **1949** *Here & Now* (N.Z.) Oct. 32/2 There are few alien hills in Mr Witheford's poems and he is not preoccupied with cultural schizophrenia. **1958** *Listener* 9 Oct. 557/1 They admire big dams and high buildings..and the *contrast* these afford to the familiar buildings... It may occur to you that the character of our environment is likely to be split in two by this schizophrenia. **1969** *Daily Tel.* 6 Oct. 9/5 Bristol's Little Theatre illustrates the same provincial schizophrenia, with the farce 'One for the Pot' next in the bill after Ibsen's 'Master Builder'.

schizophrenic (skitsofre·nik, skidz-), *a.* and *sb.* [f. prec. + -IC.] **A.** *adj.* **a.** *Psychol.* Characteristic of or having schizophrenia.

1912 [see *AUTISM]. **1927** HENDERSON & GILLESPIE *Text bk. Psychiatry* ix. 218 It is now generally recognised that although a schizophrenic type of disturbance is always most serious, there are certain cases which can, and do, readjust themselves. **1931** [see *SCHIZOID *a.* a]. **1945** *Times* 28 Sept. 7/5 He was schizophrenic long before the thing became fashionable, half of him being entirely rational, the other half living in a world in which it was taken for granted that pigs have wings. **1973** I. L. CHILD *Humanistic Psychol.* ix. 137 Laing and Esterson..argue that schizophrenic behavior appears in these patients as a somewhat sensible response to an extremely difficult situation. **1974** PASSMORE & ROBSON *Compan. Med. Stud.* III. xxxv. 55/2 Other examples are the 'schizophrenic smile', which appears without obvious external cause and is presumed to be a response to an internal hallucinatory stimulus, and the 'schizophrenic handshake', the patient's hand when grasped remaining limp. **1981** *Brit. Med. Jrnl.* 24 Jan. 313/3 While drugs have certainly facilitated the extramural care of schizophrenic patients the minimisation of prolonged inpatient treatment has, to a large extent, been due to social measures and to changes in attitude within the psychiatric services.

b. *transf.* and *fig.*, freq. with the implication of mutually contradictory or inconsistent elements.

1955 *Sci. Amer.* Oct. 113/1 The behavior of the puzzled Board reflected its schizophrenic task. The members performed as part jury, part judge, and then as part administrative agency, engaged in a part rule-making, part quasi-judicial proceeding. **1960** *Times* 13 June 14/1 It was a schizophrenic day when nearly every player seemed to live two lives. **1962** A. LURIE *Love & Friendship* viii. 155 You're not living two different lives that don't match... For me it's absolutely impossible. It's schizophrenic. *a* **1974** R. CROSSMAN *Diaries* (1977) III. 71 We are all deeply schizophrenic on this Bill, hate the interference, hate the break with the trade unions, yet we can see that without it there must be a higher level of unemployment than we can tolerate. **1978** M. SHANKS *What's Wrong with Mod. World?* iii. 45 In their reaction to inflationary pressures government have been..schizophrenic. On the one hand they have sought..to fight them. On the other hand they have felt obliged to compensate the victims. **1980** *Daily Tel.* 24 July 11/5 The work is schizophrenic in its switches of style from genuine opera-drama to operetta and then to the typical vehicle for a soprano anxious and able to sing Ophelia's mad scene.

B. *sb.* A person with schizophrenia.

1926 W. MCDOUGALL *Outl. Abnormal Psychol.* xxiii. 384 The delusions and hallucinations of the schizophrenic so commonly concern his body. **1953** W. BURROUGHS *Junkie* (1972) x. 111 One young schizophrenic had both hands fastened in front with a bandage so he could not bother the other patients. **1956** A. HUXLEY *Heaven & Hell* 84 Many schizophrenics pass most of their time..in a shadowy world of phantoms and unrealities. **1958** M. ARGYLE *Relig. Behaviour* ix. 109 Schizophrenics..are more chaotic and harbour a number of unrelated fantasies and identifications simultaneously. **1979** N. SCHEPER-HUGHES *Saints, Scholars & Schizophrenics* iii. 69/1 Interviews with Irish schizophrenics support the hypothesis that the later age of onset of the disease in rural Ireland is related to the postponed adulthood..of the Irish bachelor.

Hence **schizophre·nically** *adv.*, in a manner suggestive or characteristic of schizophrenia.

1963 *Times* 23 Apr. 16/1 Ionesco's hero—perpetually exhausted, always eating, schizophrenically incapable of action. **1975** *Gramophone* Nov. 790/1 Then there's what one might call a strange psychological world in which almost schizophrenically Sibelius uses brightness and lightness juxtaposed with the darkest and most ferocious gestures. **1979** *Times* 27 Dec. 11/5 Schizophrenically Janus-like, we offer at least two different faces towards a policeman.

schizophreniform (skitsofre·nifǭɹm, skidz-), *a. Psychol.* [f. as prec. + -FORM.] Resembling schizophrenia.

1937 G. LANGFELDT *Prognosis in Schizophrenia* i. 17 The author..is of opinion that it will be advantageous to separate *atypical* conditions, and give them their own description, such as 'Schizofreni-form' (or 'Schizophrenic reaction types'). **1951** *Practitioner* Aug. 135 Schizophreniform conditions.—Usually acute, dramatic and often running a benign course, even without much active treatment. **1976** SMYTHIES & CORBETT *Psychiatry* iv. 37 Even normal people can experience a short-lived schizophreniform psychosis as the result of unbearable stress—as in battle exhaustion—or severe sleep deprivation. **1978** P. O'BRIEN *Disordered Mind* ii. 35 If the disorganized state of mind lasts..less than 6 months, but more than one week, it is called a schizophreniform disorder.

schizophrenogenic (ski:tsofrīnodʒe·nik, ski:dz-), *a. Psychol.* [f. as prec. + -O + *-GENIC.] Tending to give rise to schizophrenia.

1949 F. FROMM-REICHMANN in *Psychiatry* XI. 265/2 The schizophrenic is painfully distrustful and resentful of other people, due to the severe early warp and rejection he encountered in important people of his infancy and childhood..mainly in a schizophrenogenic mother. **1956** *Behavioral Sci.* I. 263/1 Whenever the system is organized for hospital purposes and it is announced to the patient that the actions are for *his* benefit, then the schizophrenogenic situation is being perpetuated. **1975** HIRSCH & LEFF *Abnormalities in Parents of Schizophrenics* vi. 95 This study provides somewhat stronger evidence against the concept of the cold, aloof, hostile schizophrenogenic mother. **1979** B. INEICHEN *Mental Illness* ii. 41 The question of whether schizophrenics are downwardly mobile socially, or whether lower-class culture is schizophrenogenic, remains an open one.

schizostylis (skizostəi·lis). Pl. **-stylis.** [mod. L. (Backhouse & Harvey 1864, in *Curtis's Bot. Mag.* XC. 5422), f. SCHIZO- + L. *stilus* (*stylus*) (see STYLE *sb.* 8), in allusion to the split styles of the plant.] A rhizomatous herb of the genus so called, belonging to the family Iridaceæ, native to South Africa, and bearing linear leaves and spathes of red or pink flowers. Cf. *Kaffir lily* s.v. *KAFFIR 4.

1864 *Curtis's Bot. Mag.* XC. 5422 Crimson Schizostylis... This lovely Iridaceous plant..inhabits eastern rivers of South Africa. **1961** *Amateur Gardening* 16 Sept. 7/4 Less romantic in association but flowering later and valuable for October and November colour, are the Caffre lilies, or schizostylis. **1979** *Daily Tel.* 27 Oct. 31/2 Earlier flowering herbaceous plants, which the schizostylis have outshone.. with the onset of autumn.

schizzy, schizy: see *SCHIZ *sb.* and *a.*

‖ **schlag** (ʃlāg, ʃlāk). Abbrev. of *SCHLAGOBERS or *SCHLAGSAHNE.

1969 A. ARENT *Laying on of Hands* xii. 138 She debouched at Demel's for pastry and *Schlag.* **1977** *Time* 24 Oct. 44/3 A slavic sour cream lay over the proceedings in place of Viennese *schlag.*

schlag, var. *SCHLOCK.

‖ **schlagobers** (ʃlā·gōbers). [Ger. dial., f. *schlagen* to beat + *obers* cream.] Whipped cream; coffee with whipped cream. Also *fig.*

1938 J. FLANNER in *New Yorker* 10 Sept. 55/1 You can now get a seat and *Schlagobers* on Tomaselli's terrace. **1967** *Listener* 27 July 123/3 This *Schlagobers* made one thirsty for pop. **1969** *Harper's Bazaar* Oct. 12/1, I consumed huge quantities of their *Torte* heaped high with *Schlagobers.*

‖ **schlagsahne** (ʃlā·gzānə). [Ger., f. *schlagen* to beat + *sahne* cream.] Whipped cream.

1907 M. A. VON ARNIM *Fräulein Schmidt & Mr. Anstruther* 9 We are poor... If we were not..we should have different sorts of puddings..with *Schlagsahne* on their tops. **1936** D. BARNES *Nightwood* i. 12 The inevitable arc produced by heavy rounds of burgundy, schlagsahne, and beer. **1972** J. EASTWOOD *Henry in Silver Frame* xviii. 155 The delicious fraulein..become[s] a devotee of *schlag-sahne.*

‖ **schlamperei** (ʃla·mpĕrəi). [Ger.] Indolent slovenliness, muddleheadedness; esp. designating a supposed south German and Austrian characteristic.

1961 *Economist* 30 Dec. 1282/2 A horrific picture of Austrian *Schlamperei* in a provincial court. **1966** F. SPIEGL in F. Shaw et al. *Lern Yerself Scouse* 12 Here the Scouser's sense of humour outweighs his *Schlamperei*, for he will never use a single word when he can think of some more or less long-winded picturesque phrase in its place. **1974** *Times Lit. Suppl.* 28 June 687/3 Surely it was not all *sachertorte* and *schlamperei* among the villas of Gringing?

schlemazl, var. *SCHLIMAZEL.

schlemiel (ʃləmī·l). *colloq.* Also **schlemihl, shlemiel.** [Yiddish, possibly ad. Heb. *Shelumiel*, name of a person in the Bible (Num. i. 6) said by the Talmud to have met with an unhappy end; perh. influenced by the name of the eponymous hero of A. von Chamisso's *Peter Schlemihls wundersame Geschichte* (1814).] An awkward, clumsy person, a blunderer; a 'born loser'; a 'dope' or 'drip'. Also *attrib.*

1892 I. ZANGWILL *Childr. Ghetto* I. I. i. 30 The withered old grandmother..cursed her angrily for a *Schlemihl.* **1898** A. M. BINSTEAD *Pink 'Un & Pelican* xi. 247 He also was what the Yids call a shlemiel; no matter what he turned his hand to, nothing ever came of it. **1932** *N.Y. Times* 10 Nov. 23/7 If they expect to beat me by having their names writ in, they're schlemiels—saps, if you get me. **1941** B. SCHULBERG *What makes Sammy Run?* iv. 68 Don't talk like a schlemiel, you schlemiel. Sounds like you're letting them push you around. **1959** *Times Lit. Suppl.* 6 Nov. p. xxxv/2 Bellow's..free-swinging translation of 'Gimpel, the Fool'—probably the best *schlemiel* story in the literature. **1963** T. PYNCHON *V.* i. 37 Only something that, being a schlemihl, he'd known for years: inanimate objects and he could not live in peace. **1969** L. MICHAELS *Going Places* 21 A hundred fifty-five pounds of stomping shlemiel. **1972** *Listener* 14 Sept. 339/3 A schlemiel is a man who falls on his back and breaks his nose. Or you can say 'When a schlemiel leaves the room, you feel as if someone came in.' **1973** *New Society* 11 Oct. 95/1 The choice of making a fool of himself or being made a fool of by others, being a schmuck or a schlemihl. **1978** I. B. SINGER *Shosha* iii. 50 You should have taken the whole five hundred. To him that's a trifle. He'll think you're a shlemiel.

schlemozzle, var. *SHEMOZZLE.

schlenter (ʃle·ntəɹ), *sb.* and *a.* Also **schlanter, shlanter, shlenter, shlinter, sl-.** [Poss. ad. Afrikaans or Du. *slenter* knavery, trick.

The history of this word is obscure; the Austral. and N.Z. forms are possibly borrowed from S. Afr. English, but by what route is not clear.]

A. *sb.* **1.** *Austral.* and *N.Z. colloq.* A trick.

1864 C. R. THATCHER *Invercargill Minstrel* 15 'Twas a 'shlinter' for the tenant one morning departed Without paying his rent. **1919** W. H. DOWNING *Digger Dial.* 45 *Slanter* (or *schlanter*), a trick. 'To run a schlanter'—to make no genuine effort to win a game. **1925** A. WRIGHT *Boy from Bullarah* 133 'A shlanter' he bellowed. **1934** *Bulletin* (Sydney) 20 June 47/1 'You worked a schlenter on me, laddie,' he said, grinning at me in the wings, 'but you're forgiven.' **1945** *N.Z. Geographer* I. i. 24 Most [shearing] sheds have somebody articulate to voice their worries if any slinters are feared. **1959** G. SLATTER *Gun in Hand* xii. 166 Wilkinson..worked a slinter at the end. Ref shoulda penalised him. **1965** F. HARDY *Yarns of Billy Borker* 70 (*title*) The greatest slanter in the history of the racing game.

2. *S. Afr.* Something counterfeit; *spec.* a counterfeit diamond.

1892 J. R. COUPER *Mixed Humanity* 263 A new branch of industry had started in Kimberley, the manufacture of 'schlenter' stones, a name given to diamonds made of glass. **1898** *Cape Argus* (Weekly ed.) 16 Mar. 35 (Pettman), A small sack containing bars of gold or schlenter. **1937** H. KLEIN *Stage-Coach Dust* x. 112 Schlenters were also useful to the individual digger to drop into the pans of their rotating washing machine, to test the honesty of their native boys; and they were also useful to a more unscrupulous class to 'salt' diamondless claims. **1946** L. G. GREEN *So Few are Free* ix. 127 That is the trade in 'schlenters', bits of glass shaped roughly from bottle stoppers to resemble diamonds. They have none of the peculiar soapy feel of the genuine diamond, but they pass muster sometimes in a hurried deal at night. **1969** J. M. WHITE *Land God made in Anger* 131 *Schlenters*, or *slenters*, are false diamonds. The best Schlenters in South West are made from the marbles in the necks of the lemonade or mineral-water bottles that can be found in dozens at the old German diggings.

B. *adj.* Dishonest, crooked; pretended, counterfeit, fake. *Austral.*, *N.Z.* and *S. Afr. colloq.*

1889 WILLIAMS & REEVES *Colonial Couplets* 51 Broke! Broke! Broke! At the will of the C.J.C. For the slenter race with the favourite dead Will never come back to me. **1891** A. DE BRÉMONT *Gent. Digger* viii. 99 'Of course,' whispers the seller who had pushed his way to the side of the buyer, 'this sale was only *shlenter*.' **1900** J. SCOTT *Tales Colonial Turf* 35 [These race-course rogues] can draw deductions so beautifully, piecing together imaginary 'schlenter goes', and 'put-up jobs' with the cleverness of a whole courtful..of lawyers. **1916** C. J. DENNIS *Songs Sentimental Bloke* 55 The slanter game I'd played wiv my Doreen—.. I seen wot made me feel fair rotten mean. **1924** L. COHEN *Reminiscences of Johannesburg & London* viii. 166 Confidence men found customers in plenty for schlenter gold bricks and amalgam. **1932** *Zionist Record* 25 Our courts employ schlenter as a word requiring no further definition, in the sense of fake when applied to mineral products. **1974** *Sunday Times* (Johannesburg) 24 Nov. 4 What makes the event more gratifying still is the fact that they sold schlenter uranium.

schlep (ʃlep), *v. colloq.* Also **schlepp, shlep.** [Yiddish *shlepn*, ad. G. *schleppen* to drag.] **a.** *trans.* To haul, carry, drag. Also *transf.* and *fig.*

1922 JOYCE *Ulysses* 48 She trudges, schlepps, trains, drags..her load. **1931** L. STEFFENS *Autobiogr.* I. xix. 137 By this means the tuglike *Schlepper* schlepped a string of cargo boats up the Neckar to Heilbron. **1966** *New Statesman* 19 Aug. 261/3, I have a dread of being a martyr. Let them *schlep* Sonny Liston instead. **1973** *Jewish Chron.* 19 Jan. 11/1 The first thing you remember to do when shown the studio floor is to schlepp the book—out of the briefcase.. and at a right moment casually hold up the volume. **1973** *Publishers Weekly* 26 Feb. 125/1 The one thing you would not want to schlep along on a backpacking trip is this book, which runs to over 340 pages. **1975** *New Yorker* 11 Aug. 32/1 When her husband, Sidney, was alive he sustained a rupture, and Mrs. Singer says she had to schlepp him in and out of bed several times a day. **1975** R. H. RIMMER *Premar Experiments* (1976) i. 68 Merle schleps cocktails at the Persian Room in the Sheraton between six and midnight. **1977** G. MARTON *Alarum* 189 The CIA schlepped you from Moscow to Washington.

b. *intr.* To toil, to 'slave'; to go or travel with effort, to traipse. Also with quasi-*obj.*

1963 'R. L. PIKE' *Mute Witness* x. 172, I waste a whole evening *schlepping* around with him. **1964** W. MARKFIELD *To Early Grave* iii. 54 My destiny, my fate..to *shlepp* for her. **1964** S. BELLOW *Herzog* 136 Why should I *schlepp* out my guts? **1972** D. E. WESTLAKE *Cops & Robbers* (1973) 137 We don't both have to hang around. Why don't you shlep on back to the station. **1978** J. PASCALL *Illustr. Hist. Rock Music* 15 As he schlepped his weary way from date to date.

Hence **schle·pping** *vbl. sb.*

1977 *New Society* 3 Mar. 454/3 The endless flat-footed *schlepping* you have to do at Gatwick or Chicago O'Hare.

schlep (ʃlep), *sb.*[1] *U.S. colloq.* Also **schlepp, shlep.** Abbrev. of *SCHLEPPER.

1939 *News Letter & Wasp* 23 June 13 The name of the radio character known to thousands, Schlepperman, is evidently a personification of 'schlep', which means a poor slob. **1963** T. PYNCHON *V.* iv. 104 'Quiet, shlep,' said the doctor, scrubbing. **1977** *New Yorker* 19 Sept. 80/3 My teacher can just zero in on one phrase, and it's immediately obvious that what I've done is so immature it makes me feel like an absolute schlepp.

schlep (ʃlep), *sb.*[2] *colloq.* (chiefly *U.S.*). Also **schlepp.** [Yiddish, prob. f. *SCHLEP *v.*] A troublesome business, a piece of hard work.

1964 *Economist* 1 Aug. 449/3 It was a schlep to find out. **1973** L. SNELLING *Heresy* II. ii. 68 Who thought up this *schlepp* with the sign, anyway? **1976** *National Observer* (U.S.) 4 Dec. 19-B/3 Anybody who has ever tried to make even a small amount of a classic brown sauce from scratch would probably agree with Liederman's assessment that 'it's the ultimate schlep'.

schlepper (ʃle·pəɹ). *colloq.* (chiefly *U.S.*). Also **shlepper.** [Yiddish, f. *SCHLEP *v.*: see -ER[1].] A person of little worth, a fool, a 'jerk'; a pauper, a beggar, a scrounger; an untidy person; (see also quot. 1934).

1934 *Amer. Speech* IX. 284/1 A customer who shops from store to store continually trying on shoes but not buying is known as a *shlepper*. **1949** S. J. PERELMAN *Westward Ha!* i. 13 In vain I protested that my dependents would be reduced to beggary; the editor's face remained flinty. 'About time those *schleppers* went to work,' he grunted. **1950** G. MARX *Let.* 20 Mar. (1967) 72 The paupers, or schlepper crowd, still hang on to their portable radios, but unfortunately they're not the ones who buy Chryslers. **1954** *Ibid.* 4 Aug. 59 Women always seem so much more joyous than men when another schlepper gets hooked. **1968** L. ROSTEN *Joys of Yiddish* 346 Hike up your slip; straighten your seams; you look like a shlepper. **1973** *Jewish Chron.* 19 Jan. 10/4 A 'star', you should pardon the expression, is never short of schleppers. And schleppers are like the tides of the ocean. If you make a hit film, they come in and almost drown you. If you make a flop, they recede into the distance. **1977** *Rolling Stone* 24 Mar., I've got a message for the Penelopes of this world. It's high time they say to their Ulysseses, 'Okay Schlepper, you've been around the world, your turn to keep the home fires burning, I'm splitting on my own trip for a while.'

schlich (ʃliχ[y]). *Metallurgy.* [Ger.: see SLIKE *sb.*] = SLICK *sb.*[2]

1677 E. BROWNE *Travels Germany* 135 They have also.. *slich*, or pounded and washed ore. **1757** tr. *Keysler's Travels* IV. 65 This method of burning of the *Schlich* saves considerable charges. **1839** URE *Dict. Arts* 814 Water..is made to flow with greater or less velocity and abundance over the schlich or pasty mud spread on a table of various inclination. **1855** J. R. LEIFCHILD *Cornwall* 207 Should the product (called *schlich*) seem tolerably rich, the operative turns the table round its axis. **1920** A. H. FAY *Gloss. Mining & Mineral Industry* 595/1 Schlich, finely pulverized ore; mud.

schlicht (ʃliχ[y]t), *a. Math.* [a. G. *schlicht* simple, plain.] (See quot. 1944.)

1944 J. E. LITTLEWOOD *Lect. Theory of Functions* i. 120 A function is called 'schlicht' in D if $f'(z) \neq 0$ in D, and $f(z_1) \neq f(z_2)$ for distinct points z_1, z_2 of D. Or: if $f(z) - \alpha = 0$ has never more than one solution (counting multiplicities) for z of D. **1968** E. T. COPSON *Metric Spaces* vii. 86 An important instance of a bijection is the schlicht function of complex variable theory.

Schlieffen (ʃlī·fən). The name of Alfred, Graf von *Schlieffen* (1833–1913), German general, used *attrib.* of a plan for the invasion and defeat of France that was formulated by him before 1905 and applied, with modifications, in 1914.

1919 A. P. F. VON TIRPITZ *My Memoirs* II. xvii. 289 The Schlieffen plan of attacking France through Belgium was intended to stave off from Germany the first vital danger. **1926** *Encycl. Brit.* Suppl. III. 479/1 How armies are to be handled in the Schlieffen spirit the war on the Eastern front showed. **1931** W. S. CHURCHILL *World Crisis* VI. vi. 89 He drew up the celebrated 'Schlieffen Plan' in which the whole strength of Germany was to be directed from the outset with the utmost rapidity upon France by means of a wheeling movement through Belgium. **1965** A. J. P. TAYLOR *Eng. Hist. 1914–45* xiv. 484 He planned to attack on the extreme right, according to the Schlieffen model. **1977** *Listener* 4 Aug. 140/2 In the Schlieffen plan, the railways..took troops to Belgium and northern France.

schliere (ʃlī·rə). *rare* in *sing.* Also **Schliere.** Pl. **-n,** and erron. **schliere, schlierin.** [Ger., f. regional *schliere* (fem.) striæ, streaks, corresp. to *schlier* (masc.) marl, f. early new HG. *schlier* (masc. and neut.), f. MHG. *slier* mud, related to MHG. *slier, sliere* ulcer, f. OHG. *sclierrun* (dat. pl.).] **1. a.** *Petrol.* An irregular streak or mass in igneous rock differing transitionally from its surroundings in texture or composition, and usu. elongated by flow.

[**1885** A. GEIKIE *Text-bk. Geol.* (ed. 2) 94 Streaked, arranged in streaky inconsistent lines (Germ. Schlieren), either parallel or convergent, and often undulating.] **1888** J. J. H. TEALL *Brit. Petrogr.* ii. 40 The differential motion of the lava will tend to drag out any parts of exceptional composition into the form of streaks or elongated lenticles (schliere). **1898** *Jrnl. Geol.* VI. 794 In the granites of Essex county are found in abundance streaks (Schlieren) and rounded rock masses of darker color and of finer grain than the surrounding rock. **1937** *Mem. Geol. Soc. Amer.* No. 5. 25 Sheet-like bodies, in which certain minerals appear in abnormal proportions, are called flow layers, or schlieren. **1966** *McGraw-Hill Encycl. Sci. & Technol.* VII. 15/2 Schlieren may represent early segregation drawn out by magma flow. Some may be xenoliths more or less digested and reworked by magma. Others may represent residual magmatic liquors of different composition injected into already crystallized portions. Schlieren formed in solid rocks are more properly metamorphic or metasomatic features.

b. A zone or stratum in a transparent medium whose density differs sufficiently from that of the surrounding medium for it to be detectable by refraction anomalies, usu. in consequence of pressure or temperature differences or composition inhomogeneities.

1895 C. S. PALMER tr. *Nernst's Theoret. Chem.* I. v. 121 If one adds, by means of a capillary pipette, a drop of a strong solution of potassium ferro-cyanide to a moderately strong solution of copper sulphate, one can see with the naked eye that a *schliere* (i.e. thin layer) of concentrated solution of copper sulphate flows downwards. **1946** F. SCHNEIDER *Qualitative Organic Microanalysis* ii. 22 The appearance of schlieren indicates the presence of impurities. **1949** *Proc. R. Soc.* A. CXCVII. 485 However imperfect an electron lens may be from the point of view of theoretical optics, it can contain neither dust nor 'schlieren', as the electromagnetic field smoothes itself out automatically. **1965** G. J. WILLIAMS *Econ. Geol. N.Z.* x. 149/1 The chromite occurs as..sporadic small narrow schlierin paralleling the enstatite crystal lamination... 1 to 3 mm schlierin in dunite show a local concentration of chromite. **1967** *Oceanogr. & Marine Biol.* V. 107 These variations may appear as 'Schlieren', that is, as thin bands of water at the surface or at any depth.

2. *attrib.* uses of pl. *schlieren*, with reference to an experimental method for the observation and recording of schlieren in transparent media, in which the specimen is illuminated with a collimated beam of light, and the diffraction pattern resulting from localized refraction of light rays by the schlieren is photographed or displayed on a screen, as *schlieren apparatus* [ad. G. *schlieren-apparat* (A. Töpler *Beobachtungen nach einer neuen optischen Methode* (1864) 16)], *illumination, method, photograph, photography, picture, system, technique.*

1895 C. S. PALMER tr. *Nernst's Theoret. Chem.* I. v. 121 Tammann observed the osmotic stream produced by the changes of concentration by means of a so-called *schlieren* apparatus. [*Translator's note*] This term, for which I find no concise English equivalent, is in common use in Germany to denote a delicate apparatus of Töpler used to detect small differences in the refractive power of the different layers ('schlieren') of heterogeneous media. **1933** *Jrnl. Scientific Instr.* X. 381 (*caption*) General arrangement of 'schlieren' apparatus set up for photographic or screen observation. **1971** *Sci. Amer.* May 118/1 In its simplest form the schlieren apparatus consists of a light source, two lenses, a pair of knife-edges and a sheet of photosensitive film. **1966** D. G. BRANDON *Mod. Techniques Metallogr.* 18 Some increase in sensitivity can be obtained if the stop is displaced from the image of the condenser aperture, so that the direct beam is merely reduced to the same intensity as the diffracted beam and not completely eliminated. This system is known as schlieren illumination and can be used to give accurate information on surface tilt. [**1899** *Phil. Mag.* XLVIII. 218 (*heading*) Photography of sound-waves by the 'Schlieren-Methode'.] **1933** *Jrnl. Scientific Instr.* X. 378 The 'Schlieren' method is an old but little-known method of rendering visible either colourless fluids, which have a different refractive index from their surrounding medium, or variations of refractive index or thickness of transparent solids. **1940** *Nature* 29 June 1021/1 The differentiation of the native proteins in the [egg] white was attempted on the basis of ionic mobilities by the method of Tiselius. The migration of the boundaries was followed optically by the 'schlieren' method using a sodium vapour lamp. **1962** *New Scientist* 6 Dec. 576/1 The effects that make optical schlieren methods feasible become negligible in gases at very low pressures. **1953** *Proc. Inst. Mech. Engineers 1951–2: Automobile Div.* 97/2 Observations by Miller of schlieren photographs taken during a very violent knocking combustion show a normal progression of the flame about three-quarters of the way across the combustion chamber. **1970** *New Scientist* 18 June 581/1 Ultrasonic frequencies up to 40kHz radiated at the base of a roaring jet of burning gas have a marked effect on the flame, altering its appearance and cutting down the noise produced. This is clearly illustrated in the two sets of spark schlieren photographs of town gas diffusion flames... An acoustic frequency of 38kHz is responsible for the remarkable alteration seen in the schlieren pictures. **1931** *Trans. Inst. Mining Engin.* LXXX. 18 Experiments carried out with Schlieren photography at Buxton are being supplemented at the U.S. Bureau of Mines Explosives Station at Pittsburgh. **1937** *Jrnl. R. Aeronaut. Soc.* XLI. 621 By using 'Schlieren' photography the air flow, fuel injection and flame formation were recorded simultaneously. **1979** *Nature* 29 Mar. 384/2 Drs Clark and B. J. Mullan used Schlieren photography to look at the air flow in and around cabinets running with and without an operator. **1957** LIEPMANN & ROSHKO *Elem. Gasdynamics* vi. 161 Schlieren pictures are seldom used for a quantitative evaluation of density. They are, however, indispensable for obtaining qualitative understanding of flows. **1966** *McGraw-Hill Encycl. Sci. & Technol.* XII. 68/1 Numerical values of density can be obtained only from schlieren pictures of airflow about two-dimensional models or about simple axisymmetric models. **1970** Schlieren picture [see *schlieren photograph* above]. **1949** O. G. SUTTON *Science of Flight* 203 Two other methods, the schlieren system and the interference method, are also in common use... The schlieren system uses either lenses alone or in combination with a concave mirror. **1956** *Nature* 10 Mar. 485/1 A schlieren system has been combined with a rotating mirror camera so that the shock propagation can be recorded in the regions outside the arc as well as in the arc channel. **1966** *McGraw-Hill Encycl. Sci. & Technol.* XII. 67/2 The schlieren system is used particularly in supersonic wind tunnels because it clearly shows the density gradients created by the shock and expansion waves of the airflow around the wind tunnel model. **1962** *New Scientist* 6 Dec. 576/1 The Schlieren technique is an optical method of studying changes of density, and hence of refractive index, in transparent media.

Hence **schli·eric** *a.*

1921 *Geol. Mag.* LVIII. 550 *Mixed rocks*, rocks which must be regarded as mixtures of carbonate magma of sövite type, and of the silicate rocks already enumerated are developed as schlieric intrusions, or as dykes cutting other members of the Fen group.

schlimazel (ʃlimǫ·z'l). *colloq.* (chiefly *U.S.*). Also **schlimazzel, schlimazl, shl-**, etc. [Yiddish, f. MHG. *slim* crooked + Heb. *mazzāl* luck.] A consistently unlucky, accident-prone person, a 'born loser'. Hence as *v. trans.*, to make a schlimazel of (a person) (*nonce-use*).

1948 N. AUSUBEL *Treasury of Jewish Folklore* III. I. 344 Sholom Aleichem drew endless amusement out of the misadventures of his irrepressible, daydreaming *schlimazls*. **1960** *Encounter* May 84/1 In the *schlimazl* of Jewish tradition, I found the ancestors of Bellow's 'Angie March'. If the *schlimazl* went into the hat business, babies would be born without heads. **1962** J. ISH-KISHOR *Tales from Wise Men of Israel* 199 She shrugged. What could one make of such a *shlimmazzel*? **1963** T. PYNCHON *V.* i. 24 It seemed sometimes that he put himself deliberately in the way of hostile objects, as if he were looking to get schlimazzeled out of existence. **1968** L. ROSTEN *Joys of Yiddish* 347 A *shlimazl* wryly sighed: 'From *mazel* to *shlimazl* is but a tiny step; but from *shlimazl* to *mazel*—oy, is that far!' **1972** J. WAMBAUGH *Blue Knight* (1973) i. 15 Just bring me a cold drink, you old schlimazel. **1980** *Times* 12 June 16/8 When a waiter spills soup on a customer, the waiter is a *shlemiel* and the customer is a *shlemazl*.

schlock (ʃlǫk). *colloq.* (chiefly *N. Amer.*). Also **schlag, shlock.** [Yiddish, app. f. *shlogn* to strike.] Cheap, shoddy, or defective goods; inferior material, junk, 'trash' (freq. applied to the arts or entertainment). Also *attrib.* or as *adj.*, and *Comb.* in **schlo·ckmeister, -master** [G. *meister* master], a purveyor of cheap merchandise, 'special offers', and the like.

1915 *N.Y. Tribune* 25 July 12/1 Damaged articles..are sold..to the..'schlock' store proprietors. **1916** *Ibid.* 10 Jan. 14/1 There is nothing 'schlock' about the Goodell method. **1939** *Amer. Speech* XIV. 80/2 Schlag describes a skirt which has scant length, tightness where it should be full, is off size, has many loose threads, defective buttons, and off size button-holes. **1963** T. PYNCHON *V.* iv. 110 She loves my rhinoplasty But the others are schlock. **1965** J. M. ULLMAN *Good Night, Irene* i. 20 Public relations, an elastic term that encompasses everything from crude schlockmeisters operating out of phone booths to high-powered representatives of billion-dollar corporations. **1966** L. DEIGHTON *Billion-Dollar Brain* xv. 142 The schlock-shops were afire with sale signs and smiling suckers. **1970** *Toronto Daily Star* 24 Sept. 30/1 The most successful.. have substituted sociological satire for sentimental schlock. **1972** *Publishers Weekly* 21 Aug. 71/3 Shlock fiction with all the necessary ingredients, the result is mindlessly entertaining, if rather tasteless. **1976** *New Mus. Express* 31 July 37/1 Presley was already showing..an inclination to go in for schlock rather than rock. **1978** M. PUZO *Fools Die* xii. 131, I knew it [*sc.* magazine writing] was schlock, but still I loved it. *Ibid.* xxxiii. 388 He had signed a long-term contract with Tri-Culture and become the ace schlockmaster for Jeff Wagon. **1981** *Listener* 26 Feb. 294/1 Atkinson is more fun away from showbiz schlock.

Hence **schlo·cky** *a.*, characterized by schlock; that is schlock; shoddy, trashy.

1968 *N.Y. Times* 25 July 26 Playing the 'special guest star' in a series of schlocky European films. **1970** *Wall St. Jrnl.* (Eastern ed.) 10 Sept. 1/6 The schlocky corner gas station import dealer is gone. **1975** *Publishers Weekly* 1 Dec. 67/2 Just what the marketplace doesn't need, one more schlocky Gothic series. **1981** *Spectator* 24 Jan. 7/2 The concentration on Sinatra arises out of the suspicion that the Reagan entourage of friends and hangers-on is loaded with shabby, shady, schlocky, smarmy, shyster millionaires.

schloss. (Earlier and later examples.)

1820 D. WORDSWORTH *Jrnl.* 29 July (1941) II. 74 The rest of the company had proceeded..to the Schloss.. to be spectators of the moonlight festivities of the ruined castle. **1855** GEO. ELIOT in *Fraser's Mag.* LI. 700/1 We saw the Schloss, and discovered the labyrinthine beauties of the park. **1974** *Times Lit. Suppl.* 23 Aug. 894/1 The incessant cold, the huge, half-ruinous, unheated schloss. **1980** *Early Music* Jan. 136 (Advt.), Our inclusive prices provide the course, room and board at Breiteneich, use of the facilities at the schloss.

schlub (ʃlʊb). *U.S. slang.* Also **shlub.** [Yiddish, perh. ad. Pol. *żłób* blockhead.] A worthless person, a 'jerk', an oaf.

1964 'E. MCBAIN' *Ax* viii. 149 'Kaplowitz,' I say, 'are you a janitor or a schlub? I'm a janitor... And such a dirty basement I can't stand.' **1969** D. E. WESTLAKE *Up your Banners* (1970) v. 39 When a man..doesn't know the facts and nobody will tell him..and people keep throwing apples and unkind remarks at him, he has no choice but to look like a *shlub*. **1970** R. H. GREENAN *Nightmare in Colour* (1971) xxxii. 114 He backed out—can you imagine? Hired a couple of college shlubs. **1978** *N.Y. Times Book Rev.* 2 Apr. 22 After bearing two children of the real-estate shlub, Earl Jr.

schm- (also **shm-**). *colloq.* (chiefly *U.S.*). An element, derived from the numerous Yiddish words that begin with this sequence of sounds, fused with or replacing the initial letter(s) of a word, so as to form a nonsense-word which is added to the original word in order to convey disparagement, dismissal, or derision.

1929 I. GOLLER *Five Bks. of Mr. Moses* v. ii. 215 'I know he made Davy go to the Palace to-day with the idea of hastening on the crisis in his illness.'.. '*Crisis-shmisis!*' mocked Barnett disparagingly. **1935** A. KOBER *Thunder over Bronx* 28 Now alluva sudden is fency-shmency with forks. *Ibid.* 48 So who you rushing to see, Miss Hurry Shmurry? **1952** *Jrnl. Eng. & Gmc. Philol.* LI. 226 The morphological pattern of the jocular repetition of a word or word-ending prefixed by the cluster ʃm- seems to have become quite generalized... I have heard.. moon-schmoon, etc. **1953** I. ASIMOV *Second Foundation* xviii. 183 'Time; schmime,' said Pappa irritably. **1963** T. PYNCHON *V.* xii. 354 'It's murdering your own child, is what it is.' 'Child, schmild. A complex protein molecule, is all.' **1966** *N.Y. Herald Tribune* 20 Mar. (Sunday Mag.) 33/3 Trotsky-shmotsky, Lesbian- or adultery-wise—any way you slice *The Group* on screen it's the same old baloney about The Girls. **1967** *New Yorker* 28 Oct. 105/2 Two early Christians chanced to meet in Heaven... 'Saul of Tarsus, yet!' cried one. 'What are *you* doing here?' 'Tarsus-Schmarsus,' replied the other, 'I'm Paul already.' **1969** *Listener* 24 Apr. 569/1, I was surprised to find René Cutforth retelling the old story of the psychiatrist and the fond mother without specifying that she's a *Jewish* mother. ('I have to tell you, madam, that your son is suffering from an Oedipus complex.' 'Oedipus, Schmoedipus! What does it matter so long as he loves his mother?') **1971** D. HEFFRON *Nice Fire & Some Moonpennies* xv. 140 Gods, schmods! You can have them. **1978** F. ROSS *Sleeping Dogs* 110 'Listen, honey—' 'Listen schmisten! I tell you I won't be here.'

schmagagi, var. *SCHMEGEGGY.

schmaltz (ʃmǫlts, ʃmalts), *sb.* Also **schmalz, shmaltz**, etc. [a. G. and Yiddish *schmalz* fat, dripping.] **1.** Melted chicken fat; *schmaltz herring*, a form of pickled herring.

1935 L. ZARA *Blessed is Man* II. ii. 232 Two or three other kegs of *schmalz* herring and such for pickling. **1951** L. W. LEONARD *Jewish Cookery* vi. 42 (*heading*) Rendering chicken or goose fat (schmaltz). **1959** *20th Cent.* June 583 Shops all choked with..schmaltz herring. **1960** A. WESKER *I'm talking about Jerusalem* I. 13 All right, so it's shmultz herring and plum pudding. **1968** M. RICHLER *Cocksure* viii. 46, I don't want this apartment stinking of schmaltz herring. **1974** *New Yorker* 3 June 80/2 If a diner thinks the mashed potatoes might be improved by a bit of schmalz—liquid chicken fat—he pours some out of a dispenser. **1976** *Ibid.* 16 Feb. 58/1 The newest supermarket in Washington Avenue specializes in Cuban food instead of schmalz herring and stuffed kishke.

2. *colloq.* Sentimentality, emotionalism; excessively sentimental music, writing, etc. Also *attrib.*

1935 *Vanity Fair* (N.Y.) Nov. 71/2 *Schmaltz* (cf. the German *schmalz*, meaning grease) is a derogatory term used to describe straight jazz. **1938** *Manch. Guardian Weekly* 2 Sept. 188/3 Sometimes they play 'schmaltz' or 'salon' (ordinary jazz). **1944** [see *HAM *sb.*[1] B. 1]. **1950** *Here & Now* (N.Z.) Nov. 27/2 Howard Wyatt has an impressive technique for his age, and his greatest lack is what has come to be known as schmalz. A certain amount..of this quality is necessary, and..I'd recommend a serious study of the 'white' jazz exponents. **1956** [see *DISNEYESQUE *a.*]. **1957** J. D. SALINGER *Zooey* in *New Yorker* 4 May 37/1 Will you be content with that standard box-office schmalz? **1960** *Guardian* 7 July 6/3 A purveyor of 'Schmalz' in long-winded repetitive symphonies. **1967** *Spectator* 24 Nov. 634/2 Some Presidents could turn..these frustrations to good account by retailing their moral and physical struggles... Lyndon Johnson spares us none of this schmaltz. **1977** *Spare Rib* June 46/4 She..is saying with appalling schmaltz that 'Josh's warm, funny smile was where I lived now'. **1978** *Observer* 19 Nov. 31/1 'What we call honest sentiment,' he says in equally honest puzzlement, 'you call schmaltz.'

schmaltz (ʃmǫlts, ʃmalts), *v. colloq.* Also **schmalz, shmaltz.** [f. prec.] *trans.* To impart a sentimental atmosphere to; to play (music) in a 'corny' or sentimental manner. Also with *up*.

1936 *Amer. Mercury* May p. x, *Schmalz it*, play it long-haired. **1966** D. SKIRROW *It won't get you Anywhere* xxxi. 143 She was like the white light of early morning, before the hot sun schmalzes up the scene. **1968** L. ROSTEN *Joys of Yiddish* 351 To *shmaltz* ('to *shmaltz* it up'): to add 'corn', pathos, mawkishness. **1969** A. LASKI *Dominant Fifth* ii. 41 He..tried to lighten his touch; no use giving this—visitor—the notion that they schmaltzed it up.

schmaltzy (ʃmǫ·ltsi, ʃma·ltsi), *a. colloq.* Also **schmalzy.** [f. as prec. + -Y[1].] Sentimentalized, over-emotional; 'corny'. Hence **schma·l(t)ziness.**

1935 [see *GROOVE *v.* 5]. **1949** L. FEATHER *Inside Be-Bop* iii. 22 Edgar Hayes, a pianist whose schmaltzy record of *Stardust* had made him a Harlem juke box favorite. **1952** B. MALAMUD *Natural* 170 A heavy-set German with a schmaltzy accent. **1959** *Guardian* 27 Oct. 7/6 I'm working on something real schmaltzy for one of your women's magazines. **1962** *John o' London's* 5 July 19/1 A few weeks ago she [*sc.* the All-American Mum] turned up in *All Fall Down*, embodied with searing schmalziness by Angela Lansbury. **1974** T. P. WHITNEY tr. *Solzhenitsyn's Gulag Archipelago* I. I. v. 218 Yuri painted for nothing schmaltzy pictures such as *Nero's Feast* and the *Chorus of Elves* and the like for the German officers on the commandant's staff. **1978** P. GRIFFITHS *Conc. Hist. Mod. Music* vii. 101 In the opera *Lulu* the effect of Berg's half-tonal serialism is an over-ripe schmalzy quality. **1980** [see *SCHMUTZIG *a.*].

schmatte (ʃma·tə). *U.S. colloq.* Also **shmatte, schmottah**, etc. [a. Yiddish *schmatte*, ad. Pol. *szmata* rag.] A rag, a ragged garment; any garment. Also *fig.*

1970 L. M. FEINSILVER *Taste of Yiddish* ii. 121 A 1969 sale catalog of the Ktav Publishing Company, New York book dealers, listed Philip Roth's licentious novel *Portnoy's Complaint* with the comment: 'A shmatte.' **1972** H. KEMELMAN *Monday Rabbi took Off* xxii. 144, I mean when they wear those checkered *shmattes* around their heads, then they're Arabs. Right? **1973** J. MARKS *Mick Jagger* 128, I ran away from home in San Bernardino when I was fifteen... All I took was this *schmottah* I wore Halloween. **1977** *New Yorker* 24 Oct. 39/2 A young woman, pale, in a Victorian schmotta.

schmeck (ʃmek). *slang.* Also **smeck.** Pl. **schme·cken.** [a. Yiddish *schmeck*, sniff.] A drug; *spec.* heroin.

1932 *Evening Sun* (Baltimore) 9 Dec. 31/5 *Smeck*, dope. **1941** M. U. SCHAPPES *Lett. from Tombs* 104 'Shmeck'—dope, a drug. **1966** *Sunday Times* (Colour Suppl.) 13 Feb. 35/4 *Schmeck*, heroin. **1967** M. CALPAN *In Deadly Vein* ix. 196 'He was always wild... Anything for kicks... In the end it was schmeck.' 'Heroin?' 'Yes. Hooked.' **1970** L. SANDERS *Anderson Tapes* xxxi. 86 She's hustling right now—schmeck, tail, abortion—the whole lot. *Ibid.* xcii. 218, I have some drugs. Some schmeck. Do you want a shot? **1971** *Oz* No. 36. 40/1 Shoot enough schmeck into them and they won't even *think* of burning and looting.

Hence **schme·cker,** a drug-addict, esp. one who takes heroin.

1953 W. BURROUGHS *Junkie* (1972) viii. 77 He went on talking about some old acquaintances who got their start in junk and later turned respectable. 'Now they say, "Don't have anything to do with Sol. He's a *shmecker*".' **1955** *Publ. Amer. Dial. Soc.* XXIV. 193 If they are all schmeckers, or narcotic addicts, they have a prearranged time to fix or take a bang. **1966** C. HIMES *Heat's On* xix. 145 The skin-poppers and the schmeckers (those who used the needle and those who sniffed the powder).

schmeer (ʃmiᵊɹ). *N. Amer. colloq.* Also **shmear, shmeer.** [ad. Yiddish *schmirn* to smear, grease, flatter.] **1.** Bribery, corruption, flattery.

1961 A. BERKMAN *Singers' Gloss. of Show Bus. Jargon* 78 *Shmear*,..payola; graft. **1962** E. LACY *Freeloaders* ii. 42 Our lad didn't want the *shmear* to start with, so he ain't greedy. **1978** *Amer. Film* Apr. 57/2 He knew the *shmeer* was on when the producer invited him to lunch.. and began the meal by ordering caviar and champagne.

2. *the whole schmeer*, everything, everything possible or available, every aspect of the situation.

1969 E. STEWART *Heads* 48 Why couldn't you burrow around and ferret out the whole shmear yourself? **1970** L. SANDERS *Anderson Tapes* v. 23, I want a complete list... Any thing and everything... The whole shmear. **1971** K. WHEELER *Epitaph for Mister Wynn* (1972) xxix. 374, I picked you because you know the whole schmeer. **1972** H. KEMELMAN *Monday Rabbi took Off* xxii. 146 Some special kind of prayer maybe where you could ask for the success of our enterprise...especially the financing, but I was thinking of the whole *shmeer*. **1978** *Maledicta* 1977 I. 282 Eventually, the whole schmeer was declared a Mexican stand-off.

schmegeggy (ʃmĕge·gi). *U.S. slang.* Also **schmagagi, shmegegge**, etc. [Origin obscure; see quots. 1968, 1970 for sense 1.] **1.** A contemptible person, an idiot.

1964 S. BELLOW *Herzog* 29 He better get it this afternoon, that ludicrous schmegeggy! **1968** L. ROSTEN *Joys of Yiddish* 353 *Shmegegge*,..Ameridish slang. Origin: unknown; probably, a dazzling onomatopoetic child of the Lower East Side. 1. An unadmirable, petty person. 2. A maladroit, untalented type. 3. A sycophant, a *shlepper*, a whiner, a drip. **1970** L. M. FEINSILVER *Taste of Yiddish* 121 *Shmegegge* (*or shmegeggi*), a galoot, a bird-brain, a stupid character... The disdain involved prompts me to suggest that the term may be a combination of two other words for 'fool': the vulgar *shmok*..and *yeke* or its German antecedent *Gecke*. **1971** *Observer* 23 May 36/3 He says he's a schlemiel which is..better than being a schmagogy... Schlemiels..drop things and..they drop on schmagogys.

2. Rubbish, nonsense.

1968 L. ROSTEN *Joys of Yiddish* 353 *Shmegegge*,..a lot of 'hot air', 'baloney', a *cockamamy* story. 'Don't give me that *shmegegge*!' **1970** L. M. FEINSILVER *Taste of Yiddish* 121 *Schmegegge (or shmegeggi)*,..as picked up in American theatrical circles, this is sometimes used in the sense of 'malarkey' or 'bushwa'. **1973** BOYD & PARKES *Dark Number* ii. 23 There was a bunch of students... They had the lot, the full schmagagi: girls got up like camp grannies.. boys in kaftans.

Schmeisser (ʃmaɪ·səɹ). The name of Louis and Hugo *Schmeisser*, German small-arms designers, used *attrib.* or *absol.* to designate various German types of submachine gun, in use from 1918 onwards.

1950 G. WILSON *Brave Company* 7, I saw that he [*sc.* a German] carried a Schmeisser. **1963** D. BAGLEY *Golden Keel* ix. 268, I opened the locker under my berth and took out the Schmeisser machine pistol and all the magazines. **1976** *Valiant* 8 May 3 (*caption*) In the United States, gun shops sell every kind of weapon, from shotguns to schmeissers. **1981** E. WARD *Baltic Emerald* xiv. 117 Modern Schmeissers..the most reliable..of all the medium-range killing devices.

schmelz (ʃmelts). Also erron. **schmel(t)ze.** [a. G. *schmelz* enamel.] Any one of several varieties of decorative glass; *spec.* a variety coloured red with a metallic salt, used to flash white glass. Also *attrib.*

[**1854** C. TOMLINSON *Cycl. Useful Arts* I. 784/1 Smetz [*sic*: ? *read* Smelz] glass is formed by fusing lengths of coloured glass into each other, so that the section shall resemble carnelian and the agates.] **1859** R. HUNT *Guide Museum Pract. Geol.* (ed. 2) 111 The Bohemian ruby is thus prepared:—a preparation called schmelze is made; it is composed of silica 500, minium 800, nitre 100, calcined potash 100. **1866** *Christie, Manson & Woods Sale Catal. 9 Feb. 1867* 65 A vase, on foot, of tortoiseshell Schmeltze... A green basket, mounted with or-molu; and a Schmeltze ditto... A ball of variegated Schmeltze. **1879** *Encycl. Brit.* X. 652/1 That peculiar kind of glass usually called schmelz, an imperfect imitation of calcedony, was also made at Venice in the 15th century. **1882** *Hamilton Palace Collection Catal.* No. 846 A Fluted Tumbler, of red and white schmelz. **1907** E. DILLON *Glass* xii. 207 There are a few exceptionally fine early examples of this schmelz at South Kensington. **1961** E. M. ELVILLE *Collector's Dict. Glass* 183/1 Variegated or marbled opaque glass, commonly known by the German word *schmeltz*.

Also ‖ **Schmelzglas.**

1935 W. A. THORPE *English Glass* v. 148 Measey and Greene ordered and sold the following lines, but the list applies generally to the members of the Company, and excepting the items of opaque-white and *calcedonic* (marbled glass or *Schmelzglas*) it may be taken as a production list. **1960** H. HAYWARD *Antique Coll.* 10/2 *'Agate' glass*, a glass of several colours which have been allowed to mingle before the vessel is formed, in imitation of agate. This type of glass was popular during the Renaissance.., particularly in Venice and Germany, and is sometimes known as *Schmelzglas*. **1975** *Oxf. Compan. Decorative Arts* 398 Not only did they [the Venetians] reproduce the Roman 'mosaic' and *millefiori* glass and the material made of blended opaque colours in imitation of natural stones (*calcedonio*, sometimes miscalled *Schmelzglas*), but they seem even to have copied..typical Roman shapes.

schmendrik (ʃme·ndrik). *U.S. slang.* Also **schmendrick, shmendrik.** [The name of a character in an operetta by Abraham Goldfaden (1840–1908).] A contemptible, foolish or immature person; an upstart, a 'sucker'.

1944 M. SAMUEL *Harvest in Desert* xii. 115 The colonists called the workers *Shmendriks*, tatterdemalions, n'er-do-wells. **1951** A. HIRSCHFELD *Show Business is No Business* 47 A schmendrick with a noodle for a brain. **1970** S. ELLIN *Bind* xxx. 151 This boy is no *shmendrik*... Believe me, he knows from the real thing. **1976** L. DEIGHTON *Twinkle, twinkle, Little Spy* x. 93 Maybe if I'd been at college with Andrei Bekuv, I could even feel sorry for *that* schmendrik.

‖ **schmerz** (ʃmerts). Also **Schmerz.** [a. G. *schmerz* pain.] Grief, sorrow, regret, pain.

1911 'P. HARDING' *Corner of Harley Street* xxx. 260 So white-coat gives him a swiftly helping hand, and within five minutes is removing a decayed semitic molar that has been giving its owner *schmerz* indescribable. **1925** R. FROST *Let.* 20 June (1964) 174 What lies at the bottom of your *Schmerz* is your own dereliction. **1977** *Times* 13 July 11/8 There is much more to Schiele than terrified mirror-gazing and sexual *Schmerz*. He was a splendid..portraitist.

Schmidt¹ (ʃmit). *Org. Chem.* [The name of Karl Friedrich *Schmidt* (b. 1887), German chemist, who first employed a reaction of this kind in 1923 (*Zeitschr. f. angew. Chem.* XXXVI. 511).] *Schmidt('s) reaction*: a widely-used synthetic method in which a carbonyl compound is treated with hydrazoic acid in the presence of mineral acid, the product(s) depending on the kind of carbonyl compound used (e.g. an aldehyde gives a mixture of a nitrile and a formyl derivative of an amide, a ketone gives an amide, and a fatty acid gives an amine).

[**1936** *Proc. R. Soc.* A. CLIV. 54 The introduction of the Schmidt method leaves the Hofmann method of great historical interest but deprives it of importance for costly and delicate synthetic work.] **1937** *Jrnl. Amer. Chem. Soc.* LIX. 2658/1 Although the Schmidt reaction has been used in a few instances it has never been extensively studied. **1963** I. L. FINAR *Org. Chem.* (ed. 4) I. ix. 178 Schmidt's reaction with acids is a modification of the Curtius reaction. **1967** L. F. & M. FIESER *Reagents for Org. Synthesis* I. 447 Application of the Schmidt reaction to cyclohexanone effects ring enlargement to ε-caprolactam. **1976** STREITWIESER & HEATHCOCK *Introd. Org. Chem.* xxviii. 825 The Schmidt reaction may also be used for the synthesis of simple amino acids if it is applied to an alkylated malonic acid.

Schmidt² (ʃmit). *Astr.* The name of Bernhard Voldemar *Schmidt* (1879–1935), Estonian-born German optician, used *attrib.* with reference to an optical system invented by him, as **Schmidt camera,** an astronomical telescope, used exclusively for wide-field photography at the primary focus, in which a Schmidt correcting lens is placed at the centre of curvature of a spherical primary mirror, the combination having no spherical aberration and little chromatic aberration; **Schmidt correcting lens, corrector, (correcting) plate,** an aspheric lens of complex figure used in the Schmidt camera and other catadioptric systems that utilize the same principle; **Schmidt telescope** = *Schmidt camera.* Also *ellipt.*, = *Schmidt camera.*

1939 SKILLING & RICHARDSON *Astron.* iii. 82 The great advantages of the Schmidt telescope are that it can photograph a very large area in the sky, giving sharp focus clear to the edge of the picture; and that it is very fast. *Ibid.*, These telescopes are sometimes called Schmidt cameras, for they cannot be used visually. **1946** *Nature* 17 Aug. 222/1 A Schmidt plate presents a very different problem, since the highest optical homogeneity is required for this, and a low-expansion glass has never yet been produced in the requisite optical quality. **1961** MICZAIKA & SINTON *Tools of Astronomer* iii. 99 (*caption*) Possible shapes of Schmidt correcting lenses. *Ibid.* 100 Such solid Schmidts, as they are called, may be made with *f*-numbers as small as *f*/0·6. **1964** *Listener* 21 May 831/1 The Armagh Schmidt is employed mainly on variable star research. **1966** *McGraw-Hill Encycl. Sci. & Technol.* XIII. 452/1 A similar correction of the principal defects of the paraboloidal reflector can be obtained by replacing the thin Schmidt correcting plate with a weakly diverging meniscus lens. **1973** *Sci. Amer.* Aug. 111/1 Schmidt correctors and other aspheric surfaces are sold by the tens of thousands in quality zoom lenses for film and television. **1978** PASACHOFF & KUTNER *University Astron.* iv. 90 The 1·2-meter Schmidt has been used to map the entire sky that is visible from Palomar. *Ibid.*, The new 1-meter Schmidt camera at the European Southern Observatory and the British 1·2-meter Schmidt camera at Siding Spring, Australia, are now being used in a joint project to extend the survey to incorporate the one-quarter of the sky that cannot be seen from Palomar. **1978** *Sci. Amer.* Dec. 90/3 The lens of the scallop eye appears to perform much the same function as the corrector plate of the Schmidt telescope.

Schmidt number (ʃmit). *Physics.* [Named after Ernst Heinrich Wilhelm *Schmidt* (b. 1892), German engineer.] A dimensionless number, used in the study of convective mass transfer and evaluated as the ratio of kinematic viscosity to mass diffusivity.

1955 D. B. SPALDING *Some Fundamentals of Combustion* vi. 239 Other experimental procedures can easily be conceived with various advantages or disadvantages, the guiding principle being that the Peclet numbers based on flow velocity and on flame speed must be kept constant, and that if possible the Mach number, Prandtl number and Schmidt number..should all have equal values in the model and the original. **1957** JAKOB & HAWKINS *Elements of Heat Transfer* (ed. 3) xvi. 293 The heat transfer equation may be altered to represent the mass transfer equation by replacing the Nusselt number by the corresponding Nusselt number for mass transfer, and replacing the Prandtl number by the Schmidt number. **1975** CROOME-GALE & ROBERTS *Airconditioning & Ventilation of Buildings* iii. 92 It can be shown that the well-known result expressing *Nu* [*sc.* the Nusselt number] as a function of the Reynolds and Prandtl numbers, i.e. $Nu = f(Re, Pr)$, has an analogous form in mass transfer $Sh = f(Re, Sc)$ where *Sc* is the Schmidt number.

‖ **schmierkäse** (ʃmiː·rˌkēzə). Also **Schmierkäse.** [G.: see SMEAR-CASE.] = SMEAR-CASE. Also *fig.*

1905 W. WITTIGSCHLAGER *Minna* 104 She carried some schmierkase (cream cheese), and butter that smelt so oily..I had to turn my head away. **1931** F. HURST *Back Street* i. 13 Sturdy, unstylish women with enormous busts, who ate and drank with relish, but knew, to the penny, for how much less they could spread their groaning home-table with these luxuries of *Schmierkäse*. **1949** *Sat. Even. Post* 23 Apr. 80/3, I took large helpings of ham and potatoes, *schmierkase*, and green salad with tomatoes. **1955** H. KURNITZ *Let.* Dec. in G. Marx *Groucho Lett.* (1967) 249, I am.. whipping up a schmierkase about light love and dark doings. **1969** R. & D. DE SOLA *Dict. Cooking* 202/2 *Schmierkäse*, (German—soft cheese). To Germans, any soft cheese; to Pennsylvania-Germans, cottage cheese.

Schmitt (ʃmit). *Electronics.* The name of Otto Herbert *Schmitt* (b. 1913), American biophysicist and electronics engineer, used *attrib.* and *absol.* to designate a bistable circuit devised by him, in which the output increases to a steady maximum when the input rises above a certain threshold, and decreases almost to zero when the input voltage falls below another threshold (usu. lower than the first).

1946 *Jrnl. Inst. Electr. Engineers* XCIII. IIIA. 306/1 Positive feedback can be used to reduce the effective grid base, or even to make it negative; an example is shown. [*Note*] This is the 'Schmitt circuit'. **1953** VON TERSCH & SWAGO *Recurrent Electr. Transients* viii. 272 If both plate-to-grid coupling and cathode coupling are utilized another trigger circuit is obtained. This circuit is called the Schmitt trigger circuit. **1962** SIMPSON & RICHARDS *Physical Princ. Junction Transistors* xvi. 418 The Schmitt trigger is neither bistable nor monostable in the ordinary sense. Its behaviour is similar to that of a non-regenerative switch but it has the advantages that it switches regeneratively at very high speed and can be designed with an accurate adjustable trigger threshold. **1967** *Electronic Engin.* XXXIX. 752/1 A theory was required to account for the existence of a minimum ionization current below which the Schmitt fails to trigger, and a maximum above which the Schmitt fails to reset. **1975** D. G. FINK *Electronics Engineers' Handbk.* XVI. 45 Schmitt bistables, also called Schmitt triggers, are suitable for detecting the moment when an analog signal crosses a given dc level. They are widely used in oscilloscopes to provide time-base synchronization pulses... In some Schmitt trigger circuits it is possible to modify the switching level by electrically changing the operating points of the transistors.

schmo (ʃmōᵘ). *U.S. slang.* Also **shmo(e).** [f. *SCHMUCK.] An idiot, a fool.

1948 *Life* 15 Mar. 23/2 Schlump is a friendlier, more sympathetic term than 'schmo', which has completely replaced 'jerk'. A schmo, of course, is a person who stands watching a machine make doughnuts, and 1) cannot understand the process, 2) cannot get up will power to leave. **1955** 'H. ROBBINS' *Stone for Danny Fisher* I. vii. 56 Let some other shmoe wet-nurse a bunch of kids. **1957** S. J. PERELMAN *Road to Miltown* 125 A couple of shmos like you and me, we can't even get up our rent, whereas them dukes and earls..are rolling in dough. **1970** D. FRANCIS *Rat Race* ii. 27 'Who,' he said crossly, 'is going to give that schmo a thousand quid for breaking his ankle?' **1979** 'H. HOWARD' *Sealed Envelope* xi. 159, I was feeling like a shmoe... Paul Ingram had outsmarted me.

schmock, var. *SCHMUCK.

schmoll (ʃmǫl). *slang.* [app. ad. Yiddish *shmol* narrow.] An idiot, a fool.

1967 J. WAINWRIGHT *Worms must Wait* xl. 101 Let's say..he was killed by some *schmoll* who wanted to rob him. **1973** —— *Pride of Pigs* 103 These hot-shot scientists. .. They're schmolls—every last one of 'em..but they get away with it.

schmooze (ʃmūz, ʃmūs), *v. U.S. colloq.* Also **schmoos(e), schmuss, shmooz,** etc. [ad. Yiddish *shmuesn* to talk, converse, chat, f. as next.] *intr.* To chat, gossip, engage in a long and intimate conversation. Hence **schmoo·zer**; **schmoo·zing** *vbl. sb.*

1897 *N.Y. Times Weekly Mag.* 14 Nov. 4/1 He loves dearly to stop and chat (*Schmoos*, he calls it). **1921** J. ANTHONY *Gang* 28 When Mrs. Sinbaum comes, we *schmoos*. **1928** *Amer. Speech* III. 364 The presence of a Jewish contingent of 'producers' and managers is responsible for such New York expressions as 'mazuma' (money), 'schmuss' (talk). **1939** *New Yorker* 4 Feb. 30/1 'Schmooze' (pronounced 'shmooss') is related to the Yiddish verb 'schmooze', which means 'to talk'. But schmoozing in the garment district is more than just a lot of idle chatter. Schmoozing is a careful tradition, dear to the hearts of everyone in New York's most thickly populated business section. *Ibid.* 30/2 Everybody in the district eats fast, the better and more to schmooze. **1939** *Reader's Digest* May 106/1, The schmoozers gulp down lunch in 15 minutes and then arrange themselves according to caste and craft. **1966** H. KEMELMAN *Saturday Rabbi went Hungry* x. 60 On Friday nights or Saturdays, don't we stand around after the services and *schmoos* a while? **1973** *New Yorker* 3 Feb. 56/2 We would schmoose all afternoon, with her talking in that funny, high Pennsylvania Dutch voice: 'Dat's gute,' or 'Dat's humbug.' **1977** *Time* 25 Apr. 47/2 Neil Diamond's beach house, Linda Ronstadt's $325,000 clapboard and the sprawling nine-bedroom house Guitarist Robbie Robertson took over from Carole King are all within schmoozing distance. **1977** *New Yorker* 27 June 29/1 Had she worked here part time, returning today out of sentimentality to schmooze with the boss? **1980** W. SAFIRE in *N.Y. Times Mag.* 18 May, A 'stoop', from the Dutch word for 'step', is a description of the porch and front steps on which Brooklynites sit and schmooze.

schmooze (ʃmūz, ʃmūs), *sb. U.S. colloq.* Also **shmoos.** [ad. Yiddish *shmues* chat, gossip ad. Heb. *shĕmūʻah* rumour.] Chat; gossip; a long and intimate conversation.

1939 *Reader's Digest* May 106/2 Because of schmooze, the garment district is the most hypersensitive city of 200,000 in the world. **1956** B. HOLIDAY *Lady sings Blues* (1973) xix. 156 [Lena Horne] insisted on taking me out with her and bought me lunch, and we had a wonderful schmooze about the old days in Hollywood. **1970** S. ELLIN *Man from Nowhere* (1971) xxxix. 194 Ready to order now..or do I wait until the end of the *shmoos*? **1977** *Zigzag* Aug. 24/1 The general demeanor and schmooze level of the crowd indicates it's a predominantly invitational radio/press group, more disposed to be open-minded.

schmottah, schmozzle, varr. *SCHMATTE, *SHEMOZZLE.

schmuck (ʃmʌk). *slang.* Also **schmock** (ʃmǫk), **shmock, shmuck.** [Yiddish; originally a taboo-word meaning 'penis'.] A contemptible or objectionable person, an idiot. Hence **schmu·cky** *a.*, objectionable, obnoxious.

1892 I. ZANGWILL *Childr. of Ghetto* II. I. xvi. 45 Becky's private refusal to entertain the addresses of such a *Shmuck.* **1945** G. MARX *Let.* 16 Feb. in *Groucho Lett.* (1967) 51 He doesn't know I can write, in fact, he thinks I'm a complete schmuck. **1958** F. NORMAN *Bang to Rights* III. 132 But as I'm no shmock I deside to play along with her. **1963** *Globe & Mail* (Toronto) 10 July 9/1 Only the pay-TV concept..can break the hold of the 'Madison Ave. schmucks, the Gestapo of the television industry'. **1967** D. SKIRROW *I was following this Girl* xxxix. 241, I know that one schmucky swallow doesn't have to spoil the barrel. **1971** B. MALAMUD *Tenants* 50 Art is the glory and only a shmuck thinks otherwise. **1972** J. CAINE *Hamlet, My Boy* xi. 161 As soon as the *shmock* of a witness offered to testify on television. **1975** *Harpers & Queen* May 128/3 Schmucky agents and flacks and show-biz parasites. **1978** M. PUZO *Fools Die* xxi. 239 Cully felt some anger that this guy was treating Merlyn like such a schmuck. **1981** *Times* 2 July 15/2 Mary Gordon is extremely funny about the beautiful Robert..and about the Woody Allen-like schmuck in the apartment below whom she sleeps with.

schmutter (ʃmʌ·tə). *colloq.* Also **shmuter, shmutter.** [ad. Yiddish *schmatte*, rag; cf. *SCHMATTE.] Clothing; also *fig.*, rubbish. Also *attrib.*, esp. in *schmutter trade, business*, etc.

1959 C. MACINNES *Absolute Beginners* 138 Coming down the steps, wearing some very fancy schmutter: mauve, button-two tuxedo, laced shirt, varnished pumps with bows, and, on his arm, a nameless dame. **1962** F. NORMAN *Guntz* i. 9 There ain't all that many birds who are loaded in the shmuter trade. **1965** *New Statesman* 30 July 152/2 Jews..may prefer their son to go into the family schmutter business. **1967** G. SIMS *Last Best Friend* xiii. 114 They said it was like Buck House but it was a right load of old schmutter! You see, everyone's an antique dealer today. **1972** *Bookseller* 27 May 2358/1 Several dresses (at trade terms) were bought for Mrs. Wolfe..from small shmutter merchants. **1980** *Times* 22 July 10/6 You can always dump a load of old schmutter destined for the California leisure set onto the unsuspecting women of Nottingham.

schmutz (ʃmuts). *slang.* Also **shmutz.** [Yiddish or Ger.] Dirt, filth, rubbish. Also *fig.* So **schmu·tzig, -ik** *a.*, filthy.

1967 P. WELLES *Babyhip* xxiv. 161 She was the one at your party wearing the *schmutzik* suit. **1968** M. RICHLER *Cocksure* xix. 116 'Of my son's ability there is no question.' '—and, em, the contents of your son's novel. You see—' '*Shmutz*,' Daniels shouted at Katansky. 'Pardon?' 'Filth. Today nothing sells like filth.' **1971** O. NORTON *Corpse-Bird Cries* vi. 113 It means dropping this driver in the *schmutz* insurance-wise. I was trying to avoid that. **1972** *Last Whole Earth Catalog* 178/1 It delights them to watch us rummaging around in the schmutz. **1980** *Times Lit. Suppl.* 5 Sept. 968/3 His [*sc.* Kurt Weill's] jazz is *schmutzig*, not *schmalzy*.

schnapper. For (ʃnæ·pə) substitute (snæ·pə). Delete 'The original form is retained in some English books, but is obsolete in Australia and New Zealand.' For Latin name substitute *Chrysophrys guttulatus* or *C. auratus*. **a.** (Later examples.)

1908 E. J. BANFIELD *Confessions of Beachcomber* II. i. 243 When maybe they have caught schnapper..they drift among the turtle. **1917** *Chambers's Jrnl.* Apr. 237/2 The schnapper, a sea-bream, is a splendid fish. **1947** K. TENNANT *Lost Haven* vi. 89 The deck was littered with the pink-bronze bodies of schnapper. **1971** *Sunday Australian* 8 Aug. 5/6 Sir Henry's best catch this time was a 10 lb schnapper.

b. (Later examples.)

1944 *Living off Land* vii. 133 Cotton schnapper line. **1947** K. TENNANT *Lost Haven* i. 14 The schnapper boat moored beside..the grey skeleton of the half-built ship.

schnauzer (ʃnau·tsə). [G.] A black or pepper-and-salt wire-haired terrier belonging to the breed so called, which includes large, standard, and miniature dogs distinguished by a stocky, robust build, docked tail, blunt, bearded muzzle, and ears that droop forwards; formerly called the wire-haired pinscher.

1923 *Dog World* Aug. 14/2 A new breed has come to America—the Schnauzer. **1930** *Observer* 9 Feb. 13/2 The German Schnauzers have sterling qualities, though they may not be particularly showy in their close wiry coats. **1957** *New Yorker* 5 Oct. 34/1 For rainy weather, this miniature schnauzer is wearing our ready-made gabardine raincoat. **1968** [see *PINSCHER]. **1970** *Manch. Guardian Weekly* 14 Mar. 4/4 She bought a schnauzer, a placid beast with large brown eyes and a yelp like a police car siren. **1977** *Time Out* 28 Jan.–3 Feb. 64/2 (Advt.), Has own home, Central London and owns beautiful little schnauzer.

schneider¹ (ʃnai·də). *Skat.* Also **Schneider.** [G., lit. 'tailor'.] (See quot. 1949.) Also as *adj.* and *v. trans.*

1886 E. E. LEMCKE *Skat* 7 With 60 points only he loses; with 30 points he is '*Schneider*' or '*geschnitten*' (cut); with no count at all he is '*Schwarz*' (black = whitewashed). Consequently the two hands in opposition to the 'player', scoring jointly 60 points, win the game from player; scoring 30 are out of *Schneider*, but are *Schwarz* with no count. **1909** R. F. FOSTER *Foster's Compl. Hoyle* 420 If he can get 91 points, he wins a double game, which is called *schneider*. *Ibid.* 437 It may be played out to see if he can make schneider or schwarz. **1935** *Encycl. Sports, Games & Pastimes* 553/1 If he scores 91 points he makes his opponents schneider. **1947** *New Compl. Hoyle* 385 If the player wins 91 or more points in play, he is said to *schneider* the opponents and the value of his game is increased. **1949** A. A. OSTROW *Compl. Card Player* 645 Official laws of American skat... The player to be out of schneider must have at least 31 points, the opponents 90. **1975** *Way to Play* 109/1 If the bidder has named suits or grand, he may before the opening lead, declare: a) schneider, ie he aims to win at least 91 trick points; or b) schwarz, ie he aims to take every trick. **1976** *National Skat & Sheepshead Q.* Mar. 18 A grand scores 80 points and possibly 100 if the hand is schneidered.

Schneider² (ʃnai·də). The name of Jacques *Schneider* (1879–1928), French flying enthusiast, used *attrib.* in *Schneider trophy, cup*: the Jacques Schneider Maritime Cup, presented in 1913 by Schneider to the winner of an international competition for seaplanes comprising an air race and seaworthiness trials, and contested annually (with certain exceptions) until won outright by Great Britain in 1931.

[**1912** *Flight* 14 Dec. 1182/1 M. Schneider has offered for international competition a trophy of the value of £1,000, to go to the club which the winning pilot represents.] **1913** *Ibid.* 5 Apr. 395/1 The French team for the forthcoming international contest for the Schneider Cup at Monaco. **1927** A. HUXLEY *Let.* 8 Oct. (1969) 291 Time rushes past as though it were trying to win the Schneider Cup. **1929** *Radio Times* 8 Nov. 395/3 We were testing all the arrangements for the Schneider Trophy relay, making sure that the loudspeaker system at various points round the coast could pick up our broadcast. **1933** *Ann. Reg. 1932* I. 24 After paying a tribute to all who had been concerned in the winning of the Schneider trophy, [the minister] remarked that though in size the Royal Air Force took only fifth place..there was no other better equipped. **1977** *Times* 23 Sept. 12/4, I hope the Schneider Trophy will be given an extra loving dust down at its home in the Science Museum.

schnitzel (ʃni·tzəl). [G.] A veal cutlet, esp. in *Wiener* (vi·nər) *schnitzel*, one coated with egg and breadcrumbs, fried and often garnished with lemon, capers, anchovies, etc., in the Viennese style.

1854 *Pioneer* (San Francisco) Nov. 318 Eggs, coffee, toast, and now and then, a chop or a 'snitzel' is the order given for thousands of people. **1862** *Temple Bar* Nov. 63 After a dinner such as Vienna only can furnish; *e.g.* a delicate soup..a *Wiener Schnitzel* (a savoury cutlet greatly to be recommended)..we take rail at half-past two p.m. **1904** *Adventures of Elizabeth in Rügen* 262 Her eyes were discreetly fixed on a *Wiener Schnitzel* that she was eating with a singular mincingness. **1911** A. FILIPPINI *International Cook Bk.* 144 Arrange a thin slice of lemon, with a twisted anchovy in oil placed over each slice of lemon, on top of each schnitzel. **1936** E. AMBLER *Dark Frontier* vii. 114 They do know how *wiener schnitzel* should be cooked. **1956** [see *ESCALOPE]. **1960** *News Chron.* 23 Feb. 3/2 Swop the porridge and oatcakes for schnitzel and strudel. **1978** *Chicago* June 210/2 The entrées perk one up immediately, though. The schnitzel à la Holstein came with a perfect fried egg and a golden puff of crust.

schnockered (ʃnǫ·kəd), *ppl. a. U.S. colloq.* Humorous var. of *SNOCKERED *ppl. a.*

1955 *Amer. Speech* XXX. 303 *Schnockered; way up*,.. drunk. **1976** *Verbatim* Feb. 15/1 George really got schnockered at Judy's party. **1977** B. GARFIELD *Recoil* iii. 45 Bradleigh took the empty glass. 'That's probably enough. You don't want to get schnockered.'

schnook (ʃnuk). *U.S. colloq.* Also **schnuck, shnook.** [app. Yiddish: perh. repr. Yiddish *shnuk* snout, or f. G. *schnucke* a small sheep.] A dupe, a sucker; a simpleton, a 'dope'; a pitiful wretch.

[**1943** S. J. PERELMAN *Let.* 7 Apr. in G. Marx *Groucho Lett.* (1967) 190 It's the story of a small schnükel of a barber who accidentally brings a statue of Venus to life.] **1948** H. L. MENCKEN *Amer. Lang.* Suppl. II. 757 *Schnuck*.., a customer easily persuaded, a sucker. **1955** N. MAILER *Deer Park* xii. 136 I'd be making a stinking seven hundred and fifty a week now like all those poor exploited schnooks. **1959** R. CHANDLER in Gardiner & Walker *R. Chandler Speaking* (1962) 262 Why does he want to see me so badly that he has to send a couple of shnooks after me? **1964** S. BELLOW *Herzog* 29 This shnook of a chiropodist—what a hellcat *he* married. **1975** A. BERGMAN *Hollywood & Le Vine* xiii. 187 It was all pretty fascinating for a Sunnyside schnook like me. **1980** W. SAFIRE in *N.Y. Times Mag.* 2 Aug. 8 To be self-conscious about the possibility of error..is to be a nerd, a schnook and a wimp.

Schnorchel, schnorkel, Schnorkel, varr. *SNORKEL.

schnorrer. Delete ‖ and add: Also **shnorrer.** Now in extended *U.S.* use, a beggar, layabout, scrounger, good-for-nothing.

1934 E. POUND *Eleven New Cantos* XXXV. 24 The tale of the perfect schnorrer. **1959** [see *LAYABOUT]. **1962** J. D. SALINGER *Franny & Zooey* 136, I had lunch with him one day a couple of weeks ago. A real schnorrer, but sort of likable. **1977** *New Yorker* 24 Oct. 38/3 Investigate your own pants, you schnorrer. **1981** J. BARNETT *Firing Squad* xiv. 190 A right pair of miserable schnorrers I've got here.

So **s(c)hnorr** *v. trans.* and *intr.*, to obtain by begging; to beg, sponge (*off*).

1892 I. ZANGWILL *Childr. Ghetto* III. II. vii. 125 Your father..stood in the Lane with lemons, and *schnorred* half-crowns of my father. *Ibid.* xii. 221 But isn't it *schnorring* to be dependent on strangers? **1894** —— *King of Schnorrers* iii. 67 Even if you can prove you can *schnorr* enough to keep a wife, I do not bind myself to consent. **1964** W. MARKFIELD *To Early Grave* iv. 76 Box after box. *Shnorred*, with cunning and craft, from tough-minded Cousin Schmeilick. **1968** *Encounter* Sept. 30/1, I can go out and within an hour *shnorr* the entire amount I owe you. **1975** *Publishers Weekly* 19 May 90/1, I hope to shnorr off a couple of Scottish landowners I've met here.

schnozz (ʃnǫz). *U.S. slang.* Also **schnoz.** [app. Yiddish: cf. G. *schnauze* snout, and see next.] **a.** The nose, nostril.

1942 A. KOBER in *New Yorker* 13 June 19/1, I see she's not occupied excep' she's powderin' her schnoz. **1940** L. SHELLY *Hepcats Jive Talk Dict.* 17/1 *Schnozz*,..the nose. **1967** P. WELLES *Babyhip* xx. 131 Mr Cox stuffed a rusty paper clip up his schnozz and broke his nose. **1973** R. HAYES *Hungarian Game* iii. 28 'You remember what our boy looks like?' 'Gray hair, widow's peak, big schnozz, red ski parka and no luggage.'

b. In fig. phr. (*right*) *on the schnozz*, precisely, exactly, on the dot (of time).

1949 W. R. BURNETT *Asphalt Jungle* xx. 130 Headlights flashed into the parking-lot, and then went out. 'This is us, I think,' said Louis, 'and right on the schnoz.' **1967** 'E. QUEEN' *Face to Face* xxx. 140 Twenty minutes to twelve on the schnozz.

schnozzle (ʃnǫ·z'l). *U.S. slang.* [pseudo-Yiddish: cf. Yiddish *shnabl* beak, and see prec.] The nose. Similarly (*joc.*) **s(c)hnozzo·la** [cf. *-OLA].

Esp. applied as a nickname to the U.S. entertainer James Francis ('Jimmy') Durante (1893–1980).

1930 *Variety* 26 Feb. 24/5 It's the medium for the screen debut of Jimmy Durante, he of the large schozzola [*sic*]. *Ibid.* 56/2 'Roadhouse Night'..brings Jimmy Durante to the screen. Admirers of his peculiar madness usually fear for its reception by a general public..but the Schnozzle's first screen appearance removes any doubts that might have been entertained. **1937** J. DURANTE in *Amer. Mag.* May 61/1 A youngster like me whose schnozzle could be seen two blocks away. *Ibid.* 61/2 When we admit our schnozzles..we begin to laugh. **1937** in Wentworth & Flexner *Dict. Amer. Slang* (1960) 448/1 A broken nose epidemic hit Dennison. In early contests 5 players broke their schnozzolas. **1959** J. LUDWIG in *Tamarack Rev.* Summer 24 What a way to louse up this new magenta outfit—streaming eyes, a shiny shnozzola! **1977** *Listener* 9 June 746/2 Hebrew amens are breathed through Yiddish schnozzles. **1981** *Times Lit. Suppl.* 15 May 535/2 He is sunk in the multiplied particularities of his vivid surroundings. Not least, in the pongs to which his great schnozzle.. is peculiarly susceptible.

‖ **Schnurkeramik** (ʃnū·rkerā:mik). *Archæol.* Also with small initial. [G., f. *schnur* string, cord + *keramik* ceramics, pottery.] = *corded ware* s.v. *CORDED *ppl. a.* 3 b.

1902 J. ABERCROMBY in *Jrnl. Anthrop. Inst.* XXXII. 391 In Germany there is a class of ceramic which goes by the name of *Schnurkeramik*, from its being almost exclusively ornamented by cord-impressions. **1928, 1950** [see *CORDED *ppl. a.* 3 b]. **1954** S. PIGGOTT *Neolithic Cultures* xi. 344 Comparable ornament appears on pots in a *schnurkeramik* context from Switzerland.

Schoenbergian (ʃönbɛ̄·ɹgiăn), *a.* and *sb.* Also **Schönbergian.** [-IAN.] **A.** *adj.* Of, pertaining to, or characteristic of the Austrian composer Arnold *Schoenberg* (1874–1951) or his music. **B.** *sb.* An admirer or adherent of Schoenberg; an exponent of Schoenberg's music. Hence **Schoe·nbergism** *rare*, the advocacy or practice of Schoenbergian techniques of musical composition.

1922 C. GRAY in *Mus. & Lett.* III. 79 Side by side with a daring experiment like Op. 6, No. 1, *Traumleben*, with its characteristic late-Schönbergian voice part. **1931** [see *DIATONICISM]. **1934** C. LAMBERT *Music Ho!* v. 330 His earlier works..show signs of a Schönbergian ruthlessness. **1947** *Penguin Music Mag.* Dec. 21 An extraordinary combination of the traditional Italian lyrical *cantilena* writing with the Schönbergian technique. **1951** Schoenbergism [see *DODECAPHONIC *a.*]. **1959** *Times* 13 Feb. 13/4 Other names in these programmes are those of Egon Wellesz, a lapsed Schönbergian..and Karlheinz Stockhausen. **1976** *Gramophone* Aug. 324/1 He had been taking a crash course in early Schoenbergian expressionism. **1978** P. GRIFFITHS *Conc. Hist. Mod. Music* iv. 46 Apart from that the work is not at all Schoenbergian.

Schoenflies (ʃɔ̄·nflīs). *Cryst.* The name of Arthur *Schoenflies* (1853–1928), German mathematician, who listed the 230 space groups in 1891 (*Krystallsysteme und Krystallstruktur*), used *attrib.* with reference to the system of nomenclature which he devised for them.

1934 W. P. DAVEY *Study of Crystal Struct.* viii. 222 Of the four sets of symbols listed in the table it is recommended that only the Schoenflies and the Wyckoff be used... The Schoenflies symbols have the great advantage of world-wide use. **1961** TERPSTRA & CODD *Crystallometry* iv. 132 The symbol 1̄ thus corresponds to the Schoenflies C_i. **1970** A. J. WILSON *Elem. X-Ray Crystallogr.* 225 For space groups the Schoenflies symbols are quite inconvenient. *Ibid.*, There is also a Schoenflies notation for the Bravais lattices, which is used even less than the symmetry notation.

schoepite (sχə̄·pəit). *Min.* [f. the name of Alfred *Schoep* (1881–1966), Belgian mineralogist + -ITE[1].] A hydrated form of uranium trioxide found as yellow to brown tabular or prismatic orthorhombic crystals as an alteration product of uranium ore; three phases (schoepite I, II, and III) are known, differing slightly in composition, colour, and morphology.

1923 T. L. WALKER in *Amer. Mineralogist* VIII. 69 As this mineral appears to be quite distinct in optical and crystallographic properties from all known uranium minerals, the writer proposes to name it schoepite in honor of Professor Alfred Schoep, of the University of Ghent, who has contributed so much to our knowledge of the secondary uranium minerals from the Congo. **1960** *Ibid.* XLV. 1034 Crystals of schoepite that are apparently single yield multiple diffraction patterns... These..correspond to the presence of two out of three possible distinct orthorhombic phases in parallel intergrowth in the crystal. The three phases are designated schoepite I, II and III. **1965** *Ibid.* L. 236 Crystals of schoepite commonly occur with an amber-brown core completely or partially surrounded by a derivative golden-yellow rim which retains the morphology of the original crystal... The brown part consists chiefly of schoepite I, and the yellow part mostly of schoepite II or schoepite III.

schoff, var. SCOFF *sb.*[2] in Dict. and Suppl.

schol (skǫl). Colloq. abbreviation of SCHOLARSHIP (sense 2).

1899 *Captain* Nov. 115/2 Wardour had licked Eccles and forfeited the 'schol'. **1958** B. HAMILTON *Too Much of Water* xi. 247, I won a schol to the House. **1965** J. SYMONS *Belting Inheritance* ii. 35 'The old thing's *delighted* about the schol,' Uncle Miles had written.

‖ **schola cantorum** (skōᵘ·lă kæntǭ·rv̆m). [med.L. = school of singers.] **a.** The choir-school attached to a cathedral or monastery (orig. the Papal Choir at Rome, established by Gregory the Great (*c* 540–604)). **b.** Used as the title of various groups of singers.

1782 C. BURNEY *Gen. Hist. Mus.* II. i. 16 Fleury, in his *Hist. Eccl.*..gives a circumstantial account of the *Scola Cantorum*, instituted by St. Gregory. **1887** E. L. TAUNTON *Hist. & Growth Church Music* iv. 39 The elder members of the Schola Cantorum, as it was called, had the title of Subdeacons. **1902** E. DICKINSON *Music in Hist. of Western Church* v. 181 The Schola Cantorum of Paris..is exerting a strong influence upon church music. **1929** E. C. THOMAS *Lay Folks' Hist. Liturgy* II. xiv. 223 The members of the schola cantorum to which the lectors belonged had no other function than that of singing. **1941** G. CHASE *Music of Spain* xi. 168 Morera..has written..choral arrangements of Catalan folk songs, some of which have been performed by the Schola Cantorum of New York. **1964** P. F. ANSON *Bishops at Large* x. 475 The ladies of the *schola cantorum* looked fetching in their red gowns and caps.

scholar. Add: **5. a.** Further appositive examples, as *scholar-official, -performer, -poet, publisher*.

1978 *Nagel's Encycl.-Guide: China* 323 All the prestige and importance of the scholar-officials came from their knowledge of characters. **1978** C. HOGWOOD in J. M. Thomson *Future of Early Music in Britain* 16 Much of the scholarly evidence is so easily assimilated by the performer that you have to invent a halfway category of the scholar-performer or the research-performer. **1928** J. BAILEY *Let.* 23 July (1935) 289 Do you know Hölderlin, the scholar-poet? **1979** R. P. GRAVES (*title*) A. E. Housman: the scholar-poet. **1963** *Times Lit. Suppl.* 26 Apr. 312/2 Dr. Mardersteig's position in typographical history as at once an artist-printer and a scholar-publisher.

scholarment (skǫ·lăɹmĕnt). *nonce-wd.* [-MENT.] Scholardom; scholars collectively.

1922 JOYCE *Ulysses* 416 Toil on, labour like a bandog and let scholarment and all Malthusiasts go hang.

scholarship. Add: **2. b.** *spec.* (though *loosely*) The 'eleven-plus' examination or the entrance to a grammar school made possible by reaching a satisfactory standard.

1959 in I. & P. Opie *Lore & Lang. Schoolch.* xi. 227 On the day I went to sit the scholarship I took the little owl and wrapped it up in a handkerchief in my pocket for luck. **1959** I. & P. OPIE *Ibid.* xvi. 356 Today the sharpest feeling is between the grammar schools and the secondary moderns, that is, between those who have gained a scholarship and those who have not in the eleven-plus examination. **1966** J. PARTRIDGE *Middle School* iv. 59 In Middle School the eleven plus is still viewed as 'the scholarship'.

3. *attrib.* and *Comb.*, as (sense 2) *scholarship boy, -candidate, child, class, exam, kid, paper, system*; **scholarship level** = *S-level* s.v. *S I. 4 a.

1959 T. S. ELIOT *Elder Statesman* I. 31 A scholarship boy from an unknown grammar school. **1980** R. F. FOSTER in Lyons & Hawkins *Ireland under Union* 254 'Scholarship boys' in politics. **1965** N. COGHILL in J. Gibb *Light on C. S. Lewis* 65 What it was learned to know in 1950 will be expected of scholarship-candidates in 2000. **1964** D. HOLBROOK *English for the Rejected* 4 The attempt to turn every child into a 'scholarship child' fit for academic education. **1966** J. PARTRIDGE *Middle School* v. 79 In the Junior School a 'scholarship' class soon emerges. **1959** in I. & P. Opie *Lore & Lang. Schoolch.* xi. 227, I took it to the scholarship exam for the grammar school and I passed. **1977** M. WALKER *National Front* 8 My education as a scholarship kid who went to grammar schools and won a scholarship to Oxford. **1947, 1963** Scholarship level [see *ORDINARY *a.* 5 e]. **1832** J. ROMILLY *Diary* 26 Apr. (1967) 11 Worked at the Scholarship papers all day. **1927** CARR-SAUNDERS & JONES *Social Structure Eng. & Wales* xi. 119 We must also attempt to analyse the working of the free-place and scholarship system.

scholasticized (skolæ·stisəizd), *ppl. a.* [f. as SCHOLASTICIZING *ppl. a.*: see -ED[1].] Imbued with or influenced by scholasticism.

1923 C. SINGER in *Edin. Rev.* Jan. 101 Dioscorides, the drug-monger, appealed to scholasticised minds for centuries. **1927** W. R. INGE *Protestantism* 12 This philosophy, already scholasticised by Proclus, became..a coherent body of doctrine.

scholzite (ʃǫ·ltsəit). *Min.* [ad. G. *scholzit* (H. Strunz 1948: see H. Strunz *Mineralogische Tabellen* (ed. 2, 1949) 164, and in *Fortschritte der Mineral.* (1950) XXVII. 31), f. the name of Adolf *Scholz*, 20th-cent. German mineral collector and industrialist: see -ITE[1].] A hydrated basic phosphate of calcium and zinc, $Ca_3Zn(PO_4)_2(OH)_2.H_2O$, occurring as a secondary mineral in colourless to greyish monoclinic crystals.

1950 *Chem. Abstr.* XLIV. 9306 (*heading*) Scholzite, a new mineral. **1974** *Mineral. Mag.* XXXIX. 686 Scholzite.. is the most common and conspicuous phosphate mineral in the mineralized zones at Reaphook Hill [in the Flinders Ranges, South Australia]. It occurs in voids as sprays of radiating white to colourless prismatic needles up to 3 cm long..or as interpenetrating groups of white fibres.

Schönbergian, var. *SCHOENBERGIAN *a.* and *sb.*

Schönlein (ʃō̈·nləin). *Path.* The name of Johann Lucas *Schönlein* (1793–1864), German physician, used in the possessive and occas. *attrib.* to designate a form of purpura associated with arthritis (described by him in 1837 (*Path. und Therapie* II. 48–49)); also used in combination with the name of *Henoch* (see *HENOCH).

Schönlein's disease is now regarded as one form of Henoch–Schönlein purpura.

1892 W. OSLER *Princ. & Pract. Med.* ii. 318 The diagnosis of Schönlein's disease offers no difficulty... Schönlein's peliosis is thought by most writers to be of rheumatic origin. **1937** *Arch. Dermatol. & Syphilol.* XXXV. 847 (*caption*) Photomicrograph of a section from a lesion of purpura affecting the leg only of a patient with Schönlein–Henoch's purpura. **1943** ORMSBY & MONTGOMERY *Dis. Skin* (ed. 6) ii. 501 Peck describes the histological changes of four cases of Schönlein–Henoch's purpura as resembling those produced by venom. **1948**, etc. [see *HENOCH]. **1974** *Encycl. Brit. Micropædia* VIII. 972/1 He [*sc.* Schönlein] was the first to describe the minute hemorrhages of the skin occurring in cases of anaphylactoid (allergic) purpura (Schönlein–Henoch purpura) and purpura rheumatica (Schönlein's disease; 1837), characterized by the appearance on the skin of small purple spots, by swelling pain, and tenderness of joints, and frequently by swelling of the hands, feet, or eyelids.

school, *sb.*[1] Add: **I. 1. c.** *to go to school with*: for † read *rare* and add later example.

1959 *Listener* 3 Dec. 1005/1 Even those who cannot accept it entirely must assuredly go to school with him.

j. high school. (Examples of use in England.) Cf. *-SCHOOLER.

1875 A. MCDOWALL *Let.* 9 Oct. in V. E. Stack *Oxford High School* (1963) I. 1 At a special Council meeting..it was resolved..to open the Oxford High School on Wednesday November 3rd. **1893** WYLIE & BRISCOE *Popular Hist. of Nottingham* xii. 122 In..1868, the Free Grammar School was removed..to..Arboretum Street, and its designation was changed to that of 'The High School'. **1901** E. NESBIT *Wouldbegoods* i. 4 After the holidays the girls went to the Blackheath High School. **1933** V. BRITTAIN *Testament of Youth* I. i. 37 In the months before I went up to Oxford,.. I often privately condemned my parents for not sending me to Cheltenham, or Roedean, or even to an ordinary High School, where practised authorities would have saved me from the fret of wrestling with academic mysteries. **1970** G. TREASE *Nottingham* xviii. 213 The High School governors seemed boldly original in choosing a scientist,..an appointment for a long time almost unique among schools represented on the Headmasters' Conference. **1974** M. SPACKMAN *Hist. Oxford Central Girls' School & Cheney Girls' Grammar School* iii. 43 In most years, two or more girls..entered for and gained one of these places at either the High School or Milham Ford.

4. b. *the school of hard knocks*, the experience of a life of hardship, considered as a means of instruction. *U.S. slang.*

1912 ADE *Knocking Neighbors* 24 They had been brought up in the School of Hard Knocks. **1931** *Kansas City Star* 23 Oct. 36/5 Fraternity brothers in the school of hard knocks. **1953** *Sun* (Baltimore) 5 Sept. 10/6 He has been through the school of hard knocks, and battled his way up with his fists to the top of fistiana. **1980** G. V. HIGGINS *Kennedy for Defense* xx. 178, I learned my business in the school of hard knocks.

5. a. (Later examples.) Also, in descriptions of works of art, in phr. *school of* (an artist), used to designate an anonymous work produced in the school of a particular artist.

1891 R. FRY *Let.* 17 May (1972) I. 145, I find..the Venetian School of painting far more instructive than the Florentine. **1903** *Ibid.* 16 Mar. 207 This, which was called 'School of Lorenzo', is Piero all over. **1958** *Spectator* 15 Aug. 219/2 An American school-of-Chayevsky drama about a jailbird's wife. **1976** D. FRANCIS *In Frame* ix. 135 Although they were original oil paintings, they were basically second rate. The sort sold as 'school of' because the artists hadn't bothered to sign them. **1981** M. SPARK *Loitering with Intent* ii. 56 She said, 'Is that a real Degas you have in your room?' 'School of,' I said.

b. (Earlier example.)

1749 SMOLLETT tr. *Le Sage's Gil Blas* IV. i. 6 Mr. Doctor ..as I am a grand nephew to a physician of the old school give me leave to revolt with you against chymical medicines.

c. In extended use of sense 5 a, in phr. *school of thought* (also † *opinion*). Also used (freq. *absol.*) with 'school' considered impersonally, a particular type of doctrine or practice as followed by such a body of persons.

1864 [see sense 5 a in Dict.]. **1873** *Illustr. London News* 26 July 70/2 It will not be necessary to utter a single word that need occasion offence to either of those 'schools of thought' into which The Church of England is divided. **1892** *New Review* May 571 He is a 'gentleman and scholar', ..'trained in a liberal school of thought'. **1909** A. BERGET *Conquest of Air* II. v. 230 We are confronted by two schools of aviating apparatus: the American school..which demands everything of the aviator, and the French school.. which requires..the minimum from the pilot. **1927** *Public Opinion* 28 Feb. 179/1 There is in philosophy a school of thought christened by Professor William James with the name Pragmatism. **1940** *Manch. Guardian Weekly* 5 Apr. 270 With two schools of thought existing in France on the subject of Russia, Molotoff's speech,..has produced two different sets of reactions. **1977** R. WILLIAMS *Marxism & Lit.* II. iv. 97 The theory became at once a cultural programme and a critical school. **1979** L. KALLEN *Introducing C.B. Greenfield* xii. 148 There's a school of thought that considers benevolent paternalism a little sick.

6. a. Delete † *Obs.* and add later examples. **b.** (Earlier example.)

1842 *Impositions practised by Vagrants* 12 These lurkers generally go in schools, (companies) and will obtain from One to Two Pounds daily. **1882** *Sydney Slang Dict.* 7/2 *School*, company of gamblers, mob of sharpers, and those who prey on the public. **1911** L. STONE *Jonah* II. vi. 213 He could think of nothing but the two-up school, which had swallowed all his spare money before he was married. **1946** A. MARSHALL *These are my People* 83 If I got into a school with some of the mugs round here they'd be penniless in two hours. **1952** H. INNES *Campbell's Kingdom* II. 230 Four of the boys had started a poker school. **1976** J. R. L. ANDERSON *Death in Desert* v. 87 Sometimes a few of the chaps would get a card school going after supper.

c. A group of persons drinking together in a bar or public house, and taking turns to buy the drinks.

1890 BARRÈRE & LELAND *Dict. Slang* II. 206/2 *School*,.. any small gathering of people generally bent on pleasure, as a school of drinkers in a public house or canteen. Much used by soldiers. **1911** R. MACAIRE *Disease & Remedy* 11 A 'school' got more from those that did not drink. **1951** *Landfall* V. 22 [She] goes across to join another school by the wall. **1963** W. H. PEARSON *Coal Flat* i. 21 He came up to the school Rogers was drinking with. **1971** D. LEES *Rainbow Conspiracy* v. 72, I..ordered a pint of bitter for myself. I didn't want to get into a school and I needed to think.

II. 7. a. Now in revived use within U.S. and some British universities (esp. those of recent foundation), a department, faculty, or course of study in a college or university. (Perh. influenced by senses 9 and 10 in Dict.)

In the U.S. *school* is often used to designate either a department devoted to one subject or a grouping of several subject departments. It is also the standard designation for an institution providing postgraduate instruction in a particular subject (as *law school, medical school*, etc.). In recently founded universities in the U.K. *school* has been used to designate a department teaching a range of subjects traditionally taught separately.

1727 *Statutes Wm. & Mary Coll.* in Hofstadter & Smith *Amer. Higher Educ.* (1961) I. I. x. 43 Let there be four schools assigned within the college precincts. *Ibid.* 44 In the philosophy school we appoint two masters or professors. **1772** J. WITHERSPOON *Address Inhabitants Jamaica* in *Ibid.* II. x. 144 Two at least of the Professors of the justly celebrated Medical School lately founded in Philadelphia. **1835** J. MARTIN *Descr. of Virginia* 82 The different branches of science and literature..taught [at the University of Virginia] are styled *schools*. **1871** L. H. BAGG *Four Years at Yale* 32 Connected with the college are four professional 'schools' or 'departments', of which..the oldest is the Theological. **1894** *Rep. Commissioners Gresham Univ. London* p. xix, in *Parl. Papers 1893–4* (C. 7259) XXXI. 807 We propose that each of the teaching institutions which complies with the necessary conditions shall be admitted, either as a whole or in certain departments, as a School of the University [of London], that is as a School at which University courses of instruction are to be pursued. **1910** *Encycl. Brit.* XIII. 39/1 The medical school [of Harvard University]..dates from 1782, the law school from 1817, the divinity school..from 1819, and the dental school.. from 1867. **1949** *Cavalier Daily* (Univ. of Va.) 22 Oct. 1/3 Williams graduated from the University in 1949 and is now in his second year of medical school at Johns Hopkins University in Baltimore. **1964** A. BRIGGS in D. Daiches *Idea of New University* iv. 62 The Schools [of the University of Sussex] were envisaged not as super-departments, to which 'subjects' were attached, but as centres of linked studies, some of which would be shared with other Schools. **1971** E. Ashby *Any Person, any Study* ii. 71 Some British universities, in their enthusiasm to 'redraw the map of knowledge', have abolished departments and put in their place 'schools of study' (e.g. European studies, African studies, which include the history, economics, politics, language and literature, and geography of these regions). **1972** J. Ben-David *Amer. Higher Educ.* vi. 87 Intellectually the graduate school had become the decisive influence in higher education by the beginning of this century. **1976** *Bull. Yale Univ.* 30 Dec. 163 The courses of study in Yale University are offered in twelve schools, as follows. Yale College (1701), which is the undergraduate school, the Graduate School (1847), School of Medicine (1810), Divinity School, [etc.].

f. *U.S.* A college or university. Also in phrases *to go* († *put*) *to school*, to attend (send to) college or university.

1767 P. V. Fithian *Jrnl. & Lett.* (1900) I A letter to my Father, begging him to put me to School. **1904** *Delineator* Oct. 657 College pillows..of crimson, with 'Harvard', n white letters; of orange, with 'Princeton' in black, and similarly with the names and colours of other schools. **1957** A. Buchwald *Brave Coward* 54, I am more American than you are. I even went to school on the GI Bill of Rights, in Rome. I got an honorable discharge from the Army. **1962** —— *How much is that in Dollars?* p. ix, When friends.. assured me the streets of Paris were paved with mattresses, I decided to finish up my last year of schooling there... But while we were going to school..Congress passed the monumental Marshall Plan. **1967** *Boston Sunday Herald* 26 Mar. II. 5/6 (*caption*) Oxford crewman J. K. Mullard waves jubilantly after victory over traditional rival Cambridge... Oxford won by three lengths in 113th meeting between the schools. **1977** I. Shaw *Beggarman, Thief* I. vi. 76 The proms at which he played the trumpet in the band, to help pay his way through school. **1978** *Sci. Amer.* July 15/2 The latter experience convinced him that his interest lay in research; he therefore went back to school, acquiring his Ph.D. from Stanford University in 1965.

VI. 16. a. *school-age* (earlier and later examples), *assembly, atlas, bag, beret, blazer, blouse, bus* (also *-busing*), *cap* (hence *-capped* adj.), *curriculum, -desk, dinner, education, fee* (later examples), *holiday, librarian, -life,* (earlier example), *lunch, mag, magazine, meal, nurse, party, play, -poem, prefect, prize* (earlier example), *reader, register, rule, satchel, scarf, secretary, slang, song, subject, system, -teacher* (later examples) (hence *-teacherish* adj.), *tie, treat, trunk, uniform, wear, year* (later examples).

1741 S. Richardson *Familiar Lett.* cxxx. 168 Nor is the Consequence of this Defect confin'd to the School-age, as I may call it. **1939** M. S. Rice *Working-Class Wives* iii. 66 The children of school age come under the School medical services. **1972** G. Sereny *Case M. Bell* II. i. 80 Fernwood Reception Centre..is used for children of school age who come there primarily because of sudden family emergencies. **1974** *Sat. Rev. World* (U.S.) 2 Nov. 24/3, 95 per-cent of school-age Eskimos are in school. **1932** Mrs. J. Murray (*title*) Incidental music for use at school assembly. Arranged by I. R. Davies. **1977** J. Aiken *Last Movement* ix. 166 Opera and large gatherings ran each other close for first place among her dislikes. How did she stand school assemblies? **1815** J. A. Cummings (*title*) A school atlas, accompanying ancient and modern geography. **1885** C. M. Yonge *Two Sides of Shield* I. vi. 100 The elder boys' old school atlases. **1979** H. McLeave *Borderline Case* xvi. 155 On a school atlas Dr. Li charted the progress of the disease. **1895** *Montgomery Ward Catal.* Spring & Summer 118/3 Waterproof School Bags; made of enameled cloth, with flap and leather shoulder strap. **1913** P. Geddes *Masque of Anc. Learning* 3 Boy enters, swinging his school-bag. **1977** C. Fremlin *Spider-Orchid* xiii. 90 She'd dumped her school bag on the floor. **1967** M. Drabble *Jerusalem the Golden* iii. 51 The girls in her class..regarded her as relatively plain.. with no notion of how to twist a school beret or hitch a school skirt. **1975** 'J. Bell' *Victim* xiii. 140 A small girl stepped out. She held a school beret in one hand. **1913** J. Vaizey *College Girl* v. 62 The boys wore flannel trousers with school blazers and caps. **1978** A. Price *'44 Vintage* vi. 74 His school blazer..had been too small for him. **1932** D. C. Minter *Mod. Needlecraft* 253/1 *School or Gym Blouse*... Long sleeves for school type, short for gym blouse. **1979** K. Conlon *Move in Game* I. i. 14 Mrs Brennan wrote: 'butter, eggs, shoe polish, school blouse, [etc.].' **1908** *Suburban Life* July 48/1 (*caption*) The school bus. **1939** G. Household *Rogue Male* 110, I saw the school-bus and an occasional car. **1976** P. R. White *Planning for Public Transport* i. 25 A local authority..may also be an important customer in its own right, by allocating subsidies, and contracts for school bus services. **1974** *Times* 25 Oct. 10/5 The sensitive issue of school busing in Boston. **1908** *Magnet* I. 1, His hair was thick and curly, and there was a school-cap stuck on the back of his head. **1930** Auden *Poems* 18 The rest as jury, wearing school caps. **1975** *Listener* 4 Dec. 747/3 Tell us that story about going to St John's Wood. Well, I had a letter, and went up wearing a school cap. **1933** M. Lowry *Ultramarine* ii. 97 Mothers with warm-smelling furs are fussing with their school-capped sons. **1973** M. Russell *Double Hit* ii. 15 A school-capped boy bicycled out of the main gates. **1913** C. Mackenzie *Sinister St.* I. II. i. 156 He taught Geography and English History and English Literature, so far as the school curriculum allowed him. **1981** *Listener* 1 Jan. 22/3 His comments on the school curriculum contain a germ of truth. **1842** Dickens *Amer. Notes* I. iii. 75 A little enclosure, made of school-desks and forms. **1953** A. Clarke *Moment next to Nothing* I. ii. 29 I'll clear the table, have our school-desk ready. **1835** Dickens *Sk. by Boz* (1836) 1st Ser. I. 26 They were three long graces in drapery, with the addition—like a school-dinner—of another long grace afterwards. **1963** *New Society* 22 Aug. 5/1 That inevitable horror, the school dinner. **1973** J. Burrows *Like Evening Gone* x. 115 She used to help with school dinners..serving and washing up. **1731** J. Creichton *Mem.* 10 Having lost the Benefit of a thorough School-Education..the Reader cannot reasonably expect to be much pleased with my Style. **1848** Mill *Pol. Econ.* I. II. xiv. 463 The earnings of.. any labour which requires school education, are at a monopoly rate. **1873** C. M. Yonge *Pillars of House* I. iii. 64 The school-fee was a mere trifle, but Mr. Ryder would willingly have boarded and lodged the boy. **1958** 'Castle' & 'Hailey' *Flight into Danger* 17 Pay off the bills—the new water tank, school fees, instalments on the Chev. **1973** J. Leasor *Host of Extras* ii. 32 He'd be selling the car to pay his son's school fees. **1939** School holiday [see *nursery tea* s.v. *nursery 8 a]. **1981** J. Robin *Elmdon* xi. 224 A private house, occupied in the school holidays by the wife of a business-man in Baghdad. **1920** B. M. Peacock (*title*) A school and club librarians' handbook. **1978** J. Irving *World according to Garp* ii. 28 It was a habit among the school librarians, upon recognizing that they didn't have a book which someone sought, to say, 'Perhaps the infirmary has it.' **1721** M. Cave *Let.* 27 Nov. in M. M. Verney *Verney Lett. of Eighteenth Cent.* (1930) II. xxiii. 71 The apprehension of Tommy's weak Constitution I find very grevious, inferring that he is unable to undergo a School Life. **1949** M. Mead *Male & Female* xvi. 330 As school-lunches develop, the home with school-age children is deserted all day long. **1980** *Times* 10 Sept. 8/1 Changes [are] taking place in the school meals service... Many parents are weighing up the relative merits of school lunches versus packed ones. **1960** L. Durrell *Let.* in *Spirit of Place* (1969) 153 The boys of King's School..asked for an article for the school mag. **1976** *Listener* 8 Apr. 452/4 It is very difficult to write about school, and the tone of the school mag is not wholly avoided. **1856** C. M. Yonge *Daisy Chain* II. v. 383, I got leave to send a ballad..to that school magazine... It was actually inserted. **1939** C. Isherwood *Goodbye to Berlin* 311 The newspapers are becoming more and more like copies of a school magazine. **1963** A. Heron *Towards Quaker View of Sex* iii. 23 The occasional poems which seek entry in the columns of the school magazine. **1948** F. Le G. Clark (*title*) The social history of the School Meal service. **1973** *Times* 5 Oct. 4/5 A [parliamentary] resolution called for..free school meals. **1912** *Q. Rev.* July 57 Enormous improvements.. have been effected in the environment of the nation since that time. A full account of these is here impossible but it may be said that they include..the appointment of..district and school nurses. **1976** J. Philips *Backlash* (1977) III. i. 122 If..the school nurse..came, I was to tell her to give me some first aid. **1803** T. Lawrence *Let.* 28 Jan. in D. E. Williams *Life & Corr. Sir T. Lawrence* (1831) I. 231 We all sat down like a Rugby school party, but rather more vociferous. **1968** J. Sangster *Touchfeather* ii. 11, I went [to Berlin] with a school party... We stayed for five days..visiting the museums. **1976** H. Tracy *Death in Reserve* xviii. 136 He was told that there were parties of Boy Scouts..and a school party due next week. **1933** E. K. Chambers *Eng. Folk-Play* 187 It is not to be supposed that, after the Reformation and the growth of the professional travelling companies, local plays..ceased to be performed... Some are school-plays produced by the local Holophernes. Some are May games. **1972** *Guardian* 17 Aug. 10/6 It is impossible not to wish him well..like you would a child on sports day or in a school play. **1973** J. R. L. Anderson *Death on Rocks* iii. 62 She's gone with the kids to a school play. **1922** Joyce *Ulysses* 167 That last pagan king of Ireland Cormac in the schoolpoem choked himself. **1933** R. Tuve *Seasons & Months* iii. 75 *Cuculus*, above all *Philomela* (familiar as the subject of various 'school-poems'). **1949** E. Coxhead *Wind in West* vii. 178 He who had been the naughty child was now the school prefect. **1975** P. D. James *Black Tower* ii. 35 The old insistent arguments spoken in that confident school prefect's voice. **1853** C. Brontë *Villette* I. iii. 54 Graham, it chanced, was at that time greatly preoccupied about some school-prize, for which he was competing. **1835** H. A. Hansard (*title*) Souter's second school reader. **1940** J. Buchan *Memory Hold-the-Door* 194 *Prester John*.. has since become a school-reader in many languages. **1981** E. Hay *Sambo Sahib* viii. 110 Helen [Bannerman].. was delighted..that some of her books had been selected as school readers. **1973** J. Burrows *Like Evening Gone* vi. 73 There were forty-three names on the school register. **1943** G. Greene *Ministry of Fear* III. ii. 192 Excited like a boy breaking a school rule. **1978** F. Weldon *Praxis* vii. 36 School rules forbade conversation between girls of different age groups. **1907** *Yesterday's Shopping* (1969) 325/2 School Satchels. Waterproof Brown Canvas. **1972** J. Fleming *Alas Poor Father* i. 7 Picking up the school satchel, he hooked it over his arm. **1907** E. Nesbit *Enchanted Castle* iii. 90 The crimson school-scarf that had supported his white flannels. **1971** A. Price *Alamut Ambush* x. 119 Carelessly hung coats and school scarves on the row of wooden pegs. **1958** J. Townsend *Young Devils* vi. 52, I was shown into his room by a cheerful middle-aged school secretary. **1977** J. Aiken *Last Movement* i. 24 Mother..had asked if Gina would be interested in the job of school secretary. **1900** Farmer *Public School Word-Bk.* p. v, It would, however, seem almost necessary to emphasise that this Word-Book is not, *per se*, a dictionary of school slang. **1934** Priebsch & Collinson *German Lang.* II. v. 263 A word or two may be added on German school-slang (*Pennälersprache*). **1975** D. Durrant *With my Little Eye* xviii. 181 Patty's coarse, cruel, school slang bitchery. **1934** M. V. Hughes *London Child of Seventies* vi. 68 Another treat to me was the school song ('Homo plantat'). **1974** *Listener* 17 Jan. 84/1 E. E. Bowen and John Farmer started the collection of Harrow School Songs, in the 1870s. **1922** H. E. Palmer *Everyday Sentences in Spoken Eng.* p. v, English is no longer either an abhorred school-subject nor a fascinating literary hobby. **1977** *Grimsby Even. Tel.* 5 May 5/2 She said..that it could easily be possible to make road safety a school subject on its own merit. **1814** Jane Austen *Mansfield Park* III. iii. 63 Common neglect of the qualification..in the ordinary school-system for boys. **1869** C. L. Brace *New West* 79 The general school system of California..is more centralized. **1911** C. E. Persons et al. *Labor Laws & their Enforcement* 218 We should know how many children..the school system could no longer control, as well as those it still retains. **1976** *National Observer* (U.S.) 1 May B4/4 In America, school systems have expanded in the atmosphere of an anticipated tug-of-war with parents. **1932** G. Greene *Stamboul Train* I. i. 6, I see his passport. Richard John. Schoolteacher. **1950** C. S. Belshaw *Island Admin. in S.W. Pacific* xii. 122 In one or two cases Councils unofficially..levied their own funds, which were to be put to such purposes as paying school-teachers [etc.]. *a* **1930** D. H. Lawrence *Phoenix* (1936) 361 The heroine being one of the old-fashioned school-teacherish sort. **1978** H. Wouk *War & Remembrance* xiii. 126 She shook a schoolteacherish finger at him. **1932** School tie [see *old school tie]. **1937** G. Barker *Poems* 24 O long lost upward in the dream descending, The flying pig and the school-tie anaconda! **1977** *Times* 23 Nov. 12/8 Western society..puts children..in school uniform and school ties to make them conform. **1888** Mrs. H. Ward *Robert Elsmere* II. III. xxv. 274 Counting up the engagements of the next few weeks—the school-treat, two club field-days, a sermon. **1934** D. L. Sayers *Nine Tailors* 121 An importunate child at a school treat. **1915** Kipling *Diversity of Creatures* (1917) 429 We'll get his old school trunk to-morrow and pack his civilian clothes. **1978** *Times* 3 Aug. 9/2 Cash's name-tapes are very widely available... But get a move on if..the first school trunk is looming. **1933** A. White *Frost in May* ii. 47 She trotted sedately behind the lay-sister, wearing her school uniform. **1976** W. Trevor *Children of Dynmouth* ii. 37 They were still in their school uniforms—Stephen's grey with touches of maroon, Kate's brown and green. **1939–40** *Army & Navy Stores Catal.* p. lv/1 School wear. **1976** *Evening Post* (Nottingham) 14 Dec. 15/8 (Advt.), Derby's leading boyswear and schoolwear specialists. **1961** *Guardian Jrnl.* (Nottingham) 14 Nov. 4 The intention here is to reduce these dates in the school year from three to two. **1965** *New Society* 16 Sept. 4/2 The new school year has begun and millions of parents have heaved a sigh of relief. **1975** *Language for Life* (Dept. Educ. & Sci.) xx. 293 An additional benefit was the informal contact between teacher and parent, a valuable foundation for the coming school year.

b. *school bully, friend, -kid, -urchin.*

1907 'Mark Twain' in *N. Amer. Rev.* Jan. 7, I had had a quarrel with a big boy who was the school-bully. **1956** 'C. Blackstock' *Dewey Death* vii. 154 Mark..had something of the school bully in him... It seemed he derived a cruel satisfaction from the young man's palpable fear. **1853** C. Brontë *Villette* I. iii. 43 Graham is busy with his school-friends. **1973** 'M. Innes' *Appleby's Answer* x. 97 He recalled Judith's school friend as soon as he set eyes on her. **1938** School-kid [see *feis 2]. **1976** J. Wainwright *Who goes Next?* 164 He went to live with his boy-friend—little more than a schoolkid. **1922** Joyce *Ulysses* 201 Antiquity mentions that Stagyrite schoolurchin and bald heathen sage.

c. *school-bell* (earlier and later examples), *building* (later example), *gate, hall, library.*

1702 S. Sewall *Diary* 9 Aug. (1879) II. 61 Set out from Salem as the School-Bell rung. **1779** J. Wedgwood *Let.* 23 Nov. (1965) 247 Rise at 7 in winter, when I shall ring the school bell. **1976** C. Dexter *Last seen Wearing* xvii. 136 The school bell rang at 4.00 p.m., and the last lesson of the day was over. **1975** *Language for Life* (Dept. Educ. & Sci.) xix. 280 The class is likely to be held in a school building. **1847** C. M. Yonge *Scenes & Characters* xxiii. 280 William walked to the school gate with them. **1973** J. Mann *Only Security* iii. 23 When she left the school gates behind her, she was finished with the problems for the day. **1933** A. Thirkell *High Rising* viii. 161 Amy took Laura over to the school hall. **1980** J. Thomson *Alibi in Time* viii. 104 The school hall opened off the entrance foyer. **1854** *Rep. Trans. Pennsylvania State Agric. Soc.* 276 Another great reform would be the introducing of a school library into every district school. **1860** J. A. Symonds *Let.* 18 Aug. (1967) I. 260, I shall..get to Shrewsbury at about half past one. That will allow me time to see the MS in the School Library. **1941** M. Treadgold *We couldn't leave Dinah* i. 20 A discerning headmaster..had directed..her vivid imagination to the excellent school library. **1971** J. B. Carroll et al. *Word Freq. Bk.* p. vi, Some of these publications are normally found in the classroom, others in the school library.

e. Produced by the pupils or assistants of a master of a school of art (see sense 5 a), as *school painting, -piece, -work.*

1903 R. Fry *Let.* 16 Mar. (1972) I. 207, I have found..a tondo..which I can't help still fancying a schoolpiece. Anyhow this, which was called 'School of Lorenzo', is Piero all over. **1905** Mrs. H. Ward *Marriage of William Ashe* I. ii. 31 It was an old low-ceiled room, panelled in white and gold, showing here and there an Italian picture—Saint, or Holy Family, agreeable school-work. **1937** *Burlington Mag.* Feb. 77/1 The accidental meeting of northern and southern art-forms, as it were, in a school-piece. **1979** R. Cox *Auction* iii. 58, I would certainly not say priceless. As School paintings go, yes, it's valuable.

17. *school-based* adj.

1975 *Language for Life* (Dept. Educ. & Sci.) xxiii. 339 Up to a third of the time is normally given to school-based teaching practice. **1977** *Times Educ. Suppl.* 21 Oct. 7/1 Many people..believe school-based assessments are important in giving a comprehensive picture of the candidates' achievements.

18. *school desegregation, governor, management, manager* (earlier example), *-teaching* (later examples).

1961 J. W. Peltason (*title*) Fifty-eight lonely men: Southern federal judges and school desegregation. **1976** *Billings* (Montana) *Gaz.* 20 June 11-E/6 President Ford heard pro and con views on busing as a remedy for school desegregation from school superintendents and principals Saturday. **1976** L. Henderson *Major Enquiry* xvii. 116, I was attending a meeting of the Branton Education Committee, I am one of the school governors. **1883** J. Landon (*title*) School management. **1975** *Language for Life* (Dept. Educ. & Sci.) xii. 193 It would not be easy to argue for another post to be added to the senior level of the school management structure. **1862** *Edin. Rev.* Apr. 415 That fortunate individual has dined at the house of a school manager. **1854** C. M. Yonge *Castle Builders* v.

65 The example of their sister..made them think school-teaching the most dignified and delightful of tasks. **1950** *Sport* 7–11 Apr. 14/1 Defensive stability has been added by the signing of schoolteaching goalkeeper, Alec Grant. **1981** E. NORTH *Dames* vi. 101 You did the right thing getting out of schoolteaching when you did.

19. school attendance, attendance at a school, used *attrib.* of persons or things involved in the enforcement of compulsory school attendance; **school(s) broadcast,** a radio or television broadcast for the instruction of children in school; also **school broadcaster, broadcasting; school-butter,** (*c*) (examples): **School Cert.,** abbrev. of next; **School Certificate,** in one of several (public) examination systems, a certificate of proficiency in subjects learned at school; **school colours,** the distinctive colours of a school, esp. as conferred as a sign of sporting achievement (see *COLOUR *sb.*[1] 6 c); **school committee,** (*a*) *U.S.* = *SCHOOL BOARD 2; (*b*) *N.Z.*, a group of the parents of primary school-children elected to assist the headmaster of that school; **school crossing,** a supervised road-crossing for school-children near the entrance to a school; **school district** *N. Amer.*, a unit for the local administration of schools; † **school-feast,** a tea-party or picnic for village school-children; **school inspector,** an officer appointed to inspect and report on the condition of schools and the teaching therein; hence **school-inspectorship; school journal** *N.Z.*, a booklet prepared by the Department of Education and issued to all primary schools at regular intervals; **school land** *N. Amer.*, land set apart for the financial support of schools (cf. *school section*); **school-leaver,** one who is about to leave or has just left school (cf. *LEAVER); **school leaving age** = *leaving age* s.v. *LEAVING *vbl. sb.*; **school method,** the teaching system to be followed by a teacher in training; the practice or thoery of school-teaching; **school milk,** milk provided at reduced cost or free of charge to children in school; **school phobia** *Psychol.*, excessive anxiety about or fear of attending school; so **school-phobic** *a.* and *ellipt.* as *sb.*; **school report** = *REPORT *sb.* 2 e; **school section** (earlier and further examples); also *Canad.*; **school ship** (earlier U.S. example); **schools programme** = **school broadcast*; **schools television,** a television broadcast for schools; **school story,** a story treating of life in a school; **school-years** = *school-time* (*b*).

1876 *Act* 39 & 40 *Vict.* c. 79 § 7 The provisions of this Act..shall be enforced—(1.) In a school district within the jurisdiction of a school board, by that board; and (2.) In every other school district by a committee (in this Act referred to as a school attendance committee). **1911** G. B. SHAW *Getting Married* Pref. 185 If you pay less than £40 a year rent, you will sometimes feel tempted to say to the..school attendance officer, and the sanitary inspector: 'Is this child mine or yours?' **1944** *Act* 7 & 8 *Geo. VI* c. 31. 252 The authority shall serve upon the parent an order in the prescribed form (hereinafter referred to as a 'school attendance order') requiring him to cause the child to become a registered pupil at a school named in the order. **1971** *Reader's Digest Family Guide to Law* 219/2 The education authorities sent the school attendance officer to the home and..he found that the child had received no tuition that day. **1931** *4th Ann. Rep. B.B.C.* in *Parl. Papers 1930–31* (Cmd. 3863) X. 291 It is believed that 5,260 schools followed the school broadcasts in the year. **1949** *Radio Times* 15 July 6/1, I asked the Chief Wireless Operator if it would be possible for me to listen to the Schools Broadcast. **1962** A. NISBETT *Technique Sound Studio* 246 The BBC permits the recording of schools broadcasts. **1974** School broadcaster [see *school broadcasting* below]. **1927** *B.B.C. Handbk. 1928* 138/1 Many thousands have their school set with its loud-speaker, and School Broadcasting has become a subject for educational research. **1928** *1st Ann. Rep. B.B.C.* 6 in *Parl. Papers* (Cmd. 3123) VII. 121 The Kent Education Committee undertook an enquiry into the efficacy of schools broadcasting. **1974** *Time* 8 Apr. 13/1 This autumn radio will celebrate 50 years of school broadcasting... School broadcasters use much more sophisticated material to complement the work of the teacher. **1935** A. B. LONGSTREET *Georgia Scenes* 84, I fell down.., running after that fellow that cried 'school-butter'. **1912** *Dialect Notes* III. 588 When he yelled *school butter* at us, we yanked him off the wagon and blacked his eyes. **1937** *Discovery* Jan. p. ii/1 (Advt.), *School Cert.* and *Army.* Quick easy way if *Latin* taken for former only. **1967** H. W. SUTHERLAND *Magnie* vii. 92 She could have taken the one year course herself, but she thought you'd need a school cert. at least. **1977** D. MAY in P. Collenette *Winter's Tales 23* 90 We were doing a run-through of School Cert. **1888** KIPLING *Wee Willie Winkie* 75 They were an educated regiment, the percentage of school-certificates in their ranks were high, and most of the men could do more than read and write. **1911** *Rep. Consultative Comm. Exam. Secondary Schools* 106 in *Parl. Papers* (Cd. 6004) XVI. 159 We would suggest that the examination should be called the examination for the Secondary School Certificate. **1931** 'G. TREVOR' *Murder at School* ii. 36 He was in my junior form... I expect he'd have taken his School Certificate. **1948** *Min. of Educ. Circular* No. 168. 23 Apr. 3/1 In 1951 the Minister proposes that the existing School and Higher School Certificate examinations should be discontinued and that in their place there should be introduced an examination for the 'General Certificate of Education'. **1966** G. W. TURNER *Eng. Lang. in Australia & N.Z.* viii. 173 He [*sc.* a New Zealander] is likely to sit School Certificate (approximately equivalent to English GCE Ordinary Level). **1978** A. PRICE *'44 Vintage* iv. 46 The acquisition of School Certificate German had been the limit of his ambition. **1913** C. MACKENZIE *Sinister St.* I. II. xiv. 382 He respected the quest of School Colours. **1924** A. HUXLEY *Little Mexican* 3 Holding to my head..a speckled straw [hat], gaudy with the school colours. **1972** L. P. DAVIES *What did I do Tomorrow?* v. 63 A scarf in the school colours of narrow emerald and gold stripes on black. **1787** in C. O. Parmenter *Hist. Pelham, Mass.* (1898) 226 Voted Not to Devid the School Quarter where Dea. John Crawford is School Committee Man. **1877** *Statutes N.Z.* XXI. § 58. 122 For every school district constituted under this Act there shall be a School Committee consisting of seven householders within the school district, to be elected as hereinafter provided. **1945** *Suburban List* (Essex Junction, Vermont) 8 Feb. 10/3 The school committee could not keep the buses running. **1947** 'A. P. GASKELL' *Big Game* 87 To crown it all the damned School Committee had to pick on this Saturday for their school picnic. **1951** *Sunday Pictorial* 21 Jan. 4/3 The warning signs brandished by Bristol's school-crossing wardens are so large that wardens find it hard to keep both feet on the ground in a strong wind. **1979** *Hampstead & Highgate Express* 22 June 10/3 Most of the school crossings in the borough were without lollipop men and women. **1809** E. A. KENDALL *Travels through Northern Parts U.S.* I. 128 There are thirteen school districts [in Berlin, Conn.]. **1876** [see *school attendance* above]. **1903** A. B. HART *Actual Govt.* 542 The smallest unit of school administration is the school district, which in many States has its own board, raises its own taxes, and appoints its own teachers. **1978** *N.Y. Times* 29 Mar. A13/1 In Duarte,..the school district and a medical center are the two major employers. **1849** C. BRONTË *Shirley* II. vi. 137 (*heading*) The school-feast. **1879** M. E. BRADDON *Vixen* I. xvii. 325 The school-feast was fixed..for the Wednesday in Whitsun week. **1822** *Missionary Reg.* Dec. 501/2 (*heading*) School inspectors and village readers. **1873** C. M. YONGE *Pillars of House* IV. xli. 192 He's a school inspector! Don't you have inspections here? Not under Government? O thrice happy people! **1924** M. KENNEDY *Constant Nymph* xiv. 190 He knows too much about everything..being a school inspector. **1979** D. COOK *Winter Doves* I. 26 The School Inspectors came round..and they saw the state of the house, so they sent someone from the Council. **1911** H. S. WALPOLE *Mr. Perrin & Mr. Traill* iii. 47 He saw himself at Eton or Harrow, or a school-inspectorship. **1907** *Append. Jrnls. House Reps. N.Z.* E.1E. 6, I might mention..the *School Journal*, because it will give an opportunity of explaining the place it should occupy in the school system. **1935** J. GUTHRIE *Little Country* v. 102 The word [*sc.* Australasia] was expurgated from school journals. **1648** *Suffolk Co.* (Mass.) *Deeds* (1880) I. 91 Humphrey Johnson of Roxbury granted unto William Chenie of Roxbury twenty Acres of land in Roxbury bounded with..the school lands & Richard Peacocks northwest. **1775** *Let.* 28 Feb. in *Coll. New Hampshire Hist. Soc.* (1889) IX. 89, I might..lay out for the Clearing the School Lands to the amount of £500 Sterl[g]. **1885** *Rep. Indian Affairs* (U.S.) 147 Others claim they have purchased their lands from the State of Nevada under the school-land grant. **1952** D. F. PUTNAM *Canad. Regions* 372/2 Another factor in the land pattern was the reservation of certain parcels as school lands. **1925** *Contemp. Rev.* May 634 The problem of the unemployed 'school-leaver' complicates in many ways the problem of the boy at work. **1955** *Times* 14 July 2/6 The Student Training Scheme is designed to enable public and grammar school-leavers to qualify professionally, having particularly in view careers in design, development, production, or commercial engineering. **1980** *Listener* 19 June 803/1 Wakefield was a miner's son and his parents did not expect him to be a late school-leaver. **1920** *Circular* (Board of Educ.) No. 1180. 12 Oct. 3 The Board are prepared to consider proposals for making a byelaw under the subsection raising the school leaving age to 15. **1946** *Ann. Reg. 1945* I. iii. 75 On September 28 the Minister of Education announced that the school-leaving age would be raised to 15 on April 1, 1947, and that no attempt would be made to postpone the change beyond that date. **1955** *Times* 9 July 2/6 Many people thought that fewer pupils were now staying after school-leaving age, but that was not so. **1972** *Times* 15 Jan. 2/5 Mrs Thatcher, Secretary of State for Education and Science, said in London last night that she had signed the order-in-council to raise school-leaving age to 16 in September. **1877** F. J. GLADMAN (*title*) School method. **1917** BERESFORD & RICHMOND *W. E. Ford* ix. 194 A description of a typical staff-meeting discussion of school method. **1927** J. ADAMS *Errors in School* 35 School-method books. **1934** *Milk-in-Schools Scheme* (Milk Marketing Board) 6 Communications should be addressed to the 'School Milk' Dept., Thames House, Millbank. **1964** L. LEE *Firstborn* 11 I'd ask her to accept her faults..and not blame them..on..school-milk, or the British Railways. **1977** *Times* 10 May 4/3 Ministers will consider claiming an EEC grant worth 3p a pint on school milk. **1941** A. M. JOHNSON in *Amer. Jrnl. Orthopsychiatry* Oct. 702 The syndrome, often referred to as 'school phobia', is recognizable by the intense terror associated with being at school. **1959** *Times* 24 Nov. 13/3 Wherein is school-phobia different from the traditional reluctance which was met by old-fashioned compulsion? **1980** *Daily Tel.* 19 Nov. 15/5 By that time, the more timid boy had been brought to the verge of school-phobia by it all. **1977** *Daily Colonist* (Victoria, B.C.) 22 Oct. 28/7 A psychiatrist..said mothers of school-phobic children are over-protective. **1981** *Lancashire Life* Jan. 25/2 We now have a new word for it... The 'school-phobic' says Lancashire Education Authority, is clearly intimidated by being required to attend school. **1874** C. M. YONGE *Lady Hester* ix. 205 Feeling very happy over the best school report of our boy we had ever had. **1958** J. CANNAN *And be a Villain* iv. 109 As his school reports revealed..he was useless at games. **1975** T. ALLBEURY *Palomino Blonde* xi. 71 There were a few school reports showing that Kristina was doing average well. **1835** *Indiana Mag. Hist.* XXII. 438 This was an action brought by the Trustees of a school Section for money due on two years rent. **1881** *Edmonton Bull.* 5 Nov. 3/2 As the surveys in Manitoba are made it is found that sections which should be available for school sections are already occupied..by the Syndicate for station grounds and other purposes. **1841** *Southern Lit. Messenger* VII. 7/2 The means of creating officers [for the navy]..are to be derived from the school-ship. **1971** C. STORR *Thursday* viii. 92 'Heaps of people do say it [*sc.* 'bloody']. Even on television.' 'But not on schools programmes.' **1973** *Listener* 31 May 707/1 Of the 30 channels in the system, three are to be made available..for schools television. **1974** Schools television [see *PIP *v.*[3] 1 c]. **1895** C. M. YONGE *Long Vacation* vii. 66 He had heard enough school stories to be wary of boasting of his title. **1914** 'I. HAY' *Lighter Side School Life* vi. 151 Whereas school stories were formerly written to be read by schoolboys, they are now written to be read..by grown-up persons. **1971** 'S. SMITH' *Grave Affair* iv. 52 'Some boys from the Fifth. I don't know their names,' he lied in the best tradition of school stories. **1922** JOYCE *Ulysses* 669 Moral apothegms (e.g. *My Favourite Hero* or *Procrastination is the Thief of Time*) composed during schoolyears.

school, *v.*[1] Add: **1. b.** *intr.* To attend school. *rare.*

1934 in WEBSTER. **1972** *Straits Times* 23 Nov. 15/4 'It's incredible,' says the amiable 32-year-old Globe Silk Store proprietor who has schooled in England.

8. *intr.* To gamble in a 'school' (cf. SCHOOL *sb.*[1] 6 a). *slang.*

1935 A. J. CRONIN *Stars look Down* I. ii. 17 Some colliers.. that made up the gambling school in ordinary times—squatted upon their hunkers against the wall. They were not schoolin' now, they had no coppers for schoolin'.

school board. Add: **2.** In countries other than Great Britain, a board charged with the provision and maintenance of schools.

1836 *Chambers's Edin. Jrnl.* 27 Aug. 244/2 Over these provinces [in Prussia] is placed a consistory, or council, divided also into three sections, one of which is termed the school-board. **1838** F. B. HAWKINS *Germany* xii. 201 Every circle and parish has also its school-board. **1857** *Harper's Mag.* Sept. 571/2 Can you inform me where the president of your school board resides? **1911** *Daily Colonist* (Victoria, B.C.) 11 Apr. 7/3 The school board which recently submitted its estimates for the year to the city council will have to revise them. **1972** *Even. Telegram* (St. John's Newfoundland) 24 June 6/1 The government..tried to save a few dollars on the busing of children to school. There were immediate cries of pain from the Opposition and from some school boards. **1976** *National Observer* (U.S.) 2 Oct. 15/11 It was my job to cover the..school-board meetings of several communities.

school-book. 1. a. (Earlier U.S. example.)

1745 B. FRANKLIN *Let.* 11 Dec. in *Writings* (1905) II. 296 At present I only send for a few school books, and books of navigation.

schoolboy. Add: **1. b.** In phr. *every schoolboy knows*, referring to a matter of factual information, supposed to be elementary and generally known.

1654 [in Dict. sense 1 a]. **1721** SWIFT *Poems* (1958) I. 281 How haughtily he lifts his Nose, To tell what ev'ry School Boy knows. **1840** MACAULAY in *Edin. Rev.* Jan. 295 Every schoolboy knows who imprisoned Montezuma, and who strangled Atahualpa. **1966** *Listener* 8 Sept. 365/3 Tallis's motet *Spem in alium nunquam habui* was for years more often written about than heard. A *tour-de-force* in forty voice-parts: so much every schoolboy knew. **1977** *Times* 15 Oct. 2/8 Every schoolboy knows that the No. 3 bus from Piccadilly Circus comes to Valley Fields, Wodehouse's familiar pseudonym for Dulwich.

3. *Comb.*, as *schoolboy code* (*of honour*), *English, French, honour, humour.* (Not clearly separable from sense 2 in Dict.)

1874 C. M. YONGE *Lady Hester* vii. 169 The boy endured all the rage and scorn that a threat so contrary to all schoolboy codes of honour and friendship might deserve. **1977** P. G. WINSLOW *Witch Hill Murder* II. xviii. 248 His blue gaze fell on Capricorn expecting him to understand and accept his schoolboy code. **1835** J. ROMILLY *Diary* 6 July (1967) 82 P. George of Camb. delighted me by his returning thanks, because it was good simple schoolboy English. **1955** E. BLISHEN *Roaring Boys* III. 158 He delighted in mimicking my schoolboy French. **1977** J. CLEARY *High Road to China* ii. 41 A six months' affair with a girl in Auxi had improved his schoolboy French. **1876** C. M. YONGE *Womankind* xviii. 138 To keep up a standard of real honour, above schoolboy honour, is most needful. **1970** P. Y. CARTER *Mr Campion's Falcon* xxii. 166 He has a sense of schoolboy honour, a perfectly straightforward code. **1962** G. K. HUNTER *John Lyly* iv. 237 The inane schoolboy humour of his part, and the tradition of Ralph Roister Doister to which it belongs, both point to a juvenile rather than an adult actor. **1977** R. PERRY *Dead End* viii. 99 Just forget the schoolboy humour and do as you're told.

schoolboyish, *a.* Add: Hence **schoo·lboyishly** *adv.*, in the manner of a schoolboy; **schoo·lboyishness,** the conduct or manner of a schoolboy.

1898 G. B. SHAW *Let.* ? 2 May (1972) II. 39 Irving & I are too eminent to indulge in such schoolboyishness in public. **1901** W. J. LOCKE *Usurper* xviii. 247 He..was so schoolboyishly happy the next morning on starting for his holiday. **1972** J. POTTER *Going West* 159 His step was jaunty and his manner schoolboyishly affable. **1976** *Daily Tel.* 9 Sept. 13/1 As an example of the schoolboyishness, I would cite the fact that Ransome and a friend..had coded signals which they displayed on their respective houses..to give notice when they were going fishing.

school doctor. 3. (Examples.)

1906 R. BROOKE *Let.* 1 Apr. (1968) 47 Dukes, the school doctor, was paying us his hurried visit. **1933** A. WHITE *Frost in May* xiii. 333 The school doctor..told them..they were now perfectly well. **1963** M. KENDON *Ladies College, Goudhurst* 19 Dr. Mapleton, the school doctor,..would drive up in his dog-cart, with his wooden stethoscope inside his silk hat. **1976** J. PHILIPS *Backlash* (1977) III. ii. 148 He had a sinecure for me. School doctor.

-schooler (skū·ləɹ). *U.S.* [f. SCHOOL *sb.*[1] + -ER[1].] As the second element in Combinations, designating a pupil at a specified type of school, or stage of school-life, as *grade, high schooler; pre-schooler.*

1954 *Recreation* Apr. 241/1 Remember that pre-schoolers are people. **1960** *Parents' Mag.* July 92/2 Brevity..produces good results with preschoolers. **1971** *Sci. Amer.* Dec. 114/3 Martin Gardner's well-known learning and mathematical depth are worn lightly in this friendly, comical book for grade schoolers. **1972** *Newsweek* 25 Sept. 106/2 *(caption)* Harvard tutor..and high schoolers. **1973** *Black World* June 44/1 Ronald and Wayne are high schoolers. **1977** *Rolling Stone* 30 June 60/2 High schoolers will dye their hair gray, and buy iron-on wrinkles, and yearn for the day when their bodies begin to sag.

schoolgirl. Add: **1. a.** (Earlier examples.)

1777 E. DRAPER *Let.* 10 July in *N. & Q.* (1944) CLXXXVII. 12/2 The pertness, of the consequential School Girl, has given place to softer Manners. **1778** F. BURNEY *Evelina* I. xi. 36, I did not choose to tell him it [*sc.* my fear] was owing to my never before dancing but with a school-girl.

2. *Comb.*, as *schoolgirl complexion, crush, English, French, passion.* (Not clearly separable from sense 1 b in Dict.)

1922 *Woman's Home Compan.* Oct. 35 (Advt.), Better than jewels —— that schoolgirl complexion... Choose Palmolive, because its action is soothing. **1924** WODEHOUSE *Ukridge* x. 241 A man like myself, who finds at least eight hours of sleep essential if that schoolgirl complexion is to be preserved. **1938** G. GREENE *Brighton Rock* v. ii. 196 The long parade of posters..Guinness is Good for You, Try a Worthington, Keep that Schoolgirl Complexion. **1973** A. MACVICAR *Painted Doll Affair* iii. 39 She was an enthusiast for soap and water, as her schoolgirl complexion showed **1952** Schoolgirl crush [see *CRUSH *sb.* 2 d]. **1963** P. MOYES *Murder à la Mode* iv. 69 Olwen had a sort of schoolgirl crush on her. **1978** C. STORR *Winter's End* xiii. 143 Bran.. wondered what she'd..meant when she'd told Rosey that she loved Philip. A schoolgirl crush? A romantic fantasy? **1939** C. ISHERWOOD *Goodbye to Berlin* 32 Frl. Hippi..speaks schoolgirl English with a slight American accent. **1967** W. G. CORP tr. *L. Oriol's Short Circuit* ii. 11 She spoke a schoolgirl English which nobody could understand. **1909** W. J. LOCKE *Septimus* iv. 49 'Will a hundred francs be of any use to you?' she asked, in her schoolgirl French. **1977** J. CLEARY *High Road to China* iv. 119 Mustafa Kemal said in French,..'I apologize for not speaking English.' Eve said..'I speak only schoolgirl French.' **1936** M. MITCHELL *Gone with Wind* xvii. 312 You still cherish a romantic schoolgirl passion for him.

schoolie (skū·li). Also **scheulie.** [f. SCHOOL *sb.*[1] + -IE.] **a.** *north. dial.* and *Austral.* A schoolteacher.

1901 in *Eng. Dial. Dict.* (1904) V. 250/2 That only three children out of a hundred have been absent on an average throughout twelve months will strike the ordinary scheulie ..with astonishment. **1907** N. SPIELVOGEL *Cocky Farmer* 33 The prettiest of all the girls was the schoolie, and didn't she lead the lads a dance. **1951** E. COXHEAD *One Green Bottle* vii. 179 'What a lot I've got to teach you!' said Christopher smiling. 'Schoolie.' 'Well, of course I'm a schoolie. What else could you expect?' **1960** S. H. COURTIER *Gently dust Corpse* xiii. 189 She was away at college, being taught to be a schoolie all that time. **1980** *Globe & Laurel* July/Aug. 198/2 At Lydd and Hythe, we enjoyed such epics as the formation of the Nelson brick (Doctor, Dentist, Padre and Schoolie).

b. *slang.* In the Navy, a classroom instructor.

1946 J. IRVING *Royal Navalese* 151 *Schoolie*, a naval schoolmaster. **1964** J. HALE *Grudge Fight* vii. 97 The E.R.A. instructors, the P.T. instructors, the gunnery instructors, the schoolies began to..brace themselves for another day of ramming drill and P.T. and lathe work and chipping and filing and maths., mechanics, machine drawing, naval history..into the minds and bodies of eight divisions of apprentices. **1977** *Navy News* Dec. 12/2 The official announcement says that in meeting the needs of the Navy during the past 20 years the role of instructor officers —the schoolies—has changed significantly.

school-keeping. (Earlier examples.)

1651 *Early Rec. Dedham, Mass.* (1892) III. 191 The time of covenant in ye schoole keepeing being expired. **1829** A. SHERWOOD *Gazetteer Georgia* (ed. 2) 193 Why is it that school-keeping is so disreputable an employment in our State? **1854** C. M. YONGE *Castle Builders* v. 70 All we have ever had to do with school-keeping, was in that short visit to my sister.

school-ma'am. For *U.S.* read 'orig. *U.S.*' and add: Also **-ma'm.** The form **-marm** is now usual. **1.** (Earlier and further examples.) Now freq. implying the conventionally prim and correct behaviour of a school-mistress. Also *fig.*

1831 *Ladies' Mag.* (Boston) IV. 557 [It] obliged me to stay the longest in the houses where..there was the most work to do, and the least time to make the school Ma'am comfortable. **1840** *Spirit of Times* 8 Aug. 276/2 Them mirrors.., why what you got agin 'em? Cost me twenty-five dollars for the set—they be busters! open like a School-marm, by Jerusalem! **1841** *Picayune* (New Orleans) 23 Feb. 2/1 What will the 'school marm' say when she reads the following extract of a letter? **1888** C. M. YONGE *Our New Mistress* xii. 107 He said he supposed he should be a startling visitor for the school marm. **1924** A. E. HOUSMAN *Let.* 10 Mar. (1971) 218 A French school-ma'm wrote to me wanting to translate *A Shropshire Lad.* **1929** D. H. LAWRENCE *Phoenix II* (1968) 579 Now the funny thing is that nobody, not even the most conscientious father, ever questions the absolute rightness of these school-marms. **1951** M. MCLUHAN *Mech. Bride* (1967) 69/2 Rigid with the social cocksureness of the schoolmarm. **1974** *Times* 14 Mar. 16/1 Mrs Margaret Thatcher..had the bearing of a school ma'am, an inability to suffer fools. **1977** M. EDELMAN *Political Lang.* v. 90 Schoolmarms of both sexes behave like teachers in the living room and when reacting to novels or to public affairs.

attrib. **1965** *New Statesman* 7 May 719/1 The schoolma'am tone that husbands are quick to notice. **1972** WODEHOUSE *Pearls, Girls, & Monty Bodkin* xii. 181 Less than the dust beneath his chariot wheels, if he remembered the quotation correctly from his school-marm days. **1978** M. PUZO *Fools Die* xxix. 333 Going through a bedroom, I saw a couple head to toe and I heard a woman's very schoolmarm voice say, 'Get *up* here.'

2. *N. Amer. slang.* (See quots.)

1939 H. O'HAGAN *Tay John* 217 It was a pine. Long ago its trunk had been broken off by a slide or by the wind. Two stout branches had grown up instead, lightly tufted, to form a crotch. It was what the men there call a 'school-marm tree'. **1958** *Scope Weekly* 22 Oct. 7/1 The same situation may occur in felling a 'schoolma'am' which is essentially a forked tree, having two main trunks. **1965** M. MCINTYRE *Place of Quiet Waters* iv. 82 The 'schoolmarm' turned out to be a tree that had branched out into two separate trunks.

Hence as *v. trans.*, to treat (someone) in the manner of a school-marm, to instruct or guide patronizingly; **schoo·l-marming** *vbl. sb.*, the occupation of being a school-marm; **schoo·l-marmish, schoo·l-marmy** *adjs.*, like or suggestive of a school-marm; **schoo·l-marmishly** *adv.*, in the manner of a school-marm.

1887 H. FREDERIC *Seth's Brother's Wife* 24 She was held to be too serious and 'school-ma'am-ish' for pleasant company. **1914** KIPLING *Egypt of Magicians* iv, in *Cosmopolitan* Sept. 458/1 Our trouble in America is we're being school-marmed to death. **1920** 'O. DOUGLAS' *Penny Plain* xii. 124 Heaps of girls would think school-marming very dull, but Elspeth makes it into a sort of daily entertainment. **1921** R. MACAULAY *Dangerous Ages* vii. 132 The W.E.A. was a practical body... Dowdy, schoolmarmish, extension-lecturish, it might be. **1941** *Scrutiny* X. 115 The priggishness of the book [sc. *Mansfield Park*] is of a special kind, not just the occasional schoolmarmy effects of *Sense and Sensibility* which there are only the result of artistic inexperience. **1943** W. S. CHURCHILL *Second World War* (1951) IV. 824 Considering..that it was the Americans.. who led the world astray, it is pretty good cheek of them now coming to school-marm us into proper behaviour. **1945** R. HARGRAVES *Enemy at Gate* 234 The Radicals' itch to continue 'school-marming' the native populations of the former Boer territories. **1959** K. VONNEGUT *Sirens of Titan* (1967) x. 174 'This way, please, We haven't got all day, you know,' said Rumfoord school-marmishly. **1967** *Economist* 15 Apr. p. xvii/1 Typical of all her encounters was her inability to find the disapproving school-marmy guide, Miss Tsu, anything but likeable. **1977** good schoolmarm. **1979** *Guardian* 23 Oct. 8/1 The remarks tend to sound school-marmy and pontifical.

schoolmaster, *sb.*[1] Add: **1. f.** An experienced horse used to train horses or riders at a riding-school.

1937 in PARTRIDGE *Dict. Slang.* **1938** H. WYNMALEN *Equitation* ix. 40 Moving away from other horses must be taught him. To this end we shall ride him beside another horse, a schoolmaster. **1976** *Horse & Hound* 10 Dec. 68/4 (Advt.), This pony is one of the finest schoolmasters jumping in 12 hands 2 in. classes.

3. b. Special Comb.: **schoolmaster studentship,** in Oxford colleges, a studentship tenable by schoolmasters; hence **schoolmaster student.**

1957 *Oxf. Univ. Gaz.* 20 June 1142/1 Balliol College Elections. *To Schoolmaster Studentships.* For Michaelmas Term. **1978** *Times Educ. Suppl.* 3 Feb. 68/3 (Advt.), Merton and St. Peter's Colleges Schoolmaster Studentships 1978/ 79... The two colleges above intend to elect four *schoolmaster students* between them.

Hence **schoo·lmastery** *a.* = SCHOOLMASTERISH *a.*

1928 *Observer* (Apr. 7 In the earlier days the Staff College did not justify the expectations founded on it. It was unreal, academic, and 'schoolmastery'. **1942** J. LEES-MILNE *Ancestral Voices* (1975) 17 What an unattractive, schoolmastery fellow.

schoolmaster, *v.* Add: **1.** (Earlier example.)

1850 J. OXENFORD tr. *Eckermann's Conversations of Goethe* I. 377 [Schlegel] is permitted, upon such high authority, to fall foul of this mighty ancient [*sc.* Euripides], and to schoolmaster him as much as he can.

2. (Later examples.)

1966 *Listener* 5 May 659/2 Nicholas Urfe is school-mastering on a Greek island, seeking escape from..an oppressive love affair. **1977** *Times* 15 Nov. 14/6 Mr Rogers ..schoolmastered for a time.

schoolmistress. Add: Hence **schoolmistressy** *a.*, characteristic of or resembling a school-mistress.

1915 D. H. LAWRENCE *Rainbow* x. 251 Miss Grey..had a certain silvery, school-mistressy beauty of character. *a* **1974** R. CROSSMAN *Diaries* (1975) I. 339 In that grating voice, she gave her clear, schoolmistressy, common-sense view of the White Paper.

schoolroom. Add: **1.** (Earlier and further examples.) Also, in *fig.* phr. *in the schoolroom*: of a young lady, not yet 'out' (cf. OUT *adv.* 26 b(a).

1773 P. V. FITHIAN *Jrnl. & Lett.* (1900) 61, I have to myself in the Evening..my Liberty, either to continue in the School room, in my own Room, or to sit over at the great House. **1812** E. WEETON *Let.* July (1969) II. 58, I breakfast with Mr. & Mrs. Armitage, and then return again to the children till 9, we go into the school-room till 12. **1857** C. M. YONGE *Dynevor Terrace* I. viii. 126 'I suppose her daughters are not come out yet?' 'Her own are in the school-room; but there is a step-daughter who is much admired.' **1952** M. LASKI *Village* ii. 35 The younger daughter in the schoolroom, the elder about to blossom forth. **1977** C. FREMLIN *Spider-Orchid* vii. 51 She's not 'out' yet, she's only in the schoolroom still.

3. *attrib.*

1814 JANE AUSTEN *Mansfield Park* I. xviii. 353 Very good school-room chairs, not made for a theatre, I dare say. **1847** A. BRONTË *Agnes Grey* xv. 242 There was the bell—the odious bell for the school-room dinner. **1857** C. M. YONGE *Dynevor Terrace* I. xiv. 227 The school-room maid..was busy unpacking in a corner of the room. *Ibid.* xv. 238 She repaired to the school-room tea. **1875** L. TROUBRIDGE *Jrnl.* 25 Dec. in J. Hope-Nicholson *Life amongst Troubridges* (1966) 133, I..found everyone congregated round the school-room table. **1923** W. J. LOCKE *Moordius & Co.* ii. 17 The family can always come up if it likes for schoolroom tea. **1948** F. THOMPSON *Still glides Stream* iv. 91 They should have heard the music, the schoolroom piano and two violins. **1959** I. & P. OPIE *Lore & Lang. Schoolch.* xvi. 343 Children whose schoolroom attitude to history is antipathetic. **1969** D. HOLMAN-HUNT *My Grandfather* xviii. 232 She would get rid of the schoolroom maid and order some new dresses. **1972** W. LABOV *Lang. in Inner City* i. 30 The subjects are asked to change certain sentences to correct schoolroom English. **1975** R. PLAYER *Let's talk of Graves* iv. 118 We had schoolroom tea in deathly silence.

Hence **schoo·lroomy** *a.*, characteristic of or resembling a schoolroom.

1895 W. S. CHURCHILL *Let.* 3 Aug. in R. S. Churchill *Winston S. Churchill* (1967) I. Compan. I. viii. 581 A very lovely—but stupid and school roomy girl—to whom I talked a good deal. **1975** D. DANIELL *Interpreter's House* ii. 20 A bit schoolroomy, possibly, and a little too much the work of a *belle-lettrist.*

schoon (skūn), *v. rare.* [See etym. note at SCHOONER *sb.*[1] The modern examples represent a fanciful back-formation from this sb.] **a.** *intr.* To sail or skim over the water, esp. in the manner of a schooner. **b.** *trans.* To run or glance (one's mind) *over* (something). Hence **schoo·ning** *vbl. sb.*

With quot. 1836 cf. etym. note in Dict. s.v. SCHOONER *sb.*[1]

1836 J. R. NEWHALL *Essex Memorial* 100 Capt. R[obinson] had constructed a vessel which he masted and rigged in the manner that schooners at this day are, and on her going off the stocks into the water, a bystander cried out, 'O how she scoons!' Robinson instantly replied, 'A schooner let her be.' **1937** O. NASH in *New Yorker* 13 Feb. 20/2 Where the schooner schoons, I schoon. **1959** I. JEFFERIES *13 Days* ix. 115, I spent my time schooning my mind over the calculations.

schooner, *sb.*[1] Add: **1. b.** *schooner on the rocks* (see quots.). *Naut. slang.*

1916 'TAFFRAIL' *Carry On!* 28 A 'schooner on the rocks' does not refer to a nautical disaster, but to meat and potatoes baked in a peculiar way. **1922** *Mariner's Mirror* VIII. 222/1 *Schooner on the Rocks.* This dish consists of a joint baked in a sea of batter. **1927** P. RILEY *Memories* ii. 11 Dinner..varied from salt beef,..'Schooner on the Rocks', i.e., joint of meat roasted on potatoes, or 'toad in the hole'.

3. *schooner-rigged* (later *fig.* examples); *schooner-man, -sail* [tr. G. *schonersegel* foresail]; **schooner barge,** (*a*) *U.S.*, a short-masted vessel designed to be towed; (*b*) a flat-bottomed vessel rigged as a topsail schooner; **schooner yawl,** a variety of two-masted schooner.

1819 *Western Rev.* I. 361 The River is navigated by steam boats, barges, keel boats, schooner barges. **1867** *Mitchell's Maritime Reg.* 1620 On Monday the fine schooner-barge Edith was launched. **1900** *Bath* (Maine) *Daily Times* 22 May 5/3 The new three-masted schooner barge *Flora* for the Commercial Towboat Co. of Boston was launched yesterday. **1945** *Amer. Neptune* V. 139 In the East Coast schooner-barge fleet, only a few have been built with five masts. **1951** F. G. C. CARR *Sailing Barges* 126 As far as the hulls of these big barquentine and schooner barges were concerned, they were like very large boomies. **1914** W. D. STEELE *Storm* 270 Then he scrutinized the rank of schooner-men flanking me. **1972** F. E. BOWKER *Blue Water Coaster* 30 We thought that he had picked up an old schoonerman, but it wasn't long before we discovered that he was an unemployed shoemaker. **1924** R. CLEMENTS *Gipsy of Horn* iii. 47 All hands were working schooner-rigged, going at it with their blood up. **1935** *Amer. Speech* X. 79/1 *Schooner rigged*, unequipped with proper clothes or other necessities. **1946** R. E. HIGGINBOTHAM *Wine for My Brothers* vi. 126 The Dane travelled schooner-rigged, and philosophically heaved his mail overboard. **1930** D. MARTIN *Boy Scout with Sea Devil* 48 We hoisted up the Fores'l and the Schooners'l. **1952** G. COWAN *Log of Pelican* vi. 41 We cleaned out lockers,..bent the schooner sail and got the fore-canvas up in stops, and found a place for everything. **1889** *Forest & Stream* 4 Apr. 227/3 Adding a jigger mast..cuts off the nasty big boom and large mainsail..making the yacht a schooner yawl. **1970** *Amer. Neptune* XXX. 196 Not counting the schooner-yawl *White Cap*, which was discussed among the schooners, yawls made up 8.7 percent of American sailing yachts in 1902.

schooner, *sb.*² Add: **1. b*.** *Austral.* and *N.Z.* A large beer-glass of locally variable capacity (see quots. 1966 and 1973); the (measure of) beer contained in such a glass.

1934 *Bulletin* (Sydney) 21 Feb. 10/1 In Brisbane, a standard pint served in a long glass is a 'schooner'. **1947** D. M. Davin *Gorse grows Pale* 126 Sitting in the pub with a schooner under his nose. **1966** G. W. Turner *Eng. Lang. in Austral. & N.Z.* viii. 163 A *schooner* in New South Wales is a fifteen-ounce glass, in Adelaide a nine-ounce glass. **1969** *Advertiser* (Adelaide) 12 May 5/4 Just because someone wants to spend an arvo sinking a few schooners in his own way. **1973** *Courier-Mail* (Brisbane) 1 Dec. 17/7 The traveller finished up at the Federal with 128 schooners (the local term for an eight ounce glass). **1977** *Bulletin* (Sydney) 22 Jan. 27/2 He calculated he would consume eight schooners (15oz glasses) of beer, plus some spirits, over three hours. **1981** *Advertiser* (Adelaide) 2 July 6/6 Mr Connelly and Mr McKenzie said the second stage of the change was planned for October when the 285 ml (10 oz) glass would be introduced to replace the 255 ml (9 oz) schooner.

2. A tall, waisted sherry glass; the measure contained by this.

1967 J. Potter *Foul Play* xvii. 204 What about joining me in a schooner of sherry? **1973** *Times* 20 Oct. 14/3 The abominably proportioned waisted Elgin glass, sometimes used for sherry, or its vulgar outsize version, the schooner. **1975** [see *noshery]. **1977** *Habitat 1977/78 Catal.* 121 *Elgin schooner.* For large sherries. 3½ oz.

Schopenhauer (ʃōᵘ·pənhauəɹ, ʃǫ·p-). The name of the German philosopher, Arthur *Schopenhauer* (1788–1860), used allusively, esp. for the pessimism and concept of will for which his philosophy is noted. Hence **Scho·penhaueresque** *a.*, resembling, of the same type as, the ideas of Schopenhauer; **Scho·penhauerian** (also as *sb.*), **Scho·penhauerish** *adjs.*, characterized by the doctrines or ideas of Schopenhauer; **Scho·penhauerism,** the pessimistic and atheistic philosophy of Schopenhauer, according to which the world is governed by a blind cosmic will entailing suffering from which man finds release only through knowledge, contemplation, and compassion; **Scho·penhauerist, Scho·penhauerite,** a follower of Schopenhauer or his doctrines.

1882 W. S. Lilly in *19th Cent.* May 713 Schopenhauerism.. is little more than Buddhism vulgarized. **1882** *Mind* VII. 561 Thought, with Hegel, stands for something objective and unconscious (like the Schopenhaurian Will). **1891** G. B. Shaw *Let.* 25 Oct. (1965) I. 317 This does not make me a Schopenhaurist, or Ibsen one. **1898** —— *Perfect Wagnerite* 101 Wagner's determination to prove he had been a Schopenhaurite all along. **1906** *Academy* 10 Mar. 233/1 It is a shallow philosophy that issues in Schopenhauerism. **1906** *Daily Chron.* 26 Sept. 4/4 You would say at one glance that he is a pessimistic ass, a Schopenhauer of donkeys. **1908** *Edin. Rev.* Apr. 423 He is a Schopenhauerian. **1928** C. E. M. Joad *Diogenes* 96 We shall all be living Schopenhauerian lives. **1959** K. F. Leidecker tr. *Nietzsche's Lett.* (1960) 50 To infuse into my presentation of the science this new blood, to transfer to my hearers that Schopenhauerian seriousness which is impressed on the forehead of this grand man,—this is my desire, my audacious hope. **1965** *New Statesman* 18 June 971/1 The shuddering Schopenhaueresque preoccupation with personal annihilation. **1968** *Guardian* 30 July 4/1 The Schopenhauerish misanthropy of the essays. **1976** *Amer. N. & Q.* XV. 57/1 A rather gloomy Schopen hauerian melancholy and despair in *The White Peacock* and *The Trespasser.*

schottische, *sb.* **a.** (Earlier examples.)

1849 *Theatrical Programme* 9 July 48 The aim of whose existence appears to be that of rattling through the polka or schottische with the velocity of a spinning jenny. **1855** J. E. Cooke *Ellie* 151 This abominable German usage we have imported—the polka and the schottish too.

schottische, *v.* (Earlier example.)

1865 O. W. Norton *Army Lett.* 27 Aug. (1903) 277, I could only schottische a little.

Schottky (ʃǫ·tki). [The name of Walter *Schottky* (1886–1976), German physicist.] **1.** Used *attrib.* in *Electr.* and *Electronics*: **Schottky barrier,** an electrostatic depletion layer formed at the interface of a metal and a semiconductor in contact, causing the junction to act as an electrical rectifier; freq. *attrib.*; **Schottky diagram** = *Schottky plot*; **Schottky diode,** a solid-state diode having a metal-semiconductor junction, used in fast switching and voltage-clamping applications; **Schottky effect,** the increase in thermionic emission of a solid surface resulting from the lowering of its work function by the presence of an external electric field; *esp.* the increase in anode current in a thermionic valve beyond that predicted by the Richardson equation because of the electric field produced by the anode at the surface of the cathode; **Schottky line,** the straight line on the Schottky plot predicted by the Schottky theory; **Schottky plot,** a diagram used to illustrate the Schottky effect, obtained by plotting the logarithm of the current density against the square root of the applied electric field at constant emitter temperature; **Schottky slope,** the gradient of the Schottky line; **Schottky theory,** the theoretical basis of the Schottky effect.

1949 *Proc. Inst. Electr. Engineers* XCVI. I. 258, F_0 is the field of the Sc[h]ottky barrier at the contact with the metal. **1957** H. K. Henisch *Rectifying Semi-Conductor Contacts* vii. 195 It is desirable to examine to what extent tunnel penetration near the top of a Schottky barrier (where the barrier is thin) determines the effective barrier height. **1964** *Bell System Technical Jrnl.* XLIII. 215 GaAs Schottky barrier varactor diodes constructed on epitaxial films may be designed to yield a high cutoff frequency. **1975** Schottky barrier [see *Schottky diode* below]. **1967** *Brit. Jrnl. Appl. Physics* XVIII. 629 The saturation values were obtained from Schottky diagrams in which the logarithm of the current is plotted against the square root of the anode voltage. **1968** *Proc. Inst. Electr. & Electronics Engineers* LVI. 232/2 (*heading*) Integrated Schottky-diode clamp for transistor storage time control. **1969** *Electronics* 21 July 76/2 The Schottky diode storage time is effectively zero, in contrast to typical values of 6 nsec for the gold-doped junction diode and 30 nsec for the junction diode without gold doping. **1975** D. G. Fink *Electronics Engineers' Handbk.* viii. 39 In Schottky barrier diodes current flow is by majority carriers, rather than by minority carrier diffusion. Thus switching speeds of Schottky diodes are not limited by storage-time delays. **1925** J. B. Johnson in *Physical Rev.* XXVI. 71 When current is limited by space charge the Schottky effect decreases because of the interaction of the electrons. **1949** *Rev. Mod. Physics* XXI. 226/2 Theory and the periodic Schottky effect both indicate at most a small reflection effect for clean tungsten. **1975** D. G. Fink *Electronics Engineers' Handbk.* i. 34 The increase in current as the anode voltage is increased beyond the value at which the normal saturation value of emitted current occurs (the Schottky effect) results from reduction by the applied field of the work function. **1930** *Rev. Mod. Physics* II. 151 A quantitative estimate of the field strength that is needed to cause the emission to depart appreciably from the Schottky line..may be made by considering the..simplified case. **1949** *Ibid.* XXI. 200/1 The well-established low voltage deviation from the Schottky line for thermionic emission from polycrystal surfaces of clean metals indicates a variation in thermionic properties of the various surfaces of crystals. *Ibid.* 204/1 Generally, the experimental Schottky plots deviate from the theory..in the low voltage region. **1967** *Brit. Jrnl. Appl. Physics* XVIII. 629 The zero-field emission is obtained by prolonging the straight asymptote of the Schottky plots to the $V = 0$ line. **1939** *Physical Rev.* LVI. 664/2 The slope of the reference line.. was the Schottky slope. **1963** J. J. Brophy *Electr. Processes in Materials* xi. 317 At the larger fields, the data points fall on a straight line having the Schottky slope.., and extrapolation of this line to zero field gives the value of J. **1930** *Rev. Mod. Physics* II. 155 Reynolds..found a variation with voltage in excellent agreement with the Schottky theory for field strengths exceeding about 10,000 volts/cm. **1958** Condon & Odishaw *Handbk. of Physics* viii. vi. 77/2 The small periodic deviations of the emission current from that predicted by the Schottky theory are..a field effect but come about through the interference effect of electron waves as the shape of the barrier is changed by means of the applied field.

2. Used *attrib.* and in the possessive with reference to the **Schottky defect,** a vacancy in a crystal lattice in which the missing atom is not an interstitial one and the number of anion and cation vacancies is such as to preserve electrical neutrality; also, the smallest possible group of such vacancies that preserves neutrality.

1938 *Trans. Faraday Soc.* XXXIV. 861 In the case of Schottky-disorder an equivalent number of anions and cations have been removed from normal lattice positions leaving holes of both 'signs'. **1940** Mott & Gurney *Electronic Processes in Ionic Crystals* ii. 26 There are two ways in which..vacant lattice points and interstitial atoms or ions can arise; we shall call them 'Frenkel defects' and 'Schottky defects'. *Ibid.* 30 We now consider a crystal containing *n* Schottky holes. **1958** K. M. Hornsby tr. *P. Glafkides's Photographic Chem.* iii. 25 Schottky's defects consist of shallow vacant sites of Br^- and Ag^+ ions, in equal quantity. **1958** Condon & Odishaw *Handbk. of Physics* viii. iii. 48/2 In a crystal containing a divalent cation impurity,..there will be a temperature below which the number of Schottky cation vacancies will be smaller than the number of additional free cation vacancies. **1966** *McGraw-Hill Encycl. Sci. & Technol.* III. 583/2 In $CaCl_2$, the Schottky defect is one positive-ion vacancy and two negative-ion vacancies. **1966** C. R. Tottle *Sci. Engin. Materials* iv. 90 The Schottky defect..is not limited to the migration of an atom to the surface, but refers to the production of a vacancy whenever a migrating atom moves to some position that does not create disturbance in the remaining lattice, i.e. the surface of a void or other sink of disordered atoms. **1967** F. C. Brown *Physics of Solids* x. 303 By comparing the lattice parameter..with the observed mass and volume of the sample, it is possible to distinguish between Frenkel and Schottky disorder. **1972** B. Henderson *Defects in Crystalline Solids* i. 11 The change in thermal entropy favours the formation of Schottky vacancies.

schradan (ʃrā·dăn). Also Schradan. [f. the name of Gerhard *Schrader* (b. 1903), German chemist, who first prepared it + -an.] A viscous liquid organophosphorus compound, bis(bisdimethylamino)phosphonous anhydride, $((CH_3)_2N)_2PO.O.PO(N(CH_3)_2)_2$, used as a systemic insecticide in the form of an aqueous solution.

1951 *Jrnl. Sci. Food & Agric.* II. 310 The systemic insecticide Schradan is slowly broken down in the plant by enzymic reaction. **1953** *New Biol.* XIV. 108 Schradan.. renders plants highly toxic to sucking insects but has no appreciable effect on bees. **1964** A. H. Burgess *Hops* i. 17 Systemic insecticides, such as schradan, which was first introduced for commercial use on hops in 1949, have revolutionized the control of pests on hops. **1977** M. B. Green et al. *Chemicals for Crop Protection & Pest Control* vii. 54 The only other compound with..any commercial utility was schradan, but this..is not now used because of its high mammalian toxicity.

Schrader (ʃrēⁱ·dəɹ). The name of George H. F. *Schrader* (fl. 1895), of New York, used as a proprietary term to designate air valves of a type introduced by him and used esp. on tyres.

1895 *Official Gaz* (U.S. Patent Office) 30 Apr. 750/2 Pneumatic and tire valves. George H. F. Schrader, New York, N.Y...Essential feature.—The words 'Schrader Universal'. Used since February 12, 1895. **1920** R. T. Nicholson *Bk. of Ford Van* xvi. 100 (*caption*) Section of the Schrader tyre valve. **1921** —— *Bk. of Ford* (ed. 6) xi. 252 Most tyres fitted to the Ford have Schrader valves, which want understanding. **1940** E. Molloy *Landing Legs, Wheels, & Brakes* i. 8 (*caption*) The cap of the special Schrader valve is screwed on in reverse to release the air pressure. **1950** C. A. H. Pollitt *Air Systems for Aircraft* iv. 38 The valve has the usual Schrader-type screwed fixing sleeve. **1967** *Trade Marks Jrnl.* 10 May 588/1 Schrader. **1977** *Lancet* 23 July 175/1 Thinking, reasonably, that this was a colour-coding marker indicating nitrous oxide, she reconnected this hose to the spigot of the blue-painted nitrous-oxide Schrader valve.

Schrage (ʃrā·gə). *Electr.* The name of H. K. *Schrage* (fl. 1914), Swedish engineer, used *attrib.* and in the possessive to designate a type of three-phase a.c. motor invented by him, in which a commutator motor is combined with an induction motor to provide speed variability at high torque.

1919 R. M. Walmsley *Electr. in Service of Man* (rev. ed.) II. ii. v. 780 (*caption*) Connections of Schrage's three-phase shunt commutator motor. *Ibid.*, The brush mounting..of a Schrage motor. **1927** V. Karapetoff *Exper. Electr. Engin.* (ed. 3) II. 439 The Schrage motor belongs to the class of adjustable-speed compensated polyphase induction motors. **1945** E. Molloy *'Electr. Engineer' Ref. Bk.* viii. 51 The Schrage system of speed control requires that the primary winding (which is connected to the supply system) shall be on the rotor and the secondary winding on the stator. **1962** G. A. T. Burdett *Automatic Control Handbk.* i. 12 A Schrage motor operates on the moving brush or rotor fed principle.

Schrammel (ʃræ·mĕl). Also with small initial. The name of Johann (1850–97) and Josef (1852–94) *Schrammel*, Austrian musicians, used *attrib.* in **Schrammel quartet** [G. *Schrammelquartett*, also used], a Viennese light-music ensemble comprising two violins, guitar, and accordion (orig. clarinet) popularized by the Schrammels. Also ‖ **Schrammelmusik** [G. *Schrammelmusik*], music played by or arranged for a Schrammel quartet or orchestra; so **Schrammel band, orchestra.**

1924 E. Wellesz in A. Eaglefield-Hull *Dict. Mod. Music & Musicians* 445/2 Nearly all the comp[ositions] of popular Viennese comp[osers], especially operetta-comp[osers] are arr[anged] for this combination which is called *Schrammel quartet.* **1938** *Oxf. Compan. Music* 848/2 *Schrammel quartet*, this is a popular Viennese type of instrumental quartet for light music... Sometimes the combination expands somewhat, into a 'Schrammel Orchestra'. **1963** E.-L. Wuorio *Woman with Portuguese Basket* xix. 167 We can go to a 'nobelheurige' which is a big place with schrammel band and singers. **1967** R. M. Stern *Kessler Legacy* ii. 24 In one corner..a stringed orchestra played *Schrammel-musik.* **1969** A. Arent *Laying on of Hands* xii. 138 The new wine and *Schrammelmusik* were available in Grinzing. **1974** P. Gore-Booth *With Great Truth & Respect* 72 We sought a '*Heuriger*', a traditional garden restaurant in Grinzing, where people drink new wine to the sound of the Schrammel-Quartett, a small ensemble with violin and harmonica.

‖ **Schrecklichkeit** (ʃre·klıχʸkəit). [Ger., = 'frightfulness'.] = *frightfulness. Also *transf.* and *fig.*

1917 G. B. Shaw in *New Republic* 6 Jan. 274/1 As to the deliberate *Schrecklichkeit* of the Germans in Belgium..no man should judge unless he knows the military history of all invasions, and of that very British institution, the punitive expedition. **1944** —— *Everybody's Political What's What?* xxxv. 307 The British frightfulness of 1943 has left the German Schrecklichkeit of 1915 far behind. **1969** R. Lowell *Notebk. 1967–68* 96 Mohammed..smashed the celibates... Changed their non-activist Buddhistic rote to his clans' strict laws of *schrecklichkeit* and honor. **1972** K. Bonfiglioli *Don't point that Thing at Me* ii. 10, I embarked on the quotidian *schrecklichkeit* of getting up. **1976** *Listener* 6 May 588/3 The *Schrecklichkeit* in which the relations between parents and children are so often conducted in Britain.

schreibersite. Substitute for def.: † **a.** A chromium sulphide, Cr_2S_3, supposed to have been found in a meteorite. *Obs.*

1846 C. U. SHEPARD in *Amer. Jrnl. Sci.* LII. 383 Schreibersite, (Shepard).—Named in honor of the late Carl von Schreibers, Director of the Imperial Cabinet at Vienna, and a well known author on meteorites.

b. A strongly magnetic phosphide of iron and nickel, $(Fe,Ni)_3P$, usu. with small amounts of cobalt, that is present in iron meteorites and forms lustrous white tetragonal crystals that tarnish to yellow or brown. Cf. RHABDITE 3. [ad. G. *schreibersit* (A. Patera 1847, in *Österreichische Blätter f. Lit. und Kunst* 23 July 694/2).]

1849 *Amer. Jrnl. Sci.* LVIII. 440 Something..similar is found in the meteoric iron of Arva. Patera was enabled to collect a sufficient quantity of it to make three analyses... As Berzelius had given no name to this substance, Haidinger, in concurrence with M. Patera, proposed for it the specific name of Schreibersite. At a subsequent session.. Haidinger..says he has since learned that the American mineralogist and chemist, Prof. Shepard,..had given..*this same name* to a mineral, also of meteoric origin, which occurs in small brown striated prisms in the meteoric stone of Bishopsville, S.C., which fell in March, 1843... Haidinger..would be pleased to continue the name of Schreibersite to the Arva Species, and would propose for Shepard's new species, the name of Shepardite. **1868** [in Dict.]. **1968** *Jrnl. Geophysical Res.* LXXIII. 6963/2 The most notable feature of schreibersite is its compositional variability. **1975** *Sci. Amer.* Feb. 35/1 At 1,294 degrees gaseous molecular phosphorus reacted with the surface of the metal grains, thus forming the mineral schreibersite. **1977** A. HALLAM *Planet Earth* 27/3 Other highly significant features which must be explained are the presence within some tektites of minute grains of the meteoritic minerals kamacite, troilite and schreibersite, [etc.].

‖ **schreierpfeife** (ʃraɪ·əɹpfaɪ:fə). Also Schreierpfeife. Pl. **schreierpfeifen.** [G., lit. 'screamer pipe'.] A musical instrument of the variety collectively known as *SCHRYARI.

1939 [see *SCHRYARI]. **1957** A. BAINES *Woodwind Instr. & their Hist.* x. 258 Several German inventories.. mention a consort of *Schreierpfeifen* or *Schryari* ('crying' or 'screaming' pipes..). These do not seem to occur in any known account of a musical performance, but Praetorius says that they could be used either alone or with other instruments. **1976** D. MUNROW *Instr. Middle Ages & Renaissance* 51/1 The origin of the name *Schreierpfeife* (Italian *schryari*) is unclear: perhaps it had something to do with the instrument's 'screaming' tone quality.

schreik, var. *SKRIK.

Schreiner (ʃraɪ·nəɹ). *Textiles.* Also **schreiner.** The name of Ludwig *Schreiner* (fl. 1900), German textile manufacturer, used *attrib.* with reference to a method of finishing mercerized fabrics by passing them through a calender, one of whose rollers has engraved upon it many fine, evenly-spaced, parallel lines which are impressed on to the fabric imparting lustre to the material.

1904 *Dyer & Calico Printer* XXIV. 9 The Schreiner finish is daily growing in importance and will..become of vaster importance than is at present dreamt of. **1946** A. J. HALL *Stand. Handbk. Textiles* iv. 241 Whilst quite a high lustre can be secured in this way there is another kind of calender which can achieve even more. It is the Schreiner calender. **1960** *Times Rev. Industry* Nov. 46/2 Among the ways of finishing a standard grey rayon material of this type are durable schreiner finishes, permanent glazed finishes, and embossed finishes. **1962** J. T. MARSH *Self-Smoothing Fabrics* xiii. 201 For the schreiner effect, pressures of 20 tons or so are commonly utilised and a temperature of 170 to 180 °C; many finishers calender the impregnated and dried goods before putting them through the schreiner machine. **1963** A. J. HALL *Textile Sci.* v. 257 A light Schreiner calendering can very effectively and desirably make more opaque the gossamer sheer and transparent knitted nylon nightwear fabrics... The passage of this fabric through a Schreiner calender..just flattens the thermoplastic nylon threads so as to fill out the interstices in the fabric yet without..impairing the fabric lustre.

Hence **Schrei·ner** *v. trans.*, to finish (fabric) by this method; also *absol.*; **Schrei·nered** *ppl. a.*; **Schrei·nering, Schrei·nerizing** *vbl. sbs.*

1905 BEAN & MCCLEARY *Chem. Finishing* 375 When the 'schreinering' process is combined with 'mercerising', it gives the nearest approach to silk ever obtained. *Ibid.* 376 Plain woven Calico goods may also be 'schreinered' with advantage. **1906** *Dyer & Calico Printer* XXVI. 17 During the last few years Schreinerising has made rapid strides, and is now a very general method of finishing dyed cotton piece goods. **1929** E. MIDGLEY *Finishing of Woven Fabrics* xii. 160 The type of lustre or reflection obtained from a broken surface, such as in the case of..schreinered sateens, is shown in Fig. 51. **1945** M. D. POTTER *Fiber to Fabric* v. 96 Schreinerizing is an inexpensive method for imparting luster to low-priced cottons. **1946** A. J. HALL *Stand. Handbk. Textiles* iv. 242 The method of schreinering fabric is comparatively simple. **1962** J. T. MARSH *Self-Smoothing Fabrics* xiii. 198 The general method is to impregnate the fabric, dry to definite requirements of moisture content, and then glaze, emboss, or schreiner, before completing the final condensation of the resin. *Ibid.* 202 The final handle of the goods is affected by the amount of moisture in the fabric at the moment of schreinering.

‖ **Schriftsprache** (ʃri·ft,ʃprāχə). *Philol.* [G., = literary or standard language.] The conventional and standardized written variety of a given language (or occas. a dialect).

1931 K. MALONE in *Mod. Lang. Notes* XLVI. 8 Caxton's importance for the English language lies chiefly in the part which he played in the standardization of our *schriftsprache.* **1934** C. L. WRENN in *Trans. Philol. Soc. 1933* 85 There was a common and universally used West-Saxon *Schriftsprache* in the late tenth and early eleventh centuries, as well known in York as in Canterbury. **1935** *Ess. & Stud. in Eng.* (Univ. Michigan Publ. Lang. & Lit. XIII) 281 The rise of a literary language, divorcing to some degree spelling and pronunciation, arouses our curiosity in regard to the extent of adoption of these voiceless inflections within the *Schriftsprache.* **1959** A. CAMPBELL *Old Eng. Gram.* 11 The vernacular ninth-century charters show a steady tendency towards the development of a local *Schriftsprache*, with increasing avoidance of Anglian spellings, and care to express local sound-changes.

schrijk, schrik, varr. *SKRIK.

schröckingerite (ʃrö·kiŋərəit). *Min.* Also **schroeckingerite.** [ad. G. *schröckingerit* (A. Schrauf 1873, in *Mineral. Mitt.* 137), f. the name of Baron J. von *Schröckinger*, 19th-cent. Austrian mineralogist: see -ITE[1].] A hydrated carbonate, sulphate, and fluoride of uranyl, calcium, and sodium found as greenish-yellow scales, usu. as an alteration product of uraninite.

1875 G. J. BRUSH *Dana's Syst. Min.* (ed. 5) App. II. 50 Schröckeringite [*sic*]... Occurs at Joachimsthal on uraninite, in small, six-sided tabular crystals. **1921** *Bull. U.S. Geol. Survey* No. 679. 131 A number of other specimens labeled 'schroeckingerite' were examined, but they proved to be uranothallite, or some other uranium mineral. **1967** *Mineral. Abstr.* XVIII. 247/1 The uranium is located only in a small mineralization zone and is primarily in pitchblende form. Secondary uranium minerals are: schröckingerite, Ca-nováčekite, and meta-zeunerite.

Schröder (ʃrö·dəɹ). Also **Schroeder.** The name of H. G. F. *Schröder* (1810–85), German mathematician and physicist, used *attrib.* and in the possessive to designate an optical illusion described by him (see *Ann. der Physik und Chem.* (1858) CV. 307), in the form of a line drawing of a staircase drawn without convergence of receding parallel lines, so that one appears successively to look down at the top and up at the underside of the staircase as the perspective reverses.

1898 E. C. SANFORD *Course in Exper. Psychol.* II. vii. 256 'Schröder's Stair Figure'..generally appears first as the upper flight of steps. **1901**, etc. [see *NECKER[1]]. **1925** J. P. C. SOUTHALL tr. J. von Kries in tr. *Helmholtz's Treat. Physiol. Optics* III. 597 A similar reversal of the impressions of distance occurs in looking at Schroeder's 'staircase' diagram.., especially if it is turned round. **1957** *Acta Psychologica* XIII. 86 With the Schröder stairs, now, a new means was found to ask the subject without using the words 'Up' or 'Down'. The S was simply asked: 'From which end would you approach the stairs in order to mount them, from Right or from Left?' **1974** *Sci. Amer.* July 101/1 The Schröder stairs, another 19th-century reversible-perspective illusion,..is the theme of Escher's 1953 lithograph *Relativity.*

Schrödinger (ʃrö·diŋəɹ). *Physics.* Also **Schroedinger.** The name of Erwin *Schrödinger* (1887–1961), Austrian-born physicist, used *attrib.* and in the possessive to designate concepts developed by him, as **Schrödinger('s) (wave) equation,** a differential equation whose solution is the Schrödinger function; this equation became the basis of the quantum-mechanical description of matter; **Schrödinger (wave, ψ-) function,** a complex function ψ of space and time such that the square of its absolute value is a measure of the local spatial probability density for a particle in the state (or with the probability amplitude) ψ, i.e., $|\psi|^2$ represents the average particle density at a given location in space and time.

1927 *Proc. R. Soc.* A. CXIV. 251 The Hamiltonian function will now provide a Schrödinger wave equation. **1935** PAULING & WILSON *Introd. Quantum Mechanics* iii. 53 The function $\Psi(x, t)$ is called the Schrödinger wave function including the time. **1938** R. W. LAWSON tr. *Hevesy & Paneth's Man. Radioactivity* (ed. 2) viii. 90 In wave mechanics a vibration law is formulated for the atom which is quite similar to the law of the mechanical vibrations of strings. But here we are not dealing with the motion of material particles, but with that of an abstract quantity called the Schrödinger ψ-function, which is only mathematically intelligible. **1955** W. HEISENBERG in W. Pauli *Niels Bohr* 23 His point of attack is..the fact that the wave function representing the system changes discontinuously when the observer takes cognizance of a result of measurement. Janossy asserts that this reduction cannot be deduced from Schrödinger's equation. **1961** POWELL & CRASEMANN *Quantum Mechanics* ii. 59 Many of the properties of ψ which are of physical interest are brought out more clearly by the Schrödinger equation than by the direct representation of ψ in terms of its harmonic components. **1968** M. S. LIVINGSTON *Particle Physics* iii. 51 The Schrödinger wave equation is based on the well-known differential equation for a traveling wave in a homogeneous medium. **1968** G. LUDWIG *Wave Mech.* I. iii. 42 Hence..the Schrödinger functions $\phi(x)$ are nothing other than the representation of the Hilbert space corresponding to the position operator. **1974** GILL & WILLIS *Pericyclic Reactions* i. 17 Now the energy can be calculated by substitution into the Schrödinger equation appropriate to the system.

schronch, var. *SCRONCH.

† **schrötterite.** *Min. Obs.* [ad. G. *schrötterit* (E. F. Glocker, *Grundr. d. Mineralogie* (1839) 536), f. the name of Anton *Schrötter* (1802–75), German chemist and mineralogist: see -ITE[1].] A name formerly applied to greenish opaline specimens of allophane.

1844 J. D. DANA *Syst. Mineral.* (ed. 2) 531 Schrötterite. Resembles allophane, and has been called opal allophane. **1858** *Amer. Jrnl. Sci.* LXXVI. 79 The fragment of rock upon which the Schrötterite occurs is a dark-colored bituminous slate. **1934** *Prof. Papers U.S. Geol. Survey* No. 185. 146/2 The analyses reported in this paper and earlier studies by others have discredited all the known reported occurrences of schrötterite, including the type material... Schrötterite should be entirely discarded as a mineral name.

schrund. Substitute for pronunc.: (ʃrunt). Delete ‖ and add: *spec.* = *BERGSCHRUND; *schrund line, schrundline*: (see quot. 1904[2]). (Earlier and later examples.)

1870 A. G. GIRDLESTONE *High Alps without Guides* ii. 36 We could see into the great blue 'schrunds', in which innumerable and gigantic icicles depended from the roof. **1904** G. K. GILBERT in *Jrnl. Geol.* XII. 573 Among the numerous crevasses or schrunds of several diverse systems sharply lining the snow surface.., one master opening, the *Bergschrund* of the Swiss mountaineers, paralleled the amphitheater wall... My instant surmise..was that this curving great schrund penetrated to the foot of the wall. *Ibid.* 582 Usually in viewing a cirque it is possible to trace about its wall a somewhat definite line separating a cliff or steeper slope above from a gentler, usually scalable, slope below. This line I conceive to mark the base of the bergschrund [*sic*] at a late stage in the excavation of the cirque basin. I have called it in my notes 'the schrund line'. **1938** *Geol. Mag.* LXXV. 262 This scarp..passes into the great vertical cliffs below Y Lliwedd so that the schrundline was present only on the side wall. **1939** *Geogr. Jrnl.* XCIV. 462 Above the crevasse the surface of the glacier was covered by scree; and the material embedded in the ice, as seen in the bergschrund, is probably derived in some way from this surface material... A snow-bridge occurred 25 feet below the surface in the open part of the schrund. **1968** R. W. FAIRBRIDGE *Encycl. Geomorphol.* 741/2 Below the schrund line, where there is one, the cirque floor begins as a slope that bears marks of glacial abrasion. **1971** C. BONINGTON *Annapurna South Face* xii. 152 They were both worried by the huge overhang of snow that reared over the schrund like a breaking wave.

‖ **schryari** (ʃriā·ri). Usu. *collect.* [Of uncertain origin (see note below).] A variety of wooden double-reed wind instrument used in the sixteenth and seventeenth centuries and recently revived for the playing of early music.

Our knowledge of the *schryari* comes principally from descriptions and drawings furnished by Praetorius, who regards the term as a plural form related to *SCHREIERPFEIFE. Later authorities have suggested an Italian or Oriental origin, but satisfactory evidence is lacking.

[**1618–20** M. PRAETORIUS *Syntagma Musicum* II. xviii. 42 Schryari (Auff deutsch Schreyerpfeiffen) sennd starck vnnd frisch am Laut/können vor sich alleine/vnd auch zu andern Instrumenten gebraucht werden [etc.].] **1939** A. CARSE *Musical Wind Instr.* xi. 129 Still more shadowy are the *schryari* or *schreierpfeifen* of which Praetorius gave a brief description... Not a single specimen is known. **1940** C. SACHS *Hist. Mus. Instr.* xv. 322 *Schryari* were loud, shrill, double-reed instruments with a tapering bore and a reed-concealing cap; they had seven fingerholes in front and two in back for the two thumbs. **1964** S. MARCUSE *Mus. Instr.* 463/1 Schryari were made in consorts of soprano, alto/tenor, and bass; they had conical tubes with double reed protected by a reed cap, 7 front fingerholes, and 2 rear thumbholes. **1976** D. MUNROW *Instr. Middle Ages & Renaissance* 52/2 The most surprising feature however is that the exterior of the schryari is conical.

schtick, var. *SHTIK.

schtschi, var. STCHI in Dict. and Suppl.

Schubertiad (ʃubɜ̄·ɹtiæd). Also ‖ **Schubertiade** (ʃubertiā·də), pl. **-n.** [ad. G. *Schubertiade*: see next and -AD.] A concert party or recital devoted solely to the performance of music and songs by Schubert.

1869 A. D. COLERIDGE tr. *K. von Hellborn's Life F. Schubert* I. ix. 223 The 'Schubertiaden',—social unions of Schubert's friends, where..Schubert's own compositions formed the staple of the entertainment. **1905** E. DUNCAN *Schubert* 93 Many of Schubert's friends and acquaintances.. banded together in a kind of social union, which became known by the name of *Schubertiaden.* Games were played, dancing and speech-making were cultivated, while the heart of the whole entertainment was discovered in the performance of Schubert's latest songs, and others of his compositions. **1945** A. HUTCHINGS *Schubert* iv. 39 Netty Hönig, in whose home so many happy Schubertiads had been held. **1963** *Times* 12 Mar. 14/4 Last night he and Mr. Gerald Moore gave us a Schubertiad in the Festival Hall. **1967** M. J. E. BROWN *Schubert Songs* v. 40 His [*sc.* Schubert's] time was occupied in Vienna by..the increasing demands of the very popular *Schubertiaden*—evenings devoted to the performance of his songs. **1977** *Times* 1 Feb. 9/2 Yesterday was Schubert's birthday..suitable occasion for a Schubertiad.

Schubertian (ʃubɜ̄·ɹtiăn), *a.* and *sb.* Also **Schubertean.** [f. the name of Franz Peter *Schubert* (1797–1828), Austrian composer + -IAN.] **A.** *a.* Of, pertaining to, or characteristic of Schubert or his music. **B.** *sb.* An admirer or adherent of Schubert; a (skilled) exponent of Schubert's music.

1866 E. WILBERFORCE *Franz Schubert* iv. 83 The present biographer discovered it in a pile of Schubertian MSS. **1911** J. A. FULLER-MAITLAND *Brahms* iv. 90 The fourth ballade, after its Schubertian waverings between minor and major, strikes the same mysterious note. **1927** *Observer* 2 Oct. 14/4 The work was well chosen to follow the Schubert Quintet, for in its trio there is the germ from which sprang what is now recognised as a truly Schubertian progression. **1928** B. MARSHALL tr. *K. Kobald's F. Schubert* 276 In the streets of the city the faithful Schubertians followed their adored genius to the grave. **1945** A. HUTCHINGS *Schubert* iii. 28 Anselm had two brothers, Josef and Heinrich, who were ardent Schubertians. **1959** *Times* 9 Nov. 6/4 The long, smooth lines of the allegretto were clouded by no more than a Schubertian wistfulness. **1971** *Daily Tel.* 25 Jan. 6/2 He [*sc.* Wilhelm Kempff] plays a lovely short A-major sonata..but he cannot, I conclude, be counted among the true-blue Schubertians.

schuchardtite (ʃū·χăɹtəit). *Min.* [ad. G. *schuchardtit* (A. Schrauf 1882, in *Zeitschr. für Krist.* VI. 386), f. the name of Theodor *Schuchardt,* 19th-cent. mineral dealer: see -ITE[1].] An ill-defined green hydrated silicate of nickel, resembling chlorite.

1885 *Jrnl. Chem. Soc.* XLVIII. I. 32 Schuchardtite... This mineral is of an apple-green colour, soft, and is disintegrated by water. **1966** *Amer. Mineralogist* LI. 292 The analytical data for schuchardtite are inconclusive; they do not fall near to the composition of the serpentine group where they would be expected to be situated but suggest admixture with pimelite. **1975** *Mineral Mag.* XL. 152 We hesitate to label the Jacupiranga minerals as schuchardtites mainly because the type material was insufficiently defined.

‖ **Schuhplattler** (ʃū·platləɹ) Also **schuh-** and erron. **Schuplaettler, -platter,** etc. [G., f. *schuh* shoe + south G. dial. *plattler* (f. *platteln* to slap).] A lively Bavarian and Austrian folk-dance, characterized by the slapping of the thighs and heels. Also **Schu·hplattltanz** (*irreg.*); **Schu·hplatteln** [G. *schuhplatteln,* to perform this dance].

1874 K. STIELER in Schmid & Stieler *Bavarian Highlands* 108 The idea of the 'Schuhplattltanz' is taken from hunting-life—from the movements of the moor-cock and wood-grouse. **1895** L. GROVE *Dancing* ix. 317 An old German dance..called the 'Schuhplatteln'. **1905** W. D. MCCRACKAN *Tyrol* x. 82 The dancer extemporized as he threw down his money for the musicians. This pay gave him the privilege of the floor for his *Ländler* (waltz), or his *Schuhplattler.* **1920** D. H. LAWRENCE *Women in Love* xxix. 456 They were dancing all together, dancing the Schuhplatteln. **1958** M. WEST *Second Victory* i. 5 The orchestras played Strauss waltzes and the peasant troupes came in to dance the *Schuhplattler* and play the zither for local colour. **1960** *Guardian* 12 Apr. 8/7 Besides the yodelling..there are the frolicsome Schuplaettler dances. **1962** *Times* 10 Nov. 11/7 The dancing of the *schuhplattler* forms a cheerful accompaniment to a stein of beer. **1976** *Michigan Holiday News* (West Michigan Tourist Assoc.) May 11/1 The Schuhplatter Dancers, the Bavarian contribution to the art of dance, occupy a unique place in the central Michigan area.

Schüller–Christian (ʃüləɹ kri·stiăn). *Path.* The names of Artur *Schüller* (1874–1958), Austrian neurologist, and Henry Asbury *Christian* (1876–1951), U.S. physician, who each described the condition (in *Fortschritte a.d. Geb. d. Roentgenstrahlen* (1916) XXIII. 12 and *Contrib. Med. & Biol. Res.* (1919) I. 390 respectively), used *attrib.* to designate a pathological condition, often associated with diabetes insipidus, in which masses of lipid-laden histiocytes develop, usu. in the bones. Also in comb. with the name of Alfred *Hand* (1868–1949), U.S. pædiatrician.

[**1925** C. Q. THOMPSON et al. in *Arch. Internal Med.* XXXVI. 650 As Christian's excellent paper has formed and will continue to form the basis for studies of this baffling syndrome, it is suggested for the sake of simplicity the name Christian's syndrome be used.] **1935** *Brit. Jrnl. Surg.* XXII. 810 It is that which is known to the medical profession as Schüller-Christian's syndrome. *Ibid.* 811 An excess of cholesterol in certain body tissues is the primary factor in the production of the clinical syndrome of lipoid granulomatosis (Schüller-Christian's disease). **1953** Schüller-Christian disease [see *HISTIOCYTOSIS] **1960** Hand-Schuller-Christian disease [see *lipid storage* s.v. *LIPID 2]. **1974** R. M. KIRK et al. *Surgery* vii. 151 Schuller-Christian disease. Histiocytes contain cholesterol.

schultenite (ʃu·ltĕnəit). *Min.* [f. the name of August Benjamin Friherre at *Schultén* (1856–1912), Finnish chemist and mineralogist: see -ITE[1].] A native lead hydrogen arsenate, $PbH(AsO_4)$, found as colourless, transparent monoclinic crystals.

1926 L. J. SPENCER in *Mineral. Mag.* XXI. 149 His 'monétite arséniée de plomb' is the subject of the present note, and for it, as a mineral, the name schultenite is suggested. **1968** I. KOSTOV *Mineralogy* 467 Schultenite is found in gypsum-like crystals with distinct {010} cleavage.

Schultz–Charlton (ʃults tʃā·ɹltǫn). *Med.* The names of Werner *Schultz* (1878–1948) and Willy *Charlton* (b. 1889), German physicians, together used *attrib.* to denote the test made by intradermal injection of antibody to scarlet fever toxin, or of serum containing this; and to denote the phenomenon, characteristically diagnostic of scarlet fever, whereby such an injection causes local extinction of a rash.

1922 *Jrnl. Amer. Med. Assoc.* 12 Aug. 594/1 Rojo's experience has confirmed the specific and reliable nature of the Schultz–Charlton phenomenon in the differential diagnosis of scarlet fever. **1925** *Jrnl. Clin. Invest.* I. 275 (*heading*) The Schultz–Charlton phenomenon. *Ibid.* 293 Serum from convalescent scarlet fever patients produced the Schultz–Charlton rash extinction phenomenon in twenty-four of twenty-seven cases tested. **1974** *Encycl. Brit. Micropædia* VIII. 948/1 When an injection of a small amount of immune serum..is made into the skin while the rash is at its height, a blanched area results at the point of injection within 18 hours if the rash in question is caused by scarlet fever toxin. This reaction is known as the Schultz–Charlton test.

Schumannesque (ʃūmane·sk), *a.* [f. the name of Robert Alexander *Schumann* (1810–1856), German composer + -ESQUE.] Resembling the compositions or technique of Schumann. So **Schumannism,** a musical element in the style of Schumann; **Schumannite,** an admirer or interpreter of Schumann.

1901 G. B. SHAW in *Anglo-Saxon Rev.* Mar. 229, I doubt whether even Puccini really studies Schumann, in spite of his harmonic Schumannisms. **1947** A. EINSTEIN *Music in Romantic Era* xiv. 191 Another follower of Schumann was Robert Franz (1815–1892), a pure specialist in song—a 'Schumannite'. *Ibid.* 196 It is significant that his first, Schumannesque songs were composed to German texts. **1958** *Listener* 18 Sept. 441/2 The richly coloured, evocative scores of Lalo are few. The 'Symphonie espagnole' is among them but not his Schumannesque symphony. **1961** *Times* 20 Feb. 6/1 His account of the first movement of Beethoven's Waldstein Sonata seemed wayward and at times almost Schumannesque in its fluctuations of tempo. **1977** *Gramophone* Sept. 503/3 Several passages, in particular the long, Schumannesque interlude before the eighth (of twelve) song, that add something to our knowledge of Strauss's abilities.

Schu mine (ʃū məin). [App. an Eng. shortening of G. *Schützenmine* *S-MINE, but see quot. 1945[2].] A type of German anti-personnel mine used in the war of 1939–45.

1945 *Finito! Po Valley Campaign* (15th Army Group) 41 The 10th Mountain Division pushed forward.. across a valley studded with Teller mines, Schu mines and the glass-topped Topf mines that fooled the mine-detectors. **1945** [see *anti-personnel* s.v. *ANTI-[1] B. 4 (iii)]. **1961** W. VAUGHAN-THOMAS *Anzio* ix. 209 The Germans..discovered the path..and sowed it with *Schu* mines—those vicious, light-weight, anti-personnel mines, cased in plastic.

Schumpeterian (ʃumpĕtiᵊ·riăn), *a.* *Econ.* [f. the name of the Moravian-born economist, Joseph Alois *Schumpeter* (1883–1950) + -IAN. Applied to the economic doctrines put forward by Schumpeter, esp. those dealing with the rôle of the entrepreneur, interest, and business cycles in the capitalist system. Hence as *sb.*, an advocate of these doctrines.

1950 CLEMENCE & DOODY *Schumpeterian System* vii. 57 The innovation of mild prosperity is the innovation of the Schumpeterian System. **1970** C. FURTADO in I. L. Horowitz *Masses in Lat. Amer.* ii. 32 These urban elements were indeed the Schumpeterians of the development, 'the forward marchers' of Latin America. **1975** *New Society* 2 Oct. 28/1 The negative, Schumpeterian defence of democracy stresses the political skills of the leaders rather than the rank and file..but sees that being chosen by an appropriate constituency is the great source of legitimacy in the modern world. **1976** *Times Lit. Suppl.* 20 Feb. 206/4 Japanese businessmen have not been typical exponents of the Weberian 'spirit of capitalism' or even Schumpeterian individualists.

schungite, var. *SHUNGITE.

Schuplaettler, ¶ var. *SCHUHPLATTLER.

‖ **Schupo** (ʃū·po). Also **schupo.** [G., colloq. abbrev. of Schu*tz*po*lizei* and Schu*tz*po*lizist* security police(man).] In Germany, a policeman; also *collect.*, the police force.

1923 *Glasgow Herald* 20 Mar. 9/5 In the events which are taking place in the Ruhr daily there is hardly one in which the schupos or green police are not concerned. **1934** *New Republic* 18 July 249/2 Similar to the *Gestapo* was the *Schupo,* the former municipal police forces of Germany. **1966** *Economist* 5 Nov. 568/1 Many of these former 'schupos' hold fairly prominent positions in the Austrian police and gendarmerie today. **1979** G. MARKSTEIN *Traitor for Cause* 14 As usual, two green-uniformed Schupos were at their post, the token presence..of West German authority.

‖ **schuss** (ʃūs), *sb.* *Skiing.* [G., lit. 'a shot'.] A straight, downhill run; the slope on which such a run is executed. Also *transf.* and *attrib.*

1937 O. LANG *Downhill Skiing* ii. 19 The straight running, or 'schuss', position should be very elastic. **1947** F. A. SMYTHE *Again Switzerland* 37 Down to the broad-backed ridge beneath..the last hundred feet in a glorious 'schuss'. **1958** L. WHISHAW *As Far as you'll take Me* iii. 31 Jack [*sc.* a lorry driver] started us on another downhill schuss. **1961** *Times* 10 Jan. 14/7 There is then a final *schuss,* which will provide sufficient speed to make the bumps before the finish. **1966** M. CATTO *Bird on Wing* iv. 62 Skis close—the whang of the wind eddying in a blast up the *Schuss.* **1977** C. WOOD *James Bond* ii. 21 He..dropped to the schuss position as soon as he began to pick up speed.

‖ **schuss,** *v.* *Skiing.* [f. prec.] **1.** *trans.* To ski down (a slope, etc.) or cover (a certain distance) by means of a schuss.

1937 O. LANG *Downhill Skiing* v. 27 In practice you will find that it is impossible to take everything 'straight' or to 'schuss' it as we express it. **1947** *Sun* (Baltimore) 28 Mar. 13/3 In April, 1939, in the annual 'inferno' races from the summit, Toni 'schussed' 3.8 miles with a vertical drop of 4,300 feet in 6½ minutes. **1972** T. MCHUGH *Time of Buffalo* xii. 147 Within minutes we were schussing cornices. **1976** *National Observer* (U.S.) 20 Nov. 15/1 Schussing the Italian Alps is the newcomer on many skiers' dream list.

2. *intr.* To effect a schuss; to ski downhill. Also with *down.*

1963 I. FLEMING *On H.M. Secret Service* xvii. 188 Bond schussed easily downwards..resting his limbs. **1969** R. PETRIE *Despatch of Dove* xii. 181 Would she..assume Zoë had *schussed* down on her own? **1973** *Times* 28 Sept. 36/5 Forty miles of pistes where you can schuss, trek, slalom, langlauf. **1979** N. SLATER *Falcon* ix. 160 When he *schussed* down the shallower *pistes,* his skis were closely parallel.

Hence **schu·ssing** *vbl. sb.*, the action of the vb.

1961 R. SKEPPER *Tackle Ski-ing this Way* vi. 74 Schussing is probably where the pleasure skier and the racer come into closest contact. Everybody enjoys trying a schuss. **1969** R. PETRIE *Despatch of Dove* xii. 176 The Grand Finale will be mass *schussing.* **1977** *Time* 21 Feb. 52/2 He gave up downhill schussing, lest an accident keep him away from the boardroom, but enjoys cross-country skiing.

‖ **schussboomer** (ʃū·sbūməɹ). *U.S.* [f. as prec. + BOOM *v.*[1] + -ER[1].] A fast downhill skier. Also *attrib.* Hence **schu·ssbooming,** fast downhill skiing.

1959 *Washington Post* 11 Dec. c6/4 Expert schussboomers appear to be coming down the slopes in effortless motion. **1961** *Ski* Nov. 33 (*heading*) Can schussbooming be stopped? *Ibid.* 34/2 The various solutions proposed for the 'schussboomer problem' in the past have tended to place most of the burdens on the ski area operators. **1967** *N.Y. Times* 20 Jan. 33/6 Cervenia continues to be the schussboomer's paradise.

‖ **Schutzbund** (ʃu·tsbunt). [G., lit. 'defence alliance'.] In full *Republikanischer Schutzbund,* an Austrian Social Democratic paramilitary organization, dissolved in 1933. Also *attrib.* Hence **Schu·tzbü:ndler,** a member of the Schutzbund.

1927 *Daily Tel.* 19 July 11/5 In an encounter between the Schutzbund and Communists and criminals six persons were killed. **1955** KOESTLER *Trail of Dinosaur* 44 The few thousand foreign workers—mainly Austrian *Schutzbund* people and German Communists—who were admitted into Soviet Russia. **1973** E. OSERS tr. *K. Waldheim's Austrian Example* ii. 27 From them [*sc.* workers' militias] grew the *Republikanischer Schutzbund,* the army of the Social-Democratic Party. **1974** T. P. WHITNEY tr. *Solzhenitsyn's Gulag Archipelago* I. I. ii. 59 There were Schutzbündlers who had lost the class battles in Vienna and had come to the Fatherland of the world proletariat for refuge.

Schutzstaffel (ʃu·tsʃta:fəl). Also pl. **Schutzstaffeln,** and with lower-case initial. [G., lit. 'defence squadron'.] The internal security force of the Nazis in Germany, more usually known by its initials S.S. (see *S 4 a). Also *transf.* and *attrib.*

1930 *Times* 18 Sept. 11/1 If the Storm detachments form the potential army of an imaginary Hitler State, the defence squads (Schutzstaffeln) are its police. **1932** [see S.S. s.v. *S 4 a]. **1946** E. LINKLATER *Private Angelo* iv. 40 The Count was a prisoner of the Schutzstaffel. **1968** *Punch* 26 June 939/3 Certainly Richelieu was both cruel and sinister... But then, nobody runs a country for 18 years—single-handed except for cronies, spies and *schützstaffel* [sic]—without being ruthless. **1974** F. NOLAN *Oshawa Project* xv. 94 The black *Schutzstaffel* uniforms.

schvartze, schvartzer (ʃvā·ɹtsə, -əɹ). *slang.* Also **schw-, shv-, -ze**(**r**), **-tza,** etc. [Yiddish, f. *shvarts* black: cf. SWART *a.* (*sb.*).

Strictly, Yiddish *shvartser* represents the masculine, and *shvartse* (occas. written *schvartza,* etc.) the feminine form, but these distinctions have become blurred. The pl. *schvartzes* could, in English, correspond to a sing. form *schvartz,* but there is no evidence for the latter.]

A Negro, a Black; *spec.* (with the ending *-a* or *-e*) a black maid (in the U.S.).

Somewhat derogatory.

1961 A. SMITH *East-Enders* vi. 92 All der young generation flocks rahnd de Schwarzers. **1963** *Spectator* 19 July 79

Where Perec Rachman gained his first experience of putting in the schwarzes. **1967** P. ROTH in *Esquire* Apr. 191/4 She [*sc.* my mother] sews, she knits, she darns—she irons better than the *shvartze.* **1967** P. WELLES *Babyhip* xvi. 114 Imagine those *schwartzas.* Pretty soon they'll be living next door. *Ibid.* 115 'She's just the *schwartza,*' Mrs Green said, 'I don't call her a nigger, it isn't nice.' **1967** *Times* 11 Nov. 17/3 Marrying a girl he hardly knew, an honest-to-god peasant, and a Haitian one at that, a schvartsa yet. **1969** L. GREENBAUM *Out of Shape* xii. 78 I'm not robbing Wheeler of his civil rights or picking on him because he's a *schwarze.* **1971** B. MALAMUD *Tenants* 213 An irritable old man.., says to his sweating son: 'You should be ashamed to dance like a shvartzer, without any clothes on.' **1975** R. H. RIMMER *Premar Experiments* i. 140, I couldn't forget the whole mad business of bringing a black girl home to my unsuspecting parents. If I arrived with one who stank of sweat, it would only prove what they already suspected about *schvartzers,* that they not only look different, but they smell different too. **1976** R. B. PARKER *Promised Land* xvii. 102 'Were you aiming at an exclusive Jewish clientele?' 'Huh? Jewish? Why Jewish? Anybody was welcome. I mean we wouldn't be thrilled if the Shvartzes moved in, but we didn't care about religion.' **1979** *Guardian* 17 Mar. 13/1 'The schwartzes can't spell,' he lapsed into Yiddish, 'but..the schwartzes have good taste.'

schwa (ʃwā). Also **shwa.** [G.: see SHEVA.] The central vowel sound (ə), typically occurring in weakly stressed syllables, as in the final syllable of 'sofa' and the first syllable of 'along'; = SHEVA 2. Occas., the symbol of an inverted 'e' used to represent this sound. Also *attrib.* and *Comb.*

1895 [see SHEVA 2]. **1933** BLOOMFIELD *Language* 519 Linguists sometimes speak of this phoneme by the name *shwa*, a term taken from Hebrew grammar. **1934** PRIEBSCH & COLLINSON *German Lang.* I. iii. 51 These overshort vowels are called 'Schwa-vowels' (from the Hebrew *ševa*). **1954** W. F. LEOPOLD in Saporta & Bastian *Psycholinguistics* (1961) 354/1 Central [ə] (schwa) was learned in unstressed syllables during the second half of the second year, because its neutral character made it suitable in such a position. **1956** D. JONES *Outl. Eng. Phonetics* (ed. 8) viii. 30 The sound known as the 'neutral vowel' or 'schwa'. **1963** *English Jrnl.* May 393/1 The inverted *e* or schwa for the neutral vowel used in weakly stressed syllables. **1964** D. WARD in D. Abercrombie et al. *Daniel Jones* 393 The plosives and j being registered with a following shwa vowel for present purposes. **1973** A. H. SOMMERSTEIN *Sound Pattern Anc. Gr.* iii. 87 Though Greek has had a stress accent for about 1,600 years, unstressed vowels have firmly resisted reduction to schwa. **1975** *Language* LI. 265 The syncope of a penultimate unaccented vowel and the deletion of final shwa lead to a system in which stress invariably falls on the last syllable. **1978** *Canad. Jrnl. Ling.* 1977 XXII. 226 In the treatment of German phonology..shwas (in, e.g., *Zunge, geöffnet,* etc.) are phonemicized as /e/ with no explanation. **1979** T. BURROW (*title*) The problem of shwa in Sanskrit. **1980** *Amer. Speech* 1976 LI. 272 The schwa some speakers have in the third syllable of *medicine* is produced by a low-level phonetic rule that reduces unstressed short vowels.

Schwabacher (ʃvā·bɑχəɪ). [G., f. *Schwabach*, name of a town in central Bavaria.] A German black-letter type-face, a simplified, lighter version of bastarda, used in the late fifteenth and sixteenth centuries. Also *attrib.*

[**1910** *Encycl. Brit.* VII. 723/2 For these scanty writings the German so-called 'Schwabach' characters were used.] **1922** D. B. UPDIKE *Printing Types* I. iv. 62 The smaller type of the Indulgences, which is a rounder black-letter, has certain peculiarities later found in 'schwabacher' fonts. **1926** [see *FRAKTUR]. **1934** A. F. JOHNSON *Type Designs* i. 31 Schwabacher has the usual Bastarda characteristics, the closed, one-storeyed a, and pointed descenders to s and f; the tail of the g is open. **1969** [see *FRAKTUR]. **1972** P. GASKELL *New Introd. Bibliogr.* 18 The Schwabacher group..tended towards the rotundas.

schwaerm, ¶ var. *SCHWARM *sb.*

Schwann (ʃvan). *Anat.* The name of Theodor *Schwann* (1810–82), German physiologist, who described the neurilema in 1839 (*Mikroskop. Untersuchungen ü. d. Uebereinstimmung in d. Strukt. u. d. Wachsthum d. Thiere u. Pflanzen*), used *attrib.*, in the possessive, and with *of*: **a.** as *sheath of Schwann, Schwann's sheath*: = *NEURILEMA, NEURILEMMA C.

1874 A. E. J. BARKER tr. *Frey's Histol. & Histochem. of Man* 680/1 (Index), Schwann's sheath of nerve fibre. **1882** T. E. SATTERTHWAITE *Man. Histol.* (ed. 2) ix. 110 A delicate membrane or envelope, the sheath of Schwann or primitive sheath. *Ibid.*, The neurilemma, which by some is spoken of as synonymous with Schwann's sheath (Frey). **1892**, etc. [see *NEURILEMA, NEURILEMMA C]. **1898** *Jrnl. Compar. Neurol.* VII. 183 The terminal branches of the axis cylinder are not invested with a continuation of the sheath of Schwann. **1925** ELWYN & STRONG *Bailey's Text-bk. Histol.* (ed. 7) viii. 197 (*caption*) Ring-like thickening of Schwann's sheath at node of Ranvier. **1972** MATZKE & FOLTZ *Synopsis of Neuroanat.* (ed. 2) ii. 11 The axon may have one or two coverings: myelin and sheath of Schwann.

b. to designate the cells which enwrap the axons of peripheral nerve fibres and form the myelin sheath (when it is present); formerly, the parts of these cells containing the nucleus and cytoplasm.

1904 *Amer. Jrnl. Anat.* III. 261 [He] referred to them as 'nerve corpuscles' and 'half-moon cells', and they have since been called 'Schwann's corpuscles' from their relation to the sheath of Schwann and their supposed identity with the nucleus of that sheath in the adult peripheral nerve. **1906** *Ibid.* V. 121 If one examines a developing nerve, one sees that there are numerous spindle shaped cells (cells of Schwann, sheath cells) throughout its course. **1931** W. BLOOM *Maximow's Text-bk. Histol.* xii. 254 The nuclei of the Schwann cells usually are flattened and oval. **1960** G. CAUSEY *Cell of Schwann* i. 5 The differentiation between Schwann membrane and Schwann cell that has been made by many histologists since 1839 is not a distinction that existed in Schwann's original description. *Ibid.* iv. 45 The term Schwann cell will be now used for any cell that enfolds a nerve fibre within its cytoplasm, whether..in the somatic or visceral parts of the peripheral nervous system. **1966**, etc. [see *NEURILEMA, NEURILEMMA C]. **1967** MATZKE & FOLTZ *Synopsis of Neuroanat.* ii. 11 The Schwann cell contains a scanty amount of cytoplasm but a prominent nucleus. **1976** *Path. Ann.* XI. 355 Studies of regenerating nerve provided morphologic data suggesting that Schwann cells are capable of manufacturing fibrillar collagen.

Schwannoma (ʃvanō^u·mă). *Path.* Also **schwannoma.** [f. prec. + *-OMA.] A tumour derived from a Schwann cell.

1932 P. MASSON in *Amer. Jrnl. Path.* VIII. 367 (*heading*) Experimental and spontaneous schwannomas. **1948** [see *NEURILEMOMA, NEURILEMMOMA]. **1961** R. D. BAKER *Essent. Path.* xxii. 604 Neurilemmomas (neurinomas, Schwannomas) are tumors which arise from the nerves and are composed of tissue like that of the sheath of Schwann. **1976** J. H. LIZUKA in G. Berci *Endoscopy* lix. 756/1 Schwannomas arising from the peripherial nerve sheath..can be stereoencephaloscopically diagnosed.

‖ **schwarm** (ʃvarm), *sb.* Also erron. **schwaerm, schwärm.** [G.: see SWARM *sb.*] An enthusiasm, a 'craze'; *spec.*, an erotic attachment, as of one woman or adolescent girl for another; a 'crush'.

1926 F. M. FORD *Man could stand Up* I. iii. 58 Your *schwaerm* for my father's memory and all. **1931** E. F. BENSON *Mapp & Lucia* vi. 151 Irene..had developed a violent *schwärm* for Lucia. *a* **1956** F. LAWRENCE *Mem. & Corr.* (1961) 121 The adoration, the *Schwarm*, for somebody or other exclusively. **1968** N. MARSH *Clutch of Constables* iv. 87 The wretched woman..had developed a *schwarm* for Troy herself.

‖ **schwärm** (ʃvē̜rm), *v.* [ad. G. *schwärmen*: see next.] *intr.* To feel or display enthusiasm or passion. Also **schwä·rmer,** (fem.) **schwä·rmerin,** an enthusiast, a zealot.

1884 G. MEREDITH *Let.* 17 Sept. (1970) II. 745 The enclosed, from a Wagner Schwärmer, may induce you to visit Munich. **1913** R. BROOKE *Let.* 17 Dec. (1968) 553 They dance so well, the Fijians... I *schwärm* for it; and no white in or near Fiji cares twopence for anything except money-making. **1927** M. SADLEIR *Trollope* 211 Kate Field.. developed first into a *Schwärmerin* for all the arts, then into a blue-stocking, and finally into a champion of woman's rights. **1946** J. CARY *Moonlight* xxxiv. 276 'Oh, I saw it, a great bare barrack, and not even allowed to speak to other girls in the passages, or, walk arm-in-arm, and nowhere to go by yourself...' Amanda, mildly surprised by this explosion of anger, said, 'It's true we weren't allowed to schwärm—.'

‖ **schwärmerei, Schwärmerei** (ʃvē̜·rmərəi). [G., f. *schwärmen* to swarm, to display enthusiasm, to rave: see SWARM *v.*[1]] Religious zeal, fanaticism, extravagant enthusiasm for a cause or a person; an erotic attachment, esp. of one woman or adolescent girl for another; a 'crush'.

1845 *Edin. Rev.* LXXXII. 453 His [*sc.* Lessing's] mind is both clear and strong, free from *schwärmerei*, (a word untranslatable, because the thing itself is un-English,) free from cant and affectation of all kinds. **1857** G. H. LEWES *Biogr. Hist. Philos.* (ed. 2) II. 531 Kant's..energetic contempt for Swedenborgianism and all other *Schwärmerei* is unequivocally expressed. **1863** CROWN PRINCESS OF PRUSSIA *Let.* 21 Mar. in R. Fulford *Dearest Mama* (1968) 183, I did wrong in allowing my feelings vent in writing to you about England; I thought afterwards it would bore you and my 'schwarmerei' would make you impatient. **1880** G. GISSING *Workers in Dawn* I. xii. 261 He has no belief whatever in the heroic woman, laughing to scorn women's rights, and speaking almost as disrespectfully of that *schwärmerei* of which you are yourself such an exalted instance. **1886** *Athenæum* 3 Apr. 451/3 A few hours' *schwärmerei* over what Joan [of Arc] must have felt under certain circumstances. **1927** F. B. YOUNG *Portrait of Clare* I. vi. 63 The expression of liberty and exultant youth that her mother's mid-Victorian fantasias and Miss Boldmere's *Schwärmerei* denied her. **1930** E. SCOTT *Forgotten Image* xiii. 98 Her idiotic, schoolgirlish schwärmerei attachment. **1937** *Times Lit. Suppl.* 8 May 358/2 It would be easy to dismiss her account of how she 'read Schopenhauer and was blissfully happy' as the Schwärmerei of a pretentious blue-stocking. **1958** *Observer* 26 Jan. 16/6 Philhellenism, when it is not a mere student Schwärmerei, may sometimes develop along much the same lines as a certain type of love affair. **1971** *Times Lit. Suppl.* 23 Apr. 470/1 There were two Watts sisters, the husband of one of them and a young son for whom Swinburne had at one time a *schwärmerei*. **1976** W. GÉRIN *Elizabeth Gaskell* x. 92 Mr. Gaskell shielded himself as best he could from the Miss Winkworths' *schwärmerei*.

‖ **schwärmerisch** (ʃvē̜·rmĕriʃ), *a.* [Ger.: see prec.] Extravagantly enthusiastic; infatuated.

1894 MRS. H. WARD *Marcella* III. IV. iii. 295 Betty.. wrote..wild, '*schwärmerisch*' letters. **1927** D. L. SAYERS *Unnatural Death* II. xvi. 179 It is natural for a schoolgirl to be *schwärmerisch*—in a young woman of twenty-two it is thoroughly undesirable. **1933** J. BUCHAN *Prince of Captivity* IV. i. 321 The type of American whose mind had two compartments, realistic business and *schwärmerisch* dreams. **1980** *Country Life* 10 Dec. 2278/1 Many had adored her [*sc.* George Eliot], and not only the *schwärmerisch* women she so forcefully attracted.

schwartz (ʃvāɹts). *Skat.* Also **Schwartz, schwarz.** [a. G. *schwarz* black.] (See quot. 1880.) Also as *adj.* and *v. trans.*

1880 W. B. DICK *Amer. Hoyle* (ed. 13) 103 If he should propose to make no less than a hundred and twenty points, he would call his bid a *Schwartz. Ibid.*, With a very strong hand, a player may bid to *Schwartz* his opponents, that is, prevent them from making a single point. **1886** E. E. LEMCKE *Skat* 7 With no count at all, he is '*Schwarz*' (black = whitewashed). **1908** A. D. GRANGER *Skat & How to play It* i. 35 All the ten tricks must be taken to score Schwarz. *Ibid.* 36 Some authorities consider that in Schwarz if a trick which contains no points is lost by the player it ought not to count against him. **1949** A. A. OSTROW *Compl. Card Player* 628 If declarer wins every trick, opponents are said to be 'schwarz'. *Ibid.* 645 To make schwarz, he must take every trick. **1975** *Way to Play* 109/1 If the bidder has named suits or grand, he may before the opening lead, declare:..schwarz, ie he aims to take every trick. **1976** *National Skat & Sheepshead Q.* Mar. 18 The correct answer is to declare a club solo schwartz announced which scores 96 points.

schwartza, schwartze: see *SCHVARTZE, SCHVARTZER.

Schwarz (ʃvāɹts). *Math.* Also (*erron.*) **Schwartz.** The name of Hermann Amadeus *Schwarz* (1843–1921), German mathematician, used *attrib.* and in the possessive to designate the various forms of the theorem which states that the square of the sum of a set of products of two quantities cannot exceed the sum of the squares of the first terms multiplied by the sum of the squares of the second terms.

1955 M. LOÈVE *Probability Theory* ix. 156 Hölder's inequality with $r = s = 2$, is called the Schwarz inequality: $E^2 \mid XY \mid \leqslant E \mid X \mid ^2 . E \mid Y \mid ^2$. **1962** W. B. THOMPSON *Introd. Plasma Physics* viii. 222 This makes use of the Schwartz inequality $\int f^2 dx \int g^2 dx \geqslant [\int fg dx]^2$. **1964** MCCORD & MORONEY *Introd. Probability Theory* ix. 155 Let X_1 and X_2 be any two jointly distributed random variables which have finite, positive variances... If a and b are any real constants deduce that $[E(X_1-a)(X_2-b)]^2 \leqslant [E(X_1-a)^2][E(X_2-b)^2]$, which is a form of Schwarz's inequality. **1965** PATTERSON & RUTHERFORD *Elem. Abstr. Algebra* v. 176 In a unitary space $\|a\| \, \|b\| \geqslant |a \cdot b|$... The inequality is known as Schwartz's inequality. **1975** KARLIN & TAYLOR *First Course Stochastic Processes* (ed. 2) ix. 452, $E[|YZ|] \leqslant \surd(E[Y^2]E[Z^2]) = \|Y\| \, \|Z\|$. This is known as Schwartz' inequality.

schwarze, schwarzer: see *SCHVARTZE, SCHVARTZER.

‖ **schwarzlot** (ʃvā·rtslōt). Also with capital initial. [G., lit. 'black lead'.] A type of decoration used on Dutch and German glass of the seventeenth century, and subsequently on German and Austrian pottery and porcelain, consisting wholly or chiefly of black enamel.

1925 B. RACKHAM tr. *E. Hannover's Pottery & Porcelain* I. IV. iii. 357 At Nuremberg and Augsburg,..there lived enamel-painters who had white wares delivered to them from the factories to be decorated by them at home.., designs in purple or pictures in the so-called *Schwarzlot. Ibid.*, The glass and *Schwarzlot* painter *Johann Schaper*.. lived at Nuremberg between 1640 and 1670. **1952** J. F. HAYWARD *Viennese Porcelain of Du Paquier Period* ix. 107 The combination of hunting subjects and schwarzlot decoration must have been one of the more successful ventures of the [Vienna] factory. *Ibid.* xi. 123 The big schwarzlot-decorated services date from the 1730s. **1954** G. SAVAGE *Porcelain through Ages* v. 172 Daniel Preussler and his son Ignaz, were Bohemian decorators whose work was principally executed in black enamel—*Schwarzlot*—which was a characteristically Bohemian practice. **1971** *Daily Tel.* 6 Apr. 10/4 An early Meissen Hausmaler coffee pot and cover. .. It was decorated in schwarzlot by J. Auffenwerth at Augsburg. **1975** *Oxf. Compan. Decorative Arts* 335/2 Johann Anton Carli of Andernach (d. 1682), painted in schwarzlot a fine goblet bearing a view of Andernach and a beautifully rendered hunting scene.

Schwarzschild (ʃvā·ɹtsʃilt, ʃwǭ·ɹtstʃaild). The name of Karl *Schwarzschild* (1873–1916), German astronomer, used *attrib.* and in the possessive to designate various concepts developed by him or arising from his work. **1.** *Photogr.* Used with reference to a quantitative law of reciprocity failure in emulsions.

1920 *Jrnl. Optical Soc. Amer.* IV. 272 If Schwarzschild's law is correct, the reciprocity law does not hold for any value of the intensity, the error being the same in percentage amount for all intensities. **1942** C. E. K. MEES *Theory of Photographic Process* vi. 236 Schwarzschild (1899) confirmed Abney's results that the reciprocity law is not valid and concluded that a constant effect is produced so long as the condition It^p = constant is satisfied, in which p is constant and equal to about 0.8. This relation, with p constant, came to be generally known as Schwarzschild's law and is frequently referred to by this name today. **1960** G. E. LOCKIE tr. *K. S. Lyalikov's Chem. of Photographic Mechanisms* I. i. 58 The Schwarzschild equation is not valid for the range of exposures used in this investigation.

2. *Physics.* Denoting concepts arising out of the exact solution of Einstein's field equations described by Schwarzschild soon after the publication of the general theory of relativity (*Sitzungsber. der k. preuss. Akad. der Wissensch.* (1916) 189, 424), as *Schwarzschild coordinate, field, geometry, horizon, solution, space-time, surface*; **Schwarzschild black hole,** a static, non-rotating, and uncharged black hole, i.e., an object postulated to result from the complete gravitational collapse of an electrically neutral and non-rotating body, and which has a physical singularity at the centre of its Schwarzschild sphere to which the infalling matter inevitably proceeds and at which the curvature of space-time is infinite; **Schwarzschild line element,** (*a*) a scalar representation of the Schwarzschild metric, being an expression for the separation of two adjacent points in the space-time of Schwarzschild geometry; (*b*) *loosely* = *Schwarzschild metric* (*a*); **Schwarzschild metric,** (*a*) a mathematical description of the geometry of space-time exterior to a non-rotating body, usu. expressed as a tensor in differential geometry; (*b*) *loosely* = *Schwarzschild line element* (*a*); **Schwarzschild radius,** the radius of the Schwarzschild sphere; **Schwarzschild singularity,** a singularity in coordinates, but not a physical singularity in space-time, occurring at the Schwarzschild radius; **Schwarzschild sphere,** the effective boundary or horizon of a Schwarzschild black hole, which infalling matter reaches in an infinite time as seen by an external observer but a finite time in the reference frame of the matter, and at which the escape velocity is infinite, so that the escape of matter or radiation from the inside is impossible except by a postulated quantum-mechanical process.

1927 G. D. Birkhoff *Relativity & Mod. Physics* (ed. 2) xv. 255 The most general solution can be obtained from the Schwarzschild solution by a proper choice of coördinates. **1934** R. C. Tolman *Relativity, Thermodynamics & Cosmology* 208 There are..three consequences which can be obtained from the Schwarzschild line element which can be used to distinguish between the relativistic and Newtonian theories of gravitation. **1939** *Ann. Math.* XL. 924 In the case of a Schwarzschild field a particle is bound to follow a path with a radius greater than $(2+\sqrt{3})$ times the radius of the Schwarzschild singularity. **1957** *Physical Rev.* CVIII. 1067/2 This transformation is not acceptable..because it assumes Euclidean rather than Schwarzschild geometry for the displacement. *Ibid.*, We get the difference between the Schwarzschild metrics for the two reduced masses. *Ibid.* 1068/2 The effective potential starts from 0 at the Schwarzschild radius, rises to a maximum and then falls off again to zero at very large *r*. **1965** B. K. Harrison et al. *Gravitation Theory & Gravitational Collapse* 157 Introduce Schwarzschild coordinates ds^2 = [etc.]..as well as the baryon number coordinate. **1966** R. Akerib tr. *M. A. Tonnelat's Einstein's Unified Field Theory* v. 82 This is the Schwarzschild solution of the field equations. It defines completely the gravitational field in the neighborhood of attractive masses and permits the determination of the trajectories of particles moving in it. **1968** Robertson & Noonan *Relativity & Cosmology* ix. 236 The Schwarzschild line element has at the radius 2μ a singularity known as the Schwarzschild singularity. **1968** Sears & Brehme *Introd. Theory of Relativity* xi. 200 If the Schwarzschild singularity did exist, the Schwarzschild radius would be the radius of a spherical surface which separates the universe into two parts which are isolated from one another by the fact that local time does not elapse at the bounding surface. **1968** *Commun. Math. Physics* VIII. 245 In the special case where the gravitational coupling of the electromagnetic energy density is neglected..all solutions are computed explicitly, thus extending an earlier result of Ginzburg for a magnetic dipole in Schwarzschild's space-time. **1969** *Nature* 16 Aug. 690/1 Nothing can ever pass outwards through the Schwarzschild sphere of radius $r = 2GM/c^2$. **1970** *Ibid.* 4 Apr. 64/2 The metric used to describe the geometry of space-time in the vicinity of the collapsed object in this and other papers..has been the spherically symmetric Schwarzschild metric, which is valid only if the collapsed object has zero angular momentum. **1971** *Jrnl. Math. Physics* XII. 1846/1 We consider the problem of a point charge slowly lowered into a Schwarzschild black hole as a simple example where the final outcome can be investigated. **1973** C. W. Misner et al. *Gravitation* xxiii. 597 The above discussion identifies the Schwarzschild coordinates.. by their intrinsic geometric properties. Not only are *r* and *t* radial and time variables, respectively (in that $\partial/\partial r$ and $\partial/\partial t$ are spacelike and timelike, respectively..), but they have particular properties..that distinguish them from other possible coordinate choices... No claim is made that they are the only coordinates that might reasonably be called *r* and *t*. **1973** *Physics Bull.* Nov. 654/3 An observer falling with the surface of the collapsing star has his light cones squashed as he reaches the Schwarzschild surface of radius $2GM/c^2$; he finds it ever more difficult to signal to distant observers as collapse proceeds. He will appear to them to fall ever more slowly as he approaches the critical surface, and never actually reach it. **1974** *Nature* 5 July 37/2 There is no creation of massless particles in the exterior region of a Schwarzschild black hole, which is the static end state reached as a result of spherically symmetric gravitational collapse. *Ibid.* 17/1 In essence the significance of the Schwarzschild surface at $r = R_s$ must have been known to Eddington, certainly by the early 1930s. *Ibid.*, Once inside the Schwarzschild sphere, one cannot communicate with the world outside; and moreover, one would inexorably be propelled towards the centre: not all the King's horses nor all the King's men can prevent it from happening. **1974** *Encycl. Brit. Macropædia* XV. 587/1 The most conspicuous feature of the Schwarzschild field is that if the total mass is thought of as concentrated at the very centre, then at a finite distance from that centre, the Schwarzschild radius, the geometry of space-time changes drastically from that to which we are accustomed. **1977** *Sci. Amer.* Jan. 34/3 For a star of about 10 solar masses the Schwarzschild radius is about 30 kilometres.

Schweik (ʃwəik). A character in *The Good Soldier Schweik* by Jaroslav Hašek (1883–1923), Czech writer, pictured as an unlucky and simple-minded but resourceful little man oppressed by higher authorities; a person of this type. Hence **Schweik** *v. intr.*, to behave in the deferential, crafty manner of Schweik; **Schwei·kism,** behaviour characteristic of a Schweik; **Schwei·kist** *a.*, typical of a Schweik.

1952 M. McCarthy *Groves of Academe* vi. 128 They're the expression of a certain reactionary Schweikism which we've seen also in faculty meetings. **1965** *New Statesman* 7 May 708/1 The Berlin Battle Groups..paraded in Bebel Square to be given their medals—a bored and happy collection of shuffling, grumbling Schweiks. **1968** *Economist* 14 Sept. 27 Censorship is now operating... In a somewhat Schweikist manner, the Czech papers succeeded in getting around this by reporting, poker-faced and without comment, what the 'socialist' press is saying, trusting to their own readers' ability to read between the lines. **1973** *Libertarian Education* xi. 17/2 They will make some kind of bitter psychological adjustment and Schweik their way to retirement.

‖ **schwein(e)hund** (ʃvəi·n(ə)hunt). Also **schwine-, -hundt** and with capital initial. [G. *schweinehund*, f. *schwein* pig + *hund* dog: cf. *pig-dog* s.v. *pig *sb.*[1] 13.] A German term of abuse: filthy dog, 'swine', 'bastard'.

1941 [see *knob *sb.* 1 e]. **1959** B. Mather *Achilles Affair* i. ix 105, I heard a curt command in German—'Spread out, you *schwinehund*—spread out.' **1975** I. Melchior *Sleeper Agent* iii. vii. 154 Himmler had turned traitor!.. That back-stabbing *Schweinehund*! **1978** T. L. Smith *Money War* i. 67 He farted long and loud. Mundt giggled, 'Schweinhundt!'

‖ **Schweinerei** (ʃvəi·nərəi). Also with small initial. [G., lit. 'piggishness'.] Obnoxious behaviour, a repulsive incident or object, a scandal.

1906 G. B. Shaw *Let.* 7 May (1972) II. 620 Reinhardt took not the smallest notice of either your letter or Barker's. Barker naturally regards this as a Schweinerei of the first order. **1938** L. Bemelmans *Life Class* i. vi. 98 Whenever a student brought in a reproduction of one of her paintings, Thaddeus would..shout: 'Take it out, out with this *Schweinerei*'! **1965** *Economist* 25 Dec. 1433/3 Some Japanese producers were discovered selling out of line at the recent Canton Fair. But this *schweinerei* was swiftly stamped on. **1975** *Times* 7 Oct. 12/8 India..will outline the petty *Schweinerei* of Mrs. Gandhi.

schweinfurt green (ʃvəi·nfūᵊɹt). *Chem.* [f. *Schweinfurt*, name of a city in Germany.] A toxic green pigment that is a mixed acetate and arsenite of copper, $Cu_3(AsO_3)_2.(CH_3COO)_2Cu$, and was formerly used as an insecticide. Also called *Paris green, Vienna green.*

1852 [see *Vienna green* s.v. Vienna a]. **1874** W. Crookes *Dyeing & Calico-Printing* ii. ii. 156 Schweinfürt green or aceto-arsenite of copper. **1879** H. Carr *Our Domestic Poisons* 7 Experiments were made on a paper coloured with Schweinfurt-green, an aceto-arsenate of copper. **1930** I. J. Kligler *Epidemiology & Control of Malaria* vii. 147 Paris green or Schweinfurt green (copper aceto-arsenite) used so much as an insecticide is an efficient larvacide.

‖ **Schweizerdeutsch** (ʃvəi·tsərdoitʃ), **Schwyzertütsch** (ʃvi·tsərtūtʃ). Also **Schwei(t)zer-Deutsch, Schwyzerdütsch,** etc. [G. *Schweizerdeutsch*, Swiss G. *Schwyzertütsch*.] **a.** Swiss German dialect. **b.** A Swiss German; also *collect.*

1934 Priebsch & Collinson *German Lang.* vii. 326 The Alemannic group includes Swabian..; High Alemannic (with 'Schwyzerdütsch' and the dialects of the southern parts of the Black Forest and Vorarlberg)..; Low Alemannic. **1953** U. Weinreich *Languages in Contact* ii. 14 Schwyzertütsch, an Alemannic dialect,..spoken in the village of Thusis. **1961** [see *Luxemburgisch]. **1963** I. Fleming *On H.M. Secret Service* xxiv. 257 Swiss Air Control, in thick Schwyzerdütch, asked them politely to identify themselves. **1963** *Guardian* 22 Aug. 6/6 The cast of the Zurich opera doing 'Porgy and Bess' in black faces *and* Schweizerdeutsch. **1963** *Punch* 18 Sept. 399/2 Your single word of Schwyzertütsch will trigger a multitude of pleased smiles. **1964** 'P. Quentin' *Family Skeletons* ii. 61 The pleasure steamer on Lac Leman..the drunken Schweizer-Deutsch trying to get fresh with her. **1969** *Beaver* Summer 6/2 Three of the sailors come in and talk the harsh Schweitzer-Deutsch of Basle. **1974** F. Nolan *Oshawa Project* xxxi. 186 You speak Schweizer-Deutsch very well. **1978** Ld. Hailsham *Dilemma of Democracy* xxv. 163 Schwyzer Dütsch, Suisses Romands, and Ticinese can form one Switzerland.

schwinehund, var. *schwein(e)hund.

science. Add: **2. c.** fig. *to blind with science* (slang): to confuse by the use of polysyllabic words or involved explanations (see also quot. 1937).

1937 Partridge *Dict. Slang* 64/2 *Blinded with science*. A catch-phrase applied by brawn defeated by brains: Australian and New Zealand: C. 20. **1948** —— *Dict. Forces' Slang 1939–45* 18 *Blind with science*, to explain away an offence, a mistake, by talking at great length and very technically, thus dazzling one's interlocutor into non-pursuance of the matter. (Mostly Army.) **1973** *Daily Tel.* 17 Oct. 14/6 We are also more familiar..with the tendency for people to be blinded by science and to succumb to 'expert' medical opinion, however quackish. **1977** *Time Out* 17–23 June 11/3 It's very easy to coast and blind the office with science.

4. b. Also with preceding sb., as *life science*, and combined with a prefix, as *bio-, geo-, neuroscience*. (See under the first element.)

c. In phrases: *science of art, of expression, of mind, of religion(s)*, denoting esp. the application of scientific methods in fields of study previously considered open only to theories based on subjective, historical, or undemonstrable abstract criteria.

1828 J. S. Mill in *Westm. Rev.* IX. 140 The impugners of the school logic, as they term it, may be divided into two classes. The first class consists of men not untinctured with philosophy, including even some writers of considerable eminence in the science of mind. **1869** W. James *Let.* 21 Jan. in R. B. Perry *Tht. & Char. W. James* (1935) I. 291 Some weeks ago I read the three last articles on 'Science of Religions' by Émile Burnouf in the *Revue des deux mondes*. **1886** T. Paterson *Mental Sci.* 4 This confusion of opinion has led many to deny the possibility of any science of mind, beyond the physical or material facts of life. **1902** W. James *Var. Relig. Exper.* xviii. 433 Of late, impartial classifications and comparisons have become possible... We have the beginnings of a 'Science of Religions', so-called. **1909** D. Ainslie tr. *Croce's Aesthetic* (*subtitle*), As science of expression and general linguistic. **1933** *Burlington Mag.* May 248/2 The great problem as to whether the science of art really is a science in the sense that the word is used in relation to natural science remains, however, unsolved. **1937** H. Read *Art & Soc.* vii. 233 Though based on the science of art and a deduction from the whole range of relevant material, the facts in question are relative to the aesthetic sensibility. **1944** J. S. Huxley *On Living in Revol.* iv. 45 The science of mind developed later than biological science. **1973** N. Smart (*title*) The science of religion and the sociology of knowledge. **1976** F. McDonagh tr. *Pannenberg's Theol. & Philos. of Sci.* iv. 256 Theology then comes under the general heading of a science of religion.

5. b. (Further examples.) This is now the dominant sense in ordinary use.

1913 C. Mackenzie *Sinister St.* I. ii. vii. 253 Science is all the go nowadays... And Science is what we want. Science and Religion. **1946** R. J. C. Atkinson *Field Archaeol.* 12 One more problem..remains to be mentioned, the problem of co-operation between archaeologists and workers in other sciences. **1955** *Bull. Atomic Sci.* Apr. 141/1 Science has become a major source of the power of civilized man. **1976** *Norwich Mercury* 17 Dec. 3/8 Second year prizes—English,..mathematics,..science,..history,..geography,.. music. **1978** *Nature* 10 Aug. 522/1 Funds for lunar sample analysis have remained roughly constant over the past few years and the programme has received praise for the high quality of the science conducted.

d. Personified.

1742 [see sense 5 a in Dict.]. **1862** G. H. Lewes *Let.* 30 Aug. in *George Eliot Lett.* (1955) IV. 52 If the passions and impertinences of public speakers, and newspaper writers on *both* sides of the Atlantic are madly widening the wounds which each ought to strive to heal, it is some comfort to reflect that Science keeps aloof from such misplaced and unjustifiable criticisms. **1894** A. Lang *Cock Lane & Common-Sense* 328 It is in this way that Science makes herself disliked. **1975** J. Plamenatz *K. Marx's Philos. Man* viii. 218 Science recognizes that its hypothesis and theories are provisional and has criteria for deciding whether or not they should be discarded for bette r ones

e. (Usually with capital initial.) *U.S.* = *Christian Science.

1902 'Mark Twain' in *N. Amer. Rev.* Dec. 768 Does the Science kill a patient here and there? **1915** E. B. Holt *Freudian Wish* 21 The 'Science' healer was immediately consulted. **1916** H. Crane *Let.* 26 Jan. (1965) 3 Carry the *science* as far as you can. **1919** —— *Let.* 2 Apr. (1965) 15 Concerning me and my attitude toward Science. **1946** *Christian Sci. Jrnl.* Dec. 616 We called on a practitioner to learn what this Science was. **1980** A. Wilson *Setting World on Fire* ii. i. 51 Servants..live in a world of doctors and illnesses and death...Of course I wasn't in Science then. I believed all their nonsense.

7. *attrib.* and *Comb.*, as (sense 5 b) *science-based* adj.; **science park** orig. *U.S.*, an area of land devoted to scientific reasearch or to industrial enterprises connected with the physical sciences.

1962 *Economist* 14 Apr. 187/1 An industry can be science-based, said Lord Hailsham, and yet do little or no actual research. **1965** A. Farrer in J. Gibb *Light on C. S. Lewis* 28 Scientific formulae may be empirically verified, but no science-based picture of the sum of things is better than a symbol. **1970** *Daily Tel.* 27 Apr. 3/8 Trinity College, Cambridge, is proposing to create a 'science park' on the north-east outskirts of the city. **1973** *Nature* 22 June 430/2 In the United States, there are over 80 science parks,..but 27 of them are wholly limited to science-based industry. **1981** *Daily Tel.* 31 July 8/3 A 116-acre science park to attract high technology-based firms, and provide hundreds of jobs, is to be established in Peterborough. Lynch Wood Science Park will also include conference and sports centres and a hotel.

sci·ence fi·ction. [f. SCIENCE + FICTION.] Imaginative fiction based on postulated scientific discoveries or spectacular environmental changes, freq. set in the future or on other planets and involving space or time travel. Also *attrib.*

Quot. 1851 shows an isolated use. The expression did not come into general use until the end of the 1920s.

1851 W. WILSON *Little Earnest Bk. upon Great Old Subject* x. 137 (*heading*) Science-Fiction. *Ibid.*, We hope it will not be long before we may have other works of Science-Fiction, as we believe such works likely to fulfil a good purpose, and create an interest, where, unhappily, science alone might fail. *Ibid.* 139 Campbell says that 'Fiction in Poetry is not the reverse of truth, but her soft and enchanting resemblance.' Now this applies especially to Science-Fiction, in which the revealed truths of Science may be given, interwoven with a pleasing story which may itself be poetical and *true*—thus circulating a knowledge of the Poetry of Science, clothed in a garb of the Poetry of Life. **1929** *Science Wonder Stories* June 89 The editor of this publication [*sc.* H. Gernsback] addressed a number of letters to science fiction lovers. The editor promised to pay $50.00 for the best letter each month on the subject of 'What Science Fiction Means to Me.' **1933** *Astounding Stories* Dec. 142/1 The..science-fiction fan does not care for stories of the supernatural... Intelligent people, as a rule, will read science fiction. **1949**, etc. [see *FANTASY, PHANTASY *sb.* 4 f]. **1954** A. HUXLEY in *Encounter* Feb. 5/1 These make up a tale which no self-respecting reader, even of Science Fiction, should be asked to swallow. **1958** *Listener* 20 Feb. 334/3 *The Naked Sun* is a happy wedding of the two great pseudo-literary forms of the century—science fiction and the 'tec. **1964** C. S. LEWIS *Discarded Image* vii. 142 The theory of the Four Zones taught that the equatorial region was too hot for life. The other hemisphere of the Earth was to us wholly inaccessible. You could write science-fiction about it, but not geography. **1972** *Sci. Amer.* Sept. 38/2, I for one would rather command a computer through a keyboard than talk to it, even if that science-fiction dream were possible. **1977** *N.Y. Rev. Bks.* 13 Oct. 13/4 The mind produces meaning like a plant branching out in a science-fiction movie. **1979** *Guardian* 18 Aug. 10/1 Science Fiction fans..have chosen April 1926 as their sacred date and nominated Hugo Gernsback for the title of Father of Science Fiction. **1980** N. BABSON *Dangerous to Know* viii. 56 The long open-plan Newsroom..always gave me a science-fiction feeling of being the last man alive.

Hence **science-fictional, science-fictive** *adjs.*, pertaining to or characteristic of science fiction; **science-fictionalized** *a.*, made into science fiction; **science-fictioneer, science-fictionist**, a writer or connoisseur of science fiction; **science-fictioner**, a film script upon a science-fictional theme.

1939 *Astounding Science-Fiction* Oct. 155 The Jekyll-science-fictionist stands for experimental truth, for logic, for *proof.* **1950** *Jrnl. Brit. Interplanetary Soc.* IX. 197 In a 'science-fictionalized' review of Arthur Clarke's book 'Interplanetary Flight', the *Daily Mirror* gave the astonishing news that British atomic scientists are now waiting for the go-ahead..to build an atomic engine which could be used as a rocket propulsion unit. **1953** C. RYAN *Conquest of Moon* i. 3 The ships the explorers will use for the long journey through space will bear little resemblance to those depicted by the science-fictionists. **1954** J. W. CAMPBELL in *Astounding Science Fiction* Aug. 5 That science-fictional device 'the planet-wrecker' bomb. **1955** *Britannica Bk. of Year* 490/1 *Science Fictioner* was coined to describe a film play of the science fiction type. **1959** C. FADIMAN in A. C. Clarke *Across Sea of Stars* p. ix, Some science fictioneers are plain old-style typewriter hacks. **1960** K. AMIS *New Maps of Hell* v. 129 That science-fictional uneasiness appears, attaching itself to an existent or incipient neurosis about overcrowded streets and buildings as well as to the rational fear of global overpopulation. **1976** I. MURDOCH *Henry & Cato* II. 222 The glossy hexagonal glasses which looked here like the appurtenances of some science fictional spaceman. **1977** *Times Lit. Suppl.* 14 Jan. 26/1 Put one science-fictioneer on a desert island and he will start a magazine. **1980** *Ibid.* 7 Nov. 1265/4 Yet Silverberg's Majipoor, where humanity..finds its future home, is about as science-fictional as Tolkien's Middle Earth.

scientaster (saiˌĕntæ·stəɹ). *rare.* [f. SCIENT(IST + -ASTER after POETASTER.] A petty or inferior scientist.

1899 M. FOSTER *Claude Bernard* ix. 232 We may recognise a salient difference between..the false scientaster and the true inquirer. **1969** *Sci. Jrnl.* Sept. 91/1 Zahlen made the neat distinction that in Lebanon most advisory scientists were 'not scientists at all but just had some scientific education'. Michael Foster coined the word 'scientaster' for such people; it deserves reintroduction.

scientific, *a.* and *sb.* Add: **A.** *adj.* **4. b.** Also, more loosely: systematic, methodical. (Further examples.)

1863 GEO. ELIOT *Let.* 18 July (1956) IV. 94 He [*sc.* Renan] has always seemed to me remarkable as a French mind that is at once 'scientific' (in the German sense) and eminently tender and reverent towards the forms in which the religious sentiment has incarnated itself. **1976** *National Observer* (U.S.) 13 Mar. 1/6 The Observer tally on abortion, however, is consistent with the findings of other recent, more 'scientific' polls.

c. (Earlier and later examples.)

1792 in G. B. Buckley *Fresh Light on 18th Cent. Cricket* (1935) 231 Brighton v. Lord Winchilsea, Hon. Mr. Bligh, Mr. Smith & Mr. Hale with 7 approved scientific men from the County of Hants. *a* **1817** JANE AUSTEN *Persuasion* (1818) IV. viii. 155 She had feelings for the tender, spirits for the gay, attention for the scientific, and patience for the wearisome; and had never liked a concert better. **1833** J. NYREN *Young Cricketer's Tutor* 29 In this accomplishment lies the distinction between the scientific player and the random batsman. **1851** H. MELVILLE *Moby Dick* II. xxv. 181 This accomplished swordsman..once more makes a scientific dash at the mass. **1891** W. G. GRACE *Cricket* xi. 300 From that year [*sc.* 1859] until 1876 he [*sc.* R. Daft] was the most scientific batsman amongst the professionals.

5. Of, pertaining to, or inspired by Christian Science. *U.S.*

1875 M. B. EDDY *Science & Health* viii. 428 The spirituality that abstracts all attention from the body, never manipulates and is the only positive position of scientific healing. *Ibid.* 429 To be able to discern the cause of sickness after the scientific mode of our Master, depends on your spirituality. **1919** H. CRANE *Let.* 7 Mar. (1965) 13, I feel quite certain that Mrs. Brooks is afflicted with consumption against which she is doubtless putting up a strenuous Scientific fight.

6. Special collocations: **scientific farming,** farming conducted according to theories based on science rather than on tradition; also **scientific farmer; scientific fiction** now *rare* = *SCIENCE FICTION; **scientific humanism,** a theory that humanism should be based on scientific empiricism (see quot. 1909); a doctrine that man should direct the future and the welfare of the human race by using the scientific methods he applies to other species and to the material environment; so **scientific humanist; scientific management** orig. *U.S.*, management of a business, industry, etc., according to principles of efficiency derived from experiments in methods of work, production, payment, etc., and esp. from time-and-motion studies; **scientific method,** a method of procedure that has characterized natural science since the 17th century, consisting in systematic observation, measurement, and experiment, and the formulation, testing, and modification of hypotheses; **scientific notation,** a system of representing numbers as a product of a number between 1 and 10 (or 0·1 and 1) and a power of 10; **scientific revolution,** a rapid and far-reaching development in science; *spec.* the developments occurring in the twentieth century that have involved the introduction of automation, atomic energy, electronics, etc.

1850 C. KINGSLEY *Alton Locke* II. iv. 43 He had one scientific farmer after another, staying in his house as a friend. **1789** A. YOUNG *Jrnl.* 19 June in *Trav. France* (1792) I. 115, I wish my brethren to stick to their *scientific* farming, and leave the practical to those that understand it. **1886** C. M. YONGE *Chantry House* I. xvii. 159 [He] worked off his superfluous energy in scientific farming. **1902** A. BENNETT *Anna of Five Towns* ix. 205 A great landowner is exhibiting the beauties of scientific farming for the behoof of his villagers. **1876** W. H. L. BARNES in W. H. Rhodes *Caxton's Book* 7 The great master of scientific action, Jules Verne. **1937** *Discovery* Oct. 318 'The Man in the Moone', the fantasy of Bishop Godwin.., is an early excursion into the realms of scientific fiction. **1909** W. JAMES *Meaning of Truth* iii. 59 'Energetics', measuring the bare face of sensible phenomena so as to describe in a single formula all their changes of 'level', is the last word of this scientific humanism. **1931** J. S. HUXLEY *What dare I Think?* iv. 148 The only way in which the conflict between science and human nature can be ended is by combining science and the other fruits of the human spirit in a new alliance, a new attitude, to which we may give the name of Scientific Humanism. **1941** —— *Uniqueness of Man* xiii. 274 Scientific humanism..insists that the same scientific procedure can be applied to human life as has been applied to lifeless matter and to animals and plants—scientific survey, study, and analysis, followed by increasing practical control. **1963** V. BROME *Problem of Progress* vii. 144 If the modern scientific humanist would have no truck with the religious tinge in Huxley's creed he equally rejects any divine inspiration in Buddhism, Christianity, [etc.]. **1903** F. W. TAYLOR in *Trans. Amer. Soc. Mech. Engineers* XXIV. 1366 The choice must be made between some of the types of management in common use.. and the more modern and scientific management based on an accurate knowledge of how long it should take to do the work. **1910** L. D. BRANDEIS in *N.Y. Times* 22 Nov. 8/2 As an alternative to the practice of combining to raise rates and hence to increase prices, we offer cooperation to reduce costs... This can be done through the introduction of scientific management. **1911** F. W. TAYLOR in *Amer. Mag.* Mar. 571/2 The best management is a true science, resting upon clearly defined laws, rules, and principles, and..these fundamental principles of Scientific Management are applicable to all kinds of human activities. **1949** GILBRETH & CAREY *Cheaper by Dozen* i. 1 Dad always practised what he preached and it was just impossible to tell where his scientific management company ended and his family life began. **1972** *Scientific Management in American Industry* (Taylor Soc.) i. 2 The body of interlocking procedures which resulted from these investigations came to be known as the 'Taylor System', and to the doctrine and principles later derived from them was given the name 'Scientific Management'. **1854** T. H. HUXLEY *Educational Value of Nat. Hist. Sciences* 13 The man of business must as much avail himself of the scientific method..as the veriest bookworm. **1871** J. A. FROUDE *Short Studies on Great Subjects* (ser. 2) 485 Neither history, nor any other knowledge, could be obtained except by scientific methods. **1889** 'L. CARROLL' *Sylvie & Bruno* xviii. 255 *That*, I believe, is the true Scientific Method. **1908** W. MCDOUGALL *Introd. Soc. Psychol.* i. 4 When..the modern principles of scientific method began to be generally accepted. **1927** J. S. HUXLEY *Relig. without Revelation* iii. 83 There was a great outcry when scientific method was applied, in the form of the so-called 'Higher Criticism'. **1955** *Bull. Atomic Sci.* Oct. 295/1 Scientists possess a technique which they call the scientific method of thought, and they are impelled by circumstances to use it with the force of a new inspiration. **1959** L. W. H. HULL *Hist. & Philos. Sci.* vii. 194 The subtle blend of observation, hypothesis, mathematics and planned experiment in the Scientific Method is a more effective procedure than that of Bacon. **1961** WEBSTER, Scientific notation. **1963** W. H. WARE *Digital Computer Technol. & Design* I. ii. 22 The power of the base appearing in an expression which is in scientific notation in effect indicates the position of the point. **1973** C. W. GEAR *Introd. Computer Sci.* ii. 61 The number ·00000001 is represented as $\cdot 1 \times 10^{-7}$... We call this floating-point or scientific notation for numbers. **1975** *Physics Bull.* Mar. 135/3 The most important [feature of the calculators]..is the provision of exponential or 'scientific' notation. **1803** S. MILLER *Brief Retrospect of Eighteenth Cent.* I. II. 416 The frequency and rapidity of scientific revolutions may be accounted for in various ways. **1946** *Amer. Jrnl. Sociol.* Jan. 267/1 The use of atomic energy appears to be a beginning of the 'scientific revolution'. **1959** C. P. SNOW in *Encounter* July 22/2, I believe the industrial society of electronics, atomic energy, automation, is in cardinal respects different in kind from any that has gone before... It is this transformation that, in my view, is entitled to the name of 'scientific revolution'. **1977** G. CLARK *World Prehistory* (ed. 3) ii. 41 A Neolithic Revolution comparable in importance with the Industrial and Scientific Revolutions.

C. quasi-*adv.*, as *scientific-minded* adj.

1946 J. CARY *Moonlight* xxiii. 179 Our admirals are uneducated men who despise science, and the Germans are really scientific-minded men. **1976** I. LEVIN *Boys from Brazil* iii. 78 He's hardly a scientific-minded man.

scientifically, *adv.* Add: **2.** Systematically, methodically, thoroughly.

1922 WODEHOUSE *Jill Reckless* i. 28 Freddie poked the fire scientifically, and assisted it with coal. **1965** *Listener* 30 Dec. 1077/2 Three friends scientifically mete out to a bully the same bullying he administered to a small boy.

3. *Comb.*, as *scientifically-minded* adj.

1927 B. RUSSELL *Analysis of Matter* xiv. 130 Levers and pulleys, falling bodies, collisions of billiard balls, etc., are all familiar in everyday life, and it is a pleasure to the scientifically minded youth to find them amenable to mathematical treatment. **1931** H. N. SHENTON et al. *Internat. Communication* i. 63 Associations of scientifically-minded persons can continually bring to the problem of verbal communication the rapidly growing possibilities of social engineering. **1959** I. & P. OPIE *Lore & Lang. Schoolch.* ix. 174 Wisecracks which..scientifically minded boys, indulge in when, at about twelve years old, they begin to take up their subject in earnest. **1977** P. FITZGERALD *Knox Brothers* iv. 107 It was neither weakness nor compromise to try to reach this kind of unity with millions of the half-persuaded and the scientifically-minded.

scienti·ficism. *rare.* [f. SCIENTIFIC *a.* + -ISM.] Analysis or explanation which only admits what is considered to be scientifically demonstrable.

c **1875** W. JAMES in R. B. Perry *Tht. & Char. of W. James* (1935) I. 523 In a rough way materialism or 'scientificism' gratifies no. (1) [*sc.* an explanation of things by their cause]. **1884** —— *Will to Believe* (1897) 165 Subjectivism has three great branches,—we may call them scientificism, sentimentalism, and sensualism, respectively.

scientificity (saiˌĕntifi·sĭti). [f. SCIENTIFIC *a.* + -ITY.] The quality of being scientific; scientific character.

1970 B. BREWSTER tr. *Althusser & Balibar's Reading Capital* I. 49 The form of order required at a given moment in the history of knowledge by the existing type of scientificity, or, if you prefer, by the norms of theoretical validity recognized by science..as scientific. **1973** *Screen* Spring/Summer 209 Science..in its efforts to set itself off from *opinion* (the act of break which is scientificity itself).. is led to criticise most often the opinions which it meets most often. **1976** T. EAGLETON *Crit. & Ideology* i. 32 A mistaking of scientificity for positivism..links him..with the Romantic 'anti-scientism' of Lukács and the Frankfurt school.

scientifiction (saiˌĕntifi·kʃən). [Blend of SCIENTIFIC *a.* and *sb.* + FICTION.] Science fiction. Hence **scientifi·ctional** *a.*

1916 H. GERNSBACK in *Electr. Experimenter* Jan. 474/1, I am supposed to report Münchhaussen's doings; am supposed to be writing fiction, *scientifiction*, to be correct. **1929** *Amazing Stories Q.* Fall 575, I wish to compliment you on your choice of 'scientifictional' stories. **1930** *N. & Q.* 10 May 339/1 This class of literature is having a tremendous vogue in America just now. Quite a number of popular magazines are devoted to what they have dubbed 'Scientifiction'. **1940** *Illustr. London News* CXCVII. 32/3 'Dr. Cyclops', at the Carlton, applies Technicolor to what is called 'scientifiction'. **1940** 'G. ORWELL' in *Horizon* I. 191 H. G. Wells..is the father of 'Scientifiction'. **1943** C. S. LEWIS *Perelandra* vi. 91 He was a man obsessed with the idea which is at this moment circulating all over our planet in obscure works of 'scientifiction', in little Interplanetary Societies and Rocketry Clubs. **1955** —— *Surprised by Joy* ii. 41 That the ordinary interest in scientifiction is an affair for psychoanalysts is borne out by the fact that all who like it, like it thus ravenously. **1970** *New Scientist* 5 Feb. 264/2 In this scientifictional milieu I can still sit on the lakeshore and rationally speculate that sounds heard across the water are messages from the past.

scientism. Add: **2.** A term applied (freq. in a derogatory manner) to a belief in the omnipotence of scientific knowledge and techniques; also to the view that the methods of study appropriate to physical science can replace those used in other fields such as philosophy and, esp., human behaviour and the social sciences.

1921 G. B. SHAW *Back to Methuselah* p. lxxviii, The iconography and hagiology of Scientism are as copious as they are mostly squalid. **1937** J. LAVER *French Painting in Nineteenth Cent.* i. 73 It really appeared to many educated people that at last all the secrets of the universe would be discovered and all the problems of human life solved. This superstition..we may call 'Scientism'. **1938** G. REAVEY tr. *Berdyaev's Solitude & Society* i. 12 Science has not only progressively reduced the competence of philosophy, but it has also attempted to suppress it altogether and to replace it by its own claim to universality. This process is generally known as 'scientism'. **1942** F. A. VON HAYEK in *Economica* IX. 269 We shall wherever we are concerned, not with the general spirit of disinterested inquiry but with that slavish imitation of the method and language of science, speak of 'scientism' or the 'scientistic' prejudice. **1953** A. H. HOBBS *Social Problems & Scientism* ii. 17 Scientism, as a belief that science can furnish answers to all human problems, makes science a substitute for philosophy, religion, manners, and morals... It is a pattern of beliefs..a creed that shapes thinking and affects behavior. **1956** E. H. HUTTEN *Lang. Mod. Physics* vi. 273 This belief in the omnipotence of science is..making a mockery of science: for this scientism represents the same, superstitious, attitude which, in previous times, ascribed such power to a supernatural agency. **1957** W. H. WHYTE *Organization Man* iii. 23 *Scientism*,..the promise that with the same techniques that have worked in the physical sciences we can eventually create an exact science of man. **1969** *Encounter* Jan. 23/2 There is an aberration of science..which has come to be known as 'scientism'... It stands for the belief that science knows or will soon know all the answers. **1972** K. R. POPPER *Objective Knowl.* iv. 185 The term 'scientism' meant originally 'the slavish imitation of the method and language of (natural) science', especially by social scientists. *Ibid.* 186 But I would go even further and accuse at least some professional historians of 'scientism'. **1977** A. SHERIDAN tr. *J. Lacan's Écrits* iii. 76 The early development of psychoanalysis..expresses..nothing less than the re-creation of human meaning in an arid period of scientism. **1980** *Times Lit. Suppl.* 26 Sept. 1072/2 Naturalism, in David Thomas's usage, is equivalent to what many know as scientism: the doctrine that there is no reason to think that the study of human agents, and the study of the social systems to which human agents give rise, cannot be pursued according to a methodology drawn from natural science.

scientist. Add: (Earlier example.)

1834 *Q. Rev.* LI. 59 Science..loses all traces of unity. A curious illustration of this result may be observed in the want of any name by which we can designate the students of the knowledge of the material world collectively. We are informed that this difficulty was felt very oppressively by the members of the British Association for the Advancement of Science, at their meetings..in the last three summers... *Philosophers* was felt to be too wide and too lofty a term,..; *savans* was rather assuming,..; some ingenious gentleman proposed that, by analogy with *artist*, they might form *scientist*, and added that there could be no scruple in making free with this termination when we have such words as *sciolist*, *economist*, and *atheist*—but this was not generally palatable.

2. (Usu. with capital initial.) A Christian Scientist.

1875 M. B. EDDY *Science & Health* viii. 428 The Scientist sees more clearly the cause of disease in mind, than the anatomist can in body; the latter examines the body to learn how matter is committing suicide, and the former reads the mind to find what beliefs are destroying the body. **1902** 'MARK TWAIN' in *N. Amer. Rev.* CLXXV. 763 Where can you purchase it, at any outlay of any sort, in any Church or out of it, except the Scientist's? **1903** —— in *Ibid.* CLXXVI. 509 The Scientist hastened to Concord and told Mrs. Eddy what a disastrous mistake had been made. **1938** M. MUGGERIDGE *In Valley of this Restless Mind* ii. 8 'There's a Congregational Chapel..and a Church of England third on the right.'.. 'Do many people go to them?' 'Not many, I think... We're Scientists.' **1980** *Country Life* 17 July 243/1 There is the dowager, American..a Scientist (of the Christian kind).

3. Appositively in *Comb.*, as *scientist-administrator*, *-astronaut*, *-dietician*, *-philosopher*.

1964 M. GOWING *Britain & Atomic Energy 1939–1945* iii. 106 The two most influential American scientist-administrators..were positively anxious to have a joint Anglo-American project. **1965** M. STONE *Man in Space* (rev. ed.) 15 A second large group of astronauts..are a different breed. These newcomers are scientists... Some of these scientist-astronauts will go along on trips to the moon with the pilot-astronauts. **1971** *New Scientist* 18 Mar. 596/1 Dr Philip Chapman, the scientist-astronaut who served as mission scientist for Apollo 14. **1961** *Ann. Reg. 1960* 14 A 'scientist-dietician' and fanatical vegetarian, she believed that if we could discover the right diet we should live for ever. **1943** BLUNDEN *Return to Husbandry* 32 Whitehead, A. N... The most eloquent of modern scientist-philosophers. **1977** *Dædalus* Fall p. v, The contributors were humanists, natural scientists, and social scientists who had met to present their papers in homage to the work of two distinguished colleagues, the scientist-philosophers P. W. Bridgman and Philipp Frank.

scientistic, *a.* Restrict *rare* to sense in Dict. and add: **2.** Of or pertaining to scientism (sense *2).

1942 [see *SCIENTISM 2]. **1943** [see *HISTORICISM 3]. **1952** K. R. POPPER *Open Society & its Enemies* (ed. 2) I. 286 A typical and influential scientistic argument in favour of historicism is, in brief, this: 'We can predict eclipses; why should we not be able to predict revolutions?' **1969** *Nature* 2 Aug. 541/1 We must apply scientific method to social studies without being besotted by a scientistic philosophy and pragmatism. **1972** *Observer* 30 Apr. 36/6 They regard his [*sc.* Russell's] kind of piecemeal, logically technical, scientistic philosophy as a covert ideological support for technological civilisation. **1980** *Times Lit. Suppl.* 26 Sept. 1072/5 My remarks..should be put down to my own lack of sympathy with the scientistic vision which Thomas upholds.

scientize (sǝi·ĕntǝiz), *v.* [f. *scient-* (see SCIENTIST) + -IZE.] *trans.* To make scientific; to give (something) a scientific character, basis, or rationale; to organize on scientific principles.

1921 M. CORELLI *Secret Power* ix. 104, I was just crazy to help all the scientists..and started 'scientising' myself. **1957** W. H. WHYTE *Organization Man* iii. 29 If ethics is to be scientized, some specific people will have to do it. **1966** H. DAALDER in R. A. Dahl *Political Oppositions* vi. 209 Marxism..'scientized' hope, and thus made life more bearable in what was otherwise a relatively weak social and political position. **1976** *Survey* Spring 75 The hitherto forbidden fields of cybernetics and sociology were called upon to improve and scientize the management of Soviet society.

Hence **sci·entized** *ppl. a.*; also **scientiza·tion,** the action or result of scientizing.

1971 J. J. SHAPIRO tr. *Habermas's Toward Rational Society* v. 62 The scientization of politics is not yet a reality, but it is a real tendency. *Ibid.* 66 The decisionistic model..approximates the actual procedures of scientized politics. **1976** *Amer. Speech 1973* XLVIII. 288 As occupations become more mechanized and scientized, folk terms are often displaced by standard ones.

Scientologist (sǝi:ĕntǫ·lŏdʒist). Also with small initial. [f. *SCIENTOLOGY + -IST.] An adherent or practitioner of Scientology; a member of the 'Church of Scientology'. Also *attrib.* and *appositively*.

1952 L. R. HUBBARD *Scientology: 8–80* vi. 24 The E-Meter is available from The Hubbard Association of Scientologists. **1954** *Notes on Lectures given by L. Ron Hubbard* iv. 22 A scientologist is expected to be able to resolve problems in a great many specialized fields, of which auditing is the first field he addresses. **1956** J. F. HORNER *Summary of Scientology* i. 9 Scientologists work toward a world in which men cheerfully and willingly work together as fully free individuals able to co-operate toward the increased understanding and improvement of themselves, the race and the universe. **1965** L. R. HUBBARD *Scientology Abridged Dict.* 30 *Scientologist*, one who knows he has found the way to a better life through Scientology and who, through Scientology books, tapes, training and processing, is actively attaining it. **1968** *Time* 23 Aug. 40/3 By watching the fluctuations of a needle, Scientologist 'auditors' can supposedly discern when a student has become 'clear' and has attained 'total awareness and freedom'. **1971** *Times* 20 Nov. 3/2 After Mr Vosper had left the institution he was declared to be in a condition of enemy and fair game for scientologists. **1977** *Daily Colonist* (Victoria, B.C.) 7 Aug. 9/2 Scientologists..can hardly be termed medical researchers. **1978** G. VIDAL *Kalki* i. 18 They were perfect 'clears', to use Scientologist jargon.

Scientology (sǝi:ĕntǫ·lŏdʒi). Also **s-.** [f. *scient-* (in L. *scientia* knowledge) + -OLOGY.] A system of beliefs based on the study of knowledge and claiming to develop the highest potentialities of its members, founded in 1951 by L. Ron Hubbard (b. 1911).

Scientology is registered in the U.S. as a proprietary term.

[**1937** A. NORDENHOLZ *Scientologie* 7 Die Scientologie oder Eidologie, als eine Wissenschaft vom Wissen selbst, stellt sich ihrer Anlage nach in einen Gegensatz zu den Wissenschaften von den Dingen, die ins Wissen eingehen.] **1951** L. R. HUBBARD (*title*) Handbook for Preclears: Scientology. **1952** —— *Scientology: 8–80* 8 Scientology means knowing about knowing, or science of knowledge. **1960** *Daily Tel.* 29 Nov. 13/2 Meanwhile, I toured the town trying to discover the meaning of 'scientology' and 'creative learning', the system under which the children were instructed to imagine they were dead. **1965** L. R. HUBBARD *Scientology Abridged Dict.* 30 *Scientology*, an applied religious philosophy dealing with the study of knowledge, which, through the application of its technology can bring about desirable changes in the conditions of life. **1969** *Wall St. Jrnl.* 30 July, The Court of Claims ruled that the Founding Church of Scientology failed to show its net income didn't benefit private individuals. **1970** *Official Gaz.* (U.S. Patent Office) 1 Sept. TM 52/2 [Reg. no.] 898,018. L. Ron Hubbard, Washington, D.C...*Scientology*. For Bulletins, Books and Newsletters (Int. Cl. 16). First use Nov. 21, 1951. **1971** J. G. FOSTER *Enquiry into Pract. & Effects Scientology* iv. 42 in *Parl. Papers 1971–2* XXXVI. 917 Scientology departs from the mechanistic psychology of Dianetics by introducing a new causative agent... More usually..and especially in recent works..it is called the 'spirit' or 'thetan'... Among the goals of Scientology processing are to increase the beingness of the thetan and thus increase the creative potential of the individual personality and its analytical mind. **1973** *Daily Tel.* 31 Oct. 14/4 There was Lord Soper grudgingly admitting that Scientology was entitled to be called a religion even if it was the worst one he had come across. **1975** D. LODGE *Changing Places* v. 176 A young man distributing, without conviction, leaflets about courses in Scientology. **1980** *Daily Tel.* 14 July 3/1 A Scientology spokesman said the removal of the ban would be 'in keeping with Mrs Thatcher's beliefs in individual freedom and human rights'.

sci-fi (sǝi fǝi). Also **scifi, sci fi.** Colloq. abbrev. of *SCIENCE FICTION.

1955 *Britannica Bk. of Year* 490/1 The popularity of science fiction was reflected in the contracted form Scifi. **1957** *MD Medical Newsmag.* June 62/1 Modern sci-fi writers follow an honorable tradition. **1961** B. WELLS *Day Earth caught Fire* viii. 123 'I'm not up on my sci-fi,' hesitantly. 'So we're orbiting to the sun.' **1974** *Observer* 27 Oct. 1/7 The SF fan world abounds in language..that can baffle the novice... Most important of all, you must not say 'sci fi'—it's always SF. **1978** *N.Y. Times* 30 Mar. c 22/3 A 10-part series based on what Mr. Kotlowitz called 'speculative fiction', stories that go beyond sci-fi and deal with 'ethical and moral demands' made in new worlds to come **1980** *Verbatim* Autumn 10/1 'Sci fi' is a term used to describe bad Hollywood science fiction movies, trashy science fiction novels, and bad science fiction written by mundane writers. **1981** 'D. JORDAN' *Double Red* xiv. 61 There was a sci-fi film we didn't watch.

sci-fic (sǝi fik). *rare.* = prec.

1963 *Guardian* 4 Jan. 5/3 (*heading*) Psychic sci-fic. **1979** *Now!* 14 Sept. 6/4 Arthur C. Clarke is first of five sci-fic writers to talk about their work.

Scillonian, *sb.* (Earlier and later examples.)

1794 A. THOMAS *Newfoundland Jrnl.* (1968) ii. 19 The Scillonians (as they call themselves) have very little to fear as to a viset from a foreign power. **1976** *Sunday Post* (Glasgow) 26 Dec., The council are determined to protect Scillonians against the tourist element!

scimitar. Add: **3. scimitar-babbler,** a northern Indian or Australian bird belonging to the genus *Pomatorhinus* or *Pomatostomus*, and distinguished by a long curved bill.

1863 T. C. JERDON *Birds of India* II. 31 (*heading*) The Southern Scimitar-babbler. **1928** H. WHISTLER *Pop. Handbk. Indian Birds* 38 This Scimitar-Babbler is a gregarious species going about in small parties. **1964** R. PERRY *World of Tiger* iv. 58 Such small pests as scimitar-babblers, whose clear ringing cries are audible half a mile away in the hills.

scindapsus (sindæ·psǒs). [mod.L. (H. W. Schott *Meletemata Botanica* (1832) 21), f. Gr. σκινδαψός a plant resembling ivy.] A tropical climbing plant of the genus so called, belonging to the family Araceæ and native to Malaysia, esp. *Scindapsus pictus*, which has large variegated leaves and is often cultivated as a house plant. Cf. POTHOS, the former name of the genus *Scindapsus*.

1946 M. FREE *All about House Plants* xiii. 103 Scindapsus, Hoya, and others..attach themselves to supports by aerial roots. **1959** *Listener* 17 Dec 1094/3 Variegated scindapsus must have plenty of light. **1980** A. HUXLEY *Huxley's House of Plants* 102/1 Philodendrons, and scindapsus (devil's ivy), will do better growing around a moss cylinder.

scintigram (si·ntigræm). *Med.* Also **scinto-.** [f. SCINTI(LLATION + -GRAM.] An image or other record of part of the body obtained by measuring radiation from an introduced radioactive tracer by means of scintillation or an analogous detection method.

1952 F. K. BAUER et al. in *Jrnl. Lab. Clin. Med.* XXXIX. 153 It is suggested that this type of picture or visualization of a radioactive area be called a 'scintigram' and that specifically in this case they be called 'thyroid scintigrams'. **1963** LEADER & STELL in M. F. Campbell *Urol.* (ed. 2) I. vii. 238 The renal scintogram does not distinguish cyst from tumour, and lesions smaller than 3 cm. in diameter cannot be picked up. **1971** EMMETT & WITTEN *Clinical Urogr.* (ed. 3) III. xx. 2041/1 To localize radioactivity graphically by moving external counting probes or by scintillation camera-type detectors, producing a cartographic image known as a scintigram or scintiscan. *Ibid.* 2064/2 The hippurate scintigram reveals the presence of abnormal kidneys. **1974** R. M. KIRK et al. *Surgery* iv. 66 A scanner or gamma camera may be used to map out the distribution of radioactivity in a body, producing a diagram or 'scintigram'. **1980** *Brit. Med. Jrnl.* 29 Mar. 883/2 Bone metastases may be detected early as areas of increased isotope uptake ('hot spots') on scintigrams.

Hence **sci·ntigraph,** (*a*) a device for producing scintigrams; (*b*) a scintigram; **scintigra·phic** *a.*, of, done by, or pertaining to scintigraphy; **scintigra·phically** *adv.*, by means of scintigraphy; **scinti·graphy,** the production and use of scintigrams.

1958 *Strahlentherapy* CV. 257 Scintigraphy and the use of collimaters provide the means of portraying true size and form of the thyroid. **1960** *Radiology* LXXIV. 913/1 (*caption*) X-ray exposure is made during the scintigraphic procedure. *Ibid.* 914/1 Metastases in the right hepatic lobe can be scintigraphically demonstrated with only slightly less definition than in the left. **1961** *Med. Radiol.* VI. x. 76 Scintigraph. *A. Stefanovich.* Summary. A short description is given of a design of the apparatus used to investigate the localisation of radioactive isotopes in the human body. **1975** *Sci. Amer.* July 42/3 A scintigraph is an image constructed by a computer from the signals of many scintillation detectors arranged to detect the annihilation gamma rays in coincidence. For example, a patient can inhale nitrogen containing the positron-emitting isotope nitrogen 13. The scintigraphs clearly show how the gas enters the windpipe, passes through the bronchi and finally reaches the alveoli..in the lung. **1976** *New England Jrnl. Med.* CCXCV. 1/1 We have previously reported on scintigraphic visualization of myocardial infarction in man with use of thallium-201. **1977** *Lancet* 8 Jan. 92/2 (*caption*) Scintigraphs of left thigh showing localisation of Tc-99 diphosphonate in soft tissue. *Ibid.* 7 May 1012/2 Amyloidosis should be suspected when scintigraphy with Tc-99m diphosphonate shows a positive activity of soft tissues. **1978** *Jrnl. R. Soc. Med.* LXXI. 39 Lesions in the pubis and ischium may be very difficult to detect scintigraphically.

scintillantly (si·ntilăntli), *adv.* [f. SCINTILLANT *a.* + -LY².] In a scintillating manner.
1900 H. HARLAND *Cardinal's Snuff-Box* xix. 191 The.. buildings stood out..the white marble, palely, scintillantly amethystine. **1928** A. L. FLEMING *Dwellers in Arctic Night* 151 Flashes of light from the Aurora Borealis move scintillantly in the sky.

scintillate, *v.* Add: **1. c.** *intr. Nucl. Physics.* Of a phosphor: to fluoresce momentarily when struck by a charged particle or high-energy photon.
1958 O. R. FRISCH *Nuclear Handbk.* xiv. 20 The recent discovery that some gases scintillate will undoubtedly have many future applications. **1966** *McGraw-Hill Encycl. Sci. & Technol.* XII. 76/1 The liquid organic solvent scintillates satisfactorily. **1971** *Sci. Amer.* June 61/2 The box was.. provided with a zinc sulfide screen that would scintillate when it was struck by an alpha particle.

scintillating, *ppl. a.* Add: *scintillating scotoma* (Path.), hallucinatory flickering patterns and gaps in the visual field as seen in migraine.
1883 W. B. HADDEN tr. *J. M. Charcot's Lect. Localisation of Cerebral & Spinal Dis.* xi. 122 A particular form of megrim..characterised especially by the co-existence of scintillating scotoma. **1918** J. H. PARSONS *Diseases of Eye* (ed. 3) xix. 384 Scintillating scotomata of various kinds occur in migraine... A positive scotoma appears in the field of vision; while obscuring sight it has a peculiar shimmering character. **1950** BERENS & SIEGEL *Encycl. of Eye* 37 Visual hallucinations, such as scintillating scotoma.

scintillatingly (si·ntilēⁱtiŋli), *adv.* [f. SCINTILLATING *ppl. a.* + -LY².] In a scintillating manner; sparklingly.
1927 *Sunday Express* 6 Feb. 4 A scintillatingly funny burlesque.

scintillation. Add: **1. e.** *Nucl. Physics.* A small flash of visible or ultraviolet light emitted by fluorescence in a phosphor when it is struck by a charged particle or high-energy photon.
1903 W. CROOKES in *Science* 26 June 1002/1 Bringing the radium nearer the screen the scintillations become more numerous and brighter. **1915** *Arch. Radiol. & Electro-therapy* XX. 183 The phosphorescence observed by the naked eye is..found to consist of individual instantaneous flashes or 'scintillations', each produced by the impact of a single α particle. **1963** B. FOZARD *Instrumentation Nuclear Reactors* vi. 68 The scintillations must pass from phosphor to photocathode with minimum absorption at intervening surfaces. **1971** *Sci. Amer.* June 61/2 The screen could be moved to intercept particles scattered at any angle, and the scintillations were counted one at a time with the aid of a low-power microscope.

3. *attrib.* and *Comb.* in *Nucl. Physics*, as *scintillation fluid, method, screen*; **scintillation counter**, a particle counter consisting of a scintillation detector and an electronic counting circuit; hence **scintillation counting** *vbl. sb.*; **scintillation detector,** a detector for charged particles and gamma rays in which scintillations produced in a phosphor are detected and amplified by a photomultiplier, giving an electrical output signal; **scintillation spectrometer,** a form of scintillation counter with which the incident energy of the particle or gamma ray may be determined.
1948 *Physical Rev.* LXXIII. 1406/1 We have prepared some transparent crystalline slabs of both materials, and their behavior as scintillation counters has been compared. **1968** *New Scientist* 15 Aug. 338/2 The receiver consists of four scintillation counters, each shielded from the others and each covering a quadrant of the azimuth circle. **1975** K. H. GOULDING in Williams & Wilson *Biologist's Guide to Princ. & Techniques Pract. Biochem.* vi. 180 The fact that the pulse is directly related to the energy of the original radioactive event is a considerable advantage of scintillation counters over Geiger counters. **1949** *Nucleonics* Oct. 30/2 During the past year the technique of scintillation counting has been considerably advanced and the applications to nuclear research have become widespread. **1979** *Nature* 29 Mar. 410/1 Individual wood samples were finely chipped in preparation for chemical pretreatment and subsequent conversion to benzene for liquid scintillation counting. **1955** A. E. S. GREEN *Nuclear Physics* v. 133 In recent scintillation detectors a photomultiplier is used to change the light pulse into a large burst of electrons. **1977** *Dædalus* Fall 42 The detectors used in the balloon flights were mainly scintillation detectors, which are particularly useful for the detection of photons with energies greater than about 15 kev. **1979** Scintillation fluid [see *scintillation spectrometer* below]. **1909** *Proc. R. Soc.* A. LXXXII. 496 For the observation of the reflected particles the scintillation method was used in all experiments. **1929** *Ibid.* CXXIII. 375 An intense beam of α-particles of definite speed falls on a thin sheet of matter and the number of α-particles scattered through an angle of about 135° is counted by the scintillation method. **1953** GAYNOR & ZEPPELIN tr. *Heisenberg's Nuclear Physics* vii. 141 We shall begin with the instruments of detection and study. The oldest method is the scintillation method. **1938** R. W. LAWSON tr. *Hevesy & Paneth's Man. Radioactivity* (ed. 2) ii. 31 If we allow the α-particles from a point source to pass in a narrow pencil through thin metal foils,..and then to fall on a scintillation screen.., we find that a fraction of the α-rays is deflected through a small angle from their original direction. **1955** W. HEISENBERG in W. Pauli *Niels Bohr* 24 Schrödinger cannot hereby remove the element of discontinuity from the world, which is found everywhere in atomic physics (very obviously, for instance, on the scintillation screen). **1949** JORDAN & BELL in *Nucleonics* Oct. 38/1 The..fact that the amount of light emitted in each flash is very nearly proportional to the energy of the particle opens up the possibility of using the instrument for measurement of gamma- and beta-ray energies. We have developed such an instrument and call it a scintillation spectrometer. **1952** *Ann. Rev. Nucl. Sci.* I. 226 A γ-ray scintillation spectrometer, in conjunction with a magnetic lens spectrometer, has proven very valuable in determining decay schemes and beta–gamma angular correlations. **1979** *Nature* 25 Jan. 313/1 (*caption*) Radioactivity was assayed in a scintillation spectrometer after addition of 5 ml ACS scintillation fluid.

scintillator. Add: **2.** *Nucl. Physics.* **a.** A material that fluoresces when struck by a charged particle or high-energy photon.
1950 *Physical Rev.* LXXVIII. 81/2 Terphenyl crystals ..appear to be among the most durable of presently known organic scintillators. **1955** *Nucleonics* Feb. 10/1 (*heading*) Gaseous scintillators. **1963** B. FOZARD *Instrumentation Nuclear Reactors* vi. 63 Even in crystalline or liquid scintillators of high transparency it is usual to surround the phosphor with a reflecting surface. **1971** *Nature* 20 Aug. 574/2 Cosmic ray muons..were selected by a counter telescope consisting of one or two 2·5 cm diameter disks of plastic scintillator and a 58 cm diameter tank of liquid scintillator placed approximately 90 cm below. **1975** DAVIS & SIMPKINS in Williams & Wilson *Biologist's Guide to Princ. & Techniques Pract. Biochem.* iv. 112 The supporting medium may be cut into small sections which are then immersed in a suitable scintillator solution.
b. = *scintillation detector* s.v. *SCINTILLATION 3.
1952 *Ann. Rev. Nuclear Sci.* I. 188 The increase in scintillator signal when the plate is grounded is a measure of the beam which travels more than once around the orbit before being lost. **1958** *Times* 28 July 8/5 The radiation counters comprise two geiger counters and two scintillators, the geiger counters recording radiation within the satellite and the scintillators measuring exterior intensities. **1964** J. A. RANSOM *Range Guide to Mines & Min.* ii. 26 Anomaly maps were made originally by..flying airplanes over regions of suspected radioactivity with scintillators on long cables below the planes registering areas of abnormal gamma-ray count. **1977** *Kuwait Times* 1 Nov. 9/5 (Advt.), On display: Diagnostic and therapeutic X-ray equipments. Surgical steel instruments. Scintillators.

scintillogram (sinti·logræm). *Med.* [f. SCINTILL(ATION + -O + -GRAM.] A scintigram.
1958 *Proc. 2nd U.N. Internat. Conf. Peaceful Uses of Atomic Energy* XXVI. 245/1 Indefiniteness can be eliminated by making scintillograms in three mutually perpendicular planes. **1966** G. M. BERLYNE *Course in Renal Dis.* xvii. 348 The scintillogram using ²⁰³Hg labelled mercurial diuretics is a useful way of diagnosing small infarcted areas of the kidney.
Hence **scinti·llograph**, a scintigraph; **scintillogra·phic** *a.*, **scintillo·graphy.**
1958 *Proc. 2nd U.N. Internat. Conf. Peaceful Uses of Atomic Energy* XXVI. 243/1 Scintillography is principally used to examine objects of which the shapes and location are approximately known. *Ibid.* 245/2 A systematic search for thyroid tissue precedes all scintillographic examination. *Ibid.* 248/1 The scintillograph reveals only lesions with a diameter greater than 2 or 3 centimetres, unless they are confluent. **1965** *Biol. Abstr.* XLVI. 4558/1 (*heading*) Scintillographic study of the spleen. **1975** *Nature* 2 Oct. 426/1 The possibility that the phenomenon was due to physical migration of isotope was investigated by serial gamma camera scintillography of two specially prepared T tubes.

scintillometer. Add: **2.** A device containing a scintillator for detecting and measuring low intensities of ionizing radiation.
1955 *Times* 17 Aug. 7/6 An R.A.A.F. spokesman said today that Beaver aircraft with scintillometer and other radio gear would fly from Mawson early next year to search for a radioactive minerals map of the Antarctic coastline. **1956** *Proc. Internat. Conf. Peaceful Uses of Atomic Energy* VI. 660/1 An efficient scintillometer is about 50 times more sensitive to terrestrial gamma rays than a Geiger-Müller counter. **1977** A. HALLAM *Planet Earth* 111 The most useful geophysical surveys for mineral deposits are magnetic.., radiometric (the main prospecting tool for uranium deposits, using Geiger counters, scintillometers and gamma-ray spectrometers), electromagnetic, electrical, gravitometric, and seismic.
Hence **scintillo·metry,** study by means of the scintillometer.
1960 *Los Alamos Sci. Lab. Rep.* LAMS 2445. 337 (*heading*) Clinical applications of whole body scintillometry. **1974** *Nature* 15 Mar. p. xvi/2 (Advt.), The department has excellent modern facilities for work on tissue and organ culture, including..scintillometry.

scintilloscope (sinti·loskōᵘp). Also **scintillascope, scintilliscope.** [f. L. *scintill-a* spark + -O + -SCOPE.] An instrument in which alpha rays are detected by the flashes of light which are emitted when they strike a fluorescent screen.
1904 *Nature* 29 Sept. 535 The little instrument, which is called the 'Scintilloscope', consists of a simple magnifier of adjustable focus, as in the spinthariscope, but instead of the fixed screen and particle of radio-active substance a small double plate of glass is used. **1916** *Yukon Territory* (Canada Dept. Interior) 173 The scintilliscope is a much more convenient instrument. **1949** *New Gould Med. Dict.* 912/2 *Scintillascope*, an instrument for observing minute flashes of light upon a fluorescent screen struck by alpha particles, emitted from a small source of radioactive material. **1951** I. L. IDRIESS *Fortunes in Minerals* (ed. 2) xxxix. 250 These tiny flashes are known as scintillations, and can be seen through a magnifying glass. This is best done by a simple little instrument called a scintilliscope or spinthariscope. It is merely a small tube, probably of brass. In one end is fitted a glass prism. The outer side of the glass is coated with zinc sulphide powder... At the other end of the tube is fixed an eyepiece, which is a small magnifying glass.

scintiscan (si·ntiskæn). *Med.* [Back-formation from next.] An autoradiograph obtained with a scintiscanner.
1960 *Radiology* LXXV. 821/1 (*caption*) Bilateral renal scintiscan superimposed on abdominal radiograph. **1971** [see *SCINTIGRAM]. **1977** *Lancet* 6 Aug. 261/2 Liver scintiscans with ⁹⁹ᵐTc sulphur colloid were performed in 52 patients.

scintiscanner (si·ntiskænəɪ). *Med.* [f. SCINTI(LLATION + SCANNER.] A radiosensitive device which scans the body or part of it and creates an image of the distribution of radioactivity therein.
1953 *Radiology* LXI. 88/1 The point-by-point technique of plotting the frontal area occupied by the thyroid gland.. has been simplified by the introduction of the 'scintiscanner' for obtaining an actual size scintigram of the gland. **1956** *Jrnl. Neurosurg.* XIII. 345 (*caption*) Scintiscanner showing patient beneath the focusing collimator. **1968** *New Scientist* 12 Dec. 617/1 The computer is connected 'on-line' to a scintiscanner instrument, which measures radiation intensities as it is moved over a patient who has ingested a weakly radioactive isotope.
So **sci·ntiscanning** *vbl. sb.*, the production and use of scintiscans.
1954 *Amer. Jrnl. Roentgenol.* LXXII. 881/2 One tube stand suspends a shielded Geiger tube for uptake studies, the other tube stand supports the scintiscanning device. **1967** *Nursing Times* 18 Aug. 1095/2 The diagnostic uses of scintiscanning are extending rapidly with technical advances in radiobiology. **1980** *Nature* 17 Apr. 619/1 When bonded to the γ-emitter technetium-99..it is used clinically for scintiscanning of functioning renal cortex.

scio- (səiₗo-), comb. form of Gr. σκιά shadow, as in **scio·philous** *a. Bot.* [-PHILOUS], thriving best in shade; **sci·ophyte** *Bot.* [-PHYTE], a plant that thrives best in shade; hence **sciophy·tic** *a.* Also SCIOMANCY etc. in Dict.
1905 F. E. CLEMENTS *Res. Methods Ecol.* iii. 140 The slight development of hairs in sciophilous plants is an advantage. **1932** FULLER & CONARD tr. *Braun-Blanquet's Plant Sociol.* v. 107 In general the lower layers of stratified communities..are designated as sciophilous. **1905** F. E. CLEMENTS *Res. Methods Ecol.* iii. 144 (*heading*) Heliophytes and sciophytes. **1947** R. F. DAUBENMIRE *Plants & Environment* v. 234 Sciophytes may be at a disadvantage in full sunlight if they cannot manufacture chlorophyll at a rapid rate. **1974** *Nature* 23 Aug. 623/1 For many years it has been conventional to classify plants into sun-demanding (heliophytes) and shade-requiring (sciophytes). **1976** *Ibid.* 22 July 281/1 We provide evidence for the existence of 'sun' (heliophytic) and 'shade' (sciophytic) differences in the net photosynthesis-radiant flux intensity response of individuals of one coral species..on the same lagoon.

scioness (səi·ǫ̈nes). *joc. rare.* [f. SCION 2 + -ESS¹.] A female heir or descendant.
1928 'BRENT OF BIN BIN' *Up Country* xi. 36 Harriet Mayborn, scioness of the English aristocracy, was dumbfounded, but kept her head. **1969** T. SOUTHERN *Magic Christian* (ed. 2) xv. 120 A venerable scioness of Roman society.

Sciote (ʃi·ot), *a.* and *sb.* [f. It. *Scio* SCIO² + -OTE] **a.** *adj.* = CHIAN *a.* **b.** *sb.* A native or inhabitant of Chios.
1718 M. WORTLEY MONTAGU *Let.* 31 July (1965) I. 419 The ruins of this great City is now inhabited by poor Greek peasants who wear the Sciote habit. **1837** H. MARTINEAU *Jrnl.* 8 Sept. in *Autobiogr.* (1877) III. 190 Eastlake..must be a metaphysician to have painted his Sciote picture. **1866** *Chambers's Encycl.* VIII. 549/1 A number of the Sciotes having, in 1822, joined the Samians,..the inhabitants.. were indiscriminately massacred... Subsequently..many of the Sciote families returned.

scissile, *a.* Add: (Later examples.) Also in *Chem.*, capable of being broken. Cf. *SCISSION 3 a.
1967 *Listener* 10 Aug. 187/2 The first [play] in the series.. was...as scissile by commercials as anything on ITV. **1978** *Nature* 5 Jan. 94/3 The scissile bond in a peptide substrate.

scission. Add: **3. a.** *Chem.* Breakage of a bond, esp. in a long chain polymer such that two smaller chains result.
1923 *Jrnl. Chem. Soc.* CXXIII. I. 85 The scission of the ring..with elimination of nitrogen seems possible. **1944** *Jrnl. Appl. Physics* XV. 389/2 For the case of Hevea and GR-S, the number of places along the chain that are subject to scission is not very large. **1952** TURNER & HARRIS *Org. Chem.* xxvii. 524 Another apparently reasonable alternative is that hydrazobenzene undergoes scission at the N—N link. **1975** *Nature* 1 May 31/2 mRNA was treated with O.M NaOH for 4 min at 0°C, which gave on average about one scission per molecule.

b. *Nuclear Physics.* The event of separation of the parts of a nucleus undergoing fission, as opposed to the process as a whole.

1956 *Physical Rev.* CII. 440/1 The corresponding deformed shape roughly approximates the egg-shaped fragment resulting from scission of a dumbbell-shaped parent nucleus. **1958** *Rev. Mod. Physics* XXX. 555/1 The separation of charge centers at the moment of scission. **1964** L. Wilets *Theories Nuclear Fission* ii. 21 Of greater relevance to the fission process is the energy release to the point of scission, the time at which the fragment masses are unalterably determined. **1975** *Physics Bull.* July 307/1 Dr Specht..concentrated on a description of those fission phenomena which seem to be decided by conditions in the nucleus at the time of scission rather than at the saddle point.

scissor, *v.* Add: **2. b.** *fig.* To excise.

1890 G. B. Shaw in *Star* 19 Apr. 2/6 The first act was vigorously scissored. **1968** *Listener* 10 Oct. 462/1, I was invited by the BBC to cut a single sentence from a broadcast talk I had recorded previously... I refused to do this, and accordingly the talk was hastily scissored out of the Third Programme. **1977** *Time* 24 Oct. 23/3 The Finance Committee scissored the entire wellhead tax scheme out of the bill.

3. a. To cause (one's legs) to move like scissors. **b.** To fix (a person) in the scissors hold or with a grip resembling it (cf. *scissors *sb. pl.* 2 a).

1961 *Rogue* May 14 Feathertop watched the smooth scissoring of her slim, trim legs as she walked to the bags. **1968** A. Keith *Compl. Guide to Championship Wrestling* v. 76 Scissoring the bottom leg frees the hips. *Ibid.* 77 A scissors his right leg through underneath the left. **1973** *Funk & Wagnalls New Encycl.* XXII. 366 The legs are then scissored while the upper arm pushes toward the feet and the lower arm returns to the chest. **1974** J. Irving *158-Pound Marriage* i. 12 When he rode you with a cross-body ride—your near leg scissored, your far arm hooked—Severin said Jones cut off your circulation somewhere near your spine. **1975** R. H. Rimmer *Premar Experiments* (1976) ii. 162 With her legs scissored around me, I found it impossible not to pat her smooth black behind.

4. *intr.* *Rugby Football.* To execute a scissors movement. Cf. *scissors *sb. pl.* 2 d.

1970 *Financial Times* 23 Mar. 3/8 Robertson and Turner scissored impeccably for Turner to score a try that Brown converted. **1975** *Sunday Times* 23 Feb. 28/2 Smaje scissored with Aitchison to get the Lancashire try, converted by Gullick.

scissors, *sb. pl.* Add: **1. c.** (Later example.)

1976 *National Observer* (U.S.) 29 May 11/1 Each without the other is oniy half a scissors.

e. (Earlier and later and *attrib.* examples.) Also *transf.*

1809 *Monthly Pantheon* Apr. 266 He was to..take the scissors and paste brush in hand. **1925** T. E. Lawrence *Let.* 21 Apr. (1938) 475, I haven't much desire to undertake so difficult a scissors and paste job. **1936** [see *collage]. **1946** R. G. Collingwood *Idea of Hist.* 257 History constructed by excerpting and combining the testimonies of different authorities I call scissors-and-paste history. **1951** [see *cradle *sb.* 2]. **1977** A. Giddens *Stud. in Social & Polit. Theory* ii. 97 'Scissors and paste' ethnology of the sort which..assembled together examples from numerous different societies without regard to the social context in which they were embedded.

2. a. Now usu. a grip with the legs or ankles crossed like a pair of scissors. Also *body scissors.*

1909 Webster, *Scissors*, a hold in which one contestant clasps the other's head or body with his legs. **1921** *Daily Colonist* (Victoria, B.C.) 13 Oct. 10/7 He [*sc.* a wrestler] took the..second [fall]..with a body scissors. **1940** R. Chandler *Farewell, my Lovely* 173 The Indian threw me sideways and got a body scissors on me as I fell. **1961** J. S. Salak *Dict. Amer. Sports* 381 *Scissors hold* (wrestling), a hold which is secured by locking the legs at the ankles around a part of the opponent's body, pressure being applied. It formerly meant a grip with the wrists crossed like a pair of scissors.

b. *High jumping.* (See quots. 1961, 1976.) Also *attrib.* as *scissors jump.*

1897 *Encycl. Sport* I. 50/2 The methods of jumping are various, but two main types predominate—viz., the straight jump, and the side-way or scissors jump. **1959** *Times* 1 Oct. 3/3 Her legs..flashed over the bar in the old-fashioned scissors style. **1961** F. C. Avis *Sportsman's Gloss.* 61/2 *Scissors jump*, in high jumping, that method in which the body is in a virtually upright sitting position, and the legs move in an up-and-down motion. **1964** M. Watman *Encycl. Athletics* 79/2 There are four basic styles of high jumping: scissors, eastern cut-off, western roll and straddle... The ordinary scissors, which is taught to most schoolchildren, is the least effective of the four styles. **1976** *Webster's Sports Dict.* 371/1 *Scissors*,..a method of high jumping in which the jumper leads with the leg nearest the bar, crosses the bar in a sitting position, and then brings the trailing leg up over the bar as the lead leg is brought down on the other side.

c. *Swimming.* A movement in which the legs, held rigid, are parted slowly and brought together forcefully. Usu. *attrib.*

1904 R. Thomas *Swimming* 418/1 The simile of the scissors clip is accurate..for the breast stroke (and would be also for the English sidestroke). **1973** *Funk & Wagnalls New Encycl.* XXII. 367/1 Sidestroke. This stroke, employed on either the right or left side with a scissors kick,..is of particular value for lifesaving technique, but is not used in competition. **1974** 'G. Black' *Golden Cockatrice* xii. 200, I saw their legs..the girl doing a scissors kick that seemed to weaken as I swam towards them.

d. *Rugby Football.* (See quot. *c* 1915.) Also *attrib.* and *transf.*

c **1915** R. A. Lloyd in E. B. Poulton *Life R. Poulton* (1919) 218 The 'Scissors' trick was this: when I had the ball, and Ronald was running beside me just as if he was going to take an ordinary pass, he would suddenly change his direction and come racing straight across at me and practically take the ball out of my hands, and breaking clean through would run right across to the opposite wing. **1927** Wakefield & Marshall *Rugger* 229 The two [*sc.* a centre and wing three-quarter] may also combine when the centre still has the ball, when..they exploit the scissors movement. *Ibid.* 230 This scissors, and dummy scissors, attack may be tried also by two centres or by a centre and stand-off half. **1960** V. Jenkins *Lions down Under* 106 One forty yards' run of his, after he and Malcolm Thomas had worked a perfect dummy scissors, was a gem. **1976** *Wymondham & Attleborough Express* 3 Dec., They worked one of their excellent set pieces including two dummies, a well taken scissors and a Gary Owen.

e. *fig.* A progressive divergence between two kinds of price or income, so called from the appearance of a graph of the two indices plotted against each other; *orig.* and *spec.* used *attrib.* of a crisis in the Soviet Union in 1923 (see quots. 1926, 1965).

1924 M. Farbman *After Lenin* vii. 125 The economic crisis of the autumn and winter of 1923–24 is known as the crisis of the scissors. **1926** *Encycl. Brit.* III. 425/1 The first of these was a crisis which from an image used by Trotsky came to be known as the crisis of the 'scissors'. The two blades of the scissors represented the prices of agricultural products and the price of manufactured goods. **1965** A. Nove in B. Pearce tr. *Preobrazhensky's New Economics* p. xi, In 1923 the Soviet economy faced the so-called 'scissors crisis': the terms of trade between town and country had become so unfavourable to the latter that the peasants were reluctant to sell their produce. **1974** J. White tr. *Poulantzas's Fascism & Dictatorship* iv. ii. 193 The index of labour income shows that the scissors between the income of skilled and semi-skilled workers widened considerably. **1979** *China Now* Mar./Apr. 25/1 The closing of the price scissors (the gap between the price paid for agricultural foods and the prices paid by the peasants for manufactured goods) has not gone far enough.

f. In phr. *scissors and stones, scissors cut paper, scissors game,* a game for two players using three postures of the right hand (see quot. 1934).

Or the left hand if one is left-handed.

1934 P. Fleming *One's Company* ii. ii. 198 From a room downstairs came that sound which so often accompanies meals in China—the staccato, competitive ejaculations of a party playing the 'scissors' game. In this you and your opponent shoot out your right hands at each other simultaneously, the fingers being arranged in one of three postures. A clenched fist means 'stone'; two fingers extended mean 'scissors'; all five fingers extended mean 'paper'. Scissors cut paper but are broken on stone, and paper wins against stone because stone can be wrapped up in paper. **1952** J. B. Pick *Phoenix Dict. Games* 291 Scissors and stones. **1964** I. Fleming *You only live Twice* i. 18 It was the old game of Scissors cut Paper, Paper wraps Stone. Stone blunts Scissors, that is played by children all over the world. **1976** *Times* 2 Dec. 16/5 The Chinese hand-game Scissors Cut Paper.

5. *scissor-leg; scissor-cut, -legged* adj.; **scissor(s)-bill,** (*b*) *slang* in various senses; *esp.* a foolish, incompetent, garrulous, or objectionable person; **scissor-cut** [tr. G. *scherenschnitt*], a silhouette that has been cut freehand with scissors; also as vb.; **scissor(s)-grinder** (earlier examples); **scissor-hold** = Scissors 2 a; **scissor(s)-lift,** a surface that is raised or lowered by the closing or opening of crossed supports pivoted like the two halves of a pair of scissors; **scissor-man,** a man who wields scissors, *spec.* a censor, a surgeon, or a tailor.

1871 *Atlantic Monthly* Nov. 566/2 Pootiest band of hogs in Tulare County! There's littler of the real sissor-bill nor Mexican racer stock than any band I have ever seen in the State. **1913** *Industrial Worker* (Spokane, Washington) 1 May 5/3 Scissorbill is a localized slang term. Here it refers to the 'home-guard' worker, who is filled with bourgeoise [*sic*] ideas and ethics. It ordinarily describes a worker who has some source of income other than his wages. **1926** J. Black *You can't Win* x. 129 When a bums' 'convention' is to be held, the jungle is first cleared of all outsiders such as 'gay cats',..'jungle buzzards', and 'scissors bills'. **1931** B. Starke *Touch & Go* xvi. 259 Dick praised me for not saying anything. 'You're not a scissor-bill.' A scissor-bill was a woman who gossiped and nagged and was bad generally. **1931** 'D. Stiff' *Milk & Honey Route* xiv. 163 The line in waiting [for prostitutes] is usually monopolised by the village scissorbills. *a* **1944** J. Conroy in B. A. Botkin *Treas. Amer. Folklore* (1944) iv. 548 Some sign painters couldn't dot the letter 'i' without a pounce to go by. It was enough to make a dog laugh to see some poor scissorsbills wrastling around with a pounce. **1961** R. P. Hobson *Rancher takes Wife* iii. 56 The hell you did, you big scissorbill, you stepped on my bum leg and my hand both. **1931** *Times Lit. Suppl.* 25 June (Suppl.) p. iii/2 His many brilliant students have perhaps done more service to the book-jacket than to the page by some of their shadow, scissor-cut and engraved letter forms. *Ibid.* p. iv/2 Professor D. P. Sterenberg portrays objects of daily life in flat lithographs that resemble scissor-cuts. **1931** V. Woolf *Waves* 126, I see.. Neville, scissor-cutting, exact. **1960** *Times* 11 Feb. 3/4 The graceful and elegant animated scissor-cuts of Lotte Reiniger. **1976** *Times* 26 Nov. 4/7 An octagonal scissor-cut emerald is set in a gold and enamel ring. **1841** N. Hawthorne *Amer. Notebks.* (1932) 88 The squirrel..frequently uttered a sharp, quick, angry noise, like that of a scissors-grinder's wheel. **1855** 'Q. K. P. Doesticks' *Doesticks* 155 The loving accents of the scissor-grinder's wheel. **1974** D. Sears *Lark in Clear Air* iii. 43 She pulled my head down close, jimmied her knees around my leg so that she had a scissor hold. **1923** W. de la Mare *Riddle & Other Stories* 178 Before him stood a kind of gaping wallet, of cracked American cloth, held yawningly open by its scissor-legs. **1947** —— *Collected Stories for Children* 26 His lank scissor-legs. **1967** Flakoll & Alegria tr. *M. A. Asturias' Cyclone* ii. 22 The scissor-legged cot. **1961** *Aeroplane & Astronautics* CI. 568/2 The mobile scissor-lift intermediate-base loading platform developed by Canadair is seen here being demonstrated with a Seaboard World Airways' CL-44. **1970** *Times* (Aviation Suppl.) 4 Sept. p. xiv/8 Ready-prepared meals for the galleys on board the aircraft are..loaded by mobile scissors-lift vehicles direct to the galley hatches. **1980** *BSI News* June 5/3 Most types of scissor lift present trapping hazards to persons employed on or about them. **1848** tr. *Hoffmann's English Struwwelpeter* (ed. 4) 16 The door flew open, in he ran, The great, long, red-legged scissar-man. Oh! children, see! the tailor's come. **1932** Auden in *Rev. Eng. Stud.* (1978) Aug. 301 The hump-backed surgeons And the scissor-man. *a* **1953** Dylan Thomas *Quite Early One Morning* (1954) 22 Struwelpeter—oh! the baby-burning flames and the clacking scissorman! **1968** *Listener* 5 Sept. 292/1 Arts censorship in Britain lives on mainly through the sheer personality of its few remaining scissormen.

sclaff (sklæf), *sb. Golf.* [See Sclaff *v.*] A stroke in which the club scrapes the ground before hitting the ball. Hence **sclaˑffy** *a.*

1893 H. Hutchinson *Golfing* 82 'Tops', and 'sclaffs', and misses. **1896** W. Park *Game of Golf* 91 The sight of bare earth..gives the impression that contact between it and the club-head, which might happen with a sclaffy shot, would inevitably result in damage to the club. **1903** W. J. Travis *Pract. Golf* 20 If..the head is allowed to move, the chances are that a sclaff or a top will result. **1948** Dante & Diegel *Nine Bad Shots of Golf* x. 104 There is one other swing that will produce a sclaff. **1973** A. MacVicar *Painted Doll Affair* vii. 84 My drives would be hooks and slices, my irons sclaffy travesties.

sclareol (sklēᵊ·riǫl). *Chem.* [ad. F. *sclaréol* (Volmar & Jermstad 1928, in *Compt. Rend.* CLXXXVI. 519), f. *sauge sclarée* Clary *sb.*[2] (mod.L. *Salvia sclarea*): see -ol.] A colourless crystalline diterpenoid alcohol, $C_{20}H_{36}O_2$, found in the leaves of clary; also, one of the two constituent epimers of this.

1928 *Chem. Abstr.* XXII. 1828 The essence [of clary].. contains 42·2% of crystallizable sclareol. **1959** *Chem. & Industry* 1379/1 Since sclareol has been dehydrated to a mixture of manool and manoyl oxide, all three compounds must have the same absolute configuration at C(13). **1975** *Nature* 22 May 328/2 An epimeric mixture of the diterpenes sclareol and 13-epi-sclareol (sclareol)..has been shown to constitute 10% of the surface exudate on leaves of *Nicotiana glutinosa*. *Ibid.*, In replicate experiments, applications of.. sclareol consistently gave good control of rust on French bean, broad bean and wheat, reducing infection to less than 10% of control.

scleractinian (sklīᵊ:rækti·niăn), *sb.* and *a.* [f. mod.L. order name *Scleractinia* (coined as *Scleractineae* by G. C. Bourne, in E. R. Lankester *Treat. Zool.* (1900) II. vi. 55), f. Gr. σκληρ-ός hard + ἀκτῖν-, ἀκτίς ray + -ia[1], -an: cf. Actinia, *actinian.] **A.** *sb.* A coral of the order Scleractinia or Madreporaria, which is characterized by compact calcareous skeletons and includes all living true corals. **B.** *adj.* Of or pertaining to such a coral or the group as a whole.

1900 G. C. Bourne in E. R. Lankester *Treat. Zool.* II. vi. 61 The anatomy of any Scleractinian resembles, in essential points, that of an Actinia. *Ibid.* 80 In *Heliopora* the skeleton is not spicular but lamellar, resembling in structure that of the Scleractinian corals. **1943** *Spec. Papers Geol. Soc. Amer.* No. 44. 1 This revision is the result of a study of the genotype species..of nearly every described scleractinian genus... The distribution of fossil and recent scleractinian faunas is broadly analyzed. *Ibid.* 90 The forerunners of most of the groups of the scleractinians are found in the Middle and Upper Triassic rocks. **1952** R. C. Moore et al. *Invertebrate Fossils* iv. 143/2 The scleractinians differ from rugose corals chiefly in the mode of addition of new septa. **1973** *Nature* 27 July 201/1 The thirty-six scleractinian species of coral found on the actively growing, fringing reefs along the western coast of Barbados are complemented by varied populations of sponges, anemones,..and cucumbers.

sclereid. Add: Also **scler(e)ide.** [a. G. *sclereïd* (A. Tschirch 1885, in *Jahrb. f. Wissensch. Bot.* XVI. 308), irreg. f. Gr. σκληρ-ός hard: see -id[2].] = *stone cell* s.v. Stone *sb.* 20. (Examples.)

1896 *Ann. Bot.* X. 11 The walls of the sclereids..acquire during the ripening an increasingly dark brown colour. **1914** M. Drummond tr. *Haberlandt's Physiol. Plant Anat.* iv. 160 The coarse villi or shaggy hairs of the Melastomaceae often contain whole bundles of sclereides, which penetrate below into the mesophyll. **1919** F. O. Bower *Bot. of Living Plant* ix. 145 Such stone-cells or sclereids, give a hard gritty texture to the parts where they occur, as in the bark or pith of various woody plants. **1934** *Jrnl. Arnold Arboretum* XV. 247 Clusters of sclerides or stone cells..are of not infrequent occurrence in the pith of the redwood. **1969** E. G. Cutter *Plant Anat.* I. vi. 57 Sclerenchyma may be sub-divided into sclereids and fibres.

sclerema. Add: Also *sclerema neonatorum* [gen. pl. of mod.L. *neonātus* (cf. *NEONATE)]. (Further examples.)

1889 J. E. GRAHAM in J. M. Keating *Cycl. Diseases Children* II. I. 90 Sclerema neonatorum..is distinguished by a peculiar, œdematous, corpse-like hardening of the skin. **1962** *Lancet* 27 Jan. 226/1 Pneumonia, hæmorrhagic disease of the new-born, or sclerema neonatorum may be diagnosed. **1974** PASSMORE & ROBSON *Compan. Med. Stud.* III. xlv. 31/1 The baby's rectal temperature..falls... He becomes less active, less hungry and less vocal. The skin reddens and grows cold and the subcutaneous tissue slowly becomes hard... This state is known as sclerema.

sclero-. Add: **1.** **scle:roblaste·ma** *Anat.* [BLASTEMA], the embryonic tissue which gives rise to bone; **sclerœde·ma** (also **scleredema**) *Path.* (see quot. 1976); **scleropro·tein** *Biochem.*, any insoluble structural protein; **sclerothe·rapy**, the treatment of varicosities by the injection of a substance which induces clotting.

1934 WEBSTER, Scleroblastema. **1968** PASSMORE & ROBSON *Compan. Med. Stud.* I. xviii. 11/2 Each vertebra is laid down as a densely cellular mesenchymal precursor, the scleroblastema; this transforms into a cartilage model which is subsequently replaced by bone by the process of endochondral ossification. **1932** *Jrnl. Amer. Med. Assoc.* 3 Sept. 822/1 Scleredema adultorum is characterized by progressive induration and swelling of the deeper portions of the skin and subcutaneous tissues. *Ibid.* 825/1 Scleredema always involutes spontaneously without subsequent atrophy of the affected tissues. **1946** *New England Jrnl. Med.* 15 Aug. 209/1 The appearance of a patient with scleredema is so striking as to suggest the diagnosis immediately. **1976** *Proc. R. Soc. Med.* LXIX. 844/2 Sclerœdema is characterized by sudden onset of diffuse symmetrical hardening of the skin of the face, neck and upper arms. **1907** HALLIBURTON & HOPKINS in *Jrnl. Physiol.* XXXV. p. xix, Sclero-proteins. This new word takes the place of the word albuminoid... It includes such substances as gelatin and keratin; the prefix indicates the skeletal origin and often insoluble nature of its members. **1958** *Immunology* I. 49 Some of the scleroproteins comprising the scale plate are antigenic, but are only slowly digested by homologous recipients. **1970** R. M. BLACK *Elements Palaeont.* ii. 8 The matrix of bone consists mainly of collagen (a fibrous scleroprotein) hardened by mineral salts. **1977** A. HALLAM *Planet Earth* 241 More usually, however, only the most resistant and stable organic materials can survive long after death, as with the lignified tissues of fossil land plants and the scleroprotein skeleton of the extinct fossil graptolites. **1944** *Amer. Jrnl. Surg.* LXVI. 363 The advantages of sclerotherapy are low morbidity, almost no mortality and no necessity for hospitalization... The disadvantage is the very high incidence of recurrence. **1977** *Lancet* 25 June 1343/1 F. Bezzouni of Russia has an approach similar to that of most surgeons in Britain—injection sclerotherapy for small, below-knee varices and high ligation and stripping for gross main-stem incompetence.

scleroblast. **2.** Substitute for def.: A spicule-forming cell in sponges.

scleromyxœdema (sklīə:romiksīdī·mă). *Path.* Also **-myxedema.** [ad. G. *skleromyxödem* (H. H. Gottron 1954, in *Arch. f. Dermatol. u. Syphilis* CXCIX. 71): see SCLERO- and *myxœdema* s.v. MYXO-.] A disease characterized by the extensive proliferation of fibroblasts and deposition of mucopolysaccharides in the skin, causing distortions of the features and lichenous eruptions.

1964 *Arch. Dermatol.* LXXXIX. 446/1 Lichen myxedematosus, also known as..scleromyxedema, is a well-known clinical entity. **1968** R. J. CAIRNS in A. Rook et al. *Textbk. Dermatol.* II. lv. 1621/2 A variant of lichen myxoedematosus is scleromyxoedema..—the Arndt–Gottron syndrome—in which diffuse thickening of the skin underlies the papules... The features may be distorted by the exaggeration of the facial ridges and flexion of the fingers may be limited. **1977** *Lancet* 4 June 1208/2 Ten years previously this patient has been treated for scleromyxœdema..with melphalan.

sclerophyll (sklīə·rofil), *sb.* and *a. Bot.* [ad. G. *sklerophyll* (A. F. W. Schimper *Pflanzen-geographie* (1898) v. 538: see next word.] **A.** *sb.* A sclerophyllous plant.

1911 J. M. COULTER et al. *Textbk. Bot.* II. iii. 710 In the inclement period they [*sc.* the leaves of deciduous trees] are as well protected as are the cacti and better protected than are the sclerophylls. **1923** *Jrnl. Ecol.* XI. 287 Northwards.. the forest becomes more important, but is soon supplanted by conifer forest..into which many of the sclerophylls, both shrubs and trees, pass as subordinate members. **1939** *Nature* 11 Mar. 412/2 The 'rhenosterbush'..represents the most arid kind of sclerophyll. **1975** *Sci. Amer.* Jan. 133/1 The text itself considers one by one the 10 vegetational zones, from the evergreen tropical forests to the regions of winter-rain sclerophylls.

B. *adj.* = *SCLEROPHYLLOUS *a.*

1926 TANSLEY & CHIPP *Aims & Methods in Study of Vegetation* vi. 99 Where the rain mainly falls in the late autumn and winter, but is sufficient in quantity, and there is a hot dry summer, the vegetation is of the evergreen sclerophyll type—trees or shrubs with rather small leathery leaves. *Ibid.* 100 Sclerophyll regions always abut on desert regions. **1970** GAY & CALABY in Krishna & Weesner *Biol. Termites* II. ix. 413 Symmetrical dome mounds..are found only occasionally in the sclerophyll woodland and mallee. **1978** *Nature* 9 Mar. 160/1 A general and sustained increase in sclerophyll vegetation at the expense of drier rain forest types, probably a result of aboriginal man's activities, can explain some..of the evolutionary changes.

So **sclero·phylly,** the fact of being sclerophyllous.

1903 W. R. FISHER tr. *Schimper's Plant-Geogr.* i. 9 With increasing physiological dryness, the leaves become smaller in surface but proportionally thicker, more leathery (sclerophylly). **1909** E. WARMING *Œcol. Plants* xlvi. 194 Sclerophylly is frequent and is due to thickness of the epidermal wall, as in Andromeda polifolia. **1973** J. WIESER tr. *Walter's Vegetation of Earth* iv. iii. 121 The ecological significance of sclerophylly is..to be seen in the ability of sclerophyllous species to conduct active gaseous exchange.. in the presence of an adequate water supply, but to cut it down radically by shutting the stomata when water is scarce.

sclerophyllous (sklīəro̧·filəs), *a. Bot.* [f. Gr. σκληρό-ς hard + φύλλ-ον leaf + -OUS.] Pertaining to or designating woody evergreen plants having leaves that are hard and tough, and usu. small and thick, so reducing the rate of loss of water; characterized by such plants.

1903 W. R. FISHER tr. *Schimper's Plant-Geogr.* v. 507 The mild temperate districts with winter rain and prolonged summer drought are the home of evergreen xerophilous woody plants, which, owing to the stiffness of their thick, leathery leaves, may be termed sclerophyllous woody plants. *Ibid.* 516 The best known districts inhabited by sclerophyllous woods are the coasts of the Mediterranean Sea. **1926** TANSLEY & CHIPP *Aims & Methods & Study of Vegetation* ii. 26 The dominance of [s]clerophyllous trees or shrubs (rather small hard evergreen leaves) indicates a moderate rainfall mainly concentrated in the winter half of the year, which is mild, and a hot dry summer. **1961** *Times* 12 Apr. 3/2 (Advt.), The Department is noted for its research in..plant ecology (with emphasis on sclerophyllous and arid plants). **1973** J. WIESER tr. *Walter's Vegetation of Earth* iv. iii. 127 The roots of sclerophyllous species reach far down into the ground because the upper soil layers are usually completely dried out in summer.

sclerosant (sklīərō͞u·zănt, sklĕr-), *sb.* and *a. Med.* [f. SCLEROS(IS + -ANT¹.] **A.** *sb.* A sclerosant agent. **B.** *adj.* Producing sclerosis or hardening of tissue.

1956 *New Gould Med. Dict.* (ed. 2) 1076/1 *Sclerosant*, a chemical irritant producing an inflammatory reaction and subsequent fibrosis. **1962** *Lancet* 8 Dec. 1221/2 McEvedy seems to have had good results after the injection of a *sclerosant* solution such as ethanolamine. **1977** *Brit. Med. Jrnl.* 12 Feb. 434/2 When ligamentous pain and tenderness seem to dominate, 'sclerosant' mixtures of phenol, dextrose, and glycerine may be injected into the tender area. **1979** *Ibid.* 22 Sept. 704/2 We used two sclerosants—namely, phenol..and tetradecyl sulphate.

Scleroscope (sklīə·ro̧skō͞up). Also **scleroscope.** [f. SCLERO- + -SCOPE.] An instrument for measuring the hardness of a material, this being indicated by the height of rebound of a small diamond-tipped hammer dropped from a standard height on to the material. Also *attrib.* Hence **sclerosco·pic** *a.*

Scleroscope is a proprietary term in the U.S.

1907 A. F. SHORE in *Amer. Machinist* 14 Nov. 748/1 The instrument was named scleroscope, from the Greek words *sclerotus*, meaning hardness, and *scope*, because it is direct reading. **1908** [see *SHORE *sb.*⁶]. **1915** [see *BRINELL]. **1921** *Glasgow Herald* 23 Sept. 9 The use of the scleroscope on light specimens of metals. **1936** P. F. FOSTER *Mech. Testing of Metals & Alloys* viii. 143 A dynamic hardness test is provided by the Shore scleroscope in which a small pointed tup weighing about 0·0052 lb. is allowed to fall freely from a height of 10 in. on to the test piece. **1950** *Engineering* 31 Mar. 371/2 Scleroscopic hardness values are approximately 85 and 65. **1961** *Official Gaz.* (U.S. Patent Office) 29 Aug. TM 149/1 The Shore Instrument & Mfg. Company, Inc.,.. N.Y..*Scleroscope*... For instruments used to test hardness of metals and other substances. **1977** R. B. ROSS *Handbk. Metal Treatments & Testing* 166 The Scleroscope test is of limited use and accuracy but, because of its extreme portability, has certain advantages over other more conventional tests.

sclerosis. Add: **3.** *fig.* Rigidity, excessive resistance to change.

1954 B. & R. NORTH tr. *M. Duverger's Pol. Parties* I. ii. 89 Such a drying-up of new recruits is the symptom of a serious sclerosis. **1958** *Times* 11 Aug. 2/5 All the world knows that he was faced with the problem of revitalizing a good tradition that was beginning to suffer from sclerosis. **1966** S. H. BEAVER tr. *J. Beaujeu-Garnier's Geogr. Population* x. 228 Research work..has shown the parallelism that exists between the sclerosis of social structures and the high proportion of marriages between first cousins. **1977** *N.Y. Rev. Bks.* 14 July 35/2 Popovic saw his harassment as a symptom of the ideological sclerosis which is increasing with Tito's age.

sclerotic, *a.*¹ Add: **5.** *fig.* Unmoving, unchanging, rigid.

1965 *Listener* 20 May 737/2 Why is it, I asked myself, that so many theatre people in Russia call the Moscow Arts old-fashioned and sclerotic? **1968** *Daily Tel.* (Colour Suppl.) 13 Dec. 61/1 The sidewalks of New York seem to get harder year by year, the skyscrapers more inhumanly overbearing, the traffic more sclerotic. **1979** *Washington Star* 8 May A15/7 She [*sc.* Margaret Thatcher] has to deal with tacky little things like the secondary boycotts, repealing sclerotic tax laws, [etc.].

sclerotin (sklīə·rǫtin). *Biol.* [f. SCLERO- + *-tin* after CHITIN, KERATIN, etc.] Any of a class of structural proteins which form the exocuticles of insects and harden and darken by a natural tanning process in which protein chains become cross-linked by quinone groups.

1940 M. G. M. PRYOR in *Proc. R. Soc.* B. CXXVIII. 391, I therefore propose the name 'sclerotin' as a general term to describe proteins such as that of the cockroach ootheca, which owe their stability to a process of natural tanning. **1957** RICHARDS & DAVIES *Imms's Textbk. Ent.* (ed. 9) I. 11 Polyphenols..are the precursors of the quinones which link the arthropodin molecules to form sclerotin. **1969** R. F. CHAPMAN *Insects* xxii. 434 Part of the protein may later be tanned.., stabilised by cross-linkages between the molecules, to form a hard, inflexible and usually darkened structure. Such tanned arthropodin is called sclerotin, and this produces the hardness of the sclerites. **1976** *Sci. Amer.* Apr. 134/3 Such quinone-linked proteins, called sclerotins, are usually coloured brown or black, accounting for the hard beetle look we all know.

sclerotinia (sklīəroti·niă). [mod.L. (L. Fuckel 1870, in *Jahrb. d. Nassauischen Vereins f. Naturk.* XXIII–XXIV. 330), f. SCLEROTIUM + *-inium*, arbitrary suffix.] The name of a genus of parasitic fungi, used *attrib.* and *absol.* to designate plant diseases caused by them.

1926 *Misc. Publ. Min. Agric. & Fish.* LII. 26 Sclerotinia disease..reported from Lancashire [potatoes]. **1950** *N.Z. Jrnl. Agric.* July 79/2 Causing rapid decay, sclerotinia rot (*Sclerotinia* spp.) attacks many plants, including petunias, zinnias, stocks, and wallflowers. Dead plants are usually black, but are covered by a white growth. **1976** E. SCARROW *N.Z. Veg. Gardening Guide* 64 Fungal diseases include early and late blight sclerotinia (or white mould disease) and various other stem and leaf blights.

sclerotized (sklīə·rotəiz'd), *ppl. a. Zool.* [f. SCLEROT(IC *a.*¹ and *sb.* + -IZ(E + -ED¹.] Hardened by conversion into sclerotin.

1928 FERRIS & CHAMBERLIN in *Entomol. News* XXXIX. 215 We might very logically extend the use of the root which appears in the word 'sclerite'. This word alone is hardly sufficient to meet all our needs and we could speak of 'sclerotic areas' or of 'sclerotized areas'. **1955** P. A. BUXTON *Nat. Hist. Tsetse Flies* iii. 53 The upper wall of the labium is also sclerotized and forms the labial gutter. **1975** *Nature* 8 May 142/2 A sclerotised edge of the left wing [of the tree cricket] serves as the scraper.

So **scle:rotiza·tion** ; **scle·rotize** *v. trans.*

1957 RICHARDS & DAVIES *Imms's Textbk. Entomol.* (ed. 9) I. 9 In most insects..the greater part of the cuticle undergoes a process of sclerotization whereby it becomes hardened and darkened to form more or less tough, rigid sclerites separated from each other by membraneous zones of unchanged soft cuticle. **1963** R. P. DALES *Annelids* ii. 41 The cuticle of the earthworm gizzard is like that of the epidermis and is simply collagenous, but in polychaetes the stomodeal cuticle may be sclerotized to form teeth or jaws. **1974** *Nature* 30 Aug. 799/2 An early effect of ecdysoids at metamorphosis in some caterpillars is conversion of tryptophane into red ommochrome pigments; in fly larvae, the conversion of tyrosine into quinones to sclerotise the puparium. *Ibid.* 20 Dec. 710/2 The sclerotisation and tanning of insect cuticles is generally thought to result from a crosslinking of the cuticular proteins by quinonoid derivatives of tyrosine.

sclerotome. Add: Hence **scleroto·mal, scleroto·mic** *adjs.*, of or pertaining to a sclerotome.

1890 WEBSTER, Sclerotomic. **1925** J. S. KINGSLEY *Vertebrate Skeleton* 21 There is one great difference between Elasmobranches and higher Vertebrates; in the former cells from the sclerotomic elements..break through the elastica externa.., invade the notochordal sheath, and may chondrify there. **1971** A. J. WATERMAN *Chordate Struct. & Function* vi. 211 The sclerotomic cells form the perichordal tube. In addition, a mass of sclerotomic tissue migrates to the myoseptum to form the neural and haemal arch anlagen. *Ibid.* (*caption*) Precartilage stage; further compaction of sclerotomal tissue with establishment of basic vertebral shape... Sclerotome stage; sclerotomal cells migrate from somite and form sclerotome. **1974** D. & M. WEBSTER *Compar. Vertebr. Morphol.* v. 87 The posterior half of one sclerotomal segment and the anterior half of the segment just behind it join together, so that each presumptive vertebra forms on a level overlapping two somites.

scobberlotcher. Delete † *Obs.* and add later examples. Also **scobolotcher.**

1933 C. DAY LEWIS *Dick Willoughby* 10 Thou bed-worm, thou scobberlotcher! **1956** *Bournemouth Daily Echo* 21 Apr. 10/4 A scobolotcher, said Mr. Moore, was an undergraduate walking around a quadrangle hands in pockets and deep in thought.

scobby. Add: Also **scobbie, skobby.** (Earlier and later examples.)

1800 D. WORDSWORTH *Jrnl.* 17 May (1941) I. 39 The Skobby sate quietly in its nest. **1976** *Jrnl. Lakeland Dial. Soc.* No. 38. 39 She wes gitten weel on afoor she kent et a scobbie wes oot but a scobbie.

scoff, *sb.*² Add: Also **schoff, skoff.** (Earlier and later examples.) Also in colloq. use outside South Africa. Also *attrib.*

1846 *Swell's Night Guide* 51 It vas hout-and-hout good scoff, and no flies. **1855** J. W. COLENSO *Ten Weeks in Natal* 54 The *meat* and other *scoff* (food), which the Kafirs are so fond of. **1863** J. S. DOBIE *Jrnl.* 6 Jan. (1945) 60 The best one was consigned to the Kafirs for 'scoff'. **1902** 'COLD-STREAMER' *Ballads of Boer War* vii. 66 They gives 'im 'schoff' an' treats 'im kind, Instead o' striking 'im be'ind. **1926** *Variety* 29 Dec. 5/3 Slang, in addition to providing me with seven flops weekly and three scoffs daily, has saved me from night school. **1928** *Daily Express* 14 May 10/6 While you've had me locked up, I've eaten your scoff! **1934** *Detective Fiction Weekly* 21 Apr. 109/2 Where the criminal eats he says he scoffs, and if he goes to a restaurant it is called a beanery, chow joint or scoff joint. **1955** J. Cope *Fair House* v. 62 He treated them familiarly, shared his skoff-tin with them. **1960** [see *bevvy]. **1969** in Halpert & Story *Christmas Mumming in Newfoundland* 84 One of the men might suggest to those in his group that everyone come over to his house for a 'scoff'. **1976** *Australasian Express* 11 June 25/3 A particularly memorable scoff was had on Colitzani beach. **1977** J. Wainwright *Do Nothin'* xi. 182 A dance, all of her own, with guests and scoff and booze of her own choice. **1981** *Guardian* 24 Aug. 8 Ah! Scoff ahoy! I spy Florida Cocktail and Gammon Steak Hawaii!

scoff, *v.*¹ Add: **2. c.** To utter in a scoffing manner (with the spoken words as obj.).

1862 Mrs. H. Wood *Channings* I. v. 70 'A senior do it!' scoffed Roland Yorke. **1894** E. Fawcett *New Nero* v. 66 'I no more ruined her,' scoffed Egerton, 'than the Sultan of Turkey did!' **1898** Skeel & Brearley *King Washington* xxv. 155 'Not I,' scoffed Anne, shaking her taffeta flounces. **1921** [see *poof *int.* A]. **1976** J. Wainwright *Bastard* i. 23 'In *this* weather?' I scoff. **1977** P. G. Winslow *Witch Hill Murder* ii. xvii. 219 'Oh, come on, Supe,' Jed scoffed. 'You're really not trying to pin that murder on me, are you?'

scoff, *v.*² Add: **1. a.** (Earlier and later examples.) Also with *up, down.* Also *fig.*

1846 *Swell's Night Guide* 48 He scoffed weed; that is, chewed tobacco. *Ibid.* 50 You must grub with the grunters, and scoff cabbage without salt. **1942** *Tee Emm* (Air Ministry) II. 148 Fluorescence which he said tasted horrible, and of which he scoffed quite a fair amount while he was waiting to be lifted out of the water. **1956** I. Murdoch *Flight from Enchanter* 125, I wonder what happens to it [*sc.* a magazine]. Fay must scoff it up in her room. **1967** E. Gilzean *Murder on Sundays* ii. 33 Come on, Janet. They'll have scoffed all the beer and cider if we don't hurry. **1972** R. K. Smith *Ransom* v. 231 Scoff it up, chillun. . and you'll grow up big and strong. **1973** J. Porter *It's Murder with Dover* v. 45 In the dining room the reporters . . were. . noisily scoffing down everything that was put in front of them. **1979** *Daily Tel.* 13 Oct. 12/3 Should the farmer wish to supplement the rations of his cattle or sheep in bad weather then he must stand guard over the feeding trough to stop the horses scoffing the lot.

b. (Earlier and later examples.)

1798 A. Barnard *Jrnl.* 24 May in A. W. C. Lindsay *Lives of Lindsays* (1849) III. 464 [The Boer] concludes of course that the passengers want to *scoff* (to eat). **1850** H. Melville *White-Jacket* xv. 73 Bear a hand, and '*scoff*' (eat) away. . . Some of you fellows keep *scoffing* as if I had nothing to do but. . look on. **1855** G. H. Mason *Life with Zulus of Natal* xvi. 193 A Caffre. . entered our service. . . It soon became manifest that our new servant was a madman. . . He would commence a war-song, or call for us to get up and 'scoff' (eat) *with him.* **1926** *Clues* Nov. 158/2 Let's scoff. Get the duffer. **1931** 'D. Stiff' *Milk & Honey Route* 213 *Scoffing*, to eat. *To scoff regularly* means to miss no meals. **1944** D. Burley *Orig. Handbk. Harlem Jive* 70 Really knock yourself out as you scoff. **1965** R. Erskine *Passion Flowers in Business* xiii. 164 Can we please go and scoff? **1973** C. Himes *Black on Black* 133 Go on, baby, you can be back in an hour with 'nuff bread so we can scoff.

scoffer² (skǫ·fəɹ). *colloq.* [f. Scoff *v.*² + -er¹.] One who eats greedily.

1935 *Amer. Speech* X. 20/1 *Scoffer*, a glutton; one who has no control over his appetite. (Obs.) **1959** I. & P. Opie *Lore & Lang. Schoolch.* ix. 154 A pair of Hertfordshire 14-year-olds, . when asked about their classmates and invited to set down their epithets for them, promptly came to life and wrote: 'Phumph, lumber bontts [bonce], . . hog, scoffer, flippin kid [etc.]'. **1976** *Times* 21 Aug. 12/6 The scoffers of doughnuts, bananas and raw eggs.

scoffing (skǫ̆·fiŋ), *sb.* *U.S. Tramps' slang.* [f. Scoff *v.*²] Usu. *pl.* Food, something to eat.

1907 J. London in *Cosmopolitan* May 17/1 A hard town for 'scoffings', was what the hoboes called it [*sc.* Reno] at that time. **1914** *Sat. Even. Post* 4 Apr. 11/3 Got to throw your feet if yuh want scoffin's. *Ibid.*, You'll have to batter for handouts this mornin'. I'll get my own scoffin's.

scofflaw (skǫ·flǭ). Chiefly *U.S.* [f. Scoff *v.*¹ + Law *sb.*¹] One who treats the law with contempt, esp. a person who avoids various kinds of not easily enforceable laws. Also *attrib.*

1924 *Boston Herald* 16 Jan. 1/2 Delcevare King of Quincy last night announced that 'scofflaw' is the winning word in the contest for the $200 he offered for a word, to characterize the 'lawless drinker' of illegally made or illegally obtained liquor. 'Scofflaw' was chosen from more than 25,000 words, submitted from all the states and from several foreign countries. The word was sent by two contestants, so the prize will be equally divided between Henry Irving Dale. . and Miss Kate L. Butler. **1936** Mencken *Amer. Lang.* (ed. 4) 174 The announcement that *scofflaw*. . had won was made on Jan. 15, 1924. The word came into immediate currency, and survived until the collapse of Prohibition. **1956** *N.Y. Times* 17 Jan. 27/3 The maximum fine of $50 a ticket was imposed yesterday upon a woman scofflaw who had accumulated fifty-one parking tickets. **1961** *Observer* 1 Oct. 30/6 An unenforceable law which automatically transformed every wet citizen into a scofflaw. **1965** P. De Vries *Let Me count Ways* iv. 57 A scofflaw in such a jam could easily insist that the facts in his possession during his lifetime justified his unbelief. **1971** J. Gray *Red Lights* iii. 78 Moose Jaw became the happy hunting ground for Regina gamblers, philandering husbands. . and unclassified scofflaws. **1973** D. E. Westlake *Cops & Robbers* 25 He had New York plates. Good. If I gave him a ticket he couldn't be a scofflaw, fade away into some other state and thumb his nose at me. **1977** *Sat. Rev.* (U.S.) 3 Sept. 6/1 The illegal phone-dialing devices called 'blue boxes' are about to be put out of business. . . By. . pressing its rewired dial-tone buttons, a scofflaw could bypass phone company billing systems.

scoldingly, *adv.* (Later examples.)

1912 J. Stephens *Crock of Gold* v. xiv. 208 As they approached the door the sound of a female voice came to them scoldingly. **1933** E. O'Neill *Ah, Wilderness!* iv. iii. 152 She goes on scoldingly.

scoleces, pl. of Scolex.

scolices, pl. (*erron.*) of Scolex.

Scoline (skōᵘ·līn). *Pharm.* Also **scoline.** [f. *s(uccinyl)c(h)oline.] A proprietary name for succinylcholine.

1952 *Trade Marks Jrnl.* 30 Jan. 89/2 *Scoline*. . . Pharmaceutical preparations and substances. Allen & Hanburys Ltd, Three Colts Lane, Bethnal Green, London, E.2; wholesale Chemists and Druggists. **1952** *Lancet* 21 June 1226/2 Succinylcholine chloride ('Scoline') was given intravenously. **1965** J. Pollitt *Depression & its Treatment* iv. 50 A modern relaxant such as succeryl choline (Scoline) is given intravenously. **1965** *Daily Express* 14 Oct. 5/7 The two-inch long ampoules of scoline and of distilled water. . were kept together in a plastic bowl in a refrigerator. **1976** Smythies & Corbett *Psychiatry* xvii. 291 American psychologists treated some criminals in jail by asking them to imagine themselves reliving the circumstances of their criminal activities and then giving an injection of scoline.

scoliosis. Add: Pl. **scolioses** (-ōᵘ·sīz). (Further examples.) **scoliotic** *a.* (example).

1939 H. H. Jordan *Orthopedic Appliances* iii. 90 A group of scolioses which are suitable for treatment by forces which we can introduce by means of an active correcting brace. **1958** *Jrnl. Bone & Joint Surg.* XLa. 553 Correction and fusion of the scoliotic spine. **1976** *Lancet* 4 Dec. 1234/1 In the causation and progression of scoliosis spinal muscles may have a major role. *Ibid.*, On electronmicroscopy there are signs of dystrophy and atrophy in the spinal muscles of scoliotic patients.

scolopale (skǫ·lǫ̆pēⁱl). *Ent.* Formerly also **-pala** (pl. **-palæ**). [ad. G. *scolopal* adj. (in *scolopale körperchen*) (V. Gräber 1882, in *Arch. f. mikrosk. Anat.* XX. 516), f. Gr. σκολοπ-, σκόλοψ spike + *-al* -al.] The rod-like structure inside the sheath of a scolopidium; also, the sheath itself.

1912 J. H. Comstock *Spider Bk.* iii. 169 The failure of other observers to discover scolopalæ or auditory pins. . has made this conclusion doubtful. **1917** *Ann. Entomol. Soc. Amer.* X. 69 Its distal portion penetrates the center of the enveloping cell into the proximal end of the cap cell, where the nerve enlarges to form the peg-shaped body or scolopale. **1925** [see *scolopophore]. **1932** *Parasitology* XXIV. 457 These cells are connected with the main antennal nerve, whereas the other end gives off a long scolopala, or the sense rod. **1948** *Sci. News* VII. 19 One finds in all insects structures which consist of parallel elements—elongated spindle-shaped sensory cells whose axes are prolonged into nerve fibres on the central side while on the other side they are in contact with the so-called 'scolopales' (pointed stakes). **1964** [see *scolopophore]. **1969** R. F. Chapman *Insects* xxx. 630 The most fully studied contact chemoreceptors are the trichoid sensilla on the legs and mouthparts of *Phormia*. They are from 30 to 300 μ long. From the tip the scolopale is invaginated. **1978** H. V. Daly et al. *Introd. Insect Biol. & Diversity* vi. 107/2 In the usual arrangement [of sensilla], the dendrite of a single bipolar neuron is attached to a movable part of the body, often by a minute cuticular sheath called a scolopale.

scolopendrine, *a.* Add: Also *fig.*

1963 V. Nabokov *Gift* iv. 257 He left a scolopendrine trace in literature as the translator of foreign poets.

scolophore, var. Scolopophore in Dict. and Suppl.

scolopidium (skǫlǫ̆pi·diəm). *Ent.* Pl. **-idia.** [mod.L., coined in Ger. (F. Eggers 1923, in *Zool. Anzeiger* LVII. 239), f. Gr. σκολοπ-, σκόλοψ spike, after Ommatidium.] An elongated sensory end-organ in insects consisting chiefly of the nucleus and dendrite of a sensory nerve cell and a tubular sheath enclosing the dendrite; *spec.* each of those that compose a chordotonal organ.

1939 V. B. Wigglesworth *Princ. Insect Physiol.* vii. 135 Chordotonal sensilla or scolopidia—These sensilla are generally believed to be derived from campaniform sensilla through their component parts becoming elongated and deeply sunk within the body. **1957** *New Biol.* XXIII. 38 Applied to the inside of the membrane [of a locust's tympanal organ] are the ends of a number of special sense cells, or scolopidia, which transmit the movements of the membrane as impulses along the auditory nerve. **1971** [see *scolopoid *a.*]. **1978** H. V. Daly et al. *Introd. Insect Biol. & Diversity* vi. 107/2 Chordotonal organs are completely internal and formed by units or scolopidia consisting of three cells: a bipolar neuron, a scolopale cell, and an attachment cell.

scolopoid (skǫ·lǫ̆poid), *a.* *Ent.* [f. Gr. σκολοπ-, σκόλοψ spike + -oid.] = *scolopophorous *a.*

1963 V. G. Dethier *Physiol. Insect Senses* ii. 19 (*caption*) Different forms of scolopoid sensilla. A. Terminal peg from a grasshopper sensillum. [Etc.] **1971** E. O. Wilson *Insect Societies* (1972) xi. 202/2 Typical chordotonal sensilla—or scolopoid sensilla, or scolopidia as they are often alternatively labelled.

scolopophore. Add: Also **scolophore.** Also, the sensory end-organ of which this sheath is part, comprising in addition the enclosed rod and neurone. (Further examples.) [ad. G. *scolopophor* (V. Graber 1881, in *Zool. Anzeiger* IV. 452).]

1917 *Ann. Entomol. Soc. Amer.* X. 66 Schwabe (1906). . first showed that the nerve end-organ or scolopophore is composed of three cells with definite boundaries. **1925** A. D. Imms *Gen. Textbk. Entomol.* i. 82 An auditory or chordotonal sensilla consists of a nerve end-organ or scolophore, enclosing a hollow peg-like structure or scolopale. **1933** *Jrnl. Cellular & Compar. Physiol.* IV. 80 The scolophores are either directly connected with the tympanum or lie on a secondary membrane so situated as to move with it. They contain a chitinous rod or scolopale, one end of which projects from the cell body into one or more supporting cells which abut against the body wall. **1964** R. M. & J. W. Fox *Introd. Compar. Entomol.* vi. 193 The unit of the chordotonal organ is the scolopophore. ., composed of an apical cap cell attached to the body wall and an envelope cell; in the central part of the cap cell is a terminal ligament which forms a functional extension of the sensory rod (scolops or scolopale) in the envelope cell. **1967** C. P. Hickman *Biol. Invertebrates* xxv. 459/1 Many Orthoptera. . have sound receptors, which are spindle-shaped bundles of chordotonal sensilla attached to the integument and called scolophores.

scolopophorous (skǫ:lǫ̆pǫ·fǒrəs), *a.* *Ent.* [f. prec. + -ous, after G. *scolopofer* (V. Graber 1881, in *Zool. Anzeiger* IV. 450).] Of a sensory end-organ: having the elongated tubular form of a scolopidium.

1935 R. E. Snodgrass *Princ. Insect Morphol.* xviii. 527 Scolopophorous sense organs are widely distributed in insects, but until recently they have not been reported in other arthropods. **1973** W. S. Romoser *Sci. of Entomol.* v. 122 A type of sensillum that is rather dramatically different from those already described is the scolopophorous or chordotonal organ.

scolops (skǫ·lǫ̆ps). *Ent.* [a. Gr. σκόλοψ spike, adopted in this sense in Ger. by F. Eggers 1923, in *Zool. Anzeiger* LVII. 239.] The rod-like structure inside the sheath of a scolopidium.

1935 R. E. Snodgrass *Princ. Insect Morphol.* xviii. 526 The distinguishing feature of sensilla scolopophora is the presence of a well-differentiated, peg-shaped 'sense rod', or scolops, at the apex of each cell. **1964** [see *scolopophore].

scolytid, *sb.* and *a.* Insert in etym. after *Scolytus* (E. L. Geoffroy *Hist. Insectes de Paris* (1762) I. 309), f. Gr. σκολι-ός bent, curved. Substitute for def.: A small cylindrical bark- or wood-boring beetle of the family Scolytidæ; of or pertaining to a beetle of this kind or the family as a whole. (Earlier and later examples.)

1890 *Proc. Entomol. Soc. Washington* II. 77 (*title*) Notes on the breeding habits of some Scolytids. **1909** *Bull. U.S. Bureau Entomol.* LXXIII. 1 (*title*) Practical information on the Scolytid beetles of North American forests. **1925** A. D. Imms *Gen. Textbk. Entomol.* iii. 510 Scolytid larvæ are apodous. **1959** E. F. Linssen *Beetles Brit. Isles* II. 256 The best-known scolytid is probably. . the Large Elm Bark Beetle. **1972** *Oxf. Univ. Gaz.* CII. No. 3496 (Suppl.* 2) 22 Investigations on Scolytid beetles of timber. **1976** *Nature* 24 June 696/2 Most scolytids. . occupy temporary habitats.

scone, *sb.* Add: **1. drop-, dropped scone** (examples).

1899 E. Heddle *Marget at Manse* 100 She. . would bake drop-scones, and carry in my tea with her own hands. **1899** R. Wallace *Country Schoolmaster* 20 Potato scones, soda scones, 'droppet' scones, treacle scones. **1942** C. Spry *Come into Garden, Cook* xv. 213 Most people have a good recipe for dropped scones. . . Drop the batter from a spoon on the hot girdle and turn once. **1956** E. Grierson *Second Man* ii. 44 Some tea-cake and drop scones and jam. **1977** *Age* (Melbourne) 18 Jan. 13/4 The cheese souffle looked more like a cheese drop-scone.

3. a. (Always with pronunc. skǫn) *to do one's scone,* to lose one's head, temper. Hence *scone-doer, -doing. N.Z. slang.*

1942 *2nd N.Z.E.F. Times* 20 Apr. 6 Scone-doer. A person subject to sudden fits of excitement and irritation. *Ibid.* 19 Oct. 5 'Don't do your plurry scone, Dig!'. . 'Who's sconing?' **1944** F. I. Cooze *Kiwis in Pacific* i. 8 The camp at Pahantanui was much as all military camps. Tedious training, fatigues, and 'scone-doing' from 6 a.m. to 4 p.m. **1952** *Here & Now* (N.Z.) II. iv. 20 Everyone question Rangi. Everyone do the Scone. **1957** M. K. Joseph *I'll Soldier no More* (1958) ix. 167 Gillies finds him a bit of a nagger, but likes him for being efficient and not doing his scone.

b. The head. *Austral. slang.*

c **1945** in S. J. Baker *Austral. Lang.* (1966) viii. 172 *Scone*, head. **1957** D. Niland *Call Me when Cross turns*

Over v. 138, I can just see you running a house. I'd give you a week before you went off your scone. **1968** D. O'Grady *Bottle of Sandwiches* 58 He reckoned we weren't right in the scone to be travelling so far on a Sunday just to chase a ball around a paddock.

4. *Comb.*, as **scone-hot** *a. Austral. slang*, in phr. *to go* (someone) *scone-hot*, to reprimand (someone) severely, to lose one's temper at (someone); see also quot. 1941.

1938 X. Herbert *Capricornia* 530 Halfcaste Shillingsworth goes Copra Co scone-hot! **1941** Baker *Dict. Austral. Slang* 63 *Scone-hot*, an intensive to describe great vigour of attack, scolding or speed, e.g., 'Go for someone scone-hot', to reprimand severely. (2) Exorbitant, unreasonable. (3) Expert, proficient, e.g., 'He's scone-hot at shearing'. **1944** *Coast to Coast 1943* 116, I don't want Reg going me scone hot because his wife's not capable of looking after herself. **1967** K. Tennant *Tell Morning This* (1968) xvii. 139 When my big brother Jim come home from work, he went Dad scone hot. **1974** D. Ireland *Burn* 136 When he finds out he'll go me scone-hot.

scone (skǫn), *v. Austral.* and *N.Z. slang.* [f. dial. *scon, scun*: see *Eng. Dial. Dict.*] *trans.* To hit.

1948 *Coast to Coast 1947* 187 The bottle broke. Damn! he hadn't meant to scone the bottle first go-off. **1958** I. Cross *God Boy* iv. 30 Joe was worried in case he had really sconed the girl.

scoop, *sb.*[1] Add: **7. scoop bonnet**, a woman's bonnet shaped like a scoop; also *scoop-shovel bonnet*.

1846 E. W. Farnham *Life in Prairie Land* 102 Sometimes her scoop bonnet covered half my field of vision. **1901** W. Churchill *Crisis* I. iv. 40 Her face was in that most seductive of frames, a scoop bonnet of dark green velvet. **1905** J. C. Lincoln *Partners of Tide* 30 [Portraits] of ladies in flowered scoop bonnets..gazed down upon him with rigid disapproval. **1884** 'Mark Twain' *Huck. Finn* xvii. 154 One was a woman in a slim black dress..and a large scoop-shovel bonnet. **1941** L. I. Wilder *Little Town on Prairie* xix. 222 She wore a sweeping black gown and a scoop bonnet.

scoop, *sb.*[2] Add: **1. a.** Also, a quantity scooped up.

1832 J. P. Kennedy *Swallow Barn* I. iii. 34 Nine scoops of water in the hollow of the hand, from a sycamore spring.., will break an ague.

b. *Mus.* = Portamento.

1911 W. K. Smith *Training Village Choirs* 8 The scoop is made on the commencing note of a tune or phrase. It consists in attacking it by way of a chromatic slide from the 'fourth' below. **1967** A. L. Lloyd *Folk Song in Eng.* i. 64 The sundry ways the folk singer has of passing from note to note by means of scoops, slides, hovers and such. **1975** *Gramophone* Aug. 316/1 He pulls the *Rosamunde* 'Entr'acte' about horribly and there are all sorts of period scoops that modern listeners will find intolerable. **1977** *Early Music* July 343/2 Special techniques and playing styles that can be developed are..'scoops' on a note, e.g. D–C♯–D completely slurred and glided simply by relaxing the breath pressure and increasing it again, keeping the fingering for the upper note held all the time.

2. b. *Film* and *Television.* (See quots.)

1940 *Chambers's Techn. Dict.* 747/2 *Scoop*, one or more suspended broadsides, which are special types of incandescent flood-lights for use in motion-picture studios. **1974** *Some Technical Terms & Slang* (Granada Television), *Scoop*, 500 watt lamp suspended from studio ceiling.

3. a. (Earlier example.)

1871 F. C. Burnand *More Happy Thoughts* xxxiv. 248 'Both the nautical Cockalorums have been going on the scoop, and are slightly moppy.' By which we understand him to mean, that the two naval officers have had as much as is bad for them.

b. For *U.S.* read orig. *U.S.* and add earlier and later examples. Also *transf.*

1874 *Macomb* (Illinois) *Eagle* 23 Nov. 1/2 Owing to a slight misunderstanding, the *Sentinel* found itself without a copy of the decision, and for a time a terrible scoop seemed imminent. **1906** *Daily Chron.* 29 Jan. 4/6 The feat escaped the notice of the representatives of all other newspapers; so the item is what in Fleet-street language is styled an 'exclusive' or 'scoop'. **1913** E. Pound *Let.* Mar. (1971) 16 It's our second scoop, for I only found the man [*sc.* Robert Frost] by accident and I think I've about the only copy of the book that has left the shop. **1917** Chesterton *Short Hist. Eng.* xiv. 181 One of these scares and scoops (not to add the less technical name of lies) was the Popish Plot. **1920** *Times* 25 Oct. 15/3 The edition would have been on the streets..leaving the heartbroken editor to bewail the death of his great 'scoop'. **1930** 'Sapper' *Finger of Fate* 127 The first thing to do was to get on the 'phone to his editor, because he had intended returning to London that night. He knew there would be no difficulty—especially if he gave a hint over the wire that he was on a scoop. **1940, 1969** [see *beat *sb.*[1] 15 c]. **1973** D. Barnes *See the Woman* 75 We've got some scoop that our outstanding suspect is holed up in the Rocket Motel.

4. *attrib.* and *Comb.*, as **scoop neck**, a rounded, low-cut neck on a garment; also (with hyphen) *attrib.*; so *scoop-necked* adj.; **scoop neckline** = *scoop neck*.

1953 *New Yorker* 20 June 64/2 At Rosette Pennington, 20 East 56th Street, there's a cool little sleeveless black cotton dress with a scoop neck and a full, flounced skirt. **1956** *Ibid.* 28 Jan. 68/3 There are short beach coats and scoop-neck dresses, all of the same material. **1972** *Vogue* Jan. 22 Bell sleeves, scoop neck, pintucks on cuffs. **1978** *Detroit Free Press* 16 Apr. D 14 (Advt.), The tab closing jacket with a skirt and scoop-neck shell in pink or beige. **1955** *New Yorker* 17 Sept. 96/1 De Pinna has acquired another sleeveless, scoop-necked Trigère dress. **1977** *Daily Tel.* 4 Apr. 15/4 The scoop-necked three-quarter mohair-knit coat over scooped-necked long-torso fine-knit sweater. **1959** *Times* 21 Sept. 12/4 A gown of deep cream satin with a fitting bodice, a scoop neckline, and a full skirt.

scoop, *v.*[1] Add: **5. a.** (Earlier and later examples.) Also in various extended uses; *esp.* to defeat, destroy, get the better of. Phr. *to scoop the kitty* (or *pool*), in *Gambling*, to win all the money that is staked; also *transf.*, to gain everything, to be completely successful.

In some uses difficult to distinguish from sense *6.

1850 W. Colton *Three Years in Calif.* xxxiii. 440 A faith that could scoop up whole tribes of savages,..impressing them with the conviction that submission to the padres was obedience to God. **1866** *Harper's Mag.* Oct. 680/1 Tell him he'll have to send this other fellow some more beans, for I've got him scooped [at draw-poker]. **1867** A. D. Richardson *Beyond Mississippi* xi. 134 'Scooped' was an importation from Wall Street. 'I am badly scooped' meant [in Kansas]: 'I am used up' or 'defeated'. **1872** 'Mark Twain' *Roughing It* xlvii. 333 'It ain't no use. They've scooped him.' 'Scooped him?' 'Yes—death has.' **1903** A. Bennett *Leonora* vii. 194 Milly had shown a straight flush and scooped the kitty. **1903** Kipling *Stellenbosh* in *Five Nations* 195 The Boojers scooped the crowd, To the last survivin' bandolier an' boot. **1916** J. Buchan *Greenmantle* xxii. 297 We have won any way; and if Peter has had a slice of luck, we've scooped the pool. **1929** H. Maclaren *Private Opinions of Brit. Blue-Jacket* 100, I haves everey intentuons to make a short spich, as scoops in the old man also a fairly wheard tipe of two passingers. *Ibid.* 101 This phrase from 'scoops in the old man' is plainly to be interpreted, by any one familiar with the ways of the fo'c'sle, as 'we have persuaded the captain to come, also two weird passengers'. **1937** H. C. Bailey *Clunk's Claimant* xlvi. 315 A million to one some side-line of a next of kin would bob up and pinch their share. Josh wouldn't scoop the pool. **1939** Wodehouse *Uncle Fred in Springtime* v. 70 There was a bit of unpleasantness at the Ball, and they scooped me in. **1944** *Jrnl. R. Aeronaut. Soc.* XLVIII. 363 De Havilland engines—the Gipsy, Gipsy Six and Gipsy Twelve..—together with the Cirrus, have almost completely 'scooped the pool' for light aircraft. **1953** K. Tennant *Joyful Condemned* viii. 69 There wasn't a girl..to touch her. She could walk right in and scoop the pool. **1959** *Encounter* Aug. 37/2 The rest of them were struggling..with razors and stakes... And soon I got scooped into the thing. **1972** Wodehouse *Pearls, Girls, & Monty Bodkin* ii. 27 You will give your consent to my scooping in the girl I love. **1973** 'P. Malloch' *Kickback* xxv. 164 You've scooped the pool. If you watch your step, you shouldn't have any more worries. **1976** *Evening Post* (Nottingham) 15 Dec. 23/9 Radford Swimming Club ended the 1976 season in fine style by scooping all but one award at the Notts. ASA Medley Team Swimming League. **1978** G. Mitchell *Mingled with Venom* iii. 23 Unless we all take care, that black boy the other lot adopted is going to scoop the pool.

b. (Further examples.) Also *transf.* Also with the news as object, and occas. the person from whom information is derived.

1937 *Printers' Ink Monthly* May 42/1 *Scoop*, to gainfully outwit a rival network or station in the broadcasting of a special event or public interest program. **1938** E. Waugh *Scoop* I. v. 88 He told..how Wenlock Jakes, highest paid journalist of the United States, scooped the world with an eye-witness story of the sinking of the *Lusitania* four hours before she was hit. **1939** R. Campbell *Flowering Rifle* vi. 143 Then if some British pressman should be handy—From a safe distance, priming him with brandy, To scoop their story in his red receivers. **1948** G. V. Galwey *Lift & Drop* v. 88 The *Voice* must scoop you when you retire from Scotland Yard. **1968** J. M. Ziman *Public Knowledge* v. 98 Many scientists are so obsessed with the fear of being 'scooped'..that they issue a long succession of scrappy communications instead of waiting until the work is complete. **1974** *Times* 17 Apr. 16/7 The Israeli press..is sometimes scooped by the foreign press... The scooping..often results from ministerial indiscretions overseas. **1978** G. McDonald *Fletch's Fortune* vi. 49 Do you realize what it would be worth to a person's career to scoop the murder?.. A handful of Pulitzer Prizes.

6. To propel or to take by or as by a scooping movement. Also with *up*.

1867 *Australasian* 19 Jan. 76/3 Davis scooped a slow to Dan Wilkie, who..held it. **1882** *Sat. Rev.* 2 Sept. 313/1 The last comer scooped his first ball round to leg for 2. **1886** F. R. Stockton *Casting away of Mrs. Lecks & Mrs. Aleshine* 50 I'll never leave this place if I have to scoop myself out to sea with an oar. **1910** *Blackw. Mag.* Feb. 269/1 A very dark-coloured little man, with his arms and legs cut off, short at the knees and elbows,..scooping himself along on his stumps. **1916** 'Boyd Cable' *Action Front* 257 And he moved as if to scoop the German's head under his arm again. **1960** *Daily Tel.* 6 Dec. 1/1 Helicopters flew to the rescue of villagers trapped by floods at Hampton Bishop, near Hereford, last night. Forty men, women and children were 'scooped' from their cottages as swirling water crept towards their upstairs rooms. **1961** 'E. Lathen' *Banking on Death* xiii. 104 'I have a dinner date.' 'So do I,' replied Nicolls, hastily scooping up the letter. **1963** G. H. Thomson *Crocus Country* xix. 127 Mother never allowed anyone to 'scoop' the ball, that is, push it ahead with the mallet. **1966** *Listener* 17 Mar. 384/2 When she moves off, either she scoops the infant up to help him cling to her or else he springs to catch hold of her. **1973** N. Graham *Murder in Dark Room* ix. 60 The phone rang and I scooped up the receiver and said, 'Solo Malcolm here.' **1978** H. Wouk *War & Remembrance* ii. 20 We'd be scooped up as we stepped off the gang-plank.

7. *Mus. intr.* To perform a scoop (*scoop *sb.*[2] 1 b).

1927 H. J. Wood *Gentle Art of Singing* 35 They are very apt to make a slow slur, to connect the notes by scooping and dragging the voice. **1958** A. Jacobs *New Dict. Music* 333 *Scoop*, in singing, to glide up to a note disagreeably from below instead of attacking it cleanly. **1975** *Gramophone* Nov. 846/3 In the thirties Busch was frequently praised because he scooped so rarely; as opposed to Lener who did it all the time. **1977** *Ibid.* Jan. 1154/2 Both violin and cello scoop heavily from note to note.

scooped, *ppl. a.* Add: **1. b.** *scooped neck, neckline* = *scoop neck*(*line*) s.v. *scoop *sb.*[2]

1956 *New Yorker* 14 Jan. 53 The scooped neckline blouse has a soft bow and short sleeves. **1959** *Harrods News* Summer 5 A matalessé cocktail frock with scooped neck. **1969** *Sears Catal.* Spring/Summer 3 Long, full skirt gathered at waistline, scooped neckline on bodice.

scooping, *vbl. sb.* (Examples corresponding to *scoop *v.*[1] 7.)

1960 C. Day Lewis *Buried Day* ii. 38 She sang her favourite arias..with much *portamento*, or luscious scooping. **1978** *Amer. Speech 1975* L. 301 *Scooping*, sliding into a tone, hitting a note on the flat side and sliding up to the proper pitch, an undesirable practice on the part of one voice in a quartet.

scoopy (skū·pi), *a. Fashion slang.* [f. Scoop *sb.*[2] or *v.*[1] + -y[1].] Of the neck of a garment: rounded and low-cut. Cf. *scoop *sb.*[2] 4, *scooped *ppl. a.* 1 b.

1970 *Daily Tel.* 1 June 13 This summer's dresses are heaven-sent for this event. The voiles are in full swing, the necks are scoopy. **1974** *Country Life* 17 Jan. 107/1 A range of knitwear..that incorporates low, scoopy necklines. **1976** *Ibid.* 22 Feb. 377/1 Evening dresses have scoopy or drawstring necklines.

scoot, *sb.*[2] Add: **2.** A bout of drunkenness, a drunken spree; chiefly in phr. *on the scoot*. *Austral.* and *N.Z. colloq.*

1924 *Truth* (Sydney) 27 Apr. 6 *Scoot*, to clear out; also continued bout of drunkenness. **1936** I. L. Idriess *Cattle King* xiv. 131 'He's a man who likes his meat raw, he chews his glass when he empties it.' 'I'm sorry to hear Eureka is on the scoot.' 'He's not. They don't go on the scoot out there. They drink dynamite and bust.' **1959** G. Slatter *Gun in Hand* iii. 42, I suppose you left the wife up there [on the farm] and you're down on the scoot. **1962** S. Gore *Down Golden Mile* vi. 120 Make mine a glass this time, seein' I have to go on the scoot with you booze artists to-night. **1975** X. Herbert *Poor Fellow My Country* 1019 We could've..gone on a proper scoot.

scoot (skūt), *sb.*[3] *slang.* [Abbrev. of Scooter *sb.*] A motor-cycle or motor-car (see also quot. 1943).

1943 *Amer. Speech* XVIII. 169/1 *Scoot*, shuttletrain. **1968–70** *Current Slang* (Univ. S. Dakota) III–IV. 105 *Scoot, n.* A motorcycle, the type often used by the Hell's Angels Motorcycle Club. **1977** *Custom Car* Nov. 64/1 For this season he's gone over to a radical Volvo-engined scoot.

scoot, *v.*[1] Add: **3. b.** *trans.* To move or convey suddenly or swiftly. *slang* or *colloq.*

1905 *Automobile Topics* 27 May 462 Basle's engine had all the power necessary to scoot him up the hill on his fourth speed. **1947** J. Steinbeck *Wayward Bus* ii. 22 Juan put his little platform behind the bus and he lay on it on his back and scooted himself under with his feet. **1968** *Globe & Mail* (Toronto) 5 Feb. 22/1 Larush scooted his charge to the front from the outset to reach the quarter pole in a swift 0:30 2–5. **1975** N. Freeling *What are Bugles blowing For?* vi. 35 She scooted her wheelchair across the room.

scoot (skūt), *v.*[2] Colloq. abbrev. *scooter *v.*

1951 N. Mitford *Blessing* I. vii. 72 The happy crowd of scooting, skating children in the Tuileries gardens. **1962** A. Huxley *Island* ix. 140 'Scooters are going to become a major political issue.' Vijaya laughed. 'To scoot or not to scoot, that is the question.'.. 'Wherever I've been..they've opted wholeheartedly for scooting.'

scooter. Add: **3.** (Earlier and further examples.) In full *scooter plough*.

1820 in *Henderson's North Carolina Almanack* (1823) 25 The ridges are opened with a small plough called a scooter, something like a shovel plough. **1842** in J. A. Turner *Cotton Planter's Manual* (1857) 55 The next operation to be performed..is to plough out the middles well, the wide way, with a good shovel-plough, having first run around the young plant with a scooter-plough. **1938** M. K. Rawlings *Yearling* xxx. 385 He brought old Caesar and the scooter plow and turned in to the field, laid off and bedded up ready for the corn, to open the furrows for the planting. **1944** T. D. Clark *Pills, Petticoats & Plows* 281 By colloquial designations the various strange shapes were known to the trade as sweeps, shovels, scooters, twisters,..scrapers and subsoilers.

4. a. A boat, propelled by sails, capable of being used both on ice and in water. *N. Amer.* **b.** A fast motor-boat, used in the war of 1914–18. **c.** A motorized pleasure boat resembling a motor-scooter. In full, *sea scooter, water scooter*.

1903 *N.Y. Times* 13 Dec., The 'scooter'..is built with a bottom and a deck which are duplicates of each other. **1909** *Cent. Dict.* Suppl. s.v *Ice-scooter*. These scooters may be run alternately through water and over ice. **1919** *Times* 21 Feb. 11/2 The war has produced 'P' boats and 'Q' boats and 'U' boats, but the wildest of all wild things is the 'scooter', professionally known as the coastal motor-boat. **1927** G. Bradford *Gloss. Sea Terms* 151/1 *Scooter*, an amphibious craft, shallow and beamy, equipped with runners beneath and rigged with a jib and mainsail. It is used as an ice boat, particularly on Great South Bay, Long Island. It is capable of crossing patches of open water. **1929** F. C. Bowen *Sea Slang* 118 *Scooter*, a coastal motor boat in the war. **1948** J. Steinbeck *Russian Jrnl.* vi. 116 There were boat races on the river, little water-scooters with outboard motors. **1958** *Times* 21 Jan. 8/5 (*heading*) Man on sea scooter believed drowned. *Ibid.*, Mr. John Penn.., believed to have been drowned..while testing a water scooter at West Mersea, Essex. **1966** *Kingston* (Ont.) *Whig-Standard* 13 Jan. 2/6 A provincial police diver today located an ice-scooter owned by a local insurance agent who vanished here last night. **1976** *Vacation Fun in Dearborn* (Dearborn, Mich., Times-Herald) Summer, Pedal boats and water scooters on Lakes Three and Six.

5. a. A child's toy consisting of a footboard mounted between two tandem wheels with a long handle attached to the front wheel, operated by resting one foot on the footboard while pushing with the other and steering by the handle.

1919 *Times* 21 Feb. 11/2 The 'scooter' we knew before the war was a new terror to the pavement. **1921** *Spectator* 2 July 8/1 Must you not use first one foot then another on your scooter, lest you get 'scooter leg'. **1939** Joyce *Finnegans Wake* 191 A youth those reporters so pettitily wanted as gamefellow that they asked his mother for little earps brupper to let him tome to Tindertarten, pease, and bing his scooter 'long. **1943** D. Powell *Time to be Born* iv. 79 The first twenty years of their existence which had been wasted in marbles, dolls, hoop-rolling, and scooter-racing. **1961** *Toys & Fancy Goods* Aug. 22 Two pavement scooters.. with red frame, yellow wheels and white grips.

b. = *motor-scooter* s.v. *Motor *sb.* 6.

1917 *Autocar* 20 Jan. 60/1 For some months past it has been known in this country that the 'scooter' in America has developed into something rather beyond the child's plaything so popular in the British Isles. Until quite recently, however, the American motor-driven 'scooter' has not been seen in London. **1919** *Model Engineer & Electrician* 27 Feb. 142/1 A scooter of this type can cover 100 miles on a gallon of petrol. **1944** R. Chandler *Lady in Lake* v. 30 An anxious-looking bird thumped past on a power-scooter. **1957** *Times* 19 Nov. 11/3 The rising popularity of new types of machines—the scooter and the moped. **1971** *Daily Tel.* 16 Dec. 1/3 Safety helmets are to be made compulsory for riders and passengers of solo motor cycles, scooters and mopeds.

c. In various extended and slang uses: see quots.

1917 *Little Folks* Sept. p. vi. (Advt.), The free-wheel auto-scooter propelled by pedal. **1919** I. F. Marcosson *S.O.S.: America's Miracle in France* vi. 154 The vastness of these Depots is such that an inspection on foot..is out of the question. They are so criss-crossed with rails that you must use a 'Scooter', which is a motor-driven hand-car fitted for standard-gauge tracks... Every important official has his own 'Scooter' and you can see them scooting over the place at all hours of the day and night. **1930** A. Armstrong *Taxi!* v. 48 There were still a large umber of two-cylinder Renaults (called 'scooters') plying for hire. **1935** N. Ersine *Underworld & Prison Slang* 64 *Scooter*, a rum-running car. **1948** 'J. Evans' *Halo for Satan* vi. 78 'We'll use your scooter, Mac... Where's she parked?'..I wondered how they knew I had a car. **1953** *Sun* (Baltimore) (B ed.) 15 June 4/2 A new $1,000 'flying scooter' powered by a 12-horse-power engine for the 'people's car' (*Volkswagen*), has been making test flights from a forest clearing south of Hamburg. *Ibid.*, The scooter has five or eight vanes, radiating from a circular passenger cabin which stands on three wheels. **1961** Partridge *Dict. Slang* Suppl. 1261/1 *Scooter*.., a single-deck bus; a driver-only bus: busmen's: since ca. 1945. **1963** *Daily Progress* (Charlottesville, Va.) 28 June 1/6 An aerospace firm has come up with something it calls a space scooter, a one-man platform with handlebars designed for crater hopping and crag climbing on the moon. **1971** A. Diment *Think Inc.* iv. 70 A scooter truck, that strange bastard little vehicle with a bulbous cab married to a small, pick-up body. **1972** *N.Y. Times* 3 Nov. 14/4 Fleets of flag-bedecked scooter-buses.

6. *attrib.* and *Comb.* (sense *5 b), as *scooter-man, rider, -traffic.* (See also senses *3 and *5 c.)

1960 *Guardian* 12 Dec. 2/4 The irresponsible way in which many scootermen (and ladies) wind their way through traffic. **1959** *Times* 16 May 7/6 As a scooter-rider of some seniority I ventured to write to you some months ago about the apparent disinterest of the authorities in the parking of scooters. **1976** *Daily Mail* (Hull) 16 Dec. 1/4 Scooter-rider J. B...was admitted to Hull Royal Infirmary..after his vehicle was involved in an accident with a car. **1960** *Daily Tel.* 14 June 1/1 Accidents involving motor-scooters showed the greatest percentage increase, 61 per cent, but the scooter traffic was estimated to have gone up by 64 per cent. during the year.

scoo·ter, *v.* [f. the sb.] *intr.* To travel by scooter (senses *4 and *5). Hence **scoo·tering** *vbl. sb.*

1911 Webster, *Scooter*.., a strongly built sailboat... Hence: *scootering, n.* **1957** C. Brooke-Rose *Languages of Love* 15 He climbed on to his Lambretta and scootered off towards Oxford Street. **1957** *New Yorker* 26 Oct. 35/3 Scootering is the most economical and practical form of transportation available in New York today. **1960** *Housewife* May 46/1 When scootering, slacks are just about permissible. **1961** *Times* 9 Mar. 21/3 Scootering in Great Britain has also become a hobby.

scooterist. [f. Scooter + -ist]. One who drives, or travels on, a scooter (sense *4 or *5).

1919 *Model Engineer & Electrician* 27 Feb. 142/1 The 'scooterist' is Mr. Franklin Gunther, First Secretary U.S. Diplomatic Service. **1956** *New Yorker* 8 Dec. 44/3 One of the owners..was a young man wearing a white crash helmet and lying supine on the pavement under his blue Vespa... As each new scooterist arrived, he would extend an arm upward to shake hands. **1959** *Times* 16 May 7/6 Does a scooterist pay his sixpence or a shilling and take up the space that will hold a mammoth Cadillac? **1976** R. Hill *Another Death in Venice* I. ii. 31 A flotilla of motor-scooters went by... There was something so utterly careless about the scooterists that he felt a pang of envy. **1981** *Times* 27 July 26/2 They withstood extreme provocation by large numbers of these scooterists.

scop. Add: Now usu. with pronunc. (ʃǫp). (Further examples.)

1774 R. Henry *Hist. Gt. Brit.* II. 437 Whether this similarity was owing to the Welsh bards having imitated the Saxon scops and Danish scalds,..it is not easy to determine. **1826** J. J. Conybeare in W. D. Conybeare *Illustrations of Anglo-Saxon Poetry* 245 The following lines [from The Exile's Complaint] may therefore be considered as an unique specimen of an original attempt of this kind [*sc.* elegiac] by an Anglo-Saxon Scop. **1839** T. Wright *Ess. Lit. & Learning under Anglo-Saxons* 1 The heroic song in which the *scóp* or poet told the venerable traditions of the foreworld to the chieftains assembled on the 'mead-bench'. **1860** G. Stephens *King Waldere's Lay* 27 The less remarkable Hero names more or less connected with this Legend which may be found in Beowulf, the Scóp's Song, the Traveler's Lay, the Codex Dipl. and elsewhere. **1893** *Trans. Philol. Soc. 1891–4* 379 To compose with such a Prosody would imply at once the greatest crudity and the greatest subtlety in the ancient 'scop'. **1898** T. Arnold *Notes on Beowulf* ii. 16 Hroðgar..gives rich gifts to Beowulf, and his *scóp*, or poet, recites the lay of Hnæf and Hengest, and their great fight in Friesland. **1903** L. F. Anderson *Anglo-Saxon Scop* 5 The poem itself is an aggregation of several interesting specimens of the scop's art. **1928** W. W. Lawrence *Beowulf & Epic Trad.* 281 What, in a Christian era, were the court-poets, the *scops*, to do, except to fall in with the new ways? **1948** K. Malone in *English Studies* XXIX. 164 The scops kept the old ideals strong by singing the heroes of the past. **1968** E. B. Irving *Reading of Beowulf* iv. 169 The story of Finn, which Hrothgar's scop tells at the Great Banquet.

‖ **scopa**[2] (skō·pa). *rare.* [It.] An Italian card-game.

1965 'W. Haggard' *Hard Sell* iii. 26 There were cafés and men inside them. They were playing *scopa.* **1977** *Time* 3 Jan. 40/3 Premier Giulio Andreotti's Christmas gift to his staff last week was a single playing card—the seven of diamonds, which in the Italian game of *scopa* is worth double and thus is considered the luckiest card in the deck.

scope, *sb.*[2] Add: **8. b.** The ability of a horse to extend its stride or jump.

The semantic resemblance to Scope *v.*[1] must be coincidental in view of the chronologies of the words.

1970 A. Fielder *Vibart & Friends* xiv. 115 Britain has got to produce horses of scope over big courses..if we want to bring home more Olympic medals. **1971** Broome & Murphy *Jump-Off* x. 79 Sunsherpa..had a big jump in him ..but, unfortunately, he was nothing like his half-brother as far as style and scope were concerned. **1975** B. Froud *Better Show Jumping* viii. 63 The average horse with reasonable scope can clear a low fence of say three feet high from two feet or twelve feet away from the base. **1980** *Times* 11 July 11/1 The final Liverpool fence of sloping poles at 6ft required more scope than most of the contenders possessed.

scope (skōup), *sb.*[3] *colloq.* Also **'scope. a.** A shortened form of many words terminating in -scope, as *cystoscope, horoscope, microscope, periscope, telescope,* etc.

1603 [see Scope *sb.*[2] 12]. **1872** [see -scope]. **1914** *Dialect Notes* IV. 131 *Scope,* from *microscope.* Student slang. 'Have you a slide in your scope?' **1933** Partridge *Slang To-day & Yesterday* III. iii. 190 *Scope,* the cystoscope, an instrument used for examining the bladder. **1937** V. Woolf *Let.* 17 Aug. (1980) VI. 159 Now I must..have out the scope and see if I can pry into your bedroom. **1968** C. Helmericks *Down Wild River North* I. ii. 32, I selected a good four-power scope and a carrying sling. **1976** J. F. Panish in G. Berci *Endoscopy* xxi. 296/2 We lubricate the scope with mineral oil. If examination is going to include the right side of the colon, we begin with the longer colonoscope. **1978** W. F. Buckley *Stained Glass* xxi. 206 They can peer into the bowels of the scope all they want to.

b. Also *scope sight.* A telescopic sight for a gun.

1934 in Webster. **1966** 'A. Hall' *9th Directive* x. 96 The dealer had sent it [*sc.* a rifle]..with the scope-sight already mounted. **1968** K. Weatherly *Roo Shooter* 93 All he had to do was put on the 'scope off the ·303. **1976** *Shooting Times & Country Mag.* 16–22 Dec. 7 (Advt.), The BSA Scorpion is a super accurate air pistol even without its 'scope sight. **1978** R. Ludlum *Holcroft Covenant* xxxi. 366 Automatic repeating rifle and scope are sewn into the mattress of the bed nearest the window.

c. An oscilloscope or visual display unit; *spec.* a radar screen.

1945 *Army & Navy Jrnl.* 18 Aug. 1534/1 In using the PPI, the operator knows that the plane is the center of the circular scope and that the map which forms shows by the intensity of its light the terrain below and buildings or other targets. **1948** M. H. Nicolson *Voyages to Moon* 3 Two and one-half seconds later a returning pulse was clearly detected on a radar scope. **1958** P. Bryant *Two Hours to Doom* 106 Goldsmith peered closely at his scope. **1960** *Practical Wireless* XXXVI. 401/1 (Advt.), Compact portable 'scope ideal for servicing and general work. **1964** *Ann. N.Y. Acad. Sci.* CXV. 659 There are two distinct display channels which may be connected either to the display scope..or else to remote standard oscilloscopes. **1965** *Wireless World* July 359/1 The oscilloscope (or 'scope' as it is now commonly called) is an instrument that lets you see what is going on inside an electrical circuit. **1968** *Amer. Documentation* Jan. 72/1 Editing will be done on-line with a display scope and keyboard. Information from the central file will be retrieved, displayed on the scope, edited, and then stored in a new file which will go directly to a printer for publication. **1970** *Times Lit. Suppl.* 23 July 821/3 With his text stored on magnetic tape, the linguist can..have printed out on paper or displayed on a visual display unit (a 'scope'), the parts of the text that he wants to inspect. **1971** R. Sale *Man who raised Hell* I. i. 16 A big fat green carnation popped up on the scope where the blip had been. **1974** *Sci. Amer.* Sept. 18/2 (Advt.), Its flexible controls allow the cardiologist to keep a waveform on the scope for as long as 40 seconds.

-scope. Add: Also added to L. stems, as in *fluoroscope, oscilloscope,* and to Eng. words, as in *radarscope, sniperscope.*

scopey, var. *Scopy *a.*

Scophony (skǫ·fŏni). *Television.* [Perh. f. Gr. σκο-πεῖν to look at, examine + *-phony,* after *telephony,* etc.] A proprietary name for a television system employing an optical and mechanical method of picture scanning Freq. *attrib.*

1932 *Trade Marks Jrnl.* 20 Apr. 488/2 *Scophony*... Philosophical instruments, scientific instruments and apparatus for useful purposes; instruments and apparatus for teaching. Scophony Limited,..London W.1.; Manufacturers. **1934** J. H. Reyner *Television* xi. 135 One of the most ingenious alternative methods proposed is the Scophony system devised by G. W. Walton. **1935** *Television Today* I. 197/1 In the Scophony system the image to be transmitted is reflected on to a special stepped prism or reflector which so displaces the image laterally that the picture is spread out into a continuous line. The line is then scanned by a vibrating light spot. **1940** D. G. Fink *Princ. Television Engin.* x. 511 The heart of the Scophony system is the so-called 'supersonic light valve'. **1957** —— *Television Engin. Handbk.* iii. 49 The Scophony system employs a liquid cell containing a piezoelectric quartz crystal as the light modulator.

scopine (skǫ·pīn). *Chem.* [ad. G. *scopin* (J. F. Eijkman 1892, in *Ber. der Deut. Chem. Ges.* XXV. 3078), f. L. *Scop-olia* (see Scopol-) + *-in* -ine[5].] A colourless crystalline alkaloid, $C_8H_{13}NO_2$, formed by hydrolysis of scopolamine (a tropyl ester of scopine) and yielding scopoline on further hydrolysis.

1923 *Chem. Abstr.* XVII. 3189 According to the investigations of Gadamer & Hammer..and of Hess and Wahl.. the basic component (I) of scopolamine (II) (which, following a suggestion of Eykman, is designated scopine) is yet unknown, the known scopoline (III) being formed from it by rearrangement of the α-oxide into a γ-oxide ring. **1957** K. W. Bentley *Alkaloids* I. i. 20 Scopine, which is optically inactive and cannot be resolved, is readily converted into oscine by acids or alkalis. **1960** A. R. Pinder in E. H. Rodd *Chem. Carbon Compounds* IVc. xxiii. 1857 Scopolamine..is the (−)- or (±)-tropyl ester of scopine.

scopol-. Add: † **scopo·leine** [ad. G. *scopoleïn* (A. Langgaard 1876–80, in *Mitth. der Deutsch. Ges. für Natur- und Völkerkunde Ostasiens* II. (Beilage III) 267)], a crystalline alkaloid said to have the formula $C_{17}H_{21}NO_4$; **scopoletin,** add: [ad. F. *scopolétine* (J. F. Eijkman 1884, in *Rec. des Trav. chim. des Pays-Bas* III. 171)], 7-hydroxy-6-methoxycoumarin, $C_{10}H_8O_4$; (earlier and further examples); **sco·polin,** a glycoside of scopoletin; **sco·poline,** an alkaloid, $C_8H_{13}NO_2$, obtained from scopolamine on hydrolysis; also called *oscine.*

1885 *Jrnl. Chem. Soc.* XLVIII. I. 404 The author has isolated three principles from the root: skopoletin, $C_{12}H_{10}O_5$, ..skopoleïne, a crystalline alkaloid;..skopolin, $C_{24}H_{30}O_{15}+2H_2O$, the glucoside of skopoletin. **1911** *Chem. Abstr.* V. 2155 Halogen alkylates and alkyl nitrates of the alkaloids of the tropeine and scopoleine series are obtained by forming addition products..of the bases of the tropeine and scopoleine series with the sulfurous acid dialkyl esters. **1885** Skopoletin [see *scopoleine* above]. **1931** *Jrnl. Chem. Soc.* 1244 On cooling, the dark bluish solution deposited scopoletin in pale yellow needles. **1959** N. Campbell in E. H. Rodd *Chem. Carbon Compounds* IVb. viii. 881 Scopoletin.. occurs in the free state and as the glucoside scopolin, $C_{22}H_{28}O_{14}$..in *Solanaceae* and *Scopolia* species. **1963** T. Robinson *Org. Constituents of Higher Plants* iv. 51 Scopoletin is the most common coumarin of higher plants. **1885** Scopolin [see *scopoleine* above]. **1933** *Chem. Abstr.* XXVII. 2685 Methylated with CH_2N_2, cichorün yields a Me ether identical with scopolin. **1959** Scopolin [see *scopoletin* above]. **1892** *Jrnl. Chem. Soc.* LXII. II. 1255 The identity of scopoline is somewhat uncertain; its boiling point agrees with that of oxytropine. **1919** *Ibid.* CXV. 476 Oscine (or scopoline)..is capable of resolution into its constituents *d-* and *l*-oscine. **1960** A. R. Pinder in E. H. Rodd *Chem. Carbon Compounds* IVc. xxiii. 1856 Scopoline, $C_8H_{13}O_2N$, contains an N-methyl group and is a secondary alcohol.

scopolamine (skǒpǫ·lămīn). *Chem.* and *Pharm.* Formerly also **-in.** [ad. G. *skopolamin* (E. Schmidt 1891, in *Apotheker Zeitung* VI. 522): see Scopol- and Amine.] A syrupy liquid alkaloid, $C_{17}H_{21}NO_4$, having powerful narcotic and sedative properties, which is found in plants of the family *Solanaceæ,* notably the thorn-apple, *Datura stramonium*; hyoscine.

1892 *Jrnl. Chem. Soc.* LXII. II. 1255 Inasmuch as the name hyoscine has been misapplied to tropine, it has become somewhat ambiguous, and the author [*sc.* E. Schmidt] proposes to call the hyoscine from hyoscyamus, scopolamine, a name which is in accord with the recent isolation of this alkaloid from *Scopolia atropoides*. **1899** [in Dict. s.v. SCOPOL-]. **1925** F. J. REYNOLDS *Marvels of 1924* 44 Dr. R. E. House has experimented with inmates of prisons, who were reduced by scopolamin to a state in which only their memories functioned. **1940** R. CHANDLER *Farewell, My Lovely* xxxiii. 156 There's a drug called scopolamine, truth serum, that sometimes makes people talk without their knowing it. **1945** A. HUXLEY *Let.* 13 Oct. (1969) 535 The adumbrations of future possibilities are to be seen in the practices of contemporary dictatorships—..use of scopolamine and other drugs to extract confessions and make people more susceptible to propaganda, [etc.]. **1976** SMYTHIES & CORBETT *Psychiatry* vii. 140 Many proprietary sleeping pills.. contain small doses of scopolamine. **1977** LEWIS & ELVIN-LEWIS *Med. Bot.* ix. 223/2 *Datura fastuosa* and *D. metel* are abundant sources of scopolamine. **1981** T. BARLING *Bikini Red North* v. 114 Sedating her with enough scopolamine to keep her comatose.

scopophilia (skǫpofi·liă). *Psychol.* Also **scoptophilia** (but see quot. 1968), **skoptophilia.** [A formative element f. Gr. -σκοπία observation (cf. *-SCOPY) + *-PHILIA.] Sexual stimulation or satisfaction derived principally from looking; voyeurism. Hence **scopo-, scoptophi·liac** *a.* and *sb.*, **scopo-, scoptophi·lic** *a.* and *sb.*; also **sco·ptophile** *a.*; **scopto·philist.**

1924 J. RIVIERE tr. *Freud's Psychogenic Visual Disturbance* in *Coll. Papers* II. 111 The obscure psychical processes implicit in the repression of scoptophilia and in the outbreak of psychogenic visual disturbance. **1928** H. H. ELLIS *Stud. in Psychol. of Sex* VII. vi. 362 The failure to react to sex attractions..is a well-defined sexual perversion, with relationships to other perversions, especially scoptophilia. **1930** W. EMPSON *Seven Types of Ambiguity* ii. 69 Shakespeare's partly scoptophile desire to see him settled in love. **1931** *Times Lit. Suppl.* 21 May 402/3 An eventual future in which..nobody will wear anything at all;..and the scoptophilists will have their day. **1931** J. C. FLÜGEL in W. Rose *Outl. Mod. Knowl.* ix. 374 Those [*sc.* component instincts] connected with the activities of vision..the active or 'scoptophilic', and the passive or 'exhibitionistic'. **1937** M. HIRSCHFELD *Sexual Anomalies & Perversions* xxviii. 621 One of the principal criteria of pathological scopophilia is the *dominant* character of the urge. **1940** C. ALLEN *Sexual Perversions* iv. 75 The scoptophiliac pervert may occur in two varieties. **1957** J. STRACHEY tr. *Freud's Instincts & Viciss.* in *Compl. Wks.* XIV. 129 The instincts whose respective aim is to look at and to display oneself (scopophilia and exhibitionism, in the language of the perversions). *Ibid.* 130 For the beginning of its activity the scopophilic instinct is auto-erotic. **1960** R. HEPPENSTALL *Four Absentees* xxiii. 198 Gill was a bit of a scopophiliac, a 'voyeur'. **1960** *Spectator* 8 Apr. 506/3 Perhaps I am going ga-ga through skoptophilia. **1960** *Times Lit. Suppl.* 24 June 394/2 There appears to be a..scopophiliac streak in both. **1968** C. RYCROFT *Crit. Dict. Psychoanal.* 148 Scopophilia.., the spelling 'scoptophilia' dates from a mistake made by Freud's first translators. **1971** *Psychol. Abstr.* XLV. June 1131/2 A sexually inhibited male scopophilic.

scoptic, *a.* and *sb.* Restrict † *Obs.* to B in Dict. and add: **A.** (Later example.)

1972 P. M. FRASER *Ptolemaic Alexandria* I. x. 571 The last of the trio, Hedylus, seems to have specialized particularly in scoptic epigrams on gluttons.

scoptophile, -philia, -philiac, -philic, -philist: see *SCOPOPHILIA.

scopy (skōᵘ·pi), *a.* Also **scopey.** [f. SCOPE *sb.*² + -Y¹.] Having or displaying plenty of scope (*SCOPE *sb.*² 8 b).

1976 *Horse & Hound* 21 May 44/4 (Advt.), This very attractive pony has a big scopey jump. **1976** *Sunday Times* 30 May 31/7 Her big, scopy Mr Vee..has shown himself a bit strong for a woman rider. **1977** *Horse & Hound* 14 Jan. 37/2 (Advt.), Bay mare..proving to be fast and exceptionally bold with a big scopy jump.

-scopy, a formative element f. Gr. -σκοπία observation (f. σκοπεῖν to examine, look at: see -Y³), used to form sbs. denoting: (*a*) (formerly) divination by inspection of something (*ooscopy, ornithoscopy*); (*b*) scientific examination by means of some instrument (*stethoscopy, telescopy*); (*c*) medical examination of some part of the body (*gastroscopy, peritoneoscopy*).

scorable (skōᵊ·răb'l), *a.* [f. SCORE *v.* + -ABLE.] Capable of being scored; from which a score may be made.

1964 J. JAFFE in Rioch & Weinstein *Disorders Communication* xxvii. 389 All the indices used are completely scorable by the computer. **1977** *Linlithgowshire Jrnl. & Gaz.* 15 Apr. 16/5 Each time the threat of a scorable free kick came about, they were watching for the curve shot.

scorch, *sb.*² Add: **1. b.** A scorched appearance of foliage, symptomatic of various plant diseases.

1906 *Misc. Publ. Board Agric. & Fisheries Dis. Fruit* 13 Cherry leaf-scorch. A disease which every now and then proves destructive to the cherry crop. The leaves are attacked by a minute fungus, which causes them to turn brown and die, often quite early in the season. **1926** *Misc. Publ. Min. Agric.* LII. 63 Leaf scorch (physiological) [of apple trees]... In Lancashire the trouble appeared largely to be due to lack of potash, which is a contributory factor in many cases. **1933** *Discovery* Nov. 350/1 Scorch, due to the fungus *Kabatiella caulivora*, a disease which has come into prominence in recent years, causes considerable destruction in pure stands of red clover. **1974** *Nature* 8 Feb. 338/1 An experimental pirimiphos-methyl formulation produced localised scorch on citrus fruit.

4. *scorch-mark.*

1952 'M. COST' *Hour Awaits* 112 She would..wash this scorch-mark off her thumb. **1974** M. BIRMINGHAM *You can help Me* ii. 38 The whole landmark came down in spectacular flames. There is still rubble and scorch marks. **1978** R. BARNARD *Unruly Son* viii. 83 If she has her eyes on someone, they show the scorch-marks pretty fast.

scorch, *v.*¹ Add: **1. a.** Also (esp. in phr. *to scorch the earth*), to subject (an area) to a scorched earth policy (see *SCORCHED *ppl. a.*¹ 1 b). Also *transf.*

1941 H. G. WELLS *You can't be too Careful* v. ii. 245 The Russians, falling back slowly upon their main line of defence, 'scorching the earth' before this last convulsive thrust of the Nazi. **1943** *Ann. Reg. 1942* I. 193 Enormous quantities of petrol, which could not be made available until the Russian oil wells, also 'scorched', produced again. **1944** *Return to Attack* (Army Board, N.Z.) 9/2 There were neither women nor children, neither villages nor farms to be destroyed. Long ago nature had scorched the earth. **1945** *Yorkshire Post* 19 Apr. 1/1 The Germans are scorching towns in the way of the great armoured thrusts now threatening Hamburg.

b. (Later examples.)

1882 'MARK TWAIN' *Prince & Pauper* 225 An' I tell him this, he will scorch thee finely for it. **1884** —— *Huck. Finn* xvi. 135 It hadn't ever come home to me before, what this thing was that I was doing. But now it did; and it staid with me, and scorched me more and more. **1934** ADE *Let.* 22 June (1973) 183 To me he continues to be a revelation and a marvel although he would scorch anyone who tried to put either of those labels on him. **1965** M. SPARK *Mandelbaum Gate* v. 122 Gardnor's hushed confidence continued to scorch Freddy's ear-drums.

3. Also in extended use, and with *away, up.*

1906 SOMERVILLE & 'ROSS' *Irish Yesterdays* 150 The priest who was to have performed the Funeral Office scorched up on his bicycle, scarlet-faced, and half an hour late. **1957** A. C. CLARKE *Deep Range* iv. 48 By keeping the torp tail-heavy and nose-up he was able to scorch along on the surface like a speed-boat. **1972** *Shooting Times & Country Mag.* 27 Mar. 22/2 The favourite scorched away to win by four lengths.

scorched, *ppl. a.*¹ Add: **1. b.** *scorched earth*: used *attrib.* of a policy of destroying all means of sustenance or supply in a country that might be of use to an invading enemy, or of orders, operations, etc., designed to effect this policy; also *transf.* and *fig.*, and *absol.*

Apparently a translation of Chinese *jiāotǔ* (*zhèngcè*) scorched earth (policy).

1937 C. MCDONALD in *Times* 6 Dec. 12/2 The populace.. are still disturbed, in spite of official denials, by wild rumours of a 'scorched earth policy' of burning the city before the Japanese enter. **1938** *Times* 21 Feb. 15/6 (*heading*) Scorched earth. **1941** *Hutchinson's Pictorial Hist. of War* 1 Oct.–23 Dec. 115 The Soviet have left nothing but scorched earth and derelict, burned-out buildings to the invaders. **1941** E. SNOW *Scorched Earth* II. iv. 60 The 'scorched-earth' policy was credited to General Pai Tsung-hsi, the ablest strategist on Chiang's staff. **1945** *Daily Herald* 20 Apr. 1/3 A special 'scorched earth' order issued by Hitler. **1959** *Listener* 12 Nov. 818/2 Remember the scorched earth, too. How can Russia forget the menace of Germany? **1960** *Twentieth Century* July 63 The so-called concentration camps..were part of Kitchener's 'scorched earth' strategy. **1963** WODEHOUSE *Stiff Upper Lip, Jeeves* xvii. 135 The kitchen maid..always adopts the scorched earth policy when preparing a meal. **1976** H. WILSON *Governance of Britain* iii. 44, I was announcing in Parliament the discovery of documents envisaging an IRA offensive and virtual 'scorched earth' policy.

2. b. *Comb.*, as *scorched-looking* adj.

1970 T. HUGHES *Crow* 11 Who owns this bristly scorched-looking face?

scorcher. Add: **3. a.** (Earlier examples.)

1842 R. W. GRISWOLD *Let.* 7 Sept. (1898) 120 The review in The Examiner..is a 'scorcher'. **1869** 'MARK TWAIN' *Innocents Abroad* 453 Every time they read me a scorcher of a lecture I mean to talk back in print.

b. (Earlier and later examples.) *spec.* a very attractive girl or woman, a 'smasher'.

1881 *Punch* 29 Oct. 204/2 She was 'a Scorcher', was Lady O. **1898** [see *HOT *a.* 6 c]. **1935** WODEHOUSE *Luck of Bodkins* ix. 88 When I'd had a look at the young lady next door and seen what a scorcher she is.

c. In *Sport*, an extremely fast shot or hit.

1900 *Dialect Notes* II. 57 *Scorcher*,..a swiftly batted ball. **1943** *Amer. Speech* XVIII. 104 A batter who hits a line drive (also called a *liner* or a *scorcher*..) is said to *line it out*. **1977** *Belfast Tel.* 14 Feb. 21/8 He..diverted a scorcher from Pat Spence later in the game.

d. Something licentious or risqué (esp. a book or play).

1942 BERREY & VAN DEN BARK *Amer. Thes. Slang* §281/6 *Risqué joke or story*,..scorcher. *Ibid.* §590/4 *Scorcher, sexer*, a risqué play. **1974** P. CAVE *Dirtiest Picture Postcard* ii. 12 Then he produced a scorcher which managed to get itself banned by the country's leading booksellers and nominated for public prosecution at the Old Bailey. **1978** *Morecambe Guardian* 14 Mar. 15/3 (*heading*) It's a scorcher at the Duke's. A scorching new show opened at Lancaster's Duke's Playhouse on Friday.

scorching, *ppl. a.*¹ Add: **1. c.** Applied *transf.* to a period of excessive sunshine and heat.

1940 'GUN BUSTER' *Return via Dunkirk* II. xix. 220 It is a pale, steady dawn, breaking with a slight haze that presages another scorching day. **1962** A. WESKER *Chips with Everything* I. i. 12 This hut..is going to be your home for the next eight scorching weeks.

2. *colloq.* Astounding, sensational; licentious, risqué; in *Sport*, of a shot or hit: exceedingly fast, 'blistering'.

1890 *St. Nicholas* Sept. 945/1 The first senior to the bat made first-base on a scorching grounder past third. **1896** A. BEARDSLEY *Let. c* 20 Sept. (1970) 167 Your joke is charming and I shall do you some scorching drawings for No. 8 [of *The Savoy*]. **1897** *Referee* 24 Oct. 3/1 A said-to-be 'scorching' play entitled 'At the Foot of the Altar'. **1963** A. ROSS *Australia 63* iii. 88 The two scorching catches by Cowdrey and Jarman. **1976** *Ilkeston Advertiser* 10 Dec. 18/2 Garbett scored with a scorching left foot drive. **1978** [see *SCORCHER 3 d].

3. quasi-*adv.*, in *scorching cold, hot.*

1873 E. HOOPER *Nurseries & School Rooms* 197 The sand so scorching hot that one could not bear one's hand upon it. **1876** E. W. HEAP *Diary* 8 Sept. in *Publ. Amer. Dial. Soc.* (1969) LII. 54 Another scorching cold morning. **1883** *Century Mag.* July 428/1 The sun was scorching hot and the shade chilly.

score, *sb.* Add: **I. 1. c.** *local.* 'A vertical indentation in a hill; a gangway down a cliff; a cutting through a ridge of hills' (E.D.D.); *spec.* in East Anglia, a narrow, steep path or street leading to the sea. Used esp. in place-names. Cf. ON. *skor* in sense 'a rift in a rock or precipice'.

The place-names *Syrithescore* and *Scourton* are recorded from the 13th century and *c* 1550 respectively (A. H. Smith, *Place-Names of East Riding of Yorkshire* (1937) 328; E. Ekwall, *Place-Names of Lancashire* (1922) 164).

1790 E. GILLINGWATER *Hist. Acct. Lowestoft* viii. 356 There are several of these passages in Lowestoft called scores, leading from the High-Street to the sea side, such as the Swan Score, Salter's Score, Rant's Score, &c. **1807** J. GRIERSON *Delineations of St. Andrews* iii. 104 That space of ground which is now converted into a public walk, and known by the name of the *Scores*. **1835** J. D. CARRICK *Laird of Logan* II. 271 The hail place was in a perfect fizz.. frae the head of the Causeyside till the Score. **1858** *Hist. & Topogr. Handbk. Lowestoft* i. 3 On the land side are many narrow streets or lanes branching off into the country; whilst seaward there are, at short intervals, steep and narrow passages down the cliff, formed into steps, and leading to the *Denes*. These passages are known locally and technically as *Scores*. **1929** H. MEREDITH *E. Anglia* iii. 95 The Scores are Lowestoft's counterpart of Yarmouth's more famous Rows. **1958** *E. Anglian Mag.* Feb. 193/1 East Anglian cities and towns have each and all their picturesque narrow ways... The scores of Lowestoft have a unique character added to their picturesqueness in that they are steep as well as narrow. **1961** *Scottish Studies* V. 14 The Score is the downfall of the west edge of Edinburgh Castle.

6. c. *spec.* (A piece of) music composed for a film; the musical part of the sound-track of a film; formerly, the background music and effects of a silent film.

1927 *Kinematograph Year Book* 32 Scores to films can be recorded by the world's greatest orchestras, under the baton of conductors impossible to obtain for motion picture houses. **1935** R. SPOTTISWOODE *Grammar of Film* v. 191 The score composed by Edmund Meisel for *Ten Days*. **1957** MANVELL & HUNTLEY *Film Music* i. 23 Among the more celebrated film scores..are those by Edmund Meisel for Eisenstein's films *The Battleship Potemkin* and *October*. **1965** *Movie* Summer 40/2 Jerry Bresler had re-edited the film..adding a score that was far from Peckinpah's choosing. **1976** R. SANDERS in D. Villiers *Next Year in Jerusalem* 212 Irving Berlin..wrote the best over-all score of his career, *Annie Get Your Gun*.

II. 10. c. In *colloq.* phrases, as *to go over the score* (chiefly *Sc.*): to act (esp. drink) immoderately; *to have a few* (see *FEW *a.* 2 f) *over the score*: to drink more at one time than one should.

1768 A. ROSS *Fortunate Shepherdess* II. 100 She thinks ye hae ga'en o'er the score. **1851** W. ANDERSON *Rhymes, Reveries, & Reminiscences* 50 Lest some o' the nickums should gang owre the score. **1915** J. L. WAUGH *Betty Grier* 157 He gangs fairly ower the score baith wi' drinkin' himsel' an' treatin' ithers. **1951** N. M. GUNN *Well at World's End* xviii. 145 'You know how, when you have had a few over the score and you may not trust your legs, your brain remains as clear—' 'I know,' said Peter.

11. b. Also *to pay off, rub out*, etc., *old scores.*

1787 'P. PINDAR' *Ode upon Ode* (ed. 5) 25 A pretty Way of rubbing out old Scores! *c* **1863** T. TAYLOR *Ticket-of-Leave Man* III. 56 There's the satisfaction of doing one's duty.. but there's something better than that...Paying off old scores. **1913** E. PHILLPOTTS *Widecombe Fair* XXX. 236 This evening..promised good opportunity to pay off old scores. **1918** L. STRACHEY *Eminent Victorians* 67 The old scores, they found, were not to be paid off, but to be wiped out.

14. c. *transf. Psychol.* A numerical record of the marks allotted to individuals in the measurement of abilities, capacity to learn, or in the assessment of personality.

1910 E. L. Thorndike in *Amer. Jrnl. Psychol.* XXI. 485 *(caption)* Scores reduced to single variables by allowance for examples wrong. **1929** F. N. Freeman in C. Murchison *Found. Exper. Psychol.* xviii. 722 These two measures..do not give the same learning curve, or the same curve when the scores are plotted by ages or grades. **1951** T. Hunt in J. S. Gray *Psychol. in Use* (rev. ed.) x. 421 This test underwent extensive validation by study of the relationship between the test scores of students and their subsequent performance in the medical schools. **1977** P. J. Dunham *Exper. Psychol.* ix. 240 A score of 10 representing a very anxious individual.

d. *fig.* The essential point or crux of a matter; the state of affairs, the (present) situation; how matters stand; the full facts (*about, on*, etc. someone or something); freq. in phrases, as *to know the score*; *to ask, realize*, etc., *what the score is*; *what's the score*; etc. *colloq.*

1938 D. Nowinson in *Better English* Oct. 8/1 Dope..a guy who doesn't know the score. **1939** *Time* 16 Oct. 101/2 But when Holger begins to long for home and daughter, Anita, realizing what the score is, runs off to Paris to study. **1948** G. H. Johnston *Death takes Small Bites* i. 16 Why don't you speak to some people who can really tell you the score? **1950** E. Hemingway *Across River* xxxiii. 250 It leaves a core of certain un-killed characters who know what the score is. **1953** W. Burroughs *Junkie* xii. 121, I asked Ike what the score was on pushing in Mexico city. He said it was impossible. **1958** P. Kemp *No Colours or Crest* iv. 68 You were fully justified in breaking off the action when you did, in view of the score at the time. **1958** P. Scott *Mark of Warrior* II. 176 'What's the score about Havildar Baksh?' 'He's a prisoner.' **1959** N. Mailer *Advts. for Myself* iii. 234, I was out of fashion and that was the score; that was all the score. **1962** J. D. Salinger *Franny & Zooey* 167 You've been around schools long enough to know the score. **1971** N. Stacey *Who Cares?* xvii. 284 At least he had the courage to tell me the score as far as I was concerned, so that I did not waste time yearning and hoping. **1977** A. Scholefield *Venom* III. 86 You didn't ask the Boss what the score was, he told you.

15. c. The money or goods obtained by means of a successful crime. *Criminals' slang.*

1914 in Jackson & Hellyer *Vocab. Criminal Slang* 74. **1930** D. Runyon in *Collier's* 13 Sept. 7/4 We have a business proposition for Big Butch. It means a nice score for him. **1936** [see *have *v.* 14 i]. **1956** H. Kurnitz *Invasion of Privacy* xi. 76 He's just a few months out of the jug and he hasn't turned a trick or made a score anywhere. **1977** *New Yorker* 22 Aug. 38/1 A million dollars from a computer crime is considered a respectable but not an extraordinary score.

d. The action or process of obtaining a supply of narcotic drugs; a supplier of narcotic drugs. Cf. *score *v.* 16 d. *slang* (orig. *U.S.*).

1951 [see *hit *sb.* 1 b]. **1953** W. Burroughs *Junkie* x. 97 'It's hard to find a score now,' I said. 'Most of them have gone away.' **1976** Deakin & Willis *Johnny go Home* ii. 47 The whole day passes..going from fix to score, to ripping off enough money to support the habit.

e. A prostitute's client (cf. *score *v.* 16 f); also in homosexual use. *slang.*

1961 J. Rechy in *Evergreen Rev.* July–Aug. 15, I could spot the scores easily—the men who paid other men sexmoney. **1969** *Jeremy* I. III. 23/1 The boy will then deliberately reveal and manipulate his erect penis, thereby exciting the score. **1972** G. Baxt *Burning Sappho* ix. 153, I..got my hot tail out of there. I heard the score yelling. **1976** 'Trevanian' *Main* iv. 66 She won't be able to make a score until dark, if then.

III. 20*. *Criminals' slang.* **a.** Twenty dollars; a twenty-dollar bill. *U.S.* **b.** Twenty pounds sterling (esp. in banknotes).

1929 G. L. Hostetter *It's a Racket!* 237 *Score*, twenty dollar bill, or units thereof—hundred, two hundred. **1933** G. Ingram *Stir* xiv. 231, 'I got about £10 out of the first, then £2 and then another "score".' 'That makes £32.' **1941** *Coast to Coast 1941* 225 They only owe me a couple of quid since Christmas now. I was holdin' a score but I dropped most of it. **1958** F. Norman *Bang to Rights* III. 152 When they turned me over I had about a score on me. **1979** K. Bonfiglioli *After you with Pistol* vii. 39 You'll have to give me a score to buy an old throwaway shooter.

IV. 21. (sense 15 d) *score dough* (*dough *sb.* 2 b), *money*; **score-bid** *Contract Bridge*, a bid by a player whose side has a part-score, sufficient to give his side game; **score-board,** *(b)* also *gen.*, a master board displaying the score of any contest; also *fig.* and *attrib.*; **score-book** (earlier and later examples); **score-box** *Cricket*, a room or hut in which the official scorers work and (usu.) the telegraph is operated; **score-card,** *(a)* (earlier and later examples); also in extended uses, esp. a card issued to a competitor before a contest, on which his score (or that of his opponent) is to be recorded, or one held by a referee or judge for the same purpose; *(d) U.S. slang.*, a menu; **score draw,** a non-goalless draw (Draw *sb.* 5) counting for three points on a football-pool coupon; **scoreline,** (a line, or part of one, in a newspaper, etc., giving) the intermediate or final score in a sports contest between two persons or teams; **score-reading,** the action or process of reading a musical score; hence *score-reader*; **score-sheet** (earlier and later examples); also *transf.* and *fig.*, esp. in phrases, as *to add one's name to the score-sheet*, to score a goal (in Association Football and the like).

1928 M. C. Work *Contract Bridge* (ed. 2) iv. 76 If my side has a contract score of 60, I must put a construction on my partner's minor two bid different from the construction put upon such a bid at no score... 'Score-bids' are exceptions to the general rules. **1936** F. D. Roosevelt in *N.Y. Herald Tribune* 2 Oct. 10/2 From where I stand it looks as if the game was pretty well in the bag... It's just plain scoreboard arithmetic... Now, when the present management of your team took charge in 1933 the national scoreboard looked pretty bad. **1963** J. Joesten *They call it Intelligence* I. v. 51 What kind of record has the CIA?.. The scoreboard: 'Soviet satellites—Excellent'.. 'Missiles—Good.' **1977** *Rolling Stone* 13 Jan. 43/3 There were shouts of delight as Texas lit up in red on one of the network's scoreboards, but it was still a close race. **1977** J. Laker *One-Day Cricket* 72 A few narrow escapes kept the scoreboard officials busy. **1851** J. Pycroft *Cricket Field* iv. 69 'Seventy-two runs,' said Fennex, and the score-book attests his accuracy, 'was Beldham's first and only innings.' **1921** P. F. Warner *My Cricketing Life* vi. 111 Sixteen centuries stand to his credit in the Middlesex score-book. **1977** J. Laker *One-Day Cricket* 113 Gone are the days of the old green bound Club scorebook. **1890** in W. A. Bettesworth *Walkers of Southgate* (1900) xvi. 335 Pressmen were expected to..keep running to the score-box to ask for any information they required. **1934** W. J. Lewis *Lang. Cricket* 226 Underneath (the score-box was) a room for the printers. **1877** C. Box *Eng. Game of Cricket* xxvi. 459 *Score card*, a printed card, with the names of the players and the results of each person's innings. **1918** E. S. Farrow *Dict. Mil. Terms* 538 *Score cards*, pasteboard cards issued to competitors at competitions, giving the number of the target of each competitor firing,..and containing a blank space for the record of the shots fired. **1930** J. Dos Passos *42nd Parallel* 160 He handed her the menu. 'Here's the scorecard.' **1958** *People* 4 May 19/7 How much is a quarter of a point worth on a fight referee's score-card? **1976** *Cumberland & Westmorland Herald* 4 Dec. 13/6 The other [*sc.* dart-players'] score cards were not in at the time of writing. **1978** *Cornish Guardian* 27 Apr. 23/5 (Advt.), When you call in at our showrooms and test drive the Austin Morris range, we'll provide a detailed scorecard. First test our cars then try to match them against the competition. **1942** Berrey & Van den Bark *Amer. Thes. Slang* §510/1 *Connection* or *score dough*, the price of a 'bindle' of narcotics. **1970** *Sporting Life* 2 Nov. 12 Percentage is based on three points for a correct score draw and two for a correct no-score match against the total number of points possible. **1977** *Daily Mirror* 15 Mar. 27/1 Plan 6..guarantees a line of at least seven score draws if any eight of your selections result as score draws. **1969** B. James *England v Scotland* iii. 64 The score line was a far from accurate guide to the run of play. **1971** *Rand Daily Mail* 27 Mar. 23/6 Had Arcadia grabbed their chances the scoreline could have been reversed. **1977** *Sunday Times* 9 Jan. 30/6 It was only when he..scored three times, that the scoreline became slightly more respectable. **1953** W. Burroughs *Junkie* vi. 61 Nick had just arrived at my apartment with some score money when I was called to the hall phone by the buzzer. **1946** *Penguin Music Mag.* Dec. 75 Music does not exist until it is *performed*, whatever our armchair score-readers may say to the contrary. **1961** J. A. MacGillivray in A. Baines *Musical Instruments through Ages* 247 Music is written for the player, not for the score-reader. **1909** *Cent. Dict.* Suppl. II. 1183/2 Score-reading. **1931** G. Jacob *Orchestral Technique* i. 4 To facilitate score-reading we give below the English, Italian, French, and German names for the instruments. **1977** *Listener* 23 June 822/2 Score-reading involves two quite different activities. First, you must learn to read music... The second element..is the ability to hear in imagination, in the mind's ear. **1859** in W. A. Bettesworth *Walkers of Southgate* (1900) v. 54 *(plate)* 'Bell's Life in London' Score Sheets, &c. &c., may be had at the Tent. **1944** W. W. Elton et al. *Guide Naval Aviation* iv. 73 Dive bombers caused much of the Jap grief at Midway, where the score sheet revealed four Jap carriers sunk and other craft damaged and sunk. **1976** *Cumberland & Westmorland Herald* 4 Dec. 12/6 Ullswater managed to keep the score sheet blank up to half-time. **1976** *Norwich Mercury* 10 Dec. 8/3 They..made sure of the points when Stew Reynolds added his name to the scoresheet.

score, *v.* **I. 5.** For *U.S.* read *N. Amer.* and add earlier and later examples. Now esp. used in newspaper headlines.

1812 J. K. Paulding *John Bull & Brother Jonathan* xiv. 102 She..fell upon Beau Nappérty, and scored him at such a rate, that if poor Beau had heard her, he would have been mad enough I warrant you. **1912** J. Sandilands *Western Canad. Dict. & Phrase-Bk.* s.v. *Scored*, An Opposition newspaper came out with the heading 'Government Legislation Scored'. **1930** *Publishers' Weekly* 8 Mar. 1331/2 *(heading)* Smoot's secret session scored. **1967** *N.Y. Times* (Internat. ed.) 11–12 Feb. 3/3 *(heading)* Professor scores Reagan.

II. 9. c. To write the score for (a film). Cf. *score *sb.* 6 c.

1934 Webster, *Score*,..to add music to a picture that already has sound effects. **1967** H. Harrison *Technicolor Time Machine* (1968) xv. 156 'Is it true you scored a couple of films?' 'It is true I did the music for a ragged piece of class-X crap.' **1969** *Daily Progress* (Charlottesville, Va.) 15 May 1-c/7 Poet-singer-composer Rod McKuen has scored three movies.

III. 13. b. *Biol.* and *Med.* To examine (experimentally treated cells, bacterial colonies, or the like), making a record of the number showing some character.

1964 *Virol.* XXIII. 118/1 Subconfluent monolayers were infected with 0·5 ml of virus and transferred the following day at an inoculation density of 100 and 500 cells per plate. Transformed colonies were scored 14 days later. **1971** *Nature* 20 Aug. 559/1 After 2–3 weeks the plates were fixed, stained and the colonies scored.

15. d. *trans. Baseball.* To cause (a teammate) to score.

1912 C. Mathewson *Pitching in Pinch* v. 109 Schlei made a base hit..and scored both men. **1976** *Billings* (Montana) *Gaz.* 17 June 2–H/4 Mark Belanger singled to score May before DeCinces' fourth home run of the season.

e. *Psychol.* To obtain (results in a test designed to measure abilities, capacities, or personality traits); to record results in (a test). Also *intr.* Cf. *score *sb.* 14 c.

1922 *Jrnl. Experim. Psychol.* V. 101 College students scoring 88 to 195 in the first trial. **1952** A. G. Wesman in N. E. Gronlund *Readings in Measurement* (1968) xx. 201 It is important to know the extent of agreement between the persons who score them [*sc.* tests]. *Ibid.*, Such a correlation coefficient yields important information—it tells us how objectively the test can be scored. **1968** P. McKellar *Experience & Behaviour* xi. 277 Engineers tend to score highly on the economic (applied science) value trait. **1977** P. J. Dunham *Experim. Psychol.* ix. 240 We will not deal with the details of how the TAQ is scored. *Ibid.*, The calm collected type of person who would score around 1 on the TAQ measure.

16. a. *to score a point* (or *points*) *off* (a person) = *to score off* (see sense 16 b in Dict.).

1956 R. Braddon *Nancy Wake* xiii. 140 Fournier was ecstatic with pride and pleasure—and with delight at having scored a point off Gaspard! **1957** *Practical Wireless* XXXIII. 558/1 The episode I heard, 'Rumour is a Lying Jade', proved very amusing, with both stars scoring points off each other with satisfactory frequency.

c. *trans.* and *intr.* To make a (freq. dishonest) gain; spec. *Criminals' slang*, to commit a theft or robbery; to steal, filch, or purloin (something), esp. from an open counter or display. orig. *U.S.*

1914 Jackson & Hellyer *Vocab. Criminal Slang* 74 *Score*,..to successfully negotiate; to 'make a touch'.. 'We scored seven times in the same joint by ringing up,' i.e., disguising. **1926** J. Black *You can't Win* xiv. 191 [The thief] throws a few dollars on the bar just to..let them guess where he 'scored' and how much he got. **1930** [see *play *sb.* 10 g]. **1942** Berrey & Van den Bark *Amer. Thes. Slang* §490/8 *Steal*,..salvage, score, shark. **1972** *Last Whole Earth Catalog* 49/3 She was already plotting in her mind to stash part of their supper in her bag so they'd have something to eat the next day. She'd already scored a can of beer and a handful of cashew nuts. **1976** D. Topolski *Muzungu* vi. 99, I spotted a sugar factory, drove in, and scored a couple of kilos. **1977** D. Mackenzie *Raven & Kamikaze* xii. 146 'Where did you get it [*sc.* a newspaper]?' ..'Nicked it... It was too early to score any milk.'

d. *intr.* and *trans.* To buy or otherwise obtain a narcotic drug; by extension, to take a narcotic drug. *slang* (orig. *U.S.*). Cf. *score *sb.* 15 d.

1935 A. J. Pollock *Underworld Speaks* 101/2 *Scored*, made a purchase of dope. **1953** W. Burroughs *Junkie* 9 Junk wins by default. I tried it as a matter of curiosity. I drifted along taking shots when I could score. **1959** *Alfred Hitchcock's Mystery Mag.* Feb. 68/1 To get you out of my pad I'll let you score for a low, low forty. **1969** *Guardian* 3 Dec. 9/1 She had needed the money to score H up in the West End. **1972** J. Brown *Chancer* ii. 30 The weekend ravers and joy-poppers..who maybe score half a pill of H for kicks. **1972** *Daily Tel.* 25 Feb. 17/3 Mick the Pimp asked me if I wanted to 'score' and gave me a tablet from a matchbox and I gave him £1. **1977** *It* June 18/1 *(caption)* I can score better shit in Hendon on an off night!

e. *intr.* Of a racehorse: to win a race.

1941 *Sun* (Baltimore) 13 June 21/1 Their choice scored by a head from Epindel. **1977** *Evening Gaz.* (Middlesbrough) 11 Jan. 13/4 Shifting Gold had gone on to score again in the Tote Northern Chase at Haydock Park.

f. *intr.* and *trans.* Of a man: to achieve intercourse (*with* a woman); to have (casual) intercourse with (a woman); also occas. of a prostitute: to obtain (a client). *slang* (chiefly *U.S.*).

1960 R. G. Reisner *Jazz Titans* 164 *Score, to*, to attain success, to get what you want. Example: I scored with that chick. **1961** J. Rechy in *Evergreen Rev.* July–Aug. 19 You wanna score?..See that old cat over there... He wants us both to come over to his house. **1970** G. Greer *Female Eunuch* 249 The boys used to go to the local dance halls and stand around..until the..sexual urge prompted them to *score a chick*. **1973** W. H. Canaway *Harry doing Good* I. 36 They might begin to ball later on... He would like to score with the Cheryl chick. **1976** D. Craig *Faith, Hope & Death* ix. 42 They talk about 'taking' a woman... Or, 'Did you score last night?'—like some great goal, scheming and forcing. **1976** 'Trevanian' *Main* (1977) ii. 39 He feels particularly sorry for the whores..who can only score drunks.

scored, *ppl. a.* Add: **2.** *Mus. rare.* Of a film, or part of a film: provided with a score (see *score *sb.* 6 c); of a piece of music: written down in a score.

1957 Manvell & Huntley *Technique Film Music* i. 21 Cueing was unusually elaborate and some of the more closely-scored scenes began to approach the techniques later developed in sound film recording. **1962** *Observer* 27 May 27/1 By the late 1920s Henderson was learning how to blend scored passages into a succession of solos.

scoreless, *a.* Add: **2.** Also, of a game, a period of play, etc.: from which no score results; involving no score. Phr. *to hold* (a person or team) *scoreless*: to prevent (a stronger opponent) from scoring.

1961 *Sun* (Baltimore) 18 Mar. 18/4 Hartman..allowed no hits in his scoreless three-inning appearance. **1972** J. MOSEDALE *Football* iii. 41 The team that had held them scoreless was weak against counterplays. **1974** *Sumter* (S. Carolina) *Daily Item* 23 Apr. CA/1 Bill Paschall.. stretched his scoreless string to 23 innings. **1977** *Arab Times* 13 Dec. 9/1 N.C.C. started the first inning against Foster Wheeler with two runs but then were held scoreless throughout the remainder of the game. **1978** *Rugby World* Apr. 25/1 France..have never held Wales to a scoreless draw in the championship.

scorer. Add: **3. a.** (Earlier example.)

1732 *Applebee's Orig. Weekly Jrnl.* 16 Sept. 3/3 There wanted six Minutes of the Time by the Scorer's Watch.

b. One who allots marks or records the scores obtained in the measurement of ability, capacity, or personality traits.

1922 *Jrnl. Exper. Psychol.* V. 107 Provision must be made to free the results from the personal equations of the scorers. **1952** A. G. WESMAN in N. E. Gronlund *Readings in Measurement* (1968) xx. 201 The scorer is required to make a judgment as to the correctness or quality of the response. *Ibid.*, Two scorers should agree perfectly.. in assigning scores.

4. b. A winner, esp. of a horse-race. Cf. *SCORE *v.* 16 e.

1974 *Marlboro Herald-Advocate* (Bennettsville, S. Carolina) 18 Apr. 5/7 After dinner six tables of bridge were played. Scorers for the ladies, Mrs. Richard Fletcher..and Mrs. Robert Lockey. **1976** *Scottish Daily Express* 27 Dec. 10/3 I'm Alright Jack..a smooth Devon and Exeter scorer last month, can put up a repeat performance in the opener at Newton Abbot.

5. One who scores (i.e. composes a score for) a film. Cf. *SCORE *v.* 9 c. *rare.*

1969 *Daily Progress* (Charlottesville, Va.) 15 May 1-c/6 The talkies brought a demand for 'scorers', composer-orchestrators of background music to enhance scenic mood.

scoring, *vbl. sb.* Add: **1.** (Further examples.)

1801 T. BUSBY *Dict. Mus.*, *Scoring*, the art of forming a score by collecting and properly arranging under each other the several detached parts of any composition. **1851** C. BOX *Cricketer's Man.* (ed. 5) 51 Printed forms..for scoring are not procurable. *Ibid.* 53 The annexed score will serve to illustrate the principles of scoring. **1876** GEO. ELIOT *Dan. Der.* I. II. xi. 201 Shall we go now and hear what the scoring says? **1904** *Daily Chron.* 21 Nov. 7/2, I viewed the match from the pavilion behind the goal where all the scoring was done. **1922** *Jrnl. Experim. Psychol.* V. 107 The scoring requires judgment. **1940** *Chambers's Techn. Dict.* 747/2 *Scoring*,..the preparation of the sound-script, in which are described all music and noises to be introduced into a motion-picture. **1952** A. G. WESMAN in N. E. Gronlund *Readings in Measurement* (1968) xx. 201 Many objective tests..are not very reliable, yet the scoring is by definition objective. **1967** *Daily Mirror* 14 Aug. 9/1 This buying of heroin ('scoring' in junkie language) is being watched closely by London Drug Squad detectives. **1978** *Time* 3 July 45/1 Warren stays with a picture through editing, mixing and scoring.

3. scoring block *Card-playing*, a pad of printed score-sheets; **scoring board** (earlier and later examples); **scoring-book** (earlier example); **scoring-booth, -box** *Cricket* = *score-box* s.v. *SCORE *sb.* 21; **scoring-card** = *score-card (a)* s.v. SCORE *sb.* 21 in Dict. and Suppl.; **scoring-paper,** *(a)* = *score-paper* s.v. SCORE *sb.* 21; *(b) Mus.* printed paper on which a musical score may be entered; **scoring-sheet** (earlier example).

1907 *Yesterday's Shopping* (1969) 375/2 *Table*..with drawer divided to take cards and bridge scoring blocks, whist cards and markers, piquet scoring blocks and cards. **1933** G. D. H. & M. COLE *End of Ancient Mariner* ii. 18 On the table stood a decanter, flanked with packs of cards and scoring-blocks. **1882** *Bell's Life* 20 May 5/1 An excellent novelty was exhibited on the ground during the Oxford Match, and that was a patent scoring board. **1904** P. F. WARNER *How We recovered Ashes* iv. 60 The Melbourne Cricket Ground, with its..huge scoring-board. **1851** F. LILLYWHITE *Guide to Cricketers* 71 'Lillywhite's Registered Scoring Book' will be found extremely useful to Clubs, for the purpose of keeping the exact averages of all the members. **1867** F. GALE *Public School Matches* 29 And now let us go to the scoring booth and get a 'true and correct score to the end of the first innings'. **1960** *Cricketer Spring Annual* 58/2, 1851 A scoring booth was on view in the Great Exhibition. **1877** C. BOX *Eng. Game Cricket* xxvi. 459 *Scoring box*, a small enclosure, so situated as to command a full view of the play. **1908** W. E. W. COLLINS *Leaves from Old Country Cricketer's Diary* xii. 201 When..I passed the scoring-box, *en route* for the pavilion, I found the small telegraph boy in the act of returning my score as sixty-nine. **1891** W. G. GRACE *Cricket* iii. 94 We kept in constant touch..posting the scoring-card at the end of every day's play. **1907** *Yesterday's Shopping* (1969) 386/1 Whist scoring cards. **1912** A. A. LILLEY *Twenty-four Years of Cricket* 124 No scoring-card could be invented to equal it in its completeness. **1851** C. BOX *Cricketer's Man.* (ed. 5) 53 Some clubs make it a rule to mark the number of 'overs' that each bowler gives, at the foot of the scoring papers. **1851** F. LILLYWHITE *Guide to Cricketers* 79 Scoring Papers, per dozen... 2/6. **1908** G. B. SHAW *Let.* 27 May (1972) II. 788 You will only waste a good deal of scoring paper which you might employ far better by trying to deal, as Strauss does,.. with the modern world in a crisp and powerful style. **1859** in W. A. Bettesworth *Walkers of Southgate* (1900) v. 54 *(caption)* Scoring Books and Sheets.

scorp (skǭɹp). *Mil. slang.* Abbrev. of SCORPION (sense 7); an inhabitant of Gibraltar. Also *Rock-scorp.*

1912 *Jock Scott, Midshipman: His Log* iv. 32 By 'scorps' he meant rock scorpions, the name bestowed on the inhabitants of Gibraltar. **1957** W. TUTE *Rock* I. 16 Millingham.. married a Rock Scorp. *Ibid.* 19 Perks and privileges for the ruling classes. Fifteen in a room for the poor-quality 'Scorps' whose Rock it was. **1973** *Publishers Weekly* 17 Sept. 59/3 Covering the rock's social strata, from the native 'scorps' to the British Governor.

Scorpio. Delete ‖, for *Astr.* read '*Astr.* and *Astrol.*' and add: **2. a.** *attrib.* or as *adj.*, born under or ruled by the sign of Scorpio (24 Oct.–21 Nov.).

1894 E. KIRK *Influence of Zodiac upon Human Life* xviii. 156 When Scorpio people live on the higher plane, they are very superior individuals. **1901** M. MAYO *Our Fate & Zodiac* 104 The..astute Scorpio man is..clever in..taking advantage of the upward revolutions of the wheel. **1930** W. WILSON *Astrology* iii. 60 Scorpio people are often found devoting themselves to art. **1964** L. MACNEICE *Astrol.* iii. 95 Some modern Scorpio types excel at skin diving. **1970** 'D. HALLIDAY' *Dolly & Cookie Bird* iii. 23 He was Scorpio: I asked him.

b. A person born under the sign of Scorpio.

1968 T. WOLFE *Electric Kool-Aid Acid Test* i. 5 Black Maria, a Scorpio herself, rummages through the Zodiac. **1972** *Guardian* 15 Jan. 9/4 He and Rommel and Montgomery all shared the same birth date, November 17, and all were Scorpios. **1976** M. MILLAR *Ask for Me Tomorrow* xv. 122, I thought Scorpios were supposed to be creative.

Hence **Sco·rpian** = *SCORPIO 2 b.

1951 M. E. HONE *Mod. Text Bk. Astrol.* iv. 68 Just as this rulership brought energy and initiatory force to the Arien, it brings it to the Scorpian. **1980** R. RENDELL *Lake of Darkness* i. 7 Scorpians are magicians, astrologers, alchemists, surgeons, bondsmen and undertakers.

scorpion. Add: **1. c.** (Later example.)

1924 R. CAMPBELL *Flaming Terrapin* iii. 42 But life, a scorpion of tenacious hold, Fastened upon their spirits.

8. a. *scorpion-kiss.*

1961 R. GRAVES *More Poems* 33 Lady Morphia—Her scorpion kiss and dark gyrating dreams.

b. *scorpion whip* (earlier example).

1824 LADY BLESSINGTON *Jrnl.* May in E. Clay *Lady Blessington at Naples* (1979) 104 Byron..was..lashed into satire by the scorpion whips of envy.

c. scorpion orchid, an orchid belonging to the genus *Arachnis*, esp. *A. flos-aeris*, native to Malaysia; = *scorpion-plant (a)*.

1897 H. N. RIDLEY in *Jrnl. Straits Branch Roy. Asiatic Soc.* xxx. 68 *Bunga Kasturi. Renantha moschifera* Lindl. (*Orchideae*). 'Musk-flower.' The scorpion orchid. **1937** M. COVARRUBIAS *Island of Bali* x. 336 Their garden is filled with golden flowers that grow side by side with the pandanus, the scorpion orchids, the..pineapples. **1961** A. D. HAWKES *Orchids* 108 The multicolored flowers are generally produced in considerable numbers, and their strange form has given them the common name of 'Scorpion Orchid'. **1971** *Ceylon Observer Mag.* 19 Sept. 2/6 (Advt.), Epidendrums & Scorpion Orchids, several colours.

scorpionic, *a.* Add: **2.** *Astrol.* (With capital initial.) Of, pertaining to, or characterized by the sign of Scorpio.

1924 C. E. O. CARTER *Conc. Encycl. Psych. Astrol.* 145 Scorpionic afflictions often cause nasal obstructions, especially when the mutable element is prominent in the horoscope. **1972** *Mainichi Daily News* (Japan) 6 Nov. 12/1 Today's natives are not truly 'Scorpionic' in nature as each reflects unique qualities.

scortatory, *a.* (Later examples.)

1922 JOYCE *Ulysses* 199 Twenty years he dallied there between conjugal love and its chaste delights and scortatory love and its foul pleasures. **1942** DYLAN THOMAS *Let.* 30 Aug. (1966) 259, I hope..that the Monico made up..for the absence of one ventripotent scortatory Krut.

scorzalite (skǭ·ɹzăləit). *Min.* [f. the name of E. P. *Scorza* (b. 1899), Brazilian mineralogist + -ITE[1].] A basic phosphate of aluminium, ferrous iron, and magnesium, $(Fe^{2+},Mg)Al_2(PO_4)_2(OH)_2$, that forms an isomorphous series with lazulite and occurs in masses of brittle, blue, monoclinic crystals.

1947 PECORA & FAHEY in *Bull. Geol. Soc. Amer.* LVIII. 1217 The new minerals are named in honour of Dr. Evaristo Scorza and Dr. Antonio José Alves de Souza... Scorzalite is a massive, blue hydrous iron magnesium aluminum phosphate. **1949** *Amer. Mineralogist* XXXIV. 83 The Corrego Frio pegmatite, Minas Gerais, Brazil,..has yielded three new phosphate minerals since its discovery in 1942. Two of these new minerals, scorzalite and souzalite, are described in this paper. **1975** *Fortschritte der Mineral.* LII. Suppl. 288 Scorzalite from the Angarf-Sud pegmatite [in Morocco] is always observed intimately associated with muscovite.

Scot, *sb.*[1] Add: **4.** (Further example.) Also as *adj.*

1823 'J. BEE' *Dict.* 155 *Scot*, a butcher's designation of a fractious man, the small Scots oxen coming to their doom with little resignation to fate; indeed, all animals try harder to retain life than man. **1916** W. OWEN *Let.* 9 Dec. (1967) 417 Major Melville, a snotty, acid, scot, impatient, irritated wretch.

Scotch, *a.* and *sb.*[3] Add:

In recent years the word *Scotch* has been falling into disuse in England as well as in Scotland, out of deference to the Scotsman's supposed dislike of it; except for certain fixed collocations, *Scottish* (less frequently *Scots*) is now the usual adjective, and to designate the inhabitants of Scotland the pl. sb. *Scots* is preferred (see Gowers/Fowler *Mod. Eng. Usage* (1965)).

A. *adj.* **1. a.** (Later examples.)

1943 *Sun* (Baltimore) 25 June 12/7 My father came from Invernesshire and certainly never restricted the use of Scotch to the whiskey. It is only in recent years that certain Anglo-American friends have made me feel guilty of committing a particularly bourgeois *faux pas* by using the word. We always looked on Scottish as rather affected, overly poetic. **1976** *Times* 11 May 15/3 Professor Trevor Roper.. tries to irritate and provoke by using the word 'Scotch' knowing well that many decent Scots..have come to regard this as a demeaning adjective.

d. (Later examples.)

1906 E. DYSON *Fact'ry 'Ands* xvi. 209 Well, he's touched me three times in a week, and I'm as Scotch as most people. **1912** J. N. MCILWRAITH *Diana of Quebec* iii. 49 'You would be the first to throw me a penny..?' 'A sixpence, truly, if he be not too Scotch,' said Nelson. **1932** *Amer. Speech* VII. 403 Mr. —, if you weren't so Scotch we could have a good time here.

e. (Earlier example.) Also, with similar connotation, *Scotch sister.*

1861 J. S. MILL *Repr. Govt.* xviii. 335 The most important offices would be thrown to Scotch cousins and adventurers. **1866** MRS. GASKELL *Wives & Daughters* I. xix. 219 She called her a sister, but whether it was a Scotch sister, or a sister *à la mode de Bretagne*, would have puzzled most people.

2. a. (Further examples); *Scotch ale* (later examples), *ballad, carpet* (earlier and later examples), *reel, salmon, snuff, whisky* (earlier and later examples).

1733 *S. Carolina Gaz.* 7 Apr. 4/2 (Advt.), To be sold..cut Tobacco, Scotch Snuff, and Pigtail. **1774** Scotch carpet [see WILTON]. **1792** F. BURNEY *Jrnl.* May (1972) I. 153 Miss Cooper..gave me a relation of her having been..at Mrs. Broadhead's masquerade as *Jenny*, from the Scotch ballad. **1835** DICKENS *Sk. Boz* (1837) 2nd Ser. 39 Mr. Thomas Potter ordered the waiter to bring two goes of his best Scotch whisky, with warm water and sugar. **1891** S. M. WELCH *Home Hist.* 183 It was not uncommon to see a couple of portly old gentlemen meeting on the street offering their boxes of Maccaboy, Rappee or Scotch, each to the other. *Ibid.* 376 [In] the 'Scotch Reel',..each lad must needs have two lassies. **1893** T. HARDY *Let.* 6 Oct. in Hardy & Pinion *One Rare Fair Woman* (1972) 28 Lady J[eune].. played and sang at least a dozen Scotch ballads to me. **1953** *Word for Word* (Whitbread & Co.) 10/2 *Scotch ale*, a draught or bottled ale of the Burton type, brewed in Scotland. **1960** *Connoisseur's Handbk. Antique Collecting* 251/1 *Scotch carpets*, double-cloth or ply weavings for the floor, also known as Kidderminster or Ingrain. **1965** V. CANNING *Whip Hand* xii. 143 We had..Scotch salmon with a cucumber salad. **1969** *Daily Tel.* 30 Apr. 29/7 New definitions of whisky..are contained in the Finance Bill, published last night... 'Scotch whisky' is to mean whisky which has been distilled in Scotland. **1978** J. MANN *Sting of Death* iii. 25 Alex would probably be ordering..gulls' eggs and Scotch salmon. **1980** R. LEWIS *Certain Blindness* iii. 80 Parton put a pint of Scotch Ale in front of him.

c. (Further examples.)

1726 D. EATON *Let.* 31 Dec. (1971) 87, I think the Scotch cattell were dearer than if they had been bought in our country [i.e. district]. I mean cattel of their size might have been bought in our markets for less mony. **1980** A. BELL *Sydney Smith* 117 Scotch sheep provided material for Sydney's only contribution to agricultural literature.

e. *Typogr.* The epithet of a variety of modern typefaces deriving from one sent from an Edinburgh foundry in 1837 to the printing firm of S. N. Dickinson in Boston, Massachusetts. So *Scotch-cut* adj.

1847 S. N. DICKINSON *Hand-bk. Specimen Printing Type* Pref., Our Scotch Faces were selected from the very extensive Foundry of Alexander Wilson and Sons of Edinburgh and also from an eminent letter cutter of that city. *Ibid.*, The symmetry of the Scotch cut figures. *a* **1863** *Specimens of Borders, Ornaments, Rules, Dashes, etc. from Dickinson Type Foundry* (Boston, U.S.) Back cover, A superior collection of the Scotch-cut letter, so highly appreciated by the trade. **1900** T. L. DE VINNE *Practice of Typogr.* vi. 212 As first made the Scotch-face was a small, neat, round letter, with long ascenders, and not noticeably condensed. **1922** D. B. UPDIKE *Printing Types* II. xx. 193 As produced by Wilson it is a very handsome and serviceable letter, and in it we have another English type-family—the Scotch modern face. **1951** S. JENNETT *Making of Bks.* xiv. 248 Bodoni is an excellent letter, but capable of great degeneration, and in Scotch Roman we see the degeneration commencing. **1966** H. WILLIAMSON *Methods Bk. Design* (ed. 2) viii. 99 The original Scotch faces were a vaguely defined class, and generalization about their letter-forms is impossible.

4. a. Scotch Baronial *a.* = *Scottish Baronial* s.v. *SCOTTISH *a.* 5; **Scotch Blackface,** a sheep belonging to the breed so called, developed in mountain and moorland regions of Scotland and northern England, and distinguished by black legs and muzzle and long wool; **Scotch boiler** [so called from its having been introduced in Scottish shipyards], a fire-tube boiler in which combustion takes place inside the shell; **Scotch († barley) broth,** a soup containing meat, vegetables and pearl barley; **Scotch egg,** a hard-boiled egg enclosed in sausage-meat; **Scotch mist,** *(b)* something insubstantial, unreal, freq. used sarcastically in a retort or rhetorical question to imply that someone has imagined or failed to comprehend something; (*c*) a drink of whisky served with a twist of lemon; **Scotch pancake** = *drop-scone* s.v. SCONE I; **Scotch peg,** rhyming slang for 'leg'; **Scotch prize** (earlier example); **Scotch terrier,** for '(see TERRIER)' read: a small stocky terrier of the breed so called, usually black or brindle, with thick, shaggy fur, erect, pointed ears and tail, and a square, bearded muzzle; formerly, a terrier belonging to one of several other Scottish races, now treated as separate breeds (cf. TERRIER[2]); **Scotch woodcock**: see WOODCOCK *sb.* 3 d; **Scotch yoke,** a mechanism by which a steady circular motion can be transformed into a linear simple harmonic motion, consisting of a crank bearing a peg which, as the crank revolves, slides in a straight slot constrained to move to and fro along a straight line in a plane at right angles to the plane of the slot.

1880 J. J. STEVENSON *House Archit.* I. xiv. 360 The Scotch 'Baronial' architecture, as it is called, resembles that of the Renaissance châteaux of France. **1931** E. SACKVILLE-WEST *Simpson* II. vii. 144 Salathiel held up a glass globe, inside which was a miniature Scotch-baronial castle in china. [**1888** J. & C. SCOTT *Blackfaced Sheep* i. 1 The origin of the Scotch blackfaced sheep is shrouded in mystery.] **1945** J. F. H. THOMAS *Sheep* ii. 30 It deserves the title Scotch Blackface because in that country it is of paramount importance. **1903** H. DE B. PARSONS *Steam-Boilers* v. 97 (*caption*) Scotch boiler, single-ended, with common combustion-chamber. **1966** *McGraw-Hill Encycl. Sci. & Technol.* VIII. 119/2 Later boilers are of the express or water-tube type, burning fuel oil, though Scotch boilers are still used in some cases and may burn either coal or fuel oil. **1747** H. GLASSE *Art of Cookery* vi. 65 (*heading*) To make Scotch barley broth. **1834** T. HOOD *Tylney Hall* I. xv. 175 We shall have an ounce of mutton swimming in a tureen of barley-water—I've heard of their Scotch broths. **1969** R. & D. DE SOLA *Dict. Cooking* 203/1 *Scotch broth,* rich soup made of beef or mutton and vegetables, thickened with barley. **1809** M. E. RUNDELL *New Syst. Domestic Cookery* (new ed.) VIII. 207 *Scotch eggs.* Boil hard five pullet's eggs, and without removing the white, cover completely with a fine relishing forcemeat. *c* **1965** A. CHRISTIE *Autobiogr.* (1977) XI. iv. 525 He fed us entirely on..'Scotch eggs'; excessively indigestible. **1972** P. D. JAMES *Unsuitable Job* i. 19 Pushing a half pint of shandy and a Scotch egg across the counter. **1977** D. WILLIAMS *Treasure by Degrees* xv. 145 A lonely Scotch egg..was the only visible justification for the plastic proclamation 'Snacks at the Bar'. **1943** HUNT & PRINGLE *Service Slang* 57 *Scotch mist,* sarcastic comment on your eyesight, inferring that you are seeing things. **1962** *New Statesman* 18 May 708/2 'Are yer married?' 'Course she is. What do yer think that is? Scotch mist?' Rube points to my wedding-ring. **1965** O. A. MENDELSOHN *Dict. Drink* 303 *Scotch mist,* cocktail of Scotch whisky and lemon peel. **1974** *Pacifist* Feb. 13/1 What are all these price-rises we are suffering now? Scotch mist? **1977** W. H. MANVILLE *Good-bye* iii. 27 You can start by ordering me a Teacher's Scotch Mist on the rocks. **1930** BENNION & STEWART *Cake Manufacture* xiv. 122 Soda scones, Scotch pan cakes, and milk scones,..can be baked on the hot plate. **1977** D. WILLIAMS *Treasure by Degrees* viii. 71 Tea..could be quite a different matter. He recalled some truly outstanding Scotch pancakes. **1857** 'DUCANGE ANGLICUS' *Vulgar Tongue* 17 *Scotch peg,* leg. **1917** W. MUIR *Observat. Orderly* xiv. 225 If he had occasion to allude to his leg he would probably have called it 'Scotch peg'. **1818** 'A. BURTON' *Johnny Newcome* III. 170 'Tis but a Scotch prize he has stolen! **1810** *Sporting Mag.* XXXVI. 61/1 Portraits of a poodle and Scotch terrier. **1847** H. D. RICHARDSON *Dogs* vii. 70 There are two varieties of the common Scotch Terrier. **1863** [see TERRIER[2] 1]. **1880, 1889** [see *Aberdeen terrier* s.v. *ABERDEEN 2]. **1927** E. C. ASH *Dogs* II. ii. 422 Two kinds of terriers are described—the rough-haired Scotch and the smooth-haired English. **1927** HAM & CRANE *Mechanics of Machinery* ii. 27 Figure 36 shows an application of the Scotch yoke as it has occasionally been used on small engines and steam pumps. **1959** KARPLUS & SOROKA *Analog Methods* (ed. 2) viii. 242 Mechanical Harmonic Synthesizers... The sine and cosine components are almost invariably generated by Scotch yoke mechanisms. **1966** *McGraw-Hill Encycl. Sci. & Technol.* I. 377/2 The modification of the Scotch yoke shown in Fig. 25 can be used to generate a tangent function over a limited range of the argument.

b. Scotch elm, substitute for def.: the wych-elm, *Ulmus glabra*; (earlier and later examples); **Scotch rose** (later examples).

1799 W. NICOL *Pract. Planter* i. 34 The Scotch Elm may with propriety be reared for this purpose [*sc.* ship-building] on thin gravelly soils. **1838** J. C. LOUDON *Arboretum et Fruticetum Britannicum* III. 1399 The Scotch elm has not so upright a trunk as the English elm. **1969** T. H. EVERETT *Living Trees of World* xiv. 131/1 The Scotch elm or wych elm..forms a rather open, broad-headed specimen. **1892** C. M. YONGE *Old Woman's Outlook in Hampshire Village* 161 The little thorny Scotch roses..are creeping over the cottages. **1972** *Country Life* 23 Mar. 695/1 Possibly the toughest of the wild roses is..the Scotch or Burnet Rose which flourishes in the sand dunes of Great Britain and Germany.

B. *sb.* **1. a.** (Earlier and later examples.)

1743 M. W. MONTAGU *Let.* 16 Sept. (1966) II. 310 Several Scotch pass here often. **1979** *Jrnl. R. Soc. Arts* Jan. 107/2 Since then I have had the greatest admiration for the education offered to, or seized by, the Scotch—Miss Murray's word and her grandfather's.

3. a. (Earlier and later examples.) Also = *Scotch ale* (in sense A. 2 a), *face* (*A. 2 e).

1778 S. FOOTE *Cozeners* III. ii. 76, I have a box of Scotch in my pocket. **1906** *Linotype Bull.* Oct.–Dec. 6/2 (*heading*) 8-Point Scotch. **1945** O. SIMON *Introd. Typogr.* iii. 12 The roman lower-case letters of Scotch and Baskerville..are wide and generous. **1962** S. CHAPLIN *Watchers & Watched* x. 199 The beer was as bitter as bile... 'Is there anythin' wrong?' 'Your Scotch doesn't taste too well.' **1964** S. JENNETT *Making of Books* (ed. 3) xiv. 251 Though Scotch is a portent, it is not itself as poor as its descendants became. **1966** H. WILLIAMSON *Methods Bk. Design* (ed. 2) viii. 99 The first Scotch to be cut for machine composition was produced by the Merganthaler Linotype Co. in 1902. **1976** *Observer* (Colour Suppl.) 1 Feb. 9/3 All Scotches are blended spirits: a mix of malt and grain whiskies. The ratio can vary between 2 to 3 and 3 to 2, and a bottle of Scotch can be a mixture of 30, 40 or even more whiskies. **1977** *Listener* 3 Mar. 275/1 You could order 'a pint of Scotch'—Scotch Ale, because it is the cheapest beer, is still the majority drink on Tyneside.

b. *ellipt.* for *Scotch peg* (see sense A. 4 a above).

1859 HOTTEN *Dict. Slang* 87 *Scotches,* the legs. **1962** R. COOK *Crust on its Uppers* ii. 30 Down to wearing my head in its proper place and not between my scotches like a sporran.

scotch, *v.*[1] Add: **2. c.** To refute conclusively or stamp out (a rumour, report, etc.); to frustrate (a plan or hope); to quash, destroy, bring to nothing. (Perh. influenced by SCOTCH *v.*[2] 1 b.)

1926 in H. W. Fowler *Dict. Mod. Eng. Usage* 518/2 The contradiction of a rumour affecting any particular company ..is seldom entirely scotched by directorial statements. *Ibid.,* We hope the proposal for a Government news service for the Colonies is finally scotched by the debate. **1947** H. S. GLADWIN *Men out of Asia* xxvi. 270 The question has been raised as to whether they [*sc.* helmets] were not copies from late European models, but this idea was scotched by Captain Cook who found them in fashion in Hawaii. **1955** *Times* 27 July 13/1 He did so with sufficient force..to scotch once and for all any lingering doubts or rumours that the pound is to be devalued by stealth. **1966** *Listener* 2 June 792/2 The closing words of his book firmly scotch any hope we may have of evading the central question. **1976** *Australian* 30 June 1/7 The Prime Minister..is to meet the Russian Ambassador..next month to scotch reports of a serious rift in Soviet–Australian relations.

Scotch bonnet. 1. (Earlier example.)

1759 L. WOOD *Jrnl.* 27 June in *Essex Inst. Hist. Coll.* (1882) XIX. 70 It Came out in order this Day that no officer in ye Rigement Should wear a Scotch bonet.

Scotch cart. Chiefly *S. Afr.* Also **scotch cart.** [Prob. f. SCOTCH *a.* + CART *sb.*; S. Afr. uses may represent derivation from Afrikaans *skotskar,* ad. G. *schuttkarren,* but this is unproved.] A light and strongly built two-wheeled cart, used chiefly for transporting rough materials such as gravel, manure, etc.

1845 *Cape of Good Hope Almanac* (Advt.), Best Scotch Carts and wheelbarrows made to order. **1850** *Mary Wedlake's Priced List Farming Implements* 33 (*heading*) Scotch Carts. These very light carriages, so superior in point of draught to the old heavy dung carts used in most counties of England, are daily substituted for those ponderous machines. **1895** R. CHURCHILL *Men, Mines & Animals in S. Afr.* xiii. 210, I accordingly borrowed a Scotch cart (a light two-wheeled covered waggon) and a span of eight oxen, with which went also two 'salted' horses. **1938** D. FORBES *My Life in S. Afr.* vi. 87 He also fixed up a scotch cart to carry the alluvial ground to the stream. **1949** *Cape Argus Mag.* 14 May 2/6 At first a few skins were sent in from farms, then..they began to arrive in sugar pockets,.. and finally by the Scotch-cart load. **1970** G. E. EVANS *Where Beards wag All* i. 31 A Scotch cart was popular round here... They'd carry about a ton. *Ibid.* 34 The extra spokes and felloes on a Scotch cart were probably needed on its home ground where a strong wheel was essential on a rougher terrain than is to be found in East Anglia. **1974** *Standard Encycl. S. Afr.* X. 571/1 The Scotch-cart, with or without springs, was always popular with farmers because it could be tilted backwards to enable its load to be discharged.

Scotchgard (skǫ·tʃgāɹd). A proprietary term in the U.S. for a series of organofluorine chemicals employed as waterproof grease- and stain-resistant finishes for textiles, suede, leather, etc.

1956 *Official Gaz.* (U.S. Patent Office) 1 May TM 7/1 Minnesota Mining and Manufacturing Company, St. Paul, Minn... *Scotchgard.* For chemical composition for application to various surfaces to repel grease and oil therefrom. First use Aug. 26, 1955. **1959** *Times* 12 Jan. 11/5 Scotch-Gard: Finish..for use on wool, cotton, or synthetic fibres to improve oil, grease, and water stain-resistance. Durable for dry-cleaning. Shortly to be marketed. **1962** *N.Y. Times Mag.* 9 Sept. 106 (Advt.), Lightweight suede 'Gliders' [*sc.* shoes] Scotchgard treated to resist stains. **1969** A. J. HALL *Stand. Handbk. Textiles* (ed. 7) v. 334 One such fluorochemical is Scotchgard F.C. 208 and when this, together with..water-repellent Velan, is dried into cotton fabric and followed by a curing..at about 130°C. for 5 min., the fabric acquires a combined water and oil repellency which withstands repeated washing with soap.

Scotch-Irish, *a.* Add: **a.** (Earlier and later examples.) **b.** = *SCOTS-IRISH *a.* b. **Scotch-Irishman** (example).

1744 W. MARSHE *Jrnl.* 21 June in *Coll. Mass. Hist. Soc.* (1801) 1st Ser. VII. 177 The inhabitants [of Lancaster, Pa.] are chiefly High-Dutch, Scotch-Irish, some few English families, and unbelieving Israelites. **1789** J. MORSE *Amer. Geogr.* 313 [The Irish of Pennsylvania] have sometimes been called Scotch-Irish, to denote their double descent. **1903** J. FOX *Little Shepherd of Kingdom Come* x. 117 Broadcast, through the people, was the upright sturdiness of the Scotch-Irishman, without his narrowness and bigotry. **1916** J. WEBSTER *Dear Enemy* 187 That Scotch-Irish ancestry of mine. **1948** H. MACLENNAN *Precipice* (1949) i. 5 The Scotch and the Scotch-Irish who had flooded into Ontario. **1963** W. K. ROSE *Lett. Wyndham Lewis* 1. 1 An English girl of Scotch-Irish descent. **1980** G. M. FRASER *Mr. American* xvii. 312 Reason is the last thing you can look for in a Scotch-Irish Protestant. *Ibid.* xix. 361 The Scotch-Irish who saw their freedom threatened.

Scotchlite (skǫ·tʃləit). The proprietary name of a light-reflecting material containing a layer of minute glass lenses.

1941 *Official Gaz.* (U.S. Patent Office) 6 May 29/2 Minnesota Mining & Manufacturing Company, St. Paul, Minn... *Scotchlite* for light reflecting material in sheet form. Claims use since Dec. 1, 1939. **1947** *Daily Progress* (Charlottesville, Va.) 28 Oct. 4/1 A Minnesota motorist..conceived the idea of covering bicycle frames with Scotchlite, a material used on reflectorized highway signs. **1957** *Times Survey Brit. Aviation* Sept. 8/5 Scotchlite is a tough, plastic reflective film. **1964** *Times* 7 Feb. p. iv/1 (Advt.), Scotchlite reflective sheeting..consists essentially of a white or coloured reflecting surface covered with minute, optically-perfect glass lenses. On top of the lot goes a clear plastic protective coating. **1970** *Trade Marks Jrnl.* 17 June 961/1 *Scotchlite...* Sign faces made of or incorporating plastics embedded with light reflective substances. Minnesota Mining and Manufacturing Company.., United States of America; manufacturers. **1972** *Police Rev.* 10 Nov. 1444/1 'Scotchlite' markings on Police vehicles.

Scotchman. Add: **1. a.** (Later example.)

SCOTSMAN is now the preferred form on both sides of the border (see small-type note s.v. *SCOTCH *a.* and *sb.*[3]).

1977 K. M. E. MURRAY *Caught in Web of Words* xi. 209 For a Scotchman James was certainly extraordinarily lacking in hard-headedness.

b. (Earlier example.) Cf. SCOTSMAN in Dict. and Suppl.

1873 J. BLACKWOOD *Let.* 6 Jan. in *Geo. Eliot Lett.* (1956) V. 365 'The Flying Scotchman', the stoker's name for the train that goes between London and Edinburgh in little more than 9 hours! **1913** D. H. LAWRENCE *Sons & Lovers* vii. 165 You should see the Flying Scotchman come through.

c. (Earlier examples.)

1719 T. MARCHANT *Jrnl.* 10 June in *Sussex Arch. Coll.* (1873) XXV. 184 In all 15s. 9d., to John Gracie, a Scotchman, for M. Balcombe. **1793** C. SMITH *Old Manor House* I. vi. 138, I had not enough money..to buy my new cotton gown, when Alexander Macgill the Scotchman called here.

Scotch tape. Also **scotch tape.** The proprietary name of a make of adhesive tape; also applied *loosely* to any adhesive tape. Hence **Scotch-tape** *v. trans.,* to affix or join with adhesive tape; **Scotch-taped** *ppl. a.,* affixed or made fast with adhesive tape.

[**1945** *Official Gaz.* (U.S. Patent Office) 16 Oct. 373/1 Minnesota Mining & Manufacturing Company, St. Paul, Minn. ..Scotch for pressure-sensitive adhesive tape. Claims use since January 1928.] **1947** R. LEE *Electronic Transformers & Circuits* ii. 28 Electrical grade scotch tape is widely used for anchoring leads. **1949** R. CHANDLER *Little Sister* ix. 54 To the lining of the toupee a piece of..paper was fastened by Scotch tape. **1955** 'J. WYNDHAM' in 'E. Crispin' *Best SF* 81 There was a wire, scotch-taped to the upper side of the bag. **1957** V. NABOKOV *Pnin* iv. 99 Carrying his purchase, wrapped in brown paper and Scotch-taped, he entered a bookstore. **1961** WODEHOUSE *Ice in Bedroom* xxvi. 222 Her lips..shall be sealed, if necessary with Scotch tape. **1961** J. H. GRIFFIN *Black like Me* 86 The whites frequently..Scotch-tape these notices to the wall. **1969** K. AMIS *Green Man* i. 26 Coloured photographs.. Scotch-taped to the walls. **1976** *Observer* 24 Oct. 28 It [*sc.* Sellotape] still has 75 per cent of the market over here, though in America Scotch Tape has become the generic term. **1977** *Time* 31 Jan. 24/1 Carter wrote at least three more drafts, sometimes spreading the paragraphs out like pieces of a jigsaw puzzle and Scotch-taping them into a new arrangement.

Scotchy, *sb.* (Later example.)

1949 E. COXHEAD *Wind in West* ii. 59 Are you really such a prim little Scotchy that you don't see the difference between one chap and another?

Scotland Yard (skǫ·tlə̆nd yāɹd). The name of the head-quarters of the Metropolitan Police, situated from 1829 to 1890 in Great Scotland Yard, a short street off Whitehall in London; from then until 1967 in New Scotland Yard, on the Thames Embankment; and from 1967 in New Scotland Yard, Broadway, Westminster: used allusively to designate the detective department of the Metropolitan Police force. Also *attrib.*

1864 M. E. BRADDON *Henry Dunbar* II. xiv. 260, I have called again upon the Scotland-Yard people, and I gave them a minute description of the scene. *Ibid.* III. iv. 49 Not that anybody would try to thwart me,..if they knew that I was detective officer Henry Carter, of Scotland Yard. **1864** [see BLUEBOTTLE 2]. **1881** *Punch* 9 July 6/2 As in all great crimes, they [*sc.* criminals] are too much for Scotland Yard and the Seldom-at-Home Secretary. **1907** [see REWARD *sb.*[1] 4 d]. **1909** [see *PHONE *v.* a]. **1926** E. WALL-

ACE *Ringer* I Nobody knows, but Scotland Yard and—Henry Arthur Milton. **1939** T. S. ELIOT *Old Possum's Bk. Pract. Cats* 33 He's the bafflement of Scotland Yard, the Flying Squad's despair. **1962** J. MCCABE *Mr. Laurel & Mr. Hardy* i. 36 A backer for the troupe, a Scotland Yard detective. **1974** N. FREELING *Dressing of Diamond* 87 Just forget all the detective stories of bumbling Scotland Yard Inspectors.

Scot Nat (skǫt næt), *sb.* and *a.* Abbrev. of *SCOTTISH NATIONALIST *a.* and *sb.* Cf. *SCOTS NAT.

1970 [see *NAT[3]]. *a* **1974** R. CROSSMAN *Diaries* (1976) II. 550 He'd told me that the Scot. Nat. woman might win and the Tories would certainly lose their deposit. **1974** *Sunday Post* (Glasgow) 28 Apr. 5/5 Even by Willie Ross's standards, last weekend's attack on the Scot. Nats. was vitriolic. **1975** *Times* 8 Sept. 12/7 Both Tory and Labour politicians in Scotland..will be tempted to enter into an auction with ScotNats over devolution.

Scoto-[1]. Add: **Scotopho·bia[2]**, a morbid dread or dislike of the Scots or things Scottish; hence **Sco·tophobe.**

1974 *Listener* 25 Apr. 520/3 There is undoubtedly a strong streak of Scotophobia in the English character. **1976** *Times Lit. Suppl.* 2 July 823/3 This 'never ending clan of Macs and Donalds upon Donalds', as one Scotophobe put it in the 1760s. **1980** B. LENMAN *Jacobite Risings in Britain* 289 A glance at the huge correspondence which Sir Everard organized so meticulously for Cumberland is very revealing about the origins of his royal master's sustained Scotophobia.

scoto-[2] (skōᵘ·to), comb. form repr. Gr. σκότος darkness, as in **sco·tophase** *Biol.*, an artificially imposed period of darkness; an artificial night; **sco·tophobia[1]** *Psychol.*, fear or dislike of the dark; hence **scotopho·bic** *a.* See also SCOTOSCOPE.

1971 *Nature* 6 Aug. 401/2 Bovines restrained inside environmentally controlled stalls (24±3°C; 70±7% relative humidity; 12 h photophase: 12 h scotophase per 24 h photocycle). **1975** *Ibid.* 25 Dec. 711/2 We considered whether the insects perceive the actual duration of photophases (or scotophases). **1938** *Brit. Jrnl. Psychol.* Apr. 372 Photo-phobia (in some animals) sufficiently strong to make them go always to D; the opposite trait, 'a-photo-phobia' or 'scoto-phobia' being present in an equal proportion of the animals. **1971** *New Scientist* 3 June 559/3 The scotophobic effect seems to be very specific for this structure.

scotoma. Add: Pl. also **scotomas.** Also *fig.* (Further examples.)

1943 *Horizon* Oct. 257 As with all neurotics, the confessions of Kierkegaard only contain a grain of the truth; the analytic scotoma constantly intervenes. **1957** F. B. WALSH *Clin. Neuro-Ophthalm.* (ed. 2) ix. 606/3 Retinal lesions are not rare in cases of Leber's optic atrophy. There may be complaint of chromatopsia and ring scotomas.

scotometer (skotǫ·mĭtəɹ). *Ophthalm.* [f. SCOTO(MA + -METER.] An instrument for diagnosing and measuring scotomata.

1890 G. FERDINANDS in *Brit. Med. Jrnl.* 27 Sept. 741/1 Those who frequently meet with cases of toxic amblyopia.. must have found the small coloured squares used in detecting scotomata both an inadequate and inconvenient test... To obviate these disadvantages I have had made for me a little instrument..which I propose to call a scotometer. **1932** *Optician* LXXXIII. 397/1, I did not take the fields for white, relying on the evidence of the scotometer. **1961** S. VAN WIEN tr. *Huber's Eye Symptoms in Brain Tumors* i. 75 For a quick survey to determine the presence of a scotoma for color, the so-called scotometer is suitable.

Hence **scoto·metry**, the use of a scotometer; **scotome·tric** *a.*

1921 *Proc. R. Soc. Med.* XIV. (Ophthalm. Sect.) 49 The purpose for which scotometry is of such importance is the determining of the increase of the blind spot in cases of suspected glaucoma. **1944** *Amer. Jrnl. Ophthalm.* XXVI. 349 (*heading*) The form and character of rod scotometry. **1955** *Jrnl. Neurol., Neurosurg. & Psychiatry* XVIII. 224/2 Scotometric studies suggested small infarctions in each infracalcarine striate cortex.

scotomization (skōᵘtŏməizē[1]·ʃən). *Psychol.* [a. F. *scotomisation* (Pichon & Laforgue in R. Laforgue *Le Rêve et la Psychoanalyse* (1926) vii. 184), f. Gr. σκοτ-οῦν to darken, make dim-sighted: see -IZATION.] (See quot. 1927.) So **sco·tomize** *v. trans.*; **sco·tomized** *ppl. a.*

1927 R. LAFORGUE in *Internat. Jrnl. Psycho-Anal.* VIII. 473 In an earlier work I have defined scotomization (or the forming of mental 'blind spots') as a process of psychic depreciation, by means of which the individual attempts to deny everything which conflicts with his ego. *Ibid.* 477 If he scotomizes them [*sc.* such stimuli as do not belong to the field of consciousness],..they seek for gratification in narcissistic compensations, and force him to a compensatory activity whose scotomized sources are hidden from him. **1954** *Brit. Jrnl. Psychol.* XLV. 233 This criticism [of horrific test pictures] does not imply any scotomization of the capacity of the child..to conceive of the horrible. **1969** P. A. ROBINSON *Freudian Left* 145 The functionalists concluded from the mere fact that a culture existed that it.. functioned harmoniously. They would thus 'scotomize' all of those psychoanalytic facts which drew attention to the terrible price we pay for civilization. **1977** A. SHERIDAN tr. *J. Lacan's Écrits* ii. 22 Freud seems suddenly to fail to recognize the existence of everything that the ego neglects, scotomizes, misconstrues in the sensations that make it react to reality.

scotophase: see *SCOTO-[2].

scotophil (skōᵘ·tofil), *a. Biol.* Also **skoto-, -phile.** [ad. G. *skotophil* (E. Bünning 1944, in *Flora* CXXXVIII. 95): see *SCOTO-[2] and -PHIL, -PHILE.] Applied to that phase of the circadian cycle of a plant or animal during which light inhibits, or does not influence, reproductive activity; opp. *photophil, -phile* s.v. *PHOTO- I.

1952, etc. [see *photophil* adj. s.v. *PHOTO- I]. **1959** F. W. WENT in R. B. Withrow *Photoperiodism & Related Phenomena in Plants & Animals* VII. 554 The leaf angle..is small in the scotophil and large in the photophil phase. **1960** *Cold Spring Harbor Symp. Quantitative Biol.* XXV. 257 In this part of the rhythm the endodiurnal system is in the scotophile state according to Bünning... The second scotophile phase is hardly weaker than the first one. **1971** *New Scientist* 29 July 254/2 The circadian rhythm [of house finches] was imagined to comprise two half cycles.., one of which was reckoned to be dark-requiring (scotophil). **1972** *Nature* 21 Apr. 407/1 The state..during which light has a promotive effect on flowering..and the state during which light is innocuous..could be respectively the photophil and skotophil phases of Bünning.

Hence **scotophi·lic** *a.*, scotophile; **scoto·phily** the state of an organism in a scotophile phase.

1960 *Cold Spring Harbor Symp. Quantitative Biol.* XXV. 265/1 According to this view long and short day effects depend on whether the photoperiod of light break coincides with the 'scotophilic' phase during the second half-cycle. **1960** Scotophily [see *photophily* s.v. *PHOTO- I]. **1976** *Sci. Amer.* Feb. 115/2 He proposed that the measurement of the length of the day or the night was accomplished by an endogenous, or built-in, daily rhythm that consisted of two half-cycles, one photophilic ('light-loving') and the other scotophilic ('dark-loving').

scotophobia: see *SCOTO-[2]; **Scotophobia:** see *SCOTO-[1].

scotophobin (skotofōᵘ·bin). *Biochem.* [f. *SCOTO-[2] + φόβ-ος fear + -IN[1]; cf. *scotophobia[1]* s.v. *SCOTO-[2].] An oligopeptide isolated from the brains of rats which have been trained to avoid darkness, and which is claimed to induce dark avoidance in untrained rats and possibly also in animals of other species.

1970 G. UNGAR et al. in *Proc. Western Pharmacol. Soc.* XIII. 150 We propose to give the name 'scotophobin' to the new substance. **1971** *New Scientist* 3 June 559/3 The peptide, called scotophobin, contains only 15 amino acids. **1975** *Behavioral Biol.* XV. 470 Acceptance of these assumptions forces us to reject the hypothesis that 'fear of the dark' was encoded in scotophobin. **1976** F. WARNER *Killing Time* II. ix. 61 We could inject Scotophobin and induce a fear of the dark.

scotopic (skotǫ·pik), *a. Physiol.* [f. *SCOTO-[2] + *-OPIA + -IC.] Of, pertaining to, or designating vision in dim light, believed to involve chiefly the rods of the retina. So **scoto·pia,** the condition of scotopic eyes.

1915 J. H. PARSONS *Introd. Study Colour Vision* ii. 17 If the eye has been kept completely free from light for a considerable period it is said to be dark-adapted. I shall speak of vision under these circumstances as scotopia..and the dark-adapted eye as a scotopic eye. **1924** J. P. C. SOUTHALL tr. W. Nagel in *H. von Helmholtz's Treat. Physiol. Optics* II. 345 The so-called *Dämmerungssehen* (or twilight vision, scotopia), when the eye is dark-adapted and the light stimulus is weak. **1937** *Nature* 6 Mar. 409 It is generally accepted that visual purple plays an essential part in the process of scotopic vision. **1946** *Ibid.* 31 Aug. 303/2 S. Hecht also arrives at the conclusion that the absorption of the visual purple is less than 20 per cent, by comparing the scotopic luminosity curve with the absorption curve of visual purple. **1972** H. J. EYSENCK et al. *Encycl. Psychol.* III. 182/1 *Scotopia*, twilight vision... With twilight vision a person is insensitive to color and his peripheral vision is better for fine detail than his central vision, since there are no rods in the fovea. **1973** 'A. HALL' *Tango Briefing* xiv. 169 My eyes were adapting to scotopic vision, the torchlight growing brighter.

scotoscope. For † *Obs.* read *rare* and add later example.

1964 *Applied Optics* III. 671 The scotoscope can be arranged to give a color presentation; however, when this is done, it is at the expense of a fairly high percentage of the photons incident from the scene.

Scots-Irish, *a.* **a.** = SCOTCH-IRISH *a.* Also as *sb.* **b.** Of mixed Scots and Irish descent.

1972 *Listener* 21 Dec. 854/2 The hostility of the Catholic Irish and the Protestant Scots-Irish. *Ibid.* 854/3 The Protestant Scots-Irish community. **1973** *Guardian* 27 June 13/3 The USA has taken to calling itself 'Scots-Irish' rather than 'British'. **1973** 'D. SHANNON' *No Holiday for Crime* (1974) iv. 62 Once in a while my Scots-Irish wife uses a little ESP. **1980** —— *Felony File* i. 35 The feudal household his Scots-Irish girl had wished on him.

Scotsman. Add: **b.** (Also *Flying Scotsman.*) Now the more usual form of (*Flying*) *Scotchman*: see SCOTCHMAN I b in Dict. and Suppl.

One of British Rail's express trains from London to Edinburgh still bears this name, though the particular steam locomotive so named was withdrawn from service on 14 Jan. 1963.

1879 [in Dict.]. **1932** P. BLOOMFIELD *Imaginary Worlds* 34 Pretending..that our O gauge railway round the nursery floor is really the line taken by the 'Flying Scotsman'. **1936** J. MASEFIELD *Let. from Pontus* 57 On the railway beside us the Scotsman went by. **1952** A. ANDERSON *Flying Scotsman* 3 Our train is the Flying Scotsman which has left King's Cross at 10 a.m. daily for over 90 years. **1962** C. H. ELLIS *Flying Scotsman* i. 11 The Special Scotch Express sooner or later became the 'Flying Scotch Express', which in turn was transformed into 'Flying Scotchman' and later still, probably when English people began to read Robert Louis Stevenson, into 'Flying Scotsman'. That eventually became the official title. **1974** *Times* 7 Dec. 3/2 The Flying Scotsman..the majestic old LNER puffer... The Flying Scotsman..is at present stabled steamless at Carnforth.

Scots Nat (skǫts næt). *colloq.* [f. SCOTS *a.* + *NAT[3]; cf. *SCOT NAT *sb.* and *a.*] A member of the Scottish National Party (see *SCOTTISH *a.* 5). Hence **Scots Na·ttery** (*nonce-wd.*) Scottish Nationalism.

1974 *Undercurrents* July–Aug. 3/2 The British did take the precaution..of incorporating Rockall into the county of Inverness—which may or may not be a smart move depending on which way the Scots Nats jump. **1977** *Times* 23 June 16/1 The delectable MP for East Dumbartonshire, Margaret Bain..a good Scots Nat and true. **1978** *Times* 21 Jan. 14/4 Successive waves of Scots Nattery going back to J. M. Bannerman.

Scott (skǫt). *Electr. Engin.* [The name of Charles F. Scott (1864–1944), U.S. electrical engineer, who devised the connection in 1894 (*Electrician* 6 Apr. 640).] *Scott connection*: a way of connecting two single-phase transformers to convert a three-phase voltage to a two-phase one (or to two single-phase ones), or vice versa: on the three-phase side the mid-point of the main transformer is connected to one terminal of the second transformer; the remaining three terminals form the terminals for the three-phase supply; the two-phase supply is taken from the two pairs of terminals on the other side. So *Scott-connected* adj.

[**1911** BOHLE & ROBERTSON *Transformers* xi. 321 (*heading*) Scott's two-phase to three-phase connection.] **1926** J. L. BEAVER *Elem. Alternating Currents* ix. 200 The so-called 'Scott' connection is an arrangement of *two* single-phase transformers, whereby three-phase power may be obtained from a two-phase circuit or vice versa. **1935** MONSETH & ROBINSON *Relay Systems* x. 304 (*caption*) Scott-connected transformer differential protective scheme. **1947** R. LEE *Electronic Transformers & Circuits* viii. 214 When autotransformers are used on three-phase supply lines, they may be connected the same as two-winding transformers in star, delta, open-delta, or Scott connections. **1966** BROSAN & HAYDEN *Adv. Electr. Power & Machines* vi. 243 The Leblanc system was invented about five years after the Scott connexion when the latter had obtained a firm foothold in Britain and its use was therefore confined to the Continent. *Ibid.*, The general case of determining the regulation of a Scott-connected group is somewhat involved.

Scottie (skǫ·ti). Shortened f. *Scotch terrier* s.v. SCOTCH *a.* 4 in Dict. and Suppl.

1907 F. T. BARTON *Terriers* xviii. 131 If a Scottie has not a sound jacket to keep out the mountain dew and rain, he ought not to take a leading place at any show. **1939** *Country Life* 11 Feb. p. xxi/2 (Advt.), For Sale.—Exceptionally strong Scottie puppies. **1945** A. CHRISTIE *Sparkling Cyanide* I. iv. 40 She came out one morning with a small black Scottie dog. **1957** R. MASON *World of Suzie Wong* II. ii. 124 Her dog..was a Scottie with an absurd, sad, long face. **1971** 'L. EGAN' *Malicious Mischief* (1972) i. 4 Scotties are nice dogs. **1973** M. AMIS *Rachel Papers* 159 Glancing downwards, my rig, in its pink muff, looked unnatural, absurd, like an overdressed Scottie dog.

Scottish, *a.* and *sb.* Add: **A.** *adj.* **5.** *Scottish-American* adj.; **Scottish Baronial** *a.*, designating a style of architecture typical of the semi-fortified houses of the medieval Scottish nobility, and revived in the nineteenth century (cf. *Scotch Baronial* s.v. *SCOTCH *a.* 4 a); **Scottish Blackface** = *Scotch Blackface* s.v. *SCOTCH *a.* 4 a; **Scottish Chaucerians,** the distinguishing epithet applied to a number of fifteenth- and sixteenth-century Scottish poets influenced by and imitating the work of Geoffrey Chaucer; **Scottish National Party,** a political party formed in 1934 by an amalgamation of the National Party of Scotland and the Scottish Party, which seeks autonomous government for Scotland (cf. *SCOTTISH NATIONALIST *a.* and *sb.*); **Scottish terrier** = *Scotch terrier* s.v. *SCOTCH *a.* 4 a.

1905 W. JAMES in *McClure's Mag.* May 3/1, I wish to pay my tribute to the memory of a Scottish-American friend of mine who died five years ago. **1978** N. GOSLING *Paris 1900–14* 49 Debussy had picked the Scottish-American star Mary Garden. **1938** L. MACNEICE *I crossed Minch* vii. 98 Oban has many hotels in the Scottish Baronial style. **1956** L. E. JONES *Edwardian Youth* iv. 87 The newly-built Scottish Baronial building which contains the Main Gateway [of Balliol College, Oxford]. **1979** R. LAIDLAW *Lion is Rampant* vi. 49 The house..was a massive structure, built..in the Scottish Baronial style. **1937** A. FRASER *Sheep Farming* ii. 22 Only a few years ago I was concerned with the export of

Scottish Blackface sheep to Palestine. **1974** *Times* 23 Feb. 14/2 Several farmers may turn out their Swaledale or Scottish Blackface, Herdwick or Lonk sheep onto one moor. **1902** G. GREGORY SMITH *Specimens of Middle Scots* p. xlv, To say this of the 'Scottish Chaucerians' is almost a platitude. **1927** E. P. HAMMOND *Eng. Verse between Chaucer & Surrey* p. xi, Rhythm in Chaucer and the English Chaucerians—Verse-Forms—The Scottish Chaucerians—Vocabulary. **1935** A. BAUGH *Hist. Eng. Lang.* vi. 192 The fifteenth century is sometimes known as the Imitative Period since so much of the poetry..was written in emulation of Chaucer... In the north the Scottish Chaucerians, particularly Henryson, Dunbar, Gavin Douglas, and Lindsay, produced significant work. **1937** *Oxf. Compan. Eng. Lit.* (ed. 2) 154/1 *Chaucerians, Scottish*, name given to a group of 15th cent. Scottish writers (of whom Dunbar and Henryson are the chief) who imitated Chaucer in some of their work. **1966** *Amer. N. & Q.* May 139/1 Robbins-Cutler now include ..the so-called Scottish Chaucerians. **1934** *Times* 26 Feb. 16/5 Resolutions were unanimously passed at a conference of the National Party of Scotland in Glasgow approving of a union with the Scottish Party, subject to that Party's agreement, the united parties to be called the Scottish National Party. **1973** *Scotsman* 12 Jan. 9/2 Mr Douglas Drysdale, a former vice-chairman of the Scottish National Party, has been appointed..for liaison among other nationalist bodies in Scotland. **1980** BUTLER & SLOMAN *Brit. Polit. Facts 1900–79* (ed. 5) ii. 162 Scottish National Party. The party was formed in 1928 as the National Party of Scotland. In 1933 it merged with a body called the Scottish Party (founded 1930) and the name was then changed to the Scottish National Party. **1837** T. BELL *Hist. Brit. Quadrupeds* 230 The other [terrier] is called the Scottish or Wire-haired Terrier. **1894** R. B. LEE *Hist. & Descr. Mod. Dogs: Terriers* xi. 251 It was about the year 1874 that a newspaper controversy brought the Scottish terrier prominently before the public. **1956** D. CASPERSZ *Popular Scottish Terrier* i. 17 The Scottish Terrier descends directly from a race of small terriers of great antiquity.

Sco·ttish Na·tionalist, *a.* and *sb.* **A.** *adj.* Of or pertaining to the Scottish National Party (see *SCOTTISH *a.* 5) or its programme. **B.** *sb.* A member of this party.

1936 'H. MACDIARMID' in *Lucky Poet* (1943) iii. 145 The long confused and inefficient Scottish Nationalist groping. **1953** E. SIMON *Past Masters* IV. 246 This Scottish Nationalist you've got there. **1968** *Daily Progress* (Charlottesville, Va.) 11 July C14/1 Winifred Ewing was a noted narker in Glasgow before she became the only Scottish Nationalist in the House of Commons. **1976** LD. HOME *Way Wind Blows* xv. 206 A Scottish Nationalist Party had grown up which had begun to advocate separation from England.

So **Sco·ttish Na·tionalism,** the political programme or ideals of the Scottish National Party.

1935 N. MITCHISON *We have been Warned* I. 73 'Don't you think..there's something in Scottish Nationalism?' 'Not while it's run by ladies and gentlemen.' **1953** E. SIMON *Past Masters* IV. 246 Scottish Nationalism, as I see it, is an absurdity.

Scottishness. (Later examples.)

1933 *Times Lit. Suppl.* 3 Aug. 523/1 Henryson was sage and serious. It was part of his Scottishness. **1956** N. PEVSNER *Englishness of Eng. Art* (rev. ed.) 125 It is easy to recognize Scottishness in the Scottish castle of the seventeenth century. **1976** *Listener* 19 Feb. 209/3 The BBC in Scotland should be asked..to abandon the excessive concern with Scottishness.

Scottishry (skǫ·tiʃri). [f. SCOTTISH *a.* + -RY; cf. IRISHRY, WELSHRY, etc.] Scottish character or nationality; a Scottish trait, Scottishness.

1958 C. WATSON *Coffin, scarcely Used* iv. 44 'Ye hear tha' frae the wee booy!' he chortled... 'For heaven's sake, drop that phoney Scottishry, Rupert.' **1973** *Daily Tel.* 24 Nov. 11/1 The whole business of Highland Scottishry is so technical that an Englishman may find himself rebuked on a point of Gaelic or a question of optics. **1979** *Ibid.* 17 Aug. 14/3 Fake Scottishry of the kind which reduces the noble name of the last Lord of the Isles, Donald Dubh, to the almost indistinguishable name of the cartoon duck.

Scotty, *a.* Add: **b.** (With small initial.) (Earlier and later examples.)

1896 E. TURNER *Little Larrikin* xvii. 191 I'm *blessed* if I know what I've done this time... Don't be scotty, Marcia. **1936** M. FRANKLIN *All that Swagger* xxxv. 334 Uncle William is as scotty as a French hen with her feathers the wrong way.

scour, *sb.*[2] Add: **2.** Also, the abrading or transporting action of a current of any other material. (Further examples.)

1904 *Jrnl. Geol.* XII. 575 With these destructional effects assigned to glacial agency, a novel possibility is at once suggested as to the part played in their persistent development by glacial scour, or coarse abrasion. **1933** SCHUCHERT & DUNBAR *Textbk. Geol.* (ed. 3) xix. 425 The ice and the scour of the last glaciers removed all weak materials. **1954** *Jrnl. Geol. Soc. Australia* I. 77 The wind scour is able to drive the sand into heaps which migrate slowly down wind. **1975** *Offshore* Sept. 49-17/1 Scour is probably the greatest menace to offshore structures and pipelines.

5. By 'cattle' understand 'livestock'. Also *pl.* (chiefly *U.S.*). (Further examples.)

1848 *Rep. Comm. Patents 1847* (U.S.) 507 They say the disease called the 'scours' is the principal one to which sheep are liable. **1950** [see *BEESTINGS I]. **1970** W. H. PARKER *Health & Dis. in Farm Animals* xvii. 226 In sheep the disease causes the same wasting but without the scour. **1973** M. CROWELL *Greener Pastures* 16 Rameses II [*sc.* a sheep] has lately been having scours, or loose-bowel trouble. **1975** *N.Z. Jrnl. Agric.* Sept. 3/1 The hens..also appear to have a green scour. **1981** 'E. PETERS' *St. Peter's Fair* i. 18 They're having trouble..with scour among the calves.

7*. *Austral.* and *N.Z.* A building in which wool is scoured.

1925 L. G. D. ACLAND *Early Canterbury Runs* (1930) 1st Ser. vi. 123 The Creek Station..was leased to T. P. Bartrum from 1879 onwards, and he established a wool scour there. **1934** T. WOOD *Cobbers* xvi. 195 The scour was a long open shed on stilts, with sheep-pens leading into it and out of it.

scour, *v.*[1] **2. b.** (Earlier example.)

1882 'MARK TWAIN' *Prince & Pauper* xxv. 300 Scour and scan me to thy content.

scour, *v.*[2] Add: **1. g.** *U.S.* Of a plough, to pass through the soil easily, without earth adhering to the mould-board; freq. in negative contexts. Also *fig.*, to succeed.

1871 *Northern Vindicator* (Estherville, Iowa) 6 May 3/1 The contemptible wretch who stole the collar to the saw at the steam mill a few weeks ago, has come to the conclusion that his meanness did not 'scour', as he anticipated, and hence he placed the collar under a board pile in town where it was discovered on Monday last. **1881** J. PERIAM *Amer. Encycl. Agric.* 742/2 In the average soil there [*sc.* in eastern U.S.] the cast-iron plow would scour perfectly. **1887** W. H. LAMON in *Washington Critic* 3 Sept. 3/1 He [*sc.* Lincoln] said to me on stand, immediately after the [Gettysburg] speech: 'Lamon, that speech won't scour. It is a flat failure, and the people are disappointed.' **1948** *Sat. Even. Post* 7 Feb. 109/1 Then his old moldboard plow wouldn't scour, and after we'd sharpened it he broke the beam.

7. d. By 'cattle' understand 'livestock'.

scourer[2]. **4.** (Earlier example.)

1859 *Rep. Comm. Patents 1858* (U.S.) I. 378 Scourer G, blast spouts EF, and fan C, [are] combined and arranged relatively with each other.

scourge, *sb.* **2.** (Examples of phr. *the Scourge of God.*)

1611 CORYAT *Crudities* 162 Came that *Flagellum Dei* that scourge of God into Italy, Attila, King of the Hunnes. **1781** GIBBON *Decl. & F.* III. xxxiv. 368 If Attila equalled the hostile ravages of Tamerlane, either the Tartar or the Hun might deserve the epithet of the *Scourge of God.* **1925** D. H. LAWRENCE *Reflections on Death of Porcupine* 157 Attila, the Scourge of God, who helped to scourge the Roman world out of existence, was great with power.

Scourian (sku·riăn, skau·riăn), *a. Geol.* [f. *Scourie*, name of a crofting village on the west coast of Sutherland + -AN.] Of, pertaining to, or designating the earlier metamorphism undergone by the Lewisian rocks of the Pre-Cambrian in NW Scotland, the rocks formed by this metamorphism, and the structures to which they belong. Also *absol.*, these rocks and structures.

1950 SUTTON & WATSON in *Q. Jrnl. Geol. Soc.* CVI. 243 In the following pages the Lewisian is..regarded as belonging to two metamorphic complexes, the first, or Scourian, being older and the second, or Laxfordian, younger than the dolerite dykes. These names are taken from localities in Sutherland where the relations of the two complexes are particularly clearly displayed. **1959** *Nature* 5 Dec. 1793/1 Three samples came from the Outer Hebrides, three from the Laxfordian, and two from the Scourian. **1961** *Q. Jrnl. Geol. Soc.* CXVII. 241 The Scourian metamorphic rocks in the vicinity of Scourie are primarily hornblende- or pyroxene-bearing gneisses containing very little mica or potassium-feldspar. *Ibid.* 242 The Scourian metamorphism occurred at least 2460 m.y. ago. **1965** A. HOLMES *Princ. Physical Geol.* (ed. 2) xiii. 370 (*caption*) The peaks are of Torridonian Sandstone, resting unconformably on Lewisian Gneiss (Scourian division). **1969** BENNISON & WRIGHT *Geol. Hist. Brit. Isles* iii. 42 The trend of the Scourian is not known since no really large structures have been found associated with the granulites. **1979** *Nature* 22 Feb. 643/1 The ~2,400 Myr age for the emplacement of the Scourie dyke swarm indicates that the Scourian tectonic episode had ceased by the beginning of the Proterozoic.

scouring, *vbl. sb.*[2] Add: **4. b.** By 'cattle' understand 'livestock'.

9. *scouring cloth, machine*; **scouring powder,** an abrasive powder used for cleaning kitchenware, etc.

1907 *Yesterday's Shopping* (1969) 120/3 Scouring Cloth—yard 0/5½ Scouring or Paint Cloths—each 0/4. **1976** W. TREVOR *Children of Dynmouth* iii. 58 He reached for a scouring cloth on a line that stretched above the sink. **1882** *Encycl. Brit.* XIV. 387/2 Another machine now largely used by curriers is the scouring machine. **1969** A. J. HALL *Stand. Handbk. Textiles* (ed. 7) iii. 110 The construction and operation of scouring machines..are such as to disturb the wool as little as possible. **1949** D. SMITH *I capture Castle* v. 61 She..scrubbed her hands until she got it [*sc.* dye] all off. She used our last grains of scouring powder. **1975** N. FREELING *What are Bugles blowing For?* vi. 37 She tacked off to write 'scouring powder' on her shopping list.

scouring, *ppl. a.*[2] Add: **4.** Of livestock: suffering from diarrhœa. Cf. SCOUR *sb.*[2] 5 in Dict. and Suppl.

1752 T. BOULT *Vet. Recipe Bk.* in *Henry Bristow Ltd. Catal.* (1974) No. 206. 31 To cure a Scowering Cow. **1973** *Country Life* 8 Feb. 360/1 A scouring cow is a very highly stressed animal.

5. *U.S.* Of a plough: see *SCOUR *v.*[2] 1 g.

1856 *Rep. Comm. Patents: Agric. 1855* (U.S. Dept. Agric.) 170 It was ploughed as near it as possible with a double-shovel scouring plough. **1943** C. CROW *Great Amer. Customer* 71 He bought old sawmill blades with which he made self scouring plows which cut through the soil as clean as a razor.

Scouse. Add: **2.** Transferred uses. *slang.* **a.** A native or inhabitant of Liverpool.

1945 *Southern Daily Echo* 27 Dec. 4/3 He was stopped by his Lordship and asked to explain the meaning of three words—'oppo', 'Geordie' and 'scouse'. His interpretations were: 'oppo' slang for opposite number, friend or colleague, 'Geordie'—a native of Newcastle-upon-Tyne; 'scouse'—a native of Liverpool where they eat 'scouse' (stew). **1960** O. MANNING *Great Fortune* II. 148 'I'm a scouse,' he said. 'From the dregs of the Liverpool soup.' **1969** R. AIRTH *Snatch!* ix. 91 'Where's home?' 'Liverpool.' 'A scouse. Fancy that.' **1980** *Times* 20 June 11/6 A roly-poly, amiable Liverpudlian, with the Scouse's seemingly god-given gift of being able to send up an overblown..occasion.

b. The dialect of English spoken in Liverpool. Also, the manner of pronunciation or accent typical to the 'scouse'.

1963 *Guardian* 3 June 10/5 This rock group suddenly made Liverpool fashionable in the entertainment world. After their first two records it became necessary for people in the business in London to learn a few words of Scouse. **1966** 'L. LANE' *ABZ of Scouse* Introd., As a dialect—for it *is* a dialect and not just a regional accent—Scouse has many curious features. **1979** *Times* 20 Nov. 4 A touch of Scouse in the pronunciation will be entirely acceptable.

c. *attrib.* or as *adj.*

1960 *Spectator* 14 Oct. 565 A horrifyingly plausible spiv, even down to that awful 'scouse' accent. **1965** G. MELLY *Owning Up* vi. 67 Albert Kinder, a scouse promoter who intended to tie up jazz in the North. **1969** I. & P. OPIE *Children's Games* x. 276 'Film Stars' is the most popular guessing game in Britain... Other names: 'Initials', 'Pop Stars', 'TV Stars', and, in Liverpool, 'Filmy', a typical scouse apocope. **1973** *Guardian* 1 Aug. 1/8 Scouse House was the tongue-in-cheek name given to the Merseyside Development Office. **1976** *Observer* 8 Aug. 11 (Advt.), Ar Alf sez darrevry Scouse Big'ead's brood special fer d'Pool, like.

Scouser (skau·səɹ). *slang.* [f. prec. + -ER[1].] = *SCOUSE 2 a.

1959 *Times* 8 Dec. 13/6 Their [*sc.* Liverpool workers'] catarrhal speech would identify them as 'Scousers' wherever English is recognized. **1966** 'L. LANE' *ABZ of Scouse* 93 *Scouser*, an inhabitant of Merseyside, not necessarily a Liverpudlian. This book assumes a narrower definition, namely, a Merseysider who speaks Scouse. **1966** P. MOLONEY *Plea for Mersey* 22 A scouser lass known as R. Mury. **1973** *Guardian* 5 Mar. 8/2 Here was Ted Whitehead, born in Scotland Road and therefore a scouser of the scousers, with a real Liverpool play. **1976** *Liverpool Echo* 22 Nov. 6/6 It's pretty well established that where there's a ship there you'll find a Scouser.

scout, *sb.*[4] Add: **1.** Also, an instance of this; a scouting or reconnoitring expedition. Also *scout-round.*

1906 'MARK TWAIN' in *Harper's Mag.* Aug. 328/2 We are back at Fort Paxton once more, after a forty-day scout. **1975** P. DICKINSON *Lively Dead* xxii. 137 They'd enough reason to send a bloke to do a preliminary scout round. **1978** F. BRANSTON *Sergeant Ritchie's Conscience* i. 12 'Organized a scout-round for the weapon?' 'Only in the immediate area.' **1980** A. PRICE *Hour of Donkey* iv. 55 Wimpy's scout through the wood must..be..completed... Bastable contented himself with cautious peering round each blind bend.

2. c. (*a*) *Boy Scout* (also with small initials): now, a member of the Scout Association, or one of its associate, or parallel, organizations whose ideals of good citizenship and a healthy active life are promoted at regular meetings of scout groups in Great Britain, the British Commonwealth, the United States, and elsewhere throughout the world. Various specialized divisions of the movement are distinguished, as *cub scout, sea scout* s.v. *SEA *sb.* 23 a, *venture scout* s.v. *VENTURE *sb.*, etc. (Later examples.)

The term 'Boy' has now been officially omitted from the title of the organization in the U.K., U.S., and elsewhere. *Girl Scout* has been the official name for the U.S. equivalent to the Girl Guide since 1912: see *GUIDE *sb.* 2 d.

1910 'SCOUTMASTER' *Boy Scout* i. 1 General Sir Robert S. Baden-Powell, the founder of the Movement, recognised this when he first propounded his scheme for boy scouts... The Movement was started less than three years ago. **1924** 'A. D. SEDGWICK' *Little French Girl* I. v. 39 Alix heard of a Women's Institute, of Boy Scouts and Girl Guides. **1959** *Listener* 27 Aug. 304/1 There's something of the boy scout about M. Debré. **1978** *Broadcast* 27 Mar. 20/3 We wish that ..people would stop calling us 'Boy' Scouts. Ten years ago we adopted the title, 'Scouts', in a process of updating our appeal to young people.

(*b*) *fig.* and *transf.*, freq. with reference to the honesty, preparedness, or supposed inexperience of a (Boy) Scout (see quots.).

1918 I. S. COBB *Glory of Coming* p. xiii, The Poilus called our soldiers 'Boy Scouts' and spoke of our effort as 'The Second Children's Crusade'. **1929** F. A. POTTLE *Stretchers* 60 The noncoms (who for weeks had been calling us 'Boy Scouts') hung a blue ribbon on the bulletin board. **1945** L. SHELLY *Jive Talk Dict.* 22 *Boy scout*, an immature male. **1962** *Amer. Speech* XXXVII. 267 *Boy scout*,..a traffic policeman who spends much of his time in helping motorists with flat tires, stalled cars, empty gas tanks, and so on.

1965 A. NICOL *Truly Married Woman* 84 Bandele had said, threateningly, that he had better not mention his name, but he could go and be a Boy Scout on his own. **1969** *Sunday Mirror* (Sydney) 13 Apr. 9/4 The accused officer has always been known as a 'boy scout'—a policeman who goes strictly by the book. **1977** J. I. M. STEWART *Madonna of Astrolabe* iii. 57 It was Mark's idea. Mark's absolutely the Boy Scout.

(*c*) *attrib.* and *Comb.*

1909 *Daily Chron.* 9 July 8/2 The youth of the three kingdoms of the boy scout movement. **1914** W. OWEN *Let.* 1 June (1967) 257 Certain of my Boy-Scout acquaintance. **1936** W. R. F. COLLIS *Silver Fleece* v. xvi. 266 Above all he hated..the 'boy scout' mentality, the modern tendency to march about in mobs, wearing coloured shirts, shouting, and beating up anybody who doesn't shout with you. **1950** 'E. CRISPIN' *Frequent Hearses* iv. 198 'What about the knife?' 'An oversized boy-scout affair..ground razor-sharp.' **1967** J. PORTER *Chinks in Curtain* v. 53 All right, chum, and what would you have done? Given the Boy Scout salute? **1978** S. BRILL *Teamsters* ii. 43 His father was a teetotaler, a boy-scout husband who came home every night.

(*d*) Hence *Boy Scoutery*, *Scoutism*, the activity or attitude of a Boy Scout; also *fig.*; *Boy Scoutish* adj., characteristic of a Boy Scout. (Freq. with pejorative connotations.)

1937 WYNDHAM LEWIS *Blasting & Bombardiering* v. ii. 254 He never got us under canvas it is true—we were not the most promising material for Ezra's boyscoutery. **1938** 'G. ORWELL' *Homage to Catalonia* iv. 49 We and they used to make daylight patrols there. It was not bad fun in a Boy Scoutish way. **1942** WYNDHAM LEWIS *Let.* (1963) 325 A curiously beastly case of boyscoutism, of arrested development or cretinism. **1962** L. DEIGHTON *Ipcress File* xiv. 84 Calling me 'boy-scoutish' which he knew would hit me where it hurt. **1963** J. VAIZEY *Educ. in Class Society* 6 These and other [travel and cultural] schemes..would..tend to counterbalance people's enthusiasm for the Boy Scoutism of the Duke of Edinburgh's award. **1967** E. GRIERSON *Crime of One's Own* xi. 96 You must be mad... You've had that look about you ever since you started this boy-scoutery.

d. A bee searching for a new site for a swarm to settle or a new source of food.

1835 *Penny Cycl.* IV. 153/1 It is said that bees send out scouts before leaving the hive, to search for a convenient situation for their new abode. **1909** S. L. BENSUSAN *Children's Story of Bee* vii. 108 The scouts..might have been seen following their aërial roads to where the swarm was stationed. *Ibid.* 110 The last of the old queen's scouts had come bringing news of a hive—clean, sweet-scented and empty—in a garden across the valley. **1954** D. ILSE tr. *von Frisch's Dancing Bees* v. 28 While the main swarm hangs from a branch in quiet idleness, its 'scouts' are busily at work, searching in all directions to find a suitable abode.

e. One sent out by an organization (as a sports club, recording company, etc.) to look for suitably talented persons with a view to their employment by that organization; a talent scout.

1905 *Sporting Life* 2 Sept. 25/4 Padden..is the official scout of the St. Louis Club. **1926** WHITEMAN & MCBRIDE *Jazz* iii. 65 Vaudeville scouts approached us. Our pictures were in the papers. **1948** *Sporting Mirror* 19 Nov. 2/2 As chief scout for Derby County he will make sure that no young Midlander with real talent fails to get a chance to develop his soccer. **1952** A. LOMAX *Mister Jelly Roll* 291 'Fritz Pollard' introduced me to..Williams who was then a scout for the Paramount Recording Company. **1968** *Blues Unlimited* Sept. 15 They had their scouts out looking for anyone who could make records. **1976** E. DUNPHY *Only a Game?* iii. 92 He was being watched by Manchester City. Their scout left before the end.

f. An official of the A.A. or R.A.C. employed to assist motorists on the road. (No longer in use.)

1909 *Q. Rev.* Jan. 143 The scouts have, beyond doubt, done a great deal to check reckless driving. **1929** E. LINKLATER *Poet's Pub* xviii. 200 They passed a scout of the Automobile Association. 'You should have returned that A.A. man's salute.'

g. *slang.* A fellow, chap, person. Freq. in approbatory use, as *good scout*, etc., and as an affectionate term of address.

1912 M. NICHOLSON *Hoosier Chron.* 129 Dad's a good old scout and he's pretty sure to do it. **1921** WODEHOUSE *Indiscretions of Archie* vii. 61 You'll never be lonely with Peter around. He's a great scout. Always merry and bright. **1922** J. A. DUNN *Man Trap* xii. 168 You didn't tell me your name, old scout. **1933** E. O'NEILL *Ah, Wilderness!* (1934) III. i. 96 Nat Miller's a good scout. **1950** A. WILSON *Such Darling Dodos* 198 She had only two roles with men—tomboy and good scout. **1953** 'N. BLAKE' *Dreadful Hollow* 112 'It's time I sent him a report.' 'Pop? No need, old scout.' **1965** 'J. LE CARRÉ' *Looking-Glass War* iv. 38 I've got nothing against old Adrian. He's a good scout.

3. Delete † and add: Now only *U.S.* (Later examples.)

1798 I. ALLEN *Hist. Vermont* 92 He sent a scout of about 300, mostly Indians, to hunt at the mouth of Otter Creek. **1867** J. N. EDWARDS *Shelby & his Men* xxiii. 412 At Current river a scout of fifty were encountered. **1940** W. FAULKNER *Hamlet* II. i. 127 A scout of two or three would lurk about the Varner fence.

4. a. (Further examples.) Also *spec.*: in oil-drilling operations, one employed by a company to keep watch on the activities of other companies; in *Sport*, one employed to observe and report on the performance of rival teams or clubs. Also, † a policeman.

1789 [see *HORNY *sb.* 2]. **1821** P. EGAN *Life in London* II. iii. 231 Turning the corner of Old Bedlam, A scout laid me flat upon my face. **1838** DICKENS *O. Twist* III. xlvi. 213 They'll have him yet, for the scouts are out, and by to-morrow night there'll be a cry all through the country. **1883** [in Dict.]. **1883** *Derrick's Handbk. Petroleum* (1898) I. 357 Scouts have squatted on the Reed and Brenneman lease..and are keeping a vigilant watch on the well; efforts to dislodge the scouts have proved unavailing. **1904** *Dialect Notes* II. 388 *Scout*,..a man sent to obtain information regarding a mystery. **1949** *Athletic Jrnl.* Oct. 20/1 The scout should familiarize himself long before the season starts with the types of defense that have been used by opponents in the past. **1973** C. CALLOW *Power from Sea* i. 14 The..oil industry employs men to keep tabs on the competition and has given them the euphemistic term of 'scouts'. **1976** M. MACHLIN *Pipeline* ii. 32 There had to be a scout on that plane.

5. b. An airship or aeroplane used for reconnoitring; a lightly-armed fighter aeroplane. Also *attrib.*

1909 A. BERGET *Conquest of Air* II. vii. 260 Airships or aeroplanes? As 'combatants' or 'scouts'? **1914** *Daily Express* 31 Dec. 3/4 We have 'scouts' which can beat anything the enemy can bring against us. **1916** H. BARBER *Aeroplane Speaks* Pl. xi, The little Gnome-engined scout biplanes. **1928** E. BLUNDEN *Undertones of War* viii. 82 On account of the aforementioned ceremonial parade, with the gleaming bayonets and accoutrements not unnoticed by German flying Scouts, the town was shelled by heavy guns on the day that we departed. **1942** *R.A.F. Jrnl.* 2 May 1 Among the planes..is an approximately equal number of bombers, pursuit planes, and scouts. **1978** H. WOUK *War & Remembrance* xxx. 304 The air raid proved to be only some old-type scout bombers buzzing a battleship of the screen and then running away from the Zeroes into the light clouds.

6. a. (Earlier example in *Baseball* and later examples in *Cricket*.)

1856 *Spirit of Times* 27 Dec. 276/3 One of these swiftly-delivered balls, when stopped by a skilful batsman, is sure to give the outmost scout employment. **1898** J. A. GIBBS *Cotswold Village* xi. 241 So also one may say..after the famous Gloucestershire hitter [*sc.* Grace] has made things merry for spectators and scouts alike. **1924** N. CARDUS *Days in Sun* 49 Supposing the fieldsmen were set..with still a number of them idle on the off-side, with great gaps between the leg-side scouts.

8. *scout boat* (earlier examples), *-craft* (later examples), *hut, knife*; **scout bee** (sense *2 d); **scout car**, (*a*) *U.S.*, a police patrol car; (*b*) *Mil.*, a fast armoured vehicle used for reconnaissance and liaison; **Scout Law**, a code of conduct enjoined upon (Boy) Scouts; **Scout's honour**, the honour on which a (Boy) Scout promises to obey the Scout Law; freq. *transf.*, as an expression of one's good faith.

1924 A. M. STURGES *Pract. Beekeeping* 306/1 Scout-bees. **1935** J. C. KENLY *Cities of Wax* xvi. 165 A scout-bee..had just brought in news to her hive that she had discovered a honey gold-mine. **1963** T. A. SEBEOK in J. A. Fishman *Readings Sociol. of Lang.* (1968) 23 [M. Lindauer] traces how the scout bees announce the location of suitable nesting places by means of the dance in the cluster. **1975** *Country Life* 20 Feb. 448/2 This swarm..was resting while scout bees looked for a suitable site. **1717** in *Statutes at Large S. Carolina* (1838) III. 24 For the scout boat on Port Royal Island, a Captain and six private men. **1862** F. MOORE *Rebellion Record* V. II. 182 The scout-boats of Com. Montgomery notified him of the presence of the Federals. **1933** *Sun* (Baltimore) 5 May 11/2 Scout car No. 7..answered fifty-five calls in the Pimlico section of the Northern district. **a 1944** K. DOUGLAS *Alamein to Zem Zem* (1946) 40 A Daimler scout car, flying a red cross, was moving and halting,..collecting wounded. **1960** R. M. OGORKIEWICZ *Armour* xxxi. 434 A far more advanced Daimler scout car was also designed before the war, and the first built in December 1939. *Ibid.* 435 Originally the Daimler scout cars were intended for liaison within the tank regiments of the armoured divisions,..but after the 1940 campaign their use was extended, as was that of armoured cars. **1977** H. INNES *Big Footprints* I. ii. 47 More craters. A burned-out scout car, some lorries gaping holes, then we were clear of the battlefield. **1910** *Chambers's Jrnl.* Feb. 114/2 They are taught scout-craft, which includes the art of stalking wild creatures. **1937** *Sun* (Baltimore) 2 July 6/1 Thousands of Boy Scouts gathered in a giant arena tonight to watch a pageant of scoutcraft and history. **1977** N. ADAM *Triplehip Cracksman* v. 54 Using my entirely non-existent knowledge of scoutcraft, I snuck up it in the closing shadows. **1974** *Times* 10 Jan. 18/7 The Scout huts in New Zealand. **1976** L. HENDERSON *Major Enquiry* ix. 54 He got bored with working in the scout hut. **1937** E. GARNETT *Family from One End Street* v. 99 Hadn't he wanted a scout knife as long as he could remember. **1977** J. PORTER *Who the Heck is Sylvia?* xvi. 150 The kid..clipped his scout knife back on his scout belt. **1908** R. S. S. BADEN-POWELL *Scouting for Boys* 49 The Scout Law. **1922** *Encycl. Brit.* XXX. 487/2 The Scout Promise, to carry out, on his honour, as far as in him lies, the Scout Law, is the binding disciplinary force. **1931** E. WAUGH *Remote People* 134 A Somali boy presented himself for examination in scout law. **1972** P. BLACK *Biggest Aspidistra in World* I. vi. 51 An establishment striving..to do its best according to the Scout Law, continued to pervade the spirit of Children's Hour. **1908** R. S. S. BADEN-POWELL *Scouting for Boys* 49 A Scout's Honour is to be trusted. **1956** 'E. MCBAIN' *Cop Hater* (1958) xx. 168 'Provided it's not for publication.' 'Scout's honour,' Savage said. **1959** [see *BROWNIE[1] 2]. **1974** A. ROSS *Bradford Business* 175 'I'll try my best, Charlie,' I said, 'scout's honour.'

scout, *sb.*[6] (Later examples of sense 'a female servant'.)

1935 D. L. SAYERS *Gaudy Night* v. 91 'The scouts are all women of excellent character, so far as I know,' said the Bursar. **1972** *Oxford Times* 26 May 1/3 Miss Bootes, who has been a scout at St. Hilda's College for 25 years, was presented with the teapot on Wednesday.

scout, *v.*[1] **2.** For '? Now *dial.*' read *Obs.* and add earlier and later examples.

1786 *County Mag.* Nov. 171/3 One that can throw well, likewise scout, He for a long stroke must stand out. **1928** *Observer* 1 July 29/4 An arrangement by which Tate is required to rest from his bowling by scouting at deep square leg.

scouter. Restrict † *Obs.* to sense in Dict. and add: **1.** (Later example.)

1867 J. N. EDWARDS *Shelby & his Men* xiv. 232 One of the truest scouters who ever fired a pistol.

2. An adult member of the (Boy) Scout movement. Cf. *GUIDER s.v. *GUIDE *sb.* 2 d.

1930 H. W. BENSON *Summer Camp* 27 [The Patrol Leader] must be taught..to decentralize... A Scouter or Rover will probably be required to show him how to set about this. **1948** *Lawton* (Okla.) *Constitution* 4 July 3/5 A large number of cubbers and scouters were present with their families. **1976** *Burnham-on-Sea Gaz.* 20 Apr., A strong committee should be established, to be responsible for fund-raising activities, leaving the various scouters to carry on their roles as cub-scout leaders.

scouting, *vbl. sb.*[1] Add: **1. a.** *attrib.* (Earlier and later U.S. examples of *scouting-party*.)

1756 R. ROGERS *Jrnl.* 28 Apr. (1765) 17 They discovered a scouting party of three or four hundred Indians. **1895** A. C. HAMLIN in M. A. Jackson *Mem. Stonewall Jackson* (ed. 2) 548 A Federal scouting party could have come up the Hazel Grove road and seized him as a prisoner of war. **1941** B. SCHULBERG *What makes Sammy Run?* xi. 199 The other members of the Wall Street scouting party were punctual.

b. (Later examples.) Also, the Scout movement itself.

1966 *Listener* 20 Oct. 570/1 'Scouts go mod', the headline said—as if the cut of the new mushroom-coloured, tapering long trousers was the most important feature of the new pattern of Scouting. **1976** *Eastern Even. News* (Norwich) 9 Dec. 6/4 I'm sure there must be lots of men with souvenirs from their Scouting days. **1977** *Times* 27 June 16/8 Olave, Lady Baden-Powell..exemplified the potential of Scouting and Guiding for world peace.

c. The activity of a scout (*SCOUT *sb.*[4] 2 e or 4 a).

1908 *Baseball Mag.* Nov. 1/1 There was the reconnoitering, scouting, feints, retreats, invasions, and then preparations made by all the ball-and-bat generals for the final big battle. **1961** J. S. SALAK *Dict. Amer. Sports* 382 *Scouting*, viewing an opposing team in action before playing them. **1968** *Blues Unlimited* Nov. 5 Joe Bihari..asked him to do some scouting for Modern Reds, as well as playing on further second dates.

2. For '? *Obs.* exc. *dial.*' read *Obs.* and add earlier and later examples.

1815 *Suffolk Chron.* 2 Sept., The Needham players are remarkable for excellent scouting. **1885** F. GALE *Life of Hon. Robert Grimston* vii. 77 Lords' forty years ago was practically a country ground... There were no nets, but ground boys did the scouting. **1908** W. E. W. COLLINS *Leaves from Old County Cricketer's Diary* xi. 191 Quite a young soldier..did most of the scouting in the far country.

scoutmaster, scout-master. Add: **1. a.** Now usu. in latter sense. (Later examples.)

1910 *Chambers's Jrnl.* Feb. 117/2 Officers, called scout-masters, must be over eighteen. **1928** R. KNOX *Footsteps at Lock* v. 42 The scout-master, a man of some age and education. **1942** E. WAUGH *Put out More Flags* i. 14 His binoculars which she remembered vaguely having lent to the scout-master. **1977** S. BRETT *Star Trap* xi. 126 He's a scout-master and tends to be off camping..most weekends.

Hence **scou·tmastering**, the occupation of a scoutmaster; **scou·tmasterish, scou·tmasterly** *adjs.*, resembling or characteristic of a scout-master.

1937 'G. ORWELL' *Road to Wigan Pier* x. 192 Shouted out of existence with a few scoutmasterish bellows of good-will. **1954** E. HYAMS *Stories & Cream* 9 The stout, genial Scout-masterly fellow. **1957** L. DURRELL *Justine* II. 124 I've done quite a bit of scoutmastering. **1964** K. G. GRUBB *Layman looks at Church* v. 152 Any form of voluntary activity from local government to scout-mastering is in the same difficulty, namely that the pressures and claims of business make voluntary work impossible. **1979** K. BONFIGLIOLI *After You with Pistol* v. 21 He patted me on the shoulder in a scoutmasterly way.

scow[2]. Add: **1. b.** *U.S.* A small flat-bottomed racing yacht.

1929 B. HECKSTALL-SMITH *'Britannia' & her Contemporaries* viii. 82 The result of these changes was that ten years after the Britannia was built the type of racing yacht had developed into a scow with a fin keel. **1932** *Sun* (Baltimore) 13 Aug. 18/7 Pitted against the High Tide was the Inland Laker type sailing scow Elusive. **1970** *Globe & Mail* (Toronto) 25 Sept. 30/1 The Australian tub, Gretel, hit the American scow, Intrepid. **1976** *Oxf. Compan. Ships & Sea* 762/2 *Scow*,..used in the U.S.A. today to describe a small flat-bottomed racing yacht fitted with bilge boards or retractable bilge keels.

c. *transf.* Applied to one of several containers or vehicles used for transporting loads (see quots.).

1942 *Amer. Speech* XVII. 104/2 *Scow*, truck with extra-ordinary capacity for a big load. **1961** F. H. BURGESS *Dict. Sailing* 180 *Scow*,..A shallow tray for hoisting small packages of cargo. **1971** M. Tak *Truck Talk* 136 *Scow*,..a low-sided trailer used for hauling pipe, steel, stone, gravel, scrap and similar cargo. **1973** *Amer. Speech 1969* XLIV. 208 *Scow*, low-sided truck or rig used for hauling pipe or steel. **1977** *New Yorker* 18 July 23/2 There is even, in a projected television series, a pilot of a spaceship (an inter-planetary garbage scow) who is called Adam Quark.

3. scow schooner, sloop *U.S.* (see quot. 1885).

1885 *17th Ann. List. Merchant Vessels U.S.* p. xxx, Scows are built with flat bottoms and square bilges, but some of them have the ordinary schooner bow. They are fitted with one, two, and three masts, and are called *scow-sloop* or *scow schooner*, according to the rig they carry. **1913** J. London *Valley of Moon* 269 At the foot of Castro street.. the scow schooners, laden with sand and gravel, lay hauled to the shore in a long row. **1951** H. I. Chapelle *Amer. Small Sailing Craft* 334 A few scow schooners were built with round bilges, but they were comparatively rare. **1885** Scow sloop [see *scow schooner* above]. **1941** H. I. Chapelle *Boatbuilding* 28 The New Jersey oyster garvey, the Maine scow sloop, and the San Francisco scow schooner represent examples of the practical use of such hull forms. **1953** *Sunday Sun Mag.* (Baltimore) 18 Oct. 24/4 An oddity in the sloop rig was the scow sloop, once common at the head of the Chesapeake near Havre de Grace... The last in service..was abandoned about 1940.

scow, *v.*[1] **b.** (Examples.)

1751 J. MacSparran *Diary* 1 Oct. in *Letter Book* (1899) 58 He and a Boy..were Scowing wood. **1929** W. Heyliger *Builder of Dam* 39 From this point I will scow the supplies over to the job.

scow (skau), *v.*[3] *north. dial.* [Origin uncertain; prob. related to Scowbanker.] *intr.* To loiter, idle; to shirk work, play truant. Hence **sco·wing** *vbl. sb.*

1901 F. E. Taylor *Folk-Speech of S. Lancs.* s.v. *Scow*, to idle about. **1905** in *Eng. Dial. Dict.* V. 265/2 Now then, you're always scowing. **1959** I. & P. Opie *Lore & Lang. Schoolch.* xvii. 372 *Sagging*..is definitely the prevailing term [for playing truant] amongst delinquents in all parts of Liverpool. A student..adds 'scowing' as a Liverpudlian expression. **1966** F. Shaw et al. *Lern Yerself Scouse* 58, *I wuz scowing*, I was having an unofficial spell of leisure time.

scowbanker. Add: Also 8 **scou-, -bancker.** Also, † one who engages in unfair business practices, a dishonest or unscrupulous trader. (Earlier examples.)

1750 G. Beekman *Let.* 4 Dec. in P. H. White *Beekman Mercantile Papers 1746–1799* (1956) I. 136 You may thank a Sett of People Called Scowbanckers..that Seed has Run so high this two years past. Our town is full of them and there is Scarce a Vessell Comes along the wharffe but there is Imediately a half a Dozen of Them aboard bidding against Each other. **1764** —— *Let.* 30 Nov. in *Ibid.* 478 Our Vandue houses are Crowded with Linens for Sale belonging to the Scoubankers who are Offering of it from house to house for Less then Prime Cost which hurts the merchant much.

scowly (skau·li), *a.* [f. Scowl *sb.*[1] or *v.* + -y[1].] Given to scowling; sullen, morose.

1951 H. Giles *Harbin's Ridge* 64 He did take to drinking mighty heavy, and he got to acting sully and scowly. **1970** *Daily Tel.* (Colour Suppl.) 28 Aug. 21 Her scowly freckled face lights up when she laughs.

scrabble, *sb.* Add: **2.** *U.S.* A scramble; a confused struggle, a 'free-for-all'.

1794 *Gazette of U.S.* 21 Feb. 3/2 The Frenchman..in a scrabble swore he would have another hem to his ruffle, and in the very scrabble lost his shirt. **1849** T. T. Johnson *Sights in Gold Region* 66 We often got caught by the waves, and had a grand scrabble to reach dry land. **1911** R. D. Saunders *Colonel Todhunter of Missouri* 43 Whoever wins will win after the toughest scrabble you and me ever saw in Missouri politics.

3. The action or sound of scrabbling (Scrabble *v.* 2 a).

1894 T. B. Aldrich *Two Bites at Cherry* 145 The next sound I heard was the scrabble of the animal's four paws as he landed on the gravelled pathway. **1946** D. C. Peattie *Road of Naturalist* i. 12, I could not hear her breathing, but I heard another sound... Someone else was trying, with a faint scrabble, to find his way out.

Scrabble (skræ·b'l), *sb.*[2] Also **scrabble. a.** The proprietary name of a game in which players use tiles displaying individual letters to form words on a special board.

1950 *Official Gaz.* (U.S. Patent Office) 10 Jan. 334/2 The Production and Marketing Corporation, Newtown, Conn... *Scrabble.* For Game including Board and Playing Pieces. Claims use since Dec. 1, 1948. **1953** *New Yorker* 30 May 17/2 We present for your edification the history of Scrabble, the biggest thing in games since Monopoly and maybe the biggest thing ever. *Ibid.* 18/1 It was as if every-one alive were suddenly clamoring to play Scrabble. **1954** *Trade Marks Jrnl.* 21 July 736/1 *Scrabble*... 'Board games.' *Production and Marketing Corporation* (a Corporation organised and existing under the laws of the State of Connecticut, United States of America; Merchants). **1957** T. Girtin in *Pick of Punch* 150/1 My suspicions were first aroused while I was losing to my wife at 'Scrabble'. **1959** C. Spry *Favourite Flowers* iii. 25 For relaxation I sometimes play the spelling game of Scrabble and in consequence am wearing to ribbons the unwieldy volumes of the *Shorter Oxford English Dictionary*. **1962** A. Sampson *Anat. of Britain* xxvii. 450 He likes going home early,..and plays bridge or scrabble in the evenings. **1971** C. Bonington *Annapurna South Face* ix. 107 After the meal we played liar dice or Scrabble. **1978** J. Matson *Dear Osborne* xxii. 151 Scrabble, Shove Ha'penny and Draughts indicate the levels of skills and activities.

b. *attrib.* and *Comb.*

1954 *Newsweek* 26 Apr. 57 To help Scrabble fans, crossword-puzzle addicts, and other persons troubled for a word ending in 'x', 'y' or 'z', a 'reverse' dictionary has been compiled at the University of Massachusetts. **1956** N. Streatfeild *Judith* ii. 117 Cynthia sprawled over the Scrabble board. **1960** *Sunday Express* 11 Sept. 6/6, I leave it to Oscar, the Scrabble-playing cat, to dredge up obscure words. **1967** *Sci. Amer.* Sept. 268/1 The Double-Crostic and games of the Scrabble type can be thought of as combinatorial play in which 26 elements (letters) are arranged into sets (words). **1977** B. Garfield *Recoil* x. 103 Anna made a word on the Scrabble board and watched him enter the score.

scrabbling, *vbl. sb.* (Later examples.)

1958 *Washington Post* 31 Oct. a 3/1 The kind of digging, scrabbling and clawing that accomplished the rescue of the 12 who were brought out alive early today. **1974** D. Sears *Lark in Clear Air* v. 60 I'd never known anything other than hard times. Nor did rough scrabbling impose other than normal conditions on Brulé Township.

scrag (skræg), *sb.*[3] *slang. rare.* [f. Scrag *v.*: see sense 1 b, quot. 1897.] In Rugby football, a rough tackle.

1903 Wodehouse *Tales of St. Austin's* 105 There's all the difference between a decent tackle and a bally scrag like the one that doubled Tony up.

scrag, *v.* Add: **1. c.** To treat (someone) roughly, to manhandle.

1835 *Sessions Paper of Central Criminal Court* May 87 He did not take him by the collar and shake him—he did not collar him at all till after the blow was struck, nor push him at all—I did not hear Emerson say, 'You b——, I'll *scrag* you.' **1901** *Daily Colonist* (Victoria, B.C.) 31 Oct. 4/3 'What makes the crowd get up and yell?' inquired the fairy maid. 'They've scragged a man, they've scragged a man,' the woolly rooter said. **1938** [see *knocking-shop]. **1947** N. Balchin *Lord, I was Afraid* 52 Before he could say another word they scragged him. **1959** I. & P. Opie *Lore & Lang. Schoolch.* x. 198 The term 'scragging' is recurrent everywhere, and seems in fact to be different from giving someone a 'beating up' or 'bashing'. One boy makes the distinction: 'To scrag is a more gentle way of having a kind of hurtful revenge. You pull his hair and take his tie off and that sort of thing.' **1969** —— *Children's Games* vii. 219 The first one to get off, gets scragged by the other lads. **1977** H. Fast *Immigrants* iii. 193 Now they've scragged me, ruined me, destroyed me.

d. To kill, murder. *U.S.*

1930 D. Runyon in *Collier's* 20 Dec. 13/4 John the Boss is a very fine character, and it is a terrible blow to many citizens when he is scragged. **1938** —— *Furthermore* iii. 51, I see by the papers where three Brooklyn citizens are scragged. **1950** *Reader's Digest* Nov. 57 If they aim at me they will overshoot or undershoot and scrag some scared civilian.

2. (Not *slang*.) To subject (a spring or suspension system) to scragging (see below). Also with *out*: to shorten the normal length of a spring by (a specified amount) by means of scragging.

Orig. in a different sense (see quot. 1909).

1909 Webster, *Scrag*, Mech., to bend, as spring steel to test it. **1923** T. H. Sanders *Laminated Springs* xi. 89 That spring would be subjected to probably another 3½ ins. or even 4 ins. test to 'scrag out' the unwanted ½ in. *Ibid.* xxxvii. 396 (*caption*) The finished spring being scragged. **1958** A. D. Merriman *Dict. Metall.* 308/1 The spring is wound somewhat longer than the required length and then scragged by compressing it to closure several times. **1969** *Maxi Workshop Man.* (Brit. Leyland Motor Corp.) x. A7 After fitting a new displacer unit to the front or rear suspension, the system should be scragged by raising the fluid pressure, to above its normal pressure, for a short period. **1972** *Pract. Motorist* Oct. 87/2 If the displacer isn't scragged, it takes up a 'set' with the car's weight upon it—it becomes permanently compressed and the car assumes a list.

scragging *vbl. sb.* (later examples); also *spec.* the process of extending a new spring beyond the desired normal length, and then compressing it, in order to improve its strength and set; an analogous process applied to a hydraulic suspension system in a motor vehicle.

1923 T. H. Sanders *Laminated Springs* xi. 90 American practice invariably indulges in scragging machines of the 'bull-dozer' type. *Ibid.* xxxvii. 395 An illustration of 'scragging' as carried out in this country is shown by Fig. 201, which shows a 12-plate..spring undergoing its test. **1936** Horner & Sprague *Dict. Terms Mech. Engin.* (ed. 6) 486 *Scragging*, the process of testing carriage and locomotive springs by impulsive loading. **1949** A. Hynd *We are Public Enemies* 79 The Ash Brothers had committed the scragging. **1959** 'M. Innes' *Hare sitting Up* ii. iii. 61 We absolutely soaked them with our water jugs, and they gave us a wonderful scragging afterwards. **1969** *Maxi Workshop Man.* (Brit. Leyland Motor Corp.) x. A7 (*heading*) Displacer unit 'scragging'. **1977** R. B. Ross *Handbk. Metal Treatments & Testing* 338 Scragging... The process is that the spring, when initially formed, is made longer than the design requirements. By applying the necessary compression load, the length of the spring is reduced and at the same time compressive stresses are applied to the surfaces of the spring.

scraggly, *a.* Add: (Earlier and later examples.) Chiefly *U.S.*

1869 Mrs. Stowe *Oldtown Folks* xlii. 534 That's all we scraggly old people are good for. **1946** C. McCullers *Member of Wedding* ii. 57 A street preacher..was preaching on a corner to a group of warehouse coloured boys and scraggly children. **1959** T. Griffith *Waist-High Culture* (1960) 172 We are like an animal that casts off its skins too quickly; no wonder we look scraggly. **1976** *National Observer* (U.S.) 13 Mar. 12/3 At least I'm not spread-eagled any more in my skivvies and scraggly black socks.

scram (skræm), *sb.*[1] Var. Scran *sb.* 2

1831 S. Lover *Legends & Stories Ireland* 96 Bad scram to you, you thick-headed vagabone. *Ibid.* Gloss. *Bad scram*, bad food. **1881** J. Sargisson *Joe Scoap* 148 He cot a model eh what he thowt t'shap on't sud be, oot of a lump eh baykin-scram. *a* **1935** [see *aid *sb.* 1 b]. **1936** F. Clune *Roaming round Darling* xxiv. 246 After unloading flour, spuds, tea, sugar—every kind of scram, we lobbed inside the house.

scram (skræm), *sb.*[2] *Nucl. Physics.* [f. *scram *v.*[3]] The rapid shutting down of a nuclear reactor, usu. in an emergency. Freq. *attrib.*

Both this word and *scram *v.*[3] are possibly derived from *scram *v.*[2]

1953 *Nucleonics* June 40/2 Momentary-contact types [of push button] used to operate..scram circuits. **1955** *Ibid.* Sept. 53/2 Scram is initiated if preset power level is exceeded by 20%. **1959** *New Scientist* 26 Mar. 696/3 The [*Nautilus* submarine] Mark I had a constant plague of 'scrams' from such slight causes as vibration from a crew member's walking through the reactor compartment. **1968** F. Kertesz *Lang. Nuclear Sci.* (Oak Ridge Nat. Lab. TM 2367) 21 During the experiment that culminated on December 2, 1942 in the accomplishment of the first controlled nuclear chain reaction, a safety rod was held by a rope running through the pile and weighted on the opposite end. The young physicist in charge was told to watch the indicator; if it exceeded a certain value he was to cut the rope and scram. Since then the term *scram* is used to designate the emergency shutdown of a reactor. Today the urgency is lost and the word scram indicates simply a fast-shutdown operation. **1973** D. R. Inglis *Nuclear Energy* iv. 117 Emergency shutdown or scram equipment must be very sure to function properly.

scram (skræm), *v.*[2] *slang* (orig. *U.S.*). [Prob. abbrev. of Scramble *v.*; but cf. G. *schramm* imp. sing. of *schrammen* to go, depart, run away.] *intr.* To depart quickly. Freq. *imp.*

1928 W. Winchell in *N.Y. Evening Graphic* 4 Oct. 23 His [*sc.* Jack Conway's] popular slang creations include.. 'scram', meaning 'git out!' **1933** *Punch* 11 Jan. 29/3 Son, beat ut, d'ya get me?—Gwawn—S-C-R-R-A-M! **1937** D. L. Sayers *Busman's Honeymoon* iv. 84 Well, I must scram. **1940** N. Mitford *Pigeon Pie* iv. 75 She gave a sort of shriek ..and scrammed. **1947** D. M. Davin *Gorse blooms Pale* 172 You tell her to scram. **1952** J. Cannan *Body in Beck* vii. 146 'Perhaps you would be good enough to withdraw.'.. Sebastian said, 'He means scram.' **1962** Wodehouse *Service with Smile* vii. 97 'Go away, boy!' he boomed. 'You mean 'Scram!', don't you, chum?' said George, who liked to get these things right. **1973** A. Hunter *Gently French* xi. 96 Kindly hook it... I just want you to scram.

scram (skræm), *v.*[3] *Nucl. Physics.* [Etym. unkn., but see note s.v. *scram *sb.*[2]] **a.** *trans.* To shut down (a nuclear reactor), usu. in an emergency.

1950 *Amer. Speech* XXV. 27 The point of neutron intensity at which the reactor is 'scrammed'—shut down, automatically or otherwise. **1953** *Nucleonics* Jan. 40/2 The operator is provided with a control console from which he can change the position of rods, switch into automatic control, and scram the reactor. **1959** *New Scientist* 26 Mar. 695/3 A highly sensitive system of eighty different control circuits was designed to anticipate any dangerous instability of the reactor and within a fraction of a second initiate an emergency shutdown, or in the jargon of the nuclear engineer, 'scram' the reactor. **1973** D. R. Inglis *Nuclear Energy* iv. 95 The current can also be used, when it gets too strong, to trigger the emergency control rods and 'scram' or shut down the reactor. **1975** *Nature* 16 Oct. 526/1 At 1251, the operator decided to shut the reactor down by inserting the control rods into the core, thereby cutting off the chain reaction (in operator's parlance, he manually 'scrammed' the reactor).

b. *intr.* Of a nuclear reactor: to shut down, usu. in an emergency.

1957 *Nucleonics* Feb. 56/3 After a reactor scrams, the question immediately arises: What circuit caused the scram and what happened during shutdown? **1979** *New Scientist* 19 Apr. 174/1 At 2350 lb/sq. in, the reactor automatically 'scrammed' and seconds later the pressure began to drop.

Hence **scra·mming** *vbl. sb.*

1958 *Nucleonics* May 64 The entire basis for scramming ..may well need to be re-examined for future power reactors.

scramasax. (Later examples.)

1917 W. M. F. Petrie *Tools & Weapons* v. 27 Examples from Mainz.., termed scramasax, are likewise equal-curved. **1923** C. Fox *Archaeol. Cambridge Region* vi. 301 To the period 950–1066 probably belongs a fine scramasax from Barrington..with damascened blade. **1936** *Antiquity* X. 374 Typological studies of Saxon scramasaxes and spear-heads. **1962** H. R. Ellis Davidson *Sword in Anglo-Saxon Eng.* 41 Mention may be made of the short dagger or dirk (*scramasax* or *handseax*). *Ibid.* 43 A scramasax from the Thames bears the twenty-eight characters of the runic alphabet. **1977** J. I. M. Stewart *Madonna of Astrolabe*

xvii. 243 Although he possessed a mass of material of great archaeological interest and considerable value, the *scramasax* was his only major treasure.

scramble, *sb.* Add: **2. b.** A motor-cycle race across rough and hilly ground.

1926 in H. Golding *Wonder Bk. of Motors* 177 Such races as the 'T.T.' and the various other Trials and 'Scrambles' organized by the larger clubs afford manufacturers an opportunity of submitting their machines..to..severe tests. **1935** *Encycl. Sports* 539/2 *Scramble*, form of motor-cycle trial in which the competitors..traverse a course marked out over moorland or heath... Among a certain section of motor cyclists scramble events are very popular. **1959** *New Statesman* 14 Nov. 658/1 About 50,000 people now turn out every week to watch the dozen or so scrambles organised throughout the country. **1969** *Daily Tel.* 25 Oct. 8/8 A scramble can best be described as a motorised form of a cross-country race over a short, rough course sometimes reserved for the purpose and often adjacent to a road-racing circuit. **1977** 'E. Crispin' *Glimpses of Moon* xi. 213 The motor-cycle scramble had arrived.

c. *Mil. slang.* A rapid or operational take-off by a group of aircraft. Cf. sense *4 of the vb.

1940 G. Barclay *Diary* 2 Sept. in *Fighter Pilot* (1976) 44, I came on the state after this scrap and we had three scrambles. [**1954** I. Jones *Tiger Squadron* xxii. 228 To Sailor's dismay, his scramble order had not been received quickly enough.] **1957** G. Wallace *R.A.F. Biggin Hill* xi. 139 Three scrambles a day were common, often more. **1963** *Times* 11 June 7/1 The royal visitors watched a 'scramble' of four R.A.F. Vulcan bombers of the quick-reaction alert force. **1969** P. Richey *Fighter Pilot* p. xii, He wanted to publish it if I would finish it. I did so..in the evenings after a day spent instructing on fighters in Gloucestershire and, later, between 'scrambles' and fighter sweeps. **1976** *Derbyshire Times* (Peak ed.) 3 Sept. 24/4 Featured in the spectacular flying display will be a scramble (operational take-off) by a pair of Vulcan bombers.

d. *U.S. Football.* An impromptu movement by a quarterback to evade tacklers. Cf. sense *1 d of the vb.

1971 Tarkenton & Yates *Broken Patterns* 52 Naturally the scramble plays were the most spectacular. **1972** J. Mosedale *Football* vi. 89 A man who played as though he invented the scramble.

3. *Cookery.* A dish composed of hastily-mixed ingredients; an informal meal of such dishes. Cf. Scrambling *ppl. a.* 1.

1893 Yonge & Coleridge *Strolling Players* xxii. 187 Selva's Irish hospitality could allow no one to depart in the rain, and her Irish happy-go-luckiness saw nothing to be ashamed of in a scramble. **1898** J. D. Brayshaw *Slum Silhouettes* 42 Some of the ladies of the district, deeming the short cut to a poor man's soul was through his vitals, invited them to a free 'muffin scramble'. **1938** E. Waugh *Scoop* I. i. 18 The recipe for a dish named 'Waffle Scramble'. **1958** *Woman's Own* 17 Sept. 15/1 Halve the rolls... Fill with the tuna scramble.

4. *Comb.*, as **scramble net** *Naut.*, a heavy net down which persons may climb from a ship in an emergency; also in *gen.* use, the webbing of a child's climbing frame.

1944 *Amer. Speech* XIX. 106 The *scramble net* (a new term in this war; it is an oversize cargo net hung over the side in times of imminent peril as an aid to getting down to water level without breaking your back). **1948** A. Baron *From City from Plough* 134 Sailors pulled at cords and the wet scramble nets thumped over the sides. **1953** *Physical Educ. in Primary School* (Min. of Educ.) II. vi. 32 (*caption*) Infants using a scramble net which is supported on a fixed tubular metal frame. **1976** *Outdoor Living* (N.Z.) I. ii. 49 (*caption*) Other attachments, such as a scramble net could be put on the frame as children outgrow the present equipment. **1979** 'G. Black' *Night Run from Java* xiii. 162 The patrol boat crew [was] going down the scramble net into the lifeboat.

scramble, *v.* Add: **1. c.** Also (freq. with advbs.), to cause (something) to move in the direction or manner indicated without proper control; to deal with hastily or ill-advisedly.

1869 *Punch* 3 July 270/2 One 'Lord Hamilton' who had been scrambling away his money, at a low public in Shadwell. **1911** *Q. Rev.* July 218 Amendments hastily scrambled through committee in a House of Commons. **1931** *Times* 28 Feb. 4 The putter scrambled the ball in from a foot away. **1976** *Oadby & Wigston* (Leics.) *Advertiser* 26 Nov. 15/1 His shot hit the bar, and eventually Snee and his defence scrambled the ball free.

d. *intr. U.S. Football.* (See quot. 1976.)

1964 *Birmingham* (Alabama) *News* 26 Oct. 20/1 Campbell had to scramble to get off passes to Jimmy Martin, Scotty Long or Ronnie Baynes. **1968** *N.Y. Times* 13 Aug. 31 It was Tarkenton who engineered this monumental upheaval, mainly because he bewildered the Packers with his scrambling. **1976** *Webster's Sports Dict.* 373/2 *Scramble*, ..of a football quarterback, to run around behind the line of scrimmage dodging would-be tacklers after initial pass protection has broken down before passing or running.

3. b. *fig.* To jumble or muddle (something).

1927 G. Ade et al. *Let.* 4 Mar. (1973) 118 When you are in the native quarter [of Algiers] you can well imagine you are in the Old Testament which has been scrambled, stood on edge and saturated with all the disagreeable odors in the world. **1950** *Times Lit. Suppl.* 27 Jan. 55/4 The characters have been 'scrambled' so that none shall be recognizable. **1962** *Listener* 5 Apr. 603/1 The different arts are being run together and the borders of art and nature are being scrambled. **1977** *Time* 10 Jan. 43/1 Their landing permits had been deliberately scrambled by the Cuban government in league with the Nazis, who wanted the ship to sail from port to port searching for asylum.

c. To make (a telephone or radio signal of a voice) unintelligible by means of a scrambler (see *Scrambler 3 a); to render (a television transmission) usable only by a subscriber equipped with a suitable unscrambling device. Also *transf.* and *absol.*

1927 *Gen. Electr. Rev.* XXX. 84/2 A Hammond multiplex system may be used with seven intermediate carrier waves which are scrambled and sent out by a single transmitter and then unscrambled at the receiving station so that each controls one of the seven light beams. **1929** *Times* 9 Nov. 12/2 An improved means for ensuring the secrecy of radio-telephonic conversations by 'scrambling' the words of the message—that is, by changing high frequencies to low frequencies and *vice versa*, so that the conversation is completely unintelligible until the 'inverted' conversation has been retranslated. **1949** F. Maclean *Eastern Approaches* III. xii. 445 When we resumed our conversation [on the telephone], the Prime Minister was off on a new tack. 'Shall we scramble?' he said gaily. I replied that I thought I was scrambled. **1955** *Times* 4 June 6/6 All three work on the principle of a device attached to the subscriber's television set which 'scrambles' the programmes to be televised until a fee is paid to unscramble them. **1959** E. H. Clements *High Tension* v. 74, I was beginning to wonder..whether we ought to scramble the telephone. **1978** G. Greene *Human Factor* II. iv. 89 There was the usual confusion: one of them pressing the right button too soon and then going back to normal transmission just when the other scrambled.

4. *Mil. slang.* **a.** *intr.* Of an aircraft (as a fighter plane, etc.) or crew: to effect a rapid take-off; to become airborne quickly. orig. *R.A.F.*

1940 G. Barclay *Diary* 2 Sept. in *Fighter Pilot* (1976) 44 The squadron scrambled and intercepted some Do215s and Me110s. **1941** [see *Angel *v.* 2]. **1942** Brennan & Hesselyn *Spitfires over Malta* 15 The signal to scramble came at about eleven o'clock... We rushed to our aircraft and in less than two minutes were off the ground. **1944** *Daily Tel.* 15 May 5/3 Hardly were they past the carrier than two Corsairs 'scrambled' off the deck to 'intercept an enemy plane'. **1952** *Times* 22 Feb. 6/4 A red Very light was fired as a warning to the pilots to 'scramble', and exactly 80 seconds later the first fighter was in the air. **1962** R. W. Clark *Rise of Boffins* ii. 53 Another great time-saver was the use of a code for passing instructions to the fighters, and such R.A.F. terms as 'scramble' (for take-off)..were invented during these experiments [on radar interception, 1936]. **1977** *R.A.F. News* 5–18 Jan. 1/1 A Wessex SAR helicopter of 22 Squadron's E flight was scrambling from Manston.

b. *trans.* To cause (an aircraft) to become airborne quickly.

1940 G. Barclay *Diary* 3 Sept. in *Fighter Pilot* (1976) 46 The squadron was off the ground which was the main thing, but they were scrambled too late to intercept. **1953** *Sun* (Baltimore) 18 Sept. 2/2 Col. Richard T. Hernlund..showed reporters he could 'scramble' the interceptors and get them into the air almost instantly. **1971** *Daily Tel.* 20 July 8/7 The final decision to scramble fighters or launch nuclear missiles is..made by..highly trained officers. **1975** *Radio Times* 14 Aug. 38/1 A call to the coastguard and the nearest rescue helicopter can be scrambled within seconds. **1978** R. V. Jones *Most Secret War* xli. 383 It was clear that their technique was to 'scramble' their fighters on a raid warning and instruct them to orbit one of a number of visual and radio beacons. **1981** *Times* 9 June 6/8 The Iraqis.. gave no indication whether Iraqi jet fighters had been scrambled in an attempt to shoot down the Israeli planes.

5. *Comb.*, as **scramble button**, a button which activates a scrambler (sense *3 a) when pressed.

1962 L. Deighton *Ipcress File* xxx. 194 The wall phone rang... I saw Jay push the 'scramble' button.

scrambled, *ppl. a.* Add: **a.** (Later examples.)

1930 *Daily Express* 6 Sept. 4/6 A series of mixed or 'scrambled' wave lengths, the key to which would only be in the possession of individual subscribers to the television service. **1949** *Jrnl. R. Aeronaut. Soc.* LIII. 29/1 Subjected to the rapid change of temperature when simulating 'scrambled take-offs'. **1951** *Good Housek. Home Encycl.* 170/2 Pack..loosely rolled or 'scrambled' sheets of newspaper..over the surface. **1962** L. Deighton *Ipcress File* xi. 70, I will want to use a phone in private—a scrambled line if possible. **1975** J. I. M. Stewart *Gaudy* xii. 218, I pictured Mogridge..in some high-powered but unobtrusive car—one equipped, no doubt, with telephonic devices enabling him to hold scrambled conversations with various quarters of the globe as he went along.

c. *scrambled egg(s)* fig., the gold braid or insignia worn on an officer's dress uniform (esp. the cap); hence by metonymy, an officer. *slang* (chiefly *Forces'*).

1943 C. H. Ward-Jackson *It's Piece of Cake* 52 *Scrambled egg*,..an officer of the rank of Group Captain or above. *Ibid.* 53 *Scrambled eggs*, the gold braid or oak leaves on the peak of the dress service cap of an officer of the rank of Group Captain or above. **1946** J. Batten *Dirty Little Collier* iv. 32 Most collier men hate their 'scrambled egg' caps, and won't wear them at all. **1958** M. Dickens *Man Overboard* iv. 60, I don't care about the scrambled egg, but it may be a bit tough at first, not being an officer. **1961** C. Brooke-Rose *Middlemen* i. 7 A blue-grey uniform with three rings round his wrist. Then four. Then a big broad one and scrambled eggs. **1968** J. Lock *Lady Policeman* ix. 84 The car drivers.. don't know which one to obey..being intimidated by all that scrambled egg on their caps. **1973** R. Dougall *In & Out of Box* xiii. 157 An older pilot with some 'scrambled-egg' on his cap was produced. **1978** *Detroit Free Press* 5 Mar. (Parade Suppl.) 14A/4 (Advt.), Capture the soaring spirit of American history—proud cap has smart military styling with golden 'scrambled eggs' & braid trim hand-sewn on the visor.

scrambler. Add: **I. 1.** (Later sporting examples.)

1954 M. Connolly *Power Tennis* 66 Many times I have seen a scrambler unnerve a much better player merely by returning her best placements. **1958** *Oxford Mail* 27 Aug. 4/9 Most of Britain's leading motor-cycle scramblers will be at Brill on October 5. **1961** *Times* 29 Apr. 3/2 Can it be that his consummate skill as a scrambler is beginning to weigh on him? **1967** *Time* 17 Mar. 55 He is known in the trade as a 'scrambler', who would just as soon run as throw, who can turn a potential 10-yd. loss into a 50-yd. gain. **1972** J. Mosedale *Football* vi. 86 Quarterbacks usually identified as scramblers got that reputation because they had to run after inept teammates failed to block for them.

II. That which scrambles. **2.** A plant, often a climbing one, depending on the support of others.

1902 L. H. Bailey *Cycl. Amer. Hort.* IV. 1935/2 There are many useful climbers among the scramblers. **1953** *Brit. Commonwealth Forest Terminol.* (Empire Forestry Assoc.) I. 116 Scrambler. A plant which, owing to lack of rigidity in its stem, and absence of special climbing organs, uses other vegetation as its support. **1974** *Country Life* 21 Mar. 642/3 This large-flowered scrambler [*sc.* a Cretan Aristolochia] is probably not very hardy.

3. a. An electronic device used, esp. in telephony and radio, to make speech signals unintelligible, usu. by dividing the signal into distinct frequency ranges which are separately inverted and displaced in frequency.

1950 G. Hackforth-Jones *Worst Enemy* i. 24 This line, which linked me directly with the Rear-Admiral, was fitted with a device known as a 'scrambler' which was completely secure against listening in and it was therefore possible to speak freely and at length at all times. **1968** *New Scientist* 19 Dec. 657/3 A simple scrambler that will turn high speech frequencies into low speech frequencies and vice versa can be bought for about £100. **1973** 'I. Drummond' *Jaws of Watchdog* ii. 31 The radio..had a scrambler, so that if the message was picked up accidentally it sounded like static. **a 1974** R. Crossman *Diaries* (1975) I. 41 Having made a big fuss about national security to George Wigg I have decided to be extremely careful in everything I do personally so I've had scramblers and big safes installed in London as well as here at Prescote. **1981** A. Melville-Ross *Tightrope* vi. 36 You can get me..the Minister's Private Secretary..on the scrambler.

fig. **1958** *Listener* 13 Nov. 791/3 Your work of art..has to suffer a further change as it goes through the scrambler of your reader's prejudices.

b. *attrib.*, as *scrambler line, phone, system, telephone*.

1958 L. Durrell *Balthazar* ii. 29 His work was invisibly dictated by a scrambler telephone. **1958** *Listener* 25 Sept. 462/2 It is a variant of the scrambler system which has been long in use for confidential telephonic communication. **1965** *Times* 16 Feb. 12/2 The 'scrambler' telephone can now be bought for £50 by individual companies. **1966** J. Bingham *Double Agent* xi. 162 He lifted the scrambler telephone. .. 'A scrambled phone is safe, but not entirely safe.' **1974** G. Markstein *Cooler* lxviii. 234 He..made a call on the scrambler line to London. **1975** 'M. Sinclair' *Long Time Sleeping* ix. 115 Pringle..switched on the scrambler phone and started writing. **1977** C. Forbes *Avalanche Express* II. xi. 118 Scholten took the call on his scrambler phone.

scrambling, *vbl. sb.* Add: **a.** (Later examples.)

1930 *Engineering* 14 Nov. 626/1 The apparatus used for this scrambling, as it is called, is installed at the Central Telegraph Office. **1942** V. E. R. Blunt *Use of Air Power* viii. 72 Wireless telegraphy and radio telephony..by 'scrambling' can now be made secret. **1955** 'N. Shute' *Requiem for Wren* 166 We were in the process of scrambling when the Jerries came over. **1959** *New Statesman* 14 Nov. 658/1 The simplest definition of scrambling is: the racing of motor bikes over rough ground. **1978** *Guardian Weekly* 24 Sept. 22/5 Scrambling, as distinct from fell walking and rock climbing, is a Cinderella of a sport.

b. *scrambling club*; **scrambling net** *Mil.* = *scramble net* s.v. *Scramble *sb.* 4; also *transf.*

1961 *Guardian* 17 Mar. 3/3 Motor-cycle scrambling clubs. **1974** G. Moffat *Corpse Road* iv. 64 She belonged to a scrambling club, which means walking... It doesn't mean rock climbing. **1959** *New Scientist* 30 July 125/1 Home grown seeds are extracted from cones, sometimes collected by means of a 'scrambling net'..thrown over a tall tree. **1964** C. Willock *Enormous Zoo* v. 75 The long-forgotten sensation of climbing down the scrambling net of a troop transport into a landing craft. **1973** A. Ross *Dunfermline Affair* 36 The scrambling net which the *Hermione* put over her side.

scramblingly, *adv.* (Later examples.)

1923 D. H. Lawrence *Ladybird* 242 For some time.. Alexander gingerly and scramblingly led the way. The slope of ice was steeper, and rounded, so that it was difficult to stand up. **1949** D. L. Sayers tr. *Dante's Inferno* xxiv. 221, I..came Scramblingly up and sat down.

scrambly (skræ·mbli), *a.* [f. Scramble *sb.* + -y[1].] **1.** Of a person, limb, etc.: that scrambles, clambers, or claws. Also applied to an informal meal. Cf. Scrambling *ppl. a.* 1.

In quot. 1900 applied to a jumble of people at a meal.

1900 R. Proctor *Diary* 26 Mar. in V. Scholderer *Fifty Ess. 15th- & 16th-Cent. Bibliogr.* (1966) 34 A company of about 16... A most amusing scrambly supper in a room calculated to hold four at most. **1943** C. McCullers in *Harper's Bazaar* Aug. 140/3 The hunchback reached in the box with his scrambly little fingers. **1977** *Time* 5 Dec. 49/1 Little scrambly front legs and big thumping back legs.

2. Characterized by scrambling or clambering over rough terrain; that necessitates such action.

1900 G. Bell *Let.* 28 Feb. (1927) I. v. 65 We had a very scrambly walk back. **1932** A. Christie *Peril at End House* ii. 34 There's a scrambly cliff path down to the sea.

scramjet (skræ·mdʒet). *Aeronaut.* [f. the initial letters of *s*upersonic *c*ombustion + *ramjet.] A ramjet in which combustion takes place in a stream of gas moving at supersonic speed.

1966 *New Scientist* 19 May 429 (*caption*) Supersonic combustion ramjets ('scramjets') theoretically could extend flight speeds to at least Mach 14. **1972** D. G. Shepherd *Aerospace Propulsion* iv. 110 There is considerable interest in supersonic combustion as this is the key to the scramjet.

scran, *sb.* Add: **2. a.** Also *spec.* in *Naut. slang*, food, rations.

1916 'Taffrail' *Pincher Martin* i. 8 Them two's on watch now, but they'll be down at eight bells clamourin' for their scran like a lot o' wolves. *a* **1935** T. E. Lawrence *Mint* (1955) 135 'Scran up!' he called in his sailor's belling tone against my ear. **1974** *Sentinel* (Ottawa) X. ii. 6/3 He's the chief cook on board, responsible for the preparation and serving of food—or 'scran', according to the hands—to 280 hungry mouths about three times a day.

scrannel, *a.* (Further examples.)

1927 E. F. Benson *Lucia in London* ii. 60 It was strange.. to hear..the foe of all modern music..producing these scrannel staccato tinklings that had so often made her wince. **1934** [see *mimsey *a.*]. **1951** Auden *Nones* (1952) 54 His scrannel music-making. **1976** *New Yorker* 1 Mar. 89/1 But the music Berlioz heard in St. Peter's was scrannel stuff, and it was years before he himself received the commissions to compose.

scrap, *sb.*[1] Add: **2. a.** (*b*) *scrap of paper*: applied contemptuously to a document containing a treaty or pledge which one does not intend to honour.

The phrase is said to have been used by the German Chancellor, Bethmann-Hollweg (1856–1921), in connection with German violation of Belgian neutrality in August 1914 (cf. G. *ein Fetzen Papier*). Some later examples allude to this.

1840 *Chambers's Edin. Jrnl.* 11 Apr. 94/1 He no more dreamt of..honouring his scraps of paper..than of paying the national debt. **1914** E. Goschen *Let.* 8 Aug. in *Coll. Diplomatic Documents rel. Outbreak Europ. War* (1915) 111 The Chancellor said that..just for a word—'neutrality',—just for a scrap of paper Great Britain was going to make war on a kindred nation. **1918** *Daily Mail Year Bk.* 1919 62/1 Those familiar with the 'scrap of paper' theory need hardly be told that the pledges given by the German Emperor.. were not observed. **1932** K. Campbell *Sarah, Duchess of Marlborough* 83 James made it plainer every day..that, compared with his Church, the constitution of England and his own coronation oaths were mere scraps of paper. **1954** W. K. Hancock *Country & Calling* iv. 111 The British Empire, not so many years back, had professed itself to be at war with the doctrine that a treaty was only 'a scrap of paper'. **1974** M. Gilbert *Flash Point* vi. 50 The First World War was fought over a small thing. A scrap of paper. **1980** *Times* 3 July 17/2 The Treaty of Union..wasn't a sacrosanct document, but in empirically English fact, just a 'scrap of paper'.

d. A small person. *colloq.*

1898 H. James *Two Magics* 60 'Perhaps she likes it!' 'Likes *such* things—a scrap of an infant!' **1928** E. P. Oppenheim *Chron. Melhampton* v. 146, I wasn't here for long, and I was a scrap of a fellow those days. **1939** N. Streatfeild *Luke* 109, I didn't know the poor little scrap could look so radiant. **1958** *Woman's Jrnl.* Mar. 77/2 'The woman?'.. 'They picked her up late last night. Poor little scrap.'

6. *scrap dealer, dealing, merchant, -metal*; **scrap basket,** a waste-paper basket; **scrap-ground** = *scrapyard* below; **scrap man,** one whose business is the collection and sale of scrap-metal and its salvageable accessories; **scrap paper,** paper that may be repulped or used again; rough paper for casual jotting; **scrap screen** chiefly *Hist.*, a screen or divider (as in a nursery) decorated with scraps (sense 2 c); **scrapyard,** the site of a scrap-heap; *spec.* a place where disused motor vehicles, etc., are scrapped.

1872 C. M. Yonge *P's & Q's* ix. 94 If she put it in the scrap basket, Persis herself might look in and see the writing. **1912** E. Pound *Let.* Dec. (1971) 13, I won't quarrel with you over what you see fit to put in the scrap basket. **1976** *Loughborough Monitor* 26 Nov., He had worked as a scrap dealer while claiming supplementary benefit. **1977** *Belfast Tel.* 22 Feb. 4/1 (*caption*) For scrap dealing..two heads better than one. **1927** *Observer* 21 Aug. 19/2 Six years is about the maximum age of the cars taken for scrapping in America. Some reach the scrap-ground much earlier. *Ibid.*, The scrap man's interest in these vehicles is purely that of a replacement part merchant. **1977** *Custom Car* Nov. 5/1 When it comes to fridge pumps, beware. The scrapman is out to con you. **1978** R. V. Jones *Most Secret War* i. 5 It certainly was tough, the future of my contemporaries encompassing everything from barrow boy to millionaire scrapmerchant and trade union peer. **1941** *Proc. Prehist. Soc.* VII. 130 The Bronze Age pieces must be ..scrap-metal. **1962** A. Battersby *Guide to Stock Control* .3 The petty cash box resembles the scrap-metal example in reverse. **1885** *Encycl. Brit.* XVIII. 228/2 The materials for the commoner classes of work are old waste and scrap paper, repulped... For very delicate relief ornaments, a pulp of scrap paper is prepared. **1960** M. Spark *Bachelors* xi. 195 Marlene walked solemnly downstairs and demanded some scrap paper from the hall porter. **1969** C. Irving *Fake!* (1970) iii. 39 He..made some preliminary sketches for several hours on scrap paper. **1873** *Young Englishwoman* Jan. 51/3 Lizzie would be glad if the Editor could give her any information as to making a scrap screen. **1899** M. Beerbohm *More* 173 They will make the scrap-screen their background. **1962** N. Marsh *Hand in Glove* v. 148 The room was masked from its entrance by an old-fashioned scrap screen. **1964** S. Nowell-Smith *Edwardian England* iv. 201 The dark, cosy Victorian nursery.. brightened by the varnished scrap-screen. **1963** *Times* 11 Jan. 10/3 (*heading*) Tow breaks on way to scrapyard. **1978** T. Allbeury *Lantern Network* iv. 59 A scrapyard with big double gates.

scrap, *sb.*[2] Add: **2. a.** (Earlier and later examples.) Also *gen.*, a contest.

1846 *Swell's Night Guide* 75 By way of varying the slang, the mock combat turns into a right good scrap. **1916** [see *bandbox b]. **1959** [see *go *sb.* 4 b]. **1973** *Times* 10 Dec. 9/5 In a final that provided a keen scrap rather than a match of high quality, they beat the Etonians. **1977** J. Cleary *High Road to China* v. 158 My chaps..[are] itching for a scrap, y'know.

b. A contest of words; a row, quarrel, squabble; a heated discussion.

1890 Barrère & Leland *Dict. Slang* II. 210/1 Having a *scrap up* is having a quarrel, a row. **1900** *Dialect Notes* II. 57 *Scrap*,..a quarrel of words, sometimes good-natured. **1903** *N.Y. Tribune* 6 Sept. 2/2 In directing the proceedings ..Mr. Hill was careful to sidetrack anything containing the germ of a 'scrap'. **1928** J. Galsworthy *Swan Song* ii. xi. 199 It was his impression that they'd been having a scrap.

scrap, *v.*[2] Add: **b.** Also *fig.*

1936 L. C. Douglas *White Banners* xvi. 335, I have given him until June first to scrap it out with himself.

c. *intr.* To quarrel, squabble; to engage in heated argument or angry dispute.

1895 W. C. Gore in *Inlander* Nov. 65 *Scrap*,..to quarrel. **1900** *Dialect Notes* II. 57 *Scrap*,..to quarrel, sometimes good-naturedly. **1923** *Daily Mail* 28 June 5 Are you going on scrapping over this garden fence for the rest of your lives? **1941** B. Schulberg *What makes Sammy Run?* vii. 120 The play..was one of those things about two red-blooded guys who are always scrapping and loving each other.

scrap-book. Add: **b.** *transf.* A loosely-constructed documentary review programme, normally covering a particular year or period, presented on radio by the B.B.C.

1933 *Radio Times* 8 Dec. 719/2 Scrapbook for 1913. *Ibid.* 740/2 This is no history book—just a scrapbook of cherished fragments. **1939** H. Nicolson *Diary* 3 Dec. (1967) 47 After the news there is a B.B.C. scrap-book for 1910. **1947** L. MacNeice *Dark Tower* 69 Features..have..a great diversity of form. Some of them are as loosely constructed as scrap-books. **1959** *Listener* 23 July 150/2 The programmes ..were almost identical exercises in the well-proven genre of biographical scrap-book. **1972** P. Black *Biggest Aspidistra in World* i. v. 43 The famous Scrapbooks, in popularity and appreciation the most successful dramatised radio series ever produced in Britain..began in 1933... The title Scrapbook first appeared in *Radio Times* in 1932.

c. *attrib.*

1897 H. James *Spoils of Poynton* i. 5 Trumpery ornament and scrapbook art. **1934** C. Lambert *Music Ho!* i. 75 Diaghileff..was able to invest with a revolutionary glamour the scrapbook mentality which in his later years he exploited with so marked a success.

scrap-book *v.* (earlier example); hence **scra·p-booking** *vbl. sb.*

1879 'Mark Twain' *Let.* 12 Nov. (1917) I. 369 Put the enclosed scraps in the drawer and I will scrap-book them. *c* **1898** —— *Autobiogr.* (1924) I. 139 He usually postponed the scrap-booking until Sunday.

scrape, *sb.*[1] Add: **I. 2. d.** (Earlier example.)

c **1807** Jane Austen *Watsons* in *Minor Wks.* (1954) 327 No sound of a Ball but the first Scrape of one violin.

h. A dilatation of the cervix and curettage of the womb; *spec.* an induced abortion. *slang.*

1968 J. Hudson *Case of Need* iii. i. 172 The word got around..that she got a bad scrape. **1972** *Rochdale's Alternative Paper* No. 6. 10/2 The most common method [of abortion] in Britain for pregnancies of less than three months is D. & C. (better known to most women as a scrape). **1980** M. Drabble *Middle Ground* 62 She was having a D and C, a routine scrape.

4. c. *Ornith.* A shallow pit in the ground excavated by a bird, usu. during a courtship display; also, the action of making such a pit.

1926 *Ibis* II. 7 All the scrapes noted were within about fifty or sixty yards from a nest. **1940** H. F. Witherby et al. *Handbk. Brit. Birds* IV. 385 In more advanced scrapes female with back to male will peck in bottom of scrape. **1942** E. A. Armstrong *Bird Display* ii. 27 An unmated female red-necked phalarope makes scrapes in the herbage, and from the first day of finding a mate this 'ceremony' often follows coition... Before laying, the female visits the various scrapes and lays an egg in one of them. **1961** [see *scrape ceremony* s.v. *scrape *v.* 10 b]. **1967** B. Campbell *J. Hanzák's Pictorial Encycl. of Birds* 254/2 The nest is a shallow scrape lined with small stones or shells.

6*. On a woodwind instrument, the part of the cane that is scraped to a narrow edge in the production of a reed. Also, the style of this scraping.

1954 *Grove's Dict. Mus.* (ed. 5) VI. 161/2 According to the quality of the cane from which it is made, and the character of its 'scrape', a reel [of an oboe] may be responsive or unyielding. **1961** Sprenkle & Ledet *Art of Oboe Playing* 95/2 The French scrape has a rather long tip. **1980** *Early Music* July 363/2 There are 3 basic scrapes..of which no. 1 is the most common.

scrape, *v.* Add: **2. f.** To clean or empty *out* by scraping.

1894 'R. Andom' *We Three & Troddles* xxi. 198 When you have done with that jam you might let me have the pot to scrape out. **1919** E. Shackleton *South* xii. 237 As the cook and his 'mate' had the privilege of scraping out the saucepans, there was some anxiety to secure the job. **1925** *Morris Owner's Man.* 14 Thoroughly scrape out and oil cams until they work quite freely.

g. To draw (hair) tightly *back* from the forehead. Cf. *scraped *ppl. a.* 2 b.

1926 'O. Douglas' *Proper Place* xxxi. 280, I couldn't have believed she had such pretty, soft hair for she wore it scraped back.

5. d. In *fig.* phr. *to scrape* (*the bottom of*) *the barrel* (or *bucket*): to collect with difficulty something inferior; to obtain something (as by necessity) from a poor source. *slang* (orig. *U.S.*).

1942 *Time* 12 Jan. 57/1 The medical profession..[is] closer to scraping the bottom of the bucket..than any other occupation, trade or profession. **1955** *N.Y. Times Bk. Rev.* 30 Oct. 1/1 It was built in the spring of 1864, when the Confederacy was scraping the bottom of its barrel of men and resources. **1957** *Essays in Criticism* VII. 342, I was scraping the barrel for evidence. **1961** B. Fergusson *Watery Maze* viii. 203 The insistence of the Americans that the Casablanca assault should be much the strongest.. meant scraping the bottom of the barrel to find extra ships, craft and crews. **1970** *Times* 5 Nov. 14/4 Professor Barlow explains how necessary it is to 'scrape the barrel' for even the most minor scraps of information. **1981** *Times* 18 Aug. 1/3 We shall have to pay something. I hope to be able to scrape the barrel and come up with something.

9. a. Also with other advs. or advb. phrases in similar senses, as *to scrape by, home, in*, etc.

1927 *Observer* 18 Sept. 17/3 Mr. Blythe, who at the last election scraped home in Monaghan. **1951** *Sport* 6–12 Apr. 17/2 The Airmen just scraped through with a 3–2 win. **1958** *Times* 16 Dec. 4/4 (*heading*) Chigwell scrape home. **1958** [see *million 2 f]. **1966** *Listener* 1 Dec. 829/1 Osbert Lancaster..depends on words rather than drawing, understandably since his drawing..only just scrapes by. **1973** M. Woodhouse *Blue Bone* iv. 35 The family didn't get on with the Germans and they only just barely scraped by with the Communists. **1978** 'M. M. Kaye' *Far Pavilions* vii. 114 As long as he can shoot and ride, I suppose he'll scrape past.

c. To acquire or obtain (something) with difficulty. *colloq.*

1963 *Guardian* 9 Aug. 7/1 He read English at Oxford. 'But I only scraped a third.' **1967** *Listener* 2 Mar. 283/1 The Congress Party, which has ruled the country since independence in 1947, has just managed to scrape a majority in the central parliament. **1980** *Early Music* Apr. 234/1 Nor does *castrato* appear in the index (though Farinelli scrapes a mention).

10. b. scrape ceremony *Ornith.*, a display by a bird, involving the excavation of a shallow pit in the ground and the pressing of the bird's breast into this, freq. performed during courtship; hence **scrape-ceremonial** *a.*

1926 Huxley & Montague in *Ibis* II. 10 Nervous picking at grass..may be seen during incubation, scrape-ceremonies and before coition. **1949** *British Birds* XLII. 8 Both sexes indulge in the 'scrape' ceremony and in many of the actions characteristic of nest-building. **1961** D. A. Bannerman *Birds Brit. Isles* IX. 15 The main type of sexual behaviour preceding coition is the tail-display... At this stage the scrape-ceremony is very common, a typically male performance by which he lures the female to one scrape after another. *Ibid.* X. 247 Dotterel and red-necked phalarope..share very similar scrape-ceremonial and egg-laying behaviour.

scraped, *ppl. a.* Add: **2. a.** Also *scraped together*.

1965 *Listener* 3 June 828/1 In June 1942 the hastily scraped together force called 23rd Indian Division, with which I was serving, was isolated from the rest of the world.

b. Designating women's hair that has been drawn back tightly from the forehead. Also *scraped-back*. Cf. *scrape *v.* 2 g.

1970 'D. Halliday' *Dolly & Cookie Bird* viii. 118 Her deep-set eyes smiling gratefully under the grey, scraped-back hair. **1977** *Times* 16 Sept. 7/8 Her scraped hair, self-effacing manner, and busy hands. **1978** I. Murdoch *Sea* 156 Her scraped-back hair revealed her bulky rounded brow.

scraper. Add: **II. 4. f.** More fully *cabinet scraper*. A thin rectangular piece of metal whose sharpened long edge is pushed over the surface of wood to smooth it.

1909 Wells & Hooper *Mod. Cabinet Work* v. 72 A carefully sharpened scraper frequently permits of about twelve resharpenings in all. **1924** H. G. Phillips *Cabinetmaking* i. 14 A very fine shaving is taken off with the scraper, which leaves the surface ready to be glasspapered. **1970** *Canadian Antiques Collector* Jan. 27/2 The only satisfactory method is the use of a cabinet scraper. **1977** *Reader's Digest Bk. Do-it-Yourself Skills & Techniques* ii. 77/1 Cabinet scrapers give a satin-smooth finish to hardwood. *Ibid.*, If a scraper becomes hot and produces dust instead of shavings during use, it needs resharpening.

g. *Mus.* A simple percussion instrument.

1953 J. G. MOORE in *Dict. Jamaican Eng.* (1967) 396/1 The scraper, a corrugated stick across which is rubbed a plain stick [in pocomania and revivalist services]. **1956** M. STEARNS *Story of Jazz* (1957) v. 53 The typically African instruments, such as drums, gourd rattles, and scrapers. **1958** E. BORNEMAN in P. Gammond *Decca Bk. Jazz* xxi. 275 One of the many..indigenous African string instruments, hand drums, scrapers, shakers and gong-gong. **1961** A. BAINES *Musical Instruments through Ages* i. 27 Scrapers have survived into modern times, for instance in the folk music of Venezuela. **1976** D. MUNROW *Instr. Middle Ages & Renaissance* 32/2 Most of the instrumental types described are of very ancient origin indeed, drums, rattles, and scrapers being the commonest instruments of primitive man.

7. a. In mod. use *spec.* an earth-mover, either self-propelled or towed, that works on the principle of a scoop. (Earlier and later examples.)

1815 T. B. HAZARD *Nailer Tom's Diary* (1930) 442/2 Delivered C. R. Potter p[ai]r Scrapers and a Chain to hich horseis with. **1823** *New England Farmer* II. 9 The most expeditious, effectual, and economic mode of making a drain would undoubtedly be to use oxen, and a scraper or ox-shovel, as it is sometimes called. **1930** *Engineering* 7 Mar. 306/1 There are three of these scrapers in each warehouse, their function being to drag down the potash from the several heaps into the central longitudinal opening in the floor. **1939** C. W. TOWNE *Her Majesty Montana* 120 Abolishing the back-breaking labor of mucking, power driven scrapers and mechanical mucking machines are now usual. **1958** *Engineering* 14 Feb. 219 For outside work the three most important types of machine—all rubber tyred—are the self-propelled scrapers, mechanical shovels and the cranes. **1974** *Encycl. Brit. Micropædia* VIII. 996/2 The scraper is the dominant tool in highway construction.

c. (Earlier example.)

1881 E. INGERSOLL *Oyster-Industry* 247 *Scraper*, a small dredge. Chiefly spoken of with reference to scallops.

7*. = *PIG *sb.*[1] 8*.

1897 B. J. CREW *Practical Treat. Petroleum* xiv. 449 Under ordinary circumstances the scraper passes rapidly through the lines, cutting off all the sedimentary matter that has adhered to the pipes. **1959** *Petroleum Handbk.* (Shell Internat. Petroleum Co. Ltd.) (ed. 4) 330 A radioactive cartridge may be fitted to the scraper as a means of locating it, should the scraper become stuck in the line. **1976** M. MACHLIN *Pipeline* xlviii. 497 The oil itself, at seven miles an hour, took four and a half days to make the trip from Prudhoe to Valdez, pushing the scraper before it to separate it from the test water in the pipes.

III. 8. (Earlier example.)

1792 S. BURDY *Life of Rev. Philip Skelton* 84 The militia men..took to their scrapers to save themselves.

9. (Earlier example.)

1818 'A. BURTON' *Johnny Newcome* I. 24 And John in Uniform arrayed: Behold him! with his dirk and scraper, And new Coatee, as stiff as paper.

IV. 10. scraper board *Art* (see quot. 1972); also, a piece of this material; **scraper ring,** a piston ring whose function is to scrape oil off the cylinder wall.

1895 E. J. WALL tr. *Fritz's Photo-Lithography* i. 25 A smooth white scraper board made by Angerer and Göschl of Vienna, which has a very even film of chalk, and which takes the lines clean and vigorously, is especially suitable for pen and ink work. **1925** *Art & Publicity* (*Studio: Special Autumn No.*) (Advt., verso front cover), Scraper boards with plain, embossed, or tinted surface for drawing for reproduction of line or half-tone. **1945** J. C. TARR *Printing To-day* viii. 95 Line engravings are also made from scraper-board originals. This board is covered with a thick layer of china clay and size upon which indian ink can be drawn or brushed, and scratched away with a knife. **1972** P. CROY *Graphic Design & Reproduction Techniques* (ed. 2) 162 Scraper board technique is an interesting method of producing white-and-black drawings. Scraper board consists of a base card coated with white and black chalk layers. The surface layer is scratched..exposing the underneath layer. Scraper board can be bought with a white surface and a black underlayer. **1918** W. E. DOMMETT *Dict. Aircraft* 35 The lowest ring, when placed at the bottom of the skirt, is known as a 'Scraper Ring'. **1928** C. F. S. GAMBLE *Story North Sea Air Station* xiii. 216 In the early days considerable difficulty was experienced with these engines owing to the rapid deterioration of the scraper rings fitted on the piston heads. **1980** HAYNES & LEGG *Citroën CX Owners Workshop Man.* i. 29/1 The oil control ring is fitted to the bottom groove, the scraper ring to the middle groove, and the compression ring to the top groove.

scrap-heap. (Further examples.)

1937 V. BARTLETT *This is my Life* xv. 258, I don't know who bought that car in the end or how soon it reached the scrap heap. **1956** *Railway Mag.* Nov. 749/2 No. 6 was rescued from an inglorious demise on the scrap heap. **1967** G. F. FIENNES *I tried to run Railway* iv. 40 Engines long past their time for the scrap-heap were being kept going. **1972** *Times* 16 May 2/2 He felt he had been thrown onto the scrap heap after 20 years' service. **1977** *Times* 7 Oct. 15/6 A socialist determination to drive fewer people onto the scrap heap. **1980** A. CLARKE *Last Voyage* ix. 100 They didn't send me to the scrap-heap straight away. Gave me a little job.

scrapiana. For † *Obs.* read *rare* and add later example.

1958 E. BLUNDEN *War Poets 1914–1918* 27 That denomination 'Eye-Witness', used in the first stage of the war to cover official scrapiana from the observation posts.

scrapie (skrē[1]·pi). Also † **scrapy.** [f. SCRAPE *v.* + -IE, -Y[6].] A subacute, invariably fatal, disease of sheep and goats, characterized by degeneration of the central nervous system, leading to uncoordinated gait and itching.

1910 *Vet. Jrnl.* LXVI. 711 Shepherds and farmers..class more than one disease with totally different symptoms under the head of Scrapy. **1913** *Jrnl. Compar. Path. & Therapeut.* XXVI. 317 The term 'scrape' or 'scrapie' is a popular one which has been applied to a disease of sheep on the borders of England and Scotland. **1914** J. P. MCGOWAN *Investigation into Dis. of Sheep called 'Scrapie'* i. 11 The disease has existed in Britain since before the middle of the eighteenth century under such names as 'scrapie', 'scratchie', 'rubbers', 'rickets', 'goggles', 'shakings', 'shrew-croft', and 'cuddie-trot'. **1925** *Glasgow Herald* 22 Apr. 7 Scrapie has mainly been confined to a certain area of the country. **1952** I. E. NEWSOM *Sheep Dis.* iv. 120 Scrapie is a chronic neurosis of sheep and goats characterized by intense pruritus, progressive incoordination, weakness, paralysis and death. **1975** *Times* 25 Aug. 8/5 Scrapie, an incurable disease of the nervous system, has afflicted various breeds of sheep for many years. **1979** *Nature* 11 Jan. 127/1 Scrapie, a subacute neuromuscular disease of middle-aged sheep, has been attributed variously to an infection or to heredity. The clinical disorder follows progressive symmetrical decay of neurones in localised brain sites,..associated with a terminal axon dystrophy. **1981** *Brit. Vet. Jrnl.* CXXXVII. 108/2 Although scrapie is caused by a virus-like agent, the development of clinical disease depends on genetic factors.

scraping, *vbl. sb.* Add: Also in *fig.* phr. *scrapings of the barrel* (see *SCRAPE *v.* 5 d).

1959 *Listener* 22 Jan. 154/1, I think Bill Slim was a very great man, because he made do with practically the scrapings of the barrel.

scrap iron. Add: **2.** *fig.* An alcoholic drink of poor quality. *U.S. slang.*

1942 Z. N. HURSTON in *Amer. Mercury* July 85 Maybe a shot of scrap-iron or a reefer. **1958** *Washington Post* 1 Nov. 1/1 A trio of investigators warned the drinking public yesterday to beware of a new bootleg concoction, 'scrap iron', noted more for its voltage than vintage. **1970** C. MAJOR *Dict. Afro-Amer. Slang* 101 *Scrap iron*, bad liquor.

scraplet. (Further examples.)

1891 A. JAMES *Diary* 7 May (1964) 203 We have a good scraplet of garden. **1972** *Time* 17 Apr. 63/1 He tests every anthology to see if some scraplet of Chandler's small output will turn up.

scrappage (skræ·pėdʒ). [f. SCRAP *sb.*[1] or *v.*[3] + -AGE.] = SCRAPPING *vbl. sb.*[2]

1949 *Sun* (Baltimore) 24 Mar. 8/3 Scrappage of passenger cars in 1948 was approximately half of the normal scrappage rate. **1950** *Engineering* 6 Jan. 26/3 Internal stresses may lead to serious scrappage on account of cracking. **1960** *Economist* 22 Oct. 359/1 Apart from natural growth in the population, sales are wholly for replacement and are related to the rate of scrappage and obsolescence. **1972** *Guardian* 29 Mar. 14/2 He says that the scrappage rate for US cars is roughly stable at 40 per cent of the new registration increase. **1976** *Nature* 17 June 540/2 The causes are recognised engineering factors such as shaft seals, maintenance operations, permeation and eventual scrappage.

scrapper[2]. Add: **1. b.** *transf.* in *gen.* use.

1976 *National Observer* (U.S.) 20 Nov. 13/4 On auction day, Harry Miner..said with his country twang, 'Vivien was a scrapper.' **1977** 'D. RAMSAY' *You can't call it Murder* ii. 124 'She was a real scrapper, Judy was.' O'Shea went on to give instances of her capacity for scrapping. **1979** *Dædalus* Summer 157 This is the Dewey..who had a long and honorable record as a scrapper for the rights of citizens of the democracy.

2. *N. Amer.* A fish that is hard to land once caught.

1959 *Moosehead Gaz.* (Dexter, Maine) Feb. 18/3 Tiny dry flies in drab patterns..brought the silvered scrappers with a rush. **1968** *Globe & Mail* (Toronto) 3 Feb. 40/1 The largemouth is a right obliging and powerful scrapper. **1974** *Sunday* (Charleston, S. Carolina) 28 Apr. (Cartoon Suppl.) 8 (Advt.), This palm-size powerhouse has all the guts in the world to wear down any scrapper you're liable to hook.

scrappet. Delete *rare* and add: Also **scrappit.** (Further examples.)

1901 L. MALET *Hist. Sir Richard Calmady* v. v. 415 There's selfishness now, if you like—to appropriate a virtue *en bloc*, not leaving a rag, not the veriest scrappit of it for anybody else! **1941** E. R. EDDISON *Fish Dinner in Memison* xiii. 209 'A scrappet of ham: just half of that littlest slab,' she said. **1971** C. BONINGTON *Annapurna South Face* xv. 194 They warned me that they had very little food—just the odd scrappets that Dougal had taken up that morning.

scrapping, *vbl. sb.*[1] Add: Also *transf.* in *gen.* use.

1937 *Times Lit. Suppl.* 2 Jan. 4/3 One is apt to consider that the campaign ended, except for some hardly necessary 'scrapping', with the capture of Baghdad. **1977** [see *SCRAPPER[2] 1 b].

scrapple, *sb.*[2] (Earlier and later examples.)

1855 *Rural New Yorker* 10 Feb. 47/3, I observe a call for a recipe for making 'Scrapple', and some other homely dishes. **1910** 'O. HENRY' *Whirligigs* x. 130, I never cared especially for feuds, believing them to be even more overrated products of our country than grapefruit, scrapple, or honeymoons. **1942** H. W. VAN LOON *Van Loon's Lives* 632 Dante has become a taste that has to be acquired like a love for figs or scrapple. **1943** [see *PONHAUS]. **1975** R. STOUT *Family Affair* (1976) ii. 20 A plate of slices of home-made scrapple.

scrappy, *a.*[1] (Further examples, in sporting use.)

1930 *Daily Express* 6 Oct. 16/6 Both sides resumed their previous rough tactics, and the play became scrappy in consequence. **1976** *Milton Keynes Express* 28 May 54/3 Inter City were unlucky at the start of the second half and then play became scrappy and several unnecessary fouls were committed.

scrappy (skræ·pi), *a.*[2] orig. *U.S.* [f. SCRAP *sb.*[2] or *v.*[2] + -Y[1].] Inclined to scrap or fight; aggressive, pugnacious, quarrelsome.

1895 W. C. GORE in *Inlander* Nov. 65 *Scrappy*,..quarrelsome. **1935** F. SCOTT FITZGERALD *Let.* 11 May (1964) 264 It was fine seeing you but I was in a scrappy mood about Tom Wolfe. **1941** B. SCHULBERG *What makes Sammy Run?* v. 83 All the instinct for self-preservation of a scrappy kitten. **1977** *Rolling Stone* 7 Apr. 52/1 She was only five feet tall, but she was scrappy—her sister Rebecca Julian remembers her once beating up a bully to protect their little brother. **1977** *Time* 27 June 33/1 'This puts transatlantic air travel in the pocket of the workingman,' proclaimed Freddie Laker, the scrappy founder of Britain's Laker Airways.

scratch, *sb.*[1] Add: **I. 4. b.** Money, esp. paper money. *slang* (orig. *U.S.*).

1914 JACKSON & HELLYER *Vocab. Criminal Slang* 74 *Scratch*,..paper currency... 'He's got a bundle of scratch'. **1916** *Lit. Digest* 19 Aug. 424/2 Money is given a score of names; the most used is 'kale', 'scratch', or 'dough'. **1931** *Writer's Digest* Oct. 29 Don't mess with that iron money; get the scratch. **1939** *New Yorker* 1 Apr. 19/2 She..also had plenty of scratch, being the bank president's daughter. **1941** J. SMILEY *Hash House Lingo* 47 *Scratch*, coins. **1955** POHL & KORNBLUTH *Space Merchants* xiv. 123 Here's some scratch, and shop when you get a chance. **1957** N. MARSH *Off with his Head* xii. 269, I wouldn't have done it only I wanted the scratch like hell. **1967** I. HAMILTON *Man with Brown Paper Face* vii. 102 Alfred Mays..had enough scratch to run two homes. **1972** D. ANTHONY *Blood on Harvest Moon* xiv. 118 She runs some kind of talent agency. Probably a tax write-off... She doesn't need the scratch. **1978** G. MCDONALD *Fletch's Fortune* xv. 106 As soon as Fletch got the story from each girl..he found himself..getting up the scratch to bus her home. **1980** *Private Eye* 6 June 7/1 This state-funded legal nonsense—which is..putting even more scratch into the bulging wallets of the lawyers.

5. a. (*Fig.* examples of *up to* (*the*) *scratch*, up to the required standard.) Now usu. without *the*.

1843 DICKENS *Let.* 17 June (1974) III. 513 Pray, as a Member of the Committee, come up to the Scratch. **1848** A. BRONTË *Tenant of Wildfell Hall* II. xi. 202 Your uncle and aunt have long been wanting us to go there, you know; but somehow, there's such a repulsion between the good lady and me, that I never could bring myself up to the scratch. **1861** C. M. YONGE *Young Step-Mother* xiii. 156 The Vicar..was meditating a fresh one [*sc.* attempt], if..he could bring his churchwarden up to the scratch. **1911** G. B. SHAW *Getting Married* 226 It's about the wedding... We cant get our man up to the scratch. Cecil has locked himself in his room and wont see or speak to any one. **1934** 'G. ORWELL' *Burmese Days* ix. 142 If they won't come up to scratch you can always get hold of the ringleaders and give them a good bambooing on the Q.T. **1953** D. GARNETT *Golden Echo* vi. 133 All Edward's friends were mobilised and came loyally up to scratch. **1960** C. DAY LEWIS *Buried Day* II. viii. 164 Those of us who had pretensions to brain Maurice brought up to scratch by loosing on them the full force of his personality. **1978** *Taxi* 16 Feb. 11/4 (Advt.), Cold weather can cause you a lot of problems if your cab's electrics aren't up to scratch.

b. Also *fig.*; esp. in phr. *from scratch*, from a position of no advantage, knowledge, influence, etc., from nothing.

1922 JOYCE *Ulysses* 454 A poor foreign immigrant who started scratch as a stowaway and is now trying to turn an honest penny. **1936** *Economist* 2 May 233/1 Nazi Germany, starting her rapid re-armament 'from scratch' in 1933, was fortunate enough to have a surplus capacity in all sections of her heavy industries. **1939** 'G. ORWELL' *Coming up for Air* II. v. 103 We'd no fishing tackle of any kind, not even a pin or a bit of string. We had to start from scratch. **1953** S. KAUFFMANN *Philanderer* v. 77 He took one look at her and thought: If I want that, I must begin all over again right from scratch. **1957** L. F. R. WILLIAMS *State of Israel* 53 Another branch of communications which has been built up from scratch to a degree of efficiency. **1962** *Guardian* 21 Mar. 2/5 The whole Treasury block could..have been rebuilt from scratch for the money. **1978** *Peace News* 25 Aug. 7/2 The daily routine was a crash programme of tuition provided by civilians, mainly Russian or other Slavic emigrés, in Russian from scratch to A-level standard, which was achieved in 10 months. **1979** *Fortune* 29 Jan. 77 NASA is not exactly starting from scratch out there in space; it is building on promising experiments done on prior space flights.

c. *Sporting.* A horse or other animal withdrawn from the list of entries for a race or other competition.

1938 *Mr.* Dec. 128/2 *Scratch*,..a horse withdrawn from a race. **1947** *Sun* (Baltimore) 20 Dec. 12/1 The overnight favorite..was a late scratch. **1960** WENTWORTH & FLEXNER *Dict. Amer. Slang* 450/2 *Scratch*,..a horse that has been withdrawn from a race after midnight of the night before the race. **1979** *Arizona Daily Star* 8 Apr. c2/3 We kept hoping there would be a scratch in the fast heat... I must have asked a hundred times if there were any scratches.

6. b. A rough hiss heard from the loudspeaker (or horn) when a record is played and caused by the friction of the stylus in the groove.

1908 *Talking Machine News* I. 9/1 Scratch seems to be filtered out of the reproduction. **1926** *Punch* 2 June p. iii (Advt.), Columbia new process records. The only records without scratch. **1942** [see *ground noise* s.v. *GROUND *sb.* 18]. **1949** G. A. BRIGGS *Sound Reproduction* xix. 117 Cutting out a slice of scratch also removes a slice of music or whatever is being reproduced. **1961** E. N. Bradley *Records & Gramophone Equipment* ii. 43 Possessors of old 78 r.p.m. records who play these on new lightweight equipment may find a quite distressing amount of scratch and surface noise.

II. 8. a. Delete *rare* and add further example.

1932 H. C. Wyld *Universal Dict. Eng. Lang.* 1068/3 Dogs enjoy a good scratch.

IV. 10*. In Billiards and related games: (*a*) a lucky stroke, a fluke ? *obs.*; (*b*) a shot that incurs a penalty. Cf. *scratch *v.* 11*.

a. 1850 M. Phelan *Billiards without Master* 12 It is amusing to observe the effect produced on some players by what is technically called a 'scratch', or fortuitous stroke. **1859** G. W. Matsell *Vocabulum* 122/1 When a player wins a stroke or count by accident, without deserving it, he is said to have made a scratch. **1869** 'Mark Twain' *Innocents Abroad* xii. 116 We had played billiards..on an ancient table that made the balls..perform feats in the way of..almost impossible 'scratches'. **1907** *N. Amer. Rev.* Nov. 333, I saw nothing there in the way of science and art that was more wonderful than shots [in Billiards] which I had seen Texas Tom make..all calculated shots, and not a fluke or a scratch among them.

b. 1913 J. T. Stoddard *Science of Billiards* vii. 153 One ball is forfeited for a failure to hit any ball, or for pocketing the cue ball ('scratch'). **1974** *Rules of Game* 85/3 Scratches are also incurred during safety play on a ball frozen to a cushion, and when a player's cue ball jumps off the table. **1975** *Way to Play* 195/3 At his third scratch in succession, a player loses one point for the third scratch, plus 15 points for the three successive scratches.

V. 11. a. *scratch boat, machine, runner.*

1896 *Rudder* July 220/2 A table of time allowances has been figured out..using the 130-foot boat as 'scratch boat' (to use a foot-racing term). **1950** *Sun* (Baltimore) 18 Mar. 12/1 The Ticonderoga..was named the scratch boat. This means she is favored to finish first in the long race. **1955** *Times* 22 Aug. 4/5 The race..resolved itself in the closing stages into an exciting tussle between Mr. Clifford, in the scratch machine, and Mr. Peter Vanneck, in the longest handicap aircraft. **1976** *Star* (Sheffield) 30 Nov., Bert Oliver (Kelty), British professional 110 metres champion, is the scratch runner in the Skol Sprint 110 metres handicap on January 1 and January 3.

b. scratch-coat (later example); hence *scratch-coating* vbl. sb.; **scratch dial,** a set of marks found on the walls of old churches, usually considered to be an ancient form of sundial; **scratch filter** *Electr.*, a filter designed to reduce the audibility of scratches and hiss in sound reproduction; **scratch hardness,** the hardness of a metal or mineral as estimated by measuring the width of a scratch made on the material by a diamond point under a specified load; **scratch hit** *Baseball* (see quot. 1976); **scratch hole,** a hole or trench scratched out of the ground; **scratch paper** *N. Amer.*, scribbling paper; **scratch-plough** *v. trans.*, to plough very shallowly; **scratch sheet** *U.S. Sporting*, a printed list of the entries in the day's races and their odds; also *transf.*; **scratch stock** (see quot. 1966); **scratch-work,** (*a*) (later example); (*b*) scratched lines on an engraving plate.

1953 Van den Branden & Knowles *Plastering Skill & Practice* i. 5 Of the three coats, the first coat, or scratch coat, is a thin coat... The purpose of the scratch coat..is to ..provide a good base for the plaster coats that will follow. **1911** *Encycl. Brit.* XXI. 785/2 For the first coat a layer of well-haired coarse stuff..is put on with the laying trowel. This is termed 'pricking up' in London, and in America 'scratch coating'. **1914** *Proc. Somerset Archæol. Soc.* LIX. ii. 26 The name Scratch Dial has been given to this ancient form of sundial. **1938** *Times Lit. Suppl.* 15 Jan. 39/1 The woodwork follows—roofs, benches, pulpits; and then scratch-dials and aumbries, mural paintings and windows bring up the rear. **1960** J. Betjeman *Summoned by Bells* v. 49 Was that the reason why the pale grey slides Of tympana, scratch dials and Norfolk screens So pleased me at his lectures? **1967** C. A. Vearncombe *Hist. of Church of St. Lawrence the Martyr* (Lydeard St. Lawrence, Somerset) 19 This doorway has a scratch dial on the east, 3 ft. 9 in. above the plinth. **1929** K. Henney *Princ. Radio* xvi. 289 Similar filters are used in phonograph reproduction to eliminate the needle noise. They are called scratch filters and may tune somewhere between 3000 and 5000 cycles. **1935** Nilson & Hornung *Pract. Radio Commun.* viii. 349 It will be necessary to attenuate the high frequencies... This may be accomplished by introducing a series-resonant circuit similar to that used for scratch filters. **1977** *Rolling Stone* 5 May 80/2 Watch for this spec when you consider the usefulness of rumble and scratch filters on your next amp or receiver. **1928** *Jrnl. Iron & Steel Inst.* CXVII. 893 Annealing these cold-rolled single crystals at 250°C..gave no measurable rise of scratch hardness. **1962** R. Webster *Gems* II. 488 For the gemmologist, scratch hardness, based on the standard minerals in Mohs's list, is the only practical basis for experiment. **1972** *Jrnl. Physics* D. V. 1293 Scratch hardness measurements reflect a greater degree of anisotropy in the properties of crystals than the corresponding indentation techniques. **1917** C. Mathewson *Second Base Sloan* 166 Four men faced Chase in the third, the first getting a scratch hit. **1935** *Encycl. Sports* 63/1 *Scratch-hit*, a weak hit into the infield. **1943** *Amer. Speech* XVIII. 103 A 'single' in the third inning becomes a 'scratch hit' in the fourth. **1976** *Webster's Sports Dict.* 374/1 *Scratch hit*, a batted ball that enables a batter to reach base safely but that is neither an error nor a clean base hit. **1923** Kipling *Irish Guards in Great War* I. 6 The German trenches, which were rather in the nature of scratch-holes. **1969** G. Coppard *With Machine Gun to Cambrai* xxi. 87 We lived a mean and impoverished sort of existence in lousy scratch holes. **1899** B. Tarkington *Gentl. Indiana* xiii. 223 Sheets of blank scratch-paper lay before them, and they relaxed not their knit brows. **1934** J. O'Hara *Appointment in Samarra* (1935) vii. 214 He wanted to work.., and he tried to the extent of getting out some scratch-paper and pencils. **1971** *Islander* (Victoria, B.C.) 12 Sept. 9/5 When I take down a recipe from someone it is usually on a piece of scratch paper. **1979** *Farmington* (New Mexico) *Daily Times* 27 May 6c/4 (Advt.), Newsprint roll end paper 20c. a pound.., or else we will cut scratch paper, any length & width desired for 35c a pound. **1926** D. H. Lawrence *Plumed Serpent* x. 170 The land was being scratch-ploughed by a pair of oxen and a lump of pointed wood. **1939** *Sun* (Baltimore) 30 Nov. 24/6, I noticed that one of the girls was looking at a scratch sheet. **1956** T. Betts *Across Board* 170 William Armstrong..published the first scratch sheet that ever appeared on the newsstands of New York. The year was 1917. **1964** L. Hairston in J. H. Clarke *Harlem* 288, I..took the resumé scratch-sheet.. background..workin' experience..and such particulars. **1973** *N.Y. Law Jrnl.* 8 May 4/4 The person who reads the *New York Times* or *Daily News* or even the scratch sheets. **1934** P. A. Wells *Design in Woodwork* iii. 28 Lines or bandings round a panel,..can be pleasant..if not overdone. These are grooved in with a scratch stock, a simple tool made in the workshop. **1966** A. W. Lewis *Gloss. Woodworking Terms* 85 *Scratch stock*, tool for making small beads, mouldings, or grooves for inlays by scraping *along* the grain of the wood. **1976** F. E. Sherlock *Enjoying Home Carpentry & Woodwork* vii. 76 The scratch stock is very useful for the fine woodworker who wishes to inlay veneer lines. **1910** W. de la Mare *Three Mulla-Mulgars* i. 6 She is shown veiled on the rude pots of Assasimmon and in Mulgar scratch-work. **1977** *Times Lit. Suppl.* 14 Jan. 40/2 Reworked by Blake with scratchwork and blank ink... In this intermediate proof Blake has made these alterations through scratchwork and pen lines, in preparation for reworking the plate.

scratch, *a.* Add: **2.** (Earlier and further examples.) Of a game or match: impromptu, played by scratch teams. Freq. also of a meal.

1851 J. Pycroft *Cricket Field* x. 189 That is the time that some..batsman, whose eminence is little seen amidst the loose hitting of a scratch match, comes..to the wicket and makes a stand. **1851** *London at Table* I. 23 The butler.. giving directions to what the four-in-hand club used to call 'a scratch team' of servants. **1874** E. J. M. Collins *Frances* III. x. 234 Frances and Cecilia, coming down, found a hasty luncheon, and everybody busy at it... When this scratch luncheon was over, everybody went out. **1903** [see *cart *v.* 1 d]. **1923** J. Manchon *Le Slang* 258 *A scratch breakfast*, un déjeuner improvisé. **1942** *R.A.F. Jrnl.* 18 Apr. 10, I then commanded a scratch squadron of rather ropey machines. **1944** *Return to Attack* (Army Board, N.Z.) 15/2 Some of the men were keeping warm..by playing scratch football. **1952** [see *organize *v.* 2 d]. **1953** S. Kauffmann *Philanderer* vi. 103 They sat down to a scratch meal at about nine. **1973** 'J. Patrick' *Glasgow Gang Observed* xviii. 146 Facilities for 'scratch' games of football. **1981** J. R. L. Anderson *Death in High Latitude* v. 85 If you don't mind a scratch meal I'd be delighted if you could stay to supper.

scratch, *v.* Add: **1. a.** (Later examples: cf. sense *3 f.)

1968 B. Evans *Dict. Quotations* 602/1 Scratch a Russian, and you will wound a Tartar. **1977** 'D. Cory' *Bennett* ii. 64 Scratch a Spaniard, Hunter thought, and he oozes an offended formality instead of blood.

2. a. *to scratch one's head*: also *fig.*

1961 J. Baker *Cottage by Springs* xvii. 100 The supervisors, who occasionally arrived in shining saloon cars, scratched their heads over the problem. **1963** *Observer* 24 Nov. 21/4 We wait for the report, read it, and then scratch our heads. **1969** *Listener* 13 Nov. 667/1 We thought we'd take this year off and scratch our heads and see whether we can do something better. **1973** *Times* 26 July 33/1 The advent of the school holidays means that millions of children will soon be embarking on long car journeys to the seaside or the Continent and just as certainly many parents will be scratching their heads over the car sickness.

c. *you scratch my back and I'll scratch yours* and varr. Cf. Claw *v.* 5 b.

1704 E. Ward *All Men Mad* 18 Scratch me, says one, and I'll scratch thee. **1858** 'A. Ward' *Let.* 27 Jan. in *Maine: Guide 'Down East'* (1937) iii. 363 You scratch my back and i will scratch your back. **1885** [in Dict., sense 2 a]. **1928** *Manch. Guardian Weekly* 10 Aug. 104/1 He goes on to spoil the effect by accusing Liberals of hypocrisy and being false to the principle of justice embodied in the phrase 'Scratch me and I'll scratch you'. **1937** 'G. Orwell' *Road to Wigan Pier* ii. 33 In order that..the Nancy poets may scratch one another's backs, coal has got to be forthcoming. **1954** M. Ewer *Heart Untouched* viii. 132 It's the advertisers getting extra publicity. It's everybody scratching everybody else's back. **1961** J. Heller *Catch-22* (1962) iv. 33 A little grease is what makes this world go round. One hand washes the other. Know what I mean? You scratch my back, I'll scratch yours. **1978** P. Hill *Enthusiast* v. 61 Local farmer, got 'is own slaughter 'ouse. 'Ee scratches my back, I scratch 'is, know what I mean?

3. a. Also *fig.* Esp. in phr. *to scratch the surface* (*of*): to make only slight progress in understanding, taking effective action (on), etc.; not to penetrate very far (into). See also sense *3 f.

1915 *New Republic* 13 Feb. 41/1 With all his earnest intention Amherst merely scratches the surface of the immense field of American social endeavor. **1932** Wodehouse *Louder & Funnier* 269 But this has merely scratched the surface. **1936** L. Hellman *Days to Come* iii. 90 You haven't seen anything. They didn't scratch the surface here. **1969** *Listener* 13 Nov. 654/3 When it [*sc.* contraception] is attempted on a mass scale, as in India, it barely scratches the surface of the problem. **1971** D. Potter *Brit. Eliz. Stamps* xiii. 147 This simplified account can only scratch the surface of a story which is as intriguing and rewarding as the collecting of stamps themselves. **1977** *Time* 9 May 48/2 The industry..has been on a hot sales streak since 1973, when energy consciousness-raising really began. And the market has barely been scratched.

f. *scratch a — and find a —* and varr.: suggesting the true or fundamental character of any particular group, nation, etc.

In some cases *scratch* is interpreted as meaning 'to wound superficially': see quots. under sense *1 a.

1823 J. Gallatin *Diary* 2 Jan. (1914) 229 Very true the saying is, 'Scratch the Russian and find the Tartar.' *c* **1863** J. R. Green *Let.* in *N. & Q.* (1965) Sept. 348 They say, if you scratch a Russian you always find the Tartar beneath. **1888** Mrs. Oliphant *Second Son* I. xiv. 242 I don't put any faith in Russians... 'Scratch a Russian and you'll come to the Tartar.' **1892** I. Zangwill *Children of Ghetto* III. ii. vi. 81 Scratch the Christian and you find the pagan—spoiled. **1924** G. B. Shaw *St. Joan* iv. 52 Scratch an Englishman, and find a Protestant. **1926** D. Parker *Enough Rope* 60 Scratch a lover, and find a foe. **1966** *Listener* 10 Feb. 217/3 Scratch a Muse and as often as not you find nothing you can fathom, not even a woman. **1973** *Freedom* 2 June 3/4 'Scratch a liberal and you find a fascist,' says Westall. What bloody nonsense is this? Did he invent the saying himself to fit his present convenience? And what do you get when you scratch a Tory, a Fabian, a Social Democrat, a Marxist-Leninist? **1977** C. McCullough *Thorn Birds* xvii. 445 Scratch Justine's surface and you find a rebel.

5. a. (Later *intr.* examples.) Also *transf.*; *to scratch for oneself* (orig. *U.S.*), to fend for oneself; *to scratch* (*around*) *for* (something), to struggle for, to labour to achieve or find, to experience difficulty in acquiring, etc.

1850 H. C. Watson *Camp-Fires of Revolution* 30 Then each one had to scratch for himself. **1856** A. Cary *Married* 304 Shaking off the other child, [she] told him to scratch for hisself a time, while she began to prepare the supper. **1930** V. Palmer *Passage* I. viii. 65 He and Bob had to scratch for a living the best way they could. *Ibid.* 160 We'll have to scratch for another year or two to pay off the new boat. **1947** K. Tennant *Lost Haven* ii. 42 How much better did it look when you went off with that..moll, and left me and the kids to scratch for ourselves? **1953** T. A. G. Hungerford *Riverslake* 202 If his mob gets in next election they'll whip up a nice old depression, just like they did the last time, and we'll all be scratching for jobs again. The only difference is that there'll be a million or so of these bludgers scratching with us. **1960** Wentworth & Flexner *Dict. Amer. Slang* 451/1 *Scratch for* (*something*)..*scratch around for* (*something*), to look for an object, to try to obtain something, esp. money or a much-wanted object; fig., to scratch in the same way a chicken does in searching for food. **1961** Webster s.v., Turned out at an early age to scratch for themselves. **1962** A. Marshall *This is Grass* 202 Not that I read much. I've been too busy scratching for a crust. **1970** *Globe & Mail* (Toronto) 25 Sept. 3/5 They moved to hake and really did a job on that. Now, they're scratching for what's left of the hake. **1976** *Laurel* (Montana) *Outlook* 9 June 16/3 This leaves the city scratching for a means to financing garbage disposal. **1976** J. Snow *Cricket Rebel* 104 Walters scratched around for 42 during which he was given a life by another blunder by Rowan. **1979** 'A. Hailey' *Overload* iii. x. 239, I scratched around for more details... Here are the exact dates of the convention and a preliminary program.

c. *intr.* To depart in haste, to make off with all speed. Freq. const. *for. U.S. colloq.*

1847 J. S. Robb *Streaks of Squatter Life* 109 I'm cussed if I hadn't to turn round, too, and scratch for the snag agin! **1875** 'Mark Twain' in *Atlantic Monthly* Mar. 285/2 The moment it splits at the top..I know I've got to scratch to starboard in a hurry. **1887** *Outing* (U.S.) May 120/1 As I fired the gun and the horses scratched away from the mark. **1904** S. E. White *Blazed Trail Stories* i. 5 This little town will scratch fer th' tall timber..when the boys goes in to take her apart.

d. With *up*: to produce with difficulty, to scrape up.

1922 H. Crane *Let.* 24 Dec. (1965) 110, I am growing bald trying to scratch up new ideas in housekeeping and personal hygiene. **1930** 'Sapper' *Finger of Fate* 188 It was six o'clock before the police arrived, and by that time we had scratched up a bit of breakfast and were feeling better.

7. c. (Earlier and later examples.)

1841 *Politician's Register for 1841* 3 Messrs. Ritner and Shulze, the Harrison Senatorial Electors, were scratched by a number of voters, and ran behind their colleagues. **1847** *Knickerbocker* Apr. 382 (Th.), He never scratched the regular ticket. **1880** *Scribner's Monthly* Oct. 909/1 They sometimes take the liberty of scratching a name, but they prefer, when the nominations are not too bad, to vote the regular ticket. **1904** *N.Y. Tribune* 8 Nov. 6 Vote the straight Republican ticket, without scratching. **1949** *Western Polit. Q.* Mar. 107 Thousands of voters scratched their ballots.

10. b. To forge (banknotes or other papers). *U.S. slang.*

1859 G. W. Matsell *Vocabulum* 77/2 *Scratch*, to write; to forge. **1926** *Flynn's Mag.* 6 Nov. 518/2 Well, scratch th' note an' we'll blow. **1935** N. Ersine *Underworld & Prison Slang* 65 *Scratch, v.* to forge checks or other papers.

11*. *U.S.* In billiards and related games: (*a*) *intr.* to make a stroke that incurs a penalty; *spec.* to hit the cue ball into a pocket; (*b*) *trans.* to hit (the cue ball) badly, incurring a penalty; *spec.* to hit (the cue ball) into a pocket. Cf. *scratch *sb.*[1] 10*.

1909 in Webster s.v. scratch *v.i.* **1959** N. Mailer *Advts. for Myself* (1961) 75 He shot poorly, hit the wrong ball and scratched. **1964** Sullivan & Crane *Young Sportsman's Guide to Pocket Billiards* ix. 91 *Scratch*, a playing stroke in which the player forfeits his playing turn. Most often caused by 'scratching' a ball unintentionally into a pocket. **1974** *Rules of Game* 85/3 A player may scratch the cue ball into a pocket at the break shot or during continuous play. **1977** *New Yorker* 4 July 24/2 This kid asked me, 'Do you ever scratch?'.. I said, 'I ain't never scratched in my life.'.. Just then, I took this shot and the cue ball went right in the pocket. He said, 'Well, you've scratched now.'

scratch-back. 1. (Earlier example.)

1842 *Ainsworth's Mag.* I. 20 What is it but..a fan, lazy-tongs, parasol, or scratchback?

scratch blue (skrætʃ blū). [f. SCRATCH *v.* + BLUE *sb.*] Used *attrib.* and *absol.* to designate a decoration of incisions filled with blue pigment found on eighteenth-century stoneware or stoneware so decorated. Cf. **scratched blue*.

1924 RACKHAM & READ *Eng. Pottery* vi. 88 In the Liverpool museum there is a mug of 'scratch blue'. **1957** MANKOWITZ & HAGGAR *Conc. Encycl. Eng. Pott. & Porc.* 28/1 A salt-glazed mug with 'scratch blue' decoration is inscribed with..the date 1742. **1960** H. HAYWARD *Antique Coll.* 251/1 '*Scratch blue' ware*, a class of white salt-glazed stoneware decorated with..ornaments and inscriptions incised upon the wares in the unfired 'green state'. **1969** G. WILLS *Eng. Pott. & Porc.* 88 The incised wording was emphasised by dusting it, before firing and glazing, with powdered cobalt-blue; a type of decoration..known as 'scratch blue'. **1971** L. A. BOGER *Dict. World Pott. & Porc.* 308/2 It is thought that this scratch blue ware may also have been made at Liverpool and in other parts of England.

scratchboard (skræ·tʃ₁bōᵊɹd). *Art.* Also **scratch board.** [f. SCRATCH *v.* + BOARD *sb.*] Cardboard specially treated and coated so that the surface can be scratched away to create drawings, etc.; a board of this type. Cf. *scraper board* s.v. *SCRAPER 10.

1930 C. E. WALLACE *Commercial Art* iv. 119 *Scratchboard Drawing.*—Scratchboard is a cardboard with an enamel surface of special finish. Drawings are made on it with ink and are afterwards scratched with a knife to obtain lights and special effects. **1942** *School Arts* (U.S.) Mar. 229/1 Why not try some scratchboard in your commercial art classes?.. Scratchboard is a lightweight cardboard, coated on one side with a clay-like composition. **1948** H. MISSINGHAM *Student's Guide in Commercial Art* II. 57 Scratch boards are available in a great variety of surfaces and tones. The surface is coated with clay preparation and is drawn or scraped away where desired. **1964** TURNBULL & BAIRD *Graphics of Communication* xii. 223 Using a bristol board coated with chalk, an artist can produce a scratchboard drawing by covering an area with ink and then scratching the ink and chalk from the surface of the board. **1976** *National Observer* (U.S.) 24 Jan. 20/1 Scratchboard—clay-coated cardboard on which you draw and scratch away.

scra·tch-build, *v.* Also **scratchbuild, scratch build.** [f. SCRATCH *sb.*[1] + BUILD *v.*] *trans.* To build (a model) from scratch, using no specially prepared components. So **scra·tch-building** *vbl. sb.*; **scra·tch-built** *ppl. a.*

1961 C. J. FREEZER *Railway Modelling* x. 95 (*heading*) Scratch building. **1967** *Railway Modeller 'Shows You How' Booklet* No. 19 (*title-page*) Our cover photograph shows one of the finest scratchbuilt model railways in the world, Peter Denny's Buckingham Branch. *Ibid.*, Scratchbuilding is the craft of modelmaking from raw materials and basic components. **1974** *Times* 17 Apr. 14/2 Parren said he hoped to attract young members by encouraging the scratch building—that is, building to scale from scratch—of modern locomotives. **1975** G. SCARBOROUGH *Tank & AFV Modelling* (Airfix Magazine Guide No. 5) ii. 7/1 Conversion and scratch-built projects of most of the popular subjects. *Ibid.* 19/1 This leaves us with the basic hull to scratch-build.

scratched, *ppl. a.* Add: **1.** *scratched blue* = *SCRATCH BLUE.

1883 L. M. SOLON *Art of Old Eng. Potter* vi. 79 Some.. processes deserve special attention. The 'scratched blue' for instance enjoyed a successful run. **1940** *Chambers's Techn. Dict.* 748/2 *Scratched blue*.., incised ornament on unbaked clay, sprinkled with cobalt glass, then fused in the kiln.

scratcher. Add: **1. c.** (Earlier example.)

1880 *Scribner's Monthly* Feb. 621/2 Mr. Evarts will be obliged to look among the 'scratchers',..for the indorsement of..Civil Service Reform.

e. For *U.S.* read orig. *U.S.* and add earlier and later examples.

1859 G. W. MATSELL *Vocabulum* 77/2 *Scratcher*, a forger; a copyist. **1927** *Writer's Monthly* Nov. 387/2 Forgers, and floaters of bad money, checks or commercial paper, are 'scratchers', 'scratchmen' and 'shovers'. **1941** V. DAVIS *Phenomena in Crime* iv. 48 The actual forger, known by such names as 'the scratcher', 'the scribe', 'the penman', may consider himself extremely fortunate if his period of office exceeds two years.

2. d. A device put down an oil or gas well to clear the bore or create turbulence mechanically.

1877 J. F. CARLL *Oil Well Records & Levels* iv. 90 A 'scratcher' is a round brush..made of steel wire. When it is to be used the tubing is drawn from the well, a few barrels of benzine are poured in and the scratcher is..run down to the oil rock, where it is worked up and down..to scratch or scrub the walls of the well. **1974** D. K. SMITH in P. L. Moore et al. *Drilling Practices Manual* xvi. 426 Scratchers or wall cleaners. 1. Rotating... 2. Reciprocating. *Ibid.* 427 Install scratchers spaced according to location of permeable zones.

scratching, *vbl. sb.* **b.** **scratching post** (earlier and later examples).

1890 J. MACDONALD *Light in Africa* iii. 37 Cattle got among their tent ropes, and they erected 'scratching posts' to keep them away from their camp. **1968** *New York City* (Michelin) 73 Abercrombie and Fitch... One can find almost anything here, from a ten-cent fish hook to..a scratching post for your cat.

scratchless, *a.* Add: (Earlier example.) Also, without scratch (*SCRATCH *sb.*[1] 6 b).

1829 P. EGAN *Boxiana* 2nd Ser. II. 750 But Jack came off quite scratchless. **1978** *Gramophone* June 31/2 After the war Sterling pursued improvements on a big scale and one recalls in particular what were called the Columbia 'scratchless' records.

scratch pad. Also **scratch-pad, scratchpad.** [f. SCRATCH *sb.*[1]] **1.** A scribbling block. Also *attrib.* and *fig. colloq.* (orig. and chiefly *U.S.*).

1895 *Montgomery Ward Catal.* Spring & Summer 111/2 Desk or Scratch Pads, made from white laid, smooth finish paper for pen or pencil. **1906** *Dial. Notes* III. 155 Can you let me have a nickel to get a scratch-pad? **1931** W. G. MCADOO *Crowded Years* xv. 220 He called it a 'scratch-pad draft'..that..was not to be taken as final. **1939** R. CHANDLER in *Dime Detect. Fict.* Aug. 48/1 The paper was from a scratch pad. It would have been very nice if it had had a message on it. **1960** *News Chron.* 4 Feb. 6/4 Desk and telephone and scratch-pad and paper-clips. **1966** *Listener* 9 June 838/3 A boy in bellbottoms lamented (or was it bragged?) he had a 'scratchpad memory'. **1970** 'W. HAGGARD' *Hardliners* iii. 26 She struck out a line from her scratch-pad and the editor watched her. **1978** W. F. BUCKLEY *Stained Glass* xix. 190 Blackford sat on the couch and made motions requesting a scratch pad.

2. *Computers.* A small, very fast memory for the temporary storage of data or for indirect addressing of the main memory; usu. *attrib.*

1965 *Proc. Conf. Amer. Federation Information Processing Societies* XXVII. I. 667/2 General-purpose commercial processors with scratchpad memories did not appear on the market until 1959. *Ibid.* 676/2 The magnetic core scratch-pad has an access limitation of one register per cycle. **1970** O. DOPPING *Computers & Data Processing* x. 135 The small, fast memory, which is well suited for data and instructions that are going to be used very often, is sometimes called a scratch pad memory. **1977** *Design Engin.* July 77/2 It incorporates a 2k × 8-bit mask-programmable read-only memory, a 64 × 8-bit scratchpad random-access memory, four 8-bit input/output ports and a binary timer. **1979** *Personal Computer World* Nov. 83/2 The user program runs in a stack whose pointer is extracted from TGTSTK (FOFA in the scratchpad RAM).

scratchy, *a.* Add: **4. b.** Of sound: rough, grating. Of a sound-recording: characterized by scratch (*SCRATCH *sb.*[1] 6 b).

1889 *Cent. Dict.* s.v., A scratchy noise. **1961** WEBSTER s.v., Scratchy tune came from the phonograph. **1961** L. HUGHES *Ask your Mama* 3 In the quarter of the negroes Where the doors are doors of paper Dust of dingy atoms Blows a scratchy sound. **1976** W. TREVOR *Children of Dynmouth* ii. 43 He told Stephen to sit on it, in a voice that wasn't as scratchy as usually it was. **1977** *Film & Television Technician* Jan. 5/2 He precariously wound up the oldest gramophone this side of the Urals so that we might hear a scratchy 78 recording of some Russian choir singing the Creed. **1978** *Oxford Times* (City ed.) 17 Feb. 19 The mono recordings are primitive and scratchy.

c. *fig.* Ill-tempered, peevish, catty.

1925 E. H. YOUNG *William* xxxii. 277 I'm no heroine. I'm a nasty, scratchy, impatient little beast. **1936** L. C. DOUGLAS *White Banners* viii. 180 But if she was going to write him any more scratchy letters..it might turn out badly. **1949** N. MARSH *Swing, Brother, Swing* ix. 214 We're both scratchy. I told her I thought the unfortunate Rivera was ghastly and she thinks I'm shaking my curls at Mr. Alleyn. **1958** *Spectator* 27 June 835/2 The small, scratchy, pert, unhappy son. **1971** P. PURSER *Holy Father's Navy* I. ii. 11 Irby..was a bit scratchy. She said, 'Why is it we can never go anywhere on time?' **1977** 'J. LE CARRÉ' *Honourable Schoolboy* i. 31 Nor did the dwarf's own..version meet with much success, which made him very scratchy.

5. Also *transf.*

1933 J. B. PRIESTLEY *Wonder Hero* ii. 36 He had taken her away from her bed-sitting room and scratchy living, and had made her queen it in a fine service flat in Knightsbridge.

Hence **scra·tchily** *adv.*

1927 *Daily Express* 27 May 13/2 Wethered,..reaching the turn rather scratchily in forty-two, stood one down. **1975** R. L. DUNCAN *Dragons at Gate* (1976) i. 27 Chamber music drifting scratchily from an old Victrola.

scrattle, *v.* Delete † and add: **2.** (Earlier example.)

1817 H. L. PIOZZI *Let.* 4 Jan. in *Autobiogr. Mrs. Piozzi* (1861) II. 187 Coal carts scrattling up the hill often used to make me think—'Hinc ex audiri gemitus, et sæva sonare Verbera; tum stridor ferri, tractæque catenæ.'

Hence **scra·ttling** *ppl. a.* (example *fig.*).

1913 D. H. LAWRENCE *Sons and Lovers* iv. 75 In this flamin', scrattlin' place.

scrawled, *ppl. a.* Add: Also *transf.* and *fig*

1895 MRS. H. WARD *Bessie Costrell* ii. 27 A wide plain travelled into the sunset, its level spaces cut by the scrawled elms and hedgerows of the nearer landscape. **1910** J. BUCHAN *Prester John* xxi. 351 There..was the body of Henriques, lying scrawled on the sand. **1939** DYLAN THOMAS *Map of Love* 4 This weak house to marrow-columned heaven, Is corner-cast, breath's rag, scrawled weed,..crow stalk, puffed, cut, and blown.

scrawliness. (Earlier example.)

1867 W. JAMES *Let.* 17 Sept. (1920) I. 103 Excuse the scrawliness of this too hurriedly written letter.

scrawny, *a.* Delete *U.S.* and add later examples.

1946 D. C. PEATTIE *Road of Naturalist* iv. 43 The one where my scrawny, bronchitic body would find itself was stone-cold, a dirty grey, so I would mentally adjourn to the other. **1977** J. F. FIXX *Compl. Bk. Running* vi. 80 Frank Shorter, who won an Olympic gold medal in the 1972 marathon, is 5 feet 10½ inches and weighs a scrawny 134. **1977** *New Yorker* 27 June 59/2 This beautiful beast that I, a scrawny little thing, am destroying.

screaky. Delete *rare* and add: Also **skreaky, skreeky.** (Earlier and later examples.)

1884 'MARK TWAIN' *Huck. Finn* xxvii. 272 A melodeum —a sick one..pretty skreeky and colicky. **1909** *Dialect Notes* III. 404 'My shoes are skreaky.' 'I hate skreaky doors.' *a* **1961** in WEBSTER, Bats..making their screaky sounds.

scream, *sb.* Add: **c.** A cause of laughter; a very amusing person or situation. *colloq.*

1888 *Boston Herald* 24 Jan. 5/1 It [*sc.* 'Bewitched'] is something more than a sketch, and a good deal less than a comedy, and its designation on the bill, 'farcical scream', perhaps conveys a good idea of its character. **1906** H. GREEN *At Actors' Boarding House* 209, I thought I'd die laughing at his making love..and me with a husband doing his bit back in Auburn. It was a perfect scream, wasn't it, Kate? **1915** *Home Chat* 9 Oct. 45/2 'He's married.'.. 'It's a fact. His bailiff told our chauffeur... Isn't it a scream?' **1919** [see *PERFECT *a.* B. 5 f]. **1929** R. C. SHERRIFF *Journey's End* III. ii. 71 Oh, skipper, you *are* a scream—and no mistake! **1946** E. O'NEILL *Iceman Cometh* (1947) I. 68 Listen, it was a scream. **1974** *Guardian* 30 Jan. 11/1 Like the bearded lady, Lorna has curiosity value... 'Yes, isn't it a scream?' she says. **1977** J. FLEMING *Every Inch a Lady* III. iv. 131 They're good... That Tommy Raffles is a scream!

d. The giving of information or evidence, *spec.* against one's accomplices in crime. *slang.*

1925 E. WALLACE *Melody of Death* vii. 113 'Look here, George,..is it a scream?' 'A scream?' Mr. Wallis was puzzled innocence itself. 'Will you turn King's evidence?' said the other shortly.

e. An urgent message. *slang.*

1929 'SEAMARK' *Down River* i. 21 'Smuggling?' queried the surgeon. 'That's the line, sir. Had a scream from Headquarters about it only this morning.'

f. *Jazz.* The sound produced when a high note is played loudly on a wind instrument. Also *attrib.*

1933 *Metronome* Jan. 34 A scream is produced somewhat the same way as the rip, only in the rip the note is cut off shortly, but in the scream it is held. **1952** B. ULANOV *Hist. Jazz in Amer.* (1958) xxi. 275 The sustained scream notes. **1962** CHARTERS & KUNSTADT *Jazz: Hist. N.Y. Scene* xvi. 200 Each section answering the other in 'screams (chords) was the feature of 'Tiger Rag'.

scream, *v.* Add: **1. c.** *spec.* to travel swiftly with a noise like a scream; also hyperbolically and *transf.*, of a person.

1943 HUNT & PRINGLE *Service Slang* 57 *Screaming downhill*, making a power dive in a fighter aircraft. **1954** *Amer. Speech* XXIX. 101 'It screams!'; i.e., it really moves. **1957** P. MOORE *Science & Fiction* 60 Airmen screaming towards the ground in a steep dive. **1975** E. HILLARY *Nothing Venture, Nothing Win* x. 155 We had discussed the..likelihood of no one getting to the South Col the next day and finally decided that Tenzing and I should scream up as a booster party to make sure that the Sherpas got there. **1976** *Wymondham & Attleborough Express* 10 Dec. 24/4 Alan Green..unleashed a full-blooded volley from just inside the area that screamed into the top of the net. **1976** A. WHITE *Long Silence* vii. 53 One of the fighters [*sc.* planes] screamed down to take a closer look. **1981** *Economist* 24 Jan. 97/2 A tenth of a second is about as long as a star falling into a black hole would be expected to 'scream'.

e. To turn informer; to give evidence against one's accomplices. *slang.*

1925 E. WALLACE *Melody of Death* vii. 114, 'I don't want to hear any more about your conscience,' said the officer wearily. 'Do you scream or don't you?' 'I don't scream,' said Mr. Wallis emphatically. **1967** J. MORGAN *Involved* 114 He never got paid..and my information is he's ready to scream.

2. b. *fig.* To cry out *for.*

1906 E. DYSON *Fact'ry 'Ands* viii. 95 Ther job's simply screamin' fer a statesman iv your sort. **1930** 'SAPPER' *Finger of Fate* 147 With every nerve in his body screaming for the stuff [*sc.* whisky]. **1978** R. LUDLUM *Holcroft Covenant* xi. 131 She did not walk; she glided—an extraordinary body screaming for observation as a prelude to invasion and satisfaction.

c. *fig.* To communicate (something) strongly.

1957 [see *BEDDABLE *a.*].

d. *to scream on* (someone), to insult in 'playing the dozens' (see *PLAY *v.* 16 e). *U.S. Blacks'.*

1970 H. E. ROBERTS *Third Ear* 12/1 *Screaming on*, telling someone off;..embarrassing someone publicly. **1974** H. L. FOSTER *Ribbin', Jivin', & Playin' Dozens* v. 198 Sometimes, 'loud mouthing' or 'loud talking', 'sounding', 'screaming on someone' or even 'bogarding' are synonyms for woofing.

3. (Further examples with direct speech as object.)

1866 C. M. YONGE *Dove in Eagle's Nest* I. ix. 189 'Peace, thou fool!' screamed the old lady. **1976** B. FREEMANTLE *November Man* x. 131 'The servants can't hear, Jocelyn,' she screamed.

screamer. Add: **4.** *slang.* **b.** (Earlier example, in sense 'a person who tells exaggerated stories'; also, earlier example of sense 'a "screaming" farce'.)

1831 *Louisville Public Advertiser* 17 Oct. 2/3 The principal character in this production, is, to use his own elegant language, a *screamer*. **1849** *Theatrical Programme* 4 June 16/1 At the Adelphi crowds muster nightly to see..Wright and Bedford in a 'screamer'.

c. An exclamation mark.

1895 in *Funk's Stand. Dict.* **1908** *Bohemian* XIV. 643/2 Few of us have forgotten..the origin of 'yellow' as descriptive of that class of journalism addicted to 'screamers'. **1927** *Amer. Speech* II. 239 Exclamation points may be 'screamers', 'astonishers', or 'shouts'. **1933** D. L. SAYERS *Murder must Advertise* viii. 132 'Waste Nerve-Power!' Capital N, capital P, and screamer. Got that? **1960** *Guardian* 17 Sept. 12/6 Some newspapermen call the ! a screamer. **1972** *Ibid.* 18 Aug. 11/1, I once worked for an editor who cut out all the screamers—that's what you and I call exclamation marks.

d. A very powerful shot in a game.

1896 W. PARK *Game of Golf* 269 Screamer, a very long stroke, so called from the whistling noise made by the ball. **1926** WODEHOUSE *Heart of Goof* i. 13 He stepped off the sixteenth, after hitting a screamer down the centre of the fairway. **1959** *Sunday Times* 9 Aug. 28 (Advt.), When you hit a screamer..you'll be glad you played Slazenger 279. **1963** V. CANNING *Limbo Line* xvii. 227 Amadeo hit a screamer, dead straight and slightly left of the middle of the fairway. **1977** *Tennis World* Sept. 17/1 A 'heavy serve', one might think, means a fast serve. Wrong again. The term to denote velocity is 'big' or occasionally 'cannonball' or 'screamer'.

e. An informer, a tale-teller; a complainer.

1903 FARMER & HENLEY *Slang* VI. 126 *Screamer*,..a thief who, robbed by another thief, applies to the police. **1961** *John o' London's* 30 Nov. 610/3 An informer..is now more often referred to..as a *singer* or a *screamer*. **1968** *Telegraph* (Brisbane) 19 June 58/7 The man I was talking to said, 'Hang on a minute, I've got a screamer coming in.' When he came back I asked him what a screamer was. It turned out to be someone who complains about defects in a car he has bought.

f. In full *screamer headline*. A large headline.

1926 [see *RAP *v.*[1] 1 d]. **1945** L. SHELLY *Jive Talk Dict.* 17/1 *Screamers*, newspaper headlines. **1975** *New Yorker* 4 Aug. 20/1 'Gifts flow profusely at 124 West 42nd St. and 625 Madison Ave' was the screamer on a flyer handed to us on Forty-second. **1979** J. DRUMMOND *I saw him Die* ii. 24 The murder was on the front page. Screamer headline.

g. *Jazz.* A passage featuring loud high notes played on a wind instrument; such a note.

1940 *Swing* Nov. 28 It's another riff tune..plus (or minus) a screamer featuring the leader's horn. **1948** *Down Beat* 1 Dec. 13 *Minor* is a screamer but not without change of pace. **1958** K. GOODWIN in P. Gammond *Decca Bk. of Jazz* xiii. 149 His ability to produce stratospheric screamers with apparent ease was utilized to add bite and drive to the brass sections.

h. A bomb that makes a screaming sound as it drops.

1942 'R. CROMPTON' *William carries On* ii. 42 Her reactions to 'screamers'. **1943** HUNT & PRINGLE *Service Slang* 57 *Screamer*, a whistling bomb, i.e. a bomb with a device attached to cause a screaming sound as it descends.

i. *the screamers* = *the screaming habdabs* s.v. *HABDABS.

1948 PARTRIDGE *Dict. Forces' Slang* 163 *Screamers, the*, an evident dislike of operational flying. **1952** M. TRIPP *Faith is Windsock* i. 17 'Cut it out, you two,' said Bergen, 'you give me the screamers.'

j. *two-pot screamer*, one who easily shows the effects of alcohol. *Austral.*

1959 D. HEWETT *Bobbin Up* 21 Look at Lou. She's a two-pot screamer, always 'as been. **1972** J. DE HOOG *Skid Row Dossier* 95 It says experienced and sober, ya bloody two-pot screamer.

screaming, *ppl. a.* Add: **1. b.** *screaming eagle* (U.S. slang) = **ruptured duck* (b).

1946 *Newsweek* 18 Mar. 34/1 'Ruptured duck': GI for the discharge button which ex-service men wear in their lapels, also, 'homecoming pigeon' and 'screaming eagle'. **1948** A. M. TAYLOR *Lang. World War II* 172 Ruptured Duck... Also nicknamed Screaming Eagle.

2. b. (Further examples.) Also, blatant, obvious.

1922 J. HERGESHEIMER *Bright Shawl* (1923) 205 The shawl ..was malevolent, screaming in color. **1944** 'G. ORWELL' *Coll. Essays, Journalism & Lett.* (1968) III. 168 The 'screaming' advertisement started some time in the nineteen-twenties. **1963** *Australasian Post* 14 Mar. 51/1 I'd be a screaming nong if I didn't recognise you as a creep. **1965** *Listener* 9 Dec. 941/1 None of..the anarchy of competing posters and screaming shop signs. **1968** *Globe & Mail Magazine* (Toronto) 13 Jan. 6/3 The commonly held stereotype of a homosexual is called, in gay jargon, a screaming queen. **1972** B. RODGERS *Queens' Vernacular* 177 *Screaming*, flagrantly homosexual. **1976** *National Observer* (U.S.) 25 Sept. 13/1 Such segregation was..a screaming mockery of the Bill of Rights. **1977** *New Yorker* 15 Aug. 22/1 The *News* and the *Post* ran screaming headlines. **1981** *Daily Tel.* 20 Feb. 17/1 Spring colours are bright pink and screaming green with khaki chino skirts for women and khaki chino trousers for men.

d. *screaming habdabs*, etc.: see *HABDABS. *screaming meemies*, etc.: see *MEEMIES *sb. pl.*

3. Comb., as *screaming-scared* adj.

a **1963** C. S. LEWIS *Poems* (1964) 106 My body awakes in bed Screaming-scared.

screech (skriːtʃ), *sb.*[2] *slang.* [ult. ad. Sc. dial. *screigh* whisky.] **a.** Whisky. **b.** Any strong alcoholic liquor, freq. one of inferior quality. **c.** *Newfoundland.* A specific rum, or a specific mixture of rums.

1902 FARMER & HENLEY *Slang* VI. 126/1 *Screech, subs.* (common), whiskey. **1944** T. H. WISDOM *Triumph over Tunisia* viii. 68 The famous and kindly *Peres Blanc* from the Monastery at near-by Thibar had supplied them with drink from the monks' own cellars, and the popular drink was one that had been aptly christened 'Screech' by '111'. **1945** W. H. PUGSLEY *Saints, Sinners & Ordinary Seamen* 231 [The rating] gets hold of some bootleg scotch—'high life', they call it on the West Coast, and 'screech' in Newfie—and then he's away to..Cells or Detention. **1957** B. HUTCHISON *Canada: Tomorrow's Giant* 24 He is a little addicted to the Island's national drink called 'Screech'. **1958** *Maclean's Mag.* 27 Sept. 63/3 Screech is a mixture of rums now sold by the liquor board under a new label that displays..the legend 'Newfoundland's Famous Screech'. **1959** *Manch. Guardian* 7 July 7/4 There has been some concern at the violence during fights ashore between servicemen following the drinking of a local concoction known in the service [the Navy] as 'Screech'. It is made of a local wine, 'Imbeet', mixed with Coca Cola. **1963** [see *NEWFIE]. **1964** C. ROUGVIE *Medal from Pamplona* vi. 80 'Beer and screech.' 'Screech?'.. 'It's a term embracing all cheap Canadian wines.' **1973** *Daily Colonist* (Victoria, B.C.) 29 Aug. 2/2 The taste of beer must rank somewhere between buttermilk and Newfie Screech. **1979** *Globe & Mail* (Toronto) 17 Oct. 6/1 But allow us to explain. Screech, the hairy-chested Newfoundland libation, is based on Jamaican rum which arrives on the tight little island in 40-gallon, fire-charred oak barrels.

screech, *v.* Add: **1.** (Later example.)

1919 [see *GRAB *v.* 3 b].

3. (Later example.)

1972 'M. SINCLAIR' *Norslag* iv. 35 The ancient lift operative..had been less than polite as he had screeched the gates open for him.

screeching, *vbl. sb.* and *ppl. a.* (Later example.)

1976 *National Observer* (U.S.) 4 Dec. 15/2 A lot of this stuff is going to come to a screeching halt quickly, and we're not going to do the screeching.

screech-owl. Add: **1. b.** A small North American owl of the genus *Otus*, esp. *O. asio.*

1671 J. OGILBY *America* 147 The Birds both common and peculiar [to New England] are thus recited:..The long-liv'd Raven, th' ominous Screech-Owl. **1812** A. WILSON *Amer. Ornithol.* V. 83 Red Owl..is..well known by its common name, the Little Screech Owl. **1884** *Cent. Mag.* Nov. 121 The screech-owl would shake and shiver in the depths of the wood. **1949** *Amer. Forests* Oct. 23/2 The weird call of the more or less familiar screech owl is probably the best known of all the owls. **1960** [see **jumby-bird*]. **1975** *Islander* (Victoria, B.C.) 2 Nov. 3/1 The screech owl is the one I hear and see most often.

screed, *sb.* Add: **3. a.** More generally in *Building*, a level strip of material formed or placed on any surface (e.g. a floor or a road) as a guide for the accurate finishing of it. Also, a levelled layer of material forming part of a floor or other horizontal surface. (Further examples.)

1937 S. C. B. STUBBS *Building Encycl.* IV. 1241/2 Screeding. A cement and sand floating on a floor, laid in preparation for a subsequent paving or on a wall for wall tiling, is known as a screeding. Often it is called simply a screed, because it is brought up level by the use of screeds. *Ibid.*, In the case of floors..it is usual to use the batten itself as a screed without forming the floated strip alongside, and hence we find the battens often referred to as the screeds. **1952** D. NIELD *Building Constr. Illustr.* iii. 35 Cross reinforcement is laid over the beams and the whole covered with a layer of fine concrete (screed). **1956** DAVIES & PETTY *Building Elements* ix. 270 A screed of cement and sand is laid later to provide a smooth and level surface for whatever floor finish is to be used. **1961** *Times* 3 July (Archit. Suppl.) p. vii/3 Heating by electric wires embedded in the concrete screed is becoming quite common. **1974** W. E. KELSEY *Building Construction* v. 87 Although the term screed is applied to the whole of the final surface, it is also used to describe the narrow strips of wet cement used as a guide to the thickness of the top layer. **1978** *Cornish Guardian* 27 Apr. 33/6 (Advt.), Uneven floors made smooth with latex screed.

b. *screed board, rail, strip.*

1949 A. G. GEESON *Gen. Building Repairs* (ed. 11) I. vi. 335 By moving the screed board with a slight tamping motion, the surface will be slightly roughened. **1968** *Gloss. Formwork Terms (B.S.I.)* 25 A tamper may be constructed so that it also acts as a screed board. *Ibid.* 22 *Screed rail*, a guide fixed at the perimeter of a concrete pour to act as a datum and support for a screed board. **1977** *Club Tennis* Mar. 13/3 The actual laying of the surface is done by screed strips and straight edge and the court is rolled and trowelled to a perfect level.

screed, *v.* Add: **4.** *Building.* **a.** To level (a surface) by means of a screed; to apply (material) as a screed to a floor surface. (Cf. SCREED *sb.* 3 a in Dict. and Suppl.)

[**1825**: see SCREEDING *vbl. sb.*] **1898** F. W. MACEY *Specifications in Detail* 68 State if screeded in lime and hair mortar instead. **1944** E. LUCAS in R. Greenhalgh *Pract. Builder* ii. 104/2 The second coat must be screeded to bring the surface level. **1949** A. G. GEESON *Gen. Building Repairs* (ed. 11) I. vi. 333 The surface is finished by screeding it with a straightedge. **1970** *Daily Tel.* (Colour Suppl.) 5 June 35 Concrete can also be screeded to floors in old houses. *Ibid* 39/2 How to screed a concrete floor.

b. With advbs.: *screed in*, to finish off a surface around (an object, as a frame) by means of a screed; *screed off*, to take *off* (excess material) from a surface by means of a screed.

1898 F. W. MACEY *Specifications in Detail* 63 Hair mortar in brickwork is only used for screeding in door and window frames. **1949** K. S. WOODS *Rural Crafts of England* IV. xi. 180 The plaster was laid on very evenly, and then 'screeded off' with a long straight-edge known as a 'screeding-rule'. **1950** *N.Z. Jrnl. Agric.* Jan. 58/3 The surplus mix [of concrete] being screeded off with a straight-edge.

screeder (skriːdəɹ). [f. *SCREED *v.* + -ER[1].] A person employed to lay floor screeds.

1976 *Derbyshire Times* (Peak ed.) 3 Sept. 11/7 (Advt.), Floor screeders and quarry tilers.—One or two reliable layers required. **1977** *Evening Post* (Nottingham) 24 Jan. 11/2 (Advt.), Floor Screeders required (male–female) for long term contract in Nottingham.

screeding, *vbl. sb.* Add to def.: The action of *SCREED *v.* 4. Also *concr.*, the material of a screed. (Further examples.)

1898 F. W. MACEY *Specifications in Detail* 68 The mortar to be used in the screeding in of frames. **1936** *Archit. Rev.* LXXIX. 8 The floors are reinforced concrete slabs with two layers of cork separated by a layer of hard screeding. **1937** [see *SCREED *sb.* 3 a]. **1956** DAVIES & PETTY *Building Elements* ix. 272 Screeding is carried out by the use of fine mix, generally one part of cement to three or four of sand.

screef (skriːf), *sb.* Also **scrief**, 9 **skreef.** [dial. var. of SCURF *sb.*[1], SCRUFF *sb.*[1]] **1.** *Sc.* and *Forestry.* A layer of vegetation on the surface of the ground.

1817 J. CHRISTIE *Instructions for Hunting* 39 Without a bit of screef aboon, But bare and naked craigs o' stane. **1866** W. GREGOR *Dialect of Banffshire* 163 There's a fine skreef o' girs on that shift. **1925** R. L. CASSIE *Gangrel Muse* 33 An' swack little feeties trip licht o' the screef, I' the reelin' an' furlin' o' fairies. **1934** *Forestry* VIII. 21 Where there is a skin of peat..it is preferable to plant in a ploughed furrow, or in a screef with loosened soil. **1952** *Buchan Observer* 7 Oct., You may weel spier fa's to cast yer divots, gin sae be that ye ken o' a bittie o' gweed screef.

2. Special Comb.: **screef-mark**, an area from which surface vegetation has been cleared.

1950 R. JENKINS *So Gaily sings Lark* xxii. 203 With the spade the vegetation was scraped away, and in the black 'scrief-mark' as it was called an L notch was made, into which the tree was carefully inserted, the earth being firmed again by careful pressure of the heel.

screef (skriːf), *v. Sc.* and *Forestry.* Also **scrief.** [f. prec. Cf. SCURF *v.*, SCRUFF *v.*[1]] *trans.* To clear (surface vegetation) from the ground.

1926 *Trans. Buchan Field Club* XIII. 82 Small places had the turf skinned off or 'scriefed'. **1930** *Forestry* IV. 20 Screef the surface lightly with the flat end [of a mattock], and then loosen up the patch with the pick end. **1948** *Country Life* 8 Oct. 739/3 To screef is to clear the ground of surface vegetation (such as heather) with a mattock or comparable tool.

So **scree·fing** *vbl. sb.*

1930 *Forestry* IV. 85 Short of removing the surface layers of the fire traces by 'screefing' or turning it in with the plough ..it is usual to get rid of the surface vegetation by controlled burning. **1953** H. L. EDLIN *Forester's Handbk.* ix. 151 It is seldom necessary to remove weed growth completely, though screefing, or the paring away of surface vegetation with a mattock, may be practised where trees are very slow to get away..or where manure is applied. **1962** *Finnish Paper & Timber* XIII. 162 When the weight and efficiency of the tractor was increased and the screefing equipment made more manoeuvrable over rough going suitable machinery for the work had been found.

screel (skriːl), *sb. dial.*, *Sc.*, and *Barbados.* [f. next.] The cry of a bird, a child, etc.; the piercing note of a whistle.

1876 C. C. ROBINSON *Gloss. Mid-Yorks.* 117/2 *Screel* (skri·h'l), v. n. and sb., to cry, in a shrieking manner; gen. **1922** *Glasgow Herald* 8 Aug. 6 With nothing to mar your peace so serene Save the screel of the curlew or sunset's red sheen. **1953** G. LAMMING *In Castle of my Skin* v. 91 At the same hour every morning the whistle screel shot up like an alarm through the rumbling of cart wheels.

screel (skriːl), *v. dial.*, *Sc.*, *N. Ir.*, and *Barbados.* Also **skreel.** [Prob. imitative or ad. ME. *skrille* scream: see SKIRL *v.*[1]] *intr.* To screech, to scream, to utter a high-pitched or a discordant cry. Occas. used *transf.* of inanimate things. So **scree·ling** *vbl. sb.*

1875 W. D. PARISH *Dict. Sussex Dial.* 106 *Skreel*, e[ast], to scream. **1889** M. PEACOCK *Taales fra Linkisheere* 103 What wi' yammerin' bairns, an' what wi' screälin' wimmin. **1934** *Punch* 14 Nov. 543 Though kelpies walk both bold and free And icy winds skreel off the sea. **1953** C. DAY LEWIS *Italian Visit* vi. 61 Again again again, the frogs are screeling Down by the lilypond. **1953** G. LAMMING *In Castle of my*

Skin vi. 113 Mother..lashed me thoroughly. Bob heard the screeling, and came down to our house listening. **1965** *Dundee Courier* 10 Apr. 8 Herring gulls skreeled.

screen, *sb.*[1] Add: **1. d.** (Examples of the sense 'surface for the reception of images'.) *spec.* (*a*) a usu. large white surface for receiving the image from a film projector; (*b*) a small fluorescent screen, esp. one in a television set (so *little screen*). Also *transf.* (usually with definite article), moving pictures collectively; the cinema; the film world.

1810 *New Family Receipt-bk.* 257 To make Transparent Screens for the Exhibition of the Phantasmagoria. **1846** *Penny Cycl.* Suppl. II. 254/2 Magic lantern is a species of lucernal microscope, its object being to obtain an enlarged representation of figures, on a screen in a darkened room. **1881** [see ZOETROPE]. **1902** [see sense 6 in Dict.]. **1910** *Moving Picture World* 19 Feb. 249/1 People..like to see on the screen what they read about. **1915** *N.Y. Times* 15 Nov. 11/1 Unlike the legitimate stage, the screen does not have to wait for a dramatist to become inspired before it may present the topic of the hour. **1920** MRS. P. CAMPBELL *Let.* 20 Dec. in *B. Shaw & Mrs. Campbell* (1952) 215, I am much too aged for Eliza on the Screen! **1926** *Nature* 3 July 19/2 Every possessor of a 'televisor' will be in a position to see on his screen the performers in operas and plays as well as hearing them. **1928** E. WALLACE *Double* i. 11 'What is her name?' 'Mary Dane... Mary Dane—sounds like something off the screen, doesn't it?' **1932** *Ann. Reg. 1931* 48 Death robbed the screen of Lya de Putti, best remembered for her performance in 'Variety', and Tyrone Power, veteran character actor. **1943** K. TENNANT *Ride on Stranger* iv. 37 He's marvellous!.. Six feet tall and fair wavy hair. He ought to be on the screen. **1946** *B.B.C. Year Bk.* 20 A badly-produced programme may make you feel that the screen is small and cramped, but if the programme is good enough you will look at the screen not as a picture within a frame but as a view seen through a window. **1949** *Radio Times* 15 July 13/4 *Music from the movies.* Melodies from the screen in swingtime and symphony. **1956** R. M. LESTER *Towards Hereafter* v. 63 Personages very well known in the world of industry, politics, stage, screen and radio. **1961** I. MURDOCH *Severed Head* xxi. 179 Violence, except on the screen, is always pathetic, ludicrous and beastly. **1975** *Listener* 2 Jan. 23/1 The cumulative effect of watching the little screen for hours on end. **1976** A. DAVIS *Television: First Forty Years* 121 In the beginning, television had little or no time to devote to religion, for there were only two hours of transmissions on weekdays, and on Sundays the screen stayed blank. **1977** *Private Eye* 1 Apr. 10/3 It's all here at-a-glance—everything you want to see and know about the glamorous, dynamic world of the little screen.

f. *Photogr.* More fully *focusing screen.* A flat piece of glass on which the image formed by a camera lens is focused prior to making the exposure.

1858 [see FOCUSING *vbl. sb.* 2]. **1879** [see sense 6 in Dict.]. **1902** A. WATKINS *Photogr.* 19 With the lens full open you will probably notice the image on the screen is not quite so sharply defined at the extreme corners as it is in the centre. **1962** A. GÜNTHER *Microphotogr. in Libr.* 23 Focusing is rather critical, and a precision camera with focusing screen should therefore be used. **1977** J. HEDGECOE *Photographer's Handbk.* 14 Some photographers find focusing on a screen more difficult than focusing with an image-coinciding rangefinder.

g. Any thin extended surface set up to intercept shot in gunnery trials.

1879 *Manual Artill. Exerc.* I. 17 The shot passes through two screens placed a certain distance apart. *Ibid.*, The velocity of the shot at the various screens [is] calculated from a comparison of the screen and time records. **1880** *Encycl. Brit.* XI. 300/1 The shot, after leaving the gun, cuts the wire of the first screen, and subsequently the wire of the second screen.

h. *Cricket.* An erection of canvas or wood placed behind the bowler, outside the boundary of the playing area, to provide a white background and a shield from moving objects behind the bowler's arm. Cf. *sight-screen* s.v. *SIGHT *sb.*[1] 17.

1894 N. GALE *Cricket Songs* 31 O Bowler... He sends you clean beyond the screen. **1908** W. E. W. COLLINS *Leaves Old Country Cricketer's Diary* ix. 153 To be sure the light—this was his account—was all wrong. Anyhow we moved the screen three times to accommodate him, and even so he was not altogether happy. **1977** J. LAKER *One-Day Cricket* 107, I eventually emerged from behind the screens.

i. *N. Amer.* and *Austral.* A frame covered with a fine netting of wire or the like, used in a window or a doorway to exclude insects.

1895 *Montgomery Ward & Co. Catal.* Spring & Summer 389/1 Adjustable Window Screen, so constructed as to form a perfect joint with the parting strip, so that it is not necessary to remove the screen in order to close the window. **1956** W. R. BIRD *Off-Trail in Nova Scotia* ii. 51 As Saturday was a warm day everyone along the road was busy, putting up screens. **1971** *Sunday Australian* 8 Aug. 8A/6 (Advt.), Insect screens and screen doors that are custom-made. **1977** *Detroit Free Press* 11 Dec. 21-A 1, I opened the window, but I couldn't get the screen off and it was getting very hot.

2. e. *Geol.* A roughly tabular body of older rock separating two intrusions.

1910 W. B. WRIGHT in *Summ. Progr. Geol. Surv. 1909* 33 About a quarter of a mile further inland, in the midst of the granophyre, a vertical screen of lava occurs... This screen varies much in thickness, being as little as 10 feet in one place, but reaching 300 feet in others... The granophyre on the outside of this screen is a distinct intrusion from that inside. **1942** M. P. BILLINGS *Structural Geol.* xv. 284 If the central block subsides several times.., a number of concentric ring-dikes will form. A remnant of the older country rock left between two ring-dikes is called a screen.

3. e. *Meteorol.* A shelter that surrounds meteorological instruments and protects them from direct sunlight and precipitation, usu. painted white and louvred to provide indirect ventilation.

1881 W. MARRIOTT *Hints to Meteorol. Observers* 10 The screen should be placed over short grass in a freely exposed situation. **1902** *Encycl. Brit.* XXX. 699/1 Various forms of open lattice work and louvre screens have been devised and used.., in all of which the wind is supposed to blow freely through the screens, while the latter cut off the greater part of the direct sunshine. **1923** F. WILD *Shackleton's Last Voy.* i. 12 One large screen, containing hair hygrograph, standard thermometer and thermograph. **1975** J. SCOTT *Fun with Meteorol.* 36/1 Ideally the thermometer bulbs should be about 4 ft. above ground level and the screen should have a north opening door to eliminate direct sunlight when it is opened.

f. A windscreen of a motor vehicle; also formerly, (*a*) a secondary screen to shield the occupants of the back seat in an open car; (*b*) a screen of celluloid for protecting the sides of an open car.

1904 A. B. FILSON YOUNG *Complete Motorist* vii. 176 When a cover is used it should have a removable glass screen in front. **1912** *Motor Manual* (ed. 14) iii. 99 Most cars now have adjustable and detachable glass or celluloid windscreens as a protection against the weather, dust, etc; screens can also be made of wire gauze and waterproof material. **1925** *Morris Owner's Man.* p. xi (Advt.), There are..rear screens and rear screens. **1955** *Times* 10 May 7/7 Perhaps the only fault from the driver's point of view is that his windscreen wiper is badly located and does not clean enough of the right-hand side of the screen. **1959** *Motor Manual* (ed. 36) vi. 186 Whatever the type of motor, it is usually combined with a suitable speed-reducing mechanism so that the wiper blades shall move reasonably slowly across the screen.

g. *U.S. Sports.* (See quots. 1961 and 1976.)

1939 *Sat. Even. Post* 7 Oct. 89/2 These are the components of a good passing game: the pitcher, receivers, and screen behind which the thrower can successfully operate. **1951** [see *PICK *sb.*[3] 10]. **1961** J. S. SALAK *Dict. Amer. Sports* 383 *Screen* (basketball), term used to describe a maneuver of the offensive team in which one player, by moving in front of opponent, 'screens' or 'screens out' that opponent from his teammate. A screen generally is worked in an effort to free one of the offensive team members for a shot at the basket. *Ibid.* 384 *Screen* (handball), an assumed or retained position on the court which prevents the opponent from getting to, or playing the ball. **1967** B. STARR *Quarterbacking* 173 Screen passes are effective countermoves by the offense when the defense is applying heated pressure on the passer. **1975** *New Yorker* 7 Apr. 100/3 On offense, they zipped the ball around fast and moved with purpose, setting the picks and screens that their principal plays.. called for until someone got open for a good shot. **1976** *Webster's Sports Dict.* 374/1 *Screen*, a maneuver in various sports by which an opponent is legally cut off from the play.

6. (Further examples from *Electricity* and *Sound.*)

1915 HAWKHEAD & DOWSETT *Handbk. Wireless Telegr.* (ed. 2) 263 Some valves are fitted with an additional screen of copper gauze covering the outside of the glass bulb... This screen protects the valve from heavy spark discharges in the neighbourhood. **1931** B. BROWN *Talking Pictures* v. 127 A special sound-porous screen is used when the speakers are placed directly behind the picture. Most of the sound screens used in this country are of the woven type and of loose construction. **1950** *High Voltage Cables* (British Insulated Callender's Cables Ltd.) (ed. 2) i. 4 The screen functions as an earth conductor in close contact with the insulation. **1978** A. M. PORTIS *Electromagnetic Fields* xiv. 544 We wish..to discuss the scattering by various kinds of apertures in a two dimensional dielectric screen.

b. *Radio.* An arrangement of parallel wires located between a transmitting aerial and the earth's surface, serving to reduce the loss of power from the aerial to the earth.

1922 R. KEEN *Direction & Position Finding by Wireless* i. 5 Experiments were being carried out in Germany..in connection with the screening of a vertical aerial... In other countries work..led to the complete wire screen or reflector. **1952** E. A. LAPORT *Radio Antenna Engin.* ii. 123 It is desirable to bring the ground wires to the surface a short distance from the radiator base so as to form a good ground screen above the soil near the antenna base where the electric field strengths are high. **1961** H. JASIK *Antenna Engin. Handbk.* xxiv. 16 If a screen is designed for both high and low bands in the VHF range, the over-all size should be determined by the lowest frequency.

c. *Electronics.* = **screen grid.*

1927 *Amateur Wireless* XI. 269/1 The presence of the outer grid between the inner grid and the plate or anode naturally acts to some extent as a screen, and since this is connected to H.T. which is effectively at earth potential, we have a capacitative screen between the two electrodes. **1933** *Jrnl. Franklin Inst.* CCXVI. 418 Close to this first grid, and coaxial with it and the cathode, is a second spiral used to screen the control grid from the fields of the plate and called therefore the 'screen grid' or simply the 'screen'. **1942** *Electronic Engin.* XIV. 639/3 This formula..gives less accurate results for pentodes and tetrodes unless the trans-conductance to the screen is taken into account. **1962** D. F. SHAW *Introd. Electronics* xi. 234 The defect in the tetrode characteristics..is eliminated by the insertion of a third grid, called the suppressor grid, between the anode and the screen.

6*. *Printing.* **a.** A transparent plate, covered with two crossing sets of closely spaced parallel lines or with a uniform pattern of fine dots, behind which a photosensitive surface is exposed to obtain a half-tone image or as a step in forming the image carrier in a gravure process; also, in *Photogr.*, a patterned transparent plate or film that is combined with a negative during printing to give a textured appearance to the finished print.

1894 *Amer. Dict. Printing & Bookmaking* 465/2 Half-tone plates are made by passing the rays of light from a negative through a screen which is ruled or dotted. **1902** *Encycl. Brit.* XXIX. 411/1 This was finally accomplished by the insertion of a screen, in the camera, between the lens and the plate—the effect of which was to break up the whole surface of the negative into dots. **1940** [see *contact screen* s.v. *CONTACT *sb.* 6]. **1946** H. WHETTON *Practical Printing & Binding* xxv. 299/2 When the tissue is dry it is ready for screening. The cross-lined screen used in photogravure differs from those used in the production of half-tones. **1967** KARCH & BUBER *Offset Processes* v. 158 Coarser screens, such as the 65-line screen, are used in newspapers printed by letterpress. **1977** J. HEDGECOE *Photographer's Handbk.* 255 The picture, below left, was made by sandwiching the screen with a 2¼ ins sq..negative so that the pattern appeared relatively small.

b. The fine gauze or mesh (orig. of silk: cf. *SILK SCREEN *sb.*) used in screen printing.

1934 F. A. BAKER *Silk Screen Practice* xvii. 114 Doubtless most screen operators have had visions of the ideal screen shop. **1938** BIEGELEISEN & BUSENBARK *Silk Screen Printing Process* v. 105 Either organdy or silk may be used as the screen for film stencils. **1957** *Screen Printer & Display Producer* July 3/2 The mesh is coated with a solution to form the screen for the photographic stencil. **1967** V. STRAUSS *Printing Industry* vii. 521/1 After the screen is ready, it may either be proofed or be used for running without proofing.

6.** An instance or the action of screening (see *SCREEN *v.* 4).

1954 [see *screen test* (sense *7 a)]. **1974** M. C. GERALD *Pharmacol.* iv. 77 In a general blind screen, a range of doses of the compound a re injected into test animals..and gross behavioral observations are made with an eye toward detecting any activity. **1975** *Language for Life* (Dept. Educ. & Sci.) xvii. 263 The majority of children scoring low on the group intelligence test have already been the subjects of consultation between head teachers and psychologists; consequently this second screen is now regarded as serving no more than a 'mopping up' purpose.

7. a. (sense 1 d) *screen image*; (sense 6*) *screen test*; **screen-cloth,** (*a*): delete † and add: metal or plastic mesh, esp. for covering a window or door screen (Webster), or for sifting material; (further examples); **screen current** *Electronics*, the current flowing in the screen grid of a valve; **screen-door,** a metallic or textile outer door of a pair, used for protection against insects or storms; also *Naut.*, for protection against explosions; **screen grid** *Electronics*, a grid placed between the control grid and the anode of a valve to reduce the capacitance between these electrodes; **screen memory, -memory** *Psychol.*, a Freudian term, orig. tr. as 'concealing memory', for a childhood memory whose apparently indifferent content screens from consciousness some (usu. previous) significant emotional event; **screen-painting,** pictorial decoration of church screens; **screen** († **forward**) **pass** *N. Amer. Football* (see quot. 1976); **screen-perch** (later examples); **screen plate** *Photogr.*, an obsolete form of colour plate in which minute filters in primary colours are incorporated in the plate itself; freq. *attrib.*; **screen porch** *N. Amer.*, a veranda protected by a screen against insects; **screen print** *sb.*, (*a*) a picture or design produced by screen printing; (*b*) screen-printed fabric; **screen printer,** one who works at screen printing; **screen printing,** a printing process used esp. for pictorial matter in which the ink is transferred to the surface to be printed through a fine screen (sense 6* b) stretched in a frame, the non-printing parts of the screen having been rendered impervious; so **screen-print** *v. trans.*, to print (a surface or a design) in this way; **screen-printed** *ppl. a.*; **screen process,** the process of screen printing; freq. *attrib.*; **screen table** (see quot. 1794); **screen temperature** *Meteorol.*, the temperature as measured by a thermometer in a screen (sense *3 e); **screen voltage** *Electronics*, the voltage applied to the screen grid of a valve; **screen wall, -wall,** a wall that serves as a screen; so **screenwalling**; **screen-wash,** the cleaning of a windscreen automatically; also *attrib.*, of a substance added to water used in screenwashing; **screen-washer,** a device which washes a windscreen by directing a jet of water on to its exterior from below; **screen-wiper,** a windscreen wiper.

1946 *Sun* (Baltimore) 7 Oct. 2/5 Sales of bronze and copper screen cloth were allowed on an adjustable prices basis. 1974 G. S. Ormsby in P. L. Moore et al. *Drilling Practices Manual* vi. 152 The particle size a shale shaker can remove depends almost completely upon the size and the shape of the mesh openings in the screen cloth. 1936 E. D. McArthur *Electronics & Electron Tubes* v. 72 In this region, the screen-current characteristic is the exact opposite of the plate-current characteristic. 1962 D. F. Shaw *Introd. Electronics* xi. 232 The characteristics of a tetrode are more complex than those of a triode because of the additional variables of screen voltage and screen current. 1975 D. G. Fink *Electronics Engineers' Handbk.* xiv. 8 Multi-grid tubes require screen-grid modulation in conjunction with the control-grid modulation to achieve space-charge modulation and to minimize screen current. 1840 Screen door [in Dict.]. 1889 I. M. Rittenhouse *Maud* (1939) vii. 225 And after he'd gone I stood staring and staring out of the screen-door at nothing. 1914 'Bartimeus' *Naval Occasions* vi. 39 The screen-door..opened from the battery to the quarter-deck. 1933 E. O'Neill *Ah, Wilderness!* (1934) I. 16 *Mrs. Miller.* That boy! (*She rushes to the screen door and out on the porch, calling:*) Tommy! You mind what your Pa told you! 1974 *News & Courier* (Charleston, S. Carolina) 19 Apr. (Wickes Lumber Advt. Suppl.) 6 Screen doors in many styles, sizes & finishes. 1977 *Gay News* 24 Mar. 13/4 Such matters as who should fix the screen door, or do the cooking ..seem to fall into place as if by prearrangement. 1979 *Sunset* Apr. 56/1 The Boulevard Cafe, with open-air lunch counter, fly fans, and a banging screen door to an indoor counter, has been serving highway customers the same way for over 32 years. 1928 G. E. Sterling *Radio Man.* 167 The connection to the screen grid is made to the regular grid connection on a standard socket. 1930 *Manch. Guardian* 20 Sept. 15/7 A remarkable constructors' set known as the 'Osram Music Magnet Four', comprising two screen-grid stages, detector, and low frequency stages. 1942 *Electronic Engin.* XV. 10/1 When used as a triode the suppressor and screen grids are connected to anode. 1974 Harvey & Bohlman *Stereo F.M. Radio Handbk.* ii. 15 Carrier voltage is applied in push-pull via T_1 to the control grids of the two valves, whilst the modulating signal is supplied to the screen grids from T_2 which also provides push-pull drive. 1897 *Knowledge* 1 Sept. 217/2 Any mixture of indefinite light with the screen image has the effect of so much fog. 1937 *Discovery* Feb. 45/1 For production of the screen image a high intensity automatic arc is being used. 1924 J. Riviere tr. *Freud's Recollection, Repetition* in *Coll. Papers* II. xxxii. 368 In many cases I have had the impression that the familiar childhood-amnesia, which is theoretically so important to us, is entirely outweighed by the screen-memories. 1940 *Chambers's Techn. Dict.* 749/1 *Screen memory*, early childhood impressions and ideas which break through into consciousness, but are distorted and condensed into something which is unrecognisable to the individual. 1957 L. Durrell *Justine* i. 78 It is perhaps what the Freudians would call a screen-memory of incidents in her earliest youth. 1962 J. Strachey tr. *Freud's Screen Memories* in *Compl. Wks.* III. 320 A screen memory may be described as 'retrogressive' or as having 'pushed forward' according as the one chronological relation or the other holds between the screen and the thing screened off. 1967 Kanzer & Blum in B. B. Wolman *Psychoanal. Techniques* iv. 107 An examination of the painful episode as a nucleus (screen memory) with an infinity of ramifications, which involved the entire relationship of the patient with his father. 1906 G. E. Fox in *Victoria Hist. County Norfolk* II. 542 The screen paintings at Barton Turf, Edingthorpe, Harpley, Potter Heigham, Houghton-le-Dale, Lessingham, Ranworth, and Walpole-St.-Peter, have all been assigned to the fifteenth century. 1937 A. G. Little *Franciscan History & Legend in English Mediaeval Art* ii. 15 (*heading*) Screen Paintings... The painting of the lower panels of the rood and parclose screens of English churches with saints was confined almost entirely to the latter end of the 15th century. 1934 C. Walsh *Intercollegiate Football* 345/2, 1908-'Screen' Forward Pass (no longer legal). 1955 E. Pope *Football's Greatest Coaches* xxviii. 326 Zuppke originated the system of pulling back guards to protect the passer, the screen pass. 1970 *Globe & Mail* (Toronto) 26 Sept. 39/1 Ernie Carnegie gave the Redmen the lead with an 80-yard touchdown from a screen pass. 1976 *Webster's Sports Dict.* 374/2 *Screen pass* or *screen football*, a short forward pass to a back in the flat in front of whom a wall of interference has been formed by linemen who have moved over after the snap. 1979 *Arizona Daily Star* 5 Aug. c 9/1 Sproul.. found Ivery on a screen pass and Ivery weaved his way down the left sideline for the deciding touchdown. 1965 P. Wayre *Wind in Reeds* x. 142 Trained birds of prey are often tied to a screen-perch in their mews at night, this is a padded perch from the underneath of which hangs a sheet of thick canvas or hessian well-weighted at the bottom to keep it taut. 1971 *Country Life* 8 Apr. 799/3 Hawks have to be set to roost on a screen perch which prevents them from bating off and entangling themselves. [1898 *Sci. Trans. R. Dublin Soc.* VI. 134 The lined screen which can bring about this will only show its individual colours when placed under the microscope. It is then seen to consist of closely ruled adjacent lines in reddish-orange, yellowish-green, and blue tints. This screen, applied closely to the sensitive surface, analyses the image in the camera.] 1909 G. L. Johnson *Photogr. Optics & Colour Photogr.* v. 238 This screen plate is covered with a panchromatic emulsion. 1930 O. Wheeler *Photogr. Printing Processes* xvii. 218 Screen-plate processes for the production of transparencies..are undoubtedly of great merit. 1970 M. J. Sethna *Photography* 8 John Joly's 'screen-plate' method led to the 'autochrome' plates made in 1907 by the Lumière brothers. 1973 D. A. Spencer *Focal Dict. Photogr. Technol.* 548 *Screen plate process*, additive colour process in which the image is both recorded and viewed through a mosaic or reseau of microscopically small colour filter elements. The emulsion is exposed through the mosaic and reversal processed to yield an additive colour transparency. 1962 M. E. Murie *Two in Far North* I. iv. 36 Mother baked pies, many of them, and doughnuts. These were put out into the cache or the screen porch and frozen. 1970 *New Yorker* 28 Feb. 48/2, I went around to the side and up on the screen porch, lifted the window to the library, and climbed in. 1979 *Arizona Daily Star* 5 Aug. (Advt. Section) 14/9 Screen porch, sun deck, 2 car garage, 3 car carport. 1938 Biegeleisen & Busenbark *Silk Screen Printing Process* viii. 184 If a photograph or wash drawing is to be reproduced, it is first sent to a photoengraver, who makes a 'screen print' from it. 1957 *Observer* 1 Dec. 11/5 Chinese 'Sampan' screen-prints of water, reeds and flowers made full-skirted dresses. 1973 *Country Life* 21 June 1808 The characteristic screen print..is an edition of 100 published by Christie's Contemporary Arts at £65 each. 1976 *Dumfries & Galloway Standard* 25 Dec. 11/4 (Advt.), Screen prints 120 cm. wide. Modern designs. Metre usually £1·60. Now 99p. 1952 *Archit. Rev.* CXI. 194 (*caption*) Curtains and chair-cover privately screen-printed for Jane Drew. 1970 *Daily Tel.* (Colour Suppl.) 15 May 14 We made our real breakthrough when we screen-printed ceramic colours on to flat ware. 1957 *Screen Printer & Display Producer* July 4/2 The older type of screen printed transfers, which have been available to potters for some ten years.., have become well established as a medium for high quality multi-colour relief decoration. 1969 *Sears Catal.* Spring/Summer 43 Long-sleeve screen-printed Sweatshirts. 1938 Biegeleisen & Busenbark *Silk Screen Printing Process* i. 12 The screen printer may make prints which so closely resemble woodblock prints that only an expert can distinguish the difference. 1977 *Daily Times* (Lagos) 11 Jan. 22/5 (Advt.), Wanted. Experienced Screen-Printers. Apply..to Clem Advertising Productions. 1934 F. A. Baker *Silk Screen Printing* iii. 21 (*heading*) Silk and other gauzes used in screen printing. 1936 [see *hand block* s.v. *hand *sb.* 63]. 1958 *Observer* 17 Aug. 7/3 The firm of Taco use beautiful hand screen-printing of fruit and leaves on cotton ottoman, a process that takes twelve screens. (These days one has to say 'hand screening' because so much screen-printing is being done with the Swiss Buser automatic multicolour machine.) 1980 *Daily Tel.* 11 July 15/4 The exhibition confirms..that screen-printing has become a major medium for the living artist. 1930 B. Zahn *Silk Screen Methods of Reproduction* 37 The specification for a paint for screen process work. 1938 Biegeleisen & Busenbark *Silk Screen Printing Process* i. 7 Applicability of the screen process to the fine and applied arts has been recognized rather belatedly. 1967 Karch & Buber *Offset Processes* ii. 35 (*caption*) Screen process presses are often used for printing on glass bottles. 1970 *British Printer* July 69/1 Screen process had always been particularly versatile in handling a variety of surfaces and shapes which could not easily be printed by any of the three main printing processes. *Ibid.* 74/2 All screen-process inks contain inflammable solvents. 1794 T. Sheraton *Cabinet-Maker & Upholsterer's Drawing-Bk.* II. 395 *Of the Screen-Table.* This table is intended for a lady to write or work at near the fire; the screen part behind securing her face from its injuries. 1971 *Country Life* 30 Sept. (Suppl.) 29 (Advt.), A rare Sheraton period mahogany screen table, 17″ wide. £245. 1913 *Rep. Brit. Assoc. Adv. Sci. 1912* 740 The explanation lies in the removal of air which has been chilled by radiation from the plant, and its replacement by air at 'screen-temperature'. 1972 *Daily Tel.* 1 Sept. 12/4 In Scotland the screen temperature fell to 32 degrees F (0 degrees C) at Tummel Bridge, Perthshire. 1954 *Cancer* VII. 1184/2 Large numbers of women could receive a screen test for carcinoma of the cervix with minimal utilization of professional personnel. 1971 *Nature* 9 July 105/1 Observations suggest that it is possible to devise an *in vitro* 'screen' test for potentially carcinogenic substances. 1936 E. D. McArthur *Electronics & Electron Tubes* v. 72 This..is fulfilled when the anode voltage becomes less positive than the screen voltage. 1945 *Electronic Engin.* XVII. 332/1 To obtain best results the control grid and screen voltages must be correctly chosen. 1962 Screen voltage [see *screen current* above]. 1900 Screen wall [in Dict.]. 1936 A. W. Clapham *Romanesque Archit.* iii. 53 This eastern screen-wall..appears only in the Apulian school. 1971 *Country Life* 30 Sept. 819/3 To guard against possible intrusion a screen wall was raised. 1976 *West Lancashire Even. Gaz.* 13 Dec. 9/5 (Advt.), Very low-priced..quality fencing, wood and concrete posts, sheds, timber, screen-walling. 1970 *Times* 5 Mar. 16 Another new feature is the 'cyclic' wipers which give not only slow and fast speeds but..eight wipes in conjunction with the screen-wash. 1976 *Scotsman* 24 Dec. 11/2 Sachets of screenwash additive are useful, however, not only in preventing washers from freezing in cold weather but in dissolving the road grime and grease that can smear or even scratch the windscreen. 1958 *Observer* 17 Aug. 15/7 The test car also had the simplest and most efficient screen washer I have seen so far. 1962 [see *accessory *sb.* 1]. 1977 *Lancashire Life* Mar. 118/4 It still has cloth seats, heated rear window and electric screenwashers. 1928 E. Wallace *Double* iii. 32 With his screen-wiper swinging madly, his mackintosh black with driving rain, Dick Staines came to Brighton. 1930 *Punch* 22 Jan. 92/3 Aggie must have something, a new mascot, a screen-wiper.., a new wing. 1970 *Railway Mag.* Oct. 558/1 With the aid of..efficient screen-wipers on the locomotive, there was no difficulty in sighting the signals. 1977 *Lancashire Life* Mar. 118/4 The screenwipers have not been re-set for right hand drive.

b. *spec.* with reference to the cinema or television screen, esp. in the *transf.* sense (see *1 d above), as *screen actor, actress, adaptation, beauty, credit, début, fan, fever, kiss, rights, set, star, story, version, world, worthiness*; *screen-filling, -struck* [after *stage-struck*], *-worthy* adjs.; **screenplay**, the script from which a motion picture film is produced; formerly, the film itself; also *attrib.*; **screen test**, a filmed test of the performing abilities of a prospective film actor, or the film shot on such an occasion; hence **screen-test** *v. trans.*; **screen time**, the time allotted to or occupied by a film or television production; **screen writer**, a writer of film scripts; hence **screen-writing** *vbl. sb.* and *ppl. a.*

1915 *Film Fun* Dec. 1 The screen actor has the best of it in holiday season. 1977 *Times* 7 Oct. 11/4 Valentino..was actually a very good screen actor. 1916 *N.Y. Times* 8 May 7 It is rumored that never again is this clever screen actress to play such a rôle. 1939 A. Huxley *Let.* 18 Nov. (1969) 448, I am working at present on the screen adaptation of *Pride and Prejudice.* 1919 H. L. Wilson *Ma Pettengill* ii. 38 It is the face of one of our famous screen beauties. 1922 Screen credit [see *credit *sb.* 13 f]. 1977 R. Ludlum *Chancellor MS.* vi. 78 They're willing to..remove your name from the screen credits..not the title, of course. 1915 *N.Y. Times* 22 Nov. 12 'The Martyrs of the Alamo', the Triangle picture in which Douglas Fairbanks made his screen début. 1923 T. Lane *What's Wrong with Movies?* vi. 100 The general run of screen fans want to do very little thinking when they go to the cinema. 1915 Screen fever [see *screen-struck adj.]. *a* 1963 J. Lusby in B. James *Austral. Short Stories* (1963) 231 The Eccentric's reel..concluded with a screen-filling close-up of the stolid face of an armourer. 1951 M. McLuhan *Mech. Bride* (1967) 101/2 Shirley Temple gets her first screen kiss in a picture you'll never forget. 1971 *Petticoat* 17 July 28/3 Peter..was signed up by Walt Disney to give Hayley Mills..her first screen kiss. 1916 *N.Y. Times* 7 Feb. 9/3 (*heading*) Anna Held's debut in a screen play. 1925 *Ladies' Home Jrnl.* Jan. 37/3 Screen play by Walter Woods. 1938 A. Huxley *Let.* 18 Nov. (1969) 437 They have followed their usual procedure and handed my treatment over to several other people to make a screen-play out of. 1945 R. Chandler *Let.* 13 Oct. in *R. Chandler Speaking* (1966) 43 He has gone so long without writing—unless you count a couple of screenplay jobs. 1977 *Times Lit. Suppl.* 24 June 750/3 A screenplay..is subsumed in the completed movie. 1980 *Times* 22 Nov. 4/8 Mr Cimino has written his own screenplay. 1920 *Q. Rev.* July 185 The feverish haste exhibited at the present time to secure the screen-rights of classics in the world of fiction. 1974 *She* Jan. 83/1 Bought screen rights to *Boy Shoots Girl*... Now to find writer to do Treatment. 1948 'T. Claymore' *Nest of Vipers* x. 195 Listening critically, I felt that she needed a Hollywood screen set and a background of soft music for these speeches. 1914 R. Grau *Theatre Science* x. 211 So here we have the unique spectacle of an idolized screen star earning a prima donna's honorarium for stage appearances at night only. 1977 J. Aiken *Last Movement* ix. 167 Seeing a screen star for the first time in the flesh. 1914 R. Grau *Theatre Science* xii. 256 Thousands are impatiently awaiting the appearance of those publications which fictionize the screen stories. 1946 D. L. Sayers *Unpopular Opinions* 124 Wishing..that they too could live like the heroes and heroines of these witless million-dollar screen stories. 1915 *Film Fun* Dec. 1 Screen-struck. Everybody wants to get into motion pictures. It is an epidemic of screen fever. 1922 I. & H. Klumph *Screen Acting* xvi. 89 Then..she went back to her work of checking up on the scenes..and gave her screen test no more thought. 1933 *Sat. Even. Post* 17 June 14/1 Harry Rapf, one of the M-G-M executives, happened to see me dancing at the Winter Garden in New York City and asked me to make a screen test. 1952 M. McCarthy *Groves of Academe* (1953) iv. 57 The cold peroxided beauties who..were here while waiting for a screen-test. 1970 *Sunday Times* 26 Apr. 29/2 He screen-tested me... And I was offered one of the three star parts in the production. 1948 *Hansard Commons* 21 Jan. 219 Overseas producers..enjoy the same proportion of British screen time they have had in the past few years. 1973 *Listener* 20 Sept. 391/1 In a typical year, the BBC sells 11,000 hours of television screen-time abroad. 1978 *Broadcast* 29 May 10/1 The problem of screen-time for groups on the extreme political fringe. 1915 *N.Y. Times* 20 Sept. 9 The screen version of 'Peer Gynt' begins with the reindeer ride and ends with the rescue of Peer. 1933 *Radio Times* 14 Apr. 75/1 In *Cavalcade* (both stage and screen versions). 1981 *Listener* 1 Jan. 22/1 The screen version of *David Copperfield*..went way beyond the accepted running time of movies of that period. 1915 *Film Flashes* 11 Dec. 4 Are we to live only for ourselves, forgetting our brothers and sisters of the screen world? 1928 *Daily Express* 7 May 9/2 The production ..has been booked by Provincial Cinematograph Theatres, a booking generally regarded throughout the world as the hallmark of screen-worthiness. 1928 *Daily Tel.* 12 June 10 Rachel... Her brief meteoric career needed no fantastic embellishments to make her story screenworthy. 1980 *Times Lit. Suppl.* 23 May 582/2 Though the screen-play for *The Tin Drum* was 'revised and augmented' by Günter Grass, Volker Schlöndorff's success has relatively little to do with making phrases screenworthy. 1921 *Moving Picture Stories* 12 Aug. 26/3 A Robertson–Cole picture..written by..two well-known screen writers. 1958 *Times Lit. Suppl.* 15 Aug. p. xxviii/5 How many genuine screen-writers have achieved any success in this country? 1974 *Listener* 17 Jan. 68/1 My first opportunities as a screenwriter were..in this country, but my career..has been in Hollywood. 1941 B. Schulberg *What makes Sammy Run?* vi. 124 Have screen-writing job for you. 1973 [see *pot-boiler 2 a]. 1977 *Listener* 20 Oct. 498/1 In the 1930s, it was fairly easy to get a handle on the politics of the screenwriting community.

screen, *sb.*² (Earlier examples.)

1789 G. Parker *Life's Painter of Variegated Characters* xv. 153 *Rum screen*, a bank note. *Ibid.* 179 *Screen*, a bank note. 1795 H. Potter *New Dict. Cant & Flash Lang.* (ed. 2) 53 *Skreen*, a bank note. 1811 *Lexicon Balatronicum*, s.v. *Screen*, Queer screens; forged bank notes.

screen, *v.* **1. b.** Delete *rare* and add: Now usu. with *out*; freq. *fig.* (Further examples.)

1943 *Sun* (Baltimore) 3 Aug. 11/1 The stalks are put through a mechanical disintegrator which reduces them to a juicy puree and screens out the toughest fibers. 1946 *Cancer Res.* VI. 490/1 In resorting to histologic and cytologic studies to screen out the inactive compounds we have made the assumption that damage induced by active compounds would become evident within 48 hours after injection. 1955 *Publ. Amer. Dial. Soc.* xxiv. 51 There is an increasing tendency to screen out all argot and slang in the presence of outsiders. 1967 M. Argyle *Psychol. Interpersonal Behaviour* x. 195 The method..releases extremely powerful emotional forces, and those not able to profit from them should be screened out. 1968 *International Herald Tribune* 3 Sept. 7/3 The FBI has improved its methods of screening out inaccurate reporting. 1971 *Sci. Amer.* Oct. 42/3 The detector was located underground to screen out relatively low-energy particles produced in the atmosphere. **1975** *New Yorker* 21 Apr. 54/2 The company's instructions to its managers do seem to indicate an employment policy favoring people of conventional outlook and screening out people who might harbor tendencies towards nonconformist intellectualizing. **1979** *Bull. Amer. Acad. Arts & Sci.* Feb. 17 The committee will not screen out applications.

c. *Electr.* To protect from external electric or magnetic fields; to cover (a wire or circuit) in order to prevent it from radiating electrical interference.

1922 *Wireless World* 1 July 416/1 The problem is to screen the receiving apparatus from the effects induced directly by the oscillator. **1931** *B.B.C. Year-bk. 1932* 422 It will..be advisable to screen the coils L_1, L_2, the tuning condenser K_1, and the secondary circuit, L_3, K_2. **1950** *Engineering* 3 Feb. 140/2 On wireless-carrying vehicles electrical equipment must be screened. **1960** *Practical Wireless* XXXVI. 393/1 The lead from the input socket is screened. **1971** L. T. Agger *Introd. Electr.* viii. 119 It is sometimes necessary.. to screen a space from external electrostatic influence, as in protection against lightning of buildings containing explosives.

2. d. To surround (a nuclear reactor or other source of ionizing radiation) with a mass of material intended to absorb the radiation.

1915 Colwell & Russ *Radium, X Rays & Living Cell* vi. 160 If the radium applicator is screened by the interposition of ·5 mm. of lead..the results are different. **1931** G. E. Birkett *Radium Therapy* ii. 36 The radium in solution should be heavily screened to protect people working in adjacent rooms. **1946** *Ann. Reg. 1945* 354 The pile was not screened well enough to protect the personnel from the injurious effects of the intense radiation emitted by the unstable fission products.

e. *U.S. Sports.* To shield (a team-mate) from attack by opponents; to act as a shield against (opponents). Also *intr.* Cf. *screen *sb.*[1] 3 g.

1922 P. D. Haughton *How to watch & understand Football* 7 To stop the runner who is so thoroughly screened by interferers. **1951** *Sun* (Baltimore) 24 Dec. (B ed.) 13/2 Watch when they screen for a shooter [in Basketball]. **1961** [see *screen *sb.*[1] 3 g].

4. c. To examine systematically in order to discover suitability for admission or acceptance; *spec.* (*a*) to examine (a person) for unwanted attributes or objects, esp. political disloyalty; (*b*) to test (chemicals) for their suitability for use as drugs.

1943 *Sun* (Baltimore) 14 May 1/3 These offices 'screen' a list of prospects for the employers. **1945** *Manch. Guardian* 18 July 8/1 The recruits had come forward from the disbanded Guardia del Popolo and from most various sources and all would be screened carefully. **1949** *Cancer Res.* IX. 625/1 More than 1,000 chemical agents have been screened against Sarcoma 37 *in vivo.* **1956** W. Graham *Sleeping Partner* x. 82 When you said you were bringing an assistant to Harwell, of course we had to have her screened. **1958** *Listener* 19 June 1015/2, I am within a few yards of the Customs desk... My wife had packed all the declared trinkets in one bag, and that is all he wants to see. He screens it in fifteen seconds flat. **1962** *Sunday Times* 14 Jan. 1/7 Every flight arriving from Europe was screened by medical and immigration officials for Pakistani immigrants. **1970** *New Scientist* 11 June 538/2 Drug companies are trying to weed out drug-takers from their staffs and to screen applicants so as to avoid taking on more. **1971** *Daily Tel.* 19 Apr. 15/7 Electronic equipment at airports to 'screen' passengers for weapons and so on. **1974** M. C. Gerald *Pharmacol.* iv. 77 Of the 15,000 compounds our government screened as substitute antimalarials, only two..were found to be superior to quinine. **1979** *Daily Tel.* 21 May 12/7 Mr Corliss describes only those events which were reported in reputable scientific journals, where all material is rigorously screened, and 'mis-identifications and hoaxes are kept to a minimum'.

d. To select or separate by means of a screening process.

1943 *Sun* (Baltimore) 10 Dec. 6/7 The Attorney General said he believed it was possible to screen loyal from disloyal Japanese. **1976** *National Observer* (U.S.) 5 June 8/3 The experiment involves 20 communities, screened from an original list of 250 where some citizen efforts at decision-making already have cropped up.

e. To examine (a person, esp. as one of a large group) for disease or defects other than as a response to a request for treatment.

1944 [implied in *screening *vbl. sb.* 2 c]. **1950** *Amer. Jrnl. Public Health* XL. 275/1 A population group in one city is screened for tuberculosis. A separate program is conducted..to screen a population group for diabetes. **1970** *Observer* 12 Apr. 25/5 We could therefore soon be in a position to screen the whole population to see which recessive genes they carry. **1970** *Daily Tel.* 10 Oct. 8/4 Mass radiography is the easiest way for the man in the street to be screened.

f. To examine or search (data or an article) for any content of particular relevance or interest.

1956 A. H. Compton *Atomic Quest* 27 The committee had begun to function that soon afterwards was screening physics news for items of possible military importance. **1964** *Ann. N.Y. Acad. Sci.* CXV. 569 The system proposed.. allows the raw experimental data to be screened and digested directly by a small fast hybrid computer. **1977** *Jrnl. R. Soc. Arts* CXXV. 228/2 For the genetic resources material to be of any value to the breeder it must be evaluated or 'screened'.

5*. *Printing.* To obtain an image of (a picture, type, etc.) through a screen (*screen *sb.*[1] 6*).

1948 R. R. Karch *Graphic Arts Procedures* ix. 247 Both type matter and illustrations are screened. **1952** R. W. & E. W. Polk *Practice of Printing* (rev. ed.) xxiv. 198 In display, sometimes a heading or a block of type is screened to create a desired effect. **1972** *Physics Bull.* Sept. 532/1 Continuous tone pictures are 'screened' to allow reproduction by normal printing methods.

7. *trans.* To show (a picture) on a screen; to project on to a screen as with a magic lantern or film projector; to exhibit as a production for the cinema or television. Also *intr.*, to be (well or ill) suited for reproducing on a cinema or television screen.

1913 *Writer's Mag.* Nov. 188/2 Because you fail to sell your story, in spite of the fact that you see others of the same type screened, will not be proof that editors are prejudiced against you. **1915** *Durham County Advertiser* 18 June 8/7 'Tommy Atkins', a stirring patriotic picture..will be screened at an early date. **1919** H. L. Wilson *Ma Pettengill* ii. 67 She'll screen well, and she's one of the few that can turn on the tears when she wants to. **1962** *Rep. Comm. Broadc. 1960* 66 Programmes of national appeal screened by all or most of the companies. **1973** *Guardian* 10 Apr. 1/6 A revised version of Granada Television's controversial documentary about Mr John Poulson..will be screened on April 30. **1976** *National Observer* (U.S.) 18 Dec. 9/2 When the movie was screened, the key obscenity standard was whether a sex work was 'utterly without redeeming social value'.

screenage (skrī·nėdʒ). [f. Screen *sb.*[1] + -age.] The material used as a screen for ionizing radiation; such screens collectively; the action or the efficiency of screening.

1929 S. Cade *Radium Treatment of Cancer* i. 5 The necrosis is in inverse proportion with the screenage. **1930** *Brit. Med. Jrnl.* 8 Feb. 234 The screenage, amounting to the equivalent of just over 1 mm. of platinum, consists of monel metal, brass, aluminium, and wood. **1933** Ward & Durden-Smith *Recent Advances in Radium* vi. 67 The screenage for seeds most commonly used at the Radium Institute is 0·5 millimetre of gold. **1940** S. Cade *Malignant Dis. & Treatment by Radium* viii. 177 Screenage of eye applicators by substances of low or medium atomic weight, such as wax, rubber, and palladium, may..still further reduce the incidence of eye complications. **1956** C. W. Wilson *Radium Therapy* (ed. 2) x. 239 When lead screenage is added to a radium source filtered by 0·5 mm. platinum so as completely to surround the source, the transmission curve is virtually a straight line up to 20 cm. thickness of lead.

screened, *ppl. a.* Add: **1. a.** Also freq. with adverbs, as *screened-in*, *-off*.

1833 [in Dict.]. **1946** J. O'Hara in *New Yorker* 6 July 18 Eben Townsend was sitting on the screened-in porch smoking his after-dinner cigar. **1968** R. M. Patterson *Finlay's River* i. 39 We slept that night on the floor in the screened-in veranda, very comfortable and protected against the rain and the mosquitoes. **1973** J. Wainwright *Pride of Pigs* 78 They led him..to the ward, and pointed out the screened-off bed. **1978** P. Niesewand *Underground Connection* 1 The screened-off telephone switchboard. **1979** *Arizona Daily Star* 5 Aug. (Advt. Section) 18/3 Enjoy the breezes and mountain views from large screened-in Arizona room. **1981** P. Mallory *Killing Matter* iii. 33 A broad screened-in porch where Holly Devereaux sat in a rattan chair.

c. *Meteorol.* Placed in or measured in a screen (see *screen *sb.*[1] 3 e).

1894 [in Dict., sense 1 a]. **1920** *Westm. Gaz.* 2 Dec. 6/4 At Greenwich, a minimum screened temperature of 27 deg. was registered.

2. b. In the sense of *screen *v.* 4 c.

1957 *Economist* 26 Oct. 321/1 A drive for Party members among discreetly screened intellectuals, who responded 'sincerely' to the 'blooming-flowers' campaign by seeing, hearing and speaking no evil, is also under way; the first 25 recruits are proudly announced from the professorial staff of Tientsin university. **1962** L. Deighton *Ipcress File* xv. 86 The screened personnel available to us. **1967** *Times Rev. Industry* July 89/3 The procedures of some 41 companies suggest that the higher the level of responsibility the less frequently a manager gains important external information from publications compared with other sources. But this may merely mean that information from publications is received in a screened form from other folk. **1979** J. Gardner *Nostradamus Traitor* xlix. 242 The screened call came in from Washington.

4. a. *Electr.* Of a wire, circuit, or appliance; having a conducting cover or shield, intended to reduce the radiation or reception of interference.

1922 *Wireless World* 1 July 416/2 A design for a screened oscillator was prepared. **1926** S. O. Pearson *Dict. Wireless Techn. Terms, Screened Aerial*, an aerial beneath which is spread a network of wires to act as a counterpoise. **1927** *Amateur Wireless* XI. 269/1 Following on these lines two practical forms of screened valve have been designed. *Ibid.* 269/3 The valve can then be built into a screened circuit,.. if a slot is cut in the external screen. **1933** *Practical Wireless* 4 Feb. 962/2 The ingenious screened wiring kit manufactured by Remax Radio is the very thing for temporary or permanent screening. **1936** *Ibid.* 16 May 232/2 (*heading*) Screened leads. **1943** *Gloss. Terms Electr. Engin.* (*B.S.I.*) 82 *Screened cable*, as used for electricity supply. A multicore cable in which the insulation of each conductor is separately enclosed in a conducting film in order to ensure a radial electric field surrounding the conductor, the films being in electrical connection with one another and with the metallic sheath of the cable and usually earthed. **1970** J. Earl *Tuners & Amplifiers* vi. 134 Screened cable must be used on these low-level inputs to avoid excessive hum coupling.

† b. Electronics. *screened grid*: in a thermionic valve, a control grid having a screen grid around it. Usu. *attrib. Obs.*

1929 *Radio Times* 8 Nov. 409 (Advt.), You could not get a better 3-valve set than the Brown Screened Grid Receiver. **1930** *Manch. Guardian* 20 Sept. 15/7 Thanks to the screened-grid valve, the old monster multi-valve set is now practically a back number. **1943** C. L. Boltz *Basic Radio* x. 164 The pentode has ousted the screened-grid valve from radio circuits.

5. Projected on a screen; shown at the cinema or on television.

1917 C. N. Bennett *Kinematography* ix. 160 (*heading*) Distortion of the screened image. *Ibid.*, [It] shows the normal proportions of the screened picture. **1966** *Listener* 24 Nov. 775/3 Selectivity in exposure, perception, attention, retention, etc., means that the effect of screened violence will not be constant and will vary from person to person.

6. *Printing.* Of an image or surface: obtained with the aid of a screen (*screen *sb.*[1] 6*); bearing a pattern formed by a screen.

1946 H. Whetton *Practical Printing & Binding* xxv. 299/2 Type or pictures have now to be printed upon the screened tissue. **1952** R. W. & E. W. Polk *Practice of Printing* (rev. ed.) xxxi. 232 (*caption*) Example of surprinting on 120-line screened background of varying densities. **1973** M. Astrua *Man. Colour Reproduction* I. 106 For the preparation of screened positives or negatives, a study has been made of suitable screens.

screener. Add: **2.** In other senses of the verb (see quots.).

1913 *Dialect Notes* IV. 57 *Screener*, a person who 'screens' cranberries. **1951** *Sun* (Baltimore) 24 Dec. (B ed.) 13/2 Watch the defensive man as he hooks his arm around the screener and swings around [in Basketball]. **1967** D. Francis *Blood Sport* iv. 48 'A screener,' he said. 'How come Teller found you?' **1977** *Lancet* 16 July 131/1 In 1974 McCarthy and Widmer calculated that screening by consultants of recommended elective surgical procedures could reduce the number of operations performed, with great savings in cost. Orthopædic, urological, and gynæcological surgical procedures were the ones most usually contested by a second opinion screener.

screenful (skrī·nful). [See -ful.] As much or as many as can be displayed at one time on the screen of a cinema or of a television set or VDU, or similar device.

1966 C. Mackenzie *Paper Lives* viii. 116 Nigel was watching the last ten minutes of 'Deadwood Gulch' and a screenful of Indians. **1969** *Listener* 30 Jan. 133/2 *Sword of Swords*,..in Mandarin with English and Chinese subtitles (a screenful). **1974** *Nature* 10 May 102/1 A page is a screenful of data; there are 24 rows on each page and each row has 40 characters. **1977** *Times* 30 Nov. 16/8 The Post Office's Viewdata project..might be used to enable customers to dial up screensful of information.

screening, *vbl. sb.* Add: **1. b.** The action or practice of shielding from electric and magnetic fields, esp. by means of an enclosing cover of conducting or magnetic material. Freq. *attrib.*

1840 *Annals Electr., Magn., & Chem.* IV. 293 The screening might, in some way, be connected with an instantaneous current in the plate. *Ibid.*, A certain thickness of metal is.. required to produce the screening effect. **1891** *Electrician* 17 Apr. 722/1 Electrostatic screening is of fundamental significance throughout electric theory. **1922** *Wireless World* 1 July 416/1 Magnetic screening from a steady field can be accomplished by surrounding the apparatus by a heavy iron screen. **1929** *B.B.C. Year-bk. 1930* 339 A copper sheet shield may be fixed to the rear of the panel for screening purposes. **1951** *Good Housek. Home Encycl.* 232/2 Most modern refrigerators are provided with suitable screening arrangements to prevent interference with other electrical appliances. **1962** A. Nisbett *Technique Sound Studio* 241 Although it has no screening effect its thickness ensures that the physical separation of successive layers of the magnetic coating is sufficient to maintain printing at a low level. **1970** J. Shepherd et al. *Higher Electrical Engin.* (ed. 2) vii. 225 The object of shielding (or screening) is to prevent a magnetic field from existing at some particular point.

c. The action of an obstruction (such as a hill or a building) in attenuating or blocking broadcast signals.

1907 J. Erskine-Murray *Handbk. Wireless Telegr.* xvii. 231 That the bending of the lines and not their absence is, in part at least, the cause of this apparent screening, is rendered still more probable by the observation that though no signals could be received close to the land, in one instance, they could be obtained at a greater distance from the transmitter by moving the ship away from the land in a straight line. **1920** *Discovery* Apr. 116/1 Mountains..close to a wireless station may produce serious screening in that direction. **1926** R. W. Hutchinson *Wireless* ix. 154 An aerial passing along a passage between the gable ends of two houses..is not efficient owing to the screening effect of the houses. **1967** G. J. King *Pract. Aerial Handbk.* iv. 102 There are invariably pockets of low signal field round the area, due to heavy screening etc. (depending on frequency), where lofty outside aerials are needed to secure the full advantage of the local transmitter.

d. *Physics.* The reduction of the electric field about an atomic nucleus by the space charge of the surrounding electrons. Also in *Comb.*, as **screening constant**, the difference between the atomic number of a nucleus and its effective charge, reduced by screening.

1922 A. D. Udden tr. *Bohr's Theory of Spectra* III. iv. 121 The effect of the presence of the electrons in inner groups upon the motion of the electrons in outer groups as a first approximation may be expected to consist in a simple screening of the nucleus. **1925** G. A. Lindsay tr. *M. Siegbahn's Spectrosc. of X-Rays* vi. 163 These doublets may be roughly explained by the screening of the nuclear charge. *Ibid.* 166 The screening constants..must depend in general on the quantum number, and on the magnitude and form of the orbit determined by it. **1965** PHILLIPS & WILLIAMS *Inorg. Chem.* I. ii. 54 The magnitude of the screening constant indicates the extent to which the full nuclear charge of an element is hidden from the electrons in a particular shell of the core. **1970** G. K. WOODGATE *Elem. Atomic Struct.* v. 82 The direct Coulomb interaction e^2/r_{12} raises the degeneracy in *l* because the amount of screening depends on the eccentricity of the orbit of the outer electron.

e. *Physics.* = *SHIELDING *vbl. sb.* 2 b.

1922 F. E. SIMPSON *Radium Therapy* vi. 45 It is best to use rather simple and uniform screening until familiarity is obtained with the effects of radium on the tissues.

f. *Basketball.* Obstruction. See *SCREEN *sb.*^{1} 3 g.

1951 *Sun* (Baltimore) 24 Dec. (B ed.) 13/2 In the old American League, the ball changed hands if the referee called screening or blocking.

2. b. (Further examples.) *spec.* in *pl.*, an inferior grade of wheat or polished rice.

1824 'A. SINGLETON' *Letters from South & West* 111 Their usual fare, is, a peck of corn in the ear a week, which they must break in their hand-mills; and the *grit*, or refuse, a Rice, like the western *screenings* of wheat. **1867** P. L. SIMMONDS *Commerc. Dict. Trade Products, Screenings,* a name in the United States for the inferior wheat that is removed by the screens and fans. **1901** *Yearbk. U.S. Dept. Agric. 1900* 135, 9,400 pounds of screenings, and 3,500 pounds of brewer's rice. **1906** *Chambers's Jrnl.* June 453/1 Tons of rock are..crushed for screenings and ballast. **1923** A. BRUTTINI *Uses of Waste Materials* II. ii. 133 By the term screenings are understood the siftings of cereals and other grains. *Ibid.*, Screenings are..made into dog biscuits.

c. Systematic examination of a large number of subjects, esp. for the detection of unwanted attributes or objects.

1944 *Sun* (Baltimore) 8 Jan. 1/1 The preliminary screening physical examination will be discontinued, except for individuals with obvious physical defects. **1946** *Cancer Res.* VI. 490/2 Compounds found in the first screening to possess potency in damaging or killing cells of sarcoma 37..were subjected to further experimentation. **1958** *New Statesman* 6 Sept. 263/3 Some 3,000 Algerians, arrested immediately after the wave of terrorism, were brought there for screening. **1960** *Guardian* 11 Mar. 7/4 Dr. Glover..advocates a psychiatric 'screening' of the entire child population in order to detect pathological tendencies to violence. **1964** HUEPER & CONWAY *Chem. Carcinogenesis & Cancers* v. 177 The highest priority for carcinogenic screening should be assigned to those chemicals with which large parts of the general population have contact. **1970** *Nature* 31 Oct. 416/1 Electrophoretic mass screening of blood proteins for new mutations..would be formidable. **1974** *Times* 27 Apr. 5/7 Herr Brandt..said he was generally satisfied with the screening of Federal employees... Herr Guillaume had been thoroughly screened, but not given the highest grade of security clearance. **1974** M. C. GERALD *Pharmacol.* iv. 77 There has been very exhaustive screening of soil samples from almost all parts of the world in an attempt to discover new antibiotics.

d. With *out.* Cf. *SCREEN *v.* 1 b.

1943 *Sun* (Baltimore) 15 Mar. 5/6 The 'screening out' of school children who need medical attention.

4. The action of *SCREEN *v.*^{1} 7; *spec.*, a particular showing of a film.

1923 E. S. VAN ZILE *That Marvel—the Movie* 121 Mr. Harding..has suggested the screening of Wells's 'Outline of History'. *Ibid.* 198 The actual screening of the story was begun. **1928** H. CRANE *Let.* 5 Feb. (1965) 316 We have met some movie actors, attended some studio screenings, etc. **1954** *Recorder* 8 Jan. 1/2 The telegram..'solemnly protested' against the screening of a Mass. **1960** *Guardian* 25 Aug. 8/5, I was present ten days prior to its [*sc.* a film's] screenings at Karlovy-Vary. **1974** 'G. BLACK' *Golden Cockatrice* v. 81 The first screening was an old Disney short. **1977** *Times* 23 June 20/4 Many of the journalists who did attend the screenings revealed an uneasiness.

5. *Printing.* The process of exposing a photosensitive surface or forming an image through a screen (*SCREEN *sb.*^{1} 6*).

1946 [see *SCREEN *sb.*^{1} 6*]. **1967** KARCH & BUBER *Offset Processes* v. 168 A device..now permits direct screening of halftone copy that removes the screen dots and reduces the graininess from enlargements. **1973** M. ASTRUA *Manual of Colour Reproduction* I. 100 For printing continuous tone we have to resort to the optical device of 'screening', that is, to the conversion of the various densities of the image..into small dots.

6. *attrib.* and *Comb.*, as (sense 2 c) *screening device, experiment, method, operation, procedure, process, programme, technique, test*; (sense 4) *screening room*; **screening clinic,** a clinic at which medical screening is carried out.

1966 *Listener* 4 Aug. 151/1 Last year saw the growth of municipally run screening clinics. In Rotherham and Glasgow there were queues of citizens in the streets waiting to be X-rayed and have other simple examinations. **1977** *Spare Rib* Sept. 19/4 The aim of developing a well woman screening clinic. **1952** M. MCCARTHY *Groves of Academe* iv. 63 Despite a high tuition and other screening devices.. something..had worked to give the college a peculiarly plebeian and subversive tone. **1971** J. ANDERSON in B. de Ferranti *Living with Computer* vii. 61 New screening experiments are under way at present. **1946** *Jrnl. Amer. Med. Assoc.* 1 June 377/2 [The smear test] can be carried out on a large scale as a screening method. **1950** *Hansard Commons* 7 Nov. 769 Mr Shepherd asked the Prime Minister what inquiries he has made into the efficiency of the screening methods of M.I.5. **1974** *Times* 19 Dec. 4/3 Downing Street refused to say how long the screening operation took. **1964** *Observer* 12 July 4/6 Mammography..is thought by some to be useful as a 'screening' procedure for women without symptoms to pick up breast cancer at a very early stage. **1949** *Cavalier Daily* (Univ. of Va.) 22 Oct. 4/2 Applicants could not get their visas approved by the Hungarian government without undergoing a screening process by the American Festival Committee. **1975** *Language for Life* (Dept. Educ. & Sci.) xiv. 215 The screening process might extend across the point of transfer. **1954** *Cancer* VII. 1183/2 A screening program to detect cancer of the cervix. **1974** M. TAYLOR tr. *Metz's Film Lang.* vi. 156 Inside the screening room. **1978** *Detroit Free Press* 16 Apr. 23 A/1, I absolutely refused to allow 'Rabbit Test' to be shown to anyone in a screening room. **1945** *Amer. Assoc. Adv. Sci. Res. Conf. Cancer* 318/2 Utilizing a number of 'screening' techniques to evaluate the place of a variety of compounds as to their ability to impair the metabolism of malignant cells. **1942** *Nation* 27 Apr. 41 Since Jan. 1 Selective Service has given only what is called a 'screening test'. The registrant strips, walks to and away from the doctor and if he has all his limbs and his eyesight and no immediately apparent organic defect, is passed. **1951** *Jrnl. Amer. Med. Assoc.* 11 Aug. 1401/1 The detection center serving..as a laboratory facility to which the physician can refer his patients for screening tests. **1969** *Times* 15 Mar. 7/8 A swift and reliable system is necessary to meet the ideal of offering every woman an annual screening test for signs of cervical cancer.

screening, *ppl. a.* (Further examples.)

1936 *Practical Wireless* 16 May 232/2 Provided that the screening cans are connected to the earth terminal no interaction should be experienced between those components. **1942** *Electronic Engin.* XV. 284/3 Grid 3 is situated between two screening grids maintained at a positive potential of 100 volts. **1943** *Gloss. Terms Electr. Engin.* (*B.S.I.*) 58 *Line choking coil* (*screening reactor*), an inductor connected in series with electrical plant and serving to reduce the effects of high-frequency or steep-fronted surges by absorption or reflection. **1966** *McGraw-Hill Encycl. Sci. & Technol.* XII. 81/2 Military screening smokes.

screenless (skrī·n es), *a.* [-LESS.] Having no screen; having had no screen used in its production; unprotected.

1921 *Blackw. Mag.* Sept. 348/2 In that screenless life friendship frankly condoled with weak nerves. **1976** *National Observer* (U.S.) 3 July 14/2 As the day progressed the screenless windows admitted less breeze and more heat and insects. **1980** *Times Lit. Suppl.* 12 Sept. 988/2 A scrupulously faithful facsimile of the lithograph edition, made by a new Screenless Printing Process.

screw, *sb.*^{1} Add: **I. 2. b.** (*a*) (Earlier and later examples.) Also, used of other kinds of pressure, e.g. the pressure of competition. (*b*) Also, occas., used of blackmail.

1834 C. A. DAVIS *Lett. J. Downing* xiv. 96 And if they don't they put the screws on 'em. **1894** P. L. FORD *Honorable Peter Stirling* xli. 241 Then I can put the screws on him safely, you think? **1917** W. J. LOCKE *Red Planet* xxiii. 298 Gedge's nocturnal waylaying of him..was another unsuccessful attempt to tighten the screw. **1938** E. AMBLER *Cause for Alarm* xi. 170 Everything..was prepared. It was only a question of waiting for Vagas to begin to turn the screw. **1977** *Navy News* Sept. 39/3 David Stracey kept the screws on, lunching with figures of three for 15 off ten overs. **1981** A. MORICE *Men in her Death* viii. 93 She worked out this scheme for a phoney kidnap, to put the screws on.

3. b. (Further examples.) Now usu. with reference to persons or their mental faculties, esp. in colloq. phr. *to have a screw loose*: to be eccentric, insane, or mentally retarded. *slang.*

1873 TROLLOPE *Eustace Diamonds* III. lxiii. 128 Something crooked about Lizzie,—a screw loose, as people say. *Ibid.* lxix. 215 Folks as would have a screw loose somewheres. **1884** *St. Louis Post-Dispatch* 4 June 7/4, I really think this wonderful woman has a screw loose in her mental organization. **1928** [see *NUT *sb.*^{1} 7 c]. **1959** I. & P. OPIE *Lore & Lang. Schoolch.* x. 179 A person who is 'wanting in the upper storey'..has a screw loose. **1963** *Times* 1 Feb. 8/7 He asked Mr. Galbraith if when he came across a person who was 'limited intellectually' he normally referred to him as 'having a screw loose'. **1974** S. E. MORISON *European Discovery of America: Southern Voyages* xxx. 725 His idea of England's opening a traffic with China independent of Spain and Portugal was sound. But there was a screw loose somewhere in Cavendish. **1977** *Lancashire Life* Nov. 63/1 An endearing little chap with a screw loose.

8. (Earlier example.)

1861 in M. Willson Disher *Cowells in Amer.* (1934) 330 Destroyed the line-of-battleship New York, on the stocks, besides scuttling the Merrimac, first-class screw, the Germantown, sloop of war.

10. b. (Earlier and later examples.)

1812 P. EGAN *Boxiana* 1st Ser. I. 122 Where *flash* has been *pattered* in all that native purity of style, and richness of eloquence, which would have startled a *High Toby Gloque*, and put a *Jigger Screw* [*i.e.* a prison warder] upon the alert. **1902** *Chambers's Jrnl.* June 367/1 Should there be a superfluity of 'screws' (warders) on the spot..your door is opened and the regulation bun..is handed in. **1933** [see *gold braid* s.v. *GOLD^1 10]. **1948** [see *BENT *ppl. a.* 5 a]. **1970** G. F. NEWMAN *Sir, You Bastard* viii. 223 The lights never out, pervy screws watching every movement. **1977** *New Yorker* 24 Oct. 68/2 Men..call their keepers 'guards', 'officers',..'screws'.

II. 11. c. (Earlier and later examples.) Also a ball to which a spin has been imparted at its delivery. Also in *Lawn Tennis.*

1840 *Bell's Life* 2 Aug. 2/2 Morewood joined Morrier, who at length received a 'Winchester screw', which shattered his timber. **1865** J. PYCROFT *Cricketana* ix. 169 Clarke could put on a decided screw..with a ball well pitched up. **1868** *J. Lillywhite's Cricketers' Compan.* 62 Southerton's 'screws' were the main cause of Kent's discomfiture. **1931** A. POWELL *Afternoon Men* III. xxiii. 203 She served underhanded screws that Pringle could not take.

11*. *coarse slang.* **a.** A prostitute; a woman considered in sexual terms; a (good, bad, etc.) sexual partner (in this use, prob. *transf.* from sense b).

1725 *New Canting Dict., A screw,* a Strumpet, a common Prostitute. **1937** PARTRIDGE *Dict. Slang* 738/1 *Screw*,..a woman *qua* sexual pleasure. **1942** BERREY & VAN DEN BARK *Amer. Thes. Slang* § 507/2 *Prostitute*,..screw. **1966** 'L. LANE' *ABZ of Scouse* 93 'A bloody good screw' might refer to an attractive girl. **1969** S. COULTER *Embassy* xi. 120, I like to figure you're my regular screw, see. A whole lot more exciting. **1976** M. MACHLIN *Pipeline* xlix. 507 As a matter of fact, he's not such a great screw, but at least he isn't a nag, the way *you* are.

b. An act of sexual intercourse, esp. of a hasty and casual nature. Also *fig.*

1929 F. SCOTT FITZGERALD *Let.* 9 Sept. (1963) 307 Here's a last flicker of the old cheap pride: the *Post* now pays the old whore $4000 a screw. **1937** PARTRIDGE *Dict. Slang* 738/1 *Screw*,..an act of copulation. **1967** A. WILSON *No laughing Matter* III. 387 He felt randy as hell but he hadn't even got the price of a quick screw. **1971** P. L. CAVE *Chopper* ii. 12 Five or six Angel birds sat around over cold cups of coffee waiting for a fast ride or a quick screw. **1978** G. GREENE *Human Factor* IV. ii. 209, I like a good screw as much as the next man, but it's not all that important, is it?

13. b. *the screws*: rheumatism (cf. *SCREWMATIC *a.* and *sb.*). *slang.*

1897 G. BARTRAM *People of Clopton* 51 In bed roarin' mad wi' the screws. **1970** G. E. EVANS *Where Beards wag All* ix. 107 Now I know all about the east wind, and I can't move my left leg without having the *screws*. **1976** 'L. BLACK' *Healthy Way to Die* ii. 11 Any rheumatism? An occasional touch of the screws, she admitted.

16*. A look, stare, or gaze; esp. in phr. *to have a screw at*: to look at. *slang* (orig. *Austral.*). Cf. *SCREW *v.* 13*.

1919 W. H. DOWNING *Digger Dialects* 44 *Screw* (vb. or n.), look. **1928** [see *RUMBLE *v.*^{1} 6]. **1933** *Bulletin* (Sydney) 23 Aug. 12/2 (*caption*) *Election Canvasser*: 'Is your wife a Feminist?' *The Worm*: 'S-sh have a screw at me.' **1934** T. WOOD *Cobbers* vi. 84 Have a screw at that bullick. *a* **1966** 'M. NA GOPALEEN' *Best of Myles* (1968) 57 And of a Sunda the Frenchmen do be walkin' around the gardens havin' a screw at the statues. **1969** *New Society* 13 Nov. 762/3 The skinhead contribution to their parents' beliefs is this characteristic rigour. 'If we see any hippies, you know, they give you the screw, you know. I don't like it,' says Bill, using 'screw' to mean 'stare'.

III. 18. (Earlier and later examples.)

1858 D. BEVERIDGE *Let.* in Ld. Beveridge *India called Them* (1947) ii. 26 Their delay in announcing an augmentation of screw. **1917** A. HUXLEY *Let.* 8 Apr. (1969) 123, I go there next week—screw, they tell me, from £200 to £250. **1939** D. L. SAYERS *In Teeth of Evidence* 91 Is he in a good way of business? Good screw, I mean? Comfortable, and all that? **1959** T. S. ELIOT *Elder Statesman* III. 95 He's offered me the job With a jolly good screw, and some pickings in commissions. **1981** 'M. INNES' *Lord Mullion's Secret* ii. 20 Cyprian would have to be found... 'A niche with a good screw to it.'

IV. 20. *screw-driven* (example).

1955 *Times* 6 June 6/6 Experience has shown that paddle tugs are more efficient than screw-driven tugs for work in confined basins.

22. a. screw axis *Cryst.*, an axis such that a combination of rotation about it and translation along it constitutes a symmetry operation, but neither does so alone; **screw-barrel** *a.*, (*c*) of a microscope, having a threaded barrel by means of which the microscope is focused; **screw-block** *Basketry*, a device for holding stakes rigid during rectangular work; **screwbound** *a.*, (*a*) fastened or held by a screw or screws (sense 10 a in quot.); (*b*) (see quot. 1966); **screw bulb,** an electric light bulb having a threaded base enabling it to be screwed into a socket; **screw-cap** (later examples); also more generally, = **screw top*; hence **screw-capped** *a.*; **screw compressor** (see quot. 1967); **screw dislocation** *Cryst.*, a form of crystal defect characterized by a unit distortion of the lattice in a particular direction such that the lattice planes perpendicular to that direction form continuous spiral sheets; **screw fly** *U.S.*, a blow-fly of the genus *Cochliomyia*, *C. hominivorax* or *C. macellaria*, which deposits eggs on animal carcasses or open wounds; **screw-hammer,** an adjustable spanner with a heavy, hammer-like head; **screw-man** *U.S. Hist.*, a worker who packed bales into cotton-ships; **screw tail,** a dog's tail which is twisted or crooked; **screw top,** a round cap or lid that can be screwed on to a bottle, jar, or the like; also *attrib.*; hence **screw-topped** *a.*; **screw worm** (*b*) read: *U.S.*, the larva of a screw fly, which has spiny hairs encircling each segment; **screw worm fly** = **screw fly*; **screw-wrench** (earlier example).

1903 H. HILTON *Math. Crystallogr.* xvi. 146 The combination of a rotation about an axis and a translation parallel to it is called a screw about that axis; and if such a combination brings a figure U to self-coincidence the axis is called a screw-axis of symmetry for U. **1937** W. L. BRAGG *Atomic Struct. Minerals* i. 13 It is the possibility of screw axes and glide planes, in addition to rotation axes and reflection planes, which gives rise to the large number of space-groups. **1974** *Nature* 11 Jan. 85/2 Dark-field observation could establish the presence of centres of symmetry, glide planes and screw axes, which could lead to the establishment of the space group. **1926** *Catal. Optical & Gen. Sci. Instrum. Optical Convention 1926* 287 Ivory screw-barrel microscope: by J. Wilson, with eight powers (unsigned, *circa* 1706). **1956** *Nature* 7 Jan. 8/1 Another contemporary scientist interested in optics was the Dutch microscopist Nicolaas Hartsoeker, born on March 26, 1656. He published in 1694 an 'Essai de Dioptrique' in which he illustrated his invention, the screw-barrel microscope, generally associated with the name of Wilson, who introduced it to England. **1924** C. CRAMPTON *Cane Work* 34 *Oblong Cane Base*... This kind of base cannot be made without using a 'screw lock', which acts as a vice for holding the sticks or stakes in an upright position. The screw block consists of two wooden blocks with thumbscrews for tightening purposes. **1959** D. WRIGHT *Baskets & Basketry* ii. 45 A *Rectangular Base* is made in a screw-block. **1892** G. B. SHAW in *Pall Mall Gaz.* 22 Feb. 2/3 In order that they might secure the door on the outside and so retain my audience screwbound to the last syllable of the vote of thanks. **1966** A. W. LEWIS *Gloss. Woodworking Terms* 85 Hinge is screwbound when the heads of the screws are not sunk correctly into their countersinking. **1960** *Practical Wireless* XXXVI. 302/2 A 500mA fuse..takes the form of a 6V, 0·5A screw bulb. **1897** *Sears, Roebuck Catal.* 35/2 Ointment pots. Flint glass. Nickle screw cap. **1936** *Lancet* 3 May 1160/2 The United Glass Bottle Manufacturers, Ltd., have produced a double-shell metal cap for bottles and pots. This cap has all the advantages of the ordinary screw-cap. **1972** *Gloss. Electrotechnical, Power Terms (B.S.I.)* IV. iii. 17 *Screw cap*, cap..in the form of a screw thread. **1898** *York Glass Company (Ltd.) Price List* 3 Pomade Bottles..Metal Screw Capped. **1964** M. HYNES *Med. Bacteriol.* (ed. 8) iv. 35 They are conveniently disposed for use in quantities of about 3 ml. in 1 oz. screw-capped bottles. **1958** *S. Afr. Mining & Engin. Jrnl.* LXIX. 243/1 The rotary screw compressor is built on the principle of an invention made by Professor A. Lysholm of Stockholm. **1967** *Gloss. Terms Materials Handling (B.S.I.)* III. 17 *Screw or worm type compressor*, a rotary compressor having left hand and right hand worms in close engagement, which entrain the air or gas and eject it at a higher pressure. **1975** *Offshore Engineer* Dec. 57/1 Atlas Copco is to supply six ZR4 screw compressors and ancillary equipment to be built into two modules by the fabricating engineers. [**1940** J. M. BURGERS in *Proc. Physical Soc.* LII. 25 Dislocation lines of this character will be said to be of the screw type.] **1948** *Rep. Conf. Strength of Solids, 1947* (Physical Soc.) 46 We may take the simpler case of a screw dislocation (Burgers' second type), lying along the *x* axis. **1966** *McGraw-Hill Encycl. Sci. & Technol.* III. 585/1 Screw dislocations have been shown to be important for crystal growth from the vapor phase. **1978** P. W. ATKINS *Physical Chem.* xxviii. 931 The surface defect formed by a screw dislocation is a ledge, possibly with some kinks, where growth can occur. **1884** R. ALDRIDGE *Life on Ranch* 191 We were a good deal troubled ..by what is called 'screw fly'. **1945** J. J. MATHEWS *Talking to Moon* 20 Sometimes their hides were torn, thus inviting screw flies. **1896** H. G. WELLS *Wheels of Chance* iv. 24 Just then the screw-hammer slipped off the nut. **1909** *Chambers's Jrnl.* Jan. 61/1 The inner screws are then driven into the board to be lifted by a screw-hammer to secure a firm purchase. **1975** R. A. SALAMAN *Dict. Tools* 530/2 This smith-made example was sometimes called a 'Screw Hammer' because the upper jaw of the Wrench was made in the form of a Hammer and could be used as such. **1856** C. NORDHOFF *Merchant Vessel* iv. 38 A lighter-load of cotton came down, and with it, a stevedore and several gangs of the *screw men*, whose business it is to load cotton-ships. **1950** BLESH & JANIS *They all played Ragtime* ii. 39 The fellows who put bales in place were screwmen. **1894** R. B. LEE *Hist. & Descr. Mod. Dogs (Non-Sporting)* ix. 239 The screw tails, which are so peculiar to the [bulldog] breed, are objected to by a few authorities as indicating excessive in-breeding. **1965** JOHNSON & GALIN *Compl. Bk. Dogs* (1968) vi. 255 If your dog has a screw or twisted tail..he may suffer from infection or sores under the skin. **1895** *Montgomery Ward Catal.* Spring & Summer 195 Large size pocket flask with collapsion cup, cover screw top. *Ibid.*, Screw top, satin engraved pocket flask. **1907** E. NESBIT *Enchanted Castle* xi. 314 A beer bottle with a screw top. **1937** G. GREENE *19 Stories* (1947) 59 There's a bottle in my pocket. Have a drink... It has a screw top. **1951** *Good Housek. Home Encycl.* 335/2 Boil the angelica..dry off..store in screw-top jars. **1963** *Times* 3 June 11/6 Make a French dressing with oil, tarragon-flavoured wine vinegar, dry mustard, salt and pepper and a pinch of castor sugar and pour into a screw-topped container. **1972** Screw-topped [see *marble-stoppered* s.v. *MARBLE *sb.* 8 c]. **1879** *Investigation of Diseases of Swine* (U.S. Dept. Agric.) 208 Ticks, screw-worm, and the large horse or cow fly have destroyed many animals. **1936** E. CALDWELL in *New Yorker* 22 Aug. 22/1 He hated weeds worse than he did boll weevils or screwworms. **1955** *Sci. Amer.* Oct. 50/3 The screwworm is a major pest of cattle in the U.S. Southeast. **1973** *Nature* 20 Apr. 494/1 The formidable task of re-eradicating the screw worm from the United States. **1908** V. L. KELLOGG *Amer. Insects* 344 A flesh-fly of serious importance is the terrible screw-worm fly,..which lays its eggs on flesh..and often in the nasal passages of domestic animals and human beings. **1955** *Sci. News Let.* 29 Jan. 78/1 The screwworm fly may be eradicated from Florida and controlled in Texas, where its maggots cause millions of dollars loss to livestock men each year. **1978** *Nature* 22 June 606/2 The well publicised eradication of the screw-worm fly from Florida. **1850** *Amer. Agriculturist* Sept. 285/2 *Adjustable Screw Wrench*.—This is just about one of the most useful little farming tools ever purchased.

screw, *v.* Add: **II. 6. d.** *slang* (chiefly *N. Amer.*). To defraud (a person, esp. of money), to cheat; to deceive, to 'rook'; freq. as *pa. ppl.* in *to be* (or *get*) *screwed*.

1900 *Dialect Notes* II. 58 *Screwed*,..in phrase 'to get *screwed*'..deceived. **1936** J. STEINBECK *In Dubious Battle* vi. 94 'What you want to strike for?' ''Cause we're gettin' screwed..the company's store is takin' five per cent house-cut.' **1959** J. OSBORNE *Paul Slickey* I. v. 48 We want to screw, screw, screw the Income Tax Man. **1966** H. KEMELMAN *Saturday Rabbi went Hungry* xxxiii. 213 In the business dealings between Hirsh and Goralsky, it wasn't Goralsky that got screwed. It was the other way around. **1974** *Saturday Night* (Toronto) Feb. 12/3 Your chances of being screwed by a Canadian factory owner then were just as good as your chances of being screwed by an American factory owner now. **1979** *Tucson Mag.* Jan. 24/2 The Richard Nixon school of thought on public scandal, that being that it's all right to screw the people as long as you were given a large mandate in the previous election.

III. 10. b. (*b*) (Earlier example.)

1821 P. EGAN *Life in London* v. 278 A well-known dashing *Prig*, whose *Head* was considered to have been *screwed on* the right way.

IV. 12. b. To spoil, ruin; to pervert; to upset, disturb mentally. *U.S. colloq.*

1938 'E. QUEEN' *Four of Hearts* iv. 54 'For gossakes!' yelled Lew, jumping up. 'That screws everything!' **1955** W. GADDIS *Recognitions* I. v. 183 She got fed up with him screwing the Sunday roast, so she shot herself. **1968** *Win* 15 Oct. 4/1 Democracy has gotten screwed, not just in Chicago but long before that. **1976** *National Observer* (U.S.) 14 Aug. 1/2 Your parents' divorce can screw you all over. It did me. I was shocked.

c. *colloq.* (orig. and chiefly *U.S.*). *to screw up*: (*a*) *intr.*, to blunder, make an error; (*b*) *trans.*, to make a mess of, spoil, ruin; to confuse, upset, disturb mentally.

This use may have originated as a euphemism for *to fuck up* (see *FUCK *v.* 3) after sense 12* below.

1942 *Yank* 23 Dec. 19 You screw up on the drill field! You goof off at inspection. **1943** M. HART *Winged Victory* I. ix. 90 My father-in-law says the OPA is screwing everything up. **1946** *Amer. Jrnl. Sociol.* Mar. 419 The common obscene expression which has the meaning in some way or another to bungle a job or to make a bad choice... There are a few acceptable substitutes such as 'screw up'. **1951** J. D. SALINGER *Catcher in Rye* xix. 176 It really screws up my sex life something awful. **1955** W. GADDIS *Recognitions* I. v. 182 He's a drunk... He gets all screwed up with religion. **1967** *Melody Maker* 16 Dec. 8/6 Those people who are supposed to be propagating the Lord's word—they're screwing it all up. **1972** M. J. BOSSE *Incident at Naha* 83 Did I screw up by admitting that you knew about the package? **1978** J. IRVING *World according to Garp* xviii. 382 He said that women's lib had screwed up his wife so much that she divorced him. **1979** 'A. HAILEY' *Overload* I. i. 6 But you and your people really screwed up today! **1981** P. NIESEWAND *Word of Gentleman* xxvii. 188 Military men usually screw things up..and the people are bloody glad to see the back of them.

12*. *coarse slang.* **a.** *intr.* To copulate, have sexual intercourse (*with* a person). **b.** *trans.* Usu. of a man: to copulate with, have sexual intercourse with (someone).

1725 *New Canting Dict.*, *To Screw*, to copulate with a Woman. **1796** F. GROSE *Class. Dict. Vulgar Tongue* (ed. 3), *To screw*, to copulate. **1927** O. W. HOLMES *Let.* 1 July in *Holmes–Laski Lett.* (1953) II. v. 958 It is enough to mention his emulating a spider by screwing a woman while he killed her by biting and, put in as an extra, chewing her throat. **1937** J. T. FARRELL *Can all this Grandeur Perish* 147 Him.. picking up bums in public dance halls and screwing them in hallways and taxicabs. **1945** G. ENDORE *Methinks the Lady* vi. 120 She thinks just because she married a sailor she can screw the whole Navy. **1952** S. KAUFFMANN *Philanderer* (1953) iv. 66 The first thing we do is..to run a few signed stories in the book, instead of all that anonymous 'I-got-screwed' stuff. **1958** N. LEVINE *Canada made Me* 16 Those who cry the most saying goodbye, screw the first. **1963** T. PYNCHON *V.* i. 10 Santa's bag is filled with all your dreams come true: Nickel beers that sparkle like champagne, Barmaids who all love to screw. **1968** *Southerly* XXVIII. 38 'We have a free relationship,' Joe said. 'She's gone off to screw some old friend.' **1972** 'G. HARDING' *Skytrap* iii. 48 You've spent the afternoon screwing with *him*, haven't you? **1975** D. LODGE *Changing Places* i. 7 All women longed to be screwed by a god, it was the source of all religion.

c. In phr. *to screw around* (*AROUND *adv.* 5 a): to be sexually promiscuous, to 'sleep around'; hence in weakened sense, to mess or fool about. orig. *U.S.*

1939 J. STEINBECK *Grapes of Wrath* ii. 14 Goin' all over the world drinkin' and raisin' hell and screwin' around. **1950** H. E. GOLDIN et al. *Dict. Amer. Underworld Lingo* 186/2 *Screw around*,..to clown and play the fool, paying scant attention to business. 'Don't you screw around when you're hustling (stealing) with me.' **1964** *New Statesman* 17 Apr. 610/3 He drinks.., screws around, lives in debt, cannot get his work published. **1972** D. S. VISCOTT *Making of Psychiatrist* iii. 43 Her husband is screwing around and she feels abandoned. **1974** *Times* 1 Apr. 6/8 All right—I am going to get him over because I am not going to screw around with this thing. **1978** R. LUDLUM *Holcroft Covenant* iv. 51 They're honest guys. They wouldn't screw around. **1981** T. HEALD *Murder at Moose Jaw* vi. 67 I've been sort of screwing around a little...I don't want to upset my husband, but a girl only has one life.

d. Used in imprecations and exclamations, as an equivalent to *FUCK *v.* 2.

1949 A. MILLER *Death of Salesman* I. 61 'In the business world some of them think you're crazy.'.. 'Screw the business world!' **1960** R. DAHL *Kiss, Kiss* 298 'Don't shout. There might be keepers.' 'Screw the keepers!' he cried. **1962** 'E. MCBAIN' *Like Love* vii. 102 'You sore?' 'Yes.' 'Screw you,' Kling said. **1979** 'A. HAILEY' *Overload* II. v. 129 She was drowned out by a chorus of, 'screw the profiteers!' and 'power belongs to the people!'

13*. a. *trans.* To look at, watch (a person); *spec.*, to eye (a person) before a fight. **b.** *intr.* To look. *slang* (orig. *Austral.*).

1919 [see *SCREW *sb.*[1] 16*]. **1938** F. D. SHARPE *Sharpe of Flying Squad* 333 *Screw*..can also mean 'to look'. ('Screw over there', 'look over there'.) **1960** *Guardian* 29 Dec. 3/1 The accused..told them to stop 'screwing' him, which meant apparently to stop looking at him. **1964** *New Statesman* 10 Apr. 555/2 'No, no,' the Mods in the dance hall shouted 'screw..means to look you up and down.' **1978** P. MARSH et al. *Rules of Disorder* iv. 104 You get someone screwing you (staring) or just standing there all cocky like.

17*. To depart hastily, go away; to get *out*, push *off*. *slang* (orig. *U.S.*).

1896 ADE *Artie* iii. 26, 'Look here,' I says, 'you screw right away from here.' **1903** A. H. LEWIS *Boss* ii. 18 'Screw out!' cried he... 'We don't want any of your talk!.. Put him out!' **1912** —— *Apaches of New York* iv. 84 As I don't want no part of it, I screws out. **1947** *Horizon* Sept. 205 Come on, let's screw out of here and find something. **1974** D. RICHARDS *Coming of Winter* i. 23 Now if you don't screw off out of here, I'll use the phone.

V. 18. Also, more generally, to break into (a house, safe, etc.), to burgle.

1938 F. D. SHARPE *Sharpe of Flying Squad* 333 *Screw*, to break open houses and safes. **1953** H. CLEVELY *Public Enemy* xxvii. 219 You want to go inside for screwin' that ware'ouse. **1958** [see *BUNG *sb.*[4]]. **1973** 'J. PATRICK' *Glasgow Gang Observed* x. 88 Yir a brave wee boay that'll screw three shoaps in the wan night.

VI. 22. a. screw-in, -on *adjs.*, that may be attached by screwing into or on to something else; also as *sb.*

1924 G. L. MALLORY *Let.* 12 Apr. in E. F. Norton *Fight for Everest: 1924* (1925) 215 Pukka wooden tables with three-ply wooden tops and screw-in legs. **1966** P. O'DONNELL *Sabre-Tooth* iii. 41 Thin steel shafts made from short screw-in sections. **1976** *Alyn & Deeside Observer* 10 Dec. 3/2 A player can cost his club almost £65 a season in boots alone! Screw-ins [*i.e.* screw-in studs] cost about £17, rubbers about £14 and flats (training shoes) £7. **1928** A. L. MATTHISON *Stoving Finishes* 54 A screw-on cap for instance, involving the operations of stamp, screw and knurling machine, is easily withstood by a high grade coating lacquer. **1935** 'G. ORWELL' *Clergyman's Daughter* i. 13 The communion bell had had a screw-on clapper, which had come loose. **1967** [see O.D. s.v. *O 5 d]. **1979** *Amat. Photographer* 10 Jan. 74/1 Buy enough storage bottles, with screw-on caps, to accommodate all the liquids you use.

screwball (skrū·bǭl), *sb.* and *a.* Chiefly *U.S.* Also **screw-ball, screw ball.** [f. SCREW *sb.*[1] + BALL *sb.*[1]; for sense 2 cf. *ODDBALL.] **A.** *sb.* **1.** † **a.** *Cricket.* A ball bowled with 'screw' or spin. *Obs.* **b.** *Baseball.* A ball pitched with reverse spin against the natural curve. Also *fig.* and *attrib.*

1866 'CAPT. CRAWLEY' *Cricket* 35 A 'screw' ball, which in slow bowling would describe the arc of a circle from the pitch to the wicket, becomes in fast bowling a sharp angle. *Ibid.* 36 The dotted line shows the direction of a slow screw ball *screwing* in from the leg. **1928** *N.Y. Times* 7 Oct. XI. 2/3 Haines is a large, healthy individual with..a 'screw ball' that ducks under many a well-meant swing with a hickory bludgeon. **1933** *Ibid.* 2 Aug. 20/1 Hubbell pitched his customary shrewd game for five innings then his deceptive screw ball lost its baffling influence. **1937** *Sun* (N.Y.) 1 June 24/3 'I thought Joe Robinson was mentioned [for the Supreme Court].' 'Yes, but it seems the President insists on screwball pitching.' **1949** *Sun* (Baltimore) 15 Oct. 12/5 Buxton, a 35-year-old screwball artist, was purchased from Oakland. **1960** *Time* 3 Oct. 47/2 Spahn started to perfect a screwball and a slider. **1971** L. KOPPETT *N.Y. Times Guide Spectator Sports* i. 15 Baseball men use the term screwball for either type of reverse curve, but the pitch is used primarily by left-handers.

2. a. An eccentric; a madman, a 'nut-case'; a fool. Freq. as a term of mild abuse. *slang.*

1933 P. GALLICO in *Sat. Even. Post* 12 Aug. 56/3 McKabe was already heading for the door. He heard Billers say: 'Who is that screwball?' **1939** WODEHOUSE *Uncle Fred in Springtime* viii. 115 You are going to Blandings Castle now, no doubt, to inspect some well-connected screwball? **1944** H. S. TRUMAN *Let.* 18 Aug. in M. Truman *Harry S. Truman* (1973) ix. 184 He should have been arrested as a screwball but wasn't. **1954** J. STEINBECK *Sweet Thursday* xxv. 163 He was a scientist, but whether brilliant or a screwball nobody ever knew. **1956** E. POUND tr. *Sophocles's Women of Trachis* 20 No use bothering with this screw-ball. **1956** W. H. WHYTE *Organization Man* (1957) xviii. 239 To talk of the problem in terms of the lone genius or the screwball is to confuse the issue. **1978** S. BRILL *Teamsters* v. 186 The word one got on Carey at Teamsters headquarters..was that he was a 'screwball', 'a weirdo', a 'strange guy', or..'a naïve kid'.

b. *spec.* Used, chiefly *attrib.* or as *adj.* (esp. as *screwball comedy*) of a kind of fast-moving, irreverent comedy film produced in the U.S. in the 1930s, of which eccentric characters were the chief feature, or of persons, etc., connected with such films.

1938 *Collier's* 26 Feb. 58/3 Wellman was named 'Screwball Bill' six or seven years ago and has, beyond any doubt, lived up to his title. **1938** *N.Y. Times* 2 Sept. 21/2 Metro-Goldwyn-Mayer..has popped up with another of those screwball comedies—this one called 'Three Loves Has Nancy'. **1939** L. JACOBS *Rise of Amer. Film* 536 Among the women Carole Lombard is the most outstanding in her 'screw-ball' activity. **1959** *Times* 6 Apr. 3/4 The situation, that of girl thwarted at every turn in her moneyless search for somewhere to sleep, suggests a 1930s screwball comedy. **1974** S. H. Scheuer *Movie Bk.* 190 Perhaps James Whale's *Remember Last Night?* (1935) first brings together all of the elements of the classic screwball comedy—beautiful people with money to burn [etc.]... The pace and movement are pure screwball. *Ibid.*, [Cary] Grant developed the perfect screwball hero. **1978** *Time* 3 July 44/2 *Heaven Can Wait* is a light, screwball fantasy about a Los Angeles Rams quarter-back (Beatty) who dies and comes back to life as an eccentric millionaire.

3. *slang*. Fast jazz improvisation or unrestrained 'swing'. Also *attrib.*

1936 *Delineator* Nov. 10/2 Barrel-house, gut-bucket, screw-ball, Dixieland..the cats are lickin' their chops, *they're* friskin' their whiskers. **1938** [see *barrel-house 2]. **1947** R. P. Dodge in A. McCarthy *Jazzbook* 64 When inspiration leaves the player..he becomes what is known as a screw-ball player. I must say that I prefer the jump style to the screw-ball style.

B. *adj.* Eccentric; mad, crazy. Also *absol. slang*.

1936 *Metronome* Feb. 21/4 *Screw-ball*, crazy without knowing. **1938** E. Hemingway *Fifth Column* (1939) II. i. 53, *I* think he is screwball. **1943** R. Chandler *Lady in Lake* (1944) xxxi. 167 That purple hat.., that messed-up make-up.., the jittery screwball manner. **1948** F. Brown *Murder can be Fun* (1951) iv. 51, I know it all sounds screwball, but here we go. **1958** S. Ellin *Eighth Circle* III. i. 173 'It must have done you a lot of good.' 'If I get home in one piece from this screwball deal, I'll know it did.' **1976** *National Observer* (U.S.) 6 Mar. 11/3 You and I know that there is a correlation between the creative and the screwball. **1976** J. McClure *Rogue Eagle* ii. 34 The only whites..are two old guys who run the place—a couple of screwball recluses.

Hence as *v. intr.*, to pitch a screwball; also *transf.*, to travel like a screwball; **screw·ballism**, (*a*) screwball behaviour, lunacy; (*b*) the screwball genre in films.

1942 Berrey & Van den Bark *Amer. Thes. Slang* § 676/15 *Pitch a curve*,..put hooks on the ball, screwball. **1946** J. W. Day *Harvest Adventure* iv. 48 Partridges sky-rocketed and screwballed overhead and fled to safety. **1947** *Sun* (Baltimore) 9 Aug. 8/4 Jesse Flores was screwballing along with no signs of trouble. **1971** D. E. Westlake *I gave at the Office* 182 The dividing line between apocalyptic visions and screwballism is a very fine one indeed. **1974** S. H. Scheuer *Movie Bk.* 190 William Powell playing the servant to a whole wacky family in *My Man Godfrey*,..or Claudette Colbert smiling her way through *Midnight*,.. immediately come to mind as high points of screwballism.

screwdriver. Add: **1.** (Earlier example.)

1779 in *Dict. Amer. Eng.* (1944) IV. 2045/1, 1 doz. draw rings, screw driver, and gimlet.

3. A cocktail made of vodka and iced orange juice. orig. *U.S.*

1956 *House & Garden* Feb. 112/2 *Screwdriver*. This has become the most popular drink the West Coast has seen in years. Merely add 2 ounces of vodka to a tall glass of orange juice. Ideal for Sunday brunch. **1959** M. Dolinsky *There is no Silence* v. 79, I didn't have the *screwdriver* she wanted, but she settled for a bourbon and soda. **1967** F. Warner *Madrigals* 30 Draining down screwdrivers in topless Broadway. **1977** *Times* 10 Aug. 14/4 The men who dispense manhattans, grasshoppers and screwdrivers..by the shakerful.

screwed, *ppl. a.* Add: **1.** Also *screwed-down, screwed-on.*

1851 H. Melville *Moby Dick* II. ii. 3 You would have seen him..spread them before him on his screwed-down table. **1965** D. Francis *Odds Against* iv. 48 He..added an inch to its length in the shape of a screwed-on photo electric light meter.

4. a. (Earlier example with *up*.)

1728 Swift in *Intelligencer* (1729) No. 8. 70 Thy screw'd-up Front, thy State grimace.

6. (Earlier example.)

1837 J. S. Coyne *Queer Subject* I. ii. 7 I've been drinking.. and I'm thinking, That I'm nearly screw'd outright.

7. screwed-up, (of a condition, situation, etc.) forced (to a certain pitch); excessively intricate; (now esp. with ref. to sense *12 c of the vb.) confused, mixed up; (of a person) in trouble; muddled, upset, neurotic.

1907 M. A. von Arnim *Fräulein Schmidt & Mr. Anstruther* lxxiv. 372, I don't love you..it makes me tired just to think..of the bother of it, of the perpetual screwed-up condition of mind and body to a pitch above the normal. **1924** F. Hopman tr. *Huizinga's Waning of Middle Ages* viii. 99 The whole genre of *Les Cent Nouvelles Nouvelles*..implies, no less than the screwed-up system of courtly love, an attempt to substitute for reality the dream of a happier life. **1943** *Yank* 26 Nov. 4/3 Oh, Lord, he thought, whatever I do, I'm a screwed-up sheep. **1967** L. Forrester *Girl called Fathom* xiii. 158 The Capitán is correct to call this 'a screwed up situation'. **1970** E. Pace *Saberlegs* xvi. 150 She has every right to be screwed up—or simply to be lonely. **1974** E. Brawley *Rap* (1975) II. xviii. 308, I grew up on army bases all over the world. I'm one of your typical screwed-up army brats, I guess. **1980** *Times* 22 Mar. 5/5 Modern society is obsessed with romanticizing ancient societies... This total fantasy about them being basically modern scientists is really screwed up.

screwer. Add: **2.** A burglar; a 'screwsman'. *Criminals' slang.*

1932 'S. Wood' *Shades of Prison House* p. ii, The smash-and-grab man, the afternoon screwer of poor men's houses, the whiz-man and the homosexual pervert end up—in gaol! **1947** [see *bust *sb.*[3] d].

screwing, *vbl. sb.* Add: **a.** (Later examples, in sense *12* a and b of the verb.)

1952 S. Kauffmann *Philanderer* (1953) xv. 248, I have eaten up my honour with random screwing. I have defiled myself. **1958** A. Wilson *Middle Age of Mrs. Eliot* 262 Married to an old man. You've never had a proper screwing. **1971** C. Fick *Danziger Transcript* 70, I fail to see how an ancient screwing can be of current interest.

screwing, *ppl. a.* (Later examples, in sense 18 of the verb.)

1960 [see *blag *sb.*]. **1966** L. Southworth *Felon in Disguise* v. 81 A geezer called Teagueman..does a bit of driving for the screwing mobs.

screwless (skrū·lės), *a.* [f. Screw *sb.*[1] + -less.] Without a screw or screws.

1913 in Webster. **1962** L. S. Sasieni *Dispensing* i. 35 The 'Ilford' screwless mounting. **1976** *Golf International* 13–29 May 32/2 Most manufacturers change to what's termed the screwless face insert, for wooden clubs.

screwmatic (skrumæ·tik), *a.* and *sb. colloq.* [A humorous perversion of Rheumatic *a.* and *sb.*, after Screw *sb.*[1] (see sense *13 b).]

A. *adj.* = Rheumatic *a.* 4 b. *rare.*

1893 P. H. Emerson *On Eng. Lagoons* 50, I had the screwmatic fever three times.

B. *sb. pl.* = Rheumatic *sb.* 1.

1895 P. H. Emerson *Birds, Beasts, & Fishes Norf. Broadland* 396 'Wiper's oil' is a reputed specific for 'screwmatics'. **1916** E. V. Lucas *Vermilion Box* 209 Wet, and rats,..and dirt and screwmaticks. **1974** P. Wright *Lang. Brit. Industry* iv. 44 Sometimes corruption has been helped by folk etymology, where the speaker supplies an imagined source for the word from what it seems to say; e.g. *screwmatics* (rheumatism).

screwsman. Add def.: A thief; a house-breaker, a burglar; also, a safe-breaker. (Further examples.)

1879 [see *dead *a.* A. 18 b]. **1928** *Daily Express* 19 Sept. 1/5 When released he came to London, and was among those whom the police call 'screws men', who break into houses to steal articles easily sold. **1936** [see *dragging *vbl. sb.*]. **1955** P. Wildeblood *Against Law* III. 137 Suppose there's some screwsman that the law's got an eye on. **1963** 'J. Prescot' *Case for Hearing* iii. 49 What does our imaginary screwsman do? He gets his hands on the keys..to take impressions. **1976** J. O'Connor *Eleventh Commandment* iv. 63, I took up my old profession of being a screwsman again.

screw·-up. *colloq.* (orig. *U.S.*). Also **screwup.** [f. vbl. phr. *to screw up*: see *screw *v.* 12 c.] A blunder, muddle, or mess; a state or situation of confusion or mental disturbance.

1960 Wentworth & Flexner *Dict. Amer. Slang* 453 *Screw-up*,..a chronic blunder. **1967** G. Legman *Fake Revolt* 23 The inability to *feel*, and the fear of touch, especially in sex... This is the key to the whole sexual screw-up of our time. **1971** Laver & Collins *Education of Tennis Player* v. 84 Bad courts were just one more factor in a general screw-up. **1975** *New Yorker* 19 May 24/2 Stewart Stern..tries to equate the American woman's supposed incapacity for love with the whole American screwup of recent years. **1977** C. McFadden *Serial* iv. 14/1 Everybody knew..that the rational mind was a screw-up.

screwy, *a.* Add: **5.** *slang* (orig. *U.S.*). Mad, crazy; eccentric; foolish; ridiculous.

1887 *Lantern* (New Orleans) 8 Oct. 3/3 Do, now, please to stop them notes which are so full of screwy talk. They make me tired. **1930** D. Runyon in *Collier's* 22 Mar. 54/2 'I am wondering how much you will take to hold still and let me shoot you, Jack?' 'Why,' Handsome Jack says, very much astonished, 'you must be screwy.' **1942** E. Waugh *Put out More Flags* iii. 163 They like the little pattering feet about the house—I know it sounds screwy but it's the truth. **1948** M. Allingham *More Work for Undertaker* xiii. 166 We feel our clients are screwy but not bloodstained. **1959** 'J. Bell' *Easy Prey* viii. 87, I think the whole idea is screwy... I can't see her risking her own life to save a murderess. **1966** R. H. Rimmer *Harrad Experiment* 42 Sheila was Tom's date and I had Tom's sister, Ruth, for a date. Sound screwy? **1978** J. Wainwright *Jury People* liv. 199 The prison psychiatrist ..can be told crap. He'll believe it... If anybody's screwy, it's *him.*

scribbledehobble (skri·b'ldĭhǫ:b'l). James Joyce's nonce-formation on Scribble *sb.* or *v.*[1], prob. influenced by such a word as *hobbledehoy*, the etymology of which is obscure. Hence, the name given to one of Joyce's notebooks (see quot. 1961).

1922 Joyce in T. E. Connoly *James Joyce's Scribbledehobble* (1961) 5 Scribbledehobble..I'm feeling so funny all over the same. **1939** —— *Finnegans Wake* II. 275 That royal pair..have discusst..why lui lied to lei and hun tried to kill ham, scribbledehobbles, in whose veins runs a mixture of, are head bent and hard upon. **1961** *Times Lit. Suppl.* 20 Oct. 754/3 Of the fifty *Finnegans Wake* notebooks now in the Lockwood Memorial Library the *Scribbledehobble* book is the largest... It contains words, phrases, clichés, anecdotes, ideas, scraps of information and other memoranda. **1977** J. Garvin in D. Ó Muirithe *Eng. Lang. in Ireland* 113 *Scribbledhobble* [sic], a note-book..compiled by him [*sc.* Joyce] in 1923..contain[s] simple phrases probably culled from his wife's conversations.

scribbler[1]. Add: **2.** A scribbling-book or pad. Chiefly *N. Amer.*

1906 *Daily Colonist* (Victoria, B.C.) 11 Jan. 10/5 (Advt.), 1000 Scribblers and Exercise Books..2c each. **1913** *T. Eaton & Co. Semi-Ann. Sale Catal.* No. 36. 17/2 *School Outfit*..2 Exercise Books, 2 Scribblers, 1 Writing Pad, ruled. **1916** Joyce *Portrait of Artist* (1969) iii. 105 Stephen, leaning back and drawing idly on his scribbler, listened to the talk about him. **1939** L. M. Montgomery *Anne of Ingleside* xxxix. 309 We write each other letters in our scribblers and exchange them. **1964** L. Edel *Diary of Alice James* p. v, She kept the record of her sickroom world in two closely-written scribblers. **1969** K. Giles *Death cracks Bottle* vi. 57 [He] had taken a page from his scribbler and written on it.

scribble-scrabble, *sb.* **2.** (Earlier example.)

1760 Lady M. W. Montagu *Let.* 12 Feb. (1967) III. 232, I see you laugh..at the vanity of my supposing any thing valuable in my scribble scrabbles.

scribbling, *vbl. sb.*[1] Add: **4.** *scribbling pad.*

1938 N. Marsh *Artists in Crime* xiii. 189 Nigel had been left to write a very guarded story..on one of Troy's scribbling-pads. **1967** C. Drummond *Death at Furlong Post* i. 5 The Chairman looked doubtful; his Board appeared absorbed in their scribbling pads.

scribe, *sb.*[1] Add: **7. c.** *U.S.* A newspaper reporter.

1929 D. Runyon in *Hearst's Internat.* July 58/1 Dave grabs the scribe..and is taking him out for an airing!.. Taking a newspaper guy..out for an airing is apt to cause talk. **1930** *Amer. Speech* VI. 120 *Scribe*,..reporter, writer: Judge Quashes Police Charges Against Scribe (here, a reporter). **1962** *John o' London's* 25 Jan. 82/3 A reporter is a *scribe* or *scribbler.*

scribe, *v.* Add: **1. a.** Now done on other materials, and by means of a fine laser beam as well as pointed instruments. (Further examples.)

1967 *Electronics* 6 Mar. 218 (Advt.), Their 4-sided diamond scriber often leaves rough, chipped lines when it scribes crystalline wafers for dicing. **1975** J. B. Harley *O.S. Maps* i. 11 A second sheet of plastic material..is placed in exact registration with the first, and is then used for plotting and scribing the contours. **1977** *Engin. Materials & Design* Aug. 30/1 Blank sheets of fired alumina ceramic are accurately located on the table and, working from a datum point, the laser scribes a grid matrix system of close and regularly spaced blind holes.

scribed, *ppl. a.* **1.** (Further examples.)

1971 *Physics Bull.* July 405/2 Conventionally the individual units are separated from a block by scribing with a diamond wheel and then breaking the ceramic along the scribed line. **1977** *Engin. Materials & Design* Aug. 29/3 The new installation..will provide the electronics industry with a high speed service based on..the supply of scribed wafer from its own stock of ceramic materials.

scriber. Add: **2.** (See quot. 1968.)

1968 'B. Mather' *Springers* v. 52 A scriber is a circular piece of paper-thin copper which fits out of sight under the moving part of the [telephone] dial which has a tiny sharp point set in it. The pressure of the dialler's finger is sufficient to bring the point down on the copper... The resultant marks..can tell..what numbers have been called. **1978** J. Barnett *Head of Force* xvi. 153 We installed scribers under the dials of public phones adjacent to suspect premises.

scribing, *vbl. sb.* Add: **1.** (Further examples.)

1969 G. C. Dickinson *Maps & Air Photographs* v. 75 Scribing..consists in producing a negative-type drawing by scraping away an opaque coating applied to glass or dimensionally stable plastic sheets. **1975** J. B. Harley *O.S. Maps* i. 14 The use of scribing instead of traditional drawing was an especially important development. **1977** *Engin. Materials & Design* Aug. 29/3 The first half of 1977 also saw the introduction by Laser Cutting Ltd of what is believed to be Europe's first facility specifically designed to provide a high quality service for ceramic scribing by laser.

3. (Further examples.)

1969 *R. & E. Coordinator* Apr. 9/2 A new glass-based scribing plate for the generation of microphotography masters, precision printed circuits, and other applications requiring extremely clean, sharp lines. **1971** *Physics Bull.* Dec. 743/3 The scribing speed is 360 in min^{-1}.

Scriblerian (skribliᵊ·riăn), *sb.* (and *a.*) [f. the name of Martinus *Scriblerus*, a character invented by members of the Scriblerus Club (see below); cf. Scribbler[1] + -ian.] A member of the Scriblerus Club formed *c* 1713 by Pope, Swift, Arbuthnot, and others, who produced the *Memoirs of Martinus Scriblerus* (publ. 1741) in order to ridicule lack of taste in learning. Also as *adj.*

1935 L. M. Beattie *John Arbuthnot* iv. 271 Swift's experience as a Scriblerian must have affected the turn given to numerous observations in *Gulliver*. *Ibid.* 276 In its humor for humor's sake it is typically Scriblerian. **1950** C. Kerby-Miller *Mem. Martinus Scriblerus* 1 The activities which may be labeled Scriblerian spanned a period of almost three decades. *Ibid.* 31 The Scriblerians began collecting material of all sorts. **1969** P. Köster in *Philol. Q.* Apr. 207 Although the subtlety of this satiric segment may have been *caviare* to all but the refined taste of Arbuthnot's fellow Scriblerians, the 'String of Epithets' could not be ignored by any but the grossest ear. **1977** —— in R. A. Wisbey *Computer in Literary & Linguistic Res.*

IV. 133 Unfortunately.., there are no examples of Scriblerian collaboration in which the shares of Arbuthnot and Swift are already known.

scrick, scrief, varr. *SKRIK, *SCREEF.

scrieve (skrīv), *v.*[2] *Shipbuilding.* [Dialectal var. SCRIVE *v.* (*Eng. Dial. Dict.*); cf. SCREEVE *v.*[2]] = SCRIVE *v.* 2. Freq. in *Comb.* as **scrieve-board** = SCRIVE-BOARD.

1898 T. H. WATSON *Naval Archit.* vi. 54 The Scrieve Board is a platform of well-seasoned deals... Sometimes both sides of the ship are scrieved in. **1901** T. WALTON *Steel Ships* vii. 180 He then transfers from the mould loft floor to the scrieve board the midship section of the vessel... He also scrieves in all decks, stringers, keelsons, and floors. **1921** *Flight* XIII. 214/1 Many engineers and aircraft builders do not realise to what fine limits naval architects have to work when scrieving out the lines. **1951** *Engineering* 15 June 730/1 Beside this striking exhibit is the scrieve board corresponding to it, showing all the details of the construction. **1957** [see *LOFTSMAN].

scrieve, var. SCREEVE *sb.*

scrike, scriker, scriking. (Later examples s.vv. *SKRIKE, *SKRIKER, *SKRIKING.)

scrim. Add: **1.** Now freq. made of muslin, sacking, or similar material. Also in *Mil.* use. (Later examples.)

1936 R. HYDE *Passport to Hell* xiii. 199 The huge spoil-dumps were camouflaged with green boughs and scrim. **1942** H. A. MADDOX *Dict. Stationery* (ed. 2) 97 Scrim. The coarse textured net fabric used for attaching to the glued backs of cheap cased-in books. **1947** D. M. DAVIN *Gorse blooms Pale* 179 A man sat screened by scrim on the latrine. **1961** *Wall St. Jrnl.* 24 Jan. 1/4 Most of the testing.. involves use of knitted paper in such unglamorous jobs as backing, or 'scrim', for more costly synthetic fibers. **1964** *Weekly News* (Auckland) 29 Apr. 41/2 Later there will be shrubs that have been wrenched and their roots balled up in scrim. **1970** *New Society* 5 Mar. 386/1 One technique, SRM (scrim-reinforced material), uses heat to laminate a scrim of random-laid fibres to wadding; the heat reactivates the bonding glue.

2. A piece of scrim used as a window-covering; *spec.* a thin, gauze-like, curtain material. Usu. as *window scrim.*

1915 E. G. PILLING *Anzac Memory* (1933) 119 Look out of the broken, scrim-covered window across fields white with snow. **1969** WIDDOWSON & HALPERT in Halpert & Story *Christmas Mumming in Newfoundland* 149 Some would put on what they used to call muslin, you know. Muslin or scrim, window scrim.., you know, like you'd have for a curtain; you could see out through it. **1970** G. F. NEWMAN *Sir, you Bastard* ii. 61 Outside on the balcony was a small piece of window scrim.

3. a. *Theatr.* and *Cinemat.* Gauze cloth used for screens or for filtering theatrical lighting; a screen of this material. orig. and chiefly *U.S.*

1928 A. E. KROWS *Equipment for Stage Production* vii. 90 The foliage..is painted on a canvas drop..and, after being cut away, is mounted..to a curtain made of a coarse netting called scrim. **1937** F. NAPIER *Curtains for Stage Settings* vi. 101 The space below the aperture can be filled in with brown paper, decorated with panels outlined in paint or chalk, but it must be pasted on to butter muslin or scrim to make it more durable. **1939** N. COWARD *Play Parade* II. p. x, *Scrim*, American term for a Gauze Cloth. **1950** *People* (Austral.) 15 Mar. 46/1 She was told she would be seated behind a 'scrim' (stage jargon for a gauze screen). **1957** V. J.-R. KEHOE *Techn. Film & T.V. Make-Up* i. 17 A spotlight to add highlight to the cheekbone, with a scrim over the light to soften the beam. **1975** *New Yorker* 26 May 90/2 The Prince and the Lilac Fairy get into a boat that remains motionless as a scrim painted with leaves and branches moves sideways across the stage. **1977** *Time* 27 June 45/1 The vast (5,000 sq. ft.) shuffle area is a stage, with theatrical lighting, scrims and backdrops rising as high as 85 ft.

b. *fig.* A veil or screen; something that conceals what is happening.

a **1963** S. PLATH *Crossing Water* (1971) 37 The salt Scrim of a sea breeze. **1970** H. & F. SCHREIDER *Exploring Amazon* vii. 154 The city of Manaus shimmered through the great scrim of rain like a stage setting from the pageant of its own lost glory. **1972** *Publishers' Weekly* 12 June 16/1 France and the French did more than serve as a scrim for vagabonding Americans. **1977** *Time* 6 June 10/2 The full story of Podgorny's dismissal may remain forever behind the scrim that veils the Kremlin's backstage dramas.

scrimmage, scrummage, *sb.* Add:

This is now used primarily as a sporting term. The older *i*-form is common in all senses, and has become predominant in American Football, whilst the *u*-form is preferred in Rugby Football.

3. a. (Later examples.) Also *fig.* (freq. after sense 4 in Dict. and Suppl.).

α. **1855** [see sense 3 b in Dict.]. **1900** H. A. JONES *Mrs. Dane's Defence* I. 17 Have you made a mess of your life?.. I wonder how many poor women have been sacrificed in the—scrimmage? **1930** E. M. BRENT-DYER *Chalet Girls in Camp* vi. 93 After something like a scrimmage they got the thing right. **1957** L. DURRELL *Justine* III. 185 The whole portentous scrimmage of sex. **1979** *This England* Winter 28/2 The doors of St. Paul's revolve like Marks and Spencer's onto the scrimmage round its bookstalls.

β. **1959** A. SILLITOE *Loneliness of Long-Distance Runner* 23 Mam had forgotten to buy me one in the scrummage of shopping.

4. c. *Amer. Football.* (*a*) A sequence of play which is started when two lines of opposing players are ranked parallel to the goal-lines, and a centre holds the ball between the teams before handing or passing it to one of his backs († see also quot. 1883); *line of scrimmage, scrimmage line*: the (imaginary) line separating two teams at the beginning of such a play.

1880 *Harvard Advocate* 8 Oct. 18/2 With such a number of rushers to enter in the scrimmages..it was found almost impossible for either side to make a goal or a touch-down. **1883** *Foot-Ball Rules* (Amer. Intercollegiate Assoc.) 6 A *scrimmage* takes place when the holder of the ball puts it down on the ground and puts it in play by kicking it or snapping it back. **1896** CAMP & DELAND *Football* xiv. 412 The man who puts the ball in play in a scrimmage, and the opponent opposite him cannot pick up the ball until it has touched some third man. **1909** *Crimson-White* (Univ. of Alabama) 18 Nov. 4/2 It finds half a dozen Alabama players bunched at the end of the scrimmage line. **1910** W. CAMP *Bk. Foot-Ball* ii. 26 The American scrimmage, while coming directly from the English play, bears now no similarity to it. Instead of an indiscriminate kicking struggle we have the snap-back and quarter-back play. The snap-back snaps the ball back with his hands; the quarter seizes it and passes it to any man for whom the ball is destined in the plan of play or he may himself run with it. **1929** G. BICKLEY *Handbk. Athletics* 105 The offensive team must have *seven* men on the line of scrimmage or be penalized. **1941** *Daily Progress* (Charlottesville, Va.) 14 Jan. 11 A player can elect to run back a punt from scrimmage if the ball is caught in the end zone. **1960** P. W. BRYANT *Building Championship Football Team* 49 The defensive ends line up in a four-point stance as close to the line of scrimmage as they can get. **1972** J. MOSEDALE *Football* i. 6 On an early play from scrimmage, he spilled Thorpe for a loss. **1981** *NCAA Football Rules & Interpretations* FR-30 The neutral zone is the space between the two lines of scrimmage and is established when the ball is ready for play.

(*b*) A session in which an offensive squad practises plays against a defensive squad.

1916 *Mobile* (Alabama) *Register* 6 Oct. 12/3 Long practices with a hard scrimmage each evening..was the schedule all week. **1929** G. BICKLEY *Handbk. Athletics* 95 'Block somebody!' should be heard on the football field every time a play is run in practice scrimmage. **1954** N. STONE *Coach Tommy of Crimson Tide* 17 After two weeks of work on fundamentals and a few basic plays, the first scrimmage was held. **1968** *Birmingham* (Alabama) *News* 7 Sept. 14/1 Jordan planned a Saturday afternoon scrimmage with freshmen running the SMU offense and defense.

scrimmage, scrummage, *v.* Add: **3. b.** *Amer. Football.* To engage in a scrimmage; *spec.* to practise plays with squads of offensive and defensive players (see sense *4 c (*b*) of the sb.).

1910 *Crimson-White* (Univ. of Alabama) 6 Oct. 1/3 Then the two teams lined up and scrimmaged for quite a time. **1934** *Birmingham* (Alabama) *Age-Herald* 15 Sept. 12/7 For the third consecutive practice day, the Vanderbilt Commodores scrimmaged Monday. **1965** *Tuscaloosa* (Alabama) *News* 9 Sept. 13/6 The Bulldogs scrimmaged Wednesday.

scrimmaging, scrummaging, *vbl. sb.* **a.** (Later examples.)

1895 W. C. GORE in *Inlander* Nov. 66 *Scrummaging*,.. a term used in the old style of foot-ball to indicate a series of efforts at goal without material results. **1955** *Times* 3 Aug. 3/7 They were beaten by nine points to six by superior scrummaging, prodigious kicking, and keen tackling. **1978** *Rugby World* Apr. 44/3 The selectors..dropped Faulkner and Quinnell, reducing the efficiency of the scrummaging.

scrimmy (skri·mi), *int.* [Orig. unknown.] A child's exclamation of astonishment (preceded by *my* or *oh*).

1896 E. TURNER *Little Larrikin* xxv. 315 It's a pound to start with. My scrimmy, you never saw such a lot as were after it! **1914** D. H. LAWRENCE *Prussian Officer & Other Stories* 221 Those old geese, oh, scrimmy, they didn't know where to turn.

scrimp (skrimp), *sb.* [f. the vb.] **a.** The act or process of scrimping; shortage, meagre allowance; economy, niggardliness.

1864 R. M. BALLANTYNE *Let.* 29 Jan. in E. Quayle *Ballantyne the Brave* (1967) viii. 169 I'm sorry to hear about the scrimp with cash. Use the money I sent you. **1933** [see *DOOR-STEP b]. **1970** G. F. NEWMAN *Sir, you Bastard* viii. 243 An existence without scrimp or worry.

b. Something constrained or crabbed (in quot., of handwriting). *rare.*

1939 V. WOOLF *Let.* 14 Apr. (1980) VI. 326 You're the only one of my friends who will take the trouble to read such a scrimp of a hand.

scrimpy, *a.*[2] [f. SCRIMP *v.* + -Y[1].] Of persons: inclined to scrimp or economize; mean, niggardly.

1918 J. SULLY *My Life & Friends* i. 9 In those days wedded folk had not begun to be scrimpy in the duty of bringing children into the world. **1919** 'K. MANSFIELD' *Let.* 28 Oct. (1951) 356, I wish the printers would not be so scrimpy, cutting the noses off the words. **1979** *Amat. Photographer* Feb. 88/1 If there's a good picture don't ever be scrimpy with film.

scrimshank, *v.* Add: (Later examples.) Now also in *gen.* use. **scrimshanking** *vbl. sb.* (later examples); **scrimshank** *sb.*, add: **b.** = *scrimshanker*; **scrimshanker** (examples).

1913 *Chambers's Jrnl.* Jan. 40/1 There's nothing to be had here but a couple of nigger skrim-shankers. **1915** *Blackw. Mag.* Jan. 66/1 It means that he is trying to get his discharge. Bring him along: I'll soon find out whether he is skrim-shanking or not. **1926** T. E. LAWRENCE *Seven Pillars* (1935) IV. xliv. 254, I was furious with..Gasim, a gap-toothed, grumbling fellow, skrimshank in all our marches, bad-tempered, suspicious, brutal. **1929** R. GRAVES *Good-bye to All That* xv. 203 The Actor said he was skrimshanking and didn't want the battle. This was unfair. The Surrey-man looked properly sick. **1932** Skrimshanker [see *PASSENGER 6]. **1937** P. BOTTOME *Mortal Storm* viii. 98 One must not do their duties for them, or pet them into skrim-shanking. **1945** E. WAUGH *Brideshead Revisited* 299 Brigade expects us to clean up the house for them. I should have thought some of those half-shaven scrimshankers I see lounging round Headquarters might have saved us the trouble. **1960** *Universe* 30 Dec. 3/3 This quietly-spoken Irishman can be very firm with scrimshankers. **1966** *Listener* 28 July 127/3 Scrimshanking, when it's a question of getting a job finished. **1975** I. MURDOCH *Word Child* 147, I was just telling Hilary we saw him skrimshanking yesterday. **1978** *Verbatim* May 1/2 It exposes the shirking *scrimshank*, who presumably preserves his legs from unnecessary exertion.

scrimshaw, *sb.* Add: (Later *attrib.* examples.) **scrimshaw** *v.* (earlier and later U.S. varr. of *pres. pple.* and *vbl. sb.*).

1825–6 in *Amer. Neptune* (1952) XII. 104 All hands employed scrimshonting. **1850** N. KINGSLEY *Diary* 15 Dec. (1914) 161 There is plenty of time to tinker or read or do any kind of 'Scrimshonging' any-one feels disposed to do. **1851** H. MELVILLE *Moby Dick* II. xv. 128 The skrimshandering business. **1933** J. MASEFIELD *Bird of Dawning* 201 Narwhal's horns on which the scrimshaw worker was cutting crude designs of rope, sennits, ladies, hearts, arrows and clipper-ships. **1948** *Atlantic Monthly* Jan. 108/1 The Whaling Museum..displays a shelf of skrimshandering tools made by hand on the whaleship *Awashonks*. **1972** *Times* 16 Sept. 10/1 'Scrimshaw' stoppers, worked by sailors on whalebone.

scrip, *sb.*[3] Restrict '*Obs.* exc. *dial.*' to senses in Dict. and add: **1.** (Later example in extended sense.)

1922 J. BUCHAN *Huntingtower* i. 21 *The Compleat Angler* seemed to fit his mood... Decidedly it was the right scrip for his pilgrimage.

3. *U.S.* [Prob. influenced by SCRIP *sb.*[4]] **b.** A certificate of indebtedness issued as currency or in lieu of money.

1790 P. FRENEAU *Poems* (1795) 430 In Scrip (not Scripture) he was fond to plod, Scrip was his prayer-book, scrip his word of God: Scrip was his joy, and scrip his dear delight. **1831** *Deb. Congress U.S.* 4 Jan. 405/1 The bill..proposed an exchange of scrip for land. **1898** *Kissimmee* (Florida) *Valley Gaz.* 18 Feb. 3/5 It is suggested that scrip be issued for the amount. **1943** S. MENEFEE *Assignment: U.S.A.* III. ix. 211 The workers are no longer paid in 'scrip' usable only in the company stores.

c. = *land scrip* s.v. LAND *sb.* 12.

1837 in *Laws of Republic of Texas* (1838) I. 266 It shall be the duty of the commissioner of the general land office.. to cause so much of the vacant lands of the republic to be surveyed and sectionized..as will be sufficient to satisfy all claims against the government for scrip sold, soldiers' claims, and head rights. **1884** *Congress. Rec.* 10 June 4994/2 [The lumbermen] have long been in the habit of getting it [*sc.* pineland] under different forms of scrip, under the soldiers' additional scrip, under the Sioux half-breed scrip, [etc.]. **1935** [see *land shark* s.v. *LAND *sb.*[1] 12]. **1978** *Washington Post* 8 Apr. E2/4 The scrip bears a face value up to $200... Buyers are permitted to accumulate as much scrip as they wish, but may only use it in exchange for 15 percent or $1,000, whichever is less, of the commission on a house transaction.

scrip, *sb.*[4] Add: **1. c.** Special combination: **scrip issue** *Econ.*, the issue of additional shares free of charge to shareholders in proportion to the shares already held; an instance of this.

[**1951** M. S. RIX *Investment Arithmetic* xiv. 141 If a company..issues to the shareholders further..ordinary capital.., it will announce the issue of a capital (or scrip) bonus of one new share of 10s. for three existing 10s. shares held.] **1955** *Times* 2 May 20/6 The scrip issue of a corresponding number of fully paid Ordinary shares of 5s. each. **1964** *Financial Times* 31 Jan. 16/1 Guinness Mahon is to better its dividend forecast, aided by..a scrip issue.

scrip (skrip), *sb.*[5] *slang.* Also **'scrip.** [Shortened form of PRESCRIPTION.] = *SCRIPT *sb.*[3]

1966 O. NORTON *School of Liars* iv. 72, I wasn't to worry if I found his tablets in the bathroom, because Chris had given him a 'scrip for some more and he had had it filled on the way up. **1967** M. GLATT et al. *Drug Scene* ii. 22 In this country..he can find drugs. Say he is not due to pick up a 'scrip' (prescription) for two hours..he can usually find someone. **1973** *Guardian* 25 Apr. 16/6 Failures of execution while we [*sc.* the Labour Party] were in government... Teeth, specs, scrips. **1975** J. F. BURKE *Death Trick* (1976) ii. 29 The little cloisonné pillbox..contained some uppies for which she had no scrip. **1977** *Times* 19 Sept. 17/6 Is there not a sickness in Whitehall which needs curing by Dr Owen before he gives us a scrip for our local [Rhodesian] consumption?

scripophily (skripǫ·fili). [Arbitrarily f. SCRIP *sb.*[4] + -O + -PHILY (see -PHILOUS).] The collection of old bond and share certificates as a pursuit. Also, articles of this nature considered *collect.* Hence **scri·pophile,** one who practises scripophily.

1978 *Times* 9 May 25/1 The winner of our competition to find a name for the hobby of collecting old bonds and share certificates is Arthur Howell of Brighton. He suggested 'scripophily', a word effectively half-English and half-Greek, combining scrip (a provisional certificate as for shares, share certificates, [etc.]..) with *philein* (to love). *Ibid.* 25/5 Commander Ross..plans to start a scripophiles' club. **1978** *Daily Tel.* 18 Nov. 25/1 The first ever auction of old bond and share certificates will be held at Stanley Gibbons next Friday. 'Scripophily' is the name of the new fascination. **1979** *National Times* (Austral.) 14 July 45/1 The Wall Street Journal in a front-page article predicted a bright and sound investment future for scripophiles. **1980** *Daily Tel.* 8 Dec. 7/1 (Advt.), Thursday 11 December 2 pm Scripophily & Paper Money. Illus. Catalogue 75p by post.

script, *sb.*[1] Add: **2. d.** A style of handwriting resembling typography, both in the shape of the characters and in their not being joined together. In full *script-writing*; cf. *print-script* s.v. *PRINT *sb.* 15 a. (Freq. used in the teaching of young children.)

1920 C. W. KIMMINS in *Child Study* Dec. 18 These norms for cursive writing were obtained from London children with the same words and under the same conditions as those for script-writing. **1937** R. TANNER *Lettering for Children* 9 A..more profitable method is.. to use the infants' school script to form a simple running italic hand. **1948** H. K. F. GULL *From Two to Seven Plus* v. 146 It is not necessary to discuss the relative values of script and cursive writing, for to-day script is almost universal in the infant school. **1955** P. RUDLAND (*title*) From scribble to script. **1959** J. C. GAGG *Beginning Three R's* xii. 83 Both the 'Marion Richardson' script and 'Italic' are found in infant schools also, in unjoined forms. **1966** D. E. M. GARDNER *Experiment & Tradition in Primary Schools* iv. 156 This scale shows specimens of children's writing in script and also in cursive hand.

5. b. The typescript of a cinema or television film; the text of a broadcast announcement, talk, play, or other material.

1931 P. DIXON *Radio Writing* i. 5 It is a curious craft—writing for radio. There is little glory.., for..network regulations forbid mentioning the name of the author of a script. **1931** *Writer* May 170/1 It is also noted for the guidance of competitors that entries should take the form of a rough shooting script. **1942** *Punch* 11 Feb. 112/1 Time was I loved it not, the mystic microphone. In some confined and subterranean crypt, Cooped with its faceless visage and my script, I did my stuff. **1952** A. HUXLEY *Let.* 22 Mar. (1969) 643, I am just about to start work on the script of a film on Gandhi. **1962** A. NISBETT *Technique Sound Studio* ii. 34 (*caption*) Microphone Position. Showing a good position for speech, with head well up (and not too close). Script also held up and to side of microphone. **1976** *Encounter* June 54/2 In his preface to the scripts, however..he dissociated himself from these films. **1980** S. BRETT *Dead Side of Mike* vi. 60 He had read his [radio] script... He didn't find it particularly funny... Charles had made a brief journey into television comedy. He hadn't found much of that script very funny either.

fig. **1954** *Sun* (Baltimore) 15 May 26/1 Another 'near perfect' murder with a script paralleling Baltimore's Grammer case. **1968** *Wall St. Jrnl.* (Eastern ed.) 28 Feb. 13 It's easy to think of a dozen different scripts for events of the next few weeks.

c. *transf.* in *Soc. Psychol.* The social role or behaviour appropriate to particular situations, esp. of a sexual nature, that an individual absorbs through his culture and association with others.

1968 SIMON & GAGNON in *Etc.* June 175 All human sexual experience is scripted behavior. Without the proper elements of a script that defines the situation, names the actors, and plots the behavior, little is likely to happen... The scripts we bring to such [interpersonal] encounters are most typically non-sexual. **1973** —— *Sexual Conduct* (1974) i. 19 The term *script* might properly be invoked to describe virtually all human behavior in the sense that there is very little that can in a full measure be called spontaneous. **1979** LURIA & ROSE *Psychol. Human Sexuality* iv. 111 Boys learn a different script from girls.

6. An examinee's written answer paper or papers.

1923 P. B. BALLARD *New Examiner* i. 27 The man who sets an examination paper will 'knock it off' in an hour or two, but the man who reads the scripts will have to toil over them for days. **1936** C. BURT in Hartog & Rhodes *Marks of Examiners* 294 The assumption that those correlations are due solely to the common influence of the true value of the scripts. **1961** J. P. TUCK in *Gen. Cert. Educ.* 8 In each case scripts which had already been marked we re-allotted to other examiners. **1978** H. CARPENTER *Inklings* III. iii. 136 He has written it on the back of old examination scripts.

7. *attrib.* and *Comb.*, as (sense 5) *script conference, editor* (also *-edit* vb. trans.), *-reader, supervisor, unit, -writer, -writing*; **script † clerk, girl** orig. *Cinemat.*, an assistant to the film director, who takes details of scenes filmed and performs other administrative functions; also in *Broadcasting*.

1927 *Current Hist.* Apr. 63/2 With scenarios in hand the script clerk (always a woman, because of the feminine aptitude for detail) takes down in shorthand everything that occurs. **1950** 'E. CRISPIN' *Frequent Hearses* iv. 35 It's a role which gets more and more etiolated..as one script conference follows another. **1977** M. BABSON *Murder, Murder, Little Star* vi. 42 Turning back into the script conference, his voice rose. **1968** *Punch* 13 Nov. 684/2 I'm script-editing a marvellous new television serial. **1959** W. S. SHARPS *Dict. Cinematogr.* 127/2 *Script editor*, ..the person responsible in a film production organization for finding, selecting and adapting suitable script material. **1974** *Radio Times* 14 Mar. 33/4 A comedy series..Script editor John Chapman. **1928** *Sat. Even. Post* 3 Mar. 5/3 It was Miss Donovan, the script girl, a friend of many years. **1951** R. BENCHLEY *My Ten Years in Quandary* 82 A girl, known as the 'script-girl', holds the book of the picture and is supposed to check up. **1980** L. ST. CLAIR *Obsessions* v. 110 The..script girl..dashed into Mimeo with a stack of scripts. **1956** *B.B.C. Handbk.* *1957* 78 A number of specialist script-readers and adapters. **1957** M. KENNEDY *Heroes of Clone* II. i. 14 She's supposed to be the Script Supervisor's secretary but she really runs the whole Department. **1965** *B.B.C. Handbk.* 203 All television scripts should be submitted to: Script Supervisor, Television, BBC Television Centre. **1956** *Ibid.* *1957* 78 A Script Unit which deals with the 200–300 scripts and texts submitted every month. **1966** *Writing for B.B.C.* iv. 13 Scripts are handled centrally by a Script Unit, consisting of a script editor and a number of assistants. **1915** C. J. CAINE *How to write Photoplays* 105 A script writer should make it a point to see that wherever a leader is broken into a scene it is not only absolutely necessary, but also somewhat of a help to the artistic value of the scenario. **1939** L. JACOBS *Rise of Amer. Film* xvii. 327 The best scenarists in the industry were..the long-experienced motion picture script writers. **1948** E. WAUGH *Loved One* 4 Sir Francis, in prime middle-age, was then the only knight in Hollywood, the doyen of English society, chief script-writer in Megalopolitan Pictures and President of the Cricket Club. **1964** M. MCLUHAN *Understanding Media* II. xxx. 299 The resonating dimension of radio is unheeded by the script writers. **1972** *Guardian* 9 Feb. 12/3 The whole team, including directors, studio managers, script writers, cameramen. **1980** G. GREENE *Doctor Fischer of Geneva* xvi. 123, I wrote it myself. Not the script writer or the director. It came to me suddenly..on the set. **1945** 'G. ORWELL' in *New Saxon Pamphlets* III. 38 Films that are all wrong from the bureaucratic point of view will always have a tendency to appear. So also with painting, photography, script-writing, reportage. **1972** *Guardian* 24 June 9/4 Script writing is full of communication tricks; the walk to the door, the slow turn, then: 'Oh, and by the way—'.

script (skript), *sb.*[3] *slang* (orig. *U.S.*). Shortened form of PRESCRIPTION 2, esp. one for narcotic drugs. Cf. *SCRIP *sb.*[5]

1951 *Even. Sun* (Baltimore) 27 Mar. 4/1 He [*sc.* a drug-addict] may have found he could acquire prescriptions, or '*script*' from a doctor who had his price. **1953** W. BURROUGHS *Junkie* iii. 40, I got a codeine script from an old doctor by putting down a story about migraine headaches. **1972** J. BROWN *Chancer* ii. 33 You're just like a bloody junkie I know. Gets his script at mid-day every day, then works his fixes out. **1980** J. WINCHESTER *Solitary Man* xiv. 136 He completed the script and handed it across the desk.

script (skript), *v.* [f. SCRIPT *sb.*[1]] *trans.* To adapt (a story, novel, etc.) for broadcasting or filming; to write the script for (a broadcast or film). Also *absol.* and *fig.* Hence **scri·pting** *vbl. sb.*

1935 in A. P. Herbert *What a Word!* ii. 58 The original story has been scripted by L. du Garde Peach. **1940** *Writer's Jrnl.* Oct. 8/1 Charles Martin is again scripting for radio. **1958** *Oxf. Mag.* 6 Mar. 354 There are two bit parts..which have been scripted with far more thought than parts of that size usually receive. **1959** *Observer* 22 Mar. 22/7 Cunning scripting, polished production and team-work added up to snug fireside entertainment. **1960** K. AMIS *New Maps of Hell* (1961) iii. 67 A British writer who has since scripted two rather..horrific science-fiction films. **1974** J. WAINWRIGHT *Hard Hit* 17 It must be hell scripting a book like that for the screen. **1977** O. SCHELL *China* (1978) I. 22 And then, as if scripted by my own thoughts, a European woman walks through this flow of Chinese faces. **1980** *Times Lit. Suppl.* 26 Sept. 1062/2 Garbo's talking version [of *Anna Karenina*]..was rather grandly scripted by Clemence Dane, Salka Viertel and S. N. Behrman.

scripted (skri·ptėd), *ppl. a. Cinemat.* and *Broadcasting.* [f. SCRIPT *sb.*[1] or **v.* + -ED.] Furnished with script; read or spoken from a prepared script as opp. extempore; adapted (esp. for film from a novel or play). Also *fig.*

1949 *Richmond* (Va.) *Times-Dispatch* 26 Jan. 13/2 The current vehicle is so well scripted, so solidly performed and so neatly combined with documentary elements,.. that the audience has the impression of belonging to the police force. **1953** *Ann. Reg. 1952* IV. 449 Previously an unscripted defamatory broadcast was treated as slander whilst a scripted one was libel. **1962** A. NISBETT *Technique Sound Studio* 252 It may be a matter of supplying sufficient 'pointers' in scripted speech. **1975** *Language for Life* (Dept. Educ. & Sci.) x. 157 Some teachers will have nothing to do with the scripted play.

scripter (skri·ptəɹ). orig. *U.S.* [f. as prec. + -ER[1].] A script-writer.

1940 *Amer. Speech* XV. 205/1 *Scripter*, a film writer. **1941** *Time* 7 July 66/3 Another cinema scripter..appeared on the set. **1945** *Sat. Rev. Lit.* (U.S.) 14 Apr. 31/1 No question but that the expert scripter, dialogician, and screen playwright is the future king of Hollywood. **1960** *News Chron.* 23 Sept. 10/4 We must be grateful to the dialogue scripter. **1968** *Punch* 14 Aug. 221/1 At present I am a scripter of strip-tease shows.

scription. 2. (Later example.)

1973 *Screen* Spring/Summer 122 There exist..two types of reference to the idea of language in general cinema theory which lead to two conceptions that I shall distinguish as those of a 'cinema of speech', mode of natural expression, and of a 'cinema of writing', activity of scription, production, transformation, analysis.

scriptless (skri·ptlės), *a.* [f. SCRIPT *sb.*[1] + -LESS.] Of a film, broadcast, etc.: without a script (sense 5 in Dict. and Suppl.); unscripted, extempore.

1962 *Punch* 4 July 30/2 Almost every major scriptless programme put out by sound radio and TV. **1968** *Guardian* 22 Sept. 8/4 The film was, we are told, scriptless; the actors made up the dialogue as they went along. **1973** *Listener* 22 Mar. 393/3 The dialogue seemed largely scriptless.

scriptore. For † *Obs.* read '*Obs.* exc. *Hist.*' and add: Usu. in form **scriptor.** (Earlier and later examples.)

1683 J. LOCKE *Let.* 26 Aug. (1976) II. 602, I think you were best lock my book of accounts up in my scriptor when you go out of town. **1955** R. FASTNEDGE *Eng. Furniture Styles* iii. 87 Small walnut and mahogany fall-front writing cabinets..continued to enjoy popularity... These pieces.. were then [*c* 1700] called 'scriptors', or 'scrutoirs'. **1965** *Listener* 22 Apr. 604/1, I would like to take as the focal object a charming and famous scriptor or writing desk from Ham House.

scriptorial, *a.* Add: (Later examples.) Hence **scripto·rially** *adv.*, in a scriptorial manner, in writing.

1933 *Trans. Philol. Soc.* 73 So much of the scriptorial work appears to have been done in later O.E. times. **1970** B. M. H. STRANG *Hist. Eng.* iii. 162 Westminster, already a great ecclesiastical centre with important scriptorial resources. **1974** V. NABOKOV *Look at Harlequins* (1975) I. iv. 19 This is corroborated scriptorially.

scripturally, *adv.* (Later example.)

1977 YARNOLD & CHADWICK *Truth & Authority* 12 It is by reference to the scripturally formed 'common faith' of the community that the individual tests his own belief, rather than by an appeal to the words of the Bible as to an ultimate authority.

scripture, *sb.* Add: **1. f.** The study of the Bible and the Christian religion as a school subject; a scripture lesson.

1927 M. DE LA ROCHE *Jalna* xiv. 165 When the time came for questions and examinations in Scripture, Finch.. usually stood at the foot of the class. **1931** 'G. TREVOR' *Murder at School* ii. 32 Ellington had to rush away to take a class in scripture. **1963** BARNARD & LAUWERYS *Handbk. Brit. Educ. Terms* 162 *Religious Instruction/Education*... Other terms are 'Religious knowledge', 'Divinity', and 'Scripture'. **1968** G. MITCHELL *Three Quick & Five Dead* i. 24 'Edward teaches history and something he calls R.K.' 'Religious Knowledge,' said Laura. 'They used to call it Scripture in my young days.' **1977** D. KOSSOFF *You have a Minute, Lord?* 45, I went to a trade school,..where poetry was not offered..and 'Scripture' was unknown.

5. d. Scripture reader, (*b*) (examples). *Obs.* exc. *Hist.*

? **1854** MRS. GASKELL *Lett.* (1966) 274 'Scripture readers' are men, sent & paid by a London society to any clergyman who applies for them to help him to read the bible in his parish. **1862** H. MAYHEW *London Labour* Extra vol. (ed. 2) p. xxii, It is the special duty of the Scripture readers to visit from house to house.

scripturient, *a.* Add: (Later example.) Now *rare.*

1872 G. M. HOPKINS *Let.* 4 Jan. in *Further Lett.* (1938) 88, I was then scripturient and quickening towards letter-heat.

scritch, *sb.* (Later example.)

a **1963** S. PLATH in *Atlantic Monthly* (1968) Sept. 59/1, I hear..water sloshing, the scritch of a comb in frizzled hair.

scritch, *v.* (Later examples.)

1944 W. DE LA MARE *Coll. Rhymes & Verses* 70 Down to the shore skipped Lallerie, His parrot on his thumb, And the twain they scritched in mockery. **1957** H. NICOLSON *Journey to Java* v. 88 The evening breeze stirs the tree above us and we hear the keel birds scritching.

scritch-owl. For 'Now *arch.*' read '*arch.* exc. *Southern U.S.*' and add later examples.

1944 *Publ. Amer. Dial. Soc.* II. 49 *Scritch-owl*, screech-owl. **1960** V. WILLIAMS *Walk Egypt* 269 Mary Morning cried, 'I seen something sliding.' 'A rat. A scritch-owl.'

scritch-scratch. (Later example.)

1977 *Time* 14 Feb. 33/2 At any hour of the day or night one can hear the scritch-scratch of individual snow shovels.

scrod. Add: Also **schrod.** Also used of young forms of other fishes, esp. the haddock, or a fillet cut from one of these fishes. (Earlier and later examples.)

1841 *Spirit of Times* 16 Oct. 396/2 Supplied with a few ship biscuit [*sic*], a dried scrod, a bottle of good swizzle [etc.]. **1949** *Chicago Tribune* 25 Feb. II. 4/6 As served in famous Boston restaurants, scrod is simply a tail piece of filleted haddock or cod dipped in oil, then bread crumbs and boiled in a moderate oven. **1949** O. NASH *Versus* 54, I lunch and sup on schrod and soup. **1971** M. SMITH *Gypsy in Amber* (1975) viii. 60 She slid a fish knife down the flaccid spine of the scrod. **1978** J. CARROLL *Mortal Friends* III.

iv. 303 'The scrod, please,' Brady said when the waiter arrived. **1979** *United States 1980/81* (Penguin Travel Guides) 84 Boston is justly famous for its seafood, especially the ubiquitous scrod, which is actually young cod—or is it grown-up cod cut into fillets?

scroddy (skrǫ·di), *a.* [Orig. unknown.] Mean, paltry. (In contemptuous use of amount or condition.) (Appar. restricted to D. H. Lawrence.)

c **1909** D. H. Lawrence *Collier's Friday Night* (1934) iii. 63 Now, Beat! (*Offering the grapes.*)..Go on—have some!.. What a scroddy few! Here, have some more. **1912** —— in *Nation* 16 Mar. 982/1 Tha gets 'appen a scroddy twenty-two shillin'. **1912** —— *Let.* Oct. (1932) 69 Tell Bunny we don't believe his last scroddy letter was meant for us.

scroggin (skrǫ·gin). *Austral.* and *N.Z.* [Etym. unknown.] A nourishing snack of raisins, chocolate, nuts, etc., eaten esp. by travellers.

1949 H. Wadman *Life Sentence* 58 We've still got the scroggin with us, if we get hungry on the way down. **1966** G. W. Turner *Eng. Lang. in Austral. & N.Z.* vii. 161 A tramper..keeps going on *scroggin*, a mixture of raisins, sultanas, chocolate, boiled lollies and anything sustaining and easily carried. **1970** *Courier-Mail* (Brisbane) 10 Dec. 23/3 Scroggin, is a mixture of peanuts, almonds, mixed fruit and chocolate well-mulched together to form a high protein and calorie meal. **1971** *N.Z. Listener* 19 Apr. 56/5 It was hard yakka, nothing but a plate of burgoo and a handful of scroggin since sparrow-chirp.

scroll, *sb.* Add: **1. e.** *Scroll of the Law*: in Judaism, a scroll containing the Torah or Pentateuch; = *Sefer Torah. Also *absol.*

1887 *Jewish Rec.* 11 Mar. 6/1 The Ark, containing only two very small scrolls of the law, was simply a deal cupboard. **1907** I. Zangwill *Ghetto Comedies* 395 There was an Ark with scrolls of the Law in the room. **1949** *Spectator* 4 Nov. 595/2 The Ark was opened and the Scrolls of the Law revealed. **1976** C. Bermant *Coming Home* i. v. 63 Sacred Scrolls of the Law..prayer-shawls, and an entire kosher field kitchen..followed us south. **1978** H. Kemelman *Thursday Rabbi walked Out* (1979) xii. 73 In the morning services..we read from the Scroll.

5. c. *Physical Geogr.* A crescent-shaped strip of land formed of material deposited on the inside of a river meander. Cf. *point bar* (*b*) s.v. *point *sb.*[1] D. 14.

1902 W. M. Davis in *Bull. Mus. Compar. Zoöl. Harvard* XXXVIII. 300 The flood plain must be scoured out for a certain stretch..around the concave banks and along the up-valley side of every lobe; while a scroll of new flood plain ..is added around the end and on the down-valley side of the lobe. **1939** A. K. Lobeck *Geomorphol.* vii. 223 The following observable characteristics of mature streams may be taken to indicate that a graded profile has been established..: (*a*) Flood plain, with natural levees; (*b*) meanders, with abandoned meander scrolls, cutoffs, and oxbow lakes; [etc.]. **1960** *Geogr. Bull.* XIV. 92 The abandoned meander scars and oxbows have radii of 1 to 2 miles, a size fully equal to the meander loops and scrolls of the lower course of the modern Horton River. **1975** R. V. Ruhe *Geomorphol.* iv. 72/2 Fresh meander scars, abandoned channels, and flood-plain scrolls are in a channel belt one to two miles wide along the present channel.

6. a. *scroll back, bracket, foot*; *scroll-leaved* adj.; *scroll-wise* (earlier example).

1958 S. Spender *Engaged in Writing* 13 The guests.. in their scroll-back chairs. **1969** J. Gloag *Short Dict. Furnit.* 590 *Scroll back*, upholsterer's term for a single chair with the back curved at the top to form a scroll. **1976** *Cumberland News* 3 Dec. 29/3 (Advt.), Three piece.. scroll back suite. **1936** *Burlington Mag.* July 25/1 A baluster finial, supported by three beaded scroll-brackets. **1976** *Southern Even. Echo* (Southampton) 18 Nov. 28/4 As well as scroll brackets, the canopies can also be supported by Georgian-style columns. **1935** *Burlington Mag.* July 36/1 The same scroll-feet curved inwards and enriched with a row of silver pearls. **1960** H. Hayward *Antique Coll.* 251/2 Designs for chairs with scroll feet were included in the third edition of Chippendale's *Director.* **1977** Fleming & Honour *Penguin Dict. Decorative Arts* 715/2 *Scroll foot*, the foot especially of a mid-c 18 English chair-leg in the form of a tight scroll. **1876** G. M. Hopkins *Wreck of Deutschland* xxi, in *Poems* (1967) 58 In thy sight Storm flakes were scroll-leaved flowers. **1851** H. Melville *Moby Dick* II. xliv. 298 To the whale, his tail is the sole means of propulsion. Scroll-wise coiled forwards beneath the body, and then rapidly sprung backwards.

c. scroll painting, a painting on a scroll, of a style widely used in the East (esp. Japan); the practice of painting on scrolls; **scroll picture,** a picture on a scroll (see prec.); **scroll salt** (see quot. 1977); **scroll-saw** (earlier example).

1911, etc. Scroll painting [see *makimono]. **1936** *Burlington Mag.* Oct. 161/1 One of the most characteristic forms of Japanese pictorial art of the medieval periods, is that of treating a subject in long scroll-paintings. **1970** *Oxf. Compan. Art* 1225/1 Scroll painting with Buddhist themes was introduced to Japan from China in the 8th c. **1977** J. van de Wetering *Japanese Corpse* (1978) ix. 95 He has some very famous scroll paintings. **1899** Kipling *From Sea to Sea* I. xi. 300 The *tokonama*..held one scroll-picture of bats wheeling in the twilight. **1923** S. Merwin *Silk* (1924) 177 The larger scroll pictures were the last to appear from the bale. **1630** in W. Prideaux *Mem. Goldsmiths' Company* (1896) I. 150 Complaint by Margaret Unwin..against Mr. Dickinson..for selling her a scroll salt untouched. **1949** N. M. Penzer in *Apollo Ann.* 48/1 (*heading*) Scroll salts. *Ibid.* 48/2 So far as known examples indicate, the scroll-salt in England lasted from about 1630–1690. **1977** Fleming & Honour *Penguin Dict. Decorative Arts* 715/2 *Scroll salt*, a salt-cellar of silver or pottery surmounted by three little scrolled arms. **1851** C. Cist *Sk. Cincinnati in 1851* 206 In the first story are located..the machinery for a scroll saw..and the apparatus by which the veneering is done.

scroll, *v.* Add: **3.** (Later example.) Also *fig.*

1958 R. Macaulay *Lett. to Sister* (1964) 265 The new high altar..is very splendid... Gold leaves scrolling round the pillars. **1976** *National Observer* (U.S.) 9 Oct. 25/4 My life..had a tendency to spread, to scroll and festoon like the frame of a baroque mirror.

4. *intr.* (See quot.)

1962 A. Nisbett *Technique Sound Studio* viii. 149 An 'overlap' is made by starting to record each new disc half a minute or more before the old one is due to run out; the extent of the overlap is indicated by 'scrolling' (i.e. by momentarily increasing the cutter's rate of travel towards the centre of the disc).

Hence **scro·lling** *ppl. a.*, forming or decorated with scrolls.

1936 *Burlington Mag.* Jan. 40/1 Inlaid with mother-o'-pearl with a scrolling design. **1979** *Times* 24 Nov. 4/6 The body of the piece is richly encrusted with scrolling ormolu.

scrolloping (skrǫ·lǒpiŋ), *ppl. a.* [Fanciful portmanteau formation by Virginia Woolf, prob. combining Scroll *sb.*, Lollop *v.*, etc.] Characterized by or possessing heavy, florid, ornament. Also *transf.* and as *pres. ppl.*, proceeding in involutions, rambling.

1923 V. Woolf *Diary* 7 Feb. (1978) I. 232 Like Vita she detests the scrolloping honours of the great, calls her family dull and stupid. **1927** —— *New Dress* in *Forum* (N.Y.) May 706 Just for a second.., there looked at her, framed in the scrolloping mahogany, a gray-white..charming girl. *Ibid.* 707 The scrolloping looking-glass. **1928** —— *Orlando* ii. 96 He tore, in one rending, the scrolloping emblazoned scroll. *Ibid.* v. 208 Cucumbers 'came scrolloping across the grass to his feet'. **1931** —— *Waves* 308 Then I scoff at the floridity and absurdity of some scrolloping tomb.

scronch (skrǫntʃ). Also **schronch, scrunch.** [Orig. uncertain; perh. var. Scrunch *sb.*] Among American Blacks, a kind of slow dance (see quot. 1970).

1926 C. Van Vechten *Nigger Heaven* 286 *Scronch*, a dance. **1935** Z. N. Hurston *Mules & Men* (1970) i. x. 224 Jim Presley's melody crying like repentance as four or five couples took the floor. Doing the slow drag, doing the schronch. **1970** C. Major *Dict. Afro-Amer. Slang* 101 *Scrunch*, (1900's–30's) a slow, dragged-out dance. **1974** *Black World* Aug. 22/1 In Polk County,..place where the blues are born, place where they dance the scronch and the belly-rub.

scrooch (skrūtʃ), *v.* *dial.* and *colloq.* (orig. and chiefly *U.S.*). Also **scrouch.** [Dialectal var. of Scrouge *v.*, perh. reinforced (in later uses) by Crouch *v.*[1]; see also Scrinch *v.*, Scringe *v.*[1] and Scrunch *v.*] **1.** *intr.* = Scrouge *v.* 1 b, *c; to crouch or bend. Freq. with *down*. Also *fig.*

1844 'J. Slick' *High Life N.Y.* II. xxix. 196 When she did kinder start up, it was jest to scrouch a leetle closer to me than she was afore. **1869** [see *cut *v.* 21 d]. **1884** 'Mark Twain' *Huck. Finn* ii. 8 We scrouched down and laid still. **1922** Joyce *Ulysses* 734 Scrooching down on me like that all the time with his big hipbones. **1948** A. Lomax in A. Dundes *Mother Wit* (1973) 475/2 Natchez scrooched up on the step. **1955** *Time* 14 Nov. 116/2 The focus scrooches down pretty quickly on the kind of hot grits that generally go with the greens Hollywood loves best. **1956** B. Cleary *Fifteen* i. 31 He was..tall enough so a medium-sized girl could..not feel she had to scrooch down when she walked beside him.

2. *trans.* = *scrouge *v.* 1 d.

1929 [implied in *scrooched *ppl. a.*]. **1958** C. McCullers *Square Root of Wonderful* ii. 90 When I hear the words agony or labor, it makes me scrooch up my behind.

Hence **scrooched** *ppl. a.*; **scroo·ching** *vbl. sb.*; **scroo·chy** *a.*, characterized by scrooching, cowering.

1844 'J. Slick' *High Life N.Y.* II. 229 The white figger at t'other eend the entry was..lookin kinder scroochy. **1885** H. Jackson *Zeph* ii. 71 Sittin' all scrouched into a heap. **1929** W. Faulkner *Sartoris* iv. 282 He right dar now, watchin' dis lantern wid his eyes scrooched up. **1941** B. A. Williams *Strange Woman* vii. 521 Will accused him of scrooching down to make the hole seem deeper than it was. **1957** E. Eager *Magic by Lake* vii. 158 He marched to his appointed jar (which happened to be the one in which Katharine sat scrooched).

Scrooge (skrūdʒ). Also **scrooge.** The name of the curmudgeonly employer in Dickens' *A Christmas Carol* (1843), used allusively to designate a miserly, tight-fisted person or killjoy. Hence **Scrooge-like** *a.*

1940 *N. & Q.* CLXXIX. 87/2 Old Scrooge, for a killjoy who grudges other people the pleasures that he cannot enjoy himself, and Mr. Micawber..are both frequent types, but more definitely literary. **1953** *Sun* (Baltimore) 14 Dec. 1/6 Britons, who have been looking forward to their gayest Christmas since before the war, suddenly face the threat that a railway strike will paralyze the nation on the eve of the holiday week. A Labor party paper called union leaders who ordered the strike 'scrooges'. **1960** *Guardian* 18 Nov. 10/6 People..were heard to wonder why this nonsense had to go on... But these were a minority of Scrooges. **1976** *Monitor* (McAllen, Texas) 10 Oct. 1B/7 Jim 'Catfish' Hunter, baseball's foremost 'money' pitcher, turned in a Scrooge-like performance Saturday. **1980** *Times* 5 Dec. 5/8 Scrooges who wish to prove their repentance this Christmas should send out for woodcock, the most expensive delicacy.

scroop, *sb.*[1] Add: **b.** The rustling sound and crisp feel associated especially with silk but capable of being imparted also to other fabrics by special treatment.

1892 G. H. Hurst *Silk Dyeing* i. 9 Dilute mineral acids have no appreciable action on silk, but they have the property of imparting to it a peculiar 'scroop' or crackle. **1921** C. Salter tr. *Ganswindt's Dyeing Silk* 32 The so-called 'scroop' of silk..is only observed in scoured silk that has been treated with weak acids. **1954** *Economist* 24 Apr. 291/1 Non-cellulose synthetics may be too hot in summer.. and..it is difficult to give them such qualities as 'scroop', the trade name for the rustle that women like. **1961** Blackshaw & Brightman *Dict. Dyeing & Textile Printing* 154 Scroop... This property can be imparted to textile materials other than silk by, for example, soap in conjunction with an organic acid. **1974** *Encycl. Brit. Micropædia* IX. 208/2 Scroop..is not a natural property of the fibre [*sc.* silk] but is developed by processing treatments, and does not indicate quality.

scrotum. Add: **b.** *Comb.*, as *scrotum-tightening* adj. (now with allusion to Joyce's use).

1922 Joyce *Ulysses* 7 Isn't the sea what Algy calls it: a grey sweet mother? The snotgreen sea. The scrotum-tightening sea. *Epi oinopa ponton.* **1935** E. E. Cummings *Let.* 3 Oct. (1969) 145 & jump you out right inwardly at the Isful..quote scrotumtightening unquote omnivorously eternal thalassa pelagas or Ocean. **1976** *Listener* 22 July 80/1 The English do not like the sea unless it happens to be blue and smooth and warm... No scrotum-tightening sea, to borrow James Joyce's heroic adjective.

scrouch, var. *scrooch.

scrouge, *v.* Add: Now chiefly *U.S.* **1. a.** (Further examples.) Also, to push or squeeze (a thing). Also *fig.*

1830 *Constellation* (N.Y.) 11 Sept. 2/5 The room was so completely crowded, that one could not have scrouged the little end of nothing, sharpened, between them. **1868** F. J. Furnivall *Babees Book* p. xxxvi, By Harrison's time, A.D. 1577, rich men's sons had not only pressed into the Universities, but were scrouging poor men's sons out of the endowments meant only for the poor. **1888** E. Eggleston *Graysons* xxxiii. 348 You know what *I* am—a good, stiddy-going, hard-working farmer, shore to get my sheer of what's to be had in the world without scrouging anybody else. **1944** L. E. Smith *Strange Fruit* xxix. 362 There'll be lynchings as long as white folks and black folks scrouge each other—everybody scrambling for the same penny.

b. (Earlier and later examples.) Also *fig.*

1798 *Aurora* (Philadelphia) 13 Dec. 2/1 Upstairs I scrouged to the front. **1908** K. Grahame *Wind in Willows* i. 2 So he scraped and scratched and scrabbled and scrooged, and then he scrooged again and scrabbled and scratched and scraped, working busily with his little paws. **1949** H. Hornsby *Lonesome Valley* xxviii. 377 He was in the top of a tree that scrouged against the sky, and they were cutting the tree down and he was falling with the tree.

c. To draw oneself into a compact shape. Cf. *scrooch *v.* 1.

1905 *Dialect Notes* III. 64 There I was, all scrooged up in a corner. *a* **1930** 'H. Stone' in Murdoch & Drake-Brockman *Austral. Short Stories* (1951) 118 Derned if this ben't an errand... Don't see how I be a-goin' to scrooge through, 'tall, 'tall. **1937** S. V. Benét in *Atlantic Monthly* Dec. 685/2 So he sort of scrooged back in a corner and waited his chance. **1948** 'La Meri' *Spanish Dancing* x. 144 Since there was seldom a sidewalk, one scrooged against their chalky walls to allow the old victoria carriages to pass. **1979** G. Swarthout *Skeletons* 230, I scrooged down in my chair, laid my head back, stretched out my legs.

d. *trans.* To draw tight; to squeeze or screw *up* (the eyes, etc.). Cf. *scrooch *v.* 2.

1909 R. A. Wason *Happy Hawkins* 162 The old man looked at me with his little shiny eyes all scrouged up.

scrouger. **1.** (Earlier examples.)

1822 *Amer. Beacon* (Norfolk, Va.) 6 Sept. 4/1 The bargemen..are divided into classes, such as Tuscaloosa Roarers, Alabama Screamers, Cahawba Scrougers, and the like gentle names. **1837** *Davy Crockett's Almanack Wild Sports 1838* I. iv. 13 He found me a real scrouger. I brake three of his ribs.

scrounge (skraundʒ), *v.*[1] *colloq.* (orig. *dial.*). Also **scrunge.** [Prob. altered f. dialectal *scringe* to pry about (see *Eng. Dial. Dict.*); the word gained general currency through its widespread use amongst servicemen in the war of 1914–18.] **1.** *intr.* To sponge *on* or live at the expense of others. Also with *off*.

1909 Webster, Scrunge. **1922** *Glasgow Herald* 1 May 6, I did not see anything in front of me except scrounging on my own people. **1950** G. Greene *Third Man* ii. 20, I badly need another drink, but I can't keep on scrounging on a stranger. Could you change me a pound..into Austrian money? **1978** R. Westall *Devil on Road* xiii. 97, I could go and scrounge off the parents for the rest of the vac.

2. a. *intr.* To seek to obtain by irregular means, as by stealth or begging; to hunt about or rummage (*for* something).

1909 J. R. WARE *Passing Eng.* 217/2 *Scrunging* (Country Boys'), stealing unripe apples and pears—probably from the noise made in masticating. **1915** W. H. L. WATSON *Adv. Despatch Rider* v. 58 George and I..'scrounged' for eggs and bread. **1918** G. GOODCHILD *Behind Barrage* vi. 94 You may scrounge for rations, kit, pay, or leave. Signallers..usually scrounge for wire. Scrounging for wire is legitimized by the War Office. **1930** BROPHY & PARTRIDGE *Songs & Slang 1914–18* 160 *To scrounge about*, to go seeking an opportunity of stealing. **1961** 'E. MCBAIN' *'Til Death* xiii. 153 Facing the world outside the police department, scrounging for a job when I'm no longer a boy. **1973** M. & G. GORDON *Informant* xliv. 165 Scrounging around in her case for a freshly laundered slip, she cast curious glances at Chris.

b. *trans.* To appropriate; to acquire by irregular means, by stealth, or by begging; to 'pinch', to 'cadge'.

1917 A. G. LEE *Let.* 24 Nov. in *No Parachute* (1968) viii. 172 Now to scrounge the watch from its casing! **1919** [see *BUCKSHEE *sb.* and *a.*]. **1923** G. H. MCKNIGHT *Eng. Words & their Background* 67 British supplies were scrounged. **1939** *Star* 2 Dec. 4/1 The Southern Railway gave a staggering figure for the specially dimmed bulbs which had been stolen (I beg pardon, scrounged) from their carriages in the first weeks of the war. **1945** *Sun* (Baltimore) 14 Dec. 6/5 Food, cigarettes, chocolate, clothing, flour and canned meat which the supply team has 'scrounged' from excess military stores. **1958** *Times Lit. Suppl.* 10 Oct. 573/3 The crude overtures of Moondoggie and the other Huck Finn louts who scrounge a lazy summer from any foolish young woman whose parents can provide them with a meal. **1976** *National Observer* (U.S.) 31 Jan., Some of these [newspapers] I picked up free in the press room; others I scrounged at the lower-lobby newsstand.

Hence **scrounge** *sb.*, the action of scrounging; **scrounged** *ppl. a.*; **scrou·nger**, one who scrounges; **scrou·nging** *vbl. sb.* and *ppl. a.*

1909 WEBSTER, Scrunger. **1918** E. S. FARROW *Dict. Mil. Terms*, *Scrounger*, a slang term for a soldier with plenty of resource in getting what he wants. **1919** tr. *A. L. Vischer's Barbed Wire Dis.* 44 The complaints about 'scrounging', which are nothing but outbreaks of loss of moral judgment. **1927** *Daily Express* 17 Aug. 3 (*heading*) Suffolks on the scrounge. Village trek for recruits. **1941** *New Statesman* 29 Mar. 316/2 'Scrounged' cups, plates, cutlery and even food. **1946** *Sun* (Baltimore) 23 Oct. 4/3 There is a blunt reminder that 'pilfering' by a native is indistinguishable from 'scrounging' by an American soldier, and that 'chiseling' and resale of Post Exchange supplies is not an act peculiar to Filipinos. **1950** *Landfall* Mar. 127, I drained my fifth warm bottle-full ages ago and have been on the scrounge ever since. **1956** L. GODFREY in *Pick of Today's Short Stories* 94 'Besides,' added Trouncer.. 'it's a good scrounge.' **1956** A. L. ROWSE *Early Churchills* viii. 151 The King, who sank back into the more consoling, if hardly less scrounging, arms of the Duchess of Portsmouth and Nell Gwynn. **1959** *Times Lit. Suppl.* 26 June 382/4 A curious collection of notes assembled under the title 'Autolycism', after Autolycus, an Athenian of scrounging habits. **1968** *Science* 3 May 522 He was a talented scrounger who in the early stages of the development of the cyclotron was able to find an available 85-ton magnet. **1974** *Listener* 7 Nov. 593/3 Reading an old, scrounged *Daily Mirror*. **1978** P. MARSH et al. *Rules of Disorder* ii. 31 You learn to scrounge. Anybody's a good scrounger around here. **1981** 'J. GASH' *Vatican Rip* i. 7 I'm an antique dealer... I was on the scrounge and feeling very sorry for myself.

scrounge (skraundʒ), *v.*² *U.S. colloq.* [Cf. SCROUGE *v.*, but perh. related to dialectal *scringe*, *scrunge* to rub with force (*Eng. Dial. Dict.*: see prec.).] *trans.* To move with a rubbing or squeezing action.

1939 J. STEINBECK *Grapes of Wrath* x. 123 Ma chuckled lightly and scrounged the clothes in and out of the bucket. **1954** —— *Sweet Thursday* xxii. 139 You keep an old lemon rind, and every time you wash your hands you scrounge your fingernails around in it.

scrub, *sb.*¹ Add: **I. 2. a.** (Earlier and further examples.) Also, in Austral. and N.Z. usage, any tract of heavily wooded country, whether bearing small or large bushes or trees.

1805 P. G. KING in *Hist. Records Australia* (1915) 1st Ser. V. 586 *A Scrub*—consists of Shrubs of low growth, Soil of a bad quality with small Iron gravelly Stones, in general Rocky Scrub and Brush may..be called the Underwood of the Forest, but it is not infrequent on the Sea Coast for Scrubs to be void of trees. **1841** *N.Z. Jrnl.* II. xlviii. 285 Every part is covered with vegetation, fern, scrub, copse and forest. **1860** J. MCD. STUART *Jrnl.* 9 Apr. (1864) 153 At four miles arrived on the top, through a very thick scrub of mulga. **1911** E. M. CLOWES *On Wallaby* i. 5 These [prisoners] were packed off next day in boats, and let loose in the dense scrub where St. Kilda and Prahan now stand. **1947** K. TENNANT *Lost Haven* vii. 105 She had been leading the children in botany expeditions through the scrub. **1966** 'J. HACKSTON' *Father clears Out* 16 Chester tried to cannon off the road and pocket us in the scrub. **1977** *Weekly Times* (Melbourne) 19 Jan. 34/1 In silence the two men rode towards the river but, turning left into the scrub before the bridge, they skirted the town.

c. *The Scrubs*: ellipt. for Wormwood Scrubs Prison in Greater London. Also *erron.* **Scrubbs.**

The element *Scrubs* in the place-name is app. identical with SCRUB *sb.*¹ (see *Conc. Oxf. Dict. Eng. Place-Names* (1936) 510/1).

1923 in J. MANCHON *Le Slang*. **1930** G. BAKER *Soul of Skunk* II. ii. 161 At the end of my first temporal month, I gibed at the Scrubbs... The broadest of my prison grins must have been that which I bestowed upon the Scrubbs' librarian. **1941** G. GREENE *When Greek meets Greek* in *19 Stories* (1947) 171 Before his first stay at the Scrubs he had held a number of positions. **1966** A. PRIOR *Operators* vi. 64 He had..taken his medicine, which had turned out to be three years in the Scrubs. **1976** M. MAGUIRE *Scratchproof* iv. 58 'Catherine put him in the Scrubbs for twelve months,' Gibson continued. 'It was in all the papers, you must have read about it.'

II. 4. a. Now in extended sense (*N. Amer.*): an animal of inferior breed or pedigree; a beast of poor physique or performance.

1812 *Columbia Centinel* 31 Oct. 2/3 May the usefulness of our Institution be acknowledged;—its *speed* drive *scrubs* from the *course*. **1858** C. L. FLINT *Milch Cows* 28 We meet with good milkers of all forms, from the round close-built Devon to the coarsest-boned scrub. **1888** *Harper's Mag.* Jan. 325/1 The colonel's horse—an old 'scrub' he had borrowed—'bucked'. **1901** *Daily Colonist* (Victoria, B.C.) 26 Oct. 8/2 Mr. Wilson, manager of the Toronto Poultry farm, says he can not get enough [chickens] of superior quality, and many others say the same. No one wants 'scrubs', the days of which are numbered. **1934** J. M. CAIN *Postman always rings Twice* xiv. 157 All the really fine pumas come from Nicaragua. These California..things are just scrubs compared to them. **1936** M. MITCHELL *Gone with Wind* xxx. 509 They knew thoroughbred horses from scrubs. **1972** FREDRICKSON & EAST *Silence of North* vii. 52 We had a dog team of sorts, two scrubs that weren't worth much but could pull a load of traps and other gear on a homemade toboggan.

5. b. *slang.* A disreputable woman; a prostitute, tart.

1900 *Dialect Notes* II. 58 *Scrub*,..a disreputable woman who frequents the streets. **1964** *New Statesman* 10 Apr. 555/2 A 'scrub' is a Rocker girl; that is, someone not fond of washing, according to the Mods, and a bit of a tart.

c. *U.S. Sport.* (*a*) A player belonging to a second or weaker team (freq. in *pl.*); a team composed of such players. Also *fig.* Cf. *SCRUB *a.* 4.

1892 *College Index* (Agric. & Mech. Coll. Alabama) Nov. 23 Arranged similarly, but with darker stockings, stand the inimitable 'scrubs', and although their name is rather depreciatory, they themselves are not to be scoffed at. **1903** *N.Y. Even. Post* 28 Oct. 9/5 The halfback tries his mettle against the scrubs. **1920** W. CAMP *Football without Coach* 62 Do not let the absence of a scrub disturb you in the least. Many a team is better off without a second eleven. **1956** B. HOLIDAY *Lady sings Blues* (1973) xxi. 173, I wouldn't have known the first team from the scrubs, but Ehrlich told me the prosecutor and the judge were the best they had. **1961** J. S. SALAK *Dict. Amer. Sports* 385 *Scrub*, a player of the second, or weaker, team; one not good enough to be on the first team.

(*b*) (See quot. 1910.)

1892 *Dialect Notes* I. 214 'Scrub' in New England is that form of base ball played when there are too few players to have opposing sides. **1896** W. A. WHITE *Real Issue* 66 Just before school was called Piggy Pennington was playing 'scrub'. **1910** *Dialect Notes* III. 447 *Scrub*, a game of baseball played by a half dozen or more persons (when there are not enough to 'choose up' for two nines), in which the players move up as a batter is retired. **1917** C. MATHEWSON *Second Base Sloan* 126 At the end of a week or so they were playing 'scrub' every noon hour.

III. 6. a. (sense 2) *scrub bull, bush, fire, horse, jungle, -land* (earlier and later examples); *scrub-covered* adj.; **scrub-cutter** *Austral.* and *N.Z.*, (*a*) a machine for cutting scrub; (*b*) one who cuts scrub; hence **scrub-cutting** *vbl. sb.*; **scrub-dashing** *vbl. sb. Austral.* (see quot. 1941); **scrub-rider** *Austral.*, one who rides in search of cattle that have escaped into the scrub; **scrub tick,** either of two small, brown, hard-bodied ticks found in Australia, *Hæmaphysalis bispinosa* or *Ixodes holocyclus*, the bush tick; **scrub typhus,** an acute rickettsial fever transmitted to man by mites normally parasitic upon small rodents; cf. *mite*(*-borne*) *typhus* s.v. *MITE¹ 3.

1908 A. GUNN *We of Never-Never* xviii. 238 Tales of scrub-bulls, maddened cow-mothers. **1946** A. MARSHALL in Murdoch & Drake-Brockman *Austral. Short Stories* (1951) 317 He was an old scrub bull,..who roamed the timbered hills beyond the Murray. **1954** [see *CENTRE *sb.* II h]. **1977** *Listener* (N.Z.) 15 Jan. 34/3 Jeremy Delacy, the 'scrub bull', eccentric conservationist station-owner who has parted company with the local 'establishment'. **1897** D. MCK. WRIGHT *Old Station Days* 11 Cobwebs..jewelled the scrub-bushes o'er. **1959** *Tararua* (N.Z.) XIII. 45 One curious term is *scrub bush*. So far as I can make out it is applicable to the individual plants which go to make up tall scrub. At any rate a tall plant of teatree may be called a *scrub bush*. **1900** W. S. CHURCHILL in *Morning Post* 19 Mar. 5/7 The proper left of this position rests on the rocky scrub-covered hill of Hlangwani. **1980** S. WILSON *Dealer's War* I. ii. 26 Grey scrub-covered hills. **1886** R. STOUT *Notes Progress N.Z.* 28 The following..are manufactured in the colony—viz., ploughs, chaff-cutters..disc-harrows..scrub-cutters. *a* **1930** H. STONE in *Austral. Short Stories* (1951) 115 But them scrub-cutters... They do need constant watchin. **1937** J. WEST *Sheep Kings* ix. 87 He purchased a new block of bush land, and employed another gang of men to break it in—timber-men and scrub-cutters and post-splitters. **1965** M. SHADBOLT *Among Cinders* xxii. 210 Probably the place had been built by scrub-cutters. **1911** 'KIWI' *On Swag* iii. 7 We were on a job of scrub cutting. **1968** *Wanganui* (N.Z.) *Chron.* 15 Nov. 10/5 (Advt.), Scrub-cutting contract for 120 acres. **1977** C. MCCULLOUGH *Thorn Birds* vi. 117 The grass had lasted just long enough eked out by scrub-cutting from the more juicy trees. **1941** BAKER *Dict. Austral. Slang* 64 *Scrub-dashing*, riding through bush or scrub, esp. after strayed cattle or brumbies. **1946** F. D. DAVISON *Dusty* xv. 166 Fred had offered Tom work; odd jobs around the homestead..while Fred did the scrub-dashing. **1944** *Living off Land* vii. 148 Slower-burning scrub fires..call for strategy. **1965** S. T. OLLIVIER *Petticoat Farm* i. 1 Harry stood at the roadside and watched the white pumice dust..hanging in the air like smoke from a scrub fire on a fine day. **1893** D. FERGUSON *Bush Life in Australia & N.Z.* 301 The scrub confused and handicapped [the thoroughbred] whilst Selina was a scrub horse. **1910** *Blackw. Mag.* Jan. 113/1, I saw my first tiger in a scrub-jungle two miles from the Nepal frontier. **1934** 'G. ORWELL' *Burmese Days* iv. 69 It was scrub jungle at first, with dense stunted bushes. **1953** D. A. BANNERMAN *Birds Brit. Isles* I. 256 The buntings spread over the plains of India, chiefly affecting cultivation and scrub-jungle. **1779** W. MCKENDRY *Jrnl.* 4 Oct. in *Proc. Mass. Hist. Soc.* (1886) 2nd Ser. III. 472 Came over skrub land this day. **1955** H. KLEIN *Winged Courier* xiv. 90 All around her lay scrubland, marsh and swamp. **1955** J. THOMAS *No Banners* xxiii. 230 The road and the lane make a kind of elongated 'V', with the two arms separated by this scrub-land. **1976** K. ROYCE *Bustillo* iv. 47 Across the scrubland, the market was preparing its stalls. **1977** 'J. LE CARRÉ' *Hon. Schoolboy* xvii. 404 The perfect tarmac road ran.. over the flat scrubland. **1881** A. C. GRANT *Bush-Life in Queensland* (1882) xv. 150 A favourite plan amongst the bold scrub-riders. **1891** *Queenslander* 3 Jan. 36/3 The scrub tick is a small animal with eight legs when mature, flat, brown in colour. **1936** *Discovery* Oct. 306/2 If the camp is in the scrub..scrub ticks have to be faced. **1965** *Austral. Encycl.* VIII. 499/1 In the genus *Haemaphysalis* are.. two introduced species: a scrub tick..originally from India, and a dog tick. **1929** W. FLETCHER et al. in *Trans. R. Soc. Trop. Med. & Hygiene* XXIII. 61 The K. form has a patchy distribution, and its virus, like the virus of the tsutsugamushi disease, has its home in circumscribed areas of untilled open country, particularly in land which after being cleared of jungle has been allowed to grow up in weeds and scrub... Because cases of the K. form have their origin in such places, we propose that this kind of tropical typhus should be called scrub-typhus. *Ibid.*, The epidemiology of this rural, or scrub-typhus, is very similar to that of the sporadic typhus-like disease of India which Megaw attributes to the bites of ticks. **1961** R. D. BAKER *Essent. Path.* ix. 241 During World War II tsutsugamushi disease, scrub typhus, was prevalent among our troops in the Far East, and many fatalities occurred. **1978** *Jrnl. R. Soc. Med.* LXXI. 507 Scrub typhus is a febrile illness, endemic in much of the roughly triangular area bounded by Japan, Pakistan and Australia.

b. scrub-bird: see also *noisy scrub bird* s.v. *NOISY *a.* 1 b; **scrub-fowl,** a grey and brown mound-building bird, *Megapodius freycinet*, found in coastal areas of northern Australia; **scrub-hen,** substitute for def.: = **scrub fowl*; **scrub jay** *U.S.*, a blue jay with no white markings, *Aphelocoma cœrulescens cœrulescens*, found only in parts of Florida; **scrub-turkey,** substitute for def.: a large mound-building bird, *Alectura lathami*, found in Australian forests and having a red head and brown body; (later examples); **scrub wallaby,** one of several wallabies belonging to the genus *Macropus* and living in woodland; **scrub wren,** a small Australian bird belonging to the genus *Sericornis*.

1908 Scrub fowl [see *DEAD-ALIVE *a.*]. **1943** C. BARRETT *Austral. Animal Bk.* xvii. 151 The scrub-fowl burrows into the mass to deposit each egg. **1938** M. K. RAWLINGS *Yearling* xxiv. 302 Scrub jays flew across the road. Their solid blue feathered coats..were prettier than the bluebirds'. **1947** R. T. PETERSON *Field Guide to Birds* (ed. 2) 159 Florida, or Scrub, Jay... Look for this crestless Jay only in the stretches of 'scrub' in Florida. **1976** *Southern Evening Echo* (Southampton) 15 Nov. (Advt. Suppl.) 4/2 Scrub jays..feed their brothers and sisters. **1885** Scrub-turkey [see *CHUCKY-CHUCKY]. **1940** F. D. DAVISON *Woman at Mill* 86 The scrub turkey had her home, her nesting mounds of leaf and forest debris. **1967** *Courier Mail* (Brisbane) 26 June 8 Normal mounding activity by feverishly active scrub turkeys in South-Eastern Queensland begins late in June, ending the following March. **1896, 1926** Scrub wallaby [see *brush-wallaby* s.v. *BRUSH *sb.*¹ 4]. **1947** K. TENNANT *Lost Haven* xii. 199 The marks of a scrub wallaby fossicking the high-tide drift. **1970** W. D. L. RIDE *Guide Native Mammals Austral.* 46 Scrub wallaby..inhabiting woodland, forest edges, and coastal scrub. **1901** A. J. CAMPBELL *Nests & Eggs Austral. Birds* I. 249 This smart Scrub Wren possesses chiefly a western distribution. **1943** C. BARRETT *Austral. Animal Bk.* xxxii. 278 The Australian scrub-wrens..are fussy, plain-coloured little birds, which spend most of their time on or near the ground, keeping to the undergrowth. **1965** *Austral. Encycl.* VIII. 48/2 Most of the scrub-wrens build domed nests of soft bark and fibre in thick vegetation.

c. scrub oak, substitute for def.: (*a*) one of several North American dwarf oaks; (earlier and later examples); (*b*) *Casuarina cunninghamii*; **scrub palmetto,** a small, slow-growing palm of the genus Sabal; **scrub pine,** add: *spec.* one of several North American dwarf pines, esp. *Pinus virginiana*, or its wood; (earlier and later examples).

1766 J. BARTRAM *Jrnl.* 13 Jan. in *Trans. Amer. Philos. Soc.* (1944) XXXIII. 42/1 We came to Round-Lake,.. almost surrounded with palmetto, pine, and scrub-oak. **1918** W. CATHER *My Antonia* II. xv. 272 The dogwoods and scrub-oaks began to turn up the silvery underside of their leaves. **1947** V. H. CAHALANE *Mammals N. Amer.* 365 One pair of these pockets can carry as many as twenty-seven scrub-oak acorns. **1964** R. MURPHY *Pond* i. 9 The second-growth pine woods, had gone back to brush, greenbrier, scrub oak. **1938** M. K. RAWLINGS *Yearling* iv. 40 Pushing through the low..scrub palmettos..was less laborious. **1968** MRS. L. B. JOHNSON *White House Diary* 23 Nov. (1970) 740 The landscape was low and flat, clotted with scrub palmettos. **1791** P. FIDLER *Jrnl.* 30 Oct. in *Publ. Champlain Soc.* (1934) XXI. 517 A high point of Rocks & scrub pine. **1818** [see *NEW JERSEY]. **1832** [see *grey pine* s.v. *GREY, GRAY *a.* 8]. **1949** *Sat. Even. Post* 9 Apr. 162/3 In front of the fireplace was a coarse-haired bearskin, scarred with burns from the snapping embers of scrub pine and cotton wood. **1976** M. & G. GORDON *Ordeal* (1977) xi. 71 They walked slowly through a forest of scrub pine.

scrub, *sb.*² Add: Also **scrubb. 1. a.** (Further examples.) Also *spec.* with *up*: see *SCRUB *v.*¹ 3 d; freq. *attrib.*

a **1902** S. BUTLER *Way of All Flesh* (1903) lxxii. 331 Ellen had given it another scrub from top to bottom. **1937** *Archit. Rev.* LXXXI. 52 (*caption*) A detail in one of the surgeon's 'scrub-up' lobbies, looking through an observatory window into an operating theatre. **1953** K. TENNANT *Joyful Condemned* xxxix. 383 Rene eyed May's house possessively. 'First thing..this gets a good scrub.' **1964** G. L. COHEN *What's Wrong with Hospitals?* vii. 125 The surgeon..spared me five minutes between a thyroidectomy and his next scrub-up. **1973** *Daily Tel.* 27 July 3/5 The theatre suite, consisting of the operating room, the anaesthetic room, the scrub-up room and the doctors' rest room.

b. Movement of part of a tyre over the road surface while in contact with it.

1936 *Proc. Inst. Automobile Engineers* XXX. 733 Features in independent springing..tending to prevent 'scrub' when the suspension is functioning. **1959** *Manch. Guardian* 27 July 2/3 Braking and acceleration also cause scrub. **1973** *Country Life* 11 Oct. 1077/3 Hard cornering produces front-tyre scrub, but the back wheels stay firmly on the road.

c. *slang.* A cancellation or abandonment, *spec.* of a flying mission. Cf. *SCRUB *v.*¹ 3* a.

1952 M. TRIPP *Faith is Windsock* i. 14 We are marking time at the moment, three scrubs in a row. **1958** *N.Y. Times Mag.* 16 Mar. 10/2 The backstage crew is made up of engineers and technicians who work themselves to a frazzle during the long countdown..which may end not in a firing but in a series of 'holds' or a 'scrub'—cancellation. **1962** V. GRISSOM in *Into Orbit* 125, I was prepared for the scrub, and it was not long in coming.

2. Also *spec.* in *Glass-painting*, a brush used to scrape out lights in a coat of paint. Cf. *SCRUB *v.*¹ 4 b.

1896 H. HOLIDAY *Stained Glass as Art* I. 23 The lights are taken out..with a hoghair brush with the hairs cut short, called a scrub. **1902** E. R. SUFFLING *Treatise on Art of Glass Painting* v. 89 Hog-hair fitches are converted into what glass painters call 'scrubs'... Scrubs are made in a variety of shapes—skew, round, flat, square, pointed. **1972** R. & G. METCALF *Making Stained Glass* 134 Employing some of the longer-haired scrubs to stipple the edges of the remaining matt.

5. b. (Transfer this entry to *SCRUB *a.* 4 a).

scrub, *a.* Add: **1.** (Later U.S. examples.)

1840 J. P. KENNEDY *Quodlibet* 158 If he..makes a little fortune, we can call him a..Scrub Aristocrat. **1881** *Harper's Mag.* June 88/2 Her little scrub-class in the Sunday-school. **1901** M. E. RYAN *That Girl Montana* ix. 125 There are always a lot of scrub whites ready to take advantage of war signals.

3. Chiefly *U.S.* **a.** Of vegetation: low-growing, stunted.

Not clearly distinguishable from *Combs.* s.v. SCRUB *sb.*¹ 6 a.

1749 [see *scrub-tree* s.v. SCRUB *sb.*¹ 6 a]. **1779** W. MCKENDRY *Jrnl.* 29 Aug. in *Proc. Mass. Hist. Soc.* 2nd Ser. III. 465 Their breastwork was made of pine Logs coverd with green skrub bushes. **1816** U. BROWN *Jrnl.* 9 June in *Maryland Hist. Mag.* (1915) X. 266 Pines of a scruby kind, Jack Oaks and other Scrub wood. **1872** *Rep. Vermont Board Agric.* I. 78 Men are as choice of a little scrub apple tree..as they would be were it classed among the favorite varieties of the day. **1904** G. STRATTON-PORTER *Freckles* ix. 196 There was a swarm of wild bees settled on a scrub-thorn only a few yards away. **1975** A. BERGMAN *Hollywood & Le Vine* (1976) viii. 104 A residential street that ended in sand and scrub bush.

b. Of livestock: of inferior breed or physique.

1744 W. ELLIS *Mod. Husbandman* Apr. xviii. 118 A petty Dealer,..keeping a scrub Horse, for carrying Fish about the Country. **1839** *Jrnl. Indiana Ho. Representatives* 8 Jan. 232 The half-blooded calves of the improved Durhams will sell, at weaning, for $20, while those of our scrub breed will only bring 3. **1868** *Rep. Iowa State Agric. Soc. 1867* 130 The general idea pervades the minds of our farmers that a larger ..animal of blooded stock can be produced by the same amount of feed, than can be made with the same feed fed to scrub stock. *Ibid.*, Our stock is scrub. **1930** C. ADDISON in *Hansard Commons* 30 Oct. 269 Imported Irish stock is of an enormously higher standard than it was a few years ago. That is due to the fact that they have eliminated the 'scrub' bull. **1948** *Minneapolis Morn. Tribune* 28 Sept. 11/5 She couldn't resist givin' him a Home, even though she had to admit that he was a very *ugly* lookin' scrub cat. **1973** B. BROADFOOT *Ten Lost Years* i. 7, I slept in the barn with about six of the sorriest looking scrub horses you have ever seen. Broom tails.

4. a. (Transferred from SCRUB *sb.*² 5 b; cf. *SCRUB *sb.*¹ 5 c.) **scrub-nine** (earlier example); **scrub-race**, also *fig.*; (earlier and later examples).

1868 *N.Y. Herald* 11 Aug. 9/4 A club..presenting on the field the appearance of a 'scrub nine'. **1791** *Address of Lad who carries Connecticut Courant* (broadside), Did not our pious father S—n Run a scrub race with Mr. Chairman? **1804** *Fredericktown* (Maryland) *Herald* 10 Mar. 3/3 His antagonists seem sanguine enough for any bet, that he is either to be distanced, or will make but a scrub race for the amusement of the Gentlemen of the turf. **1894** *Outing* XXIV. 145/1 In a scrub race the helmsman cracks on until the lee gunwale is almost on a level with the water. **1947** C. PRICE *Trails I Rode* 190 He had put in most of his life travelling around the country with some kind of an old scrub race horse.

b. Hence in general sporting use. Of a team or player: not first-class, not of regular standing; of a game: played by scrub or scratch teams. Also *fig.*

1867 *Ball Player's Chron.* 7 Nov. 1/1 A scrub match was arranged with seven of the Star nine and two others against ten in the field. **1892** J. L. FORD *Dr. Dodd's School* i. 5 The school eleven..were playing a practice game of football with a scrub eleven enrolled for the occasion. **1920** W. CAMP *Football without Coach* 63 You will have your regular center playing against a scrub center. **1947** *Chicago Tribune* 29 Jan. 29/2 Perhaps football could be cleaned up if it had more scrub teams. **1951** *Daily Progress* (Charlottesville, Va.) 19 Mar. 1/3 The Chinese have employed in the past second-rate troops in the front line. Behind them are superior troops ready to take advantage of any breakthrough made by the scrub team.

scrub, *v.*¹ Add: **3. c.** *absol.* or *intr.*

1870 J. P. SMITH *Widow Goldsmith's Daughter* xxvi. 416 She began to clean the boots..while she whistled a jig and scrubbed for dear life. **1895** 'G. MORTIMER' *Like Stars that Fall* ii. 22, I must scrub and clean for you the rest of my life.

d. *intr.* for *refl.* To wash (usually with a brush) and disinfect the hands and forearms prior to performing or assisting at a surgical operation. Usu. with *up*.

1900 GOULD & WARREN *Internat. Text-bk. Surg.* I. xi. 283 While scrubbing, it is best to keep the hands and arms immersed in hot water, and particular attention should be given to the finger-nails. **1919** E. W. H. GROVES *Surg. Operations* i. 10 The sister scrubs up, covers herself in sterile gown, cap, gloves, and mask. **1944** *Brit. Jrnl. Surgery* XXXII. 25/2 The insertion was carried out by a member of the theatre staff who had 'scrubbed up' and donned the usual cap, mask, gown, and gloves. **1966** I. JEFFERIES *House-Surgeon* x. 185, I scrubbed, with Bernard alongside me asking questions about operative technique. **1976** *Lancet* 25 Dec. 1402/2 His asepsis was extraordinary. When he had spent the requisite ten minutes scrubbing up, he would dip his hands routinely into three successive bowls containing fluids of different colours.

e. *intr.* Of a horse-rider: to rub the arms and legs urgently upon a horse's neck and flanks to urge the horse to move faster.

1958 J. HISLOP *From Start to Finish* viii. 68 If you are riding a long-striding horse, you will find that you must scrub more slowly than on a short-striding horse. **1961** F. C. AVIS *Sportsman's Gloss.* 236/2 *Scrub*, of a jockey, to move the arms and legs, particularly as the end of a race is approaching. **1977** *Horse & Hound* 14 Jan. 21/1 By now the field was spreadeagled and scrubbing to keep in touch with the hounds.

3*. a. *trans.* To cancel, scrap, call off; to eliminate, erase; to reject, dismiss. Also with *out. colloq.*

The current widespread use was reinforced by the popularity of the expression amongst servicemen in the war of 1939–45 (see quot. 1945).

1828 W. SCOTT *Jrnl.* 22 Mar. (1941) 212 If I were alone, I could scrub it [*sc.* a visit to London], but there is no doing that with Anne. **1943** H. E. BATES *There's Something in Air* 77 He was worked up to a very high state of tension.. when Control informed him that the whole show would be scrubbed. **1944** *Yank* 30 June 8 At 1400 hours there was a briefing; at 1500 the mission was scrubbed. **1945** *Spectator* 25 May 478/1 The author can possibly justify the inclusion of the term 'scrub', meaning 'to cancel', in a collection of R.A.F. slang. The expression is in common use in the Royal Navy and has been for many generations. It derives from the days when all signals and orders were written on a slate. When the signals were cancelled or orders executed, the words on the slate were 'scrubbed out' or, equally correctly 'washed out'. **1953** *Sun* (Baltimore) 4 May 2/2 What do you mean that my mission is scrubbed? It's my mission and no one scrubs my mission but me. **1958** 'J. BROGAN' *Cummings Report* xix. 202 He might have told the operator to scrub it from the record. **1962** *Listener* 8 Feb. 247/2 At the end of the war some people realized that the best thing to do would be to scrub it [*sc.* the national debt] out. **1965** J. PORTER *Dover Three* xiii. 148 She doesn't sound the type of woman we're looking for. Scrub her! **1974** 'P. B. YUILL' *Bornless Keeper* ii. 17, I suggest scrubbing that thing on the Kent miners, can't see any foreign sales there. **1980** *News & Observer* (Raleigh, N. Carolina) 28 Oct. 10/1 Metropolitan Opera House musicians voted Monday to accept a new contract with the opera company, ending—at least temporarily—a strike that forced the Met. to scrub the 1980 season.

b. *intr.* To manage with difficulty, to 'scrape' *along*. Also with *on. colloq.*

1831 M. EDGEWORTH *Let.* 29 Mar. (1971) 507 He..has run through two large fortunes and is now scrubbing on upon a few thousands. **1889** W. DAVIDSON *Stories N.Z. Life* ii. 48 Dennis O'Brien had scrubbed along for many years, a miserable kind of existence, saving and hoarding, and living on the 'smell of an oil rag'. **1901** MERWIN & WEBSTER *Calumet 'K'* xi. 202 The rest of the road had to scrub along as best it could. **1905** G. BELL *Let.* 17 Apr. (1927) I. x. 212, I hope in a week or so I shall begin to scrub along.

c. *trans.* To reprimand severely; to punish *Mil. slang* (chiefly *Naut.*).

1911 [see *MATELOT I]. **1916** 'TAFFRAIL' *Pincher Martin* v. 76, I..jolly nearly got badly scrubbed for exceeding my duty and abducting the General. **1949** J. R. COLE *It was so Late* 62 That was my first station after they scrubbed me.

d. *intr.* Const. *round.* To dispense with, ignore; to drop (a subject). (See also quot. 1943.) *slang* (orig. *Mil.*). Cf. sense 3* a above.

1943 HUNT & PRINGLE *Service Slang* 58 *Scrub round*, to wash off the slate, to agree to forget, to let bygones be bygones. **1948** PARTRIDGE *Dict. Forces' Slang* 163 One declines an invitation to a party with 'Thanks very much, but you'll have to scrub round me, I'm Duty Boy to-morrow'. **1962** J. WAIN *Strike Father Dead* v. 222 'I just said I didn't want to break the contract we had at present,' I said. 'I felt it was no good trying to scrub round it.' **1964** T. WHITE tr. *P. Leullietté's St. Michael & Dragon* 189, I was required to do no less than fifteen days' cells. Reason: disobedience. Luckily, the captain had a sense of humour and finally scrubbed round it.

4. a. Substitute for def.: To treat (a material, esp. a gas or vapour) so as to remove impurities, usu. by bringing it into contact with a liquid; to wash *out* or remove (impurities) in such a way. (Further examples.)

1931 HOFFERT & CLAXTON *Motor Benzole* viii. 211 In this type of washer, the gas is scrubbed by the oil in the form of a fine spray in six or more superimposed sections or chambers, through which the gas ascends in turn. **1941** *Thorpe's Dict. Appl. Chem.* (ed. 4) V. 461/1 The [coal] gas is cooled by passage through condensers before scrubbing out the ammonia. **1961** G. CLAXTON *Benzoles* viii. 213 The greater proportion of the benzole is scrubbed out of the gas by means of wash oil. **1972** *Sci. Amer.* Oct. 26/1 Cooled and scrubbed with water to remove dust, the clean gas could be burned itself to provide the desired clean heat. **1974** *Daily Tel.* 22 Feb. 7/6 The diver inside the suit operates at ordinary surface pressures, and breathes oxygen which is continuously scrubbed and recirculated. **1979** *Sci. Amer.* Oct. 74/2 Consideration is being given to adding nitrogen-removing devices to the procedures that now 'scrub' sulfur dioxide..from stack gases.

b. *Glass-painting.* To scrape away (paint) or to scrape *out* (lights) with a scrub. Cf. *SCRUB *sb.*² 2.

1897 L. F. DAY *Windows* vi. 65 The practice in the sixteenth century was mainly, by a process of scrubbing lights out of matted or washed tints of brown, to get very considerable modelling. **1910** *Encycl. Brit.* XII. 106/2 The modelling was got by scrubbing away the paint with a dry hog-hair brush.

5. *scrub-man, -water, -woman* (earlier and later examples); (sense *3 d) *scrub nurse, room.*

1905 *Cleveland* (Ohio) *Plain Dealer* 24 Jan. 3 Once a soldier in the army of the great white czar, now a scrubman in one of the large department stores. **1927** *Amer. Speech* II. 312/2 The 'scrub nurse' is she who handles the instruments and works within the sterile field, differing from the 'dirty nurse' who may touch only contaminated or unsterilized things. **1958** F. G. SLAUGHTER *Daybreak* I. vii. 54 He stepped out of the hard white cone of the operating lights in response to a scrub nurse's signal. **1972** M. CRICHTON *Terminal Man* II. i. 57 Two scrub nurses were working in the cavernous gray-tiled space. They were setting out sterile tables and drapes. **1927** *Amer. Speech* II. 312/1 In the Operating Room one finds 'scrub rooms' where the surgeon and his assistants literally scrub their arms and hands with brushes and green soap. **1977** D. BENNETT *Jigsaw Man* 13 The surgeon..strode briskly to the scrub-room... The scrub-nurse removed his mask and gloves. **1935** Z. N. HURSTON *Mules & Men* 336 It is put in scrub water to scrub the house. **1975** *New Yorker* 28 July 31/2 He catches her scent of gray scrubwater as she passes. **1873** *N.Y. Herald* 16 Sept. 8/5 We have a specimen of this watch-dog policy in the case of a poor scrub woman. **1942** E. PAUL *Narrow St.* i. 2 Eugénie, a pale, brown-eyed scrubwoman not yet forty. **1973** E. MCGIRR *Bardel's Murder* i. 6 A scrubwoman did what was necessary in the cleaning line. **1980** G. M. FRASER *Mr American* xxii. 428 There's one way of treating a suffragette who's a scrub-woman..and another of treating a peer's daughter.

scrubbable (skrʌ·băb'l), *a.* [f. SCRUB *v.*¹ + -ABLE.] That may be scrubbed without damage or injury; capable of being cleaned by scrubbing.

1923 *Daily Mail* 29 May 10 Matone's 'scrubbable' matt finish is fadeless. **1960** *House & Garden* Oct. 150/3 Wallpaper..guaranteed scrubbable for seven years. **1976** *Woman's Day* (U.S.) Nov. 123/2 Vinyl wall covering is scrubbable.

scrubbed (skrʌbd), *ppl. a.* [f. SCRUB *v.*¹ + -ED¹.] Cleaned by scrubbing. Also *fig.*

1870 J. P. SMITH *Widow Goldsmith's Daughter* ii. 19 Chandos and Christabel were presentable children: both.. were kept scrubbed and combed, and 'cleaned up' within an inch of their lives. **1905** E. M. ALBANESI *Brown Eyes of Mary* xvi. 213 The sight of the old kitchen, with its scrubbed boards and red tiles. **1958** *Listener* 18 Dec. 1050/2 'People Today' gave us a fresh, scrubbed and shiny picture of Hawick.

scrubber¹. Add: **2. b.** More widely, any apparatus or installation for scrubbing (SCRUB *v.*¹ 4 in Dict. and Suppl.). (Further examples.)

1948 *Petroleum Handbk.* (ed. 3) xvi. 231 The crude product is then neutralized in a caustic scrubber and fractionated to remove light gases. **1974** L. DEIGHTON *Spy Story* xv. 154 The CO_2 scrubber that cleans the air in an atomic submarine before recirculating it. **1975** *N.Y. Times* 14 Apr. 49/2 The air standards..require utilities..to install costly pollution-control systems called scrubbers to clean emissions from coal with a high sulphur content. **1977** *Lancet* 9 July 76/2 The gas containing benzene was.. passed through a wet scrubber, and channelled into an activated-charcoal absorber unit, where benzene was recovered and recycled.

scrubber². Add: **1.** *Austral.* and *N.Z.* **a.** (Further examples.)

1869 in *Occas. Papers Univ. Sydney Austral. Lang. Res. Centre* (1980) No. 17. 55 'Were there any scrubbers—croppies—out here thin?'..'Four—murra [= very] wicked fellows!' **1897** D. McK. Wright in Chapman & Bennett *Anthol. N.Z. Verse* (1956) 42 New fences climb the warm brown spurs to guard the scrubber ewes. **1966** *Sunday Mail Mag.* (Brisbane) 9 Oct. 4/2 At the start of every cattle movement the 'scrubbers' (delinquent cattle) are noted, and are disciplined fast. **1978** O. White *Silent Reach* v. 54 Scrubber bulls have been turned into stud paddocks.

b. *fig.* An ill-bred or degenerate animal; an ill-favoured, despicable person.

1876 D. Kennedy *Colonial Travel* xviii. 249 We four adventurers..each..mounted on the shaggiest of small 'scrubbers', with a pannikin and a coil of rope dangling.. at his saddle-bow. **1941** Baker *Dict. Austral. Slang* 64 *Scrubbers*, cattle or horses that have run wild in the scrub and have deteriorated in condition. (2) Any weedy or unpleasant person. **1966** —— *Austral. Lang.* (ed. 2) iii. 66 *Scrubber*, a poor-looking, ill-bred horse. **1966** G. W. Turner *Eng. Lang. Austral. & N.Z.* iii. 54 *Scrubbers*, 'cattle that have run wild and deteriorated in condition', suggested figurative uses. It may mean *urchin*: I remember as a child hearing the phrase 'dirty little scrubber', and, not knowing the bush sense of the word, thinking it illogical.

c. The grey kangaroo, *Macropus giganteus*.

1968 K. Weatherly *Roo Shooter* 137 Scrubber is the name that shooters give to the grey kangaroo. **1977** J. L. Harper *Population Biol. Plants* xiii. 422 The grey kangaroo or scrubber..and..the red kangaroo..are regarded as pests by some sheep farmers.

3. *slang.* [Perh. properly related to Scrubber¹.] A prostitute, a tart (see also quot. 1965); an untidy, slatternly girl or woman.

1959 *Encounter* May 30 'The scrubbers': very young girls who follow jazz bands round the country. **1962** R. Cook *Crust on its Uppers* ii. 29 This aged scrubber, Mrs. Marengo ..she was so old, forty. **1965** G. Melly *Owning Up* xiv. 172 The word 'scrubber' has cropped up quite frequently in this story, and perhaps the time has come to attempt a precise definition of what it means, or rather meant, for I understand that in the beat world it has become debased and now means a prostitute. In our day this was not the case. A scrubber was a girl who slept with a jazzman but for her own satisfaction as much as his. **1968** J. Mitchell *Undiscovered Country* I. 134 'She's only a scrubber.' 'A what?' 'It's the new word for "short-term sexual partner".' **1970** G. Greer *Female Eunuch* 264 The most recent case in which contempt for menial labour has devised a new term of abuse for women is the usage of *scrubber* for a girl of easy virtue. **1973** B. Mather *Snowline* viii. 95 'She looked a scrubber. That means—' 'A mare that runs wild in the scrub country, copulating indiscriminately with stray stallions. Derivation Australian, but also applied to women of similar propensities in other parts of English-speaking world.' **1974** H. J. Parker *View from Boys* 213 *Scrubber*, used instead of 'tart' which has a non-derogatory meaning. 'A right scrubber' is a girl who's rough-looking, whore-like.

scrubbily (skrʌ·bili), *adv. rare.* [f. Scrubby *a.*¹ + -ly².] In a mean or paltry manner; shabbily.

1891 G. Gissing *New Grub Street* I. vi. 142 'By-the-by, how has *The Study* been in the habit of treating you?' 'Scrubbily.' 'I'll make an opportunity of talking about your books to Fadge.'

scrubbing, *vbl. sb.* Add: **2. d.** *Surg.* The action of *scrub *v.*¹ 3 d. Also with *up*.

1898 Wharton & Curtis *Pract. of Surg.* viii. 156 This scrubbing should be employed for several minutes; the hands are then rinsed to remove the soap, and are soaked for two minutes in a 1 to 1000 bichloride of mercury solution. **1910** H. A. Haubold *Preparatory & After Treatm. in Operative Cases* vi. 127 The object of the scrubbing is not to destroy the bacteria, but to remove them. **1937** 'J. Bell' *Murder in Hospital* vi. 109 The 'scrubbing up' process occupied about ten minutes. **1969** B. Weil *Dossier IX* xviii. 142 The space between the sides of the theatre and the walls had been fitted out for scrubbing up with washbasins. **1976** J. Archer *Not Penny More, not Penny Less* xii. 140 'Jean-Pierre, you scrub up as instructed.' .. Jean-Pierre appeared from the scrubbing-up room. **1978** Roaf & Hookinson *Basic Surg. Care* ix. 141 All preparation must be made beforehand to ensure that it is unnecessary to touch any unsterile surface once scrubbing is complete.

4. The action of Scrub *v.*¹ 4 in Dict. and Suppl.; removal of impurities from a material (usu. a gas or vapour).

1896 B. Redwood *Treat. Petroleum* II. 424 The scrubbing process consists in passing the gas through a series of coke towers in which it is exposed to streams of oil and water, the volatile hydrocarbons being removed by the oil, and the ammonia by the water. **1921** W. H. Fulweiler in A. Rogers *Industr. Chem.* (ed. 3) xx. 499 The gas is forced to pass in contact and bubble through the scrubbing liquid by a series of partitions arranged across the flow of gas. **1959** *Engineering* 23 Jan. 99/3, I am insufficiently informed of the details of gas scrubbing practice to say whether the systems at present in use are satisfactory. **1976** *Offshore Engineer* Apr. 61/1 There is continuous scrubbing of the air (many other subs have manual bleed-in and scrubbing) with direct readouts of O^2 and CO^2 levels as well as silica gel drying agents to remove moisture. **1976** *Physics Bull.* Apr. 160/2 A reduction of η to about zero or even slightly negative can be achieved by ion 'scrubbing' of the vacuum chamber surfaces in a high pressure argon glow discharge.

5. = *scrub *sb.*² 1 b.

1936 *Proc. Inst. Automobile Engineers* XXX. 739 Tyre wear due to lateral reaction, where location is high, offsets that which occurs in independently sprung cars due to 'scrubbing' when cornering. **1959** *Manch. Guardian* 27 July 2/3 Wear is the result of relative movement between tyre and road—'scrubbing' in other words. **1979** *Truck & Bus Transportation* Sept. 72/1 A third axle was placed between the front and rear axles to act as a turning pivot for the whole trailer. The result—no more scrubbing.

6. *Comb.*, as *scrubbing-board*.

1889 H. S. Edwards in *Century* XXXVIII. 84/1 Her great black, muscular arms drooped towards the scrubbing-board that reclined in the tub. **1969** E. H. Pinto *Treen* 155 It is believed that ribbed wooden scrubbing boards.. originated in Scandinavia and the manufacture spread to other countries during the 19th century.

scrubbing, *ppl. a.*² [f. Scrub *v.*¹ + -ing².] That scrubs (a floor, wood, etc.).

1868 M. H. Smith *Sunshine & Shadow in N.Y.* 362 The crowd is composed of the millionaire and the hod-carrier..madame flashing jewels, and the scrubbing-woman who cleans paint and washes linen. **1936** M. de la Roche *Whiteoak Harvest* xvi. 198 Two scrubbing women were sent to prepare the house for Sarah.

scrubble (skrʌ·b'l), *v.* [App. var. Scrabble *v.*] = Scrabble *v.*

c **1854** Mrs. Gaskell *Lett.* (1966) 274 It will..cost *two guineas*,..and so I must scrubble up money for that. **1920** D. H. Lawrence *Lost Girl* vi. 105 Country..now scrubbled all over with mining villages. **1927** J. Elder *Thomasina Toddy* i. 11 The blanket..comes up and scrubbles on your face, all rough and horrid. **1957** H. Nicolson *Let.* 26 Dec. (1968) 342 They played *God Save the Queen*, and all the old English boys scrubbled up on their crutches.

scrubby, *a.*¹ Add: **2.** (Later examples.) Also, consisting of or in the form of scrub.

1901 M. Franklin *My Brilliant Career* iii. 14 The school was situated on a wild scrubby hill. **1936** D. McCowan *Animals Canad. Rockies* xvi. 144 It finally reached a haven in the scrubby thicket. **1957** M. Spark *Comforters* ix. 233 He saw the bits of paper come to rest, some on the scrubby ground, some among the deep marsh weeds. **1971** *Sci. Amer.* Sept. 130/1 It takes less energy to support a pound of biomass in a mature tropical rain forest than it does in the grassy or scrubby forest stages that precede maturity. **1979** D. Kyle *Green River High* vi. 82 We were edging on to scrubby land, patches of low, tangling heather.

3. (Earlier and later examples.)

1754 J. Sackville *Let.* 4 Sept. in *16th Rep. R. Comm Hist. Manuscripts: Rep. MSS. Mrs. Stopford-Sackville* I. 40 in *Parl. Papers 1904* (Cd. 1892) I He still continues to persecute me, and acts in regard to me in a most scrubby manner. **1913** [see *honest *a.* 4 d]. **1967** *Southerly* XXVII. 75 It would work out, as it always did, under a cover of scrubby banality. **1975** *New Yorker* 5 May 18/3 (Advt.), A great deal of talent has been badly used, though James Caan has some good scenes as scrubby, anxious Billy Rose.

scruff, *sb.*¹ Add: **4. c.** A scruffy person, an oaf, a layabout; a contemptible or inferior person, someone of no breeding. Also *collect.*, scum, riff-raff.

1836 W. Carleton *Traits & Stories of Irish Peasantry* (ed. 4) II. 342 Oh, you scruff of the earth. **1896** G. F. Northall *Warwickshire Word-Book* 203 *Scruff*, a wastrel, raffish rogue. **1905** J. Wright *Eng. Dial. Dict.* V. 290/1 The village is well enough but for the scruff that comes in. **1958** *People* 4 May 12/4 'A nice class of fellow, too,' he said. 'Not one of the scruff.' **1960** D. Storey *This Sporting Life* I. v. 116 Every scruff in town's crept in. I don't like it. **1968** J. Lock *Lady Policeman* iii. 22 The 'scruff' might merely be an arty or beat type being deliberately scruffy and the very young face might belong to a grown woman. **1973** 'H. Carmichael' *Too Late for Tears* x. 121 Nature gives some of us the wrong heredity... So you're a scruff and John Piper's a gentleman. **1977** *Listener* 20 Jan. 72/2 Writing books or theatre plays is the only proper pursuit for a literary lady or gent, and..people who write for the new forms are money-grubbing scruffs who have sold their souls to the ghastly mass media.

scruff, *v.*¹ **1.** Delete † *Obs.*, for '*Sc.* and *north.*' read 'orig. *Sc.* and *north.*' and add later *lit.* examples. Also *spec.*, (*a*) in *Golf*, to graze (the turf) when striking the ball; (*b*) in *Painting*, to stroke (oil colour) lightly over a rough surface. Also *absol.* or *intr.* Hence **scru·ffing** *vbl. sb.*

Examples in *Sc.* use with various spellings (as *screef, scrief, scriff*, etc.) may be found in *S.N.D.* s.v. *scruif, n., v.* **1857** H. B. Farnie *Golfer's Man.* (1947) 74 *Scruff*, slightly razing the grass in striking. **1862** *St. Andrews Gaz.* 3 Oct. 3/3 The boy was sleeping on the cart and fell down, and..his head was a little 'scruffed' on the wheel. **1876** C. Clough Robinson *Gloss. Dial. Mid-Yorks.* 118/2 One will be told to get a besom and *scruff* the snow off the doorstone. **1896** P. A. Graham *Red Scaur* 347, I felt it scruff his chafts. **1920** C. Sandburg *Smoke & Steel* 25 Wearing leather shoes scruffed with fire. **1926** *Amer. Speech* I. 633/1 *Scruff*, to graze the grass with the club in striking. **1950** *Chambers's Encycl.* X. 310/2 The 'scruffing' trick: the brush laden with dry (light) paint is rapidly dragged over a darker tone. **1961** M. Levy *Studio Dict. of Art Terms* 100 *Scruffing*, an application of paint which skims the surface of a painting area, but does not take in the depressions of the panel or canvas texture. **1970** *Oxf. Compan. Art* 1055/1 A scumble must..be applied irregularly—dragged or scruffed—in such a way that small areas of the under colour show through.

2. [As a back-formation from Scruffy *a.*] *to scruff oneself up*: to make oneself scruffy.

1970 G. Lord *Marshmallow Pie* ii. 19 Scruff yourself up a bit over the weekend. You know, sweat a bit and that. **1970** *Guardian* 6 Apr. 9/4 The hardest thing..was to make those girls look really scruffy... You don't *look* like a plumber's wife, we kept saying... She didn't scruff herself up enough..for what the part demanded.

scruff, *v.*² Add: **b.** To seize and hold (a calf) while it is being branded or castrated. *Austral.*

1881 A. C. Grant *Bush-Life in Queensland* I. xvi. 228 The smaller calves are scruffed. **1909** *Chambers's Jrnl.* Dec. 810/2 After the calves are separated from their mothers..the former are one by one 'scruffed'—that is, seized by a couple of men and held down while knife and branding-iron are applied. **1931** F. D. Davison *Man-Shy* (1934) v. 71 It was the red heifer's turn... 'Get the ropes. She's too big to scruff,' he said.

c. To push roughly; manhandle. *rare.*

1926 J. Black *You can't Win* ix. 121 After they got done scruffing me around, two of them took me by each arm. **1941** Baker *Dict. Austral. Slang* 64 *Scruff, to*, to attack, manhandle a person.

scruffo (skrʌ·fo). *slang.* = *scruff *sb.*¹ 4 c.

1959 C. MacInnes *Absolute Beginners* 183 One of the scruffos turned and looked at his choice companions. **1976** *Tel.* (Brisbane) 10 June 40/1 They are not scruffoes, layabouts, or dole cheats.

scruffy, *a.* Add: **b.** Shabby, mean, dirty; slovenly, messy, untidy. Also *Comb.*, as *scruffy-looking* adj.

1871 'Mark Twain' *Screamers* ii. 16 When he'd got the blues, and feel kind o' scruffy, aggravated, and disgusted.. he would curl up..and go to sleep. **1925** Fraser & Gibbons *Soldier & Sailor Words* 253 *Scruffy*, dirty: slovenly: untidy in appearance. **1931** *Star* 8 May 6/3 Anyone who has travelled through lottery countries and seen the hundreds of scruffy ticket-shops in the cities. **1935** *Punch* 5 June 656/1 'Mine,' said the scruffy-looking chap who had started by borrowing a match, 'is a tragedy of jealousy.' **1940** Blunden *Poems 1930–40* 204 While I leisured it so, from the verge of the street Those scruffy old weeds in a flash had me beat. **1951** Auden *Nones* (1952) 29 A rather scruffy-looking god Descends in a machine. **1958** *Times Lit. Suppl.* 16 May 274/1 Always late, crumpled and scruffy, perpetually in debt, hourly expecting the sack, Greare takes refuge..in Mittyesque fantasies. **1967** A. N. Sherwin-White *Racial Prejudice in Imperial Rome* I. 4 It is because they..live..in a scruffy fashion, following the impulses and necessities of beasts. **1974** N. Freeling *Dressing of Diamond* 122 His chin was badly shaved: it gave him a dirty look, and sort of scruffy.

Hence **scru·ffily** *adv.*; **scru·ffiness.**

1974 *Times* 5 Oct. 13 That general 'scruffiness' could easily be rectified. **1977** *Listener* 4 Aug. 145/2 Making herself look scruffily bizarre is a time-consuming business.

scrum, *sb.* Add: **1.** (Later examples.) Also *ellipt.* for *scrum-half*.

1921 [see *fly *sb.*² 1 e]. **1930** R. Campbell *Poems* 11 See the fat nouns like porky forwards sprawl Into a scrum that never heels the ball. **1978** *Church Times* 23 Mar. 7/3 He pictured that duty as being like a forward's in a rugger scrum; he must put his head down and shove blindly.

2. *transf.* A confused, noisy throng (at a social function or the like).

1950 J. Cannan *Murder Included* ii. 23, I kept wondering where *you* were..in that awful scrum. **1959** P. Moyes *Dead Men don't Ski* i. 11 The handsome, fair-haired young man emerged from the scrum at the bar. **1965** P. O'Donnell *Modesty Blaise* iii. 32 She looked towards the manœuvring scrum at the bar. **1976** *Eastern Daily Press* (Norwich) 19 Nov. 1/4 Cindy, as the new Miss World likes to be called, was surrounded by the traditional scrum of over 100 press photographers. **1979** *Globe & Mail* (Toronto) 4 May 9/5 But he warned reporters after the second scrum yesterday, 'We're going to have to stop having these impromptu press conferences.'

3. *Comb.*, as **scrum-cap**, a cap worn to protect the head in a scrum; **scrum-half,** the half-back who puts the ball into the scrum; also, by extension, the scrum-half's position in a team.

1917 *Harrods General Catal.* 449/4 *Scrum Caps.* All Crochet Work, 3/3 each; all netting, 2/0 each; and Padded Ear Caps, 2/6. **1933** C. Day Lewis *Magnetic Mountain* in *Coll. Poems* (1935) 118 But will it suffice To wear a scrum-cap against falling skies? **1976** *Field* 18 Nov. 986/2 The headgear is authentic—more sensible than the top-hats once worn, less so than the scrum-caps which some favour now. **1906** Gallagher & Stead *Compl. Rugby Footballer* v. 69 Wallace played in every position except that of scrum half. **1922** *Somerset County Herald* 11 Feb. 4/3 As scrum-half [he] manfully overcame his disadvantage in weight. **1951** *Sport* 30 Mar.–5 Apr. 6/3 Another surprise 'cap' is that of Ike Proctor at scrum-half. **1978** *Rugby World* Apr. 3/2 The most exciting confrontation that day will be the scrum-half battle between Gareth Edwards and Jérôme Gallion.

scrum (skrʌm), *v.* [f. the sb.] *intr.* To jostle, crowd.

1925 A. S. M. Hutchinson *One Increasing Purpose* I. xxv. 153 The trouble with me is..feeding and frivoling at night and weekends where the masters live and where we scrum at shows. **1938** P. Lawlor *House of Templemore* ix. 98 Young calves 'scrumming' to dip their heads in the long troughs of milk. **1939** G. GREENE *Confidential Agent* I. i. 3 A rugger team was returning home and they scrummed boisterously for their glasses. **1948** C. DAY LEWIS *Otterbury Incident* iv. 49 Everyone was scrumming around behind him.

scrum (skrɒm), *a.* School and College slang abbrev. of SCRUMPTIOUS *a.* ? *Obs.*

1895 W. C. GORE in *Inlander* Nov. 65 *Scrum*, prob. from scrumptious, with which it is synonymous. **1913** J. VAIZEY *College Girl* xviii. 250 'Good cakes?' 'Scrum!'

scrumble (skrɒ·mb'l), *v.*[1] *rare.* [Perh. a blend of SCRAPE *v.* or SCRATCH *v.*+CRUMBLE *v.*] *trans.* To scrape or scratch *out of* or *from* (something).

The two examples perhaps represent independent nonce-formations.

1906 W. B. YEATS *King's Threshold* in *Poems, 1899–1905* 223 I'll scrumble the ermine out of his skin! **1975** P. LIVELY *Going Back* iv. 43 We scrumble the soft innards from the loaf and hold it high above us and now it snows bread upon the snow.

scrumble (skrɒ·mb'l), *v.*[2] [App. alteration of SCUMBLE *v.*] *trans.* To produce a smeary or grainy effect on (paint). Hence **scru·mbled** *ppl. a.*

1921 *Spectator* 9 Apr. 454/2 The paint has been scrumbled, i.e. if you look into it, it does not present a flat surface, it shows variations something like the grain of wood. **1937** *Sunday Times* 17 Jan. 30/3 Dining room designed in the Tudor style with scrumbled walls and beamed ceilings. **1959** *Spectator* 8 May 652/2 In his later large decorations.. the light colours, the scrumbled paint and the botanist's eye meet in something very far from mythology on one hand, and neurosis on the other.

scrummy (skrɒ·mi), *a. colloq.* [f. SCRUM(PTIOUS *a.* + -Y[1].] Excellent, fine, 'smashing'; enjoyable, delicious.

1915 MRS. H. WARD *Eltham House* i. 14 You've got to change and rest..before dinner!.. You've got to put on a scrummy frock too! **1918** GALSWORTHY *Five Tales* 122 He's promised to take mother and me to the theatre and supper afterwards. Won't it be scrummy! **1923** 'R. CROMPTON' *William Again* viii. 147 The cakes had been scrummy. **1928** —— *William—the Good* viii. 220 'Does it [*sc.* the trap-door] go out on to the roof?' called the Outlaws... 'Yes, it does. It's scrummy. Right on the edge of the roof.' **1960** *News Chron.* 8 July 8/5 Out spring the five white tubers of a corpse's hand. Scrummy! **1977** *Harper's & Queen* Nov. 52/2 Scrummy French food in cosy surroundings.

scrump, *sb.* Add: Also *spec.*, a withered or stunted apple.

1887 PARISH & SHAW *Dict. Kentish Dial.* 138 *Scrump*, a stunted, badly-grown apple. **1896** G. F. NORTHALL *Warwickshire Word-Bk.* 203 *Scrumps*, sb. pl. Apples.

scrump (skrɒmp), *v. dial.* or *slang.* [f. the sb.] *trans.* To steal (apples), esp. from orchards. Also *transf.* and *absol.*

1866 R. HALLAM *Wadsley Jack* iv. 17 Dick Greasy.. ax'd me if I'd mak' one to goa a scrumpim', that is, fetchin' apples off sumboddy's trees. **1931** 'G. ORWELL' *Hop-Picking* in *Coll. Essays* (1968) I. 71 *Scrump, to*, to steal. **1945** B. NAUGHTON in C. Madge *Pilot Papers* I. 101 They'd come scrumping..in Woolworths, or over at the market, or from the street stalls. **1951** A. BARON *Rosie Hogarth* III. i. 137 Scrumping apples, remember?.. God didn't put 'em on that tree for Mr. Moggeridge. **1966** M. TORRIE *Heavy as Lead* xiv. 169 His lordship was going scrumping... You know. Kids scrump apples, Sir G. scrumped rock garden plants. **1972** K. BONFIGLIOLI *Don't point that Thing at Me* i. 3 English policemen..dare not even spank the bottoms of little boys caught scrumping apples nowadays.

Hence **scrumped** *ppl. a.*; **scru·mper,** one who scrumps; **scru·mping** *vbl. sb.*

1946 *Scrutiny* XIII. 293 There is to be, after all, no development in Fant's moral powers: only, as it were, a schoolboy scrumping of all the redeeming fruits of experience. **1957** *Times* 20 Aug. 5/1 Scrumping is an offence which perhaps no one in this court-room has not committed. **1969** M. WIGGIN *Cottage Idyll* ii. 26 One scoundrel sent me a..message to the effect that he would like his cherished scrumping stick back. **1973** D. ORGILL *Jasius Pursuit* i. 9 If the police had to jail every hippy fruit-scrumper, the prisons would soon be overcrowded. **1976** A. HILL *Summer's End* vii. 98 Scrumped apples always taste better than bought ones. **1981** *Daily Tel.* 3 Mar. 3/1 (*heading*) Rector used stick on girl scrumper.

scrumple, *v.* Delete '*Obs.* exc. *dial.*' and add later examples. Also freq. with *up*.

1939 A. RANSOME *Secret Water* xxii. 261 She jumped up, grabbed the message, scrumpled it up and poked it into the stove. **1954** M. PROCTER *Hell is a City* I. ii. 23 It [*sc.* money in notes] came out of my bag all scrumpled up anyhow, just as I'd stuffed it in. **1961** R. M. DASHWOOD *Provincial Daughter* 83, I discover shirt scrumpled up in polythene bag at bottom of wardrobe. **1971** G. EWART *Gavin Ewart Show* I. 25 His secretary has a habit of scrumpling the top copies.

scrumpled, *ppl. a.* (Earlier example, and later example with *up*.)

1813 E. WEETON *Jrnl.* Dec. (1969) II. 115 She thrust something into my hand... It felt like a small parcel of scrumpled paper. **1947** A. RANSOME *Great Northern?* xvii. 210 He pulled the scrumpled up paper out of his knapsack and spread it out again.

scrumptious, *a.* Add: **2. b.** Now esp. of food: delicious. So **scru·mptiousness,** the state or condition of being scrumptious.

1881 *Punch* 30 July 47/2 There is a certain exquisite scrumptiousness and goloptiousness about Real Turtle. **1894** SOMERVILLE & 'ROSS' *Real Charlotte* II. xxxii. 247 The cake was scrumptious. **1922** JOYCE *Ulysses* 740 You will always think of the lovely teas we had together scrumptious currant scones and raspberry wafers I adore. **1930** *Magnet* 25 Jan. 6/2 'It's lovely butterscotch—scrumptious!' **1976** A. L. ROWSE *Cornishman Abroad* 14 The scrumptious meal she cooked, Cornish duck and Californian avocado stuffed with shrimp, our own cream from the farm with the delicious sweet.

scrumptiously (skrɒ·mpʃəsli), *adv.* [-LY[2].] In a scrumptious manner, excellently, deliciously.

1844 A. S. STEPHENS *High Life in N.Y.* I. xvi. 237 The frocks answered just as well to make bonnets out on, arter she'd dashed out in 'em once or twice, and the sleeves and waist cut up scrumptiously for ruffles and furbelows. **1927** *Observer* 1 May 8 He shows us 'Life' and 'High Life' simultaneously, so scrumptiously and yet with O such a touch of wanton wistful weariness! **1976** *New Yorker* 17 May 167/1 It is all scrumptiously pretty.

scrumpy (skrɒ·mpi). *dial.* or *colloq.* [f. SCRUMP *sb.* + -Y[6].] Rough cider, made from small or unselected apples. Also *attrib.* in *scrumpy cider.*

1904 in *Eng. Dial. Dict.* s.v., These apples are of no good but to make scrumpy of. **1932** [see *NOBBLE *v.* 3]. **1962** G. COMPTON *Too Many Murderers* xii. 87 Scrumpy was only eightpence a pint. **1973** C. BONINGTON *Next Horizon* viii. 114 A brisk five-minute walk took you to the Coronation Tap, where you could down a pint of scrumpy cider and eat home-made pies. **1977** *Times Lit. Suppl.* 4 Mar. 242/4 Another [pub] sold evil-smelling 'scrumpy', producing its own extensive Saturday-night network of vomit.

scrunch, *v.* Add: **2. c.** *U.S. intr.* for *refl.* To squeeze oneself into a compact shape; to huddle *up, together*; to cower or crouch *down.*

1884 'MARK TWAIN' *Huck. Finn* i. 4 Miss Watson would say,..'Dont scrunch up like that, Huckleberry—set [*sic*] up straight.' **1939** J. STEINBECK *Grapes of Wrath* ii. 11 'Scrunch down on the running board till we get around the bend,' he said. **1951** T. CAPOTE *Grass Harp* ii. 63 We scrunched together to make a place for Riley. **1972** D. DELMAN *Sudden Death* ii. 48 Wally knew something bad was about to happen to him; you could tell from the way he scrunched up, as a man will, sometimes, when a punch is telegraphed. **1974** K. MILLETT *Flying* (1975) IV. 394 In the North Terminal I scrunch into a bench and wait for Nell. **1978** J. IRVING *World according to Garp* xv. 311 He let her lean against him, though she was slightly taller..and in order to rest her head against him, she had to scrunch down.

scrunch, var. *SCRONCH.

scrunched, *ppl. a.* (and *pa. pple.*) Add: **a.** Also freq. with *up*.

1910 C. E. MONTAGUE *Hind let Loose* xi. 219 Some ebb.. would leave..the foreshore only littered with..tobacco-ashes, used matches, scrunched-up envelopes. **1963** C. D. SIMAK *They walked like Men* iii. 13 Balls of scrunched-up copy paper tossed onto the floor. **1974** T. P. WHITNEY tr. *Solzhenitsyn's Gulag Archipelago* I. II. i. 504 All that was left in that scrunched-up wad the engine room of the law had spewed out into the prisoner transport was a greed for life, and no understanding whatever.

b. Hunched, huddled, cowering. Usu. with *up*; occas. with *back, down*, etc. Chiefly *U.S.*

a **1902** S. BUTLER *Way of All Flesh* (1903) lv. 253 He looks that worrited and scrunched up at times. **1905** *N.Y. Sunday World* 11 June (Mag. Section) 8/2 You sit there with your shoulders scrunched up, giving an imitation of Reginald Vanderbilt driving his coach. **1931** *Virginia* (Louisiana) *Q. Rev.* Jan. 106 The twins lay upon the spare bed... 'Look at dis'n all scrunched up.' **1962** W. FAULKNER *Reivers* vii. 158 Otis was scrunched back against the wall. **1966** N. S. HAYNER *New Patterns in Old Mexico* ix. 167 One of the men approached the padre with his back scrunched up. **1976** *National Observer* (U.S.) 12 June 22/3 The wolves stayed where they were, scrunched motionless against the far wall. **1977** *Rolling Stone* 7 Apr. 58/1 That night Carl Sagan and I sat scrunched down in a sofa in his Pasadena apartment.

scru·nching, *vbl. sb.* [f. SCRUNCH *v.*+-ING[1].] The action of the verb SCRUNCH.

1869 S. R. HOLE *Bk. about Roses* 263 That yellow-bellied abomination, the grub which produces the saw-fly, in this month attacks the Rose... The process of 'scrunching' is disagreeable, but it *must* be done. **1927** A. CLARKE *Son of Learning* I. 9 The sloppiness of custard, the sourness of green apple, With crunching, munching, scrunching.

scrunchy (skrɒ·nʃi), *a.* [f. SCRUNCH *v.*+-Y[1].] That scrunches; that emits a crisp, crunching sound when crushed.

? **1905** *Eng. Dial. Dict.* Suppl. 168/2 *Scrunchy*, of frozen grass: emitting a crisp, crunching sound when trodden on. **1907** W. DE MORGAN *Alice-for-Short* xxvi. 274 Of course you may have scrunchy toast if you like. **1927** *Daily Express* 6 Dec. 11 The delicious, scrunchy crispness of 'Ovaltine' Rusks. **1937** *John o' London's Weekly* 29 Jan. 722/2 The minor roads are paved with scrunchy white shells. **1974** *Country Life* 13 June 1580/3 The vegetable..runs to flower without first making the desired, juicy, yummy, scrunchy, foliage.

scrunty (skrɒ·nti), *a.* orig. *Sc.* and *north. dial.* [f. SCRUNT.] Stunted, shrivelled, stumpy.

1811 A. SCOTT *Poems* 59 [A bird] wha, on his native scrunty thorn, 'Mang birds o' song bude hail the morn. **1849** in C. Brontë *Shirley* vii. 148 Then whudder awa' thou bitter biting blast, And sough through the scrunty tree. **1868** W. SHELLEY *Wayside Flowers* 55 He'd been sae scrimpit o' his corn His scrunty banes stood brent in sight. **1947** A. MCCORMICK *Galloway* 219 The scrunty aul' buddy has nae smeff. **1951** AUDEN *Nones* (1952) 54 A scrunty beggar With one glass eye and one hickory leg. **1963** S. PLATH *Bell Jar* i. 10 A short, scrunty fellow detached himself and came into the bar with us.

scrupulant (skrū·piulǎnt). *Eccl.* [f. L. *scrupul-us* + -ANT[1].] One who is over-scrupulous in confessing his sins; one who suffers from scrupulosity of conscience.

1938 'H. KINGSMILL' *English Genius* 199 George Fox was not what the Catholic Church calls a scrupulant. **1961** J. B. SHEERIN *Sacrament of Freedom* x. 133 The scrupulous person..breaks contact with reality when it comes to the matter of sin. In some cases, a scrupulant is sane about sin in general and has a blind spot only in regard to one particular type of sin. **1961** *Theol. Stud.* June 232 When dealing with a scrupulant..persuade him.. of the pathological element in his personality.

‖ **scrutin** (skrütæ̃n). [Fr., vote.] In Fr. combinations, referring to contrasting electoral systems: **scrutin d'arrondissement** (darondismaṅ) [lit., electoral district vote], a system of voting in France by which votes are cast for a single representative of an electoral district; **scrutin de liste** (list) = *list vote* s.v. *LIST *sb.*[6] d.

1851 *Ann. Reg. 1850* I. 230/2 According to Article 30, the election is effected in the department and by *Scrutin de liste.* **1911** J. H. HUMPHREYS *Proportional Representation* viii. 172 List systems of proportional representation are based upon the block vote or *scrutin de liste.* **1921** J. BRYCE *Mod. Democracies* I. xx. 270 Three times this method was dropped and replaced by the *Scrutin d'arrondissement* (the scheme of one-membered constituencies). Now the *Scrutin de liste* has returned once more. **1954** [see *list vote* s.v. *LIST *sb.*[6] d]. **1960** MACRIDIS & BROWN *De Gaulle Republic* xiii. 236 The cabinet decided to adopt the *scrutin d'arrondissement* with *ballottage.*

scrutineer, *sb.* Add: **1.** (Later examples in *gen.* use.) Also *spec.* in *Motor Racing* and *Motor-Boat Racing*, an official who inspects a car or boat in order to ensure that it complies with the regulations.

1932 S. C. H. DAVIS *Motor Racing* xxii. 270 Caracciola's Mercédès was rejected by the scrutineers. **1963** *Times* 4 June 14/7 The scrutineers' protest was upheld and both cars ruled ineligible. **1968** *Guardian* 19 Mar. 9/3 In the windy entrance lobby..there is a photograph of Mr Novotny... There is also a lady of the militia... Once past these two scrutineers you cross a yard.., and enter the works proper. **1972** [see next]. **1976** *Church Times* 16 July 6/5 A passport to immortality consisting of 'Cranford', 'Cousin Phillis' and 'Wives and Daughters' is convincing enough in all conscience for the most demanding of literary scrutineers.

2. (With capital initial.) A contributor to *Scrutiny*, a literary journal edited by F. R. Leavis (see *LEAVISIAN *sb.* and *a.*), and others, between 1932 and 1953; a follower of Leavis. *rare.*

1958 J. RAYMOND in *Times Lit. Suppl.* 15 Aug. p. xxxii/1 The difficulty of writing on a general theme like this is to decide at the beginning just what we are attempting to discuss... The Situation (desperate of course) of the Contemporary Writer? The Collapse of the Essay?.. Scrutineers All—and After? **1978** J. MARCUS in *Ibid.* 12 May 528/5 The Scrutineers have taught generations of British students that Virginia Woolf was a snob.

scrutineer (skrūtiniə·ɹ), *v.* [f. prec.] *trans.* In *Motor Racing* and *Motor-Boat Racing*: to inspect (a car or boat) in order to ensure that it complies with the regulations. Hence **scrutinee·ring** *vbl. sb.*

1930 E. WAUGH *Vile Bodies* x. 175 Changed the whole engine over after they'd been scrutineered. Anyone else would have been disqualified. **1932** S. C. H. DAVIS *Motor Racing* xxii. 270 That..served to emphasize..the weakness of scrutineering on the day before the race. **1971** *Sunday Express* (Johannesburg) 28 Mar. 7/1 The scrutineering area for checking whether cars comply with regulations. **1971** *E. Afr. Standard* (Nairobi) 13 Apr. 1/3 The margin on the road was four points, but the gap was narrowed when the two Datsuns went to scrutineering. **1972** C. MUDIE *Motor Boats & Boating* 150 Other boats will begin to arrive with tall tales of fantastic practice performances and all will build up to scrutineering the day before the race. Each boat has to present itself to a team of scrutineers who will check the hull and machinery. *Ibid.*, (*caption*) The scrutineering team check each boat before an important race.

scrutinization (skrūːtinəizēⁱ·ʃən). [f. SCRUTINIZE *v.* + -ATION.] The action of scrutinizing.

1922 *Autocar* 10 Nov. (Advt. Suppl.) p. lxxxv, Our unique methods of scrutinisation and the introduction of every detailed improvement. **1976** *Kybernetes* V. 36/1 If a particular scrutinization fails a logico-grammatical test, then its rejection requires the reformulation of a Postulated Hypothesis.

scrutoire. (Later examples.)
1853 J. G. M. Ramsey *Annals of Tennessee* 132 These issues of the North-Carolina Treasury..are still found in great abundance in the scrutoires and chests of the old families. **1978** W. M. Spackman *Armful of Warm Girl* 33 And he himself unpacked..a manila folder of assorted private relics, which he stowed one by one in the upstairs scrutoire.

scrutty (skrʊ·ti), *a. rare.* [Origin unknown.] Dirty, dusty, scruffy.
1914 M. Beerbohm *Let.* 27 Apr. (1964) 234 The Arnold Bennetts—very dusty and scrutty but nice—alighted from a motor-car here yesterday. **1970** T. Hughes *Crow* 68 He tried hating the sea But instantly felt like a scrutty dry rabbit dropping on the windy cliff.

scuba (skiū·bă, skū·bă). Also **SCUBA.** [f. the initials of *s*elf *c*ontained *u*nderwater *b*reathing *a*pparatus.] Self-contained apparatus designed to enable a swimmer to breathe while under the water. Also (rarely) *collect.* and *ellipt.* for *scuba-diving* vbl. sb. Freq. *attrib.* and *Comb.*, esp. in **scuba-dive** *v. intr.*, to swim under water using such apparatus; so **scuba-diver, scuba-diving** *vbl. sb.* and *ppl. a.*
1952 Hahn & Lambertsen *On using Self Contained Underwater Breathing Apparatus* (U.S. Nat. Acad. Sci.) 1 Within the last 3–5 years we have witnessed..a rapid increase in the numbers of self contained underwater breathing apparatus (SCUBA) in use... SCUBA are now in relatively large scale use by spearfishermen and sports swimmers. **1957** *Time* 25 Feb. 49/1 Most types of scuba are of the open-circuit design which supply air on demand, and discharge exhaled air into the water. **1962** (*title*) The new science of skin and scuba diving. **1963** G. L. Pickard *Descriptive Physical Oceanogr.* v. 57 In clear ocean water the superior penetration of blue and green light is evident..when SCUBA diving. **1963** *Today's Health* June 18/2 The scubacide victim is the person who tries to become a scuba diver in one fatal lesson (self-taught). **1966** T. Pynchon *Crying of Lot 49* ii. 31 It [*sc.* a housing development] was to be laced by canals with private landings for power boats, a floating social hall,.. all for the entertainment of Scuba enthusiasts. **1973** P. O'Donnell *Silver Mistress* v. 82 Under the hull..two scuba-suited figures clung to magnetic limpets clamped to the steel plates. **1975** *New Yorker* 26 May 17 (Advt.), Swimming, scuba and long beautiful beaches. **1977** *Ibid.* 4 July 83/1 In 'The Deep'..Nick Nolte plays a scuba-diving hero called David. **1980** *Nature* 4 Sept. 12/1 Scuba dive over the lost road of Atlantis.
Hence as *vb.*; also **scu·baˌing** *vbl. sb.* (in quot. spelt *scubering*).
1973 B. Mather *Snowline* xix. 234 Some of the boys are keen on scubering, water-skiing and fishing. **1977** *Rolling Stone* 16 June 74/5 (Advt.), Hike, swim, scuba, snorkel, sail.

scud, *sb.*[1] Add: **2. d.** Also of snow.
1969 N. W. Parsons *Upon Sagebrush Harp* xv. 85 Usually, at dawn the wind died and a knee-high scud sharp as glass would skitter sullenly along the surface of the hard-packed snow.
e. Also *Comb.*, as **scud-like** *a.*
1866 G. M. Hopkins *Jrnls. & Papers* (1959) 138 A 'dirty' looking kind of clouds, scud-like, rising.

scud, *sb.*[2] Add: **3.** *Tanning.* Dirt, lime, fat, and fragments of hair which must be removed from a hide. Cf. Scud *v.*[3] 2.
1885 A. Watt *Art of Leather Manufacture* xxvi. 324 The 'scud' is removed by working the pelt upon the beam with the blunt knife. **1969** T. C. Thorstensen *Pract. Leather Technol.* vi. 96 The hair-destruction system may result in uneven swelling and in the formation of scud (surface dirt) on the hides. *Ibid.* 98 The strong oxidizing action of the chlorine dioxide and chlorine results in the bleaching of the hair, and there is no dark scud left on the hide.

scud, *v.*[1] Add: **6.** *Sc.* To slap, beat, strike, spank; to beat down.
1814 W. Nicholson *Tales in Verse & Miscellaneous Poems* 123 And farmers, keen to cut the crap, Lest win's should scud it. **1866** J. Smith *Merry Bridal* (ed. 2) 23 Lassie, when I get ye I'll scud ye till I'm sair. **1925** *United Free Church Mission Record* Dec. 569/2 The risen wind scudded my cheek—wet, stinging, and with the bite of the sea. **1976** *Scotsman* 24 Dec. (Weekend Suppl.) 1/1 Any more cracks and I'll scud yer hint end for ye.

scuddy, *a.*[2] Delete † *Obs.* and ? and add later examples.
1872 Thudichum & Dupré *Treat. on Wine* xx. 633 The wines are spoiled during fermentation, become acidified, scuddy. **1964** R. Braddon *Year Angry Rabbit* xi. 94 Jacks..at once flung himself gratefully into a chair, spilling half his cold, scuddy tea into his lap as he did so.

scuff, *sb.*[1] Add: **2. b.** A mark made by scraping or rubbing.
1954 J. Steinbeck *Sweet Thursday* v. 35 Brown calf shoes.., scuff on the right toe. **1976** B. Lecomber *Dead Weight* i. 11 A thousand scuffs and scratches in the shabby wood and leather.
4. A type of slipper or sandal without a back. Chiefly *U.S.*
1909 in *Cent. Dict. Suppl.* **1938** *Sears, Roebuck Catal.* Fall/Winter 324/3 Adorable Slip-on 'Scuffs'. No trouble at all to slip in or out of these cunning, snug 'scuffs'. **1945** *Creative Footwear* Apr. 106/2 (Advt.), Shearling scuff, leather sole. **1953** S. Ransome *Drag Dark* xiv. 140 In the snow in her stocking feet, her red scuffs lost behind her. **1968** J. Ironside *Fashion Alphabet* 135 *Mule*, loose slipper with front vamp only, no back. Also called a 'scuff'. **1974** *Spartanburg* (S. Carolina) *Herald* 18 Apr. (Kmart Advt. Suppl.) 1 Soft-stepping flowered cotton terry cloth scuffs, molded rubber sole.

scuff, *v.* Add: **5.** *intr.* for *pass.* **a.** To become marked, worn, or damaged by rubbing or scraping.
1934 Webster, s.v., Soft bindings scuff easily. **1978** *Radio Times* 18–24 Mar. 80 (Advt.), For kids who play rough, shoes that won't scuff.
b. Of a metal part: to undergo scuffing (*scuffing *vbl. sb.* 3).
1959 *Engineering* 23 Jan. 117/3 The untreated mild steel rings scuffed shortly after being put under test. **1970** H. J. Watson *Mod. Gear Production* xvi. 283 The peaks [of helical gears] were prone to scuff or pit in service largely owing to the high local loading on the restricted areas.
6. *Comb.*, as **scuff-resistant** adj., resistant to scuffing; hence **scuff resistance.**
1967 *Times Rev. Industry* May 84/3 The growing demand for higher gloss and better scuff and product resistance has led to the development of synthetic resin based types [of varnish]. **1959** *Spectator* 21 Aug. 219 (Advt.), Everything from scuff-resistant flooring and unbreakable gramophone records to transparent polyethylene wrapping. **1978** *Radio Times* 18–24 Mar. 80 (Advt.), A shoe that's an astonishing 30 to 40 times more scuff-resistant than normal leather.

scuffed, *pa. pple.* and *ppl. a.* Restrict '*Sc.*, *Anglo-Irish*, and *U.S.*' to sense in Dict. and add: **1. b.** Of shoes, a floor, etc.: worn or marked by rubbing, scraping, or treading. Also with *up*.
1927 *Scribner's Mag.* Apr. 381/2 It wasn't a large room but everything in it, from the scuffed leather slippers to the stout..easy chairs, proclaimed a man who knew how to put himself at ease. **1973** R. Thomas *If you can't be Good* (1974) xii. 99 The beat-up desks..and the scuffed-up floor. **1975** J. Gores *Hammett* (1976) vii. 51 The hardwood floor waxed but well-scuffed, ready for dancers. **1978** *Morecambe Guardian* 14 Mar. 17/3 Generally speaking there are two categories of small boy..the studious, eyes-down-in-a-book type and the outdoor scuffed shoes clothes-in-a-mess variety.
c. *Engin.* Of a metal part: worn by scuffing.
1934 *Jrnl. R. Aeronaut. Soc.* XXXVIII. 310 Cases have come to one's notice where engines have suffered from troubles in the form of scored, or, as our friends in America term it, 'scuffed' pistons. **1941** [see *scuffing *vbl. sb.* 3].

scuffer[1] (skʊ·fəɹ). *dial.* or *slang* (chiefly *north.* and *Sc.*). Also **scufter.** [Origin obscure; perh. f. Scuff *sb.*[2] or *v.*] A policeman.
1860 Hotten *Dict. Slang* (ed. 2) 209 *Scufter*, a policeman. **1886** A. G. Murdoch *Scotch Readings* 1st Ser. (ed. 2) 78 The policeman..was familiar [to]..him as..'the Scufter'. **1959** I. & P. Opie *Lore & Lang. Schoolch.* xvii. 369 In Penrith children still commonly use the old northern name 'Scufty' or 'Scufter', a term which had been thought to be obsolete. **1961** Partridge *Dict. Slang* Suppl. 1263/1 *Scuffer*, a policeman: Liverpool: C. 20. Ex. dial. *scuff*, to strike... Cf. *scufter*. **1966** P. Moloney *Plea for Mersey* 45 Scuffer! Scuffer! on the beat, With thy elephantine feet, You can't see the way to go Cos yer 'at comes down too low. **1967** J. Wainwright *Talent for Murder* 17 Are you from the slops, sonny?.. The scuffers. The jacks. Are you from the coppers, sonny? **1970** T. Lewis *Jack's Return Home* 49 What do you think I should do? Go to the scuffers? **1978** *Daily Mail* 25 Jan. 12/2 The strange language of a group who call themselves 'bogeys', 'bobbies' or 'scuffers'. They are, of course, regional variations describing policemen.

scuffer[2] (skʊ·fəɹ). *N. Amer.* [f. Scuff *sb.*[1] or *v.* + -er[1].] = *scuff *sb.*[1] 4 (see also quot. 1939).
1911 *Daily Colonist* (Victoria, B.C.) 5 Apr. 7/1 (Advt.), Correct spring styles in America's best footwear..Broadwalk Scuffers for children. **1935** *Amer. Speech* X. 9/2 *Scuffers* and *ghillies* are words of the fashion page. **1939** M. P. Picken *Lang. of Fashion* 130/3 Scuffer..child's sandal-like play shoe, light-weight and flexible with sturdy sole. Also used for sportswear by adults.

scuffing, *vbl. sb.* (In Dict. s.v. Scuff *v.*) Add: **2.** (See quot. 1928.)
1928 Holt & Cooke in *Bur. Standards Jrnl. Res.* I. 25 A considerable part of tread wear may be caused by the slipping of portions of the tread over the road surface in changing from the normal to the deflected condition and vice versa. This might be termed a scuffing action. **1955** W. H. Crouse *Automotive Chassis & Body* vi. 157 High-speed operation causes much more rapid tire wear because of the high temperature and greater amount of scuffing and rapid flexing to which the tires are subjected.
3. *Engin.* The roughening of a metal surface designed to rub against another when the lubrication is inadequate to prevent local fusion and tearing of the two surfaces.
1941 *Engineering* 11 Apr. 286/1 Should a local breakdown of the lubricating-oil film occur, the two surfaces may momentarily become fused. With the reciprocating movement of the parts, a shearing action takes place,..causing disruption of the surfaces. An example of this effect, which is known as piston-ring 'scuffing', is seen in Fig. 1, which shows the surface of a scuffed piston ring. **1950** *Engineering* 17 Mar. 310/1 Failure of a gear lubricant to prevent the teeth from making metallic contact may result in destruction of the tooth surfaces by 'scuffing', 'seizing', or 'welding': all different degrees of welding. **1961** *New Scientist* 26 Jan. 218/3 'Scuffing' of valve gear cams and the tappets that run against them occurred. **1966** G. W. Michalec *Precision Gearing* viii. 354 Scoring and scuffing are associated with welding (or seizing) and plastic deformation.

scuffle, *sb.*[2] **2.** (Earlier examples.)
1797 S. Deane *Newengland Farmer* (ed. 2) 95/2 *Dutch Hoe*, sometimes called a *Scuffle*; an iron instrument, with a sharp steeled edge, nearly in the shape of the letter D. **1825** J. Lorain *Nature & Reason harmonized in Practice of Husbandry* 191 The scuffle (or D hoe as it is sometimes called) will destroy weeds growing on a level surface.

scuffle, *v.*[1] Add: **2. b.** *trans.* To obtain, collect, raise (money). Also with *up* and *intr.* (const. *up on*). *slang* (chiefly *U.S.*).
1946 Mezzrow & Wolfe *Really Blues* (1957) 378 *Scuffle up*, raise, collect, get together. **1956** B. Holiday *Lady sings Blues* (1973) vii. 66, I stayed around Philly a couple of days before I could scuffle up enough to get back to New York on the bus. **1965** 'Malcolm X' *Autobiogr.* (1966) xvi. 389 Trying to scuffle up on some bread. **1973** *Brit. Jrnl. Sociol.* XXIV. 203 It is surely of immense sociological significance that when a Ras-Tafarian 'scuffles' a fare (he might beg, borrow or steal it), he seeks to migrate not to Ethiopia, as we would expect, but to Britain or the United States.
3. b. *intr.* To survive with difficulty, to make a bare living by uncongenial or degrading means. *slang* (chiefly *U.S.*).
1939 W. Hobson *Amer. Jazz Music* (1940) 173 At the bottom of the economic pile are those musicians who have nothing which could accurately be called a job but are taking whatever one-night stand happens along; this is called 'scuffling'. **1956** S. Longstreet *Real Jazz Old & New* xviii. 147 *Scuffle* is to get by. **1956** M. Stearns *Story of Jazz* (1957) xvii. 212 The Basie band was scuffling. 'It was a cracker town but a happy time,' Basie recalls. **1961** Rigney & Smith *Real Bohemia* p. xvi, *Scuffle*, to live by one's wits, not by a gig. **1972** T. Kochman *Rappin' & stylin' Out* 164 'Scuffling' in the idiom means barely making it from day to day, generally by engaging in nonprestigious..activities such as begging, collecting and returning pop bottles for the deposit, working at odd jobs for minimum wages, etc.

scuffler[1]. (Later examples.)
1961 F. G. Cassidy *Jamaica Talk* x. 215 A *scuffler* is a thief. **1965** H. Williamson *Hustler* vi. 169 He said he was a hustler, but he really wasn't nothin' but a goddamn scuffler.

scufter, var. *scuffer[1].

scug, *sb.*[3] Add: Also in extended use. Also *attrib.* Hence **scu·ggish, scu·ggy** *adjs.*
1911 R. Nevill *Floreat Etona* iii. 98 Once it began to be considered 'scuggish', the fate of Eton pugilism was sealed. **1916** E. F. Benson *David Blaize* v. 101 These are all college houses, in-boarders, and rather scuggy compared to out-boarders. *Ibid.* viii. 143 You were such a scug, you see, that you didn't do those things when it was scuggish not to. **1922** S. Leslie *Oppidan* iv. 48 A *Tug* was something between a *scug* and a hireling chorister. *Ibid.* v. 57 The sad sight of a *Pop* wearing a *scug*-cap. **1928** *Observer* 15 Apr. 29/4 A band of what I can only describe as 'Scugs' in bowler hats. **1940** E. F. Benson *Final Edition* ii. 27 Mr. Luxmore..wrote to a friend in withering disdain of him and his official purple as a Monsignor, declaring that he was just the same 'sharp insignificant little scug as he had been at Eton'. **1962** J. P. Carstairs *Pardon my Gun* ii. 28 He was a bit of a scug but what the hell. **1980** D. Marlowe *Rich Boy from Chicago* xxi. 314 Many refused to talk..dismissing Lambert as a 'scug', a loathsome queer.

sculduddery. (See also *skulduggery.)

scull, *sb.*[1] Add: **1. a.** Also in *Comb.*, as **scull-hole** = *sculling-hole* s.v. Sculling *vbl. sb.* b.
1843 G. Little *Life on Ocean* 63 The crew got the bight of the rope fore and aft the boat, leading it from the stern over the scull-hole. **1973** W. Elmer *Terminol. Fishing* iv. 125 Many of the smallest boats are not fitted with rowlocks or tholes, but have a notch in the transom for sculling (*sculling-notch* or *scull-hole*).

scull, *v.* Add: **4.** *intr.* To skate without lifting the feet from the ice.
1895 in *Funk's Stand. Dict.* **1938** [implied in *sculling *vbl. sb.* a]. **1976** *Webster's Sports Dict.* 376/1 *Scull or skull*,..to propel oneself forward or backward by alternately moving the heels or the toes apart and together changing from an outer edge on the outward movement to an inner edge on the inward movement.
5. a. *to scull about*, to lie about; *spec.* of objects left on the deck of a ship instead of being put away. *colloq.*
1917 'Taffrail' *Sub* v. 136 You went round..with a large bag. In this you placed all..articles..found 'sculling' about. **1938** C. Morgan *Flashing Stream* iii. 263 Don't leave it [*sc.* a key] sculling about. **1943** C. S. Forester *Ship* 12, I want those mess-traps brought back... Don't leave them sculling about on the decks.
b. *to scull around* (or *about*), to move about aimlessly; also *fig. colloq.*
1921 *Daily Colonist* (Victoria, B.C.) 20 Mar. 19/7 My opposite number..has one or two questions pertaining to his own branch sculling around in his mind. **1935** M. Egan

Dominant Sex I. 12 *Angela.* Where have you been these ages? *Alec.* Oh, sculling round the country on business. **1950** [see *NUMBER *sb.* 5 c]. **1961** B. FERGUSSON *Watery Maze* vi. 151 While these ideas were sculling around Whitehall, there arrived from Moscow..M. Molotov. **1981** 'J. Ross' *Dark Blue & Dangerous* xxiii. 137 What with Wiffen and one or two others who were there sculling about, the picture is a little confusing.

sculduggery, see *SKULDUGGERY.

sculling, *vbl. sb.* Add: **a.** (Later examples, in sense *4 of the verb.)

1938 D. CUMMINGS *Figure Skating as Hobby* iii. 19 You can try sculling. Feet together, put your weight on the inside of both your skates..bend your knees, push down, move your feet apart, straighten slightly and bring them together again. **1973** R. S. OGILVIE *Basic Ice Skating Skills* II. 49 This progression across the ice by moving both feet in and out is known as *sculling*. Sculling..can be done forward as well as backward. *Ibid.* 175 *Sculling*,..a method of two-footed progression forward or backward by an in-and-out movement of the feet.

b. sculling-notch, sculling score = *sculling-hole.*

1933 BAMFIELD & PALMER *Art of Sailing* ix. 76 Have a sculling notch cut in the stern, shod with a strip of brass. **1973** Sculling-notch [see *SCULL *sb.*[1] 1 a]. **1946** F. B. COOKE *Cruising Hints* (ed. 6) xxvii. 244 Every yacht's dinghy should have a sculling score in the transom. **1960** —— *Yachting with Economy* xxi. 146 When leaving the yacht to get the kedge, place the warp in the sculling score.

sculp, *sb.*[1] **2.** (Later example.)

1883 *Daily News* 18 Jan. 5/7 Perhaps no statue, except the unfortunates in Trafalgar-square, and the melancholy meeting of 'sculps' in Parliament-square, was more sharply criticised at the time of its erection.

sculp, *sb.*[2] Add: Also, in early or *arch.* use, a human scalp.

1743 J. ISHAM *Observations on Hudsons Bay* (1949) 93 They make an offering, putting a painted Stick up, some with a cross hanging a hatchet,..or Ice Chissel, or what Else they have on the top, with the sculp of their Enemies, when they go to Warr. **1758** in *Essex Inst. Hist. Coll.* (1881) XVIII. 180 They obtained fifty-two Sculps and two Prisoners. **1804** LEWIS & CLARK *Orig. Jrnls. Lewis & Clark Exped.* (1905) VII. 64 They took the 65 of the Mahars sculps and had them hung on Small poles. **1845** W. G. SIMMS *Wigwam & Cabin* 1st Ser. 53 A pretty fellow..at his time of life to be looking after sculps of women and children. **1921** J. BUCHAN *Path of King* xii. 242 Maybe the Indians have got his sculp.

sculp, *v.*[2] Add: **a.** Also *U.S.*, to scalp (a person). Now *arch.*

1758 in *Essex Inst. Hist. Coll.* (1881) XVIII. 109 Taring his Nails out by ye Roots, Sculping alive and such like torments, they wou'd shout and yell. **1759** in *Ibid.* (1882) XIX. 188 [He] retook one of ye Prisoners and killed and sculpt one of ye Indians. **1834** W. A. CARRUTHERS *Kentuckian in New York* I. 24 But as to shootin and sculpin Injins, that's a thing there is no bones made about. **1845** W. G. SIMMS *Wigwam & Cabin* 1st Ser. 44 They'll be sculped, every human of them, in their beds. *Ibid.* 51 We heard of murders and sculpings on every side. **1884** SWEET & KNOX *On Mexican Mustang through Texas* xviii. 246 I'm a scout from the Far West, whar..the coyote sleeps in the deserted wigwams of the skulpt Indian. **1921** J. BUCHAN *Path of King* xii. 243 The Shawnees cotched me and Jim... They'd ha' sculped us if it hadn't been for Jim.

sculpt, *v.* Delete '*rare* exc. in jocular use' and add: **1.** (Later examples.)

1928 *Daily Express* 16 June 4/5 He sculpts in almost every material. **1931** *Sun (Baltimore)* 13 Mar. 12/7 Somebody proposed that instead of being depicted as astride a horse (steed, charger) this general be sculpted as a figure seated in a motor car. **1966** J. RICHARDSON *George IV* 332 The statue (known as the Copper Horse) had been sculpted by Westmacott. **1977** *Times* 5 Sept. 5/7 My uncle, my mother's brother, draws beautifully and sculpts.

2. *transf.* To shape, form, mould.

1967 *Times Rev. Industry* Apr. 86/3 Numerical control of machine tools is obtainable in a number of forms, from the simple point-to-point positioning system, through straight-line machining systems, to the complex continuous path systems which can sculpt any shape capable of being expressed numerically. **1972** *Sci. Amer.* Mar. 45/1 (Advt.), High-level signal lights, neatly sculpted into the rear deck of the car.

sculpted (skɒ·lptėd), *ppl. a.* [f. SCULPT *v.* + -ED[1].] = SCULPTURED *ppl. a.* in Dict. and Suppl. Also *fig.*

1961 in WEBSTER. **1976** *Listener* 22 Apr. 510/1 The dialogue was full of sculpted pauses, a gain for poetry but a loss for credibility. **1978** P. PORTER *Cost of Seriousness* 17 Seeing grief in formal state Upon a sculpted angel group. **1978** A. & G. RITCHIE *Anc. Monuments Orkney* 5 The landscape is typical of that produced by Old Red Sandstone, predominantly gentle and rounded, but rising to spectacularly sculpted cliffs along the west and north coasts.

sculptured, *ppl. a.* Add: **3.** Shaped in a manner resembling sculpture.

1966 J. S. COX *Illustr. Dict. Hairdressing & Wigmaking* 132/2 *Sculptured curl*, a firmly and smoothly formed curl showing the comb-teeth lines. *Sculptured hair style*, a hairdress with hard, firm, definite lines in its constituent parts; not fussy, light or tapered. **1970** *Which?* Sept. 268/1 Now, however, you will also find twists, loop-pile and sculptured pile—a pattern formed by mixing loops of different heights or looped and cut pile. **1974** *Times Lit. Suppl.* 24 May 544/3 The second president of General Motors invented the scheme of elaboration and development, bright colours, sculptured lines and rising prices. **1974** *Times-Picayune* (New Orleans) 15 Aug. v. 6/1 The bride..wore a peau de soie gown styled with a sculptured yoke of re-embroidered lace and a cameo neckline.

sculpturing, *vbl. sb.* Add: **2.** *Bot.* The structural ornamentation of the surface of a pollen grain or spore.

1943 G. ERDTMAN *Introd. Pollen Analysis* v. 43 The outer surface of the exine may sometimes be provided with some sculpturing or ornamentation. The ornamentations of sculptured pollen grains are exceedingly varied. **1967** M. E. HALE *Biol. Lichens* ii. 37 The spores are unornamented, although exospore sculpturing is reported in *Tholurna*. **1970** *Watsonia* VIII. 4 The sculpturing of the perispore of *D[ryopteris] assimilis* differs from that of *D. dilatata* and *D. carthusiana* in density and shape and size of projections.

scum, *sb.* Add: **2. b.** More generally, any undesirable surface layer or deposit, usu. but not necessarily on a liquid. (Further examples.)

1940 *Chambers's Techn. Dict.* 750/1 *Scum*,..a surface formation of lime crystals appearing on new cement work. **1941** *Thorpe's Dict. Appl. Chem.* (ed. 4) V. 573/1 Silica scum is sometimes found on the top of tank-melted glass if the melting temperature is not very high. **1967** E. CHAMBERS *Photolitho-Offset* xiv. 211 The albumen image.. may look clear and free from ink when the grain is full of scum, which will readily ink-up on the press run with the soft machine ink.

d. *coarse slang* (chiefly *U.S.*). Semen.

1967 WENTWORTH & FLEXNER *Dict. Amer. Slang* Suppl. 703/1 *Scum* (taboo),..semen... *Scumbag* (taboo),..a condom. **1972** R. A. WILSON *Playboy's Bk. of Forbidden Words* 257 *Scum*, the semen.

4. scumspittle *nonce-wd.*, ? scummy or frothy spittle.

1922 JOYCE *Ulysses* 446 The bulldog growls,..a gobbet of pig's knuckle between his molars through which rabid scumspittle dribbles.

scumbag (skɒ·mbæg). *coarse slang* (chiefly *U.S.*). Also **scum bag.** [f. SCUM *sb.* + BAG *sb.*]

1. A condom.

1967 [see *SCUM *sb.* 2 d]. **1968–70** *Current Slang* (Univ. S. Dakota) III–IV. 106 *Scum bag*, a condom. **1974** *Time Out* 6 Dec. 21/1 Young blades carried their sheaths or condoms or..'scumbags' in their wallets.

2. A base, despicable person. Also as a term of vulgar abuse.

1971 *Courier-Mail* (Brisbane) 23 Dec. 5/2 Another called him a 'scumbag' and said he should have been killed. **1973** E. BULLINS *Theme is Blackness* 80 [Ann] No, you can't think that about me! [Peter] Why can't I, scumbag? **1976** G. V. HIGGINS *Judgement of Deke Hunter* iv. 29, I had three scumbags that went to trial. **1977** *Zigzag* Apr. 34/2 What little scumbag would say something like that?

scumble, *v.* **3.** (Later example.)

1974 V. NABOKOV *Look at Harlequins* (1975) VI. i. 227 The summer tan..would scumble, I knew, the liver spots on my temples.

scumbled *ppl. a.*, **scumbling** *vbl. sb.* (Later *fig.* examples.)

1967 *Listener* 12 Jan. 48/3 A verb 'to scumble', which means to blur and soften the outlines. A great deal of our national life seems to me to be scumbled. **1977** *Times* 19 Nov. 9/2 The confusion of the times..the scumbling of boundary lines.

scummy, *a.* Delete *rare* and add: **1.** (Later examples.)

1936 A. RANSOME *Pigeon Post* xxix. 312 'What'll it look like when we see it again?'..'All scummy on the top... The pure gold'll be underneath.' **1967** E. CHAMBERS *Photolitho-Offset* xiv. 215 Under-exposure produces a weak, soft stencil, so that the image thickens-up in development and results in stencil breakdown and a scummy plate. **1979** K. M. PEYTON *Marion's Angels* ii. 29 At high-water springs the river came right up over the saltings.. and sent scummy fingers up the garden path.

3. *transf.* and *fig.* Filthy, dirty; despicable, disreputable. Also *Comb.* orig. and chiefly *U.S. colloq.*

1932 [see *PIG *sb.*[1] 5]. **1952** B. MALAMUD *Natural* 67, I don't like the scummy tricks you play on people. **1973** E. BULLINS *Theme is Blackness* 78 Hey, you white scummy-lookin' bourgeois bitch, take me to dinner? **1977** R. E. HARRINGTON *Quintain* xvii. 202 Meeting scummy little men at..squalid Parisian restaurants. **1979** *Maledicta* III. 133 The scummy millionaire Marxist profs I know don't spend one *red* penny of their own: Let the workers & peasants pay!

scunge (skɒndʒ), *sb. colloq.* (orig. *Sc.*). Also **skunge.** [Origin unknown: cf. next.] **a.** A sly or vicious person. **b.** A scrounger or sponger. **c.** As a vague term of abuse.

1824 J. MACTAGGART *Scottish Gallovidian Encycl.* 424 *Scun*, plan, craft. A scunge, a sly fellow; a maid seducer. **1900** in *Sc. Nat. Dict.* (1971) VIII. 104/1 A scunge has a crappin' for a' corns. **1912** G. CUNNINGHAM *Verse Maistly in Doric* 184 Jock, ye scunge! Come oot the dresser. **1948** *Football Times* 11 Sept., 'You great big skunge', meaning that you were always on the 'mootch'. **1967** *Comment* (N.Z.) June 14/1 He obviously thought I must be a bit of a scunge asking political questions. **1976** R. BARNARD *Death on High C's* iv. 44 'Big joke, scunge,' said Gaylene, giving him the sort of shove that would have sent a lesser man through the wall.

scunge (skɒndʒ), *v. colloq.* (orig. and chiefly *Sc.*). Also **scundge, scunje,** etc. [Origin unknown: cf. prec. and *SCROUNGE *v.*[1]] *intr.* To prowl around looking for food, etc.; to scrounge, to sponge. So **scu·nging** *ppl. a.*

1843 J. B. PRATT *Life & Death Jamie Fleeman* (ed. 9) iv. 32 Hame wi you, ye scunging tyke, hame! **1844** W. CROSS *Disruption* xxxi. 341 Neither will ye scunge after the gentry like McQuirkie. **1905** *Eng. Dial. Dict.* V. 299/2 *Scunge*, to slink about; to fawn like a dog for food. **1964** X. HERBERT *Larger than Life* 243 Senile wrecks..coveting and scundging and bickering. **1966** *Huntly Express* 30 Sept. 2 It's maybe been a scunjin' dog.

‖ **scungille** (skundʒi·le). Pl. **scungilli.** [ad. It. dial. *scunciglio* conch, seashell, prob. alteration of It. *conchiglia* seashell, shellfish.] A mollusc or conch, esp. the meat of a mollusc eaten as a delicacy.

1953 A. BONI *Talisman Italian Cookbk.* 65 Scungilli Marinara...½ pound of scungilli (pulp of conch)... Boil scungilli about 15 minutes and drain. **1963** T. PYNCHON *V.* iii. 62 He tended each seashell on his submarine scungille farm. **1972** *Village Voice* (N.Y.) 1 June 75/1 (Advt.), Italian–American fish specialties. Shrimp, calamari, scungilli, mussels, [etc.]. **1980** D. E. WESTLAKE *Castle in Air* i. 12 Stuffing scungilli and spaghetti into her mouth.

scungy (skɒ·ndʒi), *a.* Chiefly *Austral.* Also **scungey.** [f. *SCUNGE *v.* + -Y[1].] Mean, dirty, disreputable. Also *Comb.*

1966 BAKER *Austral. Lang.* (ed. 2) x. 215 *Scungey*, dirty, untidy, disreputable. **1969** *Coast to Coast 1967–8* 86 Y' hate me, don'tya? Don'tya? Don'tya, eh? Answer me, y' scungy bitch. Answer me! **1970** *Telegraph* (Brisbane) 10 Mar. 8/5 Nowadays people..talk about 'that scungy place, Bondi'. It's the truth, but it hurts. **1978** *Courier-Mail* (Brisbane) 19 May 5/5 Sometimes you see scungy-looking grapes that are worth a lot of money. **1980** R. ANSELL *To fight Wild* 56 The dressing on her leg was getting very scungy but I wasn't game to touch it until the bone had had time to begin setting.

scunner, *sb.* For '*Sc.* and *north.*' read 'orig. *Sc.* and *north.*' and add: **1.** (Later examples.) Now freq. in a milder sense: a grudge, repugnance, dislike. Also *to take a scunner to.*

1900 R. J. MUIR *Mystery Muncraig* ii. 21 He had neve told his weakness to his brother, having had a 'scunner against doing so. **1911** F. E. CRICHTON *Soundless Tide* ii. 20 He tuk some soort of a scunner til her, an' now he's just left her sittin'. **1927** J. BUCHAN *Witch Wood* i. 21 You'll give our young brother a scunner of the place. **1935** L. KERR *Woman of Glenshiels* xiii. 207 It fair gies ye the scunner the way they all grumble. **1957** V. PALMER *Seedtime* ii. 15 He remembered he had taken a scunner against McCoy when he had flown down to her wedding. **1964** *Scotsman* 12 Nov. 5 Many of them have taken a scunner at religion because they took a scunner at it at school. **1974** P. DE VRIES *Glory of Hummingbird* ix. 123 He had taken a scunner to me... What had soured him on me.. had been Jake's replacing him with me. **1977** L. MEYNELL *Hooky gets Wooden Spoon* xiii. 152 Thirty per cent of the calls..originated in personal spite, someone had taken a scunner against the next-door neighbours.

2. *Sc. dial.* **a.** Of persons: a nuisance, a pest, a good-for-nothing.

1796 J. LAUDERDALE *Poems* 91 Some poor waff detested scunner. **1899** *Shetland News* 11 Feb. 7/3 Yon black pairts is whaur som' o' da scunners o' boys is been makkin' slides. **1926** W. QUEEN *We're a' Coortin* III. i. 69 Ye wee, bowly-leggit scunner ye. **1940** *Horizon* 11 Nov. 243 He was aye sittin' in ma road. A fair scunner! **1958** *Banffshire Jrnl.* 1 Apr. 7/1 A fraisie, meally-mou'd twa-faced scunner o' a lad.

b. Of things: a nuisance, a hardship, a plague, a vexatious matter.

1865 J. HORNE *Poems* 24 Faigs, borrowed money is a sconner. **1917** A. S. NEILL *Dominie Dismissed* xi. 138 'Bairns is just a scunner,' said Sarah. 'Ye'll hae to stop yer typewriter or ye'll waken them.' **1926** W. QUEEN *We're a' Coortin* I. i. 10 It's a richt scunner walkin' up that long avenue tae the big hoose. **1947** H. W. PRYDE *1st Bk. McFlannels* i. 4 Ah thocht the room floor was bad, but this is a fair scunner.

‖ **scuola** (skwō·la). Pl. **scuole.** [It., = school.] In Venice, any of the buildings in which the medieval religious confraternities or guilds used to meet, a guild-hall; also *Hist.*, one of these guilds.

1851 J. RUSKIN *Stones of Venice* I. 340 It is the most curious in conception of all the pictures in the Scuola. **1888** *Encycl. Brit.* XXIV. 155/1 Much of the splendour of Venice..was due to the wealth and religious zeal of the various trade guilds or confraternities, called *scuole* by the Venetians. **1902** R. FRY *Let.* 14 Oct. (1972) I. 198 Jacopo Bellini is known to have painted a large number of decorative pieces for the Venetian *Scuole* and these are, I believe, part of one of these series. **1936** A. B. GREENE *Sunshine & Dust* xxiii. 397 In the Scuola, some wood-carvings of the life of St. Roche are worth study. **1961** L. MUMFORD *City in History* Note to plate 21, The architectural quality..is repeated..in the..scuola or guild hall. **1962** *Listener* 13 Sept. 386/2 The crucifix still exists..in the Church of S. Giovanni Evangelista in Venice; it was originally made for the *scuola* of that church, to house..a fragment of the True Cross. **1965** H. HONOUR *Compan. Guide to Venice* iv. 53 The members of one *scuola* visited prisoners and paid for the last rites of those who were executed. **1974** *Country Life* 25 Apr. 978/1 Most of the *Scuole* of Venice were..suppressed by the Napoleonic régime... Though teaching formed part of their function, the main aims of the *Scuole* were charitable.

scupper, *sb.* Add: **1. c.** *fig. coarse slang.* A depreciatory term for a woman, *esp.* a prostitute.

1935 A. J. POLLOCK *Underworld Speaks* 102/2 *Scupper*, a prostitute. **1970** G. GREER *Female Eunuch* 265 More familiar terms in current usage refer to women as receptacles for refuse,..as *tramp, scow, scupper.* **1972** F. WARNER *Lying Figures* IV. 40 *Sapph* You were always firm... *Laz* Your limbs and trunk were in angles of contingency. *Sapph* I was your scupper.

scupper, *v.* Add: **b.** *colloq.* To defeat, ruin, destroy, put an end to.

a **1918** [see *KNOCK *v.* 12 a]. **1948** [see *DITCH *v.*[1] 6 c]. **1957** *Economist* 19 Oct. 235/1 The suspicion is still alive that there would have been secret rejoicing in Whitehall if the French Assembly had scuppered the common market. **1957** L. DURRELL *Justine* III. 155 You can help us scupper them, old man. **1962** *Times* 2 Mar. 4/2 Underwood followed up his kick ahead and, when scuppered, found Rogers, as ever, there for a try at the post. **1974** *Times* 7 Feb. 14/8 If the Government wants to welsh on its promise, it will have to scupper Mr Money's Bill. **1981** W. WINWARD *Ball Bearing Run* iv. 51 'We're scuppered,' said Fallon... It was a crushing blow.

scuppernong. a. Substitute for def.: A cultivated grape-vine belonging to the variety of the southern muscadine, *Vitis rotundifolia*, so called, originally found in the region of the Scuppernong River; also, the fruit of a vine of this kind. Also *attrib.* (Earlier and later examples.)

1811 *Raleigh* (N. Carolina) *Star* 7 Mar. 40/2 Doctor James Mease..having seen Mr. Blount's account of the Scuppernong Grape..has requested of us to procure for him some specimens of the vine. **1829** *Free Press* (Tarboro, N. Carolina) 27 Feb. 3/3 Among them the Scuppernong, a native of North Carolina, growing in a swamp. **1857** *Harper's Mag.* May 746/1 The dwellings in the Piny Woods..almost always have..a trellis supporting an extensive scuppernong grape-vine. **1901** C. T. MOHR *Plant Life of Alabama* 136 The scuppernong grape yields its crops year after year with regular abundance. **1938** M. K. RAWLINGS *Yearling* ix. 74 The Scuppernong grapevine, a gift from his mother's kin in Carolina, was in bloom for the first time. **1944** *Clarke County Democrat* (Grove Hill, Alabama) 14 Dec. 1/5 The deer became entangled in a growth of scuppernong vines. **1949** B. A. BOTKIN *Treas. S. Folklore* II. i. 146 The poetic fable of the origin of the purple scuppernong grape in the seedling that sprouted on the edge of the pool stained with her blood from the silver arrow. **1972** J. HEWITT *N.Y. Times Cook Bk.* 308/1 Scuppernong Nectar South Carolina 12 pounds scuppernong grapes 1 cup white vinegar [etc.].

b. Wine made from the scuppernong grape. In full, **scuppernong wine.**

1825 *Catawba Jrnl.* (Charlotte, N. Carolina) 2 Aug. 3/1 The editor..having had a taste of the Scuppernong wine from North-Carolina, extols it in the highest terms. **1846** *Spirit of Times* 25 Apr. 97/1 A keg of 'Scuppernong' is on its way to us, having been shipped from Wilmington, N.C. **1862** 'E. KIRKE' *Among Pines* xvii. 280 [He] brought forth a box of Havanas, and a decanter of Scuppernong. **1887** [in Dict.]. **1936** M. MITCHELL *Gone with Wind* xxxviii. 685 It never occurred to him that a decent woman would drink anything stronger than scuppernong wine.

scuppled (skʌ·p'ld), *a. nonce-wd.* [Cf. SCUFFLE *v.*[2]] Grooved, furrowed.

1873 G. M. HOPKINS *Jrnls. & Papers* (1959) 235, I saw big smooth flinty waves, carved and scuppled in shallow grooves.

scur (skɜ̄ɹ). [Origin unknown.] A small horn found in polled cattle and sheep or their cross-bred offspring, not rooted in the skull but loosely attached by the skin. Hence **scurred** *a.*, having scurs.

1882 *Nat. Live Stock Jrnl.* (Chicago) Oct. 460/1 A heifer with only 'scurs', as the modified horns sometimes found in Polled cattle and in cross-bred offspring of Polled and horned breeds, are called in Scotland. **1902** W. BATESON *Mendel's Princ. Heredity: A Defence* 6 The offspring of the Polled Angus cow and the Shorthorn bull is almost invariably polled or with very small loose 'scurs'. **1919** J. BIGGAR *Galloway Cattle* 7 The Galloway increased the total of polled stock in the county, and knocked out the 'scurs' or abortive horns very considerably. **1960** *Farmer & Stockbreeder* 23 Feb. 81/1 Not every heterozygous bull showed scurs. *Ibid.* 22 Mar. 81/1 Some had small loose horns, some just had scurs. **1963** *Guardian* 3 Dec. 6 Only about half the ewes carry thin spiky horns, the others being polled or 'scurred'.

scurfer (skɜ̄·ɹfəɹ). [f. SCURF *v.* 3 + -ER[1].] An operative who removes incrustations of dirt from boilers, metal plates, etc.

1881 *Instructions to Census Clerks* (1885) 36 Scurfer (Ships). **1921** *Dict. Occup. Terms* (1927) § 699 *Scurfer, retort scurfer* (gas works);..chips off deposited gas carbon from sides of retorts when it gets too thick. *Ibid.* § 952 *Boiler cleaner, boiler scaler, boiler scraper, boiler scurfer,..scurfer boy*..; removes 'scale' (incrusted deposit) from inner surface of boilers and from boiler tubes.

S-curve, -curved: see *S I. 2 c.

scurvy, *sb.* Add: **1.** Now recognized as due to insufficient ascorbic acid (vitamin C) in the diet. (Further examples.)

1966 DUNLOP & ALSTEAD *Textbk. Med. Treatment* (ed. 10) 390 Scurvy is a nutritional disease which results from prolonged subsistence on diets practically devoid of fresh fruits and vegetables. **1968** PASSMORE & ROBSON *Compan. Med. Stud.* I. v. 10/1 Five major diseases: scurvy, beriberi, pellagra, keratomalacia and rickets, arise as a result of a dietary lack of one of the vitamins.

scuse, *v.* Delete † and for '*Obs.* exc. in illiterate use' read 'Now chiefly in representations of colloq. speech, esp. in form 'scuse.' (Further examples.)

1864 DICKENS *Our Mutual Friend* (1865) I. 231 'Scuse *me*, Lawyer Lightwood, it's a part of the truth. **1902** [see *EXCUSE *v.* 6 b]. **1922** JOYCE *Ulysses* 418 All poppycock, you'll scuse me saying. **1971** G. SIMS *Dead Hand* I. iv. 46 Scuse fingers.

scut, *sb.*[1] **2. b.** Delete † *Obs.* and add later examples.

1877 *Coursing Cal. 1876* 21 Handling her hare in grand style, never left the scut until she killed. *Ibid.* 78 Keeping well to the scut, she never gave her opponent a chance. **1921** GALSWORTHY *To Let* III. xi. 310 He sat there a long time dreaming his career, faithful to the scut of his possessive instinct.

scut (skʌt), *sb.*[4] *dial.* or *slang.* Also **scutt, skut.** [? Var. of SCOUT *sb.*[2]] A term of contempt for a person.

1873 TROLLOPE *Harry Heathcote* (1874) vi. 146, I thought you was ringing trees for that young scut at Gangoil? **1895** M. E. FRANCIS *Frieze & Fustian* 63 I'll pinnance ye, ye little scut! **1901** *Longman's Mag.* Sept. 405 Moran, ye scut! don't be skirmishin'. **1916** J. B. COOPER *Coo-oo-ee* viii. 95 The likes of them skuts to find fault with my cookin'—'deed it's more than O'Callaghan himself would dare do. **1929** W. DEEPING *Roper's Row* ix. 96 He always was a precocious little scut. **1936** M. FRANKLIN *All that Swagger* xxvii. 254 You speak like a low-down scut. **1970** L. SANDERS *Anderson Tapes* xii. 41 You bloody scut! Forget it! **1978** 'M. M. KAYE' *Far Pavilions* lxiii. 863 You'd think those scutts could have given us a bit more notice... It's a shabby lot they are.

scut (skʌt), *sb.*[5] *U.S. colloq.* [Origin unknown: cf. prec.] Tedious menial work. Freq. *attrib.* in *scut work.*

1960 WENTWORTH & FLEXNER *Dict. Amer. Slang* 454/1 *Scud, scut*,..hard, boring, or tedious tasks; minor details that are unrewarding and time-consuming. **1972** *Newsweek* 10 Jan. 37/2 Huber inflicted a fair amount of scut work on the boy—washing dishes, fetching books and journals from the library. **1976** *National Observer* (U.S.) 20 Mar. 14/2, I did all the scutwork: paid the bills, ran the houses, drove the children. **1978** L. PRYOR *Viper* (1979) iii. 40 The servants..were..brought from Iran and Turkey to do the scut work. **1978** *Maledicta* II. 69 *Scut*, menial medical procedures that must be carried out, usually relegated to the least senior member of the medical team.

scutching, *vbl. sb.*[1] (Later example.)

1962 H. G. GREEN *Time to pass Over* xii. 142 I'll damn well have to give you a scutching for this.

scutching, *vbl. sb.*[2] Add: **1.** (Later examples.)

1875 [see *BLOWING *vbl. sb.*[1] 1 b]. **1902** [see *DROPPING *vbl. sb.* 5 b]. **1931** S. A. G. CALDWELL *Preparation & Spinning of Flax Fibre* I. i. 15 The old method of scutching by hand has now given place to mill scutching. **1937** W. E. MORTON *Introd. Study of Spinning* I. iv. 84 It is the essential purpose of scutching to remove only the boon and the bark. **1973** *Times* 7 May 11/5 One particularly alarming process, scutching, was always done by hand, and I am surprised that a whole generation of Ulstermen have any fingers uncrushed, for to scutch you feed a hank of flax under the karate-chop action of a wooden propeller!

2. *scutching blade, machine* (later examples); **scutching knife** (later *Hist.* example).

1973 L. RUSSELL *Everyday Life Colonial Canada* ix. 111 A scutching blade, a wooden tool shaped like a butcher's knife. **1969** E. H. PINTO *Treen* 301 Old Irish, Scottish and English scutching knives are usually plain and straight bladed. **1839** Scutching machine [see *blowing-machine* s.v. *BLOWING *vbl. sb.*[1] 5]. **1901** T. THORNLEY *Cotton Spinning* I. iii. 75 The rollers..are seldom used on any scutching machines.

scute (skiūt), *sb.*[2] *Zool.* [f. SCUTE(LLAR *a.*] The name of any of a group of closely linked X-linked genes in *Drosophila* which act to reduce the number of scutellar bristles; also, a phenotype produced by these genes.

1923 BRIDGES & MORGAN *Third-Chromosome Group Mutant Characters Drosophila Melanogaster* 160 Scute arose in the line selected for increased number of scutellar bristles. **1923** *Anat. Rec.* XXVI. 397 In three of these species the closely linked [*sc.* to yellow] character 'scute' or 'scutellar' is also known. **1940** *Genetics* XXV. 566 The great phenotypic similarity of the three scutes in question is an expression of the extreme similarity of their gene arrangements. **1974** GOODENOUGH & LEVINE *Genetics* xi. 500 The *Basc* chromosome..carries the *Bar* eye gene *B*.., the *apricot* eye color gene *apr*, and a double inversion involving the *scute* (*sc*) region of the chromosome.

scutt, var. *SCUT *sb.*[4]

scutter, *sb.* (Later examples.)

1935 E. POUND *Let.* 23 May (1971) 274 The turn of the wave and the scutter of receding pebbles. **1961** H. R. F. KEATING *Rush on Ultimate* i. 9 Clearly visible from their moderate height the violent scutter of human activity—figures running up and down on the beach in short sharp bursts. **1980** *Times* 16 Jan. 14/8 The Anglo-Egyptian treaty was settled up in 1936 in a sort of scutter.

scutter, *v.*[2] For '*colloq.* and *dial.*' read 'orig. *colloq.* and *dial.*' and add later examples. Also *fig.*

1916 A. BENNETT *Lion's Share* xvii. 128 Miss Ingate scuttered to Audrey. 'Well,' she whispered. 'Here I am.' **1920** WODEHOUSE *Jill the Reckless* (1922) xxi. 313 All these people... Scuttering about and thinking they know all there is to know. **1934** E. POUND *ABC of Reading* II. 99 Inferior passages where he..has..scuttered over less interesting matter. **1947** A. RANSOME *Great Northern?* vi. 82 A family of baby water-hens scuttered across. **1948** L. MACNEICE *Holes in Sky* 38 A pebble Scutters from under the wheel. **1972** R. ADAMS *Watership Down* viii. 28 They watched him ..shake a shower of drops out of his fur and scutter into the alder bushes.

scuttle, *sb.*[1] Add: **3.** The part of a motor vehicle which connects the bonnet with the body. Also *attrib.*

1914 *Chambers's Jrnl.* Mar. 206/1 The scuttle-dash protects his body and chest from the wind. **1922** *Autocar* 10 Nov. 973 The coachwork, which now tapers from bonnet to scuttle in an unbroken sweep. **1925** *Morris Owner's Man.* 71 Under the butterfly nut at the back of the bonnet hinge (on top of the scuttle). **1963** *Times* 4 June 7/7 Above 65–70 m.p.h.., road noise was high and there was some scuttle shake. **1970** *Motoring Which?* July 109/2 Front wing to scuttle seams cracking, driver's seat had cut through carpet. **1973** 'A. HALL' *Tango Briefing* vii. 94 A hole appeared in the scuttle three inches forward of the windscreen. **1980** *Daily Tel.* 5 Mar. 12/6 Even on some of the worst French road surfaces there was hardly any sign of scuttle shake.

scuttle, *sb.*[5] Add: **1. a.** (Later example.)

1967 O. WYND *Walk Softly, Men Praying* iv. 49, I stopped a scuttle back to his den with yet another request.

b. For (See SCUTTLE *v.*[1] 2.) in Dict. read (See SCUTTLE *v.*[1] 1 b.), and add later examples.

1906 *Daily News* 16 June 6/4 The word scuttle..in the Jingo Press, where the 'policy of scuttle' is used whenever we give up something to a small Power. **1954** *Economist* 7 Aug. 428 Mr. Attlee has always been particularly offended by Tory charges of 'scuttle' during his years in office. **1967** *Daily Express* 17 Feb. 2/2 The speed-up of the scuttle is inadvertently revealed in the Defence White Paper. **1969** *Guardian* 31 July 8/1 President Nixon has ruled out both a military solution and a 'scuttle'.

scuttle, *v.*[2] Add: **1. a.** Hence, by extension: to sink (one's own vessel) deliberately; to submerge; to destroy or smash (a car, aeroplane, etc.). Also *refl.*, of a vessel.

1779 J. RAMSAY *Let.* 23 Nov. in *Parl. Papers 1910* (Cd. 5038) XXXV. 675 Captain Wilkinson is particularly celebrated for having said..he wished that all the English sugar islands were scuttled (sunk). **1939** *Times* 16 Dec. 7/3 The German steamer Adolf Leonhart (2,989 tons) was scuttled by her crew in the South Atlantic when she was intercepted by a British warship. *Ibid.* 18 Dec. 8/1 The Admiral Graf Spee the German 'pocket battleship' which was cornered by British warships, scuttled herself outside Montevideo harbour last night. **1941** *Collier's* 20 Dec. 50/1 Bruce, in a heavy sedan, had come banging out of his driveway to a collision. No one was hurt, but the flivver was scuttled. **1942** *R.A.F. Jrnl.* 13 June 10 The enemy would reveal herself by firing her guns or scuttling herself. **1955** *Times* 1 June 2/7 His Black Sea fleet had been scuttled and the war was confined to a narrowing circle round Sebastopol.

b. *fig.* (esp. in political contexts).

1888 [in Dict.]. **1940** *Star* 15 May 3/2 A favourite way of settling an argument is to exclaim, 'You go and scuttle yourself!' **1942** *Capital* 20 Jan. 1/3 The ill-concealed Axis maneuver, apparently part of a..scheme to scuttle the [Rio de] Janeiro conference. **1955** *Times* 16 May 5/1 'Now they scuttle us,' said Mr. Oatley, 'by slapping controls on what can be considered the cornerstone of every household—a domestic cooker.' **1965** MRS L. B. JOHNSON *White House Diary* 21 Oct. (1970) 329 The day..began with bad news. The Rent Subsidy Bill had been scuttled without opportunity to work on it. **1976** *National Observer* (U.S.) 24 Apr. 18/3 Earlier this month the White House, in apparent agreement, scuttled a legislative proposal to deregulate cable TV. **1977** *Time* 7 Nov. 21/3 His effort to pay off a campaign promise to maritime unions by fixing the percentage of imported oil that must be carried in U.S. ships was scuttled.

scuttle-butt, scuttlebutt (skʌ·t'lbʌt). *Naut.* [See SCUTTLED *ppl. a.*] **a.** A cask of drinking-water on board ship; a drinking-fountain. Also *fig.*

1805 J. J. MOORE *Midshipman's or Brit. Mariner's Vocab.*, *Scuttle-butt*, or cask, is a cask having a square piece sawn out of its bilge and lashed upon the deck. It is used to contain the fresh water for daily use. **1832** E. C. WINES *Two Years & Half in Navy* I. iii. 45 At sea the marines in succession all do duty as sentries in the following places;—one at the cabin door, one at the scuttle-butt, one at the brig. **1840** [see SCUTTLE *sb.*[2] 4]. **1844** J. F. COOPER *Afloat & Ashore* II. xi. 178 People never can tell so much of other person's affairs, without bailing out most of their ideas from their own scuttle-butts. **1846** [see SCUTTLED *ppl. a.*]. **1920** *U.S.S. Oklahoma Sea-Bag* 25 July 2/1 The Scuttle Butt has justified its existence as a source of prognostic rumor. The water is freezing cold—the Scuttle Butt is iced... Come down and get a drink of cold water. **1972** F. VAN W. MASON *Roads to Liberty* 104

Katie, on her way to draw water from the scuttlebutt, saw a flying fish.

b. orig. *U.S. Naut. slang.* Rumour, idle gossip, unfounded report.

1901 *Smoking Lamp* June 55/2 (*title of miscellany column*) Scuttle butt. **1933** *Leatherneck* July 18/1 We will endeavor to convey all of the scandal, scuttle-butt, dope and dopes to you through the..Editor. **1943** *Sun* (Baltimore) 20 Sept. 11/7 Also a cause for betting was the ultimate destination. In navy slang 'scuttlebutt' was rife and had the ship bound everywhere from China to Murmansk. **1950** 'D. Divine' *King of Fassarai* iv. 20 I'd got the scuttle-butt about that from the Marine Corps boys. **1966** K. Giles *Big Greed* 76 He'd heard a rumour that the Frog drank.. but he dismissed it as a scuttlebutt. **1977** *Time* 11 Apr. 17/1 Rawlings Co. now makes the official major league baseball after a 101-year Spalding reign, and the scuttlebutt is that Rawlings is turning out a rabbit ball. **1980** *Rydge's* (Sydney) Jan. 23/1 They are privy to vast amounts of corporate intelligence (and scuttlebutt) that runs daily around the Rialto.

c. *attrib.*, as **scuttle-butt gossip,** (*a*) one who exchanges gossip at a scuttle-butt; (*b*) the gossip exchanged there; **scuttle-butt yarn,** a yarn originating from talk around a scuttle-butt.

1901 *Smoking Lamp* May 18/1 (*title*) Scuttle butt gossip. **1918** R. W. Kauffman *Our Navy at Work* xiii. 198 It's wilder than anything the scuttle-butt gossips could make up! *Ibid.* 199 Ships are full of..rumours..which originate in talk exchanged around the skuttle-butt, or drinking barrel, so that all wild stories are branded as 'scuttle-butt yarns'. **1923** *Our Navy* 1 May 15/2 While these rumors are branded as of the 'scuttle butt' variety they persist as rumors. **1930** P. Buranelli *Maggie of Suicide Fleet* ii. 57 There are stories and rumors, scuttle-butt gossip.

Hence **scu·ttlebutt** *v. intr.*, to gossip, to spread unfounded stories.

1945 H. I. Phillips *Private Purkey's Private Peace* xi. 62 There were many who felt..Oscar was just scuttle-butting.

scuzzy (skʌ·zi), *a. N. Amer. colloq.* [Perh. blend of Scummy *a.* + Fuzzy *a.*] Dirty, grimy; murky. So **scuz(z)** *sb.*, a dirty, messy person.

1968 *Sunday Sun* (Baltimore) 3 Nov. D1/5, I..did 'Midnight Cowboy' where I'm *Ratso Rizzo*, a complete scuzz. **1969** *Publ. Amer. Dial. Soc.* LI. 16 *Scuzzy, groady, skoady,* and *grungy* should probably be listed also under 'Blends'.. *Scuzzy*, for example, seems to imply *fuzzy* and *scummy*: 'Your teeth are scuzzy.' **1972** J. Wambaugh *Blue Knight* vi. 78 One white, bearded scuz in a dirty buckskin vest and yellow headband. **1974** A. Fowles *Pastime* vii. 63 The scuzzy, grey, February days, neither cold nor clear. **1976** *Daily Colonist* (Victoria, B.C.) 14 Apr. 5/4 Perhaps Mr. Vander Kalm has good intentions about evicting scuzzy malingerers from the dole.

scyphozoan (sǝiːfozōᵘ·ăn), *sb.* and *a.* [f. mod. L. class name *Scyphozoa* (A. Goette 1898, in *Zeitschr. f. Wiss. Zool.* LXIII. 292), f. Scypho- + *-zoa* (see Zoon).] A jellyfish belonging to the class Scyphozoa; of or pertaining to an animal of this kind.

[**1892** J. A. Thomson *Outlines Zool.* x. 137 (*caption*) Contrast between a Hydrozoon and a Scyphozoon medusoid.] **1915** Shipley & MacBride *Zool.* (ed. 3) iii. 75 The construction of the Scyphozoan organ is quite different. *Ibid.* 78 The original Scyphozoan was probably an organism like a polyp. **1938** R. Buchsbaum *Anim. without Backbones* viii. 95 *Aurelia* is one of the commonest of the scyphozoan jellyfish. **1967** P. A. Meglitsch *Invertebrate Zool.* vi. 148/1 Stauromedusae are the most unusual scyphozoans.

Scyth. a. For 'Now *rare*' in Dict., read '*Obs.* exc. *Hist.*' and add later examples.

1914 D. G. Hogarth *Ancient East* iii. 122 The predatory Scyth..probably lacked skill to inscribe them. **1950** [see *Kimmerian]. **1964** *Listener* 6 Feb. 238/2 So we came to the plain and the Scyths. **1973** R. L. Fox *Alexander* iv. 75 The barbarian Scyths and Thracians.

b. = *Scythian *sb.* 1 b. *rare.*

1972 B. Thomson *Premature Revolution* I. vii. 130 The 'Scyths' revived the old Slavophile faith in the Russian peasantry, as a bastion of spiritual values in an age of materialism... Usually the 'Scyths' were concerned with purely Russian questions, but Blok's poem *The Scyths* (*Skify*, 1918) reveals a chauvinistic and aggressive side to the movement.

scythe, *sb.* Add: **4. a.** *scythe-stroke* (also *fig.*).

1913 D. H. Lawrence *Mowers* in *Smart Set* Nov. 12 There's four men mowing down by the river; I can hear the sound of the scythe strokes, four Sharp breaths swishing. **1940** W. S. Churchill *Into Battle* (1941) 216 This armoured scythe-stroke almost reached Dunkirk—almost but not quite.

scythe, *v.* Add: **2. b.** *fig.* To cut down swiftly and drastically.

1970 *Daily Tel.* 12 Mar. 22/3 Net attributable profits are scythed from £602,000 to £210,000.

3. Delete *nonce-use* and add later examples.

1946 J. W. Day *Harvest Adventure* vii. 107 'Pleu-eu! Pleu-eu! Pleu!' and whimbrel went scything off low across the water, putting up a mixed lot of sandpipers. **1955** E. Pound *Classic Anthol.* II. 94 Feckless Huns town'd in Tsiao, seized Huo, lacking provisions, Scythed into Hao up to its border. **1966** Gillman & Haston *Eiger Direct* v. 107 John scythed up on his skis and stopped in a spray of snow. **1978** *Antiques & Art Monitor* 28 Oct. 23/3 High-rise aerial perspectives of a motorway scything through a city.

scythed, *ppl. a.* Add: **1.** (Later example.)

1922 Joyce *Ulysses* 649 Humanely his driver waited till he (or she) had ended, patient in his scythed car.

3. *fig.* Swept over as though by a scythe.

1952 Dylan Thomas *Coll. Poems* 172 Who knows the rocketing-wind will blow The bones out of the hills, And the scythed boulders bleed.

Scythian, *a.* and *sb.* Add: Now freq. with pronunc. (si·ðiăn). **B.** *sb.* **1. b.** *Russ. Lit.* An advocate of Scythism (sense *c).

1923 *Contemp. Rev.* Aug. 193 There is an immense wealth of pride in these *Scythians*, they heartily and sincerely despise the West. **1970** M. Ginsburg tr. *Zamyatin's Soviet Heretic* 22 Ivanov-Razumnik..leader of the Scythians, a literary group that included Blok and Bely. **1974** Moore & Parry *Twentieth-Cent. Russ. Lit.* ii. 18 He was now briefly one of the Scythians, who confronted the new social events with fervor and a sense of exultation.

2. (Later examples.)

1870 [see *Babylonian *sb.* 2]. **1894** [see *Medic *sb.*[2]]. **1939** L. H. Gray *Foundations of Lang.* xiii. 425 Hesychios.. cites words..from many non-Classical languages, such as.. Scythian. **1972** W. B. Lockwood *Panorama Indo-Europ. Lang.* xii. 235 The exiguous records of the Median language are of the same character as those of Scythian and Sarmatian.

Scythianism: see *Scythism c.

scything, *ppl. a.* Add: Also, having the sweeping action of a scythe. Also *fig.*

1960 E. Hamilton *Great Teresa* i. 37 The black, scything wings of swifts dipping and swerving. **1963** *Times* 17 May 5/4 Smith's scything forehand stroke. **1978** *Daily Tel.* 18 Feb. 1 Some victims were killed by collapsing masonry and scything debris.

scything (sǝi·ðiŋ), *vbl. sb.* [f. Scythe *v.* + -ing[1].] The action of the verb; the result of this, scythed grass, etc. Also *fig.*

1969 *Gloss. Landscape Work* (*B.S.I.*) v. 21 *Scything*, 1. The cutting of grass with a scythe. 2. Now usually the cutting of long grass, or other vegetation, either with a scythe or by a machine with reciprocating blades. **1969** M. Poole in R. Blythe *Akenfield* xii. 196 Back she arrived later when I was lying on the scythings. **1978** *Maledicta* II. 232 In order to give you a taste of the 'vilest venom' of scholarly verbal aggression mentioned in our first issue..I wish to share with you excerpts from Zizi Quirk's scything of *Maledicta*.

Scythism. Restrict † *Obs.* to senses in Dict. and add pronunc. (si·þiz'm, si·ðiz'm). **c.** *Russ. Lit.* A movement among Russian men of letters soon after the Revolution of 1917 which favoured the peasant values of Asiatic Russia as against Western European civilization. Also **Scy·thianism.**

The term is a rendering of Russ. *skifstvo.*

1921 D. H. Lawrence *Sea & Sardinia* v. 164, I am glad that Russia flies back into savage Russianism, Scythism, savagely self-pivoting. **1923** *Contemp. Rev.* Aug. 193 National Bolshevism is of much more recent growth than either Bolshevism or Scythianism. **1926** *Encycl. Brit.* III. 1070/1 Moscow became the scene of a struggle between what may be called 'Europeanism' and what is known there as 'Scythism'. Scythism, which achieved the miracle of rallying to the Bolshevik standard the Russian reactionaries who were most violently opposed to it, inculcates scorn and hatred of western civilization, and aims at nothing less than Asia's vengeance on Europe. **1958** E. H. Carr *Socialism in One Country* I. ii. 60 After the publication of Blok's poem the name 'Scythism' (Skifstvo) came to be applied, not to a literary movement, but to a tendency which inspired many writers in the first years of the revolution. **1963** G. Struve in Hayward & Labedz *Lit. & Revol. in Soviet Russia* 4 R. Ivanov-Razumnik..the main ideologist, in the early days of the Revolution, of the so-called 'Scythianism'. **1972** B. Thomson *Premature Revol.* I. vii. 130 The peasant poets were..more sympathetic to the Social-Revolutionaries than to the Bolsheviks... Under the guidance of Ivanov-Razumnik they formed a movement, called *Scythianism* ('*Skifstvo*').